1992 County and City Extra

1992 County and City Extra

Annual Metro, City and County Data Book

Edited by:
Courtenay M. Slater
and George E. Hall

BERNAN PRESS
Lanham, MD

Printed in the United States of America

∞™

Bernan Press
An Imprint of Bernan Associates
4611-F Assembly Drive
Lanham, Maryland 20706-4391
(301) 459-7666

ISBN 0-89059-004-4
ISSN 1059-9096

Contents

ABOUT THE EDITORS

Dr. Courtenay M. Slater served as the Chief Economist for the U.S. Department of Commerce from 1977-1981. She has also served on the professional staffs of the President's Council of Economic Advisers and the Joint Economic Committee of Congress. Since leaving the government, Dr. Slater has directed numerous research projects pertaining to federal statistics. Through her written work, speaking appearances, and congressional testimony, she has been a leading advocate of a strengthened federal statistical system.

George E. Hall has over 30 years' experience in statistical analysis and program development. Mr. Hall has served as Associate Director for Demographic Fields at the U.S. Bureau of the Census. He was also Deputy Director of the Office of Federal Statistical Policy and Standards, and worked as a senior statistical official in other federal positions. More recently he has served on advisory councils and expert committees on statistical issues in health, education, transportation, and other areas.

Currently, Dr. Slater and Mr. Hall direct **Slater Hall Information Products (SHIP)**, a company they co-founded in 1986. Since its inception, SHIP has pioneered the publication of general purpose statistical data on compact discs (CD-ROM) and has become the medium's recognized leader in the distribution of economic and demographic statistics.

INTRODUCTION

The *County and City Extra* is an annual publication providing the most up-to-date statistical information available for every state, county, metropolitan area, city, and place in the United States. It is designed to meet the needs of libraries, businesses, organizations and individuals who desire a single convenient and timely source for the most frequently sought information about geographic entities within the United States.

This first edition of the *County and City Extra* contains recent data from the 1990 decennial census and other current statistics covering a wide array of disciplines. Future editions will contain updates of existing data, as well as the introduction of new categories to the tables. Because certain sources update their figures irregularly, some data will be repeated from one year to the next out of necessity. However, much of the data will be updated on an annual basis. This constant updating and expansion of the *County and City Extra* ensures its stature as a reliable and authoritative source for statistical information.

Volume Organization

The data in this book are arranged in four tables. Table A, beginning on page 35, contains information for states and counties, while Table B, beginning on page 737, contains similar data for metropolitan areas. Statistics for cities with a 1980 population of 25,000 or more can be found in Table C, which begins on page 811. Finally, Table D, beginning on page 947, presents more limited information for places (including cities, census designated places, towns and townships) with a 1990 population of 2,500 or more.

A contents page at the front of each of the four tables lists the page number where the data for a given geographic area begin.

Counties, cities, and places are listed alphabetically by state within each of the four tables. Metropolitan areas are listed alphabetically, except that Primary Metropolitan Statistical Areas (PMSAs) are listed alphabetically under the Consolidated Metropolitan Statistical Area (CMSA) of which they are components. (For more information on geographic divisions see Appendix A, page A-1.)

Rankings of the largest counties, metropolitan areas, and cities, by selected subjects, begin on page 2.

Detailed information about geographic codes, sources and definitions, a listing of metropolitan areas with their component counties, and maps showing the counties and metropolitan areas within each state, are found in the Appendices, beginning on page A-1.

Subjects Covered

A summary of the subjects covered in each of the four tables of this volume appears on page xi. Pages xii to xxi show the complete column headings for each table.

Symbols and Terms

The following symbols are used in this volume:

D Indicates that a figure has been withheld to avoid disclosure of information pertaining to a specific organization or individual, or because it does not meet statistical standards for publication.

NA Indicates that data are not available.

X Indicates that data are not applicable or are not meaningful for this geographic unit.

In this volume, where a figure is less than half of the unit of measure shown, it will appear as a zero.

Sources

The great majority of the data in this volume have been obtained from federal government sources. A few items have been acquired from private sources which are widely recognized as being reliable basic sources of those particular data items. For a complete list of sources, see Appendix D, page D-1.

Data included in this volume meet the publication standards established by the Census Bureau and the other federal statistical agencies from which they were obtained. Every effort has been made to select data that are accurate, meaningful and useful. All data from censuses, surveys, and administrative records are subject to error arising from factors such as sampling variability, reporting errors, incomplete coverage, nonresponse, imputations, and processing error. Responsibility of the editors and publisher of this volume is limited to reasonable care in the reproduction and presentation of data obtained from sources believed to be reliable.

An electronic version of the County and City Extra is also available. Information on the County and City Plus CD-ROM may be obtained from Bernan Press.

ACKNOWLEDGMENTS

The editors wish to thank the many federal agency personnel who not only assisted them in obtaining the data for this volume, but who also responded patiently and tirelessly to the editors' endless queries pertaining to geographic area delineations, data definitions and other technical matters.

SUBJECTS COVERED, BY TYPE OF AREA

State and county data begin on page 35; metro area data on page 737; city data on page 811; and data for places on page 947.

Subject	States and Counties	Metro Areas	Cities	Places
Land area	X	X	X	X
Population:				
Total persons	X	X	X	X
Rank	X	X	X	
Density	X	X	X	
Race	X	X	X	X
Hispanic origin	X	X	X	X
Age distribution	X	X		
Percent female	X	X		
Change	X	X	X	X
Components of change	X	X		
Households:				
Number	X	X	X	
Change	X	X		
Persons per household	X	X	X	
Female head	X	X	X	
Single person	X	X	X	
Vital statistics:				
Births – total	X	X	X	
Low birth weight	X	X		
Deaths	X	X	X	
Marriages	X	X		
Divorces	X	X		
Health:				
Physicians	X	X		
Hospitals	X	X	X	
Nursing homes	X	X		
Crime and law enforcement:				
Number of crimes	X	X	X	
Police officers	X	X	X	
Education:				
School enrollment	X	X		
Attainment	X	X	X	
Local government expenditure	X	X		
Social insurance:				
Social security program	X	X		
Supplemental security income program	X	X		
Income:				
Money income	X		X	
Poverty	X		X	
Personal income by type	X	X		
Earnings by industry	X	X		
Construction and housing:				
Total housing units	X	X	X	X
Change	X	X	X	
Median value	X		X	
Median rent	X		X	
Construction authorized:				
Residential	X	X	X	
Nonresidential	X	X	X	
Labor force and employment:				
Total	X	X	X	

Subject	States and Counties	Metro Areas	Cities	Places
Unemployed	X	X	X	
Unemployment rate	X	X	X	
Private establishments, employment, and payroll	X	X		
Employment by industry	X	X		
Agriculture:				
Farms	X	X		
Farm operators	X	X		
Acreage	X	X		
Value of land and buildings	X			
Value of sales	X	X		
Manufactures:				
Establishments	X	X	X	
Employment	X	X	X	
Payroll	X	X	X	
Average wage	X	X	X	
Value added	X	X	X	
Shipments	X	X	X	
Capital expenditures	X	X	X	
Wholesale trade:				
Establishments	X	X	X	
Sales	X	X	X	
Employment	X	X	X	
Payroll	X	X	X	
Retail trade:				
All establishments:				
Number	X	X	X	
Sales	X	X	X	
Establishments with payroll:				
Number	X	X	X	
Sales by selected type	X	X	X	
Employment	X	X	X	
Payroll	X	X	X	
Service industries:				
Establishments	X	X	X	
Receipts by selected type	X	X	X	
Employment	X	X	X	
Payroll	X	X	X	
Bank deposits	X	X	X	
Savings capital	X	X	X	
Federal funds and grants	X	X	X	
Government:				
Finances:				
Revenue by source	X	X	X	
Expenditures by function	X	X	X	
Debt	X	X	X	
Employment:	X	X	X	
State and local	X	X		
Federal civilian	X	X	X	
City			X	
Elections	X	X		
Climate and electric bills			X	

COLUMN HEADINGS FOR STATES AND COUNTIES

Table A. States and Counties — **Land Area and Population**

STATE–County code	MSA/CMSA/NECMA code[1]	STATE County	Land Area,[2] 1990 (Sq. Km.)	Population, 1990											
							Race						Age of population Percent		
				Total persons	Rank	Per square kilometer	White	Black	Am. Indian, Eskimo, Aleut	Asian & Pacific Islander	Other race	Hispanic[3]	Under 5 years	5 to 14 years	15 to 24 years
			1	2	3	4	5	6	7	8	9	10	11	12	13

1. MSA = Metropolitan Statistical Area. CMSA = Consolidated MSA. NECMA = New England county metropolitan area. PMSA = Primary MSA. See Appendix A for explanation of these concepts. See Appendix B for list of metropolitan areas identified by type, with component counties. 2. Dry land or land partially or temporarily covered by water. 3. Hispanic persons may be of any race.

Table A. States and Counties — **Population**

STATE County	Population, 1990 (cont'd)							Population–Change and components of change							
	Age of population (cont'd) Percent							Change		Components of change, 1980–1986					
								1980–1990				Net change		Natural increase	
	25 to 34 years	35 to 44 years	45 to 54 years	55 to 64 years	65 to 74 years	75 years and over	Percent female	Number	Percent	Total persons, 1986	Total persons, 1980	Number	Percent	Births	Deaths
	14	15	16	17	18	19	20	21	22	23	24	25	26	27	28

Table A. States and Counties — **Population, Households, and Vital Statistics**

STATE County	Population–(cont'd)	Households, 1990					Births, 1988			Deaths, 1987				Marriages, 1984	
	Components of change, 1980-1986 (cont'd)				Percent					Number		Rate			
	Net migration	Number	Percent change, 1980–1990	Persons per house-hold	Female family house-holder[1]	One-person	Total	Rate[2]	Low birth weight[3] (Number)	Total	Infant[4]	Total[2]	Infant[5]	Number	Rate[2]
	29	30	31	32	33	34	35	36	37	38	39	40	41	42	43

1. No spouse present. 2. Per 1,000 resident population estimated as of July 1 of the year shown. 3. Under 2,500 grams. 4. Deaths of infants under 1 year old. 5. Deaths of infants under 1 year old per 1,000 live births.

Table A. States and Counties — **Vital Statistics, Health Resources, Crime, and Education**

STATE County	Divorces, 1984		Physicians, active non–Federal, 1989		Hospitals, 1989			Nursing homes,[4] 1986		Serious crimes known to police, 1988			Education			
						Beds				Number			Public school enrollment[7]		Attainment,[8] 1980	
	Number	Rate[1]	Number[2]	Rate[3]	Number	Number	Rate[3]	Number	Beds	Total[5]	Violent[6]	Rate[3]	1986–1987	1980	Percent 12 yrs. or more	Percent 16 yrs. or more
	44	45	46	47	48	49	50	51	52	53	54	55	56	57	58	59

1. Per 1,000 resident population estimated as of July 1 of the year shown. 2. As of end of year. 3. Per 100,000 resident population as of July 1 of the year shown. 4. Preliminary. Covers nursing homes with 3 or more beds. 5. Data for serious crimes have not been adjusted for underreporting, this may affect comparability between geographic areas or over time. 6. Includes murder and nonnegligent manslaughter, forcible rape, robbery, and aggravated assault. 7. The 1986–1987 data are based on administrative reports obtained by the U.S. National Center for Education Statistics. The 1980 data are based on the 1980 Census of Population and Housing. 8. Persons 25 years old or older.

COLUMN HEADINGS FOR STATES AND COUNTIES

Table A. States and Counties — **Education, Social Security, Money Income, and Housing**

STATE County	Education (cont'd)		Social Security Program December 1988				Money income						Housing units, 1990	
	Local government expenditures for education,[1] 1982		Beneficiaries			Supplemental Security Income Program recipients June 1986	Per capita[3]			Median household income 1979 (Dollars)	Percent below poverty level, 1979			
							1987 Income, (Dollars)	1979						
	Total (Mil dol)	Per capita (Dollars)	Total	Rate[2]	Payments ($1,000)			Current dollars	Constant 1987 dollars		Persons	Families	Total	Percent change, 1980–1990
	60	61	62	63	64	65	66	67	68	69	70	71	72	73

1. Elementary and secondary. 2. Per 1,000 resident population estimated as of July 1 of the year shown. 3. Based on the resident population estimated as of July 1, 1988 for 1987 data and enumerated as of April 1, 1980 for 1979 data.

Table A. States and Counties — **Housing, Labor Force, and Employment**

STATE County	Housing units, 1990 (cont'd)				Civilian labor force, 1990				Private nonfarm establishments, 1988					
	Occupied units						Unemployment				Employment[2]			
		Owner occupied												
	Total	Percent	Median value (Dollars)	Median rent (Dollars)	Total	Percent change, 1989–1990	Total	Rate[1]	Number	Net change, 1987–1988	Total	Percent change, 1987–1988	Manufacturing	Retail trade
	74	75	76	77	78	79	80	81	82	83	84	85	86	87

1. Percent of total civilian labor force. 2. For week including March 12. Excludes government employees, self-employed persons, farm workers, domestic service workers, railroad employees subject to the Railroad Retirement Act, and employees on oceanborne vessels or in foreign countries.

Table A. States and Counties — **Employment, Personal Income, and Earnings**

STATE County	Private nonfarm establishments, 1988 (cont'd)				Personal income, 1989								Earnings, 1989		
	Employment[1] (cont'd)		Annual payroll								Per capita[3]			Percent by selected industries	
															Goods-related[4]
	Finance, insurance, and real estate	Services	Total (Mil dol)	Average per employee (Dollars)	Total (Mil dol)	Percent change, 1988–1989	Wages and salaries[2] (Mil dol)	Proprietor's income (Mil dol)	Dividends, interest, & rent (Mil dol)	Transfer payments (Mil dol)	Dollars	Rank	Total (Mil dol)	Farm	Total
	88	89	90	91	92	93	94	95	96	97	98	99	100	101	102

1. For week including March 12. Excludes government employees, self-employed persons, farm workers, domestic service workers, railroad employees subject to the Railroad Retirement Act, and employees on oceanborne vessels or in foreign countries. 2. Includes other labor income. 3. Based on the resident population estimated as of July 1 of the year shown. 4. Covers mining, construction, and manufacturing.

COLUMN HEADINGS FOR STATES AND COUNTIES

Table A. States and Counties — **Earnings and Agriculture**

STATE County	Earnings, 1989 (cont'd)						Agriculture, 1987									
	Percent by selected industries (cont'd)						Farms			Farm operators, percent		Land in farms				
	Goods-related[1]	Service-related & other[2]						Percent with						Acres		
	Manufacturing	Total	Retail trade	Finance, insurance, & real estate	Services	Government	Number	Less than 50 acres	500 acres and over	Whose principal occupation is farming	Residing on farm operated	Acreage (1,000)	Percent change, 1982–1987	Average size of farm	Total irrigated (1,000)	Total cropland (1,000)
	103	104	105	106	107	108	109	110	111	112	113	114	115	116	117	118

1. Covers mining, construction, and manufacturing. 2. Covers private sector earnings in agricultural services, forestry, and fisheries; transportation and public utilities; wholesale trade; retail trade; finance, insurance, and real estate; and services.

Table A. States and Counties — **Agriculture and Manufactures**

STATE County	Agriculture, 1987 (cont'd)								Manufactures, 1987						
	Value of land and buildings		Value of products sold				Percent of farms with sales of		Establishments		All employees			Production workers	
					Percent from										
	Average per farm ($1,000)	Average per acre (Dollars)	Total (Mil dol)	Average per farm (Dollars)	Crops	Livestock and poultry[1]	$10,000 or more	$100,000 or more	Total	Percent with 20 or more employees	Number (1,000)	Percent change, 1982–1987	Annual payroll (Mil dol)	Number (1,000)	Work hours (Mil)
	119	120	121	122	123	124	125	126	127	128	129	130	131	132	133

1. Includes livestock and poultry products.

Table A. States and Counties — **Manufactures and Construction**

STATE County	Manufactures, 1987 (cont'd)					Value of construction authorized by building permits, 1990							
	Production workers (cont'd)						Nonresidential				Residential		
	Wages							Percent					
	Total (Mil dol)	Average per worker (Dollars)	Value added by manufacture (Mil dol)	Value of shipments (Mil dol)	New capital expenditures (Mil dol)	Total[1] ($1,000)	Total ($1,000)	Office	Industrial	Stores	New construction ($1,000)	Number of housing units	Alterations and additions ($1,000)
	134	135	136	137	138	139	140	141	142	143	144	145	146

1. Includes nonresidential additions and alterations, residential nonhousekeeping buildings, and residential garages and carports not shown separately.

COLUMN HEADINGS FOR STATES AND COUNTIES

Table A. States and Counties — **Wholesale and Retail Trade**

STATE County	Wholesale trade, 1987				Retail trade, all establishments, 1987				Retail trade, establishments with payroll, 1987					
						Sales				Sales				
											Per capita[2] (Dollars)			
	Estab-lishments	Sales (Mil dol)	Paid employees[1]	Annual payroll (Mil dol)	Number	Total (Mil dol)	Percent change, 1982–1987	Per capita[2] (Dollars)	Number	Total (Mil dol)	General merchan-dise stores	Food stores	Apparel & acces-sory stores	Eating and drinking places
	147	148	149	150	151	152	153	154	155	156	157	158	159	160

1. For pay period including March 12. 2. Based on the estimated population as of July 1 of the year shown.

Table A. States and Counties — **Retail Trade, Services, and Banking**

STATE County	Retail trade, establishments with payroll, 1987 (cont'd)		Taxable service industries–establishments with payroll, 1987							Bank deposits,[2] June 1989		Savings capital,[3] September 1989	
				Receipts (Mil dol)									
					Selected kinds of business								
	Paid employees[1]	Annual payroll (Mil dol)	Number	Total	Hotels, motels and other lodg-ing places	Health services	Legal services	Paid employees	Annual payroll (Mil dol)	Total (Mil dol)	Percent change, 1988–1989	Total (Mil dol)	Percent change, 1988–1989
	161	162	163	164	165	166	167	168	169	170	171	172	173

1. For the period including March 12 of the year shown. 2. Includes deposits for all insured and reporting noninsured commercial and mutual savings banks. 3. Includes savings capital for all FSLIC insured savings institutions.

Table A. States and Counties — **Federal Funds and Local Government Finances**

STATE County	Federal funds and grants, 1989							Local government finances, 1981–1982							
	Expenditures		Per capita[1] (Dollars)					General revenue						Direct general expenditure	
									Intergovernmental		Taxes				
												Per capita[2]			
	Total (Mil dol)	Percent change, 1988–1989	Total	Direct pay-ments for indi-viduals	Procure-ment contract awards	Salaries and wages	Grant awards	Total (Mil dol)	Total (Mil dol)	Percent from state	Total (Mil dol)	Total (Dollars)	Property (Dollars)	Total (Mil dol)	Percent change, 1977–1982
	174	175	176	177	178	179	180	181	182	183	184	185	186	187	188

1. Based on the estimated population as of July 1 of the year shown. 2. Based on the estimated population as of July 1, 1982.

Table A. States and Counties — **Local Gov't. Finances, Gov't. Employment, and Elections**

STATE County	Local government finances, 1981–1982 (cont'd)								State and local government employ-ment, 1989		Federal government civilian employment 1989		Elections, 1988[3]	
	Direct general expenditure (cont'd)						Debt outstanding							
		Percent of total for–												
	Per capita[1] (Dollars)	Educa-tion	Health & hospitals	Police protec-tion	Public welfare	High-ways	Total (Mil dol)	Per capita[1] (Dollars)	Total	Rate[2]	Total	Earnings ($1,000)	Total vote cast for president	Vote for lead party (Percent)
	189	190	191	192	193	194	195	196	197	198	199	200	201	202

1. Based on the estimated population as of July 1, 1982. 2. Per 10,000 resident population estimated as of July 1 of the year shown. 3. Data subject to copyright.

COLUMN HEADINGS FOR METROPOLITAN AREAS

Table B. Metropolitan Areas — Land Area and Population

MSA/ CMSA/ NECMA/ PMSA code[1]	Area name	Land Area,[2] 1990 (Sq. Km.)	Population, 1990									Age of population Percent				
						Race										
			Total persons	Rank	Per square kilometer	White	Black	Am. Indian, Eskimo, Aleut	Asian & Pacific Islander	Other race	Hispanic[3]	Under 5 years	5 to 14 years	15 to 24 years	25 to 34 years	35 to 44 years
		1	2	3	4	5	6	7	8	9	10	11	12	13	14	15

1. MSA = Metropolitan Statistical Area. CMSA = Consolidated MSA. NECMA = New England county metropolitan area. PMSA = Primary MSA. See Appendix A for explanation of these concepts. See Appendix B for list of metropolitan areas identified by type, with component counties. 2. Dry land or land partially or temporarily covered by water. 3. Hispanic persons may be of any race.

Table B. Metropolitan Areas — Population and Households

Area name	Population, 1990 (cont'd)					Population–change and components of change									Households, 1990
	Age of population (cont'd) Percent					Change, 1980–1990		Components of change, 1980–1986							
										Net change		Natural increase			
	45 to 54 years	55 to 64 years	65 to 74 years	75 years and over	Percent female	Number	Percent	Total persons, 1986	Total persons, 1980	Number	Percent	Births	Deaths	Net migration	Total
	16	17	18	19	20	21	22	23	24	25	26	27	28	29	30

Table B. Metropolitan Areas — Households, Vital Statistics, and Health Resources

Area name	Households, 1990 (cont'd)			Births, 1988			Deaths, 1987				Marriages, 1984		Divorces, 1984		Physicians, active non-Federal, 1989	
		Percent					Number		Rate							
	Percent change, 1980–1990	Female family house-holder[1]	One-person	Total	Rate[2]	Low birth weight[3] (Number)	Total	Infant[4]	Total[2]	Infant[5]	Number	Rate[2]	Number	Rate[2]	Number[6]	Rate[7]
	31	33	34	35	36	37	38	39	40	41	42	43	44	45	46	47

1. No spouse present. 2. Per 1,000 resident population estimated as of July 1 of the year shown. 3. Under 2,500 grams. 4. Deaths of infants under 1 year old. 5. Deaths of infants under 1 year old per 1,000 live births. 6. As of end of year. 7. Per 100,000 resident population as of July 1 of the year shown.

Table B. Metropolitan Areas — Health Resources, Crime, Education, and Social Security

Area name	Hospitals, 1989			Nursing homes,[2] 1986		Serious crimes known to police, 1988			Education						Social Security Program December 1988	
		Beds				Number			Public school enrollment[6]		Attainment,[7] 1980		Local government expenditures for education,[8] 1982		Beneficiaries	
	Number	Number	Rate[1]	Number	Beds	Total[3]	Violent[4]	Rate[5]	1986–1987	1980	Percent 12 years or more	Percent 16 years or more	Total (Mil dol)	Per capita (Dol-lars)	Total	Rate[9]
	48	49	50	51	52	53	54	55	56	57	58	59	60	61	62	63

1. Per 100,000 resident population estimated as of July 1 of the year shown. 2. Covers nursing homes with 3 or more beds. 3. Data for serious crimes have not been adjusted for underreporting, this may affect comparability between geographic areas or over time. 4. Includes murder and nonnegligent manslaughter, forcible rape, robbery, and aggravated assault. 5. Per 100,000 resident population as of July 1 of the year shown. 6. The 1986–1987 data are based on administrative reports obtained by the U.S. National Center for Education Statistics. The 1980 data are based on the 1980 Census of Population and Housing. 7. Persons 25 years old or older. 8. Elementary and secondary. 9. Per 1,000 resident population estimated as of July 1 of the year shown.

COLUMN HEADINGS FOR METROPOLITAN AREAS

Table B. Metropolitan Areas — Social Security, Housing, Labor Force, and Employment

Area name	Social Security Program, Dec. 1988 (cont'd)		Housing units, 1990				Civilian labor force, 1990				Private nonfarm establishments, 1988			
					Occupied units				Unemployment				Employment[2]	
	Payments ($1,000)	Supplemental Security Income Program recipients, June 1986	Total	Percent change, 1980–1990	Total	Percent owner-occupied	Total	Percent change, 1989–1990	Total	Rate[1]	Number	Net change, 1987–1988	Total	Percent change, 1987–1988
	64	65	72	73	74	75	78	79	80	81	82	83	84	85

1. Percent of total civilian labor force. 2. For week including March 12. Excludes government employees, self-employed persons, farm workers, domestic service workers, railroad employees subject to the Railroad Retirement Act, and employees on oceanborne vessels or in foreign countries.

Table B. Metropolitan Areas — Employment and Personal Income

Area name	Private nonfarm establishments, 1987 (cont'd)						Personal income, 1989							
	Employment[1] (cont'd)				Annual payroll								Per capita[3]	
	Manufacturing	Retail trade	Finance, insurance, and real estate	Services	Total (Mil dol)	Average per employee	Total (Mil dol)	Percent change, 1988–1989	Wages and salaries[2] (Mil dol)	Proprietor's income (Mil dol)	Dividends, Interest, & rent (Mil dol)	Transfer payments (Mil dol)	Dollars	Rank (Dollars)
	86	87	88	89	90	91	92	93	94	95	96	97	98	99

1. For week including March 12. Excludes government employees, self-employed persons, farm workers, domestic service workers, railroad employees subject to the Railroad Retirement Act, and employees on oceanborne vessels or in foreign countries. 2. Includes other labor income. 3. Based on the resident population estimated as of July 1 of the year shown.

Table B. Metropolitan Areas — Earnings and Agriculture

Area name	Earnings, 1989									Agriculture, 1987									
		Percent by selected industries								Farms			Farm operators, Percent		Land in farms				
			Goods-related[1]		Service-related & other[2]						Percent with						Acres		
	Total (Mil dol)	Farm	Total	Manufacturing	Total	Retail trade	Finance, insurance, & real estate	Services	Government	Number	Less than 50 acres	500 acres and over	Whose principal occupation is farming	Residing on farm operated	Acreage (1,000)	Percent change, 1982–1987	Average size of farm	Total irrigated (1,000)	Total cropland (1,000)
	100	101	102	103	104	105	106	107	108	109	110	111	112	113	114	115	116	117	118

1. Covers mining, construction, and manufacturing. 2. Covers private sector earnings in agricultural services, forestry, and fisheries; transportation and public utilities; wholesale trade; retail trade; finance, insurance, and real estate; and services.

Table B. Metropolitan Areas — Agriculture and Manufactures

Area name	Agriculture, 1987 (cont'd)						Manufactures, 1987								
	Value of products sold				Percent of farms with sales of		Establishments		All employees		Production workers				
			Percent from										Wages		
	Total (Mil dol)	Average per farm (Dollars)	Crops	Livestock and poultry[1]	$10,000 or more	$100,000 or more	Total	Percent with 20 or more employees	Number (1,000)	Annual payroll (Mil dol)	Number (1,000)	Work hours (Millions)	Total (Mil dol)	Average per worker (Dollars)	Value added by manufacture (Mil dol)
	121	122	123	124	125	126	127	128	129	131	132	133	134	135	136

1. Includes livestock and poultry products.

COLUMN HEADINGS FOR METROPOLITAN AREAS

Table B. Metropolitan Areas — Manufactures, Construction, Wholesale and Retail Trade

Area name	Manufactures, 1987 (cont'd)		Value of construction authorized by building permits, 1990								Wholesale trade, 1987				Retail trade, all establishments, 1987
				Nonresidential				Residential							
					Percent										
	Value of shipments (Mil dol)	New capital expenditures (Mil dol)	Total[1] ($1,000)	Total ($1,000)	Office	Industrial	Stores	New construction ($1,000)	Number of housing units	Alterations and additions ($1,000)	Establishments	Sales (Mil dol)	Paid employees[2]	Annual payroll (Mil dol)	Number
	137	138	139	140	141	142	143	144	145	146	147	148	149	150	151

1. Includes nonresidential additions and alterations, residential nonhousekeeping buildings, and residential garages and carports not shown separately. 2. For pay period including March 12.

Table B. Metropolitan Areas — Retail Trade and Services

Area name	Retail trade, all establishments, 1987 (cont'd)			Retail trade, establishments with payroll, 1987								Taxable service industries–establishments with payroll, 1987				
	Sales				Sales								Receipts (Mil dol)			
						Per capita[1] (Dollars)								Selected kinds of business		
	Total (Mil dol)	Percent change, 1982–1987	Per capita[1] (Dollars)	Number	Total (Mil dol)	General merchandise stores	Food stores	Apparel and accessory stores	Eating and drinking places	Paid employees[2]	Annual payroll (Mil dol)	Number	Total	Hotels, motels & other lodging places	Health services	Legal services
	152	153	154	155	156	157	158	159	160	161	162	163	164	165	166	167

1. Based on the estimated population as of July 1 of the year shown. 2. For the period including March 12 of the year shown.

Table B. Metropolitan Areas — Services, Banking, Federal Funds, and Local Government Finances

Area name	Taxable service Industries–establishments with payroll, 1987 (cont'd)		Banking		Federal funds and grants, 1989							Local government finances, 1981–1982				
						Per capita[3] (Dollars)						General revenue				
														Taxes		
															Per capita[4]	
	Paid employees	Annual payroll (Mil dol)	Bank deposits[1], June 1989 (Mil dol)	Savings capital[2], September 1989 (Mil dol)	Expenditures (Mil dol)	Total	Direct payments for individuals	Procurement contract awards	Salaries and wages	Grant awards	Total (Mil dol)	Intergovernmental (Mil dol)	Total (Mil dol)	Total (Dollars)	Property (Dollars)
	168	169	170	172	174	176	177	178	179	180	181	182	184	185	186

1. Includes deposits for all insured and reporting noninsured commercial and mutual savings banks. 2. Includes savings capital for all FSLIC insured savings institutions. 3. Based on the estimated population as of July 1 of the year shown. 4. Based on the estimated population as of July 1, 1982.

Table B. Metropolitan Areas — Local Gov't. Finances, Gov't. Employment, and Elections

Area name	Local government finances, 1981–1982, (cont'd)										State and local government employment, 1989		Federal government civilian employment, 1989		Elections,[3] 1988	
	Direct general expenditure								Debt outstanding							
				Percent of total for–												
	Total (Mil dol)	Percent change, 1977–1982	Per capita[1] (Dollars)	Education	Health & hospitals	Police protection	Public welfare	Highways	Total (Mil dol)	Per capita[1] (Dollars)	Total	Rate[2]	Total	Earnings ($1,000)	Total vote cast for president	Vote for lead party (Percent)
	187	188	189	190	191	192	193	194	195	196	197	198	199	200	201	202

1. Based on the estimated population as of July 1, 1982. 2. Per 10,000 resident population estimated as of July 1 of the year shown. 3. Data subject to copyright.

COLUMN HEADINGS FOR CITIES

Table C. Cities — Area and Population

MSA/ CMSA Code[1]	State/ Place code	City	Land Area,[2] 1990 (Sq. Km.)	Population						Population characteristics, 1990						
				1990				Change 1980–1990		Percent						
										Race						
				Total persons	Rank	Per sq. km.	1980	Number	Per-cent	White	Black	Am. Indian, Eskimo, Aleut	Asian & Pacific Islander	Other race	His- panic[3]	65 Years and over
			1	2	3	4	5	6	7	8	9	10	11	12	13	14

1. MSA = Metropolitan Statistical Area. CMSA = Consolidated MSA. 2. Dry land or land partially or temporarily covered by water. 3. Hispanic persons may be of any race.

Table C. Cities — Households, Vital Statistics, and Hospitals

City	Households, 1990				Births, 1984			Deaths, 1984				Hospitals, 1985		
			Percent–		Number			Number		Rate			Beds	
	Number	Persons per house- hold	Female family house- holder[1]	One- person[2]	Total	To mothers under 20 yrs. old (Percent)	Rate[3]	Total	Infant[4]	Total[3]	Infant[5]	Number	Number	Rate[6]
	15	16	17	18	19	20	21	22	23	24	25	26	27	28

1. No spouse present. 2. Householder living alone. 3. Per 1,000 resident population estimated as of July 1 of the year shown. 4. Deaths of infants under 1 year old. 5. Deaths of infants under 1 year old per 1,000 live births. 6. Per 100,000 resident population estimated as of July 1, 1986.

Table C. Cities — Crime, Police Officers, Education, Money Income, and Housing

City	Serious crimes known to police, 1985			Police officers, 1985		Educational attainment,[4] 1980		Money income						Housing, 1990		
	Number							Per capita[5]				Percent below poverty level 1979				
								1985		1979						
	Total	Violent[1]	Rate[2]	Number	Rate[3]	Percent com- pleting 12 years or more	Percent com- pleting 16 years or more	Total (Dollars)	Percent of State average	Current dollars	Constant (1985) dollars	Persons	Families	Total units	Percent change, 1980–1990	Vacant units for sale or rent[6]
	29	30	31	32	33	34	35	36	37	38	39	40	41	42	43	44

1. Includes murder and nonnegligent manslaughter, forcible rape, robbery, and aggravated assault. 2. Per 100,000 resident population estimated for 1985 by the FBI. 3. Per 10,000 resident population estimated for 1985 by the FBI. 4. Persons 25 years old or older. 5. Based on the resident population estimated as of July 1, 1988 for 1987 data and enumerated as of April 1, 1980 for 1979 data. 6. Also includes units rented or sold, but not occupied.

Table C. Cities — Housing and Labor Force

City	Housing, 1990 (cont'd)					Construction authorized by building permits, 1990				Civilian labor force, 1990			
	Occupied units					New private housing units						Unemployment	
			Owner-occupied										
	Total	Percent with more than 1 person per room	Percent of total	Median values[1] (Dollars)	Median rent[2] (Dollars)	Number	Value ($1,000)	Percent single family	Non- residential, value ($1,000)	Total	Percent change, 1989–1990	Total	Rate[3]
	45	46	47	48	49	50	51	52	53	54	55	56	57

1. Specified owner-occupied units. 2. Specified renter-occupied units. 3. Percent of total civilian labor force.

COLUMN HEADINGS FOR CITIES

Table C. Cities — Labor Force and Manufactures

City	Employed,[1] 1980			Manufactures, 1987											
		Rate per 1,000 employees		Establishments		All employees			Production workers						
											Wages				
	Total	Professional, specialty, and technical	Precision production, craft, and operators	Total	Percent with 20 or more employees	Number (1,000)	Percent change, 1982–1987	Annual payroll (Mil. dol.)	Number (1,000)	Work-hours (Millions)	Total (Mil. dol.)	Average per production worker (Dollars)	Value added by manufacture (Mil. dol.)	Value of shipments (Mil. dol.)	New capital expenditures (Mil. dol.)
	58	59	60	61	62	63	64	65	66	67	68	69	70	71	72

1. Persons 16 years old and over.

Table C. Cities — Wholesale Trade and Retail Trade

City	Wholesale trade, 1987				Retail trade–all establishments, 1987				Retail trade–establishments with payroll, 1987					
						Sales				Sales				
											Per capita[2] (Dollars)			
	Establishments	Sales (Mil. dol.)	Paid employees[1]	Annual payroll ($1,000)	Number	Total (Mil. dol.)	Percent change, 1982–1987	Per capita[2] (Dollars)	Number	Total (Mil. dol.)	General merchandise group stores	Food stores	Apparel and accessory stores	Eating and drinking places
	73	74	75	76	77	78	79	80	81	82	83	84	85	86

1. For the period including March 12 of the year shown. 2. Based on resident population estimated as of July 1, 1986.

Table C. Cities — Retail Trade, Taxable Service Industries, and Federal Grants

City	Retail trade–establishments with payroll, 1987 (cont'd)			Taxable service industries–establishments with payroll, 1987							Federal grants, 1986		
	Paid employees[1]				Receipts (Mil. dol.)								
						Selected kinds of business							
	Number	Percent change, 1982–1987	Annual payroll (Mil. dol.)	Number	Total	Hotels, motels, and other lodging places	Health services	Legal services	Paid employees[1]	Annual payroll (Mil. dol.)	Procurement contract awards (Mil. dol.)	Grant awards (Mil. dol.)	Federal government civilian employment, 1984
	87	88	89	90	91	92	93	94	95	96	97	98	99

1. For the period including March 12 of the year shown.

COLUMN HEADINGS FOR CITIES

Table C. Cities — Government Employment and City Government Finances

City	City government employment, 1985 (October)			Form of government[2] (As of 1986)	City government finances, 1984–1985												
					General revenue							General expenditure					
						Intergovernmental		Taxes					Per capita[3] (Dol.)		Percent of total for–		
									Per capita[3] (Dollars)								
	Total	Rate[1]	Percent education		Total (Mil. dol.)	Total (Mil. dol.)	Percent from State government	Total (Mil. dol.)	Total	Property	Sales & gross receipts	Total (Mil. dol.)	Total	Capital outlays	Public welfare	Highways	Education
	100	101	102	103	104	105	106	107	108	109	110	111	112	113	114	115	116

1. Per 10,000 population estimated as of July 1, 1986. 2. 1 = Mayor-council; 2 = Council-manager; 3 = Commission. Data subject to copyright. 3. Based on resident population estimated as of July 1, 1986.

Table C. Cities — City Government Finances, Climate and Electric Bills

City	City government finances, 1984–1985 (cont'd)								Climate[2]							Typical monthly electric bills, 1986		
	General expenditure (cont'd)					Debt outstanding			Average daily temperature (Degrees Fahrenheit)							Residential[6]		
	Percent of total for (cont'd)								Mean		Limits							
	Health and hospitals	Police protection	Sewerage and sanitation	Parks and recreation	Housing and community development	Total (Mil. dol.)	Per capita[1] (Dollars)	Percent utility	Jan.	July	Jan.[3]	July[4]	Annual precipitation (Inches)	Heating degree days[5]	Cooling degree days[5]	Total (Dollars)	Percent change, 1980–1986	Commercial[7] (Dollars)
	117	118	119	120	121	122	123	124	125	126	127	128	129	130	131	132	133	134

1. Based on resident population estimated as of July 1, 1986. 2. Represents normal values based on the 30-year period, 1951–1980 (see text). 3. Average daily minimum. 4. Average daily maximum. 5. For definition, see text. 6. As of January 1; based on consumption of 750 kWh. 7. Based on billing demand of 30 kW and consumption of 6,000 kWh.

COLUMN HEADINGS FOR PLACES

Table D. Places — Population, Housing, Income, and Land Area

State/ Place/ MCD[1] code	Place	Population			Population characteristics, 1990						Total housing units, 1990	Per capita income, 1985 (Dollars)	Land area,[3] 1990 (Sq. Km.)
			Places of 10,000 or more		Race								
		1990	1980	Percent change, 1980–1990	White	Black	Am. Indian, Eskimo, Aleut	Asian & Pacific Islander	Other race	Hispanic[2]			
		1	2	3	4	5	6	7	8	9	10	11	12

1. Codes shown are 2-digit FIPS codes for states; 4-digit census place codes for places; and 3-digit FIPS county codes followed by 3-digit census MCD codes for minor civil divisions (MCDs). MCD names are followed by county names in parentheses. 2. Hispanic persons may be of any race. 3. Dry land or land partially or temporarily covered by water.

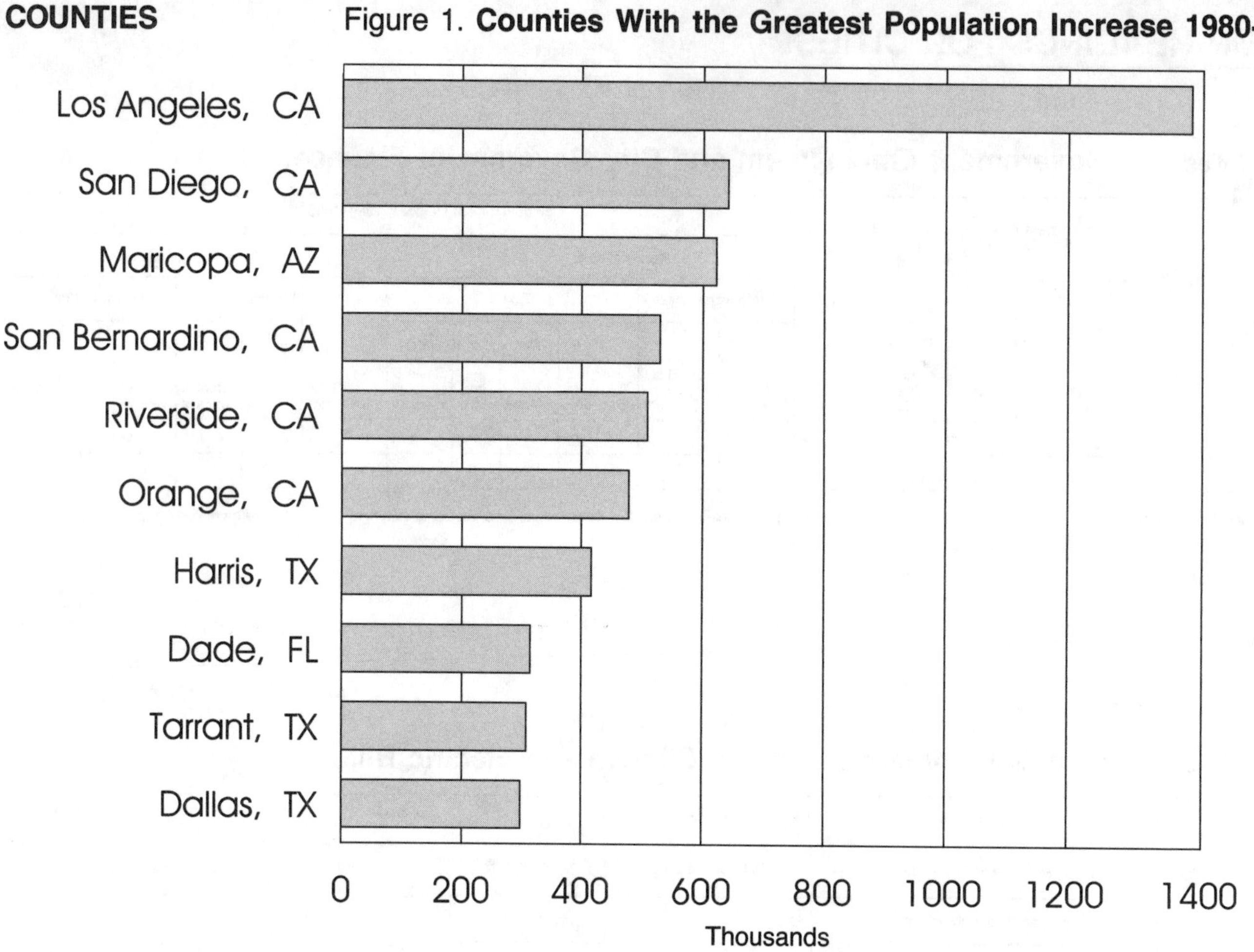

Figure 1. **Counties With the Greatest Population Increase 1980-1990**

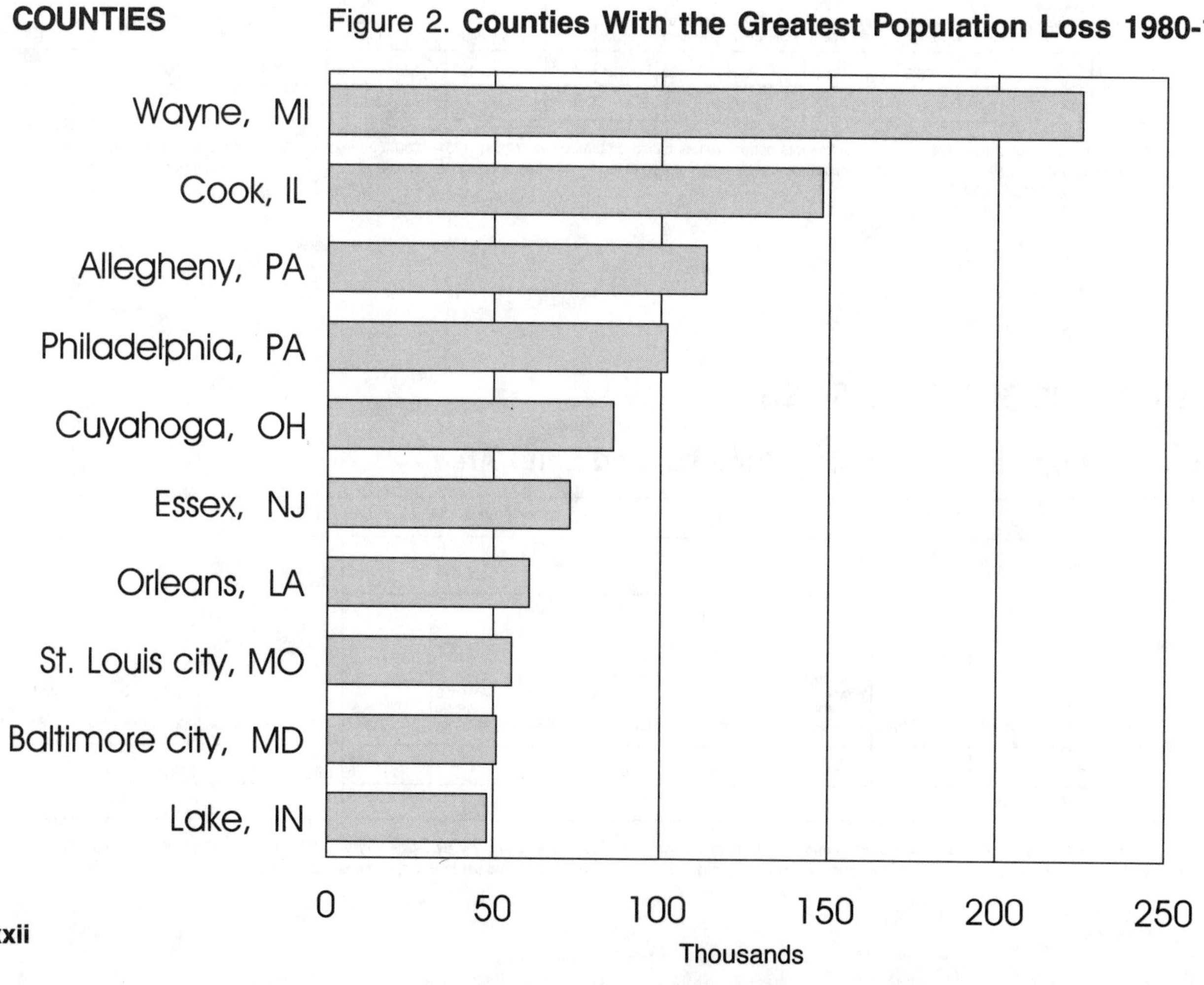

Figure 2. **Counties With the Greatest Population Loss 1980-1990**

Area Rankings:

Selected Rankings of States and Counties, Metropolitan Areas, and Cities

TABLE 1—75 Largest Counties by 1990 Population

Selected Rankings

Total Persons 1990			Population Density (per Square Kilometer) 1990				Population Change 1980–1990			
Rank	County	Population	Population Rank	Density Rank	County	Density	Population Rank	Change Rank	County	Percent Change
1	Los Angeles, CA	8,863,164	15	1	New York, NY	20,377	26	1	Riverside, CA	76.5
2	Cook, IL	5,105,067	6	2	Kings, NY	12,572	52	2	Clark, NV	60.1
3	Harris, TX	2,818,199	24	3	Bronx, NY	11,044	16	3	San Bernardino, CA	58.5
4	San Diego, CA	2,498,016	9	4	Queens, NY	6,896	37	4	Palm Beach, FL	49.7
5	Orange, CA	2,410,556	56	5	San Francisco, CA	5,983	62	5	Orange, FL	43.9
6	Kings, NY	2,300,664	12	6	Philadelphia, PA	4,530	7	6	Maricopa, AZ	40.6
7	Maricopa, AZ	2,122,101	70	7	Suffolk, MA	4,368	45	7	Fairfax, VA	37.4
8	Wayne, MI	2,111,687	53	8	Baltimore city, MD	3,522	27	8	Tarrant, TX	35.9
9	Queens, NY	1,951,598	50	9	Essex, NJ	2,380	4	9	San Diego, CA	34.2
10	Dade, FL	1,937,094	2	10	Cook, IL	2,085	29	10	Sacramento, CA	32.9
11	Dallas, TX	1,852,810	21	11	Nassau, NY	1,733	51	11	Montgomery, MD	30.7
12	Philadelphia, PA	1,585,577	34	12	Milwaukee, WI	1,532	67	12	Fresno, CA	29.7
13	King, WA	1,507,319	44	13	Bergen, NJ	1,360	41	13	Hillsborough, FL	28.9
14	Santa Clara, CA	1,497,577	8	14	Wayne, MI	1,327	66	14	Ventura, CA	26.4
15	New York, NY	1,487,536	17	15	Cuyahoga, OH	1,190	68	15	Pima, AZ	25.5
16	San Bernardino, CA	1,418,380	5	16	Orange, CA	1,179	5	16	Orange, CA	24.7
17	Cuyahoga, OH	1,412,140	39	17	Pinellas, FL	1,173	23	17	Broward, FL	23.3
18	Middlesex, MA	1,398,468	49	18	Du Page, IL	903	47	18	Contra Costa, CA	22.5
19	Allegheny, PA	1,336,449	1	19	Los Angeles, CA	843	25	19	Bexar, TX	19.9
20	Suffolk, NY	1,321,864	64	20	Middlesex, NJ	834	10	20	Dade, FL	19.2
21	Nassau, NY	1,287,348	36	21	Hamilton, OH	821	11	21	Dallas, TX	19.0
22	Alameda, CA	1,279,182	11	22	Dallas, TX	813	13	22	King, WA	18.7
23	Broward, FL	1,255,488	45	23	Fairfax, VA	799	49	23	Du Page, IL	18.6
24	Bronx, NY	1,203,789	35	24	Westchester, NY	780	1	24	Los Angeles, CA	18.5
25	Bexar, TX	1,185,394	48	25	Marion, IN	776	63	25	Duval, FL	17.9
26	Riverside, CA	1,170,413	31	26	St. Louis, MO	756	55	26	Salt Lake, UT	17.3
27	Tarrant, TX	1,170,103	30	27	Hennepin, MN	716	3	27	Harris, TX	17.0
28	Oakland, MI	1,083,592	19	28	Allegheny, PA	707	39	28	Pinellas, FL	16.9
29	Sacramento, CA	1,041,219	33	29	Franklin, OH	687	22	29	Alameda, CA	15.7
30	Hennepin, MN	1,032,431	22	30	Alameda, CA	670	14	30	Santa Clara, CA	15.6
31	St. Louis, MO	993,529	69	31	Jefferson, KY	667	64	31	Middlesex, NJ	12.7
32	Erie, NY	968,532	18	32	Middlesex, MA	656	33	32	Franklin, OH	10.6
33	Franklin, OH	961,437	3	33	Harris, TX	629	72	33	San Mateo, CA	10.6
34	Milwaukee, WI	959,275	75	34	Norfolk, MA	595	73	34	Fulton, GA	10.0
35	Westchester, NY	874,866	51	35	Montgomery, MD	591	59	35	Worcester, MA	9.8
36	Hamilton, OH	866,228	54	36	Prince George's, MD	579	54	36	Prince George's, MD	9.7
37	Palm Beach, FL	863,518	57	37	Macomb, MI	577	40	37	Honolulu, HI	9.7
38	Hartford, CT	851,783	20	38	Suffolk, NY	560	30	38	Hennepin, MN	9.7
39	Pinellas, FL	851,659	72	39	San Mateo, CA	559	28	39	Oakland, MI	7.1
40	Honolulu, HI	836,231	61	40	Montgomery, PA	542	56	40	San Francisco, CA	6.6
41	Hillsborough, FL	834,054	40	41	Honolulu, HI	538	43	41	Shelby, TN	6.3
42	Fairfield, CT	827,645	27	42	Tarrant, TX	523	65	42	Essex, MA	5.7
43	Shelby, TN	826,330	65	43	Essex, MA	519	60	43	Baltimore, MD	5.6
44	Bergen, NJ	825,380	46	44	New Haven, CT	513	46	44	New Haven, CT	5.6
45	Fairfax, VA	818,584	42	45	Fairfield, CT	511	61	45	Montgomery, PA	5.4
46	New Haven, CT	804,219	28	46	Oakland, MI	480	38	46	Hartford, CT	5.4
47	Contra Costa, CA	803,732	73	47	Fulton, GA	474	48	47	Marion, IN	4.2
48	Marion, IN	797,159	14	48	Santa Clara, CA	448	15	48	New York, NY	4.1
49	Du Page, IL	781,666	38	49	Hartford, CT	447	57	49	Macomb, MI	3.3
50	Essex, NJ	778,206	60	50	Baltimore, MD	446	9	50	Queens, NY	3.2
51	Montgomery, MD	757,027	47	51	Contra Costa, CA	431	6	51	Kings, NY	3.1
52	Clark, NV	741,459	43	52	Shelby, TN	423	24	52	Bronx, NY	3.0
53	Baltimore city, MD	736,014	58	53	Monroe, NY	418	20	53	Suffolk, NY	2.9
54	Prince George's, MD	729,268	29	54	Sacramento, CA	416	42	54	Fairfield, CT	2.5
55	Salt Lake, UT	725,956	74	55	Jackson, MO	404	18	55	Middlesex, MA	2.3
56	San Francisco, CA	723,959	23	56	Broward, FL	401	70	56	Suffolk, MA	2.1
57	Macomb, MI	717,400	10	57	Dade, FL	385	31	57	St. Louis, MO	2.0
58	Monroe, NY	713,968	55	58	Salt Lake, UT	380	58	58	Monroe, NY	1.7
59	Worcester, MA	709,705	25	59	Bexar, TX	367	75	59	Norfolk, MA	1.6
60	Baltimore, MD	692,134	32	60	Erie, NY	358	35	60	Westchester, NY	1.0
61	Montgomery, PA	678,111	63	61	Duval, FL	336	74	61	Jackson, MO	0.6
62	Orange, FL	677,491	41	62	Hillsborough, FL	306	34	62	Milwaukee, WI	-0.6
63	Duval, FL	672,971	62	63	Orange, FL	288	36	63	Hamilton, OH	-0.8
64	Middlesex, NJ	671,780	13	64	King, WA	274	44	64	Bergen, NJ	-2.4
65	Essex, MA	670,080	4	65	San Diego, CA	229	21	65	Nassau, NY	-2.6
66	Ventura, CA	669,016	71	66	Jefferson, AL	226	2	66	Cook, IL	-2.8
67	Fresno, CA	667,490	59	67	Worcester, MA	181	69	67	Jefferson, KY	-2.9
68	Pima, AZ	666,880	37	68	Palm Beach, FL	164	71	68	Jefferson, AL	-3.0
69	Jefferson, KY	664,937	66	69	Ventura, CA	140	32	69	Erie, NY	-4.6
70	Suffolk, MA	663,906	7	70	Maricopa, AZ	89	17	70	Cuyahoga, OH	-5.8
71	Jefferson, AL	651,525	26	71	Riverside, CA	63	12	71	Philadelphia, PA	-6.1
72	San Mateo, CA	649,623	67	72	Fresno, CA	43	53	72	Baltimore city, MD	-6.4
73	Fulton, GA	648,951	52	73	Clark, NV	36	19	73	Allegheny, PA	-7.8
74	Jackson, MO	633,232	68	74	Pima, AZ	28	50	74	Essex, NJ	-8.6
75	Norfolk, MA	616,087	16	75	San Bernardino, CA	27	8	75	Wayne, MI	-9.7

TABLE 1—75 Largest Counties by 1990 Population

Selected Rankings

Percent White 1990				Percent Black 1990				Percent Hispanic 1990			
Population Rank	White Rank	County	Percent White	Population Rank	Black Rank	County	Percent Black	Population Rank	Hispanic Rank	County	Percent Hispanic
57	1	Macomb, MI	96.7	53	1	Baltimore city, MD	59.2	25	1	Bexar, TX	49.7
75	2	Norfolk, MA	94.6	54	2	Prince George's, MD	50.7	10	2	Dade, FL	49.2
59	3	Worcester, MA	93.8	73	3	Fulton, GA	49.9	24	3	Bronx, NY	43.5
55	4	Salt Lake, UT	93.0	43	4	Shelby, TN	43.6	1	4	Los Angeles, CA	37.8
18	5	Middlesex, MA	92.1	50	5	Essex, NJ	40.6	67	5	Fresno, CA	35.5
65	6	Essex, MA	92.0	8	6	Wayne, MI	40.2	16	6	San Bernardino, CA	26.7
49	7	Du Page, IL	91.5	12	7	Philadelphia, PA	39.9	66	7	Ventura, CA	26.4
61	8	Montgomery, PA	91.4	6	8	Kings, NY	37.9	26	8	Riverside, CA	26.3
39	9	Pinellas, FL	90.5	24	9	Bronx, NY	37.3	15	9	New York, NY	26.0
20	10	Suffolk, NY	90.0	71	10	Jefferson, AL	35.1	68	10	Pima, AZ	24.5
28	11	Oakland, MI	89.6	2	11	Cook, IL	25.8	5	11	Orange, CA	23.4
30	12	Hennepin, MN	89.3	17	12	Cuyahoga, OH	24.8	3	12	Harris, TX	22.9
19	13	Allegheny, PA	87.5	63	13	Duval, FL	24.4	14	13	Santa Clara, CA	21.0
44	14	Bergen, NJ	87.0	70	14	Suffolk, MA	22.5	4	14	San Diego, CA	20.4
21	15	Nassau, NY	86.6	15	15	New York, NY	22.0	6	15	Kings, NY	20.1
32	16	Erie, NY	85.9	9	16	Queens, NY	21.7	9	16	Queens, NY	19.5
46	17	New Haven, CT	85.5	74	17	Jackson, MO	21.4	72	17	San Mateo, CA	17.6
60	18	Baltimore, MD	84.9	48	18	Marion, IN	21.3	11	18	Dallas, TX	17.0
13	19	King, WA	84.8	36	19	Hamilton, OH	20.9	7	19	Maricopa, AZ	16.3
37	20	Palm Beach, FL	84.8	10	20	Dade, FL	20.5	22	20	Alameda, CA	14.2
7	21	Maricopa, AZ	84.8	34	21	Milwaukee, WI	20.4	56	21	San Francisco, CA	13.9
42	22	Fairfield, CT	84.6	11	22	Dallas, TX	19.9	2	22	Cook, IL	13.6
31	23	St. Louis, MO	84.2	3	23	Harris, TX	19.2	41	23	Hillsborough, FL	12.8
58	24	Monroe, NY	84.1	22	24	Alameda, CA	17.9	50	24	Essex, NJ	12.6
38	25	Hartford, CT	83.5	69	25	Jefferson, KY	17.1	27	25	Tarrant, TX	12.0
41	26	Hillsborough, FL	82.8	33	26	Franklin, OH	15.9	29	26	Sacramento, CA	11.7
64	27	Middlesex, NJ	81.9	23	27	Broward, FL	15.4	47	27	Contra Costa, CA	11.4
69	28	Jefferson, KY	81.9	62	28	Orange, FL	15.2	52	28	Clark, NV	11.2
23	29	Broward, FL	81.7	31	29	St. Louis, MO	14.0	70	29	Suffolk, MA	11.0
33	30	Franklin, OH	81.5	35	30	Westchester, NY	13.7	35	30	Westchester, NY	9.9
45	31	Fairfax, VA	81.3	41	31	Hillsborough, FL	13.2	62	31	Orange, FL	9.6
52	32	Clark, NV	81.3	37	32	Palm Beach, FL	12.5	64	32	Middlesex, NJ	8.9
62	33	Orange, FL	79.6	60	33	Baltimore, MD	12.3	23	33	Broward, FL	8.6
35	34	Westchester, NY	79.4	51	34	Montgomery, MD	12.2	42	34	Fairfield, CT	8.6
66	35	Ventura, CA	79.1	27	35	Tarrant, TX	12.0	38	35	Hartford, CT	8.4
68	36	Pima, AZ	78.7	58	36	Monroe, NY	11.9	37	36	Palm Beach, FL	7.7
5	37	Orange, CA	78.6	32	37	Erie, NY	11.3	51	37	Montgomery, MD	7.4
27	38	Tarrant, TX	78.4	1	38	Los Angeles, CA	11.2	65	38	Essex, MA	7.2
36	39	Hamilton, OH	77.7	19	39	Allegheny, PA	11.2	40	39	Honolulu, HI	6.8
48	40	Marion, IN	77.2	56	40	San Francisco, CA	10.9	20	40	Suffolk, NY	6.6
51	41	Montgomery, MD	76.7	38	41	Hartford, CT	10.2	46	41	New Haven, CT	6.3
26	42	Riverside, CA	76.4	46	42	New Haven, CT	10.2	45	42	Fairfax, VA	6.3
47	43	Contra Costa, CA	76.0	42	43	Fairfield, CT	9.8	44	43	Bergen, NJ	6.0
74	44	Jackson, MO	75.6	52	44	Clark, NV	9.5	55	44	Salt Lake, UT	6.0
29	45	Sacramento, CA	75.1	29	45	Sacramento, CA	9.3	21	45	Nassau, NY	6.0
4	46	San Diego, CA	74.9	47	46	Contra Costa, CA	9.3	12	46	Philadelphia, PA	5.6
34	47	Milwaukee, WI	74.9	21	47	Nassau, NY	8.6	34	47	Milwaukee, WI	4.7
25	48	Bexar, TX	74.1	16	48	San Bernardino, CA	8.1	59	48	Worcester, MA	4.6
16	49	San Bernardino, CA	73.0	64	49	Middlesex, NJ	8.0	49	49	Du Page, IL	4.4
10	50	Dade, FL	72.9	45	50	Fairfax, VA	7.7	54	50	Prince George's, MD	4.1
63	51	Duval, FL	72.8	39	51	Pinellas, FL	7.7	58	51	Monroe, NY	3.7
17	52	Cuyahoga, OH	72.6	28	52	Oakland, MI	7.2	18	52	Middlesex, MA	3.4
72	53	San Mateo, CA	71.9	25	53	Bexar, TX	7.1	74	53	Jackson, MO	3.0
14	54	Santa Clara, CA	68.9	4	54	San Diego, CA	6.4	13	54	King, WA	2.9
11	55	Dallas, TX	67.0	20	55	Suffolk, NY	6.3	63	55	Duval, FL	2.6
70	56	Suffolk, MA	66.1	30	56	Hennepin, MN	5.8	8	56	Wayne, MI	2.4
3	57	Harris, TX	64.7	61	57	Montgomery, PA	5.8	39	57	Pinellas, FL	2.4
71	58	Jefferson, AL	64.2	26	58	Riverside, CA	5.4	32	58	Erie, NY	2.3
67	59	Fresno, CA	63.3	72	59	San Mateo, CA	5.4	17	59	Cuyahoga, OH	2.2
2	60	Cook, IL	62.8	13	60	King, WA	5.1	73	60	Fulton, GA	2.1
22	61	Alameda, CA	59.6	67	61	Fresno, CA	5.0	28	61	Oakland, MI	1.8
15	62	New York, NY	58.3	44	62	Bergen, NJ	4.9	75	62	Norfolk, MA	1.4
9	63	Queens, NY	57.9	14	63	Santa Clara, CA	3.8	30	63	Hennepin, MN	1.4
8	64	Wayne, MI	57.4	7	64	Maricopa, AZ	3.5	61	64	Montgomery, PA	1.2
1	65	Los Angeles, CA	56.8	68	65	Pima, AZ	3.1	60	65	Baltimore, MD	1.2
43	66	Shelby, TN	55.1	40	66	Honolulu, HI	3.1	57	66	Macomb, MI	1.1
56	67	San Francisco, CA	53.6	18	67	Middlesex, MA	2.9	48	67	Marion, IN	1.1
12	68	Philadelphia, PA	53.5	65	68	Essex, MA	2.4	53	68	Baltimore city, MD	1.0
50	69	Essex, NJ	51.1	66	69	Ventura, CA	2.3	31	69	St. Louis, MO	1.0
73	70	Fulton, GA	47.8	59	70	Worcester, MA	2.1	33	70	Franklin, OH	1.0
6	71	Kings, NY	46.9	49	71	Du Page, IL	2.0	43	71	Shelby, TN	0.9
54	72	Prince George's, MD	43.1	75	72	Norfolk, MA	2.0	69	72	Jefferson, KY	0.7
53	73	Baltimore city, MD	39.1	5	73	Orange, CA	1.8	19	73	Allegheny, PA	0.7
24	74	Bronx, NY	35.7	57	74	Macomb, MI	1.4	36	74	Hamilton, OH	0.6
40	75	Honolulu, HI	31.6	55	75	Salt Lake, UT	0.8	71	75	Jefferson, AL	0.4

TABLE 1—75 Largest Counties by 1990 Population

Selected Rankings

Percent Female 1990				Percent Under 5 Years 1990				Percent 75 Years and Over 1990			
Population Rank	Female Rank	County	Percent Female	Population Rank	Under 5 Rank	County	Percent Under 5	Population Rank	75 Plus Rank	County	Percent 75 Plus
24	1	Bronx, NY	53.9	16	1	San Bernardino, CA	9.8	39	1	Pinellas, FL	12.5
12	2	Philadelphia, PA	53.5	55	2	Salt Lake, UT	9.6	37	2	Palm Beach, FL	10.9
6	3	Kings, NY	53.4	67	3	Fresno, CA	9.4	23	3	Broward, FL	10.1
53	4	Baltimore city, MD	53.3	26	4	Riverside, CA	9.0	19	4	Allegheny, PA	7.1
71	5	Jefferson, AL	53.3	3	5	Harris, TX	8.6	56	5	San Francisco, CA	6.6
39	6	Pinellas, FL	53.3	24	6	Bronx, NY	8.5	12	6	Philadelphia, PA	6.5
19	7	Allegheny, PA	53.1	27	7	Tarrant, TX	8.5	10	7	Dade, FL	6.4
17	8	Cuyahoga, OH	53.0	11	8	Dallas, TX	8.4	35	8	Westchester, NY	6.4
15	9	New York, NY	52.9	25	9	Bexar, TX	8.4	17	9	Cuyahoga, OH	6.4
69	10	Jefferson, KY	52.8	1	10	Los Angeles, CA	8.3	61	10	Montgomery, PA	6.4
50	11	Essex, NJ	52.7	49	11	Du Page, IL	8.2	9	11	Queens, NY	6.4
36	12	Hamilton, OH	52.7	8	12	Wayne, MI	8.1	46	12	New Haven, CT	6.3
8	13	Wayne, MI	52.6	63	13	Duval, FL	8.1	75	13	Norfolk, MA	6.3
34	14	Milwaukee, WI	52.6	29	14	Sacramento, CA	8.1	32	14	Erie, NY	6.2
75	15	Norfolk, MA	52.5	43	15	Shelby, TN	8.1	44	15	Bergen, NJ	6.2
35	16	Westchester, NY	52.5	7	16	Maricopa, AZ	8.0	65	16	Essex, MA	6.2
9	17	Queens, NY	52.5	66	17	Ventura, CA	8.0	15	17	New York, NY	6.1
48	18	Marion, IN	52.5	34	18	Milwaukee, WI	7.9	34	18	Milwaukee, WI	6.1
32	19	Erie, NY	52.4	48	19	Marion, IN	7.9	59	19	Worcester, MA	6.0
74	20	Jackson, MO	52.4	6	20	Kings, NY	7.8	38	20	Hartford, CT	6.0
43	21	Shelby, TN	52.4	4	21	San Diego, CA	7.8	71	21	Jefferson, AL	6.0
73	22	Fulton, GA	52.3	36	22	Hamilton, OH	7.8	36	22	Hamilton, OH	5.9
65	23	Essex, MA	52.3	53	23	Baltimore city, MD	7.7	53	23	Baltimore city, MD	5.8
60	24	Baltimore, MD	52.3	52	24	Clark, NV	7.7	74	24	Jackson, MO	5.8
31	25	St. Louis, MO	52.3	5	25	Orange, CA	7.7	69	25	Jefferson, KY	5.6
10	26	Dade, FL	52.1	47	26	Contra Costa, CA	7.6	31	26	St. Louis, MO	5.6
23	27	Broward, FL	52.1	58	27	Monroe, NY	7.6	42	27	Fairfield, CT	5.6
44	28	Bergen, NJ	52.0	33	28	Franklin, OH	7.6	70	28	Suffolk, MA	5.5
37	29	Palm Beach, FL	52.0	54	29	Prince George's, MD	7.6	68	29	Pima, AZ	5.5
46	30	New Haven, CT	52.0	74	30	Jackson, MO	7.6	18	30	Middlesex, MA	5.5
58	31	Monroe, NY	52.0	51	31	Montgomery, MD	7.5	6	31	Kings, NY	5.4
18	32	Middlesex, MA	51.9	59	32	Worcester, MA	7.5	58	32	Monroe, NY	5.4
2	33	Cook, IL	51.9	30	33	Hennepin, MN	7.5	50	33	Essex, NJ	5.4
38	34	Hartford, CT	51.9	22	34	Alameda, CA	7.5	24	34	Bronx, NY	5.4
61	35	Montgomery, PA	51.9	68	35	Pima, AZ	7.5	60	35	Baltimore, MD	5.4
70	36	Suffolk, MA	51.9	14	36	Santa Clara, CA	7.5	26	36	Riverside, CA	5.3
42	37	Fairfield, CT	51.8	2	37	Cook, IL	7.5	21	37	Nassau, NY	5.2
33	38	Franklin, OH	51.8	62	38	Orange, FL	7.4	2	38	Cook, IL	5.1
51	39	Montgomery, MD	51.8	40	39	Honolulu, HI	7.4	30	39	Hennepin, MN	5.1
21	40	Nassau, NY	51.7	73	40	Fulton, GA	7.4	7	40	Maricopa, AZ	5.1
30	41	Hennepin, MN	51.6	12	41	Philadelphia, PA	7.3	72	41	San Mateo, CA	5.0
25	42	Bexar, TX	51.5	65	42	Essex, MA	7.3	8	42	Wayne, MI	4.9
54	43	Prince George's, MD	51.5	41	43	Hillsborough, FL	7.3	48	43	Marion, IN	4.9
57	44	Macomb, MI	51.4	10	44	Dade, FL	7.2	41	44	Hillsborough, FL	4.8
28	45	Oakland, MI	51.4	28	45	Oakland, MI	7.2	13	45	King, WA	4.6
41	46	Hillsborough, FL	51.3	17	46	Cuyahoga, OH	7.1	57	46	Macomb, MI	4.6
59	47	Worcester, MA	51.3	45	47	Fairfax, VA	7.1	20	47	Suffolk, NY	4.5
63	48	Duval, FL	51.2	50	48	Essex, NJ	7.0	4	48	San Diego, CA	4.4
20	49	Suffolk, NY	51.1	46	49	New Haven, CT	7.0	73	49	Fulton, GA	4.4
68	50	Pima, AZ	51.1	13	50	King, WA	7.0	22	50	Alameda, CA	4.4
29	51	Sacramento, CA	51.1	20	51	Suffolk, NY	7.0	28	51	Oakland, MI	4.4
47	52	Contra Costa, CA	51.0	31	52	St. Louis, MO	7.0	67	52	Fresno, CA	4.3
11	53	Dallas, TX	50.8	71	53	Jefferson, AL	6.9	47	53	Contra Costa, CA	4.3
64	54	Middlesex, NJ	50.8	42	54	Fairfield, CT	6.9	43	54	Shelby, TN	4.3
22	55	Alameda, CA	50.7	72	55	San Mateo, CA	6.9	63	55	Duval, FL	4.2
7	56	Maricopa, AZ	50.7	32	56	Erie, NY	6.9	64	56	Middlesex, NJ	4.2
13	57	King, WA	50.7	61	57	Montgomery, PA	6.8	29	57	Sacramento, CA	4.1
72	58	San Mateo, CA	50.7	60	58	Baltimore, MD	6.8	51	58	Montgomery, MD	4.1
49	59	Du Page, IL	50.7	69	59	Jefferson, KY	6.8	62	59	Orange, FL	4.1
27	60	Tarrant, TX	50.5	38	60	Hartford, CT	6.8	1	60	Los Angeles, CA	4.0
67	61	Fresno, CA	50.4	57	61	Macomb, MI	6.8	40	61	Honolulu, HI	4.0
55	62	Salt Lake, UT	50.4	64	62	Middlesex, NJ	6.7	66	62	Ventura, CA	3.9
62	63	Orange, FL	50.4	35	63	Westchester, NY	6.6	25	63	Bexar, TX	3.9
45	64	Fairfax, VA	50.3	75	64	Norfolk, MA	6.5	33	64	Franklin, OH	3.9
3	65	Harris, TX	50.3	18	65	Middlesex, MA	6.5	5	65	Orange, CA	3.8
1	66	Los Angeles, CA	50.1	70	66	Suffolk, MA	6.4	49	66	Du Page, IL	3.5
26	67	Riverside, CA	50.0	19	67	Allegheny, PA	6.3	55	67	Salt Lake, UT	3.5
16	68	San Bernardino, CA	49.9	23	68	Broward, FL	6.3	16	68	San Bernardino, CA	3.5
56	69	San Francisco, CA	49.9	9	69	Queens, NY	6.2	14	69	Santa Clara, CA	3.4
66	70	Ventura, CA	49.6	37	70	Palm Beach, FL	6.2	11	70	Dallas, TX	3.3
5	71	Orange, CA	49.6	21	71	Nassau, NY	6.1	52	71	Clark, NV	3.3
52	72	Clark, NV	49.3	44	72	Bergen, NJ	5.9	27	72	Tarrant, TX	3.3
14	73	Santa Clara, CA	49.3	15	73	New York, NY	5.3	3	73	Harris, TX	2.7
40	74	Honolulu, HI	49.1	39	74	Pinellas, FL	5.2	54	74	Prince George's, MD	2.4
4	75	San Diego, CA	49.0	56	75	San Francisco, CA	4.9	45	75	Fairfax, VA	2.1

TABLE 1—75 Largest Counties by 1990 Population

Selected Rankings

Percent Female Family Households 1990

Population Rank	Fem. HHs. Rank	County	Percent Fem. HHs.
24	1	Bronx, NY	28.0
53	2	Baltimore city, MD	24.6
6	3	Kings, NY	21.5
8	4	Wayne, MI	20.8
12	5	Philadelphia, PA	20.3
50	6	Essex, NJ	19.2
43	7	Shelby, TN	18.6
73	8	Fulton, GA	18.5
70	9	Suffolk, MA	16.6
54	10	Prince George's, MD	16.3
34	11	Milwaukee, WI	15.8
71	12	Jefferson, AL	15.7
2	13	Cook, IL	15.4
17	14	Cuyahoga, OH	14.9
10	15	Dade, FL	14.9
25	16	Bexar, TX	14.5
69	17	Jefferson, KY	14.5
9	18	Queens, NY	14.3
36	19	Hamilton, OH	14.0
67	20	Fresno, CA	13.9
48	21	Marion, IN	13.8
63	22	Duval, FL	13.7
74	23	Jackson, MO	13.6
32	24	Erie, NY	13.3
1	25	Los Angeles, CA	13.1
29	26	Sacramento, CA	13.0
22	27	Alameda, CA	12.9
15	28	New York, NY	12.8
38	29	Hartford, CT	12.7
11	30	Dallas, TX	12.7
3	31	Harris, TX	12.7
33	32	Franklin, OH	12.6
46	33	New Haven, CT	12.5
58	34	Monroe, NY	12.5
19	35	Allegheny, PA	12.5
65	36	Essex, MA	12.4
16	37	San Bernardino, CA	12.1
41	38	Hillsborough, FL	11.9
35	39	Westchester, NY	11.6
62	40	Orange, FL	11.6
42	41	Fairfield, CT	11.3
52	42	Clark, NV	11.2
59	43	Worcester, MA	11.2
60	44	Baltimore, MD	11.1
68	45	Pima, AZ	10.9
47	46	Contra Costa, CA	10.8
27	47	Tarrant, TX	10.8
4	48	San Diego, CA	10.8
31	49	St. Louis, MO	10.7
40	50	Honolulu, HI	10.5
18	51	Middlesex, MA	10.5
20	52	Suffolk, NY	10.4
14	53	Santa Clara, CA	10.3
21	54	Nassau, NY	10.2
7	55	Maricopa, AZ	10.2
57	56	Macomb, MI	10.1
55	57	Salt Lake, UT	10.1
30	58	Hennepin, MN	10.0
75	59	Norfolk, MA	10.0
64	60	Middlesex, NJ	10.0
23	61	Broward, FL	10.0
56	62	San Francisco, CA	9.9
66	63	Ventura, CA	9.8
72	64	San Mateo, CA	9.8
5	65	Orange, CA	9.7
26	66	Riverside, CA	9.6
28	67	Oakland, MI	9.6
39	68	Pinellas, FL	9.4
44	69	Bergen, NJ	9.4
51	70	Montgomery, MD	9.4
13	71	King, WA	9.0
37	72	Palm Beach, FL	8.6
45	73	Fairfax, VA	8.4
61	74	Montgomery, PA	8.3
49	75	Du Page, IL	7.3

Infant Deaths per 1,000 Live Births 1987

Population Rank	Death Rate Rank	County	Infant Death Rate
53	1	Baltimore city, MD	19.2
12	2	Philadelphia, PA	17.3
43	3	Shelby, TN	15.9
8	4	Wayne, MI	15.1
73	5	Fulton, GA	14.2
6	6	Kings, NY	13.9
2	7	Cook, IL	13.8
24	8	Bronx, NY	13.7
74	9	Jackson, MO	13.6
48	10	Marion, IN	13.5
71	11	Jefferson, AL	13.5
37	12	Palm Beach, FL	13.4
50	13	Essex, NJ	13.2
15	14	New York, NY	12.3
63	15	Duval, FL	12.2
54	16	Prince George's, MD	12.0
70	17	Suffolk, MA	11.9
19	18	Allegheny, PA	11.4
9	19	Queens, NY	11.4
17	20	Cuyahoga, OH	11.3
16	21	San Bernardino, CA	11.0
34	22	Milwaukee, WI	10.7
23	23	Broward, FL	10.6
29	24	Sacramento, CA	10.6
21	25	Nassau, NY	10.3
10	26	Dade, FL	10.3
41	27	Hillsborough, FL	10.3
36	28	Hamilton, OH	10.2
32	29	Erie, NY	10.1
7	30	Maricopa, AZ	10.0
30	31	Hennepin, MN	10.0
52	32	Clark, NV	10.0
38	33	Hartford, CT	9.9
3	34	Harris, TX	9.8
31	35	St. Louis, MO	9.8
1	36	Los Angeles, CA	9.8
26	37	Riverside, CA	9.7
60	38	Baltimore, MD	9.7
40	39	Honolulu, HI	9.6
11	40	Dallas, TX	9.5
62	41	Orange, FL	9.4
4	42	San Diego, CA	9.4
46	43	New Haven, CT	9.3
27	44	Tarrant, TX	9.3
35	45	Westchester, NY	9.2
13	46	King, WA	9.2
55	47	Salt Lake, UT	9.1
51	48	Montgomery, MD	9.0
22	49	Alameda, CA	8.9
58	50	Monroe, NY	8.9
69	51	Jefferson, KY	8.9
33	52	Franklin, OH	8.8
25	53	Bexar, TX	8.8
28	54	Oakland, MI	8.8
49	55	Du Page, IL	8.7
67	56	Fresno, CA	8.6
14	57	Santa Clara, CA	8.5
64	58	Middlesex, NJ	8.2
59	59	Worcester, MA	8.1
39	60	Pinellas, FL	8.0
61	61	Montgomery, PA	7.8
20	62	Suffolk, NY	7.8
68	63	Pima, AZ	7.8
56	64	San Francisco, CA	7.7
57	65	Macomb, MI	7.6
65	66	Essex, MA	7.6
5	67	Orange, CA	7.5
42	68	Fairfield, CT	7.4
66	69	Ventura, CA	7.4
45	70	Fairfax, VA	7.2
47	71	Contra Costa, CA	7.1
44	72	Bergen, NJ	6.1
18	73	Middlesex, MA	5.5
75	74	Norfolk, MA	5.4
72	75	San Mateo, CA	5.4

Physicians per 100,000 Population 1989

Population Rank	M.D. Rate Rank	County	M.D. Rate
15	1	New York, NY	917
70	2	Suffolk, MA	827
53	3	Baltimore city, MD	724
56	4	San Francisco, CA	644
51	5	Montgomery, MD	620
35	6	Westchester, NY	518
73	7	Fulton, GA	497
21	8	Nassau, NY	456
61	9	Montgomery, PA	454
75	10	Norfolk, MA	439
12	11	Philadelphia, PA	402
17	12	Cuyahoga, OH	389
46	13	New Haven, CT	388
44	14	Bergen, NJ	384
19	15	Allegheny, PA	382
28	16	Oakland, MI	368
18	17	Middlesex, MA	368
71	18	Jefferson, AL	364
48	19	Marion, IN	358
30	20	Hennepin, MN	357
36	21	Hamilton, OH	349
13	22	King, WA	345
58	23	Monroe, NY	340
10	24	Dade, FL	336
38	25	Hartford, CT	334
50	26	Essex, NJ	333
69	27	Jefferson, KY	316
34	28	Milwaukee, WI	295
43	29	Shelby, TN	292
42	30	Fairfield, CT	289
2	31	Cook, IL	287
32	32	Erie, NY	284
14	33	Santa Clara, CA	278
72	34	San Mateo, CA	277
55	35	Salt Lake, UT	277
68	36	Pima, AZ	275
59	37	Worcester, MA	275
33	38	Franklin, OH	271
49	39	Du Page, IL	268
1	40	Los Angeles, CA	267
3	41	Harris, TX	266
74	42	Jackson, MO	261
5	43	Orange, CA	256
22	44	Alameda, CA	250
11	45	Dallas, TX	245
64	46	Middlesex, NJ	244
9	47	Queens, NY	241
25	48	Bexar, TX	240
29	49	Sacramento, CA	235
41	50	Hillsborough, FL	234
4	51	San Diego, CA	234
40	52	Honolulu, HI	230
24	53	Bronx, NY	223
20	54	Suffolk, NY	222
63	55	Duval, FL	219
47	56	Contra Costa, CA	213
6	57	Kings, NY	211
37	58	Palm Beach, FL	210
62	59	Orange, FL	206
7	60	Maricopa, AZ	201
45	61	Fairfax, VA	198
23	62	Broward, FL	198
39	63	Pinellas, FL	191
65	64	Essex, MA	184
8	65	Wayne, MI	183
67	66	Fresno, CA	182
60	67	Baltimore, MD	175
16	68	San Bernardino, CA	173
54	69	Prince George's, MD	172
66	70	Ventura, CA	171
27	71	Tarrant, TX	143
52	72	Clark, NV	135
26	73	Riverside, CA	121
31	74	St. Louis, MO	114
57	75	Macomb, MI	101

TABLE 1—75 Largest Counties by 1990 Population

Selected Rankings

Hospital Beds per 100,000 Population 1989			
Population Rank	Bed Rate Rank	County	Bed Rate
70	1	Suffolk, MA	1,315
15	2	New York, NY	1,145
53	3	Baltimore city, MD	1,036
73	4	Fulton, GA	965
19	5	Allegheny, PA	907
20	6	Suffolk, NY	826
74	7	Jackson, MO	800
43	8	Shelby, TN	767
36	9	Hamilton, OH	746
71	10	Jefferson, AL	737
56	11	San Francisco, CA	735
17	12	Cuyahoga, OH	718
12	13	Philadelphia, PA	715
50	14	Essex, NJ	708
48	15	Marion, IN	704
39	16	Pinellas, FL	700
34	17	Milwaukee, WI	689
32	18	Erie, NY	685
25	19	Bexar, TX	657
69	20	Jefferson, KY	653
30	21	Hennepin, MN	645
8	22	Wayne, MI	587
61	23	Montgomery, PA	580
59	24	Worcester, MA	580
35	25	Westchester, NY	578
18	26	Middlesex, MA	566
24	27	Bronx, NY	561
3	28	Harris, TX	560
10	29	Dade, FL	560
38	30	Hartford, CT	560
58	31	Monroe, NY	547
41	32	Hillsborough, FL	540
2	33	Cook, IL	539
23	34	Broward, FL	536
46	35	New Haven, CT	492
33	36	Franklin, OH	491
62	37	Orange, FL	482
11	38	Dallas, TX	475
75	39	Norfolk, MA	461
6	40	Kings, NY	458
65	41	Essex, MA	444
63	42	Duval, FL	437
37	43	Palm Beach, FL	436
44	44	Bergen, NJ	435
66	45	Ventura, CA	428
27	46	Tarrant, TX	424
55	47	Salt Lake, UT	422
1	48	Los Angeles, CA	421
68	49	Pima, AZ	420
64	50	Middlesex, NJ	408
42	51	Fairfield, CT	406
9	52	Queens, NY	397
7	53	Maricopa, AZ	395
28	54	Oakland, MI	392
21	55	Nassau, NY	377
40	56	Honolulu, HI	375
51	57	Montgomery, MD	368
16	58	San Bernardino, CA	356
14	59	Santa Clara, CA	356
13	60	King, WA	341
4	61	San Diego, CA	336
52	62	Clark, NV	325
67	63	Fresno, CA	322
22	64	Alameda, CA	317
5	65	Orange, CA	301
72	66	San Mateo, CA	289
29	67	Sacramento, CA	287
47	68	Contra Costa, CA	269
26	69	Riverside, CA	262
60	70	Baltimore, MD	257
49	71	Du Page, IL	256
54	72	Prince George's, MD	228
57	73	Macomb, MI	163
45	74	Fairfax, VA	131
31	75	St. Louis, MO	108

Median Value of Owned Housing 1990			
Population Rank	Median Value Rank	County	Median Value (Dollars)
15	1	New York, NY	487,300
72	2	San Mateo, CA	343,900
56	3	San Francisco, CA	298,900
14	4	Santa Clara, CA	289,400
40	5	Honolulu, HI	283,600
35	6	Westchester, NY	283,500
5	7	Orange, CA	252,700
42	8	Fairfield, CT	249,800
66	9	Ventura, CA	245,300
44	10	Bergen, NJ	227,700
22	11	Alameda, CA	227,200
1	12	Los Angeles, CA	226,400
47	13	Contra Costa, CA	219,400
45	14	Fairfax, VA	213,800
21	15	Nassau, NY	209,500
51	16	Montgomery, MD	200,800
6	17	Kings, NY	196,100
50	18	Essex, NJ	196,100
18	19	Middlesex, MA	192,800
9	20	Queens, NY	191,000
4	21	San Diego, CA	186,700
75	22	Norfolk, MA	182,900
65	23	Essex, MA	176,200
24	24	Bronx, NY	173,900
38	25	Hartford, CT	168,900
20	26	Suffolk, NY	165,900
46	27	New Haven, CT	165,200
64	28	Middlesex, NJ	164,700
70	29	Suffolk, MA	162,100
61	30	Montgomery, PA	143,400
13	31	King, WA	140,100
59	32	Worcester, MA	140,000
26	33	Riverside, CA	139,100
49	34	Du Page, IL	137,100
29	35	Sacramento, CA	129,800
16	36	San Bernardino, CA	129,200
54	37	Prince George's, MD	122,600
2	38	Cook, IL	102,100
60	39	Baltimore, MD	99,900
37	40	Palm Beach, FL	98,400
73	41	Fulton, GA	97,700
28	42	Oakland, MI	95,400
52	43	Clark, NV	93,300
23	44	Broward, FL	91,800
30	45	Hennepin, MN	91,000
58	46	Monroe, NY	90,700
10	47	Dade, FL	86,500
7	48	Maricopa, AZ	85,300
67	49	Fresno, CA	83,600
31	50	St. Louis, MO	83,500
62	51	Orange, FL	81,400
11	52	Dallas, TX	79,200
57	53	Macomb, MI	76,800
68	54	Pima, AZ	76,500
32	55	Erie, NY	74,000
33	56	Franklin, OH	73,800
39	57	Pinellas, FL	73,800
41	58	Hillsborough, FL	73,100
27	59	Tarrant, TX	72,900
36	60	Hamilton, OH	72,200
17	61	Cuyahoga, OH	72,100
55	62	Salt Lake, UT	71,000
43	63	Shelby, TN	66,500
34	64	Milwaukee, WI	65,300
63	65	Duval, FL	64,000
3	66	Harris, TX	63,500
48	67	Marion, IN	61,400
71	68	Jefferson, AL	58,700
74	69	Jackson, MO	58,400
19	70	Allegheny, PA	57,100
69	71	Jefferson, KY	57,000
25	72	Bexar, TX	56,300
53	73	Baltimore city, MD	54,700
12	74	Philadelphia, PA	49,400
8	75	Wayne, MI	48,500

Median Rent 1990			
Population Rank	Median Rent Rank	County	Median Rent (Dollars)
45	1	Fairfax, VA	748
5	2	Orange, CA	728
14	3	Santa Clara, CA	715
72	4	San Mateo, CA	711
51	5	Montgomery, MD	698
20	6	Suffolk, NY	696
66	7	Ventura, CA	695
21	8	Nassau, NY	678
44	9	Bergen, NJ	627
40	10	Honolulu, HI	615
56	11	San Francisco, CA	613
47	12	Contra Costa, CA	613
75	13	Norfolk, MA	612
64	14	Middlesex, NJ	608
54	15	Prince George's, MD	607
42	16	Fairfield, CT	599
18	17	Middlesex, MA	598
1	18	Los Angeles, CA	570
22	19	Alameda, CA	570
49	20	Du Page, IL	568
4	21	San Diego, CA	564
70	22	Suffolk, MA	546
35	23	Westchester, NY	543
65	24	Essex, MA	522
61	25	Montgomery, PA	521
9	26	Queens, NY	513
26	27	Riverside, CA	502
37	28	Palm Beach, FL	499
23	29	Broward, FL	497
28	30	Oakland, MI	495
46	31	New Haven, CT	493
38	32	Hartford, CT	491
16	33	San Bernardino, CA	489
15	34	New York, NY	478
29	35	Sacramento, CA	462
50	36	Essex, NJ	461
52	37	Clark, NV	461
60	38	Baltimore, MD	458
13	39	King, WA	457
30	40	Hennepin, MN	452
59	41	Worcester, MA	448
62	42	Orange, FL	441
57	43	Macomb, MI	437
6	44	Kings, NY	428
10	45	Dade, FL	422
58	46	Monroe, NY	418
2	47	Cook, IL	411
31	48	St. Louis, MO	397
73	49	Fulton, GA	396
7	50	Maricopa, AZ	394
39	51	Pinellas, FL	393
24	52	Bronx, NY	392
11	53	Dallas, TX	389
41	54	Hillsborough, FL	374
27	55	Tarrant, TX	364
34	56	Milwaukee, WI	363
67	57	Fresno, CA	363
12	58	Philadelphia, PA	358
33	59	Franklin, OH	355
63	60	Duval, FL	355
48	61	Marion, IN	345
3	62	Harris, TX	339
68	63	Pima, AZ	338
74	64	Jackson, MO	322
53	65	Baltimore city, MD	321
17	66	Cuyahoga, OH	321
25	67	Bexar, TX	317
55	68	Salt Lake, UT	316
19	69	Allegheny, PA	315
36	70	Hamilton, OH	304
43	71	Shelby, TN	302
8	72	Wayne, MI	297
32	73	Erie, NY	292
69	74	Jefferson, KY	282
71	75	Jefferson, AL	263

TABLE 1—75 Largest Counties by 1990 Population

Selected Rankings

Change in Labor Force 1989–1990				Unemployment Rate 1990				Per Capita Personal Income 1989			
Population Rank	Percent Change Rank	County	Percent Change	Population Rank	Unemployment Rate Rank	County	Unemployment Rate (Percent)	Population Rank	P.C. Personal Income Rank	County	P.C. Personal Income
52	1	Clark, NV	7.1	67	1	Fresno, CA	10.2	15	1	New York, NY	35,193
1	2	Los Angeles, CA	4.9	8	2	Wayne, MI	8.3	42	2	Fairfield, CT	31,438
26	3	Riverside, CA	4.8	24	3	Bronx, NY	8.2	35	3	Westchester, NY	31,188
16	4	San Bernardino, CA	4.6	6	4	Kings, NY	7.9	44	4	Bergen, NJ	30,967
62	5	Orange, FL	4.3	53	5	Baltimore city, MD	7.7	51	5	Montgomery, MD	29,639
64	6	Middlesex, NJ	3.4	26	6	Riverside, CA	7.7	21	6	Nassau, NY	28,678
39	7	Pinellas, FL	2.6	57	7	Macomb, MI	7.5	45	7	Fairfax, VA	28,366
46	8	New Haven, CT	2.5	25	8	Bexar, TX	7.1	72	8	San Mateo, CA	27,659
3	9	Harris, TX	2.3	59	9	Worcester, MA	7.0	56	9	San Francisco, CA	26,454
41	10	Hillsborough, FL	2.2	10	10	Dade, FL	6.7	75	10	Norfolk, MA	26,379
37	11	Palm Beach, FL	2.1	37	11	Palm Beach, FL	6.5	28	11	Oakland, MI	26,052
40	12	Honolulu, HI	2.0	50	12	Essex, NJ	6.4	61	12	Montgomery, PA	25,989
23	13	Broward, FL	2.0	2	13	Cook, IL	6.3	49	13	Du Page, IL	24,958
13	14	King, WA	1.8	65	14	Essex, MA	6.2	18	14	Middlesex, MA	24,923
38	15	Hartford, CT	1.8	12	15	Philadelphia, PA	6.0	14	15	Santa Clara, CA	24,581
63	16	Duval, FL	1.7	9	16	Queens, NY	6.0	37	16	Palm Beach, FL	24,319
67	17	Fresno, CA	1.7	73	17	Fulton, GA	5.9	47	17	Contra Costa, CA	24,308
30	18	Hennepin, MN	1.6	28	18	Oakland, MI	5.8	5	18	Orange, CA	24,288
6	19	Kings, NY	1.5	1	19	Los Angeles, CA	5.8	64	19	Middlesex, NJ	24,139
24	20	Bronx, NY	1.5	15	20	New York, NY	5.8	38	20	Hartford, CT	24,040
9	21	Queens, NY	1.3	16	21	San Bernardino, CA	5.7	65	21	Essex, MA	22,793
27	22	Tarrant, TX	1.3	70	22	Suffolk, MA	5.7	20	22	Suffolk, NY	22,601
45	23	Fairfax, VA	1.3	46	23	New Haven, CT	5.6	31	23	St. Louis, MO	22,598
10	24	Dade, FL	1.2	63	24	Duval, FL	5.6	30	24	Hennepin, MN	22,584
36	25	Hamilton, OH	1.1	23	25	Broward, FL	5.5	13	25	King, WA	22,125
15	26	New York, NY	1.1	66	26	Ventura, CA	5.5	23	26	Broward, FL	21,898
7	27	Maricopa, AZ	1.1	62	27	Orange, FL	5.5	50	27	Essex, NJ	21,873
53	28	Baltimore city, MD	0.9	74	28	Jackson, MO	5.4	46	28	New Haven, CT	21,736
19	29	Allegheny, PA	0.9	11	29	Dallas, TX	5.3	60	29	Baltimore, MD	21,725
42	30	Fairfield, CT	0.8	3	30	Harris, TX	5.3	70	30	Suffolk, MA	21,676
69	31	Jefferson, KY	0.8	27	31	Tarrant, TX	5.3	73	31	Fulton, GA	21,557
33	32	Franklin, OH	0.7	69	32	Jefferson, KY	5.2	39	32	Pinellas, FL	21,255
29	33	Sacramento, CA	0.7	71	33	Jefferson, AL	5.1	58	33	Monroe, NY	21,192
66	34	Ventura, CA	0.6	38	34	Hartford, CT	5.0	22	34	Alameda, CA	20,967
73	35	Fulton, GA	0.5	52	35	Clark, NV	4.9	59	35	Worcester, MA	20,200
43	36	Shelby, TN	0.4	18	36	Middlesex, MA	4.9	66	36	Ventura, CA	20,156
50	37	Essex, NJ	0.4	39	37	Pinellas, FL	4.9	57	37	Macomb, MI	19,984
60	38	Baltimore, MD	0.4	41	38	Hillsborough, FL	4.8	1	38	Los Angeles, CA	19,906
12	39	Philadelphia, PA	0.3	17	39	Cuyahoga, OH	4.8	9	39	Queens, NY	19,835
54	40	Prince George's, MD	0.3	32	40	Erie, NY	4.8	17	40	Cuyahoga, OH	19,722
49	41	Du Page, IL	0.2	75	41	Norfolk, MA	4.8	2	41	Cook, IL	19,658
4	42	San Diego, CA	0.2	29	42	Sacramento, CA	4.7	11	42	Dallas, TX	19,602
2	43	Cook, IL	0.2	42	43	Fairfield, CT	4.7	19	43	Allegheny, PA	19,249
61	44	Montgomery, PA	0.2	48	44	Marion, IN	4.5	40	44	Honolulu, HI	19,171
17	45	Cuyahoga, OH	0.1	4	45	San Diego, CA	4.5	36	45	Hamilton, OH	19,046
31	46	St. Louis, MO	0.0	60	46	Baltimore, MD	4.5	54	46	Prince George's, MD	18,960
51	47	Montgomery, MD	-0.1	43	47	Shelby, TN	4.4	4	47	San Diego, CA	18,651
68	48	Pima, AZ	-0.2	20	48	Suffolk, NY	4.4	52	48	Clark, NV	18,508
74	49	Jackson, MO	-0.3	7	49	Maricopa, AZ	4.3	29	49	Sacramento, CA	18,194
44	50	Bergen, NJ	-0.4	47	50	Contra Costa, CA	4.3	62	50	Orange, FL	18,083
57	51	Macomb, MI	-0.5	31	51	St. Louis, MO	4.2	34	51	Milwaukee, WI	18,062
70	52	Suffolk, MA	-0.5	22	52	Alameda, CA	4.2	10	52	Dade, FL	17,963
65	53	Essex, MA	-0.6	19	53	Allegheny, PA	4.2	3	53	Harris, TX	17,948
75	54	Norfolk, MA	-0.6	64	54	Middlesex, NJ	4.2	33	54	Franklin, OH	17,917
11	55	Dallas, TX	-0.7	34	55	Milwaukee, WI	4.1	69	55	Jefferson, KY	17,783
58	56	Monroe, NY	-0.7	30	56	Hennepin, MN	4.1	48	56	Marion, IN	17,730
55	57	Salt Lake, UT	-0.7	68	57	Pima, AZ	4.1	32	57	Erie, NY	17,724
59	58	Worcester, MA	-0.8	56	58	San Francisco, CA	4.0	7	58	Maricopa, AZ	17,705
32	59	Erie, NY	-0.8	14	59	Santa Clara, CA	4.0	27	59	Tarrant, TX	17,686
71	60	Jefferson, AL	-0.9	33	60	Franklin, OH	3.9	74	60	Jackson, MO	17,328
18	61	Middlesex, MA	-1.1	54	61	Prince George's, MD	3.9	43	61	Shelby, TN	17,301
47	62	Contra Costa, CA	-1.3	36	62	Hamilton, OH	3.9	26	62	Riverside, CA	17,028
28	63	Oakland, MI	-1.4	55	63	Salt Lake, UT	3.8	8	63	Wayne, MI	16,955
72	64	San Mateo, CA	-1.5	61	64	Montgomery, PA	3.7	71	64	Jefferson, AL	16,597
22	65	Alameda, CA	-1.5	44	65	Bergen, NJ	3.7	53	65	Baltimore city, MD	16,311
25	66	Bexar, TX	-1.6	49	66	Du Page, IL	3.6	63	66	Duval, FL	16,074
8	67	Wayne, MI	-1.6	13	67	King, WA	3.4	41	67	Hillsborough, FL	16,044
56	68	San Francisco, CA	-1.8	35	68	Westchester, NY	3.4	67	68	Fresno, CA	15,927
5	69	Orange, CA	-1.9	5	69	Orange, CA	3.4	6	69	Kings, NY	15,683
35	70	Westchester, NY	-1.9	58	70	Monroe, NY	3.3	16	70	San Bernardino, CA	15,635
21	71	Nassau, NY	-2.1	21	71	Nassau, NY	3.3	12	71	Philadelphia, PA	15,479
34	72	Milwaukee, WI	-2.1	72	72	San Mateo, CA	2.8	68	72	Pima, AZ	15,203
20	73	Suffolk, NY	-2.2	51	73	Montgomery, MD	2.7	55	73	Salt Lake, UT	14,315
48	74	Marion, IN	-3.3	40	74	Honolulu, HI	2.6	24	74	Bronx, NY	14,234
14	75	Santa Clara, CA	-4.0	45	75	Fairfax, VA	2.1	25	75	Bexar, TX	14,053

TABLE 2—75 Counties with Highest Agricultural Sales–1987

Selected Rankings

Value of Agricultural Sales 1987			Average Agricultural Sales per Farm 1987				Operators Living on Farm Operated 1987			
Value of Sales Rank	County	Value of Agricultural Sales (Mil Dol)	Value of Sales Rank	Average Sales Rank	County	Average Sales (Dollars)	Value of Sales Rank	Operators Living on Farm Rank	County	Operators Living on Farm Percent
1	Fresno, CA	1,682	30	1	Hansford, TX	906,248	72	1	Marathon, WI	85.3
2	Kern, CA	1,100	52	2	Hartley, TX	899,505	74	2	Dodge, WI	85.1
3	Tulare, CA	1,030	10	3	Imperial, CA	890,790	58	3	Marion, OR	82.6
4	Weld, CO	865	5	4	Palm Beach, FL	877,100	49	4	Stearns, MN	82.4
5	Palm Beach, FL	855	13	5	Deaf Smith, TX	841,486	64	5	Grant, WI	82.3
6	Merced, CA	792	43	6	Haskell, KS	790,379	55	6	Dane, WI	81.5
7	Stanislaus, CA	786	47	7	Grant, KS	763,735	71	7	Ottawa, MI	80.2
8	Monterey, CA	731	54	8	Sherman, TX	729,019	45	8	Chester, PA	79.4
9	Riverside, CA	727	35	9	Scott, KS	716,708	12	9	Lancaster, PA	79.4
10	Imperial, CA	716	21	10	Finney, KS	714,479	42	10	Canyon, ID	79.0
11	San Joaquin, CA	634	59	11	Moore, TX	701,946	39	11	Benton, AR	78.8
12	Lancaster, PA	601	51	12	Wichita, KS	628,830	70	12	Plymouth, IA	78.0
13	Deaf Smith, TX	578	23	13	Yuma, AZ	584,812	32	13	Washington, AR	77.3
14	Maricopa, AZ	549	20	14	Pinal, AZ	551,448	16	14	Yakima, WA	77.3
15	Ventura, CA	538	8	15	Monterey, CA	535,738	4	15	Weld, CO	77.3
16	Yakima, WA	498	27	16	Parmer, TX	524,597	36	16	Rockingham, VA	76.8
17	San Bernardino, CA	489	34	17	Castro, TX	491,190	62	17	Sacramento, CA	76.2
18	Kings, CA	487	38	18	Swisher, TX	490,510	7	18	Stanislaus, CA	75.3
19	San Diego, CA	444	2	19	Kern, CA	487,821	25	19	Sioux, IA	74.9
20	Pinal, AZ	403	22	20	Texas, OK	444,265	60	20	Cullman, AL	74.7
21	Finney, KS	382	44	21	Gray, KS	432,227	37	21	Morgan, CO	73.0
22	Texas, OK	357	18	22	Kings, CA	404,412	57	22	Sonoma, CA	73.0
23	Yuma, AZ	356	68	23	Orange, CA	372,825	28	23	Cuming, NE	72.7
24	Grant, WA	351	37	24	Morgan, CO	345,288	24	24	Grant, WA	71.9
25	Sioux, IA	349	65	25	Phelps, NE	311,507	29	25	Sussex, DE	71.7
26	Madera, CA	346	31	26	Dawson, NE	307,603	66	26	Logan, CO	70.5
27	Parmer, TX	343	4	27	Weld, CO	290,623	18	27	Kings, CA	70.5
28	Cuming, NE	338	28	28	Cuming, NE	285,425	17	28	San Bernardino, CA	69.9
29	Sussex, DE	330	48	29	Ford, KS	282,121	11	29	San Joaquin, CA	69.1
30	Hansford, TX	311	6	30	Merced, CA	259,877	73	30	Adams, WA	68.8
31	Dawson, NE	300	15	31	Ventura, CA	253,547	6	31	Merced, CA	68.5
32	Washington, AR	299	17	32	San Bernardino, CA	252,187	1	32	Fresno, CA	67.8
33	Santa Barbara, CA	288	14	33	Maricopa, AZ	235,128	50	33	Hillsborough, FL	66.4
34	Castro, TX	281	73	34	Adams, WA	226,706	65	34	Phelps, NE	66.1
35	Scott, KS	280	1	35	Fresno, CA	221,545	56	35	Duplin, NC	65.6
36	Rockingham, VA	277	66	36	Logan, CO	202,311	63	36	Los Angeles, CA	65.4
37	Morgan, CO	276	26	37	Madera, CA	197,921	75	37	Yuma, CO	64.6
38	Swisher, TX	268	29	38	Sussex, DE	190,602	19	38	San Diego, CA	63.9
39	Benton, AR	263	9	39	Riverside, CA	187,636	69	39	Sampson, NC	63.8
40	Polk, FL	261	24	40	Grant, WA	186,586	31	40	Dawson, NE	61.4
41	Dade, FL	251	75	41	Yuma, CO	184,869	14	41	Maricopa, AZ	61.3
42	Canyon, ID	249	61	42	Orange, FL	175,483	3	42	Tulare, CA	61.1
43	Haskell, KS	249	3	43	Tulare, CA	174,328	67	43	Sutter, CA	60.5
44	Gray, KS	236	25	44	Sioux, IA	173,001	47	44	Grant, KS	58.7
45	Chester, PA	235	7	45	Stanislaus, CA	169,745	9	45	Riverside, CA	55.9
46	Hidalgo, TX	233	33	46	Santa Barbara, CA	163,876	41	46	Dade, FL	55.5
47	Grant, KS	231	41	47	Dade, FL	154,356	26	47	Madera, CA	55.4
48	Ford, KS	229	45	48	Chester, PA	149,149	21	48	Finney, KS	55.4
49	Stearns, MN	224	36	49	Rockingham, VA	146,263	48	49	Ford, KS	55.2
50	Hillsborough, FL	223	11	50	San Joaquin, CA	145,144	53	50	Hawaii, HI	54.9
51	Wichita, KS	223	56	51	Duplin, NC	140,343	33	51	Santa Barbara, CA	54.7
52	Hartley, TX	221	67	52	Sutter, CA	131,637	51	52	Wichita, KS	54.6
53	Hawaii, HI	220	69	53	Sampson, NC	126,833	44	53	Gray, KS	54.5
54	Sherman, TX	217	12	54	Lancaster, PA	125,816	43	54	Haskell, KS	54.0
55	Dane, WI	216	71	55	Ottawa, MI	124,378	8	55	Monterey, CA	53.8
56	Duplin, NC	215	42	56	Canyon, ID	123,977	15	56	Ventura, CA	53.1
57	Sonoma, CA	209	62	57	Sacramento, CA	123,272	61	57	Orange, FL	53.0
58	Marion, OR	208	46	58	Hidalgo, TX	120,837	22	58	Texas, OK	52.9
59	Moore, TX	208	16	59	Yakima, WA	117,496	2	59	Kern, CA	49.4
60	Cullman, AL	197	39	60	Benton, AR	107,941	27	60	Parmer, TX	48.9
61	Orange, FL	197	70	61	Plymouth, IA	105,525	46	61	Hidalgo, TX	48.6
62	Sacramento, CA	196	32	62	Washington, AR	104,696	38	62	Swisher, TX	47.3
63	Los Angeles, CA	194	40	63	Polk, FL	98,813	13	63	Deaf Smith, TX	47.2
64	Grant, WI	193	63	64	Los Angeles, CA	95,394	20	64	Pinal, AZ	45.3
65	Phelps, NE	192	60	65	Cullman, AL	89,143	68	65	Orange, CA	44.8
66	Logan, CO	191	74	66	Dodge, WI	84,216	40	66	Polk, FL	44.4
67	Sutter, CA	189	50	67	Hillsborough, FL	80,793	35	67	Scott, KS	44.2
68	Orange, CA	188	58	68	Marion, OR	80,317	5	68	Palm Beach, FL	42.6
69	Sampson, NC	187	53	69	Hawaii, HI	78,205	23	69	Yuma, AZ	42.2
70	Plymouth, IA	184	64	70	Grant, WI	78,089	34	70	Castro, TX	40.0
71	Ottawa, MI	183	55	71	Dane, WI	75,976	30	71	Hansford, TX	39.7
72	Marathon, WI	183	19	72	San Diego, CA	70,938	10	72	Imperial, CA	39.3
73	Adams, WA	182	49	73	Stearns, MN	70,484	54	73	Sherman, TX	35.4
74	Dodge, WI	181	57	74	Sonoma, CA	68,794	52	74	Hartley, TX	32.9
75	Yuma, CO	180	72	75	Marathon, WI	59,616	59	75	Moore, TX	29.3

TABLE 3—75 Counties with Largest Number of Manufacturing Employees–1987

Selected Rankings

Number of Manufacturing Employees 1987			Value Added by Manufacture 1987				New Manufacturing Capital Expenditures 1987			
Number of Employees Rank	County	Number of Manu-facturing Employees (1,000)	Number of Employees Rank	Value Added Rank	County	Value Added (Mil Dol)	Number of Employees Rank	New Capital Rank	County	New Capital Expendi-tures (Mil Dol)
1	Los Angeles, CA	881.0	1	1	Los Angeles, CA	50,905.6	1	1	Los Angeles, CA	2,995.5
2	Cook, IL	491.6	2	2	Cook, IL	31,463.1	3	2	Santa Clara, CA	1,742.9
3	Santa Clara, CA	275.7	3	3	Santa Clara, CA	20,865.3	2	3	Cook, IL	1,478.6
4	New York, NY	255.4	4	4	New York, NY	16,406.8	6	4	Wayne, MI	1,147.2
5	Orange, CA	254.6	5	5	Orange, CA	14,860.0	10	5	Harris, TX	1,017.9
6	Wayne, MI	229.7	10	6	Harris, TX	13,474.8	5	6	Orange, CA	881.6
7	Dallas, TX	182.5	6	7	Wayne, MI	12,335.3	8	7	Middlesex, MA	791.8
8	Middlesex, MA	176.6	20	8	Monroe, NY	11,173.7	9	8	Cuyahoga, OH	728.1
9	Cuyahoga, OH	163.8	8	9	Middlesex, MA	10,839.9	7	9	Dallas, TX	664.1
10	Harris, TX	150.5	7	10	Dallas, TX	10,369.7	12	10	Maricopa, AZ	655.2
11	King, WA	140.8	13	11	Hamilton, OH	9,807.3	20	11	Monroe, NY	625.4
12	Maricopa, AZ	135.8	9	12	Cuyahoga, OH	8,881.5	13	12	Hamilton, OH	582.7
13	Hamilton, OH	124.8	18	13	Oakland, MI	8,437.0	28	13	St. Louis, MO	515.6
14	Hennepin, MN	122.0	12	14	Maricopa, AZ	8,179.8	41	14	Kent, MI	509.0
15	San Diego, CA	120.0	11	15	King, WA	7,659.7	14	15	Hennepin, MN	484.6
16	Fairfield, CT	117.0	14	16	Hennepin, MN	7,034.6	11	16	King, WA	439.5
17	Hartford, CT	112.5	34	17	Alameda, CA	6,882.6	15	17	San Diego, CA	429.0
18	Oakland, MI	111.3	45	18	Jefferson, KY	6,651.4	17	18	Hartford, CT	428.1
19	Macomb, MI	110.8	17	19	Hartford, CT	6,484.2	37	19	Middlesex, NJ	410.1
20	Monroe, NY	109.6	25	20	Montgomery, PA	6,477.9	18	20	Oakland, MI	408.9
21	Milwaukee, WI	107.0	32	21	Essex, MA	6,470.9	4	21	New York, NY	391.3
22	Bergen, NJ	101.3	16	22	Fairfield, CT	6,441.4	29	22	Marion, IN	373.0
23	Suffolk, NY	98.3	15	23	San Diego, CA	6,426.8	25	23	Montgomery, PA	353.7
24	Philadelphia, PA	95.9	37	24	Middlesex, NJ	6,172.4	19	24	Macomb, MI	351.1
25	Montgomery, PA	92.5	21	25	Milwaukee, WI	6,027.2	75	25	Forsyth, NC	340.5
26	Dade, FL	89.3	29	26	Marion, IN	5,813.5	21	26	Milwaukee, WI	324.5
27	Nassau, NY	88.8	19	27	Macomb, MI	5,753.9	31	27	St. Louis city, MO	318.3
28	St. Louis, MO	86.4	23	28	Suffolk, NY	5,558.8	32	28	Essex, MA	310.9
29	Marion, IN	82.7	75	29	Forsyth, NC	5,469.7	34	29	Alameda, CA	310.2
30	Allegheny, PA	82.7	27	30	Nassau, NY	5,356.2	16	30	Fairfield, CT	303.5
31	St. Louis city, MO	82.6	33	31	Erie, NY	5,255.8	23	31	Suffolk, NY	295.7
32	Essex, MA	82.4	22	32	Bergen, NJ	5,251.2	38	32	New Haven, CT	295.5
33	Erie, NY	80.4	31	33	St. Louis city, MO	5,232.2	50	33	Sedgwick, KS	286.8
34	Alameda, CA	79.3	24	34	Philadelphia, PA	5,084.5	33	34	Erie, NY	280.8
35	Kings, NY	77.9	28	35	St. Louis, MO	4,879.6	45	35	Jefferson, KY	272.9
36	Providence, RI	77.5	42	36	Union, NJ	4,781.6	53	36	Fulton, GA	268.9
37	Middlesex, NJ	76.3	44	37	Ramsey, MN	4,606.0	54	37	Lancaster, PA	264.7
38	New Haven, CT	76.2	51	38	Franklin, OH	4,419.1	27	38	Nassau, NY	263.8
39	Montgomery, OH	75.4	41	39	Kent, MI	4,379.0	48	39	Westchester, NY	258.0
40	Queens, NY	74.6	53	40	Fulton, GA	4,342.0	63	40	Lake, IL	255.4
41	Kent, MI	73.8	38	41	New Haven, CT	4,247.5	39	41	Montgomery, OH	251.3
42	Union, NJ	69.7	39	42	Montgomery, OH	4,190.7	49	42	Essex, NJ	246.8
43	Worcester, MA	69.4	65	43	Baltimore city, MD	4,064.2	44	43	Ramsey, MN	246.1
44	Ramsey, MN	68.9	58	44	Jackson, MO	4,019.2	61	44	York, PA	241.8
45	Jefferson, KY	68.0	50	45	Sedgwick, KS	3,969.6	43	45	Worcester, MA	237.0
46	Du Page, IL	67.5	43	46	Worcester, MA	3,908.1	22	46	Bergen, NJ	236.5
47	Bristol, MA	66.8	54	47	Lancaster, PA	3,883.7	42	47	Union, NJ	234.1
48	Westchester, NY	66.5	49	48	Essex, NJ	3,802.5	46	48	Du Page, IL	230.9
49	Essex, NJ	66.0	46	49	Du Page, IL	3,628.3	51	49	Franklin, OH	221.2
50	Sedgwick, KS	64.8	66	50	Shelby, TN	3,582.5	24	50	Philadelphia, PA	213.3
51	Franklin, OH	64.6	26	51	Dade, FL	3,561.9	74	51	Hudson, NJ	212.7
52	Passaic, NJ	61.4	55	52	Guilford, NC	3,559.1	70	52	New Castle, DE	212.0
53	Fulton, GA	60.8	40	53	Queens, NY	3,452.9	71	53	Salt Lake, UT	200.2
54	Lancaster, PA	60.0	30	54	Allegheny, PA	3,442.4	59	54	Mecklenburg, NC	196.8
55	Guilford, NC	56.9	56	55	Baltimore, MD	3,431.7	47	55	Bristol, MA	196.1
56	Baltimore, MD	56.0	35	56	Kings, NY	3,295.3	65	56	Baltimore city, MD	193.4
57	Summit, OH	55.2	60	57	Norfolk, MA	3,065.3	36	57	Providence, RI	193.0
58	Jackson, MO	54.7	36	58	Providence, RI	3,045.3	60	58	Norfolk, MA	186.3
59	Mecklenburg, NC	53.6	52	59	Passaic, NJ	2,985.9	56	59	Baltimore, MD	184.9
60	Norfolk, MA	53.0	73	60	Morris, NJ	2,977.2	72	60	Berks, PA	184.5
61	York, PA	52.1	63	61	Lake, IL	2,920.7	58	61	Jackson, MO	184.0
62	Greenville, SC	51.1	47	62	Bristol, MA	2,882.9	30	62	Allegheny, PA	183.8
63	Lake, IL	50.9	69	63	Davidson, TN	2,881.8	62	63	Greenville, SC	180.0
64	San Bernardino, CA	50.8	48	64	Westchester, NY	2,789.8	68	64	Bucks, PA	170.5
65	Baltimore city, MD	50.4	64	65	San Bernardino, CA	2,780.2	69	65	Davidson, TN	165.5
66	Shelby, TN	50.3	62	66	Greenville, SC	2,728.3	57	66	Summit, OH	160.0
67	Elkhart, IN	50.0	61	67	York, PA	2,671.1	64	67	San Bernardino, CA	159.7
68	Bucks, PA	48.5	67	68	Elkhart, IN	2,640.8	52	68	Passaic, NJ	144.3
69	Davidson, TN	48.1	74	69	Hudson, NJ	2,635.9	55	69	Guilford, NC	142.5
70	New Castle, DE	47.7	72	70	Berks, PA	2,628.6	26	70	Dade, FL	132.0
71	Salt Lake, UT	47.5	68	71	Bucks, PA	2,590.3	40	71	Queens, NY	130.7
72	Berks, PA	47.3	59	72	Mecklenburg, NC	2,579.5	73	72	Morris, NJ	119.7
73	Morris, NJ	46.7	71	73	Salt Lake, UT	2,556.0	67	73	Elkhart, IN	113.5
74	Hudson, NJ	46.0	70	74	New Castle, DE	2,474.0	35	74	Kings, NY	112.4
75	Forsyth, NC	45.4	57	75	Summit, OH	2,341.6	66	75	Shelby, TN	D

TABLE 4—75 Largest Metropolitan Areas by 1990 Population

Selected Rankings

Total Persons 1990			Population Density (per Square Kilometer) 1990			
Rank	Metro Area	Population	Population Rank	Density Rank	Metro Area	Density
1	N.Y.-North N.J.-Long Island,NY-NJ-CT	17,953,372	1	1	N.Y.-North N.J.-Long Island,NY-NJ-CT	990.0
2	Los Angeles-Anaheim-Riverside, CA	14,531,529	9	2	Boston-Lawrence-Salem, MA	598.6
3	Chicago-Gary-Lake County, IL-IN-WI	8,065,633	3	3	Chicago-Gary-Lake County, IL-IN-WI	554.2
4	San Francisco-Oakland-San Jose, CA	6,253,311	51	4	Honolulu, HI	538.1
5	Phila.-Willming.-Trenton,PA-NJ-DE-MD	5,899,345	52	5	New Haven-Waterbury-Meriden, CT	512.6
6	Detroit-Ann Arbor, MI	4,665,236	5	6	Phila.-Willming.-Trenton,PA-NJ-DE-MD	426.1
7	Washington, DC-MD-VA	3,923,574	11	7	Miami-Fort Lauderdale, FL	390.9
8	Dallas-Fort Worth, TX	3,885,415	7	8	Washington, DC-MD-VA	381.9
9	Boston-Lawrence-Salem, MA	3,783,817	45	9	Providence-Pawtucket-Fall Rvr, RI-MA	376.1
10	Houston-Galveston-Brazoria, TX	3,711,043	13	10	Cleveland-Akron-Lorain, OH	366.2
11	Miami-Fort Lauderdale, FL	3,192,582	18	11	Baltimore, MD	352.5
12	Atlanta, GA	2,833,511	75	12	New Bedford, MA	351.6
13	Cleveland-Akron-Lorain, OH	2,759,823	6	13	Detroit-Ann Arbor, MI	348.0
14	Seattle-Tacoma, WA	2,559,164	24	14	Milwaukee-Racine, WI	346.0
15	San Diego, CA	2,498,016	4	15	San Francisco-Oakland-San Jose, CA	327.7
16	Minneaolis-St. Paul, MN-WI	2,464,124	28	16	Norfolk-Virginia B.-Newport News, VA	319.9
17	St. Louis, MO-IL	2,444,099	21	17	Tampa-St. Petersburg-Clearwater, FL	312.5
18	Baltimore, MD	2,382,172	33	18	Buffalo-Niagara Falls, NY	292.9
19	Pittsburgh-Beaver Valley, PA	2,242,798	35	19	Hartford-New Britain-Middletown, CT	286.4
20	Phoenix, AZ	2,122,101	23	20	Cincinnati-Hamilton, OH-KY-IN	259.7
21	Tampa-St. Petersburg-Clearwater, FL	2,067,959	37	21	Salt Lake City-Ogden, UT	255.9
22	Denver-Boulder, CO	1,848,319	15	22	San Diego, CA	229.4
23	Cincinnati-Hamilton, OH-KY-IN	1,744,124	19	23	Pittsburgh-Beaver Valley, PA	225.8
24	Milwaukee-Racine, WI	1,607,183	69	24	El Paso, TX	225.5
25	Kansas City, MO-KS	1,566,280	43	25	Dayton-Springfield, OH	218.1
26	Sacramento, CA	1,481,102	8	26	Dallas-Fort Worth, TX	215.3
27	Portland-Vancouver, OR-WA	1,477,895	12	27	Atlanta, GA	213.6
28	Norfolk-Virginia B.-Newport News, VA	1,396,107	32	28	New Orleans, LA	207.2
29	Columbus, OH	1,377,419	68	29	Springfield, MA	202.9
30	San Antonio, TX	1,302,099	10	30	Houston-Galveston-Brazoria, TX	201.6
31	Indianapolis, IN	1,249,822	30	31	San Antonio, TX	199.5
32	New Orleans, LA	1,238,816	16	32	Minneaolis-St. Paul, MN-WI	188.3
33	Buffalo-Niagara Falls, NY	1,189,288	59	33	Grand Rapids, MI	186.9
34	Charlotte-Gastonia-Rock Hill, NC-SC	1,162,093	60	34	Allentown-Bethlehem, PA-NJ	181.5
35	Hartford-New Britain-Middletown, CT	1,123,678	57	35	Worcester-Fitchburg-Leominster, MA	181.1
36	Orlando, FL	1,072,748	17	36	St. Louis, MO-IL	177.0
37	Salt Lake City-Ogden, UT	1,072,227	66	37	Toledo, OH	173.7
38	Rochester, NY	1,002,410	14	38	Seattle-Tacoma, WA	167.7
39	Nashville, TN	985,026	2	39	Los Angeles-Anaheim-Riverside, CA	165.2
40	Memphis, TN-AR-MS	981,747	40	40	Memphis, TN-AR-MS	164.6
41	Oklahoma City, OK	958,839	50	41	W. Palm Beach-Boca Raton-Delray, FL	163.9
42	Louisville, KY-IN	952,662	36	42	Orlando, FL	163.2
43	Dayton-Springfield, OH	951,270	42	43	Louisville, KY-IN	162.3
44	Greensboro-Winston-Salem-High Pt.,NC	942,091	22	44	Denver-Boulder, CO	158.5
45	Providence-Pawtucket-Fall Rvr, RI-MA	916,270	31	45	Indianapolis, IN	157.1
46	Birmingham, AL	907,810	29	46	Columbus, OH	148.6
47	Jacksonville, FL	906,727	55	47	Raleigh-Durham, NC	140.9
48	Albany-Schenectady-Troy, NY	874,304	34	48	Charlotte-Gastonia-Rock Hill, NC-SC	132.8
49	Richmond-Petersburg, VA	865,640	47	49	Jacksonville, FL	132.8
50	W. Palm Beach-Boca Raton-Delray, FL	863,518	38	50	Rochester, NY	132.0
51	Honolulu, HI	836,231	27	51	Portland-Vancouver, OR-WA	130.6
52	New Haven-Waterbury-Meriden, CT	804,219	72	52	Baton Rouge, LA	128.6
53	Austin, TX	781,572	65	53	Omaha, NE	124.6
54	Las Vegas, NV	741,459	25	54	Kansas City, MO-KS	121.2
55	Raleigh-Durham, NC	735,480	64	55	Greenville-Spartanburg, SC	117.8
56	Scranton-Wilkes Barre, PA	734,175	70	56	Harrisburg-Lebanon-Carlisle, PA	114.0
57	Worcester-Fitchburg-Leominster, MA	709,705	49	57	Richmond-Petersburg, VA	113.5
58	Tulsa, OK	708,954	26	58	Sacramento, CA	112.3
59	Grand Rapids, MI	688,399	53	59	Austin, TX	108.1
60	Allentown-Bethlehem, PA-NJ	686,688	63	60	Syracuse, NY	106.6
61	Fresno, CA	667,490	44	61	Greensboro-Winston-Salem-High Pt.,NC	105.4
62	Tucson, AZ	666,880	48	62	Albany-Schenectady-Troy, NY	103.9
63	Syracuse, NY	659,864	56	63	Scranton-Wilkes Barre, PA	99.8
64	Greenville-Spartanburg, SC	640,861	39	64	Nashville, TN	93.4
65	Omaha, NE	618,262	20	65	Phoenix, AZ	89.0
66	Toledo, OH	614,128	46	66	Birmingham, AL	88.0
67	Knoxville, TN	604,816	41	67	Oklahoma City, OK	87.2
68	Springfield, MA	602,878	67	68	Knoxville, TN	84.2
69	El Paso, TX	591,610	74	69	Charleston, SC	75.5
70	Harrisburg-Lebanon-Carlisle, PA	587,986	73	70	Little Rock-North Little Rock, AR	68.1
71	Bakersfield, CA	543,477	58	71	Tulsa, OK	54.6
72	Baton Rouge, LA	528,264	61	72	Fresno, CA	43.2
73	Little Rock-North Little Rock, AR	513,117	54	73	Las Vegas, NV	36.2
74	Charleston, SC	506,875	62	74	Tucson, AZ	28.0
75	New Bedford, MA	506,325	71	75	Bakersfield, CA	25.8

TABLE 4—75 Largest Metropolitan Areas by 1990 Population

Selected Rankings

Population Change 1980–1990

Population Rank	Change Rank	Metro Area	Percent Change
54	1	Las Vegas, NV	60.1
36	2	Orlando, FL	53.3
50	3	W. Palm Beach-Boca Raton-Delray, FL	49.7
53	4	Austin, TX	45.6
20	5	Phoenix, AZ	40.6
71	6	Bakersfield, CA	34.8
26	7	Sacramento, CA	34.7
15	8	San Diego, CA	34.2
8	9	Dallas-Fort Worth, TX	32.6
12	10	Atlanta, GA	32.5
55	11	Raleigh-Durham, NC	31.2
61	12	Fresno, CA	29.7
21	13	Tampa-St. Petersburg-Clearwater, FL	28.2
2	14	Los Angeles-Anaheim-Riverside, CA	26.4
47	15	Jacksonville, FL	25.5
62	16	Tucson, AZ	25.5
69	17	El Paso, TX	23.3
14	18	Seattle-Tacoma, WA	22.3
30	19	San Antonio, TX	21.5
11	20	Miami-Fort Lauderdale, FL	20.8
7	21	Washington, DC-MD-VA	20.7
28	22	Norfolk-Virginia B.-Newport News, VA	20.3
10	23	Houston-Galveston-Brazoria, TX	19.7
34	24	Charlotte-Gastonia-Rock Hill, NC-SC	19.6
74	25	Charleston, SC	17.8
37	26	Salt Lake City-Ogden, UT	17.8
4	27	San Francisco-Oakland-San Jose, CA	16.5
39	28	Nashville, TN	15.8
16	29	Minneapolis-St. Paul, MN-WI	15.3
59	30	Grand Rapids, MI	14.4
22	31	Denver-Boulder, CO	14.2
27	32	Portland-Vancouver, OR-WA	13.9
49	33	Richmond-Petersburg, VA	13.7
64	34	Greenville-Spartanburg, SC	12.4
41	35	Oklahoma City, OK	11.4
29	36	Columbus, OH	10.7
44	37	Greensboro-Winston-Salem-High Pt.,NC	10.6
57	38	Worcester-Fitchburg-Leominster, MA	9.8
51	39	Honolulu, HI	9.7
25	40	Kansas City, MO-KS	9.3
18	41	Baltimore, MD	8.3
60	42	Allentown-Bethlehem, PA-NJ	8.1
73	43	Little Rock-North Little Rock, AR	8.1
1	44	N.Y.-North N.J.-Long Island,NY-NJ-CT	8.1
58	45	Tulsa, OK	7.9
40	46	Memphis, TN-AR-MS	7.5
31	47	Indianapolis, IN	7.1
72	48	Baton Rouge, LA	6.9
67	49	Knoxville, TN	6.9
35	50	Hartford-New Britain-Middletown, CT	6.9
75	51	New Bedford, MA	6.7
45	52	Providence-Pawtucket-Fall Rvr, RI-MA	5.8
70	53	Harrisburg-Lebanon-Carlisle, PA	5.7
65	54	Omaha, NE	5.7
52	55	New Haven-Waterbury-Meriden, CT	5.6
23	56	Cincinnati-Hamilton, OH-KY-IN	5.1
48	57	Albany-Schenectady-Troy, NY	4.6
5	58	Phila.-Willming.-Trenton,PA-NJ-DE-MD	3.9
68	59	Springfield, MA	3.6
9	60	Boston-Lawrence-Salem, MA-NH	3.3
38	61	Rochester, NY	3.2
17	62	St. Louis, MO-IL	2.8
46	63	Birmingham, AL	2.7
63	64	Syracuse, NY	2.6
24	65	Milwaukee-Racine, WI	2.4
3	66	Chicago-Gary-Lake County, IL-IN-WI	1.6
43	67	Dayton-Springfield, OH	1.0
56	68	Scranton-Wilkes Barre, PA	0.7
42	69	Louisville, KY-IN	-0.4
66	70	Toledo, OH	-0.4
32	71	New Orleans, LA	-1.4
6	72	Detroit-Ann Arbor, MI	-1.8
13	73	Cleveland-Akron-Lorain, OH	-2.6
33	74	Buffalo-Niagara Falls, NY	-4.3
19	75	Pittsburgh-Beaver Valley, PA	-7.4

Percent White 1990

Population Rank	White Rank	Metro Area	Percent White
56	1	Scranton-Wilkes Barre, PA	98.2
75	2	New Bedford, MA	95.3
60	3	Allentown-Bethlehem, PA-NJ	94.6
57	4	Worcester-Fitchburg-Leominster, MA	93.8
37	5	Salt Lake City-Ogden, UT	93.3
48	6	Albany-Schenectady-Troy, NY	93.3
67	7	Knoxville, TN	92.8
16	8	Minneaolis-St. Paul, MN-WI	92.1
63	9	Syracuse, NY	91.8
27	10	Portland-Vancouver, OR-WA	91.4
70	11	Harrisburg-Lebanon-Carlisle, PA	91.3
45	12	Providence-Pawtucket-Fall Rvr, RI-MA	91.2
19	13	Pittsburgh-Beaver Valley, PA	91.0
59	14	Grand Rapids, MI	90.6
65	15	Omaha, NE	89.1
21	16	Tampa-St. Petersburg-Clearwater, FL	88.4
9	17	Boston-Lawrence-Salem, MA-NH	88.1
38	18	Rochester, NY	87.4
33	19	Buffalo-Niagara Falls, NY	87.2
23	20	Cincinnati-Hamilton, OH-KY-IN	87.2
68	21	Springfield, MA	87.1
22	22	Denver-Boulder, CO	86.6
14	23	Seattle-Tacoma, WA	86.4
35	24	Hartford-New Britain-Middletown, CT	86.2
29	25	Columbus, OH	86.0
42	26	Louisville, KY-IN	86.0
66	27	Toledo, OH	85.7
52	28	New Haven-Waterbury-Meriden, CT	85.5
43	29	Dayton-Springfield, OH	85.3
31	30	Indianapolis, IN	84.9
50	31	W. Palm Beach-Boca Raton-Delray, FL	84.8
20	32	Phoenix, AZ	84.8
25	33	Kansas City, MO-KS	84.3
58	34	Tulsa, OK	83.3
24	35	Milwaukee-Racine, WI	83.1
39	36	Nashville, TN	83.1
36	37	Orlando, FL	82.9
13	38	Cleveland-Akron-Lorain, OH	81.9
64	39	Greenville-Spartanburg, SC	81.6
54	40	Las Vegas, NV	81.3
17	41	St. Louis, MO-IL	81.2
41	42	Oklahoma City, OK	81.1
44	43	Greensboro-Winston-Salem-High Pt.,NC	79.4
26	44	Sacramento, CA	79.0
73	45	Little Rock-North Little Rock, AR	78.9
62	46	Tucson, AZ	78.7
34	47	Charlotte-Gastonia-Rock Hill, NC-SC	78.5
47	48	Jacksonville, FL	77.4
5	49	Phila.-Willming.-Trenton,PA-NJ-DE-MD	77.0
53	50	Austin, TX	76.8
6	51	Detroit-Ann Arbor, MI	76.5
69	52	El Paso, TX	76.5
11	53	Miami-Fort Lauderdale, FL	76.4
8	54	Dallas-Fort Worth, TX	75.3
30	55	San Antonio, TX	75.1
15	56	San Diego, CA	74.9
55	57	Raleigh-Durham, NC	72.5
46	58	Birmingham, AL	72.2
18	59	Baltimore, MD	71.8
3	60	Chicago-Gary-Lake County, IL-IN-WI	71.6
12	61	Atlanta, GA	71.3
1	62	N.Y.-North N.J.-Long Island,NY-NJ-CT	70.0
71	63	Bakersfield, CA	69.6
4	64	San Francisco-Oakland-San Jose, CA	69.3
72	65	Baton Rouge, LA	68.8
49	66	Richmond-Petersburg, VA	68.8
28	67	Norfolk-Virginia B.-Newport News, VA	67.8
74	68	Charleston, SC	67.8
10	69	Houston-Galveston-Brazoria, TX	67.6
7	70	Washington, DC-MD-VA	65.7
2	71	Los Angeles-Anaheim-Riverside, CA	64.6
61	72	Fresno, CA	63.3
32	73	New Orleans, LA	62.2
40	74	Memphis, TN-AR-MS	58.1
51	75	Honolulu, HI	31.6

TABLE 4—75 Largest Metropolitan Areas by 1990 Population

Selected Rankings

Percent Black 1990

Population Rank	Black Rank	Metro Area	Percent Black
40	1	Memphis, TN-AR-MS	40.6
32	2	New Orleans, LA	34.7
74	3	Charleston, SC	30.2
72	4	Baton Rouge, LA	29.6
49	5	Richmond-Petersburg, VA	29.2
28	6	Norfolk-Virginia B.-Newport News, VA	28.5
46	7	Birmingham, AL	27.1
7	8	Washington, DC-MD-VA	26.6
12	9	Atlanta, GA	26.0
18	10	Baltimore, MD	25.9
55	11	Raleigh-Durham, NC	24.9
6	12	Detroit-Ann Arbor, MI	20.9
47	13	Jacksonville, FL	20.0
34	14	Charlotte-Gastonia-Rock Hill, NC-SC	19.9
73	15	Little Rock-North Little Rock, AR	19.9
44	16	Greensboro-Winston-Salem-High Pt.,NC	19.3
3	17	Chicago-Gary-Lake County, IL-IN-WI	19.2
5	18	Phila.-Willming.-Trenton,PA-NJ-DE-MD	18.7
11	19	Miami-Fort Lauderdale, FL	18.5
1	20	N.Y.-North N.J.-Long Island,NY-NJ-CT	18.3
10	21	Houston-Galveston-Brazoria, TX	17.9
64	22	Greenville-Spartanburg, SC	17.4
17	23	St. Louis, MO-IL	17.3
13	24	Cleveland-Akron-Lorain, OH	16.0
39	25	Nashville, TN	15.5
8	26	Dallas-Fort Worth, TX	14.3
31	27	Indianapolis, IN	13.8
24	28	Milwaukee-Racine, WI	13.3
43	29	Dayton-Springfield, OH	13.3
42	30	Louisville, KY-IN	13.1
25	31	Kansas City, MO-KS	12.8
50	32	W. Palm Beach-Boca Raton-Delray, FL	12.5
36	33	Orlando, FL	12.4
29	34	Columbus, OH	12.0
23	35	Cincinnati-Hamilton, OH-KY-IN	11.7
66	36	Toledo, OH	11.4
41	37	Oklahoma City, OK	10.5
33	38	Buffalo-Niagara Falls, NY	10.3
52	39	New Haven-Waterbury-Meriden, CT	10.2
54	40	Las Vegas, NV	9.5
38	41	Rochester, NY	9.4
53	42	Austin, TX	9.2
21	43	Tampa-St. Petersburg-Clearwater, FL	9.0
4	44	San Francisco-Oakland-San Jose, CA	8.6
35	45	Hartford-New Britain-Middletown, CT	8.5
2	46	Los Angeles-Anaheim-Riverside, CA	8.5
65	47	Omaha, NE	8.3
58	48	Tulsa, OK	8.2
19	49	Pittsburgh-Beaver Valley, PA	8.0
26	50	Sacramento, CA	6.9
30	51	San Antonio, TX	6.8
70	52	Harrisburg-Lebanon-Carlisle, PA	6.7
15	53	San Diego, CA	6.4
9	54	Boston-Lawrence-Salem, MA-NH	6.2
68	55	Springfield, MA	6.1
67	56	Knoxville, TN	6.0
59	57	Grand Rapids, MI	6.0
63	58	Syracuse, NY	5.9
71	59	Bakersfield, CA	5.5
22	60	Denver-Boulder, CO	5.3
61	61	Fresno, CA	5.0
14	62	Seattle-Tacoma, WA	4.8
57	63	Worcester-Fitchburg-Leominster, MA	4.7
48	64	Albany-Schenectady-Troy, NY	4.7
45	65	Providence-Pawtucket-Fall Rvr, RI-MA	3.9
69	66	El Paso, TX	3.7
16	67	Minneaolis-St. Paul, MN-WI	3.6
20	68	Phoenix, AZ	3.5
62	69	Tucson, AZ	3.1
51	70	Honolulu, HI	3.1
27	71	Portland-Vancouver, OR-WA	2.8
60	72	Allentown-Bethlehem, PA-NJ	2.0
75	73	New Bedford, MA	1.6
56	74	Scranton-Wilkes Barre, PA	1.0
37	75	Salt Lake City-Ogden, UT	1.0

Percent Hispanic 1990

Population Rank	Hispanic Rank	Metro Area	Percent Hispanic
69	1	El Paso, TX	69.6
30	2	San Antonio, TX	47.6
61	3	Fresno, CA	35.5
11	4	Miami-Fort Lauderdale, FL	33.3
2	5	Los Angeles-Anaheim-Riverside, CA	32.9
71	6	Bakersfield, CA	28.0
62	7	Tucson, AZ	24.5
10	8	Houston-Galveston-Brazoria, TX	20.8
53	9	Austin, TX	20.5
15	10	San Diego, CA	20.4
20	11	Phoenix, AZ	16.3
4	12	San Francisco-Oakland-San Jose, CA	15.5
1	13	N.Y.-North N.J.-Long Island,NY-NJ-CT	15.5
8	14	Dallas-Fort Worth, TX	13.4
22	15	Denver-Boulder, CO	12.2
26	16	Sacramento, CA	11.6
54	17	Las Vegas, NV	11.2
3	18	Chicago-Gary-Lake County, IL-IN-WI	11.1
36	19	Orlando, FL	9.0
68	20	Springfield, MA	8.2
50	21	W. Palm Beach-Boca Raton-Delray, FL	7.7
35	22	Hartford-New Britain-Middletown, CT	6.8
51	23	Honolulu, HI	6.8
21	24	Tampa-St. Petersburg-Clearwater, FL	6.7
52	25	New Haven-Waterbury-Meriden, CT	6.3
37	26	Salt Lake City-Ogden, UT	5.8
7	27	Washington, DC-MD-VA	5.7
9	28	Boston-Lawrence-Salem, MA-NH	4.9
45	29	Providence-Pawtucket-Fall Rvr, RI-MA	4.8
57	30	Worcester-Fitchburg-Leominster, MA	4.6
32	31	New Orleans, LA	4.3
60	32	Allentown-Bethlehem, PA-NJ	4.2
5	33	Phila.-Willming.-Trenton,PA-NJ-DE-MD	3.8
24	34	Milwaukee-Racine, WI	3.8
41	35	Oklahoma City, OK	3.6
27	36	Portland-Vancouver, OR-WA	3.4
66	37	Toledo, OH	3.3
59	38	Grand Rapids, MI	3.3
38	39	Rochester, NY	3.1
14	40	Seattle-Tacoma, WA	3.0
25	41	Kansas City, MO-KS	2.9
75	42	New Bedford, MA	2.7
65	43	Omaha, NE	2.6
47	44	Jacksonville, FL	2.5
28	45	Norfolk-Virginia B.-Newport News, VA	2.3
58	46	Tulsa, OK	2.1
33	47	Buffalo-Niagara Falls, NY	2.0
12	48	Atlanta, GA	2.0
6	49	Detroit-Ann Arbor, MI	1.9
13	50	Cleveland-Akron-Lorain, OH	1.9
48	51	Albany-Schenectady-Troy, NY	1.8
70	52	Harrisburg-Lebanon-Carlisle, PA	1.7
16	53	Minneaolis-St. Paul, MN-WI	1.5
74	54	Charleston, SC	1.5
72	55	Baton Rouge, LA	1.4
63	56	Syracuse, NY	1.4
18	57	Baltimore, MD	1.3
55	58	Raleigh-Durham, NC	1.2
49	59	Richmond-Petersburg, VA	1.1
17	60	St. Louis, MO-IL	1.1
34	61	Charlotte-Gastonia-Rock Hill, NC-SC	0.9
31	62	Indianapolis, IN	0.9
29	63	Columbus, OH	0.8
40	64	Memphis, TN-AR-MS	0.8
73	65	Little Rock-North Little Rock, AR	0.8
64	66	Greenville-Spartanburg, SC	0.8
39	67	Nashville, TN	0.8
56	68	Scranton-Wilkes Barre, PA	0.8
43	69	Dayton-Springfield, OH	0.8
44	70	Greensboro-Winston-Salem-High Pt.,NC	0.8
42	71	Louisville, KY-IN	0.6
19	72	Pittsburgh-Beaver Valley, PA	0.6
23	73	Cincinnati-Hamilton, OH-KY-IN	0.5
67	74	Knoxville, TN	0.5
46	75	Birmingham, AL	0.4

TABLE 4—75 Largest Metropolitan Areas by 1990 Population

Selected Rankings

Percent Female 1990				Percent Under 5 Years 1990			
Population Rank	Female Rank	Metro Area	Percent Female	Population Rank	Under 5 Rank	Metro Area	Percent Under 5
19	1	Pittsburgh-Beaver Valley, PA	52.8	37	1	Salt Lake City-Ogden, UT	9.7
46	2	Birmingham, AL	52.7	71	2	Bakersfield, CA	9.6
56	3	Scranton-Wilkes Barre, PA	52.5	61	3	Fresno, CA	9.4
68	4	Springfield, MA	52.5	69	4	El Paso, TX	9.0
49	5	Richmond-Petersburg, VA	52.4	59	5	Grand Rapids, MI	8.7
32	6	New Orleans, LA	52.4	74	6	Charleston, SC	8.6
13	7	Cleveland-Akron-Lorain, OH	52.3	10	7	Houston-Galveston-Brazoria, TX	8.5
33	8	Buffalo-Niagara Falls, NY	52.3	2	8	Los Angeles-Anaheim-Riverside, CA	8.4
21	9	Tampa-St. Petersburg-Clearwater, FL	52.3	28	9	Norfolk-Virginia B.-Newport News, VA	8.4
42	10	Louisville, KY-IN	52.3	8	10	Dallas-Fort Worth, TX	8.4
40	11	Memphis, TN-AR-MS	52.2	30	11	San Antonio, TX	8.3
44	12	Greensboro-Winston-Salem-High Pt.,NC	52.2	65	12	Omaha, NE	8.1
75	13	New Bedford, MA	52.2	16	13	Minneaolis-St. Paul, MN-WI	8.1
45	14	Providence-Pawtucket-Fall Rvr, RI-MA	52.2	40	14	Memphis, TN-AR-MS	8.1
17	15	St. Louis, MO-IL	52.2	20	15	Phoenix, AZ	8.0
1	16	N.Y.-North N.J.-Long Island,NY-NJ-CT	52.2	53	16	Austin, TX	7.8
66	17	Toledo, OH	52.2	47	17	Jacksonville, FL	7.8
11	18	Miami-Fort Lauderdale, FL	52.1	72	18	Baton Rouge, LA	7.8
52	19	New Haven-Waterbury-Meriden, CT	52.0	22	19	Denver-Boulder, CO	7.8
5	20	Phila.-Willming.-Trenton,PA-NJ-DE-MD	52.0	26	20	Sacramento, CA	7.8
9	21	Boston-Lawrence-Salem, MA-NH	52.0	15	21	San Diego, CA	7.8
67	22	Knoxville, TN	52.0	23	22	Cincinnati-Hamilton, OH-KY-IN	7.8
23	23	Cincinnati-Hamilton, OH-KY-IN	52.0	25	23	Kansas City, MO-KS	7.7
73	24	Little Rock-North Little Rock, AR	52.0	31	24	Indianapolis, IN	7.7
50	25	W. Palm Beach-Boca Raton-Delray, FL	52.0	12	25	Atlanta, GA	7.7
31	26	Indianapolis, IN	51.9	32	26	New Orleans, LA	7.7
43	27	Dayton-Springfield, OH	51.9	24	27	Milwaukee-Racine, WI	7.7
6	28	Detroit-Ann Arbor, MI	51.8	54	28	Las Vegas, NV	7.7
34	29	Charlotte-Gastonia-Rock Hill, NC-SC	51.8	3	29	Chicago-Gary-Lake County, IL-IN-WI	7.7
63	30	Syracuse, NY	51.8	38	30	Rochester, NY	7.6
24	31	Milwaukee-Racine, WI	51.8	17	31	St. Louis, MO-IL	7.6
60	32	Allentown-Bethlehem, PA-NJ	51.7	58	32	Tulsa, OK	7.6
48	33	Albany-Schenectady-Troy, NY	51.7	6	33	Detroit-Ann Arbor, MI	7.6
55	34	Raleigh-Durham, NC	51.7	14	34	Seattle-Tacoma, WA	7.5
72	35	Baton Rouge, LA	51.7	18	35	Baltimore, MD	7.5
18	36	Baltimore, MD	51.7	29	36	Columbus, OH	7.5
39	37	Nashville, TN	51.7	66	37	Toledo, OH	7.5
38	38	Rochester, NY	51.7	62	38	Tucson, AZ	7.5
25	39	Kansas City, MO-KS	51.7	63	39	Syracuse, NY	7.5
70	40	Harrisburg-Lebanon-Carlisle, PA	51.7	57	40	Worcester-Fitchburg-Leominster, MA	7.5
64	41	Greenville-Spartanburg, SC	51.7	51	41	Honolulu, HI	7.4
35	42	Hartford-New Britain-Middletown, CT	51.6	41	42	Oklahoma City, OK	7.4
58	43	Tulsa, OK	51.5	27	43	Portland-Vancouver, OR-WA	7.4
65	44	Omaha, NE	51.5	73	44	Little Rock-North Little Rock, AR	7.3
30	45	San Antonio, TX	51.4	7	45	Washington, DC-MD-VA	7.3
3	46	Chicago-Gary-Lake County, IL-IN-WI	51.4	36	46	Orlando, FL	7.3
69	47	El Paso, TX	51.4	34	47	Charlotte-Gastonia-Rock Hill, NC-SC	7.3
7	48	Washington, DC-MD-VA	51.3	43	48	Dayton-Springfield, OH	7.2
12	49	Atlanta, GA	51.3	5	49	Phila.-Willming.-Trenton,PA-NJ-DE-MD	7.2
59	50	Grand Rapids, MI	51.3	49	50	Richmond-Petersburg, VA	7.2
57	51	Worcester-Fitchburg-Leominster, MA	51.3	39	51	Nashville, TN	7.2
41	52	Oklahoma City, OK	51.3	13	52	Cleveland-Akron-Lorain, OH	7.1
29	53	Columbus, OH	51.2	4	53	San Francisco-Oakland-San Jose, CA	7.1
62	54	Tucson, AZ	51.1	75	54	New Bedford, MA	7.1
47	55	Jacksonville, FL	51.1	52	55	New Haven-Waterbury-Meriden, CT	7.0
16	56	Minneaolis-St. Paul, MN-WI	51.1	46	56	Birmingham, AL	7.0
27	57	Portland-Vancouver, OR-WA	51.0	11	57	Miami-Fort Lauderdale, FL	6.9
22	58	Denver-Boulder, CO	50.8	68	58	Springfield, MA	6.9
26	59	Sacramento, CA	50.8	55	59	Raleigh-Durham, NC	6.9
20	60	Phoenix, AZ	50.7	33	60	Buffalo-Niagara Falls, NY	6.9
36	61	Orlando, FL	50.7	42	61	Louisville, KY-IN	6.8
8	62	Dallas-Fort Worth, TX	50.6	64	62	Greenville-Spartanburg, SC	6.8
14	63	Seattle-Tacoma, WA	50.5	35	63	Hartford-New Britain-Middletown, CT	6.8
61	64	Fresno, CA	50.4	1	64	N.Y.-North N.J.-Long Island,NY-NJ-CT	6.8
37	65	Salt Lake City-Ogden, UT	50.3	48	65	Albany-Schenectady-Troy, NY	6.8
10	66	Houston-Galveston-Brazoria, TX	50.2	45	66	Providence-Pawtucket-Fall Rvr, RI-MA	6.7
4	67	San Francisco-Oakland-San Jose, CA	50.2	9	67	Boston-Lawrence-Salem, MA-NH	6.7
74	68	Charleston, SC	50.1	60	68	Allentown-Bethlehem, PA-NJ	6.7
53	69	Austin, TX	50.1	70	69	Harrisburg-Lebanon-Carlisle, PA	6.6
2	70	Los Angeles-Anaheim-Riverside, CA	50.0	44	70	Greensboro-Winston-Salem-High Pt.,NC	6.6
28	71	Norfolk-Virginia B.-Newport News, VA	49.9	67	71	Knoxville, TN	6.3
71	72	Bakersfield, CA	49.6	50	72	W. Palm Beach-Boca Raton-Delray, FL	6.2
54	73	Las Vegas, NV	49.3	19	73	Pittsburgh-Beaver Valley, PA	6.2
51	74	Honolulu, HI	49.1	56	74	Scranton-Wilkes Barre, PA	6.2
15	75	San Diego, CA	49.0	21	75	Tampa-St. Petersburg-Clearwater, FL	6.0

TABLE 4—75 Largest Metropolitan Areas by 1990 Population
Selected Rankings

Percent 75 Years and Over 1990

Population Rank	75 Plus Rank	Metro Area	Percent 75 Plus
50	1	W. Palm Beach-Boca Raton-Delray, FL	10.9
21	2	Tampa-St. Petersburg-Clearwater, FL	9.4
11	3	Miami-Fort Lauderdale, FL	7.9
56	4	Scranton-Wilkes Barre, PA	7.8
19	5	Pittsburgh-Beaver Valley, PA	7.0
45	6	Providence-Pawtucket-Fall Rvr, RI-MA	6.6
60	7	Allentown-Bethlehem, PA-NJ	6.3
52	8	New Haven-Waterbury-Meriden, CT	6.3
33	9	Buffalo-Niagara Falls, NY	6.2
48	10	Albany-Schenectady-Troy, NY	6.2
75	11	New Bedford, MA	6.1
57	12	Worcester-Fitchburg-Leominster, MA	6.0
68	13	Springfield, MA	5.9
70	14	Harrisburg-Lebanon-Carlisle, PA	5.8
9	15	Boston-Lawrence-Salem, MA-NH	5.7
35	16	Hartford-New Britain-Middletown, CT	5.7
46	17	Birmingham, AL	5.6
17	18	St. Louis, MO-IL	5.6
1	19	N.Y.-North N.J.-Long Island,NY-NJ-CT	5.6
13	20	Cleveland-Akron-Lorain, OH	5.6
62	21	Tucson, AZ	5.5
5	22	Phila.-Willming.-Trenton,PA-NJ-DE-MD	5.4
38	23	Rochester, NY	5.4
24	24	Milwaukee-Racine, WI	5.4
67	25	Knoxville, TN	5.4
42	26	Louisville, KY-IN	5.3
27	27	Portland-Vancouver, OR-WA	5.2
63	28	Syracuse, NY	5.2
66	29	Toledo, OH	5.2
20	30	Phoenix, AZ	5.1
25	31	Kansas City, MO-KS	5.0
44	32	Greensboro-Winston-Salem-High Pt.,NC	5.0
23	33	Cincinnati-Hamilton, OH-KY-IN	5.0
43	34	Dayton-Springfield, OH	4.9
64	35	Greenville-Spartanburg, SC	4.8
58	36	Tulsa, OK	4.8
73	37	Little Rock-North Little Rock, AR	4.8
41	38	Oklahoma City, OK	4.7
59	39	Grand Rapids, MI	4.6
4	40	San Francisco-Oakland-San Jose, CA	4.6
18	41	Baltimore, MD	4.6
6	42	Detroit-Ann Arbor, MI	4.6
3	43	Chicago-Gary-Lake County, IL-IN-WI	4.6
31	44	Indianapolis, IN	4.6
49	45	Richmond-Petersburg, VA	4.6
65	46	Omaha, NE	4.5
39	47	Nashville, TN	4.5
14	48	Seattle-Tacoma, WA	4.4
15	49	San Diego, CA	4.4
32	50	New Orleans, LA	4.4
16	51	Minneaolis-St. Paul, MN-WI	4.4
40	52	Memphis, TN-AR-MS	4.3
61	53	Fresno, CA	4.3
34	54	Charlotte-Gastonia-Rock Hill, NC-SC	4.3
47	55	Jacksonville, FL	4.2
36	56	Orlando, FL	4.2
26	57	Sacramento, CA	4.1
29	58	Columbus, OH	4.1
30	59	San Antonio, TX	4.1
51	60	Honolulu, HI	4.0
2	61	Los Angeles-Anaheim-Riverside, CA	4.0
71	62	Bakersfield, CA	3.8
22	63	Denver-Boulder, CO	3.7
55	64	Raleigh-Durham, NC	3.7
72	65	Baton Rouge, LA	3.4
37	66	Salt Lake City-Ogden, UT	3.4
54	67	Las Vegas, NV	3.3
7	68	Washington, DC-MD-VA	3.3
28	69	Norfolk-Virginia B.-Newport News, VA	3.3
8	70	Dallas-Fort Worth, TX	3.3
12	71	Atlanta, GA	3.2
53	72	Austin, TX	3.1
74	73	Charleston, SC	3.1
69	74	El Paso, TX	3.0
10	75	Houston-Galveston-Brazoria, TX	2.8

Percent Female Family Households 1990

Population Rank	Fem. HHs. Rank	Metro Area	Percent Fem. HHs.
40	1	Memphis, TN-AR-MS	17.9
32	2	New Orleans, LA	17.5
69	3	El Paso, TX	15.8
6	4	Detroit-Ann Arbor, MI	14.7
18	5	Baltimore, MD	14.6
72	6	Baton Rouge, LA	14.4
1	7	N.Y.-North N.J.-Long Island,NY-NJ-CT	14.2
68	8	Springfield, MA	14.1
30	9	San Antonio, TX	14.0
46	10	Birmingham, AL	13.9
61	11	Fresno, CA	13.9
49	12	Richmond-Petersburg, VA	13.6
5	13	Phila.-Willming.-Trenton,PA-NJ-DE-MD	13.5
74	14	Charleston, SC	13.5
42	15	Louisville, KY-IN	13.5
3	16	Chicago-Gary-Lake County, IL-IN-WI	13.4
28	17	Norfolk-Virginia B.-Newport News, VA	13.1
13	18	Cleveland-Akron-Lorain, OH	13.0
12	19	Atlanta, GA	13.0
33	20	Buffalo-Niagara Falls, NY	12.9
24	21	Milwaukee-Racine, WI	12.9
11	22	Miami-Fort Lauderdale, FL	12.8
17	23	St. Louis, MO-IL	12.6
47	24	Jacksonville, FL	12.6
75	25	New Bedford, MA	12.5
66	26	Toledo, OH	12.5
52	27	New Haven-Waterbury-Meriden, CT	12.5
71	28	Bakersfield, CA	12.3
23	29	Cincinnati-Hamilton, OH-KY-IN	12.3
39	30	Nashville, TN	12.2
10	31	Houston-Galveston-Brazoria, TX	12.2
73	32	Little Rock-North Little Rock, AR	12.1
9	33	Boston-Lawrence-Salem, MA-NH	12.1
64	34	Greenville-Spartanburg, SC	12.0
43	35	Dayton-Springfield, OH	12.0
2	36	Los Angeles-Anaheim-Riverside, CA	12.0
34	37	Charlotte-Gastonia-Rock Hill, NC-SC	12.0
7	38	Washington, DC-MD-VA	12.0
45	39	Providence-Pawtucket-Fall Rvr, RI-MA	11.9
44	40	Greensboro-Winston-Salem-High Pt.,NC	11.8
26	41	Sacramento, CA	11.8
31	42	Indianapolis, IN	11.7
19	43	Pittsburgh-Beaver Valley, PA	11.7
38	44	Rochester, NY	11.7
29	45	Columbus, OH	11.6
35	46	Hartford-New Britain-Middletown, CT	11.6
65	47	Omaha, NE	11.4
41	48	Oklahoma City, OK	11.4
25	49	Kansas City, MO-KS	11.3
63	50	Syracuse, NY	11.3
55	51	Raleigh-Durham, NC	11.2
54	52	Las Vegas, NV	11.2
57	53	Worcester-Fitchburg-Leominster, MA	11.2
8	54	Dallas-Fort Worth, TX	11.1
36	55	Orlando, FL	11.0
56	56	Scranton-Wilkes Barre, PA	11.0
62	57	Tucson, AZ	10.9
67	58	Knoxville, TN	10.8
15	59	San Diego, CA	10.8
4	60	San Francisco-Oakland-San Jose, CA	10.7
48	61	Albany-Schenectady-Troy, NY	10.7
51	62	Honolulu, HI	10.5
58	63	Tulsa, OK	10.4
59	64	Grand Rapids, MI	10.3
22	65	Denver-Boulder, CO	10.2
53	66	Austin, TX	10.2
20	67	Phoenix, AZ	10.2
37	68	Salt Lake City-Ogden, UT	10.0
21	69	Tampa-St. Petersburg-Clearwater, FL	9.9
16	70	Minneaolis-St. Paul, MN-WI	9.7
27	71	Portland-Vancouver, OR-WA	9.7
70	72	Harrisburg-Lebanon-Carlisle, PA	9.6
14	73	Seattle-Tacoma, WA	9.4
60	74	Allentown-Bethlehem, PA-NJ	9.3
50	75	W. Palm Beach-Boca Raton-Delray, FL	8.6

TABLE 4—75 Largest Metropolitan Areas by 1990 Population

Selected Rankings

Infant Deaths per 1,000 Live Births 1987				Physicians per 100,000 Population 1989			
Population Rank	Death Rate Rank	Metro Area	Infant Death Rate	Population Rank	Rate Rank	Metro Area	M.D. Rate
28	1	Norfolk-Virginia B.-Newport News, VA	19.3	55	1	Raleigh-Durham, NC	527
40	2	Memphis, TN-AR-MS	15.3	9	2	Boston-Lawrence-Salem, MA-NH	402
72	3	Baton Rouge, LA	14.1	52	3	New Haven-Waterbury-Meriden, CT	388
55	4	Raleigh-Durham, NC	13.7	18	4	Baltimore, MD	350
50	5	W. Palm Beach-Boca Raton-Delray, FL.	13.4	7	5	Washington, DC-MD-VA	336
64	6	Greenville-Spartanburg, SC	13.2	1	6	N.Y.-North N.J.-Long Island,NY-NJ-CT	330
34	7	Charlotte-Gastonia-Rock Hill, NC-SC	12.8	32	7	New Orleans, LA	312
18	8	Baltimore, MD	12.6	73	8	Little Rock-North Little Rock, AR	299
31	9	Indianapolis, IN	12.5	4	9	San Francisco-Oakland-San Jose, CA.	298
32	10	New Orleans, LA	12.3	35	10	Hartford-New Britain-Middletown, CT	298
63	11	Syracuse, NY	12.3	49	11	Richmond-Petersburg, VA	291
3	12	Chicago-Gary-Lake County, IL-IN-WI	12.3	11	12	Miami-Fort Lauderdale, FL	282
46	13	Birmingham, AL	11.9	46	13	Birmingham, AL	281
6	14	Detroit-Ann Arbor, MI	11.8	5	14	Phila.-Willming.-Trenton,PA-NJ-DE-MD	280
5	15	Phila.-Willming.-Trenton,PA-NJ-DE-MD	11.8	39	15	Nashville, TN	278
12	16	Atlanta, GA	11.7	65	16	Omaha, NE	276
49	17	Richmond-Petersburg, VA	11.5	62	17	Tucson, AZ	275
73	18	Little Rock-North Little Rock, AR	11.5	57	18	Worcester-Fitchburg-Leominster, MA	275
25	19	Kansas City, MO-KS	11.4	31	19	Indianapolis, IN	274
44	20	Greensboro-Winston-Salem-High Pt.,NC	11.4	19	20	Pittsburgh-Beaver Valley, PA	274
74	21	Charleston, SC	11.0	13	21	Cleveland-Akron-Lorain, OH	272
47	22	Jacksonville, FL	10.9	38	22	Rochester, NY	271
7	23	Washington, DC-MD-VA	10.8	74	23	Charleston, SC	263
41	24	Oklahoma City, OK	10.8	22	24	Denver-Boulder, CO	259
67	25	Knoxville, TN	10.5	14	25	Seattle-Tacoma, WA	259
1	26	N.Y.-North N.J.-Long Island,NY-NJ-CT	10.5	45	26	Providence-Pawtucket-Fall Rvr, RI-MA	257
11	27	Miami-Fort Lauderdale, FL	10.4	63	27	Syracuse, NY	252
70	28	Harrisburg-Lebanon-Carlisle, PA	10.4	40	28	Memphis, TN-AR-MS	252
13	29	Cleveland-Akron-Lorain, OH	10.4	33	29	Buffalo-Niagara Falls, NY	252
59	30	Grand Rapids, MI	10.1	48	30	Albany-Schenectady-Troy, NY	251
69	31	El Paso, TX	10.0	17	31	St. Louis, MO-IL	249
14	32	Seattle-Tacoma, WA	10.0	42	32	Louisville, KY-IN	247
20	33	Phoenix, AZ	10.0	3	33	Chicago-Gary-Lake County, IL-IN-WI	247
54	34	Las Vegas, NV	10.0	27	34	Portland-Vancouver, OR-WA	246
17	35	St. Louis, MO-IL	9.9	10	35	Houston-Galveston-Brazoria, TX	244
26	36	Sacramento, CA	9.9	66	36	Toledo, OH	243
39	37	Nashville, TN	9.9	2	37	Los Angeles-Anaheim-Riverside, CA	241
19	38	Pittsburgh-Beaver Valley, PA	9.9	24	38	Milwaukee-Racine, WI	240
22	39	Denver-Boulder, CO	9.8	16	39	Minneaolis-St. Paul, MN-WI	236
51	40	Honolulu, HI	9.6	6	40	Detroit-Ann Arbor, MI	235
27	41	Portland-Vancouver, OR-WA	9.5	15	41	San Diego, CA	234
35	42	Hartford-New Britain-Middletown, CT	9.5	41	42	Oklahoma City, OK	232
8	43	Dallas-Fort Worth, TX	9.4	51	43	Honolulu, HI	230
33	44	Buffalo-Niagara Falls, NY	9.4	30	44	San Antonio, TX	227
24	45	Milwaukee-Racine, WI	9.4	23	45	Cincinnati-Hamilton, OH-KY-IN	227
15	46	San Diego, CA	9.4	37	46	Salt Lake City-Ogden, UT	226
2	47	Los Angeles-Anaheim-Riverside, CA	9.4	70	47	Harrisburg-Lebanon-Carlisle, PA	222
65	48	Omaha, NE	9.3	25	48	Kansas City, MO-KS	221
52	49	New Haven-Waterbury-Meriden, CT	9.3	26	49	Sacramento, CA	219
10	50	Houston-Galveston-Brazoria, TX	9.2	44	50	Greensboro-Winston-Salem-High Pt.,NC	216
37	51	Salt Lake City-Ogden, UT	9.1	29	51	Columbus, OH	214
23	52	Cincinnati-Hamilton, OH-KY-IN	9.1	50	52	W. Palm Beach-Boca Raton-Delray, FL.	210
21	53	Tampa-St. Petersburg-Clearwater, FL	9.0	68	53	Springfield, MA	206
71	54	Bakersfield, CA	8.9	67	54	Knoxville, TN	203
38	55	Rochester, NY	8.8	12	55	Atlanta, GA	202
58	56	Tulsa, OK	8.8	20	56	Phoenix, AZ	201
29	57	Columbus, OH	8.8	47	57	Jacksonville, FL	196
36	58	Orlando, FL	8.8	21	58	Tampa-St. Petersburg-Clearwater, FL	192
16	59	Minneaolis-St. Paul, MN-WI	8.7	28	59	Norfolk-Virginia B.-Newport News, VA	183
30	60	San Antonio, TX	8.6	61	60	Fresno, CA	182
61	61	Fresno, CA	8.6	8	61	Dallas-Fort Worth, TX	180
56	62	Scranton-Wilkes Barre, PA	8.6	43	62	Dayton-Springfield, OH	179
43	63	Dayton-Springfield, OH	8.5	60	63	Allentown-Bethlehem, PA-NJ	177
60	64	Allentown-Bethlehem, PA-NJ	8.5	53	64	Austin, TX	175
42	65	Louisville, KY-IN	8.5	59	65	Grand Rapids, MI	174
45	66	Providence-Pawtucket-Fall Rvr, RI-MA	8.5	36	66	Orlando, FL	172
66	67	Toledo, OH	8.3	58	67	Tulsa, OK	170
57	68	Worcester-Fitchburg-Leominster, MA	8.1	64	68	Greenville-Spartanburg, SC	168
48	69	Albany-Schenectady-Troy, NY	8.1	56	69	Scranton-Wilkes Barre, PA	168
62	70	Tucson, AZ	7.8	72	70	Baton Rouge, LA	164
4	71	San Francisco-Oakland-San Jose, CA.	7.8	34	71	Charlotte-Gastonia-Rock Hill, NC-SC	142
68	72	Springfield, MA	7.5	54	72	Las Vegas, NV	135
53	73	Austin, TX	7.3	69	73	El Paso, TX	129
9	74	Boston-Lawrence-Salem, MA-NH	7.2	71	74	Bakersfield, CA	124
75	75	New Bedford, MA	7.0	75	75	New Bedford, MA	113

TABLE 4—75 Largest Metropolitan Areas by 1990 Population

Selected Rankings

Hospital Beds per 100,000 Population 1989				Change in Labor Force 1989–1990			
Population Rank	Bed Rate Rank	Metro Area	Bed Rate	Population Rank	Percent Change Rank	Metro Area	Percent Change
73	1	Little Rock-North Little Rock, AR	903	54	1	Las Vegas, NV	7.1
65	2	Omaha, NE	759	36	2	Orlando, FL	4.1
39	3	Nashville, TN	734	74	3	Charleston, SC	3.7
49	4	Richmond-Petersburg, VA	702	2	4	Los Angeles-Anaheim-Riverside, CA	3.3
19	5	Pittsburgh-Beaver Valley, PA	694	65	5	Omaha, NE	3.0
40	6	Memphis, TN-AR-MS	681	22	6	Denver-Boulder, CO	2.9
55	7	Raleigh-Durham, NC	680	52	7	New Haven-Waterbury-Meriden, CT	2.5
43	8	Dayton-Springfield, OH	669	21	8	Tampa-St. Petersburg-Clearwater, FL	2.4
9	9	Boston-Lawrence-Salem, MA-NH	664	50	9	W. Palm Beach-Boca Raton-Delray, FL	2.1
56	10	Scranton-Wilkes Barre, PA	644	60	10	Allentown-Bethlehem, PA-NJ	2.1
33	11	Buffalo-Niagara Falls, NY	632	10	11	Houston-Galveston-Brazoria, TX	2.1
32	12	New Orleans, LA	631	51	12	Honolulu, HI	2.0
70	13	Harrisburg-Lebanon-Carlisle, PA	617	27	13	Portland-Vancouver, OR-WA	1.8
30	14	San Antonio, TX	615	14	14	Seattle-Tacoma, WA	1.7
66	15	Toledo, OH	611	47	15	Jacksonville, FL	1.7
46	16	Birmingham, AL	603	61	16	Fresno, CA	1.7
68	17	Springfield, MA	595	35	17	Hartford-New Britain-Middletown, CT	1.6
67	18	Knoxville, TN	592	16	18	Minneaolis-St. Paul, MN-WI	1.5
17	19	St. Louis, MO-IL	587	11	19	Miami-Fort Lauderdale, FL	1.5
25	20	Kansas City, MO-KS	583	58	20	Tulsa, OK	1.4
57	21	Worcester-Fitchburg-Leominster, MA	580	49	21	Richmond-Petersburg, VA	1.4
38	22	Rochester, NY	571	64	22	Greenville-Spartanburg, SC	1.3
1	23	N.Y.-North N.J.-Long Island,NY-NJ-CT	570	20	23	Phoenix, AZ	1.1
21	24	Tampa-St. Petersburg-Clearwater, FL	563	5	24	Phila.-Willming.-Trenton,PA-NJ-DE-MD	0.9
11	25	Miami-Fort Lauderdale, FL	550	34	25	Charlotte-Gastonia-Rock Hill, NC-SC	0.9
13	26	Cleveland-Akron-Lorain, OH	550	23	26	Cincinnati-Hamilton, OH-KY-IN	0.9
42	27	Louisville, KY-IN	545	28	27	Norfolk-Virginia B.-Newport News, VA	0.9
48	28	Albany-Schenectady-Troy, NY	544	59	28	Grand Rapids, MI	0.9
35	29	Hartford-New Britain-Middletown, CT	534	53	29	Austin, TX	0.9
5	30	Phila.-Willming.-Trenton,PA-NJ-DE-MD	530	48	30	Albany-Schenectady-Troy, NY	0.8
18	31	Baltimore, MD	529	55	31	Raleigh-Durham, NC	0.8
31	32	Indianapolis, IN	529	29	32	Columbus, OH	0.8
41	33	Oklahoma City, OK	523	19	33	Pittsburgh-Beaver Valley, PA	0.8
10	34	Houston-Galveston-Brazoria, TX	512	12	34	Atlanta, GA	0.7
24	35	Milwaukee-Racine, WI	511	26	35	Sacramento, CA	0.7
23	36	Cincinnati-Hamilton, OH-KY-IN	503	39	36	Nashville, TN	0.7
28	37	Norfolk-Virginia B.-Newport News, VA	501	56	37	Scranton-Wilkes Barre, PA	0.7
52	38	New Haven-Waterbury-Meriden, CT	492	42	38	Louisville, KY-IN	0.6
3	39	Chicago-Gary-Lake County, IL-IN-WI	488	18	39	Baltimore, MD	0.5
60	40	Allentown-Bethlehem, PA-NJ	482	63	40	Syracuse, NY	0.5
45	41	Providence-Pawtucket-Fall Rvr, RI-MA	474	68	41	Springfield, MA	0.5
6	42	Detroit-Ann Arbor, MI	462	25	42	Kansas City, MO-KS	0.4
74	43	Charleston, SC	445	70	43	Harrisburg-Lebanon-Carlisle, PA	0.4
58	44	Tulsa, OK	445	3	44	Chicago-Gary-Lake County, IL-IN-WI	0.4
12	45	Atlanta, GA	438	40	45	Memphis, TN-AR-MS	0.4
50	46	W. Palm Beach-Boca Raton-Delray, FL	436	1	46	N.Y.-North N.J.-Long Island,NY-NJ-CT	0.3
63	47	Syracuse, NY	433	69	47	El Paso, TX	0.2
53	48	Austin, TX	427	15	48	San Diego, CA	0.2
64	49	Greenville-Spartanburg, SC	427	13	49	Cleveland-Akron-Lorain, OH	0.1
7	50	Washington, DC-MD-VA	426	41	50	Oklahoma City, OK	0.0
62	51	Tucson, AZ	420	72	51	Baton Rouge, LA	0.0
8	52	Dallas-Fort Worth, TX	416	8	52	Dallas-Fort Worth, TX	0.0
34	53	Charlotte-Gastonia-Rock Hill, NC-SC	415	44	53	Greensboro-Winston-Salem-High Pt.,NC	0.0
4	54	San Francisco-Oakland-San Jose, CA	411	73	54	Little Rock-North Little Rock, AR	-0.1
72	55	Baton Rouge, LA	406	7	55	Washington, DC-MD-VA	-0.1
29	56	Columbus, OH	395	17	56	St. Louis, MO-IL	-0.1
20	57	Phoenix, AZ	395	62	57	Tucson, AZ	-0.2
36	58	Orlando, FL	392	43	58	Dayton-Springfield, OH	-0.3
59	59	Grand Rapids, MI	391	75	59	New Bedford, MA	-0.3
16	60	Minneaolis-St. Paul, MN-WI	388	67	60	Knoxville, TN	-0.4
44	61	Greensboro-Winston-Salem-High Pt.,NC	388	37	61	Salt Lake City-Ogden, UT	-0.6
2	62	Los Angeles-Anaheim-Riverside, CA	384	66	62	Toledo, OH	-0.7
47	63	Jacksonville, FL	383	33	63	Buffalo-Niagara Falls, NY	-0.7
69	64	El Paso, TX	382	9	64	Boston-Lawrence-Salem, MA-NH	-0.7
75	65	New Bedford, MA	380	57	65	Worcester-Fitchburg-Leominster, MA	-0.8
51	66	Honolulu, HI	375	38	66	Rochester, NY	-0.9
22	67	Denver-Boulder, CO	366	46	67	Birmingham, AL	-0.9
37	68	Salt Lake City-Ogden, UT	364	6	68	Detroit-Ann Arbor, MI	-1.1
14	69	Seattle-Tacoma, WA	362	45	69	Providence-Pawtucket-Fall Rvr, RI-MA	-1.4
27	70	Portland-Vancouver, OR-WA	348	4	70	San Francisco-Oakland-San Jose, CA	-1.5
15	71	San Diego, CA	336	30	71	San Antonio, TX	-1.6
54	72	Las Vegas, NV	325	24	72	Milwaukee-Racine, WI	-2.1
61	73	Fresno, CA	322	71	73	Bakersfield, CA	-2.2
26	74	Sacramento, CA	256	32	74	New Orleans, LA	-2.3
71	75	Bakersfield, CA	237	31	75	Indianapolis, IN	-3.3

TABLE 4—75 Largest Metropolitan Areas by 1990 Population

Selected Rankings

Unemployment Rate 1990				Per Capita Personal Income 1989			
Population Rank	Unemployment Rate Rank	Metro Area	Unemployment Rate (Percent)	Population Rank	P.C. Personal Income Rank	Metro Area	P.C. Personal Income (Dollars)
69	1	El Paso, TX	10.7	7	1	Washington, DC-MD-VA	24,845
71	2	Bakersfield, CA	10.5	50	2	W. Palm Beach-Boca Raton-Delray, FL	24,319
61	3	Fresno, CA	10.2	1	3	N.Y.-North N.J.-Long Island,NY-NJ-CT	23,841
75	4	New Bedford, MA	8.7	4	4	San Francisco-Oakland-San Jose, CA	23,778
6	5	Detroit-Ann Arbor, MI	7.3	9	5	Boston-Lawrence-Salem, MA-NH	23,746
57	6	Worcester-Fitchburg-Leominster, MA	7.0	35	6	Hartford-New Britain-Middletown, CT	23,695
56	7	Scranton-Wilkes Barre, PA	6.9	52	7	New Haven-Waterbury-Meriden, CT	21,736
66	8	Toledo, OH	6.9	18	8	Baltimore, MD	20,267
30	9	San Antonio, TX	6.9	16	9	Minneaolis-St. Paul, MN-WI	20,227
45	10	Providence-Pawtucket-Fall Rvr, RI-MA	6.8	57	10	Worcester-Fitchburg-Leominster, MA	20,200
50	11	W. Palm Beach-Boca Raton-Delray, FL	6.5	49	11	Richmond-Petersburg, VA	20,164
11	12	Miami-Fort Lauderdale, FL	6.2	3	12	Chicago-Gary-Lake County, IL-IN-WI	20,109
59	13	Grand Rapids, MI	6.1	2	13	Los Angeles-Anaheim-Riverside, CA	20,004
17	14	St. Louis, MO-IL	5.9	5	14	Phila.-Willming.-Trenton,PA-NJ-DE-MD	19,909
73	15	Little Rock-North Little Rock, AR	5.9	38	15	Rochester, NY	19,858
3	16	Chicago-Gary-Lake County, IL-IN-WI	5.8	14	16	Seattle-Tacoma, WA	19,851
32	17	New Orleans, LA	5.7	6	17	Detroit-Ann Arbor, MI	19,826
68	18	Springfield, MA	5.7	11	18	Miami-Fort Lauderdale, FL	19,526
52	19	New Haven-Waterbury-Meriden, CT	5.6	22	19	Denver-Boulder, CO	19,345
9	20	Boston-Lawrence-Salem, MA-NH	5.5	51	20	Honolulu, HI	19,171
47	21	Jacksonville, FL	5.5	12	21	Atlanta, GA	19,055
60	22	Allentown-Bethlehem, PA-NJ	5.5	17	22	St. Louis, MO-IL	18,957
2	23	Los Angeles-Anaheim-Riverside, CA	5.4	55	23	Raleigh-Durham, NC	18,945
72	24	Baton Rouge, LA	5.4	75	24	New Bedford, MA	18,845
41	25	Oklahoma City, OK	5.4	48	25	Albany-Schenectady-Troy, NY	18,802
46	26	Birmingham, AL	5.4	8	26	Dallas-Fort Worth, TX	18,721
36	27	Orlando, FL	5.3	24	27	Milwaukee-Racine, WI	18,686
10	28	Houston-Galveston-Brazoria, TX	5.3	15	28	San Diego, CA	18,651
58	29	Tulsa, OK	5.3	68	29	Springfield, MA	18,519
1	30	N.Y.-North N.J.-Long Island,NY-NJ-CT	5.3	54	30	Las Vegas, NV	18,508
43	31	Dayton-Springfield, OH	5.3	13	31	Cleveland-Akron-Lorain, OH	18,380
8	32	Dallas-Fort Worth, TX	5.2	26	32	Sacramento, CA	18,299
21	33	Tampa-St. Petersburg-Clearwater, FL	5.1	60	33	Allentown-Bethlehem, PA-NJ	18,294
42	34	Louisville, KY-IN	5.1	31	34	Indianapolis, IN	18,080
13	35	Cleveland-Akron-Lorain, OH	5.1	45	35	Providence-Pawtucket-Fall Rvr, RI-MA	17,923
18	36	Baltimore, MD	5.1	25	36	Kansas City, MO-KS	17,899
12	37	Atlanta, GA	5.1	59	37	Grand Rapids, MI	17,766
25	38	Kansas City, MO-KS	5.0	27	38	Portland-Vancouver, OR-WA	17,713
33	39	Buffalo-Niagara Falls, NY	5.0	20	39	Phoenix, AZ	17,705
19	40	Pittsburgh-Beaver Valley, PA	5.0	21	40	Tampa-St. Petersburg-Clearwater, FL	17,675
67	41	Knoxville, TN	5.0	44	41	Greensboro-Winston-Salem-High Pt.,NC	17,652
54	42	Las Vegas, NV	4.9	36	42	Orlando, FL	17,540
26	43	Sacramento, CA	4.8	10	43	Houston-Galveston-Brazoria, TX	17,538
5	44	Phila.-Willming.-Trenton,PA-NJ-DE-MD	4.8	63	44	Syracuse, NY	17,490
28	45	Norfolk-Virginia B.-Newport News, VA	4.7	19	45	Pittsburgh-Beaver Valley, PA	17,455
35	46	Hartford-New Britain-Middletown, CT	4.7	33	46	Buffalo-Niagara Falls, NY	17,439
40	47	Memphis, TN-AR-MS	4.6	34	47	Charlotte-Gastonia-Rock Hill, NC-SC	17,377
53	48	Austin, TX	4.6	23	48	Cincinnati-Hamilton, OH-KY-IN	17,365
22	49	Denver-Boulder, CO	4.5	29	49	Columbus, OH	17,178
15	50	San Diego, CA	4.5	39	50	Nashville, TN	17,134
70	51	Harrisburg-Lebanon-Carlisle, PA	4.4	43	51	Dayton-Springfield, OH	16,919
29	52	Columbus, OH	4.4	66	52	Toledo, OH	16,893
23	53	Cincinnati-Hamilton, OH-KY-IN	4.4	70	53	Harrisburg-Lebanon-Carlisle, PA	16,830
27	54	Portland-Vancouver, OR-WA	4.3	42	54	Louisville, KY-IN	16,768
16	55	Minneaolis-St. Paul, MN-WI	4.3	65	55	Omaha, NE	16,753
20	56	Phoenix, AZ	4.3	40	56	Memphis, TN-AR-MS	16,484
31	57	Indianapolis, IN	4.2	47	57	Jacksonville, FL	16,215
62	58	Tucson, AZ	4.1	53	58	Austin, TX	16,113
63	59	Syracuse, NY	4.1	58	59	Tulsa, OK	16,016
4	60	San Francisco-Oakland-San Jose, CA	4.1	61	60	Fresno, CA	15,927
37	61	Salt Lake City-Ogden, UT	4.1	46	61	Birmingham, AL	15,833
39	62	Nashville, TN	4.0	28	62	Norfolk-Virginia B.-Newport News, VA	15,721
49	63	Richmond-Petersburg, VA	3.9	64	63	Greenville-Spartanburg, SC	15,707
24	64	Milwaukee-Racine, WI	3.9	73	64	Little Rock-North Little Rock, AR	15,657
64	65	Greenville-Spartanburg, SC	3.9	41	65	Oklahoma City, OK	15,536
44	66	Greensboro-Winston-Salem-High Pt.,NC	3.7	56	66	Scranton-Wilkes Barre, PA	15,519
38	67	Rochester, NY	3.7	62	67	Tucson, AZ	15,203
14	68	Seattle-Tacoma, WA	3.7	67	68	Knoxville, TN	15,110
48	69	Albany-Schenectady-Troy, NY	3.6	71	69	Bakersfield, CA	14,856
34	70	Charlotte-Gastonia-Rock Hill, NC-SC	3.5	72	70	Baton Rouge, LA	14,757
74	71	Charleston, SC	3.4	32	71	New Orleans, LA	14,745
7	72	Washington, DC-MD-VA	3.4	30	72	San Antonio, TX	14,144
51	73	Honolulu, HI	2.6	37	73	Salt Lake City-Ogden, UT	13,962
65	74	Omaha, NE	2.6	74	74	Charleston, SC	12,351
55	75	Raleigh-Durham, NC	2.5	69	75	El Paso, TX	10,735

TABLE 5—75 Metropolitan Areas with Highest Agricultural Sales–1987

Selected Rankings

Value of Agricultural Sales 1987			Operators Living on Farm Operated 1987			
Value of Sales Rank	Metro Area	Value of Agricultural Sales (Mil Dol)	Value of Sales Rank	Operators Living on Farm Rank	Metro Area	Operators Living on Farm Percent
1	Los Angeles-Anaheim-Riverside, CA	2,135	46	1	Appleton-Oshkosh-Neenah, WI	85.8
2	Fresno, CA	1,682	24	2	Portland-Vancouver, OR-WA	85.8
3	Bakersfield, CA	1,100	48	3	Seattle-Tacoma, WA	85.8
4	Visalia-Tulare-Porterville, CA	1,030	65	4	Wausau, WI	85.3
5	San Francisco-Oakland-San Jose, CA	910	67	5	Bellingham, WA	84.8
6	Greeley, CO	865	39	6	Rochester, NY	83.1
7	W. Palm Beach-Boca Raton-Delray, FL	855	17	7	Minneaolis-St. Paul, MN-WI	83.1
8	Merced, CA	792	44	8	Salem, OR	82.8
9	Modesto, CA	786	34	9	Detroit-Ann Arbor, MI	82.8
10	Salinas-Seaside-Monterey, CA	731	26	10	St. Cloud, MN	82.6
11	Stockton, CA	634	64	11	Cleveland-Akron-Lorain, OH	82.5
12	Phila.-Willming.-Trenton,PA-NJ-DE-MD	630	42	12	Grand Rapids, MI	82.1
13	Lancaster, PA	601	54	13	Madison, WI	81.5
14	Phoenix, AZ	549	45	14	Harrisburg-Lebanon-Carlisle, PA	81.3
15	Chicago-Gary-Lake County, IL-IN-WI	521	74	15	Reading, PA	81.0
16	Yakima, WA	498	68	16	Baltimore, MD	80.7
17	Minneaolis-St. Paul, MN-WI	458	53	17	York, PA	79.6
18	San Diego, CA	444	13	18	Lancaster, PA	79.4
19	Sacramento, CA	418	58	19	Milwaukee-Racine, WI	79.3
20	N.Y.-North N.J.-Long Island,NY-NJ-CT	401	12	20	Phila.-Willming.-Trenton,PA-NJ-DE-MD	79.3
21	St. Louis, MO-IL	376	61	21	Washington, DC-MD-VA	78.9
22	Lexington-Fayette, KY	367	20	22	N.Y.-North N.J.-Long Island,NY-NJ-CT	77.4
23	Columbus, OH	364	33	23	Fayetteville-Springdale, AR	77.3
24	Portland-Vancouver, OR-WA	364	16	24	Yakima, WA	77.3
25	Yuma, AZ	356	6	25	Greeley, CO	77.3
26	St. Cloud, MN	323	60	26	Athens, GA	77.1
27	Omaha, NE	323	19	27	Sacramento, CA	76.7
28	Indianapolis, IN	318	71	28	Waterloo-Cedar Falls, IA	76.5
29	Tampa-St. Petersburg-Clearwater, FL	316	52	29	Atlanta, GA	76.0
30	Richland-Kennewick-Pasco, WA	309	31	30	Davenport-Rock Island-Moline, IA-IL	75.9
31	Davenport-Rock Island-Moline, IA-IL	301	49	31	Fargo-Moorhead, ND-MN	75.7
32	Kansas City, MO-KS	301	9	32	Modesto, CA	75.3
33	Fayetteville-Springdale, AR	299	37	33	Charlotte-Gastonia-Rock Hill, NC-SC	75.2
34	Detroit-Ann Arbor, MI	299	72	34	Denver-Boulder, CO	74.8
35	Fort Pierce, FL	296	56	35	Dayton-Springfield, OH	74.8
36	Miami-Fort Lauderdale, FL	294	23	36	Columbus, OH	74.6
37	Charlotte-Gastonia-Rock Hill, NC-SC	289	59	37	Louisville, KY-IN	74.2
38	Santa Barbara-Santa Maria-Lompoc, CA	288	30	38	Richland-Kennewick-Pasco, WA	74.2
39	Rochester, NY	277	28	39	Indianapolis, IN	74.0
40	Orlando, FL	273	32	40	Kansas City, MO-KS	73.6
41	Yuba City, CA	267	55	41	Wichita, KS	73.2
42	Grand Rapids, MI	266	27	42	Omaha, NE	73.0
43	Lakeland-Winter Haven, FL	261	15	43	Chicago-Gary-Lake County, IL-IN-WI	73.0
44	Salem, OR	255	57	44	Greensboro-Winston-Salem-High Pt.,NC	72.5
45	Harrisburg-Lebanon-Carlisle, PA	254	21	45	St. Louis, MO-IL	72.5
46	Appleton-Oshkosh-Neenah, WI	243	62	46	Des Moines, IA	72.4
47	Dallas-Fort Worth, TX	242	69	47	Toledo, OH	69.6
48	Seattle-Tacoma, WA	241	51	48	Peoria, IL	69.1
49	Fargo-Moorhead, ND-MN	234	11	49	Stockton, CA	69.1
50	McAllen-Edinburg-Mission, TX	233	8	50	Merced, CA	68.5
51	Peoria, IL	228	5	51	San Francisco-Oakland-San Jose, CA	68.2
52	Atlanta, GA	219	75	52	Bloomington-Normal, IL	68.0
53	York, PA	219	2	53	Fresno, CA	67.8
54	Madison, WI	216	29	54	Tampa-St. Petersburg-Clearwater, FL	67.1
55	Wichita, KS	211	70	55	Chico, CA	66.4
56	Dayton-Springfield, OH	209	22	56	Lexington-Fayette, KY	65.7
57	Greensboro-Winston-Salem-High Pt.,NC	207	47	57	Dallas-Fort Worth, TX	65.6
58	Milwaukee-Racine, WI	197	18	58	San Diego, CA	63.9
59	Louisville, KY-IN	197	41	59	Yuba City, CA	62.8
60	Athens, GA	192	14	60	Phoenix, AZ	61.3
61	Washington, DC-MD-VA	192	4	61	Visalia-Tulare-Porterville, CA	61.1
62	Des Moines, IA	189	1	62	Los Angeles-Anaheim-Riverside, CA	59.2
63	Amarillo, TX	184	66	63	Houston-Galveston-Brazoria, TX	57.5
64	Cleveland-Akron-Lorain, OH	183	73	64	Honolulu, HI	56.8
65	Wausau, WI	183	40	65	Orlando, FL	56.7
66	Houston-Galveston-Brazoria, TX	181	36	66	Miami-Fort Lauderdale, FL	55.6
67	Bellingham, WA	180	63	67	Amarillo, TX	55.2
68	Baltimore, MD	178	38	68	Santa Barbara-Santa Maria-Lompoc, CA	54.7
69	Toledo, OH	178	10	69	Salinas-Seaside-Monterey, CA	53.8
70	Chico, CA	176	3	70	Bakersfield, CA	49.4
71	Waterloo-Cedar Falls, IA	175	50	71	McAllen-Edinburg-Mission, TX	48.6
72	Denver-Boulder, CO	170	43	72	Lakeland-Winter Haven, FL	44.4
73	Honolulu, HI	169	7	73	W. Palm Beach-Boca Raton-Delray, FL	42.6
74	Reading, PA	168	25	74	Yuma, AZ	42.2
75	Bloomington-Normal, IL	164	35	75	Fort Pierce, FL	40.0

TABLE 6–75 Metropolitan Areas with Largest Number of Manufacturing Employees–1987

Selected Rankings

Number of Manufacturing Employees 1987

Number of Employees Rank	Metro Area	Number of Manufacturing Employees (Thousands)
1	N.Y.-North N.J.-Long Island,NY-NJ-CT	1,393.2
2	Los Angeles-Anaheim-Riverside, CA	1,255.9
3	Chicago-Gary-Lake County, IL-IN-WI	755.4
4	Detroit-Ann Arbor, MI	518.3
5	San Francisco-Oakland-San Jose, CA	507.1
6	Phila.-Willming.-Trenton,PA-NJ-DE-MD	486.8
7	Boston-Lawrence-Salem, MA-NH	377.7
8	Dallas-Fort Worth, TX	329.3
9	Cleveland-Akron-Lorain, OH	296.4
10	Minneaolis-St. Paul, MN-WI	250.1
11	St. Louis, MO-IL	221.7
12	Atlanta, GA	200.4
13	Seattle-Tacoma, WA	194.2
14	Milwaukee-Racine, WI	189.5
15	Houston-Galveston-Brazoria, TX	183.2
16	Cincinnati-Hamilton, OH-KY-IN	174.4
17	Charlotte-Gastonia-Rock Hill, NC-SC	155.4
18	Greensboro-Winston-Salem-High Pt.,NC	149.9
19	Baltimore, MD	145.2
20	Phoenix, AZ	135.8
21	Pittsburgh-Beaver Valley, PA	133.4
22	Hartford-New Britain-Middletown, CT	132.7
23	Miami-Fort Lauderdale, FL	132.6
24	Rochester, NY	130.2
25	Denver-Boulder, CO	125.9
26	San Diego, CA	120.0
27	Kansas City, MO-KS	115.4
28	Portland-Vancouver, OR-WA	109.0
29	Providence-Pawtucket-Fall Rvr, RI-MA	106.0
30	Dayton-Springfield, OH	105.9
31	Indianapolis, IN	105.6
32	Washington, DC-MD-VA	103.2
33	Buffalo-Niagara Falls, NY	103.2
34	Grand Rapids, MI	101.5
35	Greenville-Spartanburg, SC	99.2
36	Columbus, OH	98.7
37	Nashville, TN	88.6
38	Louisville, KY-IN	86.1
39	Tampa-St. Petersburg-Clearwater, FL	84.5
40	Allentown-Bethlehem, PA-NJ	78.1
41	New Haven-Waterbury-Meriden, CT	76.2
42	Worcester-Fitchburg-Leominster, MA	69.4
43	Scranton-Wilkes Barre, PA	69.3
44	Wichita, KS	69.0
45	New Bedford, MA	66.8
46	Richmond-Petersburg, VA	66.4
47	Norfolk-Virginia B.-Newport News, VA	66.0
48	Hickory, NC	65.8
49	Toledo, OH	63.2
50	Salt Lake City-Ogden, UT	61.0
51	Memphis, TN-AR-MS	60.3
52	Lancaster, PA	60.0
53	Raleigh-Durham, NC	59.4
54	York, PA	59.2
55	Harrisburg-Lebanon-Carlisle, PA	53.6
56	Johnson City-Kingsport-Bristol,TN-VA	52.8
57	Orlando, FL	51.9
58	Syracuse, NY	51.9
59	Birmingham, AL	51.6
60	Springfield, MA	51.4
61	Elkhart-Goshen, IN	50.0
62	Appleton-Oshkosh-Neenah, WI	49.7
63	Youngstown-Warren, OH	49.5
64	Knoxville, TN	48.8
65	Tulsa, OK	48.7
66	Oklahoma City, OK	48.2
67	Albany-Schenectady-Troy, NY	48.0
68	Reading, PA	47.3
69	Fort Wayne, IN	45.7
70	Chattanooga, TN-GA	44.2
71	San Antonio, TX	44.1
72	Manchester, NH	43.9
73	Rockford, IL	43.8
74	Canton, OH	43.5
75	New Orleans, LA	43.1

Value Added by Manufacture 1987

Number of Employees Rank	Value Added Rank	Metro Area	Value Added (Mil Dol)
1	1	N.Y.-North N.J.-Long Island,NY-NJ-CT	81,959.2
2	2	Los Angeles-Anaheim-Riverside, CA	72,520.5
3	3	Chicago-Gary-Lake County, IL-IN-WI	49,773.3
5	4	San Francisco-Oakland-San Jose, CA	38,913.2
4	5	Detroit-Ann Arbor, MI	31,043.7
6	6	Phila.-Willming.-Trenton,PA-NJ-DE-MD	28,940.8
7	7	Boston-Lawrence-Salem, MA-NH	24,076.4
8	8	Dallas-Fort Worth, TX	19,641.4
15	9	Houston-Galveston-Brazoria, TX	18,596.9
9	10	Cleveland-Akron-Lorain, OH	17,262.2
10	11	Minneaolis-St. Paul, MN-WI	15,732.2
11	12	St. Louis, MO-IL	14,115.0
12	13	Atlanta, GA	13,345.7
16	14	Cincinnati-Hamilton, OH-KY-IN	12,831.7
24	15	Rochester, NY	12,409.0
14	16	Milwaukee-Racine, WI	11,609.4
18	17	Greensboro-Winston-Salem-High Pt.,NC	10,910.7
13	18	Seattle-Tacoma, WA	10,895.9
19	19	Baltimore, MD	9,675.6
27	20	Kansas City, MO-KS	9,124.0
38	21	Louisville, KY-IN	8,320.8
20	22	Phoenix, AZ	8,179.8
17	23	Charlotte-Gastonia-Rock Hill, NC-SC	8,153.6
25	24	Denver-Boulder, CO	8,037.3
22	25	Hartford-New Britain-Middletown, CT	7,784.0
36	26	Columbus, OH	7,079.1
33	27	Buffalo-Niagara Falls, NY	7,025.5
46	28	Richmond-Petersburg, VA	6,833.0
31	29	Indianapolis, IN	6,806.0
32	30	Washington, DC-MD-VA	6,788.0
28	31	Portland-Vancouver, OR-WA	6,445.4
26	32	San Diego, CA	6,426.8
21	33	Pittsburgh-Beaver Valley, PA	6,322.8
30	34	Dayton-Springfield, OH	6,284.6
34	35	Grand Rapids, MI	5,967.7
23	36	Miami-Fort Lauderdale, FL	5,700.2
37	37	Nashville, TN	4,989.5
35	38	Greenville-Spartanburg, SC	4,967.5
49	39	Toledo, OH	4,925.1
53	40	Raleigh-Durham, NC	4,728.5
40	41	Allentown-Bethlehem, PA-NJ	4,693.8
29	42	Providence-Pawtucket-Fall Rvr, RI-MA	4,425.3
75	43	New Orleans, LA	4,314.7
47	44	Norfolk-Virginia B.-Newport News, VA	4,285.3
41	45	New Haven-Waterbury-Meriden, CT	4,247.5
39	46	Tampa-St. Petersburg-Clearwater, FL	4,139.8
44	47	Wichita, KS	4,122.8
51	48	Memphis, TN-AR-MS	4,114.2
42	49	Worcester-Fitchburg-Leominster, MA	3,908.1
52	50	Lancaster, PA	3,883.7
66	51	Oklahoma City, OK	3,653.4
60	52	Springfield, MA	3,586.5
43	53	Scranton-Wilkes Barre, PA	3,522.9
58	54	Syracuse, NY	3,431.6
50	55	Salt Lake City-Ogden, UT	3,395.3
57	56	Orlando, FL	3,197.8
55	57	Harrisburg-Lebanon-Carlisle, PA	3,197.4
72	58	Manchester, NH	3,112.8
67	59	Albany-Schenectady-Troy, NY	3,109.0
56	60	Johnson City-Kingsport-Bristol,TN-VA	3,105.8
62	61	Appleton-Oshkosh-Neenah, WI	3,085.7
54	62	York, PA	2,975.3
74	63	Canton, OH	2,970.4
63	64	Youngstown-Warren, OH	2,889.3
45	65	New Bedford, MA	2,882.9
73	66	Rockford, IL	2,807.7
65	67	Tulsa, OK	2,735.9
61	68	Elkhart-Goshen, IN	2,640.8
68	69	Reading, PA	2,628.6
64	70	Knoxville, TN	2,621.8
59	71	Birmingham, AL	2,613.2
69	72	Fort Wayne, IN	2,361.8
70	73	Chattanooga, TN-GA	2,298.7
48	74	Hickory, NC	2,230.7
71	75	San Antonio, TX	2,127.7

TABLE 7—75 Largest Cities by 1990 Population

Selected Rankings

Total Persons 1990			Population Density (per Square Kilometer) 1990				Population Change 1980–1990			
Rank	City	Population	Population Rank	Density Rank	City	Density	Population Rank	Change Rank	City	Percent Change
1	New York, NY	7,322,564	1	1	New York, NY	9,151	53	1	Mesa, AZ	89.0
2	Los Angeles, CA	3,485,398	14	2	San Francisco, CA	5,983	61	2	Arlington, TX	63.5
3	Chicago, IL	2,783,726	67	3	Jersey City, NJ	5,936	47	3	Fresno, CA	62.9
4	Houston, TX	1,630,553	3	4	Chicago, IL	4,730	63	4	Las Vegas, NV	56.9
5	Philadelphia, PA	1,585,577	20	5	Boston, MA	4,580	37	5	Virginia Beach, VA	49.9
6	San Diego, CA	1,110,549	5	6	Philadelphia, PA	4,530	52	6	Santa Ana, CA	44.0
7	Detroit, MI	1,027,974	56	7	Newark, NJ	4,461	74	7	Stockton, CA	42.3
8	Dallas, TX	1,006,877	52	8	Santa Ana, CA	4,184	72	8	Aurora, CO	40.1
9	Phoenix, AZ	983,403	46	9	Miami, FL	3,893	75	9	Raleigh, NC	38.4
10	San Antonio, TX	935,933	19	10	Washington, DC	3,815	27	10	Austin, TX	34.6
11	San Jose, CA	782,248	12	11	Baltimore, MD	3,517	41	11	Sacramento, CA	34.0
12	Baltimore, MD	736,014	32	12	Long Beach, CA	3,316	68	12	Riverside, CA	32.8
13	Indianapolis, IN	731,327	50	13	Buffalo, NY	3,119	54	13	Colorado Springs, CO	30.7
14	San Francisco, CA	723,959	2	14	Los Angeles, CA	2,867	69	14	Anchorage, AK	29.8
15	Jacksonville, FL	635,230	7	15	Detroit, MI	2,861	6	15	San Diego, CA	26.8
16	Columbus, OH	632,910	42	16	Minneapolis, MN	2,589	35	16	Charlotte, NC	25.5
17	Milwaukee, WI	628,088	40	17	Pittsburgh, PA	2,567	9	17	Phoenix, AZ	24.5
18	Memphis, TN	610,337	39	18	Oakland, CA	2,564	11	18	San Jose, CA	24.3
19	Washington, DC	606,900	23	19	Cleveland, OH	2,534	33	19	Tucson, AZ	22.6
20	Boston, MA	574,283	17	20	Milwaukee, WI	2,524	59	20	Anaheim, CA	21.4
21	Seattle, WA	516,259	66	21	Rochester, NY	2,499	22	21	El Paso, TX	21.2
22	El Paso, TX	515,342	34	22	St. Louis, MO	2,473	10	22	San Antonio, TX	19.1
23	Cleveland, OH	505,616	21	23	Seattle, WA	2,376	32	23	Long Beach, CA	18.8
24	New Orleans, LA	496,938	59	24	Anaheim, CA	2,323	30	24	Portland, OR	18.8
25	Nashville-Davidson, TN	488,374	57	25	St. Paul, MN	1,991	15	25	Jacksonville, FL	17.4
26	Denver, CO	467,610	62	26	Norfolk, VA	1,877	2	26	Los Angeles, CA	17.4
27	Austin, TX	465,622	45	27	Cincinnati, OH	1,820	28	27	Fort Worth, TX	16.2
28	Fort Worth, TX	447,619	11	28	San Jose, CA	1,763	38	28	Albuquerque, NM	15.6
29	Oklahoma City, OK	444,719	44	29	Honolulu, HI (CDP)	1,703	16	29	Columbus, OH	12.0
30	Portland, OR	437,319	58	30	Louisville, KY	1,672	8	30	Dallas, TX	11.3
31	Kansas City, MO	435,146	49	31	Toledo, OH	1,595	64	31	Corpus Christi, TX	10.9
32	Long Beach, CA	429,433	65	32	St. Petersburg, FL	1,557	70	32	Lexington-Fayette, KY	10.4
33	Tucson, AZ	405,390	74	33	Stockton, CA	1,549	29	33	Oklahoma City, OK	10.1
34	St. Louis, MO	396,685	41	34	Sacramento, CA	1,481	39	34	Oakland, CA	9.7
35	Charlotte, NC	395,934	71	35	Akron, OH	1,384	51	35	Wichita, KS	8.6
36	Atlanta, GA	394,017	47	36	Fresno, CA	1,379	25	36	Nashville-Davidson, TN	7.2
37	Virginia Beach, VA	393,069	30	37	Portland, OR	1,354	48	37	Omaha, NE	7.0
38	Albuquerque, NM	384,736	6	38	San Diego, CA	1,323	14	38	San Francisco, CA	6.6
39	Oakland, CA	372,242	48	39	Omaha, NE	1,288	21	39	Seattle, WA	4.5
40	Pittsburgh, PA	369,879	16	40	Columbus, OH	1,280	13	40	Indianapolis, IN	4.4
41	Sacramento, CA	369,365	63	41	Las Vegas, NV	1,197	1	41	New York, NY	3.5
42	Minneapolis, MN	368,383	26	42	Denver, CO	1,178	46	42	Miami, FL	3.4
43	Tulsa, OK	367,302	4	43	Houston, TX	1,166	55	43	Tampa, FL	3.1
44	Honolulu, HI (CDP)	365,272	36	44	Atlanta, GA	1,154	4	44	Houston, TX	2.2
45	Cincinnati, OH	364,040	73	45	Baton Rouge, LA	1,146	67	45	Jersey City, NJ	2.2
46	Miami, FL	358,548	8	46	Dallas, TX	1,135	20	46	Boston, MA	2.0
47	Fresno, CA	354,202	68	47	Riverside, CA	1,126	43	47	Tulsa, OK	1.8
48	Omaha, NE	335,795	38	48	Albuquerque, NM	1,124	57	48	St. Paul, MN	0.7
49	Toledo, OH	332,943	61	49	Arlington, TX	1,086	44	49	Honolulu, HI (CDP)	0.1
50	Buffalo, NY	328,123	10	50	San Antonio, TX	1,085	65	50	St. Petersburg, FL	0.0
51	Wichita, KS	304,011	24	51	New Orleans, LA	1,062	73	51	Baton Rouge, LA	-0.4
52	Santa Ana, CA	293,742	53	52	Mesa, AZ	1,024	42	52	Minneapolis, MN	-0.7
53	Mesa, AZ	288,091	51	53	Wichita, KS	1,019	17	53	Milwaukee, WI	-1.3
54	Colorado Springs, CO	281,140	33	54	Tucson, AZ	1,001	62	54	Norfolk, VA	-2.2
55	Tampa, FL	280,015	55	55	Tampa, FL	995	31	55	Kansas City, MO	-2.9
56	Newark, NJ	275,221	18	56	Memphis, TN	920	66	56	Rochester, NY	-4.2
57	St. Paul, MN	272,235	75	57	Raleigh, NC	911	19	57	Washington, DC	-4.9
58	Louisville, KY	269,063	9	58	Phoenix, AZ	904	26	58	Denver, CO	-5.1
59	Anaheim, CA	266,406	35	59	Charlotte, NC	877	45	59	Cincinnati, OH	-5.5
60	Birmingham, AL	265,968	27	60	Austin, TX	826	18	60	Memphis, TN	-5.5
61	Arlington, TX	261,721	22	61	El Paso, TX	811	71	61	Akron, OH	-6.0
62	Norfolk, VA	261,229	13	62	Indianapolis, IN	781	5	62	Philadelphia, PA	-6.1
63	Las Vegas, NV	258,295	43	63	Tulsa, OK	773	49	63	Toledo, OH	-6.1
64	Corpus Christi, TX	257,453	64	64	Corpus Christi, TX	736	12	64	Baltimore, MD	-6.4
65	St. Petersburg, FL	238,629	60	65	Birmingham, AL	692	60	65	Birmingham, AL	-6.5
66	Rochester, NY	231,636	72	66	Aurora, CO	647	36	66	Atlanta, GA	-7.3
67	Jersey City, NJ	228,537	28	67	Fort Worth, TX	615	3	67	Chicago, IL	-7.4
68	Riverside, CA	226,505	37	68	Virginia Beach, VA	611	50	68	Buffalo, NY	-8.3
69	Anchorage, AK	226,338	54	69	Colorado Springs, CO	592	58	69	Louisville, KY	-9.9
70	Lexington-Fayette, KY	225,366	31	70	Kansas City, MO	539	24	70	New Orleans, LA	-10.9
71	Akron, OH	223,019	25	71	Nashville-Davidson, TN	398	23	71	Cleveland, OH	-11.9
72	Aurora, CO	222,103	15	72	Jacksonville, FL	323	34	72	St. Louis, MO	-12.4
73	Baton Rouge, LA	219,531	70	73	Lexington-Fayette, KY	306	40	73	Pittsburgh, PA	-12.8
74	Stockton, CA	210,943	29	74	Oklahoma City, OK	282	7	74	Detroit, MI	-14.6
75	Raleigh, NC	207,951	69	75	Anchorage, AK	51	56	75	Newark, NJ	-16.4

TABLE 7—75 Largest Cities by 1990 Population

Selected Rankings

Percent White 1990				Percent Black 1990				Percent Hispanic 1990			
Population Rank	White Rank	City	Percent White	Population Rank	Black Rank	City	Percent Black	Population Rank	Hispanic Rank	City	Percent Hispanic
53	1	Mesa, AZ	90.07	7	1	Detroit, MI	75.67	22	1	El Paso, TX	69.02
54	2	Colorado Springs, CO	85.90	36	2	Atlanta, GA	67.07	52	2	Santa Ana, CA	65.15
30	3	Portland, OR	84.64	19	3	Washington, DC	65.84	46	3	Miami, FL	62.46
70	4	Lexington-Fayette, KY	84.51	60	4	Birmingham, AL	63.27	10	4	San Antonio, TX	55.59
48	5	Omaha, NE	83.86	24	5	New Orleans, LA	61.92	64	5	Corpus Christi, TX	50.38
61	6	Arlington, TX	82.64	12	6	Baltimore, MD	59.21	2	6	Los Angeles, CA	39.92
72	7	Aurora, CO	82.41	56	7	Newark, NJ	58.46	38	7	Albuquerque, NM	34.49
51	8	Wichita, KS	82.29	18	8	Memphis, TN	54.84	59	8	Anaheim, CA	31.44
57	9	St. Paul, MN	82.26	34	9	St. Louis, MO	47.50	47	9	Fresno, CA	29.87
9	10	Phoenix, AZ	81.69	23	10	Cleveland, OH	46.56	33	10	Tucson, AZ	29.25
69	11	Anchorage, AK	80.74	73	11	Baton Rouge, LA	43.89	4	11	Houston, TX	27.63
37	12	Virginia Beach, VA	80.50	39	12	Oakland, CA	43.88	11	12	San Jose, CA	26.64
43	13	Tulsa, OK	79.35	5	13	Philadelphia, PA	39.86	56	13	Newark, NJ	26.07
42	14	Minneapolis, MN	78.44	3	14	Chicago, IL	39.07	68	14	Riverside, CA	25.97
63	15	Las Vegas, NV	78.42	62	15	Norfolk, VA	39.05	74	15	Stockton, CA	24.96
38	16	Albuquerque, NM	78.24	45	16	Cincinnati, OH	37.94	1	16	New York, NY	24.36
65	17	St. Petersburg, FL	78.00	35	17	Charlotte, NC	31.78	67	17	Jersey City, NJ	24.24
49	18	Toledo, OH	76.96	66	18	Rochester, NY	31.53	32	18	Long Beach, CA	23.62
22	19	El Paso, TX	76.87	50	19	Buffalo, NY	30.65	26	19	Denver, CO	22.96
64	20	Corpus Christi, TX	76.14	17	20	Milwaukee, WI	30.45	27	20	Austin, TX	22.95
13	21	Indianapolis, IN	75.81	67	21	Jersey City, NJ	29.69	8	21	Dallas, TX	20.88
21	22	Seattle, WA	75.32	58	22	Louisville, KY	29.65	6	22	San Diego, CA	20.67
33	23	Tucson, AZ	75.25	31	23	Kansas City, MO	29.59	9	23	Phoenix, AZ	20.04
29	24	Oklahoma City, OK	74.78	8	24	Dallas, TX	29.50	3	24	Chicago, IL	19.61
16	25	Columbus, OH	74.42	1	25	New York, NY	28.71	28	25	Fort Worth, TX	19.51
25	26	Nashville-Davidson, TN	73.77	4	26	Houston, TX	28.09	41	26	Sacramento, CA	16.25
71	27	Akron, OH	73.76	75	27	Raleigh, NC	27.58	55	27	Tampa, FL	15.00
10	28	San Antonio, TX	72.24	46	28	Miami, FL	27.39	14	28	San Francisco, CA	13.91
40	29	Pittsburgh, PA	72.13	40	29	Pittsburgh, PA	25.78	39	29	Oakland, CA	13.89
26	30	Denver, CO	72.11	20	30	Boston, MA	25.59	63	30	Las Vegas, NV	12.53
15	31	Jacksonville, FL	71.87	15	31	Jacksonville, FL	25.23	53	31	Mesa, AZ	10.88
59	32	Anaheim, CA	71.44	55	32	Tampa, FL	25.05	20	32	Boston, MA	10.79
55	33	Tampa, FL	70.90	71	33	Akron, OH	24.51	54	33	Colorado Springs, CO	9.13
68	34	Riverside, CA	70.79	25	34	Nashville-Davidson, TN	24.29	61	34	Arlington, TX	8.91
27	35	Austin, TX	70.56	13	35	Indianapolis, IN	22.64	66	35	Rochester, NY	8.66
58	36	Louisville, KY	69.21	16	36	Columbus, OH	22.55	72	36	Aurora, CO	6.65
75	37	Raleigh, NC	69.18	28	37	Fort Worth, TX	22.01	17	37	Milwaukee, WI	6.27
52	38	Santa Ana, CA	67.99	49	38	Toledo, OH	19.70	5	38	Philadelphia, PA	5.63
6	39	San Diego, CA	67.12	65	39	St. Petersburg, FL	19.58	19	39	Washington, DC	5.39
31	40	Kansas City, MO	66.78	29	40	Oklahoma City, OK	15.98	51	40	Wichita, KS	5.02
46	41	Miami, FL	65.64	41	41	Sacramento, CA	15.30	29	41	Oklahoma City, OK	4.95
35	42	Charlotte, NC	65.61	2	42	Los Angeles, CA	13.99	50	42	Buffalo, NY	4.92
50	43	Buffalo, NY	64.75	37	43	Virginia Beach, VA	13.91	23	43	Cleveland, OH	4.59
28	44	Fort Worth, TX	63.79	32	44	Long Beach, CA	13.68	44	44	Honolulu, HI (CDP)	4.57
17	45	Milwaukee, WI	63.37	43	45	Tulsa, OK	13.57	57	45	St. Paul, MN	4.22
20	46	Boston, MA	62.84	70	46	Lexington-Fayette, KY	13.38	69	46	Anchorage, AK	4.09
11	47	San Jose, CA	62.80	48	47	Omaha, NE	13.10	49	47	Toledo, OH	3.97
66	48	Rochester, NY	61.09	42	48	Minneapolis, MN	13.02	31	48	Kansas City, MO	3.91
45	49	Cincinnati, OH	60.51	26	49	Denver, CO	12.84	21	49	Seattle, WA	3.55
41	50	Sacramento, CA	60.09	27	50	Austin, TX	12.43	24	50	New Orleans, LA	3.47
47	51	Fresno, CA	59.18	63	51	Las Vegas, NV	11.43	30	51	Portland, OR	3.17
32	52	Long Beach, CA	58.38	72	52	Aurora, CO	11.43	37	52	Virginia Beach, VA	3.09
74	53	Stockton, CA	57.54	51	53	Wichita, KS	11.28	48	53	Omaha, NE	3.06
62	54	Norfolk, VA	56.74	14	54	San Francisco, CA	10.92	62	54	Norfolk, VA	2.91
8	55	Dallas, TX	55.30	21	55	Seattle, WA	10.06	7	55	Detroit, MI	2.77
73	56	Baton Rouge, LA	53.95	74	56	Stockton, CA	9.63	65	56	St. Petersburg, FL	2.62
14	57	San Francisco, CA	53.56	6	57	San Diego, CA	9.39	43	57	Tulsa, OK	2.60
5	58	Philadelphia, PA	53.52	61	58	Arlington, TX	8.41	15	58	Jacksonville, FL	2.59
2	59	Los Angeles, CA	52.83	47	59	Fresno, CA	8.30	42	59	Minneapolis, MN	2.14
4	60	Houston, TX	52.69	30	60	Portland, OR	7.67	36	60	Atlanta, GA	1.91
1	61	New York, NY	52.26	68	61	Riverside, CA	7.39	73	61	Baton Rouge, LA	1.57
34	62	St. Louis, MO	50.94	57	62	St. Paul, MN	7.38	35	62	Charlotte, NC	1.41
23	63	Cleveland, OH	49.49	10	63	San Antonio, TX	7.04	75	63	Raleigh, NC	1.41
67	64	Jersey City, NJ	48.25	54	64	Colorado Springs, CO	7.02	34	64	St. Louis, MO	1.29
3	65	Chicago, IL	45.39	69	65	Anchorage, AK	6.43	70	65	Lexington-Fayette, KY	1.13
18	66	Memphis, TN	44.01	9	66	Phoenix, AZ	5.19	16	66	Columbus, OH	1.07
12	67	Baltimore, MD	39.10	64	67	Corpus Christi, TX	4.80	13	67	Indianapolis, IN	1.05
60	68	Birmingham, AL	35.96	11	68	San Jose, CA	4.70	12	68	Baltimore, MD	1.03
24	69	New Orleans, LA	34.92	33	69	Tucson, AZ	4.28	25	69	Nashville-Davidson, TN	0.95
39	70	Oakland, CA	32.47	22	70	El Paso, TX	3.44	40	70	Pittsburgh, PA	0.94
36	71	Atlanta, GA	31.05	38	71	Albuquerque, NM	2.98	18	71	Memphis, TN	0.73
19	72	Washington, DC	29.60	52	72	Santa Ana, CA	2.62	71	72	Akron, OH	0.72
56	73	Newark, NJ	28.62	59	73	Anaheim, CA	2.54	45	73	Cincinnati, OH	0.66
44	74	Honolulu, HI (CDP)	26.70	53	74	Mesa, AZ	1.85	58	74	Louisville, KY	0.65
7	75	Detroit, MI	21.63	44	75	Honolulu, HI (CDP)	1.32	60	75	Birmingham, AL	0.39

TABLE 7—75 Largest Cities by 1990 Population

Selected Rankings

Percent 65 Years and Over 1990				Female Family Households 1990				One Person Households 1990			
Population Rank	65 Plus Rank	City	Percent 65 Plus	Population Rank	Fem. HHs. Rank	City	Percent Fem. HHs.	Population Rank	1 person HHs. Rank	City	Percent 1 Person HHs.
65	1	St. Petersburg, FL	22.2	7	1	Detroit, MI	30.3	19	1	Washington, DC	41.5
40	2	Pittsburgh, PA	17.9	56	2	Newark, NJ	28.6	26	2	Denver, CO	40.4
58	3	Louisville, KY	16.6	12	3	Baltimore, MD	24.6	21	3	Seattle, WA	39.8
34	4	St. Louis, MO	16.6	24	4	New Orleans, LA	24.1	45	4	Cincinnati, OH	39.5
46	5	Miami, FL	16.6	36	5	Atlanta, GA	23.4	14	5	San Francisco, CA	39.3
44	6	Honolulu, HI (CDP)	16.0	23	6	Cleveland, OH	22.7	34	6	St. Louis, MO	39.2
5	7	Philadelphia, PA	15.2	18	7	Memphis, TN	21.9	42	7	Minneapolis, MN	38.5
21	8	Seattle, WA	15.2	60	8	Birmingham, AL	21.7	40	8	Pittsburgh, PA	36.2
71	9	Akron, OH	14.9	66	9	Rochester, NY	20.6	50	9	Buffalo, NY	35.6
60	10	Birmingham, AL	14.8	34	10	St. Louis, MO	20.5	20	10	Boston, MA	35.5
50	11	Buffalo, NY	14.8	67	11	Jersey City, NJ	20.4	66	11	Rochester, NY	35.3
14	12	San Francisco, CA	14.6	5	12	Philadelphia, PA	20.3	65	12	St. Petersburg, FL	35.1
30	13	Portland, OR	14.6	50	13	Buffalo, NY	20.2	36	13	Atlanta, GA	35.0
55	14	Tampa, FL	14.6	17	14	Milwaukee, WI	19.8	58	14	Louisville, KY	35.0
23	15	Cleveland, OH	14.0	3	15	Chicago, IL	19.6	30	15	Portland, OR	34.9
45	16	Cincinnati, OH	13.9	19	16	Washington, DC	19.5	57	16	St. Paul, MN	34.7
26	17	Denver, CO	13.9	46	17	Miami, FL	18.6	8	17	Dallas, TX	34.2
57	18	St. Paul, MN	13.7	39	18	Oakland, CA	18.5	27	18	Austin, TX	34.1
12	19	Baltimore, MD	13.7	58	19	Louisville, KY	18.3	23	19	Cleveland, OH	33.5
49	20	Toledo, OH	13.6	45	20	Cincinnati, OH	18.2	39	20	Oakland, CA	33.2
42	21	Minneapolis, MN	13.0	1	21	New York, NY	18.0	1	21	New York, NY	32.9
1	22	New York, NY	13.0	73	22	Baton Rouge, LA	17.7	43	22	Tulsa, OK	32.7
24	23	New Orleans, LA	13.0	40	23	Pittsburgh, PA	17.2	31	23	Kansas City, MO	32.5
48	24	Omaha, NE	12.9	20	24	Boston, MA	16.8	55	24	Tampa, FL	32.3
31	25	Kansas City, MO	12.9	71	25	Akron, OH	16.6	24	25	New Orleans, LA	32.2
19	26	Washington, DC	12.8	22	26	El Paso, TX	16.4	75	26	Raleigh, NC	32.2
43	27	Tulsa, OK	12.7	47	27	Fresno, CA	16.2	3	27	Chicago, IL	32.1
33	28	Tucson, AZ	12.6	62	28	Norfolk, VA	16.1	60	28	Birmingham, AL	31.9
17	29	Milwaukee, WI	12.4	10	29	San Antonio, TX	15.7	5	29	Philadelphia, PA	31.6
51	30	Wichita, KS	12.4	49	30	Toledo, OH	15.7	33	30	Tucson, AZ	31.3
53	31	Mesa, AZ	12.4	55	31	Tampa, FL	15.5	16	31	Columbus, OH	31.3
7	32	Detroit, MI	12.2	74	32	Stockton, CA	15.5	4	32	Houston, TX	31.0
18	33	Memphis, TN	12.2	31	33	Kansas City, MO	15.1	41	33	Sacramento, CA	30.9
41	34	Sacramento, CA	12.1	4	34	Houston, TX	14.6	32	34	Long Beach, CA	30.8
66	35	Rochester, NY	12.1	25	35	Nashville-Davidson, TN	14.5	71	35	Akron, OH	30.8
39	36	Oakland, CA	12.0	41	36	Sacramento, CA	14.3	25	36	Nashville-Davidson, TN	30.7
29	37	Oklahoma City, OK	11.9	16	37	Columbus, OH	14.2	48	37	Omaha, NE	30.6
3	38	Chicago, IL	11.9	13	38	Indianapolis, IN	14.1	12	38	Baltimore, MD	30.5
20	39	Boston, MA	11.5	35	39	Charlotte, NC	14.0	17	39	Milwaukee, WI	30.5
73	40	Baton Rouge, LA	11.5	15	40	Jacksonville, FL	13.9	29	40	Oklahoma City, OK	30.0
25	41	Nashville-Davidson, TN	11.4	8	41	Dallas, TX	13.9	51	41	Wichita, KS	30.0
13	42	Indianapolis, IN	11.4	64	42	Corpus Christi, TX	13.8	7	42	Detroit, MI	29.8
36	43	Atlanta, GA	11.3	2	43	Los Angeles, CA	13.6	49	43	Toledo, OH	29.7
28	44	Fort Worth, TX	11.2	48	44	Omaha, NE	13.3	73	44	Baton Rouge, LA	29.7
38	45	Albuquerque, NM	11.1	28	45	Fort Worth, TX	13.3	13	45	Indianapolis, IN	29.4
67	46	Jersey City, NJ	11.1	57	46	St. Paul, MN	13.0	70	46	Lexington-Fayette, KY	29.1
32	47	Long Beach, CA	10.8	32	47	Long Beach, CA	13.0	28	47	Fort Worth, TX	29.0
15	48	Jacksonville, FL	10.6	42	48	Minneapolis, MN	12.7	46	48	Miami, FL	28.9
74	49	Stockton, CA	10.5	29	49	Oklahoma City, OK	12.6	67	49	Jersey City, NJ	28.7
62	50	Norfolk, VA	10.5	68	50	Riverside, CA	12.5	2	50	Los Angeles, CA	28.5
10	51	San Antonio, TX	10.5	33	51	Tucson, AZ	12.4	18	51	Memphis, TN	28.3
63	52	Las Vegas, NV	10.3	65	52	St. Petersburg, FL	12.4	38	52	Albuquerque, NM	28.2
6	53	San Diego, CA	10.2	70	53	Lexington-Fayette, KY	12.2	72	53	Aurora, CO	28.1
47	54	Fresno, CA	10.1	38	54	Albuquerque, NM	12.1	35	54	Charlotte, NC	28.0
64	55	Corpus Christi, TX	10.1	63	55	Las Vegas, NV	12.0	56	55	Newark, NJ	27.5
2	56	Los Angeles, CA	10.0	11	56	San Jose, CA	11.9	44	56	Honolulu, HI (CDP)	27.4
70	57	Lexington-Fayette, KY	9.9	52	57	Santa Ana, CA	11.8	62	57	Norfolk, VA	26.8
35	58	Charlotte, NC	9.8	9	58	Phoenix, AZ	11.8	54	58	Colorado Springs, CO	26.7
9	59	Phoenix, AZ	9.7	72	59	Aurora, CO	11.8	6	59	San Diego, CA	26.3
8	60	Dallas, TX	9.7	43	60	Tulsa, OK	11.8	63	60	Las Vegas, NV	26.2
56	61	Newark, NJ	9.3	59	61	Anaheim, CA	11.6	9	61	Phoenix, AZ	26.1
16	62	Columbus, OH	9.2	26	62	Denver, CO	11.5	15	62	Jacksonville, FL	25.8
54	63	Colorado Springs, CO	9.2	75	63	Raleigh, NC	11.3	10	63	San Antonio, TX	25.0
68	64	Riverside, CA	8.9	6	64	San Diego, CA	11.2	61	64	Arlington, TX	24.8
75	65	Raleigh, NC	8.8	51	65	Wichita, KS	11.1	47	65	Fresno, CA	24.1
22	66	El Paso, TX	8.7	44	66	Honolulu, HI (CDP)	11.0	53	66	Mesa, AZ	24.0
59	67	Anaheim, CA	8.4	27	67	Austin, TX	11.0	74	67	Stockton, CA	23.4
4	68	Houston, TX	8.3	30	68	Portland, OR	11.0	69	68	Anchorage, AK	22.9
27	69	Austin, TX	7.4	54	69	Colorado Springs, CO	10.1	64	69	Corpus Christi, TX	22.5
11	70	San Jose, CA	7.2	69	70	Anchorage, AK	10.1	68	70	Riverside, CA	20.6
72	71	Aurora, CO	6.8	14	71	San Francisco, CA	9.9	59	71	Anaheim, CA	19.9
37	72	Virginia Beach, VA	5.9	37	72	Virginia Beach, VA	9.5	11	72	San Jose, CA	18.4
52	73	Santa Ana, CA	5.6	61	73	Arlington, TX	9.4	22	73	El Paso, TX	17.9
61	74	Arlington, TX	5.0	53	74	Mesa, AZ	9.3	37	74	Virginia Beach, VA	17.1
69	75	Anchorage, AK	3.6	21	75	Seattle, WA	9.0	52	75	Santa Ana, CA	16.6

TABLE 7—75 Largest Cities by 1990 Population

Selected Rankings

Median Value of Owned Housing 1990				Median Rent 1990				Change in Labor Force 1989-1990			
Population Rank	Median Value Rank	City	Median Value (Dollars)	Population Rank	Median Rent Rank	City	Median Rent (Dollars)	Population Rank	Percent Change Rank	City	Percent Change
44	1	Honolulu, HI (CDP)	353,900	11	1	San Jose, CA	692	63	1	Las Vegas, NV	7.1
14	2	San Francisco, CA	298,900	52	2	Santa Ana, CA	679	2	2	Los Angeles, CA	5.0
11	3	San Jose, CA	259,100	59	3	Anaheim, CA	661	32	3	Long Beach, CA	4.8
2	4	Los Angeles, CA	244,500	14	4	San Francisco, CA	613	68	4	Riverside, CA	4.8
32	5	Long Beach, CA	222,900	44	5	Honolulu, HI (CDP)	582	48	5	Omaha, NE	3.5
59	6	Anaheim, CA	218,700	6	6	San Diego, CA	560	64	6	Corpus Christi, TX	3.0
1	7	New York, NY	189,600	32	7	Long Beach, CA	551	72	7	Aurora, CO	2.9
6	8	San Diego, CA	189,400	20	8	Boston, MA	546	26	8	Denver, CO	2.8
52	9	Santa Ana, CA	185,400	2	9	Los Angeles, CA	544	65	9	St. Petersburg, FL	2.6
39	10	Oakland, CA	177,400	69	10	Anchorage, AK	528	69	10	Anchorage, AK	2.6
20	11	Boston, MA	161,400	68	11	Riverside, CA	512	4	11	Houston, TX	2.3
21	12	Seattle, WA	137,900	39	12	Oakland, CA	486	55	12	Tampa, FL	2.2
68	13	Riverside, CA	134,800	37	13	Virginia Beach, VA	484	44	13	Honolulu, HI (CDP)	2.0
67	14	Jersey City, NJ	127,700	67	14	Jersey City, NJ	464	21	14	Seattle, WA	1.7
19	15	Washington, DC	123,900	1	15	New York, NY	448	15	15	Jacksonville, FL	1.7
41	16	Sacramento, CA	115,800	19	16	Washington, DC	441	47	16	Fresno, CA	1.6
56	17	Newark, NJ	110,000	63	17	Las Vegas, NV	434	57	17	St. Paul, MN	1.6
69	18	Anchorage, AK	109,700	41	18	Sacramento, CA	429	42	18	Minneapolis, MN	1.5
74	19	Stockton, CA	107,200	21	19	Seattle, WA	425	43	19	Tulsa, OK	1.4
75	20	Raleigh, NC	96,600	74	20	Stockton, CA	404	1	20	New York, NY	1.4
37	21	Virginia Beach, VA	96,500	53	21	Mesa, AZ	396	61	21	Arlington, TX	1.3
63	22	Las Vegas, NV	89,200	75	22	Raleigh, NC	394	46	22	Miami, FL	1.3
53	23	Mesa, AZ	86,500	72	23	Aurora, CO	393	28	23	Fort Worth, TX	1.2
38	24	Albuquerque, NM	85,900	42	24	Minneapolis, MN	390	9	24	Phoenix, AZ	1.1
61	25	Arlington, TX	82,800	57	25	St. Paul, MN	389	56	25	Newark, NJ	1.1
54	26	Colorado Springs, CO	81,900	56	26	Newark, NJ	385	53	26	Mesa, AZ	1.1
35	27	Charlotte, NC	81,300	61	27	Arlington, TX	382	58	27	Louisville, KY	1.1
47	28	Fresno, CA	80,300	3	28	Chicago, IL	377	75	28	Raleigh, NC	1.0
72	29	Aurora, CO	80,200	35	29	Charlotte, NC	377	51	29	Wichita, KS	1.0
46	30	Miami, FL	79,200	66	30	Rochester, NY	377	45	30	Cincinnati, OH	1.0
26	31	Denver, CO	79,000	8	31	Dallas, TX	375	37	31	Virginia Beach, VA	1.0
8	32	Dallas, TX	78,800	9	32	Phoenix, AZ	374	12	32	Baltimore, MD	0.9
3	33	Chicago, IL	78,700	47	33	Fresno, CA	369	27	33	Austin, TX	0.9
9	34	Phoenix, AZ	77,100	62	34	Norfolk, VA	361	67	34	Jersey City, NJ	0.8
62	35	Norfolk, VA	74,500	54	35	Colorado Springs, CO	360	54	35	Colorado Springs, CO	0.8
25	36	Nashville-Davidson, TN	74,400	25	36	Nashville-Davidson, TN	358	40	36	Pittsburgh, PA	0.8
70	37	Lexington-Fayette, KY	73,900	5	37	Philadelphia, PA	358	30	37	Portland, OR	0.7
27	38	Austin, TX	72,600	38	38	Albuquerque, NM	353	16	38	Columbus, OH	0.7
42	39	Minneapolis, MN	71,700	15	39	Jacksonville, FL	353	35	39	Charlotte, NC	0.6
36	40	Atlanta, GA	71,200	65	40	St. Petersburg, FL	353	41	40	Sacramento, CA	0.6
57	41	St. Paul, MN	70,900	16	41	Columbus, OH	348	36	41	Atlanta, GA	0.5
24	42	New Orleans, LA	69,600	46	42	Miami, FL	346	18	42	Memphis, TN	0.4
73	43	Baton Rouge, LA	67,900	27	43	Austin, TX	346	70	43	Lexington-Fayette, KY	0.3
33	44	Tucson, AZ	66,800	36	44	Atlanta, GA	342	5	44	Philadelphia, PA	0.3
16	45	Columbus, OH	66,000	13	45	Indianapolis, IN	342	29	45	Oklahoma City, OK	0.2
66	46	Rochester, NY	65,200	17	46	Milwaukee, WI	342	3	46	Chicago, IL	0.2
65	47	St. Petersburg, FL	63,000	30	47	Portland, OR	340	6	47	San Diego, CA	0.2
15	48	Jacksonville, FL	62,900	26	48	Denver, CO	339	22	48	El Paso, TX	0.2
45	49	Cincinnati, OH	61,900	70	49	Lexington-Fayette, KY	338	62	49	Norfolk, VA	0.2
13	50	Indianapolis, IN	60,800	28	50	Fort Worth, TX	337	23	50	Cleveland, OH	0.1
43	51	Tulsa, OK	60,500	55	51	Tampa, FL	334	73	51	Baton Rouge, LA	0.1
28	52	Fort Worth, TX	59,900	4	52	Houston, TX	328	71	52	Akron, OH	0.1
30	53	Portland, OR	59,200	33	53	Tucson, AZ	327	33	53	Tucson, AZ	-0.2
55	54	Tampa, FL	59,000	48	54	Omaha, NE	326	38	54	Albuquerque, NM	-0.3
22	55	El Paso, TX	58,500	31	55	Kansas City, MO	324	31	55	Kansas City, MO	-0.3
4	56	Houston, TX	58,000	12	56	Baltimore, MD	321	34	56	St. Louis, MO	-0.4
51	57	Wichita, KS	56,700	10	57	San Antonio, TX	308	20	57	Boston, MA	-0.5
64	58	Corpus Christi, TX	56,500	64	58	Corpus Christi, TX	305	49	58	Toledo, OH	-0.6
31	59	Kansas City, MO	56,100	22	59	El Paso, TX	303	8	59	Dallas, TX	-0.8
18	60	Memphis, TN	55,700	51	60	Wichita, KS	299	66	60	Rochester, NY	-0.9
29	61	Oklahoma City, OK	54,900	40	61	Pittsburgh, PA	298	60	61	Birmingham, AL	-1.0
12	62	Baltimore, MD	54,700	43	62	Tulsa, OK	293	50	62	Buffalo, NY	-1.2
48	63	Omaha, NE	54,600	49	63	Toledo, OH	286	39	63	Oakland, CA	-1.5
17	64	Milwaukee, WI	53,500	45	64	Cincinnati, OH	283	10	64	San Antonio, TX	-1.6
34	65	St. Louis, MO	50,700	18	65	Memphis, TN	282	7	65	Detroit, MI	-1.6
10	66	San Antonio, TX	49,700	29	66	Oklahoma City, OK	282	14	66	San Francisco, CA	-1.8
5	67	Philadelphia, PA	49,400	71	67	Akron, OH	281	52	67	Santa Ana, CA	-1.8
49	68	Toledo, OH	48,900	24	68	New Orleans, LA	277	59	68	Anaheim, CA	-1.9
50	69	Buffalo, NY	46,700	73	69	Baton Rouge, LA	273	17	69	Milwaukee, WI	-2.1
60	70	Birmingham, AL	44,500	7	70	Detroit, MI	265	74	70	Stockton, CA	-2.3
58	71	Louisville, KY	44,300	50	71	Buffalo, NY	255	24	71	New Orleans, LA	-2.5
71	72	Akron, OH	43,800	34	72	St. Louis, MO	252	13	72	Indianapolis, IN	-3.3
40	73	Pittsburgh, PA	41,200	58	73	Louisville, KY	244	11	73	San Jose, CA	-3.9
23	74	Cleveland, OH	40,900	23	74	Cleveland, OH	237	19	74	Washington, DC	-5.4
7	75	Detroit, MI	25,600	60	75	Birmingham, AL	225	25	NA	Nashville-Davidson, TN	NA

TABLE 7—75 Largest Cities by 1990 Population

Selected Rankings

Unemployment Rate–1990				Mean January Temperature (F)				Mean July Temperature (F)			
Population Rank	Unemployment Rate Rank	City	Unemployment Rate (Percent)	Population Rank	Mean January Temp. Rank	City	Mean January Temp.	Population Rank	Mean July Temp. Rank	City	Mean July Temp.
7	1	Detroit, MI	10.9	44	1	Honolulu, HI (CDP)	72.6	9	1	Phoenix, AZ	92.3
22	2	El Paso, TX	10.6	46	2	Miami, FL	67.1	63	2	Las Vegas, NV	90.3
56	3	Newark, NJ	10.3	65	3	St. Petersburg, FL	61.9	53	3	Mesa, AZ	90.0
74	4	Stockton, CA	9.7	55	4	Tampa, FL	59.8	61	4	Arlington, TX	86.3
47	5	Fresno, CA	9.0	2	5	Los Angeles, CA	57.2	28	5	Fort Worth, TX	86.3
67	6	Jersey City, NJ	8.3	6	6	San Diego, CA	56.8	8	6	Dallas, TX	86.3
46	7	Miami, FL	8.3	64	7	Corpus Christi, TX	56.3	33	7	Tucson, AZ	86.2
34	8	St. Louis, MO	8.2	59	8	Anaheim, CA	55.9	64	8	Corpus Christi, TX	84.9
49	9	Toledo, OH	8.0	52	9	Santa Ana, CA	55.9	27	9	Austin, TX	84.7
12	10	Baltimore, MD	7.7	32	10	Long Beach, CA	55.2	10	10	San Antonio, TX	84.6
3	11	Chicago, IL	7.7	15	11	Jacksonville, FL	53.2	43	11	Tulsa, OK	83.2
23	12	Cleveland, OH	7.5	68	12	Riverside, CA	52.8	65	12	St. Petersburg, FL	83.1
68	13	Riverside, CA	7.5	24	13	New Orleans, LA	52.4	4	13	Houston, TX	83.1
10	14	San Antonio, TX	7.5	9	14	Phoenix, AZ	52.3	22	14	El Paso, TX	82.5
60	15	Birmingham, AL	7.5	4	15	Houston, TX	51.4	46	15	Miami, FL	82.4
36	16	Atlanta, GA	7.2	53	16	Mesa, AZ	51.1	55	16	Tampa, FL	82.2
50	17	Buffalo, NY	6.8	33	17	Tucson, AZ	51.1	18	17	Memphis, TN	82.1
1	18	New York, NY	6.8	73	18	Baton Rouge, LA	50.8	24	18	New Orleans, LA	82.1
64	19	Corpus Christi, TX	6.7	10	19	San Antonio, TX	50.4	73	19	Baton Rouge, LA	82.1
19	20	Washington, DC	6.6	11	20	San Jose, CA	49.5	29	20	Oklahoma City, OK	82.1
28	21	Fort Worth, TX	6.5	27	21	Austin, TX	49.1	51	21	Wichita, KS	81.4
2	22	Los Angeles, CA	6.5	39	22	Oakland, CA	49.0	15	22	Jacksonville, FL	81.3
71	23	Akron, OH	6.5	14	23	San Francisco, CA	48.5	47	23	Fresno, CA	81.0
54	24	Colorado Springs, CO	6.1	41	24	Sacramento, CA	47.1	31	24	Kansas City, MO	80.9
8	25	Dallas, TX	6.0	47	25	Fresno, CA	45.5	60	25	Birmingham, AL	80.3
5	26	Philadelphia, PA	6.0	74	26	Stockton, CA	45.2	44	26	Honolulu, HI (CDP)	80.1
24	27	New Orleans, LA	6.0	8	27	Dallas, TX	45.0	12	27	Baltimore, MD	79.9
58	28	Louisville, KY	5.9	63	28	Las Vegas, NV	44.6	25	28	Nashville-Davidson, TN	79.4
39	29	Oakland, CA	5.8	22	29	El Paso, TX	44.2	34	29	St. Louis, MO	78.9
31	30	Kansas City, MO	5.8	61	30	Arlington, TX	44.0	19	30	Washington, DC	78.9
65	31	St. Petersburg, FL	5.7	28	31	Fort Worth, TX	44.0	38	31	Albuquerque, NM	78.8
29	32	Oklahoma City, OK	5.7	60	32	Birmingham, AL	42.4	36	32	Atlanta, GA	78.6
32	33	Long Beach, CA	5.6	36	33	Atlanta, GA	41.9	35	33	Charlotte, NC	78.5
15	34	Jacksonville, FL	5.6	21	34	Seattle, WA	40.6	62	34	Norfolk, VA	78.4
4	35	Houston, TX	5.6	35	35	Charlotte, NC	40.5	37	35	Virginia Beach, VA	78.4
20	36	Boston, MA	5.5	37	36	Virginia Beach, VA	39.9	74	36	Stockton, CA	78.0
26	37	Denver, CO	5.4	62	37	Norfolk, VA	39.9	48	37	Omaha, NE	77.7
41	38	Sacramento, CA	5.4	75	38	Raleigh, NC	39.6	75	38	Raleigh, NC	77.7
73	39	Baton Rouge, LA	5.3	18	39	Memphis, TN	39.6	58	39	Louisville, KY	77.6
55	40	Tampa, FL	5.3	30	40	Portland, OR	38.9	68	40	Riverside, CA	77.2
66	41	Rochester, NY	5.3	25	41	Nashville-Davidson, TN	37.1	56	41	Newark, NJ	76.8
69	42	Anchorage, AK	5.2	29	42	Oklahoma City, OK	35.9	1	42	New York, NY	76.7
63	43	Las Vegas, NV	5.2	12	43	Baltimore, MD	35.5	41	43	Sacramento, CA	76.6
45	44	Cincinnati, OH	5.2	19	44	Washington, DC	35.2	5	44	Philadelphia, PA	76.5
17	45	Milwaukee, WI	5.0	43	45	Tulsa, OK	35.2	45	45	Cincinnati, OH	76.1
30	46	Portland, OR	5.0	38	46	Albuquerque, NM	34.8	70	46	Lexington-Fayette, KY	76.0
43	47	Tulsa, OK	4.9	58	47	Louisville, KY	32.5	13	47	Indianapolis, IN	75.1
62	48	Norfolk, VA	4.8	1	48	New York, NY	31.8	67	48	Jersey City, NJ	74.6
18	49	Memphis, TN	4.8	70	49	Lexington-Fayette, KY	31.5	2	49	Los Angeles, CA	74.1
57	50	St. Paul, MN	4.8	56	50	Newark, NJ	31.3	16	50	Columbus, OH	73.8
27	51	Austin, TX	4.8	5	51	Philadelphia, PA	31.2	20	51	Boston, MA	73.5
38	52	Albuquerque, NM	4.7	67	52	Jersey City, NJ	30.6	26	52	Denver, CO	73.3
11	53	San Jose, CA	4.7	45	53	Cincinnati, OH	30.3	72	53	Aurora, CO	73.3
51	54	Wichita, KS	4.7	51	54	Wichita, KS	29.6	57	54	St. Paul, MN	73.1
16	55	Columbus, OH	4.5	20	55	Boston, MA	29.6	42	55	Minneapolis, MN	73.1
13	56	Indianapolis, IN	4.5	26	56	Denver, CO	29.5	3	56	Chicago, IL	73.0
6	57	San Diego, CA	4.5	72	57	Aurora, CO	29.5	32	57	Long Beach, CA	72.8
9	58	Phoenix, AZ	4.5	34	58	St. Louis, MO	28.8	59	58	Anaheim, CA	72.2
42	59	Minneapolis, MN	4.5	54	59	Colorado Springs, CO	28.8	52	59	Santa Ana, CA	72.2
40	60	Pittsburgh, PA	4.5	31	60	Kansas City, MO	28.4	40	60	Pittsburgh, PA	72.0
52	61	Santa Ana, CA	4.4	16	61	Columbus, OH	27.1	7	61	Detroit, MI	71.9
72	62	Aurora, CO	4.3	40	62	Pittsburgh, PA	26.7	49	62	Toledo, OH	71.8
61	63	Arlington, TX	4.3	13	63	Indianapolis, IN	26.0	23	63	Cleveland, OH	71.6
53	64	Mesa, AZ	4.1	23	64	Cleveland, OH	25.5	71	64	Akron, OH	71.6
33	65	Tucson, AZ	4.1	71	65	Akron, OH	25.1	66	65	Rochester, NY	71.3
37	66	Virginia Beach, VA	4.0	66	66	Rochester, NY	23.6	54	66	Colorado Springs, CO	71.2
14	67	San Francisco, CA	4.0	50	67	Buffalo, NY	23.5	50	67	Buffalo, NY	70.7
59	68	Anaheim, CA	3.8	7	68	Detroit, MI	23.4	17	68	Milwaukee, WI	70.5
21	69	Seattle, WA	3.7	49	69	Toledo, OH	23.1	6	69	San Diego, CA	70.3
70	70	Lexington-Fayette, KY	3.2	3	70	Chicago, IL	21.4	11	70	San Jose, CA	68.8
35	71	Charlotte, NC	3.1	48	71	Omaha, NE	20.2	30	71	Portland, OR	67.7
75	72	Raleigh, NC	2.9	17	72	Milwaukee, WI	18.7	21	72	Seattle, WA	65.3
44	73	Honolulu, HI (CDP)	2.6	69	73	Anchorage, AK	13.0	39	73	Oakland, CA	63.7
48	74	Omaha, NE	2.6	57	74	St. Paul, MN	11.2	14	74	San Francisco, CA	62.2
25	NA	Nashville-Davidson, TN	NA	42	75	Minneapolis, MN	11.2	69	75	Anchorage, AK	58.1

TABLE 8—75 Cities with Largest Number of Manufacturing Employees–1987

Selected Rankings

Number of Manufacturing Employees			Value Added by Manufacture				New Manufacturing Capital Expenditures			
Number of Employees Rank	City	Number of Manufacturing Employees (1,000)	Number of Employees Rank	Value Added Rank	City	Value Added (Mil Dol)	Number of Employees Rank	New Capital Rank	City	New Capital Expenditures (Mil Dol)
1	New York, NY	436.1	1	1	New York, NY	24,542.8	1	1	New York, NY	697.6
2	Los Angeles, CA	301.9	2	2	Los Angeles, CA	16,084.6	2	2	Los Angeles, CA	695.1
3	Chicago, IL	220.6	3	3	Chicago, IL	14,333.2	15	3	Sunnyvale, CA	553.3
4	Houston, TX	112.8	4	4	Houston, TX	7,192.9	13	4	Rochester, NY	521.8
5	Dallas, TX	105.8	15	5	Sunnyvale, CA	6,864.0	3	5	Chicago, IL	504.8
6	Detroit, MI	102.2	5	6	Dallas, TX	6,023.1	5	6	Dallas, TX	403.0
7	Philadelphia, PA	95.9	20	7	Louisville, KY	5,319.0	16	7	San Jose, CA	384.2
8	St. Louis, MO	82.6	12	8	Indianapolis, IN	5,268.9	4	8	Houston, TX	374.9
9	San Diego, CA	77.5	13	9	Rochester, NY	5,249.2	12	9	Indianapolis, IN	352.6
10	Phoenix, AZ	75.7	8	10	St. Louis, MO	5,232.2	36	10	Winston-Salem, NC	327.1
11	Cleveland, OH	75.6	32	11	Richmond, VA	5,206.6	8	11	St. Louis, MO	318.3
12	Indianapolis, IN	74.3	36	12	Winston-Salem, NC	5,187.3	9	12	San Diego, CA	314.6
13	Rochester, NY	72.3	7	13	Philadelphia, PA	5,084.5	10	13	Phoenix, AZ	299.1
14	Fort Worth, TX	71.9	6	14	Detroit, MI	4,829.0	53	14	Torrance, CA	287.8
15	Sunnyvale, CA	71.6	10	15	Phoenix, AZ	4,665.3	23	15	Santa Clara, CA	284.1
16	San Jose, CA	68.3	16	16	San Jose, CA	4,645.1	6	16	Detroit, MI	257.8
17	Milwaukee, WI	63.9	14	17	Fort Worth, TX	4,616.4	14	17	Fort Worth, TX	247.1
18	Cincinnati, OH	57.8	9	18	San Diego, CA	4,302.9	19	18	Wichita, KS	240.0
19	Wichita, KS	56.5	21	19	Baltimore, MD	4,064.2	49	19	Austin, TX	238.5
20	Louisville, KY	51.4	11	20	Cleveland, OH	3,974.6	11	20	Cleveland, OH	235.6
21	Baltimore, MD	50.4	23	21	Santa Clara, CA	3,741.3	34	21	Long Beach, CA	220.0
22	Anaheim, CA	50.0	19	22	Wichita, KS	3,554.5	7	22	Philadelphia, PA	213.3
23	Santa Clara, CA	48.8	37	23	Toledo, OH	3,355.6	27	23	Minneapolis, MN	210.4
24	Warren, MI	47.2	17	24	Milwaukee, WI	3,353.6	32	24	Richmond, VA	203.1
25	Columbus, OH	47.1	25	25	Columbus, OH	3,353.0	41	25	Grand Rapids, MI	201.6
26	Kansas City, MO	45.0	18	26	Cincinnati, OH	3,349.8	21	26	Baltimore, MD	193.4
27	Minneapolis, MN	44.3	22	27	Anaheim, CA	3,188.3	33	27	Atlanta, GA	191.8
28	Charlotte, NC	44.0	26	28	Kansas City, MO	3,185.1	42	28	Irvine, CA	190.6
29	San Francisco, CA	43.8	30	29	Memphis, TN	3,138.7	22	29	Anaheim, CA	188.9
30	Memphis, TN	43.4	35	30	Oklahoma City, OK	3,089.5	20	30	Louisville, KY	187.4
31	Boston, MA	42.5	46	31	St. Paul, MN	2,938.9	37	31	Toledo, OH	184.4
32	Richmond, VA	41.5	29	32	San Francisco, CA	2,745.0	25	32	Columbus, OH	180.6
33	Atlanta, GA	40.3	31	33	Boston, MA	2,517.4	30	33	Memphis, TN	180.2
34	Long Beach, CA	40.1	42	34	Irvine, CA	2,423.2	28	34	Charlotte, NC	172.2
35	Winston-Salem, NC	39.7	33	35	Atlanta, GA	2,413.3	18	35	Cincinnati, OH	167.8
36	Winston-Salem	39.7	55	36	Jacksonville, FL	2,384.2	46	36	St. Paul, MN	157.7
37	Toledo, OH	39.5	27	37	Minneapolis, MN	2,343.0	17	37	Milwaukee, WI	155.2
38	Santa Ana, CA	39.1	45	38	Buffalo, NY	2,339.8	70	38	Huntsville, AL	155.0
39	Denver, CO	37.9	58	39	Greensboro, NC	2,258.8	26	39	Kansas City, MO	140.6
40	Dayton, OH	36.4	49	40	Austin, TX	2,212.4	63	40	Orlando, FL	134.7
41	Grand Rapids, MI	35.8	47	41	Burbank, CA	2,187.6	55	41	Jacksonville, FL	130.0
42	Irvine, CA	35.4	41	42	Grand Rapids, MI	2,145.8	31	42	Boston, MA	123.6
43	Seattle, WA	35.2	34	43	Long Beach, CA	2,091.0	61	43	Newark, NJ	120.8
44	San Antonio, TX	34.9	28	44	Charlotte, NC	2,079.0	47	44	Burbank, CA	120.6
45	Buffalo, NY	34.9	53	45	Torrance, CA	2,070.0	40	45	Dayton, OH	119.9
46	St. Paul, MN	34.6	24	46	Warren, MI	2,051.8	35	46	Oklahoma City, OK	116.9
47	Burbank, CA	33.7	39	47	Denver, CO	2,034.8	38	47	Santa Ana, CA	114.6
48	Tulsa, OK	33.4	60	48	Omaha, NE	2,004.1	48	48	Tulsa, OK	112.8
49	Austin, TX	33.2	38	49	Santa Ana, CA	1,974.9	39	49	Denver, CO	109.1
50	El Paso, TX	33.0	63	50	Orlando, FL	1,959.3	64	50	Tucson, AZ	106.5
51	Portland, OR	32.7	40	51	Dayton, OH	1,935.1	60	51	Omaha, NE	100.3
52	Pittsburgh, PA	30.8	48	52	Tulsa, OK	1,864.9	45	52	Buffalo, NY	95.7
53	Torrance, CA	30.6	43	53	Seattle, WA	1,852.2	59	53	Fort Wayne, IN	89.6
54	Newport News, VA	30.1	51	54	Portland, OR	1,831.0	72	54	Elk Grove Village, IL	89.3
55	Jacksonville, FL	29.7	64	55	Tucson, AZ	1,745.3	69	55	Providence, RI	87.9
56	Akron, OH	28.8	70	56	Huntsville, AL	1,718.2	24	56	Warren, MI	86.1
57	Salt Lake City, UT	27.6	71	57	Fullerton, CA	1,648.2	65	57	Palo Alto, CA	85.8
58	Fort Wayne, IN	26.8	44	58	San Antonio, TX	1,636.2	43	58	Seattle, WA	85.6
59	Fort Wayne	26.8	65	59	Palo Alto, CA	1,635.4	29	59	San Francisco, CA	84.3
60	Omaha, NE	26.7	62	60	Rockford, IL	1,581.4	57	60	Salt Lake City, UT	80.1
61	Newark, NJ	26.7	61	61	Newark, NJ	1,568.7	51	61	Portland, OR	78.1
62	Rockford, IL	26.6	74	62	Stamford, CT	1,529.2	75	62	Tampa, FL	77.9
63	Orlando, FL	26.4	57	63	Salt Lake City, UT	1,495.0	66	63	Birmingham, AL	73.9
64	Tucson, AZ	26.3	73	64	Elkhart, IN	1,443.7	58	64	Greensboro, NC	71.4
65	Palo Alto, CA	26.1	67	65	Chattanooga, TN	1,416.6	71	65	Fullerton, CA	69.2
66	Birmingham, AL	25.4	72	66	Elk Grove Village, IL	1,389.0	73	66	Elkhart, IN	66.5
67	Chattanooga, TN	25.3	54	67	Newport News, VA	1,380.7	67	67	Chattanooga, TN	62.0
68	High Point, NC	25.0	50	68	El Paso, TX	1,377.8	44	68	San Antonio, TX	61.4
69	Providence, RI	24.6	59	69	Fort Wayne, IN	1,348.9	50	69	El Paso, TX	61.1
70	Huntsville, AL	23.9	66	70	Birmingham, AL	1,244.0	56	70	Akron, OH	56.5
71	Fullerton, CA	23.8	52	71	Pittsburgh, PA	1,185.7	74	71	Stamford, CT	55.2
72	Elk Grove Village, IL	23.6	56	72	Akron, OH	1,131.3	52	72	Pittsburgh, PA	54.0
73	Elkhart, IN	22.9	75	73	Tampa, FL	1,087.9	68	73	High Point, NC	47.8
74	Stamford, CT	22.9	68	74	High Point, NC	932.0	54	NA	Newport News, VA	NA
75	Tampa, FL	22.9	69	75	Providence, RI	870.4	62	NA	Rockford, IL	NA

TABLE 9—States by 1987 Agricultural Sales

Selected Rankings

Value of Agricultural Sales 1987			Average Agricultural Sales per Farm 1987				Operators Living on Farm Operated 1987			
Value of Sales Rank	State	Value of Agricultural Sales (Mil Dol)	Value of Sales Rank	Average Sales Rank	State	Average Sales (Dollars)	Value of Sales Rank	Operators Living on Farm Rank	State	Operators Living on Farm Percent
X	UNITED STATES	136,049	X	X	UNITED STATES	65,165	X	X	UNITED STATES	71.3
1	CALIFORNIA	13,922	29	1	ARIZONA	212,354	48	1	NEW HAMPSHIRE	87.5
2	TEXAS	10,549	1	2	CALIFORNIA	167,300	43	2	VERMONT	87.1
3	IOWA	8,927	41	3	DELAWARE	149,553	8	3	WISCONSIN	84.8
4	NEBRASKA	6,667	39	4	HAWAII	125,203	22	4	NEW YORK	84.5
5	KANSAS	6,477	9	5	FLORIDA	119,033	42	5	MAINE	84.2
6	ILLINOIS	6,377	15	6	COLORADO	115,201	28	6	OREGON	83.3
7	MINNESOTA	5,676	4	7	NEBRASKA	110,197	16	7	PENNSYLVANIA	82.2
8	WISCONSIN	4,910	44	8	CONNECTICUT	99,917	21	8	MICHIGAN	82.0
9	FLORIDA	4,351	5	9	KANSAS	94,441	7	9	MINNESOTA	80.0
10	INDIANA	4,068	23	10	IDAHO	94,002	44	10	CONNECTICUT	79.8
11	MISSOURI	3,645	17	11	WASHINGTON	87,000	17	11	WASHINGTON	79.7
12	NORTH CAROLINA	3,541	3	12	IOWA	84,872	40	12	NEW JERSEY	79.4
13	OHIO	3,434	47	13	NEVADA	82,741	45	13	MASSACHUSETTS	79.1
14	ARKANSAS	3,320	19	14	SOUTH DAKOTA	74,761	35	14	MARYLAND	77.1
15	COLORADO	3,143	34	15	NEW MEXICO	74,399	49	15	RHODE ISLAND	77.0
16	PENNSYLVANIA	3,078	37	16	WYOMING	73,517	46	16	WEST VIRGINIA	76.8
17	WASHINGTON	2,920	6	17	ILLINOIS	71,822	13	17	OHIO	76.4
18	GEORGIA	2,815	14	18	ARKANSAS	68,825	47	18	NEVADA	75.8
19	SOUTH DAKOTA	2,719	35	19	MARYLAND	66,937	23	19	IDAHO	75.5
20	OKLAHOMA	2,715	7	20	MINNESOTA	66,719	37	20	WYOMING	75.4
21	MICHIGAN	2,545	8	21	WISCONSIN	65,351	10	21	INDIANA	75.0
22	NEW YORK	2,442	22	22	NEW YORK	64,697	3	22	IOWA	74.8
23	IDAHO	2,269	42	23	MAINE	64,681	32	23	MONTANA	74.3
24	NORTH DAKOTA	2,188	18	24	GEORGIA	64,626	50	24	ALASKA	73.9
25	KENTUCKY	2,076	43	25	VERMONT	63,899	19	25	SOUTH DAKOTA	73.4
26	ALABAMA	1,908	32	26	MONTANA	62,980	41	26	DELAWARE	73.3
27	MISSISSIPPI	1,863	24	27	NORTH DAKOTA	62,007	11	27	MISSOURI	73.1
28	OREGON	1,846	12	28	NORTH CAROLINA	59,737	15	28	COLORADO	72.8
29	ARIZONA	1,629	16	29	PENNSYLVANIA	59,701	31	29	VIRGINIA	72.3
30	TENNESSEE	1,618	10	30	INDIANA	57,693	6	30	ILLINOIS	71.4
31	VIRGINIA	1,589	28	31	OREGON	57,664	30	31	TENNESSEE	70.9
32	MONTANA	1,547	2	32	TEXAS	55,877	24	32	NORTH DAKOTA	70.7
33	LOUISIANA	1,340	40	33	NEW JERSEY	54,916	18	33	GEORGIA	70.2
34	NEW MEXICO	1,060	45	34	MASSACHUSETTS	54,772	26	34	ALABAMA	69.7
35	MARYLAND	989	27	35	MISSISSIPPI	54,672	36	35	SOUTH CAROLINA	69.6
36	SOUTH CAROLINA	879	49	36	RHODE ISLAND	53,903	14	36	ARKANSAS	69.0
37	WYOMING	677	21	37	MICHIGAN	49,736	12	37	NORTH CAROLINA	68.7
38	UTAH	618	33	38	LOUISIANA	49,000	4	38	NEBRASKA	67.9
39	HAWAII	610	26	39	ALABAMA	44,053	25	39	KENTUCKY	67.7
40	NEW JERSEY	496	38	40	UTAH	43,927	27	40	MISSISSIPPI	67.3
41	DELAWARE	444	13	41	OHIO	43,317	5	41	KANSAS	66.4
42	MAINE	405	36	42	SOUTH CAROLINA	42,827	20	42	OKLAHOMA	66.1
43	VERMONT	376	48	43	NEW HAMPSHIRE	42,585	1	43	CALIFORNIA	65.9
44	CONNECTICUT	358	20	44	OKLAHOMA	38,658	34	44	NEW MEXICO	64.8
45	MASSACHUSETTS	340	31	45	VIRGINIA	35,464	33	45	LOUISIANA	63.8
46	WEST VIRGINIA	271	11	46	MISSOURI	34,353	38	46	UTAH	62.7
47	NEVADA	250	50	47	ALASKA	31,309	9	47	FLORIDA	62.5
48	NEW HAMPSHIRE	107	25	48	KENTUCKY	22,450	29	48	ARIZONA	61.0
49	RHODE ISLAND	38	30	49	TENNESSEE	20,294	39	49	HAWAII	56.5
50	ALASKA	18	46	50	WEST VIRGINIA	15,701	2	50	TEXAS	54.9

TABLE 10—States and the District of Columbia by Largest Number of Manufacturing Employees–1987 — Selected Rankings

Number of Manufacturing Employees 1987			Value Added by Manufacture 1987				New Manufacturing Capital Expenditures 1987			
Number of Employees Rank	State	Number of Manufacturing Employees (1,000)	Number of Employees Rank	Value Added Rank	State	Value Added (Mil Dol)	Number of Employees Rank	New Capital Rank	State	New Capital Expenditures (Mil Dol)
X	UNITED STATES	18,950.3	X	X	UNITED STATES	1,165,746.8	X	X	UNITED STATES	78,647.8
1	CALIFORNIA	2,104.3	1	1	CALIFORNIA	132,637.5	1	1	CALIFORNIA	8,571.7
2	NEW YORK	1,278.7	2	2	NEW YORK	80,033.3	6	2	MICHIGAN	4,793.5
3	OHIO	1,100.2	3	3	OHIO	71,707.4	3	3	OHIO	4,742.2
4	PENNSYLVANIA	1,037.5	7	4	TEXAS	63,899.1	7	4	TEXAS	4,548.0
5	ILLINOIS	989.6	5	5	ILLINOIS	63,350.1	5	5	ILLINOIS	4,425.8
6	MICHIGAN	980.1	6	6	MICHIGAN	60,258.6	2	6	NEW YORK	4,296.5
7	TEXAS	914.0	4	7	PENNSYLVANIA	57,605.2	4	7	PENNSYLVANIA	3,440.5
8	NORTH CAROLINA	842.4	8	8	NORTH CAROLINA	47,007.4	10	8	INDIANA	3,363.9
9	NEW JERSEY	690.8	9	9	NEW JERSEY	42,526.6	8	9	NORTH CAROLINA	2,958.7
10	INDIANA	602.0	10	10	INDIANA	39,278.8	12	10	GEORGIA	2,471.5
11	MASSACHUSETTS	591.3	11	11	MASSACHUSETTS	35,769.7	9	11	NEW JERSEY	2,312.5
12	GEORGIA	569.9	12	12	GEORGIA	33,708.1	11	12	MASSACHUSETTS	2,169.0
13	WISCONSIN	514.0	13	13	WISCONSIN	31,653.0	13	13	WISCONSIN	2,027.4
14	FLORIDA	499.3	14	14	FLORIDA	27,574.2	14	14	FLORIDA	1,910.7
15	TENNESSEE	484.9	15	15	TENNESSEE	27,049.7	15	15	TENNESSEE	1,904.7
16	VIRGINIA	429.2	16	16	VIRGINIA	26,857.3	19	16	MINNESOTA	1,765.5
17	MISSOURI	418.8	17	17	MISSOURI	25,916.7	23	17	KENTUCKY	1,746.0
18	CONNECTICUT	388.9	19	18	MINNESOTA	23,322.1	17	18	MISSOURI	1,620.1
19	MINNESOTA	374.2	18	19	CONNECTICUT	22,348.9	20	19	SOUTH CAROLINA	1,586.0
20	SOUTH CAROLINA	365.8	20	20	SOUTH CAROLINA	19,111.9	16	20	VIRGINIA	1,542.7
21	ALABAMA	347.3	22	21	WASHINGTON	19,016.1	32	21	LOUISIANA	1,419.8
22	WASHINGTON	309.7	21	22	ALABAMA	18,652.1	21	22	ALABAMA	1,360.1
23	KENTUCKY	251.6	23	23	KENTUCKY	18,091.7	18	23	CONNECTICUT	1,293.3
24	MARYLAND	230.4	32	24	LOUISIANA	16,425.8	22	24	WASHINGTON	1,244.8
25	MISSISSIPPI	218.9	26	25	IOWA	14,469.0	29	25	KANSAS	1,011.2
26	IOWA	206.1	24	26	MARYLAND	14,020.0	27	26	ARKANSAS	891.5
27	ARKANSAS	205.5	29	27	KANSAS	12,908.8	24	27	MARYLAND	875.2
28	OREGON	202.9	31	28	COLORADO	12,045.8	30	28	ARIZONA	836.9
29	KANSAS	189.1	28	29	OREGON	11,610.3	26	29	IOWA	834.2
30	ARIZONA	184.1	30	30	ARIZONA	11,299.0	31	30	COLORADO	791.5
31	COLORADO	183.8	27	31	ARKANSAS	10,826.9	28	31	OREGON	735.4
32	LOUISIANA	161.4	25	32	MISSISSIPPI	10,502.6	25	32	MISSISSIPPI	647.7
33	OKLAHOMA	151.2	33	33	OKLAHOMA	9,856.9	36	33	MAINE	539.4
34	RHODE ISLAND	112.0	35	34	NEW HAMPSHIRE	8,188.6	33	34	OKLAHOMA	538.4
35	NEW HAMPSHIRE	107.9	37	35	NEBRASKA	5,819.2	39	35	WEST VIRGINIA	434.8
36	MAINE	101.6	39	36	WEST VIRGINIA	5,404.4	38	36	UTAH	403.5
37	NEBRASKA	90.7	36	37	MAINE	5,270.6	35	37	NEW HAMPSHIRE	339.8
38	UTAH	88.8	38	38	UTAH	4,882.9	42	38	VERMONT	334.4
39	WEST VIRGINIA	83.8	34	39	RHODE ISLAND	4,787.5	37	39	NEBRASKA	317.9
40	DELAWARE	66.6	40	40	DELAWARE	3,866.0	40	40	DELAWARE	276.9
41	IDAHO	52.9	41	41	IDAHO	3,057.0	34	41	RHODE ISLAND	276.4
42	VERMONT	48.5	42	42	VERMONT	2,543.1	41	42	IDAHO	234.8
43	NEW MEXICO	34.7	43	43	NEW MEXICO	1,652.9	43	43	NEW MEXICO	196.4
44	SOUTH DAKOTA	27.5	48	44	DISTRICT OF COLUMBIA	1,525.4	45	44	NEVADA	114.0
45	NEVADA	23.7	44	45	SOUTH DAKOTA	1,476.1	46	45	HAWAII	102.0
46	HAWAII	22.2	46	46	HAWAII	1,405.3	47	46	MONTANA	97.0
47	MONTANA	20.1	45	47	NEVADA	1,279.3	44	47	SOUTH DAKOTA	79.3
48	DISTRICT OF COLUMBIA	17.0	47	48	MONTANA	1,112.0	50	48	ALASKA	68.6
49	NORTH DAKOTA	15.4	49	49	NORTH DAKOTA	979.0	51	49	WYOMING	65.3
50	ALASKA	11.1	50	50	ALASKA	834.0	49	50	NORTH DAKOTA	47.0
51	WYOMING	7.7	51	51	WYOMING	492.8	48	51	DISTRICT OF COLUMBIA	43.6

TABLE 11—States and the District of Columbia by 1990 Population

Selected Rankings

Total Persons 1990			Population Density (per Square Kilometer) 1990				Population Change 1980-1990			
Rank	State	Population	Population Rank	Density Rank	State	Density	Population Rank	Change Rank	State	Percent Change
X	UNITED STATES	248,709,873	X	X	UNITED STATES	27	X	X	UNITED STATES	9.8
1	CALIFORNIA	29,760,021	48	1	DISTRICT OF COLUMBIA	3,817	39	1	NEVADA	50.2
2	NEW YORK	17,990,455	9	2	NEW JERSEY	402	50	2	ALASKA	36.8
3	TEXAS	16,986,510	43	3	RHODE ISLAND	371	24	3	ARIZONA	34.9
4	FLORIDA	12,937,926	13	4	MASSACHUSETTS	296	4	4	FLORIDA	32.8
5	PENNSYLVANIA	11,881,643	27	5	CONNECTICUT	262	1	5	CALIFORNIA	25.7
6	ILLINOIS	11,430,602	19	6	MARYLAND	189	40	6	NEW HAMPSHIRE	20.4
7	OHIO	10,847,115	2	7	NEW YORK	147	3	7	TEXAS	19.4
8	MICHIGAN	9,295,297	46	8	DELAWARE	132	11	8	GEORGIA	18.6
9	NEW JERSEY	7,730,188	7	9	OHIO	102	35	9	UTAH	17.9
10	NORTH CAROLINA	6,628,637	5	10	PENNSYLVANIA	102	18	10	WASHINGTON	17.8
11	GEORGIA	6,478,216	4	11	FLORIDA	92	37	11	NEW MEXICO	16.3
12	VIRGINIA	6,187,358	6	12	ILLINOIS	79	12	12	VIRGINIA	15.7
13	MASSACHUSETTS	6,016,425	1	13	CALIFORNIA	74	41	13	HAWAII	14.8
14	INDIANA	5,544,159	41	14	HAWAII	67	26	14	COLORADO	14.0
15	MISSOURI	5,117,073	8	15	MICHIGAN	63	19	15	MARYLAND	13.4
16	WISCONSIN	4,891,769	12	16	VIRGINIA	60	10	16	NORTH CAROLINA	12.7
17	TENNESSEE	4,877,185	14	17	INDIANA	60	46	17	DELAWARE	12.1
18	WASHINGTON	4,866,692	10	18	NORTH CAROLINA	52	25	18	SOUTH CAROLINA	11.7
19	MARYLAND	4,781,468	40	19	NEW HAMPSHIRE	48	49	19	VERMONT	10.1
20	MINNESOTA	4,375,099	17	20	TENNESSEE	46	38	20	MAINE	9.1
21	LOUISIANA	4,219,973	25	21	SOUTH CAROLINA	45	29	21	OREGON	7.9
22	ALABAMA	4,040,587	11	22	GEORGIA	43	20	22	MINNESOTA	7.3
23	KENTUCKY	3,685,296	21	23	LOUISIANA	37	42	23	IDAHO	6.6
24	ARIZONA	3,665,228	23	24	KENTUCKY	36	17	24	TENNESSEE	6.2
25	SOUTH CAROLINA	3,486,703	16	25	WISCONSIN	35	43	25	RHODE ISLAND	6.0
26	COLORADO	3,294,394	22	26	ALABAMA	31	27	26	CONNECTICUT	5.8
27	CONNECTICUT	3,287,116	34	27	WEST VIRGINIA	29	9	27	NEW JERSEY	5.0
28	OKLAHOMA	3,145,585	15	28	MISSOURI	29	13	28	MASSACHUSETTS	4.9
29	OREGON	2,842,321	18	29	WASHINGTON	28	32	29	KANSAS	4.8
30	IOWA	2,776,755	3	30	TEXAS	25	15	30	MISSOURI	4.1
31	MISSISSIPPI	2,573,216	49	31	VERMONT	24	28	31	OKLAHOMA	4.0
32	KANSAS	2,477,574	20	32	MINNESOTA	21	16	32	WISCONSIN	3.9
33	ARKANSAS	2,350,725	31	33	MISSISSIPPI	21	22	33	ALABAMA	3.8
34	WEST VIRGINIA	1,793,477	30	34	IOWA	19	33	34	ARKANSAS	2.8
35	UTAH	1,722,850	28	35	OKLAHOMA	18	2	35	NEW YORK	2.5
36	NEBRASKA	1,578,385	33	36	ARKANSAS	17	31	36	MISSISSIPPI	2.1
37	NEW MEXICO	1,515,069	38	37	MAINE	15	44	37	MONTANA	1.5
38	MAINE	1,227,928	32	38	KANSAS	12	14	38	INDIANA	1.0
39	NEVADA	1,201,833	26	39	COLORADO	12	45	39	SOUTH DAKOTA	0.7
40	NEW HAMPSHIRE	1,109,252	24	40	ARIZONA	12	23	40	KENTUCKY	0.7
41	HAWAII	1,108,229	29	41	OREGON	11	7	41	OHIO	0.5
42	IDAHO	1,006,749	36	42	NEBRASKA	8	36	42	NEBRASKA	0.5
43	RHODE ISLAND	1,003,464	35	43	UTAH	8	8	43	MICHIGAN	0.4
44	MONTANA	799,065	37	44	NEW MEXICO	5	21	44	LOUISIANA	0.3
45	SOUTH DAKOTA	696,004	42	45	IDAHO	5	5	45	PENNSYLVANIA	0.1
46	DELAWARE	666,168	39	46	NEVADA	4	6	46	ILLINOIS	0.0
47	NORTH DAKOTA	638,800	47	47	NORTH DAKOTA	4	47	47	NORTH DAKOTA	-2.2
48	DISTRICT OF COLUMBIA	606,900	45	48	SOUTH DAKOTA	4	51	48	WYOMING	-3.5
49	VERMONT	562,758	51	49	WYOMING	2	30	49	IOWA	-4.7
50	ALASKA	550,043	44	50	MONTANA	2	48	50	DISTRICT OF COLUMBIA	-4.9
51	WYOMING	453,588	50	51	ALASKA	0	34	51	WEST VIRGINIA	-8.0

TABLE 11—States and the District of Columbia by 1990 Population
Selected Rankings

Percent White 1990				Percent Black 1990				Percent Hispanic 1990			
Population Rank	White Rank	State	Percent White	Population Rank	Black Rank	State	Percent Black	Population Rank	Hispanic Rank	State	Percent Hispanic
X	X	UNITED STATES	80.3	X	X	UNITED STATES	12.1	X	X	UNITED STATES	9.0
49	1	VERMONT	98.6	48	1	DISTRICT OF COLUMBIA	65.8	37	1	NEW MEXICO	38.2
38	2	MAINE	98.4	31	2	MISSISSIPPI	35.6	1	2	CALIFORNIA	25.8
40	3	NEW HAMPSHIRE	98.0	21	3	LOUISIANA	30.8	3	3	TEXAS	25.5
30	4	IOWA	96.6	25	4	SOUTH CAROLINA	29.8	24	4	ARIZONA	18.8
34	5	WEST VIRGINIA	96.2	11	5	GEORGIA	27.0	26	5	COLORADO	12.9
47	6	NORTH DAKOTA	94.6	22	6	ALABAMA	25.3	2	6	NEW YORK	12.3
42	7	IDAHO	94.4	19	7	MARYLAND	24.9	4	7	FLORIDA	12.2
20	8	MINNESOTA	94.4	10	8	NORTH CAROLINA	22.0	39	8	NEVADA	10.4
51	9	WYOMING	94.2	12	9	VIRGINIA	18.8	9	9	NEW JERSEY	9.6
36	10	NEBRASKA	93.8	46	10	DELAWARE	16.9	6	10	ILLINOIS	7.9
35	11	UTAH	93.8	17	11	TENNESSEE	16.0	41	11	HAWAII	7.3
29	12	OREGON	92.8	33	12	ARKANSAS	15.9	27	12	CONNECTICUT	6.5
44	13	MONTANA	92.7	2	13	NEW YORK	15.9	51	13	WYOMING	5.7
16	14	WISCONSIN	92.2	6	14	ILLINOIS	14.8	48	14	DISTRICT OF COLUMBIA	5.4
23	15	KENTUCKY	92.0	8	15	MICHIGAN	13.9	42	15	IDAHO	5.3
45	16	SOUTH DAKOTA	91.6	4	16	FLORIDA	13.6	35	16	UTAH	4.9
43	17	RHODE ISLAND	91.4	9	17	NEW JERSEY	13.4	13	17	MASSACHUSETTS	4.8
14	18	INDIANA	90.6	3	18	TEXAS	11.9	43	18	RHODE ISLAND	4.6
32	19	KANSAS	90.1	15	19	MISSOURI	10.7	18	19	WASHINGTON	4.4
13	20	MASSACHUSETTS	89.8	7	20	OHIO	10.6	29	20	OREGON	4.0
5	21	PENNSYLVANIA	88.5	5	21	PENNSYLVANIA	9.2	32	21	KANSAS	3.8
18	22	WASHINGTON	88.5	27	22	CONNECTICUT	8.3	50	22	ALASKA	3.2
26	23	COLORADO	88.2	14	23	INDIANA	7.8	28	23	OKLAHOMA	2.7
7	24	OHIO	87.8	28	24	OKLAHOMA	7.4	19	24	MARYLAND	2.6
15	25	MISSOURI	87.7	1	25	CALIFORNIA	7.4	12	25	VIRGINIA	2.6
27	26	CONNECTICUT	87.0	23	26	KENTUCKY	7.1	46	26	DELAWARE	2.4
39	27	NEVADA	84.3	39	27	NEVADA	6.6	36	27	NEBRASKA	2.3
8	28	MICHIGAN	83.4	32	28	KANSAS	5.8	21	28	LOUISIANA	2.2
4	29	FLORIDA	83.1	16	29	WISCONSIN	5.0	8	29	MICHIGAN	2.2
17	30	TENNESSEE	83.0	13	30	MASSACHUSETTS	5.0	5	30	PENNSYLVANIA	2.0
33	31	ARKANSAS	82.7	50	31	ALASKA	4.1	16	31	WISCONSIN	1.9
28	32	OKLAHOMA	82.1	26	32	COLORADO	4.0	14	32	INDIANA	1.8
24	33	ARIZONA	80.8	43	33	RHODE ISLAND	3.9	11	33	GEORGIA	1.7
46	34	DELAWARE	80.3	36	34	NEBRASKA	3.6	44	34	MONTANA	1.5
9	35	NEW JERSEY	79.3	34	35	WEST VIRGINIA	3.1	7	35	OHIO	1.3
6	36	ILLINOIS	78.3	18	36	WASHINGTON	3.1	20	36	MINNESOTA	1.2
12	37	VIRGINIA	77.4	24	37	ARIZONA	3.0	15	37	MISSOURI	1.2
37	38	NEW MEXICO	75.6	41	38	HAWAII	2.5	30	38	IOWA	1.2
10	39	NORTH CAROLINA	75.6	20	39	MINNESOTA	2.2	10	39	NORTH CAROLINA	1.2
50	40	ALASKA	75.5	37	40	NEW MEXICO	2.0	40	40	NEW HAMPSHIRE	1.0
3	41	TEXAS	75.2	30	41	IOWA	1.7	25	41	SOUTH CAROLINA	0.9
2	42	NEW YORK	74.4	29	42	OREGON	1.6	33	42	ARKANSAS	0.8
22	43	ALABAMA	73.6	51	43	WYOMING	0.8	45	43	SOUTH DAKOTA	0.8
11	44	GEORGIA	71.0	35	44	UTAH	0.7	47	44	NORTH DAKOTA	0.7
19	45	MARYLAND	71.0	40	45	NEW HAMPSHIRE	0.6	17	45	TENNESSEE	0.7
25	46	SOUTH CAROLINA	69.0	47	46	NORTH DAKOTA	0.6	49	46	VERMONT	0.7
1	47	CALIFORNIA	69.0	45	47	SOUTH DAKOTA	0.5	31	47	MISSISSIPPI	0.6
21	48	LOUISIANA	67.3	38	48	MAINE	0.4	22	48	ALABAMA	0.6
31	49	MISSISSIPPI	63.5	49	49	VERMONT	0.3	23	49	KENTUCKY	0.6
41	50	HAWAII	33.4	42	50	IDAHO	0.3	38	50	MAINE	0.6
48	51	DISTRICT OF COLUMBIA	29.6	44	51	MONTANA	0.3	34	51	WEST VIRGINIA	0.5

TABLE 11—States and the District of Columbia by 1990 Population

Selected Rankings

Percent Female 1990				Percent Under 5 Years 1990				Percent 75 Years and Over 1990			
Population Rank	Female Rank	State	Percent Female	Population Rank	Under 5 Rank	State	Percent Under 5	Population Rank	75 Plus Rank	State	Percent 75 Plus
X	X	UNITED STATES	51.3	X	X	UNITED STATES	7.4	X	X	UNITED STATES	5.3
48	1	DISTRICT OF COLUMBIA	53.4	50	1	ALASKA	10.0	4	1	FLORIDA	7.7
31	2	MISSISSIPPI	52.2	35	2	UTAH	9.8	30	2	IOWA	7.2
5	3	PENNSYLVANIA	52.1	37	3	NEW MEXICO	8.3	45	3	SOUTH DAKOTA	6.9
22	4	ALABAMA	52.1	3	4	TEXAS	8.2	47	4	NORTH DAKOTA	6.8
2	5	NEW YORK	52.1	1	5	CALIFORNIA	8.1	36	5	NEBRASKA	6.7
43	6	RHODE ISLAND	52.0	42	6	IDAHO	8.0	33	6	ARKANSAS	6.6
13	7	MASSACHUSETTS	52.0	24	7	ARIZONA	8.0	43	7	RHODE ISLAND	6.5
34	8	WEST VIRGINIA	52.0	21	8	LOUISIANA	7.9	32	8	KANSAS	6.4
21	9	LOUISIANA	51.9	45	9	SOUTH DAKOTA	7.8	5	9	PENNSYLVANIA	6.4
17	10	TENNESSEE	51.8	20	10	MINNESOTA	7.7	34	10	WEST VIRGINIA	6.3
15	11	MISSOURI	51.8	51	11	WYOMING	7.7	15	11	MISSOURI	6.3
33	12	ARKANSAS	51.8	39	12	NEVADA	7.7	28	12	OKLAHOMA	6.0
7	13	OHIO	51.8	26	13	COLORADO	7.7	16	13	WISCONSIN	6.0
9	14	NEW JERSEY	51.7	32	14	KANSAS	7.6	13	14	MASSACHUSETTS	6.0
23	15	KENTUCKY	51.6	31	15	MISSISSIPPI	7.6	29	15	OREGON	5.9
4	16	FLORIDA	51.6	11	16	GEORGIA	7.6	20	16	MINNESOTA	5.8
30	17	IOWA	51.6	40	17	NEW HAMPSHIRE	7.6	38	17	MAINE	5.8
25	18	SOUTH CAROLINA	51.6	8	18	MICHIGAN	7.6	27	18	CONNECTICUT	5.8
46	19	DELAWARE	51.5	36	19	NEBRASKA	7.6	44	19	MONTANA	5.7
14	20	INDIANA	51.5	19	20	MARYLAND	7.5	2	20	NEW YORK	5.6
27	21	CONNECTICUT	51.5	47	21	NORTH DAKOTA	7.5	22	21	ALABAMA	5.5
10	22	NORTH CAROLINA	51.5	18	22	WASHINGTON	7.5	48	22	DISTRICT OF COLUMBIA	5.5
11	23	GEORGIA	51.5	41	23	HAWAII	7.5	9	23	NEW JERSEY	5.5
8	24	MICHIGAN	51.5	44	24	MONTANA	7.4	31	24	MISSISSIPPI	5.5
19	25	MARYLAND	51.5	25	25	SOUTH CAROLINA	7.4	23	25	KENTUCKY	5.4
6	26	ILLINOIS	51.4	16	26	WISCONSIN	7.4	17	26	TENNESSEE	5.4
38	27	MAINE	51.3	6	27	ILLINOIS	7.4	6	27	ILLINOIS	5.4
36	28	NEBRASKA	51.3	49	28	VERMONT	7.3	14	28	INDIANA	5.3
28	29	OKLAHOMA	51.3	46	29	DELAWARE	7.3	7	29	OHIO	5.3
16	30	WISCONSIN	51.1	15	30	MISSOURI	7.2	49	30	VERMONT	5.2
40	31	NEW HAMPSHIRE	51.0	7	31	OHIO	7.2	42	31	IDAHO	5.1
49	32	VERMONT	51.0	12	32	VIRGINIA	7.2	24	32	ARIZONA	5.1
12	33	VIRGINIA	51.0	14	33	INDIANA	7.2	8	33	MICHIGAN	4.9
20	34	MINNESOTA	51.0	28	34	OKLAHOMA	7.2	18	34	WASHINGTON	4.9
32	35	KANSAS	51.0	29	35	OREGON	7.1	10	35	NORTH CAROLINA	4.8
29	36	OREGON	50.8	38	36	MAINE	7.0	40	36	NEW HAMPSHIRE	4.8
37	37	NEW MEXICO	50.8	22	37	ALABAMA	7.0	46	37	DELAWARE	4.7
45	38	SOUTH DAKOTA	50.8	2	38	NEW YORK	7.0	21	38	LOUISIANA	4.6
3	39	TEXAS	50.7	33	39	ARKANSAS	7.0	1	39	CALIFORNIA	4.3
24	40	ARIZONA	50.6	30	40	IOWA	7.0	12	40	VIRGINIA	4.3
44	41	MONTANA	50.5	27	41	CONNECTICUT	6.9	25	41	SOUTH CAROLINA	4.3
26	42	COLORADO	50.5	10	42	NORTH CAROLINA	6.9	51	42	WYOMING	4.3
18	43	WASHINGTON	50.4	13	43	MASSACHUSETTS	6.9	37	43	NEW MEXICO	4.3
35	44	UTAH	50.3	9	44	NEW JERSEY	6.9	19	44	MARYLAND	4.2
47	45	NORTH DAKOTA	50.2	17	45	TENNESSEE	6.8	41	45	HAWAII	4.2
42	46	IDAHO	50.2	23	46	KENTUCKY	6.8	3	46	TEXAS	4.2
51	47	WYOMING	50.0	5	47	PENNSYLVANIA	6.7	26	47	COLORADO	4.1
1	48	CALIFORNIA	49.9	43	48	RHODE ISLAND	6.7	11	48	GEORGIA	4.1
39	49	NEVADA	49.1	4	49	FLORIDA	6.6	35	49	UTAH	3.6
41	50	HAWAII	49.1	48	50	DISTRICT OF COLUMBIA	6.2	39	50	NEVADA	3.5
50	51	ALASKA	47.3	34	51	WEST VIRGINIA	5.9	50	51	ALASKA	1.2

TABLE 11—States and the District of Columbia by 1990 Population

Selected Rankings

Percent Female Family Households 1990				Infant Deaths per 1,000 Live Births 1987				Physicians per 100,000 Population 1989			
Population Rank	Fem. HHs. Rank	State	Percent Fem. HHs.	Population Rank	Death Rate Rank	State	Infant Death Rate	Population Rank	M.D. Rate Rank	State	M.D. Rate
X	X	UNITED STATES	11.6	X	X	UNITED STATES	10.1	X	X	UNITED STATES	210
48	1	DISTRICT OF COLUMBIA	19.5	48	1	DISTRICT OF COLUMBIA	19.3	48	1	DISTRICT OF COLUMBIA	601
31	2	MISSISSIPPI	15.9	31	2	MISSISSIPPI	13.7	13	2	MASSACHUSETTS	330
21	3	LOUISIANA	15.6	25	3	SOUTH CAROLINA	12.7	19	3	MARYLAND	323
25	4	SOUTH CAROLINA	14.0	11	4	GEORGIA	12.7	2	4	NEW YORK	310
11	5	GEORGIA	13.9	22	5	ALABAMA	12.2	27	5	CONNECTICUT	298
2	6	NEW YORK	13.8	10	6	NORTH CAROLINA	11.9	43	6	RHODE ISLAND	247
22	7	ALABAMA	13.4	21	7	LOUISIANA	11.8	49	7	VERMONT	247
19	8	MARYLAND	13.3	17	8	TENNESSEE	11.7	9	8	NEW JERSEY	239
8	9	MICHIGAN	12.9	46	9	DELAWARE	11.7	1	9	CALIFORNIA	236
17	10	TENNESSEE	12.6	6	10	ILLINOIS	11.6	5	10	PENNSYLVANIA	231
10	11	NORTH CAROLINA	12.3	19	11	MARYLAND	11.5	41	11	HAWAII	215
9	12	NEW JERSEY	12.1	8	12	MICHIGAN	10.7	20	12	MINNESOTA	215
13	13	MASSACHUSETTS	12.1	2	13	NEW YORK	10.7	6	13	ILLINOIS	211
6	14	ILLINOIS	12.0	4	14	FLORIDA	10.6	26	14	COLORADO	204
37	15	NEW MEXICO	11.9	50	15	ALASKA	10.4	18	15	WASHINGTON	203
46	16	DELAWARE	11.8	42	16	IDAHO	10.4	12	16	VIRGINIA	200
43	17	RHODE ISLAND	11.7	29	17	OREGON	10.4	4	17	FLORIDA	200
7	18	OHIO	11.7	5	18	PENNSYLVANIA	10.4	29	18	OREGON	197
23	19	KENTUCKY	11.6	33	19	ARKANSAS	10.3	15	19	MISSOURI	193
3	20	TEXAS	11.6	15	20	MISSOURI	10.2	7	20	OHIO	193
1	21	CALIFORNIA	11.5	12	21	VIRGINIA	10.2	24	21	ARIZONA	190
27	22	CONNECTICUT	11.4	14	22	INDIANA	10.1	40	22	NEW HAMPSHIRE	190
5	23	PENNSYLVANIA	11.3	44	23	MONTANA	10.0	17	23	TENNESSEE	190
33	24	ARKANSAS	11.1	45	24	SOUTH DAKOTA	9.9	46	24	DELAWARE	189
12	25	VIRGINIA	11.1	34	25	WEST VIRGINIA	9.8	21	25	LOUISIANA	187
34	26	WEST VIRGINIA	10.7	26	26	COLORADO	9.8	16	26	WISCONSIN	184
4	27	FLORIDA	10.7	23	27	KENTUCKY	9.7	8	27	MICHIGAN	182
15	28	MISSOURI	10.6	18	28	WASHINGTON	9.7	10	28	NORTH CAROLINA	180
41	29	HAWAII	10.5	39	29	NEVADA	9.6	35	29	UTAH	179
14	30	INDIANA	10.5	28	30	OKLAHOMA	9.6	38	30	MAINE	176
28	31	OKLAHOMA	10.4	32	31	KANSAS	9.5	37	31	NEW MEXICO	175
24	32	ARIZONA	10.4	24	32	ARIZONA	9.5	32	32	KANSAS	172
39	33	NEVADA	10.2	9	33	NEW JERSEY	9.4	3	33	TEXAS	170
26	34	COLORADO	9.7	7	34	OHIO	9.3	36	34	NEBRASKA	169
16	35	WISCONSIN	9.6	51	35	WYOMING	9.2	34	35	WEST VIRGINIA	168
50	36	ALASKA	9.6	3	36	TEXAS	9.1	11	36	GEORGIA	167
38	37	MAINE	9.5	30	37	IOWA	9.1	47	37	NORTH DAKOTA	167
18	38	WASHINGTON	9.4	1	38	CALIFORNIA	9.0	23	38	KENTUCKY	164
49	39	VERMONT	9.2	41	39	HAWAII	8.9	25	39	SOUTH CAROLINA	155
29	40	OREGON	9.2	35	40	UTAH	8.8	22	40	ALABAMA	154
35	41	UTAH	9.1	27	41	CONNECTICUT	8.8	44	41	MONTANA	154
44	42	MONTANA	8.6	47	42	NORTH DAKOTA	8.7	14	42	INDIANA	153
20	43	MINNESOTA	8.6	20	43	MINNESOTA	8.7	39	43	NEVADA	149
32	44	KANSAS	8.6	36	44	NEBRASKA	8.6	30	44	IOWA	148
40	45	NEW HAMPSHIRE	8.5	16	45	WISCONSIN	8.6	33	45	ARKANSAS	145
36	46	NEBRASKA	8.3	49	46	VERMONT	8.5	28	46	OKLAHOMA	145
51	47	WYOMING	8.3	43	47	RHODE ISLAND	8.4	51	47	WYOMING	141
42	48	IDAHO	8.0	38	48	MAINE	8.3	45	48	SOUTH DAKOTA	139
30	49	IOWA	8.0	37	49	NEW MEXICO	8.1	50	49	ALASKA	135
45	50	SOUTH DAKOTA	8.0	40	50	NEW HAMPSHIRE	7.8	31	50	MISSISSIPPI	128
47	51	NORTH DAKOTA	7.3	13	51	MASSACHUSETTS	7.2	42	51	IDAHO	120

TABLE 11—States and the District of Columbia by 1990 Population

Selected Rankings

Hospital Beds per 100,000 Population 1989				Median Value of Owned Housing 1990				Median Rent 1990			
Population Rank	Bed Rate Rank	State	Bed Rate	Population Rank	Median Value Rank	State	Median Value	Population Rank	Median Rent Rank	State	Median Rent
X	X	UNITED STATES	499	X	X	UNITED STATES	79,100	X	X	UNITED STATES	374
48	1	DISTRICT OF COLUMBIA	1,336	41	1	HAWAII	245,300	41	1	HAWAII	599
47	2	NORTH DAKOTA	851	1	2	CALIFORNIA	195,500	1	2	CALIFORNIA	561
45	3	SOUTH DAKOTA	747	27	3	CONNECTICUT	177,800	9	3	NEW JERSEY	521
31	4	MISSISSIPPI	688	13	4	MASSACHUSETTS	162,800	27	4	CONNECTICUT	510
36	5	NEBRASKA	682	9	5	NEW JERSEY	162,300	13	5	MASSACHUSETTS	506
32	6	KANSAS	651	43	6	RHODE ISLAND	133,500	50	6	ALASKA	503
51	7	WYOMING	637	2	7	NEW YORK	131,600	40	7	NEW HAMPSHIRE	479
44	8	MONTANA	618	40	8	NEW HAMPSHIRE	129,400	19	8	MARYLAND	473
30	9	IOWA	611	48	9	DISTRICT OF COLUMBIA	123,900	39	9	NEVADA	445
17	10	TENNESSEE	602	19	10	MARYLAND	116,500	48	10	DISTRICT OF COLUMBIA	441
13	11	MASSACHUSETTS	601	46	11	DELAWARE	100,100	2	11	NEW YORK	428
2	12	NEW YORK	598	39	12	NEVADA	95,700	46	12	DELAWARE	425
15	13	MISSOURI	594	49	13	VERMONT	95,500	43	13	RHODE ISLAND	416
34	14	WEST VIRGINIA	580	50	14	ALASKA	94,400	12	14	VIRGINIA	411
22	15	ALABAMA	579	18	15	WASHINGTON	93,400	4	15	FLORIDA	402
20	16	MINNESOTA	572	12	16	VIRGINIA	91,000	20	16	MINNESOTA	384
5	17	PENNSYLVANIA	567	38	17	MAINE	87,400	18	17	WASHINGTON	383
11	18	GEORGIA	557	26	18	COLORADO	82,700	49	18	VERMONT	378
21	19	LOUISIANA	554	6	19	ILLINOIS	80,900	24	19	ARIZONA	370
33	20	ARKANSAS	538	24	20	ARIZONA	80,100	6	20	ILLINOIS	369
16	21	WISCONSIN	512	4	21	FLORIDA	77,100	26	21	COLORADO	362
6	22	ILLINOIS	511	20	22	MINNESOTA	74,000	38	22	MAINE	358
23	23	KENTUCKY	510	11	23	GEORGIA	71,300	11	23	GEORGIA	344
7	24	OHIO	500	37	24	NEW MEXICO	70,100	29	24	OREGON	344
9	25	NEW JERSEY	499	5	25	PENNSYLVANIA	69,700	8	25	MICHIGAN	343
4	26	FLORIDA	496	35	26	UTAH	68,900	16	26	WISCONSIN	331
38	27	MAINE	492	29	27	OREGON	67,100	3	27	TEXAS	328
12	28	VIRGINIA	491	10	28	NORTH CAROLINA	65,800	5	28	PENNSYLVANIA	322
14	29	INDIANA	480	7	29	OHIO	63,500	37	29	NEW MEXICO	312
3	30	TEXAS	480	16	30	WISCONSIN	62,500	35	30	UTAH	300
28	31	OKLAHOMA	478	51	31	WYOMING	61,600	7	31	OHIO	296
37	32	NEW MEXICO	466	25	32	SOUTH CAROLINA	61,100	14	32	INDIANA	291
27	33	CONNECTICUT	462	8	33	MICHIGAN	60,600	32	33	KANSAS	285
10	34	NORTH CAROLINA	462	15	34	MISSOURI	59,800	10	34	NORTH CAROLINA	284
40	35	NEW HAMPSHIRE	458	3	35	TEXAS	59,600	15	35	MISSOURI	282
43	36	RHODE ISLAND	456	21	36	LOUISIANA	58,500	36	36	NEBRASKA	282
8	37	MICHIGAN	449	17	37	TENNESSEE	58,400	25	37	SOUTH CAROLINA	276
19	38	MARYLAND	442	42	38	IDAHO	58,200	17	38	TENNESSEE	273
46	39	DELAWARE	430	44	39	MONTANA	56,600	51	39	WYOMING	270
25	40	SOUTH CAROLINA	428	14	40	INDIANA	53,900	47	40	NORTH DAKOTA	266
49	41	VERMONT	409	22	41	ALABAMA	53,700	42	41	IDAHO	261
26	42	COLORADO	398	32	42	KANSAS	52,200	30	42	IOWA	261
42	43	IDAHO	386	47	43	NORTH DAKOTA	50,800	21	43	LOUISIANA	260
24	44	ARIZONA	381	23	44	KENTUCKY	50,500	28	44	OKLAHOMA	259
41	45	HAWAII	372	36	45	NEBRASKA	50,400	44	45	MONTANA	251
39	46	NEVADA	372	28	46	OKLAHOMA	48,100	23	46	KENTUCKY	250
1	47	CALIFORNIA	367	34	47	WEST VIRGINIA	47,900	45	47	SOUTH DAKOTA	242
50	48	ALASKA	367	33	48	ARKANSAS	46,300	33	48	ARKANSAS	230
29	49	OREGON	365	30	49	IOWA	45,900	22	49	ALABAMA	229
35	50	UTAH	342	31	50	MISSISSIPPI	45,600	34	50	WEST VIRGINIA	221
18	51	WASHINGTON	338	45	51	SOUTH DAKOTA	45,200	31	51	MISSISSIPPI	215

TABLE 11—States and the District of Columbia by 1990 Population

Selected Rankings

Change in Labor Force 1989–1990			
Population Rank	Percent Change Rank	State	Percent Change
X	X	UNITED STATES	0.7
39	1	NEVADA	4.0
26	2	COLORADO	3.6
36	3	NEBRASKA	3.3
40	4	NEW HAMPSHIRE	3.1
38	5	MAINE	3.1
51	6	WYOMING	2.9
4	7	FLORIDA	2.8
41	8	HAWAII	2.7
20	9	MINNESOTA	2.6
18	10	WASHINGTON	2.1
25	11	SOUTH CAROLINA	1.7
50	12	ALASKA	1.6
27	13	CONNECTICUT	1.6
12	14	VIRGINIA	1.6
31	15	MISSISSIPPI	1.5
9	16	NEW JERSEY	1.5
23	17	KENTUCKY	1.4
42	18	IDAHO	1.4
32	19	KANSAS	1.2
29	20	OREGON	1.2
17	21	TENNESSEE	1.2
24	22	ARIZONA	1.1
28	23	OKLAHOMA	1.1
1	24	CALIFORNIA	1.0
5	25	PENNSYLVANIA	0.8
15	26	MISSOURI	0.8
49	27	VERMONT	0.7
11	28	GEORGIA	0.7
34	29	WEST VIRGINIA	0.7
19	30	MARYLAND	0.5
35	31	UTAH	0.4
10	32	NORTH CAROLINA	0.3
37	33	NEW MEXICO	0.3
7	34	OHIO	0.3
3	35	TEXAS	0.2
6	36	ILLINOIS	0.2
46	37	DELAWARE	0.0
2	38	NEW YORK	-0.1
33	39	ARKANSAS	-0.2
8	40	MICHIGAN	-0.3
45	41	SOUTH DAKOTA	-0.3
13	42	MASSACHUSETTS	-0.4
44	43	MONTANA	-0.7
22	44	ALABAMA	-0.8
16	45	WISCONSIN	-0.9
30	46	IOWA	-1.1
21	47	LOUISIANA	-1.4
14	48	INDIANA	-1.7
43	49	RHODE ISLAND	-1.7
47	50	NORTH DAKOTA	-1.8
48	51	DISTRICT OF COLUMBIA	-5.4

Unemployment Rate 1990			
Population Rank	Unemployment Rate Rank	State	Unemployment Rate
X	X	UNITED STATES	5.5
34	1	WEST VIRGINIA	8.3
8	2	MICHIGAN	7.5
31	3	MISSISSIPPI	7.5
50	4	ALASKA	6.9
33	5	ARKANSAS	6.9
22	6	ALABAMA	6.8
43	7	RHODE ISLAND	6.7
48	8	DISTRICT OF COLUMBIA	6.6
37	9	NEW MEXICO	6.3
21	10	LOUISIANA	6.2
3	11	TEXAS	6.2
6	12	ILLINOIS	6.2
13	13	MASSACHUSETTS	6.0
4	14	FLORIDA	5.9
23	15	KENTUCKY	5.8
44	16	MONTANA	5.8
42	17	IDAHO	5.8
7	18	OHIO	5.7
15	19	MISSOURI	5.7
1	20	CALIFORNIA	5.6
28	21	OKLAHOMA	5.6
40	22	NEW HAMPSHIRE	5.6
29	23	OREGON	5.5
11	24	GEORGIA	5.4
5	25	PENNSYLVANIA	5.4
51	26	WYOMING	5.4
14	27	INDIANA	5.3
24	28	ARIZONA	5.3
2	29	NEW YORK	5.2
17	30	TENNESSEE	5.2
38	31	MAINE	5.1
27	32	CONNECTICUT	5.1
46	33	DELAWARE	5.1
49	34	VERMONT	5.0
9	35	NEW JERSEY	5.0
39	36	NEVADA	4.9
26	37	COLORADO	4.9
18	38	WASHINGTON	4.9
20	39	MINNESOTA	4.8
25	40	SOUTH CAROLINA	4.7
19	41	MARYLAND	4.6
32	42	KANSAS	4.4
16	43	WISCONSIN	4.4
12	44	VIRGINIA	4.3
35	45	UTAH	4.3
30	46	IOWA	4.2
10	47	NORTH CAROLINA	4.1
47	48	NORTH DAKOTA	3.9
45	49	SOUTH DAKOTA	3.7
41	50	HAWAII	2.8
36	51	NEBRASKA	2.2

Per capita Personal Income 1989			
Population Rank	P.C. Personal Income Rank	State	P.C. Personal Income
X	X	UNITED STATES	17,592
27	1	CONNECTICUT	24,798
9	2	NEW JERSEY	23,726
48	3	DISTRICT OF COLUMBIA	22,998
13	4	MASSACHUSETTS	22,236
50	5	ALASKA	21,375
19	6	MARYLAND	20,929
2	7	NEW YORK	20,817
40	8	NEW HAMPSHIRE	20,312
1	9	CALIFORNIA	19,840
39	10	NEVADA	18,989
12	11	VIRGINIA	18,979
6	12	ILLINOIS	18,870
46	13	DELAWARE	18,750
41	14	HAWAII	18,379
43	15	RHODE ISLAND	18,113
4	16	FLORIDA	17,715
18	17	WASHINGTON	17,696
20	18	MINNESOTA	17,649
8	19	MICHIGAN	17,535
26	20	COLORADO	17,504
5	21	PENNSYLVANIA	17,387
32	22	KANSAS	16,526
49	23	VERMONT	16,514
7	24	OHIO	16,462
16	25	WISCONSIN	16,454
15	26	MISSOURI	16,447
38	27	MAINE	16,422
11	28	GEORGIA	16,050
29	29	OREGON	16,009
14	30	INDIANA	15,830
24	31	ARIZONA	15,829
36	32	NEBRASKA	15,697
30	33	IOWA	15,664
3	34	TEXAS	15,512
10	35	NORTH CAROLINA	15,287
17	36	TENNESSEE	14,736
51	37	WYOMING	14,554
44	38	MONTANA	14,149
28	39	OKLAHOMA	14,111
45	40	SOUTH DAKOTA	13,852
23	41	KENTUCKY	13,823
42	42	IDAHO	13,760
47	43	NORTH DAKOTA	13,693
22	44	ALABAMA	13,669
25	45	SOUTH CAROLINA	13,624
37	46	NEW MEXICO	13,221
35	47	UTAH	13,104
33	48	ARKANSAS	13,000
21	49	LOUISIANA	12,923
34	50	WEST VIRGINIA	12,434
31	51	MISSISSIPPI	11,806

TABLE A:

States and Counties

(For explanation of symbols, see page ix)

STATE–County code	MSA/CMSA/NECMA code[1]	STATE County	Land Area,[2] 1990 (Sq. Km.)	Population, 1990: Total persons	Population, 1990: Rank	Population, 1990: Per square kilometer	Race: White	Race: Black	Race: Am. Indian, Eskimo, Aleut	Race: Asian & Pacific Islander	Race: Other race	Hispanic[3]	Age of population, Percent: Under 5 years	Age of population, Percent: 5 to 14 years	Age of population, Percent: 15 to 24 years
			1	2	3	4	5	6	7	8	9	10	11	12	13
00 000	...	UNITED STATES	9 159 127	248 709 873	X	27.2	199 686 070	29 986 060	1 959 234	7 273 662	9 804 847	22 354 059	7.4	14.2	14.8
01 000	...	ALABAMA	131 443	4 040 587	X	30.7	2 975 797	1 020 705	16 506	21 797	5 782	24 629	7.0	14.7	15.5
01 001	5240	Autauga	1 544	34 222	1 158	22.2	27 144	6 845	71	120	42	230	7.8	16.5	14.9
01 003	5160	Baldwin	4 135	98 280	467	23.8	84 565	12 640	630	221	224	1 022	6.9	14.6	13.0
01 005	...	Barbour	2 292	25 417	1 449	11.1	14 118	11 194	46	44	15	124	7.4	16.8	14.5
01 007	...	Bibb	1 612	16 576	1 881	10.3	13 052	3 478	25	11	10	39	7.1	16.3	16.3
01 009	1000	Blount	1 672	39 248	1 019	23.5	38 397	521	133	33	164	286	6.7	14.1	14.8
01 011	...	Bullock	1 619	11 042	2 289	6.8	3 036	7 986	8	10	2	65	8.6	17.0	14.2
01 013	...	Butler	2 012	21 892	1 583	10.9	13 049	8 798	24	19	2	65	7.5	17.4	13.7
01 015	0450	Calhoun	1 576	116 034	396	73.6	92 873	21 578	296	869	418	1 282	6.4	14.1	17.4
01 017	...	Chambers	1 547	36 876	1 078	23.8	23 575	13 221	41	13	26	127	6.6	14.6	15.0
01 019	...	Cherokee	1 433	19 543	1 696	13.6	18 154	1 291	51	24	23	57	5.8	13.6	14.4
01 021	...	Chilton	1 798	32 458	1 201	18.1	28 647	3 674	63	38	36	116	6.8	15.1	14.5
01 023	...	Choctaw	2 366	16 018	1 921	6.8	8 913	7 077	10	12	6	53	7.1	16.4	15.4
01 025	...	Clarke	3 208	27 240	1 382	8.5	15 527	11 625	45	35	8	103	7.2	17.3	15.8
01 027	...	Clay	1 567	13 252	2 116	8.5	11 044	2 166	23	13	6	27	5.9	14.1	14.9
01 029	...	Cleburne	1 451	12 730	2 163	8.8	12 084	587	20	13	26	38	6.7	14.6	14.9
01 031	...	Coffee	1 759	40 240	994	22.9	32 702	6 917	163	317	141	471	6.7	14.2	14.8
01 033	2650	Colbert	1 540	51 666	818	33.5	42 820	8 568	137	93	48	187	6.6	13.6	13.7
01 035	...	Conecuh	2 204	14 054	2 052	6.4	8 063	5 925	43	13	10	82	6.7	16.2	13.8
01 037	...	Coosa	1 690	11 063	2 287	6.5	7 242	3 782	34	4	1	18	7.1	14.2	15.0
01 039	...	Covington	2 680	36 478	1 091	13.6	31 551	4 777	72	48	30	130	6.4	14.5	13.4
01 041	...	Crenshaw	1 579	13 635	2 089	8.6	10 048	3 544	27	11	5	30	6.6	15.2	13.8
01 043	...	Cullman	1 913	67 613	657	35.3	66 744	560	134	117	58	272	6.6	14.1	14.3
01 045	2180	Dale	1 453	49 633	845	34.2	39 365	8 847	239	731	451	1 215	8.6	15.1	17.4
01 047	...	Dallas	2 540	48 130	867	18.9	20 121	27 825	41	129	14	131	8.0	17.8	15.6
01 049	...	De Kalb	2 015	54 651	789	27.1	52 980	1 028	481	77	85	215	6.2	14.5	14.4
01 051	5240	Elmore	1 610	49 210	854	30.6	37 850	11 039	137	129	55	270	6.8	14.6	15.2
01 053	...	Escambia	2 454	35 518	1 110	14.5	24 326	10 046	1 047	58	41	169	6.5	15.1	14.9
01 055	2880	Etowah	1 385	99 840	459	72.1	85 274	13 799	250	419	98	331	6.0	13.9	14.5
01 057	...	Fayette	1 626	17 962	1 790	11.0	15 717	2 190	9	19	27	78	6.1	14.7	14.4
01 059	...	Franklin	1 646	27 814	1 358	16.9	26 463	1 249	57	35	10	101	6.5	14.0	14.0
01 061	...	Geneva	1 493	23 647	1 507	15.8	20 682	2 824	93	15	33	121	6.4	13.8	14.2
01 063	...	Greene	1 673	10 153	2 373	6.1	1 966	8 181	3	0	3	24	7.8	19.6	14.3
01 065	...	Hale	1 667	15 498	1 953	9.3	6 255	9 214	20	9	0	57	8.0	18.1	14.4
01 067	...	Henry	1 455	15 374	1 966	10.6	9 918	5 395	31	6	24	92	6.6	15.1	14.4
01 069	2180	Houston	1 503	81 331	559	54.1	61 513	18 954	287	470	107	464	7.4	15.4	14.3
01 071	...	Jackson	2 794	47 796	879	17.1	44 696	1 968	1 020	90	22	208	6.2	14.6	14.7
01 073	1000	Jefferson	2 882	651 525	71	226.1	418 317	228 521	889	3 222	576	2 745	6.9	14.0	13.9
01 075	...	Lamar	1 567	15 715	1 940	10.0	13 805	1 862	24	10	14	71	6.4	14.3	14.4
01 077	2650	Lauderdale	1 734	79 661	572	45.9	71 560	7 695	165	196	45	313	6.4	13.4	15.5
01 079	2030	Lawrence	1 796	31 513	1 229	17.5	24 563	4 798	2 124	19	9	102	7.3	15.2	16.0
01 081	...	Lee	1 577	87 146	524	55.3	64 889	20 407	132	1 584	134	552	6.2	12.1	29.7
01 083	...	Limestone	1 471	54 135	794	36.8	46 658	7 127	148	158	44	261	6.8	14.0	15.0
01 085	...	Lowndes	1 860	12 658	2 170	6.8	3 185	9 456	10	4	3	60	9.0	19.7	16.5
01 087	...	Macon	1 581	24 928	1 466	15.8	3 443	21 340	24	99	22	103	7.2	14.3	23.6
01 089	3440	Madison	2 085	238 912	209	114.6	184 197	48 116	1 601	4 232	766	2 984	7.3	13.5	15.4
01 091	...	Marengo	2 531	23 084	1 534	9.1	11 314	11 745	11	11	3	75	7.8	16.9	15.0
01 093	...	Marion	1 920	29 830	1 301	15.5	28 759	967	57	35	12	65	6.3	13.6	14.9
01 095	...	Marshall	1 469	70 832	625	48.2	69 361	1 087	231	111	42	289	6.5	13.6	14.1
01 097	5160	Mobile	3 194	378 643	134	118.5	254 853	117 872	1 940	3 398	580	3 164	7.8	16.0	15.1
01 099	...	Monroe	2 657	23 968	1 493	9.0	14 320	9 372	215	54	7	94	7.8	17.2	15.7
01 101	5240	Montgomery	2 046	209 085	239	102.2	119 420	87 312	414	1 533	406	1 624	7.7	15.2	15.9
01 103	2030	Morgan	1 508	100 043	458	66.3	89 122	10 081	310	370	160	584	6.9	14.7	13.8
01 105	...	Perry	1 864	12 759	2 160	6.8	4 503	8 219	16	14	7	36	7.6	17.7	18.6
01 107	...	Pickens	2 283	20 699	1 644	9.1	12 002	8 645	24	27	1	50	7.1	16.6	13.8
01 109	...	Pike	1 738	27 595	1 369	15.9	17 814	9 548	146	68	19	108	6.7	13.6	23.0
01 111	...	Randolph	1 505	19 881	1 683	13.2	15 138	4 686	29	21	7	53	6.4	14.8	14.5
01 113	1800	Russell	1 661	46 860	893	28.2	28 473	18 088	90	117	92	301	7.5	14.5	15.2
01 115	1000	St. Clair	1 642	50 009	842	30.5	45 138	4 561	136	77	97	209	7.2	14.8	14.4
01 117	1000	Shelby	2 059	99 358	462	48.3	90 715	7 718	264	575	86	525	8.0	15.3	14.4
01 119	...	Sumter	2 344	16 174	1 912	6.9	4 759	11 369	6	30	10	78	7.6	17.5	19.6
01 121	...	Talladega	1 916	74 107	608	38.7	50 970	22 773	174	113	77	490	6.9	15.6	15.8
01 123	...	Tallapoosa	1 860	38 826	1 027	20.9	28 493	10 212	62	37	22	71	6.4	14.2	14.7
01 125	8600	Tuscaloosa	3 432	150 522	310	43.9	109 398	39 377	253	1 264	230	948	6.4	13.2	21.6
01 127	1000	Walker	2 058	67 670	656	32.9	63 042	4 405	84	107	32	224	6.2	14.4	14.5

1. MSA = Metropolitan Statistical Area. CMSA = Consolidated MSA. NECMA = New England county metropolitan area. PMSA = Primary MSA. See Appendix A for explanation of these concepts. See Appendix B for list of metropolitan areas identified by type, with component counties. 2. Dry land or land partially or temporarily covered by water. 3. Hispanic persons may be of any race.

STATE County	Population, 1990 (cont'd)							Population–Change and components of change							
	Age of population (cont'd) Percent						Percent female	Change		Components of change, 1980–1986					
								1980–1990		Total persons, 1986	Total persons, 1980	Net change		Natural increase	
	25 to 34 years	35 to 44 years	45 to 54 years	55 to 64 years	65 to 74 years	75 years and over		Number	Percent			Number	Percent	Births	Deaths
	14	15	16	17	18	19	20	21	22	23	24	25	26	27	28
UNITED STATES	17.4	15.1	10.1	8.5	7.3	5.3	51.3	22 163 873	9.8	241 078 000	226 546 000	14 532 000	6.4	22 922 000	12 633 000
ALABAMA	16.0	14.4	10.4	9.0	7.5	5.5	52.1	146 587	3.8	4 052 000	3 894 000	159 000	4.1	377 000	226 000
Autauga	16.2	14.8	11.4	8.5	5.7	4.1	51.3	1 963	6.1	35 600	32 259	3 400	10.5	3 100	1 600
Baldwin	14.7	14.4	11.0	10.3	9.2	6.0	51.4	19 724	25.1	92 300	78 556	13 700	17.5	8 000	4 700
Barbour	14.4	14.2	9.2	8.8	8.2	6.4	52.5	661	2.7	25 300	24 756	500	2.2	2 600	1 700
Bibb	14.9	13.7	10.7	8.5	6.7	6.0	51.1	853	5.4	16 000	15 723	300	1.8	1 500	1 100
Blount	15.1	14.7	12.0	9.5	7.4	5.6	51.2	2 789	7.6	39 000	36 459	2 500	6.8	2 800	1 900
Bullock	15.3	12.9	8.6	7.3	8.5	7.6	51.7	446	4.2	10 100	10 596	-500	-4.6	1 300	800
Butler	13.5	12.9	9.2	8.9	8.8	8.0	53.2	212	1.0	21 800	21 680	200	0.7	2 500	1 600
Calhoun	15.9	14.5	10.2	9.1	7.4	5.0	51.7	-3 727	-3.1	123 800	119 761	4 100	3.4	10 700	6 300
Chambers	14.1	13.4	10.0	9.6	9.2	7.7	52.9	-2 315	-5.9	39 800	39 191	600	1.6	3 400	2 700
Cherokee	14.4	14.3	11.9	10.8	8.9	5.8	50.8	783	4.2	19 200	18 760	500	2.6	1 400	1 100
Chilton	15.2	14.0	11.1	9.6	7.8	6.1	51.4	1 846	6.0	31 100	30 612	500	1.7	2 600	2 000
Choctaw	14.1	13.2	11.0	8.9	7.5	6.4	52.6	-821	-4.9	17 000	16 839	100	0.7	1 500	1 000
Clarke	14.6	12.9	10.5	8.5	7.1	6.0	52.2	-462	-1.7	27 500	27 702	-200	-0.6	3 000	1 800
Clay	14.2	12.9	11.2	10.0	8.6	8.3	52.0	-451	-3.3	13 100	13 703	-600	-4.5	1 200	1 000
Cleburne	15.1	13.9	11.8	9.6	7.7	5.7	50.9	135	1.1	12 900	12 595	300	2.2	1 100	800
Coffee	15.9	14.8	11.2	9.4	7.6	5.6	51.1	1 707	4.4	40 200	38 533	1 700	4.4	3 700	2 100
Colbert	15.1	14.2	11.8	10.4	9.0	5.7	52.0	-2 853	-5.2	54 500	54 519	0	-0.1	4 500	3 000
Conecuh	14.0	12.7	9.5	9.7	9.3	8.0	52.8	-1 830	-11.5	15 500	15 884	-400	-2.4	1 500	1 100
Coosa	15.2	12.9	10.5	10.6	8.3	6.2	50.9	-314	-2.8	10 700	11 377	-700	-6.1	900	700
Covington	14.1	13.2	10.7	10.4	9.5	7.7	52.7	-372	-1.0	36 400	36 850	-400	-1.1	3 300	2 800
Crenshaw	13.3	13.1	10.0	9.7	10.0	8.3	52.6	-475	-3.4	13 400	14 110	-700	-5.2	1 200	1 100
Cullman	15.2	14.1	11.2	10.0	8.2	6.2	51.4	5 971	9.7	66 000	61 642	4 400	7.1	5 200	3 700
Dale	19.7	13.3	9.2	7.4	5.5	3.9	49.5	1 812	3.8	49 600	47 821	1 800	3.7	5 500	1 900
Dallas	14.3	12.8	9.3	8.5	7.5	6.2	54.4	-5 851	-10.8	52 700	53 981	-1 300	-2.4	6 300	3 500
De Kalb	15.0	14.3	11.1	9.9	8.2	6.4	51.7	993	1.9	53 900	53 658	200	0.4	4 400	3 300
Elmore	17.1	15.3	10.8	8.6	6.7	5.0	49.4	5 820	13.4	47 900	43 390	4 600	10.5	4 100	2 500
Escambia	15.3	14.0	10.9	9.4	7.6	6.3	50.8	-2 922	-7.6	36 400	38 440	-2 100	-5.3	3 400	2 300
Etowah	14.2	14.6	10.8	10.3	9.4	6.5	52.7	-3 217	-3.1	102 300	103 057	-800	-0.7	8 700	6 600
Fayette	13.9	14.0	11.1	9.5	8.6	7.7	52.3	-847	-4.5	19 000	18 809	100	0.7	1 600	1 200
Franklin	14.5	13.7	11.6	10.4	8.6	6.8	52.2	-536	-1.9	28 000	28 350	-400	-1.4	2 500	1 900
Geneva	13.7	13.4	11.4	10.4	9.2	7.6	51.8	-606	-2.5	23 900	24 253	-300	-1.3	2 000	1 700
Greene	13.6	11.9	8.4	8.8	7.4	8.2	54.1	-868	-7.9	10 600	11 021	-400	-3.6	1 300	800
Hale	14.3	12.2	8.9	8.2	8.3	7.7	53.3	-106	-0.7	14 800	15 604	-800	-5.1	1 800	1 100
Henry	13.3	14.1	10.4	9.8	9.0	7.3	52.7	72	0.5	14 800	15 302	-500	-3.1	1 400	1 100
Houston	16.0	15.0	10.6	8.9	7.3	5.1	52.5	6 699	9.0	80 300	74 632	5 600	7.5	7 800	4 000
Jackson	15.1	15.0	12.2	9.8	7.5	5.1	51.7	-3 611	-7.0	49 900	51 407	-1 500	-2.8	4 400	2 800
Jefferson	16.8	15.3	9.9	9.2	8.0	6.0	53.3	-19 846	-3.0	676 400	671 371	5 000	0.7	64 300	41 800
Lamar	14.4	13.6	11.1	10.1	8.2	7.5	52.2	-738	-4.5	16 400	16 453	-100	-0.4	1 400	1 100
Lauderdale	15.2	14.2	11.1	9.9	8.4	5.9	52.3	-885	-1.1	83 200	80 546	2 700	3.4	6 700	4 100
Lawrence	16.1	13.7	11.1	8.8	7.0	4.9	50.8	1 343	4.5	31 500	30 170	1 300	4.3	2 900	1 700
Lee	15.6	12.5	8.6	6.7	5.0	3.6	50.4	10 863	14.2	80 800	76 283	4 600	6.0	6 800	3 200
Limestone	18.2	14.8	11.1	8.8	6.5	4.8	50.0	8 130	17.7	51 800	46 005	5 800	12.5	4 100	2 500
Lowndes	14.4	11.6	8.5	7.6	6.7	6.0	53.7	-595	-4.5	12 700	13 253	-500	-3.8	1 700	800
Macon	12.6	11.7	7.9	7.4	8.4	6.9	53.7	-1 901	-7.1	26 200	26 829	-600	-2.3	2 500	1 700
Madison	19.9	14.8	11.3	8.8	5.6	3.3	50.7	41 946	21.3	233 700	196 966	36 700	18.6	19 400	8 600
Marengo	13.8	13.0	9.7	9.2	7.7	6.9	52.8	-1 963	-7.8	24 200	25 047	-800	-3.3	2 600	1 700
Marion	14.3	13.9	11.8	9.9	8.2	7.0	51.1	-211	-0.7	31 100	30 041	1 000	3.5	2 500	1 800
Marshall	15.4	14.4	11.6	10.4	8.1	5.9	52.1	5 210	7.9	71 500	65 622	5 900	9.0	5 800	4 100
Mobile	16.3	14.6	10.0	8.3	7.0	4.8	52.6	13 663	3.7	377 700	364 980	12 800	3.5	41 900	19 700
Monroe	14.6	13.2	9.8	8.5	7.1	6.1	51.7	1 317	5.8	22 400	22 651	-200	-0.9	2 500	1 400
Montgomery	17.0	15.0	9.6	8.0	6.7	4.9	52.9	12 047	6.1	215 400	197 038	18 400	9.3	21 200	10 900
Morgan	16.9	15.4	11.4	9.1	6.9	4.8	51.3	9 812	10.9	98 800	90 231	8 500	9.5	8 500	4 700
Perry	12.0	10.7	9.1	8.4	7.7	8.1	53.4	-2 253	-15.0	14 600	15 012	-400	-3.0	1 500	900
Pickens	13.6	12.1	10.2	10.3	8.7	7.7	53.3	-782	-3.6	21 400	21 481	-100	-0.5	2 300	1 500
Pike	13.4	11.7	9.2	7.8	7.7	6.9	53.1	-455	-1.6	27 700	28 050	-300	-1.2	2 600	1 700
Randolph	14.4	13.0	10.0	10.2	9.2	7.4	51.6	-194	-1.0	19 900	20 075	-200	-0.8	1 800	1 400
Russell	15.9	13.8	10.8	9.6	7.6	5.1	52.2	-496	-1.0	48 700	47 356	1 300	2.8	4 700	3 200
St. Clair	16.3	15.2	11.3	9.3	7.1	4.5	49.8	8 804	21.4	46 900	41 205	5 700	13.9	3 900	2 200
Shelby	19.4	17.9	10.5	6.9	4.6	3.0	51.1	33 060	49.9	81 200	66 298	14 900	22.5	7 500	2 800
Sumter	14.1	11.1	7.8	7.7	7.4	7.2	53.8	-734	-4.3	16 100	16 908	-800	-4.7	1 800	1 100
Talladega	14.8	14.5	10.2	9.3	7.6	5.3	51.7	281	0.4	76 500	73 826	2 700	3.6	7 300	4 300
Tallapoosa	14.0	13.9	10.5	10.2	9.1	7.0	53.0	60	0.2	38 800	38 766	0	0.1	3 200	2 700
Tuscaloosa	15.7	14.2	9.2	8.3	6.6	4.8	51.7	12 981	9.4	141 300	137 541	3 700	2.7	12 100	6 600
Walker	14.9	14.5	11.4	9.7	8.2	6.2	52.0	-990	-1.4	67 500	68 660	-1 100	-1.6	5 600	4 300

STATE County	Population—(cont'd): Components of change, 1980-1986 (cont'd)	Households, 1990			Households, 1990: Percent		Births, 1988			Deaths, 1987: Number		Deaths, 1987: Rate		Marriages, 1984	
	Net migration	Number	Percent change, 1980–1990	Persons per house-hold	Female family house-holder[1]	One-person	Total	Rate[2]	Low birth weight[3] (Number)	Total	Infant[4]	Total[2]	Infant[5]	Number	Rate[2]
	29	30	31	32	33	34	35	36	37	38	39	40	41	42	43
UNITED STATES	4 244 000	91 947 410	14.4	2.63	11.6	24.6	3 909 510	15.9	270 681	2 123 323	38 408	8.7	10.1	2 477 192	10.5
ALABAMA	8 000	1 506 790	12.3	2.62	13.4	23.8	60 745	14.8	4 866	37 708	727	9.2	12.2	47 541	11.9
Autauga	1 900	11 826	16.0	2.88	12.2	17.7	536	15.0	40	279	5	7.9	9.6	451	13.4
Baldwin	10 500	37 044	38.4	2.62	10.0	21.4	1 360	14.1	87	844	13	8.9	9.2	1 473	17.1
Barbour	-400	9 218	10.1	2.70	16.5	25.4	386	15.0	37	258	5	10.1	12.9	237	9.4
Bibb	-200	5 745	11.2	2.84	11.3	20.3	239	14.1	21	170	1	10.1	4.2	154	9.4
Blount	1 700	14 644	15.5	2.67	7.9	19.0	460	12.0	21	353	4	9.3	8.9	377	10.3
Bullock	-900	3 787	9.6	2.74	25.9	27.0	214	19.5	28	118	1	10.8	5.1	89	8.3
Butler	-700	7 935	6.2	2.73	16.2	25.0	341	15.4	27	260	1	11.6	2.9	212	9.5
Calhoun	-300	42 983	8.4	2.59	12.4	23.2	1 645	13.3	117	1 010	21	8.2	12.6	1 413	11.3
Chambers	-100	13 786	2.0	2.65	15.7	23.9	529	13.3	50	434	10	10.9	19.3	445	11.0
Cherokee	300	7 466	14.8	2.61	8.9	20.4	210	10.5	13	199	1	10.1	4.6	185	9.3
Chilton	-100	12 114	12.8	2.66	10.1	21.1	463	14.4	29	317	10	10.0	23.0	381	12.3
Choctaw	-400	5 747	6.3	2.77	14.5	23.8	244	14.4	15	166	2	9.8	8.0	310	18.2
Clarke	-1 400	9 506	6.6	2.83	14.8	23.0	382	13.8	32	295	5	10.6	11.0	273	9.8
Clay	-800	5 003	5.0	2.62	9.9	23.0	183	14.0	17	161	3	12.3	18.1	241	17.7
Cleburne	0	4 776	9.2	2.65	8.1	20.0	169	13.1	13	123	4	9.5	25.0	217	17.0
Coffee	100	15 260	13.6	2.61	10.7	21.7	589	14.6	53	392	9	9.7	15.4	570	14.2
Colbert	-1 600	20 096	4.8	2.56	11.3	22.9	680	12.8	58	534	8	10.0	12.5	581	10.7
Conecuh	-800	5 259	-3.6	2.65	15.4	24.8	207	13.8	21	149	2	9.7	9.4	168	10.5
Coosa	-900	4 017	3.0	2.72	11.8	21.3	145	13.1	11	127	2	11.3	14.8	108	9.5
Covington	-900	14 444	5.1	2.50	11.3	25.7	478	13.1	29	443	7	12.2	14.9	780	21.1
Crenshaw	-800	5 262	4.7	2.56	14.2	26.7	177	12.7	10	174	4	12.6	22.7	112	8.0
Cullman	2 900	25 605	17.7	2.61	8.2	20.6	872	13.2	74	639	10	9.7	12.8	745	11.7
Dale	-1 800	17 574	15.9	2.69	11.7	21.1	944	18.8	66	360	10	7.3	11.3	567	12.2
Dallas	-4 100	17 033	-3.2	2.77	23.7	25.4	900	17.2	86	573	11	10.8	12.7	492	9.0
De Kalb	-900	20 968	8.9	2.58	9.2	21.8	699	12.7	45	586	7	10.7	10.0	478	8.7
Elmore	3 000	16 532	17.9	2.77	11.2	19.4	762	15.1	59	433	11	8.8	15.1	543	11.6
Escambia	-3 100	12 899	1.9	2.65	14.3	24.2	433	12.1	42	393	4	10.8	8.5	607	16.9
Etowah	-2 800	38 675	4.9	2.55	11.8	24.3	1 323	12.9	99	1 159	15	11.3	11.7	1 107	10.7
Fayette	-200	6 859	2.2	2.59	9.7	23.1	209	11.3	17	197	1	10.5	4.7	163	8.7
Franklin	-1 000	10 850	6.3	2.53	9.0	23.3	385	13.8	14	369	5	13.1	12.6	351	12.3
Geneva	-600	9 231	7.7	2.55	9.9	24.2	298	12.7	12	240	5	10.2	17.0	310	13.0
Greene	-900	3 512	1.7	2.87	25.5	26.1	161	14.8	22	115	2	10.6	11.1	86	7.7
Hale	-1 500	5 397	11.3	2.82	20.3	24.4	264	16.9	23	186	8	12.1	33.3	116	7.4
Henry	-700	5 769	9.7	2.65	13.5	23.3	222	14.8	17	175	3	11.7	14.6	132	8.6
Houston	1 800	30 844	17.8	2.61	13.3	24.1	1 229	15.2	88	679	13	8.5	10.4	996	12.8
Jackson	-3 100	18 020	1.9	2.63	9.3	20.7	615	12.4	48	480	8	9.7	13.5	512	9.9
Jefferson	-17 500	251 479	3.0	2.54	15.7	26.5	10 094	14.9	916	6 892	136	10.1	13.5	7 551	11.2
Lamar	-400	6 005	3.8	2.59	9.5	23.6	202	12.5	18	163	1	9.9	4.8	322	19.6
Lauderdale	100	30 905	9.5	2.53	10.1	23.4	1 069	13.0	63	710	8	8.6	7.7	1 703	20.9
Lawrence	200	11 410	16.3	2.75	10.4	19.5	455	14.6	35	294	8	9.5	18.2	356	11.4
Lee	900	33 097	22.7	2.50	11.1	26.1	1 214	14.9	100	507	14	6.3	12.5	829	10.7
Limestone	4 200	19 685	28.2	2.66	9.8	20.7	750	14.2	60	397	8	7.7	11.6	534	11.2
Lowndes	-1 500	4 056	8.7	3.11	26.3	21.0	255	19.5	30	92	2	7.0	7.5	100	7.6
Macon	-1 400	8 483	2.5	2.67	24.2	29.3	391	14.9	36	278	7	10.5	15.9	193	7.4
Madison	25 900	91 208	36.0	2.56	10.5	24.0	3 722	15.7	228	1 519	30	6.6	8.6	3 059	14.3
Marengo	-1 800	8 156	0.5	2.81	17.8	24.2	423	17.4	49	219	5	8.9	13.2	228	9.0
Marion	300	11 521	6.8	2.54	8.8	23.0	383	12.5	26	288	5	9.4	12.8	331	10.7
Marshall	4 200	27 761	18.2	2.53	10.1	22.8	932	12.7	61	708	6	9.8	6.4	840	12.3
Mobile	-9 400	136 899	11.0	2.71	16.7	23.3	6 376	16.4	531	3 336	80	8.6	12.0	3 786	10.0
Monroe	-1 300	8 412	16.2	2.83	15.0	22.8	374	16.2	37	240	3	10.5	8.1	220	9.7
Montgomery	8 000	77 173	12.7	2.61	17.2	26.7	3 711	17.3	321	1 726	51	8.1	14.5	2 318	11.3
Morgan	4 800	37 799	20.5	2.60	10.3	22.1	1 417	14.0	110	848	7	8.5	4.9	1 162	12.4
Perry	-1 000	4 201	-8.6	2.89	22.5	25.0	228	15.5	16	134	4	9.0	17.9	107	7.1
Pickens	-900	7 568	8.2	2.70	16.3	24.1	335	15.6	23	236	5	10.9	16.0	216	9.9
Pike	-1 200	10 314	8.3	2.50	15.6	28.0	421	15.0	38	271	7	9.7	18.7	337	12.2
Randolph	-600	7 553	7.2	2.60	11.6	24.0	301	15.0	26	257	5	12.8	19.8	254	12.5
Russell	-200	17 499	7.7	2.65	17.4	24.5	743	14.8	61	529	16	10.6	20.5	880	18.2
St. Clair	4 000	17 666	27.6	2.74	9.0	18.5	710	14.5	54	426	6	8.9	8.4	521	11.8
Shelby	10 200	35 985	64.9	2.71	8.0	19.5	1 591	18.1	93	509	8	5.9	5.5	619	8.5
Sumter	-1 500	5 545	5.6	2.78	23.2	26.6	289	17.8	35	170	3	10.2	13.0	308	18.0
Talladega	-300	26 448	9.9	2.71	14.2	21.9	1 081	14.3	99	723	10	9.6	9.5	1 297	17.2
Tallapoosa	-500	14 700	10.7	2.60	13.9	23.4	559	14.1	51	448	11	11.3	21.5	428	10.9
Tuscaloosa	-1 800	55 354	18.2	2.55	13.0	25.8	2 098	14.4	169	1 119	27	7.7	14.1	1 514	10.9
Walker	-2 400	25 554	7.3	2.62	10.7	21.9	872	12.6	78	697	7	10.1	8.2	898	13.0

1. No spouse present. 2. Per 1,000 resident population estimated as of July 1 of the year shown. 3. Under 2,500 grams. 4. Deaths of infants under 1 year old. 5. Deaths of infants under 1 year old per 1,000 live births.

STATE County	Divorces, 1984		Physicians, active non-Federal, 1989		Hospitals, 1989			Nursing homes,[4] 1986		Serious crimes known to police, 1988			Education			
						Beds				Number			Public school enrollment[7]		Attainment,[8] 1980	
	Number	Rate[1]	Number[2]	Rate[3]	Number	Number	Rate[3]	Number	Beds	Total[5]	Violent[6]	Rate[3]	1986–1987	1980	Percent 12 yrs. or more	Percent 16 yrs. or more
	44	45	46	47	48	49	50	51	52	53	54	55	56	57	58	59
UNITED STATES	1 169 000	4.9	522 138	210	6 882	1 237 719	499	26 383	1 770 967	12 292 580	1 376 000	5 557	40 024 299	42 121 836	66.5	16.2
ALABAMA	25 413	6.4	6 356	154	142	23 827	579	288	23 559	177 236	21 680	4 453	733 735	770 528	56.5	12.2
Autauga	163	4.9	20	56	2	134	373	3	101	1 247	206	3 515	6 829	7 380	59.4	12.1
Baldwin	642	7.5	96	98	3	241	245	8	733	3 231	240	3 396	16 417	15 527	60.3	12.1
Barbour	130	5.2	18	70	1	74	287	1	180	607	103	2 337	5 071	5 463	44.9	9.2
Bibb	48	2.9	8	47	1	128	749	1	103	7	1	275	3 557	3 532	40.5	4.9
Blount	172	4.7	11	29	1	75	195	3	118	646	84	1 647	7 319	7 771	46.1	5.3
Bullock	42	3.9	6	54	1	62	559	1	32	235	2	5 416	2 014	2 307	41.0	8.8
Butler	146	6.6	9	40	2	96	430	2	179	708	162	3 402	4 640	4 058	45.0	8.2
Calhoun	1 088	8.7	136	111	5	584	475	7	593	5 529	888	4 469	20 939	23 279	56.7	11.0
Chambers	254	6.3	27	68	1	172	434	6	282	820	155	2 044	7 109	8 034	45.4	7.4
Cherokee	118	5.9	7	35	1	60	297	1	53	431	31	2 176	3 789	3 900	43.2	6.3
Chilton	212	6.8	12	37	1	60	185	2	132	672	72	2 091	6 151	6 117	46.0	6.5
Choctaw	66	3.9	5	29	1	65	380	1	49	134	9	872	3 418	3 432	44.7	7.0
Clarke	152	5.4	20	72	3	127	460	2	141	233	40	2 118	5 976	6 128	49.4	8.9
Clay	74	5.4	6	46	1	116	885	4	158	21	1	1 139	2 906	2 916	46.6	5.9
Cleburne	74	5.8	5	39	1	70	543	1	40	136	8	1 043	2 419	2 644	38.3	5.8
Coffee	354	8.8	39	97	3	341	846	1	151	1 557	215	3 813	8 470	8 740	56.6	12.2
Colbert	276	5.1	57	109	2	251	478	3	264	1 582	136	2 995	9 065	11 227	55.8	9.4
Conecuh	73	4.6	4	27	1	42	284	1	51	81	12	1 974	2 817	3 233	42.5	6.2
Coosa	75	6.6	2	18	0	0	0	1	42	163	8	1 440	2 098	2 545	43.1	3.6
Covington	179	4.9	24	66	3	195	536	2	227	783	95	2 117	7 141	7 594	44.3	7.1
Crenshaw	68	4.9	7	50	1	65	464	1	137	121	14	952	2 839	2 800	37.6	6.8
Cullman	435	6.8	50	75	2	224	338	8	513	944	66	1 402	11 294	12 507	46.6	7.3
Dale	421	9.1	24	48	2	124	246	2	237	1 320	212	2 860	7 959	9 874	64.9	11.6
Dallas	281	5.2	69	133	2	283	544	3	269	2 817	655	5 239	11 188	11 793	53.5	11.3
De Kalb	434	7.9	28	51	1	103	186	4	420	961	122	1 741	10 516	10 744	42.7	5.7
Elmore	217	4.6	20	39	2	135	264	3	281	1 513	215	3 055	9 222	8 691	57.7	10.3
Escambia	192	5.3	22	62	3	172	486	1	100	964	100	2 620	7 366	8 156	50.8	7.2
Etowah	683	6.6	153	149	3	570	554	7	814	3 679	525	3 541	18 288	20 502	54.9	8.9
Fayette	109	5.8	11	60	1	162	880	2	113	267	28	1 383	3 246	3 945	43.6	7.3
Franklin	68	2.4	22	79	2	131	470	5	290	199	35	1 515	5 439	5 771	45.1	6.0
Geneva	109	4.6	6	26	1	169	725	1	86	282	42	1 172	4 599	5 313	46.0	5.9
Greene	25	2.2	8	74	1	72	667	1	52	327	77	2 968	2 367	2 725	39.9	9.6
Hale	33	2.1	6	38	1	28	177	2	160	126	16	810	3 475	3 743	38.2	6.7
Henry	62	4.1	3	20	0	0	0	2	76	222	19	1 464	3 139	3 170	44.0	8.6
Houston	687	8.8	172	212	3	675	831	7	308	5 640	592	6 949	15 362	15 268	58.3	12.7
Jackson	298	5.8	30	61	2	231	470	2	145	1 039	125	2 170	10 039	10 778	47.8	6.8
Jefferson	4 564	6.8	2 470	364	19	4 995	737	56	4 258	46 705	5 991	6 863	110 697	121 606	64.7	15.8
Lamar	78	4.8	5	31	1	70	435	2	144	3	0	141	3 432	3 564	43.0	5.9
Lauderdale	497	6.1	110	134	2	648	791	7	568	2 629	179	3 157	13 748	15 914	57.6	13.0
Lawrence	184	5.9	12	39	1	71	228	1	136	303	61	963	6 599	7 338	42.9	4.0
Lee	419	5.4	99	121	1	290	355	2	278	5 382	395	6 542	13 342	12 911	62.1	21.6
Limestone	208	4.4	27	51	2	129	242	2	228	888	126	1 699	9 654	10 017	50.7	8.7
Lowndes	23	1.8	3	23	0	0	0	0	0	176	13	1 319	2 992	3 383	42.5	6.8
Macon	73	2.8	27	103	1	838	3 186	2	209	1 756	293	6 606	4 779	5 200	54.3	18.1
Madison	1 701	8.0	386	162	5	1 068	447	8	610	14 974	1 025	6 400	37 098	40 061	70.1	21.4
Marengo	99	3.9	12	49	1	99	407	2	135	602	100	2 431	5 219	5 470	48.2	8.8
Marion	227	7.3	19	62	2	189	622	3	243	223	8	749	5 755	6 229	42.3	6.1
Marshall	635	9.3	46	62	3	198	269	5	474	1 822	141	2 500	13 438	13 586	50.1	8.6
Mobile	2 600	6.9	843	215	9	2 692	685	22	2 000	27 379	4 308	7 110	68 612	64 313	61.7	12.4
Monroe	42	1.9	13	56	1	94	405	2	129	517	108	2 234	5 442	5 266	50.6	8.7
Montgomery	1 596	7.8	420	196	7	1 443	672	14	1 259	11 405	549	5 290	36 789	36 575	66.8	20.0
Morgan	682	7.3	119	116	4	530	516	7	654	4 298	333	4 257	18 337	19 016	59.9	11.8
Perry	36	2.4	5	34	0	0	0	2	102	342	100	2 256	2 869	3 548	43.1	9.7
Pickens	45	2.1	13	60	1	56	260	3	179	340	71	1 536	4 179	4 425	43.8	7.0
Pike	170	6.1	24	85	1	97	345	1	164	974	177	3 442	5 036	5 450	47.4	11.3
Randolph	105	5.1	8	40	2	84	418	2	152	283	68	1 359	3 954	4 304	41.2	7.2
Russell	440	9.1	33	65	1	234	460	4	264	2 522	458	4 941	8 347	8 956	42.8	5.7
St. Clair	149	3.4	17	34	1	72	145	5	413	956	148	2 056	8 818	8 612	49.9	6.4
Shelby	396	5.4	58	64	2	180	198	1	226	1 279	103	1 596	14 314	12 731	63.6	17.8
Sumter	71	4.2	7	43	1	33	205	1	100	209	17	1 238	3 296	3 651	46.5	9.9
Talladega	569	7.6	52	69	2	299	398	4	392	2 078	301	2 720	15 401	17 335	49.1	7.8
Tallapoosa	151	3.9	29	73	2	121	303	6	491	1 102	178	2 767	7 693	8 036	48.3	8.3
Tuscaloosa	625	4.5	292	199	5	2 811	1 912	9	1 131	7 059	920	4 843	24 252	24 658	60.1	16.6
Walker	287	4.1	46	66	1	267	383	8	545	1 497	152	2 281	13 447	14 617	45.6	6.4

1. Per 1,000 resident population estimated as of July 1 of the year shown. 2. As of end of year. 3. Per 100,000 resident population as of July 1 of the year shown. 4. Preliminary. Covers nursing homes with 3 or more beds. 5. Data for serious crimes have not been adjusted for underreporting, this may affect comparability between geographic areas or over time. 6. Includes murder and nonnegligent manslaughter, forcible rape, robbery, and aggravated assault. 7. The 1986–1987 data are based on administrative reports obtained by the U.S. National Center for Education Statistics. The 1980 data are based on the 1980 Census of Population and Housing. 8. Persons 25 years old or older.

STATE County	Education (cont'd) — Local government expenditures for education,[1] 1982 — Total (Mil dol)	Education (cont'd) — Local government expenditures for education,[1] 1982 — Per capita (Dollars)	Social Security Program December 1988 — Beneficiaries — Total	Social Security Program December 1988 — Beneficiaries — Rate[2]	Social Security Program December 1988 — Payments ($1,000)	Supplemental Security Income Program recipients June 1986	Money income — Per capita[3] — 1987 Income, (Dollars)	Money income — Per capita[3] — 1979 — Current dollars	Money income — Per capita[3] — 1979 — Constant 1987 dollars	Money income — Median household income 1979 (Dollars)	Money income — Percent below poverty level, 1979 — Persons	Money income — Percent below poverty level, 1979 — Families	Housing units, 1990 — Total	Housing units, 1990 — Percent change, 1980–1990
	60	61	62	63	64	65	66	67	68	69	70	71	72	73
UNITED STATES	104 707.7	451	37 705 973	153.4	18 408 795	4 268 581	11 923	7 295	11 414	16 841	12.4	9.6	102 263 678	15.7
ALABAMA	1 277.1	324	686 970	167.5	295 500	131 057	9 615	5 892	9 219	13 669	18.9	14.8	1 670 379	13.8
Autauga	11.0	339	4 570	128.0	1 913	1 092	9 563	5 774	9 035	16 524	16.6	13.5	12 732	16.1
Baldwin	24.1	292	17 380	180.3	7 804	1 736	9 763	5 960	9 326	14 614	16.2	13.2	50 933	53.1
Barbour	10.1	408	4 525	176.1	1 708	1 560	7 586	4 544	7 110	10 058	30.8	24.4	10 705	14.8
Bibb	5.4	336	3 025	179.0	1 214	684	7 388	4 859	7 603	12 299	21.2	17.5	6 404	11.2
Blount	11.5	314	5 420	141.1	2 216	1 130	8 143	5 213	8 157	12 657	18.0	15.3	15 790	14.0
Bullock	4.5	424	2 320	210.9	804	1 000	6 515	3 961	6 198	8 204	35.4	28.4	4 458	14.5
Butler	7.1	322	4 560	205.4	1 713	1 278	7 106	4 594	7 188	10 206	27.2	20.3	8 745	7.7
Calhoun	35.6	288	20 075	162.8	8 325	3 212	9 137	5 596	8 756	13 665	16.3	12.6	46 753	9.8
Chambers	12.3	311	7 885	198.6	3 573	1 298	8 797	5 171	8 091	12 304	17.8	13.1	14 910	3.3
Cherokee	6.8	352	3 435	171.8	1 423	628	8 892	5 436	8 506	12 004	18.6	15.1	9 379	14.4
Chilton	9.4	310	5 795	180.0	2 391	1 140	8 332	5 153	8 063	11 879	19.8	15.6	13 883	7.9
Choctaw	5.8	351	3 040	178.8	1 090	1 086	7 874	4 657	7 287	10 134	31.5	27.5	6 789	11.6
Clarke	10.9	386	5 320	192.1	2 055	1 468	7 922	5 041	7 888	12 091	26.4	20.2	10 853	8.3
Clay	4.8	352	2 780	212.2	1 057	616	7 854	4 579	7 165	10 984	21.0	16.8	5 608	5.3
Cleburne	4.0	309	2 320	179.8	877	502	8 198	5 013	7 844	12 782	16.7	13.7	5 232	9.0
Coffee	14.2	358	6 535	161.8	2 612	1 360	9 918	5 699	8 917	14 148	16.3	14.1	16 951	16.2
Colbert	20.1	369	10 050	188.9	4 684	1 596	8 941	6 256	9 789	15 445	14.5	11.0	21 812	4.9
Conecuh	5.4	343	2 975	198.3	1 087	948	7 138	4 504	7 047	9 211	29.4	24.3	6 207	3.5
Coosa	3.6	315	2 075	186.9	830	406	8 072	4 912	7 686	10 968	24.7	20.6	5 113	3.6
Covington	12.2	334	8 525	232.9	3 434	1 700	8 502	5 186	8 115	11 209	19.9	15.5	16 178	6.3
Crenshaw	4.7	339	3 055	219.8	1 133	958	7 473	4 339	6 789	8 906	29.8	24.8	5 938	7.9
Cullman	21.2	340	12 910	195.0	5 175	2 534	9 144	5 444	8 518	12 117	17.5	15.4	28 369	14.7
Dale	13.6	282	6 430	128.3	2 485	1 280	9 260	5 313	8 313	12 627	16.5	14.1	19 432	17.4
Dallas	18.5	337	9 600	183.2	3 698	3 298	7 248	4 654	7 282	10 565	32.3	25.4	19 045	-1.6
De Kalb	16.2	300	10 400	188.7	4 001	2 440	8 510	5 294	8 284	11 475	19.5	16.4	22 939	9.8
Elmore	14.7	328	8 230	163.6	3 439	1 462	9 385	5 742	8 985	14 985	18.2	13.1	19 497	13.3
Escambia	14.8	396	6 735	188.1	2 779	1 334	8 122	5 034	7 877	11 580	21.0	16.4	14 356	5.9
Etowah	29.0	282	21 310	207.1	9 652	3 518	9 448	6 105	9 552	13 320	16.1	12.9	41 787	4.8
Fayette	5.3	279	3 440	185.9	1 337	840	8 338	5 300	8 293	11 878	18.1	15.4	7 555	0.5
Franklin	9.7	341	6 205	221.6	2 549	1 414	8 181	5 454	8 534	12 112	17.1	14.5	11 772	4.7
Geneva	7.6	321	5 135	218.5	1 936	1 230	9 133	5 585	8 739	10 866	20.8	17.4	10 416	11.5
Greene	6.3	569	1 985	182.1	679	1 008	5 715	3 532	5 527	7 406	45.7	36.1	4 162	8.5
Hale	6.3	404	3 270	209.6	1 165	1 200	6 173	3 735	5 844	8 236	39.5	33.0	6 370	14.4
Henry	5.8	382	3 090	206.0	1 178	792	8 489	4 880	7 636	11 627	22.7	17.7	7 056	13.3
Houston	26.2	340	12 725	157.1	5 284	2 704	10 283	6 094	9 535	14 075	16.9	13.4	33 196	16.2
Jackson	16.3	316	8 995	181.0	3 614	2 036	8 346	5 452	8 531	13 772	15.7	13.7	19 768	0.8
Jefferson	218.6	327	122 640	180.6	59 371	15 382	11 249	7 070	11 062	15 656	15.3	12.0	273 097	5.1
Lamar	5.8	353	3 235	199.7	1 228	774	7 901	5 098	7 977	12 695	18.2	14.3	6 617	3.7
Lauderdale	28.1	346	14 850	180.4	6 790	2 306	9 833	6 283	9 831	15 093	14.8	11.4	33 522	9.7
Lawrence	11.0	356	4 565	146.3	1 781	1 300	7 816	4 804	7 517	12 097	23.6	19.4	12 212	11.4
Lee	22.3	284	9 365	114.9	4 133	1 862	9 521	5 638	8 822	11 655	23.6	13.9	36 636	23.5
Limestone	17.5	376	7 280	137.9	2 863	1 662	9 803	5 579	8 729	14 223	17.0	14.0	21 455	30.1
Lowndes	6.7	528	1 950	148.9	658	834	5 252	3 318	5 192	8 383	45.0	36.6	4 792	13.5
Macon	7.9	294	3 925	149.2	1 469	1 324	6 407	4 046	6 331	8 843	33.0	28.3	9 818	6.4
Madison	70.2	346	26 165	110.5	10 869	4 010	12 858	7 050	11 031	16 957	13.8	10.8	97 855	37.6
Marengo	8.4	341	4 135	170.2	1 581	1 432	7 818	4 739	7 415	10 494	33.4	25.5	9 144	2.6
Marion	9.6	316	5 790	189.2	2 306	1 168	8 098	5 164	8 080	11 964	16.1	13.7	12 597	8.6
Marshall	20.9	312	14 375	196.6	5 727	2 870	8 857	5 439	8 510	12 433	16.6	13.9	30 225	13.3
Mobile	109.6	292	59 035	151.7	26 684	8 894	9 395	6 047	9 462	14 702	18.8	15.4	151 220	14.6
Monroe	9.6	426	4 215	182.5	1 622	1 262	7 994	4 913	7 687	11 596	25.9	19.3	9 633	19.2
Montgomery	56.8	280	31 250	145.5	13 738	6 088	10 790	6 579	10 294	14 877	19.4	14.7	84 525	14.6
Morgan	32.8	362	16 010	157.7	6 980	2 876	10 469	6 323	9 894	15 790	13.9	10.8	40 419	19.5
Perry	5.8	382	2 410	163.9	853	1 004	5 410	3 562	5 573	7 856	43.8	32.8	4 807	-4.3
Pickens	7.7	356	4 275	198.8	1 614	1 402	7 166	4 451	6 964	10 436	27.1	22.6	8 379	7.5
Pike	10.7	380	5 445	194.5	2 078	1 710	7 359	4 503	7 046	9 748	27.4	20.1	11 506	12.8
Randolph	6.3	313	4 355	216.7	1 716	982	7 317	4 362	6 825	10 398	23.2	18.1	8 728	11.2
Russell	15.4	328	8 660	172.5	3 548	1 880	8 104	4 832	7 561	11 344	24.7	19.6	19 633	10.0
St. Clair	12.6	298	6 715	137.3	2 879	944	8 726	5 617	8 789	14 485	15.6	12.6	20 382	30.5
Shelby	19.9	285	8 370	95.3	3 797	1 120	11 772	6 891	10 782	18 272	12.4	9.9	39 201	59.1
Sumter	6.1	361	2 810	173.5	1 001	1 150	6 925	4 383	6 858	9 185	33.6	28.7	6 545	7.2
Talladega	26.3	352	14 360	190.2	6 075	2 990	8 107	4 981	7 794	12 625	20.8	16.3	29 861	14.6
Tallapoosa	11.7	302	7 725	194.6	3 371	1 442	9 190	5 311	8 310	12 476	17.4	13.3	17 312	12.8
Tuscaloosa	40.2	293	21 455	147.6	9 539	4 170	9 223	5 684	8 894	13 119	20.9	14.6	58 740	16.7
Walker	22.1	319	15 140	218.8	6 516	2 316	8 442	5 524	8 643	13 185	16.4	13.8	28 427	5.1

1. Elementary and secondary. 2. Per 1,000 resident population estimated as of July 1 of the year shown. 3. Based on the resident population estimated as of July 1, 1988 for 1987 data and enumerated as of April 1, 1980 for 1979 data.

STATE County	Housing units, 1990 (cont'd): Occupied units: Total	Owner occupied: Percent	Owner occupied: Median value (Dollars)	Median rent (Dollars)	Civilian labor force, 1990: Total	Percent change, 1989–1990	Unemployment: Total	Unemployment: Rate[1]	Private nonfarm establishments, 1988: Number	Net change, 1987–1988	Employment[2]: Total	Per-cent change, 1987–1988	Manu-facturing	Retail trade
	74	75	76	77	78	79	80	81	82	83	84	85	86	87
UNITED STATES	91 947 410	64.2	79 100	374	124 787 000	0.7	6 876 000	5.5	6 018 600	81 540	87 881 632	2.8	19 261 691	18 801 521
ALABAMA	1 506 790	70.5	53 700	229	1 892 000	-0.8	128 000	6.8	X	X	1 222 484	2.0	353 712	258 926
Autauga	11 826	79.7	59 200	257	16 061	-0.9	1 085	6.8	540	6	6 156	7.6	2 435	1 649
Baldwin	37 044	78.4	64 200	265	40 485	0.2	2 390	5.9	2 215	13	20 376	3.1	5 280	6 258
Barbour	9 218	70.4	41 400	146	12 387	0.9	939	7.6	506	13	6 454	3.1	2 882	1 221
Bibb	5 745	78.5	39 500	140	7 065	-1.9	609	8.6	256	6	3 104	2.6	1 817	453
Blount	14 644	81.8	46 500	164	17 071	1.5	1 268	7.4	517	21	4 151	4.3	1 165	939
Bullock	3 787	72.1	32 300	102	4 045	-4.5	505	12.5	152	-6	1 827	6.0	823	432
Butler	7 935	72.9	34 000	133	8 431	-4.4	1 024	12.1	418	-6	5 316	-6.7	2 873	942
Calhoun	42 983	70.3	51 600	218	50 774	-1.7	3 569	7.0	2 200	20	30 650	2.0	10 474	7 537
Chambers	13 786	76.0	37 900	154	16 842	1.4	1 222	7.3	535	0	11 803	2.5	0	1 474
Cherokee	7 466	79.8	44 700	148	8 316	0.2	862	10.4	275	3	3 286	7.1	1 634	569
Chilton	12 114	81.2	42 800	157	14 769	-3.3	1 305	8.8	600	22	4 974	1.7	1 824	1 274
Choctaw	5 747	84.8	37 200	99	6 598	-5.4	755	11.4	310	-11	4 921	6.1	0	607
Clarke	9 506	79.6	40 300	147	11 229	-1.1	919	8.2	621	-14	6 822	-1.0	3 094	1 531
Clay	5 003	75.6	35 500	116	6 526	0.9	403	6.2	212	-5	2 398	-1.9	1 379	426
Cleburne	4 776	81.7	42 600	147	5 457	-2.4	391	7.2	148	-6	1 804	-13.7	1 101	292
Coffee	15 260	70.9	53 300	234	17 956	-1.6	1 236	6.9	882	0	10 547	7.8	4 399	2 635
Colbert	20 096	75.3	46 300	191	23 989	-0.6	1 899	7.9	1 230	2	16 206	1.2	6 665	3 388
Conecuh	5 259	80.1	33 300	110	5 853	3.1	556	9.5	237	2	2 375	6.0	928	428
Coosa	4 017	82.7	35 600	137	4 964	-0.3	308	6.2	125	-1	1 467	2.0	1 098	86
Covington	14 444	75.7	34 800	147	16 857	-1.6	1 305	7.7	837	-5	11 111	1.5	4 953	2 048
Crenshaw	5 262	74.6	31 200	118	6 293	-3.7	457	7.3	235	5	2 878	-4.2	1 567	471
Cullman	25 605	77.8	48 100	184	32 378	-1.1	2 288	7.1	1 292	21	17 199	9.3	6 999	4 121
Dale	17 574	61.0	49 400	238	18 188	-0.7	1 338	7.4	721	3	9 849	8.7	1 652	2 113
Dallas	17 033	62.2	43 800	151	19 828	-1.6	2 105	10.6	1 049	1	13 249	1.3	5 098	2 614
De Kalb	20 968	78.2	39 700	161	30 446	-0.8	2 121	7.0	1 002	21	14 952	6.0	8 559	2 379
Elmore	16 532	80.3	58 100	197	21 975	0.1	1 329	6.0	687	2	6 543	6.2	2 191	1 665
Escambia	12 899	76.4	41 100	153	15 187	-4.0	1 307	8.6	775	-16	9 211	-0.8	3 554	1 970
Etowah	38 675	74.0	42 700	186	42 291	-0.8	4 532	10.7	1 949	30	30 266	1.3	11 223	6 800
Fayette	6 859	76.8	36 800	132	7 688	-0.6	725	9.4	325	8	4 752	6.8	2 617	815
Franklin	10 850	75.1	38 300	146	13 887	-5.5	1 452	10.5	522	-17	6 943	-5.3	3 526	1 330
Geneva	9 231	78.1	35 800	130	10 956	-0.8	628	5.7	364	1	4 265	2.3	1 947	846
Greene	3 512	71.1	35 800	99	3 534	-4.3	400	11.3	153	5	1 344	8.5	270	293
Hale	5 397	79.1	34 900	99	6 342	0.7	474	7.5	204	-10	2 226	-2.1	1 239	357
Henry	5 769	78.4	41 300	134	7 274	2.5	426	5.9	305	5	3 824	6.9	2 066	596
Houston	30 844	67.6	52 600	215	40 482	-0.7	2 021	5.0	2 401	-3	32 587	-4.7	7 551	8 571
Jackson	18 020	76.7	43 200	169	20 925	1.9	2 061	9.8	797	21	10 565	1.8	5 936	2 204
Jefferson	251 479	65.2	58 700	263	328 843	-0.9	16 744	5.1	17 271	184	304 181	2.6	42 755	58 237
Lamar	6 005	75.6	38 900	110	7 980	-3.9	602	7.5	283	-12	5 085	-3.0	3 494	407
Lauderdale	30 905	73.4	52 700	217	37 509	0.6	2 493	6.6	1 726	46	19 983	9.5	6 320	5 334
Lawrence	11 410	80.8	44 300	143	12 877	0.2	1 253	9.7	310	-17	3 759	-8.6	0	633
Lee	33 097	58.1	64 900	266	40 727	-1.2	2 516	6.2	1 485	33	23 350	4.3	9 062	5 891
Limestone	19 685	76.2	56 300	214	30 308	-1.0	1 782	5.9	831	25	14 220	13.4	6 689	2 579
Lowndes	4 056	80.5	34 800	99	5 299	-20.5	712	13.4	127	12	1 281	-4.3	693	252
Macon	8 483	66.9	43 400	186	9 477	-3.4	742	7.8	246	-4	4 271	3.8	383	775
Madison	91 208	65.1	77 900	332	133 346	-0.2	6 227	4.7	5 534	181	87 676	2.9	25 188	19 531
Marengo	8 156	77.1	41 800	117	9 916	1.1	654	6.6	455	23	6 164	2.2	3 382	1 103
Marion	11 521	75.3	38 300	132	14 695	-3.7	1 811	12.3	493	-13	8 833	5.1	5 569	1 021
Marshall	27 761	74.2	48 100	200	39 331	0.8	3 040	7.7	1 716	76	23 431	5.2	11 635	5 314
Mobile	136 899	66.8	53 300	233	170 739	-0.8	12 185	7.1	8 690	62	116 438	0.7	19 367	27 419
Monroe	8 412	77.3	43 200	169	10 925	5.9	1 046	9.6	440	4	6 926	5.8	3 919	1 149
Montgomery	77 173	62.3	62 600	292	99 297	-0.6	6 124	6.2	5 404	114	86 776	-2.0	14 540	19 499
Morgan	37 799	71.8	60 900	261	48 487	1.4	3 212	6.6	2 321	8	33 429	0.3	11 936	6 441
Perry	4 201	70.1	31 600	99	5 079	-7.3	556	10.9	165	-9	2 186	-12.3	882	414
Pickens	7 568	76.9	38 000	99	7 052	-1.9	728	10.3	357	-8	3 176	-1.7	1 213	616
Pike	10 314	66.4	43 500	177	12 676	-0.3	766	6.0	598	10	7 289	4.7	2 651	1 599
Randolph	7 553	79.0	36 500	133	8 655	-4.7	718	8.3	343	6	4 289	4.9	2 510	734
Russell	17 499	65.0	46 200	195	22 872	1.5	1 644	7.2	796	22	8 247	5.3	3 102	1 969
St. Clair	17 666	83.1	53 400	199	21 888	-0.5	1 315	6.0	656	42	6 156	7.8	2 267	1 124
Shelby	35 985	75.6	88 300	379	42 812	-1.0	1 674	3.9	1 411	12	15 036	-10.9	4 979	3 191
Sumter	5 545	71.0	34 700	115	6 061	1.9	514	8.5	235	-5	2 732	19.1	877	448
Talladega	26 448	75.2	44 800	163	30 911	-4.1	2 964	9.6	1 193	26	17 353	1.1	8 154	3 672
Tallapoosa	14 700	75.1	43 200	160	18 180	-2.0	1 118	6.1	705	17	15 506	5.5	9 755	2 075
Tuscaloosa	55 354	61.5	62 100	254	73 097	1.3	3 693	5.1	3 101	64	39 442	5.2	9 159	10 826
Walker	25 554	79.3	42 100	175	28 571	-2.5	2 650	9.3	1 301	3	14 446	-5.3	2 717	3 649

1. Percent of total civilian labor force. 2. For week including March 12. Excludes government employees, self-employed persons, farm workers, domestic service workers, railroad employees subject to the Railroad Retirement Act, and employees on oceanborne vessels or in foreign countries.

STATE County	Private nonfarm establishments, 1988 (cont'd)				Personal income, 1989								Earnings, 1989		
	Employment[1] (cont'd)		Annual payroll								Per capita[3]			Percent by selected industries	
	Finance, insurance, and real estate	Services	Total (Mil dol)	Average per employee (Dollars)	Total (Mil dol)	Percent change, 1988–1989	Wages and salaries[2] (Mil dol)	Proprietor's income (Mil dol)	Dividends, interest, & rent (Mil dol)	Transfer payments (Mil dol)	Dollars	Rank	Total (Mil dol)	Farm	Goods-related[4] Total
	88	89	90	91	92	93	94	95	96	97	98	99	100	101	102
UNITED STATES	6 659 618	25 142 715	1 859 530	21 159	4 367 401	7.6	2 804 223	372 901	765 847	637 134	17 592	X	3 177 124	1.6	26.9
ALABAMA	72 728	276 423	22 018	X	56 287	6.7	36 007	4 848	7 678	9 750	13 669	X	40 855	2.4	30.6
Autauga	199	1 024	106	17 238	484	7.0	166	26	46	84	13 470	1 702	192	1.3	41.9
Baldwin	1 123	4 714	266	13 072	1 310	8.5	442	113	262	253	13 306	1 769	554	0.7	24.3
Barbour	317	908	99	15 284	312	4.2	175	30	41	66	12 110	2 284	205	5.5	43.1
Bibb	109	220	39	12 456	186	5.3	64	14	20	39	10 910	2 682	77	3.0	40.6
Blount	236	872	56	13 516	473	9.6	118	69	42	69	12 292	2 200	188	23.1	24.8
Bullock	73	135	22	12 076	103	2.3	50	17	18	28	9 212	2 989	67	16.9	NA
Butler	141	708	76	14 385	228	2.4	113	24	32	56	10 247	2 845	137	5.2	41.9
Calhoun	1 160	6 386	465	15 185	1 518	5.2	1 049	102	185	311	12 353	2 182	1 151	1.5	23.2
Chambers	210	1 472	184	15 624	468	4.5	277	27	54	91	11 833	2 384	304	1.2	56.5
Cherokee	110	537	40	12 236	236	4.1	68	32	34	41	11 675	2 451	100	22.5	NA
Chilton	222	781	64	12 896	365	5.9	107	36	39	72	11 241	2 582	143	7.4	33.9
Choctaw	95	505	120	24 361	175	6.6	168	14	25	37	10 230	2 849	182	2.0	72.8
Clarke	413	851	101	14 868	321	6.1	166	30	44	65	11 665	2 456	195	1.9	43.3
Clay	85	250	33	13 791	158	7.6	70	22	18	31	12 125	2 274	92	12.0	NA
Cleburne	64	108	22	11 927	144	8.4	43	21	15	26	11 130	2 629	64	21.6	33.8
Coffee	586	1 716	138	13 080	542	6.0	402	72	76	103	13 441	1 716	474	7.1	19.5
Colbert	544	2 794	317	19 554	650	4.0	573	51	91	124	12 381	2 168	624	2.2	42.1
Conecuh	63	431	30	12 796	156	2.3	67	15	17	39	10 506	2 788	82	6.6	28.0
Coosa	0	101	23	15 883	113	4.8	39	10	13	23	10 112	2 865	49	7.1	NA
Covington	428	1 503	148	13 352	439	6.8	231	49	72	103	12 055	2 309	280	4.9	32.6
Crenshaw	81	249	34	11 883	154	2.7	59	25	20	38	11 057	2 650	84	17.1	27.0
Cullman	613	2 464	262	15 259	872	8.6	380	151	104	151	13 156	1 836	531	14.9	NA
Dale	358	1 649	132	13 369	651	6.5	429	50	57	115	12 930	1 938	479	4.0	35.6
Dallas	635	3 115	203	15 286	536	3.5	310	39	84	137	10 313	2 832	350	1.5	34.6
De Kalb	385	1 973	216	14 451	729	9.5	323	116	72	114	13 175	1 826	439	16.5	42.6
Elmore	282	1 272	87	13 308	665	6.6	179	42	67	129	12 979	1 913	221	4.2	27.0
Escambia	508	1 413	140	15 237	410	3.2	242	34	64	86	11 581	2 479	276	1.0	42.7
Etowah	1 250	6 421	579	19 127	1 286	4.3	792	97	184	261	12 514	2 107	888	1.3	42.0
Fayette	180	357	78	16 335	210	8.1	128	17	32	39	11 452	2 521	144	3.3	59.2
Franklin	274	983	94	13 540	359	3.6	148	40	46	74	12 844	1 982	188	4.7	37.1
Geneva	155	250	58	13 568	313	8.0	100	66	38	61	13 453	1 712	166	27.7	24.4
Greene	0	521	16	12 182	91	1.5	45	13	11	26	8 376	3 050	58	13.9	19.2
Hale	52	336	25	11 210	129	4.6	48	9	17	40	8 179	3 063	57	3.3	28.0
Henry	132	355	54	14 128	190	3.9	79	20	28	38	12 706	2 033	99	8.1	45.2
Houston	1 289	7 363	534	16 389	1 188	7.1	848	111	164	181	14 635	1 152	959	2.3	26.0
Jackson	411	953	171	16 142	550	1.3	305	49	65	105	11 176	2 612	353	4.0	42.8
Jefferson	29 343	82 859	6 400	21 040	11 254	6.6	8 700	889	1 794	1 715	16 597	505	9 588	0.0	20.6
Lamar	154	423	79	15 507	190	5.1	106	18	27	36	11 797	2 402	124	1.2	52.7
Lauderdale	981	4 450	289	14 456	1 055	5.9	470	89	173	184	12 890	1 956	559	1.8	29.3
Lawrence	107	318	89	23 645	331	6.0	153	29	28	57	10 652	2 750	182	6.7	NA
Lee	1 050	3 971	385	16 469	1 106	8.5	732	82	140	148	13 554	1 659	814	0.8	36.1
Limestone	231	3 265	304	21 345	726	4.2	615	66	74	105	13 596	1 633	681	2.9	41.4
Lowndes	54	134	25	19 187	139	11.0	81	17	13	27	10 628	2 766	98	13.5	NA
Macon	104	2 495	52	12 199	232	5.2	140	8	23	73	8 825	3 022	148	0.8	4.8
Madison	3 519	26 785	1 884	21 486	4 201	8.6	3 712	226	495	557	17 577	359	3 938	0.3	32.1
Marengo	249	511	123	19 962	261	2.5	132	26	37	54	10 729	2 735	158	7.5	37.1
Marion	276	1 090	131	14 851	315	2.8	208	31	41	69	10 374	2 817	239	1.3	56.5
Marshall	696	2 473	347	14 827	995	7.8	531	143	115	175	13 517	1 670	674	5.6	42.3
Mobile	6 509	34 298	2 091	17 954	5 071	7.0	3 316	452	724	899	12 904	1 953	3 769	1.5	26.1
Monroe	202	513	127	18 368	267	6.4	199	31	32	50	11 495	2 499	230	4.2	53.1
Montgomery	7 610	24 762	1 509	17 394	3 366	6.6	2 672	250	546	556	15 685	742	2 922	0.6	17.5
Morgan	1 785	7 288	620	18 542	1 516	7.1	917	118	179	232	14 744	1 109	1 035	2.2	45.4
Perry	100	407	23	10 519	111	1.9	46	7	16	35	7 643	3 088	53	5.7	NA
Pickens	188	596	40	12 508	214	7.8	73	36	29	54	9 956	2 [illegible]88	109	19.4	25.9
Pike	388	902	108	14 877	330	6.1	192	32	50	73	11 752	2 421	224	4.2	30.3
Randolph	241	460	58	13 435	225	4.6	94	29	29	49	11 187	2 608	123	14.0	38.2
Russell	432	1 474	119	14 482	559	6.9	237	34	55	123	10 981	2 668	271	0.8	41.9
St. Clair	280	1 038	101	16 341	601	9.1	172	72	59	90	12 050	2 312	244	14.7	31.3
Shelby	407	2 802	269	17 889	1 435	9.9	617	74	140	125	15 743	724	690	0.7	37.8
Sumter	108	364	44	16 054	158	5.3	88	19	17	43	9 803	2 908	107	9.7	NA
Talladega	660	2 530	313	18 021	861	5.9	505	59	96	184	11 466	2 515	564	3.2	47.6
Tallapoosa	472	2 240	234	15 079	517	6.7	319	27	74	96	12 946	1 930	346	0.7	60.7
Tuscaloosa	2 415	8 347	693	17 563	2 041	8.1	1 373	166	274	364	13 886	1 485	1 538	0.8	34.6
Walker	816	3 012	257	17 802	918	6.0	432	71	127	198	13 172	1 827	503	1.8	38.5

1. For week including March 12. Excludes government employees, self-employed persons, farm workers, domestic service workers, railroad employees subject to the Railroad Retirement Act, and employees on oceanborne vessels or in foreign countries. 2. Includes other labor income. 3. Based on the resident population estimated as of July 1 of the year shown. 4. Covers mining, construction, and manufacturing.

STATE County	Earnings, 1989 (cont'd): Percent by selected industries (cont'd): Goods-related[1]: Manu-facturing	Service-related & other[2]: Total	Retail trade	Finance, insur-ance, & real estate	Services	Govern-ment	Agriculture, 1987: Farms: Number	Percent with: Less than 50 acres	500 acres and over	Farm operators, percent: Whose principal occu-pation is farming	Residing on farm operated	Land in farms: Acreage (1,000)	Percent change, 1982–1987	Acres: Average size of farm	Total irrigated (1,000)	Total cropland (1,000)
	103	104	105	106	107	108	109	110	111	112	113	114	115	116	117	118
UNITED STATES	19.7	55.8	9.5	7.0	25.5	15.7	2 087 759	28.5	17.7	54.5	71.3	964 471	-2.3	462	46 386	443 318
ALABAMA	23.9	47.7	9.1	4.5	20.8	19.3	43 318	34.5	9.4	37.9	69.7	9 146	-10.3	211	84	4 497
Autauga	35.2	42.4	12.2	4.3	17.1	14.4	388	27.3	15.2	41.5	72.7	116	-20.0	299	1	62
Baldwin	17.9	57.3	15.2	4.7	24.6	17.7	991	44.4	10.3	45.9	75.4	192	-14.1	194	14	137
Barbour	38.5	36.8	7.9	3.0	11.4	14.6	498	16.5	23.5	47.4	54.4	208	-6.4	417	4	79
Bibb	33.4	36.0	8.8	3.1	12.3	20.4	202	23.3	12.4	25.2	66.3	51	2.4	252	0	19
Blount	17.4	35.2	8.2	3.5	12.0	14.1	1 199	38.2	3.5	37.9	77.2	140	-14.4	117	1	71
Bullock	24.5	NA	8.6	2.1	9.7	23.0	275	16.7	34.5	48.0	61.5	156	-15.6	568	1	56
Butler	38.6	39.5	9.8	3.3	16.9	13.4	520	30.4	7.5	39.4	76.0	100	-19.7	192	0	45
Calhoun	19.7	35.1	9.6	2.3	13.4	40.2	685	41.3	2.2	35.9	75.2	90	-3.0	132	0	41
Chambers	53.7	32.7	8.3	1.5	11.8	9.5	365	15.1	15.6	32.9	67.1	102	-15.6	280	0	33
Cherokee	24.5	35.0	8.9	2.8	10.4	14.7	487	23.0	14.4	44.8	68.2	120	-16.5	246	1	73
Chilton	24.3	41.4	11.9	3.9	14.9	17.4	704	32.8	4.4	33.9	77.0	104	-9.3	148	1	49
Choctaw	68.7	18.2	4.9	0.7	7.2	7.0	299	23.7	10.0	31.4	70.6	85	-21.3	283	0	24
Clarke	37.4	37.8	10.4	4.2	13.1	16.9	331	27.5	10.6	26.6	58.3	95	-18.5	286	0	25
Clay	45.9	24.0	6.4	2.3	8.6	15.0	439	18.7	6.2	31.7	71.8	84	6.2	192	0	29
Cleburne	25.7	25.2	6.7	2.4	10.6	19.5	366	33.6	3.6	43.4	70.5	49	-0.1	134	D	19
Coffee	16.9	24.7	6.8	2.4	10.7	48.7	842	27.6	10.5	47.7	64.1	179	-7.8	213	5	98
Colbert	36.0	32.0	7.2	2.3	13.1	23.6	563	35.0	14.7	34.1	68.4	145	-10.1	258	2	93
Conecuh	24.9	NA	6.3	1.6	14.5	21.3	405	26.9	10.1	30.6	64.2	102	-24.2	251	0	47
Coosa	50.4	NA	3.4	0.6	11.4	17.0	256	17.6	9.0	23.0	57.8	59	-4.3	231	0	16
Covington	26.5	48.8	10.2	3.3	17.7	13.7	870	26.8	7.0	43.7	72.2	176	-9.1	202	1	81
Crenshaw	24.1	39.9	9.9	3.4	10.1	16.1	494	26.1	11.5	43.1	73.3	118	-12.1	239	3	46
Cullman	24.7	NA	16.8	2.2	12.7	12.0	2 210	51.1	1.4	43.9	74.7	194	-6.0	88	1	100
Dale	33.0	26.9	5.5	1.5	14.8	33.5	490	22.2	15.7	41.8	73.3	129	-4.2	263	2	63
Dallas	29.6	47.9	10.1	3.4	22.1	15.9	486	27.2	28.0	47.3	55.1	250	-18.2	514	1	129
De Kalb	39.5	31.0	8.3	2.3	14.1	9.9	2 047	46.0	2.4	39.7	76.9	213	-3.6	104	1	122
Elmore	20.0	41.6	11.1	3.1	17.4	27.2	622	26.2	9.6	33.9	71.2	129	-9.3	207	1	70
Escambia	32.8	37.7	10.3	4.2	12.0	18.6	414	32.9	8.7	43.5	62.1	91	-11.5	219	2	64
Etowah	37.2	44.9	9.5	3.4	21.6	11.8	928	52.5	2.6	33.2	72.8	101	-14.5	108	0	47
Fayette	41.0	23.3	8.2	1.6	7.4	14.1	350	26.3	8.0	30.0	70.6	67	-7.4	192	D	29
Franklin	34.2	41.7	10.3	3.5	15.3	16.6	834	28.1	5.2	33.5	67.6	128	-6.7	153	0	65
Geneva	21.9	NA	8.4	2.1	11.5	10.8	881	29.3	10.4	53.2	70.5	200	-7.3	227	4	135
Greene	11.9	44.8	7.0	1.3	16.8	22.1	351	25.9	19.9	39.9	59.0	137	-18.7	390	1	39
Hale	24.8	41.8	10.6	3.2	15.9	26.9	441	20.2	17.0	50.3	61.0	155	-13.9	351	1	75
Henry	41.5	33.1	10.3	3.2	10.9	13.7	421	18.3	25.9	54.2	61.8	171	-11.9	407	4	101
Houston	17.4	58.6	12.1	3.7	23.2	13.0	862	28.9	14.0	52.3	65.2	208	2.4	241	7	142
Jackson	39.3	29.2	8.3	2.6	10.6	23.9	1 224	40.0	8.3	38.2	71.2	208	-8.2	170	1	121
Jefferson	13.0	65.8	8.8	8.1	27.1	13.6	520	57.3	2.1	28.7	67.1	45	-7.9	87	0	23
Lamar	48.8	36.0	5.5	2.4	12.8	10.2	362	27.3	7.5	31.8	67.7	60	-17.2	165	D	24
Lauderdale	23.8	49.4	13.5	4.4	22.8	19.5	1 254	38.1	7.1	32.6	70.7	200	-6.4	159	0	127
Lawrence	47.2	NA	6.1	1.1	10.3	17.2	1 123	38.3	6.9	31.6	72.8	188	-6.5	168	1	134
Lee	30.9	35.4	9.7	2.5	15.5	27.8	402	33.3	8.5	24.4	68.4	80	-20.9	199	0	34
Limestone	37.3	22.2	5.6	0.9	12.3	33.5	1 090	38.6	11.7	34.7	68.7	223	-8.0	205	1	167
Lowndes	25.4	NA	5.0	1.1	6.3	12.0	378	25.7	27.0	42.6	61.9	208	-8.4	550	3	81
Macon	1.9	43.8	6.6	1.6	30.6	50.6	370	19.2	19.5	31.4	59.2	145	-12.6	392	2	52
Madison	28.4	40.7	6.8	2.3	25.2	26.9	977	40.8	12.2	39.5	68.4	235	-19.6	241	1	170
Marengo	33.8	38.4	8.9	3.6	12.0	17.0	471	16.3	24.4	35.5	60.5	221	-4.6	468	0	90
Marion	53.7	29.8	6.5	2.3	11.5	12.3	658	28.1	5.2	30.9	72.3	106	-7.1	160	D	46
Marshall	38.2	39.9	12.8	2.9	13.1	12.2	1 582	53.9	1.7	34.5	71.1	137	-9.9	86	0	78
Mobile	19.1	57.4	10.8	4.4	27.3	15.0	754	56.5	7.4	41.4	76.8	111	-6.3	148	3	65
Monroe	47.8	31.3	7.7	1.8	8.3	11.4	455	31.9	12.1	34.9	58.7	149	-2.4	328	1	55
Montgomery	11.6	52.4	9.3	7.0	23.9	29.5	712	26.4	19.5	35.5	63.5	269	-16.8	378	1	102
Morgan	36.2	39.7	9.9	3.6	16.6	12.7	1 243	41.7	3.9	32.6	72.8	160	-4.6	129	0	95
Perry	30.3	37.1	8.5	3.1	20.5	24.1	341	20.8	18.8	44.6	59.8	160	-18.2	469	0	75
Pickens	22.5	38.3	7.1	2.7	18.3	16.5	417	20.6	10.3	37.2	63.1	109	-18.6	261	1	48
Pike	25.2	43.1	8.5	4.0	12.2	22.4	605	21.5	17.5	40.0	64.6	180	-13.2	297	4	82
Randolph	35.2	29.9	9.7	3.0	10.7	17.9	646	25.1	4.3	33.1	74.9	100	0.5	154	0	31
Russell	32.6	39.1	10.6	2.8	16.0	18.2	276	23.6	21.4	35.5	68.5	144	1.8	520	1	51
St. Clair	20.3	37.0	10.7	3.0	11.9	16.9	634	34.1	4.7	35.0	72.6	89	-6.5	141	3	40
Shelby	27.3	49.3	8.1	4.5	15.5	12.2	526	37.8	6.8	32.5	74.5	81	-6.6	155	0	38
Sumter	20.9	45.5	6.4	1.6	12.7	22.0	456	23.7	25.7	42.8	52.6	208	-0.7	457	1	88
Talladega	39.7	31.0	8.8	2.4	12.4	18.1	552	32.2	10.1	38.0	73.9	115	-10.6	208	0	64
Tallapoosa	56.2	28.2	7.0	3.4	14.0	10.5	365	18.9	6.8	28.2	66.3	85	-4.2	232	0	25
Tuscaloosa	20.3	37.9	9.3	3.0	17.3	26.7	521	28.0	12.3	36.5	67.8	121	-10.5	231	1	48
Walker	12.9	48.0	11.6	3.3	19.8	11.6	559	41.3	3.4	23.8	74.2	65	7.2	116	D	29

1. Covers mining, construction, and manufacturing. 2. Covers private sector earnings in agricultural services, forestry, and fisheries; transportation and public utilities; wholesale trade; retail trade; finance, insurance, and real estate; and services.

STATE County	Agriculture, 1987 (cont'd): Value of land and buildings: Average per farm ($1,000)	Average per acre (Dollars)	Value of products sold: Total (Mil dol)	Average per farm (Dollars)	Percent from: Crops	Livestock and poultry[1]	Percent of farms with sales of: $10,000 or more	$100,000 or more	Manufactures, 1987: Establishments: Total	Percent with 20 or more em-ployees	All employees: Number (1,000)	Percent change, 1982–1987	Annual payroll (Mil dol)	Production workers: Number (1,000)	Work hours (Mil)
	119	120	121	122	123	124	125	126	127	128	129	130	131	132	133
UNITED STATES	289	627	136 049	65 165	43.3	56.7	50.8	14.2	368 897	34.2	18 950.3	-0.8	475 651.0	12 242.7	24 300.6
ALABAMA	168	800	1 908	44 053	26.1	73.9	32.3	10.4	5 843	35.4	347.3	5.4	6 962.5	268.8	530.7
Autauga	182	573	11	29 503	45.5	54.5	34.5	8.0	36	27.8	2.2	10.0	50.6	1.6	2.9
Baldwin	265	1 275	50	50 236	75.4	24.6	37.9	9.3	112	30.4	5.2	20.9	79.6	4.2	8.0
Barbour	213	494	20	39 562	55.3	44.7	48.4	9.4	53	41.5	2.9	52.6	49.7	2.2	4.5
Bibb	130	616	2	11 209	15.0	85.0	17.3	4.0	54	33.3	1.9	26.7	22.4	1.8	3.0
Blount	124	1 013	71	59 497	7.4	92.6	32.8	14.1	47	17.0	1.1	-8.3	13.0	0.9	1.6
Bullock	356	638	12	43 912	63.7	36.3	43.6	7.6	22	18.2	0.8	-11.1	10.1	0.7	1.5
Butler	125	682	18	35 369	13.9	86.1	30.8	6.9	73	13.7	3.1	0.0	46.4	2.7	5.5
Calhoun	143	1 122	27	39 186	9.5	90.5	20.4	7.9	143	46.9	10.7	8.1	176.6	8.3	16.3
Chambers	139	535	4	12 024	12.1	87.9	21.1	2.5	55	45.5	D	D	D	D	D
Cherokee	193	769	27	54 606	61.5	38.5	34.3	10.7	34	20.6	1.5	-6.3	17.6	1.2	2.3
Chilton	145	1 005	9	13 429	58.5	41.5	23.2	1.4	71	28.2	1.7	-26.1	24.4	1.4	2.7
Choctaw	140	518	4	13 865	8.4	91.6	17.1	2.7	40	22.5	D	D	D	D	D
Clarke	200	724	3	8 508	18.0	82.0	20.5	0.6	90	17.8	3.0	15.4	55.7	2.5	5.1
Clay	121	580	15	34 381	1.5	98.5	26.2	10.3	25	32.0	1.5	-11.8	19.4	1.3	2.5
Cleburne	101	810	23	62 414	5.4	94.6	32.2	16.7	25	24.0	1.1	-8.3	11.6	1.0	1.8
Coffee	145	632	73	86 844	20.6	79.4	51.8	22.1	59	37.3	4.5	36.4	64.7	3.5	6.6
Colbert	213	862	24	42 066	63.6	36.4	30.4	12.8	110	40.0	6.4	-15.8	164.3	4.8	9.5
Conecuh	186	715	6	15 683	44.4	55.6	25.4	3.7	45	20.0	0.8	-20.0	11.3	0.7	1.4
Coosa	119	483	1	5 675	D	D	11.3	0.0	32	21.9	1.1	22.2	18.7	1.0	2.1
Covington	138	762	36	41 612	33.5	66.5	37.6	10.5	63	36.5	5.0	13.6	62.3	4.3	8.3
Crenshaw	150	630	40	80 427	12.7	87.3	40.9	18.8	41	24.4	1.8	50.0	20.0	1.5	2.6
Cullman	118	1 314	197	89 143	4.0	96.0	41.4	23.6	95	36.8	5.9	13.5	101.9	4.8	9.3
Dale	199	817	23	47 263	47.4	52.6	41.0	11.2	41	29.3	1.6	60.0	18.8	1.3	2.6
Dallas	245	459	22	45 127	42.4	57.6	41.4	10.7	76	39.5	4.9	-5.8	81.4	3.7	7.2
De Kalb	116	1 055	120	58 569	10.8	89.2	36.2	17.4	166	39.8	8.0	17.6	118.1	6.8	13.4
Elmore	152	758	17	27 811	51.8	48.2	29.3	7.4	54	29.6	2.2	83.3	35.8	1.8	3.4
Escambia	189	966	38	91 259	D	D	37.9	8.0	72	27.8	3.5	9.4	59.9	3.1	5.9
Etowah	108	1 027	25	27 108	9.8	90.2	21.8	7.3	110	41.8	11.1	3.7	287.3	9.0	18.9
Fayette	99	571	5	14 176	28.7	71.3	18.0	3.4	46	37.0	2.4	-7.7	41.1	2.1	4.1
Franklin	112	863	28	33 288	6.4	93.6	29.6	9.8	70	40.0	3.7	27.6	58.6	3.1	5.7
Geneva	172	733	53	60 620	37.7	62.3	53.9	13.3	29	31.0	1.9	5.6	24.9	1.7	3.2
Greene	184	468	8	21 805	17.9	82.1	27.1	3.1	14	35.7	0.3	-25.0	4.1	0.2	0.4
Hale	175	531	18	40 296	12.2	87.8	39.2	10.9	27	33.3	1.1	120.0	13.7	1.0	1.7
Henry	262	656	29	68 992	81.1	18.9	61.0	20.2	34	29.4	2.0	17.6	28.8	1.8	3.6
Houston	188	800	38	43 535	72.2	27.8	55.3	11.1	107	39.3	8.6	-12.2	159.6	6.6	13.7
Jackson	148	828	33	26 907	27.3	72.7	28.9	7.3	66	40.9	5.7	5.6	102.5	4.6	8.7
Jefferson	171	2 480	9	17 164	21.9	78.1	19.2	3.1	841	37.8	41.0	-6.0	916.1	27.6	55.1
Lamar	90	552	4	9 859	26.1	73.9	14.1	2.2	42	42.9	3.5	40.0	52.0	3.1	5.9
Lauderdale	142	859	24	19 207	46.4	53.6	23.7	5.1	104	37.5	5.8	38.1	99.5	4.7	9.4
Lawrence	166	956	55	48 871	28.7	71.3	28.0	11.0	31	35.5	D	D	D	D	D
Lee	167	906	7	18 474	49.3	50.7	24.4	2.2	85	37.6	9.1	4.6	183.7	7.1	12.0
Limestone	268	1 341	42	38 147	63.3	36.7	30.2	8.3	51	45.1	6.8	61.9	189.5	5.9	11.9
Lowndes	266	470	25	65 178	14.0	86.0	41.3	11.6	28	21.4	0.6	50.0	7.3	0.5	0.7
Macon	201	517	9	24 128	60.1	39.9	27.3	4.1	17	29.4	0.3	50.0	2.3	0.2	0.4
Madison	330	1 355	35	35 698	63.9	36.1	32.1	8.8	293	36.9	25.6	7.6	705.2	16.1	32.6
Marengo	218	443	15	31 504	20.0	80.0	35.0	7.0	42	35.7	3.3	3.1	77.5	2.7	5.9
Marion	123	654	11	16 601	12.7	87.3	18.1	5.0	68	39.7	5.6	0.0	83.3	4.6	7.7
Marshall	120	1 396	105	66 356	3.2	96.8	29.3	13.2	130	38.5	11.0	29.4	169.4	9.3	17.2
Mobile	215	1 442	44	58 289	81.9	18.1	29.6	8.1	405	30.9	19.9	-16.4	518.9	14.1	28.4
Monroe	200	656	12	26 894	55.6	44.4	36.9	6.4	49	30.6	3.8	8.6	74.8	3.1	6.3
Montgomery	286	775	31	43 173	27.3	72.7	36.0	6.6	247	39.3	14.2	18.3	263.1	10.8	22.6
Morgan	146	1 280	55	43 921	11.6	88.4	27.9	9.9	180	39.4	12.1	6.1	296.0	9.2	18.6
Perry	207	457	12	34 674	27.5	72.5	34.9	9.4	17	29.4	0.9	50.0	10.2	0.9	1.7
Pickens	186	692	47	113 395	6.8	93.2	40.3	21.1	39	33.3	1.3	-18.8	17.8	1.1	2.3
Pike	153	543	30	49 657	34.6	65.4	46.6	15.4	54	24.1	2.3	0.0	37.4	1.9	3.6
Randolph	111	690	24	36 900	1.3	98.7	25.9	10.5	44	22.7	2.2	-8.3	31.8	1.8	3.5
Russell	316	617	7	26 599	46.8	53.2	31.5	5.4	46	37.0	3.1	19.2	65.3	2.7	5.6
St. Clair	166	1 056	24	37 494	25.1	74.9	25.1	9.9	65	32.3	2.0	25.0	37.1	1.5	3.1
Shelby	193	1 495	10	19 041	30.0	70.0	21.1	4.6	114	46.5	4.8	6.7	93.8	3.7	7.6
Sumter	214	505	12	26 239	25.2	74.8	28.7	3.9	28	28.6	0.7	-41.7	9.6	0.6	1.1
Talladega	184	975	17	30 062	12.0	88.0	30.1	7.1	92	48.9	8.2	0.0	170.2	6.5	13.4
Tallapoosa	144	587	8	20 742	37.1	62.9	19.7	3.6	69	43.5	9.5	17.3	143.6	7.8	16.2
Tuscaloosa	151	731	13	24 906	34.3	65.7	23.8	6.1	152	36.8	8.7	22.5	214.5	6.5	13.0
Walker	111	884	20	35 419	4.3	95.7	17.5	7.3	83	31.3	2.7	17.4	33.1	2.3	4.0

1. Includes livestock and poultry products.

STATE County	Manufactures, 1987 (cont'd): Production workers (cont'd): Wages: Total (Mil dol)	Manufactures, 1987 (cont'd): Production workers (cont'd): Wages: Average per worker (Dollars)	Manufactures, 1987 (cont'd): Value added by manufacture (Mil dol)	Manufactures, 1987 (cont'd): Value of shipments (Mil dol)	Manufactures, 1987 (cont'd): New capital expenditures (Mil dol)	Value of construction authorized by building permits, 1990: Total[1] ($1,000)	Nonresidential: Total ($1,000)	Nonresidential: Percent: Office	Nonresidential: Percent: Industrial	Nonresidential: Percent: Stores	Residential: New construction ($1,000)	Residential: Number of housing units	Residential: Alterations and additions ($1,000)
	134	135	136	137	138	139	140	141	142	143	144	145	146
UNITED STATES	251 432.6	20 537	1 165 746.8	2 475 901.0	78 647.8	171 406 129	43 741 712	25.1	17.9	27.7	84 336 296	1 077 853	13 176 993
ALABAMA	4 745.6	17 655	18 652.1	40 901.4	1 360.1	1 703 163	514 807	17.6	13.9	34.8	683 799	12 564	105 608
Autauga	31.2	19 500	183.6	336.6	D	5 287	462	0.0	0.0	0.0	4 492	87	237
Baldwin	57.3	13 643	168.7	422.7	10.1	41 100	11 900	24.6	4.0	32.5	23 865	328	1 355
Barbour	30.2	13 727	117.0	275.2	13.6	20 452	13 573	0.0	73.8	24.4	5 233	94	342
Bibb	18.4	10 222	64.3	131.2	3.6	NA	NA	NA	NA	NA	NA	NA	NA
Blount	9.7	10 778	46.5	106.9	1.0	2 300	30	0.0	0.0	0.0	1 422	22	0
Bullock	8.1	11 571	23.9	74.0	0.7	548	12	0.0	0.0	0.0	146	8	177
Butler	37.0	13 704	143.7	347.8	8.0	3 824	3 236	0.0	0.0	84.1	444	10	82
Calhoun	122.5	14 759	352.9	773.5	16.7	27 399	9 717	15.2	33.2	30.3	10 312	231	2 646
Chambers	D	D	D	D	D	3 480	1 656	55.4	0.0	43.2	1 398	17	386
Cherokee	13.0	10 833	33.9	94.9	1.6	3 401	542	5.5	0.0	87.8	2 327	85	264
Chilton	18.6	13 286	56.5	127.5	1.8	5 634	1 455	5.8	9.9	43.4	2 497	61	650
Choctaw	D	D	D	D	D	584	485	0.0	0.0	44.0	69	1	24
Clarke	41.4	16 560	128.7	307.1	9.4	4 929	196	93.9	0.0	0.0	4 007	112	128
Clay	15.0	11 538	40.8	84.0	2.6	504	252	0.0	8.7	84.9	202	3	8
Cleburne	10.2	10 200	25.8	59.4	0.8	414	0	NA	NA	NA	414	10	0
Coffee	45.7	13 057	186.1	480.2	5.3	10 675	2 370	47.8	2.0	25.7	4 798	79	705
Colbert	114.2	23 792	365.3	1 607.7	32.4	10 185	2 426	13.3	3.0	51.9	3 474	74	1 841
Conecuh	8.3	11 857	28.4	64.5	7.8	5 093	3 598	0.0	93.9	2.8	284	8	0
Coosa	15.1	15 100	30.2	89.2	2.7	121	0	NA	NA	NA	121	3	0
Covington	46.7	10 860	146.0	262.5	D	6 110	1 243	30.9	0.0	5.8	3 322	40	424
Crenshaw	15.1	10 067	34.1	71.1	1.6	261	62	0.0	0.0	0.0	168	4	11
Cullman	72.7	15 146	230.1	523.4	9.9	10 304	5 471	3.7	7.1	72.0	1 767	37	242
Dale	14.4	11 077	36.4	69.2	1.9	5 897	2 594	4.0	43.2	29.1	2 467	69	394
Dallas	50.5	13 649	254.8	622.5	22.5	6 607	5 233	0.0	2.6	85.6	314	11	186
De Kalb	86.8	12 765	233.2	513.2	22.1	7 800	3 662	5.0	72.0	3.4	2 469	45	72
Elmore	26.1	14 500	73.7	129.3	D	9 328	5 938	0.0	24.2	31.9	596	10	832
Escambia	46.5	15 000	287.6	493.2	10.7	8 006	3 482	0.0	10.1	86.6	1 359	18	1 028
Etowah	221.0	24 556	677.4	1 341.1	19.4	18 877	8 948	4.4	11.2	80.4	6 974	132	596
Fayette	34.0	16 190	120.7	221.3	21.2	3 363	2 989	0.0	21.2	71.4	256	6	8
Franklin	43.4	14 000	107.5	274.7	3.0	3 255	1 620	0.9	0.0	93.5	1 230	25	163
Geneva	20.9	12 294	59.9	109.0	2.8	1 269	630	0.0	0.0	97.5	367	12	124
Greene	3.3	16 500	10.7	24.4	0.5	1 967	277	0.0	0.0	28.9	1 198	26	109
Hale	9.8	9 800	43.9	112.0	2.8	413	341	0.0	0.0	44.0	45	1	6
Henry	23.4	13 000	103.3	311.8	2.9	3 895	389	46.2	9.2	2.1	1 988	39	568
Houston	103.3	15 652	387.2	825.8	36.2	46 197	15 368	6.0	15.9	42.8	18 062	307	2 858
Jackson	75.8	16 478	322.4	708.3	14.7	6 604	1 716	1.2	61.3	19.0	2 611	51	266
Jefferson	539.2	19 536	2 175.7	4 816.2	130.8	561 368	171 467	12.9	6.3	25.2	204 195	2 855	36 468
Lamar	41.1	13 258	115.6	291.8	5.2	438	214	0.0	0.0	100.0	207	3	0
Lauderdale	68.3	14 532	214.3	429.5	9.2	30 337	9 328	20.1	14.2	62.0	11 009	292	2 221
Lawrence	D	D	D	D	D	4 051	3 231	25.3	0.0	24.4	606	8	157
Lee	138.6	19 521	376.6	874.9	29.6	38 410	5 354	28.9	7.0	38.0	26 239	584	1 978
Limestone	161.6	27 390	431.1	826.1	20.4	12 407	2 633	12.9	38.2	31.7	4 851	99	548
Lowndes	3.6	7 200	14.8	31.4	0.7	10 727	8 850	0.0	4.0	96.0	830	24	15
Macon	1.7	8 500	5.9	10.4	0.1	4 217	98	61.5	0.0	0.0	1 856	61	132
Madison	380.6	23 640	1 881.9	3 427.2	158.5	187 250	58 592	53.7	0.5	22.5	57 311	1 865	8 809
Marengo	55.6	20 593	231.9	494.7	19.2	2 424	654	12.2	0.0	37.8	1 280	21	92
Marion	60.0	13 043	211.5	476.2	16.9	1 642	1 147	0.0	55.1	18.6	454	12	16
Marshall	128.1	13 774	492.2	1 167.7	20.6	23 720	8 022	5.9	2.0	47.2	10 614	192	2 475
Mobile	336.5	23 865	1 945.2	4 170.2	177.5	118 173	19 639	19.6	0.3	57.9	35 734	496	11 455
Monroe	53.3	17 194	283.6	604.9	D	5 645	1 504	14.0	0.0	86.0	3 501	57	112
Montgomery	175.1	16 213	677.8	1 429.3	34.6	131 226	41 415	27.7	12.6	34.6	45 271	839	10 185
Morgan	194.8	21 174	1 098.3	2 642.3	58.8	49 869	7 192	14.7	16.4	34.1	33 806	573	2 420
Perry	9.1	10 111	23.9	39.6	1.0	1 453	90	0.0	0.0	0.0	1 277	86	1
Pickens	14.7	13 364	54.3	97.1	4.2	1 172	800	0.0	93.8	6.2	372	6	0
Pike	27.7	14 579	53.4	170.6	4.8	5 703	1 703	15.2	0.0	56.2	2 566	53	463
Randolph	24.2	13 444	89.9	170.1	2.2	397	397	46.2	0.0	53.8	0	0	0
Russell	51.1	18 926	223.5	541.6	16.9	14 281	3 564	5.5	58.9	16.9	6 461	151	3 649
St. Clair	26.3	17 533	98.5	211.6	8.7	19 455	11 012	6.8	69.3	2.2	6 563	128	466
Shelby	62.5	16 892	209.0	443.4	14.7	107 614	25 108	6.3	41.6	40.2	71 754	950	1 881
Sumter	7.1	11 833	31.3	53.7	1.3	2 373	451	17.5	43.3	0.0	1 115	35	0
Talladega	119.4	18 369	424.1	929.6	38.8	12 038	5 607	12.3	6.2	55.0	3 021	54	552
Tallapoosa	106.2	13 615	230.4	635.5	D	9 138	2 186	35.4	0.0	4.4	4 720	115	872
Tuscaloosa	149.2	22 954	579.6	1 392.2	44.7	54 188	10 327	7.6	0.8	43.2	33 621	886	3 544
Walker	23.7	10 304	83.5	169.8	2.6	6 374	1 848	36.4	0.0	55.8	3 612	36	359

1. Includes nonresidential additions and alterations, residential nonhousekeeping buildings, and residential garages and carports not shown separately.

STATE County	Wholesale trade, 1987: Establishments	Wholesale trade, 1987: Sales (Mil dol)	Wholesale trade, 1987: Paid employees[1]	Wholesale trade, 1987: Annual payroll (Mil dol)	Retail trade, all establishments, 1987: Number	Retail trade, all establishments, 1987: Sales: Total (Mil dol)	Retail trade, all establishments, 1987: Sales: Percent change, 1982–1987	Retail trade, all establishments, 1987: Sales: Per capita[2] (Dollars)	Retail trade, establishments with payroll, 1987: Number	Retail trade, establishments with payroll, 1987: Sales: Total (Mil dol)	Sales: Per capita[2] (Dollars): General merchandise stores	Sales: Per capita[2] (Dollars): Food stores	Sales: Per capita[2] (Dollars): Apparel & accessory stores	Sales: Per capita[2] (Dollars): Eating and drinking places
	147	148	149	150	151	152	153	154	155	156	157	158	159	160
UNITED STATES	469 539	2 524 726.8	5 609 024	133 359.4	2 419 641	1 540 263.3	44.5	6 328	1 503 593	1 493 308.8	744	1 240	318	611
ALABAMA	6 671	24 343.6	77 559	1 548.5	40 218	22 268.2	53.8	5 453	24 092	21 260.9	649	1 096	282	445
Autauga	23	13.6	100	1.8	270	171.9	83.9	4 897	162	165.2	D	1 064	101	383
Baldwin	133	283.1	990	15.8	1 120	510.3	57.5	5 389	701	489.8	579	1 313	115	538
Barbour	39	59.5	437	5.6	272	103.7	63.1	4 049	153	97.3	260	1 315	144	351
Bibb	8	14.6	115	1.5	136	47.2	54.2	2 811	64	43.2	D	797	58	141
Blount	33	71.7	312	4.6	283	117.8	67.1	3 091	153	108.7	D	679	118	152
Bullock	13	17.0	182	1.6	106	31.2	38.1	2 861	60	28.7	D	761	157	221
Butler	26	95.2	184	2.8	263	85.4	16.8	3 812	153	78.5	232	910	174	348
Calhoun	139	528.4	1 549	28.0	1 258	645.4	50.1	5 243	672	615.0	701	814	255	487
Chambers	27	45.3	188	3.7	321	131.1	24.5	3 294	158	119.4	123	835	44	205
Cherokee	27	33.6	211	2.5	194	54.2	37.9	2 751	87	47.0	281	453	63	159
Chilton	39	44.6	242	3.1	316	133.1	52.1	4 198	170	123.6	443	1 122	65	216
Choctaw	19	32.3	115	1.7	191	52.2	56.8	3 073	117	47.6	164	1 060	72	223
Clarke	30	28.5	109	2.3	336	127.9	27.3	4 602	217	122.7	256	1 407	181	249
Clay	10	D	D	D	175	42.9	31.2	3 272	76	37.0	D	813	D	110
Cleburne	10	5.4	32	0.3	135	37.9	94.4	2 938	43	31.7	185	D	D	78
Coffee	50	68.5	269	3.1	445	245.4	63.3	6 090	293	235.0	575	1 333	301	362
Colbert	113	277.8	1 032	20.2	551	289.7	36.9	5 435	346	277.1	602	1 279	133	511
Conecuh	15	17.8	111	1.8	135	37.6	3.9	2 461	66	34.3	140	668	77	198
Coosa	10	10.5	52	0.9	75	10.4	62.5	926	26	6.6	D	D	0	D
Covington	73	266.5	988	14.0	484	187.6	41.9	5 153	277	171.5	150	1 506	262	283
Crenshaw	21	82.6	296	4.0	158	35.5	33.0	2 573	69	30.0	D	746	33	151
Cullman	93	183.3	710	10.0	755	348.8	62.2	5 285	382	319.2	520	1 054	259	376
Dale	34	198.6	703	8.1	412	151.9	34.2	3 075	246	143.8	D	765	76	506
Dallas	72	244.7	686	11.5	495	235.8	35.1	4 440	311	226.6	614	1 093	162	248
De Kalb	54	153.2	628	9.1	644	233.3	71.8	4 265	308	206.2	413	783	150	289
Elmore	39	43.1	246	3.2	415	147.3	50.6	2 981	196	135.4	D	967	61	167
Escambia	56	57.0	336	5.1	425	174.6	27.0	4 811	280	166.6	412	832	178	297
Etowah	137	333.0	1 340	24.8	1 110	566.3	43.1	5 520	616	537.0	724	1 215	277	443
Fayette	25	39.2	182	1.8	165	68.4	28.8	3 636	96	64.1	D	1 043	140	183
Franklin	28	57.3	310	3.4	353	146.8	52.0	5 222	165	134.3	458	1 009	90	258
Geneva	37	403.5	882	14.0	219	71.9	41.5	3 060	122	63.3	270	959	72	47
Greene	10	18.8	96	1.1	74	23.7	-15.4	2 171	49	22.2	193	601	57	162
Hale	13	22.1	85	1.0	138	41.7	40.4	2 709	69	37.4	80	950	24	56
Henry	28	88.7	356	4.6	154	46.8	17.9	3 119	92	43.7	D	1 094	D	174
Houston	226	560.5	2 611	46.3	1 055	717.2	62.1	8 932	749	701.6	D	1 507	491	682
Jackson	49	81.2	364	4.9	622	212.3	45.7	4 272	259	188.2	448	847	165	273
Jefferson	1 799	9 903.2	26 742	630.4	6 365	4 791.5	55.0	7 056	4 237	4 673.5	906	1 240	513	632
Lamar	9	11.2	67	0.9	205	44.4	15.0	2 707	94	37.7	D	732	158	102
Lauderdale	100	155.2	917	14.6	951	462.2	44.3	5 623	533	438.5	1 075	1 099	299	392
Lawrence	24	23.0	164	1.6	238	73.3	39.4	2 358	98	59.3	D	648	95	112
Lee	92	208.8	787	13.4	661	495.8	65.7	6 143	446	481.1	903	1 295	181	523
Limestone	50	82.5	415	6.5	478	218.4	66.0	4 225	258	201.1	437	1 058	124	326
Lowndes	4	D	D	D	58	26.2	29.7	1 983	31	24.6	D	833	D	D
Macon	11	23.4	85	1.6	164	72.7	61.9	2 755	92	68.8	D	572	97	250
Madison	404	1 506.2	4 155	90.7	2 248	1 586.7	77.6	6 866	1 460	1 547.7	1 003	1 236	433	681
Marengo	33	99.7	318	5.4	231	92.1	18.1	3 743	147	88.2	459	1 232	130	224
Marion	38	66.6	300	4.6	319	103.9	41.7	3 372	151	89.6	415	895	121	187
Marshall	144	557.0	1 548	25.7	1 082	596.7	110.8	8 287	585	520.6	689	1 492	730	466
Mobile	784	2 607.6	9 300	183.1	3 424	2 283.5	40.5	5 869	2 281	2 224.9	754	1 201	272	522
Monroe	31	75.4	358	5.0	261	117.6	87.3	5 160	161	109.7	153	1 068	936	279
Montgomery	459	2 429.7	6 701	137.8	1 893	1 508.2	56.5	7 054	1 289	1 480.1	1 029	999	377	674
Morgan	173	449.3	1 770	33.5	1 174	634.1	68.9	6 348	650	600.2	700	1 054	300	506
Perry	13	38.0	223	1.9	110	30.4	45.5	2 038	63	28.5	102	662	126	153
Pickens	26	44.5	203	3.3	195	60.0	54.2	2 763	118	53.4	156	846	48	115
Pike	58	106.5	470	7.6	305	132.7	43.1	4 740	187	125.5	D	1 208	191	464
Randolph	20	40.3	134	1.5	218	69.9	46.8	3 496	97	62.2	388	922	100	186
Russell	33	64.9	209	3.5	411	142.5	27.7	2 850	223	132.8	D	916	86	D
St. Clair	42	85.8	370	5.3	378	150.0	71.6	3 132	180	138.8	D	631	38	203
Shelby	118	330.7	1 492	36.7	616	306.7	92.9	3 550	357	293.0	D	903	53	260
Sumter	14	23.3	131	2.0	147	42.3	20.9	2 550	91	39.1	414	761	D	158
Talladega	66	106.5	485	9.8	725	341.5	47.5	4 541	412	323.4	468	1 131	214	308
Tallapoosa	41	44.1	235	3.4	373	172.0	60.9	4 354	217	158.6	D	1 074	215	252
Tuscaloosa	167	392.0	1 596	27.0	1 357	881.9	52.4	6 094	920	857.2	816	1 120	316	524
Walker	76	219.1	543	11.2	813	393.5	58.9	5 712	437	371.6	469	1 241	308	321

1. For pay period including March 12. 2. Based on the estimated population as of July 1 of the year shown.

STATE County	Retail trade, establishments with payroll, 1987 (cont'd): Paid employees[1]	Retail trade, establishments with payroll, 1987 (cont'd): Annual payroll (Mil dol)	Taxable service industries–establishments with payroll, 1987: Number	Receipts (Mil dol): Total	Receipts, selected kinds of business: Hotels, motels and other lodging places	Receipts, selected kinds of business: Health services	Receipts, selected kinds of business: Legal services	Paid employees	Annual payroll (Mil dol)	Bank deposits,[2] June 1989: Total (Mil dol)	Bank deposits, June 1989: Percent change, 1988–1989	Savings capital,[3] September 1989: Total (Mil dol)	Savings capital, September 1989: Percent change, 1988–1989
	161	162	163	164	165	166	167	168	169	170	171	172	173
UNITED STATES	17 779 942	177 547.9	1 626 017	772 194.1	51 864.7	182 289.2	66 997.5	16 054 738	289 806.5	2 341 259	5.0	932 695.3	-1.4
ALABAMA	249 847	2 357.5	20 474	8 397.2	350.7	2 874.5	562.0	189 566	3 066.9	27 552	9.1	6 322.4	-4.7
Autauga	1 779	15.6	115	31.9	D	14.5	3.3	778	10.1	150	11.1	24.7	-0.8
Baldwin	6 281	55.6	495	116.8	30.2	29.4	6.6	3 282	40.3	557	17.3	199.1	-8.4
Barbour	1 179	10.9	109	19.2	2.1	7.9	1.5	564	6.0	182	9.5	17.9	-12.1
Bibb	548	4.5	36	4.8	D	1.6	0.5	135	1.6	75	8.3	7.5	11.9
Blount	1 049	9.8	96	13.8	D	4.6	1.1	396	4.9	192	12.9	10.9	-25.1
Bullock	381	3.3	29	5.2	D	3.0	D	131	1.3	54	4.3	13.3	0.3
Butler	1 020	8.7	68	20.1	1.2	13.9	1.1	451	7.3	136	6.2	15.9	-6.5
Calhoun	7 785	71.2	542	142.9	11.8	56.1	10.1	3 985	51.5	749	9.3	94.3	7.3
Chambers	1 331	13.2	117	22.2	D	12.1	0.6	666	8.1	119	6.2	65.4	-8.8
Cherokee	590	4.7	55	8.4	0.3	3.0	0.3	272	3.3	93	0.3	17.8	1.7
Chilton	1 233	12.2	92	20.2	D	10.1	0.7	641	7.1	143	7.2	48.2	-0.6
Choctaw	626	5.2	56	7.9	1.0	2.6	0.8	246	2.6	95	11.7	13.1	1.6
Clarke	1 410	13.1	109	21.7	1.0	12.6	2.1	618	6.2	189	0.6	35.4	2.5
Clay	388	3.4	37	5.1	D	2.9	0.4	168	1.7	75	9.0	13.7	7.6
Cleburne	234	2.1	33	7.6	D	5.0	0.3	182	2.1	72	8.2	0.0	NA
Coffee	2 447	24.0	215	54.9	D	31.4	2.5	1 377	19.5	299	5.8	30.1	-1.1
Colbert	3 366	29.0	292	82.3	3.8	46.5	D	2 037	28.2	302	13.3	97.4	-4.8
Conecuh	413	3.7	45	8.2	D	4.1	0.7	277	2.8	56	-3.1	0.0	NA
Coosa	81	0.6	22	2.5	0.0	0.9	0.5	94	0.9	7	-27.0	0.0	NA
Covington	1 951	19.1	178	46.7	1.7	22.7	2.5	1 160	15.2	308	7.9	48.1	-8.5
Crenshaw	344	3.3	30	5.9	0.0	3.7	0.6	190	2.0	91	5.7	0.0	NA
Cullman	3 321	30.9	252	73.0	2.0	34.2	3.9	1 953	24.0	395	7.5	134.8	-2.1
Dale	2 192	16.9	183	42.3	5.2	10.4	2.3	1 259	14.0	178	7.2	25.8	1.9
Dallas	2 440	23.3	257	79.4	3.0	49.6	3.9	1 961	27.3	306	3.8	36.5	-12.7
De Kalb	2 335	21.2	213	51.7	4.9	16.4	2.3	1 410	17.2	309	5.3	41.9	3.6
Elmore	1 457	13.5	154	29.0	D	12.1	4.6	1 008	11.8	235	8.7	5.3	-14.6
Escambia	1 893	17.7	140	35.5	2.4	12.5	2.1	890	10.4	296	3.9	52.7	8.3
Etowah	6 539	56.0	495	141.3	4.2	78.6	9.9	3 920	58.7	595	9.0	103.7	-3.7
Fayette	747	6.7	42	8.1	D	3.3	0.4	192	3.4	128	0.2	23.3	25.4
Franklin	1 324	12.3	121	33.7	D	23.7	1.3	898	10.8	220	10.5	53.3	-3.7
Geneva	708	6.1	67	6.6	0.0	2.6	0.8	177	2.0	186	2.3	0.0	NA
Greene	303	2.3	32	24.1	D	D	0.2	436	5.9	24	-1.0	7.7	66.0
Hale	389	3.7	31	5.3	0.0	4.0	0.3	217	2.0	83	5.8	0.0	NA
Henry	534	4.8	50	11.5	0.0	5.1	D	302	3.7	127	11.3	11.4	4.3
Houston	8 391	80.6	629	268.5	12.9	151.3	8.3	5 662	103.5	776	17.0	191.3	-4.1
Jackson	2 078	19.8	177	30.3	1.6	11.6	2.2	781	10.7	270	5.6	46.0	-0.6
Jefferson	55 560	545.3	4 667	2 769.6	77.3	773.0	232.2	54 417	981.2	7 105	9.7	1 692.7	-6.7
Lamar	484	4.0	51	14.1	D	6.4	D	384	4.3	152	11.3	4.8	-18.0
Lauderdale	5 194	46.3	455	123.7	2.7	68.5	6.7	2 932	44.7	641	11.5	185.5	-2.7
Lawrence	686	5.4	64	13.4	0.0	8.4	0.8	373	4.5	92	9.4	21.3	11.9
Lee	5 865	52.4	330	98.4	5.2	37.9	6.1	2 413	35.8	574	9.3	33.2	6.1
Limestone	2 325	22.0	180	58.9	1.1	17.9	3.5	1 400	24.2	201	14.6	82.2	-3.8
Lowndes	235	2.7	18	2.6	0.0	D	D	64	0.9	45	0.5	0.0	NA
Macon	922	7.4	61	53.0	D	4.4	1.4	1 053	9.5	53	5.9	29.0	-0.4
Madison	18 683	181.5	1 582	1 247.6	49.2	254.1	D	25 086	476.9	1 406	14.2	360.4	7.7
Marengo	1 084	9.8	79	13.5	1.6	6.3	0.7	391	4.3	175	7.4	11.2	-5.6
Marion	1 024	8.5	106	22.0	D	14.1	1.4	736	8.4	245	6.7	23.0	-9.5
Marshall	4 918	45.4	368	70.4	4.7	26.4	3.4	2 119	23.5	580	9.5	132.4	-17.6
Mobile	27 622	262.6	2 307	944.3	32.7	354.0	88.7	22 495	357.7	2 178	13.0	853.8	-6.4
Monroe	1 200	11.0	74	15.4	1.0	7.6	0.8	418	5.3	136	7.6	21.6	-2.1
Montgomery	17 146	171.2	1 489	625.8	D	227.7	52.3	14 626	247.0	1 815	5.6	285.9	-17.9
Morgan	6 602	66.5	586	196.5	7.6	87.4	9.0	5 894	79.4	645	12.8	179.7	2.2
Perry	412	3.3	25	7.6	D	6.5	D	207	2.4	73	8.4	0.0	NA
Pickens	622	5.7	62	14.2	D	4.4	0.6	349	3.5	135	4.5	7.3	-1.3
Pike	1 665	13.5	105	26.5	D	8.5	1.5	595	6.6	254	3.0	18.0	-2.3
Randolph	718	6.7	68	14.0	D	7.3	0.5	395	4.6	129	4.5	18.7	-1.1
Russell	1 778	15.2	181	34.0	1.7	13.0	3.4	1 073	11.1	171	-3.0	125.5	1.0
St. Clair	1 139	10.8	106	17.0	1.2	8.6	1.4	491	5.5	148	7.0	58.0	4.2
Shelby	3 170	29.8	289	71.3	D	19.1	2.5	1 582	25.0	325	10.8	23.4	-8.5
Sumter	517	4.0	37	5.7	D	2.1	0.5	257	2.5	65	10.4	13.3	-4.8
Talladega	3 814	33.3	248	65.3	1.8	23.3	4.1	1 569	22.0	329	4.5	120.1	-2.2
Tallapoosa	1 698	17.4	155	41.4	2.2	20.6	3.2	1 336	17.4	271	9.6	62.9	-3.8
Tuscaloosa	10 433	97.7	744	244.8	13.1	112.5	17.2	5 801	91.1	774	3.9	278.1	-5.2
Walker	3 682	35.8	271	76.0	D	40.3	5.8	1 733	32.7	448	8.0	177.0	-1.1

1. For the period including March 12 of the year shown. 2. Includes deposits for all insured and reporting noninsured commercial and mutual savings banks. 3. Includes savings capital for all FSLIC insured savings institutions.

STATE County	Federal funds and grants, 1989 — Expenditures — Total (Mil dol)	Federal funds and grants, 1989 — Expenditures — Percent change, 1988–1989	Federal funds and grants, 1989 — Per capita[1] (Dollars) — Total	Per capita[1] — Direct payments for individuals	Per capita[1] — Procurement contract awards	Per capita[1] — Salaries and wages	Per capita[1] — Grant awards	Local government finances, 1981–1982 — General revenue — Total (Mil dol)	General revenue — Intergovernmental — Total (Mil dol)	General revenue — Intergovernmental — Percent from state	General revenue — Taxes — Total (Mil dol)	Taxes — Per capita[2] — Total (Dollars)	Taxes — Per capita[2] — Property (Dollars)	Direct general expenditure — Total (Mil dol)	Direct general expenditure — Percent change, 1977–1982
	174	175	176	177	178	179	180	181	182	183	184	185	186	187	188
UNITED STATES	929 603.3	5.7	X	1 811	727	572	523	281 044.7	116 618.7	81.8	103 782.7	447	340	264 355.4	54.6
ALABAMA	15 131.1	4.1	X	1 917	558	668	469	3 188.6	1 338.3	81.8	776.8	197	76	3 153.2	65.5
Autauga	77.5	12.1	2 159	1 696	22	154	198	18.7	11.5	88.1	4.5	139	37	18.4	74.2
Baldwin	242.7	13.4	2 466	1 998	15	95	315	52.7	22.8	91.1	8.5	103	51	58.0	133.7
Barbour	75.5	12.3	2 927	2 108	10	134	563	19.2	10.8	85.6	3.9	158	51	17.8	56.7
Bibb	38.0	6.2	2 224	1 722	37	191	249	11.6	6.6	91.9	1.4	87	30	10.8	57.8
Blount	69.2	13.3	1 802	1 362	14	87	304	21.2	10.9	94.8	4.3	118	53	20.7	42.2
Bullock	30.3	-12.0	2 734	1 754	11	156	567	8.6	4.9	93.0	1.7	159	72	8.3	55.8
Butler	54.6	7.5	2 446	1 891	14	114	393	14.3	9.1	82.5	2.5	113	40	14.1	92.6
Calhoun	752.6	18.4	6 123	2 080	981	2 830	226	100.1	36.3	84.3	18.0	146	57	97.4	66.2
Chambers	91.0	15.1	2 299	1 821	44	67	354	23.0	12.8	83.4	4.7	118	40	22.5	75.8
Cherokee	52.9	-8.4	2 620	1 557	628	90	211	14.5	6.5	96.0	2.0	103	46	13.9	62.6
Chilton	69.5	5.2	2 140	1 676	144	84	185	15.1	9.8	92.4	3.2	106	45	14.6	41.2
Choctaw	39.6	-9.9	2 314	1 637	210	98	350	10.7	8.1	94.3	1.7	100	66	9.5	-1.1
Clarke	62.3	4.3	2 258	1 740	40	146	314	24.7	10.2	95.3	3.4	120	37	23.8	117.0
Clay	30.5	5.1	2 325	1 868	25	179	236	10.2	5.1	90.2	0.8	61	31	11.5	74.9
Cleburne	26.0	3.2	2 012	1 594	21	161	215	9.2	4.8	96.0	1.0	76	47	8.5	58.7
Coffee	195.3	-59.9	4 846	2 113	2 202	227	252	25.0	13.3	90.3	5.7	144	57	23.7	46.1
Colbert	220.5	-3.8	4 201	2 080	160	1 615	233	49.8	17.8	88.7	9.4	172	78	57.0	100.5
Conecuh	43.9	13.1	2 968	2 006	15	131	729	9.1	6.3	94.7	1.6	99	43	9.4	67.3
Coosa	23.4	7.4	2 090	1 591	81	146	254	5.6	4.1	96.4	0.8	70	37	5.7	38.2
Covington	104.1	5.8	2 861	2 324	23	158	279	22.9	11.9	88.4	5.5	151	54	20.7	46.6
Crenshaw	38.1	1.5	2 724	2 033	32	172	377	10.7	5.4	93.7	1.2	89	40	10.1	132.6
Cullman	158.6	9.0	2 392	1 790	75	130	374	51.2	21.6	86.8	8.1	130	33	50.8	44.3
Dale	452.2	130.0	8 972	1 882	178	6 667	211	28.6	14.2	83.8	5.0	103	29	26.8	76.6
Dallas	161.4	-9.2	3 105	1 973	418	124	475	40.2	23.9	72.0	9.4	171	79	42.4	69.7
De Kalb	123.1	13.6	2 221	1 610	21	113	428	30.8	17.7	85.8	6.1	112	45	29.5	81.0
Elmore	110.1	6.7	2 150	1 755	30	117	174	24.8	12.9	95.4	4.1	92	33	25.2	73.0
Escambia	86.5	7.5	2 442	1 905	74	99	298	26.1	13.1	92.3	4.8	129	55	26.3	48.9
Etowah	266.8	-3.1	2 596	2 007	209	156	211	69.7	33.8	84.0	24.3	236	71	64.0	60.2
Fayette	45.0	15.3	2 446	1 593	417	127	264	13.5	6.7	93.1	2.4	128	50	12.4	56.9
Franklin	74.8	9.0	2 681	2 087	131	105	326	18.5	9.6	93.3	4.0	141	54	17.0	59.8
Geneva	62.1	3.9	2 667	2 099	14	141	265	15.5	8.2	92.2	2.4	100	45	15.4	60.9
Greene	33.2	-14.5	3 075	1 743	14	139	1 052	14.9	9.6	67.9	2.2	197	60	13.9	120.0
Hale	44.3	6.1	2 802	1 820	34	165	636	12.0	7.6	94.1	1.1	74	33	10.0	31.6
Henry	39.4	-7.3	2 630	1 948	17	155	293	12.1	6.9	85.2	1.9	129	60	12.1	70.5
Houston	220.9	20.5	2 720	1 767	483	172	256	88.8	26.9	79.5	18.5	241	113	93.1	99.4
Jackson	135.1	-27.3	2 746	1 736	29	668	274	54.0	16.3	95.9	7.0	136	48	40.4	76.7
Jefferson	2 018.6	3.6	2 977	2 016	156	434	360	626.6	230.3	70.0	223.9	335	136	606.5	51.7
Lamar	36.8	8.7	2 285	1 729	102	166	250	12.5	7.1	92.0	2.0	123	59	11.9	70.6
Lauderdale	192.3	5.3	2 348	1 913	41	139	181	71.4	24.3	85.8	13.0	160	70	73.1	41.6
Lawrence	68.0	20.4	2 186	1 364	24	124	409	29.0	11.0	96.1	3.0	97	28	26.5	121.5
Lee	175.1	5.3	2 145	1 287	144	206	492	57.9	21.2	85.7	13.8	175	62	66.5	79.7
Limestone	108.2	-6.5	2 026	1 422	37	101	213	31.6	14.9	95.0	5.9	127	38	31.2	59.3
Lowndes	34.7	20.3	2 646	1 391	11	118	963	9.0	7.4	88.8	1.0	75	51	9.3	68.5
Macon	123.3	8.0	4 689	2 079	226	1 491	816	14.9	10.7	82.8	2.4	88	31	14.5	27.1
Madison	2 711.1	1.7	11 343	1 839	6 289	2 869	310	221.9	68.8	74.1	49.7	245	109	201.3	72.6
Marengo	55.2	-19.2	2 272	1 528	49	170	425	23.5	11.8	74.2	3.5	140	62	19.9	49.4
Marion	70.1	7.9	2 306	1 785	24	126	342	20.2	11.5	79.0	3.9	129	36	17.7	34.8
Marshall	169.3	4.2	2 300	1 907	40	137	196	56.5	22.7	85.5	9.8	146	43	56.9	94.0
Mobile	1 027.0	0.5	2 613	1 726	265	313	298	250.6	110.6	84.2	86.6	231	91	254.1	46.3
Monroe	54.5	10.1	2 351	1 645	11	114	465	20.9	9.2	94.8	2.6	115	69	20.8	57.3
Montgomery	1 190.1	1.7	5 546	1 990	330	1 576	1 632	144.6	69.1	69.1	50.1	247	57	135.2	62.5
Morgan	340.1	-6.4	3 309	1 618	221	1 250	205	86.2	29.8	80.6	19.7	217	103	86.2	53.5
Perry	37.4	5.1	2 560	1 746	18	147	485	12.0	8.1	79.1	1.7	112	37	12.2	63.8
Pickens	62.5	19.4	2 907	1 870	326	138	502	17.4	9.8	85.9	2.2	103	49	17.8	98.7
Pike	75.0	5.0	2 670	1 939	62	205	386	23.1	10.7	88.7	4.4	157	52	23.2	111.4
Randolph	56.9	7.5	2 832	1 959	462	115	282	14.3	6.4	93.8	1.7	85	45	14.5	68.9
Russell	121.9	7.1	2 394	1 951	10	77	321	58.1	17.4	78.9	6.2	132	55	52.7	72.6
St. Clair	85.1	9.0	1 709	1 383	10	108	202	26.7	13.0	92.6	5.1	120	62	25.2	86.9
Shelby	135.2	20.9	1 484	1 012	206	76	176	55.8	16.8	93.5	12.7	181	92	52.9	121.5
Sumter	46.2	2.4	2 873	1 868	217	145	555	12.7	8.9	78.2	1.6	95	47	12.2	59.1
Talladega	189.6	1.6	2 525	1 888	125	204	292	56.0	25.5	86.5	9.4	126	45	56.0	71.4
Tallapoosa	90.7	3.0	2 272	1 805	65	93	292	25.5	13.6	80.2	5.1	132	49	24.5	84.8
Tuscaloosa	366.9	-10.6	2 496	1 631	221	370	258	142.5	41.8	78.2	31.7	231	66	128.0	27.8
Walker	185.8	-19.5	2 665	2 302	24	124	208	39.0	22.5	86.6	10.5	151	52	40.4	52.1

1. Based on the estimated population as of July 1, of the year shown. 2. Based on the estimated population as of July 1, 1982.

STATE County	Local government finances, 1981–1982 (cont'd): Direct general expenditure (cont'd): Per capita[1] (Dollars)	Percent of total for– Education	Percent of total for– Health & hospitals	Percent of total for– Police protection	Percent of total for– Public welfare	Percent of total for– Highways	Debt outstanding: Total (Mil dol)	Debt outstanding: Per capita[1] (Dollars)	State and local government employment, 1989: Total	State and local government employment, 1989: Rate[2]	Federal government civilian employment 1989: Total	Federal government civilian employment 1989: Earnings ($1,000)	Elections, 1988[3]: Total vote cast for president	Elections, 1988[3]: Vote for lead party (Percent)
	189	190	191	192	193	194	195	196	197	198	199	200	201	202
UNITED STATES	1 139	42.4	8.1	5.3	5.6	5.5	257 108.9	1 108	14 771 000	595.0	3 198 000	102 688 000	91 595 000	R–53.4
ALABAMA	800	40.5	16.0	4.9	0.3	7.0	3 762.2	954	246 959	599.7	65 050	2 117 653	1 378 476	R–59.2
Autauga	569	59.6	0.3	5.4	0.5	9.9	7.5	232	1 232	343.2	78	2 018	11 661	R–67.1
Baldwin	703	41.5	29.6	4.0	0.0	6.5	51.1	620	4 748	482.5	201	5 457	35 598	R–72.8
Barbour	719	56.7	0.5	3.2	1.0	7.3	19.4	785	1 477	572.5	81	2 062	8 900	R–55.7
Bibb	668	50.2	22.1	2.6	0.6	11.2	8.8	544	731	427.5	97	2 207	5 146	R–56.1
Blount	566	55.5	17.9	3.5	0.4	8.6	8.1	223	1 219	317.4	86	2 348	13 548	R–64.6
Bullock	771	54.9	14.2	3.9	0.0	10.8	2.5	237	788	709.9	50	1 333	4 584	D–68.1
Butler	635	50.6	0.4	4.5	0.0	10.3	17.3	781	854	383.0	59	1 514	7 460	R–52.6
Calhoun	788	36.5	31.0	3.6	0.1	6.7	74.8	605	6 614	538.2	7 205	221 740	33 970	R–58.3
Chambers	568	54.8	8.6	5.2	0.0	7.8	14.0	354	1 372	346.5	66	1 735	12 956	R–59.4
Cherokee	717	49.1	25.7	3.2	0.3	8.3	2.0	105	744	368.3	52	1 228	6 101	D–52.1
Chilton	479	64.7	0.5	5.7	0.3	14.0	5.4	177	1 126	346.5	72	1 944	12 623	R–69.4
Choctaw	574	61.1	0.0	3.7	0.1	11.2	1.2	73	706	412.9	43	1 035	7 131	R–50.9
Clarke	842	45.9	27.2	4.1	0.0	10.5	21.0	742	1 593	577.2	78	2 111	10 021	R–57.0
Clay	840	42.0	26.2	2.5	0.0	16.6	5.4	396	724	552.7	47	1 194	5 239	R–66.7
Cleburne	655	47.1	27.8	3.7	0.1	11.0	1.2	90	589	456.6	78	1 846	4 491	R–68.4
Coffee	596	60.0	4.2	4.9	0.2	8.8	9.2	233	2 131	528.8	140	3 892	13 357	R–66.6
Colbert	1 046	35.3	32.7	3.4	0.1	6.0	50.6	929	2 953	562.5	2 431	84 394	18 409	D–56.5
Conecuh	596	57.5	0.1	4.3	0.0	16.4	3.1	198	845	570.9	51	1 409	6 357	R–51.2
Coosa	501	62.9	0.3	6.4	0.1	19.8	2.8	250	414	369.6	30	759	4 283	R–56.2
Covington	566	58.9	0.3	5.2	0.3	11.1	18.4	505	1 770	486.3	154	3 869	12 075	R–67.3
Crenshaw	725	46.8	24.8	2.6	0.3	13.2	2.6	183	683	487.9	53	1 184	4 478	R–58.4
Cullman	816	41.7	27.1	3.0	0.3	8.9	55.7	894	3 028	456.7	188	5 186	23 197	R–61.9
Dale	556	50.6	15.0	4.4	0.4	5.6	31.3	649	2 641	524.0	4 279	112 233	12 909	R–71.8
Dallas	772	43.6	1.1	4.3	0.0	4.7	51.3	935	2 749	528.7	145	4 045	17 423	D–55.4
De Kalb	545	55.1	0.3	5.6	0.5	8.7	29.1	538	2 070	373.6	155	3 861	18 971	R–60.5
Elmore	562	58.4	16.0	4.8	0.3	7.2	12.1	270	2 822	551.2	100	2 633	15 540	R–69.8
Escambia	705	56.2	18.0	4.5	0.4	9.4	7.2	192	2 554	721.5	79	2 197	10 954	R–62.1
Etowah	622	45.3	1.0	6.3	0.2	5.7	45.8	445	4 553	442.9	356	11 060	35 891	R–49.7
Fayette	659	42.3	26.0	3.3	0.0	12.9	2.9	152	990	538.0	50	1 219	7 557	R–57.4
Franklin	600	56.8	8.6	4.9	0.2	9.1	13.7	483	1 415	507.2	88	2 286	10 241	R–50.2
Geneva	652	49.3	20.6	4.1	0.2	8.9	5.7	240	882	378.5	78	1 994	8 472	R–67.3
Greene	1 249	45.5	0.3	2.8	0.1	8.5	18.9	1 700	776	718.5	38	927	4 377	D–75.3
Hale	644	62.7	10.4	3.3	0.1	13.0	2.5	163	754	477.2	55	1 336	5 652	D–56.4
Henry	801	47.8	21.2	3.4	0.0	8.8	3.4	226	671	447.3	52	1 370	5 844	R–61.8
Houston	1 208	28.1	32.7	3.7	0.2	4.0	129.7	1 684	5 376	662.1	391	11 906	27 061	R–73.9
Jackson	781	40.4	22.2	3.6	0.3	6.7	150.4	2 909	2 589	526.2	1 077	34 205	13 671	D–54.3
Jefferson	908	36.0	7.2	6.6	1.0	7.0	878.1	1 315	44 986	663.4	8 948	282 965	258 062	R–57.7
Lamar	724	48.7	14.8	3.6	0.1	14.9	4.0	242	612	380.1	49	1 133	5 499	R–58.4
Lauderdale	899	38.5	31.0	3.6	0.2	4.3	61.0	750	4 900	598.3	266	8 016	26 190	R–49.4
Lawrence	861	41.4	12.8	3.0	0.5	5.1	159.9	5 191	1 446	465.0	148	3 894	8 417	D–55.2
Lee	845	33.5	28.4	5.0	0.1	5.1	124.9	1 587	9 833	1 205.0	329	10 467	26 685	R–64.4
Limestone	672	56.0	17.3	3.8	0.3	7.8	23.1	498	3 312	620.2	3 874	161 027	14 760	R–61.6
Lowndes	735	71.9	0.4	3.1	0.2	15.0	2.2	173	716	546.6	36	791	4 776	D–69.7
Macon	538	54.7	0.2	7.0	0.0	12.0	6.7	248	1 357	516.0	1 521	49 063	7 756	D–81.9
Madison	991	34.9	25.0	3.7	0.0	5.3	226.1	1 114	14 347	600.3	17 052	643 421	79 894	R–67.1
Marengo	808	42.3	29.2	3.6	0.1	8.2	10.6	430	1 330	547.3	61	1 609	8 725	D–50.5
Marion	581	54.4	0.7	2.8	0.0	12.9	33.9	1 112	1 250	411.2	66	1 655	10 497	R–56.7
Marshall	851	36.6	27.7	3.7	0.0	7.0	64.3	961	3 840	521.7	304	8 594	19 947	R–60.9
Mobile	677	43.1	2.3	7.8	0.1	6.5	588.7	1 567	20 402	519.1	3 031	101 521	118 688	R–60.8
Monroe	922	46.2	29.0	2.7	0.1	6.7	16.7	741	1 351	582.3	65	1 562	8 954	R–60.1
Montgomery	665	42.0	0.8	8.3	0.6	8.3	115.6	569	21 972	1 023.9	7 193	193 688	70 482	R–58.4
Morgan	949	38.1	24.1	3.3	0.2	6.0	54.8	603	5 938	577.6	305	9 030	29 407	R–63.5
Perry	807	47.3	14.3	3.0	0.2	11.6	2.8	187	592	405.5	45	1 157	5 758	D–62.1
Pickens	823	43.2	18.2	2.6	0.0	14.7	12.8	593	868	403.7	57	1 499	6 982	R–55.2
Pike	825	46.1	21.9	3.8	0.1	8.8	13.3	475	2 534	901.8	79	2 056	9 822	R–60.0
Randolph	717	43.6	32.1	2.3	0.0	8.9	8.6	425	1 142	568.2	56	1 429	7 224	R–64.0
Russell	1 124	29.2	44.7	2.3	0.0	3.5	74.2	1 582	2 508	492.7	91	2 376	13 087	D–50.3
St. Clair	595	50.2	23.2	4.4	0.5	8.2	9.4	221	1 970	395.6	88	2 203	14 997	R–70.7
Shelby	758	37.6	32.5	4.9	0.5	4.6	66.2	948	3 831	420.5	159	4 191	34 314	R–78.8
Sumter	715	50.5	9.4	4.3	0.0	11.6	6.4	375	1 228	762.7	45	1 077	6 635	D–66.2
Talladega	750	46.9	20.5	4.0	0.8	4.3	42.1	563	4 847	645.4	497	14 969	21 507	R–60.3
Tallapoosa	630	47.9	6.3	4.3	0.1	7.2	31.9	821	1 655	414.8	97	2 565	13 298	R–63.9
Tuscaloosa	931	31.4	34.6	5.6	0.0	5.0	72.4	526	15 882	1 080.4	1 882	53 061	45 758	R–59.9
Walker	584	54.7	0.8	4.8	0.0	10.4	48.8	706	2 543	364.8	207	5 853	22 700	D–49.9

1. Based on the estimated population as of July 1, 1982. 2. Per 10,000 resident population estimated as of July 1 of the year shown. 3. Data subject to copyright.

STATE–County code	MSA/CMSA/NECMA code[1]	STATE County	Land Area,[2] 1990 (Sq. Km.)	Population, 1990												
				Total persons	Rank	Per square kilometer	Race					Hispanic[3]	Age of population Percent		
							White	Black	Am. Indian, Eskimo, Aleut	Asian & Pacific Islander	Other race		Under 5 years	5 to 14 years	15 to 24 years
			1	2	3	4	5	6	7	8	9	10	11	12	13
		ALABAMA—Con.													
01 129	...	Washington	2 799	16 694	1 869	6.0	10 984	4 623	1 068	14	5	51	7.4	17.7	15.3
01 131	...	Wilcox	2 302	13 568	2 096	5.9	4 203	9 353	6	6	0	40	7.9	19.6	15.6
01 133	...	Winston	1 592	22 053	1 572	13.9	21 925	57	42	26	3	59	6.4	13.6	14.5
02 000	...	ALASKA*	1 477 268	550 043	X	0.4	415 492	22 451	85 698	19 728	6 674	17 803	10.0	17.3	14.2
02 010	...	Aleutian Islands	NA	NA	X	NA	NA	NA	NA	NA	NA	NA	NA	NA	NA
02 013	...	Aleutians East Borough	18 091	2 464	3 024	0.1	827	16	1 042	463	116	180	7.3	12.3	18.7
02 016	...	Aleutians West Census Area	11 401	9 478	2 436	0.8	6 360	662	1 076	979	401	742	8.2	10.1	24.8
02 020	0380	Anchorage	4 397	226 338	218	51.5	182 736	14 544	14 569	10 910	3 579	9 258	9.5	16.0	14.6
02 050	...	Bethel	106 416	13 656	2 085	0.1	2 105	62	11 370	91	28	80	13.7	20.5	15.7
02 060	...	Bristol Bay	1 345	1 410	3 100	1.0	894	38	455	12	11	33	8.7	15.0	13.8
02 070	...	Dillingham	47 829	4 012	2 918	0.1	1 019	8	2 925	27	33	49	14.0	19.6	12.5
02 090	...	Fairbanks North Star	19 069	77 720	583	4.1	63 751	5 553	5 330	1 998	1 088	2 899	10.4	17.2	16.8
02 100	...	Haines	6 105	2 117	3 062	0.3	1 802	1	279	17	18	27	7.3	16.1	10.9
02 110	...	Juneau	6 717	26 751	1 399	4.0	21 570	292	3 462	1 154	273	749	9.0	16.5	11.9
02 122	...	Kenai Peninsula	41 644	40 802	981	1.0	37 089	203	2 935	428	147	726	9.3	18.6	12.3
02 130	...	Ketchikan Gateway	3 159	13 828	2 072	4.4	11 316	55	1 898	493	66	285	8.8	16.9	12.8
02 140	...	Kobuk	NA	NA	X	NA	NA	NA	NA	NA	NA	NA	NA	NA	NA
02 150	...	Kodiak Island	16 738	13 309	2 113	0.8	9 289	135	2 126	1 492	267	663	10.5	16.8	14.6
02 164	...	Lake and Peninsula Borough	61 208	1 668	3 088	0.0	389	0	1 261	12	6	32	12.8	21.6	11.8
02 170	...	Matanuska-Susitna	63 957	39 683	1 008	0.6	36 949	307	1 939	297	191	752	9.8	20.9	10.8
02 180	...	Nome	59 603	8 288	2 538	0.1	2 023	9	6 148	55	53	106	12.9	20.4	14.2
02 185	...	North Slope	227 559	5 979	2 761	0.0	1 274	41	4 336	285	43	124	13.9	19.7	13.2
02 188	...	Northwest Arctic Borough	92 884	6 113	2 741	0.1	841	12	5 209	48	3	36	15.7	22.3	15.5
02 201	...	Prince of Wales-Outer Ketchikan	18 970	6 278	2 727	0.3	3 859	9	2 358	28	24	121	9.3	19.0	12.4
02 220	...	Sitka	7 463	8 588	2 505	1.2	6 359	39	1 797	333	60	209	8.9	17.8	13.2
02 231	...	Skagway-Yakutat-Angoon	33 361	4 385	2 883	0.1	2 649	7	1 670	32	27	67	8.9	18.9	11.6
02 240	...	Southeast Fairbanks	67 325	5 913	2 770	0.1	4 670	290	770	82	101	177	10.2	21.0	12.9
02 261	...	Valdez-Cordova	95 688	9 952	2 391	0.1	8 247	57	1 245	324	79	270	8.9	16.4	12.0
02 270	...	Wade Hampton	44 351	5 791	2 780	0.1	346	12	5 405	23	5	17	18.0	22.1	16.9
02 280	...	Wrangell-Petersburg	15 044	7 042	2 654	0.5	5 544	11	1 367	94	26	119	9.8	16.8	11.9
02 290	...	Yukon-Koyukuk	406 944	8 478	2 514	0.0	3 584	88	4 726	51	29	82	11.0	19.2	11.9
04 000	...	ARIZONA	294 333	3 665 228	X	12.5	2 963 186	110 524	203 527	55 206	332 785	688 338	8.0	14.7	14.8
04 001	...	Apache	29 023	61 591	708	2.1	12 456	100	47 803	94	1 138	2 599	12.2	23.5	16.5
04 003	...	Cochise	15 980	97 624	471	6.1	79 724	5 078	790	2 247	9 785	28 379	7.7	15.6	15.0
04 005	...	Coconino	48 224	96 591	477	2.0	61 836	1 419	28 233	861	4 242	9 696	8.9	17.3	21.8
04 007	...	Gila	12 349	40 216	995	3.3	30 776	99	5 238	140	3 963	7 486	7.1	15.0	11.3
04 009	...	Graham	11 991	26 554	1 406	2.2	20 603	502	3 951	106	1 392	6 682	8.8	19.2	15.9
04 011	...	Greenlee	4 784	8 008	2 566	1.7	6 835	28	183	16	946	3 456	7.5	20.8	12.2
04 012	...	La Paz	11 654	13 844	2 068	1.2	10 335	118	2 402	102	887	3 139	7.8	14.8	11.5
04 013	6200	Maricopa	23 838	2 122 101	7	89.0	1 799 420	74 257	38 017	36 294	174 113	345 498	8.0	14.3	14.6
04 015	...	Mohave	34 479	93 497	495	2.7	88 834	303	2 145	569	1 646	4 919	6.5	12.6	10.2
04 017	...	Navajo	25 780	77 658	585	3.0	34 205	703	40 417	264	2 069	5 652	11.1	21.6	15.2
04 019	8520	Pima	23 794	666 880	68	28.0	524 976	20 795	20 330	11 964	88 815	163 262	7.5	13.7	15.6
04 021	...	Pinal	13 908	116 379	395	8.4	87 219	3 648	10 785	502	14 225	34 062	8.3	16.5	13.7
04 023	...	Santa Cruz	3 206	29 676	1 307	9.3	22 159	97	64	164	7 192	23 221	9.3	19.4	15.2
04 025	...	Yavapai	21 040	107 714	429	5.1	103 106	321	1 740	490	2 057	6 899	5.6	12.5	10.5
04 027	9360	Yuma	14 282	106 895	432	7.5	80 702	3 056	1 429	1 393	20 315	43 388	8.5	16.5	16.0
05 000	...	ARKANSAS	134 875	2 350 725	X	17.4	1 944 744	373 912	12 773	12 530	6 766	19 876	7.0	14.9	14.6
05 001	...	Arkansas	2 560	21 653	1 594	8.5	16 816	4 738	53	35	11	61	6.8	15.9	12.6
05 003	...	Ashley	2 386	24 319	1 485	10.2	17 511	6 616	46	48	98	220	7.1	16.0	14.4
05 005	...	Baxter	1 436	31 186	1 238	21.7	30 964	4	123	61	34	171	4.7	11.4	9.4
05 007	...	Benton	2 184	97 499	472	44.6	94 968	124	1 435	455	517	1 359	6.8	14.1	12.8
05 009	...	Boone	1 531	28 297	1 345	18.5	28 038	5	176	44	34	171	6.4	14.1	13.2
05 011	...	Bradley	1 685	11 793	2 230	7.0	8 012	3 648	13	2	118	191	6.6	14.5	13.7
05 013	...	Calhoun	1 627	5 826	2 778	3.6	4 357	1 447	5	7	10	31	7.1	15.6	13.1
05 015	...	Carroll	1 642	18 654	1 755	11.4	18 416	6	146	54	32	194	6.1	14.0	12.0
05 017	...	Chicot	1 668	15 713	1 941	9.4	6 692	8 859	22	57	83	159	7.9	18.5	15.1
05 019	...	Clark	2 242	21 437	1 605	9.6	16 344	4 913	55	76	49	127	5.9	12.5	22.2
05 021	...	Clay	1 656	18 107	1 785	10.9	18 031	6	45	14	11	70	5.7	12.9	12.7
05 023	...	Cleburne	1 433	19 411	1 710	13.5	19 292	6	72	22	19	105	5.2	12.5	10.9
05 025	...	Cleveland	1 548	7 781	2 598	5.0	6 681	1 059	13	14	14	47	6.5	14.9	14.3
05 027	...	Columbia	1 984	25 691	1 432	12.9	16 564	8 992	53	62	20	77	7.0	15.1	15.7

1. MSA = Metropolitan Statistical Area. CMSA = Consolidated MSA. NECMA = New England county metropolitan area. PMSA = Primary MSA. See Appendix A for explanation of these concepts. See Appendix B for list of metropolitan areas identified by type, with component counties. 2. Dry land or land partially or temporarily covered by water. 3. Hispanic persons may be of any race.

STATE County	Population, 1990 (cont'd): Age of population (cont'd) Percent: 25 to 34 years	35 to 44 years	45 to 54 years	55 to 64 years	65 to 74 years	75 years and over	Percent female	Population–Change and components of change: Change 1980–1990: Number	Percent	Components of change, 1980–1986: Total persons, 1986	Total persons, 1980	Net change: Number	Net change: Percent	Natural increase: Births	Natural increase: Deaths
	14	15	16	17	18	19	20	21	22	23	24	25	26	27	28
ALABAMA—Con.															
Washington	15.1	13.5	10.5	8.5	6.7	5.3	51.2	-127	-0.8	16 700	16 821	-100	-0.8	1 800	1 000
Wilcox	12.8	11.4	8.5	8.3	8.3	7.5	53.5	-1 187	-8.0	14 000	14 755	-700	-5.0	2 000	1 100
Winston	14.9	14.3	12.1	10.1	8.2	5.9	51.2	100	0.5	21 900	21 953	-100	-0.4	1 900	1 300
ALASKA*	20.5	18.7	9.8	5.4	2.8	1.2	47.3	148 043	36.8	534 000	402 000	132 000	32.8	73 000	12 000
Aleutian Islands	NA	NA	NA	NA	NA	NA	NA	NA	NA	8 000	7 768	200	2.7	1 000	200
Aleutians East Borough	26.6	17.4	9.6	5.7	2.1	0.3	35.8	NA	NA	NA	NA	NA	NA	NA	NA
Aleutians West Census Area	30.9	16.8	5.9	2.5	0.6	0.3	34.2	NA	NA	NA	NA	NA	NA	NA	NA
Anchorage	21.5	19.2	10.3	5.3	2.7	1.0	48.6	51 907	29.8	235 000	174 431	60 600	34.7	29 900	4 100
Bethel	18.7	13.5	8.1	5.0	3.0	1.8	47.6	2 657	24.2	12 100	10 999	1 100	10.4	2 200	400
Bristol Bay	27.9	18.0	9.0	4.5	2.2	0.8	40.1	316	28.9	1 200	1 094	100	6.8	100	0
Dillingham	19.1	15.5	8.4	5.7	3.2	1.9	48.3	-604	-13.1	5 500	4 616	900	18.5	900	200
Fairbanks North Star	21.8	17.9	8.3	4.4	2.3	1.0	46.6	23 737	44.0	67 600	53 983	13 600	25.3	10 400	1 400
Haines	16.8	20.6	12.2	7.6	6.1	2.5	46.6	437	26.0	1 700	1 680	0	2.4	300	100
Juneau	19.3	21.5	11.2	5.5	3.3	1.8	49.3	7 223	37.0	25 000	19 528	5 400	27.8	3 200	600
Kenai Peninsula	17.8	20.2	10.5	6.3	3.7	1.3	47.0	15 520	61.4	43 200	25 282	17 900	70.7	4 800	800
Ketchikan Gateway	18.2	18.7	11.5	6.5	4.2	2.4	47.8	2 512	22.2	12 300	11 316	1 000	8.4	1 600	500
Kobuk	NA	NA	NA	NA	NA	NA	NA	NA	NA	5 500	4 831	600	13.1	1 100	200
Kodiak Island	22.7	19.3	8.5	4.5	2.2	1.0	44.4	3 370	33.9	13 800	9 939	3 900	38.7	1 800	300
Lake and Peninsula Borough	20.8	13.4	8.2	6.5	3.5	1.6	45.4	NA	NA	NA	NA	NA	NA	NA	NA
Matanuska-Susitna	17.8	20.4	9.9	5.8	3.3	1.4	48.1	21 867	122.7	39 000	17 816	21 200	119.0	4 100	600
Nome	18.5	15.0	8.5	5.5	3.0	2.1	45.9	1 751	26.8	7 400	6 537	800	12.7	1 300	400
North Slope	19.6	15.2	9.6	5.5	2.1	1.2	45.5	1 780	42.4	4 800	4 199	600	15.2	900	200
Northwest Arctic Borough	17.7	12.2	6.7	5.2	2.5	2.1	47.3	NA	NA	NA	NA	NA	NA	NA	NA
Prince of Wales-Outer Ketchikan	19.2	19.1	11.7	5.8	2.4	1.1	43.5	2 456	64.3	5 000	3 822	1 200	31.7	700	100
Sitka	19.6	17.5	11.2	6.1	3.4	2.3	47.6	785	10.1	7 700	7 803	-100	-1.8	1 200	300
Skagway-Yakutat-Angoon	18.9	19.6	10.6	6.1	3.6	1.8	44.8	907	26.1	3 500	3 478	100	1.6	500	200
Southeast Fairbanks	18.5	18.3	10.2	5.2	2.6	1.2	46.1	237	4.2	6 600	5 676	900	15.9	1 000	100
Valdez-Cordova	19.6	21.1	11.1	6.4	3.2	1.4	45.0	1 604	19.2	8 600	8 348	300	3.2	1 200	300
Wade Hampton	16.3	10.7	6.4	5.2	3.1	1.4	48.1	1 126	24.1	4 800	4 665	200	3.4	1 100	200
Wrangell-Petersburg	18.5	18.6	10.6	6.7	4.5	2.7	46.4	875	14.2	6 200	6 167	100	1.2	900	200
Yukon-Koyukuk	18.8	18.1	10.2	6.0	2.8	1.9	43.5	605	7.7	9 100	7 873	1 300	16.1	1 300	300
ARIZONA	17.3	14.4	9.5	8.2	7.9	5.1	50.6	947 228	34.9	3 279 000	2 718 000	561 000	22.1	338 000	143 000
Apache	15.0	11.7	8.3	6.1	4.0	2.7	50.9	9 483	18.2	59 400	52 108	7 300	13.9	11 100	1 900
Cochise	15.5	14.0	10.2	9.3	8.1	4.7	49.1	11 938	13.9	96 500	85 686	10 900	12.7	9 900	4 100
Coconino	17.1	14.9	8.4	5.8	3.7	2.0	50.2	21 583	28.8	86 100	75 008	11 100	14.8	11 400	2 100
Gila	11.6	12.9	10.8	11.9	12.2	7.2	51.1	3 136	8.5	39 700	37 080	2 600	7.1	4 400	2 400
Graham	14.1	12.6	8.6	8.1	7.3	5.3	48.7	3 692	16.1	23 700	22 862	800	3.6	2 900	1 100
Greenlee	13.9	14.5	10.5	9.4	7.2	4.0	49.4	-3 398	-29.8	8 600	11 406	-2 900	-25.0	1 400	400
La Paz	13.0	12.3	10.2	11.3	12.2	6.9	48.7	1 287	10.2	14 100	12 557	1 600	12.4	1 400	900
Maricopa	18.5	14.8	9.6	7.7	7.4	5.1	50.7	612 874	40.6	1 900 200	1 509 227	391 000	25.9	186 600	79 300
Mohave	13.2	12.8	11.1	13.1	14.2	6.5	50.2	37 632	67.4	75 800	55 865	19 900	35.7	5 800	3 900
Navajo	15.0	12.6	9.0	7.3	5.3	2.9	50.2	10 029	14.8	71 100	67 629	3 500	5.1	11 700	2 600
Pima	17.1	14.7	9.3	8.4	8.2	5.5	51.1	135 437	25.5	602 400	531 443	71 000	13.4	59 700	28 300
Pinal	15.2	13.5	9.6	9.4	8.8	4.9	48.7	25 461	28.0	102 400	90 918	11 500	12.7	12 000	4 800
Santa Cruz	14.6	13.5	9.2	8.2	6.7	3.9	52.4	9 217	45.1	23 100	20 459	2 600	12.8	3 100	900
Yavapai	11.3	13.5	10.4	12.5	15.2	8.6	51.1	39 569	58.1	88 100	68 145	19 900	29.2	6 400	5 800
Yuma	16.0	12.4	8.3	8.4	8.9	4.9	49.1	30 690	40.3	88 500	76 205	12 300	16.1	10 900	3 800
ARKANSAS	15.3	13.9	10.4	9.1	8.3	6.6	51.8	64 725	2.8	2 372 000	2 286 000	86 000	3.8	221 000	145 000
Arkansas	14.0	14.3	10.1	9.5	9.0	7.8	52.8	-2 522	-10.4	23 100	24 175	-1 100	-4.6	2 200	1 800
Ashley	14.1	13.7	11.0	9.1	8.0	6.6	52.0	-2 219	-8.4	26 200	26 538	-300	-1.2	2 500	1 600
Baxter	10.6	11.7	10.1	13.0	16.5	12.7	52.4	3 777	13.8	30 300	27 409	2 900	10.7	1 800	2 600
Benton	15.0	13.4	9.9	10.1	10.9	7.0	51.2	19 384	24.8	89 000	78 115	10 800	13.9	7 200	5 100
Boone	14.3	13.5	10.9	10.4	9.2	8.0	52.2	2 230	8.6	27 900	26 067	1 900	7.2	2 300	1 800
Bradley	13.1	12.5	10.5	10.2	9.9	8.9	52.5	-2 010	-14.6	13 200	13 803	-600	-4.4	1 100	1 100
Calhoun	15.3	13.0	10.3	9.1	8.9	7.6	51.7	-253	-4.2	6 100	6 079	0	0.3	500	400
Carroll	13.5	14.4	11.2	10.7	10.2	7.9	51.7	2 451	15.1	18 100	16 203	1 900	11.7	1 300	1 200
Chicot	12.4	11.3	9.4	9.1	8.1	8.1	54.0	-2 080	-11.7	17 200	17 793	-600	-3.5	2 000	1 300
Clark	12.9	11.8	9.3	8.7	8.7	8.0	52.6	-1 889	-8.1	22 700	23 326	-700	-2.9	1 800	1 500
Clay	13.1	12.2	11.3	11.4	10.9	9.8	52.2	-2 509	-12.2	19 400	20 616	-1 200	-6.1	1 500	1 600
Cleburne	13.0	12.2	11.9	13.3	12.4	8.5	51.5	2 502	14.8	19 300	16 909	2 400	14.3	1 200	1 300
Cleveland	13.5	14.3	11.9	9.7	7.9	7.0	51.4	-87	-1.1	8 300	7 868	400	5.5	600	500
Columbia	14.4	12.1	9.7	9.3	8.5	8.3	53.1	-953	-3.6	26 900	26 644	200	0.9	2 500	1 900

STATE County	Population—(cont'd) Components of change, 1980-1986 (cont'd) Net migration	Households, 1990 Number	Households, 1990 Percent change, 1980–1990	Households, 1990 Persons per household	Households, 1990 Percent Female family householder[1]	Households, 1990 Percent One-person	Births, 1988 Total	Births, 1988 Rate[2]	Births, 1988 Low birth weight[3] (Number)	Deaths, 1987 Number Total	Deaths, 1987 Number Infant[4]	Deaths, 1987 Rate Total[2]	Deaths, 1987 Rate Infant[5]	Marriages, 1984 Number	Marriages, 1984 Rate[2]
	29	30	31	32	33	34	35	36	37	38	39	40	41	42	43
ALABAMA—Con.															
Washington	-1 000	5 709	8.3	2.91	12.7	19.2	278	16.2	12	176	5	10.2	18.4	278	16.0
Wilcox	-1 700	4 415	1.2	3.02	23.4	23.9	259	18.5	31	171	8	12.0	32.1	84	5.5
Winston	-700	8 544	10.7	2.55	8.3	21.5	259	12.1	18	235	3	11.0	12.1	286	12.8
ALASKA*	71 000	188 915	43.7	2.80	9.6	22.1	11 232	21.4	558	2 055	121	3.9	10.4	6 499	12.9
Aleutian Islands	-600	NA	NA	NA	NA	NA	NA	NA	NA	NA	NA	NA	NA	67	8.7
Aleutians East Borough	NA	533	NA	2.97	9.6	22.5	NA	NA	NA	NA	NA	NA	NA	NA	NA
Aleutians West Census Area	NA	1 845	NA	3.02	5.1	14.3	NA	NA	NA	NA	NA	NA	NA	NA	NA
Anchorage	34 800	82 702	36.8	2.68	10.1	22.9	NA	NA	NA	NA	NA	NA	NA	3 168	13.9
Bethel	-700	3 605	34.3	3.72	14.7	18.2	NA	NA	NA	NA	NA	NA	NA	98	8.4
Bristol Bay	0	407	65.4	2.81	6.1	27.0	NA	NA	NA	NA	NA	NA	NA	0	0.0
Dillingham	100	1 215	0.1	3.30	13.3	18.6	NA	NA	NA	NA	NA	NA	NA	36	7.2
Fairbanks North Star	4 600	26 693	46.5	2.76	8.1	22.4	NA	NA	NA	NA	NA	NA	NA	957	15.2
Haines	-200	791	38.3	2.59	5.1	24.4	NA	NA	NA	NA	NA	NA	NA	22	12.2
Juneau	2 800	9 902	40.8	2.66	10.2	23.6	NA	NA	NA	NA	NA	NA	NA	314	13.1
Kenai Peninsula	13 900	14 250	66.7	2.79	8.4	21.8	NA	NA	NA	NA	NA	NA	NA	463	12.1
Ketchikan Gateway	-100	5 030	26.2	2.70	9.2	24.0	NA	NA	NA	NA	NA	NA	NA	193	15.0
Kobuk	-200	NA	NA	NA	NA	NA	NA	NA	NA	NA	NA	NA	NA	42	8.1
Kodiak Island	2 300	4 083	34.9	3.03	8.1	18.4	NA	NA	NA	NA	NA	NA	NA	150	10.1
Lake and Peninsula Borough	NA	509	NA	3.22	11.0	21.6	NA	NA	NA	NA	NA	NA	NA	NA	NA
Matanuska-Susitna	17 700	13 394	135.0	2.92	8.7	19.0	NA	NA	NA	NA	NA	NA	NA	395	13.4
Nome	-100	2 371	36.2	3.41	14.6	21.7	NA	NA	NA	NA	NA	NA	NA	43	6.1
North Slope	-100	1 673	70.7	3.44	14.8	20.8	NA	NA	NA	NA	NA	NA	NA	50	11.1
Northwest Arctic Borough	NA	1 526	NA	3.96	17.8	17.6	NA	NA	NA	NA	NA	NA	NA	NA	NA
Prince of Wales-Outer Ketchikan	700	2 061	83.9	2.92	9.1	21.4	NA	NA	NA	NA	NA	NA	NA	44	9.6
Sitka	-1 000	2 939	20.5	2.81	9.1	20.9	NA	NA	NA	NA	NA	NA	NA	95	12.7
Skagway-Yakutat-Angoon	-300	1 422	30.8	2.94	8.6	23.5	NA	NA	NA	NA	NA	NA	NA	47	13.4
Southeast Fairbanks	0	1 909	14.6	2.96	7.0	19.7	NA	NA	NA	NA	NA	NA	NA	78	12.6
Valdez-Cordova	-700	3 425	27.4	2.73	7.5	24.2	NA	NA	NA	NA	NA	NA	NA	92	10.1
Wade Hampton	-700	1 368	44.5	4.23	15.8	16.9	NA	NA	NA	NA	NA	NA	NA	24	5.1
Wrangell-Petersburg	-500	2 514	21.3	2.73	7.6	22.9	NA	NA	NA	NA	NA	NA	NA	58	9.1
Yukon-Koyukuk	300	2 748	20.5	2.88	12.6	27.7	NA	NA	NA	NA	NA	NA	NA	63	7.6
ARIZONA	365 000	1 368 843	43.0	2.62	10.4	24.7	65 623	18.8	4 088	26 969	601	7.9	9.5	33 321	10.8
Apache	-1 900	15 981	26.5	3.80	20.4	16.8	1 895	30.8	115	344	16	5.8	8.6	192	3.6
Cochise	5 100	34 546	19.2	2.68	10.2	23.3	1 638	16.3	98	765	11	7.7	6.8	961	10.2
Coconino	1 800	29 918	36.7	2.99	11.5	19.9	1 967	20.9	117	397	16	4.4	8.0	624	7.5
Gila	600	15 438	20.2	2.56	8.8	24.3	659	16.2	50	411	3	10.4	5.3	411	10.6
Graham	-900	7 930	20.4	3.09	12.2	19.9	418	17.1	26	193	4	8.1	9.0	261	10.8
Greenlee	-3 800	2 809	-22.1	2.85	8.0	22.7	112	14.2	4	67	0	8.4	0.0	63	6.2
La Paz	1 000	5 348	NA	2.56	9.5	24.6	(6)	(6)	(6)	(6)	(6)	(6)	(6)	NA	NA
Maricopa	283 600	807 560	48.2	2.59	10.2	25.0	38 125	18.8	2 362	14 889	368	7.5	10.0	19 408	11.0
Mohave	18 100	36 801	74.3	2.47	7.5	21.8	1 269	15.2	94	984	11	12.5	9.2	531	7.7
Navajo	-5 600	22 189	21.2	3.44	15.3	16.8	1 955	26.0	114	464	31	6.3	15.6	517	7.4
Pima	39 600	261 792	33.9	2.49	10.9	27.8	11 222	17.6	675	5 313	85	8.5	7.8	6 292	11.0
Pinal	4 300	39 154	37.8	2.83	11.4	19.9	2 091	19.5	137	923	19	8.8	8.9	920	9.5
Santa Cruz	300	8 808	46.8	3.35	14.9	16.6	664	27.2	58	161	7	6.8	12.8	325	14.6
Yavapai	19 300	44 778	68.3	2.35	7.0	24.9	1 284	13.4	95	1 220	11	13.3	9.4	743	9.1
Yuma	5 200	35 791	19.9	2.87	9.4	19.0	[6]2 324	[6]21.7	[6]143	[6]838	[6]19	[6]8.0	[6]8.8	2 073	21.6
ARKANSAS	10 000	891 179	9.2	2.57	11.1	24.0	35 035	14.6	2 870	24 429	356	10.2	10.3	32 878	14.0
Arkansas	-1 500	8 389	-5.8	2.54	12.1	25.8	255	11.3	22	267	2	11.7	7.2	283	11.9
Ashley	-1 200	8 890	-1.9	2.70	11.9	21.9	380	14.7	31	262	5	10.1	13.7	416	15.7
Baxter	3 800	13 486	20.6	2.28	6.1	24.5	290	9.3	15	464	1	15.1	3.4	421	14.3
Benton	8 700	37 555	31.2	2.55	6.9	20.0	1 312	13.7	96	924	21	9.9	16.5	1 209	14.3
Boone	1 400	11 131	13.8	2.50	7.9	23.2	393	13.7	27	303	6	10.7	16.6	524	19.1
Bradley	-600	4 545	-9.8	2.54	13.3	25.2	148	11.5	19	178	1	13.7	6.4	156	11.6
Calhoun	0	2 185	3.0	2.63	10.5	24.0	72	12.0	10	75	0	12.3	0.0	68	11.1
Carroll	1 700	7 550	17.4	2.45	8.4	24.4	263	14.3	8	211	3	11.5	14.9	551	31.7
Chicot	-1 400	5 557	-7.3	2.81	21.7	26.8	278	16.6	37	182	5	10.7	19.8	239	13.4
Clark	-1 100	7 907	-2.8	2.42	11.2	27.4	292	13.4	21	216	5	9.8	18.7	244	10.7
Clay	-1 100	7 504	-5.1	2.38	7.7	26.5	217	11.3	12	270	2	14.0	9.0	277	13.9
Cleburne	2 500	7 926	23.7	2.41	6.7	22.0	172	8.7	14	256	3	13.1	16.5	271	14.5
Cleveland	300	2 868	3.6	2.69	9.5	19.5	92	11.2	2	83	0	10.1	0.0	55	6.8
Columbia	-300	9 638	1.1	2.57	13.8	26.8	346	12.9	23	327	8	12.2	20.8	309	11.3

1. No spouse present. 2. Per 1,000 resident population estimated as of July 1 of the year shown. 3. Under 2,500 grams. 4. Deaths of infants under 1 year old. 5. Deaths of infants under 1 year old per 1,000 live births. 6. La Paz County included with Yuma County.

STATE County	Divorces, 1984		Physicians, active non–Federal, 1989		Hospitals, 1989			Nursing homes,[4] 1986		Serious crimes known to police, 1988			Education			
						Beds				Number			Public school enrollment[7]		Attainment,[8] 1980	
	Number	Rate[1]	Number[2]	Rate[3]	Number	Number	Rate[3]	Number	Beds	Total[5]	Violent[6]	Rate[3]	1986–1987	1980	Percent 12 yrs. or more	Percent 16 yrs. or more
	44	45	46	47	48	49	50	51	52	53	54	55	56	57	58	59
ALABAMA—Con.																
Washington	87	5.0	5	29	1	103	595	1	73	NA	NA	NA	4 069	4 040	46.5	5.5
Wilcox	37	2.4	4	29	1	32	230	1	75	67	33	551	3 057	3 360	41.6	9.5
Winston	157	7.0	9	42	1	47	221	3	297	222	13	1 060	4 587	4 749	42.9	5.2
ALASKA*	3 850	7.6	710	135	27	1 932	367	17	1 203	X	2 607	4 925	102 872	86 887	82.5	21.1
Aleutian Islands	1	0.1	NA	NA	NA	NA	NA	0	0	X	1	3 314	1 239	1 305	77.1	15.3
Aleutians East Borough	NA	NA	NA	NA	NA	NA	NA	NA	NA	X	0	0	NA	NA	NA	NA
Aleutians West Census Area	NA	NA	NA	NA	NA	NA	NA	NA	NA	NA	NA	NA	NA	NA	NA	NA
Anchorage	1 989	8.7	NA	NA	NA	NA	NA	2	456	12 534	1 122	5 765	39 785	36 008	88.3	23.6
Bethel	29	2.5	NA	NA	NA	NA	NA	0	0	292	178	7 797	3 206	3 361	45.9	13.7
Bristol Bay	0	0.0	NA	NA	NA	NA	NA	0	0	63	7	5 464	603	196	81.9	16.5
Dillingham	2	0.4	NA	NA	NA	NA	NA	0	0	NA	NA	NA	933	1 347	56.4	16.2
Fairbanks North Star	753	12.0	NA	NA	NA	NA	NA	2	155	2 529	261	3 688	13 155	10 285	86.6	22.0
Haines	0	0.0	NA	NA	NA	NA	NA	0	0	34	2	3 307	350	416	77.9	19.8
Juneau	229	9.6	NA	NA	NA	NA	NA	1	42	1 028	46	4 002	4 594	3 870	91.1	33.9
Kenai Peninsula	239	6.2	NA	NA	NA	NA	NA	2	82	1 090	53	6 630	8 262	5 801	82.0	16.2
Ketchikan Gateway	165	12.8	NA	NA	NA	NA	NA	2	91	NA	NA	NA	2 891	2 446	82.2	17.7
Kobuk	19	3.7	NA	NA	NA	NA	NA	0	0	NA	NA	NA	1 560	1 385	48.2	13.4
Kodiak Island	57	3.9	NA	NA	NA	NA	NA	1	19	604	54	8 809	2 250	1 932	78.3	17.7
Lake and Peninsula Borough	NA	NA	NA	NA	NA	NA	NA	NA	NA	NA	NA	NA	NA	NA	NA	NA
Matanuska-Susitna	180	6.1	NA	NA	NA	NA	NA	2	186	201	23	5 720	8 930	4 133	81.4	17.7
Nome	22	3.1	NA	NA	NA	NA	NA	1	6	287	21	10 563	2 000	1 839	54.4	13.7
North Slope	6	1.3	NA	NA	NA	NA	NA	0	0	294	55	6 379	1 149	1 034	56.4	12.6
Northwest Arctic Borough	NA	NA	NA	NA	NA	NA	NA	NA	NA	331	28	14 790	NA	NA	NA	NA
Prince of Wales-Outer Ketchikan	0	0.0	NA	NA	NA	NA	NA	0	0	241	84	14 597	905	893	69.1	10.0
Sitka	61	8.1	NA	NA	NA	NA	NA	1	130	NA	NA	NA	1 752	1 756	81.1	21.2
Skagway-Yakutat-Angoon	0	0.0	NA	NA	NA	NA	NA	0	0	38	1	6 485	902	811	70.9	14.7
Southeast Fairbanks	1	0.2	NA	NA	NA	NA	NA	0	0	NA	NA	NA	1 519	1 323	79.6	15.3
Valdez-Cordova	53	5.8	NA	NA	NA	NA	NA	1	8	122	3	5 596	1 880	1 788	80.3	15.6
Wade Hampton	0	0.0	NA	NA	NA	NA	NA	0	0	NA	NA	NA	1 577	1 620	34.6	7.7
Wrangell-Petersburg	44	6.9	NA	NA	NA	NA	NA	2	28	327	53	6 717	1 303	1 312	77.1	17.7
Yukon-Koyukuk	0	0.0	NA	NA	NA	NA	NA	0	0	NA	NA	NA	2 127	2 026	66.9	13.4
ARIZONA	20 009	6.5	6 759	190	94	13 581	381	166	13 410	X	20 864	7 498	609 411	524 962	72.4	17.4
Apache	97	1.8	58	94	4	172	277	2	145	508	62	817	13 160	13 847	49.3	10.4
Cochise	701	7.5	68	67	6	332	327	9	323	4 010	245	3 991	55 848	19 467	68.8	13.8
Coconino	429	5.2	144	150	4	251	261	1	80	5 700	542	6 239	17 638	16 117	74.4	23.2
Gila	289	7.5	40	98	4	234	575	1	22	748	87	1 849	7 364	8 008	61.7	7.8
Graham	152	6.3	12	49	1	36	148	2	134	613	85	2 536	5 064	5 421	60.5	10.0
Greenlee	32	3.1	1	13	0	0	0	0	0	111	15	2 358	2 079	3 015	68.3	9.9
La Paz	NA	NA	(9)	(9)	(9)	(9)	(9)			861	151	5 758	2 477	0	0.0	0.0
Maricopa	11 626	6.6	4 187	201	41	8 208	395	102	8 247	155 742	12 845	7 760	320 411	279 863	75.0	18.3
Mohave	482	7.0	80	92	3	199	230	5	390	5 446	368	6 589	12 036	9 646	69.1	8.8
Navajo	273	3.9	73	96	5	183	242	1	38	2 551	221	3 432	15 969	17 740	59.7	11.2
Pima	3 747	6.5	1 778	275	16	2 708	420	23	2 678	62 325	4 475	9 825	96 300	95 851	74.6	20.7
Pinal	699	7.2	61	56	3	324	297	7	482	6 452	749	5 915	22 070	20 725	55.0	9.3
Santa Cruz	97	4.3	21	85	1	73	294	0	0	1 701	108	7 520	6 033	5 355	54.0	13.2
Yavapai	629	7.7	116	118	3	547	555	9	649	4 377	303	4 610	14 266	11 184	73.9	16.2
Yuma	756	7.9	[9]120	[9]110	[9]3	[9]314	[9]288	4	222	5 546	593	9 201	18 696	18 723	61.6	10.9
ARKANSAS	15 337	6.5	3 492	145	99	12 941	538	271	22 678	101 903	10 200	4 207	429 260	459 251	55.5	10.8
Arkansas	135	5.7	16	72	2	133	599	5	399	476	15	2 059	4 272	4 660	48.8	8.1
Ashley	210	7.9	14	54	1	38	148	4	284	787	89	2 985	5 182	6 169	52.3	7.7
Baxter	183	6.2	39	124	1	117	371	4	352	425	39	1 361	4 667	4 354	57.3	9.0
Benton	520	6.1	98	99	4	334	338	11	799	2 561	70	2 736	14 454	14 637	61.8	11.8
Boone	218	7.9	40	138	1	148	510	3	309	575	27	1 990	5 261	5 057	59.7	9.8
Bradley	59	4.4	5	39	1	49	386	2	204	130	13	994	2 515	2 831	46.6	8.0
Calhoun	34	5.6	2	33	0	0	0	1	74	6	0	97	897	1 227	47.3	4.1
Carroll	127	7.3	16	86	2	67	360	3	170	668	78	3 600	2 941	2 827	57.1	9.8
Chicot	100	5.6	15	91	2	83	506	1	85	483	49	2 818	3 942	4 097	41.1	6.8
Clark	122	5.3	13	60	1	57	265	3	249	310	35	1 377	3 683	3 961	55.9	15.8
Clay	91	4.6	5	26	2	75	395	3	262	390	21	1 982	3 243	3 973	38.0	4.7
Cleburne	108	5.8	15	75	1	49	246	5	267	332	6	1 670	3 016	3 259	49.5	7.2
Cleveland	20	2.5	3	37	0	0	0	1	67	35	4	416	1 459	1 752	45.6	6.0
Columbia	147	5.4	18	68	1	86	323	3	284	326	44	1 195	5 017	5 640	52.6	9.8

1. Per 1,000 resident population estimated as of July 1 of the year shown. 2. As of end of year. 3. Per 100,000 resident population as of July 1 of the year shown. 4. Preliminary. Covers nursing homes with 3 or more beds. 5. Data for serious crimes have not been adjusted for underreporting, this may affect comparability between geographic areas or over time. 6. Includes murder and nonnegligent manslaughter, forcible rape, robbery, and aggravated assault. 7. The 1986–1987 data are based on administrative reports obtained by the U.S. National Center for Education Statistics. The 1980 data are based on the 1980 Census of Population and Housing. 8. Persons 25 years old or older. 9. La Paz County included with Yuma County.

STATE / County	Education (cont'd): Local government expenditures for education,[1] 1982: Total (Mil dol)	Education (cont'd): Local government expenditures for education,[1] 1982: Per capita (Dollars)	Social Security Program December 1988: Beneficiaries: Total	Social Security Program December 1988: Beneficiaries: Rate[2]	Social Security Program December 1988: Payments ($1,000)	Supplemental Security Income Program recipients June 1986	Money income: Per capita[3]: 1987 Income, (Dollars)	Money income: Per capita[3]: 1979: Current dollars	Money income: Per capita[3]: 1979: Constant 1987 dollars	Money income: Median household income 1979 (Dollars)	Money income: Percent below poverty level, 1979: Persons	Money income: Percent below poverty level, 1979: Families	Housing units, 1990: Total	Housing units, 1990: Percent change, 1980–1990
	60	61	62	63	64	65	66	67	68	69	70	71	72	73
ALABAMA—Con.														
Washington	8.0	460	2 795	162.5	1 083	844	7 120	4 578	7 163	12 745	23.5	19.4	6 625	12.0
Wilcox	5.5	366	3 015	215.4	968	1 522	5 954	3 624	5 670	8 261	45.3	36.2	5 119	1.6
Winston	7.8	359	4 220	197.2	1 628	1 048	8 032	5 219	8 166	11 995	18.2	15.6	10 254	17.9
ALASKA*	469.6	1 055	30 576	58.3	14 457	3 605	13 263	10 193	15 949	25 414	10.7	8.6	232 608	42.9
Aleutian Islands	5.6	714	165	NA	73	20	12 780	10 540	16 492	19 389	12.4	9.6	NA	NA
Aleutians East Borough	NA	NA	X	X	X	NA	16 714	NA	NA	NA	NA	NA	693	NA
Aleutians West Census Area	NA	NA	NA	NA	NA	NA	NA	NA	NA	NA	NA	NA	2 051	NA
Anchorage	148.9	729	10 895	49.9	5 323	1 094	15 386	11 339	17 742	27 375	7.4	6.1	94 153	33.8
Bethel	0.0	0	NA	NA	NA	NA	6 660	4 917	7 694	13 656	31.3	28.3	4 362	32.3
Bristol Bay	3.5	2 938	155	110.7	82	12	18 557	14 948	23 389	33 516	4.1	0.0	596	61.5
Dillingham	7.4	1 564	380	63.3	146	90	9 807	7 462	11 676	18 977	22.7	24.2	1 691	-13.4
Fairbanks North Star	66.6	1 130	3 740	53.4	1 883	306	11 986	9 823	15 370	23 647	9.5	8.1	31 823	40.1
Haines	3.6	1 979	265	155.9	126	12	11 740	8 407	13 154	20 893	14.0	10.0	1 112	49.7
Juneau	23.4	1 022	1 840	70.0	940	114	16 186	12 421	19 435	30 834	4.1	3.3	10 638	38.9
Kenai Peninsula	37.5	1 172	2 975	72.6	1 412	202	11 966	9 636	15 077	23 660	11.7	8.8	19 364	64.9
Ketchikan Gateway	12.3	985	1 210	100.8	658	76	14 212	10 829	16 944	27 015	7.4	5.6	5 463	23.3
Kobuk	0.0	0	0	0.0	NA	122	NA	5 171	8 091	17 756	27.0	24.5	NA	NA
Kodiak Island	18.1	1 447	595	43.1	292	56	12 552	10 415	16 296	26 421	10.6	7.5	4 885	37.3
Lake and Peninsula Borough	NA	NA	0	0.0	X	NA	8 954	NA	NA	NA	NA	NA	991	NA
Matanuska-Susitna	32.8	1 549	2 380	61.3	1 111	120	10 701	8 682	13 585	23 483	13.8	11.0	20 953	107.5
Nome	7.6	1 157	600	76.9	205	162	7 648	5 496	8 600	14 550	28.4	25.0	3 684	41.3
North Slope	52.9	1 259	310	57.4	136	50	15 125	11 006	17 221	31 378	11.2	10.8	2 153	85.9
Northwest Arctic Borough	NA	NA	440	72.1	144	NA	7 633	NA	NA	NA	NA	NA	1 998	NA
Prince of Wales-Outer Ketchikan	3.3	786	280	51.9	125	26	12 279	8 327	13 029	21 947	11.0	10.8	2 543	83.6
Sitka	8.8	1 127	585	75.0	311	26	13 602	10 744	16 811	31 133	4.9	4.3	3 222	19.6
Skagway-Yakutat-Angoon	4.7	1 348	295	77.6	132	38	10 713	8 179	12 798	21 396	13.1	10.0	2 102	35.4
Southeast Fairbanks	0.0	0	305	46.9	129	62	8 927	6 751	10 563	15 903	16.5	13.6	3 149	28.5
Valdez-Cordova	17.1	1 904	595	67.6	294	100	14 984	11 638	18 210	27 469	12.1	7.9	5 196	25.4
Wade Hampton	4.0	840	465	83.0	113	182	4 724	3 203	5 012	11 373	38.1	36.3	1 882	60.4
Wrangell-Petersburg	7.3	1 106	590	85.5	310	20	13 206	10 087	15 783	24 403	6.5	5.4	3 005	27.2
Yukon-Koyukuk	4.2	520	NA	NA	NA	NA	8 673	7 137	11 167	12 371	29.3	25.8	4 899	53.5
ARIZONA	1 313.2	453	551 690	158.2	272 937	35 076	11 521	7 042	11 019	16 448	13.2	9.5	1 659 430	49.4
Apache	54.4	1 035	5 950	96.7	1 856	2 784	4 824	3 338	5 223	11 057	40.0	35.3	26 731	41.6
Cochise	41.2	461	15 300	152.4	6 783	1 154	9 369	5 738	8 978	13 668	14.9	11.8	40 238	23.6
Coconino	43.6	563	10 510	111.7	4 770	1 514	9 002	5 631	8 811	15 962	20.4	15.2	42 914	41.8
Gila	25.4	642	9 940	244.8	4 938	526	7 981	5 511	8 623	13 828	16.2	12.8	22 961	22.4
Graham	10.7	458	4 235	173.6	1 965	404	6 687	4 623	7 234	12 479	19.3	15.2	9 112	23.1
Greenlee	13.3	1 133	1 305	165.2	666	62	8 004	6 567	10 275	21 396	8.8	6.8	3 582	-17.5
La Paz	NA	NA	2 540	177.6	1 145	NA	8 263	5 063	7 922	0	0.0	0.0	10 182	NA
Maricopa	672.5	417	301 660	148.6	154 041	15 484	12 780	7 717	12 075	17 728	10.5	7.5	952 041	55.9
Mohave	29.7	478	22 395	268.5	11 079	496	9 994	6 673	10 441	14 160	11.2	8.7	50 822	76.4
Navajo	51.5	756	8 365	111.4	3 488	1 756	6 684	4 485	7 018	13 593	29.7	24.1	38 967	37.2
Pima	226.5	400	104 435	164.2	52 032	6 656	11 499	7 147	11 183	15 796	13.0	9.1	298 207	36.4
Pinal	53.6	556	19 555	182.4	9 027	1 834	8 042	5 313	8 313	14 478	18.2	14.3	52 732	54.7
Santa Cruz	15.1	710	4 070	166.8	1 702	596	9 082	5 447	8 523	14 575	18.1	13.4	9 595	49.9
Yavapai	30.2	395	25 695	269.1	12 500	792	9 838	6 450	10 092	13 076	13.0	9.4	54 805	62.3
Yuma	45.5	477	15 085	162.2	6 707	894	8 810	5 782	9 047	13 589	16.0	12.3	46 541	24.1
ARKANSAS	807.8	350	458 160	191.3	193 941	73 817	9 061	5 613	8 783	12 214	19.0	14.9	1 000 667	11.4
Arkansas	7.8	323	4 740	209.7	2 097	870	8 885	6 054	9 473	12 189	19.6	14.4	9 575	-3.0
Ashley	10.9	408	4 845	187.1	2 058	1 024	8 172	5 203	8 141	12 704	20.9	17.8	9 820	0.5
Baxter	7.5	266	10 755	345.8	5 110	466	9 859	5 719	8 949	11 432	12.1	9.7	15 549	20.3
Benton	24.9	311	21 130	221.0	9 882	1 046	10 498	6 100	9 545	13 930	11.1	8.8	41 444	28.7
Boone	8.3	310	6 685	232.9	2 766	736	8 868	5 434	8 503	11 336	17.3	13.7	12 380	15.8
Bradley	5.0	368	3 005	232.9	1 275	548	7 408	4 563	7 140	10 024	26.2	21.8	5 092	-8.9
Calhoun	2.4	398	1 035	172.5	429	224	6 600	4 257	6 661	9 822	24.7	20.0	2 437	2.7
Carroll	4.4	267	4 090	222.3	1 718	340	8 696	5 238	8 196	10 898	18.5	14.9	8 740	19.0
Chicot	8.2	454	3 415	204.5	1 224	1 276	5 859	4 091	6 401	7 455	40.0	33.0	6 191	-6.0
Clark	6.8	297	4 665	214.0	1 961	758	8 237	5 546	8 678	11 478	18.1	13.7	8 807	-0.2
Clay	6.5	324	5 110	266.1	1 968	1 012	7 984	4 794	7 501	9 363	22.5	19.4	8 362	-3.8
Cleburne	5.4	307	4 980	252.8	2 068	526	8 425	5 093	7 969	10 891	20.1	17.4	10 802	25.8
Cleveland	2.8	355	1 460	178.0	563	288	7 372	4 833	7 562	11 108	17.5	13.3	3 322	7.9
Columbia	9.5	350	5 770	215.3	2 459	1 132	9 048	5 526	8 647	11 354	22.8	17.1	10 690	2.3

1. Elementary and secondary. 2. Per 1,000 resident population estimated as of July 1 of the year shown. 3. Based on the resident population estimated as of July 1, 1988 for 1987 data and enumerated as of April 1, 1980 for 1979 data.

STATE County	Housing units, 1990 (cont'd): Occupied units: Total	Owner occupied: Percent	Owner occupied: Median value (Dollars)	Median rent (Dollars)	Civilian labor force, 1990: Total	Percent change, 1989–1990	Unemployment: Total	Unemployment: Rate[1]	Private nonfarm establishments, 1988: Number	Net change, 1987–1988	Employment[2]: Total	Percent change, 1987–1988	Manu-facturing	Retail trade
	74	75	76	77	78	79	80	81	82	83	84	85	86	87
ALABAMA—Con.														
Washington	5 709	87.2	34 300	112	6 442	2.5	660	10.2	241	8	3 038	1.9	0	398
Wilcox	4 415	77.1	34 000	99	4 195	0.2	483	11.5	261	2	1 644	0.2	632	353
Winston	8 544	79.9	37 700	140	10 405	-1.1	1 161	11.2	473	4	7 238	6.2	4 722	849
ALASKA*	188 915	56.1	94 400	503	257 000	1.6	18 000	6.9	X	X	134 432	-2.8	10 167	33 728
Aleutian Islands	NA	NA	NA	NA	2 584	-0.6	32	1.2	X	X	X	X	X	X
Aleutians East Borough	533	61.4	85 700	518	920	-1.1	9	1.0	X	X	X	X	X	X
Aleutians West Census Area	1 845	17.9	80 100	428	NA	NA	NA	NA	NA	NA	NA	NA	NA	NA
Anchorage	82 702	52.8	109 700	528	117 230	2.6	6 141	5.2	6 569	-113	73 502	-6.0	1 709	17 906
Bethel	3 605	58.8	51 900	460	5 029	-0.2	312	6.2	179	-5	1 560	-2.7	0	310
Bristol Bay	407	48.6	102 000	464	505	-0.6	24	4.8	56	3	300	-4.2	75	61
Dillingham	1 215	63.2	63 300	518	2 373	-0.3	120	5.1	X	X	X	X	X	X
Fairbanks North Star	26 693	49.0	87 300	471	30 922	-0.3	2 651	8.6	1 827	-41	15 046	-2.0	752	4 749
Haines	791	65.0	81 000	405	878	0.2	72	8.2	91	3	480	35.2	0	151
Juneau	9 902	58.2	113 500	587	16 093	0.9	761	4.7	820	-3	6 241	1.2	312	1 855
Kenai Peninsula	14 250	67.9	85 100	410	18 961	-1.2	2 065	10.9	1 133	-24	6 890	-1.3	754	1 900
Ketchikan Gateway	5 030	56.0	112 600	533	6 826	1.6	543	8.0	476	6	4 376	-5.9	1 059	946
Kobuk	NA	NA	NA	NA	NA	NA	NA	NA	NA	NA	NA	NA	NA	NA
Kodiak Island	4 083	50.0	111 500	602	6 777	-2.5	339	5.0	343	4	3 871	25.6	1 783	780
Lake and Peninsula Borough	509	69.5	67 100	417	NA	NA	NA	NA	X	X	X	X	X	X
Matanuska-Susitna	13 394	73.3	71 500	430	15 649	6.3	1 912	12.2	705	-16	3 786	-9.8	69	1 412
Nome	2 371	56.8	56 700	546	3 069	1.8	272	8.9	146	-6	1 284	18.2	0	336
North Slope	1 673	40.0	80 700	600	2 999	1.7	107	3.6	74	-7	884	7.0	0	339
Northwest Arctic Borough	1 526	57.9	62 800	627	2 237	5.9	280	12.5	NA	NA	NA	NA	NA	NA
Prince of Wales-Outer Ketchikan	2 061	60.5	63 300	329	2 794	0.0	294	10.5	100	12	1 079	20.8	636	194
Sitka	2 939	55.9	120 000	520	4 213	0.9	219	5.2	302	-29	2 155	-13.2	0	548
Skagway-Yakutat-Angoon	1 422	54.2	65 200	306	1 798	1.6	237	13.2	128	5	728	58.6	0	246
Southeast Fairbanks	1 909	60.8	54 900	389	2 058	1.3	251	12.2	110	-10	480	-4.6	15	140
Valdez-Cordova	3 425	64.5	97 100	457	4 773	1.9	532	11.1	275	10	1 683	-3.7	194	411
Wade Hampton	1 368	67.9	42 400	359	1 700	1.0	170	10.0	54	0	323	17.0	0	197
Wrangell-Petersburg	2 514	66.7	91 700	422	3 721	-0.2	294	7.9	224	-2	1 722	42.3	768	418
Yukon-Koyukuk	2 748	71.1	31 800	279	2 891	-1.5	364	12.6	153	-6	1 298	54.5	0	327
ARIZONA	1 368 843	64.2	80 100	370	1 726 000	1.1	92 000	5.3	X	X	1 174 821	3.3	183 427	X
Apache	15 981	73.2	19 400	162	14 851	-1.8	2 240	15.1	429	1	5 587	0.4	746	1 578
Cochise	34 546	63.6	60 600	287	36 070	2.3	2 378	6.6	1 758	61	15 260	4.3	1 398	5 102
Coconino	29 918	60.5	82 800	371	45 166	3.0	3 102	6.9	2 208	33	24 288	6.2	2 477	8 834
Gila	15 438	77.4	58 300	246	13 145	4.9	1 186	9.0	845	19	8 628	14.1	0	2 315
Graham	7 930	73.7	51 300	221	8 523	0.3	592	6.9	398	19	3 088	13.2	209	1 420
Greenlee	2 809	49.7	40 900	162	3 022	7.9	233	7.7	94	0	0	0.0	0	230
La Paz	5 348	72.5	57 000	259	5 555	-5.7	406	7.3	275	10	1 782	10.1	102	925
Maricopa	807 560	63.3	85 300	394	1 074 542	1.1	46 422	4.3	53 030	513	802 077	3.1	133 471	176 787
Mohave	36 801	72.1	75 600	375	37 511	10.2	2 225	5.9	2 183	136	18 885	11.3	3 116	6 181
Navajo	22 189	74.5	51 900	213	27 533	2.2	3 024	11.0	1 244	-1	11 572	7.0	1 378	3 683
Pima	261 792	60.9	76 500	338	313 679	-0.2	12 924	4.1	15 466	181	209 786	2.6	31 618	52 459
Pinal	39 154	72.0	53 200	283	38 514	-3.5	2 862	7.4	1 665	46	17 440	-5.5	2 819	5 442
Santa Cruz	8 808	66.0	71 500	280	11 813	2.1	1 720	14.6	900	82	7 962	4.9	1 008	2 734
Yavapai	44 778	72.1	84 500	342	40 492	4.0	1 940	4.8	3 000	136	22 448	7.5	2 215	7 407
Yuma	35 791	66.0	64 000	336	55 587	3.4	10 747	19.3	1 885	-5	22 502	1.1	1 725	7 337
ARKANSAS	891 179	69.6	46 300	230	1 133 000	-0.2	78 000	6.9	X	X	690 943	3.3	212 363	147 639
Arkansas	8 389	67.0	40 600	179	10 580	-1.7	521	4.9	619	-6	7 196	7.0	2 577	1 214
Ashley	8 890	77.0	39 200	182	11 353	-0.9	694	6.1	411	-11	7 013	1.8	4 124	908
Baxter	13 486	80.5	51 800	240	11 195	-2.5	742	6.6	819	7	8 339	-3.0	3 241	1 751
Benton	37 555	73.1	58 700	286	53 857	1.9	1 890	3.5	1 917	46	34 730	3.4	11 814	9 150
Boone	11 131	76.1	45 900	230	14 918	-1.9	829	5.6	749	15	12 240	34.9	3 131	1 750
Bradley	4 545	74.9	30 500	132	5 063	-3.0	468	9.2	271	5	2 812	-4.7	1 345	470
Calhoun	2 185	81.2	34 400	177	4 536	-10.4	277	6.1	88	-5	548	2.8	205	91
Carroll	7 550	75.6	47 700	227	10 523	0.7	630	6.0	563	-12	5 477	-1.3	2 701	933
Chicot	5 557	69.2	28 700	140	5 702	-3.1	633	11.1	294	-6	2 210	4.6	0	630
Clark	7 907	68.8	40 000	185	9 673	1.9	569	5.9	528	7	5 158	2.2	1 560	1 440
Clay	7 504	74.0	28 900	149	9 556	4.4	596	6.2	352	2	3 648	4.7	1 788	616
Cleburne	7 926	81.3	50 700	200	8 979	4.2	675	7.5	403	-1	3 576	6.7	1 349	845
Cleveland	2 868	83.1	33 900	129	3 673	4.0	238	6.5	83	4	521	13.5	140	85
Columbia	9 638	71.9	39 200	172	12 453	-2.3	765	6.1	622	0	7 286	6.5	2 962	1 501

1. Percent of total civilian labor force. 2. For week including March 12. Excludes government employees, self-employed persons, farm workers, domestic service workers, railroad employees subject to the Railroad Retirement Act, and employees on oceanborne vessels or in foreign countries.

STATE / County	Private nonfarm establishments, 1988 (cont'd) — Employment[1] (cont'd) — Finance, insurance, and real estate	Employment[1] (cont'd) — Services	Annual payroll — Total (Mil dol)	Annual payroll — Average per employee (Dollars)	Personal income, 1989 — Total (Mil dol)	Percent change, 1988–1989	Wages and salaries[2] (Mil dol)	Proprietor's income (Mil dol)	Dividends, interest, & rent (Mil dol)	Transfer payments (Mil dol)	Per capita[3] — Dollars	Per capita[3] — Rank	Earnings, 1989 — Total (Mil dol)	Percent by selected industries — Farm	Percent by selected industries — Goods-related[4] — Total
	88	89	90	91	92	93	94	95	96	97	98	99	100	101	102
ALABAMA—Con.															
Washington	86	149	75	24 626	185	3.3	135	19	20	37	10 694	2 741	154	5.6	NA
Wilcox	88	288	19	11 309	131	1.0	89	21	17	38	9 448	2 966	110	8.9	NA
Winston	221	412	112	15 458	260	11.1	148	57	33	50	12 220	2 221	205	15.6	45.1
ALASKA*	9 267	39 970	3 651	X	11 254	12.4	8 043	1 410	1 427	1 625	21 375	X	9 452	0.1	21.1
Aleutian Islands	X	X	X	X	0	0.0	0	0	0	0	0	0	NA	0.0	0.0
Aleutians East Borough	X	X	X	X	40	18.6	36	3	2	4	22 255	86	40	0.0	NA
Aleutians West Census Area	NA	NA	NA	NA	147	6.8	156	14	9	11	21 482	112	170	0.6	NA
Anchorage	6 438	24 014	2 062	28 056	5 313	12.1	3 793	612	665	659	24 773	42	4 405	0.0	19.6
Bethel	68	836	25	16 193	172	9.8	107	12	12	49	12 820	1 990	119	0.0	5.6
Bristol Bay	0	9	11	36 013	44	17.9	46	11	3	4	29 755	16	58	0.0	NA
Dillingham	X	X	X	X	114	9.7	64	29	11	17	18 171	276	94	0.0	27.5
Fairbanks North Star	970	4 817	342	22 714	1 326	11.2	969	148	186	210	18 507	249	1 116	0.2	14.2
Haines	0	73	10	20 121	63	14.3	44	6	8	7	37 548	1	50	0.0	60.2
Juneau	372	2 234	144	23 008	674	10.3	428	87	99	96	25 075	39	515	NA	8.1
Kenai Peninsula	252	2 075	178	25 804	797	20.1	458	124	114	124	19 453	196	583	0.2	32.1
Ketchikan Gateway	195	1 126	126	28 721	316	12.3	232	32	47	42	26 530	26	264	0.0	31.7
Kobuk	NA	NA	NA	NA	0	0.0	0	0	0	0	0	0	0	0.0	0.0
Kodiak Island	77	650	73	18 782	284	16.8	197	73	35	32	20 537	144	271	0.0	18.1
Lake and Peninsula Borough	X	X	X	X	0	0.0	0	0	0	0	0	0	0	0.0	0.0
Matanuska-Susitna	187	1 069	79	20 749	581	12.6	179	65	84	111	14 565	1 180	243	2.7	10.5
Nome	50	501	30	23 156	120	8.8	83	7	9	31	15 103	941	89	0.0	NA
North Slope	0	50	27	30 026	126	17.8	396	5	10	18	22 219	87	401	0.0	NA
Northwest Arctic Borough	NA	NA	NA	NA	94	12.5	58	10	9	24	14 711	1 121	68	0.0	NA
Prince of Wales-Outer Ketchikan	0	46	30	27 580	95	11.8	68	9	8	16	16 986	441	76	0.0	44.5
Sitka	97	550	52	24 006	190	11.2	120	40	30	24	23 995	52	161	0.0	27.2
Skagway-Yakutat-Angoon	0	128	16	21 794	84	14.8	56	13	10	15	21 207	120	68	0.0	NA
Southeast Fairbanks	0	137	7	14 096	84	5.2	53	4	9	18	12 956	1 925	57	0.0	3.9
Valdez-Cordova	46	447	54	31 959	247	21.3	312	41	25	31	27 727	21	352	0.0	7.7
Wade Hampton	0	61	6	17 412	56	12.4	32	7	2	22	9 548	2 953	40	0.0	NA
Wrangell-Petersburg	35	198	48	27 814	162	3.0	77	49	24	21	22 862	73	125	0.0	27.5
Yukon-Koyukuk	74	147	49	37 463	125	6.6	79	7	16	39	13 022	1 898	87	0.0	15.0
ARIZONA	90 145	356 933	22 327	X	56 353	7.6	35 322	3 942	10 987	8 637	15 829	X	39 264	1.5	23.9
Apache	325	1 745	88	15 732	459	8.8	334	35	26	138	7 406	3 091	369	4.9	14.5
Cochise	847	5 081	211	13 806	1 174	6.0	679	83	166	290	11 564	2 481	762	3.1	7.9
Coconino	660	7 221	375	15 432	1 150	5.2	742	94	173	192	11 947	2 343	837	1.7	16.4
Gila	250	1 633	178	20 656	459	8.5	252	35	100	128	11 272	2 571	287	1.2	43.7
Graham	114	793	34	10 858	251	7.7	102	37	34	65	10 312	2 834	139	15.0	7.5
Greenlee	0	102	D	D	94	5.7	86	6	9	18	12 512	2 109	92	1.5	74.5
La Paz	103	247	22	12 206	183	5.7	79	16	27	29	12 812	1 994	95	19.4	16.0
Maricopa	70 083	243 566	16 228	20 232	36 804	7.8	24 296	2 376	7 099	4 768	17 705	335	26 672	0.8	24.4
Mohave	936	4 618	274	14 513	1 043	10.3	443	89	240	258	12 046	2 314	532	1.1	24.4
Navajo	407	2 649	204	17 602	701	4.4	448	57	73	170	9 261	2 983	505	2.3	26.1
Pima	12 837	71 527	3 565	16 995	9 814	7.3	5 657	648	2 143	1 707	15 203	908	6 305	0.4	25.3
Pinal	714	3 598	307	17 590	1 316	7.8	728	175	209	280	12 064	2 305	903	14.4	30.6
Santa Cruz	408	1 142	108	13 596	319	10.4	194	29	58	54	12 845	1 981	223	2.1	13.9
Yavapai	1 259	6 439	320	14 238	1 383	10.6	505	137	436	318	14 020	1 428	642	1.8	24.7
Yuma	969	6 541	315	14 001	1 204	2.3	778	124	194	222	12 725	2 024	902	11.4	9.9
ARKANSAS	35 647	159 295	11 281	X	31 261	7.1	17 991	3 984	4 899	6 076	13 000	X	21 975	6.9	29.5
Arkansas	338	1 036	114	15 840	308	2.3	168	53	62	61	13 887	1 484	221	14.1	NA
Ashley	294	853	158	22 486	323	5.2	209	43	33	60	12 593	2 075	253	6.5	NA
Baxter	331	1 981	117	14 026	445	9.3	171	50	152	116	14 130	1 379	221	4.4	38.0
Benton	1 536	5 353	637	18 350	1 458	9.8	851	162	335	239	14 770	1 096	1 012	6.6	36.7
Boone	309	1 722	191	15 609	378	8.8	217	64	73	74	13 054	1 888	280	7.0	27.3
Bradley	128	344	39	13 813	158	12.0	75	28	20	41	12 478	2 127	104	9.3	45.4
Calhoun	0	56	7	13 664	56	3.5	102	8	6	14	9 348	2 974	110	1.1	NA
Carroll	146	941	71	13 012	243	9.9	100	48	58	45	13 105	1 861	149	16.4	32.5
Chicot	125	369	26	11 611	155	0.1	61	30	22	45	9 485	2 961	91	22.2	15.3
Clark	217	1 210	67	13 006	255	7.4	124	33	40	68	11 875	2 366	157	4.7	26.8
Clay	107	372	47	12 968	222	2.2	84	40	37	56	11 693	2 444	124	16.5	31.2
Cleburne	176	753	48	13 545	228	10.2	81	34	53	56	11 475	2 510	115	12.1	35.8
Cleveland	0	74	6	10 827	100	7.8	15	19	10	18	12 107	2 286	34	35.0	15.3
Columbia	230	1 439	119	16 329	350	8.4	190	43	63	69	13 146	1 841	233	6.1	48.6

1. For week including March 12. Excludes government employees, self-employed persons, farm workers, domestic service workers, railroad employees subject to the Railroad Retirement Act, and employees on oceanborne vessels or in foreign countries. 2. Includes other labor income. 3. Based on the resident population estimated as of July 1 of the year shown. 4. Covers mining, construction, and manufacturing.

STATE County	Earnings, 1989 (cont'd)						Agriculture, 1987									
	Percent by selected industries (cont'd)						Farms			Farm operators, percent		Land in farms				
	Goods-related[1]	Service-related & other[2]						Percent with						Acres		
	Manu-facturing	Total	Retail trade	Finance, insur-ance, & real estate	Services	Govern-ment	Number	Less than 50 acres	500 acres and over	Whose principal occu-pation is farming	Residing on farm operated	Acreage (1,000)	Percent change, 1982–1987	Average size of farm	Total irrigated (1,000)	Total cropland (1,000)
	103	104	105	106	107	108	109	110	111	112	113	114	115	116	117	118
ALABAMA—Con.																
Washington	51.0	NA	3.4	1.3	17.3	9.4	416	32.7	9.6	30.0	70.7	87	-10.8	208	0	20
Wilcox	49.6	23.0	5.5	1.6	11.1	13.4	322	29.5	22.4	32.3	54.0	157	-17.0	487	D	46
Winston	40.6	28.8	6.6	2.1	8.0	10.5	591	40.6	2.5	38.2	78.2	58	-8.7	98	D	24
ALASKA*	5.6	48.3	8.2	3.4	18.5	30.5	574	36.4	16.7	43.2	73.9	1 027	-22.4	1 789	2	66
Aleutian Islands	0.0	0.0	0.0	0.0	0.0	0.0	27	25.9	70.4	37.0	29.6	727	-5.0	26 911	D	D
Aleutians East Borough	64.3	NA	2.6	0.8	1.6	16.9	NA	NA	NA	NA	NA	NA	NA	NA	NA	NA
Aleutians West Census Area	21.5	20.7	2.2	1.5	2.6	50.4	NA	NA	NA	NA	NA	NA	NA	NA	NA	NA
Anchorage	1.4	52.8	9.6	4.7	22.6	27.6	245	38.8	7.8	45.3	75.1	59	-76.9	242	1	17
Bethel	3.3	40.0	5.7	3.6	16.8	54.4	NA	NA	NA	NA	NA	NA	NA	NA	NA	NA
Bristol Bay	28.3	NA	3.3	NA	1.7	31.4	NA	NA	NA	NA	NA	NA	NA	NA	NA	NA
Dillingham	23.6	54.2	4.3	2.0	16.0	18.3	NA	NA	NA	NA	NA	NA	NA	NA	NA	NA
Fairbanks North Star	2.0	42.5	9.1	2.4	20.2	43.2	175	28.6	20.0	49.7	73.7	155	-24.3	885	1	43
Haines	55.5	29.7	6.3	1.5	7.0	10.0	NA	NA	NA	NA	NA	NA	NA	NA	NA	NA
Juneau	2.5	40.4	8.0	4.4	18.1	51.4	8	87.5	0.0	25.0	100.0	0	68.5	27	D	D
Kenai Peninsula	11.3	47.8	6.8	1.3	16.5	19.9	119	42.0	19.3	31.9	79.8	86	-12.6	720	D	5
Ketchikan Gateway	24.1	43.5	9.4	2.9	15.6	24.8	NA	NA	NA	NA	NA	NA	NA	NA	NA	NA
Kobuk	0.0	0.0	0.0	0.0	0.0	0.0	NA	NA	NA	NA	NA	NA	NA	NA	NA	NA
Kodiak Island	13.4	58.4	6.4	1.1	12.3	23.5	NA	NA	NA	NA	NA	NA	NA	NA	NA	NA
Lake and Peninsula Borough	0.0	0.0	0.0	0.0	0.0	0.0	NA	NA	NA	NA	NA	NA	NA	NA	NA	NA
Matanuska-Susitna	0.3	54.6	13.5	2.4	19.5	32.2	NA	NA	NA	NA	NA	NA	NA	NA	NA	NA
Nome	NA	NA	7.1	2.1	19.5	43.5	NA	NA	NA	NA	NA	NA	NA	NA	NA	NA
North Slope	NA	NA	3.8	1.5	12.8	19.3	NA	NA	NA	NA	NA	NA	NA	NA	NA	NA
Northwest Arctic Borough	0.0	NA	7.4	4.8	19.2	39.5	NA	NA	NA	NA	NA	NA	NA	NA	NA	NA
Prince of Wales-Outer Ketchikan	40.3	31.5	6.9	2.0	6.1	24.0	NA	NA	NA	NA	NA	NA	NA	NA	NA	NA
Sitka	20.0	49.1	6.6	1.6	16.7	23.7	NA	NA	NA	NA	NA	NA	NA	NA	NA	NA
Skagway-Yakutat-Angoon	25.0	NA	5.6	NA	6.7	19.8	NA	NA	NA	NA	NA	NA	NA	NA	NA	NA
Southeast Fairbanks	0.5	23.2	6.1	0.9	11.2	72.8	NA	NA	NA	NA	NA	NA	NA	NA	NA	NA
Valdez-Cordova	6.0	77.9	3.2	1.2	7.9	14.4	NA	NA	NA	NA	NA	NA	NA	NA	NA	NA
Wade Hampton	NA	NA	6.3	2.0	5.7	50.1	NA	NA	NA	NA	NA	NA	NA	NA	NA	NA
Wrangell-Petersburg	22.7	52.4	6.3	1.4	6.2	20.1	NA	NA	NA	NA	NA	NA	NA	NA	NA	NA
Yukon-Koyukuk	0.0	26.6	4.3	1.4	8.1	58.5	NA	NA	NA	NA	NA	NA	NA	NA	NA	NA
ARIZONA	15.5	56.8	11.1	7.0	26.1	17.8	7 669	47.8	25.5	49.3	61.0	36 288	-3.9	4 732	914	1 454
Apache	4.3	NA	5.8	2.0	23.9	38.1	380	38.2	38.9	36.6	59.7	5 780	-7.3	15 209	14	37
Cochise	3.7	37.2	8.4	2.0	16.7	51.8	836	25.6	38.5	54.5	68.5	2 078	0.3	2 485	49	139
Coconino	8.8	47.4	13.2	2.3	23.6	34.5	294	52.7	29.6	44.2	60.9	5 906	-0.5	20 087	3	11
Gila	18.8	34.9	10.5	2.3	16.1	20.3	157	45.2	19.1	49.0	71.3	1 189	3.3	7 574	1	6
Graham	2.6	36.8	11.7	2.3	14.9	40.7	323	34.1	28.8	57.0	57.9	1 853	-3.9	5 736	38	54
Greenlee	1.8	11.6	3.1	0.9	3.5	12.3	102	26.5	22.5	58.8	71.6	140	-1.2	1 371	4	9
La Paz	6.2	44.1	15.3	2.0	18.9	20.5	109	33.9	36.7	68.8	54.1	227	NA	2 082	82	89
Maricopa	17.1	60.8	11.0	8.7	27.2	14.0	2 334	65.9	11.7	44.6	61.3	1 391	-2.7	596	276	424
Mohave	11.0	57.8	17.3	4.7	25.6	16.7	236	46.2	39.4	47.5	58.1	1 907	-16.0	8 079	12	21
Navajo	9.3	47.8	9.1	1.8	19.9	23.9	376	44.1	32.2	38.0	68.6	7 687	5.1	20 445	9	25
Pima	16.1	52.4	11.3	4.4	28.3	21.9	520	64.0	20.2	39.4	73.1	3 195	-8.1	6 144	27	39
Pinal	11.8	29.6	8.5	2.2	11.6	25.3	730	27.0	39.7	69.7	45.3	1 958	-18.5	2 683	190	339
Santa Cruz	10.0	64.4	17.9	3.2	17.0	19.5	179	24.6	36.3	53.1	67.6	346	-8.9	1 934	7	10
Yavapai	7.6	53.3	14.8	3.7	26.6	20.2	484	45.2	30.2	49.2	73.1	2 359	-6.0	4 873	7	28
Yuma	5.0	47.8	10.7	2.6	18.2	30.9	609	49.8	20.0	52.4	42.2	272	-46.6	447	194	223
ARKANSAS	23.6	48.4	10.1	4.4	19.4	15.2	48 242	24.8	15.6	50.2	69.0	14 356	-2.2	298	2 406	9 950
Arkansas	24.6	NA	9.1	3.2	NA	9.5	572	9.3	57.5	83.4	53.0	455	2.1	795	245	383
Ashley	55.1	NA	6.2	2.2	11.0	7.7	368	28.8	26.6	47.8	53.3	155	-2.1	420	53	133
Baxter	29.4	48.3	12.9	3.2	24.7	9.3	484	24.2	8.9	37.8	75.2	103	1.5	213	0	37
Benton	31.7	50.4	20.3	3.7	14.6	6.3	2 441	43.5	2.9	45.8	78.8	303	2.4	124	1	165
Boone	21.5	NA	10.4	2.8	NA	14.0	1 193	23.8	8.3	40.4	73.3	242	0.1	203	0	100
Bradley	40.7	31.4	6.8	2.5	13.5	14.0	266	35.7	3.8	39.8	77.4	32	-18.0	120	1	14
Calhoun	75.4	NA	1.7	NA	4.1	7.9	127	25.2	4.7	34.6	63.8	20	-15.7	155	0	9
Carroll	28.0	40.4	11.7	3.8	15.6	10.7	1 045	18.9	10.0	51.5	75.9	241	-4.6	230	0	105
Chicot	13.2	43.3	7.7	6.0	13.2	19.3	409	14.4	48.4	74.6	50.1	321	-0.8	784	69	284
Clark	23.7	47.3	11.8	3.3	20.5	21.2	408	21.3	13.5	40.7	65.4	114	-12.4	280	2	59
Clay	28.2	41.0	7.4	3.5	12.9	11.3	670	18.1	31.9	65.2	61.6	310	2.8	463	88	277
Cleburne	28.4	41.0	12.4	2.3	17.6	11.1	717	25.7	4.3	50.1	76.3	117	-1.1	163	0	50
Cleveland	9.0	33.6	4.2	1.6	9.6	16.0	261	32.2	3.8	41.8	73.9	37	-12.5	141	D	16
Columbia	37.2	32.1	9.1	2.6	13.2	13.1	411	25.1	5.1	34.8	65.0	66	-18.0	161	0	28

1. Covers mining, construction, and manufacturing. 2. Covers private sector earnings in agricultural services, forestry, and fisheries; transportation and public utilities; wholesale trade; retail trade; finance, insurance, and real estate; and services.

STATE County	Agriculture, 1987 (cont'd)								Manufactures, 1987						
	Value of land and buildings		Value of products sold				Percent of farms with sales of		Establishments		All employees			Production workers	
					Percent from										
	Average per farm ($1,000)	Average per acre (Dollars)	Total (Mil dol)	Average per farm (Dollars)	Crops	Livestock and poultry[1]	$10,000 or more	$100,000 or more	Total	Percent with 20 or more employees	Number (1,000)	Percent change, 1982–1987	Annual payroll (Mil dol)	Number (1,000)	Work hours (Mil)
	119	120	121	122	123	124	125	126	127	128	129	130	131	132	133
ALABAMA—Con.															
Washington	171	726	14	33 405	7.6	92.4	27.9	7.7	42	11.9	D	D	D	D	D
Wilcox	228	424	8	23 952	20.3	79.7	27.0	5.0	49	16.3	0.6	20.0	7.5	0.5	0.9
Winston	110	1 109	51	87 140	0.4	99.6	37.4	24.9	99	46.5	4.1	-16.3	59.7	3.3	6.1
ALASKA*	553	309	18	31 309	59.9	40.1	29.1	6.8	427	24.8	11.1	-13.3	271.7	8.4	16.7
Aleutian Islands	3 341	124	1	24 662	D	D	33.3	11.1	7	57.1	0.4	-42.9	8.9	0.4	1.0
Aleutians East Borough	NA	NA	NA	NA	NA	NA	NA	NA	NA	NA	NA	NA	NA	NA	NA
Aleutians West Census Area	NA	NA	NA	NA	NA	NA	NA	NA	NA	NA	NA	NA	NA	NA	NA
Anchorage	353	1 460	13	53 600	59.0	41.0	32.7	11.0	146	15.1	2.3	-17.9	59.8	1.3	2.4
Bethel	NA	NA	NA	NA	NA	NA	NA	NA	3	0.0	D	D	D	D	D
Bristol Bay	NA	NA	NA	NA	NA	NA	NA	NA	4	75.0	0.6	100.0	6.1	0.2	0.4
Dillingham	NA	NA	NA	NA	NA	NA	NA	NA	14	42.9	0.4	-42.9	7.9	0.3	0.6
Fairbanks North Star	512	579	3	19 938	72.3	27.7	35.4	4.6	42	14.3	D	D	D	D	D
Haines	NA	NA	NA	NA	NA	NA	NA	NA	4	25.0	D	D	D	D	D
Juneau	129	4 822	0	2 375	D	D	0.0	0.0	24	8.3	0.3	50.0	7.9	0.2	0.5
Kenai Peninsula	420	583	1	5 592	63.0	37.1	13.4	0.8	48	25.0	1.2	-42.9	32.2	1.0	1.9
Ketchikan Gateway	NA	NA	NA	NA	NA	NA	NA	NA	24	50.0	1.4	16.7	42.5	1.2	2.7
Kobuk	NA	NA	NA	NA	NA	NA	NA	NA	NA	NA	NA	NA	NA	NA	NA
Kodiak Island	NA	NA	NA	NA	NA	NA	NA	NA	19	47.4	1.1	-21.4	18.0	1.0	1.8
Lake and Peninsula Borough	NA	NA	NA	NA	NA	NA	NA	NA	NA	NA	NA	NA	NA	NA	NA
Matanuska-Susitna	NA	NA	NA	NA	NA	NA	NA	NA	22	9.1	D	D	D	D	D
Nome	NA	NA	NA	NA	NA	NA	NA	NA	1	0.0	D	D	D	D	D
North Slope	NA	NA	NA	NA	NA	NA	NA	NA	1	100.0	D	D	D	D	D
Northwest Arctic Borough	NA	NA	NA	NA	NA	NA	NA	NA	NA	NA	NA	NA	NA	NA	NA
Prince of Wales-Outer Ketchikan	NA	NA	NA	NA	NA	NA	NA	NA	14	50.0	0.5	25.0	15.4	0.5	1.0
Sitka	NA	NA	NA	NA	NA	NA	NA	NA	8	37.5	D	D	D	D	D
Skagway-Yakutat-Angoon	NA	NA	NA	NA	NA	NA	NA	NA	3	33.3	D	D	D	D	D
Southeast Fairbanks	NA	NA	NA	NA	NA	NA	NA	NA	5	0.0	0.0	0.0	0.3	0.0	0.0
Valdez-Cordova	NA	NA	NA	NA	NA	NA	NA	NA	10	50.0	0.6	100.0	11.2	0.6	1.0
Wade Hampton	NA	NA	NA	NA	NA	NA	NA	NA	2	50.0	D	D	D	D	D
Wrangell-Petersburg	NA	NA	NA	NA	NA	NA	NA	NA	23	30.4	0.7	-36.4	13.4	0.6	1.0
Yukon-Koyukuk	NA	NA	NA	NA	NA	NA	NA	NA	1	0.0	D	D	D	D	D
ARIZONA	1 318	279	1 629	212 354	55.1	44.9	46.7	22.3	4 151	27.2	184.1	22.9	4 669.0	105.9	214.2
Apache	1 869	126	18	46 300	7.8	92.2	27.6	5.5	17	23.5	D	D	D	D	D
Cochise	795	309	54	64 498	41.8	58.2	46.5	13.6	53	26.4	D	D	D	D	D
Coconino	3 049	149	15	52 388	4.9	95.1	30.3	10.2	89	20.2	2.3	0.0	50.4	1.6	3.3
Gila	1 802	237	5	33 695	5.5	94.5	40.1	8.3	28	28.6	D	D	D	D	D
Graham	1 548	270	30	94 308	62.9	37.1	60.4	23.5	13	15.4	0.1	0.0	1.4	0.1	0.1
Greenlee	451	311	5	48 623	25.2	74.8	46.1	7.8	1	0.0	D	D	D	D	D
La Paz	3 217	1 521	68	623 509	99.3	0.7	67.0	46.8	7	28.6	0.1	0.0	1.3	0.1	0.2
Maricopa	839	1 416	549	235 128	56.2	43.8	45.1	25.7	2 803	28.9	135.8	25.7	3 541.5	78.7	160.9
Mohave	953	118	14	57 222	45.0	55.0	40.3	11.4	93	22.6	2.7	28.6	47.2	1.7	3.2
Navajo	3 092	150	29	77 288	4.5	95.5	29.8	7.4	58	22.4	1.4	0.0	32.5	1.2	2.2
Pima	914	148	57	108 978	62.8	37.2	31.5	14.4	686	23.6	30.7	16.3	793.3	14.6	28.9
Pinal	1 838	722	403	551 448	43.1	56.9	73.8	53.8	67	38.8	2.7	12.5	60.0	2.1	4.3
Santa Cruz	1 277	654	7	37 659	6.6	93.4	48.6	11.2	42	21.4	D	D	D	D	D
Yavapai	783	162	19	40 253	8.2	91.8	38.4	11.0	138	13.8	2.4	50.0	41.7	1.6	3.2
Yuma	1 452	3 356	356	584 812	72.0	28.0	63.1	32.3	56	39.3	1.6	14.3	23.3	1.2	2.1
ARKANSAS	226	761	3 320	68 825	37.5	62.5	44.4	18.9	3 390	35.7	205.5	8.3	3 814.6	161.7	326.3
Arkansas	672	882	81	141 503	98.9	1.1	84.4	51.6	32	46.9	2.6	-3.7	46.3	1.8	3.9
Ashley	282	722	33	88 351	92.7	7.3	49.5	29.1	44	50.0	D	D	D	D	D
Baxter	170	602	15	31 130	1.2	98.8	31.6	5.4	46	28.3	3.3	13.8	56.9	2.6	5.6
Benton	181	1 434	263	107 941	1.5	98.5	44.1	20.1	164	42.7	11.5	16.2	196.3	8.6	16.4
Boone	139	714	26	21 390	2.1	97.9	32.9	4.4	56	30.4	2.7	12.5	43.8	2.3	4.4
Bradley	101	798	10	35 956	29.1	70.9	30.8	9.8	38	26.3	1.6	0.0	25.9	1.4	2.7
Calhoun	97	620	1	8 329	9.4	90.6	15.0	1.6	19	15.8	D	D	D	D	D
Carroll	178	723	80	77 022	1.0	99.0	49.3	16.7	37	24.3	D	D	D	D	D
Chicot	542	697	54	132 713	87.6	12.4	73.6	36.7	9	33.3	0.7	0.0	7.4	0.6	1.3
Clark	176	625	9	22 142	34.2	65.8	29.9	4.9	60	20.0	1.4	-22.2	25.4	1.2	2.7
Clay	340	831	46	68 456	94.4	5.6	63.4	22.1	24	50.0	1.6	23.1	21.8	1.4	2.7
Cleburne	126	668	34	47 850	0.8	99.2	39.7	19.4	30	36.7	1.2	50.0	19.2	0.9	1.8
Cleveland	97	953	26	101 146	1.1	98.9	32.6	17.2	18	5.6	0.1	-50.0	1.5	0.1	0.2
Columbia	124	790	20	48 134	10.1	89.9	25.8	11.4	57	31.6	2.7	3.8	59.0	2.1	8.1

1. Includes livestock and poultry products.

STATE County	Manufactures, 1987 (cont'd): Production workers (cont'd): Wages: Total (Mil dol)	Manufactures, 1987 (cont'd): Production workers (cont'd): Wages: Average per worker (Dollars)	Manufactures, 1987 (cont'd): Value added by manufacture (Mil dol)	Manufactures, 1987 (cont'd): Value of shipments (Mil dol)	Manufactures, 1987 (cont'd): New capital expenditures (Mil dol)	Value of construction authorized by building permits, 1990: Total[1] ($1,000)	Nonresidential: Total ($1,000)	Nonresidential: Percent: Office	Nonresidential: Percent: Industrial	Nonresidential: Percent: Stores	Residential: New construction ($1,000)	Residential: Number of housing units	Residential: Alterations and additions ($1,000)
	134	135	136	137	138	139	140	141	142	143	144	145	146
ALABAMA—Con.													
Washington	D	D	D	D	D	291	0	NA	NA	NA	55	1	8
Wilcox	5.9	11 800	13.1	29.5	1.3	0	0	NA	NA	NA	0	0	0
Winston	39.3	11 909	139.6	323.2	6.1	704	504	12.3	0.0	7.8	200	16	0
ALASKA*	191.4	22 786	834.0	2 710.7	68.6	240 710	59 144	2.7	12.2	57.7	102 115	876	17 434
Aleutian Islands	7.8	19 500	38.1	104.7	D	NA	NA	NA	NA	NA	NA	NA	NA
Aleutians East Borough	NA	NA	NA	NA	NA	0	0	NA	NA	NA	0	0	0
Aleutians West Census Area	NA	NA	NA	NA	NA	0	0	NA	NA	NA	0	0	0
Anchorage	30.0	23 077	234.8	714.1	9.3	122 642	20 612	2.1	1.7	80.0	62 476	399	8 930
Bethel	D	D	D	D	D	0	0	NA	NA	NA	0	0	0
Bristol Bay	3.5	17 500	14.0	45.8	0.9	6 269	4 824	0.0	78.7	8.9	1 407	17	32
Dillingham	5.7	19 000	21.1	68.9	D	0	0	NA	NA	NA	0	0	0
Fairbanks North Star	D	D	D	D	D	18 962	11 354	0.1	3.3	89.4	2 031	26	723
Haines	D	D	D	D	D	1 523	590	0.0	0.0	44.7	624	9	47
Juneau	5.2	26 000	20.2	27.7	D	18 869	5 032	10.4	0.0	22.7	4 570	38	2 329
Kenai Peninsula	23.4	23 400	124.8	473.1	3.3	6 683	1 246	2.4	0.0	86.5	2 044	26	762
Ketchikan Gateway	34.9	29 083	103.1	234.3	5.1	21 936	5 476	3.4	36.4	39.0	10 404	147	1 407
Kobuk	NA	NA	NA	NA	NA	NA	NA	NA	NA	NA	NA	NA	NA
Kodiak Island	15.5	15 500	28.5	166.2	8.6	13 332	2 494	0.0	0.0	10.9	7 610	75	1 187
Lake and Peninsula Borough	NA	NA	NA	NA	NA	NA	NA	NA	NA	NA	NA	NA	NA
Matanuska-Susitna	D	D	D	D	D	2 288	911	0.0	0.0	70.3	248	3	440
Nome	D	D	D	D	D	1 852	93	0.0	0.0	0.0	1 594	25	145
North Slope	D	D	D	D	D	0	0	NA	NA	NA	0	0	0
Northwest Arctic Borough	NA	NA	NA	NA	NA	3 100	800	0.0	0.0	0.0	0	0	0
Prince of Wales-Outer Ketchikan	13.1	26 200	54.2	114.9	3.8	3 031	1 861	0.0	0.0	57.4	813	10	97
Sitka	D	D	D	D	D	4 052	344	0.0	0.0	27.4	3 006	42	483
Skagway-Yakutat-Angoon	D	D	D	D	D	2 025	114	0.0	0.0	0.0	690	14	154
Southeast Fairbanks	0.2	NA	1.0	1.4	0.0	NA	NA	NA	NA	NA	NA	NA	NA
Valdez-Cordova	8.6	14 333	21.6	87.4	2.7	10 808	2 863	3.7	18.9	13.5	2 965	25	409
Wade Hampton	D	D	D	D	D	0	0	NA	NA	NA	0	0	0
Wrangell-Petersburg	10.7	17 833	30.6	87.5	6.2	3 339	531	61.1	32.6	0.0	1 632	20	290
Yukon-Koyukuk	D	D	D	D	D	NA	NA	NA	NA	NA	NA	NA	NA
ARIZONA	2 148.8	20 291	11 299.0	20 757.7	836.9	3 223 773	678 003	18.7	17.1	36.2	1 963 013	23 031	108 448
Apache	D	D	D	D	D	5 766	888	0.0	5.9	2.4	3 577	49	486
Cochise	D	D	D	D	D	33 016	11 886	29.1	8.9	16.3	16 133	312	1 810
Coconino	31.3	19 562	192.5	390.7	9.8	76 941	13 636	5.2	29.0	44.8	45 580	591	4 136
Gila	D	D	D	D	D	19 356	4 578	8.3	0.0	75.8	11 278	164	1 879
Graham	0.9	9 000	3.2	6.7	D	4 418	278	0.0	0.0	0.0	2 551	47	618
Greenlee	D	D	D	D	D	295	52	38.5	0.0	0.0	188	3	40
La Paz	0.9	9 000	1.8	3.9	0.1	7 672	3 208	1.3	0.0	34.3	1 835	24	388
Maricopa	1 673.3	21 262	8 179.8	14 061.8	655.2	2 167 246	469 475	17.8	19.4	35.6	1 285 519	12 950	62 131
Mohave	27.1	15 941	106.7	291.7	8.1	254 487	32 712	14.6	6.9	41.2	198 979	3 187	5 354
Navajo	24.5	20 417	115.6	238.0	9.0	26 503	6 680	0.4	0.0	89.1	13 418	250	2 569
Pima	254.0	17 397	1 947.0	3 608.8	126.1	345 807	72 735	41.2	10.3	23.8	195 457	2 678	16 264
Pinal	42.5	20 238	322.3	1 022.5	7.8	42 029	5 883	10.2	23.7	12.8	29 182	428	3 264
Santa Cruz	D	D	D	D	D	20 151	3 899	2.9	0.0	40.1	13 940	243	872
Yavapai	28.0	17 500	100.8	185.0	3.7	143 326	27 325	2.0	16.6	55.3	102 057	1 286	5 884
Yuma	15.0	12 500	67.4	144.6	3.8	76 760	24 768	11.7	15.8	45.1	43 321	819	2 752
ARKANSAS	2 651.6	16 398	10 826.9	25 307.6	891.5	825 229	328 103	17.1	23.3	25.2	343 289	6 000	31 708
Arkansas	27.8	15 444	83.2	473.0	12.8	1 366	304	7.9	4.9	46.4	738	13	197
Ashley	D	D	D	D	D	5 726	2 201	1.4	0.0	45.7	2 744	62	131
Baxter	38.9	14 962	118.8	221.4	9.2	7 487	1 790	77.4	0.0	21.6	3 506	61	165
Benton	126.6	14 721	570.0	1 293.1	53.9	69 809	30 208	3.8	46.1	21.4	32 036	576	1 591
Boone	31.6	13 739	127.7	222.6	3.0	10 945	4 611	1.6	43.3	0.0	6 013	109	229
Bradley	20.2	14 429	77.3	134.4	2.8	2 540	995	20.5	20.1	1.8	1 127	24	200
Calhoun	D	D	D	D	D	282	273	0.0	0.0	0.0	0	0	8
Carroll	D	D	D	D	D	8 285	1 049	7.6	0.0	89.5	1 350	21	86
Chicot	4.8	8 000	14.2	19.1	D	2 138	212	0.0	0.0	87.2	1 405	46	215
Clark	21.0	17 500	60.3	160.2	5.4	6 541	4 102	15.9	23.7	15.8	2 158	31	202
Clay	17.1	12 214	42.8	72.4	D	1 948	234	20.3	50.4	0.0	1 488	46	132
Cleburne	12.6	14 000	45.2	103.4	2.9	2 326	132	0.0	100.0	0.0	1 501	33	183
Cleveland	1.2	12 000	2.5	5.6	0.3	0	0	NA	NA	NA	0	0	0
Columbia	40.3	19 190	159.4	332.1	D	4 423	2 228	81.0	0.0	6.7	1 419	23	483

1. Includes nonresidential additions and alterations, residential nonhousekeeping buildings, and residential garages and carports not shown separately.

STATE County	Wholesale trade, 1987: Establishments	Wholesale trade, 1987: Sales (Mil dol)	Wholesale trade, 1987: Paid employees[1]	Wholesale trade, 1987: Annual payroll (Mil dol)	Retail trade, all establishments, 1987: Number	Retail trade, all establishments, 1987: Sales: Total (Mil dol)	Retail trade, all establishments, 1987: Sales: Percent change, 1982–1987	Retail trade, all establishments, 1987: Sales: Per capita[2] (Dollars)	Retail trade, establishments with payroll, 1987: Number	Retail trade, establishments with payroll, 1987: Sales: Total (Mil dol)	Sales: Per capita[2] (Dollars): General merchandise stores	Sales: Per capita[2] (Dollars): Food stores	Sales: Per capita[2] (Dollars): Apparel & accessory stores	Sales: Per capita[2] (Dollars): Eating and drinking places
	147	148	149	150	151	152	153	154	155	156	157	158	159	160
ALABAMA—Con.														
Washington	17	17.8	98	1.2	142	46.6	58.0	2 709	63	40.1	D	520	26	151
Wilcox	22	16.8	114	1.4	138	33.6	13.9	2 347	84	29.9	D	934	57	107
Winston	44	95.1	417	7.1	278	72.3	13.5	3 378	127	61.7	448	1 137	31	206
ALASKA*	778	2 685.5	7 176	204.9	6 266	3 728.1	15.5	7 111	3 522	3 606.2	998	1 740	368	875
Aleutian Islands	3	D	D	D	61	25.2	108.3	3 116	27	24.3	729	1 283	0	800
Aleutians East Borough	NA	NA	NA	NA	NA	NA	NA	NA	NA	NA	NA	NA	NA	NA
Aleutians West Census Area	NA	NA	NA	NA	NA	NA	NA	NA	NA	NA	NA	NA	NA	NA
Anchorage	479	1 708.5	4 965	146.8	2 314	1 994.3	11.1	9 012	1 403	1 952.5	1 672	1 702	571	1 265
Bethel	7	D	D	D	121	42.9	58.3	3 402	52	38.6	982	1 183	0	D
Bristol Bay	1	D	D	D	25	7.9	8.2	6 090	20	7.6	0	2 842	0	1 096
Dillingham	5	3.5	8	0.2	74	15.7	55.4	2 662	26	13.2	1 107	169	0	160
Fairbanks North Star	98	298.3	1 085	28.1	795	504.8	8.4	7 359	441	492.0	678	1 879	384	767
Haines	1	D	D	D	67	12.3	8.8	7 237	29	10.7	D	D	D	722
Juneau	27	56.9	211	6.2	348	188.4	9.0	7 058	234	184.4	D	1 502	324	788
Kenai Peninsula	53	D	D	D	606	235.7	24.9	5 694	326	222.6	73	1 859	250	646
Ketchikan Gateway	22	43.0	126	4.2	219	103.1	25.6	8 810	140	99.1	D	D	346	801
Kobuk	NA	NA	NA	NA	NA	NA	NA	NA	NA	NA	NA	NA	NA	NA
Kodiak Island	15	22.7	113	1.9	147	79.3	12.8	5 962	81	76.3	0	2 045	31	551
Lake and Peninsula Borough	NA	NA	NA	NA	NA	NA	NA	NA	NA	NA	NA	NA	NA	NA
Matanuska-Susitna	22	31.1	126	2.9	427	179.6	79.1	4 536	192	172.4	D	1 685	188	307
Nome	2	D	D	D	93	41.2	31.2	5 415	55	38.2	327	2 531	D	475
North Slope	5	11.3	25	0.8	41	34.1	0.9	6 566	25	33.5	2 486	2 878	0	D
Northwest Arctic Borough	0	0.0	0	0.0	53	24.6	NA	4 092	28	22.4	1 228	1 530	0	367
Prince of Wales-Outer Ketchikan	1	D	D	D	69	20.9	80.2	4 014	35	18.7	D	2 023	41	194
Sitka	13	15.5	32	0.8	140	53.5	27.4	7 042	85	51.1	98	D	633	886
Skagway-Yakutat-Angoon	2	D	D	D	100	19.0	65.2	5 004	54	17.6	D	1 929	0	1 017
Southeast Fairbanks	0	0.0	0	0.0	85	15.8	21.5	2 426	41	13.3	D	694	D	364
Valdez-Cordova	8	24.3	53	1.8	189	53.5	5.7	6 006	87	47.3	D	1 760	171	847
Wade Hampton	1	D	D	D	40	14.8	22.3	2 746	25	14.1	1 103	1 176	0	D
Wrangell-Petersburg	9	7.1	10	0.2	129	40.4	25.1	6 024	67	38.1	D	3 084	291	743
Yukon-Koyukuk	4	D	D	D	123	21.1	-14.2	2 265	49	18.1	426	434	D	D
ARIZONA	5 874	20 776.8	64 687	1 420.3	31 519	22 359.9	60.9	6 579	19 798	21 778.4	729	1 466	246	650
Apache	8	13.0	34	0.5	277	135.1	62.2	2 281	159	128.8	411	676	26	110
Cochise	71	93.4	511	6.6	969	416.2	48.0	4 171	571	401.3	439	984	191	299
Coconino	109	589.5	949	16.4	937	604.0	41.0	6 682	678	590.8	852	1 545	171	908
Gila	42	32.9	146	2.6	445	180.6	26.4	4 584	261	172.5	243	1 470	93	446
Graham	32	32.1	170	2.6	190	100.9	9.8	4 238	135	98.2	227	1 300	166	324
Greenlee	4	3.1	14	0.2	67	18.5	-11.1	2 317	35	17.2	D	D	D	194
La Paz	14	17.4	65	1.4	177	67.7	0.0	4 802	98	62.4	D	D	D	485
Maricopa	3 984	16 991.1	49 119	1 141.4	17 682	14 229.8	66.7	7 194	11 133	13 889.3	777	1 551	277	729
Mohave	105	106.9	563	8.9	1 096	510.9	61.8	6 509	599	486.0	362	1 694	118	533
Navajo	61	111.4	407	6.6	686	317.7	26.6	4 282	408	302.0	303	1 278	52	342
Pima	911	1 607.4	8 470	161.4	5 464	3 980.9	53.5	6 391	3 675	3 900.9	848	1 340	268	637
Pinal	84	164.7	505	9.7	817	445.4	59.9	4 259	509	434.4	298	1 410	86	349
Santa Cruz	180	627.8	1 726	29.5	323	190.2	43.8	8 026	211	185.5	2 176	1 752	1 069	484
Yavapai	110	96.8	538	7.6	1 577	565.7	81.2	6 182	780	523.3	434	1 627	123	571
Yuma	159	289.3	1 470	24.8	812	596.1	39.4	6 594	546	585.9	826	1 390	184	546
ARKANSAS	4 024	12 780.7	38 940	705.5	27 040	12 318.7	35.2	5 159	15 096	11 631.7	719	1 044	211	381
Arkansas	70	D	D	D	308	104.8	9.2	4 596	196	99.8	588	1 096	273	351
Ashley	29	D	D	D	241	89.8	17.7	3 454	135	83.8	D	926	125	164
Baxter	34	38.1	197	2.5	456	170.4	54.1	5 533	251	159.9	D	1 382	163	394
Benton	132	503.5	981	17.6	1 019	479.7	59.7	5 164	522	446.6	D	1 110	130	358
Boone	61	D	D	D	402	187.0	46.6	6 585	205	175.2	845	1 235	327	434
Bradley	22	19.1	95	1.4	127	43.5	13.3	3 345	74	40.1	165	981	181	166
Calhoun	5	D	D	D	51	11.2	7.7	1 829	29	9.1	D	505	D	56
Carroll	33	27.8	194	2.6	405	102.2	70.9	5 586	204	92.0	D	1 273	46	526
Chicot	34	53.3	233	3.4	163	46.5	7.6	2 733	97	40.7	109	740	114	133
Clark	33	45.8	260	4.5	261	139.5	36.2	6 312	158	133.3	D	1 067	203	514
Clay	34	72.2	273	3.4	254	61.0	32.9	3 159	108	52.1	D	812	40	133
Cleburne	28	38.2	143	2.2	255	82.0	48.6	4 206	116	74.3	D	900	44	193
Cleveland	8	13.0	95	0.8	63	7.3	17.7	895	18	4.5	0	287	D	D
Columbia	38	51.8	236	3.3	318	123.2	28.2	4 596	186	114.2	768	920	342	312

1. For pay period including March 12. 2. Based on the estimated population as of July 1 of the year shown.

STATE / County	Retail trade, establishments with payroll, 1987 (cont'd): Paid employees[1]	Retail trade, establishments with payroll, 1987 (cont'd): Annual payroll (Mil dol)	Taxable service industries–establishments with payroll, 1987: Number	Taxable service industries: Receipts (Mil dol): Total	Receipts: Selected kinds of business: Hotels, motels and other lodging places	Receipts: Selected kinds of business: Health services	Receipts: Selected kinds of business: Legal services	Taxable service industries: Paid employees	Taxable service industries: Annual payroll (Mil dol)	Bank deposits,[2] June 1989: Total (Mil dol)	Bank deposits,[2] June 1989: Percent change, 1988–1989	Savings capital,[3] September 1989: Total (Mil dol)	Savings capital,[3] September 1989: Percent change, 1988–1989
	161	162	163	164	165	166	167	168	169	170	171	172	173
ALABAMA—Con.													
Washington	370	3.5	28	3.5	D	0.7	D	95	1.2	66	7.0	0.0	NA
Wilcox	358	3.3	46	5.9	0.3	2.7	0.1	201	2.1	66	2.9	0.0	NA
Winston	834	6.7	78	12.1	D	4.1	1.0	365	3.4	186	2.4	16.9	13.9
ALASKA*	35 967	483.5	3 949	1 544.3	174.4	369.0	205.2	27 555	591.6	3 566	-4.8	330.5	-12.7
Aleutian Islands	196	3.0	10	D	D	D	0.0	D	D	X	X	0.0	NA
Aleutians East Borough	NA	NA	NA	NA	NA	NA	NA	NA	NA	X	X	X	X
Aleutians West Census Area	NA	NA	NA	NA	NA	NA	NA	NA	NA	NA	NA	NA	NA
Anchorage	19 703	267.0	2 123	1 064.1	85.8	241.6	169.2	18 302	420.4	2 024	-13.7	171.5	-10.3
Bethel	304	3.4	17	3.3	D	D	D	100	1.3	26	11.4	0.0	NA
Bristol Bay	69	1.1	7	1.4	1.3	0.0	D	12	0.3	NA	NA	0.0	NA
Dillingham	122	1.5	21	5.6	4.3	0.0	D	105	1.3	X	X	0.0	NA
Fairbanks North Star	4 640	67.9	532	179.9	19.7	60.2	13.2	3 338	70.3	386	5.0	18.2	-23.1
Haines	141	1.4	18	2.3	0.9	0.3	D	34	0.6	13	-0.5	0.0	NA
Juneau	1 885	25.7	240	74.3	10.9	17.7	10.7	1 255	29.3	153	-12.0	54.8	-7.9
Kenai Peninsula	2 428	26.7	293	72.2	12.8	12.6	2.5	1 389	24.9	203	23.5	22.6	-20.9
Ketchikan Gateway	950	13.0	109	26.6	3.4	7.0	3.0	539	9.0	168	-4.4	18.7	-12.2
Kobuk	NA	NA	NA	NA	NA	NA	NA	NA	NA	NA	NA	NA	NA
Kodiak Island	673	10.3	79	17.3	3.4	5.7	1.5	341	5.6	83	28.6	11.5	-31.3
Lake and Peninsula Borough	NA	NA	NA	NA	NA	NA	NA	NA	NA	X	X	X	X
Matanuska-Susitna	1 706	21.9	208	35.9	3.9	13.5	2.3	871	11.2	79	25.0	10.4	-22.3
Nome	375	4.7	17	4.3	D	D	D	61	1.2	34	5.3	0.0	NA
North Slope	297	4.7	14	7.0	1.6	0.0	0.0	91	1.9	16	44.5	0.0	NA
Northwest Arctic Borough	253	3.2	6	1.8	D	0.0	D	41	0.7	12	39.9	0.0	NA
Prince of Wales-Outer Ketchikan	173	2.3	7	1.6	D	D	0.0	17	0.2	27	33.3	0.0	NA
Sitka	517	6.9	75	9.7	0.4	4.3	0.6	288	3.5	68	1.0	17.2	-6.3
Skagway-Yakutat-Angoon	220	2.3	26	9.9	7.5	D	0.0	152	2.2	21	-5.8	0.0	NA
Southeast Fairbanks	161	1.7	25	4.3	2.5	1.2	0.0	99	1.3	9	14.3	0.0	NA
Valdez-Cordova	420	6.0	57	13.1	7.6	2.0	D	227	3.5	116	84.8	0.0	NA
Wade Hampton	161	1.5	2	D	D	0.0	0.0	D	D	NA	NA	0.0	NA
Wrangell-Petersburg	417	5.4	35	4.0	0.8	1.6	D	98	1.2	68	1.1	5.5	-6.2
Yukon-Koyukuk	156	1.9	28	4.4	2.8	D	0.0	135	1.2	3	10.6	0.0	NA
ARIZONA	260 512	2 624.3	25 250	10 639.5	1 072.7	2 570.9	888.7	243 999	4 011.3	22 375	-4.1	16 716.6	5.6
Apache	1 329	12.2	83	16.6	6.5	3.3	0.8	430	4.4	86	16.0	0.0	NA
Cochise	4 809	44.8	417	98.7	14.3	25.4	4.2	2 936	36.6	433	3.4	139.3	0.2
Coconino	8 086	74.5	594	220.4	86.4	32.1	7.9	4 876	59.2	359	-2.3	111.0	8.8
Gila	2 081	19.8	179	39.8	4.1	19.5	2.0	1 046	13.0	249	6.4	71.3	14.2
Graham	1 228	10.8	84	16.6	D	9.0	0.4	510	5.3	100	3.2	34.1	16.0
Greenlee	213	1.7	17	1.4	D	0.5	0.0	64	0.4	41	-8.6	0.0	NA
La Paz	838	7.4	55	9.2	2.0	2.5	0.2	184	2.8	12	21.0	X	X
Maricopa	163 886	1 703.1	16 684	7 765.1	681.0	1 723.7	703.4	170 803	2 963.6	14 585	-6.3	11 189.5	8.1
Mohave	5 465	50.1	481	115.0	27.4	36.9	3.8	2 923	35.9	526	14.1	281.8	7.4
Navajo	3 374	32.3	272	61.2	17.7	14.6	1.3	1 483	17.4	258	5.5	17.4	5.4
Pima	48 624	473.5	4 703	1 915.2	171.3	590.6	144.4	48 712	740.9	3 429	-2.6	4 243.9	0.6
Pinal	5 048	46.9	354	74.8	15.9	20.3	4.1	1 971	24.5	450	-2.7	91.7	-4.1
Santa Cruz	2 249	20.2	126	21.4	5.1	4.2	0.9	646	7.0	540	-8.0	16.9	-6.0
Yavapai	6 288	62.6	692	129.2	18.0	45.7	8.5	3 283	43.7	686	8.7	366.5	-4.6
Yuma	6 994	64.4	509	155.0	21.3	42.6	6.8	4 132	56.4	621	3.2	X	X
ARKANSAS	138 671	1 245.8	12 437	3 703.2	237.8	1 515.5	241.1	93 960	1 365.9	16 435	3.7	6 548.5	-1.2
Arkansas	1 190	11.1	128	19.3	1.3	8.9	0.8	554	6.9	323	8.0	60.7	-2.0
Ashley	882	8.2	72	14.0	D	5.3	2.0	428	4.6	156	4.6	0.0	NA
Baxter	1 872	17.3	242	49.9	8.2	23.8	2.1	1 354	17.7	249	8.6	261.3	-5.5
Benton	4 905	45.4	464	108.4	5.3	41.3	5.1	2 911	41.4	764	10.1	290.3	-8.4
Boone	1 842	18.3	213	51.0	11.0	17.2	2.3	1 145	14.9	165	-1.8	183.6	4.1
Bradley	431	4.1	46	8.8	D	4.9	0.5	283	3.0	125	1.5	19.6	1.5
Calhoun	88	0.7	5	2.7	0.0	D	0.0	111	0.9	23	4.8	0.0	NA
Carroll	1 001	8.7	142	27.3	11.3	6.3	0.5	750	7.3	179	9.2	44.3	-13.9
Chicot	475	4.2	57	9.3	0.6	4.7	1.4	267	3.3	105	5.2	0.0	NA
Clark	1 549	12.4	111	18.8	2.5	7.8	1.6	624	6.7	182	3.1	77.7	5.3
Clay	620	5.0	51	9.4	D	6.8	0.5	298	3.3	92	5.4	75.1	0.9
Cleburne	730	7.5	99	24.6	2.1	9.3	D	714	8.0	160	2.4	43.3	-1.1
Cleveland	63	0.5	3	D	0.0	D	0.0	D	D	17	3.9	0.0	NA
Columbia	1 506	12.6	134	23.9	D	8.1	1.4	720	9.5	310	0.4	36.0	-2.5

1. For the period including March 12 of the year shown. 2. Includes deposits for all insured and reporting noninsured commercial and mutual savings banks. 3. Includes savings capital for all FSLIC insured savings institutions.

STATE County	Federal funds and grants, 1989: Expenditures: Total (Mil dol)	Expenditures: Percent change, 1988–1989	Per capita[1] (Dollars): Total	Per capita: Direct payments for individuals	Per capita: Procurement contract awards	Per capita: Salaries and wages	Per capita: Grant awards	Local government finances, 1981–1982: General revenue: Total (Mil dol)	Intergovernmental: Total (Mil dol)	Intergovernmental: Percent from state	Taxes: Total (Mil dol)	Taxes: Per capita[2]: Total (Dollars)	Taxes: Per capita[2]: Property (Dollars)	Direct general expenditure: Total (Mil dol)	Direct general expenditure: Percent change, 1977–1982
	174	175	176	177	178	179	180	181	182	183	184	185	186	187	188
ALABAMA—Con.															
Washington	60.9	-1.4	3 522	2 208	31	763	489	11.9	7.7	95.6	2.9	165	136	11.3	82.6
Wilcox	49.5	12.3	3 561	1 966	473	274	748	15.5	7.7	88.8	1.0	66	31	74.6	1 199.0
Winston	47.1	-5.3	2 210	1 739	37	160	255	23.1	10.1	78.9	2.6	119	34	20.5	148.7
ALASKA*	3 159.8	13.1	X	1 050	1 195	2 159	1 577	1 455.1	747.2	91.6	274.0	616	491	1 459.4	169.8
Aleutian Islands	179.6	14.3	NA	NA	NA	NA	NA	14.9	11.7	91.6	2.6	325	142	14.7	NA
Aleutians East Borough	1.9	7.8	1 063	11	12	0	668	NA	NA	NA	NA	NA	NA	NA	NA
Aleutians West Census Area	0.0	0.0	0	0	0	0	0	NA	NA	NA	NA	NA	NA	NA	NA
Anchorage	1 151.1	8.1	5 366	917	720	2 881	835	430.8	225.8	91.9	63.5	311	271	398.1	76.7
Bethel	71.4	25.5	5 328	466	818	824	3 206	23.3	17.6	85.3	1.6	136	0	48.3	NA
Bristol Bay	17.8	24.0	11 864	841	985	6 035	3 991	9.1	6.2	96.0	2.0	1 653	449	10.2	582.5
Dillingham	21.5	-44.0	3 411	404	84	421	2 486	15.8	12.4	86.9	0.7	156	34	17.0	NA
Fairbanks North Star	619.5	31.8	8 640	797	2 929	3 781	1 124	148.6	101.5	94.1	20.1	342	209	143.7	52.7
Haines	4.3	-10.4	2 524	1 521	169	301	526	7.3	6.2	95.8	0.8	438	146	7.2	97.1
Juneau	261.7	4.7	9 729	851	269	1 551	7 047	65.1	37.2	90.5	9.2	402	178	65.6	160.8
Kenai Peninsula	84.9	14.5	2 070	796	689	285	279	99.6	68.7	93.5	17.4	545	329	85.4	206.1
Ketchikan Gateway	36.7	-7.9	3 082	1 083	187	1 054	750	49.1	31.2	92.3	5.9	473	140	35.8	74.6
Kobuk	0.0	0.0	0	0	0	0	0	13.0	9.3	96.9	0.7	143	0	9.8	NA
Kodiak Island	27.2	-39.1	1 971	531	625	393	416	37.5	24.8	88.5	5.4	429	125	41.3	118.6
Lake and Peninsula Borough	0.0	0.0	0	0	0	0	0	NA	NA	NA	NA	NA	NA	NA	NA
Matanuska-Susitna	57.3	18.7	1 436	855	26	185	366	65.9	47.6	94.9	8.3	389	363	55.4	200.6
Nome	58.9	22.4	7 356	1 089	1 029	761	4 462	23.6	19.1	94.8	1.4	212	65	16.5	NA
North Slope	12.9	13.5	2 259	475	446	392	939	216.3	38.9	77.6	114.4	27 233	26 126	277.9	710.9
Northwest Arctic Borough	66.7	7.3	10 425	507	772	784	8 345	NA	NA	NA	NA	NA	NA	NA	NA
Prince of Wales-Outer Ketchikan	20.9	-6.6	3 731	433	701	499	2 091	4.4	3.4	95.4	0.4	84	19	5.1	NA
Sitka	24.4	8.1	3 084	1 022	216	1 482	358	45.5	22.8	80.7	3.7	469	128	28.6	155.5
Skagway-Yakutat-Angoon	11.7	7.3	2 917	847	527	544	987	7.6	4.3	95.5	1.0	273	90	11.3	NA
Southeast Fairbanks	55.1	-13.0	8 473	808	1 404	2 711	3 539	0.2	0.2	89.6	0.0	0	0	0.3	NA
Valdez-Cordova	23.1	21.2	2 598	670	485	594	829	129.8	24.1	98.3	12.1	1 342	1 206	141.3	NA
Wade Hampton	20.9	21.7	3 542	407	83	190	2 852	10.2	7.7	95.1	0.2	42	0	12.2	NA
Wrangell-Petersburg	17.9	31.2	2 526	928	299	721	573	21.6	15.0	91.2	2.5	375	86	18.6	NA
Yukon-Koyukuk	104.9	-1.5	10 924	714	6 531	2 008	1 651	15.7	11.3	94.4	0.4	44	6	15.1	NA
ARIZONA	13 510.4	9.5	X	1 880	899	539	427	3 411.0	1 524.8	83.4	1 032.8	357	268	3 397.1	73.9
Apache	257.4	9.1	4 152	1 039	171	877	2 056	67.3	37.7	79.8	15.7	299	286	70.0	148.2
Cochise	666.1	9.1	6 563	2 209	1 200	2 847	234	100.2	55.7	83.4	27.5	308	254	110.3	104.6
Coconino	257.6	3.7	2 675	1 209	175	688	594	90.9	50.8	70.2	24.5	316	247	90.9	59.9
Gila	135.6	10.8	3 332	2 418	158	273	476	54.9	20.9	83.7	17.3	437	384	58.4	108.3
Graham	71.4	10.2	2 940	1 835	275	337	380	27.5	17.6	86.5	4.9	210	167	29.1	74.2
Greenlee	15.2	6.3	2 022	1 670	23	130	150	12.8	5.4	95.7	5.7	487	467	19.7	190.1
La Paz	136.5	146.3	9 543	5 552	3 203	110	390	NA	NA	NA	NA	NA	NA	NA	NA
Maricopa	6 642.0	7.3	3 195	1 695	797	393	282	1 926.3	827.0	84.4	553.4	343	246	1 885.2	78.4
Mohave	271.2	15.5	3 132	2 647	29	143	297	71.5	25.1	88.2	28.4	458	417	72.7	84.7
Navajo	231.5	21.1	3 058	1 581	158	614	696	86.0	47.6	70.4	19.9	293	249	90.2	120.1
Pima	3 071.9	6.0	4 759	1 969	1 875	554	351	655.3	283.7	82.0	231.3	408	299	652.3	52.8
Pinal	364.1	6.4	3 338	1 717	758	183	438	109.5	53.3	89.3	37.4	388	345	109.1	46.2
Santa Cruz	66.6	22.4	2 687	1 591	116	524	452	26.6	15.6	89.1	8.4	396	305	26.7	96.2
Yavapai	322.1	8.7	3 267	2 742	44	295	178	76.3	29.6	88.4	30.6	399	333	77.4	74.1
Yuma	417.4	7.7	4 412	1 797	219	2 038	292	105.9	54.9	86.2	27.7	290	224	105.2	57.8
ARKANSAS	7 986.8	5.8	X	2 021	221	363	509	1 678.9	774.7	81.3	403.2	175	153	1 601.9	69.7
Arkansas	112.0	28.9	5 043	2 097	1 135	260	423	25.6	12.1	58.6	4.4	181	162	19.5	46.7
Ashley	71.4	14.4	2 777	1 727	12	118	390	24.3	9.2	89.9	4.3	163	150	19.1	31.4
Baxter	117.0	4.8	3 714	3 304	72	177	140	19.7	6.0	87.2	5.3	187	164	19.8	113.8
Benton	237.3	1.8	2 405	2 088	55	115	110	47.4	17.1	91.3	16.2	202	185	45.7	78.8
Boone	82.3	10.2	2 839	2 079	243	208	255	23.5	8.2	88.0	4.1	153	142	22.8	82.2
Bradley	40.6	8.8	3 201	2 175	15	138	813	9.8	5.5	80.4	2.0	145	134	9.4	48.9
Calhoun	60.1	-63.1	10 014	1 629	7 824	96	439	3.8	2.4	93.0	1.0	164	158	3.9	66.5
Carroll	47.0	8.2	2 525	2 001	13	225	186	10.4	4.0	89.9	2.6	156	125	9.3	49.6
Chicot	62.5	3.2	3 811	1 888	22	125	765	17.4	8.1	90.5	2.6	145	134	16.7	88.8
Clark	70.3	21.0	3 271	2 342	50	206	612	14.2	5.8	91.6	3.5	150	133	13.7	50.4
Clay	74.0	9.6	3 897	2 223	28	142	471	13.4	6.0	91.8	2.4	119	106	11.7	58.5
Cleburne	59.7	11.0	2 998	2 380	46	171	367	9.7	4.9	87.1	2.2	126	118	9.5	65.9
Cleveland	17.5	11.2	2 138	1 706	9	75	312	4.2	2.9	91.0	0.7	89	87	4.1	49.0
Columbia	73.3	-12.0	2 756	1 978	232	114	418	19.4	9.0	95.2	3.7	136	121	19.5	60.9

1. Based on the estimated population as of July 1 of the year shown. 2. Based on the estimated population as of July 1, 1982.

STATE County	Local government finances, 1981–1982 (cont'd): Direct general expenditure (cont'd): Per capita[1] (Dollars)	Percent of total for– Educa-tion	Health & hospitals	Police protec-tion	Public welfare	High-ways	Debt outstanding: Total (Mil dol)	Per capita[1] (Dollars)	State and local government employment, 1989: Total	Rate[2]	Federal government civilian employment 1989: Total	Earnings ($1,000)	Elections, 1988[3]: Total vote cast for president	Vote for lead party (Percent)
	189	190	191	192	193	194	195	196	197	198	199	200	201	202
ALABAMA—Con.														
Washington	654	70.3	0.3	3.6	0.3	9.0	2.6	152	797	460.7	48	1 085	7 164	R–52.2
Wilcox	4 941	7.4	1.4	0.4	0.0	1.4	104.9	6 946	773	556.1	58	1 272	5 118	D–65.8
Winston	945	38.0	36.2	3.2	0.2	8.3	9.1	422	1 014	476.1	110	2 687	9 225	R–67.6
ALASKA*	3 280	32.2	3.5	5.1	0.2	5.7	3 139.8	7 056	47 728	906.5	18 249	620 915	200 116	R–59.6
Aleutian Islands	1 855	38.5	0.3	5.7	1.8	7.3	4.9	623	NA	NA	NA	NA	NA	NA
Aleutians East Borough	NA	NA	NA	NA	NA	NA	NA	NA	182	1 011.1	31	1 360	NA	NA
Aleutians West Census Area	NA	NA	NA	NA	NA	NA	NA	NA	404	594.1	814	15 649	NA	NA
Anchorage	1 950	37.4	2.5	5.6	0.0	4.6	552.3	2 705	14 832	691.5	10 210	362 288	NA	NA
Bethel	4 131	0.0	1.6	2.6	0.1	2.1	33.5	2 867	1 939	1 447.0	284	9 609	NA	NA
Bristol Bay	8 492	34.6	1.7	0.8	0.0	0.5	3.9	3 246	307	2 046.7	92	2 706	NA	NA
Dillingham	3 611	43.3	0.0	3.1	0.0	1.8	9.7	2 055	529	839.7	86	2 874	NA	NA
Fairbanks North Star	2 439	46.3	1.1	5.7	0.5	3.4	95.7	1 626	6 465	901.7	3 080	96 460	NA	NA
Haines	4 020	49.2	0.0	3.8	0.0	3.9	1.5	833	157	923.5	NA	364	NA	NA
Juneau	2 866	35.7	14.8	2.6	1.1	4.3	76.0	3 318	5 736	2 132.3	1 089	44 361	NA	NA
Kenai Peninsula	2 669	43.9	2.2	3.0	0.0	2.3	70.3	2 197	3 000	731.7	269	9 751	NA	NA
Ketchikan Gateway	2 866	34.4	4.3	3.7	1.1	0.8	66.4	5 312	1 421	1 194.1	273	9 941	NA	NA
Kobuk	1 959	0.0	0.0	6.8	0.2	40.6	4.9	982	0	0.0	0	0	NA	NA
Kodiak Island	3 306	43.8	2.9	3.7	0.4	5.0	27.4	2 190	913	661.6	160	6 024	NA	NA
Lake and Peninsula Borough	NA	NA	NA	NA	NA	NA	NA	NA	0	0.0	0	0	NA	NA
Matanuska-Susitna	2 614	59.3	1.7	1.1	0.2	10.9	65.9	3 110	2 206	552.9	105	3 649	NA	NA
Nome	2 496	46.4	2.4	5.4	0.2	8.4	1.5	228	1 147	1 433.8	96	3 530	NA	NA
North Slope	6 616	19.0	3.3	9.2	0.0	11.8	587.4	139 857	1 716	3 010.5	102	2 729	NA	NA
Northwest Arctic Borough	NA	NA	NA	NA	NA	NA	NA	NA	865	1 351.6	89	3 115	NA	NA
Prince of Wales-Outer Ketchikan	1 208	65.1	0.0	4.0	0.0	3.2	0.3	61	569	1 016.1	123	3 529	NA	NA
Sitka	3 668	30.7	30.5	2.8	0.0	1.4	78.0	9 994	698	883.5	260	9 014	NA	NA
Skagway-Yakutat-Angoon	3 233	41.7	0.0	2.1	0.9	2.0	1.7	473	366	915.0	125	3 892	NA	NA
Southeast Fairbanks	44	0.0	0.0	0.0	17.9	13.7	0.0	0	412	633.8	354	11 061	NA	NA
Valdez-Cordova	1 570	12.1	1.8	1.2	0.0	2.1	1 446.2	160 683	1 234	1 386.5	107	3 678	NA	NA
Wade Hampton	2 548	33.0	0.0	7.7	0.5	5.3	0.1	20	855	1 449.2	25	479	NA	NA
Wrangell-Petersburg	2 820	39.2	15.0	4.8	0.0	4.2	8.8	1 336	586	825.4	179	6 130	NA	NA
Yukon-Koyukuk	1 884	27.6	0.0	5.2	0.7	8.9	3.4	430	1 189	1 238.5	287	8 722	NA	NA
ARIZONA	1 173	44.0	5.5	6.5	2.0	5.9	7 070.0	2 440	207 252	582.1	44 405	1 334 280	1 171 873	R–60.0
Apache	1 333	77.7	0.9	1.4	0.8	2.5	319.8	6 091	2 937	473.7	2 202	56 837	14 544	D–61.5
Cochise	1 236	45.1	6.3	5.5	0.0	4.8	63.2	708	4 739	466.9	5 147	154 097	28 050	R–56.4
Coconino	1 173	48.0	2.4	6.3	4.4	7.8	48.8	630	8 559	888.8	2 889	78 953	32 140	R–51.8
Gila	1 474	43.6	9.7	4.9	1.0	6.2	112.4	2 839	2 055	504.9	497	12 172	15 299	R–51.4
Graham	1 249	63.9	1.2	3.2	3.3	4.4	14.4	620	2 083	857.2	290	9 131	8 652	R–59.2
Greenlee	1 681	67.4	1.3	3.0	2.2	5.9	11.1	949	505	673.3	31	807	3 302	D–52.5
La Paz	NA	NA	NA	NA	NA	NA	NA	NA	656	458.7	166	4 638	4 376	R–58.5
Maricopa	1 169	40.4	5.4	7.2	1.3	5.8	5 245.2	3 254	115 221	554.3	18 691	588 648	681 518	R–64.9
Mohave	1 170	45.9	11.6	6.3	5.0	5.9	45.1	726	3 448	398.2	366	11 192	28 286	R–62.4
Navajo	1 324	72.9	1.9	3.2	1.3	4.0	53.3	782	3 697	488.4	1 530	36 645	19 677	R–52.8
Pima	1 152	39.1	5.9	6.9	2.8	7.2	974.5	1 720	42 936	665.2	8 058	241 059	234 473	R–50.3
Pinal	1 132	58.9	6.1	6.1	3.4	5.5	38.8	403	9 788	897.2	711	19 626	29 180	R–51.3
Santa Cruz	1 252	56.7	3.4	5.2	5.6	5.8	11.7	548	1 319	531.9	418	14 967	6 690	R–49.6
Yavapai	1 010	50.8	10.2	4.4	4.2	4.8	24.1	314	4 576	464.1	989	29 171	43 206	R–64.4
Yuma	1 103	52.1	4.7	4.8	5.5	4.8	107.7	1 128	4 733	500.3	2 420	76 337	22 480	R–59.0
ARKANSAS	694	50.4	11.6	4.0	0.3	6.4	1 903.9	825	129 302	537.7	22 557	664 895	827 738	R–56.4
Arkansas	803	40.2	22.8	3.3	0.0	7.6	16.4	673	998	449.5	162	4 185	7 205	R–55.6
Ashley	717	57.0	0.4	3.3	0.1	9.4	53.6	2 013	987	384.0	89	2 239	8 659	D–51.6
Baxter	704	37.7	38.3	3.1	3.7	6.3	8.1	288	886	281.3	162	4 586	13 597	R–63.4
Benton	570	54.5	7.9	4.5	0.2	5.5	62.6	780	2 931	297.0	326	8 994	34 110	R–71.2
Boone	856	36.2	45.1	2.4	0.1	5.5	6.2	234	2 118	730.3	204	5 782	11 816	R–64.0
Bradley	693	53.1	14.5	3.7	0.2	6.9	4.5	332	769	605.5	47	1 248	4 269	D–50.8
Calhoun	645	61.7	3.6	3.6	0.0	13.8	1.1	180	592	986.7	19	474	2 344	R–56.1
Carroll	562	47.6	18.0	3.6	0.1	8.4	10.5	636	729	391.9	108	3 031	7 253	R–62.8
Chicot	924	49.1	29.8	3.0	0.1	5.8	7.4	407	939	572.6	61	1 659	4 346	D–55.8
Clark	597	49.8	18.5	4.7	0.1	10.0	8.8	383	1 805	839.5	123	3 106	8 130	D–57.5
Clay	580	55.8	18.7	2.5	0.1	8.4	9.6	476	740	389.5	82	2 104	6 240	D–55.2
Cleburne	542	56.7	19.3	4.0	0.2	7.8	2.6	149	547	274.9	106	2 479	8 381	R–58.8
Cleveland	517	68.7	2.4	3.8	0.2	10.4	1.5	186	287	350.0	21	548	2 881	R–50.7
Columbia	718	48.7	26.4	2.7	0.1	10.2	6.6	244	1 615	607.1	67	1 819	9 802	R–59.3

1. Based on the estimated population as of July 1, 1982. 2. Per 10,000 resident population estimated as of July 1 of the year shown. 3. Data subject to copyright.

STATE–County code	MSA/ CMSA/ NECMA code[1]	STATE County	Land Area,[2] 1990 (Sq. Km.)	Population, 1990 Total persons	Rank	Per square kilometer	Race White	Black	Am. Indian, Eskimo, Aleut	Asian & Pacific Islander	Other race	Hispanic[3]	Age of population Percent Under 5 years	5 to 14 years	15 to 24 years
			1	2	3	4	5	6	7	8	9	10	11	12	13
		ARKANSAS—Con.													
05 029	...	Conway	1 441	19 151	1 724	13.3	16 139	2 876	73	30	33	119	7.0	15.6	13.3
05 031	...	Craighead	1 841	68 956	642	37.5	64 449	3 778	200	393	136	386	7.0	13.7	18.5
05 033	2720	Crawford	1 542	42 493	946	27.6	40 974	374	658	389	98	459	7.5	16.7	13.7
05 035	4920	Crittenden	1 581	49 939	843	31.6	28 152	21 401	90	181	115	336	8.8	18.0	15.2
05 037	...	Cross	1 595	19 225	1 718	12.1	14 343	4 782	40	40	20	109	7.5	17.3	14.8
05 039	...	Dallas	1 729	9 614	2 423	5.6	5 873	3 698	16	11	16	32	6.6	15.1	13.1
05 041	...	Desha	1 981	16 798	1 860	8.5	9 500	7 139	48	37	74	152	8.0	18.4	14.5
05 043	...	Drew	2 145	17 369	1 830	8.1	12 530	4 754	27	23	35	92	7.0	16.1	17.2
05 045	4400	Faulkner	1 677	60 006	724	35.8	54 644	4 778	256	226	102	341	7.0	14.3	20.7
05 047	...	Franklin	1 579	14 897	1 995	9.4	14 644	99	98	24	32	179	6.4	14.7	14.2
05 049	...	Fulton	1 601	10 037	2 381	6.3	9 969	10	47	9	2	28	5.8	13.4	11.7
05 051	...	Garland	1 756	73 397	613	41.8	66 770	5 604	484	228	311	777	5.8	12.0	11.6
05 053	...	Grant	1 636	13 948	2 061	8.5	13 491	377	38	21	21	82	6.8	15.1	13.9
05 055	...	Greene	1 496	31 804	1 217	21.3	31 627	20	79	41	37	167	6.7	14.1	14.0
05 057	...	Hempstead	1 888	21 621	1 596	11.5	14 888	6 464	74	37	158	291	7.0	16.1	12.8
05 059	...	Hot Spring	1 593	26 115	1 418	16.4	23 066	2 865	126	33	25	115	6.5	14.8	12.9
05 061	...	Howard	1 522	13 569	2 094	8.9	10 504	2 919	53	60	33	94	6.9	16.1	13.6
05 063	...	Independence	1 978	31 192	1 237	15.8	30 344	595	80	115	58	172	6.5	15.1	13.8
05 065	...	Izard	1 504	11 364	2 265	7.6	11 266	11	64	18	5	71	5.6	12.0	10.7
05 067	...	Jackson	1 641	18 944	1 739	11.5	16 081	2 759	66	23	15	66	6.3	14.5	12.8
05 069	6240	Jefferson	2 292	85 487	537	37.3	47 878	36 877	227	352	153	427	7.3	16.0	16.5
05 071	...	Johnson	1 715	18 221	1 777	10.6	17 632	309	109	77	94	221	6.3	14.1	15.0
05 073	...	Lafayette	1 364	9 643	2 420	7.1	5 884	3 711	20	17	11	41	6.4	16.3	14.1
05 075	...	Lawrence	1 519	17 457	1 825	11.5	17 223	88	126	16	4	60	6.3	13.9	14.1
05 077	...	Lee	1 558	13 053	2 137	8.4	5 449	7 487	11	47	59	174	8.2	19.1	15.1
05 079	...	Lincoln	1 454	13 690	2 082	9.4	8 611	4 935	65	20	59	152	6.0	13.2	14.9
05 081	...	Little River	1 377	13 966	2 059	10.1	10 820	2 931	116	17	82	160	6.8	16.2	14.6
05 083	...	Logan	1 839	20 557	1 651	11.2	20 083	273	125	28	48	143	6.8	15.0	13.8
05 085	4400	Lonoke	1 983	39 268	1 018	19.8	35 395	3 536	166	114	57	246	7.0	17.4	13.7
05 087	...	Madison	2 168	11 618	2 247	5.4	11 435	3	140	13	27	111	7.1	15.2	12.8
05 089	...	Marion	1 548	12 001	2 220	7.8	11 899	6	53	24	19	48	5.2	12.8	10.5
05 091	8360	Miller	1 616	38 467	1 041	23.8	29 464	8 625	148	143	87	310	7.5	16.3	14.5
05 093	...	Mississippi	2 327	57 525	756	24.7	40 689	16 006	168	352	310	745	8.9	17.5	15.9
05 095	...	Monroe	1 571	11 333	2 272	7.2	6 862	4 422	26	22	1	32	7.6	16.8	13.1
05 097	...	Montgomery	2 023	7 841	2 592	3.9	7 718	8	93	11	11	56	5.7	13.0	12.1
05 099	...	Nevada	1 606	10 101	2 377	6.3	6 856	3 196	27	5	17	64	6.4	15.6	13.9
05 101	...	Newton	2 132	7 666	2 606	3.6	7 582	0	51	19	14	43	6.4	16.8	12.5
05 103	...	Ouachita	1 897	30 574	1 261	16.1	19 702	10 739	44	67	22	133	7.0	15.5	12.6
05 105	...	Perry	1 427	7 969	2 575	5.6	7 780	119	42	17	11	47	6.2	14.1	14.1
05 107	...	Phillips	1 794	28 838	1 335	16.1	12 915	15 753	40	72	58	237	9.0	19.6	14.3
05 109	...	Pike	1 562	10 086	2 379	6.5	9 621	378	56	6	25	56	6.7	14.5	13.3
05 111	...	Poinsett	1 963	24 664	1 475	12.6	22 797	1 773	43	28	23	124	7.2	14.9	13.8
05 113	...	Polk	2 226	17 347	1 831	7.8	17 035	0	186	33	93	301	6.5	14.5	12.6
05 115	...	Pope	2 103	45 883	906	21.8	44 126	1 129	319	200	109	423	7.3	14.6	17.3
05 117	...	Prairie	1 673	9 518	2 432	5.7	8 170	1 294	38	4	12	38	6.7	14.5	13.2
05 119	4400	Pulaski	1 997	349 660	147	175.1	252 554	92 200	1 163	2 762	981	3 199	7.5	14.5	14.4
05 121	...	Randolph	1 688	16 558	1 883	9.8	16 322	146	52	19	19	75	6.5	14.5	13.3
05 123	...	St. Francis	1 642	28 497	1 343	17.4	14 722	13 521	47	116	91	202	8.4	19.0	14.4
05 125	4400	Saline	1 877	64 183	684	34.2	62 215	1 348	285	245	90	378	6.7	15.7	13.8
05 127	...	Scott	2 315	10 205	2 371	4.4	10 035	1	106	51	12	42	7.2	13.8	13.6
05 129	...	Searcy	1 728	7 841	2 591	4.5	7 750	2	66	15	8	32	5.9	14.0	11.8
05 131	2720	Sebastian	1 389	99 590	461	71.7	88 719	5 666	1 396	3 291	518	1 362	7.3	14.6	13.8
05 133	...	Sevier	1 461	13 637	2 088	9.3	12 081	787	222	16	531	632	6.4	15.3	13.5
05 135	...	Sharp	1 565	14 109	2 046	9.0	13 908	66	105	17	13	57	4.9	12.5	10.9
05 137	...	Stone	1 571	9 775	2 407	6.2	9 687	8	54	20	6	42	5.7	14.4	10.8
05 139	...	Union	2 691	46 719	895	17.4	32 414	14 061	79	91	74	222	7.2	15.7	12.9
05 141	...	Van Buren	1 843	14 008	2 054	7.6	13 845	41	76	22	24	98	5.1	13.1	10.9
05 143	2580	Washington	2 461	113 409	405	46.1	108 743	1 676	1 486	1 043	461	1 526	6.9	13.9	19.1
05 145	...	White	2 678	54 676	788	20.4	52 509	1 703	233	119	112	372	6.5	14.2	17.8
05 147	...	Woodruff	1 519	9 520	2 431	6.3	6 502	2 991	15	11	1	17	7.3	16.2	13.9
05 149	...	Yell	2 403	17 759	1 800	7.4	17 172	371	75	98	43	177	6.9	14.2	13.7
06 000	...	CALIFORNIA	403 970	29 760 021	X	73.7	20 524 327	2 208 801	242 164	2 845 659	3 939 070	7 687 938	8.1	14.1	15.3
06 001	7362	Alameda	1 910	1 279 182	22	669.7	761 815	229 249	8 894	192 554	86 670	181 805	7.5	12.7	14.7
06 003	...	Alpine	1 913	1 113	3 109	0.6	806	6	281	5	15	74	7.1	15.5	11.9
06 005	...	Amador	1 535	30 039	1 293	19.6	26 894	1 682	493	218	752	2 520	4.9	11.0	13.2

1. MSA = Metropolitan Statistical Area. CMSA = Consolidated MSA. NECMA = New England county metropolitan area. PMSA = Primary MSA. See Appendix A for explanation of these concepts. See Appendix B for list of metropolitan areas identified by type, with component counties. 2. Dry land or land partially or temporarily covered by water. 3. Hispanic persons may be of any race.

Table A. States and Counties — **Population**

STATE County	Population, 1990 (cont'd)							Population–Change and components of change							
	Age of population (cont'd) Percent						Percent female	Change		Components of change, 1980–1986					
								1980–1990		Total persons, 1986	Total persons, 1980	Net change		Natural increase	
	25 to 34 years	35 to 44 years	45 to 54 years	55 to 64 years	65 to 74 years	75 years and over		Number	Percent			Number	Percent	Births	Deaths
	14	15	16	17	18	19	20	21	22	23	24	25	26	27	28
ARKANSAS—Con.															
Conway	14.6	12.7	10.5	9.9	9.2	7.2	52.1	-354	-1.8	19 200	19 505	-300	-1.4	1 800	1 300
Craighead	16.2	13.9	10.3	8.4	6.8	5.4	51.9	5 717	9.0	63 400	63 239	100	0.2	5 600	3 500
Crawford	16.1	14.5	11.1	8.4	6.8	5.1	51.1	5 601	15.2	41 900	36 892	5 000	13.5	3 600	2 100
Crittenden	16.2	13.6	9.9	7.6	6.1	4.5	52.8	440	0.9	50 400	49 499	900	1.8	6 000	2 800
Cross	14.3	13.4	10.5	8.3	7.6	6.3	52.0	-1 209	-5.9	20 400	20 434	0	-0.2	2 200	1 300
Dallas	13.2	13.6	10.3	9.8	9.5	8.8	52.1	-901	-8.6	10 400	10 515	-100	-0.9	1 000	900
Desha	14.1	13.0	9.4	7.8	7.6	7.2	53.3	-2 962	-15.0	19 400	19 760	-400	-1.9	2 300	1 300
Drew	14.5	13.5	10.0	8.3	7.1	6.4	51.9	-541	-3.0	18 000	17 910	100	0.3	1 700	1 000
Faulkner	16.5	14.0	9.5	7.3	6.1	4.6	51.6	13 814	29.9	52 900	46 192	6 700	14.5	4 500	2 300
Franklin	14.1	13.5	10.7	9.5	9.1	7.7	50.4	192	1.3	15 700	14 705	1 000	6.7	1 300	1 000
Fulton	11.9	13.0	11.1	12.0	12.2	9.0	52.2	62	0.6	10 300	9 975	300	3.2	700	800
Garland	13.0	13.1	10.5	11.9	12.9	9.2	52.4	2 866	4.1	75 300	70 531	4 700	6.7	5 700	5 900
Grant	15.1	15.0	12.4	8.8	7.1	5.7	50.8	940	7.2	13 500	13 008	500	4.0	1 100	800
Greene	14.5	13.9	11.5	9.9	8.6	6.9	51.6	1 060	3.4	31 700	30 744	900	3.0	2 500	2 000
Hempstead	15.0	13.0	10.1	9.3	8.4	8.2	52.5	-2 014	-8.5	23 000	23 635	-600	-2.6	2 100	1 700
Hot Spring	13.8	14.2	10.9	10.3	9.6	7.1	51.7	-704	-2.6	27 400	26 819	500	2.0	2 200	1 700
Howard	14.2	12.8	10.5	8.7	8.6	8.6	52.0	110	0.8	13 500	13 459	0	0.1	1 400	1 000
Independence	14.9	14.5	10.9	9.5	8.1	6.6	51.4	1 045	3.5	32 300	30 147	2 100	7.1	2 800	1 900
Izard	11.5	11.7	11.0	11.8	14.3	11.6	52.0	596	5.5	11 000	10 768	200	1.9	700	900
Jackson	14.1	13.6	11.0	10.1	9.5	8.2	52.3	-2 702	-12.5	20 700	21 646	-900	-4.2	1 700	1 500
Jefferson	15.0	13.7	9.8	8.3	7.5	6.0	51.9	-5 231	-5.8	90 000	90 718	-700	-0.8	9 400	5 400
Johnson	14.3	12.5	10.4	10.0	9.2	8.1	51.3	798	4.6	18 600	17 423	1 100	6.5	1 600	1 300
Lafayette	13.1	12.5	10.8	9.1	9.2	8.5	52.3	-570	-5.6	9 800	10 213	-400	-4.3	1 000	900
Lawrence	13.6	12.8	10.8	9.9	9.8	8.9	52.0	-990	-5.4	18 100	18 447	-300	-1.7	1 600	1 400
Lee	11.4	11.9	9.4	9.3	8.3	7.4	52.8	-2 486	-16.0	15 000	15 539	-500	-3.5	1 800	1 100
Lincoln	21.6	15.1	9.6	7.6	6.1	5.9	41.2	321	2.4	13 200	13 369	-200	-1.3	1 100	700
Little River	14.1	13.9	11.3	9.0	7.7	6.4	51.5	14	0.1	14 100	13 952	200	1.3	1 200	800
Logan	14.0	13.2	10.9	9.3	9.0	8.0	50.7	413	2.1	20 900	20 144	800	3.9	1 800	1 400
Lonoke	16.1	14.9	11.4	7.9	6.5	5.1	50.9	4 750	13.8	38 400	34 518	3 800	11.1	3 400	2 000
Madison	13.6	14.0	11.1	9.9	9.2	7.2	50.9	245	2.2	11 900	11 373	600	4.9	1 100	800
Marion	11.7	12.8	11.4	12.8	13.5	9.3	51.3	667	5.9	12 600	11 334	1 300	11.2	800	800
Miller	15.2	13.7	10.1	8.8	7.8	6.2	52.2	701	1.9	38 900	37 766	1 200	3.1	3 800	2 400
Mississippi	16.4	13.1	8.8	7.6	6.5	5.2	51.7	-1 992	-3.3	58 000	59 517	-1 500	-2.5	7 600	3 600
Monroe	13.1	11.6	10.0	9.8	9.6	8.4	53.1	-2 719	-19.3	12 900	14 052	-1 100	-8.1	1 400	1 100
Montgomery	12.6	12.5	12.0	12.1	11.4	8.5	50.7	70	0.9	7 900	7 771	100	1.9	500	600
Nevada	13.3	13.5	10.0	8.9	9.6	8.7	52.2	-996	-9.0	10 800	11 097	-300	-2.6	900	900
Newton	13.2	14.3	12.1	9.7	8.9	6.1	49.9	-90	-1.2	8 200	7 756	500	6.0	700	400
Ouachita	14.6	14.0	9.9	10.0	8.9	7.6	52.8	33	0.1	33 800	30 541	3 200	10.6	3 200	2 400
Perry	13.6	13.6	11.3	10.8	9.9	6.3	50.8	703	9.7	7 900	7 266	600	8.1	600	500
Phillips	12.6	11.5	9.4	8.6	8.1	7.0	54.3	-5 934	-17.1	33 100	34 772	-1 700	-4.9	4 600	2 500
Pike	13.8	12.9	11.1	9.5	10.1	8.2	51.3	-287	-2.8	10 000	10 373	-300	-3.2	900	800
Poinsett	14.6	13.3	11.4	9.5	8.7	6.6	51.9	-2 368	-8.8	26 000	27 032	-1 000	-3.6	2 400	1 700
Polk	12.4	12.8	11.1	10.7	10.3	9.0	51.3	340	2.0	17 100	17 007	100	0.4	1 500	1 300
Pope	15.7	14.4	10.0	8.3	6.9	5.5	50.6	6 919	17.8	43 400	38 964	4 500	11.5	3 800	2 100
Prairie	14.3	13.3	11.3	10.2	9.4	7.2	50.9	-622	-6.1	10 100	10 140	0	-0.3	900	700
Pulaski	18.4	15.7	10.1	7.9	6.6	4.9	52.4	9 062	2.7	356 300	340 598	15 700	4.6	38 400	17 900
Randolph	13.5	12.8	11.2	11.0	9.5	7.7	51.7	-276	-1.6	16 700	16 834	-100	-0.7	1 300	1 100
St. Francis	13.9	13.2	9.5	8.3	7.4	6.0	53.6	-2 361	-7.7	31 500	30 858	700	2.2	3 800	2 000
Saline	16.5	15.7	11.6	8.9	6.7	4.4	50.6	11 027	20.7	58 000	53 156	4 800	9.1	4 600	2 300
Scott	14.0	12.0	12.1	10.5	8.8	8.0	50.9	520	5.4	10 300	9 685	600	6.3	700	700
Searcy	11.8	13.9	11.2	11.6	10.9	8.9	51.2	-1 006	-11.4	8 900	8 847	0	0.2	600	600
Sebastian	16.4	14.7	10.7	8.5	7.8	6.2	51.7	4 418	4.6	99 200	95 172	4 000	4.3	9 500	5 500
Sevier	14.9	13.6	10.6	9.2	8.8	7.6	50.6	-423	-3.0	14 200	14 060	100	0.8	1 200	1 000
Sharp	10.7	11.3	10.0	12.6	15.5	11.6	52.5	-498	-3.4	15 500	14 607	900	6.3	1 000	1 200
Stone	13.1	13.9	12.4	12.3	10.1	7.3	51.1	753	8.3	10 000	9 022	1 000	11.4	700	600
Union	15.0	14.0	9.7	8.9	9.0	7.6	52.7	-1 854	-3.8	49 000	48 573	500	1.0	4 800	3 500
Van Buren	11.0	11.9	10.4	13.7	15.1	8.7	50.7	651	4.9	15 000	13 357	1 700	12.5	900	900
Washington	16.8	14.4	9.8	7.7	6.3	4.9	50.6	12 915	12.9	107 400	100 494	6 900	6.8	9 900	5 000
White	14.2	13.1	10.6	9.0	8.1	6.6	51.5	3 841	7.6	53 200	50 835	2 300	4.6	4 700	3 100
Woodruff	13.6	13.3	9.5	8.6	9.3	8.3	53.0	-1 702	-15.2	10 500	11 222	-800	-6.8	1 100	900
Yell	14.5	12.9	11.3	10.1	9.3	7.2	51.3	733	4.3	17 700	17 026	700	4.2	1 400	1 200
CALIFORNIA	19.1	15.6	9.8	7.5	6.2	4.3	49.9	6 092 021	25.7	26 981 000	23 668 000	3 313 000	14.0	2 739 000	1 204 000
Alameda	19.6	17.2	10.3	7.4	6.2	4.4	50.7	173 803	15.7	1 208 700	1 105 379	103 300	9.3	116 800	58 800
Alpine	19.0	18.2	11.5	9.3	4.3	3.2	47.0	16	1.5	1 300	1 097	200	17.1	100	0
Amador	16.0	15.9	10.6	10.8	10.9	6.7	43.7	10 725	55.5	23 700	19 314	4 400	22.9	1 600	1 500

STATE County	Population–(cont'd) Components of change, 1980-1986 (cont'd) Net migration	Households, 1990 Number	Households, 1990 Percent change, 1980–1990	Households, 1990 Persons per household	Households, 1990 Percent Female family householder[1]	Households, 1990 Percent One-person	Births, 1988 Total	Births, 1988 Rate[2]	Births, 1988 Low birth weight[3] (Number)	Deaths, 1987 Number Total	Deaths, 1987 Number Infant[4]	Deaths, 1987 Rate Total[2]	Deaths, 1987 Rate Infant[5]	Marriages, 1984 Number	Marriages, 1984 Rate[2]
	29	30	31	32	33	34	35	36	37	38	39	40	41	42	43
ARKANSAS—Con.															
Conway	-800	7 179	5.6	2.62	10.9	23.5	300	15.8	14	219	1	11.5	3.6	272	13.9
Craighead	-2 000	26 285	17.7	2.53	10.5	23.5	959	14.7	66	584	5	9.1	5.5	996	15.8
Crawford	3 500	15 251	21.4	2.75	9.9	17.9	679	15.5	46	392	4	9.2	6.2	657	16.5
Crittenden	-2 300	17 120	9.0	2.89	18.7	21.3	974	19.0	111	461	16	9.1	16.8	1 129	22.6
Cross	-1 000	6 754	1.9	2.81	12.8	20.8	308	15.2	26	180	2	8.9	6.6	250	12.1
Dallas	-200	3 600	-3.6	2.61	11.6	25.3	153	14.9	23	146	0	14.0	0.0	135	12.7
Desha	-1 400	5 957	-10.3	2.78	17.5	24.3	293	15.6	38	191	5	10.0	17.3	157	8.0
Drew	-600	6 342	2.3	2.63	13.6	23.7	280	15.9	29	162	1	9.2	4.3	212	11.8
Faulkner	4 600	21 325	37.7	2.65	9.3	20.5	804	14.3	40	418	9	7.7	11.1	719	14.5
Franklin	700	5 578	8.0	2.58	8.0	22.2	210	13.4	14	163	1	10.4	4.7	256	16.6
Fulton	400	4 010	6.5	2.47	7.0	23.3	104	9.9	6	123	2	11.8	18.2	94	9.0
Garland	5 000	30 836	9.5	2.32	9.5	27.6	971	12.7	71	1 031	8	13.5	8.6	1 218	16.4
Grant	300	5 118	13.6	2.70	7.2	19.1	176	12.6	13	123	3	9.0	14.9	192	14.5
Greene	400	12 325	9.8	2.54	8.5	22.0	387	12.2	17	319	6	10.0	14.3	496	15.9
Hempstead	-1 000	8 212	-4.3	2.58	13.4	25.0	310	13.7	35	242	3	10.6	9.0	287	12.2
Hot Spring	0	10 115	4.5	2.55	10.0	23.2	320	11.8	28	300	2	10.9	5.9	301	11.1
Howard	-400	4 975	3.3	2.65	11.5	23.4	201	15.0	19	190	1	14.1	4.7	206	15.1
Independence	1 300	11 846	8.7	2.58	8.2	22.8	432	13.5	36	314	3	9.8	7.4	406	12.6
Izard	400	4 684	9.3	2.37	6.9	24.2	106	9.5	4	193	1	17.4	9.7	100	9.1
Jackson	-1 200	7 361	-5.5	2.54	12.2	25.0	234	11.5	19	250	4	12.2	17.0	287	13.3
Jefferson	-4 800	30 001	-1.9	2.70	16.0	24.2	1 463	16.1	163	897	13	9.9	9.3	1 013	11.2
Johnson	800	7 059	10.4	2.50	8.6	24.4	236	12.8	13	207	4	11.2	17.2	205	11.1
Lafayette	-500	3 584	-0.1	2.66	13.9	26.6	112	11.8	11	132	0	13.6	0.0	122	12.1
Lawrence	-600	6 857	0.9	2.49	9.3	24.9	220	12.4	11	240	1	13.3	4.2	231	12.6
Lee	-1 200	4 578	-7.4	2.82	20.1	25.6	227	15.7	32	169	3	11.4	12.9	191	12.4
Lincoln	-600	3 796	-3.1	2.76	14.0	23.4	177	13.3	17	133	0	9.9	0.0	117	8.8
Little River	-200	5 150	8.8	2.68	11.5	22.1	185	13.2	17	145	0	10.4	0.0	164	11.6
Logan	400	7 628	8.1	2.60	8.6	23.6	288	13.9	24	262	0	12.6	0.0	261	12.7
Lonoke	2 400	13 866	21.5	2.80	9.4	18.5	509	12.9	51	342	11	8.8	20.6	489	13.3
Madison	300	4 392	7.3	2.63	6.2	20.7	149	12.3	13	131	2	10.8	11.2	146	12.4
Marion	1 300	4 970	15.3	2.40	6.8	23.3	128	9.8	7	137	1	10.7	7.7	111	9.0
Miller	-300	14 273	5.9	2.64	14.9	23.7	654	16.6	54	399	4	10.1	6.6	732	18.7
Mississippi	-5 500	20 420	3.4	2.76	15.3	22.4	1 171	20.5	108	614	10	10.7	8.7	890	15.0
Monroe	-1 500	4 361	-11.4	2.57	15.8	28.7	209	16.7	13	165	2	12.9	9.7	130	9.7
Montgomery	300	3 062	4.8	2.46	6.9	23.2	98	12.3	5	91	2	11.4	19.8	92	11.8
Nevada	-300	3 798	-4.6	2.60	12.3	26.0	121	11.4	11	145	1	13.4	8.3	130	11.9
Newton	200	2 818	3.7	2.70	6.1	20.5	129	15.7	9	85	1	10.4	11.4	54	6.7
Ouachita	2 500	11 712	4.6	2.57	13.0	25.8	532	15.7	57	394	2	11.7	3.7	407	12.4
Perry	500	3 055	19.1	2.58	6.9	22.8	87	10.7	4	96	1	12.0	9.8	82	10.6
Phillips	-3 700	10 183	-10.9	2.80	22.1	26.8	571	18.0	54	397	11	12.3	18.0	373	11.1
Pike	-400	3 855	0.4	2.57	6.8	22.5	139	13.4	10	113	2	11.1	14.6	96	9.5
Poinsett	-1 700	9 368	-1.0	2.60	11.4	23.1	367	14.2	25	322	4	12.4	10.8	281	10.8
Polk	-200	6 827	8.1	2.51	7.5	24.0	207	11.9	12	223	1	13.0	4.6	251	14.4
Pope	2 800	16 828	23.6	2.61	8.7	21.8	705	15.7	46	375	5	8.5	7.6	546	13.1
Prairie	-200	3 661	0.1	2.58	8.9	24.1	122	12.3	5	107	2	10.7	16.8	107	10.7
Pulaski	-4 800	137 209	10.2	2.49	13.5	27.5	5 978	16.7	530	2 969	67	8.3	11.1	4 799	13.7
Randolph	-300	6 445	6.0	2.54	8.5	23.1	212	12.8	15	201	1	12.0	5.2	217	13.2
St. Francis	-1 200	9 958	0.3	2.83	19.2	23.8	496	16.2	45	344	5	11.0	9.5	357	11.4
Saline	2 600	23 037	31.1	2.73	8.1	17.6	818	13.5	64	415	7	7.0	8.9	828	14.9
Scott	600	3 957	12.0	2.55	8.1	22.0	154	14.7	5	113	1	10.8	6.8	149	15.1
Searcy	0	3 117	-4.3	2.49	5.5	23.6	86	10.0	2	99	1	11.2	10.1	82	9.2
Sebastian	100	39 298	9.8	2.49	9.8	26.7	1 561	15.5	131	961	19	9.6	12.2	1 853	19.0
Sevier	-100	5 118	1.2	2.62	8.8	23.2	154	11.0	15	175	3	12.4	17.8	247	17.3
Sharp	1 100	5 819	3.1	2.39	6.5	24.0	145	9.2	7	222	0	14.1	0.0	145	9.4
Stone	1 000	3 866	17.9	2.50	7.0	22.0	108	10.6	9	110	0	10.9	0.0	115	12.0
Union	-800	17 819	-1.4	2.57	13.0	25.8	764	15.7	67	565	9	11.5	12.7	661	13.4
Van Buren	1 700	5 698	13.6	2.43	6.5	22.8	137	8.7	5	155	0	10.1	0.0	132	9.0
Washington	2 000	43 372	20.2	2.52	8.1	24.4	1 732	15.7	115	906	14	8.3	8.6	1 811	17.4
White	800	19 823	13.8	2.60	8.5	21.4	741	13.7	60	518	4	9.7	5.4	642	12.3
Woodruff	-1 000	3 630	-9.6	2.59	16.3	26.8	151	15.3	19	127	1	12.5	7.3	119	11.1
Yell	600	6 907	11.1	2.55	8.4	22.8	281	15.4	17	209	2	11.7	7.5	107	6.1
CALIFORNIA	1 778 000	10 381 206	20.3	2.79	11.5	23.4	533 148	18.8	32 001	209 424	4 546	7.6	9.0	227 968	8.8
Alameda	45 300	479 518	12.5	2.59	12.9	26.8	21 866	17.6	1 590	9 718	186	8.0	8.9	7 441	6.3
Alpine	100	450	16.6	2.47	10.2	29.8	20	16.7	1	5	0	4.2	0.0	12	10.0
Amador	4 300	10 518	40.8	2.41	6.0	22.3	234	8.5	18	299	1	11.8	3.8	128	5.8

1. No spouse present. 2. Per 1,000 resident population estimated as of July 1 of the year shown. 3. Under 2,500 grams. 4. Deaths of infants under 1 year old. 5. Deaths of infants under 1 year old per 1,000 live births.

STATE County	Divorces, 1984: Number	Divorces, 1984: Rate[1]	Physicians, active non–Federal, 1989: Number[2]	Physicians: Rate[3]	Hospitals, 1989: Number	Hospitals, 1989: Beds: Number	Hospitals, 1989: Beds: Rate[3]	Nursing homes,[4] 1986: Number	Nursing homes: Beds	Serious crimes known to police, 1988: Number: Total[5]	Serious crimes: Number: Violent[6]	Serious crimes: Rate[3]	Education: Public school enrollment[7]: 1986–1987	Public school enrollment[7]: 1980	Attainment,[8] 1980: Percent 12 yrs. or more	Attainment,[8] 1980: Percent 16 yrs. or more
	44	45	46	47	48	49	50	51	52	53	54	55	56	57	58	59
ARKANSAS—Con.																
Conway	91	4.7	13	69	1	84	444	2	175	250	11	1 291	3 507	4 085	50.9	7.6
Craighead	309	4.9	157	238	3	455	690	8	602	2 891	91	4 420	11 904	11 879	54.0	13.3
Crawford	323	8.1	17	38	1	100	222	3	372	1 063	46	2 455	8 260	8 031	52.5	5.1
Crittenden	326	6.5	33	64	1	123	238	5	274	2 716	367	5 283	10 831	12 036	46.2	7.3
Cross	NA	NA	10	50	1	53	265	4	352	450	37	2 186	4 595	5 009	43.5	7.4
Dallas	56	5.3	5	49	1	79	775	4	250	250	60	2 371	2 051	2 221	51.9	8.8
Desha	46	2.3	9	48	2	69	371	2	220	828	41	4 275	4 518	4 702	46.2	8.8
Drew	117	6.5	8	46	1	50	287	1	124	151	9	832	3 334	3 717	51.6	12.8
Faulkner	353	7.1	46	80	1	116	201	5	353	1 948	159	3 525	9 061	8 325	61.9	14.5
Franklin	85	5.5	5	32	1	22	140	2	211	228	40	1 441	3 296	2 979	51.1	6.1
Fulton	40	3.8	7	67	1	51	486	1	125	147	10	1 407	1 662	1 939	48.7	5.3
Garland	496	6.7	129	168	3	435	565	9	710	3 997	289	5 152	11 788	12 244	59.9	11.3
Grant	84	6.4	4	28	0	0	0	1	110	229	17	1 648	3 776	2 967	53.4	7.3
Greene	238	7.6	27	85	1	129	406	5	374	941	56	2 927	5 718	6 178	44.8	7.3
Hempstead	137	5.8	19	84	1	75	333	2	203	700	38	3 014	4 264	4 624	56.2	8.8
Hot Spring	211	7.8	13	48	1	77	283	3	268	581	38	2 076	5 478	5 659	54.0	8.2
Howard	100	7.4	9	67	1	63	470	5	365	222	20	1 634	2 935	2 796	48.1	7.1
Independence	250	7.8	34	107	1	130	408	3	306	901	36	2 734	5 709	5 960	50.2	8.2
Izard	48	4.4	5	44	1	26	230	3	259	52	3	462	1 617	1 886	51.1	8.6
Jackson	125	5.8	18	89	2	218	1 079	3	245	459	23	2 219	3 351	4 653	41.2	8.0
Jefferson	546	6.0	138	152	1	425	468	6	505	4 757	668	5 183	18 487	19 441	57.6	11.9
Johnson	110	6.0	13	71	1	68	370	3	159	357	13	1 893	3 312	3 451	47.8	8.7
Lafayette	64	6.3	3	32	0	0	0	1	116	49	2	503	1 937	2 275	41.2	5.7
Lawrence	NA	NA	9	51	1	170	971	5	284	171	0	932	3 369	3 809	41.0	5.5
Lee	84	5.5	6	42	0	0	0	3	192	518	37	3 428	3 213	4 029	31.9	7.1
Lincoln	69	5.2	0	0	0	0	0	2	159	85	4	640	2 174	2 668	41.6	5.7
Little River	95	6.7	5	36	1	42	300	2	129	322	42	2 252	3 058	3 335	52.2	7.7
Logan	109	5.3	12	58	2	47	228	4	232	366	8	1 735	3 415	4 096	46.5	6.3
Lonoke	247	6.7	13	32	0	0	0	11	544	679	32	1 708	8 041	8 103	53.3	8.0
Madison	66	5.6	6	50	1	42	347	1	70	220	20	1 793	2 297	2 299	47.9	6.2
Marion	79	6.4	11	83	1	48	361	1	61	135	0	1 040	2 011	2 151	56.2	7.2
Miller	226	5.8	36	91	1	229	577	4	268	4 339	297	10 943	7 983	7 928	54.9	7.8
Mississippi	482	8.1	45	80	4	298	527	7	519	3 573	537	6 138	12 109	13 427	46.9	8.6
Monroe	56	4.2	11	89	0	0	0	2	105	328	18	2 527	2 554	3 147	39.8	6.1
Montgomery	50	6.4	2	25	0	0	0	2	87	56	3	699	1 339	1 403	47.5	7.8
Nevada	60	5.5	6	58	1	65	625	2	181	139	14	1 269	2 364	2 280	48.0	6.7
Newton	35	4.3	2	24	0	0	0	1	42	40	1	481	1 397	1 629	45.3	6.9
Ouachita	234	7.1	22	65	1	150	442	4	387	1 457	510	4 238	6 376	6 237	52.0	9.1
Perry	NA	NA	2	24	0	0	0	1	65	119	8	1 467	1 585	1 716	51.2	5.6
Phillips	160	4.7	21	67	1	121	388	3	318	1 140	52	3 491	7 575	8 469	41.7	8.3
Pike	46	4.6	5	48	1	32	308	2	145	50	1	483	1 906	2 127	48.2	7.2
Poinsett	182	7.0	8	31	0	0	0	3	301	622	26	2 368	5 105	5 957	39.4	6.2
Polk	134	7.7	15	86	1	51	293	2	174	236	18	1 369	3 168	3 524	49.9	8.1
Pope	148	3.6	60	132	1	144	316	4	408	1 663	92	3 719	8 120	7 849	57.5	11.8
Prairie	51	5.1	2	20	0	0	0	1	80	82	5	809	1 802	2 316	42.8	6.5
Pulaski	2 862	8.2	1 442	403	13	4 383	1 226	21	2 440	33 943	4 310	9 347	60 022	62 475	71.7	18.8
Randolph	82	5.0	10	60	1	50	301	3	164	208	13	1 221	2 740	3 433	42.2	6.3
St. Francis	210	6.7	19	62	1	118	387	5	294	2 049	366	6 476	7 639	7 509	45.1	8.0
Saline	405	7.3	46	74	2	171	277	5	969	1 817	15	3 001	10 168	11 499	60.2	8.2
Scott	66	6.7	6	56	1	113	1 056	1	85	110	10	1 023	1 574	1 982	42.4	3.7
Searcy	16	1.8	3	35	0	0	0	1	77	62	9	695	1 419	1 783	41.6	7.1
Sebastian	795	8.1	252	248	4	951	936	8	797	6 163	624	6 065	16 490	17 125	64.4	11.9
Sevier	110	7.7	11	80	1	90	652	1	105	364	21	2 528	2 444	3 083	52.5	8.5
Sharp	75	4.9	10	63	1	34	215	3	212	145	14	911	2 902	2 737	53.7	8.2
Stone	55	5.7	7	68	1	48	466	1	86	41	2	393	1 602	1 859	41.9	7.0
Union	387	7.9	88	181	1	301	621	6	617	1 657	146	3 342	9 703	9 458	58.0	10.7
Van Buren	NA	NA	9	57	1	32	201	1	83	147	16	947	2 230	2 709	52.4	6.8
Washington	807	7.8	202	180	5	837	746	9	701	5 200	231	4 674	18 220	17 551	63.8	18.0
White	396	7.6	49	90	2	205	378	5	453	1 535	83	2 824	9 804	9 951	48.6	8.8
Woodruff	66	6.2	5	52	0	0	0	1	105	65	3	628	2 113	2 620	38.4	7.0
Yell	163	9.3	13	71	2	85	462	3	256	386	48	2 126	3 426	3 477	48.7	5.0
CALIFORNIA	142 972	5.5	68 519	236	566	106 768	367	4 262	168 325	1 864 212	261 279	6 620	4 621 126	4 173 201	73.5	19.6
Alameda	7 470	6.3	3 145	250	24	3 995	317	255	9 245	103 708	10 963	8 328	184 707	183 421	76.0	22.3
Alpine	3	2.5	0	0	0	0	0	0	0	171	2	13 993	146	228	86.1	32.4
Amador	126	5.7	33	113	1	87	298	3	134	754	73	3 028	3 630	3 500	76.8	12.6

1. Per 1,000 resident population estimated as of July 1 of the year shown. 2. As of end of year. 3. Per 100,000 resident population as of July 1 of the year shown. 4. Preliminary. Covers nursing homes with 3 or more beds. 5. Data for serious crimes have not been adjusted for underreporting, this may affect comparability between geographic areas or over time. 6. Includes murder and nonnegligent manslaughter, forcible rape, robbery, and aggravated assault. 7. The 1986–1987 data are based on administrative reports obtained by the U.S. National Center for Education Statistics. The 1980 data are based on the 1980 Census of Population and Housing. 8. Persons 25 years old or older.

STATE County	Education (cont'd) Local government expenditures for education,[1] 1982: Total (Mil dol)	Education (cont'd) Local government expenditures for education,[1] 1982: Per capita (Dollars)	Social Security Program December 1988 Beneficiaries: Total	Social Security Program December 1988 Beneficiaries: Rate[2]	Social Security Program December 1988: Payments ($1,000)	Supplemental Security Income Program recipients June 1986	Money income Per capita[3]: 1987 Income, (Dollars)	Money income Per capita[3] 1979: Current dollars	Money income Per capita[3] 1979: Constant 1987 dollars	Money income: Median household income 1979 (Dollars)	Money income Percent below poverty level, 1979: Persons	Money income Percent below poverty level, 1979: Families	Housing units, 1990: Total	Housing units, 1990: Percent change, 1980–1990
	60	61	62	63	64	65	66	67	68	69	70	71	72	73
ARKANSAS—Con.														
Conway	6.7	350	4 080	214.7	1 641	840	8 242	5 091	7 966	11 681	17.5	14.1	8 009	7.4
Craighead	19.8	317	11 210	171.9	4 767	1 952	9 562	5 839	9 136	13 040	15.0	12.5	28 434	17.8
Crawford	11.7	310	7 210	164.2	2 936	882	8 376	5 166	8 083	12 932	16.1	13.7	16 711	21.4
Crittenden	18.8	379	7 530	146.8	2 927	2 554	7 600	4 942	7 733	11 687	31.4	23.8	18 875	11.2
Cross	7.9	380	3 625	179.5	1 394	900	7 772	5 160	8 074	12 171	22.4	17.3	7 254	0.9
Dallas	3.7	345	2 395	232.5	1 003	468	8 871	5 547	8 679	11 473	17.3	12.6	4 049	-4.4
Desha	9.5	478	3 195	169.9	1 229	914	7 219	5 063	7 922	10 167	27.0	20.9	6 706	-7.7
Drew	6.2	342	3 195	181.5	1 278	652	8 067	5 283	8 266	11 908	17.8	14.6	7 159	7.7
Faulkner	13.6	287	8 290	147.5	3 570	1 286	9 081	5 574	8 722	13 500	13.6	9.7	23 397	39.2
Franklin	5.4	359	3 340	212.7	1 337	374	7 736	4 684	7 329	11 465	18.1	15.2	6 228	9.5
Fulton	2.8	283	2 475	235.7	929	402	6 901	4 272	6 684	9 454	21.7	18.2	4 839	11.0
Garland	20.4	285	20 270	265.0	9 507	1 748	10 151	6 357	9 947	12 132	15.5	10.7	37 966	11.3
Grant	5.8	447	2 320	165.7	965	278	9 064	5 674	8 878	14 233	15.5	13.3	5 540	13.0
Greene	9.8	317	6 370	200.3	2 522	1 132	8 228	5 143	8 047	11 503	18.0	14.7	13 216	10.6
Hempstead	10.2	433	4 345	191.4	1 826	706	8 273	5 095	7 972	11 161	19.1	15.5	9 690	-0.1
Hot Spring	8.8	332	5 550	204.0	2 460	678	7 754	5 463	8 548	12 412	16.9	13.4	11 378	6.3
Howard	4.8	355	3 125	233.2	1 286	470	8 076	5 280	8 262	11 590	16.1	12.1	5 600	8.9
Independence	11.8	374	6 185	193.3	2 469	1 064	8 094	5 092	7 967	11 763	15.6	12.4	12 838	10.4
Izard	3.3	305	3 560	317.9	1 479	432	8 227	4 784	7 486	9 620	21.2	17.4	5 535	9.1
Jackson	6.9	318	4 470	219.1	1 747	1 132	7 956	5 197	8 132	10 960	23.2	19.9	8 086	-2.6
Jefferson	33.7	373	14 950	164.6	6 074	3 378	8 409	5 476	8 568	12 761	22.7	18.0	33 311	0.8
Johnson	5.5	307	4 195	228.0	1 697	622	8 050	5 132	8 030	10 562	18.0	15.0	7 984	11.2
Lafayette	4.1	409	1 955	205.8	768	546	6 815	4 362	6 825	9 228	32.0	25.6	4 523	0.5
Lawrence	6.1	329	4 750	268.4	1 834	954	7 199	4 617	7 224	9 679	22.6	19.0	7 692	2.8
Lee	7.1	451	2 780	191.7	888	1 148	4 942	3 447	5 394	7 376	44.3	36.6	5 085	-3.5
Lincoln	4.4	335	2 000	150.4	732	616	6 160	4 157	6 504	10 384	26.7	21.1	4 295	1.6
Little River	5.7	404	2 525	180.4	1 013	472	9 181	5 723	8 955	13 516	19.4	14.9	6 171	7.7
Logan	5.6	275	4 895	236.5	1 918	746	7 630	4 604	7 204	10 023	22.3	18.6	8 539	8.1
Lonoke	11.9	338	5 895	149.2	2 425	970	8 779	5 434	8 503	13 493	17.8	14.2	15 009	20.6
Madison	4.0	356	2 510	207.4	939	346	7 396	4 381	6 855	10 171	21.2	17.9	5 182	9.2
Marion	3.3	281	3 230	248.5	1 370	334	9 311	4 940	7 730	9 935	23.5	19.4	6 139	13.9
Miller	13.2	342	6 735	170.5	2 752	1 204	8 845	5 428	8 493	12 518	19.2	15.5	16 172	10.1
Mississippi	24.7	417	9 700	169.6	3 764	2 674	7 562	4 791	7 496	11 207	26.3	20.5	22 232	3.1
Monroe	5.2	377	2 840	227.2	1 060	900	6 258	4 292	6 716	8 515	34.7	28.2	5 063	-11.7
Montgomery	2.9	379	1 820	227.5	713	220	7 387	4 548	7 116	9 845	22.7	19.6	4 269	18.6
Nevada	4.3	388	2 290	216.0	928	432	7 865	4 976	7 786	10 380	22.2	18.7	4 287	-3.4
Newton	3.2	404	1 590	193.9	570	436	6 064	3 554	5 561	7 849	31.7	26.8	3 439	11.6
Ouachita	11.1	352	6 935	205.2	3 014	1 330	8 631	5 335	8 348	11 312	21.0	16.4	13 204	9.0
Perry	2.8	376	1 895	234.0	745	310	7 877	4 781	7 481	11 483	16.7	12.8	3 702	16.6
Phillips	15.2	444	6 845	215.3	2 450	2 680	6 232	4 177	6 536	8 580	39.8	31.2	11 094	-10.5
Pike	3.9	384	2 345	225.5	956	300	8 059	5 166	8 083	11 062	18.5	15.2	4 550	7.0
Poinsett	9.5	360	5 450	210.4	2 102	1 482	8 144	5 138	8 039	11 200	22.5	18.6	10 271	0.6
Polk	5.5	323	4 605	264.7	1 848	508	8 479	5 238	8 196	10 056	23.0	18.8	7 732	10.5
Pope	15.9	392	7 880	175.9	3 266	1 222	9 307	5 574	8 722	12 792	16.4	13.3	18 430	23.7
Prairie	4.2	409	1 800	181.8	725	338	6 925	4 900	7 667	10 089	23.6	20.2	4 340	6.9
Pulaski	129.0	374	53 165	149.0	24 450	6 576	11 797	7 133	11 161	15 652	12.7	9.4	151 538	14.1
Randolph	4.8	292	3 620	218.1	1 459	644	7 739	4 841	7 575	10 785	19.2	16.7	7 343	9.3
St. Francis	12.6	402	5 720	186.3	2 135	2 124	6 439	4 380	6 853	9 653	33.8	27.8	10 958	2.8
Saline	14.4	264	6 820	112.7	3 211	750	9 557	6 416	10 039	17 536	9.6	7.5	24 602	30.5
Scott	3.5	364	2 350	223.8	914	314	7 154	4 374	6 844	9 109	23.9	20.8	4 485	16.8
Searcy	3.0	342	2 255	262.2	793	552	5 993	3 765	5 891	7 602	30.6	27.3	3 739	1.5
Sebastian	32.4	341	17 945	177.8	8 245	1 520	11 054	6 834	10 693	13 762	13.3	10.8	43 621	11.5
Sevier	4.3	301	2 770	197.9	1 130	322	7 834	5 198	8 133	11 992	17.1	13.7	5 880	6.4
Sharp	5.6	380	5 180	329.9	2 256	516	7 489	4 792	7 498	9 940	23.7	18.8	7 617	5.7
Stone	3.0	318	2 075	203.4	773	502	6 345	4 038	6 318	8 224	30.2	24.8	4 548	17.9
Union	18.1	371	10 585	216.9	4 888	1 766	9 402	5 878	9 197	12 016	20.2	15.6	20 276	2.8
Van Buren	4.2	300	3 885	247.5	1 651	422	8 345	4 770	7 464	10 668	19.5	17.3	7 580	25.1
Washington	33.7	332	17 360	157.0	7 568	1 440	9 781	5 852	9 157	12 800	14.9	10.3	47 349	23.0
White	17.8	345	10 775	199.9	4 423	1 688	7 827	4 860	7 604	11 249	18.5	16.0	21 658	17.2
Woodruff	4.3	392	2 290	231.3	865	646	6 866	4 572	7 154	9 107	32.9	26.6	4 169	-7.0
Yell	5.9	344	4 280	235.2	1 673	748	7 988	4 801	7 512	10 508	19.8	15.5	7 868	14.4
CALIFORNIA	11 417.0	461	3 552 588	125.5	1 768 539	710 575	13 197	8 294	12 978	18 243	11.4	8.7	11 182 882	20.5
Alameda	508.2	445	154 360	124.4	77 728	37 094	13 753	8 537	13 358	18 700	11.3	8.7	504 109	13.4
Alpine	0.9	751	150	125.0	73	12	13 240	7 669	12 000	15 912	18.8	18.1	1 319	41.4
Amador	8.3	402	6 185	224.9	3 045	428	10 486	6 988	10 934	15 370	9.0	7.5	12 814	35.7

1. Elementary and secondary. 2. Per 1,000 resident population estimated as of July 1 of the year shown. 3. Based on the resident population estimated as of July 1, 1988 for 1987 data and enumerated as of April 1, 1980 for 1979 data.

STATE County	Housing units, 1990 (cont'd): Occupied units: Total	Owner occupied: Percent	Owner occupied: Median value (Dollars)	Median rent (Dollars)	Civilian labor force, 1990: Total	Percent change, 1989–1990	Unemployment: Total	Unemployment: Rate[1]	Private nonfarm establishments, 1988: Number	Net change, 1987–1988	Employment[2]: Total	Per-cent change, 1987–1988	Manu-facturing	Retail trade
	74	75	76	77	78	79	80	81	82	83	84	85	86	87
ARKANSAS—Con.														
Conway	7 179	76.4	38 200	179	7 739	-1.9	586	7.6	345	-2	4 378	4.8	1 664	827
Craighead	26 285	65.4	50 200	261	36 976	-0.8	1 986	5.4	1 730	0	23 072	4.5	5 966	5 392
Crawford	15 251	76.4	43 500	218	21 691	-0.3	1 732	8.0	665	11	8 220	5.2	3 410	1 625
Crittenden	17 120	61.0	48 900	228	22 483	-2.7	1 725	7.7	905	-8	10 417	4.8	1 869	3 090
Cross	6 754	69.7	39 100	176	8 596	-0.7	754	8.8	338	7	4 224	10.2	2 019	889
Dallas	3 600	77.9	33 600	162	4 400	-2.0	362	8.2	252	-16	2 807	-5.8	1 289	587
Desha	5 957	66.0	36 700	144	6 950	-4.4	771	11.1	370	2	3 675	1.6	1 459	955
Drew	6 342	72.0	38 700	179	8 091	-2.1	706	8.7	327	-13	4 453	5.0	2 377	966
Faulkner	21 325	70.5	55 400	247	28 479	-0.3	2 295	8.1	1 068	29	15 551	2.9	6 449	2 998
Franklin	5 578	79.0	36 600	181	5 971	-3.2	561	9.4	241	-3	2 362	-0.3	902	474
Fulton	4 010	81.7	34 000	152	3 884	-2.9	276	7.1	170	-16	1 104	1.7	461	189
Garland	30 836	70.8	53 500	235	31 516	-1.1	2 116	6.7	2 010	-52	22 903	-1.4	3 600	6 110
Grant	5 118	82.9	43 000	200	7 185	2.0	383	5.3	212	-13	2 298	15.1	1 348	404
Greene	12 325	73.0	39 400	199	15 227	1.9	1 143	7.5	644	-6	8 310	1.0	3 917	1 636
Hempstead	8 212	73.6	34 900	188	10 387	0.7	919	8.8	430	-5	5 557	2.9	2 634	1 142
Hot Spring	10 115	77.7	39 200	179	11 399	3.9	1 089	9.6	456	-13	4 297	1.0	1 606	1 025
Howard	4 975	73.6	36 200	187	6 213	-0.7	515	8.3	291	0	5 522	3.1	3 553	498
Independence	11 846	75.3	40 600	186	15 726	2.9	1 215	7.7	714	-7	11 174	-1.7	4 236	1 605
Izard	4 684	79.8	37 300	146	5 710	5.6	269	4.7	194	4	1 668	8.7	403	337
Jackson	7 361	68.6	34 100	151	8 543	-0.5	987	11.6	439	-1	4 349	0.2	1 504	913
Jefferson	30 001	67.1	43 300	218	37 676	-0.3	3 147	8.4	1 724	-63	24 287	3.8	6 877	5 707
Johnson	7 059	75.2	38 200	186	7 483	3.9	646	8.6	296	16	3 955	6.2	2 068	749
Lafayette	3 584	76.3	24 300	138	3 334	-0.8	290	8.7	165	-5	1 352	-9.9	0	210
Lawrence	6 857	75.1	31 000	165	7 943	-5.3	859	10.8	325	-18	3 651	3.1	1 603	777
Lee	4 578	62.8	31 500	127	4 290	-1.3	530	12.4	145	-4	1 189	0.1	386	294
Lincoln	3 796	75.5	30 300	120	4 611	3.5	393	8.5	119	-5	883	6.5	255	163
Little River	5 150	76.6	40 100	202	6 722	16.9	369	5.5	211	11	2 913	0.6	0	484
Logan	7 628	78.2	34 200	166	9 502	-3.0	580	6.1	351	-3	3 311	4.1	1 394	832
Lonoke	13 866	74.4	52 700	217	18 049	-0.5	1 185	6.6	596	21	5 443	7.8	2 060	1 254
Madison	4 392	80.0	34 800	163	5 278	3.6	311	5.9	139	5	1 214	7.9	596	227
Marion	4 970	80.4	41 800	196	6 143	-0.1	401	6.5	175	-3	2 151	13.6	1 202	258
Miller	14 273	68.3	43 200	245	17 866	-1.8	1 119	6.3	662	-22	9 901	2.2	2 788	2 116
Mississippi	20 420	54.4	41 800	192	21 623	-0.7	2 267	10.5	999	-18	13 135	3.6	6 324	2 796
Monroe	4 361	63.1	32 300	133	4 864	0.8	385	7.9	270	4	1 768	17.6	341	613
Montgomery	3 062	82.5	32 600	142	2 809	0.3	153	5.4	189	0	1 144	4.5	508	196
Nevada	3 798	76.3	30 000	153	3 874	-8.3	462	11.9	174	-7	1 925	-2.1	800	320
Newton	2 818	83.2	32 200	143	3 781	2.5	262	6.9	89	10	332	14.1	86	66
Ouachita	11 712	73.2	38 900	189	13 572	-1.2	1 947	14.3	699	-9	10 933	8.2	6 273	1 723
Perry	3 055	83.6	34 800	158	4 816	6.2	343	7.1	82	-6	470	2.0	0	203
Phillips	10 183	53.7	36 900	135	9 841	-2.4	1 138	11.6	596	13	5 459	4.8	1 428	1 479
Pike	3 855	79.9	32 800	162	4 495	-2.8	418	9.3	196	3	1 928	6.3	825	338
Poinsett	9 368	65.2	34 500	129	10 505	-2.5	1 190	11.3	435	-10	4 725	3.3	2 322	936
Polk	6 827	76.2	36 300	173	7 310	2.3	418	5.7	322	7	3 268	10.5	1 456	773
Pope	16 828	70.8	48 000	228	24 491	0.7	1 485	6.1	1 050	36	13 632	3.4	3 477	3 087
Prairie	3 661	73.2	35 200	131	4 638	-2.6	329	7.1	173	-1	1 370	18.2	727	257
Pulaski	137 209	60.3	61 300	303	191 312	0.0	10 519	5.5	10 675	72	161 843	3.0	21 559	35 459
Randolph	6 445	74.9	31 300	161	6 929	-2.1	713	10.3	269	-5	3 819	4.9	2 284	642
St. Francis	9 958	61.1	38 600	158	9 641	-6.4	1 344	13.9	558	-25	5 911	-9.1	1 632	1 420
Saline	23 037	80.6	59 000	241	30 873	0.3	1 880	6.1	839	-24	7 295	4.4	1 899	2 176
Scott	3 957	78.0	34 100	169	5 649	0.4	334	5.9	155	0	2 177	-5.4	1 360	356
Searcy	3 117	79.6	29 400	135	3 278	-1.9	310	9.5	122	3	1 366	-19.3	588	194
Sebastian	39 298	65.2	48 600	244	53 914	-0.9	3 839	7.1	3 099	-54	57 949	5.3	22 607	9 818
Sevier	5 118	76.3	35 000	176	7 188	6.2	337	4.7	264	-4	3 201	0.8	1 575	599
Sharp	5 819	82.5	37 100	181	6 718	6.2	406	6.0	233	11	1 582	19.5	67	767
Stone	3 866	78.5	36 900	150	4 453	0.9	345	7.7	189	-3	1 475	17.2	551	399
Union	17 819	73.8	40 500	196	20 854	-1.5	1 438	6.9	1 329	-17	16 431	4.9	5 368	2 942
Van Buren	5 698	82.3	44 300	190	6 216	2.9	584	9.4	256	9	2 419	21.8	530	513
Washington	43 372	61.6	56 500	274	64 170	1.3	2 224	3.5	2 844	81	38 391	3.9	10 201	9 234
White	19 823	73.3	43 200	194	25 491	0.8	2 282	9.0	1 085	-21	12 591	0.9	4 110	3 492
Woodruff	3 630	63.2	29 700	127	3 824	-5.0	440	11.5	155	-2	1 497	-11.6	772	251
Yell	6 907	73.5	37 000	182	8 754	0.5	468	5.3	274	-7	4 662	-10.4	3 011	473
CALIFORNIA	10 381 206	55.6	195 500	561	14 670 000	1.0	823 000	5.6	X	X	10 436 477	3.5	2 140 959	2 152 280
Alameda	479 518	53.3	227 200	570	675 648	-1.5	28 080	4.2	31 903	615	470 890	3.4	81 839	99 927
Alpine	450	57.3	113 200	349	595	-12.5	34	5.7	42	4	1 023	7.6	0	29
Amador	10 518	74.6	118 500	411	11 124	2.8	618	5.6	746	13	4 989	-0.3	859	1 611

1. Percent of total civilian labor force. 2. For week including March 12. Excludes government employees, self-employed persons, farm workers, domestic service workers, railroad employees subject to the Railroad Retirement Act, and employees on oceanborne vessels or in foreign countries.

STATE County	Private nonfarm establishments, 1988 (cont'd)				Personal income, 1989								Earnings, 1989		
	Employment[1] (cont'd)		Annual payroll								Per capita[3]			Percent by selected industries	
	Finance, insurance, and real estate	Services	Total (Mil dol)	Average per employee (Dollars)	Total (Mil dol)	Percent change, 1988–1989	Wages and salaries[2] (Mil dol)	Proprietor's income (Mil dol)	Dividends, interest, & rent (Mil dol)	Transfer payments (Mil dol)	Dollars	Rank	Total (Mil dol)	Farm	Goods-related[4] Total
	88	89	90	91	92	93	94	95	96	97	98	99	100	101	102
ARKANSAS—Con.															
Conway	171	1 020	78	17 734	237	7.0	118	48	30	51	12 550	2 095	166	17.8	36.8
Craighead	983	6 747	363	15 750	888	6.9	573	124	117	152	13 479	1 697	697	6.0	29.6
Crawford	228	1 413	122	14 795	492	7.4	203	68	53	89	10 945	2 675	271	7.7	34.8
Crittenden	451	2 773	155	14 871	565	4.4	246	56	51	105	10 940	2 676	302	7.0	19.1
Cross	180	576	61	14 540	236	2.3	102	36	31	47	11 800	2 399	138	20.1	29.3
Dallas	77	431	40	14 373	120	5.9	64	14	16	30	11 773	2 414	78	2.3	51.7
Desha	177	528	57	15 473	200	0.7	100	44	28	46	10 725	2 737	143	22.2	23.2
Drew	147	480	59	13 289	199	5.6	102	32	25	41	11 424	2 534	134	12.6	38.6
Faulkner	443	3 409	238	15 294	792	9.7	373	70	86	149	13 699	1 579	443	3.0	39.2
Franklin	95	503	31	12 945	180	9.2	61	33	28	40	11 411	2 537	93	24.2	NA
Fulton	57	115	13	11 541	95	8.2	23	21	19	27	9 057	3 002	44	20.9	17.1
Garland	1 303	8 030	315	13 766	1 097	8.0	480	107	301	252	14 244	1 303	587	2.1	25.6
Grant	80	159	31	13 532	185	8.7	59	21	16	30	12 975	1 917	79	5.5	NA
Greene	288	1 559	119	14 353	360	5.9	184	61	50	73	11 314	2 564	245	9.6	43.5
Hempstead	186	942	83	14 962	258	9.9	125	45	38	54	11 438	2 523	170	18.9	30.9
Hot Spring	191	648	65	15 214	289	8.0	131	29	43	70	10 628	2 764	160	3.2	44.9
Howard	100	871	78	14 036	196	20.0	118	58	25	36	14 646	1 150	176	23.0	45.8
Independence	470	2 815	170	15 239	395	8.7	254	67	55	76	12 390	2 165	321	9.2	36.8
Izard	96	528	19	11 308	139	11.2	45	24	27	38	12 356	2 180	69	16.4	29.9
Jackson	201	1 048	69	15 828	230	2.2	110	38	31	62	11 429	2 531	148	14.2	29.3
Jefferson	1 563	6 492	417	17 175	1 103	5.2	775	78	154	228	12 134	2 269	854	2.6	27.0
Johnson	123	747	50	12 725	204	10.1	81	37	35	54	11 076	2 644	117	14.8	36.5
Lafayette	67	209	19	13 771	131	9.3	34	49	15	25	14 026	1 424	83	49.2	17.9
Lawrence	108	694	43	11 897	215	4.5	77	51	31	54	12 266	2 207	128	24.8	NA
Lee	52	251	16	13 400	119	-1.1	39	21	15	39	8 368	3 051	60	28.0	14.6
Lincoln	0	203	14	15 701	119	2.7	44	23	12	28	8 894	3 014	66	27.3	21.2
Little River	106	328	75	25 769	173	9.4	121	27	19	32	12 428	2 150	148	11.2	NA
Logan	128	599	42	12 759	253	9.4	89	45	38	65	12 247	2 211	135	16.4	35.0
Lonoke	206	1 048	77	14 181	512	6.9	133	64	55	90	12 725	2 025	197	18.9	29.9
Madison	55	207	14	11 825	140	11.9	33	40	19	26	11 606	2 472	73	39.1	18.4
Marion	64	356	28	12 833	150	7.9	43	18	41	37	11 286	2 569	61	8.3	38.6
Miller	539	2 619	186	18 776	491	6.0	264	64	64	93	12 384	2 167	328	7.0	36.9
Mississippi	493	1 790	197	14 975	632	1.6	421	63	72	133	11 156	2 619	484	6.0	33.9
Monroe	139	380	21	12 062	131	0.0	44	33	18	36	10 647	2 752	77	29.8	14.8
Montgomery	37	117	13	11 119	89	10.3	19	27	16	22	11 131	2 628	46	41.5	15.3
Nevada	44	346	27	13 961	119	6.6	44	23	19	28	11 398	2 541	68	24.4	30.9
Newton	0	94	4	11 789	73	7.9	13	9	12	18	8 875	3 017	21	22.9	12.3
Ouachita	250	1 205	203	18 553	382	5.3	198	36	58	85	11 277	2 570	233	3.0	44.7
Perry	0	138	6	11 726	83	8.3	18	12	11	22	10 099	2 867	30	24.9	NA
Phillips	253	1 106	70	12 761	299	2.6	135	39	41	95	9 578	2 947	174	13.8	21.5
Pike	80	182	22	11 431	127	10.2	40	37	17	27	12 187	2 241	76	21.1	24.0
Poinsett	240	392	63	13 245	292	1.5	116	55	41	65	11 342	2 555	171	22.9	32.7
Polk	134	644	40	12 244	193	9.6	71	45	34	51	11 061	2 648	116	23.7	28.2
Pope	401	3 264	221	16 178	567	9.5	376	88	74	102	12 457	2 140	463	7.8	30.3
Prairie	46	117	19	13 890	105	-1.0	33	23	17	23	10 635	2 759	57	31.1	NA
Pulaski	14 122	52 200	2 990	18 474	5 966	6.9	4 906	476	854	883	16 685	487	5 382	0.2	15.7
Randolph	110	400	50	13 135	171	4.3	75	32	26	41	10 291	2 837	107	13.2	39.2
St. Francis	281	1 604	83	13 994	278	1.8	147	35	36	78	9 122	2 995	181	8.7	24.8
Saline	339	1 539	123	16 850	831	9.1	241	51	75	134	13 445	1 714	292	1.2	37.1
Scott	105	191	25	11 559	118	7.0	38	33	18	25	11 083	2 641	70	33.5	NA
Searcy	36	145	12	8 672	82	7.9	21	25	12	23	9 587	2 945	46	28.4	NA
Sebastian	2 201	13 208	1 021	17 620	1 500	5.2	1 294	152	261	242	14 773	1 092	1 446	1.0	41.8
Sevier	94	574	42	13 065	181	18.0	72	48	21	34	13 041	1 891	121	28.3	NA
Sharp	144	367	17	10 719	156	8.8	37	20	40	53	9 845	2 902	58	13.7	12.3
Stone	42	295	16	10 820	95	13.5	29	23	15	27	9 232	2 987	53	29.5	20.8
Union	649	3 341	286	17 408	705	7.4	409	77	151	131	14 529	1 198	487	1.3	45.8
Van Buren	134	405	30	12 339	165	10.2	44	36	35	44	10 364	2 821	81	21.0	17.7
Washington	1 639	7 159	602	15 677	1 546	9.5	1 062	161	256	240	13 775	1 547	1 224	2.3	30.2
White	419	2 479	186	14 793	610	8.9	301	89	85	133	11 233	2 588	390	8.5	30.7
Woodruff	0	113	20	13 476	108	-1.2	45	22	18	30	11 243	2 581	66	29.8	18.3
Yell	129	569	58	12 352	213	8.9	90	46	31	49	11 602	2 473	136	21.0	39.2
CALIFORNIA	814 775	3 115 547	244 400	X	576 433	8.1	374 840	54 526	98 987	75 520	19 840	X	429 366	1.6	25.2
Alameda	27 963	142 434	11 316	24 030	26 393	6.6	17 831	1 934	3 916	3 588	20 967	125	19 765	0.2	23.2
Alpine	12	0	7	7 130	25	20.5	16	2	4	5	20 220	157	19	0.0	5.1
Amador	399	1 071	75	14 979	426	9.0	183	50	119	86	14 573	1 177	232	1.5	21.5

1. For week including March 12. Excludes government employees, self-employed persons, farm workers, domestic service workers, railroad employees subject to the Railroad Retirement Act, and employees on oceanborne vessels or in foreign countries. 2. Includes other labor income. 3. Based on the resident population estimated as of July 1 of the year shown. 4. Covers mining, construction, and manufacturing.

STATE County	Earnings, 1989 (cont'd): Percent by selected industries (cont'd): Goods-related[1]: Manufacturing	Service-related & other[2]: Total	Service-related & other[2]: Retail trade	Service-related & other[2]: Finance, insurance, & real estate	Service-related & other[2]: Services	Government	Agriculture, 1987: Farms: Number	Farms: Percent with: Less than 50 acres	Farms: Percent with: 500 acres and over	Farm operators, percent: Whose principal occupation is farming	Farm operators, percent: Residing on farm operated	Land in farms: Acreage (1,000)	Land in farms: Percent change, 1982–1987	Land in farms: Acres: Average size of farm	Land in farms: Acres: Total irrigated (1,000)	Land in farms: Acres: Total cropland (1,000)
	103	104	105	106	107	108	109	110	111	112	113	114	115	116	117	118
ARKANSAS—Con.																
Conway	29.4	36.8	9.0	4.1	16.3	8.5	721	23.2	8.7	50.1	72.5	169	-1.0	234	5	97
Craighead	24.1	51.0	10.8	3.8	24.6	13.3	902	21.3	29.6	65.4	51.3	351	1.5	389	117	324
Crawford	26.8	47.2	9.6	2.5	15.5	10.3	902	38.6	5.1	41.1	76.5	131	-8.5	145	5	72
Crittenden	13.7	59.8	14.1	3.7	23.3	14.1	315	16.8	53.3	73.3	46.0	326	-12.7	1 036	44	314
Cross	26.6	36.2	9.1	2.9	11.2	14.3	492	14.6	46.3	75.4	55.9	340	3.0	691	137	311
Dallas	46.9	35.3	9.5	2.0	14.1	10.7	128	22.7	2.3	27.3	64.8	19	-26.4	148	D	10
Desha	21.1	42.1	9.9	3.0	11.8	12.4	406	14.0	49.0	81.5	46.6	295	-0.3	725	108	271
Drew	35.0	29.2	9.2	2.7	11.3	19.6	380	21.6	18.4	46.3	61.6	112	-23.3	294	24	83
Faulkner	32.1	40.4	10.1	2.4	21.7	17.4	1 103	22.6	9.0	36.6	70.4	224	-1.8	203	4	127
Franklin	16.7	NA	7.3	2.8	12.8	20.2	721	21.9	9.8	51.3	72.1	165	3.5	230	1	82
Fulton	11.1	44.6	9.8	3.3	18.4	17.3	712	14.3	12.5	40.7	75.1	197	-10.1	277	0	69
Garland	15.1	60.4	13.9	4.6	32.1	11.9	389	40.9	1.5	30.3	75.3	41	3.4	106	0	19
Grant	36.5	NA	8.0	1.9	10.5	14.1	235	30.6	3.4	32.8	83.0	34	-3.9	144	0	17
Greene	39.6	37.0	10.0	3.0	17.2	9.9	847	22.6	21.4	56.8	63.9	253	3.2	299	63	221
Hempstead	27.7	37.4	8.8	2.7	14.4	12.8	802	25.9	10.2	46.1	67.2	183	1.9	228	1	94
Hot Spring	34.7	37.9	9.2	2.3	12.5	14.0	526	28.7	4.6	34.4	75.3	80	11.2	153	3	38
Howard	44.1	24.4	5.7	1.6	9.2	6.8	656	33.1	5.6	48.9	72.7	102	-8.2	156	D	50
Independence	33.0	45.0	7.2	2.2	18.3	9.0	961	22.3	12.9	43.6	70.9	268	-2.8	279	9	150
Izard	23.7	40.5	8.6	2.3	16.4	13.2	664	10.7	11.9	40.2	70.9	174	-0.3	261	D	71
Jackson	25.0	46.9	9.6	3.3	19.8	9.6	469	9.8	48.0	74.0	50.5	360	1.0	768	122	327
Jefferson	21.4	49.8	8.7	3.3	19.4	20.6	417	27.3	40.3	63.8	51.3	280	-5.4	671	121	252
Johnson	32.6	34.0	9.8	2.4	12.6	14.7	611	20.9	6.9	47.5	75.9	114	2.5	187	2	58
Lafayette	10.7	23.6	4.4	3.1	6.5	9.4	257	20.2	20.2	56.4	65.8	110	-9.1	429	10	67
Lawrence	23.9	NA	8.5	2.1	11.4	12.6	709	12.4	29.8	65.7	63.2	291	3.5	411	74	231
Lee	12.1	36.9	7.9	3.4	14.2	20.5	393	18.6	40.2	72.0	55.0	297	1.8	756	62	276
Lincoln	16.0	25.3	5.5	1.6	8.0	26.2	356	16.6	33.1	57.0	60.4	213	-2.4	598	73	175
Little River	48.2	NA	4.9	1.8	5.5	8.5	402	17.4	15.7	36.3	66.2	146	4.5	364	3	80
Logan	29.5	32.5	9.2	2.3	14.7	16.1	995	23.1	5.9	43.2	74.5	188	0.2	189	1	93
Lonoke	21.8	37.6	9.1	3.7	13.7	13.6	908	22.9	31.9	62.0	61.9	383	-7.8	421	167	322
Madison	15.4	30.2	7.0	1.4	13.5	12.3	1 201	17.7	9.2	52.0	74.7	260	2.3	217	1	103
Marion	34.1	37.9	7.8	1.8	17.2	15.2	544	17.8	11.9	40.8	77.9	137	-6.9	251	0	51
Miller	29.7	46.7	10.2	3.5	22.8	9.4	539	26.3	14.3	42.3	68.3	175	-7.9	324	5	109
Mississippi	31.1	31.0	8.2	2.9	9.8	29.1	615	16.7	47.0	76.7	56.7	488	-1.1	794	52	475
Monroe	13.0	42.7	12.3	3.4	13.0	12.8	306	11.4	56.5	82.4	51.0	235	-0.3	767	86	212
Montgomery	9.4	26.8	6.3	1.8	12.0	16.4	435	20.0	6.0	53.8	75.2	78	-3.2	179	0	36
Nevada	25.8	29.0	6.6	1.9	9.6	15.7	447	21.7	6.3	43.6	70.9	80	-3.9	179	0	39
Newton	6.0	NA	7.9	1.7	16.7	32.3	562	19.9	4.8	36.5	74.7	98	-8.6	175	0	36
Ouachita	38.7	38.3	10.0	2.4	12.3	13.9	234	34.2	8.1	30.3	62.8	44	6.3	188	0	21
Perry	8.8	NA	5.4	NA	15.8	23.3	396	26.0	6.8	44.7	71.7	70	7.3	176	2	41
Phillips	17.1	46.7	10.7	4.0	17.7	18.0	441	16.3	47.4	78.2	51.0	344	-5.9	779	41	315
Pike	17.9	42.0	9.0	2.7	9.0	12.8	443	37.2	5.4	45.4	71.8	68	-16.4	154	D	33
Poinsett	28.1	32.8	7.4	3.7	8.1	11.5	643	11.0	51.0	82.3	48.5	404	0.9	629	190	380
Polk	24.2	35.1	8.0	2.7	12.7	13.1	814	35.3	4.8	55.8	80.2	112	-1.3	138	0	49
Pope	20.5	50.4	9.3	2.1	18.0	11.4	964	32.2	5.0	44.0	69.1	156	-1.7	162	1	77
Prairie	15.9	36.7	10.5	2.6	10.3	13.4	486	10.7	44.0	79.4	59.3	313	3.9	644	143	269
Pulaski	10.7	63.6	9.8	8.2	25.6	20.5	507	43.4	12.0	36.7	64.7	142	-3.3	280	21	98
Randolph	34.9	36.6	8.7	2.5	14.8	10.9	709	15.9	22.3	49.5	68.7	250	4.7	353	21	148
St. Francis	21.1	46.1	11.3	2.9	17.1	20.5	422	13.0	39.1	65.4	48.8	275	-11.1	653	76	245
Saline	26.1	42.3	12.6	2.7	17.4	19.4	427	39.6	4.2	32.6	77.3	55	-6.3	129	0	30
Scott	24.8	28.6	7.6	2.2	8.6	11.3	667	22.8	4.9	49.3	75.3	113	-2.8	169	D	51
Searcy	15.5	36.8	9.3	2.1	15.2	14.5	714	17.1	12.6	40.5	70.4	196	-0.6	275	0	70
Sebastian	35.0	48.9	9.1	4.0	24.3	8.2	738	33.5	7.0	31.6	69.2	119	-13.6	161	0	58
Sevier	24.5	NA	8.2	2.4	11.1	9.5	558	33.5	8.1	48.2	76.2	126	3.5	227	D	59
Sharp	4.4	53.2	12.1	4.5	21.1	20.9	537	13.6	13.6	37.4	71.1	152	-12.6	284	0	55
Stone	13.3	33.8	11.5	2.2	14.2	15.9	628	21.0	8.4	51.3	78.8	134	17.4	214	0	46
Union	30.7	43.6	8.6	3.0	18.6	9.3	333	43.2	1.2	36.6	70.3	35	-19.7	104	0	13
Van Buren	12.6	50.6	9.4	10.4	12.6	10.7	553	16.3	8.7	51.7	78.1	123	-8.2	222	D	57
Washington	25.0	48.0	10.3	3.2	17.3	19.5	2 853	40.2	4.1	44.2	77.3	363	5.0	127	1	182
White	24.1	49.0	13.8	2.3	20.6	11.7	1 529	22.8	11.1	44.9	72.0	382	-5.9	250	36	267
Woodruff	14.1	38.8	4.9	2.4	7.1	13.1	309	15.5	53.1	74.8	48.2	270	-0.5	872	106	250
Yell	33.7	25.8	5.6	2.3	8.6	14.0	937	27.3	8.0	49.4	71.9	197	-4.0	210	3	113
CALIFORNIA	18.0	58.1	9.5	7.4	28.1	15.0	83 217	61.5	10.8	50.4	65.9	30 598	-4.8	368	7 596	10 895
Alameda	15.0	56.3	10.5	4.7	25.3	20.3	692	52.7	11.1	37.7	58.1	241	-18.9	349	8	56
Alpine	0.7	NA	1.8	10.4	65.4	16.4	8	25.0	50.0	37.5	37.5	7	-5.0	873	2	1
Amador	12.6	43.9	11.3	3.6	19.0	33.0	371	38.0	19.7	45.3	67.4	219	10.3	589	5	27

1. Covers mining, construction, and manufacturing. 2. Covers private sector earnings in agricultural services, forestry, and fisheries; transportation and public utilities; wholesale trade; retail trade; finance, insurance, and real estate; and services.

STATE County	Agriculture, 1987 (cont'd): Value of land and buildings: Average per farm ($1,000)	Value of land and buildings: Average per acre (Dollars)	Value of products sold: Total (Mil dol)	Value of products sold: Average per farm (Dollars)	Value of products sold: Percent from: Crops	Value of products sold: Percent from: Livestock and poultry[1]	Percent of farms with sales of: $10,000 or more	Percent of farms with sales of: $100,000 or more	Manufactures, 1987: Establishments: Total	Establishments: Percent with 20 or more em- ployees	All employees: Number (1,000)	All employees: Percent change, 1982–1987	All employees: Annual payroll (Mil dol)	Production workers: Number (1,000)	Production workers: Work hours (Mil)
	119	120	121	122	123	124	125	126	127	128	129	130	131	132	133
ARKANSAS—Con.															
Conway	163	716	47	65 043	8.9	91.1	42.3	22.3	18	38.9	1.6	-46.7	35.1	1.2	2.5
Craighead	350	933	70	77 124	94.7	5.3	67.2	26.9	108	40.7	6.6	8.2	123.2	5.0	10.2
Crawford	140	951	36	40 413	20.4	79.6	28.9	11.0	50	44.0	D	D	D	D	D
Crittenden	781	760	49	157 103	99.6	0.4	75.6	43.5	48	41.7	1.9	5.6	31.5	1.4	2.7
Cross	511	744	56	114 443	98.4	1.6	72.4	37.6	21	38.1	D	D	D	D	D
Dallas	114	776	1	7 751	15.7	84.3	12.5	0.8	51	19.6	1.4	0.0	24.4	1.2	2.5
Desha	497	710	57	139 407	98.2	1.8	79.3	45.3	15	53.3	D	D	D	D	D
Drew	184	682	15	40 590	82.6	17.4	39.7	13.9	35	37.1	2.4	9.1	36.3	2.0	3.8
Faulkner	160	708	19	16 968	16.8	83.2	25.2	4.4	70	35.7	5.6	14.3	99.5	4.2	8.4
Franklin	184	863	52	71 657	5.3	94.7	40.2	16.2	23	34.8	0.9	-10.0	12.8	0.7	1.4
Fulton	117	417	13	17 642	1.7	98.3	33.1	3.7	11	27.3	0.4	33.3	6.6	0.4	0.7
Garland	112	1 206	12	30 513	6.4	93.6	15.7	4.6	96	31.2	3.7	-5.1	68.1	2.8	5.4
Grant	134	848	5	19 155	7.1	92.9	18.7	6.0	31	32.3	0.9	12.5	14.9	0.7	1.5
Greene	220	807	38	44 305	90.5	9.5	51.1	15.6	40	32.5	3.6	-14.3	66.4	3.0	6.0
Hempstead	172	725	108	134 182	2.4	97.6	42.9	21.9	28	46.4	2.6	-3.7	46.8	2.2	4.5
Hot Spring	144	847	8	14 447	12.8	87.2	20.9	3.0	52	36.5	1.6	14.3	33.9	1.2	2.6
Howard	117	789	70	106 834	0.3	99.7	55.8	32.0	32	40.6	3.3	0.0	47.1	2.9	5.1
Independence	188	639	47	48 798	19.7	80.3	37.7	10.9	44	40.9	4.1	13.9	70.0	3.3	6.6
Izard	102	376	17	26 285	1.1	98.8	30.7	7.7	18	27.8	0.5	66.7	5.5	0.4	0.8
Jackson	525	688	52	111 352	96.5	3.5	70.6	32.6	27	44.4	1.4	0.0	27.0	1.1	2.3
Jefferson	492	757	57	136 353	93.6	6.4	60.7	36.2	87	43.7	5.8	3.6	142.8	4.5	9.6
Johnson	138	771	43	70 651	2.9	97.1	37.0	14.1	32	50.0	2.1	16.7	31.4	1.9	3.8
Lafayette	306	619	33	126 912	21.7	78.3	54.9	28.8	18	16.7	0.5	-16.7	7.1	0.5	0.8
Lawrence	262	664	41	57 546	90.2	9.8	58.8	20.7	32	31.2	1.6	23.1	22.0	1.4	2.5
Lee	483	632	43	108 524	98.3	1.7	63.9	29.5	4	75.0	D	D	D	D	D
Lincoln	443	706	49	138 585	68.8	31.2	53.9	35.4	9	11.1	0.2	-60.0	4.3	0.1	0.3
Little River	173	558	16	40 660	23.3	76.7	38.1	7.7	21	23.8	D	D	D	D	D
Logan	138	682	38	37 838	3.8	96.2	34.3	11.5	28	39.3	1.5	7.1	20.8	1.3	2.4
Lonoke	331	830	85	93 873	69.8	30.2	57.2	30.5	30	30.0	1.9	-5.0	32.7	1.6	3.0
Madison	157	763	76	63 498	0.8	99.2	45.4	19.9	12	33.3	D	D	D	D	D
Marion	165	617	11	20 949	1.4	98.6	33.1	2.9	13	30.8	1.1	57.1	13.7	0.9	1.2
Miller	248	790	31	57 498	22.5	77.5	38.6	16.0	29	31.0	2.4	0.0	64.9	1.8	3.5
Mississippi	678	894	90	146 171	99.1	0.9	77.2	43.1	56	57.1	6.3	-8.7	105.5	5.2	9.7
Monroe	487	638	33	109 391	97.8	2.2	78.4	38.9	13	23.1	0.2	-50.0	2.2	0.1	0.2
Montgomery	151	767	27	62 181	0.7	99.3	42.1	20.2	35	5.7	0.5	25.0	5.8	0.4	0.8
Nevada	129	683	27	59 781	3.1	96.9	36.2	15.7	20	20.0	D	D	D	D	D
Newton	108	595	5	8 641	2.5	97.5	21.5	0.7	16	0.0	0.1	0.0	0.6	0.1	0.1
Ouachita	137	673	8	34 246	5.0	95.0	23.9	8.5	63	38.1	5.8	52.6	127.8	3.9	8.1
Perry	141	851	26	65 510	7.8	92.2	43.9	17.7	1	0.0	D	D	D	D	D
Phillips	510	672	48	109 072	96.6	3.4	69.8	29.3	27	44.4	1.2	20.0	19.4	1.0	2.1
Pike	120	893	31	70 238	1.9	98.1	49.0	25.1	34	8.8	0.6	20.0	8.5	0.6	1.1
Poinsett	496	794	80	124 266	98.1	1.9	79.8	48.4	29	48.3	2.1	-8.7	29.0	1.6	3.1
Polk	137	787	64	78 399	0.4	99.6	49.5	27.8	38	34.2	1.3	-7.1	17.3	1.1	2.2
Pope	167	921	73	75 290	2.5	97.5	37.4	20.3	57	35.1	3.2	3.2	58.9	2.5	5.0
Prairie	480	739	54	110 546	87.5	12.5	75.1	38.3	15	26.7	0.6	200.0	8.3	0.5	0.9
Pulaski	256	903	16	30 684	69.8	30.2	28.2	9.3	424	38.4	21.8	-9.5	452.4	14.4	28.1
Randolph	185	562	21	29 174	69.5	30.5	35.3	8.7	34	29.4	2.0	11.1	28.4	1.8	3.7
St. Francis	447	726	37	88 518	98.5	1.5	63.0	30.8	31	25.8	D	D	D	D	D
Saline	158	1 307	4	8 561	27.7	72.3	15.0	1.6	66	22.7	1.8	-37.9	47.4	1.4	2.6
Scott	130	732	43	64 431	0.5	99.5	39.3	18.9	21	23.8	D	D	D	D	D
Searcy	142	474	10	13 642	2.8	97.2	29.1	2.7	11	54.5	0.6	50.0	7.1	0.5	1.0
Sebastian	148	942	20	27 100	5.2	94.8	24.9	7.5	227	43.6	21.8	30.5	465.3	17.3	34.4
Sevier	174	832	58	104 087	0.2	99.8	54.1	29.2	18	27.8	D	D	D	D	D
Sharp	149	573	11	19 848	2.7	97.3	27.2	3.9	13	7.7	0.1	0.0	0.9	0.1	0.1
Stone	118	522	29	46 964	0.9	99.1	42.4	18.9	25	12.0	0.5	66.7	4.5	0.4	0.8
Union	103	972	31	94 073	1.0	99.0	33.6	21.3	97	33.0	5.3	-8.6	115.8	4.1	8.6
Van Buren	140	641	17	30 377	2.4	97.6	34.4	9.6	15	26.7	0.5	0.0	6.0	0.4	0.8
Washington	160	1 271	299	104 696	1.0	99.0	44.7	22.2	140	44.3	9.8	24.1	165.3	7.6	15.1
White	192	726	53	34 723	34.0	66.0	33.7	8.2	60	40.0	3.8	46.2	63.7	3.0	5.2
Woodruff	579	687	40	128 139	98.5	1.5	73.1	43.7	9	44.4	0.9	-18.2	10.9	0.8	1.3
Yell	153	705	75	80 379	4.4	95.6	47.7	24.0	28	28.6	3.5	0.0	44.8	3.3	10.2
CALIFORNIA	584	1 575	13 922	167 300	66.6	33.4	51.5	20.5	49 930	31.4	2 104.3	5.0	57 147.8	1 240.2	2 432.9
Alameda	814	2 483	54	77 532	75.5	24.5	36.1	9.2	2 452	30.1	79.3	3.8	2 212.9	47.3	93.3
Alpine	D	D	0	56 305	0.0	100.0	62.5	12.5	NA	NA	NA	NA	NA	NA	NA
Amador	432	883	25	68 272	12.7	87.3	35.8	5.1	53	18.9	1.0	11.1	24.5	0.7	1.5

1. Includes livestock and poultry products.

STATE County	Manufactures, 1987 (cont'd) — Production workers (cont'd) — Wages — Total (Mil dol)	Average per worker (Dollars)	Value added by manufacture (Mil dol)	Value of shipments (Mil dol)	New capital expenditures (Mil dol)	Value of construction authorized by building permits, 1990 — Total[1] ($1,000)	Nonresidential — Total ($1,000)	Nonresidential — Percent — Office	Industrial	Stores	Residential — New construction ($1,000)	Number of housing units	Alterations and additions ($1,000)
	134	135	136	137	138	139	140	141	142	143	144	145	146
ARKANSAS—Con.													
Conway	23.4	19 500	131.3	260.6	D	2 051	450	14.4	63.7	10.0	509	12	96
Craighead	85.3	17 060	415.2	790.5	31.2	42 245	18 470	3.2	62.3	10.8	16 692	351	1 490
Crawford	D	D	D	D	D	13 658	2 916	55.5	0.0	5.8	9 161	178	308
Crittenden	20.6	14 714	77.5	250.1	8.4	21 442	5 990	7.8	46.0	22.3	12 393	223	989
Cross	D	D	D	D	D	3 170	1 429	9.4	11.4	11.8	1 075	30	130
Dallas	19.9	16 583	61.8	136.1	3.2	459	185	0.0	0.0	0.0	274	9	0
Desha	D	D	D	D	D	2 579	1 534	17.0	0.0	48.2	476	19	229
Drew	27.5	13 750	76.7	172.4	5.7	1 798	866	15.7	15.0	0.0	912	10	20
Faulkner	65.7	15 643	309.6	536.7	17.7	35 577	8 507	6.7	49.1	23.9	22 916	352	788
Franklin	9.0	12 857	58.9	119.5	1.5	2 709	52	100.0	0.0	0.0	2 601	68	25
Fulton	5.3	13 250	10.6	11.8	0.2	0	0	NA	NA	NA	0	0	0
Garland	43.6	15 571	139.7	522.0	8.8	56 386	48 159	17.6	0.2	7.8	4 352	70	1 085
Grant	11.5	16 429	47.7	114.2	1.4	1 366	1 060	17.3	0.0	20.1	306	8	0
Greene	51.8	17 267	330.9	528.1	9.9	6 914	976	4.5	28.4	32.0	5 114	128	497
Hempstead	34.0	15 455	80.2	242.9	6.6	2 347	858	0.0	16.8	54.2	1 122	21	49
Hot Spring	23.0	19 167	91.9	223.3	18.6	3 002	2 371	1.3	18.4	67.3	410	7	128
Howard	38.3	13 207	137.8	464.6	10.6	645	87	23.0	0.0	0.0	514	9	23
Independence	52.5	15 909	172.6	428.0	30.6	4 960	1 380	10.7	21.5	31.6	1 598	24	139
Izard	4.6	11 500	15.3	22.7	0.3	1 557	25	0.0	0.0	0.0	1 254	18	45
Jackson	20.9	19 000	65.1	163.0	1.1	1 850	791	18.3	0.0	24.1	806	17	170
Jefferson	102.9	22 867	388.7	902.9	68.6	33 158	24 500	4.9	69.4	22.8	2 770	103	1 689
Johnson	24.0	12 632	81.6	204.6	5.0	2 092	616	3.2	4.9	20.9	1 097	28	53
Lafayette	5.4	10 800	15.8	30.6	0.2	0	0	NA	NA	NA	0	0	0
Lawrence	17.1	12 214	73.9	191.4	D	5 004	3 120	0.0	35.1	41.1	1 185	22	230
Lee	D	D	D	D	D	256	38	0.0	0.0	26.0	217	8	0
Lincoln	2.9	29 000	5.6	12.6	0.3	791	13	0.0	0.0	0.0	68	6	69
Little River	D	D	D	D	D	1 938	596	0.0	0.0	0.0	1 214	34	104
Logan	16.8	12 923	65.9	147.6	7.2	879	479	52.6	0.0	31.3	162	5	41
Lonoke	23.0	14 375	88.1	171.5	D	14 525	5 372	5.2	0.0	44.7	7 945	174	425
Madison	D	D	D	D	D	3 230	2 873	2.8	0.0	3.0	357	8	0
Marion	9.8	10 889	54.2	78.2	D	1 956	130	0.0	0.0	0.0	1 163	31	187
Miller	46.9	26 056	193.8	347.3	D	10 121	2 486	23.3	6.9	2.5	3 130	44	1 654
Mississippi	77.5	14 904	381.1	831.8	35.6	6 379	3 170	12.0	0.0	87.1	3 101	64	43
Monroe	1.2	12 000	3.7	8.0	0.2	2 169	1 592	39.9	52.7	5.7	186	3	183
Montgomery	4.5	11 250	10.4	24.5	0.5	NA	NA	NA	NA	NA	NA	NA	NA
Nevada	D	D	D	D	D	1 121	595	0.0	0.0	35.9	192	4	56
Newton	0.5	5 000	1.3	2.6	0.0	0	0	NA	NA	NA	0	0	0
Ouachita	74.4	19 077	387.6	1 014.5	27.3	4 305	1 811	3.6	0.0	73.8	1 344	15	513
Perry	D	D	D	D	D	1 255	46	0.0	0.0	0.0	1 129	32	0
Phillips	13.1	13 100	60.5	246.4	5.4	1 639	878	0.0	41.0	18.9	348	9	214
Pike	7.4	12 333	15.7	54.4	1.4	NA	NA	NA	NA	NA	NA	NA	NA
Poinsett	18.9	11 812	112.9	196.1	6.5	4 430	1 352	41.2	3.7	6.1	2 919	74	107
Polk	13.6	12 364	53.4	123.0	3.6	2 046	346	50.5	0.0	0.0	836	22	0
Pope	38.2	15 280	157.6	378.4	12.0	17 478	2 080	17.8	8.6	9.5	11 282	213	509
Prairie	6.1	12 200	18.6	32.0	1.0	5	0	NA	NA	NA	0	0	5
Pulaski	265.7	18 451	1 277.3	2 863.6	79.4	197 131	79 379	24.7	18.1	29.4	74 429	796	10 350
Randolph	21.1	11 722	78.1	141.6	3.7	5	0	NA	NA	NA	0	0	0
St. Francis	D	D	D	D	D	4 048	1 669	7.3	4.2	84.3	1 011	27	624
Saline	32.2	23 000	86.0	213.2	D	21 304	2 882	46.5	0.0	19.4	16 679	237	365
Scott	D	D	D	D	D	231	93	0.0	0.0	46.9	29	1	0
Searcy	4.8	9 600	9.7	15.3	0.2	832	35	0.0	0.0	100.0	80	1	23
Sebastian	319.5	18 468	1 391.3	3 001.5	68.6	45 307	7 647	3.5	1.8	41.2	22 191	466	1 360
Sevier	D	D	D	D	D	1 265	952	10.5	2.9	81.3	120	2	49
Sharp	0.6	6 000	2.1	4.3	0.1	82	75	0.0	0.0	53.3	0	0	0
Stone	3.8	9 500	8.8	23.3	0.3	967	522	5.7	5.2	49.6	385	13	34
Union	79.2	19 317	392.9	1 162.2	25.4	4 095	1 562	16.0	38.5	16.2	793	24	382
Van Buren	4.4	11 000	18.2	50.8	0.5	70	70	0.0	0.0	0.0	0	0	0
Washington	117.1	15 408	409.3	1 027.1	37.9	81 463	26 555	41.4	0.9	34.7	40 000	753	1 883
White	42.1	14 033	210.4	410.9	11.4	19 244	5 724	6.8	0.0	90.5	7 822	148	358
Woodruff	8.6	10 750	35.2	64.0	1.3	3 660	3 500	0.0	100.0	0.0	140	5	20
Yell	38.0	11 515	62.6	306.6	9.5	2 214	904	12.3	0.0	48.1	995	29	141
CALIFORNIA	25 697.0	20 720	132 637.5	252 728.8	8 571.7	32 809 140	7 600 432	23.7	20.0	28.5	17 233 076	163 175	3 085 086
Alameda	1 086.9	22 979	6 882.6	13 439.7	310.2	1 096 626	345 928	7.4	58.9	18.4	333 972	2 706	128 839
Alpine	NA	NA	NA	NA	NA	2 183	0	NA	NA	NA	2 173	15	10
Amador	16.2	23 143	64.1	140.5	2.2	49 086	8 156	2.6	1.3	55.0	35 119	353	2 262

1. Includes nonresidential additions and alterations, residential nonhousekeeping buildings, and residential garages and carports not shown separately.

STATE County	Wholesale trade, 1987				Retail trade, all establishments, 1987				Retail trade, establishments with payroll, 1987					
						Sales				Sales				
											Per capita[2] (Dollars)			
	Establishments	Sales (Mil dol)	Paid employees[1]	Annual payroll (Mil dol)	Number	Total (Mil dol)	Percent change, 1982–1987	Per capita[2] (Dollars)	Number	Total (Mil dol)	General merchandise stores	Food stores	Apparel & accessory stores	Eating and drinking places
	147	148	149	150	151	152	153	154	155	156	157	158	159	160
ARKANSAS—Con.														
Conway	24	48.6	181	2.3	230	90.8	5.2	4 756	126	84.0	D	962	164	217
Craighead	137	239.9	1 304	20.8	821	447.0	42.9	6 942	489	426.1	1 215	1 159	445	452
Crawford	42	59.1	215	3.4	407	152.7	67.6	3 577	181	139.0	D	980	31	297
Crittenden	80	182.9	660	13.6	461	330.5	23.4	6 518	280	321.2	492	1 082	138	426
Cross	29	56.3	245	3.9	211	69.9	6.2	3 444	118	65.4	D	951	67	163
Dallas	15	11.7	78	1.2	129	47.2	29.7	4 540	80	43.1	D	891	208	149
Desha	35	78.8	251	4.5	225	78.9	-15.4	4 132	131	73.5	D	860	74	189
Drew	23	41.9	120	1.9	184	79.1	43.8	4 467	111	75.3	D	1 008	105	359
Faulkner	54	147.9	531	7.5	547	270.0	51.3	4 954	307	255.5	503	1 038	278	441
Franklin	18	10.8	101	1.0	155	40.1	4.2	2 569	75	35.4	D	381	D	210
Fulton	12	4.1	28	0.3	144	22.5	9.2	2 168	73	19.2	70	598	58	114
Garland	124	668.4	1 031	21.4	1 046	500.1	35.6	6 538	587	479.4	990	1 264	236	615
Grant	12	13.7	61	1.1	129	35.4	24.2	2 580	66	31.9	D	661	15	140
Greene	55	86.1	370	5.0	426	139.3	33.8	4 381	200	119.9	D	693	263	346
Hempstead	25	44.8	202	2.8	259	83.9	20.7	3 664	138	76.5	135	1 107	143	307
Hot Spring	26	37.1	162	2.3	265	92.9	9.7	3 368	120	85.9	442	748	41	269
Howard	23	44.7	138	2.0	175	53.7	-1.5	3 976	94	51.1	D	955	66	149
Independence	55	74.8	469	6.0	382	154.9	42.0	4 809	187	141.6	713	925	146	343
Izard	5	1.9	26	0.3	133	35.3	24.3	3 182	56	30.9	D	997	D	107
Jackson	31	43.0	228	3.6	254	81.5	6.4	3 975	146	75.7	D	574	252	296
Jefferson	124	272.2	1 193	20.1	914	464.4	25.3	5 109	560	446.0	724	997	225	382
Johnson	16	13.0	57	0.7	208	81.0	54.9	4 379	104	73.9	D	872	98	170
Lafayette	8	2.3	17	0.2	101	22.1	11.6	2 280	53	19.4	170	809	D	117
Lawrence	23	33.6	150	2.4	241	76.0	33.8	4 197	106	65.5	D	843	74	204
Lee	19	31.3	93	1.8	110	28.2	14.6	1 905	48	24.5	D	572	32	42
Lincoln	9	14.0	48	0.7	88	16.8	-17.6	1 254	47	15.2	68	515	D	25
Little River	17	14.2	72	1.0	148	48.9	34.7	3 490	65	44.2	D	955	D	205
Logan	18	39.6	78	1.2	231	73.1	23.3	3 513	116	66.1	D	761	144	265
Lonoke	48	84.1	378	5.9	406	123.3	16.8	3 162	184	110.1	D	820	78	132
Madison	8	3.7	38	0.4	117	29.4	26.7	2 430	40	24.3	D	D	D	117
Marion	10	5.4	86	0.7	111	21.6	56.5	1 687	44	18.4	D	782	D	103
Miller	60	138.7	590	11.4	387	185.6	19.5	4 711	233	172.3	D	1 499	169	437
Mississippi	74	113.7	538	9.1	629	236.7	23.4	4 117	350	222.5	604	861	137	293
Monroe	21	20.9	119	1.3	168	53.3	4.1	4 166	95	48.6	D	1 152	88	400
Montgomery	11	16.6	48	0.8	145	18.0	44.0	2 252	44	13.2	120	D	0	124
Nevada	12	24.1	64	0.9	95	29.8	14.6	2 758	55	27.9	96	650	72	82
Newton	4	3.2	17	0.2	51	7.6	24.6	930	15	6.2	D	D	0	35
Ouachita	43	102.6	369	8.0	388	165.3	29.9	4 905	233	155.8	462	1 216	252	279
Perry	5	4.5	12	0.2	69	19.2	178.3	2 395	28	17.4	0	712	0	D
Phillips	47	80.2	315	5.3	364	125.4	8.9	3 881	206	115.9	439	896	178	298
Pike	11	31.4	109	0.9	151	37.4	23.8	3 665	62	30.9	237	743	D	109
Poinsett	34	67.6	306	4.7	301	82.5	16.5	3 172	156	76.4	D	667	15	166
Polk	19	36.5	123	1.2	179	64.7	14.7	3 783	104	60.0	D	990	64	196
Pope	72	209.4	711	12.4	566	285.6	47.1	6 462	304	271.2	800	1 292	230	510
Prairie	18	18.5	104	1.7	106	31.7	22.4	3 169	63	29.4	D	569	50	161
Pulaski	997	5 853.1	13 228	277.1	3 852	2 699.9	42.0	7 531	2 515	2 630.8	1 183	1 195	447	666
Randolph	22	38.7	158	1.7	179	60.0	55.8	3 591	85	53.2	D	1 069	82	154
St. Francis	44	100.4	344	5.3	333	122.0	3.2	3 910	190	114.1	579	946	140	256
Saline	41	71.0	265	5.3	453	205.2	36.2	3 466	250	196.5	D	880	101	240
Scott	8	13.0	67	0.5	94	30.9	55.3	2 943	47	27.7	D	664	37	168
Searcy	11	17.1	72	0.5	104	22.0	30.2	2 504	43	17.9	212	620	D	57
Sebastian	291	684.5	2 713	50.1	1 332	776.3	36.5	7 755	885	751.9	D	1 428	367	753
Sevier	23	29.3	154	2.6	165	61.5	54.5	4 363	94	56.1	D	1 154	71	279
Sharp	6	5.5	20	0.3	186	52.4	78.8	3 337	66	46.2	D	1 469	14	162
Stone	10	11.8	61	0.4	148	32.5	26.0	3 213	58	28.4	130	925	17	169
Union	96	129.6	633	10.8	623	295.6	38.8	6 033	365	281.0	534	1 260	328	293
Van Buren	11	5.8	36	0.3	171	49.6	40.5	3 220	82	43.5	D	960	D	113
Washington	225	904.4	2 813	52.6	1 208	776.3	55.8	7 129	732	750.2	1 431	1 317	269	498
White	85	132.6	588	9.3	708	274.1	33.4	5 124	365	255.6	616	1 093	169	336
Woodruff	20	46.5	185	3.1	108	29.6	21.3	2 905	51	24.6	250	732	D	64
Yell	17	31.5	97	1.1	196	49.4	34.6	2 761	89	42.6	D	592	D	135
CALIFORNIA	53 773	327 370.4	684 516	17 653.6	268 873	185 958.6	50.0	6 725	157 760	179 801.4	778	1 320	347	723
Alameda	2 697	21 363.4	42 945	1 157.7	11 363	8 386.4	49.3	6 864	7 044	8 160.9	803	1 355	262	716
Alpine	0	0.0	0	0.0	8	1.6	-48.4	1 362	4	1.1	D	0	0	D
Amador	30	265.1	189	4.1	457	134.1	23.3	5 301	229	122.7	D	1 782	127	510

1. For pay period including March 12. 2. Based on the estimated population as of July 1 of the year shown.

STATE County	Retail trade, establishments with payroll, 1987 (cont'd) — Paid employees[1]	Retail trade, establishments with payroll, 1987 (cont'd) — Annual payroll (Mil dol)	Taxable service industries–establishments with payroll, 1987 — Number	Receipts (Mil dol) — Total	Receipts — Selected kinds of business — Hotels, motels and other lodging places	Receipts — Selected kinds of business — Health services	Receipts — Selected kinds of business — Legal services	Paid employees	Annual payroll (Mil dol)	Bank deposits,[2] June 1989 — Total (Mil dol)	Bank deposits — Percent change, 1988–1989	Savings capital,[3] September 1989 — Total (Mil dol)	Savings capital — Percent change, 1988–1989
	161	162	163	164	165	166	167	168	169	170	171	172	173
ARKANSAS—Con.													
Conway	898	8.0	84	17.7	1.3	9.9	1.2	702	6.4	90	-2.1	52.3	-15.4
Craighead	4 871	44.7	436	144.0	2.5	72.4	9.3	3 531	58.9	517	5.8	164.2	-6.9
Crawford	1 641	15.3	127	37.2	1.8	19.4	0.8	959	12.0	185	7.8	68.3	-0.3
Crittenden	3 378	28.9	209	85.0	D	19.7	2.6	1 547	23.3	199	0.7	71.9	-4.1
Cross	765	6.4	59	13.5	D	6.2	0.4	491	5.1	170	13.6	36.3	1.8
Dallas	449	4.1	41	8.4	D	5.6	0.6	233	2.8	75	1.2	16.7	7.4
Desha	815	7.2	63	11.9	D	5.9	0.5	350	3.7	144	0.1	5.3	-7.6
Drew	939	7.4	58	11.9	1.2	6.0	0.8	297	3.2	115	3.6	20.1	16.0
Faulkner	2 936	25.7	249	76.0	2.2	21.3	1.8	1 844	26.7	300	-0.3	107.8	-1.0
Franklin	494	3.8	41	7.3	D	5.1	0.3	254	3.0	104	3.8	24.0	2.8
Fulton	239	1.8	36	4.8	0.5	2.7	D	172	1.6	65	1.1	16.2	-2.8
Garland	6 519	55.7	542	188.8	24.4	82.0	6.2	5 474	67.0	515	-1.7	264.2	0.4
Grant	383	3.5	44	4.9	D	1.3	0.3	111	1.3	49	8.1	37.0	15.9
Greene	1 695	13.9	159	31.5	0.2	11.1	1.7	826	8.8	220	3.5	56.8	-3.4
Hempstead	1 022	8.6	109	30.0	3.1	15.0	0.7	805	9.5	209	5.4	37.5	2.9
Hot Spring	1 024	9.2	105	13.5	D	5.6	0.6	432	4.8	134	4.0	77.8	-2.0
Howard	531	4.6	58	13.4	D	5.9	0.4	597	6.0	104	7.3	24.7	8.6
Independence	1 610	14.4	180	48.6	2.2	15.2	2.9	1 377	16.5	210	6.3	132.5	39.8
Izard	341	2.7	38	8.3	D	4.8	D	296	3.6	69	13.6	21.3	6.7
Jackson	891	8.0	105	34.1	D	24.8	1.6	847	12.4	128	7.9	46.1	-11.5
Jefferson	5 575	50.3	455	128.4	6.6	58.5	8.0	2 839	49.2	609	0.7	424.3	-7.6
Johnson	691	6.3	47	7.7	D	4.4	D	270	3.0	105	3.3	37.4	-4.9
Lafayette	251	2.1	26	5.0	0.0	2.2	0.5	151	1.7	79	0.6	0.0	NA
Lawrence	723	6.3	68	8.7	D	2.9	0.6	216	2.6	122	17.0	45.9	-3.2
Lee	291	2.4	31	4.4	0.0	2.2	1.0	148	1.2	41	1.3	19.4	-6.6
Lincoln	161	1.5	18	4.5	0.0	3.9	D	173	1.6	38	-0.4	0.0	NA
Little River	538	4.1	37	6.4	D	2.2	D	193	2.4	84	7.7	29.6	20.2
Logan	752	6.6	70	10.0	0.0	5.8	0.8	360	3.2	131	2.8	47.4	-0.4
Lonoke	1 254	10.5	106	19.9	D	12.3	0.9	652	7.5	206	5.8	40.0	-1.4
Madison	251	2.2	29	3.5	D	2.1	0.2	94	1.6	59	6.0	11.9	-4.4
Marion	213	1.7	50	8.1	1.6	4.1	0.2	234	2.4	63	3.8	23.4	-4.7
Miller	2 215	18.9	132	57.7	D	31.6	3.5	1 253	16.8	368	-0.9	116.6	-0.7
Mississippi	2 664	23.8	217	42.3	5.7	19.4	2.5	1 308	15.2	321	7.6	49.6	-21.6
Monroe	602	5.2	52	7.9	3.0	2.5	0.7	275	2.6	103	3.1	14.8	-6.4
Montgomery	164	1.3	31	5.3	3.3	0.8	D	147	1.2	38	3.4	0.0	NA
Nevada	339	2.7	30	5.1	D	2.8	D	225	2.0	41	5.3	25.6	-9.0
Newton	60	0.5	15	3.3	D	D	D	58	1.1	33	9.1	0.0	NA
Ouachita	1 874	16.8	130	22.6	D	8.9	1.3	744	9.3	179	-3.3	103.4	3.3
Perry	192	2.2	15	2.6	0.0	1.3	D	86	0.8	37	2.5	0.0	NA
Phillips	1 461	13.0	123	20.3	D	11.4	1.7	610	7.6	212	4.5	29.5	-27.5
Pike	365	2.6	22	3.7	0.5	2.4	D	147	1.3	100	3.8	0.0	NA
Poinsett	896	7.6	68	7.7	D	4.1	0.9	275	2.6	161	2.7	36.9	-3.4
Polk	757	5.6	66	13.8	D	4.1	0.7	309	3.4	121	4.9	30.6	-6.6
Pope	3 334	28.0	268	91.9	5.3	49.3	2.6	2 614	35.8	281	4.1	111.7	6.7
Prairie	240	2.2	22	2.7	0.0	0.4	D	69	0.6	51	11.0	19.4	-0.6
Pulaski	32 020	304.1	3 077	1 252.8	58.4	427.4	115.0	29 559	500.0	2 825	2.5	1 582.7	5.0
Randolph	671	5.3	49	10.6	D	6.6	0.7	241	2.9	79	5.7	66.4	4.2
St. Francis	1 379	11.9	128	28.7	8.7	9.5	1.8	903	9.2	135	3.1	40.2	-2.4
Saline	2 199	20.9	202	51.0	D	27.2	2.8	1 074	15.8	180	-2.7	138.5	1.9
Scott	349	2.8	24	2.5	D	1.5	D	63	0.5	85	6.3	9.1	-5.1
Searcy	165	1.4	21	3.0	0.6	1.4	D	110	1.0	31	7.3	10.0	19.5
Sebastian	9 661	88.0	741	325.4	18.7	136.7	15.0	7 957	122.0	813	1.3	508.0	-6.3
Sevier	731	5.6	63	14.0	0.6	8.6	0.6	451	4.6	119	4.1	13.4	-2.7
Sharp	487	4.2	49	4.9	D	1.3	0.4	120	1.5	120	8.2	24.0	-9.2
Stone	332	3.0	42	7.4	1.0	5.0	D	223	2.2	40	8.1	20.3	11.2
Union	3 461	29.4	289	74.5	3.6	31.1	6.5	1 856	25.7	470	-0.2	135.8	-3.3
Van Buren	536	4.4	52	6.9	D	1.5	D	210	1.9	80	8.3	31.8	6.5
Washington	8 585	80.9	751	191.2	9.0	81.3	14.1	4 378	68.4	834	4.2	252.8	-9.3
White	2 796	23.4	247	67.3	1.4	43.6	3.2	1 647	25.4	335	7.4	112.6	-10.6
Woodruff	243	2.2	20	D	0.0	0.9	D	D	D	84	6.4	5.0	-8.8
Yell	598	4.2	44	7.8	0.3	5.4	D	292	2.9	171	6.4	7.5	10.8
CALIFORNIA	2 022 068	22 731.7	222 636	128 546.0	6 028.5	28 009.4	10 419.4	2 248 466	47 369.0	213 076	5.3	225 572.8	1.0
Alameda	89 283	1 086.2	9 408	5 219.3	177.0	1 325.2	296.0	93 674	2 015.1	8 910	4.7	6 861.6	0.5
Alpine	31	0.2	11	D	2.3	0.0	0.0	D	D	NA	NA	0.0	NA
Amador	1 454	15.5	167	D	4.9	12.5	0.6	D	D	258	10.6	112.1	4.3

1. For the period including March 12 of the year shown. 2. Includes deposits for all insured and reporting noninsured commercial and mutual savings banks. 3. Includes savings capital for all FSLIC insured savings institutions.

STATE County	Federal funds and grants, 1989: Expenditures: Total (Mil dol)	Expenditures: Percent change, 1988–1989	Per capita[1] (Dollars): Total	Per capita: Direct payments for individuals	Per capita: Procurement contract awards	Per capita: Salaries and wages	Per capita: Grant awards	Local government finances, 1981–1982: General revenue: Total (Mil dol)	Intergovernmental: Total (Mil dol)	Intergovernmental: Percent from state	Taxes: Total (Mil dol)	Taxes: Per capita[2]: Total (Dollars)	Taxes: Per capita[2]: Property (Dollars)	Direct general expenditure: Total (Mil dol)	Direct general expenditure: Percent change, 1977–1982
	174	175	176	177	178	179	180	181	182	183	184	185	186	187	188
ARKANSAS–Con.															
Conway	50.1	5.7	2 650	2 082	20	132	347	10.7	6.9	80.6	2.5	130	120	10.4	57.2
Craighead	167.1	3.3	2 536	1 719	39	128	292	47.6	23.5	64.0	10.3	164	145	38.4	59.6
Crawford	97.3	10.4	2 163	1 495	15	88	536	18.7	11.8	85.8	4.3	114	101	18.9	93.1
Crittenden	125.6	10.6	2 430	1 444	84	102	598	42.0	24.4	74.0	7.3	146	125	37.9	65.1
Cross	75.9	-9.9	3 796	1 653	658	143	347	14.7	7.7	90.6	2.9	139	128	15.0	71.6
Dallas	29.2	6.7	2 868	2 188	192	116	349	8.4	4.2	80.7	1.7	162	150	7.6	28.3
Desha	62.2	9.4	3 345	1 675	103	126	508	16.7	8.5	86.1	4.2	210	193	16.4	50.5
Drew	50.8	9.8	2 922	1 733	183	174	411	12.1	5.9	90.8	2.5	141	128	12.1	64.3
Faulkner	117.2	15.6	2 027	1 543	14	115	300	20.0	10.9	94.9	5.3	111	104	19.7	69.0
Franklin	52.1	-9.6	3 317	1 972	423	605	210	8.8	5.6	82.3	2.1	138	130	8.2	44.2
Fulton	26.6	9.9	2 532	1 945	15	120	332	6.8	3.0	89.4	0.9	94	89	6.6	62.8
Garland	268.5	6.6	3 488	2 807	179	227	267	52.2	19.7	74.9	15.3	214	157	49.0	32.0
Grant	27.2	9.5	1 900	1 543	13	98	232	7.8	4.9	96.5	1.9	150	146	7.6	68.7
Greene	83.6	4.3	2 628	1 757	11	103	266	18.7	9.7	86.6	3.3	107	102	15.5	87.5
Hempstead	53.8	1.1	2 391	1 834	23	142	324	16.2	7.2	87.3	2.9	122	118	18.2	148.5
Hot Spring	70.5	18.4	2 591	1 965	12	107	475	17.7	7.4	90.1	4.2	158	146	16.6	55.7
Howard	34.8	11.5	2 597	2 031	36	164	341	10.1	4.4	93.5	2.1	158	152	9.8	74.9
Independence	80.7	6.0	2 529	1 830	18	193	376	17.8	9.6	82.5	4.9	156	148	19.4	119.8
Izard	40.2	17.1	3 557	2 809	15	128	515	5.6	3.5	86.6	1.3	122	111	5.6	85.6
Jackson	83.9	15.5	4 156	2 203	11	108	892	12.9	7.6	76.2	3.1	145	131	11.6	45.5
Jefferson	370.9	-5.8	4 080	1 920	790	689	455	69.6	29.2	86.6	22.1	244	213	64.6	64.0
Johnson	61.4	18.9	3 336	2 219	538	163	387	10.2	6.6	76.9	1.9	107	103	11.3	128.7
Lafayette	32.9	17.7	3 537	1 929	386	103	641	8.6	5.1	72.6	1.6	154	148	8.6	58.7
Lawrence	71.6	14.9	4 091	2 438	38	167	533	15.1	7.4	73.8	2.0	106	97	15.2	70.0
Lee	51.8	2.8	3 651	1 766	39	148	1 028	11.0	8.0	90.0	1.8	115	103	10.2	17.0
Lincoln	37.3	15.4	2 785	1 402	18	79	495	6.6	4.5	94.2	1.2	92	89	6.5	35.3
Little River	31.6	-11.0	2 258	1 758	18	113	260	14.8	5.0	88.9	2.7	193	187	12.1	66.0
Logan	58.5	11.4	2 837	2 144	20	231	346	10.8	6.5	77.9	1.8	91	87	10.4	67.2
Lonoke	107.3	16.1	2 669	1 620	44	102	333	19.0	12.3	88.7	4.0	112	104	16.9	76.0
Madison	30.0	15.0	2 481	1 697	33	140	525	5.7	4.1	95.5	1.0	88	83	5.5	71.1
Marion	41.8	18.8	3 145	2 350	42	96	603	5.7	3.7	79.1	1.6	132	125	5.4	49.2
Miller	97.3	13.8	2 451	1 817	157	59	280	28.4	15.8	84.7	6.9	180	138	30.1	63.6
Mississippi	241.0	12.5	4 258	1 699	380	1 354	509	61.4	27.4	84.6	8.5	143	127	55.6	54.4
Monroe	52.0	12.3	4 229	2 176	14	131	786	10.7	6.6	82.7	1.6	114	100	8.7	26.5
Montgomery	23.1	8.0	2 889	2 219	50	246	344	4.2	3.1	92.4	0.6	82	79	4.2	75.9
Nevada	29.9	14.0	2 873	1 937	30	181	658	8.6	4.3	94.4	1.4	126	124	8.9	75.5
Newton	19.8	0.8	2 420	1 696	38	192	445	4.1	3.2	91.5	0.5	69	66	4.0	69.9
Ouachita	163.6	-54.1	4 827	1 916	2 396	184	319	30.2	15.1	62.3	4.7	151	132	24.7	50.9
Perry	23.1	0.0	2 813	2 159	42	200	309	4.0	2.8	93.5	0.8	106	103	3.9	51.2
Phillips	109.2	10.8	3 500	2 066	137	100	853	27.2	14.8	88.3	6.2	182	165	23.7	27.9
Pike	26.8	8.8	2 573	1 949	29	238	319	4.9	3.1	95.3	1.1	109	103	5.5	62.1
Poinsett	97.0	18.1	3 759	1 869	166	119	467	17.3	11.0	75.5	3.5	133	121	16.2	53.2
Polk	50.0	-3.7	2 873	2 407	30	176	238	12.5	6.0	83.8	2.0	116	113	13.4	128.8
Pope	108.3	-4.7	2 380	1 743	90	267	254	28.6	10.1	84.7	12.7	314	301	26.8	72.9
Prairie	40.2	14.1	4 060	1 694	16	178	508	6.5	3.6	94.3	1.7	162	154	6.5	40.6
Pulaski	1 432.8	3.1	4 008	1 901	171	1 143	772	297.2	114.9	67.6	94.3	273	221	299.0	92.2
Randolph	45.2	6.4	2 722	1 936	26	84	316	9.1	5.1	91.3	1.8	112	102	8.9	63.8
St. Francis	97.5	16.2	3 198	1 834	86	119	738	26.4	12.5	92.7	4.1	131	118	25.2	55.5
Saline	84.7	3.1	1 371	1 147	7	66	142	29.9	13.0	88.4	6.3	115	107	28.0	73.9
Scott	27.4	8.6	2 561	1 865	82	208	351	8.3	5.8	51.7	0.6	64	59	9.1	214.7
Searcy	24.6	-7.5	2 897	2 113	17	137	484	4.3	3.2	93.0	0.7	79	76	4.2	33.3
Sebastian	274.3	13.7	2 700	1 986	98	406	196	62.0	27.8	79.2	18.8	197	177	58.6	74.3
Sevier	37.0	16.8	2 682	1 928	167	185	372	7.6	4.3	84.3	1.7	118	111	7.1	79.3
Sharp	54.5	8.5	3 447	2 893	101	109	304	9.1	4.7	91.7	3.3	224	219	9.2	119.9
Stone	26.0	8.9	2 527	1 868	14	157	435	4.3	3.3	88.9	0.7	78	73	4.3	57.2
Union	130.5	12.4	2 690	2 044	117	156	367	41.6	15.3	92.1	8.8	181	162	40.6	71.1
Van Buren	44.2	8.6	2 782	2 326	12	96	292	6.1	3.9	90.8	1.5	106	104	6.1	78.7
Washington	289.2	15.4	2 578	1 662	190	296	409	87.2	27.2	80.5	18.6	182	151	82.9	80.0
White	194.7	47.3	3 585	1 904	1 109	130	242	31.6	15.5	92.6	6.8	132	122	31.5	76.5
Woodruff	43.3	10.4	4 508	2 243	16	154	678	9.5	4.9	80.7	1.6	149	144	8.7	77.4
Yell	53.4	10.8	2 901	2 093	60	281	399	10.5	6.3	92.2	1.8	105	98	10.2	58.6
CALIFORNIA	108 071.3	4.7	X	1 608	1 014	606	437	38 152.4	19 296.0	88.1	10 633.8	429	306	35 375.4	55.8
Alameda	5 371.7	0.0	4 267	1 623	1 193	903	485	2 131.8	1 019.5	83.8	603.7	529	353	1 798.4	45.9
Alpine	2.3	-2.2	1 939	1 315	42	101	478	4.8	2.2	96.4	1.3	1 078	878	3.9	125.9
Amador	82.5	27.9	2 826	2 098	406	104	205	28.8	10.5	87.7	8.9	431	366	29.9	105.7

1. Based on the estimated population as of July 1 of the year shown. 2. Based on the estimated population as of July 1, 1982.

STATE County	Local government finances, 1981–1982 (cont'd): Direct general expenditure (cont'd): Per capita[1] (Dollars)	Percent of total for– Education	Percent of total for– Health & hospitals	Percent of total for– Police protection	Percent of total for– Public welfare	Percent of total for– Highways	Debt outstanding: Total (Mil dol)	Debt outstanding: Per capita[1] (Dollars)	State and local government employment, 1989: Total	State and local government employment, 1989: Rate[2]	Federal government civilian employment 1989: Total	Federal government civilian employment 1989: Earnings ($1,000)	Elections, 1988[3]: Total vote cast for president	Elections, 1988[3]: Vote for lead party (Percent)
	189	190	191	192	193	194	195	196	197	198	199	200	201	202
ARKANSAS—Con.														
Conway	543	64.4	1.8	4.4	0.9	7.3	9.4	488	750	396.8	73	1 881	8 239	D—50.2
Craighead	614	51.7	0.9	3.4	0.0	5.9	125.2	2 000	4 343	659.0	387	11 855	21 615	R—55.0
Crawford	499	62.1	1.6	3.2	0.1	6.8	12.6	332	1 240	275.6	93	2 537	12 832	R—70.9
Crittenden	763	49.7	1.3	5.6	0.9	5.3	61.5	1 238	1 975	382.0	125	3 644	14 384	R—51.7
Cross	725	52.4	18.8	3.7	0.0	6.3	4.8	230	986	493.0	89	2 551	6 212	R—51.3
Dallas	716	48.1	24.1	4.5	0.2	7.1	5.5	515	486	476.5	30	756	3 958	D—50.3
Desha	830	57.6	10.5	3.8	0.0	6.2	12.4	625	912	490.3	79	2 113	5 435	D—52.6
Drew	670	51.0	20.6	5.0	0.2	6.8	6.9	384	1 353	777.6	90	2 622	5 620	R—53.3
Faulkner	417	68.9	0.9	5.1	0.3	8.6	20.3	429	4 138	715.9	152	4 003	18 279	R—58.4
Franklin	547	65.7	1.5	2.1	2.1	12.5	4.3	287	742	472.6	188	4 734	6 089	R—58.9
Fulton	665	42.5	35.0	1.8	0.1	9.2	3.4	337	413	393.3	36	811	3 957	D—51.0
Garland	685	41.6	19.0	4.9	0.3	6.1	29.2	408	2 752	357.4	538	15 692	31 642	R—60.9
Grant	590	75.8	1.0	3.4	0.0	8.4	3.9	303	616	430.8	35	908	4 904	R—55.4
Greene	499	63.5	1.0	3.7	0.1	6.3	25.6	825	1 137	357.5	98	2 628	10 310	R—50.1
Hempstead	774	56.0	17.3	2.8	0.0	6.0	8.9	379	1 092	485.3	110	2 894	7 799	R—50.5
Hot Spring	623	53.3	24.9	3.2	0.2	6.5	10.5	394	1 170	430.1	68	1 774	9 405	D—54.1
Howard	732	48.6	26.4	4.2	0.2	7.0	5.4	406	575	429.1	71	1 809	4 337	R—57.9
Independence	613	61.0	1.1	3.2	0.2	6.0	13.0	410	1 279	400.9	197	5 590	11 208	R—59.2
Izard	517	59.0	3.0	4.9	0.2	11.7	2.0	186	507	448.7	48	1 061	5 517	R—51.2
Jackson	538	59.2	1.6	4.8	0.4	9.1	11.8	544	776	384.2	71	1 735	7 276	D—57.7
Jefferson	714	52.2	1.5	4.8	0.2	5.3	161.8	1 788	5 369	590.6	2 144	68 347	29 752	D—56.0
Johnson	630	48.7	1.8	3.3	0.1	7.7	9.2	513	813	441.8	111	2 825	6 941	R—58.3
Lafayette	852	48.0	12.6	3.2	0.1	9.0	3.9	384	433	465.6	31	821	3 800	D—50.4
Lawrence	822	40.0	28.7	3.2	0.0	5.3	6.3	343	845	482.9	87	2 133	6 421	R—49.9
Lee	649	69.6	1.7	4.1	0.3	9.1	4.7	296	648	456.3	84	1 910	4 812	D—59.8
Lincoln	493	67.9	1.8	4.1	0.5	10.3	1.9	147	931	694.8	45	1 168	3 794	D—58.1
Little River	863	46.8	15.5	2.2	4.0	7.5	25.5	1 823	679	485.0	60	1 502	5 119	D—53.5
Logan	515	53.5	13.0	3.3	0.2	7.6	5.0	245	1 075	521.8	153	3 740	3 504	R—62.9
Lonoke	478	70.7	1.6	4.8	0.0	5.7	9.5	268	1 395	347.0	110	2 789	12 090	R—59.7
Madison	490	72.6	1.3	3.3	0.0	12.4	1.2	103	442	365.3	57	1 370	5 223	R—58.7
Marion	460	61.0	1.6	4.1	0.3	11.6	4.2	357	460	345.9	50	1 173	5 178	R—57.8
Miller	780	43.8	1.3	5.8	0.2	6.9	39.4	1 019	1 420	357.7	65	2 036	12 629	R—56.3
Mississippi	937	44.5	19.1	4.5	0.7	4.5	84.0	1 416	3 268	577.4	798	17 646	14 888	R—52.7
Monroe	628	60.0	12.0	3.8	0.0	8.2	3.7	265	485	394.3	53	1 338	3 972	D—51.7
Montgomery	548	69.2	1.6	3.5	0.0	12.9	1.1	142	345	431.2	87	2 018	3 129	R—56.0
Nevada	799	48.5	23.9	4.3	0.1	9.1	3.3	294	581	558.7	51	1 244	3 459	D—50.1
Newton	510	79.2	1.3	0.7	0.3	9.3	1.4	183	343	418.3	71	1 445	4 039	R—62.0
Ouachita	783	44.9	26.0	4.3	0.6	7.7	23.1	734	1 620	477.9	110	3 195	12 043	R—52.3
Perry	518	72.6	1.1	2.7	0.0	8.2	2.3	312	366	446.3	54	1 235	3 128	R—52.0
Phillips	694	63.9	2.0	4.6	0.0	7.5	23.2	679	1 696	543.6	103	2 601	9 861	D—56.6
Pike	540	71.0	4.1	3.3	0.0	13.3	2.9	288	481	462.5	108	2 625	3 797	R—55.4
Poinsett	615	58.5	1.5	4.3	0.3	6.7	13.1	496	1 086	420.9	87	2 218	7 566	D—51.2
Polk	781	41.3	22.1	2.3	0.1	7.9	4.3	253	792	455.2	102	2 574	6 595	R—62.2
Pope	663	59.2	1.3	4.7	0.0	10.8	35.8	884	2 183	479.8	353	10 455	15 123	R—66.7
Prairie	634	64.5	1.0	5.2	0.2	10.4	3.8	369	371	374.7	54	1 283	3 656	R—53.3
Pulaski	866	43.1	2.4	4.6	0.3	4.4	584.7	1 694	30 312	847.9	9 609	298 762	128 333	R—55.0
Randolph	544	53.7	14.1	3.0	0.0	9.7	5.9	360	618	372.3	50	1 294	5 418	D—51.3
St. Francis	804	50.0	24.3	3.7	0.7	5.5	15.8	503	1 941	636.4	116	3 106	8 980	D—51.8
Saline	514	51.5	26.1	3.3	0.1	5.1	10.6	194	2 835	458.7	85	2 415	20 977	R—58.9
Scott	938	38.8	16.6	0.8	0.2	8.3	1.2	124	310	289.7	92	2 468	4 262	R—58.8
Searcy	472	72.4	1.7	2.8	0.0	14.9	1.3	143	337	396.5	34	786	4 143	R—66.2
Sebastian	616	55.3	1.1	5.6	0.0	4.4	68.3	718	3 733	367.4	1 404	44 240	34 432	R—70.9
Sevier	506	59.6	1.6	4.2	0.1	11.1	4.2	298	543	393.5	96	2 383	4 327	R—52.1
Sharp	627	60.6	0.9	2.0	0.3	9.3	3.9	267	665	420.9	55	1 319	6 612	R—54.8
Stone	463	68.6	1.9	1.9	0.5	12.4	2.0	217	397	385.4	84	1 719	3 962	R—55.2
Union	832	44.5	25.6	3.5	0.3	6.9	43.5	892	2 209	455.5	215	6 245	17 256	R—61.3
Van Buren	433	69.2	2.0	3.2	0.2	9.4	3.9	277	407	256.0	55	1 348	6 209	R—57.4
Washington	815	40.7	31.8	3.3	0.1	4.8	83.7	823	9 940	885.9	1 052	34 092	36 658	R—64.4
White	612	56.4	20.7	3.2	0.4	6.6	11.8	229	2 413	444.4	182	4 863	18 234	R—60.8
Woodruff	803	48.9	24.5	3.1	0.2	7.7	5.2	477	465	484.4	51	1 272	3 034	D—63.4
Yell	595	57.9	13.9	3.9	0.0	9.2	7.9	458	865	470.1	194	5 040	6 331	R—55.8
CALIFORNIA	1 427	37.6	9.3	5.9	11.6	3.7	19 019.5	767	1 637 329	563.5	357 962	11 249 444	9 887 065	R—51.1
Alameda	1 576	33.3	10.8	5.2	11.9	3.5	1 611.1	1 412	99 776	792.6	22 514	733 969	478 998	D—64.8
Alpine	3 240	23.2	2.9	7.9	7.2	13.2	1.1	921	118	983.3	18	326	552	R—55.4
Amador	1 442	27.9	25.5	5.1	6.8	5.6	6.8	329	2 447	838.0	128	3 192	12 338	R—55.9

1. Based on the estimated population as of July 1, 1982. 2. Per 10,000 resident population estimated as of July 1 of the year shown. 3. Data subject to copyright.

STATE–County code	MSA/CMSA/NECMA code[1]	STATE County	Land Area,[2] 1990 (Sq. Km.)	Population, 1990									Age of population Percent		
							Race								
				Total persons	Rank	Per square kilometer	White	Black	Am. Indian, Eskimo, Aleut	Asian & Pacific Islander	Other race	Hispanic[3]	Under 5 years	5 to 14 years	15 to 24 years
			1	2	3	4	5	6	7	8	9	10	11	12	13
		CALIFORNIA—Con.													
06 007	1620	Butte	4 247	182 120	266	42.9	165 200	2 361	3 241	5 170	6 148	13 606	6.8	13.4	17.1
06 009	...	Calaveras	2 642	31 998	1 210	12.1	30 609	184	682	203	320	1 714	6.5	14.4	9.0
06 011	...	Colusa	2 981	16 275	1 905	5.5	12 442	96	343	357	3 037	5 424	8.2	17.8	13.6
06 013	7362	Contra Costa	1 866	803 732	47	430.7	611 003	74 577	5 336	77 012	35 804	91 282	7.6	13.8	12.8
06 015	...	Del Norte	2 610	23 460	1 517	9.0	20 210	858	1 494	450	448	2 414	7.4	15.9	12.9
06 017	6920	El Dorado	4 433	125 995	368	28.4	119 118	606	1 351	2 456	2 464	8 777	7.4	15.2	10.6
06 019	2840	Fresno	15 445	667 490	67	43.2	422 839	33 423	7 119	57 239	146 870	236 634	9.4	17.5	15.7
06 021	...	Glenn	3 406	24 798	1 472	7.3	21 176	137	511	821	2 153	4 958	8.4	17.4	13.1
06 023	...	Humboldt	9 254	119 118	388	12.9	107 881	960	6 568	2 315	1 394	4 989	7.2	14.8	14.8
06 025	...	Imperial	10 813	109 303	421	10.1	73 615	2 622	1 859	2 135	29 072	71 935	9.1	19.5	15.8
06 027	...	Inyo	26 397	18 281	1 775	0.7	15 777	79	1 826	178	421	1 536	6.5	14.3	9.1
06 029	0680	Kern	21 087	543 477	88	25.8	378 479	30 131	7 026	16 541	111 300	151 995	9.6	17.5	14.4
06 031	...	Kings	3 599	101 469	451	28.2	65 166	8 243	1 133	3 594	23 333	34 551	9.3	16.8	16.9
06 033	...	Lake	3 259	50 631	832	15.5	46 486	933	1 159	475	1 578	3 633	6.7	14.0	9.0
06 035	...	Lassen	11 804	27 598	1 368	2.3	24 215	1 719	854	310	500	2 883	6.6	14.4	15.3
06 037	4472	Los Angeles	10 515	8 863 164	1	842.9	5 035 103	992 974	45 508	954 485	1 835 094	3 351 242	8.3	13.9	16.3
06 039	...	Madera	5 539	88 090	518	15.9	63 369	2 494	1 418	1 264	19 545	30 400	8.3	18.0	13.9
06 041	7362	Marin	1 346	230 096	212	170.9	204 128	8 172	789	9 442	7 565	17 930	5.9	10.2	10.6
06 043	...	Mariposa	3 759	14 302	2 031	3.8	13 221	122	639	128	192	697	6.2	13.3	9.8
06 045	...	Mendocino	9 089	80 345	568	8.8	72 026	507	3 304	925	3 583	8 248	7.3	15.9	11.7
06 047	4940	Merced	4 996	178 403	272	35.7	120 280	8 523	1 516	15 128	32 956	58 107	10.2	19.1	15.6
06 049	...	Modoc	10 216	9 678	2 414	0.9	8 803	78	406	40	351	701	6.5	16.2	10.7
06 051	...	Mono	7 885	9 956	2 390	1.3	9 229	43	368	131	185	1 126	8.2	13.1	12.7
06 053	7120	Monterey	8 604	355 660	144	41.3	227 008	22 849	3 017	27 856	74 930	119 570	8.8	14.9	17.0
06 055	7362	Napa	1 953	110 765	417	56.7	98 469	1 204	828	3 604	6 660	15 941	6.7	13.0	12.8
06 057	...	Nevada	2 480	78 510	576	31.7	76 371	180	849	635	475	3 269	6.2	14.4	9.2
06 059	4472	Orange	2 045	2 410 556	5	1 178.8	1 894 593	42 681	12 165	249 192	211 925	564 828	7.7	12.9	16.4
06 061	6920	Placer	3 637	172 796	280	47.5	161 948	1 033	1 861	3 806	4 148	13 871	7.3	15.0	11.6
06 063	...	Plumas	6 615	19 739	1 688	3.0	18 590	152	604	118	275	907	6.4	15.2	8.9
06 065	4472	Riverside	18 669	1 170 413	26	62.7	894 767	63 591	11 494	41 591	158 970	307 514	9.0	15.6	13.7
06 067	6920	Sacramento	2 501	1 041 219	29	416.3	782 326	97 129	12 068	96 344	53 352	121 544	8.1	14.6	14.0
06 069	...	San Benito	3 598	36 697	1 081	10.2	25 617	204	353	804	9 719	16 800	8.7	17.8	14.6
06 071	4472	San Bernardino	51 960	1 418 380	16	27.3	1 035 328	114 934	13 411	59 201	195 506	378 582	9.8	17.0	15.1
06 073	7320	San Diego	10 890	2 498 016	4	229.4	1 872 256	159 306	20 066	198 311	248 077	510 781	7.8	13.1	17.0
06 075	7362	San Francisco	121	723 959	56	5 983.1	387 783	79 039	3 456	210 876	42 805	100 717	4.9	8.5	13.0
06 077	8120	San Joaquin	3 625	480 628	101	132.6	353 169	27 094	5 085	59 690	35 590	112 673	8.8	16.5	14.7
06 079	...	San Luis Obispo	8 559	217 162	229	25.4	193 619	5 727	2 203	6 195	9 418	28 923	6.4	12.3	17.7
06 081	7362	San Mateo	1 163	649 623	72	558.6	466 885	35 283	2 987	109 281	35 187	114 627	6.9	11.7	12.8
06 083	7480	Santa Barbara	7 093	369 608	139	52.1	285 461	10 402	3 351	16 429	53 965	98 199	7.3	12.6	18.0
06 085	7362	Santa Clara	3 344	1 497 577	14	447.8	1 032 190	56 211	9 269	261 466	138 441	314 564	7.5	12.8	15.1
06 087	7362	Santa Cruz	1 155	229 734	214	198.9	192 849	2 632	1 821	8 512	23 920	46 797	7.2	13.1	15.8
06 089	6690	Shasta	9 805	147 036	320	15.0	137 977	1 081	3 954	2 684	1 340	5 652	7.7	15.6	12.3
06 091	...	Sierra	2 469	3 318	2 971	1.3	3 175	6	73	12	52	184	6.9	15.6	8.2
06 093	...	Siskiyou	16 284	43 531	931	2.7	40 105	691	1 797	383	555	2 549	6.7	15.9	10.8
06 095	7362	Solano	2 145	340 421	149	158.7	227 292	45 839	3 070	43 440	20 780	45 517	8.7	16.0	14.3
06 097	7362	Sonoma	4 082	388 222	130	95.1	351 650	5 547	4 397	10 774	15 854	41 223	7.3	13.9	12.5
06 099	5170	Stanislaus	3 871	370 522	137	95.7	297 315	6 450	4 039	19 223	43 495	80 897	9.1	17.2	14.1
06 101	9340	Sutter	1 561	64 415	677	41.3	49 521	1 041	941	6 079	6 833	10 592	8.4	15.9	13.7
06 103	...	Tehama	7 643	49 625	846	6.5	45 593	256	966	353	2 457	5 124	7.3	15.8	11.5
06 105	...	Trinity	8 233	13 063	2 135	1.6	12 133	53	624	100	153	431	6.8	15.4	10.0
06 107	8780	Tulare	12 495	311 921	160	25.0	204 835	4 618	3 992	13 319	85 157	120 893	9.3	18.9	15.1
06 109	...	Tuolumne	5 790	48 456	863	8.4	43 792	1 551	980	395	1 738	3 726	5.7	13.4	11.1
06 111	4472	Ventura	4 781	669 016	66	139.9	529 166	15 629	4 909	34 579	84 733	176 952	8.0	15.1	15.0
06 113	6920	Yolo	2 622	141 092	337	53.8	107 113	3 172	1 741	11 914	17 152	28 182	7.3	13.4	22.1
06 115	9340	Yuba	1 633	58 228	744	35.7	45 541	2 437	1 675	4 917	3 658	6 728	10.4	17.3	14.7
08 000	...	COLORADO	268 660	3 294 394	X	12.3	2 905 474	133 146	27 776	59 862	168 136	424 302	7.7	14.6	14.1
08 001	2082	Adams	3 087	265 038	186	85.9	229 808	8 833	2 396	6 876	17 125	49 179	8.7	16.2	14.1
08 003	...	Alamosa	1 872	13 617	2 091	7.3	11 219	69	126	120	2 083	5 254	8.6	16.2	20.3
08 005	2082	Arapahoe	2 080	391 511	129	188.2	349 314	23 279	2 099	11 115	5 704	21 743	7.9	15.2	13.0
08 007	...	Archuleta	3 495	5 345	2 815	1.5	4 664	7	107	29	538	1 244	8.3	17.0	9.8
08 009	...	Baca	6 620	4 556	2 868	0.7	4 320	1	64	10	161	255	6.6	14.6	9.8
08 011	...	Bent	3 921	5 048	2 837	1.3	4 588	33	37	30	360	1 371	6.7	15.2	10.3
08 013	2082	Boulder	1 923	225 339	221	117.2	210 190	1 959	1 313	5 508	6 369	15 195	7.0	12.7	17.9
08 015	...	Chaffee	2 625	12 684	2 166	4.8	12 100	202	118	38	226	1 200	5.5	13.4	12.4
08 017	...	Cheyenne	4 614	2 397	3 032	0.5	2 358	0	4	3	32	83	9.0	18.1	10.2

1. MSA = Metropolitan Statistical Area. CMSA = Consolidated MSA. NECMA = New England county metropolitan area. PMSA = Primary MSA. See Appendix A for explanation of these concepts. See Appendix B for list of metropolitan areas identified by type, with component counties. 2. Dry land or land partially or temporarily covered by water. 3. Hispanic persons may be of any race.

STATE County	Population, 1990 (cont'd): Age of population (cont'd) Percent: 25 to 34 years	35 to 44 years	45 to 54 years	55 to 64 years	65 to 74 years	75 years and over	Percent female	Population–Change and components of change: Change 1980–1990: Number	Percent	Components of change, 1980–1986: Total persons, 1986	Total persons, 1980	Net change: Number	Percent	Natural increase: Births	Deaths
	14	15	16	17	18	19	20	21	22	23	24	25	26	27	28
CALIFORNIA—Con.															
Butte	14.5	13.9	8.7	8.4	10.1	7.2	51.0	38 269	26.6	166 700	143 851	22 800	15.9	14 100	9 600
Calaveras	12.6	16.1	11.8	11.9	11.6	6.1	50.4	11 288	54.5	28 300	20 710	7 600	36.9	1 700	1 500
Colusa	15.1	14.4	9.4	8.7	7.8	5.1	48.9	3 484	27.2	15 000	12 791	2 200	17.2	1 600	900
Contra Costa	17.5	17.6	11.8	8.1	6.6	4.3	51.0	147 401	22.5	725 100	656 331	68 800	10.5	63 300	30 500
Del Norte	18.9	14.3	9.5	8.2	8.0	4.9	45.7	5 243	28.8	19 200	18 217	1 000	5.6	2 200	1 100
El Dorado	16.2	19.0	10.8	8.9	7.7	4.1	50.0	40 183	46.8	108 200	85 812	22 400	26.1	8 900	3 900
Fresno	17.1	14.1	8.8	7.1	6.1	4.3	50.4	152 869	29.7	587 600	514 621	73 000	14.2	70 100	25 300
Glenn	14.9	14.2	9.5	8.4	8.0	6.0	50.1	3 448	16.1	23 100	21 350	1 800	8.3	2 500	1 400
Humboldt	16.4	17.0	9.6	7.9	7.2	5.1	50.3	10 593	9.8	114 200	108 525	5 600	5.2	11 500	6 100
Imperial	15.4	13.3	8.6	8.1	6.5	3.7	50.8	17 193	18.7	107 000	92 110	14 900	16.2	13 900	4 600
Inyo	13.3	15.9	11.3	11.0	10.7	7.8	51.0	386	2.2	18 200	17 895	300	1.5	1 700	1 200
Kern	18.2	14.3	9.0	7.2	5.9	3.8	49.6	140 388	34.8	494 200	403 089	91 100	22.6	58 900	21 300
Kings	21.1	14.1	8.1	6.0	4.6	3.1	46.0	27 731	37.6	85 900	73 738	12 100	16.5	11 600	3 400
Lake	12.3	14.4	9.8	11.1	13.9	8.7	51.1	14 265	39.2	49 100	36 366	12 700	35.0	3 600	3 700
Lassen	19.8	16.6	9.2	7.8	6.5	3.8	41.6	5 937	27.4	25 000	21 661	3 300	15.4	2 200	1 100
Los Angeles	19.8	15.1	9.5	7.3	5.7	4.0	50.1	1 385 925	18.5	8 295 900	7 477 239	818 700	10.9	894 400	377 100
Madera	14.7	14.8	9.6	8.5	7.5	4.8	49.8	24 974	39.6	77 900	63 116	14 800	23.4	8 400	3 400
Marin	17.1	20.7	14.1	9.2	7.3	5.0	50.5	7 504	3.4	225 500	222 592	2 900	1.3	15 300	10 500
Mariposa	14.2	15.3	11.8	11.7	11.2	6.3	49.5	3 194	28.8	13 700	11 108	2 600	23.5	900	700
Mendocino	14.1	17.9	11.0	8.5	8.0	5.5	50.2	13 607	20.4	74 800	66 738	8 100	12.1	7 600	4 100
Merced	17.4	13.2	8.3	7.0	5.7	3.5	49.5	43 846	32.6	163 500	134 557	29 000	21.5	20 900	6 000
Modoc	13.1	15.3	10.9	10.4	10.3	6.6	49.0	1 068	12.4	9 400	8 610	800	9.3	1 000	600
Mono	22.4	19.7	10.4	7.3	4.1	2.1	45.6	1 379	16.1	9 200	8 577	600	7.2	900	200
Monterey	19.5	14.7	8.4	7.0	5.8	4.0	48.1	65 216	22.5	339 700	290 444	49 200	17.0	40 600	13 100
Napa	15.2	16.0	11.0	8.8	9.0	7.5	50.4	11 566	11.7	104 700	99 199	5 500	5.6	8 400	5 900
Nevada	12.3	18.5	10.9	10.4	11.5	6.6	50.8	26 865	52.0	71 100	51 645	19 400	37.6	5 500	3 500
Orange	20.1	15.6	10.6	7.5	5.4	3.8	49.6	477 635	24.7	2 166 800	1 932 921	233 900	12.1	213 000	79 700
Placer	15.8	18.2	11.7	8.4	7.2	4.8	50.5	55 549	47.4	142 500	117 247	25 300	21.6	11 500	6 300
Plumas	12.5	16.7	11.4	11.9	11.0	5.9	50.3	2 399	13.8	19 500	17 340	2 200	12.5	1 700	900
Riverside	18.1	14.1	8.6	7.6	7.9	5.3	50.0	507 214	76.5	862 000	663 199	198 800	30.0	85 500	43 700
Sacramento	19.4	15.9	9.7	7.8	6.5	4.1	51.1	257 838	32.9	914 700	783 381	131 300	16.8	91 000	39 700
San Benito	17.1	15.3	9.3	7.4	6.0	3.9	49.5	11 692	46.8	31 800	25 005	6 800	27.1	3 300	1 300
San Bernardino	19.2	15.0	8.6	6.5	5.3	3.5	49.9	523 364	58.5	1 139 100	895 016	244 100	27.3	120 300	46 600
San Diego	20.0	15.2	8.8	7.1	6.5	4.4	49.0	636 170	34.2	2 201 300	1 861 846	339 500	18.2	216 700	89 100
San Francisco	21.9	17.9	10.3	8.8	7.9	6.6	49.9	44 985	6.6	749 000	678 974	70 000	10.3	57 900	48 500
San Joaquin	17.3	14.9	9.3	7.4	6.5	4.6	49.4	133 286	38.4	432 700	347 342	85 300	24.6	45 400	20 200
San Luis Obispo	16.9	15.8	8.8	7.9	8.4	5.7	48.4	61 727	39.7	196 700	155 435	41 200	26.5	15 200	9 000
San Mateo	18.9	17.0	11.5	8.9	7.3	5.0	50.7	62 294	10.6	613 500	587 329	26 200	4.5	55 000	28 600
Santa Barbara	18.2	14.5	9.3	7.8	6.9	5.4	49.8	70 914	23.7	339 400	298 694	40 700	13.6	30 500	15 000
Santa Clara	21.2	16.3	10.9	7.5	5.3	3.4	49.3	202 506	15.6	1 401 600	1 295 071	106 600	8.2	144 600	49 400
Santa Cruz	17.7	18.8	9.7	6.6	6.1	5.2	50.3	41 593	22.1	218 500	188 141	30 400	16.1	21 600	10 500
Shasta	14.7	15.6	11.0	9.1	8.6	5.5	51.0	31 423	27.2	133 100	115 613	17 500	15.1	12 400	6 900
Sierra	12.8	17.1	12.2	9.7	10.2	7.2	49.8	245	8.0	3 400	3 073	400	12.0	300	200
Siskiyou	12.7	16.4	10.7	10.3	9.9	6.6	50.8	3 799	9.6	42 600	39 732	2 900	7.3	4 400	2 500
Solano	19.4	17.2	9.5	6.6	5.2	3.0	48.8	105 218	44.7	287 600	235 203	52 300	22.3	30 100	10 300
Sonoma	16.8	18.4	10.4	7.4	7.5	5.9	51.0	88 541	29.5	343 600	299 681	43 900	14.6	30 000	18 400
Stanislaus	17.6	14.7	9.3	7.2	6.3	4.5	50.8	104 622	39.3	316 600	265 900	50 700	19.1	33 000	14 600
Sutter	16.2	14.2	10.7	9.0	7.0	4.8	50.5	12 169	23.3	59 400	52 246	7 100	13.6	6 300	2 800
Tehama	14.0	13.7	10.7	10.2	10.0	6.8	50.8	10 737	27.6	44 800	38 888	5 900	15.2	4 000	2 700
Trinity	12.7	17.9	11.0	11.2	9.8	5.2	49.0	1 205	10.2	13 500	11 858	1 700	13.9	1 100	800
Tulare	16.1	13.6	9.0	7.2	6.2	4.6	50.1	66 183	26.9	287 300	245 738	41 600	16.9	35 300	13 000
Tuolumne	16.0	16.5	10.2	10.6	10.6	5.9	47.0	14 528	42.8	42 300	33 928	8 400	24.8	3 000	2 100
Ventura	18.1	16.4	10.7	7.4	5.5	3.9	49.6	139 842	26.4	611 000	529 174	81 800	15.5	61 800	21 100
Yolo	17.7	14.3	8.9	6.8	5.6	4.0	50.4	27 718	24.4	126 000	113 374	12 600	11.1	11 600	5 500
Yuba	17.3	13.0	8.8	7.9	6.5	4.0	50.0	8 495	17.1	54 800	49 733	5 100	10.2	6 800	2 500
COLORADO	18.6	17.2	10.2	7.6	5.9	4.1	50.5	404 394	14.0	3 267 000	2 890 000	377 000	13.1	336 000	124 000
Adams	19.7	16.0	9.9	7.8	4.9	2.7	50.4	19 094	7.8	278 300	245 944	32 400	13.2	31 900	8 200
Alamosa	15.8	14.3	8.9	6.6	4.9	4.4	50.9	1 818	15.4	12 600	11 799	800	6.5	1 600	500
Arapahoe	19.4	19.1	11.1	6.9	4.8	2.6	51.2	98 219	33.5	383 500	293 292	90 200	30.7	36 300	9 300
Archuleta	14.2	17.1	10.6	11.4	8.2	3.4	49.0	1 681	45.9	5 000	3 664	1 400	37.1	600	200
Baca	12.7	14.3	10.4	11.0	11.6	9.0	50.5	-863	-15.9	5 000	5 419	-500	-8.6	500	300
Bent	11.8	14.8	10.5	11.8	10.8	8.0	48.0	-897	-15.1	5 800	5 945	-100	-2.3	500	400
Boulder	19.6	18.7	10.2	6.2	4.3	3.3	49.9	35 714	18.8	214 400	189 625	24 700	13.0	19 400	6 300
Chaffee	15.3	15.7	10.6	10.7	9.7	6.8	46.4	-543	-4.1	12 900	13 227	-400	-2.8	1 300	700
Cheyenne	17.2	13.7	8.1	7.9	7.8	7.9	49.1	244	11.3	2 400	2 153	300	12.1	300	100

STATE County	Population—(cont'd) Components of change, 1980-1986 (cont'd): Net migration	Households, 1990: Number	Households, 1990: Percent change, 1980–1990	Households, 1990: Persons per household	Households, 1990: Percent: Female family householder[1]	Households, 1990: Percent: One-person	Births, 1988: Total	Births, 1988: Rate[2]	Births, 1988: Low birth weight[3] (Number)	Deaths, 1987: Number: Total	Deaths, 1987: Number: Infant[4]	Deaths, 1987: Rate: Total[2]	Deaths, 1987: Rate: Infant[5]	Marriages, 1984: Number	Marriages, 1984: Rate[2]
	29	30	31	32	33	34	35	36	37	38	39	40	41	42	43
CALIFORNIA—Con.															
Butte	18 400	71 665	25.9	2.48	9.7	25.4	2 493	14.3	154	1 770	25	10.5	10.5	1 071	6.8
Calaveras	7 400	12 649	58.0	2.50	7.1	21.2	336	10.8	22	296	0	10.0	0.0	128	5.0
Colusa	1 400	5 612	19.7	2.84	9.3	22.5	292	19.1	9	140	3	9.4	11.5	75	5.3
Contra Costa	36 000	300 288	24.3	2.64	10.8	22.3	12 068	15.8	767	5 551	81	7.5	7.1	4 233	6.0
Del Norte	-100	7 987	17.6	2.63	10.8	23.0	343	17.1	14	202	6	10.4	20.8	208	11.3
El Dorado	17 400	46 845	44.1	2.66	7.8	18.3	1 785	14.7	115	855	13	7.5	7.7	8 038	81.0
Fresno	28 200	220 933	23.8	2.96	13.9	21.0	13 095	21.3	851	4 604	107	7.7	8.6	6 146	10.9
Glenn	700	8 821	14.5	2.77	10.0	23.2	429	18.3	19	270	5	11.8	12.6	146	6.4
Humboldt	300	46 420	11.7	2.49	10.6	26.2	1 765	15.2	88	1 046	16	9.2	9.0	980	8.8
Imperial	5 700	32 842	16.6	3.26	15.0	18.0	2 504	22.2	106	685	17	6.3	7.5	630	6.1
Inyo	-300	7 565	4.9	2.35	8.7	29.0	217	12.1	9	240	4	13.4	17.2	117	6.4
Kern	53 500	181 480	29.8	2.92	12.3	20.3	11 078	21.3	716	3 756	93	7.4	8.9	3 963	8.5
Kings	4 000	29 082	23.8	3.08	12.9	17.4	2 028	21.9	120	545	13	6.2	6.6	695	8.4
Lake	12 900	20 805	36.9	2.38	9.5	26.3	722	14.0	47	655	6	13.0	9.2	217	4.8
Lassen	2 200	8 543	15.4	2.66	9.5	21.3	394	14.5	30	187	2	7.1	5.3	149	6.2
Los Angeles	301 400	2 989 552	9.5	2.91	13.1	25.0	175 332	20.4	11 088	64 118	1 630	7.6	9.8	71 257	8.9
Madera	9 700	28 370	35.4	3.05	10.9	17.0	1 529	18.4	103	620	12	7.7	8.3	374	5.1
Marin	-2 000	95 006	7.1	2.33	8.5	28.4	2 796	12.2	120	1 727	21	7.6	7.5	1 901	8.4
Mariposa	2 500	5 604	35.6	2.42	7.1	23.9	170	11.6	10	154	1	11.0	6.1	118	9.2
Mendocino	4 600	30 419	21.3	2.57	10.7	24.6	1 161	15.2	46	699	10	9.3	8.7	518	7.2
Merced	14 000	55 331	24.2	3.17	12.5	17.7	3 771	22.2	190	1 171	30	7.1	8.1	955	6.2
Modoc	400	3 711	16.0	2.49	8.0	25.1	132	14.3	9	87	2	9.5	15.6	47	4.9
Mono	0	3 961	14.7	2.48	6.1	25.0	173	18.2	11	36	1	3.9	6.7	78	8.7
Monterey	21 800	112 965	18.0	2.96	10.4	20.4	7 166	20.5	396	2 202	59	6.4	8.5	4 088	12.7
Napa	3 000	41 312	12.8	2.54	9.2	24.7	1 373	12.9	67	1 062	9	10.1	6.6	576	5.6
Nevada	17 500	30 758	53.7	2.51	7.6	20.8	943	12.2	41	619	11	8.4	12.3	505	7.8
Orange	100 600	827 066	20.5	2.87	9.7	20.7	42 287	18.7	2 096	14 155	295	6.4	7.5	19 486	9.3
Placer	20 100	64 101	50.0	2.66	8.7	19.5	2 321	14.9	137	1 181	18	7.9	8.5	1 036	7.8
Plumas	1 400	8 125	22.4	2.41	8.1	24.1	241	12.0	18	160	2	8.1	7.9	110	5.9
Riverside	157 100	402 067	65.5	2.85	9.6	20.6	19 852	20.2	1 253	8 438	170	9.2	9.7	6 192	7.9
Sacramento	79 900	394 530	31.6	2.58	13.0	25.3	17 339	17.7	1 088	7 336	178	7.7	10.6	6 831	7.9
San Benito	4 700	11 422	44.9	3.15	9.8	16.0	692	20.1	36	205	7	6.2	11.8	392	13.5
San Bernardino	170 300	464 737	50.6	2.97	12.1	19.0	28 039	21.7	1 866	8 931	281	7.4	11.0	9 189	8.9
San Diego	211 900	887 403	32.4	2.69	10.8	22.9	44 096	18.6	2 539	16 113	388	7.0	9.4	20 358	9.8
San Francisco	60 600	305 584	2.2	2.29	9.9	39.3	10 034	13.7	693	8 256	75	11.2	7.7	8 188	11.4
San Joaquin	60 200	158 156	26.9	2.94	12.7	20.9	8 974	19.7	607	3 704	76	8.3	8.7	2 188	5.5
San Luis Obispo	35 100	80 281	37.9	2.53	8.5	23.8	2 809	13.5	123	1 638	21	8.1	7.9	1 604	8.9
San Mateo	-100	241 914	7.4	2.64	9.8	25.1	9 843	15.7	509	4 844	52	7.8	5.4	3 694	6.1
Santa Barbara	25 200	129 802	18.7	2.73	9.3	23.0	5 887	17.2	273	2 507	40	7.3	7.4	3 364	10.4
Santa Clara	11 400	520 180	13.4	2.81	10.3	21.7	26 292	18.4	1 414	8 324	209	5.9	8.5	11 766	8.5
Santa Cruz	19 300	83 566	16.4	2.66	9.6	24.1	3 976	17.5	191	1 749	16	7.9	4.2	1 923	9.3
Shasta	12 000	55 966	30.1	2.58	11.0	22.3	2 184	15.6	87	1 374	29	10.1	14.6	958	7.5
Sierra	200	1 336	4.9	2.45	5.7	26.3	32	9.1	1	14	0	4.1	0.0	24	7.1
Siskiyou	1 000	17 306	14.5	2.48	9.6	25.7	594	13.7	24	451	5	10.6	8.4	284	6.7
Solano	32 600	113 429	41.0	2.88	11.5	18.5	5 751	18.3	363	1 913	46	6.4	8.5	1 550	5.8
Sonoma	32 300	149 011	30.2	2.55	9.8	24.6	5 475	15.0	269	3 098	42	8.7	7.9	2 469	7.6
Stanislaus	32 300	125 375	32.4	2.91	11.5	19.9	6 590	19.3	411	2 777	58	8.5	9.6	2 354	7.9
Sutter	3 600	23 111	22.9	2.75	10.9	21.6	1 086	17.5	43	498	8	8.2	7.6	391	6.9
Tehama	4 600	18 704	28.7	2.60	9.9	22.3	735	15.8	41	469	3	10.3	4.6	251	5.8
Trinity	1 300	5 156	14.6	2.49	8.4	24.6	152	10.9	8	117	1	8.7	6.0	79	6.0
Tulare	19 300	97 861	21.3	3.12	12.8	18.1	6 072	20.4	349	2 299	53	7.9	9.0	1 812	6.6
Tuolumne	7 500	17 959	39.6	2.46	8.5	22.5	565	12.2	35	425	2	9.5	3.9	357	9.2
Ventura	41 100	217 298	25.8	3.02	9.8	17.5	11 481	17.7	566	3 769	80	6.0	7.4	5 294	9.0
Yolo	6 500	50 972	23.4	2.63	10.2	23.1	2 216	16.8	125	917	15	7.2	7.5	680	5.6
Yuba	800	19 776	13.0	2.85	12.8	20.6	1 318	23.3	79	443	12	8.0	9.7	350	6.6
COLORADO	165 000	1 282 489	20.8	2.51	9.7	26.6	53 367	16.2	4 186	21 093	527	6.4	9.8	35 072	11.0
Adams	8 700	96 353	14.4	2.72	12.2	21.7	5 026	17.9	443	1 536	61	5.5	12.1	2 381	8.7
Alamosa	-300	4 721	20.4	2.67	12.3	24.7	264	20.3	16	90	2	7.0	7.3	144	11.4
Arapahoe	63 100	154 710	45.9	2.51	10.1	26.3	6 275	16.0	487	1 659	68	4.3	10.8	4 403	12.2
Archuleta	1 000	2 010	62.0	2.66	8.0	19.8	91	17.5	3	30	0	5.9	0.0	59	10.9
Baca	-700	1 872	-8.5	2.39	5.0	28.4	77	15.7	7	48	0	9.8	0.0	28	5.4
Bent	-300	1 865	-6.7	2.51	8.7	28.6	76	14.1	5	55	0	9.8	0.0	37	6.3
Boulder	11 600	88 402	28.2	2.45	7.9	26.3	3 232	14.8	200	1 062	17	4.9	5.2	2 686	12.8
Chaffee	-900	4 848	1.9	2.38	7.2	27.5	148	11.6	9	107	0	8.3	0.0	128	10.0
Cheyenne	100	904	11.2	2.60	5.1	29.0	48	20.0	2	27	1	11.7	27.0	21	8.8

1. No spouse present. 2. Per 1,000 resident population estimated as of July 1 of the year shown. 3. Under 2,500 grams. 4. Deaths of infants under 1 year old. 5. Deaths of infants under 1 year old per 1,000 live births.

Table A. States and Counties — **Vital Statistics, Health Resources, Crime, and Education**

STATE County	Divorces, 1984 Number	Divorces, 1984 Rate[1]	Physicians, active non-Federal, 1989 Number[2]	Physicians Rate[3]	Hospitals, 1989 Number	Hospitals Beds Number	Hospitals Beds Rate[3]	Nursing homes,[4] 1986 Number	Nursing homes Beds	Serious crimes known to police, 1988 Number Total[5]	Serious crimes Number Violent[6]	Serious crimes Rate[3]	Education Public school enrollment[7] 1986–1987	Public school enrollment 1980	Attainment,[8] 1980 Percent 12 yrs. or more	Attainment, 1980 Percent 16 yrs. or more
	44	45	46	47	48	49	50	51	52	53	54	55	56	57	58	59
CALIFORNIA—Con.																
Butte	1 095	6.9	331	185	5	592	331	54	1 323	10 554	745	6 133	26 097	22 479	71.6	16.9
Calaveras	162	6.4	26	79	1	33	100	5	148	1 042	108	3 445	5 185	3 796	76.3	13.8
Colusa	80	5.7	11	71	1	36	231	3	80	555	52	3 683	3 135	2 516	64.6	12.3
Contra Costa	4 311	6.1	1 673	213	12	2 106	269	157	4 449	50 536	5 705	6 662	124 804	124 720	81.7	25.5
Del Norte	158	8.6	16	77	1	44	213	2	112	1 195	226	6 080	3 773	3 278	67.1	10.1
El Dorado	662	6.7	146	114	2	171	134	22	530	5 016	455	4 329	20 105	15 729	81.2	17.4
Fresno	3 187	5.6	1 143	182	15	2 028	322	87	3 925	50 435	6 171	8 358	126 617	104 489	63.7	15.2
Glenn	114	5.0	7	30	1	30	127	6	123	1 084	168	4 649	5 631	4 469	63.0	9.3
Humboldt	890	8.0	204	173	5	248	210	46	931	6 317	593	5 461	20 427	18 315	76.4	18.0
Imperial	556	5.4	82	71	4	235	204	5	277	8 736	683	8 047	26 114	22 725	50.9	9.6
Inyo	107	5.8	39	217	2	92	511	4	136	718	61	3 939	3 993	3 351	74.2	12.2
Kern	2 923	6.3	666	124	12	1 268	237	63	2 162	36 756	4 547	7 155	100 462	81 814	62.1	11.8
Kings	534	6.5	81	85	5	201	211	10	639	3 769	476	4 235	18 503	15 907	58.7	10.2
Lake	228	5.0	52	98	2	103	195	15	163	2 409	300	4 703	8 152	5 657	66.4	10.2
Lassen	194	8.0	31	110	1	59	209	2	127	767	182	2 875	5 065	4 292	73.1	11.9
Los Angeles	34 368	4.3	23 363	267	169	36 881	421	919	58 377	594 139	120 668	6 861	1 368 386	1 276 117	69.8	18.5
Madera	77	1.1	62	72	2	106	123	17	389	4 275	927	5 341	16 697	12 929	60.1	10.7
Marin	1 569	7.0	985	424	5	523	225	41	2 022	8 436	743	3 638	29 197	33 102	89.9	38.3
Mariposa	90	7.0	17	113	1	34	225	1	23	376	57	2 637	2 062	1 867	73.7	15.4
Mendocino	562	7.8	158	204	4	212	274	38	742	3 935	434	5 159	18 857	12 340	76.4	17.6
Merced	739	4.8	187	107	6	361	207	21	677	8 298	949	4 915	36 955	29 356	60.4	10.5
Modoc	55	5.7	4	44	2	46	505	8	117	265	63	2 829	2 074	1 662	72.3	12.4
Mono	62	6.9	12	124	2	40	412	0	0	745	94	7 953	1 292	1 405	88.2	22.7
Monterey	2 172	6.7	505	142	6	807	227	82	1 727	18 845	2 648	5 394	60 358	52 011	71.0	19.6
Napa	608	6.0	330	306	4	2 371	2 197	48	1 362	4 580	473	4 280	16 257	16 547	75.4	17.8
Nevada	395	6.1	128	158	2	180	222	14	431	2 357	249	3 141	10 420	8 966	82.0	18.0
Orange	12 335	5.9	5 911	256	41	6 931	301	147	9 651	131 837	10 643	5 834	378 000	359 838	80.4	22.6
Placer	1 064	8.0	297	184	2	323	200	18	847	7 397	642	4 885	27 581	23 073	77.4	16.7
Plumas	16	0.9	20	98	4	108	527	4	93	1 222	65	6 123	4 159	3 298	78.4	14.5
Riverside	4 820	6.2	1 266	121	16	2 750	262	130	4 921	78 027	11 144	8 376	169 481	122 337	68.9	12.8
Sacramento	6 512	7.5	2 375	235	14	2 896	287	170	5 719	75 972	7 322	7 893	163 042	138 737	78.0	19.3
San Benito	163	5.6	20	55	1	90	249	4	167	1 294	300	3 851	6 572	5 250	56.5	10.6
San Bernardino	6 180	6.0	2 382	173	24	4 895	356	126	5 183	87 161	12 576	7 108	235 579	174 410	71.0	13.1
San Diego	9 100	4.4	5 755	234	35	8 251	336	377	12 384	171 804	17 024	7 381	353 115	316 060	78.0	20.9
San Francisco	3 750	5.2	4 722	644	18	5 393	735	200	4 701	67 672	9 801	8 976	67 439	61 166	74.0	28.2
San Joaquin	2 475	6.2	670	142	8	1 086	231	136	3 619	36 506	3 173	8 084	88 704	66 466	62.6	11.5
San Luis Obispo	1 085	6.0	410	191	7	1 557	725	24	1 140	7 726	595	3 758	27 727	23 012	76.8	19.0
San Mateo	5 176	8.5	1 758	277	9	1 830	289	147	3 686	30 424	3 597	4 805	80 555	88 202	81.6	25.5
Santa Barbara	2 084	6.4	864	248	11	1 185	341	72	2 464	18 554	1 723	5 345	50 904	48 089	79.1	24.6
Santa Clara	8 739	6.3	4 024	278	16	5 152	356	263	7 129	71 015	7 765	4 929	232 530	244 087	79.5	26.4
Santa Cruz	1 404	6.8	415	179	4	597	257	57	1 798	13 443	1 067	5 955	37 449	28 955	77.8	23.5
Shasta	1 136	8.9	260	182	3	440	307	24	732	8 626	1 307	6 247	26 350	23 004	75.6	12.4
Sierra	17	5.0	3	83	1	40	1 111	0	0	126	36	3 640	687	546	78.1	18.0
Siskiyou	369	8.8	57	130	2	132	301	9	244	1 820	204	4 267	8 319	7 706	75.6	14.1
Solano	1 884	7.1	435	132	7	1 024	311	66	1 341	20 370	2 516	6 686	53 692	47 768	76.8	13.7
Sonoma	2 161	6.6	781	207	9	2 220	587	111	2 768	18 149	1 326	5 035	57 076	52 239	77.6	19.3
Stanislaus	2 163	7.3	530	149	8	1 317	371	78	3 224	22 566	2 463	6 769	67 256	52 470	62.0	11.8
Sutter	0	0.0	89	141	1	128	202	14	360	4 016	583	6 541	13 929	10 649	67.7	14.4
Tehama	312	7.3	40	84	1	92	193	14	331	2 319	234	4 994	8 879	7 642	69.5	9.1
Trinity	103	7.8	13	92	1	71	500	1	46	512	99	3 724	2 384	2 446	74.5	13.6
Tulare	1 617	5.9	364	120	8	1 874	615	41	1 397	16 699	2 087	5 624	64 722	54 719	55.8	10.1
Tuolumne	260	6.7	80	165	2	220	455	10	136	1 559	98	3 433	6 554	5 753	77.3	13.7
Ventura	3 303	5.6	1 139	171	11	2 845	428	67	2 756	22 469	2 345	3 512	108 831	110 075	75.9	18.2
Yolo	775	6.4	328	244	3	286	212	14	913	10 174	964	7 763	19 512	18 017	73.5	27.0
Yuba	472	8.9	74	128	2	146	253	9	200	3 980	765	7 043	10 997	10 199	63.8	9.3
COLORADO	18 430	5.8	6 763	204	90	13 201	398	313	20 432	X	15 541	6 177	555 678	546 738	78.6	23.0
Adams	1 250	4.6	432	153	4	756	268	26	1 495	18 685	1 342	6 679	44 002	53 216	73.5	10.8
Alamosa	110	8.7	25	191	1	50	382	1	60	782	60	6 121	2 528	2 451	70.9	20.6
Arapahoe	1 691	4.7	550	139	7	924	233	15	1 358	25 085	2 714	6 497	73 883	60 994	88.6	31.9
Archuleta	30	5.6	4	75	0	0	0	0	0	195	15	3 907	1 034	906	72.3	22.3
Baca	23	4.4	2	42	1	65	1 354	0	0	97	15	1 983	883	1 169	62.2	12.4
Bent	17	2.9	7	132	1	379	7 151	1	10	105	5	1 879	1 072	1 249	60.9	9.9
Boulder	1 286	6.1	430	196	4	480	219	9	820	12 953	711	5 986	35 647	33 195	87.4	36.4
Chaffee	102	8.0	15	118	1	38	299	1	120	388	27	3 013	2 196	2 463	72.8	13.3
Cheyenne	9	3.8	2	87	1	32	1 391	1	40	65	11	2 831	442	440	71.9	12.7

1. Per 1,000 resident population estimated as of July 1 of the year shown. 2. As of end of year. 3. Per 100,000 resident population as of July 1 of the year shown. 4. Preliminary. Covers nursing homes with 3 or more beds. 5. Data for serious crimes have not been adjusted for underreporting, this may affect comparability between geographic areas or over time. 6. Includes murder and nonnegligent manslaughter, forcible rape, robbery, and aggravated assault. 7. The 1986–1987 data are based on administrative reports obtained by the U.S. National Center for Education Statistics. The 1980 data are based on the 1980 Census of Population and Housing. 8. Persons 25 years old or older.

STATE / County	Education (cont'd): Local government expenditures for education,[1] 1982: Total (Mil dol)	Education (cont'd): Local government expenditures for education,[1] 1982: Per capita (Dollars)	Social Security Program December 1988: Beneficiaries: Total	Social Security Program December 1988: Beneficiaries: Rate[2]	Social Security Program December 1988: Payments ($1,000)	Supplemental Security Income Program recipients June 1986	Money income: Per capita[3]: 1987 Income, (Dollars)	Money income: Per capita[3]: 1979: Current dollars	Money income: Per capita[3]: 1979: Constant 1987 dollars	Money income: Median household income 1979 (Dollars)	Money income: Percent below poverty level, 1979: Persons	Money income: Percent below poverty level, 1979: Families	Housing units, 1990: Total	Housing units, 1990: Percent change, 1980–1990
	60	61	62	63	64	65	66	67	68	69	70	71	72	73
CALIFORNIA—Con.														
Butte	70.4	462	37 505	214.9	18 018	6 342	9 963	6 708	10 496	13 012	15.0	9.5	76 115	24.0
Calaveras	14.7	631	6 660	213.5	3 307	588	10 992	7 152	11 191	15 266	10.1	7.5	19 153	50.3
Colusa	8.1	586	2 710	177.1	1 319	454	9 531	7 280	11 391	15 379	10.7	8.8	6 295	18.0
Contra Costa	307.3	452	99 705	130.3	52 274	14 806	16 101	9 821	15 367	22 870	7.6	6.1	316 170	25.5
Del Norte	10.4	564	4 150	206.5	1 924	932	8 147	6 287	9 837	13 783	12.7	11.4	9 091	19.9
El Dorado	50.4	536	18 690	154.1	9 121	1 652	12 498	7 968	12 468	17 513	8.7	6.7	61 451	36.6
Fresno	293.7	547	83 400	135.7	38 571	22 742	10 298	6 967	10 901	15 726	14.5	11.4	235 563	21.6
Glenn	14.4	650	4 355	186.1	1 998	718	9 151	6 534	10 224	14 664	13.1	10.5	9 329	10.7
Humboldt	53.7	488	19 070	164.1	9 290	3 882	9 800	6 890	10 781	14 774	14.3	9.4	51 134	12.7
Imperial	65.4	668	15 920	141.1	6 599	4 982	7 671	5 775	9 036	14 673	15.3	12.7	36 559	13.9
Inyo	11.5	626	4 235	235.3	2 009	572	11 087	6 987	10 933	14 572	10.2	7.3	8 712	2.7
Kern	236.6	544	68 775	132.3	32 024	16 448	10 003	6 990	10 937	16 358	12.6	10.2	198 636	27.6
Kings	43.2	553	10 320	111.6	4 543	2 974	8 369	5 843	9 143	14 518	14.6	12.4	30 843	20.0
Lake	18.0	442	14 190	275.5	6 791	2 226	9 365	6 292	9 845	11 172	13.3	11.2	28 822	25.3
Lassen	13.8	588	4 160	152.9	1 860	720	9 515	6 406	10 023	15 595	10.3	7.1	10 358	16.4
Los Angeles	3 513.2	456	885 925	103.2	452 837	240 902	13 357	8 303	12 992	17 551	13.4	10.5	3 163 343	10.8
Madera	41.7	604	13 065	157.4	5 873	3 422	8 850	6 361	9 953	15 339	15.7	12.4	30 831	25.3
Marin	90.9	406	30 295	131.7	16 665	2 798	21 611	12 332	19 296	24 554	7.0	4.9	99 757	7.7
Mariposa	7.0	579	2 895	198.3	1 370	262	10 348	6 676	10 446	13 320	11.5	9.6	7 700	33.6
Mendocino	43.2	622	13 750	180.4	6 565	2 614	9 869	6 809	10 654	15 013	12.3	9.5	33 649	16.0
Merced	89.9	631	20 040	117.9	8 886	5 852	9 056	6 267	9 806	14 665	14.7	11.9	58 410	16.7
Modoc	6.9	754	1 865	202.7	843	320	9 397	6 563	10 269	13 394	14.5	11.8	4 672	25.0
Mono	5.3	564	695	73.2	326	74	13 241	8 590	13 441	16 930	11.2	6.4	10 664	27.0
Monterey	146.5	480	39 465	113.1	18 890	6 076	11 220	7 495	11 727	17 658	11.4	8.9	121 224	17.1
Napa	42.4	420	19 340	181.4	9 304	2 048	13 446	8 376	13 106	18 887	8.1	6.0	44 199	10.4
Nevada	23.6	394	14 945	193.3	7 339	1 322	11 562	7 484	11 710	16 125	8.7	6.5	37 352	50.9
Orange	876.4	434	241 775	107.1	128 104	29 616	16 037	9 567	14 969	22 557	7.3	5.2	875 072	21.3
Placer	66.9	530	23 505	151.4	11 225	3 078	12 968	8 167	12 779	18 685	8.6	7.0	77 879	44.2
Plumas	11.5	629	3 900	194.0	1 875	526	10 137	6 857	10 729	15 205	9.7	8.2	11 942	26.4
Riverside	329.9	460	166 520	169.0	82 462	22 528	11 499	7 477	11 699	16 037	11.3	8.8	483 847	64.0
Sacramento	376.8	453	128 425	131.5	59 780	27 978	12 457	7 950	12 439	17 390	11.2	8.9	417 574	29.0
San Benito	14.9	554	4 210	122.0	1 958	644	9 933	6 208	9 714	16 998	13.0	10.8	12 230	39.8
San Bernardino	453.3	468	151 330	117.1	71 843	28 594	10 815	7 090	11 094	17 463	11.1	9.1	542 332	46.5
San Diego	851.8	433	306 440	129.3	148 668	46 216	12 764	7 960	12 455	17 106	11.3	8.4	946 240	31.4
San Francisco	205.9	297	111 285	152.1	57 734	34 112	15 137	9 265	14 497	15 866	13.7	10.3	328 471	3.7
San Joaquin	184.3	495	63 880	140.2	29 974	16 334	10 366	7 016	10 978	16 071	13.3	10.8	166 274	22.3
San Luis Obispo	61.6	369	35 155	169.4	17 067	3 884	11 199	7 048	11 028	14 805	13.7	8.0	90 200	35.1
San Mateo	243.1	411	83 665	133.2	46 165	10 272	17 656	10 666	16 689	23 172	6.1	4.5	251 782	8.0
Santa Barbara	134.5	435	49 895	145.4	24 856	6 006	13 633	8 400	13 143	17 962	10.6	6.7	138 149	20.2
Santa Clara	712.2	534	140 385	98.0	73 138	24 914	16 086	9 518	14 893	23 369	7.1	5.3	540 240	14.0
Santa Cruz	82.1	418	30 920	136.4	15 111	4 746	13 152	8 197	12 826	16 877	12.2	8.2	91 878	13.6
Shasta	70.0	575	27 355	195.8	12 968	4 854	10 225	6 791	10 626	14 699	10.9	8.8	60 552	27.6
Sierra	2.9	880	820	234.3	378	122	10 771	7 120	11 141	14 468	12.9	9.3	2 166	14.4
Siskiyou	24.0	579	9 520	218.9	4 448	1 588	9 162	6 535	10 225	14 472	12.1	9.6	20 141	15.1
Solano	118.0	463	31 795	101.2	14 325	5 836	11 674	7 407	11 590	19 264	9.4	8.1	119 533	41.8
Sonoma	133.8	426	59 960	163.8	29 815	8 006	13 024	8 087	12 654	17 732	9.5	7.1	161 062	29.7
Stanislaus	135.9	483	50 205	147.2	23 452	12 534	10 657	7 094	11 100	16 074	11.9	10.0	132 027	28.8
Sutter	29.9	541	9 340	150.9	4 341	1 960	10 004	7 108	11 122	15 683	11.3	9.0	24 163	18.3
Tehama	21.1	511	9 485	203.5	4 433	1 658	8 885	6 137	9 603	13 425	12.9	11.0	20 403	23.2
Trinity	13.1	1 047	2 610	186.4	1 245	320	9 526	6 295	9 850	14 175	11.4	9.1	7 540	18.7
Tulare	159.1	615	43 335	145.5	19 031	13 742	8 690	6 038	9 448	14 150	16.5	13.2	105 013	18.3
Tuolumne	15.8	435	9 780	211.7	4 842	970	10 241	6 745	10 554	14 178	11.9	9.2	25 175	30.0
Ventura	272.9	488	73 130	113.0	36 058	10 114	13 429	8 015	12 541	21 236	8.0	6.1	228 478	24.6
Yolo	47.2	403	14 945	113.5	7 190	3 154	11 211	7 277	11 386	15 398	15.9	9.1	53 000	21.5
Yuba	28.5	559	8 750	154.6	3 843	2 852	8 013	5 539	8 667	12 032	16.1	14.4	21 245	10.4
COLORADO	1 606.2	523	396 855	120.2	189 125	31 341	12 271	7 998	12 514	18 056	10.1	7.4	1 477 349	23.7
Adams	128.7	491	32 880	117.0	15 942	2 414	10 993	7 259	11 358	19 511	7.6	6.0	106 947	19.8
Alamosa	9.4	767	1 690	130.0	669	320	8 471	5 694	8 909	11 945	21.2	18.1	5 254	18.5
Arapahoe	212.0	639	28 755	73.5	14 856	1 154	15 545	10 199	15 958	23 861	4.6	3.3	168 665	49.0
Archuleta	2.6	558	885	170.2	390	58	7 566	5 550	8 684	13 079	18.6	15.9	3 951	93.3
Baca	4.0	753	1 055	215.3	458	94	7 889	5 607	8 773	11 049	20.6	15.5	2 434	-1.9
Bent	3.4	580	995	184.3	380	118	9 285	5 811	9 092	12 991	12.9	10.5	2 332	-1.5
Boulder	98.9	494	21 625	99.2	10 743	1 090	13 924	8 607	13 467	19 774	10.1	5.0	94 621	26.8
Chaffee	6.0	443	2 480	193.8	1 113	162	8 328	6 244	9 770	15 204	7.8	6.4	6 547	13.3
Cheyenne	2.3	992	410	170.8	183	28	9 279	5 663	8 861	11 733	17.9	13.4	1 083	13.0

1. Elementary and secondary. 2. Per 1,000 resident population estimated as of July 1 of the year shown. 3. Based on the resident population estimated as of July 1, 1988 for 1987 data and enumerated as of April 1, 1980 for 1979 data.

STATE County	Housing units, 1990 (cont'd): Occupied units: Total	Owner occupied: Percent	Owner occupied: Median value (Dollars)	Median rent (Dollars)	Civilian labor force, 1990: Total	Percent change, 1989–1990	Unemployment: Total	Unemployment: Rate[1]	Private nonfarm establishments, 1988: Number	Net change, 1987–1988	Employment[2]: Total	Per-cent change, 1987–1988	Manu-facturing	Retail trade
	74	75	76	77	78	79	80	81	82	83	84	85	86	87
CALIFORNIA—Con.														
Butte	71 665	60.9	94 000	369	74 502	-3.0	5 625	7.6	4 337	51	40 959	4.9	5 645	12 551
Calaveras	12 649	76.1	113 700	384	10 868	-0.9	894	8.2	777	47	4 174	8.2	325	1 262
Colusa	5 612	63.5	68 900	272	8 199	-1.6	1 019	12.4	367	-5	2 817	-1.6	343	919
Contra Costa	300 288	67.6	219 400	613	416 629	-1.3	17 776	4.3	19 078	468	247 511	5.1	28 297	60 178
Del Norte	7 987	65.4	84 600	341	8 385	5.0	1 056	12.6	586	29	4 024	15.0	797	1 132
El Dorado	46 845	70.4	155 000	478	66 467	0.8	2 854	4.3	3 005	57	21 838	11.3	2 049	7 160
Fresno	220 933	54.3	83 600	363	318 441	1.7	32 571	10.2	14 355	23	170 922	5.0	21 827	42 743
Glenn	8 821	61.8	67 400	278	10 345	-3.0	1 295	12.5	512	8	4 694	8.0	1 198	1 104
Humboldt	46 420	58.8	88 000	344	50 662	-3.4	3 880	7.7	3 377	41	31 074	5.6	6 834	8 504
Imperial	32 842	57.6	72 500	313	45 663	-5.5	8 733	19.1	2 035	82	18 835	8.8	1 634	6 196
Inyo	7 565	66.3	115 800	317	8 036	-6.9	492	6.1	584	-1	4 577	-1.4	313	1 893
Kern	181 480	59.3	82 800	365	232 418	-2.2	24 378	10.5	10 407	10	119 973	4.2	8 256	32 434
Kings	29 082	52.9	70 700	335	35 171	-7.2	3 834	10.9	1 406	-9	13 981	1.3	2 833	4 536
Lake	20 805	71.2	93 300	351	17 611	-3.4	1 652	9.4	1 114	-21	7 394	2.9	330	2 644
Lassen	8 543	69.4	70 400	296	9 821	-2.1	878	8.9	545	6	3 728	-10.6	770	1 189
Los Angeles	2 989 552	48.2	226 400	570	4 428 000	4.9	255 000	5.8	216 117	3 146	3 628 164	2.3	891 105	622 070
Madera	28 370	64.9	86 500	333	38 240	-0.6	4 713	12.3	1 485	61	13 053	-0.2	3 468	3 598
Marin	95 006	62.1	354 200	763	126 928	-1.6	3 403	2.7	9 050	155	82 441	2.4	5 721	22 576
Mariposa	5 604	69.3	99 800	311	7 322	2.7	380	5.2	332	0	2 612	8.0	106	625
Mendocino	30 419	62.1	123 900	384	36 571	1.6	2 954	8.1	2 531	30	19 824	2.7	4 567	5 473
Merced	55 331	54.4	90 800	358	73 095	-1.9	8 478	11.6	2 716	32	30 243	5.4	7 101	8 218
Modoc	3 711	69.6	49 600	225	3 950	-4.5	379	9.6	217	-5	1 346	-4.7	132	407
Mono	3 961	51.9	159 900	450	5 467	-6.8	347	6.3	475	4	5 333	11.9	34	1 682
Monterey	112 965	50.6	198 200	566	160 646	-2.3	14 142	8.8	8 012	220	79 157	1.9	8 562	23 269
Napa	41 312	64.5	183 600	561	55 154	2.1	2 577	4.7	3 032	105	29 969	5.5	5 042	7 623
Nevada	30 758	74.4	154 700	489	32 255	-0.7	1 780	5.5	2 258	39	16 387	9.7	2 728	4 702
Orange	827 066	60.1	252 700	728	1 382 849	-1.9	46 443	3.4	68 128	1 607	1 098 300	3.3	251 736	217 890
Placer	64 101	70.7	169 000	496	80 303	1.1	3 821	4.8	4 826	248	44 412	4.3	5 886	13 330
Plumas	8 125	67.5	89 900	272	8 700	-4.5	909	10.4	599	-6	3 495	-2.4	1 017	952
Riverside	402 067	67.4	139 100	502	466 214	4.8	35 931	7.7	20 050	939	246 031	8.6	37 361	65 742
Sacramento	394 530	56.6	129 800	462	520 943	0.7	24 486	4.7	23 249	307	305 804	6.3	28 961	81 356
San Benito	11 422	61.1	206 600	491	17 689	-0.2	2 203	12.5	704	40	6 266	8.8	1 542	1 624
San Bernardino	464 737	63.3	129 200	489	605 421	4.6	34 698	5.7	23 136	643	320 552	7.6	54 581	83 693
San Diego	887 403	53.8	186 700	564	1 174 417	0.2	52 771	4.5	57 667	1 768	767 646	4.5	124 379	184 606
San Francisco	305 584	34.5	298 900	613	393 245	-1.8	15 695	4.0	31 664	-6	504 187	0.1	45 053	77 676
San Joaquin	158 156	57.6	121 700	417	196 738	-2.3	19 238	9.8	9 532	114	118 224	4.9	24 073	28 984
San Luis Obispo	80 281	59.8	215 300	510	98 617	-1.5	3 997	4.1	5 785	179	52 966	-0.4	6 089	16 850
San Mateo	241 914	60.2	343 900	711	353 026	-1.5	9 845	2.8	18 239	333	277 317	3.6	33 520	54 236
Santa Barbara	129 802	54.7	250 000	606	180 500	-1.3	8 109	4.5	10 210	102	121 331	0.7	20 831	30 395
Santa Clara	520 180	59.1	289 400	715	813 569	-4.0	32 854	4.0	38 070	699	769 907	4.3	286 410	120 608
Santa Cruz	83 566	59.9	256 100	651	134 510	0.8	8 551	6.4	6 384	160	67 153	8.7	13 284	19 012
Shasta	55 966	64.5	91 300	358	61 526	-0.8	5 270	8.6	4 209	50	37 182	4.4	5 006	10 167
Sierra	1 336	68.1	79 300	280	1 685	1.4	170	10.1	80	-8	457	8.3	0	100
Siskiyou	17 306	67.2	68 300	270	18 923	-2.5	2 194	11.6	1 234	6	8 837	3.3	1 967	2 671
Solano	113 429	62.9	147 300	521	145 347	2.1	8 126	5.6	5 457	139	62 105	5.9	7 008	20 055
Sonoma	149 011	62.9	201 400	576	209 955	3.3	9 155	4.4	11 024	284	109 801	4.5	18 939	28 657
Stanislaus	125 375	60.7	124 300	417	163 563	-0.8	18 552	11.3	7 280	171	91 621	4.8	21 819	22 863
Sutter	23 111	58.7	91 900	321	29 514	0.7	4 059	13.8	1 436	10	12 652	-0.2	1 883	3 781
Tehama	18 704	68.6	68 700	288	17 581	-5.9	1 888	10.7	938	14	8 713	-10.6	2 667	2 506
Trinity	5 156	69.6	81 800	292	5 421	-2.9	659	12.2	327	13	1 874	6.7	700	546
Tulare	97 861	60.1	73 900	324	136 767	-2.8	15 467	11.3	5 529	63	59 830	1.1	11 869	15 766
Tuolumne	17 959	70.6	120 400	392	19 294	0.0	1 320	6.8	1 422	29	9 642	8.3	1 017	3 003
Ventura	217 298	65.5	245 300	695	374 422	0.6	20 768	5.5	14 332	537	186 813	5.7	33 248	46 346
Yolo	50 972	51.9	137 800	459	71 421	0.6	4 311	6.0	3 014	27	38 877	5.3	6 054	10 121
Yuba	19 776	52.8	67 600	312	19 717	-0.5	2 078	10.5	873	11	8 053	-1.7	1 187	2 475
COLORADO	1 282 489	62.2	82 700	362	1 756 000	3.6	87 000	4.9	X	X	1 168 580	0.0	184 893	270 368
Adams	96 353	65.5	71 500	373	150 710	2.6	8 095	5.4	5 640	-109	78 511	-1.5	13 015	19 425
Alamosa	4 721	62.5	48 100	241	6 253	4.2	374	6.0	408	-15	3 253	2.0	91	1 189
Arapahoe	154 710	63.6	93 000	404	216 538	3.0	8 000	3.7	11 434	-21	142 898	-1.7	13 793	36 643
Archuleta	2 010	70.7	79 600	285	2 500	-2.0	165	6.6	189	-28	862	-30.6	23	325
Baca	1 872	72.9	31 100	148	2 154	8.8	65	3.0	113	-9	382	-21.9	0	167
Bent	1 865	69.3	24 300	207	2 081	3.7	95	4.6	81	-13	373	-10.3	0	113
Boulder	88 402	61.1	102 800	449	138 920	3.7	5 092	3.7	6 935	15	90 546	1.5	29 704	20 585
Chaffee	4 848	70.9	62 900	247	6 778	1.1	393	5.8	433	-7	2 499	-5.0	185	900
Cheyenne	904	70.0	38 200	224	1 081	9.6	26	2.4	62	-1	350	-6.2	0	99

1. Percent of total civilian labor force. 2. For week including March 12. Excludes government employees, self-employed persons, farm workers, domestic service workers, railroad employees subject to the Railroad Retirement Act, and employees on oceanborne vessels or in foreign countries.

STATE County	Private nonfarm establishments, 1988 (cont'd): Employment[1] (cont'd): Finance, insurance, and real estate	Private nonfarm establishments, 1988 (cont'd): Employment[1] (cont'd): Services	Private nonfarm establishments, 1988 (cont'd): Annual payroll: Total (Mil dol)	Private nonfarm establishments, 1988 (cont'd): Annual payroll: Average per employee (Dollars)	Personal income, 1989: Total (Mil dol)	Personal income, 1989: Percent change, 1988–1989	Personal income, 1989: Wages and salaries[2] (Mil dol)	Personal income, 1989: Proprietor's income (Mil dol)	Personal income, 1989: Dividends, interest, & rent (Mil dol)	Personal income, 1989: Transfer payments (Mil dol)	Personal income, 1989: Per capita[3]: Dollars	Personal income, 1989: Per capita[3]: Rank	Earnings, 1989: Total (Mil dol)	Earnings, 1989: Percent by selected industries: Farm	Earnings, 1989: Percent by selected industries: Goods-related[4]: Total
	88	89	90	91	92	93	94	95	96	97	98	99	100	101	102
CALIFORNIA–Con.															
Butte	2 348	12 950	643	15 694	2 590	9.4	1 175	296	559	614	14 471	1 224	1 471	4.2	18.1
Calaveras	213	984	71	17 030	416	11.1	137	65	112	97	12 607	2 070	202	2.6	35.2
Colusa	107	510	52	18 419	281	13.2	116	72	57	44	17 998	294	188	36.6	12.8
Contra Costa	28 392	67 920	5 929	23 956	19 054	8.3	8 958	1 456	3 414	2 019	24 308	47	10 414	0.2	25.7
Del Norte	148	1 112	64	15 872	251	11.0	119	22	47	74	12 139	2 266	141	3.3	26.6
El Dorado	1 483	6 396	370	16 950	2 208	12.0	638	193	376	321	17 264	403	831	0.6	22.6
Fresno	12 466	49 184	3 204	18 744	10 023	8.2	5 706	1 491	1 567	1 828	15 927	667	7 197	10.1	16.6
Glenn	110	614	97	20 596	382	7.4	149	104	69	71	16 185	598	253	34.2	21.5
Humboldt	1 431	8 640	544	17 507	1 833	8.4	994	240	340	360	15 546	787	1 233	2.3	26.0
Imperial	828	3 583	289	15 328	1 467	4.1	803	307	153	326	12 712	2 031	1 110	25.5	9.6
Inyo	163	1 396	65	14 287	307	9.6	149	37	73	66	17 045	428	185	2.1	14.8
Kern	5 997	34 962	2 306	19 222	7 948	5.9	4 873	1 173	1 066	1 388	14 856	1 052	6 046	9.2	24.0
Kings	534	3 420	242	17 285	1 326	11.1	773	227	156	233	13 907	1 469	1 000	18.6	18.7
Lake	523	2 147	108	14 599	749	10.3	217	67	169	218	14 166	1 363	284	2.7	18.2
Lassen	161	965	59	15 891	342	8.2	192	32	50	84	12 126	2 273	224	3.4	17.9
Los Angeles	285 731	1 124 051	89 414	24 644	174 366	7.7	131 725	16 244	29 841	21 908	19 906	173	147 969	0.1	25.8
Madera	486	2 925	233	17 857	1 130	3.6	490	204	181	243	13 121	1 852	694	20.2	25.3
Marin	10 136	28 865	1 845	22 379	8 124	8.0	2 704	1 287	1 878	579	34 983	4	3 991	0.3	12.7
Mariposa	177	1 330	40	15 377	207	8.2	89	17	47	45	13 735	1 558	107	2.6	11.5
Mendocino	1 011	5 085	332	16 750	1 226	10.8	579	182	271	240	15 858	693	762	4.9	27.8
Merced	2 330	6 218	508	16 797	2 335	7.7	1 172	376	333	506	13 387	1 735	1 548	18.8	NA
Modoc	52	386	19	14 322	132	4.3	49	26	26	32	14 494	1 217	75	18.4	6.1
Mono	379	2 640	62	11 594	182	9.3	120	22	27	16	18 855	226	142	2.2	NA
Monterey	4 526	25 440	1 492	18 844	6 274	5.2	3 448	976	1 251	858	17 622	350	4 424	13.4	12.4
Napa	1 497	10 086	560	18 671	2 311	9.0	986	256	501	360	21 417	113	1 242	5.4	23.6
Nevada	1 536	4 567	272	16 577	1 295	10.4	440	169	350	228	15 987	648	609	0.5	31.4
Orange	98 506	303 982	26 178	23 835	56 000	8.9	35 398	4 594	9 339	4 895	24 288	48	39 992	0.2	30.9
Placer	3 138	13 185	821	18 476	3 130	11.7	1 418	331	527	463	19 337	203	1 749	1.3	29.1
Plumas	207	730	66	18 811	302	8.8	144	34	70	66	14 726	1 113	178	2.0	26.5
Riverside	14 244	67 333	4 519	18 366	17 872	10.2	7 376	1 461	3 186	2 883	17 028	431	8 837	3.3	25.5
Sacramento	26 856	98 138	6 073	19 860	18 359	10.1	13 051	1 458	2 628	3 420	18 194	272	14 509	0.3	14.3
San Benito	286	1 131	118	18 806	551	6.2	220	95	104	73	15 279	879	315	20.7	NA
San Bernardino	14 573	88 236	6 062	18 912	21 473	9.2	10 204	1 568	2 360	3 302	15 635	766	11 772	1.7	23.2
San Diego	64 541	243 821	16 145	21 032	45 868	9.6	28 784	3 633	8 709	6 614	18 651	242	32 417	1.1	22.6
San Francisco	81 178	190 115	13 912	27 592	19 398	6.0	20 166	2 741	4 197	2 428	26 454	27	22 906	0.0	10.7
San Joaquin	8 769	29 922	2 277	19 257	6 998	7.7	3 891	793	1 190	1 411	14 861	1 049	4 683	5.7	23.8
San Luis Obispo	2 961	14 926	868	16 392	3 498	10.0	1 643	448	862	555	16 290	572	2 092	5.8	18.4
San Mateo	24 903	79 609	7 396	26 670	17 529	8.0	9 869	1 364	3 905	1 534	27 659	22	11 234	0.7	21.2
Santa Barbara	9 246	39 094	2 518	20 753	7 478	9.0	4 163	910	1 911	905	21 504	110	5 073	4.9	25.2
Santa Clara	31 173	208 860	23 116	30 025	35 544	7.4	29 885	2 348	5 190	3 043	24 581	44	32 233	0.3	45.5
Santa Cruz	3 191	19 951	1 301	19 367	4 322	-0.1	1 986	485	615	572	18 637	243	2 471	6.3	26.1
Shasta	1 784	10 538	709	19 066	2 229	9.8	1 175	292	402	475	15 567	784	1 467	1.1	24.6
Sierra	21	121	9	19 024	55	9.4	23	4	11	12	15 235	892	27	4.5	29.9
Siskiyou	505	1 992	133	15 084	628	6.3	283	89	132	151	14 300	1 289	372	7.5	20.4
Solano	3 373	17 294	1 189	19 142	5 315	8.0	2 751	334	605	857	16 154	603	3 085	1.9	18.8
Sonoma	9 207	28 554	2 181	19 863	7 883	9.3	3 384	831	1 668	1 014	20 860	132	4 215	3.4	27.5
Stanislaus	3 944	23 306	1 750	19 098	5 212	8.8	2 864	587	873	962	14 689	1 136	3 451	7.1	30.2
Sutter	823	3 057	232	18 317	961	9.7	369	115	182	193	15 185	914	483	10.7	20.6
Tehama	426	2 047	146	16 746	594	6.6	254	73	123	152	12 471	2 129	327	9.4	30.0
Trinity	49	257	33	17 660	178	9.2	71	20	35	45	12 495	2 119	91	1.7	26.8
Tulare	2 688	13 048	986	16 478	4 164	6.6	1 976	730	632	868	13 668	1 595	2 706	18.0	17.7
Tuolumne	592	2 570	152	15 752	681	10.0	294	78	172	145	14 080	1 397	372	1.3	24.3
Ventura	12 960	52 681	3 870	20 717	13 396	7.9	6 401	1 197	1 928	1 456	20 156	161	7 598	4.9	24.5
Yolo	1 913	8 056	783	20 139	2 533	11.0	1 519	306	388	386	18 816	232	1 825	5.6	19.7
Yuba	503	1 967	140	17 361	680	7.1	450	77	89	200	11 801	2 398	527	9.7	12.8
COLORADO	95 731	349 265	24 062	X	58 077	7.1	37 644	5 752	10 020	7 347	17 504	X	43 396	1.9	23.2
Adams	3 447	13 623	1 663	21 177	4 036	6.0	2 300	283	363	560	14 306	1 285	2 583	1.0	24.4
Alamosa	161	1 022	42	12 899	163	10.4	87	29	25	34	12 437	2 145	116	12.7	NA
Arapahoe	19 047	42 926	3 112	21 775	8 192	7.6	4 522	615	1 329	677	20 663	141	5 138	0.2	16.8
Archuleta	76	309	10	11 262	59	7.5	25	10	16	13	11 109	2 633	35	6.0	NA
Baca	43	66	5	12 034	85	4.6	17	39	18	12	17 625	349	56	65.9	NA
Bent	38	57	4	11 887	69	12.8	32	11	13	21	13 171	1 828	43	18.6	4.0
Boulder	4 785	24 213	1 974	21 799	4 428	6.9	2 867	393	769	382	20 203	158	3 260	0.8	39.5
Chaffee	149	908	29	11 471	173	7.0	68	19	41	37	13 669	1 594	87	3.1	12.7
Cheyenne	64	70	4	12 714	73	17.9	13	44	12	5	31 117	12	57	69.0	NA

1. For week including March 12. Excludes government employees, self-employed persons, farm workers, domestic service workers, railroad employees subject to the Railroad Retirement Act, and employees on oceanborne vessels or in foreign countries. 2. Includes other labor income. 3. Based on the resident population estimated as of July 1 of the year shown. 4. Covers mining, construction, and manufacturing.

STATE County	Earnings, 1989 (cont'd): Percent by selected industries (cont'd): Goods-related[1]: Manu-facturing	Service-related & other[2]: Total	Service-related & other[2]: Retail trade	Service-related & other[2]: Finance, insur-ance, & real estate	Service-related & other[2]: Services	Govern-ment	Agriculture, 1987: Farms: Number	Farms: Percent with: Less than 50 acres	Farms: Percent with: 500 acres and over	Farm operators, percent: Whose principal occu-pation is farming	Farm operators, percent: Residing on farm operated	Land in farms: Acreage (1,000)	Land in farms: Percent change, 1982–1987	Land in farms: Acres: Average size of farm	Acres: Total irrigated (1,000)	Acres: Total cropland (1,000)
	103	104	105	106	107	108	109	110	111	112	113	114	115	116	117	118
CALIFORNIA—Con.																
Butte	9.8	59.1	13.8	4.9	29.1	18.5	2 030	60.1	9.9	55.2	66.4	495	5.8	244	179	256
Calaveras	4.5	40.8	11.1	2.5	19.0	21.4	431	42.9	20.6	46.2	70.8	253	17.9	588	13	26
Colusa	9.0	37.6	9.5	2.0	9.8	13.0	764	24.6	24.3	70.0	46.1	456	2.8	597	207	303
Contra Costa	13.7	61.9	10.9	9.4	27.7	12.2	840	66.8	9.9	40.0	71.0	200	-24.5	238	25	54
Del Norte	16.5	44.3	12.5	1.8	19.1	25.8	84	50.0	6.0	46.4	77.4	13	-23.9	156	6	9
El Dorado	7.0	57.1	14.3	4.3	31.2	19.7	738	68.0	4.7	37.3	82.8	128	-12.6	174	9	19
Fresno	8.8	55.8	10.8	5.1	23.1	17.5	7 590	62.7	8.4	56.5	67.8	1 975	-4.7	260	1 011	1 231
Glenn	16.7	29.5	6.8	1.1	9.3	14.8	1 170	45.0	18.4	63.2	68.1	491	-6.0	419	182	266
Humboldt	17.3	52.2	13.1	2.7	22.1	19.6	890	38.3	17.8	54.7	73.7	616	-5.0	692	13	57
Imperial	3.0	42.1	9.3	1.9	13.7	22.8	804	30.2	33.1	69.7	39.3	543	-2.9	675	413	468
Inyo	2.8	53.7	15.5	1.9	25.7	29.4	94	40.4	25.5	48.9	71.3	220	-26.9	2 338	13	18
Kern	6.3	44.7	8.9	3.2	19.2	22.1	2 255	39.5	26.5	56.4	49.4	3 037	-3.3	1 347	747	974
Kings	15.1	29.2	8.1	1.5	12.1	33.4	1 204	50.3	14.0	62.5	70.5	702	-13.1	583	476	566
Lake	2.5	56.6	16.1	4.3	25.6	22.5	873	60.3	7.1	38.1	64.6	155	0.9	177	21	37
Lassen	12.2	34.7	10.7	3.2	12.9	44.0	413	34.9	31.5	49.2	78.2	518	-6.8	1 254	81	116
Los Angeles	20.6	62.8	8.7	8.1	31.9	11.2	2 035	85.2	3.7	33.8	65.4	280	-11.8	138	23	64
Madera	18.4	39.1	9.0	2.3	16.1	15.4	1 746	45.0	14.0	54.0	55.4	757	13.8	434	240	324
Marin	4.2	78.7	11.7	11.3	46.8	8.3	285	32.6	37.5	58.6	70.9	168	1.0	588	1	21
Mariposa	3.9	55.5	7.0	2.7	42.8	30.3	255	26.3	32.9	45.1	73.3	237	2.4	928	8	22
Mendocino	20.8	51.2	12.3	2.7	23.0	16.0	1 067	42.6	18.7	46.9	74.7	777	-0.7	728	21	64
Merced	13.8	NA	8.9	3.7	13.5	25.1	3 048	55.1	10.7	59.0	68.5	1 049	-9.8	344	423	517
Modoc	3.7	41.1	8.9	1.8	16.1	34.3	495	14.5	38.6	66.1	71.9	729	-2.5	1 473	146	196
Mono	0.3	NA	15.4	4.1	36.1	19.7	76	34.2	38.2	60.5	68.4	73	-6.2	959	22	17
Monterey	6.7	49.0	10.2	3.6	21.4	25.2	1 364	44.4	26.6	66.1	53.8	1 385	2.9	1 015	181	316
Napa	12.5	53.7	11.4	4.3	29.6	17.2	1 197	61.6	8.4	46.4	63.9	258	11.8	216	30	70
Nevada	15.0	52.3	12.6	4.5	29.3	15.7	386	69.2	7.8	39.4	84.2	56	-29.2	146	4	14
Orange	22.7	59.8	10.6	9.6	28.3	9.0	504	79.6	2.4	42.1	44.8	109	-34.1	216	17	24
Placer	14.2	56.5	13.0	5.4	24.9	13.2	1 233	71.9	5.6	38.3	83.8	168	-8.0	136	29	60
Plumas	19.2	45.1	10.7	3.3	16.7	26.4	109	33.0	30.3	55.0	74.3	88	-14.7	809	20	24
Riverside	11.7	52.6	12.0	4.9	25.4	18.6	3 874	77.3	4.6	37.9	55.9	491	-2.1	127	197	293
Sacramento	6.6	50.7	9.7	6.8	23.5	34.6	1 586	64.0	10.7	43.3	76.2	412	-2.4	260	117	186
San Benito	19.2	34.2	9.1	2.1	11.4	15.3	704	50.4	23.4	55.0	66.1	632	2.0	898	31	90
San Bernardino	13.2	52.9	12.0	3.8	23.8	22.1	1 938	79.5	2.7	45.2	69.9	1 682	-20.7	868	37	62
San Diego	14.3	52.7	9.9	6.9	26.4	23.6	6 259	87.7	1.9	37.9	63.9	530	-15.1	85	73	123
San Francisco	6.6	75.1	7.3	18.3	35.5	14.3	5	100.0	0.0	60.0	20.0	D	D	D	0	0
San Joaquin	15.4	52.4	9.9	6.3	20.8	18.2	4 366	63.1	7.4	54.9	69.1	824	-7.6	189	449	551
San Luis Obispo	7.2	55.3	14.0	4.5	23.7	20.5	1 991	50.5	19.6	50.8	69.6	1 444	-5.6	725	48	337
San Mateo	13.4	69.6	10.4	8.0	27.1	8.5	330	63.3	9.4	48.8	60.3	64	-9.2	192	5	23
Santa Barbara	16.9	54.4	10.4	5.6	28.8	15.6	1 756	62.4	15.2	55.2	54.7	870	3.5	495	76	145
Santa Clara	40.2	45.6	7.0	3.6	25.0	8.6	1 312	75.2	5.7	48.1	68.9	348	5.5	265	24	45
Santa Cruz	16.2	52.5	12.0	3.0	28.6	15.0	813	75.4	2.1	59.8	61.1	55	-3.9	68	19	27
Shasta	12.0	56.8	12.0	3.0	27.1	17.4	899	57.4	14.2	43.3	82.2	377	-6.9	420	49	60
Sierra	27.2	NA	5.0	NA	10.6	47.6	46	17.4	28.3	50.0	58.7	51	-3.8	1 116	8	8
Siskiyou	14.5	47.1	10.2	3.0	18.6	25.0	765	26.0	29.3	61.8	76.1	669	-5.9	875	129	188
Solano	8.2	40.3	11.9	2.8	17.2	39.0	895	59.3	16.0	48.9	70.5	321	-9.6	359	95	177
Sonoma	14.5	54.2	12.5	6.3	24.1	14.9	3 039	65.1	7.9	45.1	73.0	550	-6.3	181	36	160
Stanislaus	21.1	48.7	11.3	4.1	21.2	14.0	4 630	68.6	5.0	50.9	75.3	720	-10.8	155	312	361
Sutter	10.8	51.9	11.2	3.8	23.8	16.7	1 438	49.6	12.0	62.8	60.5	356	1.2	248	212	296
Tehama	23.7	41.5	11.9	3.1	18.5	19.1	1 420	57.1	13.3	50.7	76.2	1 105	-5.4	778	90	160
Trinity	17.4	33.9	9.1	1.3	17.6	37.5	133	37.6	17.3	39.1	81.2	104	-18.0	782	1	7
Tulare	11.6	45.9	9.7	3.0	16.1	18.4	5 911	61.5	8.2	54.0	61.1	1 410	5.5	239	597	762
Tuolumne	9.8	51.3	13.6	4.9	25.8	23.1	271	40.2	19.6	42.4	72.3	121	9.4	447	3	13
Ventura	14.3	52.8	10.5	5.3	24.4	17.8	2 120	70.8	5.5	44.6	53.1	329	9.4	155	104	134
Yolo	10.5	45.5	9.0	3.0	17.5	29.2	1 011	46.7	20.8	57.1	64.3	506	-6.7	500	233	376
Yuba	5.8	36.7	8.5	3.5	13.3	40.8	654	47.6	13.0	53.5	67.7	223	4.8	341	74	98
COLORADO	15.0	57.2	9.6	6.7	25.9	17.7	27 284	25.9	37.5	60.5	72.8	34 048	1.5	1 248	3 014	10 989
Adams	16.8	56.2	12.2	2.8	17.7	18.3	701	38.7	30.5	60.3	70.9	712	-2.2	1 016	29	533
Alamosa	1.8	NA	14.0	4.0	25.5	24.0	327	15.3	30.3	64.2	75.2	210	-7.2	641	108	108
Arapahoe	7.7	72.8	11.1	12.5	32.3	10.3	285	39.6	35.1	46.0	66.7	295	3.4	1 036	2	155
Archuleta	2.4	NA	14.3	4.5	NA	19.5	152	13.8	37.5	53.9	69.7	161	17.0	1 059	14	22
Baca	NA	17.7	5.6	-1.0	5.3	14.4	612	4.7	72.1	73.4	50.3	1 305	1.7	2 132	40	680
Bent	2.0	18.7	4.5	2.2	6.5	58.7	292	14.4	50.3	71.9	73.3	856	12.4	2 930	55	103
Boulder	33.9	43.5	8.8	3.2	25.5	16.3	752	55.7	6.8	37.5	79.1	155	-3.7	207	39	69
Chaffee	2.8	50.0	16.3	3.3	20.2	34.2	160	26.9	22.5	50.6	78.8	105	-4.7	658	15	20
Cheyenne	NA	NA	2.3	1.6	2.9	7.9	325	1.2	81.5	81.2	52.6	863	-8.8	2 655	19	D

1. Covers mining, construction, and manufacturing. 2. Covers private sector earnings in agricultural services, forestry, and fisheries; transportation and public utilities; wholesale trade; retail trade; finance, insurance, and real estate; and services.

STATE County	Agriculture, 1987 (cont'd) — Value of land and buildings — Average per farm ($1,000)	Value of land and buildings — Average per acre (Dollars)	Value of products sold — Total (Mil dol)	Value of products sold — Average per farm (Dollars)	Value of products sold — Percent from — Crops	Value of products sold — Percent from — Livestock and poultry[1]	Percent of farms with sales of — $10,000 or more	Percent of farms with sales of — $100,000 or more	Manufactures, 1987 — Establishments — Total	Establishments — Percent with 20 or more employees	All employees — Number (1,000)	All employees — Percent change, 1982–1987	All employees — Annual payroll (Mil dol)	Production workers — Number (1,000)	Production workers — Work hours (Mil)
	119	120	121	122	123	124	125	126	127	128	129	130	131	132	133
CALIFORNIA—Con.															
Butte	432	1 807	176	86 559	92.8	7.2	54.3	20.2	222	23.0	5.7	29.5	107.7	4.4	8.5
Calaveras	371	749	18	41 378	4.7	95.3	28.1	3.7	45	6.7	0.3	-25.0	6.0	0.2	0.4
Colusa	870	1 340	133	174 551	94.0	6.0	78.8	38.4	15	33.3	D	D	D	D	D
Contra Costa	475	2 213	52	62 428	73.8	26.2	36.4	9.3	759	25.6	27.8	-1.8	855.9	14.7	29.4
Del Norte	473	3 067	14	164 821	47.0	53.0	42.9	22.6	40	22.5	0.8	-11.1	18.2	0.7	1.4
El Dorado	350	1 827	9	12 221	60.2	39.8	19.9	1.9	135	13.3	1.7	54.5	37.5	1.2	2.5
Fresno	563	2 180	1 682	221 545	72.8	27.2	68.1	25.2	678	30.2	21.1	-0.5	442.4	14.8	28.7
Glenn	542	1 412	148	126 329	74.0	26.0	64.7	27.8	32	25.0	1.3	8.3	28.4	1.0	2.1
Humboldt	422	556	54	60 369	18.6	81.4	46.6	16.7	264	20.8	6.7	19.6	160.2	5.1	10.7
Imperial	1 349	2 013	716	890 790	52.1	47.9	81.2	51.7	63	30.2	1.8	38.5	32.6	1.3	2.6
Inyo	1 204	515	5	50 161	18.2	81.8	39.4	13.8	18	16.7	0.3	50.0	3.6	0.2	0.2
Kern	1 291	946	1 100	487 821	87.1	12.9	64.5	40.6	357	22.4	7.7	-8.3	174.0	5.1	9.8
Kings	1 041	1 794	487	404 412	67.6	32.4	69.0	39.6	51	47.1	2.9	-3.3	63.0	2.1	4.3
Lake	318	1 389	24	27 663	90.4	9.6	32.0	6.1	37	13.5	0.4	100.0	6.3	0.3	0.5
Lassen	714	493	31	74 720	55.8	44.2	48.4	13.1	33	18.2	0.7	40.0	16.9	0.6	1.2
Los Angeles	474	3 216	194	95 394	82.1	17.9	28.8	10.1	19 753	35.2	881.0	1.7	23 114.7	557.2	1 089.9
Madera	669	1 692	346	197 921	69.9	30.1	69.2	31.5	75	40.0	3.4	-2.9	79.8	2.6	5.0
Marin	863	1 375	42	146 531	4.0	96.0	56.8	27.4	386	15.3	5.9	18.0	139.9	3.0	5.9
Mariposa	563	581	15	58 176	2.6	97.4	35.7	7.1	9	11.1	D	D	D	D	D
Mendocino	512	710	38	35 497	72.1	27.9	40.6	8.6	201	21.4	4.7	0.0	105.7	3.8	7.2
Merced	605	1 736	792	259 877	40.2	59.8	67.1	31.2	120	44.2	7.3	-3.9	137.9	5.8	11.8
Modoc	851	556	46	92 188	54.0	46.0	69.5	23.6	14	7.1	0.1	0.0	2.7	0.1	0.2
Mono	665	694	5	66 878	51.2	48.8	48.7	15.8	7	0.0	0.0	0.0	0.3	0.0	0.0
Monterey	1 316	1 204	731	535 738	94.1	5.9	65.2	38.0	252	23.8	7.8	-7.1	182.7	4.9	9.0
Napa	678	3 320	73	60 749	92.1	7.9	44.1	13.2	198	24.2	4.7	4.4	113.0	2.7	5.0
Nevada	247	2 539	3	8 034	26.5	73.5	15.3	1.6	131	16.8	2.4	33.3	60.2	1.4	2.8
Orange	1 516	7 186	188	372 825	98.4	1.6	44.8	25.0	5 855	31.4	254.6	9.6	6 786.3	147.0	294.4
Placer	294	2 199	35	28 575	32.7	67.3	20.4	4.9	206	18.9	5.7	111.1	131.6	3.5	6.8
Plumas	472	641	6	54 845	25.6	74.4	43.1	11.9	44	22.7	1.0	25.0	24.5	0.9	1.7
Riverside	484	3 759	727	187 636	46.1	53.9	40.9	16.3	979	29.0	34.9	34.7	759.9	23.3	45.6
Sacramento	520	2 030	196	123 272	44.6	55.4	37.9	17.0	902	24.6	28.1	24.9	695.6	16.4	32.3
San Benito	778	681	84	119 280	66.9	33.1	50.9	17.5	53	30.2	1.9	46.2	37.0	1.3	2.4
San Bernardino	450	520	489	252 187	8.4	91.6	41.8	20.9	1 515	33.5	50.8	39.2	1 164.9	34.4	68.8
San Diego	309	3 451	444	70 938	77.8	22.2	32.3	8.9	3 041	26.3	120.0	7.6	3 236.3	67.4	129.2
San Francisco	D	D	2	402 010	100.0	0.0	100.0	60.0	1 695	27.8	43.8	-16.4	1 174.9	25.5	46.0
San Joaquin	536	2 894	634	145 144	65.5	34.5	60.6	23.5	535	38.9	25.8	32.3	581.1	19.4	37.6
San Luis Obispo	723	994	160	80 449	73.4	26.6	39.2	11.0	234	24.8	5.3	43.2	100.1	3.4	6.4
San Mateo	813	3 193	88	267 007	98.0	2.0	53.0	23.3	1 072	26.4	32.2	-10.3	955.1	16.6	33.7
Santa Barbara	740	1 455	288	163 876	84.9	15.1	48.4	17.8	523	24.3	20.2	2.5	563.0	8.6	17.1
Santa Clara	432	1 699	132	100 623	80.4	19.6	35.7	15.2	3 298	34.4	275.7	-0.3	9 742.1	104.6	208.9
Santa Cruz	445	9 652	162	198 677	96.9	3.1	50.9	24.5	375	21.6	12.2	8.0	288.2	8.4	15.2
Shasta	358	861	27	29 708	48.3	51.7	28.6	6.0	239	22.6	5.0	16.3	117.6	3.7	7.1
Sierra	576	516	2	37 735	11.9	88.1	45.7	8.7	12	8.3	D	D	D	D	D
Siskiyou	543	733	51	67 135	52.9	47.1	54.9	18.3	90	26.7	1.7	41.7	37.9	1.5	3.1
Solano	645	1 796	96	107 566	80.5	19.5	46.3	18.4	232	27.2	6.3	5.0	164.1	4.3	8.3
Sonoma	473	2 902	209	68 794	47.4	52.6	40.3	13.1	657	25.0	19.2	35.2	467.1	12.0	23.0
Stanislaus	446	2 832	786	169 745	38.5	61.5	59.1	22.1	379	35.4	23.2	5.9	531.9	17.4	34.1
Sutter	555	2 159	189	131 637	96.1	3.9	68.4	28.8	73	21.9	1.8	-10.0	38.9	1.4	2.7
Tehama	404	532	82	57 886	56.7	43.3	43.0	12.1	71	31.0	2.9	61.1	66.1	2.4	4.8
Trinity	308	394	2	12 994	5.7	94.3	17.3	2.3	38	15.8	0.6	100.0	15.2	0.6	1.2
Tulare	580	2 476	1 030	174 328	63.9	36.1	66.2	27.8	301	30.9	11.2	3.7	216.7	8.4	16.3
Tuolumne	305	526	9	34 344	16.3	83.7	28.4	4.8	59	18.6	0.9	50.0	24.3	0.7	1.5
Ventura	733	3 996	538	253 547	89.5	10.5	55.8	23.3	836	30.7	34.6	28.6	920.2	19.9	39.6
Yolo	936	1 979	178	175 975	94.7	5.3	53.5	24.8	172	32.0	6.1	17.3	138.1	4.2	8.1
Yuba	564	1 610	78	119 428	80.2	19.8	50.9	21.4	44	25.0	1.3	18.2	28.3	1.0	1.8
COLORADO	459	369	3 143	115 201	24.9	75.1	55.3	16.2	4 718	23.4	183.8	-4.0	4 958.4	103.3	204.0
Adams	626	579	91	129 181	46.4	53.6	53.1	17.5	372	28.2	11.9	-22.7	297.2	7.8	15.3
Alamosa	447	654	34	104 604	87.7	12.3	58.7	24.2	10	10.0	0.1	0.0	1.2	0.0	0.1
Arapahoe	407	416	14	48 403	67.7	32.3	41.1	9.8	476	21.8	14.3	5.1	391.0	7.8	15.7
Archuleta	731	646	9	60 064	1.5	98.5	40.1	14.5	10	0.0	0.0	0.0	0.5	0.0	0.1
Baca	424	193	72	118 370	23.0	77.0	70.9	16.8	1	0.0	D	D	D	D	D
Bent	474	157	37	126 635	17.8	82.2	67.8	21.2	5	20.0	D	D	D	D	D
Boulder	549	2 308	40	52 692	29.7	70.3	31.1	6.9	507	27.4	29.5	-6.1	776.0	11.6	23.4
Chaffee	477	712	5	28 858	24.4	75.6	44.4	8.1	16	25.0	0.2	100.0	2.1	0.1	0.2
Cheyenne	571	211	27	82 701	40.8	59.2	77.8	19.7	2	0.0	D	D	D	D	D

1. Includes livestock and poultry products.

STATE County	Manufactures, 1987 (cont'd)					Value of construction authorized by building permits, 1990							
	Production workers (cont'd)						Nonresidential				Residential		
	Wages							Percent					
	Total (Mil dol)	Average per worker (Dollars)	Value added by manu- facture (Mil dol)	Value of shipments (Mil dol)	New capital expend- itures (Mil dol)	Total[1] ($1,000)	Total ($1,000)	Office	Industrial	Stores	New construction ($1,000)	Number of housing units	Alterations and additions ($1,000)
	134	135	136	137	138	139	140	141	142	143	144	145	146
CALIFORNIA—Con.													
Butte	78.5	17 841	274.3	671.0	20.5	199 001	36 337	19.9	8.2	43.5	141 182	1 912	9 411
Calaveras	3.8	19 000	13.4	26.9	1.2	89 672	6 940	5.3	4.5	32.7	75 550	645	4 261
Colusa	D	D	D	D	D	10 135	1 862	0.0	0.0	74.8	6 254	99	995
Contra Costa	403.8	27 469	2 596.7	9 189.4	488.0	813 356	155 237	12.9	23.0	32.2	467 546	4 281	93 367
Del Norte	15.2	21 714	50.4	130.1	1.6	25 145	3 953	26.9	0.0	23.7	17 029	206	2 039
El Dorado	26.4	22 000	78.2	183.2	9.3	332 842	29 699	26.1	1.4	46.0	236 170	1 948	19 865
Fresno	262.5	17 736	1 309.9	3 172.6	71.9	687 317	183 956	12.3	22.6	19.3	431 534	5 353	16 485
Glenn	21.4	21 400	91.7	253.6	2.5	12 758	2 364	7.9	0.0	48.7	7 329	93	1 456
Humboldt	119.0	23 333	469.8	986.1	48.6	87 860	11 340	17.6	21.9	33.1	59 097	875	6 763
Imperial	21.7	16 692	93.4	189.3	D	97 145	22 093	2.9	4.8	66.0	64 653	1 087	3 646
Inyo	2.0	10 000	6.9	11.2	0.2	14 347	2 973	16.0	51.3	26.4	7 501	69	1 739
Kern	98.3	19 275	532.5	1 455.2	51.2	662 266	153 977	14.7	15.0	29.1	445 351	4 954	16 182
Kings	42.6	20 286	191.6	552.4	15.7	70 194	9 723	2.3	8.1	49.8	53 078	627	2 706
Lake	3.8	12 667	14.7	28.7	1.1	71 726	3 004	4.9	38.8	8.3	59 957	532	6 540
Lassen	12.9	21 500	43.3	128.0	5.7	14 423	1 926	26.0	9.4	29.7	9 909	176	1 148
Los Angeles	11 239.9	20 172	50 905.6	99 888.6	2 995.5	7 892 454	2 115 588	29.0	13.3	25.2	2 978 493	25 125	1 106 222
Madera	55.5	21 346	270.1	567.4	13.5	133 502	27 163	8.6	19.1	51.0	94 960	1 558	3 073
Marin	55.3	18 433	275.8	481.3	13.5	210 144	19 753	67.2	5.4	4.8	107 969	811	57 553
Mariposa	D	D	D	D	D	19 550	1 513	14.8	7.1	17.1	14 701	173	815
Mendocino	82.5	21 711	243.8	491.7	12.5	68 861	11 082	4.3	35.3	24.5	44 288	562	7 030
Merced	102.2	17 621	379.6	1 322.6	21.9	141 154	21 077	15.1	10.0	26.1	101 691	1 178	7 208
Modoc	2.3	23 000	6.7	25.6	0.4	2 193	683	0.0	0.0	19.4	640	8	108
Mono	0.1	NA	0.8	1.6	D	48 397	40 920	0.1	0.0	0.0	6 679	77	454
Monterey	101.7	20 755	603.6	1 195.1	30.7	274 255	61 556	33.2	12.7	24.0	132 562	1 183	44 502
Napa	55.8	20 667	404.5	638.8	30.7	201 545	29 852	6.6	47.4	18.3	117 849	707	21 533
Nevada	30.7	21 929	155.2	253.9	11.2	155 265	15 832	27.8	2.6	32.8	118 009	1 145	12 741
Orange	3 081.8	20 965	14 860.0	25 887.4	881.6	2 492 261	723 737	26.4	8.4	38.2	1 149 251	11 983	218 632
Placer	70.8	20 229	412.0	779.4	28.4	538 992	80 069	24.6	16.3	35.7	418 495	2 888	21 464
Plumas	20.3	22 556	53.6	123.5	3.4	25 390	1 008	14.0	33.2	0.0	20 698	297	1 151
Riverside	423.8	18 189	1 773.5	3 427.2	113.5	2 327 281	476 297	14.3	25.1	35.6	1 647 630	15 362	66 351
Sacramento	329.7	20 104	1 784.9	3 457.2	116.0	1 644 521	305 595	47.1	10.9	28.1	1 129 733	10 395	62 009
San Benito	22.8	17 538	127.1	213.8	4.5	42 189	8 231	4.9	28.4	48.1	30 056	282	2 182
San Bernardino	657.3	19 108	2 780.2	6 018.1	159.7	2 171 380	551 282	12.1	31.0	38.6	1 363 226	13 250	112 915
San Diego	1 369.1	20 313	6 426.8	10 996.6	429.0	3 008 354	566 216	26.2	19.0	28.5	1 820 448	15 732	226 345
San Francisco	458.4	17 976	2 745.0	4 727.9	84.3	790 487	164 032	60.6	0.0	3.1	143 432	1 077	172 978
San Joaquin	400.3	20 634	1 880.9	3 974.3	139.0	588 474	185 031	17.4	10.4	54.2	338 037	3 187	23 240
San Luis Obispo	56.3	16 559	283.8	624.9	12.2	245 407	28 101	24.6	18.0	17.7	178 529	1 605	20 654
San Mateo	373.8	22 518	2 353.8	3 843.8	126.7	524 788	85 359	47.8	4.0	13.5	160 015	827	149 160
Santa Barbara	163.9	19 058	1 023.6	1 733.6	53.8	350 342	91 545	17.1	57.2	12.3	168 325	1 279	49 336
Santa Clara	2 562.7	24 500	20 865.3	32 056.6	1 742.9	1 433 337	349 747	21.8	39.5	18.1	498 957	4 983	172 117
Santa Cruz	147.6	17 571	995.7	2 076.7	64.7	139 449	26 470	32.1	13.4	13.5	70 773	553	26 130
Shasta	84.9	22 946	338.7	732.1	17.3	286 451	58 005	22.0	10.6	22.0	204 371	2 368	8 866
Sierra	D	D	D	D	D	1 739	201	48.2	0.0	0.0	1 089	11	223
Siskiyou	31.6	21 067	93.4	236.4	6.8	29 956	4 734	26.9	9.3	10.0	16 449	175	4 365
Solano	101.5	23 605	703.7	2 036.7	54.9	395 643	76 039	22.3	21.3	36.0	266 525	2 314	30 675
Sonoma	252.0	21 000	1 090.2	2 088.0	58.6	483 189	74 549	33.0	8.6	26.0	325 178	3 645	41 894
Stanislaus	354.9	20 397	2 209.2	4 625.4	130.6	463 755	94 054	5.9	25.7	46.3	316 625	3 957	14 994
Sutter	28.1	20 071	148.9	308.8	4.4	137 885	34 207	9.2	59.5	2.7	92 442	1 070	4 803
Tehama	51.7	21 542	126.0	364.0	8.8	58 895	23 579	0.5	35.2	38.5	29 216	319	2 206
Trinity	13.5	22 500	34.0	85.9	4.6	5 345	512	0.0	0.0	45.3	3 702	65	682
Tulare	150.5	17 917	705.9	1 688.6	32.4	305 796	79 283	16.5	28.7	34.5	171 520	2 138	13 455
Tuolumne	18.4	26 286	40.4	121.9	2.3	55 614	6 729	21.4	19.2	11.7	43 813	848	3 761
Ventura	414.7	20 839	2 201.3	3 671.9	98.2	607 715	162 397	18.8	26.3	28.9	326 632	2 620	45 307
Yolo	86.1	20 500	527.3	1 076.0	22.5	128 253	12 202	22.4	31.9	7.9	97 919	1 114	7 706
Yuba	18.9	18 900	48.7	203.8	5.6	42 851	6 732	6.0	54.1	5.6	28 744	373	2 532
COLORADO	2 285.6	22 126	12 045.8	23 235.9	791.5	1 996 358	225 314	20.5	17.6	29.3	1 172 594	12 012	149 467
Adams	168.3	21 577	866.1	2 503.7	54.9	64 641	11 658	4.6	15.7	42.6	36 362	433	2 447
Alamosa	0.7	NA	2.4	4.9	0.1	4 307	1 677	28.6	0.0	53.1	1 297	29	151
Arapahoe	161.6	20 718	794.3	1 272.2	31.9	218 336	25 977	45.1	0.7	36.0	100 101	656	25 094
Archuleta	0.3	NA	0.9	1.8	0.0	8 052	915	0.0	7.8	30.8	6 560	72	267
Baca	D	D	D	D	D	239	184	99.5	0.0	0.0	25	1	12
Bent	D	D	D	D	D	419	0	NA	NA	NA	172	2	217
Boulder	211.3	18 216	1 451.0	2 744.2	144.1	214 465	21 593	17.4	51.0	4.0	136 978	1 460	20 092
Chaffee	1.3	13 000	4.1	10.2	D	5 547	802	43.8	0.0	24.7	2 628	36	1 346
Cheyenne	D	D	D	D	D	339	20	0.0	100.0	0.0	209	4	44

1. Includes nonresidential additions and alterations, residential nonhousekeeping buildings, and residential garages and carports not shown separately.

STATE County	Wholesale trade, 1987				Retail trade, all establishments, 1987				Retail trade, establishments with payroll, 1987					
						Sales				Sales				
											Per capita[2] (Dollars)			
	Establishments	Sales (Mil dol)	Paid employees[1]	Annual payroll (Mil dol)	Number	Total (Mil dol)	Percent change, 1982–1987	Per capita[2] (Dollars)	Number	Total (Mil dol)	General merchandise stores	Food stores	Apparel & accessory stores	Eating and drinking places
	147	148	149	150	151	152	153	154	155	156	157	158	159	160
CALIFORNIA—Con.														
Butte	238	569.2	1 849	36.8	1 848	944.2	36.3	5 584	1 145	913.8	576	1 366	184	565
Calaveras	24	22.9	87	1.3	394	105.1	42.6	3 540	196	95.8	106	1 086	51	349
Colusa	42	192.7	446	9.8	157	60.8	43.4	4 081	102	57.9	D	1 584	D	527
Contra Costa	1 187	8 943.3	10 834	288.6	6 837	5 071.4	44.4	6 808	3 880	4 915.8	906	1 444	406	599
Del Norte	24	D	D	D	269	90.4	24.0	4 661	177	87.4	D	1 545	153	578
El Dorado	111	123.6	644	12.7	1 311	632.4	47.1	5 548	718	604.1	D	1 493	188	616
Fresno	1 129	4 557.5	12 845	294.7	5 352	3 641.3	42.0	6 088	3 403	3 526.1	665	1 315	253	569
Glenn	48	92.3	451	7.5	249	88.7	13.7	3 873	150	84.7	101	1 263	135	383
Humboldt	179	758.7	1 741	31.0	1 474	668.8	27.2	5 862	976	648.9	403	1 482	306	563
Imperial	206	607.3	1 652	32.7	927	490.0	15.6	4 475	565	476.9	565	1 313	263	366
Inyo	36	47.0	197	3.9	298	148.4	14.4	8 290	198	143.9	272	1 775	317	1 137
Kern	752	3 335.5	8 292	191.8	4 510	2 851.0	36.9	5 637	2 745	2 762.8	569	1 287	196	519
Kings	78	227.6	756	16.4	622	352.6	33.8	4 038	427	344.2	365	1 002	167	456
Lake	39	58.1	182	5.2	547	230.4	42.4	4 589	339	220.3	253	1 598	51	394
Lassen	27	26.5	154	2.1	283	105.3	18.3	3 975	165	99.6	109	930	146	498
Los Angeles	19 688	141 729.2	266 696	6 929.9	79 297	56 140.7	46.2	6 619	43 606	54 071.8	738	1 250	393	719
Madera	81	209.6	705	11.8	716	310.3	36.8	3 874	387	296.6	142	1 231	122	399
Marin	547	1 645.5	4 447	115.7	3 188	1 999.7	46.1	8 778	1 900	1 919.8	781	1 777	589	954
Mariposa	11	5.3	30	0.6	185	59.3	53.2	4 238	102	56.0	D	1 012	231	575
Mendocino	137	198.4	1 199	20.5	1 092	469.1	41.6	6 247	692	448.4	289	1 850	194	671
Merced	154	578.4	1 588	33.6	1 192	715.1	33.9	4 339	765	686.7	441	1 059	119	366
Modoc	13	14.9	87	1.6	140	35.0	24.6	3 804	88	32.8	32	959	48	446
Mono	8	3.1	26	0.4	209	77.0	12.2	8 281	143	72.8	0	2 067	335	2 343
Monterey	460	1 680.2	5 025	120.1	3 393	1 970.4	38.2	5 736	2 220	1 905.1	623	975	327	710
Napa	149	249.1	1 084	24.7	1 082	611.2	43.1	5 805	713	591.4	426	1 405	185	765
Nevada	66	58.0	357	5.6	930	396.2	51.5	5 362	534	377.8	221	1 416	188	495
Orange	6 055	47 128.5	77 218	2 134.8	24 061	18 099.1	54.9	8 167	13 385	17 426.8	1 000	1 414	457	941
Placer	223	326.1	1 329	26.5	1 909	1 222.1	80.6	8 213	1 110	1 185.6	251	1 620	262	797
Plumas	20	45.4	131	2.3	329	96.0	17.9	4 873	210	90.6	109	1 424	94	490
Riverside	980	2 958.3	9 924	223.4	8 275	6 032.0	74.3	6 546	4 850	5 839.2	698	1 438	230	642
Sacramento	1 471	5 738.3	20 026	466.2	8 434	6 752.8	54.3	7 128	5 331	6 594.3	1 106	1 369	295	726
San Benito	39	86.5	466	9.3	291	132.1	57.3	3 990	165	125.4	D	1 142	179	353
San Bernardino	1 328	5 397.8	15 084	335.5	10 242	7 289.0	79.5	6 024	5 839	7 056.1	899	1 221	240	557
San Diego	3 415	9 950.2	37 917	894.1	21 117	15 641.6	65.0	6 841	12 733	15 213.1	895	1 239	363	729
San Francisco	2 257	13 943.4	28 131	759.1	10 194	5 726.7	34.7	7 766	6 884	5 513.0	778	1 328	684	1 517
San Joaquin	631	2 672.7	7 176	164.0	3 629	2 443.1	53.0	5 505	2 261	2 371.2	624	1 156	197	532
San Luis Obispo	217	316.1	1 928	34.0	2 587	1 277.7	69.2	6 319	1 579	1 229.4	447	1 495	204	801
San Mateo	1 817	11 693.5	24 218	693.4	6 308	5 137.8	47.0	8 275	3 671	4 980.7	1 166	1 471	456	928
Santa Barbara	538	1 114.3	4 991	118.2	3 914	2 376.6	28.7	6 963	2 512	2 301.5	549	1 644	381	829
Santa Clara	2 886	21 700.5	47 875	1 488.0	13 339	10 501.9	40.3	7 432	7 991	10 226.2	944	1 321	444	763
Santa Cruz	328	893.0	3 343	75.6	2 646	1 578.0	59.3	7 102	1 541	1 518.4	473	1 603	226	759
Shasta	262	651.1	2 118	44.5	1 621	904.2	50.0	6 663	972	871.8	659	1 578	191	527
Sierra	1	D	D	D	51	8.2	30.2	2 416	27	6.3	0	786	0	D
Siskiyou	48	67.6	350	4.9	629	216.4	39.4	5 068	375	204.7	66	1 602	174	500
Solano	250	1 290.1	3 336	80.6	2 344	1 620.0	56.4	5 389	1 467	1 582.4	663	1 192	167	551
Sonoma	596	1 690.5	6 024	137.2	3 973	2 562.4	58.8	7 234	2 427	2 480.9	827	1 609	271	660
Stanislaus	469	1 331.0	5 246	107.4	2 914	2 036.8	56.2	6 217	1 812	1 977.7	775	1 344	224	535
Sutter	95	209.1	796	17.3	556	337.9	42.9	5 595	337	325.7	D	1 707	191	485
Tehama	37	117.7	232	3.3	441	240.4	39.7	5 271	286	231.9	180	1 325	85	461
Trinity	9	D	D	D	176	40.0	32.5	2 966	104	37.9	159	1 155	D	405
Tulare	390	1 558.6	6 075	104.6	2 575	1 368.1	27.0	4 692	1 558	1 318.5	446	1 266	179	355
Tuolumne	58	100.8	357	6.8	659	238.2	66.0	5 329	385	226.9	D	1 504	236	643
Ventura	867	6 306.1	9 877	233.8	5 803	4 376.6	69.0	6 957	3 328	4 251.3	929	1 301	249	607
Yolo	278	2 427.5	5 218	118.6	1 089	687.5	40.2	5 397	735	669.1	D	1 394	169	598
Yuba	47	59.9	407	6.3	437	228.1	22.4	4 118	272	218.9	D	937	94	316
COLORADO	7 100	29 972.0	76 393	1 770.9	36 131	21 287.1	28.4	6 464	22 389	20 688.6	768	1 298	273	723
Adams	670	4 131.4	9 808	236.8	2 286	1 777.9	30.4	6 332	1 407	1 745.6	D	1 207	D	518
Alamosa	40	74.5	339	3.9	177	84.7	18.8	6 615	118	82.2	D	D	271	702
Arapahoe	894	7 176.4	10 309	302.8	3 908	3 347.5	41.9	8 616	2 468	3 285.7	1 378	1 380	391	668
Archuleta	6	D	D	D	112	32.6	41.1	6 400	68	31.2	0	2 351	261	508
Baca	14	14.2	56	1.0	78	20.1	-9.0	4 107	40	19.0	D	589	D	154
Bent	4	D	D	D	56	13.5	-9.4	2 409	33	12.3	D	747	44	96
Boulder	395	1 062.6	3 912	96.9	2 546	1 638.1	44.7	7 570	1 585	1 599.6	720	1 571	298	819
Chaffee	11	D	D	D	246	71.6	-1.4	5 550	137	66.6	775	1 182	134	460
Cheyenne	11	D	D	D	38	5.5	-17.9	2 377	18	4.2	0	D	0	343

1. For pay period including March 12. 2. Based on the estimated population as of July 1 of the year shown.

STATE County	Retail trade, establishments with payroll, 1987 (cont'd) — Paid employees[1]	Retail trade — Annual payroll (Mil dol)	Taxable service industries–establishments with payroll, 1987 — Number	Receipts (Mil dol) — Total	Receipts — Selected kinds of business — Hotels, motels and other lodging places	Receipts — Selected kinds of business — Health services	Receipts — Selected kinds of business — Legal services	Paid employees	Annual payroll (Mil dol)	Bank deposits,[2] June 1989 — Total (Mil dol)	Bank deposits — Percent change, 1988–1989	Savings capital,[3] September 1989 — Total (Mil dol)	Savings capital — Percent change, 1988–1989
	161	162	163	164	165	166	167	168	169	170	171	172	173
CALIFORNIA—Con.													
Butte	12 031	115.3	1 235	343.3	11.7	173.6	17.8	8 463	126.1	972	8.8	834.2	3.5
Calaveras	1 205	11.4	166	D	3.2	7.0	1.1	D	D	143	11.5	67.4	-10.0
Colusa	839	7.4	89	14.1	1.4	D	1.4	427	4.4	153	3.3	35.7	6.7
Contra Costa	52 635	648.1	5 902	2 574.5	47.0	681.6	152.9	49 879	1 019.4	7 794	25.7	4 721.7	2.7
Del Norte	1 051	10.4	129	D	4.8	7.6	1.2	D	D	80	3.6	70.3	-2.3
El Dorado	6 913	75.5	864	179.8	38.6	51.6	7.0	4 462	57.7	511	16.0	373.5	0.7
Fresno	39 975	422.6	4 135	1 448.9	56.0	477.3	112.3	31 678	533.4	3 040	-2.4	2 525.1	-5.5
Glenn	969	10.4	109	19.6	2.9	4.3	1.9	427	4.6	162	7.2	41.5	1.5
Humboldt	8 224	85.0	867	230.1	22.8	106.3	13.7	5 855	79.1	605	3.8	416.4	-0.5
Imperial	5 640	57.2	475	145.1	12.0	45.0	10.2	3 321	50.0	794	4.9	161.0	-9.0
Inyo	1 892	18.6	172	42.0	11.6	10.5	1.6	1 049	11.4	116	7.8	95.3	4.9
Kern	32 031	335.2	2 795	1 185.4	54.8	329.7	61.0	25 142	459.4	2 078	4.2	1 533.8	1.3
Kings	4 265	40.8	349	91.9	3.0	36.9	7.2	1 977	27.6	360	3.9	318.4	7.8
Lake	2 553	28.0	316	58.8	5.5	21.5	2.1	1 596	19.5	231	10.6	282.2	3.8
Lassen	1 190	13.0	121	D	D	D	D	D	D	97	0.3	45.6	2.9
Los Angeles	591 714	6 740.6	73 951	52 548.6	1 504.9	10 095.0	4 784.9	822 432	19 188.7	74 684	3.5	90 929.4	-1.1
Madera	3 582	35.1	326	91.3	7.2	30.6	3.2	1 956	27.9	321	7.9	203.5	-2.2
Marin	22 183	277.4	2 981	1 223.9	20.2	277.1	64.6	20 148	461.4	2 035	4.9	1 973.9	-1.2
Mariposa	647	6.6	80	56.0	D	2.1	0.1	921	12.8	48	10.9	34.7	0.5
Mendocino	5 533	56.7	638	139.4	32.3	50.9	5.5	3 468	42.2	544	4.0	241.3	5.8
Merced	7 907	81.8	694	169.4	7.6	73.8	10.3	4 037	58.8	706	7.1	366.1	-6.1
Modoc	402	3.4	36	5.3	0.7	1.8	D	168	1.8	35	1.0	33.7	6.6
Mono	1 633	11.6	131	61.5	19.3	D	1.2	2 131	21.6	47	12.2	0.0	NA
Monterey	22 953	256.7	2 293	933.5	236.5	183.9	51.0	19 067	333.4	1 762	2.3	1 597.3	-2.0
Napa	7 377	84.2	889	273.0	55.8	96.5	10.9	5 875	97.7	859	9.4	548.1	1.1
Nevada	4 513	49.0	586	118.7	8.8	40.1	6.9	3 422	42.1	505	16.9	399.7	8.2
Orange	197 763	2 177.0	21 771	13 959.7	716.8	3 326.5	798.5	241 866	4 900.5	17 093	6.3	23 125.7	4.0
Placer	12 671	140.3	1 242	475.5	20.2	135.8	12.8	9 371	148.1	863	9.7	751.7	4.9
Plumas	1 121	10.9	135	D	4.4	6.1	0.5	D	D	110	6.7	63.0	7.0
Riverside	61 886	688.1	5 317	2 240.4	250.3	683.0	103.0	51 352	776.2	4 618	10.3	5 531.4	8.2
Sacramento	74 382	811.6	7 350	3 118.8	105.4	820.5	319.5	64 170	1 190.6	6 038	4.4	4 726.3	3.4
San Benito	1 569	15.5	130	D	0.7	D	1.0	D	D	195	12.8	145.1	7.1
San Bernardino	75 754	819.8	6 075	2 475.2	95.8	827.9	97.9	54 480	896.1	4 384	12.0	4 780.2	6.1
San Diego	174 403	1 867.1	17 874	8 938.0	679.8	2 148.0	665.8	172 878	3 386.6	13 624	4.0	21 799.4	5.1
San Francisco	74 733	910.3	10 538	8 794.5	794.6	829.4	1 706.6	139 602	3 444.7	20 468	1.4	13 686.3	-8.1
San Joaquin	26 246	285.0	2 550	865.2	23.1	344.5	54.6	20 858	331.8	2 758	4.5	5 026.3	46.8
San Luis Obispo	16 297	164.0	1 542	534.5	82.3	218.0	34.0	11 827	177.8	1 153	18.5	1 158.2	0.2
San Mateo	52 238	662.0	5 440	3 360.5	212.3	599.9	118.8	59 300	1 201.2	5 120	-1.7	6 006.2	-0.4
Santa Barbara	30 106	314.9	3 034	1 447.5	101.9	354.9	78.2	27 572	539.9	2 484	7.6	3 165.4	1.8
Santa Clara	114 281	1 346.7	12 323	8 516.4	260.7	1 411.2	506.8	144 637	3 375.7	12 010	9.3	8 394.9	1.2
Santa Cruz	17 858	194.8	1 756	601.5	40.0	190.5	31.3	13 884	221.2	1 243	2.3	1 265.0	1.3
Shasta	9 345	103.4	1 162	348.8	28.4	135.7	26.4	7 951	125.5	793	2.1	504.7	-3.1
Sierra	97	0.8	19	5.8	0.6	D	D	117	1.7	NA	NA	6.6	-3.9
Siskiyou	2 603	22.8	292	46.6	7.4	18.4	2.0	1 332	15.1	272	5.1	142.3	1.1
Solano	18 068	203.4	1 430	509.8	13.6	201.2	20.3	11 481	190.2	1 241	12.6	809.1	-1.9
Sonoma	27 526	317.9	3 161	931.9	46.7	326.2	55.0	21 323	345.1	2 403	7.7	2 585.0	1.9
Stanislaus	21 461	238.6	1 943	747.8	20.0	361.8	32.2	17 383	279.4	1 998	8.9	1 352.9	4.3
Sutter	3 799	38.8	393	99.3	3.2	39.1	5.7	2 455	37.0	342	5.2	267.3	-0.2
Tehama	2 441	25.7	226	D	5.2	14.2	2.0	D	D	236	8.8	126.6	-0.2
Trinity	506	4.6	82	D	3.1	2.6	0.5	D	D	44	10.3	28.4	1.9
Tulare	15 668	155.3	1 349	397.1	18.3	170.3	20.1	10 302	148.3	1 324	10.6	823.2	-2.7
Tuolumne	2 939	30.3	337	64.6	7.5	21.7	2.1	1 736	22.6	231	-13.3	227.5	8.1
Ventura	44 843	487.9	4 269	1 910.4	75.7	555.7	84.2	37 377	697.6	3 242	9.6	3 735.3	3.5
Yolo	8 396	84.9	775	318.0	9.4	70.9	8.0	5 846	96.6	731	5.5	427.5	-42.6
Yuba	2 443	25.4	206	53.9	1.9	27.6	3.9	1 119	17.8	206	6.3	87.7	5.4
COLORADO	267 899	2 668.0	28 596	11 532.8	824.8	2 430.7	972.9	256 147	4 341.8	20 649	2.2	13 746.6	-4.9
Adams	19 039	196.0	1 400	517.8	D	133.9	8.1	11 089	171.6	536	-0.9	426.2	-15.5
Alamosa	1 199	10.1	110	23.8	4.8	8.6	1.8	682	8.4	60	4.2	60.7	-1.2
Arapahoe	35 588	386.7	3 724	1 913.5	51.5	415.4	81.3	35 748	710.2	1 646	1.5	3 084.4	43.4
Archuleta	416	3.7	43	6.4	0.5	0.7	0.4	242	1.8	35	2.7	6.4	-30.5
Baca	177	1.4	27	2.0	0.1	0.5	D	74	0.4	44	2.3	10.7	-12.6
Bent	135	1.1	16	1.3	D	0.3	D	50	0.3	32	3.9	13.9	3.0
Boulder	20 555	205.0	2 244	847.2	26.2	149.9	48.3	17 715	315.6	1 247	7.0	835.0	8.8
Chaffee	981	8.5	119	22.5	7.1	5.5	0.9	719	7.1	37	10.8	87.6	3.2
Cheyenne	72	0.5	12	2.0	D	D	0.0	85	0.6	48	1.7	0.0	NA

1. For the period including March 12 of the year shown. 2. Includes deposits for all insured and reporting noninsured commercial and mutual savings banks. 3. Includes savings capital for all FSLIC insured savings institutions.

STATE County	Federal funds and grants, 1989							Local government finances, 1981–1982							
	Expenditures		Per capita[1] (Dollars)					General revenue						Direct general expenditure	
									Intergovernmental		Taxes				
												Per capita[2]			
	Total (Mil dol)	Percent change, 1988–1989	Total	Direct payments for individuals	Procurement contract awards	Salaries and wages	Grant awards	Total (Mil dol)	Total (Mil dol)	Percent from state	Total (Mil dol)	Total (Dollars)	Property (Dollars)	Total (Mil dol)	Percent change, 1977–1982
	174	175	176	177	178	179	180	181	182	183	184	185	186	187	188
CALIFORNIA—Con.															
Butte	494.8	4.8	2 764	2 214	31	103	267	176.0	103.5	92.3	49.8	327	248	171.6	66.8
Calaveras	81.9	9.7	2 483	1 993	80	109	279	33.3	16.2	95.1	9.6	412	349	34.0	101.3
Colusa	69.5	10.9	4 456	1 797	88	169	274	26.4	9.4	92.4	8.9	647	527	23.1	77.8
Contra Costa	1 851.2	-0.4	2 362	1 505	261	387	198	1 056.2	522.1	87.2	285.5	420	336	1 013.7	49.2
Del Norte	58.0	13.6	2 800	2 025	118	226	426	34.7	18.3	95.9	5.1	278	203	36.6	86.9
El Dorado	245.4	6.9	1 918	1 507	53	185	167	135.2	70.0	88.9	44.0	468	370	128.7	90.4
Fresno	1 433.3	2.5	2 278	1 376	75	417	315	869.1	488.7	91.2	207.9	387	297	834.9	56.5
Glenn	83.8	4.8	3 551	1 841	30	284	316	35.6	15.3	95.1	10.7	484	401	38.2	59.4
Humboldt	311.9	-2.4	2 645	1 748	171	331	329	167.7	108.2	85.7	36.8	335	263	168.7	56.4
Imperial	266.9	3.6	2 313	1 380	121	327	420	197.1	94.6	91.1	29.5	301	216	206.3	76.4
Inyo	135.7	23.1	7 539	2 316	4 184	489	528	38.4	14.3	80.6	10.3	562	436	35.9	59.7
Kern	1 891.3	1.1	3 535	1 445	794	941	262	721.1	309.6	91.3	240.5	553	445	703.7	52.4
Kings	308.0	3.7	3 229	1 194	57	1 425	291	116.1	64.2	90.1	24.0	307	236	116.1	53.9
Lake	180.5	7.3	3 412	2 895	45	105	347	53.3	28.7	86.7	15.2	374	318	55.5	97.7
Lassen	108.8	19.0	3 860	1 762	325	1 240	493	42.2	26.7	93.2	7.1	302	243	39.7	89.0
Los Angeles	30 039.3	-1.5	3 429	1 380	1 396	329	314	12 155.8	6 554.0	89.6	3 323.6	432	292	11 169.8	50.8
Madera	176.6	3.5	2 051	1 463	85	107	279	90.1	49.8	95.0	25.2	364	297	88.8	84.4
Marin	502.1	8.6	2 162	1 629	118	217	188	319.7	124.9	83.2	103.1	460	372	301.2	40.1
Mariposa	44.2	-7.9	2 928	1 930	98	691	167	15.7	7.5	92.5	5.3	443	304	16.5	139.7
Mendocino	231.5	25.3	2 994	1 784	101	152	948	111.2	64.5	90.8	26.0	374	290	113.9	68.9
Merced	516.5	1.5	2 961	1 398	259	780	348	264.2	142.8	90.2	45.4	319	255	254.1	72.2
Modoc	32.5	-24.1	3 572	2 056	183	814	316	16.8	9.6	91.0	4.5	485	423	18.3	93.7
Mono	29.5	72.7	3 042	754	377	791	1 111	22.4	5.9	94.3	9.8	1 041	762	20.2	53.2
Monterey	1 553.2	19.9	4 363	1 486	254	2 398	214	458.2	232.7	82.2	116.5	381	266	455.7	71.3
Napa	295.6	3.9	2 740	2 341	23	118	250	114.3	59.9	91.0	36.6	362	280	116.3	58.0
Nevada	208.4	9.6	2 573	1 947	221	155	246	73.8	30.6	92.0	23.0	384	311	68.4	118.0
Orange	7 516.5	2.6	3 260	1 323	1 342	344	243	2 583.1	1 152.2	85.9	943.1	467	357	2 344.1	54.3
Placer	395.4	5.9	2 444	1 884	67	290	161	182.2	86.2	93.1	60.4	478	381	183.1	45.5
Plumas	63.0	1.3	3 074	2 061	134	513	353	37.2	16.8	77.7	8.8	480	411	37.7	100.5
Riverside	2 493.1	5.9	2 375	1 777	106	277	204	1 165.2	555.3	89.8	293.3	409	314	1 110.1	93.9
Sacramento	6 779.3	13.3	6 718	1 760	1 211	1 04[illegible]	2 685	1 276.4	720.0	92.2	278.6	335	243	1 202.5	54.4
San Benito	60.7	0.8	1 681	1 064	271	101	158	37.4	18.2	93.2	8.5	314	251	34.1	58.7
San Bernardino	3 879.2	-0.7	2 825	1 308	598	702	213	1 366.4	792.6	89.2	311.8	322	242	1 279.3	79.4
San Diego	11 531.7	5.2	4 689	1 731	1 009	1 637	306	2 726.8	1 329.9	86.4	718.7	365	273	2 500.2	72.9
San Francisco	3 576.4	3.1	4 877	2 170	530	1 435	714	1 710.5	752.9	72.5	506.9	731	368	1 306.9	43.8
San Joaquin	1 109.7	-0.8	2 357	1 528	143	357	305	596.8	343.0	92.7	132.6	356	257	602.5	50.0
San Luis Obispo	461.5	6.8	2 148	1 735	56	123	205	191.1	77.6	88.3	74.9	448	351	188.6	59.3
San Mateo	1 598.4	1.9	2 522	1 612	411	302	191	836.6	300.8	89.7	296.4	501	387	791.3	36.8
Santa Barbara	1 526.0	1.0	4 388	1 744	1 794	579	260	432.2	192.6	85.6	137.1	443	334	411.4	40.9
Santa Clara	7 369.2	1.8	5 096	1 180	3 173	424	311	2 169.5	1 006.5	87.4	690.6	518	352	2 031.7	45.9
Santa Cruz	431.5	5.9	1 861	1 433	93	94	236	228.9	115.2	89.3	72.3	368	266	240.4	63.2
Shasta	431.3	18.2	3 012	1 984	189	270	560	180.3	101.4	92.6	45.5	373	293	184.6	75.7
Sierra	11.8	-40.9	3 266	2 239	109	462	426	7.6	4.0	96.7	2.3	712	648	7.5	53.5
Siskiyou	154.2	5.9	3 512	2 184	238	562	465	63.9	39.2	94.5	15.0	363	295	66.0	75.8
Solano	1 484.4	-3.7	4 512	1 623	516	2 187	172	334.6	178.7	89.2	83.9	329	247	340.6	69.4
Sonoma	877.9	5.9	2 323	1 754	97	226	234	431.3	191.1	92.0	132.7	423	321	405.1	53.7
Stanislaus	732.5	6.6	2 065	1 451	131	106	274	415.1	224.9	88.2	98.1	349	259	396.0	60.9
Sutter	170.9	17.6	2 700	1 674	43	96	512	80.6	39.0	95.4	19.9	360	283	80.7	58.4
Tehama	124.2	2.0	2 609	2 014	26	170	327	47.9	26.7	93.3	12.8	311	243	52.2	60.1
Trinity	40.0	-26.6	2 814	1 815	221	556	217	26.7	16.3	98.0	3.5	283	236	26.5	121.7
Tulare	678.4	-8.2	2 227	1 355	57	115	375	438.7	255.4	91.0	74.6	288	209	433.0	72.2
Tuolumne	131.2	0.9	2 712	2 093	51	250	310	48.0	22.3	91.6	13.2	365	296	47.9	68.8
Ventura	2 129.3	14.5	3 204	1 339	932	757	172	792.8	404.1	87.6	220.3	394	312	774.8	68.0
Yolo	326.3	-4.9	2 424	1 380	150	165	638	147.7	76.8	86.4	43.8	374	283	149.0	58.4
Yuba	275.9	4.4	4 790	1 902	276	1 968	490	87.1	52.0	90.1	16.5	324	266	85.6	45.6
COLORADO	14 163.0	8.8	X	1 585	1 202	855	521	4 114.6	1 344.2	80.9	1 752.4	570	392	3 829.0	71.4
Adams	751.8	7.7	2 665	1 275	158	970	234	304.3	114.9	87.9	113.5	433	305	308.5	85.5
Alamosa	36.8	4.6	2 806	1 517	97	403	727	18.5	9.4	87.7	5.5	447	291	18.0	156.3
Arapahoe	700.0	12.3	1 766	1 125	375	179	77	425.4	114.1	92.5	209.5	632	421	407.4	74.7
Archuleta	14.3	26.3	2 689	1 664	631	180	199	4.9	1.9	94.4	2.4	521	462	5.9	77.4
Baca	30.5	-22.7	6 355	1 920	25	238	306	9.4	3.7	74.7	3.3	631	580	8.1	34.7
Bent	41.6	-3.4	7 854	3 629	209	3 159	384	7.7	3.6	92.7	2.2	373	334	7.6	53.6
Boulder	740.5	11.0	3 378	1 167	981	486	734	215.6	71.0	83.2	106.2	530	394	205.8	49.9
Chaffee	32.9	9.3	2 589	2 020	36	251	267	15.1	5.7	88.3	5.2	382	269	14.7	73.8
Cheyenne	14.8	-32.2	6 416	1 706	25	267	53	3.9	1.0	93.6	2.3	1 020	1 009	4.3	86.0

1. Based on the estimated population as of July 1 of the year shown. 2. Based on the estimated population as of July 1, 1982.

STATE County	Local government finances, 1981–1982 (cont'd) — Direct general expenditure (cont'd) — Per capita[1] (Dollars)	Percent of total for– Education	Percent of total for– Health & hospitals	Percent of total for– Police protection	Percent of total for– Public welfare	Percent of total for– Highways	Debt outstanding — Total (Mil dol)	Debt outstanding — Per capita[1] (Dollars)	State and local government employment, 1989 — Total	State and local government employment, 1989 — Rate[2]	Federal government civilian employment 1989 — Total	Federal government civilian employment 1989 — Earnings ($1,000)	Elections, 1988[3] — Total vote cast for president	Elections, 1988[3] — Vote for lead party (Percent)
	189	190	191	192	193	194	195	196	197	198	199	200	201	202
CALIFORNIA—Con.														
Butte	1 126	48.6	3.5	5.2	13.0	6.3	113.8	746	10 903	609.1	572	16 584	71 631	R—56.0
Calaveras	1 461	43.2	13.0	4.1	8.5	7.2	9.2	394	1 782	540.0	148	3 778	13 574	R—56.3
Colusa	1 677	34.9	3.8	6.5	6.4	7.3	12.7	923	1 076	689.7	126	3 024	5 172	R—59.5
Contra Costa	1 492	35.0	16.0	5.0	10.3	3.2	638.6	940	35 365	451.2	7 061	243 869	331 511	D—51.1
Del Norte	1 977	28.5	24.5	3.9	11.7	7.8	5.7	308	1 284	620.3	163	4 589	7 468	R—49.7
El Dorado	1 367	41.2	2.7	8.1	8.8	5.2	66.4	705	5 395	421.8	962	24 244	50 603	R—59.3
Fresno	1 554	40.1	11.8	4.8	13.5	4.3	331.1	616	39 022	620.1	10 198	265 100	189 870	R—49.9
Glenn	1 729	37.6	13.8	6.0	7.6	7.9	40.8	1 846	1 583	670.8	239	7 044	7 966	R—62.1
Humboldt	1 534	42.1	4.7	5.6	12.7	6.4	50.9	462	8 277	702.0	985	26 449	52 146	D—57.1
Imperial	2 107	36.3	17.7	4.2	7.0	3.2	41.6	425	7 802	676.1	1 213	37 739	23 365	R—55.2
Inyo	1 953	32.1	25.0	4.4	8.8	5.7	4.4	238	1 817	1 009.4	395	10 182	7 837	R—64.3
Kern	1 618	39.3	9.7	5.0	9.4	4.0	304.4	700	30 137	563.2	12 125	410 775	147 293	R—61.5
Kings	1 487	37.2	7.4	4.7	13.1	4.4	32.0	409	6 638	695.8	1 535	29 645	21 482	R—56.4
Lake	1 364	32.4	14.9	5.2	14.4	3.8	10.2	250	2 375	449.0	183	4 983	19 502	D—50.4
Lassen	1 698	48.0	11.1	4.3	10.4	6.7	3.4	146	2 170	769.5	1 196	32 790	8 802	R—58.6
Los Angeles	1 451	36.1	8.4	7.2	12.9	2.9	6 856.8	890	444 584	507.5	74 627	2 504 949	2 644 671	D—51.9
Madera	1 287	46.9	5.2	4.8	13.0	4.8	30.2	438	4 313	500.9	410	10 152	24 281	R—54.6
Marin	1 345	36.8	13.4	5.2	5.3	4.1	140.3	627	10 863	467.8	962	31 598	117 920	D—58.8
Mariposa	1 379	42.0	14.2	6.5	9.6	8.3	0.1	6	818	541.7	578	13 639	6 910	R—54.5
Mendocino	1 639	43.1	10.8	4.3	13.1	5.5	8.8	126	4 228	547.0	363	10 036	30 947	D—55.4
Merced	1 782	41.3	11.2	3.3	13.0	3.3	87.0	610	10 513	602.8	1 339	30 207	42 414	R—51.2
Modoc	1 986	38.0	10.5	2.5	7.3	11.5	10.2	1 107	871	957.1	279	7 513	4 017	R—62.7
Mono	2 144	26.3	20.9	6.8	3.1	9.0	8.1	857	733	755.7	174	3 649	3 547	R—61.4
Monterey	1 492	37.5	13.8	5.2	8.6	4.3	95.2	312	16 426	461.4	8 784	221 194	100 381	R—49.8
Napa	1 150	45.6	3.8	6.4	8.8	6.0	41.9	415	7 716	715.1	328	10 480	46 290	R—50.2
Nevada	1 142	34.5	15.4	5.0	9.8	6.3	84.9	1 418	3 274	404.2	472	12 550	37 023	R—57.8
Orange	1 161	46.0	2.1	6.9	7.3	5.4	1 400.8	694	98 671	427.9	16 091	499 325	865 307	R—67.7
Placer	1 450	43.2	2.7	4.8	9.4	4.6	180.9	1 432	8 888	549.3	632	18 397	70 642	R—59.6
Plumas	2 059	30.5	20.1	4.2	6.9	10.1	1.8	97	1 475	719.5	604	15 278	9 015	R—51.1
Riverside	1 549	33.0	19.3	5.0	10.7	4.5	573.1	800	54 009	514.6	5 548	149 242	336 348	R—59.5
Sacramento	1 447	36.9	2.4	5.0	18.0	2.2	1 064.8	1 282	128 377	1 272.2	28 072	898 471	395 690	R—51.0
San Benito	1 267	43.7	19.4	3.9	9.0	0.8	27.8	1 032	1 874	519.1	116	3 189	10 308	R—54.1
San Bernardino	1 321	39.8	7.5	5.4	14.4	3.5	637.7	659	61 470	447.6	14 857	424 379	392 008	R—60.0
San Diego	1 271	40.5	10.0	4.6	11.1	3.0	927.6	471	125 687	511.1	46 047	1 353 428	869 195	R—60.2
San Francisco	1 885	20.3	11.9	6.3	11.0	1.5	895.1	1 291	64 613	881.1	29 054	960 855	277 394	D—72.8
San Joaquin	1 617	35.1	9.7	5.1	17.4	4.3	135.6	364	25 449	540.4	5 949	167 317	138 453	R—54.4
San Luis Obispo	1 129	37.3	8.3	6.9	8.9	5.0	43.0	258	13 871	645.8	712	20 379	83 467	R—55.8
San Mateo	1 336	36.6	17.4	6.2	6.4	4.3	261.4	442	24 917	393.1	5 707	203 828	254 480	D—55.7
Santa Barbara	1 330	40.5	7.5	5.1	7.4	3.5	126.3	408	25 574	735.3	4 319	122 573	142 940	R—54.2
Santa Clara	1 524	41.5	9.8	4.8	9.6	4.4	685.6	514	75 110	519.4	13 894	469 719	541 528	D—51.3
Santa Cruz	1 225	41.5	4.4	5.1	12.0	4.7	84.6	431	15 025	647.9	572	18 176	102 611	D—61.5
Shasta	1 516	44.8	9.1	4.4	14.8	5.6	51.3	421	8 754	611.3	1 306	39 940	54 585	R—59.4
Sierra	2 278	38.6	13.4	6.9	4.3	17.5	0.5	162	464	1 288.9	95	2 129	1 696	R—50.7
Siskiyou	1 591	43.9	1.9	4.3	9.0	11.7	9.9	239	3 097	705.5	1 193	29 975	17 797	R—50.9
Solano	1 336	38.8	1.6	6.6	11.0	7.6	305.2	1 197	14 279	434.0	15 539	534 676	106 088	D—51.2
Sonoma	1 291	39.1	12.6	5.2	10.5	6.2	165.9	529	20 541	543.6	1 906	60 312	161 583	D—56.5
Stanislaus	1 409	40.9	10.9	5.2	14.8	3.2	142.9	508	19 609	552.7	876	27 259	97 315	R—53.1
Sutter	1 463	37.0	13.9	5.8	10.5	4.1	24.8	449	2 894	457.2	177	5 053	20 898	R—67.5
Tehama	1 267	40.4	10.3	4.9	11.9	7.5	7.8	189	2 197	461.6	298	8 624	17 434	R—56.5
Trinity	2 121	49.4	12.4	3.1	8.2	13.6	1.8	145	1 066	750.7	516	11 774	5 980	R—54.6
Tulare	1 672	39.6	17.1	4.5	15.6	4.0	70.7	273	19 068	626.0	1 316	34 400	78 669	R—59.6
Tuolumne	1 319	33.0	15.2	4.7	10.2	5.8	10.1	277	2 601	537.4	550	14 613	19 715	R—54.0
Ventura	1 384	40.1	7.8	5.8	7.5	4.1	342.1	611	29 755	447.7	11 944	391 332	239 473	R—61.6
Yolo	1 271	31.7	7.1	5.1	13.1	4.4	40.9	349	21 862	1 624.2	598	19 346	53 372	D—57.0
Yuba	1 678	53.5	2.7	3.5	16.1	2.8	151.8	2 976	3 826	664.2	1 397	31 206	14 563	R—61.4
COLORADO	1 246	42.7	6.6	5.0	7.0	6.6	4 679.5	1 523	216 182	651.5	56 274	1 765 763	1 372 395	R—53.1
Adams	1 178	41.7	3.7	4.3	7.4	5.4	500.7	1 911	11 464	406.4	3 870	118 630	94 094	D—52.6
Alamosa	1 467	52.3	1.8	4.2	9.7	12.3	7.7	623	1 140	870.2	194	5 530	4 780	R—53.7
Arapahoe	1 228	52.0	0.5	5.7	2.8	5.3	638.7	1 926	19 079	481.3	1 971	52 791	159 245	R—60.2
Archuleta	1 292	43.2	0.8	3.0	6.3	10.4	8.1	1 762	314	592.5	46	1 072	2 262	R—63.7
Baca	1 532	49.2	21.2	3.5	4.3	4.7	2.0	381	480	1 000.0	51	1 041	2 556	R—65.3
Bent	1 281	45.3	15.4	3.9	9.9	11.2	1.0	167	372	701.9	674	19 089	2 167	D—50.2
Boulder	1 028	48.0	2.1	5.5	6.3	6.5	126.6	632	22 720	1 036.5	2 674	105 834	107 223	D—53.4
Chaffee	1 089	40.7	21.4	4.0	9.0	8.0	3.1	232	1 270	1 000.0	79	2 185	5 714	R—53.9
Cheyenne	1 865	53.2	2.1	3.1	4.0	17.4	1.9	839	271	1 178.3	22	500	1 186	R—64.1

1. Based on the estimated population as of July 1, 1982. 2. Per 10,000 resident population estimated as of July 1 of the year shown. 3. Data subject to copyright.

STATE–County code	MSA/CMSA/NECMA code[1]	STATE County	Land Area,[2] 1990 (Sq. Km.)	Population, 1990 Total persons	Rank	Per square kilometer	Race: White	Black	Am. Indian, Eskimo, Aleut	Asian & Pacific Islander	Other race	Hispanic[3]	Age of population Percent: Under 5 years	5 to 14 years	15 to 24 years
			1	2	3	4	5	6	7	8	9	10	11	12	13
		COLORADO—Con.													
08 019	...	Clear Creek	1 024	7 619	2 609	7.4	7 444	20	32	39	84	254	7.0	15.4	9.0
08 021	...	Conejos	3 334	7 453	2 619	2.2	6 387	12	31	23	1 000	4 463	8.5	20.5	13.0
08 023	...	Costilla	3 178	3 190	2 985	1.0	2 664	8	18	40	460	2 452	7.2	17.1	12.0
08 025	...	Crowley	2 044	3 946	2 922	1.9	3 462	262	72	31	119	912	5.6	12.5	11.9
08 027	...	Custer	1 914	1 926	3 072	1.0	1 886	0	27	3	10	55	5.9	16.3	8.3
08 029	...	Delta	2 958	20 980	1 629	7.1	20 144	60	129	54	593	1 915	5.9	14.4	10.1
08 031	2082	Denver	397	467 610	105	1 177.9	337 198	60 046	5 381	11 005	53 980	107 382	7.4	11.6	12.8
08 033	...	Dolores	2 764	1 504	3 096	0.5	1 445	0	41	1	17	48	6.4	16.6	10.8
08 035	2082	Douglas	2 176	60 391	718	27.8	58 682	407	267	508	527	1 910	9.5	17.2	9.9
08 037	...	Eagle	4 372	21 928	1 580	5.0	20 078	46	113	100	1 591	2 917	8.9	13.9	12.8
08 039	...	Elbert	4 794	9 646	2 419	2.0	9 419	47	68	43	69	211	7.3	18.7	10.1
08 041	1720	El Paso	5 508	397 014	125	72.1	341 400	28 593	3 242	9 841	13 938	34 473	8.5	15.0	16.2
08 043	...	Fremont	3 971	32 273	1 206	8.1	30 555	848	329	112	429	2 759	5.5	13.2	11.5
08 045	...	Garfield	7 634	29 974	1 298	3.9	29 148	82	215	124	405	1 673	8.1	15.9	12.1
08 047	...	Gilpin	388	3 070	2 996	7.9	2 993	14	36	13	14	109	6.2	13.4	9.0
08 049	...	Grand	4 791	7 966	2 576	1.7	7 762	16	29	38	121	243	6.6	14.8	12.3
08 051	...	Gunnison	8 389	10 273	2 362	1.2	10 009	63	69	48	84	366	6.5	11.7	26.1
08 053	...	Hinsdale	2 895	467	3 135	0.2	463	1	3	0	0	4	3.9	11.8	7.5
08 055	...	Huerfano	4 121	6 009	2 756	1.5	5 569	27	78	14	321	2 428	6.0	15.2	10.7
08 057	...	Jackson	4 178	1 605	3 090	0.4	1 480	0	26	1	98	118	7.4	14.3	11.7
08 059	2082	Jefferson	2 000	438 430	113	219.2	414 542	3 231	2 428	7 630	10 599	30 791	7.6	14.8	12.6
08 061	...	Kiowa	4 587	1 688	3 086	0.4	1 648	0	11	0	29	55	6.0	18.1	9.2
08 063	...	Kit Carson	5 597	7 140	2 639	1.3	6 794	9	23	11	303	468	7.7	17.0	10.5
08 065	...	Lake	976	6 007	2 757	6.2	5 483	13	49	21	441	1 434	8.2	15.7	14.1
08 067	...	La Plata	4 383	32 284	1 205	7.4	29 022	71	1 602	179	1 410	3 586	6.9	15.0	18.1
08 069	2670	Larimer	6 738	186 136	260	27.6	175 971	1 114	1 063	2 777	5 211	12 227	7.3	14.3	18.0
08 071	...	Las Animas	12 362	13 765	2 076	1.1	11 924	34	122	66	1 619	6 080	6.4	14.6	13.1
08 073	...	Lincoln	6 698	4 529	2 872	0.7	4 444	4	29	12	40	75	7.6	14.9	9.7
08 075	...	Logan	4 762	17 567	1 817	3.7	16 842	20	49	42	614	1 393	7.0	15.4	13.1
08 077	...	Mesa	8 619	93 145	497	10.8	88 177	391	659	632	3 286	7 563	7.1	15.6	13.0
08 079	...	Mineral	2 268	558	3 132	0.2	547	0	5	0	6	27	8.8	10.9	6.3
08 081	...	Moffat	12 283	11 357	2 266	0.9	10 923	11	87	40	296	698	8.6	19.4	11.3
08 083	...	Montezuma	5 276	18 672	1 752	3.5	15 943	12	2 141	46	530	1 612	8.3	18.1	11.9
08 085	...	Montrose	5 804	24 423	1 480	4.2	23 407	68	136	72	740	2 736	6.4	16.9	10.4
08 087	...	Morgan	3 329	21 939	1 579	6.6	19 320	61	124	83	2 351	4 034	8.3	17.1	12.1
08 089	...	Otero	3 271	20 185	1 664	6.2	16 727	118	199	120	3 021	7 104	7.3	16.8	12.6
08 091	...	Ouray	1 404	2 295	3 040	1.6	2 249	0	10	2	34	103	5.5	15.8	7.8
08 093	...	Park	5 700	7 174	2 635	1.3	7 031	40	52	16	35	206	6.6	16.9	7.9
08 095	...	Phillips	1 781	4 189	2 900	2.4	4 174	0	2	9	4	170	6.7	15.1	9.9
08 097	...	Pitkin	2 514	12 661	2 169	5.0	12 328	41	48	142	102	475	5.6	9.1	11.1
08 099	...	Prowers	4 249	13 347	2 110	3.1	11 397	43	95	36	1 776	3 102	8.2	18.3	13.3
08 101	6560	Pueblo	6 187	123 051	374	19.9	104 304	2 253	991	729	14 774	44 090	6.9	15.1	13.6
08 103	...	Rio Blanco	8 343	5 972	2 762	0.7	5 807	9	42	22	92	236	7.5	17.6	14.1
08 105	...	Rio Grande	2 364	10 770	2 310	4.6	9 675	7	81	15	992	4 342	7.8	17.6	12.4
08 107	...	Routt	6 117	14 088	2 049	2.3	13 913	8	64	41	62	353	7.1	14.9	13.3
08 109	...	Saguache	8 207	4 619	2 866	0.6	3 699	11	140	7	762	2 106	8.2	18.7	12.7
08 111	...	San Juan	1 003	745	3 127	0.7	711	1	4	2	27	118	6.3	18.7	11.8
08 113	...	San Miguel	3 332	3 653	2 945	1.1	3 609	5	13	10	16	102	7.0	12.8	11.4
08 115	...	Sedgwick	1 420	2 690	3 015	1.9	2 614	10	15	32	19	230	5.3	14.9	9.1
08 117	...	Summit	1 575	12 881	2 149	8.2	12 574	32	79	96	100	323	7.3	10.8	15.0
08 119	...	Teller	1 443	12 468	2 183	8.6	12 189	24	106	52	97	322	7.6	16.8	9.5
08 121	...	Washington	6 530	4 812	2 856	0.7	4 721	1	13	8	69	139	6.5	16.4	10.0
08 123	3060	Weld	10 341	131 821	350	12.7	117 247	567	785	1 133	12 089	27 502	7.9	16.0	17.4
08 125	...	Yuma	6 128	8 954	2 475	1.5	8 769	2	39	12	132	284	6.6	17.4	11.0
09 000	...	CONNECTICUT	12 550	3 287 116	X	261.9	2 859 353	274 269	6 654	50 698	96 142	213 116	6.9	12.3	14.1
09 001	5602	Fairfield	1 621	827 645	42	510.6	700 350	81 519	1 226	17 332	27 218	70 818	6.9	12.0	13.2
09 003	3283	Hartford	1 905	851 783	38	447.1	711 315	87 255	1 425	13 347	38 441	71 575	6.8	12.2	14.0
09 005	...	Litchfield	2 383	174 092	278	73.1	170 361	1 631	327	1 411	362	1 907	6.9	12.9	12.2
09 007	3283	Middlesex	956	143 196	332	149.8	134 489	6 002	230	1 538	937	2 881	6.7	11.7	13.8
09 009	5483	New Haven	1 569	804 219	46	512.6	687 491	82 011	1 536	10 484	22 697	51 003	7.0	12.2	14.2
09 011	5523	New London	1 725	254 957	195	147.8	234 274	12 123	1 338	3 389	3 833	8 455	7.4	12.7	15.4
09 013	3283	Tolland	1 062	128 699	361	121.2	122 785	2 625	221	2 446	622	2 216	6.8	12.2	19.7
09 015	...	Windham	1 328	102 525	450	77.2	98 288	1 103	351	751	2 032	4 261	7.4	14.5	14.9

1. MSA = Metropolitan Statistical Area. CMSA = Consolidated MSA. NECMA = New England county metropolitan area. PMSA = Primary MSA. See Appendix A for explanation of these concepts. See Appendix B for list of metropolitan areas identified by type, with component counties. 2. Dry land or land partially or temporarily covered by water. 3. Hispanic persons may be of any race.

STATE County	Population, 1990 (cont'd): Age of population (cont'd) Percent: 25 to 34 years	35 to 44 years	45 to 54 years	55 to 64 years	65 to 74 years	75 years and over	Percent female	Population–Change and components of change: Change 1980–1990: Number	Percent	Components of change, 1980–1986: Total persons, 1986	Total persons, 1980	Net change: Number	Percent	Natural increase: Births	Deaths
	14	15	16	17	18	19	20	21	22	23	24	25	26	27	28
COLORADO—Con.															
Clear Creek	16.1	24.8	12.9	7.5	4.6	2.6	48.1	311	4.3	7 300	7 308	0	0.4	1 000	200
Conejos	12.9	12.8	8.9	9.4	8.0	6.0	50.3	-341	-4.4	7 900	7 794	100	1.4	1 000	400
Costilla	13.1	12.8	10.5	11.0	9.6	6.7	50.0	119	3.9	3 700	3 071	600	20.7	300	200
Crowley	21.8	16.1	9.1	8.4	7.6	7.0	37.6	958	32.1	3 200	2 988	200	6.7	300	200
Custer	12.4	15.7	13.8	12.9	9.2	5.6	49.9	398	26.0	1 900	1 528	300	21.9	200	100
Delta	11.5	13.8	10.8	11.1	12.3	10.1	50.7	-245	-1.2	23 100	21 225	1 900	8.8	2 200	1 600
Denver	20.5	16.5	9.1	8.2	7.6	6.2	51.3	-25 084	-5.1	505 000	492 694	12 300	2.5	55 600	28 500
Dolores	14.1	14.0	12.2	11.2	8.5	6.1	49.2	-154	-9.3	1 600	1 658	0	-2.0	200	100
Douglas	20.0	22.0	11.7	5.5	2.8	1.3	49.8	35 238	140.1	38 800	25 153	13 600	54.2	3 300	700
Eagle	27.2	21.9	8.3	3.8	2.2	1.0	47.3	8 608	64.6	16 400	13 320	3 100	23.2	2 300	300
Elbert	16.4	21.2	11.7	6.9	4.4	3.3	49.9	2 796	40.8	8 600	6 850	1 800	25.9	700	300
El Paso	19.6	16.1	9.6	7.0	5.0	3.0	49.8	87 590	28.3	380 400	309 424	71 000	22.9	41 000	11 200
Fremont	15.5	15.3	10.2	10.0	10.1	8.7	48.1	3 597	12.5	31 800	28 676	3 200	11.0	2 400	2 400
Garfield	18.4	18.7	9.6	7.2	5.8	4.2	49.1	7 460	33.1	27 100	22 514	4 600	20.5	3 200	1 000
Gilpin	18.1	26.3	12.6	7.2	4.6	2.6	47.1	629	25.8	2 700	2 441	300	11.3	300	100
Grand	20.9	19.7	9.1	8.9	5.1	2.5	46.9	491	6.6	8 800	7 475	1 300	17.7	900	200
Gunnison	17.9	16.9	8.6	6.0	3.8	2.6	47.0	-416	-3.9	10 200	10 689	-500	-4.6	900	300
Hinsdale	17.3	20.3	12.4	14.1	9.0	3.6	47.3	59	14.5	500	408	100	20.3	0	0
Huerfano	11.5	13.6	10.9	11.2	11.2	9.8	51.3	-431	-6.7	6 900	6 440	500	7.4	500	500
Jackson	15.7	16.6	12.8	10.7	5.7	5.0	46.7	-258	-13.8	1 700	1 863	-200	-9.8	200	100
Jefferson	18.5	18.9	11.8	7.7	5.0	3.0	50.7	66 677	17.9	427 400	371 753	55 700	15.0	39 300	12 700
Kiowa	13.3	14.8	10.2	8.8	11.1	8.5	51.2	-248	-12.8	1 900	1 936	-100	-2.8	200	100
Kit Carson	15.0	13.6	10.4	9.7	8.8	7.4	50.5	-459	-6.0	7 600	7 599	0	0.4	800	500
Lake	19.1	17.3	9.9	7.6	4.9	3.3	48.4	-2 823	-32.0	6 700	8 830	-2 100	-23.9	1 000	200
La Plata	15.3	17.7	9.6	7.4	6.0	4.0	49.6	5 089	18.7	31 500	27 195	4 300	15.7	3 300	1 200
Larimer	17.9	16.9	9.4	6.5	5.5	4.1	50.5	36 952	24.8	174 600	149 184	25 400	17.0	16 400	5 600
Las Animas	12.0	13.7	10.0	10.3	10.1	9.7	51.3	-1 132	-7.6	14 200	14 897	-700	-4.9	1 400	1 100
Lincoln	15.4	12.1	10.6	10.3	10.4	9.1	51.0	-134	-2.9	4 700	4 663	0	0.1	500	400
Logan	15.1	13.8	10.1	9.9	8.5	7.1	51.2	-2 233	-11.3	19 400	19 800	-400	-1.8	2 100	1 100
Mesa	14.9	15.7	10.2	9.1	8.6	5.9	51.5	11 615	14.2	89 000	81 530	7 500	9.2	10 300	4 300
Mineral	19.4	14.9	12.9	11.8	9.7	5.4	48.6	-246	-30.6	700	804	-100	-13.1	100	0
Moffat	17.3	17.5	10.5	7.4	4.6	3.4	49.4	-1 776	-13.5	12 700	13 133	-400	-3.1	1 900	400
Montezuma	14.4	15.2	10.2	9.4	7.6	4.8	51.3	2 162	13.1	19 300	16 510	2 800	16.8	2 100	800
Montrose	13.1	15.2	11.6	10.0	9.5	6.9	51.2	71	0.3	24 600	24 352	300	1.2	2 500	1 300
Morgan	15.7	13.5	9.3	8.9	7.8	7.3	51.0	-574	-2.5	22 500	22 513	0	-0.2	2 800	1 400
Otero	13.4	13.3	10.0	9.5	9.0	8.1	51.8	-2 382	-10.6	21 900	22 567	-700	-3.0	2 400	1 500
Ouray	12.5	19.0	15.5	10.8	8.5	4.6	49.5	370	19.2	2 000	1 925	100	5.2	200	100
Park	17.3	22.6	13.1	8.2	5.4	2.0	48.8	1 841	34.5	7 000	5 333	1 700	31.1	700	200
Phillips	13.4	12.8	10.1	10.9	10.0	11.0	52.8	-353	-7.8	4 400	4 542	-200	-3.3	400	400
Pitkin	24.7	26.1	13.0	6.0	3.1	1.3	47.5	2 323	22.5	10 300	10 338	0	-0.2	900	200
Prowers	15.0	14.3	9.7	8.5	7.1	5.6	51.2	277	2.1	14 200	13 070	1 100	8.4	1 900	800
Pueblo	14.9	14.6	9.8	10.0	8.8	6.4	51.6	-2 921	-2.3	127 100	125 972	1 100	0.9	12 200	6 800
Rio Blanco	15.6	16.5	11.2	7.9	5.5	4.1	49.2	-283	-4.5	6 600	6 255	400	5.7	900	200
Rio Grande	14.2	14.1	10.1	9.3	8.0	6.6	50.6	259	2.5	11 700	10 511	1 200	11.1	1 400	700
Routt	20.9	23.6	9.4	5.1	3.6	2.1	46.5	684	5.1	13 300	13 404	-100	-0.8	1 600	400
Saguache	15.5	15.1	9.8	7.5	7.5	4.9	48.7	684	17.4	4 100	3 935	200	5.1	600	200
San Juan	16.1	23.2	10.6	6.8	5.5	0.9	44.3	-88	-10.6	900	833	100	6.5	200	0
San Miguel	23.2	25.8	10.4	5.0	2.3	2.0	47.0	461	14.4	3 200	3 192	0	-0.7	400	100
Sedgwick	12.4	13.6	10.1	11.6	11.9	11.2	51.3	-576	-17.6	3 000	3 266	-300	-7.9	300	200
Summit	30.6	21.3	7.9	4.8	1.8	0.5	45.6	4 033	45.6	11 100	8 848	2 200	25.4	1 400	100
Teller	16.8	22.4	11.6	8.0	5.0	2.2	49.2	4 434	55.2	11 600	8 034	3 600	44.8	1 100	300
Washington	13.8	13.7	10.5	11.5	10.0	7.6	50.0	-492	-9.3	5 300	5 304	0	0.6	500	400
Weld	16.4	15.3	9.6	7.2	5.7	4.5	50.6	8 383	6.8	135 000	123 438	11 600	9.4	14 200	5 000
Yuma	13.8	14.2	10.6	9.6	8.8	8.0	51.1	-728	-7.5	9 700	9 682	100	0.5	1 100	600
CONNECTICUT	17.8	15.5	10.8	9.0	7.8	5.8	51.5	179 116	5.8	3 189 000	3 108 000	81 000	2.6	259 000	171 000
Fairfield	17.1	15.7	12.0	9.8	7.7	5.6	51.8	20 502	2.5	821 000	807 143	13 900	1.7	64 400	43 500
Hartford	17.9	15.3	10.6	9.2	8.1	6.0	51.9	44 017	5.4	825 200	807 766	17 400	2.2	66 200	43 900
Litchfield	16.8	17.1	11.4	8.7	7.9	6.2	51.0	17 323	11.1	162 200	156 769	5 400	3.5	12 300	9 000
Middlesex	18.3	16.9	11.1	8.5	7.3	5.8	51.2	14 179	11.0	136 700	129 017	7 700	6.0	10 400	6 900
New Haven	18.0	15.1	10.1	8.7	8.4	6.3	52.0	42 894	5.6	778 900	761 325	17 600	2.3	64 200	45 500
New London	19.3	14.9	9.9	8.4	7.0	4.9	49.4	16 548	6.9	246 400	238 409	8 000	3.4	23 100	12 300
Tolland	17.7	16.6	10.7	7.3	5.4	3.6	50.0	13 876	12.1	121 500	114 823	6 700	5.9	9 700	4 300
Windham	17.6	15.2	10.2	7.8	7.0	5.5	51.3	10 213	11.1	96 800	92 312	4 500	4.9	8 400	5 200

STATE County	Population—(cont'd): Components of change, 1980-1986 (cont'd): Net migration	Households, 1990: Number	Households, 1990: Percent change, 1980–1990	Households, 1990: Persons per household	Households, 1990: Percent: Female family householder[1]	Households, 1990: Percent: One-person	Births, 1988: Total	Births, 1988: Rate[2]	Births, 1988: Low birth weight[3] (Number)	Deaths, 1987: Number: Total	Deaths, 1987: Number: Infant[4]	Deaths, 1987: Rate: Total[2]	Deaths, 1987: Rate: Infant[5]	Marriages, 1984: Number	Marriages, 1984: Rate[2]
	29	30	31	32	33	34	35	36	37	38	39	40	41	42	43
COLORADO—Con.															
Clear Creek	-700	3 153	11.2	2.40	6.2	27.5	112	15.6	11	26	0	3.6	0.0	102	13.6
Conejos	-500	2 492	5.8	2.98	10.6	21.6	133	16.4	11	71	1	8.8	7.3	49	6.0
Costilla	500	1 192	16.3	2.67	11.9	23.9	43	13.0	4	24	0	7.3	0.0	0	0.0
Crowley	200	1 165	3.1	2.50	9.0	27.0	41	12.4	4	33	1	10.6	23.8	25	8.1
Custer	300	770	34.6	2.50	5.5	23.4	17	8.9	1	6	0	3.2	0.0	0	0.0
Delta	1 200	8 372	5.7	2.45	6.7	24.5	236	10.8	17	267	3	12.1	11.6	203	8.5
Denver	-14 700	210 952	-0.3	2.17	11.5	40.4	8 379	17.0	837	4 523	102	9.0	11.5	6 623	13.0
Dolores	-100	581	-0.5	2.59	3.1	24.3	24	16.0	4	14	0	9.3	0.0	19	11.2
Douglas	11 000	20 844	165.3	2.89	5.5	12.4	992	21.9	55	134	7	3.2	8.2	252	7.6
Eagle	1 100	8 354	59.9	2.61	7.0	22.0	370	21.9	25	61	3	3.7	8.1	247	15.5
Elbert	1 300	3 377	48.3	2.84	4.9	14.7	125	13.2	7	40	0	4.4	0.0	42	5.1
El Paso	41 200	146 965	36.3	2.60	9.8	23.7	7 659	19.4	620	2 119	85	5.4	11.1	4 839	13.7
Fremont	3 100	11 713	16.5	2.42	9.5	26.4	350	10.7	28	358	2	10.8	5.5	308	9.8
Garfield	2 400	11 266	38.6	2.60	7.6	22.3	418	14.5	27	193	5	7.0	11.8	329	12.2
Gilpin	0	1 308	36.5	2.35	5.4	27.2	41	14.6	8	10	0	3.6	0.0	38	14.1
Grand	600	3 168	13.3	2.49	5.1	23.9	104	12.4	8	37	0	4.3	0.0	110	12.5
Gunnison	-1 100	3 855	1.9	2.38	5.7	26.8	130	13.1	13	58	2	5.8	15.9	118	11.2
Hinsdale	0	214	31.3	2.18	2.8	28.5	3	6.0	0	2	0	4.0	0.0	7	14.0
Huerfano	400	2 446	1.8	2.41	11.2	30.2	78	11.6	3	69	1	10.1	14.1	20	2.8
Jackson	-300	632	-4.5	2.52	4.6	25.0	17	10.6	3	12	0	7.1	0.0	12	6.7
Jefferson	29 000	166 545	28.3	2.59	9.2	22.1	6 587	15.3	459	2 159	48	5.1	7.3	3 541	8.6
Kiowa	-100	657	-8.5	2.50	5.5	26.9	22	11.6	0	16	0	8.4	0.0	17	8.5
Kit Carson	-300	2 785	0.7	2.54	6.2	25.7	119	15.9	7	51	0	6.7	0.0	70	8.9
Lake	-2 900	2 382	-20.6	2.51	8.4	27.5	82	13.9	8	32	3	5.1	33.7	71	9.9
La Plata	2 200	11 976	22.9	2.56	8.8	23.6	456	14.5	35	192	3	6.1	6.2	457	14.8
Larimer	14 600	70 472	30.3	2.55	7.6	23.0	2 773	15.2	170	1 015	22	5.7	8.3	1 803	10.9
Las Animas	-1 000	5 421	1.0	2.47	12.2	29.3	183	13.3	15	197	2	14.1	10.5	108	7.3
Lincoln	-200	1 817	-0.3	2.43	6.4	28.5	81	17.6	5	51	1	10.9	14.9	51	11.1
Logan	-1 300	6 978	-2.4	2.46	7.4	27.5	232	12.5	13	170	1	9.0	3.9	203	10.1
Mesa	1 500	36 250	22.2	2.50	9.8	24.8	1 210	13.3	90	751	12	8.4	10.2	964	10.1
Mineral	-200	247	-21.3	2.26	5.7	30.4	7	11.7	0	1	0	1.4	0.0	13	16.3
Moffat	-1 800	4 178	-8.7	2.69	7.4	23.5	152	12.7	10	63	1	5.2	5.4	131	9.3
Montezuma	1 400	6 762	19.4	2.74	10.4	21.5	321	17.1	12	143	5	7.5	15.6	189	9.8
Montrose	-900	9 405	11.6	2.55	8.1	22.5	299	11.9	26	229	8	9.1	29.0	228	8.8
Morgan	-1 500	8 139	2.0	2.64	7.9	24.6	371	16.3	30	230	4	10.0	11.5	213	9.0
Otero	-1 500	7 593	-4.3	2.59	11.7	25.7	322	15.0	12	238	3	11.0	9.0	191	8.5
Ouray	0	947	31.0	2.42	5.2	24.3	26	12.4	2	15	1	7.1	41.7	25	11.9
Park	1 100	2 775	49.4	2.59	4.0	19.9	101	13.8	10	41	1	5.7	10.5	46	6.9
Phillips	-200	1 712	-2.3	2.41	6.5	28.9	54	12.6	2	56	0	13.0	0.0	22	4.8
Pitkin	-700	5 877	30.1	2.13	5.4	35.4	153	14.0	12	27	0	2.5	0.0	259	25.1
Prowers	0	4 984	7.0	2.64	10.6	25.7	242	17.7	20	148	2	10.6	8.2	162	11.3
Pueblo	-4 200	47 057	4.4	2.55	13.7	25.8	1 752	13.7	135	1 205	10	9.5	5.6	1 111	8.8
Rio Blanco	-300	2 181	3.7	2.67	5.9	22.1	92	14.6	5	37	0	5.7	0.0	57	8.3
Rio Grande	500	3 930	11.6	2.69	10.8	21.8	181	15.6	18	114	0	9.7	0.0	142	12.6
Routt	-1 300	5 483	11.1	2.54	6.5	23.3	199	15.1	12	60	2	4.5	11.0	198	14.1
Saguache	-200	1 643	20.8	2.76	11.0	23.4	65	15.1	1	31	0	7.4	0.0	18	4.4
San Juan	-100	287	-9.7	2.60	7.7	26.1	10	11.1	2	4	0	4.0	0.0	19	19.0
San Miguel	-300	1 489	19.1	2.42	6.4	26.5	64	18.8	8	8	1	2.4	21.3	34	11.3
Sedgwick	-300	1 141	-9.4	2.33	5.2	28.7	35	12.1	0	38	0	13.1	0.0	49	15.3
Summit	1 000	5 295	48.3	2.42	4.6	23.7	203	18.5	23	16	2	1.5	10.6	242	23.0
Teller	2 900	4 720	63.8	2.63	6.6	19.3	179	14.3	15	57	2	4.7	10.5	76	7.2
Washington	-100	1 915	-5.1	2.50	4.8	26.1	52	9.8	9	54	1	10.0	13.3	38	6.8
Weld	2 300	47 470	11.0	2.69	9.1	22.3	2 122	15.6	157	873	30	6.4	14.0	1 018	7.6
Yuma	-400	3 472	-3.7	2.54	5.6	26.9	111	11.4	5	100	1	10.4	8.0	76	7.7
CONNECTICUT	-6 000	1 230 479	12.5	2.59	11.4	24.2	48 077	14.9	3 238	28 327	411	8.8	8.8	27 236	8.6
Fairfield	-7 000	305 011	8.7	2.66	11.3	22.9	11 943	14.6	797	6 938	87	8.5	7.4	7 151	8.8
Hartford	-4 900	324 691	12.1	2.55	12.7	25.0	12 321	14.6	884	7 421	121	8.9	9.9	7 030	8.6
Litchfield	2 100	66 371	19.2	2.59	8.4	23.1	2 302	13.8	129	1 435	11	8.8	4.9	1 425	9.0
Middlesex	4 200	54 651	19.0	2.51	9.0	24.4	1 977	14.2	126	1 192	17	8.7	9.0	1 194	8.9
New Haven	-1 200	304 730	12.2	2.55	12.5	25.9	12 090	15.2	890	7 663	110	9.7	9.3	6 267	8.1
New London	-2 800	93 245	14.0	2.59	9.6	23.1	4 151	16.8	239	1 997	41	8.1	10.3	2 495	10.2
Tolland	1 400	44 309	22.2	2.66	7.6	20.1	1 773	14.1	84	756	13	6.1	7.4	840	7.1
Windham	1 300	37 471	16.3	2.66	10.8	22.2	1 520	15.4	89	925	11	9.5	8.0	834	8.8

1. No spouse present. 2. Per 1,000 resident population estimated as of July 1 of the year shown. 3. Under 2,500 grams. 4. Deaths of infants under 1 year old. 5. Deaths of infants under 1 year old per 1,000 live births.

STATE County	Divorces, 1984		Physicians, active non-Federal, 1989		Hospitals, 1989			Nursing homes,[4] 1986		Serious crimes known to police, 1988			Education			
						Beds				Number			Public school enrollment[7]		Attainment,[8] 1980	
	Number	Rate[1]	Number[2]	Rate[3]	Number	Number	Rate[3]	Number	Beds	Total[5]	Violent[6]	Rate[3]	1986–1987	1980	Percent 12 yrs. or more	Percent 16 yrs. or more
	44	45	46	47	48	49	50	51	52	53	54	55	56	57	58	59
COLORADO—Con.																
Clear Creek	39	5.2	4	56	0	0	0	0	0	601	36	8 137	1 462	1 201	87.7	29.9
Conejos	25	3.1	4	49	1	49	598	0	0	152	6	1 880	1 980	2 117	52.0	9.7
Costilla	0	0.0	0	0	0	0	0	0	0	50	9	1 354	703	749	45.9	10.1
Crowley	7	2.3	1	30	0	0	0	1	59	105	19	3 287	523	536	55.9	8.6
Custer	0	0.0	2	105	0	0	0	0	0	43	4	2 393	309	297	79.0	16.8
Delta	141	5.9	16	75	1	38	178	4	186	448	58	2 013	3 914	4 186	68.0	12.2
Denver	4 167	8.2	2 852	588	16	4 359	899	57	4 079	42 413	3 637	8 473	60 578	64 116	74.7	24.8
Dolores	6	3.5	0	0	0	0	0	0	0	33	0	2 066	345	350	64.4	7.7
Douglas	120	3.6	32	65	0	0	0	1	80	1 519	78	3 572	9 693	6 645	88.5	27.2
Eagle	103	6.5	25	146	1	30	175	0	0	1 835	102	11 210	2 212	1 939	89.6	34.6
Elbert	14	1.7	5	51	0	0	0	1	32	108	18	1 176	1 869	1 699	76.7	15.0
El Paso	2 503	7.1	537	133	6	1 373	341	26	1 636	25 816	1 542	6 634	69 625	60 963	82.7	20.9
Fremont	291	9.3	32	97	2	274	828	11	672	1 400	77	4 370	5 694	5 181	66.9	11.7
Garfield	154	5.7	42	144	2	146	502	2	117	1 072	24	3 863	5 682	4 152	80.4	20.2
Gilpin	12	4.4	2	71	0	0	0	0	0	150	16	5 367	371	454	87.0	25.6
Grand	57	6.5	6	72	1	21	253	0	0	622	24	7 163	1 639	1 354	83.7	21.2
Gunnison	55	5.2	10	102	1	24	245	1	51	680	40	6 745	1 403	1 414	89.9	39.6
Hinsdale	5	10.0	1	200	0	0	0	0	0	20	2	4 008	41	76	86.9	30.6
Huerfano	31	4.4	6	92	1	35	538	1	50	180	7	2 652	1 076	1 291	52.6	11.3
Jackson	0	0.0	3	188	0	0	0	0	0	61	3	3 595	326	409	76.4	13.4
Jefferson	2 046	5.0	537	124	1	301	69	26	2 896	23 421	1 434	5 414	75 760	79 660	86.2	26.8
Kiowa	3	1.5	0	0	1	42	2 211	2	49	8	0	401	366	300	71.5	8.9
Kit Carson	25	3.2	4	54	1	24	324	2	66	178	5	2 346	1 595	1 624	69.9	12.4
Lake	58	8.1	3	54	1	23	411	0	0	239	20	3 801	1 212	1 861	74.3	13.5
La Plata	213	6.9	79	252	2	180	575	6	171	1 495	73	4 816	5 359	4 908	79.8	22.1
Larimer	821	4.9	270	146	3	384	207	17	1 183	8 941	583	4 990	29 505	26 160	82.7	28.8
Las Animas	50	3.4	13	96	1	38	279	1	226	562	67	4 022	2 447	2 810	61.4	11.3
Lincoln	29	6.3	2	43	1	56	1 217	4	131	55	2	1 172	722	867	68.8	9.4
Logan	75	3.7	18	99	1	45	249	2	198	653	4	3 480	3 405	4 074	70.0	12.4
Mesa	669	7.0	154	170	4	555	611	16	892	4 234	278	4 734	15 918	15 452	74.5	16.3
Mineral	4	5.0	0	0	0	0	0	0	0	14	2	2 003	110	162	83.5	22.9
Moffat	76	5.4	9	78	1	27	233	1	60	461	55	3 817	2 558	2 650	75.5	14.7
Montezuma	113	5.9	13	70	1	137	737	3	96	721	55	3 782	4 173	3 574	64.2	13.6
Montrose	186	7.2	29	116	1	75	300	6	309	1 021	42	4 244	4 777	5 261	69.9	13.8
Morgan	117	5.0	14	62	2	69	308	5	349	836	23	3 690	4 496	4 747	65.2	12.4
Otero	119	5.3	30	142	1	218	1 033	5	305	1 023	98	4 745	4 570	5 061	60.0	12.0
Ouray	7	3.3	4	190	0	0	0	1	8	3	0	143	389	409	77.2	24.6
Park	33	4.9	1	13	0	0	0	0	0	279	35	3 829	1 434	1 141	82.3	18.8
Phillips	22	4.8	3	71	2	51	1 214	1	51	27	0	629	810	894	69.0	12.9
Pitkin	49	4.8	34	306	1	49	441	0	0	1 054	68	9 869	946	1 204	94.9	46.2
Prowers	26	1.8	8	59	1	40	294	2	112	678	35	4 784	3 006	2 999	65.4	12.8
Pueblo	587	4.7	259	203	3	1 224	957	26	1 037	8 858	1 223	6 966	23 143	26 399	66.5	13.2
Rio Blanco	38	5.5	3	48	2	63	1 016	1	25	166	7	2 559	1 580	1 291	79.3	18.0
Rio Grande	77	6.8	11	95	1	69	595	5	175	380	44	3 226	2 583	2 397	62.0	15.3
Routt	77	5.5	13	100	1	71	546	1	50	642	51	4 873	2 406	2 317	88.1	31.7
Saguache	14	3.4	1	23	0	0	0	0	0	116	5	2 767	916	869	59.3	11.2
San Juan	5	5.0	0	0	0	0	0	0	0	69	6	7 684	195	168	81.7	24.3
San Miguel	0	0.0	4	114	0	0	0	0	0	91	0	2 763	617	557	85.1	35.9
Sedgwick	8	2.5	2	71	1	56	2 000	1	32	44	6	1 470	548	661	66.9	11.2
Summit	0	0.0	18	162	0	0	0	0	0	2 408	50	21 933	1 482	1 217	95.3	38.7
Teller	21	2.0	7	54	0	0	0	1	59	356	17	2 900	2 445	1 829	83.3	19.5
Washington	18	3.2	0	0	1	11	212	1	24	113	6	2 096	1 001	1 068	65.5	10.9
Weld	559	4.2	169	124	1	281	206	14	872	7 971	636	5 907	22 127	24 920	68.8	16.8
Yuma	37	3.7	4	42	2	39	411	4	191	202	9	2 108	1 945	2 015	65.8	11.5
CONNECTICUT	11 763	3.7	9 643	298	65	14 969	462	350	29 709	X	14 749	5 907	445 646	565 152	70.3	20.7
Fairfield	2 663	3.3	2 347	289	13	3 299	406	56	5 461	41 516	3 319	5 181	113 090	146 984	73.0	25.9
Hartford	2 778	3.4	2 826	334	16	4 740	560	82	9 222	46 870	4 541	5 678	120 717	147 154	69.7	19.8
Litchfield	530	3.3	278	166	6	459	274	24	1 330	2 614	184	2 618	22 362	29 965	70.6	18.6
Middlesex	529	4.0	336	239	4	912	648	30	1 820	3 557	252	4 244	19 393	23 887	73.1	20.4
New Haven	3 083	4.0	3 100	388	15	3 928	492	103	8 503	49 746	4 519	6 618	106 990	131 483	67.8	17.9
New London	1 110	4.5	472	191	5	1 109	449	31	2 068	7 435	488	4 723	34 677	45 090	71.0	16.9
Tolland	683	5.8	155	122	4	298	235	8	419	1 647	83	4 222	17 452	22 427	76.8	24.4
Windham	387	4.1	129	130	2	224	225	16	886	1 837	91	4 842	15 511	18 162	59.4	13.1

1. Per 1,000 resident population estimated as of July 1 of the year shown. 2. As of end of year. 3. Per 100,000 resident population as of July 1 of the year shown. 4. Preliminary. Covers nursing homes with 3 or more beds. 5. Data for serious crimes have not been adjusted for underreporting, this may affect comparability between geographic areas or over time. 6. Includes murder and nonnegligent manslaughter, forcible rape, robbery, and aggravated assault. 7. The 1986–1987 data are based on administrative reports obtained by the U.S. National Center for Education Statistics. The 1980 data are based on the 1980 Census of Population and Housing. 8. Persons 25 years old or older.

STATE County	Education (cont'd) Local government expenditures for education,[1] 1982: Total (Mil dol)	Education (cont'd) Local government expenditures for education,[1] 1982: Per capita (Dollars)	Social Security Program December 1988 Beneficiaries: Total	Social Security Program December 1988 Beneficiaries: Rate[2]	Social Security Program December 1988: Payments ($1,000)	Supplemental Security Income Program recipients June 1986	Money income Per capita[3]: 1987 Income, (Dollars)	Money income Per capita[3] 1979: Current dollars	Money income Per capita[3] 1979: Constant 1987 dollars	Money income: Median household income 1979 (Dollars)	Money income Percent below poverty level, 1979: Persons	Money income Percent below poverty level, 1979: Families	Housing units, 1990: Total	Housing units, 1990: Percent change, 1980–1990
	60	61	62	63	64	65	66	67	68	69	70	71	72	73
COLORADO—Con.														
Clear Creek	5.7	766	535	74.3	261	22	12 364	9 393	14 697	21 110	5.8	3.1	4 811	14.6
Conejos	5.4	681	1 360	167.9	469	402	4 940	3 285	5 140	9 167	30.4	27.1	3 574	14.7
Costilla	2.4	735	725	219.7	243	246	6 257	3 680	5 758	7 358	36.1	32.3	1 743	21.3
Crowley	1.5	496	735	222.7	291	90	6 833	4 675	7 315	9 974	17.1	14.1	1 415	4.0
Custer	0.8	489	365	192.1	148	18	8 001	5 331	8 341	12 106	18.5	15.2	2 216	100.0
Delta	19.3	819	5 810	265.3	2 514	454	7 778	5 519	8 636	11 377	14.5	10.7	10 082	9.1
Denver	203.9	403	78 975	160.5	39 439	8 100	12 980	8 553	13 383	15 506	13.7	10.3	239 636	5.2
Dolores	1.1	674	375	250.0	160	16	7 065	5 381	8 420	13 164	22.7	18.2	947	3.8
Douglas	21.6	749	2 500	55.1	1 239	66	16 437	10 522	16 464	28 380	4.1	3.2	22 291	157.0
Eagle	7.1	456	930	55.0	442	42	14 184	9 888	15 472	21 336	9.4	6.5	15 226	37.7
Elbert	4.5	603	810	85.3	365	32	11 272	6 940	10 859	18 148	7.3	6.7	3 997	46.8
El Paso	159.4	481	40 035	101.6	18 226	2 788	11 461	7 027	10 995	16 236	10.3	8.1	165 056	40.4
Fremont	12.8	431	7 425	226.4	3 257	518	8 843	5 901	9 233	12 992	13.4	9.9	13 683	19.1
Garfield	16.4	570	3 770	130.9	1 777	178	10 260	7 704	12 054	18 692	8.9	6.0	12 517	33.9
Gilpin	0.8	294	195	69.6	92	8	11 322	7 920	12 392	19 436	10.0	7.7	2 438	21.2
Grand	6.4	766	795	94.6	387	24	10 596	7 768	12 155	18 538	8.6	6.8	9 985	38.5
Gunnison	4.1	371	880	88.9	383	44	8 935	6 630	10 374	15 313	18.1	6.3	7 294	27.2
Hinsdale	0.3	538	50	100.0	26	0	14 753	7 806	12 214	15 484	11.1	5.3	1 254	79.9
Huerfano	3.0	441	1 500	223.9	608	244	7 162	5 159	8 072	10 285	20.2	14.6	3 913	12.9
Jackson	1.4	771	220	137.5	99	6	9 246	6 864	10 740	16 853	8.5	7.4	1 326	25.0
Jefferson	220.3	561	34 760	80.8	17 764	1 640	14 610	9 469	14 816	24 044	4.6	3.3	178 611	28.9
Kiowa	1.7	851	365	192.1	165	22	10 798	6 452	10 095	13 596	14.6	13.4	878	5.1
Kit Carson	5.2	663	1 370	182.7	642	82	9 138	5 950	9 310	13 707	18.2	16.4	3 224	-2.0
Lake	6.4	742	695	117.8	356	30	9 212	7 733	12 100	22 204	4.5	3.2	3 527	-6.0
La Plata	14.3	483	4 155	132.3	1 840	346	9 945	6 721	10 516	15 246	13.9	9.2	15 412	26.8
Larimer	72.7	459	21 150	116.2	9 987	1 124	11 431	7 458	11 670	17 169	11.0	5.9	77 811	25.1
Las Animas	8.0	520	3 300	239.1	1 341	530	6 941	5 110	7 996	11 229	20.4	15.3	6 975	8.5
Lincoln	3.7	800	890	193.5	401	62	9 105	6 357	9 947	12 808	12.8	10.1	2 204	2.8
Logan	13.3	665	3 320	179.5	1 563	248	9 429	6 600	10 327	15 289	10.7	8.3	7 824	0.1
Mesa	44.3	468	15 955	175.3	7 375	1 368	9 705	7 167	11 214	16 592	9.7	7.1	39 208	20.4
Mineral	0.7	732	75	125.0	36	4	10 277	7 104	11 116	15 259	8.5	4.7	1 201	72.3
Moffat	12.6	863	1 200	100.0	563	82	10 349	8 003	12 522	21 176	5.6	3.5	5 235	-0.6
Montezuma	10.4	578	3 085	164.1	1 319	278	8 333	5 963	9 330	13 971	14.6	10.5	8 050	23.9
Montrose	13.8	536	4 795	191.0	2 085	448	9 688	6 379	9 981	15 273	10.4	8.5	10 353	10.4
Morgan	13.6	599	3 815	168.1	1 758	322	8 519	6 431	10 063	15 004	11.7	8.9	9 230	2.3
Otero	14.0	621	4 080	190.7	1 671	624	7 763	5 123	8 016	11 600	20.3	16.3	8 739	-1.2
Ouray	1.2	585	350	166.7	175	8	11 013	6 770	10 593	14 229	12.4	9.2	1 507	26.7
Park	5.1	830	655	89.7	312	8	10 456	7 095	11 102	18 051	11.9	10.5	7 247	48.7
Phillips	4.4	932	1 070	248.8	515	60	9 231	6 325	9 897	12 531	13.5	11.5	1 960	-2.7
Pitkin	4.0	383	575	52.8	301	10	18 861	12 035	18 831	20 979	9.7	6.4	9 837	15.7
Prowers	10.3	765	2 130	155.5	955	256	8 380	5 641	8 826	12 762	18.6	15.1	5 855	7.4
Pueblo	68.3	543	23 105	181.1	10 426	2 750	8 947	6 669	10 435	15 479	13.7	10.9	50 872	3.6
Rio Blanco	5.2	728	720	114.3	334	20	10 357	7 679	12 015	20 853	5.9	4.0	2 803	11.1
Rio Grande	7.0	630	2 020	174.1	846	292	8 109	5 448	8 524	13 016	18.9	15.5	5 277	18.8
Routt	15.2	1 084	1 010	76.5	473	42	11 897	8 972	14 038	21 487	7.1	3.9	9 252	27.1
Saguache	3.0	720	815	189.5	323	134	6 831	4 504	7 047	9 862	26.8	23.3	2 306	22.4
San Juan	0.7	657	80	88.9	39	2	9 585	6 061	9 484	14 688	11.4	6.6	481	1.3
San Miguel	2.2	717	245	72.1	105	16	9 980	6 346	9 930	13 601	16.7	12.2	2 635	51.5
Sedgwick	2.1	625	755	260.3	371	42	9 161	5 913	9 252	12 867	9.8	8.1	1 414	-2.3
Summit	4.6	438	430	39.1	207	6	13 939	10 152	15 885	21 410	8.3	3.3	17 091	66.6
Teller	4.7	506	1 300	104.0	602	36	11 657	7 052	11 034	16 882	11.3	8.9	7 565	48.3
Washington	4.0	742	935	176.4	432	46	8 499	5 754	9 003	13 648	16.5	13.7	2 307	-4.4
Weld	58.7	464	16 430	120.6	7 577	1 564	9 547	6 505	10 178	15 805	14.1	10.0	51 138	10.0
Yuma	6.0	596	1 775	183.0	775	88	8 726	5 958	9 322	11 832	17.8	14.9	4 082	-1.8
CONNECTICUT	1 493.0	477	512 452	158.5	279 780	28 242	16 094	8 511	13 317	20 077	8.0	6.2	1 320 850	14.0
Fairfield	410.1	506	121 535	148.7	68 722	6 428	20 093	10 408	16 285	22 961	7.5	5.9	324 355	9.9
Hartford	410.5	506	140 885	167.1	76 720	8 858	15 604	8 342	13 053	20 140	8.2	6.3	341 812	13.7
Litchfield	76.3	481	27 995	168.3	15 354	774	15 479	8 179	12 798	19 813	5.2	4.0	74 274	20.2
Middlesex	63.5	487	21 405	153.2	11 751	972	15 505	8 036	12 574	20 345	6.4	4.2	61 593	20.3
New Haven	329.7	432	135 165	170.1	72 986	7 764	14 307	7 609	11 906	18 424	9.4	7.4	327 079	13.9
New London	111.7	465	36 410	147.1	19 028	1 942	13 666	7 307	11 433	18 125	8.2	6.4	104 461	15.7
Tolland	50.8	436	12 435	99.2	6 746	434	14 229	7 506	11 745	21 305	6.0	4.1	46 677	22.7
Windham	40.5	432	16 435	166.0	8 374	1 046	11 814	6 418	10 042	16 185	9.5	7.2	40 599	17.2

1. Elementary and secondary. 2. Per 1,000 resident population estimated as of July 1 of the year shown. 3. Based on the resident population estimated as of July 1, 1988 for 1987 data and enumerated as of April 1, 1980 for 1979 data.

STATE County	Housing units, 1990 (cont'd)				Civilian labor force, 1990				Private nonfarm establishments, 1988					
	Occupied units						Unemployment				Employment[2]			
		Owner occupied												
	Total	Percent	Median value (Dollars)	Median rent (Dollars)	Total	Percent change, 1989–1990	Total	Rate[1]	Number	Net change, 1987–1988	Total	Percent change, 1987–1988	Manu-facturing	Retail trade
	74	75	76	77	78	79	80	81	82	83	84	85	86	87
COLORADO—Con.														
Clear Creek	3 153	71.9	90 800	335	2 890	7.0	179	6.2	173	-6	1 688	-18.6	44	487
Conejos	2 492	79.2	35 400	150	2 545	0.7	320	12.6	89	-5	576	5.9	69	121
Costilla	1 192	77.3	35 400	116	1 187	7.4	132	11.1	26	-3	257	10.8	0	24
Crowley	1 165	69.9	26 500	167	1 652	6.5	61	3.7	39	-5	200	-2.9	0	48
Custer	770	73.9	58 900	223	766	2.5	40	5.2	58	5	194	14.8	9	49
Delta	8 372	74.5	51 200	219	8 771	6.3	647	7.4	467	-2	2 717	-0.3	380	740
Denver	210 952	49.2	79 000	339	266 954	2.8	14 482	5.4	19 402	-329	319 438	-0.9	35 201	49 914
Dolores	581	80.0	40 400	202	988	-3.4	47	4.8	30	0	157	31.9	0	63
Douglas	20 844	85.2	119 500	520	23 603	3.1	957	4.1	1 165	33	7 923	7.5	808	2 029
Eagle	8 354	57.5	135 900	544	15 037	10.2	753	5.0	1 182	66	12 665	2.8	316	4 384
Elbert	3 377	82.9	92 400	370	4 095	3.4	232	5.7	173	-9	1 223	-0.8	152	180
El Paso	146 965	57.4	81 700	364	189 614	0.7	11 931	6.3	9 854	-277	122 359	0.4	21 994	30 057
Fremont	11 713	72.9	57 900	265	11 671	0.1	794	6.8	685	-23	5 686	-4.2	1 009	1 486
Garfield	11 266	57.9	90 400	359	17 550	11.6	900	5.1	1 074	8	8 147	-0.5	424	2 365
Gilpin	1 308	75.5	74 600	351	1 548	-1.1	59	3.8	60	3	146	-11.5	0	68
Grand	3 168	57.7	81 400	367	5 107	0.4	212	4.2	434	-47	3 779	-2.8	199	1 058
Gunnison	3 855	51.3	79 000	297	5 936	5.1	288	4.9	478	22	3 750	-0.4	73	1 061
Hinsdale	214	59.3	84 200	275	503	-3.6	11	2.2	31	0	51	-7.3	0	12
Huerfano	2 446	70.0	36 100	173	2 216	-0.2	188	8.5	159	-8	711	-13.6	16	250
Jackson	632	65.3	49 800	223	885	-0.9	37	4.2	46	-3	262	-9.0	0	69
Jefferson	166 545	70.1	93 600	416	236 528	2.8	9 534	4.0	10 407	-29	128 418	1.8	33 189	33 155
Kiowa	657	68.9	31 300	179	916	1.8	22	2.4	49	-6	125	-37.5	0	42
Kit Carson	2 785	71.2	46 700	206	3 964	6.4	77	1.9	224	-9	1 354	-0.4	113	385
Lake	2 382	64.4	48 700	271	1 618	3.2	170	10.5	170	6	1 048	-3.9	0	329
La Plata	11 976	65.3	85 100	354	17 476	4.8	847	4.8	1 195	-38	9 492	-3.4	342	2 831
Larimer	70 472	62.9	83 900	368	102 596	5.8	4 484	4.4	5 168	-43	50 613	0.9	12 258	13 945
Las Animas	5 421	67.0	44 700	167	4 863	1.9	379	7.8	293	-3	1 653	-8.1	44	632
Lincoln	1 817	70.2	43 800	226	2 289	1.3	79	3.5	135	10	914	10.5	0	489
Logan	6 978	66.7	43 200	214	9 146	4.0	324	3.5	566	-3	4 990	1.3	774	1 448
Mesa	36 250	64.9	62 700	275	44 767	7.3	2 649	5.9	2 412	-40	22 628	0.6	2 394	6 444
Mineral	247	70.4	53 800	231	236	-0.4	19	8.1	38	3	76	-24.0	0	30
Moffat	4 178	66.7	52 900	251	5 094	1.1	340	6.7	301	-16	2 408	-1.9	90	672
Montezuma	6 762	74.2	58 100	257	10 197	7.5	711	7.0	516	-25	3 650	-7.8	482	1 062
Montrose	9 405	72.0	60 000	257	12 215	6.1	842	6.9	725	4	5 573	3.1	616	1 633
Morgan	8 139	62.5	52 000	245	9 915	3.3	562	5.7	568	-21	5 619	-0.2	1 755	1 259
Otero	7 593	66.9	38 200	201	8 565	5.1	639	7.5	519	-4	4 272	0.7	701	1 064
Ouray	947	74.6	91 800	291	1 864	1.4	131	7.0	104	-3	437	6.1	36	135
Park	2 775	80.6	80 100	366	2 985	-8.1	188	6.3	114	-4	350	-18.4	25	122
Phillips	1 712	72.3	41 600	171	2 236	9.6	61	2.7	129	2	592	-17.0	41	182
Pitkin	5 877	52.4	452 800	663	10 378	13.8	539	5.2	1 055	61	11 738	6.2	234	4 397
Prowers	4 984	65.5	39 400	196	6 266	3.3	332	5.3	417	13	3 424	-3.5	743	940
Pueblo	47 057	67.9	51 300	252	53 671	8.8	3 575	6.7	2 720	-53	30 159	6.5	3 981	9 529
Rio Blanco	2 181	66.1	57 400	249	2 871	4.3	118	4.1	180	4	1 753	9.4	24	327
Rio Grande	3 930	68.3	47 400	214	4 846	-1.6	449	9.3	331	-10	2 500	-5.2	341	539
Routt	5 483	61.2	94 900	396	9 046	8.1	442	4.9	657	18	8 507	8.2	116	2 165
Saguache	1 643	67.1	39 000	174	1 537	-1.9	239	15.5	81	-8	472	-5.0	0	100
San Juan	287	61.7	51 000	276	604	5.0	46	7.6	41	4	367	491.9	0	41
San Miguel	1 489	55.5	151 800	447	3 346	16.7	174	5.2	197	21	1 223	14.6	0	607
Sedgwick	1 141	71.1	29 200	138	1 472	6.6	49	3.3	92	-5	402	-13.0	0	169
Summit	5 295	48.2	121 500	492	10 259	11.9	388	3.8	851	31	9 588	8.6	103	3 307
Teller	4 720	77.1	83 300	387	5 472	0.1	313	5.7	332	-22	1 358	-13.1	41	546
Washington	1 915	72.2	37 100	167	2 493	6.0	81	3.2	115	-12	695	10.7	83	198
Weld	47 470	61.2	67 500	307	71 008	5.8	3 498	4.9	2 718	-59	34 501	3.0	8 440	7 269
Yuma	3 472	70.2	47 000	203	4 732	7.2	128	2.7	300	5	1 522	3.3	90	464
CONNECTICUT	1 230 479	65.6	177 800	510	1 789 000	1.6	91 000	5.1	X	X	1 496 366	1.9	383 455	285 931
Fairfield	305 011	68.2	249 800	599	466 634	0.8	21 979	4.7	27 513	547	419 079	2.7	115 854	78 447
Hartford	324 691	62.7	168 900	491	468 752	1.8	23 264	5.0	24 294	621	477 602	-0.1	107 435	82 920
Litchfield	66 371	73.2	166 300	481	96 007	2.3	4 905	5.1	5 186	179	56 263	4.8	19 080	11 352
Middlesex	54 651	70.4	175 100	537	81 389	-0.4	3 398	4.2	3 958	73	58 437	1.3	14 929	11 737
New Haven	304 730	62.8	165 200	493	425 041	2.5	23 647	5.6	21 999	483	335 133	2.8	77 020	65 479
New London	93 245	64.7	149 200	493	127 125	0.4	7 124	5.6	6 014	178	96 009	3.3	33 448	21 964
Tolland	44 309	72.0	165 000	531	71 150	2.1	2 789	3.9	2 460	68	23 403	2.9	4 520	7 221
Windham	37 471	66.6	126 800	406	52 897	3.2	3 889	7.4	2 193	89	29 936	8.5	11 159	6 811

1. Percent of total civilian labor force. 2. For week including March 12. Excludes government employees, self-employed persons, farm workers, domestic service workers, railroad employees subject to the Railroad Retirement Act, and employees on oceanborne vessels or in foreign countries.

Table A. States and Counties — **Employment, Personal Income, and Earnings**

STATE County	Private nonfarm establishments, 1988 (cont'd)				Personal income, 1989								Earnings, 1989		
	Employment[1] (cont'd)		Annual payroll								Per capita[3]			Percent by selected industries	
															Goods-related[4]
	Finance, insurance, and real estate	Services	Total (Mil dol)	Average per employee (Dollars)	Total (Mil dol)	Percent change, 1988–1989	Wages and salaries[2] (Mil dol)	Proprietor's income (Mil dol)	Dividends, interest, & rent (Mil dol)	Transfer payments (Mil dol)	Dollars	Rank	Total (Mil dol)	Farm	Total
	88	89	90	91	92	93	94	95	96	97	98	99	100	101	102
COLORADO—Con.															
Clear Creek	37	623	34	20 432	116	3.5	54	9	16	11	16 379	551	63	0.0	44.0
Conejos	0	153	7	11 932	67	10.3	22	14	8	20	8 157	3 067	36	30.5	9.5
Costilla	0	0	2	8 424	39	9.9	10	9	5	11	12 379	2 171	19	50.1	NA
Crowley	0	70	2	10 815	45	15.1	17	6	9	11	13 569	1 650	23	28.8	2.9
Custer	0	50	3	13 784	26	2.2	5	6	7	5	13 513	1 673	11	17.9	28.1
Delta	214	670	40	14 650	256	6.9	78	38	68	70	12 019	2 322	116	8.1	15.1
Denver	33 002	106 725	7 496	23 467	9 727	6.2	11 376	1 144	2 065	1 493	20 059	164	12 520	0.0	15.0
Dolores	0	0	2	12 688	25	1.0	9	7	4	4	16 951	446	16	33.3	NA
Douglas	658	1 579	154	19 469	1 075	10.1	247	89	150	54	21 972	95	335	2.4	24.5
Eagle	1 167	5 115	171	13 464	389	13.7	281	43	57	20	22 790	76	324	0.9	20.6
Elbert	44	318	18	14 522	162	5.7	20	28	21	15	16 390	547	48	30.7	22.9
El Paso	8 752	42 876	2 249	18 378	6 479	6.7	4 183	475	1 067	984	16 105	618	4 658	0.2	23.1
Fremont	263	1 979	80	14 059	403	6.2	164	36	92	104	12 157	2 256	200	2.0	20.6
Garfield	449	2 426	148	18 213	432	9.9	234	57	86	59	14 828	1 061	290	1.2	26.1
Gilpin	0	48	2	12 452	41	7.1	6	3	6	4	14 796	1 078	9	0.0	NA
Grand	330	1 790	40	10 469	135	6.2	72	19	26	14	16 301	569	90	1.4	13.1
Gunnison	378	1 669	40	10 711	131	7.3	76	16	30	17	13 331	1 763	93	2.4	16.7
Hinsdale	10	20	1	14 059	8	9.3	2	2	3	1	17 441	373	5	15.6	NA
Huerfano	43	265	7	9 582	72	5.6	20	11	17	22	10 977	2 670	31	12.5	9.6
Jackson	0	9	5	18 176	25	0.8	11	6	5	3	15 492	805	17	28.8	31.3
Jefferson	7 240	35 604	2 882	22 444	8 614	6.0	4 372	641	1 317	691	19 891	175	5 013	0.2	38.6
Kiowa	0	27	1	9 376	50	6.7	7	30	9	4	26 916	23	37	75.0	NA
Kit Carson	84	339	17	12 747	146	3.7	41	57	34	18	19 676	184	98	42.8	NA
Lake	50	346	17	15 839	57	9.3	39	4	12	11	10 208	2 854	43	0.0	32.7
La Plata	472	3 855	137	14 459	455	8.1	230	58	103	66	14 522	1 202	288	2.0	14.0
Larimer	2 743	12 739	913	18 043	2 954	9.3	1 647	279	534	355	15 925	668	1 926	1.5	33.9
Las Animas	119	564	18	11 031	166	7.2	67	17	35	52	12 216	2 224	84	8.7	15.3
Lincoln	53	64	13	14 118	85	9.9	26	32	19	12	18 487	252	57	47.6	3.0
Logan	312	1 283	71	14 156	261	6.1	125	43	58	44	14 415	1 245	168	8.2	15.7
Mesa	1 305	7 743	388	17 132	1 292	9.5	690	144	256	239	14 232	1 315	834	2.1	18.5
Mineral	0	11	1	16 461	8	3.0	4	1	2	1	12 793	2 002	5	2.6	NA
Moffat	121	389	50	20 880	162	4.3	118	18	23	20	13 984	1 441	136	3.7	38.9
Montezuma	211	643	54	14 924	237	9.6	108	33	45	43	12 752	2 015	141	5.4	23.9
Montrose	330	1 532	86	15 414	329	6.5	157	45	74	64	13 150	1 838	202	4.3	20.5
Morgan	221	1 320	75	13 425	296	8.0	139	56	69	49	13 201	1 813	195	15.2	24.8
Otero	214	1 368	56	13 074	267	3.6	117	36	51	71	12 649	2 055	153	11.2	10.7
Ouray	38	67	7	15 908	36	9.2	12	5	11	6	16 840	462	17	12.1	NA
Park	17	94	6	16 231	101	6.1	20	8	16	12	13 582	1 641	28	5.8	23.9
Phillips	63	127	8	13 252	74	5.2	21	22	22	13	17 629	348	42	41.9	6.1
Pitkin	1 560	4 278	160	13 627	369	11.5	274	60	98	13	33 108	5	334	0.2	17.7
Prowers	241	638	44	12 888	196	7.5	84	50	35	34	14 439	1 237	135	25.5	NA
Pueblo	1 426	10 104	462	15 324	1 659	7.6	856	127	314	443	12 974	1 918	984	1.4	21.9
Rio Blanco	67	111	42	23 748	92	4.2	58	18	15	11	14 866	1 044	76	3.8	47.2
Rio Grande	133	518	34	13 444	149	10.2	67	30	30	30	12 882	1 964	97	20.3	17.0
Routt	887	2 787	156	18 343	252	10.6	163	35	48	19	19 412	199	198	2.9	28.9
Saguache	29	60	8	16 839	50	27.7	17	14	7	11	11 614	2 468	31	43.1	NA
San Juan	0	0	9	25 771	13	4.0	11	1	1	1	13 557	1 657	12	0.0	73.9
San Miguel	220	150	12	9 776	52	14.4	31	7	12	4	14 803	1 076	38	3.1	20.6
Sedgwick	0	94	5	11 794	48	4.1	13	12	13	9	17 175	413	25	36.0	5.0
Summit	772	4 337	103	10 697	258	12.5	187	22	35	13	23 220	70	209	0.2	9.4
Teller	135	348	16	11 653	182	6.0	31	20	33	25	14 003	1 435	50	0.6	21.1
Washington	62	96	9	13 573	103	9.6	22	47	21	12	19 768	181	70	61.6	3.6
Weld	3 057	7 596	698	20 243	1 943	6.9	1 027	223	303	269	14 230	1 317	1 250	6.6	32.6
Yuma	117	365	19	12 710	188	12.8	44	94	35	20	19 698	183	138	58.1	5.5
CONNECTICUT	146 826	409 400	37 414	X	80 333	6.7	52 172	5 248	15 415	8 524	24 798	X	57 420	0.3	31.1
Fairfield	34 663	110 470	12 211	29 138	25 545	6.6	15 549	1 881	5 456	2 068	31 438	9	17 430	0.0	33.0
Hartford	74 175	128 761	11 999	25 123	20 360	7.0	17 266	1 173	3 741	2 373	24 040	50	18 439	0.2	28.9
Litchfield	1 950	13 625	1 190	21 146	4 223	7.0	1 687	374	864	392	25 183	37	2 061	0.8	41.7
Middlesex	8 352	14 805	1 318	22 554	3 314	6.5	1 884	249	597	322	23 542	64	2 133	0.7	32.4
New Haven	21 953	103 519	7 601	22 679	17 345	6.6	10 601	1 042	3 240	2 241	21 736	103	11 643	0.2	28.0
New London	3 558	25 162	2 076	21 620	5 051	6.6	3 439	273	908	637	20 429	149	3 712	1.0	36.2
Tolland	1 016	6 128	441	18 839	2 733	7.7	916	153	355	225	21 563	108	1 069	1.0	23.5
Windham	997	6 901	568	18 974	1 762	6.9	830	103	254	268	17 706	334	933	1.5	38.8

1. For week including March 12. Excludes government employees, self-employed persons, farm workers, domestic service workers, railroad employees subject to the Railroad Retirement Act, and employees on oceanborne vessels or in foreign countries. 2. Includes other labor income. 3. Based on the resident population estimated as of July 1 of the year shown. 4. Covers mining, construction, and manufacturing.

STATE County	Earnings, 1989 (cont'd): Percent by selected industries (cont'd): Goods-related[1]: Manu-facturing	Earnings, 1989 (cont'd): Percent by selected industries (cont'd): Service-related & other[2]: Total	Service-related & other[2]: Retail trade	Service-related & other[2]: Finance, insur-ance, & real estate	Service-related & other[2]: Services	Govern-ment	Agriculture, 1987: Farms: Number	Farms: Percent with: Less than 50 acres	Farms: Percent with: 500 acres and over	Farm operators, percent: Whose principal occu-pation is farming	Farm operators, percent: Residing on farm operated	Land in farms: Acreage (1,000)	Land in farms: Percent change, 1982–1987	Land in farms: Acres: Average size of farm	Acres: Total irrigated (1,000)	Acres: Total cropland (1,000)
	103	104	105	106	107	108	109	110	111	112	113	114	115	116	117	118
COLORADO—Con.																
Clear Creek	2.1	35.0	10.4	1.9	17.3	20.9	11	27.3	36.4	45.5	72.7	8	107.8	767	0	0
Conejos	5.6	33.0	5.7	2.8	13.8	27.0	439	17.3	28.9	61.7	71.3	302	-4.9	687	105	126
Costilla	NA	NA	3.3	NA	5.8	25.1	191	25.1	18.8	46.1	63.4	292	8.0	1 529	31	D
Crowley	0.0	NA	4.9	1.7	6.3	52.7	187	19.3	47.1	69.5	75.4	409	-9.3	2 185	21	59
Custer	0.7	NA	8.0	4.4	9.4	19.0	130	11.5	46.9	61.5	71.5	150	-32.8	1 156	21	29
Delta	5.3	52.7	11.6	4.1	18.0	24.2	900	45.0	10.7	55.3	81.9	269	10.7	299	66	77
Denver	8.3	69.7	6.9	9.4	29.2	15.3	17	100.0	0.0	35.3	29.4	0	NA	3	0	0
Dolores	NA	NA	6.6	NA	3.8	25.3	130	3.1	65.4	70.8	72.3	160	-4.5	1 230	1	70
Douglas	6.9	56.4	11.5	6.7	28.1	16.7	454	41.4	21.6	38.1	80.6	212	-6.7	467	5	32
Eagle	2.5	68.5	19.1	8.2	34.5	10.0	147	19.7	32.7	50.3	78.9	213	5.8	1 452	26	26
Elbert	2.4	27.5	5.4	1.9	13.5	18.9	679	17.8	46.7	53.6	77.9	1 015	0.5	1 495	5	197
El Paso	16.9	46.9	9.1	5.0	24.7	29.7	711	26.6	39.5	46.8	77.6	918	2.4	1 291	13	90
Fremont	11.5	41.7	11.2	3.1	22.3	35.7	412	57.8	22.3	43.7	79.1	305	-9.2	741	12	20
Garfield	2.1	55.8	13.8	4.7	26.9	17.0	480	31.9	30.6	57.9	77.1	484	5.7	1 008	54	78
Gilpin	1.2	NA	19.7	1.6	29.3	27.8	15	13.3	33.3	33.3	53.3	16	65.9	1 036	D	D
Grand	5.1	66.2	16.4	9.4	33.0	19.3	163	11.7	62.6	58.3	77.3	320	12.4	1 961	49	54
Gunnison	1.4	55.2	15.9	6.2	24.8	25.7	173	17.9	50.3	77.5	80.3	225	-11.1	1 302	45	47
Hinsdale	NA	NA	14.0	6.0	18.7	20.5	16	0.0	50.0	62.5	87.5	10	-9.3	619	2	2
Huerfano	2.3	48.9	14.5	-0.7	21.0	29.0	243	10.7	58.0	62.1	61.3	643	-8.8	2 646	14	35
Jackson	22.3	NA	8.7	2.3	4.0	17.7	126	15.9	74.6	67.5	69.0	460	2.4	3 651	109	103
Jefferson	30.7	44.5	10.5	4.6	23.5	16.7	446	65.0	11.0	37.2	74.9	92	-19.3	207	3	21
Kiowa	0.3	NA	2.0	1.1	5.2	9.4	328	6.1	73.2	72.9	47.9	997	9.5	3 039	3	501
Kit Carson	2.0	NA	7.8	3.0	14.5	11.8	793	7.6	71.4	77.2	60.0	1 416	9.1	1 785	124	860
Lake	0.6	NA	9.8	1.9	13.9	27.1	14	42.9	21.4	28.6	85.7	11	7.2	789	D	1
La Plata	2.6	62.7	14.3	3.7	31.9	21.4	682	28.3	20.4	48.1	81.5	614	4.1	900	61	109
Larimer	25.7	40.9	10.5	3.3	20.8	23.7	1 233	48.6	13.5	43.4	76.5	575	4.9	466	80	142
Las Animas	1.0	47.0	11.4	3.1	14.7	29.1	481	12.3	59.9	57.2	67.6	2 150	0.6	4 469	32	82
Lincoln	0.8	33.4	10.3	2.7	7.1	16.1	489	5.9	77.9	78.9	69.9	1 615	8.2	3 303	5	473
Logan	7.6	60.5	11.5	4.5	21.5	15.6	945	13.1	51.4	74.1	70.5	1 082	1.0	1 145	95	557
Mesa	8.1	61.5	13.9	4.1	29.8	18.0	1 223	59.6	10.1	49.7	81.8	437	-0.9	357	82	98
Mineral	NA	NA	10.8	NA	39.1	26.2	11	9.1	63.6	36.4	36.4	12	4.0	1 094	2	D
Moffat	0.5	NA	8.1	2.3	NA	17.4	330	19.4	53.3	53.6	71.8	1 033	-1.7	3 129	42	125
Montezuma	5.7	46.0	13.6	3.5	16.8	24.6	623	29.9	20.9	48.2	80.9	844	-0.3	1 355	36	108
Montrose	7.9	52.4	12.7	3.6	19.4	22.9	826	34.3	16.7	59.4	80.6	431	0.9	521	87	104
Morgan	17.1	44.4	8.6	2.9	18.5	15.6	800	14.0	37.6	74.0	73.0	743	6.7	929	119	344
Otero	6.9	57.4	9.9	3.3	22.1	20.7	491	27.9	25.7	60.3	74.1	732	17.2	1 490	56	D
Ouray	2.7	NA	13.0	4.4	12.2	19.8	88	13.6	46.6	67.0	78.4	D	D	D	13	16
Park	2.0	35.8	7.4	1.9	17.7	34.5	162	16.0	44.4	50.0	71.6	400	-1.2	2 470	14	22
Phillips	1.5	36.3	7.7	3.0	8.4	15.7	417	8.9	60.0	77.7	61.2	450	-2.8	1 080	70	366
Pitkin	1.8	73.9	18.8	9.3	39.8	8.2	70	30.0	32.9	47.1	87.1	33	-27.5	477	14	14
Prowers	9.1	NA	9.8	4.0	11.8	18.0	510	16.7	53.7	76.9	66.3	882	-5.2	1 730	105	468
Pueblo	15.4	51.5	11.9	4.3	24.7	25.2	615	33.0	32.4	50.4	73.3	892	-8.5	1 451	32	103
Rio Blanco	0.2	25.5	5.4	1.7	7.1	23.5	231	21.2	47.6	62.8	71.0	505	17.8	2 188	27	60
Rio Grande	6.5	44.7	8.1	3.6	15.3	18.1	345	12.8	36.8	68.1	79.4	221	-6.9	641	117	120
Routt	1.2	55.9	13.7	5.7	25.5	12.3	405	24.9	43.2	50.4	76.0	589	-3.3	1 455	44	115
Saguache	NA	33.1	6.0	1.8	6.0	21.4	254	7.9	54.7	74.8	68.1	472	-2.7	1 859	137	155
San Juan	3.1	NA	9.2	NA	4.3	10.2	3	0.0	66.7	66.7	33.3	D	NA	D	D	D
San Miguel	3.0	59.4	16.5	10.8	26.2	17.0	84	20.2	47.6	61.9	70.2	169	7.8	2 015	11	22
Sedgwick	1.7	40.8	10.1	3.7	13.6	18.3	263	7.2	64.6	75.7	58.9	324	-0.2	1 233	40	223
Summit	0.9	79.0	21.0	9.6	42.8	11.4	21	9.5	57.1	90.5	61.9	34	-9.8	1 637	10	10
Teller	1.8	53.5	14.0	6.6	22.4	24.7	67	28.4	37.3	37.3	68.7	83	10.4	1 243	1	3
Washington	0.3	24.8	4.4	2.5	5.6	10.0	854	8.8	66.2	73.7	63.6	1 391	1.9	1 629	40	841
Weld	23.5	45.5	8.8	4.5	18.8	15.3	2 975	25.7	24.4	66.7	77.3	2 105	6.2	708	359	957
Yuma	1.0	26.7	5.7	3.4	6.9	9.6	975	8.1	65.4	74.3	64.6	1 478	4.4	1 516	246	710
CONNECTICUT	24.1	57.1	9.4	10.3	24.8	11.5	3 580	48.5	3.4	51.5	79.8	398	-10.3	111	7	210
Fairfield	26.7	59.7	9.1	9.8	27.0	7.3	261	69.7	0.0	49.4	79.7	14	-23.3	52	0	7
Hartford	22.4	59.4	8.6	16.5	21.7	11.5	656	57.5	2.6	54.9	73.2	60	-10.8	92	5	38
Litchfield	29.1	47.3	10.5	2.2	24.4	10.1	619	39.1	5.8	51.4	82.9	95	-8.3	154	0	48
Middlesex	25.6	55.6	9.5	13.4	23.1	11.3	259	54.1	3.1	38.2	83.0	24	2.4	92	1	11
New Haven	20.3	59.8	10.7	5.8	28.7	11.9	407	63.4	1.2	52.8	73.5	26	-12.7	64	1	15
New London	29.6	40.0	9.5	2.4	19.7	22.8	556	34.4	3.2	55.8	79.5	74	-10.5	133	0	34
Tolland	12.2	40.6	10.8	2.7	21.0	34.9	338	44.4	5.0	45.3	79.0	41	-9.2	121	0	23
Windham	30.6	43.8	11.0	2.6	22.4	15.8	484	40.5	4.3	53.3	89.3	64	-13.1	133	0	34

1. Covers mining, construction, and manufacturing. 2. Covers private sector earnings in agricultural services, forestry, and fisheries; transportation and public utilities; wholesale trade; retail trade; finance, insurance, and real estate; and services.

STATE County	Agriculture, 1987 (cont'd) — Value of land and buildings — Average per farm ($1,000)	Average per acre (Dollars)	Value of products sold — Total (Mil dol)	Average per farm (Dollars)	Percent from — Crops	Livestock and poultry[1]	Percent of farms with sales of — $10,000 or more	$100,000 or more	Manufactures, 1987 — Establishments — Total	Percent with 20 or more employees	All employees — Number (1,000)	Percent change, 1982–1987	Annual payroll (Mil dol)	Production workers — Number (1,000)	Work hours (Mil)
	119	120	121	122	123	124	125	126	127	128	129	130	131	132	133
COLORADO—Con.															
Clear Creek	645	842	D	D	NA	NA	27.3	0.0	8	12.5	0.1	0.0	1.1	0.0	0.1
Conejos	391	549	19	42 953	34.4	65.7	53.1	10.5	8	25.0	0.1	0.0	1.0	0.1	0.1
Costilla	421	263	12	61 390	83.2	16.8	39.8	9.9	NA	NA	NA	NA	NA	NA	NA
Crowley	312	178	88	469 027	3.1	96.9	64.2	21.9	1	0.0	D	D	D	D	D
Custer	415	481	5	38 956	21.7	78.3	56.2	9.2	2	0.0	D	D	D	D	D
Delta	228	720	30	33 197	42.3	57.7	38.0	7.3	31	19.4	D	D	D	D	D
Denver	181	D	2	118 446	D	D	47.1	29.4	1 146	26.9	37.9	-14.3	935.9	20.4	39.0
Dolores	355	304	4	33 934	60.4	39.6	63.1	5.4	2	0.0	D	D	D	D	D
Douglas	623	1 342	9	19 512	24.2	75.8	27.1	4.2	61	23.0	0.9	0.0	19.2	0.5	1.0
Eagle	1 068	689	6	42 259	4.9	95.1	41.5	9.5	29	20.7	0.3	50.0	5.8	0.2	0.4
Elbert	453	312	26	38 654	12.6	87.4	48.6	10.8	7	28.6	0.1	0.0	1.7	0.1	0.2
El Paso	413	336	24	33 132	26.4	73.6	38.3	7.6	419	23.9	22.2	20.0	532.9	13.3	25.6
Fremont	244	353	10	24 087	24.2	75.8	30.1	3.6	51	27.5	1.2	0.0	21.2	0.9	1.7
Garfield	497	481	17	34 871	15.9	84.1	47.9	8.1	37	18.9	0.4	0.0	7.9	0.2	0.4
Gilpin	463	447	0	6 337	0.0	100.0	13.3	0.0	2	0.0	D	D	D	D	D
Grand	884	452	8	49 895	8.7	91.3	56.4	10.4	21	9.5	0.2	100.0	4.4	0.1	0.3
Gunnison	706	546	10	55 614	3.1	96.9	53.8	13.9	14	0.0	0.1	0.0	1.0	0.0	0.1
Hinsdale	789	1 275	0	25 201	1.2	99.0	62.5	0.0	1	0.0	D	D	D	D	D
Huerfano	542	226	8	31 695	3.8	96.2	48.1	8.6	3	0.0	0.0	0.0	0.2	0.0	0.0
Jackson	1 664	464	14	109 416	11.1	88.9	69.0	27.0	11	9.1	0.1	0.0	3.6	0.1	0.3
Jefferson	356	1 208	15	33 682	83.3	16.7	24.4	7.0	451	18.8	31.5	5.4	1 183.7	19.6	39.6
Kiowa	615	189	21	64 978	49.4	50.6	71.3	19.5	2	0.0	D	D	D	D	D
Kit Carson	512	268	127	159 613	35.1	64.9	78.2	30.9	11	9.1	0.1	0.0	1.6	0.1	0.1
Lake	658	834	1	38 671	D	D	28.6	7.1	4	0.0	0.0	0.0	0.1	0.0	0.0
La Plata	518	570	16	23 520	17.6	82.4	35.2	4.8	40	15.0	D	D	D	D	D
Larimer	351	798	90	73 146	20.0	80.0	36.0	10.7	274	24.8	12.5	-1.6	336.5	6.3	13.2
Las Animas	524	112	21	43 339	10.0	90.0	49.7	11.0	5	0.0	0.0	-100.0	0.3	0.0	0.0
Lincoln	493	154	57	116 706	24.6	75.4	76.5	24.3	1	0.0	D	D	D	D	D
Logan	337	311	191	202 311	16.8	83.2	76.7	21.0	26	30.8	D	D	D	D	D
Mesa	291	783	39	32 096	38.2	61.8	36.4	6.8	107	19.6	2.3	-20.7	40.7	1.5	2.8
Mineral	591	540	0	16 491	D	D	36.4	0.0	1	0.0	D	D	D	D	D
Moffat	566	182	15	43 958	16.2	83.8	48.5	10.0	12	8.3	0.1	0.0	1.6	0.0	0.1
Montezuma	350	263	11	17 831	38.2	61.8	36.4	3.0	38	18.4	0.5	66.7	6.0	0.4	0.7
Montrose	272	535	46	55 633	27.3	72.7	48.5	10.4	34	26.5	0.8	33.3	11.7	0.6	1.2
Morgan	361	369	276	345 288	13.9	86.1	78.2	29.6	26	23.1	D	D	D	D	D
Otero	349	257	79	161 427	15.7	84.3	56.0	17.7	28	25.0	0.8	-33.3	12.0	0.6	1.2
Ouray	1 101	606	3	38 428	5.8	94.2	53.4	10.2	8	12.5	D	D	D	D	D
Park	793	361	4	22 183	10.6	89.4	37.0	4.3	11	0.0	0.0	0.0	0.3	0.0	0.0
Phillips	440	398	55	133 073	56.0	44.0	79.4	30.0	5	20.0	0.1	0.0	1.0	0.0	0.0
Pitkin	646	1 353	2	23 254	9.6	90.4	35.7	2.9	26	7.7	0.2	0.0	2.7	0.1	0.2
Prowers	564	314	144	282 330	16.7	83.3	72.2	21.0	18	44.4	0.9	28.6	16.1	0.7	1.4
Pueblo	336	253	38	62 422	23.4	76.6	39.7	10.9	95	17.9	3.6	-36.8	85.7	2.4	5.2
Rio Blanco	569	274	15	63 875	6.9	93.1	53.2	19.9	8	0.0	0.0	-100.0	0.5	0.0	0.0
Rio Grande	669	937	35	102 186	85.4	14.6	68.4	28.1	19	15.8	0.3	-25.0	4.3	0.2	0.4
Routt	668	444	20	48 782	8.8	91.2	49.1	10.9	20	5.0	0.1	0.0	1.6	0.1	0.1
Saguache	713	377	36	142 066	72.3	27.7	67.3	29.1	3	0.0	0.0	0.0	0.1	0.0	0.0
San Juan	214	D	D	D	NA	NA	100.0	0.0	1	0.0	D	D	D	D	D
San Miguel	765	379	3	39 947	10.5	89.5	46.4	13.1	3	0.0	D	D	D	D	D
Sedgwick	374	345	31	119 427	53.2	46.8	84.8	30.8	3	0.0	D	D	D	D	D
Summit	1 223	747	1	54 939	5.9	94.0	52.4	19.0	13	7.7	0.1	0.0	1.1	0.0	0.1
Teller	596	479	1	16 630	2.1	97.9	40.3	1.5	11	0.0	0.0	0.0	0.6	0.0	0.0
Washington	451	287	84	98 769	46.7	53.3	78.7	21.9	8	12.5	D	D	D	D	D
Weld	438	621	865	290 623	14.0	86.0	66.6	24.9	142	22.5	7.9	16.2	202.0	5.0	9.7
Yuma	509	341	180	184 869	40.6	59.4	80.9	34.1	12	8.3	0.1	0.0	1.2	0.1	0.1
CONNECTICUT	468	4 171	358	99 917	46.0	54.0	41.5	14.8	6 747	36.5	388.9	-8.4	11 110.6	216.5	440.6
Fairfield	465	8 170	15	58 530	42.7	57.3	35.6	10.7	1 796	36.9	117.0	-11.7	3 813.6	52.5	105.6
Hartford	497	5 701	89	135 411	76.0	24.0	46.6	15.9	1 733	38.0	112.5	-8.2	3 230.6	62.7	128.4
Litchfield	560	3 474	28	45 771	22.9	77.1	41.0	12.1	488	30.3	18.3	-8.5	414.5	13.4	26.5
Middlesex	490	4 343	30	115 755	80.8	19.2	23.2	9.3	335	35.2	15.8	-6.5	416.9	10.8	22.5
New Haven	428	6 506	30	73 181	76.4	23.6	42.8	12.5	1 795	36.8	76.2	-8.4	1 943.7	47.8	97.3
New London	397	3 152	99	177 176	29.4	70.6	41.4	16.5	255	38.0	34.2	-2.6	973.6	18.3	39.0
Tolland	458	3 832	21	63 104	19.8	80.2	37.3	14.2	161	24.8	4.4	37.5	94.4	3.0	6.1
Windham	421	3 216	46	94 339	8.7	91.3	50.4	22.1	184	41.8	10.4	-4.6	223.3	8.0	15.3

1. Includes livestock and poultry products.

STATE County	Manufactures, 1987 (cont'd) — Production workers (cont'd) — Wages — Total (Mil dol)	Average per worker (Dollars)	Value added by manu-facture (Mil dol)	Value of shipments (Mil dol)	New capital expend-itures (Mil dol)	Value of construction authorized by building permits, 1990 — Total[1] ($1,000)	Nonresidential — Total ($1,000)	Nonresidential — Percent — Office	Industrial	Stores	Residential — New construction ($1,000)	Number of housing units	Alterations and additions ($1,000)
	134	135	136	137	138	139	140	141	142	143	144	145	146
COLORADO—Con.													
Clear Creek	0.6	NA	2.4	4.0	0.1	2 809	75	0.0	0.0	100.0	1 517	24	492
Conejos	0.7	7 000	2.9	5.7	D	35	0	NA	NA	NA	20	1	6
Costilla	NA	NA	NA	NA	NA	NA	NA	NA	NA	NA	NA	NA	NA
Crowley	D	D	D	D	D	48	0	NA	NA	NA	40	1	8
Custer	D	D	D	D	D	387	0	NA	NA	NA	0	0	72
Delta	D	D	D	D	D	2 175	1 663	0.0	0.0	94.4	191	5	134
Denver	397.6	19 490	2 034.8	3 798.2	109.1	167 427	15 310	18.9	5.8	22.0	15 852	198	19 772
Dolores	D	D	D	D	D	NA	NA	NA	NA	NA	NA	NA	NA
Douglas	9.7	19 400	53.1	98.4	3.9	194 460	5 515	30.3	6.5	4.1	183 248	1 587	2 490
Eagle	3.4	17 000	10.2	18.0	0.4	102 405	8 968	13.1	5.1	42.2	79 471	643	1 903
Elbert	1.3	13 000	3.7	7.4	0.1	9 830	1 587	7.9	0.0	0.4	7 665	97	492
El Paso	258.2	19 414	1 136.6	2 111.9	97.9	152 459	17 632	38.0	1.8	12.8	87 655	1 049	7 802
Fremont	13.8	15 333	74.2	118.3	3.2	8 761	385	10.4	0.0	0.0	6 563	132	1 326
Garfield	4.8	24 000	17.5	31.4	0.7	24 270	1 677	13.1	12.1	16.7	16 006	220	1 710
Gilpin	D	D	D	D	D	1 861	9	0.0	0.0	0.0	1 260	16	415
Grand	3.4	34 000	7.4	21.6	0.5	8 155	526	0.0	0.0	65.6	4 074	63	1 703
Gunnison	0.6	NA	2.4	4.3	D	16 808	1 717	33.6	2.7	52.6	13 238	164	1 137
Hinsdale	D	D	D	D	D	1 495	0	NA	NA	NA	1 252	13	133
Huerfano	0.1	NA	0.3	0.5	0.0	1 092	184	0.0	0.0	0.0	445	11	181
Jackson	3.3	33 000	5.5	12.0	0.1	1 289	104	0.0	0.0	0.0	531	11	542
Jefferson	641.1	32 709	2 838.0	4 447.5	241.9	218 070	25 913	29.0	3.6	37.9	155 860	1 622	12 616
Kiowa	D	D	D	D	D	38	1	0.0	0.0	0.0	0	0	26
Kit Carson	1.1	11 000	3.9	12.0	0.2	631	267	84.2	3.7	0.0	203	3	54
Lake	0.1	NA	0.3	0.4	0.0	1 103	34	0.0	19.1	0.0	249	3	273
La Plata	D	D	D	D	D	24 338	2 692	3.8	36.1	18.3	17 826	249	2 593
Larimer	149.1	23 667	694.6	1 124.3	40.4	149 840	16 406	10.1	31.0	28.0	85 567	1 236	6 427
Las Animas	0.1	NA	0.8	1.2	0.0	3 180	992	57.2	0.0	29.8	2 003	46	125
Lincoln	D	D	D	D	D	2 090	951	9.2	0.0	87.6	725	11	161
Logan	D	D	D	D	D	2 840	297	0.0	0.0	36.1	741	12	129
Mesa	21.1	14 067	103.2	169.1	7.6	43 759	10 575	2.9	43.9	19.2	20 995	267	4 924
Mineral	D	D	D	D	D	1 024	190	0.0	0.0	0.0	448	10	79
Moffat	0.7	NA	2.8	4.5	0.1	1 861	721	29.8	0.0	0.0	598	7	354
Montezuma	4.7	11 750	19.5	32.1	0.4	1 547	350	0.0	0.0	42.8	605	10	184
Montrose	8.2	13 667	36.1	66.9	0.7	7 927	1 510	0.0	17.8	18.9	5 139	104	542
Morgan	D	D	D	D	D	3 303	1 096	4.6	0.0	49.9	858	9	117
Otero	8.2	13 667	21.2	54.4	0.6	1 921	247	11.0	0.0	0.0	210	5	287
Ouray	D	D	D	D	D	4 169	229	0.0	0.0	93.7	2 590	32	746
Park	0.2	NA	0.6	1.0	0.0	11 809	821	4.5	0.0	31.5	9 154	124	1 099
Phillips	0.3	NA	2.0	2.9	D	938	498	0.0	0.0	0.0	253	6	106
Pitkin	1.3	13 000	5.9	9.5	0.3	90 236	2 413	0.0	1.7	38.9	60 652	176	15 958
Prowers	10.5	15 000	38.4	115.6	0.6	551	44	35.3	54.4	0.0	100	1	10
Pueblo	57.4	23 917	230.7	467.2	12.3	23 526	4 243	3.6	23.2	27.6	10 355	224	1 491
Rio Blanco	0.3	NA	0.7	1.1	0.0	1 509	828	0.0	67.0	0.0	389	8	218
Rio Grande	3.4	17 000	14.9	29.5	2.2	400	132	0.0	0.0	98.9	0	0	82
Routt	0.8	8 000	3.8	6.4	0.2	29 204	6 141	0.0	22.5	76.6	17 104	187	2 271
Saguache	0.1	NA	0.2	0.5	0.0	301	53	0.0	47.2	0.0	0	0	31
San Juan	D	D	D	D	D	225	0	NA	NA	NA	74	2	107
San Miguel	D	D	D	D	D	52 986	1 482	0.0	0.0	86.5	22 596	137	1 908
Sedgwick	D	D	D	D	D	891	607	0.0	0.0	35.2	155	2	40
Summit	0.6	NA	2.8	4.7	0.1	45 953	10 666	24.6	0.0	71.9	29 428	248	1 864
Teller	0.3	NA	1.6	2.5	0.0	5 682	812	56.1	0.0	8.5	3 678	68	336
Washington	D	D	D	D	D	176	0	NA	NA	NA	140	3	7
Weld	104.2	20 840	1 457.4	3 037.1	33.6	50 230	14 244	11.9	65.2	5.3	20 458	271	4 174
Yuma	0.6	6 000	3.5	6.0	0.1	1 985	1 681	0.0	9.3	0.9	80	1	135
CONNECTICUT	4 825.6	22 289	22 348.9	37 400.3	1 293.3	1 834 908	309 974	21.6	9.4	23.2	648 770	7 584	350 261
Fairfield	1 201.1	22 878	6 441.4	10 833.0	303.5	531 463	78 256	22.7	5.6	24.1	149 925	1 461	139 468
Hartford	1 475.0	23 525	6 484.2	10 832.6	428.1	453 398	109 675	31.1	10.2	14.3	129 381	1 468	67 925
Litchfield	260.4	19 433	1 311.4	2 228.8	94.4	140 923	23 942	17.1	5.4	28.6	72 821	851	29 182
Middlesex	256.3	23 731	1 089.9	1 800.6	44.4	76 525	5 731	15.2	8.0	13.0	38 786	401	18 169
New Haven	983.3	20 571	4 247.5	7 374.4	295.5	386 153	58 811	11.9	10.6	35.5	129 173	1 875	52 737
New London	440.1	24 049	1 985.0	2 930.9	87.3	131 249	22 630	6.6	17.1	33.3	62 450	751	25 126
Tolland	55.4	18 467	209.9	379.4	16.1	55 544	5 706	18.3	25.0	12.8	35 500	357	9 711
Windham	154.0	19 250	579.6	1 020.5	24.1	59 654	5 223	12.8	7.2	13.1	30 733	420	7 944

1. Includes nonresidential additions and alterations, residential nonhousekeeping buildings, and residential garages and carports not shown separately.

STATE County	Wholesale trade, 1987: Establishments	Wholesale trade, 1987: Sales (Mil dol)	Wholesale trade, 1987: Paid employees[1]	Wholesale trade, 1987: Annual payroll (Mil dol)	Retail trade, all establishments, 1987: Number	Retail trade, all establishments, 1987: Sales: Total (Mil dol)	Retail trade, all establishments, 1987: Sales: Percent change, 1982–1987	Retail trade, all establishments, 1987: Sales: Per capita[2] (Dollars)	Retail trade, establishments with payroll, 1987: Number	Retail trade, establishments with payroll, 1987: Sales: Total (Mil dol)	Sales: Per capita[2] (Dollars): General merchandise stores	Sales: Per capita[2] (Dollars): Food stores	Sales: Per capita[2] (Dollars): Apparel & accessory stores	Sales: Per capita[2] (Dollars): Eating and drinking places
	147	148	149	150	151	152	153	154	155	156	157	158	159	160
COLORADO—Con.														
Clear Creek	11	13.5	53	1.3	145	26.8	-6.3	3 675	71	23.8	D	D	63	900
Conejos	6	7.2	132	0.8	82	14.4	12.5	1 782	30	12.2	D	681	0	56
Costilla	2	D	D	D	37	2.2	-31.2	678	10	1.3	D	D	0	D
Crowley	3	D	D	D	33	4.6	35.3	1 476	10	3.8	0	D	D	121
Custer	0	0.0	0	0.0	42	4.7	27.0	2 461	19	3.9	D	D	0	139
Delta	29	83.2	244	3.5	283	70.9	-10.6	3 223	144	65.6	285	1 027	D	211
Denver	2 028	11 108.0	28 205	685.5	5 115	3 300.8	16.8	6 584	3 527	3 224.0	686	1 448	364	1 077
Dolores	4	D	D	D	21	4.4	10.0	2 909	10	3.7	0	D	0	151
Douglas	70	64.3	321	5.8	404	156.5	123.6	3 718	181	147.1	D	1 178	D	330
Eagle	25	20.1	135	2.0	449	219.6	29.6	13 308	345	213.0	53	2 521	1 540	3 113
Elbert	19	35.9	115	1.3	78	12.4	121.4	1 365	21	10.3	0	328	0	D
El Paso	537	986.4	4 483	88.8	3 825	2 423.3	46.6	6 191	2 458	2 362.3	786	1 010	262	615
Fremont	35	22.6	177	2.6	372	105.8	13.4	3 207	190	97.8	215	913	92	387
Garfield	48	61.4	289	4.8	455	218.8	9.0	7 899	290	212.0	417	1 755	175	769
Gilpin	1	D	D	D	54	5.2	33.3	1 846	26	3.9	0	0	D	D
Grand	12	6.7	40	0.6	216	55.8	14.3	6 412	146	53.3	D	1 812	197	1 128
Gunnison	6	D	D	D	222	60.3	-3.8	6 031	136	58.1	387	D	214	941
Hinsdale	0	0.0	0	0.0	28	2.7	8.0	5 434	12	2.2	0	D	0	1 194
Huerfano	6	D	D	D	113	22.5	-3.0	3 307	61	20.0	0	1 173	41	277
Jackson	5	D	D	D	45	6.6	-4.3	3 868	12	5.2	0	D	D	422
Jefferson	658	1 661.3	4 401	108.3	4 171	2 808.0	23.5	6 573	2 408	2 734.9	781	1 403	276	686
Kiowa	13	D	D	D	22	3.4	-24.4	1 786	11	2.5	0	D	0	D
Kit Carson	37	95.2	326	4.8	109	43.6	15.6	5 740	66	41.8	D	1 494	165	189
Lake	5	D	D	D	99	23.5	-21.7	3 725	60	22.4	D	1 267	25	531
La Plata	68	89.2	503	8.2	509	218.6	24.3	6 961	319	209.1	373	1 856	223	857
Larimer	293	522.9	2 006	39.1	2 154	1 136.8	47.0	6 347	1 269	1 101.9	611	1 275	214	656
Las Animas	16	22.4	136	1.6	189	53.1	31.1	3 796	104	50.4	D	1 141	D	216
Lincoln	13	22.8	76	1.1	81	37.7	-3.8	8 025	47	35.9	0	1 098	D	1 568
Logan	55	192.0	517	9.3	248	110.8	7.6	5 894	148	105.6	914	840	288	510
Mesa	198	348.4	1 557	28.4	971	545.4	-8.0	6 101	597	526.3	782	975	200	904
Mineral	0	0.0	0	0.0	23	3.1	-3.1	4 369	12	2.8	0	D	0	D
Moffat	27	29.5	138	2.5	154	63.7	-28.8	5 219	87	61.5	D	1 668	231	453
Montezuma	32	24.9	154	2.2	242	109.8	7.2	5 782	151	105.0	D	1 013	134	583
Montrose	38	48.0	264	3.9	310	135.7	13.4	5 384	180	130.6	396	1 496	170	502
Morgan	59	499.1	1 286	18.2	284	98.1	-15.2	4 284	169	91.3	477	1 123	166	388
Otero	52	127.6	359	5.3	251	80.1	4.3	3 693	156	76.9	D	986	122	329
Ouray	0	0.0	0	0.0	65	10.4	85.7	4 968	43	8.4	D	516	D	1 153
Park	7	D	D	D	101	12.7	29.6	1 760	30	9.9	D	D	D	243
Phillips	15	55.4	126	2.7	69	21.8	18.5	5 065	37	20.5	D	1 215	0	199
Pitkin	21	31.6	149	3.4	409	192.7	42.4	18 009	298	186.0	D	2 350	2 383	5 182
Prowers	43	76.3	372	6.3	188	78.3	10.4	5 591	118	75.0	D	1 386	224	401
Pueblo	137	247.8	1 347	23.3	1 252	690.9	27.7	5 423	842	671.7	786	1 246	170	548
Rio Blanco	11	6.1	41	0.7	83	18.8	-17.9	2 894	44	17.3	0	1 382	D	328
Rio Grande	36	95.6	739	7.7	148	47.2	8.0	3 998	89	45.1	158	1 324	120	273
Routt	22	24.7	144	2.9	319	121.6	37.9	9 141	195	115.5	150	1 956	856	1 544
Saguache	13	22.4	180	2.0	55	11.9	63.0	2 841	24	11.0	D	D	D	105
San Juan	0	0.0	0	0.0	38	4.3	10.3	4 286	19	3.1	0	D	D	1 034
San Miguel	2	D	D	D	101	22.3	79.8	6 761	57	20.2	0	1 616	327	1 702
Sedgwick	13	26.2	59	1.1	57	18.7	9.4	6 448	31	17.9	D	1 226	D	604
Summit	21	14.3	69	1.5	421	160.6	40.1	14 738	295	155.4	D	2 652	913	3 319
Teller	9	D	D	D	222	46.6	52.8	3 849	117	41.9	D	1 337	50	570
Washington	18	35.3	136	2.5	67	12.2	-17.0	2 264	32	10.3	136	D	D	237
Weld	241	583.1	1 970	35.0	1 100	591.0	29.3	4 355	672	570.2	591	1 051	117	418
Yuma	35	102.8	279	4.7	153	43.8	0.2	4 561	89	40.7	153	1 246	140	252
CONNECTICUT	6 138	49 235.6	84 714	2 384.5	32 816	25 785.1	62.9	8 029	21 688	25 101.8	815	1 402	470	651
Fairfield	1 926	29 767.2	28 151	922.9	8 627	7 465.6	61.3	9 119	5 838	7 272.6	931	1 579	638	676
Hartford	1 672	9 233.2	26 806	727.2	8 055	6 926.4	59.5	8 270	5 500	6 780.8	912	1 279	494	721
Litchfield	253	897.6	2 057	46.9	2 027	1 162.5	77.5	7 101	1 175	1 115.9	436	1 385	233	486
Middlesex	211	512.1	1 863	41.2	1 557	1 113.6	78.3	8 093	969	1 081.0	636	1 410	309	659
New Haven	1 577	7 734.3	21 518	548.8	7 817	5 981.1	62.3	7 580	5 222	5 811.3	831	1 400	443	625
New London	261	636.5	2 701	63.7	2 687	1 882.3	62.7	7 680	1 822	1 833.6	775	1 348	404	672
Tolland	120	231.0	688	15.2	1 061	642.8	64.7	5 222	580	620.5	437	1 202	182	445
Windham	118	223.7	930	18.6	985	610.8	76.0	6 297	582	586.1	334	1 387	222	523

1. For pay period including March 12. 2. Based on the estimated population as of July 1 of the year shown.

STATE County	Retail trade, establishments with payroll, 1987 (cont'd)		Taxable service industries–establishments with payroll, 1987							Bank deposits,[2] June 1989		Savings capital,[3] September 1989	
				Receipts (Mil dol)									
					Selected kinds of business								
	Paid employees[1]	Annual payroll (Mil dol)	Number	Total	Hotels, motels and other lodging places	Health services	Legal services	Paid employees	Annual payroll (Mil dol)	Total (Mil dol)	Percent change, 1988–1989	Total (Mil dol)	Percent change, 1988–1989
	161	162	163	164	165	166	167	168	169	170	171	172	173
COLORADO—Con.													
Clear Creek	595	3.7	41	16.6	1.4	0.8	D	561	7.1	17	9.2	0.0	NA
Conejos	117	1.2	17	1.6	0.2	D	D	49	0.6	16	5.2	0.0	NA
Costilla	22	0.1	4	0.2	D	0.0	D	9	0.1	4	0.8	0.0	NA
Crowley	53	0.3	5	0.3	0.0	D	0.0	11	0.1	17	74.1	0.0	NA
Custer	48	0.3	7	0.7	D	D	0.0	22	0.2	6	5.4	0.0	NA
Delta	793	6.9	104	13.8	D	5.9	0.9	358	4.0	124	2.9	89.5	-2.7
Denver	48 853	505.5	6 471	3 927.6	261.6	695.7	619.4	78 075	1 517.6	7 407	1.1	2 687.8	-37.8
Dolores	50	0.4	1	D	0.0	0.0	0.0	D	D	10	2.2	0.0	NA
Douglas	1 778	17.2	294	52.7	D	11.2	2.4	1 172	18.3	170	3.9	220.4	29.6
Eagle	4 026	35.9	242	153.0	52.2	8.8	1.9	5 100	51.0	185	9.0	2.3	-53.8
Elbert	101	1.1	45	7.4	0.0	0.4	D	362	2.9	24	-4.9	0.0	NA
El Paso	29 251	302.5	3 094	1 181.1	98.6	273.0	64.3	27 353	475.2	1 727	-1.3	1 663.0	7.5
Fremont	1 464	12.5	183	40.4	5.4	14.3	1.6	1 168	13.7	157	1.2	146.4	-2.0
Garfield	2 455	24.5	309	69.8	14.8	16.3	6.4	1 836	26.2	212	13.1	68.8	-3.4
Gilpin	69	0.8	17	2.5	D	D	0.0	60	0.6	NA	NA	0.0	NA
Grand	1 110	8.1	139	37.5	5.6	3.1	2.1	1 529	13.3	53	-9.7	6.2	-16.3
Gunnison	1 113	7.8	122	32.5	12.9	3.2	1.4	1 353	10.5	63	2.6	47.5	3.0
Hinsdale	24	0.2	7	0.8	D	0.0	0.0	14	0.1	7	12.5	0.0	NA
Huerfano	261	2.3	32	4.4	1.1	1.8	0.4	204	1.6	21	-5.7	27.3	-2.3
Jackson	75	0.6	5	0.3	D	D	D	6	0.1	8	-1.2	0.0	NA
Jefferson	33 780	338.7	3 390	1 069.2	33.8	247.4	41.3	26 457	432.0	1 792	-0.3	1 673.8	-0.5
Kiowa	49	0.3	11	0.8	D	0.4	D	23	0.2	11	5.5	0.0	NA
Kit Carson	422	4.0	46	7.8	1.8	2.5	1.1	236	2.2	92	0.7	36.1	-1.0
Lake	314	2.8	37	6.3	1.8	1.7	0.7	199	1.9	26	1.5	7.5	-2.0
La Plata	2 986	28.1	396	102.2	30.6	22.7	5.5	2 985	34.9	199	5.2	55.5	-23.3
Larimer	14 593	138.7	1 558	358.0	23.0	105.5	19.5	9 854	135.4	879	1.6	516.3	-7.3
Las Animas	700	5.3	66	9.6	2.0	2.9	D	272	2.5	80	12.2	58.2	0.4
Lincoln	432	4.6	18	2.8	1.9	D	D	40	0.5	60	-0.4	6.9	14.0
Logan	1 393	11.8	146	28.8	3.1	10.1	1.1	776	9.9	160	-3.2	81.7	5.3
Mesa	7 225	70.5	717	183.1	16.8	53.5	14.1	4 835	72.1	430	7.3	419.9	1.6
Mineral	44	0.4	8	0.9	D	0.0	0.0	14	0.3	NA	NA	0.0	NA
Moffat	753	7.0	92	12.5	2.3	5.6	0.8	370	3.7	47	-2.6	25.6	-32.7
Montezuma	1 229	12.4	132	19.3	4.9	5.0	1.4	466	5.6	162	2.6	19.3	-22.8
Montrose	1 561	15.4	207	36.5	3.3	13.9	2.3	955	11.9	196	23.0	67.4	-3.4
Morgan	1 244	10.7	133	29.9	2.5	16.1	1.9	912	10.6	159	0.1	107.8	6.8
Otero	1 104	8.7	118	16.7	1.5	8.2	1.4	467	5.7	134	-6.0	110.4	-4.7
Ouray	176	1.2	26	3.1	1.9	D	D	79	0.6	14	-0.6	0.0	NA
Park	140	1.2	24	2.4	0.8	D	D	78	0.6	8	11.6	0.0	NA
Phillips	203	1.8	24	2.3	D	1.2	D	90	0.7	48	1.7	20.9	0.9
Pitkin	3 930	34.8	308	149.3	38.9	8.2	9.3	4 134	42.7	210	23.0	97.1	50.9
Prowers	929	8.7	90	16.3	3.1	4.3	1.9	502	5.1	140	5.1	44.2	-7.1
Pueblo	8 621	81.4	804	193.4	12.4	90.6	11.3	5 333	72.1	608	5.8	388.8	-25.4
Rio Blanco	278	2.1	31	3.1	0.8	0.8	D	80	0.9	39	-11.3	5.5	NA
Rio Grande	567	4.9	92	12.0	2.4	3.5	1.0	320	3.9	52	26.1	57.7	0.4
Routt	2 132	16.5	165	66.8	16.0	4.6	2.8	2 119	20.2	133	11.8	21.5	-37.0
Saguache	113	1.0	6	0.6	D	D	D	15	0.1	15	17.6	0.0	NA
San Juan	31	0.4	4	D	D	0.0	0.0	D	D	2	-21.0	0.0	NA
San Miguel	494	3.4	37	7.2	1.9	D	0.6	122	1.7	26	3.2	0.0	NA
Sedgwick	194	1.8	21	2.1	D	0.5	D	58	0.4	20	-2.9	36.7	3.8
Summit	3 250	25.3	207	124.7	44.6	4.9	2.6	3 859	36.7	87	12.5	37.4	3.3
Teller	619	4.7	74	10.1	3.2	2.5	D	257	3.0	44	10.3	16.1	7.5
Washington	147	1.1	18	1.4	0.1	0.4	D	43	0.5	57	0.2	25.7	1.8
Weld	7 381	69.2	697	165.6	5.3	57.7	7.5	4 326	61.7	702	3.2	286.6	6.6
Yuma	445	4.0	59	7.8	0.4	3.5	0.3	214	2.2	105	-0.5	38.1	5.0
CONNECTICUT	267 611	3 081.1	25 756	12 692.3	458.0	2 819.4	1 033.1	250 198	4 888.4	60 168	6.9	4 810.7	-5.3
Fairfield	71 464	918.8	8 304	4 791.6	158.9	775.8	338.3	75 232	1 732.6	17 702	-4.2	763.0	-0.8
Hartford	74 544	839.1	6 718	3 892.6	136.1	846.3	361.1	78 582	1 568.7	19 322	21.3	2 523.3	-15.1
Litchfield	11 034	130.1	1 225	329.5	15.9	99.6	26.7	7 591	114.6	2 456	3.9	274.9	12.6
Middlesex	11 476	131.0	1 005	330.3	17.5	118.2	17.9	7 585	127.0	2 118	2.8	8.8	1.0
New Haven	64 042	693.8	5 933	2 409.1	70.3	730.2	209.8	59 858	975.3	13 701	7.4	728.6	21.5
New London	20 955	226.3	1 506	639.9	51.9	159.1	61.0	14 532	266.7	2 767	3.9	317.7	0.4
Tolland	7 449	73.7	605	172.9	5.4	38.5	9.0	3 694	59.7	1 202	6.8	63.9	44.9
Windham	6 647	68.2	460	126.3	2.2	51.6	9.3	3 124	43.7	899	3.8	130.5	3.2

1. For the period including March 12 of the year shown. 2. Includes deposits for all insured and reporting noninsured commercial and mutual savings banks. 3. Includes savings capital for all FSLIC insured savings institutions.

STATE County	Federal funds and grants, 1989: Expenditures: Total (Mil dol)	Expenditures: Percent change, 1988–1989	Per capita[1] (Dollars): Total	Per capita: Direct payments for individuals	Per capita: Procurement contract awards	Per capita: Salaries and wages	Per capita: Grant awards	Local government finances, 1981–1982: General revenue: Total (Mil dol)	Intergovernmental: Total (Mil dol)	Intergovernmental: Percent from state	Taxes: Total (Mil dol)	Taxes: Per capita[2]: Total (Dollars)	Taxes: Per capita[2]: Property (Dollars)	Direct general expenditure: Total (Mil dol)	Direct general expenditure: Percent change, 1977–1982
	174	175	176	177	178	179	180	181	182	183	184	185	186	187	188
COLORADO—Con.															
Clear Creek	12.1	3.4	1 702	819	12	149	717	11.0	1.8	81.7	7.5	1 011	864	10.3	99.7
Conejos	19.7	-1.1	2 405	1 516	14	147	682	11.9	7.5	96.4	1.5	193	169	11.8	72.8
Costilla	11.2	-3.5	3 516	2 173	30	167	1 055	5.4	3.3	95.6	1.7	525	494	5.3	61.9
Crowley	10.7	-5.7	3 232	2 149	22	161	401	3.0	1.7	95.3	1.0	318	291	3.1	57.2
Custer	5.3	8.6	2 771	2 210	19	158	339	2.1	0.9	85.8	0.8	490	455	2.1	93.3
Delta	70.6	3.6	3 313	2 415	147	261	356	29.1	10.5	91.7	8.3	353	266	38.4	195.8
Denver	4 428.5	4.6	9 133	2 228	4 309	1 373	1 191	931.6	272.5	61.3	426.3	842	431	717.1	33.1
Dolores	12.1	101.5	8 085	2 010	4 345	174	359	2.7	1.7	94.7	0.8	469	430	2.8	52.7
Douglas	51.3	11.3	1 049	686	74	83	200	34.6	10.2	96.5	15.9	552	516	42.1	218.5
Eagle	23.4	52.7	1 366	568	30	202	555	40.8	5.6	53.6	22.5	1 450	944	43.9	165.3
Elbert	16.4	-18.0	1 655	923	99	112	217	7.6	3.3	95.7	3.3	436	423	7.5	72.8
El Paso	2 445.2	12.0	6 078	1 775	1 543	2 564	186	348.8	135.6	79.9	126.2	381	288	327.2	70.7
Fremont	93.6	5.0	2 826	2 333	27	148	306	32.4	16.3	68.3	9.8	328	263	32.6	133.2
Garfield	197.4	210.9	6 784	1 477	30	272	4 982	39.0	17.8	84.9	13.8	480	342	38.4	135.4
Gilpin	3.0	-47.7	1 057	668	11	84	289	2.8	0.9	90.1	1.6	588	472	2.5	141.1
Grand	18.2	3.0	2 191	1 116	604	337	122	19.5	5.4	40.7	8.7	1 050	845	22.9	158.8
Gunnison	18.4	10.4	1 883	1 048	80	300	444	13.8	3.3	83.5	6.4	577	362	15.9	157.2
Hinsdale	1.0	-24.5	2 096	1 652	78	222	130	0.9	0.4	98.5	0.4	782	602	1.0	148.1
Huerfano	21.8	10.0	3 357	2 437	10	80	783	9.1	4.8	82.6	3.1	453	389	7.8	55.2
Jackson	3.3	10.6	2 056	1 491	38	390	114	3.7	1.6	89.0	1.4	799	680	3.3	75.8
Jefferson	1 494.2	5.3	3 450	1 012	1 405	899	131	416.0	129.6	91.3	206.5	526	397	397.0	84.6
Kiowa	14.7	-31.8	7 752	1 749	62	270	143	4.3	1.0	95.1	2.1	1 053	1 036	4.2	100.5
Kit Carson	37.0	-20.1	4 995	1 740	63	235	163	12.2	4.0	85.9	5.0	638	586	12.4	47.3
Lake	9.6	-19.1	1 719	1 276	57	281	101	22.9	7.1	86.2	10.6	1 233	1 162	22.8	65.1
La Plata	68.7	6.6	2 194	1 433	90	324	305	38.3	11.0	87.4	14.9	504	331	38.9	101.3
Larimer	391.7	7.8	2 111	1 247	154	315	383	201.4	52.6	85.1	76.9	486	353	189.6	91.3
Las Animas	51.2	5.6	3 762	2 642	62	227	721	16.3	9.4	95.3	5.2	339	266	17.5	46.9
Lincoln	21.0	-8.5	4 576	1 900	20	256	869	8.8	3.0	95.3	3.2	693	601	8.1	87.3
Logan	50.8	-18.7	2 806	1 793	59	194	284	31.7	12.4	71.3	11.4	572	493	35.1	103.9
Mesa	298.5	7.2	3 287	1 884	773	395	200	105.7	38.1	85.0	38.5	407	308	106.4	165.5
Mineral	1.3	-66.2	2 100	1 337	193	490	63	1.5	0.4	82.0	0.9	950	838	1.4	86.5
Moffat	21.9	-3.7	1 891	999	14	416	173	37.7	8.1	90.3	12.9	885	741	34.0	191.6
Montezuma	56.1	16.9	3 016	1 552	583	430	360	24.6	10.5	81.5	6.3	350	249	26.3	58.0
Montrose	94.2	34.0	3 767	1 831	396	438	1 038	36.1	13.2	90.4	9.8	380	296	36.9	83.6
Morgan	52.6	-13.3	2 347	1 489	15	173	231	27.3	10.0	92.8	12.7	558	478	26.2	69.2
Otero	68.2	5.1	3 231	2 154	185	238	543	27.7	16.2	87.1	7.0	312	262	27.2	62.3
Ouray	5.3	-46.6	2 547	1 755	32	150	593	3.0	1.1	90.9	1.3	602	477	2.8	72.7
Park	10.5	-10.0	1 399	1 061	23	187	116	10.2	4.1	91.4	4.0	653	626	9.8	128.4
Phillips	23.2	-20.2	5 512	2 439	55	236	198	8.7	2.5	96.7	2.8	602	561	8.8	49.8
Pitkin	12.2	7.7	1 100	524	59	315	182	30.3	2.4	61.8	16.1	1 537	781	30.3	77.6
Prowers	41.6	-1.7	3 055	1 531	14	145	627	21.0	8.7	95.1	6.5	486	354	21.5	80.0
Pueblo	396.2	-1.8	3 098	2 148	163	321	444	165.9	72.6	86.2	61.0	485	363	153.6	57.6
Rio Blanco	51.6	57.2	8 319	1 135	5 777	291	910	22.2	6.0	92.2	10.2	1 431	1 337	20.4	62.8
Rio Grande	29.9	-1.6	2 577	1 761	33	291	411	13.0	6.7	85.8	3.4	306	217	12.8	65.5
Routt	20.9	-18.9	1 611	837	55	321	291	27.1	5.7	72.2	14.8	1 058	777	32.0	229.0
Saguache	12.5	-13.8	2 907	1 703	146	291	566	6.2	3.5	86.3	1.9	474	448	6.1	62.8
San Juan	1.2	35.0	1 324	784	12	83	441	1.7	0.7	60.3	0.8	758	583	1.7	91.9
San Miguel	3.8	-2.0	1 093	555	27	253	179	5.2	2.1	87.3	2.4	761	640	5.3	101.6
Sedgwick	15.0	-23.6	5 375	2 496	271	257	166	5.8	1.6	90.1	2.1	632	535	5.4	32.3
Summit	8.6	-12.2	777	523	11	135	102	27.2	2.8	84.2	14.1	1 356	785	23.0	148.0
Teller	54.8	211.2	4 212	1 367	2 413	76	354	10.8	3.7	90.9	4.7	515	437	10.0	96.3
Washington	23.3	-29.3	4 472	1 618	23	265	262	7.3	2.6	93.4	3.9	722	693	7.2	38.6
Weld	244.6	-5.9	1 791	1 167	77	110	296	168.4	56.5	78.5	61.9	489	409	164.1	75.6
Yuma	35.8	-47.8	3 764	1 541	63	344	186	13.4	4.0	89.6	5.7	567	523	13.9	66.2
CONNECTICUT	15 817.4	13.2	X	1 788	2 003	372	597	3 045.8	878.1	77.1	1 812.2	580	573	3 028.3	45.0
Fairfield	3 723.8	-1.2	4 583	1 608	2 416	235	305	881.5	200.2	75.9	582.9	719	710	880.1	46.3
Hartford	4 044.0	8.5	4 775	1 723	1 872	340	798	848.0	263.3	77.2	478.7	590	584	836.0	43.0
Litchfield	351.2	8.2	2 094	1 655	119	122	189	127.0	36.3	83.9	80.1	505	501	127.6	57.7
Middlesex	335.9	4.8	2 386	1 523	221	125	510	116.3	36.3	70.5	66.9	513	510	123.3	86.0
New Haven	2 313.7	12.6	2 899	1 763	228	280	617	724.1	220.8	75.5	414.7	543	536	711.7	40.8
New London	3 613.2	38.6	14 617	1 655	10 877	1 774	301	200.8	66.7	78.1	109.9	457	452	206.5	36.3
Tolland	190.0	3.3	1 500	1 051	48	118	264	81.6	27.5	88.9	46.4	398	394	77.8	34.1
Windham	219.1	8.6	2 202	1 612	117	120	342	66.6	27.0	84.9	32.7	350	347	65.3	61.3

1. Based on the estimated population as of July 1 of the year shown. 2. Based on the estimated population as of July 1, 1982.

STATE County	Local government finances, 1981–1982 (cont'd)								State and local government employment, 1989		Federal government civilian employment 1989		Elections, 1988[3]	
	Direct general expenditure (cont'd)						Debt outstanding							
	Per capita[1] (Dollars)	Percent of total for– Education	Health & hospitals	Police protection	Public welfare	Highways	Total (Mil dol)	Per capita[1] (Dollars)	Total	Rate[2]	Total	Earnings ($1,000)	Total vote cast for president	Vote for lead party (Percent)
	189	190	191	192	193	194	195	196	197	198	199	200	201	202
COLORADO—Con.														
Clear Creek	1 398	54.8	0.8	6.3	2.5	10.1	7.4	1 004	544	766.2	42	916	3 632	R–50.1
Conejos	1 498	45.5	17.8	2.5	19.3	5.2	3.9	499	455	554.9	60	1 225	3 447	D–57.3
Costilla	1 649	44.6	2.0	2.3	22.3	13.4	1.1	335	353	1 103.1	18	355	1 581	D–70.8
Crowley	1 001	49.6	0.7	2.3	19.1	12.6	1.1	368	476	1 442.4	16	356	1 500	R–57.5
Custer	1 231	39.8	0.0	4.3	5.2	17.9	0.9	552	113	594.7	NA	209	1 084	R–69.5
Delta	1 628	50.3	15.9	2.1	5.7	6.4	44.8	1 897	1 225	575.1	193	5 403	9 144	R–59.6
Denver	1 416	28.4	11.2	6.9	10.6	3.3	535.8	1 058	44 688	921.6	17 300	568 722	209 430	D–60.7
Dolores	1 622	41.6	1.0	4.9	8.9	29.2	0.7	424	250	1 666.7	10	229	732	R–66.7
Douglas	1 462	51.2	0.3	2.3	1.3	7.2	50.1	1 740	2 347	480.0	92	2 597	24 350	R–70.0
Eagle	2 833	16.1	0.5	6.7	1.2	15.6	73.1	4 714	1 283	750.3	109	2 880	7 809	R–55.9
Elbert	1 000	60.4	0.8	1.8	4.4	19.0	2.6	348	496	501.0	35	793	4 448	R–63.1
El Paso	988	48.7	6.7	5.1	6.3	5.7	426.5	1 288	20 104	499.7	9 783	252 748	138 466	R–70.0
Fremont	1 095	39.4	0.7	4.0	12.0	6.6	28.5	957	2 704	816.9	150	4 409	13 088	R–58.2
Garfield	1 337	42.6	7.8	5.6	3.2	13.8	20.3	706	2 018	693.5	256	7 844	11 114	R–57.2
Gilpin	921	32.0	1.1	7.4	7.6	16.7	2.5	929	121	432.1	NA	247	1 590	D–50.6
Grand	2 757	27.8	9.5	3.7	1.2	7.5	22.1	2 661	682	821.7	152	3 944	3 838	R–60.1
Gunnison	1 436	25.8	10.9	5.5	3.0	23.1	4.1	373	941	960.2	123	2 922	4 523	R–55.7
Hinsdale	1 960	27.4	0.4	7.0	0.0	41.4	0.1	222	50	1 000.0	NA	199	407	R–72.5
Huerfano	1 148	38.4	2.5	3.7	19.6	10.6	4.0	586	449	690.8	20	497	2 971	D–63.1
Jackson	1 850	41.7	1.7	4.4	3.2	22.0	1.6	914	127	793.8	35	729	891	R–65.5
Jefferson	1 011	55.5	1.1	4.8	4.1	8.1	313.4	798	17 932	414.0	10 581	370 666	196 511	R–56.4
Kiowa	2 107	40.4	25.7	1.8	3.7	16.5	0.1	31	212	1 115.8	22	461	1 053	R–61.3
Kit Carson	1 588	41.7	18.1	2.9	4.3	14.6	2.6	332	654	883.8	63	1 541	3 512	R–64.4
Lake	2 645	79.3	0.8	1.9	2.3	4.2	5.7	662	503	898.2	64	1 946	2 543	D–59.6
La Plata	1 318	36.7	10.5	5.5	8.1	6.4	43.7	1 480	2 421	773.5	396	10 990	13 362	R–57.7
Larimer	1 199	38.3	14.7	3.9	5.9	6.4	594.2	3 756	16 382	883.1	1 931	65 205	83 066	R–55.3
Las Animas	1 142	45.6	1.0	4.0	17.6	10.2	5.7	370	1 279	940.4	79	2 333	6 331	D–64.4
Lincoln	1 750	45.7	17.7	2.7	5.7	15.2	5.5	1 192	465	1 010.9	46	1 104	2 249	R–60.3
Logan	1 756	54.5	2.6	2.7	3.7	7.2	30.9	1 546	1 244	687.3	104	2 790	7 975	R–56.2
Mesa	1 126	41.6	1.7	3.7	7.3	6.5	164.7	1 743	4 863	535.6	1 194	36 853	37 155	R–59.6
Mineral	1 521	48.1	0.7	3.4	0.1	28.4	0.4	482	58	966.7	22	416	394	R–55.1
Moffat	2 329	37.0	10.3	3.6	2.9	11.5	115.4	7 903	859	740.5	185	5 314	4 519	R–61.0
Montezuma	1 462	39.5	19.3	3.1	6.2	5.7	6.9	382	1 342	721.5	361	9 809	6 551	R–64.2
Montrose	1 434	37.4	24.1	3.1	6.1	7.5	24.8	967	1 727	690.8	318	10 978	9 993	R–60.2
Morgan	1 155	51.9	1.0	4.5	8.9	12.5	11.8	520	1 590	709.8	109	3 004	8 680	R–55.2
Otero	1 209	51.4	2.4	3.1	15.9	5.3	19.5	867	1 543	731.3	118	3 247	8 299	R–51.4
Ouray	1 315	44.5	1.1	5.2	3.8	17.9	1.6	763	174	828.6	NA	252	1 274	R–63.9
Park	1 573	52.8	7.5	3.4	2.5	13.9	4.4	704	446	594.7	62	1 251	3 357	R–56.9
Phillips	1 881	49.6	18.7	2.3	4.4	8.9	1.9	411	398	947.6	34	778	2 278	R–57.8
Pitkin	2 884	13.3	15.9	7.0	0.6	11.3	33.7	3 210	999	900.0	83	2 575	6 326	D–54.1
Prowers	1 602	47.8	11.9	3.9	9.3	8.6	5.5	408	1 196	879.4	61	1 522	5 286	R–56.3
Pueblo	1 221	44.4	1.6	5.0	15.6	4.3	436.0	3 466	8 946	699.5	1 286	38 864	53 318	D–61.5
Rio Blanco	2 877	44.2	12.2	3.0	1.0	16.7	3.7	518	807	1 301.6	65	1 898	2 662	R–68.4
Rio Grande	1 150	54.8	0.7	5.0	13.0	10.4	2.1	185	729	628.4	152	3 817	4 235	R–62.0
Routt	2 287	47.4	1.0	5.1	2.0	12.3	26.1	1 868	975	750.0	164	4 207	6 319	R–51.7
Saguache	1 491	48.3	4.5	4.3	12.6	13.2	4.2	1 030	358	832.6	40	877	2 014	D–51.3
San Juan	1 668	39.4	0.7	5.5	4.0	24.2	0.4	401	66	733.3	NA	75	417	R–50.4
San Miguel	1 698	42.2	1.6	5.2	4.7	20.2	1.8	578	267	762.9	38	804	1 839	D–52.3
Sedgwick	1 625	38.4	11.2	2.1	11.0	12.2	3.0	920	285	1 017.9	26	584	1 545	R–59.6
Summit	2 216	19.8	1.7	6.7	1.5	13.2	64.5	6 198	891	802.7	54	1 485	5 624	R–51.4
Teller	1 088	46.5	6.3	5.6	5.5	12.3	6.1	668	577	443.8	41	978	5 500	R–68.4
Washington	1 336	55.6	2.9	3.7	5.0	19.2	0.7	137	355	682.7	56	1 285	2 715	R–62.9
Weld	1 295	40.0	17.5	4.3	7.9	6.8	212.7	1 678	8 387	614.0	442	12 430	47 807	R–55.4
Yuma	1 390	42.8	18.6	3.1	4.8	14.3	4.6	465	716	753.7	64	1 528	4 414	R–56.9
CONNECTICUT	968	49.3	1.6	5.7	2.5	5.1	2 164.8	692	185 636	573.0	25 568	835 792	1 443 387	R–52.0
Fairfield	1 085	46.6	2.5	6.2	2.8	4.8	543.1	669	36 738	452.1	4 910	161 585	374 878	R–59.0
Hartford	1 030	49.1	0.8	6.0	3.2	4.6	522.3	643	59 732	705.3	8 296	275 867	376 536	D–53.1
Litchfield	804	59.8	0.8	3.9	0.4	8.9	60.8	384	7 332	437.2	430	13 270	79 757	R–56.0
Middlesex	946	51.5	0.9	4.2	1.5	9.8	78.0	599	8 614	611.8	344	10 981	69 344	R–50.0
New Haven	933	46.3	2.2	5.9	2.3	4.2	741.5	972	41 432	519.2	6 326	215 614	342 361	R–50.9
New London	859	54.1	1.3	4.9	2.3	6.2	132.0	549	14 126	571.4	4 805	144 328	102 851	R–51.2
Tolland	669	65.2	0.8	3.5	1.0	7.1	49.3	423	12 228	965.1	225	7 164	55 861	R–50.8
Windham	698	62.0	0.9	2.9	1.8	6.1	37.8	404	5 434	546.1	232	6 983	41 799	R–50.9

1. Based on the estimated population as of July 1, 1982. 2. Per 10,000 resident population estimated as of July 1 of the year shown. 3. Data subject to copyright.

STATE-County code	MSA/CMSA/NECMA code[1]	STATE County	Land Area,[2] 1990 (Sq. Km.)	Population, 1990: Total persons	Rank	Per square kilometer	Race: White	Black	Am. Indian, Eskimo, Aleut	Asian & Pacific Islander	Other race	Hispanic[3]	Age of population Percent: Under 5 years	5 to 14 years	15 to 24 years
			1	2	3	4	5	6	7	8	9	10	11	12	13
10 000	...	DELAWARE	5 062	666 168	X	131.6	535 094	112 460	2 019	9 057	7 538	15 820	7.3	13.5	15.1
10 001	...	Kent	1 530	110 993	414	72.5	87 300	20 631	614	1 420	1 028	2 540	8.4	14.8	16.0
10 003	6162	New Castle	1 104	441 946	112	400.3	355 399	72 834	760	7 048	5 905	11 804	7.2	13.2	15.7
10 005	...	Sussex	2 429	113 229	407	46.6	92 395	18 995	645	589	605	1 476	6.8	13.5	12.1
11 000	8840	DISTRICT OF COLUMBIA	159	606 900	X	3 817.0	179 667	399 604	1 466	11 214	14 949	32 710	6.2	10.1	16.6
11 001	8840	District of Columbia	159	606 900	76	3 817.0	179 667	399 604	1 466	11 214	14 949	32 710	6.2	10.1	16.6
12 000	...	FLORIDA	139 852	12 937 926	X	92.5	10 749 285	1 759 534	36 335	154 302	238 470	1 574 143	6.6	12.1	12.9
12 001	2900	Alachua	2 264	181 596	269	80.2	140 787	34 427	362	4 556	1 464	6 779	6.5	12.1	25.2
12 003	...	Baker	1 516	18 486	1 763	12.2	15 579	2 768	60	50	29	200	7.8	17.5	15.4
12 005	6015	Bay	1 978	126 994	365	64.2	109 570	13 713	949	2 229	533	2 256	7.3	14.0	14.0
12 007	2900	Bradford	759	22 515	1 555	29.7	17 692	4 555	81	100	87	426	6.3	13.7	13.4
12 009	4900	Brevard	2 638	398 978	124	151.2	358 391	31 417	1 369	5 379	2 422	12 261	6.6	12.0	12.1
12 011	4992	Broward	3 131	1 255 488	23	401.0	1 025 583	193 447	2 634	17 130	16 694	108 439	6.3	11.0	11.3
12 013	...	Calhoun	1 470	11 011	2 291	7.5	9 164	1 658	133	13	43	118	7.1	14.7	14.8
12 015	...	Charlotte	1 797	110 975	415	61.8	105 401	4 243	216	738	377	2 764	4.4	8.7	8.4
12 017	...	Citrus	1 512	93 515	494	61.8	90 411	2 206	283	395	220	1 702	4.7	9.9	8.5
12 019	3600	Clay	1 557	105 986	437	68.1	97 691	5 513	367	1 780	635	2 764	7.6	16.2	14.6
12 021	5345	Collier	5 246	152 099	305	29.0	139 073	6 986	428	584	5 028	20 734	6.0	10.9	10.8
12 023	...	Columbia	2 065	42 613	943	20.6	34 423	7 678	105	261	146	619	7.3	16.0	13.8
12 025	4992	Dade	5 036	1 937 094	10	384.6	1 413 015	397 993	3 066	26 307	96 713	953 407	7.2	13.0	14.0
12 027	...	De Soto	1 651	23 865	1 497	14.5	19 141	3 726	97	99	802	2 282	6.9	12.6	13.6
12 029	...	Dixie	1 824	10 585	2 329	5.8	9 594	920	36	16	19	96	6.7	13.9	12.5
12 031	3600	Duval	2 004	672 971	63	335.8	489 604	163 902	1 904	12 940	4 621	17 333	8.1	14.0	15.1
12 033	6080	Escambia	1 719	262 798	191	152.9	201 235	52 618	2 632	5 048	1 265	5 013	7.4	13.9	16.1
12 035	...	Flagler	1 256	28 701	1 338	22.9	25 831	2 366	52	283	169	1 260	5.1	10.8	9.3
12 037	...	Franklin	1 383	8 967	2 473	6.5	7 776	1 112	49	20	10	65	6.3	13.5	11.9
12 039	8240	Gadsden	1 337	41 105	978	30.7	16 686	23 700	68	94	557	964	7.7	16.9	15.0
12 041	...	Gilchrist	904	9 667	2 417	10.7	8 761	825	30	18	33	150	6.7	13.8	18.1
12 043	...	Glades	2 003	7 591	2 611	3.8	5 987	922	431	16	235	605	6.4	13.8	11.3
12 045	...	Gulf	1 463	11 504	2 256	7.9	9 253	2 162	56	25	8	86	6.1	14.0	13.6
12 047	...	Hamilton	1 334	10 930	2 303	8.2	6 448	4 256	42	18	166	295	7.4	16.0	16.7
12 049	...	Hardee	1 651	19 499	1 702	11.8	16 382	1 034	82	42	1 959	4 562	7.8	16.7	14.7
12 051	...	Hendry	2 985	25 773	1 429	8.6	18 592	4 311	543	99	2 228	5 757	9.0	17.3	15.4
12 053	8280	Hernando	1 239	101 115	454	81.6	96 108	3 895	244	406	462	2 962	5.0	10.3	9.1
12 055	...	Highlands	2 664	68 432	645	25.7	59 735	6 848	227	390	1 232	3 500	5.1	10.6	8.7
12 057	8280	Hillsborough	2 722	834 054	41	306.4	690 352	110 283	2 454	11 379	19 586	106 908	7.3	13.1	14.5
12 059	...	Holmes	1 250	15 778	1 935	12.6	14 740	782	174	50	32	176	6.2	14.0	14.2
12 061	...	Indian River	1 303	90 208	507	69.2	81 418	7 660	136	473	521	2 704	5.5	10.8	10.0
12 063	...	Jackson	2 372	41 375	972	17.4	30 085	10 845	228	87	130	974	5.9	14.0	16.0
12 065	...	Jefferson	1 548	11 296	2 275	7.3	6 334	4 897	17	28	20	130	7.4	16.9	13.7
12 067	...	Lafayette	1 406	5 578	2 793	4.0	4 629	785	17	9	138	226	5.8	14.2	15.7
12 069	...	Lake	2 469	152 104	304	61.6	135 619	14 191	384	566	1 344	4 305	5.6	11.0	10.0
12 071	2700	Lee	2 081	335 113	154	161.0	306 200	22 184	672	1 894	4 163	15 094	5.9	10.7	10.3
12 073	8240	Leon	1 727	192 493	249	111.5	141 712	46 527	500	2 694	1 060	4 715	6.4	12.5	24.0
12 075	...	Levy	2 897	25 923	1 425	8.9	22 346	3 211	108	134	124	490	6.4	13.8	11.9
12 077	...	Liberty	2 165	5 569	2 794	2.6	4 508	982	29	12	38	108	6.0	13.7	15.6
12 079	...	Madison	1 792	16 569	1 882	9.2	9 545	6 915	54	9	46	231	7.8	14.9	15.5
12 081	1140	Manatee	1 920	211 707	237	110.3	190 328	16 400	501	1 227	3 251	9 424	5.8	10.4	10.2
12 083	5790	Marion	4 090	194 833	247	47.6	167 094	24 844	638	945	1 312	5 860	6.3	12.3	11.2
12 085	2710	Martin	1 439	100 900	455	70.1	92 119	6 043	179	534	2 025	4 728	5.1	9.6	9.6
12 087	...	Monroe	2 583	78 024	580	30.2	71 840	4 203	258	630	1 093	9 580	5.7	9.2	10.2
12 089	3600	Nassau	1 688	43 941	926	26.0	39 069	4 522	134	133	83	480	7.4	14.9	13.9
12 091	2750	Okaloosa	2 424	143 776	330	59.3	125 191	13 007	776	3 658	1 144	4 427	7.8	14.2	14.9
12 093	...	Okeechobee	2 006	29 627	1 309	14.8	24 984	1 898	145	154	2 446	3 493	7.7	14.7	13.8
12 095	5960	Orange	2 351	677 491	62	288.2	539 061	103 092	2 036	13 994	19 308	64 946	7.4	12.9	16.3
12 097	5960	Osceola	3 424	107 728	428	31.5	96 231	5 902	360	1 637	3 598	12 866	7.3	13.9	13.9
12 099	8960	Palm Beach	5 269	863 518	37	163.9	732 231	107 705	1 211	9 020	13 351	66 613	6.2	10.5	10.4
12 101	8280	Pasco	1 930	281 131	176	145.7	270 658	5 457	784	1 480	2 752	9 309	5.2	9.8	9.5
12 103	8280	Pinellas	726	851 659	39	1 173.1	770 374	65 868	1 985	9 790	3 642	20 069	5.2	9.6	10.4
12 105	3980	Polk	4 856	405 382	122	83.5	341 952	54 385	1 158	2 486	5 401	16 600	7.0	13.2	13.1
12 107	...	Putnam	1 870	65 070	673	34.8	52 019	11 940	129	275	707	1 688	6.8	14.4	12.2
12 109	3600	St. Johns	1 577	83 829	547	53.2	75 547	7 328	182	509	263	1 902	6.4	12.3	12.6
12 111	2710	St. Lucie	1 483	150 171	313	101.3	122 159	24 666	347	1 031	1 968	5 952	7.0	12.6	11.0
12 113	6080	Santa Rosa	2 631	81 608	557	31.0	76 385	3 275	715	973	260	1 223	7.8	15.1	13.5
12 115	7510	Sarasota	1 481	277 776	178	187.6	262 836	12 073	483	1 430	954	5 882	4.6	8.6	8.8
12 117	5960	Seminole	798	287 529	170	360.3	253 621	24 314	803	4 843	3 948	18 606	7.0	14.1	13.8

1. MSA = Metropolitan Statistical Area. CMSA = Consolidated MSA. NECMA = New England county metropolitan area. PMSA = Primary MSA. See Appendix A for explanation of these concepts. See Appendix B for list of metropolitan areas identified by type, with component counties. 2. Dry land or land partially or temporarily covered by water. 3. Hispanic persons may be of any race.

Table A. States and Counties — **Population**

STATE County	Population, 1990 (cont'd): Age of population (cont'd) Percent: 25 to 34 years	35 to 44 years	45 to 54 years	55 to 64 years	65 to 74 years	75 years and over	Percent female	Population–Change and components of change: Change 1980–1990: Number	Percent	Components of change, 1980–1986: Total persons, 1986	Total persons, 1980	Net change: Number	Percent	Natural increase: Births	Deaths
	14	15	16	17	18	19	20	21	22	23	24	25	26	27	28
DELAWARE	17.9	14.8	10.2	9.0	7.4	4.7	51.5	72 168	12.1	633 000	594 000	38 000	6.5	56 000	30 000
Kent	17.8	14.2	10.1	8.4	6.1	4.2	51.1	12 774	13.0	105 200	98 219	7 000	7.1	11 200	4 500
New Castle	18.5	15.2	10.3	8.6	7.0	4.4	51.6	43 831	11.0	417 800	398 115	19 700	5.0	36 200	20 700
Sussex	15.5	14.1	10.2	11.1	10.6	6.2	51.6	15 225	15.5	109 700	98 004	11 700	12.0	8 700	6 100
DISTRICT OF COLUMBIA	20.0	15.7	10.2	8.4	7.3	5.5	53.4	-31 532	-4.9	626 100	638 432	-12 400	-1.9	59 200	41 900
District of Columbia	20.0	15.7	10.2	8.4	7.3	5.5	53.4	-31 532	-4.9	626 100	638 432	-12 400	-1.9	59 200	41 900
FLORIDA	16.4	14.0	10.0	9.8	10.6	7.7	51.6	3 191 926	32.8	11 675 000	9 746 000	1 928 000	19.8	931 000	707 000
Alachua	18.1	14.4	8.2	6.3	5.5	3.8	50.9	30 227	20.0	176 000	151 369	24 600	16.3	15 700	6 100
Baker	18.3	15.4	10.2	7.4	4.8	3.2	47.8	3 197	20.9	17 800	15 289	2 500	16.3	1 800	700
Bay	17.8	14.5	10.8	9.6	7.7	4.3	50.7	29 254	29.9	122 300	97 740	24 600	25.2	11 200	5 300
Bradford	19.4	15.3	10.9	8.8	7.3	4.8	44.8	2 492	12.4	23 800	20 023	3 800	18.8	2 000	1 200
Brevard	17.5	13.6	10.5	11.0	10.8	5.8	50.6	126 019	46.2	361 200	272 959	88 300	32.3	25 300	16 700
Broward	17.1	14.8	9.9	8.8	10.6	10.1	52.1	237 231	23.3	1 142 400	1 018 257	124 200	12.2	82 100	78 300
Calhoun	15.9	13.5	10.8	8.7	7.8	6.7	48.2	1 717	18.5	9 700	9 294	400	4.0	900	700
Charlotte	10.8	10.3	8.7	15.0	20.9	12.9	51.8	52 515	89.8	84 100	58 460	25 600	43.8	3 700	6 600
Citrus	10.5	10.7	9.7	14.6	19.8	11.5	52.2	38 812	71.0	80 200	54 703	25 500	46.5	4 000	6 000
Clay	16.8	17.3	11.7	7.4	5.2	3.3	50.7	38 934	58.1	91 400	67 052	24 300	36.3	7 200	3 300
Collier	14.6	12.8	10.0	12.1	14.4	8.4	50.4	66 128	76.9	121 400	85 971	35 500	41.2	9 400	6 400
Columbia	15.1	14.2	10.6	9.6	8.5	4.8	50.9	7 214	20.4	40 700	35 399	5 300	14.9	4 000	2 100
Dade	17.1	14.4	10.9	9.4	7.5	6.4	52.1	311 585	19.2	1 769 500	1 625 509	144 000	8.9	161 700	105 700
De Soto	14.9	12.8	9.9	10.1	11.8	7.6	48.4	4 826	25.3	22 000	19 039	3 000	15.6	2 100	1 400
Dixie	14.4	13.7	11.8	12.3	9.9	4.9	48.2	2 834	36.6	9 500	7 751	1 800	23.1	800	500
Duval	19.4	15.2	9.5	7.9	6.5	4.2	51.2	101 968	17.9	646 400	571 003	75 400	13.2	68 100	32 400
Escambia	17.1	14.1	10.5	9.1	7.4	4.5	51.4	29 004	12.4	270 600	233 794	36 800	15.7	25 700	11 600
Flagler	11.4	12.0	9.7	16.0	19.1	6.4	52.1	17 788	163.0	18 200	10 913	7 300	66.5	1 000	900
Franklin	13.3	12.7	12.4	11.8	10.7	7.3	51.2	1 306	17.0	8 400	7 661	800	10.1	900	600
Gadsden	15.6	14.1	9.8	8.4	7.2	5.4	52.5	-569	-1.4	45 200	41 674	3 500	8.4	5 000	2 400
Gilchrist	13.6	13.3	10.4	10.4	9.0	4.8	47.2	3 900	67.6	7 200	5 767	1 500	25.7	700	400
Glades	12.2	11.8	11.8	13.1	13.0	6.7	49.3	1 599	26.7	6 800	5 992	900	14.3	500	400
Gulf	15.4	12.6	11.3	11.8	9.2	6.1	49.8	846	7.9	11 700	10 658	1 100	10.1	900	600
Hamilton	16.9	14.1	9.6	7.9	6.5	4.9	47.6	2 169	24.8	9 300	8 761	500	5.7	1 000	600
Hardee	13.8	12.7	9.8	9.4	9.4	5.8	49.3	-858	-4.2	21 600	20 357	1 200	6.1	2 400	1 100
Hendry	15.7	13.0	10.2	8.4	6.8	4.2	49.3	7 174	38.6	23 400	18 599	4 800	25.6	2 900	1 100
Hernando	10.5	10.8	9.1	14.5	21.1	9.6	52.1	56 646	127.4	77 700	44 469	33 300	74.8	3 800	5 000
Highlands	10.6	9.7	8.2	13.6	20.6	12.9	52.6	20 906	44.0	60 600	47 526	13 100	27.5	4 100	4 700
Hillsborough	18.7	15.4	10.3	8.4	7.4	4.8	51.3	187 115	28.9	775 900	646 939	128 900	19.9	69 600	38 300
Holmes	14.9	13.7	11.6	9.7	9.1	6.6	49.2	1 055	7.2	16 100	14 723	1 400	9.7	1 200	1 000
Indian River	12.9	12.0	9.1	12.5	17.1	10.1	51.7	30 312	50.6	81 000	59 896	21 100	35.2	5 400	5 000
Jackson	15.3	14.1	10.5	9.3	8.2	6.7	49.3	2 221	5.7	41 900	39 154	2 700	6.9	3 500	2 600
Jefferson	13.8	14.5	9.9	9.1	8.2	6.6	52.2	593	5.5	11 700	10 703	1 000	9.5	1 200	700
Lafayette	19.7	14.4	10.3	8.9	6.9	4.0	42.4	1 543	38.2	4 600	4 035	600	14.1	400	200
Lake	12.2	11.4	9.6	12.6	16.2	11.3	52.1	47 234	45.0	132 500	104 870	27 700	26.4	9 400	9 800
Lee	14.1	12.5	9.5	12.1	15.3	9.4	51.7	129 847	63.3	279 100	205 266	73 800	36.0	19 000	17 200
Leon	18.0	15.7	8.9	6.2	5.0	3.2	51.9	43 838	29.5	172 800	148 655	24 100	16.2	14 600	5 500
Levy	13.2	13.1	10.9	11.7	12.3	6.6	52.2	6 053	30.5	24 100	19 870	4 200	21.3	2 000	1 600
Liberty	19.7	14.7	9.7	9.3	6.8	4.5	43.0	1 309	30.7	4 500	4 260	300	6.2	400	300
Madison	16.1	13.0	10.0	8.5	7.7	6.4	48.8	1 675	11.2	15 600	14 894	700	4.9	1 600	1 000
Manatee	13.7	12.0	8.8	11.0	15.6	12.5	52.7	63 262	42.6	177 100	148 445	28 700	19.3	13 300	14 900
Marion	13.8	12.5	9.8	11.9	14.4	7.7	51.8	72 345	59.1	171 000	122 488	48 500	39.6	13 200	9 900
Martin	13.6	12.7	9.7	12.2	16.7	10.8	50.9	36 886	57.6	85 300	64 014	21 300	33.2	5 400	5 800
Monroe	17.8	17.3	12.1	11.8	10.5	5.4	47.5	14 836	23.5	72 500	63 188	9 300	14.7	5 700	3 700
Nassau	16.6	15.7	12.0	9.3	6.4	3.7	50.5	11 047	33.6	42 000	32 894	9 100	27.6	3 500	1 500
Okaloosa	19.8	14.6	10.4	9.1	6.3	3.0	49.4	33 856	30.8	141 300	109 920	31 400	28.6	13 500	4 400
Okeechobee	14.8	12.4	9.7	10.7	10.7	5.5	48.9	9 363	46.2	27 300	20 264	7 100	34.8	2 800	1 500
Orange	20.5	14.9	9.4	8.0	6.5	4.1	50.4	206 624	43.9	575 200	470 867	104 400	22.2	51 100	25 900
Osceola	17.0	14.7	10.3	8.9	8.3	5.6	51.1	58 441	118.6	83 100	49 287	33 900	68.7	6 100	4 200
Palm Beach	15.8	13.6	9.3	9.8	13.5	10.9	52.0	286 764	49.7	755 600	576 754	178 800	31.0	53 700	49 800
Pasco	11.8	10.9	8.6	11.9	18.9	13.4	52.6	87 470	45.2	245 500	193 661	51 900	26.8	13 300	20 500
Pinellas	14.9	13.6	9.7	10.5	13.5	12.5	53.3	123 128	16.9	815 100	728 531	86 600	11.9	49 100	74 800
Polk	14.7	13.1	10.0	10.3	11.3	7.3	51.5	83 730	26.0	377 200	321 652	55 500	17.3	33 700	21 500
Putnam	13.6	12.9	10.2	11.8	11.7	6.4	51.2	14 521	28.7	59 400	50 549	8 800	17.5	5 200	3 800
St. Johns	15.5	15.5	10.8	10.4	10.4	6.1	51.5	32 526	63.4	72 900	51 303	21 600	42.1	5 100	4 000
St. Lucie	15.3	12.8	9.1	11.1	13.7	7.3	51.1	62 989	72.3	120 400	87 182	33 200	38.1	10 600	7 000
Santa Rosa	18.2	15.3	11.6	9.0	6.1	3.4	50.2	25 620	45.8	66 500	55 988	10 500	18.8	6 500	2 500
Sarasota	12.0	12.0	9.5	12.4	17.9	14.2	53.2	75 525	37.3	247 600	202 251	45 300	22.4	13 500	20 900
Seminole	18.3	17.4	11.1	8.0	6.3	4.0	51.1	107 777	60.0	240 100	179 752	60 300	33.6	17 300	8 900

STATE County	Population–(cont'd): Components of change, 1980-1986 (cont'd)	Households, 1990					Births, 1988			Deaths, 1987				Marriages, 1984	
					Percent					Number		Rate			
	Net migration	Number	Percent change, 1980–1990	Persons per house-hold	Female family house-holder[1]	One-person	Total	Rate[2]	Low birth weight[3] (Number)	Total	Infant[4]	Total[2]	Infant[5]	Number	Rate[2]
	29	30	31	32	33	34	35	36	37	38	39	40	41	42	43
DELAWARE	13 000	247 497	19.5	2.61	11.8	23.2	10 406	15.8	765	5 603	116	8.6	11.7	5 455	8.9
Kent	300	39 655	21.1	2.70	11.9	21.2	1 918	17.7	139	920	19	8.6	9.9	1 037	10.2
New Castle	4 200	164 161	18.1	2.61	12.1	24.0	6 875	15.8	512	3 467	78	8.1	12.2	3 430	8.4
Sussex	9 100	43 681	23.4	2.54	10.9	22.3	1 613	13.9	114	1 216	19	10.7	12.1	988	9.5
DISTRICT OF COLUMBIA	-29 600	249 634	-1.4	2.26	19.5	41.5	10 540	17.1	1 507	7 430	197	12.0	19.3	5 488	8.8
District of Columbia	-29 600	249 634	-1.4	2.26	19.5	41.5	10 540	17.1	1 507	7 430	197	12.0	19.3	5 488	8.8
FLORIDA	1 704 000	5 134 869	37.1	2.46	10.7	25.5	184 119	14.9	14 119	127 290	1 848	10.6	10.6	126 449	11.4
Alachua	14 900	71 258	30.5	2.40	12.0	28.1	2 612	14.3	182	1 174	23	6.5	8.8	1 719	10.2
Baker	1 400	5 554	30.9	3.00	12.4	15.8	324	17.4	15	126	2	7.0	6.9	164	9.6
Bay	18 700	48 938	40.8	2.54	11.1	23.0	2 070	16.5	125	998	16	8.1	8.1	1 658	15.0
Bradford	3 000	7 193	14.2	2.68	12.3	20.4	314	12.7	20	196	3	8.0	9.3	230	10.0
Brevard	79 600	161 365	58.5	2.43	9.1	23.7	5 273	13.6	357	3 244	44	8.7	8.9	3 728	11.3
Broward	120 400	528 442	26.6	2.35	10.0	29.5	17 078	14.4	1 390	13 944	169	12.0	10.6	10 858	9.9
Calhoun	100	3 793	17.8	2.64	13.3	24.3	163	16.0	9	124	2	12.7	13.3	108	11.3
Charlotte	28 500	48 433	86.8	2.23	6.0	23.0	835	8.8	34	1 345	5	15.0	6.5	740	9.8
Citrus	27 400	40 573	76.5	2.27	6.8	23.1	832	9.1	70	1 298	6	14.9	7.8	701	9.6
Clay	20 400	36 663	69.4	2.86	9.1	15.2	1 508	15.0	99	585	7	6.1	4.6	821	10.0
Collier	32 400	61 703	81.7	2.41	7.1	22.6	2 012	14.5	141	1 338	27	10.2	14.4	1 219	10.9
Columbia	3 300	15 611	28.1	2.67	13.0	22.7	606	14.4	49	358	6	8.6	9.6	457	11.6
Dade	88 100	692 355	13.5	2.75	14.9	24.9	31 560	17.4	2 590	17 654	308	9.9	10.3	22 819	13.2
De Soto	2 300	8 222	31.4	2.62	10.9	22.1	367	16.2	24	274	9	12.3	23.1	272	13.0
Dixie	1 400	3 916	47.1	2.56	10.0	22.4	141	13.7	8	93	1	9.3	6.9	98	10.8
Duval	39 700	257 245	23.5	2.54	13.7	26.0	12 437	18.5	960	5 601	151	8.4	12.2	6 257	10.2
Escambia	22 700	98 608	21.6	2.57	14.2	23.6	4 403	15.8	347	2 236	52	8.1	12.0	3 510	13.6
Flagler	7 200	11 880	172.5	2.40	7.1	18.9	248	10.7	20	234	2	11.2	10.0	156	10.0
Franklin	500	3 628	31.2	2.42	9.6	25.4	135	15.9	9	109	1	13.0	7.7	132	15.9
Gadsden	900	13 405	10.9	2.90	22.5	21.5	731	16.0	80	445	17	9.8	24.0	330	7.6
Gilchrist	1 200	3 284	63.7	2.65	9.4	19.0	115	15.1	9	91	0	12.3	0.0	84	11.8
Glades	800	2 885	29.7	2.57	7.0	22.1	81	11.7	4	76	0	11.0	0.0	59	8.8
Gulf	800	4 324	17.4	2.56	11.1	22.6	143	11.5	15	117	0	9.7	0.0	137	12.0
Hamilton	100	3 488	20.1	2.81	18.4	22.2	173	17.7	18	104	4	11.1	28.4	81	8.7
Hardee	0	6 391	2.2	2.95	10.4	17.6	393	18.0	24	181	4	8.3	10.9	263	12.5
Hendry	2 900	8 402	41.0	2.99	12.1	17.6	550	21.9	41	208	9	8.5	17.3	523	23.8
Hernando	34 500	42 300	138.5	2.37	6.9	19.7	894	9.5	71	1 068	1	12.3	1.3	700	10.2
Highlands	13 700	29 544	55.8	2.28	7.0	24.2	822	12.4	53	929	10	14.5	13.3	623	11.0
Hillsborough	97 600	324 872	36.5	2.51	11.9	25.3	13 599	16.7	1 139	6 853	133	8.6	10.3	8 710	11.9
Holmes	1 300	5 800	10.6	2.56	11.2	23.6	179	10.7	14	162	1	10.0	4.9	159	10.1
Indian River	20 800	38 057	63.1	2.33	7.8	23.9	1 039	12.0	88	906	1	10.9	1.0	848	11.2
Jackson	1 800	14 465	8.5	2.56	12.9	25.3	493	11.6	48	454	7	10.7	14.6	305	7.5
Jefferson	500	3 982	14.2	2.79	16.7	22.1	151	12.6	18	105	3	8.9	19.9	124	10.6
Lafayette	400	1 721	21.8	2.74	10.7	19.6	47	8.7	5	53	0	10.0	0.0	49	11.1
Lake	28 100	63 616	52.7	2.35	8.0	23.8	1 863	13.1	133	1 852	8	13.4	4.5	1 351	10.9
Lee	72 000	140 124	69.8	2.35	8.2	23.0	4 148	13.4	295	3 431	41	11.6	10.7	2 856	11.2
Leon	15 000	74 828	38.3	2.43	12.3	27.0	2 593	14.2	202	1 004	36	5.7	14.2	1 762	10.6
Levy	3 800	10 079	38.7	2.52	11.1	22.4	330	12.6	31	304	1	11.9	2.8	256	10.9
Liberty	100	1 706	14.9	2.69	11.3	21.9	64	13.9	2	42	1	8.9	15.9	63	14.0
Madison	100	5 522	11.0	2.75	17.1	22.9	251	15.9	29	163	2	10.4	7.5	139	9.0
Manatee	30 200	91 060	46.9	2.29	8.4	27.0	2 695	14.4	190	2 655	38	14.5	14.8	1 890	11.1
Marion	45 200	78 177	72.0	2.44	10.3	22.9	2 640	13.9	200	2 045	24	11.2	9.1	1 858	11.9
Martin	21 600	43 022	66.3	2.28	6.5	25.0	1 117	11.7	72	1 094	19	11.9	16.7	829	10.4
Monroe	7 200	33 583	27.5	2.24	6.4	27.8	946	12.3	48	666	12	8.9	12.1	1 119	16.0
Nassau	7 100	16 192	47.5	2.68	9.5	21.2	730	16.2	49	282	5	6.5	7.2	298	7.8
Okaloosa	22 200	53 313	42.0	2.60	9.5	20.9	2 505	16.6	181	850	24	5.8	9.7	1 881	14.5
Okeechobee	5 800	10 214	46.3	2.75	9.3	19.1	576	19.4	54	271	6	9.5	11.7	332	13.3
Orange	79 100	254 852	49.3	2.56	11.6	23.7	10 739	17.6	822	4 547	95	7.7	9.4	7 610	14.2
Osceola	32 000	39 150	110.3	2.68	9.5	19.2	1 497	16.7	95	785	13	9.3	9.3	1 017	14.4
Palm Beach	174 800	365 558	56.0	2.32	8.6	27.5	12 001	14.7	947	9 400	150	12.0	13.4	7 279	10.5
Pasco	59 100	121 674	49.6	2.26	7.3	25.7	2 916	11.0	198	3 940	21	15.3	8.2	1 887	8.2
Pinellas	112 300	380 635	19.1	2.18	9.4	31.9	9 792	11.9	678	12 571	74	15.4	8.0	8 556	10.8
Polk	43 300	155 969	36.3	2.53	10.8	22.4	6 122	15.5	493	3 826	68	9.9	12.0	4 439	12.4
Putnam	7 400	25 070	36.3	2.55	11.8	23.1	962	15.4	70	705	18	11.2	20.1	600	10.4
St. Johns	20 500	33 426	79.5	2.44	9.3	24.1	1 138	14.4	86	680	7	9.1	7.1	843	13.2
St. Lucie	29 600	58 174	79.0	2.54	9.9	20.3	2 109	15.5	197	1 445	24	11.2	11.7	1 073	9.6
Santa Rosa	6 600	29 900	60.8	2.68	9.8	18.3	1 254	17.6	84	498	17	7.1	15.2	686	10.8
Sarasota	52 800	125 493	41.4	2.18	7.3	27.7	2 567	9.9	154	3 866	26	15.1	10.5	2 567	10.8
Seminole	51 900	107 657	70.2	2.64	10.1	21.2	3 967	14.7	260	1 686	25	6.5	7.0	2 087	9.4

1. No spouse present. 2. Per 1,000 resident population estimated as of July 1 of the year shown. 3. Under 2,500 grams. 4. Deaths of infants under 1 year old. 5. Deaths of infants under 1 year old per 1,000 live births.

STATE County	Divorces, 1984: Number	Divorces, 1984: Rate[1]	Physicians, active non-Federal, 1989: Number[2]	Physicians, active non-Federal, 1989: Rate[3]	Hospitals, 1989: Number	Hospitals, 1989: Beds: Number	Hospitals, 1989: Beds: Rate[3]	Nursing homes,[4] 1986: Number	Nursing homes,[4] 1986: Beds	Serious crimes known to police, 1988: Number: Total[5]	Serious crimes known to police, 1988: Number: Violent[6]	Serious crimes known to police, 1988: Rate[3]	Education: Public school enrollment[7]: 1986–1987	Education: Public school enrollment[7]: 1980	Education: Attainment,[8] 1980: Percent 12 yrs. or more	Education: Attainment,[8] 1980: Percent 16 yrs. or more
	44	45	46	47	48	49	50	51	52	53	54	55	56	57	58	59
DELAWARE	2 907	4.7	1 271	189	13	2 893	430	48	4 165	31 674	2 981	4 799	98 111	103 949	68.6	17.5
Kent	602	5.9	111	101	2	208	188	10	1 040	4 876	475	4 463	22 425	20 412	65.4	12.6
New Castle	1 785	4.4	997	225	8	2 289	517	29	2 488	21 784	1 999	5 003	57 653	64 097	72.4	20.6
Sussex	520	5.0	163	136	3	396	331	9	637	5 014	507	4 348	18 033	19 440	57.1	9.9
DISTRICT OF COLUMBIA	3 057	4.9	3 651	601	18	8 118	1 336	35	3 033	61 471	11 914	9 915	85 612	97 345	67.1	27.5
District of Columbia	3 057	4.9	3 651	601	18	8 118	1 336	35	3 033	61 471	11 914	9 915	85 612	97 345	67.1	27.5
FLORIDA	75 332	6.8	25 376	200	300	62 816	496	1 246	70 578	NA	NA	NA	1 607 115	1 571 197	66.7	14.9
Alachua	1 018	6.0	1 150	619	5	1 685	906	12	843	NA	NA	NA	23 345	23 019	75.5	29.4
Baker	86	5.1	22	116	2	831	4 374	1	68	NA	NA	NA	3 747	3 519	50.7	5.7
Bay	1 072	9.7	163	126	3	505	391	10	644	NA	NA	NA	21 341	20 384	65.8	13.2
Bradford	180	7.8	13	52	1	54	216	3	141	NA	NA	NA	3 974	4 064	53.6	7.6
Brevard	2 089	6.3	543	135	10	1 356	337	18	1 410	NA	NA	NA	48 154	49 200	75.4	17.1
Broward	6 642	6.0	2 394	198	27	6 477	536	128	6 591	NA	NA	NA	131 725	140 003	70.4	15.1
Calhoun	81	8.4	6	58	1	36	346	7	254	NA	NA	NA	1 986	1 983	47.0	6.9
Charlotte	305	4.1	170	169	3	674	670	15	545	NA	NA	NA	8 788	6 771	66.7	12.8
Citrus	371	5.1	100	103	2	283	293	18	657	NA	NA	NA	9 763	7 868	55.3	7.1
Clay	398	4.8	155	148	2	238	227	5	475	NA	NA	NA	19 412	16 999	73.7	16.8
Collier	646	5.8	256	175	2	543	371	7	473	NA	NA	NA	16 087	13 110	71.2	18.5
Columbia	282	7.2	54	126	3	656	1 536	3	133	NA	NA	NA	7 628	7 795	58.9	9.3
Dade	12 980	7.5	6 175	336	37	10 270	560	148	8 383	NA	NA	NA	243 690	245 600	64.0	16.8
De Soto	173	8.2	42	182	2	1 031	4 463	2	63	NA	NA	NA	3 654	3 578	50.6	8.2
Dixie	64	7.0	3	28	0	0	0	0	0	NA	NA	NA	1 632	1 629	49.4	4.9
Duval	5 893	9.6	1 503	219	14	3 008	437	59	4 040	NA	NA	NA	102 966	104 002	66.8	14.0
Escambia	2 097	8.1	494	174	5	1 683	593	30	1 355	NA	NA	NA	41 666	44 592	67.3	14.1
Flagler	112	7.2	17	66	1	81	314	6	146	NA	NA	NA	2 614	1 658	70.8	13.7
Franklin	65	7.8	5	59	1	29	341	1	60	NA	NA	NA	1 572	1 594	44.0	9.0
Gadsden	197	4.5	45	97	2	1 417	3 060	2	79	NA	NA	NA	8 355	9 228	47.1	8.6
Gilchrist	46	6.5	1	13	0	0	0	1	90	NA	NA	NA	1 595	1 359	56.5	7.1
Glades	11	1.6	0	0	0	0	0	0	0	NA	NA	NA	811	1 180	53.0	7.8
Gulf	79	6.9	7	56	1	45	360	2	142	NA	NA	NA	2 262	2 417	58.6	6.8
Hamilton	52	5.6	7	71	1	42	424	1	60	NA	NA	NA	2 274	2 186	49.4	5.9
Hardee	146	7.0	12	55	1	50	228	2	92	NA	NA	NA	3 937	4 651	44.9	7.4
Hendry	361	16.4	17	65	1	66	254	1	120	NA	NA	NA	5 188	4 715	50.5	7.6
Hernando	263	3.8	90	89	2	236	233	6	375	NA	NA	NA	9 727	7 153	59.9	8.6
Highlands	349	6.1	92	133	3	306	442	16	685	NA	NA	NA	7 787	7 181	57.2	9.7
Hillsborough	5 379	7.4	1 953	234	22	4 507	540	69	3 944	NA	NA	NA	115 373	115 576	65.8	14.5
Holmes	127	8.0	6	36	1	34	201	2	66	NA	NA	NA	3 194	3 347	43.7	6.0
Indian River	544	7.2	174	193	3	453	503	6	380	NA	NA	NA	10 137	9 365	66.6	15.5
Jackson	269	6.6	33	77	2	129	301	4	316	NA	NA	NA	7 482	8 807	51.1	8.1
Jefferson	372	31.8	4	33	0	0	0	2	96	NA	NA	NA	2 068	2 372	51.7	11.3
Lafayette	25	5.7	2	34	0	0	0	0	0	NA	NA	NA	1 019	937	53.9	8.5
Lake	960	7.8	160	109	4	675	459	21	1 018	NA	NA	NA	18 609	16 923	61.8	12.6
Lee	1 745	6.8	501	154	5	1 318	406	27	1 675	NA	NA	NA	35 309	30 009	67.4	13.3
Leon	1 057	6.4	404	216	3	819	438	8	526	NA	NA	NA	24 106	24 024	78.8	32.0
Levy	144	6.2	16	60	1	40	149	2	230	NA	NA	NA	4 216	4 036	53.8	7.8
Liberty	22	4.9	1	22	0	0	0	1	32	NA	NA	NA	1 001	891	47.7	8.0
Madison	78	5.1	9	57	1	37	233	3	110	NA	NA	NA	3 177	3 305	43.5	8.3
Manatee	1 041	6.1	305	160	2	895	469	31	1 789	NA	NA	NA	22 873	20 920	66.5	12.4
Marion	1 147	7.4	213	107	4	612	308	21	831	NA	NA	NA	25 456	22 078	59.5	9.6
Martin	482	6.1	190	189	1	236	235	2	302	NA	NA	NA	10 253	8 834	70.4	16.0
Monroe	447	6.4	102	129	4	269	341	4	395	NA	NA	NA	7 528	8 161	72.3	15.9
Nassau	188	4.9	31	66	1	54	115	2	128	NA	NA	NA	7 840	7 853	58.1	9.1
Okaloosa	1 100	8.5	175	112	5	627	402	8	551	NA	NA	NA	23 889	24 205	77.4	16.6
Okeechobee	176	7.1	27	87	1	101	326	1	20	NA	NA	NA	5 281	4 479	50.6	5.7
Orange	3 524	6.6	1 299	206	9	3 039	482	57	2 863	NA	NA	NA	84 125	85 680	70.4	15.7
Osceola	985	14.0	90	95	5	515	546	8	612	NA	NA	NA	13 133	8 817	61.4	9.2
Palm Beach	4 012	5.8	1 791	210	22	3 711	436	64	4 670	NA	NA	NA	84 685	73 748	70.7	17.1
Pasco	1 200	5.2	292	106	5	941	342	36	1 985	NA	NA	NA	29 347	25 721	55.8	6.8
Pinellas	4 987	6.3	1 580	191	23	5 782	700	177	9 332	NA	NA	NA	88 934	93 576	68.3	14.6
Polk	2 553	7.1	555	137	8	1 519	375	39	2 564	NA	NA	NA	59 233	60 487	59.8	11.4
Putnam	369	6.4	47	74	1	161	253	9	293	NA	NA	NA	10 851	10 168	55.3	8.1
St. Johns	323	5.1	124	150	2	237	286	5	302	NA	NA	NA	9 593	9 285	66.0	14.4
St. Lucie	620	5.5	169	118	5	570	397	7	562	NA	NA	NA	17 131	14 011	62.7	10.9
Santa Rosa	389	6.1	77	105	4	194	264	4	206	NA	NA	NA	13 315	12 769	69.5	14.4
Sarasota	1 499	6.3	626	235	6	1 466	551	28	1 899	NA	NA	NA	25 436	24 294	73.4	17.7
Seminole	792	3.6	345	121	3	406	143	15	1 226	NA	NA	NA	41 626	36 743	76.2	19.5

1. Per 1,000 resident population estimated as of July 1 of the year shown. 2. As of end of year. 3. Per 100,000 resident population as of July 1 of the year shown. 4. Preliminary. Covers nursing homes with 3 or more beds. 5. Data for serious crimes have not been adjusted for underreporting, this may affect comparability between geographic areas or over time. 6. Includes murder and nonnegligent manslaughter, forcible rape, robbery, and aggravated assault. 7. The 1986–1987 data are based on administrative reports obtained by the U.S. National Center for Education Statistics. The 1980 data are based on the 1980 Census of Population and Housing. 8. Persons 25 years old or older.

STATE County	Education (cont'd) Local government expenditures for education,[1] 1982: Total (Mil dol)	Education (cont'd) Local government expenditures for education,[1] 1982: Per capita (Dollars)	Social Security Program December 1988 Beneficiaries: Total	Social Security Program December 1988 Beneficiaries: Rate[2]	Social Security Program December 1988: Payments ($1,000)	Supplemental Security Income Program recipients June 1986	Money income Per capita[3]: 1987 Income, (Dollars)	Money income Per capita[3] 1979: Current dollars	Money income Per capita[3] 1979: Constant 1987 dollars	Money income: Median household income 1979 (Dollars)	Money income Percent below poverty level, 1979: Persons	Money income Percent below poverty level, 1979: Families	Housing units, 1990: Total	Housing units, 1990: Percent change, 1980–1990
	60	61	62	63	64	65	66	67	68	69	70	71	72	73
DELAWARE	252.4	421	100 203	151.8	51 316	7 699	12 785	7 449	11 655	17 846	11.9	8.9	289 919	21.5
Kent	41.6	420	14 050	129.4	6 652	1 552	10 445	6 126	9 585	15 342	13.6	11.1	42 106	19.1
New Castle	160.5	400	61 350	140.9	32 596	4 180	13 891	8 067	12 622	19 656	11.0	8.0	173 560	16.8
Sussex	50.3	506	24 660	212.2	11 999	1 964	10 829	6 262	9 798	14 483	13.6	10.1	74 253	35.8
DISTRICT OF COLUMBIA	324.6	519	78 774	127.7	33 589	16 383	14 778	8 959	14 018	16 211	18.6	15.1	278 489	0.5
District of Columbia	324.6	519	78 630	127.4	33 518	16 383	14 778	8 959	14 018	16 211	18.6	15.1	278 489	0.5
FLORIDA	4 019.2	384	2 503 546	203.0	1 238 374	189 217	12 456	7 260	11 360	14 675	13.5	9.9	6 100 262	39.3
Alachua	52.6	327	22 645	123.8	10 348	3 416	10 928	6 094	9 535	12 354	23.5	13.9	79 022	34.1
Baker	7.9	482	2 140	115.1	895	290	8 033	4 727	7 396	14 391	16.6	12.3	5 975	31.4
Bay	47.3	454	18 855	150.2	8 358	1 914	9 689	5 968	9 338	13 271	16.2	12.8	65 999	53.8
Bradford	8.9	410	3 230	130.8	1 360	470	7 892	4 813	7 531	11 816	19.8	17.9	8 099	11.7
Brevard	115.2	381	69 235	178.3	33 725	2 648	12 775	7 448	11 654	16 858	9.7	7.3	185 150	62.6
Broward	360.6	337	267 120	225.0	143 139	8 994	14 914	8 621	13 489	16 580	9.1	6.3	628 660	29.3
Calhoun	4.5	480	2 000	196.1	785	460	7 815	4 710	7 370	10 657	23.7	19.6	4 468	25.4
Charlotte	19.7	292	32 000	337.2	16 376	342	12 554	7 547	11 809	13 190	8.9	6.7	64 641	85.8
Citrus	21.0	329	30 295	330.7	15 058	718	10 487	6 055	9 474	11 258	13.6	10.0	49 854	70.8
Clay	33.9	459	10 675	106.2	4 880	544	11 556	6 741	10 548	18 407	10.0	8.6	40 249	65.4
Collier	47.8	475	32 215	232.6	17 261	846	16 466	9 424	14 746	16 620	13.6	9.5	94 165	85.6
Columbia	15.6	417	6 955	165.2	2 904	1 166	9 213	5 702	8 922	12 794	19.7	15.3	17 818	30.7
Dade	682.4	398	265 040	146.1	126 399	69 446	12 401	7 722	12 083	15 571	15.0	11.9	771 288	15.9
De Soto	9.4	466	4 920	216.7	2 261	370	8 139	4 913	7 687	11 292	21.1	16.1	10 310	38.2
Dixie	3.9	463	2 005	194.7	857	238	7 334	4 690	7 338	9 631	25.2	22.3	6 445	60.7
Duval	247.4	419	88 775	131.8	41 177	10 876	11 614	6 822	10 674	14 938	15.8	12.7	284 673	25.4
Escambia	103.8	418	37 430	134.4	16 075	4 706	10 316	6 183	9 675	14 442	17.4	14.0	112 230	26.6
Flagler	10.4	785	6 320	272.4	3 245	154	11 529	6 920	10 828	14 562	15.5	11.8	15 215	158.3
Franklin	4.5	569	1 815	213.5	742	324	7 648	4 653	7 281	9 444	28.3	23.6	5 891	31.0
Gadsden	20.3	475	7 655	167.1	2 859	1 952	6 990	4 172	6 528	11 110	32.6	26.3	14 859	11.2
Gilchrist	3.7	554	1 530	201.3	653	148	8 743	4 804	7 517	10 778	19.3	16.1	4 071	53.8
Glades	2.9	466	835	121.0	394	42	7 667	4 615	7 221	10 074	21.0	16.6	4 624	33.1
Gulf	5.8	524	2 175	175.4	971	358	8 153	4 932	7 717	12 089	21.3	18.3	6 339	33.7
Hamilton	5.6	620	1 840	187.8	714	458	7 172	4 350	6 806	10 565	26.6	21.8	4 119	23.2
Hardee	11.0	527	3 390	155.5	1 428	506	7 832	5 130	8 027	12 028	25.8	19.3	7 941	12.5
Hendry	10.9	531	3 200	127.5	1 461	322	8 939	5 738	8 978	14 565	21.5	16.8	9 945	41.4
Hernando	18.4	330	32 570	347.2	16 278	726	9 780	5 881	9 202	12 366	13.4	9.7	50 018	121.9
Highlands	18.7	353	21 630	325.3	10 572	784	10 024	5 964	9 332	11 283	18.8	12.6	40 114	54.3
Hillsborough	282.5	412	121 995	149.7	57 641	12 578	11 752	6 683	10 457	14 868	14.0	10.7	367 740	39.5
Holmes	7.3	470	3 215	192.5	1 196	716	8 203	4 741	7 418	9 880	26.9	21.5	6 785	18.0
Indian River	28.8	423	27 105	311.9	14 040	618	13 722	7 976	12 480	15 101	12.3	8.3	47 128	60.2
Jackson	17.5	435	8 545	200.6	3 315	2 084	7 961	4 672	7 310	10 636	23.0	18.5	16 320	11.9
Jefferson	6.4	568	2 025	168.8	779	520	7 713	4 570	7 151	9 786	28.3	23.7	4 395	14.4
Lafayette	2.3	549	685	126.9	280	88	8 815	4 934	7 720	11 090	21.4	18.1	2 266	28.5
Lake	43.7	384	44 060	310.1	21 521	1 592	11 837	6 449	10 091	12 489	14.0	9.9	75 707	49.9
Lee	89.9	390	84 660	273.9	43 127	2 310	12 948	7 554	11 820	14 612	11.0	7.7	189 051	70.3
Leon	60.1	380	19 250	105.3	9 072	2 340	11 923	6 862	10 737	14 369	17.8	11.8	81 325	36.6
Levy	9.5	430	5 200	199.2	2 300	562	8 579	5 100	7 980	10 686	20.8	16.6	12 307	35.7
Liberty	2.4	557	900	195.7	354	214	8 309	4 730	7 401	10 541	22.1	17.9	2 157	6.4
Madison	7.9	518	3 140	198.7	1 214	928	6 943	4 205	6 580	10 169	30.2	26.4	6 275	12.9
Manatee	54.2	336	54 425	291.2	27 283	1 554	12 357	7 206	11 275	13 568	11.0	7.9	115 245	37.9
Marion	56.7	407	49 265	259.6	23 599	2 630	9 707	5 813	9 096	11 797	17.9	14.0	94 567	70.9
Martin	30.4	418	28 170	294.1	14 734	560	15 256	8 099	12 673	15 749	11.1	7.3	54 199	59.4
Monroe	22.7	338	10 060	130.8	4 841	722	14 184	7 755	12 134	13 713	13.4	10.0	46 215	21.3
Nassau	16.3	459	5 235	115.8	2 434	570	11 039	6 416	10 039	16 948	12.4	10.1	18 726	40.8
Okaloosa	52.8	444	16 755	111.3	7 233	1 468	11 192	6 422	10 049	15 151	10.9	8.7	62 569	45.2
Okeechobee	11.5	493	6 525	219.7	3 077	472	9 224	5 478	8 571	12 074	17.5	13.2	13 266	38.1
Orange	203.0	405	90 665	148.3	43 254	6 812	12 501	6 985	10 929	15 298	13.2	10.0	282 686	53.0
Osceola	21.4	358	15 875	177.0	7 625	526	10 770	6 055	9 474	12 984	11.8	9.3	47 959	101.3
Palm Beach	227.3	352	203 305	248.4	111 467	5 674	15 964	8 899	13 924	16 665	10.1	6.7	461 665	56.1
Pasco	67.2	310	93 675	353.2	46 729	2 090	10 797	6 063	9 487	11 645	10.9	7.7	148 965	47.7
Pinellas	232.6	307	233 480	284.4	116 685	6 676	13 451	7 610	11 907	13 404	9.8	6.5	458 341	21.6
Polk	142.1	417	80 120	202.4	38 396	5 464	10 393	6 445	10 084	14 248	14.6	10.3	186 225	38.1
Putnam	24.1	450	13 365	214.2	5 984	1 372	9 109	5 387	8 429	11 438	21.3	17.1	31 840	34.7
St. Johns	26.3	460	14 405	182.6	6 941	1 008	12 315	6 665	10 429	14 213	15.6	11.0	40 712	78.1
St. Lucie	37.8	373	30 300	222.8	15 094	1 496	10 623	6 460	10 108	13 878	17.1	12.3	73 843	80.5
Santa Rosa	37.7	631	9 400	131.7	4 086	928	10 501	6 057	9 477	15 085	16.2	13.9	32 831	61.3
Sarasota	68.3	311	97 575	374.4	50 971	1 480	14 848	8 449	13 220	15 069	9.1	6.1	157 055	38.6
Seminole	79.3	398	29 955	111.0	14 372	1 916	13 594	7 672	12 004	18 289	9.2	7.0	117 845	72.9

1. Elementary and secondary. 2. Per 1,000 resident population estimated as of July 1 of the year shown. 3. Based on the resident population estimated as of July 1, 1988 for 1987 data and enumerated as of April 1, 1980 for 1979 data.

STATE County	Housing units, 1990 (cont'd): Occupied units: Total	Owner occupied: Percent	Owner occupied: Median value (Dollars)	Median rent (Dollars)	Civilian labor force, 1990: Total	Percent change, 1989–1990	Unemployment: Total	Unemployment: Rate[1]	Private nonfarm establishments, 1988: Number	Net change, 1987–1988	Employment[2]: Total	Per-cent change, 1987–1988	Manu-facturing	Retail trade
	74	75	76	77	78	79	80	81	82	83	84	85	86	87
DELAWARE	247 497	70.2	100 100	425	362 000	0.0	19 000	5.1	X	X	288 288	5.4	67 621	59 869
Kent	39 655	69.2	80 800	343	52 226	1.3	3 232	6.2	2 426	62	32 831	10.5	7 988	10 005
New Castle	164 161	68.3	110 900	460	246 387	0.1	12 631	5.1	11 445	512	216 656	5.4	47 690	40 805
Sussex	43 681	78.6	79 800	278	64 387	0.1	3 137	4.9	3 533	52	38 641	1.4	11 943	9 059
DISTRICT OF COLUMBIA	249 634	38.9	123 900	441	298 000	-5.4	20 000	6.6	19 842	166	408 974	3.1	16 193	55 267
District of Columbia	249 634	38.9	123 900	441	298 000	-5.4	20 000	6.6	19 842	166	408 974	3.1	16 193	55 267
FLORIDA	5 134 869	67.2	77 100	402	6 365 000	2.8	378 000	5.9	X	X	4 273 861	4.6	517 930	1 101 174
Alachua	71 258	54.1	66 000	316	98 808	3.1	3 330	3.4	4 459	65	57 253	2.8	5 762	17 539
Baker	5 554	79.3	53 400	225	8 091	3.8	524	6.5	228	9	1 542	7.6	224	457
Bay	48 938	65.5	61 600	289	60 531	-0.1	5 130	8.5	3 663	75	37 651	2.5	3 090	13 285
Bradford	7 193	77.0	49 300	223	10 261	4.0	473	4.6	396	11	3 339	5.5	785	1 211
Brevard	161 365	69.2	75 200	404	195 550	4.3	10 811	5.5	9 113	270	126 107	5.2	25 352	31 217
Broward	528 442	68.0	91 800	497	660 159	2.0	36 231	5.5	37 956	1 456	426 412	2.7	44 740	116 148
Calhoun	3 793	79.4	33 200	149	3 924	2.8	314	8.0	226	-1	1 780	-3.1	401	428
Charlotte	48 433	79.6	77 200	412	39 294	10.5	2 065	5.3	2 097	119	19 962	10.3	694	6 288
Citrus	40 573	83.2	66 100	297	36 783	7.8	2 547	6.9	1 790	44	16 591	8.3	913	5 327
Clay	36 663	73.4	82 100	404	45 903	1.7	2 218	4.8	2 142	67	21 333	3.6	1 437	8 026
Collier	61 703	70.2	121 400	495	78 307	8.7	4 225	5.4	5 323	416	51 027	11.3	1 814	15 329
Columbia	15 611	73.7	47 300	222	19 869	1.6	1 649	8.3	935	6	11 492	7.2	3 598	3 597
Dade	692 355	54.3	86 500	422	952 318	1.2	63 849	6.7	58 752	716	727 290	2.1	94 379	152 735
De Soto	8 222	74.0	49 600	272	9 160	14.2	844	9.2	391	0	3 351	5.9	0	1 184
Dixie	3 916	82.6	37 500	160	3 932	2.7	280	7.1	184	-4	1 310	5.4	479	395
Duval	257 245	62.0	64 000	355	351 209	1.7	19 628	5.6	18 254	374	293 253	4.6	30 074	64 513
Escambia	98 608	64.7	57 800	305	119 439	1.5	6 929	5.8	6 264	65	82 020	1.5	9 135	23 040
Flagler	11 880	76.5	97 500	435	11 334	10.7	700	6.2	513	36	5 585	33.6	1 014	1 374
Franklin	3 628	80.5	51 700	206	5 459	-6.7	321	5.9	220	-6	1 261	5.9	83	404
Gadsden	13 405	75.6	39 500	168	20 834	3.3	1 220	5.9	617	-24	7 098	-2.5	2 001	1 394
Gilchrist	3 284	85.4	45 900	198	3 677	6.0	230	6.3	135	7	843	22.0	78	250
Glades	2 885	78.2	57 200	255	3 156	5.6	280	8.9	65	4	591	71.3	167	147
Gulf	4 324	78.5	43 200	193	4 458	-1.2	336	7.5	197	-2	2 457	2.6	0	444
Hamilton	3 488	76.2	36 300	143	3 843	2.9	320	8.3	157	-6	1 106	-9.1	154	493
Hardee	6 391	75.8	40 300	257	9 056	4.0	990	10.9	389	6	2 648	4.7	187	893
Hendry	8 402	70.8	61 200	302	11 151	2.0	1 444	12.9	463	8	3 943	2.5	771	1 275
Hernando	42 300	84.5	71 200	341	38 673	2.8	2 631	6.8	1 789	119	15 380	7.7	866	5 101
Highlands	29 544	78.0	58 500	282	26 052	6.9	2 055	7.9	1 548	21	12 526	-4.2	913	4 194
Hillsborough	324 872	63.1	73 100	374	466 230	2.2	22 441	4.8	22 815	278	344 857	5.8	35 979	75 636
Holmes	5 800	80.8	36 200	181	6 550	0.0	471	7.2	214	-8	1 890	-5.5	533	613
Indian River	38 057	75.0	78 800	422	42 752	7.1	3 919	9.2	2 731	110	26 951	6.0	2 217	7 389
Jackson	14 465	77.0	41 400	165	19 411	2.7	1 309	6.7	737	9	7 690	3.3	1 655	2 288
Jefferson	3 982	76.7	43 900	199	5 195	6.1	265	5.1	185	2	1 694	20.9	344	491
Lafayette	1 721	80.7	43 700	175	2 793	2.1	154	5.5	67	-2	610	19.6	266	61
Lake	63 616	78.3	67 800	311	59 799	3.7	4 695	7.9	3 332	116	33 757	4.4	3 997	10 369
Lee	140 124	72.1	84 300	417	152 616	4.9	6 739	4.4	9 525	413	98 786	8.7	6 014	30 623
Leon	74 828	56.9	75 200	351	116 364	3.1	4 470	3.8	5 220	143	60 282	7.1	2 823	19 014
Levy	10 079	81.8	49 100	214	10 698	4.1	630	5.9	481	-20	3 562	2.7	370	1 295
Liberty	1 706	80.8	39 600	158	3 060	15.1	111	3.6	71	5	781	12.1	160	111
Madison	5 522	76.0	38 800	148	7 835	2.8	583	7.4	285	12	2 823	3.4	1 199	635
Manatee	91 060	70.9	79 400	397	93 021	7.6	4 316	4.6	4 289	-29	50 686	-1.2	6 194	15 990
Marion	78 177	75.6	61 800	297	80 781	2.9	5 583	6.9	4 510	136	49 432	9.0	8 347	14 652
Martin	43 022	76.9	112 700	442	42 953	3.5	3 137	7.3	3 289	194	33 067	7.2	3 827	9 639
Monroe	33 583	62.1	151 200	523	44 370	5.6	1 479	3.3	2 757	65	25 068	4.2	526	9 804
Nassau	16 192	78.5	72 600	327	22 624	2.1	1 320	5.8	887	8	8 355	0.9	1 992	2 274
Okaloosa	53 313	62.2	70 600	342	64 813	2.2	4 047	6.2	3 708	83	38 493	6.1	4 580	12 472
Okeechobee	10 214	72.4	55 600	312	12 678	4.5	1 142	9.0	615	5	4 970	0.3	275	1 838
Orange	254 852	59.3	81 400	441	408 016	4.3	22 279	5.5	19 137	627	334 860	6.7	40 217	69 922
Osceola	39 150	65.7	75 700	438	53 474	3.7	2 719	5.1	2 030	107	28 788	7.9	1 894	10 338
Palm Beach	365 558	71.9	98 400	499	430 148	2.1	28 086	6.5	26 188	1 229	311 676	5.7	38 396	80 806
Pasco	121 674	80.9	59 000	329	100 253	2.8	6 912	6.9	5 034	174	49 899	5.3	4 074	16 863
Pinellas	380 635	69.2	73 800	393	412 718	2.6	20 124	4.9	23 961	388	307 693	3.7	46 471	81 317
Polk	155 969	70.5	61 000	300	182 628	1.6	17 738	9.7	8 906	191	130 560	8.2	21 720	34 109
Putnam	25 070	79.0	49 900	222	25 232	1.7	1 745	6.9	1 066	3	11 364	5.7	3 157	3 844
St. Johns	33 426	70.4	85 800	394	40 011	1.8	2 250	5.6	1 901	108	20 221	5.5	2 117	6 964
St. Lucie	58 174	71.9	73 400	410	66 197	5.5	8 280	12.5	3 013	149	32 367	8.1	2 855	9 763
Santa Rosa	29 900	75.3	65 900	285	30 375	1.7	2 075	6.8	1 261	-2	11 620	6.0	1 608	3 560
Sarasota	125 493	76.2	87 200	458	126 594	3.9	5 188	4.1	9 835	300	99 952	6.0	12 021	29 409
Seminole	107 657	66.9	91 500	471	179 038	3.8	8 996	5.0	7 052	296	77 479	6.9	11 395	23 284

1. Percent of total civilian labor force. 2. For week including March 12. Excludes government employees, self-employed persons, farm workers, domestic service workers, railroad employees subject to the Railroad Retirement Act, and employees on oceanborne vessels or in foreign countries.

STATE County	Private nonfarm establishments, 1988 (cont'd): Employment[1] (cont'd): Finance, insurance, and real estate	Employment[1] (cont'd): Services	Annual payroll: Total (Mil dol)	Annual payroll: Average per employee (Dollars)	Personal income, 1989: Total (Mil dol)	Percent change, 1988–1989	Wages and salaries[2] (Mil dol)	Proprietor's income (Mil dol)	Dividends, interest, & rent (Mil dol)	Transfer payments (Mil dol)	Per capita[3]: Dollars	Per capita[3]: Rank	Earnings, 1989: Total (Mil dol)	Percent by selected industries: Farm	Percent by selected industries: Goods-related[4]: Total
	88	89	90	91	92	93	94	95	96	97	98	99	100	101	102
DELAWARE	27 499	77 300	6 400	X	12 611	8.8	9 281	1 005	2 209	1 558	18 750	X	10 286	1.8	39.1
Kent	1 469	7 624	511	15 555	1 552	7.6	1 013	111	205	271	14 054	1 411	1 125	3.8	21.2
New Castle	23 798	61 525	5 263	24 294	9 256	9.0	7 329	668	1 648	974	20 907	128	7 996	0.2	42.4
Sussex	2 220	8 108	623	16 112	1 803	9.2	939	226	356	314	15 095	944	1 165	10.7	33.8
DISTRICT OF COLUMBIA	40 494	251 125	10 563	25 828	13 973	4.6	24 619	1 471	2 255	2 713	22 998	X	26 090	0.0	4.6
District of Columbia	40 494	251 125	10 563	25 828	13 973	4.6	24 619	1 471	2 255	2 713	22 998	72	26 090	0.0	4.6
FLORIDA	365 336	1 330 684	78 002	X	224 410	9.7	123 500	15 979	57 524	35 843	17 715	X	139 479	1.8	18.4
Alachua	4 295	20 271	888	15 514	2 736	9.7	1 892	202	440	438	14 719	1 116	2 094	1.0	11.5
Baker	97	248	23	15 165	221	8.1	80	20	17	38	11 670	2 452	100	10.4	NA
Bay	3 252	10 539	530	14 075	1 747	8.1	1 054	150	276	364	13 524	1 667	1 204	0.0	15.2
Bradford	119	748	43	12 905	250	10.5	98	23	28	55	10 029	2 877	121	7.2	NA
Brevard	5 260	45 054	2 624	20 811	6 618	10.5	4 100	327	1 297	1 127	16 445	536	4 428	0.4	30.1
Broward	42 365	131 110	8 323	19 518	26 470	9.2	12 086	1 396	7 970	3 652	21 898	96	13 482	0.2	18.4
Calhoun	53	293	22	12 349	96	7.8	42	13	13	29	9 243	2 986	54	2.7	NA
Charlotte	1 702	6 333	313	15 680	1 670	14.1	506	105	666	419	16 600	504	611	1.7	18.0
Citrus	1 070	4 350	253	15 233	1 214	12.4	409	79	424	342	12 559	2 090	488	0.7	14.8
Clay	989	5 791	309	14 475	1 658	9.0	491	93	187	222	15 785	715	585	1.2	21.8
Collier	4 363	17 662	863	16 915	3 413	14.6	1 361	306	1 503	391	23 322	69	1 667	4.8	18.7
Columbia	430	1 919	201	17 465	510	8.3	260	36	70	112	11 947	2 342	296	2.2	19.1
Dade	69 871	223 340	14 700	20 212	32 964	8.1	22 415	2 448	7 187	4 734	17 963	300	24 862	0.7	13.5
De Soto	208	846	41	12 383	271	7.9	119	24	53	68	11 712	2 436	143	8.2	11.2
Dixie	44	181	16	12 466	103	12.0	47	9	15	28	9 690	2 928	56	2.3	NA
Duval	35 922	83 332	5 723	19 515	11 056	7.2	9 318	569	1 532	1 617	16 074	627	9 888	0.1	15.7
Escambia	4 231	26 941	1 344	16 385	3 793	7.8	2 618	276	549	794	13 375	1 745	2 894	0.0	17.5
Flagler	780	1 448	87	15 633	348	12.8	140	26	93	83	13 506	1 679	166	6.2	29.9
Franklin	92	318	15	11 695	103	9.3	35	16	21	28	12 100	2 290	51	0.0	8.7
Gadsden	315	1 381	100	14 148	483	9.3	245	44	57	113	10 445	2 802	289	9.0	NA
Gilchrist	109	178	9	10 811	101	8.8	29	18	15	23	12 947	1 929	47	28.0	NA
Glades	33	23	7	12 555	61	5.1	21	13	13	13	8 776	3 027	35	41.9	NA
Gulf	94	437	52	21 065	136	5.9	82	8	17	34	10 824	2 709	90	0.0	NA
Hamilton	35	240	13	11 806	106	9.2	119	7	10	27	10 733	2 734	126	1.8	NA
Hardee	194	573	39	14 578	266	4.6	102	51	46	45	12 128	2 272	153	27.7	NA
Hendry	367	846	63	16 099	357	4.7	160	89	52	48	13 728	1 564	249	30.8	19.1
Hernando	985	4 135	218	14 163	1 281	12.7	367	81	349	352	12 676	2 044	448	2.9	19.0
Highlands	811	3 863	170	13 575	964	9.8	324	109	320	243	13 932	1 458	433	14.8	14.5
Hillsborough	30 337	113 150	6 479	18 788	13 402	9.1	10 192	970	2 108	1 882	16 044	635	11 162	1.6	15.9
Holmes	61	487	20	10 557	171	10.4	51	21	23	46	10 096	2 870	71	13.7	16.6
Indian River	2 119	8 735	435	16 126	1 881	13.4	708	139	790	316	20 880	130	847	5.4	21.2
Jackson	474	1 290	97	12 623	481	8.8	234	37	63	133	11 205	2 600	271	4.3	17.2
Jefferson	106	453	20	11 553	129	4.5	46	14	19	29	10 628	2 765	59	17.9	13.5
Lafayette	0	61	7	12 133	67	11.9	17	20	8	12	11 554	2 484	37	48.8	NA
Lake	2 718	8 795	491	14 550	2 600	9.9	881	307	747	513	17 698	337	1 188	14.9	18.2
Lee	8 797	28 656	1 647	16 671	5 858	12.4	2 570	429	1 966	1 032	18 063	286	3 000	1.7	18.1
Leon	4 413	21 833	937	15 537	2 943	10.4	2 268	188	400	370	15 724	731	2 455	0.1	8.2
Levy	294	642	43	11 992	292	9.8	92	32	59	71	10 884	2 689	124	8.7	NA
Liberty	0	219	11	13 570	56	11.0	23	4	6	17	12 110	2 283	28	0.5	NA
Madison	88	503	38	13 469	174	8.8	76	16	30	44	10 934	2 678	92	5.9	25.2
Manatee	3 625	16 855	803	15 836	3 530	11.6	1 392	284	1 177	647	18 482	253	1 676	6.4	23.8
Marion	2 765	12 309	731	14 778	2 525	10.8	1 194	187	603	572	12 699	2 035	1 381	1.8	25.6
Martin	3 081	8 886	575	17 382	2 394	11.7	868	186	979	314	23 832	55	1 054	6.8	25.2
Monroe	1 789	8 132	345	13 776	1 418	10.9	664	141	506	169	17 986	296	805	0.0	9.2
Nassau	1 164	1 415	139	16 603	721	8.3	282	44	86	90	15 316	869	325	1.1	30.4
Okaloosa	3 392	11 892	533	13 856	2 124	8.7	1 378	133	320	449	13 619	1 620	1 512	0.1	12.6
Okeechobee	266	1 388	68	13 639	347	9.1	129	39	61	79	11 193	2 603	168	14.1	13.0
Orange	23 694	129 226	6 552	19 567	11 409	9.9	10 424	877	1 769	1 430	18 083	284	11 300	1.6	19.7
Osceola	1 497	10 858	381	13 220	1 662	13.0	657	103	242	217	17 596	358	761	2.8	19.9
Palm Beach	32 392	94 341	6 378	20 463	20 707	11.3	9 322	1 308	8 282	2 555	24 319	46	10 630	3.0	21.4
Pasco	3 345	15 485	700	14 032	3 770	9.4	1 119	260	1 129	985	13 710	1 575	1 379	3.0	17.4
Pinellas	26 319	103 243	5 346	17 374	17 554	10.2	7 678	1 362	5 351	3 128	21 255	119	9 040	0.1	22.3
Polk	9 217	33 078	2 198	16 837	5 768	8.9	3 341	566	1 218	1 015	14 246	1 302	3 908	4.8	25.6
Putnam	501	2 180	186	16 359	719	7.2	326	58	121	190	11 304	2 566	384	4.8	34.4
St. Johns	1 194	5 932	286	14 130	1 528	11.8	484	114	339	218	18 436	257	598	5.6	19.4
St. Lucie	2 642	8 613	529	16 337	1 914	9.6	916	178	449	408	13 349	1 757	1 094	6.0	15.1
Santa Rosa	593	3 608	152	13 094	1 031	7.9	375	65	141	191	14 023	1 426	441	0.6	21.1
Sarasota	7 996	31 072	1 650	16 504	6 402	11.5	2 371	404	2 867	1 148	24 039	51	2 775	0.4	20.0
Seminole	4 233	18 719	1 371	17 694	4 634	10.0	1 879	375	602	518	16 316	564	2 255	1.0	25.1

1. For week including March 12. Excludes government employees, self-employed persons, farm workers, domestic service workers, railroad employees subject to the Railroad Retirement Act, and employees on oceanborne vessels or in foreign countries. 2. Includes other labor income. 3. Based on the resident population estimated as of July 1 of the year shown. 4. Covers mining, construction, and manufacturing.

STATE County	Earnings, 1989 (cont'd) — Percent by selected industries (cont'd) — Goods-related[1] — Manu-facturing	Service-related & other[2] — Total	Retail trade	Finance, insur-ance, & real estate	Services	Govern-ment	Agriculture, 1987 — Farms — Number	Percent with — Less than 50 acres	500 acres and over	Farm operators, percent — Whose principal occu-pation is farming	Residing on farm operated	Land in farms — Acreage (1,000)	Percent change, 1982–1987	Acres — Average size of farm	Total irrigated (1,000)	Total cropland (1,000)
	103	104	105	106	107	108	109	110	111	112	113	114	115	116	117	118
DELAWARE	30.8	46.3	8.6	7.8	20.1	12.7	2 966	46.6	10.7	59.8	73.3	608	-7.2	205	61	501
Kent	16.5	36.7	10.8	2.3	16.7	38.3	857	37.8	12.0	56.4	75.6	201	-4.1	235	19	170
New Castle	33.5	48.0	7.7	8.9	21.1	9.3	380	39.2	14.5	55.5	75.5	94	-7.9	247	2	78
Sussex	26.0	44.4	12.5	5.3	16.4	11.2	1 729	52.5	9.1	62.5	71.7	313	-8.9	181	40	253
DISTRICT OF COLUMBIA	2.7	53.3	3.6	5.4	37.6	42.0	NA	NA	NA	NA	NA	NA	NA	NA	NA	NA
District of Columbia	2.7	53.3	3.6	5.4	37.6	42.0	NA	NA	NA	NA	NA	NA	NA	NA	NA	NA
FLORIDA	10.7	63.9	12.4	7.6	30.1	16.0	36 556	56.5	9.0	43.3	62.5	11 194	-12.6	306	1 623	3 791
Alachua	6.2	50.0	10.3	4.4	29.3	37.5	1 161	54.3	7.6	37.9	74.8	192	-12.3	166	9	83
Baker	6.9	31.3	9.3	2.2	7.1	49.2	220	57.7	6.8	35.0	75.9	28	-13.1	127	0	10
Bay	8.3	53.2	14.8	4.5	24.9	31.6	85	57.6	3.5	32.9	68.2	11	-38.7	135	D	4
Bradford	9.0	NA	13.0	2.7	17.0	40.7	349	56.4	4.0	34.1	75.1	41	1.2	118	0	17
Brevard	23.8	53.9	10.4	2.9	34.6	15.6	495	78.6	5.9	32.3	55.8	165	-14.9	333	17	28
Broward	9.8	69.7	14.0	8.9	33.2	11.7	448	82.1	3.6	38.8	55.8	36	-52.1	80	6	D
Calhoun	9.7	49.7	13.0	1.7	18.0	31.8	159	28.9	17.0	42.8	72.3	48	-14.0	303	1	32
Charlotte	2.8	67.3	17.4	6.4	35.5	13.0	197	46.2	17.8	44.2	58.4	214	-1.3	1 088	9	24
Citrus	3.2	69.0	14.8	4.5	28.0	15.5	331	58.0	7.9	38.1	74.6	74	-20.3	224	1	19
Clay	6.9	61.6	18.8	3.8	27.0	15.4	244	66.4	7.0	33.2	78.7	84	-21.0	344	0	8
Collier	3.6	67.0	14.4	7.5	34.2	9.5	224	43.3	34.4	61.2	38.4	332	18.7	1 483	43	60
Columbia	12.5	48.2	15.4	3.3	18.3	30.6	535	40.4	9.3	40.0	76.4	99	-15.4	184	2	50
Dade	8.5	71.4	11.2	8.9	31.9	14.4	1 623	84.8	2.3	44.3	55.5	83	-5.0	51	53	66
De Soto	5.0	42.1	10.4	2.8	16.7	38.4	654	52.1	13.6	39.1	53.2	351	1.0	537	48	87
Dixie	30.7	NA	11.4	1.0	11.2	31.5	114	36.8	13.2	26.3	70.2	56	-77.9	495	0	6
Duval	9.2	62.8	9.9	11.8	23.3	21.4	434	77.4	3.5	36.4	76.0	42	-41.6	96	1	12
Escambia	10.8	50.6	10.3	3.8	25.9	31.9	502	54.8	6.2	39.4	76.9	65	-16.7	130	1	45
Flagler	18.8	49.7	11.9	9.2	22.3	14.3	104	30.8	25.0	52.9	74.0	83	-19.0	801	6	11
Franklin	5.5	67.7	12.5	3.2	23.1	23.6	6	66.7	0.0	0.0	50.0	D	NA	D	0	D
Gadsden	12.4	NA	8.1	1.9	10.6	41.5	348	35.3	8.0	36.5	67.8	62	-20.2	178	2	28
Gilchrist	4.0	29.1	5.9	1.9	12.5	34.3	336	34.5	11.3	42.6	72.9	88	-9.0	260	4	44
Glades	0.8	NA	5.5	NA	5.9	19.8	194	34.5	26.3	52.1	58.8	222	-54.6	1 146	50	32
Gulf	46.9	34.1	6.1	2.7	11.9	16.3	35	45.7	17.1	25.7	48.6	34	-32.7	961	D	10
Hamilton	65.6	12.7	4.1	0.6	4.6	18.1	256	23.0	16.0	45.3	61.7	74	-7.8	288	3	35
Hardee	3.6	44.9	9.0	2.7	17.3	17.4	1 130	50.5	11.3	46.3	49.9	304	-4.7	269	44	103
Hendry	12.1	33.0	7.7	2.0	10.0	17.1	396	43.7	21.7	51.0	41.9	545	1.3	1 377	145	141
Hernando	4.8	59.8	13.8	4.3	30.8	18.2	431	62.2	7.9	41.3	75.9	66	-29.7	154	1	23
Highlands	6.3	53.1	15.3	4.3	23.0	17.7	735	49.4	14.1	43.8	39.9	413	8.0	562	72	102
Hillsborough	9.3	67.5	10.7	8.7	28.9	15.0	2 754	75.8	3.8	42.2	66.4	288	-12.6	105	38	108
Holmes	13.7	40.0	10.9	2.5	21.1	29.8	572	28.3	4.0	46.7	77.8	87	-18.3	152	1	46
Indian River	9.2	62.1	14.0	5.5	32.3	11.3	539	57.9	8.9	52.5	34.9	196	-6.5	363	84	88
Jackson	13.5	41.5	12.4	4.3	13.8	37.0	910	26.7	14.1	50.9	70.5	270	0.2	296	16	163
Jefferson	8.5	46.6	10.6	4.0	18.3	21.9	296	38.9	17.6	38.2	64.5	130	-5.1	440	7	46
Lafayette	6.3	NA	3.1	NA	5.6	27.9	273	26.4	8.4	53.5	78.0	95	36.7	347	2	27
Lake	9.8	53.7	12.4	4.6	22.7	13.2	1 285	61.2	7.5	42.5	55.3	233	-25.0	181	29	112
Lee	4.8	66.5	16.4	6.9	31.7	13.7	415	61.0	9.9	45.5	61.2	133	11.9	320	17	33
Leon	2.9	50.4	10.1	5.3	27.6	41.3	302	49.7	7.0	27.2	66.2	102	-11.6	337	1	26
Levy	6.6	NA	14.6	3.6	18.1	23.1	540	34.6	13.9	41.3	75.4	180	-7.2	333	4	68
Liberty	18.6	NA	6.8	1.7	19.8	37.1	80	50.0	7.5	31.2	63.7	18	5.3	219	0	2
Madison	23.0	42.7	11.9	2.3	17.9	26.3	482	24.3	12.0	46.3	72.6	132	-24.7	274	2	63
Manatee	17.2	57.8	13.8	4.2	30.9	12.1	766	50.4	14.5	48.6	58.5	329	-6.9	430	41	93
Marion	16.7	56.6	14.2	4.9	24.1	16.0	1 707	55.7	5.6	45.7	74.6	311	-6.5	182	6	112
Martin	9.8	59.3	14.2	6.7	28.7	8.7	316	59.2	19.0	44.0	45.6	232	-13.0	733	59	85
Monroe	1.5	64.5	17.2	4.0	31.6	26.3	16	100.0	0.0	43.8	62.5	0	NA	2	0	D
Nassau	21.6	45.0	11.6	2.3	19.8	23.5	317	56.2	7.9	29.3	81.7	49	-9.5	155	0	12
Okaloosa	7.4	42.6	10.7	3.8	22.1	44.8	322	43.2	6.8	39.1	79.8	63	-11.3	195	1	29
Okeechobee	4.6	55.8	15.9	3.4	25.8	17.2	400	37.0	25.8	40.8	56.5	384	0.6	960	19	65
Orange	12.7	66.0	10.6	7.2	33.4	12.6	1 125	79.9	5.3	48.3	53.0	162	-33.6	144	34	64
Osceola	8.7	64.1	19.9	4.1	34.1	13.3	503	55.3	16.1	49.3	63.2	787	-15.2	1 565	26	67
Palm Beach	12.5	64.8	12.2	8.1	33.0	10.8	975	71.7	11.3	54.6	42.6	659	-1.3	676	423	573
Pasco	6.3	65.8	17.0	4.8	32.8	13.8	1 011	62.6	8.3	39.5	66.7	219	-20.1	217	9	64
Pinellas	15.0	66.7	13.7	11.6	31.6	10.8	166	85.5	3.6	39.8	57.2	9	-36.3	52	0	3
Polk	15.5	57.3	13.9	4.9	25.2	12.4	2 638	64.4	7.7	40.4	44.4	602	-11.4	228	115	201
Putnam	28.1	40.3	12.3	2.8	16.6	20.5	421	53.7	9.5	38.2	67.7	107	-26.1	254	8	27
St. Johns	12.4	59.4	15.1	3.6	32.2	15.5	172	40.7	15.1	62.2	62.2	49	-32.0	287	22	25
St. Lucie	5.1	63.7	14.0	5.3	26.2	15.2	522	60.7	13.2	49.2	36.6	297	-1.8	570	110	112
Santa Rosa	11.5	43.5	9.5	2.3	22.0	34.7	435	40.2	10.3	49.2	75.4	82	-11.3	188	0	59
Sarasota	7.9	67.8	16.5	6.6	35.9	11.7	352	69.3	8.8	36.4	69.6	167	-19.4	474	5	13
Seminole	13.4	62.6	15.2	6.3	28.4	11.3	390	73.3	4.6	40.3	59.2	60	-9.7	154	4	9

1. Covers mining, construction, and manufacturing. 2. Covers private sector earnings in agricultural services, forestry, and fisheries; transportation and public utilities; wholesale trade; retail trade; finance, insurance, and real estate; and services.

STATE County	Agriculture, 1987 (cont'd)								Manufactures, 1987						
	Value of land and buildings		Value of products sold				Percent of farms with sales of		Establishments		All employees			Production workers	
					Percent from										
	Average per farm ($1,000)	Average per acre (Dollars)	Total (Mil dol)	Average per farm (Dollars)	Crops	Livestock and poultry[1]	$10,000 or more	$100,000 or more	Total	Percent with 20 or more em-ployees	Number (1,000)	Percent change, 1982–1987	Annual payroll (Mil dol)	Number (1,000)	Work hours (Mil)
	119	120	121	122	123	124	125	126	127	128	129	130	131	132	133
DELAWARE	370	1 765	444	149 553	21.7	78.3	62.7	37.4	673	38.9	66.6	-1.9	2 090.8	32.8	65.2
Kent	403	1 568	84	97 557	46.5	53.5	50.4	21.7	86	36.0	6.5	-12.2	129.3	4.8	9.8
New Castle	670	2 769	30	80 044	70.1	29.9	51.6	16.8	424	39.9	47.7	-4.0	1 738.3	18.3	37.1
Sussex	287	1 607	330	190 602	10.9	89.1	71.2	49.6	163	38.0	12.4	14.8	223.2	9.7	18.3
DISTRICT OF COLUMBIA	NA	NA	NA	NA	NA	NA	NA	NA	486	25.5	17.0	1.8	494.1	5.2	10.7
District of Columbia	NA	NA	NA	NA	NA	NA	NA	NA	486	25.5	17.0	1.8	494.1	5.2	10.7
FLORIDA	544	1 790	4 351	119 033	76.2	23.8	40.1	13.1	15 603	25.9	499.3	9.9	10 954.0	308.7	614.7
Alachua	284	1 612	32	27 561	46.8	53.2	27.9	5.8	169	25.4	D	D	D	D	D
Baker	177	1 600	21	95 274	50.5	49.5	30.5	13.6	15	13.3	0.2	100.0	4.2	0.2	0.4
Bay	161	1 198	D	D	NA	NA	18.8	2.4	114	19.3	2.8	-26.3	64.8	2.2	4.6
Bradford	190	1 840	15	43 850	10.7	89.3	27.2	10.6	29	27.6	D	D	D	D	D
Brevard	424	1 358	22	43 472	77.1	22.9	31.9	6.9	387	25.1	24.3	6.1	665.0	10.5	19.7
Broward	395	6 371	43	96 748	81.7	18.3	43.5	14.7	1 790	22.2	43.3	7.4	936.0	26.2	51.9
Calhoun	298	945	9	55 030	77.4	22.6	36.5	12.6	40	12.5	0.5	66.7	5.6	0.4	0.6
Charlotte	1 144	1 093	19	93 950	74.7	25.3	47.2	14.2	69	15.9	0.6	50.0	9.0	0.4	0.8
Citrus	280	1 494	6	18 544	27.0	73.0	22.1	3.0	51	15.7	0.9	125.0	12.1	0.6	1.2
Clay	581	1 470	29	117 710	3.4	96.6	18.9	9.0	73	21.9	1.4	40.0	25.1	1.0	2.2
Collier	1 756	1 212	119	530 599	94.3	5.7	62.5	34.4	136	15.4	1.5	50.0	29.2	0.9	1.7
Columbia	210	1 185	16	30 582	34.2	65.8	28.2	4.9	47	34.0	1.7	-26.1	28.9	1.3	2.4
Dade	343	6 853	251	154 356	97.2	2.8	47.2	18.5	3 395	27.7	89.3	-9.2	1 568.4	62.2	119.0
De Soto	721	1 335	73	110 988	73.1	26.9	46.5	12.5	14	7.1	D	D	D	D	D
Dixie	388	760	1	12 875	27.8	72.2	21.1	3.5	25	16.0	0.5	25.0	8.0	0.4	0.8
Duval	248	2 193	22	51 299	19.1	80.9	24.2	8.5	743	32.8	29.9	9.1	693.4	20.4	41.3
Escambia	194	1 261	12	23 398	55.4	44.6	29.1	4.6	217	22.6	D	D	D	D	D
Flagler	713	946	11	102 905	89.8	10.2	47.1	22.1	22	31.8	0.8	60.0	16.4	0.7	1.4
Franklin	D	D	0	4 667	0.0	100.0	16.7	0.0	15	6.7	0.1	0.0	1.1	0.1	0.1
Gadsden	243	1 165	39	112 726	90.4	9.6	27.6	6.9	63	34.9	2.0	25.0	30.9	1.7	3.2
Gilchrist	414	1 336	15	44 916	23.4	76.6	33.3	5.4	6	0.0	0.1	0.0	0.6	0.0	0.1
Glades	1 054	940	37	188 549	48.1	51.9	42.3	16.0	7	0.0	0.0	0.0	0.7	0.0	0.1
Gulf	564	587	1	41 250	D	D	31.4	8.6	12	33.3	D	D	D	D	D
Hamilton	245	856	12	47 015	55.9	44.1	41.4	12.9	12	25.0	D	D	D	D	D
Hardee	493	1 848	93	82 188	72.5	27.5	56.3	14.7	17	29.4	0.2	0.0	3.7	0.1	0.3
Hendry	2 216	1 612	162	408 212	86.3	13.7	54.3	22.7	15	33.3	D	D	D	D	D
Hernando	297	2 280	25	57 104	3.9	96.1	19.0	6.0	59	22.0	0.7	16.7	12.0	0.5	1.0
Highlands	871	1 673	138	188 059	77.0	23.0	58.0	21.0	55	20.0	1.0	42.9	17.2	0.7	1.4
Hillsborough	325	3 186	223	80 793	61.8	38.2	37.2	12.5	1 034	30.6	36.1	2.3	764.5	23.0	46.6
Holmes	119	753	28	49 555	16.4	83.6	39.2	16.6	24	25.0	0.7	-12.5	7.2	0.6	1.1
Indian River	1 189	3 436	139	257 838	96.1	3.9	68.1	24.1	85	18.8	2.4	4.3	45.9	1.6	2.8
Jackson	257	797	49	53 375	63.4	36.6	52.4	12.4	46	37.0	2.0	17.6	30.7	1.7	3.1
Jefferson	434	942	17	56 540	45.0	55.0	38.9	10.1	24	8.3	0.3	-25.0	4.3	0.3	0.6
Lafayette	256	706	39	142 609	8.9	91.1	52.0	32.6	9	33.3	0.2	0.0	2.3	0.2	0.3
Lake	447	2 176	76	59 069	79.6	20.4	34.6	9.6	155	23.2	3.3	17.9	54.0	2.7	5.4
Lee	634	1 878	73	176 893	96.6	3.4	41.7	14.9	305	23.6	5.6	40.0	100.8	3.6	7.1
Leon	452	1 356	4	14 769	28.9	71.1	18.9	2.0	142	18.3	2.6	0.0	45.4	1.7	3.3
Levy	384	1 233	16	30 194	41.8	58.2	36.9	6.7	38	10.5	0.3	-40.0	5.1	0.3	0.5
Liberty	122	556	1	8 874	6.2	93.8	28.7	0.0	17	5.9	0.2	-33.3	2.7	0.1	0.3
Madison	209	810	24	50 569	22.9	77.1	41.9	11.4	35	20.0	D	D	D	D	D
Manatee	759	1 680	149	194 067	84.7	15.3	49.2	19.8	215	27.0	9.3	60.3	198.9	6.6	14.4
Marion	476	2 534	94	54 894	14.2	85.8	28.4	6.9	208	28.8	6.5	12.1	113.4	4.6	8.9
Martin	1 882	2 598	130	411 051	88.6	11.4	55.1	26.9	132	24.2	3.7	32.1	78.8	2.5	5.0
Monroe	D	D	D	D	NA	NA	56.2	12.5	87	9.2	0.5	-37.5	9.3	0.3	0.6
Nassau	245	2 208	22	69 872	4.6	95.4	23.0	10.4	59	18.6	2.3	-17.9	63.7	1.7	3.5
Okaloosa	274	1 387	5	16 946	41.7	58.3	22.7	4.0	115	27.0	4.7	56.7	75.6	3.6	7.1
Okeechobee	1 004	1 057	115	287 367	14.3	85.7	50.2	18.8	19	15.8	0.2	0.0	4.2	0.1	0.3
Orange	490	3 770	197	175 483	97.5	2.5	48.4	22.2	836	30.7	40.4	39.3	1 057.4	19.7	39.5
Osceola	1 640	1 037	57	113 292	62.9	37.1	43.3	15.3	69	30.4	2.3	15.0	47.1	1.4	2.9
Palm Beach	2 202	3 233	855	877 100	99.0	1.0	59.8	32.1	861	23.2	38.5	24.6	1 189.6	13.6	28.4
Pasco	478	2 328	59	58 796	23.9	76.1	24.7	8.9	155	18.1	3.6	-2.7	59.9	2.3	4.3
Pinellas	220	3 051	9	56 433	D	D	31.9	6.6	1 298	25.0	44.0	15.2	998.1	25.4	52.1
Polk	569	2 610	261	98 813	84.0	16.0	48.1	11.4	469	40.7	20.7	6.2	416.4	14.9	30.4
Putnam	348	1 308	27	64 420	83.3	16.7	33.5	11.2	61	29.5	3.2	3.2	77.6	2.5	5.0
St. Johns	486	1 589	39	228 455	96.4	3.6	55.8	39.5	67	19.4	1.8	50.0	25.6	1.4	2.4
St. Lucie	1 597	2 914	166	317 678	93.7	6.3	67.0	24.1	99	32.3	2.6	30.0	46.1	1.6	3.4
Santa Rosa	223	1 231	20	45 180	81.3	18.7	40.7	12.9	45	17.8	D	D	D	D	D
Sarasota	624	1 365	15	43 293	65.0	35.0	36.4	8.8	427	21.1	8.9	17.1	180.2	5.6	11.3
Seminole	360	2 919	19	48 742	90.5	9.5	29.5	10.8	344	23.3	9.1	16.7	198.4	5.8	11.6

1. Includes livestock and poultry products.

STATE County	Manufactures, 1987 (cont'd)					Value of construction authorized by building permits, 1990							
	Production workers (cont'd)						Nonresidential				Residential		
	Wages							Percent					
	Total (Mil dol)	Average per worker (Dollars)	Value added by manufacture (Mil dol)	Value of shipments (Mil dol)	New capital expenditures (Mil dol)	Total[1] ($1,000)	Total ($1,000)	Office	Industrial	Stores	New construction ($1,000)	Number of housing units	Alterations and additions ($1,000)
	134	135	136	137	138	139	140	141	142	143	144	145	146
DELAWARE	760.0	23 171	3 866.0	10 729.7	276.9	667 530	187 368	33.6	6.6	38.7	274 461	5 142	54 692
Kent	84.6	17 625	706.1	1 249.4	21.9	87 865	23 008	28.6	9.8	33.3	44 662	822	7 975
New Castle	526.8	28 787	2 474.0	7 619.3	212.0	402 188	128 321	42.4	6.8	43.0	133 279	2 988	20 586
Sussex	148.6	15 320	685.9	1 860.9	43.0	177 477	36 039	5.7	4.2	26.9	96 520	1 332	26 131
DISTRICT OF COLUMBIA	118.8	22 846	1 525.4	2 128.3	43.6	111 076	19 378	42.1	0.0	28.1	20 801	368	19 601
District of Columbia	118.8	22 846	1 525.4	2 128.3	43.6	111 076	19 378	42.1	0.0	28.1	20 801	368	19 601
FLORIDA	5 222.7	16 918	27 574.2	56 612.7	1 910.7	13 876 675	2 654 097	17.5	6.5	31.8	8 426 844	126 384	887 217
Alachua	D	D	D	D	D	93 449	18 462	13.3	2.7	23.7	57 702	1 137	5 057
Baker	3.3	16 500	10.6	43.0	D	5 929	850	6.9	0.7	9.4	3 946	98	314
Bay	47.9	21 773	170.3	447.2	D	96 490	25 199	9.3	6.9	56.6	53 326	725	5 769
Bradford	D	D	D	D	D	7 002	1 272	1.6	19.4	27.9	4 230	74	753
Brevard	206.6	19 676	1 412.6	2 500.1	92.1	499 832	85 601	27.4	9.4	17.0	359 764	4 759	17 704
Broward	446.1	17 027	2 138.3	3 746.3	122.0	1 243 736	242 029	16.0	7.2	53.0	810 513	10 749	63 793
Calhoun	4.4	11 000	16.3	34.5	0.8	2 956	123	0.0	0.0	46.4	2 479	51	264
Charlotte	5.1	12 750	21.0	43.1	1.0	257 688	61 749	20.6	0.0	63.7	177 031	2 717	11 288
Citrus	7.1	11 833	35.6	57.2	1.1	170 097	95 074	1.4	0.0	13.0	46 946	1 359	8 247
Clay	15.1	15 100	67.7	178.6	9.8	88 437	4 929	11.1	0.0	50.6	76 378	1 010	2 940
Collier	14.5	16 111	73.8	129.7	5.5	534 561	78 111	25.3	7.4	16.9	415 803	5 846	19 351
Columbia	19.2	14 769	52.2	123.1	4.2	14 542	2 569	7.4	0.0	63.5	9 901	278	348
Dade	880.1	14 150	3 561.9	6 734.4	132.0	1 300 893	209 748	17.9	11.0	29.0	661 535	10 855	115 119
De Soto	D	D	D	D	D	11 723	2 904	15.3	13.8	31.1	6 114	138	1 182
Dixie	6.2	15 500	16.5	43.2	2.6	8 034	2 610	11.3	0.0	3.1	3 370	64	1 405
Duval	414.6	20 324	2 395.5	4 874.4	130.2	628 414	183 996	34.1	9.2	16.9	306 260	5 573	22 930
Escambia	D	D	D	D	D	119 563	32 437	34.3	19.9	20.7	60 886	1 093	8 677
Flagler	12.5	17 857	39.0	95.3	3.8	73 466	12 743	15.4	0.9	8.9	57 159	891	1 504
Franklin	0.8	8 000	2.6	8.4	0.1	10 697	1 986	37.8	0.0	25.7	7 365	80	887
Gadsden	22.3	13 118	73.4	148.4	6.2	16 049	1 491	6.6	3.0	29.9	10 917	160	2 388
Gilchrist	0.5	NA	1.6	3.5	D	3 122	733	11.1	0.0	2.0	2 166	49	117
Glades	0.6	NA	0.9	4.2	D	3 761	1 209	13.9	0.0	2.2	1 326	24	935
Gulf	D	D	D	D	D	6 404	652	0.0	0.0	18.4	5 197	85	495
Hamilton	D	D	D	D	D	2 338	745	19.1	45.7	0.6	1 238	26	221
Hardee	2.1	21 000	7.1	20.3	0.3	8 983	3 472	0.0	0.7	17.5	3 961	57	1 129
Hendry	D	D	D	D	D	15 013	5 717	6.7	40.0	23.1	6 052	113	1 513
Hernando	6.8	13 600	49.5	102.1	2.1	145 981	43 407	26.3	0.8	12.1	88 901	1 750	6 994
Highlands	9.9	14 143	53.3	120.1	3.1	59 601	10 737	9.1	12.6	26.4	38 075	847	4 581
Hillsborough	388.5	16 891	1 732.5	4 317.3	122.3	627 357	158 464	10.4	2.1	48.1	324 562	5 529	35 606
Holmes	5.6	9 333	11.7	20.5	0.7	3 900	627	0.0	12.4	10.4	2 469	65	534
Indian River	28.3	17 688	165.6	255.0	6.4	188 533	26 937	28.4	1.4	22.4	136 536	1 266	12 156
Jackson	23.9	14 059	69.5	151.8	2.7	12 882	1 465	30.5	0.0	59.5	7 883	152	918
Jefferson	3.1	10 333	9.7	23.8	0.4	5 006	665	37.7	0.0	24.6	3 458	47	537
Lafayette	1.8	9 000	4.7	10.3	0.6	1 654	302	4.0	25.8	6.6	1 231	37	80
Lake	37.6	13 926	187.1	535.1	21.0	189 803	32 159	15.3	9.8	4.7	134 449	2 205	11 961
Lee	55.1	15 306	239.3	452.0	13.2	526 687	118 551	13.0	6.7	35.2	342 640	4 915	34 353
Leon	25.5	15 000	106.0	194.6	6.2	222 831	47 606	42.3	10.6	20.2	149 441	2 829	5 314
Levy	3.8	12 667	11.8	25.1	D	17 158	2 559	13.5	0.9	21.0	11 923	188	655
Liberty	2.2	22 000	6.7	18.1	0.4	1 684	25	0.0	0.0	0.0	1 322	14	48
Madison	D	D	D	D	D	4 448	522	59.8	11.9	0.0	2 020	46	863
Manatee	115.8	17 545	671.0	1 502.8	38.6	188 805	36 598	23.6	8.7	24.3	125 327	2 381	15 451
Marion	69.3	15 065	247.7	545.9	23.5	119 542	18 806	25.9	4.4	42.9	72 988	1 988	5 156
Martin	47.4	18 960	164.7	307.8	7.7	219 000	33 049	12.8	20.4	9.4	141 663	1 199	6 709
Monroe	5.2	17 333	21.3	47.0	2.4	154 064	19 689	6.6	0.0	48.0	54 015	791	2 332
Nassau	45.7	26 882	302.3	737.6	27.9	40 095	4 448	24.6	0.0	6.1	30 932	407	1 268
Okaloosa	48.8	13 556	180.1	290.8	8.5	84 606	19 005	27.6	3.3	31.9	54 353	1 065	4 222
Okeechobee	2.2	22 000	13.0	71.6	0.7	8 926	1 496	10.7	0.0	17.4	6 473	111	235
Orange	348.2	17 675	2 713.1	4 734.1	173.2	1 254 404	266 598	12.2	5.3	36.6	635 927	9 647	50 779
Osceola	21.8	15 571	95.2	182.4	9.2	289 976	29 313	10.2	0.4	23.0	241 898	3 867	4 059
Palm Beach	282.8	20 794	2 685.6	6 405.7	160.0	1 353 935	185 910	13.4	3.5	30.0	731 379	9 861	219 797
Pasco	31.4	13 652	189.9	503.4	8.4	168 851	49 453	16.5	5.4	28.2	98 912	1 536	9 519
Pinellas	427.5	16 831	2 167.8	3 624.1	146.4	685 895	133 379	20.7	5.7	39.8	350 160	4 290	56 165
Polk	253.4	17 007	1 517.4	4 109.3	83.8	263 744	72 157	16.4	11.8	33.4	150 976	2 785	18 805
Putnam	55.8	22 320	203.0	514.4	D	29 626	7 516	35.0	9.7	18.1	13 506	229	5 136
St. Johns	16.1	11 500	69.3	145.7	2.2	136 923	14 750	20.9	0.6	32.2	108 454	1 168	7 259
St. Lucie	24.8	15 500	201.9	392.4	4.3	194 745	28 470	12.7	8.5	39.4	153 765	2 579	7 118
Santa Rosa	D	D	D	D	D	51 468	0	NA	NA	NA	51 468	904	0
Sarasota	88.5	15 804	433.1	692.2	24.9	439 327	82 541	12.3	6.2	26.2	290 064	3 487	27 305
Seminole	96.2	16 586	389.5	738.8	21.0	462 732	66 893	13.8	4.2	34.0	358 793	5 317	10 845

1. Includes nonresidential additions and alterations, residential nonhousekeeping buildings, and residential garages and carports not shown separately.

STATE County	Wholesale trade, 1987: Establishments	Wholesale trade, 1987: Sales (Mil dol)	Wholesale trade, 1987: Paid employees[1]	Wholesale trade, 1987: Annual payroll (Mil dol)	Retail trade, all establishments, 1987: Number	Retail trade, all establishments, 1987: Sales: Total (Mil dol)	Retail trade, all establishments, 1987: Sales: Percent change, 1982–1987	Retail trade, all establishments, 1987: Sales: Per capita[2] (Dollars)	Retail trade, establishments with payroll, 1987: Number	Retail trade, establishments with payroll, 1987: Sales: Total (Mil dol)	Sales: Per capita[2] (Dollars): General merchandise stores	Sales: Per capita[2] (Dollars): Food stores	Sales: Per capita[2] (Dollars): Apparel & accessory stores	Sales: Per capita[2] (Dollars): Eating and drinking places
	147	148	149	150	151	152	153	154	155	156	157	158	159	160
DELAWARE	999	7 899.6	15 526	452.6	6 380	5 076.8	62.2	7 836	4 416	4 975.7	1 074	1 391	338	677
Kent	149	575.4	1 998	45.1	1 091	874.6	60.5	8 159	752	855.8	1 251	1 289	268	630
New Castle	674	6 895.5	12 110	380.8	3 655	3 415.3	62.4	7 995	2 584	3 357.3	1 170	1 458	333	658
Sussex	176	428.7	1 418	26.7	1 634	786.9	63.1	6 933	1 080	762.6	546	1 237	424	793
DISTRICT OF COLUMBIA	554	2 846.2	8 856	231.6	4 478	3 464.9	30.5	5 578	3 681	3 423.0	506	951	525	1 347
District of Columbia	554	2 846.2	8 856	231.6	4 478	3 464.9	30.5	5 578	3 681	3 423.0	506	951	525	1 347
FLORIDA	25 636	97 360.0	261 765	5 554.7	130 508	90 295.0	62.8	7 510	83 808	87 925.6	824	1 414	333	756
Alachua	215	435.5	2 223	38.5	1 727	1 275.7	51.9	7 075	1 208	1 248.7	933	1 511	267	731
Baker	11	D	D	D	137	43.5	32.6	2 404	77	39.7	119	981	29	162
Bay	198	379.9	1 781	27.9	1 670	950.7	63.9	7 717	1 136	924.2	985	1 616	293	1 015
Bradford	24	26.0	108	1.8	178	99.6	46.0	4 048	130	98.2	114	1 018	55	391
Brevard	456	1 158.8	3 992	75.7	3 779	2 514.0	68.9	6 724	2 387	2 446.7	885	1 258	169	680
Broward	3 064	11 773.1	26 350	634.8	13 790	10 410.9	55.0	8 949	8 625	10 140.8	829	1 546	419	940
Calhoun	13	D	D	D	110	38.2	29.5	3 901	62	35.1	230	990	48	241
Charlotte	63	D	D	D	835	505.2	60.4	5 632	492	481.4	518	1 358	185	511
Citrus	61	40.2	335	4.5	936	445.6	82.8	5 098	481	424.8	343	1 212	130	368
Clay	87	269.6	1 162	19.1	888	628.6	96.1	6 514	565	616.4	1 320	1 139	397	573
Collier	214	346.6	1 378	25.3	1 886	1 174.3	73.6	8 985	1 236	1 133.1	837	1 901	563	889
Columbia	81	148.5	534	8.5	448	292.3	54.6	7 060	306	286.5	852	1 589	116	724
Dade	6 860	21 772.3	63 030	1 373.9	19 581	13 325.8	41.6	7 457	13 136	13 047.3	884	1 280	522	739
De Soto	21	D	D	D	199	105.4	30.1	4 727	118	101.3	D	1 445	76	284
Dixie	8	7.6	42	0.4	121	36.6	37.6	3 662	63	33.7	D	1 361	D	198
Duval	1 554	14 935.8	23 301	538.3	6 150	4 933.1	62.6	7 440	4 408	4 862.9	679	1 220	284	749
Escambia	436	1 141.3	4 756	90.2	2 690	1 795.0	52.3	6 501	1 793	1 753.2	869	1 135	262	633
Flagler	16	D	D	D	244	106.1	165.2	5 100	121	99.9	D	1 415	21	375
Franklin	28	D	D	D	126	32.8	54.7	3 904	71	30.6	144	1 886	D	304
Gadsden	30	349.1	618	13.2	348	154.5	59.4	3 388	183	145.6	300	946	71	146
Gilchrist	14	12.8	74	1.2	72	19.6	104.2	2 648	43	18.8	D	1 092	D	193
Glades	1	D	D	D	38	10.0	40.8	1 449	19	9.1	D	1 027	0	90
Gulf	7	11.8	42	0.6	131	38.1	53.0	3 151	69	34.0	188	1 180	D	380
Hamilton	4	D	D	D	102	46.7	59.4	4 966	70	45.4	D	1 230	41	261
Hardee	29	85.7	527	4.4	205	94.5	58.6	4 333	112	91.6	363	1 505	120	132
Hendry	25	40.1	126	2.5	253	122.1	28.5	5 006	151	116.2	451	1 733	78	368
Hernando	69	76.8	442	6.6	825	413.0	123.1	4 742	430	398.7	537	1 253	47	384
Highlands	77	149.9	741	11.0	679	405.4	88.6	6 315	406	394.1	650	1 398	116	388
Hillsborough	2 259	14 607.3	33 148	750.4	8 158	5 728.8	58.2	7 199	5 265	5 600.6	913	1 413	282	754
Holmes	12	9.7	76	0.8	145	44.9	34.0	2 769	65	39.4	90	632	13	373
Indian River	130	214.6	1 108	17.5	955	611.3	66.3	7 320	634	590.0	639	1 793	285	634
Jackson	61	193.5	714	10.2	438	216.6	58.7	5 095	258	206.3	307	1 065	353	234
Jefferson	9	10.7	51	0.6	109	40.4	33.3	3 421	54	37.0	73	940	22	113
Lafayette	6	2.6	10	0.1	47	7.0	1.4	1 321	22	6.1	0	604	0	D
Lake	207	515.7	2 048	33.4	1 533	894.4	68.2	6 491	923	865.0	717	1 360	191	501
Lee	538	954.1	4 487	83.9	3 769	2 597.6	85.5	8 770	2 369	2 522.5	978	1 644	346	858
Leon	273	639.1	2 847	60.2	1 661	1 330.9	61.5	7 494	1 215	1 305.7	1 049	1 330	340	796
Levy	18	24.5	139	2.3	290	109.4	67.0	4 291	163	103.4	128	1 338	29	373
Liberty	2	D	D	D	35	10.2	72.9	2 168	13	8.8	0	928	0	D
Madison	14	48.2	150	2.4	134	55.6	38.3	3 540	83	52.8	126	913	57	119
Manatee	197	1 058.2	2 001	37.4	1 863	1 367.9	54.4	7 483	1 172	1 320.8	818	1 570	251	769
Marion	311	1 075.9	3 780	71.0	1 951	1 204.1	64.1	6 602	1 216	1 165.3	766	1 346	186	564
Martin	125	167.8	784	14.8	1 280	806.2	85.8	8 773	792	775.9	549	1 661	349	715
Monroe	114	139.8	799	13.2	1 345	654.1	70.5	8 722	859	625.3	732	1 999	361	1 631
Nassau	29	53.0	221	3.7	429	223.2	75.7	5 107	271	216.5	462	1 315	129	431
Okaloosa	163	328.3	1 173	18.4	1 650	961.9	70.7	6 584	1 142	933.3	895	1 080	219	812
Okeechobee	33	138.9	299	5.4	337	160.4	61.7	5 607	207	153.8	D	1 822	105	628
Orange	1 634	9 251.9	22 072	502.2	6 220	5 703.3	94.3	9 597	4 193	5 586.7	980	1 535	388	1 124
Osceola	62	504.1	845	16.5	958	709.1	110.1	8 391	629	693.0	795	1 670	215	1 406
Palm Beach	1 440	4 101.6	12 664	279.1	9 115	6 801.2	76.8	8 655	5 938	6 622.1	943	1 558	528	868
Pasco	211	231.6	1 467	22.5	2 296	1 527.8	82.7	5 931	1 321	1 486.1	692	1 443	161	424
Pinellas	1 447	3 078.5	12 828	254.8	9 028	6 791.9	67.0	8 325	5 743	6 625.3	901	1 507	297	805
Polk	634	2 462.6	9 347	153.6	3 720	2 431.8	49.3	6 292	2 329	2 357.2	758	1 285	213	518
Putnam	56	78.1	363	6.2	564	288.3	47.7	4 597	320	275.1	600	1 276	129	299
St. Johns	86	167.0	662	13.0	936	486.1	90.0	6 508	581	471.1	586	1 327	120	889
St. Lucie	184	492.0	2 000	36.8	1 300	907.3	79.9	7 012	771	880.1	815	1 408	198	585
Santa Rosa	59	52.0	261	3.8	646	289.8	67.2	4 151	361	278.0	463	1 135	66	321
Sarasota	470	788.6	3 208	62.3	3 528	2 431.5	69.8	9 528	2 217	2 360.1	1 044	1 623	388	966
Seminole	610	1 677.1	4 921	107.6	2 630	1 883.7	76.8	7 290	1 566	1 815.7	921	1 365	382	705

1. For pay period including March 12. 2. Based on the estimated population as of July 1 of the year shown.

STATE County	Retail trade, establishments with payroll, 1987 (cont'd): Paid employees[1]	Retail trade, establishments with payroll, 1987 (cont'd): Annual payroll (Mil dol)	Taxable service industries–establishments with payroll, 1987: Number	Taxable service industries: Receipts (Mil dol): Total	Receipts: Selected kinds of business: Hotels, motels and other lodging places	Receipts: Selected kinds of business: Health services	Receipts: Selected kinds of business: Legal services	Taxable service industries: Paid employees	Taxable service industries: Annual payroll (Mil dol)	Bank deposits,[2] June 1989: Total (Mil dol)	Bank deposits,[2] June 1989: Percent change, 1988–1989	Savings capital,[3] September 1989: Total (Mil dol)	Savings capital,[3] September 1989: Percent change, 1988–1989
	161	162	163	164	165	166	167	168	169	170	171	172	173
DELAWARE	56 077	565.7	4 447	2 108.1	95.4	497.3	171.5	46 209	767.0	26 808	14.1	483.3	7.6
Kent	9 502	94.6	587	181.1	9.0	45.9	12.0	4 782	67.1	1 382	6.7	17.4	36.3
New Castle	37 768	380.5	3 150	1 769.1	68.3	402.0	149.9	37 077	641.8	23 948	15.0	374.2	2.3
Sussex	8 807	90.5	710	157.8	18.1	49.3	9.7	4 350	58.1	1 478	6.8	91.7	30.0
DISTRICT OF COLUMBIA	54 549	575.4	7 486	7 882.5	679.4	564.6	2 992.4	120 844	2 993.0	12 515	5.3	4 104.0	4.4
District of Columbia	54 549	575.4	7 486	7 882.5	679.4	564.6	2 992.4	120 844	2 993.0	12 515	5.3	4 104.0	4.4
FLORIDA	1 022 862	10 297.0	98 713	45 530.9	4 474.6	12 901.0	3 697.5	974 746	16 909.6	102 213	10.0	78 470.3	-0.1
Alachua	16 483	145.6	1 381	500.1	21.6	211.2	29.8	11 518	197.7	902	8.9	319.8	-4.8
Baker	405	3.5	49	7.2	0.0	4.6	0.3	172	2.3	64	8.8	9.4	9.2
Bay	12 495	106.9	976	328.9	60.7	107.3	15.1	8 176	117.7	505	-2.5	411.9	-2.2
Bradford	1 099	10.4	85	15.6	2.0	5.4	1.2	484	5.4	86	3.6	27.4	7.2
Brevard	29 636	284.3	2 533	1 751.4	79.5	266.1	45.3	34 426	791.0	2 206	14.4	1 340.8	-1.8
Broward	109 968	1 162.1	11 840	5 457.1	442.7	1 751.6	448.6	110 484	1 978.8	8 055	7.5	14 910.1	-1.7
Calhoun	389	3.5	45	7.2	D	4.4	0.4	247	2.8	40	5.8	10.5	-3.5
Charlotte	5 782	52.8	524	180.0	7.9	109.5	9.1	3 745	66.7	863	19.0	827.5	1.1
Citrus	4 983	45.2	481	146.9	14.3	58.1	4.3	3 697	53.2	715	19.9	563.1	0.2
Clay	7 461	68.3	585	186.4	3.9	92.5	5.3	4 530	64.7	378	9.5	147.0	-2.6
Collier	13 328	139.3	1 261	522.4	164.4	102.4	37.2	12 608	189.2	1 708	15.4	978.5	-3.6
Columbia	3 556	31.3	233	65.1	12.8	27.1	5.0	1 319	19.4	204	13.6	89.7	-3.1
Dade	141 703	1 573.3	17 972	7 934.6	676.0	2 200.9	1 127.8	165 893	3 137.6	21 746	8.3	18 157.5	2.8
De Soto	1 212	10.7	85	15.2	1.2	4.9	0.6	380	4.4	152	13.3	55.4	-0.2
Dixie	366	3.1	31	4.3	0.7	D	D	116	1.2	26	8.9	6.6	-6.2
Duval	55 164	570.3	5 145	2 537.4	94.9	527.0	193.0	56 715	1 021.0	5 575	6.5	1 758.3	-5.2
Escambia	22 098	203.6	1 676	675.4	35.2	265.4	56.2	17 058	264.8	1 723	3.5	255.2	-2.4
Flagler	1 066	11.1	97	40.9	0.6	17.7	0.8	1 017	13.9	167	23.5	152.5	13.3
Franklin	388	3.3	39	8.5	1.7	4.2	0.4	220	3.0	41	11.5	9.0	9.1
Gadsden	1 693	14.5	129	25.1	0.8	7.1	1.2	712	7.5	180	7.5	0.0	NA
Gilchrist	228	2.0	20	2.5	D	0.0	0.4	48	0.5	41	23.2	6.3	2.8
Glades	96	0.8	5	0.3	0.0	0.0	0.0	9	0.1	15	19.8	0.0	NA
Gulf	506	4.0	34	4.2	D	1.8	0.4	219	1.7	44	2.7	21.8	7.3
Hamilton	498	4.6	29	5.6	2.5	1.9	0.3	227	1.9	30	8.6	9.7	-0.8
Hardee	864	8.7	75	13.3	D	5.3	0.8	328	4.2	166	13.1	0.0	NA
Hendry	1 322	12.6	102	24.8	2.7	7.8	1.1	804	8.2	151	12.6	47.5	-4.4
Hernando	4 546	43.3	397	120.7	4.4	65.9	3.9	2 692	41.7	759	17.2	568.7	3.4
Highlands	4 225	40.1	377	95.5	5.5	49.5	5.0	2 266	31.7	625	11.1	340.7	4.8
Hillsborough	68 343	666.8	6 807	3 763.1	161.5	882.9	294.7	83 310	1 432.9	6 152	5.2	1 794.9	3.8
Holmes	574	4.7	47	10.8	0.8	6.1	0.3	310	3.6	61	-0.1	12.7	4.4
Indian River	7 029	71.3	701	252.8	17.1	98.4	15.1	5 904	93.6	1 054	13.4	662.5	-0.8
Jackson	2 128	20.7	157	33.2	3.5	16.6	1.4	849	10.8	219	3.7	44.1	6.0
Jefferson	449	3.8	41	8.1	D	2.4	0.7	200	2.5	58	7.9	9.6	4.5
Lafayette	67	0.5	9	1.7	D	D	0.0	32	0.6	22	12.4	4.5	32.2
Lake	9 759	97.0	820	226.2	25.8	88.3	13.0	5 578	83.3	1 301	16.7	598.1	-5.5
Lee	28 903	300.8	2 339	975.2	125.4	345.8	60.1	21 368	371.0	3 073	16.4	1 763.5	-3.1
Leon	17 756	154.6	1 652	645.4	39.3	164.9	107.6	14 404	242.4	1 219	13.9	450.2	-5.3
Levy	1 261	10.8	93	13.5	0.6	5.1	0.6	498	4.8	141	8.4	33.0	-8.2
Liberty	108	0.8	9	3.1	0.0	D	0.0	169	1.6	17	6.0	0.0	NA
Madison	520	5.3	50	8.8	D	4.2	0.8	285	3.2	72	1.6	30.6	-2.9
Manatee	15 890	152.1	1 201	462.5	29.1	217.8	24.8	11 407	187.7	1 705	12.6	1 283.6	-10.8
Marion	13 986	134.8	1 110	376.2	38.2	135.5	25.1	8 240	129.4	1 210	14.8	733.6	-0.5
Martin	8 964	93.0	858	266.4	14.4	74.8	25.1	6 658	109.7	1 129	11.4	607.6	-6.8
Monroe	9 307	86.4	733	304.2	132.7	51.0	13.6	7 522	91.7	754	11.4	193.5	-6.8
Nassau	2 577	22.2	189	34.4	5.1	13.1	1.3	1 032	12.1	168	17.8	44.9	11.3
Okaloosa	12 694	110.7	995	424.4	63.2	138.6	15.8	9 063	139.4	892	4.8	159.4	10.1
Okeechobee	1 932	16.8	122	53.6	1.8	38.9	1.7	867	13.1	179	11.8	74.1	1.7
Orange	61 223	643.5	5 814	5 398.9	870.9	726.2	279.0	93 091	1 661.0	4 943	8.3	2 637.8	6.1
Osceola	9 551	86.2	545	401.9	247.0	86.5	3.7	9 230	108.8	560	22.4	289.0	-2.0
Palm Beach	76 125	812.8	7 627	3 262.1	229.4	985.3	371.6	70 529	1 290.1	7 595	9.4	8 761.1	5.8
Pasco	16 780	161.2	1 327	497.3	40.5	298.0	22.1	11 452	182.3	2 079	15.8	2 036.7	-1.0
Pinellas	78 507	769.7	7 482	3 145.6	291.3	1 146.3	171.0	71 416	1 146.8	7 960	12.1	7 570.1	-3.9
Polk	27 872	264.4	2 198	842.0	100.0	254.7	57.0	20 429	321.3	2 746	9.2	964.9	2.3
Putnam	2 977	28.1	259	63.2	4.2	33.9	3.0	1 657	21.0	235	9.0	151.9	0.6
St. Johns	6 533	55.7	467	242.3	54.5	46.1	4.4	4 601	63.3	506	13.6	166.1	-7.9
St. Lucie	9 332	95.8	732	306.4	20.9	144.3	18.0	7 391	113.8	651	24.0	716.4	-2.7
Santa Rosa	3 419	28.2	313	102.9	18.8	42.0	2.5	2 791	39.2	376	11.6	21.1	-1.7
Sarasota	27 670	288.6	2 896	1 046.3	75.3	375.7	84.4	24 838	403.5	3 696	7.6	2 188.6	-3.3
Seminole	21 731	216.4	1 909	652.8	30.3	221.4	20.7	13 854	238.2	1 253	21.9	949.0	-2.8

1. For the period including March 12 of the year shown. 2. Includes deposits for all insured and reporting noninsured commercial and mutual savings banks. 3. Includes savings capital for all FSLIC insured savings institutions.

STATE County	Federal funds and grants, 1989							Local government finances, 1981–1982							
	Expenditures		Per capita[1] (Dollars)					General revenue						Direct general expenditure	
									Intergovernmental		Taxes				
												Per capita[2]			
	Total (Mil dol)	Percent change, 1988–1989	Total	Direct payments for individuals	Procurement contract awards	Salaries and wages	Grant awards	Total (Mil dol)	Total (Mil dol)	Percent from state	Total (Mil dol)	Total (Dollars)	Property (Dollars)	Total (Mil dol)	Percent change, 1977–1982
	174	175	176	177	178	179	180	181	182	183	184	185	186	187	188
DELAWARE	2 140.5	3.4	X	1 757	315	539	533	518.1	269.4	74.5	127.3	212	183	506.2	33.5
Kent	460.6	5.9	4 172	1 662	397	1 397	685	66.1	47.8	76.3	8.3	84	80	64.4	39.9
New Castle	1 214.9	-4.2	2 744	1 538	364	426	392	378.5	172.5	70.0	104.6	261	219	371.0	32.4
Sussex	333.0	16.5	2 786	2 097	58	162	438	73.5	49.1	88.5	14.4	145	136	70.9	33.8
DISTRICT OF COLUMBIA	X	5.5	X	3 050	4 859	14 040	3 466	2 782.2	1 342.0	0.0	1 227.4	1 962	542	2 164.1	44.8
District of Columbia	16 161.6	5.5	26 599	3 050	4 859	14 040	3 466	2 782.2	1 342.0	0.0	1 227.4	1 962	542	2 164.1	44.8
FLORIDA	46 871.1	8.6	X	2 345	495	481	346	11 862.6	4 754.9	78.5	3 666.2	350	289	11 417.3	79.1
Alachua	520.5	6.3	2 800	1 499	199	493	590	167.3	78.6	79.8	40.6	253	214	152.0	29.1
Baker	30.9	16.2	1 629	1 357	8	79	176	14.7	9.5	87.7	1.8	109	95	14.1	80.0
Bay	584.9	7.5	4 527	2 136	561	1 664	160	145.7	64.1	75.3	24.7	237	161	136.1	86.1
Bradford	47.8	7.4	1 911	1 476	10	211	195	18.0	10.5	90.5	2.4	112	92	17.1	59.0
Brevard	3 182.7	23.0	7 907	2 321	4 720	754	107	313.1	128.5	83.7	84.3	279	220	299.0	62.3
Broward	3 690.1	6.1	3 053	2 564	94	193	187	1 252.2	350.8	79.5	488.3	456	364	1 150.3	84.0
Calhoun	25.6	5.1	2 464	1 886	9	105	396	9.8	6.1	86.8	1.2	128	115	9.1	40.6
Charlotte	370.1	9.7	3 679	3 510	14	87	58	50.4	14.7	83.4	24.8	368	324	43.4	104.3
Citrus	308.4	11.4	3 190	3 010	10	72	94	53.2	18.5	89.8	18.6	291	278	57.9	156.3
Clay	227.2	18.4	2 163	1 843	135	108	73	55.8	32.7	95.1	14.0	189	170	52.8	86.7
Collier	443.8	22.6	3 033	2 242	161	135	485	107.5	29.8	86.4	56.2	559	511	98.1	91.2
Columbia	114.9	10.9	2 690	1 860	32	601	165	41.3	22.5	93.3	6.0	162	135	41.1	55.1
Dade	5 376.7	8.5	2 930	1 923	87	406	506	2 747.4	1 165.4	70.0	825.8	482	385	2 553.8	89.2
De Soto	57.2	9.0	2 478	2 131	10	92	237	21.6	9.5	91.1	4.6	227	197	21.1	92.4
Dixie	24.8	11.9	2 318	1 962	5	93	235	7.4	5.2	96.1	1.5	183	169	7.1	51.0
Duval	2 967.6	8.3	4 315	1 809	402	1 747	343	626.3	305.5	87.0	152.2	258	202	638.0	52.8
Escambia	1 357.3	8.6	4 786	2 139	483	1 925	228	277.9	126.3	84.8	49.2	198	171	270.6	74.7
Flagler	76.0	7.4	2 946	2 716	43	103	78	12.8	3.2	90.8	6.9	522	481	15.7	199.3
Franklin	23.9	5.2	2 809	2 336	13	147	310	9.9	5.8	79.2	2.2	273	245	9.6	54.9
Gadsden	91.4	0.0	1 975	1 418	35	99	404	32.8	23.7	89.1	3.7	87	77	33.6	62.7
Gilchrist	18.8	8.5	2 416	2 037	13	72	192	5.7	4.0	94.3	1.1	166	150	5.9	49.9
Glades	11.5	13.9	1 664	1 323	103	47	182	6.0	3.1	93.1	2.4	386	380	5.7	57.8
Gulf	36.0	39.1	2 883	1 953	34	57	833	14.6	6.2	94.6	2.9	260	236	14.5	91.9
Hamilton	26.2	7.7	2 646	1 923	16	94	427	14.0	7.4	90.6	2.9	319	297	11.5	87.0
Hardee	43.2	13.3	1 971	1 501	9	96	272	22.1	9.9	92.9	7.0	333	317	20.6	85.0
Hendry	42.7	0.9	1 642	1 229	101	138	171	29.3	11.4	94.4	8.7	426	403	30.3	64.8
Hernando	329.5	19.8	3 259	3 069	17	91	76	79.9	27.9	56.1	23.5	422	405	70.9	97.6
Highlands	241.9	12.9	3 496	3 073	75	192	145	50.4	20.9	84.4	15.2	288	258	47.2	72.2
Hillsborough	2 299.3	5.9	2 753	1 700	265	574	197	785.6	327.4	78.2	218.7	319	242	776.4	55.0
Holmes	47.3	14.4	2 802	2 068	11	132	478	13.0	8.7	90.9	1.6	102	91	13.0	17.1
Indian River	319.4	13.8	3 545	3 158	91	165	120	74.8	13.5	92.5	25.1	369	340	79.9	104.8
Jackson	122.7	16.1	2 861	1 923	83	311	436	37.8	22.2	95.1	4.5	112	92	37.5	43.1
Jefferson	26.9	1.4	2 224	1 535	12	89	473	9.9	7.7	87.2	1.4	126	113	10.1	77.2
Lafayette	10.7	24.7	1 839	1 280	144	77	203	4.9	3.8	69.9	0.8	185	175	5.4	111.6
Lake	473.0	5.8	3 220	2 941	46	118	108	88.5	47.6	82.1	23.1	203	179	87.4	70.8
Lee	981.6	9.9	3 027	2 706	22	164	119	268.5	75.3	80.3	95.5	414	376	252.4	118.9
Leon	1 080.0	4.0	5 772	1 247	75	306	4 134	161.1	79.0	72.6	37.3	236	201	187.2	60.2
Levy	63.9	11.0	2 383	2 004	13	104	206	17.6	10.2	89.8	3.8	170	154	16.4	57.9
Liberty	12.9	18.5	2 811	1 870	26	211	691	4.7	3.9	90.3	0.3	77	71	5.0	104.2
Madison	41.6	9.7	2 614	1 906	13	124	500	16.0	11.0	90.7	2.0	130	110	19.1	85.8
Manatee	620.2	16.4	3 247	2 956	40	112	128	194.8	63.1	87.5	53.9	334	295	161.0	37.9
Marion	563.7	12.5	2 836	2 449	116	106	152	126.9	64.3	88.3	25.8	186	173	123.7	90.1
Martin	338.9	21.0	3 375	2 712	484	106	67	57.0	20.0	94.9	28.2	388	355	53.1	103.0
Monroe	261.1	-1.1	3 310	1 672	297	1 216	119	67.7	23.8	69.6	23.9	357	335	68.2	73.0
Nassau	106.5	7.6	2 261	1 343	97	660	148	34.8	15.4	94.1	9.6	271	249	32.9	56.2
Okaloosa	1 170.4	15.8	7 502	2 298	1 791	3 294	108	101.7	63.7	83.0	18.3	154	123	93.2	45.2
Okeechobee	71.6	15.7	2 310	1 998	50	82	167	17.5	11.4	92.8	4.9	210	192	17.7	47.5
Orange	3 212.8	-6.4	5 092	1 781	2 191	897	211	583.6	245.6	73.4	163.7	326	268	646.8	118.6
Osceola	192.7	6.7	2 041	1 814	71	85	67	48.9	20.7	87.9	16.9	283	228	44.9	92.3
Palm Beach	3 040.2	-8.3	3 570	2 551	710	194	104	713.0	196.7	72.5	328.1	509	445	709.3	105.2
Pasco	978.7	9.2	3 560	3 279	72	94	108	137.3	64.7	87.2	42.5	196	175	130.4	82.3
Pinellas	3 564.3	8.6	4 316	3 281	624	279	121	724.8	281.5	70.9	252.2	333	263	690.6	77.7
Polk	1 009.8	19.0	2 494	1 959	226	131	171	286.1	138.6	86.5	84.0	246	213	277.7	54.6
Putnam	156.4	3.3	2 460	2 077	17	96	255	53.5	30.1	90.8	14.9	278	258	54.6	72.4
St. Johns	227.3	18.3	2 742	2 106	107	190	333	48.8	25.2	86.1	15.1	264	231	45.5	97.2
St. Lucie	364.1	13.8	2 539	2 298	17	106	113	93.4	38.7	87.4	33.8	333	298	100.9	96.0
Santa Rosa	257.9	13.4	3 509	1 992	239	1 092	129	63.3	28.0	94.1	13.9	233	221	63.8	76.3
Sarasota	1 105.8	14.8	4 152	3 778	125	148	90	224.5	47.9	80.1	83.7	381	312	207.3	82.7
Seminole	454.1	12.2	1 599	1 341	56	80	117	171.2	85.2	89.7	50.5	253	212	159.4	94.7

1. Based on the estimated population as of July 1 of the year shown. 2. Based on the estimated population as of July 1, 1982.

STATE County	Local government finances, 1981–1982 (cont'd): Direct general expenditure (cont'd): Per capita[1] (Dollars)	Percent of total for– Education	Percent of total for– Health & hospitals	Percent of total for– Police protection	Percent of total for– Public welfare	Percent of total for– Highways	Debt outstanding: Total (Mil dol)	Debt outstanding: Per capita[1] (Dollars)	State and local government employment, 1989: Total	State and local government employment, 1989: Rate[2]	Federal government civilian employment 1989: Total	Federal government civilian employment 1989: Earnings ($1,000)	Elections, 1988[3]: Total vote cast for president	Elections, 1988[3]: Vote for lead party (Percent)
	189	190	191	192	193	194	195	196	197	198	199	200	201	202
DELAWARE	844	49.9	0.1	6.1	0.1	4.6	655.2	1 092	40 997	609.5	5 948	185 281	249 891	R–55.9
Kent	650	64.6	0.6	4.2	0.3	1.2	49.4	499	10 717	970.7	2 314	59 579	33 113	R–60.2
New Castle	924	43.3	0.0	6.9	0.0	5.7	553.8	1 379	25 491	575.8	3 156	112 017	173 003	R–53.5
Sussex	713	71.0	0.2	3.7	0.1	2.1	52.0	523	4 789	400.8	478	13 685	43 775	R–62.0
DISTRICT OF COLUMBIA	3 459	18.1	9.3	5.8	16.3	4.1	2 833.0	4 528	56 074	922.9	213 193	8 444 256	192 877	D–82.6
District of Columbia	3 459	18.1	9.3	5.8	16.3	4.1	2 833.0	4 528	56 074	922.9	213 193	8 444 256	192 877	D–82.6
FLORIDA	1 090	39.5	9.8	6.6	0.8	4.5	11 119.2	1 061	681 844	538.2	120 816	3 803 067	4 302 313	R–60.9
Alachua	945	48.1	0.9	7.0	1.0	4.8	330.2	2 053	31 013	1 668.3	2 946	100 297	60 213	R–50.1
Baker	866	55.6	20.1	4.2	0.2	4.4	7.5	461	2 635	1 386.8	63	1 522	4 781	R–71.5
Bay	1 306	40.9	22.4	4.5	0.4	4.1	61.4	589	7 239	560.3	3 754	104 335	43 851	R–72.5
Bradford	789	51.9	17.3	4.1	0.0	5.1	21.7	999	2 285	914.0	42	1 139	6 636	R–63.6
Brevard	989	47.0	8.6	5.3	0.6	4.6	454.3	1 502	16 588	412.1	6 372	220 558	149 159	R–70.3
Broward	1 075	34.4	16.7	9.9	0.2	5.6	931.7	870	57 163	472.9	5 928	197 008	440 605	R–50.0
Calhoun	975	49.3	22.3	4.6	0.0	6.6	1.7	184	807	776.0	40	1 078	3 784	R–64.0
Charlotte	644	45.4	2.2	7.1	1.0	10.3	17.7	262	3 304	328.4	237	7 229	45 159	R–64.0
Citrus	906	36.3	16.4	3.5	0.1	12.1	107.9	1 689	3 511	363.1	171	4 778	33 474	R–63.0
Clay	714	64.3	5.2	5.3	0.7	6.3	63.3	856	3 479	331.3	344	9 971	33 837	R–76.7
Collier	977	48.7	1.9	8.0	0.4	14.0	111.7	1 111	5 652	386.3	496	16 080	51 980	R–74.9
Columbia	1 099	57.2	19.6	3.6	0.0	6.0	12.9	344	2 986	699.3	1 014	28 193	11 916	R–65.1
Dade	1 491	30.6	8.8	6.3	0.8	2.4	2 370.4	1 384	97 900	533.5	19 412	673 329	490 265	R–55.3
De Soto	1 042	44.7	18.7	5.5	0.4	6.9	8.5	419	2 973	1 287.0	51	1 411	6 464	R–65.6
Dixie	848	54.6	0.6	4.7	0.2	22.3	1.9	223	866	809.3	35	1 117	3 397	R–59.8
Duval	1 081	46.6	8.3	5.9	0.1	4.3	948.2	1 607	34 479	501.3	16 769	501 366	203 980	R–62.8
Escambia	1 091	48.0	5.5	4.3	0.6	3.1	310.8	1 253	14 754	520.2	11 035	335 501	95 459	R–68.0
Flagler	1 186	66.2	1.8	5.2	0.2	6.9	11.9	904	1 094	424.0	65	2 256	10 782	R–60.3
Franklin	1 212	46.9	12.8	5.8	0.5	8.3	7.3	923	591	695.3	34	1 041	3 269	R–58.5
Gadsden	784	60.6	7.3	5.1	0.3	6.9	20.0	466	6 053	1 307.3	121	3 475	12 577	D–50.7
Gilchrist	888	62.5	0.2	5.3	0.4	12.9	0.8	114	800	1 025.6	19	485	3 012	R–61.6
Glades	899	51.8	1.3	7.7	1.1	11.9	1.6	255	340	492.8	11	305	2 593	R–59.7
Gulf	1 317	39.8	9.2	3.9	0.2	16.9	16.2	1 476	772	617.6	19	623	4 872	R–62.4
Hamilton	1 259	49.3	18.3	5.0	0.1	11.6	4.8	524	1 138	1 149.5	29	725	3 396	R–60.7
Hardee	985	53.5	13.6	6.2	0.2	8.3	8.7	414	1 313	599.5	53	1 522	5 436	R–67.0
Hendry	1 479	35.9	13.7	5.5	0.3	5.5	18.3	894	1 870	719.2	106	3 092	6 035	R–65.7
Hernando	1 270	26.0	30.8	3.1	0.0	2.5	12.6	226	3 482	344.4	250	6 797	36 863	R–57.5
Highlands	894	46.7	16.2	6.7	0.6	9.3	24.5	464	3 256	470.5	308	8 539	24 941	R–67.1
Hillsborough	1 131	38.9	10.5	5.9	0.9	3.6	726.8	1 059	48 637	582.3	10 725	341 241	250 716	R–59.9
Holmes	831	56.5	13.0	3.4	0.8	10.7	5.0	319	1 037	613.6	63	1 501	5 900	R–71.6
Indian River	1 173	36.1	27.1	5.6	0.5	3.9	71.3	1 047	3 524	391.1	339	10 837	35 333	R–69.7
Jackson	934	58.5	17.8	3.5	0.6	6.4	28.3	704	4 707	1 097.2	430	12 642	13 513	R–62.2
Jefferson	894	63.5	0.3	4.6	0.4	11.3	1.4	126	642	530.6	36	961	4 398	R–52.9
Lafayette	1 276	43.0	0.8	4.1	0.4	7.7	3.1	740	519	894.8	15	417	2 185	R–66.4
Lake	769	54.5	5.7	6.4	0.7	6.2	40.3	355	6 630	451.3	469	13 127	54 582	R–68.4
Lee	1 095	38.8	14.9	4.2	0.9	6.8	302.8	1 313	17 138	528.5	1 352	43 562	128 936	R–67.7
Leon	1 183	35.7	0.9	5.2	0.6	4.7	270.3	1 709	42 669	2 280.5	1 508	50 653	70 148	R–51.4
Levy	744	57.7	12.8	5.3	0.5	7.1	7.8	355	1 373	512.3	69	1 823	8 791	R–59.8
Liberty	1 145	48.6	0.3	3.8	0.8	29.9	4.7	1 077	459	997.8	56	1 076	2 177	R–65.3
Madison	1 257	57.2	7.4	3.3	0.5	17.6	8.3	543	1 157	727.7	55	1 407	4 529	R–56.6
Manatee	999	40.2	19.6	5.6	0.5	5.7	240.7	1 493	9 012	471.8	567	17 398	78 113	R–65.5
Marion	890	52.7	18.2	6.2	0.3	3.4	41.4	297	10 320	519.1	604	16 175	62 520	R–66.4
Martin	731	57.2	1.6	8.7	1.2	7.3	121.7	1 674	4 157	414.0	266	8 028	43 083	R–72.6
Monroe	1 018	39.0	12.3	8.1	1.9	3.2	105.2	1 570	4 387	556.0	1 305	37 415	26 405	R–60.3
Nassau	925	49.6	15.6	5.5	0.2	6.3	28.9	813	2 030	431.0	624	33 090	12 575	R–66.6
Okaloosa	785	64.3	0.5	3.9	0.1	6.3	43.5	367	6 272	402.1	6 721	174 670	50 462	R–80.0
Okeechobee	760	64.9	1.7	7.5	0.2	6.7	6.2	268	1 232	397.4	73	2 189	7 791	R–60.8
Orange	1 290	34.5	1.8	6.6	1.0	3.2	775.3	1 546	36 748	582.5	8 606	257 645	172 770	R–67.9
Osceola	752	47.6	0.7	10.4	1.7	8.8	63.1	1 058	4 208	445.8	202	6 542	31 381	R–68.1
Palm Beach	1 099	34.4	7.1	7.7	2.1	4.3	579.9	899	40 226	472.4	4 063	132 899	327 217	R–55.5
Pasco	602	56.5	7.5	6.2	1.0	5.5	126.8	585	7 938	288.8	600	17 575	114 803	R–55.6
Pinellas	911	38.3	0.4	8.0	1.6	5.6	643.5	848	30 750	372.3	6 170	196 008	365 369	R–57.8
Polk	814	54.4	8.2	6.9	1.0	5.6	266.3	781	19 850	490.2	1 360	41 969	116 041	R–66.4
Putnam	1 019	50.0	1.7	5.1	3.7	6.2	98.6	1 839	3 596	565.4	167	4 673	20 307	R–57.2
St. Johns	794	57.9	1.7	8.2	0.6	7.7	47.7	833	3 884	468.5	354	10 212	27 347	R–70.2
St. Lucie	994	55.4	0.9	6.9	0.7	5.5	105.7	1 041	6 794	473.8	434	14 204	50 004	R–64.5
Santa Rosa	1 068	59.1	18.4	3.5	0.1	6.9	24.3	406	3 240	440.8	750	19 395	24 423	R–77.9
Sarasota	944	32.9	27.5	6.5	0.4	4.9	115.6	526	12 158	456.6	1 074	34 961	127 483	R–66.4
Seminole	799	59.1	9.4	6.6	0.2	4.5	56.6	284	9 998	352.0	607	19 897	83 674	R–72.2

1. Based on the estimated population as of July 1, 1982. 2. Per 10,000 resident population estimated as of July 1 of the year shown. 3. Data subject to copyright.

STATE–County code	MSA/CMSA/NECMA code[1]	STATE County	Land Area,[2] 1990 (Sq. Km.)	Population, 1990											
							Race						Age of population Percent		
				Total persons	Rank	Per square kilometer	White	Black	Am. Indian, Eskimo, Aleut	Asian & Pacific Islander	Other race	Hispanic[3]	Under 5 years	5 to 14 years	15 to 24 years
			1	2	3	4	5	6	7	8	9	10	11	12	13
		FLORIDA—Con.													
12 119	...	Sumter	1 413	31 577	1 227	22.3	26 088	5 102	164	55	168	762	6.0	12.5	12.4
12 121	...	Suwannee	1 781	26 780	1 397	15.0	22 524	3 949	104	65	138	417	6.2	15.4	13.3
12 123	...	Taylor	2 699	17 111	1 846	6.3	13 791	3 083	159	39	39	174	7.8	15.4	13.8
12 125	...	Union	622	10 252	2 363	16.5	7 697	2 379	58	38	80	335	6.6	14.8	13.2
12 127	2020	Volusia	2 864	370 712	136	129.4	328 530	33 455	915	2 739	5 073	14 840	5.7	10.8	12.7
12 129	...	Wakulla	1 571	14 202	2 037	9.0	12 226	1 837	96	32	11	83	7.0	16.3	13.1
12 131	...	Walton	2 739	27 760	1 361	10.1	25 300	1 885	417	130	28	244	6.3	13.3	11.9
12 133	...	Washington	1 502	16 919	1 855	11.3	14 029	2 459	279	84	68	180	6.4	14.0	13.5
13 000	...	GEORGIA	150 010	6 478 216	X	43.2	4 600 148	1 746 565	13 348	75 781	42 374	108 922	7.6	14.7	15.7
13 001	...	Appling	1 318	15 744	1 936	11.9	12 356	3 268	17	41	62	138	6.9	16.6	15.6
13 003	...	Atkinson	876	6 213	2 732	7.1	4 427	1 658	2	3	123	154	8.0	17.0	16.0
13 005	...	Bacon	738	9 566	2 427	13.0	8 030	1 480	11	19	26	83	7.5	17.1	15.7
13 007	...	Baker	889	3 615	2 950	4.1	1 747	1 861	1	2	4	21	7.4	17.2	15.4
13 009	...	Baldwin	669	39 530	1 012	59.1	22 451	16 706	44	271	58	349	6.0	12.8	17.7
13 011	...	Banks	605	10 308	2 357	17.0	9 874	364	18	31	21	52	6.6	14.9	15.6
13 013	0520	Barrow	420	29 721	1 305	70.8	25 962	3 354	67	228	110	253	8.5	15.2	14.8
13 015	...	Bartow	1 191	55 911	774	46.9	50 413	5 026	125	143	204	521	8.2	14.9	15.3
13 017	...	Ben Hill	652	16 245	1 911	24.9	11 098	5 088	16	34	9	78	8.0	17.4	14.2
13 019	...	Berrien	1 172	14 153	2 041	12.1	12 407	1 648	27	30	41	277	7.6	15.2	15.2
13 021	4680	Bibb	648	149 967	314	231.4	86 252	62 526	190	791	208	916	7.6	14.6	15.3
13 023	...	Bleckley	563	10 430	2 346	18.5	8 000	2 332	6	79	13	43	6.8	14.9	17.2
13 025	...	Brantley	1 151	11 077	2 285	9.6	10 438	596	32	5	6	36	7.6	17.4	15.7
13 027	...	Brooks	1 279	15 398	1 964	12.0	8 893	6 390	27	27	61	253	8.4	16.5	14.9
13 029	...	Bryan	1 144	15 438	1 959	13.5	13 018	2 293	27	73	27	136	8.5	18.8	14.7
13 031	...	Bulloch	1 768	43 125	936	24.4	31 464	11 226	60	227	148	360	6.4	12.7	29.4
13 033	...	Burke	2 151	20 579	1 650	9.6	9 762	10 756	13	27	21	67	9.1	18.6	15.2
13 035	0520	Butts	483	15 326	1 970	31.7	9 770	5 438	38	49	31	113	7.0	14.5	15.3
13 037	...	Calhoun	726	5 013	2 842	6.9	2 047	2 953	12	1	0	8	7.2	16.6	14.3
13 039	...	Camden	1 632	30 167	1 290	18.5	23 284	6 079	150	405	249	622	10.4	16.0	18.0
13 043	...	Candler	640	7 744	2 600	12.1	5 238	2 405	7	9	85	138	7.4	14.5	15.3
13 045	...	Carroll	1 293	71 422	620	55.2	59 646	11 231	149	230	166	592	7.3	14.9	18.8
13 047	1560	Catoosa	420	42 464	947	101.1	41 822	357	91	152	42	205	6.7	14.6	14.5
13 049	...	Charlton	2 022	8 496	2 513	4.2	6 094	2 355	33	10	4	35	9.1	16.8	15.1
13 051	7520	Chatham	1 141	216 935	230	190.1	130 607	82 608	461	2 352	907	2 782	7.9	14.6	15.1
13 053	1800	Chattahoochee	644	16 934	1 853	26.3	10 091	5 235	106	480	1 022	1 793	8.0	16.7	35.0
13 055	...	Chattooga	813	22 242	1 566	27.4	20 220	1 941	40	24	17	75	6.8	14.1	14.8
13 057	0520	Cherokee	1 098	90 204	508	82.2	87 690	1 693	251	309	261	1 059	9.1	14.9	13.4
13 059	0500	Clarke	313	87 594	520	279.9	61 929	22 935	134	2 155	441	1 491	6.0	10.9	32.0
13 061	...	Clay	506	3 364	2 967	6.6	1 310	2 044	5	3	2	19	7.3	17.3	13.6
13 063	0520	Clayton	369	182 052	267	493.4	131 729	43 403	456	5 046	1 418	3 746	8.3	15.0	16.3
13 065	...	Clinch	2 096	6 160	2 736	2.9	4 456	1 682	8	6	8	60	7.9	16.4	15.9
13 067	0520	Cobb	881	447 745	111	508.2	391 959	44 154	957	7 918	2 757	9 403	7.6	13.8	14.3
13 069	...	Coffee	1 552	29 592	1 312	19.1	21 558	7 504	31	114	385	557	8.1	16.8	16.2
13 071	...	Colquitt	1 430	36 645	1 084	25.6	27 047	8 861	75	42	620	1 588	7.3	16.2	15.4
13 073	0600	Columbia	751	66 031	664	87.9	56 785	7 282	156	1 547	261	962	8.2	17.6	13.7
13 075	...	Cook	593	13 456	2 104	22.7	9 311	4 031	34	30	50	217	7.9	15.7	15.8
13 077	0520	Coweta	1 148	53 853	798	46.9	41 322	12 194	107	149	81	385	8.4	15.5	14.3
13 079	...	Crawford	842	8 991	2 471	10.7	6 090	2 757	33	14	97	149	7.9	15.5	15.0
13 081	...	Crisp	709	20 011	1 677	28.2	11 783	8 153	36	27	12	62	7.7	17.0	14.3
13 083	1560	Dade	450	13 147	2 128	29.2	12 972	101	42	26	6	64	6.7	14.5	16.8
13 085	...	Dawson	547	9 429	2 439	17.2	9 328	4	82	7	8	39	7.7	15.3	14.0
13 087	...	Decatur	1 546	25 511	1 446	16.5	15 228	10 070	66	41	106	472	7.5	16.9	15.5
13 089	0520	De Kalb	695	545 837	87	785.4	292 310	230 425	998	16 266	5 838	15 619	7.1	12.8	15.6
13 091	...	Dodge	1 297	17 607	1 813	13.6	12 620	4 864	16	35	72	148	7.0	14.2	15.4
13 093	...	Dooly	1 018	9 901	2 398	9.7	4 991	4 852	3	40	15	77	7.8	17.6	13.7
13 095	0120	Dougherty	854	96 311	479	112.8	47 034	48 387	250	452	188	816	8.4	16.7	17.2
13 097	0520	Douglas	516	71 120	622	137.8	64 734	5 597	176	386	227	749	7.9	15.8	15.2
13 099	...	Early	1 324	11 854	2 227	9.0	6 579	5 226	31	16	2	45	7.7	17.2	14.4
13 101	...	Echols	1 047	2 334	3 037	2.2	2 007	264	40	2	21	45	7.5	17.2	15.6
13 103	7520	Effingham	1 242	25 687	1 435	20.7	21 906	3 620	54	60	47	169	8.0	18.0	15.0
13 105	...	Elbert	955	18 949	1 738	19.8	13 153	5 718	8	49	21	134	7.2	15.4	13.5
13 107	...	Emanuel	1 777	20 546	1 652	11.6	13 772	6 681	20	44	29	82	7.8	17.5	14.4
13 109	...	Evans	479	8 724	2 492	18.2	5 654	2 963	2	19	86	109	8.0	16.1	14.8
13 111	...	Fannin	999	15 992	1 922	16.0	15 927	5	38	15	7	62	5.8	13.1	12.2
13 113	0520	Fayette	511	62 415	696	122.1	57 729	3 380	82	1 053	171	994	7.0	17.1	13.1

1. MSA = Metropolitan Statistical Area. CMSA = Consolidated MSA. NECMA = New England county metropolitan area. PMSA = Primary MSA. See Appendix A for explanation of these concepts. See Appendix B for list of metropolitan areas identified by type, with component counties. 2. Dry land or land partially or temporarily covered by water. 3. Hispanic persons may be of any race.

STATE County	Population, 1990 (cont'd)							Population–Change and components of change							
	Age of population (cont'd) Percent							Change		Components of change, 1980–1986					
								1980–1990				Net change		Natural increase	
	25 to 34 years	35 to 44 years	45 to 54 years	55 to 64 years	65 to 74 years	75 years and over	Percent female	Number	Percent	Total persons, 1986	Total persons, 1980	Number	Percent	Births	Deaths
	14	15	16	17	18	19	20	21	22	23	24	25	26	27	28
FLORIDA—Con.															
Sumter	13.1	11.5	10.0	12.3	14.6	7.7	49.8	7 305	30.1	29 400	24 272	5 100	21.1	2 300	1 900
Suwannee	13.1	13.3	11.1	10.7	9.3	7.6	51.7	4 493	20.2	25 800	22 287	3 500	15.8	2 300	1 600
Taylor	15.4	13.4	10.6	10.3	8.0	5.2	51.5	579	3.5	18 400	16 532	1 900	11.3	1 700	1 000
Union	23.9	17.4	9.6	7.0	4.8	2.7	38.2	86	0.8	10 600	10 166	500	4.7	900	500
Volusia	14.8	13.0	9.4	10.9	13.3	9.5	51.6	111 950	43.3	320 900	258 762	62 100	24.0	20 800	24 300
Wakulla	14.9	16.5	11.4	9.1	6.8	4.8	51.1	3 315	30.4	13 500	10 887	2 600	24.0	1 000	600
Walton	14.5	13.4	11.5	12.6	10.4	6.1	50.9	6 460	30.3	26 700	21 300	5 400	25.3	1 800	1 400
Washington	13.1	13.2	11.3	10.9	10.1	7.5	51.6	2 410	16.6	15 600	14 509	1 100	7.7	1 300	1 000
GEORGIA	18.1	15.7	10.3	7.7	6.0	4.1	51.5	1 015 216	18.6	6 104 000	5 463 000	641 000	11.7	574 000	287 000
Appling	15.3	14.6	10.4	8.4	7.1	5.1	51.8	179	1.2	16 300	15 565	700	4.8	1 600	900
Atkinson	15.1	13.3	11.0	7.9	7.1	4.7	51.4	72	1.2	6 500	6 141	400	6.4	700	400
Bacon	14.7	14.2	10.1	8.5	7.4	4.8	52.5	187	2.0	9 400	9 379	100	0.6	1 000	500
Baker	14.7	13.4	9.6	9.0	7.5	5.7	54.0	-193	-5.1	3 700	3 808	-100	-3.8	400	300
Baldwin	19.4	15.1	10.2	8.0	6.3	4.4	48.3	4 844	14.0	38 200	34 686	3 600	10.3	3 400	1 800
Banks	16.1	15.8	11.3	8.2	6.9	4.5	49.5	1 606	18.5	10 100	8 702	1 400	16.4	700	400
Barrow	18.8	14.1	10.0	7.7	6.2	4.8	51.1	8 367	39.2	26 300	21 354	5 000	23.3	2 300	1 300
Bartow	17.8	15.1	10.7	8.0	6.1	4.0	50.7	15 151	37.2	48 100	40 760	7 300	18.0	4 500	2 200
Ben Hill	14.5	14.1	9.6	8.2	7.8	6.2	54.0	245	1.5	17 300	16 000	1 300	8.4	1 800	1 200
Berrien	15.1	13.9	10.9	9.3	7.4	5.3	51.3	628	4.6	13 800	13 525	200	1.7	1 300	900
Bibb	16.7	14.6	9.7	8.7	7.6	5.3	53.4	-289	-0.2	156 500	150 256	6 200	4.1	14 800	9 300
Bleckley	14.5	13.2	10.9	9.1	7.9	5.5	51.9	-337	-3.1	10 600	10 767	-100	-1.3	900	600
Brantley	15.6	15.4	10.8	8.5	5.5	3.5	50.3	2 376	27.3	10 200	8 701	1 500	16.8	800	500
Brooks	14.4	12.6	9.3	8.8	8.1	7.1	52.8	143	0.9	15 000	15 255	-200	-1.6	1 600	1 100
Bryan	17.0	17.4	9.7	6.7	4.7	2.5	50.7	5 263	51.7	13 200	10 175	3 000	29.5	1 400	500
Bulloch	13.9	12.0	8.4	7.0	5.9	4.3	51.4	7 340	20.5	37 500	35 785	1 700	4.7	3 400	1 800
Burke	15.7	13.4	9.0	7.6	6.6	4.9	52.8	1 230	6.4	21 200	19 349	1 900	9.7	2 400	1 200
Butts	17.9	15.3	10.3	8.2	6.6	5.0	47.1	1 661	12.2	15 500	13 665	1 800	13.5	1 400	800
Calhoun	14.2	12.9	8.8	9.0	8.6	8.4	54.8	-704	-12.3	5 500	5 717	-200	-3.4	600	500
Camden	23.8	14.5	7.4	4.8	3.2	1.9	46.7	16 796	125.6	19 400	13 371	6 000	45.1	2 100	600
Candler	13.4	13.7	10.5	8.9	9.1	7.3	52.5	226	3.0	7 600	7 518	100	1.5	600	600
Carroll	16.5	14.4	10.4	7.4	5.8	4.4	51.6	15 076	26.8	64 900	56 346	8 600	15.2	5 900	3 000
Catoosa	16.0	15.8	12.1	9.6	6.7	4.2	51.7	5 473	14.8	39 300	36 991	2 400	6.4	3 000	1 600
Charlton	16.8	12.5	10.6	8.5	5.9	4.5	51.4	1 153	15.7	7 700	7 343	300	4.3	700	400
Chatham	17.4	14.3	9.6	8.5	7.8	5.0	52.1	14 709	7.3	217 700	202 226	15 500	7.6	23 400	12 100
Chattahoochee	23.5	11.6	2.6	1.3	0.9	0.5	34.1	-4 798	-22.1	20 900	21 732	-900	-4.0	2 000	200
Chattooga	14.5	13.7	10.9	10.3	8.9	5.9	52.0	386	1.8	21 400	21 856	-500	-2.2	1 800	1 400
Cherokee	21.6	17.8	10.2	6.0	4.2	2.8	49.7	38 505	74.5	73 800	51 699	22 100	42.8	6 900	2 200
Clarke	17.0	12.3	7.4	5.7	4.9	3.7	52.3	13 096	17.6	78 800	74 498	4 300	5.8	6 500	3 000
Clay	13.0	12.9	8.3	9.5	10.0	8.2	55.2	-189	-5.3	3 200	3 553	-300	-9.7	300	300
Clayton	20.7	16.6	10.6	6.6	3.8	2.0	51.3	31 695	21.1	170 500	150 357	20 100	13.4	16 400	4 900
Clinch	14.9	14.3	10.2	8.8	6.9	4.7	51.7	-500	-7.5	6 900	6 660	200	3.0	700	400
Cobb	21.3	19.0	11.2	6.5	4.1	2.2	50.8	150 027	50.4	392 400	297 718	94 700	31.8	32 300	10 600
Coffee	16.3	14.0	10.1	7.5	6.5	4.5	51.9	2 698	10.0	29 800	26 894	2 900	10.6	3 000	1 500
Colquitt	14.5	13.6	10.4	8.5	8.1	6.0	51.5	1 269	3.6	36 500	35 376	1 100	3.1	3 600	2 200
Columbia	18.0	19.3	11.0	6.4	3.9	2.0	50.1	25 913	64.6	56 400	40 118	16 300	40.6	5 300	1 500
Cook	14.3	12.9	10.8	8.9	7.9	5.9	51.9	-34	-0.3	13 900	13 490	400	3.1	1 400	800
Coweta	16.9	15.5	11.1	8.0	5.9	4.2	51.7	14 585	37.1	46 400	39 268	7 200	18.2	4 500	2 400
Crawford	17.6	14.6	11.6	7.7	5.8	4.3	50.6	1 307	17.0	7 500	7 684	-200	-2.3	700	400
Crisp	14.3	14.1	9.7	9.0	7.8	6.2	54.2	522	2.7	20 200	19 489	700	3.8	2 400	1 400
Dade	15.8	14.8	11.8	8.6	6.7	4.2	51.2	829	6.7	11 800	12 318	-500	-4.4	1 000	500
Dawson	18.8	15.4	11.3	8.6	6.1	2.8	49.5	4 655	97.5	6 700	4 774	1 900	39.4	600	300
Decatur	15.4	13.8	9.3	8.6	7.6	5.4	52.3	16	0.1	26 600	25 495	1 100	4.5	2 700	1 600
De Kalb	20.9	17.2	10.5	7.5	5.2	3.3	52.1	62 813	13.0	529 300	483 024	46 300	9.6	45 100	19 000
Dodge	15.3	14.1	10.9	9.1	8.1	6.1	50.9	652	3.8	16 900	16 955	0	-0.2	1 500	1 200
Dooly	13.9	13.1	10.2	8.7	8.3	6.7	54.5	-925	-8.5	10 200	10 826	-600	-5.7	1 200	800
Dougherty	15.5	14.4	9.5	8.1	6.2	4.0	53.1	-4 399	-4.4	102 700	100 710	2 000	2.0	12 000	4 700
Douglas	18.5	17.5	11.2	6.8	4.3	2.8	50.4	16 547	30.3	68 200	54 573	13 600	25.0	5 800	2 200
Early	12.9	13.2	9.6	9.1	8.3	7.6	53.9	-1 304	-9.9	12 800	13 158	-300	-2.4	1 400	900
Echols	16.7	13.6	10.4	9.2	6.1	3.9	48.9	37	1.6	2 400	2 297	100	4.3	200	100
Effingham	17.8	15.5	10.7	7.1	5.0	2.9	49.9	7 360	40.2	22 000	18 327	3 700	20.2	1 900	900
Elbert	14.7	13.8	10.9	9.3	8.3	6.8	52.3	191	1.0	19 000	18 758	200	1.2	1 900	1 300
Emanuel	14.3	13.6	9.8	8.3	8.4	6.0	52.4	-249	-1.2	21 600	20 795	800	3.7	2 500	1 500
Evans	15.5	13.1	9.5	8.6	7.9	6.4	51.4	296	3.5	8 200	8 428	-200	-2.5	900	600
Fannin	13.2	14.2	11.0	12.6	11.1	6.8	51.8	1 244	8.4	15 700	14 748	900	6.4	1 100	1 000
Fayette	14.2	20.9	13.7	6.7	4.6	2.5	50.6	33 372	114.9	47 300	29 043	18 300	62.9	3 000	1 100

STATE County	Population—(cont'd): Components of change, 1980-1986 (cont'd): Net migration	Households, 1990: Number	Households, 1990: Percent change, 1980–1990	Households, 1990: Persons per household	Households, 1990: Percent: Female family householder[1]	Households, 1990: Percent: One-person	Births, 1988: Total	Births, 1988: Rate[2]	Births, 1988: Low birth weight[3] (Number)	Deaths, 1987: Number: Total	Deaths, 1987: Number: Infant[4]	Deaths, 1987: Rate: Total[2]	Deaths, 1987: Rate: Infant[5]	Marriages, 1984: Number	Marriages, 1984: Rate[2]
	29	30	31	32	33	34	35	36	37	38	39	40	41	42	43
FLORIDA—Con.															
Sumter	4 700	12 119	41.2	2.46	10.9	23.4	382	12.1	35	372	7	12.0	17.9	255	9.1
Suwannee	2 900	10 034	29.7	2.61	11.3	23.2	328	12.2	17	298	3	11.3	9.7	253	10.1
Taylor	1 200	6 401	9.9	2.67	12.2	21.4	295	15.4	29	174	5	9.2	15.8	216	12.1
Union	200	2 658	25.4	2.91	12.4	18.7	121	11.6	9	89	0	8.4	0.0	61	5.7
Volusia	65 600	153 416	45.0	2.33	9.5	26.4	4 401	12.6	323	4 465	45	13.3	10.7	3 180	10.6
Wakulla	2 200	5 210	39.7	2.70	12.5	19.0	195	13.7	17	122	4	8.9	22.0	160	12.6
Walton	5 000	11 294	40.4	2.44	10.1	24.5	350	12.4	34	266	2	9.6	6.1	222	9.0
Washington	900	6 443	23.1	2.55	11.1	23.2	197	11.9	9	213	3	13.1	14.5	182	11.6
GEORGIA	354 000	2 366 615	26.4	2.66	13.9	22.7	105 923	16.7	8 858	50 199	1 306	8.1	12.7	74 159	12.7
Appling	0	5 834	14.0	2.67	11.8	24.6	215	12.9	15	158	2	9.6	8.8	184	11.3
Atkinson	100	2 210	10.0	2.81	12.1	23.4	116	18.1	13	61	2	9.5	15.9	85	13.5
Bacon	-400	3 442	10.5	2.74	15.7	21.6	140	14.4	12	97	3	9.9	21.0	109	11.6
Baker	-200	1 300	7.6	2.78	16.9	25.1	42	11.4	4	36	0	9.5	0.0	21	5.7
Baldwin	1 900	12 165	19.8	2.65	17.9	22.8	530	13.7	60	302	8	7.8	15.3	288	7.7
Banks	1 200	3 775	24.4	2.73	7.5	19.2	122	11.3	8	82	1	7.7	8.2	44	4.6
Barrow	4 000	10 676	46.0	2.76	10.8	18.9	521	18.9	51	219	6	8.2	11.4	268	11.2
Bartow	5 000	20 091	45.5	2.76	10.7	19.2	938	18.1	66	421	8	8.4	8.9	460	10.5
Ben Hill	800	5 972	5.3	2.67	16.9	25.2	268	15.5	19	211	5	12.3	17.7	186	10.9
Berrien	-200	5 149	10.7	2.69	11.1	21.5	183	13.0	13	115	2	8.2	9.2	186	13.4
Bibb	700	56 307	7.1	2.58	19.1	26.4	2 462	15.6	259	1 498	47	9.6	18.8	1 590	10.2
Bleckley	-400	3 816	7.4	2.62	14.0	23.2	148	13.8	18	107	0	10.1	0.0	121	11.4
Brantley	1 100	3 811	36.9	2.90	10.1	16.5	149	14.3	10	99	1	9.7	7.0	125	13.3
Brooks	-700	5 392	8.1	2.79	18.1	22.7	236	15.4	21	209	3	13.8	12.1	142	9.3
Bryan	2 100	5 070	57.7	3.02	10.9	14.5	270	17.1	17	98	2	6.8	7.4	107	9.2
Bulloch	100	14 984	32.1	2.63	11.9	23.3	596	15.7	46	289	6	7.7	10.4	288	7.8
Burke	700	7 037	13.3	2.89	21.9	22.4	391	18.4	38	195	7	9.2	17.6	130	6.4
Butts	1 300	4 696	17.8	2.89	14.6	18.6	236	14.2	23	141	5	8.5	22.9	112	7.6
Calhoun	-300	1 794	-2.1	2.74	20.4	27.4	75	14.2	5	66	1	12.5	13.2	34	6.1
Camden	4 600	9 459	115.6	2.89	10.6	17.0	524	23.2	35	162	9	7.5	20.0	2 084	120.5
Candler	100	2 828	11.9	2.63	14.7	25.4	118	15.7	11	114	4	15.4	37.0	75	9.7
Carroll	5 700	25 370	33.5	2.71	11.7	21.1	1 115	16.1	107	531	14	7.9	13.0	742	12.0
Catoosa	900	15 745	24.5	2.67	10.3	19.3	559	13.4	36	305	9	7.5	16.9	4 632	119.4
Charlton	0	2 911	30.8	2.88	14.0	19.7	178	21.7	12	64	2	7.8	12.5	2 607	343.0
Chatham	4 100	81 111	13.7	2.59	16.0	25.9	3 880	17.6	388	2 103	68	9.6	17.6	2 081	9.8
Chattahoochee	-2 700	2 884	-4.2	3.68	7.4	7.5	234	12.9	21	34	1	1.9	4.0	70	3.3
Chattooga	-900	8 467	9.5	2.61	12.6	22.6	297	13.6	24	257	4	11.8	14.5	189	8.8
Cherokee	17 400	31 309	85.8	2.86	7.4	14.1	1 639	18.9	91	436	13	5.4	8.4	553	8.7
Clarke	800	33 170	24.8	2.40	13.3	28.8	1 131	14.5	89	526	7	6.8	6.3	736	9.5
Clay	-400	1 210	1.4	2.72	21.3	26.3	52	14.9	5	39	1	11.5	18.5	22	6.5
Clayton	8 600	65 523	29.9	2.75	14.1	19.9	3 076	17.8	237	946	32	5.6	11.1	2 353	14.3
Clinch	-100	2 173	2.5	2.78	14.4	21.9	107	16.0	7	80	1	11.6	8.3	67	10.0
Cobb	73 000	171 288	60.7	2.60	9.1	22.5	7 189	16.9	425	1 989	80	4.9	11.5	4 694	13.2
Coffee	1 400	10 541	18.4	2.75	15.3	22.0	498	16.5	52	234	6	7.8	12.8	338	11.9
Colquitt	-400	12 980	6.8	2.69	16.0	22.8	568	15.3	55	375	6	10.1	11.9	419	11.6
Columbia	12 400	21 841	70.2	2.97	9.4	13.5	1 086	17.4	62	289	18	4.8	17.7	301	6.1
Cook	-100	4 825	7.8	2.73	13.5	23.1	226	16.0	27	153	5	10.9	22.9	149	10.9
Coweta	5 000	18 930	42.3	2.82	13.1	17.9	876	17.3	73	397	6	8.2	6.7	516	12.0
Crawford	-500	3 069	30.2	2.87	12.9	18.8	146	19.5	17	70	0	9.5	0.0	77	10.5
Crisp	-300	7 287	11.1	2.69	20.5	24.8	344	16.9	35	214	4	10.5	12.2	204	10.1
Dade	-1 000	4 661	16.6	2.70	9.2	18.4	165	13.8	3	99	0	8.3	0.0	1 642	140.3
Dawson	1 600	3 360	102.0	2.79	8.0	16.0	149	18.0	6	67	5	8.6	34.5	50	8.8
Decatur	0	8 962	7.8	2.76	18.2	23.2	426	15.8	33	288	6	10.7	14.3	327	12.3
De Kalb	20 200	208 690	20.7	2.57	15.0	25.2	8 640	15.9	763	3 341	97	6.2	11.8	5 710	11.3
Dodge	-300	6 387	8.9	2.60	14.9	25.2	240	13.8	27	206	2	11.9	9.6	181	10.5
Dooly	-1 000	3 557	0.8	2.74	19.5	25.7	139	13.6	18	116	3	11.3	21.4	89	8.5
Dougherty	-5 300	34 163	3.4	2.72	22.0	23.3	1 791	17.8	215	783	25	7.7	14.4	1 195	11.5
Douglas	10 000	24 277	43.6	2.90	9.9	15.0	1 171	15.9	66	378	12	5.3	11.0	747	11.8
Early	-900	4 263	-0.9	2.73	17.4	25.0	200	15.4	16	149	6	11.4	29.1	108	8.2
Echols	0	816	11.0	2.84	9.6	18.8	38	16.5	1	13	0	5.7	0.0	80	34.8
Effingham	2 600	8 759	51.4	2.93	10.6	16.2	378	15.5	35	138	2	5.9	6.0	147	7.2
Elbert	-400	7 115	8.6	2.62	14.2	23.6	306	16.0	21	205	2	10.8	7.7	128	6.7
Emanuel	-200	7 420	6.1	2.72	16.2	24.2	354	16.0	25	239	8	10.9	21.8	246	11.5
Evans	-500	3 144	10.0	2.66	16.3	24.8	159	18.5	15	90	0	10.7	0.0	76	8.8
Fannin	900	6 334	14.7	2.50	8.3	22.1	184	11.2	12	170	2	10.5	9.7	129	8.5
Fayette	16 400	21 054	128.6	2.96	6.8	12.5	714	12.7	34	272	4	5.2	5.9	299	7.6

1. No spouse present. 2. Per 1,000 resident population estimated as of July 1 of the year shown. 3. Under 2,500 grams. 4. Deaths of infants under 1 year old. 5. Deaths of infants under 1 year old per 1,000 live births.

STATE County	Divorces, 1984		Physicians, active non–Federal, 1989		Hospitals, 1989			Nursing homes,[4] 1986		Serious crimes known to police, 1988			Education			
						Beds				Number			Public school enrollment[7]		Attainment,[8] 1980	
	Number	Rate[1]	Number[2]	Rate[3]	Number	Number	Rate[3]	Number	Beds	Total[5]	Violent[6]	Rate[3]	1986–1987	1980	Percent 12 yrs. or more	Percent 16 yrs. or more
	44	45	46	47	48	49	50	51	52	53	54	55	56	57	58	59
FLORIDA–Con.																
Sumter	166	5.9	4	12	1	106	327	1	120	NA	NA	NA	4 722	4 559	51.3	7.0
Suwannee	145	5.8	15	55	1	60	220	3	234	NA	NA	NA	4 982	4 910	53.3	6.5
Taylor	100	5.6	11	57	1	48	247	1	120	NA	NA	NA	3 376	3 788	52.6	8.6
Union	42	3.9	14	136	2	180	1 748	0	0	NA	NA	NA	1 703	1 552	56.9	5.9
Volusia	1 870	6.2	472	131	8	1 399	387	64	2 768	NA	NA	NA	40 192	37 538	66.5	13.0
Wakulla	82	6.5	3	21	0	0	0	2	144	NA	NA	NA	2 724	2 487	56.7	8.4
Walton	182	7.3	11	38	1	29	100	3	168	NA	NA	NA	4 190	4 238	50.8	9.6
Washington	131	8.3	9	53	1	45	266	5	177	NA	NA	NA	3 326	3 266	51.0	6.3
GEORGIA	30 905	5.3	10 765	167	215	35 830	557	601	35 209	X	41 313	6 188	1 089 412	1 101 032	56.4	14.6
Appling	86	5.3	7	42	1	40	240	2	101	407	31	2 413	3 562	3 794	41.6	6.5
Atkinson	28	4.4	1	16	0	0	0	0	0	75	12	1 664	1 381	1 456	35.1	5.0
Bacon	53	5.6	8	82	1	40	412	1	88	363	39	3 601	2 156	2 247	41.7	6.9
Baker	14	3.8	0	0	0	0	0	0	0	1	1	26	705	801	29.0	4.9
Baldwin	183	4.9	120	309	2	2 096	5 402	3	197	1 902	227	4 741	5 760	5 962	52.8	15.4
Banks	37	3.9	4	36	0	0	0	0	0	133	5	1 243	1 804	1 775	39.5	5.0
Barrow	110	4.6	13	46	1	60	214	3	162	836	60	3 067	4 948	4 425	37.7	7.5
Bartow	324	7.4	33	61	1	80	149	3	135	1 616	87	3 196	9 958	9 264	39.9	6.3
Ben Hill	97	5.7	10	58	1	75	436	2	245	898	85	5 075	3 565	3 243	43.1	8.1
Berrien	49	3.5	7	50	1	59	418	1	54	365	38	2 553	2 789	2 963	41.1	5.9
Bibb	1 024	6.6	414	263	7	1 191	756	13	1 331	11 943	798	7 428	24 461	27 609	55.8	13.0
Bleckley	54	5.1	5	47	1	45	425	1	75	197	24	1 807	1 823	2 363	47.0	9.0
Brantley	29	3.1	0	0	0	0	0	0	0	155	14	1 492	2 403	2 158	47.9	4.8
Brooks	78	5.1	6	39	1	31	204	3	278	250	38	1 609	3 059	3 267	39.5	7.5
Bryan	48	4.1	6	35	0	0	0	0	0	496	54	3 325	2 976	2 358	41.9	4.4
Bulloch	168	4.5	42	111	2	159	418	4	316	1 732	154	4 587	6 554	6 635	51.9	15.6
Burke	91	4.5	11	51	1	40	187	6	184	486	68	2 275	4 382	4 177	38.6	7.9
Butts	68	4.6	10	58	1	28	164	1	196	304	21	1 904	2 625	2 637	43.6	6.4
Calhoun	6	1.1	2	39	1	84	1 647	1	60	88	12	1 584	1 151	1 343	34.7	7.2
Camden	153	8.8	15	62	1	34	140	1	69	815	84	3 809	4 178	3 196	51.5	8.2
Candler	32	4.2	5	68	1	47	635	4	308	73	8	946	1 512	1 645	40.7	9.0
Carroll	391	6.3	68	96	3	284	402	4	350	3 248	235	4 763	12 654	12 058	46.9	11.2
Catoosa	151	3.9	31	73	2	293	694	5	179	1 399	73	3 366	7 795	7 744	55.7	7.3
Charlton	39	5.1	4	48	1	46	548	1	92	138	14	1 656	1 699	1 930	43.6	5.5
Chatham	1 376	6.5	481	218	5	1 452	659	29	1 043	15 598	1 302	6 952	31 954	33 626	60.6	14.1
Chattahoochee	24	1.1	9	52	1	347	2 017	0	0	90	4	503	942	3 163	81.8	20.4
Chattooga	81	3.8	5	23	1	116	532	2	96	627	34	2 985	4 102	4 218	34.3	5.9
Cherokee	342	5.4	32	34	2	105	113	4	243	2 118	136	2 547	13 756	11 386	52.1	9.7
Clarke	312	4.0	189	244	4	604	778	7	460	5 366	409	6 722	10 383	10 372	67.4	35.0
Clay	8	2.4	3	86	0	0	0	2	53	27	6	772	664	816	37.2	9.8
Clayton	846	5.2	190	110	1	340	196	3	386	14 294	1 032	8 212	32 340	33 547	66.5	10.3
Clinch	36	5.4	5	75	1	39	582	2	95	33	3	465	1 434	1 667	34.4	6.5
Cobb	2 794	7.9	612	139	6	1 184	268	28	1 175	24 605	1 627	5 854	66 951	59 283	72.3	23.0
Coffee	124	4.4	33	109	1	145	477	3	156	1 264	165	4 123	6 069	5 880	43.4	8.2
Colquitt	171	4.7	35	94	2	214	574	3	169	1 460	182	3 805	7 510	7 833	45.1	8.4
Columbia	310	6.3	125	190	0	0	0	6	150	1 485	127	2 418	11 597	9 274	67.2	15.4
Cook	28	2.0	9	63	1	147	1 035	1	80	555	73	3 854	2 734	3 117	38.7	5.7
Coweta	230	5.3	55	105	2	244	465	3	198	1 517	76	3 053	9 336	8 579	46.1	9.8
Crawford	29	4.0	1	14	0	0	0	2	106	95	7	1 283	1 531	1 745	40.5	6.5
Crisp	112	5.6	16	79	1	70	345	2	243	1 893	294	9 065	4 296	4 238	45.1	9.0
Dade	66	5.6	11	92	2	26	217	2	70	276	30	2 236	2 239	2 532	43.7	7.8
Dawson	46	8.1	3	33	0	0	0	0	0	407	32	5 607	1 544	1 027	36.7	4.4
Decatur	124	4.7	18	67	1	187	695	6	136	1 001	133	3 723	6 055	5 659	45.4	8.4
De Kalb	2 905	5.8	1 020	185	8	2 147	390	49	2 107	55 820	4 665	10 073	74 831	93 446	76.9	27.9
Dodge	0	0.0	11	63	1	87	500	3	215	340	42	1 982	3 430	3 884	40.2	6.6
Dooly	36	3.4	7	69	1	38	376	2	106	226	27	2 215	1 939	2 339	33.9	7.9
Dougherty	691	6.7	170	171	2	624	628	18	657	9 641	1 013	9 206	19 335	22 614	58.5	14.2
Douglas	123	1.9	56	74	3	811	1 067	6	287	2 874	173	3 957	13 338	12 452	57.4	9.1
Early	60	4.6	5	38	1	176	1 354	1	127	340	77	2 523	2 783	3 196	38.8	8.6
Echols	15	6.5	0	0	0	0	0	0	0	19	3	803	520	546	41.0	3.9
Effingham	84	4.1	6	24	1	97	383	1	56	534	53	2 218	4 931	4 149	46.6	5.2
Elbert	92	4.8	13	68	1	52	274	5	202	612	48	3 298	3 602	3 955	41.4	7.9
Emanuel	53	2.5	9	41	1	122	550	7	292	519	94	2 363	4 440	4 497	38.4	7.2
Evans	13	1.5	7	81	1	36	419	2	109	54	6	625	1 659	1 887	43.1	7.2
Fannin	66	4.4	11	66	1	51	305	1	101	363	29	2 192	2 776	2 911	40.9	5.2
Fayette	112	2.8	48	79	0	0	0	2	25	1 349	58	2 522	10 384	6 947	73.3	16.5

1. Per 1,000 resident population estimated as of July 1 of the year shown. 2. As of end of year. 3. Per 100,000 resident population as of July 1 of the year shown. 4. Preliminary. Covers nursing homes with 3 or more beds. 5. Data for serious crimes have not been adjusted for underreporting, this may affect comparability between geographic areas or over time. 6. Includes murder and nonnegligent manslaughter, forcible rape, robbery, and aggravated assault. 7. The 1986–1987 data are based on administrative reports obtained by the U.S. National Center for Education Statistics. The 1980 data are based on the 1980 Census of Population and Housing. 8. Persons 25 years old or older.

STATE County	Education (cont'd): Local government expenditures for education,[1] 1982: Total (Mil dol)	Education (cont'd): Local government expenditures for education,[1] 1982: Per capita (Dollars)	Social Security Program December 1988: Beneficiaries: Total	Social Security Program December 1988: Beneficiaries: Rate[2]	Social Security Program December 1988: Payments ($1,000)	Supplemental Security Income Program recipients June 1986	Money income: Per capita[3]: 1987 Income, (Dollars)	Money income: Per capita[3]: 1979: Current dollars	Money income: Per capita[3]: 1979: Constant 1987 dollars	Money income: Median household income 1979 (Dollars)	Money income: Percent below poverty level, 1979: Persons	Money income: Percent below poverty level, 1979: Families	Housing units, 1990: Total	Housing units, 1990: Percent change, 1980–1990
	60	61	62	63	64	65	66	67	68	69	70	71	72	73
FLORIDA–Con.														
Sumter	10.4	400	7 700	244.4	3 495	598	8 576	5 153	8 063	11 232	20.6	15.7	15 298	38.0
Suwannee	11.2	469	5 695	211.7	2 368	784	8 395	4 908	7 680	10 964	23.9	19.0	11 699	33.5
Taylor	8.0	462	3 295	172.5	1 415	522	9 358	5 718	8 947	12 285	22.2	18.0	7 908	13.3
Union	3.8	343	1 025	98.6	412	232	6 511	3 703	5 794	12 321	17.2	13.4	2 975	27.7
Volusia	96.4	342	92 620	265.8	45 178	3 994	11 420	6 588	10 308	12 393	14.1	9.7	180 972	45.4
Wakulla	6.2	540	1 885	132.7	787	248	8 769	5 111	7 997	12 158	18.1	15.9	6 587	29.9
Walton	8.3	364	4 465	157.8	1 824	730	8 252	5 218	8 165	10 687	23.0	19.3	18 728	71.5
Washington	10.8	713	3 800	228.9	1 512	804	7 825	4 526	7 082	10 028	25.0	20.7	7 703	28.8
GEORGIA	2 198.0	389	845 012	133.2	371 147	154 491	11 406	6 380	9 983	15 033	16.6	13.2	2 638 418	30.1
Appling	8.3	531	2 405	144.0	888	864	7 999	4 544	7 110	10 675	29.0	22.9	6 629	14.1
Atkinson	2.5	417	1 165	182.0	406	412	6 808	3 844	6 015	9 397	31.3	26.9	2 449	5.7
Bacon	3.5	375	1 590	163.9	589	438	7 876	4 538	7 101	10 942	23.1	20.3	3 859	13.0
Baker	1.3	350	475	128.4	164	192	7 583	4 431	6 933	10 928	27.4	25.4	1 499	17.7
Baldwin	11.4	310	5 360	138.1	2 353	1 228	9 562	5 583	8 736	14 831	16.4	10.8	14 200	16.1
Banks	2.3	252	1 195	110.6	459	262	9 434	5 497	8 601	13 237	11.6	9.9	4 193	27.8
Barrow	6.8	303	4 465	162.4	1 914	866	9 613	5 554	8 690	14 060	16.8	13.1	11 812	51.9
Bartow	19.0	451	7 465	144.1	3 276	990	9 916	5 702	8 922	14 493	12.9	10.8	21 757	46.7
Ben Hill	5.5	333	3 080	178.0	1 194	826	8 185	5 083	7 953	10 589	24.6	17.9	6 875	10.9
Berrien	5.0	362	2 430	172.3	909	510	8 967	5 113	8 000	12 212	20.1	17.1	5 858	14.4
Bibb	61.5	401	26 615	168.6	11 378	5 288	10 827	6 137	9 603	14 355	19.5	15.1	61 462	10.6
Bleckley	3.6	341	1 905	178.0	702	420	9 706	5 520	8 637	13 655	18.3	14.5	4 268	8.8
Brantley	6.1	667	1 345	129.3	517	320	7 413	4 505	7 049	12 597	18.6	14.1	4 404	39.7
Brooks	6.4	418	2 635	172.2	986	730	7 392	4 135	6 470	9 495	32.2	26.8	5 972	11.4
Bryan	5.3	489	1 895	119.9	747	418	8 532	4 883	7 640	13 628	20.0	15.2	5 549	58.0
Bulloch	13.0	348	5 445	143.3	2 232	1 206	8 871	4 982	7 795	12 479	21.8	16.1	16 541	30.4
Burke	7.6	379	3 255	152.8	1 216	1 120	7 497	4 493	7 030	10 568	28.5	23.3	8 329	22.3
Butts	5.0	337	2 430	146.4	1 018	506	8 895	5 363	8 391	13 939	16.5	12.8	5 536	11.3
Calhoun	2.8	486	1 370	258.5	496	438	7 306	4 072	6 371	10 132	29.2	26.4	2 061	5.0
Camden	8.0	505	2 065	91.4	893	330	8 893	5 404	8 456	13 480	21.8	17.9	10 885	102.3
Candler	2.6	344	1 565	208.7	597	558	8 037	4 713	7 374	9 892	28.9	22.5	3 203	12.7
Carroll	21.8	368	10 640	154.0	4 598	1 738	9 428	5 460	8 543	13 981	15.7	12.0	27 736	36.5
Catoosa	11.1	289	4 440	106.7	2 082	576	9 736	5 919	9 261	16 017	11.2	9.2	16 762	25.1
Charlton	5.8	772	1 240	151.2	499	312	7 814	4 504	7 047	13 156	21.3	17.2	3 222	28.6
Chatham	66.5	315	34 640	157.5	16 320	5 626	11 090	6 385	9 991	14 242	18.4	14.7	91 178	17.7
Chattahoochee	0.7	33	385	21.3	141	96	8 040	4 817	7 537	13 465	11.8	9.4	3 108	-2.9
Chattooga	7.6	353	4 625	212.2	2 027	738	8 602	5 054	7 908	12 908	16.4	12.4	9 142	10.3
Cherokee	19.9	345	6 865	79.4	3 077	756	11 813	6 341	9 922	17 715	10.7	8.7	33 840	89.1
Clarke	26.6	352	9 880	126.8	4 524	1 732	10 814	6 192	9 689	12 381	20.7	12.7	35 971	30.3
Clay	0.9	257	590	168.6	222	210	7 444	4 084	6 390	7 333	40.7	32.8	1 586	18.4
Clayton	59.6	377	15 190	88.1	7 249	1 402	12 306	7 308	11 435	19 960	8.0	6.9	71 926	35.7
Clinch	3.0	448	1 090	162.7	410	330	6 987	4 402	6 888	10 992	26.4	21.6	2 423	3.0
Cobb	119.4	369	35 940	84.5	18 152	2 408	15 700	8 580	13 425	21 420	6.3	4.8	189 872	67.6
Coffee	14.3	519	4 535	150.7	1 716	1 228	8 034	4 615	7 221	10 845	24.0	20.5	11 650	19.0
Colquitt	13.7	382	6 835	183.7	2 710	1 552	8 886	5 088	7 961	11 872	19.5	14.8	14 350	10.8
Columbia	16.7	377	4 670	74.7	2 025	568	12 433	6 739	10 545	18 353	10.9	9.4	23 745	68.4
Cook	5.4	392	2 445	173.4	924	566	8 354	4 735	7 409	11 767	19.1	14.8	5 340	9.9
Coweta	16.0	389	7 275	143.5	3 276	1 152	10 968	6 324	9 895	15 329	16.7	12.6	20 413	44.6
Crawford	3.1	430	845	112.7	307	266	8 801	4 807	7 522	14 720	18.5	16.1	3 279	27.4
Crisp	8.1	404	3 685	181.5	1 455	1 122	8 901	5 217	8 163	11 672	28.6	23.2	8 318	12.7
Dade	3.9	327	1 860	155.0	799	336	8 009	5 003	7 828	13 116	17.3	14.9	4 998	16.4
Dawson	2.3	458	1 240	149.4	496	226	9 666	5 084	7 955	12 236	19.0	16.5	4 321	80.0
Decatur	9.4	357	4 615	170.9	1 768	1 286	8 436	4 869	7 619	11 854	23.7	18.3	10 120	11.6
De Kalb	190.9	388	59 355	109.0	30 083	6 072	14 875	8 443	13 211	19 861	9.7	7.3	231 520	27.3
Dodge	7.5	436	3 175	182.5	1 156	970	7 868	4 616	7 223	10 483	27.4	22.0	7 094	10.9
Dooly	5.6	530	1 910	187.3	708	614	7 310	4 050	6 337	10 316	33.9	27.5	4 003	6.1
Dougherty	39.9	387	13 445	133.4	5 627	3 324	9 850	5 988	9 369	15 276	20.8	16.4	37 373	7.6
Douglas	20.9	356	6 630	90.2	3 081	718	11 289	6 520	10 202	20 059	7.9	6.2	26 495	49.2
Early	5.4	404	2 245	172.7	829	726	8 080	4 684	7 329	9 943	31.1	25.1	4 714	0.7
Echols	1.1	462	255	110.9	95	80	7 102	4 273	6 686	11 536	25.6	21.3	942	13.9
Effingham	8.6	454	2 325	95.3	1 010	366	9 191	5 425	8 488	15 567	16.9	12.6	9 492	50.1
Elbert	6.5	338	3 870	202.6	1 620	836	8 406	5 023	7 859	12 123	19.7	15.1	7 891	11.9
Emanuel	9.4	442	4 215	190.7	1 559	1 444	7 754	4 755	7 440	10 600	26.5	21.5	8 344	6.9
Evans	3.2	372	1 530	177.9	581	464	8 499	4 664	7 298	10 863	25.4	20.6	3 512	10.1
Fannin	4.9	332	3 620	220.7	1 524	662	7 942	4 670	7 307	9 925	23.1	19.1	8 363	24.3
Fayette	15.1	443	4 580	81.5	2 285	230	15 738	8 782	13 741	25 586	5.3	4.7	22 428	133.2

1. Elementary and secondary. 2. Per 1,000 resident population estimated as of July 1 of the year shown. 3. Based on the resident population estimated as of July 1, 1988 for 1987 data and enumerated as of April 1, 1980 for 1979 data.

STATE County	Housing units, 1990 (cont'd): Occupied units: Total	Housing units, 1990 (cont'd): Occupied units: Owner occupied: Percent	Housing units, 1990 (cont'd): Occupied units: Owner occupied: Median value (Dollars)	Housing units, 1990 (cont'd): Occupied units: Median rent (Dollars)	Civilian labor force, 1990: Total	Civilian labor force, 1990: Percent change, 1989–1990	Civilian labor force, 1990: Unemployment: Total	Civilian labor force, 1990: Unemployment: Rate[1]	Private nonfarm establishments, 1988: Number	Private nonfarm establishments, 1988: Net change, 1987–1988	Private nonfarm establishments, 1988: Employment[2]: Total	Private nonfarm establishments, 1988: Employment[2]: Per-cent change, 1987–1988	Private nonfarm establishments, 1988: Employment[2]: Manu-facturing	Private nonfarm establishments, 1988: Employment[2]: Retail trade
	74	75	76	77	78	79	80	81	82	83	84	85	86	87
FLORIDA—Con.														
Sumter	12 119	80.1	49 900	235	12 044	-1.0	976	8.1	463	26	4 671	10.0	688	1 703
Suwannee	10 034	79.2	45 100	182	11 678	2.1	922	7.9	489	10	5 341	8.2	1 100	1 364
Taylor	6 401	78.5	43 600	188	9 203	1.3	941	10.2	430	15	5 353	-1.2	2 474	1 277
Union	2 658	69.9	43 800	152	4 176	3.5	168	4.0	112	11	1 484	15.2	0	250
Volusia	153 416	71.9	69 400	382	160 040	2.6	8 899	5.6	9 177	160	101 107	5.0	12 956	32 158
Wakulla	5 210	83.4	51 800	245	6 507	0.8	317	4.9	204	12	1 818	4.4	0	564
Walton	11 294	78.4	49 700	233	13 932	7.4	879	6.3	459	7	4 165	0.2	1 103	1 187
Washington	6 443	80.5	40 100	177	7 222	3.5	513	7.1	281	-15	2 567	7.5	608	573
GEORGIA	2 366 615	64.9	71 300	344	3 216 000	0.7	175 000	5.4	X	X	2 358 191	2.9	580 809	519 484
Appling	5 834	76.6	39 200	175	7 562	-4.7	837	11.1	310	4	4 689	0.1	1 366	817
Atkinson	2 210	72.9	30 300	123	4 197	-0.8	222	5.3	84	1	1 005	2.1	650	197
Bacon	3 442	71.8	40 500	166	4 331	-1.7	279	6.4	206	-13	2 848	-0.1	1 640	530
Baker	1 300	73.0	36 600	125	1 477	-4.3	92	6.2	26	1	306	-6.7	0	59
Baldwin	12 165	68.3	54 900	227	17 136	2.5	722	4.2	692	-5	9 569	1.5	3 619	2 886
Banks	3 775	81.2	51 100	202	5 134	5.0	282	5.5	102	-7	1 967	21.0	834	212
Barrow	10 676	72.3	64 000	281	14 368	0.6	1 164	8.1	524	22	7 049	1.1	3 294	1 553
Bartow	20 091	71.7	63 100	308	25 014	2.2	2 132	8.5	1 053	22	16 928	3.9	7 595	3 684
Ben Hill	5 972	66.3	42 300	163	7 710	2.1	434	5.6	405	16	5 040	-1.9	2 242	1 044
Berrien	5 149	73.9	40 400	164	7 088	-3.1	473	6.7	235	2	4 815	5.1	3 387	536
Bibb	56 307	57.6	57 900	253	75 789	1.3	3 657	4.8	4 357	24	65 974	3.3	13 726	15 738
Bleckley	3 816	75.1	41 000	158	6 013	-1.3	236	3.9	200	6	2 456	-15.7	0	470
Brantley	3 811	84.6	36 400	172	4 488	-0.6	396	8.8	134	5	703	1.9	214	144
Brooks	5 392	72.0	42 200	143	6 967	0.5	287	4.1	203	3	2 531	14.7	1 151	488
Bryan	5 070	79.8	70 200	226	6 257	4.9	343	5.5	210	8	2 098	13.2	568	585
Bulloch	14 984	60.1	59 900	248	19 347	4.3	740	3.8	874	18	10 531	7.1	2 695	3 510
Burke	7 037	70.8	43 500	139	8 143	-3.8	863	10.6	300	-14	5 401	0.5	1 472	881
Butts	4 696	71.8	55 500	242	7 459	-0.7	510	6.8	249	2	3 209	4.9	1 332	834
Calhoun	1 794	69.1	29 400	99	1 930	-3.3	107	5.5	112	-1	904	6.1	345	161
Camden	9 459	63.0	66 700	352	12 194	-1.1	657	5.4	444	48	5 950	0.8	0	1 370
Candler	2 828	71.7	44 700	153	3 651	-1.7	174	4.8	169	-4	1 591	2.3	360	378
Carroll	25 370	69.4	60 300	264	32 526	0.6	2 009	6.2	1 408	91	22 675	8.3	10 602	4 444
Catoosa	15 745	75.9	56 500	271	21 341	-0.9	897	4.2	529	33	8 134	7.7	2 992	2 214
Charlton	2 911	78.8	41 200	206	3 052	0.1	180	5.9	142	12	1 265	-0.5	510	359
Chatham	81 111	58.8	63 300	296	106 116	2.8	5 268	5.0	5 835	75	91 196	1.4	19 993	19 712
Chattahoochee	2 884	20.2	42 600	415	1 537	-0.3	220	14.3	23	-3	276	61.4	0	54
Chattooga	8 467	74.7	34 700	174	9 141	-0.7	704	7.7	306	10	5 143	2.6	3 304	937
Cherokee	31 309	82.5	86 600	415	45 304	0.2	1 980	4.4	1 350	147	11 176	3.3	2 479	2 834
Clarke	33 170	44.2	73 200	313	41 075	-1.0	1 637	4.0	2 332	106	36 579	-0.8	11 130	10 434
Clay	1 210	66.4	31 300	99	1 180	3.5	66	5.6	52	0	370	13.1	0	83
Clayton	65 523	58.8	70 100	441	97 751	0.8	5 584	5.7	3 689	169	52 979	0.8	5 172	18 087
Clinch	2 173	68.2	33 600	115	2 349	1.7	142	6.0	107	-19	1 598	-9.1	625	324
Cobb	171 288	64.6	97 700	483	253 438	0.4	10 481	4.1	12 283	615	176 781	6.2	30 655	47 355
Coffee	10 541	72.6	45 600	184	14 714	0.7	1 014	6.9	661	15	8 723	5.0	3 917	2 496
Colquitt	12 980	68.5	40 700	167	16 650	-1.2	936	5.6	803	17	9 294	-4.6	3 687	1 992
Columbia	21 841	79.3	83 700	362	31 095	3.7	961	3.1	1 051	26	10 988	5.0	3 087	2 825
Cook	4 825	75.0	39 500	168	6 310	-1.0	444	7.0	261	-11	3 979	18.6	1 871	568
Coweta	18 930	72.8	68 700	287	25 368	1.8	1 604	6.3	853	45	13 993	2.4	5 462	3 282
Crawford	3 069	81.3	49 500	155	3 632	-0.7	285	7.8	73	5	505	42.7	0	50
Crisp	7 287	61.1	47 100	173	9 450	-1.3	637	6.7	530	-9	6 221	4.2	1 762	2 019
Dade	4 661	79.1	45 100	213	5 537	-0.6	344	6.2	127	-4	1 775	13.9	609	510
Dawson	3 360	85.2	80 900	290	3 036	-4.1	259	8.5	113	10	550	0.5	180	149
Decatur	8 962	72.0	42 700	173	11 393	-0.8	545	4.8	542	-4	7 741	1.2	3 786	1 455
De Kalb	208 690	57.8	91 600	468	326 890	0.8	16 282	5.0	16 845	308	286 055	0.2	36 780	62 082
Dodge	6 387	74.3	33 700	144	6 612	1.1	429	6.5	378	15	3 266	-8.1	717	1 258
Dooly	3 557	68.7	39 200	116	4 452	-1.9	266	6.0	197	7	1 834	-1.4	682	409
Dougherty	34 163	52.3	57 500	224	46 424	0.7	3 171	6.8	2 640	-19	36 077	0.3	7 868	9 178
Douglas	24 277	77.8	73 400	445	37 913	0.7	1 812	4.8	1 354	84	14 418	7.7	1 774	4 436
Early	4 263	69.2	40 100	105	5 250	-1.4	342	6.5	229	0	3 232	3.3	0	516
Echols	816	81.4	40 000	155	906	25.5	48	5.3	12	0	32	-25.6	0	14
Effingham	8 759	78.8	61 300	266	10 978	3.2	483	4.4	252	3	2 200	12.1	787	743
Elbert	7 115	73.2	44 600	157	8 823	0.5	693	7.9	518	-1	5 598	-2.8	2 608	965
Emanuel	7 420	69.9	35 200	146	9 570	0.8	768	8.0	398	2	6 230	10.2	3 312	1 184
Evans	3 144	67.6	44 100	160	4 347	0.3	181	4.2	205	-1	2 248	-21.3	1 004	546
Fannin	6 334	83.8	48 000	179	6 985	-0.2	518	7.4	312	-12	2 502	8.2	719	858
Fayette	21 054	86.1	116 700	487	30 015	0.6	920	3.1	1 166	89	13 206	11.8	2 674	3 729

1. Percent of total civilian labor force. 2. For week including March 12. Excludes government employees, self-employed persons, farm workers, domestic service workers, railroad employees subject to the Railroad Retirement Act, and employees on oceanborne vessels or in foreign countries.

STATE County	Private nonfarm establishments, 1988 (cont'd) — Employment[1] (cont'd) — Finance, insurance, and real estate	Employment[1] (cont'd) — Services	Annual payroll — Total (Mil dol)	Annual payroll — Average per employee (Dollars)	Personal income, 1989 — Total (Mil dol)	Percent change, 1988–1989	Wages and salaries[2] (Mil dol)	Proprietor's income (Mil dol)	Dividends, interest, & rent (Mil dol)	Transfer payments (Mil dol)	Per capita[3] — Dollars	Per capita[3] — Rank	Earnings, 1989 — Total (Mil dol)	Percent by selected industries — Farm	Percent by selected industries — Goods-related[4] — Total
	88	89	90	91	92	93	94	95	96	97	98	99	100	101	102
FLORIDA—Con.															
Sumter	169	964	61	13 109	373	10.6	118	38	71	104	11 517	2 492	155	11.4	NA
Suwannee	335	1 279	72	13 429	307	9.4	128	39	55	78	11 225	2 593	167	10.8	19.5
Taylor	205	811	97	18 119	227	7.9	150	14	26	46	11 700	2 441	163	0.9	NA
Union	51	190	19	13 099	97	6.2	68	12	9	18	9 452	2 965	80	8.4	NA
Volusia	6 634	31 462	1 463	14 468	5 553	10.5	2 317	420	1 587	1 194	15 364	851	2 737	2.4	20.4
Wakulla	66	276	30	16 281	167	10.1	50	13	18	32	11 438	2 524	62	1.3	36.5
Walton	248	620	53	12 673	298	10.1	117	23	48	84	10 245	2 846	141	1.6	20.7
Washington	73	509	34	13 337	182	7.2	74	21	28	58	10 741	2 730	94	6.6	15.2
GEORGIA	161 075	553 285	46 530	X	103 339	6.7	71 497	8 363	14 931	13 417	16 050	X	79 861	1.7	24.6
Appling	127	381	95	20 292	196	4.4	138	15	23	35	11 727	2 429	153	3.9	NA
Atkinson	0	64	13	13 279	81	7.9	26	20	9	16	12 714	2 029	46	35.6	NA
Bacon	92	271	40	14 128	121	9.3	65	16	14	22	12 505	2 114	82	8.5	NA
Baker	0	0	3	9 958	44	0.7	12	12	5	7	11 909	2 357	24	52.8	NA
Baldwin	343	1 447	160	16 709	536	7.0	354	36	68	123	13 800	1 535	391	0.5	27.4
Banks	0	233	31	15 980	134	6.9	36	23	12	16	12 075	2 299	59	27.7	NA
Barrow	302	924	107	15 114	399	7.8	179	43	55	57	14 214	1 331	222	8.2	NA
Bartow	507	2 004	287	16 942	737	9.8	440	64	90	90	13 698	1 581	504	2.8	46.0
Ben Hill	211	869	78	15 404	209	7.8	127	23	34	48	12 156	2 258	150	2.8	42.5
Berrien	211	362	71	14 744	165	2.1	93	16	25	35	11 754	2 420	109	6.2	49.8
Bibb	6 251	17 443	1 292	19 579	2 503	7.1	1 858	206	395	453	15 887	684	2 064	0.1	26.9
Bleckley	71	260	37	15 197	139	5.1	61	10	18	33	13 098	1 864	71	5.1	NA
Brantley	17	71	11	15 714	112	11.4	26	17	9	20	10 632	2 762	42	26.4	NA
Brooks	90	538	32	12 638	150	7.7	54	24	24	37	9 837	2 905	78	23.0	NA
Bryan	0	523	28	13 408	192	8.1	298	12	18	27	11 263	2 573	310	0.7	NA
Bulloch	514	1 876	144	13 638	493	9.0	276	53	75	83	12 975	1 916	330	4.0	27.4
Burke	133	474	111	20 529	222	-4.3	159	22	28	55	10 380	2 815	182	5.6	17.1
Butts	141	534	38	11 842	206	8.4	67	12	24	36	12 099	2 291	80	2.3	25.1
Calhoun	29	109	10	10 826	62	-2.4	22	12	12	17	12 203	2 231	34	24.3	NA
Camden	125	946	108	18 128	310	13.2	298	11	23	37	12 755	2 013	309	0.4	NA
Candler	71	477	19	12 202	93	6.5	36	10	16	23	12 573	2 080	47	10.2	NA
Carroll	881	2 735	376	16 578	982	7.1	558	91	135	137	13 897	1 476	649	2.7	45.6
Catoosa	199	1 320	125	15 411	510	6.0	220	40	47	63	12 075	2 300	260	2.7	31.7
Charlton	0	171	15	11 943	97	5.3	31	9	11	19	11 607	2 471	40	11.2	NA
Chatham	5 446	25 552	1 734	19 009	3 559	7.5	2 560	248	606	571	16 164	601	2 808	0.4	28.6
Chattahoochee	172	25	3	9 638	190	-1.5	495	1	5	10	11 007	2 664	496	0.0	NA
Chattooga	177	245	71	13 754	254	5.7	129	22	29	52	11 650	2 460	151	2.5	NA
Cherokee	607	2 077	170	15 202	1 480	8.6	299	126	134	102	15 903	673	425	7.5	29.4
Clarke	1 577	7 831	592	16 189	1 234	7.1	1 157	83	214	176	15 907	671	1 241	0.6	23.5
Clay	0	187	3	8 868	31	5.0	8	5	6	10	8 875	3 018	14	22.2	NA
Clayton	1 399	10 403	973	18 358	2 764	4.6	2 401	136	252	280	15 953	659	2 537	0.0	11.4
Clinch	29	146	23	14 404	62	5.5	37	7	9	16	9 334	2 977	44	4.1	NA
Cobb	11 367	44 855	3 739	21 149	9 179	5.4	5 128	518	1 115	600	20 781	135	5 646	0.1	22.9
Coffee	342	914	130	14 861	369	10.5	211	53	54	66	12 149	2 261	264	10.2	34.0
Colquitt	439	1 648	133	14 338	483	6.7	226	69	73	93	12 952	1 926	295	10.6	28.9
Columbia	486	2 335	175	15 887	1 002	8.4	443	62	100	102	15 232	895	505	0.9	22.4
Cook	241	769	52	13 173	158	5.5	69	20	23	32	11 178	2 611	89	10.4	NA
Coweta	479	2 621	262	18 722	784	7.6	395	51	104	105	14 929	1 016	446	1.3	36.5
Crawford	0	144	6	11 743	104	5.4	16	7	9	18	13 996	1 438	23	14.6	NA
Crisp	300	1 112	81	12 957	237	6.5	137	26	38	55	11 713	2 435	162	5.9	25.5
Dade	50	437	22	12 237	129	3.9	41	9	15	24	10 757	2 727	51	3.8	31.9
Dawson	37	99	9	15 600	121	10.9	26	15	16	14	13 295	1 774	40	14.6	NA
Decatur	227	659	124	16 067	321	6.8	200	44	44	65	11 910	2 356	243	10.0	NA
De Kalb	23 533	80 728	6 573	22 979	10 927	4.9	7 909	729	1 752	963	19 860	177	8 638	0.0	17.4
Dodge	174	582	34	10 417	205	9.3	73	22	31	50	11 813	2 395	96	7.9	26.2
Dooly	94	373	25	13 746	125	3.6	47	30	19	32	12 435	2 148	78	32.0	NA
Dougherty	2 022	8 182	659	18 274	1 350	6.0	1 096	96	184	258	13 594	1 635	1 192	0.5	26.9
Douglas	620	4 223	220	15 268	1 147	7.9	369	73	95	108	15 094	945	441	0.5	NA
Early	110	297	73	22 534	155	5.7	117	19	25	36	11 897	2 360	135	8.3	51.0
Echols	0	0	0	6 188	25	3.8	4	2	4	5	10 979	2 669	6	18.8	NA
Effingham	115	224	37	16 792	285	6.0	87	17	27	38	11 261	2 574	104	2.4	50.5
Elbert	204	560	78	14 017	253	7.4	124	31	44	50	13 321	1 766	155	4.1	42.1
Emanuel	257	865	75	11 976	239	7.9	126	17	37	61	10 792	2 718	143	2.9	NA
Evans	81	312	32	14 314	124	9.3	55	16	19	23	14 390	1 251	71	6.6	NA
Fannin	111	414	30	11 812	188	3.9	53	21	34	46	11 298	2 568	73	2.2	23.8
Fayette	499	3 416	223	16 919	1 327	14.3	366	69	152	77	21 789	100	435	0.6	31.9

1. For week including March 12. Excludes government employees, self-employed persons, farm workers, domestic service workers, railroad employees subject to the Railroad Retirement Act, and employees on oceanborne vessels or in foreign countries. 2. Includes other labor income. 3. Based on the resident population estimated as of July 1 of the year shown. 4. Covers mining, construction, and manufacturing.

STATE County	Earnings, 1989 (cont'd): Percent by selected industries (cont'd): Goods-related[1]: Manu-facturing	Service-related & other[2]: Total	Service-related & other[2]: Retail trade	Service-related & other[2]: Finance, insur-ance, & real estate	Service-related & other[2]: Services	Govern-ment	Agriculture, 1987: Farms: Number	Farms: Percent with: Less than 50 acres	Farms: Percent with: 500 acres and over	Farm operators, percent: Whose principal occu-pation is farming	Farm operators, percent: Residing on farm operated	Land in farms: Acreage (1,000)	Land in farms: Percent change, 1982–1987	Land in farms: Acres: Average size of farm	Land in farms: Acres: Total irrigated (1,000)	Land in farms: Acres: Total cropland (1,000)
	103	104	105	106	107	108	109	110	111	112	113	114	115	116	117	118
FLORIDA–Con.																
Sumter	9.8	NA	13.5	1.6	17.9	22.8	705	45.8	8.4	41.3	71.3	254	-14.2	360	4	53
Suwannee	12.3	52.0	16.6	4.4	17.2	17.7	985	34.3	8.0	48.6	76.9	182	-9.1	185	11	102
Taylor	44.1	31.2	9.6	2.3	12.8	12.9	158	32.3	13.3	36.7	76.6	77	-23.7	490	0	8
Union	15.0	NA	3.5	1.3	11.7	49.5	205	38.0	7.8	35.1	80.0	67	6.6	328	1	18
Volusia	11.3	60.9	16.1	4.9	31.0	16.3	920	71.0	5.1	47.3	66.6	193	-12.9	210	5	27
Wakulla	31.7	38.4	9.9	2.0	17.1	23.8	87	56.3	4.6	29.9	67.8	D	D	D	D	D
Walton	14.6	57.7	14.3	2.8	28.7	20.0	430	32.8	7.2	45.1	74.9	104	-9.6	242	1	65
Washington	10.5	43.5	8.1	0.7	21.6	34.7	318	28.3	8.2	43.4	79.2	62	-22.6	194	0	29
GEORGIA	18.3	57.0	9.9	6.6	21.9	16.6	43 552	31.8	12.1	44.7	70.2	10 745	-12.6	247	640	5 780
Appling	16.2	NA	6.5	1.7	7.6	13.9	519	26.0	10.2	54.5	75.9	110	-18.0	211	1	62
Atkinson	37.4	13.4	5.5	1.3	4.1	12.0	255	18.4	14.5	63.1	65.9	78	-14.0	307	3	30
Bacon	38.7	37.5	10.5	2.7	10.4	13.3	345	25.2	9.3	49.0	69.6	81	-10.5	236	1	38
Baker	9.0	NA	2.4	NA	5.4	12.9	155	12.9	36.1	69.0	57.4	117	-23.6	756	25	76
Baldwin	24.0	27.0	9.0	1.9	13.4	45.0	135	21.5	11.9	35.6	72.6	36	-17.9	270	D	11
Banks	30.0	NA	9.5	NA	7.7	11.4	477	34.4	1.9	47.2	78.2	54	15.3	113	0	21
Barrow	35.6	NA	12.4	3.7	13.9	12.1	411	48.9	2.9	41.8	75.7	40	1.9	98	0	18
Bartow	36 3	38.9	8.7	2.1	14.0	12.3	429	35.4	6.5	44.3	72.5	88	-15.4	204	0	40
Ben Hill	39.1	38.6	7.6	4.5	13.8	16.0	195	24.6	18.5	58.5	66.2	58	-12.1	295	7	33
Berrien	47.0	32.4	14.2	5.0	9.1	11.6	477	21.0	13.0	57.9	66.0	130	-17.1	273	8	69
Bibb	21.9	59.5	10.9	8.1	25.4	13.5	140	43.6	2.1	33.6	73.6	17	-30.3	119	0	9
Bleckley	38.1	29.5	9.8	2.6	11.4	21.5	206	15.0	20.9	42.7	74.3	69	-6.3	334	7	50
Brantley	10.3	NA	4.4	NA	7.4	20.6	234	31.6	2.1	30.8	78.6	29	-26.9	125	0	9
Brooks	25.2	29.5	8.1	2.8	10.1	18.7	438	25.1	19.4	60.5	64.8	170	-14.1	388	9	95
Bryan	2.6	8.7	2.6	0.9	3.0	86.8	62	40.3	11.3	33.9	62.9	20	-21.2	319	0	6
Bulloch	21.4	43.2	11.7	3.3	19.3	25.4	592	25.2	21.8	52.2	70.4	217	-8.1	366	4	143
Burke	13.0	NA	6.8	1.9	NA	13.4	335	19.4	31.9	49.3	66.0	203	-25.4	606	7	135
Butts	19.5	NA	13.6	3.3	15.7	29.3	146	26.7	9.6	31.5	76.7	29	-2.9	200	0	12
Calhoun	12.7	35.3	6.8	2.8	10.8	23.1	127	13.4	51.2	74.0	62.2	115	1.9	906	18	75
Camden	29.2	24.2	6.0	1.2	14.4	37.7	54	53.7	18.5	24.1	68.5	23	-32.9	423	D	3
Candler	16.4	51.4	12.3	3.3	18.5	20.0	234	15.0	15.8	56.8	67.5	62	-11.8	265	3	39
Carroll	38.5	38.8	10.0	3.6	17.7	13.0	824	31.7	1.6	33.4	77.8	88	-9.6	107	D	39
Catoosa	25.7	46.1	12.2	2.3	13.7	19.5	256	41.4	3.9	32.4	77.7	32	-17.8	126	0	19
Charlton	30.3	NA	12.3	4.5	10.3	24.0	90	34.4	11.1	28.9	74.4	26	-30.3	286	D	6
Chatham	20.2	55.1	10.1	4.7	25.3	15.9	51	54.9	9.8	47.1	68.6	11	-16.3	209	0	3
Chattahoochee	NA	NA	2.5	NA	0.7	96.4	13	7.7	23.1	46.2	46.2	4	-16.1	328	D	D
Chattooga	49.7	NA	10.1	2.1	10.6	13.6	296	21.3	7.8	31.1	73.0	55	-11.2	187	0	25
Cherokee	11.7	47.4	13.6	4.1	18.3	15.7	551	62.6	1.1	37.9	78.8	38	-17.2	69	0	14
Clarke	19.3	42.3	9.6	3.5	19.2	33.5	86	40.7	5.8	37.2	62.8	14	-6.8	164	0	7
Clay	6.9	37.8	6.9	1.9	18.2	24.9	60	6.7	43.3	61.7	83.3	46	-16.7	768	4	25
Clayton	6.6	76.9	13.2	2.5	12.4	11.7	73	45.2	1.4	37.0	65.8	8	12.5	110	0	3
Clinch	41.8	NA	5.3	NA	11.4	17.8	115	53.9	4.3	36.5	62.6	15	-29.4	128	0	3
Cobb	14.5	66.2	12.2	7.2	23.7	10.8	180	63.3	2.8	28.9	76.7	13	-23.2	75	0	7
Coffee	29.8	39.6	18.1	2.5	11.8	16.2	649	20.2	16.6	63.0	71.3	179	-10.8	276	10	90
Colquitt	25.6	44.2	10.0	2.7	18.7	16.3	706	24.8	15.7	60.1	68.8	196	-9.7	278	21	119
Columbia	14.3	26.4	6.2	3.0	13.2	50.3	187	47.1	5.3	31.0	74.3	27	-35.0	145	0	10
Cook	34.9	34.8	9.2	2.5	14.1	14.9	293	24.2	12.6	56.7	67.2	65	-27.9	223	5	40
Coweta	31.5	51.7	17.3	3.2	19.6	10.5	366	35.5	5.2	29.8	73.5	52	-22.8	142	0	21
Crawford	9.0	NA	9.7	NA	19.6	26.5	136	24.3	11.8	44.1	69.9	40	-11.3	295	1	17
Crisp	19.8	49.7	15.6	3.9	17.3	18.9	192	15.6	35.9	66.7	58.9	112	-8.7	586	7	82
Dade	27.3	47.1	11.6	2.8	20.8	17.2	167	39.5	6.6	32.9	76.6	28	-20.6	167	0	9
Dawson	9.5	45.6	14.4	2.9	15.7	18.6	182	57.7	3.3	48.9	65.9	18	-0.7	98	D	8
Decatur	30.3	NA	8.0	3.4	NA	18.2	376	25.8	23.7	51.9	69.7	163	-16.2	434	33	102
De Kalb	11.0	70.9	10.4	8.1	29.1	11.6	59	64.4	0.0	33.9	64.4	4	-24.4	65	D	2
Dodge	20.8	40.4	13.1	4.0	13.7	25.6	428	19.4	12.9	44.6	69.9	109	-17.2	256	9	63
Dooly	19.5	31.2	7.8	2.3	8.8	15.9	295	22.4	39.0	68.1	64.1	158	-3.5	536	11	120
Dougherty	21.5	47.0	9.6	4.3	19.7	25.6	165	47.9	17.6	37.0	63.6	82	-23.9	499	11	42
Douglas	6.7	NA	15.8	3.5	26.6	16.0	134	53.7	1.5	27.6	77.6	11	-26.1	80	D	4
Early	49.0	28.0	5.1	1.8	9.9	12.7	336	19.9	28.3	65.2	65.2	179	-6.8	534	21	112
Echols	11.7	NA	5.0	NA	11.3	34.0	80	37.5	10.0	43.8	73.8	14	-23.6	172	0	5
Effingham	28.9	26.4	8.7	2.3	8.5	20.7	202	27.2	13.4	30.2	68.8	56	-24.8	278	D	27
Elbert	35.1	36.7	8.8	3.6	14.9	17.1	331	21.1	6.9	38.4	68.0	60	-5.4	180	0	31
Emanuel	36.1	37.3	10.0	4.7	10.7	22.0	423	18.0	17.0	48.0	64.3	130	-23.9	307	3	70
Evans	32.4	37.0	10.0	3.5	15.5	16.7	181	30.4	14.4	54.7	64.6	44	-20.9	244	2	26
Fannin	15.9	NA	16.6	3.1	19.0	18.8	196	34.7	0.5	40.8	71.9	19	-8.5	99	D	7
Fayette	19.1	55.7	10.5	4.1	25.9	11.8	248	45.6	2.4	31.0	78.6	27	-15.1	109	0	14

1. Covers mining, construction, and manufacturing. 2. Covers private sector earnings in agricultural services, forestry, and fisheries; transportation and public utilities; wholesale trade; retail trade; finance, insurance, and real estate; and services.

STATE County	Agriculture, 1987 (cont'd)								Manufactures, 1987						
	Value of land and buildings		Value of products sold				Percent of farms with sales of		Establishments		All employees			Production workers	
					Percent from										
	Average per farm ($1,000)	Average per acre (Dollars)	Total (Mil dol)	Average per farm (Dollars)	Crops	Livestock and poultry[1]	$10,000 or more	$100,000 or more	Total	Percent with 20 or more employees	Number (1,000)	Percent change, 1982–1987	Annual payroll (Mil dol)	Number (1,000)	Work hours (Mil)
	119	120	121	122	123	124	125	126	127	128	129	130	131	132	133
FLORIDA—Con.															
Sumter	347	998	31	43 654	26.5	73.5	29.4	6.5	24	25.0	0.6	20.0	11.0	0.4	0.8
Suwannee	222	1 196	64	65 039	26.4	73.6	38.2	13.9	21	28.6	1.1	-8.3	15.0	0.9	1.8
Taylor	256	540	2	15 487	28.2	71.8	19.6	3.2	49	28.6	2.7	12.5	62.3	2.2	4.5
Union	386	1 230	9	42 928	22.7	77.3	26.3	6.8	9	33.3	0.6	50.0	8.5	0.6	1.1
Volusia	346	1 807	64	69 341	84.4	15.6	43.2	14.5	359	21.2	12.6	37.0	264.3	7.6	15.9
Wakulla	D	D	1	16 180	37.7	62.3	19.5	1.1	12	33.3	0.6	0.0	15.2	0.4	1.0
Walton	154	706	18	42 992	22.2	77.8	34.4	8.4	22	36.4	1.2	300.0	11.8	0.9	1.2
Washington	124	584	8	25 663	27.1	72.9	30.5	6.0	30	6.7	0.6	200.0	7.0	0.5	0.9
GEORGIA	226	920	2 815	64 626	35.7	64.3	41.6	15.8	9 187	38.4	569.9	13.3	11 933.1	409.4	820.1
Appling	122	651	24	45 691	36.1	63.9	48.6	12.3	31	41.9	1.5	15.4	19.9	1.2	2.2
Atkinson	205	698	27	104 858	24.4	75.6	63.1	26.3	20	35.0	0.7	0.0	11.5	0.6	1.2
Bacon	175	696	17	48 634	40.1	59.9	49.6	10.7	23	47.8	1.5	36.4	20.5	1.4	2.7
Baker	694	924	24	152 252	80.5	19.5	78.1	34.8	1	100.0	D	D	D	D	D
Baldwin	207	751	2	13 315	15.9	84.1	20.7	3.7	28	39.3	3.7	2.8	74.3	3.2	6.6
Banks	176	1 448	44	91 205	1.3	98.7	45.1	27.0	16	31.2	0.6	0.0	9.4	0.5	0.9
Barrow	205	2 344	38	92 173	0.5	99.5	36.5	25.3	39	56.4	3.3	-13.2	54.9	2.6	4.9
Bartow	218	1 087	24	57 066	11.3	88.7	34.0	16.6	94	54.3	7.4	-1.3	133.3	5.7	11.4
Ben Hill	219	761	11	56 604	81.9	18.1	57.9	17.9	39	46.2	2.3	15.0	41.8	1.8	3.8
Berrien	222	782	25	51 915	73.7	26.3	54.7	15.5	20	45.0	2.9	70.6	47.2	2.6	5.6
Bibb	106	1 002	3	23 878	16.7	83.2	26.4	7.9	168	38.7	13.2	3.9	351.5	9.5	20.1
Bleckley	178	574	10	47 476	72.8	27.2	43.2	15.5	12	33.3	D	D	D	D	D
Brantley	102	797	17	70 704	11.6	88.4	28.6	9.8	21	9.5	0.2	0.0	3.0	0.2	0.3
Brooks	322	719	39	88 321	51.3	48.7	56.6	18.9	16	31.2	0.9	28.6	11.0	0.8	1.6
Bryan	188	591	1	20 930	72.1	27.8	33.9	6.5	20	15.0	0.5	150.0	9.8	0.4	0.9
Bulloch	257	748	42	71 554	65.8	34.2	60.1	19.1	44	36.4	2.4	-4.0	45.1	1.9	3.9
Burke	350	623	22	65 369	63.5	36.5	51.6	19.4	24	33.3	1.3	0.0	16.6	1.0	1.9
Butts	209	1 166	2	16 111	21.9	78.1	24.7	5.5	25	44.0	1.3	30.0	17.4	1.0	1.9
Calhoun	687	800	21	165 613	90.9	9.1	74.0	44.1	5	60.0	D	D	D	D	D
Camden	249	589	0	7 319	35.7	64.3	20.4	0.0	20	30.0	1.9	0.0	59.2	1.3	2.8
Candler	157	611	12	52 849	45.1	54.9	55.6	14.1	19	15.8	0.5	66.7	6.0	0.4	0.7
Carroll	150	1 425	35	42 371	4.1	95.9	23.3	10.3	101	46.5	9.6	37.1	165.3	7.3	14.6
Catoosa	186	1 742	9	35 461	8.3	91.7	27.7	9.8	53	50.9	2.9	0.0	50.4	2.4	4.8
Charlton	216	732	5	60 981	8.8	91.2	26.7	8.9	19	15.8	0.4	-20.0	6.4	0.3	0.7
Chatham	278	1 332	3	52 724	92.7	7.3	35.3	13.7	213	33.8	15.2	2.0	417.3	9.9	21.6
Chattahoochee	218	663	0	8 163	25.5	74.5	30.8	0.0	1	0.0	D	D	D	D	D
Chattooga	159	734	5	17 912	8.7	91.3	22.3	4.1	29	41.4	3.4	-17.1	55.7	3.1	6.4
Cherokee	282	3 379	41	75 260	6.2	93.8	39.9	22.9	84	22.6	2.5	19.0	30.3	2.0	3.4
Clarke	317	1 684	20	238 263	12.7	87.3	45.3	15.1	105	49.5	11.6	10.5	198.9	9.0	15.7
Clay	455	592	7	121 868	79.9	20.1	70.0	35.0	5	0.0	D	D	D	D	D
Clayton	245	2 231	1	8 655	38.9	61.1	13.7	1.4	162	35.8	5.7	3.6	127.5	4.2	8.8
Clinch	111	892	2	20 875	28.9	71.1	36.5	5.2	24	20.8	0.8	-11.1	12.8	0.7	1.5
Cobb	182	5 010	3	17 308	64.7	35.4	13.3	2.2	483	26.1	30.9	47.8	934.2	19.7	41.0
Coffee	192	643	56	86 629	36.7	63.3	63.2	17.9	57	38.6	3.6	20.0	57.2	3.0	5.8
Colquitt	222	804	62	88 128	68.5	31.5	60.5	22.8	58	41.4	3.7	27.6	58.4	2.7	5.4
Columbia	140	1 257	2	13 341	39.0	61.0	15.5	3.2	45	26.7	2.8	40.0	57.4	1.9	3.9
Cook	182	727	17	56 576	85.4	14.6	55.3	15.7	29	41.4	1.5	7.1	22.0	1.2	2.4
Coweta	199	1 488	6	15 092	44.0	56.0	18.9	2.5	55	50.9	5.1	6.2	98.4	4.0	7.3
Crawford	205	696	6	46 028	51.6	48.4	32.4	8.8	11	0.0	0.0	-100.0	0.4	0.0	0.0
Crisp	479	827	25	130 978	87.6	12.4	68.8	35.4	34	47.1	1.7	-15.0	28.5	1.4	2.5
Dade	166	1 056	4	23 047	7.2	92.8	24.6	8.4	11	36.4	0.7	0.0	13.1	0.6	1.1
Dawson	215	2 625	22	119 855	0.8	99.2	56.0	35.2	9	22.2	0.2	0.0	2.3	0.2	0.3
Decatur	352	760	33	87 281	83.9	16.1	56.6	21.5	37	48.6	3.8	2.7	66.9	2.9	5.1
De Kalb	217	3 335	0	8 392	63.2	36.8	13.6	3.4	894	32.9	36.0	15.0	911.7	21.1	41.1
Dodge	127	586	14	31 573	55.4	44.6	44.6	8.2	22	27.3	0.9	-30.8	11.5	0.8	1.3
Dooly	350	680	32	108 947	87.7	12.3	71.2	34.2	13	53.8	0.8	0.0	11.6	0.7	1.3
Dougherty	532	1 097	13	81 461	92.7	7.3	37.6	16.4	94	43.6	D	D	D	D	D
Douglas	198	2 192	1	7 859	30.6	69.5	12.7	1.5	73	34.2	D	D	D	D	D
Early	340	644	29	86 647	84.8	15.2	67.6	24.4	20	30.0	1.7	0.0	53.0	1.2	2.6
Echols	108	601	1	18 187	66.0	34.0	32.5	5.0	NA	NA	NA	NA	NA	NA	NA
Effingham	252	970	5	26 960	50.5	49.5	35.6	7.4	31	19.4	0.7	133.3	13.2	0.5	1.2
Elbert	122	717	7	20 414	20.6	79.4	21.1	6.9	113	28.3	2.6	4.0	40.5	2.1	4.0
Emanuel	186	574	13	31 845	56.3	43.7	39.7	6.6	46	45.7	3.0	20.0	36.0	2.6	5.0
Evans	191	1 086	18	100 240	24.9	75.0	49.7	17.1	18	27.8	1.0	-9.1	11.8	0.9	1.9
Fannin	129	1 298	2	8 837	41.4	58.6	10.2	1.5	25	20.0	0.7	-22.2	8.1	0.6	1.0
Fayette	192	2 330	2	6 968	29.6	70.4	14.1	1.2	55	41.8	2.7	125.0	56.7	1.8	3.7

1. Includes livestock and poultry products.

STATE County	Manufactures, 1987 (cont'd): Production workers (cont'd): Wages: Total (Mil dol)	Average per worker (Dollars)	Value added by manufacture (Mil dol)	Value of shipments (Mil dol)	New capital expenditures (Mil dol)	Value of construction authorized by building permits, 1990: Total[1] ($1,000)	Nonresidential: Total ($1,000)	Nonresidential: Percent: Office	Industrial	Stores	Residential: New construction ($1,000)	Number of housing units	Alterations and additions ($1,000)
	134	135	136	137	138	139	140	141	142	143	144	145	146
FLORIDA—Con.													
Sumter	6.5	16 250	25.1	88.9	D	12 659	3 054	8.7	20.1	9.4	6 892	156	1 191
Suwannee	11.5	12 778	19.8	91.4	0.9	20 047	9 331	2.1	0.6	5.4	8 104	133	870
Taylor	44.5	20 227	216.6	416.1	15.5	8 572	1 567	0.4	54.7	1.0	4 787	136	520
Union	7.3	12 167	19.1	35.4	0.5	1 512	51	0.0	0.0	0.0	1 329	26	75
Volusia	118.0	15 526	603.7	1 029.7	42.3	410 941	42 153	14.4	6.5	27.8	304 875	3 860	20 255
Wakulla	9.1	22 750	36.4	77.1	D	10 178	1 389	0.0	0.0	42.4	7 145	112	1 108
Walton	6.4	7 111	18.0	81.6	1.6	28 802	5 111	5.3	4.3	26.2	21 458	340	1 213
Washington	5.8	11 600	25.1	47.7	0.8	6 598	935	0.0	9.1	32.5	4 723	108	894
GEORGIA	7 239.9	17 684	33 708.1	75 709.2	2 471.5	5 562 565	1 534 764	30.6	14.0	31.1	2 847 696	43 265	274 446
Appling	14.2	11 833	38.7	106.4	2.3	1 660	663	7.5	60.3	0.0	635	10	55
Atkinson	8.2	13 667	32.9	76.8	2.4	NA	NA	NA	NA	NA	NA	NA	NA
Bacon	16.6	11 857	44.2	118.5	D	1 024	809	37.1	54.0	3.0	147	3	27
Baker	D	D	D	D	D	NA	NA	NA	NA	NA	NA	NA	NA
Baldwin	58.7	18 344	239.4	445.8	D	9 838	6 613	51.5	0.0	43.1	1 483	22	1 665
Banks	4.6	9 200	9.3	17.4	D	495	0	NA	NA	NA	495	22	0
Barrow	36.4	14 000	125.8	304.1	7.2	11 782	1 605	22.4	43.6	3.1	9 451	257	696
Bartow	93.8	16 456	448.3	1 146.3	18.9	73 008	7 966	46.5	16.0	33.6	37 968	554	1 166
Ben Hill	31.5	17 500	110.0	287.6	D	5 458	1 124	0.0	26.5	0.0	1 811	35	972
Berrien	33.9	13 038	90.1	203.0	9.2	3 588	1 306	0.0	0.0	98.1	868	17	282
Bibb	239.3	25 189	2 072.3	3 215.6	67.6	116 734	17 300	48.5	3.2	34.1	52 507	800	8 153
Bleckley	D	D	D	D	D	3 615	1 007	0.0	0.0	42.4	649	28	941
Brantley	2.3	11 500	11.0	22.8	D	226	214	0.0	0.0	100.0	0	0	0
Brooks	8.8	11 000	19.3	59.0	1.0	3 774	1 071	0.0	0.0	27.8	1 823	43	292
Bryan	7.7	19 250	45.4	75.0	0.9	16 917	186	0.0	0.0	0.0	16 105	261	369
Bulloch	31.6	16 632	115.5	216.0	9.8	20 932	3 512	5.9	0.9	47.6	15 962	354	985
Burke	10.9	10 900	34.7	67.5	1.1	3 654	520	10.6	0.0	41.3	2 781	79	129
Butts	12.8	12 800	48.9	94.7	D	7 975	1 714	13.3	0.0	73.0	5 283	152	497
Calhoun	D	D	D	D	D	NA	NA	NA	NA	NA	NA	NA	NA
Camden	35.1	27 000	190.8	425.6	D	28 450	7 000	9.8	1.5	76.4	21 033	454	292
Candler	4.6	11 500	15.8	27.9	D	1 619	1 121	0.4	5.6	69.1	390	11	54
Carroll	107.5	14 726	936.9	1 856.6	13.6	38 982	8 590	14.0	8.0	24.0	26 591	439	1 920
Catoosa	34.1	14 208	217.7	869.4	6.8	2 733	1 207	23.0	0.0	35.5	1 284	57	82
Charlton	4.7	15 667	10.5	31.5	0.6	474	95	0.0	0.0	100.0	191	2	106
Chatham	252.8	25 535	1 065.8	3 095.3	D	168 037	63 385	50.5	4.0	27.9	67 987	1 073	9 983
Chattahoochee	D	D	D	D	D	0	0	NA	NA	NA	0	0	0
Chattooga	47.4	15 290	127.0	360.8	D	965	635	0.0	0.0	33.6	285	7	0
Cherokee	20.0	10 000	103.5	256.0	5.7	71 202	16 688	34.0	12.5	8.2	49 489	1 061	1 985
Clarke	130.8	14 533	492.0	1 022.2	25.4	78 670	33 338	8.6	49.5	18.8	28 083	462	3 480
Clay	D	D	D	D	D	0	0	NA	NA	NA	0	0	0
Clayton	80.0	19 048	441.3	892.4	27.5	154 479	42 608	16.0	26.0	41.1	106 316	1 400	586
Clinch	11.3	16 143	23.5	73.3	1.2	1 181	410	52.4	0.0	0.0	319	7	24
Cobb	488.2	24 782	2 359.1	4 099.5	57.9	484 549	114 883	12.5	4.1	60.2	275 971	2 845	11 796
Coffee	40.7	13 567	155.4	370.8	6.3	10 114	4 102	8.9	2.8	83.3	5 711	121	129
Colquitt	37.3	13 815	129.7	388.3	5.0	6 164	1 807	0.0	16.8	25.7	1 309	16	2 146
Columbia	32.1	16 895	140.8	272.9	12.8	87 540	18 394	6.2	42.8	33.1	64 918	812	1 330
Cook	16.6	13 833	47.8	118.3	2.8	2 200	1 304	4.6	0.0	94.4	690	10	145
Coweta	65.5	16 375	218.9	518.1	19.7	59 735	5 602	17.2	19.5	13.5	50 791	817	2 241
Crawford	0.3	NA	0.8	1.7	D	2 858	463	0.0	0.0	35.6	2 275	38	50
Crisp	18.4	13 143	87.6	186.2	3.4	4 735	712	52.3	0.0	0.0	2 258	40	587
Dade	10.2	17 000	27.4	76.5	2.8	472	271	0.0	0.0	1.8	115	3	58
Dawson	1.7	8 500	8.4	13.0	0.2	13 469	2 769	34.6	0.0	13.4	9 978	155	555
Decatur	45.5	15 690	246.7	467.1	17.9	13 522	2 051	17.9	46.4	20.8	5 661	118	1 563
De Kalb	480.2	22 758	2 425.7	5 068.1	278.8	479 865	116 171	35.8	1.6	14.5	243 983	3 646	18 745
Dodge	8.7	10 875	28.5	67.2	0.7	4 178	2 182	30.7	0.0	66.4	501	6	54
Dooly	8.9	12 714	32.7	78.3	D	37	0	NA	NA	NA	37	1	0
Dougherty	D	D	D	D	D	37 576	10 838	18.5	41.9	28.1	16 020	273	2 872
Douglas	D	D	D	D	D	45 133	12 475	0.2	10.4	35.5	26 636	559	1 819
Early	34.8	29 000	228.1	439.2	D	727	40	0.0	100.0	0.0	645	36	16
Echols	NA	NA	NA	NA	NA	NA	NA	NA	NA	NA	NA	NA	NA
Effingham	10.2	20 400	44.3	99.2	D	12 981	2 091	9.9	7.7	1.5	10 166	156	527
Elbert	29.8	14 190	76.6	143.2	4.5	228	0	NA	NA	NA	228	5	0
Emanuel	28.8	11 077	97.5	210.9	9.0	1 117	244	0.0	18.0	82.0	676	8	0
Evans	9.6	10 667	25.3	58.9	4.4	578	55	0.0	0.0	72.7	302	28	200
Fannin	6.7	11 167	45.0	66.3	D	1 486	1 350	13.6	46.9	31.6	0	0	40
Fayette	33.0	18 333	167.4	424.0	D	114 473	26 659	24.5	4.0	54.1	82 873	817	1 962

1. Includes nonresidential additions and alterations, residential nonhousekeeping buildings, and residential garages and carports not shown separately.

STATE County	Wholesale trade, 1987: Establishments	Wholesale trade, 1987: Sales (Mil dol)	Wholesale trade, 1987: Paid employees[1]	Wholesale trade, 1987: Annual payroll (Mil dol)	Retail trade, all establishments, 1987: Number	Retail trade, all establishments, 1987: Sales: Total (Mil dol)	Retail trade, all establishments, 1987: Sales: Percent change, 1982–1987	Retail trade, all establishments, 1987: Sales: Per capita[2] (Dollars)	Retail trade, establishments with payroll, 1987: Number	Retail trade, establishments with payroll, 1987: Sales: Total (Mil dol)	Retail trade, establishments with payroll, 1987: Sales: Per capita[2] (Dollars): General merchandise stores	Per capita[2] (Dollars): Food stores	Per capita[2] (Dollars): Apparel & accessory stores	Per capita[2] (Dollars): Eating and drinking places
	147	148	149	150	151	152	153	154	155	156	157	158	159	160
FLORIDA—Con.														
Sumter	20	31.8	117	1.3	242	135.2	42.6	4 374	145	129.2	270	1 156	D	471
Suwannee	39	61.0	307	4.8	246	113.8	30.1	4 309	146	106.6	244	1 309	95	294
Taylor	21	39.6	176	2.9	221	105.4	57.3	5 549	147	100.2	D	1 398	142	439
Union	1	D	D	D	56	17.0	28.8	1 608	31	16.1	0	646	0	D
Volusia	449	662.3	3 627	63.9	3 972	2 452.4	63.2	7 323	2 440	2 372.5	817	1 589	262	797
Wakulla	10	D	D	D	115	35.4	107.0	2 586	68	32.4	148	1 072	D	240
Walton	25	45.4	218	3.2	267	96.6	49.8	3 488	155	90.9	76	1 254	79	299
Washington	11	26.7	94	0.7	171	45.1	12.5	2 766	86	41.0	D	1 200	D	250
GEORGIA	13 678	86 854.0	178 235	4 116.6	61 686	41 186.2	68.7	6 614	39 782	39 994.9	790	1 238	299	639
Appling	24	D	D	D	154	70.4	51.7	4 293	85	66.6	106	1 097	198	387
Atkinson	5	6.0	20	0.3	56	14.9	35.5	2 326	30	13.2	D	1 080	D	64
Bacon	19	D	D	D	94	47.9	74.2	4 889	69	46.9	96	1 221	227	260
Baker	3	D	D	D	21	2.8	-28.2	734	10	2.4	D	D	0	0
Baldwin	30	D	D	D	370	213.2	52.0	5 524	251	208.2	651	1 299	274	454
Banks	5	D	D	D	76	24.1	170.8	2 277	34	20.1	D	177	D	288
Barrow	26	66.4	267	4.0	265	153.9	70.1	5 786	140	147.7	D	1 285	160	387
Bartow	86	169.6	751	14.7	494	288.6	69.1	5 773	295	273.5	513	1 188	121	500
Ben Hill	33	45.5	260	3.9	206	80.0	42.1	4 650	126	75.8	D	1 616	209	268
Berrien	23	D	D	D	141	62.9	45.3	4 492	82	59.7	D	1 434	117	168
Bibb	346	1 275.1	4 426	91.2	1 589	1 243.0	51.0	7 938	1 196	1 222.4	1 168	1 279	400	748
Bleckley	10	5.8	42	0.5	112	39.2	35.6	3 700	66	36.6	D	D	204	254
Brantley	6	9.9	29	0.4	75	12.3	75.7	1 207	34	10.8	0	521	0	69
Brooks	15	15.3	81	1.5	122	40.6	15.3	2 671	63	38.6	56	978	75	92
Bryan	6	33.1	37	0.6	132	50.4	140.0	3 475	65	46.9	D	1 309	0	271
Bulloch	78	188.3	741	11.5	382	216.3	31.7	5 768	261	209.9	1 015	1 278	226	564
Burke	27	D	D	D	166	66.6	17.7	3 155	101	63.3	D	1 107	125	210
Butts	15	43.0	112	1.8	137	90.7	214.9	5 497	89	88.4	D	1 862	107	251
Calhoun	18	D	D	D	70	14.1	30.6	2 651	35	12.6	D	1 260	D	28
Camden	12	7.1	65	0.8	222	120.8	163.2	5 620	152	118.3	D	1 313	72	525
Candler	18	27.0	105	1.6	101	38.8	40.6	5 241	66	37.9	D	1 444	206	216
Carroll	77	219.2	687	11.4	749	371.2	76.0	5 524	426	349.8	582	1 543	149	397
Catoosa	26	80.7	476	8.8	286	197.1	49.1	4 831	161	188.7	D	1 436	D	458
Charlton	13	10.3	60	0.8	91	29.7	50.0	3 619	55	28.2	240	1 135	63	272
Chatham	447	1 742.9	5 507	115.8	2 106	1 597.3	53.1	7 320	1 586	1 571.8	D	1 318	389	782
Chattahoochee	0	0.0	0	0.0	14	3.1	-3.1	172	6	2.8	0	D	0	D
Chattooga	10	7.6	36	0.5	219	104.2	67.3	4 800	111	92.3	594	1 301	158	214
Cherokee	87	232.6	799	13.1	503	270.1	106.0	3 343	286	256.1	434	671	36	276
Clarke	152	715.9	1 944	42.9	901	693.9	53.5	8 988	716	685.5	1 418	1 488	401	1 010
Clay	7	3.0	24	0.3	33	7.4	76.2	2 184	21	6.7	D	872	D	152
Clayton	305	2 191.1	5 222	118.8	1 483	1 621.5	84.2	9 589	1 020	1 597.4	1 612	1 459	380	707
Clinch	11	D	D	D	65	20.0	75.4	2 895	43	19.3	150	991	D	53
Cobb	1 150	8 274.3	14 458	395.9	4 342	3 773.1	93.5	9 225	2 788	3 700.4	1 419	1 386	472	880
Coffee	62	D	D	D	322	173.9	74.4	5 816	204	166.7	527	1 756	247	380
Colquitt	71	D	D	D	363	170.2	42.1	4 576	229	163.0	542	1 117	182	293
Columbia	36	129.9	532	9.8	424	261.4	167.0	4 357	239	251.3	D	1 166	32	310
Cook	26	D	D	D	130	57.1	59.5	4 076	90	54.8	71	932	269	329
Coweta	55	158.8	437	8.4	420	257.8	74.0	5 337	235	245.8	531	1 115	192	340
Crawford	6	D	D	D	46	6.6	43.5	886	15	4.3	0	420	D	D
Crisp	62	232.8	737	11.9	273	148.3	29.9	7 269	197	145.7	846	1 666	351	672
Dade	5	3.2	23	0.2	116	50.4	50.9	4 234	47	44.2	D	1 559	D	228
Dawson	1	D	D	D	74	11.7	56.0	1 497	26	8.8	0	247	0	25
Decatur	54	195.5	546	8.2	281	119.2	54.6	4 447	207	116.7	308	1 068	261	284
De Kalb	2 015	18 694.6	31 225	849.2	5 323	4 780.1	56.7	8 877	3 568	4 701.3	1 086	1 340	480	841
Dodge	21	22.7	95	1.2	217	85.5	25.4	4 940	143	79.1	471	1 139	153	590
Dooly	22	31.7	126	2.5	97	31.3	-9.0	3 039	55	30.0	D	467	D	76
Dougherty	258	931.9	3 229	61.0	1 071	743.2	43.8	7 301	761	725.9	1 133	1 551	D	631
Douglas	72	814.2	766	15.9	553	447.4	113.5	6 319	344	435.7	D	1 270	126	515
Early	24	166.3	472	5.0	122	45.6	26.0	3 480	85	43.7	107	1 099	181	143
Echols	1	D	D	D	5	D	D	D	4	0.6	0	D	0	D
Effingham	17	9.6	61	0.9	130	73.1	156.5	3 124	71	70.8	D	1 039	41	84
Elbert	49	54.6	715	7.5	239	128.6	68.8	6 770	129	120.7	244	1 131	62	301
Emanuel	36	72.6	250	3.0	218	101.0	40.7	4 592	128	94.5	D	1 189	302	268
Evans	14	21.5	110	1.5	104	46.1	45.0	5 492	71	44.3	125	932	D	204
Fannin	16	15.3	91	1.6	224	71.6	68.9	4 422	123	63.4	652	1 155	211	321
Fayette	78	140.7	641	14.7	505	225.7	173.9	4 341	247	214.9	437	1 471	127	359

1. For pay period including March 12. 2. Based on the estimated population as of July 1 of the year shown.

STATE County	Retail trade, establishments with payroll, 1987 (cont'd)		Taxable service industries–establishments with payroll, 1987							Bank deposits,[2] June 1989		Savings capital,[3] September 1989	
				Receipts (Mil dol)									
					Selected kinds of business								
	Paid employees[1]	Annual payroll (Mil dol)	Number	Total	Hotels, motels and other lodging places	Health services	Legal services	Paid employees	Annual payroll (Mil dol)	Total (Mil dol)	Percent change, 1988–1989	Total (Mil dol)	Percent change, 1988–1989
	161	162	163	164	165	166	167	168	169	170	171	172	173
FLORIDA–Con.													
Sumter	1 614	13.5	88	25.9	4.6	9.3	1.5	830	8.9	112	9.4	50.3	-2.4
Suwannee	1 222	11.8	92	18.9	0.7	5.0	2.3	498	5.7	150	10.4	72.0	6.5
Taylor	1 201	11.0	90	18.5	2.7	6.2	0.9	567	5.8	66	7.9	41.2	3.9
Union	179	1.7	17	4.9	0.0	4.2	D	134	1.9	27	14.6	0.0	NA
Volusia	31 065	279.4	2 538	925.0	180.8	315.1	56.3	22 549	320.0	2 493	16.2	2 197.3	-3.3
Wakulla	472	3.4	34	10.3	2.1	2.5	D	337	3.9	49	32.0	40.4	-20.1
Walton	1 092	9.2	78	12.8	D	4.9	0.6	407	4.2	78	18.4	68.3	-5.5
Washington	490	4.3	68	12.5	D	4.0	D	339	4.4	42	-0.6	23.1	15.3
GEORGIA	486 992	4 791.6	39 189	18 645.8	1 234.8	4 756.6	1 346.7	414 969	6 908.9	46 850	10.2	14 478.9	0.9
Appling	834	7.2	53	10.1	D	2.7	D	237	2.8	68	2.5	35.1	5.1
Atkinson	174	1.0	10	0.7	0.0	D	D	23	0.2	21	7.5	0.0	NA
Bacon	620	4.5	47	8.0	D	3.9	0.9	328	2.8	66	5.5	0.0	NA
Baker	33	0.3	1	D	0.0	0.0	D	D	D	12	10.4	0.0	NA
Baldwin	2 957	25.0	177	36.9	2.7	17.8	2.8	1 004	13.2	295	14.4	49.5	-1.3
Banks	224	1.7	19	5.3	D	D	D	198	1.7	30	-6.8	0.0	NA
Barrow	1 551	15.9	103	28.7	D	16.4	1.3	774	10.1	181	15.1	62.0	1.1
Bartow	3 340	31.3	227	58.3	5.9	22.7	2.1	1 595	20.9	303	26.9	82.3	0.8
Ben Hill	1 025	7.9	86	18.8	D	7.9	1.9	588	6.1	165	26.5	2.5	-88.1
Berrien	570	5.5	41	10.1	D	7.5	D	303	4.2	70	-0.5	15.7	4.9
Bibb	15 510	145.8	1 180	554.3	17.9	287.3	34.6	11 970	194.5	1 043	11.8	533.0	-2.7
Bleckley	474	4.0	39	5.6	0.0	2.6	0.3	197	1.8	60	12.9	22.1	19.1
Brantley	157	1.1	18	0.6	0.0	0.0	D	31	0.2	24	11.9	0.0	NA
Brooks	445	3.6	42	6.2	D	1.2	1.2	138	1.6	54	4.3	26.4	8.6
Bryan	580	4.9	30	13.5	10.1	1.3	0.3	394	3.5	34	4.6	0.0	NA
Bulloch	3 033	24.2	203	52.2	3.2	25.8	3.7	1 537	20.7	265	9.7	82.6	-0.5
Burke	886	7.2	57	12.1	D	5.5	0.2	330	4.4	90	7.2	26.6	-6.7
Butts	841	8.5	44	8.6	0.0	4.3	0.9	327	3.8	91	6.7	0.0	NA
Calhoun	134	1.2	11	0.6	D	D	D	20	0.3	43	-24.0	0.0	NA
Camden	1 443	12.1	92	33.9	9.3	4.0	1.4	867	9.3	81	18.8	3.8	7.2
Candler	341	3.1	22	7.8	D	5.2	D	360	3.8	67	8.7	0.0	NA
Carroll	4 399	38.6	297	88.8	3.1	40.3	6.0	2 270	33.7	391	14.6	226.4	1.4
Catoosa	2 097	18.9	118	34.8	D	17.6	D	763	14.6	121	12.9	80.0	9.4
Charlton	393	3.3	17	3.4	D	2.1	0.5	128	1.4	53	17.0	3.6	-4.3
Chatham	19 833	186.7	1 499	620.6	D	207.8	44.9	14 450	237.3	1 575	14.6	553.5	-4.0
Chattahoochee	40	0.4	2	D	0.0	0.0	0.0	D	D	51	-4.3	0.0	NA
Chattooga	953	8.7	53	6.1	D	1.7	1.3	160	1.7	107	9.6	34.9	-3.5
Cherokee	2 893	28.8	252	56.9	D	17.9	5.5	1 425	19.9	467	10.4	62.9	2.2
Clarke	9 860	85.0	608	199.5	9.9	88.9	12.5	6 186	80.3	551	6.3	357.0	1.5
Clay	73	0.6	7	1.1	0.0	D	0.0	33	0.5	13	-10.9	0.0	NA
Clayton	16 276	174.5	975	396.6	18.0	129.0	11.2	10 462	150.3	659	13.8	310.4	-0.8
Clinch	222	1.7	18	4.6	0.0	1.8	1.3	151	1.6	28	17.5	0.0	NA
Cobb	42 737	452.4	3 575	1 890.8	80.5	353.6	82.1	37 340	691.4	3 018	29.2	1 100.4	8.5
Coffee	1 927	17.6	154	32.0	D	10.8	3.2	887	9.7	200	1.4	73.7	1.3
Colquitt	2 120	19.2	179	46.3	1.9	18.8	2.2	1 202	16.0	215	14.5	68.6	-14.7
Columbia	2 784	26.9	238	50.2	D	10.7	1.7	1 589	23.6	166	15.5	62.3	3.3
Cook	637	5.6	57	15.4	1.2	8.4	0.5	554	6.1	64	8.7	21.0	-4.4
Coweta	2 644	27.5	172	76.4	D	38.9	2.8	1 693	27.1	308	17.5	81.3	-15.7
Crawford	40	0.4	12	3.0	D	1.7	D	123	1.0	21	13.6	0.0	NA
Crisp	2 218	18.4	113	23.2	6.6	7.4	1.5	792	7.0	98	2.9	58.5	1.8
Dade	440	3.9	27	3.9	D	1.5	D	151	1.2	42	14.7	0.0	NA
Dawson	109	1.1	19	4.9	0.0	0.6	0.0	72	1.7	34	3.8	0.0	NA
Decatur	1 469	11.9	102	19.8	D	8.2	1.6	484	6.2	141	8.8	34.2	-0.3
De Kalb	54 307	599.5	4 940	3 236.2	122.6	677.2	169.0	60 428	1 149.8	3 104	8.2	2 218.5	0.9
Dodge	1 322	9.1	77	14.5	D	8.2	0.8	493	5.2	128	16.4	0.0	NA
Dooly	347	3.7	34	6.4	1.4	3.7	D	250	2.2	66	6.8	4.9	-9.9
Dougherty	9 356	84.6	721	286.2	D	D	D	6 799	109.7	480	10.0	222.7	-2.0
Douglas	4 397	46.0	328	118.1	0.2	62.6	4.7	2 885	44.8	295	16.4	119.2	3.2
Early	516	4.4	38	5.8	D	3.3	0.7	141	1.9	60	10.8	13.0	-14.3
Echols	8	0.1	0	0.0	0.0	0.0	0.0	0	0.0	NA	NA	0.0	NA
Effingham	619	6.3	44	5.2	D	1.6	0.3	139	1.6	76	29.9	0.0	NA
Elbert	1 011	9.6	85	20.3	D	7.2	2.4	466	5.4	183	-5.3	19.5	0.2
Emanuel	1 206	10.7	86	16.0	0.3	7.0	1.1	483	5.6	136	5.4	31.0	11.4
Evans	425	4.7	47	8.7	D	3.0	D	252	2.5	59	5.1	17.5	-1.8
Fannin	750	6.3	66	17.0	D	9.2	0.7	378	6.2	78	22.2	44.9	5.8
Fayette	2 887	26.2	262	72.4	D	13.3	4.3	2 424	32.8	307	15.8	77.3	11.3

1. For the period including March 12 of the year shown. 2. Includes deposits for all insured and reporting noninsured commercial and mutual savings banks. 3. Includes savings capital for all FSLIC insured savings institutions.

STATE County	Federal funds and grants, 1989: Expenditures: Total (Mil dol)	Expenditures: Percent change, 1988–1989	Per capita[1] (Dollars): Total	Per capita: Direct payments for individuals	Per capita: Procurement contract awards	Per capita: Salaries and wages	Per capita: Grant awards	Local government finances, 1981–1982: General revenue: Total (Mil dol)	Intergovernmental: Total (Mil dol)	Intergovernmental: Percent from state	Taxes: Total (Mil dol)	Taxes: Per capita[2]: Total (Dollars)	Taxes: Per capita[2]: Property (Dollars)	Direct general expenditure: Total (Mil dol)	Direct general expenditure: Percent change, 1977–1982
	174	175	176	177	178	179	180	181	182	183	184	185	186	187	188
FLORIDA—Con.															
Sumter	89.1	0.7	2 751	2 340	55	83	219	18.2	12.3	83.5	3.8	144	126	17.8	33.9
Suwannee	75.8	14.6	2 776	2 290	28	116	248	20.2	12.0	93.9	4.1	172	144	19.1	21.7
Taylor	55.8	-16.9	2 875	1 607	915	90	256	19.6	8.6	96.3	3.5	203	174	20.1	64.1
Union	15.2	11.9	1 473	1 100	9	65	204	5.4	3.9	93.1	0.9	79	67	5.6	62.2
Volusia	1 206.9	1.6	3 339	2 711	380	120	116	326.6	112.2	77.4	94.4	335	276	303.7	90.0
Wakulla	28.4	-31.2	1 946	1 364	264	116	190	10.5	7.9	84.0	1.6	143	134	9.9	78.9
Walton	77.6	-16.3	2 665	2 069	14	251	289	18.9	9.0	88.7	4.9	216	197	19.4	94.3
Washington	51.8	8.6	3 067	2 480	10	108	405	25.1	12.4	93.9	2.1	141	126	23.8	55.0
GEORGIA	20 148.6	10.1	X	1 532	328	753	457	5 818.9	1 999.2	75.8	1 870.4	331	243	5 485.0	77.6
Appling	34.0	7.4	2 037	1 298	116	117	421	18.7	8.6	63.0	6.7	428	411	14.1	56.6
Atkinson	16.1	3.6	2 561	1 660	12	83	536	4.2	2.5	92.9	1.4	226	169	4.0	52.3
Bacon	21.4	-0.5	2 210	1 538	14	88	444	8.7	3.7	84.4	2.3	248	170	8.5	69.5
Baker	8.0	9.0	2 168	1 131	10	86	498	2.3	1.1	88.7	1.1	283	259	2.1	45.2
Baldwin	72.2	-0.3	1 861	1 421	27	76	330	35.7	12.1	81.6	7.8	211	127	37.3	90.2
Banks	13.5	0.5	1 213	984	5	44	159	4.0	2.0	92.5	1.7	189	148	3.5	-28.3
Barrow	56.8	9.9	2 023	1 445	74	274	216	14.0	5.7	89.7	4.5	200	128	13.9	68.3
Bartow	84.7	9.7	1 575	1 190	40	106	221	43.3	12.2	90.6	12.9	306	283	43.4	64.6
Ben Hill	42.5	7.5	2 469	1 795	157	83	376	15.4	5.4	89.9	3.2	192	158	15.6	109.3
Berrien	34.2	9.9	2 427	1 779	10	81	323	9.0	4.9	92.2	3.1	225	146	8.3	59.3
Bibb	459.5	5.4	2 915	2 113	98	355	338	180.2	50.6	73.7	61.8	403	270	173.8	70.7
Bleckley	30.4	7.8	2 865	2 248	9	77	345	8.8	3.4	92.8	2.3	213	141	8.5	62.0
Brantley	19.3	11.0	1 841	1 397	10	74	342	6.2	3.8	96.2	1.6	180	168	7.6	163.7
Brooks	41.1	3.0	2 701	1 598	12	87	448	11.0	5.2	88.3	2.8	180	138	11.8	52.3
Bryan	502.8	56.2	29 578	1 220	1 869	26 246	230	7.4	4.3	90.8	2.5	235	144	7.6	137.8
Bulloch	79.1	7.2	2 080	1 465	20	152	349	31.7	13.5	92.6	7.1	191	168	31.5	99.5
Burke	52.3	-3.0	2 444	1 436	47	114	521	15.1	6.8	89.9	4.8	240	220	15.0	71.0
Butts	30.4	-1.4	1 776	1 326	10	118	310	7.2	3.6	89.5	2.7	179	119	8.3	58.4
Calhoun	18.9	4.0	3 709	2 386	19	132	653	6.3	2.6	91.4	1.6	285	252	6.0	45.9
Camden	157.3	-44.2	6 473	1 030	780	4 462	196	16.3	7.6	83.6	7.5	475	355	14.2	113.4
Candler	20.0	-2.5	2 702	1 878	15	121	484	5.0	2.8	88.0	1.8	233	150	4.7	19.1
Carroll	125.7	3.1	1 778	1 429	20	96	226	55.3	18.9	85.5	12.9	217	125	52.6	79.5
Catoosa	59.8	22.3	1 418	1 085	22	53	250	42.6	9.5	92.4	6.9	180	125	39.4	87.4
Charlton	17.2	7.1	2 050	1 553	8	129	351	7.2	2.8	86.2	2.5	331	265	9.1	91.1
Chatham	960.1	28.0	4 360	1 891	1 021	1 073	367	221.0	71.3	67.7	63.7	302	238	231.0	78.5
Chattahoochee	85.7	-18.5	4 980	314	4 587	9	69	1.4	0.8	71.1	0.4	20	11	1.2	7.0
Chattooga	49.1	5.4	2 251	1 778	52	82	316	14.2	6.2	91.2	5.1	238	209	13.7	55.0
Cherokee	81.4	-0.6	875	741	10	69	49	33.5	15.7	93.6	9.4	162	146	33.0	87.6
Clarke	245.4	-2.7	3 163	1 394	81	786	891	87.8	28.3	72.4	26.4	349	216	83.8	81.7
Clay	12.0	-3.0	3 442	1 610	425	515	661	3.6	1.3	70.8	0.6	183	140	3.3	35.2
Clayton	266.1	4.1	1 536	1 096	73	260	103	139.0	44.0	85.2	51.3	325	295	134.9	68.0
Clinch	20.8	37.0	3 109	1 660	682	89	656	7.0	2.9	90.1	2.0	301	239	6.5	63.8
Cobb	1 349.6	19.3	3 056	953	1 601	328	168	291.6	83.1	83.0	104.9	324	294	262.9	73.2
Coffee	59.9	6.6	1 970	1 450	10	120	308	30.3	13.0	77.4	6.0	218	142	32.5	130.8
Colquitt	93.0	10.5	2 493	1 765	10	92	397	34.3	14.5	76.7	6.5	180	158	32.4	70.9
Columbia	488.9	46.7	7 430	1 138	1 057	5 124	107	21.6	10.6	95.0	8.3	187	137	23.1	102.1
Cook	32.3	10.5	2 274	1 485	9	66	442	8.6	4.4	93.0	3.0	219	164	8.3	9.1
Coweta	93.1	7.4	1 774	1 453	14	91	206	38.2	12.2	91.5	11.9	288	186	36.7	65.9
Crawford	13.0	-25.0	1 760	1 270	7	52	298	4.3	2.5	91.6	1.5	203	154	4.5	20.3
Crisp	49.6	3.0	2 444	1 631	52	103	495	14.5	7.8	82.0	5.7	285	176	14.9	80.1
Dade	21.3	7.9	1 771	1 430	11	61	263	5.8	3.2	94.0	2.2	181	125	6.1	83.5
Dawson	14.6	8.4	1 606	1 145	135	70	235	3.8	1.8	91.9	1.8	345	324	3.7	79.2
Decatur	96.4	62.6	3 584	1 446	1 528	80	385	28.7	9.0	87.8	5.8	220	151	27.3	139.2
De Kalb	1 273.2	10.8	2 314	1 063	74	608	563	531.0	180.6	66.1	206.3	420	309	508.3	53.8
Dodge	48.7	7.9	2 798	1 960	11	102	581	12.8	5.9	91.0	2.8	166	132	14.2	73.2
Dooly	40.0	-39.2	3 960	2 076	14	98	629	8.0	4.9	79.7	2.6	249	175	10.9	79.8
Dougherty	360.4	4.2	3 630	1 665	317	1 188	440	118.8	38.3	86.3	29.3	284	171	136.9	117.4
Douglas	94.0	7.1	1 237	971	10	71	180	45.7	17.8	92.0	15.1	256	192	44.3	56.3
Early	32.7	-1.2	2 517	1 559	20	114	589	13.2	6.7	94.5	3.0	226	180	13.5	84.0
Echols	4.0	-28.0	1 806	1 163	5	34	362	1.6	0.9	93.9	0.7	293	293	1.5	46.5
Effingham	32.7	-8.6	1 292	1 017	6	78	169	13.4	6.6	94.8	3.9	205	161	13.6	77.4
Elbert	56.9	7.7	2 993	1 905	285	307	444	14.3	7.7	75.4	3.8	197	176	14.7	104.5
Emanuel	60.6	5.8	2 732	1 796	45	189	560	23.0	10.2	85.8	6.0	283	212	24.1	77.5
Evans	21.1	-5.0	2 451	1 768	13	143	427	10.6	4.9	59.3	1.8	206	123	8.9	70.9
Fannin	43.8	10.6	2 620	2 013	14	101	482	9.7	5.1	80.9	2.9	192	143	8.9	61.8
Fayette	67.6	11.2	1 110	961	10	94	40	22.1	9.4	93.6	10.3	303	264	22.1	150.3

1. Based on the estimated population as of July 1 of the year shown. 2. Based on the estimated population as of July 1, 1982.

STATE County	Local government finances, 1981–1982 (cont'd) — Direct general expenditure (cont'd) — Per capita[1] (Dollars)	Percent of total for– Education	Health & hospitals	Police protection	Public welfare	Highways	Debt outstanding — Total (Mil dol)	Per capita[1] (Dollars)	State and local government employment, 1989 — Total	Rate[2]	Federal government civilian employment 1989 — Total	Earnings ($1,000)	Elections, 1988[3] — Total vote cast for president	Vote for lead party (Percent)
	189	190	191	192	193	194	195	196	197	198	199	200	201	202
FLORIDA—Con.														
Sumter	680	58.8	2.3	7.3	2.9	5.4	7.2	275	1 667	514.5	67	1 831	9 896	R–60.0
Suwannee	800	58.6	13.6	4.0	0.2	7.8	3.8	160	1 309	479.5	91	2 454	9 122	R–64.3
Taylor	1 157	39.9	20.3	4.5	0.1	7.6	43.7	2 514	1 006	518.6	39	1 087	5 875	R–69.1
Union	509	67.4	0.9	5.6	0.7	7.5	3.6	326	1 816	1 763.1	20	544	2 349	R–70.0
Volusia	1 078	39.4	20.9	6.4	0.2	5.1	187.9	667	18 924	523.6	1 025	34 207	131 182	R–56.6
Wakulla	862	62.7	1.9	5.6	0.0	7.5	5.0	431	731	500.7	54	1 477	4 805	R–65.7
Walton	848	42.9	25.6	3.8	0.0	10.3	11.0	480	1 311	450.5	81	2 166	10 808	R–69.3
Washington	1 568	45.5	38.9	2.4	0.0	4.3	7.6	500	1 445	855.0	51	1 337	6 564	R–66.6
GEORGIA	971	40.4	24.0	4.7	0.3	4.6	5 904.8	1 045	404 956	629.0	101 462	3 013 950	1 809 657	R–59.8
Appling	895	59.3	3.1	3.2	0.5	10.8	18.4	1 174	1 077	644.9	55	1 372	4 859	R–61.7
Atkinson	655	63.6	5.2	5.9	0.3	11.0	0.6	95	289	458.7	19	463	2 025	R–55.6
Bacon	910	41.2	23.6	3.7	0.1	5.1	5.6	603	576	593.8	31	825	2 194	R–64.1
Baker	543	64.5	1.5	4.6	2.3	10.0	0.2	61	179	483.8	12	288	1 348	D–52.4
Baldwin	1 012	30.7	44.6	4.2	0.3	4.6	9.7	264	8 236	2 122.7	68	1 931	9 911	R–59.0
Banks	385	65.6	2.4	4.2	0.6	11.8	1.2	133	358	322.5	19	459	2 582	R–61.6
Barrow	621	48.9	21.3	6.5	0.1	8.0	5.2	232	1 185	421.7	144	3 992	7 218	R–65.6
Bartow	1 030	43.8	16.6	3.2	0.1	6.8	133.2	3 157	2 735	508.4	185	5 169	13 044	R–61.6
Ben Hill	945	35.2	36.4	3.9	0.1	6.6	6.1	372	1 281	744.8	41	1 088	3 918	R–51.2
Berrien	606	59.8	3.1	7.1	0.2	11.7	1.8	134	626	444.0	41	1 027	3 420	R–59.4
Bibb	1 134	35.4	28.9	6.0	0.2	2.8	107.6	702	10 481	665.0	1 261	41 886	44 396	R–50.0
Bleckley	793	42.9	34.4	4.4	0.3	7.5	1.6	151	778	734.0	33	797	3 138	R–62.1
Brantley	839	79.4	0.9	2.9	0.1	5.2	2.6	288	459	437.1	26	572	3 007	R–51.2
Brooks	764	54.8	18.4	4.4	0.1	8.0	2.9	185	791	520.4	43	1 062	3 649	R–58.5
Bryan	701	69.7	3.8	5.1	0.4	7.5	2.2	206	742	436.5	29	683	4 235	R–66.2
Bulloch	844	41.2	35.0	3.2	0.2	3.7	12.2	327	3 985	1 048.7	144	4 047	9 794	R–64.9
Burke	748	50.7	20.5	6.6	0.8	6.9	1.8	89	1 227	573.4	69	1 691	5 872	R–50.9
Butts	554	60.7	3.5	7.3	0.0	7.2	3.4	231	1 023	598.2	52	1 397	3 924	R–55.7
Calhoun	1 050	46.3	29.7	5.0	0.2	4.7	4.1	713	442	866.7	23	494	1 551	D–58.1
Camden	899	56.2	2.2	7.0	0.1	11.3	5.6	355	1 271	523.0	766	17 497	5 050	R–57.7
Candler	607	56.7	1.5	7.6	0.1	7.9	2.5	329	476	643.2	27	685	2 144	R–58.8
Carroll	887	41.4	36.5	3.4	0.0	5.3	22.7	383	3 823	540.7	193	5 373	15 541	R–69.2
Catoosa	1 027	28.2	55.3	2.3	0.1	5.3	12.8	333	2 358	558.8	71	1 937	12 940	R–72.0
Charlton	1 217	63.4	21.6	2.4	0.0	2.6	5.4	717	462	550.0	41	1 155	2 304	R–57.6
Chatham	1 096	28.8	30.1	5.3	1.2	5.4	253.7	1 203	12 134	551.0	2 950	88 427	61 289	R–58.1
Chattahoochee	56	59.3	1.4	5.9	0.3	8.5	0.4	17	143	83.1	5 029	143 224	817	R–55.6
Chattooga	635	55.6	9.8	4.8	0.2	9.2	17.9	832	1 081	495.9	52	1 374	5 895	R–62.2
Cherokee	571	60.4	18.0	3.3	0.0	7.6	15.0	259	2 869	308.2	154	4 227	19 088	R–76.5
Clarke	1 105	31.8	32.3	5.1	1.7	2.3	48.4	638	13 413	1 728.5	1 966	67 163	22 452	D–49.7
Clay	951	27.0	48.5	3.2	0.2	9.0	1.0	293	182	520.0	11	301	994	D–59.9
Clayton	854	44.2	25.7	5.9	0.1	3.1	125.8	796	10 028	578.6	3 032	69 711	43 137	R–65.4
Clinch	971	46.2	32.3	3.4	0.3	7.2	2.4	351	406	606.0	17	462	1 465	R–58.9
Cobb	813	45.4	23.2	5.5	0.1	3.6	318.0	983	20 630	467.1	3 454	105 974	146 658	R–72.7
Coffee	1 176	44.2	27.0	3.1	0.1	5.9	14.8	534	2 098	690.1	126	3 424	6 822	R–58.9
Colquitt	901	42.4	29.1	3.9	0.1	5.6	10.0	278	2 263	606.7	119	3 096	8 691	R–65.0
Columbia	521	72.3	2.4	4.5	0.1	5.9	18.6	420	2 087	317.2	113	3 364	21 094	R–77.8
Cook	609	64.4	5.0	6.6	0.3	8.6	4.1	302	653	459.9	36	922	2 792	R–55.7
Coweta	891	43.7	24.1	4.1	0.1	4.1	46.8	1 135	1 990	379.0	121	3 292	13 929	R–69.4
Crawford	623	69.1	1.9	4.9	0.1	9.8	1.4	189	330	445.9	13	295	2 597	D–51.6
Crisp	746	54.2	3.6	6.8	0.1	9.4	9.9	493	1 530	753.7	59	1 621	4 633	R–62.9
Dade	506	64.6	1.5	3.8	0.4	11.3	0.3	23	434	361.7	20	559	3 671	R–69.2
Dawson	725	63.1	1.8	6.5	0.2	13.3	0.2	34	398	437.4	17	428	2 686	R–71.0
Decatur	1 039	34.3	43.4	3.2	0.2	5.1	6.9	263	2 332	866.9	68	1 676	6 241	R–61.9
De Kalb	1 034	41.1	32.1	4.6	0.2	2.5	268.0	545	26 570	482.9	10 715	307 109	184 250	D–50.2
Dodge	829	52.6	23.1	3.1	0.2	6.0	2.4	143	1 232	708.0	49	1 172	4 872	R–54.9
Dooly	1 025	51.8	4.4	4.1	0.1	7.7	1.2	111	649	642.6	48	1 066	3 021	D–53.4
Dougherty	1 329	29.2	18.1	4.5	0.1	3.0	48.4	470	8 382	844.1	3 503	112 231	30 517	R–50.9
Douglas	751	47.3	26.9	5.4	0.4	4.7	38.4	652	3 019	397.2	129	3 560	18 678	R–72.2
Early	1 015	39.8	34.2	3.5	0.1	7.3	4.7	354	940	723.1	55	1 291	3 281	R–58.5
Echols	671	68.8	2.6	2.9	0.1	10.0	0.4	170	124	563.6	NA	NA	670	R–63.0
Effingham	717	63.4	12.7	2.7	0.1	10.9	1.3	67	1 227	485.0	39	940	5 859	R–67.1
Elbert	767	44.1	25.7	3.9	0.6	8.2	2.2	118	1 213	638.4	153	4 739	4 925	R–56.8
Emanuel	1 136	38.9	36.4	3.2	2.3	6.0	13.8	652	1 486	669.4	128	3 292	5 988	R–59.0
Evans	1 021	36.5	39.4	3.5	0.1	6.3	8.5	974	563	654.7	40	1 040	2 753	R–62.0
Fannin	595	55.8	2.7	3.7	0.6	11.3	3.3	224	695	416.2	71	1 514	6 427	R–66.5
Fayette	650	68.2	1.3	6.0	0.0	6.7	25.4	748	2 183	358.5	118	3 450	21 123	R–77.8

1. Based on the estimated population as of July 1, 1982. 2. Per 10,000 resident population estimated as of July 1 of the year shown. 3. Data subject to copyright.

STATE–County code	MSA/CMSA/NECMA code[1]	STATE County	Land Area,[2] 1990 (Sq. Km.)	Population, 1990											
				Total persons	Rank	Per square kilometer	Race					Hispanic[3]	Age of population Percent		
							White	Black	Am. Indian, Eskimo, Aleut	Asian & Pacific Islander	Other race		Under 5 years	5 to 14 years	15 to 24 years
			1	2	3	4	5	6	7	8	9	10	11	12	13
		GEORGIA–Con.													
13 115	...	Floyd	1 329	81 251	561	61.1	69 338	11 106	138	409	260	831	6.7	13.1	15.6
13 117	0520	Forsyth	585	44 083	923	75.4	43 573	14	98	81	317	635	7.7	13.8	14.1
13 119	...	Franklin	682	16 650	1 873	24.4	14 906	1 681	29	27	7	77	6.5	12.9	15.2
13 121	0520	Fulton	1 369	648 951	73	474.0	309 901	324 008	981	8 380	5 681	13 373	7.4	13.0	15.8
13 123	...	Gilmer	1 105	13 368	2 108	12.1	13 258	37	16	20	37	102	6.5	14.3	14.0
13 125	...	Glascock	373	2 357	3 036	6.3	2 055	298	2	0	2	6	5.5	14.1	12.7
13 127	...	Glynn	1 094	62 496	695	57.1	45 989	15 941	120	301	145	585	7.3	14.4	13.8
13 129	...	Gordon	920	35 072	1 127	38.1	33 487	1 321	86	124	54	200	7.1	14.9	15.5
13 131	...	Grady	1 187	20 279	1 661	17.1	13 664	6 395	77	22	121	289	7.3	15.8	14.9
13 133	...	Greene	1 006	11 793	2 229	11.7	5 860	5 887	13	1	32	96	7.6	18.2	14.0
13 135	0520	Gwinnett	1 121	352 910	146	314.8	320 971	18 175	715	10 219	2 830	8 470	8.6	15.2	13.7
13 137	...	Habersham	721	27 621	1 367	38.3	25 324	1 554	76	512	155	342	6.3	13.2	17.9
13 139	...	Hall	1 020	95 428	484	93.6	83 108	8 195	180	659	3 286	4 558	7.5	13.9	15.5
13 141	...	Hancock	1 226	8 908	2 479	7.3	1 802	7 077	6	1	22	63	7.8	18.1	15.2
13 143	...	Haralson	731	21 966	1 577	30.0	20 438	1 427	30	49	22	84	7.5	14.6	14.6
13 145	...	Harris	1 201	17 788	1 798	14.8	13 103	4 571	52	39	23	97	6.4	14.3	13.3
13 147	...	Hart	601	19 712	1 690	32.8	15 646	4 002	17	35	12	76	6.8	13.5	14.2
13 149	...	Heard	767	8 628	2 501	11.2	7 418	1 163	12	22	13	68	7.2	16.0	15.5
13 151	0520	Henry	836	58 741	741	70.3	52 112	6 068	110	329	122	463	8.1	15.3	13.8
13 153	4680	Houston	976	89 208	514	91.4	68 097	19 376	277	1 030	428	1 459	8.2	15.5	14.6
13 155	...	Irwin	924	8 649	2 499	9.4	5 992	2 630	6	13	8	53	7.9	16.2	14.3
13 157	0500	Jackson	887	30 005	1 294	33.8	26 942	2 904	60	55	44	160	7.2	14.9	14.6
13 159	...	Jasper	960	8 453	2 518	8.8	5 481	2 940	15	10	7	57	7.4	16.1	13.4
13 161	...	Jeff Davis	864	12 032	2 216	13.9	10 084	1 834	10	24	80	144	7.4	15.7	16.2
13 163	...	Jefferson	1 367	17 408	1 827	12.7	7 660	9 700	14	16	18	41	8.1	16.8	16.0
13 165	...	Jenkins	906	8 247	2 544	9.1	4 811	3 412	5	16	3	13	8.1	16.6	14.1
13 167	...	Johnson	788	8 329	2 532	10.6	5 474	2 839	3	8	5	35	7.7	16.7	14.3
13 169	4680	Jones	1 020	20 739	1 642	20.3	15 318	5 317	32	48	24	79	7.6	15.7	14.3
13 171	...	Lamar	479	13 038	2 139	27.2	8 559	4 442	19	11	7	49	6.9	14.7	15.7
13 173	...	Lanier	484	5 531	2 798	11.4	3 978	1 470	37	21	25	68	8.0	16.5	15.3
13 175	...	Laurens	2 105	39 988	1 000	19.0	26 485	13 304	37	137	25	180	7.4	16.1	14.3
13 177	0120	Lee	922	16 250	1 909	17.6	13 007	3 135	31	46	31	112	7.5	19.0	15.1
13 179	...	Liberty	1 345	52 745	804	39.2	28 935	20 655	254	1 195	1 706	3 236	11.4	15.6	26.3
13 181	...	Lincoln	547	7 442	2 621	13.6	4 600	2 826	3	9	4	56	6.7	15.2	14.5
13 183	...	Long	1 039	6 202	2 733	6.0	4 685	1 342	23	41	111	189	10.3	15.3	20.5
13 185	...	Lowndes	1 306	75 981	591	58.2	50 566	24 241	230	647	297	991	8.2	15.4	19.2
13 187	...	Lumpkin	737	14 573	2 015	19.8	14 002	238	237	45	51	213	6.8	13.6	20.3
13 189	0600	McDuffie	673	20 119	1 669	29.9	12 720	7 320	38	29	12	84	8.0	16.5	14.6
13 191	...	McIntosh	1 123	8 634	2 500	7.7	4 880	3 719	13	5	17	63	7.5	15.2	14.9
13 193	...	Macon	1 045	13 114	2 131	12.5	5 358	7 694	15	27	20	57	7.9	18.4	15.0
13 195	0500	Madison	737	21 050	1 625	28.6	19 051	1 849	30	54	66	182	7.2	14.9	14.6
13 197	...	Marion	951	5 590	2 792	5.9	3 250	2 306	18	11	5	23	7.7	16.1	14.6
13 199	...	Meriwether	1 304	22 411	1 560	17.2	12 357	9 989	26	17	22	121	7.8	16.1	15.7
13 201	...	Miller	733	6 280	2 726	8.6	4 542	1 726	6	4	2	20	6.8	15.6	14.5
13 205	...	Mitchell	1 326	20 275	1 662	15.3	10 414	9 647	53	16	145	260	7.8	18.2	15.8
13 207	...	Monroe	1 025	17 113	1 845	16.7	11 597	5 406	39	39	32	96	7.0	15.2	15.0
13 209	...	Montgomery	635	7 163	2 636	11.3	4 998	2 026	5	14	120	142	6.6	14.9	18.4
13 211	...	Morgan	906	12 883	2 148	14.2	8 355	4 459	12	26	31	117	7.4	15.4	14.4
13 213	...	Murray	892	26 147	1 415	29.3	25 956	41	44	57	49	136	7.6	16.0	16.1
13 215	1800	Muscogee	560	179 278	271	320.1	105 762	68 161	569	2 510	2 276	5 294	8.2	14.5	16.8
13 217	0520	Newton	716	41 808	960	58.4	32 171	9 357	91	107	82	390	8.1	15.3	16.3
13 219	0500	Oconee	481	17 618	1 812	36.6	16 154	1 315	33	88	28	178	7.9	16.3	13.5
13 221	...	Oglethorpe	1 143	9 763	2 408	8.5	7 294	2 419	23	7	20	66	7.3	14.4	14.3
13 223	0520	Paulding	812	41 611	967	51.2	39 711	1 648	114	75	63	269	9.3	15.4	15.1
13 225	4680	Peach	391	21 189	1 620	54.2	10 716	10 075	72	72	254	378	7.1	15.5	19.8
13 227	...	Pickens	601	14 432	2 022	24.0	14 119	247	36	19	11	46	7.2	13.4	14.5
13 229	...	Pierce	888	13 328	2 111	15.0	11 683	1 569	20	10	46	104	6.7	15.9	15.3
13 231	...	Pike	566	10 224	2 368	18.1	8 122	2 053	11	21	17	54	7.3	15.4	13.9
13 233	...	Polk	806	33 815	1 168	42.0	28 561	4 791	59	87	317	483	7.1	14.6	15.0
13 235	...	Pulaski	641	8 108	2 555	12.6	5 397	2 632	7	16	56	83	6.7	15.6	13.5
13 237	...	Putnam	892	14 137	2 043	15.8	9 300	4 748	21	42	26	97	6.8	14.6	14.1
13 239	...	Quitman	393	2 209	3 055	5.6	1 093	1 107	6	3	0	1	7.3	14.3	14.4
13 241	...	Rabun	961	11 648	2 241	12.1	11 524	41	33	17	33	67	5.8	11.7	13.1
13 243	...	Randolph	1 112	8 023	2 563	7.2	3 310	4 645	4	46	18	39	7.1	17.3	16.4
13 245	0600	Richmond	839	189 719	253	226.1	104 612	79 639	529	3 317	1 622	3 707	8.0	14.8	17.1
13 247	0520	Rockdale	339	54 091	795	159.6	48 915	4 355	114	515	192	594	7.6	16.0	14.5

1. MSA = Metropolitan Statistical Area. CMSA = Consolidated MSA. NECMA = New England county metropolitan area. PMSA = Primary MSA. See Appendix A for explanation of these concepts. See Appendix B for list of metropolitan areas identified by type, with component counties. 2. Dry land or land partially or temporarily covered by water. 3. Hispanic persons may be of any race.

STATE County	Population, 1990 (cont'd) — Age of population (cont'd) Percent — 25 to 34 years	35 to 44 years	45 to 54 years	55 to 64 years	65 to 74 years	75 years and over	Percent female	Population–Change and components of change — Change 1980–1990 — Number	Percent	Components of change, 1980–1986 — Total persons, 1986	Total persons, 1980	Net change — Number	Percent	Natural increase — Births	Deaths
	14	15	16	17	18	19	20	21	22	23	24	25	26	27	28
GEORGIA—Con.															
Floyd	15.4	14.1	10.7	9.8	8.4	6.2	52.4	1 451	1.8	78 700	79 800	-1 100	-1.4	6 900	4 800
Forsyth	18.5	17.0	11.9	8.0	5.5	3.4	49.9	16 125	57.7	37 600	27 958	9 600	34.5	2 900	1 300
Franklin	14.2	13.5	11.6	10.6	9.2	6.4	52.2	1 465	9.6	16 000	15 185	800	5.2	1 300	1 000
Fulton	19.6	16.8	10.3	7.0	5.6	4.4	52.3	59 047	10.0	622 700	589 904	32 800	5.6	61 800	35 200
Gilmer	14.7	14.4	11.8	10.9	8.0	5.6	50.8	2 258	20.3	12 400	11 110	1 300	11.4	1 000	600
Glascock	14.7	13.4	11.5	10.4	9.0	8.8	53.3	-25	-1.0	2 400	2 382	0	-0.3	200	200
Glynn	15.9	14.5	10.9	9.2	8.4	5.5	52.5	7 515	13.7	59 800	54 981	4 900	8.8	5 500	3 300
Gordon	16.7	14.9	11.7	8.5	6.3	4.4	50.8	5 002	16.6	32 900	30 070	2 900	9.5	2 900	1 600
Grady	15.1	13.5	10.2	8.7	7.9	6.6	52.5	434	2.2	21 400	19 845	1 600	7.8	1 900	1 300
Greene	13.7	13.4	10.1	8.7	8.1	6.1	53.4	402	3.5	11 900	11 391	500	4.1	1 400	800
Gwinnett	22.9	19.4	10.2	5.2	3.0	1.7	50.3	186 095	111.6	276 800	166 815	110 000	65.9	23 100	5 500
Habersham	15.1	13.8	10.7	9.8	7.8	5.4	48.9	2 601	10.4	27 300	25 020	2 300	9.0	2 000	1 300
Hall	17.9	15.1	11.0	8.3	6.5	4.3	50.7	19 779	26.1	87 100	75 649	11 500	15.2	7 300	3 800
Hancock	14.5	13.1	9.0	8.5	7.7	6.0	54.6	-558	-5.9	9 400	9 466	0	-0.5	1 000	600
Haralson	15.5	14.0	11.2	9.3	7.6	5.8	52.0	3 544	19.2	20 300	18 422	1 900	10.2	1 700	1 100
Harris	15.1	16.2	11.5	9.9	8.4	4.9	50.7	2 324	15.0	17 400	15 464	2 000	12.8	1 400	1 000
Hart	14.6	13.6	10.8	10.5	9.3	6.6	51.8	1 127	6.1	19 500	18 585	900	5.1	1 400	1 200
Heard	15.8	14.2	11.2	8.1	7.0	5.0	51.2	2 108	32.3	7 200	6 520	700	10.6	600	500
Henry	18.8	16.3	11.4	8.0	5.1	3.3	50.6	22 432	61.8	46 700	36 309	10 400	28.8	4 000	1 800
Houston	19.1	15.3	11.1	8.3	5.3	2.5	50.9	11 603	15.0	86 900	77 605	9 300	12.0	8 400	2 900
Irwin	14.0	12.4	10.6	9.1	8.4	7.2	53.0	-339	-3.8	8 800	8 988	-200	-2.5	900	600
Jackson	16.7	14.7	11.4	8.4	7.0	5.0	50.4	4 662	18.4	28 200	25 343	2 900	11.3	2 400	1 500
Jasper	14.8	15.4	10.0	9.3	7.8	5.9	51.8	900	11.9	7 700	7 553	100	1.4	700	500
Jeff Davis	15.5	14.6	10.7	8.9	6.7	4.4	50.7	559	4.9	11 900	11 473	400	3.8	1 100	700
Jefferson	14.1	13.3	9.0	8.0	8.0	6.6	53.8	-995	-5.4	18 800	18 403	400	2.2	2 000	1 200
Jenkins	14.5	13.3	9.9	9.3	8.6	5.6	53.0	-594	-6.7	8 400	8 841	-500	-5.3	1 000	600
Johnson	14.8	12.0	9.8	9.3	8.6	6.7	53.5	-331	-3.8	8 800	8 660	100	1.6	800	500
Jones	17.3	16.3	11.7	7.7	5.9	3.4	51.4	4 160	25.1	18 800	16 579	2 200	13.3	1 700	700
Lamar	15.0	14.3	10.8	9.2	7.8	5.6	52.7	823	6.7	12 400	12 215	200	1.5	1 100	800
Lanier	15.8	13.6	10.5	8.5	6.4	5.4	51.4	-123	-2.2	5 700	5 654	100	1.4	600	300
Laurens	15.3	14.1	10.0	8.9	8.3	5.6	52.1	2 998	8.1	38 300	36 990	1 300	3.5	3 800	2 500
Lee	18.7	18.1	9.1	5.9	4.2	2.3	49.2	4 566	39.1	14 500	11 684	2 800	23.7	1 400	500
Liberty	23.4	11.2	5.2	3.2	2.3	1.4	44.6	15 162	40.3	42 300	37 583	4 700	12.5	8 200	1 000
Lincoln	14.4	13.9	10.8	10.3	8.9	5.3	51.7	726	10.8	7 100	6 716	400	6.1	600	400
Long	16.7	13.1	8.9	6.7	5.5	3.0	49.7	1 678	37.1	5 600	4 524	1 100	23.9	800	300
Lowndes	17.7	14.0	9.0	6.9	5.6	3.9	51.0	8 009	11.8	73 700	67 972	5 700	8.4	7 800	3 400
Lumpkin	17.1	13.6	10.2	8.2	5.9	4.3	50.4	3 811	35.4	12 300	10 762	1 600	14.5	900	500
McDuffie	15.5	15.0	10.1	8.5	7.2	4.7	52.8	1 573	8.5	20 300	18 546	1 700	9.2	2 000	1 100
McIntosh	15.6	13.8	10.6	9.6	7.6	5.2	51.6	588	7.3	8 200	8 046	100	1.5	800	500
Macon	14.5	13.7	9.3	7.5	7.4	6.4	53.5	-889	-6.3	14 100	14 003	100	0.9	1 500	900
Madison	17.0	15.5	11.4	8.3	6.3	4.7	51.1	3 303	18.6	19 600	17 747	1 800	10.2	1 700	900
Marion	16.3	14.2	10.7	7.5	7.6	5.3	52.0	293	5.5	5 500	5 297	200	3.1	500	300
Meriwether	14.9	13.3	10.1	8.5	7.8	5.7	52.2	1 182	5.6	20 700	21 229	-500	-2.3	2 100	1 400
Miller	13.4	12.2	11.6	9.3	8.9	7.8	52.6	-758	-10.8	6 900	7 038	-100	-1.9	700	400
Mitchell	14.3	12.8	9.9	8.1	7.3	5.8	53.1	-839	-4.0	21 600	21 114	500	2.3	2 500	1 300
Monroe	16.1	15.9	11.0	8.5	6.4	4.9	51.0	2 503	17.1	15 900	14 610	1 300	8.6	1 300	800
Montgomery	16.5	13.7	9.6	8.1	6.8	5.5	50.7	152	2.2	7 100	7 011	100	1.1	600	400
Morgan	16.2	14.3	10.7	8.3	7.4	5.8	51.8	1 311	11.3	12 500	11 572	900	7.9	1 200	700
Murray	18.6	14.9	11.1	7.6	4.9	3.3	50.5	6 462	32.8	22 500	19 685	2 800	14.1	1 900	900
Muscogee	18.1	13.9	9.1	8.6	6.5	4.3	51.4	9 170	5.4	181 000	170 108	10 900	6.4	19 700	9 500
Newton	16.5	14.3	10.8	8.1	6.1	4.5	52.1	7 319	21.2	40 300	34 489	5 800	16.8	3 800	1 900
Oconee	16.9	18.1	11.2	6.9	5.1	4.1	51.3	5 191	41.8	14 900	12 427	2 400	19.7	1 300	500
Oglethorpe	16.5	15.0	11.4	9.0	6.8	5.3	51.8	834	9.3	9 600	8 929	600	7.1	800	500
Paulding	21.1	15.4	9.7	6.7	4.4	2.9	50.1	15 501	59.4	32 500	26 110	6 400	24.6	2 900	1 300
Peach	15.4	13.6	10.3	8.3	6.0	4.0	52.4	2 038	10.6	20 000	19 151	800	4.3	2 000	1 100
Pickens	15.8	14.4	11.5	9.8	8.1	5.4	51.1	2 780	23.9	13 600	11 652	1 900	16.4	1 100	800
Pierce	14.7	15.2	11.4	9.1	7.0	4.7	51.5	1 431	12.0	13 000	11 897	1 100	9.2	1 100	700
Pike	15.7	14.4	11.8	9.0	7.1	5.3	50.6	1 287	14.4	8 900	8 937	0	-0.4	800	500
Polk	15.2	13.6	11.0	9.4	8.0	6.1	52.0	1 433	4.4	33 900	32 382	1 500	4.6	3 100	2 200
Pulaski	13.9	13.5	11.3	10.0	8.7	6.9	53.2	-842	-9.4	8 800	8 950	-200	-2.0	800	700
Putnam	15.8	13.9	11.6	10.8	7.8	4.5	51.0	3 842	37.3	12 100	10 295	1 800	17.4	1 200	600
Quitman	13.0	12.0	10.4	11.2	11.2	6.3	53.6	-148	-6.3	2 200	2 357	-100	-5.0	200	200
Rabun	13.1	14.5	11.9	11.8	10.6	7.6	51.7	1 182	11.3	11 000	10 466	500	5.1	800	700
Randolph	12.9	12.2	8.3	8.6	9.5	7.8	54.5	-1 576	-16.4	9 100	9 599	-500	-4.8	1 000	700
Richmond	18.4	14.4	9.3	8.0	6.1	3.9	51.5	8 090	4.5	194 800	181 629	13 200	7.2	21 000	9 500
Rockdale	17.2	17.1	12.0	7.6	5.0	3.0	50.7	17 344	47.2	47 200	36 747	10 400	28.3	3 600	1 500

STATE County	Population–(cont'd): Components of change, 1980-1986 (cont'd): Net migration	Households, 1990: Number	Households, 1990: Percent change, 1980–1990	Households, 1990: Persons per household	Households, 1990: Percent: Female family householder[1]	Households, 1990: Percent: One-person	Births, 1988: Total	Births, 1988: Rate[2]	Births, 1988: Low birth weight[3] (Number)	Deaths, 1987: Number: Total	Deaths, 1987: Number: Infant[4]	Deaths, 1987: Rate: Total[2]	Deaths, 1987: Rate: Infant[5]	Marriages, 1984: Number	Marriages, 1984: Rate[2]
	29	30	31	32	33	34	35	36	37	38	39	40	41	42	43
GEORGIA—Con.															
Floyd	-3 200	30 518	7.2	2.55	12.6	23.6	1 235	15.3	99	829	22	10.3	18.8	854	10.9
Forsyth	8 100	15 938	69.6	2.75	7.0	16.3	652	15.3	44	252	2	6.3	3.2	379	11.4
Franklin	400	6 365	18.7	2.56	9.9	23.3	244	14.8	20	182	3	11.1	13.9	104	6.8
Fulton	6 200	257 140	14.1	2.44	18.5	31.0	11 625	18.1	1 176	5 967	160	9.4	14.2	6 853	11.2
Gilmer	900	5 072	28.8	2.60	9.0	20.4	193	14.7	18	123	6	9.6	34.5	142	11.9
Glascock	0	867	3.7	2.59	9.7	22.6	27	12.3	5	28	0	12.2	0.0	17	7.1
Glynn	2 700	23 947	20.8	2.57	14.0	23.6	931	15.4	75	527	11	8.9	11.5	794	13.7
Gordon	1 600	12 778	24.3	2.72	10.3	19.8	555	16.2	45	279	8	8.3	14.7	320	9.9
Grady	900	7 354	11.1	2.72	15.2	22.3	293	13.8	30	224	8	10.5	27.9	191	9.2
Greene	-100	4 083	8.7	2.86	19.4	23.9	166	13.7	12	140	2	11.9	9.4	92	7.7
Gwinnett	92 400	126 971	129.9	2.77	8.3	17.7	6 124	18.9	345	1 153	53	3.8	9.3	2 595	11.3
Habersham	1 600	9 966	18.7	2.59	8.5	21.2	382	13.5	24	239	3	8.6	8.7	200	7.5
Hall	8 000	34 721	33.2	2.70	11.1	20.0	1 554	17.3	102	733	16	8.3	11.1	842	10.3
Hancock	-400	2 969	6.4	2.95	26.5	24.4	149	16.0	19	114	4	12.1	25.2	72	7.7
Haralson	1 300	8 248	26.8	2.63	10.9	22.2	311	15.0	23	192	4	9.3	12.7	282	14.4
Harris	1 600	6 454	23.3	2.73	11.1	19.1	234	13.2	14	150	3	8.7	13.1	139	8.5
Hart	700	7 459	18.7	2.60	12.1	22.0	232	11.7	14	187	0	9.5	0.0	162	8.4
Heard	600	3 093	40.3	2.75	11.8	19.8	107	13.9	10	83	3	11.1	28.3	79	11.8
Henry	8 200	20 012	72.1	2.91	8.9	13.2	883	16.4	55	366	8	7.3	9.2	437	10.4
Houston	3 800	32 433	27.1	2.71	12.3	20.6	1 433	16.1	110	504	15	5.8	11.0	1 010	12.0
Irwin	-500	3 142	4.3	2.71	15.6	23.9	103	11.4	12	95	1	10.6	7.4	91	10.3
Jackson	2 000	10 721	24.4	2.73	10.2	19.5	444	14.8	38	228	4	7.8	8.5	282	10.5
Jasper	-200	3 036	18.9	2.76	14.1	21.2	115	14.2	8	92	0	11.5	0.0	54	7.0
Jeff Davis	0	4 357	15.5	2.74	13.6	20.0	172	14.2	16	95	2	8.0	11.8	124	10.6
Jefferson	-400	6 093	2.5	2.79	22.2	24.6	302	16.3	31	219	6	11.7	20.7	116	6.3
Jenkins	-800	2 951	1.5	2.75	17.8	23.4	143	16.8	13	106	1	12.5	7.1	91	10.8
Johnson	-100	3 010	1.9	2.71	17.1	24.8	109	12.5	7	89	1	10.3	8.1	94	10.8
Jones	1 300	7 300	38.5	2.81	12.8	18.4	276	14.3	19	134	7	7.0	25.1	163	9.0
Lamar	-100	4 669	16.4	2.73	15.1	21.4	200	15.3	20	141	2	10.8	10.3	102	8.4
Lanier	-200	1 965	7.8	2.78	15.1	21.3	101	17.4	12	66	2	11.2	21.1	50	8.8
Laurens	0	14 514	16.6	2.68	15.8	23.2	631	16.1	71	423	16	10.8	26.2	366	9.6
Lee	1 800	5 199	42.8	3.00	13.2	15.0	255	16.5	21	71	4	4.6	16.2	115	8.4
Liberty	-2 500	15 136	57.2	2.99	12.1	14.8	1 455	34.6	106	169	16	4.1	10.7	642	15.2
Lincoln	200	2 702	23.7	2.74	14.1	21.9	104	14.4	14	87	1	12.1	10.3	40	5.9
Long	500	2 196	43.0	2.79	9.9	20.4	111	21.3	8	45	0	9.0	0.0	77	14.0
Lowndes	1 300	26 311	16.4	2.72	15.2	21.8	1 291	17.7	114	607	14	8.3	11.4	1 348	18.6
Lumpkin	1 200	4 976	46.9	2.68	8.8	19.3	174	13.4	6	95	4	7.5	19.1	107	9.1
McDuffie	800	7 270	15.9	2.73	17.7	21.4	308	15.2	30	199	2	9.9	6.7	182	9.4
McIntosh	-200	3 186	21.1	2.71	16.9	22.9	130	14.0	13	73	1	7.8	7.6	88	11.1
Macon	-500	4 388	0.4	2.92	23.8	22.6	221	16.0	21	164	4	12.0	18.2	111	7.9
Madison	1 000	7 740	26.4	2.70	9.7	18.9	263	12.6	23	161	4	7.9	13.3	154	8.2
Marion	0	1 962	16.3	2.81	16.2	20.0	90	17.0	11	62	1	11.7	11.9	37	7.0
Meriwether	-1 200	7 637	11.1	2.87	17.8	22.1	348	16.0	38	207	5	9.6	14.9	145	7.0
Miller	-400	2 336	-2.9	2.65	13.7	23.7	96	13.7	4	60	1	8.6	9.2	49	7.1
Mitchell	-700	6 798	4.8	2.94	21.4	20.8	389	18.1	43	198	2	9.1	5.6	179	8.3
Monroe	800	5 838	25.1	2.83	13.7	19.4	240	15.2	19	153	3	9.9	12.3	144	9.6
Montgomery	-100	2 493	12.6	2.69	13.0	24.0	81	11.2	7	79	0	10.8	0.0	75	10.7
Morgan	300	4 399	20.1	2.89	15.5	19.4	228	17.5	21	102	1	8.0	4.9	112	9.2
Murray	1 700	9 363	43.2	2.77	9.5	17.4	391	16.1	14	166	5	7.1	13.7	238	11.2
Muscogee	700	65 858	11.4	2.61	17.9	24.5	3 485	19.5	320	1 656	56	9.3	16.2	2 475	14.0
Newton	3 800	14 401	31.2	2.85	13.3	18.3	778	18.0	53	352	8	8.4	11.0	463	12.2
Oconee	1 600	6 156	45.3	2.84	9.0	16.0	266	16.8	18	99	0	6.5	0.0	113	7.9
Oglethorpe	300	3 581	21.5	2.70	12.5	20.6	149	15.4	8	100	0	10.3	0.0	80	8.5
Paulding	4 800	14 326	63.8	2.88	8.5	13.7	691	19.0	53	258	6	7.5	9.4	292	10.0
Peach	-100	7 142	15.6	2.79	19.4	20.0	322	15.6	33	200	4	10.0	13.3	180	9.3
Pickens	1 600	5 386	29.4	2.65	8.4	19.5	213	14.8	7	134	3	9.6	13.0	126	9.7
Pierce	700	4 807	22.4	2.76	10.5	20.4	175	13.2	21	149	2	11.4	10.6	163	13.0
Pike	-300	3 526	24.1	2.86	9.0	18.3	161	17.1	16	104	1	11.4	7.6	71	8.2
Polk	600	12 519	9.7	2.67	13.0	22.6	515	15.1	47	385	6	11.4	11.5	438	13.2
Pulaski	-300	3 098	1.0	2.58	16.3	27.2	98	11.4	8	131	1	14.9	9.3	87	9.7
Putnam	1 300	5 229	53.9	2.65	13.4	21.4	181	14.1	12	118	1	9.4	5.8	105	9.3
Quitman	-200	857	11.0	2.57	19.5	25.0	43	18.7	4	21	1	9.5	35.7	19	8.6
Rabun	400	4 630	19.0	2.48	8.9	22.4	113	10.1	9	127	1	11.5	7.6	101	9.4
Randolph	-800	2 815	-9.9	2.73	21.1	27.5	123	13.7	10	127	4	14.0	35.1	69	7.4
Richmond	1 700	68 675	15.4	2.61	18.0	26.1	3 582	18.7	354	1 689	49	8.8	14.1	1 462	7.8
Rockdale	8 300	18 337	58.2	2.92	9.9	14.4	799	15.4	66	282	7	5.7	9.6	522	12.3

1. No spouse present. 2. Per 1,000 resident population estimated as of July 1 of the year shown. 3. Under 2,500 grams. 4. Deaths of infants under 1 year old. 5. Deaths of infants under 1 year old per 1,000 live births.

STATE County	Divorces, 1984 Number	Divorces, 1984 Rate[1]	Physicians, active non-Federal, 1989 Number[2]	Physicians Rate[3]	Hospitals, 1989 Number	Hospitals Beds Number	Hospitals Beds Rate[3]	Nursing homes,[4] 1986 Number	Nursing homes Beds	Serious crimes known to police, 1988 Number Total[5]	Serious crimes Number Violent[6]	Serious crimes Rate[3]	Education Public school enrollment[7] 1986–1987	Public school enrollment 1980	Attainment,[8] 1980 Percent 12 yrs. or more	Attainment, 1980 Percent 16 yrs. or more
	44	45	46	47	48	49	50	51	52	53	54	55	56	57	58	59
GEORGIA—Con.																
Floyd	557	7.1	201	248	3	907	1 121	7	571	3 736	258	4 637	13 719	15 149	48.8	11.8
Forsyth	173	5.2	18	40	1	36	80	2	203	1 601	59	3 901	6 650	6 236	50.8	8.7
Franklin	78	5.1	14	84	1	222	1 329	1	144	298	43	1 822	2 904	3 058	37.9	7.9
Fulton	1 916	3.1	3 204	497	28	6 223	965	53	3 225	94 224	16 269	14 334	105 528	103 064	66.0	23.0
Gilmer	74	6.2	6	44	1	134	993	2	58	192	9	1 447	2 329	2 151	37.5	6.6
Glascock	8	3.3	0	0	0	0	0	2	114	NA	NA	NA	426	470	31.8	4.8
Glynn	443	7.6	120	197	2	429	706	5	376	5 608	778	9 132	10 061	10 488	61.9	14.9
Gordon	140	4.3	26	75	1	65	188	3	221	1 229	50	3 642	6 602	6 627	42.1	6.8
Grady	97	4.7	13	61	1	45	212	2	112	483	67	2 105	4 045	4 510	40.7	7.0
Greene	42	3.5	8	67	1	29	242	3	79	246	20	2 435	2 289	2 375	34.9	6.3
Gwinnett	1 329	5.8	258	74	2	426	122	5	525	16 051	745	5 367	53 730	36 821	71.7	18.9
Habersham	145	5.5	15	53	1	143	502	3	211	169	11	589	4 478	4 816	43.5	9.3
Hall	462	5.6	152	166	2	462	505	8	415	5 203	327	5 794	15 477	15 243	48.1	12.2
Hancock	0	0.0	2	22	1	42	462	2	152	23	3	240	1 967	2 493	33.6	6.4
Haralson	105	5.4	13	62	1	59	281	3	242	558	75	3 353	4 005	4 095	42.0	6.9
Harris	55	3.4	6	34	0	0	0	1	100	578	41	3 305	2 708	3 139	49.7	11.8
Hart	105	5.5	7	35	1	98	490	2	209	397	62	1 959	3 583	4 057	38.1	7.7
Heard	47	7.0	1	13	1	198	2 506	2	88	90	1	1 167	1 488	1 381	35.5	4.4
Henry	219	5.2	17	30	1	106	185	3	202	1 793	96	3 716	8 368	7 043	54.4	9.4
Houston	589	7.0	84	94	3	249	278	8	447	5 107	547	5 700	14 697	17 425	68.8	13.2
Irwin	37	4.2	3	33	1	64	703	2	113	314	50	3 469	1 696	1 994	39.5	5.7
Jackson	154	5.7	12	39	1	138	450	2	122	791	95	2 666	5 392	5 412	40.7	8.0
Jasper	26	3.4	2	24	1	72	878	1	44	76	9	935	1 396	1 285	41.4	9.2
Jeff Davis	90	7.7	6	49	1	56	459	1	73	244	13	1 977	2 537	2 638	40.5	7.4
Jefferson	67	3.6	10	55	1	37	202	2	213	290	47	1 508	3 659	3 969	36.4	6.8
Jenkins	46	5.5	5	59	1	38	447	4	109	206	22	2 328	1 786	1 891	35.2	7.0
Johnson	8	0.9	2	23	0	0	0	2	153	63	21	772	1 603	1 861	35.0	6.2
Jones	71	3.9	4	21	0	0	0	2	162	301	25	1 532	3 559	3 472	54.2	10.6
Lamar	60	4.9	6	45	0	0	0	1	117	375	72	2 804	2 202	2 561	45.7	8.0
Lanier	0	0.0	2	35	1	40	702	2	71	204	37	3 361	1 140	1 395	39.4	5.3
Laurens	95	2.5	56	142	3	718	1 827	10	619	1 878	238	4 693	7 936	7 821	45.7	9.8
Lee	80	5.8	2	13	0	0	0	0	0	287	26	1 812	3 504	2 755	54.1	9.3
Liberty	299	7.1	23	55	2	142	339	1	169	1 642	151	3 981	6 891	6 710	69.4	12.3
Lincoln	15	2.2	3	41	0	0	0	3	35	144	7	1 944	1 413	1 505	41.1	7.3
Long	26	4.7	0	0	0	0	0	0	0	81	2	1 544	1 025	941	46.1	6.3
Lowndes	387	5.3	114	157	4	449	618	3	248	5 108	379	6 756	13 842	13 983	57.1	13.2
Lumpkin	76	6.5	10	75	1	46	346	1	102	263	19	2 029	2 138	2 114	43.2	9.8
McDuffie	117	6.1	16	79	1	41	203	4	171	179	8	2 371	3 960	3 974	41.9	8.2
McIntosh	46	5.8	1	10	0	0	0	0	0	171	12	1 787	1 789	2 005	41.4	6.0
Macon	39	2.8	5	37	1	50	370	3	248	404	59	2 888	2 686	3 144	35.2	8.0
Madison	79	4.2	5	23	0	0	0	1	100	282	9	1 375	3 694	3 859	42.6	7.5
Marion	14	2.6	3	58	1	80	1 538	1	50	26	6	477	1 097	1 329	36.0	6.1
Meriwether	95	4.6	8	37	2	173	790	2	171	103	8	1 535	4 283	4 636	39.4	7.1
Miller	42	6.1	4	56	1	121	1 704	1	83	42	5	583	1 253	1 578	41.6	7.1
Mitchell	107	5.0	7	33	1	52	243	2	144	695	84	3 128	4 517	4 952	39.4	7.5
Monroe	46	3.1	6	38	1	40	255	4	300	704	87	4 387	2 746	2 717	45.5	9.4
Montgomery	48	6.9	2	28	0	0	0	0	0	41	4	546	1 249	1 497	41.9	7.1
Morgan	58	4.8	7	53	1	26	198	1	67	349	26	2 889	2 419	2 622	41.1	9.6
Murray	165	7.8	8	32	1	42	168	1	120	665	18	2 775	4 854	4 489	36.2	5.1
Muscogee	1 329	7.5	332	187	6	1 357	765	13	1 155	11 464	890	6 289	29 555	33 352	60.9	12.9
Newton	239	6.3	27	61	1	90	202	5	215	2 120	182	5 140	7 799	7 715	45.1	8.6
Oconee	65	4.5	12	75	0	0	0	1	100	118	8	770	2 924	2 556	60.1	21.2
Oglethorpe	32	3.4	2	21	0	0	0	2	17	208	14	2 106	1 739	1 851	42.6	9.5
Paulding	165	5.6	8	21	1	181	473	1	136	1 020	66	2 908	6 650	5 934	41.7	4.3
Peach	39	2.0	21	100	1	75	357	1	75	312	35	2 698	3 765	4 241	51.0	14.4
Pickens	78	6.0	9	61	1	91	619	3	149	98	2	718	2 429	2 319	37.9	6.9
Pierce	78	6.2	4	30	1	65	485	1	29	280	25	2 078	2 773	2 559	46.5	6.9
Pike	0	0.0	2	21	0	0	0	1	50	143	6	1 575	1 826	1 837	46.9	8.7
Polk	216	6.5	16	47	2	79	231	4	295	809	67	2 313	6 407	6 758	39.7	5.7
Pulaski	22	2.4	8	94	1	55	647	1	102	188	22	2 101	1 578	1 970	45.8	8.6
Putnam	0	0.0	7	53	1	50	379	1	92	253	16	2 033	1 957	1 884	46.3	9.2
Quitman	3	1.4	0	0	0	0	0	0	0	NA	NA	NA	343	534	35.8	6.6
Rabun	49	4.6	10	89	3	97	866	2	132	233	18	2 078	1 868	2 106	46.3	11.4
Randolph	18	1.9	3	34	1	120	1 348	1	80	156	24	1 685	1 564	1 693	35.6	6.7
Richmond	1 419	7.5	1 023	538	9	3 636	1 913	33	1 244	14 065	1 393	7 092	32 264	32 190	61.4	14.8
Rockdale	127	3.0	44	81	1	100	184	2	179	2 872	219	5 640	9 758	8 706	63.4	12.6

1. Per 1,000 resident population estimated as of July 1 of the year shown. 2. As of end of year. 3. Per 100,000 resident population as of July 1 of the year shown. 4. Preliminary. Covers nursing homes with 3 or more beds. 5. Data for serious crimes have not been adjusted for underreporting, this may affect comparability between geographic areas or over time. 6. Includes murder and nonnegligent manslaughter, forcible rape, robbery, and aggravated assault. 7. The 1986–1987 data are based on administrative reports obtained by the U.S. National Center for Education Statistics. The 1980 data are based on the 1980 Census of Population and Housing. 8. Persons 25 years old or older.

STATE County	Education (cont'd) — Local government expenditures for education,[1] 1982 — Total (Mil dol)	Education (cont'd) — Local government expenditures for education,[1] 1982 — Per capita (Dollars)	Social Security Program December 1988 — Beneficiaries — Total	Social Security Program December 1988 — Beneficiaries — Rate[2]	Social Security Program December 1988 — Payments ($1,000)	Supplemental Security Income Program recipients June 1986	Money income — Per capita[3] — 1987 Income, (Dollars)	Money income — Per capita[3] — 1979 — Current dollars	Money income — Per capita[3] — 1979 — Constant 1987 dollars	Money income — Median household income 1979 (Dollars)	Money income — Percent below poverty level, 1979 — Persons	Money income — Percent below poverty level, 1979 — Families	Housing units, 1990 — Total	Housing units, 1990 — Percent change, 1980–1990
	60	61	62	63	64	65	66	67	68	69	70	71	72	73
GEORGIA—Con.														
Floyd	32.0	403	15 260	189.1	7 110	2 158	10 578	6 218	9 729	14 674	12.3	10.1	32 821	8.5
Forsyth	12.7	416	3 860	90.8	1 711	514	12 646	6 656	10 415	16 845	10.7	9.7	17 869	62.9
Franklin	5.0	329	3 650	221.2	1 471	748	8 605	4 963	7 766	11 716	19.8	16.5	7 613	23.0
Fulton	292.4	489	82 075	128.1	38 891	15 712	14 048	7 611	11 909	13 988	21.2	17.5	297 503	20.7
Gilmer	3.7	328	2 455	187.4	989	506	8 936	4 932	7 717	11 205	20.4	16.8	6 986	57.9
Glascock	1.0	430	520	236.4	203	152	9 155	5 390	8 434	11 567	20.7	16.9	1 036	13.8
Glynn	23.1	408	10 650	175.7	5 111	1 272	11 821	6 840	10 703	15 109	16.1	12.6	27 724	24.0
Gordon	12.3	399	5 215	152.5	2 224	688	9 953	5 571	8 717	14 078	12.9	10.7	13 777	26.0
Grady	6.8	338	3 610	169.5	1 368	854	7 781	4 418	6 913	10 654	25.8	22.3	8 129	14.1
Greene	6.9	601	2 245	185.5	904	572	7 748	4 308	6 741	10 813	26.6	20.6	4 699	13.3
Gwinnett	79.8	418	18 380	56.8	8 981	1 394	14 375	8 168	12 780	22 572	5.6	4.5	137 608	136.7
Habersham	7.9	300	4 660	165.2	1 978	794	9 465	5 371	8 404	12 701	14.7	12.9	11 076	24.0
Hall	28.2	360	13 605	151.2	6 043	1 764	11 564	6 469	10 122	15 838	10.9	8.7	38 315	37.1
Hancock	4.1	434	1 635	175.8	577	622	6 583	3 776	5 908	9 811	39.3	32.2	3 396	7.4
Haralson	6.8	358	3 760	180.8	1 645	582	8 897	5 426	8 490	12 956	15.2	11.6	9 016	29.0
Harris	4.8	308	2 580	145.8	1 064	482	11 127	6 206	9 711	15 253	17.2	14.1	7 814	29.1
Hart	6.1	319	3 180	159.8	1 373	722	9 177	5 056	7 911	12 201	16.6	12.8	8 942	18.8
Heard	3.5	527	1 155	150.0	464	238	8 675	5 223	8 172	12 738	16.8	12.0	3 536	43.8
Henry	14.0	360	6 130	113.5	2 822	648	12 139	6 857	10 729	18 893	10.5	8.2	21 275	73.3
Houston	26.7	327	8 525	96.0	3 163	1 338	11 151	6 703	10 488	18 598	11.2	8.8	34 785	26.8
Irwin	3.2	368	1 515	168.3	553	450	8 238	4 814	7 532	10 675	24.7	19.4	3 479	4.1
Jackson	8.2	312	5 130	171.0	2 143	962	9 454	5 401	8 451	13 479	14.1	11.3	11 775	29.3
Jasper	2.7	357	1 230	151.9	510	266	9 373	5 277	8 257	12 789	20.4	16.2	3 637	18.0
Jeff Davis	4.5	388	2 030	167.8	780	446	8 850	5 092	7 967	13 137	17.1	14.2	4 792	18.4
Jefferson	6.7	363	3 440	185.9	1 270	1 264	6 911	4 183	6 545	9 638	30.4	25.0	7 065	8.4
Jenkins	3.6	425	1 655	194.7	604	572	7 249	4 112	6 434	9 115	33.8	26.6	3 365	0.6
Johnson	2.7	310	1 550	178.2	578	502	7 893	4 548	7 116	10 574	26.1	21.5	3 389	1.9
Jones	5.9	337	1 720	89.1	702	364	10 442	5 833	9 127	16 553	14.9	11.7	7 722	32.4
Lamar	4.2	343	2 290	174.8	977	392	9 001	5 258	8 227	13 543	16.3	12.5	5 066	16.9
Lanier	2.2	399	820	141.4	293	300	7 166	4 078	6 381	10 313	28.4	23.8	2 202	8.2
Laurens	15.4	409	6 950	177.3	2 686	1 858	9 167	5 337	8 351	12 378	20.1	15.6	16 504	22.4
Lee	5.3	421	1 360	87.7	553	266	9 673	5 856	9 163	17 759	16.7	13.4	5 537	42.8
Liberty	9.8	234	2 490	59.1	928	626	8 145	4 910	7 683	11 675	20.9	17.5	16 776	55.3
Lincoln	2.5	380	1 430	198.6	566	306	9 038	5 352	8 374	13 301	18.3	13.9	3 870	25.3
Long	1.6	320	515	99.0	181	166	7 294	4 513	7 061	10 881	24.5	19.3	2 638	52.1
Lowndes	24.2	349	10 315	141.3	4 344	2 178	9 383	5 609	8 776	12 760	19.2	15.3	28 906	18.8
Lumpkin	3.4	302	1 630	125.4	656	382	9 716	5 384	8 424	12 140	16.6	13.2	5 729	49.4
McDuffie	6.7	354	3 095	153.2	1 248	846	8 265	5 166	8 083	12 328	20.5	16.7	8 043	16.6
McIntosh	3.2	399	1 575	169.4	621	406	7 119	4 260	6 666	10 273	31.4	25.8	4 276	17.4
Macon	5.7	402	2 135	154.7	794	832	7 230	4 306	6 738	10 223	32.5	27.2	4 848	3.7
Madison	6.3	341	3 225	154.3	1 284	630	8 883	5 266	8 240	12 790	16.1	12.8	8 428	30.1
Marion	1.9	353	775	146.2	273	326	7 130	3 933	6 154	10 600	29.8	26.2	2 152	16.9
Meriwether	7.3	344	3 665	168.9	1 459	908	8 040	4 907	7 678	12 204	20.9	17.5	8 409	10.6
Miller	3.1	444	1 235	176.4	453	312	7 965	4 557	7 130	10 729	27.3	23.5	2 602	1.6
Mitchell	9.1	423	3 585	166.7	1 349	1 096	7 542	4 612	7 216	11 692	29.5	23.4	7 443	5.6
Monroe	5.8	389	2 245	142.1	930	438	9 497	5 388	8 431	14 067	15.9	12.6	6 401	28.1
Montgomery	2.2	314	1 200	166.7	432	414	8 046	4 381	6 855	10 156	23.5	16.9	2 885	13.6
Morgan	4.5	372	2 055	158.1	852	476	8 898	4 886	7 645	12 976	21.7	15.2	4 814	22.9
Murray	7.1	348	2 890	118.9	1 185	478	9 353	5 580	8 731	14 761	14.1	11.2	10 207	47.0
Muscogee	68.4	391	25 540	143.1	11 212	4 178	10 355	6 044	9 457	13 343	18.0	14.5	70 902	11.1
Newton	13.1	359	6 270	144.8	2 796	940	9 944	5 659	8 855	15 516	14.2	10.7	15 494	28.6
Oconee	4.6	348	1 855	117.4	805	230	11 988	6 708	10 496	17 236	10.1	6.8	6 561	45.8
Oglethorpe	3.5	382	1 190	122.7	473	310	8 933	5 046	7 895	12 937	18.8	14.7	3 936	25.0
Paulding	9.5	340	3 560	97.8	1 559	528	10 306	5 650	8 841	15 427	12.4	10.7	15 237	66.2
Peach	6.0	318	3 065	148.1	1 180	702	9 366	5 337	8 351	12 859	26.2	21.6	7 537	13.5
Pickens	4.0	329	2 510	174.3	1 082	402	10 208	5 474	8 565	12 515	17.1	13.4	6 403	32.5
Pierce	6.1	495	2 355	177.1	896	512	7 736	4 485	7 018	11 682	22.8	19.7	5 271	22.7
Pike	3.2	368	1 680	178.7	707	316	10 333	5 629	8 808	15 308	14.8	10.9	3 797	22.6
Polk	11.8	360	6 805	199.0	2 951	1 236	8 899	5 327	8 335	12 997	16.0	12.5	13 585	12.6
Pulaski	3.1	347	1 660	193.0	625	466	8 978	5 063	7 922	12 125	25.1	20.5	3 470	1.9
Putnam	4.2	389	2 035	159.0	875	386	9 661	5 421	8 482	13 874	20.1	16.5	7 113	35.3
Quitman	0.7	299	540	234.8	201	164	6 589	3 436	5 376	8 314	40.7	32.1	1 346	38.1
Rabun	3.9	357	2 460	219.6	1 028	504	9 033	5 469	8 557	11 536	17.1	14.0	7 883	27.9
Randolph	3.3	348	1 695	188.3	646	586	8 332	4 669	7 306	8 975	33.7	28.4	3 225	-9.4
Richmond	76.3	417	26 165	136.7	11 294	5 466	10 424	5 873	9 189	13 635	18.3	14.4	77 288	19.2
Rockdale	17.0	422	4 945	95.3	2 380	470	12 474	7 136	11 166	20 845	8.2	6.8	19 963	64.1

1. Elementary and secondary. 2. Per 1,000 resident population estimated as of July 1 of the year shown. 3. Based on the resident population estimated as of July 1, 1988 for 1987 data and enumerated as of April 1, 1980 for 1979 data.

STATE County	Housing units, 1990 (cont'd) — Occupied units — Total	Owner occupied — Percent	Owner occupied — Median value (Dollars)	Median rent (Dollars)	Civilian labor force, 1990 — Total	Percent change, 1989–1990	Unemployment — Total	Unemployment — Rate[1]	Private nonfarm establishments, 1988 — Number	Net change, 1987–1988	Employment[2] — Total	Percent change, 1987–1988	Manu-facturing	Retail trade
	74	75	76	77	78	79	80	81	82	83	84	85	86	87
GEORGIA—Con.														
Floyd	30 518	66.1	50 100	228	40 276	0.0	2 859	7.1	1 817	25	29 313	1.7	11 347	6 090
Forsyth	15 938	81.9	96 200	397	22 525	1.1	1 072	4.8	809	37	8 144	4.8	2 579	1 957
Franklin	6 365	78.0	49 500	163	9 781	5.5	623	6.4	385	9	4 128	10.0	1 256	1 051
Fulton	257 140	49.5	97 700	396	331 747	0.5	19 607	5.9	23 568	500	498 210	2.3	59 717	83 198
Gilmer	5 072	80.4	56 800	197	6 597	1.5	449	6.8	270	1	3 579	-8.2	1 779	659
Glascock	867	77.9	30 700	111	1 145	0.9	63	5.5	29	0	385	-4.7	0	32
Glynn	23 947	65.1	67 200	295	31 068	-1.5	1 531	4.9	1 973	30	24 935	4.9	4 844	7 569
Gordon	12 778	72.1	53 100	260	22 388	0.8	1 394	6.2	905	21	18 898	8.9	11 451	2 207
Grady	7 354	73.0	41 400	166	10 077	-3.0	508	5.0	351	4	3 881	-6.7	1 704	896
Greene	4 083	77.2	38 800	152	5 557	-1.5	348	6.3	227	2	3 129	-2.0	1 883	510
Gwinnett	126 971	68.4	95 900	483	188 852	1.1	8 115	4.3	8 807	585	124 715	7.9	25 081	28 778
Habersham	9 966	76.7	57 800	219	13 633	1.8	583	4.3	590	21	9 187	5.0	4 972	1 692
Hall	34 721	69.4	75 400	340	48 028	-1.1	2 676	5.6	2 456	49	36 655	7.4	13 077	7 556
Hancock	2 969	77.1	29 200	108	3 988	4.2	243	6.1	88	-1	881	-8.6	320	156
Haralson	8 248	76.2	47 100	212	8 497	-0.1	664	7.8	394	12	6 214	-14.8	3 376	1 006
Harris	6 454	82.4	64 500	191	9 196	-4.5	411	4.5	227	20	2 481	-2.1	847	364
Hart	7 459	79.3	51 700	173	11 005	-1.8	625	5.7	322	2	6 138	5.4	4 064	697
Heard	3 093	78.9	43 900	179	3 284	1.9	198	6.0	83	-1	1 185	11.5	627	121
Henry	20 012	83.4	81 200	408	28 283	0.9	1 427	5.0	783	61	9 326	22.7	2 551	2 519
Houston	32 433	65.1	62 100	315	40 386	1.4	1 756	4.3	1 637	47	16 905	3.3	2 451	6 601
Irwin	3 142	73.3	40 900	125	3 411	-3.5	231	6.8	154	13	2 055	66.3	1 095	226
Jackson	10 721	75.1	55 300	230	16 044	0.1	899	5.6	491	3	6 160	6.9	2 736	1 485
Jasper	3 036	76.5	51 100	170	2 742	2.7	209	7.6	105	-4	1 365	0.1	874	195
Jeff Davis	4 357	73.1	39 200	164	6 286	4.4	393	6.3	276	1	4 186	-2.4	2 435	581
Jefferson	6 093	69.1	38 300	133	7 455	-3.2	545	7.3	318	-4	5 236	11.0	2 828	673
Jenkins	2 951	71.1	39 500	111	3 402	-1.5	328	9.6	149	8	1 660	-3.1	882	260
Johnson	3 010	78.0	31 600	105	4 003	2.0	227	5.7	132	-5	2 123	18.7	1 445	264
Jones	7 300	83.7	63 500	231	9 351	1.5	425	4.5	162	8	1 272	5.4	166	193
Lamar	4 669	70.0	47 600	190	5 096	-0.7	299	5.9	182	-11	2 826	4.7	1 520	474
Lanier	1 965	71.5	37 500	168	3 039	1.0	147	4.8	105	-7	1 025	10.9	319	280
Laurens	14 514	70.9	46 500	182	17 539	-6.6	998	5.7	981	28	13 611	3.2	5 424	3 183
Lee	5 199	77.9	65 300	267	7 659	1.5	373	4.9	87	6	771	5.6	0	80
Liberty	15 136	43.5	60 400	345	11 799	1.7	772	6.5	501	3	4 427	-0.7	308	2 125
Lincoln	2 702	80.3	46 000	122	3 419	0.0	177	5.2	115	10	644	10.8	275	173
Long	2 196	67.1	40 500	259	1 380	0.8	102	7.4	29	-3	116	3.6	0	26
Lowndes	26 311	59.7	60 800	262	36 889	-0.4	1 712	4.6	2 079	14	25 123	0.1	6 133	7 486
Lumpkin	4 976	76.0	66 400	283	6 898	0.2	267	3.9	204	0	2 345	5.1	805	579
McDuffie	7 270	68.6	48 000	182	10 099	3.1	519	5.1	464	6	6 623	10.5	3 001	1 751
McIntosh	3 186	83.5	37 500	170	3 947	1.5	275	7.0	148	20	1 568	15.5	698	414
Macon	4 388	68.7	35 900	147	4 669	-1.0	458	9.8	235	1	3 335	7.4	1 810	554
Madison	7 740	82.1	53 900	214	10 986	0.4	670	6.1	258	10	1 840	4.0	740	238
Marion	1 962	78.8	38 400	126	3 722	-6.8	277	7.4	68	-3	1 515	29.7	0	120
Meriwether	7 637	74.8	39 900	172	8 883	-3.4	627	7.1	309	-2	4 203	0.6	2 471	754
Miller	2 336	75.7	41 200	130	2 762	-2.4	122	4.4	119	0	730	-13.5	0	263
Mitchell	6 798	70.1	40 800	141	9 297	-5.4	833	9.0	397	7	4 662	0.5	2 000	841
Monroe	5 838	74.6	62 400	208	7 494	2.9	459	6.1	261	10	4 346	6.0	1 442	932
Montgomery	2 493	74.1	40 100	121	3 305	9.7	207	6.3	129	-2	1 694	3.8	532	451
Morgan	4 399	76.4	55 000	220	6 688	2.8	463	6.9	282	11	3 634	7.5	1 596	880
Murray	9 363	75.0	52 000	248	12 791	1.1	919	7.2	215	-4	6 245	9.9	4 925	669
Muscogee	65 858	53.9	58 900	275	76 197	0.9	4 191	5.5	4 236	40	65 570	-0.1	15 720	16 920
Newton	14 401	70.9	65 400	315	21 902	1.6	1 475	6.7	683	3	8 966	1.1	3 743	2 428
Oconee	6 156	77.5	77 900	335	8 959	-0.8	298	3.3	338	26	2 767	6.1	732	419
Oglethorpe	3 581	82.3	52 500	181	5 514	-4.4	318	5.8	118	-2	769	27.3	155	158
Paulding	14 326	81.5	68 600	337	17 608	0.5	1 067	6.1	450	19	3 569	8.5	496	1 260
Peach	7 142	69.1	56 700	204	9 304	1.9	552	5.9	388	18	4 912	9.5	0	1 145
Pickens	5 386	80.2	59 500	234	5 457	-1.4	547	10.0	285	-1	3 559	-5.0	1 400	611
Pierce	4 807	80.0	41 700	162	5 808	3.0	389	6.7	265	3	2 308	15.2	766	504
Pike	3 526	80.7	51 600	218	4 294	1.5	276	6.4	109	11	770	-6.1	0	157
Polk	12 519	72.4	41 600	216	13 229	-1.5	1 535	11.6	549	9	8 274	3.1	3 990	1 523
Pulaski	3 098	70.5	44 900	141	3 917	-0.1	206	5.3	197	4	1 629	-13.3	402	358
Putnam	5 229	74.9	59 000	191	5 471	3.8	264	4.8	214	4	2 584	-5.2	1 140	487
Quitman	857	73.5	36 400	99	650	-5.1	68	10.5	23	0	114	-30.5	35	31
Rabun	4 630	81.5	65 900	205	6 240	-2.0	304	4.9	389	-7	3 775	1.6	1 480	796
Randolph	2 815	66.7	33 000	99	3 778	-0.9	213	5.6	166	-9	1 532	-4.5	669	333
Richmond	68 675	56.4	58 500	305	90 009	3.3	4 562	5.1	4 483	-59	70 803	0.1	13 273	18 974
Rockdale	18 337	75.2	86 200	447	27 302	0.9	1 256	4.6	1 299	5	17 123	-0.7	5 872	3 945

1. Percent of total civilian labor force. 2. For week including March 12. Excludes government employees, self-employed persons, farm workers, domestic service workers, railroad employees subject to the Railroad Retirement Act, and employees on oceanborne vessels or in foreign countries.

STATE County	Private nonfarm establishments, 1988 (cont'd) — Employment[1] (cont'd) — Finance, insurance, and real estate	Employment[1] (cont'd) — Services	Annual payroll — Total (Mil dol)	Annual payroll — Average per employee (Dollars)	Personal income, 1989 — Total (Mil dol)	Per-cent change, 1988–1989	Wages and salaries[2] (Mil dol)	Propri-etor's income (Mil dol)	Dividends, interest, & rent (Mil dol)	Transfer payments (Mil dol)	Per capita[3] — Dollars	Per capita[3] — Rank	Earnings, 1989 — Total (Mil dol)	Percent by selected industries — Farm	Goods-related[4] — Total
	88	89	90	91	92	93	94	95	96	97	98	99	100	101	102
GEORGIA—Con.															
Floyd	1 290	6 129	544	18 546	1 228	6.0	813	91	189	198	15 171	917	904	1.0	36.9
Forsyth	487	998	125	15 342	793	8.5	237	111	98	56	17 601	356	347	10.6	NA
Franklin	201	988	56	13 660	232	6.8	89	42	37	47	13 885	1 487	131	16.8	26.4
Fulton	58 967	155 079	12 483	25 056	13 906	6.0	18 684	1 310	2 815	1 582	21 557	109	19 995	0.0	13.1
Gilmer	251	466	52	14 427	193	7.1	84	23	30	34	14 308	1 282	108	6.8	NA
Glascock	0	0	4	10 161	32	3.8	11	3	4	8	14 604	1 164	14	7.5	NA
Glynn	1 265	7 406	393	15 769	1 013	7.1	636	74	220	160	16 664	491	710	0.1	28.5
Gordon	282	2 236	326	17 273	497	8.1	360	70	54	61	14 404	1 247	430	5.8	NA
Grady	193	561	53	13 696	245	7.3	95	25	50	46	11 548	2 486	120	6.6	NA
Greene	153	274	42	13 368	150	8.2	73	17	24	31	12 458	2 138	90	8.2	NA
Gwinnett	6 710	25 944	2 737	21 944	6 527	10.4	3 614	362	613	320	18 692	239	3 976	0.3	30.4
Habersham	310	793	140	15 289	395	7.1	219	52	64	61	13 865	1 497	271	8.7	42.4
Hall	2 137	7 192	621	16 937	1 517	7.2	935	184	237	174	16 583	508	1 119	4.1	35.8
Hancock	50	285	8	9 479	97	8.5	26	7	12	27	10 596	2 770	33	6.8	NA
Haralson	142	893	103	16 581	283	4.7	129	34	41	49	13 474	1 701	164	4.3	41.3
Harris	0	733	32	12 715	255	7.7	57	18	39	38	14 300	1 288	75	5.4	22.5
Hart	116	508	102	16 589	290	8.7	154	43	44	40	14 501	1 211	197	8.0	NA
Heard	0	127	15	12 532	89	5.5	39	6	8	16	11 315	2 563	44	3.6	NA
Henry	401	2 183	134	14 374	945	8.4	298	51	108	94	16 479	533	349	1.5	31.1
Houston	1 063	4 725	234	13 824	1 302	6.4	1 006	73	144	222	14 551	1 188	1 079	0.7	11.9
Irwin	63	198	21	10 029	96	-1.1	33	15	19	20	10 587	2 774	47	21.1	NA
Jackson	175	394	97	15 774	438	13.5	170	66	49	62	14 296	1 291	237	17.1	37.9
Jasper	69	111	24	17 628	112	4.9	42	14	18	18	13 730	1 563	55	13.0	NA
Jeff Davis	52	317	65	15 520	158	9.0	109	20	21	24	13 029	1 895	129	6.8	NA
Jefferson	216	536	82	15 671	211	5.2	110	13	29	52	11 495	2 500	123	3.8	NA
Jenkins	57	201	22	13 308	94	5.2	39	14	13	22	11 078	2 643	53	14.2	NA
Johnson	0	231	22	10 307	99	2.9	31	13	15	21	11 539	2 487	44	9.2	NA
Jones	33	277	19	14 695	266	7.4	50	14	28	31	13 662	1 596	63	2.8	NA
Lamar	100	340	37	13 007	172	5.2	61	9	20	28	12 948	1 928	70	3.6	42.2
Lanier	38	216	10	9 617	66	7.7	18	12	8	15	11 453	2 520	30	22.2	NA
Laurens	502	2 438	211	15 477	571	14.3	374	53	73	102	14 536	1 196	427	2.2	41.2
Lee	0	62	10	12 460	188	3.9	37	12	16	22	11 816	2 392	49	17.0	NA
Liberty	315	839	49	11 078	497	5.1	194	20	29	66	11 857	2 377	214	0.5	14.0
Lincoln	0	105	7	10 634	87	7.6	26	10	12	17	11 932	2 346	36	10.1	NA
Long	0	28	1	8 336	49	1.4	7	3	5	10	9 760	2 916	10	7.8	NA
Lowndes	1 381	5 225	380	15 127	1 013	8.6	695	88	146	179	13 955	1 452	782	1.5	25.2
Lumpkin	153	598	36	15 452	193	10.1	68	27	27	24	14 458	1 230	95	16.1	NA
McDuffie	198	684	93	14 078	256	9.0	116	25	37	49	12 628	2 063	140	2.1	NA
McIntosh	0	224	24	15 369	101	8.4	30	9	11	22	10 345	2 827	39	0.1	NA
Macon	95	497	57	17 165	158	6.7	94	10	24	39	11 714	2 434	104	4.8	53.5
Madison	66	234	24	13 023	255	6.4	40	38	32	40	11 923	2 352	79	27.4	19.6
Marion	0	305	17	11 167	65	6.3	26	10	9	13	12 329	2 188	37	18.8	NA
Meriwether	123	393	70	16 629	245	4.6	126	19	33	52	11 154	2 620	145	3.3	43.9
Miller	47	82	9	12 159	77	3.3	22	8	16	19	10 918	2 681	30	16.3	8.6
Mitchell	184	587	60	12 799	225	5.2	106	20	36	51	10 515	2 786	127	4.1	32.4
Monroe	86	751	70	16 083	222	2.0	109	18	31	34	14 125	1 381	127	3.4	NA
Montgomery	117	268	21	12 285	82	2.9	26	9	13	18	11 392	2 543	35	11.6	NA
Morgan	123	405	55	15 000	189	5.8	94	24	34	30	14 448	1 233	118	11.8	39.7
Murray	128	177	100	15 945	306	7.0	191	18	31	35	12 233	2 216	208	3.1	NA
Muscogee	5 835	15 734	1 093	16 676	2 555	5.4	1 598	155	420	501	14 409	1 246	1 753	0.0	29.4
Newton	409	1 175	167	18 624	616	7.1	275	53	70	84	13 861	1 499	328	2.2	45.8
Oconee	168	559	45	16 170	265	9.1	53	40	33	27	16 531	522	93	23.4	31.6
Oglethorpe	0	228	9	11 182	124	13.0	23	21	14	17	12 807	1 996	44	35.4	19.2
Paulding	282	446	48	13 537	528	8.0	103	45	41	57	13 802	1 534	148	5.6	NA
Peach	203	504	86	17 511	316	6.7	160	27	57	58	15 073	955	187	5.0	47.2
Pickens	256	371	58	16 343	208	3.9	77	25	30	31	14 192	1 346	102	9.8	32.9
Pierce	124	391	26	11 423	139	7.9	44	17	19	30	10 432	2 805	61	13.2	NA
Pike	57	118	9	12 217	124	2.2	23	11	17	20	13 202	1 811	34	7.2	33.5
Polk	230	1 128	124	14 960	416	2.8	188	27	53	84	12 162	2 254	214	1.6	NA
Pulaski	77	534	21	13 033	113	8.5	41	13	19	25	13 386	1 737	55	12.2	NA
Putnam	78	370	44	16 936	156	8.4	91	12	25	31	11 839	2 382	103	2.5	36.6
Quitman	0	0	1	10 035	26	4.1	3	4	4	8	11 239	2 585	7	31.1	NA
Rabun	76	1 014	55	14 510	139	8.1	67	16	34	30	12 396	2 162	83	3.1	39.2
Randolph	67	229	19	12 239	91	5.6	41	13	18	23	10 222	2 851	54	9.2	29.0
Richmond	4 128	23 024	1 257	17 752	2 812	7.3	2 247	157	381	544	14 791	1 081	2 403	0.1	25.6
Rockdale	481	2 738	327	19 110	946	6.4	441	60	110	79	17 388	378	502	0.4	45.5

1. For week including March 12. Excludes government employees, self-employed persons, farm workers, domestic service workers, railroad employees subject to the Railroad Retirement Act, and employees on oceanborne vessels or in foreign countries. 2. Includes other labor income. 3. Based on the resident population estimated as of July 1 of the year shown. 4. Covers mining, construction, and manufacturing.

Table A. States and Counties — **Earnings and Agriculture**

STATE County	Earnings, 1989 (cont'd) — Percent by selected industries (cont'd) — Goods-related[1] — Manufacturing	Earnings, 1989 (cont'd) — Service-related & other[2] — Total	Service-related & other[2] — Retail trade	Service-related & other[2] — Finance, insurance, & real estate	Service-related & other[2] — Services	Government	Agriculture, 1987 — Farms — Number	Farms — Percent with — Less than 50 acres	Farms — Percent with — 500 acres and over	Farm operators, percent — Whose principal occupation is farming	Farm operators, percent — Residing on farm operated	Land in farms — Acreage (1,000)	Land in farms — Percent change, 1982–1987	Land in farms — Acres — Average size of farm	Land in farms — Acres — Total irrigated (1,000)	Land in farms — Acres — Total cropland (1,000)
	103	104	105	106	107	108	109	110	111	112	113	114	115	116	117	118
GEORGIA—Con.																
Floyd	32.1	46.3	10.5	3.8	21.3	15.8	478	30.5	6.5	32.0	70.9	83	-11.5	174	1	41
Forsyth	19.5	NA	10.6	2.7	16.2	9.4	567	64.7	3.2	42.5	79.0	43	-12.3	76	0	19
Franklin	20.4	45.4	12.7	3.4	18.7	11.4	677	35.9	3.1	44.3	75.3	75	-7.1	111	0	36
Fulton	9.4	73.1	7.9	11.9	27.8	13.8	344	59.6	2.9	34.6	71.5	33	-22.8	95	0	12
Gilmer	34.6	NA	10.3	6.4	NA	13.5	248	39.1	1.2	51.6	75.4	27	-12.7	111	0	8
Glascock	23.2	NA	2.8	1.8	NA	16.2	79	5.1	16.5	43.0	65.8	27	-4.0	344	D	13
Glynn	21.1	51.4	12.4	3.9	27.4	20.0	48	47.9	14.6	20.8	77.1	10	4.0	214	0	1
Gordon	52.5	NA	6.7	1.8	9.9	7.5	548	41.2	4.7	43.4	72.8	72	-15.2	132	1	41
Grady	31.7	42.5	13.1	3.3	15.5	15.3	544	26.5	14.9	55.5	69.7	143	-11.7	263	4	83
Greene	41.3	NA	8.6	5.4	12.8	15.2	203	22.2	14.8	44.3	65.5	54	-6.7	265	0	23
Gwinnett	21.5	60.3	11.6	6.2	18.8	9.0	441	60.3	1.1	32.2	73.5	29	-12.8	67	0	11
Habersham	37.3	32.8	10.9	2.9	9.9	16.1	452	57.3	1.8	48.9	72.8	40	-5.1	88	0	15
Hall	29.5	48.9	10.2	5.2	22.2	11.2	821	57.5	1.6	46.2	75.3	61	-8.7	74	0	27
Hancock	17.0	NA	6.0	5.1	26.8	25.9	138	8.7	15.9	33.3	64.5	45	-6.5	323	D	13
Haralson	36.8	42.5	8.6	1.3	16.2	11.8	295	35.9	5.1	28.1	79.7	37	-4.8	124	D	14
Harris	15.0	55.4	15.2	2.1	31.8	16.7	214	30.4	7.9	30.8	74.8	39	-38.1	180	0	15
Hart	50.6	NA	7.0	NA	11.3	10.0	507	33.1	3.9	38.3	75.5	62	-8.5	123	1	38
Heard	29.1	NA	2.6	NA	9.1	18.8	192	22.4	4.2	35.9	75.5	33	-7.8	173	1	11
Henry	21.4	38.9	9.2	4.3	14.2	28.5	388	42.0	4.6	32.0	74.0	49	-16.4	127	D	26
Houston	7.9	24.8	7.4	2.1	11.1	62.5	264	39.8	16.7	39.8	55.7	80	-21.6	302	7	53
Irwin	9.4	38.2	5.0	3.3	15.8	18.2	371	14.6	25.1	65.2	66.6	143	-5.7	386	15	89
Jackson	30.7	34.1	9.6	2.0	10.0	10.9	770	41.7	3.9	41.7	76.6	87	0.1	113	0	42
Jasper	47.1	20.1	4.5	2.2	10.1	14.7	204	19.6	14.7	41.2	61.8	61	-9.3	300	D	22
Jeff Davis	49.6	31.7	8.2	1.2	8.8	9.5	284	25.4	11.6	52.8	70.1	76	-28.7	267	3	34
Jefferson	39.8	NA	7.2	2.9	11.3	16.2	339	15.6	26.3	51.0	62.2	142	-10.1	418	14	97
Jenkins	32.8	31.8	5.6	2.1	9.5	18.5	208	18.8	26.0	55.3	67.8	85	-21.1	406	6	53
Johnson	37.9	33.2	10.2	1.4	12.3	14.9	273	15.0	16.1	37.4	67.4	85	0.6	313	1	49
Jones	8.1	NA	7.3	1.4	18.3	19.3	164	26.2	9.8	36.0	76.2	32	-18.9	197	0	13
Lamar	39.0	36.1	13.7	4.0	10.8	18.2	210	32.9	6.7	32.9	73.3	38	-9.3	181	1	20
Lanier	14.4	NA	4.9	3.2	15.4	16.7	130	23.1	19.2	50.8	56.9	51	-2.5	389	4	18
Laurens	22.6	38.0	10.3	2.6	17.3	18.5	622	20.1	15.3	44.4	68.3	179	-15.6	288	5	119
Lee	9.5	NA	3.9	0.7	8.0	33.9	162	22.2	38.3	45.1	54.3	133	-20.7	819	23	75
Liberty	10.3	32.9	10.3	3.4	11.7	52.6	41	26.8	19.5	39.0	80.5	18	-8.6	445	D	2
Lincoln	36.8	30.6	8.5	1.6	9.7	16.5	156	25.6	12.2	34.6	69.2	36	-17.2	233	D	15
Long	4.0	NA	6.5	0.8	14.5	42.3	75	41.3	10.7	34.7	70.7	12	-23.7	165	0	4
Lowndes	18.3	45.7	12.3	3.8	18.1	27.6	411	38.2	8.0	33.3	65.9	72	-40.8	176	2	40
Lumpkin	19.1	35.3	10.2	3.7	13.0	25.1	269	51.7	3.0	43.1	77.7	26	-12.6	96	0	8
McDuffie	31.4	NA	11.5	3.5	17.2	16.5	186	30.1	9.1	29.6	72.6	39	-27.5	207	1	17
McIntosh	17.0	50.9	14.4	1.9	14.0	26.6	23	30.4	17.4	13.0	73.9	5	-0.7	220	D	1
Macon	45.7	28.9	6.8	1.6	13.0	12.8	252	12.3	26.2	54.4	60.3	133	-4.8	527	10	83
Madison	4.8	35.4	5.9	2.3	16.6	17.7	593	38.6	2.2	41.3	79.6	63	-1.6	106	1	32
Marion	34.8	24.8	6.8	0.7	11.9	16.3	128	22.7	18.0	41.4	65.6	42	-7.4	324	1	17
Meriwether	41.2	30.1	7.9	2.2	8.5	22.7	301	18.3	14.6	39.5	63.8	78	-14.4	259	0	31
Miller	6.5	46.4	10.3	2.0	13.9	28.8	311	19.6	27.0	64.3	73.6	131	5.0	422	30	90
Mitchell	27.1	44.0	9.4	3.6	15.0	19.5	496	23.8	28.2	59.9	61.7	224	-5.4	451	46	148
Monroe	19.5	NA	8.1	1.3	13.9	17.5	160	23.1	15.6	33.1	65.0	39	-32.8	246	1	17
Montgomery	17.2	NA	11.1	5.6	17.3	23.0	247	22.3	17.0	40.5	65.6	82	-1.5	333	1	27
Morgan	37.1	37.7	10.4	2.7	10.5	10.7	368	25.5	13.6	49.5	71.5	102	-7.1	278	2	46
Murray	61.5	NA	4.9	1.5	6.3	10.4	240	32.9	2.5	33.3	70.0	34	-14.6	141	0	17
Muscogee	22.8	55.1	12.0	9.7	23.7	15.5	49	44.9	4.1	30.6	75.5	5	-55.3	108	0	2
Newton	35.7	38.0	9.5	2.4	15.5	14.0	277	35.7	5.4	26.0	75.5	44	-13.3	158	0	20
Oconee	13.7	30.8	3.3	3.0	18.0	14.2	295	38.0	6.1	44.7	77.6	51	-16.5	171	1	28
Oglethorpe	5.8	29.3	5.0	1.9	14.6	16.2	314	27.7	8.6	39.8	76.1	63	-9.4	202	0	28
Paulding	7.9	42.9	12.7	4.3	18.3	22.0	275	48.7	1.8	32.0	81.5	26	-10.2	94	D	11
Peach	44.2	28.2	6.7	3.0	10.7	19.7	170	33.5	15.9	44.7	61.2	55	0.5	322	5	37
Pickens	12.7	42.2	11.7	4.2	12.7	15.1	217	52.1	0.9	41.9	70.5	18	-18.6	82	D	6
Pierce	13.8	50.4	9.5	4.0	21.1	16.9	376	27.7	11.7	52.7	72.3	96	-7.1	254	4	41
Pike	18.5	37.5	6.4	4.3	17.2	21.7	282	33.3	7.4	34.0	78.0	48	-13.2	172	0	24
Polk	43.7	NA	9.7	2.9	12.9	15.6	314	37.3	5.4	31.2	74.5	47	-0.8	150	D	25
Pulaski	13.8	53.9	9.1	4.0	27.6	14.9	163	18.4	29.4	60.7	58.9	86	-3.5	530	15	59
Putnam	34.0	NA	7.0	1.2	NA	15.1	174	20.1	13.8	47.7	63.8	42	-6.4	243	0	19
Quitman	1.8	NA	7.7	NA	13.4	23.5	25	8.0	32.0	64.0	52.0	18	-24.4	706	D	D
Rabun	26.8	44.9	14.9	4.9	19.1	12.9	151	50.3	1.3	36.4	64.2	14	23.6	95	1	5
Randolph	26.4	41.7	8.0	3.0	18.8	20.2	117	9.4	44.4	76.9	68.4	102	-17.3	874	17	61
Richmond	17.7	48.5	10.5	4.1	24.9	25.7	130	47.7	4.6	29.2	65.4	18	-28.6	137	0	11
Rockdale	32.5	42.2	11.1	3.4	14.7	11.9	112	58.9	5.4	21.4	82.1	13	-6.0	119	0	4

1. Covers mining, construction, and manufacturing. 2. Covers private sector earnings in agricultural services, forestry, and fisheries; transportation and public utilities; wholesale trade; retail trade; finance, insurance, and real estate; and services.

Table A. States and Counties — **Agriculture and Manufactures**

STATE County	Agriculture, 1987 (cont'd): Value of land and buildings: Average per farm ($1,000)	Value of land and buildings: Average per acre (Dollars)	Value of products sold: Total (Mil dol)	Value of products sold: Average per farm (Dollars)	Value of products sold: Percent from: Crops	Value of products sold: Percent from: Livestock and poultry[1]	Percent of farms with sales of: $10,000 or more	Percent of farms with sales of: $100,000 or more	Manufactures, 1987: Establishments: Total	Establishments: Percent with 20 or more employees	All employees: Number (1,000)	All employees: Percent change, 1982–1987	All employees: Annual payroll (Mil dol)	Production workers: Number (1,000)	Production workers: Work hours (Mil)
	119	120	121	122	123	124	125	126	127	128	129	130	131	132	133
GEORGIA—Con.															
Floyd	184	898	11	23 568	11.1	88.9	22.4	4.8	118	55.1	11.5	5.5	245.4	9.2	18.4
Forsyth	207	3 375	59	104 394	0.9	99.1	50.4	29.5	58	37.9	2.5	66.7	42.2	2.1	4.1
Franklin	147	1 167	61	90 552	0.6	99.4	39.1	24.1	29	44.8	1.2	0.0	16.6	1.0	1.9
Fulton	227	2 470	7	19 096	35.7	64.3	20.9	3.2	1 143	39.5	60.8	10.3	1 680.0	32.6	65.9
Gilmer	133	1 333	25	102 515	4.5	95.5	44.0	25.8	30	30.0	2.1	61.5	29.6	1.8	3.6
Glascock	181	527	2	21 975	29.2	70.8	30.4	7.6	6	33.3	0.2	0.0	2.3	0.2	0.4
Glynn	238	1 113	0	4 272	18.5	81.5	10.4	0.0	74	40.5	5.6	3.7	131.2	4.3	8.8
Gordon	223	1 545	54	99 285	3.7	96.3	43.1	25.2	150	46.0	10.1	77.2	191.7	7.9	16.9
Grady	230	860	51	93 438	70.7	29.3	50.6	15.1	35	28.6	1.7	-10.5	24.7	1.4	3.1
Greene	245	831	16	81 213	3.4	96.6	42.4	22.2	36	33.3	1.9	11.8	26.6	1.7	3.2
Gwinnett	278	3 984	13	30 076	32.7	67.3	16.3	6.8	524	34.2	26.3	64.4	676.8	13.6	26.5
Habersham	188	2 060	74	162 934	1.4	98.6	56.0	39.6	62	40.3	4.6	4.5	70.4	4.0	8.1
Hall	194	2 249	134	163 710	0.4	99.6	43.7	25.7	162	51.2	12.9	4.0	229.6	10.4	20.8
Hancock	207	561	2	14 229	17.6	82.3	24.6	2.9	10	30.0	0.4	33.3	3.4	0.3	0.5
Haralson	119	1 129	13	43 539	1.6	98.4	24.4	9.5	33	63.6	4.7	-16.1	72.3	4.1	7.3
Harris	176	1 182	2	8 630	26.0	74.0	16.8	1.4	24	20.8	0.9	50.0	10.9	0.8	1.5
Hart	180	1 233	26	51 496	6.0	94.0	30.2	14.4	34	47.1	3.7	12.1	64.5	3.1	5.7
Heard	118	667	5	25 934	5.2	94.8	18.8	5.7	11	54.5	0.6	20.0	9.3	0.6	1.0
Henry	237	1 890	5	13 073	39.2	60.8	16.0	2.8	28	53.6	2.5	47.1	42.5	2.0	3.7
Houston	261	870	15	57 738	52.5	47.5	39.4	13.3	58	34.5	2.6	4.0	63.5	2.0	4.0
Irwin	325	855	28	75 049	79.5	20.5	74.9	21.6	12	8.3	0.3	50.0	3.5	0.2	0.4
Jackson	173	1 608	80	103 248	1.4	98.6	47.3	27.9	37	35.1	2.5	0.0	37.5	2.1	4.1
Jasper	261	826	20	96 876	1.8	98.2	39.7	17.2	13	53.8	0.9	-10.0	17.0	0.8	1.6
Jeff Davis	139	535	12	43 484	47.7	52.3	48.2	12.7	29	27.6	2.5	-7.4	37.7	2.0	4.2
Jefferson	254	624	18	53 701	52.3	47.7	48.1	17.4	40	35.0	2.7	35.0	39.8	2.3	4.3
Jenkins	259	652	18	87 257	28.0	72.0	60.6	25.5	9	33.3	0.9	12.5	11.1	0.8	1.5
Johnson	135	510	7	24 300	32.1	67.9	33.7	4.0	19	57.9	1.5	36.4	14.7	1.4	2.6
Jones	200	1 021	8	50 523	6.4	93.6	26.8	13.4	13	23.1	D	D	D	D	D
Lamar	206	1 042	5	24 880	13.1	86.9	21.4	6.7	16	37.5	1.5	0.0	22.7	1.0	2.2
Lanier	212	557	12	89 696	73.8	26.2	46.2	15.4	7	14.3	0.3	200.0	2.7	0.3	0.5
Laurens	201	685	25	40 463	62.8	37.2	40.7	8.7	58	50.0	5.5	14.6	84.4	4.4	8.5
Lee	764	946	26	158 664	81.3	18.7	67.3	34.0	3	33.3	D	D	D	D	D
Liberty	373	838	1	19 967	13.7	86.3	29.3	4.9	19	21.1	0.3	-62.5	4.3	0.3	0.5
Lincoln	174	854	5	33 422	2.0	98.0	36.5	7.7	10	30.0	0.3	-50.0	3.0	0.2	0.4
Long	184	817	2	30 849	21.8	78.2	26.7	6.7	5	0.0	0.0	0.0	0.1	0.0	0.0
Lowndes	183	1 113	11	27 892	80.2	19.8	38.2	7.3	107	33.6	6.1	5.2	105.5	4.8	9.5
Lumpkin	226	2 185	36	135 020	1.3	98.8	53.9	32.3	11	36.4	0.7	0.0	12.6	0.7	1.4
McDuffie	225	1 069	8	41 052	63.3	36.7	16.7	4.8	41	56.1	2.8	16.7	43.6	2.0	3.8
McIntosh	248	1 125	0	2 288	7.5	90.6	0.0	0.0	6	83.3	D	D	D	D	D
Macon	351	646	28	111 809	41.8	58.2	60.7	27.8	25	28.0	1.9	-5.0	36.9	1.7	3.7
Madison	130	1 208	52	87 626	0.9	99.1	40.3	26.0	27	18.5	0.7	0.0	9.1	0.6	1.2
Marion	159	651	8	66 001	24.3	75.7	46.1	14.1	8	25.0	D	D	D	D	D
Meriwether	228	838	5	16 415	19.8	80.2	26.6	3.7	29	44.8	2.5	-21.9	44.6	2.2	5.5
Miller	280	656	24	77 680	79.2	20.8	74.6	22.5	5	20.0	D	D	D	D	D
Mitchell	379	868	51	102 185	83.4	16.6	61.7	26.0	34	41.2	2.2	22.2	28.9	1.9	3.6
Monroe	259	912	11	66 365	2.1	97.9	33.1	13.1	29	27.6	1.5	7.1	21.2	1.3	2.5
Montgomery	235	672	7	27 504	46.3	53.7	42.1	5.3	14	35.7	0.5	0.0	6.0	0.4	0.8
Morgan	312	1 100	32	87 556	5.0	95.0	50.3	28.3	29	34.5	1.3	8.3	27.0	1.1	2.7
Murray	204	1 301	9	38 695	8.4	91.6	27.5	10.0	55	52.7	4.6	21.1	88.5	3.7	8.4
Muscogee	319	2 946	0	6 710	10.6	89.4	16.3	0.0	157	51.0	D	D	D	D	D
Newton	250	1 647	10	34 336	5.0	95.0	19.9	4.3	43	41.9	3.8	15.2	92.1	2.3	4.7
Oconee	290	1 817	40	137 235	6.2	93.8	43.7	25.1	28	17.9	0.5	25.0	9.5	0.4	0.8
Oglethorpe	202	1 115	29	92 901	3.6	96.4	38.5	21.0	17	23.5	0.2	0.0	2.2	0.2	0.3
Paulding	199	2 643	10	34 700	2.5	97.5	25.1	10.2	29	27.6	0.7	16.7	8.6	0.5	0.9
Peach	347	1 096	9	54 415	89.8	10.2	38.8	15.9	23	26.1	D	D	D	D	D
Pickens	146	1 806	20	92 920	0.5	99.5	41.5	29.0	32	31.2	1.4	-6.7	21.7	1.2	2.2
Pierce	213	839	16	43 125	50.0	50.0	38.6	10.6	31	38.7	0.7	40.0	7.9	0.6	1.2
Pike	184	914	6	20 805	23.2	76.8	25.2	3.5	2	50.0	D	D	D	D	D
Polk	131	981	7	21 009	24.4	75.6	22.6	6.7	41	46.3	4.0	0.0	70.5	3.2	6.5
Pulaski	361	714	16	96 891	83.0	17.0	65.6	27.0	10	20.0	0.4	0.0	4.3	0.4	0.7
Putnam	214	852	20	117 615	1.7	98.3	46.0	30.5	23	43.5	1.2	0.0	22.4	1.1	2.3
Quitman	487	690	1	34 850	80.6	19.5	48.0	8.0	7	0.0	0.0	0.0	0.4	0.0	0.1
Rabun	229	2 351	5	35 861	30.5	69.5	21.2	9.9	31	29.0	1.5	0.0	23.8	1.3	2.5
Randolph	588	690	17	148 796	82.8	17.2	72.6	39.3	22	27.3	0.6	0.0	9.8	0.5	1.0
Richmond	199	1 442	2	16 919	61.3	38.7	21.5	3.8	165	47.9	13.4	8.1	326.8	8.8	18.4
Rockdale	359	2 874	1	10 470	30.3	69.7	10.7	3.6	86	43.0	5.7	46.2	128.6	4.2	8.8

1. Includes livestock and poultry products.

STATE County	Manufactures, 1987 (cont'd): Production workers (cont'd): Wages: Total (Mil dol)	Average per worker (Dollars)	Value added by manufacture (Mil dol)	Value of shipments (Mil dol)	New capital expenditures (Mil dol)	Value of construction authorized by building permits, 1990: Total[1] ($1,000)	Nonresidential: Total ($1,000)	Percent: Office	Industrial	Stores	Residential: New construction ($1,000)	Number of housing units	Alterations and additions ($1,000)
	134	135	136	137	138	139	140	141	142	143	144	145	146
GEORGIA—Con.													
Floyd	175.4	19 065	627.5	1 387.2	31.2	53 906	15 433	4.1	21.6	46.0	20 457	306	4 095
Forsyth	29.5	14 048	133.1	292.8	5.0	95 616	33 053	1.3	0.1	77.1	58 607	678	1 973
Franklin	11.8	11 800	37.2	103.1	0.7	1 618	969	9.0	0.0	42.6	478	10	50
Fulton	753.3	23 107	4 342.0	10 347.6	268.9	1 266 560	414 855	59.1	14.9	11.4	448 476	6 192	116 007
Gilmer	23.1	12 833	85.4	178.1	2.2	24 757	5 720	0.0	11.1	11.2	18 891	276	121
Glascock	2.0	10 000	6.5	13.1	D	795	280	0.0	0.0	0.0	515	19	0
Glynn	88.0	20 465	299.3	834.4	39.4	45 350	11 574	5.1	1.6	41.5	27 733	365	3 498
Gordon	125.7	15 911	491.7	1 359.9	49.2	33 588	7 180	11.8	30.1	35.8	21 842	450	642
Grady	18.3	13 071	85.6	154.4	4.0	4 778	1 640	49.1	42.7	1.1	1 710	30	798
Greene	21.5	12 647	54.6	141.3	D	13 015	1 170	0.0	0.0	85.5	11 700	156	115
Gwinnett	289.5	21 287	1 762.7	3 030.3	133.1	444 266	121 509	16.1	9.1	53.2	258 058	4 022	5 345
Habersham	52.9	13 225	144.3	252.2	17.9	19 544	5 616	5.0	25.4	7.4	11 956	221	445
Hall	162.4	15 615	678.1	1 678.7	41.1	83 421	16 198	14.1	2.1	52.4	43 815	631	4 745
Hancock	2.9	9 667	5.7	8.9	0.2	3 504	659	0.0	0.0	64.8	1 850	53	817
Haralson	52.6	12 829	196.4	374.1	4.2	10 003	2 309	0.0	39.2	9.2	7 663	113	0
Harris	9.1	11 375	33.0	89.9	1.0	19 494	1 700	0.0	0.0	0.0	16 417	199	1 271
Hart	49.5	15 968	211.1	480.3	10.9	952	16	0.0	0.0	0.0	381	8	150
Heard	7.2	12 000	21.8	49.2	0.8	377	250	0.0	0.0	0.0	100	1	0
Henry	27.1	13 550	142.4	281.1	6.0	119 268	16 282	11.6	0.0	59.4	96 832	1 292	1 800
Houston	45.6	22 800	138.7	358.2	7.9	43 487	11 792	12.7	0.6	46.4	24 167	518	1 660
Irwin	2.3	11 500	6.4	13.0	0.2	121	6	0.0	0.0	0.0	34	1	80
Jackson	27.6	13 143	90.9	185.4	6.9	19 644	6 241	0.0	12.3	24.2	11 695	169	593
Jasper	14.4	18 000	44.0	116.1	D	2 237	27	0.0	0.0	55.0	2 173	42	11
Jeff Davis	28.0	14 000	111.4	218.2	D	859	306	0.0	86.5	9.8	282	6	38
Jefferson	30.8	13 391	86.1	179.0	D	8 662	6 316	4.0	95.0	0.8	1 281	25	358
Jenkins	8.2	10 250	33.3	55.8	D	296	150	0.0	0.0	86.7	65	1	54
Johnson	11.8	8 429	23.2	37.3	0.8	494	426	0.0	0.0	87.9	0	0	0
Jones	D	D	D	D	D	6 492	497	15.1	0.0	20.1	5 579	90	302
Lamar	15.9	15 900	65.0	179.8	D	3 501	725	0.0	0.0	0.0	2 586	49	148
Lanier	2.5	8 333	6.1	11.2	0.1	282	191	0.0	0.0	0.0	55	5	0
Laurens	56.5	12 841	187.4	455.0	14.3	13 397	8 908	28.5	18.3	41.0	3 131	43	668
Lee	D	D	D	D	D	5 924	362	23.2	0.0	42.7	4 814	111	431
Liberty	2.9	9 667	8.5	16.7	D	31 846	5 757	0.8	32.9	45.4	17 508	266	1 032
Lincoln	2.3	11 500	5.1	8.1	0.1	3 055	725	0.0	30.3	58.9	2 040	49	0
Long	0.1	NA	0.2	0.5	0.0	NA	NA	NA	NA	NA	NA	NA	NA
Lowndes	73.6	15 333	321.7	781.4	30.4	48 909	9 709	37.9	26.1	19.5	19 270	403	2 009
Lumpkin	10.6	15 143	24.1	76.3	D	12 449	707	46.5	0.0	26.4	10 858	229	32
McDuffie	24.1	12 050	100.0	249.8	6.8	3 291	1 780	0.0	0.0	87.6	183	5	213
McIntosh	D	D	D	D	D	5 838	817	0.0	0.0	8.0	4 439	70	308
Macon	28.1	16 529	163.6	316.5	D	2 453	770	0.0	82.2	0.0	1 490	50	146
Madison	7.5	12 500	17.5	42.4	1.0	12 684	812	0.0	0.0	48.6	11 145	146	262
Marion	D	D	D	D	D	0	0	NA	NA	NA	0	0	0
Meriwether	34.0	15 455	122.9	231.9	3.3	18 270	8 235	4.5	46.1	7.8	8 933	165	386
Miller	D	D	D	D	D	141	0	NA	NA	NA	0	0	24
Mitchell	20.7	10 895	61.0	135.8	2.1	4 486	2 294	1.5	2.3	6.5	1 164	26	228
Monroe	15.7	12 077	39.8	160.2	2.2	1 359	360	0.0	0.0	97.2	797	16	96
Montgomery	4.1	10 250	16.4	24.5	D	0	0	NA	NA	NA	0	0	0
Morgan	19.8	18 000	47.3	131.0	3.7	4 673	736	0.0	0.0	23.8	3 355	85	43
Murray	66.5	17 973	248.4	786.3	16.4	17 656	11 676	6.3	75.8	16.5	5 877	146	0
Muscogee	D	D	D	D	D	102 921	39 938	55.7	0.0	7.1	23 491	461	7 579
Newton	44.8	19 478	364.4	635.1	7.9	53 369	9 019	2.0	8.1	65.6	41 115	660	1 578
Oconee	5.9	14 750	16.1	89.0	0.7	18 459	1 268	19.3	0.4	25.3	16 591	180	437
Oglethorpe	1.6	8 000	4.4	10.4	0.4	NA	NA	NA	NA	NA	NA	NA	NA
Paulding	5.8	11 600	12.0	32.4	D	42 757	3 695	9.5	33.0	3.8	38 250	969	746
Peach	D	D	D	D	D	8 914	3 174	0.0	26.1	26.1	5 135	108	282
Pickens	16.3	13 583	47.8	76.0	1.8	13 276	2 087	0.0	13.6	15.4	10 802	170	264
Pierce	6.0	10 000	22.6	58.2	0.9	1 934	1 480	0.0	85.5	0.0	261	6	61
Pike	D	D	D	D	D	5 478	464	22.4	1.5	0.0	4 388	79	370
Polk	51.0	15 938	234.4	435.0	5.5	14 012	6 336	0.0	82.5	3.4	6 405	153	795
Pulaski	3.7	9 250	10.0	12.3	D	2 504	730	4.1	0.0	31.2	1 057	36	351
Putnam	18.9	17 182	23.2	156.2	0.8	223	0	NA	NA	NA	223	10	0
Quitman	0.2	NA	0.8	2.5	0.2	759	690	0.0	91.7	0.0	69	1	0
Rabun	17.6	13 538	68.0	193.1	D	19 208	3 892	1.0	0.0	0.2	14 896	237	166
Randolph	6.4	12 800	24.2	65.9	0.7	45	0	NA	NA	NA	45	3	0
Richmond	179.3	20 375	1 104.7	2 351.5	125.8	119 156	47 491	23.3	1.4	69.1	28 050	615	10 476
Rockdale	86.4	20 571	326.5	897.4	22.6	83 335	13 823	24.5	23.7	18.7	53 301	635	1 310

1. Includes nonresidential additions and alterations, residential nonhousekeeping buildings, and residential garages and carports not shown separately.

STATE County	Wholesale trade, 1987				Retail trade, all establishments, 1987				Retail trade, establishments with payroll, 1987					
						Sales				Sales				
											Per capita[2] (Dollars)			
	Establishments	Sales (Mil dol)	Paid employees[1]	Annual payroll (Mil dol)	Number	Total (Mil dol)	Percent change, 1982–1987	Per capita[2] (Dollars)	Number	Total (Mil dol)	General merchandise stores	Food stores	Apparel & accessory stores	Eating and drinking places
	147	148	149	150	151	152	153	154	155	156	157	158	159	160
GEORGIA—Con.														
Floyd	144	336.3	1 202	23.3	880	499.9	66.4	6 240	558	481.0	950	1 155	284	560
Forsyth	65	132.1	490	9.8	336	171.0	110.3	4 255	179	162.2	D	1 055	86	351
Franklin	30	72.0	189	3.3	266	122.8	80.6	7 491	129	98.7	183	1 552	116	307
Fulton	2 599	28 528.1	39 108	1 028.0	6 557	5 511.4	53.6	8 648	4 707	5 423.6	1 010	1 223	532	1 448
Gilmer	18	27.9	94	1.8	179	68.4	103.6	5 347	99	63.0	716	1 084	87	436
Glascock	0	0.0	0	0.0	20	3.0	42.9	1 286	9	2.3	D	D	0	D
Glynn	103	203.8	948	15.3	820	491.2	62.1	8 256	636	483.0	935	1 572	584	962
Gordon	77	130.9	743	9.8	517	205.5	88.7	6 135	246	187.7	366	1 187	175	588
Grady	31	86.6	331	4.2	179	113.1	66.6	5 285	117	110.6	D	1 111	126	181
Greene	14	34.7	120	1.6	126	42.1	66.4	3 570	71	37.2	51	1 288	D	135
Gwinnett	1 202	9 611.5	21 973	532.6	2 909	2 439.3	224.7	8 085	1 796	2 385.1	1 044	1 549	330	771
Habersham	37	65.9	593	9.4	322	151.6	53.4	5 452	173	138.4	371	998	293	390
Hall	223	907.0	3 150	58.1	1 020	648.0	84.7	7 380	617	621.4	1 126	1 317	307	615
Hancock	5	5.9	35	0.3	61	12.4	0.8	1 314	29	9.8	D	429	D	D
Haralson	18	68.5	261	6.9	244	96.4	115.2	4 682	132	89.6	508	1 169	182	221
Harris	5	11.2	74	1.3	134	28.2	76.2	1 638	63	25.6	38	452	D	123
Hart	28	42.3	215	2.7	180	71.2	82.6	3 614	92	64.0	138	809	338	265
Heard	4	D	D	D	54	14.9	129.2	1 985	20	13.2	D	1 231	0	60
Henry	37	40.9	253	5.2	344	178.1	101.2	3 554	180	170.2	D	833	20	408
Houston	60	122.6	418	8.4	710	534.6	60.0	6 130	506	527.2	679	1 184	146	535
Irwin	14	16.4	101	1.6	69	22.9	95.7	2 541	43	21.3	D	500	134	D
Jackson	26	86.8	454	7.2	321	132.7	72.6	4 528	180	124.5	144	1 145	93	347
Jasper	2	D	D	D	64	19.8	83.3	2 478	35	17.6	D	954	D	113
Jeff Davis	25	94.8	233	4.3	152	53.3	30.0	4 477	91	50.6	381	1 351	235	138
Jefferson	24	30.0	199	2.4	170	58.5	33.3	3 128	96	55.5	162	943	104	129
Jenkins	13	23.9	89	1.2	84	24.0	17.1	2 824	50	21.9	155	1 190	117	55
Johnson	11	12.3	46	0.6	76	18.8	55.4	2 188	41	16.4	D	790	D	105
Jones	4	1.7	17	0.1	71	24.7	76.4	1 295	35	22.7	D	397	D	80
Lamar	12	6.1	36	0.7	119	42.8	41.7	3 270	58	39.3	D	922	D	283
Lanier	10	10.0	44	0.5	57	18.8	123.8	3 186	30	17.8	156	793	D	71
Laurens	74	152.2	721	10.6	436	247.4	51.7	6 328	295	239.7	793	1 244	303	435
Lee	6	6.1	50	0.4	68	10.5	43.8	682	26	8.3	0	314	D	10
Liberty	17	11.8	108	1.4	307	153.4	53.9	3 733	213	150.3	D	732	165	418
Lincoln	2	D	D	D	83	12.9	46.6	1 792	38	10.4	46	407	141	96
Long	1	D	D	D	26	3.0	0.0	598	10	1.8	0	258	0	D
Lowndes	156	351.6	1 549	26.6	882	565.2	58.1	7 710	657	554.1	945	1 374	498	689
Lumpkin	7	3.6	29	0.4	135	57.1	101.1	4 529	69	54.3	D	821	D	454
McDuffie	23	32.2	163	2.6	231	126.0	54.0	6 271	149	121.8	D	1 410	239	672
McIntosh	8	10.8	33	0.3	93	35.5	76.6	3 813	53	33.7	D	1 366	D	129
Macon	27	50.4	155	2.8	112	44.8	55.0	3 269	71	41.8	D	1 057	D	181
Madison	15	10.1	70	1.2	154	26.2	81.9	1 284	44	18.7	0	387	D	D
Marion	7	8.4	50	0.6	38	11.1	13.3	2 100	27	10.3	111	506	D	D
Meriwether	16	19.3	120	1.8	192	98.8	57.3	4 576	116	96.0	205	1 528	77	198
Miller	14	100.8	213	3.4	81	21.6	40.3	3 090	49	20.1	D	1 051	164	24
Mitchell	42	95.1	316	5.0	209	68.2	19.6	3 142	124	62.9	D	982	140	181
Monroe	12	9.5	56	0.6	133	70.2	88.2	4 531	80	68.2	D	1 188	35	530
Montgomery	8	9.7	57	1.1	78	49.6	55.5	6 798	49	48.8	D	2 720	316	250
Morgan	23	66.7	358	5.8	138	62.8	39.2	4 910	87	59.1	109	1 211	50	444
Murray	19	74.7	403	7.3	100	74.9	37.4	3 199	76	72.6	97	1 784	48	224
Muscogee	268	867.8	3 026	54.8	1 692	1 361.1	63.8	7 604	1 256	1 343.1	D	D	404	D
Newton	36	51.3	285	3.6	359	191.6	80.2	4 552	206	183.3	615	1 116	231	384
Oconee	25	82.0	321	5.4	121	34.4	88.0	2 265	54	32.0	0	73	D	D
Oglethorpe	8	2.6	23	0.3	65	20.6	25.6	2 121	31	18.7	0	456	D	33
Paulding	26	37.7	139	1.7	217	159.5	179.3	4 637	115	154.1	D	1 183	31	235
Peach	21	23.9	104	1.8	185	110.8	77.8	5 540	118	107.1	D	1 044	D	356
Pickens	22	35.8	111	2.1	149	120.9	189.2	8 699	80	116.4	168	1 166	D	291
Pierce	20	30.9	130	1.8	136	48.3	79.6	3 683	78	44.4	86	687	77	240
Pike	5	2.5	22	0.4	73	11.7	120.8	1 290	22	9.3	D	525	0	D
Polk	22	153.8	502	8.9	333	141.7	46.2	4 180	192	134.4	D	1 163	102	247
Pulaski	15	47.6	133	2.0	104	35.3	26.5	4 015	66	34.0	D	1 390	175	219
Putnam	10	49.4	154	2.8	125	37.0	39.6	2 964	66	34.3	128	1 295	D	164
Quitman	1	D	D	D	20	D	D	D	9	3.2	D	D	0	D
Rabun	14	11.6	50	0.7	202	70.2	64.8	6 379	103	63.1	136	1 607	132	535
Randolph	18	18.7	98	1.4	84	24.0	27.0	2 639	60	22.8	D	1 030	52	295
Richmond	330	998.8	4 074	79.4	1 806	1 478.6	61.3	7 697	1 332	1 453.8	1 271	1 166	358	757
Rockdale	96	613.5	1 094	25.4	459	398.6	124.1	8 021	309	390.6	D	1 551	139	640

1. For pay period including March 12. 2. Based on the estimated population as of July 1 of the year shown.

STATE County	Retail trade, establishments with payroll, 1987 (cont'd)		Taxable service industries–establishments with payroll, 1987							Bank deposits,[2] June 1989		Savings capital,[3] September 1989	
				Receipts (Mil dol)									
					Selected kinds of business								
	Paid employees[1]	Annual payroll (Mil dol)	Number	Total	Hotels, motels and other lodging places	Health services	Legal services	Paid employees	Annual payroll (Mil dol)	Total (Mil dol)	Percent change, 1988–1989	Total (Mil dol)	Percent change, 1988–1989
	161	162	163	164	165	166	167	168	169	170	171	172	173
GEORGIA–Con.													
Floyd	5 946	57.8	419	170.8	2.4	103.3	8.9	4 938	68.1	479	12.9	283.2	-0.9
Forsyth	1 921	17.1	155	40.5	D	16.5	2.0	930	12.2	259	2.6	43.2	5.0
Franklin	954	9.2	73	15.6	D	3.0	0.5	311	4.4	155	13.2	11.2	-3.6
Fulton	75 574	790.3	7 561	5 698.4	486.4	904.7	677.6	119 294	2 178.3	13 973	6.7	2 264.7	2.3
Gilmer	755	6.0	48	16.9	D	9.8	0.4	372	5.5	119	3.7	16.4	9.6
Glascock	37	0.2	3	D	0.0	D	0.0	D	D	4	1.0	0.0	NA
Glynn	7 549	60.0	510	219.8	76.5	61.6	12.8	5 664	82.5	340	5.0	262.6	3.0
Gordon	2 042	19.8	155	36.0	8.1	9.9	1.4	1 031	12.5	190	37.7	76.0	-10.0
Grady	1 322	11.3	68	9.9	0.0	3.4	D	288	3.1	102	15.1	29.6	-18.6
Greene	503	4.3	38	5.3	D	2.1	0.4	226	2.0	137	11.8	0.0	NA
Gwinnett	27 994	286.5	2 176	1 050.2	26.5	167.8	24.0	20 333	386.2	1 415	14.9	604.1	11.1
Habersham	1 429	15.1	113	20.9	D	5.4	2.1	818	6.4	308	6.0	110.2	16.7
Hall	6 797	72.4	614	213.2	20.1	95.4	12.3	5 215	77.9	938	14.5	245.9	5.1
Hancock	135	1.0	23	4.2	0.0	3.0	D	173	1.8	43	12.2	0.0	NA
Haralson	950	8.3	80	34.2	D	6.7	2.1	751	8.1	119	5.6	73.7	9.5
Harris	337	2.8	34	D	D	1.8	D	D	D	42	0.8	0.0	NA
Hart	757	7.5	63	15.1	D	5.9	1.1	434	4.9	132	11.9	32.1	-2.3
Heard	123	1.2	17	2.1	D	D	D	121	0.8	21	14.1	0.0	NA
Henry	1 970	18.8	186	43.0	6.6	10.3	3.2	1 551	15.9	262	11.2	37.1	-7.6
Houston	6 101	57.3	432	131.1	17.3	44.0	D	3 691	46.7	340	15.5	239.0	-11.0
Irwin	248	2.3	23	4.7	D	1.8	D	145	2.1	48	-0.3	11.8	-10.2
Jackson	1 418	13.0	77	18.6	D	5.0	0.7	313	4.9	134	2.5	47.9	14.3
Jasper	204	2.0	19	1.6	D	0.7	0.2	45	0.4	54	6.1	0.0	NA
Jeff Davis	564	4.9	56	14.9	D	3.6	0.9	291	3.5	50	19.7	27.7	7.4
Jefferson	639	5.9	56	10.3	0.7	5.8	D	422	3.6	111	10.4	5.0	7.1
Jenkins	270	2.3	29	2.9	D	1.2	0.3	87	1.0	43	9.4	0.0	NA
Johnson	217	1.8	25	4.2	D	D	D	149	1.5	47	7.8	0.0	NA
Jones	190	2.0	25	4.8	D	D	D	184	2.1	45	34.1	0.0	-100.0
Lamar	505	4.1	34	5.3	0.2	2.5	0.3	226	1.7	86	10.9	4.2	-7.2
Lanier	205	2.1	24	2.0	0.0	D	D	70	0.5	36	7.5	0.0	NA
Laurens	2 969	25.3	238	82.9	3.5	54.6	2.8	2 097	29.3	363	15.0	63.9	4.3
Lee	107	0.7	13	0.9	0.0	D	D	15	0.3	9	2.1	0.0	NA
Liberty	2 218	16.9	114	23.7	2.6	5.9	3.9	729	7.8	97	8.9	27.2	12.7
Lincoln	139	1.2	18	2.6	0.0	D	D	39	0.7	33	9.1	0.0	NA
Long	28	0.2	2	D	0.0	0.0	0.0	D	D	5	-3.4	0.0	NA
Lowndes	7 328	62.3	536	160.1	16.8	68.4	7.1	4 293	58.6	450	13.4	156.2	3.6
Lumpkin	540	5.3	40	14.7	D	11.4	D	334	4.2	114	2.2	15.4	9.4
McDuffie	1 473	13.5	110	16.9	D	6.6	1.5	510	5.9	148	10.9	28.3	12.5
McIntosh	340	3.2	21	3.7	D	D	0.2	147	0.8	31	8.0	0.0	NA
Macon	501	4.8	40	13.7	0.0	9.4	0.5	382	4.6	65	-3.2	9.2	-6.2
Madison	211	1.8	32	5.3	0.0	1.9	0.3	157	1.4	45	12.3	0.0	NA
Marion	126	1.3	8	1.1	0.0	0.7	D	31	0.2	18	5.9	0.0	NA
Meriwether	805	9.0	60	8.6	D	3.5	0.9	219	2.7	98	5.5	19.3	-12.4
Miller	242	2.3	22	2.2	0.0	1.0	D	57	0.6	62	6.5	0.0	NA
Mitchell	845	7.6	81	11.6	D	1.6	1.0	380	3.4	132	13.0	26.6	5.6
Monroe	884	7.4	47	17.2	8.5	4.9	1.0	654	5.5	82	5.3	17.0	1.2
Montgomery	513	5.0	15	4.0	D	D	D	109	1.2	92	5.5	0.0	NA
Morgan	782	6.8	49	13.5	2.7	3.7	D	348	4.8	96	4.6	0.0	NA
Murray	652	7.3	28	7.6	0.0	1.7	0.6	121	2.2	86	2.6	14.7	37.6
Muscogee	16 345	160.7	1 123	D	19.8	160.6	29.4	D	D	1 207	9.0	372.4	-2.8
Newton	2 304	20.3	162	33.2	1.7	14.9	2.8	1 106	12.3	214	12.4	65.5	-12.8
Oconee	473	3.3	73	13.4	D	1.2	0.3	315	3.8	89	14.5	15.1	5.7
Oglethorpe	124	1.3	30	3.8	0.0	1.1	0.1	116	1.6	35	4.5	0.0	NA
Paulding	1 166	12.0	84	13.8	0.0	4.0	1.6	369	4.4	184	13.3	32.1	-12.7
Peach	946	7.7	80	11.7	D	D	D	348	3.3	116	0.3	22.7	10.8
Pickens	635	7.5	44	8.4	D	2.4	0.8	190	2.8	107	5.0	11.4	2.3
Pierce	512	4.5	46	6.2	D	2.1	D	152	2.4	77	10.3	9.5	8.2
Pike	149	1.0	17	1.7	0.0	D	0.3	80	0.7	62	11.9	0.0	NA
Polk	1 501	14.0	125	20.3	D	7.2	3.7	596	6.1	166	8.2	54.7	4.6
Pulaski	406	3.4	43	8.2	D	4.4	0.4	266	3.4	71	-0.6	0.0	NA
Putnam	487	3.6	44	7.1	D	4.3	0.5	247	2.4	83	11.3	0.0	NA
Quitman	32	0.3	0	0.0	0.0	0.0	0.0	0	0.0	NA	NA	0.0	NA
Rabun	717	7.1	102	26.8	8.9	10.4	0.8	707	8.3	136	-1.3	3.7	-8.8
Randolph	287	2.7	22	3.0	D	D	D	76	0.7	49	7.1	12.1	3.5
Richmond	19 656	179.9	1 328	617.0	32.4	245.2	32.4	14 807	249.4	1 038	2.1	657.0	-6.0
Rockdale	4 015	39.5	301	81.0	D	19.8	3.2	3 632	31.7	267	12.0	127.1	5.9

1. For the period including March 12 of the year shown. 2. Includes deposits for all insured and reporting noninsured commercial and mutual savings banks. 3. Includes savings capital for all FSLIC insured savings institutions.

STATE County	Federal funds and grants, 1989: Expenditures: Total (Mil dol)	Federal funds and grants, 1989: Expenditures: Percent change, 1988–1989	Per capita[1] (Dollars): Total	Per capita[1] (Dollars): Direct payments for individuals	Per capita[1] (Dollars): Procurement contract awards	Per capita[1] (Dollars): Salaries and wages	Per capita[1] (Dollars): Grant awards	Local government finances, 1981–1982: General revenue: Total (Mil dol)	General revenue: Intergovernmental: Total (Mil dol)	General revenue: Intergovernmental: Percent from state	General revenue: Taxes: Total (Mil dol)	Taxes: Per capita[2]: Total (Dollars)	Taxes: Per capita[2]: Property (Dollars)	Direct general expenditure: Total (Mil dol)	Direct general expenditure: Percent change, 1977–1982
	174	175	176	177	178	179	180	181	182	183	184	185	186	187	188
GEORGIA—Con.															
Floyd	175.0	5.0	2 163	1 699	22	115	315	89.3	26.0	77.1	30.1	379	267	85.9	85.9
Forsyth	50.7	20.8	1 124	901	11	66	139	21.6	7.8	95.8	8.9	292	235	23.1	121.7
Franklin	38.8	10.7	2 326	1 784	21	111	372	8.6	4.6	87.0	2.6	171	145	8.1	60.5
Fulton	3 122.2	-2.0	4 840	1 821	383	1 514	1 082	1 175.7	320.7	49.7	444.9	744	517	899.1	66.7
Gilmer	28.7	-0.8	2 124	1 712	13	114	255	6.6	3.5	91.1	2.6	229	166	6.0	39.6
Glascock	6.6	4.6	3 005	2 207	24	172	485	1.6	1.0	96.0	0.4	167	155	1.8	67.3
Glynn	200.1	14.7	3 291	1 964	438	634	250	72.9	16.8	81.7	25.0	442	296	80.0	104.1
Gordon	55.8	6.8	1 619	1 299	13	103	185	23.4	8.9	93.4	9.1	296	245	22.1	55.7
Grady	47.3	19.6	2 232	1 490	7	66	519	15.6	6.0	87.6	4.5	222	179	15.3	81.1
Greene	34.4	28.1	2 864	1 779	327	174	520	13.7	9.5	64.2	2.1	184	155	13.3	191.6
Gwinnett	427.9	21.0	1 226	586	410	134	91	152.2	56.5	74.3	56.8	297	272	148.9	128.1
Habersham	61.9	-13.8	2 174	1 496	346	108	209	18.6	7.8	77.9	5.1	196	172	16.8	79.1
Hall	193.4	11.4	2 114	1 380	316	185	217	83.3	25.1	85.9	24.4	311	202	83.7	108.8
Hancock	25.2	11.4	2 772	1 806	8	108	830	6.0	4.0	92.0	1.7	184	163	6.1	44.6
Haralson	43.4	8.4	2 068	1 707	43	77	229	16.5	6.1	87.2	5.5	293	218	16.3	51.5
Harris	36.1	3.8	2 016	1 709	8	70	223	7.6	3.9	95.3	3.3	209	160	7.6	66.7
Hart	42.2	3.9	2 110	1 503	110	136	283	12.9	5.9	91.7	3.6	189	170	12.5	47.3
Heard	15.9	21.3	2 008	1 454	9	59	470	8.1	2.3	90.7	3.9	592	375	7.9	192.5
Henry	121.1	9.3	2 109	1 187	31	722	159	36.2	8.5	92.8	11.4	292	225	39.3	163.4
Houston	893.4	14.1	9 982	1 866	1 679	6 207	206	72.9	23.3	86.5	20.1	246	211	66.1	71.6
Irwin	21.9	12.0	2 406	1 461	71	88	483	6.9	4.1	92.4	1.5	171	131	5.9	50.7
Jackson	56.0	8.2	1 824	1 462	12	86	241	20.1	7.4	91.1	5.7	218	155	19.5	151.7
Jasper	17.2	4.2	2 099	1 554	36	139	326	5.6	2.7	84.9	1.9	258	238	6.2	64.5
Jeff Davis	24.1	6.4	1 978	1 468	10	74	308	11.0	4.0	89.0	3.5	303	193	11.7	118.4
Jefferson	72.1	1.7	3 941	1 857	1 262	97	594	11.1	6.7	91.6	3.6	194	128	11.4	67.8
Jenkins	23.6	4.5	2 778	1 732	26	99	594	7.6	3.7	92.1	1.8	211	187	7.9	94.0
Johnson	20.1	-2.3	2 343	1 640	12	73	472	4.7	2.9	90.6	1.5	171	123	4.5	84.3
Jones	22.1	-23.0	1 139	874	13	50	179	8.6	4.9	89.3	2.2	128	92	8.7	109.6
Lamar	27.4	3.3	2 063	1 609	11	80	317	7.4	3.6	89.1	2.7	223	168	6.8	46.4
Lanier	15.1	21.9	2 649	1 689	9	71	795	3.4	2.2	91.0	1.0	179	134	3.5	37.8
Laurens	123.4	6.3	3 140	1 810	180	675	394	29.4	16.8	80.9	9.9	265	161	27.4	50.3
Lee	20.7	6.8	1 299	914	7	49	158	7.9	4.5	90.9	2.8	221	188	7.4	24.6
Liberty	111.8	0.9	2 667	1 018	16	1 338	291	21.3	9.8	81.2	5.6	134	77	20.1	103.3
Lincoln	17.2	11.0	2 362	1 831	8	115	375	3.8	2.3	94.6	1.2	183	139	3.6	53.7
Long	8.8	6.6	1 755	1 328	7	57	328	2.9	1.5	89.3	1.1	222	208	2.8	105.6
Lowndes	251.8	10.9	3 468	1 668	276	1 175	317	71.1	23.9	86.2	17.6	253	141	68.2	79.1
Lumpkin	26.9	25.8	2 024	1 250	27	482	254	9.7	3.8	85.2	2.4	214	195	8.6	146.8
McDuffie	44.0	5.6	2 178	1 683	9	80	390	13.5	6.8	87.3	3.0	158	82	13.7	83.3
McIntosh	39.1	-25.3	4 028	1 644	1 406	79	894	5.8	3.4	73.7	1.6	206	140	5.7	94.3
Macon	35.7	6.9	2 643	1 604	24	94	740	16.3	11.5	43.9	4.0	281	192	13.6	126.8
Madison	37.0	7.2	1 729	1 330	14	77	274	8.7	5.3	95.7	2.7	144	138	8.6	73.5
Marion	13.5	8.3	2 601	1 788	8	134	584	5.7	2.6	93.1	1.2	220	165	4.6	0.9
Meriwether	49.8	13.4	2 275	1 699	36	71	438	12.7	7.2	92.3	4.0	187	156	12.6	65.7
Miller	15.0	-3.4	2 107	1 327	10	88	406	6.2	2.4	87.1	1.8	259	227	6.0	50.1
Mitchell	55.2	14.4	2 580	1 538	20	94	573	18.4	8.9	85.5	4.0	186	164	19.0	77.6
Monroe	31.4	-18.0	2 001	1 372	10	187	398	12.8	5.1	94.2	4.1	280	162	12.7	76.3
Montgomery	19.6	10.6	2 716	1 886	14	102	524	4.7	2.9	73.4	1.5	217	196	3.3	59.4
Morgan	27.2	11.9	2 077	1 484	23	89	326	7.7	3.8	90.9	2.7	222	131	7.3	56.0
Murray	33.7	1.2	1 349	943	131	128	138	13.2	6.2	93.3	3.4	164	147	12.7	70.2
Muscogee	1 099.3	21.2	6 200	2 118	53	3 632	392	188.1	57.8	68.2	61.1	349	204	209.4	94.9
Newton	76.1	7.3	1 710	1 368	26	91	213	28.7	10.7	91.6	8.7	237	166	28.9	61.3
Oconee	23.7	13.3	1 484	1 149	11	159	105	6.4	3.5	94.7	2.3	174	161	6.3	100.7
Oglethorpe	18.6	6.9	1 914	1 199	9	66	568	4.4	2.8	94.2	1.4	152	132	4.6	70.0
Paulding	46.1	-15.3	1 205	964	7	63	164	21.1	8.0	91.5	5.9	212	165	19.9	93.6
Peach	58.0	-3.2	2 761	1 844	110	191	564	13.5	5.6	92.6	3.5	184	118	13.7	56.8
Pickens	30.9	3.9	2 103	1 584	163	95	255	10.5	3.8	79.6	3.3	273	256	10.1	53.8
Pierce	30.6	12.0	2 282	1 674	11	96	346	9.5	4.2	90.4	2.9	235	173	10.8	107.2
Pike	24.0	21.3	2 549	2 063	12	95	319	4.7	2.8	92.6	1.3	150	135	4.5	32.6
Polk	93.3	1.5	2 727	1 822	489	92	295	25.2	11.0	88.8	7.4	225	157	27.0	59.2
Pulaski	24.4	-14.3	2 867	1 714	211	101	467	7.5	5.2	54.3	1.7	192	159	5.5	68.8
Putnam	30.7	14.3	2 325	1 757	12	119	340	8.2	3.7	84.2	3.9	360	330	7.6	10.2
Quitman	8.2	6.1	3 574	2 597	20	146	722	1.2	0.8	80.1	0.4	162	123	1.0	32.7
Rabun	30.1	10.2	2 689	2 101	80	146	322	8.5	3.7	83.4	3.1	283	252	11.2	67.4
Randolph	23.8	1.5	2 676	1 800	10	81	589	8.5	4.0	82.4	1.6	170	131	8.1	109.6
Richmond	641.6	0.4	3 375	1 972	81	921	394	231.7	59.5	77.1	51.1	279	165	224.9	114.4
Rockdale	65.5	12.1	1 204	975	12	71	140	34.7	10.4	92.2	13.8	343	316	34.6	111.6

1. Based on the estimated population as of July 1 of the year shown. 2. Based on the estimated population as of July 1, 1982.

STATE County	Local government finances, 1981–1982 (cont'd) — Direct general expenditure (cont'd) — Per capita[1] (Dollars)	Percent of total for– Education	Percent of total for– Health & hospitals	Percent of total for– Police protection	Percent of total for– Public welfare	Percent of total for– Highways	Debt outstanding — Total (Mil dol)	Debt outstanding — Per capita[1] (Dollars)	State and local government employment, 1989 — Total	State and local government employment, 1989 — Rate[2]	Federal government civilian employment 1989 — Total	Federal government civilian employment 1989 — Earnings ($1,000)	Elections, 1988[3] — Total vote cast for president	Elections, 1988[3] — Vote for lead party (Percent)
	189	190	191	192	193	194	195	196	197	198	199	200	201	202
GEORGIA—Con.														
Floyd	1 082	37.2	30.9	4.1	0.1	4.3	63.4	799	6 354	785.4	234	7 319	23 386	R–62.8
Forsyth	757	55.0	23.3	3.9	0.3	5.6	13.2	432	1 402	310.9	85	2 458	10 344	R–76.8
Franklin	530	62.2	1.6	6.8	0.0	11.3	4.5	293	743	444.9	57	1 383	4 465	R–58.6
Fulton	1 504	32.6	8.9	5.6	0.4	2.8	2 966.9	4 962	70 057	1 086.0	24 482	828 190	214 689	D–56.2
Gilmer	530	61.9	1.1	4.5	0.1	11.5	1.8	157	736	545.2	50	1 403	4 746	R–70.6
Glascock	741	58.0	2.4	3.3	0.8	12.4	0.2	86	120	545.5	NA	217	790	R–73.4
Glynn	1 413	28.9	35.1	6.1	0.1	4.3	44.6	788	5 011	824.2	1 039	38 661	17 611	R–63.2
Gordon	717	55.7	13.9	5.1	0.1	10.5	23.0	745	1 358	393.6	93	2 556	8 445	R–71.7
Grady	763	44.2	24.2	4.3	0.0	5.4	9.6	476	969	457.1	55	1 292	4 892	R–61.1
Greene	1 159	51.9	9.7	2.6	0.1	3.6	5.9	516	707	589.2	36	963	3 260	D–55.8
Gwinnett	780	53.6	13.1	5.4	0.1	5.5	189.7	993	13 559	388.3	1 390	35 889	87 940	R–75.5
Habersham	643	46.7	27.5	4.4	0.0	6.8	7.5	288	2 119	743.5	117	2 870	7 014	R–69.4
Hall	1 068	33.7	37.6	4.0	0.4	4.6	26.1	333	5 080	555.2	497	15 480	25 344	R–68.7
Hancock	653	66.4	7.6	4.9	0.3	4.8	2.6	277	451	495.6	20	565	2 589	D–75.2
Haralson	861	41.5	19.7	4.9	0.2	9.8	10.2	541	966	460.0	43	1 176	6 950	R–65.2
Harris	482	63.9	5.2	5.3	0.1	1.7	6.3	398	603	336.9	39	991	5 339	R–63.9
Hart	659	48.4	24.1	4.6	0.3	5.4	3.7	197	868	434.0	90	2 501	5 547	R–54.9
Heard	1 195	44.1	26.5	2.8	0.3	15.3	1.7	261	419	530.4	12	313	2 432	R–63.8
Henry	1 009	35.7	39.1	4.5	0.1	3.9	40.1	1 030	2 544	443.2	835	44 522	15 304	R–71.1
Houston	809	40.4	31.8	5.1	0.3	3.7	26.3	322	4 494	502.1	16 799	480 012	24 597	R–64.0
Irwin	668	55.1	19.9	5.0	0.3	6.3	0.7	76	465	511.0	35	824	2 151	R–57.0
Jackson	745	41.9	32.8	4.3	0.2	5.4	8.2	315	1 246	405.9	80	2 104	7 045	R–62.6
Jasper	825	43.2	21.3	5.1	0.2	13.7	0.7	89	415	506.1	49	1 036	2 676	R–55.1
Jeff Davis	1 006	38.6	20.5	3.3	0.1	11.9	5.5	476	609	499.2	33	803	3 305	R–62.0
Jefferson	618	58.7	4.2	8.2	0.1	3.5	1.6	88	985	538.3	55	1 212	5 151	R–54.1
Jenkins	931	45.7	29.6	3.7	0.2	7.9	1.2	137	537	631.8	34	817	2 248	R–57.3
Johnson	519	59.8	7.1	3.5	0.2	13.1	0.6	71	345	401.2	24	577	2 494	R–62.8
Jones	502	67.1	3.3	3.7	0.1	9.5	2.1	119	557	287.1	29	842	6 302	R–57.4
Lamar	565	60.8	4.2	5.7	0.1	6.8	3.5	293	596	448.1	31	826	3 519	R–57.8
Lanier	632	63.1	6.2	4.9	0.1	7.7	0.7	127	240	421.1	22	485	1 427	R–50.8
Laurens	730	56.1	6.8	4.9	0.1	8.7	6.0	161	2 295	584.0	1 030	34 061	11 970	R–57.9
Lee	594	70.9	0.6	3.7	0.1	8.3	1.7	138	805	506.3	28	683	3 883	R–74.0
Liberty	479	48.8	17.7	4.2	0.1	5.1	6.0	143	1 774	423.4	3 549	80 896	6 050	R–51.2
Lincoln	544	69.8	1.8	3.9	0.1	8.8	1.6	243	312	427.4	23	807	2 324	R–61.0
Long	541	59.1	2.1	7.5	4.5	12.5	0.2	32	226	452.0	11	256	1 551	R–55.3
Lowndes	983	35.5	37.2	3.8	0.1	5.3	27.2	392	5 804	799.4	1 037	23 861	17 333	R–62.6
Lumpkin	763	39.5	35.3	3.0	0.2	7.8	3.7	325	858	645.1	51	1 172	4 000	R–67.2
McDuffie	721	49.2	19.3	3.7	0.2	8.0	9.3	489	1 105	547.0	50	1 294	4 968	R–65.0
McIntosh	709	56.2	4.7	9.1	0.2	8.1	1.4	177	548	564.9	26	630	2 824	D–54.1
Macon	957	42.0	2.5	4.3	0.1	5.2	2.6	185	662	490.4	42	970	3 697	D–61.3
Madison	463	73.6	4.2	3.1	0.2	9.0	0.4	24	696	325.2	45	1 090	5 389	R–69.1
Marion	875	40.3	36.5	2.6	0.2	8.8	1.4	258	318	611.5	27	743	1 652	D–51.1
Meriwether	595	57.8	4.3	5.9	0.3	12.3	5.9	279	1 631	744.7	45	1 210	6 044	R–51.3
Miller	856	51.9	26.9	3.9	0.1	5.7	3.0	435	429	604.2	32	724	1 625	R–68.0
Mitchell	884	47.9	21.8	3.5	0.2	5.4	10.4	484	1 278	597.2	81	2 053	4 860	R–53.3
Monroe	855	45.5	19.9	7.7	0.0	8.0	11.9	805	1 069	680.9	43	1 157	4 558	R–56.4
Montgomery	484	65.0	9.5	5.2	0.0	8.1	1.8	263	373	518.1	26	571	2 136	R–57.5
Morgan	612	60.7	2.5	5.7	0.2	9.3	11.7	973	603	460.3	35	896	3 628	R–58.1
Murray	618	56.4	20.0	4.4	0.1	9.5	0.9	42	997	398.8	94	2 312	5 700	R–70.1
Muscogee	1 198	32.6	34.6	3.4	1.1	4.0	121.4	695	11 413	643.7	2 086	37 310	42 000	R–54.9
Newton	791	45.4	14.2	5.2	0.2	8.0	12.7	348	2 062	463.4	96	2 611	8 969	R–64.8
Oconee	473	73.6	1.3	4.0	0.9	6.5	0.1	4	541	338.1	73	2 306	6 282	R–67.9
Oglethorpe	501	76.2	1.5	3.3	0.1	11.1	0.3	35	333	343.3	20	504	3 116	R–62.6
Paulding	717	47.5	30.3	3.9	0.3	6.6	6.0	216	1 534	400.5	57	1 566	10 091	R–72.6
Peach	724	44.0	29.8	5.6	0.4	2.7	2.0	106	1 526	726.7	98	2 904	5 796	D–51.3
Pickens	828	39.7	28.2	3.9	0.4	8.2	5.2	423	847	576.2	39	998	4 474	R–67.5
Pierce	871	56.9	15.7	4.2	0.1	7.6	4.2	338	489	364.9	46	1 148	3 509	R–55.5
Pike	515	71.4	1.2	4.6	0.0	9.1	0.5	62	372	395.7	26	609	3 274	R–63.3
Polk	823	43.7	19.0	4.8	0.1	5.8	8.1	247	1 602	468.4	90	2 548	8 461	R–64.5
Pulaski	606	57.3	4.3	6.1	0.3	9.4	0.7	83	405	476.5	24	654	2 888	D–51.1
Putnam	703	55.3	4.4	8.1	0.2	13.7	3.6	331	743	562.9	62	1 264	3 656	R–57.7
Quitman	450	66.4	2.9	7.1	0.6	5.6	0.2	74	85	369.6	NA	165	738	D–59.1
Rabun	1 031	34.7	9.4	2.6	0.1	36.6	3.6	335	549	490.2	65	1 474	3 608	R–63.1
Randolph	853	40.8	28.8	3.3	0.1	7.4	3.7	387	656	737.1	26	708	2 695	D–50.8
Richmond	1 228	33.9	41.4	3.1	0.1	2.3	178.4	974	18 860	992.1	7 488	209 996	48 258	R–57.1
Rockdale	860	49.0	24.0	4.6	0.0	2.9	39.6	985	2 591	476.3	102	2 974	16 826	R–73.8

1. Based on the estimated population as of July 1, 1982. 2. Per 10,000 resident population estimated as of July 1 of the year shown. 3. Data subject to copyright.

STATE–County code	MSA/CMSA/NECMA code[1]	STATE County	Land Area,[2] 1990 (Sq. Km.)	Population, 1990 Total persons	Rank	Per square kilometer	Race White	Black	Am. Indian, Eskimo, Aleut	Asian & Pacific Islander	Other race	Hispanic[3]	Age of population Percent Under 5 years	5 to 14 years	15 to 24 years
			1	2	3	4	5	6	7	8	9	10	11	12	13
		GEORGIA—Con.													
13 249	...	Schley	434	3 588	2 952	8.3	2 317	1 222	3	0	46	55	7.4	16.0	16.5
13 251	...	Screven	1 680	13 842	2 069	8.2	7 598	6 209	14	15	6	51	7.9	16.7	13.5
13 253	...	Seminole	617	9 010	2 468	14.6	6 031	2 943	22	10	4	530	6.8	14.8	15.8
13 255	0520	Spalding	513	54 457	792	106.2	38 281	15 785	88	233	70	316	7.9	15.4	15.1
13 257	...	Stephens	464	23 257	1 527	50.1	20 300	2 787	32	101	37	144	6.7	13.1	16.0
13 259	...	Stewart	1 188	5 654	2 789	4.8	2 041	3 578	16	16	3	26	6.7	15.7	15.2
13 261	...	Sumter	1 257	30 228	1 285	24.0	15 910	14 045	100	113	60	189	8.0	16.2	17.5
13 263	...	Talbot	1 019	6 524	2 707	6.4	2 436	4 067	13	3	5	51	6.9	15.2	14.3
13 265	...	Taliaferro	506	1 915	3 074	3.8	736	1 167	1	4	7	21	6.9	15.9	13.4
13 267	...	Tattnall	1 253	17 722	1 802	14.1	12 087	5 177	23	51	384	547	6.6	13.6	14.3
13 269	...	Taylor	978	7 642	2 607	7.8	4 292	3 300	2	11	37	58	7.2	15.6	15.7
13 271	...	Telfair	1 143	11 000	2 293	9.6	7 202	3 773	9	6	10	41	6.9	16.3	13.8
13 273	...	Terrell	869	10 653	2 322	12.3	4 251	6 377	8	15	2	40	7.9	17.2	13.5
13 275	...	Thomas	1 420	38 986	1 022	27.5	23 971	14 759	100	65	91	289	7.6	16.2	13.9
13 277	...	Tift	687	34 998	1 131	50.9	24 941	9 371	42	183	461	1 233	7.9	15.9	17.2
13 279	...	Toombs	950	24 072	1 490	25.3	17 596	5 637	37	148	654	824	7.9	16.6	14.4
13 281	...	Towns	431	6 754	2 680	15.7	6 734	0	13	4	3	18	4.6	9.6	14.5
13 283	...	Treutlen	520	5 994	2 758	11.5	4 001	1 984	2	0	7	16	7.1	15.9	15.6
13 285	...	Troup	1 072	55 536	779	51.8	38 458	16 694	56	288	40	289	7.8	15.4	15.1
13 287	...	Turner	741	8 703	2 493	11.7	5 129	3 534	10	20	10	35	8.2	18.1	15.5
13 289	...	Twiggs	933	9 806	2 404	10.5	5 290	4 501	8	6	1	46	7.9	18.0	14.6
13 291	...	Union	836	11 993	2 221	14.3	11 925	19	27	21	1	49	5.6	12.8	12.6
13 293	...	Upson	843	26 300	1 411	31.2	18 897	7 272	34	70	27	98	6.8	14.3	14.1
13 295	1560	Walker	1 156	58 340	743	50.5	55 779	2 246	133	131	51	214	6.5	14.7	13.9
13 297	0520	Walton	853	38 586	1 038	45.2	31 177	7 105	89	143	72	338	7.8	15.5	15.1
13 299	...	Ware	2 338	35 471	1 111	15.2	26 007	9 238	58	123	45	190	6.9	15.0	14.4
13 301	...	Warren	740	6 078	2 748	8.2	2 413	3 656	2	7	0	2	8.2	15.7	13.7
13 303	...	Washington	1 762	19 112	1 726	10.8	9 198	9 874	10	25	5	65	8.0	16.5	14.2
13 305	...	Wayne	1 670	22 356	1 562	13.4	17 884	4 358	41	44	29	177	7.7	16.4	14.2
13 307	...	Webster	543	2 263	3 047	4.2	1 127	1 132	4	0	0	1	6.8	16.2	14.4
13 309	...	Wheeler	771	4 903	2 845	6.4	3 352	1 474	4	5	68	101	7.5	15.7	15.3
13 311	...	White	626	13 006	2 142	20.8	12 522	360	37	71	16	98	6.0	12.8	14.3
13 313	...	Whitfield	751	72 462	617	96.5	67 533	2 901	172	323	1 533	2 321	7.1	14.4	16.1
13 315	...	Wilcox	985	7 008	2 658	7.1	4 757	2 225	9	2	15	30	7.3	16.3	13.9
13 317	...	Wilkes	1 221	10 597	2 328	8.7	5 650	4 909	16	13	9	44	6.5	15.6	12.7
13 319	...	Wilkinson	1 157	10 228	2 367	8.8	5 910	4 302	5	7	4	30	7.7	17.1	15.2
13 321	...	Worth	1 476	19 745	1 686	13.4	13 540	6 051	55	37	62	222	8.2	16.8	15.3
15 000	...	HAWAII	16 636	1 108 229	X	66.6	369 616	27 195	5 099	685 236	21 083	81 390	7.5	14.0	14.7
15 001	...	Hawaii	10 433	120 317	383	11.5	47 736	615	868	68 699	2 399	11 134	7.9	16.6	11.7
15 003	3320	Honolulu	1 554	836 231	40	538.1	264 372	25 875	3 532	526 459	15 993	56 884	7.4	13.4	15.6
15 005	...	Kalawao	34	130	3 139	3.8	30	0	0	100	0	11	0.0	0.0	0.8
15 007	...	Kauai	1 612	51 177	823	31.7	17 712	211	178	32 093	983	5 580	7.8	15.8	12.2
15 009	...	Maui	3 002	100 374	457	33.4	39 766	494	521	57 885	1 708	7 781	7.8	14.9	12.5
16 000	...	IDAHO	214 325	1 006 749	X	4.7	950 451	3 370	13 780	9 365	29 783	52 927	8.0	17.9	14.5
16 001	1080	Ada	2 733	205 775	242	75.3	198 888	958	1 382	2 887	1 660	5 556	7.7	16.3	14.1
16 003	...	Adams	3 535	3 254	2 980	0.9	3 203	2	41	1	7	38	7.4	16.3	10.6
16 005	...	Bannock	2 883	66 026	665	22.9	61 742	431	1 678	712	1 463	2 740	8.4	19.2	15.7
16 007	...	Bear Lake	2 516	6 084	2 747	2.4	5 999	0	25	5	55	136	8.9	23.5	10.9
16 009	...	Benewah	2 010	7 937	2 580	3.9	7 278	6	602	28	23	124	7.5	16.9	12.8
16 011	...	Bingham	5 426	37 583	1 057	6.9	32 439	39	2 615	273	2 217	3 614	9.4	23.3	13.8
16 013	...	Blaine	6 850	13 552	2 097	2.0	13 241	10	53	104	144	397	7.5	15.6	10.7
16 015	...	Boise	4 927	3 509	2 957	0.7	3 431	2	35	14	27	84	7.0	16.7	10.8
16 017	...	Bonner	4 500	26 622	1 402	5.9	26 210	37	220	71	84	352	7.0	17.1	10.2
16 019	...	Bonneville	4 840	72 207	618	14.9	69 246	297	391	687	1 586	3 010	9.5	20.5	14.2
16 021	...	Boundary	3 286	8 332	2 531	2.5	7 950	3	150	26	203	310	7.6	18.7	13.7
16 023	...	Butte	5 783	2 918	3 005	0.5	2 829	0	22	5	62	101	7.4	21.4	11.2
16 025	...	Camas	2 784	727	3 128	0.3	712	2	8	3	2	4	7.8	15.7	11.0
16 027	...	Canyon	1 527	90 076	510	59.0	80 445	175	687	987	7 782	11 838	8.2	17.6	14.8
16 029	...	Caribou	4 574	6 963	2 665	1.5	6 824	7	22	13	97	192	8.1	24.2	11.8
16 031	...	Cassia	6 647	19 532	1 698	2.9	17 580	3	170	96	1 683	2 623	9.2	21.8	13.8
16 033	...	Clark	4 571	762	3 126	0.2	688	0	5	0	69	79	7.0	20.1	11.0
16 035	...	Clearwater	6 375	8 505	2 510	1.3	8 262	10	180	21	32	112	5.3	15.3	10.7
16 037	...	Custer	12 757	4 133	2 904	0.3	4 044	2	33	19	35	90	8.0	17.4	10.5
16 039	...	Elmore	7 971	21 205	1 619	2.7	18 898	777	171	453	906	1 597	10.5	17.0	16.2

1. MSA = Metropolitan Statistical Area. CMSA = Consolidated MSA. NECMA = New England county metropolitan area. PMSA = Primary MSA. See Appendix A for explanation of these concepts. See Appendix B for list of metropolitan areas identified by type, with component counties. 2. Dry land or land partially or temporarily covered by water. 3. Hispanic persons may be of any race.

STATE County	Population, 1990 (cont'd)							Population–Change and components of change							
	Age of population (cont'd) Percent							Change		Components of change, 1980–1986					
								1980–1990				Net change		Natural increase	
	25 to 34 years	35 to 44 years	45 to 54 years	55 to 64 years	65 to 74 years	75 years and over	Percent female	Number	Percent	Total persons, 1986	Total persons, 1980	Number	Percent	Births	Deaths
	14	15	16	17	18	19	20	21	22	23	24	25	26	27	28
GEORGIA—Con.															
Schley	13.9	13.4	12.0	7.6	7.9	5.5	51.8	155	4.5	3 500	3 433	0	0.6	300	200
Screven	14.9	14.1	9.3	8.6	8.5	6.4	52.6	-201	-1.4	15 100	14 043	1 000	7.4	1 400	1 000
Seminole	14.8	12.8	9.9	10.4	9.0	5.8	50.6	-47	-0.5	8 900	9 057	-100	-1.2	800	600
Spalding	16.4	14.6	10.5	8.3	6.9	4.9	52.1	6 558	13.7	53 000	47 899	5 100	10.7	4 700	2 900
Stephens	14.5	14.3	11.1	9.2	9.2	5.8	51.7	1 496	6.9	22 500	21 761	700	3.4	2 000	1 300
Stewart	13.9	12.7	9.5	9.1	9.8	7.4	51.9	-242	-4.1	5 600	5 896	-300	-4.5	600	400
Sumter	15.1	13.2	9.2	7.4	7.0	6.3	53.9	868	3.0	30 200	29 360	800	2.8	3 300	2 000
Talbot	15.8	14.7	10.1	9.5	7.1	6.4	52.6	-12	-0.2	6 600	6 536	100	1.7	500	400
Taliaferro	13.4	11.5	10.7	9.0	10.3	8.9	52.8	-117	-5.8	2 100	2 032	0	0.9	200	200
Tattnall	19.1	14.2	10.4	8.4	7.8	5.6	46.3	-412	-2.3	17 900	18 134	-300	-1.5	1 800	1 100
Taylor	15.0	12.4	11.1	8.6	8.6	5.8	53.2	-260	-3.3	8 100	7 902	200	1.9	700	600
Telfair	14.4	13.1	8.9	9.1	9.5	8.0	54.2	-445	-3.9	11 100	11 445	-300	-2.8	1 300	900
Terrell	14.1	12.7	10.4	9.2	8.3	6.7	54.1	-1 364	-11.4	11 600	12 017	-500	-3.8	1 300	700
Thomas	15.2	13.9	10.4	8.9	8.0	5.9	53.5	888	2.3	38 100	38 098	0	-0.1	4 200	2 500
Tift	15.9	14.2	9.7	7.8	6.5	4.8	51.3	2 136	6.5	34 300	32 862	1 400	4.3	3 500	1 700
Toombs	15.8	14.3	10.5	8.0	7.2	5.3	52.5	1 480	6.6	24 100	22 592	1 500	6.7	2 500	1 400
Towns	11.7	11.9	9.9	13.9	13.8	10.1	51.5	1 116	19.8	6 200	5 638	600	10.7	400	400
Treutlen	14.1	12.9	10.1	8.9	8.3	7.0	53.9	-93	-1.5	6 000	6 087	-100	-1.9	600	400
Troup	15.7	14.4	9.3	8.6	7.7	6.0	52.9	5 533	11.1	54 200	50 003	4 200	8.4	5 200	3 300
Turner	13.1	12.7	10.0	8.6	7.9	6.2	52.7	-807	-8.5	9 500	9 510	0	0.4	1 100	600
Twiggs	16.6	13.3	10.2	8.3	6.6	4.5	52.0	452	4.8	10 100	9 354	700	7.6	1 000	500
Union	12.9	13.6	11.2	12.9	10.8	7.6	50.3	2 603	27.7	10 800	9 390	1 400	15.2	700	700
Upson	15.2	13.4	10.8	9.5	9.0	7.0	52.7	302	1.2	26 700	25 998	700	2.6	2 100	1 900
Walker	15.6	14.7	11.5	9.7	8.0	5.3	51.5	1 870	3.3	56 400	56 470	-100	-0.1	4 600	3 100
Walton	17.0	14.6	11.0	7.9	6.5	4.7	51.6	7 375	23.6	33 800	31 211	2 600	8.3	3 200	1 700
Ware	14.7	14.4	9.9	9.7	8.7	6.4	51.7	-1 709	-4.6	37 000	37 180	-200	-0.4	3 700	2 300
Warren	14.7	13.0	9.3	9.0	8.4	8.1	54.6	-505	-7.7	6 200	6 583	-400	-5.7	600	500
Washington	16.1	13.8	9.5	8.1	7.4	6.3	53.0	270	1.4	19 300	18 842	500	2.5	2 000	1 300
Wayne	15.3	15.1	10.4	9.1	6.8	4.9	51.4	1 606	7.7	22 000	20 750	1 300	6.1	2 200	1 300
Webster	15.1	13.5	9.8	9.7	8.7	5.8	53.3	-78	-3.3	2 200	2 341	-200	-7.2	200	200
Wheeler	12.5	14.0	10.5	8.4	9.3	6.9	51.5	-252	-4.9	5 100	5 155	0	-0.2	400	300
White	14.2	14.5	12.3	10.9	8.9	6.0	51.3	2 886	28.5	11 600	10 120	1 400	14.2	900	600
Whitfield	17.2	15.4	11.5	8.5	6.0	3.9	50.8	6 687	10.2	69 300	65 775	3 500	5.3	6 400	3 100
Wilcox	12.9	13.5	9.8	9.0	9.9	7.4	52.9	-674	-8.8	7 600	7 682	-100	-1.7	700	500
Wilkes	14.6	13.4	10.5	9.5	9.7	7.3	52.3	-354	-3.2	11 100	10 951	100	1.0	1 100	800
Wilkinson	16.4	13.1	10.3	8.7	6.7	4.8	52.4	-140	-1.4	10 800	10 368	400	4.0	1 100	600
Worth	15.3	14.2	10.6	7.9	7.0	4.6	51.8	1 681	9.3	18 700	18 064	600	3.3	2 000	1 000
HAWAII	18.1	16.1	9.8	8.5	7.1	4.2	49.1	143 229	14.8	1 062 000	965 000	98 000	10.1	116 000	33 000
Hawaii	15.0	17.6	9.9	8.9	7.8	4.8	49.6	28 264	30.7	111 800	92 053	19 700	21.4	12 000	4 000
Honolulu	18.7	15.6	9.8	8.5	7.0	4.0	49.1	73 666	9.7	816 700	762 565	54 200	7.1	88 900	24 700
Kalawao	6.9	11.5	18.5	28.5	20.0	13.8	38.5	NA	NA	0	0	0	0.0	0	0
Kauai	16.0	17.0	9.8	8.3	7.7	5.4	49.3	12 095	30.9	46 300	39 082	7 200	18.5	4 900	1 600
Maui	17.7	17.8	9.9	7.9	7.0	4.3	49.0	29 383	41.4	87 500	70 991	16 600	23.3	9 500	2 900
IDAHO	15.2	14.8	9.8	7.7	6.9	5.1	50.2	62 749	6.6	1 002 000	944 000	58 000	6.2	117 000	44 000
Ada	17.7	16.9	10.0	6.8	6.0	4.4	50.8	32 650	18.9	193 800	173 125	20 700	12.0	20 000	7 300
Adams	13.7	15.1	12.0	10.3	8.6	6.0	48.5	-93	-2.8	3 300	3 347	-100	-2.6	300	200
Bannock	15.8	14.8	9.0	6.9	5.9	4.3	50.4	605	0.9	68 100	65 421	2 700	4.1	9 100	2 600
Bear Lake	12.8	11.3	9.1	8.5	8.6	6.4	50.6	-847	-12.2	6 600	6 931	-300	-4.4	1 100	400
Benewah	13.4	15.8	11.4	9.1	7.2	5.9	49.3	-355	-4.3	8 700	8 292	400	4.9	1 000	500
Bingham	14.1	13.0	9.0	7.4	5.9	4.2	49.8	1 094	3.0	38 300	36 489	1 800	5.0	5 700	1 400
Blaine	20.0	22.1	11.1	6.3	4.2	2.5	48.1	3 711	37.7	13 200	9 841	3 400	34.2	1 200	300
Boise	14.3	17.8	12.0	10.4	7.5	3.5	47.3	510	17.0	3 100	2 999	100	2.9	300	100
Bonner	13.2	17.7	10.9	9.6	8.7	5.6	50.3	2 459	10.2	25 900	24 163	1 700	7.1	2 700	1 300
Bonneville	16.1	14.1	9.5	7.2	5.4	3.6	49.7	6 227	9.4	70 600	65 980	4 600	7.0	9 700	2 500
Boundary	13.1	16.2	9.3	9.2	6.7	5.6	49.0	1 043	14.3	7 600	7 289	300	4.7	900	400
Butte	12.5	14.3	10.6	9.7	7.4	5.4	49.6	-424	-12.7	3 100	3 342	-200	-6.4	400	200
Camas	13.1	15.4	13.5	9.9	7.6	6.1	46.6	-91	-11.1	700	818	-100	-15.4	100	0
Canyon	14.4	13.9	9.7	7.7	7.6	6.1	50.7	6 320	7.5	90 200	83 756	6 400	7.6	9 700	4 400
Caribou	13.3	13.1	9.7	8.1	6.5	5.2	49.8	-1 732	-19.9	8 000	8 695	-700	-8.0	1 300	300
Cassia	13.4	12.7	8.7	8.0	7.2	5.2	49.7	105	0.5	20 300	19 427	900	4.5	3 000	800
Clark	15.4	12.7	13.0	8.7	8.0	4.2	45.1	-36	-4.5	700	798	-100	-8.1	100	0
Clearwater	14.6	15.4	12.9	10.8	9.0	6.0	47.8	-1 885	-18.1	9 400	10 390	-1 000	-9.6	1 000	500
Custer	14.7	17.0	11.7	8.7	7.3	4.7	48.4	748	22.1	5 100	3 385	1 700	49.7	600	200
Elmore	21.0	13.6	8.1	6.0	4.6	2.9	47.8	-360	-1.7	22 000	21 565	400	1.9	3 500	600

STATE County	Population–(cont'd)	Households, 1990					Births, 1988			Deaths, 1987				Marriages, 1984	
	Components of change, 1980-1986 (cont'd)				Percent					Number		Rate			
	Net migration	Number	Percent change, 1980–1990	Persons per house-hold	Female family house-holder[1]	One-person	Total	Rate[2]	Low birth weight[3] (Number)	Total	Infant[4]	Total[2]	Infant[5]	Number	Rate[2]
	29	30	31	32	33	34	35	36	37	38	39	40	41	42	43
GEORGIA—Con.															
Schley	-100	1 315	16.9	2.72	13.5	24.6	56	16.0	5	32	0	8.9	0.0	35	10.3
Screven	600	5 048	5.9	2.70	17.1	24.5	274	18.0	29	168	1	10.9	4.8	95	6.6
Seminole	-300	3 137	2.8	2.68	16.5	23.8	132	15.2	14	93	1	10.7	8.1	1 255	142.6
Spalding	3 300	19 426	20.1	2.76	16.6	19.9	878	16.0	88	514	15	9.5	18.0	443	8.8
Stephens	100	8 949	14.9	2.54	10.7	23.8	305	13.1	26	243	4	10.6	12.2	147	6.7
Stewart	-400	1 982	4.8	2.80	21.4	25.5	67	12.0	6	76	0	13.3	0.0	38	6.6
Sumter	-500	10 484	10.8	2.75	21.7	24.3	508	17.2	41	250	5	8.4	9.6	290	9.6
Talbot	0	2 345	12.4	2.78	20.2	23.2	93	13.1	8	92	1	13.1	11.6	0	0.0
Taliaferro	0	727	-4.1	2.63	16.4	31.6	18	9.0	3	33	0	16.5	0.0	9	4.3
Tattnall	-1 000	5 845	4.6	2.61	14.1	24.6	252	13.8	10	186	1	10.2	3.7	151	8.5
Taylor	0	2 804	5.7	2.72	18.9	24.1	129	16.3	8	92	1	11.5	7.8	67	8.4
Telfair	-700	4 017	2.8	2.65	17.1	26.0	164	14.9	16	147	3	13.4	18.1	121	10.8
Terrell	-1 000	3 738	-2.6	2.81	21.5	23.7	171	14.7	29	113	5	9.6	27.5	98	8.3
Thomas	-1 800	14 323	12.0	2.68	17.9	23.3	679	17.4	52	422	9	10.8	13.7	487	12.7
Tift	-400	12 184	13.5	2.75	15.7	22.4	614	17.8	73	330	11	9.7	19.4	359	10.7
Toombs	400	8 804	14.8	2.69	15.4	24.8	414	17.0	40	222	5	9.2	13.3	349	14.9
Towns	600	2 812	38.9	2.26	6.5	25.3	58	8.7	7	61	1	9.1	15.6	51	8.4
Treutlen	-300	2 158	4.1	2.74	17.0	23.8	99	16.0	8	65	0	10.5	0.0	74	12.1
Troup	2 300	20 371	16.7	2.68	16.2	23.4	930	17.4	74	607	12	11.4	14.0	553	10.5
Turner	-400	3 043	-1.1	2.82	18.9	22.1	187	19.9	30	91	0	9.6	0.0	74	7.6
Twiggs	300	3 296	17.2	2.93	16.8	20.2	136	14.0	17	90	1	9.2	6.0	88	9.2
Union	1 400	4 709	39.8	2.50	7.5	20.8	136	11.9	10	124	1	11.3	9.1	115	11.2
Upson	400	9 911	8.1	2.61	15.5	24.0	364	13.4	26	299	1	11.0	2.8	313	11.9
Walker	-1 600	21 697	10.5	2.65	10.8	20.1	859	14.7	58	530	16	9.2	20.1	378	6.8
Walton	1 100	13 433	34.2	2.85	12.0	17.4	601	16.8	57	304	10	8.7	17.5	300	9.3
Ware	-1 600	13 046	2.0	2.59	14.9	25.4	545	14.8	49	397	4	10.7	6.8	446	12.1
Warren	-500	2 130	0.9	2.80	21.9	22.9	93	14.3	18	80	3	12.1	28.8	35	5.4
Washington	-200	6 739	10.9	2.79	19.7	23.8	325	16.8	25	215	4	11.1	12.7	132	6.9
Wayne	400	7 922	15.2	2.75	13.3	21.1	315	14.1	18	229	6	10.3	16.7	199	9.1
Webster	-200	798	5.6	2.84	16.4	21.6	27	12.9	3	24	1	10.9	43.5	17	7.7
Wheeler	-100	1 786	3.1	2.70	13.2	24.7	60	12.0	6	64	1	12.8	14.9	52	10.2
White	1 100	4 907	40.2	2.55	7.8	20.8	173	13.7	15	104	3	8.5	19.1	121	11.0
Whitfield	200	26 859	19.6	2.67	10.9	20.3	1 181	16.7	76	549	13	7.9	11.4	630	9.3
Wilcox	-300	2 511	-3.3	2.71	14.3	25.5	100	13.2	12	77	0	10.1	0.0	54	7.1
Wilkes	-200	4 022	3.7	2.61	16.1	25.1	131	11.9	14	144	1	13.0	7.4	95	8.5
Wilkinson	-100	3 619	8.0	2.81	17.0	21.8	166	15.1	12	95	0	8.7	0.0	83	7.8
Worth	-400	6 895	18.7	2.85	15.3	19.5	353	18.8	39	171	2	9.1	6.4	156	8.5
HAWAII	16 000	356 267	21.2	3.01	10.5	19.4	19 045	17.3	1 311	6 224	166	5.8	8.9	14 982	14.4
Hawaii	11 700	41 461	41.8	2.86	11.5	20.6	1 978	16.8	140	795	14	6.9	7.3	1 234	11.5
Honolulu	-10 000	265 304	15.2	3.02	10.5	19.2	14 538	17.3	1 000	4 591	137	5.5	9.6	10 009	12.5
Kalawao	0	62	-12.7	1.37	0.0	62.9	([6])	([6])	([6])	([6])	([6])	([6])	([6])	NA	NA
Kauai	4 000	16 295	35.6	3.10	9.8	17.4	873	17.7	61	308	4	6.4	4.6	1 693	38.3
Maui	9 900	33 145	47.2	2.99	9.9	19.8	[6]1 656	[6]17.8	[6]110	[6]530	[6]11	[6]5.9	[6]6.8	2 044	24.5
IDAHO	-15 000	360 723	11.3	2.73	8.0	22.4	15 741	15.7	808	7 343	165	7.3	10.4	13 264	13.3
Ada	8 000	77 471	22.7	2.60	9.2	23.6	3 065	15.3	153	1 282	38	6.5	12.4	1 993	10.6
Adams	-200	1 251	3.2	2.59	4.9	20.5	40	12.9	2	27	0	8.4	0.0	39	11.5
Bannock	-3 800	23 412	4.1	2.78	8.8	23.9	1 150	17.0	54	429	10	6.3	8.5	593	8.7
Bear Lake	-1 000	2 005	-9.3	3.01	4.4	22.1	112	18.7	7	55	1	9.0	10.2	38	5.5
Benewah	-100	2 991	2.0	2.63	7.8	21.8	146	17.4	7	69	1	8.2	7.6	75	8.6
Bingham	-2 400	11 513	6.9	3.23	9.2	16.5	663	17.3	28	238	8	6.2	10.5	275	7.2
Blaine	2 400	5 506	38.4	2.43	7.2	28.0	198	14.0	9	72	1	5.1	5.3	183	14.4
Boise	-100	1 357	22.6	2.59	5.2	22.5	47	15.7	5	22	1	7.3	24.4	27	9.0
Bonner	300	10 269	16.5	2.58	7.2	23.2	324	12.9	13	223	4	9.0	10.7	340	13.3
Bonneville	-2 600	24 289	14.0	2.94	7.8	20.3	1 360	18.6	85	432	17	5.9	11.6	949	13.7
Boundary	-200	2 857	15.2	2.78	7.4	21.0	115	14.9	4	62	2	8.2	18.3	78	10.0
Butte	-500	997	-7.0	2.87	6.5	22.6	51	17.0	0	19	1	6.3	28.6	34	10.0
Camas	-200	275	-5.5	2.64	4.0	20.7	8	13.3	0	2	0	3.3	0.0	1	1.4
Canyon	1 100	31 288	9.9	2.79	9.3	21.2	1 464	16.3	70	708	19	7.9	13.2	901	10.2
Caribou	-1 700	2 262	-15.4	3.06	3.7	19.7	105	14.2	4	53	1	7.2	10.4	63	7.3
Cassia	-1 300	6 373	4.2	3.04	7.2	20.4	338	16.9	24	145	3	7.1	7.8	204	9.8
Clark	-200	277	5.7	2.67	4.7	26.0	12	15.0	1	12	0	17.1	0.0	11	13.8
Clearwater	-1 500	3 213	-11.6	2.51	6.6	21.6	83	8.9	3	81	2	8.5	20.8	95	9.2
Custer	1 300	1 561	26.2	2.63	4.9	24.1	65	14.8	1	27	0	5.9	0.0	27	5.2
Elmore	-2 500	7 136	4.4	2.81	6.3	18.6	486	22.0	26	103	3	4.7	5.4	254	11.3

1. No spouse present. 2. Per 1,000 resident population estimated as of July 1 of the year shown. 3. Under 2,500 grams. 4. Deaths of infants under 1 year old. 5. Deaths of infants under 1 year old per 1,000 live births. 6. Kalawao County included with Maui County.

STATE County	Divorces, 1984		Physicians, active non-Federal, 1989		Hospitals, 1989			Nursing homes,[4] 1986		Serious crimes known to police, 1988			Education			
						Beds				Number			Public school enrollment[7]		Attainment,[8] 1980	
	Number	Rate[1]	Number[2]	Rate[3]	Number	Number	Rate[3]	Number	Beds	Total[5]	Violent[6]	Rate[3]	1986–1987	1980	Percent 12 yrs. or more	Percent 16 yrs. or more
	44	45	46	47	48	49	50	51	52	53	54	55	56	57	58	59
GEORGIA—Con.																
Schley	15	4.4	0	0	0	0	0	0	0	44	12	1 188	647	807	44.3	8.4
Screven	61	4.3	6	39	1	40	261	1	128	278	24	1 813	2 981	2 987	41.5	7.4
Seminole	39	4.4	5	59	1	62	729	2	66	198	29	2 212	1 759	2 167	42.9	7.3
Spalding	347	6.9	59	106	1	149	268	4	351	3 385	336	6 082	10 307	10 435	44.4	9.0
Stephens	95	4.3	33	140	1	96	409	3	201	770	52	3 269	3 951	4 342	43.3	9.9
Stewart	10	1.7	4	71	1	32	571	0	0	60	14	1 041	1 009	1 334	35.9	7.7
Sumter	153	5.1	35	119	1	140	478	7	420	1 517	190	4 932	5 479	5 623	46.9	14.0
Talbot	24	3.7	0	0	0	0	0	0	0	5	1	77	1 238	1 446	40.3	8.0
Taliaferro	9	4.3	0	0	0	0	0	0	0	30	0	1 458	298	371	25.1	5.4
Tattnall	56	3.2	8	44	1	40	219	4	261	195	19	1 042	3 018	3 071	44.4	5.2
Taylor	20	2.5	3	38	0	0	0	0	0	86	22	1 243	1 618	1 712	36.0	7.4
Telfair	51	4.6	8	74	1	52	481	3	234	162	4	1 432	2 308	2 379	39.6	8.1
Terrell	27	2.3	4	34	1	28	241	1	74	268	28	2 331	2 042	2 457	37.3	9.0
Thomas	199	5.2	88	224	2	777	1 977	13	324	2 278	236	5 881	7 859	8 137	48.6	11.2
Tift	25	0.7	54	157	1	168	488	2	278	2 690	466	7 805	7 133	6 810	45.5	11.5
Toombs	149	6.4	22	90	1	122	498	2	309	354	31	1 422	4 913	5 362	44.0	9.2
Towns	33	5.4	5	72	1	98	1 420	1	30	29	0	477	785	967	45.0	9.9
Treutlen	0	0.0	3	48	0	0	0	1	50	195	33	3 057	1 290	1 319	33.0	6.2
Troup	324	6.1	76	143	1	361	679	7	458	3 354	317	6 094	10 167	10 179	41.8	10.9
Turner	36	3.7	2	21	0	0	0	1	76	162	28	1 641	2 080	2 248	39.8	7.8
Twiggs	31	3.2	1	11	0	0	0	1	131	70	2	702	1 847	2 010	33.6	5.1
Union	21	2.0	7	60	1	145	1 250	1	96	98	3	866	1 779	1 910	38.6	8.0
Upson	154	5.8	33	121	1	119	436	4	306	792	82	2 841	4 814	5 291	41.5	7.1
Walker	180	3.2	16	27	0	0	0	4	219	1 637	113	2 772	10 594	11 364	44.6	6.0
Walton	201	6.2	27	74	1	113	310	4	234	1 090	76	3 036	6 949	7 039	38.0	7.3
Ware	114	3.1	55	151	1	171	468	4	449	2 170	247	5 686	7 137	8 089	47.2	10.0
Warren	15	2.3	0	0	0	0	0	1	110	1	0	22	1 212	1 341	31.2	7.5
Washington	29	1.5	14	73	1	110	570	4	214	448	63	2 323	3 466	3 978	37.9	8.7
Wayne	129	5.9	24	108	1	123	552	5	237	457	34	2 097	4 417	4 723	48.6	7.2
Webster	8	3.6	0	0	0	0	0	0	0	15	2	634	427	466	36.5	6.7
Wheeler	10	2.0	3	60	1	40	800	1	62	47	10	896	1 082	1 136	36.8	7.5
White	41	3.7	9	69	0	0	0	1	89	279	8	2 223	2 022	1 800	48.1	9.6
Whitfield	690	10.2	99	140	1	256	362	8	381	4 051	298	5 650	13 366	13 782	44.7	9.7
Wilcox	13	1.7	3	39	0	0	0	2	203	71	11	980	1 362	1 577	36.4	6.1
Wilkes	47	4.2	7	64	1	51	468	1	47	260	23	2 277	2 073	2 026	40.3	10.1
Wilkinson	50	4.7	3	27	0	0	0	0	0	144	19	1 284	2 117	2 458	40.5	7.3
Worth	21	1.1	7	37	1	50	265	1	60	573	51	2 995	4 042	4 099	43.4	7.8
HAWAII	4 769	4.6	2 394	215	27	4 147	372	190	3 617	65 460	2 810	5 989	164 336	165 489	73.8	20.3
Hawaii	427	4.0	177	147	5	406	338	26	222	5 909	202	5 116	NA	18 401	68.9	15.2
Honolulu	3 779	4.7	1 947	230	15	3 176	375	147	2 880	49 469	2 186	5 899	164 336	126 860	75.6	21.7
Kalawao	NA	NA	(9)	(9)	(9)	(9)	(9)			NA	NA	NA	NA	0	28.2	3.5
Kauai	179	4.0	88	174	3	277	546	8	232	2 524	87	5 252	NA	7 505	64.1	15.7
Maui	384	4.6	[9]182	[9]190	[9]4	[9]288	[9]301	9	283	7 558	335	8 326	NA	12 723	67.7	15.3
IDAHO	6 210	6.2	1 218	120	49	3 911	386	122	6 235	39 319	2 474	4 026	211 360	199 793	73.7	15.8
Ada	1 443	7.6	356	173	5	816	397	23	1 318	9 454	642	4 829	37 359	34 608	81.7	22.1
Adams	18	5.3	1	32	1	21	677	1	20	51	5	1 545	593	803	68.9	11.8
Bannock	323	4.7	93	136	2	248	364	3	290	3 222	169	4 709	14 931	13 543	79.2	18.4
Bear Lake	3	0.4	4	69	1	64	1 103	2	46	94	1	1 492	1 652	1 627	73.9	11.2
Benewah	56	6.4	5	60	1	33	393	1	59	127	8	1 494	1 776	1 935	65.3	10.0
Bingham	142	3.7	14	36	2	287	740	8	170	829	39	2 204	11 084	9 456	72.0	12.0
Blaine	99	7.8	36	247	2	64	438	1	25	605	48	4 383	2 079	1 528	88.1	30.4
Boise	56	18.7	1	32	0	0	0	0	0	129	1	4 030	562	592	71.7	13.0
Bonner	191	7.5	31	124	1	54	215	1	89	1 096	92	4 314	4 969	4 640	72.0	12.1
Bonneville	535	7.7	121	161	1	260	346	5	386	3 107	158	4 314	16 287	15 516	80.6	21.1
Boundary	25	3.2	7	90	1	52	667	2	74	153	10	2 039	1 494	1 494	67.7	11.4
Butte	1	0.3	0	0	1	26	897	2	25	9	0	300	787	765	71.0	14.5
Camas	7	10.0	0	0	0	0	0	0	0	8	1	1 143	165	203	83.8	17.7
Canyon	541	6.1	103	113	3	482	529	13	763	4 511	176	4 978	18 082	17 198	65.2	12.0
Caribou	34	4.0	4	56	1	68	958	1	37	100	4	1 369	2 221	2 040	76.2	14.4
Cassia	136	6.5	16	80	1	87	435	2	102	1 166	73	5 714	5 175	4 566	70.5	11.4
Clark	2	2.5	0	0	0	0	0	0	0	22	1	2 750	170	181	75.6	16.4
Clearwater	58	5.6	4	44	2	58	637	1	61	215	10	2 239	1 940	2 276	68.2	10.6
Custer	20	3.8	2	49	0	0	0	0	0	39	3	848	1 074	723	75.3	13.4
Elmore	164	7.3	14	63	2	114	511	0	0	443	34	1 995	4 218	4 735	76.2	13.5

1. Per 1,000 resident population estimated as of July 1 of the year shown. 2. As of end of year. 3. Per 100,000 resident population as of July 1 of the year shown. 4. Preliminary. Covers nursing homes with 3 or more beds. 5. Data for serious crimes have not been adjusted for underreporting, this may affect comparability between geographic areas or over time. 6. Includes murder and nonnegligent manslaughter, forcible rape, robbery, and aggravated assault. 7. The 1986–1987 data are based on administrative reports obtained by the U.S. National Center for Education Statistics. The 1980 data are based on the 1980 Census of Population and Housing. 8. Persons 25 years old or older. 9. Kalawao County included with Maui County.

STATE County	Education (cont'd): Local government expenditures for education,[1] 1982: Total (Mil dol)	Education (cont'd): Local government expenditures for education,[1] 1982: Per capita (Dollars)	Social Security Program December 1988: Beneficiaries: Total	Social Security Program December 1988: Beneficiaries: Rate[2]	Social Security Program December 1988: Payments ($1,000)	Supplemental Security Income Program recipients June 1986	Money income: Per capita[3]: 1987 Income, (Dollars)	Money income: Per capita[3]: 1979: Current dollars	Money income: Per capita[3]: 1979: Constant 1987 dollars	Money income: Median household income 1979 (Dollars)	Money income: Percent below poverty level, 1979: Persons	Money income: Percent below poverty level, 1979: Families	Housing units, 1990: Total	Housing units, 1990: Percent change, 1980–1990
	60	61	62	63	64	65	66	67	68	69	70	71	72	73
GEORGIA–Con.														
Schley	0.9	266	555	158.6	220	162	8 474	4 516	7 066	11 496	26.8	21.9	1 447	16.2
Screven	6.0	431	2 680	176.3	1 015	828	7 407	4 500	7 041	9 410	34.1	27.4	5 861	6.4
Seminole	3.8	420	1 730	198.9	671	422	7 989	4 641	7 262	11 064	23.4	18.3	3 962	2.8
Spalding	17.0	342	9 065	165.1	4 018	1 624	9 663	5 758	9 010	13 598	17.6	13.7	20 702	21.5
Stephens	7.0	319	4 940	212.0	2 146	850	9 128	5 524	8 643	12 579	14.8	11.6	10 254	19.6
Stewart	4.5	781	1 065	190.2	377	400	6 423	3 517	5 503	8 308	38.8	33.8	2 156	3.2
Sumter	13.1	437	4 905	165.7	2 003	1 272	8 610	5 001	7 825	11 965	23.2	18.1	11 726	15.3
Talbot	2.1	319	1 120	157.7	417	336	8 737	4 784	7 486	11 964	20.6	17.2	2 645	10.8
Taliaferro	0.5	249	475	237.5	183	184	7 250	4 083	6 389	8 879	32.4	27.2	886	1.7
Tattnall	4.8	273	3 370	184.2	1 197	948	7 643	4 110	6 431	9 482	28.3	23.7	6 756	6.4
Taylor	3.0	372	1 640	207.6	595	472	9 157	5 290	8 277	11 460	28.1	22.8	3 162	10.4
Telfair	5.5	489	2 555	232.3	940	760	7 741	4 398	6 882	10 003	26.5	22.4	4 756	8.5
Terrell	3.2	274	1 895	163.4	719	668	7 437	4 314	6 750	10 636	31.1	24.8	4 069	-1.9
Thomas	16.8	438	7 690	196.7	3 178	1 818	8 838	5 168	8 086	12 377	21.4	17.2	15 936	15.5
Tift	10.4	310	5 655	163.9	2 209	1 334	9 275	5 259	8 229	12 068	22.6	18.8	13 359	21.4
Toombs	8.6	374	4 295	176.0	1 669	1 194	8 554	4 808	7 523	10 812	26.0	23.7	9 952	17.2
Towns	1.5	254	1 785	266.4	740	284	9 483	5 106	7 989	9 480	22.7	20.4	4 577	34.0
Treutlen	2.2	352	1 200	193.5	433	376	8 390	4 840	7 573	10 274	29.3	23.3	2 437	3.9
Troup	22.3	434	10 465	195.2	4 646	1 866	9 661	5 707	8 930	13 033	18.0	13.9	22 426	22.2
Turner	3.9	410	1 685	179.3	609	446	8 256	4 696	7 348	10 850	32.0	23.7	3 426	6.8
Twiggs	3.2	332	1 290	133.0	480	410	8 197	4 459	6 977	12 817	18.5	14.8	3 648	16.0
Union	3.1	315	2 580	226.3	1 020	452	8 545	4 408	6 897	9 242	26.2	22.6	6 624	50.9
Upson	12.7	476	5 520	202.9	2 457	810	9 377	5 615	8 786	12 890	13.0	11.1	10 667	9.5
Walker	20.3	359	11 205	192.2	5 201	1 216	9 648	5 671	8 873	13 968	12.3	9.9	23 347	11.6
Walton	11.1	351	5 740	160.8	2 511	964	9 651	5 412	8 468	13 809	16.9	14.1	14 514	39.0
Ware	14.7	397	6 580	178.8	2 640	1 512	8 956	5 388	8 431	11 938	21.1	17.0	14 628	6.0
Warren	2.3	347	1 135	174.6	428	386	7 172	4 257	6 661	10 572	28.3	23.3	2 443	5.1
Washington	7.4	388	3 240	167.0	1 284	1 028	8 302	4 863	7 609	11 335	25.3	20.8	7 416	11.9
Wayne	7.5	351	3 530	158.3	1 473	904	8 840	5 423	8 485	12 120	20.2	16.6	8 812	15.3
Webster	0.8	338	340	161.9	133	102	8 263	4 492	7 029	9 702	31.0	27.9	898	8.2
Wheeler	2.2	423	1 025	205.0	346	378	6 628	3 854	6 030	8 511	30.4	25.0	2 148	11.8
White	3.5	327	2 265	179.8	923	344	9 937	5 652	8 844	12 868	16.4	15.5	6 082	48.7
Whitfield	27.0	410	10 400	147.3	4 697	1 346	11 316	6 579	10 294	16 148	11.9	9.9	28 832	20.9
Wilcox	2.7	344	1 510	198.7	509	514	7 677	4 420	6 916	10 680	30.4	23.3	2 865	2.5
Wilkes	4.0	354	2 320	210.9	919	566	8 986	5 247	8 210	11 367	20.6	17.8	4 548	8.4
Wilkinson	4.1	392	1 770	160.9	769	346	8 919	5 206	8 146	13 953	17.6	14.9	4 151	9.2
Worth	6.6	358	2 555	135.9	954	664	8 198	4 881	7 637	13 031	23.7	19.1	7 597	18.7
HAWAII	0.3	0	141 730	129.1	67 493	11 789	12 290	7 740	12 111	20 473	9.9	7.8	389 810	16.6
Hawaii	0.0	0	19 190	163.3	9 107	1 452	9 825	6 554	10 255	16 975	13.2	10.3	48 253	41.0
Honolulu	0.0	0	100 455	119.8	47 849	9 002	12 734	7 912	12 380	21 077	9.5	7.5	281 683	11.8
Kalawao	NA	NA	13 810	148.5	48	NA	X	0	0	5 750	31.9	13.3	101	-16.5
Kauai	0.1	4	8 060	163.5	3 785	566	10 882	7 022	10 987	19 066	8.9	6.9	17 613	18.8
Maui	0.2	2	0	0.0	6 595	740	X	7 816	12 230	20 237	9.6	7.6	42 160	27.6
IDAHO	371.6	380	151 106	150.7	71 524	8 713	9 159	6 248	9 776	15 285	12.6	9.6	413 327	10.2
Ada	61.6	339	25 805	128.6	12 766	1 382	11 427	7 748	12 123	17 510	8.5	6.3	80 849	19.2
Adams	1.4	435	620	200.0	274	20	7 773	5 873	9 189	14 785	15.0	11.5	1 778	12.5
Bannock	23.6	348	7 535	111.1	3 651	540	9 024	6 692	10 471	17 458	9.4	7.3	25 694	3.5
Bear Lake	5.1	693	1 145	190.8	491	60	7 339	5 442	8 515	15 598	10.6	10.0	2 934	5.1
Benewah	3.5	415	1 485	176.8	663	88	9 015	6 484	10 146	16 975	10.5	7.7	3 731	6.6
Bingham	16.8	449	4 970	129.8	2 292	392	7 629	5 155	8 066	15 357	13.6	11.6	12 664	4.8
Blaine	3.6	311	1 115	79.1	534	28	12 183	7 992	12 505	14 608	11.9	8.3	9 500	29.8
Boise	1.5	505	565	188.3	264	18	8 683	6 308	9 870	15 527	10.6	10.3	2 894	22.0
Bonner	8.1	324	4 920	196.0	2 227	234	7 569	5 315	8 316	12 201	17.6	15.0	15 152	16.1
Bonneville	27.0	400	8 315	113.4	4 122	430	9 889	6 568	10 277	18 167	8.5	7.0	26 049	10.9
Boundary	2.9	392	1 375	178.6	604	84	7 053	4 958	7 758	12 459	17.5	14.8	3 242	17.7
Butte	1.7	475	540	180.0	260	56	8 304	5 484	8 581	13 590	13.8	10.5	1 265	-1.2
Camas	0.5	636	145	241.7	73	2	9 852	5 861	9 171	13 199	12.6	10.9	481	-8.7
Canyon	30.0	349	15 045	167.4	6 800	1 398	8 166	5 761	9 014	13 831	15.0	11.7	33 137	8.2
Caribou	4.6	513	1 020	137.8	512	20	8 245	5 798	9 072	17 685	12.5	10.0	2 867	-7.7
Cassia	8.0	395	3 010	150.5	1 399	158	7 762	5 245	8 207	13 740	14.6	11.9	7 212	2.9
Clark	0.6	723	125	156.2	54	2	5 611	4 591	7 184	11 463	16.6	13.9	502	12.8
Clearwater	4.5	431	1 555	167.2	742	110	8 872	6 612	10 346	17 269	8.7	6.8	3 805	-7.5
Custer	3.6	697	665	151.1	284	22	7 557	5 237	8 194	11 746	18.7	15.9	2 437	16.0
Elmore	9.7	437	2 010	91.0	870	116	7 921	5 324	8 330	13 347	13.7	10.1	8 430	4.7

1. Elementary and secondary. 2. Per 1,000 resident population estimated as of July 1 of the year shown. 3. Based on the resident population estimated as of July 1, 1988 for 1987 data and enumerated as of April 1, 1980 for 1979 data.

STATE County	Housing units, 1990 (cont'd)				Civilian labor force, 1990				Private nonfarm establishments, 1988					
	Occupied units						Unemployment				Employment[2]			
		Owner occupied												
	Total	Percent	Median value (Dollars)	Median rent (Dollars)	Total	Percent change, 1989–1990	Total	Rate[1]	Number	Net change, 1987–1988	Total	Percent change, 1987–1988	Manu-facturing	Retail trade
	74	75	76	77	78	79	80	81	82	83	84	85	86	87
GEORGIA—Con.														
Schley	1 315	72.2	40 400	150	1 476	-1.8	135	9.1	59	3	874	-6.4	678	114
Screven	5 048	73.5	41 800	160	5 541	2.0	470	8.5	211	-12	3 002	-0.1	1 692	476
Seminole	3 137	78.6	42 800	159	3 736	-3.1	191	5.1	200	2	1 524	1.9	0	409
Spalding	19 426	61.4	57 700	250	27 229	0.6	1 544	5.7	1 040	11	15 587	2.5	6 316	4 081
Stephens	8 949	72.9	49 900	200	11 017	-1.2	764	6.9	579	17	9 669	6.9	5 367	1 607
Stewart	1 982	70.8	30 400	99	2 001	1.8	168	8.4	106	-1	728	1.7	297	141
Sumter	10 484	64.1	45 300	189	14 415	-2.7	1 103	7.7	660	2	10 228	2.7	3 780	2 259
Talbot	2 345	77.8	35 100	99	2 710	2.8	196	7.2	78	6	352	-3.0	73	71
Taliaferro	727	79.4	28 600	99	749	1.8	45	6.0	30	0	155	12.3	0	0
Tattnall	5 845	68.9	43 500	156	7 761	5.8	378	4.9	293	-16	3 276	14.1	970	718
Taylor	2 804	73.2	35 800	130	3 032	5.6	263	8.7	143	2	1 134	8.1	357	228
Telfair	4 017	76.5	31 100	138	5 288	4.2	406	7.7	226	2	3 554	-6.7	2 147	475
Terrell	3 738	63.6	41 200	125	4 620	-2.1	386	8.4	192	3	2 532	-1.1	1 314	444
Thomas	14 323	68.5	46 400	213	18 577	-0.5	1 017	5.5	1 025	-6	13 884	1.2	4 781	2 833
Tift	12 184	66.2	51 600	194	17 817	-1.1	1 139	6.4	937	27	11 529	3.2	4 311	3 181
Toombs	8 804	64.6	49 100	162	11 262	3.1	711	6.3	677	2	7 800	9.4	2 718	2 169
Towns	2 812	87.6	69 400	189	3 779	11.8	140	3.7	135	8	1 043	23.3	228	290
Treutlen	2 158	72.6	33 300	113	2 761	1.5	191	6.9	99	-2	815	-3.3	313	193
Troup	20 371	64.1	54 600	234	30 052	2.1	1 671	5.6	1 276	5	22 909	6.4	10 435	4 658
Turner	3 043	66.4	37 000	148	3 104	-1.7	264	8.5	178	2	1 618	9.5	589	427
Twiggs	3 296	80.0	37 300	145	3 595	-0.1	218	6.1	72	-2	1 433	5.3	126	71
Union	4 709	82.6	58 300	212	5 375	2.8	251	4.7	210	10	1 842	10.5	825	389
Upson	9 911	70.5	41 300	183	11 542	0.9	670	5.8	502	16	8 258	1.2	4 552	1 803
Walker	21 697	77.3	45 800	236	27 513	-0.7	1 731	6.3	858	3	13 417	0.7	7 870	1 900
Walton	13 433	70.6	66 700	273	17 905	2.3	1 335	7.5	518	6	7 168	4.4	3 346	1 739
Ware	13 046	69.7	41 200	192	15 871	-1.3	951	6.0	979	8	10 568	1.7	2 644	3 211
Warren	2 130	74.3	33 200	121	2 600	-5.2	209	8.0	82	-2	1 568	-17.5	1 045	152
Washington	6 739	72.0	39 600	148	8 952	-1.4	528	5.9	360	3	5 511	1.8	1 422	942
Wayne	7 922	72.3	44 500	166	9 769	6.9	683	7.0	443	10	5 707	2.4	1 858	1 436
Webster	798	79.8	30 900	99	835	0.5	84	10.1	23	2	193	14.9	0	25
Wheeler	1 786	75.9	29 700	106	2 579	-7.8	154	6.0	59	-2	629	1.1	303	87
White	4 907	82.0	69 700	251	6 865	2.5	307	4.5	355	9	3 772	19.5	967	1 032
Whitfield	26 859	66.9	61 200	289	45 356	1.2	2 236	4.9	2 171	76	47 387	3.9	27 556	6 256
Wilcox	2 511	76.3	32 000	125	3 783	13.4	152	4.0	104	-11	929	-2.2	385	120
Wilkes	4 022	77.4	42 200	124	4 638	0.3	263	5.7	274	-2	3 542	4.2	2 053	637
Wilkinson	3 619	81.1	40 000	135	4 676	-1.7	208	4.4	150	-6	3 067	2.2	1 012	236
Worth	6 895	73.9	45 700	149	6 798	-0.9	515	7.6	256	4	2 435	5.3	777	607
HAWAII	356 267	53.9	245 300	599	539 000	2.7	15 000	2.8	X	X	382 943	5.4	22 467	107 072
Hawaii	41 461	61.1	113 000	428	61 538	7.5	2 362	3.8	3 187	166	32 679	8.6	2 444	9 578
Honolulu	265 304	52.0	283 600	615	391 387	2.0	9 999	2.6	20 395	383	297 324	4.5	16 613	79 379
Kalawao	62	0.0	0	99	NA	NA	NA	NA	0	0	0	NA	0	0
Kauai	16 295	58.8	171 500	532	28 398	3.9	1 023	3.6	1 389	17	17 089	8.9	1 023	5 536
Maui	33 145	57.6	202 100	658	57 678	3.8	1 616	2.8	2 958	91	35 781	8.4	2 387	12 574
IDAHO	360 723	70.1	58 200	261	496 000	1.4	29 000	5.8	X	X	265 606	4.8	54 316	65 548
Ada	77 471	69.1	70 500	340	116 504	2.6	4 471	3.8	6 028	236	76 912	8.0	12 386	17 812
Adams	1 251	75.3	43 900	180	1 668	-0.3	218	13.1	71	4	290	12.0	95	76
Bannock	23 412	68.7	53 300	237	30 493	-2.2	1 945	6.4	1 540	-10	16 365	-0.2	3 160	4 913
Bear Lake	2 005	83.2	38 700	175	2 283	-7.7	135	5.9	108	1	679	3.0	148	267
Benewah	2 991	76.4	44 500	172	3 535	1.5	380	10.7	191	-7	1 845	4.4	921	332
Bingham	11 513	76.7	50 700	207	16 564	-0.8	1 130	6.8	574	2	6 601	-0.8	2 377	1 270
Blaine	5 506	64.2	127 400	410	8 805	13.9	325	3.7	788	22	6 017	11.1	165	1 741
Boise	1 357	79.2	59 700	201	1 414	3.8	96	6.8	57	1	337	-10.6	116	56
Bonner	10 269	75.8	60 500	251	12 302	1.8	1 075	8.7	813	14	6 836	10.6	2 388	1 570
Bonneville	24 289	71.5	63 700	293	36 965	2.7	1 716	4.6	1 924	34	26 577	6.6	2 618	6 376
Boundary	2 857	78.3	49 500	217	4 491	8.4	345	7.7	211	-2	1 369	14.3	399	361
Butte	997	74.6	41 400	158	1 645	-4.1	82	5.0	58	-5	201	-9.0	0	88
Camas	275	75.6	35 500	171	396	-10.2	40	10.1	13	0	64	-22.9	0	0
Canyon	31 288	68.7	51 900	232	43 467	0.8	3 247	7.5	1 748	16	21 915	4.2	6 574	5 027
Caribou	2 262	80.2	48 200	190	3 017	-7.3	153	5.1	185	13	1 784	21.7	0	263
Cassia	6 373	71.4	46 100	193	7 933	-0.7	690	8.7	500	1	4 764	-4.7	1 285	1 388
Clark	277	62.8	37 300	189	730	23.7	19	2.6	13	0	43	19.4	0	19
Clearwater	3 213	74.3	43 000	194	4 177	-2.0	525	12.6	243	-3	1 777	0.8	827	380
Custer	1 561	71.0	49 800	219	2 936	-1.9	112	3.8	100	-5	708	-0.8	0	189
Elmore	7 136	54.4	57 900	242	8 536	4.9	517	6.1	341	11	2 369	4.5	339	981

1. Percent of total civilian labor force. 2. For week including March 12. Excludes government employees, self-employed persons, farm workers, domestic service workers, railroad employees subject to the Railroad Retirement Act, and employees on oceanborne vessels or in foreign countries.

Table A. States and Counties — **Employment, Personal Income, and Earnings**

STATE County	Private nonfarm establishments, 1988 (cont'd): Employment[1] (cont'd): Finance, insurance, and real estate	Employment[1] (cont'd): Services	Annual payroll: Total (Mil dol)	Annual payroll: Average per employee (Dollars)	Personal income, 1989: Total (Mil dol)	Percent change, 1988–1989	Wages and salaries[2] (Mil dol)	Proprietor's income (Mil dol)	Dividends, interest, & rent (Mil dol)	Transfer payments (Mil dol)	Per capita[3]: Dollars	Per capita[3]: Rank	Earnings, 1989: Total (Mil dol)	Percent by selected industries: Farm	Goods-related[4]: Total
	88	89	90	91	92	93	94	95	96	97	98	99	100	101	102
GEORGIA—Con.															
Schley	0	15	15	16 759	43	7.5	21	6	5	8	12 115	2 280	27	10.1	NA
Screven	97	443	47	15 668	161	6.5	76	16	25	38	10 543	2 780	92	10.6	46.5
Seminole	112	292	18	11 758	108	5.6	37	21	17	23	12 685	2 040	58	23.6	NA
Spalding	712	2 449	227	14 586	749	5.8	372	44	106	114	13 457	1 710	415	0.9	33.4
Stephens	212	1 293	140	14 526	300	7.6	200	30	48	56	12 786	2 003	230	1.8	NA
Stewart	40	109	9	11 931	56	2.2	19	8	9	16	9 959	2 887	27	10.5	NA
Sumter	339	1 826	160	15 596	388	5.8	248	34	70	74	13 260	1 789	282	3.1	NA
Talbot	42	33	5	14 571	74	7.4	15	5	10	15	10 349	2 826	20	13.4	NA
Taliaferro	0	21	2	12 135	29	6.3	4	4	6	6	15 087	948	8	32.6	NA
Tattnall	131	510	39	11 762	225	8.6	89	39	27	49	12 316	2 193	129	16.5	NA
Taylor	50	130	19	16 917	93	6.4	33	10	14	22	11 902	2 359	43	7.6	21.7
Telfair	90	454	48	13 611	123	7.1	75	15	19	35	11 402	2 539	90	8.8	NA
Terrell	83	236	30	11 701	110	3.7	50	11	21	27	9 538	2 955	61	9.6	28.3
Thomas	579	3 164	231	16 655	541	4.8	336	87	85	105	13 785	1 541	423	4.3	NA
Tift	405	1 847	182	15 747	493	8.4	319	89	71	79	14 331	1 275	408	12.2	27.7
Toombs	201	1 299	108	13 787	328	7.0	157	42	47	64	13 395	1 728	199	4.3	27.5
Towns	58	234	13	12 433	75	7.1	24	7	19	19	10 872	2 693	31	0.4	NA
Treutlen	0	121	7	9 063	59	5.9	18	8	9	16	9 557	2 951	26	12.0	NA
Troup	830	3 774	412	17 977	810	11.2	615	56	132	132	15 215	902	671	0.6	53.1
Turner	44	218	19	11 737	99	2.5	30	22	20	22	10 559	2 777	53	29.2	NA
Twiggs	0	177	37	26 152	103	1.9	58	4	7	20	10 854	2 697	62	1.3	72.0
Union	91	273	22	12 055	130	6.8	46	20	29	31	11 182	2 610	66	13.2	29.1
Upson	191	974	109	13 239	336	6.7	178	35	49	69	12 316	2 194	213	2.5	44.1
Walker	572	1 338	209	15 570	733	6.5	306	53	104	131	12 509	2 110	359	1.9	50.7
Walton	264	801	107	14 894	489	5.3	174	51	66	74	13 376	1 744	225	5.6	37.2
Ware	541	2 124	145	13 702	459	6.1	296	49	76	110	12 571	2 081	346	2.3	19.6
Warren	26	190	20	12 448	65	3.9	30	7	10	18	9 804	2 907	37	9.1	NA
Washington	136	696	102	18 521	271	8.4	187	16	43	47	14 088	1 393	203	2.5	49.3
Wayne	141	1 612	87	15 180	277	8.8	164	22	35	57	12 395	2 163	186	2.7	NA
Webster	0	29	3	14 316	30	5.7	8	5	7	5	14 170	1 360	12	29.9	NA
Wheeler	0	17	8	12 959	51	5.9	17	7	6	14	10 339	2 829	24	17.5	NA
White	479	818	44	11 665	183	9.2	64	34	37	27	14 143	1 373	97	18.8	19.1
Whitfield	964	5 458	843	17 800	1 195	6.0	1 065	85	166	125	16 876	457	1 150	0.7	52.2
Wilcox	50	207	11	11 699	89	6.4	21	15	13	21	11 688	2 445	36	31.9	NA
Wilkes	80	335	49	13 848	149	6.7	77	23	29	29	13 731	1 562	100	11.6	41.8
Wilkinson	55	196	60	19 719	140	7.3	97	8	16	25	12 714	2 028	105	0.7	NA
Worth	141	369	32	12 991	213	4.6	57	26	30	40	11 305	2 565	83	23.0	9.9
HAWAII	32 784	131 179	7 243	X	20 477	11.2	14 110	1 556	3 147	2 660	18 379	X	15 666	1.6	12.7
Hawaii	1 470	11 512	490	15 003	1 800	14.2	982	219	335	309	14 969	1 000	1 201	8.5	13.9
Honolulu	28 088	101 289	5 905	19 860	16 251	10.5	11 488	1 098	2 408	2 043	19 171	213	12 585	0.4	12.3
Kalawao	0	0	0	NA	(5)	(5)	(5)	(5)	(5)	(5)	(5)	(5)	(5)	(5)	(5)
Kauai	1 178	5 701	274	16 009	790	14.0	540	75	131	114	15 585	777	615	5.4	13.8
Maui	2 024	12 669	573	16 000	[5]1 638	[5]14.4	[5]1 100	[5]164	[5]273	[5]194	[5]17 121	[5]418	(5)	[5]4.4	[5]15.5
IDAHO	15 459	69 012	4 680	X	13 953	9.4	7 872	2 270	2 251	2 154	13 760	X	10 142	8.6	26.2
Ada	6 323	20 755	1 579	20 527	3 538	10.0	2 323	448	542	429	17 194	411	2 772	1.1	29.7
Adams	0	23	11	39 179	46	10.3	19	9	11	8	14 908	1 023	28	11.1	49.4
Bannock	1 665	3 832	284	17 362	838	8.0	497	76	106	141	12 288	2 202	573	1.7	16.1
Bear Lake	56	99	7	10 931	67	3.1	18	11	9	14	11 669	2 453	29	24.1	9.2
Benewah	52	228	40	21 920	108	4.9	58	24	15	21	12 854	1 978	82	9.3	NA
Bingham	208	801	100	15 109	444	10.1	234	103	53	66	11 462	2 518	337	23.0	NA
Blaine	431	2 538	84	14 011	264	13.8	135	51	76	17	18 055	288	185	3.9	25.2
Boise	0	34	5	15 632	36	5.3	14	5	5	7	11 859	2 375	19	12.0	35.9
Bonner	308	1 221	96	14 055	318	8.6	144	55	64	66	12 658	2 053	199	3.0	38.3
Bonneville	1 147	11 449	580	21 837	1 068	10.1	602	135	143	125	14 212	1 333	737	5.5	16.1
Boundary	49	321	22	15 814	89	10.4	41	18	14	19	11 372	2 549	59	9.1	35.6
Butte	0	27	2	11 269	38	7.8	257	10	5	7	12 929	1 940	266	2.5	NA
Camas	0	18	1	9 031	12	0.1	4	5	3	2	19 349	202	9	44.9	NA
Canyon	721	5 215	332	15 171	1 108	9.8	581	185	182	208	12 166	2 250	765	10.1	30.0
Caribou	86	115	38	21 268	108	6.1	70	25	15	13	15 204	906	94	11.1	59.7
Cassia	215	972	68	14 310	257	10.8	121	73	42	37	12 801	1 997	194	28.1	21.0
Clark	0	0	0	9 419	18	6.9	5	10	2	2	23 775	58	15	65.5	NA
Clearwater	60	277	31	17 321	117	7.9	66	20	17	22	12 832	1 986	86	4.5	NA
Custer	29	66	17	24 105	62	13.7	43	10	9	8	15 060	962	53	8.2	NA
Elmore	151	484	26	10 907	264	8.0	166	38	26	44	11 859	2 376	204	13.5	4.5

1. For week including March 12. Excludes government employees, self-employed persons, farm workers, domestic service workers, railroad employees subject to the Railroad Retirement Act, and employees on oceanborne vessels or in foreign countries. 2. Includes other labor income. 3. Based on the resident population estimated as of July 1 of the year shown. 4. Covers mining, construction, and manufacturing. 5. Kalawao County included with Maui County.

STATE County	Earnings, 1989 (cont'd)						Agriculture, 1987									
	Percent by selected industries (cont'd)						Farms			Farm operators, percent		Land in farms				
	Goods-related[1]	Service-related & other[2]						Percent with						Acres		
	Manu-facturing	Total	Retail trade	Finance, insur-ance, & real estate	Services	Govern-ment	Number	Less than 50 acres	500 acres and over	Whose principal occu-pation is farming	Residing on farm operated	Acreage (1,000)	Percent change, 1982–1987	Average size of farm	Total irrigated (1,000)	Total cropland (1,000)
	103	104	105	106	107	108	109	110	111	112	113	114	115	116	117	118
GEORGIA—Con.																
Schley	54.3	NA	4.7	NA	8.9	12.2	94	14.9	19.1	31.9	62.8	38	0.5	404	1	17
Screven	44.0	24.8	6.1	2.8	8.9	18.1	304	14.8	27.3	53.0	69.7	145	-21.3	477	9	96
Seminole	7.2	52.5	12.9	3.3	19.0	14.7	210	24.3	29.0	56.7	64.8	100	0.4	475	27	69
Spalding	28.4	48.3	13.4	4.1	19.9	17.4	247	38.9	6.1	27.1	78.5	36	-12.8	146	0	17
Stephens	44.1	NA	9.6	2.9	13.6	11.5	198	46.5	1.0	38.4	76.8	15	-10.5	77	D	7
Stewart	25.1	40.5	9.7	2.4	16.8	21.0	99	14.1	25.3	48.5	47.5	48	-29.2	484	2	24
Sumter	28.6	NA	10.2	2.2	14.8	19.1	314	22.3	34.7	60.5	61.8	175	-9.4	559	27	125
Talbot	3.0	NA	6.1	4.5	11.3	26.7	128	10.9	16.4	32.0	71.9	39	-6.6	304	D	11
Taliaferro	NA	NA	8.8	4.0	10.6	19.1	63	12.7	25.4	39.7	57.1	19	-14.0	303	D	7
Tattnall	12.1	34.6	8.5	2.5	12.3	32.2	525	33.7	10.7	50.9	63.0	117	-9.8	222	4	65
Taylor	13.2	48.2	7.5	3.6	12.2	22.5	172	16.3	24.4	44.2	59.3	77	-14.3	448	3	37
Telfair	37.7	37.3	6.3	3.0	12.8	14.3	324	24.7	11.7	54.3	67.9	69	-30.8	214	5	42
Terrell	26.7	43.0	9.2	3.1	15.1	19.1	197	17.8	38.6	62.4	61.4	154	-0.5	781	14	100
Thomas	23.8	NA	9.5	3.2	27.6	16.1	507	28.8	19.3	51.5	66.3	217	0.8	428	6	100
Tift	23.3	41.2	10.8	2.5	17.9	18.9	351	27.9	14.0	59.3	65.8	108	-1.9	306	20	66
Toombs	18.9	53.8	18.7	3.4	19.0	14.5	325	24.3	11.1	47.7	68.9	84	-14.4	260	3	47
Towns	8.0	58.3	16.0	4.5	21.4	22.1	149	46.3	0.0	35.6	71.8	11	-21.9	71	0	5
Treutlen	25.6	NA	10.1	4.6	12.3	22.1	121	22.3	12.4	49.6	72.7	36	-33.2	299	D	14
Troup	46.9	33.9	9.3	3.3	13.9	12.4	281	30.2	10.3	29.5	69.0	53	-4.9	187	0	21
Turner	9.9	39.9	10.0	2.6	16.2	18.3	285	18.6	25.3	68.1	66.3	114	-0.3	401	12	69
Twiggs	2.4	NA	2.0	0.5	8.3	12.3	112	35.7	15.2	33.9	68.8	32	-21.1	283	1	15
Union	16.3	36.1	10.7	4.4	14.8	21.6	263	48.7	1.5	44.1	69.6	23	-17.8	88	0	11
Upson	41.3	39.7	11.8	2.4	19.9	13.6	214	28.5	6.1	33.2	68.2	41	-18.5	189	1	16
Walker	45.7	34.0	8.0	3.3	15.2	13.3	563	33.7	5.0	36.8	74.8	95	-9.2	169	0	40
Walton	26.2	40.5	10.7	3.1	16.0	16.7	469	38.0	5.8	33.0	73.6	65	-18.9	139	0	34
Ware	15.6	60.5	10.7	3.4	23.5	17.6	313	40.6	9.9	33.9	70.0	62	-8.1	199	1	23
Warren	49.1	NA	7.1	1.7	8.5	13.4	146	12.3	24.7	41.8	64.4	53	-12.0	360	0	22
Washington	14.0	33.0	7.3	1.6	11.5	15.2	308	15.9	21.8	34.4	59.4	115	-13.4	374	4	64
Wayne	34.8	30.2	9.7	1.4	12.2	20.2	315	30.2	8.3	35.9	67.0	60	-13.4	190	1	30
Webster	25.8	NA	1.3	NA	15.5	14.3	94	13.8	34.0	61.7	55.3	60	1.3	636	5	33
Wheeler	18.2	38.9	3.9	2.6	14.0	22.6	195	19.5	14.9	43.1	66.7	51	-35.4	260	2	28
White	12.1	47.2	14.5	8.6	18.1	14.9	304	56.6	0.7	45.1	70.1	23	-1.4	76	0	10
Whitfield	48.9	39.6	8.3	2.6	16.3	7.4	382	40.6	3.1	32.2	65.2	43	-9.1	113	0	23
Wilcox	14.1	33.2	4.6	2.7	11.9	17.7	274	17.9	27.7	58.4	54.7	115	1.0	419	13	71
Wilkes	38.7	33.0	7.6	2.0	13.4	13.6	331	17.5	17.8	33.5	71.3	104	-14.1	315	0	36
Wilkinson	27.6	NA	3.2	1.8	NA	8.4	121	22.3	15.7	28.9	72.7	43	-8.7	357	0	11
Worth	6.7	46.5	9.5	3.1	20.3	20.6	478	24.7	23.6	63.8	66.3	198	0.7	414	14	119
HAWAII	4.3	59.3	11.8	7.1	27.6	26.4	4 870	87.4	3.0	57.8	56.5	1 722	-12.1	353	149	327
Hawaii	5.0	59.0	12.6	4.2	31.4	18.6	2 810	88.4	2.6	55.0	54.9	1 007	-14.1	358	13	138
Honolulu	4.2	58.2	11.1	7.6	26.2	29.1	938	92.0	2.5	70.4	56.8	131	3.8	139	36	50
Kalawao	(3)	(3)	(3)	(3)	(3)	(3)	NA	NA	NA	NA	NA	NA	NA	NA	NA	NA
Kauai	4.2	65.6	15.0	6.3	31.0	15.3	400	80.0	4.5	53.2	53.5	224	-12.4	560	32	50
Maui	[3]4.5	[3]67.9	[3]15.7	[3]6.2	[3]36.2	[3]12.2	722	81.4	4.2	55.1	63.7	359	-10.9	498	67	89
IDAHO	17.6	48.6	9.9	4.1	21.4	16.6	24 142	34.3	22.6	60.3	75.5	13 932	0.1	577	3 219	6 742
Ada	18.7	53.3	10.8	6.9	21.8	15.9	1 293	63.9	5.6	44.0	80.4	247	-0.1	191	86	D
Adams	44.3	NA	5.7	0.9	NA	19.8	257	36.6	30.4	51.8	84.4	208	32.8	808	20	42
Bannock	10.8	60.7	11.4	6.5	19.3	21.5	655	45.0	21.1	40.9	74.0	358	1.7	547	41	204
Bear Lake	5.6	41.0	14.8	4.7	8.6	25.7	446	24.2	29.4	54.5	66.6	269	-8.1	604	45	142
Benewah	44.6	NA	4.7	1.6	10.7	14.2	205	26.8	29.8	54.6	81.0	115	-7.3	561	1	77
Bingham	15.5	NA	5.6	NA	19.1	15.2	1 466	39.1	22.1	58.1	76.0	1 407	39.8	960	306	D
Blaine	3.3	61.5	15.4	4.6	33.3	9.4	221	24.0	35.3	62.0	69.7	247	-17.4	1 117	54	75
Boise	33.4	28.2	4.6	1.5	15.0	23.9	73	23.3	26.0	49.3	71.2	67	-16.0	915	3	8
Bonner	31.3	43.7	11.6	2.6	18.2	15.0	516	28.5	10.5	47.5	86.0	137	-11.4	265	5	46
Bonneville	5.5	65.4	12.1	3.7	37.7	12.9	905	38.9	22.1	58.0	72.9	505	-1.7	558	147	351
Boundary	29.5	35.4	8.9	1.8	11.4	19.9	297	31.0	14.8	51.9	79.5	79	-5.9	267	1	52
Butte	NA	NA	0.7	0.1	59.5	12.3	224	23.7	37.1	67.4	79.9	161	-12.2	721	66	85
Camas	0.0	NA	5.9	NA	7.0	18.4	117	18.8	61.5	66.7	63.2	175	-7.7	1 494	14	112
Canyon	23.5	48.7	10.4	2.9	19.6	11.2	2 009	49.8	6.7	58.5	79.0	328	1.8	163	213	248
Caribou	30.5	19.1	4.4	1.3	6.2	10.1	428	15.0	50.0	68.7	67.3	587	1.1	1 372	66	247
Cassia	16.4	38.9	11.3	2.6	15.0	12.0	873	25.4	34.9	69.8	71.6	654	-6.6	749	237	413
Clark	NA	NA	3.2	NA	1.8	14.9	103	7.8	70.9	75.7	48.5	363	15.3	3 520	71	D
Clearwater	41.2	23.8	6.2	1.4	8.5	26.1	216	14.8	26.4	47.7	81.5	135	9.0	624	0	40
Custer	0.2	NA	4.5	1.0	NA	14.0	261	26.8	27.6	65.5	73.9	137	-7.5	525	56	68
Elmore	1.7	22.3	7.5	1.7	8.1	59.7	341	35.5	30.5	58.9	69.2	402	8.2	1 178	75	D

1. Covers mining, construction, and manufacturing. 2. Covers private sector earnings in agricultural services, forestry, and fisheries; transportation and public utilities; wholesale trade; retail trade; finance, insurance, and real estate; and services. 3. Kalawao County included with Maui County.

STATE County	Agriculture, 1987 (cont'd): Value of land and buildings: Average per farm ($1,000)	Value of land and buildings: Average per acre (Dollars)	Value of products sold: Total (Mil dol)	Value of products sold: Average per farm (Dollars)	Value of products sold: Percent from: Crops	Value of products sold: Percent from: Livestock and poultry[1]	Percent of farms with sales of: $10,000 or more	Percent of farms with sales of: $100,000 or more	Manufactures, 1987: Establishments: Total	Establishments: Percent with 20 or more employees	All employees: Number (1,000)	All employees: Percent change, 1982–1987	All employees: Annual payroll (Mil dol)	Production workers: Number (1,000)	Production workers: Work hours (Mil)
	119	120	121	122	123	124	125	126	127	128	129	130	131	132	133
GEORGIA—Con.															
Schley	196	522	5	53 298	44.5	55.5	33.0	13.8	12	66.7	0.8	100.0	13.9	0.6	1.2
Screven	322	728	19	62 865	62.0	38.0	59.2	16.8	26	15.4	1.7	-5.6	30.6	1.5	2.9
Seminole	485	937	23	107 426	85.0	15.0	71.9	28.1	7	28.6	0.3	0.0	3.3	0.2	0.4
Spalding	283	1 726	5	18 678	17.7	82.2	19.4	3.2	64	48.4	5.8	-19.4	96.2	4.6	9.3
Stephens	118	1 430	13	65 457	0.8	99.3	31.3	18.2	75	42.7	4.7	14.6	79.4	3.7	7.2
Stewart	257	550	7	70 964	61.6	38.4	49.5	17.2	14	28.6	0.3	0.0	4.5	0.2	0.4
Sumter	392	715	35	112 617	75.7	24.3	63.1	26.1	43	44.2	3.4	25.9	58.7	2.6	5.2
Talbot	189	631	2	16 274	21.7	78.3	24.2	4.7	9	11.1	0.1	0.0	0.9	0.1	0.1
Taliaferro	161	531	3	42 957	2.2	97.8	28.6	11.1	2	0.0	D	D	D	D	D
Tattnall	175	823	52	99 485	23.5	76.5	53.3	23.0	34	23.5	0.9	-30.8	8.0	0.8	1.3
Taylor	266	555	15	85 036	53.9	46.1	45.3	12.8	12	16.7	0.3	-40.0	3.0	0.2	0.4
Telfair	133	571	13	38 778	49.5	50.5	48.5	9.0	16	31.2	1.3	0.0	16.9	1.2	2.3
Terrell	564	697	24	121 353	93.8	6.2	69.5	29.4	12	50.0	1.2	9.1	12.5	0.9	1.8
Thomas	377	822	30	59 310	66.2	33.8	44.8	16.6	77	49.4	5.2	15.6	84.6	3.6	7.2
Tift	286	1 018	39	110 613	86.4	13.6	68.7	20.2	45	53.3	4.1	20.6	62.8	3.2	6.3
Toombs	158	626	16	49 105	54.4	45.6	44.6	12.0	49	46.9	2.5	13.6	31.8	1.8	3.3
Towns	145	2 132	2	11 183	12.1	87.9	15.4	2.7	6	33.3	0.1	0.0	0.6	0.1	0.1
Treutlen	141	458	2	19 499	50.7	49.4	29.8	4.1	8	25.0	0.3	-25.0	2.9	0.3	0.5
Troup	149	908	5	19 363	7.7	92.3	21.7	5.0	93	54.8	10.2	4.1	203.7	7.6	15.9
Turner	302	807	25	88 801	81.9	18.1	75.8	23.2	8	62.5	0.6	-25.0	6.2	0.5	1.0
Twiggs	109	511	2	18 117	62.1	37.9	35.7	2.7	13	7.7	0.1	0.0	1.7	0.1	0.2
Union	181	1 854	12	46 931	5.7	94.3	23.2	4.2	15	26.7	0.7	-12.5	6.7	0.6	1.1
Upson	190	1 021	7	34 059	8.6	91.4	21.0	5.6	29	37.9	4.5	-8.2	69.2	3.7	7.7
Walker	139	867	14	24 809	5.3	94.7	25.6	5.2	82	51.2	7.8	52.9	130.3	6.2	13.2
Walton	271	1 778	16	33 092	12.3	87.7	27.7	9.8	33	69.7	3.2	-13.5	48.6	2.5	4.8
Ware	147	677	11	34 260	43.5	56.5	32.6	8.6	66	40.9	2.7	-3.6	37.3	2.1	3.9
Warren	224	657	5	33 740	8.9	91.1	32.9	11.0	6	100.0	1.0	25.0	15.0	0.9	1.6
Washington	203	515	8	27 575	58.3	41.7	38.6	8.1	33	36.4	1.5	15.4	22.5	1.2	2.3
Wayne	164	823	7	22 064	66.9	33.1	34.6	5.7	36	25.0	D	D	D	D	D
Webster	323	532	8	84 722	84.1	15.9	67.0	27.7	4	25.0	D	D	D	D	D
Wheeler	146	521	6	33 163	61.2	38.8	44.6	6.2	10	10.0	0.3	0.0	3.3	0.3	0.5
White	166	2 270	38	124 429	0.6	99.4	47.4	33.2	28	28.6	1.1	-15.4	12.6	0.8	1.7
Whitfield	158	1 671	22	56 756	3.8	96.2	26.2	10.5	330	45.2	25.6	43.8	498.6	18.8	38.0
Wilcox	282	709	19	69 054	84.0	16.0	60.2	20.8	13	23.1	0.6	100.0	4.8	0.5	0.9
Wilkes	195	548	16	48 389	7.2	92.8	32.3	10.3	41	36.6	2.0	17.6	28.2	1.7	3.6
Wilkinson	202	566	1	11 915	34.3	65.7	21.5	1.7	23	30.4	1.1	266.7	19.8	0.8	1.6
Worth	307	769	42	87 958	77.8	22.2	66.3	27.0	17	52.9	0.8	-20.0	10.3	0.7	1.2
HAWAII	603	1 707	610	125 203	81.7	18.3	42.1	7.7	1 022	22.0	22.2	-5.9	440.2	15.2	28.8
Hawaii	574	1 600	220	78 205	88.8	11.2	40.4	5.3	100	21.0	2.2	-8.3	40.7	1.6	3.2
Honolulu	440	3 159	169	179 983	59.4	40.6	53.5	12.7	800	22.8	16.5	-7.8	330.7	10.9	19.9
Kalawao	NA	NA	NA	NA	NA	NA	NA	NA	NA	NA	NA	NA	NA	NA	NA
Kauai	709	1 266	68	169 619	91.5	8.5	31.5	5.2	34	17.6	0.7	0.0	13.8	0.5	1.1
Maui	873	1 754	153	212 345	91.8	8.2	39.8	12.0	88	18.2	2.8	7.7	54.9	2.2	4.6
IDAHO	337	572	2 269	94 002	48.3	51.7	56.6	18.4	1 491	24.9	52.9	11.1	1 148.5	38.3	72.4
Ada	207	975	113	87 283	17.0	83.0	36.8	12.2	284	25.7	11.1	20.7	293.3	6.1	12.0
Adams	272	369	10	37 580	5.0	95.0	46.3	7.8	16	18.8	0.2	0.0	3.9	0.2	0.3
Bannock	215	353	20	30 341	51.7	48.3	35.6	6.9	56	25.0	3.2	-13.5	85.8	2.0	3.9
Bear Lake	193	325	14	30 989	17.2	82.8	49.6	9.2	4	25.0	D	D	D	D	D
Benewah	435	710	9	44 769	84.7	15.3	38.0	13.7	45	24.4	1.2	33.3	26.1	1.0	2.0
Bingham	506	502	148	100 939	73.2	26.8	60.0	22.8	27	33.3	2.2	10.0	38.7	1.8	3.3
Blaine	553	467	19	84 666	37.9	62.1	58.8	20.4	33	9.1	0.2	0.0	3.6	0.2	0.3
Boise	348	380	2	28 691	36.8	63.2	45.2	5.5	11	18.2	0.1	0.0	3.5	0.1	0.3
Bonner	277	1 223	5	10 645	19.9	80.1	21.1	1.9	110	21.8	1.8	38.5	35.7	1.4	3.0
Bonneville	339	719	89	98 578	63.5	36.5	56.6	18.6	66	31.8	2.7	22.7	80.3	1.6	3.0
Boundary	293	948	9	29 463	64.9	35.1	36.0	8.1	38	7.9	0.4	0.0	9.1	0.3	0.6
Butte	323	436	15	66 234	57.2	42.8	69.6	19.2	2	0.0	D	D	D	D	D
Camas	446	303	7	58 778	52.0	48.0	62.4	18.8	NA	NA	NA	NA	NA	NA	NA
Canyon	231	1 438	249	123 977	44.7	55.3	53.3	18.7	114	32.5	6.8	33.3	118.2	4.9	9.0
Caribou	446	334	32	75 385	59.6	40.4	71.7	22.2	8	25.0	D	D	D	D	D
Cassia	465	632	175	200 239	51.3	48.7	74.1	32.2	23	39.1	1.5	7.1	24.7	1.2	2.1
Clark	1 514	430	26	253 643	61.2	38.8	71.8	37.9	NA	NA	NA	NA	NA	NA	NA
Clearwater	217	364	4	18 669	63.9	36.1	33.3	2.8	59	18.6	0.9	-18.2	20.1	0.8	1.6
Custer	311	551	11	42 713	12.0	88.0	55.6	10.0	2	0.0	D	D	D	D	D
Elmore	453	372	133	389 651	25.4	74.6	54.8	22.6	9	55.6	0.2	100.0	2.6	0.2	0.4

1. Includes livestock and poultry products.

STATE County	Manufactures, 1987 (cont'd): Production workers (cont'd): Wages: Total (Mil dol)	Manufactures, 1987 (cont'd): Production workers (cont'd): Wages: Average per worker (Dollars)	Manufactures, 1987 (cont'd): Value added by manu-facture (Mil dol)	Manufactures, 1987 (cont'd): Value of shipments (Mil dol)	Manufactures, 1987 (cont'd): New capital expend-itures (Mil dol)	Value of construction authorized by building permits, 1990: Total[1] ($1,000)	Nonresidential: Total ($1,000)	Nonresidential: Percent: Office	Nonresidential: Percent: Industrial	Nonresidential: Percent: Stores	Residential: New construction ($1,000)	Residential: Number of housing units	Residential: Alterations and additions ($1,000)
	134	135	136	137	138	139	140	141	142	143	144	145	146
GEORGIA—Con.													
Schley	9.9	16 500	25.6	68.6	D	249	126	100.0	0.0	0.0	91	2	0
Screven	23.0	15 333	82.0	157.8	3.3	278	44	0.0	0.0	0.0	185	3	19
Seminole	2.2	11 000	7.4	15.0	0.1	2 738	1 852	0.0	73.9	25.9	835	18	24
Spalding	64.2	13 957	208.2	467.0	D	26 177	6 514	11.6	12.7	61.9	13 084	261	1 494
Stephens	55.2	14 919	207.6	462.1	11.7	11 980	1 519	6.9	0.0	36.2	7 043	136	322
Stewart	3.2	16 000	8.4	25.4	0.7	860	0	NA	NA	NA	860	34	0
Sumter	37.5	14 423	140.6	367.8	13.6	5 740	673	0.0	49.3	10.2	3 543	64	483
Talbot	0.7	7 000	1.7	3.5	0.1	30	0	NA	NA	NA	30	1	0
Taliaferro	D	D	D	D	D	NA	NA	NA	NA	NA	NA	NA	NA
Tattnall	6.8	8 500	14.3	29.9	D	1 327	775	0.0	69.7	20.7	394	9	72
Taylor	2.3	11 500	15.3	24.7	0.4	437	37	0.0	0.0	0.0	352	13	42
Telfair	13.8	11 500	72.8	193.2	2.5	548	77	0.0	0.0	0.0	187	4	43
Terrell	9.1	10 111	11.5	61.4	1.7	592	70	0.0	0.0	0.0	298	13	97
Thomas	45.5	12 639	196.1	523.7	7.7	20 040	4 004	9.8	1.0	26.2	7 625	119	2 400
Tift	46.6	14 562	145.1	385.7	13.8	18 626	5 424	8.3	1.1	77.5	6 242	105	1 621
Toombs	16.8	9 333	72.3	150.6	2.2	10 815	7 599	0.5	13.5	65.1	3 213	49	0
Towns	0.5	5 000	1.2	2.0	0.0	65	0	NA	NA	NA	65	1	0
Treutlen	2.4	8 000	7.5	12.3	0.1	630	214	0.0	0.0	100.0	276	4	8
Troup	128.6	16 921	594.4	1 334.3	47.2	46 529	21 348	0.9	92.4	0.5	15 156	235	3 658
Turner	4.8	9 600	14.1	36.3	0.3	1 561	1 022	0.0	61.9	20.9	195	9	217
Twiggs	1.1	11 000	3.1	6.8	0.3	309	78	0.0	0.0	0.0	138	3	8
Union	5.5	9 167	13.2	25.2	0.3	NA	NA	NA	NA	NA	NA	NA	NA
Upson	50.6	13 676	105.2	282.3	11.0	24 748	6 428	0.0	68.4	4.3	11 123	193	1 100
Walker	96.3	15 532	305.1	1 015.2	44.0	13 260	1 674	13.9	25.8	17.9	10 578	257	426
Walton	35.4	14 160	106.2	293.0	6.8	37 319	4 895	22.7	11.7	30.1	29 409	565	1 871
Ware	25.3	12 048	71.7	194.3	5.4	9 388	1 795	6.3	0.0	77.6	5 144	56	446
Warren	11.9	13 222	27.8	75.4	0.8	207	3	0.0	0.0	0.0	180	1	18
Washington	16.2	13 500	59.3	119.0	D	3 637	233	23.6	0.0	25.7	2 992	80	187
Wayne	D	D	D	D	D	4 579	541	0.0	0.0	39.5	2 886	102	250
Webster	D	D	D	D	D	NA	NA	NA	NA	NA	NA	NA	NA
Wheeler	2.6	8 667	7.7	16.9	0.2	0	0	NA	NA	NA	0	0	0
White	10.2	12 750	55.8	119.5	3.0	23 595	211	0.0	0.0	94.8	22 697	291	303
Whitfield	322.4	17 149	1 290.9	4 212.0	124.2	71 181	45 199	22.0	0.2	41.7	12 336	296	2 057
Wilcox	4.3	8 600	8.7	24.2	0.2	0	0	NA	NA	NA	0	0	0
Wilkes	22.3	13 118	79.2	205.6	6.2	7 782	3 172	0.0	19.9	74.2	3 085	94	148
Wilkinson	14.5	18 125	66.3	108.5	3.0	71	0	NA	NA	NA	63	2	8
Worth	7.1	10 143	50.9	131.6	D	6 390	3 259	0.0	0.0	98.0	1 230	64	142
HAWAII	254.2	16 724	1 405.3	3 447.9	102.0	2 008 248	460 524	19.3	4.8	32.8	1 007 598	8 718	157 711
Hawaii	27.5	17 188	117.4	250.5	11.6	417 461	65 802	20.6	3.3	27.3	256 497	2 669	12 395
Honolulu	178.2	16 349	1 077.1	2 783.8	66.1	917 553	212 819	20.1	8.9	23.1	401 876	2 977	110 626
Kalawao	NA	NA	NA	NA	NA	NA	NA	NA	NA	NA	NA	NA	NA
Kauai	9.5	19 000	51.8	99.5	5.9	238 968	24 039	33.2	0.0	17.0	160 985	1 196	13 952
Maui	39.0	17 727	159.0	314.2	18.5	434 266	157 864	15.5	0.6	50.5	188 240	1 876	20 738
IDAHO	698.3	18 232	3 057.0	7 004.7	234.8	773 112	175 775	22.8	25.0	23.7	445 609	5 712	42 002
Ada	117.5	19 262	633.7	1 473.7	48.4	310 645	65 155	41.2	27.1	17.5	183 212	2 570	10 108
Adams	3.4	17 000	8.7	19.6	0.1	366	214	0.0	0.0	100.0	55	1	32
Bannock	51.6	25 800	238.8	603.3	16.5	22 326	2 587	0.9	0.0	35.1	8 657	125	800
Bear Lake	D	D	D	D	D	71	0	0.0	0.0	0.0	30	1	0
Benewah	21.2	21 200	35.8	129.0	3.4	1 663	128	0.0	0.0	0.0	1 258	35	154
Bingham	26.8	14 889	149.9	262.0	7.6	13 027	7 253	2.3	28.5	20.8	4 314	71	654
Blaine	2.3	11 500	13.5	36.4	0.4	92 135	6 538	36.6	4.4	36.3	74 369	425	8 884
Boise	3.1	31 000	6.3	21.9	0.1	0	0	NA	NA	NA	0	0	0
Bonner	27.3	19 500	85.9	258.7	6.1	17 439	1 966	0.0	0.0	44.9	10 035	215	1 140
Bonneville	38.3	23 937	182.6	247.8	D	54 097	12 148	14.7	45.9	13.9	33 685	469	1 842
Boundary	7.7	25 667	19.2	49.8	1.2	588	0	NA	NA	NA	478	12	81
Butte	D	D	D	D	D	43	0	NA	NA	NA	38	1	5
Camas	NA	NA	NA	NA	NA	469	11	0.0	0.0	0.0	432	6	18
Canyon	70.8	14 449	402.3	989.2	19.7	45 919	12 459	11.9	15.7	6.9	27 118	414	1 549
Caribou	D	D	D	D	D	577	107	0.0	0.0	29.9	315	5	77
Cassia	19.0	15 833	112.2	209.5	D	5 132	1 787	0.0	6.6	1.4	2 617	31	564
Clark	NA	NA	NA	NA	NA	0	0	NA	NA	NA	0	0	0
Clearwater	17.0	21 250	45.4	82.8	2.6	1 457	257	0.0	0.0	0.0	746	15	111
Custer	D	D	D	D	D	929	269	14.9	0.0	10.4	369	7	21
Elmore	1.9	9 500	7.5	16.7	0.3	3 821	912	0.0	12.1	35.3	2 170	47	259

1. Includes nonresidential additions and alterations, residential nonhousekeeping buildings, and residential garages and carports not shown separately.

STATE County	Wholesale trade, 1987				Retail trade, all establishments, 1987				Retail trade, establishments with payroll, 1987					
						Sales				Sales				
											Per capita[2] (Dollars)			
	Estab-lishments	Sales (Mil dol)	Paid employees[1]	Annual payroll (Mil dol)	Number	Total (Mil dol)	Percent change, 1982–1987	Per capita[2] (Dollars)	Number	Total (Mil dol)	General merchan-dise stores	Food stores	Apparel & acces-sory stores	Eating and drinking places
	147	148	149	150	151	152	153	154	155	156	157	158	159	160
GEORGIA—Con.														
Schley	2	D	D	D	33	10.4	9.5	2 887	20	9.5	D	1 014	0	D
Screven	16	47.5	178	2.4	145	42.8	15.4	2 777	79	40.1	127	932	105	135
Seminole	26	71.9	236	3.5	101	35.4	33.1	4 074	64	33.1	189	1 443	D	204
Spalding	70	324.5	764	14.6	509	344.1	63.1	6 373	332	335.7	856	1 321	321	428
Stephens	38	34.6	200	2.4	285	158.6	85.1	6 894	162	150.0	524	1 350	101	416
Stewart	10	7.4	40	0.7	78	14.1	20.5	2 474	38	12.0	D	1 003	D	109
Sumter	59	145.7	708	11.3	306	177.3	38.2	5 949	221	171.7	D	1 209	407	393
Talbot	4	D	D	D	54	8.7	22.5	1 246	21	7.8	D	548	0	0
Taliaferro	3	D	D	D	16	2.4	0.0	1 192	6	1.8	0	D	D	D
Tattnall	28	45.8	367	4.8	176	56.2	35.1	3 086	97	51.2	120	957	D	100
Taylor	12	D	D	D	77	22.5	27.8	2 811	43	19.9	D	578	D	85
Telfair	18	69.1	397	7.4	133	40.0	14.0	3 634	77	35.9	208	1 106	182	257
Terrell	23	159.0	323	4.9	108	37.8	14.9	3 203	72	36.2	D	1 104	228	108
Thomas	86	253.7	898	15.3	442	231.2	59.3	5 912	289	219.3	684	1 291	247	352
Tift	90	171.7	719	12.1	410	257.2	43.0	7 543	290	250.8	660	1 385	322	649
Toombs	58	138.3	365	6.8	308	127.4	61.9	5 264	195	121.1	1 054	1 111	252	346
Towns	1	D	D	D	113	23.2	54.7	3 468	45	18.9	D	376	54	489
Treutlen	5	1.1	10	0.1	52	12.3	33.7	1 977	29	11.7	D	962	48	227
Troup	88	255.2	858	16.2	657	356.5	58.9	6 701	403	343.4	714	1 182	382	609
Turner	20	123.4	164	2.8	93	33.8	2.7	3 555	55	32.2	198	1 248	85	205
Twiggs	4	0.6	7	0.1	51	7.9	16.2	803	21	6.0	0	396	D	D
Union	7	11.5	50	0.9	144	43.2	131.0	3 925	63	37.8	D	1 037	66	263
Upson	25	33.2	166	2.2	300	121.8	36.1	4 495	187	115.7	539	1 118	155	452
Walker	73	135.8	750	11.2	576	207.5	36.1	3 608	273	187.7	157	939	198	135
Walton	29	44.4	230	3.2	232	126.1	67.9	3 604	142	121.0	D	899	117	315
Ware	75	124.3	755	11.2	463	238.7	28.4	6 435	301	229.5	1 005	1 573	230	457
Warren	5	4.6	30	0.4	47	11.3	14.1	1 717	27	10.4	D	619	D	D
Washington	23	28.9	138	2.2	190	93.8	64.9	4 859	121	89.6	270	1 156	182	242
Wayne	23	36.3	139	2.0	233	119.2	38.3	5 368	149	115.1	336	1 014	210	363
Webster	4	3.1	12	0.2	6	D	D	D	5	1.9	D	0	0	0
Wheeler	2	D	D	D	46	8.0	150.0	1 592	17	6.3	0	D	0	67
White	14	17.2	87	1.2	251	84.7	206.9	6 884	138	73.6	411	1 162	424	790
Whitfield	321	1 948.7	3 981	79.5	922	558.1	69.1	8 019	537	534.7	1 069	1 552	290	610
Wilcox	10	35.7	133	1.9	74	11.5	71.6	1 510	30	8.6	162	581	D	D
Wilkes	21	47.3	192	2.9	147	57.2	42.3	5 156	88	54.9	289	1 182	218	208
Wilkinson	8	7.6	30	0.6	75	22.8	19.4	2 087	35	20.2	D	754	0	100
Worth	31	99.4	298	4.3	132	57.8	48.6	3 093	75	55.2	152	981	D	145
HAWAII	1 998	5 362.5	20 157	415.1	11 143	8 267.4	59.2	7 641	7 195	8 084.4	1 159	1 453	535	1 248
Hawaii	191	347.2	1 534	26.4	1 323	746.8	51.7	6 505	842	721.8	410	1 919	350	716
Honolulu	1 577	4 501.8	16 907	357.5	7 814	6 207.7	56.7	7 488	4 918	6 079.6	1 357	1 219	517	1 247
Kalawao	NA	NA	NA	NA	0	0.0	0.0	0	0	0.0	0	0	0	0
Kauai	73	124.9	506	8.4	666	372.9	70.0	7 784	464	362.5	428	2 334	490	1 384
Maui	157	388.6	1 210	22.9	1 340	940.1	81.1	10 411	971	920.6	682	2 535	952	1 868
IDAHO	2 128	5 078.2	20 814	353.4	10 953	5 082.2	25.2	5 083	6 587	4 891.0	484	1 133	194	448
Ada	536	1 746.1	5 479	115.4	1 961	1 217.3	36.5	6 164	1 233	1 186.2	676	1 341	255	656
Adams	2	D	D	D	54	7.1	12.7	2 215	25	6.1	0	D	D	220
Bannock	123	358.2	1 160	21.8	733	388.2	23.6	5 684	459	378.2	741	1 167	228	511
Bear Lake	11	9.8	62	0.9	80	20.2	-17.9	3 306	45	19.0	240	D	D	135
Benewah	9	10.3	40	0.5	108	31.7	33.2	3 773	56	29.6	0	1 302	D	215
Bingham	68	185.3	1 337	15.1	295	119.0	33.7	3 108	161	111.2	131	1 063	31	163
Blaine	40	41.9	183	3.5	323	105.0	25.4	7 500	196	98.3	D	1 720	575	1 253
Boise	0	0.0	0	0.0	39	4.3	53.6	1 433	18	3.5	D	D	0	513
Bonner	29	39.2	154	2.5	375	123.9	28.8	4 975	230	117.2	171	1 208	209	651
Bonneville	203	470.0	2 264	39.7	808	489.6	24.8	6 725	514	476.4	1 004	1 310	297	548
Boundary	15	13.8	87	1.4	98	30.7	10.8	4 037	49	28.1	D	D	D	216
Butte	7	5.2	29	0.3	46	9.2	12.2	3 083	25	7.8	0	D	D	196
Camas	0	0.0	0	0.0	13	D	D	D	5	0.3	0	D	0	D
Canyon	152	343.5	1 541	26.0	847	465.9	27.1	5 189	491	450.8	743	945	167	371
Caribou	25	21.9	102	1.5	75	20.1	-22.7	2 716	49	19.2	D	1 011	D	160
Cassia	64	212.9	443	6.6	224	112.0	-7.7	5 515	150	107.9	D	1 411	316	354
Clark	1	D	D	D	9	D	D	D	5	1.1	D	0	0	D
Clearwater	8	5.0	32	0.5	116	34.4	19.4	3 620	61	31.3	D	1 279	55	285
Custer	8	8.1	53	1.3	82	13.2	-7.0	2 859	36	11.1	0	607	D	142
Elmore	19	13.1	84	1.1	187	68.9	3.3	3 118	113	66.2	D	387	112	204

1. For pay period including March 12. 2. Based on the estimated population as of July 1 of the year shown.

STATE County	Retail trade, establishments with payroll, 1987 (cont'd): Paid employees[1]	Retail trade, establishments with payroll, 1987 (cont'd): Annual payroll (Mil dol)	Taxable service industries–establishments with payroll, 1987: Number	Receipts (Mil dol): Total	Receipts (Mil dol), Selected kinds of business: Hotels, motels and other lodging places	Receipts (Mil dol), Selected kinds of business: Health services	Receipts (Mil dol), Selected kinds of business: Legal services	Paid employees	Annual payroll (Mil dol)	Bank deposits,[2] June 1989: Total (Mil dol)	Bank deposits,[2] June 1989: Percent change, 1988–1989	Savings capital,[3] September 1989: Total (Mil dol)	Savings capital,[3] September 1989: Percent change, 1988–1989
	161	162	163	164	165	166	167	168	169	170	171	172	173
GEORGIA—Con.													
Schley	104	1.0	5	0.5	0.0	0.0	0.0	13	0.1	20	18.6	0.0	NA
Screven	434	4.2	42	8.7	D	4.2	0.4	292	3.0	79	5.3	20.4	-3.1
Seminole	402	3.3	40	6.7	0.3	3.1	0.3	158	2.9	51	8.0	23.4	1.9
Spalding	4 017	38.7	254	69.8	2.7	23.2	3.7	1 864	26.0	328	5.4	106.8	2.7
Stephens	1 394	13.2	108	24.1	D	13.0	1.9	602	7.2	134	3.1	46.7	1.6
Stewart	146	1.1	14	4.9	D	D	D	102	1.5	20	-1.9	0.0	NA
Sumter	2 192	19.7	135	36.0	D	12.6	4.5	1 121	14.5	213	21.1	46.6	-9.1
Talbot	68	0.5	10	0.5	0.0	0.0	D	18	0.1	32	4.4	0.0	NA
Taliaferro	28	0.3	4	0.6	0.0	D	0.0	12	0.2	14	-30.6	0.0	NA
Tattnall	606	4.9	51	13.1	D	3.6	0.8	375	4.1	95	2.0	8.7	41.6
Taylor	189	2.3	17	4.2	0.0	1.1	D	84	1.4	43	4.5	0.0	NA
Telfair	471	4.1	54	14.8	D	10.2	0.5	510	4.5	63	10.6	29.2	-4.5
Terrell	478	3.9	37	5.4	D	2.0	D	167	1.8	89	-1.5	9.7	-12.1
Thomas	2 665	24.9	255	63.1	D	33.5	3.4	1 486	24.3	272	15.9	117.5	-3.9
Tift	3 049	28.1	207	72.0	10.4	28.2	4.0	1 798	27.8	268	18.8	60.3	-10.3
Toombs	1 422	13.4	153	34.5	D	13.6	1.9	970	13.1	137	10.1	70.8	0.5
Towns	272	2.3	25	4.3	0.3	1.9	0.5	119	1.6	71	14.0	0.0	NA
Treutlen	189	1.4	15	2.2	0.0	D	0.0	98	0.8	25	3.9	0.0	NA
Troup	4 223	40.5	265	84.4	6.2	30.5	4.6	2 855	35.4	401	17.6	212.2	0.6
Turner	405	2.9	43	5.9	0.5	2.3	0.4	189	1.9	78	7.2	34.3	35.3
Twiggs	63	0.6	9	2.2	0.0	D	D	127	0.9	9	41.5	0.0	NA
Union	438	3.7	46	6.0	D	3.0	0.5	146	2.1	121	18.3	0.0	NA
Upson	1 761	15.0	115	21.8	0.9	12.6	1.7	707	7.7	170	13.9	36.1	-5.3
Walker	1 818	17.3	171	45.3	D	14.2	4.5	1 137	15.2	179	4.0	155.3	1.8
Walton	1 514	14.3	127	23.5	D	9.0	1.6	656	8.3	215	7.8	35.5	1.2
Ware	3 291	28.0	227	53.1	2.5	23.4	5.0	1 252	20.0	205	12.6	93.4	-3.6
Warren	127	1.3	13	2.8	0.0	2.5	D	138	1.2	21	-0.2	0.0	NA
Washington	1 030	9.2	72	14.0	D	5.8	0.5	498	5.5	124	7.7	19.7	3.8
Wayne	1 415	12.7	99	23.4	D	9.9	1.1	781	8.4	89	11.7	33.7	-10.5
Webster	22	0.2	1	D	0.0	0.0	0.0	D	D	3	-26.0	0.0	NA
Wheeler	99	0.6	5	0.2	0.0	D	D	8	0.1	12	2.4	0.0	NA
White	897	8.3	75	12.1	2.6	4.4	0.4	379	3.7	144	-4.0	2.2	NA
Whitfield	5 664	58.8	398	141.3	5.7	40.2	9.1	3 041	57.3	540	7.5	251.4	5.1
Wilcox	104	0.9	15	4.6	0.0	2.9	D	345	1.8	41	15.9	5.4	-1.6
Wilkes	608	5.6	48	7.5	D	2.9	0.3	208	2.5	107	6.9	13.1	9.2
Wilkinson	257	2.1	24	2.8	0.0	0.9	D	63	0.8	49	7.1	0.0	NA
Worth	529	5.2	52	9.0	D	4.6	0.3	291	2.9	66	4.8	20.9	-1.8
HAWAII	101 969	1 016.1	7 458	4 456.0	1 562.0	742.5	315.5	91 673	1 499.5	11 642	10.9	4 848.8	11.9
Hawaii	9 456	87.9	736	382.2	191.9	69.7	14.4	8 670	126.2	790	12.1	247.8	2.3
Honolulu	74 485	752.8	5 704	3 234.3	868.9	601.3	283.7	66 533	1 124.0	9 663	10.1	4 189.1	13.3
Kalawao	0	0.0	NA	NA	NA	NA	NA	NA	NA	NA	NA	0.0	NA
Kauai	5 173	47.1	293	186.6	98.5	26.4	3.1	4 001	58.6	368	12.8	102.8	7.4
Maui	12 855	128.3	725	652.8	402.8	45.2	14.3	12 469	190.7	821	19.0	309.1	3.6
IDAHO	62 535	556.1	6 239	2 063.9	131.6	574.6	145.5	47 621	789.5	6 129	6.9	1 179.1	-4.9
Ada	15 793	143.5	1 691	566.3	36.2	151.2	62.0	14 169	213.1	1 463	14.1	261.4	-13.1
Adams	107	0.7	8	D	D	D	0.0	D	D	16	9.8	0.0	NA
Bannock	5 182	43.6	410	105.4	6.2	43.4	12.0	2 875	40.4	314	3.7	17.1	-3.9
Bear Lake	258	1.9	23	D	D	D	D	D	D	54	2.8	0.0	NA
Benewah	325	2.8	33	4.7	D	2.1	0.7	150	1.8	49	6.7	0.0	NA
Bingham	1 315	11.2	108	20.9	D	6.3	2.6	540	6.2	162	6.4	8.5	31.0
Blaine	1 701	14.4	187	45.1	7.0	8.0	3.4	1 133	16.6	88	14.4	60.7	17.4
Boise	123	0.4	10	D	0.3	D	0.0	D	D	NA	NA	0.0	NA
Bonner	1 624	13.8	165	28.6	6.5	10.5	2.6	985	9.1	150	7.3	27.9	9.7
Bonneville	6 024	52.9	535	541.4	D	97.5	15.2	8 190	232.7	452	1.7	85.9	-3.5
Boundary	321	3.0	37	4.4	D	1.1	D	155	1.1	57	1.6	0.0	NA
Butte	103	0.9	13	D	D	D	D	D	D	17	4.6	0.0	NA
Camas	21	0.1	1	D	D	0.0	0.0	D	D	2	0.5	0.0	NA
Canyon	5 276	50.0	425	103.2	D	53.6	4.1	2 893	39.5	406	3.4	199.2	-3.3
Caribou	275	1.9	34	D	0.0	D	D	D	D	52	0.9	19.1	-13.4
Cassia	1 258	12.0	122	20.5	D	7.4	1.4	751	6.9	191	9.3	21.7	-9.0
Clark	14	0.1	2	D	D	0.0	0.0	D	D	3	9.1	0.0	NA
Clearwater	438	3.4	48	6.1	0.8	1.7	0.5	202	1.9	52	10.4	0.0	NA
Custer	146	1.3	26	D	1.3	0.7	0.0	D	D	24	14.5	0.0	NA
Elmore	958	7.6	78	11.2	1.2	3.1	0.6	394	3.3	56	2.1	12.2	-10.9

1. For the period including March 12 of the year shown. 2. Includes deposits for all insured and reporting noninsured commercial and mutual savings banks. 3. Includes savings capital for all FSLIC insured savings institutions.

STATE County	Federal funds and grants, 1989							Local government finances, 1981–1982							
	Expenditures		Per capita[1] (Dollars)					General revenue						Direct general expenditure	
									Intergovernmental		Taxes				
												Per capita[2]			
	Total (Mil dol)	Percent change, 1988–1989	Total	Direct payments for individuals	Procurement contract awards	Salaries and wages	Grant awards	Total (Mil dol)	Total (Mil dol)	Percent from state	Total (Mil dol)	Total (Dollars)	Property (Dollars)	Total (Mil dol)	Percent change, 1977–1982
	174	175	176	177	178	179	180	181	182	183	184	185	186	187	188
GEORGIA—Con.															
Schley	8.0	-3.8	2 212	1 554	32	70	428	2.4	1.6	93.1	0.7	194	131	2.4	127.4
Screven	36.1	5.0	2 362	1 638	11	98	433	11.5	5.1	93.8	3.3	236	174	11.3	69.7
Seminole	24.4	5.8	2 873	1 989	11	96	416	5.8	3.0	92.0	2.2	242	171	5.5	73.4
Spalding	110.8	12.3	1 990	1 565	71	91	255	43.5	15.5	89.2	10.4	209	176	43.7	58.4
Stephens	53.1	-2.8	2 261	1 827	45	106	271	19.3	6.6	84.2	4.7	216	163	18.7	65.7
Stewart	16.7	-3.7	2 982	2 009	14	104	782	6.4	4.0	90.8	1.1	186	161	8.4	136.7
Sumter	69.7	-0.9	2 378	1 661	17	162	410	34.8	14.9	81.4	6.3	210	111	37.3	96.4
Talbot	14.2	11.5	1 975	1 454	12	89	386	5.3	3.9	52.4	1.2	175	132	3.6	42.6
Taliaferro	7.2	15.2	3 813	2 586	22	160	867	0.9	0.5	87.7	0.3	152	136	0.9	8.4
Tattnall	46.0	11.1	2 515	1 829	14	108	470	11.4	4.7	89.0	3.1	178	123	10.7	83.7
Taylor	23.3	10.7	2 952	2 035	56	143	544	5.2	3.2	85.1	1.6	203	144	4.8	44.1
Telfair	33.0	1.4	3 059	2 213	15	116	587	10.8	5.6	76.5	3.0	261	159	10.7	75.3
Terrell	51.7	56.1	4 461	1 578	1 881	205	562	6.1	3.6	90.9	2.1	176	108	5.8	-11.9
Thomas	101.1	5.9	2 572	1 862	16	190	370	30.5	17.4	81.7	8.5	223	196	30.7	59.0
Tift	70.8	5.1	2 058	1 413	38	238	300	36.2	10.0	87.3	7.0	207	108	36.5	108.9
Toombs	58.4	8.2	2 383	1 657	61	112	477	21.3	8.0	87.7	4.2	185	150	21.0	73.0
Towns	19.1	8.7	2 766	2 327	12	88	326	4.5	2.0	63.7	0.9	146	119	3.6	19.2
Treutlen	14.9	-5.9	2 399	1 667	11	84	516	3.8	2.4	92.1	1.0	160	111	3.9	67.2
Troup	130.3	-10.9	2 449	1 825	166	112	336	58.4	19.9	78.6	14.3	278	173	61.9	193.0
Turner	25.3	11.6	2 695	1 816	54	143	377	8.9	4.9	72.5	2.4	255	178	9.5	89.9
Twiggs	18.3	6.2	1 928	1 370	15	81	405	4.8	2.9	92.9	1.7	175	165	4.5	54.2
Union	30.3	8.0	2 613	2 087	15	146	346	9.7	3.8	85.7	1.4	144	143	8.8	116.5
Upson	60.2	0.2	2 205	1 713	70	77	329	26.3	8.9	89.4	6.5	246	204	27.8	115.9
Walker	129.1	6.7	2 203	1 887	23	79	199	31.5	17.9	78.9	9.8	173	126	30.5	52.6
Walton	65.3	1.2	1 790	1 433	15	92	224	28.1	11.1	84.6	6.7	212	146	26.4	77.6
Ware	103.8	7.3	2 843	2 148	19	205	438	46.4	17.5	86.1	9.6	260	156	43.8	95.9
Warren	18.4	10.0	2 794	1 721	115	102	763	4.3	2.3	90.6	1.3	201	146	4.2	52.0
Washington	60.3	35.3	3 124	2 421	13	97	501	17.5	7.1	87.2	5.3	281	191	16.6	53.3
Wayne	47.7	-45.5	2 141	1 632	18	80	344	23.0	6.7	89.9	5.7	265	226	21.9	88.2
Webster	5.7	6.5	2 717	1 552	97	142	620	1.5	0.8	91.3	0.6	265	253	1.3	47.9
Wheeler	14.8	13.0	2 961	1 948	19	87	645	3.7	1.8	92.8	0.8	150	139	4.0	41.2
White	26.1	10.7	2 011	1 544	16	91	330	5.5	3.0	86.8	1.9	184	158	5.7	69.9
Whitfield	112.2	5.6	1 585	1 256	53	94	176	73.9	19.9	89.4	23.6	359	227	72.7	79.2
Wilcox	23.8	13.3	3 132	2 156	15	109	550	4.8	3.2	78.6	1.3	171	155	4.3	49.7
Wilkes	28.5	8.0	2 611	1 855	13	146	459	10.2	4.4	73.5	2.1	192	167	10.4	54.0
Wilkinson	22.3	2.2	2 023	1 575	9	69	344	7.0	4.0	88.8	2.6	253	196	6.3	56.3
Worth	42.0	10.5	2 222	1 562	9	74	370	10.8	6.0	91.8	3.6	195	147	10.8	24.7
HAWAII	5 570.9	10.0	X	1 691	560	2 051	635	525.5	119.8	28.1	315.0	316	255	456.2	13.9
Hawaii	260.9	1.9	2 171	1 633	46	227	259	59.4	17.9	40.5	36.3	363	303	57.4	21.5
Honolulu	4 784.6	9.0	5 645	1 667	661	2 627	683	389.9	82.4	20.8	236.2	304	244	330.7	8.5
Kalawao	0.0	0.0	0	0	0	0	0	NA	NA	NA	0.0	NA	0	NA	NA
Kauai	131.2	34.6	2 587	1 463	522	308	290	29.4	10.6	40.0	15.4	367	297	25.7	63.3
Maui	190.2	5.3	1 987	1 312	331	158	181	46.8	8.9	56.7	27.0	351	284	42.4	28.5
IDAHO	3 776.3	9.1	X	1 641	916	474	551	859.7	375.2	84.0	235.3	241	231	835.0	61.6
Ada	674.6	6.0	3 278	1 524	151	753	823	141.2	55.1	81.2	50.5	278	266	133.0	39.7
Adams	9.7	-77.6	3 118	1 907	109	541	451	3.1	1.6	84.4	0.6	185	180	3.3	66.7
Bannock	150.9	8.4	2 213	1 521	67	271	285	60.9	22.9	81.8	16.0	236	226	59.5	98.1
Bear Lake	22.7	37.6	3 913	1 875	640	250	593	9.1	2.9	87.4	1.9	264	262	11.6	201.6
Benewah	25.3	-1.9	3 018	1 820	234	334	472	7.3	3.2	93.3	2.1	252	247	7.3	47.5
Bingham	101.0	13.4	2 602	1 147	782	249	309	33.3	17.3	88.4	7.6	202	196	30.2	40.1
Blaine	15.8	2.1	1 083	740	62	145	82	15.2	2.4	76.0	6.5	557	448	14.1	105.0
Boise	22.6	46.6	7 294	1 794	215	489	4 713	2.8	1.7	95.5	0.8	266	263	3.2	83.2
Bonner	65.2	2.3	2 596	1 995	70	227	289	18.4	7.4	91.4	3.9	155	148	18.5	59.1
Bonneville	934.9	44.5	12 433	1 122	10 275	761	207	46.5	22.3	92.6	15.5	230	221	47.9	43.2
Boundary	26.1	21.5	3 349	1 775	953	363	191	7.3	3.3	79.2	1.7	226	223	6.8	33.0
Butte	10.1	1.4	3 471	1 668	36	284	1 202	3.3	1.7	85.5	0.6	183	178	3.3	27.5
Camas	4.9	47.5	8 115	2 155	53	902	830	1.3	0.8	75.5	0.3	374	368	1.0	18.5
Canyon	208.5	-5.7	2 289	1 670	29	105	310	60.3	30.3	82.8	17.8	207	199	60.5	61.5
Caribou	18.1	-8.2	2 550	1 320	12	174	167	10.8	3.8	89.5	2.8	318	312	10.5	72.2
Cassia	47.1	-6.0	2 353	1 310	131	234	227	16.6	9.2	80.3	3.9	192	186	16.5	60.0
Clark	31.8	118.3	39 705	1 589	71	1 124	33 802	1.5	0.8	88.9	0.4	484	463	1.3	43.4
Clearwater	28.6	-6.5	3 138	1 651	357	827	266	10.0	5.4	84.2	2.0	193	188	10.3	47.8
Custer	28.5	87.6	6 956	1 525	4 370	622	190	5.5	2.6	86.1	0.9	179	170	5.3	86.4
Elmore	146.9	3.7	6 587	1 453	511	4 177	322	18.4	9.9	78.6	3.3	150	142	17.3	50.9

1. Based on the estimated population as of July 1 of the year shown. 2. Based on the estimated population as of July 1, 1982.

STATE County	Local government finances, 1981–1982 (cont'd) — Direct general expenditure (cont'd) — Per capita[1] (Dollars)	Percent of total for– Educa-tion	Percent of total for– Health & hospitals	Percent of total for– Police protec-tion	Percent of total for– Public welfare	Percent of total for– High-ways	Debt outstanding — Total (Mil dol)	Debt outstanding — Per capita[1] (Dollars)	State and local government employ-ment, 1989 — Total	State and local government employ-ment, 1989 — Rate[2]	Federal government civilian employment 1989 — Total	Federal government civilian employment 1989 — Earnings ($1,000)	Elections, 1988[3] — Total vote cast for president	Elections, 1988[3] — Vote for lead party (Percent)
	189	190	191	192	193	194	195	196	197	198	199	200	201	202
GEORGIA—Con.														
Schley	698	38.1	10.0	5.1	0.1	13.4	1.0	305	172	477.8	11	252	1 078	R–58.9
Screven	807	53.4	17.6	4.2	0.1	10.7	0.8	55	831	543.1	52	1 206	3 659	R–59.5
Seminole	608	69.0	1.3	5.1	0.2	6.4	1.5	164	408	480.0	32	740	2 645	R–55.5
Spalding	878	38.9	32.7	5.4	0.0	3.5	8.4	168	3 437	617.1	142	4 339	12 138	R–63.7
Stephens	860	37.1	36.5	3.6	0.1	4.8	14.4	660	1 217	517.9	61	1 694	6 550	R–66.1
Stewart	1 450	53.9	29.3	2.3	0.3	6.3	0.6	107	304	542.9	22	478	1 973	D–57.6
Sumter	1 243	35.2	33.3	3.7	0.1	3.7	12.0	399	2 628	896.9	123	4 045	7 668	R–55.9
Talbot	543	58.8	1.4	2.7	0.1	10.4	1.5	220	293	406.9	20	490	2 060	D–60.6
Taliaferro	447	55.7	5.5	5.4	0.7	13.8	0.2	90	87	457.9	NA	135	777	D–60.4
Tattnall	609	44.9	26.2	3.4	0.7	8.4	3.3	186	1 940	1 060.1	51	1 203	4 878	R–65.0
Taylor	603	61.8	5.1	6.1	0.4	7.0	1.6	195	492	622.8	31	653	2 284	R–50.1
Telfair	944	51.7	19.0	4.2	0.3	6.1	5.0	443	643	595.4	48	1 072	3 595	R–50.2
Terrell	487	56.3	8.0	10.1	0.3	4.4	1.9	160	513	442.2	80	2 197	2 905	R–52.2
Thomas	801	54.7	5.7	4.7	0.1	8.0	5.0	130	2 981	758.5	212	7 049	10 145	R–64.8
Tift	1 087	28.5	41.9	3.2	0.0	4.7	43.7	1 301	3 569	1 037.5	239	7 615	7 234	R–65.8
Toombs	918	40.8	37.8	3.2	0.0	3.2	4.5	198	1 380	563.3	87	2 246	5 619	R–78.9
Towns	595	42.7	33.5	2.4	0.3	11.1	0.9	158	412	597.1	18	457	2 738	R–65.1
Treutlen	622	56.5	8.2	5.1	0.2	10.6	0.2	37	307	495.2	18	497	1 696	R–57.2
Troup	1 205	36.1	34.0	4.6	0.1	5.4	14.9	290	3 994	750.8	173	5 125	14 089	R–67.3
Turner	1 013	40.4	17.4	4.6	0.1	6.0	4.3	456	437	464.9	43	1 130	2 597	R–50.5
Twiggs	471	70.3	5.1	3.6	0.2	7.7	0.6	65	399	420.0	31	665	3 005	D–57.6
Union	879	35.8	43.5	1.3	0.0	10.8	3.5	349	705	607.8	71	1 655	3 664	R–65.4
Upson	1 046	45.5	33.9	3.3	0.1	4.0	10.6	399	1 316	482.1	55	1 454	7 318	R–63.1
Walker	540	66.5	3.6	4.5	0.1	6.4	22.5	399	2 124	362.5	150	4 386	15 280	R–68.6
Walton	837	41.9	29.6	4.4	0.1	5.5	10.2	323	1 720	471.2	86	2 432	9 112	R–65.6
Ware	1 184	33.5	38.8	3.5	0.1	4.5	18.5	500	2 776	760.5	188	5 700	9 163	R–52.6
Warren	630	55.1	1.7	5.6	0.9	11.6	6.5	989	276	418.2	18	402	2 003	D–54.5
Washington	875	44.4	23.9	4.6	0.2	11.2	4.1	214	1 489	771.5	53	1 320	5 383	R–51.1
Wayne	1 021	34.4	41.8	3.7	0.3	4.9	14.1	655	1 826	818.8	72	2 242	5 766	R–57.9
Webster	580	58.2	2.8	5.5	0.1	16.9	0.2	78	112	533.3	NA	165	790	D–54.1
Wheeler	775	54.6	27.1	3.8	0.3	4.9	0.5	90	292	584.0	22	434	1 373	R–51.6
White	534	61.2	1.3	5.8	0.3	11.4	0.8	80	725	557.7	31	722	3 696	R–71.6
Whitfield	1 103	37.2	38.2	2.9	0.1	4.4	27.9	424	3 694	521.8	196	5 741	17 451	R–73.1
Wilcox	552	62.4	5.4	5.4	0.2	6.8	0.6	73	328	431.6	31	701	2 319	R–53.3
Wilkes	929	38.1	29.5	3.3	0.1	5.3	2.5	225	694	636.7	46	1 081	3 370	R–53.7
Wilkinson	610	64.3	6.3	5.2	0.2	9.8	1.2	112	453	411.8	26	627	3 413	D–53.6
Worth	587	61.0	2.0	5.0	0.2	9.9	2.3	124	892	472.0	55	1 307	4 009	R–66.6
HAWAII	457	0.1	1.1	15.7	1.0	10.8	337.5	338	67 161	602.8	33 973	1 086 334	354 461	D–54.3
Hawaii	573	0.0	0.0	17.1	0.0	11.3	49.9	499	7 578	630.4	778	23 574	41 768	D–57.7
Honolulu	425	0.0	1.6	15.6	0.0	10.8	248.6	320	51 284	605.0	32 479	1 039 629	261 577	D–53.1
Kalawao	NA	0.0	NA	0.0	NA	NA	NA	NA	0	0.0	0	0	NA	NA
Kauai	613	0.6	0.0	14.9	1.4	12.8	19.1	455	3 013	594.3	320	10 376	20 266	D–58.1
Maui	551	0.4	0.0	15.4	9.8	9.0	19.9	259	5 286	552.4	396	12 755	30 850	D–56.8
IDAHO	854	46.7	11.6	4.9	0.6	8.5	541.4	554	64 730	638.4	12 745	362 200	408 968	R–62.1
Ada	732	46.3	0.4	7.3	0.0	8.4	78.8	433	14 271	693.4	4 135	135 514	87 334	R–62.9
Adams	990	44.0	17.5	4.7	0.3	12.6	0.4	129	148	477.4	144	3 012	1 799	R–61.5
Bannock	878	39.6	23.2	5.1	0.3	4.7	16.9	249	5 754	843.7	558	16 538	28 601	R–52.4
Bear Lake	1 584	43.8	34.3	1.0	0.7	5.6	5.9	812	422	727.6	59	1 262	2 980	R–69.9
Benewah	864	48.0	17.6	3.2	0.2	10.8	2.7	317	532	633.3	105	2 789	3 238	R–51.0
Bingham	807	55.7	15.0	3.7	0.5	6.4	11.6	310	2 298	592.3	330	10 349	14 705	R–68.9
Blaine	1 211	25.6	26.0	5.7	7.0	7.0	8.5	733	782	535.6	96	2 383	5 755	R–54.4
Boise	1 081	46.7	0.0	7.3	0.5	16.9	0.7	238	174	561.3	99	2 015	1 710	R–61.1
Bonner	741	43.7	23.8	5.5	0.4	8.1	3.9	158	1 339	533.5	257	6 150	11 455	R–49.9
Bonneville	710	56.4	1.4	5.8	0.2	5.7	60.9	902	3 368	447.9	723	25 992	30 147	R–75.0
Boundary	920	42.7	23.5	4.7	0.9	9.3	2.9	395	549	703.8	154	3 631	3 202	R–56.2
Butte	953	49.9	21.3	3.0	0.6	10.6	0.2	48	168	579.3	40	821	1 444	R–62.3
Camas	1 209	52.6	1.1	4.8	0.7	14.7	0.4	545	74	1 233.3	22	545	437	R–65.9
Canyon	703	49.6	0.9	4.8	0.5	7.0	22.3	260	4 335	475.9	237	6 742	32 396	R–66.1
Caribou	1 175	43.6	18.3	2.9	0.4	11.7	18.3	2 055	521	733.8	55	1 299	3 144	R–71.2
Cassia	819	48.3	2.6	5.1	0.6	13.1	6.8	337	1 087	543.5	169	5 037	7 288	R–73.3
Clark	1 635	44.2	0.7	5.0	0.2	31.4	0.3	385	81	1 012.5	49	1 225	421	R–66.7
Clearwater	976	44.1	19.3	4.6	0.3	13.6	1.8	176	793	871.4	339	8 752	3 617	D–51.5
Custer	1 044	66.7	1.9	3.3	0.2	9.1	4.3	843	254	619.5	160	3 564	1 896	R–66.1
Elmore	784	55.7	13.4	4.3	0.4	9.2	4.7	215	952	426.9	987	20 816	5 919	R–63.5

1. Based on the estimated population as of July 1, 1982. 2. Per 10,000 resident population estimated as of July 1 of the year shown. 3. Data subject to copyright.

STATE–County code	MSA/ CMSA/ NECMA code[1]	STATE County	Land Area,[2] 1990 (Sq. Km.)	Population, 1990												
				Total persons	Rank	Per square kilometer	Race					Hispanic[3]	Age of population Percent		
							White	Black	Am. Indian, Eskimo, Aleut	Asian & Pacific Islander	Other race		Under 5 years	5 to 14 years	15 to 24 years
			1	2	3	4	5	6	7	8	9	10	11	12	13
		IDAHO—Con.													
16 041	...	Franklin	1 724	9 232	2 452	5.4	9 052	5	38	12	125	237	9.3	24.0	13.9
16 043	...	Fremont	4 835	10 937	2 300	2.3	10 273	9	68	37	550	762	8.7	22.5	15.0
16 045	...	Gem	1 457	11 844	2 228	8.1	11 322	13	139	53	317	615	7.1	16.2	12.1
16 047	...	Gooding	1 893	11 633	2 244	6.1	10 886	7	43	31	666	1 021	7.3	17.9	11.8
16 049	...	Idaho	21 977	13 783	2 073	0.6	13 378	3	346	34	22	124	6.6	16.5	10.9
16 051	...	Jefferson	2 836	16 543	1 887	5.8	15 627	7	122	40	747	1 155	10.0	24.2	14.0
16 053	...	Jerome	1 554	15 138	1 978	9.7	14 304	9	115	54	656	1 018	8.2	19.1	12.0
16 055	...	Kootenai	3 225	69 795	635	21.6	68 461	94	675	326	239	1 052	7.1	15.7	12.7
16 057	...	Latah	2 789	30 617	1 259	11.0	29 388	174	206	709	140	449	6.5	13.0	26.2
16 059	...	Lemhi	11 822	6 899	2 673	0.6	6 773	2	49	23	52	140	6.9	16.2	10.1
16 061	...	Lewis	1 241	3 516	2 956	2.8	3 322	4	169	18	3	42	7.4	16.5	10.2
16 063	...	Lincoln	3 122	3 308	2 976	1.1	3 231	3	22	12	40	195	7.1	19.3	12.9
16 065	...	Madison	1 221	23 674	1 505	19.4	22 741	43	108	296	486	753	8.1	19.2	39.0
16 067	...	Minidoka	1 968	19 361	1 712	9.8	16 540	43	201	100	2 477	3 735	8.4	21.2	13.2
16 069	...	Nez Perce	2 199	33 754	1 169	15.3	31 681	48	1 692	211	122	419	6.5	14.4	13.2
16 071	...	Oneida	3 109	3 492	2 958	1.1	3 431	4	19	8	30	56	9.5	22.8	10.2
16 073	...	Owyhee	19 887	8 392	2 522	0.4	6 935	22	276	76	1 083	1 408	8.4	18.5	16.1
16 075	...	Payette	1 055	16 434	1 895	15.6	15 210	14	189	158	863	1 200	7.9	17.6	12.7
16 077	...	Power	3 641	7 086	2 648	1.9	6 157	7	203	40	679	937	8.5	20.4	14.1
16 079	...	Shoshone	6 822	13 931	2 063	2.0	13 620	16	182	40	73	247	5.7	15.2	12.3
16 081	...	Teton	1 167	3 439	2 961	2.9	3 360	2	13	1	63	237	9.7	19.0	13.7
16 083	...	Twin Falls	4 986	53 580	801	10.7	51 202	65	309	524	1 480	3 106	7.7	17.5	13.1
16 085	...	Valley	9 527	6 109	2 742	0.6	5 988	8	60	27	26	107	6.9	16.5	9.3
16 087	...	Washington	3 772	8 550	2 509	2.3	7 660	7	46	130	707	915	6.9	17.2	11.1
17 000	...	ILLINOIS	143 987	11 430 602	X	79.4	8 952 978	1 694 273	21 836	285 311	476 204	904 446	7.4	14.3	14.7
17 001	...	Adams	2 219	66 090	661	29.8	63 917	1 702	98	249	124	265	7.0	14.7	13.2
17 003	...	Alexander	612	10 626	2 324	17.4	7 054	3 496	19	48	9	54	8.4	15.8	12.5
17 005	...	Bond	985	14 991	1 988	15.2	14 477	429	35	16	34	80	6.3	14.0	15.5
17 007	6880	Boone	729	30 806	1 248	42.3	29 344	127	46	150	1 139	2 065	7.6	15.6	14.2
17 009	...	Brown	792	5 836	2 777	7.4	5 264	547	14	5	6	104	5.6	13.0	14.2
17 011	...	Bureau	2 250	35 688	1 105	15.9	35 157	50	65	195	221	1 003	6.5	15.3	12.5
17 013	...	Calhoun	657	5 322	2 816	8.1	5 298	1	8	15	0	12	6.2	13.8	12.6
17 015	...	Carroll	1 151	16 805	1 859	14.6	16 519	111	30	61	84	296	6.4	14.3	11.9
17 017	...	Cass	974	13 437	2 105	13.8	13 384	16	8	23	6	56	6.6	14.9	12.8
17 019	1400	Champaign	2 583	173 025	279	67.0	146 506	16 559	331	8 033	1 596	3 485	6.8	11.8	25.8
17 021	...	Christian	1 836	34 418	1 151	18.7	34 176	82	51	89	20	103	6.9	14.1	12.6
17 023	...	Clark	1 299	15 921	1 929	12.3	15 842	10	26	36	7	42	6.5	14.0	12.1
17 025	...	Clay	1 215	14 460	2 019	11.9	14 403	4	17	29	7	57	6.3	15.0	12.0
17 027	7040	Clinton	1 228	33 944	1 163	27.6	32 688	1 021	48	104	83	336	6.9	15.8	14.0
17 029	...	Coles	1 317	51 644	819	39.2	50 177	925	92	341	109	405	5.5	12.0	26.2
17 031	1602	Cook	2 449	5 105 067	2	2 084.6	3 204 947	1 317 147	10 289	188 565	384 119	694 194	7.5	13.6	14.7
17 033	...	Crawford	1 149	19 464	1 704	16.9	19 300	63	34	48	19	80	6.4	14.2	11.8
17 035	...	Cumberland	896	10 670	2 320	11.9	10 627	5	6	26	6	39	7.5	16.0	13.4
17 037	...	De Kalb	1 643	77 932	582	47.4	72 968	2 069	123	1 751	1 021	2 329	6.3	12.0	28.4
17 039	...	De Witt	1 030	16 516	1 891	16.0	16 387	25	37	43	24	80	6.8	14.9	12.1
17 041	...	Douglas	1 080	19 464	1 705	18.0	19 280	16	19	41	108	292	7.3	16.4	12.1
17 043	1602	Du Page	866	781 666	49	902.6	714 905	15 462	962	39 634	10 703	34 567	8.2	14.4	13.4
17 045	...	Edgar	1 615	19 595	1 693	12.1	19 469	68	24	24	10	52	6.4	14.6	12.3
17 047	...	Edwards	576	7 440	2 622	12.9	7 401	6	8	19	6	30	6.3	14.7	11.6
17 049	...	Effingham	1 240	31 704	1 221	25.6	31 523	12	45	95	29	121	8.7	17.1	12.8
17 051	...	Fayette	1 856	20 893	1 633	11.3	20 148	599	40	35	71	154	6.4	14.4	12.9
17 053	...	Ford	1 259	14 275	2 032	11.3	14 157	43	14	40	21	81	6.6	15.1	11.3
17 055	...	Franklin	1 067	40 319	992	37.8	40 068	36	106	84	25	110	6.1	13.4	13.0
17 057	...	Fulton	2 242	38 080	1 051	17.0	37 117	668	83	105	107	244	5.8	14.4	12.7
17 059	...	Gallatin	838	6 909	2 672	8.2	6 842	42	10	11	4	16	5.9	13.3	13.1
17 061	...	Greene	1 407	15 317	1 971	10.9	15 231	14	50	17	5	44	6.9	15.2	12.5
17 063	1602	Grundy	1 088	32 337	1 204	29.7	31 864	21	45	113	294	748	7.3	15.8	13.4
17 065	...	Hamilton	1 127	8 499	2 511	7.5	8 462	3	11	21	2	29	5.9	14.2	11.0
17 067	...	Hancock	2 058	21 373	1 614	10.4	21 272	26	25	37	13	58	6.3	15.1	11.6
17 069	...	Hardin	462	5 189	2 827	11.2	5 062	85	16	13	13	30	5.4	14.4	12.9
17 071	...	Henderson	981	8 096	2 556	8.3	8 037	8	29	10	12	56	6.3	14.6	11.5
17 073	1960	Henry	2 132	51 159	824	24.0	49 969	657	63	128	342	797	6.7	15.8	12.3
17 075	...	Iroquois	2 892	30 787	1 251	10.6	30 154	164	43	69	357	660	6.5	14.9	11.7
17 077	...	Jackson	1 523	61 067	713	40.1	51 991	6 342	109	2 178	447	1 082	5.5	10.7	31.1
17 079	...	Jasper	1 281	10 609	2 327	8.3	10 574	1	11	17	6	32	7.3	16.5	12.0

1. MSA = Metropolitan Statistical Area. CMSA = Consolidated MSA. NECMA = New England county metropolitan area. PMSA = Primary MSA. See Appendix A for explanation of these concepts. See Appendix B for list of metropolitan areas identified by type, with component counties. 2. Dry land or land partially or temporarily covered by water. 3. Hispanic persons may be of any race.

STATE County	Population, 1990 (cont'd): Age of population (cont'd), Percent: 25 to 34 years	35 to 44 years	45 to 54 years	55 to 64 years	65 to 74 years	75 years and over	Percent female	Population–Change and components of change: Change 1980–1990: Number	Percent	Components of change, 1980–1986: Total persons, 1986	Total persons, 1980	Net change: Number	Percent	Natural increase: Births	Deaths
	14	15	16	17	18	19	20	21	22	23	24	25	26	27	28
IDAHO—Con.															
Franklin	12.2	11.3	8.3	7.1	7.2	6.7	49.7	337	3.8	9 500	8 895	600	6.8	1 500	500
Fremont	13.0	12.2	9.1	8.1	6.6	4.7	49.1	124	1.1	10 500	10 813	-300	-3.1	1 500	500
Gem	13.1	13.1	11.0	9.4	10.4	7.5	50.1	-128	-1.1	11 500	11 972	-400	-3.6	1 200	700
Gooding	13.4	12.6	10.2	9.5	9.3	8.0	50.1	-241	-2.0	12 000	11 874	200	1.4	1 300	700
Idaho	13.6	15.0	11.3	10.5	8.7	6.9	49.2	-986	-6.7	14 200	14 769	-500	-3.6	1 500	800
Jefferson	13.4	12.8	9.0	6.8	5.7	4.1	49.2	1 239	8.1	16 500	15 304	1 200	7.6	2 500	600
Jerome	14.7	13.8	9.6	8.6	8.4	5.7	50.0	298	2.0	15 300	14 840	500	3.1	1 800	700
Kootenai	14.6	16.4	11.2	8.9	8.0	5.4	50.9	10 025	16.8	67 500	59 770	7 700	13.0	6 300	3 100
Latah	16.8	13.6	8.3	5.9	4.9	4.7	49.0	1 868	6.5	30 600	28 749	1 900	6.5	3 000	1 200
Lemhi	11.9	15.2	11.9	10.2	10.9	6.6	50.4	-561	-7.5	7 200	7 460	-300	-4.1	900	400
Lewis	13.7	13.2	11.3	10.2	10.2	7.3	49.2	-602	-14.6	3 800	4 118	-300	-7.7	400	300
Lincoln	12.4	14.7	9.7	9.6	8.1	6.3	49.1	-128	-3.7	3 400	3 436	0	-0.1	400	200
Madison	10.0	8.3	5.8	3.9	3.2	2.6	52.6	4 194	21.5	22 000	19 480	2 500	13.1	3 400	500
Minidoka	14.4	12.9	9.6	7.9	8.0	4.5	49.8	-357	-1.8	20 900	19 718	1 200	5.8	2 900	800
Nez Perce	15.0	14.7	10.7	9.4	9.0	7.1	50.9	534	1.6	33 000	33 220	-200	-0.6	3 000	2 000
Oneida	13.0	11.3	8.2	7.3	9.5	8.2	50.3	234	7.2	3 500	3 258	300	8.4	400	200
Owyhee	13.4	12.5	9.7	8.6	7.1	5.7	47.8	120	1.5	8 600	8 272	300	3.4	1 000	400
Payette	13.0	13.4	10.8	8.6	8.8	7.3	50.8	609	3.8	16 300	15 825	500	3.3	1 700	1 000
Power	14.1	15.2	9.5	8.0	5.8	4.4	50.3	242	3.5	6 900	6 844	100	1.0	800	300
Shoshone	13.3	15.1	11.5	10.2	9.5	7.3	50.2	-5 295	-27.5	16 400	19 226	-2 800	-14.8	1 700	1 100
Teton	15.4	15.1	8.9	7.2	6.9	4.2	47.3	542	18.7	3 300	2 897	400	12.5	500	200
Twin Falls	14.2	14.1	9.8	8.3	8.4	6.9	51.0	653	1.2	55 800	52 927	2 800	5.4	6 200	2 900
Valley	12.9	19.7	11.9	10.0	8.8	4.0	49.0	505	9.0	6 900	5 604	1 300	22.5	700	300
Washington	11.6	12.9	10.1	10.3	10.6	9.3	51.7	-253	-2.9	8 200	8 803	-600	-6.9	900	600
ILLINOIS	17.4	14.9	10.2	8.5	7.2	5.4	51.4	3 602	0.0	11 552 000	11 427 000	126 000	1.1	1 139 000	637 000
Adams	14.5	13.5	10.0	9.5	9.3	8.3	52.5	-5 532	-7.7	68 100	71 622	-3 500	-4.9	6 600	5 400
Alexander	13.5	12.0	9.8	9.8	9.6	8.5	53.0	-1 638	-13.4	11 400	12 264	-900	-7.4	1 200	1 100
Bond	14.2	13.5	9.3	9.7	9.1	8.3	51.7	-1 233	-7.6	16 000	16 224	-200	-1.3	1 300	1 100
Boone	15.7	15.5	11.6	8.2	6.6	5.1	50.6	2 176	7.6	29 400	28 630	700	2.6	2 800	1 400
Brown	19.3	14.1	9.1	7.9	8.3	8.5	43.7	425	7.9	5 100	5 411	-300	-5.5	500	400
Bureau	13.8	13.9	10.4	9.4	9.7	8.5	52.2	-3 426	-8.8	37 100	39 114	-2 000	-5.0	3 400	2 700
Calhoun	13.2	12.3	10.9	11.1	10.2	9.7	50.0	-545	-9.3	5 600	5 867	-300	-4.6	500	400
Carroll	13.7	13.6	10.7	10.7	10.2	8.4	51.6	-1 974	-10.5	17 700	18 779	-1 100	-5.8	1 600	1 300
Cass	14.5	13.8	10.5	9.7	9.2	8.0	51.4	-1 647	-10.9	14 100	15 084	-1 000	-6.7	1 300	1 100
Champaign	18.9	13.6	7.9	6.4	5.0	3.8	49.4	4 633	2.8	171 100	168 392	2 700	1.6	16 300	5 900
Christian	14.5	13.6	10.5	9.9	9.4	8.5	52.8	-2 028	-5.6	35 500	36 446	-1 000	-2.7	3 100	2 600
Clark	14.7	13.0	10.4	10.0	10.3	9.1	52.0	-992	-5.9	16 500	16 913	-400	-2.6	1 400	1 300
Clay	14.3	13.3	10.2	9.6	10.0	9.4	52.7	-823	-5.4	14 900	15 283	-400	-2.7	1 400	1 300
Clinton	17.1	13.9	9.6	9.0	7.5	6.2	49.1	1 327	4.1	33 600	32 617	1 000	3.1	3 200	1 800
Coles	13.7	12.3	8.7	7.9	7.4	6.4	52.9	-616	-1.2	52 000	52 260	-300	-0.5	4 100	3 000
Cook	18.5	14.6	10.1	8.7	7.3	5.1	51.9	-148 561	-2.8	5 297 900	5 253 628	44 300	0.8	543 100	301 300
Crawford	14.6	13.7	10.5	10.5	9.7	8.6	51.7	-1 354	-6.5	20 500	20 818	-300	-1.7	1 800	1 500
Cumberland	14.8	13.1	10.0	9.4	8.8	6.8	50.7	-392	-3.5	10 900	11 062	-200	-1.9	1 100	700
De Kalb	15.6	12.5	8.4	6.6	5.6	4.6	50.8	3 304	4.4	74 100	74 628	-500	-0.7	5 900	3 200
De Witt	15.6	13.5	11.1	9.4	9.2	7.5	51.0	-1 592	-8.8	17 400	18 108	-700	-3.8	1 600	1 200
Douglas	15.1	13.5	10.1	10.2	8.6	6.6	51.6	-310	-1.6	19 500	19 774	-300	-1.3	2 000	1 200
Du Page	19.5	17.3	11.1	7.5	5.2	3.5	50.7	122 790	18.6	727 700	658 876	68 800	10.4	70 300	24 600
Edgar	13.5	13.7	10.7	10.0	10.2	8.8	52.6	-2 130	-9.8	20 800	21 725	-900	-4.3	1 800	1 700
Edwards	14.0	14.1	10.2	9.3	10.6	9.3	52.1	-521	-6.5	8 200	7 961	200	2.4	700	600
Effingham	16.4	13.6	9.4	8.1	7.5	6.4	51.3	760	2.5	31 700	30 944	800	2.5	3 600	1 800
Fayette	15.9	13.2	9.9	9.4	9.4	8.5	49.2	-1 274	-5.7	21 800	22 167	-400	-1.8	1 900	1 600
Ford	14.4	13.2	10.0	10.4	9.8	9.3	52.2	-990	-6.5	14 800	15 265	-500	-3.2	1 300	1 100
Franklin	13.5	13.6	10.7	9.4	11.1	9.1	52.6	-2 882	-6.7	42 600	43 201	-600	-1.3	3 400	3 700
Fulton	14.4	14.0	9.9	9.9	10.0	8.9	50.9	-5 607	-12.8	38 100	43 687	-5 500	-12.7	3 200	3 000
Gallatin	12.5	13.3	12.2	10.1	10.2	9.4	52.2	-681	-9.0	7 500	7 590	-100	-1.8	700	600
Greene	14.0	12.5	9.9	10.0	10.0	8.9	51.4	-1 344	-8.1	15 800	16 661	-900	-5.3	1 500	1 200
Grundy	16.4	15.4	10.6	8.2	7.2	5.7	50.4	1 755	5.7	31 700	30 582	1 100	3.7	3 100	1 500
Hamilton	13.4	12.8	10.6	10.4	11.5	10.2	52.6	-673	-7.3	9 000	9 172	-200	-2.2	800	700
Hancock	13.8	13.8	10.2	10.5	10.0	8.7	52.5	-2 504	-10.5	23 000	23 877	-900	-3.7	2 000	1 600
Hardin	13.8	14.2	10.7	11.0	10.2	7.4	49.8	-194	-3.6	5 300	5 383	-100	-1.6	400	500
Henderson	14.1	14.0	12.4	10.7	9.6	6.7	51.1	-1 018	-11.2	8 800	9 114	-300	-3.7	800	500
Henry	13.8	14.6	11.0	9.5	8.8	7.6	51.2	-6 809	-11.7	54 700	57 968	-3 300	-5.7	5 100	3 400
Iroquois	14.0	13.5	10.7	10.3	10.0	8.3	51.6	-2 189	-6.6	31 900	32 976	-1 100	-3.2	3 000	2 200
Jackson	16.1	11.9	7.5	6.4	5.8	5.0	48.6	-582	-0.9	60 500	61 649	-1 100	-1.8	5 000	2 800
Jasper	15.1	12.9	9.6	9.0	9.3	8.3	51.1	-709	-6.3	11 200	11 318	-100	-0.8	1 200	800

STATE County	Population–(cont'd) Components of change, 1980-1986 (cont'd) Net migration	Households, 1990 Number	Households, 1990 Percent change, 1980–1990	Households, 1990 Persons per household	Households, 1990 Percent Female family householder[1]	Households, 1990 Percent One-person	Births, 1988 Total	Births, 1988 Rate[2]	Births, 1988 Low birth weight[3] (Number)	Deaths, 1987 Number Total	Deaths, 1987 Number Infant[4]	Deaths, 1987 Rate Total[2]	Deaths, 1987 Rate Infant[5]	Marriages, 1984 Number	Marriages, 1984 Rate[2]
	29	30	31	32	33	34	35	36	37	38	39	40	41	42	43
IDAHO—Con.															
Franklin	-400	2 824	6.1	3.25	4.9	18.5	173	18.8	15	56	2	6.1	12.7	60	6.2
Fremont	-1 400	3 453	5.4	3.12	6.5	19.5	177	17.2	11	76	1	7.4	6.3	94	8.7
Gem	-1 000	4 424	4.9	2.64	7.8	22.0	154	13.9	10	133	2	11.9	11.7	119	10.2
Gooding	-400	4 320	4.3	2.63	6.6	24.7	120	10.4	11	111	2	9.6	11.8	73	5.9
Idaho	-1 200	5 187	0.7	2.57	5.4	24.0	166	12.2	1	152	2	11.1	11.6	118	8.1
Jefferson	-700	4 871	9.8	3.38	6.6	15.4	364	21.8	14	83	2	5.0	6.1	112	6.9
Jerome	-700	5 325	4.7	2.79	7.2	21.0	232	15.9	15	128	3	8.7	11.7	105	6.8
Kootenai	4 500	26 942	25.9	2.57	8.5	23.0	958	14.3	51	550	4	8.3	4.5	3 809	58.2
Latah	100	11 229	9.5	2.45	6.1	25.6	413	13.5	17	183	7	6.0	16.4	326	10.7
Lemhi	-700	2 769	3.3	2.47	6.9	26.4	98	14.4	3	64	1	9.4	10.5	110	13.9
Lewis	-500	1 393	-7.7	2.51	6.2	25.8	38	10.6	1	35	0	9.7	0.0	24	6.2
Lincoln	-200	1 191	0.5	2.75	4.3	24.5	45	14.1	2	28	2	8.8	36.4	18	5.1
Madison	-300	5 801	15.8	3.84	5.5	11.5	470	20.7	15	80	1	3.6	2.4	218	10.0
Minidoka	-900	6 472	4.5	2.96	7.7	19.0	332	16.5	22	145	6	7.2	20.6	134	6.3
Nez Perce	-1 300	13 618	9.0	2.43	8.3	26.7	414	12.4	17	342	2	10.2	4.6	506	15.2
Oneida	100	1 159	5.9	2.97	4.2	23.0	67	19.1	2	33	0	9.4	0.0	32	9.4
Owyhee	-300	2 820	6.6	2.84	7.7	23.5	130	15.1	9	86	1	10.0	8.1	18	2.1
Payette	-200	6 040	8.3	2.70	9.0	21.9	233	14.6	13	142	3	8.8	12.0	232	14.3
Power	-500	2 370	8.0	2.97	7.4	19.2	121	17.8	6	49	1	7.1	9.4	79	11.4
Shoshone	-3 500	5 691	-17.2	2.42	8.9	27.4	156	10.6	5	179	2	11.9	14.0	133	7.8
Teton	0	1 123	26.0	3.03	3.7	20.4	49	15.3	2	20	0	6.2	0.0	33	10.3
Twin Falls	-400	19 737	4.5	2.66	8.0	23.4	779	14.0	52	480	8	8.6	10.0	542	9.6
Valley	800	2 404	16.5	2.51	6.1	22.5	88	12.9	10	32	0	4.8	0.0	80	11.8
Washington	-900	3 257	2.9	2.59	7.0	24.6	132	16.3	8	95	1	11.7	8.5	109	13.0
ILLINOIS	-377 000	4 202 240	3.9	2.65	12.0	25.7	184 841	15.9	13 793	102 314	2 102	8.8	11.6	102 432	8.9
Adams	-4 800	25 515	-3.4	2.50	9.3	27.7	916	13.6	42	776	11	11.5	11.0	596	8.5
Alexander	-1 000	4 234	-10.9	2.46	18.0	29.9	193	16.8	18	167	1	14.4	5.5	74	6.2
Bond	-400	5 652	-3.2	2.53	7.7	25.1	183	11.4	10	163	4	10.1	20.4	149	9.3
Boone	-600	10 950	12.7	2.78	8.3	18.7	419	13.9	36	242	0	8.2	0.0	269	9.3
Brown	-300	1 991	-5.1	2.45	6.1	29.2	52	10.4	1	66	1	12.9	17.5	60	10.9
Bureau	-2 700	13 790	-3.2	2.55	7.6	25.8	446	12.1	18	435	5	11.8	10.3	301	7.9
Calhoun	-300	2 048	-2.2	2.56	5.2	24.5	74	13.2	6	73	0	13.0	0.0	51	8.8
Carroll	-1 300	6 638	-4.6	2.49	7.2	25.4	243	13.9	21	183	2	10.4	9.4	157	8.6
Cass	-1 200	5 195	-8.2	2.53	8.3	25.6	163	11.7	11	150	2	10.8	14.3	144	9.9
Champaign	-7 700	63 900	9.4	2.43	8.4	28.7	2 615	15.2	168	969	25	5.7	9.6	1 636	9.6
Christian	-1 500	13 591	-0.7	2.49	8.4	27.0	519	14.6	31	440	4	12.3	8.6	360	9.9
Clark	-500	6 394	-1.4	2.45	7.6	26.3	203	12.4	14	170	3	10.4	13.9	196	11.7
Clay	-600	5 708	-1.6	2.47	7.9	26.1	176	11.8	10	179	0	12.0	0.0	121	7.9
Clinton	-400	11 583	7.6	2.76	8.0	22.2	431	12.6	19	270	1	7.9	2.2	251	7.4
Coles	-1 400	18 957	1.8	2.41	8.1	28.2	581	11.1	37	486	2	9.3	3.4	473	9.0
Cook	-197 500	1 879 488	0.0	2.67	15.4	28.2	91 305	17.3	8 089	48 192	1 221	9.1	13.8	45 330	8.6
Crawford	-600	7 792	-3.2	2.46	7.4	26.3	216	10.7	16	256	0	12.6	0.0	234	11.3
Cumberland	-600	4 029	0.7	2.63	7.4	24.1	138	12.7	5	101	1	9.4	6.1	91	8.3
De Kalb	-3 300	26 413	8.5	2.56	7.3	25.2	913	12.0	39	514	12	6.8	13.2	572	7.8
De Witt	-1 100	6 488	-5.2	2.51	8.0	25.6	209	11.9	11	180	2	10.3	9.1	155	8.7
Douglas	-1 000	7 206	0.2	2.66	7.0	23.0	299	15.3	18	186	1	9.4	3.4	190	9.7
Du Page	23 200	279 344	25.8	2.76	7.3	20.4	12 797	16.8	579	4 192	107	5.6	8.7	6 042	8.6
Edgar	-1 000	7 859	-5.7	2.45	8.9	27.8	237	11.6	12	293	2	14.1	7.6	216	10.1
Edwards	100	3 016	-2.9	2.44	6.4	26.7	83	10.5	9	65	1	8.1	11.0	81	9.9
Effingham	-1 000	11 465	7.8	2.73	8.4	23.8	516	15.8	24	321	5	10.0	9.5	314	10.0
Fayette	-700	7 719	-3.4	2.53	7.7	26.1	274	12.5	21	244	4	11.1	13.7	186	8.4
Ford	-600	5 602	-2.4	2.49	7.1	26.7	187	12.7	10	214	4	14.6	21.4	131	8.7
Franklin	-300	16 564	-2.4	2.40	9.2	28.9	457	10.9	32	618	3	14.5	6.0	419	9.8
Fulton	-5 800	14 893	-8.5	2.45	8.9	26.8	394	10.2	23	461	4	12.0	10.0	340	8.3
Gallatin	-200	2 784	-1.6	2.42	8.9	26.8	72	10.0	3	92	0	12.4	0.0	114	15.0
Greene	-1 100	5 910	-4.6	2.56	8.2	25.8	207	12.9	21	201	0	12.6	0.0	142	8.8
Grundy	-400	11 979	11.2	2.67	6.8	22.8	474	14.6	26	251	1	7.8	2.4	259	8.3
Hamilton	-200	3 476	-4.5	2.41	7.2	27.8	90	10.1	9	102	1	11.5	9.3	81	8.9
Hancock	-1 300	8 409	-5.3	2.50	7.2	25.7	260	11.4	6	230	2	10.0	7.4	151	6.4
Hardin	0	2 049	-1.5	2.43	10.2	27.7	41	7.7	4	64	0	11.9	0.0	62	11.5
Henderson	-600	3 237	-4.1	2.49	6.3	26.1	84	9.4	7	72	0	8.2	0.0	54	5.9
Henry	-5 000	19 514	-4.9	2.59	7.9	24.0	672	12.6	28	512	5	9.5	7.6	486	8.9
Iroquois	-1 800	11 788	-2.3	2.56	7.2	24.1	397	12.6	17	372	5	11.7	13.3	237	7.3
Jackson	-3 300	23 466	4.0	2.30	8.9	32.1	709	11.9	43	478	9	8.0	11.8	461	7.5
Jasper	-500	3 962	-0.9	2.66	6.2	22.8	150	13.4	7	92	2	8.2	11.7	109	9.6

1. No spouse present. 2. Per 1,000 resident population estimated as of July 1 of the year shown. 3. Under 2,500 grams. 4. Deaths of infants under 1 year old. 5. Deaths of infants under 1 year old per 1,000 live births.

STATE County	Divorces, 1984		Physicians, active non–Federal, 1989		Hospitals, 1989			Nursing homes,[4] 1986		Serious crimes known to police, 1988			Education			
						Beds				Number			Public school enrollment[7]		Attainment,[8] 1980	
	Number	Rate[1]	Number[2]	Rate[3]	Number	Number	Rate[3]	Number	Beds	Total[5]	Violent[6]	Rate[3]	1986–1987	1980	Percent 12 yrs. or more	Percent 16 yrs. or more
	44	45	46	47	48	49	50	51	52	53	54	55	56	57	58	59
IDAHO—Con.																
Franklin	31	3.2	3	33	1	65	707	1	45	234	13	2 515	2 713	2 326	77.4	11.4
Fremont	31	2.9	4	38	0	0	0	1	12	128	2	1 242	2 642	2 540	71.5	12.0
Gem	77	6.6	6	55	1	39	355	4	144	251	4	2 221	2 336	2 628	63.1	8.1
Gooding	76	6.1	5	44	1	19	167	2	50	234	24	1 999	2 550	2 576	66.0	12.8
Idaho	78	5.4	8	59	2	52	382	3	103	229	19	1 683	2 430	3 240	68.6	12.4
Jefferson	39	2.4	3	18	0	0	0	1	23	345	30	2 129	5 141	3 846	70.6	10.3
Jerome	80	5.2	7	48	1	80	552	2	48	450	38	3 019	3 333	3 214	66.0	10.8
Kootenai	504	7.7	92	136	1	178	263	6	454	3 317	233	4 927	12 627	12 362	75.6	13.8
Latah	153	5.0	36	117	1	40	130	3	230	853	32	2 805	4 479	4 575	81.5	29.6
Lemhi	47	5.9	5	75	1	35	522	2	48	31	3	1 050	1 395	1 532	70.3	12.8
Lewis	17	4.4	2	56	0	0	0	2	18	66	3	1 783	1 045	840	67.2	11.8
Lincoln	18	5.1	2	62	0	0	0	1	40	NA	NA	NA	732	737	72.2	11.8
Madison	74	3.4	17	73	1	52	224	0	0	660	9	5 415	5 477	3 646	81.3	18.7
Minidoka	118	5.6	10	50	1	103	515	2	95	677	57	3 318	4 617	4 096	64.2	10.5
Nez Perce	248	7.5	79	234	1	121	358	6	318	1 982	211	5 932	5 759	6 810	72.3	13.1
Oneida	11	3.2	1	28	1	35	972	2	49	NA	NA	NA	946	756	71.8	12.6
Owyhee	13	1.5	0	0	0	0	0	2	93	189	12	2 249	2 223	1 824	53.1	7.4
Payette	128	7.9	7	43	0	0	0	1	103	486	45	3 018	3 580	3 279	61.1	9.1
Power	36	5.2	2	29	1	40	588	1	20	272	15	3 999	1 837	1 617	70.5	11.1
Shoshone	80	4.7	10	71	2	79	560	2	165	550	64	3 715	3 303	4 412	63.9	9.7
Teton	17	5.3	1	31	1	13	406	0	0	48	0	1 500	847	699	78.5	17.0
Twin Falls	398	7.1	96	170	2	172	305	8	542	2 422	137	4 517	11 498	10 776	68.2	13.4
Valley	29	4.3	8	116	2	31	449	1	64	260	29	3 767	1 332	1 166	80.3	21.1
Washington	53	6.3	2	25	1	23	284	3	106	255	19	3 187	1 900	1 867	60.8	13.0
ILLINOIS	48 910	4.2	24 576	211	251	59 628	511	818	99 883	642 276	89 041	5 573	1 810 530	2 053 063	66.5	16.2
Adams	366	5.2	126	188	2	519	773	9	1 140	2 945	97	4 365	9 971	12 123	64.2	10.6
Alexander	70	5.8	6	52	0	0	0	2	90	556	169	4 894	2 079	2 428	47.0	6.8
Bond	68	4.3	8	49	1	204	1 259	2	242	216	4	1 355	2 454	3 042	55.3	11.2
Boone	143	4.9	19	62	2	98	321	3	278	1 103	42	3 764	5 391	6 388	66.8	9.6
Brown	30	5.5	0	0	0	0	0	1	87	82	4	1 613	781	943	56.7	7.7
Bureau	170	4.5	39	107	2	221	604	6	487	447	5	1 285	6 587	8 134	66.3	10.6
Calhoun	14	2.4	3	54	0	0	0	1	87	46	2	824	684	1 009	46.8	5.8
Carroll	71	3.9	7	40	1	34	195	3	263	417	16	2 405	3 315	3 873	65.3	9.5
Cass	59	4.1	5	36	0	0	0	4	277	128	4	931	2 348	3 050	61.7	8.1
Champaign	875	5.2	382	221	4	1 032	597	13	1 399	9 393	1 001	5 486	23 263	25 200	80.9	30.0
Christian	157	4.3	18	51	2	199	561	6	641	424	10	1 202	6 275	7 206	62.3	7.8
Clark	86	5.1	10	61	0	0	0	3	271	257	8	1 602	2 890	3 339	60.1	7.7
Clay	85	5.5	8	54	1	40	270	3	267	320	7	2 169	2 753	2 999	50.9	6.0
Clinton	68	2.0	17	49	1	93	270	4	365	445	23	1 325	5 164	6 063	55.3	6.5
Coles	221	4.2	57	109	1	176	337	7	912	1 277	61	2 474	7 739	7 969	66.2	16.4
Cook	20 545	3.9	15 195	287	87	28 499	539	225	38 002	397 691	71 331	7 545	746 499	874 463	64.3	17.1
Crawford	102	4.9	18	90	1	107	538	5	264	307	5	1 525	3 791	3 900	64.6	9.3
Cumberland	46	4.2	7	64	0	0	0	1	60	110	1	1 013	2 010	2 374	56.8	7.6
De Kalb	256	3.5	76	99	3	232	302	7	708	2 870	70	3 824	11 837	12 456	75.2	22.2
De Witt	81	4.5	10	57	1	52	297	3	244	428	21	2 482	3 244	3 581	65.4	9.7
Douglas	72	3.7	6	30	1	43	218	3	322	335	6	1 715	3 415	3 788	66.4	9.4
Du Page	2 791	4.0	2 085	268	9	1 994	256	32	4 649	25 893	835	3 496	113 969	125 260	83.1	29.0
Edgar	109	5.1	10	49	1	49	240	3	275	611	34	2 962	3 847	4 222	61.9	9.6
Edwards	44	5.4	1	13	0	0	0	2	82	18	1	229	1 294	1 482	58.9	6.8
Effingham	130	4.1	38	115	1	146	442	4	494	988	23	3 088	5 634	5 665	62.4	9.4
Fayette	106	4.8	9	41	1	144	658	4	378	254	7	1 174	3 508	4 265	53.0	6.6
Ford	55	3.7	11	75	1	82	558	5	292	244	7	1 677	1 549	2 979	69.3	8.6
Franklin	135	3.1	29	69	2	229	548	8	556	542	47	1 289	7 511	8 295	52.2	6.7
Fulton	182	4.4	33	86	1	121	316	7	461	734	23	1 954	8 156	8 950	62.5	7.8
Gallatin	27	3.6	2	28	0	0	0	2	178	59	15	811	1 245	1 464	45.8	4.8
Greene	74	4.6	6	38	1	73	456	4	214	263	9	1 803	2 598	3 398	56.8	7.2
Grundy	209	6.7	28	85	1	82	248	2	221	860	25	2 680	7 024	6 353	66.7	9.7
Hamilton	36	4.0	4	45	1	104	1 182	3	146	108	3	1 218	1 478	1 666	47.0	6.4
Hancock	94	4.0	11	48	1	67	295	4	290	241	8	1 061	4 337	4 635	68.0	11.3
Hardin	36	6.7	1	19	1	48	906	1	50	17	0	420	1 027	1 080	42.0	5.6
Henderson	61	6.7	5	56	0	0	0	0	0	117	6	1 349	1 273	1 868	62.1	7.6
Henry	210	3.9	27	51	2	165	313	5	576	1 109	34	2 076	10 364	12 371	67.8	11.1
Iroquois	113	3.5	23	73	2	150	476	8	523	418	30	1 323	5 727	6 640	63.5	8.7
Jackson	220	3.6	111	188	2	213	360	3	709	3 994	203	6 624	8 041	8 580	69.7	26.4
Jasper	36	3.2	3	27	0	0	0	1	92	199	4	1 783	1 913	2 292	54.5	7.6

1. Per 1,000 resident population estimated as of July 1 of the year shown. 2. As of end of year. 3. Per 100,000 resident population as of July 1 of the year shown. 4. Preliminary. Covers nursing homes with 3 or more beds. 5. Data for serious crimes have not been adjusted for underreporting, this may affect comparability between geographic areas or over time. 6. Includes murder and nonnegligent manslaughter, forcible rape, robbery, and aggravated assault. 7. The 1986–1987 data are based on administrative reports obtained by the U.S. National Center for Education Statistics. The 1980 data are based on the 1980 Census of Population and Housing. 8. Persons 25 years old or older.

STATE County	Education (cont'd): Local government expenditures for education,[1] 1982: Total (Mil dol)	Education (cont'd): Local government expenditures for education,[1] 1982: Per capita (Dollars)	Social Security Program December 1988: Beneficiaries: Total	Social Security Program December 1988: Beneficiaries: Rate[2]	Social Security Program December 1988: Payments ($1,000)	Supplemental Security Income Program recipients June 1986	Money income: Per capita[3]: 1987 Income, (Dollars)	Money income: Per capita[3]: 1979: Current dollars	Money income: Per capita[3]: 1979: Constant 1987 dollars	Money income: Median household income 1979 (Dollars)	Money income: Percent below poverty level, 1979: Persons	Money income: Percent below poverty level, 1979: Families	Housing units, 1990: Total	Housing units, 1990: Percent change, 1980–1990
	60	61	62	63	64	65	66	67	68	69	70	71	72	73
IDAHO—Con.														
Franklin	3.9	420	1 585	172.3	711	56	7 181	4 771	7 465	14 435	12.0	8.5	3 240	6.3
Fremont	4.7	433	1 635	158.7	746	54	7 198	4 724	7 392	13 204	16.7	14.4	5 961	10.9
Gem	3.7	320	2 610	235.1	1 170	134	8 484	5 801	9 077	13 345	14.9	12.9	4 725	3.2
Gooding	4.3	348	2 410	209.6	1 083	126	8 011	5 353	8 376	12 060	17.8	13.4	4 800	4.6
Idaho	5.7	387	2 800	205.9	1 301	158	8 663	5 873	9 189	14 483	14.5	11.7	6 346	0.0
Jefferson	7.2	459	2 190	131.1	988	90	6 716	4 577	7 162	14 176	17.0	14.3	5 353	7.2
Jerome	5.2	335	2 705	185.3	1 258	124	8 683	5 638	8 822	13 783	12.9	10.0	5 886	6.4
Kootenai	20.2	324	12 170	181.9	5 852	604	9 223	6 346	9 930	15 154	11.9	9.4	31 964	18.6
Latah	11.7	387	3 755	122.7	1 904	134	9 547	6 441	10 078	14 025	14.6	8.5	11 870	7.8
Lemhi	2.9	364	1 570	230.9	688	72	8 146	5 565	8 708	12 512	17.0	13.1	3 752	8.7
Lewis	2.8	689	1 125	312.5	540	102	9 315	5 782	9 047	14 145	11.8	8.9	1 681	-7.0
Lincoln	1.7	475	545	170.3	246	24	6 822	4 853	7 593	12 007	18.3	14.5	1 386	3.2
Madison	7.1	343	1 715	75.6	804	62	5 898	4 098	6 412	13 039	27.5	10.9	6 133	10.8
Minidoka	8.2	407	3 070	152.7	1 412	144	7 760	5 368	8 399	14 652	14.4	10.9	7 044	2.4
Nez Perce	11.7	354	6 140	183.8	3 057	456	10 238	6 990	10 937	15 862	11.9	9.0	14 463	7.1
Oneida	1.9	584	710	202.9	321	14	7 486	4 353	6 811	11 460	19.2	14.0	1 496	1.4
Owyhee	4.2	498	1 265	147.1	532	108	6 077	4 377	6 849	10 583	28.0	21.3	3 332	10.5
Payette	5.8	367	3 245	202.8	1 417	178	7 811	5 074	7 939	11 654	18.1	13.9	6 520	6.6
Power	3.7	544	835	122.8	405	36	8 655	5 971	9 343	15 684	13.9	12.8	2 701	5.6
Shoshone	10.8	560	3 375	229.6	1 740	156	8 105	6 531	10 219	16 879	9.5	7.9	6 923	-9.8
Teton	1.4	457	530	165.6	234	44	6 679	4 297	6 724	11 565	18.0	16.7	1 645	32.1
Twin Falls	17.8	326	9 925	177.9	4 773	526	9 280	6 405	10 022	14 529	12.0	8.7	21 158	3.1
Valley	2.7	409	1 030	151.5	484	34	8 733	6 615	10 350	15 802	9.0	7.2	6 640	30.0
Washington	4.0	463	2 045	252.5	906	106	7 725	5 112	7 999	10 833	20.1	15.8	3 685	2.2
ILLINOIS	5 078.1	442	1 725 153	148.5	897 920	145 268	12 437	8 064	12 618	19 321	11.0	8.4	4 506 275	4.3
Adams	22.4	313	14 030	207.5	6 786	1 220	9 582	6 667	10 432	15 426	11.0	8.8	28 021	-2.0
Alexander	6.1	509	2 590	225.2	1 086	604	7 373	4 987	7 803	9 569	26.5	18.2	4 902	-6.9
Bond	4.9	300	3 010	187.0	1 390	202	9 197	6 376	9 977	14 197	13.2	10.9	6 136	-3.8
Boone	11.0	382	4 220	140.2	2 226	106	11 463	7 555	11 821	20 729	6.6	5.4	11 477	14.1
Brown	2.1	391	1 235	247.0	543	60	8 617	5 705	8 927	11 826	16.4	13.3	2 357	-1.2
Bureau	17.3	450	7 610	206.8	3 835	186	10 867	7 408	11 591	17 311	7.9	5.3	14 762	-2.6
Calhoun	2.2	383	1 275	227.7	557	104	8 417	5 606	8 772	12 440	13.9	9.9	2 951	-2.5
Carroll	8.9	483	3 475	198.6	1 570	142	10 389	6 785	10 616	15 744	10.3	7.9	7 481	-1.8
Cass	6.1	413	2 850	205.0	1 373	204	9 690	6 809	10 654	16 253	10.2	7.9	5 698	-6.3
Champaign	61.1	355	17 375	101.0	8 219	1 208	10 948	7 306	11 432	16 436	13.2	6.9	68 416	9.4
Christian	14.7	409	7 450	209.3	3 735	398	10 213	6 983	10 926	15 915	9.7	7.2	14 640	0.3
Clark	7.2	421	3 870	236.0	1 812	170	9 610	6 655	10 413	14 077	11.7	9.8	7 115	-1.8
Clay	7.6	488	3 485	233.9	1 544	268	8 267	5 592	8 750	12 156	14.6	11.5	6 270	-3.3
Clinton	10.9	329	4 910	143.6	2 255	306	9 826	6 259	9 793	16 907	8.8	6.5	12 746	7.1
Coles	18.0	345	8 380	160.5	3 935	650	10 174	6 686	10 462	15 108	13.5	6.5	20 329	1.3
Cook	2 330.8	443	744 380	140.9	399 550	86 188	12 810	8 229	12 876	19 187	13.6	10.8	2 021 833	1.4
Crawford	8.6	410	4 485	223.1	2 185	180	10 237	7 020	10 984	15 595	8.2	5.5	8 464	-2.7
Cumberland	4.6	421	2 060	189.0	928	110	8 902	6 174	9 660	14 612	11.4	8.9	4 448	0.9
De Kalb	32.1	430	9 515	125.2	4 992	300	10 737	7 214	11 288	18 345	11.2	4.9	27 351	8.1
De Witt	8.2	459	3 045	174.0	1 534	154	10 789	7 528	11 779	17 630	9.8	7.7	6 942	-5.3
Douglas	8.7	442	2 980	152.0	1 487	134	10 549	7 397	11 574	18 014	9.3	6.9	7 607	-1.7
Du Page	326.4	478	82 190	108.0	46 954	2 320	16 924	10 464	16 373	27 509	3.0	2.3	292 537	24.6
Edgar	8.5	392	4 430	216.1	2 136	278	9 292	6 560	10 264	13 888	12.2	9.4	8 733	-4.3
Edwards	2.7	342	1 550	196.2	700	58	9 401	6 289	9 840	13 761	11.2	8.7	3 260	-4.2
Effingham	11.6	374	5 540	169.9	2 557	348	10 343	6 941	10 861	16 982	8.1	6.2	12 189	4.3
Fayette	8.5	384	4 440	202.7	2 000	316	9 095	6 044	9 457	13 510	12.7	10.5	8 551	-4.2
Ford	6.8	447	3 040	206.8	1 542	78	10 627	7 530	11 782	16 989	6.9	5.2	6 118	-3.3
Franklin	18.9	438	10 265	244.4	4 803	752	8 937	6 384	9 989	12 627	14.1	11.1	18 430	-2.7
Fulton	19.8	464	8 975	233.1	4 429	398	9 151	6 852	10 721	16 331	10.7	8.4	16 480	-6.0
Gallatin	3.3	431	1 615	224.3	703	212	8 553	5 594	8 753	12 032	18.1	13.7	3 197	0.2
Greene	6.3	382	3 485	217.8	1 596	302	8 552	5 721	8 952	12 796	17.5	13.9	6 575	-3.5
Grundy	20.1	660	5 060	155.7	2 722	94	12 072	8 109	12 688	21 678	5.4	4.4	12 652	9.7
Hamilton	4.0	434	2 265	254.5	947	196	8 473	5 688	8 900	11 582	16.2	12.2	4 013	-3.9
Hancock	10.9	458	4 905	215.1	2 303	202	9 421	6 505	10 178	15 147	11.6	8.8	9 692	-3.1
Hardin	2.7	499	1 140	215.1	507	160	7 546	4 976	7 786	10 398	19.3	16.7	2 403	-2.9
Henderson	3.3	361	1 485	166.9	743	70	9 846	6 638	10 386	15 975	11.1	9.1	4 089	-3.9
Henry	22.7	413	9 855	184.9	4 959	306	10 279	7 486	11 713	18 947	7.5	6.2	20 881	-3.6
Iroquois	16.9	514	6 555	207.4	3 263	204	9 902	7 032	11 003	16 382	9.7	7.6	12 819	-4.9
Jackson	20.9	336	7 960	133.6	3 511	884	8 922	6 044	9 457	11 765	22.3	11.2	25 539	4.3
Jasper	5.4	466	2 230	199.1	992	112	9 543	6 370	9 967	14 614	10.8	8.3	4 297	-3.1

1. Elementary and secondary. 2. Per 1,000 resident population estimated as of July 1 of the year shown. 3. Based on the resident population estimated as of July 1, 1988 for 1987 data and enumerated as of April 1, 1980 for 1979 data.

STATE County	Housing units, 1990 (cont'd)				Civilian labor force, 1990				Private nonfarm establishments, 1988					
	Occupied units						Unemployment				Employment[2]			
		Owner occupied												
	Total	Percent	Median value (Dollars)	Median rent (Dollars)	Total	Percent change, 1989–1990	Total	Rate[1]	Number	Net change, 1987–1988	Total	Percent change, 1987–1988	Manufacturing	Retail trade
	74	75	76	77	78	79	80	81	82	83	84	85	86	87
IDAHO—Con.														
Franklin	2 824	80.2	46 800	192	3 474	-5.2	153	4.4	151	2	976	0.8	139	356
Fremont	3 453	80.2	46 200	192	4 679	-2.6	395	8.4	185	7	1 184	-0.4	220	342
Gem	4 424	77.7	46 700	192	4 993	-0.4	385	7.7	200	6	1 827	6.3	667	353
Gooding	4 320	69.9	40 600	180	5 286	-0.1	227	4.3	251	6	1 545	6.6	28	404
Idaho	5 187	75.5	45 700	188	6 443	0.5	508	7.9	362	7	2 432	1.5	1 006	465
Jefferson	4 871	80.5	54 300	221	6 943	0.8	457	6.6	227	9	2 221	-7.0	802	403
Jerome	5 325	70.4	42 100	189	6 630	6.5	394	5.9	287	-2	2 887	8.5	899	543
Kootenai	26 942	71.3	64 800	296	34 827	3.0	2 460	7.1	1 897	34	16 420	8.8	3 228	4 311
Latah	11 229	56.4	63 500	264	14 821	1.7	584	3.9	758	-3	6 063	2.5	617	2 281
Lemhi	2 769	73.6	47 500	196	3 222	1.2	285	8.8	208	7	1 033	6.4	215	393
Lewis	1 393	71.2	38 500	164	2 016	2.6	132	6.5	98	5	452	-12.2	90	118
Lincoln	1 191	72.0	37 000	171	1 825	-0.7	93	5.1	42	1	341	-1.2	0	72
Madison	5 801	59.9	68 700	239	8 495	-1.4	461	5.4	398	2	6 407	0.9	1 316	1 224
Minidoka	6 472	74.5	41 400	184	10 091	-0.3	771	7.6	313	4	4 022	-8.3	1 958	691
Nez Perce	13 618	66.2	56 700	249	16 673	0.1	811	4.9	1 094	-2	13 046	5.8	3 295	3 483
Oneida	1 159	81.8	43 100	201	1 214	-7.5	51	4.2	58	2	348	-10.3	0	124
Owyhee	2 820	68.4	39 900	172	3 512	-6.5	189	5.4	98	-15	602	-9.2	25	163
Payette	6 040	70.9	43 800	208	8 500	3.2	584	6.9	274	6	2 970	-5.0	1 077	355
Power	2 370	73.8	50 400	190	2 682	-1.6	283	10.6	131	4	1 849	8.7	0	271
Shoshone	5 691	70.9	32 500	169	5 185	4.9	526	10.1	350	-12	3 105	22.7	326	692
Teton	1 123	74.0	59 000	229	1 635	0.1	93	5.7	74	2	277	8.2	13	123
Twin Falls	19 737	67.8	50 700	235	26 750	0.6	1 290	4.8	1 631	-33	15 218	-2.8	2 572	4 455
Valley	2 404	70.6	70 700	265	4 033	8.2	324	8.0	271	18	1 368	4.2	198	520
Washington	3 257	72.5	43 700	183	4 215	3.0	329	7.8	179	1	1 360	13.3	187	270
ILLINOIS	4 202 240	64.2	80 900	369	6 029 000	0.2	371 000	6.2	X	X	4 375 618	3.7	1 033 272	881 624
Adams	25 515	71.1	43 400	198	33 287	0.9	1 898	5.7	1 707	0	23 161	4.4	5 649	5 595
Alexander	4 234	68.4	23 900	124	3 400	-1.2	529	15.6	212	-12	1 878	3.4	421	489
Bond	5 652	77.8	40 400	180	7 213	0.4	596	8.3	307	4	3 428	13.5	618	748
Boone	10 950	72.3	67 900	306	17 048	2.0	1 364	8.0	546	29	11 237	22.1	7 038	1 617
Brown	1 991	73.7	30 600	155	2 232	2.4	172	7.7	127	-3	886	14.3	0	157
Bureau	13 790	72.7	41 800	220	17 187	0.2	1 016	5.9	817	-31	8 270	-1.6	2 586	1 844
Calhoun	2 048	80.2	35 000	143	1 784	-1.5	281	15.8	104	-8	905	-7.7	0	187
Carroll	6 638	71.8	38 300	196	8 272	-3.6	557	6.7	394	-27	3 110	-10.8	985	762
Cass	5 195	74.1	32 900	188	6 477	-1.5	636	9.8	314	5	3 178	5.6	1 264	508
Champaign	63 900	54.5	67 700	336	91 966	0.7	3 577	3.9	3 726	22	53 659	2.5	9 728	16 557
Christian	13 591	73.9	37 400	200	16 593	0.0	1 049	6.3	727	0	7 055	0.1	1 052	1 955
Clark	6 394	78.2	34 200	167	7 078	0.4	700	9.9	381	2	2 891	-6.2	847	845
Clay	5 708	78.9	31 900	162	7 465	3.3	718	9.6	358	-10	3 016	0.3	1 257	599
Clinton	11 583	79.5	55 000	218	16 478	-0.6	1 099	6.7	702	-17	6 219	7.0	942	1 474
Coles	18 957	64.7	44 600	238	26 168	0.0	1 441	5.5	1 185	11	17 176	3.6	5 776	4 206
Cook	1 879 488	55.5	102 100	411	2 754 255	0.2	174 290	6.3	117 716	785	2 277 668	2.9	504 871	405 863
Crawford	7 792	78.4	36 700	190	7 667	-1.1	796	10.4	424	-8	4 924	-3.8	2 037	928
Cumberland	4 029	80.7	37 700	169	4 971	1.4	500	10.1	157	6	1 058	4.6	116	366
De Kalb	26 413	58.1	81 200	354	36 691	-3.3	1 566	4.3	1 577	33	21 334	7.2	7 563	5 488
De Witt	6 488	70.9	43 700	203	8 374	-3.3	566	6.8	350	10	4 923	-5.0	1 007	905
Douglas	7 206	74.5	44 000	217	9 084	-3.0	503	5.5	491	2	4 934	-3.4	1 622	1 114
Du Page	279 344	74.4	137 100	568	447 414	0.2	16 251	3.6	23 931	1 213	419 760	6.6	76 392	88 800
Edgar	7 859	72.8	33 200	187	7 872	-5.6	821	10.4	445	-1	4 380	0.8	1 357	1 044
Edwards	3 016	81.2	32 000	158	3 961	-2.1	311	7.9	230	-3	2 790	1.1	0	314
Effingham	11 465	76.5	54 400	214	18 946	1.7	1 371	7.2	874	34	14 070	12.6	4 637	3 245
Fayette	7 719	77.3	34 600	175	8 004	2.7	911	11.4	428	-19	3 670	4.4	970	832
Ford	5 602	73.3	42 500	213	7 085	-3.2	403	5.7	424	3	3 505	-4.3	876	749
Franklin	16 564	76.4	30 000	184	16 916	2.9	2 431	14.4	830	-44	8 182	-3.1	739	2 044
Fulton	14 893	72.2	31 100	189	16 629	-2.7	1 447	8.7	716	-6	6 246	0.8	613	2 061
Gallatin	2 784	78.8	32 600	124	2 592	-2.8	256	9.9	159	-2	1 313	-4.9	0	156
Greene	5 910	74.2	29 000	157	6 635	-5.2	514	7.7	301	-5	2 147	6.9	382	500
Grundy	11 979	69.8	71 900	319	17 834	0.5	1 517	8.5	716	7	9 472	9.2	3 125	1 917
Hamilton	3 476	79.4	29 400	139	2 358	-9.9	420	17.8	175	1	1 059	-8.4	57	259
Hancock	8 409	76.2	34 500	175	10 956	-3.0	666	6.1	493	10	3 568	3.5	993	671
Hardin	2 049	78.4	25 100	131	1 783	-3.8	169	9.5	103	3	922	16.6	0	173
Henderson	3 237	76.3	32 900	176	4 174	-3.4	281	6.7	135	-2	552	-2.8	0	209
Henry	19 514	75.1	40 500	217	24 681	0.6	1 833	7.4	1 099	14	11 852	1.5	4 078	3 220
Iroquois	11 788	73.8	40 100	202	14 927	-3.1	909	6.1	681	-12	6 547	5.1	1 845	1 368
Jackson	23 466	52.7	47 100	249	27 843	-0.6	1 859	6.7	1 289	-19	13 869	-3.9	1 238	5 428
Jasper	3 962	82.6	39 400	162	5 907	0.3	378	6.4	225	-1	2 189	9.9	777	360

1. Percent of total civilian labor force. 2. For week including March 12. Excludes government employees, self-employed persons, farm workers, domestic service workers, railroad employees subject to the Railroad Retirement Act, and employees on oceanborne vessels or in foreign countries.

STATE County	Private nonfarm establishments, 1988 (cont'd): Employment[1] (cont'd): Finance, insurance, and real estate	Private nonfarm establishments, 1988 (cont'd): Employment[1] (cont'd): Services	Private nonfarm establishments, 1988 (cont'd): Annual payroll: Total (Mil dol)	Private nonfarm establishments, 1988 (cont'd): Annual payroll: Average per employee (Dollars)	Personal income, 1989: Total (Mil dol)	Personal income, 1989: Percent change, 1988–1989	Personal income, 1989: Wages and salaries[2] (Mil dol)	Personal income, 1989: Proprietor's income (Mil dol)	Personal income, 1989: Dividends, interest, & rent (Mil dol)	Personal income, 1989: Transfer payments (Mil dol)	Personal income, 1989: Per capita[3]: Dollars	Personal income, 1989: Per capita[3]: Rank	Earnings, 1989: Total (Mil dol)	Earnings, 1989: Percent by selected industries: Farm	Earnings, 1989: Percent by selected industries: Goods-related[4]: Total
	88	89	90	91	92	93	94	95	96	97	98	99	100	101	102
IDAHO—Con.															
Franklin	53	189	12	12 515	88	6.4	28	15	16	17	9 516	2 959	43	23.1	NA
Fremont	41	198	17	13 986	131	9.8	43	31	21	20	12 563	2 087	74	34.1	13.7
Gem	40	369	27	14 829	140	6.2	47	26	27	31	12 692	2 038	73	16.3	37.6
Gooding	57	397	18	11 417	147	6.7	50	35	28	28	12 820	1 991	85	31.8	12.0
Idaho	107	354	42	17 425	174	8.1	72	41	37	31	12 843	1 983	113	17.2	28.6
Jefferson	40	239	23	10 190	176	8.1	53	34	22	26	10 344	2 828	87	27.9	14.8
Jerome	69	508	38	13 322	170	8.4	61	43	32	31	11 760	2 419	104	27.7	16.0
Kootenai	743	4 490	273	16 607	950	9.8	438	124	171	172	14 032	1 421	562	2.0	27.7
Latah	284	1 761	77	12 755	393	9.9	197	56	73	64	12 743	2 018	253	8.7	15.1
Lemhi	40	236	12	11 814	87	7.4	32	18	20	19	12 859	1 975	50	13.4	18.9
Lewis	33	30	8	16 777	64	10.4	20	25	10	12	18 048	292	46	39.7	NA
Lincoln	0	70	4	13 132	51	15.3	19	18	6	7	15 989	647	37	50.4	NA
Madison	124	2 715	82	12 766	231	12.5	123	53	34	23	9 997	2 881	176	15.5	15.2
Minidoka	88	394	64	15 879	228	7.8	116	46	35	37	11 384	2 545	162	16.9	32.7
Nez Perce	707	3 336	237	18 130	509	8.2	368	86	93	89	15 052	969	453	5.0	36.4
Oneida	0	62	4	11 129	40	0.5	11	7	7	8	11 198	2 601	17	28.3	NA
Owyhee	36	116	9	14 485	90	11.7	38	29	13	16	10 352	2 824	67	42.0	NA
Payette	215	436	47	15 755	189	8.3	78	36	31	38	11 701	2 440	113	18.4	30.0
Power	33	131	26	14 125	116	12.6	83	41	13	13	16 941	447	124	28.3	NA
Shoshone	147	529	59	18 918	181	9.5	114	13	29	43	12 858	1 977	126	0.2	51.7
Teton	0	73	3	9 354	40	17.3	10	15	7	6	12 520	2 105	25	51.1	NA
Twin Falls	786	3 258	238	15 632	762	9.0	392	136	147	125	13 514	1 672	529	10.9	20.5
Valley	82	377	16	11 944	94	9.3	47	14	20	16	13 682	1 592	62	5.5	28.9
Washington	61	261	14	10 373	100	10.5	34	21	20	25	12 319	2 190	55	28.3	19.5
ILLINOIS	375 184	1 229 040	101 291	X	220 021	7.5	142 923	19 546	39 783	28 830	18 870	X	162 470	1.4	27.1
Adams	1 069	7 257	391	16 893	1 077	7.2	578	138	265	186	16 041	636	716	4.5	30.5
Alexander	82	364	27	14 412	123	8.3	52	18	17	40	10 694	2 742	70	8.8	NA
Bond	138	1 462	38	11 027	230	6.9	54	32	45	40	14 152	1 368	86	16.4	22.5
Boone	283	1 413	300	26 678	518	5.4	410	44	80	57	16 978	442	454	2.3	NA
Brown	78	234	13	14 414	80	12.0	21	20	17	14	16 140	605	41	24.2	NA
Bureau	456	1 882	137	16 626	587	6.7	213	98	143	94	16 057	633	311	12.9	26.6
Calhoun	50	162	11	12 201	75	6.9	11	9	17	17	13 355	1 753	20	19.8	NA
Carroll	228	628	44	14 153	260	6.0	101	44	66	49	14 928	1 017	144	9.9	15.8
Cass	159	491	59	18 593	196	14.1	85	36	47	39	14 210	1 339	121	16.6	32.2
Champaign	2 956	15 070	891	16 613	2 777	6.7	1 868	276	494	372	16 063	630	2 144	2.6	15.3
Christian	545	1 715	119	16 797	558	10.1	209	89	116	107	15 713	737	299	13.4	25.8
Clark	201	427	38	13 260	232	14.7	65	54	56	43	14 234	1 312	120	23.9	24.0
Clay	142	385	46	15 111	206	11.5	85	42	42	44	13 915	1 463	127	11.9	37.4
Clinton	319	1 405	102	16 398	548	8.0	187	113	98	76	15 899	675	299	10.1	24.2
Coles	747	3 856	302	17 554	751	9.5	484	95	142	133	14 361	1 263	578	5.0	35.5
Cook	240 089	685 920	57 010	25 030	103 965	6.5	80 875	8 364	19 288	14 053	19 658	186	89 239	0.0	23.9
Crawford	308	722	103	20 854	299	2.6	146	38	74	58	14 991	992	183	10.5	41.3
Cumberland	61	314	12	11 647	143	12.7	25	27	31	24	13 091	1 868	52	28.1	9.2
De Kalb	851	4 319	401	18 775	1 228	9.1	621	146	230	153	15 975	652	768	5.4	30.0
De Witt	158	719	115	23 399	279	16.7	130	41	53	44	15 984	649	172	13.8	19.8
Douglas	239	711	90	18 248	282	14.0	140	61	58	43	14 308	1 283	201	15.0	NA
Du Page	26 745	118 682	10 441	24 874	19 405	10.0	11 794	1 227	3 016	1 280	24 958	40	13 021	0.0	25.5
Edgar	239	1 015	66	15 024	302	11.6	102	62	68	57	14 781	1 088	165	22.7	21.5
Edwards	170	271	43	15 507	118	10.2	62	25	32	18	15 097	943	87	12.4	54.2
Effingham	478	3 486	256	18 218	531	13.2	332	80	105	73	16 113	613	412	5.0	37.0
Fayette	198	841	51	14 007	271	10.5	95	53	58	56	12 380	2 169	148	16.4	25.4
Ford	191	782	57	16 303	247	8.7	86	39	61	45	16 782	474	125	15.8	23.6
Franklin	336	1 580	173	21 093	553	6.4	231	69	99	148	13 241	1 796	300	4.2	41.1
Fulton	302	2 064	82	13 162	531	8.7	163	73	113	122	13 874	1 494	237	11.2	9.3
Gallatin	64	246	30	22 594	101	15.0	48	23	20	23	14 242	1 305	71	19.6	NA
Greene	129	514	26	11 935	208	12.3	58	40	45	45	13 027	1 897	98	24.4	13.9
Grundy	498	1 492	224	23 691	590	6.4	371	55	102	70	17 897	308	426	4.5	22.5
Hamilton	82	217	12	11 710	115	14.5	24	29	28	29	12 976	1 915	53	38.8	7.4
Hancock	206	933	55	15 387	328	10.9	95	57	75	59	14 467	1 226	153	17.7	24.2
Hardin	33	337	13	14 537	55	4.8	19	6	12	17	10 216	2 852	25	5.0	NA
Henderson	78	105	6	11 301	119	8.7	14	20	23	19	13 449	1 713	34	44.9	NA
Henry	585	1 895	178	15 058	800	6.9	278	98	176	126	15 189	913	376	9.6	30.0
Iroquois	397	1 685	97	14 760	480	10.5	136	98	115	84	15 232	896	234	23.4	16.9
Jackson	726	4 149	200	14 405	779	7.8	516	89	125	162	13 152	1 837	605	3.0	11.5
Jasper	124	238	36	16 365	168	14.0	63	43	40	25	14 887	1 031	106	22.4	22.5

1. For week including March 12. Excludes government employees, self-employed persons, farm workers, domestic service workers, railroad employees subject to the Railroad Retirement Act, and employees on oceanborne vessels or in foreign countries. 2. Includes other labor income. 3. Based on the resident population estimated as of July 1 of the year shown. 4. Covers mining, construction, and manufacturing.

STATE County	Earnings, 1989 (cont'd): Percent by selected industries (cont'd): Goods-related[1]: Manu-facturing	Service-related & other[2]: Total	Retail trade	Finance, insur-ance, & real estate	Services	Govern-ment	Agriculture, 1987: Farms: Number	Percent with: Less than 50 acres	500 acres and over	Farm operators, percent: Whose principal occu-pation is farming	Residing on farm operated	Land in farms: Acreage (1,000)	Percent change, 1982–1987	Acres: Average size of farm	Total irrigated (1,000)	Total cropland (1,000)
	103	104	105	106	107	108	109	110	111	112	113	114	115	116	117	118
IDAHO—Con.																
Franklin	8.6	NA	10.5	3.0	14.1	20.6	641	31.4	20.6	58.2	76.0	242	2.1	378	49	145
Fremont	10.9	28.7	6.3	1.2	8.6	23.5	546	23.6	31.0	63.2	68.1	384	-3.4	703	106	195
Gem	31.6	32.3	9.4	1.6	10.6	13.7	539	46.2	11.9	55.3	80.7	223	-9.4	414	35	53
Gooding	5.9	40.6	7.2	2.3	11.9	15.6	729	36.9	11.5	69.8	76.5	239	-1.2	328	108	128
Idaho	22.2	31.6	7.6	1.7	13.3	22.6	774	18.5	42.0	58.3	76.6	803	-0.3	1 037	4	265
Jefferson	7.9	38.9	5.5	1.8	8.0	18.4	823	34.5	18.3	53.1	77.2	332	-12.6	403	170	210
Jerome	10.2	45.4	9.1	1.4	13.7	10.9	909	38.1	11.3	64.6	78.2	205	-12.4	226	135	162
Kootenai	18.3	52.8	12.4	4.0	23.1	17.6	611	40.3	14.6	45.0	84.0	171	-14.4	279	18	96
Latah	11.1	38.0	10.8	2.3	17.7	38.1	644	21.0	36.3	60.9	73.3	353	-0.7	548	3	264
Lemhi	13.1	41.2	12.6	2.1	17.3	26.5	365	31.2	29.3	66.0	80.5	201	-1.6	551	78	86
Lewis	22.4	24.4	5.9	2.4	4.9	12.0	191	8.9	67.5	74.9	64.9	223	-1.8	1 166	D	158
Lincoln	9.1	16.3	2.1	1.0	4.3	23.1	338	16.6	23.1	75.7	81.1	145	-10.5	430	65	91
Madison	11.1	58.3	8.8	4.0	33.2	11.1	510	32.5	25.5	59.8	77.1	240	-2.6	470	117	186
Minidoka	28.1	37.6	6.4	1.8	11.2	12.9	858	34.3	11.2	73.3	76.7	208	-0.8	242	146	181
Nez Perce	30.9	47.4	10.8	4.4	21.1	11.2	405	26.2	45.9	64.9	73.3	474	0.3	1 170	3	217
Oneida	0.8	NA	9.2	5.7	11.4	27.6	363	15.2	49.3	62.3	60.6	309	-1.6	852	31	211
Owyhee	2.2	NA	4.8	1.0	5.4	13.2	573	25.0	25.5	76.3	72.3	717	-8.1	1 251	117	142
Payette	24.9	40.6	6.2	3.1	12.4	10.9	572	49.5	7.9	60.7	78.8	135	-7.2	237	50	62
Power	44.8	NA	3.5	0.8	4.7	7.7	350	22.0	52.3	66.9	66.0	436	-1.4	1 247	94	327
Shoshone	6.9	30.7	7.7	2.0	14.5	17.4	46	52.2	2.2	41.3	78.3	5	3.6	112	D	2
Teton	1.1	24.8	7.9	1.3	8.7	16.6	268	14.9	35.8	64.9	70.1	149	-4.6	556	55	117
Twin Falls	14.6	55.3	13.0	4.0	22.4	13.3	1 576	33.7	13.6	68.8	73.6	553	-4.5	351	272	327
Valley	9.8	38.7	11.5	2.1	18.7	26.9	113	24.8	29.2	55.8	69.9	82	-28.3	724	18	21
Washington	14.9	36.0	8.8	2.4	12.4	16.2	492	30.1	33.1	66.3	73.0	523	0.3	1 063	38	119
ILLINOIS	20.5	59.2	8.8	8.5	26.0	12.3	88 786	21.3	21.8	64.3	71.4	28 527	-0.7	321	208	25 102
Adams	24.2	54.5	12.3	2.8	26.9	10.5	1 662	21.7	18.8	63.2	71.9	467	0.2	281	0	358
Alexander	16.0	NA	9.8	2.9	18.4	19.7	184	13.0	21.7	53.8	68.5	73	-7.1	397	1	60
Bond	16.5	53.7	9.7	2.8	25.6	7.5	714	25.9	15.5	55.6	72.5	187	-3.3	262	0	165
Boone	68.6	NA	4.9	0.9	9.2	5.5	560	24.1	15.9	66.6	81.1	153	-6.1	273	1	142
Brown	0.5	NA	7.2	5.4	16.0	10.9	442	20.1	24.4	60.4	64.0	157	3.5	356	D	105
Bureau	18.0	48.7	7.6	4.3	21.9	11.8	1 517	14.4	23.1	72.9	69.1	517	1.1	341	3	469
Calhoun	NA	47.7	17.1	4.4	16.4	26.1	491	22.4	10.6	49.3	69.9	101	-8.2	206	D	60
Carroll	9.5	52.0	13.7	4.2	16.6	22.3	775	17.2	20.5	73.9	74.5	260	-3.9	335	4	219
Cass	27.8	41.1	6.3	2.9	13.1	10.1	500	15.6	36.2	70.6	64.0	227	2.8	453	2	188
Champaign	10.0	45.5	8.6	3.3	23.2	36.7	1 671	16.8	26.3	71.2	64.7	594	-1.0	356	2	574
Christian	7.7	51.0	10.2	3.9	18.4	9.8	1 051	21.7	31.5	71.0	70.1	426	3.3	405	0	398
Clark	14.6	44.3	9.1	5.0	17.5	7.8	818	24.8	23.1	57.0	68.7	272	-4.8	333	3	229
Clay	28.2	38.8	8.7	1.6	16.2	11.8	719	21.3	20.9	59.1	75.1	219	3.2	305	D	190
Clinton	5.3	52.4	10.4	2.6	18.8	13.3	1 115	22.3	9.3	60.8	72.6	241	-1.9	217	0	219
Coles	29.6	40.5	8.1	2.8	17.8	19.0	833	25.5	26.4	65.4	65.9	286	0.9	343	D	263
Cook	18.6	65.2	8.2	11.5	27.9	10.9	389	60.4	7.5	48.3	55.5	47	-5.2	121	1	41
Crawford	32.5	36.9	8.7	3.7	11.3	11.3	595	23.5	28.4	59.3	76.6	220	-2.4	370	1	190
Cumberland	3.9	46.5	14.6	3.8	17.4	16.1	710	26.1	14.5	55.2	74.1	178	-2.3	251	D	155
De Kalb	23.8	39.2	9.0	3.0	18.1	25.5	1 063	18.4	25.0	72.4	75.7	384	-2.9	362	0	365
De Witt	16.7	55.5	9.0	2.6	15.7	11.0	565	17.3	31.0	73.6	67.1	222	3.0	393	D	211
Douglas	29.5	NA	8.7	3.4	12.5	8.1	807	22.6	25.5	70.3	68.2	271	-1.9	336	0	259
Du Page	16.6	67.8	10.4	6.0	32.7	6.7	161	60.2	8.7	46.0	64.0	25	-21.9	158	0	23
Edgar	16.5	39.2	9.8	3.3	16.4	16.5	965	16.2	30.4	71.2	67.6	383	4.3	397	0	347
Edwards	46.9	26.7	6.3	2.0	11.4	6.7	387	23.8	25.3	63.3	76.5	133	10.1	343	D	115
Effingham	31.5	49.5	11.4	2.8	20.1	8.5	1 228	24.6	9.2	55.0	71.7	258	0.9	210	0	221
Fayette	17.2	38.5	10.8	2.9	15.1	19.7	1 208	25.1	16.8	52.3	70.1	318	-5.6	263	0	267
Ford	15.4	49.7	9.9	2.7	18.3	10.9	729	11.1	30.0	77.0	65.7	297	2.7	407	D	284
Franklin	5.3	39.8	10.2	2.8	17.7	14.9	586	34.0	15.4	40.1	75.1	167	-9.3	285	D	147
Fulton	3.4	62.5	12.2	3.1	26.9	16.9	1 371	20.6	21.7	62.4	68.5	459	8.8	335	D	339
Gallatin	NA	NA	5.2	2.0	14.5	8.7	287	22.0	38.3	66.9	67.2	170	2.2	593	5	153
Greene	7.0	42.3	7.6	3.2	15.3	19.4	827	22.5	26.5	68.6	66.4	297	-5.0	359	1	235
Grundy	15.7	NA	7.5	4.3	NA	8.1	598	14.5	29.8	68.1	67.6	237	3.9	396	0	220
Hamilton	0.8	35.7	9.0	3.6	11.7	18.1	581	19.3	22.0	57.8	76.4	205	-4.9	353	D	176
Hancock	16.0	45.7	7.9	4.2	22.3	12.3	1 391	17.1	21.6	69.8	71.4	448	2.1	322	1	372
Hardin	5.0	NA	7.4	2.3	NA	20.7	198	18.2	4.5	26.3	73.2	37	-10.8	185	D	22
Henderson	NA	37.5	10.4	4.9	13.4	13.8	522	12.8	30.7	76.1	71.3	213	0.4	407	9	181
Henry	22.3	47.2	12.1	3.5	17.0	13.3	1 696	19.7	17.7	72.8	75.7	485	-2.1	286	4	442
Iroquois	10.6	48.6	9.4	4.1	18.8	11.1	1 745	11.3	30.3	75.3	69.5	685	0.8	393	1	651
Jackson	4.1	42.8	11.7	3.0	20.4	42.6	720	21.2	14.0	46.8	73.3	205	-4.1	284	0	160
Jasper	16.5	45.1	5.5	3.4	8.5	10.0	894	20.9	21.1	63.4	74.6	262	-1.0	293	0	233

1. Covers mining, construction, and manufacturing. 2. Covers private sector earnings in agricultural services, forestry, and fisheries; transportation and public utilities; wholesale trade; retail trade; finance, insurance, and real estate; and services.

STATE County	Agriculture, 1987 (cont'd): Value of land and buildings: Average per farm ($1,000)	Value of land and buildings: Average per acre (Dollars)	Value of products sold: Total (Mil dol)	Value of products sold: Average per farm (Dollars)	Value of products sold: Percent from: Crops	Value of products sold: Percent from: Livestock and poultry[1]	Percent of farms with sales of: $10,000 or more	Percent of farms with sales of: $100,000 or more	Manufactures, 1987: Establishments: Total	Establishments: Percent with 20 or more employees	All employees: Number (1,000)	All employees: Percent change, 1982–1987	All employees: Annual payroll (Mil dol)	Production workers: Number (1,000)	Production workers: Work hours (Mil)
	119	120	121	122	123	124	125	126	127	128	129	130	131	132	133
IDAHO—Con.															
Franklin	194	518	40	63 161	15.4	84.6	57.6	15.9	10	40.0	0.2	0.0	2.3	0.2	0.3
Fremont	351	547	62	112 830	60.0	40.0	65.8	23.4	13	15.4	0.2	0.0	4.2	0.2	0.4
Gem	187	479	22	40 417	38.1	61.9	48.1	10.6	15	53.3	D	D	D	D	D
Gooding	271	846	113	154 600	25.9	74.1	64.2	23.3	9	0.0	0.0	0.0	0.4	0.0	0.0
Idaho	362	358	34	43 659	53.1	46.9	57.8	12.4	50	18.0	1.1	57.1	21.9	1.0	1.8
Jefferson	287	670	66	80 452	46.9	53.1	58.4	20.2	16	12.5	D	D	D	D	D
Jerome	246	1 016	129	142 020	34.6	65.4	68.0	21.1	12	33.3	D	D	D	D	D
Kootenai	314	911	17	28 356	83.8	16.2	20.6	6.7	153	21.6	3.6	28.6	67.7	2.7	4.9
Latah	444	731	34	53 169	89.3	10.7	54.3	17.9	42	19.0	0.6	0.0	12.6	0.6	1.1
Lemhi	317	570	16	44 087	6.0	94.0	61.4	11.2	9	33.3	0.2	0.0	3.2	0.2	0.3
Lewis	701	535	20	107 020	92.6	7.4	79.6	41.9	8	25.0	0.1	0.0	2.2	0.1	0.2
Lincoln	242	578	29	86 631	39.7	60.3	74.6	22.5	2	50.0	D	D	D	D	D
Madison	419	848	51	100 570	82.2	17.8	60.0	25.5	15	53.3	1.1	22.2	15.1	0.9	1.8
Minidoka	267	1 141	83	97 292	71.2	28.8	72.0	30.4	13	61.5	2.1	16.7	36.3	1.9	3.5
Nez Perce	612	493	30	74 863	82.9	17.1	58.5	23.7	50	22.0	3.0	-16.7	89.4	2.2	4.1
Oneida	299	312	12	33 614	54.5	45.5	55.9	8.5	3	0.0	D	D	D	D	D
Owyhee	515	393	75	130 998	34.8	65.2	72.4	26.2	3	0.0	D	D	D	D	D
Payette	222	933	49	85 079	56.3	43.7	53.7	16.3	19	42.1	1.1	83.3	19.2	0.8	1.7
Power	709	601	66	189 235	75.0	25.0	66.0	36.3	6	33.3	D	D	D	D	D
Shoshone	114	1 018	0	6 049	36.0	64.0	13.0	0.0	36	16.7	0.3	50.0	4.8	0.2	0.5
Teton	442	736	17	65 221	67.2	32.8	65.7	16.0	4	0.0	0.0	0.0	0.1	0.0	0.0
Twin Falls	285	814	162	102 574	48.3	51.7	69.5	20.2	69	29.0	2.9	7.4	48.8	2.3	4.0
Valley	328	532	8	70 769	8.3	91.7	46.0	13.3	18	11.1	0.2	0.0	3.3	0.1	0.3
Washington	365	300	42	85 419	32.2	67.8	58.3	16.9	9	22.2	0.2	0.0	2.7	0.1	0.3
ILLINOIS	403	1 262	6 377	71 822	65.2	34.8	70.6	22.1	18 404	39.1	989.6	-8.1	26 234.7	609.3	1 227.5
Adams	250	892	100	59 933	46.8	53.2	66.4	18.2	79	40.5	5.7	-29.6	136.5	3.5	6.9
Alexander	293	717	8	44 464	85.4	14.6	54.9	11.4	10	40.0	D	D	D	D	D
Bond	231	881	34	47 226	54.7	45.3	60.9	14.6	16	25.0	0.6	0.0	10.0	0.4	0.7
Boone	382	1 444	38	68 258	59.2	40.8	72.3	24.5	47	46.8	4.7	-25.4	160.8	3.5	7.5
Brown	222	609	23	52 265	50.7	49.3	63.6	12.9	2	0.0	D	D	D	D	D
Bureau	473	1 325	146	96 491	68.4	31.6	84.3	26.5	49	44.9	2.9	0.0	60.7	2.0	3.6
Calhoun	129	760	17	34 440	41.0	59.0	49.3	8.6	7	14.3	D	D	D	D	D
Carroll	374	1 127	102	131 993	31.0	69.0	78.8	36.3	26	30.8	1.2	20.0	23.3	0.9	1.6
Cass	529	1 079	60	120 501	52.6	47.4	82.2	33.2	16	43.8	1.0	0.0	21.1	0.7	1.2
Champaign	645	1 835	135	80 550	91.0	9.0	82.0	27.0	141	41.1	9.4	28.8	189.7	6.4	12.1
Christian	564	1 438	101	95 952	87.2	12.8	76.5	33.3	26	46.2	1.2	-14.3	24.0	0.9	1.9
Clark	367	1 128	52	64 116	75.7	24.3	63.4	20.2	22	36.4	0.8	-33.3	13.2	0.6	1.1
Clay	257	768	33	45 823	73.5	26.5	64.3	12.5	27	44.4	1.3	85.7	23.1	0.9	1.9
Clinton	237	1 059	82	73 398	30.7	69.3	73.6	23.2	40	32.5	D	D	D	D	D
Coles	502	1 492	59	70 242	85.7	14.3	68.9	24.1	60	45.0	5.8	16.0	126.6	4.8	9.3
Cook	425	4 251	23	58 250	92.0	8.0	43.7	11.3	9 450	40.7	491.6	-11.5	13 180.7	290.3	589.3
Crawford	347	945	42	70 629	72.2	27.8	64.9	24.0	24	41.7	D	D	D	D	D
Cumberland	340	1 264	39	55 370	61.0	39.0	64.1	16.1	10	20.0	0.1	-66.7	1.6	0.1	0.2
De Kalb	613	1 700	143	134 226	48.6	51.4	82.8	33.7	120	45.8	7.0	-2.8	174.2	4.4	8.6
De Witt	587	1 581	48	85 114	93.1	6.9	78.6	32.4	15	66.7	1.5	66.7	32.2	1.1	2.2
Douglas	601	1 714	68	84 219	82.8	17.2	79.7	29.9	35	31.4	1.6	0.0	39.0	1.1	2.2
Du Page	1 376	6 577	19	115 756	93.3	6.6	51.6	19.9	1 857	35.3	67.5	5.5	1 820.8	38.1	76.3
Edgar	476	1 207	78	80 817	82.2	17.8	79.3	26.6	24	54.2	1.4	-17.6	27.7	1.1	2.3
Edwards	252	914	26	66 900	54.5	45.5	68.0	22.7	14	35.7	D	D	D	D	D
Effingham	253	1 247	61	49 965	49.2	50.8	66.4	16.0	48	39.6	3.8	15.2	99.2	2.9	5.8
Fayette	213	852	49	40 365	72.1	27.9	54.8	12.3	19	26.3	1.0	0.0	16.4	0.8	1.4
Ford	519	1 320	67	91 935	79.7	20.3	87.5	31.0	23	39.1	0.8	-11.1	15.0	0.6	1.2
Franklin	193	748	21	35 390	73.1	26.9	43.0	9.9	38	15.8	0.7	40.0	13.7	0.6	1.1
Fulton	298	869	71	52 101	66.9	33.1	63.8	15.2	26	23.1	D	D	D	D	D
Gallatin	619	990	29	100 246	88.0	12.0	70.4	30.7	5	40.0	0.1	-50.0	1.9	0.1	0.1
Greene	346	1 012	57	68 388	62.4	37.6	72.4	22.2	14	35.7	0.4	0.0	6.6	0.3	0.6
Grundy	576	1 480	45	75 326	86.5	13.5	81.4	25.9	44	52.3	2.9	-6.5	86.7	2.0	4.3
Hamilton	270	746	26	43 982	86.1	13.9	57.8	11.7	7	0.0	0.1	0.0	0.8	0.0	0.1
Hancock	367	1 108	93	67 080	52.9	47.1	74.8	18.8	23	26.1	1.0	42.9	17.0	0.7	1.2
Hardin	99	532	2	7 627	31.5	68.5	16.7	1.0	4	25.0	D	D	D	D	D
Henderson	411	1 043	48	91 822	60.6	39.4	83.0	31.0	2	0.0	D	D	D	D	D
Henry	350	1 221	175	102 893	35.7	64.3	80.1	30.2	59	42.4	4.3	87.0	76.0	3.2	6.5
Iroquois	508	1 319	164	94 071	75.9	24.1	87.0	29.1	44	40.9	1.9	0.0	31.7	1.5	3.2
Jackson	218	768	27	37 426	75.3	24.7	47.6	10.0	34	32.4	1.4	0.0	23.6	1.1	2.0
Jasper	318	1 124	60	67 169	58.6	41.4	71.4	21.0	14	28.6	0.6	20.0	7.3	0.5	1.1

1. Includes livestock and poultry products.

STATE County	Manufactures, 1987 (cont'd): Production workers (cont'd): Wages: Total (Mil dol)	Manufactures, 1987 (cont'd): Production workers (cont'd): Wages: Average per worker (Dollars)	Manufactures, 1987 (cont'd): Value added by manufacture (Mil dol)	Manufactures, 1987 (cont'd): Value of shipments (Mil dol)	Manufactures, 1987 (cont'd): New capital expenditures (Mil dol)	Value of construction authorized by building permits, 1990: Total[1] ($1,000)	Nonresidential: Total ($1,000)	Nonresidential: Percent: Office	Nonresidential: Percent: Industrial	Nonresidential: Percent: Stores	Residential: New construction ($1,000)	Residential: Number of housing units	Residential: Alterations and additions ($1,000)
	134	135	136	137	138	139	140	141	142	143	144	145	146
IDAHO—Con.													
Franklin	1.7	8 500	11.8	22.7	D	1 610	687	0.0	0.0	78.3	879	9	44
Fremont	3.7	18 500	12.1	26.6	0.8	3 680	1 027	0.0	0.0	9.6	2 250	51	356
Gem	D	D	D	D	D	3 282	504	0.0	29.8	0.0	1 874	26	588
Gooding	0.2	NA	0.7	1.7	0.0	2 805	950	0.0	0.0	88.9	895	12	235
Idaho	19.4	19 400	45.6	113.6	D	2 108	154	0.0	0.0	55.4	405	6	276
Jefferson	D	D	D	D	D	8 534	4 320	0.2	78.7	0.0	2 893	35	392
Jerome	D	D	D	D	D	3 792	1 519	6.4	9.5	44.8	1 439	14	425
Kootenai	40.5	15 000	148.0	294.3	13.4	85 481	27 481	17.3	8.0	56.8	45 574	574	4 496
Latah	10.2	17 000	25.7	58.2	1.4	10 585	329	0.0	0.0	0.0	6 887	80	2 040
Lemhi	2.4	12 000	6.4	18.1	0.3	2 763	241	0.0	24.9	6.6	1 605	35	470
Lewis	1.9	19 000	4.6	13.7	D	1 013	277	0.0	0.0	0.0	29	1	241
Lincoln	D	D	D	D	D	241	8	0.0	0.0	100.0	0	0	39
Madison	11.7	13 000	38.9	77.1	1.6	4 264	2 222	22.3	0.0	4.7	1 778	24	138
Minidoka	29.7	15 632	88.0	254.4	4.4	6 622	3 579	5.4	13.5	1.3	969	15	880
Nez Perce	63.2	28 727	213.6	461.2	D	18 341	8 187	3.2	60.4	17.1	5 995	75	1 519
Oneida	D	D	D	D	D	0	0	NA	NA	NA	0	0	0
Owyhee	D	D	D	D	D	114	0	NA	NA	NA	70	1	26
Payette	11.5	14 375	35.8	119.1	1.8	4 539	1 432	0.0	27.9	18.2	1 987	34	283
Power	D	D	D	D	D	2 730	1 070	0.0	0.0	0.0	662	6	297
Shoshone	3.6	18 000	10.7	26.2	0.5	1 251	203	35.5	18.7	0.0	541	8	150
Teton	0.1	NA	0.2	0.4	0.0	96	0	NA	NA	NA	85	1	0
Twin Falls	33.9	14 739	151.5	401.4	10.7	24 771	8 370	16.4	49.0	18.5	10 878	136	1 571
Valley	2.9	29 000	7.4	23.7	D	12 237	1 040	12.6	0.0	19.1	7 818	115	1 019
Washington	2.1	21 000	6.1	16.4	0.1	1 550	383	0.0	72.3	2.6	199	4	218
ILLINOIS	13 401.4	21 995	63 350.1	132 204.3	4 425.8	8 295 905	2 434 138	35.6	14.0	23.9	3 517 201	38 289	596 922
Adams	70.6	20 171	320.3	1 042.7	14.9	17 459	5 978	10.3	28.5	44.4	10 632	105	226
Alexander	D	D	D	D	D	290	284	0.0	57.0	38.7	0	0	0
Bond	6.4	16 000	32.0	60.8	0.8	4 903	474	0.0	0.0	67.9	1 914	33	103
Boone	111.1	31 743	267.9	889.5	D	39 878	7 096	65.9	10.8	4.0	29 943	300	1 258
Brown	D	D	D	D	D	194	2	0.0	0.0	0.0	160	5	5
Bureau	38.9	19 450	148.7	302.8	D	6 882	1 927	0.0	4.4	39.0	3 170	38	622
Calhoun	D	D	D	D	D	6 744	5 025	0.0	88.1	8.5	1 325	21	145
Carroll	14.0	15 556	61.2	113.4	D	8 582	1 460	18.7	5.9	12.5	6 417	63	316
Cass	15.2	21 714	36.4	126.4	0.8	1 296	507	0.0	0.0	59.2	594	15	116
Champaign	117.5	18 359	676.5	1 685.7	34.7	65 068	13 273	20.3	24.3	8.6	29 114	529	3 907
Christian	14.5	16 111	69.6	278.6	D	5 904	2 239	2.9	0.0	12.0	2 191	44	364
Clark	8.4	14 000	30.3	54.3	D	1 033	26	0.0	100.0	0.0	795	16	0
Clay	17.1	19 000	70.2	151.0	D	NA	NA	NA	NA	NA	NA	NA	NA
Clinton	D	D	D	D	D	4 904	886	9.0	11.3	17.6	3 374	43	201
Coles	97.6	20 333	481.6	893.7	32.6	14 386	3 972	16.7	60.6	1.6	6 440	92	512
Cook	6 315.2	21 754	31 463.1	60 440.1	1 478.6	3 222 856	1 051 604	46.4	4.5	18.3	857 685	9 542	305 826
Crawford	D	D	D	D	D	2 193	1 759	10.4	0.0	72.8	236	4	113
Cumberland	1.0	10 000	3.0	5.3	0.1	152	0	NA	NA	NA	115	2	8
De Kalb	89.9	20 432	323.8	669.4	19.1	48 740	5 809	4.4	35.1	13.0	37 982	468	2 740
De Witt	20.3	18 455	103.7	174.3	10.1	7 537	2 414	0.0	9.0	35.2	2 740	36	653
Douglas	23.8	21 636	69.6	224.8	5.6	3 331	960	19.1	14.3	42.8	1 765	34	225
Du Page	770.1	20 213	3 628.3	6 252.4	230.9	1 175 090	346 542	40.7	24.2	19.3	545 234	4 805	59 399
Edgar	18.0	16 364	78.3	149.4	D	2 997	1 668	0.0	80.5	4.2	839	10	190
Edwards	D	D	D	D	D	NA	NA	NA	NA	NA	NA	NA	NA
Effingham	63.9	22 034	220.5	461.6	14.4	21 026	11 211	3.7	4.6	52.7	7 105	112	293
Fayette	11.9	14 875	39.0	75.1	6.5	3 456	2 425	0.0	61.9	0.0	728	12	153
Ford	10.2	17 000	46.5	161.5	D	2 288	838	0.0	8.8	8.2	1 022	16	128
Franklin	9.6	16 000	43.3	67.0	D	3 174	1 541	0.0	0.8	49.3	1 136	16	211
Fulton	D	D	D	D	D	4 642	432	0.0	3.5	20.5	2 490	40	585
Gallatin	0.9	9 000	2.6	9.5	0.1	0	0	NA	NA	NA	0	0	0
Greene	4.7	15 667	12.2	25.6	D	NA	NA	NA	NA	NA	NA	NA	NA
Grundy	52.6	26 300	298.8	791.0	D	27 257	2 977	0.0	21.8	25.6	21 231	239	749
Hamilton	0.6	NA	5.2	8.9	0.0	NA	NA	NA	NA	NA	NA	NA	NA
Hancock	9.3	13 286	37.5	101.9	D	2 731	1 752	0.0	2.3	25.8	352	9	244
Hardin	D	D	D	D	D	124	25	100.0	0.0	0.0	63	1	12
Henderson	D	D	D	D	D	997	183	38.3	0.0	0.0	645	18	85
Henry	51.8	16 187	125.3	1 189.0	D	12 830	2 388	22.7	4.2	31.9	5 323	64	1 657
Iroquois	23.3	15 533	86.5	199.1	D	9 870	3 328	7.5	38.5	45.1	2 838	49	565
Jackson	16.2	14 727	51.1	133.6	3.7	21 042	3 298	11.3	0.0	74.5	3 156	83	792
Jasper	5.9	11 800	23.5	39.2	0.4	0	0	NA	NA	NA	0	0	0

1. Includes nonresidential additions and alterations, residential nonhousekeeping buildings, and residential garages and carports not shown separately.

STATE County	Wholesale trade, 1987				Retail trade, all establishments, 1987				Retail trade, establishments with payroll, 1987					
						Sales				Sales				
											Per capita[2] (Dollars)			
	Estab-lishments	Sales (Mil dol)	Paid employees[1]	Annual payroll (Mil dol)	Number	Total (Mil dol)	Percent change, 1982–1987	Per capita[2] (Dollars)	Number	Total (Mil dol)	General merchandise stores	Food stores	Apparel & accessory stores	Eating and drinking places
	147	148	149	150	151	152	153	154	155	156	157	158	159	160
IDAHO—Con.														
Franklin	12	22.1	118	1.6	85	30.6	28.6	3 327	46	28.9	D	D	21	154
Fremont	21	40.4	259	2.6	95	24.5	-3.9	2 377	51	22.9	D	489	D	184
Gem	14	15.2	108	1.7	110	31.3	9.1	2 795	61	29.8	D	1 063	D	113
Gooding	22	48.4	193	2.9	120	34.5	0.9	2 971	74	32.8	91	709	D	193
Idaho	25	36.3	198	3.3	184	42.5	23.9	3 103	113	37.9	98	886	58	445
Jefferson	26	51.1	441	4.5	145	31.4	-9.0	1 901	62	28.3	D	548	21	90
Jerome	36	78.7	366	4.4	135	47.9	17.1	3 260	76	45.0	D	931	18	255
Kootenai	100	177.0	828	15.3	836	385.7	47.4	5 827	480	366.6	339	1 463	171	512
Latah	61	85.2	337	6.1	361	155.3	18.2	5 058	240	151.1	584	1 150	278	470
Lemhi	12	5.6	26	0.3	123	27.3	-7.8	4 013	65	25.5	D	628	D	316
Lewis	16	33.6	142	2.7	71	9.1	-16.5	2 526	33	7.9	0	1 025	85	176
Lincoln	3	D	D	D	36	4.9	-39.5	1 537	15	3.4	0	467	0	216
Madison	41	56.4	484	5.1	168	96.3	17.7	4 280	113	94.1	379	1 015	197	258
Minidoka	39	104.5	602	9.2	171	61.4	35.8	3 054	93	57.7	D	597	68	231
Nez Perce	83	265.8	776	14.3	433	254.5	24.4	7 621	293	249.8	928	1 687	267	687
Oneida	4	D	D	D	41	10.8	28.6	3 082	26	10.3	D	D	D	203
Owyhee	19	26.3	128	2.3	70	19.8	14.5	2 305	36	18.1	0	883	D	101
Payette	24	48.5	254	3.1	126	36.3	11.3	2 242	60	32.5	D	769	D	139
Power	18	96.0	146	1.9	61	19.8	52.3	2 876	35	18.1	D	937	D	273
Shoshone	13	4.7	38	0.5	208	66.1	3.3	4 375	118	62.9	D	1 256	117	243
Teton	7	4.3	11	0.2	52	13.1	35.1	4 108	29	11.5	D	1 152	D	242
Twin Falls	187	336.3	1 914	29.7	626	369.4	30.8	6 621	422	362.8	753	1 065	375	488
Valley	7	5.9	20	0.4	139	31.5	5.0	4 708	75	29.2	D	1 159	104	624
Washington	18	37.0	314	2.7	84	15.6	-24.3	1 930	50	13.9	189	454	52	196
ILLINOIS	23 620	167 460.9	319 497	8 081.0	99 468	69 937.2	37.8	6 037	63 945	68 263.9	694	1 075	351	602
Adams	173	D	D	D	722	394.8	15.5	5 840	459	385.2	962	1 229	337	522
Alexander	19	D	D	D	126	42.8	10.9	3 692	85	41.3	D	1 048	24	343
Bond	23	D	D	D	168	50.1	4.4	3 093	86	47.0	96	633	101	292
Boone	42	75.5	265	5.0	247	144.9	53.8	4 895	132	139.3	398	1 156	D	512
Brown	17	D	D	D	53	11.1	-3.5	2 177	32	10.2	D	D	D	215
Bureau	82	D	D	D	449	143.4	8.6	3 876	245	135.1	D	849	156	299
Calhoun	9	D	D	D	73	17.2	17.8	3 065	45	16.1	D	425	D	549
Carroll	29	D	D	D	201	58.0	33.0	3 296	127	54.6	70	950	22	409
Cass	33	D	D	D	152	45.2	12.4	3 251	87	43.1	D	1 166	D	202
Champaign	229	1 490.0	3 160	70.5	1 491	1 137.0	43.5	6 634	1 032	1 117.7	944	1 108	317	798
Christian	69	D	D	D	413	177.1	29.6	4 962	227	169.8	D	1 175	178	366
Clark	31	D	D	D	208	61.9	29.8	3 797	110	57.0	D	851	58	360
Clay	34	D	D	D	202	54.4	18.3	3 648	106	46.6	D	771	61	194
Clinton	60	131.5	471	8.0	343	132.5	29.4	3 897	232	127.7	D	810	73	280
Coles	93	240.7	804	17.2	573	321.1	39.9	6 163	356	312.0	999	893	244	632
Cook	11 278	92 995.4	184 170	4 784.6	40 043	31 572.1	36.5	5 958	26 437	30 847.0	657	1 053	452	669
Crawford	30	124.8	196	3.6	222	94.0	14.2	4 629	112	89.4	D	1 073	67	265
Cumberland	23	46.7	139	2.3	103	29.8	28.4	2 758	50	27.7	D	703	D	120
De Kalb	100	185.7	701	15.9	696	407.0	47.6	5 419	439	396.6	D	1 002	223	526
De Witt	36	80.2	194	4.1	173	82.1	30.9	4 689	102	79.1	D	985	33	394
Douglas	45	391.6	323	4.8	256	92.2	14.4	4 681	143	87.9	86	1 113	389	444
Du Page	2 813	32 087.9	41 915	1 250.1	6 304	7 131.7	55.1	9 577	4 377	7 038.1	1 070	1 260	624	803
Edgar	49	101.5	312	4.5	247	104.4	37.5	5 020	141	100.3	D	1 424	97	320
Edwards	20	D	D	D	111	26.4	1.9	3 303	60	24.3	D	1 242	41	110
Effingham	74	285.8	921	18.9	412	271.0	28.0	8 415	250	265.5	D	1 160	380	700
Fayette	48	107.4	510	7.0	224	79.1	8.1	3 594	122	73.6	D	657	50	256
Ford	52	249.1	477	8.8	211	64.1	23.3	4 362	116	60.0	221	903	105	403
Franklin	59	73.2	444	8.1	541	204.5	27.2	4 800	298	191.3	D	1 073	146	405
Fulton	51	79.0	308	4.4	451	172.5	26.1	4 480	248	163.0	321	1 534	172	340
Gallatin	17	20.4	136	2.1	96	16.1	3.9	2 178	50	15.0	D	527	106	117
Greene	30	62.2	190	2.3	162	40.8	3.0	2 568	100	39.1	54	873	20	215
Grundy	52	198.3	479	9.8	315	155.7	28.3	4 851	187	149.3	D	924	94	513
Hamilton	16	33.4	66	1.3	115	32.7	33.5	3 671	51	30.0	D	731	D	126
Hancock	52	120.3	328	5.6	303	56.7	9.0	2 465	145	51.4	44	452	D	186
Hardin	4	1.3	5	0.1	63	11.2	60.0	2 083	32	10.1	D	662	D	81
Henderson	18	41.9	101	1.5	84	13.9	-9.2	1 575	44	11.9	0	387	0	291
Henry	91	351.7	672	11.7	527	249.5	38.2	4 647	330	241.3	481	915	144	423
Iroquois	88	242.4	547	9.2	383	111.7	9.3	3 500	195	104.3	D	826	79	291
Jackson	67	74.5	390	6.4	626	396.9	16.5	6 615	433	389.2	1 111	1 212	456	690
Jasper	32	86.4	202	3.4	108	39.2	-6.7	3 497	58	35.7	D	756	72	152

1. For pay period including March 12. 2. Based on the estimated population as of July 1 of the year shown.

STATE County	Retail trade, establishments with payroll, 1987 (cont'd)		Taxable service industries–establishments with payroll, 1987							Bank deposits,[2] June 1989		Savings capital,[3] September 1989	
				Receipts (Mil dol)									
					Selected kinds of business								
	Paid employees[1]	Annual payroll (Mil dol)	Number	Total	Hotels, motels and other lodging places	Health services	Legal services	Paid employees	Annual payroll (Mil dol)	Total (Mil dol)	Percent change, 1988–1989	Total (Mil dol)	Percent change, 1988–1989
	161	162	163	164	165	166	167	168	169	170	171	172	173
IDAHO—Con.													
Franklin	335	2.6	33	5.4	D	1.4	0.5	151	1.1	47	4.1	0.0	NA
Fremont	277	2.2	35	5.0	1.1	1.1	D	132	1.5	53	2.1	0.0	NA
Gem	355	3.3	41	6.3	D	4.1	0.4	218	1.9	81	4.1	6.5	-20.3
Gooding	390	3.3	46	7.2	D	3.4	0.3	318	2.6	79	3.8	9.7	3.5
Idaho	474	3.8	82	8.9	1.6	2.8	0.3	260	2.2	109	1.2	8.5	-3.5
Jefferson	395	3.0	34	6.9	0.0	1.9	D	181	3.0	65	7.7	0.0	NA
Jerome	546	4.8	61	8.5	0.3	3.4	1.0	230	2.5	89	8.1	8.2	-16.1
Kootenai	4 099	39.5	503	118.6	23.3	39.8	9.9	3 521	43.1	340	5.9	124.1	1.2
Latah	2 175	18.1	166	32.7	D	11.4	1.3	1 035	11.1	203	2.4	19.0	-6.8
Lemhi	369	3.0	52	6.6	2.0	2.3	0.2	221	2.0	54	5.8	10.7	1.5
Lewis	128	0.8	14	D	D	D	0.2	D	D	38	1.9	0.0	NA
Lincoln	64	0.4	7	D	0.0	0.8	0.0	D	D	18	8.0	0.0	NA
Madison	1 140	9.4	89	18.6	D	7.0	1.9	466	6.2	126	7.2	11.1	-27.0
Minidoka	723	6.1	77	11.2	D	2.9	1.3	302	3.0	90	4.1	10.2	-1.4
Nez Perce	3 067	28.9	297	77.4	2.8	36.6	6.6	1 980	27.9	265	2.3	59.1	-2.9
Oneida	126	0.9	12	D	D	0.5	D	D	D	29	2.2	0.0	NA
Owyhee	162	1.5	17	D	D	D	D	D	D	39	4.7	0.0	NA
Payette	343	3.2	64	8.5	D	3.6	0.7	294	2.6	89	5.2	15.1	-7.3
Power	246	1.9	27	3.0	0.3	0.8	D	85	0.6	42	-2.1	0.0	NA
Shoshone	661	6.1	74	11.2	1.4	3.7	1.2	355	4.0	118	5.0	11.8	7.8
Teton	143	1.2	13	D	D	0.4	0.0	D	D	16	3.7	0.0	NA
Twin Falls	4 268	41.4	439	121.4	7.4	51.8	11.2	3 105	47.4	405	8.3	164.6	-4.9
Valley	512	3.7	60	8.4	3.5	2.3	0.8	263	2.5	43	7.1	6.7	-3.4
Washington	275	1.7	40	6.5	0.2	2.5	1.0	190	2.1	80	1.7	0.0	NA
ILLINOIS	820 197	8 078.4	70 738	36 499.6	1 695.4	7 270.4	3 771.9	729 655	13 682.5	122 872	6.8	55 198.0	-3.0
Adams	5 284	44.6	393	103.8	5.9	34.0	6.6	2 755	39.0	598	1.4	407.7	-8.0
Alexander	508	4.0	34	4.9	D	1.0	0.7	163	1.7	57	1.3	0.0	NA
Bond	631	4.8	64	8.3	1.1	2.3	0.5	217	2.6	119	3.9	24.7	-12.1
Boone	1 795	16.3	110	28.3	D	14.7	1.8	923	9.9	171	1.2	74.2	-4.6
Brown	157	1.2	29	2.6	D	0.5	0.6	70	0.6	62	1.8	6.3	-12.3
Bureau	1 841	14.6	164	36.5	D	16.3	2.7	964	13.9	477	5.1	91.1	-5.3
Calhoun	211	1.6	15	2.9	D	D	D	118	1.0	70	5.6	0.0	NA
Carroll	797	5.0	72	11.3	0.7	4.6	0.7	356	3.3	241	3.9	7.3	0.5
Cass	525	4.3	56	7.7	D	4.2	D	257	2.4	153	13.0	24.3	0.2
Champaign	15 749	130.6	958	416.7	33.7	156.5	26.3	10 195	165.6	1 342	5.4	496.1	-0.9
Christian	1 969	16.9	141	26.9	D	14.3	1.9	818	9.6	356	5.3	124.5	-3.8
Clark	790	5.9	70	8.4	0.6	3.1	0.9	207	1.8	172	0.8	25.5	18.5
Clay	619	4.6	60	9.1	D	3.1	1.1	259	3.0	163	2.5	20.2	-25.1
Clinton	1 460	12.9	127	37.6	D	22.1	1.3	1 008	14.5	358	3.0	43.1	-17.0
Coles	4 140	33.5	268	71.7	4.7	32.6	7.3	1 986	24.9	395	2.2	251.2	-1.6
Cook	370 039	3 843.4	35 276	22 831.1	1 079.0	3 606.0	3 020.6	425 041	8 690.9	72 219	8.4	32 369.1	-3.1
Crawford	964	9.0	97	21.2	D	8.3	1.7	655	8.0	259	-1.2	48.3	-9.2
Cumberland	321	2.4	27	3.7	D	2.1	D	129	1.3	79	0.8	0.0	NA
De Kalb	5 360	44.8	350	78.7	3.5	38.3	4.2	2 275	26.8	691	8.7	216.9	-9.7
De Witt	938	8.1	61	18.7	D	4.7	1.3	410	5.2	128	0.9	57.8	-1.4
Douglas	1 168	9.3	91	17.3	1.1	7.6	0.8	548	5.2	160	-0.8	56.8	2.2
Du Page	77 553	828.0	6 753	4 228.9	200.1	616.2	104.0	77 449	1 472.7	6 384	9.7	4 305.5	1.5
Edgar	1 118	10.5	72	14.2	D	4.7	1.9	363	4.4	182	3.1	99.8	-3.3
Edwards	305	2.7	34	5.2	D	3.2	0.3	193	1.6	86	11.8	27.9	3.2
Effingham	3 178	30.1	176	69.3	15.7	17.1	2.7	1 867	26.0	380	10.4	139.6	-4.0
Fayette	845	7.0	85	13.5	1.8	4.2	1.6	492	5.3	159	1.5	37.1	17.6
Ford	808	6.5	69	16.1	D	6.4	0.9	505	5.0	166	-1.0	100.6	2.8
Franklin	2 237	19.5	181	33.0	D	12.4	2.9	921	11.7	432	2.4	8.6	-80.6
Fulton	2 074	17.7	148	29.1	0.2	16.1	2.8	1 042	10.7	327	2.3	119.3	-6.7
Gallatin	192	1.4	13	3.0	D	2.4	D	161	1.2	69	5.2	0.0	NA
Greene	547	4.4	59	7.2	D	3.5	0.9	263	2.3	179	2.3	2.6	7.9
Grundy	1 822	16.4	162	42.1	2.8	9.0	3.9	936	17.5	300	8.2	94.8	1.6
Hamilton	256	2.4	24	3.2	0.0	1.9	0.6	95	1.1	108	4.3	0.0	NA
Hancock	692	5.4	68	11.7	0.3	6.2	1.3	352	3.8	191	-10.7	39.4	4.9
Hardin	79	0.7	18	1.9	D	1.4	D	61	0.8	31	8.7	0.0	NA
Henderson	225	1.5	17	1.4	0.0	0.4	D	41	0.4	91	1.5	4.8	-6.1
Henry	3 141	27.2	209	33.4	3.1	12.9	3.5	950	10.2	502	6.8	181.2	-2.9
Iroquois	1 483	12.8	110	18.5	D	7.9	1.2	451	6.0	313	1.5	133.8	-14.8
Jackson	5 636	47.0	313	91.6	4.6	39.7	7.7	2 628	36.5	373	-1.0	125.0	-5.2
Jasper	360	3.7	30	5.8	0.0	0.8	0.3	134	1.7	142	1.7	11.6	7.0

1. For the period including March 12 of the year shown. 2. Includes deposits for all insured and reporting noninsured commercial and mutual savings banks. 3. Includes savings capital for all FSLIC insured savings institutions.

STATE County	Federal funds and grants, 1989: Expenditures: Total (Mil dol)	Expenditures: Percent change, 1988–1989	Per capita[1] (Dollars): Total	Per capita: Direct payments for individuals	Per capita: Procurement contract awards	Per capita: Salaries and wages	Per capita: Grant awards	Local government finances, 1981–1982: General revenue: Total (Mil dol)	Intergovernmental: Total (Mil dol)	Intergovernmental: Percent from state	Taxes: Total (Mil dol)	Taxes: Per capita[2]: Total (Dollars)	Taxes: Per capita[2]: Property (Dollars)	Direct general expenditure: Total (Mil dol)	Direct general expenditure: Percent change, 1977–1982
	174	175	176	177	178	179	180	181	182	183	184	185	186	187	188
IDAHO—Con.															
Franklin	19.4	-5.0	2 113	1 416	13	153	130	6.8	4.2	88.6	1.6	172	170	6.5	38.6
Fremont	28.5	9.3	2 743	1 458	388	511	177	8.5	5.2	93.1	2.3	208	204	8.1	60.8
Gem	30.3	7.3	2 758	2 139	32	237	243	8.0	3.8	92.6	1.4	122	118	7.7	50.9
Gooding	29.2	0.5	2 563	1 895	35	187	281	10.4	5.0	90.7	2.3	185	179	10.0	69.0
Idaho	47.4	6.2	3 482	1 662	362	778	460	13.2	8.8	84.0	1.8	119	115	13.5	74.9
Jefferson	26.3	-22.5	1 544	1 121	39	114	108	10.3	6.9	92.2	2.3	146	143	10.2	57.2
Jerome	30.1	-52.6	2 079	1 616	11	108	210	12.3	6.7	78.8	3.1	202	173	12.3	74.7
Kootenai	203.5	3.9	3 006	1 897	91	245	754	65.5	23.8	90.8	17.6	282	270	61.4	85.2
Latah	76.2	-35.2	2 474	1 379	105	261	593	21.0	9.7	78.6	7.3	242	230	21.5	92.6
Lemhi	23.6	12.0	3 526	2 204	19	750	400	6.5	3.2	87.0	1.3	163	160	6.2	60.6
Lewis	19.8	-15.3	5 489	2 650	21	308	1 625	4.7	2.6	94.2	1.4	351	348	4.5	36.3
Lincoln	10.5	-9.3	3 270	1 718	48	640	165	3.0	2.0	86.1	0.7	187	182	2.9	66.8
Madison	26.6	4.3	1 145	816	7	85	147	19.1	8.8	63.0	4.2	200	197	19.8	49.2
Minidoka	35.4	-20.4	1 769	1 360	20	128	150	18.1	6.9	91.8	3.7	182	175	17.6	49.3
Nez Perce	97.5	1.9	2 886	2 006	146	261	373	32.8	12.1	76.5	10.5	319	312	31.6	75.1
Oneida	16.9	10.1	4 685	1 852	12	216	780	4.0	1.7	86.4	1.1	328	325	4.5	83.0
Owyhee	21.2	3.7	2 436	1 289	244	253	343	9.0	5.3	78.1	1.8	216	213	7.5	33.9
Payette	36.5	-1.3	2 251	1 764	33	94	289	9.7	5.7	89.4	2.9	181	174	9.2	52.3
Power	22.6	-15.8	3 316	1 159	12	118	617	13.1	4.2	73.2	3.7	549	543	11.8	119.0
Shoshone	46.9	-24.1	3 327	2 313	142	224	643	21.5	8.0	91.1	7.5	390	386	23.1	69.5
Teton	11.5	19.5	3 588	1 470	29	287	1 120	2.6	1.5	90.4	0.5	157	153	2.7	69.7
Twin Falls	126.0	-18.8	2 234	1 672	46	219	216	68.7	25.8	81.8	12.1	221	214	64.1	66.4
Valley	20.8	18.0	3 020	1 808	194	878	124	7.7	3.7	76.5	2.7	417	371	7.6	91.7
Washington	25.8	-5.2	3 186	2 344	51	170	385	10.5	4.7	71.7	2.5	288	281	9.3	71.9
ILLINOIS	34 543.3	6.8	X	1 776	214	385	439	13 691.3	4 965.5	71.9	6 267.5	546	414	12 431.0	44.2
Adams	183.6	-1.5	2 736	2 069	82	182	256	65.1	28.5	71.8	21.4	299	245	65.7	-11.8
Alexander	37.4	-4.0	3 254	2 328	31	157	671	11.2	6.9	90.1	2.5	205	147	11.8	48.3
Bond	45.8	4.0	2 826	1 806	72	118	540	11.5	4.9	93.9	4.7	290	251	10.5	42.3
Boone	56.1	0.8	1 839	1 274	19	75	52	25.0	8.2	94.3	11.8	407	358	20.8	60.0
Brown	20.1	-13.0	4 023	2 085	628	162	290	4.9	2.2	81.8	2.1	396	346	4.4	43.2
Bureau	114.8	3.0	3 137	1 940	27	139	86	46.6	12.5	83.3	18.4	480	429	47.7	66.2
Calhoun	48.0	89.1	8 564	2 141	5 796	169	161	4.5	2.2	90.7	1.6	283	254	4.0	-48.7
Carroll	82.0	9.7	4 713	2 197	283	1 038	136	17.3	6.0	92.2	7.8	422	383	16.9	58.0
Cass	40.2	2.9	2 911	2 053	27	189	107	14.8	4.5	92.9	4.6	313	273	14.9	79.0
Champaign	597.3	-0.2	3 454	1 240	355	915	769	183.3	51.3	73.8	73.1	425	347	174.8	60.1
Christian	105.7	-1.1	2 977	2 240	15	112	148	32.4	11.9	79.8	15.4	427	362	30.6	44.9
Clark	49.3	9.5	3 026	2 045	203	124	164	12.6	5.9	92.4	4.5	264	221	12.7	53.0
Clay	41.6	2.5	2 808	2 058	39	149	188	15.3	5.7	88.6	5.4	345	284	15.6	26.7
Clinton	66.9	3.5	1 938	1 500	39	112	110	19.9	8.6	89.6	8.6	259	224	18.2	57.6
Coles	136.0	17.2	2 601	1 666	475	106	130	49.6	17.7	81.0	20.8	398	331	46.4	58.0
Cook	14 872.6	1.2	2 812	1 739	222	395	413	7 374.8	2 920.6	62.6	3 421.6	650	437	6 525.1	42.1
Crawford	53.7	-3.4	2 697	2 143	16	111	107	20.9	8.2	66.0	7.7	364	308	20.5	64.4
Cumberland	25.9	-9.3	2 380	1 614	14	107	149	9.6	4.6	92.5	3.6	326	298	9.3	57.2
De Kalb	133.2	-5.6	1 733	1 250	-7	102	117	69.5	19.3	82.6	34.0	454	386	65.5	59.0
De Witt	49.1	1.4	2 807	1 900	15	120	249	25.1	4.0	89.5	13.5	752	704	20.4	75.5
Douglas	47.2	-1.7	2 396	1 504	22	124	94	20.1	4.5	91.2	10.0	510	442	18.0	49.7
Du Page	1 165.0	2.1	1 498	1 141	71	214	64	792.0	153.0	84.8	452.3	662	573	691.4	53.6
Edgar	59.3	-5.7	2 905	1 974	20	154	135	17.5	6.1	87.7	9.1	423	368	16.9	39.4
Edwards	18.9	2.6	2 429	1 718	49	121	92	4.5	2.1	96.5	1.7	213	177	4.6	50.2
Effingham	75.1	-0.7	2 276	1 546	165	193	146	24.4	9.0	89.0	11.1	357	279	23.3	54.4
Fayette	53.3	1.3	2 435	1 754	27	114	113	21.4	7.2	89.4	6.7	303	258	18.7	35.9
Ford	60.8	0.0	4 135	2 324	8	145	203	15.7	5.0	93.3	8.2	542	489	13.8	20.1
Franklin	149.0	19.8	3 564	2 557	511	170	234	42.1	17.0	93.0	11.9	276	225	39.0	42.6
Fulton	114.3	3.6	2 985	2 350	84	134	102	45.7	18.0	83.3	19.9	467	421	42.4	30.9
Gallatin	23.6	-9.1	3 324	2 174	33	144	253	6.3	2.9	84.7	2.4	314	261	7.0	62.7
Greene	45.5	-1.1	2 844	2 048	18	139	179	12.7	6.0	81.0	4.7	289	253	12.8	41.4
Grundy	76.0	9.3	2 304	1 533	143	130	52	36.6	7.0	86.9	23.3	764	711	33.8	50.3
Hamilton	29.9	-2.3	3 400	2 378	19	157	279	11.3	3.4	90.9	2.8	308	271	10.5	50.3
Hancock	66.5	-0.4	2 930	1 930	21	158	109	19.1	7.8	93.6	8.7	367	334	18.1	33.3
Hardin	14.7	3.9	2 770	2 182	16	179	300	5.0	3.0	88.3	0.9	160	138	4.4	70.4
Henderson	29.6	-11.0	3 321	1 601	31	155	116	6.3	2.4	81.7	2.9	323	295	6.6	58.0
Henry	137.1	-3.1	2 602	1 749	24	135	74	58.2	16.2	94.0	20.7	376	322	54.1	72.3
Iroquois	113.6	2.9	3 605	2 032	93	146	77	30.0	8.8	90.1	17.5	532	488	30.8	47.6
Jackson	141.7	4.4	2 393	1 656	65	267	343	55.6	26.2	65.4	16.0	257	186	52.1	50.8
Jasper	28.9	-4.9	2 553	1 652	18	126	144	10.3	3.1	92.7	5.7	496	454	9.0	63.5

1. Based on the estimated population as of July 1 of the year shown. 2. Based on the estimated population as of July 1, 1982.

STATE County	Local government finances, 1981–1982 (cont'd)								State and local government employment, 1989		Federal government civilian employment 1989		Elections, 1988[3]	
	Direct general expenditure (cont'd)						Debt outstanding							
	Per capita[1] (Dollars)	Percent of total for– Education	Health & hospitals	Police protection	Public welfare	Highways	Total (Mil dol)	Per capita[1] (Dollars)	Total	Rate[2]	Total	Earnings ($1,000)	Total vote cast for president	Vote for lead party (Percent)
	189	190	191	192	193	194	195	196	197	198	199	200	201	202
IDAHO—Con.														
Franklin	690	60.8	1.9	4.4	0.4	14.0	1.0	111	523	568.5	41	1 061	3 871	R–77.3
Fremont	742	58.3	7.8	4.8	0.8	11.5	2.8	258	657	631.7	236	5 959	4 652	R–73.1
Gem	658	48.7	20.4	4.8	0.4	8.8	1.3	115	507	460.9	84	2 407	5 142	R–56.9
Gooding	809	43.0	12.4	4.2	0.3	10.4	2.3	187	720	631.6	67	1 897	4 876	R–59.6
Idaho	915	42.3	10.1	3.9	3.6	22.4	2.1	141	721	530.1	625	13 834	5 871	R–60.3
Jefferson	654	70.1	0.6	3.7	0.5	9.0	1.2	79	876	515.3	66	1 595	6 649	R–79.6
Jerome	791	42.4	0.4	4.6	0.2	9.2	4.2	272	617	425.5	51	1 309	5 955	R–64.3
Kootenai	985	47.8	24.4	3.9	0.2	5.5	31.0	497	4 255	628.5	545	14 863	27 130	R–55.6
Latah	713	54.3	0.4	4.8	3.1	13.0	7.3	241	5 089	1 652.3	297	7 893	13 136	D–49.8
Lemhi	777	46.8	22.6	3.4	0.4	12.3	3.2	399	429	640.3	272	6 090	3 590	R–66.2
Lewis	1 108	62.2	1.2	6.3	0.3	15.4	0.7	168	293	813.9	50	1 193	1 612	D–50.1
Lincoln	806	58.9	0.4	5.0	0.6	10.9	0.6	168	363	1 134.4	102	2 723	1 525	R–60.2
Madison	951	36.1	19.7	4.0	0.0	8.2	5.3	254	1 070	461.2	51	1 388	7 302	R–84.9
Minidoka	869	46.8	17.1	3.8	1.2	6.1	13.6	673	1 117	558.5	85	2 500	7 033	R–65.7
Nez Perce	958	36.9	0.0	5.7	0.6	7.8	82.2	2 491	2 230	659.8	258	7 960	15 020	D–51.6
Oneida	1 352	43.2	17.8	2.1	0.1	11.8	3.5	1 052	268	744.4	37	955	1 810	R–70.1
Owyhee	887	56.2	0.0	3.2	0.6	12.2	6.7	790	402	462.1	86	2 194	2 634	R–64.8
Payette	577	63.5	0.0	6.7	0.4	7.4	3.1	192	723	446.3	39	1 131	5 809	R–65.2
Power	1 742	31.2	18.7	4.9	0.2	15.2	19.5	2 865	488	717.6	29	718	2 981	R–61.7
Shoshone	1 204	46.5	14.9	4.4	0.8	12.4	5.1	267	968	686.5	207	4 184	5 586	D–60.5
Teton	872	52.4	12.3	3.3	0.6	14.9	0.4	132	211	659.4	45	967	1 527	R–64.3
Twin Falls	1 173	42.5	26.7	3.3	0.1	6.1	84.4	1 545	3 240	574.5	381	11 484	20 734	R–63.9
Valley	1 171	34.9	6.8	5.9	0.6	13.6	3.7	572	567	821.7	310	7 979	3 195	R–59.4
Washington	1 072	43.2	13.8	4.1	0.5	9.6	3.7	425	494	609.9	63	1 480	3 840	R–62.0
ILLINOIS	1 083	45.0	5.3	6.9	1.4	6.0	9 848.3	858	638 206	547.4	110 975	3 588 568	4 559 120	R–50.7
Adams	917	41.2	1.3	4.3	0.2	13.3	65.8	918	3 404	507.3	307	9 369	29 710	R–53.3
Alexander	979	52.0	0.9	5.6	5.8	12.1	3.4	281	591	513.9	51	1 204	4 663	D–57.8
Bond	646	46.5	4.8	4.6	0.2	11.0	7.4	454	298	184.0	61	1 425	7 105	R–50.8
Boone	721	53.0	0.1	5.5	4.9	11.2	4.0	137	1 119	366.9	74	1 948	11 222	R–61.7
Brown	811	48.3	4.2	4.7	0.3	19.6	2.1	380	260	520.0	26	637	2 646	R–51.9
Bureau	1 242	36.2	31.2	2.7	3.6	10.7	24.7	644	2 160	590.2	158	4 130	16 351	R–54.4
Calhoun	705	54.3	3.3	4.1	0.1	16.3	1.1	201	235	419.6	30	665	2 790	D–55.3
Carroll	914	52.9	8.3	3.4	0.1	8.8	5.2	284	794	456.3	646	18 143	7 512	R–59.4
Cass	1 016	40.7	25.9	2.3	0.5	10.1	4.3	292	641	464.5	77	2 121	6 267	D–52.9
Champaign	1 015	43.0	13.7	4.6	2.7	7.4	100.8	586	29 229	1 690.5	2 923	78 957	63 499	R–52.4
Christian	851	48.0	0.8	4.4	0.5	18.1	21.0	582	1 403	395.2	112	2 941	15 436	D–53.7
Clark	744	56.6	1.5	4.3	0.3	17.4	9.3	545	526	322.7	67	1 658	7 811	R–57.7
Clay	1 000	48.8	14.4	3.5	0.5	12.9	7.7	497	750	506.8	70	1 793	6 279	R–55.6
Clinton	550	59.9	1.1	3.5	0.1	13.2	9.7	293	1 813	525.5	122	3 064	13 680	R–56.1
Coles	887	54.9	1.2	5.9	0.4	9.0	21.9	418	5 460	1 044.0	143	4 199	19 504	R–56.6
Cook	1 240	39.5	5.1	8.7	1.1	3.9	5 512.8	1 048	277 535	524.8	58 751	1 971 796	2 026 144	D–55.8
Crawford	978	42.0	26.5	4.0	0.3	10.4	2.8	135	1 090	547.7	66	1 710	8 571	R–57.8
Cumberland	857	49.1	0.5	3.1	0.5	19.8	3.5	321	418	383.5	36	851	4 600	R–58.0
De Kalb	877	49.1	7.3	5.6	4.7	9.0	44.7	598	10 289	1 338.0	206	5 926	29 190	R–58.9
De Witt	1 140	40.2	19.6	4.8	4.1	12.7	7.4	414	967	552.6	56	1 497	6 645	R–59.3
Douglas	917	48.2	12.2	4.5	0.4	15.9	4.3	219	812	412.2	73	1 948	7 598	R–57.6
Du Page	1 012	51.5	3.0	5.5	1.9	6.1	628.6	920	30 636	394.0	2 959	95 976	314 054	R–69.4
Edgar	784	50.0	0.8	3.8	0.6	19.1	10.7	494	1 195	585.8	80	1 972	9 459	R–58.5
Edwards	581	58.9	2.6	5.7	0.1	16.5	0.6	69	249	319.2	36	810	3 450	R–64.1
Effingham	752	49.7	1.8	6.5	0.6	16.9	8.7	280	1 263	382.7	186	5 422	13 066	R–64.5
Fayette	843	45.5	29.8	2.7	0.1	10.1	3.8	169	1 356	619.2	76	1 938	10 118	R–53.9
Ford	908	49.2	1.2	4.7	0.4	17.7	6.0	392	702	477.6	69	1 752	6 145	R–66.1
Franklin	902	48.6	16.2	4.7	2.1	7.6	32.5	751	1 992	476.6	186	5 166	18 783	D–58.7
Fulton	996	55.6	2.7	4.2	1.9	10.8	29.1	684	2 080	543.1	127	3 390	16 108	D–56.2
Gallatin	918	47.0	0.5	4.0	1.6	9.9	5.8	766	331	466.2	37	799	4 063	D–60.4
Greene	778	49.1	5.3	4.1	3.5	10.6	7.4	451	1 020	637.5	66	1 649	6 203	R–50.6
Grundy	1 107	59.6	1.1	4.8	4.4	12.8	16.6	543	1 495	453.0	119	3 314	14 361	R–60.9
Hamilton	1 138	38.2	36.7	2.4	0.6	12.1	4.4	482	516	586.4	55	1 189	5 256	R–49.9
Hancock	765	59.9	0.4	2.1	1.7	20.0	4.9	205	1 143	503.5	103	2 340	9 378	D–50.5
Hardin	816	61.2	0.2	4.4	4.3	7.5	2.9	539	235	443.4	37	727	2 824	R–53.3
Henderson	731	49.4	1.6	4.2	0.4	22.7	1.8	193	275	309.0	48	1 076	3 821	D–54.6
Henry	984	42.0	9.2	2.8	1.9	10.9	27.6	502	2 736	519.2	187	4 946	23 048	D–50.3
Iroquois	937	54.9	3.2	4.1	0.1	20.0	10.1	307	1 344	426.7	131	3 341	13 886	R–69.1
Jackson	835	40.2	3.6	5.1	3.9	9.0	78.9	1 265	12 667	2 139.7	435	13 173	21 185	D–53.5
Jasper	784	59.5	0.0	2.5	1.0	24.0	1.3	110	533	471.7	50	1 171	5 189	R–58.3

1. Based on the estimated population as of July 1, 1982. 2. Per 10,000 resident population estimated as of July 1 of the year shown. 3. Data subject to copyright.

STATE–County code	MSA/CMSA/NECMA code[1]	STATE County	Land Area,[2] 1990 (Sq. Km.)	Population, 1990: Total persons	Rank	Per square kilometer	Race: White	Black	Am. Indian, Eskimo, Aleut	Asian & Pacific Islander	Other race	Hispanic[3]	Age of population Percent: Under 5 years	5 to 14 years	15 to 24 years
			1	2	3	4	5	6	7	8	9	10	11	12	13
		ILLINOIS—Con.													
17 081	...	Jefferson	1 479	37 020	1 071	25.0	34 856	1 924	56	129	55	157	7.4	15.3	12.6
17 083	7040	Jersey	956	20 539	1 653	21.5	20 346	96	43	32	22	103	6.9	15.4	15.3
17 085	...	Jo Daviess	1 557	21 821	1 588	14.0	21 732	14	20	29	26	94	6.4	15.2	12.5
17 087	...	Johnson	896	11 347	2 268	12.7	10 230	1 046	26	14	31	189	4.8	11.4	13.8
17 089	1602	Kane	1 349	317 471	159	235.3	269 675	19 006	620	4 474	23 696	43 535	8.8	16.6	14.4
17 091	3740	Kankakee	1 755	96 255	480	54.8	80 194	14 399	150	644	868	1 946	7.6	15.9	14.5
17 093	1602	Kendall	830	39 413	1 014	47.5	38 019	210	73	224	887	1 805	7.7	17.3	14.1
17 095	...	Knox	1 855	56 393	771	30.4	52 413	2 860	85	320	715	1 416	6.0	13.8	13.5
17 097	1602	Lake	1 160	516 418	90	445.2	450 666	34 771	1 198	12 588	17 195	38 570	8.5	15.1	14.9
17 099	...	La Salle	2 940	106 913	431	36.4	103 805	1 153	206	523	1 226	3 249	6.8	14.6	12.9
17 101	...	Lawrence	963	15 972	1 925	16.6	15 759	151	31	21	10	56	6.0	14.0	11.4
17 103	...	Lee	1 879	34 392	1 152	18.3	32 530	1 222	84	181	375	727	6.9	14.9	12.6
17 105	...	Livingston	2 703	39 301	1 017	14.5	36 551	2 115	62	131	442	826	6.6	14.2	12.8
17 107	...	Logan	1 601	30 798	1 249	19.2	29 223	1 291	37	143	104	348	6.4	13.7	13.9
17 109	...	McDonough	1 526	35 244	1 123	23.1	32 992	1 254	65	802	131	358	5.0	10.4	31.5
17 111	1602	McHenry	1 565	183 241	262	117.1	178 895	310	299	1 293	2 444	6 066	8.6	16.3	12.5
17 113	1040	McLean	3 066	129 180	358	42.1	121 057	5 563	203	1 624	733	1 671	6.6	13.0	24.1
17 115	2040	Macon	1 504	117 206	394	77.9	102 197	14 135	157	506	211	540	6.8	14.8	13.6
17 117	...	Macoupin	2 237	47 679	880	21.3	47 077	379	94	88	41	184	6.4	15.1	13.0
17 119	7040	Madison	1 878	249 238	200	132.7	230 217	16 136	683	1 420	782	2 713	7.2	14.3	13.8
17 121	...	Marion	1 482	41 561	969	28.0	39 647	1 519	106	232	57	232	7.0	15.2	12.7
17 123	...	Marshall	1 000	12 846	2 152	12.8	12 752	17	30	28	19	79	5.9	14.7	12.5
17 125	...	Mason	1 396	16 269	1 906	11.7	16 180	8	27	38	16	58	6.6	14.9	12.5
17 127	...	Massac	619	14 752	2 003	23.8	13 804	870	37	31	10	44	5.8	13.7	12.3
17 129	7880	Menard	814	11 164	2 280	13.7	11 101	9	29	14	11	37	6.9	16.1	11.5
17 131	...	Mercer	1 453	17 290	1 835	11.9	17 155	30	33	35	37	109	6.6	15.5	12.4
17 133	7040	Monroe	1 006	22 422	1 558	22.3	22 262	13	53	57	37	166	7.3	15.5	12.3
17 135	...	Montgomery	1 823	30 728	1 255	16.9	29 956	559	49	66	98	235	6.6	14.8	12.3
17 137	...	Morgan	1 473	36 397	1 093	24.7	34 561	1 510	48	130	148	286	6.3	14.1	15.0
17 139	...	Moultrie	869	13 930	2 064	16.0	13 884	8	22	13	3	38	6.9	15.0	11.6
17 141	...	Ogle	1 966	45 957	904	23.4	44 895	66	87	136	773	1 379	7.3	15.8	12.6
17 143	6120	Peoria	1 605	182 827	263	113.9	154 298	24 892	312	2 225	1 100	2 596	7.0	14.7	15.1
17 145	...	Perry	1 142	21 412	1 609	18.7	20 901	399	26	63	23	120	6.8	15.1	13.0
17 147	...	Piatt	1 140	15 548	1 950	13.6	15 508	8	16	11	5	35	6.2	15.2	11.6
17 149	...	Pike	2 151	17 577	1 816	8.2	17 499	8	24	32	14	69	6.4	14.5	11.8
17 151	...	Pope	961	4 373	2 887	4.6	4 072	266	15	6	14	57	5.1	12.6	17.7
17 153	...	Pulaski	520	7 523	2 615	14.5	5 032	2 466	8	7	10	29	7.2	17.2	12.2
17 155	...	Putnam	414	5 730	2 785	13.8	5 616	9	7	7	91	138	6.9	14.9	12.3
17 157	...	Randolph	1 498	34 583	1 147	23.1	31 532	2 852	54	83	62	345	6.1	14.2	13.8
17 159	...	Richland	933	16 545	1 886	17.7	16 442	17	24	43	19	74	6.8	15.1	12.1
17 161	1960	Rock Island	1 105	148 723	318	134.6	133 428	10 488	354	1 017	3 436	8 084	6.9	14.5	13.7
17 163	7040	St. Clair	1 719	262 852	190	152.9	187 866	71 275	585	2 007	1 119	3 861	8.0	15.9	14.5
17 165	...	Saline	993	26 551	1 407	26.7	25 452	931	66	40	62	135	6.1	13.4	12.8
17 167	7880	Sangamon	2 249	178 386	273	79.3	162 013	14 364	290	1 377	342	1 274	7.2	14.5	12.5
17 169	...	Schuyler	1 133	7 498	2 617	6.6	7 479	2	9	6	2	7	6.0	14.4	12.1
17 171	...	Scott	650	5 644	2 790	8.7	5 634	1	6	3	0	15	6.5	15.3	12.1
17 173	...	Shelby	1 965	22 261	1 564	11.3	22 190	14	27	27	3	45	6.8	14.7	12.4
17 175	...	Stark	746	6 534	2 705	8.8	6 496	8	8	21	1	30	6.2	15.1	11.5
17 177	...	Stephenson	1 461	48 052	870	32.9	44 524	3 081	58	304	85	283	7.1	14.6	12.8
17 179	6120	Tazewell	1 681	123 692	372	73.6	122 639	186	221	432	214	825	6.8	15.1	13.2
17 181	...	Union	1 078	17 619	1 811	16.3	17 313	122	34	53	97	182	6.1	12.9	12.3
17 183	...	Vermilion	2 329	88 257	516	37.9	78 956	7 841	165	507	788	1 405	6.7	14.8	12.8
17 185	...	Wabash	579	13 111	2 132	22.6	12 955	40	11	80	25	73	6.5	15.4	13.3
17 187	...	Warren	1 405	19 181	1 721	13.7	18 630	356	20	70	105	207	6.4	15.3	14.5
17 189	...	Washington	1 457	14 965	1 990	10.3	14 856	46	31	26	6	48	6.7	15.4	11.6
17 191	...	Wayne	1 849	17 241	1 840	9.3	17 141	9	31	44	16	72	6.3	14.1	12.5
17 193	...	White	1 282	16 522	1 890	12.9	16 397	41	37	35	12	58	6.1	13.8	10.8
17 195	...	Whiteside	1 774	60 186	721	33.9	57 135	417	85	187	2 362	4 462	7.0	15.2	13.4
17 197	1602	Will	2 169	357 313	143	164.7	303 420	38 361	692	4 774	10 066	19 973	8.2	16.9	14.7
17 199	...	Williamson	1 099	57 733	753	52.5	56 135	1 147	112	252	87	448	6.4	13.4	13.2
17 201	6880	Winnebago	1 331	252 913	198	190.0	222 439	23 256	651	2 986	3 581	7 771	7.6	14.4	13.8
17 203	6120	Woodford	1 368	32 653	1 197	23.9	32 388	64	54	102	45	221	7.2	16.9	13.2
18 000	...	INDIANA	92 904	5 544 159	X	59.7	5 020 700	432 092	12 720	37 617	41 030	98 788	7.2	14.7	15.2
18 001	...	Adams	879	31 095	1 242	35.4	30 530	36	42	60	427	810	8.7	18.1	14.9
18 003	2760	Allen	1 702	300 836	164	176.8	264 086	30 314	892	2 644	2 900	5 821	7.9	15.5	14.3

1. MSA = Metropolitan Statistical Area. CMSA = Consolidated MSA. NECMA = New England county metropolitan area. PMSA = Primary MSA. See Appendix A for explanation of these concepts. See Appendix B for list of metropolitan areas identified by type, with component counties. 2. Dry land or land partially or temporarily covered by water. 3. Hispanic persons may be of any race.

STATE County	Population, 1990 (cont'd): Age of population (cont'd) Percent: 25 to 34 years	35 to 44 years	45 to 54 years	55 to 64 years	65 to 74 years	75 years and over	Percent female	Population–Change and components of change: Change 1980–1990: Number	Percent	Total persons, 1986	Total persons, 1980	Components of change, 1980–1986: Net change: Number	Percent	Natural increase: Births	Deaths
	14	15	16	17	18	19	20	21	22	23	24	25	26	27	28
ILLINOIS—Con.															
Jefferson	15.0	14.4	10.0	9.0	9.1	7.4	52.0	462	1.3	38 100	36 558	1 600	4.3	3 800	2 500
Jersey	15.3	13.7	10.4	9.2	7.8	6.0	51.1	1	0.0	20 200	20 538	-300	-1.7	1 900	1 200
Jo Daviess	14.2	13.9	10.9	10.3	9.7	7.0	50.7	-1 699	-7.2	23 100	23 520	-400	-1.8	2 000	1 300
Johnson	18.6	15.5	11.2	9.3	8.7	6.8	42.2	1 723	17.9	10 900	9 624	1 300	13.2	700	600
Kane	17.9	16.1	10.0	7.0	5.3	4.0	50.4	39 066	14.0	305 800	278 405	27 400	9.9	33 000	13 400
Kankakee	15.3	14.3	10.1	8.6	7.9	5.8	51.6	-6 671	-6.5	98 000	102 926	-5 000	-4.8	10 300	5 600
Kendall	16.1	16.9	12.1	7.2	5.3	3.4	50.0	2 211	5.9	37 100	37 202	-100	-0.2	3 500	1 300
Knox	14.4	14.7	10.5	10.0	9.2	7.9	51.0	-5 214	-8.5	56 300	61 607	-5 300	-8.6	5 000	4 000
Lake	18.0	16.9	10.8	7.5	5.1	3.3	49.4	76 031	17.3	480 200	440 387	39 800	9.0	46 800	17 200
La Salle	15.1	13.5	10.2	9.7	9.4	7.8	51.1	-5 120	-4.6	108 200	112 033	-3 900	-3.5	9 800	7 200
Lawrence	14.2	13.2	9.8	10.3	10.1	10.8	53.2	-1 835	-10.3	17 500	17 807	-300	-1.7	1 500	1 500
Lee	16.9	14.8	10.1	9.1	8.0	6.7	49.6	-1 936	-5.3	34 700	36 328	-1 700	-4.6	3 300	2 200
Livingston	17.5	14.3	9.8	8.9	8.1	7.7	49.8	-2 080	-5.0	40 200	41 381	-1 200	-3.0	3 800	2 400
Logan	16.7	14.2	10.3	8.8	8.3	7.7	49.9	-1 004	-3.2	31 200	31 802	-600	-1.7	2 700	2 200
McDonough	12.9	11.0	8.1	7.4	7.1	6.6	50.3	-2 223	-5.9	34 800	37 467	-2 700	-7.1	2 700	1 900
McHenry	18.0	17.3	10.9	6.9	5.4	4.0	50.0	35 344	23.9	162 400	147 897	14 500	9.8	15 100	6 900
McLean	16.3	14.0	8.6	6.9	5.7	4.8	52.3	10 031	8.4	122 700	119 149	3 600	3.0	11 000	5 500
Macon	14.8	14.9	10.8	9.6	8.2	6.3	52.3	-14 169	-10.8	126 700	131 375	-4 700	-3.6	11 600	7 300
Macoupin	14.0	13.6	9.8	10.0	9.5	8.5	52.1	-1 705	-3.5	49 100	49 384	-300	-0.6	4 400	3 600
Madison	16.5	14.5	10.4	9.5	7.9	6.0	52.0	1 574	0.6	250 200	247 664	2 600	1.0	22 400	14 500
Marion	14.9	13.6	10.3	9.2	9.0	8.0	52.4	-1 962	-4.5	43 500	43 523	-100	-0.1	4 300	3 200
Marshall	13.0	14.0	10.7	9.7	10.5	9.0	51.8	-1 633	-11.3	13 200	14 479	-1 300	-9.1	1 200	900
Mason	13.9	13.9	11.0	9.7	9.6	7.9	51.3	-3 223	-16.5	17 400	19 492	-2 100	-10.6	1 500	1 100
Massac	14.6	12.8	10.9	10.6	10.3	9.0	53.0	-238	-1.6	14 900	14 990	-100	-0.7	1 200	1 200
Menard	14.9	15.6	11.1	8.9	7.7	7.4	51.9	-536	-4.6	11 700	11 700	0	-0.2	1 100	800
Mercer	14.1	14.5	11.6	9.3	8.8	7.4	51.5	-1 996	-10.3	18 300	19 286	-1 000	-5.2	1 600	1 100
Monroe	16.8	14.4	10.7	9.5	7.2	6.2	50.8	2 305	11.5	21 200	20 117	1 100	5.4	1 800	1 300
Montgomery	15.8	13.6	9.4	9.2	9.6	8.7	50.2	-958	-3.0	31 800	31 686	100	0.5	2 900	2 400
Morgan	15.6	13.8	10.2	9.2	8.3	7.5	51.4	-1 105	-2.9	37 200	37 502	-300	-0.8	3 400	2 500
Moultrie	14.0	13.7	10.3	9.3	9.1	10.1	52.4	-616	-4.2	14 500	14 546	-100	-0.6	1 300	1 000
Ogle	16.0	14.5	10.9	8.9	7.7	6.4	51.0	-381	-0.8	45 300	46 338	-1 000	-2.2	4 200	2 500
Peoria	15.2	14.7	10.2	8.9	7.9	6.3	52.1	-17 639	-8.8	183 400	200 466	-17 100	-8.5	19 400	10 900
Perry	14.4	14.2	10.0	9.4	9.1	7.9	51.9	-302	-1.4	22 000	21 714	300	1.2	1 900	1 600
Piatt	15.2	15.0	11.7	9.7	8.6	6.8	51.3	-1 033	-6.2	16 100	16 581	-500	-2.8	1 400	1 000
Pike	13.2	13.3	9.9	10.2	10.6	10.0	51.9	-1 319	-7.0	18 000	18 896	-900	-4.9	1 600	1 500
Pope	13.6	12.6	10.7	9.4	10.1	8.3	46.5	-31	-0.7	4 400	4 404	0	-0.6	300	300
Pulaski	13.7	11.5	9.7	9.7	9.9	8.9	53.4	-1 317	-14.9	8 500	8 840	-400	-4.4	900	800
Putnam	14.7	14.1	12.2	9.5	9.0	6.4	49.8	-355	-5.8	5 900	6 085	-200	-3.7	600	300
Randolph	17.7	14.6	9.8	8.5	7.9	7.4	46.7	-1 069	-3.0	35 300	35 652	-400	-1.1	3 000	2 300
Richland	15.2	12.7	10.8	9.9	8.9	8.6	52.3	-1 042	-5.9	17 600	17 587	0	0.2	1 700	1 200
Rock Island	15.2	14.6	10.6	9.6	8.5	6.5	51.9	-18 036	-10.8	159 700	166 759	-7 000	-4.2	15 800	9 400
St. Clair	16.8	14.2	9.2	8.8	7.2	5.5	52.2	-4 679	-1.7	269 700	267 531	2 100	0.8	30 000	16 300
Saline	13.5	13.0	10.7	10.1	10.5	9.9	52.8	-1 897	-6.7	28 400	28 448	0	-0.1	2 300	2 700
Sangamon	17.1	16.0	10.3	8.7	7.5	6.3	52.9	2 316	1.3	178 900	176 070	2 900	1.6	17 400	10 300
Schuyler	14.1	13.5	10.3	10.3	10.1	9.2	51.3	-867	-10.4	7 800	8 365	-600	-7.2	600	600
Scott	14.9	13.1	10.5	9.7	8.9	8.9	52.2	-498	-8.1	6 000	6 142	-100	-2.0	500	400
Shelby	14.4	13.2	10.5	10.2	9.8	8.1	50.8	-1 662	-6.9	23 500	23 923	-400	-1.7	2 100	1 500
Stark	13.6	13.5	10.7	10.1	10.2	9.2	52.0	-855	-11.6	6 800	7 389	-600	-7.9	700	500
Stephenson	15.5	14.1	10.7	9.2	8.8	7.1	51.7	-1 484	-3.0	49 400	49 536	-200	-0.3	4 500	2 900
Tazewell	15.2	15.3	11.1	10.0	7.4	5.8	51.5	-8 386	-6.3	124 700	132 078	-7 400	-5.6	12 200	6 100
Union	14.1	14.2	11.5	9.8	9.9	9.0	51.3	-146	-0.8	18 000	17 765	300	1.6	1 400	1 300
Vermilion	15.0	14.4	10.6	9.8	9.1	6.8	51.3	-6 965	-7.3	91 300	95 222	-3 900	-4.1	8 700	6 200
Wabash	15.0	14.2	9.9	9.7	8.9	7.3	52.0	-602	-4.4	13 900	13 713	200	1.5	1 400	1 000
Warren	13.5	13.5	10.2	9.3	9.1	8.2	51.8	-2 762	-12.6	20 500	21 943	-1 400	-6.5	1 900	1 400
Washington	14.9	13.4	10.0	9.3	9.8	8.8	51.3	-507	-3.3	15 200	15 472	-300	-1.6	1 400	1 200
Wayne	14.0	12.6	10.9	10.2	10.2	9.3	51.9	-818	-4.5	18 100	18 059	0	0.2	1 600	1 400
White	14.4	13.2	10.4	10.5	10.7	9.9	52.9	-1 342	-7.5	17 800	17 864	0	-0.2	1 500	1 600
Whiteside	15.0	14.4	10.6	9.7	8.4	6.5	51.3	-5 784	-8.8	62 800	65 970	-3 200	-4.8	5 800	3 500
Will	17.4	16.8	10.5	6.8	5.1	3.5	50.1	32 853	10.1	338 400	324 460	14 000	4.3	33 500	13 200
Williamson	15.3	14.5	11.1	9.2	9.4	7.5	51.9	1 195	2.1	58 000	56 538	1 400	2.6	4 800	4 100
Winnebago	17.0	15.3	10.6	8.8	7.4	5.3	51.5	2 029	0.8	250 900	250 884	100	0.0	24 400	12 800
Woodford	14.1	15.6	10.4	8.6	7.4	6.7	51.1	-667	-2.0	32 300	33 320	-1 000	-3.1	3 100	1 700
INDIANA	16.5	14.8	10.3	8.7	7.3	5.3	51.5	54 159	1.0	5 504 000	5 490 000	13 000	0.2	516 000	297 000
Adams	15.0	13.3	9.2	7.4	7.3	6.2	51.0	1 476	5.0	30 300	29 619	700	2.4	3 600	1 500
Allen	17.5	15.6	9.8	8.1	6.6	4.8	51.5	6 501	2.2	295 300	294 335	1 000	0.3	30 200	14 000

STATE County	Population–(cont'd): Components of change, 1980-1986 (cont'd): Net migration	Households, 1990: Number	Households, 1990: Percent change, 1980–1990	Households, 1990: Persons per household	Households, 1990: Percent: Female family householder[1]	Households, 1990: Percent: One-person	Births, 1988: Total	Births, 1988: Rate[2]	Births, 1988: Low birth weight[3] (Number)	Deaths, 1987: Number: Total	Deaths, 1987: Number: Infant[4]	Deaths, 1987: Rate: Total[2]	Deaths, 1987: Rate: Infant[5]	Marriages, 1984: Number	Marriages, 1984: Rate[2]
	29	30	31	32	33	34	35	36	37	38	39	40	41	42	43
ILLINOIS—Con.															
Jefferson	300	14 606	4.6	2.51	10.1	26.3	545	14.6	33	349	11	9.3	20.4	430	11.3
Jersey	-1 100	7 344	7.7	2.68	8.1	22.0	257	12.5	17	217	3	10.5	10.4	193	9.5
Jo Daviess	-1 200	8 371	0.5	2.59	7.0	23.9	293	12.7	13	221	1	9.6	3.8	195	8.4
Johnson	1 200	3 725	12.8	2.48	6.7	24.1	90	8.0	4	98	1	8.8	9.6	80	7.8
Kane	7 900	107 176	14.3	2.90	9.9	19.9	5 783	18.3	373	2 257	71	7.3	12.9	3 005	10.2
Kankakee	-9 700	34 623	-0.9	2.68	12.5	24.3	1 600	16.3	136	965	16	9.9	10.7	900	9.0
Kendall	-2 300	13 301	10.5	2.94	7.0	16.1	564	14.6	28	219	5	5.8	9.4	285	7.7
Knox	-6 300	21 909	-4.1	2.42	9.6	28.3	673	12.0	52	655	7	11.6	9.8	549	9.4
Lake	10 200	173 966	24.5	2.85	8.7	18.5	8 693	17.6	512	2 971	73	6.1	8.8	4 842	10.6
La Salle	-6 500	41 284	0.8	2.53	8.7	26.4	1 332	12.4	77	1 157	15	10.7	10.8	965	8.8
Lawrence	-300	6 320	-6.4	2.43	9.0	27.4	186	11.0	14	246	3	14.3	14.4	202	11.0
Lee	-2 800	12 475	-1.4	2.59	8.0	25.1	490	14.1	25	345	9	10.0	18.9	353	10.3
Livingston	-2 600	13 737	-2.4	2.58	7.8	24.7	534	13.2	23	364	6	9.1	10.2	373	9.1
Logan	-1 000	11 033	-2.3	2.49	8.6	26.9	384	12.2	17	344	1	10.9	2.4	282	9.0
McDonough	-3 400	12 255	-2.1	2.35	7.5	29.6	349	10.2	19	311	7	9.0	19.3	278	7.7
McHenry	6 300	62 940	28.2	2.89	7.1	16.9	2 838	16.6	155	1 178	21	7.1	7.7	1 527	9.8
McLean	-1 900	46 796	12.2	2.52	8.3	26.1	1 758	14.1	89	912	15	7.4	9.0	1 138	9.3
Macon	-9 000	45 996	-4.8	2.49	11.4	26.4	1 735	14.0	135	1 105	19	8.9	10.9	1 293	10.0
Macoupin	-1 200	18 176	0.0	2.56	8.9	24.3	608	12.4	38	606	8	12.3	13.9	384	7.8
Madison	-5 400	94 857	6.6	2.59	11.2	23.9	3 738	14.8	267	2 375	32	9.5	8.8	2 411	9.7
Marion	-1 200	16 272	-1.0	2.51	10.7	26.7	579	13.4	32	499	3	11.5	4.7	437	9.9
Marshall	-1 600	4 900	-5.4	2.57	6.0	23.6	139	10.5	11	151	2	11.5	13.3	123	8.9
Mason	-2 400	6 342	-12.0	2.54	7.9	24.2	208	12.0	12	189	1	10.8	5.0	136	7.5
Massac	-200	5 908	3.1	2.44	10.2	26.7	150	10.0	13	173	0	11.6	0.0	188	12.6
Menard	-300	4 199	0.0	2.61	8.0	22.0	151	12.9	8	115	0	9.8	0.0	101	8.7
Mercer	-1 500	6 572	-3.2	2.60	6.8	22.8	209	11.5	9	188	1	10.3	5.0	143	7.4
Monroe	500	8 189	16.8	2.70	6.4	21.0	302	13.6	13	197	1	9.0	3.5	188	9.0
Montgomery	-400	11 480	-4.0	2.53	8.0	25.8	390	12.2	18	383	7	12.0	17.2	279	8.7
Morgan	-1 100	13 678	0.4	2.44	8.8	28.6	466	12.5	21	383	2	10.2	4.7	324	8.8
Moultrie	-400	5 122	-0.5	2.61	7.0	23.0	195	13.5	12	195	3	13.5	15.2	120	8.3
Ogle	-2 700	17 132	5.0	2.65	7.1	22.2	625	13.5	34	405	5	8.8	8.0	434	9.5
Peoria	-25 500	70 797	-3.5	2.49	12.3	28.1	2 592	14.2	203	1 700	35	9.3	13.4	1 882	9.8
Perry	0	8 306	2.1	2.54	9.1	25.5	275	12.7	17	245	3	11.1	11.2	197	8.9
Piatt	-800	5 934	-0.1	2.58	6.5	21.7	193	11.9	13	169	0	10.5	0.0	136	8.3
Pike	-1 000	7 016	-4.1	2.47	6.9	26.5	231	12.9	11	248	2	13.9	8.7	148	8.0
Pope	0	1 611	4.0	2.45	7.3	26.3	33	7.7	1	53	0	12.3	0.0	37	8.4
Pulaski	-500	2 957	-10.7	2.52	14.1	29.4	118	13.9	8	123	2	14.5	16.5	65	7.6
Putnam	-500	2 204	2.3	2.60	6.8	22.9	65	11.4	6	54	0	9.3	0.0	50	8.2
Randolph	-1 100	11 949	1.0	2.57	8.3	25.3	393	11.0	22	355	3	10.0	6.5	313	8.8
Richland	-500	6 503	-3.2	2.49	8.1	26.0	217	12.8	17	207	1	12.0	5.5	164	9.0
Rock Island	-13 400	59 317	-2.8	2.44	11.5	28.6	2 064	13.3	115	1 530	22	9.7	10.1	1 526	9.2
St. Clair	-11 600	95 333	4.8	2.71	16.4	24.4	4 584	17.0	394	2 640	44	9.8	9.5	2 191	8.2
Saline	400	10 839	-3.7	2.36	10.0	30.1	319	11.4	14	385	2	13.7	6.2	305	10.7
Sangamon	-4 200	72 146	6.1	2.43	11.3	29.4	2 759	15.3	223	1 650	28	9.2	10.7	1 709	9.6
Schuyler	-600	3 002	-5.7	2.46	7.0	25.1	87	11.2	5	89	0	11.4	0.0	62	7.7
Scott	-200	2 190	-4.9	2.55	8.4	24.3	64	10.5	4	73	1	12.2	14.3	52	8.7
Shelby	-1 000	8 563	-1.7	2.58	6.1	22.7	304	12.9	18	242	2	10.3	6.5	211	8.9
Stark	-700	2 512	-5.3	2.55	6.2	25.3	73	11.1	3	83	0	12.2	0.0	62	8.9
Stephenson	-1 800	18 920	2.6	2.50	8.3	26.0	699	14.2	48	462	9	9.4	14.3	477	9.6
Tazewell	-13 500	47 171	1.7	2.59	8.3	22.8	1 599	12.8	91	1 063	14	8.6	9.0	1 124	8.7
Union	200	6 838	2.9	2.43	8.0	27.0	199	11.1	11	224	1	12.4	4.5	206	11.4
Vermilion	-6 400	34 072	-3.7	2.50	11.2	27.0	1 177	13.0	85	948	10	10.4	8.4	931	10.0
Wabash	-200	5 032	-2.5	2.56	7.9	25.3	169	12.2	8	125	0	9.1	0.0	171	12.1
Warren	-2 000	7 393	-6.3	2.48	8.4	27.5	250	12.4	14	222	1	11.0	4.4	180	8.5
Washington	-400	5 658	0.9	2.59	5.8	25.3	203	13.0	8	183	2	11.9	9.9	120	7.9
Wayne	-200	6 935	-0.6	2.46	7.1	25.4	217	12.2	11	211	2	11.8	9.6	201	10.9
White	0	6 845	-2.9	2.36	7.3	28.0	176	10.2	13	213	3	12.1	13.8	173	9.6
Whiteside	-5 500	22 740	-2.0	2.60	8.3	23.6	809	12.9	44	641	13	10.3	16.4	551	8.6
Will	-6 200	116 933	13.4	2.98	9.9	17.7	5 666	16.3	335	2 261	48	6.6	9.0	2 425	7.3
Williamson	800	23 120	5.9	2.44	9.4	27.5	729	12.5	47	624	6	10.7	8.1	599	10.3
Winnebago	-11 600	96 727	8.2	2.57	10.9	24.5	3 874	15.4	268	2 154	41	8.6	10.6	2 454	9.8
Woodford	-2 400	11 395	3.1	2.78	6.0	19.5	444	13.5	25	292	5	9.0	13.3	257	7.8
INDIANA	-206 000	2 065 355	7.2	2.61	10.5	24.1	81 643	14.7	5 365	48 906	790	8.8	10.1	53 719	9.8
Adams	-1 400	10 470	8.8	2.92	7.6	20.9	535	17.0	26	268	9	8.6	15.9	252	8.4
Allen	-15 200	113 333	8.6	2.61	10.9	24.9	5 063	16.7	327	2 354	46	7.8	9.3	2 741	9.5

1. No spouse present. 2. Per 1,000 resident population estimated as of July 1 of the year shown. 3. Under 2,500 grams. 4. Deaths of infants under 1 year old. 5. Deaths of infants under 1 year old per 1,000 live births.

STATE County	Divorces, 1984 Number	Divorces, 1984 Rate[1]	Physicians, active non–Federal, 1989 Number[2]	Physicians, active non–Federal, 1989 Rate[3]	Hospitals, 1989 Number	Hospitals, 1989 Beds Number	Hospitals, 1989 Beds Rate[3]	Nursing homes,[4] 1986 Number	Nursing homes,[4] 1986 Beds	Serious crimes known to police, 1988 Number Total[5]	Serious crimes known to police, 1988 Number Violent[6]	Serious crimes known to police, 1988 Rate[3]	Education Public school enrollment[7] 1986–1987	Education Public school enrollment[7] 1980	Education Attainment,[8] 1980 Percent 12 yrs. or more	Education Attainment,[8] 1980 Percent 16 yrs. or more
	44	45	46	47	48	49	50	51	52	53	54	55	56	57	58	59
ILLINOIS—Con.																
Jefferson	266	7.0	43	116	2	211	569	4	315	1 794	71	4 787	7 068	7 225	56.3	10.7
Jersey	105	5.2	9	43	1	67	322	4	276	472	12	2 310	2 970	3 967	59.3	8.2
Jo Daviess	69	3.0	10	43	1	89	385	3	120	308	10	1 344	4 494	4 943	64.7	9.9
Johnson	60	5.9	2	18	0	0	0	1	71	28	2	253	1 738	1 895	53.1	7.9
Kane	1 457	5.0	463	143	6	2 091	647	19	2 177	16 938	1 177	5 400	68 619	54 851	70.6	16.7
Kankakee	354	3.5	132	135	2	556	569	11	1 197	5 351	694	5 490	17 609	20 484	61.0	10.6
Kendall	91	2.5	10	26	0	0	0	2	151	835	33	2 234	7 415	8 647	76.9	14.4
Knox	320	5.5	87	155	2	361	645	7	771	2 285	83	4 116	9 723	11 314	68.4	11.1
Lake	2 071	4.5	1 042	206	9	2 987	591	22	3 277	20 754	1 221	4 213	84 057	87 144	77.6	25.1
La Salle	552	5.0	106	99	4	504	471	10	1 158	2 354	97	2 191	16 124	20 129	62.1	8.9
Lawrence	88	4.8	13	78	1	46	277	3	524	263	2	1 543	3 056	3 422	61.9	7.8
Lee	180	5.2	34	97	1	121	346	5	477	733	23	2 113	5 515	7 394	67.8	9.9
Livingston	216	5.3	31	77	2	210	520	8	744	917	26	2 295	6 646	7 814	63.3	10.1
Logan	127	4.1	22	69	2	570	1 798	6	542	961	38	3 081	3 988	5 396	66.4	11.9
McDonough	129	3.6	37	109	1	155	457	6	377	1 224	25	3 591	4 691	5 426	74.4	21.7
McHenry	713	4.6	156	89	3	367	209	7	864	4 301	123	2 604	26 760	31 751	74.9	17.1
McLean	537	4.4	171	136	2	662	528	11	1 103	5 847	277	4 739	18 668	18 675	76.0	22.8
Macon	755	5.9	170	139	3	906	741	10	1 185	7 323	625	5 945	21 608	25 078	68.5	12.9
Macoupin	243	4.9	20	41	2	109	221	10	773	560	29	1 149	9 721	9 559	60.3	7.9
Madison	1 044	4.2	281	111	7	1 450	571	21	2 043	11 336	571	4 523	41 777	46 439	62.8	11.0
Marion	204	4.6	53	123	2	320	742	6	547	1 395	79	3 255	8 293	8 281	56.4	8.8
Marshall	52	3.8	8	61	0	0	0	3	234	63	1	486	2 376	3 182	67.7	9.6
Mason	66	3.6	8	46	1	36	208	1	89	150	4	880	3 602	4 354	60.3	8.3
Massac	127	8.5	7	46	1	57	377	3	273	422	35	2 880	2 618	2 969	53.1	8.4
Menard	33	2.8	5	43	0	0	0	2	182	88	4	761	2 494	2 483	67.0	12.7
Mercer	63	3.3	3	17	1	51	282	2	195	92	6	523	3 847	4 481	67.5	8.6
Monroe	65	3.1	9	40	0	0	0	2	299	316	23	1 461	3 074	3 551	59.8	8.1
Montgomery	153	4.8	23	72	2	238	744	7	658	440	21	1 397	5 282	5 883	58.0	8.1
Morgan	165	4.5	44	118	1	168	450	6	676	1 425	60	3 854	5 837	6 804	67.5	14.1
Moultrie	33	2.3	7	49	0	0	0	5	561	205	13	1 428	1 996	2 709	59.1	9.2
Ogle	188	4.1	20	43	1	42	91	6	484	908	23	2 029	8 756	10 441	66.8	10.4
Peoria	985	5.1	568	313	4	1 533	846	15	1 927	12 194	1 352	6 762	29 252	35 408	69.3	16.1
Perry	120	5.4	14	65	2	152	704	4	243	431	26	1 984	3 422	4 200	55.0	8.1
Piatt	107	6.5	13	81	1	18	112	2	162	200	9	1 254	3 482	3 569	70.0	13.9
Pike	63	3.4	8	45	1	59	331	3	224	230	4	1 311	3 229	3 775	61.3	7.7
Pope	12	2.7	1	24	0	0	0	1	59	70	7	1 633	749	900	48.8	5.3
Pulaski	49	5.7	1	12	0	0	0	1	64	27	12	323	1 725	1 800	46.9	6.8
Putnam	24	3.9	1	18	0	0	0	0	0	34	1	588	1 028	1 356	65.8	9.3
Randolph	160	4.5	25	70	4	533	1 493	5	495	418	17	1 185	5 287	5 663	55.4	6.8
Richland	112	6.1	31	188	1	124	752	2	248	426	23	2 500	2 703	3 347	60.1	10.3
Rock Island	994	6.0	209	136	3	780	508	11	1 468	6 781	438	4 354	25 232	30 204	69.7	12.2
St. Clair	1 308	4.9	308	114	5	1 492	551	21	2 506	14 146	2 734	5 338	47 919	56 299	59.1	11.4
Saline	226	7.9	26	94	2	124	446	9	753	746	14	2 664	4 942	5 339	50.7	6.8
Sangamon	987	5.5	596	330	4	1 549	857	14	1 634	9 623	960	5 438	32 991	27 971	72.4	18.7
Schuyler	35	4.3	5	64	1	58	744	2	119	90	3	1 173	1 229	1 686	60.7	7.9
Scott	23	3.8	1	16	0	0	0	1	64	28	2	658	1 098	1 219	60.3	7.4
Shelby	95	4.0	13	55	1	70	295	3	198	233	2	1 003	4 003	4 837	60.7	7.5
Stark	15	2.1	3	45	0	0	0	1	136	66	3	1 003	1 383	1 624	68.7	9.3
Stephenson	200	4.0	64	130	1	178	361	5	523	1 751	136	3 571	7 973	9 708	67.5	11.2
Tazewell	660	5.1	101	81	2	352	283	11	1 196	3 213	119	2 617	22 178	27 720	68.7	11.8
Union	122	6.7	19	106	2	595	3 306	6	338	235	33	1 310	3 442	3 078	50.0	7.8
Vermilion	460	5.0	119	132	3	1 434	1 590	7	782	4 068	392	4 461	16 459	18 237	62.3	9.7
Wabash	78	5.5	12	87	1	64	464	2	269	368	8	2 676	2 327	2 619	62.2	8.7
Warren	67	3.2	12	60	1	49	246	3	251	621	23	3 209	3 014	4 442	65.3	12.7
Washington	32	2.1	3	19	1	68	433	1	230	273	9	1 790	2 187	2 578	49.9	6.9
Wayne	91	4.9	8	45	1	82	466	2	128	122	1	684	3 098	3 539	49.9	6.1
White	112	6.2	10	59	1	49	288	3	313	257	9	1 474	3 272	3 077	55.7	7.9
Whiteside	348	5.4	58	93	2	217	348	10	698	1 489	56	2 387	11 487	13 899	62.3	8.7
Will	1 048	3.2	301	86	3	813	231	16	2 299	16 829	1 496	4 892	60 005	67 463	70.2	14.3
Williamson	303	5.2	61	104	3	422	723	8	656	1 956	118	3 378	9 921	10 408	58.5	10.5
Winnebago	1 224	4.9	492	195	4	1 223	484	19	2 363	18 493	1 413	7 363	41 338	47 552	67.5	13.5
Woodford	71	2.1	13	39	0	0	0	8	602	304	12	924	6 573	7 062	70.4	13.5
INDIANA	32 701	6.0	8 580	153	138	26 823	480	472	48 480	196 911	18 621	4 451	965 071	1 077 905	66.4	12.5
Adams	117	3.9	15	47	1	100	312	3	251	520	61	1 670	5 198	5 731	66.4	8.5
Allen	1 357	4.7	534	173	5	1 688	546	19	2 485	19 494	1 187	6 405	48 389	52 108	73.3	15.0

1. Per 1,000 resident population estimated as of July 1 of the year shown. 2. As of end of year. 3. Per 100,000 resident population as of July 1 of the year shown. 4. Preliminary. Covers nursing homes with 3 or more beds. 5. Data for serious crimes have not been adjusted for underreporting, this may affect comparability between geographic areas or over time. 6. Includes murder and nonnegligent manslaughter, forcible rape, robbery, and aggravated assault. 7. The 1986–1987 data are based on administrative reports obtained by the U.S. National Center for Education Statistics. The 1980 data are based on the 1980 Census of Population and Housing. 8. Persons 25 years old or older.

STATE County	Education (cont'd): Local government expenditures for education,[1] 1982: Total (Mil dol)	Education (cont'd): Local government expenditures for education,[1] 1982: Per capita (Dollars)	Social Security Program December 1988: Beneficiaries: Total	Social Security Program December 1988: Beneficiaries: Rate[2]	Social Security Program December 1988: Payments ($1,000)	Supplemental Security Income Program recipients June 1986	Money income: Per capita[3]: 1987 Income, (Dollars)	Money income: Per capita[3]: 1979: Current dollars	Money income: Per capita[3]: 1979: Constant 1987 dollars	Money income: Median household income 1979 (Dollars)	Money income: Percent below poverty level, 1979: Persons	Money income: Percent below poverty level, 1979: Families	Housing units, 1990: Total	Housing units, 1990: Percent change, 1980–1990
	60	61	62	63	64	65	66	67	68	69	70	71	72	73
ILLINOIS—Con.														
Jefferson	16.8	446	7 565	202.3	3 508	582	10 022	6 941	10 861	14 759	13.0	10.6	16 075	4.6
Jersey	6.7	327	3 155	153.2	1 511	226	9 921	6 557	10 260	17 342	8.0	5.8	8 216	3.4
Jo Daviess	9.7	412	4 335	187.7	2 040	132	10 452	6 720	10 515	16 800	7.8	5.8	10 757	11.2
Johnson	4.0	403	2 330	206.2	984	214	7 835	5 245	8 207	12 434	16.2	12.8	4 671	11.6
Kane	156.6	556	38 845	122.6	21 107	1 856	13 086	8 467	13 248	22 102	6.1	4.6	111 496	13.1
Kankakee	42.7	418	17 645	180.2	8 833	1 750	10 104	6 812	10 659	17 382	12.4	9.8	37 001	-1.6
Kendall	15.4	416	3 205	83.0	1 734	54	12 742	8 490	13 284	24 513	4.2	3.3	13 747	9.8
Knox	21.4	357	11 260	200.4	5 641	746	10 612	7 340	11 485	17 084	9.0	7.2	23 722	-3.7
Lake	239.8	531	51 325	103.6	28 168	2 492	16 856	10 103	15 808	25 210	5.3	3.9	183 283	21.8
La Salle	47.9	436	22 695	211.5	11 958	740	10 872	7 614	11 914	18 593	7.0	5.5	43 827	0.8
Lawrence	7.7	425	4 055	239.9	1 905	274	9 386	6 423	10 050	14 040	12.1	9.9	6 980	-5.1
Lee	15.0	423	6 490	186.5	3 258	364	10 699	7 258	11 357	18 545	7.0	5.2	13 314	-0.3
Livingston	21.7	529	6 925	171.4	3 583	368	10 902	7 558	11 826	19 260	7.4	5.2	14 365	-4.1
Logan	12.0	385	5 840	184.8	2 924	484	10 547	7 163	11 208	17 194	8.2	6.3	11 638	-3.4
McDonough	12.1	320	5 390	157.6	2 574	276	8 898	6 195	9 693	14 119	15.9	9.1	13 257	-4.9
McHenry	64.9	431	20 715	121.1	11 282	446	13 685	8 641	13 521	23 473	4.2	3.3	65 985	24.6
McLean	48.6	403	16 055	128.7	8 360	772	11 872	7 794	12 195	18 545	10.4	5.1	49 164	8.3
Macon	49.4	380	20 865	168.7	10 771	1 638	11 631	7 893	12 350	18 682	9.9	7.8	50 049	-3.0
Macoupin	22.6	462	10 825	220.0	5 210	524	9 294	6 491	10 156	15 578	9.6	7.3	20 068	-0.1
Madison	107.0	436	44 420	176.1	22 522	3 202	10 900	7 293	11 411	18 364	9.8	7.4	101 098	7.9
Marion	20.2	458	9 110	210.4	4 183	774	9 777	6 605	10 335	14 534	11.5	9.3	18 123	1.7
Marshall	6.4	451	2 685	203.4	1 366	70	10 617	7 338	11 482	18 392	7.1	5.8	5 317	-6.5
Mason	8.8	468	3 685	211.8	1 828	184	10 044	7 038	11 012	16 660	11.2	9.6	7 684	-9.3
Massac	8.2	554	3 450	230.0	1 574	370	9 065	6 216	9 726	13 144	15.4	11.6	6 446	3.7
Menard	5.2	451	1 980	169.2	983	116	10 670	7 434	11 632	18 832	7.8	6.6	4 650	0.9
Mercer	9.0	462	3 185	175.0	1 547	104	9 904	7 024	10 990	17 950	9.9	7.8	7 244	-4.7
Monroe	7.0	345	3 475	156.5	1 730	110	11 812	7 650	11 970	20 057	5.6	4.1	8 774	17.8
Montgomery	14.0	433	6 855	214.9	3 319	378	9 086	6 683	10 457	14 814	10.3	7.7	12 456	-3.6
Morgan	16.0	433	6 745	180.8	3 292	756	11 009	7 279	11 389	16 208	10.5	8.0	14 724	1.1
Moultrie	4.5	311	3 225	224.0	1 598	118	10 128	6 938	10 856	17 339	8.8	6.2	5 384	-1.9
Ogle	26.5	582	7 325	158.5	3 730	192	11 295	7 371	11 533	19 170	6.9	5.7	18 052	4.4
Peoria	80.7	405	33 135	181.4	17 401	2 158	11 797	8 343	13 054	19 399	9.6	7.3	75 211	-5.2
Perry	8.1	372	4 310	198.6	2 067	208	9 585	7 191	11 252	16 218	8.8	7.4	9 235	2.5
Piatt	9.4	575	2 910	179.6	1 506	86	11 458	7 888	12 342	19 428	6.4	4.8	6 227	-1.4
Pike	8.0	428	4 390	245.3	1 951	300	8 874	6 079	9 512	12 392	15.4	12.2	8 057	-2.6
Pope	2.0	476	820	190.7	348	98	7 793	5 070	7 933	11 992	20.5	14.1	2 154	11.5
Pulaski	8.1	920	1 990	234.1	807	420	7 148	4 683	7 327	9 424	29.9	22.4	3 410	-6.8
Putnam	3.5	587	1 105	193.9	570	18	10 966	7 774	12 164	20 216	6.7	5.3	2 600	5.6
Randolph	12.9	363	6 735	189.2	3 217	292	9 660	6 630	10 374	17 660	8.7	6.2	13 179	2.0
Richland	6.8	371	3 600	213.0	1 646	248	10 312	6 790	10 624	14 425	10.0	7.4	7 142	-4.0
Rock Island	66.4	396	27 955	179.7	14 219	1 526	11 318	8 234	12 884	19 942	8.4	6.2	63 327	-0.3
St. Clair	132.4	495	41 870	155.2	20 321	5 534	9 896	6 453	10 097	16 119	17.7	14.1	103 432	6.1
Saline	13.4	466	6 810	244.1	3 109	770	8 996	6 411	10 031	12 396	15.1	11.6	12 350	0.2
Sangamon	62.3	353	31 000	172.2	15 381	2 056	12 446	8 179	12 798	18 085	8.6	6.2	76 873	5.5
Schuyler	2.8	342	1 605	205.8	733	98	8 716	6 366	9 961	14 202	12.2	9.6	3 329	-7.7
Scott	2.7	439	1 120	183.6	529	58	9 835	6 431	10 063	14 693	12.6	10.4	2 442	-3.7
Shelby	9.7	411	4 750	201.3	2 240	256	9 774	6 671	10 438	15 890	10.6	7.7	9 329	-5.6
Stark	4.1	564	1 510	228.8	754	62	10 674	7 076	11 072	17 182	8.9	7.2	2 716	-5.5
Stephenson	19.5	393	9 305	188.7	4 689	424	11 375	7 419	11 609	17 615	7.1	5.5	20 378	5.5
Tazewell	49.3	376	20 740	166.2	10 943	958	11 276	8 237	12 888	21 146	6.0	4.8	49 315	0.9
Union	9.1	510	4 085	226.9	1 728	710	9 550	6 389	9 997	13 520	14.6	11.5	7 408	4.8
Vermilion	40.3	432	17 600	194.3	8 569	1 298	9 973	6 950	10 875	16 193	11.5	9.1	37 061	-3.4
Wabash	5.4	389	2 590	187.7	1 269	172	10 569	7 379	11 546	16 316	11.0	7.7	5 572	-2.4
Warren	8.8	409	3 910	194.5	1 967	222	9 762	6 927	10 839	15 959	12.0	9.3	8 229	-4.0
Washington	4.7	308	3 110	199.4	1 439	150	9 944	6 608	10 340	15 656	9.5	7.5	6 261	-0.1
Wayne	8.0	435	3 945	221.6	1 809	234	9 287	6 301	9 859	13 005	13.7	10.5	7 622	-2.2
White	8.3	456	4 435	257.8	2 053	298	10 323	6 912	10 815	13 824	10.7	7.9	7 797	-0.6
Whiteside	31.9	491	11 630	186.1	5 953	534	10 565	7 696	12 042	20 111	6.8	5.5	24 000	-0.4
Will	155.7	476	35 250	101.7	18 532	1 808	11 807	7 993	12 507	23 329	6.4	4.9	122 870	12.0
Williamson	22.5	394	11 595	199.2	5 496	884	9 292	6 513	10 191	14 305	11.8	8.9	25 183	3.7
Winnebago	105.4	420	40 345	160.0	21 586	2 684	11 818	7 935	12 416	20 213	8.3	6.5	101 666	9.1
Woodford	14.7	440	4 840	147.1	2 507	144	10 765	7 775	12 166	21 231	5.6	4.2	11 932	1.1
INDIANA	2 311.5	422	890 585	160.3	453 599	50 891	11 078	7 141	11 174	17 582	9.7	7.3	2 246 046	7.4
Adams	12.5	427	4 815	152.9	2 529	304	9 660	6 459	10 106	17 586	10.4	6.8	10 931	7.2
Allen	124.9	430	43 415	142.9	22 916	2 370	12 237	7 766	12 151	19 090	8.1	6.2	122 923	11.0

1. Elementary and secondary. 2. Per 1,000 resident population estimated as of July 1 of the year shown. 3. Based on the resident population estimated as of July 1, 1988 for 1987 data and enumerated as of April 1, 1980 for 1979 data.

Table A. States and Counties — **Housing, Labor Force, and Employment**

STATE County	Housing units, 1990 (cont'd) — Occupied units — Total	Owner occupied — Percent	Owner occupied — Median value (Dollars)	Median rent (Dollars)	Civilian labor force, 1990 — Total	Percent change, 1989–1990	Unemployment — Total	Unemployment — Rate[1]	Private nonfarm establishments, 1988 — Number	Net change, 1987–1988	Employment[2] — Total	Per-cent change, 1987–1988	Manu-facturing	Retail trade
	74	75	76	77	78	79	80	81	82	83	84	85	86	87
ILLINOIS—Con.														
Jefferson	14 606	73.0	41 500	197	18 546	2.0	1 908	10.3	958	-23	13 014	9.3	3 030	2 717
Jersey	7 344	76.1	45 400	209	9 873	-1.7	607	6.1	333	3	3 109	6.6	51	1 221
Jo Daviess	8 371	74.9	48 700	212	11 348	-3.0	630	5.6	527	19	4 667	15.1	1 401	1 090
Johnson	3 725	81.7	36 800	150	4 238	1.6	460	10.9	160	-13	806	-3.2	58	284
Kane	107 176	69.5	102 500	439	169 586	2.5	10 070	5.9	7 649	299	122 134	6.5	39 480	26 951
Kankakee	34 623	66.8	54 700	273	47 600	2.8	3 388	7.1	1 935	-1	27 329	0.9	6 732	6 055
Kendall	13 301	76.9	99 700	416	21 021	2.1	989	4.7	570	9	5 721	12.6	1 545	1 309
Knox	21 909	69.1	37 100	215	27 803	0.9	1 922	6.9	1 228	20	17 701	0.6	4 621	4 097
Lake	173 966	74.2	136 700	487	309 130	1.8	12 128	3.9	12 087	553	183 018	7.1	49 906	43 470
La Salle	41 284	73.2	50 500	236	51 459	1.3	4 503	8.8	2 804	22	31 759	1.6	7 648	8 409
Lawrence	6 320	76.5	32 800	172	6 967	1.0	664	9.5	330	-24	4 141	1.6	564	716
Lee	12 475	69.6	46 600	228	15 216	-1.1	952	6.3	764	12	9 516	0.7	3 437	1 734
Livingston	13 737	70.9	46 700	238	18 615	-3.8	836	4.5	914	0	10 454	1.2	4 337	1 985
Logan	11 033	67.8	48 700	223	15 378	-3.5	912	5.9	684	3	8 394	3.7	1 983	1 813
McDonough	12 255	62.2	36 000	223	16 175	-3.1	842	5.2	739	7	8 066	15.3	1 957	2 969
McHenry	62 940	79.9	111 000	461	92 975	0.7	4 937	5.3	4 051	197	54 307	7.0	23 444	9 920
McLean	46 796	63.5	65 900	326	75 503	1.7	3 005	4.0	2 868	42	50 505	-1.7	6 241	12 096
Macon	45 996	70.2	45 400	250	60 229	-1.1	4 247	7.1	2 745	5	47 978	3.5	14 637	10 540
Macoupin	18 176	77.4	39 700	194	21 514	0.2	1 628	7.6	930	-3	8 351	-4.0	1 153	2 107
Madison	94 857	72.0	51 400	282	124 579	-0.8	8 139	6.5	5 286	15	71 433	2.1	19 946	17 192
Marion	16 272	76.2	36 000	189	19 514	-0.9	2 289	11.7	1 203	12	13 919	-1.5	4 545	2 891
Marshall	4 900	76.1	44 000	196	5 961	-2.6	340	5.7	304	2	2 432	2.9	781	552
Mason	6 342	73.8	35 800	185	7 342	-2.4	648	8.8	344	-3	2 016	1.6	356	624
Massac	5 908	77.6	35 700	157	4 678	0.5	463	9.9	253	-10	2 810	1.7	690	550
Menard	4 199	76.6	51 500	210	6 342	0.3	329	5.2	225	11	1 185	0.1	38	365
Mercer	6 572	74.7	34 900	189	8 463	-3.6	614	7.3	312	9	1 883	8.7	257	649
Monroe	8 189	78.6	72 100	295	11 275	0.0	758	6.7	443	0	4 007	1.3	256	1 018
Montgomery	11 480	76.6	35 300	182	14 265	1.1	1 239	8.7	726	-24	7 381	0.4	1 892	1 928
Morgan	13 678	67.7	47 700	231	17 256	-0.9	912	5.3	908	4	12 621	1.9	3 645	2 497
Moultrie	5 122	75.8	41 200	210	6 724	-1.7	486	7.2	269	1	2 889	6.7	1 077	561
Ogle	17 132	71.2	57 200	252	23 499	-2.9	1 491	6.3	910	6	12 581	1.3	5 834	1 819
Peoria	70 797	64.0	49 100	272	90 045	1.1	5 573	6.2	4 550	8	89 099	10.7	26 273	16 631
Perry	8 306	78.1	40 400	173	7 990	4.1	1 167	14.6	480	-7	5 892	-2.2	1 411	1 070
Piatt	5 934	76.5	51 200	232	7 969	-3.7	463	5.8	347	-7	2 758	2.1	599	627
Pike	7 016	73.7	28 500	144	8 000	1.4	651	8.1	387	-13	2 570	4.9	337	715
Pope	1 611	75.5	29 700	121	1 465	-0.3	156	10.6	48	-3	421	-25.5	0	41
Pulaski	2 957	75.8	24 000	133	2 354	-2.0	332	14.1	129	4	1 052	7.5	0	121
Putnam	2 204	77.5	48 400	199	2 792	1.8	217	7.8	119	4	1 476	3.3	0	141
Randolph	11 949	78.5	45 000	202	14 187	-2.4	1 295	9.1	729	-9	9 424	-2.6	3 636	2 004
Richland	6 503	76.6	35 800	180	7 974	1.2	694	8.7	471	-9	4 226	4.0	1 057	1 081
Rock Island	59 317	66.9	47 800	253	76 630	-0.1	4 821	6.3	3 379	-21	57 990	3.0	13 228	13 736
St. Clair	95 333	64.7	55 500	285	117 955	-0.7	9 269	7.9	4 950	51	60 872	3.2	8 199	18 169
Saline	10 839	75.2	33 400	173	11 439	-0.8	1 002	8.8	692	-15	7 516	0.8	403	1 662
Sangamon	72 146	66.5	60 900	310	108 514	0.2	4 774	4.4	4 515	-1	65 192	0.7	4 593	15 878
Schuyler	3 002	76.0	35 100	183	3 564	-1.2	331	9.3	183	-6	1 091	-11.7	133	407
Scott	2 190	73.9	32 800	148	2 679	-0.5	202	7.5	125	-11	966	-11.0	86	149
Shelby	8 563	78.9	39 100	188	12 657	6.8	854	6.7	428	11	3 837	12.0	1 096	744
Stark	2 512	74.2	31 200	184	2 971	-2.1	230	7.7	126	-1	833	2.7	270	117
Stephenson	18 920	71.2	50 700	231	25 141	-1.0	1 745	6.9	1 047	6	19 198	10.7	8 950	3 226
Tazewell	47 171	71.6	48 700	243	60 918	0.4	3 669	6.0	2 406	34	34 234	11.2	9 131	8 717
Union	6 838	72.2	36 700	168	8 309	1.7	956	11.5	332	3	3 069	-2.1	766	706
Vermilion	34 072	71.2	38 700	223	40 548	0.8	4 013	9.9	1 910	-6	28 052	4.9	9 473	6 112
Wabash	5 032	75.8	42 200	187	6 506	-2.6	498	7.7	374	-17	5 411	0.4	1 276	901
Warren	7 393	69.4	33 700	197	9 460	-4.4	654	6.9	425	-7	4 980	14.8	867	1 066
Washington	5 658	80.2	46 000	206	8 176	1.5	607	7.4	339	7	2 715	-8.5	368	643
Wayne	6 935	79.1	34 500	157	7 484	-2.3	847	11.3	414	-11	3 416	2.4	0	715
White	6 845	74.8	34 500	158	7 541	-0.2	727	9.6	435	5	3 062	-9.2	196	859
Whiteside	22 740	71.7	44 400	240	29 464	-0.3	1 977	6.7	1 273	14	17 986	1.4	7 555	4 494
Will	116 933	77.4	89 900	377	192 094	0.8	12 373	6.4	5 969	174	81 393	2.5	18 465	19 052
Williamson	23 120	73.7	40 800	210	26 158	1.3	2 529	9.7	1 276	10	12 830	-1.9	2 663	3 455
Winnebago	96 727	68.0	60 600	301	139 611	0.1	8 688	6.2	6 338	85	113 288	5.0	41 858	21 339
Woodford	11 395	78.3	57 700	244	15 472	0.2	597	3.9	542	18	5 280	11.0	1 195	1 359
INDIANA	2 065 355	70.2	53 900	291	2 832 000	-1.7	150 000	5.3	X	X	1 999 805	3.4	620 193	430 707
Adams	10 470	78.4	51 100	229	15 091	-5.7	1 114	7.4	690	5	11 550	9.1	6 796	2 025
Allen	113 333	70.2	59 900	320	170 412	-1.0	8 664	5.1	7 818	32	156 134	3.5	40 053	30 553

1. Percent of total civilian labor force. 2. For week including March 12. Excludes government employees, self-employed persons, farm workers, domestic service workers, railroad employees subject to the Railroad Retirement Act, and employees on oceanborne vessels or in foreign countries.

STATE County	Private nonfarm establishments, 1988 (cont'd): Employment[1] (cont'd): Finance, insurance, and real estate	Employment[1] (cont'd): Services	Annual payroll: Total (Mil dol)	Annual payroll: Average per employee (Dollars)	Personal income, 1989: Total (Mil dol)	Percent change, 1988–1989	Wages and salaries[2] (Mil dol)	Proprietor's income (Mil dol)	Dividends, interest, & rent (Mil dol)	Transfer payments (Mil dol)	Per capita[3]: Dollars	Per capita[3]: Rank	Earnings, 1989: Total (Mil dol)	Percent by selected industries: Farm	Goods-related[4]: Total
	88	89	90	91	92	93	94	95	96	97	98	99	100	101	102
ILLINOIS—Con.															
Jefferson	604	4 147	247	18 946	584	7.7	384	77	100	108	15 726	730	461	4.4	40.2
Jersey	156	1 256	32	10 437	295	8.8	59	38	52	43	14 172	1 359	97	19.3	6.5
Jo Daviess	246	836	67	14 265	365	8.7	121	57	95	50	15 819	706	178	11.8	31.1
Johnson	56	181	8	10 238	109	8.6	30	17	21	29	9 593	2 944	48	16.1	NA
Kane	7 131	29 155	2 650	21 701	6 331	7.4	3 275	420	956	616	19 577	190	3 695	0.7	37.1
Kankakee	1 453	8 441	503	18 418	1 474	6.5	770	134	251	281	15 078	949	904	3.6	28.8
Kendall	180	1 021	91	15 847	771	10.1	330	79	96	47	19 670	185	410	5.3	62.9
Knox	871	5 326	301	17 001	857	9.0	483	89	171	174	15 315	871	572	4.4	32.9
Lake	13 626	47 474	4 484	24 500	13 039	9.5	6 483	1 007	2 296	880	25 804	32	7 490	0.1	30.3
La Salle	1 482	7 798	595	18 744	1 691	8.2	799	200	394	298	15 804	710	999	5.5	28.4
Lawrence	0	760	65	15 765	245	8.2	81	44	64	54	14 790	1 083	125	11.6	22.8
Lee	484	2 451	165	17 289	564	6.3	294	75	125	87	16 099	619	369	6.9	21.0
Livingston	428	2 243	209	20 020	656	8.3	306	88	156	94	16 244	581	394	9.4	39.2
Logan	567	2 375	142	16 912	497	8.6	231	73	100	86	15 685	743	304	11.2	NA
McDonough	628	1 431	112	13 876	452	13.3	243	63	96	85	13 342	1 758	305	8.8	21.5
McHenry	2 236	9 656	1 101	20 280	3 645	8.7	1 442	318	508	299	20 742	136	1 760	2.1	47.5
McLean	12 124	11 896	1 035	20 493	2 302	12.6	1 557	232	379	254	18 357	260	1 789	3.1	18.3
Macon	2 518	10 787	1 103	22 991	2 051	6.2	1 472	203	376	316	16 767	477	1 674	2.0	42.8
Macoupin	460	2 042	143	17 097	720	9.8	230	85	150	143	14 617	1 158	316	7.8	30.7
Madison	3 647	18 430	1 499	20 980	4 278	6.4	2 186	364	716	705	16 858	459	2 551	1.0	41.7
Marion	717	3 446	242	17 358	609	8.2	346	87	118	143	14 126	1 380	433	4.8	33.2
Marshall	119	450	42	17 410	216	9.4	63	32	54	33	16 540	518	95	16.1	32.9
Mason	168	294	31	15 168	244	10.8	64	33	53	49	14 082	1 395	97	21.8	14.2
Massac	124	603	60	21 189	188	9.5	83	22	34	48	12 491	2 121	104	7.3	24.8
Menard	106	227	17	14 071	183	8.3	36	30	34	30	15 568	783	66	24.3	13.1
Mercer	160	355	24	12 641	265	8.2	49	43	54	42	14 608	1 162	91	23.4	13.5
Monroe	250	1 012	72	18 041	426	9.8	100	38	81	47	18 742	236	138	11.4	23.1
Montgomery	405	1 899	118	16 034	462	10.4	181	73	112	93	14 446	1 235	254	10.6	23.5
Morgan	776	3 771	211	16 683	605	9.7	296	98	124	97	16 231	587	394	7.7	30.9
Moultrie	112	750	42	14 602	215	10.7	52	30	42	39	14 872	1 040	82	21.5	20.7
Ogle	425	1 821	246	19 546	750	8.2	345	87	145	91	16 197	595	432	6.3	42.7
Peoria	5 901	26 927	2 010	22 554	3 192	7.8	2 317	256	639	501	17 602	355	2 573	0.8	30.5
Perry	202	1 012	125	21 250	313	8.5	164	39	68	61	14 521	1 203	203	6.4	54.3
Piatt	183	557	43	15 554	278	12.3	69	55	54	40	17 224	408	124	23.8	16.4
Pike	189	608	33	12 776	251	15.2	67	60	59	50	14 135	1 378	127	24.3	11.2
Pope	0	99	8	19 952	45	13.2	13	8	8	12	10 645	2 755	22	12.5	NA
Pulaski	43	538	14	13 659	96	18.0	36	15	13	28	11 426	2 533	51	16.9	NA
Putnam	54	112	41	28 077	103	10.1	71	17	22	14	18 205	271	88	11.4	54.5
Randolph	365	1 585	185	19 683	506	10.1	307	62	102	89	14 173	1 357	369	5.7	34.4
Richland	198	1 002	56	13 347	246	10.7	108	50	58	47	14 889	1 028	158	9.9	23.4
Rock Island	4 305	14 892	1 273	21 957	2 494	7.1	2 018	188	507	428	16 247	578	2 206	0.5	32.3
St. Clair	3 474	19 278	1 080	17 745	4 085	5.7	1 982	319	648	794	15 097	942	2 301	1.0	19.7
Saline	400	2 698	124	16 512	416	7.5	193	56	73	102	14 989	993	249	6.6	34.3
Sangamon	7 200	24 466	1 190	18 251	3 301	5.7	2 237	347	556	523	18 268	267	2 584	2.1	10.0
Schuyler	52	230	14	13 187	108	13.8	28	22	25	20	13 904	1 472	50	25.7	NA
Scott	65	65	34	34 965	93	14.5	48	19	19	15	15 193	911	67	23.0	NA
Shelby	182	929	59	15 360	354	13.0	87	71	76	57	14 917	1 019	158	24.8	23.7
Stark	75	264	11	13 303	113	15.6	31	23	30	18	17 202	409	53	26.2	21.4
Stephenson	2 373	3 169	391	20 358	853	7.2	499	93	185	113	17 292	398	592	4.3	48.9
Tazewell	1 740	6 556	776	22 678	2 127	8.6	1 451	159	369	290	17 092	422	1 609	1.9	59.9
Union	126	936	44	14 421	243	9.2	98	33	43	59	13 476	1 698	131	9.0	NA
Vermilion	1 356	7 294	526	18 761	1 298	6.8	806	152	227	261	14 390	1 252	957	4.9	40.9
Wabash	191	792	123	22 664	217	9.2	135	39	51	34	15 730	729	174	4.7	54.8
Warren	250	1 260	79	15 854	290	5.5	117	55	67	52	14 550	1 189	172	12.7	13.0
Washington	266	723	35	13 026	268	16.6	80	50	56	41	17 058	426	130	18.7	25.5
Wayne	178	679	54	15 679	266	10.5	98	63	61	49	15 150	925	161	15.4	21.2
White	198	753	53	17 470	263	10.4	85	58	62	55	15 431	822	143	12.0	24.4
Whiteside	750	2 943	361	20 058	956	4.9	475	110	213	148	15 353	858	585	3.7	46.4
Will	3 494	21 338	1 759	21 616	6 252	7.2	2 424	422	830	627	17 788	320	2 846	1.2	34.0
Williamson	911	3 144	235	18 279	819	5.5	350	93	142	179	14 037	1 418	444	1.7	25.1
Winnebago	5 359	30 212	2 442	21 556	4 440	6.4	3 159	354	762	557	17 560	362	3 513	0.4	46.1
Woodford	198	1 485	85	16 044	532	9.0	130	48	114	61	16 081	624	178	10.9	22.0
INDIANA	114 303	482 823	40 082	X	88 499	7.6	58 103	7 048	14 187	12 274	15 830	X	65 151	1.7	39.3
Adams	276	1 444	211	18 297	439	8.7	275	48	89	55	13 719	1 572	323	5.1	NA
Allen	12 403	39 887	3 305	21 169	5 471	7.5	4 325	343	909	606	17 711	333	4 668	0.4	37.7

1. For week including March 12. Excludes government employees, self-employed persons, farm workers, domestic service workers, railroad employees subject to the Railroad Retirement Act, and employees on oceanborne vessels or in foreign countries. 2. Includes other labor income. 3. Based on the resident population estimated as of July 1 of the year shown. 4. Covers mining, construction, and manufacturing.

STATE County	Earnings, 1989 (cont'd): Percent by selected industries (cont'd): Goods-related[1]: Manufacturing	Service-related & other[2]: Total	Service-related & other[2]: Retail trade	Service-related & other[2]: Finance, insurance, & real estate	Service-related & other[2]: Services	Government	Agriculture, 1987: Farms: Number	Farms: Percent with: Less than 50 acres	Farms: Percent with: 500 acres and over	Farm operators, percent: Whose principal occupation is farming	Farm operators, percent: Residing on farm operated	Land in farms: Acreage (1,000)	Land in farms: Percent change, 1982–1987	Land in farms: Acres: Average size of farm	Land in farms: Acres: Total irrigated (1,000)	Land in farms: Acres: Total cropland (1,000)
	103	104	105	106	107	108	109	110	111	112	113	114	115	116	117	118
ILLINOIS—Con.																
Jefferson	25.1	46.0	10.1	8.3	18.9	9.4	1 031	27.2	12.5	45.4	76.1	235	-6.3	228	0	196
Jersey	1.6	54.6	13.3	4.3	24.6	19.7	619	23.7	22.1	57.4	72.2	197	-2.6	318	0	152
Jo Daviess	24.1	46.5	10.1	6.5	17.2	10.6	1 070	14.1	14.2	74.0	79.9	314	0.2	293	0	212
Johnson	0.5	NA	11.7	3.0	12.3	36.3	476	24.6	9.7	41.4	72.3	100	-8.3	209	0	68
Kane	27.9	52.0	11.0	5.6	24.3	10.2	824	28.6	16.5	64.9	70.4	228	-5.0	277	1	211
Kankakee	21.0	50.9	10.0	3.3	26.0	16.8	1 086	18.2	23.9	67.1	69.3	389	2.7	358	8	370
Kendall	53.8	24.9	5.5	1.3	11.2	6.9	535	18.7	23.4	65.8	74.8	186	0.2	348	0	176
Knox	27.9	50.3	10.3	3.1	22.9	12.4	1 165	20.9	24.0	69.0	72.2	405	-0.7	347	0	330
Lake	23.1	52.7	10.1	4.6	24.4	16.8	448	57.6	9.4	45.3	72.5	82	-10.6	184	0	69
La Salle	19.7	54.8	11.6	3.9	22.4	11.3	1 978	13.9	20.9	67.3	68.6	642	0.7	324	0	600
Lawrence	3.7	52.6	8.3	7.7	24.3	13.1	435	26.2	28.0	65.3	73.3	168	-0.9	387	6	152
Lee	17.1	53.0	7.0	3.6	23.3	19.2	1 148	10.7	25.6	71.9	65.4	422	0.8	368	6	395
Livingston	32.0	37.0	7.7	2.8	16.5	14.4	1 760	13.2	26.9	75.9	68.8	648	3.2	368	1	620
Logan	18.9	44.0	9.4	3.2	22.6	16.9	949	15.0	31.2	76.4	72.5	376	3.3	396	D	355
McDonough	17.0	34.5	9.2	3.4	15.3	35.2	1 018	20.2	23.6	66.6	70.0	349	1.5	342	0	302
McHenry	34.0	41.7	9.0	2.6	20.2	8.7	1 136	37.1	12.9	59.1	80.0	266	-1.6	234	8	240
McLean	13.7	65.7	8.9	24.0	21.5	12.9	1 906	16.8	30.0	72.2	68.0	741	-0.6	389	1	707
Macon	35.1	47.2	8.2	3.6	20.1	8.0	850	23.3	32.1	66.8	65.4	329	1.1	387	0	316
Macoupin	12.5	49.5	9.8	5.9	15.6	12.0	1 509	21.5	19.8	62.0	71.6	445	-4.8	295	0	369
Madison	33.0	44.5	8.7	4.1	21.7	12.8	1 500	30.9	11.1	51.7	74.2	322	-1.9	214	2	289
Marion	27.3	49.7	7.0	2.9	21.0	12.3	950	23.9	17.8	50.8	71.1	252	-5.6	265	0	213
Marshall	28.3	41.1	10.9	5.1	16.3	9.9	611	13.1	25.0	68.2	70.7	212	2.6	346	2	187
Mason	10.8	NA	10.9	NA	14.3	18.0	581	14.1	42.9	78.0	69.5	300	-1.5	517	60	274
Massac	20.6	50.6	9.0	2.0	12.4	17.3	414	23.2	12.3	54.6	75.4	104	-0.4	251	3	86
Menard	0.7	43.9	7.3	4.5	13.6	18.6	437	23.3	34.3	68.6	72.3	190	-2.8	434	0	170
Mercer	6.2	46.3	9.7	4.8	18.8	16.8	933	20.7	24.1	69.5	74.5	325	0.1	348	1	276
Monroe	5.5	52.4	12.3	4.2	24.8	13.1	660	24.2	20.3	56.7	74.7	203	0.3	308	1	167
Montgomery	17.7	55.0	12.7	3.2	21.9	10.9	1 246	20.1	19.6	64.3	71.4	373	-2.5	300	0	336
Morgan	24.1	49.3	8.3	4.3	25.1	12.1	944	20.6	25.6	70.4	71.3	331	-2.6	351	2	281
Moultrie	11.3	46.5	9.3	3.7	19.1	11.3	561	25.0	24.1	65.1	65.4	185	0.4	329	D	175
Ogle	36.6	40.8	7.2	2.1	12.4	10.2	1 312	19.3	19.9	68.8	74.2	416	-4.4	317	2	373
Peoria	23.6	59.1	9.5	5.4	31.6	9.6	1 102	28.1	17.2	53.4	69.5	290	3.0	263	5	247
Perry	16.1	29.6	7.4	2.7	14.1	9.8	591	20.1	17.1	52.3	74.6	174	-14.1	295	1	146
Piatt	12.1	46.3	9.4	4.9	20.5	13.6	604	13.2	38.6	75.7	62.9	274	-1.2	453	0	263
Pike	4.9	54.2	8.6	6.2	29.8	10.2	1 193	18.2	27.0	63.7	68.3	455	-1.5	381	2	335
Pope	1.2	37.3	6.5	1.6	21.2	32.1	279	14.3	11.1	50.5	74.6	75	-6.4	270	D	50
Pulaski	10.9	NA	4.4	2.4	NA	23.5	244	16.8	18.9	49.6	70.5	82	-6.6	337	D	69
Putnam	48.8	29.6	4.5	2.6	4.8	4.6	242	17.8	26.0	70.7	71.5	85	0.7	352	0	73
Randolph	25.3	43.7	8.2	2.7	12.3	16.2	1 019	24.2	15.4	53.0	74.4	274	-2.2	269	0	216
Richland	16.3	50.4	10.4	1.6	24.7	16.3	617	24.5	22.4	60.9	77.3	197	1.6	319	0	174
Rock Island	28.6	44.0	9.5	4.5	17.8	23.2	723	27.1	16.2	60.0	75.0	187	7.8	259	3	155
St. Clair	10.0	52.0	11.1	3.3	24.9	27.3	1 101	26.9	15.5	61.2	73.5	280	-3.9	254	1	251
Saline	1.3	45.2	10.9	3.1	19.8	14.0	465	27.3	21.5	48.4	68.2	140	-7.6	300	D	123
Sangamon	4.3	59.2	10.5	8.0	28.8	28.8	1 277	27.7	28.5	67.7	68.5	493	4.0	386	0	457
Schuyler	4.6	NA	10.7	2.2	18.6	16.8	594	13.6	29.0	69.2	66.8	234	1.2	393	D	155
Scott	2.2	21.1	2.7	2.1	5.0	9.9	410	22.2	26.1	68.3	63.9	150	6.0	367	2	122
Shelby	17.7	40.1	7.2	3.9	18.5	11.3	1 431	21.5	20.8	63.1	69.7	422	0.5	295	0	381
Stark	17.1	41.6	4.4	4.9	11.8	10.8	434	17.1	32.9	74.2	70.0	179	0.1	413	D	166
Stephenson	42.2	39.0	7.5	9.5	14.6	7.7	1 290	16.2	13.4	76.4	83.4	339	-0.9	263	D	299
Tazewell	53.3	31.3	6.6	3.2	11.5	7.0	1 182	26.7	21.6	63.9	72.8	353	1.8	299	16	324
Union	16.5	NA	8.8	1.7	17.4	28.8	580	22.2	11.0	46.9	76.7	130	-5.9	223	0	93
Vermilion	35.6	39.3	8.1	2.9	18.1	14.9	1 225	20.3	31.0	70.8	71.0	488	-2.4	398	0	457
Wabash	24.1	32.3	6.0	2.3	17.9	8.1	286	24.5	30.1	65.0	66.8	118	0.9	414	D	107
Warren	9.2	62.4	13.3	3.5	18.4	11.9	904	17.8	27.9	73.9	72.1	327	2.0	362	D	290
Washington	20.2	46.7	9.5	2.9	20.1	9.1	987	18.0	20.0	64.3	72.8	316	4.3	320	1	282
Wayne	15.1	43.3	8.2	2.9	19.0	20.2	1 061	20.3	22.5	61.4	70.6	343	-3.4	323	0	305
White	2.4	49.4	11.9	3.9	21.2	14.2	545	18.2	33.9	65.9	69.2	274	1.4	503	4	244
Whiteside	40.0	38.1	8.9	3.2	15.2	11.9	1 276	19.7	19.8	71.3	76.3	393	-1.4	308	14	358
Will	22.8	51.0	8.9	2.8	24.0	13.8	1 239	28.3	16.4	60.5	72.0	329	-7.0	265	3	309
Williamson	14.5	50.5	10.8	3.1	21.5	22.7	607	32.6	7.6	36.6	77.3	102	4.2	168	0	78
Winnebago	40.4	45.6	8.4	3.7	22.1	8.0	808	32.1	14.5	61.3	76.9	204	-8.2	253	1	183
Woodford	13.3	53.0	10.0	0.1	22.6	14.2	1 103	22.0	16.7	61.7	64.8	298	-0.4	270	0	272
INDIANA	32.6	46.3	9.4	4.7	19.4	12.7	70 506	29.0	13.1	52.0	75.0	16 171	-0.8	229	170	13 593
Adams	54.1	NA	8.9	1.6	8.4	8.8	1 195	33.8	8.1	51.6	75.0	206	7.5	172	0	187
Allen	31.3	54.0	9.4	7.8	20.3	7.9	1 649	31.0	7.9	48.4	75.4	291	-3.2	177	1	257

1. Covers mining, construction, and manufacturing. 2. Covers private sector earnings in agricultural services, forestry, and fisheries; transportation and public utilities; wholesale trade; retail trade; finance, insurance, and real estate; and services.

STATE County	Agriculture, 1987 (cont'd) — Value of land and buildings — Average per farm ($1,000)	Value of land and buildings — Average per acre (Dollars)	Value of products sold — Total (Mil dol)	Value of products sold — Average per farm (Dollars)	Value of products sold — Percent from — Crops	Value of products sold — Percent from — Livestock and poultry[1]	Percent of farms with sales of — $10,000 or more	Percent of farms with sales of — $100,000 or more	Manufactures, 1987 — Establishments — Total	Establishments — Percent with 20 or more employees	All employees — Number (1,000)	All employees — Percent change, 1982–1987	All employees — Annual payroll (Mil dol)	Production workers — Number (1,000)	Production workers — Work hours (Mil)
	119	120	121	122	123	124	125	126	127	128	129	130	131	132	133
ILLINOIS—Con.															
Jefferson	161	750	31	29 741	70.1	29.9	45.5	7.8	41	36.6	2.9	20.8	74.5	2.2	3.7
Jersey	335	967	36	57 720	67.1	32.9	60.9	19.1	12	16.7	0.2	100.0	2.1	0.1	0.2
Jo Daviess	220	785	74	69 571	18.3	81.7	77.5	23.6	22	50.0	1.3	18.2	24.0	1.1	2.1
Johnson	112	614	11	22 470	34.5	65.5	32.1	4.0	7	0.0	0.0	0.0	0.4	0.0	0.1
Kane	661	2 312	81	98 153	64.2	35.8	73.3	25.5	749	42.2	37.4	-6.3	954.7	24.8	50.2
Kankakee	511	1 434	94	86 251	85.9	14.1	80.4	25.5	111	40.5	7.0	-13.6	170.7	4.7	9.1
Kendall	679	1 902	48	90 579	72.3	27.7	80.7	26.9	51	29.4	1.4	16.7	23.1	1.1	2.1
Knox	382	1 134	99	84 666	51.3	48.7	72.6	24.0	55	41.8	4.6	-13.2	107.7	3.6	6.7
Lake	561	3 269	29	64 603	72.8	27.2	45.3	17.0	760	38.0	50.9	11.6	1 476.1	22.1	44.2
La Salle	523	1 621	150	75 974	77.5	22.5	82.9	23.1	153	43.8	8.1	-5.8	204.1	5.9	12.1
Lawrence	341	941	28	63 986	79.0	21.0	65.5	21.8	24	16.7	0.5	0.0	7.4	0.4	0.6
Lee	516	1 397	102	88 547	65.4	34.6	87.7	26.5	51	51.0	3.6	16.1	72.7	2.5	5.0
Livingston	557	1 511	140	79 431	75.5	24.5	86.4	27.7	56	48.2	4.2	13.5	105.6	3.3	6.4
Logan	638	1 622	90	94 833	78.3	21.7	84.4	33.6	21	52.4	1.9	11.8	44.5	1.5	2.6
McDonough	394	1 163	67	65 513	68.2	31.8	73.5	21.2	30	53.3	1.9	18.7	38.6	1.6	3.0
McHenry	458	1 971	96	84 361	54.9	45.1	62.4	20.5	435	37.0	20.8	15.6	457.2	15.4	31.9
McLean	655	1 647	164	86 208	83.1	16.9	82.2	31.2	99	34.3	6.4	0.0	132.9	3.5	6.9
Macon	647	1 618	72	84 631	93.0	7.0	74.4	32.6	129	36.4	13.1	-17.1	428.2	8.2	16.7
Macoupin	306	1 042	96	63 396	57.0	43.0	67.9	18.6	35	37.1	1.0	0.0	21.6	0.6	1.3
Madison	248	1 195	68	45 267	66.1	33.9	55.3	12.1	217	32.7	19.5	-9.3	596.3	13.9	28.9
Marion	196	774	37	39 441	68.4	31.6	54.5	10.3	68	36.8	4.7	11.9	107.1	3.7	7.1
Marshall	490	1 414	42	69 548	76.2	23.8	80.7	21.4	16	43.8	0.7	0.0	20.0	0.5	1.0
Mason	548	1 057	51	87 931	84.0	16.0	84.2	28.7	20	20.0	0.2	-33.3	4.2	0.1	0.3
Massac	182	678	15	36 539	48.5	51.5	52.4	11.8	12	33.3	D	D	D	D	D
Menard	607	1 480	42	97 216	66.0	34.0	73.7	31.1	7	14.3	0.1	0.0	1.4	0.1	0.1
Mercer	356	1 112	72	76 762	57.7	42.3	75.0	24.8	16	18.8	0.2	0.0	4.0	0.2	0.4
Monroe	353	1 046	40	60 217	52.8	47.2	64.1	17.9	19	21.1	0.2	100.0	4.5	0.1	0.2
Montgomery	327	1 139	77	61 782	67.4	32.6	70.5	19.5	43	34.9	1.6	0.0	35.4	1.2	2.5
Morgan	446	1 201	77	81 639	64.4	35.6	74.2	26.8	38	31.6	3.5	12.9	74.4	2.6	5.4
Moultrie	501	1 588	44	78 593	81.5	18.5	76.5	26.6	19	21.1	1.0	100.0	19.5	0.8	1.7
Ogle	464	1 375	131	99 809	43.5	56.5	77.8	27.4	66	48.5	5.7	39.0	117.9	4.2	8.2
Peoria	358	1 357	58	52 332	73.5	26.5	58.6	14.2	185	44.9	20.4	-36.8	672.1	9.2	18.5
Perry	234	711	21	36 082	69.0	31.0	56.7	11.3	29	24.1	1.5	25.0	26.4	1.1	2.3
Piatt	779	1 798	63	104 300	91.1	8.9	86.3	38.9	16	31.2	0.5	-16.7	11.4	0.4	0.8
Pike	283	806	87	73 186	47.0	53.0	69.9	21.4	19	21.1	0.3	-40.0	4.8	0.2	0.4
Pope	153	606	6	20 259	42.9	57.1	40.1	3.6	2	0.0	D	D	D	D	D
Pulaski	185	627	12	48 184	68.9	31.1	54.1	13.5	3	66.7	D	D	D	D	D
Putnam	441	1 361	27	110 656	75.0	25.0	81.4	28.1	10	40.0	D	D	D	D	D
Randolph	200	767	39	38 742	57.2	42.8	56.4	11.9	30	46.7	3.6	5.9	85.9	2.7	5.8
Richland	333	1 059	34	54 677	68.7	31.3	66.9	16.4	23	21.7	1.0	-47.4	15.1	0.8	1.3
Rock Island	307	1 181	45	62 680	51.6	48.4	66.1	17.2	200	36.0	14.9	-33.2	481.3	8.5	15.8
St. Clair	341	1 420	55	49 509	70.7	29.3	65.2	14.2	194	31.4	7.7	-1.3	188.9	5.4	10.4
Saline	254	773	17	37 515	82.1	17.9	51.4	12.3	17	47.1	0.4	33.3	4.6	0.3	0.6
Sangamon	601	1 632	122	95 220	77.2	22.8	69.9	29.2	126	30.2	4.3	0.0	91.2	2.7	5.2
Schuyler	314	749	32	53 938	60.2	39.8	67.7	17.7	10	20.0	0.1	0.0	2.1	0.1	0.2
Scott	393	1 018	29	71 559	60.9	39.1	72.0	22.9	8	37.5	0.1	0.0	1.2	0.1	0.1
Shelby	352	1 246	86	60 428	73.7	26.3	70.2	19.2	16	25.0	D	D	D	D	D
Stark	599	1 386	38	87 468	78.8	21.2	82.7	30.0	6	33.3	0.2	0.0	4.0	0.2	0.4
Stephenson	288	1 112	121	93 757	23.5	76.5	79.8	34.3	63	39.7	7.9	-2.5	195.8	5.6	11.1
Tazewell	493	1 640	91	76 605	66.9	33.1	69.9	24.9	97	36.1	8.3	-32.5	284.5	5.9	12.1
Union	144	727	17	29 958	64.9	35.1	39.0	6.4	12	66.7	0.8	-11.1	12.8	0.7	1.2
Vermilion	539	1 321	102	83 404	85.5	14.5	75.8	28.3	108	45.4	8.8	-12.0	247.9	6.5	13.2
Wabash	357	903	20	71 272	77.6	22.4	68.9	23.4	15	46.7	1.4	27.3	30.4	1.1	2.1
Warren	519	1 442	80	89 014	56.8	43.2	79.6	30.1	22	22.7	0.7	16.7	8.7	0.6	1.0
Washington	301	969	65	65 842	52.3	47.7	70.5	20.7	13	38.5	0.2	100.0	3.9	0.2	0.4
Wayne	245	717	52	48 692	72.5	27.5	60.6	15.0	17	11.8	D	D	D	D	D
White	419	871	38	70 602	84.5	15.5	67.5	22.4	11	45.5	0.3	50.0	3.9	0.2	0.4
Whiteside	379	1 239	119	93 360	46.2	53.8	80.9	28.8	65	33.8	7.1	-1.4	196.7	5.4	11.5
Will	500	1 779	81	65 769	82.4	17.6	70.8	15.5	361	36.3	17.6	-17.8	508.7	12.2	25.4
Williamson	122	884	10	16 530	58.6	41.4	31.3	4.1	60	30.0	2.8	-6.7	59.8	2.1	3.6
Winnebago	323	1 284	56	69 766	45.8	54.2	64.7	20.8	725	37.9	39.1	-2.2	1 068.9	24.3	48.9
Woodford	454	1 741	80	72 090	63.6	36.4	72.5	20.7	37	27.0	1.0	-9.1	22.8	0.7	1.5
INDIANA	265	1 158	4 068	57 693	52.3	47.7	57.4	15.5	8 641	41.8	602.0	2.9	15 756.5	426.7	858.9
Adams	275	1 627	74	62 071	37.4	62.6	72.3	16.9	76	51.3	6.4	30.6	136.3	5.3	10.0
Allen	287	1 575	74	45 169	50.8	49.2	59.5	12.2	532	39.8	36.6	1.4	990.9	22.7	44.5

1. Includes livestock and poultry products.

STATE County	Manufactures, 1987 (cont'd)					Value of construction authorized by building permits, 1990							
	Production workers (cont'd)						Nonresidential				Residential		
	Wages							Percent					
	Total (Mil dol)	Average per worker (Dollars)	Value added by manu- facture (Mil dol)	Value of shipments (Mil dol)	New capital expend- itures (Mil dol)	Total[1] ($1,000)	Total ($1,000)	Office	Industrial	Stores	New construction ($1,000)	Number of housing units	Alterations and additions ($1,000)
	134	135	136	137	138	139	140	141	142	143	144	145	146
ILLINOIS—Con.													
Jefferson	52.5	23 864	225.5	403.1	D	10 475	5 749	16.7	1.4	35.7	2 617	25	112
Jersey	1.4	14 000	4.9	12.3	D	13 641	4 993	8.5	0.0	41.4	7 996	108	334
Jo Daviess	19.1	17 364	109.4	226.5	4.4	4 005	1 064	10.5	11.5	11.8	2 453	46	178
Johnson	0.3	NA	1.4	3.2	0.1	NA	NA	NA	NA	NA	NA	NA	NA
Kane	542.9	21 891	2 643.6	5 019.7	D	599 231	139 585	26.1	27.4	35.5	372 573	3 623	28 227
Kankakee	108.0	22 979	606.5	1 301.6	32.0	64 942	19 043	2.4	40.5	44.2	33 221	449	2 786
Kendall	14.3	13 000	79.5	128.0	D	46 482	15 889	20.4	14.2	45.9	26 465	225	2 276
Knox	78.9	21 917	290.9	639.3	8.2	13 569	6 006	10.8	11.1	6.0	4 205	50	689
Lake	450.4	20 380	2 920.7	4 816.3	255.4	730 276	145 861	36.6	14.2	21.0	446 775	4 121	67 756
La Salle	139.2	23 593	626.9	1 325.9	39.6	35 447	16 973	3.0	35.1	26.1	11 410	155	2 725
Lawrence	4.0	10 000	23.2	33.2	D	670	375	0.0	0.0	0.0	95	2	125
Lee	46.7	18 680	214.3	427.0	15.6	21 728	6 883	0.4	9.9	36.4	6 326	92	644
Livingston	76.6	23 212	273.7	575.2	23.3	16 316	7 558	2.6	8.4	67.0	4 803	81	519
Logan	33.7	22 467	242.4	373.3	10.3	6 795	3 064	8.0	0.2	76.5	2 574	44	291
McDonough	28.0	17 500	92.2	164.4	D	3 782	1 588	26.7	0.0	10.8	668	10	150
McHenry	284.4	18 468	1 127.6	2 243.0	71.0	343 864	54 422	16.6	50.6	18.6	244 136	2 319	11 892
McLean	74.3	21 229	323.1	786.3	D	102 456	33 163	36.1	4.9	30.8	46 220	747	4 727
Macon	254.7	31 061	1 281.8	3 345.0	135.6	55 132	18 544	16.2	20.4	32.2	23 513	242	2 375
Macoupin	10.5	17 500	36.8	115.7	3.0	1 055	202	0.0	0.0	0.0	705	11	71
Madison	384.5	27 662	1 308.5	5 455.5	D	137 176	28 944	19.8	15.3	14.6	80 829	1 077	5 633
Marion	75.1	20 297	298.2	469.2	17.4	7 036	2 913	6.5	3.4	72.4	2 089	26	240
Marshall	13.0	26 000	68.9	162.4	D	832	23	0.0	0.0	96.5	515	6	96
Mason	2.3	23 000	17.1	25.5	0.3	3 855	428	42.9	18.7	11.0	1 020	16	292
Massac	D	D	D	D	D	355	60	0.0	0.0	0.0	241	8	54
Menard	1.1	11 000	6.2	12.6	0.1	2 722	54	0.0	0.0	23.0	2 413	47	248
Mercer	2.7	13 500	10.8	33.6	0.6	829	108	0.0	0.0	0.0	571	10	10
Monroe	2.1	21 000	9.8	16.3	D	22 496	6 282	14.0	36.5	1.0	14 569	185	1 130
Montgomery	23.1	19 250	95.5	194.2	9.0	2 884	328	4.7	0.0	0.0	544	19	230
Morgan	50.3	19 346	286.2	740.8	42.3	11 807	6 405	2.8	13.4	51.4	2 791	44	553
Moultrie	14.4	18 000	44.8	85.5	D	5 007	2 259	2.7	3.9	13.5	2 450	39	88
Ogle	77.1	18 357	293.7	833.2	33.9	18 131	2 959	0.0	13.4	18.3	12 211	193	900
Peoria	264.4	28 739	1 204.2	2 588.7	D	183 508	87 739	47.7	3.4	28.6	37 736	398	6 115
Perry	18.4	16 727	52.9	178.6	D	NA	NA	NA	NA	NA	NA	NA	NA
Piatt	8.4	21 000	31.0	69.8	D	6 972	2 406	0.0	79.2	2.8	3 932	43	342
Pike	3.4	17 000	13.5	85.9	0.3	3 494	1 399	3.6	45.2	0.0	1 887	32	72
Pope	D	D	D	D	D	115	82	90.9	0.0	9.1	0	0	0
Pulaski	D	D	D	D	D	830	740	0.0	0.0	0.0	31	1	28
Putnam	D	D	D	D	D	1 969	107	46.6	0.0	0.0	1 526	19	47
Randolph	59.8	22 148	202.2	516.0	21.6	7 711	2 079	15.6	5.3	15.4	4 364	102	115
Richland	8.5	10 625	35.4	131.7	D	1 256	298	0.0	41.3	31.5	525	7	141
Rock Island	227.9	26 812	1 089.7	1 915.5	D	85 329	27 226	34.0	6.6	24.5	16 387	146	17 045
St. Clair	120.2	22 259	557.3	1 376.4	D	88 796	25 110	24.3	34.3	23.6	51 597	670	2 887
Saline	3.4	11 333	8.3	17.1	D	100	100	0.0	0.0	0.0	0	0	0
Sangamon	47.9	17 741	197.5	483.8	D	142 619	39 786	38.4	3.1	25.1	69 426	1 221	6 179
Schuyler	1.2	12 000	1.9	15.9	D	NA	NA	NA	NA	NA	NA	NA	NA
Scott	0.7	7 000	3.5	5.4	D	0	0	NA	NA	NA	0	0	0
Shelby	D	D	D	D	D	7 108	2 324	12.2	0.0	9.2	4 180	76	191
Stark	3.1	15 500	15.2	24.3	0.1	544	245	0.0	16.3	0.0	93	2	126
Stephenson	122.8	21 929	488.0	899.8	D	14 995	3 429	0.9	18.4	23.6	7 880	165	483
Tazewell	192.4	32 610	593.9	1 378.0	D	49 076	13 210	9.5	42.6	21.0	24 823	277	3 001
Union	9.7	13 857	37.2	78.7	1.7	2 791	1 838	24.8	0.0	0.0	844	15	54
Vermilion	176.4	27 138	659.7	1 473.7	29.6	40 736	24 754	1.4	30.9	10.8	4 011	50	1 979
Wabash	23.6	21 455	56.9	83.0	D	1 870	639	0.0	0.0	81.3	858	24	138
Warren	5.7	9 500	15.3	160.9	D	1 019	235	10.6	25.5	0.0	323	5	119
Washington	2.8	14 000	4.1	19.2	0.4	4 456	1 715	0.0	36.9	0.0	1 428	24	105
Wayne	D	D	D	D	D	598	335	0.0	0.0	4.5	135	1	55
White	2.7	13 500	8.5	23.4	0.4	49	12	0.0	0.0	0.0	0	0	0
Whiteside	141.0	26 111	431.9	881.4	40.1	20 104	8 417	1.7	13.5	36.7	7 405	94	832
Will	323.6	26 525	1 617.3	5 223.1	139.8	387 081	92 593	6.4	29.8	43.6	245 045	2 535	28 247
Williamson	37.0	17 619	160.4	376.5	D	49 031	38 175	1.8	0.0	96.3	8 237	152	295
Winnebago	558.5	22 984	2 539.8	4 384.6	D	141 234	40 040	36.9	18.8	33.6	63 909	1 172	9 840
Woodford	15.2	21 714	104.7	198.7	D	19 661	3 074	5.5	19.7	0.8	14 862	174	730
INDIANA	9 874.1	23 141	39 278.8	83 787.9	3 363.9	4 682 559	1 855 379	16.7	44.7	21.9	2 038 260	25 065	172 127
Adams	99.7	18 811	322.7	898.0	15.4	16 206	4 712	0.0	0.0	55.9	8 404	120	1 315
Allen	507.0	22 335	1 918.8	4 020.0	127.2	300 082	129 885	61.2	9.7	18.9	149 323	1 469	15 181

1. Includes nonresidential additions and alterations, residential nonhousekeeping buildings, and residential garages and carports not shown separately.

STATE County	Wholesale trade, 1987				Retail trade, all establishments, 1987				Retail trade, establishments with payroll, 1987					
						Sales				Sales				
											Per capita[2] (Dollars)			
	Establishments	Sales (Mil dol)	Paid employees[1]	Annual payroll (Mil dol)	Number	Total (Mil dol)	Percent change, 1982–1987	Per capita[2] (Dollars)	Number	Total (Mil dol)	General merchandise stores	Food stores	Apparel & accessory stores	Eating and drinking places
	147	148	149	150	151	152	153	154	155	156	157	158	159	160
ILLINOIS—Con.														
Jefferson	94	151.6	698	13.0	449	243.7	30.8	6 464	275	234.2	1 099	943	232	599
Jersey	27	76.7	195	3.3	181	93.0	63.7	4 517	119	91.4	D	D	123	397
Jo Daviess	40	172.5	419	6.9	368	77.8	22.7	3 381	169	71.1	54	757	6	355
Johnson	16	38.0	138	1.5	101	25.1	18.4	2 238	50	22.8	93	560	D	171
Kane	579	3 394.9	6 021	157.9	2 636	2 128.2	59.0	6 896	1 781	2 086.7	D	1 265	427	619
Kankakee	140	530.6	1 786	34.4	779	552.3	31.9	5 642	487	539.2	687	1 088	167	485
Kendall	45	116.5	428	7.6	224	103.8	29.9	2 738	122	99.6	D	628	89	263
Knox	97	455.8	997	18.2	582	340.2	18.8	6 000	381	331.7	1 011	1 199	262	460
Lake	872	5 398.3	9 342	259.7	4 130	3 681.3	60.3	7 581	2 786	3 614.6	703	1 189	370	655
La Salle	207	703.6	1 862	34.0	1 356	697.0	30.6	6 466	843	674.5	759	1 317	244	482
Lawrence	30	47.1	181	3.1	172	62.4	13.7	3 631	95	58.8	D	864	58	200
Lee	82	235.2	633	12.2	347	148.4	49.9	4 290	207	140.5	166	980	120	376
Livingston	88	208.0	516	9.8	387	176.4	21.6	4 387	255	172.3	377	1 029	116	365
Logan	72	236.4	838	14.2	314	155.1	30.1	4 923	200	150.4	560	889	121	442
McDonough	62	111.5	379	5.1	383	171.3	12.1	4 981	241	165.2	713	896	309	661
McHenry	285	737.1	2 664	59.0	1 411	891.3	55.6	5 369	842	867.8	411	1 044	140	461
McLean	241	1 111.3	3 526	73.3	1 202	849.7	41.9	6 880	811	832.8	938	1 072	282	763
Macon	189	3 662.4	2 038	42.9	1 149	783.6	28.0	6 279	748	766.0	965	1 072	255	595
Macoupin	88	167.7	719	13.3	546	205.4	35.2	4 166	292	195.8	246	733	87	260
Madison	282	1 476.1	2 687	57.6	2 287	1 459.5	32.9	5 813	1 478	1 426.2	D	1 368	130	524
Marion	82	158.9	606	11.9	582	252.6	18.0	5 807	342	242.9	772	1 283	145	491
Marshall	38	119.3	216	4.3	145	41.5	39.7	3 165	76	38.5	93	798	22	337
Mason	35	191.6	245	4.3	212	51.0	-13.0	2 916	113	47.9	D	800	D	356
Massac	11	15.6	32	0.5	145	48.3	17.8	3 240	87	46.4	D	705	55	237
Menard	27	52.8	140	2.9	116	31.3	35.5	2 674	55	29.8	D	943	D	100
Mercer	36	65.8	182	3.3	183	46.4	22.4	2 534	92	42.0	D	540	34	239
Monroe	28	51.9	169	3.2	192	103.7	79.7	4 757	114	95.9	D	D	42	505
Montgomery	63	155.6	425	7.5	394	149.6	20.1	4 689	250	142.8	D	1 045	121	480
Morgan	85	351.5	608	11.5	410	229.7	30.4	6 141	248	223.0	894	1 137	251	491
Moultrie	24	75.5	199	3.2	151	47.7	22.6	3 312	79	44.0	D	750	91	367
Ogle	71	426.2	1 041	18.2	452	160.3	24.3	3 499	270	152.3	D	908	83	260
Peoria	416	3 066.3	5 299	124.8	1 819	1 269.4	29.5	6 971	1 232	1 243.2	1 078	1 126	339	661
Perry	33	71.3	350	6.0	256	84.5	7.8	3 840	147	81.1	D	909	122	293
Piatt	43	124.7	304	5.8	159	63.6	45.9	3 953	83	60.6	D	826	20	293
Pike	50	101.6	321	4.6	197	61.8	23.8	3 473	110	57.1	D	725	104	272
Pope	4	D	D	D	34	3.9	-13.3	903	14	3.3	D	D	0	D
Pulaski	11	D	D	D	84	12.5	3.3	1 471	38	10.5	D	541	D	D
Putnam	15	172.5	104	2.3	63	16.6	23.9	2 864	27	15.0	0	864	0	154
Randolph	51	69.3	321	4.8	416	175.9	42.1	4 968	248	167.7	D	1 183	35	427
Richland	46	57.7	212	3.7	224	88.8	-1.6	5 162	135	85.0	906	784	219	416
Rock Island	283	1 959.8	4 184	98.7	1 426	960.6	17.9	6 111	993	944.2	770	1 168	232	688
St. Clair	259	1 182.8	2 567	53.6	2 202	1 419.9	34.5	5 245	1 418	1 393.9	1 087	875	258	501
Saline	43	182.4	382	7.3	362	157.8	14.3	5 597	219	151.5	D	1 439	147	411
Sangamon	334	1 488.5	3 595	86.1	1 817	1 258.7	35.2	7 044	1 167	1 234.7	D	1 204	D	751
Schuyler	18	69.0	127	2.4	86	30.4	30.5	3 901	58	29.4	D	1 050	217	350
Scott	20	163.5	151	3.6	59	14.3	26.5	2 385	27	13.1	D	D	42	209
Shelby	54	233.5	417	7.6	252	60.8	5.6	2 589	117	56.2	D	713	67	146
Stark	19	18.5	80	1.1	83	12.9	7.5	1 901	33	11.1	0	463	0	67
Stephenson	74	118.3	469	9.1	440	258.3	34.3	5 240	290	250.2	418	1 205	178	422
Tazewell	183	1 524.2	2 777	77.5	1 154	738.2	31.6	5 944	720	723.9	667	1 294	140	475
Union	23	22.8	131	2.2	159	68.3	27.7	3 795	105	66.0	D	833	74	293
Vermilion	156	511.4	1 604	31.7	851	479.2	27.4	5 237	536	462.7	809	1 119	221	492
Wabash	26	38.8	175	2.6	154	67.4	-1.6	4 886	98	66.4	D	1 115	111	613
Warren	45	108.7	373	7.9	195	86.4	20.5	4 278	121	84.3	520	949	73	323
Washington	36	83.4	233	4.0	167	53.6	47.3	3 479	97	49.9	D	568	36	242
Wayne	42	91.0	348	6.1	223	75.0	-10.1	4 192	108	69.0	D	1 491	235	187
White	46	60.4	200	4.0	194	78.7	6.6	4 473	112	74.7	D	1 275	37	296
Whiteside	100	464.9	1 294	29.3	599	319.1	24.7	5 105	381	311.1	808	994	140	479
Will	374	1 590.2	3 729	88.4	2 358	1 665.1	44.9	4 876	1 474	1 624.9	D	886	152	407
Williamson	82	137.4	656	11.9	625	332.8	37.4	5 690	373	322.7	D	847	133	414
Winnebago	564	1 360.0	6 002	136.0	2 360	1 634.9	38.6	6 503	1 531	1 600.2	939	1 246	D	605
Woodford	46	119.7	480	11.7	267	133.5	33.1	4 107	144	129.0	55	621	25	282
INDIANA	9 678	40 500.7	108 208	2 344.0	53 633	33 992.3	43.3	6 147	33 083	33 097.1	735	1 096	234	589
Adams	49	147.7	372	6.7	362	183.0	72.8	5 883	200	173.6	310	1 076	114	499
Allen	782	5 266.2	11 566	264.4	2 803	2 234.5	58.1	7 394	1 842	2 185.2	1 049	1 125	319	744

1. For pay period including March 12. 2. Based on the estimated population as of July 1 of the year shown.

STATE County	Retail trade, establishments with payroll, 1987 (cont'd): Paid employees[1]	Retail trade, establishments with payroll, 1987 (cont'd): Annual payroll (Mil dol)	Taxable service industries–establishments with payroll, 1987: Number	Receipts (Mil dol): Total	Receipts (Mil dol), Selected kinds of business: Hotels, motels and other lodging places	Receipts (Mil dol), Selected kinds of business: Health services	Receipts (Mil dol), Selected kinds of business: Legal services	Paid employees	Annual payroll (Mil dol)	Bank deposits,[2] June 1989: Total (Mil dol)	Bank deposits,[2] June 1989: Percent change, 1988–1989	Savings capital,[3] September 1989: Total (Mil dol)	Savings capital,[3] September 1989: Percent change, 1988–1989
	161	162	163	164	165	166	167	168	169	170	171	172	173
ILLINOIS—Con.													
Jefferson	2 780	26.1	227	79.1	7.2	22.8	6.7	2 180	27.6	316	4.1	173.2	8.5
Jersey	1 073	9.4	66	11.9	0.2	5.8	1.3	444	3.7	109	7.2	25.2	-19.5
Jo Daviess	986	6.7	91	18.3	5.8	3.5	1.4	533	5.6	330	6.0	0.0	-100.0
Johnson	270	2.4	28	4.0	0.1	1.6	0.0	129	1.3	101	13.4	0.0	NA
Kane	25 443	245.8	1 907	649.9	D	205.4	42.1	14 835	248.8	2 234	11.7	1 430.3	-5.0
Kankakee	6 243	59.0	537	146.6	3.9	57.6	6.2	3 774	57.0	629	4.5	402.3	-1.8
Kendall	1 261	10.7	112	21.7	D	7.7	0.7	630	7.2	219	5.7	57.7	68.8
Knox	4 064	37.0	263	73.7	3.4	36.3	3.9	1 905	31.9	349	6.5	275.4	-7.1
Lake	38 873	409.3	3 349	1 636.9	67.3	381.7	52.7	29 808	592.4	3 692	7.9	1 581.0	-4.6
La Salle	7 979	72.2	653	144.6	7.9	54.1	11.8	3 791	53.9	972	2.7	746.6	1.9
Lawrence	695	6.3	62	10.2	D	4.8	1.4	360	3.9	135	3.2	57.4	-1.0
Lee	1 715	15.2	159	53.8	2.7	22.0	1.8	1 109	18.1	360	0.9	87.1	-5.2
Livingston	2 145	18.6	173	34.5	0.7	12.9	3.5	808	11.6	415	2.6	199.3	0.9
Logan	1 856	17.4	119	20.5	1.1	8.1	1.7	539	7.0	275	-2.3	145.5	-1.9
McDonough	2 882	18.9	179	31.7	2.3	15.9	1.8	847	11.6	196	2.8	163.4	-13.1
McHenry	9 728	93.2	944	277.6	3.6	74.5	19.0	6 164	95.2	1 213	8.3	527.5	-2.6
McLean	11 471	94.7	679	239.7	11.2	78.5	15.9	5 835	89.1	821	6.4	779.8	2.0
Macon	9 947	92.7	678	235.0	10.4	69.2	15.1	5 505	92.6	969	-29.6	406.4	-4.1
Macoupin	2 092	19.0	161	29.3	0.0	11.7	2.0	825	8.7	450	2.7	59.7	-3.8
Madison	16 946	160.9	1 397	412.6	19.2	132.5	45.8	9 823	139.3	1 690	5.0	1 145.3	-2.1
Marion	2 916	26.4	263	75.4	5.7	41.2	4.6	2 093	27.6	375	0.8	102.8	-10.5
Marshall	575	3.9	55	7.5	D	4.9	0.8	215	2.8	129	3.8	42.0	-8.1
Mason	700	5.2	55	7.8	D	3.2	0.9	228	2.4	179	4.5	28.4	-4.1
Massac	554	4.4	52	10.0	D	4.7	0.9	336	3.6	142	-0.8	6.2	-40.4
Menard	310	2.6	29	4.8	D	1.7	1.1	166	1.4	137	11.5	0.0	NA
Mercer	605	4.3	43	7.5	D	3.7	0.4	250	2.6	126	-12.8	28.3	-2.9
Monroe	1 201	9.9	99	26.0	D	4.7	2.8	711	9.9	276	5.4	34.0	-10.3
Montgomery	1 876	15.0	146	36.3	D	13.7	2.1	1 106	13.4	367	4.6	90.6	-1.4
Morgan	2 559	22.6	203	53.7	4.7	15.5	3.1	1 652	17.3	352	2.2	156.3	-4.1
Moultrie	492	4.5	45	6.6	D	2.9	0.8	219	2.0	141	-1.8	20.4	9.5
Ogle	1 847	16.1	168	39.0	1.5	8.9	2.4	2 096	18.7	352	1.1	86.5	-3.9
Peoria	15 527	142.9	1 230	541.2	22.9	171.5	55.7	12 365	230.3	1 447	7.2	880.0	-10.1
Perry	1 088	9.2	98	16.0	D	8.3	0.9	484	4.9	226	-0.7	35.8	-3.9
Piatt	657	5.3	69	18.0	D	4.1	1.2	355	5.7	235	2.8	26.0	-7.3
Pike	759	5.6	81	9.4	0.6	4.8	0.9	309	3.3	212	1.8	34.9	0.5
Pope	40	0.3	8	1.0	0.0	D	D	64	0.4	20	-0.5	0.0	NA
Pulaski	125	1.0	18	3.9	0.0	D	D	89	1.1	34	2.7	0.0	NA
Putnam	122	0.9	17	4.5	D	0.0	D	97	1.3	64	1.4	0.0	NA
Randolph	1 864	16.2	147	23.7	0.4	12.1	2.1	749	7.8	323	2.0	202.6	1.3
Richland	1 072	9.7	93	23.4	0.7	12.6	1.8	696	9.4	143	5.1	92.8	-2.3
Rock Island	12 774	116.9	882	299.0	12.3	91.1	22.1	7 215	111.8	1 250	2.8	335.4	-9.4
St. Clair	17 406	162.5	1 301	460.0	D	159.8	64.1	10 612	176.2	1 794	8.3	774.2	-7.0
Saline	1 688	15.2	159	39.0	0.8	22.8	3.0	1 096	14.0	369	9.9	45.2	-23.7
Sangamon	15 376	142.4	1 214	542.5	D	172.0	36.6	13 013	207.6	1 711	3.5	643.5	-3.7
Schuyler	430	3.6	44	5.4	D	2.0	0.9	182	1.7	66	4.3	27.9	-5.0
Scott	167	1.4	20	1.1	D	D	0.4	34	0.3	79	0.5	0.0	NA
Shelby	702	5.6	77	10.6	D	4.3	0.8	294	3.3	198	11.8	46.2	-29.4
Stark	134	1.0	21	2.1	D	0.6	0.6	64	0.5	93	8.5	4.1	-27.3
Stephenson	2 858	26.9	218	54.3	1.8	26.0	3.5	1 513	22.5	516	6.6	131.0	-6.1
Tazewell	7 844	76.8	546	148.6	7.4	42.9	6.1	3 897	54.1	645	5.5	524.3	-2.5
Union	766	6.7	70	26.3	D	4.6	1.2	739	7.6	163	5.7	16.2	-17.6
Vermilion	5 937	52.4	411	155.2	5.9	44.1	9.3	3 320	52.0	621	-0.8	205.5	-2.4
Wabash	1 001	7.4	80	12.4	D	4.5	1.3	417	4.3	210	-2.5	34.9	0.8
Warren	918	8.5	91	15.5	D	6.3	1.8	461	4.9	180	-0.2	99.0	-2.8
Washington	636	5.3	50	11.0	1.2	4.1	D	363	3.4	181	6.9	13.2	-7.4
Wayne	823	7.1	75	10.9	D	1.9	1.0	209	2.4	224	-2.6	18.7	3.3
White	955	7.6	77	12.8	0.0	2.6	0.9	264	2.9	255	3.0	28.3	6.3
Whiteside	4 494	35.2	243	55.7	D	27.3	4.4	1 724	21.6	618	2.3	154.2	0.1
Will	18 644	175.4	1 465	475.5	11.7	153.3	29.1	11 565	180.2	1 698	9.0	1 218.0	2.1
Williamson	3 515	33.4	306	79.8	3.6	33.5	6.4	1 849	29.7	429	5.0	126.4	3.2
Winnebago	20 565	190.5	1 596	646.7	D	189.9	39.0	18 113	255.9	1 937	3.3	733.0	-4.4
Woodford	1 409	12.6	85	11.7	0.0	5.2	1.0	329	3.5	197	4.3	111.4	-5.6
INDIANA	412 466	3 726.7	30 336	11 204.5	516.3	3 649.7	631.5	282 483	4 239.8	44 530	6.6	11 590.7	0.0
Adams	2 003	16.6	130	22.0	0.7	8.8	1.3	665	6.4	359	7.8	27.2	2.6
Allen	28 285	262.2	2 045	916.0	D	259.8	47.7	23 066	355.7	3 401	9.6	406.6	6.1

1. For the period including March 12 of the year shown. 2. Includes deposits for all insured and reporting noninsured commercial and mutual savings banks. 3. Includes savings capital for all FSLIC insured savings institutions.

STATE County	Federal funds and grants, 1989: Expenditures: Total (Mil dol)	Expenditures: Percent change, 1988–1989	Per capita[1] (Dollars): Total	Per capita: Direct payments for individuals	Per capita: Procurement contract awards	Per capita: Salaries and wages	Per capita: Grant awards	Local government finances, 1981–1982: General revenue: Total (Mil dol)	Intergovernmental: Total (Mil dol)	Intergovernmental: Percent from state	Taxes: Total (Mil dol)	Taxes: Per capita[2]: Total (Dollars)	Taxes: Per capita[2]: Property (Dollars)	Direct general expenditure: Total (Mil dol)	Direct general expenditure: Percent change, 1977–1982
	174	175	176	177	178	179	180	181	182	183	184	185	186	187	188
ILLINOIS—Con.															
Jefferson	98.9	4.8	2 665	2 066	39	176	253	37.2	17.4	86.0	13.3	353	277	35.8	27.3
Jersey	38.5	0.2	1 851	1 458	11	90	100	18.8	6.4	91.9	4.8	237	201	17.3	35.2
Jo Daviess	62.9	14.7	2 722	1 753	15	111	55	20.8	7.5	88.4	8.8	377	325	20.1	50.8
Johnson	27.8	5.7	2 440	1 837	19	178	211	7.0	4.0	82.0	2.1	211	184	6.4	43.9
Kane	822.3	6.5	2 543	1 389	799	233	83	334.8	97.8	90.1	166.7	592	524	314.2	43.0
Kankakee	267.0	4.7	2 733	1 949	58	167	231	87.2	38.5	86.9	34.7	340	276	84.6	54.4
Kendall	47.3	-6.8	1 206	830	62	63	28	28.5	9.3	94.5	15.7	424	386	24.7	17.7
Knox	166.2	2.1	2 968	2 204	35	174	161	55.4	17.1	88.2	26.0	436	375	49.7	10.2
Lake	1 413.9	-2.2	2 798	1 205	159	1 270	153	536.0	126.7	81.9	320.9	711	633	460.0	43.1
La Salle	334.5	21.4	3 126	2 087	459	151	118	99.2	29.7	88.6	52.9	481	424	94.0	38.8
Lawrence	49.8	-1.3	3 002	2 242	16	131	187	15.9	5.9	94.8	4.9	270	234	15.2	74.7
Lee	99.2	-1.8	2 835	1 710	14	116	129	35.7	12.1	88.6	16.1	453	409	33.8	36.2
Livingston	126.0	10.5	3 119	1 665	37	115	43	38.9	11.2	87.0	20.0	488	437	37.6	51.8
Logan	86.5	2.5	2 729	1 831	14	112	117	27.9	7.4	87.6	15.5	498	451	24.1	31.2
McDonough	77.8	0.0	2 296	1 657	17	132	128	39.7	9.1	80.7	12.8	337	289	38.7	91.0
McHenry	273.7	10.2	1 558	1 184	71	100	109	133.9	37.8	89.1	72.2	480	429	120.9	42.1
McLean	284.4	12.7	2 268	1 365	88	232	109	108.4	26.5	79.2	57.3	475	403	105.0	52.2
Macon	284.4	-0.8	2 325	1 809	73	150	160	117.0	43.8	77.7	51.0	392	315	117.4	60.2
Macoupin	131.9	3.5	2 676	2 203	13	114	123	35.9	16.8	91.6	13.9	284	239	37.0	55.0
Madison	647.1	-2.9	2 550	1 999	194	127	202	226.1	87.1	91.1	86.2	352	290	219.6	26.8
Marion	123.2	-2.0	2 858	2 371	30	186	148	47.7	20.3	87.3	16.1	364	294	49.5	87.1
Marshall	40.4	6.9	3 085	1 913	15	113	126	12.1	3.7	94.3	7.1	499	463	10.4	24.6
Mason	54.9	4.1	3 176	2 127	21	133	128	18.9	5.6	87.7	8.9	471	430	17.0	20.4
Massac	46.1	9.6	3 056	2 237	160	117	340	15.8	6.9	84.8	4.4	298	264	17.4	66.9
Menard	32.6	0.2	2 789	1 730	14	122	115	12.1	4.1	88.9	5.2	450	418	11.3	60.3
Mercer	60.5	5.3	3 342	1 735	280	138	102	20.4	7.0	92.2	7.5	386	352	18.6	25.2
Monroe	44.5	-16.4	1 959	1 550	10	82	136	13.1	4.6	94.3	6.2	306	267	12.7	53.7
Montgomery	93.9	3.4	2 934	2 101	165	153	137	27.0	9.3	85.3	13.5	417	360	24.5	16.8
Morgan	90.2	-1.1	2 417	1 817	16	116	173	29.1	10.2	81.0	13.6	367	307	29.0	47.2
Moultrie	42.2	-13.4	2 933	2 074	13	126	61	9.7	2.5	86.2	5.9	404	372	9.6	45.9
Ogle	107.3	-0.3	2 317	1 385	20	117	147	50.6	14.9	92.5	27.5	602	557	49.0	66.1
Peoria	531.0	3.3	2 929	1 942	298	405	208	235.5	77.3	78.0	101.8	511	432	233.2	48.7
Perry	53.4	2.6	2 471	2 099	13	93	128	18.3	6.2	87.5	6.3	289	227	18.5	70.9
Piatt	46.5	-7.2	2 886	1 825	19	146	56	18.7	6.6	92.9	8.3	507	468	17.6	26.3
Pike	55.5	0.4	3 119	2 153	29	156	244	15.3	7.2	82.0	6.1	330	288	14.9	29.7
Pope	13.5	2.2	3 217	1 909	93	543	308	3.7	2.5	81.3	0.7	174	159	4.2	87.2
Pulaski	28.6	-0.5	3 411	2 312	24	168	700	12.1	10.0	84.9	1.4	164	132	11.3	96.0
Putnam	20.0	31.3	3 503	1 814	21	152	762	6.2	2.2	90.2	3.1	523	491	5.6	28.3
Randolph	79.6	2.1	2 231	1 820	46	130	113	27.1	9.6	90.2	10.1	284	213	24.1	0.4
Richland	45.2	1.3	2 739	2 068	26	135	175	36.7	12.8	92.3	7.7	419	345	35.7	42.9
Rock Island	732.5	6.3	4 772	2 072	532	1 899	198	205.8	59.6	82.7	68.0	406	333	201.3	50.3
St. Clair	1 027.7	1.2	3 798	1 967	245	1 223	342	280.1	153.8	83.1	72.5	271	206	271.8	55.6
Saline	89.0	-4.2	3 200	2 616	38	172	271	27.3	15.0	82.3	8.2	284	225	26.7	60.7
Sangamon	1 073.4	2.8	5 940	1 851	53	468	3 464	160.8	56.2	79.4	73.9	419	354	159.7	52.3
Schuyler	22.7	0.6	2 914	1 838	21	183	278	7.0	2.8	92.2	2.7	330	296	6.1	-3.5
Scott	17.0	-6.1	2 794	1 711	74	164	161	5.4	2.1	92.5	2.0	320	282	5.1	20.6
Shelby	66.7	-2.5	2 816	1 856	48	138	152	21.0	8.5	91.4	8.7	368	335	19.1	55.4
Stark	25.2	-13.5	3 825	2 064	24	183	80	7.5	1.8	92.6	4.7	649	616	6.6	37.1
Stephenson	122.1	7.8	2 477	1 712	37	119	194	45.2	18.0	89.5	18.3	368	319	40.7	42.7
Tazewell	258.9	2.7	2 081	1 642	65	74	153	125.8	34.3	88.7	62.4	475	420	102.9	47.1
Union	47.0	2.2	2 609	2 018	13	122	306	20.3	9.0	90.3	4.8	270	235	21.1	60.2
Vermilion	306.6	1.5	3 399	2 115	325	517	191	96.0	41.2	85.8	36.0	386	334	90.7	40.4
Wabash	31.8	-0.5	2 307	1 770	61	97	123	15.7	4.0	88.7	4.1	298	233	17.2	92.6
Warren	69.7	-0.4	3 501	1 895	20	142	129	21.8	7.0	74.2	7.0	327	285	21.1	41.4
Washington	38.8	-12.1	2 470	1 866	19	149	54	14.8	3.4	90.8	5.8	374	333	13.0	34.1
Wayne	52.4	9.5	2 980	2 023	17	137	268	15.7	6.9	88.8	6.1	329	275	15.1	59.8
White	147.6	172.0	8 681	2 350	5 562	150	282	20.5	6.7	95.0	5.9	321	237	21.6	89.0
Whiteside	156.6	7.8	2 513	1 678	31	117	133	68.8	24.9	91.2	24.0	370	319	66.8	82.8
Will	579.0	12.0	1 647	1 153	269	80	86	327.3	105.7	90.7	143.3	438	383	307.2	49.5
Williamson	203.2	-11.4	3 479	2 130	563	516	234	53.9	20.9	89.0	15.0	262	199	51.5	46.2
Winnebago	582.5	2.3	2 303	1 533	378	171	155	241.1	97.9	85.6	102.4	409	335	228.6	41.9
Woodford	67.8	4.1	2 048	1 340	11	91	59	26.6	8.2	92.7	14.8	442	407	24.0	41.2
INDIANA	16 068.6	7.2	X	1 659	347	306	422	5 323.1	2 415.3	84.2	1 765.4	322	309	4 936.7	54.2
Adams	62.4	14.6	1 951	1 305	22	79	356	29.4	13.6	85.0	9.2	313	309	24.2	64.3
Allen	1 033.6	16.6	3 346	1 395	1 476	223	226	267.6	138.6	76.9	91.6	315	313	245.3	33.3

1. Based on the estimated population as of July 1 of the year shown. 2. Based on the estimated population as of July 1, 1982.

STATE County	Local government finances, 1981–1982 (cont'd): Direct general expenditure (cont'd): Per capita[1] (Dollars)	Percent of total for– Education	Percent of total for– Health & hospitals	Percent of total for– Police protection	Percent of total for– Public welfare	Percent of total for– Highways	Debt outstanding: Total (Mil dol)	Debt outstanding: Per capita[1] (Dollars)	State and local government employment, 1989: Total	State and local government employment, 1989: Rate[2]	Federal government civilian employment 1989: Total	Federal government civilian employment 1989: Earnings ($1,000)	Elections, 1988[3]: Total vote cast for president	Elections, 1988[3]: Vote for lead party (Percent)
	189	190	191	192	193	194	195	196	197	198	199	200	201	202
ILLINOIS—Con.														
Jefferson	951	63.4	0.0	4.0	1.1	6.7	21.1	561	1 856	500.3	171	5 020	15 426	D—50.1
Jersey	846	38.6	35.7	3.7	0.8	8.8	6.7	326	949	456.2	55	1 308	8 752	D—50.0
Jo Daviess	854	48.2	13.8	3.3	0.3	10.3	10.0	424	1 063	460.2	82	2 025	9 137	R—53.9
Johnson	649	62.0	0.2	1.9	1.8	10.8	4.5	453	654	573.7	72	1 591	4 692	R—59.6
Kane	1 116	56.4	0.4	4.7	0.2	7.1	195.9	696	12 914	399.3	1 841	74 670	103 412	R—64.1
Kankakee	828	60.7	0.4	5.9	0.5	9.0	36.6	359	6 327	647.6	429	13 943	35 755	R—56.8
Kendall	666	62.4	0.9	4.7	0.1	10.6	10.3	278	1 209	308.4	71	1 887	15 084	R—70.6
Knox	832	52.9	0.1	5.6	4.3	10.8	57.7	966	3 236	577.9	252	7 393	23 700	D—53.8
Lake	1 019	55.5	1.6	5.9	1.9	6.6	300.2	665	22 200	439.3	9 058	266 546	179 633	R—63.5
La Salle	856	57.5	1.3	4.8	2.8	12.4	40.4	368	4 896	457.6	426	12 254	44 650	D—49.9
Lawrence	837	50.8	20.5	3.0	0.2	12.0	2.7	148	818	492.8	66	1 620	6 823	R—53.6
Lee	951	58.4	1.4	4.1	3.1	10.0	10.6	300	3 211	917.4	109	2 902	13 596	R—65.5
Livingston	919	57.6	0.6	4.1	5.1	11.9	13.3	324	2 486	615.3	141	3 503	15 405	R—67.0
Logan	774	49.7	1.5	6.6	0.4	10.7	8.8	282	2 074	654.3	100	2 630	13 286	R—63.9
McDonough	1 022	31.3	31.8	3.6	0.4	8.8	30.9	816	6 014	1 774.0	111	3 045	12 493	R—57.4
McHenry	803	57.1	4.9	6.8	1.1	7.8	57.1	379	6 690	380.8	453	13 273	65 499	R—70.4
McLean	870	46.3	1.2	5.3	1.7	12.1	84.5	700	10 174	811.3	936	23 452	49 511	R—61.7
Macon	903	47.0	1.3	4.9	1.9	6.0	127.8	983	5 567	455.2	401	12 649	49 489	D—51.3
Macoupin	754	61.2	1.2	5.0	0.4	11.8	21.1	431	1 953	396.1	153	3 988	21 669	D—56.3
Madison	895	52.4	7.7	5.0	1.1	6.4	152.0	619	14 008	551.9	706	21 327	99 695	D—54.3
Marion	1 123	50.4	9.4	3.6	1.0	8.9	16.6	377	2 374	550.8	220	6 577	17 373	R—50.0
Marshall	732	61.6	0.0	5.5	0.5	16.2	4.6	327	517	394.7	51	1 214	6 367	R—56.4
Mason	905	51.8	17.5	3.1	0.3	9.9	9.2	488	933	539.3	67	1 660	6 855	R—49.9
Massac	1 165	47.5	19.4	4.2	1.3	4.3	9.8	659	820	543.0	67	1 838	6 763	R—51.9
Menard	976	46.2	1.8	3.0	8.9	7.9	13.0	1 121	623	532.5	40	974	5 705	R—62.4
Mercer	956	48.3	19.8	2.6	0.3	12.7	8.8	452	912	503.9	84	2 064	7 929	D—53.0
Monroe	624	55.4	1.8	6.2	1.0	11.4	5.4	265	942	415.0	52	1 396	10 851	R—57.8
Montgomery	757	57.2	0.7	4.8	0.4	13.5	17.4	537	1 274	398.1	122	3 068	13 759	D—53.0
Morgan	785	55.1	2.0	6.0	0.3	11.0	15.5	418	2 189	586.9	121	3 446	14 886	R—59.2
Moultrie	659	47.2	1.5	4.6	0.8	15.9	5.4	370	446	309.7	55	1 444	6 212	R—51.0
Ogle	1 074	63.1	0.4	3.7	0.6	12.4	25.5	559	1 965	424.4	164	4 272	17 394	R—66.9
Peoria	1 172	42.6	1.6	5.0	1.6	7.1	207.5	1 043	8 514	469.6	1 641	55 745	73 230	R—51.4
Perry	852	43.7	21.5	3.7	0.4	11.2	6.1	281	940	435.2	56	1 557	9 781	D—52.8
Piatt	1 074	53.5	0.3	3.5	8.7	15.5	5.8	355	912	566.5	69	1 708	7 277	R—56.9
Pike	802	53.4	2.7	3.4	0.7	16.8	7.7	413	644	361.8	87	2 026	8 599	D—53.7
Pope	987	48.2	0.2	6.3	1.8	9.9	1.1	256	232	552.4	105	2 454	2 208	R—54.4
Pulaski	1 285	71.6	0.7	1.7	3.1	5.7	2.0	225	608	723.8	42	1 058	3 478	D—51.6
Putnam	929	63.1	0.2	3.9	0.2	9.1	3.2	528	247	433.3	22	534	3 139	D—51.0
Randolph	677	53.6	13.9	3.7	0.5	8.9	17.7	497	2 534	709.8	112	2 993	15 318	D—51.2
Richland	1 939	48.9	31.8	2.0	0.1	6.1	17.4	943	1 491	903.6	69	1 775	7 153	R—59.6
Rock Island	1 200	39.8	19.0	4.8	1.5	6.0	138.9	828	7 055	459.6	9 427	345 279	67 901	D—59.2
St. Clair	1 016	54.2	4.7	5.6	5.0	6.0	136.7	511	12 401	458.3	5 200	143 043	97 313	D—57.0
Saline	928	65.8	0.2	2.8	3.2	5.9	14.6	508	1 540	554.0	145	4 258	12 521	D—53.3
Sangamon	906	46.0	1.9	5.8	1.2	7.2	294.5	1 671	24 081	1 332.7	2 247	72 090	88 403	R—56.8
Schuyler	742	46.0	2.2	2.6	1.1	25.8	0.5	58	466	597.4	44	1 090	4 066	R—53.6
Scott	837	52.5	0.0	4.5	11.7	9.0	0.8	132	349	572.1	35	876	2 790	R—55.0
Shelby	804	51.1	3.6	2.8	0.4	12.3	7.9	335	907	382.7	131	3 250	10 078	R—53.3
Stark	923	61.2	0.1	1.8	0.9	13.8	1.5	204	311	471.2	38	883	3 153	R—58.4
Stephenson	821	60.1	0.8	3.9	3.7	8.5	17.1	345	2 213	448.9	176	4 831	18 945	R—59.9
Tazewell	784	47.9	0.9	5.9	1.7	8.4	144.8	1 103	5 275	424.0	232	6 790	53 727	R—53.7
Union	1 185	56.3	20.4	2.1	0.2	7.6	12.8	717	1 539	855.0	78	1 863	8 479	R—50.1
Vermilion	972	50.5	1.0	4.4	1.2	6.9	58.9	631	4 296	476.3	1 877	60 754	35 067	D—51.1
Wabash	1 237	31.5	44.6	3.9	0.1	4.2	9.6	693	781	565.9	39	1 055	5 726	R—60.3
Warren	983	41.6	21.0	3.1	0.2	12.1	10.8	502	1 058	531.7	71	1 661	8 254	R—55.5
Washington	844	36.4	23.6	1.9	0.3	13.7	5.3	341	702	447.1	74	1 714	6 874	R—60.0
Wayne	814	53.4	0.7	3.6	0.3	14.7	11.0	595	1 513	859.7	73	1 885	8 660	R—63.3
White	1 179	38.7	35.3	2.2	3.0	9.3	2.1	114	1 144	672.9	68	1 738	8 531	R—51.0
Whiteside	1 029	47.7	19.6	4.5	1.6	6.9	24.5	378	3 241	520.2	202	5 548	24 462	R—53.1
Will	939	55.3	1.1	6.1	1.2	6.4	459.0	1 403	16 003	455.3	643	19 968	123 731	R—59.1
Williamson	902	52.7	19.2	3.5	1.0	5.3	26.0	455	3 153	539.9	1 081	32 650	25 130	D—50.6
Winnebago	912	50.3	1.4	6.8	2.2	7.4	122.0	486	9 934	392.8	1 096	36 414	101 550	R—54.8
Woodford	715	61.5	0.3	4.0	1.2	14.5	12.2	366	1 266	382.5	77	1 966	14 155	R—66.9
INDIANA	900	46.8	10.7	3.9	5.9	5.0	3 517.5	642	310 511	555.4	46 106	1 451 339	2 168 621	R—59.8
Adams	823	51.8	14.8	2.5	3.7	5.5	16.6	564	1 471	459.7	80	2 142	11 997	R—67.8
Allen	844	50.9	0.5	5.6	8.5	3.5	190.5	655	13 457	435.6	1 851	61 713	114 935	R—64.9

1. Based on the estimated population as of July 1, 1982. 2. Per 10,000 resident population estimated as of July 1 of the year shown. 3. Data subject to copyright.

STATE–County code	MSA/CMSA/NECMA code[1]	STATE County	Land Area,[2] 1990 (Sq. Km.)	Population, 1990: Total persons	Rank	Per square kilometer	Race: White	Black	Am. Indian, Eskimo, Aleut	Asian & Pacific Islander	Other race	Hispanic[3]	Age of population Percent: Under 5 years	5 to 14 years	15 to 24 years
			1	2	3	4	5	6	7	8	9	10	11	12	13
		INDIANA—Con.													
18 005	...	Bartholomew	1 054	63 657	687	60.4	61 774	1 005	97	610	171	435	7.2	14.1	14.1
18 007	...	Benton	1 052	9 441	2 438	9.0	9 389	6	16	1	29	108	7.4	16.3	12.2
18 009	...	Blackford	428	14 067	2 051	32.9	13 978	7	44	16	22	90	6.9	13.7	13.5
18 011	3480	Boone	1 095	38 147	1 050	34.8	37 814	83	90	94	66	250	7.5	15.5	12.0
18 013	...	Brown	809	14 080	2 050	17.4	13 968	13	47	18	34	94	6.2	14.0	12.3
18 015	...	Carroll	964	18 809	1 747	19.5	18 720	19	22	3	45	121	7.0	14.9	13.1
18 017	...	Cass	1 069	38 413	1 042	35.9	37 765	330	138	114	66	230	6.7	15.0	13.0
18 019	4520	Clark	972	87 777	519	90.3	82 289	4 703	192	356	237	560	6.6	14.6	14.1
18 021	8320	Clay	926	24 705	1 474	26.7	24 522	113	41	15	14	66	6.8	14.9	13.0
18 023	...	Clinton	1 049	30 974	1 245	29.5	30 657	36	51	61	169	453	7.4	15.6	13.0
18 025	...	Crawford	792	9 914	2 393	12.5	9 868	9	26	11	0	16	6.9	15.4	14.3
18 027	...	Daviess	1 116	27 533	1 373	24.7	27 372	99	26	20	16	86	7.9	16.3	13.2
18 029	1642	Dearborn	791	38 835	1 026	49.1	38 440	252	53	75	15	125	7.4	16.6	13.4
18 031	...	Decatur	965	23 645	1 508	24.5	23 444	39	19	129	14	92	7.3	16.6	14.3
18 033	2760	De Kalb	940	35 324	1 119	37.6	35 009	37	91	88	99	321	7.7	16.5	14.0
18 035	5280	Delaware	1 019	119 659	386	117.4	111 232	7 167	274	641	345	853	6.1	12.1	22.8
18 037	...	Dubois	1 114	36 616	1 086	32.9	36 466	33	30	55	32	244	8.1	15.8	13.6
18 039	2330	Elkhart	1 201	156 198	300	130.1	146 505	7 106	453	997	1 137	2 932	8.5	15.6	14.6
18 041	...	Fayette	557	26 015	1 420	46.7	25 462	435	37	69	12	83	6.2	15.0	14.7
18 043	4520	Floyd	383	64 404	678	168.2	61 415	2 642	92	175	80	254	6.9	15.1	13.6
18 045	...	Fountain	1 025	17 808	1 797	17.4	17 726	4	25	27	26	88	6.7	14.6	13.1
18 047	...	Franklin	1 000	19 580	1 694	19.6	19 496	10	34	27	13	52	7.4	16.9	14.3
18 049	...	Fulton	954	18 840	1 743	19.7	18 555	151	47	36	51	135	6.8	15.4	12.0
18 051	...	Gibson	1 266	31 913	1 214	25.2	31 146	596	38	104	29	133	6.6	14.8	13.0
18 053	...	Grant	1 072	74 169	607	69.2	67 817	5 047	298	373	634	1 514	6.5	13.8	15.8
18 055	...	Greene	1 404	30 410	1 273	21.7	30 248	10	47	65	40	146	6.4	14.7	12.9
18 057	3480	Hamilton	1 031	108 936	423	105.7	106 764	676	163	1 190	143	725	8.2	16.3	12.1
18 059	3480	Hancock	793	45 527	909	57.4	45 173	44	59	176	75	333	6.6	16.0	13.7
18 061	4520	Harrison	1 257	29 890	1 300	23.8	29 641	124	58	36	31	126	6.8	16.6	13.5
18 063	3480	Hendricks	1 058	75 717	594	71.6	74 519	685	157	275	81	353	7.0	15.7	13.9
18 065	...	Henry	1 018	48 139	866	47.3	47 446	474	78	78	63	214	6.1	13.7	13.7
18 067	3850	Howard	759	80 827	564	106.5	75 420	4 398	226	457	326	1 057	7.1	14.8	13.8
18 069	...	Huntington	991	35 427	1 114	35.7	35 012	52	154	133	76	281	7.5	15.9	14.0
18 071	...	Jackson	1 319	37 730	1 055	28.6	37 289	138	66	189	48	122	6.9	15.4	14.0
18 073	...	Jasper	1 450	24 960	1 464	17.2	24 659	111	60	40	90	317	7.1	16.6	16.2
18 075	...	Jay	994	21 512	1 602	21.6	21 313	30	32	67	70	151	7.0	14.9	13.8
18 077	...	Jefferson	936	29 797	1 303	31.8	29 181	363	58	122	73	123	6.4	14.3	16.0
18 079	...	Jennings	977	23 661	1 506	24.2	23 347	209	31	51	23	90	7.0	14.9	14.9
18 081	3480	Johnson	829	88 109	517	106.3	86 455	845	139	534	136	627	7.1	15.2	15.2
18 083	...	Knox	1 336	39 884	1 007	29.9	39 107	486	69	178	44	205	6.1	13.3	18.7
18 085	...	Kosciusko	1 392	65 294	671	46.9	64 058	309	118	322	487	1 258	8.2	16.3	13.9
18 087	...	Lagrange	983	29 477	1 315	30.0	29 156	44	59	92	126	362	10.0	19.3	16.1
18 089	1602	Lake	1 287	475 594	103	369.5	334 203	116 688	865	2 772	21 066	44 526	7.2	16.1	14.2
18 091	...	La Porte	1 550	107 066	430	69.1	96 286	9 580	259	431	510	1 576	6.7	14.4	13.8
18 093	...	Lawrence	1 163	42 836	940	36.8	42 536	109	88	77	26	145	6.5	14.4	13.8
18 095	0400	Madison	1 171	130 669	355	111.6	119 734	9 870	299	415	351	885	6.4	13.9	14.8
18 097	3480	Marion	1 027	797 159	48	776.2	615 039	169 654	1 698	7 579	3 189	8 450	7.9	13.8	14.3
18 099	...	Marshall	1 151	42 182	955	36.6	41 508	76	72	151	375	830	7.7	16.3	13.2
18 101	...	Martin	871	10 369	2 351	11.9	10 321	12	14	14	8	14	7.0	15.4	13.7
18 103	...	Miami	973	36 897	1 076	37.9	34 784	1 115	571	224	203	544	7.9	15.9	15.1
18 105	1020	Monroe	1 021	108 978	422	106.7	102 752	2 835	216	2 713	462	1 367	5.5	10.2	31.8
18 107	...	Montgomery	1 307	34 436	1 150	26.3	33 971	201	68	138	58	159	7.0	14.0	14.6
18 109	3480	Morgan	1 053	55 920	773	53.1	55 635	9	137	91	48	228	7.1	15.7	14.6
18 111	...	Newton	1 041	13 551	2 098	13.0	13 436	9	39	24	43	177	7.0	17.1	12.9
18 113	...	Noble	1 065	37 877	1 053	35.6	37 456	58	83	98	182	625	8.1	16.4	14.5
18 115	...	Ohio	225	5 315	2 818	23.6	5 255	41	8	9	2	7	6.9	15.4	12.7
18 117	...	Orange	1 035	18 409	1 769	17.8	18 213	127	40	21	8	59	7.0	15.0	13.4
18 119	...	Owen	998	17 281	1 836	17.3	17 167	44	46	18	6	55	7.0	15.2	13.2
18 121	...	Parke	1 152	15 410	1 963	13.4	15 222	118	42	16	12	95	6.5	13.8	13.3
18 123	...	Perry	988	19 107	1 727	19.3	18 819	210	32	32	14	66	6.3	15.1	14.3
18 125	...	Pike	871	12 509	2 181	14.4	12 469	3	16	19	2	40	6.3	13.7	12.9
18 127	1602	Porter	1 083	128 932	359	119.1	126 329	454	243	944	962	3 858	6.8	16.1	15.5
18 129	2440	Posey	1 058	25 968	1 422	24.5	25 588	283	38	34	25	104	7.6	16.0	12.8
18 131	...	Pulaski	1 123	12 643	2 173	11.3	12 509	65	21	20	28	106	7.6	16.4	13.1
18 133	...	Putnam	1 244	30 315	1 278	24.4	29 196	826	77	154	62	182	6.0	13.2	20.1
18 135	...	Randolph	1 173	27 148	1 385	23.1	26 947	56	49	37	59	192	6.5	14.4	13.9

1. MSA = Metropolitan Statistical Area. CMSA = Consolidated MSA. NECMA = New England county metropolitan area. PMSA = Primary MSA. See Appendix A for explanation of these concepts. See Appendix B for list of metropolitan areas identified by type, with component counties. 2. Dry land or land partially or temporarily covered by water. 3. Hispanic persons may be of any race.

STATE County	Population, 1990 (cont'd)							Population–Change and components of change							
	Age of population (cont'd) Percent							Change		Components of change, 1980–1986					
								1980–1990				Net change		Natural increase	
	25 to 34 years	35 to 44 years	45 to 54 years	55 to 64 years	65 to 74 years	75 years and over	Percent female	Number	Percent	Total persons, 1986	Total persons, 1980	Number	Percent	Births	Deaths
	14	15	16	17	18	19	20	21	22	23	24	25	26	27	28
INDIANA—Con.															
Bartholomew	16.0	15.8	12.2	9.0	6.7	4.8	51.4	-1 431	-2.2	64 500	65 088	-600	-0.9	5 300	3 000
Benton	14.6	13.1	10.2	9.5	9.4	7.2	51.1	-777	-7.6	9 800	10 218	-400	-4.0	1 000	600
Blackford	14.8	14.1	11.5	10.1	8.7	6.5	51.5	-1 503	-9.7	15 000	15 570	-500	-3.5	1 300	1 000
Boone	16.1	16.3	11.5	8.3	6.8	6.0	51.8	1 701	4.7	38 400	36 446	2 000	5.4	3 500	2 100
Brown	15.0	16.6	12.8	10.4	7.9	4.8	50.0	1 703	13.8	12 800	12 377	400	3.5	1 000	600
Carroll	15.0	14.5	11.2	9.6	8.8	6.0	51.0	-913	-4.6	19 100	19 722	-600	-3.1	1 600	1 100
Cass	15.3	14.5	10.8	9.5	8.9	6.3	52.0	-2 523	-6.2	39 700	40 936	-1 200	-3.0	3 500	2 400
Clark	16.9	15.8	10.9	9.1	7.1	5.0	52.3	-1 061	-1.2	88 800	88 838	0	0.0	7 800	4 600
Clay	15.0	13.5	10.2	9.6	9.2	7.7	52.0	-157	-0.6	24 700	24 862	-200	-0.7	2 300	1 900
Clinton	15.4	14.1	10.0	8.9	8.4	7.1	51.7	-571	-1.8	31 100	31 545	-400	-1.3	2 900	2 200
Crawford	14.9	14.4	10.6	9.2	7.6	6.6	50.4	94	1.0	10 300	9 820	500	4.6	800	700
Daviess	14.6	13.5	9.5	8.9	8.9	7.1	51.6	-303	-1.1	28 700	27 836	900	3.3	2 900	1 800
Dearborn	15.6	15.6	10.8	8.6	7.0	4.9	51.0	4 544	13.3	37 200	34 291	2 900	8.4	3 300	2 000
Decatur	15.8	13.9	10.2	8.5	7.4	6.0	50.7	-196	-0.8	23 500	23 841	-300	-1.2	2 200	1 400
De Kalb	17.1	14.7	9.8	8.1	6.6	5.3	51.0	1 718	5.1	33 800	33 606	200	0.6	3 000	1 800
Delaware	13.9	13.0	10.6	8.8	7.3	5.4	52.5	-8 928	-6.9	120 900	128 587	-7 700	-6.0	9 800	6 400
Dubois	17.8	14.4	9.8	8.3	6.6	5.7	50.9	2 378	6.9	36 000	34 238	1 800	5.2	3 700	1 700
Elkhart	16.6	15.2	10.3	8.0	6.4	4.8	51.1	18 868	13.7	146 400	137 330	9 100	6.6	14 800	6 700
Fayette	13.9	15.1	10.9	9.6	8.4	6.1	51.6	-2 257	-8.0	27 500	28 272	-800	-2.8	2 400	1 600
Floyd	16.1	16.1	10.7	8.8	7.4	5.4	52.3	3 199	5.2	63 000	61 205	1 800	2.9	5 500	3 300
Fountain	14.3	13.2	11.6	9.8	9.5	7.2	51.7	-1 225	-6.4	18 600	19 033	-400	-2.3	1 600	1 200
Franklin	15.3	14.5	10.3	8.9	6.9	5.5	50.5	-32	-0.2	20 100	19 612	500	2.6	1 800	1 000
Fulton	15.3	13.5	10.8	10.1	9.1	6.9	51.4	-495	-2.6	18 700	19 335	-600	-3.2	1 700	1 200
Gibson	15.4	14.1	10.5	9.8	8.5	7.2	52.0	-1 243	-3.7	33 500	33 156	400	1.1	3 100	2 100
Grant	14.2	14.2	11.6	10.2	8.1	5.7	51.9	-6 765	-8.4	77 100	80 934	-3 900	-4.8	6 600	4 400
Greene	14.7	14.2	11.0	9.7	9.1	7.3	51.5	-6	0.0	30 400	30 416	0	-0.1	2 400	2 100
Hamilton	17.5	18.5	11.7	7.5	5.0	3.2	51.1	26 909	32.8	94 200	82 027	12 200	14.8	7 500	3 200
Hancock	15.0	17.1	12.6	8.6	6.1	4.3	50.8	1 588	3.6	44 900	43 939	1 000	2.3	3 600	2 100
Harrison	16.0	16.1	10.8	8.7	6.5	4.9	50.4	2 614	9.6	29 100	27 276	1 800	6.8	2 700	1 400
Hendricks	16.6	16.9	12.0	8.2	6.0	3.7	49.6	5 913	8.5	74 500	69 804	4 700	6.7	6 100	2 900
Henry	14.9	14.9	11.8	10.1	8.5	6.2	52.0	-5 197	-9.7	50 100	53 336	-3 200	-6.0	3 900	3 200
Howard	15.6	15.2	12.2	9.6	7.0	4.8	52.2	-6 069	-7.0	85 200	86 896	-1 700	-1.9	8 000	4 300
Huntington	16.3	14.0	9.9	8.3	7.7	6.5	51.5	-169	-0.5	35 500	35 596	-100	-0.1	3 400	2 300
Jackson	16.1	14.3	10.7	9.0	7.4	6.2	51.5	1 207	3.3	37 100	36 523	600	1.7	3 400	2 200
Jasper	14.7	14.2	10.7	8.1	7.2	5.1	50.5	-1 178	-4.5	26 300	26 138	100	0.5	2 500	1 300
Jay	14.4	13.8	11.3	9.6	8.7	6.6	51.4	-1 727	-7.4	21 800	23 239	-1 500	-6.3	2 000	1 400
Jefferson	15.4	14.5	11.0	9.0	7.8	5.7	51.3	-622	-2.0	29 300	30 419	-1 100	-3.8	2 500	1 700
Jennings	16.2	15.0	11.6	8.8	6.8	4.7	50.5	807	3.5	22 800	22 854	0	-0.2	1 900	1 100
Johnson	16.6	16.4	11.2	7.8	5.8	4.8	51.5	10 869	14.1	83 200	77 240	6 000	7.7	7 100	3 600
Knox	14.0	12.9	9.7	9.3	8.4	7.5	51.4	-1 954	-4.7	41 400	41 838	-500	-1.1	3 600	3 000
Kosciusko	16.3	14.7	10.3	8.4	7.0	4.9	51.0	5 739	9.6	63 600	59 555	4 000	6.8	6 900	3 000
Lagrange	14.7	13.1	9.2	7.5	6.0	4.2	50.1	3 927	15.4	28 000	25 550	2 400	9.5	3 600	1 100
Lake	16.0	14.5	10.4	9.3	7.7	4.6	52.0	-47 323	-9.0	491 700	522 917	-31 200	-6.0	52 000	27 000
La Porte	16.6	15.7	10.6	9.2	7.9	5.2	49.1	-1 566	-1.4	106 100	108 632	-2 600	-2.4	9 900	6 200
Lawrence	14.9	14.8	11.5	9.7	8.1	6.4	51.6	364	0.9	42 400	42 472	0	-0.1	3 400	2 600
Madison	15.2	14.8	11.2	9.5	8.2	5.8	51.1	-8 667	-6.2	132 700	139 336	-6 600	-4.8	11 000	7 700
Marion	20.1	14.6	9.3	8.3	6.8	4.9	52.5	31 926	4.2	785 000	765 233	19 700	2.6	83 000	42 600
Marshall	15.7	14.6	10.2	9.0	7.4	5.9	50.9	3 027	7.7	41 300	39 155	2 100	5.5	4 000	2 300
Martin	15.2	14.4	10.9	9.5	8.6	5.3	50.7	-632	-5.7	11 000	11 001	0	0.2	1 100	600
Miami	16.8	14.5	9.8	8.4	6.8	4.8	50.7	-2 923	-7.3	38 000	39 820	-1 900	-4.7	4 100	2 000
Monroe	16.8	12.8	8.0	6.5	4.9	3.7	51.7	10 193	10.3	101 700	98 785	2 900	2.9	7 400	3 400
Montgomery	16.0	13.8	11.0	9.3	7.9	6.4	50.4	-1 065	-3.0	35 300	35 501	-200	-0.6	3 000	2 100
Morgan	16.1	15.6	11.9	8.6	6.1	4.2	50.9	3 921	7.5	53 000	51 999	1 000	1.9	4 800	2 500
Newton	15.1	14.5	11.2	8.8	7.3	6.0	50.8	-1 293	-8.7	13 900	14 844	-900	-6.4	1 300	800
Noble	16.1	14.7	9.9	8.2	6.9	5.2	50.7	2 434	6.9	37 200	35 443	1 700	4.9	3 700	1 900
Ohio	16.6	13.9	11.1	9.5	7.6	6.4	51.4	201	3.9	5 300	5 114	200	3.7	500	300
Orange	15.2	14.3	10.4	9.5	8.8	6.4	51.3	-268	-1.4	19 300	18 677	700	3.5	1 600	1 200
Owen	15.0	14.8	11.3	10.2	7.7	5.7	50.7	1 440	9.1	16 900	15 841	1 000	6.4	1 300	900
Parke	14.4	14.0	11.4	10.7	8.8	7.1	51.5	-962	-5.9	15 900	16 372	-500	-2.8	1 300	1 100
Perry	16.8	14.0	9.7	9.1	8.4	6.2	49.5	-239	-1.2	19 000	19 346	-400	-1.9	1 700	1 200
Pike	15.2	14.3	11.6	10.2	8.6	7.1	50.8	-956	-7.1	13 200	13 465	-300	-1.9	1 100	1 000
Porter	15.6	16.9	11.2	8.0	6.0	3.8	51.1	9 116	7.6	123 100	119 816	3 200	2.7	11 300	4 700
Posey	16.6	15.8	10.6	8.6	6.8	5.2	50.6	-446	-1.7	25 800	26 414	-600	-2.2	2 600	1 400
Pulaski	14.9	13.3	9.7	9.5	8.9	6.7	50.7	-615	-4.6	13 200	13 258	0	-0.2	1 300	900
Putnam	15.3	13.4	10.2	9.2	7.0	5.7	48.7	1 152	4.0	30 000	29 163	800	2.8	2 200	1 700
Randolph	14.4	14.2	11.0	10.3	8.6	6.7	51.6	-2 849	-9.5	28 000	29 997	-2 000	-6.6	2 300	1 700

STATE County	Population–(cont'd): Components of change, 1980-1986 (cont'd): Net migration	Households, 1990: Number	Households, 1990: Percent change, 1980–1990	Households, 1990: Persons per household	Households, 1990: Percent: Female family householder[1]	Households, 1990: Percent: One-person	Births, 1988: Total	Births, 1988: Rate[2]	Births, 1988: Low birth weight[3] (Number)	Deaths, 1987: Number: Total	Deaths, 1987: Number: Infant[4]	Deaths, 1987: Rate: Total[2]	Deaths, 1987: Rate: Infant[5]	Marriages, 1984: Number	Marriages, 1984: Rate[2]
	29	30	31	32	33	34	35	36	37	38	39	40	41	42	43
INDIANA—Con.															
Bartholomew	-2 900	24 192	6.1	2.60	9.2	21.7	866	13.4	50	498	3	7.7	3.4	666	10.3
Benton	-800	3 524	-3.5	2.65	7.3	23.9	131	13.4	9	114	4	11.8	31.7	72	7.2
Blackford	-800	5 436	-2.5	2.56	8.6	23.2	163	11.2	8	143	2	9.8	10.9	168	11.1
Boone	600	13 922	10.1	2.69	6.9	19.7	546	14.0	28	359	3	9.3	5.6	357	9.4
Brown	0	5 370	21.2	2.61	5.7	20.4	174	13.2	7	97	2	7.5	12.0	195	15.9
Carroll	-1 200	7 067	1.1	2.63	6.1	21.4	259	13.4	15	161	3	8.4	12.4	207	10.7
Cass	-2 400	14 659	-0.4	2.55	9.7	24.5	493	12.4	22	398	3	9.9	5.5	399	10.0
Clark	-3 100	33 292	7.3	2.59	12.2	23.3	1 182	13.3	67	758	6	8.5	5.6	808	9.0
Clay	-600	9 382	1.6	2.60	8.6	24.0	367	14.6	22	315	3	12.5	8.9	251	10.2
Clinton	-1 100	11 450	1.1	2.65	8.4	22.1	456	14.3	27	378	1	11.9	2.3	308	9.8
Crawford	300	3 660	5.7	2.69	8.1	22.4	122	12.0	9	91	2	8.9	14.6	99	9.9
Daviess	-100	10 012	1.4	2.70	8.3	24.2	434	15.0	24	287	5	9.9	12.1	254	8.8
Dearborn	1 600	13 642	18.8	2.81	9.1	19.2	493	12.9	29	320	2	8.5	3.8	355	9.7
Decatur	-1 100	8 427	4.4	2.77	8.6	20.9	341	14.1	16	234	2	9.8	6.2	239	10.1
De Kalb	-1 000	12 725	11.3	2.75	8.3	21.3	515	14.5	25	301	7	8.6	13.3	343	10.3
Delaware	-11 100	45 177	1.1	2.47	10.6	25.9	1 458	12.1	86	1 080	15	9.0	10.0	1 170	9.5
Dubois	-200	13 023	16.3	2.75	6.7	21.9	571	15.6	26	302	7	8.3	11.8	368	10.4
Elkhart	1 000	56 713	17.8	2.71	9.1	21.6	2 722	18.0	160	1 162	24	7.8	9.4	1 592	11.1
Fayette	-1 500	9 945	-0.2	2.58	11.0	24.1	327	12.0	19	277	4	10.0	12.9	246	8.8
Floyd	-400	24 085	12.2	2.63	12.6	21.9	893	13.8	62	596	7	9.3	8.5	575	9.2
Fountain	-800	6 858	-1.6	2.57	7.3	23.8	211	11.5	10	230	4	12.4	18.7	169	9.0
Franklin	-300	6 636	8.1	2.90	6.8	18.2	280	13.9	14	143	1	7.1	3.4	151	7.4
Fulton	-1 100	7 345	2.0	2.54	7.6	24.2	260	13.9	12	226	1	12.1	4.3	174	9.3
Gibson	-600	12 299	1.0	2.56	7.9	24.5	452	13.7	30	294	4	8.9	9.8	323	9.5
Grant	-6 100	27 701	-0.9	2.56	11.4	23.7	1 009	13.3	72	731	7	9.6	7.4	772	9.9
Greene	-300	11 910	3.4	2.52	8.2	24.8	363	11.8	17	364	1	11.8	2.8	310	10.2
Hamilton	7 800	38 834	42.4	2.78	6.9	17.0	1 504	14.7	87	578	15	5.9	10.1	757	8.5
Hancock	-600	15 959	10.3	2.82	6.8	17.0	556	12.2	24	364	8	8.1	14.8	453	10.2
Harrison	500	10 618	16.9	2.79	8.3	18.2	348	11.8	24	262	1	9.0	2.7	267	9.4
Hendricks	1 500	26 109	15.1	2.81	7.1	16.4	975	12.7	54	543	15	7.2	15.4	614	8.5
Henry	-3 900	18 642	-0.8	2.55	9.3	22.8	621	12.6	33	482	6	9.8	10.5	534	10.6
Howard	-5 400	31 523	1.5	2.54	11.3	25.0	1 123	13.6	74	686	7	8.2	6.1	945	11.1
Huntington	-1 200	12 830	3.8	2.68	8.1	21.9	574	15.7	31	381	1	10.5	1.9	367	10.5
Jackson	-600	14 032	8.3	2.66	9.1	21.2	540	14.5	24	333	2	9.0	3.9	312	8.4
Jasper	-1 100	8 527	2.9	2.80	7.5	19.1	349	13.3	17	217	3	8.3	9.8	264	9.9
Jay	-2 100	8 161	-2.4	2.61	8.4	23.7	306	13.9	27	256	2	11.6	7.2	189	8.5
Jefferson	-1 900	10 897	5.9	2.57	10.5	23.4	385	12.9	19	277	3	9.3	7.8	257	8.4
Jennings	-800	8 351	14.2	2.75	8.7	20.0	314	13.5	24	189	2	8.3	6.2	219	9.6
Johnson	2 500	31 354	23.7	2.71	8.6	19.3	1 221	14.2	81	664	13	7.8	11.0	813	10.0
Knox	-1 100	15 145	-2.2	2.45	9.5	27.9	448	11.0	15	464	4	11.4	8.8	422	10.0
Kosciusko	200	23 449	12.4	2.74	7.2	20.1	1 116	17.1	64	493	11	7.6	10.4	651	10.5
Lagrange	0	9 209	18.5	3.15	5.7	16.6	633	21.9	27	191	10	6.7	17.4	274	10.1
Lake	-56 200	170 748	-2.5	2.76	15.9	23.2	7 445	15.3	644	4 371	73	9.0	11.3	4 173	8.3
La Porte	-6 300	38 488	2.9	2.63	10.9	23.6	1 404	13.3	93	936	20	8.9	14.3	1 057	9.9
Lawrence	-800	16 235	4.6	2.60	8.3	22.5	550	12.8	43	428	4	10.0	8.3	453	10.7
Madison	-10 000	49 804	-0.4	2.52	11.4	24.9	1 678	12.7	132	1 253	25	9.5	15.0	1 393	10.4
Marion	-20 700	319 471	12.1	2.45	13.8	29.3	14 161	17.9	1 120	6 947	181	8.8	13.5	8 577	11.1
Marshall	500	15 146	11.0	2.74	7.5	21.0	617	14.8	33	347	4	8.4	6.3	432	10.6
Martin	-400	3 836	1.1	2.64	7.9	23.9	163	14.4	10	127	0	11.2	0.0	120	10.9
Miami	-4 000	13 484	-1.5	2.68	8.6	21.2	626	16.6	23	275	3	7.3	4.7	401	10.6
Monroe	-1 000	39 351	15.9	2.39	8.3	28.5	1 278	12.4	75	571	10	5.6	8.7	977	9.6
Montgomery	-1 100	13 235	2.1	2.51	7.8	24.4	487	13.7	19	331	4	9.3	9.3	380	10.7
Morgan	-1 300	19 600	14.2	2.83	8.4	16.2	560	10.2	42	415	6	7.6	8.1	546	10.2
Newton	-1 400	4 839	-4.3	2.77	7.5	20.4	174	12.6	10	126	2	9.2	12.6	108	7.7
Noble	-100	13 418	11.2	2.78	8.1	19.8	630	16.3	31	308	1	8.0	1.6	387	10.7
Ohio	100	1 980	8.9	2.66	7.6	21.6	82	14.9	5	65	0	11.8	0.0	63	11.9
Orange	200	6 950	3.5	2.61	8.8	22.8	251	13.0	16	186	3	9.7	12.1	176	9.3
Owen	500	6 394	13.5	2.68	7.5	19.6	259	14.6	18	142	2	8.2	9.4	159	9.7
Parke	-700	5 845	-1.8	2.55	8.3	23.6	217	13.9	16	168	0	10.7	0.0	174	10.6
Perry	-800	6 845	1.3	2.66	9.1	23.0	221	11.7	12	178	2	9.4	8.5	188	9.8
Pike	-400	4 925	-2.5	2.52	7.5	23.5	165	12.8	9	122	2	9.4	11.6	129	9.6
Porter	-3 300	45 159	15.4	2.77	8.4	19.6	1 558	12.5	88	806	8	6.6	5.3	1 050	8.5
Posey	-1 800	9 508	4.8	2.71	7.2	20.4	390	14.8	18	239	3	9.1	8.5	246	9.3
Pulaski	-500	4 722	0.7	2.65	6.4	23.8	187	14.1	12	145	3	10.9	17.3	143	10.7
Putnam	300	9 996	6.3	2.62	6.9	21.7	352	11.7	17	263	4	8.7	11.7	269	9.0
Randolph	-2 600	10 451	-2.4	2.57	8.4	22.9	362	13.1	19	276	4	9.9	12.5	257	9.0

1. No spouse present. 2. Per 1,000 resident population estimated as of July 1 of the year shown. 3. Under 2,500 grams. 4. Deaths of infants under 1 year old. 5. Deaths of infants under 1 year old per 1,000 live births.

STATE County	Divorces, 1984 Number	Divorces, 1984 Rate[1]	Physicians, active non–Federal, 1989 Number[2]	Physicians Rate[3]	Hospitals, 1989 Number	Hospitals Beds Number	Hospitals Beds Rate[3]	Nursing homes,[4] 1986 Number	Nursing homes Beds	Serious crimes known to police, 1988 Number Total[5]	Serious crimes Number Violent[6]	Serious crimes Rate[3]	Education Public school enrollment[7] 1986–1987	Public school enrollment 1980	Attainment,[8] 1980 Percent 12 yrs. or more	Attainment, 1980 Percent 16 yrs. or more
	44	45	46	47	48	49	50	51	52	53	54	55	56	57	58	59
INDIANA—Con.																
Bartholomew	494	7.6	93	143	3	282	434	6	474	2 831	87	4 321	11 628	13 758	68.5	14.8
Benton	38	3.8	6	61	0	0	0	2	96	139	12	1 407	2 134	2 200	70.1	9.4
Blackford	127	8.4	6	42	1	60	417	2	138	310	56	2 107	2 858	3 399	63.1	7.1
Boone	261	6.9	69	176	2	111	282	4	339	551	9	4 605	7 073	8 085	74.5	15.7
Brown	43	3.5	3	22	0	0	0	1	70	96	4	727	2 256	2 515	66.6	14.3
Carroll	53	2.7	8	41	0	0	0	2	126	310	46	1 884	3 050	4 280	68.1	8.1
Cass	343	8.6	48	120	2	642	1 605	1	233	1 090	79	6 184	7 656	8 579	69.9	8.9
Clark	1 096	12.2	100	112	3	327	366	7	777	3 313	323	3 673	16 321	18 151	63.6	9.2
Clay	175	7.1	12	47	1	78	308	3	234	385	71	4 961	4 492	4 902	65.2	8.3
Clinton	140	4.5	16	50	1	53	165	6	498	862	72	5 602	6 086	6 420	65.3	9.3
Crawford	63	6.3	2	20	0	0	0	1	78	99	16	NA	2 004	2 106	49.1	5.6
Daviess	125	4.3	18	62	1	148	510	5	470	225	12	775	4 345	4 727	58.2	7.1
Dearborn	181	5.0	25	65	1	131	339	2	236	244	42	5 712	7 651	7 421	60.7	9.6
Decatur	146	6.2	17	70	1	80	329	3	351	182	7	1 211	4 833	5 043	61.6	8.1
De Kalb	183	5.5	22	60	1	56	154	4	349	445	42	1 269	6 769	7 290	68.3	8.5
Delaware	409	3.3	214	179	1	552	461	11	1 066	4 348	291	3 580	21 440	25 300	66.4	14.9
Dubois	130	3.7	32	86	2	207	558	5	484	582	37	1 591	6 486	7 516	58.3	10.2
Elkhart	960	6.7	159	104	3	605	394	9	1 100	7 573	384	5 019	26 856	27 890	65.6	12.3
Fayette	186	6.6	20	74	1	93	343	3	190	1 009	77	6 101	5 625	5 808	56.7	7.2
Floyd	396	6.3	88	135	1	266	407	5	634	2 283	164	5 723	11 188	12 094	62.6	10.6
Fountain	100	5.3	7	38	0	0	0	1	143	43	4	352	3 444	4 038	63.2	8.0
Franklin	81	4.0	4	20	0	0	0	1	48	104	11	610	2 975	4 370	53.6	7.8
Fulton	79	4.2	12	64	1	49	262	2	197	17	4	NA	2 856	3 894	68.5	8.5
Gibson	161	4.7	13	40	2	143	436	5	434	17	3	NA	5 445	6 154	62.1	9.0
Grant	499	6.4	92	122	2	856	1 134	7	597	1 958	237	2 536	13 539	16 827	62.7	9.7
Greene	238	7.8	13	42	1	76	245	4	318	260	11	3 115	5 820	6 020	58.7	7.3
Hamilton	429	4.8	242	227	1	122	114	5	500	2 308	156	2 334	18 721	19 040	80.6	25.7
Hancock	365	8.2	43	93	1	120	259	4	391	1 119	24	2 467	9 184	10 418	73.5	11.3
Harrison	74	2.6	21	70	1	68	228	2	180	435	16	1 678	5 607	5 875	62.5	6.8
Hendricks	227	3.1	74	95	1	127	162	7	687	623	52	3 564	11 547	15 519	76.4	14.4
Henry	281	5.6	40	82	1	107	218	9	675	793	63	4 326	9 863	11 808	60.8	7.4
Howard	841	9.9	94	115	2	349	426	5	627	2 999	221	3 526	15 740	19 304	68.5	11.0
Huntington	185	5.3	24	65	1	69	186	4	518	695	28	4 056	6 688	6 932	71.2	10.3
Jackson	217	5.8	31	83	1	106	284	3	328	833	60	2 216	6 705	6 811	59.8	7.4
Jasper	65	2.4	13	50	1	73	279	1	180	218	20	826	4 465	5 575	64.3	9.3
Jay	146	6.6	14	63	1	65	294	3	200	249	25	2 679	4 558	5 119	60.0	6.9
Jefferson	170	5.6	42	140	2	560	1 860	3	307	212	11	1 188	5 223	5 979	62.3	12.2
Jennings	113	5.0	8	34	1	48	206	2	104	433	15	1 868	4 490	4 831	58.2	6.8
Johnson	467	5.8	84	96	2	280	320	11	1 851	1 215	56	2 668	17 107	17 630	70.8	13.3
Knox	203	4.8	54	134	1	281	699	4	474	134	13	832	6 395	7 100	62.5	9.9
Kosciusko	280	4.5	48	72	1	113	170	5	433	474	21	3 342	13 337	11 892	68.4	12.1
Lagrange	114	4.2	10	34	1	62	211	2	242	347	45	1 191	5 729	5 036	52.6	6.9
Lake	2 372	4.7	714	147	6	2 616	538	20	2 711	25 668	3 536	5 509	89 981	105 246	63.3	10.1
La Porte	545	5.1	153	145	4	574	544	7	774	4 559	202	4 387	19 444	21 296	63.7	10.6
Lawrence	229	5.4	53	123	2	254	588	5	602	986	54	2 555	7 823	8 999	57.8	6.7
Madison	890	6.7	137	104	4	655	498	11	1 095	4 982	443	6 243	23 814	29 246	64.5	10.4
Marion	5 812	7.5	2 853	358	15	5 619	704	62	6 170	48 478	6 626	6 088	122 505	136 110	67.5	16.3
Marshall	205	5.0	31	74	2	86	205	5	377	136	12	3 415	7 122	7 923	67.1	10.4
Martin	58	5.3	4	35	0	0	0	1	36	71	12	2 340	2 044	2 541	58.3	7.3
Miami	235	6.2	22	59	1	145	387	2	238	89	12	NA	8 683	8 445	70.2	7.8
Monroe	536	5.3	167	161	1	285	275	4	601	3 744	199	3 586	12 855	14 246	74.7	31.3
Montgomery	152	4.3	36	101	1	86	242	5	431	983	139	2 724	6 253	7 313	71.7	10.9
Morgan	351	6.5	40	72	2	168	304	5	412	642	37	3 543	10 993	12 298	64.9	9.5
Newton	111	7.9	6	43	0	0	0	2	133	223	35	1 603	2 948	3 385	64.8	8.3
Noble	193	5.3	19	48	1	51	130	4	314	458	52	3 984	7 277	7 687	63.4	7.4
Ohio	36	6.8	0	0	0	0	0	1	58	13	1	NA	986	1 070	54.2	7.9
Orange	163	8.6	9	47	1	38	197	3	180	121	13	629	3 506	3 742	54.2	7.0
Owen	70	4.3	5	27	0	0	0	3	146	24	5	NA	2 637	3 592	57.3	7.0
Parke	112	6.8	8	52	0	0	0	3	334	326	24	2 034	2 748	3 536	67.2	8.1
Perry	153	8.0	10	53	1	55	293	1	165	128	14	1 487	3 758	4 092	52.0	6.3
Pike	71	5.3	3	23	0	0	0	1	134	30	4	1 054	2 341	2 656	56.6	6.3
Porter	486	3.9	168	134	1	379	303	5	727	3 215	223	2 591	24 332	25 605	74.5	14.7
Posey	131	5.0	8	30	0	0	0	4	260	32	6	NA	4 682	5 193	64.1	9.7
Pulaski	67	5.0	6	45	1	47	353	2	79	101	15	753	2 482	2 930	63.2	8.0
Putnam	205	6.9	18	59	1	85	281	6	338	119	11	NA	5 577	5 814	70.0	12.1
Randolph	182	6.4	11	40	2	68	247	3	198	380	73	4 334	5 915	6 494	64.4	7.8

1. Per 1,000 resident population estimated as of July 1 of the year shown. 2. As of end of year. 3. Per 100,000 resident population as of July 1 of the year shown. 4. Preliminary. Covers nursing homes with 3 or more beds. 5. Data for serious crimes have not been adjusted for underreporting, this may affect comparability between geographic areas or over time. 6. Includes murder and nonnegligent manslaughter, forcible rape, robbery, and aggravated assault. 7. The 1986–1987 data are based on administrative reports obtained by the U.S. National Center for Education Statistics. The 1980 data are based on the 1980 Census of Population and Housing. 8. Persons 25 years old or older.

STATE County	Education (cont'd): Local government expenditures for education,[1] 1982: Total (Mil dol)	Education (cont'd): Local government expenditures for education,[1] 1982: Per capita (Dollars)	Social Security Program December 1988: Beneficiaries: Total	Social Security Program December 1988: Beneficiaries: Rate[2]	Social Security Program December 1988: Payments ($1,000)	Supplemental Security Income Program recipients June 1986	Money income: Per capita[3]: 1987 Income, (Dollars)	Money income: Per capita[3]: 1979: Current dollars	Money income: Per capita[3]: 1979: Constant 1987 dollars	Money income: Median household income 1979 (Dollars)	Money income: Percent below poverty level, 1979: Persons	Money income: Percent below poverty level, 1979: Families	Housing units, 1990: Total	Housing units, 1990: Percent change, 1980–1990
	60	61	62	63	64	65	66	67	68	69	70	71	72	73
INDIANA—Con.														
Bartholomew	33.5	518	9 560	147.5	4 889	640	12 302	7 947	12 435	19 504	8.7	7.0	25 432	6.0
Benton	6.0	597	2 020	206.1	1 015	60	9 908	6 906	10 806	16 529	8.6	6.6	3 833	-3.1
Blackford	6.0	389	2 775	191.4	1 411	100	9 388	6 157	9 634	15 686	9.7	8.3	5 856	-3.6
Boone	14.2	375	5 375	137.8	2 800	150	13 283	8 030	12 565	19 435	7.1	5.4	14 516	7.7
Brown	5.2	420	1 255	95.1	629	58	10 292	6 690	10 468	16 481	10.9	8.6	6 997	16.0
Carroll	7.6	384	2 945	152.6	1 493	76	10 574	6 976	10 915	17 324	7.5	5.2	8 431	0.4
Cass	21.3	530	7 230	181.2	3 634	402	10 457	7 031	11 001	17 567	7.5	6.1	15 633	-0.9
Clark	34.9	392	13 850	155.4	6 746	940	10 253	6 552	10 252	17 014	8.8	7.3	35 313	6.7
Clay	10.7	442	5 605	223.3	2 706	298	9 306	6 218	9 729	14 885	10.9	8.4	10 606	3.1
Clinton	15.1	475	5 730	180.2	2 866	230	10 515	6 960	10 890	16 150	9.5	7.4	12 100	-0.5
Crawford	3.5	357	2 020	198.0	845	210	7 701	5 115	8 003	11 738	18.8	15.2	4 374	6.0
Daviess	9.2	319	4 850	167.8	2 137	320	8 708	5 565	8 708	12 579	16.7	12.8	10 985	4.1
Dearborn	15.4	441	6 005	157.6	2 982	320	10 431	6 567	10 275	17 699	8.3	6.9	14 532	17.1
Decatur	8.8	365	4 100	170.1	1 937	232	9 618	6 013	9 409	15 717	11.0	9.1	9 098	4.0
De Kalb	13.4	407	5 005	141.0	2 534	202	10 476	6 760	10 577	18 220	6.7	4.6	13 601	10.7
Delaware	49.3	392	19 870	165.4	10 245	1 502	10 461	6 716	10 509	16 455	12.6	9.0	48 793	2.5
Dubois	15.7	458	5 495	149.7	2 691	148	11 498	6 926	10 837	17 657	6.7	4.6	13 964	18.2
Elkhart	60.9	445	20 965	138.7	11 188	940	11 471	7 222	11 300	17 593	7.9	5.8	60 182	16.0
Fayette	12.3	441	5 025	184.7	2 527	320	10 053	6 072	9 501	15 111	11.4	8.7	10 525	-1.0
Floyd	27.6	442	10 385	160.8	5 049	722	11 072	6 843	10 707	17 298	9.1	7.4	25 238	10.8
Fountain	7.3	382	3 960	216.4	1 938	180	9 825	6 505	10 178	15 896	8.3	6.2	7 344	-5.0
Franklin	5.1	250	2 710	134.2	1 210	186	9 740	5 757	9 008	15 660	10.1	7.4	7 176	7.5
Fulton	5.9	305	3 610	193.0	1 786	92	10 244	6 717	10 510	15 822	8.9	7.2	8 656	0.3
Gibson	13.3	388	6 155	186.5	3 031	264	10 398	6 940	10 859	16 456	9.8	7.4	13 454	3.0
Grant	39.2	501	13 540	178.6	6 798	918	10 388	6 703	10 488	17 031	10.2	7.9	29 904	-0.9
Greene	10.6	344	6 130	199.0	2 769	296	9 226	6 017	9 415	13 253	12.2	9.3	13 337	5.6
Hamilton	38.4	455	9 740	95.2	5 163	420	16 360	9 426	14 749	24 407	4.2	3.2	41 074	41.3
Hancock	17.9	409	5 695	124.6	2 929	204	12 024	7 609	11 906	21 724	6.2	5.0	16 495	8.8
Harrison	10.8	379	4 505	152.7	2 038	248	9 510	6 028	9 432	16 197	8.5	6.8	11 456	14.9
Hendricks	28.3	395	8 330	108.5	4 401	242	12 569	7 925	12 400	22 679	4.0	3.4	26 962	14.1
Henry	23.1	448	9 665	196.0	4 879	582	9 985	6 401	10 016	16 168	10.1	8.3	19 835	-0.8
Howard	38.8	455	13 235	160.2	6 947	710	11 695	7 656	11 979	19 220	8.1	6.5	33 820	2.7
Huntington	13.1	382	6 550	179.0	3 325	164	10 580	6 764	10 584	17 047	7.0	5.2	13 629	2.6
Jackson	16.0	428	6 770	182.0	3 285	382	9 643	6 243	9 768	15 749	9.6	7.8	14 820	6.7
Jasper	9.5	354	4 150	158.4	2 086	130	9 989	6 855	10 726	18 810	7.8	6.2	8 984	2.7
Jay	9.9	442	4 365	198.4	2 181	180	9 243	5 925	9 271	14 636	10.9	8.3	8 905	-1.8
Jefferson	15.8	517	5 285	176.8	2 410	444	9 377	6 050	9 466	14 726	12.7	9.8	11 921	6.8
Jennings	7.8	344	3 780	162.9	1 708	302	9 133	5 802	9 078	15 951	11.6	10.0	9 129	16.8
Johnson	30.0	377	11 350	132.3	5 889	460	12 039	7 520	11 767	20 800	6.7	5.1	33 289	22.3
Knox	13.2	310	8 125	200.1	3 849	578	9 179	6 166	9 648	13 193	13.3	10.3	16 730	1.9
Kosciusko	24.5	410	9 390	143.6	4 813	258	11 305	6 864	10 740	16 754	8.3	6.6	30 516	4.0
Lagrange	13.1	506	3 335	115.4	1 678	112	8 903	5 638	8 822	15 612	16.6	11.7	12 218	15.5
Lake	240.3	468	81 315	166.7	43 004	5 738	10 748	7 725	12 087	21 307	11.0	9.2	183 014	-1.8
La Porte	44.6	411	17 725	167.9	9 344	790	10 796	7 279	11 389	18 708	8.3	6.1	42 268	4.2
Lawrence	16.8	405	7 700	179.1	3 609	504	9 814	6 302	9 861	14 756	8.8	7.1	17 587	6.1
Madison	53.1	393	24 540	186.2	12 874	1 448	10 947	7 161	11 205	17 887	9.4	7.3	53 353	0.0
Marion	341.6	443	124 165	156.8	64 705	9 064	12 212	7 677	12 012	17 400	11.1	8.4	349 403	12.9
Marshall	14.3	361	6 680	159.8	3 340	162	10 405	6 705	10 491	16 519	8.9	7.2	16 820	9.4
Martin	4.2	385	1 905	168.6	786	152	8 671	5 377	8 413	13 934	12.2	8.5	4 116	0.0
Miami	20.3	537	5 370	142.8	2 559	272	9 364	6 222	9 736	15 649	8.4	7.4	14 639	0.2
Monroe	29.2	289	11 240	109.0	5 816	662	10 324	6 303	9 862	13 721	15.0	8.1	41 948	15.8
Montgomery	14.2	404	6 255	176.2	3 154	258	10 822	6 968	10 903	16 748	6.6	4.7	13 957	1.4
Morgan	20.8	396	7 540	137.3	3 777	416	10 928	7 018	10 981	19 742	8.8	7.0	20 500	12.3
Newton	6.6	436	2 080	150.7	1 046	70	9 522	6 690	10 468	18 034	9.0	7.2	5 276	-4.1
Noble	13.1	371	5 755	149.1	2 835	188	9 648	6 235	9 756	16 455	8.7	6.9	15 516	7.6
Ohio	1.5	298	835	151.8	387	48	9 575	6 259	9 793	15 315	9.7	8.9	2 161	-0.4
Orange	6.9	371	3 570	185.0	1 567	310	8 385	5 318	8 321	12 282	14.8	11.3	7 732	3.8
Owen	6.0	379	2 755	155.6	1 277	156	9 365	5 769	9 027	14 012	12.8	10.0	8 011	14.8
Parke	5.9	352	3 190	204.5	1 514	186	9 438	6 172	9 657	14 795	11.8	8.9	7 189	-3.5
Perry	7.1	371	3 735	197.6	1 768	226	8 918	5 921	9 265	15 107	10.6	8.4	7 404	0.9
Pike	5.7	425	2 480	192.2	1 175	154	9 907	6 535	10 225	14 855	9.4	7.5	5 487	0.9
Porter	54.4	442	15 455	124.3	8 385	548	11 870	8 459	13 236	24 201	4.9	3.8	47 240	13.8
Posey	11.6	432	3 875	147.3	1 894	226	11 025	6 924	10 834	18 790	8.5	7.3	10 401	4.7
Pulaski	8.7	656	2 590	194.7	1 237	82	9 559	6 336	9 914	14 954	11.4	8.8	5 541	2.3
Putnam	11.9	403	4 800	158.9	2 400	214	10 074	6 482	10 142	17 318	8.7	6.7	10 981	7.1
Randolph	15.2	525	5 585	202.4	2 769	196	9 605	6 149	9 621	15 664	10.8	8.8	11 327	-1.8

1. Elementary and secondary. 2. Per 1,000 resident population estimated as of July 1 of the year shown. 3. Based on the resident population estimated as of July 1, 1988 for 1987 data and enumerated as of April 1, 1980 for 1979 data.

STATE County	Housing units, 1990 (cont'd) — Occupied units — Total	Owner occupied — Percent	Owner occupied — Median value (Dollars)	Median rent (Dollars)	Civilian labor force, 1990 — Total	Percent change, 1989–1990	Unemployment — Total	Unemployment — Rate[1]	Private nonfarm establishments, 1988 — Number	Net change, 1987–1988	Employment[2] — Total	Per-cent change, 1987–1988	Manu-facturing	Retail trade
	74	75	76	77	78	79	80	81	82	83	84	85	86	87
INDIANA—Con.														
Bartholomew	24 192	73.2	57 200	305	31 116	-4.2	1 622	5.2	1 589	19	30 340	-2.1	15 817	4 964
Benton	3 524	72.9	38 100	196	4 352	-1.0	186	4.3	236	-13	2 021	0.6	380	363
Blackford	5 436	77.3	32 300	181	6 883	-2.9	574	8.3	289	5	3 462	-3.2	1 890	656
Boone	13 922	76.2	71 100	297	20 739	-3.5	566	2.7	912	6	8 393	3.6	1 541	2 320
Brown	5 370	82.6	64 900	278	6 011	-3.9	317	5.3	291	17	1 585	0.8	105	684
Carroll	7 067	78.0	45 400	210	8 223	-3.1	401	4.9	370	6	3 375	0.0	1 017	789
Cass	14 659	74.4	40 300	219	19 582	-3.4	1 188	6.1	884	1	12 246	4.6	5 622	2 481
Clark	33 292	68.4	50 000	285	47 956	-0.8	2 684	5.6	1 871	20	26 928	-1.6	7 260	8 017
Clay	9 382	79.3	35 500	197	10 890	-0.3	530	4.9	455	-2	4 274	1.7	1 454	1 049
Clinton	11 450	72.0	40 900	241	15 655	-0.2	869	5.6	698	-12	8 013	0.0	3 513	1 792
Crawford	3 660	85.2	31 800	142	5 183	-1.5	409	7.9	147	4	970	5.0	169	315
Daviess	10 012	78.0	40 600	188	14 003	2.5	654	4.7	644	12	5 804	-4.5	1 407	1 516
Dearborn	13 642	78.3	59 900	248	19 308	0.8	1 595	8.3	654	-5	8 813	9.2	2 592	1 666
Decatur	8 427	75.6	44 900	227	12 565	-0.6	602	4.8	519	-7	6 727	10.4	3 209	1 426
De Kalb	12 725	81.2	49 700	259	18 733	-1.5	1 186	6.3	764	2	13 275	3.9	7 234	2 041
Delaware	45 177	66.8	42 300	254	60 611	-0.3	3 175	5.2	2 557	-52	41 732	4.1	11 200	10 396
Dubois	13 023	78.7	58 000	240	21 270	-1.0	847	4.0	1 032	6	19 675	6.0	9 897	3 329
Elkhart	56 713	71.8	62 300	335	94 095	-3.9	5 364	5.7	4 522	165	94 211	4.8	54 015	12 222
Fayette	9 945	69.9	41 100	225	11 482	-0.4	1 381	12.0	487	9	10 477	8.9	6 223	1 463
Floyd	24 085	71.8	57 600	267	34 100	-0.6	1 626	4.8	1 281	-25	16 057	6.0	5 382	3 639
Fountain	6 858	76.7	37 000	183	7 367	-2.2	469	6.4	379	10	3 949	-5.6	1 750	1 088
Franklin	6 636	79.5	53 300	200	10 328	2.7	769	7.4	252	6	2 223	6.8	702	522
Fulton	7 345	77.3	42 200	225	9 690	-2.6	506	5.2	447	-1	5 551	0.3	2 969	965
Gibson	12 299	78.6	44 400	192	16 412	-1.7	976	5.9	696	-12	8 033	7.4	2 620	1 750
Grant	27 701	71.3	40 400	231	35 237	-0.4	2 336	6.6	1 585	3	26 537	0.2	10 457	5 212
Greene	11 910	80.4	36 800	190	15 560	-0.8	1 089	7.0	585	11	4 402	0.5	1 017	1 434
Hamilton	38 834	76.9	106 500	412	55 944	-3.4	1 492	2.7	2 720	151	33 017	6.3	5 490	6 808
Hancock	15 959	80.0	72 000	299	24 058	-2.9	890	3.7	893	28	7 792	-8.1	2 107	2 128
Harrison	10 618	85.3	51 800	219	14 668	-1.1	793	5.4	470	5	4 637	2.3	1 197	1 201
Hendricks	26 109	82.4	75 700	327	40 401	-3.3	1 077	2.7	1 179	12	10 717	0.2	1 038	3 306
Henry	18 642	75.2	36 800	210	21 873	-2.4	1 921	8.8	930	-5	10 691	6.7	3 477	2 904
Howard	31 523	72.1	51 700	279	39 731	-1.9	2 634	6.6	1 820	-13	35 692	-1.5	17 437	7 842
Huntington	12 830	76.7	44 200	266	19 329	-1.8	994	5.1	758	15	11 663	0.5	5 264	2 292
Jackson	14 032	77.1	43 900	237	19 310	1.4	1 179	6.1	845	28	12 402	4.0	4 387	2 691
Jasper	8 527	75.4	55 100	228	13 309	-2.0	733	5.5	587	53	5 996	2.0	1 491	1 299
Jay	8 161	77.6	32 400	181	9 454	1.9	812	8.6	407	8	5 661	1.1	3 112	1 001
Jefferson	10 897	73.2	44 900	215	14 349	-0.5	804	5.6	642	-20	8 405	1.2	3 287	1 842
Jennings	8 351	80.0	43 700	221	12 474	3.2	688	5.5	330	6	3 514	6.8	1 432	809
Johnson	31 354	74.0	72 200	339	45 750	-3.5	1 625	3.6	1 852	77	22 298	1.9	4 505	7 891
Knox	15 145	70.6	39 800	226	18 333	-1.7	971	5.3	1 039	-8	9 957	-2.0	1 694	2 913
Kosciusko	23 449	79.0	60 600	280	36 984	-0.7	1 688	4.6	1 610	17	24 759	1.0	12 167	3 992
Lagrange	9 209	81.4	55 100	244	14 495	1.6	928	6.4	519	9	7 822	-8.7	3 988	1 282
Lake	170 748	67.8	54 800	287	207 805	0.4	12 862	6.2	8 830	95	155 604	5.0	44 703	35 620
La Porte	38 488	73.1	52 700	266	50 650	-2.6	2 883	5.7	2 227	22	34 787	0.1	12 366	7 464
Lawrence	16 235	79.7	42 000	222	20 786	-0.6	1 831	8.8	774	22	10 746	8.3	4 701	2 613
Madison	49 804	73.1	43 700	250	59 535	-1.8	3 805	6.4	2 548	-42	41 748	0.0	16 386	9 536
Marion	319 471	57.0	61 400	345	434 632	-3.3	19 395	4.5	21 457	498	433 780	5.6	84 465	89 372
Marshall	15 146	76.7	49 600	263	22 865	1.5	1 271	5.6	976	-2	12 762	-2.3	5 797	2 301
Martin	3 836	81.7	38 700	172	5 442	-1.8	331	6.1	193	7	2 041	10.9	839	501
Miami	13 484	70.6	40 300	238	15 459	-1.5	958	6.2	632	13	6 664	1.1	2 563	1 666
Monroe	39 351	54.8	66 600	339	60 553	-0.7	2 004	3.3	2 427	91	34 735	5.6	8 559	10 383
Montgomery	13 235	72.2	48 100	253	19 598	-0.5	828	4.2	801	-13	12 073	2.0	5 604	2 380
Morgan	19 600	78.9	59 700	287	27 502	-3.3	1 456	5.3	939	29	10 148	0.5	3 085	3 093
Newton	4 839	76.9	43 300	207	6 966	-1.9	330	4.7	255	-6	2 722	14.6	1 048	578
Noble	13 418	78.1	49 100	253	22 726	-1.5	1 598	7.0	857	16	14 058	9.3	8 709	1 869
Ohio	1 980	78.6	45 400	193	2 306	-4.1	159	6.9	61	0	339	-8.9	0	123
Orange	6 950	81.1	37 400	188	9 070	-3.0	876	9.7	330	-1	5 854	1.0	2 508	749
Owen	6 394	83.0	43 000	206	10 868	-0.6	501	4.6	220	6	2 021	14.1	589	594
Parke	5 845	79.0	37 900	193	7 544	-3.9	411	5.4	289	-5	2 027	-8.1	525	536
Perry	6 845	79.8	42 600	190	7 856	0.5	759	9.7	355	8	3 863	5.1	1 890	750
Pike	4 925	82.6	35 700	174	5 497	1.0	397	7.2	204	4	1 594	9.0	114	295
Porter	45 159	75.2	69 600	340	55 946	0.1	2 104	3.8	2 261	58	34 360	6.7	11 058	7 710
Posey	9 508	80.3	58 800	213	12 717	-1.0	610	4.8	493	-3	5 909	0.6	2 530	936
Pulaski	4 722	77.5	40 300	198	6 990	1.1	384	5.5	278	0	2 877	-3.8	1 303	579
Putnam	9 996	75.9	51 600	242	12 717	-0.5	454	3.6	544	3	6 058	-14.3	1 014	1 356
Randolph	10 451	75.6	35 500	185	11 594	-7.0	1 157	10.0	575	-15	7 701	-2.5	4 427	1 170

1. Percent of total civilian labor force. 2. For week including March 12. Excludes government employees, self-employed persons, farm workers, domestic service workers, railroad employees subject to the Railroad Retirement Act, and employees on oceanborne vessels or in foreign countries.

STATE County	Private nonfarm establishments, 1988 (cont'd)				Personal income, 1989								Earnings, 1989		
	Employment[1] (cont'd)		Annual payroll								Per capita[3]			Percent by selected industries	
	Finance, insurance, and real estate	Services	Total (Mil dol)	Average per employee (Dollars)	Total (Mil dol)	Percent change, 1988–1989	Wages and salaries[2] (Mil dol)	Proprietor's income (Mil dol)	Dividends, interest, & rent (Mil dol)	Transfer payments (Mil dol)	Dollars	Rank	Total (Mil dol)	Farm	Goods-related[4] Total
	88	89	90	91	92	93	94	95	96	97	98	99	100	101	102
INDIANA—Con.															
Bartholomew	1 388	4 227	781	25 730	1 033	5.6	895	97	184	124	15 891	683	993	1.4	57.3
Benton	135	310	32	15 999	145	12.6	40	26	34	23	14 880	1 033	66	27.2	15.2
Blackford	166	422	61	17 643	206	8.9	93	16	28	34	14 312	1 280	109	4.8	53.1
Boone	595	1 724	136	16 215	788	8.3	214	77	133	69	20 025	168	291	5.7	28.7
Brown	33	628	17	10 426	172	8.0	32	18	29	19	12 828	1 988	49	2.7	17.1
Carroll	268	474	52	15 362	297	8.4	75	39	57	36	15 232	897	113	19.5	28.6
Cass	456	1 938	205	16 774	599	7.6	313	51	103	101	15 002	987	364	3.6	43.1
Clark	712	5 917	468	17 363	1 298	5.2	721	107	181	204	14 529	1 197	828	0.8	30.8
Clay	186	766	75	17 456	335	9.2	127	36	60	65	13 242	1 794	163	6.5	40.8
Clinton	347	1 213	129	16 056	483	9.4	201	54	84	72	15 040	974	254	10.1	44.2
Crawford	58	168	11	11 791	110	6.6	23	11	14	24	10 806	2 715	34	8.1	23.3
Daviess	283	1 229	81	13 965	373	9.4	155	60	74	73	12 864	1 972	215	10.2	34.3
Dearborn	436	1 437	163	18 528	560	6.0	220	41	78	79	14 458	1 229	261	1.1	40.0
Decatur	232	871	123	18 256	359	8.9	184	40	63	51	14 750	1 106	225	5.5	50.1
De Kalb	264	2 418	247	18 593	535	7.6	369	39	90	63	14 702	1 127	408	2.3	64.8
Delaware	1 627	10 903	804	19 274	1 768	6.6	1 146	130	287	281	14 770	1 095	1 276	0.9	36.9
Dubois	520	2 852	347	17 642	648	9.7	463	70	136	68	17 470	371	532	3.3	53.6
Elkhart	2 154	13 584	1 888	20 043	2 524	6.5	2 395	221	423	265	16 442	537	2 617	0.7	61.7
Fayette	290	1 804	230	21 990	379	6.6	302	32	61	66	13 981	1 445	334	2.2	66.6
Floyd	792	3 691	256	15 966	1 029	6.9	400	79	162	150	15 732	727	479	0.9	33.6
Fountain	167	556	63	16 073	256	10.5	84	27	45	45	14 012	1 432	111	12.5	38.1
Franklin	141	470	32	14 380	267	8.5	56	32	47	32	13 195	1 817	88	13.2	31.2
Fulton	279	546	97	17 399	263	6.2	126	30	50	42	14 064	1 403	156	6.6	48.7
Gibson	306	1 768	142	17 737	500	6.4	204	58	99	80	15 229	899	262	7.5	33.3
Grant	1 388	6 964	553	20 834	1 115	8.1	822	74	159	180	14 778	1 090	896	1.4	54.4
Greene	274	768	54	12 297	386	7.8	134	30	70	81	12 438	2 144	164	4.3	37.6
Hamilton	2 602	7 031	704	21 323	2 551	10.2	944	202	386	155	23 928	53	1 146	0.9	25.2
Hancock	325	1 491	138	17 740	802	8.6	241	70	99	80	17 328	391	311	4.3	39.3
Harrison	308	772	68	14 583	398	9.3	112	37	64	54	13 365	1 748	149	6.4	28.9
Hendricks	583	2 533	183	17 051	1 358	8.6	374	97	167	115	17 361	384	471	3.2	18.0
Henry	469	2 419	196	18 368	727	7.9	294	58	111	134	14 828	1 062	352	3.1	42.4
Howard	1 125	6 168	980	27 446	1 395	7.6	1 362	86	187	185	17 033	429	1 448	0.8	65.9
Huntington	501	2 432	187	16 054	562	7.5	278	42	99	77	15 161	923	320	3.2	51.5
Jackson	672	2 504	187	15 071	548	10.1	303	52	94	82	14 673	1 143	356	5.8	42.0
Jasper	383	1 144	106	17 702	384	9.5	168	43	67	52	14 682	1 139	211	8.5	24.4
Jay	202	732	86	15 243	293	10.9	130	36	50	51	13 296	1 773	166	10.1	46.0
Jefferson	241	1 882	148	17 568	362	8.3	249	43	61	74	12 022	2 321	292	3.2	36.9
Jennings	130	712	54	15 290	303	10.9	114	28	36	68	12 970	1 919	141	7.6	NA
Johnson	1 078	5 661	335	15 016	1 535	8.3	495	125	215	154	17 562	361	620	1.4	30.1
Knox	575	2 555	146	14 690	560	7.9	281	64	111	117	13 934	1 457	345	6.7	17.7
Kosciusko	790	4 879	516	20 859	1 099	9.3	686	115	180	112	16 553	514	801	3.1	57.7
Lagrange	276	981	132	16 839	375	9.1	179	52	61	41	12 736	2 019	230	9.2	48.1
Lake	6 565	42 367	3 525	22 650	7 301	6.8	5 156	394	1 054	1 214	15 017	984	5 550	0.2	44.5
La Porte	1 189	8 088	651	18 716	1 678	7.0	944	120	253	236	15 905	672	1 064	1.6	40.4
Lawrence	382	1 962	210	19 500	601	7.1	315	46	84	109	13 910	1 467	361	1.5	51.5
Madison	1 508	10 149	949	22 731	2 048	8.1	1 377	122	314	335	15 558	785	1 499	0.9	56.6
Marion	40 655	126 011	9 485	21 865	14 143	7.3	13 805	978	2 162	1 934	17 730	329	14 783	0.1	28.5
Marshall	407	2 631	211	16 520	618	7.2	316	65	108	76	14 698	1 129	381	3.9	47.9
Martin	92	301	34	16 563	128	7.8	223	9	20	27	11 249	2 578	232	0.8	NA
Miami	370	1 116	99	14 817	506	6.5	267	34	71	82	13 486	1 691	301	3.7	25.5
Monroe	1 708	8 390	567	16 337	1 444	8.1	1 042	126	235	186	13 905	1 471	1 167	0.2	29.2
Montgomery	372	2 223	239	19 826	572	10.1	353	48	95	78	16 111	614	401	3.5	53.1
Morgan	465	1 995	149	14 680	818	7.5	227	61	93	102	14 822	1 068	288	2.8	28.5
Newton	96	489	42	15 510	195	6.5	68	26	34	27	14 138	1 376	94	14.0	NA
Noble	356	1 491	233	16 600	549	9.6	316	43	82	67	13 975	1 446	358	3.2	61.7
Ohio	0	90	4	10 392	68	5.9	8	4	9	11	12 190	2 238	13	7.8	NA
Orange	208	1 320	81	13 858	230	6.9	114	27	34	44	11 912	2 355	141	4.3	NA
Owen	95	276	30	14 834	214	9.8	45	19	32	33	11 777	2 413	64	6.8	29.6
Parke	93	507	25	12 369	212	7.1	51	25	36	39	13 640	1 608	76	12.1	20.6
Perry	218	532	60	15 642	243	5.9	98	22	44	44	12 890	1 955	120	2.1	42.0
Pike	131	331	28	17 712	177	4.7	89	15	33	33	13 807	1 532	105	6.3	38.6
Porter	1 536	9 027	737	21 457	2 079	7.5	1 141	146	287	215	16 618	499	1 287	0.6	47.6
Posey	219	937	141	23 851	391	6.8	223	44	72	50	14 830	1 059	266	6.8	53.9
Pulaski	166	363	55	19 242	200	11.4	86	25	44	28	15 053	967	111	12.3	41.6
Putnam	299	2 554	79	12 964	413	8.3	165	40	69	61	13 610	1 625	205	4.7	26.4
Randolph	263	940	146	18 971	358	6.5	195	37	70	64	13 020	1 900	232	4.2	56.3

1. For week including March 12. Excludes government employees, self-employed persons, farm workers, domestic service workers, railroad employees subject to the Railroad Retirement Act, and employees on oceanborne vessels or in foreign countries. 2. Includes other labor income. 3. Based on the resident population estimated as of July 1 of the year shown. 4. Covers mining, construction, and manufacturing.

STATE County	Earnings, 1989 (cont'd) — Percent by selected industries (cont'd) — Goods-related[1] — Manu-facturing	Service-related & other[2] — Total	Retail trade	Finance, insur-ance, & real estate	Services	Govern-ment	Agriculture, 1987 — Farms — Number	Percent with — Less than 50 acres	500 acres and over	Farm operators, percent — Whose principal occu-pation is farming	Residing on farm operated	Land in farms — Acreage (1,000)	Percent change, 1982–1987	Acres — Average size of farm	Total irrigated (1,000)	Total cropland (1,000)
	103	104	105	106	107	108	109	110	111	112	113	114	115	116	117	118
INDIANA—Con.																
Bartholomew	52.0	32.1	7.0	4.7	12.0	9.2	748	33.4	15.2	50.9	77.8	176	3.3	235	2	154
Benton	11.8	NA	6.8	3.6	NA	17.3	614	9.8	34.0	80.5	64.7	272	6.0	442	D	259
Blackford	51.0	28.7	7.9	2.5	12.9	13.3	364	25.5	14.0	50.5	71.4	91	6.6	250	D	81
Boone	16.5	53.5	11.7	4.1	23.2	12.2	822	31.1	19.1	56.3	71.7	228	1.0	277	D	208
Brown	2.7	58.0	20.5	0.8	29.9	22.3	200	30.0	4.0	36.0	77.5	26	-20.9	128	0	13
Carroll	21.6	39.2	7.3	3.4	13.9	12.7	770	27.8	18.3	61.9	70.3	230	3.6	299	0	210
Cass	37.6	36.4	9.1	3.0	12.9	17.0	920	29.8	15.8	52.2	74.2	222	-0.3	241	2	196
Clark	24.5	51.5	13.3	2.3	17.8	16.9	691	31.0	7.1	42.0	80.3	119	-7.2	172	1	84
Clay	25.2	38.7	11.5	3.0	13.9	14.0	646	28.8	18.1	51.4	71.7	163	-4.9	252	D	136
Clinton	36.5	32.9	9.1	2.8	12.4	12.8	801	27.8	20.7	65.0	72.9	247	3.0	308	D	229
Crawford	5.9	NA	15.8	3.8	15.7	22.0	418	23.2	5.3	35.4	77.5	72	-8.7	171	D	33
Daviess	13.6	41.8	10.1	2.6	13.7	13.7	1 257	35.2	9.9	55.7	74.1	228	-0.1	182	1	196
Dearborn	30.2	43 9	10.1	2.9	15.9	15.0	796	26.1	1.9	33.0	77.6	90	-9.3	113	0	49
Decatur	46.1	34.6	8.3	2.4	10.9	9.8	816	23.0	16.2	60.2	75.0	210	5.0	257	D	182
De Kalb	61.2	25.2	6.3	1.5	10.7	7.8	824	26.9	11.0	46.2	77.3	175	-7.5	213	1	152
Delaware	32.1	45.6	11.1	2.9	22.3	16.5	834	37.1	12.0	46.6	71.8	179	-6.2	215	0	163
Dubois	46.5	36.4	9.5	2.6	12.1	6.7	982	23.2	9.5	51.2	69.9	195	-1.4	199	0	140
Elkhart	56.7	32.5	6.9	2.7	12.3	5.1	1 556	42.4	4.7	49.8	79.3	205	-4.1	131	20	179
Fayette	64.1	23.1	5.4	1.8	11.4	8.1	514	28.0	13.8	54.5	70.8	119	8.0	232	D	92
Floyd	25.1	46.8	11.0	5.1	20.2	18.7	394	43.7	0.8	31.7	85.3	32	-16.4	82	0	20
Fountain	34.9	35.0	10.7	3.0	11.4	14.4	693	20.2	25.3	62.3	68.3	235	9.8	339	0	199
Franklin	17.8	39.6	10.0	3.6	14.3	16.0	921	21.5	6.0	50.6	76.4	161	-5.3	175	0	108
Fulton	41.1	32.9	8.2	2.9	12.7	11.8	773	26.1	14.6	53.0	77.4	202	8.7	261	11	180
Gibson	26.8	48.8	9.3	2.3	15.4	10.4	846	29.7	18.7	58.3	70.1	248	5.9	293	D	219
Grant	51.2	32.0	7.9	2.7	15.0	12.2	744	29.4	16.8	56.7	73.8	196	-6.1	264	D	180
Greene	15.9	39.2	9.9	3.1	16.1	18.8	987	27.3	10.0	45.1	74.8	203	-3.9	205	0	144
Hamilton	13.2	65.2	10.2	9.2	22.6	8.8	772	39.5	13.7	50.5	73.4	172	1.1	223	0	155
Hancock	30.6	40.7	10.6	3.1	17.5	15.8	698	37.1	14.2	50.4	76.5	167	2.5	239	0	156
Harrison	21.4	47.4	11.3	3.6	15.0	17.3	1 297	31.1	4.9	43.7	79.0	185	4.8	142	0	122
Hendricks	5.9	60.8	12.0	3.4	18.6	18.0	926	38.0	11.4	49.5	74.7	182	-0.1	196	0	160
Henry	35.7	36.3	10.4	2.9	16.5	18.2	938	33.8	11.0	52.2	73.3	186	-4.8	198	D	167
Howard	63.2	25.9	7.0	1.9	12.0	7.3	677	33.7	13.0	58.8	72.8	154	0.9	227	0	141
Huntington	46.2	33.8	9.5	2.4	14.2	11.4	818	25.2	14.9	52.8	75.6	195	-0.5	238	0	174
Jackson	36.2	40.6	12.8	2.7	11.8	11.6	963	24.9	12.6	51.8	75.3	216	4.3	225	0	168
Jasper	14.7	54.4	10.2	2.4	13.2	12.7	780	23.5	28.1	69.9	70.3	306	1.1	392	9	276
Jay	42.8	30.6	9.7	2.1	11.5	13.3	922	28.1	10.7	51.4	75.9	189	-7.7	205	0	163
Jefferson	32.9	NA	9.0	2.3	NA	19.7	962	33.9	4.4	39.0	70.0	137	-3.2	143	0	86
Jennings	26.7	29.0	8.6	3.1	10.1	29.0	671	28.5	9.5	42.9	77.9	131	-5.5	196	0	92
Johnson	20.4	54.7	17.2	4.3	24.1	13.8	650	35.4	15.1	51.7	77.2	140	-5.4	215	D	124
Knox	11.6	50.5	11.0	4.8	19.7	25.2	833	21.5	24.6	69.6	75.9	309	6.2	371	5	274
Kosciusko	53.1	33.0	8.4	1.9	13.1	6.2	1 327	31.7	10.6	48.5	78.1	268	-2.2	202	9	228
Lagrange	43.1	32.6	9.4	2.5	11.1	10.2	1 437	34.9	5.6	57.4	81.9	191	-1.4	133	19	155
Lake	35.5	45.1	8.7	2.8	21.0	10.2	551	34.3	17.6	57.4	73.7	146	-1.7	264	6	134
La Porte	34.8	44.4	9.7	2.7	20.3	13.5	914	27.6	18.4	55.5	73.2	259	-6.4	283	16	231
Lawrence	45.6	34.7	9.2	2.5	16.1	12.3	865	24.6	8.3	37.5	78.0	172	-2.5	199	0	104
Madison	53.5	32.9	8.5	2.3	16.7	9.5	956	39.1	15.0	50.1	74.8	226	1.6	236	1	206
Marion	22.4	57.4	9.4	8.2	23.8	14.0	361	59.3	8.0	43.2	69.5	57	-8.0	157	1	48
Marshall	41.7	38.6	8.9	3.5	14.6	9.6	1 090	27.8	10.3	53.1	76.1	222	-2.6	204	4	194
Martin	6.2	NA	2.4	0.9	3.3	77.2	361	26.6	9.7	39.6	73.4	67	-8.2	187	D	41
Miami	22.0	29.3	7.6	2.4	8.3	41.4	818	27.3	14.9	57.1	79.6	196	-1.2	240	2	175
Monroe	22.7	41.7	10.6	3.3	19.2	28.9	583	31.0	3.1	31.7	76.5	73	-3.0	125	0	42
Montgomery	49.3	34.2	8.7	2.3	13.9	9.2	942	27.2	21.4	60.7	74.5	289	1.2	307	0	255
Morgan	19.2	51.8	13.5	3.6	23.6	16.8	713	37.2	10.5	46.7	74.6	145	1.4	204	0	117
Newton	27.5	NA	8.3	2.8	13.8	14.2	480	15.8	36.0	77.5	66.9	227	2.4	473	10	210
Noble	55.5	25.3	6.9	1.6	9.5	9.8	1 057	26.1	8.1	48.0	79.8	198	-1.7	187	2	164
Ohio	2.7	52.5	13.0	3.1	22.1	30.4	283	27.2	2.8	27.6	77.4	37	4.2	132	0	19
Orange	36.0	NA	7.7	3.0	15.8	12.8	566	17.7	9.0	46.8	81.1	112	-5.5	198	D	72
Owen	22.6	44.4	11.9	3.3	17.0	19.2	665	25.4	7.7	40.8	74.4	115	-2.7	174	0	74
Parke	10.8	45.5	11.3	3.0	15.3	21.8	587	21.1	20.1	54.0	69.8	192	-0.1	327	0	141
Perry	34.3	35.3	10.5	3.9	13.3	20.6	526	21.7	6.5	36.7	78.9	92	-2.0	175	0	53
Pike	3.0	NA	5.0	2.6	7.8	10.8	382	24.1	13.9	47.6	70.7	99	2.2	259	0	83
Porter	42.0	40.4	8.2	2.1	18.7	11.4	597	33.2	17.9	56.8	77.7	163	0.8	272	4	147
Posey	44.7	30.8	4.6	1.6	12.6	8.5	551	21.4	24.9	61.9	75.3	217	-1.6	394	D	191
Pulaski	36.6	32.0	7.0	2.9	9.8	14.1	718	19.9	23.7	63.9	69.2	243	1.1	339	8	217
Putnam	18.8	48.0	11.6	3.1	23.6	20.9	891	29.2	13.8	51.5	74.6	211	-3.9	237	0	157
Randolph	51.9	28.1	7.0	2.1	10.6	11.4	1 074	28.7	13.2	52.2	75.7	244	-3.7	227	D	217

1. Covers mining, construction, and manufacturing. 2. Covers private sector earnings in agricultural services, forestry, and fisheries; transportation and public utilities; wholesale trade; retail trade; finance, insurance, and real estate; and services.

STATE County	Agriculture, 1987 (cont'd): Value of land and buildings: Average per farm ($1,000)	Agriculture, 1987 (cont'd): Value of land and buildings: Average per acre (Dollars)	Value of products sold: Total (Mil dol)	Value of products sold: Average per farm (Dollars)	Value of products sold: Percent from: Crops	Value of products sold: Percent from: Livestock and poultry[1]	Percent of farms with sales of: $10,000 or more	Percent of farms with sales of: $100,000 or more	Manufactures, 1987: Establishments: Total	Establishments: Percent with 20 or more employees	All employees: Number (1,000)	All employees: Percent change, 1982–1987	All employees: Annual payroll (Mil dol)	Production workers: Number (1,000)	Production workers: Work hours (Mil)
	119	120	121	122	123	124	125	126	127	128	129	130	131	132	133
INDIANA—Con.															
Bartholomew	311	1 357	37	49 658	65.7	34.3	57.2	16.0	110	43.6	15.0	2.7	447.7	8.6	16.6
Benton	563	1 266	56	91 343	88.5	11.5	87.5	34.2	14	50.0	0.4	100.0	5.0	0.3	0.6
Blackford	196	880	21	56 580	65.2	34.8	59.3	15.7	34	55.9	2.0	17.6	38.6	1.5	2.8
Boone	395	1 436	59	72 313	65.6	34.4	67.8	22.6	63	28.6	1.5	15.4	28.8	1.0	1.9
Brown	125	1 029	2	9 280	58.1	41.9	24.0	0.5	18	5.6	0.1	0.0	1.3	0.1	0.1
Carroll	402	1 364	92	119 878	40.2	59.8	74.0	27.7	26	34.6	1.2	20.0	22.7	1.0	1.9
Cass	286	1 196	60	64 827	57.7	42.3	66.1	19.1	59	55.9	5.5	25.0	112.7	4.4	8.2
Clark	182	1 093	16	23 249	67.2	32.8	37.2	5.1	112	39.3	7.1	7.6	178.2	5.3	10.6
Clay	246	1 057	29	45 537	73.7	26.3	56.0	14.4	31	22.6	1.2	50.0	31.5	0.9	2.2
Clinton	451	1 440	82	102 743	51.9	48.1	74.7	27.2	45	46.7	3.6	33.3	67.0	2.9	5.3
Crawford	111	641	5	10 773	27.1	72.9	22.0	1.7	17	11.8	0.1	0.0	1.4	0.1	0.2
Daviess	228	1 274	92	73 274	29.5	70.5	66.0	19.3	42	31.0	1.5	25.0	20.5	1.3	3.1
Dearborn	123	930	9	10 920	41.5	58.5	21.7	2.1	35	40.0	2.8	-3.4	73.7	2.2	4.3
Decatur	321	1 229	70	85 343	39.9	60.1	71.3	23.7	38	31.6	2.8	16.7	68.4	2.4	5.7
De Kalb	196	913	35	43 033	46.7	53.3	54.7	10.6	92	51.1	6.8	65.9	151.3	5.2	10.3
Delaware	246	1 168	39	47 305	75.0	25.0	54.9	13.1	188	39.9	11.2	7.7	327.3	7.9	16.1
Dubois	225	1 170	123	124 823	11.0	89.0	62.2	27.2	105	56.2	9.7	34.7	187.5	7.8	16.5
Elkhart	207	1 620	86	55 381	27.8	72.2	62.4	16.6	855	51.0	50.0	44.5	1 100.8	36.1	70.2
Fayette	236	962	27	51 669	44.4	55.6	60.1	16.3	33	39.4	5.5	-3.5	163.6	4.4	9.3
Floyd	178	1 904	6	15 031	48.2	51.8	18.5	3.3	102	48.0	D	D	D	D	D
Fountain	340	996	43	62 491	75.5	24.5	67.1	20.2	27	29.6	1.8	-18.2	39.0	1.3	2.3
Franklin	184	1 034	34	36 628	32.9	67.1	49.8	11.6	12	41.7	0.7	16.7	12.8	0.6	1.2
Fulton	246	966	46	59 229	56.0	44.0	66.9	18.2	50	60.0	2.8	16.7	51.1	2.2	4.3
Gibson	352	1 151	55	64 944	65.5	34.5	64.3	18.7	36	41.7	2.1	0.0	43.2	1.7	3.5
Grant	352	1 260	52	69 718	65.8	34.2	64.2	20.4	91	38.5	10.8	-5.3	323.8	8.6	18.0
Greene	180	892	33	33 195	50.4	49.6	38.0	6.4	26	26.9	0.9	28.6	12.7	0.7	1.3
Hamilton	384	1 733	47	61 501	72.1	27.9	59.5	15.2	138	29.0	5.0	28.2	107.2	3.2	6.8
Hancock	346	1 435	40	57 745	72.6	27.4	59.5	16.2	63	30.2	3.5	66.7	98.8	1.4	2.6
Harrison	134	982	51	39 620	17.5	82.5	30.0	4.5	28	39.3	D	D	D	D	D
Hendricks	280	1 415	41	43 961	72.1	27.9	53.2	13.5	53	30.2	1.3	85.7	17.8	0.9	1.6
Henry	200	1 045	46	48 581	59.2	40.8	59.9	13.1	54	37.0	3.4	13.3	87.6	2.6	5.1
Howard	367	1 601	48	70 465	59.8	40.2	68.4	19.5	75	37.3	18.1	0.0	667.0	13.4	28.8
Huntington	294	1 243	50	60 739	57.5	42.5	65.0	16.0	74	47.3	7.9	51.9	207.9	6.2	12.9
Jackson	242	1 081	67	69 387	33.2	66.8	56.2	13.9	76	44.7	4.3	26.5	75.2	3.4	6.8
Jasper	401	1 024	86	110 406	59.9	40.1	78.5	31.9	23	39.1	1.3	18.2	23.3	1.1	2.2
Jay	212	1 012	56	60 592	38.9	61.1	63.0	14.0	32	56.2	3.0	-3.2	53.1	2.2	4.2
Jefferson	112	807	18	19 082	67.3	32.7	36.0	3.7	41	48.8	3.3	26.9	68.8	2.8	5.1
Jennings	169	913	29	43 005	41.5	58.5	43.1	7.0	28	57.1	1.4	16.7	25.7	1.2	2.3
Johnson	307	1 421	32	48 956	71.0	29.0	56.0	14.6	109	33.9	4.4	18.9	94.8	3.4	6.5
Knox	355	986	66	79 279	71.9	28.1	73.9	24.8	45	33.3	1.7	-10.5	34.9	1.3	2.2
Kosciusko	239	1 122	116	87 364	25.0	75.0	59.8	18.3	174	49.4	12.1	19.8	281.4	8.6	17.5
Lagrange	169	1 244	81	56 669	26.3	73.7	68.7	11.9	69	49.3	4.1	41.4	75.9	3.1	5.8
Lake	346	1 377	33	59 080	81.3	18.7	61.0	18.3	379	42.0	42.1	-34.0	1 344.1	31.0	64.3
La Porte	311	1 099	65	71 504	64.4	35.6	62.7	21.8	188	46.3	11.8	-9.9	265.5	8.1	16.6
Lawrence	130	661	16	18 146	36.7	63.3	35.5	3.7	64	32.8	4.4	29.4	122.8	3.6	7.4
Madison	360	1 499	58	60 274	75.3	24.7	57.5	17.3	132	31.8	16.8	1.2	599.0	12.5	25.5
Marion	324	2 295	22	61 071	68.8	31.2	41.8	12.5	1 254	37.2	82.7	-13.1	2 544.1	50.6	103.0
Marshall	210	988	51	47 139	53.1	46.9	59.9	14.2	122	52.5	5.7	16.3	110.1	4.7	9.7
Martin	136	702	23	65 094	13.3	86.7	45.2	14.7	13	30.8	0.7	75.0	14.1	0.5	1.2
Miami	256	1 078	63	76 516	42.1	57.9	65.8	21.8	47	42.6	2.6	0.0	49.1	1.8	3.5
Monroe	165	1 226	7	12 635	41.9	58.1	25.4	2.6	108	32.4	8.2	3.8	184.8	6.9	13.4
Montgomery	359	1 174	83	88 511	53.5	46.5	69.4	22.6	41	43.9	5.5	25.0	127.7	4.2	8.4
Morgan	228	1 169	26	36 862	65.8	34.2	44.0	9.4	58	36.2	2.9	45.0	48.5	2.3	4.1
Newton	554	1 198	59	123 318	65.3	34.7	81.5	32.1	13	30.8	D	D	D	D	D
Noble	162	919	46	43 852	40.3	59.7	56.1	11.6	143	53.1	7.6	46.2	140.1	6.2	12.5
Ohio	117	842	3	9 523	52.0	48.0	24.0	0.7	2	0.0	D	D	D	D	D
Orange	168	832	17	30 352	31.6	68.4	39.0	8.1	33	51.5	2.6	52.9	40.9	2.2	4.1
Owen	159	891	12	18 768	56.9	43.1	34.0	4.2	19	31.6	0.5	150.0	9.4	0.4	0.7
Parke	276	854	30	51 685	67.7	32.3	60.0	16.2	22	31.8	0.5	0.0	7.4	0.4	0.8
Perry	122	686	9	16 720	27.0	73.0	31.0	3.0	32	37.5	1.6	-20.0	31.2	1.4	2.7
Pike	246	952	19	48 634	54.5	45.5	58.9	13.1	11	18.2	0.1	0.0	2.1	0.1	0.2
Porter	348	1 322	33	55 733	78.3	21.7	60.0	17.8	104	31.7	10.7	-9.3	352.4	7.7	15.8
Posey	446	1 173	41	74 775	74.9	25.1	73.3	25.8	30	36.7	D	D	D	D	D
Pulaski	325	962	67	93 985	54.6	45.4	75.5	26.2	17	41.2	1.2	100.0	26.9	0.9	1.8
Putnam	257	1 054	38	43 004	56.3	43.7	48.0	13.4	24	33.3	0.9	-43.8	17.7	0.7	1.3
Randolph	232	987	55	51 065	57.4	42.6	64.9	15.1	56	46.4	4.6	21.1	103.0	3.7	7.6

1. Includes livestock and poultry products.

STATE County	Manufactures, 1987 (cont'd): Production workers (cont'd): Wages: Total (Mil dol)	Manufactures, 1987 (cont'd): Production workers (cont'd): Wages: Average per worker (Dollars)	Manufactures, 1987 (cont'd): Value added by manufacture (Mil dol)	Manufactures, 1987 (cont'd): Value of shipments (Mil dol)	Manufactures, 1987 (cont'd): New capital expenditures (Mil dol)	Value of construction authorized by building permits, 1990: Total[1] ($1,000)	Nonresidential: Total ($1,000)	Nonresidential: Percent: Office	Nonresidential: Percent: Industrial	Nonresidential: Percent: Stores	Residential: New construction ($1,000)	Residential: Number of housing units	Residential: Alterations and additions ($1,000)
	134	135	136	137	138	139	140	141	142	143	144	145	146
INDIANA—Con.													
Bartholomew	229.8	26 721	1 101.4	2 079.8	59.7	61 199	32 670	0.0	45.9	53.9	19 088	208	1 444
Benton	3.5	11 667	14.6	30.4	D	3 353	1 268	0.0	49.9	16.8	1 308	21	167
Blackford	25.7	17 133	108.4	227.4	11.0	3 818	711	50.3	0.0	0.0	1 902	57	208
Boone	16.5	16 500	52.2	88.3	3.1	40 466	5 260	3.2	23.8	14.2	30 771	186	2 771
Brown	1.0	10 000	2.2	4.4	0.2	13 056	3 271	0.0	0.0	26.5	7 060	115	336
Carroll	17.5	17 500	55.6	115.5	3.5	6 661	1 656	0.0	49.5	0.0	2 661	59	722
Cass	80.8	18 364	278.5	722.2	16.3	10 143	3 818	2.6	55.0	29.5	4 096	55	67
Clark	122.7	23 151	805.1	1 298.0	26.3	67 913	36 983	6.2	0.0	79.3	25 737	384	1 198
Clay	21.3	23 667	70.2	224.1	D	3 654	2 502	0.0	2.6	81.7	706	17	316
Clinton	48.2	16 621	310.6	629.8	33.7	11 398	2 834	0.0	23.5	0.0	6 748	96	798
Crawford	1.2	12 000	5.3	10.9	D	287	274	21.9	0.0	78.1	0	0	10
Daviess	16.7	12 846	52.5	171.5	D	3 940	896	0.0	0.0	36.7	2 656	47	151
Dearborn	52.1	23 682	199.3	390.7	D	41 590	12 054	27.4	9.5	26.4	28 166	305	615
Decatur	56.4	23 500	252.1	434.7	15.0	13 236	1 955	0.0	0.0	21.2	6 156	152	707
De Kalb	102.8	19 769	351.3	747.1	22.3	24 929	9 675	0.0	65.4	24.1	11 276	196	430
Delaware	216.5	27 405	611.3	1 177.3	44.9	43 861	12 462	17.5	3.0	45.3	20 414	258	1 633
Dubois	132.1	16 936	378.4	757.6	20.6	34 453	13 433	7.5	16.2	58.4	18 941	227	280
Elkhart	646.9	17 920	2 640.8	5 760.2	113.5	108 529	26 840	2.4	31.8	32.0	55 067	744	7 138
Fayette	120.3	27 341	396.3	770.4	D	7 000	1 983	0.0	0.0	88.8	3 154	96	255
Floyd	D	D	D	D	D	49 162	4 977	47.7	11.8	26.7	36 079	485	1 747
Fountain	22.7	17 462	66.6	119.2	3.0	2 129	664	2.5	75.2	0.0	492	10	189
Franklin	10.6	17 667	31.6	80.2	2.2	7 305	132	0.0	0.0	0.0	5 505	85	574
Fulton	35.1	15 955	155.7	301.4	D	3 543	1 680	17.3	0.0	59.5	1 540	20	19
Gibson	31.9	18 765	111.5	261.9	3.2	3 114	1 657	2.1	0.0	90.5	982	8	184
Grant	251.9	29 291	456.1	1 202.7	D	25 817	2 557	0.0	0.0	67.5	9 009	131	2 461
Greene	9.8	14 000	21.5	47.0	1.4	0	0	NA	NA	NA	0	0	0
Hamilton	58.6	18 312	252.7	470.5	14.4	310 755	56 650	29.6	5.8	24.8	223 594	1 778	6 967
Hancock	19.8	14 143	70.7	132.5	D	44 863	14 708	16.7	10.6	30.1	26 859	300	1 515
Harrison	D	D	D	D	D	16 161	2 683	30.5	0.0	29.4	10 791	189	726
Hendricks	10.6	11 778	33.6	77.9	D	82 552	12 251	15.9	1.6	32.0	65 220	660	2 183
Henry	65.2	25 077	182.3	354.0	9.7	13 431	2 111	0.0	19.3	50.7	6 789	162	2 202
Howard	470.7	35 127	1 141.7	2 494.1	D	52 933	29 780	33.2	18.1	1.8	19 690	200	1 209
Huntington	152.6	24 613	511.2	1 947.8	D	20 451	3 449	0.0	18.3	49.6	8 941	120	811
Jackson	52.9	15 559	189.8	400.9	D	20 207	10 284	4.4	43.7	34.4	8 810	180	563
Jasper	18.4	16 727	53.0	124.2	3.5	7 140	427	16.4	0.0	0.0	5 997	101	323
Jay	36.1	16 409	138.3	237.1	6.2	1 493	180	33.3	66.7	0.0	1 175	16	0
Jefferson	47.3	16 893	206.7	317.0	12.3	14 658	8 144	0.0	87.7	0.1	4 187	78	826
Jennings	21.4	17 833	54.4	107.1	3.8	7 132	1 626	8.0	60.2	19.9	4 384	85	340
Johnson	66.6	19 588	230.2	496.9	16.2	85 546	13 132	39.0	12.4	24.3	66 584	644	2 971
Knox	23.0	17 692	87.5	217.0	4.1	16 949	3 307	27.8	58.4	1.2	4 686	92	786
Kosciusko	170.4	19 814	831.5	1 444.5	42.9	61 513	30 123	48.5	25.3	15.1	26 649	356	4 101
Lagrange	50.1	16 161	171.8	413.6	9.6	18 192	5 217	2.1	22.7	7.5	9 507	183	2 267
Lake	944.2	30 458	3 760.9	10 297.9	458.8	296 870	68 279	11.1	32.5	32.7	147 442	1 385	19 335
La Porte	159.1	19 642	654.6	1 368.9	28.8	40 850	7 254	17.1	27.7	19.2	23 834	344	3 258
Lawrence	96.2	26 722	244.5	637.2	19.2	5 744	1 715	20.3	13.0	30.9	1 832	47	554
Madison	433.3	34 664	973.4	2 119.1	45.4	30 953	10 675	19.1	11.9	33.3	16 584	221	1 725
Marion	1 374.8	27 170	5 813.5	11 358.2	373.0	1 040 509	420 185	26.5	28.1	31.8	341 798	4 328	24 546
Marshall	79.4	16 894	277.4	681.9	22.9	21 492	6 947	3.3	57.4	24.9	11 296	191	1 315
Martin	11.0	22 000	56.2	104.0	2.6	NA	NA	NA	NA	NA	NA	NA	NA
Miami	31.1	17 278	121.2	220.3	2.8	4 883	115	86.7	0.0	0.0	2 760	50	682
Monroe	140.7	20 391	763.5	1 616.2	D	72 497	16 835	20.0	27.6	21.4	45 869	541	3 156
Montgomery	84.1	20 024	314.0	589.4	18.9	21 764	12 405	17.9	29.0	43.5	6 425	205	1 773
Morgan	32.1	13 957	120.6	208.3	19.0	31 147	3 169	16.4	14.0	33.4	25 294	349	1 137
Newton	D	D	D	D	D	3 797	995	18.4	76.1	2.0	2 043	39	295
Noble	102.2	16 484	331.0	677.2	19.1	24 952	6 647	4.8	35.6	42.6	11 683	214	1 614
Ohio	D	D	D	D	D	2 616	61	0.0	0.0	0.0	2 163	72	64
Orange	29.2	13 273	82.2	227.9	3.2	1 115	663	0.0	0.0	0.0	351	11	67
Owen	5.2	13 000	29.7	40.4	D	3 320	1 720	29.7	5.8	52.3	993	34	79
Parke	5.5	13 750	19.1	38.9	D	3 992	1 703	10.8	37.1	16.1	1 892	33	143
Perry	25.3	18 071	69.7	121.6	2.2	4 014	546	0.0	0.0	8.2	2 990	56	331
Pike	1.5	15 000	D	10.2	0.1	29	6	0.0	0.0	100.0	0	0	10
Porter	246.2	31 974	1 438.3	2 891.6	91.8	153 451	45 995	4.5	70.4	10.3	92 770	908	6 336
Posey	D	D	D	D	D	18 869	8 663	9.8	83.9	1.0	7 387	74	1 387
Pulaski	17.6	19 556	64.7	122.1	4.9	539	100	100.0	0.0	0.0	352	5	66
Putnam	12.3	17 571	50.6	96.1	2.5	30 132	26 756	1.4	2.4	93.5	2 459	58	261
Randolph	80.3	21 703	205.6	397.7	14.5	3 341	1 309	0.0	0.0	11.3	1 265	23	472

1. Includes nonresidential additions and alterations, residential nonhousekeeping buildings, and residential garages and carports not shown separately.

STATE County	Wholesale trade, 1987				Retail trade, all establishments, 1987				Retail trade, establishments with payroll, 1987					
						Sales				Sales				
											Per capita[2] (Dollars)			
	Estab-lishments	Sales (Mil dol)	Paid employees[1]	Annual payroll (Mil dol)	Number	Total (Mil dol)	Percent change, 1982–1987	Per capita[2] (Dollars)	Number	Total (Mil dol)	General merchan-dise stores	Food stores	Apparel & acces-sory stores	Eating and drinking places
	147	148	149	150	151	152	153	154	155	156	157	158	159	160
INDIANA—Con.														
Bartholomew	115	303.7	1 039	20.7	675	409.3	39.7	6 336	406	399.5	812	1 225	253	697
Benton	43	D	D	D	136	36.3	43.5	3 744	71	33.9	0	753	D	194
Blackford	16	38.2	174	3.0	147	54.2	22.6	3 712	95	52.3	194	967	54	307
Boone	86	224.1	565	11.8	401	188.7	27.7	4 901	234	182.6	232	772	151	489
Brown	8	7.4	23	0.7	206	31.4	82.6	2 413	119	28.4	49	504	103	454
Carroll	50	175.4	495	8.8	182	53.9	17.4	2 808	100	51.9	D	633	33	197
Cass	87	183.7	744	12.8	439	197.8	26.0	4 921	272	192.5	585	952	109	449
Clark	123	298.6	1 196	23.1	864	703.4	53.6	7 930	569	693.3	1 231	1 158	D	716
Clay	21	41.8	138	2.6	285	106.3	23.3	4 234	139	102.6	D	D	D	363
Clinton	72	170.1	429	8.1	369	136.4	38.8	4 304	206	132.5	D	742	132	477
Crawford	4	3.3	27	0.2	127	29.6	72.1	2 902	61	25.7	D	670	D	258
Daviess	41	71.1	380	7.0	291	122.2	17.5	4 227	192	119.7	546	838	102	283
Dearborn	37	47.5	219	3.4	337	172.8	68.8	4 607	187	166.0	353	970	68	351
Decatur	62	135.3	400	6.5	215	105.0	29.3	4 375	135	100.3	306	872	104	401
De Kalb	40	102.7	312	6.1	339	168.6	61.8	4 817	204	161.7	D	1 044	163	457
Delaware	163	445.4	1 905	37.1	1 184	719.8	25.9	5 969	758	697.8	775	1 111	252	631
Dubois	87	395.7	1 105	24.9	466	279.8	57.5	7 707	291	272.9	940	1 212	190	558
Elkhart	397	1 640.4	5 285	120.0	1 562	1 090.4	43.2	7 313	960	1 061.3	665	1 278	266	625
Fayette	26	59.7	346	5.5	241	120.4	17.7	4 347	134	114.8	404	963	157	499
Floyd	83	227.5	710	13.2	535	280.8	35.6	4 394	311	275.4	D	1 178	D	415
Fountain	30	44.5	150	2.1	236	75.8	10.3	4 098	126	72.2	114	920	D	514
Franklin	21	32.7	145	2.2	162	48.9	44.2	2 435	81	44.6	D	717	D	177
Fulton	47	127.7	254	4.9	215	81.3	27.0	4 348	120	77.5	207	1 207	54	442
Gibson	50	157.5	297	6.1	357	134.4	1.9	4 073	206	130.1	D	1 124	86	347
Grant	101	133.4	738	12.3	730	444.9	40.5	5 831	477	433.9	652	1 037	242	538
Greene	46	69.2	247	3.0	341	118.6	31.8	3 851	189	113.1	599	1 048	73	268
Hamilton	306	1 202.2	2 829	74.3	936	543.1	88.2	5 554	527	527.4	407	947	113	598
Hancock	66	168.4	418	8.7	402	185.2	21.0	4 106	204	178.9	D	812	74	350
Harrison	39	69.4	386	5.9	291	112.4	61.5	3 863	139	104.2	D	943	D	291
Hendricks	70	90.4	399	6.5	559	295.3	52.1	3 901	295	283.2	D	1 021	64	353
Henry	63	86.8	384	6.4	540	240.9	34.7	4 876	297	230.9	405	1 023	122	417
Howard	113	241.5	981	17.7	938	620.1	41.1	7 444	593	607.6	1 067	D	D	743
Huntington	56	206.6	414	6.9	355	160.6	36.3	4 423	216	155.3	D	851	144	492
Jackson	47	284.7	861	15.5	418	202.2	28.1	5 435	224	194.2	646	1 065	220	471
Jasper	47	148.5	396	7.0	266	114.0	11.7	4 366	155	106.9	174	811	165	374
Jay	27	84.0	202	3.1	234	73.5	5.9	3 339	120	68.4	123	897	41	341
Jefferson	44	33.9	256	2.8	376	144.4	18.8	4 862	223	139.6	517	1 368	116	429
Jennings	22	19.5	88	1.7	209	73.1	37.4	3 206	100	69.6	140	848	33	235
Johnson	118	165.4	770	14.5	853	596.3	62.7	6 999	517	577.3	1 832	797	429	546
Knox	99	261.9	986	18.6	500	233.4	24.5	5 720	319	226.5	942	1 124	214	505
Kosciusko	125	267.6	1 037	18.6	710	348.9	56.7	5 409	426	330.0	450	1 029	252	505
Lagrange	35	137.0	407	7.8	304	93.9	32.4	3 296	150	85.8	121	681	17	355
Lake	492	2 462.7	6 060	128.0	3 938	2 821.3	20.9	5 798	2 579	2 751.8	742	1 144	273	551
La Porte	144	229.2	1 147	22.3	942	573.9	29.6	5 445	625	561.1	671	1 085	292	463
Lawrence	41	98.2	331	6.4	457	205.5	37.3	4 825	256	196.2	767	1 142	111	417
Madison	127	274.5	1 370	26.0	1 256	768.9	33.8	5 820	773	752.4	690	1 154	209	531
Marion	2 031	14 481.2	30 180	747.3	7 338	6 979.9	59.2	8 860	5 070	6 874.9	1 121	1 229	378	931
Marshall	82	162.5	524	10.7	473	216.0	48.9	5 230	268	200.7	279	917	188	525
Martin	11	34.6	82	1.2	122	41.4	27.8	3 668	62	36.7	D	949	D	281
Miami	41	144.5	269	4.3	344	144.9	29.4	3 823	193	139.0	244	740	127	302
Monroe	117	458.0	1 577	30.5	996	632.0	45.1	6 153	680	617.0	916	1 211	383	731
Montgomery	61	407.1	753	13.9	396	198.4	42.4	5 589	248	193.4	586	1 296	139	475
Morgan	59	69.7	278	4.6	487	251.2	48.6	4 585	269	244.5	223	1 072	133	524
Newton	34	61.9	277	8.5	142	38.9	6.6	2 837	84	36.8	D	695	122	234
Noble	76	207.3	712	11.8	346	166.7	61.7	4 331	204	161.2	291	1 007	99	347
Ohio	2	D	D	D	34	10.6	20.5	1 919	19	10.1	0	D	D	251
Orange	24	27.2	128	1.9	232	61.9	27.4	3 225	107	54.1	169	1 184	46	225
Owen	10	5.4	31	0.5	135	48.4	44.9	2 796	63	43.3	D	719	0	239
Parke	23	22.0	89	1.2	211	56.5	59.6	3 596	87	52.9	D	755	D	225
Perry	17	12.7	100	1.4	208	74.1	13.5	3 898	111	68.8	310	1 123	211	248
Pike	13	21.5	72	1.4	124	28.5	3.3	2 190	61	25.6	D	776	22	126
Porter	136	339.5	1 281	27.3	976	584.7	41.2	4 766	598	569.2	423	1 114	101	506
Posey	32	248.4	319	6.9	236	78.5	18.8	2 986	126	74.0	D	686	67	197
Pulaski	39	97.3	330	6.0	135	47.6	17.0	3 582	72	44.2	D	623	D	236
Putnam	35	36.6	149	2.2	302	111.6	33.7	3 709	162	107.4	D	823	133	294
Randolph	55	66.4	281	4.0	288	94.4	21.8	3 371	153	88.9	167	842	63	317

1. For pay period including March 12. 2. Based on the estimated population as of July 1 of the year shown.

STATE County	Retail trade, establishments with payroll, 1987 (cont'd): Paid employees[1]	Retail trade, establishments with payroll, 1987 (cont'd): Annual payroll (Mil dol)	Taxable service industries–establishments with payroll, 1987: Number	Taxable service industries: Receipts (Mil dol): Total	Receipts: Selected kinds of business: Hotels, motels and other lodging places	Receipts: Selected kinds of business: Health services	Receipts: Selected kinds of business: Legal services	Taxable service industries: Paid employees	Taxable service industries: Annual payroll (Mil dol)	Bank deposits,[2] June 1989: Total (Mil dol)	Bank deposits,[2] June 1989: Percent change, 1988–1989	Savings capital,[3] September 1989: Total (Mil dol)	Savings capital,[3] September 1989: Percent change, 1988–1989
	161	162	163	164	165	166	167	168	169	170	171	172	173
INDIANA—Con.													
Bartholomew	5 431	44.8	405	127.5	10.1	50.8	5.8	2 954	45.6	409	4.4	213.7	-0.8
Benton	350	2.7	43	6.6	D	3.9	0.3	218	2.3	128	-1.0	14.0	10.9
Blackford	702	5.7	61	12.6	D	5.1	0.8	345	3.3	94	3.1	23.6	-1.5
Boone	2 436	21.6	199	48.0	2.6	19.0	2.8	1 391	17.7	260	8.0	77.1	-7.8
Brown	564	4.2	53	19.8	9.9	1.0	0.3	627	6.6	31	1.1	17.4	15.0
Carroll	681	5.9	61	6.8	D	2.3	1.0	227	2.0	160	-13.7	39.9	2.4
Cass	2 520	22.3	170	41.0	1.8	19.8	3.3	1 205	15.9	354	3.6	102.5	-5.1
Clark	8 094	76.2	464	151.5	D	71.0	5.1	3 891	50.3	588	9.2	151.1	-2.1
Clay	1 101	10.0	105	14.9	D	7.4	1.1	475	5.0	204	1.6	42.8	-6.3
Clinton	1 810	14.9	138	21.2	0.9	10.0	1.7	662	7.0	257	4.6	60.4	-6.9
Crawford	323	2.4	23	3.7	D	2.1	D	143	1.2	65	10.6	0.0	NA
Daviess	1 581	12.7	125	23.8	0.5	10.6	1.4	804	8.4	202	2.7	55.4	-2.0
Dearborn	1 642	14.7	133	32.4	0.3	14.4	1.7	987	13.9	181	7.9	205.6	3.2
Decatur	1 258	10.8	105	18.3	D	9.0	0.9	509	6.4	196	5.3	34.9	-10.0
De Kalb	2 109	16.9	190	47.4	D	16.5	3.6	1 923	15.5	222	4.3	99.8	3.0
Delaware	10 007	82.4	688	206.3	4.3	78.8	10.3	5 561	81.6	725	6.0	338.4	-4.5
Dubois	3 063	28.8	201	56.9	D	23.2	2.2	1 363	19.0	618	6.4	33.3	2.3
Elkhart	12 002	116.6	887	387.0	18.3	75.8	14.6	8 377	111.7	1 609	4.9	99.5	-14.3
Fayette	1 508	12.8	121	29.1	1.1	15.1	1.1	839	10.9	154	0.2	88.3	-2.5
Floyd	3 604	33.3	315	94.1	D	41.5	7.3	2 425	35.3	440	12.6	225.2	3.0
Fountain	1 203	7.8	67	11.0	D	5.3	0.8	421	3.7	193	6.7	6.8	-12.3
Franklin	514	4.4	43	6.5	D	2.5	0.7	206	2.2	148	6.5	15.5	10.4
Fulton	1 019	8.3	79	13.8	D	6.3	0.8	388	4.9	161	-1.7	28.4	-0.9
Gibson	1 629	14.0	133	19.7	0.5	10.0	1.4	589	5.9	279	1.2	97.7	18.1
Grant	5 360	46.3	371	93.6	2.4	45.8	4.5	2 820	36.2	460	11.4	184.2	-1.2
Greene	1 524	11.7	103	11.0	D	5.5	0.6	298	3.1	287	3.0	43.5	4.0
Hamilton	6 270	61.9	647	220.3	0.9	65.5	7.1	4 986	84.9	638	4.9	150.6	-5.7
Hancock	2 135	18.5	203	42.5	0.9	21.0	3.2	1 297	15.9	263	6.4	36.8	-7.6
Harrison	1 341	10.1	92	18.9	D	6.9	0.6	551	5.5	300	0.3	38.4	5.5
Hendricks	3 479	30.6	308	60.3	D	29.2	2.8	2 204	22.7	429	10.2	87.5	1.8
Henry	2 977	24.8	218	50.3	3.1	21.4	1.9	1 524	18.2	264	0.6	209.7	-7.7
Howard	7 610	66.7	474	130.2	D	61.6	6.7	3 616	51.2	501	5.5	192.6	-1.0
Huntington	2 287	19.1	147	28.7	D	11.9	2.0	863	8.6	290	1.3	73.8	3.9
Jackson	2 161	20.4	183	38.5	3.3	13.1	3.0	1 132	13.5	266	8.0	161.5	-1.7
Jasper	1 308	11.4	101	25.1	2.1	10.2	0.6	858	8.0	258	5.7	30.3	-4.5
Jay	959	7.7	74	12.8	D	7.7	0.8	363	3.8	158	-2.4	11.2	-10.5
Jefferson	1 863	15.5	135	31.5	1.5	16.2	2.5	858	9.7	174	0.5	88.2	2.7
Jennings	736	6.4	56	12.5	D	6.1	0.6	400	3.9	118	3.6	31.6	7.8
Johnson	7 639	65.5	433	124.7	D	46.8	5.6	3 579	42.6	556	7.3	174.8	15.9
Knox	2 948	24.8	241	61.3	D	29.6	3.2	1 648	23.0	359	5.3	197.8	-5.3
Kosciusko	4 065	38.7	339	85.6	3.0	31.5	3.3	2 377	31.0	556	7.5	39.6	-3.2
Lagrange	1 149	10.0	105	29.4	3.9	12.7	1.0	740	9.3	300	13.3	7.5	2.0
Lake	34 228	309.9	2 578	958.9	23.9	339.8	56.3	23 570	391.2	2 717	3.4	1 418.3	-0.1
La Porte	6 923	62.6	550	182.9	9.6	79.4	6.2	4 967	67.5	723	6.5	200.8	4.0
Lawrence	2 418	21.1	163	43.6	2.0	21.3	1.7	1 042	16.0	334	5.7	44.6	-1.7
Madison	9 666	84.4	722	178.9	3.9	77.5	7.3	5 231	71.3	698	4.5	387.7	-9.9
Marion	79 913	791.0	6 026	3 404.6	199.4	858.9	242.9	79 326	1 361.5	8 814	11.4	1 546.6	0.1
Marshall	2 601	20.1	200	49.0	2.3	13.9	2.2	1 524	14.3	338	5.6	58.5	-2.7
Martin	496	3.7	31	5.7	D	2.7	D	184	2.3	77	5.2	8.0	-0.9
Miami	1 733	14.9	123	20.1	D	10.7	1.4	651	6.4	220	1.8	76.7	-1.9
Monroe	9 986	76.9	629	168.3	7.7	63.5	9.9	4 367	60.6	500	7.7	206.2	1.6
Montgomery	2 316	20.9	191	53.0	D	32.0	2.0	1 801	16.3	281	4.9	139.0	2.5
Morgan	3 202	28.2	211	53.1	D	22.2	2.1	1 414	19.8	255	2.7	113.1	1.9
Newton	567	4.0	44	14.2	D	1.5	1.1	328	4.1	125	1.6	8.2	-1.1
Noble	1 894	16.8	149	26.9	D	6.7	1.3	955	9.3	279	4.8	38.6	5.2
Ohio	126	1.1	12	1.8	0.0	D	D	83	0.7	23	5.2	0.0	NA
Orange	767	5.5	53	35.6	D	4.8	D	954	10.5	213	0.4	0.0	NA
Owen	642	4.6	38	7.3	D	2.6	0.9	227	2.4	82	5.9	17.1	-0.4
Parke	568	4.9	66	12.4	D	6.6	0.6	392	3.7	106	-0.9	12.9	5.9
Perry	908	6.8	59	12.0	0.7	5.5	0.9	371	3.3	199	5.3	39.4	6.0
Pike	292	2.4	31	5.7	D	2.9	0.6	185	1.7	125	0.2	4.6	19.1
Porter	7 646	63.4	601	224.0	4.8	60.1	11.7	4 427	78.1	555	7.2	363.1	-2.7
Posey	1 038	8.3	95	35.9	D	D	1.0	800	11.1	273	4.4	38.0	-2.4
Pulaski	605	4.2	52	8.9	D	3.2	0.9	241	3.3	176	3.7	17.5	-2.2
Putnam	1 370	11.9	106	21.2	D	9.2	1.1	732	7.6	216	3.7	50.9	-3.5
Randolph	1 229	9.7	107	18.4	0.2	8.7	1.2	670	6.1	213	0.6	30.3	12.4

1. For the period including March 12 of the year shown. 2. Includes deposits for all insured and reporting noninsured commercial and mutual savings banks. 3. Includes savings capital for all FSLIC insured savings institutions.

STATE County	Federal funds and grants, 1989: Expenditures: Total (Mil dol)	Expenditures: Percent change, 1988–1989	Per capita[1] (Dollars): Total	Per capita: Direct payments for individuals	Per capita: Procurement contract awards	Per capita: Salaries and wages	Per capita: Grant awards	Local government finances, 1981–1982: General revenue: Total (Mil dol)	Intergovernmental: Total (Mil dol)	Intergovernmental: Percent from state	Taxes: Total (Mil dol)	Taxes: Per capita[2]: Total (Dollars)	Taxes: Per capita[2]: Property (Dollars)	Direct general expenditure: Total (Mil dol)	Direct general expenditure: Percent change, 1977–1982
	174	175	176	177	178	179	180	181	182	183	184	185	186	187	188
INDIANA—Con.															
Bartholomew	189.7	14.7	2 918	1 382	971	219	253	94.0	28.2	87.8	26.0	402	345	91.4	52.4
Benton	34.0	-3.2	3 472	1 896	19	152	118	10.8	4.9	89.7	4.8	475	429	8.9	38.2
Blackford	34.4	3.1	2 389	1 827	12	93	186	15.1	6.1	91.3	4.1	266	245	12.8	59.7
Boone	70.3	0.0	1 790	1 310	39	112	125	34.7	12.8	91.9	10.0	264	263	29.1	64.5
Brown	14.9	0.9	1 115	912	6	48	109	7.0	3.9	96.4	2.5	201	179	7.4	71.1
Carroll	40.3	-2 940.7	2 067	1 351	13	115	97	14.2	6.6	92.8	5.9	301	256	13.5	75.6
Cass	123.6	19.5	3 090	1 850	666	130	246	42.2	16.2	87.6	11.3	280	234	45.2	72.0
Clark	299.6	1.3	3 352	1 616	927	465	308	84.8	34.8	90.2	22.5	252	250	77.1	58.2
Clay	67.9	2.9	2 685	2 040	17	148	299	20.5	8.3	95.1	5.1	210	209	20.8	110.8
Clinton	73.5	-3.7	2 288	1 744	19	96	168	34.3	12.5	88.7	10.0	315	268	34.3	94.0
Crawford	24.1	-15.9	2 362	1 723	17	126	407	6.9	4.8	76.8	1.8	191	191	6.7	70.2
Daviess	70.1	-5.0	2 419	1 787	44	151	189	25.8	9.5	89.4	5.5	192	183	24.9	63.0
Dearborn	68.4	3.0	1 767	1 481	11	75	174	39.7	13.9	92.5	11.0	316	315	32.4	103.9
Decatur	55.5	-1.3	2 285	1 586	16	91	256	23.7	8.8	91.6	6.3	264	222	21.6	62.7
De Kalb	96.9	22.4	2 662	1 291	949	80	171	28.4	14.0	85.0	10.1	306	255	22.9	49.0
Delaware	265.5	-6.4	2 218	1 687	50	149	281	103.8	55.9	83.1	34.7	276	276	106.2	40.5
Dubois	69.4	-6.5	1 870	1 319	185	127	105	25.8	12.2	96.4	9.2	270	269	23.6	30.0
Elkhart	249.2	5.0	1 623	1 269	45	82	195	120.2	53.2	88.1	50.6	370	311	111.6	46.4
Fayette	62.2	3.0	2 296	1 749	42	99	263	29.6	10.8	92.0	7.8	281	278	28.1	123.7
Floyd	135.4	8.1	2 070	1 622	55	96	286	70.2	24.0	90.0	14.8	237	236	74.8	100.0
Fountain	52.1	3.2	2 860	2 031	31	128	173	14.0	6.5	96.2	5.7	298	275	12.5	21.8
Franklin	32.1	1.4	1 590	1 118	10	79	222	9.3	5.6	95.1	2.8	136	135	7.9	22.4
Fulton	46.0	1.3	2 461	1 783	15	101	143	15.8	5.7	94.1	5.0	258	258	14.0	61.9
Gibson	77.6	-1.2	2 367	1 822	22	101	172	27.3	12.0	92.5	11.9	345	343	23.0	25.9
Grant	198.5	4.0	2 630	1 755	48	480	269	68.5	36.4	83.0	23.5	301	299	65.0	63.9
Greene	83.1	-2.1	2 680	2 022	150	131	235	28.4	12.0	84.1	7.1	232	231	25.9	68.8
Hamilton	144.1	10.9	1 352	981	114	114	86	80.9	29.9	91.3	30.5	361	360	72.6	67.0
Hancock	74.0	4.5	1 598	1 230	49	99	116	42.4	15.1	96.5	14.1	321	267	37.4	50.4
Harrison	51.9	5.4	1 740	1 343	14	116	175	20.5	10.5	94.5	4.4	155	154	19.4	63.1
Hendricks	99.4	-1.0	1 271	1 036	10	75	76	57.9	22.4	96.5	20.2	283	253	53.2	52.9
Henry	114.8	4.9	2 344	1 854	12	87	242	57.1	23.4	87.9	14.5	281	279	53.2	62.7
Howard	182.6	-13.0	2 229	1 746	25	166	219	89.2	36.5	90.7	27.6	323	323	81.1	42.4
Huntington	77.9	5.1	2 099	1 637	25	120	119	30.6	12.7	89.8	10.5	308	254	27.6	55.3
Jackson	83.7	6.1	2 244	1 630	25	111	300	36.5	15.4	78.9	9.0	242	241	37.0	76.2
Jasper	63.8	-11.3	2 435	1 507	12	132	134	24.3	8.3	92.8	7.8	291	249	21.9	76.7
Jay	55.3	5.6	2 502	1 764	12	88	246	28.6	12.4	67.1	6.3	282	238	25.4	98.1
Jefferson	82.8	1.1	2 752	1 734	132	489	293	27.2	12.4	96.2	10.6	349	348	24.3	84.4
Jennings	47.7	3.0	2 046	1 498	24	106	274	16.9	10.4	79.3	5.0	219	219	12.4	41.9
Johnson	156.3	8.1	1 789	1 324	159	126	126	73.5	29.3	94.6	23.8	299	250	60.5	49.4
Knox	121.8	4.9	3 029	2 085	17	171	467	60.2	16.0	83.2	9.7	228	225	54.6	30.7
Kosciusko	126.9	14.8	1 910	1 262	219	101	204	54.7	21.0	91.8	19.1	320	319	50.2	83.8
Lagrange	40.2	-0.1	1 366	1 018	13	80	109	22.3	8.8	95.5	7.8	298	298	21.1	52.8
Lake	1 141.0	6.3	2 347	1 762	45	149	364	630.2	319.2	85.1	223.3	435	430	550.5	50.6
La Porte	229.1	6.2	2 171	1 666	57	102	245	96.7	41.4	93.2	41.7	384	383	87.7	34.5
Lawrence	101.7	7.1	2 355	1 843	29	153	247	40.2	15.7	90.2	11.2	271	230	39.5	66.5
Madison	323.6	7.6	2 459	1 934	40	112	299	115.1	62.7	83.2	37.9	281	279	100.8	48.9
Marion	3 375.8	3.5	4 232	1 777	811	933	691	849.1	403.8	76.1	291.3	378	367	812.1	45.1
Marshall	76.5	3.8	1 821	1 387	14	100	166	35.0	14.0	89.0	12.8	323	272	31.7	50.1
Martin	191.3	4.5	16 782	1 888	1 775	12 435	543	7.6	4.6	93.3	2.4	223	206	7.0	45.7
Miami	157.1	6.5	4 189	1 656	11	2 146	219	36.3	17.0	92.1	9.1	240	239	36.7	56.1
Monroe	235.1	7.9	2 265	1 223	86	150	791	62.9	31.3	78.8	21.7	215	214	54.9	44.9
Montgomery	83.9	2.1	2 364	1 601	74	141	251	32.0	13.1	92.1	9.5	269	268	27.7	33.6
Morgan	95.4	5.4	1 727	1 345	38	83	181	42.4	18.3	94.9	11.1	211	166	40.5	32.2
Newton	40.5	4.0	2 935	1 397	15	112	292	13.8	5.4	95.1	5.3	352	310	12.6	54.3
Noble	64.9	3.3	1 652	1 284	23	86	124	31.3	13.1	87.1	9.4	265	223	30.8	69.9
Ohio	10.5	11.3	1 870	1 411	12	88	301	3.1	1.9	96.1	0.9	169	136	2.6	28.9
Orange	43.9	3.1	2 274	1 656	51	87	324	21.6	12.0	59.2	4.6	248	247	17.4	56.9
Owen	33.7	9.6	1 852	1 324	13	103	249	9.7	5.0	95.9	3.5	219	218	8.6	67.8
Parke	42.7	0.8	2 757	1 903	27	143	271	10.9	6.1	92.5	3.9	231	230	9.5	15.5
Perry	43.1	3.4	2 293	1 694	81	158	310	15.9	8.2	88.4	3.7	195	193	14.4	29.0
Pike	48.1	45.4	3 761	1 954	984	104	487	13.1	4.8	91.2	7.4	550	549	9.5	57.3
Porter	194.1	5.0	1 552	1 246	30	96	123	140.2	48.4	83.2	44.2	359	346	122.1	77.8
Posey	52.0	2.8	1 978	1 345	26	89	295	18.4	9.0	89.2	7.7	285	283	18.1	51.9
Pulaski	36.6	-1.0	2 749	1 681	28	114	167	15.0	5.2	91.3	4.8	364	324	16.7	87.8
Putnam	62.1	5.0	2 050	1 514	18	112	195	27.1	12.6	78.0	7.3	246	245	26.7	83.4
Randolph	68.4	-4.6	2 489	1 869	35	128	219	25.7	11.8	89.3	7.5	258	218	26.0	42.2

1. Based on the estimated population as of July 1 of the year shown. 2. Based on the estimated population as of July 1, 1982.

STATE County	Local government finances, 1981–1982 (cont'd): Direct general expenditure (cont'd): Per capita[1] (Dollars)	Percent of total for– Education	Percent of total for– Health & hospitals	Percent of total for– Police protection	Percent of total for– Public welfare	Percent of total for– Highways	Debt outstanding: Total (Mil dol)	Debt outstanding: Per capita[1] (Dollars)	State and local government employment, 1989: Total	State and local government employment, 1989: Rate[2]	Federal government civilian employment 1989: Total	Federal government civilian employment 1989: Earnings ($1,000)	Elections, 1988[3]: Total vote cast for president	Elections, 1988[3]: Vote for lead party (Percent)
	189	190	191	192	193	194	195	196	197	198	199	200	201	202
INDIANA—Con.														
Bartholomew	1 413	36.7	33.0	2.2	4.1	3.1	40.7	629	3 903	600.5	243	7 432	26 291	R–66.0
Benton	883	67.6	0.0	1.6	0.8	11.6	7.7	762	532	542.9	41	1 050	4 069	R–66.3
Blackford	830	46.9	21.7	2.2	4.3	6.5	4.8	310	737	511.8	37	1 050	5 608	R–59.5
Boone	767	48.9	21.9	2.1	2.5	4.4	31.4	828	1 524	387.8	109	2 928	15 806	R–73.4
Brown	604	69.5	1.7	2.9	6.6	4.0	3.3	270	525	391.8	20	533	5 501	R–60.9
Carroll	685	56.0	0.5	2.9	3.3	10.5	5.4	277	654	335.4	60	1 451	7 964	R–62.5
Cass	1 122	47.2	20.9	2.3	2.7	5.3	34.9	867	2 900	725.0	128	3 610	16 851	R–65.1
Clark	864	45.3	26.3	2.8	5.7	2.6	22.7	254	4 375	489.4	2 211	48 926	31 192	R–53.0
Clay	859	51.5	20.6	2.3	2.4	4.5	2.4	98	1 151	454.9	79	1 905	9 629	R–60.8
Clinton	1 079	44.0	13.9	2.6	2.8	8.1	17.3	544	1 525	475.1	85	2 245	13 021	R–65.8
Crawford	690	51.7	1.0	0.6	3.3	22.7	6.7	688	360	352.9	37	839	4 596	R–55.1
Daviess	866	36.9	24.7	1.8	3.8	5.9	10.0	348	1 294	446.2	112	3 377	10 294	R–65.7
Dearborn	927	47.6	27.7	2.7	3.1	2.8	14.8	424	1 688	436.2	73	2 007	13 309	R–61.6
Decatur	900	40.5	29.9	2.4	3.9	5.2	10.9	456	1 050	432.1	71	1 728	9 272	R–67.4
De Kalb	695	58.6	0.8	3.8	4.7	7.8	21.1	640	1 410	387.4	93	2 456	13 716	R–65.7
Delaware	846	46.4	1.6	3.4	7.6	4.4	29.9	238	9 326	779.1	477	15 433	48 112	R–56.8
Dubois	691	66.3	0.5	1.9	3.3	6.8	21.2	620	1 460	393.5	124	3 290	16 048	R–62.3
Elkhart	815	54.6	0.8	5.8	6.4	4.0	61.9	452	5 292	344.8	361	11 056	48 200	R–70.1
Fayette	1 011	43.6	0.8	3.1	3.2	3.8	10.1	363	1 189	438.7	68	1 822	10 108	R–58.9
Floyd	1 200	36.9	30.3	2.7	3.8	3.8	89.0	1 429	4 121	630.1	148	4 750	25 393	R–56.3
Fountain	659	57.9	0.4	2.6	3.0	13.6	11.9	624	791	434.6	70	1 805	8 441	R–60.6
Franklin	389	64.3	0.5	2.4	5.1	13.3	1.3	65	610	302.0	46	1 163	7 271	R–65.7
Fulton	727	41.9	22.0	2.5	3.2	10.0	10.2	529	893	477.5	54	1 397	8 051	R–65.0
Gibson	669	58.0	0.2	3.7	4.8	12.6	7.9	229	1 105	336.9	105	2 817	14 684	R–51.8
Grant	830	60.4	0.4	3.8	6.3	3.7	30.7	392	2 855	378.1	1 445	46 817	29 371	R–62.8
Greene	842	40.8	18.5	1.6	2.1	9.4	15.4	502	1 449	467.4	113	2 837	13 746	R–55.9
Hamilton	860	53.0	15.0	2.9	1.7	4.5	49.9	591	3 926	368.3	287	8 589	45 615	R–80.4
Hancock	854	47.9	25.7	2.8	1.8	4.5	17.7	404	2 227	481.0	112	2 866	18 780	R–71.2
Harrison	679	55.8	19.4	1.2	1.0	7.9	6.0	210	1 193	400.3	103	2 424	11 661	R–57.5
Hendricks	744	53.1	17.1	2.6	2.4	5.6	33.5	469	3 854	492.8	156	4 226	29 803	R–74.1
Henry	1 031	43.4	25.0	2.5	3.8	4.0	37.3	724	3 144	641.6	117	3 218	19 116	R–59.0
Howard	952	47.8	15.4	4.5	6.0	4.2	27.8	326	4 455	544.0	333	10 402	31 620	R–63.2
Huntington	807	47.3	14.5	3.7	3.4	6.5	17.9	524	1 637	441.2	107	2 860	15 594	R–74.9
Jackson	992	43.2	21.0	2.0	4.9	3.9	32.3	866	1 866	500.3	125	3 262	15 088	R–62.8
Jasper	816	43.4	20.8	2.0	2.9	7.8	247.6	9 240	1 328	506.9	89	2 302	9 292	R–64.7
Jay	1 136	38.9	18.3	2.4	3.5	5.8	3.0	136	1 035	468.3	59	1 627	8 620	R–62.2
Jefferson	798	64.8	0.5	3.5	4.3	4.8	28.2	925	2 005	666.1	542	18 202	12 268	R–56.6
Jennings	547	62.9	0.3	2.5	5.8	9.8	3.7	164	2 071	888.8	69	1 854	9 348	R–60.3
Johnson	760	49.6	19.9	3.4	2.6	3.4	24.6	309	3 756	429.7	296	6 849	33 778	R–73.0
Knox	1 285	24.1	53.6	1.6	4.2	3.5	40.2	946	4 332	1 077.6	200	5 969	16 881	R–58.1
Kosciusko	839	48.9	0.6	2.3	2.3	6.3	22.1	370	2 180	328.3	191	4 969	23 163	R–76.7
Lagrange	813	62.2	16.8	1.0	2.2	7.4	3.4	131	1 030	350.3	71	1 916	6 546	R–68.7
Lake	1 072	43.6	2.5	5.2	12.0	3.4	498.0	970	23 350	480.3	1 770	58 031	185 735	D–56.5
La Porte	809	50.8	0.5	5.1	5.8	5.4	76.7	708	6 201	587.8	270	7 774	38 285	R–53.6
Lawrence	955	42.4	22.7	3.0	2.5	5.4	33.2	803	2 006	464.4	181	4 939	16 599	R–64.7
Madison	746	52.7	0.5	4.2	6.5	4.2	58.8	435	5 745	436.6	369	10 884	57 241	R–56.9
Marion	1 053	42.1	11.7	5.3	6.7	4.3	536.7	696	58 111	728.5	18 712	626 081	315 095	R–58.6
Marshall	799	45.1	12.6	3.4	4.5	7.6	26.3	664	1 595	379.8	111	3 047	16 038	R–65.4
Martin	646	59.6	0.8	3.7	5.4	12.7	1.5	142	402	352.6	4 952	169 400	5 219	R–58.7
Miami	972	55.2	16.2	2.1	3.8	7.5	15.5	411	1 745	465.3	1 266	31 525	13 236	R–64.5
Monroe	542	53.3	0.6	4.1	4.3	4.0	29.2	288	16 233	1 563.9	367	11 224	37 038	R–56.0
Montgomery	786	51.4	13.9	2.9	3.9	7.1	9.7	273	1 608	453.0	120	3 166	14 472	R–74.6
Morgan	770	51.4	20.6	1.9	4.1	6.1	23.4	445	2 176	394.2	112	3 102	19 736	R–72.4
Newton	837	52.1	13.3	2.6	3.4	7.9	8.8	585	637	461.6	46	1 132	5 035	R–65.0
Noble	871	42.6	24.4	2.5	2.5	6.2	17.6	498	1 710	435.1	101	2 509	12 089	R–65.3
Ohio	504	59.2	1.1	4.9	6.4	8.6	1.6	306	176	314.3	17	409	2 531	R–55.8
Orange	934	39.7	16.5	1.1	2.5	7.0	13.0	701	864	447.7	54	1 473	8 015	R–65.4
Owen	544	69.7	0.6	2.0	4.1	9.7	2.3	145	624	342.9	48	1 226	6 363	R–60.3
Parke	568	62.0	0.3	2.6	7.2	8.0	5.9	352	798	514.8	58	1 351	7 053	R–63.2
Perry	754	49.3	16.1	2.4	4.9	8.7	11.4	597	1 112	591.5	74	1 692	9 580	D–50.1
Pike	705	60.2	0.1	1.6	2.6	11.4	6.4	475	527	411.7	45	1 060	6 371	R–51.7
Porter	993	44.6	25.4	3.6	2.2	5.0	96.4	784	6 267	501.0	382	10 529	49 345	R–60.4
Posey	674	64.1	0.3	3.0	5.2	8.6	11.2	415	1 019	387.5	62	1 614	10 490	R–57.1
Pulaski	1 265	51.9	19.3	1.3	2.2	8.8	12.6	955	784	589.5	48	1 213	5 917	R–62.1
Putnam	904	44.6	20.4	1.5	1.7	7.9	12.9	439	2 087	688.8	95	2 541	11 021	R–64.6
Randolph	895	58.7	11.9	2.1	4.6	5.1	11.2	386	1 237	449.8	95	2 399	10 908	R–62.9

1. Based on the estimated population as of July 1, 1982. 2. Per 10,000 resident population estimated as of July 1 of the year shown. 3. Data subject to copyright.

STATE-County code	MSA/CMSA/NECMA code[1]	STATE County	Land Area,[2] 1990 (Sq. Km.)	Population, 1990: Total persons	Rank	Per square kilometer	Race: White	Black	Am. Indian, Eskimo, Aleut	Asian & Pacific Islander	Other race	Hispanic[3]	Age of population Percent: Under 5 years	5 to 14 years	15 to 24 years
			1	2	3	4	5	6	7	8	9	10	11	12	13
		INDIANA—Con.													
18 137	...	Ripley	1 156	24 616	1 476	21.3	24 501	16	44	38	17	62	7.4	16.1	14.3
18 139	...	Rush	1 058	18 129	1 781	17.1	17 901	142	15	60	11	61	6.9	15.6	14.6
18 141	7800	St. Joseph	1 185	247 052	203	208.5	216 984	24 190	846	2 507	2 525	5 201	7.3	14.1	16.3
18 143	...	Scott	493	20 991	1 628	42.6	20 850	16	25	50	50	148	7.2	15.5	15.1
18 145	3480	Shelby	1 069	40 307	993	37.7	39 743	330	67	142	25	118	7.3	15.2	13.9
18 147	...	Spencer	1 033	19 490	1 703	18.9	19 295	111	37	33	14	89	6.9	15.8	13.1
18 149	...	Starke	801	22 747	1 546	28.4	22 446	73	86	48	94	367	7.3	15.7	14.3
18 151	...	Steuben	800	27 446	1 378	34.3	27 146	51	64	132	53	193	7.2	14.5	15.4
18 153	...	Sullivan	1 158	18 993	1 735	16.4	18 905	15	39	15	19	59	6.1	14.9	12.7
18 155	...	Switzerland	573	7 738	2 601	13.5	7 695	15	16	10	2	22	6.6	15.9	12.7
18 157	3920	Tippecanoe	1 295	130 598	356	100.8	122 013	2 660	320	4 821	784	2 078	6.3	11.5	29.2
18 159	3850	Tipton	674	16 119	1 915	23.9	15 990	10	20	51	48	121	6.3	15.1	13.4
18 161	...	Union	418	6 976	2 664	16.7	6 915	20	15	21	5	25	6.7	15.9	14.4
18 163	2440	Vanderburgh	608	165 058	289	271.5	151 216	12 410	284	917	231	883	6.9	13.4	13.7
18 165	...	Vermillion	665	16 773	1 863	25.2	16 690	15	32	28	8	61	6.0	14.5	13.0
18 167	8320	Vigo	1 045	106 107	436	101.5	98 411	5 916	297	1 161	322	997	6.2	13.0	18.5
18 169	...	Wabash	1 070	35 069	1 128	32.8	34 462	138	259	123	87	321	6.7	14.8	15.7
18 171	...	Warren	945	8 176	2 548	8.7	8 140	1	17	15	3	23	7.0	14.7	12.8
18 173	2440	Warrick	995	44 920	913	45.1	44 274	371	83	157	35	168	7.0	16.3	13.6
18 175	...	Washington	1 332	23 717	1 502	17.8	23 625	23	28	18	23	108	6.8	15.8	14.2
18 177	...	Wayne	1 045	71 951	619	68.9	67 532	3 795	153	296	175	374	6.6	14.0	14.8
18 179	...	Wells	958	25 948	1 423	27.1	25 758	10	40	41	99	262	7.7	16.4	12.8
18 181	...	White	1 309	23 265	1 526	17.8	23 127	2	50	41	45	175	6.8	15.6	12.4
18 183	2760	Whitley	869	27 651	1 365	31.8	27 473	29	73	37	39	126	7.5	16.0	13.7
19 000	...	IOWA	144 716	2 776 755	X	19.2	2 683 090	48 090	7 349	25 476	12 750	32 647	7.0	14.9	14.3
19 001	...	Adair	1 475	8 409	2 520	5.7	8 377	1	5	19	7	35	6.6	14.7	10.1
19 003	...	Adams	1 097	4 866	2 847	4.4	4 847	3	7	3	6	18	7.0	13.1	10.1
19 005	...	Allamakee	1 657	13 855	2 067	8.4	13 791	5	21	28	10	42	7.2	15.8	11.0
19 007	...	Appanoose	1 285	13 743	2 077	10.7	13 582	79	26	36	20	72	6.3	14.6	11.8
19 009	...	Audubon	1 148	7 334	2 626	6.4	7 324	1	3	6	0	22	6.9	14.5	9.7
19 011	...	Benton	1 856	22 429	1 557	12.1	22 317	20	31	42	19	93	7.4	16.2	11.6
19 013	8920	Black Hawk	1 469	123 798	370	84.3	113 656	8 514	226	1 005	397	912	6.7	14.8	17.8
19 015	...	Boone	1 480	25 186	1 455	17.0	25 003	62	19	78	24	99	6.6	14.3	11.2
19 017	8920	Bremer	1 134	22 813	1 541	20.1	22 580	70	11	132	20	72	6.0	14.8	16.1
19 019	...	Buchanan	1 480	20 844	1 637	14.1	20 695	38	24	43	44	112	7.8	18.2	12.1
19 021	...	Buena Vista	1 489	19 965	1 679	13.4	19 458	56	16	396	39	160	7.1	15.0	15.2
19 023	...	Butler	1 503	15 731	1 938	10.5	15 681	4	12	25	9	37	6.2	15.7	11.0
19 025	...	Calhoun	1 477	11 508	2 255	7.8	11 433	30	11	23	11	40	6.0	15.2	9.2
19 027	...	Carroll	1 475	21 423	1 607	14.5	21 325	7	19	56	16	57	7.9	17.6	11.4
19 029	...	Cass	1 462	15 128	1 979	10.3	15 074	9	22	15	8	46	6.4	15.2	10.1
19 031	...	Cedar	1 501	17 381	1 829	11.6	17 274	16	17	49	25	109	6.3	16.3	10.9
19 033	...	Cerro Gordo	1 472	46 733	894	31.7	45 738	303	44	260	388	994	6.8	14.2	12.7
19 035	...	Cherokee	1 495	14 098	2 048	9.4	14 000	20	37	32	9	51	6.6	15.9	10.6
19 037	...	Chickasaw	1 307	13 295	2 115	10.2	13 264	4	4	18	5	40	6.7	16.7	11.2
19 039	...	Clarke	1 117	8 287	2 539	7.4	8 252	3	8	21	3	19	6.8	15.2	11.1
19 041	...	Clay	1 474	17 585	1 815	11.9	17 449	8	31	82	15	44	7.1	16.4	11.3
19 043	...	Clayton	2 017	19 054	1 730	9.4	18 996	6	16	27	9	61	7.0	16.2	11.4
19 045	...	Clinton	1 800	51 040	827	28.4	49 882	732	125	202	99	294	7.0	15.3	12.4
19 047	...	Crawford	1 850	16 775	1 862	9.1	16 569	59	33	88	26	98	7.0	15.4	12.9
19 049	2120	Dallas	1 519	29 755	1 304	19.6	29 534	63	42	70	46	176	7.1	16.5	11.3
19 051	...	Davis	1 304	8 312	2 533	6.4	8 246	2	25	21	18	41	7.3	15.5	11.9
19 053	...	Decatur	1 379	8 338	2 530	6.0	8 197	35	16	71	19	45	6.1	13.2	18.0
19 055	...	Delaware	1 497	18 035	1 789	12.0	17 959	11	15	32	18	68	7.8	18.3	12.0
19 057	...	Des Moines	1 078	42 614	942	39.5	40 809	1 327	69	225	184	492	6.6	15.1	12.4
19 059	...	Dickinson	987	14 909	1 993	15.1	14 830	16	22	26	15	52	5.5	14.2	9.8
19 061	2200	Dubuque	1 575	86 403	528	54.9	85 367	354	77	437	168	437	7.0	15.7	15.2
19 063	...	Emmet	1 025	11 569	2 250	11.3	11 484	19	12	31	23	63	6.1	15.7	14.0
19 065	...	Fayette	1 893	21 843	1 586	11.5	21 673	48	16	48	58	195	6.8	15.3	12.3
19 067	...	Floyd	1 297	17 058	1 848	13.2	16 953	8	13	44	40	92	6.6	15.1	11.7
19 069	...	Franklin	1 509	11 364	2 264	7.5	11 253	6	8	17	80	152	6.4	15.3	10.3
19 071	...	Fremont	1 324	8 226	2 546	6.2	8 177	4	9	16	20	53	6.3	15.5	10.6
19 073	...	Greene	1 472	10 045	2 380	6.8	9 994	5	10	30	6	30	6.3	14.5	10.0
19 075	...	Grundy	1 302	12 029	2 217	9.2	11 986	7	9	21	6	34	6.4	14.9	10.0
19 077	...	Guthrie	1 530	10 935	2 301	7.1	10 883	7	19	14	12	35	5.8	15.0	10.2
19 079	...	Hamilton	1 494	16 071	1 918	10.8	15 902	9	21	90	49	116	6.6	14.6	11.1

1. MSA = Metropolitan Statistical Area. CMSA = Consolidated MSA. NECMA = New England county metropolitan area. PMSA = Primary MSA. See Appendix A for explanation of these concepts. See Appendix B for list of metropolitan areas identified by type, with component counties. 2. Dry land or land partially or temporarily covered by water. 3. Hispanic persons may be of any race.

STATE County	Population, 1990 (cont'd): Age of population (cont'd), Percent: 25 to 34 years	35 to 44 years	45 to 54 years	55 to 64 years	65 to 74 years	75 years and over	Percent female	Population–Change and components of change: Change, 1980–1990: Number	Percent	Components of change, 1980–1986: Total persons, 1986	Total persons, 1980	Net change: Number	Percent	Natural increase: Births	Deaths
	14	15	16	17	18	19	20	21	22	23	24	25	26	27	28
INDIANA–Con.															
Ripley	15.3	14.0	10.2	8.6	7.6	6.6	51.0	218	0.9	25 400	24 398	1 000	4.1	2 300	1 400
Rush	15.0	13.8	10.1	9.3	8.2	6.5	51.6	-1 475	-7.5	18 800	19 604	-800	-4.2	1 600	1 300
St. Joseph	15.9	14.5	9.1	8.8	8.0	6.1	51.8	5 435	2.2	241 400	241 617	-200	-0.1	22 600	13 800
Scott	15.9	14.4	11.5	8.5	6.5	5.3	51.5	569	2.8	20 400	20 422	0	-0.1	1 800	1 100
Shelby	16.7	15.0	10.7	8.9	6.9	5.3	51.4	420	1.1	39 500	39 887	-400	-1.0	3 600	2 100
Spencer	16.3	14.8	10.8	9.1	7.2	5.8	50.0	129	0.7	20 300	19 361	900	4.8	1 800	1 200
Starke	15.4	13.1	10.2	9.6	8.2	6.2	50.8	750	3.4	21 400	21 997	-600	-2.5	2 100	1 400
Steuben	15.5	14.5	10.7	9.2	7.8	5.3	50.1	2 752	11.1	26 500	24 694	1 800	7.2	2 200	1 300
Sullivan	13.6	14.7	10.5	9.7	9.8	8.0	52.1	-2 114	-10.0	20 600	21 107	-500	-2.2	1 700	1 700
Switzerland	14.5	13.8	11.7	9.8	8.2	6.9	50.9	585	8.2	7 300	7 153	100	2.1	600	500
Tippecanoe	16.3	12.7	8.1	6.4	5.4	4.1	49.3	8 896	7.3	124 400	121 702	2 700	2.2	10 900	5 100
Tipton	14.8	15.0	11.7	8.9	8.0	6.8	51.4	-700	-4.2	16 200	16 819	-600	-3.8	1 400	900
Union	15.0	14.7	11.1	8.4	7.5	6.4	51.5	116	1.7	7 000	6 860	100	2.0	600	400
Vanderburgh	16.9	14.2	9.8	9.4	8.8	6.9	52.9	-2 457	-1.5	167 600	167 515	100	0.1	15 600	11 000
Vermillion	14.3	14.5	11.3	9.2	9.4	7.9	52.6	-1 456	-8.0	17 600	18 229	-600	-3.4	1 300	1 400
Vigo	15.4	13.9	9.3	8.5	8.5	6.6	51.0	-6 278	-5.6	109 500	112 385	-2 900	-2.6	9 700	7 300
Wabash	14.7	13.8	10.4	9.1	7.9	6.9	51.6	-1 571	-4.3	35 200	36 640	-1 500	-4.0	3 200	2 100
Warren	13.9	14.7	12.1	9.9	8.8	6.1	50.7	-800	-8.9	8 500	8 976	-500	-5.1	600	500
Warrick	16.0	17.4	11.7	7.7	6.0	4.3	50.8	3 446	8.3	45 400	41 474	3 900	9.5	3 900	1 900
Washington	16.0	14.3	10.7	8.7	7.7	5.8	50.3	1 785	8.1	22 500	21 932	500	2.4	1 900	1 300
Wayne	14.7	13.9	10.9	9.9	8.5	6.6	52.3	-4 107	-5.4	72 200	76 058	-3 800	-5.1	6 400	4 600
Wells	16.4	14.4	10.2	8.5	7.5	6.0	51.5	547	2.2	24 400	25 401	-1 000	-4.1	2 400	1 300
White	15.0	14.6	9.9	9.9	9.3	6.5	51.7	-602	-2.5	23 300	23 867	-600	-2.4	2 200	1 600
Whitley	15.8	15.5	9.7	8.9	7.1	5.8	50.9	1 436	5.5	27 000	26 215	800	2.9	2 500	1 400
IOWA	15.4	14.2	9.9	9.0	8.2	7.2	51.6	-137 245	-4.7	2 851 000	2 914 000	-63 000	-2.2	274 000	171 000
Adair	13.3	11.7	10.0	10.1	11.2	12.4	51.9	-1 100	-11.6	8 800	9 509	-700	-7.3	800	700
Adams	13.5	12.4	10.9	11.3	11.2	10.5	50.9	-865	-15.1	5 400	5 731	-300	-5.7	500	400
Allamakee	13.8	12.9	9.9	10.0	10.1	9.4	51.1	-1 253	-8.3	15 100	15 108	0	0.0	1 400	1 100
Appanoose	13.5	12.6	9.9	9.8	10.9	10.5	52.4	-1 768	-11.4	14 300	15 511	-1 200	-8.0	1 300	1 200
Audubon	12.0	12.1	10.5	11.2	11.7	11.4	52.0	-1 225	-14.3	7 900	8 559	-600	-7.4	800	600
Benton	15.4	13.6	10.0	9.3	8.8	7.8	51.0	-1 220	-5.2	22 700	23 649	-1 000	-4.1	2 000	1 400
Black Hawk	14.1	14.6	9.8	8.6	7.7	5.9	52.4	-14 163	-10.3	127 600	137 961	-10 400	-7.5	13 400	6 600
Boone	15.1	15.0	10.1	9.6	8.9	9.1	52.3	-998	-3.8	25 700	26 184	-500	-2.0	2 200	1 800
Bremer	12.7	13.8	11.2	8.6	8.6	8.1	51.4	-2 007	-8.1	23 900	24 820	-900	-3.7	2 100	1 300
Buchanan	14.3	13.7	9.9	8.5	8.7	6.9	51.0	-2 056	-9.0	21 900	22 900	-1 000	-4.2	2 600	1 200
Buena Vista	14.4	12.8	8.0	9.5	9.3	8.6	51.5	-809	-3.9	20 500	20 774	-300	-1.5	2 000	1 500
Butler	12.9	13.7	9.9	10.1	10.6	9.9	51.3	-1 937	-11.0	16 700	17 668	-900	-5.2	1 500	1 100
Calhoun	12.6	13.1	9.9	10.4	12.2	11.6	52.4	-2 034	-15.0	12 200	13 542	-1 300	-9.7	1 100	1 100
Carroll	14.5	12.5	9.0	9.4	9.3	8.4	51.7	-1 528	-6.7	22 500	22 951	-400	-1.9	2 500	1 500
Cass	13.7	13.2	10.3	10.2	10.3	10.7	52.4	-1 804	-10.7	16 100	16 932	-900	-5.1	1 500	1 300
Cedar	14.8	14.9	10.5	9.5	9.0	7.8	51.2	-1 254	-6.7	18 500	18 635	-100	-0.6	1 600	1 100
Cerro Gordo	15.8	14.2	9.7	9.8	9.1	7.8	52.7	-1 725	-3.6	48 800	48 458	400	0.8	4 500	3 000
Cherokee	13.5	13.8	9.9	11.1	9.6	8.9	51.7	-2 140	-13.2	15 200	16 238	-1 000	-6.3	1 400	1 100
Chickasaw	14.4	13.1	10.7	9.3	9.3	8.6	50.4	-2 142	-13.9	14 800	15 437	-600	-4.0	1 400	900
Clarke	14.3	14.0	10.1	10.0	8.7	9.9	52.2	-325	-3.8	8 600	8 612	0	-0.3	700	600
Clay	15.0	14.5	9.5	9.7	9.0	7.5	52.4	-1 991	-10.2	18 300	19 576	-1 300	-6.6	1 900	1 100
Clayton	14.2	13.0	10.0	10.2	9.4	8.7	50.8	-2 044	-9.7	20 700	21 098	-400	-2.1	1 900	1 500
Clinton	15.1	14.2	10.6	9.4	8.9	7.1	52.0	-6 082	-10.6	53 600	57 122	-3 500	-6.2	5 100	3 400
Crawford	14.2	13.1	10.4	9.7	9.3	8.1	51.1	-2 160	-11.4	18 700	18 935	-200	-1.3	1 800	1 200
Dallas	15.8	15.8	10.5	8.3	7.7	6.9	51.2	242	0.8	29 800	29 513	300	0.9	2 700	1 700
Davis	13.7	12.9	10.4	9.6	8.9	9.9	51.1	-792	-8.7	8 900	9 104	-200	-2.0	900	700
Decatur	12.1	11.3	9.1	9.6	10.1	10.4	51.7	-1 456	-14.9	8 900	9 794	-900	-9.3	700	700
Delaware	15.7	12.7	9.7	9.1	8.2	6.5	50.9	-898	-4.7	19 100	18 933	100	0.6	2 100	1 100
Des Moines	14.5	15.0	10.7	9.5	8.7	7.5	52.2	-3 589	-7.8	44 600	46 203	-1 600	-3.6	4 300	2 900
Dickinson	12.8	14.9	10.4	11.6	11.7	9.1	52.1	-720	-4.6	15 200	15 629	-400	-2.6	1 200	1 000
Dubuque	15.2	14.1	10.0	8.7	7.6	6.5	51.7	-7 342	-7.8	91 100	93 745	-2 700	-2.9	8 800	5 100
Emmet	12.5	13.3	9.3	10.2	9.7	9.1	51.6	-1 767	-13.2	11 900	13 336	-1 500	-11.1	1 200	900
Fayette	13.6	13.0	9.9	9.9	10.0	9.2	51.4	-3 645	-14.3	23 500	25 488	-1 900	-7.6	2 200	1 800
Floyd	12.5	13.3	11.2	10.1	10.4	9.3	52.4	-2 539	-13.0	18 600	19 597	-1 000	-5.1	1 600	1 400
Franklin	13.4	13.8	10.1	10.6	10.1	9.9	51.6	-1 672	-12.8	12 300	13 036	-800	-5.9	1 100	900
Fremont	12.2	13.7	9.7	10.5	11.2	10.4	52.7	-1 175	-12.5	8 900	9 401	-500	-5.4	800	800
Greene	12.8	13.1	9.8	10.9	10.9	11.6	52.5	-2 074	-17.1	11 200	12 119	-1 000	-7.9	1 100	900
Grundy	13.1	14.0	11.3	10.2	10.6	9.4	52.0	-2 337	-16.3	13 200	14 366	-1 200	-8.0	1 100	800
Guthrie	12.3	13.3	10.7	11.7	11.1	9.9	52.0	-1 048	-8.7	11 400	11 983	-600	-4.9	900	1 000
Hamilton	14.6	13.8	10.3	10.5	10.0	8.4	51.5	-1 791	-10.0	17 000	17 862	-800	-4.7	1 500	1 100

STATE County	Population–(cont'd) Components of change, 1980-1986 (cont'd)	Households, 1990					Births, 1988			Deaths, 1987				Marriages, 1984	
					Percent					Number		Rate			
	Net migration	Number	Percent change, 1980–1990	Persons per house-hold	Female family house-holder[1]	One-person	Total	Rate[2]	Low birth weight[3] (Number)	Total	Infant[4]	Total[2]	Infant[5]	Number	Rate[2]
	29	30	31	32	33	34	35	36	37	38	39	40	41	42	43
INDIANA—Con.															
Ripley	100	8 778	7.0	2.76	7.6	22.2	345	13.6	28	244	5	9.7	15.2	172	6.9
Rush	-1 200	6 504	-2.1	2.71	8.2	21.1	229	12.4	13	194	1	10.5	4.0	160	8.5
St. Joseph	-8 900	92 365	7.1	2.54	11.4	26.4	3 717	15.2	228	2 367	40	9.7	11.1	2 358	9.8
Scott	-700	7 593	12.9	2.73	11.2	20.1	305	14.6	25	213	0	10.1	0.0	238	11.7
Shelby	-1 800	14 761	6.8	2.70	8.2	21.0	565	14.1	39	357	2	8.9	3.7	367	9.2
Spencer	300	6 962	8.5	2.72	6.7	20.8	248	12.3	18	197	2	9.8	7.5	168	8.3
Starke	-1 200	8 141	9.1	2.75	9.2	21.1	335	15.1	24	245	1	11.1	3.1	183	8.6
Steuben	900	10 194	16.4	2.62	6.9	22.8	409	14.6	23	208	4	7.5	9.5	313	12.4
Sullivan	-500	7 364	-7.3	2.54	7.5	25.6	244	12.1	18	246	1	12.1	4.5	231	11.2
Switzerland	0	2 839	11.5	2.69	7.0	23.0	105	14.2	6	82	3	11.1	33.7	54	7.3
Tippecanoe	-3 200	45 618	12.1	2.50	7.9	25.4	1 761	14.0	91	841	12	6.8	6.9	1 147	9.2
Tipton	-1 100	6 026	0.6	2.64	7.7	21.8	177	10.9	11	151	1	9.3	4.8	151	9.3
Union	0	2 576	6.9	2.67	8.7	21.2	73	10.6	3	54	0	7.8	0.0	70	10.1
Vanderburgh	-4 400	66 780	4.3	2.40	11.4	29.2	2 338	14.1	166	1 765	25	10.6	10.6	1 660	9.9
Vermillion	-500	6 638	-4.1	2.49	8.8	27.2	197	11.3	8	207	0	11.8	0.0	154	8.7
Vigo	-5 300	39 804	-1.2	2.45	10.7	28.3	1 439	13.4	89	1 180	19	10.9	13.6	1 071	9.7
Wabash	-2 600	12 630	0.3	2.62	7.6	22.4	483	13.6	23	344	3	9.7	6.1	343	9.7
Warren	-600	3 015	-2.5	2.68	6.0	19.1	117	13.9	6	85	1	10.2	10.5	92	10.6
Warrick	1 900	15 817	15.2	2.80	7.7	16.8	643	13.9	44	309	6	6.7	9.9	318	7.1
Washington	-100	8 664	14.7	2.70	9.0	21.2	318	13.7	22	230	1	10.0	3.3	229	10.3
Wayne	-5 700	27 587	0.6	2.52	11.3	24.9	951	13.2	54	791	13	10.9	13.1	713	9.7
Wells	-2 200	9 438	6.7	2.70	7.5	20.9	407	15.4	23	225	2	8.6	5.1	252	10.4
White	-1 200	8 926	1.5	2.58	7.1	23.5	301	12.7	19	243	0	10.3	0.0	234	9.9
Whitley	-300	10 010	10.4	2.72	6.8	20.3	420	15.1	35	242	3	8.8	7.5	281	10.6
IOWA	-166 000	1 064 325	1.1	2.52	8.0	25.9	38 119	13.5	2 072	27 234	343	9.6	9.1	26 366	9.1
Adair	-800	3 419	-5.4	2.41	4.8	27.6	86	10.1	4	124	1	14.4	10.6	62	6.7
Adams	-400	2 005	-9.5	2.37	4.5	28.5	74	14.0	1	55	0	10.2	0.0	38	6.8
Allamakee	-300	5 268	1.0	2.55	5.7	27.1	201	13.5	6	185	1	12.4	5.0	152	9.7
Appanoose	-1 300	5 609	-6.7	2.41	8.5	28.8	167	11.7	7	197	3	13.8	18.4	100	6.7
Audubon	-800	2 936	-8.0	2.43	4.5	26.8	82	10.8	4	96	2	12.5	21.1	69	8.2
Benton	-1 600	8 518	-0.5	2.59	6.8	23.5	286	12.6	18	235	1	10.4	3.5	141	6.0
Black Hawk	-17 200	46 932	-2.6	2.51	10.4	25.6	1 628	13.1	99	1 082	15	8.7	9.2	1 230	9.1
Boone	-900	9 827	1.0	2.46	7.2	25.8	347	13.7	22	281	3	11.1	9.4	245	9.5
Bremer	-1 800	8 394	-0.7	2.55	5.0	24.0	233	10.0	9	236	0	10.1	0.0	220	8.7
Buchanan	-2 300	7 506	-2.2	2.71	7.4	23.6	310	14.2	20	183	3	8.5	9.2	176	7.4
Buena Vista	-800	7 515	-2.1	2.49	5.4	27.5	302	15.0	23	221	4	10.9	15.2	195	9.4
Butler	-1 300	6 036	-5.0	2.55	5.4	23.8	188	11.5	5	192	2	11.8	11.2	85	4.7
Calhoun	-1 200	4 684	-8.4	2.36	5.1	30.8	111	9.2	9	169	0	14.0	0.0	89	6.8
Carroll	-1 500	7 964	1.2	2.63	6.3	27.0	311	13.9	7	227	3	10.2	8.9	210	9.0
Cass	-1 000	6 177	-5.3	2.39	5.5	29.6	190	12.3	6	199	1	12.8	6.1	186	10.9
Cedar	-700	6 684	-1.3	2.57	6.1	23.2	198	10.9	9	169	2	9.3	10.5	107	5.6
Cerro Gordo	-1 100	19 061	2.0	2.37	8.5	29.3	623	13.0	25	484	4	10.1	6.4	436	9.2
Cherokee	-1 300	5 514	-8.1	2.48	6.0	27.8	169	11.5	7	177	0	11.9	0.0	119	7.4
Chickasaw	-1 100	5 040	-6.0	2.59	5.8	24.9	170	11.9	10	169	3	11.7	19.5	283	18.0
Clarke	-100	3 343	-0.4	2.45	6.8	26.8	112	12.7	6	93	0	10.7	0.0	77	8.8
Clay	-2 100	7 074	-4.1	2.45	6.7	27.9	222	12.6	6	189	7	10.7	29.3	175	9.2
Clayton	-900	7 218	-3.6	2.59	5.2	25.2	235	11.6	6	232	2	11.5	8.0	153	7.1
Clinton	-5 200	19 757	-2.9	2.53	9.2	25.6	676	12.8	33	501	4	9.5	5.8	532	9.5
Crawford	-800	6 397	-4.0	2.54	6.2	27.2	256	13.9	10	173	1	9.4	3.6	161	8.3
Dallas	-800	11 204	4.8	2.61	7.7	22.1	385	12.7	16	304	7	10.2	16.5	246	8.2
Davis	-400	3 093	-5.6	2.63	5.6	23.3	115	13.2	6	89	0	10.1	0.0	70	7.4
Decatur	-900	3 207	-7.3	2.38	5.6	29.8	99	11.5	5	105	0	12.1	0.0	76	8.1
Delaware	-900	6 389	2.7	2.78	6.3	21.8	290	15.6	17	153	4	8.2	14.1	162	8.1
Des Moines	-3 100	16 874	-2.7	2.48	9.9	27.0	561	12.7	26	440	6	10.0	11.1	492	10.9
Dickinson	-700	6 160	2.1	2.34	6.1	27.7	148	9.7	6	147	1	9.7	5.7	133	8.6
Dubuque	-6 400	30 799	2.6	2.67	8.5	24.4	1 192	13.1	66	782	7	8.6	5.6	924	9.9
Emmet	-1 800	4 461	-7.9	2.49	6.9	26.7	140	12.1	7	132	1	11.4	6.9	121	9.5
Fayette	-2 400	8 490	-6.6	2.50	5.9	27.4	297	13.1	8	268	1	11.8	3.8	156	6.2
Floyd	-1 200	6 721	-5.1	2.46	6.7	26.6	197	10.9	4	177	1	9.7	4.8	155	8.0
Franklin	-1 000	4 579	-8.6	2.44	5.7	27.7	136	11.5	4	157	0	13.1	0.0	101	8.0
Fremont	-500	3 217	-10.3	2.50	6.5	26.1	103	11.7	8	144	1	16.2	9.7	81	8.7
Greene	-1 100	4 195	-10.4	2.36	6.0	29.4	117	10.9	4	148	0	13.6	0.0	95	8.1
Grundy	-1 400	4 776	-8.6	2.48	4.7	24.8	142	11.2	1	128	1	10.0	8.3	104	7.5
Guthrie	-500	4 407	-3.6	2.42	6.0	26.1	117	10.6	1	165	0	15.0	0.0	76	6.6
Hamilton	-1 200	6 358	-4.0	2.49	6.8	25.0	199	11.8	8	169	2	10.0	10.1	131	7.6

1. No spouse present. 2. Per 1,000 resident population estimated as of July 1 of the year shown. 3. Under 2,500 grams. 4. Deaths of infants under 1 year old. 5. Deaths of infants under 1 year old per 1,000 live births.

STATE County	Divorces, 1984		Physicians, active non–Federal, 1989		Hospitals, 1989			Nursing homes,[4] 1986		Serious crimes known to police, 1988			Education			
						Beds				Number			Public school enrollment[7]		Attainment,[8] 1980	
	Number	Rate[1]	Number[2]	Rate[3]	Number	Number	Rate[3]	Number	Beds	Total[5]	Violent[6]	Rate[3]	1986–1987	1980	Percent 12 yrs. or more	Percent 16 yrs. or more
	44	45	46	47	48	49	50	51	52	53	54	55	56	57	58	59
INDIANA—Con.																
Ripley	140	5.6	18	71	1	106	417	4	304	312	41	1 224	5 070	5 037	56.5	7.7
Rush	121	6.4	9	49	1	52	284	2	198	258	29	1 391	3 169	4 578	62.5	7.5
St. Joseph	1 424	5.9	415	169	4	1 114	453	18	2 201	17 059	998	6 983	37 838	41 804	67.6	14.6
Scott	179	8.8	13	62	1	65	308	4	246	281	18	5 307	4 287	4 788	48.6	5.3
Shelby	214	5.4	26	64	1	73	180	4	324	79	7	NA	7 749	8 752	63.4	8.5
Spencer	79	3.9	5	25	0	0	0	2	120	72	17	NA	3 708	4 087	58.8	8.4
Starke	106	5.0	7	31	1	47	207	2	278	249	6	1 353	4 368	4 976	52.6	6.5
Steuben	125	5.0	17	59	1	61	210	3	199	974	92	3 527	4 247	5 011	71.9	9.7
Sullivan	107	5.2	7	35	1	56	280	2	215	66	5	NA	3 955	4 322	62.7	7.8
Switzerland	40	5.4	2	27	0	0	0	2	118	29	7	384	1 506	1 509	51.0	5.6
Tippecanoe	572	4.6	226	179	5	770	611	11	1 591	4 501	157	3 578	16 871	18 627	76.8	25.5
Tipton	103	6.4	9	55	1	136	829	3	244	14	2	NA	3 285	3 529	67.6	8.2
Union	41	5.9	2	29	0	0	0	1	22	34	5	NA	1 522	1 532	62.2	9.0
Vanderburgh	1 473	8.8	404	243	5	1 984	1 194	15	2 007	7 533	678	4 484	22 717	25 540	64.2	12.5
Vermillion	85	4.8	9	52	1	56	322	2	161	26	4	NA	3 311	3 720	60.5	7.8
Vigo	609	5.5	178	167	3	573	536	10	972	3 323	293	5 550	17 533	19 384	68.3	16.3
Wabash	166	4.7	28	78	1	92	256	6	640	472	22	1 319	6 825	7 626	67.0	11.8
Warren	63	7.2	2	24	1	35	422	1	108	25	3	NA	1 401	2 073	65.0	8.3
Warrick	292	6.6	37	79	1	41	87	4	345	299	48	4 046	9 224	9 322	71.3	13.6
Washington	185	8.3	10	42	1	70	297	1	138	202	22	1 136	3 145	4 833	52.0	6.0
Wayne	493	6.7	104	144	2	821	1 137	8	693	2 458	147	3 373	13 435	15 768	63.8	10.1
Wells	103	4.3	59	217	2	193	710	3	264	353	25	1 342	5 173	5 379	69.0	8.9
White	116	4.9	10	42	1	59	247	2	230	361	69	7 017	5 430	4 919	66.7	8.5
Whitley	142	5.4	12	42	1	55	194	3	236	46	3	NA	4 820	5 835	71.3	7.2
IOWA	10 509	3.6	4 218	148	135	17 363	611	499	36 563	115 533	7 279	4 077	482 051	548 925	71.5	13.9
Adair	39	4.2	2	24	1	31	369	3	180	92	1	1 083	1 222	1 816	68.6	8.8
Adams	9	1.6	4	77	1	22	423	1	64	84	0	1 556	792	1 127	70.0	9.9
Allamakee	33	2.1	8	54	2	66	443	5	293	196	1	1 307	2 809	3 218	62.5	9.4
Appanoose	55	3.7	7	49	1	60	420	3	207	435	16	3 064	2 532	2 900	62.0	9.1
Audubon	21	2.5	0	0	1	29	387	2	208	108	4	1 385	1 266	1 798	63.4	9.0
Benton	45	1.9	7	31	1	89	389	4	234	449	7	1 970	4 349	5 184	68.2	8.6
Black Hawk	564	4.2	198	161	3	709	575	15	1 297	6 743	389	5 361	19 116	24 284	73.9	15.4
Boone	95	3.7	14	55	2	502	1 969	5	606	661	22	2 593	3 937	4 690	70.6	12.1
Bremer	76	3.0	15	65	2	74	320	4	346	397	74	1 690	5 857	5 109	71.4	13.9
Buchanan	61	2.6	20	92	2	364	1 677	3	215	616	23	2 866	3 252	5 030	70.3	9.3
Buena Vista	54	2.6	15	75	1	67	333	5	407	445	27	2 182	3 222	3 607	74.4	14.6
Butler	42	2.3	4	25	0	0	0	6	314	137	3	836	2 780	3 741	63.0	7.2
Calhoun	32	2.5	13	108	1	49	408	4	278	148	1	1 223	2 530	2 724	68.0	9.6
Carroll	52	2.2	18	80	2	173	772	6	405	429	9	1 924	2 666	2 923	63.2	9.6
Cass	67	3.9	14	92	1	71	464	6	345	335	7	2 121	3 208	3 331	70.6	9.9
Cedar	39	2.1	7	39	0	0	0	5	255	246	32	1 352	3 525	4 031	70.1	10.6
Cerro Gordo	191	4.0	119	247	2	321	666	5	631	2 875	159	5 978	7 364	8 572	72.5	13.8
Cherokee	63	3.9	29	200	2	301	2 076	4	292	263	9	1 754	2 866	3 308	74.2	11.7
Chickasaw	32	2.0	6	43	1	50	355	3	158	180	4	1 233	2 485	3 390	67.1	8.5
Clarke	30	3.4	3	33	1	48	533	2	111	221	7	2 570	1 666	1 702	66.7	7.9
Clay	63	3.3	18	103	1	96	552	3	259	670	19	3 765	3 267	3 690	75.5	12.8
Clayton	43	2.0	11	55	2	58	289	5	305	288	19	1 412	3 764	4 336	62.5	8.8
Clinton	218	3.9	58	110	2	372	705	6	491	2 628	61	4 969	9 659	11 608	70.6	10.8
Crawford	66	3.4	9	49	1	92	503	3	254	527	12	2 865	3 586	3 923	64.7	8.6
Dallas	118	3.9	14	45	1	53	172	7	447	577	26	1 937	6 305	6 076	75.7	13.3
Davis	28	3.0	6	70	1	80	930	2	119	129	2	1 466	1 483	1 693	63.7	7.2
Decatur	29	3.1	8	94	1	53	624	3	203	174	11	2 000	1 556	1 705	64.4	13.8
Delaware	34	1.7	10	54	1	86	462	2	143	321	10	1 726	3 416	4 026	65.8	8.1
Des Moines	182	4.0	68	153	1	388	872	9	690	2 348	209	5 313	7 903	9 042	70.7	11.5
Dickinson	50	3.2	14	91	1	49	318	3	188	449	2	2 994	2 772	2 968	74.9	13.7
Dubuque	261	2.8	146	160	2	558	611	13	1 265	3 030	269	3 341	13 239	14 631	68.6	15.0
Emmet	44	3.4	9	78	1	58	504	4	251	299	6	2 578	2 303	2 765	69.8	10.8
Fayette	67	2.7	13	58	2	79	354	4	275	459	34	1 987	4 531	5 320	67.8	11.3
Floyd	56	2.9	12	67	1	38	211	6	425	290	46	1 585	3 266	4 022	70.4	11.5
Franklin	37	2.9	3	26	1	92	786	3	209	248	22	2 033	1 808	2 543	68.8	10.2
Fremont	26	2.8	3	34	1	40	460	2	163	238	8	2 675	1 745	1 836	69.1	10.5
Greene	22	1.9	9	86	1	127	1 210	2	132	166	1	1 523	1 940	2 477	71.4	10.8
Grundy	30	2.2	5	40	1	88	704	4	202	125	1	954	2 388	2 969	70.3	10.0
Guthrie	34	2.9	3	28	1	25	229	4	272	134	2	1 176	2 585	2 410	66.0	7.2
Hamilton	55	3.2	13	76	1	50	294	4	243	434	68	2 539	3 065	3 404	72.9	11.2

1. Per 1,000 resident population estimated as of July 1 of the year shown. 2. As of end of year. 3. Per 100,000 resident population as of July 1 of the year shown. 4. Preliminary. Covers nursing homes with 3 or more beds. 5. Data for serious crimes have not been adjusted for underreporting, this may affect comparability between geographic areas or over time. 6. Includes murder and nonnegligent manslaughter, forcible rape, robbery, and aggravated assault. 7. The 1986–1987 data are based on administrative reports obtained by the U.S. National Center for Education Statistics. The 1980 data are based on the 1980 Census of Population and Housing. 8. Persons 25 years old or older.

STATE County	Education (cont'd): Local government expenditures for education,[1] 1982: Total (Mil dol)	Education (cont'd): Local government expenditures for education,[1] 1982: Per capita (Dollars)	Social Security Program December 1988: Beneficiaries: Total	Social Security Program December 1988: Beneficiaries: Rate[2]	Social Security Program December 1988: Payments ($1,000)	Supplemental Security Income Program recipients June 1986	Money income: Per capita[3]: 1987 Income, (Dollars)	Money income: Per capita[3]: 1979: Current dollars	Money income: Per capita[3]: 1979: Constant 1987 dollars	Money income: Median household income 1979 (Dollars)	Money income: Percent below poverty level, 1979: Persons	Money income: Percent below poverty level, 1979: Families	Housing units, 1990: Total	Housing units, 1990: Percent change, 1980–1990
	60	61	62	63	64	65	66	67	68	69	70	71	72	73
INDIANA—Con.														
Ripley	11.2	453	4 800	189.7	2 226	284	9 365	5 739	8 980	14 755	10.7	8.6	9 587	4.4
Rush	6.9	363	3 260	177.2	1 605	144	9 427	6 019	9 418	15 511	11.2	9.0	7 014	-1.7
St. Joseph	94.6	395	44 045	180.4	23 397	2 032	11 697	7 322	11 457	17 570	9.2	6.7	97 956	7.4
Scott	8.5	421	3 950	189.0	1 754	456	8 539	5 410	8 465	14 562	13.0	10.6	8 078	11.0
Shelby	15.3	383	5 720	142.3	2 834	344	10 792	6 926	10 837	18 032	7.9	6.1	15 654	4.8
Spencer	7.3	365	3 255	161.1	1 513	182	9 390	6 246	9 773	16 436	10.9	7.9	7 636	9.5
Starke	9.4	438	3 735	168.2	1 787	180	8 020	5 641	8 826	14 896	12.5	10.3	9 888	7.0
Steuben	7.8	318	4 930	175.4	2 459	136	11 056	6 833	10 692	16 371	9.2	6.8	15 768	5.1
Sullivan	13.7	654	4 425	219.1	2 082	250	9 076	6 303	9 862	14 317	10.3	7.5	8 487	-3.8
Switzerland	2.5	337	1 360	183.8	564	148	7 970	5 196	8 130	12 060	13.9	12.4	3 732	16.5
Tippecanoe	41.1	332	15 185	121.1	7 973	656	10 907	6 929	10 842	16 428	11.1	6.1	48 134	11.6
Tipton	7.5	460	2 790	171.2	1 437	96	11 774	7 520	11 767	18 789	6.3	4.6	6 427	-0.2
Union	3.3	479	1 075	155.8	518	60	9 092	5 903	9 236	14 731	10.9	9.2	2 813	7.1
Vanderburgh	60.2	360	32 735	196.7	16 709	2 122	11 735	7 480	11 704	16 070	10.3	7.1	72 637	7.6
Vermillion	6.1	340	3 540	202.3	1 701	190	9 155	6 151	9 624	14 119	10.7	8.1	7 288	-2.4
Vigo	45.7	408	20 255	188.4	10 010	1 404	10 220	6 671	10 438	15 224	10.7	7.5	44 203	2.6
Wabash	14.9	422	6 535	183.6	3 300	332	10 516	6 722	10 518	16 466	7.9	6.0	13 394	-0.5
Warren	3.2	357	1 215	144.6	605	50	9 814	6 600	10 327	17 180	10.1	7.9	3 275	-3.7
Warrick	19.3	439	5 905	127.3	2 954	296	11 162	7 520	11 767	21 379	6.9	5.8	16 926	14.7
Washington	8.8	392	3 890	167.7	1 758	268	8 667	5 457	8 539	13 698	14.6	11.0	9 520	11.8
Wayne	33.5	448	14 210	196.5	7 199	962	10 114	6 512	10 189	15 658	11.2	8.6	29 586	1.0
Wells	11.2	447	3 925	148.7	2 040	118	11 051	7 194	11 256	18 271	5.3	3.9	9 928	4.5
White	16.6	691	4 940	208.4	2 479	106	9 807	6 816	10 665	16 490	7.3	5.3	11 875	6.4
Whitley	9.5	364	4 705	168.6	2 382	82	10 557	6 793	10 629	18 298	5.6	4.0	10 852	6.2
IOWA	1 394.9	480	516 529	182.3	253 392	28 763	11 198	7 136	11 166	16 799	10.1	7.5	1 143 669	1.1
Adair	3.5	379	1 950	229.4	880	162	9 905	5 946	9 304	12 527	16.9	14.5	3 714	-6.3
Adams	2.5	448	1 225	231.1	526	102	9 601	5 797	9 071	12 844	14.4	11.0	2 234	-9.8
Allamakee	8.6	578	3 250	218.1	1 392	162	8 641	5 314	8 315	13 098	14.5	11.9	6 603	0.4
Appanoose	7.0	463	3 650	255.2	1 573	310	8 333	5 483	8 579	11 352	17.3	14.8	6 402	-4.5
Audubon	4.0	478	1 905	250.7	839	72	10 019	6 167	9 650	13 722	13.0	9.0	3 247	-7.9
Benton	14.5	618	4 290	189.0	2 071	150	10 799	6 870	10 749	16 742	11.5	9.0	9 125	0.4
Black Hawk	57.5	416	22 220	178.5	11 481	1 570	10 872	7 735	12 103	19 494	9.3	6.6	49 688	-1.2
Boone	10.8	414	4 955	195.1	2 452	368	11 120	7 089	11 092	16 471	9.1	6.4	10 371	-0.5
Bremer	17.5	701	4 500	193.1	2 182	150	10 770	6 984	10 928	18 102	7.6	6.4	8 847	0.4
Buchanan	9.5	413	4 010	183.9	1 913	206	9 755	6 268	9 808	16 066	11.8	9.3	8 272	0.6
Buena Vista	8.9	428	4 370	217.4	2 156	198	11 092	7 373	11 537	16 222	8.4	5.8	8 140	-0.7
Butler	8.2	467	3 735	229.1	1 723	194	9 710	6 356	9 945	15 698	9.7	7.7	6 483	-4.4
Calhoun	9.0	676	3 175	262.4	1 533	136	10 103	6 946	10 868	15 036	10.4	8.0	5 362	-7.3
Carroll	7.6	333	4 680	208.9	2 203	230	10 637	6 674	10 443	16 109	8.8	6.8	8 356	-0.3
Cass	9.0	532	3 855	248.7	1 818	200	10 678	6 654	10 412	14 136	11.7	8.2	6 788	-3.4
Cedar	11.8	638	3 175	175.4	1 532	88	10 745	7 016	10 978	17 292	10.6	8.1	7 146	-2.3
Cerro Gordo	21.3	441	9 835	204.5	4 948	556	11 104	7 371	11 533	16 443	8.7	5.6	20 954	0.1
Cherokee	8.4	526	3 105	211.2	1 520	150	10 734	7 196	11 260	15 609	10.7	8.8	5 973	-7.8
Chickasaw	8.9	584	2 885	201.7	1 317	112	9 736	6 087	9 524	15 541	11.4	9.4	5 486	-3.8
Clarke	4.2	482	1 810	205.7	781	112	9 258	5 733	8 970	12 158	16.4	13.0	3 599	-3.1
Clay	9.5	491	3 450	196.0	1 679	190	11 615	7 470	11 688	16 222	9.7	7.7	7 659	-4.8
Clayton	10.9	521	4 400	217.8	1 861	252	9 500	5 875	9 193	13 356	13.9	10.7	8 344	-2.5
Clinton	28.0	495	10 100	190.9	5 130	424	10 579	7 175	11 227	18 516	7.7	5.7	21 296	-0.3
Crawford	9.8	512	3 550	192.9	1 594	200	9 870	6 435	10 069	15 633	12.3	10.1	6 920	-2.5
Dallas	15.6	532	5 380	177.0	2 631	216	11 682	7 503	11 740	18 661	7.2	5.5	11 812	2.2
Davis	3.7	402	1 820	209.2	804	142	9 239	5 843	9 143	13 015	22.0	16.9	3 365	-6.0
Decatur	4.2	444	2 040	237.2	852	170	7 928	5 007	7 834	11 074	19.5	14.7	3 692	-7.1
Delaware	9.8	523	2 955	158.9	1 340	168	9 798	5 961	9 327	15 991	13.4	10.5	7 408	13.2
Des Moines	21.8	478	8 320	187.8	4 268	478	11 012	7 498	11 732	17 252	8.4	6.5	18 248	-1.7
Dickinson	7.2	461	3 665	239.5	1 799	126	11 392	7 341	11 486	16 032	8.5	5.9	9 723	-4.6
Dubuque	41.4	447	15 370	169.1	7 699	858	10 294	7 063	11 051	19 396	8.3	6.1	32 053	1.7
Emmet	7.1	535	2 655	228.9	1 292	132	10 523	6 823	10 676	16 338	12.7	8.6	4 914	-6.7
Fayette	14.6	583	4 915	217.5	2 169	288	9 716	6 297	9 853	14 815	10.8	8.2	9 262	-4.7
Floyd	10.2	529	4 005	221.3	1 963	270	10 200	6 636	10 383	16 031	9.2	7.4	7 233	-4.7
Franklin	6.3	495	2 545	215.7	1 235	136	10 656	6 770	10 593	15 365	12.1	9.1	5 018	-7.4
Fremont	5.7	612	2 085	236.9	984	122	10 538	6 169	9 653	13 201	16.6	13.6	3 607	-10.2
Greene	6.3	532	2 675	250.0	1 330	100	10 897	6 823	10 676	14 464	13.1	10.9	4 707	-6.2
Grundy	9.1	646	2 745	216.1	1 367	64	11 817	7 592	11 879	18 006	6.3	5.0	5 158	-5.9
Guthrie	7.3	628	2 925	265.9	1 341	136	10 187	6 190	9 685	13 352	14.9	12.1	5 179	-2.0
Hamilton	9.6	543	3 510	207.7	1 728	148	11 797	7 108	11 122	16 304	9.4	7.4	6 879	-3.7

1. Elementary and secondary. 2. Per 1,000 resident population estimated as of July 1 of the year shown. 3. Based on the resident population estimated as of July 1, 1988 for 1987 data and enumerated as of April 1, 1980 for 1979 data.

STATE County	Housing units, 1990 (cont'd): Occupied units: Total	Owner occupied: Percent	Owner occupied: Median value (Dollars)	Median rent (Dollars)	Civilian labor force, 1990: Total	Percent change, 1989–1990	Unemployment: Total	Unemployment: Rate[1]	Private nonfarm establishments, 1988: Number	Net change, 1987–1988	Employment[2]: Total	Percent change, 1987–1988	Manufacturing	Retail trade
	74	75	76	77	78	79	80	81	82	83	84	85	86	87
INDIANA—Con.														
Ripley	8 778	75.9	49 000	215	13 421	1.7	772	5.8	561	5	8 398	8.9	4 022	1 403
Rush	6 504	71.9	41 200	199	8 098	-0.5	530	6.5	360	12	3 174	-1.4	944	746
St. Joseph	92 365	72.0	50 800	325	130 699	-1.0	7 104	5.4	6 153	39	102 432	4.6	23 957	22 889
Scott	7 593	77.2	38 000	221	10 675	-1.4	763	7.1	348	14	4 154	17.3	1 666	1 418
Shelby	14 761	73.5	51 300	271	21 645	-2.2	1 517	7.0	787	-2	10 927	2.3	4 804	2 141
Spencer	6 962	81.3	47 000	191	10 244	-8.0	656	6.4	367	-11	4 449	4.6	1 728	588
Starke	8 141	77.9	40 900	204	9 443	-1.8	727	7.7	328	5	3 193	2.0	991	1 148
Steuben	10 194	79.0	59 800	271	19 140	-2.8	855	4.5	718	6	11 476	8.6	5 055	2 277
Sullivan	7 364	80.0	32 300	164	7 779	0.6	553	7.1	360	15	2 997	2.0	346	829
Switzerland	2 839	79.1	37 700	174	3 117	-1.9	240	7.7	93	5	1 004	2.1	548	111
Tippecanoe	45 618	57.1	66 000	335	68 642	-1.1	1 967	2.9	2 610	29	44 580	1.8	12 034	12 303
Tipton	6 026	76.9	50 900	238	7 858	-0.8	445	5.7	300	1	2 337	-1.6	401	788
Union	2 576	72.3	41 800	188	3 285	-2.8	230	7.0	131	4	731	-0.1	0	258
Vanderburgh	66 780	64.8	52 100	265	87 130	-1.0	4 734	5.4	4 960	-15	86 861	-0.7	21 100	19 731
Vermillion	6 638	80.2	32 300	186	8 718	-1.7	482	5.5	264	4	2 679	-2.3	672	821
Vigo	39 804	69.3	40 000	236	50 133	-0.1	2 262	4.5	2 396	29	39 579	3.4	9 623	11 093
Wabash	12 630	74.3	43 400	233	16 834	-1.7	964	5.7	788	1	12 543	0.8	6 327	2 130
Warren	3 015	78.6	39 700	176	3 714	-1.6	176	4.7	109	8	704	14.1	85	93
Warrick	15 817	81.7	64 800	266	22 578	-2.1	1 037	4.6	813	-6	10 023	0.4	0	1 920
Washington	8 664	80.0	40 000	200	12 691	-0.7	809	6.4	358	8	4 299	5.9	2 446	860
Wayne	27 587	67.6	42 400	231	33 929	-3.2	2 611	7.7	1 617	13	25 025	0.3	7 973	5 806
Wells	9 438	78.9	53 000	236	14 333	-0.9	689	4.8	565	17	7 988	4.0	3 311	1 409
White	8 926	76.0	46 900	217	11 778	-7.3	697	5.9	574	14	5 997	1.8	2 474	1 313
Whitley	10 010	82.5	57 300	247	15 179	-0.7	886	5.8	536	7	6 526	8.2	2 448	1 575
IOWA	1 064 325	70.0	45 900	261	1 496 000	-1.1	63 000	4.2	X	X	920 042	5.2	219 610	215 693
Adair	3 419	73.5	29 400	164	4 538	-0.3	139	3.1	226	1	1 862	8.4	0	474
Adams	2 005	72.5	28 700	174	2 991	-3.5	114	3.8	122	4	1 016	-22.4	0	179
Allamakee	5 268	75.8	39 700	172	7 327	-4.6	442	6.0	396	5	3 371	-0.6	1 131	742
Appanoose	5 609	74.5	25 600	174	6 407	-1.9	456	7.1	318	13	2 908	7.6	724	742
Audubon	2 936	76.1	25 300	149	3 594	2.5	141	3.9	197	2	1 087	-3.2	74	289
Benton	8 518	74.8	38 600	189	10 646	-1.3	627	5.9	530	-9	3 323	8.6	677	824
Black Hawk	46 932	67.3	44 100	255	61 871	0.7	3 082	5.0	2 950	-6	42 766	6.6	11 641	10 880
Boone	9 827	71.9	40 300	230	12 592	-1.6	460	3.7	521	-10	4 680	2.4	901	1 586
Bremer	8 394	75.0	45 900	203	10 765	0.9	375	3.5	567	3	6 767	15.0	1 536	1 261
Buchanan	7 506	75.0	36 300	188	9 818	-1.4	542	5.5	446	12	3 266	7.9	705	919
Buena Vista	7 515	67.8	41 400	218	10 634	-6.3	211	2.0	624	1	6 394	0.0	1 872	1 550
Butler	6 036	77.6	31 600	162	7 283	-2.2	377	5.2	372	10	1 903	-1.7	256	511
Calhoun	4 684	71.7	26 700	165	5 492	-0.3	146	2.7	331	-8	2 042	0.8	260	441
Carroll	7 964	73.4	42 000	207	11 514	-1.7	491	4.3	718	-9	7 000	6.6	1 013	1 543
Cass	6 177	71.8	34 700	186	8 201	-3.8	453	5.5	488	-1	4 782	5.0	1 330	1 282
Cedar	6 684	73.1	45 700	220	9 545	-1.3	290	3.0	438	1	2 940	8.4	640	800
Cerro Gordo	19 061	68.8	45 400	253	26 031	-1.3	1 320	5.1	1 405	-29	17 725	5.2	3 101	5 490
Cherokee	5 514	70.8	32 500	167	6 882	-1.8	206	3.0	380	-9	3 430	-7.0	824	1 069
Chickasaw	5 040	78.4	37 200	183	7 120	-2.8	435	6.1	374	17	3 286	7.2	1 327	603
Clarke	3 343	72.4	36 400	219	4 604	0.3	241	5.2	210	2	2 188	-0.4	1 105	479
Clay	7 074	65.4	41 000	208	9 010	-2.8	232	2.6	595	-10	5 728	10.0	1 160	1 681
Clayton	7 218	74.9	37 200	173	9 896	-3.0	547	5.5	509	5	4 002	4.5	1 404	721
Clinton	19 757	71.2	39 100	235	23 354	-1.9	1 530	6.6	1 190	-3	15 864	5.7	4 332	3 659
Crawford	6 397	71.5	33 900	198	8 418	-6.3	482	5.7	477	21	4 951	0.9	0	938
Dallas	11 204	74.4	50 100	242	16 597	-2.4	600	3.6	592	1	5 156	5.5	1 421	1 128
Davis	3 093	77.6	28 900	173	3 784	-1.5	160	4.2	179	4	1 147	8.3	264	329
Decatur	3 207	70.8	22 700	163	3 909	-0.6	213	5.4	175	12	1 897	-10.6	0	305
Delaware	6 389	75.7	44 600	186	8 885	0.1	421	4.7	398	-2	2 797	13.5	797	708
Des Moines	16 874	72.8	41 600	242	22 452	-2.8	1 196	5.3	1 181	-8	18 214	5.1	6 571	4 011
Dickinson	6 160	75.8	49 400	210	10 083	3.1	294	2.9	561	10	4 340	1.4	1 217	1 328
Dubuque	30 799	71.2	53 600	252	44 513	-0.9	2 467	5.5	2 255	38	40 225	9.8	12 694	7 990
Emmet	4 461	72.0	27 800	178	5 016	-0.7	273	5.4	280	-8	2 603	-2.7	372	685
Fayette	8 490	74.4	30 100	169	10 382	-1.6	481	4.6	626	18	4 870	11.6	919	1 197
Floyd	6 721	73.2	36 200	182	8 539	-2.2	494	5.8	440	-1	4 504	6.9	1 419	1 028
Franklin	4 579	72.0	30 500	186	5 218	-1.3	273	5.2	317	-11	2 339	2.7	545	481
Fremont	3 217	72.3	32 000	168	4 102	-4.6	147	3.6	177	-2	1 183	-4.5	0	369
Greene	4 195	71.7	27 200	171	4 834	-7.6	278	5.8	290	-4	2 137	3.0	417	627
Grundy	4 776	74.4	38 100	179	6 776	0.1	188	2.8	313	-10	2 076	7.2	441	545
Guthrie	4 407	75.5	29 200	174	5 307	-1.6	257	4.8	234	-23	1 650	2.5	355	367
Hamilton	6 358	71.0	39 900	214	9 776	-6.0	431	4.4	445	4	5 694	6.4	2 538	1 049

1. Percent of total civilian labor force. 2. For week including March 12. Excludes government employees, self-employed persons, farm workers, domestic service workers, railroad employees subject to the Railroad Retirement Act, and employees on oceanborne vessels or in foreign countries.

STATE County	Private nonfarm establishments, 1988 (cont'd)				Personal income, 1989								Earnings, 1989		
	Employment[1] (cont'd)		Annual payroll								Per capita[3]			Percent by selected industries	
	Finance, insurance, and real estate	Services	Total (Mil dol)	Average per employee (Dollars)	Total (Mil dol)	Percent change, 1988–1989	Wages and salaries[2] (Mil dol)	Proprietor's income (Mil dol)	Dividends, interest, & rent (Mil dol)	Transfer payments (Mil dol)	Dollars	Rank	Total (Mil dol)	Farm	Goods-related[4] Total
	88	89	90	91	92	93	94	95	96	97	98	99	100	101	102
INDIANA—Con.															
Ripley	344	1 401	180	21 469	373	9.7	233	39	65	56	14 692	1 135	273	4.1	56.7
Rush	242	479	47	14 773	263	8.8	86	31	49	42	14 369	1 259	117	13.0	29.2
St. Joseph	5 350	33 620	1 954	19 077	4 067	6.2	2 641	282	682	555	16 545	516	2 922	0.6	32.1
Scott	161	536	56	13 540	243	5.2	89	20	32	52	11 478	2 507	109	3.6	38.8
Shelby	257	2 060	181	16 528	629	8.4	275	68	92	84	15 509	800	343	5.4	47.2
Spencer	177	585	83	18 588	274	10.2	141	29	44	40	13 557	1 658	170	7.6	37.3
Starke	161	575	40	12 590	265	7.0	72	30	39	49	11 699	2 442	102	11.2	25.1
Steuben	259	2 199	209	18 244	468	7.1	284	41	68	55	16 136	608	325	2.0	50.8
Sullivan	181	699	52	17 404	279	9.1	90	32	52	57	13 909	1 468	123	12.7	18.2
Switzerland	70	149	12	11 911	78	8.1	23	7	12	18	10 506	2 789	30	10.4	NA
Tippecanoe	3 316	11 625	838	18 787	1 936	9.2	1 465	155	340	239	15 366	848	1 620	1.3	34.3
Tipton	193	505	39	16 798	284	8.8	73	34	46	37	17 248	405	107	18.1	19.7
Union	48	144	10	13 063	94	7.5	19	13	18	14	13 723	1 569	31	19.4	9.8
Vanderburgh	4 663	24 668	1 717	19 763	2 799	6.1	2 100	237	591	447	16 840	463	2 337	0.3	34.6
Vermillion	121	362	52	19 284	231	7.4	135	26	35	46	13 219	1 806	162	7.4	54.2
Vigo	1 757	10 815	719	18 174	1 515	8.3	1 027	113	278	291	14 177	1 355	1 140	0.9	31.2
Wabash	433	2 447	213	17 020	519	8.9	292	49	96	80	14 457	1 231	341	5.5	50.3
Warren	85	269	9	13 055	116	8.1	35	20	20	16	13 946	1 453	55	26.7	31.2
Warrick	344	1 658	253	25 232	764	6.3	385	70	107	80	16 283	574	454	1.5	60.5
Washington	194	443	68	15 911	285	9.3	110	31	47	48	12 076	2 296	140	6.0	NA
Wayne	1 159	6 728	448	17 916	1 056	7.0	691	89	183	178	14 620	1 157	780	1.5	41.4
Wells	224	1 705	133	16 705	402	8.9	189	45	75	48	14 810	1 072	233	5.4	39.9
White	327	753	107	17 857	353	13.1	177	42	71	57	14 807	1 075	218	8.2	42.2
Whitley	282	1 325	116	17 791	435	9.7	245	34	70	55	15 311	872	279	2.8	57.6
IOWA	73 080	246 528	16 108	X	44 537	8.6	24 816	6 323	8 521	6 723	15 664	X	31 139	7.8	26.6
Adair	81	362	27	14 332	123	9.9	38	28	32	20	14 586	1 173	66	27.5	NA
Adams	54	653	13	13 196	74	13.1	26	18	16	13	14 138	1 377	43	24.0	NA
Allamakee	152	663	40	11 821	192	9.5	74	47	44	33	12 869	1 970	121	15.0	22.6
Appanoose	113	694	42	14 398	187	9.1	72	32	37	47	13 064	1 882	104	8.0	NA
Audubon	75	325	13	11 845	104	9.6	27	28	29	19	13 911	1 464	56	31.4	7.3
Benton	232	671	47	14 009	342	11.1	83	60	69	49	14 961	1 005	143	20.7	12.9
Black Hawk	2 396	12 260	867	20 282	1 891	8.4	1 355	146	320	331	15 335	861	1 501	1.9	40.7
Boone	258	1 222	68	14 620	377	8.3	155	43	75	67	14 761	1 104	198	10.8	13.2
Bremer	1 553	1 575	112	16 575	342	8.7	144	47	76	48	14 782	1 086	191	6.6	28.6
Buchanan	207	539	45	13 727	282	8.9	91	42	61	48	12 981	1 912	133	15.0	18.8
Buena Vista	487	1 565	93	14 551	320	10.2	147	65	70	49	15 896	677	212	17.5	25.4
Butler	126	504	23	12 331	228	9.6	47	52	54	39	14 122	1 383	99	33.1	10.7
Calhoun	135	759	26	12 682	188	13.2	52	64	45	33	15 667	750	115	35.9	8.7
Carroll	291	2 073	99	14 178	359	8.7	148	91	87	50	16 025	640	239	17.1	14.7
Cass	199	962	68	14 251	252	10.9	105	50	64	43	16 425	538	156	16.7	23.4
Cedar	178	654	38	12 804	280	6.2	76	45	67	36	15 477	810	120	18.9	18.4
Cerro Gordo	1 124	5 388	271	15 270	759	8.3	437	92	158	122	15 748	723	528	4.8	26.5
Cherokee	241	746	51	14 953	215	10.1	93	50	49	36	14 781	1 087	143	22.1	22.1
Chickasaw	119	624	50	15 067	201	6.9	80	45	45	31	14 211	1 334	126	11.7	32.8
Clarke	68	322	33	15 279	121	12.9	60	21	24	21	13 547	1 662	81	13.1	39.7
Clay	283	1 524	83	14 535	279	10.1	139	61	59	41	16 057	634	200	17.1	19.0
Clayton	208	790	56	14 020	263	8.5	93	56	64	46	13 118	1 855	149	20.1	24.5
Clinton	753	5 207	269	16 963	768	5.9	415	85	146	135	14 536	1 195	500	4.5	36.6
Crawford	224	1 031	75	15 191	239	7.5	110	54	54	41	13 078	1 874	165	20.2	28.6
Dallas	355	1 073	80	15 525	467	4.9	140	46	83	71	15 189	912	186	7.7	24.5
Davis	63	243	15	13 426	104	8.1	31	19	22	22	11 996	2 329	50	11.5	16.2
Decatur	55	994	18	9 679	93	11.4	38	15	19	24	10 882	2 690	53	12.6	17.4
Delaware	176	462	44	15 898	242	7.6	88	53	58	34	13 037	1 893	141	23.3	NA
Des Moines	764	4 203	331	18 185	682	7.7	473	71	123	114	15 316	870	544	2.3	43.4
Dickinson	188	855	63	14 468	256	11.3	100	47	68	39	16 696	483	147	13.6	24.7
Dubuque	1 430	13 086	725	18 036	1 299	7.4	939	134	273	198	14 207	1 341	1 073	3.1	40.7
Emmet	153	839	34	13 084	168	10.1	66	42	38	32	14 590	1 171	108	23.9	18.5
Fayette	270	1 377	68	13 919	293	9.6	119	53	67	57	13 149	1 840	172	14.7	15.7
Floyd	208	1 208	68	15 137	255	8.9	106	49	61	46	14 187	1 350	155	18.7	29.4
Franklin	109	594	35	14 907	179	10.0	62	56	44	27	15 306	873	118	35.5	18.4
Fremont	81	388	14	11 802	144	10.4	51	39	29	24	16 511	525	90	30.3	25.1
Greene	190	492	28	12 911	170	11.3	50	46	46	29	16 236	584	97	33.4	14.9
Grundy	141	431	29	13 826	205	7.6	54	46	49	29	16 423	539	100	31.2	14.6
Guthrie	146	438	19	11 467	164	7.2	38	35	37	31	14 953	1 008	73	28.6	9.9
Hamilton	187	908	87	15 354	292	7.4	131	55	61	42	17 178	412	187	14.6	NA

1. For week including March 12. Excludes government employees, self-employed persons, farm workers, domestic service workers, railroad employees subject to the Railroad Retirement Act, and employees on oceanborne vessels or in foreign countries. 2. Includes other labor income. 3. Based on the resident population estimated as of July 1 of the year shown. 4. Covers mining, construction, and manufacturing.

STATE County	Earnings, 1989 (cont'd)						Agriculture, 1987									
	Percent by selected industries (cont'd)						Farms			Farm operators, percent		Land in farms				
	Goods-related[1]	Service-related & other[2]						Percent with						Acres		
	Manu-facturing	Total	Retail trade	Finance, insur-ance, & real estate	Services	Govern-ment	Number	Less than 50 acres	500 acres and over	Whose principal occu-pation is farming	Residing on farm operated	Acreage (1,000)	Percent change, 1982–1987	Average size of farm	Total irrigated (1,000)	Total cropland (1,000)
	103	104	105	106	107	108	109	110	111	112	113	114	115	116	117	118
INDIANA—Con.																
Ripley	52.4	31.1	8.1	1.6	11.2	8.0	1 071	27.4	5.8	45.0	76.3	174	0.1	162	D	130
Rush	23.4	39.0	9.2	3.0	12.8	18.8	834	19.2	18.7	70.0	72.8	240	4.5	287	D	213
St. Joseph	25.1	58.0	10.2	5.3	28.4	9.2	897	37.9	10.6	50.2	80.8	174	0.2	194	11	156
Scott	31.9	38.3	13.9	2.7	14.6	19.3	390	30.3	7.9	35.4	71.3	64	-12.4	163	D	46
Shelby	38.5	36.1	9.2	2.3	14.6	11.3	876	32.8	15.4	58.9	73.2	218	-2.3	249	1	201
Spencer	22.3	45.9	6.1	1.7	14.5	9.3	808	26.9	10.4	45.7	73.1	179	3.3	221	0	141
Starke	19.5	43.5	14.4	3.1	16.7	20.2	449	28.5	19.8	51.2	71.3	141	-1.0	314	9	120
Steuben	45.6	40.2	10.0	1.8	12.9	7.0	573	23.4	12.4	52.4	81.7	132	-7.4	231	2	107
Sullivan	5.7	51.5	10.2	2.9	11.2	17.5	599	25.0	18.9	54.8	71.6	189	2.2	315	2	162
Switzerland	29.5	NA	6.1	3.1	12.4	20.8	660	25.3	2.0	41.8	71.8	86	-5.2	131	0	41
Tippecanoe	28.3	39.9	9.2	5.3	18.9	24.5	881	31.9	18.5	52.3	74.1	247	-5.1	280	1	222
Tipton	14.1	42.2	11.8	3.6	15.7	20.0	551	26.1	21.1	63.3	70.8	161	-2.0	292	0	150
Union	3.5	49.5	14.6	5.2	15.1	21.2	300	16.7	18.0	65.3	77.0	88	0.3	293	0	73
Vanderburgh	24.8	56.6	11.2	4.3	27.0	8.5	378	37.8	11.9	50.8	71.7	86	5.0	227	D	79
Vermillion	41.0	27.5	7.5	1.5	6.7	10.9	393	24.7	21.6	59.0	67.9	128	9.3	325	D	108
Vigo	24.5	51.0	13.5	3.4	22.1	16.9	623	37.1	14.0	48.6	73.4	148	0.1	237	0	125
Wabash	46.8	33.3	8.4	2.4	13.1	10.9	865	24.5	11.9	57.5	77.1	203	-2.6	234	2	176
Warren	28.2	30.0	6.2	1.5	11.6	12.2	486	17.9	30.7	64.4	70.0	205	-2.7	421	0	180
Warrick	42.6	30.1	6.0	1.9	13.1	7.9	432	31.7	14.1	46.3	71.1	100	-8.3	231	0	84
Washington	40.8	NA	9.3	2.7	11.0	15.8	1 034	24.8	8.8	45.8	76.1	195	-6.2	189	0	133
Wayne	36.2	45.3	10.8	3.7	20.1	11.8	888	26.8	12.3	53.2	78.3	197	-1.9	222	0	162
Wells	34.6	43.4	8.6	1.8	21.5	11.3	875	24.9	14.4	55.3	76.5	209	2.6	239	0	190
White	37.4	38.5	8.6	3.2	12.1	11.1	786	21.9	28.5	68.4	71.5	293	0.0	373	2	267
Whitley	52.7	28.3	7.3	2.2	11.8	11.3	880	31.6	9.2	43.3	79.5	165	-7.2	188	D	142
IOWA	21.7	50.6	9.2	5.9	21.4	14.9	105 180	18.0	18.6	71.6	74.8	31 638	-3.0	301	92	27 291
Adair	12.3	NA	9.1	3.5	NA	12.1	970	13.4	23.6	73.5	74.5	353	-0.5	364	0	298
Adams	15.8	NA	8.5	3.1	20.8	12.3	688	13.5	26.0	70.6	73.8	244	-4.1	354	0	191
Allamakee	18.8	49.0	10.3	3.7	15.1	13.4	1 062	10.8	14.1	80.1	80.0	321	-8.7	302	0	196
Appanoose	21.1	NA	9.2	2.4	22.8	14.7	891	15.9	16.8	59.5	74.2	245	3.5	275	D	177
Audubon	1.5	47.4	9.2	3.6	16.5	13.9	851	16.1	17.9	73.9	73.8	268	-5.4	315	D	236
Benton	6.4	49.2	8.6	4.2	17.2	17.2	1 434	17.6	18.0	70.2	75.4	419	-5.1	293	D	377
Black Hawk	36.8	42.2	9.2	3.5	20.2	15.3	1 269	27.6	14.6	58.5	75.1	306	-1.1	241	0	279
Boone	9.8	51.8	13.5	2.3	16.3	24.2	1 029	19.0	22.2	67.3	75.2	337	1.1	327	0	303
Bremer	24.3	52.8	9.0	11.3	23.4	12.1	1 140	25.3	8.4	63.1	78.1	235	-6.1	206	0	211
Buchanan	13.7	42.6	10.2	3.6	13.5	23.6	1 332	19.1	14.9	72.7	75.6	337	0.5	253	0	307
Buena Vista	22.4	45.1	9.3	4.5	19.0	11.9	1 097	13.3	21.4	78.8	75.2	359	-0.6	327	D	331
Butler	5.9	42.9	6.9	3.1	16.0	13.2	1 294	21.9	13.8	72.8	79.0	328	-2.3	254	D	296
Calhoun	5.5	43.5	5.7	4.0	19.4	12.0	992	13.3	24.1	80.0	70.7	342	-2.6	345	1	323
Carroll	10.3	59.9	10.1	4.2	20.8	8.3	1 319	16.5	15.1	80.1	72.8	367	0.9	278	D	337
Cass	17.1	44.3	9.8	3.7	17.9	15.6	942	16.0	24.2	74.3	71.5	333	-3.7	354	D	291
Cedar	12.5	48.0	9.2	3.9	13.0	14.7	1 170	17.2	17.7	77.5	77.1	345	-1.1	295	D	303
Cerro Gordo	22.0	56.7	11.0	4.0	29.1	12.0	929	21.4	24.8	70.0	71.2	318	-2.9	342	0	297
Cherokee	17.4	38.1	11.2	2.6	14.7	17.7	1 091	16.7	18.4	77.3	76.0	339	-0.6	310	0	293
Chickasaw	28.5	45.4	6.8	2.8	24.9	10.1	1 054	16.9	13.3	71.3	77.2	276	-4.6	262	1	246
Clarke	37.8	34.0	8.3	2.4	14.4	13.2	697	14.6	21.5	68.9	77.2	229	-3.1	329	D	165
Clay	13.6	50.6	10.8	3.8	20.0	13.2	877	16.2	26.0	78.0	75.7	316	-9.2	360	0	288
Clayton	16.6	38.9	8.0	3.8	13.8	16.5	1 705	13.8	13.0	78.2	79.2	451	0.8	264	D	330
Clinton	29.6	49.0	9.0	3.3	22.5	9.9	1 437	20.0	14.9	69.7	74.3	377	-5.3	262	0	337
Crawford	25.7	36.9	7.6	2.8	15.3	14.4	1 339	20.1	19.1	74.8	75.4	407	-4.6	304	D	359
Dallas	17.3	52.0	9.1	5.9	21.4	15.7	1 081	25.3	20.4	59.7	71.0	328	-5.1	304	0	289
Davis	13.0	52.2	11.4	5.1	21.1	20.1	921	15.5	16.8	61.3	81.5	267	-4.3	290	D	186
Decatur	12.8	50.6	7.5	2.4	21.3	19.4	715	13.8	24.8	59.2	71.3	279	-7.3	390	D	178
Delaware	19.7	NA	7.5	3.4	12.8	14.9	1 452	13.9	10.2	83.5	81.8	354	0.6	244	D	307
Des Moines	38.4	44.7	9.2	3.0	19.6	9.7	753	19.8	15.8	59.1	71.6	211	-6.2	280	D	173
Dickinson	19.1	50.3	13.5	4.8	22.9	11.3	593	17.4	25.8	79.1	73.9	211	-7.3	356	D	193
Dubuque	36.0	48.5	9.1	3.5	25.2	7.7	1 689	18.5	5.7	75.5	81.2	334	-1.4	198	0	267
Emmet	14.0	42.4	8.8	2.8	18.9	15.2	609	14.1	28.1	83.7	77.8	228	-7.1	374	0	212
Fayette	12.1	56.6	9.9	3.7	20.5	13.1	1 510	15.1	13.4	76.4	80.3	421	-3.7	279	0	363
Floyd	25.5	38.9	8.0	3.2	19.4	13.0	985	20.1	19.9	69.2	73.2	296	-1.7	301	1	272
Franklin	14.0	35.6	6.0	2.5	15.2	10.5	1 012	15.2	22.6	80.2	77.1	346	-5.6	342	0	319
Fremont	22.2	35.3	5.8	2.4	12.0	9.3	719	16.3	32.5	77.7	65.2	309	0.7	429	1	269
Greene	10.8	37.3	7.1	4.1	14.3	14.4	948	17.5	27.6	76.3	67.1	353	-1.6	373	1	320
Grundy	11.0	41.7	5.5	3.2	15.8	12.5	1 037	17.9	18.0	73.5	71.6	320	-0.3	308	0	298
Guthrie	0.6	43.2	7.5	5.6	14.5	18.3	960	16.5	22.7	68.3	72.6	317	-3.0	330	D	260
Hamilton	29.3	NA	7.0	3.2	13.3	11.1	1 026	15.5	22.2	74.1	70.6	347	-3.0	339	D	326

1. Covers mining, construction, and manufacturing. 2. Covers private sector earnings in agricultural services, forestry, and fisheries; transportation and public utilities; wholesale trade; retail trade; finance, insurance, and real estate; and services.

STATE County	Agriculture, 1987 (cont'd)								Manufactures, 1987						
	Value of land and buildings		Value of products sold				Percent of farms with sales of		Establishments		All employees			Production workers	
					Percent from										
	Average per farm ($1,000)	Average per acre (Dollars)	Total (Mil dol)	Average per farm (Dollars)	Crops	Livestock and poultry[1]	$10,000 or more	$100,000 or more	Total	Percent with 20 or more employees	Number (1,000)	Percent change, 1982–1987	Annual payroll (Mil dol)	Number (1,000)	Work hours (Mil)
	119	120	121	122	123	124	125	126	127	128	129	130	131	132	133
INDIANA—Con.															
Ripley	154	984	31	28 646	55.4	44.6	47.2	6.3	35	42.9	3.7	8.8	91.1	2.3	4.9
Rush	351	1 238	67	79 786	51.3	48.7	82.0	25.8	27	37.0	1.0	-9.1	18.7	0.8	1.5
St. Joseph	257	1 312	47	52 787	60.1	39.9	51.8	13.4	489	38.7	23.2	-2.1	599.5	14.8	28.9
Scott	158	1 016	9	22 393	71.1	28.9	35.6	5.9	29	34.5	1.5	25.0	29.7	1.1	2.6
Shelby	306	1 192	50	56 871	70.4	29.6	63.5	16.4	75	44.0	4.4	18.9	93.6	3.2	6.8
Spencer	213	1 032	35	42 806	44.9	55.1	50.5	12.0	24	33.3	1.3	8.3	22.9	1.0	2.1
Starke	274	883	25	56 375	76.6	23.4	57.7	16.5	20	45.0	0.9	50.0	13.9	0.7	1.3
Steuben	183	783	23	40 159	41.1	58.9	54.1	11.2	83	59.0	4.7	88.0	100.2	3.6	7.2
Sullivan	297	891	32	53 665	81.3	18.7	62.4	15.4	27	25.9	0.5	0.0	6.8	0.4	0.7
Switzerland	107	833	10	15 447	43.1	56.9	27.0	2.6	8	37.5	0.5	0.0	6.2	0.5	0.9
Tippecanoe	394	1 351	60	68 452	65.1	34.9	62.0	21.0	106	44.3	11.7	13.6	328.9	8.1	16.1
Tipton	483	1 602	51	92 853	69.7	30.3	73.5	26.3	10	40.0	0.4	0.0	10.1	0.3	0.6
Union	472	1 502	23	75 027	45.4	54.6	77.0	26.0	5	20.0	D	D	D	D	D
Vanderburgh	397	1 794	18	47 601	82.8	17.2	57.1	11.4	272	38.2	21.1	-6.2	595.3	13.0	25.7
Vermillion	338	1 057	23	58 875	74.6	25.4	54.7	17.3	15	46.7	0.7	0.0	15.9	0.4	0.7
Vigo	240	1 097	24	38 080	80.0	20.0	48.2	10.8	130	44.6	9.7	-12.6	264.9	6.1	13.0
Wabash	255	1 129	100	115 312	26.1	73.9	68.4	24.3	79	55.7	5.8	16.0	121.9	4.4	8.8
Warren	486	1 173	37	75 877	89.8	10.2	70.2	25.5	6	33.3	0.1	0.0	1.1	0.1	0.1
Warrick	275	1 165	16	37 349	68.4	31.6	46.1	12.3	44	31.8	D	D	D	D	D
Washington	155	832	39	37 583	27.2	72.8	40.9	9.6	32	34.4	2.3	21.1	41.1	2.0	4.0
Wayne	218	973	57	64 660	52.3	47.7	60.4	16.4	130	45.4	8.8	-10.2	201.3	6.7	13.6
Wells	326	1 309	55	62 539	59.7	40.3	69.0	19.2	43	51.2	3.1	19.2	59.5	2.4	4.9
White	462	1 223	90	113 988	54.7	45.3	78.9	30.4	39	46.2	2.4	14.3	39.3	1.9	3.5
Whitley	206	1 100	38	42 687	44.2	55.8	53.3	11.4	50	52.0	2.3	0.0	45.1	1.8	3.6
IOWA	284	947	8 927	84 872	41.0	59.0	78.6	25.5	3 569	35.3	206.1	-3.4	4 971.1	140.1	277.5
Adair	244	652	71	73 277	43.6	56.4	79.6	21.5	11	9.1	D	D	D	D	D
Adams	172	505	40	57 983	41.1	58.9	75.1	16.4	4	50.0	D	D	D	D	D
Allamakee	183	653	77	72 916	13.2	86.8	81.5	26.1	21	19.0	1.1	37.5	16.1	0.9	1.9
Appanoose	135	466	26	28 628	36.2	63.8	57.4	5.6	11	36.4	0.7	0.0	14.3	0.6	1.2
Audubon	294	880	80	94 216	36.6	63.4	83.0	26.0	8	25.0	0.1	0.0	1.1	0.1	0.1
Benton	323	1 125	141	98 279	42.3	57.7	82.3	29.2	23	34.8	0.6	100.0	11.8	0.5	1.0
Black Hawk	257	1 106	100	78 750	50.0	50.0	75.6	24.2	154	33.1	10.6	-41.8	338.1	7.2	13.7
Boone	386	1 134	91	88 676	59.2	40.8	77.5	25.5	27	44.4	0.9	0.0	16.6	0.6	1.2
Bremer	250	1 148	75	65 815	41.5	58.5	74.5	18.9	34	35.3	1.2	9.1	31.7	0.9	2.0
Buchanan	279	1 071	109	81 851	42.5	57.5	82.2	25.2	26	38.5	0.6	0.0	10.3	0.5	1.0
Buena Vista	354	1 102	132	120 577	38.1	61.9	88.7	33.0	26	30.8	D	D	D	D	D
Butler	237	925	105	81 305	41.1	58.9	82.3	25.3	17	17.6	0.2	100.0	3.4	0.2	0.3
Calhoun	408	1 213	98	98 971	58.8	41.2	87.2	33.6	15	20.0	0.2	0.0	3.8	0.2	0.4
Carroll	306	1 088	171	129 358	28.9	71.1	89.5	37.2	32	25.0	0.9	12.5	19.6	0.8	1.4
Cass	264	753	83	88 135	43.5	56.5	82.1	24.9	25	36.0	1.2	140.0	22.6	0.7	1.2
Cedar	338	1 209	105	89 497	40.2	59.8	82.7	29.4	23	34.8	0.6	20.0	10.2	0.5	0.9
Cerro Gordo	336	1 040	83	89 346	60.3	39.7	81.1	29.7	65	40.0	3.2	18.5	64.6	2.3	4.2
Cherokee	337	1 028	119	109 306	34.5	65.5	86.1	31.4	20	30.0	0.7	-30.0	16.2	0.6	1.2
Chickasaw	229	850	85	80 799	38.2	61.8	78.2	22.3	19	36.8	1.3	8.3	25.6	1.1	2.0
Clarke	169	489	27	39 139	33.1	66.9	64.1	9.3	17	47.1	D	D	D	D	D
Clay	369	1 013	94	106 844	48.1	51.9	86.1	32.4	31	29.0	1.0	-16.7	18.7	0.8	1.5
Clayton	238	905	145	84 937	16.8	83.2	81.1	29.4	35	37.1	1.2	71.4	16.2	0.9	1.9
Clinton	261	980	116	80 527	37.1	62.9	79.7	24.9	47	48.9	4.0	-32.2	101.2	3.1	6.6
Crawford	232	782	111	82 968	38.7	61.3	82.4	26.1	19	26.3	D	D	D	D	D
Dallas	362	1 151	78	72 613	61.9	38.1	68.0	19.9	27	44.4	D	D	D	D	D
Davis	128	453	33	36 261	30.8	69.2	59.0	9.3	8	37.5	0.2	0.0	3.6	0.2	0.3
Decatur	184	459	36	49 749	31.6	68.4	62.4	11.2	6	50.0	0.4	33.3	5.8	0.3	0.7
Delaware	261	1 100	168	115 392	17.2	82.8	88.0	43.3	24	37.5	0.8	33.3	17.9	0.6	1.2
Des Moines	293	1 075	44	58 139	58.4	41.6	68.8	16.7	63	47.6	6.6	4.8	170.5	5.0	9.8
Dickinson	344	975	64	108 329	44.8	55.2	83.8	29.2	25	28.0	1.2	20.0	22.8	0.7	1.2
Dubuque	216	1 135	153	90 636	8.8	91.2	81.9	31.1	143	40.6	12.2	2.5	318.4	8.3	16.2
Emmet	391	1 036	57	93 472	63.2	36.8	85.7	31.7	11	36.4	0.3	0.0	4.5	0.3	0.5
Fayette	253	906	135	89 647	35.3	64.7	86.1	30.2	30	30.0	0.8	0.0	15.4	0.6	1.2
Floyd	270	947	79	80 151	57.5	42.5	78.9	24.8	17	29.4	1.3	0.0	26.3	0.9	1.7
Franklin	356	1 080	111	109 623	50.5	49.5	88.4	33.0	18	33.3	D	D	D	D	D
Fremont	358	815	68	94 452	55.0	45.0	80.4	25.5	5	20.0	D	D	D	D	D
Greene	389	1 037	90	94 916	65.5	34.5	82.2	30.7	17	29.4	0.5	25.0	9.2	0.4	0.8
Grundy	387	1 227	121	116 584	47.3	52.7	87.6	32.9	18	22.2	D	D	D	D	D
Guthrie	238	769	65	67 487	47.5	52.5	76.6	18.6	9	33.3	0.4	300.0	4.1	0.4	0.5
Hamilton	420	1 251	134	130 473	43.1	56.9	85.9	31.4	33	45.5	2.3	43.7	41.7	1.7	3.2

1. Includes livestock and poultry products.

STATE County	Manufactures, 1987 (cont'd): Production workers (cont'd): Wages: Total (Mil dol)	Manufactures, 1987 (cont'd): Production workers (cont'd): Wages: Average per worker (Dollars)	Manufactures, 1987 (cont'd): Value added by manufacture (Mil dol)	Manufactures, 1987 (cont'd): Value of shipments (Mil dol)	Manufactures, 1987 (cont'd): New capital expenditures (Mil dol)	Value of construction authorized by building permits, 1990: Total[1] ($1,000)	Nonresidential: Total ($1,000)	Nonresidential: Percent: Office	Nonresidential: Percent: Industrial	Nonresidential: Percent: Stores	Residential: New construction ($1,000)	Residential: Number of housing units	Residential: Alterations and additions ($1,000)
	134	135	136	137	138	139	140	141	142	143	144	145	146
INDIANA—Con.													
Ripley	44.2	19 217	258.6	379.6	D	16 369	2 446	30.0	0.0	10.4	8 219	114	396
Rush	13.5	16 875	65.8	120.7	2.1	4 719	1 109	10.8	23.1	22.3	2 575	40	263
St. Joseph	313.2	21 162	1 189.9	2 887.6	79.6	654 537	505 130	1.3	89.3	1.6	111 052	1 490	8 680
Scott	21.8	19 818	97.1	223.9	5.6	26 384	22 490	1.9	95.1	0.9	3 208	66	293
Shelby	60.3	18 844	232.5	442.1	D	35 008	10 333	1.9	69.9	20.5	15 060	233	1 038
Spencer	15.4	15 400	49.7	102.2	2.1	7 761	3 968	0.0	51.7	0.3	3 407	57	275
Starke	9.1	13 000	32.8	56.9	1.5	5 064	1 102	16.3	9.2	7.4	2 244	59	437
Steuben	69.9	19 417	275.5	528.1	23.6	35 389	16 019	15.9	18.4	58.9	14 033	199	2 482
Sullivan	5.3	13 250	15.9	27.4	D	2 781	974	0.0	0.0	65.8	1 573	53	88
Switzerland	5.1	10 200	32.3	52.6	D	600	0	NA	NA	NA	488	36	0
Tippecanoe	200.8	24 790	941.4	1 965.0	100.6	108 814	36 327	11.9	50.9	28.5	45 701	752	6 209
Tipton	6.9	23 000	27.3	52.5	D	5 866	1 613	3.4	0.0	0.0	2 510	36	316
Union	D	D	D	D	D	1 227	309	27.5	14.9	20.2	684	14	157
Vanderburgh	285.5	21 962	2 006.4	3 234.1	D	69 409	21 604	29.1	4.1	3.8	29 059	600	4 907
Vermillion	6.8	17 000	44.3	76.4	D	33 186	31 077	18.1	36.4	1.5	1 889	31	55
Vigo	154.8	25 377	942.6	1 810.5	D	50 250	19 234	5.4	47.4	35.2	21 016	354	1 982
Wabash	77.9	17 705	302.3	671.5	12.2	15 526	7 964	0.0	92.1	5.0	4 234	63	190
Warren	0.8	8 000	4.7	6.4	D	1 421	152	0.0	0.0	0.0	997	21	163
Warrick	D	D	D	D	D	29 294	936	35.4	8.3	29.6	26 545	322	747
Washington	31.6	15 800	97.6	178.2	3.9	4 487	2 648	0.0	58.5	14.0	1 638	50	115
Wayne	145.7	21 746	381.5	822.8	22.0	20 209	2 951	36.8	44.7	2.0	9 915	135	2 648
Wells	38.3	15 958	171.8	279.5	7.0	16 650	5 146	7.1	61.4	16.6	5 978	97	585
White	29.1	15 316	88.7	202.2	6.6	7 786	994	0.0	30.2	45.0	4 591	62	668
Whitley	32.7	18 167	91.8	288.2	6.2	32 126	7 228	14.5	14.2	37.1	21 061	298	2 120
IOWA	3 043.4	21 723	14 469.0	35 408.6	834.2	1 238 803	354 194	18.9	24.3	25.3	530 765	7 637	66 853
Adair	D	D	D	D	D	1 154	271	0.0	27.7	0.0	598	8	141
Adams	D	D	D	D	D	972	859	0.0	100.0	0.0	100	1	0
Allamakee	13.7	15 222	48.2	135.1	1.8	5 254	3 448	0.0	58.6	2.0	1 275	23	87
Appanoose	9.5	15 833	53.4	84.9	D	1 374	1 194	0.0	0.0	96.5	70	2	14
Audubon	0.6	6 000	2.6	7.4	0.1	857	625	0.0	0.0	22.4	0	0	70
Benton	8.3	16 600	28.0	63.5	D	5 125	2 499	16.4	10.7	2.4	1 694	25	157
Black Hawk	207.3	28 792	745.1	1 339.8	D	71 569	23 326	10.4	45.2	22.0	15 756	180	5 922
Boone	9.4	15 667	28.4	55.8	1.6	4 528	1 111	0.0	58.6	21.2	1 985	27	411
Bremer	23.3	25 889	112.4	219.9	D	13 144	4 639	3.4	11.8	3.6	4 837	56	910
Buchanan	7.3	14 600	45.1	111.4	1.9	2 409	242	0.0	0.0	31.0	1 040	18	257
Buena Vista	D	D	D	D	D	7 175	1 773	3.4	0.0	20.5	2 523	36	487
Butler	2.1	10 500	6.8	14.1	D	1 111	131	19.1	45.2	0.0	596	9	156
Calhoun	2.4	12 000	7.6	12.6	0.3	3 237	1 150	16.0	6.8	0.0	1 157	18	286
Carroll	15.0	18 750	64.5	163.6	2.1	11 927	4 649	6.6	56.5	14.1	4 875	73	348
Cass	11.1	15 857	41.6	92.8	D	3 250	1 930	31.7	0.0	0.0	908	17	173
Cedar	7.1	14 200	27.2	73.6	D	1 754	332	39.2	17.2	2.4	848	12	237
Cerro Gordo	40.8	17 739	232.7	514.9	9.3	13 990	1 251	24.5	0.0	0.4	6 578	85	1 379
Cherokee	12.5	20 833	18.3	121.6	D	5 272	260	0.0	0.0	0.0	583	7	44
Chickasaw	19.6	17 818	92.3	279.5	2.5	1 671	66	0.0	0.0	0.0	251	4	341
Clarke	D	D	D	D	D	4 029	2 592	0.0	38.6	30.9	1 260	23	102
Clay	13.6	17 000	58.0	102.8	6.3	7 409	993	39.3	22.1	12.1	3 100	47	1 083
Clayton	11.8	13 111	49.9	152.4	2.3	2 870	90	0.0	0.0	38.8	1 763	28	204
Clinton	72.8	23 484	513.0	1 048.6	29.7	18 469	4 360	0.0	13.1	76.8	6 135	62	587
Crawford	D	D	D	D	D	1 898	588	0.0	19.1	58.4	216	3	75
Dallas	D	D	D	D	D	24 123	7 219	0.2	62.4	27.9	14 897	133	517
Davis	2.6	13 000	11.5	25.9	0.4	257	111	0.0	0.0	0.0	85	2	24
Decatur	4.5	15 000	7.5	15.8	D	446	100	49.9	0.0	23.9	214	4	16
Delaware	12.9	21 500	52.5	149.5	4.1	4 831	1 159	0.0	0.0	87.8	2 028	42	89
Des Moines	124.5	24 900	615.5	1 106.6	26.7	17 075	8 310	23.1	1.5	45.2	2 667	31	1 539
Dickinson	12.2	17 429	58.9	114.4	D	13 274	5 440	4.7	43.9	9.0	6 078	85	1 042
Dubuque	199.9	24 084	775.1	1 893.4	38.2	66 614	17 518	32.0	23.0	18.9	26 184	346	3 639
Emmet	3.0	10 000	12.8	43.8	0.5	1 592	1 158	0.0	54.6	0.0	83	2	185
Fayette	11.3	18 833	49.9	97.2	2.1	8 574	925	0.0	82.7	3.0	1 087	14	845
Floyd	14.0	15 556	50.5	118.8	D	6 020	842	0.0	2.4	17.9	1 150	32	882
Franklin	D	D	D	D	D	746	340	0.0	29.5	8.0	300	24	32
Fremont	D	D	D	D	D	212	18	0.0	0.0	0.0	84	2	74
Greene	6.8	17 000	20.5	49.6	D	596	77	0.0	32.5	0.0	379	6	26
Grundy	D	D	D	D	D	1 337	379	0.0	15.8	0.0	586	10	219
Guthrie	2.9	7 250	7.3	19.0	0.1	3 098	442	36.9	20.3	0.0	1 863	20	124
Hamilton	27.4	16 118	32.5	252.7	14.6	5 426	4 267	4.4	0.0	94.2	849	30	120

1. Includes nonresidential additions and alterations, residential nonhousekeeping buildings, and residential garages and carports not shown separately.

STATE County	Wholesale trade, 1987: Establishments	Wholesale trade, 1987: Sales (Mil dol)	Wholesale trade, 1987: Paid employees[1]	Wholesale trade, 1987: Annual payroll (Mil dol)	Retail trade, all establishments, 1987: Number	Retail trade, all establishments, 1987: Sales: Total (Mil dol)	Retail trade, all establishments, 1987: Sales: Percent change, 1982–1987	Retail trade, all establishments, 1987: Sales: Per capita[2] (Dollars)	Retail trade, establishments with payroll, 1987: Number	Retail trade, establishments with payroll, 1987: Sales: Total (Mil dol)	Sales: Per capita[2] (Dollars): General merchandise stores	Sales: Per capita[2] (Dollars): Food stores	Sales: Per capita[2] (Dollars): Apparel & accessory stores	Sales: Per capita[2] (Dollars): Eating and drinking places
	147	148	149	150	151	152	153	154	155	156	157	158	159	160
INDIANA—Con.														
Ripley	36	34.0	225	2.7	309	112.2	55.2	4 452	170	107.2	360	1 400	70	345
Rush	42	106.7	291	4.4	171	64.8	8.5	3 503	90	61.7	266	758	16	245
St. Joseph	501	1 597.5	6 098	136.0	2 383	1 715.1	49.0	7 055	1 571	1 686.9	1 030	1 242	289	689
Scott	25	35.5	189	3.2	245	90.9	40.7	4 331	116	84.9	214	1 056	55	462
Shelby	59	131.1	495	9.9	350	170.4	30.5	4 240	201	165.2	623	1 017	115	396
Spencer	32	149.2	326	6.8	209	62.1	24.7	3 089	107	57.4	43	741	D	132
Starke	26	48.2	136	2.0	221	89.9	18.3	4 087	119	84.4	338	867	D	216
Steuben	45	63.7	289	4.8	391	161.8	42.4	5 862	219	152.0	D	1 014	379	703
Sullivan	28	103.6	243	3.7	214	91.7	78.8	4 515	99	87.0	D	616	38	192
Switzerland	3	0.9	12	0.1	54	11.2	6.7	1 520	27	9.8	D	633	D	99
Tippecanoe	143	261.9	1 433	27.1	1 068	864.4	46.0	6 943	743	851.3	1 133	1 128	277	727
Tipton	27	120.7	207	3.5	142	95.7	86.5	5 869	82	93.5	104	D	94	377
Union	10	21.0	64	1.0	69	21.6	35.0	3 137	35	20.4	D	D	D	167
Vanderburgh	463	1 867.5	5 944	132.8	1 736	1 356.4	33.4	8 146	1 234	1 337.0	1 285	1 375	474	895
Vermillion	18	28.1	102	1.3	188	76.1	37.9	4 347	96	72.4	D	899	D	228
Vigo	183	480.9	1 938	35.5	1 049	1 177.2	70.7	10 879	678	1 161.7	D	D	D	693
Wabash	69	132.1	478	8.5	379	173.3	41.9	4 868	220	166.8	563	1 041	90	413
Warren	16	27.6	79	1.3	59	8.0	-3.6	964	24	6.2	0	D	0	70
Warrick	43	120.7	327	5.5	366	139.5	32.1	3 045	183	132.9	D	861	34	266
Washington	18	17.5	84	1.4	209	88.9	45.7	3 882	103	82.9	D	786	40	261
Wayne	94	445.5	1 184	24.1	793	490.6	24.8	6 785	462	478.6	1 080	1 210	169	631
Wells	41	525.5	647	10.4	248	103.9	30.4	3 982	147	96.9	D	1 129	82	405
White	51	73.4	318	5.6	293	111.4	26.2	4 719	157	106.5	D	1 156	60	519
Whitley	39	51.3	299	5.4	271	113.9	33.2	4 141	140	108.4	D	1 407	37	391
IOWA	7 015	24 483.5	65 941	1 281.0	32 338	15 581.5	23.2	5 519	20 311	15 081.6	685	1 165	221	485
Adair	23	57.7	179	3.2	118	30.7	-11.8	3 566	70	28.3	D	1 010	58	459
Adams	13	9.4	49	0.5	58	14.9	21.1	2 764	36	14.0	D	D	D	146
Allamakee	39	141.9	395	4.3	219	64.1	15.5	4 301	124	59.3	195	1 195	126	279
Appanoose	25	32.3	125	1.7	197	65.4	14.5	4 573	105	61.3	436	1 473	275	236
Audubon	27	D	D	D	106	30.8	11.2	4 000	54	28.4	D	745	65	155
Benton	66	174.1	449	7.4	251	76.0	13.8	3 364	158	73.2	D	725	93	251
Black Hawk	223	534.5	2 313	46.2	1 287	774.0	16.0	6 197	852	759.2	995	1 104	211	564
Boone	29	D	D	D	255	107.7	23.5	4 240	165	104.8	206	1 115	173	319
Bremer	55	146.4	341	5.8	259	91.3	22.6	3 900	160	88.7	386	880	146	324
Buchanan	53	125.1	373	6.9	250	85.9	26.0	3 979	123	80.8	D	727	27	222
Buena Vista	58	174.5	560	10.3	277	110.9	11.3	5 490	187	107.3	568	1 214	296	473
Butler	48	117.3	291	5.1	215	38.4	10.0	2 356	117	33.8	D	382	37	134
Calhoun	44	121.8	288	5.0	152	40.1	0.0	3 318	97	38.7	D	693	78	155
Carroll	82	327.0	926	21.2	315	134.0	9.1	6 009	201	128.9	603	1 427	285	342
Cass	53	130.4	527	7.1	257	97.9	10.2	6 275	163	92.9	621	1 068	281	383
Cedar	54	120.5	357	5.7	199	73.8	15.5	4 076	120	70.4	D	1 057	67	199
Cerro Gordo	124	518.9	1 181	23.1	631	376.2	29.5	7 837	432	369.5	1 473	1 512	357	679
Cherokee	35	D	D	D	195	77.0	4.6	5 171	122	73.7	502	1 148	153	319
Chickasaw	39	115.7	315	4.6	190	45.6	11.8	3 169	107	41.8	109	913	39	268
Clarke	10	35.0	40	0.7	118	45.8	20.8	5 267	69	44.1	D	D	33	341
Clay	68	176.8	529	10.9	267	115.3	7.1	6 550	170	111.5	982	1 305	649	369
Clayton	63	190.2	441	6.5	263	68.2	10.7	3 377	145	63.5	D	574	56	196
Clinton	94	193.6	623	9.7	574	301.4	10.2	5 708	379	292.3	608	1 276	219	461
Crawford	47	618.5	1 043	18.4	241	69.5	9.8	3 756	145	64.0	D	719	203	382
Dallas	52	133.9	422	7.3	281	114.7	10.3	3 849	159	109.0	D	1 007	94	157
Davis	24	73.6	164	2.5	93	25.4	0.8	2 885	45	23.3	D	D	24	126
Decatur	19	71.1	128	1.7	106	22.8	-16.5	2 622	60	21.5	D	760	D	161
Delaware	46	108.7	300	5.7	207	61.5	3.9	3 289	119	57.3	300	695	110	305
Des Moines	103	347.9	1 049	19.4	522	276.0	22.5	6 259	344	269.2	1 227	1 303	292	649
Dickinson	30	83.1	283	4.5	289	102.4	39.1	6 781	179	98.2	321	1 339	282	703
Dubuque	191	506.2	2 025	34.5	982	572.9	31.8	6 323	650	556.2	1 204	1 187	231	601
Emmet	23	50.8	191	3.4	144	57.3	5.3	4 938	91	54.4	D	1 201	162	354
Fayette	67	209.5	568	9.5	292	103.9	12.9	4 557	182	99.8	379	1 159	191	237
Floyd	50	125.9	358	6.0	221	75.2	0.4	4 130	128	72.1	529	1 022	142	333
Franklin	38	91.7	234	4.1	131	35.2	-13.7	2 931	77	33.1	D	553	53	205
Fremont	24	85.6	230	3.4	115	24.3	-20.3	2 736	55	22.3	D	1 532	D	D
Greene	25	42.8	163	2.7	139	48.3	19.0	4 430	79	45.8	D	951	112	183
Grundy	38	100.2	257	5.1	148	35.6	-9.0	2 779	83	33.7	0	785	44	255
Guthrie	25	66.6	185	2.4	139	27.4	27.4	2 489	75	24.3	68	427	39	192
Hamilton	49	307.8	845	15.0	202	77.2	22.5	4 568	124	74.1	D	1 091	349	295

1. For pay period including March 12. 2. Based on the estimated population as of July 1 of the year shown.

STATE County	Retail trade, establishments with payroll, 1987 (cont'd)		Taxable service industries–establishments with payroll, 1987							Bank deposits,[2] June 1989		Savings capital,[3] September 1989	
				Receipts (Mil dol)									
					Selected kinds of business								
	Paid employees[1]	Annual payroll (Mil dol)	Number	Total	Hotels, motels and other lodging places	Health services	Legal services	Paid employees	Annual payroll (Mil dol)	Total (Mil dol)	Percent change, 1988–1989	Total (Mil dol)	Percent change, 1988–1989
	161	162	163	164	165	166	167	168	169	170	171	172	173
INDIANA—Con.													
Ripley	1 292	10.8	114	19.0	D	10.2	1.5	677	6.4	318	6.1	20.0	32.6
Rush	728	6.7	72	16.1	D	6.6	1.3	413	4.1	144	2.9	45.6	-2.0
St. Joseph	22 445	203.8	1 687	705.5	23.5	211.1	32.0	17 168	273.1	1 900	5.0	483.0	-3.8
Scott	1 088	9.1	60	10.7	D	3.9	0.9	379	3.3	98	4.2	56.7	0.9
Shelby	2 234	18.0	161	35.7	D	15.5	3.7	1 166	12.7	304	5.5	51.9	7.5
Spencer	599	5.3	59	16.2	D	4.4	0.9	473	5.5	132	8.1	9.2	11.5
Starke	1 126	9.6	63	9.9	D	5.6	0.9	299	3.5	133	2.0	33.4	8.5
Steuben	2 032	18.2	161	36.1	4.4	8.6	0.9	1 671	14.1	214	2.5	38.9	10.8
Sullivan	765	6.4	63	14.1	D	7.9	0.7	451	5.5	179	6.2	33.4	-5.9
Switzerland	134	1.0	15	2.5	D	0.6	D	204	0.9	46	5.0	0.0	NA
Tippecanoe	11 746	95.9	654	277.9	17.0	94.7	13.2	6 811	97.4	998	17.0	223.4	9.3
Tipton	755	7.7	68	11.9	D	6.9	0.5	339	4.3	140	-6.8	68.7	-3.4
Union	274	2.5	23	2.8	D	1.6	D	118	0.9	96	6.4	5.1	6.0
Vanderburgh	18 162	169.3	1 295	552.5	D	173.2	27.5	13 209	214.0	1 649	4.6	657.7	3.6
Vermillion	823	7.1	48	9.5	D	6.0	0.3	320	3.2	111	5.1	20.2	-0.8
Vigo	10 848	101.9	596	231.2	D	116.7	10.6	5 653	79.0	1 008	3.5	187.2	-4.0
Wabash	2 054	18.9	158	30.2	D	18.2	2.1	1 001	11.9	254	5.2	55.9	3.9
Warren	94	0.7	15	3.1	0.0	D	0.4	141	0.8	39	-2.2	5.0	2.9
Warrick	1 887	15.0	191	37.9	D	16.7	1.4	1 103	13.8	252	12.1	71.8	0.9
Washington	823	7.0	62	10.5	D	5.4	1.0	331	3.1	172	7.4	48.3	1.2
Wayne	5 986	55.1	382	122.3	6.8	44.9	4.5	3 547	46.8	484	3.0	272.6	6.1
Wells	1 371	10.7	106	29.2	0.2	18.3	1.6	717	13.3	211	0.1	35.6	6.1
White	1 308	12.8	125	24.6	0.7	7.3	1.0	562	7.0	246	1.2	46.8	0.2
Whitley	1 508	12.2	107	37.9	D	9.0	1.9	913	16.6	250	5.0	35.4	4.9
IOWA	203 517	1 705.2	16 387	5 121.0	262.0	1 568.0	382.1	131 041	1 828.7	25 926	1.2	7 392.1	-2.4
Adair	465	3.0	40	5.3	0.6	D	0.9	183	1.7	91	-0.5	14.3	-3.0
Adams	209	1.6	26	3.6	0.2	2.2	D	161	1.3	46	-2.9	11.3	-3.8
Allamakee	773	5.7	80	11.7	D	5.1	0.8	308	3.9	195	7.0	5.8	-13.0
Appanoose	721	6.1	69	11.6	D	5.8	0.6	366	3.9	118	3.7	31.8	-4.4
Audubon	303	2.3	34	4.0	D	1.8	0.5	159	1.3	80	4.8	17.3	0.1
Benton	885	6.9	98	13.5	D	4.9	1.5	424	4.2	220	-4.8	26.3	-4.0
Black Hawk	10 257	87.8	772	244.0	D	92.7	16.8	6 604	98.7	820	5.0	389.9	-8.5
Boone	1 305	11.0	116	17.4	D	5.3	2.6	545	5.9	167	-0.9	98.6	-1.0
Bremer	1 249	9.5	103	19.4	D	5.7	1.9	598	5.6	246	0.8	35.4	0.4
Buchanan	851	7.7	69	12.0	0.0	5.7	0.8	368	3.6	183	0.7	29.3	-5.9
Buena Vista	1 530	12.0	138	24.6	D	10.5	2.5	810	9.0	257	-2.6	76.2	-5.5
Butler	467	3.1	66	11.1	D	4.8	1.3	472	3.9	140	-2.5	15.4	9.7
Calhoun	428	3.2	59	12.7	D	6.9	1.1	361	4.1	137	-0.6	36.2	-3.2
Carroll	1 525	13.1	144	23.5	D	10.0	2.5	658	5.7	238	1.4	101.2	-3.8
Cass	1 181	9.4	91	20.2	D	8.9	1.2	650	6.9	180	-2.0	42.3	1.4
Cedar	843	6.2	80	12.5	D	4.1	0.8	421	3.2	216	-0.4	11.0	13.0
Cerro Gordo	5 307	43.3	331	107.2	5.9	40.2	6.6	2 527	36.9	376	-1.0	208.5	-6.0
Cherokee	912	7.9	80	13.1	D	6.3	1.2	485	4.4	174	0.4	62.1	29.2
Chickasaw	551	4.1	69	11.9	0.4	4.2	1.4	344	3.5	198	6.0	15.3	3.6
Clarke	491	4.8	47	10.6	D	2.3	0.7	251	2.4	85	7.4	55.8	0.3
Clay	1 534	13.9	130	36.5	2.2	14.0	2.7	997	12.1	187	-1.5	98.9	-12.4
Clayton	752	5.7	96	13.2	0.9	6.7	0.7	435	4.1	190	5.8	11.5	-12.7
Clinton	3 797	31.9	278	115.7	D	26.9	D	2 742	34.7	407	1.5	142.7	-8.7
Crawford	985	6.6	101	24.4	D	5.9	1.7	625	6.8	179	4.2	50.3	-11.3
Dallas	1 109	10.5	139	20.2	D	8.1	2.3	638	6.3	226	-1.8	42.7	-8.8
Davis	264	2.1	40	6.9	D	3.6	0.8	243	2.2	52	-3.6	22.6	-2.4
Decatur	284	2.2	30	6.7	D	4.7	0.3	243	2.2	45	1.7	7.5	-9.7
Delaware	712	6.1	76	9.6	D	3.3	1.7	250	3.0	160	1.4	24.7	2.0
Des Moines	3 888	33.1	268	80.5	4.7	26.0	4.8	1 822	28.0	364	3.7	158.2	-8.3
Dickinson	1 329	10.9	135	29.7	8.1	8.3	1.0	845	8.5	114	2.5	41.0	-14.8
Dubuque	7 436	67.0	481	217.0	11.0	97.4	8.2	5 152	91.1	770	-1.0	178.4	3.8
Emmet	734	5.7	71	14.9	D	7.0	2.2	405	5.0	105	-5.6	41.2	-5.4
Fayette	1 173	10.0	126	20.3	D	8.1	1.1	654	7.4	229	4.2	44.1	-4.8
Floyd	1 087	8.3	106	21.1	1.0	10.6	1.6	682	7.7	203	2.0	28.5	-3.1
Franklin	480	3.4	63	8.6	D	3.4	1.8	290	2.9	106	-1.6	37.5	-4.4
Fremont	339	2.7	39	7.0	D	3.3	1.0	305	2.6	106	0.8	3.3	NA
Greene	526	4.1	63	9.2	D	3.8	1.1	307	2.8	181	-3.2	19.0	-9.5
Grundy	540	3.6	65	10.5	D	3.7	1.2	319	3.7	177	1.0	12.0	-6.2
Guthrie	361	2.6	47	7.7	0.2	4.4	0.7	346	2.5	116	0.0	30.1	1.0
Hamilton	1 055	7.7	99	18.2	0.6	8.6	1.3	673	6.4	188	0.8	104.9	1.7

1. For the period including March 12 of the year shown. 2. Includes deposits for all insured and reporting noninsured commercial and mutual savings banks. 3. Includes savings capital for all FSLIC insured savings institutions.

STATE County	Federal funds and grants, 1989							Local government finances, 1981–1982								
	Expenditures		Per capita[1] (Dollars)					General revenue							Direct general expenditure	
									Intergovernmental		Taxes					
												Per capita[2]				
	Total (Mil dol)	Percent change, 1988–1989	Total	Direct payments for individuals	Procurement contract awards	Salaries and wages	Grant awards	Total (Mil dol)	Total (Mil dol)	Percent from state	Total (Mil dol)	Total (Dollars)	Property (Dollars)	Total (Mil dol)	Percent change, 1977–1982
	174	175	176	177	178	179	180	181	182	183	184	185	186	187	188
INDIANA–Con.															
Ripley	63.9	2.4	2 517	1 645	339	117	254	18.3	9.8	92.9	6.0	242	219	15.7	58.0
Rush	44.5	-6.5	2 430	1 631	17	122	198	17.7	6.5	92.7	5.4	284	256	15.4	30.3
St. Joseph	867.5	5.5	3 529	1 712	1 278	202	305	202.2	94.8	89.5	76.8	321	320	193.9	42.3
Scott	50.1	7.5	2 376	1 733	13	117	416	21.1	11.6	71.9	3.8	187	187	17.0	85.2
Shelby	82.6	-5.5	2 033	1 449	33	202	156	35.3	14.0	96.0	10.7	268	267	30.6	39.2
Spencer	42.2	5.5	2 090	1 452	76	121	270	12.4	6.7	90.5	4.2	210	208	12.5	52.1
Starke	50.4	1.7	2 219	1 574	11	101	214	18.4	8.3	92.0	5.5	257	237	17.8	69.2
Steuben	54.7	2.4	1 885	1 476	15	89	131	16.0	6.8	94.9	7.2	292	243	13.2	45.7
Sullivan	58.0	3.5	2 902	2 128	63	134	285	21.3	7.7	92.5	7.8	372	371	23.1	152.8
Switzerland	17.5	8.2	2 367	1 729	17	133	351	5.5	3.2	96.3	2.0	271	271	4.3	36.5
Tippecanoe	314.4	10.1	2 495	1 332	108	195	780	99.9	45.0	88.1	40.7	328	327	95.2	91.8
Tipton	38.2	-5.8	2 327	1 759	59	106	132	27.0	9.7	61.4	6.1	374	314	23.0	166.9
Union	15.4	-2.8	2 230	1 436	13	102	186	5.4	2.9	95.9	1.8	270	232	5.3	44.9
Vanderburgh	482.7	10.5	2 904	2 000	216	213	450	158.0	77.0	82.4	53.6	320	319	159.0	64.1
Vermillion	57.2	1.6	3 289	1 995	700	119	210	14.5	6.0	94.6	3.8	209	208	14.0	68.8
Vigo	338.9	11.3	3 170	2 197	120	428	385	85.2	42.3	86.3	32.9	294	293	88.2	60.6
Wabash	87.5	3.8	2 438	1 619	309	98	181	33.7	13.5	94.4	10.0	283	236	32.7	48.5
Warren	22.2	-15.4	2 669	1 394	12	106	129	7.4	3.6	83.4	2.9	315	248	6.1	53.9
Warrick	74.1	10.1	1 580	1 215	29	84	189	35.5	13.0	94.1	16.8	383	382	32.6	99.9
Washington	49.5	5.6	2 099	1 475	10	104	307	20.1	8.9	95.6	5.7	255	237	18.5	97.1
Wayne	197.5	15.5	2 736	1 819	177	107	514	88.7	55.7	51.1	24.0	320	277	83.1	117.0
Wells	48.1	4.3	1 767	1 301	18	101	106	22.8	9.0	96.3	7.4	295	269	21.5	35.8
White	70.2	8.6	2 936	1 925	17	125	376	25.6	9.3	95.0	10.3	428	384	27.3	90.8
Whitley	64.5	-6.8	2 270	1 481	412	101	83	23.0	9.1	96.2	6.1	236	235	19.6	32.2
IOWA	9 871.1	2.1	X	1 843	225	243	458	3 477.4	1 358.4	86.2	1 297.0	446	438	3 209.6	49.0
Adair	32.7	-12.3	3 891	1 909	18	149	346	9.8	3.5	93.1	3.9	415	411	8.3	3.3
Adams	22.5	4.6	4 330	1 995	30	269	462	6.4	3.0	87.7	2.6	464	459	5.7	18.3
Allamakee	52.3	28.4	3 510	1 739	674	130	198	19.7	8.0	89.3	6.3	424	420	17.9	70.6
Appanoose	52.6	10.7	3 680	2 406	172	212	440	15.4	8.7	77.5	4.8	314	311	14.1	66.1
Audubon	30.1	-9.1	4 014	2 064	23	212	237	9.3	4.0	93.2	3.7	443	438	8.8	18.3
Benton	70.3	5.3	3 071	1 669	15	110	152	29.3	14.1	75.5	10.6	453	447	28.7	89.1
Black Hawk	355.6	-5.5	2 884	1 883	89	184	567	151.9	61.3	83.4	57.1	413	405	147.0	60.1
Boone	81.9	5.8	3 210	2 023	176	218	175	28.9	8.9	94.6	10.4	400	395	25.8	42.6
Bremer	74.7	-2.9	3 234	1 673	710	100	170	29.3	12.9	97.5	10.5	422	418	28.6	58.9
Buchanan	67.5	1.9	3 111	1 636	16	121	342	23.0	9.2	92.0	7.9	344	340	21.1	57.4
Buena Vista	64.4	-5.2	3 203	2 015	132	197	159	24.1	7.0	90.9	9.3	445	442	21.9	43.3
Butler	52.7	1.9	3 256	1 948	17	127	201	15.7	7.0	95.9	7.1	403	398	14.2	36.2
Calhoun	45.0	-13.5	3 754	2 266	22	164	182	16.1	5.7	94.4	8.5	638	630	16.3	67.2
Carroll	62.5	-5.2	2 791	1 818	20	167	206	23.4	7.6	87.1	10.3	451	444	19.7	32.5
Cass	59.6	-2.9	3 897	2 205	45	165	646	22.7	7.6	95.1	7.2	427	422	21.6	30.4
Cedar	60.5	0.9	3 342	1 508	102	170	155	19.8	8.3	96.9	7.9	428	424	18.8	49.2
Cerro Gordo	136.7	-3.2	2 836	1 950	65	163	249	53.0	21.3	86.0	22.9	474	467	47.9	32.4
Cherokee	46.2	-14.1	3 186	1 948	22	147	210	16.8	6.9	90.9	7.1	444	441	15.5	39.7
Chickasaw	49.1	-56.1	3 485	1 762	297	131	188	15.8	6.9	89.4	5.9	386	383	16.4	46.1
Clarke	29.3	-50.0	3 251	1 725	14	147	438	10.1	4.0	92.1	3.7	417	414	9.3	64.0
Clay	55.7	-2.6	3 204	1 819	43	189	241	26.8	7.0	91.9	9.0	466	461	26.0	23.7
Clayton	67.7	6.9	3 369	1 832	21	164	277	24.8	12.8	81.3	8.4	403	399	21.7	52.5
Clinton	151.2	5.3	2 864	1 921	19	119	181	64.9	24.0	90.5	24.1	426	420	52.9	19.9
Crawford	58.3	-2.3	3 188	1 722	260	205	225	22.9	8.5	95.0	7.8	406	402	20.5	41.3
Dallas	78.8	-21.5	2 557	1 731	14	126	191	33.0	12.0	94.9	13.9	474	470	30.8	62.9
Davis	28.4	3.9	3 303	1 906	18	149	298	13.8	4.3	95.3	3.3	361	356	12.8	50.6
Decatur	38.0	18.6	4 476	2 217	25	192	1 081	13.2	5.2	78.5	3.5	364	362	12.2	81.9
Delaware	58.1	10.6	3 126	1 357	14	120	182	23.1	9.8	83.9	6.8	360	356	21.4	40.7
Des Moines	181.4	7.3	4 075	1 881	1 671	171	109	64.3	32.7	63.0	18.9	415	408	61.1	76.6
Dickinson	46.0	-2.9	2 989	2 072	46	119	166	29.2	11.3	44.6	9.3	590	584	24.2	98.3
Dubuque	251.1	19.6	2 747	1 676	85	165	622	92.8	39.8	84.9	36.0	389	377	88.8	60.7
Emmet	42.0	-10.0	3 649	2 256	18	165	268	22.0	10.7	81.7	6.5	493	488	20.4	7.9
Fayette	83.3	-7.9	3 733	2 066	32	168	298	27.9	12.7	93.2	10.3	409	404	25.5	47.1
Floyd	60.9	-2.4	3 382	2 072	15	125	282	24.9	9.1	86.9	8.4	436	431	22.9	26.7
Franklin	47.5	-20.0	4 058	1 882	253	165	176	17.1	5.1	81.7	6.7	520	516	16.5	49.5
Fremont	32.9	-11.0	3 785	2 224	21	159	267	10.7	4.1	92.0	5.0	542	534	10.3	67.8
Greene	44.0	-7.0	4 190	2 226	21	172	275	17.8	5.1	94.0	6.6	551	547	16.0	42.8
Grundy	42.6	-37.5	3 411	1 890	18	134	90	17.1	6.1	87.2	7.7	548	541	17.3	48.3
Guthrie	41.2	-2.8	3 779	2 267	24	179	297	15.5	5.9	94.2	6.4	548	545	13.6	35.5
Hamilton	60.1	-3.3	3 537	1 973	16	135	246	25.7	7.6	88.8	9.8	553	547	22.8	42.8

1. Based on the estimated population as of July 1 of the year shown. 2. Based on the estimated population as of July 1, 1982.

STATE County	Local government finances, 1981–1982 (cont'd) — Direct general expenditure (cont'd) — Per capita[1] (Dollars)	Percent of total for– Education	Health & hospitals	Police protection	Public welfare	Highways	Debt outstanding — Total (Mil dol)	Per capita[1] (Dollars)	State and local government employment, 1989 — Total	Rate[2]	Federal government civilian employment 1989 — Total	Earnings ($1,000)	Elections, 1988[3] — Total vote cast for president	Vote for lead party (Percent)
	189	190	191	192	193	194	195	196	197	198	199	200	201	202
INDIANA—Con.														
Ripley	635	71.4	0.4	1.9	3.5	6.3	10.2	414	989	389.4	91	2 193	10 051	R–63.8
Rush	809	44.8	23.9	3.8	3.8	6.9	1.7	90	1 034	565.0	62	1 566	7 583	R–67.4
St. Joseph	809	48.8	4.4	6.0	6.9	4.7	163.6	683	10 354	421.2	1 225	40 829	97 864	R–50.6
Scott	842	50.0	22.9	2.3	5.5	5.0	11.2	555	1 026	486.3	61	1 645	6 854	R–50.4
Shelby	766	50.1	21.9	3.4	3.5	4.5	21.7	544	1 694	417.2	166	4 002	15 621	R–65.1
Spencer	627	58.1	0.5	1.9	3.3	8.7	13.4	670	660	326.7	87	1 963	9 055	R–54.8
Starke	832	52.7	18.7	2.5	5.0	5.2	5.8	271	1 026	452.0	66	1 622	8 606	R–51.8
Steuben	535	59.4	0.6	5.5	4.3	8.4	4.8	194	1 082	373.1	69	1 756	10 000	R–68.5
Sullivan	1 104	59.2	14.0	0.9	3.3	6.5	54.5	2 607	1 043	521.5	73	1 707	8 597	D–50.3
Switzerland	584	57.8	0.8	2.0	6.8	8.9	1.9	256	332	448.6	28	667	3 059	R–51.4
Tippecanoe	768	43.2	0.5	4.1	3.7	5.6	42.8	345	16 748	1 329.2	588	18 835	44 364	R–62.9
Tipton	1 420	32.4	38.1	1.4	1.9	6.1	9.7	596	1 001	610.4	47	1 128	7 666	R–67.2
Union	775	61.8	0.6	3.0	4.4	10.3	1.1	166	358	518.8	23	584	2 770	R–65.5
Vanderburgh	950	37.9	1.0	4.3	7.4	4.8	84.8	507	7 074	425.6	923	30 781	70 453	R–55.3
Vermillion	776	43.8	26.6	2.0	4.9	7.3	7.8	434	921	529.3	51	1 182	7 772	D–52.0
Vigo	789	51.8	0.5	3.3	5.2	7.2	67.9	608	7 896	738.6	1 266	43 244	41 293	R–53.1
Wabash	923	45.7	19.1	3.4	4.6	7.2	16.8	475	1 763	491.1	95	2 541	13 384	R–68.4
Warren	675	52.8	0.3	2.1	5.7	10.4	5.9	643	335	403.6	29	679	3 799	R–59.0
Warrick	740	59.4	0.2	3.0	3.4	5.8	40.8	928	1 371	292.3	98	2 500	18 564	R–56.6
Washington	824	47.5	20.6	1.2	4.1	10.1	16.6	742	1 062	450.0	70	1 649	8 416	R–59.4
Wayne	1 109	40.4	0.8	2.8	6.4	4.2	35.3	471	4 240	587.3	193	5 592	26 702	R–61.4
Wells	858	52.1	17.8	2.1	2.9	8.1	21.6	860	1 222	449.3	68	1 757	11 188	R–68.9
White	1 136	60.8	11.9	1.5	1.4	5.0	21.6	901	1 177	492.5	83	2 106	9 513	R–65.4
Whitley	754	48.3	27.4	2.6	2.7	4.6	9.4	363	1 403	494.0	91	2 376	11 386	R–67.4
IOWA	1 104	48.3	8.7	3.8	2.2	10.7	2 375.3	817	192 698	677.7	20 920	625 489	1 225 612	D–54.7
Adair	897	42.2	16.6	2.6	3.1	20.0	3.8	409	429	510.7	52	1 245	4 123	D–54.8
Adams	1 022	43.8	3.5	3.9	5.5	23.9	1.5	259	247	475.0	47	1 090	2 380	D–53.9
Allamakee	1 198	48.2	16.4	3.2	4.5	12.1	11.7	788	875	587.2	71	1 784	5 995	R–53.1
Appanoose	931	49.7	0.9	4.4	3.0	12.2	8.9	585	699	488.8	97	2 564	6 088	D–52.7
Audubon	1 046	45.7	11.7	3.5	0.3	19.5	1.0	124	402	536.0	49	1 261	3 371	D–55.3
Benton	1 228	50.3	7.2	2.7	1.6	11.3	12.8	546	1 389	606.6	81	2 051	9 977	D–58.9
Black Hawk	1 064	45.5	7.4	5.0	3.0	7.4	92.8	672	10 132	821.7	550	17 491	56 171	D–56.4
Boone	991	41.8	22.0	3.8	3.5	11.2	9.5	366	2 197	861.6	121	3 345	11 686	D–61.9
Bremer	1 149	61.0	8.1	2.9	2.1	10.3	9.2	368	1 172	507.4	76	2 080	10 099	R–50.3
Buchanan	917	45.0	15.8	3.9	2.7	15.1	3.0	128	1 469	677.0	87	2 142	8 321	D–57.4
Buena Vista	1 052	40.7	20.6	3.8	2.2	12.0	9.5	458	1 197	595.5	126	3 654	8 825	D–51.9
Butler	808	57.8	1.0	3.2	0.3	20.5	4.7	264	698	430.9	66	1 461	6 146	R–57.3
Calhoun	1 228	55.1	3.4	3.2	2.4	18.4	7.4	559	677	564.2	62	1 500	5 505	D–54.3
Carroll	864	38.5	4.6	4.3	5.9	17.4	11.8	517	1 005	448.7	109	2 980	9 273	D–58.6
Cass	1 280	41.6	27.6	2.7	1.7	12.4	14.6	861	1 135	741.8	82	2 170	6 968	R–56.9
Cedar	1 015	62.9	1.3	2.1	2.0	14.5	6.4	348	835	461.3	114	2 669	7 479	D–53.9
Cerro Gordo	991	58.3	1.0	5.0	1.3	9.4	12.3	255	2 743	569.1	244	7 297	22 365	D–57.5
Cherokee	966	54.4	1.3	3.3	1.5	13.5	5.2	323	1 103	760.7	68	1 697	6 855	D–52.1
Chickasaw	1 082	54.0	1.9	2.8	1.4	14.8	9.7	637	592	419.9	73	1 767	6 136	D–57.5
Clarke	1 056	45.7	15.1	3.6	0.7	15.6	4.4	498	518	575.6	55	1 434	3 934	D–57.5
Clay	1 350	36.4	23.2	3.0	2.6	12.6	27.4	1 421	1 206	693.1	111	3 028	7 870	D–53.0
Clayton	1 037	50.3	6.5	2.7	3.8	13.6	4.3	207	1 165	579.6	139	2 856	8 242	D–52.4
Clinton	933	53.0	1.8	4.4	3.0	8.6	88.9	1 567	2 350	445.1	172	4 970	23 002	D–54.6
Crawford	1 071	47.8	19.6	3.1	1.1	14.3	4.5	238	1 115	609.3	126	3 317	7 311	D–52.9
Dallas	1 049	50.7	13.7	3.4	3.8	9.5	14.2	483	1 401	454.9	113	2 926	12 419	D–60.4
Davis	1 394	28.9	38.7	1.8	2.8	12.9	3.4	370	526	611.6	42	1 023	3 849	D–58.4
Decatur	1 281	34.7	25.6	3.7	0.4	16.2	1.7	181	534	628.2	51	1 270	3 627	D–60.4
Delaware	1 136	46.1	17.9	2.9	1.4	15.4	9.6	512	1 025	551.1	79	1 930	7 432	D–53.1
Des Moines	1 339	46.8	1.6	3.0	1.5	7.0	38.4	843	2 197	493.7	229	6 605	19 374	D–59.8
Dickinson	1 542	29.9	12.8	2.8	2.4	8.3	18.9	1 202	825	535.7	62	1 580	7 101	R–51.8
Dubuque	959	46.7	4.9	3.9	1.5	8.0	57.7	623	3 167	346.5	363	11 240	38 547	D–61.7
Emmet	1 548	67.4	1.7	2.9	1.2	7.3	7.6	578	943	820.0	60	1 587	4 977	D–55.8
Fayette	1 016	57.4	6.5	2.9	2.5	12.1	8.6	343	1 050	470.9	114	2 997	10 287	D–51.6
Floyd	1 187	44.6	19.2	2.8	0.8	10.7	7.2	371	989	549.4	73	1 898	7 733	D–56.6
Franklin	1 292	38.3	21.6	2.9	1.0	17.4	2.9	230	626	535.0	65	1 500	4 951	D–52.4
Fremont	1 109	55.2	0.6	2.4	1.8	20.2	3.0	318	434	498.9	52	1 212	3 527	R–55.2
Greene	1 347	39.5	27.7	2.8	1.7	14.1	5.9	496	752	716.2	61	1 429	5 164	D–58.3
Grundy	1 225	52.7	11.1	2.7	0.3	13.3	8.5	605	695	556.0	54	1 349	5 682	R–60.4
Guthrie	1 166	53.8	8.7	2.4	2.9	14.4	3.9	336	692	634.9	74	1 717	4 983	D–58.4
Hamilton	1 286	42.2	15.7	3.1	2.0	12.6	18.8	1 061	1 005	591.2	78	2 100	7 494	D–55.5

1. Based on the estimated population as of July 1, 1982. 2. Per 10,000 resident population estimated as of July 1 of the year shown. 3. Data subject to copyright.

STATE–County code	MSA/CMSA/NECMA code[1]	STATE County	Land Area,[2] 1990 (Sq. Km.)	Population, 1990										Age of population Percent		
							Race									
				Total persons	Rank	Per square kilometer	White	Black	Am. Indian, Eskimo, Aleut	Asian & Pacific Islander	Other race	Hispanic[3]	Under 5 years	5 to 14 years	15 to 24 years
			1	2	3	4	5	6	7	8	9	10	11	12	13
		IOWA—Con.													
19 081	...	Hancock	1 479	12 638	2 174	8.5	12 524	1	5	26	82	129	7.2	16.5	11.0
19 083	...	Hardin	1 475	19 094	1 728	12.9	18 844	117	25	53	55	106	5.9	14.3	12.8
19 085	...	Harrison	1 805	14 730	2 004	8.2	14 649	10	15	51	5	50	7.0	15.6	11.3
19 087	...	Henry	1 125	19 226	1 717	17.1	18 710	211	44	215	46	127	6.6	14.5	13.9
19 089	...	Howard	1 226	9 809	2 402	8.0	9 768	5	7	20	9	24	6.9	15.8	10.2
19 091	...	Humboldt	1 125	10 756	2 311	9.6	10 701	9	15	27	4	37	6.6	15.0	10.0
19 093	...	Ida	1 118	8 365	2 527	7.5	8 331	1	5	19	9	23	7.5	16.0	10.2
19 095	...	Iowa	1 519	14 630	2 010	9.6	14 566	7	11	34	12	39	7.2	14.7	10.4
19 097	...	Jackson	1 648	19 950	1 681	12.1	19 867	16	23	24	20	96	7.1	16.1	12.4
19 099	...	Jasper	1 891	34 795	1 138	18.4	34 446	65	62	175	47	194	6.4	14.8	12.0
19 101	...	Jefferson	1 128	16 310	1 901	14.5	16 027	93	23	139	28	141	6.5	14.3	10.9
19 103	3500	Johnson	1 592	96 119	482	60.4	89 649	1 979	176	3 837	478	1 435	6.4	11.1	27.5
19 105	...	Jones	1 490	19 444	1 706	13.0	19 056	299	35	22	32	95	6.5	14.9	13.2
19 107	...	Keokuk	1 500	11 624	2 246	7.7	11 565	6	19	27	7	19	6.5	15.5	10.6
19 109	...	Kossuth	2 520	18 591	1 759	7.4	18 463	8	7	59	54	94	7.0	16.5	10.3
19 111	...	Lee	1 340	38 687	1 036	28.9	36 990	1 112	61	135	389	732	6.6	15.1	11.9
19 113	1360	Linn	1 858	168 767	284	90.8	163 164	3 334	363	1 401	505	1 591	7.1	14.1	14.9
19 115	...	Louisa	1 041	11 592	2 248	11.1	11 206	86	36	18	246	425	6.9	15.8	13.2
19 117	...	Lucas	1 115	9 070	2 463	8.1	9 004	4	20	17	25	53	6.3	14.4	11.1
19 119	...	Lyon	1 522	11 952	2 223	7.9	11 896	2	15	35	4	11	7.9	17.7	11.6
19 121	...	Madison	1 453	12 483	2 182	8.6	12 402	5	37	16	23	67	6.7	16.1	11.9
19 123	...	Mahaska	1 479	21 522	1 601	14.6	21 254	42	16	179	31	92	7.1	14.9	13.6
19 125	...	Marion	1 436	30 001	1 295	20.9	29 550	104	42	283	22	162	6.6	14.9	15.6
19 127	...	Marshall	1 482	38 276	1 047	25.8	37 472	279	105	302	118	292	6.5	14.4	12.2
19 129	...	Mills	1 131	13 202	2 122	11.7	13 110	22	28	17	25	72	6.3	16.2	12.3
19 131	...	Mitchell	1 215	10 928	2 304	9.0	10 896	2	1	21	8	45	6.5	15.1	11.1
19 133	...	Monona	1 795	10 034	2 383	5.6	9 982	5	26	13	8	30	6.0	14.4	9.7
19 135	...	Monroe	1 123	8 114	2 554	7.2	8 039	19	16	33	7	18	6.3	14.9	11.3
19 137	...	Montgomery	1 098	12 076	2 212	11.0	12 038	5	11	12	10	52	6.0	14.6	10.8
19 139	...	Muscatine	1 136	39 907	1 006	35.1	37 745	208	90	300	1 564	2 900	7.4	16.1	13.4
19 141	...	O'Brien	1 484	15 444	1 958	10.4	15 343	8	32	52	9	39	6.6	15.9	10.9
19 143	...	Osceola	1 033	7 267	2 629	7.0	7 228	3	9	16	11	16	7.4	15.5	11.4
19 145	...	Page	1 385	16 870	1 858	12.2	16 586	84	52	80	68	197	5.9	14.8	11.3
19 147	...	Palo Alto	1 460	10 669	2 321	7.3	10 616	8	23	18	4	24	6.4	15.9	11.8
19 149	...	Plymouth	2 237	23 388	1 520	10.5	23 260	48	14	53	13	58	7.3	17.2	13.1
19 151	...	Pocahontas	1 496	9 525	2 430	6.4	9 485	4	10	17	9	32	6.8	15.2	9.1
19 153	2120	Polk	1 475	327 140	156	221.8	303 168	14 799	922	6 003	2 248	6 161	7.6	13.8	14.6
19 155	5920	Pottawattamie	2 472	82 628	550	33.4	81 205	464	240	284	435	1 516	7.5	15.5	13.2
19 157	...	Poweshiek	1 515	19 033	1 733	12.6	18 705	87	22	191	28	68	6.1	14.2	16.7
19 159	...	Ringgold	1 393	5 420	2 806	3.9	5 390	1	10	18	1	16	5.4	14.6	9.4
19 161	...	Sac	1 491	12 324	2 192	8.3	12 276	4	14	20	10	44	6.8	15.8	9.8
19 163	1960	Scott	1 186	150 979	309	127.3	139 408	7 970	485	1 357	1 759	4 253	7.8	16.0	14.0
19 165	...	Shelby	1 530	13 230	2 118	8.6	13 177	5	20	20	8	44	6.7	15.9	10.8
19 167	...	Sioux	1 989	29 903	1 299	15.0	29 608	25	32	209	29	66	7.7	17.9	17.0
19 169	...	Story	1 484	74 252	606	50.0	69 143	1 191	106	3 464	348	840	5.9	11.0	31.6
19 171	...	Tama	1 868	17 419	1 826	9.3	16 465	31	812	65	46	128	6.5	15.3	11.6
19 173	...	Taylor	1 383	7 114	2 643	5.1	7 070	1	7	18	18	46	6.1	15.1	10.4
19 175	...	Union	1 099	12 750	2 162	11.6	12 650	10	22	49	19	42	6.3	15.0	13.0
19 177	...	Van Buren	1 257	7 676	2 604	6.1	7 638	10	8	18	2	29	7.1	15.2	10.8
19 179	...	Wapello	1 118	35 687	1 106	31.9	35 063	270	95	168	91	224	6.5	13.5	12.8
19 181	2120	Warren	1 481	36 033	1 098	24.3	35 684	90	51	145	63	277	7.2	16.4	14.9
19 183	...	Washington	1 473	19 612	1 692	13.3	19 403	90	16	54	49	196	7.4	15.3	11.3
19 185	...	Wayne	1 361	7 067	2 650	5.2	7 036	1	8	16	6	29	6.3	13.4	9.4
19 187	...	Webster	1 853	40 342	989	21.8	39 022	883	113	159	165	490	7.3	14.8	12.5
19 189	...	Winnebago	1 037	12 122	2 206	11.7	11 965	31	17	77	32	97	6.5	14.9	13.4
19 191	...	Winneshiek	1 786	20 847	1 635	11.7	20 577	43	5	195	27	61	6.8	14.1	20.0
19 193	7720	Woodbury	2 260	98 276	468	43.5	92 098	1 877	1 697	1 266	1 338	2 712	7.6	16.2	14.0
19 195	...	Worth	1 036	7 991	2 568	7.7	7 918	15	2	14	42	91	6.3	14.5	10.7
19 197	...	Wright	1 504	14 269	2 033	9.5	14 175	10	15	41	28	92	6.7	13.8	10.3
20 000	...	KANSAS	211 922	2 477 574	X	11.7	2 231 986	143 076	21 965	31 750	48 797	93 670	7.6	15.2	14.2
20 001	...	Allen	1 303	14 638	2 008	11.2	14 128	270	100	46	94	258	6.9	16.3	12.3
20 003	...	Anderson	1 510	7 803	2 596	5.2	7 672	40	67	10	14	51	6.6	15.3	11.5
20 005	...	Atchison	1 120	16 932	1 854	15.1	15 598	957	84	131	162	370	7.0	15.5	15.8
20 007	...	Barber	2 938	5 874	2 774	2.0	5 791	13	31	3	36	73	6.7	16.4	9.1
20 009	...	Barton	2 316	29 382	1 316	12.7	28 392	348	141	109	392	816	7.6	15.7	11.6

1. MSA = Metropolitan Statistical Area. CMSA = Consolidated MSA. NECMA = New England county metropolitan area. PMSA = Primary MSA. See Appendix A for explanation of these concepts. See Appendix B for list of metropolitan areas identified by type, with component counties. 2. Dry land or land partially or temporarily covered by water. 3. Hispanic persons may be of any race.

STATE County	Population, 1990 (cont'd): Age of population (cont'd), Percent: 25 to 34 years	35 to 44 years	45 to 54 years	55 to 64 years	65 to 74 years	75 years and over	Percent female	Population–Change and components of change: Change, 1980–1990: Number	Percent	Total persons, 1986	Total persons, 1980	Components of change, 1980–1986: Net change: Number	Percent	Natural increase: Births	Deaths
	14	15	16	17	18	19	20	21	22	23	24	25	26	27	28
IOWA—Con.															
Hancock	14.6	13.7	9.5	9.4	9.3	8.8	51.4	-1 195	-8.6	13 300	13 833	-500	-3.6	1 300	900
Hardin	13.0	12.9	9.7	10.2	10.6	10.6	51.6	-2 682	-12.3	20 800	21 776	-1 000	-4.7	1 900	1 500
Harrison	14.1	12.6	10.1	9.9	9.8	9.7	51.8	-1 618	-9.9	15 800	16 348	-500	-3.2	1 400	1 200
Henry	15.5	14.8	9.9	8.2	8.4	8.2	50.1	336	1.8	18 600	18 890	-300	-1.7	1 700	1 200
Howard	13.7	11.7	9.7	10.4	10.4	11.3	51.4	-1 305	-11.7	10 600	11 114	-500	-4.5	1 000	900
Humboldt	13.4	12.8	10.0	11.2	11.4	9.6	51.6	-1 490	-12.2	11 600	12 246	-700	-5.5	1 100	800
Ida	13.7	12.9	9.0	10.6	10.3	10.0	51.6	-543	-6.1	8 900	8 908	0	0.0	900	600
Iowa	15.4	13.5	9.9	10.0	9.8	9.1	51.7	-799	-5.2	15 000	15 429	-400	-2.8	1 300	1 000
Jackson	14.3	13.0	10.4	10.1	8.8	7.8	51.0	-2 553	-11.3	22 100	22 503	-400	-1.6	2 200	1 400
Jasper	15.1	14.6	10.7	10.4	8.7	7.3	51.2	-1 630	-4.5	35 900	36 425	-600	-1.6	3 000	2 100
Jefferson	14.3	21.2	10.1	8.0	7.4	7.3	51.2	-6	0.0	16 500	16 316	200	1.0	1 400	1 000
Johnson	20.3	14.5	7.5	5.4	4.1	3.4	50.5	14 402	17.6	85 300	81 717	3 600	4.4	8 200	2 700
Jones	15.9	14.3	10.0	9.1	8.4	7.6	48.3	-957	-4.7	20 000	20 401	-400	-2.1	1 800	1 100
Keokuk	14.2	12.4	9.7	10.4	10.2	10.6	51.5	-1 297	-10.0	12 300	12 921	-600	-4.6	1 100	1 100
Kossuth	13.9	12.8	10.1	10.4	9.8	9.2	51.4	-3 300	-15.1	20 300	21 891	-1 600	-7.1	2 000	1 300
Lee	15.0	14.6	10.4	9.5	9.2	7.6	51.1	-4 419	-10.3	41 300	43 106	-1 800	-4.1	3 900	2 700
Linn	17.2	15.5	10.6	8.4	6.8	5.4	51.4	-1 008	-0.6	168 800	169 775	-1 000	-0.6	15 900	7 700
Louisa	15.3	14.4	10.3	9.1	7.7	7.3	49.7	-463	-3.8	12 000	12 055	0	-0.4	1 100	700
Lucas	12.9	12.9	10.9	10.9	10.4	10.3	52.3	-1 243	-12.1	9 800	10 313	-500	-5.3	800	800
Lyon	13.1	12.8	8.7	10.3	9.3	8.7	51.1	-944	-7.3	12 500	12 896	-400	-3.0	1 300	700
Madison	13.4	14.6	10.4	8.9	8.9	9.1	51.3	-114	-0.9	12 400	12 597	-200	-1.2	1 000	900
Mahaska	14.7	13.6	9.3	9.1	9.6	8.1	51.3	-1 345	-5.9	22 300	22 867	-600	-2.6	2 100	1 600
Marion	14.1	13.8	9.9	9.0	8.5	7.7	50.3	332	1.1	29 700	29 669	0	0.0	2 700	1 800
Marshall	14.2	14.9	10.8	9.5	9.4	8.1	51.1	-3 376	-8.1	40 500	41 652	-1 200	-2.8	3 800	2 700
Mills	15.1	16.8	10.7	8.9	7.3	6.4	50.4	-204	-1.5	13 400	13 406	0	0.0	1 200	800
Mitchell	13.0	12.0	9.9	10.5	10.7	11.2	51.4	-1 401	-11.4	11 600	12 329	-700	-5.9	1 000	1 000
Monona	12.3	12.3	10.4	11.1	11.5	12.3	52.4	-1 658	-14.2	10 600	11 692	-1 000	-8.9	900	1 000
Monroe	13.6	13.1	9.7	10.4	10.8	9.8	51.9	-1 095	-11.9	8 600	9 209	-600	-6.7	700	700
Montgomery	13.5	13.7	9.3	10.3	10.2	11.6	52.9	-1 337	-10.0	12 600	13 413	-800	-6.2	1 100	1 000
Muscatine	16.3	14.9	10.3	8.3	7.2	6.2	51.1	-529	-1.3	41 300	40 436	800	2.1	4 300	2 300
O'Brien	13.7	12.6	9.1	10.5	10.3	10.4	51.9	-1 528	-9.0	16 000	16 972	-1 000	-5.9	1 600	1 200
Osceola	14.2	12.2	9.3	10.6	9.5	9.8	51.5	-1 104	-13.2	7 900	8 371	-500	-5.5	800	600
Page	13.2	13.7	9.9	10.2	10.5	10.5	51.6	-2 193	-11.5	17 700	19 063	-1 400	-7.2	1 500	1 600
Palo Alto	12.7	11.7	9.4	11.5	9.9	10.6	51.7	-2 052	-16.1	11 700	12 721	-1 000	-7.9	1 200	900
Plymouth	13.8	13.3	9.4	9.7	8.3	8.0	50.9	-1 355	-5.5	23 900	24 743	-800	-3.4	2 500	1 500
Pocahontas	13.3	12.4	10.6	10.8	11.3	10.5	51.6	-1 844	-16.2	10 900	11 369	-500	-4.3	1 000	900
Polk	18.7	15.6	10.0	8.1	6.5	5.1	52.3	23 970	7.9	315 800	303 170	12 600	4.2	31 400	15 300
Pottawattamie	16.3	14.1	10.3	9.7	7.7	5.7	51.9	-3 933	-4.5	88 000	86 561	1 400	1.6	8 700	4 900
Poweshiek	13.7	13.3	10.0	9.1	8.7	8.0	51.9	-273	-1.4	18 700	19 306	-700	-3.4	1 500	1 200
Ringgold	11.7	12.4	10.1	12.2	12.1	12.1	52.4	-692	-11.3	5 600	6 112	-600	-9.1	500	500
Sac	13.2	12.6	9.1	10.8	11.0	11.0	51.2	-1 794	-12.7	12 800	14 118	-1 300	-9.1	1 200	1 100
Scott	16.7	15.7	10.3	8.1	6.6	4.8	51.6	-9 043	-5.7	156 900	160 022	-3 100	-1.9	16 800	7 300
Shelby	13.4	12.8	9.7	10.4	10.4	9.9	51.2	-1 813	-12.1	14 400	15 043	-600	-4.2	1 300	1 000
Sioux	13.2	12.3	8.7	8.3	7.9	6.8	51.5	-910	-3.0	30 500	30 813	-300	-1.0	3 500	1 500
Story	16.1	12.2	7.6	6.0	5.0	4.6	48.3	1 926	2.7	72 500	72 326	100	0.2	6 500	2 400
Tama	13.4	12.8	10.7	10.3	9.8	9.7	51.6	-2 114	-10.8	18 800	19 533	-700	-3.5	1 700	1 300
Taylor	11.6	12.7	9.3	10.6	11.8	12.4	52.7	-1 239	-14.8	7 800	8 353	-600	-6.9	700	700
Union	13.6	13.9	9.8	9.2	9.6	9.7	53.0	-1 108	-8.0	13 200	13 858	-700	-4.8	1 200	1 100
Van Buren	13.1	12.8	10.5	10.1	10.5	9.9	50.7	-950	-11.0	8 200	8 626	-400	-4.6	700	700
Wapello	14.0	14.1	9.9	10.5	9.8	8.9	52.3	-4 554	-11.3	38 000	40 241	-2 200	-5.5	3 300	2 900
Warren	15.1	16.1	11.4	8.0	5.9	5.0	51.3	1 155	3.3	35 800	34 878	900	2.6	3 200	1 500
Washington	15.0	13.7	9.6	9.1	9.2	9.4	51.9	-529	-2.6	19 800	20 141	-300	-1.7	1 800	1 300
Wayne	12.2	11.6	9.5	11.3	13.1	13.1	52.8	-1 132	-13.8	7 400	8 199	-800	-9.5	600	800
Webster	14.6	13.5	9.6	10.1	9.3	8.4	52.3	-5 611	-12.2	42 700	45 953	-3 300	-7.1	4 200	3 000
Winnebago	13.7	13.8	9.2	9.2	9.0	10.1	51.6	-888	-6.8	12 700	13 010	-300	-2.4	1 100	900
Winneshiek	14.1	12.0	8.9	8.7	8.2	7.3	51.1	-1 029	-4.7	22 000	21 876	100	0.7	1 900	1 300
Woodbury	15.6	14.2	8.9	8.8	8.1	6.6	51.9	-2 608	-2.6	98 600	100 884	-2 200	-2.2	10 500	6 000
Worth	13.5	13.3	10.5	10.4	9.9	10.9	51.4	-1 084	-11.9	8 800	9 075	-300	-2.8	800	600
Wright	13.4	13.2	9.8	10.6	11.4	10.7	52.4	-2 050	-12.6	15 200	16 319	-1 100	-6.6	1 300	1 200
KANSAS	16.7	14.6	9.5	8.4	7.5	6.4	51.0	113 574	4.8	2 460 000	2 364 000	97 000	4.1	252 000	137 000
Allen	13.8	12.9	9.4	9.4	9.6	9.4	51.9	-1 016	-6.5	15 700	15 654	0	0.1	1 600	1 200
Anderson	12.8	11.9	10.1	9.8	10.9	11.1	51.8	-946	-10.8	8 200	8 749	-600	-6.4	800	800
Atchison	14.0	12.1	9.6	9.2	8.5	8.4	51.2	-1 465	-8.0	17 900	18 397	-500	-2.6	1 700	1 300
Barber	14.4	12.6	9.0	10.5	11.4	10.0	52.0	-674	-10.3	6 900	6 548	400	6.0	800	500
Barton	15.4	13.4	9.5	10.0	9.1	7.6	51.8	-1 961	-6.3	32 800	31 343	1 500	4.7	3 800	2 000

STATE County	Population– (cont'd)	Households, 1990					Births, 1988			Deaths, 1987				Marriages, 1984	
	Components of change, 1980-1986 (cont'd)				Percent					Number		Rate			
	Net migration	Number	Percent change, 1980–1990	Persons per household	Female family householder[1]	One-person	Total	Rate[2]	Low birth weight[3] (Number)	Total	Infant[4]	Total[2]	Infant[5]	Number	Rate[2]
	29	30	31	32	33	34	35	36	37	38	39	40	41	42	43
IOWA—Con.															
Hancock	-900	4 867	-2.7	2.55	5.6	24.9	159	12.0	11	135	0	10.2	0.0	90	6.5
Hardin	-1 400	7 611	-6.7	2.38	5.5	28.0	224	11.3	7	243	2	12.1	9.2	174	8.1
Harrison	-700	5 656	-5.1	2.55	6.8	25.7	194	12.2	3	212	1	13.4	4.4	126	7.7
Henry	-800	7 089	5.7	2.51	7.0	25.8	248	13.2	17	219	2	11.6	8.5	178	9.6
Howard	-600	3 856	-3.9	2.48	5.1	28.5	112	10.7	3	154	0	14.5	0.0	99	8.8
Humboldt	-1 000	4 339	-6.1	2.44	5.4	26.6	143	12.7	7	113	4	10.0	29.0	108	8.9
Ida	-200	3 222	-4.4	2.53	4.3	26.4	122	14.2	12	115	1	13.4	8.9	71	7.9
Iowa	-700	5 713	2.1	2.51	6.0	24.9	179	12.2	12	196	3	13.2	16.7	121	8.0
Jackson	-1 200	7 527	-1.4	2.61	7.5	24.8	275	12.7	16	237	1	10.9	3.4	156	6.8
Jasper	-1 500	13 632	0.5	2.50	6.6	23.7	446	12.3	33	343	5	9.6	11.4	294	8.1
Jefferson	-200	6 309	10.4	2.42	7.4	28.2	208	12.5	12	162	0	9.8	0.0	162	9.9
Johnson	-1 900	36 067	19.3	2.41	6.7	27.8	1 330	15.3	55	450	9	5.3	7.0	961	11.7
Jones	-1 100	6 917	-0.2	2.60	7.1	23.6	240	12.1	12	178	3	9.0	13.9	124	6.0
Keokuk	-700	4 573	-6.4	2.50	6.3	25.9	159	13.2	5	152	0	12.7	0.0	89	7.1
Kossuth	-2 200	7 194	-7.8	2.53	5.1	27.3	243	12.3	11	195	1	9.8	4.0	141	6.5
Lee	-2 900	14 936	-4.4	2.49	9.7	26.8	512	12.7	33	435	9	10.7	16.5	429	10.1
Linn	-9 200	65 501	6.0	2.51	8.5	25.0	2 465	14.4	139	1 269	19	7.5	8.0	1 614	9.6
Louisa	-400	4 296	1.8	2.65	7.3	22.0	141	11.8	9	107	1	9.0	6.0	77	6.2
Lucas	-600	3 766	-6.9	2.35	6.6	29.9	111	11.7	2	106	1	11.0	9.9	76	7.5
Lyon	-1 000	4 289	-4.4	2.74	4.0	22.4	183	15.0	7	117	0	9.6	0.0	114	8.6
Madison	-300	4 715	3.1	2.59	6.4	23.6	161	12.8	6	141	1	11.3	7.2	94	7.5
Mahaska	-1 100	8 306	-3.5	2.51	6.9	25.0	297	13.3	15	230	4	10.4	13.5	231	10.2
Marion	-900	10 815	4.8	2.55	6.5	24.7	364	12.1	27	276	3	9.2	7.4	258	8.5
Marshall	-2 300	14 890	-3.4	2.47	8.3	26.0	489	12.4	37	459	5	11.6	11.0	389	9.4
Mills	-400	4 665	2.8	2.65	8.9	22.7	154	11.5	15	148	3	11.2	17.4	104	7.6
Mitchell	-800	4 253	-4.0	2.48	4.7	26.7	138	12.0	7	166	1	14.4	7.5	104	8.6
Monona	-1 000	4 098	-8.3	2.38	6.6	28.7	105	10.1	2	144	1	13.7	9.1	77	6.8
Monroe	-600	3 196	-8.9	2.48	7.6	27.9	88	10.5	4	112	3	13.3	28.0	76	8.6
Montgomery	-900	4 955	-6.0	2.37	7.4	29.0	148	12.1	7	175	0	14.3	0.0	108	8.2
Muscatine	-1 200	14 806	4.2	2.65	9.2	23.0	615	15.0	35	383	5	9.4	8.9	402	9.5
O'Brien	-1 400	5 980	-4.4	2.49	4.6	27.1	173	11.1	6	210	1	13.5	5.4	91	5.4
Osceola	-600	2 817	-7.6	2.54	4.5	26.6	104	13.7	1	100	1	13.0	11.5	67	8.1
Page	-1 300	6 687	-8.6	2.41	7.3	28.7	209	12.2	16	240	1	14.0	5.3	152	8.3
Palo Alto	-1 300	4 183	-9.5	2.48	5.1	29.5	133	12.0	3	145	0	12.9	0.0	66	5.3
Plymouth	-1 800	8 417	-0.1	2.70	5.6	23.6	311	12.9	16	243	4	10.1	11.3	168	6.8
Pocahontas	-500	3 820	-10.5	2.44	4.4	27.9	135	13.1	12	128	1	12.3	9.2	91	8.2
Polk	-3 500	129 237	12.6	2.47	10.2	27.0	4 999	15.4	316	2 485	60	7.8	12.0	3 413	11.2
Pottawattamie	-2 400	31 262	1.5	2.60	11.2	23.3	1 297	14.7	94	823	18	9.4	14.4	1 156	13.1
Poweshiek	-1 000	7 158	4.3	2.48	6.4	25.9	203	10.7	16	187	1	10.0	5.3	139	7.4
Ringgold	-600	2 218	-7.9	2.38	5.0	27.6	56	10.4	2	78	2	14.4	33.3	58	9.7
Sac	-1 400	4 914	-8.2	2.46	5.4	28.1	142	11.3	4	168	1	13.2	6.7	73	5.4
Scott	-12 500	57 438	1.3	2.58	11.1	24.9	2 398	15.4	135	1 219	17	7.8	7.4	1 555	9.7
Shelby	-1 000	5 024	-3.7	2.56	5.4	24.7	170	12.1	10	148	0	10.4	0.0	113	7.4
Sioux	-2 300	9 925	0.1	2.80	3.7	22.0	473	15.7	17	238	3	7.9	6.6	217	6.7
Story	-3 900	25 941	9.6	2.45	5.8	25.4	949	13.2	40	411	7	5.8	7.5	624	8.7
Tama	-1 000	6 768	-4.5	2.51	6.6	24.8	207	11.2	8	199	0	10.8	0.0	107	5.5
Taylor	-600	2 859	-12.9	2.42	5.6	27.7	73	9.7	2	119	0	15.7	0.0	48	5.7
Union	-800	5 173	-2.7	2.41	8.5	28.9	143	11.1	7	175	0	13.5	0.0	114	8.3
Van Buren	-500	3 056	-4.4	2.47	5.7	27.0	123	15.0	8	107	0	13.0	0.0	41	4.8
Wapello	-2 500	14 555	-5.7	2.40	9.4	27.1	420	11.5	28	445	7	12.0	15.7	388	9.8
Warren	-800	12 659	10.0	2.75	8.0	18.3	483	13.2	16	242	5	6.6	10.3	230	6.3
Washington	-800	7 454	3.3	2.55	6.4	25.9	280	13.9	20	219	0	11.0	0.0	167	8.3
Wayne	-600	2 953	-10.9	2.35	4.7	28.5	89	12.5	6	107	0	14.7	0.0	65	8.2
Webster	-4 500	15 963	-5.5	2.44	9.1	27.9	589	14.1	42	491	7	11.7	11.8	415	9.5
Winnebago	-500	4 704	-2.9	2.43	6.0	28.2	164	13.2	10	148	1	11.9	6.5	139	10.7
Winneshiek	-500	7 256	2.7	2.58	5.1	25.6	271	12.4	9	181	1	8.3	3.7	165	7.2
Woodbury	-6 700	36 899	0.7	2.59	10.5	25.9	1 582	16.1	109	946	21	9.7	13.6	874	8.7
Worth	-400	3 239	-6.2	2.43	5.8	27.2	101	11.7	7	102	1	12.0	10.1	80	8.9
Wright	-1 200	5 899	-5.5	2.37	5.6	28.3	174	11.8	12	181	1	12.2	5.6	139	8.7
KANSAS	-18 000	944 726	8.3	2.53	8.6	25.9	38 792	15.5	2 379	22 113	364	8.9	9.5	24 737	10.1
Allen	-300	5 705	-4.9	2.50	7.7	27.3	186	12.4	11	201	4	13.1	20.3	170	10.5
Anderson	-600	3 067	-7.5	2.50	6.6	26.3	91	11.1	2	119	1	14.5	9.8	68	7.7
Atchison	-900	6 129	-1.5	2.56	9.4	26.3	231	13.0	9	202	3	11.3	11.9	180	9.9
Barber	200	2 358	-10.3	2.44	4.9	27.9	95	15.1	3	78	0	12.2	0.0	52	7.3
Barton	-400	11 561	-2.0	2.48	7.7	27.3	455	15.0	26	303	5	9.7	10.6	398	12.0

1. No spouse present. 2. Per 1,000 resident population estimated as of July 1 of the year shown. 3. Under 2,500 grams. 4. Deaths of infants under 1 year old. 5. Deaths of infants under 1 year old per 1,000 live births.

STATE County	Divorces, 1984		Physicians, active non-Federal, 1989		Hospitals, 1989			Nursing homes,[4] 1986		Serious crimes known to police, 1988			Education			
						Beds				Number			Public school enrollment[7]		Attainment,[8] 1980	
	Number	Rate[1]	Number[2]	Rate[3]	Number	Number	Rate[3]	Number	Beds	Total[5]	Violent[6]	Rate[3]	1986–1987	1980	Percent 12 yrs. or more	Percent 16 yrs. or more
	44	45	46	47	48	49	50	51	52	53	54	55	56	57	58	59
IOWA—Con.																
Hancock	32	2.3	3	23	1	30	226	4	219	232	7	1 745	2 381	2 831	69.9	9.2
Hardin	58	2.7	14	72	2	76	390	6	424	381	6	1 877	4 301	4 380	68.1	11.0
Harrison	56	3.4	8	50	1	36	224	4	414	219	3	1 386	3 051	3 587	69.6	8.2
Henry	64	3.4	13	68	2	226	1 183	6	285	376	31	1 979	3 688	3 712	70.5	12.5
Howard	22	2.0	6	58	1	42	404	5	255	152	5	1 434	2 080	2 060	59.9	7.7
Humboldt	39	3.2	5	45	1	49	438	2	150	186	5	1 646	1 898	2 443	70.3	9.6
Ida	17	1.9	3	35	1	35	412	2	121	198	4	2 303	1 495	1 797	67.1	10.8
Iowa	45	3.0	6	41	1	44	301	4	225	81	1	537	2 658	3 033	67.8	9.5
Jackson	48	2.1	13	60	1	61	281	7	321	432	25	1 991	3 755	4 832	62.5	8.5
Jasper	117	3.2	17	46	1	61	166	6	354	1 028	29	2 864	6 428	7 196	69.2	9.8
Jefferson	82	5.0	22	130	1	67	396	2	175	458	1	2 776	2 044	2 957	74.1	18.5
Johnson	289	3.5	1 211	1 378	4	1 443	1 642	6	434	5 144	443	5 997	10 420	11 618	85.6	38.6
Jones	65	3.1	7	35	2	76	384	2	179	287	9	1 443	3 433	4 440	67.5	9.4
Keokuk	21	1.7	5	42	1	33	277	3	195	149	0	1 242	2 404	2 572	67.4	7.3
Kossuth	49	2.3	5	26	1	32	165	4	257	252	2	1 267	2 591	3 575	67.9	8.6
Lee	186	4.4	43	107	2	163	404	6	501	1 630	121	3 996	6 594	7 417	68.7	9.5
Linn	576	3.4	249	143	2	928	534	14	1 137	9 243	345	5 451	29 107	32 778	77.6	16.7
Louisa	37	3.0	1	8	0	0	0	3	160	393	10	3 303	2 839	2 634	68.1	8.5
Lucas	38	3.7	1	11	1	56	596	3	172	240	1	2 501	1 654	1 986	67.7	7.8
Lyon	13	1.0	3	25	1	30	246	2	99	69	0	561	2 288	2 478	60.7	9.3
Madison	27	2.1	3	23	1	31	242	4	275	272	11	2 194	2 843	2 694	71.8	8.5
Mahaska	107	4.7	11	49	1	53	236	7	359	706	55	3 167	3 268	3 747	64.6	11.0
Marion	122	4.0	17	56	3	822	2 686	8	367	659	68	2 197	5 284	5 409	63.6	10.5
Marshall	152	3.7	56	143	1	176	449	7	1 296	1 501	147	3 772	6 977	8 155	74.7	14.2
Mills	59	4.3	7	52	1	604	4 474	3	178	310	17	2 314	2 547	2 611	66.4	10.2
Mitchell	24	2.0	7	61	1	40	351	6	355	157	5	1 354	1 811	2 591	68.8	8.5
Monona	26	2.3	6	58	1	48	466	4	283	278	5	2 648	1 852	2 260	64.1	8.2
Monroe	27	3.1	1	12	1	46	554	3	153	224	14	2 636	1 376	1 810	65.2	6.5
Montgomery	62	4.7	9	74	1	49	405	4	270	540	6	4 391	2 226	2 443	68.9	10.4
Muscatine	225	5.3	26	63	1	80	193	6	521	1 316	35	3 187	7 622	8 334	66.4	11.8
O'Brien	32	1.9	7	45	3	160	1 039	7	315	288	7	1 812	2 812	3 003	64.4	11.7
Osceola	12	1.4	4	53	1	32	421	2	115	100	6	1 282	951	1 528	59.8	8.5
Page	63	3.4	17	100	3	253	1 488	4	313	435	5	2 515	3 150	3 589	69.4	10.8
Palo Alto	34	2.7	6	55	1	54	495	4	277	263	14	2 328	2 015	2 467	69.5	11.4
Plymouth	63	2.5	9	37	1	44	180	5	339	416	12	1 719	3 949	4 308	67.2	11.9
Pocahontas	27	2.4	4	40	1	20	198	5	268	98	3	925	1 683	2 231	69.3	9.7
Polk	1 578	5.2	637	192	7	2 312	698	30	2 359	25 472	1 846	7 979	51 294	55 199	78.8	19.2
Pottawattamie	434	4.9	106	120	2	485	547	8	629	5 163	328	5 848	16 127	18 187	68.3	9.2
Poweshiek	58	3.1	17	89	1	53	279	5	291	240	4	1 291	3 103	3 782	73.2	14.8
Ringgold	28	4.7	3	57	1	40	755	2	150	56	0	1 018	983	1 077	67.5	8.4
Sac	30	2.2	8	64	1	54	432	4	237	107	1	836	2 373	2 689	65.2	10.6
Scott	736	4.6	207	133	3	632	406	15	1 312	8 980	964	5 754	28 480	31 997	74.2	18.4
Shelby	33	2.2	8	57	1	52	371	3	286	235	14	1 632	2 379	3 162	70.0	9.6
Sioux	46	1.4	17	56	4	277	914	5	321	230	9	764	3 752	4 360	59.1	12.0
Story	207	2.9	106	147	3	378	524	8	573	2 856	115	3 979	9 551	10 304	85.6	33.9
Tama	56	2.9	2	11	0	0	0	5	314	313	22	1 692	3 537	4 184	66.3	10.1
Taylor	25	3.0	2	27	0	0	0	3	154	132	13	1 737	1 440	1 579	64.5	7.1
Union	60	4.4	14	109	1	53	411	3	205	435	11	3 347	2 496	2 525	68.1	9.2
Van Buren	22	2.6	1	12	1	40	482	2	123	128	6	1 581	1 488	1 625	65.8	8.4
Wapello	224	5.7	48	133	1	220	608	7	616	1 978	56	5 304	6 909	7 675	65.0	9.9
Warren	120	3.3	10	27	0	0	0	8	489	966	37	2 684	6 998	8 306	78.4	13.9
Washington	66	3.3	7	35	1	76	376	6	385	454	28	2 305	3 421	3 770	69.1	11.8
Wayne	31	3.9	2	29	1	28	400	2	130	93	0	1 274	1 244	1 415	63.1	7.8
Webster	168	3.9	54	130	1	178	429	7	680	2 180	138	5 167	6 325	8 190	71.4	12.6
Winnebago	49	3.8	4	32	1	45	363	4	268	198	10	1 572	2 788	2 591	68.7	10.6
Winneshiek	48	2.1	14	64	1	83	377	3	243	341	6	1 572	2 605	3 922	61.5	13.3
Woodbury	431	4.3	180	182	2	795	803	12	1 176	7 270	568	7 443	17 220	18 126	71.7	14.9
Worth	19	2.1	2	23	0	0	0	2	150	182	4	2 092	1 246	1 722	67.1	8.2
Wright	61	3.8	9	62	2	54	372	5	329	217	18	1 467	2 792	3 103	70.6	10.2
KANSAS	12 905	5.3	4 312	172	161	16 361	651	399	26 544	116 589	8 734	4 747	415 105	422 884	73.3	17.0
Allen	108	6.7	9	61	1	50	340	6	359	329	19	2 142	2 785	2 858	65.4	12.0
Anderson	39	4.4	6	73	1	58	707	2	78	120	21	1 457	1 306	1 537	59.7	8.6
Atchison	98	5.4	19	107	1	141	792	2	150	539	19	3 033	2 541	3 137	69.0	13.1
Barber	27	3.8	2	33	2	66	1 082	1	50	93	9	1 403	1 203	1 141	70.1	12.3
Barton	180	5.4	35	119	3	370	1 254	4	379	991	77	3 143	5 013	5 641	70.8	12.4

1. Per 1,000 resident population estimated as of July 1 of the year shown. 2. As of end of year. 3. Per 100,000 resident population as of July 1 of the year shown. 4. Preliminary. Covers nursing homes with 3 or more beds. 5. Data for serious crimes have not been adjusted for underreporting, this may affect comparability between geographic areas or over time. 6. Includes murder and nonnegligent manslaughter, forcible rape, robbery, and aggravated assault. 7. The 1986–1987 data are based on administrative reports obtained by the U.S. National Center for Education Statistics. The 1980 data are based on the 1980 Census of Population and Housing. 8. Persons 25 years old or older.

STATE County	Education (cont'd) Local government expenditures for education,[1] 1982 Total (Mil dol)	Education (cont'd) Local government expenditures for education,[1] 1982 Per capita (Dollars)	Social Security Program December 1988 Beneficiaries Total	Social Security Program December 1988 Beneficiaries Rate[2]	Social Security Program December 1988 Payments ($1,000)	Supplemental Security Income Program recipients June 1986	Money income Per capita[3] 1987 Income, (Dollars)	Money income Per capita[3] 1979 Current dollars	Money income Per capita[3] 1979 Constant 1987 dollars	Money income Median household income 1979 (Dollars)	Money income Percent below poverty level, 1979 Persons	Money income Percent below poverty level, 1979 Families	Housing units, 1990 Total	Housing units, 1990 Percent change, 1980–1990
	60	61	62	63	64	65	66	67	68	69	70	71	72	73
IOWA—Con.														
Hancock	7.0	513	2 540	191.0	1 233	78	10 140	6 778	10 606	15 967	8.2	6.5	5 236	-3.2
Hardin	12.5	580	4 915	248.2	2 410	182	11 003	6 867	10 745	15 541	10.5	7.9	8 419	-4.3
Harrison	8.9	549	3 280	206.3	1 521	200	9 936	5 989	9 371	13 895	15.6	13.0	6 175	-2.9
Henry	10.5	560	3 780	201.1	1 867	154	10 374	6 689	10 466	15 662	8.2	6.1	7 507	3.7
Howard	6.6	600	2 445	232.9	1 026	154	10 531	6 398	10 011	13 795	14.8	10.6	4 155	-2.7
Humboldt	6.7	550	2 565	227.0	1 296	104	11 290	7 187	11 245	15 843	8.4	6.5	4 670	-6.9
Ida	4.0	465	2 010	233.7	917	94	10 840	6 764	10 584	13 632	14.2	11.7	3 473	-4.4
Iowa	8.3	542	3 135	213.3	1 506	78	11 499	6 965	10 898	17 063	8.0	6.6	6 003	2.2
Jackson	11.0	495	4 165	191.9	1 879	270	9 844	6 313	9 878	16 308	12.8	9.4	8 426	-1.6
Jasper	20.4	565	6 775	187.2	3 404	320	11 828	7 100	11 109	16 986	8.1	6.3	14 338	-0.8
Jefferson	6.2	382	2 790	167.1	1 350	124	10 147	6 185	9 678	14 162	12.3	9.5	6 739	11.7
Johnson	28.0	334	8 125	93.7	4 335	462	12 412	7 627	11 934	16 253	14.9	5.6	37 210	17.8
Jones	10.0	491	3 635	183.6	1 709	144	10 010	6 247	9 775	16 297	10.6	8.6	7 366	0.2
Keokuk	6.7	530	3 110	259.2	1 438	146	10 170	6 214	9 723	13 501	12.7	9.6	5 024	-6.9
Kossuth	9.1	419	4 100	208.1	1 975	166	9 659	6 544	10 239	15 373	12.0	10.1	7 765	-5.8
Lee	18.1	423	7 610	188.4	3 784	392	10 411	7 052	11 034	16 590	8.9	6.4	16 443	-1.4
Linn	87.6	519	25 815	150.5	13 599	1 376	12 382	8 094	12 665	20 084	6.8	4.9	68 357	5.5
Louisa	8.7	718	2 060	171.7	1 028	94	10 637	6 606	10 336	16 674	11.3	8.9	5 044	4.5
Lucas	4.2	409	2 295	241.6	1 028	202	9 774	5 949	9 308	12 073	15.9	11.9	4 179	-7.2
Lyon	6.1	483	2 485	203.7	1 131	80	9 350	6 251	9 781	14 776	13.3	10.6	4 561	-4.5
Madison	9.2	728	2 530	200.8	1 193	136	10 523	6 354	9 942	15 591	12.5	9.9	4 995	0.6
Mahaska	8.1	354	4 425	197.5	2 084	286	10 252	6 319	9 887	14 245	12.5	9.7	8 977	-3.7
Marion	14.0	465	5 640	186.8	2 608	266	10 550	6 553	10 253	16 549	9.6	7.7	11 420	3.6
Marshall	20.6	492	7 750	196.7	3 964	430	11 682	7 542	11 801	17 856	8.0	5.6	15 862	-2.9
Mills	6.3	466	2 480	185.1	1 157	506	11 080	6 469	10 122	16 417	9.2	7.3	5 004	3.6
Mitchell	5.6	466	2 800	243.5	1 312	92	11 252	6 881	10 767	14 450	12.8	9.9	4 514	-4.7
Monona	5.8	500	2 765	265.9	1 257	160	9 980	6 165	9 646	13 438	15.3	12.8	4 555	-6.6
Monroe	3.8	417	2 030	241.7	905	144	9 493	6 031	9 437	13 190	13.7	9.0	3 740	-2.1
Montgomery	5.9	448	3 030	248.4	1 449	160	10 734	6 797	10 635	14 830	9.4	6.8	5 363	-7.5
Muscatine	19.2	461	6 820	165.9	3 454	274	11 462	7 338	11 482	18 233	9.1	7.5	16 044	5.2
O'Brien	8.6	507	3 755	240.7	1 778	242	10 180	6 738	10 543	14 718	10.4	8.2	6 476	-2.7
Osceola	3.0	368	1 725	227.0	805	58	9 783	6 672	10 440	15 215	11.0	9.8	2 998	-8.2
Page	8.3	438	4 310	252.0	2 044	284	10 265	6 387	9 994	13 805	11.1	8.6	7 339	-9.1
Palo Alto	6.5	521	2 680	241.4	1 272	186	9 824	6 425	10 053	14 590	12.1	7.9	4 826	-8.0
Plymouth	11.5	471	4 580	190.0	2 153	186	11 257	6 714	10 505	15 889	11.8	9.1	8 806	-0.6
Pocahontas	6.1	552	2 490	241.7	1 218	92	10 245	6 928	10 840	14 611	12.4	9.5	4 193	-10.0
Polk	143.6	469	47 435	146.1	24 982	3 180	13 054	8 305	12 995	18 849	8.4	6.1	135 979	11.3
Pottawattamie	44.2	509	13 330	151.5	6 403	924	10 466	6 801	10 642	16 930	9.6	7.7	32 831	1.3
Poweshiek	8.6	451	3 690	195.2	1 842	140	11 266	6 519	10 200	15 566	11.6	8.9	8 199	1.5
Ringgold	3.2	538	1 405	260.2	583	126	8 628	5 318	8 321	10 011	24.7	20.8	2 713	-8.8
Sac	7.1	515	3 205	254.4	1 518	148	9 817	6 730	10 530	14 781	10.7	7.5	5 648	-7.0
Scott	80.1	498	21 675	139.5	11 134	1 346	12 165	8 226	12 871	20 767	7.9	5.9	61 379	2.7
Shelby	7.7	519	2 910	206.4	1 372	158	10 380	6 327	9 900	15 214	12.6	9.9	5 430	-3.2
Sioux	10.7	345	5 270	174.5	2 479	262	9 220	6 111	9 562	16 163	10.4	7.5	10 333	-0.8
Story	26.7	367	8 310	115.6	4 388	266	11 317	6 991	10 939	17 006	12.2	5.9	26 847	6.7
Tama	10.6	550	4 030	219.0	1 890	172	10 096	6 395	10 006	15 448	11.2	8.8	7 417	-3.9
Taylor	4.2	503	2 090	278.7	881	90	8 800	5 570	8 715	11 747	17.8	13.9	3 307	-10.2
Union	6.4	464	3 035	235.3	1 343	240	10 204	6 224	9 739	13 661	13.4	10.1	5 622	-2.2
Van Buren	4.4	518	1 995	243.3	870	106	8 635	5 156	8 068	11 569	19.6	15.0	3 529	1.3
Wapello	19.1	483	8 460	231.1	4 112	682	9 845	6 866	10 743	14 915	10.2	7.0	15 640	-4.3
Warren	17.4	495	4 525	123.3	2 227	174	11 030	7 035	11 008	20 087	6.6	5.4	13 157	8.0
Washington	9.3	460	4 275	212.7	2 064	148	10 819	6 631	10 376	15 043	13.0	10.2	7 866	2.2
Wayne	3.4	421	2 115	297.9	895	146	8 448	5 460	8 543	10 828	18.8	15.8	3 334	-13.4
Webster	19.7	435	8 795	210.9	4 474	498	10 825	7 164	11 210	16 369	9.4	7.1	17 063	-4.1
Winnebago	7.6	597	2 785	224.6	1 312	130	11 252	6 613	10 347	14 873	7.3	5.7	5 030	-4.2
Winneshiek	7.5	341	3 695	168.7	1 641	166	9 764	5 682	8 891	13 718	13.5	10.0	7 726	4.1
Woodbury	46.8	464	18 635	189.2	9 212	1 256	10 503	6 917	10 823	16 054	11.4	9.2	39 071	0.1
Worth	3.8	427	1 885	219.2	876	68	11 498	7 134	11 163	15 617	8.5	5.8	3 443	-7.5
Wright	8.8	550	3 675	250.0	1 833	162	11 436	7 214	11 288	15 633	10.3	7.5	6 636	-4.4
KANSAS	1 106.2	459	401 192	160.8	200 003	21 882	11 520	7 349	11 499	16 362	10.1	7.4	1 044 112	9.3
Allen	6.9	434	3 240	216.0	1 497	296	9 473	6 222	9 736	12 865	12.2	8.8	6 454	-5.6
Anderson	3.8	437	2 075	253.0	931	74	8 831	5 829	9 121	12 319	13.3	10.4	3 514	-3.1
Atchison	8.7	470	3 375	189.6	1 588	152	8 797	5 910	9 247	14 314	12.2	8.8	6 691	-3.2
Barber	3.7	531	1 470	233.3	743	74	10 185	7 612	11 910	14 581	11.7	8.6	3 120	2.9
Barton	13.7	416	5 685	187.6	2 957	168	10 611	7 217	11 292	16 292	8.4	6.2	13 144	2.1

1. Elementary and secondary. 2. Per 1,000 resident population estimated as of July 1 of the year shown. 3. Based on the resident population estimated as of July 1, 1988 for 1987 data and enumerated as of April 1, 1980 for 1979 data.

Table A. States and Counties — **Housing, Labor Force, and Employment**

STATE County	Housing units, 1990 (cont'd) — Occupied units — Total	Owner occupied — Percent	Owner occupied — Median value (Dollars)	Median rent (Dollars)	Civilian labor force, 1990 — Total	Percent change, 1989–1990	Unemployment — Total	Unemployment — Rate[1]	Private nonfarm establishments, 1988 — Number	Net change, 1987–1988	Employment[2] — Total	Per-cent change, 1987–1988	Manu-facturing	Retail trade
	74	75	76	77	78	79	80	81	82	83	84	85	86	87
IOWA—Con.														
Hancock	4 867	73.0	36 800	191	6 353	-1.2	406	6.4	319	-12	2 838	8.8	1 067	472
Hardin	7 611	71.9	33 800	192	9 561	-0.2	399	4.2	656	26	5 077	-4.8	1 040	1 303
Harrison	5 656	74.5	33 600	182	6 955	0.0	314	4.5	338	13	2 169	2.1	153	719
Henry	7 089	73.5	43 800	229	12 068	-1.7	375	3.1	473	3	7 160	6.8	1 850	1 741
Howard	3 856	78.0	30 400	152	4 933	-1.9	208	4.2	241	-7	1 736	-5.8	460	382
Humboldt	4 339	72.8	34 600	189	5 343	0.2	182	3.4	314	3	2 407	8.2	633	608
Ida	3 222	71.7	29 900	167	4 663	-1.6	125	2.7	242	2	2 443	15.2	857	489
Iowa	5 713	76.1	43 600	207	8 260	-4.2	237	2.9	407	2	5 972	-3.3	3 164	1 419
Jackson	7 527	73.7	41 200	189	10 802	-0.8	668	6.2	485	-16	3 554	5.6	825	1 072
Jasper	13 632	74.6	46 000	240	17 745	-1.1	698	3.9	747	-7	10 645	6.8	4 506	2 122
Jefferson	6 309	66.7	47 000	243	8 939	-3.0	386	4.3	515	-20	5 797	12.3	1 641	1 061
Johnson	36 067	52.7	76 900	360	61 922	-0.1	1 020	1.6	1 997	13	25 941	6.3	3 764	9 010
Jones	6 917	73.6	40 800	193	9 444	0.1	451	4.8	443	2	3 245	3.9	806	856
Keokuk	4 573	78.0	23 900	154	5 548	-4.6	286	5.2	277	-7	1 587	-10.1	225	351
Kossuth	7 194	73.1	33 900	175	8 989	-2.8	460	5.1	526	0	4 581	2.2	1 146	1 163
Lee	14 936	74.1	36 300	208	18 344	-0.5	1 302	7.1	1 022	-10	12 820	2.7	5 435	2 635
Linn	65 501	70.4	58 500	308	96 835	-0.9	4 989	5.2	4 411	63	78 591	2.5	24 527	16 498
Louisa	4 296	74.5	39 400	217	8 001	2.6	312	3.9	224	-2	2 654	34.4	0	433
Lucas	3 766	74.3	30 200	179	4 970	0.7	283	5.7	192	3	2 433	0.7	328	0
Lyon	4 289	77.1	31 800	144	6 162	-0.1	133	2.2	283	-5	1 650	3.3	266	436
Madison	4 715	73.5	42 800	218	6 164	-0.1	291	4.7	286	10	1 831	4.9	63	687
Mahaska	8 306	70.0	36 400	209	10 553	0.5	443	4.2	551	-7	5 274	6.4	958	1 643
Marion	10 815	73.9	48 200	240	16 217	-0.9	542	3.3	653	12	9 914	5.1	4 678	1 763
Marshall	14 890	71.2	42 100	241	19 979	-1.5	739	3.7	946	-5	12 978	1.9	4 579	2 862
Mills	4 665	74.8	47 000	229	5 432	-3.1	235	4.3	223	5	1 719	2.0	43	529
Mitchell	4 253	78.3	34 700	163	5 763	-1.2	210	3.6	326	12	2 153	-0.4	457	474
Monona	4 098	74.2	27 400	153	4 643	-2.9	194	4.2	285	-6	1 905	-0.8	141	550
Monroe	3 196	76.9	27 800	183	4 041	1.0	234	5.8	180	1	1 244	-6.7	186	361
Montgomery	4 955	71.7	35 200	184	6 320	-2.1	313	5.0	322	1	3 656	3.7	1 206	874
Muscatine	14 806	72.0	50 600	262	21 632	0.0	1 108	5.1	945	-31	16 538	3.8	8 673	2 761
O'Brien	5 980	75.0	32 700	171	8 006	-0.9	182	2.3	519	9	4 529	11.0	533	1 188
Osceola	2 817	74.7	28 000	167	3 531	-0.4	120	3.4	199	0	1 385	8.8	434	268
Page	6 687	70.6	33 700	173	8 504	0.7	422	5.0	496	-8	5 079	-1.6	1 571	1 467
Palo Alto	4 183	70.9	28 000	171	5 056	-3.5	169	3.3	315	7	1 923	1.3	205	509
Plymouth	8 417	74.8	48 800	214	12 571	0.5	374	3.0	617	-16	5 624	-1.6	801	1 458
Pocahontas	3 820	74.3	27 000	156	4 908	-0.9	122	2.5	299	-10	2 143	6.5	486	572
Polk	129 237	65.2	59 700	369	198 430	-0.4	6 465	3.3	9 638	55	184 627	7.4	25 940	36 853
Pottawattamie	31 262	71.1	46 900	299	48 198	-1.0	2 157	4.5	1 758	-18	21 601	4.7	3 755	6 665
Poweshiek	7 158	70.5	47 500	232	10 696	-2.1	374	3.5	528	4	6 913	9.1	1 703	1 192
Ringgold	2 218	75.4	22 000	155	2 456	-4.7	132	5.4	128	4	759	5.6	0	220
Sac	4 914	72.5	27 100	160	5 480	-3.7	274	5.0	362	-20	2 104	0.3	238	579
Scott	57 438	66.4	54 400	286	80 868	-2.4	4 118	5.1	3 943	40	58 830	1.7	12 841	14 644
Shelby	5 024	73.8	36 500	176	6 672	-2.6	291	4.4	388	7	3 261	1.4	337	783
Sioux	9 925	78.2	44 700	191	16 474	0.5	284	1.7	801	10	9 810	12.0	3 728	1 643
Story	25 941	56.0	63 900	334	42 145	-0.9	811	1.9	1 602	54	18 541	0.8	2 570	6 647
Tama	6 768	75.2	32 100	185	8 431	-4.9	412	4.9	381	16	3 054	2.5	664	849
Taylor	2 859	75.6	23 000	157	3 328	-0.9	134	4.0	181	2	1 475	32.8	477	364
Union	5 173	68.7	32 900	213	6 611	-0.2	308	4.7	342	5	3 670	7.8	698	1 087
Van Buren	3 056	77.7	21 300	143	3 395	-6.6	179	5.3	169	4	1 024	3.4	412	189
Wapello	14 555	75.6	27 000	219	15 669	-1.1	996	6.4	804	7	9 866	4.4	2 504	2 504
Warren	12 659	76.8	59 300	287	20 555	-0.2	559	2.7	582	8	4 828	1.9	392	1 339
Washington	7 454	71.8	43 000	215	9 495	-0.2	344	3.6	581	24	4 212	3.2	849	1 272
Wayne	2 953	75.8	19 900	137	3 231	-1.6	110	3.4	168	1	1 189	4.3	433	246
Webster	15 963	68.9	37 000	216	20 485	-1.5	1 007	4.9	1 147	-2	13 536	3.4	2 599	3 720
Winnebago	4 704	74.6	39 300	194	7 395	-3.2	429	5.8	327	8	6 267	13.9	0	697
Winneshiek	7 256	71.0	49 700	211	13 470	2.7	503	3.7	545	3	6 571	16.3	1 082	1 240
Woodbury	36 899	68.5	41 000	255	51 851	-0.8	2 119	4.1	2 646	-9	36 854	6.2	5 390	9 136
Worth	3 239	76.3	33 500	173	5 123	2.9	270	5.3	180	4	1 222	12.6	0	201
Wright	5 899	72.2	32 700	184	7 681	-3.7	282	3.7	436	3	3 994	2.5	1 267	820
KANSAS	944 726	67.9	52 200	285	1 300 000	1.2	57 000	4.4	X	X	834 617	2.9	192 883	189 031
Allen	5 705	75.1	27 600	174	7 259	2.7	400	5.5	372	-14	4 094	6.7	1 653	936
Anderson	3 067	77.9	27 200	159	3 819	1.4	230	6.0	195	-7	1 212	4.7	278	276
Atchison	6 129	73.1	32 400	184	7 480	-0.2	424	5.7	369	14	4 633	6.2	1 561	912
Barber	2 358	75.1	28 400	193	2 890	0.1	95	3.3	207	-15	1 500	23.6	22	359
Barton	11 561	72.3	37 700	211	14 605	1.2	581	4.0	1 050	-37	9 835	-0.7	1 857	2 429

1. Percent of total civilian labor force. 2. For week including March 12. Excludes government employees, self-employed persons, farm workers, domestic service workers, railroad employees subject to the Railroad Retirement Act, and employees on oceanborne vessels or in foreign countries.

STATE County	Private nonfarm establishments, 1988 (cont'd): Employment[1] (cont'd): Finance, insurance, and real estate	Employment[1] (cont'd): Services	Annual payroll: Total (Mil dol)	Annual payroll: Average per employee (Dollars)	Personal income, 1989: Total (Mil dol)	Percent change, 1988–1989	Wages and salaries[2] (Mil dol)	Proprietor's income (Mil dol)	Dividends, interest, & rent (Mil dol)	Transfer payments (Mil dol)	Per capita[3]: Dollars	Per capita[3]: Rank	Earnings, 1989: Total (Mil dol)	Percent by selected industries: Farm	Goods-related[4]: Total
	88	89	90	91	92	93	94	95	96	97	98	99	100	101	102
IOWA—Con.															
Hancock	147	591	43	15 291	198	11.2	65	54	48	27	14 864	1 045	119	32.8	24.6
Hardin	288	901	69	13 678	302	6.1	122	52	79	56	15 502	803	174	12.9	20.9
Harrison	145	571	27	12 542	216	12.2	55	50	42	42	13 439	1 717	105	33.6	8.5
Henry	239	2 522	116	16 231	308	10.0	170	32	58	44	16 115	611	202	5.2	29.4
Howard	116	437	24	13 563	149	8.5	48	36	39	25	14 237	1 309	83	26.6	20.5
Humboldt	151	467	35	14 365	183	13.7	58	56	43	28	16 383	550	114	33.1	16.8
Ida	82	500	39	15 953	131	6.1	56	33	31	20	15 328	864	89	21.6	29.7
Iowa	175	658	105	17 521	226	5.3	150	40	55	31	15 408	834	190	7.9	50.2
Jackson	229	893	41	11 400	292	9.1	82	56	66	51	13 475	1 699	139	19.5	20.6
Jasper	781	1 605	203	19 067	582	7.4	281	76	118	82	15 866	688	358	8.4	45.3
Jefferson	292	1 874	93	16 075	240	6.5	135	42	49	34	14 205	1 342	177	6.7	31.2
Johnson	1 464	8 457	385	14 853	1 572	9.9	1 131	150	230	149	17 890	309	1 281	1.3	14.6
Jones	149	657	44	13 489	254	8.2	90	42	62	41	12 831	1 987	132	14.3	NA
Keokuk	136	307	22	13 778	175	6.7	42	39	48	34	14 692	1 134	80	17.9	NA
Kossuth	372	889	67	14 547	299	11.9	103	94	70	43	15 386	840	197	32.5	18.9
Lee	445	2 696	240	18 730	574	8.4	380	65	112	105	14 232	1 314	445	2.2	46.4
Linn	5 264	19 027	1 669	21 242	2 980	7.8	2 237	217	508	355	17 143	416	2 454	0.7	39.1
Louisa	112	359	38	14 485	178	8.9	63	26	32	25	14 679	1 140	89	13.0	38.4
Lucas	152	310	42	17 283	135	9.1	65	14	29	28	14 350	1 268	79	7.5	11.0
Lyon	110	405	21	12 808	168	10.1	48	54	37	24	13 814	1 527	101	37.5	15.1
Madison	131	585	22	11 838	185	9.0	43	26	35	31	14 497	1 213	68	13.3	NA
Mahaska	287	1 363	70	13 315	305	6.0	107	50	68	53	13 529	1 666	157	15.5	21.4
Marion	249	2 034	187	18 814	494	7.3	300	76	95	74	16 108	616	376	5.2	44.1
Marshall	559	3 148	254	19 587	624	7.8	388	80	123	98	15 915	670	468	5.0	39.7
Mills	104	691	20	11 456	203	8.6	66	32	31	33	15 043	972	98	20.7	3.1
Mitchell	134	626	28	13 196	179	12.6	49	47	50	27	15 651	759	96	26.2	NA
Monona	115	691	24	12 345	153	10.4	42	48	32	32	14 789	1 084	90	37.3	7.7
Monroe	58	309	15	12 435	113	8.1	43	19	21	26	13 603	1 628	62	8.6	34.4
Montgomery	147	627	53	14 368	193	9.8	89	35	43	36	15 939	663	123	17.0	26.5
Muscatine	549	2 921	352	21 303	684	7.8	465	54	142	91	16 508	526	520	2.8	57.7
O'Brien	305	1 368	54	11 888	245	9.3	84	69	58	38	15 862	690	153	30.2	9.3
Osceola	84	271	19	13 944	117	13.8	31	40	27	17	15 522	795	71	40.3	17.9
Page	233	923	73	14 437	255	12.2	105	52	61	50	15 031	978	157	18.4	20.1
Palo Alto	111	668	22	11 686	174	12.3	48	54	38	29	15 971	653	102	38.6	6.3
Plymouth	321	1 180	90	15 991	350	12.3	131	75	82	48	14 348	1 269	206	16.3	22.5
Pocahontas	108	451	28	13 219	167	13.6	52	56	40	25	16 482	532	108	39.1	NA
Polk	31 973	50 617	3 673	19 897	6 187	8.8	5 027	540	930	759	18 679	241	5 567	0.3	18.0
Pottawattamie	1 191	6 284	318	14 711	1 287	7.3	546	130	181	216	14 509	1 208	676	7.1	16.7
Poweshiek	723	1 707	130	18 786	303	6.6	175	52	64	42	15 949	661	227	8.8	25.4
Ringgold	46	214	9	11 580	71	5.6	20	17	18	15	13 335	1 761	36	24.0	NA
Sac	138	544	24	11 639	197	8.4	47	64	49	34	15 741	725	111	40.5	6.4
Scott	3 523	17 221	1 176	19 985	2 634	7.8	1 593	281	408	375	16 930	451	1 874	0.7	31.2
Shelby	210	1 200	42	12 799	199	5.0	66	45	53	32	14 163	1 364	111	19.6	12.4
Sioux	375	2 660	122	12 475	424	14.5	187	114	90	55	13 996	1 437	301	20.3	27.8
Story	1 225	5 201	258	13 907	1 088	8.4	724	108	193	139	15 062	960	832	3.6	12.7
Tama	246	630	49	16 018	268	9.2	88	48	66	43	14 665	1 145	137	18.5	20.7
Taylor	63	238	16	11 110	94	11.2	21	23	24	21	12 813	1 993	43	29.8	NA
Union	199	1 062	49	13 315	182	8.0	97	22	41	39	14 088	1 394	119	5.4	26.3
Van Buren	78	162	12	12 005	95	5.6	27	16	21	21	11 503	2 495	42	17.3	NA
Wapello	413	3 197	177	17 898	505	8.8	299	52	86	117	13 934	1 456	351	2.6	35.5
Warren	248	1 906	59	12 277	550	8.3	111	56	69	63	14 712	1 120	167	12.5	13.8
Washington	283	960	60	14 127	289	7.1	98	57	77	45	14 283	1 294	156	15.4	24.2
Wayne	54	253	16	13 286	96	9.3	32	18	25	24	13 701	1 578	51	14.9	NA
Webster	535	4 153	211	15 606	627	9.1	332	93	132	116	15 105	940	425	10.2	21.3
Winnebago	125	909	104	16 523	214	7.1	137	47	47	28	17 253	404	184	16.8	49.4
Winneshiek	204	3 048	82	12 550	298	10.5	138	64	67	42	13 548	1 661	202	16.8	22.6
Woodbury	2 356	12 596	625	16 948	1 532	7.6	934	204	265	266	15 479	808	1 139	2.5	21.5
Worth	71	244	16	12 714	136	14.2	31	38	28	21	15 924	669	69	40.6	21.7
Wright	278	735	64	16 084	262	11.5	109	61	62	41	18 048	291	170	24.8	27.5
KANSAS	59 126	210 867	15 727	X	41 511	6.0	24 243	4 336	7 892	5 894	16 526	X	28 579	3.7	25.6
Allen	156	757	64	15 542	201	8.1	98	27	46	41	13 616	1 622	125	6.5	38.7
Anderson	85	282	14	11 820	113	9.1	29	18	29	23	13 900	1 475	47	16.8	17.8
Atchison	160	1 232	78	16 807	238	6.2	122	20	49	45	13 378	1 743	142	5.4	NA
Barber	100	394	22	14 445	101	0.4	40	23	26	18	16 560	512	63	19.2	20.9
Barton	437	2 312	157	15 981	473	2.8	248	60	114	76	16 038	637	308	4.7	27.5

1. For week including March 12. Excludes government employees, self-employed persons, farm workers, domestic service workers, railroad employees subject to the Railroad Retirement Act, and employees on oceanborne vessels or in foreign countries. 2. Includes other labor income. 3. Based on the resident population estimated as of July 1 of the year shown. 4. Covers mining, construction, and manufacturing.

STATE County	Earnings, 1989 (cont'd): Percent by selected industries (cont'd): Goods-related[1]: Manufacturing	Service-related & other[2]: Total	Service-related & other[2]: Retail trade	Service-related & other[2]: Finance, insurance, & real estate	Service-related & other[2]: Services	Government	Agriculture, 1987: Farms: Number	Farms: Percent with: Less than 50 acres	Farms: Percent with: 500 acres and over	Farm operators, percent: Whose principal occupation is farming	Farm operators, percent: Residing on farm operated	Land in farms: Acreage (1,000)	Land in farms: Percent change, 1982–1987	Acres: Average size of farm	Acres: Total irrigated (1,000)	Acres: Total cropland (1,000)
	103	104	105	106	107	108	109	110	111	112	113	114	115	116	117	118
IOWA—Con.																
Hancock	21.4	31.0	5.5	2.5	9.0	11.6	1 052	11.9	21.4	80.4	75.2	348	-1.0	331	1	328
Hardin	14.9	48.5	9.0	3.2	16.5	17.6	1 065	18.9	21.4	75.0	74.5	338	-5.0	317	D	305
Harrison	3.6	43.6	10.2	3.6	15.0	14.4	1 024	15.4	27.7	75.8	70.3	387	-5.2	378	16	329
Henry	24.8	49.0	18.5	2.5	17.0	16.5	893	19.0	15.2	63.7	71.7	232	-3.3	259	D	191
Howard	17.2	39.1	6.5	2.9	16.8	13.8	938	16.0	15.7	78.1	77.6	269	-3.4	287	D	241
Humboldt	13.8	38.8	6.8	3.9	14.3	11.2	754	11.4	23.6	77.9	70.3	275	0.0	365	0	259
Ida	25.0	39.6	7.0	3.0	12.8	9.1	787	16.1	21.9	77.8	71.5	260	0.2	330	0	234
Iowa	46.1	34.5	10.4	1.7	12.0	7.4	1 057	15.5	16.9	75.3	75.3	330	-8.8	312	D	287
Jackson	14.8	43.3	10.4	3.3	16.2	16.6	1 354	18.1	13.7	67.1	78.9	346	-0.5	255	0	246
Jasper	41.6	35.3	7.7	2.7	14.6	10.9	1 465	23.8	19.0	67.2	75.7	427	-4.5	292	D	367
Jefferson	27.5	50.9	9.8	4.8	26.8	11.2	775	15.9	19.1	67.6	73.2	235	-5.3	303	0	190
Johnson	10.1	37.4	7.8	2.7	20.2	46.7	1 356	23.7	11.9	65.4	75.7	306	-6.9	225	0	265
Jones	17.5	NA	10.3	3.4	17.2	18.6	1 161	18.2	16.8	72.6	77.1	322	-4.3	278	D	266
Keokuk	6.7	NA	7.7	4.4	21.5	13.0	1 036	17.6	21.9	72.9	74.8	343	-2.1	331	0	281
Kossuth	14.1	39.1	7.7	4.9	12.4	9.5	1 718	10.3	20.7	82.0	75.5	599	-2.0	349	0	563
Lee	42.4	40.2	8.1	2.3	16.4	11.2	989	18.5	15.5	57.1	77.4	266	-0.2	269	1	201
Linn	33.4	50.5	9.2	5.4	21.9	9.6	1 690	27.6	11.5	57.9	76.9	356	-3.4	211	0	308
Louisa	34.3	33.5	5.8	3.3	12.0	15.1	634	17.7	20.2	72.9	73.5	199	-4.7	314	3	168
Lucas	8.1	64.6	40.9	3.3	10.7	16.9	690	16.4	16.5	61.0	76.2	207	-5.9	299	D	148
Lyon	11.2	36.3	6.6	2.4	14.2	11.1	1 234	16.9	14.2	81.0	76.7	343	-4.1	278	1	312
Madison	5.3	NA	10.3	3.6	22.9	19.5	1 059	22.1	16.9	58.1	70.5	294	-6.4	277	0	213
Mahaska	14.7	50.0	11.2	4.2	22.2	13.1	1 193	18.4	15.9	73.8	75.7	328	-2.4	275	D	277
Marion	39.9	35.6	6.2	1.7	14.3	15.0	1 131	24.7	13.8	59.4	74.5	279	-4.5	247	0	223
Marshall	35.9	41.2	7.4	2.5	19.7	14.2	1 073	20.9	21.8	71.1	75.6	330	-2.3	308	0	294
Mills	0.5	36.2	7.3	2.7	16.2	40.0	641	19.8	28.7	73.2	71.5	245	-3.5	383	1	219
Mitchell	13.8	NA	7.8	3.9	18.9	11.6	939	19.9	16.9	72.0	75.9	271	-0.9	288	1	248
Monona	3.8	42.6	8.9	3.3	19.7	12.5	854	11.9	31.6	76.7	64.9	377	-0.4	441	25	321
Monroe	21.6	42.5	8.8	3.5	18.3	14.5	736	13.7	18.8	58.0	70.8	225	1.3	306	D	147
Montgomery	19.1	43.8	8.1	3.3	14.1	12.6	701	14.6	26.0	75.5	72.8	248	-2.2	354	D	218
Muscatine	53.7	28.8	6.3	1.8	13.2	10.7	901	24.5	16.4	60.6	76.5	233	-2.1	259	3	199
O'Brien	4.3	49.0	9.5	4.3	17.8	11.5	1 232	15.7	16.2	79.3	74.7	362	-0.2	294	0	332
Osceola	13.2	33.9	5.1	4.0	13.3	7.9	731	14.8	16.8	79.5	79.2	231	-6.3	316	1	216
Page	16.1	44.3	12.2	3.5	17.4	17.1	1 015	15.5	24.1	68.9	71.9	338	1.4	333	2	285
Palo Alto	3.3	38.5	6.1	3.3	15.5	16.6	934	12.4	27.3	78.1	71.1	344	-0.4	368	5	321
Plymouth	17.8	50.4	9.7	4.6	18.2	10.8	1 740	16.0	17.4	75.9	78.0	521	0.7	300	2	465
Pocahontas	13.0	NA	4.2	2.9	12.1	10.3	987	10.5	24.9	80.6	72.6	349	-2.2	354	D	331
Polk	13.3	68.5	9.2	16.0	25.3	13.2	1 001	38.9	14.2	51.9	70.2	238	-3.6	238	D	214
Pottawattamie	11.8	60.8	12.7	3.7	25.0	15.4	1 652	22.7	23.6	69.4	73.1	544	-2.1	329	2	488
Poweshiek	19.3	58.0	7.3	8.7	24.8	7.9	1 047	17.8	21.9	73.0	74.5	335	-5.7	320	D	296
Ringgold	4.4	46.6	10.1	2.9	20.4	19.8	701	11.3	28.4	74.6	73.2	285	-9.1	407	D	225
Sac	2.9	42.3	6.8	3.6	14.9	10.8	1 035	13.1	23.1	80.0	71.5	360	0.1	348	1	322
Scott	25.8	58.9	10.9	4.5	28.1	9.2	973	24.4	12.7	65.4	77.0	230	-3.6	237	0	210
Shelby	4.7	53.3	9.6	4.2	20.7	14.7	1 177	15.5	18.5	78.2	74.3	351	-1.5	299	D	322
Sioux	23.1	43.2	7.9	3.3	17.5	8.7	2 015	24.2	10.5	73.9	74.9	472	0.5	234	9	439
Story	8.2	35.9	8.9	2.5	18.1	47.8	1 138	24.3	20.5	63.9	69.3	327	-3.3	287	0	302
Tama	16.7	NA	7.9	3.1	NA	15.0	1 404	17.3	19.0	72.8	76.8	417	-0.6	297	D	368
Taylor	5.0	42.3	7.7	3.4	19.0	18.2	774	11.1	26.6	71.8	71.6	291	-0.4	376	0	229
Union	22.4	46.6	11.8	2.9	16.9	21.6	693	19.5	21.9	62.9	78.1	234	-0.8	337	D	177
Van Buren	17.8	NA	8.0	3.9	14.7	21.5	783	13.7	19.7	61.0	74.1	245	-9.5	313	0	166
Wapello	31.1	46.8	9.8	2.4	23.1	15.0	899	23.0	14.0	53.9	78.9	212	-5.0	235	D	162
Warren	6.0	55.7	11.5	3.6	27.7	18.0	1 310	28.3	13.8	48.5	75.2	304	-5.3	232	0	235
Washington	16.2	46.8	10.8	4.1	17.8	13.6	1 158	20.5	16.9	75.3	75.4	322	-4.8	278	0	279
Wayne	17.9	46.8	8.6	2.8	15.5	16.8	743	13.5	28.1	72.7	70.9	281	-3.1	379	0	218
Webster	17.3	54.7	10.9	3.1	25.1	13.7	1 235	15.6	22.9	73.0	67.5	417	-0.7	337	D	384
Winnebago	47.0	25.4	4.4	2.4	11.2	8.4	742	13.9	21.6	78.4	75.5	242	-1.7	327	D	225
Winneshiek	13.9	45.9	8.5	2.8	22.7	14.7	1 633	15.8	8.5	77.5	80.2	377	-5.9	231	D	301
Woodbury	15.5	64.2	10.0	5.2	31.2	11.8	1 360	21.5	21.7	69.3	73.2	452	-5.6	332	5	399
Worth	15.3	27.7	4.4	3.1	9.4	10.0	667	18.9	24.9	77.8	78.9	222	-5.4	332	D	206
Wright	23.8	37.9	6.7	3.5	12.3	9.8	882	11.6	28.9	79.5	72.6	344	-4.6	390	D	323
KANSAS	19.1	53.1	9.6	5.5	22.0	17.6	68 579	14.5	38.6	62.1	66.4	46 629	-0.9	680	2 463	31 385
Allen	32.5	37.1	9.1	3.1	17.4	17.7	665	13.8	24.1	61.2	74.1	277	-2.6	416	D	189
Anderson	9.9	43.8	9.3	4.7	17.5	21.6	727	14.6	32.2	59.1	70.7	352	-2.5	484	1	231
Atchison	31.8	NA	7.6	2.8	19.0	14.9	694	18.2	21.0	61.4	72.2	234	-0.5	337	0	178
Barber	12.4	44.4	7.8	3.5	14.5	15.5	535	13.1	56.8	68.6	50.3	700	0.2	1 309	3	255
Barton	13.1	55.0	11.1	4.3	22.4	12.7	937	14.8	40.6	64.9	62.9	556	-0.6	594	29	487

1. Covers mining, construction, and manufacturing. 2. Covers private sector earnings in agricultural services, forestry, and fisheries; transportation and public utilities; wholesale trade; retail trade; finance, insurance, and real estate; and services.

STATE County	Agriculture, 1987 (cont'd): Value of land and buildings: Average per farm ($1,000)	Value of land and buildings: Average per acre (Dollars)	Value of products sold: Total (Mil dol)	Value of products sold: Average per farm (Dollars)	Value of products sold: Percent from Crops	Value of products sold: Percent from Livestock and poultry[1]	Percent of farms with sales of $10,000 or more	Percent of farms with sales of $100,000 or more	Manufactures, 1987: Establishments: Total	Establishments: Percent with 20 or more employees	All employees: Number (1,000)	All employees: Percent change, 1982–1987	All employees: Annual payroll (Mil dol)	Production workers: Number (1,000)	Production workers: Work hours (Mil)
	119	120	121	122	123	124	125	126	127	128	129	130	131	132	133
IOWA—Con.															
Hancock	376	1 117	98	92 920	54.1	45.9	88.2	32.8	22	40.9	0.9	28.6	16.7	0.7	1.3
Hardin	343	1 026	115	108 422	46.7	53.3	86.5	34.4	33	42.4	1.2	0.0	20.0	0.9	1.8
Harrison	313	839	82	79 604	61.2	38.8	80.6	24.6	11	36.4	0.1	0.0	2.5	0.1	0.2
Henry	274	979	56	62 367	41.5	58.5	68.0	18.0	26	38.5	1.6	60.0	32.4	1.2	2.4
Howard	209	737	67	71 186	42.7	57.3	83.2	21.0	19	10.5	0.4	33.3	8.7	0.3	0.6
Humboldt	396	1 089	78	103 164	58.2	41.8	90.8	32.5	21	38.1	0.5	25.0	9.6	0.4	0.8
Ida	340	956	80	102 026	37.0	63.0	87.5	29.4	12	33.3	0.7	75.0	15.9	0.4	1.1
Iowa	263	873	91	86 376	37.4	62.6	80.3	24.6	27	29.6	D	D	D	D	D
Jackson	188	794	94	69 219	15.6	84.4	75.3	20.0	32	40.6	0.8	33.3	12.9	0.7	1.4
Jasper	264	928	120	81 697	42.3	57.7	75.6	27.4	48	29.2	D	D	D	D	D
Jefferson	242	818	44	56 936	46.6	53.4	67.6	16.4	44	34.1	1.4	-17.6	27.5	1.0	2.0
Johnson	254	1 167	95	69 959	29.5	70.5	71.3	19.9	76	23.7	3.7	12.1	84.5	2.5	4.6
Jones	273	977	110	94 343	25.4	74.6	80.0	28.3	31	32.3	0.7	0.0	14.1	0.5	1.1
Keokuk	299	843	85	82 373	39.7	60.3	74.6	28.0	16	6.2	D	D	D	D	D
Kossuth	405	1 158	173	100 952	57.7	42.3	91.6	33.1	17	35.3	1.1	22.2	24.6	0.9	1.8
Lee	227	810	57	57 389	32.9	67.1	61.5	16.3	60	43.3	5.0	-24.2	129.0	3.6	7.1
Linn	245	1 147	93	54 922	46.2	53.8	65.7	14.9	234	38.9	23.4	-7.9	669.8	11.4	23.0
Louisa	345	1 104	42	66 674	54.7	45.3	76.8	22.6	15	20.0	D	D	D	D	D
Lucas	146	468	23	33 503	32.5	67.5	55.4	10.0	7	57.1	0.3	0.0	5.3	0.2	0.4
Lyon	284	981	136	109 897	28.6	71.4	89.5	31.6	16	18.8	0.2	0.0	3.8	0.2	0.4
Madison	221	778	57	54 144	37.2	62.8	59.7	13.4	7	14.3	0.1	0.0	1.0	0.0	0.1
Mahaska	291	1 059	112	93 704	32.1	67.9	79.7	29.1	25	32.0	0.8	-20.0	16.6	0.6	1.2
Marion	183	785	64	56 336	41.3	58.7	65.3	17.2	35	37.1	4.4	25.7	111.7	3.5	7.2
Marshall	314	1 041	90	84 146	55.0	45.0	78.2	26.3	50	40.0	4.5	-25.0	131.2	2.7	5.3
Mills	278	773	55	85 976	57.4	42.6	75.0	26.2	5	0.0	D	D	D	D	D
Mitchell	259	923	96	102 443	35.3	64.7	81.6	31.9	17	17.6	D	D	D	D	D
Monona	357	773	75	87 869	57.6	42.4	81.9	27.4	8	12.5	0.1	0.0	2.0	0.1	0.1
Monroe	139	432	27	37 322	25.6	74.4	59.4	8.7	8	62.5	0.2	-66.7	2.9	0.2	0.3
Montgomery	237	672	54	77 273	52.9	47.1	79.7	24.4	14	42.9	1.2	9.1	21.6	1.0	1.8
Muscatine	289	1 145	54	60 275	45.7	54.3	67.9	19.1	81	53.1	8.3	5.1	217.9	5.9	11.9
O'Brien	362	1 199	157	127 204	33.8	66.2	90.2	32.6	23	34.8	0.5	25.0	6.9	0.3	0.7
Osceola	340	1 063	74	101 739	47.1	52.9	90.3	30.0	11	36.4	0.4	33.3	5.9	0.3	0.6
Page	211	624	73	71 746	50.6	49.4	75.7	21.4	24	33.3	1.4	7.7	31.7	1.1	2.2
Palo Alto	378	1 096	92	98 145	57.5	42.5	89.0	32.5	13	30.8	D	D	D	D	D
Plymouth	292	1 047	184	105 525	29.7	70.3	84.5	31.4	23	30.4	D	D	D	D	D
Pocahontas	402	1 123	94	95 364	55.5	44.5	90.4	29.1	27	25.9	0.5	25.0	9.2	0.3	0.6
Polk	314	1 211	55	55 436	71.7	28.3	57.9	17.5	425	32.7	D	D	D	D	D
Pottawattamie	297	909	149	90 047	48.9	51.1	75.1	27.0	75	34.7	D	D	D	D	D
Poweshiek	289	928	81	77 490	44.6	55.4	79.6	27.5	34	41.2	1.6	14.3	32.6	1.2	2.2
Ringgold	186	480	39	55 093	33.8	66.2	71.9	15.5	4	25.0	0.1	-50.0	1.1	0.1	0.1
Sac	357	1 071	130	125 547	35.4	64.6	90.2	34.5	25	12.0	0.2	-50.0	3.2	0.2	0.3
Scott	362	1 527	82	83 792	39.7	60.3	75.2	25.3	193	32.1	13.5	-16.1	421.6	9.5	19.4
Shelby	278	915	109	92 263	40.9	59.1	87.7	27.3	11	36.4	D	D	D	D	D
Sioux	282	1 181	349	173 001	15.8	84.2	88.3	39.1	59	32.2	3.1	19.2	48.2	2.4	4.2
Story	350	1 237	102	89 445	54.3	45.7	77.8	25.1	58	32.8	2.5	-13.8	52.6	1.7	3.3
Tama	287	977	106	75 244	51.9	48.1	79.4	24.5	20	20.0	D	D	D	D	D
Taylor	181	511	40	52 244	45.5	54.5	72.9	14.3	7	28.6	0.2	-33.3	2.9	0.2	0.3
Union	186	556	40	57 186	33.0	67.0	66.4	13.7	16	43.8	0.7	-41.7	15.4	0.5	0.9
Van Buren	161	531	33	42 084	41.4	58.6	62.6	11.1	12	50.0	0.4	33.3	5.9	0.3	0.6
Wapello	156	723	35	39 416	48.0	52.0	54.7	11.6	26	46.2	2.1	0.0	69.5	1.5	3.0
Warren	182	806	55	41 961	42.2	57.8	52.8	11.2	22	31.8	0.4	33.3	6.8	0.2	0.4
Washington	267	1 044	113	97 829	29.2	70.8	80.4	30.6	26	26.9	0.8	-20.0	18.4	0.6	1.2
Wayne	184	488	35	46 608	41.7	58.3	68.9	12.0	10	50.0	0.4	0.0	6.7	0.2	0.5
Webster	432	1 289	112	90 805	64.1	35.9	83.7	27.0	57	42.1	2.7	-18.2	58.4	1.5	3.3
Winnebago	367	1 132	58	77 548	63.6	36.4	85.6	26.7	17	35.3	D	D	D	D	D
Winneshiek	192	846	121	73 828	17.5	82.5	80.1	25.7	26	34.6	1.1	57.1	17.1	0.9	1.3
Woodbury	256	769	127	93 709	37.5	62.5	75.1	25.4	101	50.5	D	D	D	D	D
Worth	318	1 043	56	83 964	57.1	42.8	81.0	28.8	12	16.7	0.3	50.0	5.1	0.3	0.6
Wright	505	1 235	85	96 409	69.1	30.9	90.2	32.4	31	41.9	1.1	22.2	22.9	0.8	1.4
KANSAS	278	413	6 477	94 441	26.1	73.9	62.3	13.7	3 275	34.8	189.1	10.8	4 597.2	120.7	245.3
Allen	178	445	23	34 624	51.0	49.0	53.5	8.4	25	32.0	1.6	6.7	30.0	1.1	2.2
Anderson	172	352	34	47 078	49.0	51.0	61.1	11.3	12	33.3	0.3	0.0	3.0	0.2	0.4
Atchison	176	564	26	37 842	53.8	46.2	62.1	9.4	21	57.1	1.6	-5.9	37.6	1.3	2.3
Barber	371	298	46	85 448	21.1	78.9	71.2	21.1	3	0.0	0.0	0.0	0.1	0.0	0.0
Barton	260	451	125	133 529	19.2	80.8	65.8	9.4	44	22.7	1.9	-5.0	32.6	1.2	2.2

1. Includes livestock and poultry products.

STATE County	Manufactures, 1987 (cont'd) — Production workers (cont'd) — Wages — Total (Mil dol)	Manufactures, 1987 (cont'd) — Production workers (cont'd) — Wages — Average per worker (Dollars)	Value added by manufacture (Mil dol)	Value of shipments (Mil dol)	New capital expenditures (Mil dol)	Value of construction authorized by building permits, 1990 — Total[1] ($1,000)	Nonresidential — Total ($1,000)	Nonresidential — Percent — Office	Nonresidential — Percent — Industrial	Nonresidential — Percent — Stores	Residential — New construction ($1,000)	Residential — Number of housing units	Residential — Alterations and additions ($1,000)
	134	135	136	137	138	139	140	141	142	143	144	145	146
IOWA—Con.													
Hancock	10.9	15 571	24.0	68.8	2.0	865	159	0.0	31.5	0.0	610	11	43
Hardin	13.7	15 222	59.8	275.3	1.6	5 676	3 477	0.0	0.0	63.4	458	7	375
Harrison	1.5	15 000	5.8	10.0	0.2	1 397	256	39.1	0.0	46.5	689	14	138
Henry	21.6	18 000	165.2	290.3	10.8	5 773	1 597	0.0	38.8	53.5	3 449	63	237
Howard	6.5	21 667	28.5	72.1	0.9	1 703	781	0.0	89.0	0.0	649	10	96
Humboldt	6.3	15 750	20.1	39.1	1.0	2 629	1 147	0.0	66.4	0.0	1 034	15	158
Ida	8.3	20 750	47.1	101.8	3.3	3 293	2 271	12.9	85.1	0.0	749	21	83
Iowa	D	D	D	D	D	1 508	690	0.0	0.0	92.9	524	9	88
Jackson	9.5	13 571	33.2	105.2	1.0	4 954	2 636	3.6	54.9	16.2	1 034	18	189
Jasper	D	D	D	D	D	8 781	1 581	17.1	31.8	24.4	4 775	87	838
Jefferson	18.5	18 500	64.1	116.5	3.4	2 793	512	29.3	0.0	55.5	795	11	178
Johnson	54.3	21 720	614.1	985.1	21.6	77 750	17 948	44.9	5.9	5.7	47 680	619	2 589
Jones	9.3	18 600	57.5	107.1	2.4	2 135	919	66.4	3.3	8.7	838	12	158
Keokuk	D	D	D	D	D	1 099	593	0.0	0.0	0.0	266	4	47
Kossuth	18.8	20 889	51.5	139.2	2.9	4 853	1 871	0.0	6.9	17.1	264	5	144
Lee	86.7	24 083	427.4	964.7	14.7	7 096	3 103	7.2	10.3	75.4	883	15	635
Linn	289.3	25 377	2 110.7	3 862.5	117.1	103 405	24 086	15.0	31.5	37.3	43 797	682	8 638
Louisa	D	D	D	D	D	1 937	311	0.0	23.5	3.2	1 282	35	118
Lucas	3.5	17 500	9.3	16.3	0.3	635	167	0.0	75.0	7.2	286	3	71
Lyon	2.7	13 500	7.3	13.4	0.3	1 533	558	0.0	3.6	76.6	721	10	68
Madison	0.7	NA	2.0	3.7	0.1	2 069	592	0.0	0.0	1.0	1 159	25	124
Mahaska	9.6	16 000	56.1	89.8	2.9	2 308	277	0.0	0.0	36.1	1 501	21	238
Marion	86.6	24 743	350.4	654.4	16.6	5 516	1 766	6.8	27.0	24.6	3 165	49	208
Marshall	68.0	25 185	235.5	652.1	11.6	9 537	2 567	3.0	0.0	25.0	3 014	37	829
Mills	D	D	D	D	D	448	0	NA	NA	NA	270	6	80
Mitchell	D	D	D	D	D	2 420	741	0.0	73.0	27.0	1 115	22	229
Monona	1.0	10 000	5.1	9.0	D	2 618	1 648	28.7	0.0	2.7	644	8	212
Monroe	2.3	11 500	6.8	9.1	0.1	497	35	0.0	0.0	100.0	305	5	2
Montgomery	15.6	15 600	60.2	118.0	2.5	1 441	517	24.2	42.2	8.4	551	7	145
Muscatine	137.0	23 220	682.2	1 614.5	29.7	16 799	8 860	4.4	73.6	1.7	5 278	73	1 114
O'Brien	4.6	15 333	27.1	135.1	1.1	3 169	713	9.8	16.0	16.8	2 256	26	89
Osceola	4.7	15 667	45.2	116.2	D	2 557	890	0.0	84.3	0.0	238	5	47
Page	23.3	21 182	157.4	239.6	5.3	3 548	2 214	0.0	90.4	1.1	998	40	100
Palo Alto	D	D	D	D	D	468	27	0.0	0.0	0.0	265	4	64
Plymouth	D	D	D	D	D	9 581	4 672	0.0	24.0	8.7	4 120	78	274
Pocahontas	4.8	16 000	17.8	53.9	0.4	2 272	1 266	0.0	99.9	0.0	399	4	42
Polk	D	D	D	D	D	293 929	77 997	39.3	0.6	26.6	154 469	2 280	10 284
Pottawattamie	D	D	D	D	D	28 965	6 110	22.0	7.2	39.9	12 098	169	2 640
Poweshiek	19.2	16 000	74.8	141.6	4.8	4 895	905	0.0	7.7	28.1	2 635	48	469
Ringgold	0.7	7 000	2.2	3.9	D	146	20	0.0	0.0	0.0	85	2	22
Sac	2.2	11 000	16.2	29.1	0.3	2 527	1 948	0.0	0.0	2.0	240	3	90
Scott	274.9	28 937	929.8	2 801.5	106.8	113 976	32 943	5.0	59.6	21.7	45 816	439	3 781
Shelby	D	D	D	D	D	1 848	370	37.8	0.0	4.9	889	11	176
Sioux	32.3	13 458	98.6	453.4	8.7	12 484	3 611	0.0	37.2	35.6	6 054	100	441
Story	32.5	19 118	203.5	405.4	7.8	33 046	5 637	54.7	14.5	14.9	17 127	290	1 273
Tama	D	D	D	D	D	2 405	424	20.5	0.0	0.0	1 409	35	226
Taylor	2.1	10 500	5.0	10.3	0.2	164	0	NA	NA	NA	110	2	15
Union	8.4	16 800	26.3	55.5	1.3	1 845	965	9.8	20.2	10.4	135	2	451
Van Buren	4.5	15 000	11.2	20.5	D	706	15	0.0	0.0	0.0	460	11	182
Wapello	44.4	29 600	306.2	643.9	D	7 504	3 200	12.5	3.3	68.2	1 458	29	1 139
Warren	3.4	17 000	23.2	45.1	1.1	21 920	922	14.1	7.8	19.5	17 974	256	564
Washington	11.7	19 500	46.1	102.1	1.0	4 928	1 446	0.0	11.8	87.6	2 473	57	314
Wayne	3.0	15 000	28.3	59.5	2.1	0	0	NA	NA	NA	0	0	0
Webster	30.9	20 600	221.7	394.3	13.2	10 513	1 269	3.9	6.3	0.0	2 078	28	1 096
Winnebago	D	D	D	D	D	3 390	2 133	3.5	11.7	1.6	900	11	72
Winneshiek	12.3	13 667	40.1	129.7	2.1	8 184	2 616	3.4	39.1	27.1	2 652	36	353
Woodbury	D	D	D	D	D	32 455	11 935	10.0	3.0	30.0	8 128	202	1 638
Worth	3.8	12 667	13.6	23.1	D	389	70	0.0	100.0	0.0	244	9	17
Wright	15.3	19 125	42.3	248.5	2.4	2 856	1 531	0.0	11.9	63.2	588	9	78
KANSAS	2 608.5	21 611	12 908.8	31 055.8	1 011.2	1 384 068	307 969	20.6	24.5	26.8	661 281	8 496	65 512
Allen	20.0	18 182	79.8	161.4	3.1	1 756	524	35.0	0.0	0.0	656	10	176
Anderson	2.4	12 000	7.8	20.0	0.1	970	456	71.4	11.0	1.4	422	7	41
Atchison	25.8	19 846	73.5	166.9	2.0	2 344	1 226	0.0	41.4	15.2	887	13	108
Barber	0.1	NA	0.3	0.5	0.0	159	56	0.0	0.0	17.7	0	0	54
Barton	18.4	15 333	83.5	148.9	D	5 491	610	27.0	0.0	0.0	774	8	773

1. Includes nonresidential additions and alterations, residential nonhousekeeping buildings, and residential garages and carports not shown separately.

STATE County	Wholesale trade, 1987				Retail trade, all establishments, 1987				Retail trade, establishments with payroll, 1987					
						Sales				Sales				
											Per capita[2] (Dollars)			
	Establishments	Sales (Mil dol)	Paid employees[1]	Annual payroll (Mil dol)	Number	Total (Mil dol)	Percent change, 1982–1987	Per capita[2] (Dollars)	Number	Total (Mil dol)	General merchandise stores	Food stores	Apparel & accessory stores	Eating and drinking places
	147	148	149	150	151	152	153	154	155	156	157	158	159	160
IOWA—Con.														
Hancock	53	130.0	348	7.1	151	33.8	17.4	2 560	81	31.4	25	625	186	198
Hardin	69	314.3	858	16.6	310	92.1	-7.7	4 584	192	89.2	D	1 230	151	281
Harrison	34	96.9	296	4.8	201	72.1	18.6	4 562	115	67.9	D	466	13	271
Henry	43	78.3	337	5.1	223	89.1	22.4	4 716	134	86.6	D	1 111	115	377
Howard	27	95.0	267	4.0	124	32.9	-2.9	3 103	79	31.4	180	1 005	88	224
Humboldt	40	113.9	250	4.8	155	45.3	4.6	4 011	89	43.1	D	1 273	175	317
Ida	27	77.5	175	3.3	104	37.4	28.5	4 354	67	35.5	D	985	74	250
Iowa	40	54.3	275	4.2	243	83.1	29.6	5 617	152	80.4	D	1 254	218	1 096
Jackson	57	89.9	322	4.1	299	87.2	31.7	3 998	158	81.8	D	1 078	129	289
Jasper	63	258.2	685	12.3	356	163.6	24.1	4 557	218	159.5	451	1 048	180	357
Jefferson	49	76.0	374	6.1	240	86.7	35.7	5 254	133	81.9	800	1 247	279	318
Johnson	91	300.2	1 004	20.4	831	540.1	46.1	6 310	597	527.1	803	1 426	267	748
Jones	55	84.9	404	5.7	245	71.1	22.2	3 608	133	67.5	532	758	13	178
Keokuk	56	100.2	277	5.3	161	37.8	23.1	3 146	71	32.5	D	541	41	136
Kossuth	78	284.4	560	9.4	250	84.9	-0.9	4 289	155	80.6	D	936	156	415
Lee	81	143.0	599	9.0	469	221.8	24.1	5 464	302	216.3	668	1 459	118	372
Linn	432	1 731.6	4 639	101.5	1 700	1 162.2	39.9	6 868	1 100	1 138.1	1 098	1 299	277	680
Louisa	17	54.1	160	2.9	144	32.9	2.8	2 763	74	30.5	D	564	26	216
Lucas	15	31.8	146	1.5	120	31.7	-25.9	3 304	66	30.5	D	D	167	323
Lyon	35	92.2	214	3.6	137	32.7	6.5	2 684	80	29.7	D	474	130	210
Madison	23	40.9	144	2.5	149	52.8	19.2	4 220	90	50.9	D	935	130	459
Mahaska	62	206.1	562	10.0	286	109.6	24.7	4 936	167	103.3	570	1 318	357	427
Marion	53	128.1	428	6.8	329	122.4	39.1	4 093	203	115.2	437	927	168	347
Marshall	86	141.7	730	14.7	450	217.0	17.3	5 493	283	211.4	859	1 279	216	487
Mills	20	27.8	117	1.8	123	42.2	12.5	3 200	63	40.8	D	865	D	227
Mitchell	41	100.9	290	4.5	146	40.2	10.7	3 496	91	38.8	57	766	94	365
Monona	38	82.8	253	4.0	153	43.8	-0.9	4 168	96	41.5	D	766	64	334
Monroe	17	41.1	86	1.1	102	32.0	26.0	3 807	55	29.8	D	1 124	62	116
Montgomery	37	95.6	258	3.6	155	59.4	4.4	4 869	96	56.9	707	1 251	106	361
Muscatine	76	162.9	415	7.2	435	203.7	12.3	4 980	275	198.4	626	1 143	222	451
O'Brien	58	233.0	464	9.1	241	87.5	17.4	5 610	148	83.8	D	1 241	290	416
Osceola	22	36.5	153	2.1	94	20.0	-4.8	2 604	54	18.6	D	528	110	177
Page	40	89.8	491	4.6	255	97.7	16.2	5 681	171	93.6	764	775	311	316
Palo Alto	28	121.4	225	4.3	148	42.9	3.6	3 828	95	39.0	117	962	64	207
Plymouth	76	406.3	880	16.8	272	113.2	18.9	4 718	184	110.5	332	1 006	187	381
Pocahontas	33	166.2	361	7.8	176	45.1	52.9	4 334	92	42.4	D	2 679	62	210
Polk	953	5 186.0	12 808	306.7	3 367	2 518.4	38.2	7 900	2 298	2 474.3	1 145	1 566	398	783
Pottawattamie	142	D	D	D	825	523.5	25.4	5 976	545	511.8	593	833	160	513
Poweshiek	51	94.6	351	5.5	220	95.4	4.4	5 100	144	91.0	D	1 172	142	359
Ringgold	16	40.8	60	1.0	70	23.0	32.9	4 262	33	19.7	D	804	D	D
Sac	60	92.7	355	5.7	176	44.8	6.4	3 530	104	40.9	D	933	69	280
Scott	436	2 108.6	4 462	99.1	1 509	1 061.4	25.0	6 834	1 057	1 043.2	943	1 303	309	671
Shelby	48	95.4	392	5.0	191	56.2	4.3	3 956	108	52.0	358	1 011	130	349
Sioux	79	249.6	761	13.7	357	105.6	7.8	3 521	209	99.0	109	770	92	264
Story	108	258.7	1 029	19.0	723	415.7	27.8	5 831	487	408.4	860	1 240	250	682
Tama	45	281.7	285	4.5	219	56.6	6.6	3 061	121	52.5	D	701	36	246
Taylor	23	75.0	209	2.5	107	17.3	-9.4	2 281	59	15.4	D	722	122	247
Union	27	84.5	220	3.3	171	72.5	11.5	5 580	107	70.3	D	1 512	147	778
Van Buren	19	14.9	60	0.7	125	16.3	5.2	1 990	52	12.2	D	564	0	126
Wapello	65	123.9	534	9.1	406	193.7	7.8	5 221	239	187.5	709	1 259	219	364
Warren	54	90.7	321	5.9	286	148.4	65.4	4 078	139	141.5	D	1 025	92	209
Washington	73	136.2	475	7.5	280	93.4	21.9	4 693	154	87.5	328	1 197	227	294
Wayne	19	61.8	128	1.5	106	22.6	3.2	3 094	48	19.1	D	1 010	66	141
Webster	109	233.3	868	17.0	516	265.2	11.4	6 330	335	256.3	1 381	1 093	273	509
Winnebago	27	D	D	D	175	52.1	7.2	4 204	105	49.8	301	939	68	320
Winneshiek	52	165.9	411	6.7	289	93.7	30.9	4 298	172	87.4	D	940	277	368
Woodbury	294	D	D	D	1 014	667.6	25.7	6 854	701	650.7	D	1 421	D	587
Worth	25	45.4	148	2.4	97	17.9	-16.4	2 111	46	15.4	0	522	D	178
Wright	42	129.7	328	5.2	227	57.1	1.8	3 856	138	54.6	147	1 102	74	241
KANSAS	5 754	30 239.8	60 810	1 282.8	27 556	13 863.4	27.9	5 601	16 797	13 396.6	724	1 132	225	520
Allen	26	36.3	209	2.7	209	53.9	-2.2	3 525	117	50.3	D	932	136	591
Anderson	18	D	D	D	109	23.0	16.2	2 807	55	20.8	D	575	53	225
Atchison	26	243.5	473	8.7	167	68.3	23.7	3 818	100	66.1	D	922	90	262
Barber	19	D	D	D	112	29.5	-8.4	4 606	72	27.2	194	910	43	272
Barton	115	157.8	867	16.2	421	187.9	-8.0	6 041	269	180.4	844	1 424	207	594

1. For pay period including March 12. 2. Based on the estimated population as of July 1 of the year shown.

STATE County	Retail trade, establishments with payroll, 1987 (cont'd)		Taxable service industries–establishments with payroll, 1987							Bank deposits,[2] June 1989		Savings capital,[3] September 1989	
				Receipts (Mil dol)									
					Selected kinds of business								
	Paid employees[1]	Annual payroll (Mil dol)	Number	Total	Hotels, motels and other lodging places	Health services	Legal services	Paid employees	Annual payroll (Mil dol)	Total (Mil dol)	Percent change, 1988–1989	Total (Mil dol)	Percent change, 1988–1989
	161	162	163	164	165	166	167	168	169	170	171	172	173
IOWA—Con.													
Hancock	515	2.9	60	7.2	D	3.6	0.7	315	2.4	136	0.5	26.5	-7.3
Hardin	1 189	9.0	116	18.0	0.4	8.3	2.4	610	5.8	276	1.3	46.4	-6.5
Harrison	705	6.4	54	9.7	D	5.4	0.6	393	3.5	138	-2.7	11.0	-4.4
Henry	1 205	9.8	97	56.0	D	7.4	2.3	1 523	27.0	161	1.9	47.5	-15.2
Howard	388	2.9	44	5.7	D	2.3	0.6	182	1.8	126	0.3	0.0	NA
Humboldt	578	4.7	58	8.7	D	3.5	D	295	2.6	122	-1.8	24.2	-13.4
Ida	432	3.3	50	7.3	D	3.5	1.1	255	2.3	112	2.1	17.2	-12.4
Iowa	1 708	10.9	69	13.1	3.8	5.1	1.4	524	4.0	147	-2.4	0.0	NA
Jackson	1 038	8.0	101	16.6	0.9	7.4	1.2	566	5.2	229	1.6	12.1	9.0
Jasper	2 067	17.8	152	27.7	2.3	11.8	2.4	992	9.6	273	1.1	135.1	0.4
Jefferson	1 080	8.7	137	41.9	1.6	6.3	1.4	1 024	16.0	139	2.1	35.2	-4.3
Johnson	8 633	67.5	520	211.6	14.1	38.7	8.2	4 518	72.8	763	2.6	46.7	7.4
Jones	805	6.4	78	12.2	0.1	6.3	1.7	395	3.6	257	-0.2	13.9	8.1
Keokuk	428	2.8	36	6.5	D	3.5	0.4	284	2.2	156	2.5	15.9	11.9
Kossuth	1 199	8.5	100	11.9	D	4.2	2.5	307	2.9	220	-1.4	87.2	-8.6
Lee	2 549	22.5	215	42.0	3.3	18.6	2.9	1 595	14.3	318	-3.4	157.8	-0.4
Linn	15 459	135.2	1 167	545.3	25.4	111.4	34.9	11 320	174.6	1 426	7.8	530.0	-2.0
Louisa	385	2.7	41	6.9	D	3.6	0.8	311	2.3	116	0.7	11.7	-12.7
Lucas	496	3.6	36	8.7	D	4.2	1.0	248	2.8	77	-0.7	37.7	-7.7
Lyon	457	2.8	50	8.7	D	D	0.7	276	3.2	121	1.6	28.1	-5.2
Madison	699	6.0	62	9.2	D	4.3	0.9	363	3.0	104	-3.6	32.1	8.3
Mahaska	1 381	11.2	113	26.7	0.9	9.1	2.3	781	8.7	187	-3.0	93.7	6.0
Marion	1 781	13.1	122	24.6	0.7	10.7	1.7	713	8.2	249	0.8	83.6	-7.4
Marshall	2 862	24.6	218	59.5	2.4	27.0	5.2	1 370	20.4	334	-1.7	148.3	-2.0
Mills	553	4.0	51	13.5	D	5.6	0.3	502	5.5	98	1.8	16.1	-2.5
Mitchell	537	3.7	46	6.7	D	2.6	0.9	209	2.2	199	5.7	27.4	-4.6
Monona	541	4.1	59	18.2	D	5.5	1.1	468	4.2	125	-0.2	35.3	0.3
Monroe	298	2.7	41	7.5	D	2.8	0.7	295	2.3	76	-1.9	0.0	NA
Montgomery	802	6.2	55	13.0	D	6.0	0.6	364	4.8	124	-2.0	36.5	-2.9
Muscatine	2 602	22.0	203	65.7	2.6	15.2	4.9	1 942	29.5	437	3.4	50.2	-6.1
O'Brien	1 259	8.3	105	14.7	D	6.4	1.7	472	4.6	184	-1.3	52.0	-2.2
Osceola	259	2.0	29	4.0	D	1.9	0.8	137	1.2	89	4.2	22.8	-9.3
Page	1 259	9.9	91	16.5	D	6.7	1.2	454	5.4	188	-3.7	53.3	2.2
Palo Alto	505	3.9	56	8.8	D	4.4	0.4	339	3.2	136	-2.9	25.9	-3.1
Plymouth	1 479	11.4	109	19.4	D	8.0	0.9	672	6.3	257	0.7	52.8	-7.0
Pocahontas	533	3.4	61	7.7	0.3	3.4	0.9	305	2.6	130	-1.1	25.8	-1.0
Polk	32 736	297.9	2 687	1 258.2	67.2	285.0	120.5	28 391	466.6	3 017	0.9	1 267.9	2.4
Pottawattamie	6 371	56.1	439	133.8	D	39.1	11.7	3 377	47.0	548	0.4	114.0	-10.0
Poweshiek	1 188	9.3	115	25.5	D	10.5	1.5	576	7.7	190	1.0	37.9	-9.7
Ringgold	212	1.7	22	4.3	0.0	2.6	D	188	1.5	49	-3.8	4.4	-16.3
Sac	653	3.7	62	8.2	D	4.2	1.0	292	2.6	150	-1.0	36.6	-0.4
Scott	13 676	127.4	1 059	357.7	19.7	113.4	20.6	9 535	134.3	1 477	0.8	353.2	-3.3
Shelby	795	5.6	67	16.3	D	4.9	1.3	603	6.5	185	2.6	43.7	-2.4
Sioux	1 460	9.2	152	22.2	0.2	8.6	1.9	672	6.5	322	6.4	58.0	1.4
Story	6 526	48.3	379	128.1	10.4	43.8	4.7	3 382	46.7	497	0.7	234.1	1.9
Tama	749	5.5	65	11.1	0.2	5.2	0.7	397	3.2	209	-0.8	19.0	-0.8
Taylor	272	1.8	30	5.4	0.0	3.5	D	245	2.1	54	-4.1	15.7	-7.4
Union	983	7.7	72	16.9	D	7.5	0.7	543	6.2	119	-3.1	54.5	-6.3
Van Buren	184	1.4	26	2.7	0.0	D	0.4	60	0.7	76	2.5	0.0	NA
Wapello	2 379	20.9	183	49.2	1.8	25.5	4.0	1 243	18.6	260	1.5	118.5	-2.1
Warren	1 251	12.3	146	31.8	D	10.7	1.2	936	9.5	170	-0.9	39.0	2.8
Washington	1 182	9.6	84	14.9	D	6.4	1.9	499	4.5	227	2.2	53.1	-6.6
Wayne	256	1.7	29	4.5	D	2.8	0.2	175	1.5	59	-0.7	21.7	-6.2
Webster	3 550	30.3	261	61.9	4.4	22.8	6.2	1 939	23.8	345	1.9	159.9	-1.1
Winnebago	723	4.6	57	8.3	D	4.5	0.8	297	2.6	161	2.3	34.0	-0.8
Winneshiek	1 238	8.9	109	16.9	D	5.1	1.9	510	6.2	225	7.1	30.1	-12.5
Woodbury	8 794	75.1	672	278.1	D	89.1	20.9	6 608	103.8	808	1.9	242.6	-1.5
Worth	215	1.5	25	3.7	D	D	0.4	137	1.1	67	1.4	6.3	4.4
Wright	820	5.3	79	12.4	D	5.7	1.0	449	4.6	213	-0.2	24.6	6.4
KANSAS	174 947	1 569.5	15 523	5 250.9	264.0	1 799.4	337.7	128 013	1 967.7	22 370	4.0	15 737.9	5.3
Allen	918	6.5	80	14.8	D	7.7	0.8	493	4.9	112	3.2	129.9	8.3
Anderson	251	1.9	49	5.7	D	2.9	0.4	221	1.7	104	9.1	18.0	-5.1
Atchison	948	7.5	74	12.3	D	6.8	1.5	363	5.2	148	9.1	84.9	1.7
Barber	368	2.8	46	7.3	D	3.9	0.6	309	2.6	98	-1.0	41.4	-5.9
Barton	2 463	21.0	228	52.4	2.6	19.0	7.4	1 412	20.2	376	-0.3	133.7	-2.6

1. For the period including March 12 of the year shown. 2. Includes deposits for all insured and reporting noninsured commercial and mutual savings banks. 3. Includes savings capital for all FSLIC insured savings institutions.

STATE County	Federal funds and grants, 1989							Local government finances, 1981–1982							
	Expenditures		Per capita[1] (Dollars)					General revenue						Direct general expenditure	
									Intergovernmental		Taxes				
												Per capita[2]			
	Total (Mil dol)	Percent change, 1988–1989	Total	Direct payments for individuals	Procurement contract awards	Salaries and wages	Grant awards	Total (Mil dol)	Total (Mil dol)	Percent from state	Total (Mil dol)	Total (Dollars)	Property (Dollars)	Total (Mil dol)	Percent change, 1977–1982
	174	175	176	177	178	179	180	181	182	183	184	185	186	187	188
IOWA—Con.															
Hancock	41.2	-12.2	3 096	1 624	18	143	119	16.3	5.1	92.2	7.5	546	539	15.1	34.2
Hardin	73.1	-1.1	3 751	2 309	19	151	230	28.3	9.2	96.1	11.8	546	537	26.1	55.9
Harrison	56.3	-4.3	3 495	2 031	20	191	421	17.2	8.1	92,5	6.9	425	422	15.0	36.1
Henry	53.8	2.0	2 818	1 757	26	149	171	21.9	8.4	90.9	7.9	424	419	20.7	43.6
Howard	40.6	0.2	3 906	1 956	75	122	259	14.0	6.2	84.4	4.9	442	438	12.7	35.2
Humboldt	39.3	-9.9	3 509	2 063	22	186	207	14.8	4.9	93.6	6.5	533	528	14.2	42.2
Ida	30.1	-14.5	3 536	1 903	15	145	278	9.3	3.8	90.1	4.2	485	481	8.6	29.0
Iowa	53.8	3.7	3 687	1 764	27	170	125	18.3	7.4	90.4	7.5	492	488	17.0	44.3
Jackson	68.3	10.5	3 146	1 791	112	133	266	27.8	12.1	85.8	7.4	331	324	25.9	59.2
Jasper	93.5	0.1	2 548	1 695	13	106	226	41.2	15.9	88.8	15.3	425	421	39.8	60.2
Jefferson	44.3	9.2	2 622	1 493	21	205	220	17.8	6.4	89.3	5.8	353	349	16.5	45.7
Johnson	281.8	9.4	3 205	1 054	459	437	1 030	71.1	27.6	77.7	31.3	375	369	66.1	68.1
Jones	61.7	9.6	3 117	1 600	15	113	167	17.1	9.1	93.8	6.4	317	311	16.9	41.7
Keokuk	56.8	6.3	4 777	2 271	30	212	339	14.4	5.7	94.8	6.2	491	488	13.5	34.7
Kossuth	69.5	-22.8	3 585	1 814	17	152	198	22.7	6.9	91.1	10.5	485	477	20.4	35.8
Lee	103.8	8.7	2 576	1 887	20	133	249	48.2	16.3	85.8	17.9	418	414	41.1	36.7
Linn	624.9	-8.4	3 596	1 470	1 452	241	211	235.1	94.0	83.2	94.0	557	548	211.3	45.7
Louisa	39.0	0.4	3 223	1 536	16	177	208	14.9	5.9	95.3	6.7	552	547	13.2	56.5
Lucas	33.7	5.3	3 581	2 306	38	180	377	14.6	5.0	86.5	4.1	395	391	13.0	44.5
Lyon	36.5	-47.2	2 989	1 603	18	137	150	12.8	5.4	94.7	5.5	435	432	10.4	33.9
Madison	38.3	0.7	2 995	1 927	17	146	188	18.0	6.7	93.0	6.6	522	517	16.9	70.0
Mahaska	67.9	7.1	3 018	1 798	15	139	273	22.2	7.6	90.3	7.6	335	331	20.3	63.2
Marion	106.5	-0.1	3 479	1 936	125	884	265	31.4	15.7	76.7	10.5	349	343	28.1	71.2
Marshall	115.9	5.4	2 958	1 919	15	125	385	51.3	21.9	88.9	20.1	479	474	49.0	37.5
Mills	42.3	-1.4	3 130	1 832	16	147	478	16.1	8.7	63.7	5.9	432	429	16.2	109.1
Mitchell	41.2	-3.7	3 616	2 009	20	148	198	15.0	4.7	90.8	5.4	454	450	12.9	36.3
Monona	46.0	-9.7	4 466	2 472	43	210	402	12.9	5.3	93.7	5.7	495	488	11.7	43.5
Monroe	30.9	7.2	3 718	2 447	17	140	438	11.2	5.0	88.4	3.5	380	371	15.6	126.9
Montgomery	43.5	-4.1	3 596	2 448	20	181	227	19.5	5.4	95.2	5.9	446	442	17.6	124.1
Muscatine	101.2	5.0	2 444	1 545	225	113	183	66.8	16.7	90.0	17.3	417	409	47.4	31.5
O'Brien	53.2	-12.2	3 456	2 080	24	188	256	24.1	10.1	72.3	8.9	528	524	23.8	51.9
Osceola	27.2	-41.9	3 578	1 817	17	149	185	7.7	2.8	89.4	3.6	437	426	7.4	43.6
Page	59.5	4.2	3 502	2 371	27	197	328	22.8	7.8	92.5	9.0	474	470	20.3	50.8
Palo Alto	46.8	-40.2	4 292	2 179	22	181	470	16.7	5.2	91.2	6.5	517	512	14.9	25.8
Plymouth	71.1	1.6	2 913	1 608	16	165	207	25.6	9.8	93.5	9.1	372	368	22.3	49.4
Pocahontas	40.4	-14.4	3 998	2 038	26	177	267	17.9	5.4	78.2	6.2	556	554	14.6	79.9
Polk	1 446.5	23.0	4 367	1 638	222	619	897	395.3	147.6	85.4	153.1	500	481	373.3	53.9
Pottawattamie	220.6	-23.7	2 488	1 765	45	113	334	100.7	46.9	91.7	34.4	396	388	92.3	35.4
Poweshiek	71.9	27.0	3 786	1 785	19	109	174	18.3	7.6	98.2	7.9	416	413	16.9	42.0
Ringgold	26.2	9.2	4 942	2 189	36	295	390	9.2	3.3	92.7	3.6	597	591	7.9	51.7
Sac	44.4	-10.3	3 548	2 139	21	175	189	13.7	5.7	94.9	6.3	455	451	13.3	36.5
Scott	364.2	0.3	2 341	1 672	157	135	257	188.4	76.0	83.6	77.1	479	470	179.8	51.9
Shelby	48.0	-14.8	3 429	1 780	18	158	404	19.5	7.4	92.7	6.2	422	415	18.1	23.4
Sioux	89.1	7.1	2 941	1 509	345	120	264	32.8	10.9	83.9	10.5	340	336	26.6	68.5
Story	230.3	3.4	3 189	1 385	353	416	783	85.8	23.3	88.9	25.6	352	347	74.7	58.3
Tama	64.9	-1.3	3 549	1 834	53	170	371	20.8	9.7	89.1	9.0	467	460	18.5	43.4
Taylor	32.7	1.8	4 421	2 266	28	231	447	8.3	4.2	92.1	3.1	368	362	8.4	51.5
Union	45.6	4.0	3 532	2 303	24	247	403	22.6	9.4	86.8	6.2	447	445	20.6	53.7
Van Buren	30.3	5.2	3 651	1 934	31	188	386	10.1	4.3	94.3	3.3	391	388	9.6	43.7
Wapello	121.2	4.2	3 347	2 476	27	178	425	50.9	21.8	94.8	15.4	388	380	47.7	36.3
Warren	65.7	-32.1	1 756	1 218	23	103	161	31.0	15.6	95.4	10.5	299	295	28.0	58.0
Washington	67.8	9.3	3 356	1 782	15	156	171	22.3	8.3	95.6	8.4	420	416	20.5	54.4
Wayne	36.0	2.3	5 140	2 811	36	253	464	9.6	3.4	91.8	3.4	415	412	9.2	65.5
Webster	133.7	1.9	3 221	2 107	25	288	314	55.0	23.2	83.8	21.0	464	459	53.6	61.4
Winnebago	42.1	-14.0	3 394	1 882	19	140	196	18.1	6.0	92.5	6.9	543	534	14.8	7.7
Winneshiek	59.0	2.0	2 682	1 562	18	150	165	27.7	11.4	90.6	8.0	364	361	26.6	41.8
Woodbury	300.8	8.3	3 039	1 969	191	313	347	124.1	50.8	81.1	48.4	480	459	117.0	41.9
Worth	34.6	-7.0	4 028	1 889	19	138	445	8.7	3.4	94.4	4.0	446	443	8.9	62.0
Wright	57.1	-5.9	3 939	2 269	21	188	275	19.7	6.9	90.4	9.2	573	569	21.2	82.7
KANSAS	9 222.7	2.8	X	1 882	473	636	383	2 779.3	810.2	80.4	1 090.0	453	412	2 676.9	65.7
Allen	41.8	5.3	2 842	2 139	16	219	305	21.6	6.1	78.3	6.6	418	411	20.5	87.1
Anderson	24.1	4.1	2 935	2 217	22	189	114	9.1	2.4	92.4	3.6	419	414	9.2	65.6
Atchison	53.8	8.0	3 020	1 906	510	126	229	16.8	7.2	77.0	6.0	327	293	15.9	60.5
Barber	19.6	-14.7	3 220	2 383	25	198	114	12.2	1.2	82.6	5.2	751	732	11.3	113.1
Barton	81.4	-0.2	2 758	1 969	57	312	110	38.1	10.7	67.5	18.0	548	524	34.3	70.9

1. Based on the estimated population as of July 1 of the year shown. 2. Based on the estimated population as of July 1, 1982.

STATE County	Local government finances, 1981–1982 (cont'd): Direct general expenditure (cont'd): Per capita[1] (Dollars)	Percent of total for– Education	Percent of total for– Health & hospitals	Percent of total for– Police protection	Percent of total for– Public welfare	Percent of total for– Highways	Debt outstanding: Total (Mil dol)	Debt outstanding: Per capita[1] (Dollars)	State and local government employment, 1989: Total	State and local government employment, 1989: Rate[2]	Federal government civilian employment 1989: Total	Federal government civilian employment 1989: Earnings ($1,000)	Elections, 1988[3]: Total vote cast for president	Elections, 1988[3]: Vote for lead party (Percent)
	189	190	191	192	193	194	195	196	197	198	199	200	201	202
IOWA—Con.														
Hancock	1 105	46.4	10.2	3.5	3.7	20.0	6.5	476	725	545.1	67	1 690	5 593	D-50.6
Hardin	1 207	48.0	18.9	2.9	1.4	12.6	10.6	493	1 613	827.2	101	2 337	9 001	D-56.5
Harrison	928	59.1	2.4	3.1	0.8	16.7	5.7	352	673	418.0	107	2 712	6 027	R-51.6
Henry	1 106	50.6	14.2	2.7	2.0	11.9	8.5	455	1 526	799.0	80	2 168	7 758	R-50.9
Howard	1 155	52.0	13.6	3.2	2.8	12.5	4.3	388	628	603.8	50	1 205	4 325	D-53.9
Humboldt	1 171	46.9	17.1	3.8	0.5	15.2	3.6	301	628	560.7	74	1 761	5 357	D-50.6
Ida	986	47.2	4.2	4.5	2.3	15.6	2.0	232	417	490.6	51	1 201	3 779	R-51.6
Iowa	1 114	48.7	11.1	2.5	3.7	17.0	4.0	261	723	495.2	83	1 941	6 685	D-49.9
Jackson	1 162	42.6	22.9	2.8	1.4	11.6	10.8	482	1 140	525.3	99	2 466	8 233	D-59.1
Jasper	1 102	51.3	11.2	3.0	5.8	10.5	11.1	306	1 879	512.0	115	2 969	15 733	D-56.8
Jefferson	1 012	37.8	21.0	2.7	3.1	13.6	5.6	346	924	546.7	94	2 516	7 296	R-49.5
Johnson	791	42.3	3.2	4.7	3.4	10.5	60.4	722	22 217	2 527.5	1 612	47 554	44 647	D-64.4
Jones	833	59.0	2.0	3.3	2.1	16.7	2.1	103	1 110	560.6	78	1 859	8 185	D-56.7
Keokuk	1 070	49.5	11.7	2.4	0.6	20.2	5.8	456	532	447.1	81	1 724	5 230	D-55.4
Kossuth	942	44.5	12.2	2.7	2.2	20.2	12.8	593	1 019	525.3	107	2 525	9 107	D-55.9
Lee	961	44.0	1.5	4.6	3.1	9.1	69.3	1 618	2 116	525.1	132	3 566	17 290	D-63.1
Linn	1 252	56.5	1.9	3.7	1.9	6.8	142.3	843	9 383	539.9	1 120	37 481	76 718	D-56.0
Louisa	1 087	66.1	1.7	2.8	3.4	11.5	3.4	284	558	461.2	77	2 054	4 380	D-51.8
Lucas	1 262	32.4	31.7	2.7	2.5	12.7	5.3	513	608	646.8	58	1 430	4 243	D-57.8
Lyon	820	58.8	2.8	3.6	0.9	16.2	3.0	238	564	462.3	60	1 381	5 264	R-66.8
Madison	1 338	54.4	12.7	2.2	0.8	14.4	12.8	1 015	701	547.7	67	1 609	5 862	D-58.4
Mahaska	892	39.7	22.6	2.6	2.4	13.1	3.9	171	981	436.0	96	2 420	9 320	R-51.5
Marion	936	49.7	1.9	3.7	1.7	11.7	16.5	551	1 202	392.8	1 088	33 780	12 954	D-53.4
Marshall	1 169	58.3	1.9	3.8	3.5	12.5	32.2	769	3 245	827.8	146	3 890	17 549	D-55.6
Mills	1 194	39.0	1.1	3.1	0.5	14.9	5.0	370	1 789	1 325.2	57	1 414	5 369	R-59.8
Mitchell	1 071	43.4	21.3	3.5	1.3	15.0	2.9	241	576	505.3	61	1 439	5 251	D-54.7
Monona	1 021	49.0	3.4	3.1	0.9	23.0	17.5	1 525	573	556.3	70	1 666	4 491	D-53.6
Monroe	1 720	24.3	42.5	2.1	2.3	16.9	6.4	703	449	541.0	44	1 023	3 667	D-63.8
Montgomery	1 330	33.7	20.9	2.3	21.8	10.5	3.4	257	756	624.8	65	1 660	5 100	R-62.1
Muscatine	1 142	40.4	16.7	3.4	2.4	6.4	287.6	6 931	2 446	590.8	142	3 904	14 102	D-50.1
O'Brien	1 410	52.9	6.4	3.0	1.9	10.2	5.2	308	886	575.3	83	2 217	7 072	R-60.0
Osceola	908	40.5	2.0	5.6	1.1	20.1	5.7	696	256	336.8	46	1 099	3 264	R-59.8
Page	1 074	40.8	21.1	4.0	2.3	13.7	13.5	715	1 181	694.7	98	2 646	6 803	R-67.4
Palo Alto	1 194	43.7	21.7	2.6	0.8	14.5	3.3	266	940	862.4	71	1 675	5 463	D-61.8
Plymouth	913	51.6	14.5	2.5	2.3	12.6	8.6	352	1 125	461.1	104	2 535	9 607	R-55.3
Pocahontas	1 317	41.9	19.9	2.8	0.6	13.8	4.7	426	602	596.0	63	1 442	4 652	D-58.5
Polk	1 220	43.5	7.5	5.6	1.9	7.6	335.0	1 095	22 588	682.0	5 590	188 779	143 144	D-59.0
Pottawattamie	1 062	60.3	1.2	4.2	1.0	7.2	75.6	870	4 515	509.0	291	8 593	32 405	R-53.1
Poweshiek	887	50.8	3.0	3.0	2.5	15.3	10.4	544	866	455.8	68	1 762	8 625	D-56.5
Ringgold	1 318	40.8	21.7	1.7	0.5	19.1	5.5	919	374	705.7	52	1 131	2 729	D-59.0
Sac	960	53.6	2.8	5.1	1.1	17.6	3.2	230	643	514.4	69	1 663	5 077	D-51.5
Scott	1 116	51.7	2.9	4.1	1.1	7.3	185.4	1 151	6 863	441.1	562	17 275	66 035	D-52.1
Shelby	1 225	42.4	19.7	1.8	1.8	16.0	13.2	894	794	567.1	80	1 942	5 860	R-51.5
Sioux	859	40.2	12.2	3.5	0.5	12.8	26.6	858	1 417	467.7	107	3 002	13 288	R-77.3
Story	1 029	35.7	27.9	3.5	1.6	8.2	66.4	915	16 614	2 301.1	911	29 762	33 105	D-57.5
Tama	959	57.3	3.7	3.0	1.7	17.0	6.6	342	972	531.1	109	2 685	8 012	D-57.2
Taylor	1 005	50.0	1.3	2.8	2.3	21.7	4.5	533	419	566.2	59	1 350	3 332	D-50.2
Union	1 482	49.0	18.8	2.4	0.9	9.0	6.1	436	1 176	911.6	110	3 081	6 041	D-53.6
Van Buren	1 124	46.1	17.7	1.6	4.6	16.1	2.1	253	525	632.5	54	1 220	3 334	R-50.7
Wapello	1 205	60.7	0.5	2.1	3.6	6.8	45.8	1 155	2 227	615.2	188	5 759	15 673	D-64.9
Warren	798	62.0	1.0	3.5	1.5	12.8	16.9	482	1 323	353.7	116	2 968	16 131	D-59.7
Washington	1 020	45.1	17.2	3.6	2.3	15.2	7.9	394	1 085	537.1	83	2 146	7 616	D-49.6
Wayne	1 139	37.0	23.2	2.2	1.7	21.0	2.2	275	450	642.9	59	1 279	3 477	D-57.2
Webster	1 185	56.9	0.7	3.7	3.3	10.4	29.6	655	2 417	582.4	348	11 244	17 393	D-59.0
Winnebago	1 162	51.4	9.6	3.3	2.3	14.7	11.3	893	782	630.6	64	1 529	5 703	R-50.2
Winneshiek	1 210	53.1	17.5	2.8	4.1	11.6	6.2	281	1 579	717.7	106	2 655	8 725	D-50.9
Woodbury	1 161	45.7	1.3	4.2	2.7	10.6	118.3	1 173	5 004	505.5	869	27 243	39 225	D-51.4
Worth	1 000	42.6	2.5	3.5	4.5	20.9	2.7	305	342	397.7	47	1 173	3 982	D-61.3
Wright	1 325	41.5	8.6	3.2	1.7	17.0	11.6	722	821	566.2	83	2 073	6 054	D-55.4
KANSAS	1 112	45.0	7.6	4.1	0.3	10.0	4 542.9	1 887	179 951	716.4	29 556	870 546	993 044	R-55.8
Allen	1 296	40.7	23.5	2.7	0.0	6.4	18.1	1 144	1 102	749.7	66	1 585	5 898	R-58.1
Anderson	1 063	41.1	26.2	2.6	0.0	10.4	4.9	564	531	647.6	45	1 058	3 283	R-54.2
Atchison	863	54.5	0.0	5.1	2.8	9.9	13.8	752	1 083	608.4	69	1 683	6 614	R-49.0
Barber	1 633	32.5	37.7	2.4	0.0	12.2	4.9	712	556	911.5	43	943	2 706	R-56.9
Barton	1 042	53.3	1.1	5.0	0.1	9.9	58.5	1 779	2 028	687.5	126	3 359	13 075	R-59.2

1. Based on the estimated population as of July 1, 1982. 2. Per 10,000 resident population estimated as of July 1 of the year shown. 3. Data subject to copyright.

STATE–County code	MSA/CMSA/NECMA code[1]	STATE County	Land Area,[2] 1990 (Sq. Km.)	Population, 1990											
							Race						Age of population Percent		
				Total persons	Rank	Per square kilometer	White	Black	Am. Indian, Eskimo, Aleut	Asian & Pacific Islander	Other race	Hispanic[3]	Under 5 years	5 to 14 years	15 to 24 years
			1	2	3	4	5	6	7	8	9	10	11	12	13
		KANSAS—Con.													
20 011	...	Bourbon	1 650	14 966	1 989	9.1	14 438	419	60	22	27	79	7.2	14.7	12.5
20 013	...	Brown	1 478	11 128	2 281	7.5	10 190	132	719	16	71	192	7.3	16.0	10.9
20 015	9040	Butler	3 699	50 580	833	13.7	49 311	367	459	169	274	742	7.6	16.9	12.3
20 017	...	Chase	2 010	3 021	2 999	1.5	2 995	5	11	1	9	40	6.5	14.5	9.8
20 019	...	Chautauqua	1 662	4 407	2 881	2.7	4 202	23	152	13	17	44	6.1	13.4	9.4
20 021	...	Cherokee	1 521	21 374	1 613	14.1	20 442	116	760	24	32	175	6.7	15.3	13.4
20 023	...	Cheyenne	2 642	3 243	2 981	1.2	3 224	5	1	9	4	20	6.2	13.9	8.8
20 025	...	Clark	2 525	2 418	3 030	1.0	2 355	0	27	7	29	42	5.5	15.6	8.9
20 027	...	Clay	1 668	9 158	2 455	5.5	9 078	18	17	27	18	38	6.5	15.1	10.3
20 029	...	Cloud	1 854	11 023	2 290	5.9	10 917	37	17	5	47	76	6.0	13.4	12.9
20 031	...	Coffey	1 632	8 404	2 521	5.1	8 315	9	54	18	8	61	6.7	15.9	11.1
20 033	...	Comanche	2 042	2 313	3 039	1.1	2 291	6	12	0	4	13	6.6	14.3	9.1
20 035	...	Cowley	2 917	36 915	1 075	12.7	34 290	1 060	714	330	521	1 097	7.0	15.3	13.4
20 037	...	Crawford	1 536	35 568	1 109	23.2	34 250	476	305	422	115	325	6.1	13.6	16.8
20 039	...	Decatur	2 314	4 021	2 916	1.7	4 001	2	9	1	8	13	7.0	15.2	7.6
20 041	...	Dickinson	2 197	18 958	1 737	8.6	18 589	123	65	54	127	341	6.8	15.0	11.0
20 043	...	Doniphan	1 016	8 134	2 552	8.0	7 839	155	97	18	25	48	6.6	15.0	14.8
20 045	4150	Douglas	1 184	81 798	554	69.1	72 885	3 324	2 161	2 581	847	2 138	6.3	11.3	30.9
20 047	...	Edwards	1 611	3 787	2 933	2.4	3 646	4	12	8	117	197	5.9	15.6	8.8
20 049	...	Elk	1 678	3 327	2 969	2.0	3 238	5	57	3	24	59	5.9	12.0	9.3
20 051	...	Ellis	2 331	26 004	1 421	11.2	25 635	109	45	151	64	205	6.8	15.3	18.7
20 053	...	Ellsworth	1 854	6 586	2 701	3.6	6 347	134	26	10	69	186	5.6	13.8	11.5
20 055	...	Finney	3 367	33 070	1 186	9.8	26 460	443	253	1 203	4 711	8 353	10.6	19.2	15.9
20 057	...	Ford	2 845	27 463	1 377	9.7	22 873	473	155	663	3 299	4 083	9.0	15.9	16.3
20 059	...	Franklin	1 486	21 994	1 575	14.8	21 202	282	187	100	223	471	8.0	15.8	13.2
20 061	...	Geary	995	30 453	1 270	30.6	20 938	7 198	203	1 224	890	1 853	11.1	15.1	20.5
20 063	...	Gove	2 775	3 231	2 982	1.2	3 219	4	5	2	1	9	6.8	15.7	9.9
20 065	...	Graham	2 327	3 543	2 955	1.5	3 407	103	13	12	8	23	6.0	16.1	8.6
20 067	...	Grant	1 489	7 159	2 637	4.8	6 059	2	78	41	979	1 543	9.0	20.5	13.4
20 069	...	Gray	2 251	5 396	2 809	2.4	5 168	7	22	1	198	229	8.6	18.8	12.1
20 071	...	Greeley	2 015	1 774	3 080	0.9	1 687	11	2	2	72	107	8.6	18.6	9.2
20 073	...	Greenwood	2 952	7 847	2 589	2.7	7 719	9	77	0	42	91	6.0	13.6	10.6
20 075	...	Hamilton	2 581	2 388	3 033	0.9	2 244	5	8	28	103	139	6.8	14.7	9.8
20 077	...	Harper	2 076	7 124	2 641	3.4	7 036	13	46	5	24	105	6.6	15.0	9.4
20 079	9040	Harvey	1 397	31 028	1 244	22.2	29 300	551	145	212	820	1 616	6.9	15.4	13.7
20 081	...	Haskell	1 495	3 886	2 927	2.6	3 413	2	23	5	443	557	9.0	18.6	12.9
20 083	...	Hodgeman	2 227	2 177	3 056	1.0	2 137	22	3	1	14	32	8.1	16.1	8.1
20 085	...	Jackson	1 701	11 525	2 254	6.8	10 705	41	722	9	48	126	7.3	17.0	11.9
20 087	...	Jefferson	1 389	15 905	1 931	11.5	15 603	73	129	65	35	132	6.8	16.3	11.4
20 089	...	Jewell	2 355	4 251	2 895	1.8	4 233	0	12	5	1	8	6.5	13.7	8.2
20 091	3760	Johnson	1 235	355 054	145	287.5	338 770	6 917	1 246	5 840	2 281	7 005	7.9	15.0	12.3
20 093	...	Kearny	2 253	4 027	2 914	1.8	3 602	4	26	5	390	671	9.3	19.4	12.4
20 095	...	Kingman	2 237	8 292	2 536	3.7	8 213	9	24	10	36	77	7.1	16.1	10.3
20 097	...	Kiowa	1 871	3 660	2 943	2.0	3 600	7	17	11	25	39	6.5	14.8	11.1
20 099	...	Labette	1 681	23 693	1 504	14.1	21 956	1 030	409	97	201	516	7.2	15.1	13.3
20 101	...	Lane	1 858	2 375	3 035	1.3	2 354	1	5	0	15	44	6.7	16.7	9.1
20 103	3760	Leavenworth	1 200	64 371	679	53.6	55 063	7 132	418	937	821	2 192	7.0	15.6	12.2
20 105	...	Lincoln	1 862	3 653	2 946	2.0	3 635	1	11	1	5	15	5.6	14.2	8.5
20 107	...	Linn	1 551	8 254	2 543	5.3	8 151	37	44	6	16	34	6.3	15.1	10.8
20 109	...	Logan	2 779	3 081	2 995	1.1	3 047	11	8	0	15	26	6.8	15.4	9.9
20 111	...	Lyon	2 204	34 732	1 141	15.8	31 828	731	215	686	1 272	2 114	7.7	15.4	20.0
20 113	...	McPherson	2 331	27 268	1 381	11.7	26 663	211	108	125	161	325	7.0	15.5	13.7
20 115	...	Marion	2 443	12 888	2 147	5.3	12 687	82	38	32	49	118	5.8	13.9	12.1
20 117	...	Marshall	2 338	11 705	2 233	5.0	11 632	10	34	11	18	49	7.1	15.9	8.9
20 119	...	Meade	2 534	4 247	2 896	1.7	4 092	0	11	12	132	198	6.9	15.8	10.7
20 121	3760	Miami	1 494	23 466	1 516	15.7	22 635	565	137	38	91	276	7.2	16.1	12.3
20 123	...	Mitchell	1 813	7 203	2 631	4.0	7 123	44	18	10	8	29	6.3	15.1	12.2
20 125	...	Montgomery	1 671	38 816	1 029	23.2	35 000	2 437	898	154	327	751	7.2	14.7	12.5
20 127	...	Morris	1 806	6 198	2 734	3.4	6 101	20	31	11	35	90	6.5	14.4	10.3
20 129	...	Morton	1 891	3 480	2 959	1.8	3 297	3	31	38	111	352	7.8	17.4	12.2
20 131	...	Nemaha	1 862	10 446	2 342	5.6	10 378	37	13	16	2	14	7.9	16.7	10.6
20 133	...	Neosho	1 481	17 035	1 849	11.5	16 544	190	134	40	127	361	7.0	15.1	11.9
20 135	...	Ness	2 784	4 033	2 913	1.4	4 016	0	4	5	8	23	5.9	16.7	8.2
20 137	...	Norton	2 274	5 947	2 766	2.6	5 724	135	16	20	52	82	5.7	12.5	11.8
20 139	...	Osage	1 822	15 248	1 974	8.4	15 035	34	107	18	54	187	6.8	15.9	11.0
20 141	...	Osborne	2 312	4 867	2 846	2.1	4 835	4	20	6	2	17	6.8	13.7	8.5

1. MSA = Metropolitan Statistical Area. CMSA = Consolidated MSA. NECMA = New England county metropolitan area. PMSA = Primary MSA. See Appendix A for explanation of these concepts. See Appendix B for list of metropolitan areas identified by type, with component counties. 2. Dry land or land partially or temporarily covered with water. 3. Hispanic persons may be of any race.

STATE County	Population, 1990 (cont'd) — Age of population (cont'd) Percent — 25 to 34 years	35 to 44 years	45 to 54 years	55 to 64 years	65 to 74 years	75 years and over	Percent female	Population–Change and components of change — Change 1980–1990 — Number	Percent	Components of change, 1980–1986 — Total persons, 1986	Total persons, 1980	Net change — Number	Percent	Natural increase — Births	Deaths
	14	15	16	17	18	19	20	21	22	23	24	25	26	27	28
KANSAS—Con.															
Bourbon	13.3	13.0	9.3	9.6	9.9	10.5	53.0	-1 003	-6.3	15 600	15 969	-400	-2.6	1 500	1 400
Brown	13.6	12.2	8.9	9.3	10.3	11.4	52.1	-827	-6.9	11 300	11 955	-600	-5.2	1 200	1 000
Butler	15.4	15.6	9.9	9.1	7.3	6.1	50.9	5 798	12.9	48 000	44 782	3 200	7.2	4 500	2 400
Chase	13.2	12.6	10.1	10.1	11.6	11.6	50.4	-288	-8.7	3 100	3 309	-200	-5.1	300	300
Chautauqua	12.0	10.9	11.4	10.3	13.8	12.7	51.4	-609	-12.1	4 600	5 016	-400	-7.8	400	500
Cherokee	13.6	13.4	10.8	9.3	9.4	8.3	52.3	-930	-4.2	22 200	22 304	-100	-0.6	1 800	1 800
Cheyenne	11.3	13.8	8.5	13.4	12.8	11.3	52.1	-435	-11.8	3 600	3 678	-100	-1.6	300	300
Clark	12.2	13.3	9.9	10.6	11.3	12.8	51.5	-181	-7.0	2 600	2 599	0	1.2	200	200
Clay	12.2	13.7	9.2	10.2	11.0	12.0	51.6	-644	-6.6	9 300	9 802	-500	-5.2	800	800
Cloud	12.0	11.7	9.6	9.6	11.1	13.6	53.0	-1 471	-11.8	11 700	12 494	-800	-6.3	1 100	1 100
Coffey	14.5	14.2	9.7	8.3	9.3	10.4	50.5	-966	-10.3	8 900	9 370	-500	-5.1	900	700
Comanche	12.0	11.8	10.3	9.8	11.6	14.5	52.1	-241	-9.4	2 500	2 554	0	-0.5	200	200
Cowley	14.7	13.8	10.1	9.4	8.2	8.1	51.5	91	0.2	37 000	36 824	200	0.5	3 500	2 700
Crawford	14.3	12.4	8.9	8.2	9.6	10.0	52.0	-2 348	-6.2	37 600	37 916	-300	-0.8	3 300	3 100
Decatur	13.7	11.7	9.0	11.4	11.4	13.1	51.4	-488	-10.8	4 300	4 509	-200	-3.6	400	400
Dickinson	14.0	13.0	10.1	10.2	9.6	10.3	51.9	-1 217	-6.0	19 800	20 175	-400	-2.0	1 600	1 500
Doniphan	13.3	13.5	9.5	9.1	9.4	8.7	50.9	-1 134	-12.2	9 100	9 268	-100	-1.5	900	600
Douglas	17.6	13.1	7.3	5.5	4.4	3.7	50.2	14 158	20.9	72 600	67 640	5 000	7.3	6 100	2 400
Edwards	14.1	11.7	10.2	10.3	11.9	11.5	51.7	-484	-11.3	4 000	4 271	-300	-6.9	400	400
Elk	10.0	10.7	10.9	11.6	13.8	15.9	52.2	-591	-15.1	3 600	3 918	-400	-9.0	300	400
Ellis	15.4	14.1	8.3	8.0	7.3	6.0	51.0	-94	-0.4	27 700	26 098	1 600	6.3	3 100	1 200
Ellsworth	14.8	13.2	9.0	9.7	10.2	12.0	48.2	-54	-0.8	6 300	6 640	-400	-5.6	600	600
Finney	19.2	14.0	7.7	5.8	4.4	3.3	49.2	9 245	38.8	30 300	23 825	6 400	27.0	4 400	1 000
Ford	16.8	13.1	8.8	7.6	7.0	5.6	49.5	3 148	12.9	26 300	24 315	1 900	8.0	3 400	1 300
Franklin	15.6	13.1	9.8	8.8	7.7	7.9	51.6	-68	-0.3	21 900	22 062	-100	-0.6	2 100	1 500
Geary	19.8	12.2	7.3	6.2	4.6	3.0	48.7	601	2.0	31 100	29 852	1 300	4.3	7 900	1 200
Gove	13.2	13.2	9.3	11.8	10.0	10.1	50.4	-495	-13.3	3 500	3 726	-200	-4.8	400	200
Graham	13.6	12.1	11.0	12.2	9.5	10.9	50.9	-452	-11.3	4 000	3 995	0	0.4	400	300
Grant	16.5	14.7	9.4	7.7	5.0	3.7	50.0	182	2.6	6 900	6 977	-100	-1.6	1 000	300
Gray	15.1	14.9	9.5	7.7	6.8	6.5	50.9	258	5.0	5 400	5 138	200	4.2	700	300
Greeley	17.2	12.5	8.1	10.1	9.0	6.7	50.3	-71	-3.8	1 800	1 845	-100	-3.7	200	100
Greenwood	12.1	12.3	9.1	11.0	12.6	12.7	51.5	-917	-10.5	8 200	8 764	-600	-6.5	700	800
Hamilton	14.2	13.2	10.3	11.1	9.2	10.6	52.5	-126	-5.0	2 500	2 514	0	-0.8	200	200
Harper	12.9	12.6	9.6	10.7	11.0	12.2	51.8	-654	-8.4	7 500	7 778	-300	-3.4	700	700
Harvey	14.5	14.4	9.8	9.0	8.0	8.4	51.5	497	1.6	30 800	30 531	300	1.0	3 000	1 800
Haskell	17.6	14.1	9.9	7.7	6.0	4.3	49.5	72	1.9	3 900	3 814	100	2.4	500	200
Hodgeman	14.8	12.2	10.0	11.5	9.0	10.0	50.4	-92	-4.1	2 300	2 269	0	1.2	300	200
Jackson	13.9	13.9	10.9	8.8	8.1	8.1	50.9	-119	-1.0	11 700	11 644	100	0.9	1 200	800
Jefferson	15.1	14.9	11.7	8.9	7.9	6.8	49.7	698	4.6	16 000	15 207	800	4.9	1 400	1 000
Jewell	11.9	12.5	9.4	13.1	11.8	13.0	50.5	-990	-18.9	4 700	5 241	-500	-9.4	400	500
Johnson	19.1	18.1	10.7	7.5	5.8	3.6	51.7	84 785	31.4	318 300	270 269	48 000	17.8	26 600	9 900
Kearny	16.2	14.5	8.7	8.2	6.3	5.1	49.2	592	17.2	3 900	3 435	500	13.7	500	200
Kingman	13.7	12.9	9.9	10.2	10.4	9.5	51.4	-668	-7.5	8 900	8 960	0	-0.5	900	700
Kiowa	12.3	13.5	9.3	11.4	10.7	10.4	52.1	-386	-9.5	3 800	4 046	-200	-5.3	400	300
Labette	14.5	13.2	9.5	8.9	9.4	9.1	52.0	-1 989	-7.7	25 400	25 682	-300	-1.1	2 400	1 900
Lane	13.3	13.0	10.3	10.1	10.7	10.0	49.5	-97	-3.9	2 500	2 472	0	0.2	300	200
Leavenworth	19.1	19.8	9.7	7.0	5.5	4.1	44.9	9 562	17.4	60 600	54 809	5 800	10.7	5 000	2 700
Lincoln	11.6	13.3	9.2	11.7	11.7	14.3	52.3	-492	-11.9	3 700	4 145	-400	-10.8	300	400
Linn	12.2	12.3	10.2	11.1	11.7	10.2	50.9	20	0.2	8 200	8 234	-100	-0.7	700	700
Logan	13.4	13.0	9.5	11.7	10.6	9.5	50.7	-397	-11.4	3 200	3 478	-200	-6.7	300	200
Lyon	16.6	13.4	8.0	6.7	6.0	6.2	51.2	-376	-1.1	35 100	35 108	0	0.0	4 100	1 800
McPherson	14.3	13.9	9.4	8.9	8.5	8.9	51.4	413	1.5	27 600	26 855	800	2.9	2 000	1 400
Marion	12.2	12.3	9.7	10.5	11.2	12.2	52.1	-634	-4.7	13 100	13 522	-400	-3.1	1 100	1 100
Marshall	13.6	11.9	9.4	10.3	10.8	12.2	51.1	-1 082	-8.5	12 800	12 787	0	-0.2	1 900	1 300
Meade	13.8	13.5	9.6	10.7	9.3	9.8	50.9	-541	-11.3	4 600	4 788	-200	-4.8	500	300
Miami	15.7	14.8	11.1	9.1	7.0	6.8	50.8	1 848	8.5	22 600	21 618	1 000	4.7	2 000	1 400
Mitchell	12.5	13.7	8.7	9.5	9.3	12.6	51.7	-914	-11.3	7 700	8 117	-500	-5.6	700	600
Montgomery	13.7	12.9	10.3	9.5	10.0	9.4	52.8	-3 465	-8.2	41 200	42 281	-1 100	-2.6	4 100	3 200
Morris	13.0	12.9	9.6	11.1	11.1	11.0	51.2	-221	-3.4	6 300	6 419	-100	-1.5	600	600
Morton	15.5	13.5	10.0	9.9	7.5	6.1	50.8	26	0.8	3 500	3 454	100	2.2	400	200
Nemaha	14.0	11.7	8.4	10.1	9.9	10.7	50.6	-765	-6.8	10 900	11 211	-300	-2.6	1 200	800
Neosho	14.2	13.0	9.9	9.9	9.7	9.3	52.0	-1 932	-10.2	18 800	18 967	-200	-1.1	1 900	1 400
Ness	14.4	12.6	9.1	10.8	10.6	11.7	50.8	-465	-10.3	4 500	4 498	0	-0.5	500	400
Norton	14.3	12.8	10.1	10.4	10.3	12.1	48.0	-742	-11.1	6 300	6 689	-400	-5.7	500	600
Osage	14.9	13.9	10.1	9.9	8.8	8.8	51.3	-71	-0.5	15 600	15 319	200	1.6	1 400	1 100
Osborne	11.7	11.6	9.3	11.4	12.6	14.4	52.1	-1 092	-18.3	5 400	5 959	-500	-8.9	500	600

STATE County	Population–(cont'd): Components of change, 1980-1986 (cont'd): Net migration	Households, 1990: Number	Households, 1990: Percent change, 1980–1990	Households, 1990: Persons per household	Households, 1990: Percent: Female family householder[1]	Households, 1990: Percent: One-person	Births, 1988: Total	Births, 1988: Rate[2]	Births, 1988: Low birth weight[3] (Number)	Deaths, 1987: Number: Total	Deaths, 1987: Number: Infant[4]	Deaths, 1987: Rate: Total[2]	Deaths, 1987: Rate: Infant[5]	Marriages, 1984: Number	Marriages, 1984: Rate[2]
	29	30	31	32	33	34	35	36	37	38	39	40	41	42	43
KANSAS—Con.															
Bourbon	-600	5 897	-7.7	2.46	8.4	28.3	222	14.6	11	179	4	11.6	20.0	145	9.1
Brown	-700	4 347	-5.7	2.50	6.1	29.1	161	14.1	6	164	2	14.4	11.9	100	8.5
Butler	1 100	18 488	14.9	2.69	7.5	20.5	615	12.3	25	394	7	8.0	9.5	394	8.4
Chase	-100	1 214	-6.8	2.43	5.4	26.9	51	16.5	6	30	0	9.7	0.0	17	5.2
Chautauqua	-300	1 835	-9.8	2.32	6.7	30.9	54	12.0	7	71	0	15.1	0.0	48	9.6
Cherokee	-200	8 396	-1.8	2.51	9.6	26.3	272	12.3	15	278	2	12.5	7.7	161	7.2
Cheyenne	-100	1 389	-8.4	2.30	4.8	30.5	39	11.5	2	43	0	12.3	0.0	28	7.8
Clark	0	1 006	-4.1	2.34	3.7	31.4	26	10.4	4	42	0	16.2	0.0	22	8.1
Clay	-500	3 641	-4.9	2.45	4.8	27.0	114	12.5	6	117	0	12.6	0.0	86	9.0
Cloud	-800	4 483	-5.8	2.36	5.5	29.9	144	12.6	13	165	1	14.3	7.6	112	9.3
Coffey	-700	3 311	-6.1	2.49	5.6	26.0	108	12.3	5	124	1	13.9	9.4	90	9.1
Comanche	0	950	-5.1	2.33	5.4	30.5	38	15.8	3	35	1	14.0	33.3	31	11.9
Cowley	-600	14 047	1.1	2.50	8.8	26.2	547	14.7	31	397	6	10.7	11.3	402	10.8
Crawford	-600	14 606	-4.0	2.34	8.4	31.7	444	12.0	18	489	3	13.0	6.8	287	7.5
Decatur	-200	1 651	-8.0	2.35	5.2	30.5	40	9.8	1	64	0	15.2	0.0	50	10.9
Dickinson	-500	7 542	-2.3	2.46	6.5	27.0	258	12.8	18	267	1	13.4	4.0	176	8.8
Doniphan	-400	3 074	-8.4	2.56	7.7	25.5	95	10.6	5	102	0	11.3	0.0	85	9.3
Douglas	1 300	30 138	26.5	2.42	7.6	27.0	1 041	13.6	68	413	5	5.5	5.0	706	10.1
Edwards	-300	1 585	-8.1	2.33	4.9	30.9	50	12.8	1	45	0	11.5	0.0	43	10.5
Elk	-200	1 436	-12.4	2.25	5.2	31.5	40	11.4	5	52	0	14.4	0.0	33	8.9
Ellis	-300	10 096	9.7	2.46	7.7	29.0	359	13.5	20	160	1	6.0	2.9	285	10.2
Ellsworth	-300	2 522	-3.8	2.35	5.5	31.7	79	12.7	5	76	0	12.3	0.0	45	7.0
Finney	3 100	10 836	33.7	3.01	9.3	19.4	750	24.3	57	149	4	4.9	5.3	318	10.9
Ford	-100	9 872	12.5	2.69	8.2	24.4	508	19.6	32	213	2	8.1	3.6	316	12.2
Franklin	-700	8 308	2.0	2.58	7.6	24.2	322	14.3	22	253	2	11.3	5.9	222	9.9
Geary	-5 400	10 676	6.0	2.71	10.2	19.6	1 124	38.5	85	193	13	6.4	11.5	761	25.2
Gove	-300	1 284	-6.8	2.48	3.7	27.3	43	12.6	0	39	0	11.1	0.0	34	9.2
Graham	-100	1 435	-5.2	2.43	5.1	28.2	50	13.9	4	32	0	8.6	0.0	36	8.8
Grant	-800	2 393	2.7	2.96	6.9	17.8	118	17.1	7	55	2	8.1	15.5	83	12.2
Gray	-200	1 913	7.2	2.77	5.2	22.5	78	14.2	5	40	1	7.4	9.0	41	7.7
Greeley	-200	656	-2.1	2.65	4.6	24.2	33	19.4	0	14	0	7.8	0.0	19	10.6
Greenwood	-500	3 285	-8.1	2.33	6.1	31.1	93	11.8	4	133	1	16.4	9.7	83	9.5
Hamilton	-100	986	1.2	2.36	7.3	32.4	40	17.4	2	33	3	13.8	107.1	27	10.8
Harper	-200	3 007	-7.0	2.32	6.1	31.3	93	12.7	4	101	2	13.5	25.6	80	10.3
Harvey	-900	11 581	5.8	2.54	7.0	25.2	382	12.4	20	315	1	10.3	2.4	354	11.5
Haskell	-300	1 372	6.2	2.81	4.3	21.1	68	17.4	1	32	0	8.2	0.0	40	10.3
Hodgeman	0	826	-4.3	2.58	3.4	23.8	33	15.0	0	26	0	11.8	0.0	19	8.3
Jackson	-300	4 277	3.1	2.66	6.3	23.2	164	13.9	8	130	0	11.1	0.0	97	8.4
Jefferson	300	5 778	9.1	2.68	5.2	20.1	232	13.7	15	146	1	8.8	4.7	134	8.4
Jewell	-400	1 806	-14.3	2.34	4.5	28.5	59	13.4	8	73	0	15.9	0.0	40	8.2
Johnson	31 300	136 433	40.8	2.58	7.8	23.0	5 435	15.7	236	1 794	45	5.4	8.7	2 584	8.7
Kearny	100	1 379	17.2	2.89	7.5	20.2	84	21.0	5	32	2	8.0	23.5	44	11.6
Kingman	-300	3 175	-5.6	2.55	6.0	25.1	111	12.6	1	100	0	11.4	0.0	85	9.3
Kiowa	-300	1 466	-7.0	2.39	5.1	29.4	57	15.8	2	54	2	14.2	35.7	34	8.5
Labette	-800	9 377	-3.3	2.44	9.3	29.0	346	13.7	24	358	5	14.0	14.6	191	7.4
Lane	-100	966	-0.5	2.41	5.1	29.6	25	10.4	0	23	1	9.2	30.3	22	8.8
Leavenworth	3 600	19 715	15.8	2.79	9.0	20.2	846	12.7	55	437	12	6.7	14.1	485	8.3
Lincoln	-300	1 531	-10.6	2.33	4.2	29.7	39	11.1	1	57	0	15.8	0.0	26	6.7
Linn	-100	3 215	1.9	2.51	5.6	24.1	125	15.1	6	127	1	15.5	11.1	56	6.7
Logan	-300	1 221	-9.0	2.47	5.2	28.3	35	11.3	0	50	0	15.6	0.0	35	10.3
Lyon	-2 300	13 059	0.4	2.51	7.7	28.3	551	15.8	20	259	4	7.4	6.9	443	11.8
McPherson	200	10 230	4.3	2.51	5.3	25.5	374	13.8	25	282	1	10.3	2.6	227	8.2
Marion	-500	4 975	-3.2	2.43	4.9	26.6	148	11.6	4	180	1	14.1	7.1	106	7.9
Marshall	-600	4 689	-7.2	2.43	4.9	29.8	175	14.2	0	172	1	13.9	6.0	126	9.8
Meade	-400	1 667	-8.1	2.49	3.8	27.6	68	15.5	8	62	0	14.1	0.0	61	13.0
Miami	400	8 402	11.0	2.67	7.3	21.8	348	14.6	18	255	1	11.0	2.8	192	8.6
Mitchell	-500	2 846	-9.6	2.41	4.5	30.5	76	10.3	7	102	1	13.6	11.5	98	12.3
Montgomery	-2 000	15 670	-4.4	2.42	9.2	28.9	554	13.5	42	505	9	12.3	15.5	394	9.3
Morris	-100	2 528	-1.2	2.41	5.6	26.4	81	12.5	2	83	1	13.0	12.2	48	7.6
Morton	-200	1 290	4.6	2.65	5.3	23.8	51	14.6	3	28	0	8.0	0.0	43	12.3
Nemaha	-600	3 996	-0.6	2.59	4.3	28.1	167	15.5	3	134	0	12.3	0.0	98	8.8
Neosho	-700	6 748	-6.8	2.45	7.2	27.3	217	12.0	10	212	0	11.6	0.0	167	8.6
Ness	-200	1 670	-6.7	2.38	4.7	30.3	54	12.9	0	44	0	10.2	0.0	41	8.7
Norton	-300	2 330	-10.0	2.31	5.0	31.3	58	9.4	4	88	0	14.2	0.0	81	12.3
Osage	0	5 806	3.7	2.57	6.6	23.1	202	12.5	14	148	0	9.2	0.0	153	9.5
Osborne	-400	2 057	-13.8	2.30	5.4	31.4	54	10.4	3	96	3	18.1	52.6	49	8.6

1. No spouse present. 2. Per 1,000 resident population estimated as of July 1 of the year shown. 3. Under 2,500 grams. 4. Deaths of infants under 1 year old. 5. Deaths of infants under 1 year old per 1,000 live births.

STATE County	Divorces, 1984		Physicians, active non–Federal, 1989		Hospitals, 1989			Nursing homes,[4] 1986		Serious crimes known to police, 1988			Education			
						Beds				Number			Public school enrollment[7]		Attainment,[8] 1980	
	Number	Rate[1]	Number[2]	Rate[3]	Number	Number	Rate[3]	Number	Beds	Total[5]	Violent[6]	Rate[3]	1986–1987	1980	Percent 12 yrs. or more	Percent 16 yrs. or more
	44	45	46	47	48	49	50	51	52	53	54	55	56	57	58	59
KANSAS—Con.																
Bourbon	86	5.4	24	160	1	106	707	4	279	385	24	2 490	2 636	2 592	63.4	10.6
Brown	51	4.4	7	61	2	70	614	3	259	156	14	1 375	1 790	2 218	66.9	9.8
Butler	209	4.4	29	57	2	223	436	7	550	1 310	65	2 689	10 117	9 192	73.6	13.2
Chase	7	2.1	1	33	0	0	0	1	73	31	1	1 029	576	599	67.1	12.0
Chautauqua	25	5.0	3	67	2	73	1 622	2	133	91	5	1 970	727	849	59.9	7.5
Cherokee	121	5.4	5	23	2	88	398	5	301	572	23	2 667	3 757	4 500	58.6	8.2
Cheyenne	15	4.2	2	61	1	23	697	1	57	5	0	252	693	667	63.3	11.3
Clark	2	0.7	2	80	2	31	1 240	2	86	12	0	460	465	498	75.3	13.6
Clay	41	4.3	9	99	1	36	396	4	203	124	5	1 328	1 604	1 800	70.4	10.2
Cloud	53	4.4	15	134	1	53	473	6	347	260	10	2 252	1 658	2 089	71.5	12.9
Coffey	84	8.5	4	47	1	26	302	2	152	120	8	1 328	1 627	1 750	62.1	9.4
Comanche	7	2.7	1	42	1	14	583	2	102	2	0	83	433	453	73.9	12.4
Cowley	267	7.2	41	110	3	653	1 751	7	516	1 348	64	3 688	6 405	6 637	68.5	11.7
Crawford	205	5.4	29	79	2	190	515	6	596	1 823	76	5 016	5 971	5 891	65.1	15.7
Decatur	24	5.2	4	100	1	73	1 825	2	117	30	4	711	739	809	68.1	10.8
Dickinson	87	4.4	13	65	2	84	418	7	351	256	14	1 337	3 976	3 872	68.5	10.5
Doniphan	47	5.2	4	44	0	0	0	2	110	115	9	1 273	1 431	1 955	62.1	8.7
Douglas	385	5.5	104	133	1	200	255	7	497	4 862	230	6 448	9 535	9 215	82.3	35.1
Edwards	27	6.6	2	53	1	49	1 289	1	94	40	2	1 021	583	705	72.5	12.4
Elk	14	3.8	1	29	0	0	0	2	91	65	1	1 798	668	657	60.7	7.0
Ellis	143	5.1	49	188	2	245	942	4	267	918	29	3 399	4 237	4 097	73.3	20.9
Ellsworth	17	2.7	2	33	2	48	787	2	166	33	0	602	1 276	1 195	68.6	11.6
Finney	188	6.5	32	103	1	99	317	2	171	2 795	179	9 156	6 598	4 803	71.2	15.9
Ford	171	6.6	42	163	2	126	488	3	188	931	50	3 512	4 699	4 309	73.7	16.9
Franklin	104	4.6	12	53	1	65	288	5	288	588	36	2 638	4 187	4 230	65.1	11.7
Geary	363	12.0	17	60	2	179	628	3	222	2 005	275	6 701	6 928	4 924	74.2	12.6
Gove	4	1.1	3	91	1	64	1 939	1	43	41	3	1 201	735	814	69.0	12.1
Graham	26	6.3	2	57	1	42	1 200	1	55	17	0	445	644	788	71.0	11.9
Grant	45	6.6	4	57	1	45	643	1	71	233	10	3 412	1 522	1 481	69.4	11.7
Gray	21	4.0	0	0	0	0	0	2	94	23	1	443	1 207	912	66.1	11.9
Greeley	11	6.1	2	118	1	18	1 059	1	32	8	0	443	339	380	73.5	11.1
Greenwood	42	4.8	3	39	1	46	597	3	193	97	1	1 347	1 209	1 598	66.6	9.2
Hamilton	14	5.6	3	130	1	56	2 435	2	48	20	3	797	471	518	71.2	11.8
Harper	39	5.0	8	111	3	140	1 944	2	107	54	6	1 052	1 243	1 322	68.0	11.2
Harvey	27	0.9	80	260	3	261	847	7	789	711	31	2 407	5 405	5 373	72.7	16.5
Haskell	13	3.3	2	53	1	42	1 105	1	27	33	4	1 187	900	842	70.2	12.6
Hodgeman	8	3.5	0	0	1	51	2 318	0	0	10	0	453	402	459	74.1	15.9
Jackson	54	4.7	5	42	1	15	127	2	111	76	8	641	2 216	2 625	72.9	9.4
Jefferson	53	3.3	10	58	1	118	682	4	234	387	11	2 530	3 555	3 389	71.0	10.9
Jewell	19	3.9	1	23	1	61	1 419	1	49	16	1	346	769	934	73.1	9.7
Johnson	1 182	4.0	1 118	311	6	1 143	318	16	1 360	14 756	824	4 408	53 162	51 185	88.8	33.3
Kearny	12	3.2	0	0	1	20	488	1	40	191	17	4 756	974	769	68.4	12.6
Kingman	35	3.8	3	34	1	49	557	2	171	110	10	1 231	1 429	1 630	66.5	10.4
Kiowa	12	3.0	3	86	1	24	686	1	50	66	6	1 730	622	709	74.3	14.3
Labette	122	4.7	32	128	3	413	1 652	9	446	711	50	2 766	4 541	5 260	65.7	10.2
Lane	10	4.0	2	83	1	31	1 292	1	21	36	4	1 494	507	457	73.4	12.2
Leavenworth	358	6.2	57	83	5	547	793	5	324	2 316	191	3 565	10 670	10 841	72.1	16.8
Lincoln	9	2.3	2	57	1	34	971	2	93	33	0	913	649	648	66.2	9.9
Linn	41	4.9	4	48	0	0	0	4	196	86	6	1 057	1 733	1 616	63.3	7.8
Logan	19	5.6	2	67	1	39	1 300	1	45	53	5	1 599	607	671	68.7	10.3
Lyon	184	4.9	39	114	2	191	557	3	243	1 838	141	5 245	5 821	5 423	76.4	20.4
McPherson	121	4.4	20	75	3	110	410	9	613	436	25	1 675	4 436	4 370	71.4	15.6
Marion	48	3.6	10	79	2	113	897	8	501	90	0	700	2 155	2 297	62.9	11.2
Marshall	31	2.4	6	49	1	55	451	5	250	127	7	1 075	2 375	2 114	66.6	9.4
Meade	19	4.0	4	93	1	26	605	2	94	55	1	1 245	561	934	70.9	14.3
Miami	100	4.5	21	86	2	393	1 617	6	442	631	52	2 720	3 637	4 316	68.4	10.0
Mitchell	18	2.3	6	83	1	89	1 236	2	141	119	13	1 580	1 437	1 313	71.2	14.0
Montgomery	289	6.8	32	79	2	168	413	9	576	1 866	125	4 544	6 982	7 614	64.5	10.5
Morris	23	3.7	4	62	1	28	431	1	100	91	2	1 439	1 023	1 150	67.4	10.8
Morton	19	5.4	6	176	1	90	2 647	0	0	61	14	1 736	831	743	76.4	13.2
Nemaha	28	2.5	6	56	2	57	528	5	327	128	5	1 180	1 668	2 210	64.0	8.3
Neosho	78	4.0	11	62	1	60	339	6	346	404	14	2 187	3 247	3 627	66.9	10.4
Ness	17	3.6	2	49	2	103	2 512	3	64	17	0	394	811	789	68.6	11.9
Norton	20	3.0	4	66	2	115	1 885	1	100	65	4	996	1 139	1 241	65.8	10.7
Osage	54	3.4	7	43	0	0	0	5	331	202	22	1 265	2 937	3 168	68.7	8.5
Osborne	19	3.3	1	20	1	29	569	2	170	6	0	263	494	1 037	66.2	10.4

1. Per 1,000 resident population estimated as of July 1 of the year shown. 2. As of end of year. 3. Per 100,000 resident population as of July 1 of the year shown. 4. Preliminary. Covers nursing homes with 3 or more beds. 5. Data for serious crimes have not been adjusted for underreporting, this may affect comparability between geographic areas or over time. 6. Includes murder and nonnegligent manslaughter, forcible rape, robbery, and aggravated assault. 7. The 1986–1987 data are based on administrative reports obtained by the U.S. National Center for Education Statistics. The 1980 data are based on the 1980 Census of Population and Housing. 8. Persons 25 years old or older.

STATE County	Education (cont'd): Local government expenditures for education,[1] 1982: Total (Mil dol)	Education (cont'd): Local government expenditures for education,[1] 1982: Per capita (Dollars)	Social Security Program December 1988: Beneficiaries: Total	Social Security Program December 1988: Beneficiaries: Rate[2]	Social Security Program December 1988: Payments ($1,000)	Supplemental Security Income Program recipients June 1986	Money income: Per capita[3]: 1987 Income, (Dollars)	Money income: Per capita[3]: 1979: Current dollars	Money income: Per capita[3]: 1979: Constant 1987 dollars	Money income: Median household income 1979 (Dollars)	Money income: Percent below poverty level, 1979: Persons	Money income: Percent below poverty level, 1979: Families	Housing units, 1990: Total	Housing units, 1990: Percent change, 1980–1990
	60	61	62	63	64	65	66	67	68	69	70	71	72	73
KANSAS—Con.														
Bourbon	6.3	393	3 520	231.6	1 602	230	9 377	6 278	9 823	12 127	13.5	8.7	6 920	-3.8
Brown	4.9	413	2 780	243.9	1 273	132	9 104	5 958	9 322	12 329	14.5	11.2	4 890	-6.4
Butler	27.1	579	7 260	144.6	3 714	234	11 425	7 456	11 666	18 457	6.9	5.0	20 072	16.4
Chase	1.7	545	730	235.5	329	28	9 961	6 332	9 908	13 457	14.5	11.5	1 547	-1.3
Chautauqua	1.9	378	1 230	273.3	551	76	8 805	6 075	9 506	11 326	15.2	13.0	2 249	-3.1
Cherokee	9.4	425	4 840	219.0	2 260	458	8 411	5 643	8 830	12 125	15.0	11.4	9 428	1.2
Cheyenne	2.7	727	910	267.6	443	38	9 637	6 700	10 483	12 978	14.1	11.4	1 687	-5.3
Clark	2.1	770	630	252.0	325	16	9 798	7 207	11 277	14 668	8.8	6.1	1 327	3.8
Clay	4.4	463	2 340	257.1	1 093	88	9 427	6 113	9 565	12 895	12.6	10.3	4 138	-2.6
Cloud	5.5	444	3 120	273.7	1 458	158	8 565	5 720	8 950	12 060	14.3	10.2	5 198	-5.4
Coffey	5.2	538	1 885	214.2	836	70	9 545	6 510	10 186	13 915	12.3	9.3	3 712	-3.9
Comanche	2.1	814	665	277.1	341	20	9 717	6 882	10 768	14 277	8.9	7.5	1 256	7.3
Cowley	16.3	435	7 185	192.6	3 554	598	10 314	6 969	10 904	14 997	9.3	6.9	15 569	2.9
Crawford	15.1	397	8 225	221.7	3 876	612	8 950	5 913	9 252	11 486	14.8	9.9	16 526	-1.8
Decatur	2.6	549	1 070	261.0	527	30	9 765	6 681	10 454	13 525	12.2	7.4	2 063	-4.2
Dickinson	11.4	571	4 220	210.0	1 959	198	10 521	6 341	9 922	13 672	12.6	9.3	8 415	-3.1
Doniphan	4.7	515	1 790	198.9	827	106	8 812	5 572	8 719	13 204	14.2	11.4	3 337	-12.3
Douglas	20.5	296	7 695	100.6	3 954	422	10 295	6 473	10 128	14 156	16.5	7.7	31 782	24.7
Edwards	2.1	522	1 050	269.2	516	52	9 605	6 372	9 970	12 929	11.8	8.3	1 867	-6.2
Elk	2.1	550	1 050	300.0	471	64	8 714	5 455	8 535	10 281	16.1	12.2	1 743	-11.7
Ellis	9.8	356	4 300	162.3	2 014	216	9 503	6 603	10 332	15 623	10.6	6.1	11 115	8.5
Ellsworth	4.7	705	1 620	261.3	773	54	8 578	5 863	9 174	12 358	12.3	9.3	3 317	1.4
Finney	13.0	489	3 215	104.0	1 599	200	9 890	7 133	11 161	17 511	9.2	6.1	11 696	30.0
Ford	10.5	420	4 115	158.9	2 075	200	10 767	7 006	10 962	16 505	9.5	6.9	10 842	10.3
Franklin	10.4	473	4 245	188.7	1 985	252	9 801	6 643	10 394	14 218	10.0	8.1	8 926	1.9
Geary	16.5	539	2 895	99.1	1 267	212	9 452	5 947	9 305	12 764	17.0	15.1	11 952	7.8
Gove	3.1	828	755	222.1	368	10	8 317	5 867	9 180	12 273	17.1	14.9	1 494	-6.4
Graham	2.9	710	825	229.2	387	42	9 430	6 479	10 138	12 493	15.4	12.8	1 753	-3.1
Grant	4.0	587	785	113.8	412	24	10 779	7 148	11 184	18 049	9.3	7.0	2 599	-0.1
Gray	4.1	785	830	150.9	414	38	10 470	6 739	10 545	16 392	9.4	7.8	2 114	5.2
Greeley	1.3	696	280	164.7	155	16	9 581	6 785	10 616	15 986	11.0	8.9	801	-1.7
Greenwood	4.5	505	2 325	294.3	1 095	110	8 806	6 109	9 559	12 087	12.4	10.2	4 243	-4.7
Hamilton	1.6	647	545	237.0	290	18	10 579	6 229	9 747	13 567	11.1	7.0	1 214	-4.6
Harper	3.6	461	1 895	259.6	961	58	9 719	6 752	10 565	13 652	13.2	10.3	3 481	-2.3
Harvey	14.1	453	5 355	173.9	2 669	188	10 751	7 008	10 965	16 817	9.0	5.6	12 290	6.3
Haskell	3.3	881	440	112.8	242	14	9 871	6 433	10 066	16 403	11.7	9.6	1 586	6.1
Hodgeman	1.7	777	425	193.2	216	6	9 040	6 850	10 718	15 352	14.6	10.7	1 022	-3.0
Jackson	6.6	562	2 245	190.3	1 003	98	9 470	6 169	9 653	15 725	9.9	7.9	4 564	1.6
Jefferson	9.8	629	2 705	160.1	1 242	96	9 963	6 635	10 382	17 234	8.2	7.1	6 314	8.5
Jewell	3.0	587	1 200	272.7	553	44	7 937	5 597	8 758	11 429	18.7	15.2	2 409	-13.7
Johnson	132.8	474	36 620	105.9	20 677	894	17 259	10 680	16 711	25 173	3.6	2.6	144 155	40.2
Kearny	3.1	820	535	133.8	268	26	10 633	6 815	10 663	17 051	12.0	9.0	1 561	10.8
Kingman	4.6	510	1 815	206.2	886	52	9 668	6 688	10 465	14 887	10.3	7.4	3 645	-1.0
Kiowa	2.8	691	905	251.4	465	34	10 775	6 868	10 746	14 237	12.0	9.0	1 738	1.5
Labette	11.3	438	5 055	200.6	2 299	540	9 407	5 975	9 349	13 330	12.2	9.3	10 641	0.2
Lane	1.7	693	535	222.9	278	14	10 465	6 825	10 679	14 004	8.8	7.7	1 117	-3.6
Leavenworth	23.5	421	6 735	101.3	3 011	340	10 093	6 642	10 393	18 511	9.8	6.8	21 264	15.3
Lincoln	2.0	498	1 100	314.3	504	32	9 045	5 947	9 305	11 833	13.0	8.5	1 864	-11.7
Linn	5.2	639	2 150	259.0	958	138	8 877	5 929	9 277	12 153	15.6	12.1	4 811	21.0
Logan	2.5	717	710	229.0	364	16	9 126	6 292	9 845	14 065	11.4	9.2	1 466	-9.3
Lyon	14.7	403	4 745	136.4	2 278	220	10 005	6 959	10 889	15 933	10.7	6.3	14 346	2.6
McPherson	13.4	491	5 360	197.8	2 748	132	10 978	6 973	10 911	16 162	7.7	5.8	10 941	4.6
Marion	6.5	482	3 295	257.4	1 542	148	9 600	6 182	9 673	13 412	11.9	8.8	5 659	-3.5
Marshall	7.0	535	2 985	242.7	1 321	124	9 810	6 437	10 072	12 607	14.3	11.8	5 269	-5.6
Meade	2.3	482	940	213.6	495	28	9 247	6 101	9 546	13 818	11.0	9.7	2 049	0.0
Miami	10.8	491	3 655	152.9	1 709	246	10 193	6 975	10 914	16 654	7.6	5.9	8 971	6.1
Mitchell	5.1	644	1 875	253.4	916	68	9 608	6 139	9 606	13 201	11.6	7.6	3 359	-4.3
Montgomery	16.9	389	9 295	227.3	4 457	668	9 572	6 587	10 307	13 755	11.2	8.0	17 920	-1.3
Morris	2.5	384	1 465	225.4	664	48	9 649	6 196	9 695	12 192	15.1	12.6	3 149	-1.2
Morton	2.9	823	535	152.9	278	18	9 923	6 895	10 789	16 380	11.6	8.1	1 515	4.2
Nemaha	5.0	451	2 595	240.3	1 146	102	9 109	5 684	8 894	12 306	16.5	12.7	4 319	-2.5
Neosho	8.2	422	3 850	212.7	1 831	226	9 439	6 496	10 164	13 919	9.2	7.3	7 726	-2.0
Ness	3.5	759	1 090	259.5	541	22	10 262	6 836	10 696	13 389	9.8	8.4	2 048	-2.8
Norton	3.6	530	1 625	262.1	787	86	9 675	6 232	9 751	11 758	16.3	12.5	2 798	-6.2
Osage	8.7	554	2 970	184.5	1 350	130	9 595	6 398	10 011	15 203	9.8	7.7	6 324	2.8
Osborne	1.7	289	1 520	292.3	721	54	8 246	5 729	8 964	11 552	14.7	10.8	2 496	-10.0

1. Elementary and secondary. 2. Per 1,000 resident population estimated as of July 1 of the year shown. 3. Based on the resident population estimated as of July 1, 1988 for 1987 data and enumerated as of April 1, 1980 for 1979 data.

STATE County	Housing units, 1990 (cont'd)				Civilian labor force, 1990				Private nonfarm establishments, 1988					
	Occupied units						Unemployment				Employment[2]			
		Owner occupied												
	Total	Percent	Median value (Dollars)	Median rent (Dollars)	Total	Percent change, 1989–1990	Total	Rate[1]	Number	Net change, 1987–1988	Total	Percent change, 1987–1988	Manu-facturing	Retail trade
	74	75	76	77	78	79	80	81	82	83	84	85	86	87
KANSAS—Con.														
Bourbon	5 897	73.8	29 800	179	6 989	-2.5	336	4.8	990	-17	6 397	6.1	935	1 245
Brown	4 347	70.6	28 000	159	5 389	2.8	221	4.1	274	-2	2 639	10.9	612	583
Butler	18 488	75.4	51 800	243	25 391	1.0	924	3.6	997	4	8 582	8.8	1 429	2 386
Chase	1 214	75.6	22 400	151	1 813	5.8	91	5.0	76	6	555	7.8	42	127
Chautauqua	1 835	79.9	18 900	141	1 810	-0.1	78	4.3	89	-6	643	6.8	0	85
Cherokee	8 396	76.5	27 000	166	10 267	2.6	716	7.0	347	-8	3 937	3.4	1 398	758
Cheyenne	1 389	75.6	31 900	144	1 447	-1.4	34	2.3	110	-7	611	2.9	0	198
Clark	1 006	75.3	29 500	189	1 082	-2.3	34	3.1	87	0	341	-11.0	0	94
Clay	3 641	73.4	33 800	169	4 011	-3.3	171	4.3	263	5	1 955	3.6	509	465
Cloud	4 483	72.4	25 600	152	5 450	1.5	188	3.4	324	-17	2 798	0.1	273	638
Coffey	3 311	77.3	34 800	194	4 477	9.7	223	5.0	219	-1	1 175	-40.8	131	438
Comanche	950	71.8	24 300	153	1 271	0.7	34	2.7	83	0	398	-9.8	51	80
Cowley	14 047	71.2	37 500	213	18 171	1.0	1 065	5.9	793	-40	9 544	0.6	3 843	2 143
Crawford	14 606	67.5	30 700	207	18 048	3.1	951	5.3	871	-9	10 250	-0.6	2 910	2 285
Decatur	1 651	75.1	28 800	166	1 909	-3.6	63	3.3	152	-4	963	5.9	76	215
Dickinson	7 542	73.5	35 600	190	9 353	0.7	410	4.4	527	-2	3 873	2.8	494	1 304
Doniphan	3 074	75.4	29 200	164	4 025	0.9	231	5.7	154	1	1 485	0.3	427	252
Douglas	30 138	52.5	68 000	343	44 397	3.9	1 617	3.6	1 813	27	21 742	6.3	4 429	6 784
Edwards	1 585	75.3	24 900	160	1 644	-1.6	51	3.1	110	-1	732	-1.6	201	157
Elk	1 436	80.0	14 999	111	1 502	1.3	66	4.4	77	0	226	0.4	0	83
Ellis	10 096	64.4	49 600	227	14 453	2.5	463	3.2	921	-5	8 024	0.7	267	2 676
Ellsworth	2 522	77.4	28 300	166	3 023	2.9	92	3.0	196	7	1 268	1.6	0	256
Finney	10 836	61.5	50 800	300	19 768	1.9	664	3.4	897	-4	11 823	7.2	4 351	2 303
Ford	9 872	64.9	48 900	263	15 693	3.7	460	2.9	794	0	9 860	4.8	2 704	2 400
Franklin	8 308	72.7	37 700	216	10 840	1.5	678	6.3	471	-23	5 287	17.2	1 207	1 308
Geary	10 676	45.5	55 400	283	11 545	-0.3	690	6.0	632	15	6 369	5.4	587	2 673
Gove	1 284	79.7	30 300	148	1 721	1.4	48	2.8	101	-3	564	-0.2	55	207
Graham	1 435	76.8	24 900	145	1 775	0.1	54	3.0	115	-9	549	2.0	20	165
Grant	2 393	69.2	53 200	263	3 547	5.7	97	2.7	236	-6	1 796	6.3	351	472
Gray	1 913	72.4	45 500	204	2 266	2.1	70	3.1	174	6	1 015	1.2	29	141
Greeley	656	70.1	39 500	206	966	1.5	30	3.1	65	2	372	7.8	0	92
Greenwood	3 285	74.2	21 900	156	3 683	-0.6	191	5.2	238	-5	1 333	1.2	104	319
Hamilton	986	70.8	37 800	197	1 133	-1.5	35	3.1	81	-2	381	-1.8	0	89
Harper	3 007	73.3	32 300	183	3 820	1.2	103	2.7	240	-3	1 400	1.4	255	389
Harvey	11 581	68.4	47 100	231	16 090	-0.7	551	3.4	761	-9	10 233	1.1	2 592	2 196
Haskell	1 372	70.0	45 900	229	1 742	0.6	66	3.8	96	-1	494	4.7	0	80
Hodgeman	826	81.0	26 800	158	1 010	-2.9	36	3.6	38	4	128	-2.3	0	44
Jackson	4 277	81.4	34 300	183	5 120	-0.4	344	6.7	239	10	1 446	11.1	0	464
Jefferson	5 778	83.9	47 100	223	8 162	2.8	454	5.6	256	-4	1 380	-1.1	50	332
Jewell	1 806	78.7	14 999	116	1 642	-3.5	57	3.5	103	0	472	11.3	24	168
Johnson	136 433	69.4	91 500	438	206 718	2.4	6 249	3.0	10 944	417	157 106	3.1	20 968	35 735
Kearny	1 379	69.4	45 900	254	1 581	-0.4	61	3.9	75	3	300	7.1	0	120
Kingman	3 175	75.6	34 600	199	4 195	2.5	143	3.4	220	12	1 455	-5.2	251	361
Kiowa	1 466	71.6	33 600	173	1 853	1.0	39	2.1	111	-5	662	-2.5	0	175
Labette	9 377	73.3	29 000	187	12 470	-3.7	788	6.3	553	1	7 569	6.7	3 709	1 420
Lane	966	74.9	32 600	169	1 090	-0.1	28	2.6	72	2	303	0.0	0	105
Leavenworth	19 715	65.2	64 000	342	27 705	1.4	1 307	4.7	882	15	9 265	-6.1	1 338	2 662
Lincoln	1 531	78.8	17 200	112	1 673	2.1	75	4.5	99	-5	418	-11.4	0	141
Linn	3 215	80.2	26 800	151	3 385	-3.2	289	8.5	182	9	1 339	9.0	58	244
Logan	1 221	76.7	30 800	157	1 440	-0.3	43	3.0	136	3	574	-0.2	3	205
Lyon	13 059	61.3	45 800	234	19 833	1.1	896	4.5	839	14	11 984	1.2	4 841	2 808
McPherson	10 230	73.1	47 900	224	14 802	0.8	430	2.9	813	-36	10 108	1.0	2 838	1 887
Marion	4 975	79.1	30 700	176	6 219	0.5	197	3.2	365	12	2 685	5.5	410	596
Marshall	4 689	78.0	26 300	156	6 240	-0.1	140	2.2	337	-4	2 593	3.6	651	611
Meade	1 667	72.5	35 900	192	2 028	1.3	54	2.7	119	-1	564	-4.2	34	154
Miami	8 402	77.1	47 700	235	11 801	1.6	613	5.2	461	11	3 703	4.7	689	998
Mitchell	2 846	74.0	28 800	174	3 874	3.3	105	2.7	251	6	1 830	-0.5	291	418
Montgomery	15 670	72.3	29 400	192	18 562	2.2	1 090	5.9	1 062	20	12 592	3.0	4 886	2 827
Morris	2 528	75.8	33 500	176	3 258	-2.2	116	3.6	141	2	1 060	7.5	192	270
Morton	1 290	72.7	44 700	218	1 617	-3.1	54	3.3	98	-6	565	0.9	0	167
Nemaha	3 996	80.6	35 400	163	5 819	-0.3	115	2.0	356	15	2 892	9.7	605	585
Neosho	6 748	74.8	28 600	180	9 012	3.6	428	4.7	510	-16	4 847	3.7	1 794	877
Ness	1 670	80.0	29 900	163	2 074	0.2	51	2.5	149	4	763	2.4	0	145
Norton	2 330	74.9	25 700	163	2 876	1.6	69	2.4	180	-10	1 159	1.8	81	360
Osage	5 806	79.2	38 300	189	8 426	2.8	567	6.7	291	12	2 121	8.2	0	603
Osborne	2 057	78.6	18 400	138	2 295	0.0	52	2.3	167	-12	1 065	-4.7	222	268

1. Percent of total civilian labor force. 2. For week including March 12. Excludes government employees, self-employed persons, farm workers, domestic service workers, railroad employees subject to the Railroad Retirement Act, and employees on oceanborne vessels or in foreign countries.

STATE County	Private nonfarm establishments, 1988 (cont'd): Employment[1] (cont'd): Finance, insurance, and real estate	Employment[1] (cont'd): Services	Annual payroll: Total (Mil dol)	Annual payroll: Average per employee (Dollars)	Personal income, 1989: Total (Mil dol)	Percent change, 1988–1989	Wages and salaries[2] (Mil dol)	Proprietor's income (Mil dol)	Dividends, interest, & rent (Mil dol)	Transfer payments (Mil dol)	Per capita[3]: Dollars	Per capita[3]: Rank	Earnings, 1989: Total (Mil dol)	Percent by selected industries: Farm	Goods-related[4]: Total
	88	89	90	91	92	93	94	95	96	97	98	99	100	101	102
KANSAS—Con.															
Bourbon	1 158	1 203	90	14 042	219	3.4	119	20	49	45	14 611	1 160	139	2.2	22.4
Brown	255	818	35	13 129	161	7.1	65	22	44	37	14 140	1 375	87	12.8	20.8
Butler	576	2 104	133	15 451	827	7.4	247	96	134	112	16 192	596	343	6.2	29.5
Chase	32	84	7	13 137	49	2.2	11	10	12	9	16 244	582	21	36.7	7.1
Chautauqua	0	290	9	13 960	57	6.9	14	11	15	17	12 672	2 047	25	14.9	13.4
Cherokee	157	649	64	16 148	268	6.2	106	26	49	61	12 163	2 253	133	5.8	28.0
Cheyenne	41	162	7	11 511	55	-0.4	15	15	18	9	16 449	535	29	25.6	NA
Clark	49	76	5	15 798	47	3.9	12	14	13	9	18 818	231	26	46.3	3.3
Clay	81	415	22	11 504	132	4.3	41	23	39	25	14 561	1 184	64	9.7	19.5
Cloud	156	1 016	38	13 427	158	3.6	65	18	46	35	14 081	1 396	83	4.8	8.6
Coffey	74	260	12	10 159	128	5.1	83	19	33	22	14 798	1 077	102	9.5	9.2
Comanche	36	149	4	9 510	37	-0.3	10	9	12	7	15 580	779	19	32.7	8.8
Cowley	408	1 910	165	17 313	559	7.5	296	65	106	101	14 993	990	361	2.8	30.0
Crawford	524	2 680	160	15 617	530	6.8	246	52	116	120	14 372	1 257	298	4.1	24.1
Decatur	52	352	11	11 327	87	3.9	20	32	22	13	21 502	111	52	51.3	7.0
Dickinson	236	941	51	13 131	285	4.0	102	28	65	62	14 154	1 367	130	3.1	12.6
Doniphan	75	221	25	16 844	105	4.6	49	11	24	21	11 677	2 449	59	8.3	31.0
Douglas	999	6 126	332	15 291	1 087	8.8	647	93	200	129	13 886	1 486	740	0.2	24.7
Edwards	73	159	10	13 738	68	-13.2	20	20	17	12	17 831	317	40	41.4	11.2
Elk	36	35	2	10 748	51	12.7	10	12	13	12	14 696	1 131	22	24.8	NA
Ellis	454	2 728	109	13 543	386	6.5	191	53	86	62	14 863	1 046	245	4.1	14.3
Ellsworth	84	385	17	13 799	90	7.5	39	9	28	16	14 764	1 102	48	6.1	25.9
Finney	538	2 591	193	16 282	470	5.0	313	70	69	52	15 056	965	382	6.0	32.8
Ford	381	2 339	157	15 965	439	2.6	247	67	81	63	16 989	440	313	5.9	25.2
Franklin	491	1 362	74	13 922	312	6.5	118	36	59	54	13 820	1 523	154	6.3	27.0
Geary	331	1 522	79	12 353	347	6.4	500	27	58	70	12 164	2 252	528	1.0	4.4
Gove	42	95	6	11 266	60	12.7	17	22	15	8	17 915	307	39	48.8	7.3
Graham	68	133	7	12 495	52	2.3	20	9	15	10	14 912	1 022	29	10.3	NA
Grant	74	201	33	18 421	136	0.5	62	47	20	14	19 564	191	108	32.2	23.7
Gray	324	177	17	16 760	82	-9.7	33	28	14	10	14 863	1 047	61	31.5	4.8
Greeley	0	115	4	10 516	41	21.4	10	21	6	4	23 620	63	31	64.8	NA
Greenwood	127	466	17	12 565	115	3.3	32	23	29	27	14 858	1 051	55	13.9	15.5
Hamilton	0	77	4	10 751	50	-15.7	13	19	12	7	21 727	104	32	50.8	NA
Harper	107	286	19	13 636	122	4.6	40	24	32	26	16 855	460	64	22.1	16.2
Harvey	348	3 796	170	16 643	458	4.8	245	48	90	73	14 870	1 043	293	4.0	29.6
Haskell	49	55	10	21 144	70	-16.2	25	26	14	6	18 274	266	51	44.0	8.3
Hodgeman	35	8	2	15 367	31	-15.2	8	7	10	5	14 070	1 401	15	38.4	NA
Jackson	93	238	16	10 762	161	6.0	39	13	31	27	13 631	1 611	52	5.2	20.0
Jefferson	79	528	19	13 560	233	6.8	49	17	42	36	13 515	1 671	66	4.1	14.4
Jewell	58	79	5	10 288	58	0.4	14	11	20	12	13 647	1 602	25	24.8	6.7
Johnson	19 685	42 145	3 331	21 200	8 397	8.0	4 649	602	1 573	579	23 346	67	5 251	0.1	18.3
Kearny	27	72	3	11 243	70	-4.2	23	24	13	8	17 031	430	47	47.8	NA
Kingman	93	393	20	13 741	117	1.6	39	14	33	22	13 297	1 772	53	7.2	21.1
Kiowa	39	278	9	12 959	63	-3.4	22	16	16	11	17 744	327	37	27.6	9.6
Labette	352	1 072	126	16 584	354	3.4	205	38	59	76	14 182	1 353	244	6.1	37.6
Lane	0	53	4	14 531	41	13.5	12	10	12	7	16 954	445	22	31.1	6.7
Leavenworth	749	2 944	137	14 769	875	7.5	527	66	120	136	12 674	2 045	593	2.8	10.0
Lincoln	46	110	4	10 378	49	1.3	14	5	17	12	14 191	1 348	19	11.7	NA
Linn	106	330	25	18 507	111	4.3	51	15	24	23	13 383	1 738	66	5.1	19.6
Logan	0	164	6	10 963	49	15.5	17	13	13	8	16 357	559	30	29.3	6.3
Lyon	475	2 245	199	16 569	507	7.0	326	39	92	81	14 769	1 099	365	2.2	35.9
McPherson	621	3 247	157	15 538	442	5.3	233	66	86	64	16 469	534	299	6.2	39.4
Marion	129	1 147	30	11 178	181	5.3	53	30	44	39	14 430	1 243	83	15.0	15.6
Marshall	193	579	37	14 272	180	6.0	71	28	53	36	14 849	1 053	99	9.1	22.9
Meade	43	149	7	12 246	68	-3.0	22	14	19	11	15 653	758	36	23.1	5.9
Miami	250	946	52	14 075	342	6.4	113	28	66	55	14 064	1 404	141	4.2	20.4
Mitchell	124	519	26	14 428	101	-1.2	46	9	31	23	14 010	1 434	55	-2.2	16.5
Montgomery	571	2 248	191	15 174	555	6.9	319	48	114	118	13 642	1 606	366	1.4	37.9
Morris	76	210	14	12 757	82	4.9	26	10	19	20	12 663	2 051	35	8.0	18.7
Morton	59	63	9	15 331	55	0.7	25	11	12	9	15 928	666	35	20.2	13.7
Nemaha	117	761	40	13 934	159	5.2	66	22	51	27	14 771	1 094	87	2.2	24.6
Neosho	235	864	76	15 732	251	7.4	126	29	49	56	14 152	1 369	155	3.8	35.5
Ness	62	100	11	14 312	75	1.5	24	21	21	12	18 579	245	44	18.8	15.9
Norton	100	267	17	14 299	88	1.1	37	12	25	18	14 485	1 221	48	6.7	13.7
Osage	91	592	25	11 794	217	6.0	52	18	44	39	13 387	1 736	69	5.0	18.8
Osborne	96	246	12	11 463	74	1.3	24	10	25	17	14 603	1 167	33	10.2	14.9

1. For week including March 12. Excludes government employees, self-employed persons, farm workers, domestic service workers, railroad employees subject to the Railroad Retirement Act, and employees on oceanborne vessels or in foreign countries. 2. Includes other labor income. 3. Based on the resident population estimated as of July 1 of the year shown. 4. Covers mining, construction, and manufacturing.

STATE County	Earnings, 1989 (cont'd)						Agriculture, 1987									
	Percent by selected industries (cont'd)						Farms			Farm operators, percent		Land in farms				
	Goods-related[1]	Service-related & other[2]						Percent with						Acres		
	Manufacturing	Total	Retail trade	Finance, insurance, & real estate	Services	Government	Number	Less than 50 acres	500 acres and over	Whose principal occupation is farming	Residing on farm operated	Acreage (1,000)	Percent change, 1982–1987	Average size of farm	Total irrigated (1,000)	Total cropland (1,000)
	103	104	105	106	107	108	109	110	111	112	113	114	115	116	117	118
KANSAS—Con.																
Bourbon	17.8	61.2	9.5	12.0	20.9	14.2	842	13.9	22.1	50.6	69.6	319	-5.4	379	1	168
Brown	17.5	49.1	7.4	8.0	21.2	17.3	728	13.7	30.6	74.6	70.1	340	-1.9	467	D	272
Butler	15.8	46.8	10.1	3.9	22.9	17.5	1 300	19.5	28.8	50.5	74.7	699	1.2	538	2	341
Chase	2.1	39.0	10.4	4.0	10.6	17.2	288	11.1	47.9	65.6	66.0	329	-20.7	1 142	0	85
Chautauqua	2.0	54.3	9.9	3.0	30.0	17.4	421	9.7	35.9	52.7	66.0	321	-3.9	762	0	73
Cherokee	24.5	48.4	6.9	3.1	15.5	17.7	841	22.5	21.3	52.1	74.9	281	-5.4	334	0	211
Cheyenne	NA	57.0	9.4	6.8	22.6	13.8	493	6.3	66.1	75.7	60.9	620	2.8	1 257	41	404
Clark	0.2	29.8	5.9	4.2	9.5	20.7	290	7.6	64.1	70.0	49.3	588	-0.1	2 026	6	198
Clay	11.9	52.1	10.4	4.0	22.1	18.7	672	10.9	43.0	74.0	67.9	392	7.5	584	11	284
Cloud	2.8	67.4	11.4	12.7	22.3	19.2	659	11.4	40.2	68.1	63.3	397	-1.5	603	10	293
Coffey	2.8	NA	6.2	2.3	NA	13.6	606	11.7	36.0	60.7	70.1	330	-1.4	545	0	208
Comanche	4.3	38.6	9.3	4.1	13.2	19.9	277	12.3	64.3	72.2	52.7	481	4.0	1 737	4	187
Cowley	24.5	46.4	7.9	2.6	27.2	20.8	997	16.3	32.9	51.8	70.5	620	-11.4	622	1	269
Crawford	16.9	50.0	9.7	3.4	23.1	21.7	809	17.3	19.4	55.3	70.0	284	-12.8	351	1	182
Decatur	0.9	32.2	5.5	1.7	12.5	9.5	486	8.2	64.8	78.6	59.7	543	1.6	1 118	10	356
Dickinson	5.0	65.7	11.9	9.1	23.1	18.5	1 028	12.5	34.8	65.2	71.7	514	-2.6	500	3	393
Doniphan	23.7	NA	7.0	3.2	NA	19.5	530	20.9	28.3	68.7	69.2	216	-3.7	408	D	169
Douglas	17.6	46.9	11.6	3.9	23.9	28.1	852	24.1	14.0	42.3	75.9	223	0.3	262	1	155
Edwards	9.0	35.6	5.4	3.6	14.6	11.8	361	5.5	58.7	78.7	55.4	387	1.3	1 073	83	316
Elk	NA	41.5	6.3	3.3	15.4	24.3	409	8.1	42.1	59.9	62.6	341	-6.6	833	D	85
Ellis	3.2	60.1	13.7	4.5	30.8	21.4	795	12.1	40.0	59.2	53.0	569	11.8	716	1	333
Ellsworth	15.5	43.5	8.1	3.8	19.1	24.5	499	7.2	51.7	69.9	63.3	424	9.3	849	1	247
Finney	25.5	48.6	9.4	3.8	20.9	12.7	534	11.6	61.8	71.0	55.4	723	0.2	1 353	184	582
Ford	19.6	54.7	11.5	4.0	21.7	14.1	812	12.9	50.7	64.3	55.2	675	-2.4	831	78	549
Franklin	19.2	48.6	10.4	7.0	19.2	18.1	979	21.3	17.8	44.0	74.5	313	2.6	319	2	208
Geary	2.4	18.2	6.2	1.3	7.2	76.5	295	18.6	34.9	56.3	75.6	170	8.7	577	2	77
Gove	3.1	29.6	7.1	3.0	6.9	14.3	534	12.7	61.8	73.2	58.2	677	0.3	1 267	16	445
Graham	NA	NA	12.1	5.6	17.1	25.1	452	8.0	59.3	73.2	53.1	504	-3.7	1 114	9	320
Grant	3.1	33.8	5.5	1.8	11.3	10.3	303	8.3	60.1	75.2	58.7	323	-3.0	1 066	99	277
Gray	0.9	52.1	5.2	12.2	9.0	11.5	547	9.0	55.2	77.3	54.5	532	-0.9	973	154	465
Greeley	NA	NA	3.8	1.9	8.7	9.0	294	5.8	59.9	73.5	51.0	475	6.6	1 617	25	430
Greenwood	2.4	53.9	10.8	4.8	22.6	16.7	587	13.1	37.5	55.2	67.5	550	-8.7	936	1	128
Hamilton	NA	NA	5.8	2.7	9.7	16.0	279	6.5	75.3	72.0	53.0	538	-1.2	1 930	19	404
Harper	7.8	41.3	9.3	3.8	13.3	20.4	648	11.4	48.0	69.8	58.8	484	-1.2	748	1	350
Harvey	24.4	55.8	8.9	2.7	30.6	10.6	874	25.7	23.9	54.8	75.7	309	-3.7	354	21	275
Haskell	2.3	33.6	4.5	3.6	6.7	14.1	315	7.6	68.3	79.4	54.0	370	2.4	1 174	154	334
Hodgeman	NA	NA	4.4	3.6	9.1	28.1	423	9.0	63.6	74.7	57.9	495	2.6	1 170	23	343
Jackson	10.1	46.3	13.8	5.4	16.7	28.5	1 082	16.5	18.9	46.2	78.6	335	-10.9	310	2	209
Jefferson	1.3	48.0	7.5	3.8	20.7	33.5	1 017	21.1	14.1	45.2	77.3	264	-3.0	259	2	178
Jewell	0.7	42.6	6.9	5.0	15.5	26.0	736	11.7	45.0	79.2	64.0	502	-1.6	682	7	354
Johnson	11.0	72.2	11.4	10.6	27.8	9.4	659	35.8	12.3	41.4	73.3	152	-10.7	230	0	107
Kearny	NA	31.5	3.4	1.4	7.7	16.2	291	8.2	66.7	77.3	52.9	549	3.3	1 888	83	393
Kingman	6.4	51.7	9.9	4.9	20.1	20.0	818	11.4	41.0	66.7	69.3	518	5.2	633	15	364
Kiowa	0.7	47.4	6.4	2.3	18.3	15.5	310	5.8	65.8	74.2	60.3	392	-7.2	1 265	37	262
Labette	33.6	35.7	7.8	2.5	11.9	20.6	971	14.2	23.5	47.9	72.5	350	-1.3	360	2	230
Lane	2.0	41.3	7.0	6.0	9.4	20.9	322	5.6	66.1	75.2	50.6	467	0.9	1 450	15	342
Leavenworth	5.0	26.7	5.7	2.7	14.4	60.5	1 144	31.6	9.0	40.0	79.3	211	-7.0	185	0	145
Lincoln	NA	NA	7.3	5.8	17.9	32.6	578	9.2	47.6	75.6	64.9	454	3.1	786	1	272
Linn	1.1	60.2	5.8	3.2	9.4	15.1	688	14.0	24.6	49.6	71.7	273	-2.6	397	D	156
Logan	1.4	43.6	11.2	3.8	13.5	20.8	382	6.0	68.1	69.6	45.8	610	4.7	1 598	11	349
Lyon	32.3	42.3	9.1	2.4	15.1	19.6	872	14.9	28.0	52.8	74.3	470	-6.1	539	D	249
McPherson	31.8	44.3	7.9	5.1	19.1	10.1	1 357	15.6	26.3	57.2	69.9	533	-4.3	393	24	432
Marion	9.8	51.5	9.1	4.4	26.1	17.8	1 119	14.7	33.2	65.0	72.8	578	1.0	516	2	391
Marshall	17.6	54.9	7.7	5.0	17.2	13.2	1 061	11.2	39.3	72.3	68.2	553	4.7	522	2	409
Meade	0.5	52.3	5.7	4.6	21.0	18.7	464	6.2	64.0	74.1	52.2	582	-1.9	1 255	100	395
Miami	12.9	46.9	9.8	3.8	16.9	28.5	1 151	26.6	11.4	37.6	74.9	272	-11.8	237	0	177
Mitchell	11.1	62.0	10.0	4.3	26.8	23.8	622	11.9	48.9	71.1	60.1	474	5.8	762	5	383
Montgomery	33.0	46.3	9.4	2.8	16.6	14.4	974	18.5	16.6	42.8	73.8	327	0.7	336	2	186
Morris	9.2	52.3	12.3	4.2	14.5	21.0	550	10.9	41.1	68.4	72.0	397	-1.6	721	0	195
Morton	1.2	42.0	6.2	2.8	10.0	24.1	226	6.6	65.9	73.5	52.7	457	6.4	2 024	36	291
Nemaha	17.2	58.9	9.6	3.6	19.4	14.3	1 127	11.5	27.4	71.2	71.1	437	5.4	388	0	331
Neosho	25.0	41.7	9.1	4.0	14.7	18.9	751	12.5	24.8	57.4	71.2	305	-4.0	407	1	197
Ness	0.4	46.9	6.2	3.9	18.5	18.3	597	4.5	60.8	71.4	53.3	673	-0.9	1 128	3	465
Norton	7.0	50.1	10.6	7.3	17.6	29.4	470	10.0	60.6	74.5	61.1	508	-1.1	1 080	6	323
Osage	10.6	51.0	13.1	4.4	17.5	25.2	885	18.0	24.6	46.0	72.7	357	-6.0	404	D	215
Osborne	11.8	55.3	9.8	7.7	17.5	19.6	607	8.4	54.4	73.6	58.5	545	6.6	899	8	348

1. Covers mining, construction, and manufacturing. 2. Covers private sector earnings in agricultural services, forestry, and fisheries; transportation and public utilities; wholesale trade; retail trade; finance, insurance, and real estate; and services.

STATE County	Agriculture, 1987 (cont'd)								Manufactures, 1987						
	Value of land and buildings		Value of products sold				Percent of farms with sales of		Establishments		All employees			Production workers	
					Percent from										
	Average per farm ($1,000)	Average per acre (Dollars)	Total (Mil dol)	Average per farm (Dollars)	Crops	Livestock and poultry[1]	$10,000 or more	$100,000 or more	Total	Percent with 20 or more employees	Number (1,000)	Percent change, 1982–1987	Annual payroll (Mil dol)	Number (1,000)	Work hours (Mil)
	119	120	121	122	123	124	125	126	127	128	129	130	131	132	133
KANSAS—Con.															
Bourbon	146	393	23	27 389	26.3	73.7	44.8	5.6	28	53.6	1.1	37.5	17.3	0.7	1.5
Brown	309	654	63	85 944	42.7	57.3	74.6	19.5	14	21.4	0.6	20.0	8.9	0.6	1.0
Butler	262	497	99	76 376	14.6	85.4	50.0	12.8	42	28.6	D	D	D	D	D
Chase	320	288	34	118 098	10.8	89.2	73.3	19.8	3	33.3	0.0	0.0	0.6	0.0	0.0
Chautauqua	187	239	16	37 309	31.2	68.8	45.1	7.1	4	0.0	D	D	D	D	D
Cherokee	174	541	22	26 194	66.1	33.9	44.5	5.5	34	32.4	1.4	27.3	22.0	1.0	1.9
Cheyenne	397	311	52	104 549	36.4	63.6	77.9	16.8	1	0.0	D	D	D	D	D
Clark	521	242	55	189 456	11.1	88.9	79.0	31.7	2	0.0	D	D	D	D	D
Clay	243	426	40	59 040	40.5	59.5	72.6	15.3	15	40.0	0.6	0.0	8.8	0.5	0.9
Cloud	263	407	31	46 847	55.7	44.3	66.2	11.7	13	23.1	0.3	0.0	5.5	0.2	0.4
Coffey	195	357	32	53 563	43.5	56.5	66.7	12.5	7	14.3	D	D	D	D	D
Comanche	418	266	29	105 220	19.3	80.7	73.6	30.3	6	16.7	0.0	0.0	0.7	0.0	0.1
Cowley	230	385	56	56 075	20.4	79.6	50.1	8.3	48	47.9	3.9	69.6	89.3	3.0	6.2
Crawford	154	436	22	26 873	47.2	52.8	46.5	4.6	65	36.9	2.2	-18.5	42.6	1.5	3.0
Decatur	351	292	73	149 300	24.1	75.9	80.5	21.8	8	12.5	0.1	0.0	0.7	0.0	0.1
Dickinson	210	446	65	63 458	27.3	72.7	64.2	14.1	25	24.0	0.5	-16.7	9.4	0.4	0.7
Doniphan	279	741	35	65 378	63.9	36.1	69.6	20.0	10	20.0	0.4	33.3	7.6	0.2	0.5
Douglas	196	827	28	32 892	44.1	55.9	39.1	8.0	82	35.4	4.5	7.1	98.8	3.1	6.5
Edwards	456	423	58	160 296	42.1	57.9	78.4	31.6	9	11.1	0.2	0.0	2.4	0.1	0.2
Elk	237	277	18	43 777	11.7	88.3	55.3	8.8	1	0.0	D	D	D	D	D
Ellis	265	381	47	59 111	20.3	79.7	55.3	6.4	21	23.8	D	D	D	D	D
Ellsworth	277	338	21	42 978	42.7	57.3	71.1	9.0	8	25.0	0.2	-33.3	3.8	0.1	0.2
Finney	657	499	382	714 479	11.3	88.7	78.8	33.7	42	33.3	D	D	D	D	D
Ford	342	429	229	282 121	12.9	87.1	71.3	20.7	33	36.4	D	D	D	D	D
Franklin	182	565	33	33 718	41.4	58.6	41.9	7.7	20	45.0	1.1	10.0	18.5	0.8	1.7
Geary	238	429	17	55 952	25.2	74.8	60.3	14.2	16	43.8	0.5	-28.6	9.8	0.4	0.8
Gove	351	297	94	175 887	16.7	83.3	76.8	20.8	4	25.0	D	D	D	D	D
Graham	413	317	28	60 859	42.8	57.2	73.5	13.5	3	0.0	D	D	D	D	D
Grant	536	513	231	763 735	8.8	91.2	79.2	29.0	9	33.3	0.2	0.0	4.6	0.2	0.3
Gray	479	518	236	432 227	16.1	83.9	81.9	38.0	4	0.0	0.0	0.0	0.2	0.0	0.0
Greeley	668	419	82	277 445	20.2	79.8	73.5	26.5	2	0.0	D	D	D	D	D
Greenwood	314	320	35	60 276	11.5	88.5	60.5	12.3	13	15.4	0.1	0.0	1.2	0.1	0.1
Hamilton	569	306	80	287 289	16.0	84.0	76.7	23.7	1	0.0	D	D	D	D	D
Harper	314	425	55	85 280	29.4	70.6	72.8	22.4	14	28.6	0.2	100.0	4.1	0.2	0.3
Harvey	254	658	52	59 919	36.9	63.1	57.9	13.4	58	39.7	D	D	D	D	D
Haskell	757	654	249	790 379	12.2	87.8	85.4	47.3	2	0.0	D	D	D	D	D
Hodgeman	386	312	89	211 527	14.7	85.3	79.0	24.3	1	0.0	D	D	D	D	D
Jackson	128	427	28	25 684	28.3	71.7	47.9	4.1	8	12.5	0.1	0.0	2.1	0.1	0.1
Jefferson	169	619	25	24 878	47.3	52.7	41.5	6.5	10	0.0	0.0	-100.0	0.5	0.0	0.0
Jewell	247	389	44	59 882	42.3	57.7	73.8	15.8	4	0.0	0.0	0.0	0.1	0.0	0.0
Johnson	323	1 334	23	34 716	46.4	53.6	39.6	7.3	522	35.2	21.5	13.2	491.8	12.2	24.7
Kearny	741	378	119	408 900	22.4	77.6	78.4	33.0	1	0.0	D	D	D	D	D
Kingman	270	434	36	43 984	44.1	55.9	65.6	10.5	10	20.0	0.2	0.0	3.3	0.1	0.3
Kiowa	405	340	25	79 330	53.4	46.6	75.5	25.2	4	0.0	D	D	D	D	D
Labette	153	430	49	50 424	23.1	76.9	47.1	5.7	45	55.6	3.4	41.7	67.3	2.5	4.6
Lane	592	371	88	273 955	16.1	83.9	76.4	26.4	2	0.0	D	D	D	D	D
Leavenworth	170	939	27	23 341	47.7	52.3	34.1	4.9	31	32.3	D	D	D	D	D
Lincoln	254	326	39	66 844	29.4	70.6	71.8	12.6	4	0.0	D	D	D	D	D
Linn	157	407	22	31 545	36.9	63.1	50.6	8.3	10	0.0	0.1	0.0	0.8	0.0	0.1
Logan	382	243	22	58 692	50.9	49.1	74.9	18.3	3	0.0	D	D	D	D	D
Lyon	178	320	58	66 718	20.6	79.4	54.7	9.9	27	55.6	4.8	6.7	106.3	3.2	6.9
McPherson	222	562	78	57 451	34.1	65.9	62.9	11.1	76	38.2	2.8	12.0	70.5	1.9	3.9
Marion	215	436	59	52 396	29.6	70.4	65.3	12.3	27	22.2	0.4	-20.0	5.7	0.3	0.5
Marshall	238	451	54	50 700	44.7	55.3	74.6	12.3	14	35.7	0.6	200.0	12.5	0.5	1.0
Meade	483	412	55	119 161	41.1	58.9	80.2	25.6	6	0.0	0.0	0.0	0.3	0.0	0.0
Miami	193	854	25	21 651	53.1	46.9	34.9	4.9	24	33.3	D	D	D	D	D
Mitchell	346	445	60	96 319	36.0	64.0	76.5	17.8	12	33.3	0.3	0.0	4.8	0.2	0.3
Montgomery	154	470	23	23 601	40.9	59.1	35.9	4.3	79	35.4	4.7	-6.0	90.4	3.6	6.9
Morris	242	336	39	71 326	16.8	83.2	66.2	12.2	8	37.5	0.2	0.0	3.0	0.1	0.3
Morton	564	280	20	89 342	48.4	51.6	71.7	23.0	5	0.0	0.0	0.0	0.7	0.0	0.1
Nemaha	167	442	61	54 499	26.1	73.9	74.2	14.1	21	28.6	0.6	50.0	9.1	0.4	0.8
Neosho	158	380	26	34 768	43.0	57.0	50.5	8.0	46	52.2	1.8	-5.3	34.9	1.2	2.4
Ness	285	257	28	46 932	48.8	51.2	72.2	13.7	3	33.3	D	D	D	D	D
Norton	341	322	33	71 101	41.0	59.0	78.7	15.7	6	16.7	0.1	0.0	1.7	0.1	0.1
Osage	155	399	31	34 762	42.5	57.5	48.8	7.1	11	27.3	D	D	D	D	D
Osborne	279	309	33	54 800	45.1	54.9	75.5	14.0	9	33.3	0.2	0.0	3.2	0.2	0.3

1. Includes livestock and poultry products.

STATE County	Manufactures, 1987 (cont'd)					Value of construction authorized by building permits, 1990							
	Production workers (cont'd)						Nonresidential				Residential		
	Wages							Percent					
	Total (Mil dol)	Average per worker (Dollars)	Value added by manu-facture (Mil dol)	Value of shipments (Mil dol)	New capital expend-itures (Mil dol)	Total[1] ($1,000)	Total ($1,000)	Office	Industrial	Stores	New construction ($1,000)	Number of housing units	Alterations and additions ($1,000)
	134	135	136	137	138	139	140	141	142	143	144	145	146
KANSAS—Con.													
Bourbon	10.0	14 286	31.5	74.1	2.2	3 110	1 284	0.0	49.3	0.0	185	4	620
Brown	6.6	11 000	19.9	35.3	D	734	63	0.0	0.0	23.7	320	6	81
Butler	D	D	D	D	D	12 178	2 262	10.5	40.2	11.4	8 562	163	748
Chase	0.4	NA	1.1	2.1	D	20	0	NA	NA	NA	0	0	0
Chautauqua	D	D	D	D	D	NA	NA	NA	NA	NA	NA	NA	NA
Cherokee	13.2	13 200	44.6	98.2	2.7	2 702	1 715	0.0	98.2	0.8	812	18	65
Cheyenne	D	D	D	D	D	262	3	0.0	0.0	0.0	180	2	42
Clark	D	D	D	D	D	297	191	0.0	0.0	0.0	80	1	6
Clay	5.5	11 000	19.6	40.2	0.4	976	261	0.0	0.0	0.0	568	10	79
Cloud	4.5	22 500	9.2	16.3	0.3	397	0	NA	NA	NA	90	1	127
Coffey	D	D	D	D	D	2 235	1 196	13.4	0.0	74.4	788	13	54
Comanche	0.4	NA	1.8	3.5	0.1	132	25	0.0	0.0	0.0	63	1	8
Cowley	63.9	21 300	275.4	1 033.4	18.3	9 205	5 057	4.9	0.1	94.3	1 748	20	1 774
Crawford	24.2	16 133	83.5	322.2	D	8 513	3 230	0.0	79.9	9.6	2 817	56	457
Decatur	0.4	NA	1.5	4.0	D	177	58	10.4	0.0	73.0	0	0	0
Dickinson	6.1	15 250	19.2	61.2	1.6	3 259	1 209	0.0	46.6	22.3	1 699	28	149
Doniphan	3.8	19 000	27.2	65.9	D	1 374	427	0.0	0.0	80.8	663	11	128
Douglas	60.5	19 516	549.4	864.4	D	80 065	14 715	36.3	24.8	7.9	48 613	710	2 216
Edwards	1.4	14 000	8.2	16.9	0.1	383	286	97.8	0.0	0.0	50	1	36
Elk	D	D	D	D	D	NA	NA	NA	NA	NA	NA	NA	NA
Ellis	D	D	D	D	D	3 132	444	54.1	0.0	31.5	1 417	17	266
Ellsworth	2.1	21 000	9.9	16.2	D	20	14	0.0	0.0	0.0	0	0	0
Finney	D	D	D	D	D	8 620	1 066	58.0	4.2	25.2	2 574	57	952
Ford	D	D	D	D	D	5 594	2 070	0.0	0.0	56.5	2 486	33	313
Franklin	13.0	16 250	51.2	104.1	0.7	5 162	1 685	10.6	47.5	2.4	1 811	43	697
Geary	6.4	16 000	23.3	56.9	1.2	2 296	40	93.9	0.0	0.0	2 177	41	41
Gove	D	D	D	D	D	NA	NA	NA	NA	NA	NA	NA	NA
Graham	D	D	D	D	D	294	1	0.0	0.0	0.0	256	5	0
Grant	2.7	13 500	22.1	56.5	D	3 845	896	22.9	69.2	0.0	1 144	14	260
Gray	0.1	NA	0.5	0.7	0.0	592	23	0.0	0.0	66.4	515	7	10
Greeley	D	D	D	D	D	NA	NA	NA	NA	NA	NA	NA	NA
Greenwood	0.8	8 000	2.8	8.6	D	527	0	NA	NA	NA	439	11	30
Hamilton	D	D	D	D	D	282	2	0.0	0.0	0.0	235	3	24
Harper	2.7	13 500	8.1	52.0	0.2	1 867	895	0.0	70.7	23.9	0	0	64
Harvey	D	D	D	D	D	12 111	4 623	2.6	10.3	1.8	5 464	56	553
Haskell	D	D	D	D	D	15	0	NA	NA	NA	0	0	9
Hodgeman	D	D	D	D	D	0	0	NA	NA	NA	0	0	0
Jackson	0.9	9 000	4.6	6.7	D	4 331	790	77.0	0.0	0.0	2 458	43	86
Jefferson	0.3	NA	0.9	2.0	0.0	5 231	653	0.0	0.0	0.0	3 722	66	384
Jewell	0.0	NA	0.1	0.4	D	68	0	NA	NA	NA	0	0	10
Johnson	218.8	17 934	1 580.8	2 781.6	D	502 568	100 391	10.5	41.2	33.3	301 473	2 836	14 597
Kearny	D	D	D	D	D	337	5	0.0	0.0	0.0	165	2	70
Kingman	2.4	24 000	12.3	26.7	0.2	2 054	784	0.0	93.8	0.0	1 145	15	4
Kiowa	D	D	D	D	D	107	40	0.0	0.0	0.0	0	0	17
Labette	38.6	15 440	145.5	221.8	1.9	3 688	976	34.4	0.0	11.3	616	15	245
Lane	D	D	D	D	D	584	18	0.0	0.0	0.0	564	6	0
Leavenworth	D	D	D	D	D	39 897	4 141	2.7	4.2	67.9	31 049	379	2 795
Lincoln	D	D	D	D	D	NA	NA	NA	NA	NA	NA	NA	NA
Linn	0.5	NA	2.5	4.7	0.1	478	0	NA	NA	NA	165	5	40
Logan	D	D	D	D	D	459	39	0.0	0.0	0.0	330	3	33
Lyon	65.5	20 469	294.3	1 614.0	10.4	11 538	4 429	27.9	0.0	56.7	1 668	19	2 541
McPherson	42.9	22 579	487.9	1 214.7	D	11 229	4 261	5.3	0.7	7.4	4 580	83	695
Marion	3.7	12 333	12.8	50.9	1.1	1 702	544	0.0	59.7	2.9	574	8	218
Marshall	8.2	16 400	29.0	65.1	D	2 512	1 976	0.0	0.0	0.0	190	3	118
Meade	0.1	NA	0.7	1.2	0.0	2 899	2 864	0.0	0.0	0.0	0	0	13
Miami	D	D	D	D	D	4 604	913	45.8	9.2	7.6	3 173	54	326
Mitchell	2.6	13 000	13.4	36.4	0.7	1 039	378	0.0	29.1	0.0	479	5	89
Montgomery	62.5	17 361	446.1	962.1	12.8	4 427	1 138	19.8	0.0	50.3	777	10	325
Morris	1.8	18 000	7.1	14.2	D	1 066	689	0.0	30.0	56.8	279	6	90
Morton	0.4	NA	6.8	10.2	0.1	2 066	1 692	0.0	74.8	25.2	0	0	64
Nemaha	5.5	13 750	30.6	102.9	1.4	4 195	1 932	9.5	32.7	14.2	1 320	17	25
Neosho	21.1	17 583	81.4	154.1	D	1 219	336	83.3	0.0	15.6	336	6	239
Ness	D	D	D	D	D	183	1	0.0	0.0	0.0	150	2	0
Norton	0.8	8 000	5.6	7.9	0.1	461	312	6.4	0.0	0.0	15	1	51
Osage	D	D	D	D	D	1 232	124	0.0	0.0	0.0	698	20	144
Osborne	1.9	9 500	7.1	50.5	D	196	101	0.0	19.5	74.0	35	1	11

1. Includes nonresidential additions and alterations, residential nonhousekeeping buildings, and residential garages and carports not shown separately.

STATE County	Wholesale trade, 1987: Establishments	Wholesale trade, 1987: Sales (Mil dol)	Wholesale trade, 1987: Paid employees[1]	Wholesale trade, 1987: Annual payroll (Mil dol)	Retail trade, all establishments, 1987: Number	Retail trade, all establishments, 1987: Sales: Total (Mil dol)	Retail trade, all establishments, 1987: Sales: Percent change, 1982–1987	Retail trade, all establishments, 1987: Sales: Per capita[2] (Dollars)	Retail trade, establishments with payroll, 1987: Number	Retail trade, establishments with payroll, 1987: Sales: Total (Mil dol)	Per capita[2] (Dollars): General merchandise stores	Per capita[2] (Dollars): Food stores	Per capita[2] (Dollars): Apparel & accessory stores	Per capita[2] (Dollars): Eating and drinking places
	147	148	149	150	151	152	153	154	155	156	157	158	159	160
KANSAS—Con.														
Bourbon	29	D	D	D	184	77.9	24.6	5 059	107	74.4	D	1 249	121	618
Brown	27	48.7	158	2.4	132	38.3	7.3	3 358	66	35.6	D	958	D	184
Butler	64	87.0	350	5.4	477	185.5	17.3	3 778	269	175.5	D	787	80	352
Chase	5	4.2	22	0.2	36	8.0	9.6	2 586	22	7.2	D	D	D	321
Chautauqua	10	D	D	D	60	8.8	-22.1	1 882	24	7.9	D	781	7	106
Cherokee	23	34.4	139	2.0	219	57.3	-1.5	2 569	116	53.1	D	991	18	228
Cheyenne	15	45.1	141	2.3	77	14.1	2.2	4 040	40	12.5	D	1 328	197	213
Clark	3	D	D	D	49	10.0	16.3	3 832	20	8.9	0	928	152	282
Clay	31	41.8	189	2.5	120	35.6	-9.0	3 832	77	33.9	D	978	185	197
Cloud	28	111.3	337	6.5	163	52.7	21.1	4 584	95	50.2	D	987	307	314
Coffey	14	21.6	61	0.9	124	29.9	12.0	3 358	72	27.4	D	826	34	218
Comanche	8	D	D	D	39	6.9	-6.8	2 770	24	6.3	0	D	D	212
Cowley	52	D	D	D	446	172.9	17.8	4 659	247	165.2	616	956	198	433
Crawford	64	137.7	661	11.0	414	168.4	22.9	4 490	238	160.5	648	1 163	168	461
Decatur	21	34.9	147	1.7	62	14.7	-27.6	3 497	39	13.2	D	D	D	363
Dickinson	41	D	D	D	269	68.1	9.5	3 406	160	65.6	D	941	82	347
Doniphan	14	191.2	380	7.4	88	25.3	21.1	2 814	41	22.2	D	682	0	D
Douglas	96	127.3	703	11.1	720	392.3	39.0	5 245	488	383.3	621	1 102	218	661
Edwards	10	31.7	100	1.5	60	10.7	-0.9	2 754	35	9.3	D	934	104	251
Elk	7	4.2	18	0.2	53	6.6	-22.4	1 833	27	5.0	0	446	0	113
Ellis	72	159.8	649	10.4	387	196.4	0.5	7 327	262	192.0	1 199	1 432	413	776
Ellsworth	16	24.9	104	1.8	97	22.5	-0.9	3 622	63	20.8	D	1 065	50	248
Finney	95	228.3	679	14.0	345	208.6	21.3	6 860	224	203.2	1 135	1 525	320	482
Ford	87	385.6	951	17.4	348	188.1	11.7	7 154	226	182.0	1 091	1 370	358	667
Franklin	28	104.9	339	5.2	268	94.3	33.9	4 228	142	88.5	D	1 092	108	394
Geary	20	45.8	193	2.3	315	156.0	10.9	5 182	228	153.4	840	D	108	852
Gove	16	28.5	99	1.8	56	14.4	26.3	4 115	30	13.5	0	D	0	521
Graham	17	33.9	106	1.1	60	16.6	-11.2	4 488	37	16.0	D	1 163	D	304
Grant	24	60.6	163	2.9	90	34.4	-0.6	5 052	57	33.7	D	D	94	530
Gray	26	106.4	225	5.0	73	10.4	-8.8	1 924	31	9.0	0	349	D	124
Greeley	9	14.0	52	0.9	22	6.9	38.0	3 814	16	6.6	0	D	D	193
Greenwood	20	41.3	90	1.2	141	25.9	2.0	3 193	71	22.2	D	891	45	248
Hamilton	9	71.0	117	1.4	40	6.3	-10.0	2 606	22	5.4	D	0	D	222
Harper	20	63.3	148	2.4	128	31.5	-1.3	4 197	82	29.6	331	1 104	174	344
Harvey	46	164.1	1 349	26.5	362	147.0	19.8	4 790	217	141.6	D	1 150	176	517
Haskell	15	67.6	126	2.8	47	7.4	7.2	1 889	27	6.7	0	913	D	163
Hodgeman	4	D	D	D	29	4.3	43.3	1 958	14	3.7	0	D	0	D
Jackson	22	23.7	130	1.1	150	39.8	40.6	3 399	67	36.0	D	798	D	169
Jefferson	13	12.6	54	0.8	148	24.9	6.0	1 510	79	20.0	33	414	0	85
Jewell	9	18.4	83	1.0	66	9.0	11.1	1 958	30	7.1	D	541	0	181
Johnson	1 300	13 614.0	14 484	389.0	3 471	2 837.4	65.9	8 554	2 149	2 778.2	1 247	1 441	429	690
Kearny	7	7.4	29	0.5	41	8.1	20.9	2 031	18	6.5	0	828	D	20
Kingman	24	38.4	125	2.3	121	28.9	25.1	3 284	66	26.3	251	962	D	264
Kiowa	9	29.2	81	1.5	64	14.7	0.0	3 871	37	13.7	D	1 004	D	442
Labette	49	99.2	321	4.2	287	105.1	2.4	4 123	165	100.6	D	1 025	138	333
Lane	11	24.9	67	1.3	37	8.4	86.7	3 358	17	7.3	0	D	0	171
Leavenworth	30	30.5	180	2.3	449	234.9	50.3	3 625	258	227.7	D	779	77	286
Lincoln	15	31.8	91	1.1	66	10.8	18.7	2 998	32	9.3	129	761	0	241
Linn	11	11.4	53	0.7	102	20.9	16.1	2 552	40	17.5	D	852	0	137
Logan	16	25.4	76	1.1	71	23.4	-10.3	7 305	43	22.3	D	1 697	113	213
Lyon	49	116.8	458	8.1	368	195.6	17.6	5 589	239	188.1	795	1 138	193	551
McPherson	50	652.6	426	9.7	350	133.3	23.3	4 882	204	129.4	D	1 094	139	449
Marion	24	55.6	192	3.5	175	44.9	18.5	3 510	106	42.2	69	605	50	236
Marshall	35	114.0	271	4.2	175	51.6	12.2	4 162	97	48.5	D	927	179	196
Meade	12	34.1	88	1.8	77	11.6	-23.7	2 629	37	9.3	D	614	D	267
Miami	26	32.5	106	1.7	205	91.6	43.3	3 949	121	88.1	D	973	40	278
Mitchell	33	84.3	265	4.8	144	45.5	11.5	6 065	78	41.7	D	1 135	129	262
Montgomery	78	124.4	598	8.8	527	217.2	7.6	5 273	312	209.3	681	1 453	190	457
Morris	8	9.8	20	0.3	88	22.6	28.4	3 533	46	21.3	D	851	83	211
Morton	9	31.5	104	1.8	50	11.8	-15.1	3 381	33	11.4	D	1 002	111	177
Nemaha	38	50.0	223	3.4	162	41.1	1.2	3 773	106	39.4	86	991	85	323
Neosho	42	278.4	324	6.1	224	89.9	5.4	4 913	136	85.9	D	959	149	338
Ness	17	29.7	125	2.3	67	14.9	-17.7	3 459	34	13.0	0	516	D	148
Norton	16	26.2	101	1.2	91	31.6	3.6	5 093	60	30.0	D	1 330	147	302
Osage	16	33.3	124	1.6	183	47.0	16.3	2 936	91	42.7	D	906	D	193
Osborne	21	49.6	130	2.2	94	20.2	-0.5	3 819	59	18.8	D	1 131	85	277

1. For pay period including March 12. 2. Based on the estimated population as of July 1 of the year shown.

Table A. States and Counties — **Retail Trade, Services, and Banking**

STATE County	Retail trade, establishments with payroll, 1987 (cont'd)		Taxable service industries–establishments with payroll, 1987							Bank deposits,[2] June 1989		Savings capital,[3] September 1989	
				Receipts (Mil dol)									
					Selected kinds of business								
	Paid employees[1]	Annual payroll (Mil dol)	Number	Total	Hotels, motels and other lodging places	Health services	Legal services	Paid employees	Annual payroll (Mil dol)	Total (Mil dol)	Percent change, 1988–1989	Total (Mil dol)	Percent change, 1988–1989
	161	162	163	164	165	166	167	168	169	170	171	172	173
KANSAS—Con.													
Bourbon	1 060	8.5	156	28.5	1.2	13.8	1.2	776	10.7	141	-4.2	55.7	3.8
Brown	452	3.2	52	9.6	D	4.9	0.8	301	3.4	306	94.8	53.1	18.8
Butler	2 289	19.3	229	35.3	0.8	15.6	1.7	1 069	11.3	359	0.9	140.3	1.5
Chase	133	0.8	9	1.7	0.0	D	D	80	0.7	31	4.2	9.9	-5.8
Chautauqua	97	0.6	18	7.5	D	6.7	D	187	2.7	41	-1.7	0.0	NA
Cherokee	749	5.9	68	13.1	D	5.9	0.3	446	4.5	176	3.9	28.6	0.1
Cheyenne	176	1.3	20	1.4	D	0.5	0.3	43	0.3	64	2.6	0.0	-100.0
Clark	111	0.8	18	1.9	D	D	0.4	60	0.7	60	5.6	0.0	NA
Clay	471	3.3	52	8.5	D	4.2	0.7	301	2.6	112	5.3	42.2	-7.3
Cloud	674	5.2	63	10.7	D	4.8	0.7	364	3.9	125	-0.5	71.8	2.0
Coffey	431	2.9	46	6.3	D	2.1	0.6	258	2.4	117	2.1	7.7	-1.4
Comanche	90	0.6	14	2.1	D	1.1	D	125	0.9	40	-1.1	0.0	NA
Cowley	2 374	18.9	184	34.7	0.6	18.4	2.7	1 087	12.3	282	6.7	169.9	1.8
Crawford	2 342	18.4	212	52.4	2.1	22.0	3.5	1 584	19.7	337	5.2	165.2	-9.1
Decatur	186	1.4	29	4.7	D	1.9	0.4	101	1.5	66	-1.6	23.5	6.8
Dickinson	1 024	7.0	107	16.4	1.3	5.5	1.0	477	4.6	206	0.4	54.9	11.0
Doniphan	243	1.9	27	3.2	D	1.9	0.3	144	1.2	89	1.9	18.8	6.9
Douglas	6 070	48.2	463	121.8	6.7	35.7	5.4	3 034	45.0	343	4.5	364.2	4.2
Edwards	182	1.1	19	2.7	0.0	2.0	0.3	93	0.8	46	0.3	17.3	-4.4
Elk	72	0.4	9	0.8	D	D	0.2	21	0.1	27	1.5	0.0	NA
Ellis	2 845	21.0	208	53.8	5.6	21.3	3.2	1 220	18.6	202	-2.1	239.2	4.6
Ellsworth	308	2.1	31	5.4	D	1.5	D	151	1.6	86	4.9	8.8	-12.8
Finney	2 252	21.9	214	60.4	8.3	19.7	3.0	1 476	22.1	271	4.3	84.5	-5.5
Ford	2 304	20.6	184	61.2	4.7	28.9	3.5	1 430	23.3	242	6.4	89.2	-6.2
Franklin	1 256	9.4	115	19.7	1.0	7.5	1.6	575	7.1	131	1.5	3 169.0	22.4
Geary	2 416	20.3	156	32.0	3.5	8.2	2.7	975	11.7	134	-1.6	69.3	0.4
Gove	196	1.5	13	1.9	D	D	D	70	0.5	52	8.1	0.0	NA
Graham	165	1.7	19	2.3	D	D	D	38	0.7	60	-0.7	12.0	-0.8
Grant	480	3.7	49	6.5	D	2.3	0.2	159	1.8	85	-0.9	1.4	-24.3
Gray	143	1.0	24	2.8	D	D	D	83	0.8	64	0.5	0.0	NA
Greeley	98	0.9	16	2.3	D	0.8	D	83	0.7	18	-3.4	0.0	NA
Greenwood	311	2.2	41	6.2	0.3	3.8	0.5	204	1.9	72	0.6	62.4	-12.7
Hamilton	88	0.5	23	1.9	D	0.6	0.3	81	0.5	46	6.9	0.9	6.4
Harper	387	3.0	52	7.2	0.2	3.5	0.7	249	2.3	129	5.1	3.4	-9.9
Harvey	2 077	17.2	151	51.6	3.0	34.2	2.4	1 204	24.0	244	-1.3	144.2	-64.3
Haskell	103	0.7	19	2.8	D	D	D	49	0.7	69	8.4	0.0	NA
Hodgeman	38	0.3	4	0.2	0.0	0.0	D	8	0.1	27	6.1	0.0	NA
Jackson	485	3.4	38	4.1	D	1.8	0.2	142	1.2	110	7.8	38.5	-2.9
Jefferson	310	2.0	54	8.8	0.0	5.2	0.3	319	2.9	92	2.3	11.1	8.2
Jewell	124	0.9	17	2.6	D	D	D	57	0.6	56	-0.8	0.0	NA
Johnson	32 056	331.5	3 027	1 459.9	67.1	364.5	67.4	32 730	545.9	3 198	6.8	2 524.7	-3.6
Kearny	100	0.6	16	1.9	D	D	D	56	0.4	47	0.4	0.0	NA
Kingman	364	3.0	35	6.4	D	3.6	1.0	266	2.4	91	5.1	26.1	-3.6
Kiowa	242	1.7	23	3.2	0.0	D	D	129	1.3	37	-2.0	11.6	5.0
Labette	1 500	11.9	112	25.9	D	14.3	1.0	788	9.6	191	7.5	94.4	-11.9
Lane	106	0.9	12	1.6	D	D	D	35	0.3	51	1.9	0.0	NA
Leavenworth	2 542	23.3	221	60.8	3.5	15.0	2.0	2 267	26.2	337	5.7	198.6	21.1
Lincoln	146	0.9	20	1.8	D	D	D	89	0.6	54	0.2	0.0	NA
Linn	243	1.7	33	5.9	0.0	3.3	0.3	177	1.5	68	-18.7	18.5	NA
Logan	211	2.2	24	3.9	1.0	1.2	D	126	1.0	35	2.1	18.6	-2.0
Lyon	2 565	21.7	227	50.2	4.8	22.5	3.1	1 527	19.7	220	-0.5	269.7	19.0
McPherson	1 701	14.7	150	20.0	1.8	6.3	1.7	599	5.9	293	3.6	128.6	1.7
Marion	553	3.9	66	9.8	D	6.1	0.7	331	3.1	131	1.5	24.0	-7.0
Marshall	556	4.1	57	9.0	0.9	3.6	0.6	293	2.4	208	3.5	50.8	-7.2
Meade	158	1.1	19	2.1	0.0	0.9	D	43	0.5	64	4.3	2.6	-8.8
Miami	1 087	8.5	108	16.5	0.3	6.8	1.1	608	5.6	216	4.2	50.7	-3.7
Mitchell	457	4.1	44	8.1	D	3.5	0.7	272	2.8	89	-2.7	74.7	8.4
Montgomery	2 892	24.0	214	45.9	3.0	20.5	2.9	1 412	17.9	347	1.1	170.4	-15.8
Morris	241	2.1	32	3.9	D	2.2	0.3	143	1.1	60	0.3	23.4	-2.3
Morton	148	1.2	21	2.7	D	1.4	D	70	0.7	51	6.3	2.3	-18.6
Nemaha	570	4.1	56	10.8	D	4.6	D	330	3.0	177	7.9	59.1	2.3
Neosho	1 028	8.5	114	22.2	0.5	11.8	1.8	823	8.1	139	-0.2	66.8	4.6
Ness	151	1.6	36	3.5	D	1.5	0.2	86	1.2	66	-4.5	0.0	NA
Norton	433	3.1	35	4.4	D	2.1	0.5	107	1.1	75	-0.2	40.1	10.8
Osage	594	4.3	59	9.9	0.0	6.5	0.7	473	4.0	102	8.8	56.4	6.1
Osborne	293	2.1	27	4.2	D	2.6	0.2	239	1.7	94	3.8	15.3	-1.7

1. For the period including March 12 of the year shown. 2. Includes deposits for all insured and reporting noninsured commercial and mutual savings banks. 3. Includes savings capital for all FSLIC insured savings institutions.

STATE County	Federal funds and grants, 1989: Expenditures: Total (Mil dol)	Expenditures: Percent change, 1988–1989	Per capita[1] (Dollars): Total	Per capita: Direct payments for individuals	Per capita: Procurement contract awards	Per capita: Salaries and wages	Per capita: Grant awards	Local government finances, 1981–1982: General revenue: Total (Mil dol)	Intergovernmental: Total (Mil dol)	Intergovernmental: Percent from state	Taxes: Total (Mil dol)	Taxes: Per capita[2]: Total (Dollars)	Taxes: Per capita[2]: Property (Dollars)	Direct general expenditure: Total (Mil dol)	Direct general expenditure: Percent change, 1977–1982
	174	175	176	177	178	179	180	181	182	183	184	185	186	187	188
KANSAS—Con.															
Bourbon	46.8	3.2	3 118	2 350	42	274	242	15.9	6.1	83.1	6.0	377	356	15.1	69.0
Brown	61.7	-7.2	5 413	3 906	85	290	393	11.4	4.0	68.9	5.3	446	418	10.4	43.8
Butler	106.8	11.2	2 090	1 627	72	101	206	52.2	21.2	85.4	20.1	430	413	49.7	86.5
Chase	10.9	18.4	3 645	2 382	91	292	660	3.7	0.8	73.1	2.5	787	773	3.2	27.1
Chautauqua	15.2	2.1	3 379	2 634	35	172	278	5.0	1.3	92.3	2.1	418	395	4.7	117.5
Cherokee	59.3	-1.0	2 682	2 125	38	102	321	22.1	7.8	92.2	5.6	256	241	20.9	106.5
Cheyenne	16.5	-23.6	4 991	2 404	16	136	147	4.1	0.8	88.8	2.6	711	698	4.0	117.4
Clark	10.9	-16.5	4 366	2 634	17	148	114	5.6	0.7	77.8	2.8	1 055	1 046	5.6	70.4
Clay	31.3	-2.6	3 439	2 358	16	139	158	10.6	2.8	79.2	4.8	497	472	9.9	56.3
Cloud	41.4	-5.0	3 697	2 587	19	198	278	13.4	4.8	87.6	6.2	503	484	13.2	48.8
Coffey	25.2	1.8	2 926	2 078	92	194	181	33.0	2.2	91.8	7.3	749	731	14.5	218.0
Comanche	13.3	-7.9	5 548	2 495	145	1 053	398	4.8	0.7	90.7	2.9	1 131	1 095	4.1	38.5
Cowley	96.3	5.4	2 582	2 058	123	125	197	50.2	12.8	82.1	15.3	409	382	53.1	108.4
Crawford	112.9	4.3	3 061	2 413	39	165	362	31.3	13.5	78.2	11.5	303	275	30.6	68.6
Decatur	19.8	-6.6	4 949	2 418	28	207	1 007	5.0	1.0	85.0	3.0	637	629	4.9	27.6
Dickinson	87.3	17.5	4 343	2 266	1 321	191	215	22.5	7.8	93.5	9.3	465	448	22.2	67.7
Doniphan	34.9	24.7	3 875	1 922	27	181	1 131	10.8	4.4	88.4	4.8	526	514	9.5	36.3
Douglas	198.5	0.9	2 536	1 177	708	254	361	71.9	14.4	84.7	24.5	352	307	66.4	32.1
Edwards	20.9	-13.1	5 496	2 749	29	232	344	7.3	1.1	56.3	3.5	850	830	6.5	83.9
Elk	13.4	9.5	3 935	2 917	28	213	439	4.6	1.2	91.2	2.3	595	582	4.8	3.6
Ellis	61.0	4.7	2 347	1 718	22	222	194	20.9	5.4	91.2	10.8	393	375	21.0	74.5
Ellsworth	23.0	2.1	3 770	2 249	357	152	111	7.7	1.8	85.9	4.7	717	694	7.5	42.3
Finney	110.1	3.2	3 530	1 083	1 496	181	178	42.4	8.5	87.1	15.6	587	569	43.2	194.8
Ford	77.4	-2.9	3 001	2 083	22	285	201	31.8	8.0	84.6	12.6	503	472	33.4	72.8
Franklin	54.1	-8.0	2 396	1 853	17	154	229	23.5	7.4	89.8	8.3	378	348	21.0	39.1
Geary	670.6	9.4	23 530	1 841	1 169	19 648	823	32.1	13.6	81.3	6.8	221	160	32.6	56.0
Gove	14.4	-62.0	4 369	2 088	29	219	75	6.3	1.1	89.4	3.5	932	924	5.9	46.8
Graham	18.1	-5.4	5 160	2 399	26	254	358	7.3	1.0	88.7	3.8	933	920	7.0	61.0
Grant	19.3	-19.2	2 759	1 284	13	106	129	10.1	1.3	84.9	6.6	965	956	8.6	43.0
Gray	22.9	-26.8	4 165	1 417	17	138	147	7.4	1.4	71.9	5.2	993	977	7.1	59.6
Greeley	11.9	-23.6	6 989	1 874	15	165	278	2.8	0.4	86.7	2.0	1 132	1 117	2.6	47.0
Greenwood	28.7	4.8	3 731	3 066	55	241	211	9.1	2.7	88.7	5.2	587	570	8.0	56.8
Hamilton	16.3	-18.9	7 083	2 476	48	177	128	5.6	0.5	81.2	2.3	920	902	5.5	60.5
Harper	34.1	-3.4	4 731	2 862	783	215	315	10.9	1.2	83.6	5.6	703	689	10.2	37.8
Harvey	77.2	2.4	2 508	1 923	228	95	94	32.7	10.3	82.8	13.7	442	421	31.6	54.7
Haskell	18.8	-29.9	4 945	1 282	11	153	117	6.3	0.7	84.5	4.6	1 222	1 202	5.6	46.6
Hodgeman	11.3	-22.1	5 137	1 988	26	216	270	4.6	0.7	88.9	3.5	1 585	1 576	4.3	82.0
Jackson	31.6	11.9	2 679	1 792	27	214	313	11.9	5.1	90.8	3.4	289	280	12.1	118.6
Jefferson	36.3	6.2	2 100	1 601	21	139	95	14.0	7.2	94.7	5.1	324	316	13.8	59.8
Jewell	19.8	-20.4	4 599	2 381	34	299	245	6.5	1.7	87.8	3.2	626	615	6.1	68.4
Johnson	742.6	6.4	2 065	1 241	108	456	147	302.5	92.2	78.7	130.2	464	365	295.4	78.2
Kearny	15.2	-19.0	3 706	1 314	9	82	163	8.9	0.8	82.4	5.6	1 466	1 454	7.1	116.5
Kingman	28.9	-13.2	3 280	2 100	51	389	135	9.6	1.3	81.2	6.4	707	698	8.7	75.5
Kiowa	16.7	-13.1	4 770	2 517	33	258	317	5.4	1.0	81.2	3.6	883	866	4.9	47.0
Labette	80.7	-0.5	3 229	2 199	460	193	283	32.9	11.1	80.7	9.4	366	351	33.4	72.4
Lane	13.4	-16.9	5 585	2 293	20	163	263	4.5	0.5	85.5	2.7	1 078	1 069	3.8	16.9
Leavenworth	412.1	-7.0	5 972	1 566	1 041	3 118	207	44.0	20.3	82.6	14.2	254	227	42.2	65.6
Lincoln	15.5	-17.7	4 437	2 691	26	292	131	4.4	0.8	84.7	2.9	703	689	4.8	74.4
Linn	29.9	17.6	3 597	2 295	43	197	677	20.5	2.7	91.0	6.4	784	774	15.6	162.5
Logan	15.0	-15.1	5 007	2 423	21	193	49	5.2	0.7	83.9	3.1	872	863	4.9	45.8
Lyon	82.9	15.7	2 416	1 750	20	164	354	41.7	10.3	87.3	12.6	344	325	41.3	89.9
McPherson	69.9	-7.1	2 608	1 933	186	124	123	30.1	5.7	89.5	14.0	512	504	29.0	83.8
Marion	39.9	-6.6	3 169	2 372	24	187	180	14.0	4.9	81.0	6.9	513	502	11.5	43.2
Marshall	46.5	-31.6	3 812	2 410	93	197	260	12.5	4.2	82.5	6.7	512	501	12.0	49.0
Meade	19.2	-20.6	4 473	2 064	11	117	205	6.0	0.7	82.5	3.6	740	725	5.4	49.9
Miami	47.2	1.7	1 942	1 567	22	107	139	19.5	7.2	90.9	7.3	331	313	18.9	93.6
Mitchell	29.1	-9.1	4 036	2 543	22	210	315	9.5	2.4	79.0	5.0	631	614	10.0	93.9
Montgomery	122.5	8.8	3 009	2 286	209	169	277	47.5	14.2	85.4	15.0	346	325	49.9	71.8
Morris	25.7	1.4	3 952	3 161	26	207	117	6.4	1.6	90.6	2.8	433	417	5.7	61.1
Morton	15.4	-17.9	4 536	1 736	15	154	107	8.3	0.9	86.9	4.4	1 250	1 231	7.7	135.5
Nemaha	42.9	-17.7	3 970	2 047	187	219	194	11.0	4.9	69.6	4.2	377	369	9.1	39.7
Neosho	49.3	-2.2	2 783	2 229	55	145	188	26.7	7.7	75.6	7.9	405	366	26.4	79.4
Ness	18.3	-17.6	4 457	2 499	28	261	110	9.0	0.9	85.0	4.6	992	982	9.5	56.5
Norton	23.9	-14.2	3 917	2 493	20	273	130	8.9	2.2	93.0	3.4	514	507	8.4	55.8
Osage	39.9	3.0	2 464	1 887	16	193	130	14.8	6.8	94.2	4.5	284	277	12.5	84.7
Osborne	23.0	-10.0	4 510	2 761	28	229	197	4.7	0.8	74.7	2.7	461	446	4.8	71.1

1. Based on the estimated population as of July 1 of the year shown. 2. Based on the estimated population as of July 1, 1982.

STATE County	Local government finances, 1981–1982 (cont'd)								State and local government employment, 1989		Federal government civilian employment 1989		Elections, 1988[3]	
	Direct general expenditure (cont'd)						Debt outstanding							
	Per capita[1] (Dollars)	Percent of total for– Education	Health & hospitals	Police protection	Public welfare	Highways	Total (Mil dol)	Per capita[1] (Dollars)	Total	Rate[2]	Total	Earnings ($1,000)	Total vote cast for president	Vote for lead party (Percent)
	189	190	191	192	193	194	195	196	197	198	199	200	201	202
KANSAS—Con.														
Bourbon	951	55.0	0.7	2.5	0.0	11.9	16.0	1 005	930	620.0	127	3 190	6 332	R–57.8
Brown	882	46.8	1.0	4.7	5.6	15.6	8.1	688	733	643.0	97	2 349	4 812	R–63.6
Butler	1 061	67.0	1.2	3.2	0.1	8.4	37.9	810	2 961	579.5	146	3 617	19 056	R–57.6
Chase	1 002	54.4	0.5	3.1	0.0	12.4	2.1	664	211	703.3	32	723	1 458	R–60.6
Chautauqua	925	40.9	22.9	2.0	0.0	10.4	3.3	650	246	546.7	26	575	1 934	R–64.5
Cherokee	952	44.7	22.8	3.0	0.3	8.2	20.0	909	1 204	544.8	70	1 783	8 402	R–51.0
Cheyenne	1 088	66.8	1.7	1.7	0.0	12.6	0.5	135	228	690.9	25	511	1 743	R–63.4
Clark	2 058	37.4	26.7	1.2	0.0	11.8	1.2	457	357	1 428.0	17	362	1 315	R–66.6
Clay	1 030	44.9	13.9	3.4	0.0	13.2	4.3	449	650	714.3	47	1 142	4 157	R–72.1
Cloud	1 077	57.7	1.2	2.9	0.0	15.6	5.4	442	836	746.4	74	1 975	5 128	R–59.3
Coffey	1 491	36.1	7.2	2.9	0.1	11.5	49.4	5 089	724	841.9	52	1 184	3 870	R–66.7
Comanche	1 579	51.5	13.9	2.2	0.2	15.2	0.5	198	252	1 050.0	16	363	1 123	R–65.7
Cowley	1 421	37.4	22.0	3.0	0.0	5.2	63.5	1 698	3 756	1 007.0	128	3 436	14 286	R–54.4
Crawford	805	49.3	6.4	2.5	0.2	12.0	26.5	696	3 215	871.3	178	4 628	14 850	D–52.4
Decatur	1 041	52.7	3.8	2.3	0.8	17.6	1.2	263	277	692.5	33	738	2 148	R–60.1
Dickinson	1 116	51.1	13.1	3.3	0.5	11.2	10.4	522	1 285	639.3	86	2 073	8 092	R–63.3
Doniphan	1 034	73.1	0.4	1.7	0.0	7.8	7.8	852	664	737.8	48	1 004	3 514	R–61.5
Douglas	957	30.9	23.2	4.4	1.9	9.6	69.6	1 003	9 546	1 219.2	544	15 268	32 361	R–49.9
Edwards	1 591	32.8	25.7	2.9	0.0	13.1	1.1	262	252	663.2	33	746	1 843	R–53.9
Elk	1 269	43.3	2.9	2.5	15.9	12.9	3.4	904	365	1 073.5	24	551	1 706	R–63.0
Ellis	762	46.8	2.8	4.8	0.0	20.2	26.6	968	2 550	980.8	176	5 131	10 672	D–49.6
Ellsworth	1 129	62.4	1.6	3.1	0.3	14.3	0.9	134	627	1 027.9	38	876	3 000	R–57.0
Finney	1 631	41.7	0.6	3.2	0.0	9.8	274.9	10 375	2 235	716.3	204	6 065	8 947	R–60.1
Ford	1 331	45.8	4.1	3.1	0.1	11.7	63.2	2 517	2 094	811.6	236	6 956	9 697	R–58.6
Franklin	955	49.6	19.5	3.7	0.0	11.5	23.3	1 061	1 337	591.6	91	2 353	8 465	R–56.4
Geary	1 063	50.7	19.2	5.5	0.0	5.0	24.5	798	1 795	629.8	3 368	81 229	6 573	R–57.5
Gove	1 583	52.3	18.3	1.6	0.0	16.5	2.0	527	329	997.0	29	620	1 684	R–57.4
Graham	1 719	41.3	24.3	2.6	0.3	16.3	2.8	691	413	1 180.0	44	919	1 868	R–61.0
Grant	1 272	46.2	6.9	4.4	2.3	14.1	6.2	913	605	864.3	28	706	2 597	R–63.7
Gray	1 369	57.3	6.0	2.0	0.1	14.5	2.6	502	358	650.9	36	770	1 917	R–61.6
Greeley	1 436	48.5	3.9	5.8	1.6	11.6	1.6	902	176	1 035.3	19	388	853	R–59.3
Greenwood	900	56.1	2.1	5.6	0.0	15.2	5.7	642	452	587.0	59	1 449	3 716	R–59.7
Hamilton	2 203	29.4	39.9	3.7	2.6	9.4	1.1	443	330	1 434.8	27	474	1 335	R–60.0
Harper	1 292	35.7	30.6	3.9	0.0	10.9	5.5	698	755	1 048.6	55	1 286	3 268	R–59.4
Harvey	1 021	44.4	2.6	3.5	0.0	10.6	64.1	2 067	1 434	465.6	90	2 467	12 711	R–54.2
Haskell	1 465	60.2	0.2	3.1	0.0	21.4	3.0	787	359	944.7	24	704	1 430	R–67.4
Hodgeman	1 975	39.3	6.4	2.6	0.0	18.0	1.1	519	268	1 218.2	21	455	1 212	R–60.4
Jackson	1 031	54.5	17.8	2.0	0.0	8.6	10.3	880	731	619.5	82	1 975	5 075	R–54.4
Jefferson	888	70.8	1.8	2.7	0.0	9.7	10.5	671	1 140	659.0	82	2 126	6 492	R–55.5
Jewell	1 193	49.2	16.0	2.8	0.0	15.6	2.8	543	384	893.0	49	980	2 274	R–68.0
Johnson	1 053	50.2	1.3	5.5	0.5	10.0	587.6	2 095	14 805	411.6	3 458	118 326	152 199	R–62.8
Kearny	1 862	44.0	14.6	3.3	0.0	15.6	4.3	1 123	438	1 068.3	20	425	1 625	R–66.0
Kingman	957	53.3	3.1	4.1	0.0	17.9	10.1	1 106	548	622.7	54	1 198	3 754	R–58.7
Kiowa	1 198	57.7	1.5	3.6	0.0	17.0	0.9	229	328	937.1	32	671	1 795	R–71.1
Labette	1 296	42.2	19.7	2.5	0.0	4.8	69.9	2 710	2 630	1 052.0	97	2 597	9 684	R–52.9
Lane	1 505	46.0	18.1	4.0	0.0	12.3	1.2	476	296	1 233.3	19	393	1 250	R–61.4
Leavenworth	756	55.7	0.8	5.0	2.4	9.5	74.1	1 325	3 206	464.6	5 266	146 318	18 870	R–52.5
Lincoln	1 178	42.3	4.0	2.8	0.1	31.4	2.7	662	385	1 100.0	48	1 188	2 060	R–59.7
Linn	1 901	33.6	3.7	1.3	0.0	11.5	95.6	11 653	505	608.4	47	1 071	3 691	R–58.6
Logan	1 396	51.4	14.7	4.0	0.0	8.3	2.2	635	332	1 106.7	29	619	1 535	R–64.4
Lyon	1 129	35.7	27.6	3.5	0.0	6.3	28.0	766	3 424	998.3	174	4 883	12 334	R–55.3
McPherson	1 061	46.3	1.4	3.1	0.0	12.1	120.7	4 422	1 390	518.7	111	2 883	11 164	R–58.8
Marion	860	56.1	4.6	3.1	0.0	14.2	9.9	739	771	611.9	86	2 077	5 850	R–63.0
Marshall	925	57.8	1.3	2.9	0.0	16.7	5.4	413	675	553.3	86	1 994	5 790	R–54.2
Meade	1 121	43.0	7.2	3.6	0.4	23.6	4.1	846	390	907.0	28	600	2 028	R–65.2
Miami	865	56.8	12.1	4.3	0.0	9.6	12.8	586	1 912	786.8	80	2 045	9 306	R–51.7
Mitchell	1 255	51.3	2.5	2.9	0.2	22.1	15.5	1 936	660	916.7	54	1 268	3 462	R–65.2
Montgomery	1 151	42.5	20.8	3.3	0.0	6.0	33.4	770	2 505	615.5	176	4 856	14 628	R–62.0
Morris	895	42.9	17.7	4.8	0.0	15.2	0.8	118	391	601.5	45	1 142	2 894	R–58.1
Morton	2 188	37.6	28.6	3.8	1.0	10.3	3.4	971	493	1 450.0	26	581	1 669	R–64.3
Nemaha	808	55.7	1.5	4.3	0.3	12.5	9.4	838	630	583.3	78	1 731	5 182	R–55.0
Neosho	1 351	38.7	19.2	2.8	0.0	5.6	31.4	1 612	1 438	812.4	79	2 113	7 222	R–51.8
Ness	2 058	36.9	37.8	1.8	0.0	9.9	1.3	287	461	1 124.4	48	1 024	2 174	R–56.6
Norton	1 248	42.4	26.6	3.1	0.4	8.8	2.7	406	731	1 198.4	50	1 092	2 847	R–67.5
Osage	796	69.7	1.2	3.6	0.0	10.2	8.1	518	905	558.6	98	2 317	6 435	R–54.3
Osborne	819	35.3	2.9	6.6	0.0	17.1	7.1	1 225	376	737.3	47	1 092	2 544	R–60.6

1. Based on the estimated population as of July 1, 1982. 2. Per 10,000 resident population estimated as of July 1 of the year shown. 3. Data subject to copyright.

STATE–County code	MSA/CMSA/NECMA code[1]	STATE County	Land Area,[2] 1990 (Sq. Km.)	Population, 1990											
				Total persons	Rank	Per square kilometer	Race					Hispanic[3]	Age of population Percent		
							White	Black	Am. Indian, Eskimo, Aleut	Asian & Pacific Islander	Other race		Under 5 years	5 to 14 years	15 to 24 years
			1	2	3	4	5	6	7	8	9	10	11	12	13
		KANSAS—Con.													
20 143	...	Ottawa	1 868	5 634	2 791	3.0	5 599	4	16	8	7	34	6.5	15.4	9.1
20 145	...	Pawnee	1 953	7 555	2 612	3.9	7 079	239	27	57	153	256	6.0	14.7	11.6
20 147	...	Phillips	2 295	6 590	2 700	2.9	6 524	16	12	28	10	32	6.5	14.8	8.9
20 149	...	Pottawatomie	2 187	16 128	1 914	7.4	15 799	93	115	61	60	239	8.2	17.0	12.4
20 151	...	Pratt	1 904	9 702	2 412	5.1	9 358	116	64	30	134	183	6.4	15.3	11.6
20 153	...	Rawlins	2 770	3 404	2 965	1.2	3 382	3	7	8	4	27	6.1	16.5	8.9
20 155	...	Reno	3 249	62 389	697	19.2	58 612	1 712	359	210	1 496	2 478	6.9	14.8	12.7
20 157	...	Republic	1 856	6 482	2 712	3.5	6 452	3	12	12	3	15	6.1	13.0	7.9
20 159	...	Rice	1 882	10 610	2 326	5.6	10 222	117	53	19	199	279	7.2	15.2	11.9
20 161	...	Riley	1 579	67 139	658	42.5	55 866	6 807	482	2 400	1 584	2 799	7.5	11.6	35.7
20 163	...	Rooks	2 301	6 039	2 752	2.6	5 974	35	12	5	13	25	7.3	15.6	9.4
20 165	...	Rush	1 860	3 842	2 930	2.1	3 814	0	5	5	18	35	5.8	13.7	7.8
20 167	...	Russell	2 291	7 835	2 593	3.4	7 734	43	35	6	17	45	5.5	14.1	8.8
20 169	...	Saline	1 864	49 301	851	26.4	46 272	1 515	239	531	744	1 222	7.4	15.0	13.3
20 171	...	Scott	1 859	5 289	2 821	2.8	5 144	5	9	22	109	138	7.7	16.4	11.5
20 173	9040	Sedgwick	2 591	403 662	123	155.8	345 173	36 061	4 556	8 728	9 144	17 435	8.5	15.3	13.7
20 175	...	Seward	1 656	18 743	1 748	11.3	14 495	1 108	143	449	2 548	3 660	9.2	18.1	15.4
20 177	8440	Shawnee	1 424	160 976	297	113.0	141 189	13 365	1 836	1 179	3 407	7 785	7.2	14.6	13.2
20 179	...	Sheridan	2 322	3 043	2 998	1.3	3 019	0	8	6	10	26	7.3	16.7	9.3
20 181	...	Sherman	2 735	6 926	2 669	2.5	6 569	17	8	16	316	474	7.8	14.9	13.0
20 183	...	Smith	2 319	5 078	2 835	2.2	5 063	4	7	3	1	7	5.3	13.2	8.0
20 185	...	Stafford	2 052	5 365	2 812	2.6	5 271	10	26	9	49	112	7.0	15.1	9.1
20 187	...	Stanton	1 761	2 333	3 038	1.3	2 015	2	17	8	291	392	9.2	18.4	12.1
20 189	...	Stevens	1 884	5 048	2 838	2.7	4 552	26	42	15	413	552	8.6	17.5	11.9
20 191	...	Sumner	3 061	25 841	1 428	8.4	24 869	140	288	72	472	888	7.6	16.8	11.3
20 193	...	Thomas	2 784	8 258	2 542	3.0	8 109	29	17	35	68	101	7.5	16.6	15.5
20 195	...	Trego	2 301	3 694	2 942	1.6	3 668	2	6	17	1	9	5.7	16.2	8.7
20 197	...	Wabaunsee	2 065	6 603	2 699	3.2	6 493	41	24	7	38	116	6.8	16.0	11.2
20 199	...	Wallace	2 367	1 821	3 077	0.8	1 785	6	5	4	21	79	8.0	16.5	12.5
20 201	...	Washington	2 327	7 073	2 649	3.0	7 050	4	7	0	12	22	5.9	14.3	10.0
20 203	...	Wichita	1 861	2 758	3 013	1.5	2 455	1	9	8	285	326	8.6	18.8	10.3
20 205	...	Wilson	1 486	10 289	2 359	6.9	10 150	20	70	16	33	76	6.6	14.7	10.6
20 207	...	Woodson	1 297	4 116	2 907	3.2	4 059	15	30	5	7	25	6.0	14.2	9.1
20 209	3760	Wyandotte	392	161 993	293	413.2	108 728	44 469	1 110	1 876	5 810	10 997	8.3	15.9	14.1
21 000	...	KENTUCKY	102 907	3 685 296	X	35.8	3 391 832	262 907	5 769	17 812	6 976	21 984	6.8	14.7	15.3
21 001	...	Adair	1 054	15 360	1 967	14.6	14 853	459	15	24	9	89	5.8	14.2	15.8
21 003	...	Allen	897	14 628	2 011	16.3	14 433	165	17	6	7	24	7.0	14.8	13.5
21 005	...	Anderson	525	14 571	2 016	27.8	14 089	432	4	20	26	68	7.1	14.8	13.8
21 007	...	Ballard	651	7 902	2 582	12.1	7 638	240	14	6	4	41	5.6	13.6	12.8
21 009	...	Barren	1 272	34 001	1 161	26.7	32 208	1 680	33	58	22	94	6.4	14.2	12.9
21 011	...	Bath	724	9 692	2 413	13.4	9 393	277	8	7	7	31	6.5	14.2	13.9
21 013	...	Bell	934	31 506	1 230	33.7	30 570	804	39	83	10	77	6.6	15.3	15.7
21 015	1642	Boone	638	57 589	755	90.3	56 716	361	88	355	69	318	8.1	16.9	13.8
21 017	4280	Bourbon	755	19 236	1 716	25.5	17 504	1 662	20	25	25	81	6.9	14.8	14.0
21 019	3400	Boyd	415	51 150	825	123.3	49 851	1 040	66	148	45	443	5.8	13.5	12.7
21 021	...	Boyle	470	25 641	1 436	54.6	23 084	2 444	15	80	18	108	5.9	13.8	15.6
21 023	...	Bracken	526	7 766	2 599	14.8	7 710	47	8	1	0	12	6.6	14.7	14.1
21 025	...	Breathitt	1 283	15 703	1 943	12.2	15 637	33	12	20	1	26	6.7	16.7	16.4
21 027	...	Breckinridge	1 483	16 312	1 900	11.0	15 672	584	29	15	12	44	6.4	15.6	13.0
21 029	4520	Bullitt	775	47 567	882	61.4	47 152	206	84	93	32	164	7.2	16.5	16.2
21 031	...	Butler	1 109	11 245	2 278	10.1	11 156	55	18	14	2	38	6.5	15.5	13.8
21 033	...	Caldwell	899	13 232	2 117	14.7	12 416	771	34	9	2	30	6.1	13.4	12.9
21 035	...	Calloway	1 000	30 735	1 253	30.7	29 558	961	30	134	52	160	5.3	11.0	23.6
21 037	1642	Campbell	393	83 866	546	213.4	82 582	851	104	258	71	319	7.7	15.0	14.4
21 039	...	Carlisle	499	5 238	2 825	10.5	5 164	55	12	3	4	21	5.8	14.0	13.2
21 041	...	Carroll	337	9 292	2 445	27.6	9 057	199	17	15	4	22	6.8	15.8	13.5
21 043	3400	Carter	1 064	24 340	1 484	22.9	24 270	20	24	17	9	60	6.2	15.4	16.7
21 045	...	Casey	1 154	14 211	2 035	12.3	14 105	37	26	17	26	47	6.5	14.8	14.3
21 047	1660	Christian	1 868	68 941	643	36.9	49 465	16 929	294	881	1 372	2 339	8.6	13.9	21.4
21 049	4280	Clark	659	29 496	1 314	44.8	27 740	1 615	74	44	23	98	6.7	14.7	13.7
21 051	...	Clay	1 220	21 746	1 590	17.8	21 329	335	34	32	16	46	7.5	17.4	16.2
21 053	...	Clinton	511	9 135	2 457	17.9	9 118	6	3	8	0	37	6.0	14.1	13.9
21 055	...	Crittenden	938	9 196	2 454	9.8	9 097	78	13	8	0	24	6.2	14.2	13.2
21 057	...	Cumberland	792	6 784	2 678	8.6	6 460	307	12	4	1	23	6.1	14.0	12.3
21 059	5990	Daviess	1 198	87 189	522	72.8	83 168	3 619	101	229	72	312	7.3	15.4	14.2

1. MSA = Metropolitan Statistical Area. CMSA = Consolidated MSA. NECMA = New England county metropolitan area. PMSA = Primary MSA. See Appendix A for explanation of these concepts. See Appendix B for list of metropolitan areas identified by type, with component counties. 2. Dry land or land partially or temporarily covered by water. 3. Hispanic persons may be of any race.

STATE County	Population, 1990 (cont'd): Age of population (cont'd), Percent: 25 to 34 years	35 to 44 years	45 to 54 years	55 to 64 years	65 to 74 years	75 years and over	Percent female	Population–Change and components of change: Change 1980–1990: Number	Percent	Components of change, 1980–1986: Total persons, 1986	Total persons, 1980	Net change: Number	Percent	Natural increase: Births	Deaths
	14	15	16	17	18	19	20	21	22	23	24	25	26	27	28
KANSAS—Con.															
Ottawa	13.8	13.4	10.2	11.0	9.6	11.1	51.6	-337	-5.6	5 800	5 971	-100	-2.4	500	500
Pawnee	13.8	14.6	10.5	9.6	10.4	8.8	49.5	-510	-6.3	7 600	8 065	-400	-5.2	800	600
Phillips	12.4	13.5	10.3	10.4	11.4	11.7	51.4	-816	-11.0	6 900	7 406	-500	-6.3	600	700
Pottawatomie	16.1	14.5	9.2	8.0	7.3	7.3	50.2	1 346	9.1	15 600	14 782	900	5.8	1 700	900
Pratt	13.8	13.8	9.8	10.2	9.7	9.5	51.6	-573	-5.6	10 900	10 275	600	5.6	1 100	700
Rawlins	12.8	13.1	10.0	11.3	10.7	10.6	50.6	-701	-17.1	3 800	4 105	-300	-7.5	400	300
Reno	15.6	14.4	10.1	9.3	8.6	7.7	50.9	-2 594	-4.0	65 300	64 983	300	0.5	6 200	3 800
Republic	11.9	11.6	10.0	11.8	13.1	14.7	52.2	-1 087	-14.4	7 100	7 569	-500	-6.3	600	700
Rice	13.1	12.1	10.0	10.4	9.7	10.4	52.2	-1 290	-10.8	11 200	11 900	-700	-5.9	1 100	900
Riley	19.1	10.8	5.1	4.0	3.5	2.8	45.0	3 634	5.7	63 400	63 505	-100	-0.1	6 300	1 500
Rooks	14.0	12.3	9.3	10.4	10.7	11.0	51.7	-967	-13.8	6 800	7 006	-200	-3.2	800	600
Rush	12.6	12.3	9.6	13.1	12.9	12.3	51.7	-674	-14.9	4 200	4 516	-300	-7.1	400	400
Russell	13.3	12.9	9.8	11.8	12.1	11.6	51.8	-1 033	-11.6	8 600	8 868	-300	-2.9	900	700
Saline	16.9	14.6	10.0	8.7	7.8	6.3	51.7	396	0.8	50 000	48 905	1 100	2.2	5 000	2 600
Scott	14.4	14.6	10.2	9.0	8.4	7.8	50.4	-493	-8.5	5 800	5 782	0	0.4	600	300
Sedgwick	18.7	15.0	9.2	8.2	6.8	4.6	51.0	36 574	10.0	391 100	367 088	24 000	6.6	45 100	17 800
Seward	18.5	13.4	8.5	7.6	5.4	4.0	49.5	1 672	9.8	18 900	17 071	1 800	10.8	2 500	800
Shawnee	17.0	15.5	10.2	9.1	7.2	5.9	51.8	6 060	3.9	160 800	154 916	5 900	3.8	15 200	8 500
Sheridan	13.7	13.3	9.6	12.3	9.2	8.7	49.1	-501	-14.1	3 300	3 544	-200	-6.1	400	200
Sherman	13.5	13.0	10.8	10.3	9.2	7.5	51.1	-833	-10.7	7 200	7 759	-600	-7.6	800	500
Smith	11.7	11.8	9.7	12.4	12.7	15.2	52.0	-869	-14.6	5 500	5 947	-500	-7.8	400	500
Stafford	12.9	12.9	9.7	10.1	11.5	11.7	51.9	-329	-5.8	5 700	5 694	0	-0.5	500	500
Stanton	16.8	12.2	10.8	9.7	5.8	5.1	50.3	-6	-0.3	2 400	2 339	100	3.7	300	100
Stevens	15.9	13.3	10.3	8.3	8.1	6.2	51.0	312	6.6	4 900	4 736	200	3.4	500	300
Sumner	14.4	14.1	9.8	9.3	8.7	8.0	51.3	913	3.7	25 500	24 928	600	2.3	2 500	1 800
Thomas	14.6	13.7	9.0	8.4	8.0	6.6	51.3	-193	-2.3	8 600	8 451	100	1.8	900	400
Trego	13.2	12.7	9.4	10.4	11.5	12.2	50.7	-471	-11.3	4 100	4 165	-100	-2.0	400	300
Wabaunsee	14.1	13.6	10.4	10.3	9.4	8.2	50.6	-264	-3.8	6 700	6 867	-100	-1.7	600	500
Wallace	13.6	13.1	9.3	10.5	8.6	7.8	49.1	-224	-11.0	1 900	2 045	-100	-4.8	200	100
Washington	11.7	11.2	9.2	11.4	12.0	14.3	51.0	-1 470	-17.2	7 500	8 543	-1 000	-11.7	600	700
Wichita	14.4	14.2	9.4	9.2	7.4	7.7	50.3	-283	-9.3	2 900	3 041	-100	-4.8	400	100
Wilson	12.3	13.1	10.2	10.5	11.2	10.8	52.1	-1 839	-15.2	11 800	12 128	-400	-3.0	1 000	1 000
Woodson	12.0	12.9	8.3	11.2	13.3	13.1	51.5	-484	-10.5	4 300	4 600	-300	-7.3	400	400
Wyandotte	17.5	13.5	9.1	8.6	7.4	5.6	52.3	-10 342	-6.0	174 100	172 335	1 800	1.0	20 700	10 500
KENTUCKY	16.6	14.9	10.4	8.8	7.3	5.4	51.6	24 296	0.7	3 729 000	3 661 000	68 000	1.9	345 000	212 000
Adair	14.4	13.5	11.1	9.6	8.9	6.8	51.1	127	0.8	15 800	15 233	600	3.8	1 200	1 000
Allen	14.2	13.3	11.1	9.9	9.2	6.9	51.5	500	3.5	14 600	14 128	500	3.4	1 200	1 000
Anderson	16.8	16.0	10.9	8.2	6.8	5.6	51.2	2 004	15.9	13 800	12 567	1 200	9.8	1 100	700
Ballard	13.9	14.4	11.8	9.8	9.5	8.6	51.2	-896	-10.2	8 100	8 798	-700	-7.6	600	700
Barren	15.6	14.0	11.0	10.0	8.7	7.3	52.6	-8	0.0	33 700	34 009	-300	-0.8	2 800	2 200
Bath	15.5	14.5	10.5	9.7	8.0	7.2	51.3	-333	-3.3	10 100	10 025	100	0.8	900	600
Bell	15.6	14.4	10.4	8.7	7.7	5.5	51.8	-2 824	-8.2	33 900	34 330	-400	-1.2	3 200	2 100
Boone	18.3	16.7	10.4	7.5	5.0	3.3	51.2	11 747	25.6	51 900	45 842	6 100	13.2	5 200	1 900
Bourbon	15.6	15.2	11.0	8.9	7.8	5.9	51.5	-169	-0.9	19 600	19 405	200	0.8	1 600	1 200
Boyd	15.6	15.3	11.7	10.7	8.7	6.1	51.5	-4 363	-7.9	53 300	55 513	-2 200	-4.0	4 500	3 400
Boyle	14.8	15.1	10.7	9.6	8.2	6.3	50.9	575	2.3	25 500	25 066	500	1.9	2 000	1 500
Bracken	14.9	13.4	10.7	10.1	8.4	7.0	51.6	28	0.4	7 600	7 738	-200	-2.2	600	600
Breathitt	15.5	15.2	10.1	8.4	6.0	4.9	50.5	-1 301	-7.7	16 700	17 004	-300	-1.9	1 600	900
Breckinridge	14.3	14.5	11.2	9.8	8.9	6.2	50.4	-549	-3.3	17 000	16 861	100	0.7	1 500	1 100
Bullitt	17.4	16.7	11.9	7.2	4.4	2.5	50.2	4 221	9.7	46 400	43 346	3 000	7.0	3 900	1 400
Butler	15.1	14.1	11.4	8.7	8.2	6.6	50.5	181	1.6	11 100	11 064	100	0.6	1 000	800
Caldwell	13.3	14.0	10.9	10.6	10.1	8.8	52.8	-241	-1.8	13 300	13 473	-200	-1.3	1 100	1 100
Calloway	13.2	12.5	9.9	8.5	8.9	7.2	51.9	704	2.3	28 700	30 031	-1 300	-4.3	2 000	1 900
Campbell	17.3	14.2	9.6	8.9	7.6	5.3	52.2	549	0.7	81 700	83 317	-1 600	-1.9	8 000	5 300
Carlisle	13.0	13.4	10.9	11.0	9.9	8.8	51.9	-249	-4.5	5 000	5 487	-500	-8.5	500	400
Carroll	15.7	14.0	10.9	9.4	8.2	5.7	51.5	22	0.2	9 600	9 270	300	3.7	900	600
Carter	14.8	14.2	10.7	8.8	7.2	5.5	51.0	-720	-2.9	25 400	25 060	400	1.5	2 400	1 400
Casey	14.2	14.2	11.3	10.0	8.4	6.7	51.2	-607	-4.1	15 000	14 818	100	1.0	1 400	900
Christian	19.7	12.0	10.9	6.7	5.4	4.5	46.1	2 063	3.1	63 300	66 878	-3 600	-5.4	8 900	3 200
Clark	16.1	16.0	7.8	9.0	7.2	5.3	51.9	1 174	4.1	29 100	28 322	700	2.6	2 600	1 400
Clay	16.5	14.2	11.2	7.7	6.0	4.6	50.7	-1 006	-4.4	23 600	22 752	900	3.8	2 500	1 100
Clinton	15.2	13.9	9.8	9.8	8.6	6.7	52.3	-186	-2.0	9 900	9 321	600	6.1	800	600
Crittenden	14.1	13.5	11.7	9.5	9.4	8.2	51.7	-11	-0.1	8 800	9 207	-400	-4.2	700	700
Cumberland	14.7	12.9	11.6	11.4	9.7	8.4	52.8	-505	-6.9	7 500	7 289	200	3.3	600	600
Daviess	16.1	14.5	10.6	9.3	7.5	5.4	52.2	1 240	1.4	87 500	85 949	1 600	1.8	9 100	4 700

STATE County	Population–(cont'd)	Households, 1990					Births, 1988			Deaths, 1987				Marriages, 1984	
	Components of change, 1980-1986 (cont'd)				Percent					Number		Rate			
	Net migration	Number	Percent change, 1980–1990	Persons per house-hold	Female family house-holder[1]	One-person	Total	Rate[2]	Low birth weight[3] (Number)	Total	Infant[4]	Total[2]	Infant[5]	Number	Rate[2]
	29	30	31	32	33	34	35	36	37	38	39	40	41	42	43
KANSAS—Con.															
Ottawa	-100	2 266	-1.1	2.43	5.7	26.6	69	11.9	1	79	1	13.4	15.6	53	9.0
Pawnee	-600	2 923	-4.7	2.34	7.2	31.6	100	13.3	5	87	2	11.4	24.4	73	9.0
Phillips	-400	2 695	-6.5	2.38	4.9	28.9	92	13.3	4	82	0	11.7	0.0	72	10.0
Pottawatomie	100	5 938	9.9	2.66	6.0	22.6	244	15.0	17	134	1	8.3	4.1	124	7.8
Pratt	200	3 937	-3.5	2.40	5.9	29.1	124	12.2	4	105	0	10.1	0.0	103	9.4
Rawlins	-400	1 361	-13.5	2.46	4.6	29.0	40	10.8	0	54	0	14.6	0.0	36	9.2
Reno	-2 000	24 239	-0.9	2.46	8.4	26.7	813	12.6	37	663	15	10.2	16.6	713	11.0
Republic	-300	2 769	-11.1	2.27	3.6	31.4	78	11.3	2	110	2	15.7	22.7	80	11.0
Rice	-900	4 165	-8.0	2.43	6.5	27.9	143	13.1	12	155	0	14.0	0.0	94	8.1
Riley	-4 800	21 280	10.4	2.58	6.4	23.6	930	14.8	56	256	4	4.1	3.8	483	7.4
Rooks	-400	2 444	-9.4	2.40	5.5	29.9	78	12.6	5	89	1	13.9	11.8	76	10.9
Rush	-300	1 642	-10.1	2.29	4.4	30.4	38	10.0	4	63	0	15.8	0.0	39	8.9
Russell	-400	3 371	-6.7	2.28	6.1	32.1	92	11.6	10	122	2	14.9	20.4	93	10.2
Saline	-1 200	19 826	6.5	2.44	9.3	27.3	757	15.1	41	455	8	9.1	11.1	582	11.6
Scott	-300	2 022	-2.5	2.57	4.9	24.5	82	15.2	4	48	1	8.6	13.9	61	10.3
Sedgwick	-3 200	156 571	13.7	2.54	10.2	26.7	7 496	18.6	532	2 964	75	7.5	10.3	4 440	11.6
Seward	100	6 614	8.0	2.79	10.3	21.1	389	21.0	29	118	2	6.3	5.0	248	13.7
Shawnee	-900	63 768	8.4	2.46	10.5	27.6	2 494	15.1	174	1 399	32	8.6	13.4	1 706	10.7
Sheridan	-300	1 171	-7.0	2.57	3.1	25.2	35	10.9	3	41	1	12.4	23.8	21	6.2
Sherman	-900	2 733	-4.5	2.47	7.5	27.1	122	17.9	6	78	2	11.1	20.4	73	9.7
Smith	-400	2 165	-9.8	2.28	4.5	30.0	55	10.4	3	100	1	18.5	21.7	47	8.4
Stafford	-100	2 203	-4.5	2.36	5.4	29.9	77	14.5	6	70	1	13.0	14.5	54	9.3
Stanton	-100	831	4.7	2.77	5.9	21.9	34	14.2	3	17	1	7.1	23.8	22	9.2
Stevens	-100	1 885	11.3	2.65	5.4	24.6	80	16.3	3	31	0	6.3	0.0	41	8.5
Sumner	-100	9 689	2.9	2.62	6.7	24.5	373	14.6	21	277	1	10.9	2.8	267	10.6
Thomas	-400	3 124	1.7	2.56	6.5	25.9	140	16.7	8	74	0	8.8	0.0	62	7.0
Trego	-200	1 464	-8.3	2.46	4.6	27.0	40	10.3	5	48	0	12.3	0.0	27	6.3
Wabaunsee	-200	2 482	-0.2	2.62	5.0	23.0	84	12.5	2	84	1	12.5	13.0	53	7.8
Wallace	-200	677	-8.5	2.65	3.7	26.3	24	12.0	2	20	0	10.5	0.0	18	9.0
Washington	-900	2 862	-12.5	2.42	3.9	29.9	79	10.5	3	105	2	13.8	23.0	56	7.0
Wichita	-400	996	-5.1	2.73	5.4	22.5	45	15.5	2	22	0	7.6	0.0	23	7.9
Wilson	-400	4 194	-12.1	2.41	6.2	28.7	135	12.1	7	159	1	13.8	6.8	116	9.8
Woodson	-400	1 699	-7.3	2.33	5.7	30.8	38	9.5	0	55	0	13.4	0.0	35	7.6
Wyandotte	-8 400	61 514	-3.0	2.60	16.4	27.5	3 046	17.6	275	1 680	38	9.7	12.5	1 939	11.3
KENTUCKY	-66 000	1 379 782	9.2	2.60	11.6	23.3	51 058	13.7	3 421	34 598	499	9.3	9.7	42 149	11.3
Adair	400	5 800	6.6	2.57	9.5	22.4	168	10.8	5	174	1	11.2	5.7	152	9.5
Allen	300	5 595	8.3	2.59	8.6	22.1	208	14.5	14	168	4	11.6	23.8	146	10.1
Anderson	800	5 438	23.2	2.66	9.0	20.0	191	13.5	13	125	3	9.0	14.6	134	10.1
Ballard	-500	3 191	-2.3	2.44	7.6	25.2	85	10.6	3	107	0	13.2	0.0	119	14.3
Barren	-800	13 136	7.1	2.54	9.5	23.0	396	11.4	29	378	5	10.9	11.2	407	11.7
Bath	-100	3 659	6.5	2.61	10.1	22.1	134	13.3	10	94	0	9.3	0.0	87	8.6
Bell	-1 500	11 512	0.9	2.69	15.6	22.0	463	14.0	29	354	4	10.5	8.0	465	13.4
Boone	2 800	20 127	35.6	2.84	9.5	18.4	853	15.3	43	324	6	6.0	7.1	616	12.3
Bourbon	-200	7 250	6.4	2.63	12.2	21.2	258	13.3	23	192	3	9.8	12.2	195	10.1
Boyd	-3 300	19 876	-0.4	2.50	10.9	24.0	543	10.4	25	513	5	9.8	7.9	736	13.6
Boyle	0	9 483	7.6	2.49	11.3	24.4	306	11.7	22	259	3	10.0	9.1	294	11.7
Bracken	-200	2 872	6.1	2.68	9.7	21.9	93	12.2	6	115	2	15.1	21.1	54	7.1
Breathitt	-1 000	5 555	6.6	2.78	13.3	19.6	207	12.9	15	169	3	10.4	13.5	167	10.1
Breckinridge	-200	6 159	4.7	2.63	8.8	22.8	193	11.4	9	209	2	12.2	9.2	59	3.5
Bullitt	600	15 965	23.3	2.97	9.2	13.5	571	11.9	30	232	7	5.0	11.7	438	9.8
Butler	-100	4 180	8.9	2.64	8.6	21.4	153	13.8	12	128	1	11.6	6.2	103	9.0
Caldwell	-200	5 274	4.6	2.46	10.2	25.6	150	11.4	12	183	3	13.8	19.5	154	11.6
Calloway	-1 400	11 607	7.8	2.34	7.8	27.1	295	9.6	21	329	3	10.8	9.0	377	12.7
Campbell	-4 400	31 169	8.9	2.66	11.7	25.3	1 335	16.2	58	836	13	10.2	9.8	1 414	17.2
Carlisle	-500	2 106	2.3	2.49	8.4	25.1	56	11.7	3	72	1	14.7	18.2	59	11.3
Carroll	100	3 505	3.8	2.61	12.0	24.4	133	13.7	7	105	0	10.9	0.0	166	17.1
Carter	-600	8 679	5.7	2.75	10.6	19.2	314	12.5	21	223	4	8.9	12.6	46	1.8
Casey	-300	5 436	5.4	2.59	9.7	22.1	172	11.9	11	144	1	9.9	5.6	50	3.3
Christian	-9 300	21 636	10.1	2.73	12.9	20.6	1 289	20.8	90	516	11	8.2	8.9	750	11.6
Clark	-500	10 973	10.9	2.66	11.0	20.1	407	13.8	27	272	7	9.3	17.9	350	12.0
Clay	-600	7 367	8.0	2.93	12.5	16.2	346	15.0	28	185	4	7.9	10.6	287	12.2
Clinton	400	3 591	10.2	2.52	10.7	24.1	125	13.0	14	116	0	12.0	0.0	112	11.3
Crittenden	-400	3 646	5.2	2.48	8.2	25.6	103	12.0	6	122	0	14.2	0.0	110	12.1
Cumberland	200	2 714	1.6	2.47	12.7	24.0	105	14.6	9	83	2	11.5	25.6	70	9.3
Daviess	-2 800	33 036	9.4	2.58	11.5	24.8	1 248	14.2	70	747	8	8.5	6.0	990	11.3

1. No spouse present. 2. Per 1,000 resident population estimated as of July 1 of the year shown. 3. Under 2,500 grams. 4. Deaths of infants under 1 year old. 5. Deaths of infants under 1 year old per 1,000 live births.

Table A. States and Counties — **Vital Statistics, Health Resources, Crime, and Education**

STATE County	Divorces, 1984		Physicians, active non-Federal, 1989		Hospitals, 1989			Nursing homes,[4] 1986		Serious crimes known to police, 1988			Education			
						Beds				Number			Public school enrollment[7]		Attainment,[8] 1980	
	Number	Rate[1]	Number[2]	Rate[3]	Number	Number	Rate[3]	Number	Beds	Total[5]	Violent[6]	Rate[3]	1986–1987	1980	Percent 12 yrs. or more	Percent 16 yrs. or more
	44	45	46	47	48	49	50	51	52	53	54	55	56	57	58	59
KANSAS—Con.																
Ottawa	25	4.2	4	68	1	43	729	3	147	20	6	343	1 129	1 147	72.2	9.5
Pawnee	41	5.1	29	392	1	475	6 419	1	100	146	8	3 231	1 286	1 355	74.9	16.0
Phillips	19	2.6	1	15	1	62	912	3	179	11	0	307	1 197	1 428	68.2	8.3
Pottawatomie	58	3.7	8	48	3	53	321	5	218	261	20	1 671	3 324	2 894	72.6	14.0
Pratt	65	6.0	15	150	1	84	840	2	140	357	22	3 419	1 740	1 702	72.0	15.1
Rawlins	6	1.5	1	28	1	24	667	1	48	43	1	1 157	571	808	67.3	12.7
Reno	414	6.4	89	138	1	172	267	8	645	3 524	299	5 399	10 995	11 466	71.4	13.2
Republic	28	3.8	4	59	1	86	1 265	3	206	42	3	598	1 083	1 262	70.8	11.6
Rice	21	1.8	5	46	1	44	407	4	205	192	9	1 788	1 957	2 180	71.7	14.0
Riley	201	3.1	70	113	2	159	256	4	274	2 532	125	4 074	6 821	7 835	85.5	31.6
Rooks	17	2.4	3	50	1	27	450	2	102	40	1	622	1 200	1 351	67.0	10.6
Rush	11	2.5	2	56	1	50	1 389	2	86	20	2	511	760	772	63.2	12.8
Russell	41	4.5	5	65	1	37	481	3	168	232	14	2 784	1 543	1 533	67.4	10.5
Saline	365	7.3	95	190	3	402	804	7	413	2 448	83	4 837	7 693	8 659	76.4	15.6
Scott	35	5.9	3	57	1	27	509	1	84	123	5	2 187	1 153	1 334	74.5	13.9
Sedgwick	2 847	7.4	926	228	7	2 132	524	27	2 492	25 616	1 841	6 492	63 177	62 290	76.5	18.6
Seward	129	7.1	18	98	1	86	467	1	100	1 722	60	9 122	4 078	3 316	70.9	13.3
Shawnee	851	5.4	439	264	7	2 191	1 316	32	1 918	12 370	930	7 638	25 425	27 696	78.3	19.9
Sheridan	2	0.6	2	65	1	59	1 903	1	40	12	0	362	575	800	67.3	11.7
Sherman	45	6.0	3	45	1	49	731	1	60	326	29	4 638	1 303	1 634	72.2	12.3
Smith	11	2.0	5	98	1	52	1 020	3	150	31	0	561	893	1 034	66.3	8.8
Stafford	22	3.8	3	59	2	59	1 157	3	180	32	0	813	1 050	977	72.4	14.1
Stanton	15	6.3	2	83	1	46	1 917	1	28	18	1	747	526	530	67.3	13.9
Stevens	32	6.7	3	61	1	17	347	1	56	90	7	1 829	1 110	923	76.1	10.1
Sumner	76	3.0	12	47	3	142	550	9	497	551	40	2 169	4 253	4 757	68.4	8.9
Thomas	44	5.0	7	85	1	30	366	2	116	249	14	2 952	1 578	1 593	74.1	17.2
Trego	14	3.3	5	132	1	72	1 895	2	86	46	2	1 175	653	775	62.5	9.2
Wabaunsee	20	2.9	4	60	0	0	0	2	160	96	1	1 537	1 086	1 378	68.9	9.7
Wallace	5	2.5	1	50	0	0	0	1	28	4	0	199	445	441	71.2	11.9
Washington	21	2.6	4	54	2	75	1 014	4	186	76	3	1 023	1 492	1 472	59.3	7.9
Wichita	11	3.8	2	69	1	43	1 483	1	30	26	1	893	630	709	65.8	13.9
Wilson	80	6.8	7	64	2	74	673	3	164	267	12	2 292	2 143	2 291	64.0	10.3
Woodson	21	4.6	2	53	0	0	0	0	0	84	2	2 040	588	746	60.5	8.4
Wyandotte	873	5.1	483	280	4	1 164	675	12	1 109	17 813	2 307	10 219	30 419	31 409	61.8	9.0
KENTUCKY	17 110	4.6	6 105	164	124	18 995	510	623	28 294	NA	NA	NA	651 370	689 582	53.1	11.1
Adair	76	4.8	10	65	1	74	481	8	125	NA	NA	NA	2 671	3 114	34.6	5.3
Allen	43	3.0	5	35	1	52	366	3	160	NA	NA	NA	2 535	2 634	38.5	5.0
Anderson	32	2.4	6	42	0	0	0	2	77	NA	NA	NA	2 708	2 767	50.3	7.3
Ballard	43	5.2	4	50	0	0	0	4	99	NA	NA	NA	1 563	1 778	53.4	7.7
Barren	216	6.2	44	127	1	218	628	6	555	NA	NA	NA	6 579	6 570	44.0	8.0
Bath	42	4.2	6	59	0	0	0	4	128	NA	NA	NA	1 877	2 051	35.6	6.4
Bell	172	5.0	53	162	2	251	768	2	186	NA	NA	NA	7 337	7 510	36.2	6.5
Boone	61	1.2	54	94	0	0	0	3	304	NA	NA	NA	9 801	9 860	65.3	11.8
Bourbon	93	4.8	14	72	1	60	308	2	90	NA	NA	NA	3 739	3 816	53.6	9.2
Boyd	413	7.6	102	196	1	313	602	19	289	NA	NA	NA	9 207	10 757	59.0	9.8
Boyle	93	3.7	48	182	1	149	564	8	275	NA	NA	NA	4 856	5 344	55.6	12.6
Bracken	25	3.3	2	26	0	0	0	7	110	NA	NA	NA	1 484	1 599	43.7	5.4
Breathitt	47	2.8	4	25	0	0	0	1	122	NA	NA	NA	3 693	3 626	37.0	8.9
Breckinridge	58	3.5	8	47	1	45	263	2	103	NA	NA	NA	3 016	3 151	42.1	5.7
Bullitt	247	5.5	11	23	0	0	0	4	81	NA	NA	NA	10 285	11 295	53.0	5.8
Butler	52	4.5	4	36	0	0	0	2	172	NA	NA	NA	2 259	2 276	34.6	3.1
Caldwell	66	5.0	7	53	1	38	290	4	206	NA	NA	NA	2 356	2 383	49.5	7.6
Calloway	89	3.0	40	127	1	174	552	3	301	NA	NA	NA	4 294	4 631	59.8	18.1
Campbell	349	4.2	114	138	1	259	313	3	589	NA	NA	NA	12 219	13 766	55.6	9.8
Carlisle	21	4.0	0	0	0	0	0	1	3	NA	NA	NA	934	1 041	52.5	4.6
Carroll	64	6.6	9	92	1	49	500	5	146	NA	NA	NA	1 812	1 942	46.5	7.6
Carter	83	3.3	3	12	0	0	0	8	24	NA	NA	NA	5 295	5 522	38.0	5.4
Casey	NA	NA	5	35	1	24	168	5	36	NA	NA	NA	2 733	3 104	33.2	5.8
Christian	421	6.5	67	110	3	769	1 259	11	678	NA	NA	NA	13 366	12 679	60.5	8.7
Clark	213	7.3	28	94	1	100	336	3	202	NA	NA	NA	5 340	5 803	55.9	9.6
Clay	125	5.3	12	52	1	50	217	2	129	NA	NA	NA	4 918	5 309	27.6	7.3
Clinton	NA	NA	3	32	1	42	442	0	0	NA	NA	NA	1 722	2 031	30.5	4.7
Crittenden	49	5.4	3	35	1	37	435	1	107	NA	NA	NA	1 532	1 665	45.4	5.9
Cumberland	NA	NA	2	29	1	31	443	5	92	NA	NA	NA	1 174	1 369	29.0	6.7
Daviess	527	6.0	134	153	3	545	621	14	925	NA	NA	NA	13 278	14 581	61.3	11.0

1. Per 1,000 resident population estimated as of July 1 of the year shown. 2. As of end of year. 3. Per 100,000 resident population as of July 1 of the year shown. 4. Preliminary. Covers nursing homes with 3 or more beds. 5. Data for serious crimes have not been adjusted for underreporting, this may affect comparability between geographic areas or over time. 6. Includes murder and nonnegligent manslaughter, forcible rape, robbery, and aggravated assault. 7. The 1986–1987 data are based on administrative reports obtained by the U.S. National Center for Education Statistics. The 1980 data are based on the 1980 Census of Population and Housing. 8. Persons 25 years old or older.

STATE County	Education (cont'd): Local government expenditures for education,[1] 1982: Total (Mil dol)	Education (cont'd): Local government expenditures for education,[1] 1982: Per capita (Dollars)	Social Security Program December 1988: Beneficiaries: Total	Social Security Program December 1988: Beneficiaries: Rate[2]	Social Security Program December 1988: Payments ($1,000)	Supplemental Security Income Program recipients June 1986	Money income: Per capita[3]: 1987 Income, (Dollars)	Money income: Per capita[3]: 1979: Current dollars	Money income: Per capita[3]: 1979: Constant 1987 dollars	Money income: Median household income 1979 (Dollars)	Money income: Percent below poverty level, 1979: Persons	Money income: Percent below poverty level, 1979: Families	Housing units, 1990: Total	Housing units, 1990: Percent change, 1980–1990
	60	61	62	63	64	65	66	67	68	69	70	71	72	73
KANSAS—Con.														
Ottawa	3.0	517	1 330	229.3	626	58	9 580	5 920	9 263	12 579	12.5	10.3	2 591	-2.8
Pawnee	5.2	634	1 675	223.3	872	62	10 907	6 771	10 595	14 480	9.4	7.1	3 412	-0.9
Phillips	4.8	647	1 705	247.1	807	84	9 302	6 119	9 574	13 165	11.0	9.9	3 264	-6.8
Pottawatomie	9.8	634	2 740	168.1	1 220	98	9 477	6 145	9 615	14 909	11.0	8.8	6 472	7.3
Pratt	4.3	397	2 000	196.1	1 038	46	10 848	7 182	11 238	15 441	9.8	7.1	4 620	3.8
Rawlins	2.3	540	830	224.3	395	48	8 947	6 093	9 534	12 467	13.9	10.3	1 744	-4.5
Reno	28.8	443	11 850	183.2	6 062	520	10 631	7 114	11 131	15 949	9.3	7.0	26 607	0.1
Republic	3.9	525	1 965	284.8	879	74	9 751	5 906	9 241	10 973	14.4	10.8	3 283	-13.6
Rice	6.6	563	2 550	233.9	1 303	56	10 673	6 907	10 807	15 475	9.3	7.1	4 868	-2.1
Riley	15.2	239	4 885	77.9	2 416	216	9 106	5 732	8 969	12 359	16.5	9.6	22 868	9.6
Rooks	3.9	536	1 575	254.0	751	52	9 003	6 286	9 836	13 789	9.5	6.9	2 979	-5.0
Rush	3.0	670	1 170	307.9	562	40	9 126	6 131	9 593	12 589	12.0	9.7	1 999	-4.8
Russell	5.8	640	2 170	274.7	1 071	98	10 385	7 474	11 695	13 589	10.6	8.0	4 079	-1.2
Saline	22.6	460	8 400	168.0	4 190	438	11 392	7 416	11 604	16 201	8.2	5.8	21 129	4.0
Scott	3.4	590	960	177.8	517	26	11 048	6 942	10 862	15 468	10.7	8.6	2 305	-1.7
Sedgwick	160.7	425	56 660	140.9	30 032	3 510	12 480	8 160	12 768	18 223	9.1	6.6	170 159	16.9
Seward	9.5	521	2 155	116.5	1 127	142	10 570	7 804	12 211	17 630	9.7	6.7	7 572	12.9
Shawnee	68.9	439	25 000	151.7	12 464	1 994	12 155	7 858	12 295	17 713	7.8	5.5	68 991	7.1
Sheridan	1.8	517	590	184.4	300	26	7 826	5 576	8 725	12 702	16.4	13.1	1 324	-8.3
Sherman	3.9	525	1 320	194.1	669	82	9 638	6 554	10 255	14 221	10.4	7.7	3 177	-3.5
Smith	3.1	531	1 500	283.0	700	48	8 517	5 347	8 366	10 875	17.1	13.0	2 615	-7.1
Stafford	4.1	699	1 500	283.0	759	24	10 272	6 477	10 135	13 162	11.9	10.0	2 666	-1.6
Stanton	2.0	816	315	131.2	169	14	9 468	6 122	9 579	14 145	15.2	14.0	956	-0.4
Stevens	4.0	858	810	165.3	436	18	11 367	7 182	11 238	16 973	7.2	5.9	2 116	7.0
Sumner	11.7	459	5 100	199.2	2 559	196	11 071	7 213	11 286	16 656	7.5	5.4	10 769	4.0
Thomas	4.5	517	1 380	164.3	737	52	9 926	6 762	10 581	15 244	10.7	6.6	3 534	1.1
Trego	2.0	476	915	234.6	422	36	9 020	6 472	10 127	13 880	10.6	9.2	1 851	-7.0
Wabaunsee	3.4	506	1 280	191.0	568	36	10 107	6 381	9 984	14 641	9.0	6.9	2 853	-1.3
Wallace	1.5	759	355	177.5	180	8	7 391	5 353	8 376	12 337	17.7	17.1	840	-5.8
Washington	5.0	608	2 195	292.7	943	98	8 976	5 664	8 862	11 470	17.9	13.7	3 355	-6.3
Wichita	2.0	679	455	156.9	243	28	10 053	5 975	9 349	14 722	16.7	13.2	1 190	-8.0
Wilson	5.7	470	2 625	234.4	1 216	150	8 729	5 686	8 897	12 147	14.4	11.8	5 091	-5.2
Woodson	1.6	350	1 255	313.8	553	66	8 707	5 561	8 701	11 185	12.6	9.2	2 199	-4.1
Wyandotte	72.8	423	26 740	154.7	13 291	2 720	9 377	6 444	10 083	15 454	13.9	11.0	69 102	0.9
KENTUCKY	1 161.7	314	629 565	169.0	271 071	100 623	9 380	5 973	9 346	13 965	17.6	14.6	1 506 845	10.1
Adair	4.6	295	3 155	203.5	1 080	1 040	7 395	4 482	7 013	9 381	28.5	23.7	6 434	4.4
Allen	4.3	308	3 005	210.1	1 096	688	8 072	4 982	7 795	10 872	20.7	16.1	6 381	6.2
Anderson	4.0	313	2 210	156.7	975	244	10 061	6 117	9 571	15 920	9.3	7.9	5 804	20.8
Ballard	3.1	369	2 160	270.0	938	212	8 717	5 798	9 072	12 492	14.8	11.7	3 553	0.3
Barren	10.7	311	6 535	188.9	2 467	1 328	8 701	5 500	8 606	12 476	17.7	14.1	14 202	5.2
Bath	3.4	340	1 850	183.2	647	528	6 669	4 309	6 742	9 937	28.3	22.7	4 021	8.8
Bell	12.7	371	7 030	212.4	2 646	1 652	6 372	4 573	7 155	9 869	30.5	26.0	12 568	4.3
Boone	14.8	307	6 350	113.6	3 045	390	11 477	7 200	11 266	20 494	6.8	6.2	21 476	33.6
Bourbon	6.8	352	3 090	159.3	1 308	478	8 897	5 694	8 909	12 555	19.6	15.7	7 781	7.9
Boyd	16.5	300	10 235	195.3	4 954	1 108	10 191	6 973	10 911	16 285	13.5	11.0	21 365	-0.4
Boyle	8.5	342	4 530	173.6	1 983	732	9 682	6 225	9 740	13 649	16.3	12.9	10 191	7.1
Bracken	2.8	363	1 515	199.3	579	258	8 496	5 014	7 845	12 682	17.9	14.5	3 166	6.2
Breathitt	6.5	383	2 705	168.0	936	1 328	6 001	4 277	6 692	9 362	36.0	31.4	6 127	10.5
Breckinridge	5.5	330	3 120	183.5	1 187	606	7 697	4 859	7 603	10 840	22.9	21.1	8 261	15.6
Bullitt	15.3	349	4 040	84.5	1 823	450	9 064	5 677	8 883	18 110	9.9	8.6	16 629	21.7
Butler	3.9	357	2 065	186.0	746	498	6 928	4 545	7 112	10 726	20.8	17.9	4 698	9.9
Caldwell	4.1	304	3 060	231.8	1 280	424	8 635	5 845	9 146	12 555	12.2	9.1	5 794	8.2
Calloway	8.8	295	6 070	197.1	2 734	492	9 112	5 885	9 208	12 707	15.3	11.9	13 242	10.3
Campbell	23.8	287	13 975	169.4	6 891	990	10 658	6 564	10 271	16 891	9.8	7.8	32 910	8.7
Carlisle	1.7	320	1 270	264.6	536	142	8 952	5 590	8 747	12 606	15.7	13.6	2 295	3.8
Carroll	3.6	375	1 845	190.2	750	350	9 058	5 667	8 867	12 517	17.8	14.0	3 870	1.3
Carter	8.7	346	4 485	178.7	1 702	1 134	6 540	4 453	6 968	10 745	25.9	21.3	9 290	5.9
Casey	4.5	297	2 635	181.7	869	866	6 312	3 775	5 907	8 318	35.9	31.4	6 046	4.0
Christian	15.7	238	8 790	142.0	3 579	1 568	8 188	5 240	8 199	12 061	20.2	16.2	23 429	10.5
Clark	8.7	302	4 560	154.1	1 943	692	10 385	6 485	10 147	15 915	16.2	13.0	11 635	11.7
Clay	8.8	380	3 890	168.4	1 216	1 896	5 173	3 481	5 447	7 897	42.4	37.1	7 930	7.1
Clinton	3.2	332	1 925	200.5	632	720	5 161	3 330	5 210	7 238	39.4	34.9	4 189	3.9
Crittenden	2.9	323	1 995	232.0	857	286	7 985	5 468	8 556	12 153	17.3	12.2	4 039	5.5
Cumberland	2.2	294	1 620	225.0	507	542	6 501	4 177	6 536	8 461	30.6	26.9	3 051	-3.1
Daviess	27.2	313	15 310	174.4	7 174	1 456	9 725	6 543	10 238	15 917	12.5	10.2	35 041	10.7

1. Elementary and secondary. 2. Per 1,000 resident population estimated as of July 1 of the year shown. 3. Based on the resident population estimated as of July 1, 1988 for 1987 data and enumerated as of April 1, 1980 for 1979 data.

STATE County	Housing units, 1990 (cont'd): Occupied units: Total	Owner occupied: Percent	Owner occupied: Median value (Dollars)	Median rent (Dollars)	Civilian labor force, 1990: Total	Percent change, 1989–1990	Unemployment: Total	Unemployment: Rate[1]	Private nonfarm establishments, 1988: Number	Net change, 1987–1988	Employment[2]: Total	Employment: Percent change, 1987–1988	Manu-facturing	Retail trade
	74	75	76	77	78	79	80	81	82	83	84	85	86	87
KANSAS—Con.														
Ottawa	2 266	78.7	27 500	162	2 614	-7.7	162	6.2	129	-4	1 512	6.4	0	233
Pawnee	2 923	71.3	35 300	197	3 703	0.4	80	2.2	203	-2	1 180	1.8	64	399
Phillips	2 695	76.4	26 800	155	3 165	-1.3	78	2.5	215	12	1 573	-15.5	0	340
Pottawatomie	5 938	77.4	46 400	219	8 828	1.8	445	5.0	313	7	2 838	5.3	413	644
Pratt	3 937	73.9	37 500	222	4 943	-3.7	148	3.0	377	11	2 398	0.2	147	946
Rawlins	1 361	76.3	27 500	168	1 742	-5.0	51	2.9	101	-2	659	7.7	122	135
Reno	24 239	69.9	40 100	233	31 231	1.0	1 434	4.6	1 678	-19	21 202	2.2	5 363	5 467
Republic	2 769	78.4	18 900	135	3 568	2.4	66	1.8	209	3	1 724	4.1	462	309
Rice	4 165	75.2	27 200	165	4 821	-0.5	182	3.8	289	-3	2 403	-3.1	324	426
Riley	21 280	44.1	63 500	323	29 426	3.4	1 074	3.6	1 237	16	13 723	5.6	921	5 432
Rooks	2 444	77.6	25 800	153	2 770	0.8	103	3.7	232	4	1 129	2.8	133	318
Rush	1 642	81.0	19 200	143	1 878	3.2	61	3.2	109	-1	604	0.7	183	92
Russell	3 371	75.8	28 000	169	3 591	-0.3	112	3.1	305	-3	2 419	5.8	277	532
Saline	19 826	66.7	45 500	249	28 454	1.7	1 193	4.2	1 561	9	20 590	4.6	4 336	5 366
Scott	2 022	73.9	44 000	225	2 501	-1.3	78	3.1	177	-9	1 255	5.6	65	321
Sedgwick	156 571	63.7	58 500	302	215 887	1.0	9 749	4.5	10 784	125	196 676	1.5	66 347	37 043
Seward	6 614	64.6	48 800	285	9 718	-0.7	423	4.4	659	4	7 836	-1.2	0	1 863
Shawnee	63 768	66.6	55 700	307	92 966	0.7	4 490	4.8	4 382	111	67 491	6.6	9 848	17 572
Sheridan	1 171	79.6	27 600	147	1 446	-2.5	45	3.1	97	-6	429	2.4	0	119
Sherman	2 733	69.7	37 900	197	3 407	2.2	108	3.2	261	-7	1 718	-2.1	22	675
Smith	2 165	79.6	20 700	125	2 521	-0.8	56	2.2	177	0	1 034	3.5	170	242
Stafford	2 203	75.7	24 000	160	2 289	0.9	70	3.1	152	-2	715	6.4	91	168
Stanton	831	64.6	44 500	207	1 155	0.7	41	3.5	55	-3	275	-2.5	0	49
Stevens	1 885	74.1	48 800	233	2 313	-0.6	67	2.9	137	0	726	10.0	0	134
Sumner	9 689	76.6	39 300	201	11 560	0.6	530	4.6	528	-7	4 009	0.1	1 079	1 017
Thomas	3 124	68.2	45 400	205	4 380	-0.2	126	2.9	303	-6	2 029	-0.9	47	723
Trego	1 464	78.8	27 900	153	1 751	-1.2	56	3.2	120	3	715	-1.5	32	199
Wabaunsee	2 482	80.8	34 600	168	3 235	-0.9	143	4.4	113	0	544	-0.4	130	155
Wallace	677	74.0	28 400	157	803	-1.7	35	4.4	53	-6	222	-1.3	0	50
Washington	2 862	78.3	18 500	124	3 533	-3.2	95	2.7	234	9	1 225	-3.8	38	309
Wichita	996	70.6	37 900	183	952	-3.3	34	3.6	79	-4	311	-1.3	0	74
Wilson	4 194	77.7	23 500	160	4 837	-1.3	258	5.3	258	-1	2 797	-2.3	1 383	359
Woodson	1 699	78.0	18 800	142	1 535	-9.1	79	5.1	109	1	505	-10.3	0	130
Wyandotte	61 514	62.9	42 300	285	89 145	-0.8	6 915	7.8	3 380	-10	63 039	4.0	16 733	10 442
KENTUCKY	1 379 782	69.6	50 500	250	1 767 000	1.4	103 000	5.8	X	X	1 093 856	3.9	262 052	254 237
Adair	5 800	79.9	35 100	162	8 437	-0.2	542	6.4	269	-8	2 758	3.5	1 156	547
Allen	5 595	76.7	35 600	144	7 087	3.0	925	13.1	193	-12	2 797	-3.5	0	1 231
Anderson	5 438	82.1	51 500	244	6 830	-1.4	418	6.1	219	3	2 332	1.3	1 168	502
Ballard	3 191	82.3	33 000	136	3 514	5.2	318	9.0	155	-3	1 843	1.4	0	322
Barren	13 136	70.8	43 300	188	16 947	-0.3	1 074	6.3	728	-25	10 866	8.0	4 562	2 368
Bath	3 659	76.5	31 000	125	5 584	6.4	552	9.9	130	5	838	16.4	0	246
Bell	11 512	65.8	34 200	163	10 371	-0.2	939	9.1	741	5	8 321	-0.4	1 010	2 031
Boone	20 127	72.0	74 500	356	30 919	1.2	1 045	3.4	1 490	81	27 461	11.2	5 954	8 188
Bourbon	7 250	62.6	51 300	241	10 066	1.2	560	5.6	387	2	4 466	7.7	1 267	1 022
Boyd	19 876	72.7	45 400	221	21 618	1.6	1 251	5.8	1 371	27	22 762	3.6	7 211	4 702
Boyle	9 483	68.5	54 700	245	12 049	1.9	729	6.1	667	-22	11 635	-5.1	4 804	2 473
Bracken	2 872	75.4	39 400	135	3 164	-1.4	250	7.9	99	-7	573	3.1	0	123
Breathitt	5 555	71.8	28 700	143	4 913	-0.4	445	9.1	268	-35	2 940	9.8	0	716
Breckinridge	6 159	80.5	37 700	164	7 125	-0.9	516	7.2	257	-6	1 581	-2.2	206	516
Bullitt	15 965	84.3	51 000	249	22 644	1.3	1 138	5.0	538	14	5 067	-2.8	1 791	1 368
Butler	4 180	79.3	33 700	151	7 678	4.4	510	6.6	147	-3	2 224	35.7	1 424	230
Caldwell	5 274	75.5	33 800	155	5 534	2.0	469	8.5	292	9	2 913	7.4	886	883
Calloway	11 607	72.4	51 800	204	16 759	4.7	723	4.3	698	-1	7 493	3.9	2 378	2 065
Campbell	31 169	68.2	62 300	298	41 593	0.8	1 601	3.8	1 396	28	16 573	4.6	2 680	5 195
Carlisle	2 106	84.3	30 300	117	1 995	3.2	197	9.9	74	-7	415	-9.0	0	134
Carroll	3 505	65.6	41 700	194	4 949	-1.6	239	4.8	191	-1	3 221	-8.8	1 724	515
Carter	8 679	80.0	37 100	183	9 414	2.4	1 267	13.5	368	-14	3 890	16.1	962	1 296
Casey	5 436	80.0	30 900	127	5 304	3.2	406	7.7	178	-10	2 275	32.7	826	602
Christian	21 636	53.4	42 400	253	20 197	2.2	1 382	6.8	1 193	0	15 454	1.2	3 959	4 068
Clark	10 973	68.3	56 900	264	15 568	0.5	1 044	6.7	640	-6	8 596	2.0	3 300	1 965
Clay	7 367	71.6	27 800	139	5 164	-5.2	424	8.2	273	-7	2 050	-0.3	185	666
Clinton	3 591	75.9	27 400	122	4 046	0.4	404	10.0	160	-6	1 811	-6.7	1 021	296
Crittenden	3 646	79.2	30 900	144	3 789	-5.3	307	8.1	172	-2	1 626	10.8	583	289
Cumberland	2 714	75.0	27 700	122	3 518	-4.2	261	7.4	116	-3	1 433	16.1	731	283
Daviess	33 036	68.8	48 000	230	45 051	1.6	2 487	5.5	2 294	-34	32 094	9.4	7 963	7 190

1. Percent of total civilian labor force. 2. For week including March 12. Excludes government employees, self-employed persons, farm workers, domestic service workers, railroad employees subject to the Railroad Retirement Act, and employees on oceanborne vessels or in foreign countries.

STATE County	Private nonfarm establishments, 1988 (cont'd)				Personal income, 1989								Earnings, 1989		
	Employment[1] (cont'd)		Annual payroll								Per capita[3]			Percent by selected industries	
														Goods-related[4]	
	Finance, insurance, and real estate	Services	Total (Mil dol)	Average per employee (Dollars)	Total (Mil dol)	Percent change, 1988–1989	Wages and salaries[2] (Mil dol)	Proprietor's income (Mil dol)	Dividends, interest, & rent (Mil dol)	Transfer payments (Mil dol)	Dollars	Rank	Total (Mil dol)	Farm	Total
	88	89	90	91	92	93	94	95	96	97	98	99	100	101	102
KANSAS—Con.															
Ottawa	66	290	21	13 651	70	-11.9	23	3	22	16	12 033	2 319	25	-7.6	22.4
Pawnee	106	399	15	13 021	125	0.6	53	27	30	22	17 007	434	80	21.6	6.3
Phillips	84	328	25	16 038	104	2.8	46	14	30	20	15 253	886	59	8.9	28.7
Pottawatomie	189	631	44	15 403	227	5.2	104	28	43	40	13 723	1 570	132	7.8	25.3
Pratt	127	605	34	14 334	161	-2.2	74	25	39	30	16 191	597	100	10.5	11.7
Rawlins	55	202	8	11 426	54	3.2	15	14	16	10	14 937	1 015	29	38.4	6.5
Reno	1 276	5 159	384	18 125	957	3.9	535	104	214	154	14 829	1 060	638	3.4	28.4
Republic	70	374	22	12 487	102	-0.8	35	21	31	19	15 022	982	55	23.6	12.6
Rice	142	805	31	13 043	154	0.7	64	16	43	32	14 363	1 262	80	7.0	24.7
Riley	1 187	4 227	168	12 274	845	6.7	384	59	127	106	13 583	1 640	443	0.1	10.4
Rooks	77	188	15	13 537	84	0.1	31	16	26	17	14 057	1 408	47	6.6	23.0
Rush	36	109	8	13 649	59	5.1	20	7	17	15	16 135	609	27	5.5	25.5
Russell	133	424	33	13 544	131	1.9	53	20	42	25	17 062	425	73	7.1	25.9
Saline	1 074	6 116	338	16 428	850	6.6	501	109	172	125	17 017	432	610	-0.3	26.0
Scott	0	372	17	13 389	91	1.4	36	20	24	14	17 091	423	55	24.9	6.2
Sedgwick	9 957	45 891	4 416	22 454	7 215	6.9	5 475	610	1 152	910	17 727	330	6 085	0.3	39.5
Seward	318	1 103	143	18 271	290	3.2	191	54	49	34	15 752	720	245	9.6	29.7
Shawnee	6 489	21 453	1 246	18 467	2 977	7.4	2 150	225	534	462	17 886	311	2 375	0.6	18.4
Sheridan	52	77	6	12 979	46	-2.8	15	11	15	7	14 781	1 089	25	21.9	9.1
Sherman	101	516	20	11 916	111	-0.4	42	23	26	22	16 648	495	65	22.6	4.1
Smith	68	331	11	11 006	77	-0.7	21	15	26	15	14 916	1 021	36	12.8	11.5
Stafford	81	195	9	12 488	91	-9.2	24	23	26	18	17 724	331	47	35.0	9.8
Stanton	0	32	5	16 564	49	-10.7	14	18	10	5	20 267	156	32	56.1	2.4
Stevens	0	117	11	14 523	116	0.5	36	50	20	10	23 417	65	87	49.8	7.1
Sumner	324	1 023	57	14 215	402	5.8	115	44	69	71	15 594	775	159	8.8	22.7
Thomas	138	537	25	12 558	139	9.2	56	38	30	19	16 891	455	94	29.9	NA
Trego	42	269	8	10 586	57	0.5	16	12	19	11	14 981	995	28	21.9	7.8
Wabaunsee	47	92	6	11 307	90	3.3	17	11	20	16	13 460	1 708	28	8.2	13.9
Wallace	0	62	3	11 905	31	0.9	9	10	8	5	15 648	762	19	36.9	NA
Washington	98	351	12	9 672	95	2.9	30	9	31	22	12 912	1 951	40	5.9	10.4
Wichita	0	53	5	15 248	57	23.6	15	28	10	6	19 646	188	43	65.3	3.5
Wilson	80	353	44	15 735	147	4.6	59	22	32	32	13 273	1 783	81	13.3	33.8
Woodson	25	109	5	10 376	55	10.3	15	9	15	13	14 273	1 298	24	21.8	13.3
Wyandotte	2 231	14 495	1 399	22 186	2 199	4.7	2 121	119	270	423	12 752	2 016	2 240	0.0	31.6
KENTUCKY	61 254	272 135	19 876	X	51 513	7.5	31 248	5 461	7 931	8 904	13 823	X	36 709	3.4	32.1
Adair	94	502	33	11 832	168	6.9	57	29	25	42	10 931	2 679	86	16.0	27.9
Allen	112	238	44	15 665	165	5.8	65	29	20	33	11 661	2 458	94	16.6	34.3
Anderson	0	306	40	17 149	198	7.5	64	22	28	27	13 911	1 465	87	8.0	43.4
Ballard	49	401	43	23 390	115	11.6	63	18	17	24	14 515	1 204	80	9.0	NA
Barren	377	1 614	183	16 817	418	7.6	282	56	66	74	12 063	2 307	338	4.2	48.0
Bath	64	156	11	12 591	101	9.3	24	16	12	24	10 006	2 879	40	24.1	NA
Bell	416	1 879	132	15 820	315	5.2	188	30	47	100	9 638	2 939	218	0.2	35.4
Boone	737	5 024	499	18 174	955	10.5	816	71	88	92	16 609	500	887	1.1	28.7
Bourbon	212	731	69	15 512	277	5.8	111	50	53	42	14 232	1 316	161	26.5	24.2
Boyd	968	4 771	550	24 163	803	9.7	736	60	135	143	15 442	816	796	0.1	48.1
Boyle	353	2 690	194	16 652	346	6.8	252	37	69	58	13 118	1 856	289	2.1	34.9
Bracken	0	109	8	13 824	85	5.6	24	13	12	17	11 183	2 609	36	17.8	NA
Breathitt	122	719	53	18 044	155	6.6	84	23	17	47	9 653	2 937	107	2.0	NA
Breckinridge	129	410	19	12 200	191	7.0	39	32	30	41	11 164	2 616	71	22.9	13.1
Bullitt	197	703	84	16 593	608	7.0	130	42	47	63	12 513	2 108	172	4.6	38.9
Butler	75	224	29	12 845	124	14.4	60	18	11	27	11 259	2 576	78	11.7	54.0
Caldwell	136	687	36	12 422	156	5.5	57	15	31	37	11 873	2 367	72	5.9	NA
Calloway	272	1 203	108	14 382	413	8.2	202	63	72	79	13 112	1 857	264	3.9	26.3
Campbell	887	4 877	272	16 424	1 264	6.8	446	70	197	185	15 277	880	516	0.5	26.8
Carlisle	0	78	5	11 475	64	10.1	11	12	13	14	13 566	1 652	23	30.3	NA
Carroll	55	372	64	19 965	126	8.6	101	14	15	25	12 875	1 966	116	4.4	54.3
Carter	166	872	40	10 387	230	6.7	68	25	24	60	9 254	2 985	93	6.2	23.4
Casey	59	401	21	9 448	135	8.4	41	32	15	33	9 435	2 969	72	24.3	NA
Christian	955	3 671	226	14 616	754	6.3	845	68	103	131	12 331	2 187	913	1.3	15.4
Clark	307	1 389	155	18 076	401	1.1	217	46	58	65	13 466	1 704	263	7.2	38.9
Clay	151	564	29	14 220	181	6.9	94	16	21	65	7 869	3 080	110	2.4	40.1
Clinton	0	208	16	8 753	76	4.5	28	13	9	28	8 023	3 075	41	13.2	29.4
Crittenden	61	480	24	14 895	98	9.9	33	12	15	25	11 514	2 493	45	11.2	31.3
Cumberland	54	300	14	10 067	64	6.6	24	12	10	20	9 061	3 001	36	15.8	NA
Daviess	1 806	7 645	589	18 348	1 296	9.1	715	132	225	208	14 769	1 098	847	2.8	29.0

1. For week including March 12. Excludes government employees, self-employed persons, farm workers, domestic service workers, railroad employees subject to the Railroad Retirement Act, and employees on oceanborne vessels or in foreign countries. 2. Includes other labor income. 3. Based on the resident population estimated as of July 1 of the year shown. 4. Covers mining, construction, and manufacturing.

STATE County	Earnings, 1989 (cont'd)						Agriculture, 1987									
	Percent by selected industries (cont'd)						Farms			Farm operators, percent		Land in farms				
	Goods-related[1]	Service-related & other[2]						Percent with						Acres		
	Manu-facturing	Total	Retail trade	Finance, insur-ance, & real estate	Services	Govern-ment	Number	Less than 50 acres	500 acres and over	Whose principal occu-pation is farming	Residing on farm operated	Acreage (1,000)	Percent change, 1982–1987	Average size of farm	Total irrigated (1,000)	Total cropland (1,000)
	103	104	105	106	107	108	109	110	111	112	113	114	115	116	117	118
KANSAS—Con.																
Ottawa	13.1	59.0	10.4	7.2	24.2	26.2	523	13.6	46.8	64.8	65.4	386	-2.0	737	2	245
Pawnee	1.7	33.3	6.5	3.8	14.4	38.7	530	10.8	55.8	75.1	57.5	487	3.9	919	65	404
Phillips	22.5	44.3	6.6	3.3	17.3	18.0	591	9.0	55.5	76.0	71.1	543	-0.3	918	5	334
Pottawatomie	17.0	52.2	13.5	2.5	14.2	14.7	790	16.7	34.8	55.7	70.3	444	-4.5	562	10	188
Pratt	2.8	56.5	11.1	4.5	23.7	21.3	517	5.8	56.9	71.2	63.1	466	6.3	902	72	392
Rawlins	3.6	36.2	7.4	4.4	13.6	18.9	541	7.0	66.0	79.1	63.0	642	-6.5	1 186	12	415
Reno	23.3	53.5	15.6	4.3	22.8	14.7	1 557	19.4	30.7	59.5	71.1	718	2.3	461	26	583
Republic	8.3	46.4	7.9	5.1	17.3	17.4	833	10.7	40.8	73.1	62.2	440	-0.2	528	45	343
Rice	10.3	49.9	7.6	3.7	19.7	18.3	604	12.1	47.8	66.4	67.5	429	-0.2	710	15	348
Riley	2.7	46.9	10.2	7.7	22.8	42.6	546	20.5	32.1	59.5	73.6	248	-2.1	453	2	133
Rooks	6.8	48.7	11.6	4.1	20.1	21.6	473	6.3	60.0	69.6	57.5	548	2.9	1 158	3	322
Rush	19.9	45.1	6.9	4.1	13.8	23.9	546	7.5	52.4	70.3	53.5	423	-0.3	774	8	347
Russell	8.3	49.3	11.0	5.0	21.7	17.7	534	7.1	48.3	69.1	52.4	461	-2.2	863	0	288
Saline	19.8	62.9	11.5	3.4	31.2	11.4	743	16.0	35.8	55.7	65.5	404	1.8	543	3	289
Scott	1.1	55.3	7.8	3.7	19.1	13.7	391	11.3	58.3	75.4	44.2	471	-7.6	1 204	55	376
Sedgwick	34.1	49.3	9.2	4.6	23.3	10.9	1 589	28.9	20.9	47.3	70.5	524	0.2	330	30	445
Seward	18.3	48.0	10.9	3.1	15.9	12.7	285	7.0	61.4	74.4	53.0	331	1.9	1 163	78	247
Shawnee	12.8	59.3	9.9	7.7	24.3	21.7	852	26.5	15.0	43.3	75.4	221	-3.8	260	11	150
Sheridan	0.6	49.6	7.9	7.2	15.8	19.4	518	8.9	59.5	76.1	55.4	504	-1.9	972	51	374
Sherman	0.5	54.4	12.9	4.3	20.6	18.9	524	6.3	63.4	73.3	57.1	626	-6.9	1 195	83	497
Smith	5.5	58.6	7.9	4.8	26.6	17.1	692	9.4	54.8	77.5	66.2	556	1.8	803	8	382
Stafford	4.0	34.8	4.2	5.0	13.1	20.4	540	8.9	54.6	73.3	62.2	461	0.6	854	66	376
Stanton	0.4	27.2	2.6	2.1	5.5	14.3	280	8.6	70.4	85.0	52.9	425	-4.5	1 518	113	380
Stevens	0.6	31.5	3.2	1.8	7.6	11.6	300	4.3	75.7	74.0	53.7	461	1.0	1 537	120	393
Sumner	17.5	49.3	8.8	4.9	21.3	19.2	1 271	14.5	38.0	58.3	68.5	705	-4.1	555	3	599
Thomas	1.7	NA	10.4	4.4	15.4	17.1	644	5.9	61.3	69.9	50.5	677	2.8	1 052	74	586
Trego	2.8	53.8	11.0	3.5	25.0	16.5	482	7.9	62.2	72.8	63.5	480	-3.9	996	3	324
Wabaunsee	7.5	52.9	10.9	5.5	29.4	24.9	633	15.3	34.9	58.8	70.1	460	4.0	727	7	149
Wallace	NA	42.3	6.2	1.6	7.7	15.9	330	10.3	66.1	74.2	55.8	530	4.7	1 605	46	300
Washington	2.4	54.8	10.4	6.2	18.9	28.9	939	13.7	38.9	78.9	68.1	519	-2.2	552	8	379
Wichita	1.2	20.8	4.2	1.4	5.6	10.4	355	9.3	62.0	73.8	54.6	440	3.0	1 241	73	368
Wilson	28.8	34.8	7.0	3.0	14.4	18.0	610	12.0	33.9	62.8	72.1	299	-10.0	491	2	184
Woodson	4.9	44.9	9.8	1.8	18.2	20.0	369	11.4	37.1	61.2	67.2	254	-8.0	688	D	123
Wyandotte	25.8	48.7	6.5	2.6	16.5	19.6	199	59.3	5.0	30.7	73.9	24	-5.5	120	0	17
KENTUCKY	22.2	48.2	10.1	4.2	20.6	16.3	92 453	33.9	5.3	44.8	67.7	14 013	-1.2	152	38	8 900
Adair	22.1	40.2	10.5	1.8	19.7	15.8	1 491	34.2	2.0	48.5	63.8	174	0.4	117	0	103
Allen	30.5	37.2	17.6	2.2	8.0	11.9	1 195	30.8	3.1	42.5	65.4	157	-2.0	132	0	96
Anderson	34.9	36.4	10.9	1.9	11.7	12.2	759	32.9	1.6	29.9	64.0	90	-6.0	119	0	56
Ballard	43.2	33.3	6.0	2.0	15.4	8.6	433	32.3	13.4	46.9	74.1	105	-5.5	243	1	87
Barren	36.6	38.7	9.1	2.0	16.8	9.1	2 232	37.6	2.9	48.6	68.5	253	1.5	113	0	185
Bath	6.2	39.3	10.4	3.7	14.2	19.7	883	33.4	5.9	52.5	60.5	131	5.1	148	0	86
Bell	8.6	48.4	12.5	3.5	21.1	16.0	60	38.3	0.0	25.0	60.0	5	23.8	84	0	2
Boone	24.0	61.7	12.1	1.9	15.1	8.4	810	46.0	2.3	32.7	74.2	85	-19.6	105	1	49
Bourbon	17.3	39.4	7.2	2.4	11.7	9.9	1 070	32.5	9.8	58.6	67.9	218	12.7	204	1	163
Boyd	35.7	43.6	7.8	2.7	18.7	8.2	235	34.0	3.8	31.1	74.5	32	-5.5	137	0	12
Boyle	30.6	52.5	10.7	2.2	22.1	10.5	765	38.8	5.0	43.4	69.5	103	-1.1	135	0	74
Bracken	13.4	36.1	7.7	2.8	11.7	15.7	734	23.8	3.3	54.2	69.5	109	0.4	149	0	63
Breathitt	1.4	NA	10.1	2.9	15.1	16.5	296	33.1	5.4	31.1	66.9	44	-15.8	148	0	9
Breckinridge	3.0	45.6	12.4	4.3	17.3	18.4	1 473	30.5	6.9	45.9	66.5	268	-4.7	182	0	151
Bullitt	29.2	39.0	11.6	2.5	15.0	17.5	596	44.5	2.3	37.1	73.8	67	-7.8	113	0	38
Butler	41.0	22.3	5.0	1.8	7.6	11.9	651	18.9	8.0	42.2	69.0	147	0.7	226	0	76
Caldwell	18.7	NA	16.5	4.0	19.4	19.1	570	20.2	13.7	45.6	68.9	135	0.9	237	D	92
Calloway	19.2	45.8	12.6	2.2	16.0	24.1	749	37.2	9.7	51.3	69.3	138	-9.5	184	1	108
Campbell	16.1	54.5	14.8	3.3	28.3	18.1	512	37.9	0.6	29.3	82.6	41	-4.7	81	0	25
Carlisle	9.5	39.5	10.6	4.4	16.7	17.0	375	28.5	10.9	37.9	69.6	85	-5.1	226	0	70
Carroll	48.9	29.7	6.3	1.2	7.0	11.6	399	27.8	4.3	47.1	61.2	67	3.1	167	0	32
Carter	13.2	48.8	15.0	3.6	16.9	21.6	1 025	32.5	1.5	35.8	68.9	118	0.3	115	0	44
Casey	24.6	NA	9.5	1.7	8.3	14.9	1 563	36.1	3.6	50.5	64.6	202	-0.1	129	0	100
Christian	12.5	23.1	5.8	1.6	10.4	60.2	1 187	27.1	13.6	49.5	67.4	302	-6.2	255	1	224
Clark	32.7	44.5	10.5	2.2	15.0	9.3	947	37.4	7.3	44.1	65.5	155	5.6	164	0	109
Clay	4.5	NA	13.7	1.7	14.4	19.5	537	33.1	4.3	35.4	64.4	74	-1.3	139	0	21
Clinton	17.8	39.6	11.8	2.2	18.9	17.8	777	43.2	3.2	49.2	71.8	86	-1.8	111	0	46
Crittenden	26.6	44.1	12.8	2.8	22.7	13.3	502	14.9	10.4	45.4	72.5	128	-6.0	255	D	78
Cumberland	24.6	NA	11.9	2.7	21.4	14.7	646	28.2	7.6	54.8	63.0	116	0.3	179	0	45
Daviess	19.3	54.8	11.5	4.0	23.1	13.4	1 288	43.7	9.5	45.2	66.1	249	3.6	193	1	208

1. Covers mining, construction, and manufacturing. 2. Covers private sector earnings in agricultural services, forestry, and fisheries; transportation and public utilities; wholesale trade; retail trade; finance, insurance, and real estate; and services.

STATE County	Agriculture, 1987 (cont'd)								Manufactures, 1987						
	Value of land and buildings		Value of products sold				Percent of farms with sales of		Establishments		All employees			Production workers	
					Percent from										
	Average per farm ($1,000)	Average per acre (Dollars)	Total (Mil dol)	Average per farm (Dollars)	Crops	Livestock and poultry[1]	$10,000 or more	$100,000 or more	Total	Percent with 20 or more employees	Number (1,000)	Percent change, 1982–1987	Annual payroll (Mil dol)	Number (1,000)	Work hours (Mil)
	119	120	121	122	123	124	125	126	127	128	129	130	131	132	133
KANSAS—Con.															
Ottawa	266	392	38	71 777	30.4	69.6	67.7	12.6	3	33.3	D	D	D	D	D
Pawnee	398	423	91	172 515	27.6	72.4	76.0	18.7	7	14.3	0.1	0.0	1.0	0.0	0.1
Phillips	274	321	35	58 581	39.7	60.3	72.4	13.9	3	33.3	D	D	D	D	D
Pottawatomie	204	374	39	49 741	23.5	76.5	57.7	10.6	15	33.3	D	D	D	D	D
Pratt	419	466	98	188 914	27.7	72.3	75.6	21.3	13	15.4	0.2	0.0	3.1	0.1	0.2
Rawlins	326	272	32	58 795	53.7	46.3	78.2	15.0	6	16.7	0.1	0.0	0.9	0.1	0.1
Reno	263	565	83	53 259	40.0	60.0	58.2	10.7	92	42.4	5.2	-23.5	115.0	3.6	7.3
Republic	262	482	97	116 801	30.8	69.2	75.3	15.1	9	22.2	0.4	100.0	4.8	0.3	0.6
Rice	315	448	70	115 204	29.8	70.2	69.0	16.4	16	25.0	0.4	-20.0	7.0	0.3	0.6
Riley	184	448	25	46 601	28.3	71.7	59.5	11.4	21	38.1	D	D	D	D	D
Rooks	328	310	25	52 713	51.8	48.2	71.0	14.0	5	20.0	D	D	D	D	D
Rush	237	322	20	36 734	63.5	36.5	67.6	8.1	8	50.0	D	D	D	D	D
Russell	241	280	20	38 043	46.6	53.4	63.9	9.6	15	33.3	0.3	-25.0	4.5	0.2	0.4
Saline	249	471	31	41 318	39.9	60.1	53.7	10.0	85	36.5	4.2	-4.5	88.8	3.4	6.8
Scott	444	373	280	716 708	6.7	93.3	80.8	31.5	5	0.0	D	D	D	D	D
Sedgwick	290	861	59	37 336	51.4	48.6	49.7	9.4	597	34.3	64.8	24.9	1 852.6	32.4	71.2
Seward	562	461	130	457 508	11.8	88.2	73.0	28.4	17	29.4	D	D	D	D	D
Shawnee	190	804	22	25 656	58.5	41.5	39.8	6.8	130	38.5	9.0	0.0	234.6	6.6	12.8
Sheridan	360	370	54	104 419	40.9	59.1	81.5	19.7	4	0.0	D	D	D	D	D
Sherman	404	360	67	128 681	44.7	55.3	78.1	24.6	6	0.0	D	D	D	D	D
Smith	283	347	51	73 486	39.4	60.6	80.2	16.0	8	12.5	0.1	0.0	1.6	0.1	0.2
Stafford	428	492	72	133 432	32.9	67.1	73.0	23.7	5	60.0	0.1	0.0	1.3	0.1	0.1
Stanton	592	409	87	310 613	27.3	72.7	78.6	37.1	NA	NA	NA	NA	NA	NA	NA
Stevens	682	438	97	322 138	25.6	74.4	80.3	32.7	2	0.0	D	D	D	D	D
Sumner	298	535	53	42 021	57.8	42.2	60.7	11.0	37	24.3	1.1	22.2	26.0	0.8	1.7
Thomas	410	396	74	115 150	47.7	52.3	76.6	20.5	9	11.1	0.0	-100.0	0.5	0.0	0.0
Trego	249	256	36	73 760	30.1	69.9	79.0	8.3	4	0.0	0.0	0.0	0.4	0.0	0.0
Wabaunsee	287	385	34	54 045	18.3	81.7	56.4	10.7	7	28.6	0.1	0.0	1.7	0.1	0.1
Wallace	558	351	29	86 671	52.7	47.3	77.9	23.6	2	0.0	D	D	D	D	D
Washington	217	406	63	66 920	31.4	68.6	75.2	17.0	8	12.5	0.0	0.0	0.4	0.0	0.0
Wichita	489	373	223	628 830	8.8	91.2	79.4	29.0	3	0.0	0.0	0.0	0.3	0.0	0.0
Wilson	179	365	20	33 120	55.5	44.5	56.2	7.2	29	51.7	1.4	27.3	24.9	1.1	2.2
Woodson	228	309	21	57 189	33.5	66.5	60.4	11.9	3	33.3	D	D	D	D	D
Wyandotte	160	1 609	5	25 202	75.0	25.0	20.6	4.5	300	42.7	17.0	-1.7	480.0	12.4	23.8
KENTUCKY	136	896	2 076	22 450	42.9	57.1	36.8	3.8	3 693	41.0	251.6	2.0	5 865.2	184.8	356.2
Adair	86	661	23	15 592	28.7	71.3	32.3	2.7	27	37.0	1.1	57.1	14.2	1.0	1.5
Allen	96	759	21	17 867	24.7	75.3	29.1	1.6	17	41.2	1.3	18.2	23.8	1.2	2.1
Anderson	125	1 110	10	13 799	38.7	61.3	35.7	1.7	16	56.2	1.1	10.0	25.5	0.7	1.5
Ballard	171	740	17	38 466	59.9	40.1	48.0	10.2	10	20.0	D	D	D	D	D
Barren	90	832	45	20 097	34.4	65.6	40.5	3.7	41	56.1	4.1	5.1	79.0	3.4	6.5
Bath	104	702	16	17 876	49.7	50.3	46.0	1.4	4	25.0	D	D	D	D	D
Bell	75	897	0	5 656	31.3	69.0	18.3	0.0	26	53.8	1.1	22.2	17.0	0.8	1.4
Boone	193	1 737	11	13 914	55.0	45.0	27.3	2.7	87	48.3	5.3	0.0	122.8	3.4	6.9
Bourbon	340	1 670	71	66 723	25.8	74.2	63.9	10.0	16	43.8	1.1	-8.3	21.5	0.8	1.6
Boyd	111	830	4	18 022	9.4	90.6	14.0	1.3	46	41.3	D	D	D	D	D
Boyle	156	1 158	17	22 838	31.2	68.8	40.3	3.5	33	54.5	4.9	19.5	102.0	3.8	6.8
Bracken	95	609	12	16 749	55.4	44.6	46.7	1.8	5	40.0	D	D	D	D	D
Breathitt	86	716	2	5 623	87.3	12.7	11.1	0.0	6	33.3	0.0	-100.0	0.5	0.0	0.1
Breckinridge	114	652	26	17 831	46.9	53.1	38.6	2.7	10	30.0	0.2	-33.3	2.6	0.2	0.3
Bullitt	159	1 226	7	12 216	38.9	61.1	24.8	2.2	28	32.1	1.7	30.8	37.6	1.3	2.4
Butler	122	547	11	16 912	52.8	47.2	33.0	3.8	11	54.5	0.9	50.0	9.3	0.8	1.3
Caldwell	135	552	16	27 357	44.6	55.4	41.1	5.6	17	23.5	0.5	-61.5	9.1	0.4	0.9
Calloway	151	804	22	29 263	75.2	24.8	49.1	7.2	32	25.0	2.2	83.3	38.5	2.0	3.7
Campbell	111	1 395	3	6 729	47.9	52.2	12.7	0.6	64	42.2	2.5	25.0	62.9	1.8	3.6
Carlisle	150	676	13	34 531	55.9	44.1	48.5	10.4	6	33.3	D	D	D	D	D
Carroll	111	695	7	16 599	68.7	31.3	41.1	1.5	12	75.0	1.9	72.7	43.7	1.4	2.9
Carter	73	546	8	8 225	45.1	54.9	15.8	1.1	18	50.0	D	D	D	D	D
Casey	85	612	21	13 417	41.8	58.2	32.1	2.0	19	31.6	D	D	D	D	D
Christian	186	765	37	31 121	71.7	28.3	47.6	8.0	47	48.9	4.0	29.0	72.6	3.2	6.2
Clark	207	1 342	26	27 637	39.4	60.6	44.9	4.8	40	45.0	3.2	6.7	75.9	2.6	5.1
Clay	75	727	3	6 256	77.0	23.0	18.6	0.0	9	33.3	0.1	0.0	1.6	0.1	0.2
Clinton	73	817	9	11 278	36.3	63.7	28.1	1.0	17	47.1	1.1	37.5	9.6	1.1	1.8
Crittenden	122	469	8	16 341	33.1	66.9	34.7	3.4	15	33.3	0.5	-16.7	10.2	0.5	0.9
Cumberland	76	499	6	9 797	47.6	52.4	29.9	0.3	12	33.3	0.8	33.3	7.6	0.7	1.1
Daviess	220	1 140	45	35 068	84.3	15.7	44.2	9.2	97	44.3	7.5	13.6	194.0	5.2	10.1

1. Includes livestock and poultry products.

STATE County	Manufactures, 1987 (cont'd): Production workers (cont'd): Wages: Total (Mil dol)	Average per worker (Dollars)	Value added by manufacture (Mil dol)	Value of shipments (Mil dol)	New capital expenditures (Mil dol)	Value of construction authorized by building permits, 1990: Total[1] ($1,000)	Nonresidential: Total ($1,000)	Nonresidential: Percent: Office	Industrial	Stores	Residential: New construction ($1,000)	Number of housing units	Alterations and additions ($1,000)
	134	135	136	137	138	139	140	141	142	143	144	145	146
KANSAS—Con.													
Ottawa	D	D	D	D	D	75	3	0.0	0.0	0.0	0	0	19
Pawnee	0.6	NA	2.4	5.1	0.1	502	16	0.0	0.0	0.0	185	2	51
Phillips	D	D	D	D	D	267	212	86.7	0.0	0.0	0	0	21
Pottawatomie	D	D	D	D	D	6 557	612	35.3	0.0	21.4	5 275	75	407
Pratt	1.8	18 000	7.4	13.8	0.2	2 193	751	56.8	10.7	0.0	168	3	76
Rawlins	0.7	7 000	1.7	3.1	0.1	110	0	NA	NA	NA	60	1	15
Reno	74.3	20 639	277.8	573.2	19.3	19 018	1 734	23.9	40.4	0.0	5 216	123	7 489
Republic	3.2	10 667	9.1	18.0	0.4	110	8	0.0	100.0	0.0	0	0	45
Rice	5.5	18 333	22.3	36.4	1.3	988	229	80.3	0.0	0.0	214	3	36
Riley	D	D	D	D	D	23 238	1 392	1.4	18.3	24.6	15 649	278	526
Rooks	D	D	D	D	D	493	146	0.0	0.0	0.0	100	1	70
Rush	D	D	D	D	D	2	0	NA	NA	NA	0	0	1
Russell	3.1	15 500	7.3	20.8	0.2	320	12	0.0	0.0	0.0	133	2	85
Saline	65.9	19 382	287.7	582.4	16.7	40 623	5 601	4.9	13.4	27.1	9 711	186	1 003
Scott	D	D	D	D	D	946	110	0.0	0.0	100.0	0	0	718
Sedgwick	875.7	27 028	3 969.6	7 494.1	286.8	369 842	92 716	35.9	12.9	23.5	120 728	2 071	16 522
Seward	D	D	D	D	D	2 672	198	0.0	0.0	0.0	513	5	552
Shawnee	160.5	24 318	980.9	1 632.6	35.2	88 413	21 149	24.4	10.3	25.2	44 137	546	2 613
Sheridan	D	D	D	D	D	NA	NA	NA	NA	NA	NA	NA	NA
Sherman	D	D	D	D	D	184	90	100.0	0.0	0.0	33	1	0
Smith	1.3	13 000	2.5	6.2	D	155	5	0.0	0.0	0.0	0	0	68
Stafford	0.8	8 000	2.9	6.3	D	140	74	0.0	0.0	0.0	0	0	24
Stanton	NA	NA	NA	NA	NA	80	6	0.0	0.0	0.0	55	1	6
Stevens	D	D	D	D	D	952	279	43.0	0.0	0.0	384	5	50
Sumner	18.4	23 000	56.6	108.7	3.3	2 453	766	0.0	27.4	30.4	619	10	168
Thomas	0.2	NA	1.2	2.0	0.0	2 298	1 237	14.2	0.0	26.8	119	1	71
Trego	0.2	NA	0.9	1.5	0.0	51	23	0.0	87.0	0.0	0	0	6
Wabaunsee	1.1	11 000	4.3	13.0	0.1	1 267	301	0.0	44.9	15.6	858	15	47
Wallace	D	D	D	D	D	102	52	0.0	0.0	0.0	50	1	0
Washington	0.2	NA	1.2	1.9	0.0	0	0	NA	NA	NA	0	0	0
Wichita	0.1	NA	2.0	7.5	D	678	14	0.0	0.0	0.0	110	2	4
Wilson	16.7	15 182	62.7	162.7	1.3	281	11	0.0	0.0	72.7	205	2	14
Woodson	D	D	D	D	D	124	98	0.0	0.0	0.0	25	1	0
Wyandotte	331.5	26 734	1 483.5	3 493.2	407.4	27 474	3 987	11.2	25.2	35.3	12 283	186	617
KENTUCKY	3 752.3	20 305	18 091.7	41 827.1	1 746.0	1 510 474	482 341	18.2	26.8	33.5	778 348	11 944	47 014
Adair	12.4	12 400	35.0	70.0	1.7	436	210	59.5	0.0	0.0	100	6	0
Allen	20.8	17 333	47.4	98.2	D	0	0	NA	NA	NA	0	0	0
Anderson	14.7	21 000	109.2	195.9	D	1 644	49	0.0	0.0	0.0	1 415	41	40
Ballard	D	D	D	D	D	NA	NA	NA	NA	NA	NA	NA	NA
Barren	60.4	17 765	131.7	352.1	D	14 289	8 382	4.7	5.1	72.9	1 980	54	345
Bath	D	D	D	D	D	1 812	1 105	31.7	0.0	13.6	650	23	57
Bell	9.7	12 125	35.2	86.9	D	3 824	475	11.6	0.0	47.4	2 593	63	218
Boone	69.7	20 500	286.7	620.9	24.6	119 266	38 906	12.1	22.2	48.4	63 131	861	943
Bourbon	12.6	15 750	55.2	98.8	D	2 205	20	0.0	0.0	0.0	2 028	53	85
Boyd	D	D	D	D	D	6 634	1 848	10.4	0.0	83.0	1 742	26	684
Boyle	68.7	18 079	632.5	861.6	22.7	13 180	4 115	8.7	56.0	22.0	7 052	99	453
Bracken	D	D	D	D	D	NA	NA	NA	NA	NA	NA	NA	NA
Breathitt	0.5	NA	1.1	1.8	0.0	0	0	NA	NA	NA	0	0	0
Breckinridge	1.8	9 000	5.2	8.0	0.1	274	35	0.0	0.0	100.0	121	3	60
Bullitt	23.3	17 923	359.9	375.2	6.8	43 501	5 347	0.9	53.2	31.8	35 749	641	262
Butler	7.1	8 875	22.5	42.8	D	860	100	0.0	0.0	0.0	710	27	0
Caldwell	6.8	17 000	34.1	53.7	D	2 360	1 257	0.0	0.0	79.6	772	14	110
Calloway	30.9	15 450	313.8	475.2	10.1	4 892	942	3.7	45.0	37.1	2 990	65	173
Campbell	39.4	21 889	168.2	362.4	D	42 522	7 710	0.2	68.9	8.5	31 953	450	1 893
Carlisle	D	D	D	D	D	NA	NA	NA	NA	NA	NA	NA	NA
Carroll	27.2	19 429	143.1	374.5	D	1 055	410	0.0	91.5	8.5	573	16	28
Carter	D	D	D	D	D	16 630	15 989	0.8	93.8	2.5	439	10	0
Casey	D	D	D	D	D	3 366	217	0.0	0.0	86.9	38	1	0
Christian	52.4	16 375	165.9	396.3	D	8 668	1 720	58.7	0.0	29.1	4 879	80	285
Clark	54.4	20 923	231.9	469.5	D	24 692	14 283	2.8	66.4	20.7	7 333	126	730
Clay	0.9	9 000	4.8	8.3	D	1 104	246	0.0	0.0	0.0	858	33	0
Clinton	8.2	7 455	14.2	31.1	0.4	0	0	NA	NA	NA	0	0	0
Crittenden	8.1	16 200	25.0	32.2	1.6	0	0	NA	NA	NA	0	0	0
Cumberland	6.4	9 143	18.5	30.2	D	364	300	0.0	0.0	0.0	39	1	25
Daviess	127.7	24 558	635.6	2 046.0	86.4	31 102	6 676	15.5	20.3	35.5	17 647	315	2 460

1. Includes nonresidential additions and alterations, residential nonhousekeeping buildings, and residential garages and carports not shown separately.

STATE County	Wholesale trade, 1987				Retail trade, all establishments, 1987				Retail trade, establishments with payroll, 1987					
						Sales				Sales				
											Per capita[2] (Dollars)			
	Estab-lishments	Sales (Mil dol)	Paid employees[1]	Annual payroll (Mil dol)	Number	Total (Mil dol)	Percent change, 1982–1987	Per capita[2] (Dollars)	Number	Total (Mil dol)	General merchan-dise stores	Food stores	Apparel & acces-sory stores	Eating and drinking places
	147	148	149	150	151	152	153	154	155	156	157	158	159	160
KANSAS—Con.														
Ottawa	12	46.6	74	1.3	88	21.5	17.5	3 638	45	20.5	D	559	D	109
Pawnee	24	38.0	144	2.7	96	29.3	-4.2	3 859	66	28.4	D	D	100	303
Phillips	19	23.5	104	1.9	102	26.3	-4.4	3 762	59	24.4	353	1 346	208	207
Pottawatomie	21	28.9	169	2.6	180	41.8	16.8	2 578	99	38.6	31	729	D	212
Pratt	32	150.8	259	4.5	172	65.3	-6.4	6 281	100	63.6	1 040	D	216	740
Rawlins	16	32.0	105	1.2	55	10.3	7.3	2 781	31	9.0	D	981	D	161
Reno	145	411.1	1 401	25.0	783	395.3	27.6	6 073	465	383.3	887	1 206	306	529
Republic	33	60.7	206	2.6	102	21.1	-6.6	3 012	56	20.0	D	739	47	152
Rice	19	31.6	142	2.6	140	32.7	-4.9	2 948	78	30.6	D	1 073	D	281
Riley	57	118.2	501	9.0	534	324.1	38.6	5 177	387	318.5	713	871	301	485
Rooks	25	45.6	116	2.0	124	21.4	-25.2	3 347	72	20.3	D	618	153	167
Rush	18	43.5	108	1.6	71	7.7	-13.5	1 926	31	6.1	D	593	0	120
Russell	33	62.1	184	2.3	150	40.4	-7.8	4 931	75	37.8	D	1 192	152	468
Saline	133	729.5	1 814	34.0	616	374.8	24.0	7 496	414	366.4	1 042	1 295	474	671
Scott	20	154.1	241	3.7	74	26.7	-10.1	4 769	47	26.3	D	D	47	444
Sedgwick	892	4 190.6	12 220	256.5	4 050	2 689.2	28.4	6 817	2 607	2 619.1	1 002	1 286	312	738
Seward	68	77.9	392	7.2	293	145.6	9.6	7 786	188	140.0	1 332	1 420	406	611
Shawnee	270	806.8	2 986	62.4	1 634	1 088.7	34.7	6 704	1 088	1 063.3	941	1 270	244	674
Sheridan	15	33.8	106	1.5	44	8.9	-5.3	2 689	23	8.0	D	865	D	D
Sherman	24	40.7	167	2.6	131	54.9	9.8	7 840	94	53.8	769	1 168	389	650
Smith	23	42.3	158	2.2	91	18.7	-7.0	3 462	56	17.9	D	965	64	180
Stafford	17	35.5	87	2.0	74	11.4	-41.8	2 115	36	9.9	D	728	D	173
Stanton	19	47.5	130	2.5	30	5.6	16.7	2 350	14	5.4	0	D	D	73
Stevens	19	50.3	121	2.4	57	14.8	0.0	3 018	28	13.1	D	968	D	165
Sumner	36	64.0	202	3.4	283	91.7	15.3	3 610	143	86.7	D	1 077	68	229
Thomas	39	80.5	248	4.0	153	50.2	12.3	5 976	89	47.7	D	1 251	118	722
Trego	8	19.8	51	0.7	67	18.2	7.1	4 665	35	16.6	0	1 087	D	261
Wabaunsee	10	8.2	48	0.6	72	16.3	33.6	2 437	38	14.9	D	357	0	230
Wallace	13	29.3	77	1.3	23	4.4	-10.2	2 334	10	4.0	0	D	D	D
Washington	32	38.9	198	2.8	106	21.3	6.0	2 800	69	19.6	D	661	D	221
Wichita	17	29.2	93	1.6	37	7.1	-43.2	2 445	19	6.8	0	D	D	88
Wilson	13	34.4	107	1.2	138	36.2	40.9	3 144	75	32.8	D	935	57	178
Woodson	9	11.0	40	0.6	71	11.8	19.2	2 890	34	8.4	D	D	D	182
Wyandotte	343	3 516.6	6 658	160.1	1 244	775.1	28.8	4 465	797	753.2	531	935	122	443
KENTUCKY	5 650	24 461.5	63 606	1 240.0	38 507	19 871.7	36.4	5 338	21 731	18 939.9	690	1 151	201	485
Adair	24	21.6	159	1.7	188	50.5	60.3	3 255	82	42.4	D	798	78	197
Allen	15	11.4	66	0.9	146	52.9	29.3	3 647	74	48.6	118	1 208	61	197
Anderson	10	4.9	34	0.4	133	58.4	75.9	4 203	69	54.6	D	889	85	210
Ballard	11	9.9	51	0.8	122	42.6	60.2	5 261	54	39.3	D	1 375	320	125
Barren	60	108.3	570	7.2	440	186.1	36.8	5 347	255	175.7	865	1 241	138	514
Bath	4	4.0	27	0.3	123	23.2	62.2	2 296	48	18.2	D	854	17	61
Bell	56	100.0	443	7.0	363	189.0	27.0	5 626	223	180.8	1 397	1 251	197	486
Boone	80	526.6	1 479	42.5	609	609.2	64.0	11 220	462	600.9	2 064	1 425	567	980
Bourbon	19	160.4	426	7.7	187	79.1	51.8	4 057	108	75.5	D	1 020	89	261
Boyd	103	294.1	1 349	22.4	591	387.0	35.0	7 357	375	377.2	1 334	1 356	263	601
Boyle	43	65.6	420	5.9	351	186.1	48.1	7 158	212	179.8	1 180	1 363	173	594
Bracken	7	4.4	34	0.4	85	12.3	0.8	1 615	38	10.1	D	371	D	75
Breathitt	11	35.3	100	2.3	198	70.6	48.9	4 359	92	63.9	720	948	142	275
Breckinridge	21	21.1	100	1.6	172	58.7	32.8	3 432	85	52.8	471	973	63	152
Bullitt	26	23.4	215	3.3	287	93.7	24.1	2 001	146	88.6	D	664	D	217
Butler	11	16.3	92	1.2	94	22.9	18.7	2 079	40	19.4	D	891	D	29
Caldwell	16	13.0	62	1.0	166	83.7	54.4	6 293	102	80.4	D	1 329	182	369
Calloway	65	176.8	661	10.7	401	201.3	18.8	6 600	215	176.0	D	1 065	396	376
Campbell	65	165.9	554	11.8	646	383.4	34.4	4 665	423	374.8	395	1 256	215	624
Carlisle	5	6.2	16	0.2	73	14.8	8.8	3 028	30	13.0	D	596	D	68
Carroll	16	35.9	87	1.1	121	48.3	37.2	5 033	63	45.9	264	1 508	73	413
Carter	28	17.0	113	1.1	280	88.7	12.7	3 547	140	81.2	445	713	89	255
Casey	12	9.8	102	1.1	163	36.3	27.4	2 483	64	30.5	197	692	53	197
Christian	105	299.0	1 098	17.6	606	312.3	32.3	4 964	375	299.1	537	889	187	486
Clark	38	57.6	251	4.1	297	174.8	44.0	5 945	180	168.2	890	1 132	126	466
Clay	17	16.9	72	1.0	232	78.2	29.9	3 355	84	71.4	D	722	130	143
Clinton	11	13.4	78	0.9	125	32.1	32.6	3 310	52	25.2	77	1 163	36	45
Crittenden	13	23.3	73	0.7	108	23.4	-2.5	2 726	43	21.1	238	998	66	153
Cumberland	6	3.0	30	0.3	100	22.4	61.2	3 108	49	18.6	117	1 076	D	225
Daviess	184	531.3	1 946	33.7	1 095	565.2	29.1	6 437	697	545.2	1 083	1 281	262	582

1. For pay period including March 12. 2. Based on the estimated population as of July 1 of the year shown.

STATE County	Retail trade, establishments with payroll, 1987 (cont'd) — Paid employees[1]	Retail trade (cont'd) — Annual payroll (Mil dol)	Taxable service industries–establishments with payroll, 1987 — Number	Receipts (Mil dol) — Total	Receipts, selected kinds of business — Hotels, motels and other lodging places	Receipts, selected kinds of business — Health services	Receipts, selected kinds of business — Legal services	Paid employees	Annual payroll (Mil dol)	Bank deposits,[2] June 1989 — Total (Mil dol)	Bank deposits — Percent change, 1988–1989	Savings capital,[3] September 1989 — Total (Mil dol)	Savings capital — Percent change, 1988–1989
	161	162	163	164	165	166	167	168	169	170	171	172	173
KANSAS—Con.													
Ottawa	199	1.7	25	4.3	0.0	3.1	D	131	1.9	74	-31.9	0.0	NA
Pawnee	386	3.6	44	6.5	0.3	3.4	0.5	196	2.2	107	3.4	19.5	-2.7
Phillips	360	2.6	40	5.2	D	2.3	0.5	226	1.7	111	4.4	13.1	4.9
Pottawatomie	615	5.0	61	9.0	D	5.0	0.4	284	2.7	143	7.7	24.4	8.0
Pratt	1 019	8.4	92	21.3	0.7	7.9	1.4	531	6.6	148	4.9	43.0	-8.1
Rawlins	136	0.9	10	1.4	0.0	0.7	D	43	0.5	55	-7.4	0.0	NA
Reno	5 233	46.0	358	107.3	9.7	37.6	6.2	2 945	44.8	519	2.6	303.3	-5.9
Republic	294	2.3	39	4.9	D	2.2	0.3	273	2.2	88	1.1	47.9	1.4
Rice	478	3.5	53	6.7	D	2.6	0.4	185	2.2	116	-0.3	36.4	-4.0
Riley	4 849	36.6	291	76.9	4.9	25.3	2.1	2 110	27.5	263	3.9	361.1	2.6
Rooks	279	2.0	34	3.6	D	0.7	0.6	96	1.0	62	-0.3	32.0	-9.3
Rush	86	0.6	18	1.8	0.0	D	0.2	55	0.6	48	2.0	12.8	10.9
Russell	557	4.1	56	8.9	D	2.7	0.9	267	3.1	135	-11.1	28.8	-7.5
Saline	4 851	42.7	384	128.9	9.8	40.7	9.8	3 138	52.2	373	7.4	348.7	4.3
Scott	293	2.5	47	9.0	0.4	1.4	0.7	171	2.1	93	6.7	1.5	-8.5
Sedgwick	34 981	323.8	2 864	1 384.8	49.5	538.6	95.9	29 706	523.0	3 369	5.7	1 940.3	15.8
Seward	1 783	15.8	141	32.6	4.0	7.7	3.0	759	11.2	215	10.8	98.4	-6.6
Shawnee	13 504	126.7	1 158	425.1	23.7	141.0	39.5	10 423	169.9	1 162	1.3	2 149.9	13.1
Sheridan	96	1.0	17	1.6	D	D	D	56	0.4	76	9.2	0.0	NA
Sherman	651	5.7	59	11.3	2.3	2.4	1.2	347	3.4	87	3.7	80.9	-5.7
Smith	233	1.8	31	4.0	0.2	1.3	0.2	121	1.1	99	-0.6	17.7	14.4
Stafford	162	1.2	33	3.8	0.0	2.0	0.5	149	1.4	104	0.3	0.0	NA
Stanton	51	0.8	7	0.6	D	D	D	27	0.2	27	4.7	0.0	NA
Stevens	151	1.2	27	5.1	D	0.5	1.5	96	1.0	53	-9.6	17.7	4.6
Sumner	1 050	8.4	112	18.8	3.4	8.6	1.3	515	5.3	255	0.2	34.7	4.0
Thomas	694	6.1	63	12.7	D	4.0	0.7	393	3.4	132	4.8	40.6	-1.3
Trego	221	1.8	27	4.7	1.0	1.4	1.1	115	1.2	30	-3.4	31.8	-3.9
Wabaunsee	184	1.4	14	2.2	D	D	D	101	0.6	45	2.1	0.0	NA
Wallace	53	0.4	10	1.1	D	D	0.0	53	0.3	12	-1.7	0.0	NA
Washington	313	2.1	30	4.2	0.0	2.5	0.2	156	1.1	106	-2.1	17.0	-0.3
Wichita	84	0.6	13	1.4	0.0	D	D	28	0.4	40	24.9	0.0	NA
Wilson	395	2.8	49	8.4	D	3.9	0.7	222	2.6	107	2.1	30.6	-6.2
Woodson	142	1.0	19	3.7	D	3.1	0.3	146	1.4	33	-7.7	0.0	NA
Wyandotte	9 067	93.7	809	345.3	12.6	105.8	25.3	8 008	133.1	1 644	2.6	513.9	-0.7
KENTUCKY	243 641	2 132.2	18 415	6 325.3	377.1	2 443.0	459.1	166 228	2 315.5	28 869	6.0	6 813.7	-2.4
Adair	535	4.2	51	6.9	0.3	4.2	D	271	2.5	77	10.0	35.5	-1.2
Allen	513	4.5	41	7.0	D	2.4	0.5	202	2.0	92	4.0	14.5	5.1
Anderson	540	4.9	50	7.1	0.0	2.8	0.4	248	2.4	103	5.8	27.1	2.6
Ballard	350	2.9	21	9.2	D	1.9	D	317	3.2	77	7.8	0.0	NA
Barren	2 197	19.1	175	38.9	3.6	20.9	2.7	1 026	16.0	201	8.0	91.3	-2.5
Bath	204	1.6	22	2.5	D	1.5	D	110	0.8	59	14.1	0.0	NA
Bell	2 350	20.4	154	35.3	D	12.5	2.7	820	11.7	147	2.0	138.1	0.9
Boone	7 115	65.7	345	166.5	9.8	29.7	6.0	8 335	55.7	354	18.7	77.7	-6.4
Bourbon	892	7.4	81	14.5	D	8.0	0.6	393	4.4	144	3.8	18.7	-0.8
Boyd	4 961	42.4	381	107.7	4.6	44.2	8.1	2 384	44.5	491	7.0	151.7	-0.9
Boyle	2 406	20.2	169	30.5	D	15.7	2.2	825	12.5	222	3.6	71.5	2.0
Bracken	145	0.9	17	2.3	0.0	1.2	D	83	0.6	67	2.7	0.0	NA
Breathitt	748	6.2	46	5.0	0.7	1.3	0.6	116	1.2	106	-2.6	0.0	NA
Breckinridge	543	4.9	50	6.3	D	3.0	0.7	176	1.8	109	3.8	15.0	-6.5
Bullitt	1 290	10.5	123	18.3	2.4	4.7	1.8	495	5.4	129	8.7	34.0	0.0
Butler	190	1.7	27	5.4	0.0	4.0	0.5	209	1.9	67	4.2	0.3	NA
Caldwell	927	8.0	59	7.2	D	2.9	0.4	229	2.2	130	3.5	20.6	-10.3
Calloway	2 057	17.2	180	38.4	1.2	17.7	2.4	1 072	14.6	333	5.4	36.8	0.9
Campbell	5 372	45.1	326	87.1	0.8	30.3	4.1	1 848	33.8	509	12.8	381.4	-3.4
Carlisle	120	1.0	20	1.9	0.0	0.6	0.2	62	0.7	51	7.2	0.0	NA
Carroll	563	4.7	36	5.9	D	2.5	D	208	2.0	44	4.8	11.2	2.2
Carter	1 041	8.6	74	D	D	D	0.5	D	D	154	9.7	5.0	-6.8
Casey	436	2.8	30	2.7	D	1.2	0.4	77	0.7	57	6.4	21.1	7.9
Christian	4 254	36.7	282	62.2	D	25.0	4.4	1 860	23.5	329	1.1	128.0	2.3
Clark	2 129	18.0	164	28.6	1.6	11.0	2.4	783	10.7	240	5.8	71.2	3.6
Clay	634	6.4	55	13.0	D	6.3	0.8	299	3.4	132	6.5	0.0	NA
Clinton	263	2.1	32	6.4	2.8	1.6	0.3	216	1.7	62	2.7	0.0	NA
Crittenden	282	2.2	33	6.1	D	3.9	D	194	1.7	57	9.2	5.0	-16.1
Cumberland	297	2.0	22	3.8	D	1.3	0.5	109	1.3	55	7.2	0.0	NA
Daviess	7 289	64.7	569	176.1	17.7	67.2	11.5	4 906	70.2	590	6.9	315.4	-1.4

1. For the period including March 12 of the year shown. 2. Includes deposits for all insured and reporting noninsured commercial and mutual savings banks. 3. Includes savings capital for all FSLIC insured savings institutions.

STATE County	Federal funds and grants, 1989 — Expenditures — Total (Mil dol)	Federal funds and grants, 1989 — Expenditures — Percent change, 1988–1989	Per capita[1] (Dollars) — Total	Per capita[1] (Dollars) — Direct payments for individuals	Per capita[1] (Dollars) — Procurement contract awards	Per capita[1] (Dollars) — Salaries and wages	Per capita[1] (Dollars) — Grant awards	Local government finances, 1981–1982 — General revenue — Total (Mil dol)	General revenue — Intergovernmental — Total (Mil dol)	General revenue — Intergovernmental — Percent from state	General revenue — Taxes — Total (Mil dol)	Taxes — Per capita[2] — Total (Dollars)	Taxes — Per capita[2] — Property (Dollars)	Direct general expenditure — Total (Mil dol)	Direct general expenditure — Percent change, 1977–1982
	174	175	176	177	178	179	180	181	182	183	184	185	186	187	188
KANSAS—Con.															
Ottawa	19.1	-10.9	3 239	2 145	20	152	369	6.2	1.6	86.4	3.3	563	551	6.1	24.8
Pawnee	26.7	-10.8	3 614	2 159	30	223	115	8.6	2.0	92.6	4.8	581	568	8.4	56.6
Phillips	24.8	-4.8	3 642	2 375	24	221	184	8.9	2.7	91.2	4.4	591	579	8.8	64.7
Pottawatomie	39.2	8.7	2 379	1 642	16	128	380	30.5	5.1	91.9	10.4	674	665	26.3	193.9
Pratt	35.9	-18.7	3 595	2 397	18	164	126	12.7	2.9	91.0	6.4	593	582	14.0	79.4
Rawlins	15.8	-29.0	4 402	2 250	26	204	148	4.0	1.0	87.8	2.6	615	604	4.4	16.7
Reno	157.0	-2.8	2 434	1 838	21	175	219	65.7	19.2	93.6	31.7	489	436	69.4	58.7
Republic	28.3	-13.7	4 165	2 334	27	200	108	8.5	1.9	88.1	4.7	633	623	7.7	43.2
Rice	36.2	-9.3	3 352	2 384	21	169	132	14.4	3.5	87.7	7.0	600	586	13.4	55.1
Riley	125.1	10.5	2 012	1 184	36	206	520	37.5	14.3	75.3	14.3	225	197	33.4	37.4
Rooks	21.8	-8.1	3 632	2 347	24	185	141	8.2	1.5	86.8	4.3	594	580	8.0	75.2
Rush	19.7	-8.7	5 475	3 063	39	297	358	7.0	1.0	80.8	3.9	863	852	6.7	53.1
Russell	30.6	-2.4	3 979	2 735	62	199	170	15.5	2.0	91.6	7.7	847	832	13.9	87.1
Saline	124.7	5.2	2 494	1 805	96	300	200	47.1	14.8	92.9	18.8	381	356	45.4	28.6
Scott	19.9	-74.2	3 757	1 845	16	155	128	7.6	1.3	92.4	3.8	652	637	7.5	70.9
Sedgwick	1 738.9	4.4	4 272	1 680	1 776	567	222	430.5	130.6	74.5	151.3	400	355	424.6	72.9
Seward	56.6	13.5	3 077	1 252	914	170	302	33.7	6.8	78.5	11.5	631	509	32.4	101.7
Shawnee	740.0	14.1	4 444	2 027	370	624	1 228	189.7	59.1	78.1	70.5	449	395	184.8	34.6
Sheridan	16.2	-32.7	5 241	1 866	14	112	339	5.5	0.9	60.9	2.9	826	813	4.9	60.6
Sherman	29.6	-17.5	4 414	2 258	16	236	162	11.0	1.6	88.1	4.7	629	618	9.6	42.4
Smith	22.4	-14.2	4 398	2 541	32	274	138	5.7	1.6	91.4	3.1	542	527	5.7	56.3
Stafford	26.2	-18.3	5 140	2 963	44	235	99	10.8	1.4	88.5	5.3	912	894	9.9	87.1
Stanton	16.3	-25.7	6 778	1 271	11	99	92	5.8	0.6	81.7	3.4	1 437	1 423	5.1	66.4
Stevens	20.4	-18.4	4 170	1 575	14	139	99	10.6	1.0	87.2	7.9	1 688	1 659	8.0	12.3
Sumner	78.3	-8.8	3 036	2 222	222	168	168	25.6	6.8	89.9	10.8	426	400	27.0	71.4
Thomas	34.1	-15.4	4 155	2 168	24	203	223	15.3	3.1	88.4	6.6	757	746	15.0	69.9
Trego	14.7	-13.5	3 874	2 366	19	158	149	4.6	1.1	73.8	2.9	679	649	4.5	66.2
Wabaunsee	24.2	38.8	3 610	2 346	19	160	682	5.7	2.1	92.6	2.9	423	416	5.6	51.7
Wallace	13.2	-16.6	6 616	1 896	24	196	213	2.5	0.4	84.7	1.8	887	875	2.5	48.7
Washington	33.2	-5.0	4 487	2 500	34	281	221	11.9	2.3	86.3	5.1	624	616	11.7	64.7
Wichita	18.1	-3.2	6 255	1 580	1 147	164	383	4.7	0.6	86.6	2.7	914	901	4.1	26.7
Wilson	33.6	1.7	3 055	2 334	56	165	255	12.2	4.4	89.1	4.3	359	348	10.9	71.6
Woodson	21.4	33.6	5 639	3 127	84	233	1 717	3.8	0.9	82.8	2.3	498	485	3.7	56.0
Wyandotte	482.7	0.1	2 798	1 802	91	424	467	220.9	86.9	69.3	63.9	371	311	219.2	53.9
KENTUCKY	12 442.8	16.8	X	1 789	322	626	526	2 437.3	1 344.9	82.2	645.6	175	98	2 322.7	49.5
Adair	40.6	9.9	2 635	1 910	12	113	478	7.4	5.6	91.5	1.2	77	69	6.5	64.1
Allen	33.1	-1.1	2 330	1 710	13	100	403	9.9	5.5	93.5	1.8	127	81	8.8	47.8
Anderson	23.1	6.9	1 627	1 308	25	80	184	6.4	4.2	94.4	1.4	108	92	6.8	50.3
Ballard	25.0	-1.4	3 130	2 366	28	163	251	4.8	3.4	96.7	1.0	122	78	9.0	147.9
Barren	71.2	9.0	2 053	1 504	41	137	303	18.9	11.7	85.9	4.6	133	87	17.4	28.3
Bath	23.1	12.3	2 286	1 586	12	117	517	5.0	4.1	95.7	0.6	57	52	4.9	62.8
Bell	100.0	-7.8	3 059	2 157	153	170	572	20.7	14.7	86.7	3.6	106	57	20.0	69.8
Boone	155.1	56.9	2 697	1 135	523	484	543	40.7	14.1	84.2	10.3	214	131	38.1	110.4
Bourbon	49.5	9.9	2 537	1 602	534	79	244	14.7	9.7	64.9	3.0	154	94	14.7	58.2
Boyd	374.9	126.9	7 210	2 088	4 383	351	378	38.5	22.8	61.8	9.5	174	118	40.1	87.9
Boyle	52.6	2.5	1 994	1 597	19	112	244	15.6	8.7	93.9	4.3	172	107	14.0	6.8
Bracken	17.2	3.7	2 265	1 673	19	156	322	4.5	3.1	92.5	0.7	97	86	4.3	18.7
Breathitt	47.5	5.2	2 971	1 882	27	200	852	10.5	8.7	89.5	0.9	56	48	9.5	62.5
Breckinridge	42.3	0.7	2 473	1 730	15	144	387	10.5	6.4	85.1	1.2	75	57	9.7	66.2
Bullitt	117.8	3.5	2 424	895	1 346	40	127	20.6	15.4	97.5	3.4	77	57	19.5	52.5
Butler	-225.7	-888.7	-20 517	1 601	-22 768	125	373	5.9	4.4	94.2	0.8	73	43	5.6	77.3
Caldwell	39.0	7.7	2 978	2 182	117	161	276	7.5	5.1	88.0	1.5	113	56	6.6	32.3
Calloway	74.7	8.9	2 372	1 869	26	113	170	25.5	9.9	83.0	3.7	124	78	26.1	48.5
Campbell	167.7	-1.2	2 028	1 702	19	136	166	56.9	35.0	60.5	16.8	202	133	51.1	53.8
Carlisle	15.4	-1.8	3 216	2 303	18	149	326	2.9	2.2	96.1	0.5	90	66	2.5	37.0
Carroll	22.2	10.9	2 266	1 710	12	127	370	15.1	3.7	91.3	1.8	188	132	14.1	158.3
Carter	59.4	4.4	2 394	1 687	129	107	457	12.7	10.8	86.5	0.8	31	25	14.6	135.3
Casey	33.9	14.0	2 370	1 483	10	81	711	7.2	5.1	95.2	0.7	47	41	8.0	131.8
Christian	867.2	37.1	14 193	1 535	949	11 288	262	46.4	35.8	45.3	6.0	91	41	44.6	134.1
Clark	61.6	6.2	2 068	1 554	21	140	314	16.5	9.5	91.3	4.3	149	84	17.6	56.9
Clay	216.7	261.0	9 420	1 815	6 729	96	769	14.6	13.3	87.4	0.7	28	22	10.3	12.6
Clinton	26.9	7.6	2 831	1 956	11	88	654	4.8	4.2	94.9	0.3	35	28	4.3	6.3
Crittenden	23.6	-0.4	2 774	2 072	16	164	293	5.0	3.4	93.9	1.0	107	63	4.6	63.3
Cumberland	18.8	2.9	2 686	1 866	25	127	581	5.0	3.3	93.3	0.4	56	42	4.2	60.1
Daviess	193.2	7.6	2 203	1 668	125	132	228	79.2	25.3	85.8	17.3	199	116	87.8	81.2

1. Based on the estimated population as of July 1 of the year shown. 2. Based on the estimated population as of July 1, 1982.

STATE County	Local government finances, 1981–1982 (cont'd): Direct general expenditure (cont'd): Per capita[1] (Dollars)	Percent of total for– Education	Percent of total for– Health & hospitals	Percent of total for– Police protection	Percent of total for– Public welfare	Percent of total for– Highways	Debt outstanding: Total (Mil dol)	Debt outstanding: Per capita[1] (Dollars)	State and local government employment, 1989: Total	State and local government employment, 1989: Rate[2]	Federal government civilian employment 1989: Total	Federal government civilian employment 1989: Earnings ($1,000)	Elections, 1988[3]: Total vote cast for president	Elections, 1988[3]: Vote for lead party (Percent)
	189	190	191	192	193	194	195	196	197	198	199	200	201	202
KANSAS—Con.														
Ottawa	1 033	50.0	1.1	3.6	0.0	23.3	3.8	652	366	620.3	34	754	2 834	R–64.8
Pawnee	1 025	61.9	1.5	3.3	0.0	12.1	4.8	591	1 534	2 073.0	64	1 289	3 373	R–54.1
Phillips	1 184	54.7	4.3	2.8	4.0	10.9	4.9	667	646	950.0	47	1 078	3 315	R–69.9
Pottawatomie	1 698	37.4	8.1	2.3	0.0	11.3	130.1	8 393	1 048	635.2	63	1 498	6 549	R–59.5
Pratt	1 293	51.5	2.7	2.7	0.0	8.3	18.4	1 706	1 148	1 148.0	61	1 480	4 245	R–59.0
Rawlins	1 037	52.1	2.0	2.2	0.7	25.1	0.8	189	365	1 013.9	32	638	1 983	R–66.5
Reno	1 069	51.7	1.0	3.8	0.5	12.6	73.8	1 137	4 186	649.0	297	8 884	24 954	R–51.1
Republic	1 045	50.2	3.6	4.0	0.0	16.7	17.1	2 317	551	810.3	55	1 176	3 462	R–67.8
Rice	1 149	49.0	15.8	2.9	0.0	12.2	7.0	595	793	734.3	64	1 566	4 645	R–53.9
Riley	525	45.6	2.3	5.4	0.5	7.6	52.2	821	8 825	1 418.8	748	26 977	17 007	R–55.9
Rooks	1 112	48.2	10.9	2.7	5.9	15.1	3.9	535	575	958.3	41	949	3 007	R–64.4
Rush	1 482	45.2	16.5	2.4	0.0	13.6	3.2	709	334	927.8	46	891	2 153	R–48.5
Russell	1 532	41.8	23.5	3.5	0.0	15.5	7.0	765	669	868.8	55	1 230	3 926	R–61.2
Saline	923	49.8	1.6	4.6	0.4	8.4	76.1	1 547	2 926	585.2	377	11 843	19 618	R–58.0
Scott	1 292	45.7	22.7	3.5	0.0	8.5	1.0	170	331	624.5	58	1 534	2 375	R–66.9
Sedgwick	1 123	37.8	3.1	4.2	0.0	9.6	968.7	2 563	19 534	480.0	4 337	140 453	155 745	R–55.3
Seward	1 779	37.7	24.3	3.2	0.0	8.5	86.8	4 769	1 506	818.5	91	2 503	5 797	R–70.5
Shawnee	1 177	46.7	1.8	5.8	0.0	6.9	279.6	1 781	18 867	1 133.2	2 983	96 700	70 197	R–50.6
Sheridan	1 386	37.3	31.3	1.8	0.0	14.0	1.5	429	310	1 000.0	22	462	1 556	R–57.9
Sherman	1 286	40.8	31.6	3.6	0.1	10.4	6.7	898	616	919.4	55	1 507	3 065	R–62.9
Smith	979	54.2	1.9	2.6	0.0	21.1	2.4	411	302	592.2	55	1 168	2 988	R–65.3
Stafford	1 701	41.1	27.6	2.3	0.0	13.7	2.9	492	543	1 064.7	44	953	2 738	R–56.0
Stanton	2 105	38.8	19.5	4.3	0.8	13.6	4.6	1 900	273	1 137.5	17	359	950	R–62.3
Stevens	1 696	50.6	2.0	4.2	0.8	21.7	3.4	731	558	1 138.8	33	760	2 307	R–71.2
Sumner	1 063	43.2	18.7	3.5	0.6	14.4	16.5	651	1 547	599.6	120	3 059	10 042	R–53.7
Thomas	1 718	54.8	17.5	2.4	0.2	8.3	8.1	936	906	1 104.9	55	1 356	3 870	R–60.5
Trego	1 061	44.9	4.0	5.0	0.0	16.4	2.2	531	229	602.6	26	584	1 831	R–53.5
Wabaunsee	825	61.4	1.3	3.2	0.4	15.2	2.5	362	393	586.6	35	740	2 967	R–58.5
Wallace	1 239	61.3	1.9	2.7	0.2	13.5	0.4	183	195	975.0	21	387	941	R–69.6
Washington	1 432	42.5	27.4	1.9	0.0	15.0	3.3	407	676	913.5	75	1 559	3 380	R–67.1
Wichita	1 422	47.7	17.3	3.8	0.9	9.7	2.6	884	280	965.5	24	516	1 148	R–62.8
Wilson	900	52.2	15.3	4.8	0.0	10.9	7.9	649	767	697.3	60	1 317	4 346	R–63.1
Woodson	794	44.1	3.1	5.8	0.0	16.6	1.7	364	254	668.4	34	732	1 847	R–57.5
Wyandotte	1 273	36.7	2.1	4.5	0.2	7.2	629.2	3 656	14 909	864.3	2 181	76 365	58 399	D–66.2
KENTUCKY	629	50.0	6.9	4.8	0.6	4.6	5 009.5	1 356	193 265	518.6	43 514	1 201 220	1 322 517	R–55.5
Adair	421	69.9	2.6	1.4	0.0	9.8	4.9	314	603	391.6	56	1 382	6 113	R–71.1
Allen	628	49.0	28.0	3.7	0.0	6.8	6.3	450	533	375.4	42	1 040	4 923	R–67.9
Anderson	524	59.7	3.7	3.1	0.3	6.2	6.9	534	502	353.5	36	985	5 450	R–59.2
Ballard	1 062	34.8	1.4	0.9	0.0	4.0	95.7	11 256	323	403.7	42	963	3 629	D–59.6
Barren	504	61.6	0.2	3.3	0.1	8.6	27.0	782	1 430	412.1	136	3 406	11 506	R–57.8
Bath	480	70.8	6.7	2.4	0.2	7.5	2.9	290	374	370.3	40	931	3 724	D–56.4
Bell	583	63.7	0.5	5.2	0.0	5.5	6.9	202	1 453	444.3	171	4 787	11 193	R–51.5
Boone	791	38.8	0.3	3.7	0.9	4.8	243.8	5 058	2 305	400.9	1 129	28 933	18 157	R–69.8
Bourbon	765	46.0	3.4	3.0	0.0	5.8	25.1	1 307	731	374.9	48	1 272	6 175	R–53.6
Boyd	730	41.2	0.5	3.5	0.1	3.7	192.3	3 502	2 290	440.4	538	17 433	18 988	D–50.3
Boyle	564	60.7	2.5	4.3	0.1	5.2	26.0	1 047	1 489	564.0	74	2 139	8 354	R–56.8
Bracken	565	64.2	4.8	2.1	0.1	9.6	3.8	506	291	382.9	39	863	2 824	R–57.7
Breathitt	562	68.2	6.5	1.4	0.1	9.3	12.1	718	838	523.8	73	1 639	5 580	D–60.7
Breckinridge	583	56.6	22.9	1.8	0.1	7.5	5.4	326	572	334.5	92	2 039	6 623	R–58.0
Bullitt	443	78.7	1.1	2.8	0.1	3.6	29.6	672	1 407	289.5	55	1 418	15 013	R–59.0
Butler	506	70.7	1.6	1.3	0.0	6.5	2.1	187	522	474.5	41	889	4 539	R–72.2
Caldwell	490	62.0	1.4	4.0	0.2	8.9	7.3	543	650	496.2	68	1 879	5 577	R–52.9
Calloway	869	33.9	39.8	2.2	0.1	4.5	31.3	1 044	3 001	952.7	88	2 339	11 546	R–53.9
Campbell	616	46.5	1.6	5.2	0.4	4.3	65.6	790	4 114	497.5	318	9 661	29 104	R–66.6
Carlisle	473	67.5	7.7	0.9	0.0	10.2	2.6	484	190	395.8	23	534	2 564	D–55.7
Carroll	1 471	25.5	16.5	1.4	0.1	2.0	115.0	11 980	718	732.7	33	857	3 636	D–52.6
Carter	577	59.9	3.2	1.6	0.0	5.1	19.9	785	944	380.6	67	1 658	8 944	D–51.1
Casey	530	56.0	24.7	0.8	0.0	10.0	5.9	393	570	398.6	41	858	5 117	R–75.4
Christian	677	35.2	2.4	3.3	0.1	3.3	67.8	1 028	2 685	439.4	4 046	86 406	15 008	R–61.6
Clark	612	49.5	0.0	4.0	0.3	4.2	107.2	3 723	1 059	355.4	129	4 165	9 622	R–55.4
Clay	447	84.9	1.9	1.5	0.7	4.6	2.9	125	1 019	443.0	73	1 722	5 884	R–70.6
Clinton	452	73.3	2.3	2.2	0.0	9.3	3.4	355	410	431.6	30	712	4 175	R–77.8
Crittenden	520	62.1	5.9	3.5	0.1	7.6	5.7	637	325	382.4	36	777	3 666	R–60.3
Cumberland	571	51.5	24.2	1.8	0.0	5.7	2.6	356	268	382.9	31	637	2 995	R–74.5
Daviess	1 009	31.0	39.8	5.0	0.6	2.4	230.5	2 650	4 935	562.7	304	9 339	32 445	R–53.5

1. Based on the estimated population as of July 1, 1982. 2. Per 10,000 resident population estimated as of July 1 of the year shown. 3. Data subject to copyright.

STATE–County code	MSA/CMSA/NECMA code[1]	STATE County	Land Area,[2] 1990 (Sq. Km.)	Population, 1990											
				Total persons	Rank	Per square kilometer	Race					Hispanic[3]	Age of population Percent		
							White	Black	Am. Indian, Eskimo, Aleut	Asian & Pacific Islander	Other race		Under 5 years	5 to 14 years	15 to 24 years
			1	2	3	4	5	6	7	8	9	10	11	12	13
		KENTUCKY—Con.													
21 061	...	Edmonson	784	10 357	2 353	13.2	10 165	169	14	7	2	25	6.1	14.6	15.8
21 063	...	Elliott	606	6 455	2 714	10.7	6 451	1	3	0	0	15	7.0	17.1	15.3
21 065	...	Estill	658	14 614	2 012	22.2	14 593	8	7	3	3	46	6.1	15.5	15.6
21 067	4280	Fayette	737	225 366	220	305.8	190 448	30 143	351	3 713	711	2 556	6.8	12.2	18.0
21 069	...	Fleming	909	12 292	2 197	13.5	12 060	216	4	8	4	56	6.3	14.4	14.7
21 071	...	Floyd	1 021	43 586	930	42.7	43 155	306	32	78	15	129	7.1	16.3	15.6
21 073	...	Franklin	545	43 781	927	80.3	40 130	3 304	67	225	55	178	6.4	13.5	14.4
21 075	...	Fulton	541	8 271	2 540	15.3	6 700	1 537	12	16	6	25	6.2	14.6	13.2
21 077	...	Gallatin	256	5 393	2 810	21.1	5 281	93	5	7	7	8	7.6	15.9	14.4
21 079	...	Garrard	599	11 579	2 249	19.3	11 099	453	15	10	2	31	6.0	13.6	13.3
21 081	...	Grant	673	15 737	1 937	23.4	15 670	27	13	19	8	36	7.3	16.6	14.9
21 083	...	Graves	1 439	33 550	1 174	23.3	31 937	1 519	36	44	14	93	6.2	13.8	12.6
21 085	...	Grayson	1 305	21 050	1 626	16.1	20 900	71	35	34	10	89	6.3	15.3	13.8
21 087	...	Green	748	10 371	2 350	13.9	9 988	349	11	11	12	60	5.6	13.6	12.5
21 089	3400	Greenup	897	36 742	1 080	41.0	36 416	147	40	115	24	76	5.7	15.0	13.9
21 091	...	Hancock	489	7 864	2 586	16.1	7 732	94	14	17	7	30	7.2	16.4	14.8
21 093	...	Hardin	1 627	89 240	513	54.8	75 918	9 914	360	1 843	1 205	2 506	8.2	15.6	20.7
21 095	...	Harlan	1 210	36 574	1 088	30.2	35 259	1 212	34	54	15	109	7.0	16.3	15.3
21 097	...	Harrison	802	16 248	1 910	20.3	15 709	479	24	14	22	42	6.5	15.4	13.5
21 099	...	Hart	1 077	14 890	1 996	13.8	13 781	1 067	22	8	12	65	6.5	14.6	14.0
21 101	2440	Henderson	1 140	43 044	937	37.8	39 754	3 051	72	129	38	166	6.9	15.5	13.5
21 103	...	Henry	749	12 823	2 154	17.1	12 255	538	15	10	5	29	6.8	14.1	13.7
21 105	...	Hickman	633	5 566	2 795	8.8	5 051	503	5	2	5	19	6.2	12.9	11.7
21 107	...	Hopkins	1 426	46 126	900	32.3	42 847	3 057	53	136	33	188	6.7	14.7	13.6
21 109	...	Jackson	897	11 955	2 222	13.3	11 935	2	13	2	3	31	7.0	16.4	15.4
21 111	4520	Jefferson	997	664 937	69	666.9	544 365	113 435	1 048	4 766	1 323	4 365	6.8	13.6	13.7
21 113	4280	Jessamine	448	30 508	1 267	68.1	29 274	988	67	125	54	184	7.4	15.6	16.6
21 115	...	Johnson	677	23 248	1 528	34.3	23 113	33	20	75	7	38	6.1	15.9	15.3
21 117	1642	Kenton	421	142 031	335	337.4	136 849	4 158	180	635	209	704	8.1	15.4	14.2
21 119	...	Knott	912	17 906	1 793	19.6	17 759	113	10	18	6	34	6.6	17.2	17.0
21 121	...	Knox	1 004	29 676	1 308	29.6	29 267	291	71	26	21	78	7.1	16.1	16.5
21 123	...	Larue	682	11 679	2 239	17.1	11 150	489	26	10	4	55	6.1	14.5	12.5
21 125	...	Laurel	1 128	43 438	932	38.5	42 969	245	127	76	21	166	6.7	16.1	15.0
21 127	...	Lawrence	1 085	13 998	2 057	12.9	13 926	22	23	23	4	24	6.5	16.5	15.0
21 129	...	Lee	544	7 422	2 623	13.6	7 389	26	7	0	0	10	6.9	16.7	13.7
21 131	...	Leslie	1 046	13 642	2 087	13.0	13 611	12	9	8	2	40	7.6	17.3	16.0
21 133	...	Letcher	878	27 000	1 389	30.8	26 737	190	38	30	5	64	6.2	17.2	14.9
21 135	...	Lewis	1 255	13 029	2 140	10.4	12 976	27	22	4	0	25	6.2	16.1	15.3
21 137	...	Lincoln	872	20 045	1 674	23.0	19 345	621	50	12	17	43	6.8	15.1	14.5
21 139	...	Livingston	819	9 062	2 465	11.1	9 023	14	17	7	1	30	5.7	13.0	13.1
21 141	...	Logan	1 439	24 416	1 481	17.0	22 234	2 085	56	26	15	79	6.5	15.3	13.1
21 143	...	Lyon	559	6 624	2 694	11.8	6 153	433	22	12	4	28	3.9	9.2	12.2
21 145	...	McCracken	650	62 879	693	96.7	56 194	6 320	96	189	80	324	6.2	14.1	12.2
21 147	...	McCreary	1 108	15 603	1 946	14.1	15 416	124	59	3	1	24	7.5	16.8	17.3
21 149	...	McLean	659	9 628	2 422	14.6	9 571	46	8	3	0	15	6.1	14.5	13.8
21 151	...	Madison	1 141	57 508	757	50.4	54 101	2 920	82	321	84	191	5.9	12.6	25.4
21 153	...	Magoffin	801	13 077	2 134	16.3	13 049	4	18	5	1	15	7.2	18.2	16.7
21 155	...	Marion	898	16 499	1 892	18.4	14 986	1 471	18	21	3	42	6.5	16.6	14.6
21 157	...	Marshall	790	27 205	1 383	34.4	27 085	10	50	30	30	118	5.9	13.4	11.7
21 159	...	Martin	598	12 526	2 180	20.9	12 499	8	9	7	3	21	7.6	18.7	16.2
21 161	...	Mason	625	16 666	1 871	26.7	15 356	1 267	11	23	9	76	6.7	14.4	13.8
21 163	...	Meade	799	24 170	1 488	30.3	21 154	2 382	85	258	291	578	10.1	18.7	14.1
21 165	...	Menifee	528	5 092	2 833	9.6	4 987	87	5	4	9	27	6.6	15.3	16.8
21 167	...	Mercer	650	19 148	1 725	29.5	18 217	817	21	83	10	87	6.1	14.1	13.4
21 169	...	Metcalfe	753	8 963	2 474	11.9	8 708	223	16	10	6	27	6.2	14.1	14.0
21 171	...	Monroe	857	11 401	2 261	13.3	11 025	350	8	10	8	64	6.1	14.1	13.5
21 173	...	Montgomery	514	19 561	1 695	38.1	18 686	816	21	19	19	56	6.3	15.0	14.9
21 175	...	Morgan	988	11 648	2 242	11.8	11 533	100	9	6	0	42	6.5	15.7	14.9
21 177	...	Muhlenberg	1 230	31 318	1 234	25.5	29 928	1 287	40	33	30	82	6.1	14.7	14.9
21 179	...	Nelson	1 095	29 710	1 306	27.1	27 781	1 811	22	69	27	131	7.4	17.2	14.3
21 181	...	Nicholas	509	6 725	2 685	13.2	6 610	88	6	17	4	16	5.8	14.9	13.6
21 183	...	Ohio	1 538	21 105	1 624	13.7	20 849	179	40	31	6	80	6.7	15.6	13.4
21 185	4520	Oldham	490	33 263	1 183	67.9	31 818	1 197	76	124	48	206	6.5	17.4	13.0
21 187	...	Owen	912	9 035	2 466	9.9	8 853	158	14	5	5	14	6.2	15.8	12.9
21 189	...	Owsley	513	5 036	2 841	9.8	5 017	14	4	1	0	13	6.3	15.4	14.9
21 191	...	Pendleton	725	12 036	2 214	16.6	11 955	43	23	7	8	29	8.0	16.4	14.6

1. MSA = Metropolitan Statistical Area. CMSA = Consolidated MSA. NECMA = New England county metropolitan area. PMSA = Primary MSA. See Appendix A for explanation of these concepts. See Appendix B for list of metropolitan areas identified by type, with component counties. 2. Dry land or land partially or temporarily covered by water. 3. Hispanic persons may be of any race.

STATE County	Population, 1990 (cont'd) — Age of population (cont'd) Percent — 25 to 34 years	35 to 44 years	45 to 54 years	55 to 64 years	65 to 74 years	75 years and over	Percent female	Population–Change and components of change — Change 1980–1990 — Number	Percent	Components of change, 1980–1986 — Total persons, 1986	Total persons, 1980	Net change — Number	Percent	Natural increase — Births	Deaths
	14	15	16	17	18	19	20	21	22	23	24	25	26	27	28
KENTUCKY—Con.															
Edmonson	13.7	13.7	12.0	10.4	8.2	5.5	50.7	395	4.0	10 800	9 962	900	8.7	800	600
Elliott	15.2	14.1	10.4	8.4	6.8	5.7	50.4	-453	-6.6	6 600	6 908	-300	-4.0	500	300
Estill	15.1	14.0	10.9	9.0	7.4	6.4	52.0	119	0.8	15 000	14 495	500	3.6	1 300	900
Fayette	20.3	15.9	9.5	7.4	5.8	4.1	52.2	21 201	10.4	212 900	204 165	8 700	4.3	19 300	9 500
Fleming	15.0	13.9	10.6	9.6	8.5	7.0	51.0	-31	-0.3	12 400	12 323	100	0.6	1 100	800
Floyd	15.8	15.3	10.0	8.3	6.8	4.7	51.2	-5 178	-10.6	51 000	48 764	2 300	4.6	4 700	2 600
Franklin	16.6	16.7	11.3	9.1	7.2	5.0	52.0	1 951	4.7	44 000	41 830	2 200	5.2	3 700	2 300
Fulton	13.5	12.6	9.7	9.9	10.6	9.8	54.2	-700	-7.8	8 000	8 971	-1 000	-10.7	800	800
Gallatin	15.3	14.9	11.1	8.3	7.0	5.5	50.4	551	11.4	4 900	4 842	100	1.3	400	300
Garrard	15.8	14.1	11.3	10.3	8.4	7.1	51.7	726	6.7	11 800	10 853	900	8.3	900	700
Grant	15.9	14.2	11.5	8.1	6.8	4.8	50.8	2 429	18.3	14 100	13 308	800	6.2	1 300	800
Graves	14.5	14.1	11.1	9.4	9.9	8.4	52.2	-499	-1.5	32 900	34 049	-1 200	-3.4	2 700	2 700
Grayson	15.0	14.1	11.1	10.0	8.5	6.0	51.2	196	0.9	21 600	20 854	700	3.6	1 900	1 300
Green	14.9	13.7	11.3	10.6	9.9	8.0	51.4	-672	-6.1	10 700	11 043	-300	-2.9	800	700
Greenup	14.5	15.9	12.5	10.3	7.6	4.6	51.7	-2 390	-6.1	38 000	39 132	-1 100	-2.9	3 100	1 900
Hancock	15.5	16.2	11.3	8.2	6.2	4.2	49.9	122	1.6	8 000	7 742	300	3.6	800	400
Hardin	18.5	13.8	8.8	6.7	4.6	3.1	47.4	323	0.4	93 800	88 917	4 900	5.5	12 100	2 900
Harlan	15.2	15.1	9.8	8.4	7.6	5.3	51.8	-5 315	-12.7	41 900	41 889	0	0.1	4 400	2 600
Harrison	15.0	14.2	10.6	9.2	8.2	7.4	51.6	1 082	7.1	15 800	15 166	600	3.9	1 400	1 200
Hart	15.1	13.8	11.1	9.7	9.2	6.1	51.8	-512	-3.3	15 700	15 402	300	2.0	1 300	1 000
Henderson	16.8	15.2	10.7	8.8	7.3	5.5	52.1	2 195	5.4	42 300	40 849	1 500	3.6	4 200	2 400
Henry	15.6	14.5	11.8	9.3	8.2	6.0	50.9	83	0.7	13 300	12 740	600	4.4	1 100	900
Hickman	14.3	13.1	11.0	9.9	10.4	10.5	52.8	-499	-8.2	5 600	6 065	-400	-7.2	400	500
Hopkins	15.5	15.2	10.7	8.9	8.1	6.6	52.0	-48	-0.1	46 600	46 174	400	0.9	4 300	3 100
Jackson	15.3	14.3	10.0	8.4	7.5	5.7	50.6	-41	-0.3	12 500	11 996	500	4.6	1 200	700
Jefferson	17.4	15.4	10.2	9.4	7.8	5.6	52.8	-19 711	-2.9	680 700	684 648	-3 900	-0.6	63 300	40 500
Jessamine	18.2	16.1	10.2	7.2	5.2	3.5	51.0	4 443	17.0	29 200	26 065	3 100	12.0	2 700	1 100
Johnson	15.7	15.8	10.9	8.5	6.9	4.9	51.1	-1 184	-4.8	25 800	24 432	1 400	5.7	2 500	1 400
Kenton	18.2	15.1	9.5	8.0	6.7	4.8	51.9	4 973	3.6	137 600	137 058	600	0.4	14 200	8 000
Knott	16.5	15.1	9.8	7.4	6.1	4.4	50.8	-34	-0.2	18 400	17 940	500	2.8	1 800	900
Knox	14.9	14.1	10.5	7.8	7.3	5.7	52.0	-563	-1.9	29 900	30 239	-300	-1.0	3 000	1 800
Larue	15.2	14.1	11.7	9.9	9.0	7.1	51.2	-243	-2.0	12 200	11 922	300	2.5	1 000	800
Laurel	16.5	15.2	10.5	8.6	6.6	4.8	51.0	4 456	11.4	42 400	38 982	3 400	8.8	4 000	2 100
Lawrence	15.0	14.5	10.6	8.9	7.4	5.6	50.7	-123	-0.9	14 400	14 121	300	2.1	1 400	1 000
Lee	14.8	14.0	10.0	9.6	7.7	6.7	51.7	-332	-4.3	8 000	7 754	200	3.1	800	600
Leslie	17.2	14.8	9.7	7.9	5.2	4.1	50.5	-1 240	-8.3	15 200	14 882	400	2.5	1 500	600
Letcher	16.0	15.3	10.3	8.4	6.9	4.8	51.5	-3 687	-12.0	30 100	30 687	-600	-2.0	3 000	1 600
Lewis	15.3	14.1	10.7	8.7	7.8	5.7	50.2	-1 516	-10.4	14 200	14 545	-400	-2.6	1 200	800
Lincoln	15.5	13.8	10.7	9.3	8.3	5.9	50.7	992	5.2	19 300	19 053	300	1.4	1 600	1 300
Livingston	15.4	15.2	11.9	10.2	8.9	6.6	51.0	-157	-1.7	9 000	9 219	-200	-2.4	700	600
Logan	15.3	13.8	11.4	9.5	8.4	6.7	51.9	278	1.2	25 800	24 138	1 600	6.7	2 200	1 600
Lyon	19.2	15.3	11.8	10.8	9.8	7.9	43.8	134	2.1	6 400	6 490	-100	-1.8	300	500
McCracken	15.6	15.1	10.7	9.8	9.0	7.2	53.0	1 569	2.6	60 300	61 310	-1 000	-1.6	5 300	4 300
McCreary	14.6	14.4	10.2	8.1	6.7	4.5	50.9	-31	-0.2	16 400	15 634	800	4.9	1 700	900
McLean	14.0	14.9	11.8	9.2	8.7	7.0	50.8	-462	-4.6	9 900	10 090	-200	-1.7	900	700
Madison	15.5	13.5	9.5	7.3	5.9	4.4	52.4	4 156	7.8	54 900	53 352	1 500	2.9	4 200	2 300
Magoffin	16.7	14.2	9.7	7.1	6.0	4.2	50.6	-438	-3.2	14 300	13 515	800	5.8	1 600	600
Marion	16.7	14.4	9.6	8.6	7.0	6.0	50.1	-1 411	-7.9	17 700	17 910	-200	-1.3	1 700	1 000
Marshall	14.4	14.2	12.0	11.2	9.9	7.4	51.2	1 568	6.1	25 800	25 637	200	0.8	1 900	1 600
Martin	16.8	15.5	9.3	7.3	5.3	3.4	51.0	-1 399	-10.0	14 400	13 925	400	3.1	1 600	600
Mason	15.2	14.0	10.0	10.0	9.2	6.7	52.0	-1 094	-6.2	17 000	17 760	-700	-4.0	1 500	1 200
Meade	22.5	13.3	8.3	6.2	4.2	2.7	50.3	1 316	5.8	23 000	22 854	100	0.4	2 100	700
Menifee	15.4	14.2	10.8	8.8	7.6	4.6	49.9	-25	-0.5	5 300	5 117	200	3.6	500	300
Mercer	15.0	14.8	11.6	10.0	8.5	6.5	52.2	137	0.7	19 200	19 011	200	0.9	1 600	1 200
Metcalfe	15.0	13.4	11.2	10.4	8.8	6.9	52.1	-521	-5.5	9 700	9 484	200	2.2	700	600
Monroe	15.1	13.6	11.6	9.9	8.5	7.6	52.2	-952	-7.7	12 200	12 353	-200	-1.6	1 100	900
Montgomery	15.1	15.8	10.7	9.2	7.4	5.6	51.8	-485	-2.4	20 600	20 046	600	3.0	1 700	1 100
Morgan	16.6	14.7	10.1	9.1	6.7	5.7	48.8	-455	-3.8	12 000	12 103	-100	-1.0	1 100	700
Muhlenberg	14.6	14.4	10.9	9.3	8.5	6.7	51.8	-920	-2.9	31 900	32 238	-400	-1.1	2 800	2 200
Nelson	17.1	15.0	9.9	7.9	6.4	4.8	51.4	2 126	7.7	29 600	27 584	2 000	7.3	3 000	1 400
Nicholas	14.4	14.3	11.2	9.9	9.0	7.0	51.6	-432	-6.0	7 200	7 157	0	0.5	600	400
Ohio	14.3	14.1	11.2	9.2	8.4	7.0	51.9	-660	-3.0	21 400	21 765	-400	-1.9	1 900	1 400
Oldham	17.0	20.5	12.4	6.5	4.1	2.6	47.9	5 468	19.7	30 700	27 795	2 900	10.4	2 300	900
Owen	15.1	14.1	10.6	9.9	8.5	6.9	50.3	111	1.2	9 400	8 924	400	4.9	700	600
Owsley	14.2	13.9	10.7	9.0	8.3	7.1	49.4	-673	-11.8	5 600	5 709	-100	-1.7	500	300
Pendleton	16.6	13.6	9.8	8.9	6.9	5.2	51.1	1 047	9.5	10 900	10 989	-100	-0.5	1 000	700

STATE County	Population—(cont'd): Components of change, 1980-1986 (cont'd): Net migration	Households, 1990: Number	Households, 1990: Percent change, 1980–1990	Households, 1990: Persons per household	Households, 1990: Percent: Female family householder[1]	Households, 1990: Percent: One-person	Births, 1988: Total	Births, 1988: Rate[2]	Births, 1988: Low birth weight[3] (Number)	Deaths, 1987: Number: Total	Deaths, 1987: Number: Infant[4]	Deaths, 1987: Rate: Total[2]	Deaths, 1987: Rate: Infant[5]	Marriages, 1984: Number	Marriages, 1984: Rate[2]
	29	30	31	32	33	34	35	36	37	38	39	40	41	42	43
KENTUCKY—Con.															
Edmonson	700	3 843	14.5	2.64	9.3	18.6	111	11.2	6	91	1	8.9	10.8	105	9.2
Elliott	-400	2 324	4.5	2.78	12.0	19.3	86	12.8	8	57	1	8.5	14.3	61	9.1
Estill	0	5 357	9.4	2.71	12.9	20.5	191	12.8	17	171	4	11.4	20.4	151	10.1
Fayette	-1 000	89 529	18.7	2.38	12.2	29.1	3 323	14.7	211	1 581	25	7.1	7.4	2 448	11.7
Fleming	-100	4 626	7.3	2.62	9.0	22.6	174	14.1	9	134	1	11.0	6.9	128	10.4
Floyd	100	15 664	-1.9	2.76	12.1	19.5	671	13.8	49	446	7	9.1	10.1	439	8.7
Franklin	800	17 385	10.9	2.44	12.0	27.0	555	12.4	39	356	7	8.0	12.8	541	12.3
Fulton	-900	3 378	-0.2	2.42	14.5	29.4	105	13.6	12	128	2	16.4	17.1	166	20.2
Gallatin	0	1 941	17.7	2.75	9.6	20.7	86	16.5	5	54	0	10.6	0.0	67	13.7
Garrard	800	4 435	12.6	2.59	9.8	20.0	144	12.4	7	109	0	9.6	0.0	117	10.2
Grant	300	5 585	26.3	2.78	9.5	19.5	250	17.1	12	147	3	10.4	13.8	191	13.7
Graves	-1 200	13 377	4.7	2.47	8.8	24.8	395	11.8	32	430	9	12.8	21.8	374	11.4
Grayson	100	7 991	10.6	2.61	8.9	21.5	255	11.5	12	198	4	9.0	17.2	214	9.8
Green	-400	4 089	2.7	2.49	8.0	22.4	115	10.7	10	119	2	11.0	18.0	111	10.1
Greenup	-2 300	13 414	3.8	2.71	9.1	18.1	352	9.4	16	310	3	8.3	7.1	474	12.3
Hancock	-100	2 795	9.5	2.79	7.9	17.6	91	11.5	7	59	1	7.5	9.0	87	10.7
Hardin	-4 300	29 358	19.3	2.78	10.2	18.6	1 781	20.6	119	502	26	5.9	14.2	1 154	12.6
Harlan	-1 700	13 269	-4.2	2.74	13.3	21.9	539	13.8	49	453	8	11.4	13.9	201	4.8
Harrison	400	6 086	11.4	2.62	10.4	22.5	201	12.6	16	187	0	11.7	0.0	163	10.4
Hart	100	5 740	5.6	2.58	9.9	22.8	182	12.4	8	162	2	10.9	10.3	19	1.2
Henderson	-300	16 558	12.7	2.56	11.4	23.5	609	14.4	55	387	8	9.2	14.0	932	22.0
Henry	400	4 896	7.3	2.61	9.8	21.8	140	10.4	4	160	1	11.9	5.9	122	9.1
Hickman	-400	2 188	-1.8	2.47	9.7	23.8	74	14.0	11	60	1	11.1	15.2	46	7.9
Hopkins	-800	17 760	7.3	2.56	11.1	23.0	640	13.9	51	502	3	10.8	4.8	565	12.2
Jackson	0	4 381	8.7	2.71	10.6	20.2	148	11.8	13	122	2	9.8	14.1	129	10.4
Jefferson	-26 700	264 138	5.4	2.48	14.5	27.5	9 453	14.0	713	6 649	83	9.8	8.9	7 938	11.6
Jessamine	1 500	10 601	26.0	2.77	10.1	16.6	435	14.2	23	192	4	6.4	8.5	302	10.7
Johnson	400	8 469	3.3	2.71	10.9	20.5	321	13.1	23	223	3	9.0	9.1	250	9.7
Kenton	-5 600	52 690	9.6	2.66	12.2	25.2	2 413	17.2	144	1 298	19	9.3	7.9	2 138	15.7
Knott	-400	6 086	11.4	2.86	12.6	18.2	217	12.1	20	164	0	9.1	0.0	51	2.8
Knox	-1 400	10 718	7.8	2.72	14.8	20.9	436	14.6	34	331	4	11.0	9.0	287	9.6
Larue	100	4 503	5.5	2.56	9.0	22.4	147	12.3	11	123	1	10.2	7.6	114	9.3
Laurel	1 500	15 585	21.6	2.75	11.2	17.7	569	13.0	34	365	7	8.5	12.0	422	10.3
Lawrence	-100	5 007	7.4	2.77	10.4	20.2	168	11.6	14	140	5	9.7	23.9	196	13.3
Lee	0	2 760	4.9	2.65	12.1	21.7	100	13.2	5	86	2	11.2	28.2	86	10.9
Leslie	-500	4 711	3.1	2.88	12.7	16.0	237	15.7	15	122	5	8.0	22.1	141	9.2
Letcher	-2 000	9 731	-2.8	2.76	11.8	19.7	334	11.4	20	276	4	9.5	10.1	109	3.6
Lewis	-800	4 713	0.9	2.74	9.7	19.7	162	11.7	5	127	0	9.1	0.0	153	10.7
Lincoln	0	7 431	14.0	2.67	9.7	20.2	252	13.0	20	215	3	11.1	12.7	190	9.9
Livingston	-300	3 593	5.1	2.49	7.5	22.7	91	10.2	6	93	0	10.3	0.0	79	8.7
Logan	1 000	9 302	8.8	2.60	9.9	23.0	334	13.1	12	273	4	10.8	11.6	232	9.1
Lyon	0	2 355	6.5	2.31	7.3	27.2	50	7.8	6	71	0	11.3	0.0	74	11.6
McCracken	-2 100	25 625	9.2	2.41	11.7	27.0	816	13.6	36	691	5	11.5	7.0	1 002	16.4
McCreary	0	5 479	12.9	2.80	14.4	20.1	244	15.2	30	155	2	9.6	8.7	200	12.3
McLean	-400	3 672	0.0	2.59	8.2	21.6	117	11.9	5	105	2	10.7	17.1	112	11.3
Madison	-400	20 012	19.1	2.56	10.6	21.8	670	11.7	44	432	8	7.6	11.1	583	10.7
Magoffin	-200	4 440	7.0	2.90	10.5	16.8	224	16.4	8	121	4	8.8	21.1	153	10.9
Marion	-1 000	5 688	1.6	2.77	12.7	21.3	223	12.9	20	171	3	9.7	12.4	142	8.0
Marshall	-100	10 789	14.4	2.48	6.9	21.5	279	10.4	13	283	2	10.6	6.6	302	11.8
Martin	-600	4 300	2.8	2.91	12.2	16.6	187	13.8	13	98	1	7.1	4.8	165	11.5
Mason	-1 000	6 537	2.8	2.52	11.5	25.3	221	12.6	12	192	1	11.0	4.8	224	12.9
Meade	-1 200	8 080	12.8	2.98	7.9	14.4	258	10.3	22	131	4	5.3	15.2	203	8.9
Menifee	100	1 842	10.3	2.68	9.6	19.8	63	11.9	5	48	1	9.1	12.2	34	6.4
Mercer	-300	7 413	8.9	2.56	9.9	22.1	274	13.8	21	224	2	11.2	8.3	182	9.6
Metcalfe	100	3 433	5.1	2.57	8.9	22.0	113	11.3	12	123	0	12.3	0.0	80	8.1
Monroe	-300	4 505	2.0	2.50	10.1	23.9	146	12.2	13	130	2	10.7	14.8	113	9.0
Montgomery	0	7 312	6.2	2.64	10.8	20.9	273	13.3	10	177	0	8.7	0.0	239	11.7
Morgan	-500	4 089	2.3	2.74	9.4	19.6	132	11.3	9	119	3	10.1	20.5	134	11.1
Muhlenberg	-1 000	11 683	5.1	2.62	9.9	21.5	384	12.5	20	366	5	11.8	12.2	329	10.3
Nelson	500	10 417	20.4	2.80	11.8	19.7	428	14.4	20	241	2	8.2	5.1	294	10.2
Nicholas	-100	2 621	0.9	2.54	9.4	23.9	77	10.5	4	80	0	10.8	0.0	79	11.0
Ohio	-900	7 816	3.0	2.66	8.3	20.8	271	13.0	24	254	6	12.1	20.6	233	10.6
Oldham	1 500	10 673	33.0	2.93	8.5	13.8	377	10.7	24	162	5	4.8	12.7	229	7.8
Owen	400	3 412	6.9	2.61	8.2	22.8	104	11.1	5	95	2	10.1	20.0	77	8.3
Owsley	-300	1 848	-2.2	2.67	11.0	19.6	54	10.0	5	73	0	13.0	0.0	40	7.1
Pendleton	-400	4 332	16.0	2.76	8.7	20.7	167	14.8	10	109	1	9.7	5.8	71	6.6

1. No spouse present. 2. Per 1,000 resident population estimated as of July 1 of the year shown. 3. Under 2,500 grams. 4. Deaths of infants under 1 year old. 5. Deaths of infants under 1 year old per 1,000 live births.

STATE County	Divorces, 1984		Physicians, active non–Federal, 1989		Hospitals, 1989			Nursing homes,[4] 1986		Serious crimes known to police, 1988			Education			
						Beds				Number			Public school enrollment[7]		Attainment,[8] 1980	
	Number	Rate[1]	Number[2]	Rate[3]	Number	Number	Rate[3]	Number	Beds	Total[5]	Violent[6]	Rate[3]	1986–1987	1980	Percent 12 yrs. or more	Percent 16 yrs. or more
	44	45	46	47	48	49	50	51	52	53	54	55	56	57	58	59
KENTUCKY—Con.																
Edmonson	NA	NA	3	32	0	0	0	1	37	NA	NA	NA	2 083	2 222	35.5	5.3
Elliott	20	3.0	2	30	0	0	0	1	3	NA	NA	NA	1 453	1 572	31.3	7.1
Estill	73	4.9	6	41	1	26	176	1	96	NA	NA	NA	3 096	3 286	38.4	6.5
Fayette	1 277	6.1	1 206	523	10	3 072	1 333	23	1 354	NA	NA	NA	30 619	32 135	71.6	25.6
Fleming	55	4.5	7	57	1	52	426	17	197	NA	NA	NA	2 315	2 650	40.2	6.3
Floyd	14	0.3	48	100	3	283	587	6	267	NA	NA	NA	9 304	10 188	39.9	6.0
Franklin	342	7.8	58	129	1	153	342	8	129	NA	NA	NA	7 222	7 634	64.0	18.0
Fulton	52	6.3	9	118	1	70	921	2	80	NA	NA	NA	1 621	1 745	45.2	6.6
Gallatin	21	4.3	2	37	0	0	0	0	0	NA	NA	NA	982	1 105	43.2	5.5
Garrard	66	5.7	4	34	1	131	1 129	3	40	NA	NA	NA	1 877	1 957	44.5	7.2
Grant	29	2.1	5	34	1	30	203	4	119	NA	NA	NA	2 973	3 033	49.0	5.6
Graves	96	2.9	24	71	1	89	263	6	438	NA	NA	NA	5 617	6 326	50.0	7.9
Grayson	1	NA	16	71	1	75	335	2	170	NA	NA	NA	4 067	4 285	37.2	5.6
Green	43	3.9	9	85	1	64	604	4	158	NA	NA	NA	1 802	2 194	35.6	3.9
Greenup	67	1.7	18	48	1	157	420	4	269	NA	NA	NA	7 759	8 998	57.1	9.1
Hancock	30	3.7	2	26	0	0	0	1	78	NA	NA	NA	1 600	1 780	57.2	6.3
Hardin	720	7.8	115	136	3	501	592	8	266	NA	NA	NA	17 862	15 833	66.5	10.9
Harlan	249	5.9	33	86	1	103	270	2	193	NA	NA	NA	8 332	9 029	38.2	5.7
Harrison	74	4.7	12	75	1	99	623	7	280	NA	NA	NA	2 955	3 018	46.9	7.3
Hart	85	5.3	8	56	1	30	210	2	57	NA	NA	NA	2 421	3 175	37.2	6.4
Henderson	13	0.3	56	133	1	213	505	3	435	NA	NA	NA	7 675	7 721	57.2	10.2
Henry	70	5.2	5	37	0	0	0	3	66	NA	NA	NA	2 514	2 746	50.9	7.4
Hickman	31	5.3	2	38	0	0	0	4	210	NA	NA	NA	941	1 138	53.2	7.5
Hopkins	311	6.7	117	254	1	410	889	7	660	NA	NA	NA	8 990	9 085	49.7	7.5
Jackson	58	4.7	2	16	0	0	0	1	3	NA	NA	NA	2 523	2 488	25.3	4.2
Jefferson	3 906	5.7	2 130	316	16	4 398	653	123	5 913	NA	NA	NA	93 384	102 834	63.6	15.3
Jessamine	146	5.2	25	80	0	0	0	6	132	NA	NA	NA	5 388	4 996	59.7	17.3
Johnson	122	4.7	30	124	1	72	299	2	91	NA	NA	NA	5 414	5 295	42.8	7.4
Kenton	103	0.8	258	183	4	800	567	7	956	NA	NA	NA	21 030	21 606	59.0	12.2
Knott	NA	NA	4	22	0	0	0	1	82	NA	NA	NA	4 062	4 057	36.2	6.1
Knox	3	0.1	10	33	1	58	194	4	246	NA	NA	NA	5 939	6 604	36.0	7.3
Larue	45	3.7	2	17	0	0	0	3	128	NA	NA	NA	2 219	2 366	43.9	5.0
Laurel	233	5.7	19	43	1	67	151	5	213	NA	NA	NA	8 715	8 316	42.5	6.7
Lawrence	65	4.4	12	83	1	90	625	1	120	NA	NA	NA	3 034	3 074	36.0	5.5
Lee	25	3.2	4	53	0	0	0	2	108	NA	NA	NA	1 526	1 688	34.6	5.7
Leslie	5	0.3	10	67	1	40	267	0	0	NA	NA	NA	3 424	3 554	30.6	7.0
Letcher	147	4.8	28	97	2	131	455	1	44	NA	NA	NA	6 282	6 805	37.9	6.7
Lewis	9	0.6	2	14	0	0	0	2	113	NA	NA	NA	2 990	3 539	33.0	5.3
Lincoln	14	0.7	8	41	1	73	376	19	211	NA	NA	NA	3 911	4 150	37.0	4.7
Livingston	61	6.7	6	68	1	26	295	2	88	NA	NA	NA	1 641	1 784	50.9	5.4
Logan	17	0.7	16	63	1	100	395	5	187	NA	NA	NA	4 566	4 764	45.1	6.6
Lyon	6	0.9	2	31	0	0	0	1	128	NA	NA	NA	872	1 005	54.1	6.4
McCracken	467	7.7	144	242	3	781	1 310	8	570	NA	NA	NA	10 647	11 162	62.9	11.5
McCreary	69	4.3	8	50	0	0	0	1	49	NA	NA	NA	3 796	4 013	28.8	5.2
McLean	84	8.5	4	41	1	18	186	2	116	NA	NA	NA	1 953	2 182	47.1	5.6
Madison	315	5.8	67	115	2	207	355	8	139	NA	NA	NA	8 992	8 544	54.9	17.8
Magoffin	15	1.1	4	29	0	0	0	4	205	NA	NA	NA	3 138	3 127	30.1	5.5
Marion	62	3.5	10	58	1	113	657	6	226	NA	NA	NA	3 107	4 049	44.9	6.7
Marshall	68	2.6	17	63	1	80	296	4	238	NA	NA	NA	4 517	4 902	56.4	8.4
Martin	64	4.5	7	52	0	0	0	0	0	NA	NA	NA	3 386	3 469	34.5	5.9
Mason	88	5.1	21	119	1	111	631	6	117	NA	NA	NA	2 973	3 421	49.2	9.7
Meade	62	2.7	3	12	0	0	0	1	64	NA	NA	NA	3 530	5 349	64.2	12.2
Menifee	39	7.4	1	19	0	0	0	2	6	NA	NA	NA	1 038	1 097	31.8	4.2
Mercer	109	5.7	10	50	1	80	396	8	136	NA	NA	NA	3 571	3 696	52.3	9.2
Metcalfe	43	4.3	3	30	0	0	0	3	135	NA	NA	NA	1 738	1 952	33.1	5.2
Monroe	16	1.3	7	58	1	49	408	1	120	NA	NA	NA	2 193	2 543	32.4	5.2
Montgomery	108	5.3	22	108	1	103	505	3	93	NA	NA	NA	4 206	4 435	46.8	8.0
Morgan	33	2.7	9	78	1	45	391	3	47	NA	NA	NA	2 435	2 502	30.5	6.3
Muhlenberg	197	6.2	20	66	1	135	446	9	371	NA	NA	NA	6 443	6 643	44.8	6.5
Nelson	116	4.0	18	60	1	52	174	3	191	NA	NA	NA	5 214	5 662	56.0	10.0
Nicholas	34	4.7	6	82	1	83	1 137	1	55	NA	NA	NA	1 327	1 426	42.0	6.3
Ohio	138	6.3	7	34	1	68	332	4	307	NA	NA	NA	4 301	4 504	44.1	5.1
Oldham	128	4.4	24	65	2	147	396	1	94	NA	NA	NA	6 392	6 273	69.3	16.4
Owen	34	3.7	3	32	1	50	532	2	103	NA	NA	NA	1 815	1 772	41.6	7.0
Owsley	21	3.8	0	0	0	0	0	1	101	NA	NA	NA	1 064	1 275	29.3	6.9
Pendleton	64	5.9	2	18	0	0	0	4	101	NA	NA	NA	2 361	2 590	47.5	6.0

1. Per 1,000 resident population estimated as of July 1 of the year shown. 2. As of end of year. 3. Per 100,000 resident population as of July 1 of the year shown. 4. Preliminary. Covers nursing homes with 3 or more beds. 5. Data for serious crimes have not been adjusted for underreporting, this may affect comparability between geographic areas or over time. 6. Includes murder and nonnegligent manslaughter, forcible rape, robbery, and aggravated assault. 7. The 1986–1987 data are based on administrative reports obtained by the U.S. National Center for Education Statistics. The 1980 data are based on the 1980 Census of Population and Housing. 8. Persons 25 years old or older.

STATE County	Education (cont'd)		Social Security Program December 1988				Money income						Housing units, 1990	
	Local government expenditures for education,[1] 1982		Beneficiaries			Supplemental Security Income Program recipients June 1986	Per capita[3]			Median household income 1979 (Dollars)	Percent below poverty level, 1979			
								1979						
	Total (Mil dol)	Per capita (Dollars)	Total	Rate[2]	Payments ($1,000)		1987 Income, (Dollars)	Current dollars	Constant 1987 dollars		Persons	Families	Total	Percent change, 1980–1990
	60	61	62	63	64	65	66	67	68	69	70	71	72	73
KENTUCKY—Con.														
Edmonson	3.2	309	1 705	172.2	605	378	6 036	4 150	6 494	10 081	22.6	19.9	5 009	18.7
Elliott	2.5	359	930	138.8	321	356	5 191	3 906	6 112	9 715	32.3	27.4	2 639	5.6
Estill	5.5	376	2 535	170.1	907	760	6 758	4 440	6 947	10 720	28.1	24.6	5 863	11.7
Fayette	66.5	319	27 230	120.6	13 010	3 080	12 411	7 395	11 571	15 915	13.5	9.5	97 742	19.6
Fleming	4.4	356	2 445	198.8	888	560	7 527	4 721	7 387	10 929	23.9	19.4	5 163	11.6
Floyd	14.6	294	9 280	190.2	3 543	1 622	6 883	4 982	7 795	12 372	22.3	18.4	17 169	-1.1
Franklin	12.0	280	8 305	186.2	3 804	2 138	11 246	7 309	11 436	16 281	10.6	7.9	18 543	9.3
Fulton	3.4	391	2 445	317.5	1 007	486	8 416	5 435	8 504	10 883	27.1	21.2	3 684	1.5
Gallatin	1.6	333	880	169.2	362	146	8 466	5 531	8 654	13 693	17.7	15.6	2 290	28.7
Garrard	3.2	284	2 225	191.8	842	364	7 844	4 965	7 769	11 513	21.7	17.6	4 929	13.8
Grant	4.5	328	2 815	192.8	1 171	356	8 513	5 648	8 837	15 434	13.1	11.6	6 543	22.2
Graves	10.4	312	8 100	241.1	3 546	948	9 610	6 048	9 463	13 636	13.9	11.9	14 528	6.6
Grayson	6.2	291	4 435	199.8	1 656	882	7 366	4 653	7 281	10 745	23.1	20.3	10 446	9.4
Green	3.1	287	2 270	212.1	786	432	7 117	4 636	7 254	10 456	24.3	21.2	4 523	5.7
Greenup	13.1	340	4 695	124.9	2 011	768	9 738	6 425	10 053	17 374	13.1	10.9	14 657	5.8
Hancock	3.4	430	1 160	146.8	487	176	8 858	5 629	8 808	15 625	14.6	13.0	3 080	9.6
Hardin	20.2	224	9 650	111.7	3 804	1 162	8 867	5 448	8 524	13 742	15.1	13.5	32 375	19.1
Harlan	13.8	323	8 115	207.0	3 328	1 472	6 532	4 952	7 748	11 175	25.8	22.1	14 735	-0.5
Harrison	5.5	360	3 150	198.1	1 304	476	8 419	5 369	8 401	12 519	19.3	15.3	6 488	8.4
Hart	4.3	280	2 950	200.7	1 009	708	6 785	4 383	6 858	9 672	28.2	24.3	6 501	1.1
Henderson	13.4	323	7 170	169.9	3 365	802	10 709	6 972	10 909	16 477	11.0	8.5	17 932	15.5
Henry	4.4	337	2 670	199.3	1 115	394	8 604	5 369	8 401	12 655	20.0	16.0	5 447	6.7
Hickman	2.0	332	1 070	201.9	440	160	9 338	5 985	9 365	13 080	18.0	14.7	2 374	-1.3
Hopkins	15.9	341	9 245	200.1	4 222	984	9 796	6 562	10 268	15 269	14.5	11.6	19 325	9.3
Jackson	4.4	358	2 275	182.0	714	856	5 372	3 560	5 570	7 428	39.2	36.0	4 895	12.1
Jefferson	219.0	320	116 305	172.1	57 789	11 154	11 783	7 324	11 460	16 664	12.2	9.7	282 578	6.3
Jessamine	7.3	270	3 425	111.9	1 479	472	9 668	5 781	9 046	14 817	14.7	11.9	11 209	23.8
Johnson	9.0	362	4 580	186.9	1 803	1 010	7 137	5 215	8 160	11 944	22.9	19.7	9 381	6.4
Kenton	38.4	280	21 035	150.0	10 354	1 720	11 287	6 867	10 745	17 195	10.1	8.2	56 086	9.5
Knott	6.4	354	2 880	160.0	1 007	942	6 473	4 335	6 783	10 527	30.9	27.3	6 718	14.5
Knox	9.9	328	4 940	165.2	1 698	1 684	6 076	3 988	6 240	8 850	37.1	31.4	11 731	8.4
Larue	3.7	312	2 290	190.8	861	366	8 491	5 093	7 969	11 632	22.5	19.5	4 824	3.8
Laurel	12.5	309	6 585	150.7	2 436	1 474	7 238	4 807	7 522	11 961	21.1	18.7	16 923	19.6
Lawrence	4.7	326	2 600	179.3	967	720	6 683	4 584	7 173	9 415	29.9	25.2	5 684	8.8
Lee	2.6	343	1 555	204.6	554	488	5 759	4 004	6 265	8 420	33.4	29.9	3 025	8.1
Leslie	5.5	360	2 155	142.7	730	772	6 033	4 055	6 345	9 419	34.1	30.9	5 038	3.7
Letcher	9.6	313	5 255	180.0	2 094	1 030	6 352	4 546	7 113	10 927	27.4	22.9	10 808	1.4
Lewis	5.1	348	2 345	168.7	836	676	5 922	4 014	6 281	9 957	31.2	26.2	5 328	5.3
Lincoln	6.2	329	3 970	204.6	1 385	998	7 280	4 431	6 933	10 474	27.9	24.5	7 985	11.0
Livingston	2.8	297	1 990	223.6	859	240	8 793	5 743	8 986	13 211	14.7	12.6	4 177	8.7
Logan	7.9	322	4 800	189.0	1 858	944	8 281	5 316	8 318	12 225	16.2	13.3	10 303	8.8
Lyon	1.8	270	1 360	212.5	618	120	8 994	5 826	9 116	14 051	13.5	11.8	3 460	36.3
McCracken	19.8	323	12 650	211.2	5 958	1 354	10 700	6 931	10 845	15 172	12.9	9.0	27 581	11.2
McCreary	6.1	382	2 980	185.1	1 056	890	4 885	3 226	5 048	7 534	39.5	34.3	6 039	16.7
McLean	3.4	345	2 040	208.2	871	220	8 053	5 646	8 834	13 471	15.2	14.2	4 042	4.9
Madison	13.1	243	7 600	132.6	3 029	1 526	8 133	5 114	8 002	12 381	21.1	17.6	21 456	19.4
Magoffin	4.6	331	2 160	157.7	741	930	5 398	4 016	6 284	9 091	35.0	29.9	4 800	7.0
Marion	5.8	326	3 065	177.2	1 162	660	7 441	4 547	7 115	11 587	23.0	19.5	6 115	3.3
Marshall	7.2	279	5 940	222.5	2 767	402	9 568	6 354	9 942	15 255	9.8	8.8	12 528	17.7
Martin	5.2	360	2 175	159.9	827	560	6 865	5 261	8 232	13 686	27.0	23.4	4 697	5.6
Mason	5.2	300	3 390	193.7	1 408	516	8 530	5 490	8 590	12 904	19.8	15.6	7 089	4.9
Meade	5.5	245	1 960	78.4	822	234	7 774	4 971	7 778	14 093	13.6	12.4	8 907	16.6
Menifee	1.6	293	935	176.4	315	290	5 638	3 698	5 786	9 155	28.9	25.7	2 421	29.6
Mercer	6.2	325	3 770	189.4	1 585	434	9 164	5 752	9 000	13 861	16.7	13.3	8 212	8.7
Metcalfe	3.0	304	1 985	198.5	639	548	6 166	4 134	6 468	9 034	30.8	28.6	3 793	6.4
Monroe	4.3	351	2 515	209.6	822	852	7 107	4 243	6 639	8 955	29.1	25.1	4 882	-5.1
Montgomery	6.9	340	3 370	164.4	1 339	680	7 949	5 152	8 061	12 022	21.7	18.6	7 759	7.2
Morgan	4.3	355	2 050	175.2	698	712	5 838	3 976	6 221	8 061	36.7	32.0	4 562	5.4
Muhlenberg	10.9	342	6 395	208.3	2 803	784	8 309	6 054	9 473	14 540	15.0	11.5	12 754	10.1
Nelson	9.8	349	4 985	167.8	2 093	620	8 718	5 362	8 390	14 297	16.8	13.6	11 078	20.1
Nicholas	2.2	308	1 400	191.8	507	310	7 901	5 000	7 824	11 177	21.0	17.3	2 930	5.7
Ohio	6.9	324	4 305	207.0	1 804	572	7 814	5 643	8 830	13 805	17.1	15.8	8 680	7.5
Oldham	10.1	357	2 690	76.6	1 268	210	11 489	7 196	11 260	21 243	6.5	5.0	11 202	28.8
Owen	2.8	306	1 460	155.3	561	252	7 461	4 738	7 414	10 620	23.2	19.5	4 723	18.9
Owsley	1.8	322	1 155	213.9	347	564	4 747	2 946	4 610	6 673	48.3	40.8	2 137	4.8
Pendleton	3.5	325	1 925	170.4	779	238	7 908	5 152	8 061	13 344	17.3	14.7	4 782	14.1

1. Elementary and secondary. 2. Per 1,000 resident population estimated as of July 1 of the year shown. 3. Based on the resident population estimated as of July 1, 1988 for 1987 data and enumerated as of April 1, 1980 for 1979 data.

STATE County	Housing units, 1990 (cont'd) — Occupied units — Total	Owner occupied — Percent	Owner occupied — Median value (Dollars)	Median rent (Dollars)	Civilian labor force, 1990 — Total	Percent change, 1989–1990	Unemployment — Total	Unemployment — Rate[1]	Private nonfarm establishments, 1988 — Number	Net change, 1987–1988	Employment[2] — Total	Per-cent change, 1987–1988	Manu-facturing	Retail trade
	74	75	76	77	78	79	80	81	82	83	84	85	86	87
KENTUCKY—Con.														
Edmonson	3 843	85.6	33 000	142	4 274	6.3	377	8.8	91	-2	509	-34.4	36	179
Elliott	2 324	78.8	32 300	116	1 499	-3.4	260	17.3	48	-10	242	-17.4	0	92
Estill	5 357	74.5	30 400	158	4 926	-0.1	600	12.2	208	8	1 714	3.8	0	492
Fayette	89 529	53.0	73 900	338	134 047	0.3	4 228	3.2	7 102	241	115 831	7.3	17 768	27 647
Fleming	4 626	76.2	36 500	140	5 555	-4.0	423	7.6	212	3	2 027	2.9	723	508
Floyd	15 664	74.6	37 800	198	15 793	-2.1	1 090	6.9	847	-13	8 952	4.2	416	1 957
Franklin	17 385	64.0	60 200	285	24 930	3.7	1 025	4.1	994	-5	14 216	6.5	4 314	3 311
Fulton	3 378	66.5	33 900	159	3 386	4.0	292	8.6	208	4	1 887	-11.8	595	603
Gallatin	1 941	75.6	45 300	168	2 141	9.1	129	6.0	73	2	412	26.0	0	128
Garrard	4 435	74.5	45 800	180	5 078	-1.2	371	7.3	179	-7	1 499	18.1	430	367
Grant	5 585	77.0	49 600	217	8 300	1.8	415	5.0	273	5	2 655	0.9	480	1 195
Graves	13 377	77.9	38 500	166	15 950	-1.1	1 482	9.3	587	2	9 052	3.9	4 041	1 585
Grayson	7 991	79.6	35 700	172	9 595	1.7	833	8.7	377	0	4 517	6.9	2 468	715
Green	4 089	78.9	31 700	135	5 655	9.1	344	6.1	156	6	1 181	-6.0	468	284
Greenup	13 414	81.6	44 100	228	14 797	1.7	891	6.0	389	13	4 675	-0.9	296	873
Hancock	2 795	80.5	43 600	188	2 910	-2.6	275	9.5	109	2	1 757	-34.3	0	142
Hardin	29 358	63.5	58 300	289	36 645	3.1	1 835	5.0	1 600	40	18 736	4.9	4 045	7 088
Harlan	13 269	70.8	29 400	161	11 950	2.1	912	7.6	663	12	7 462	4.2	160	1 814
Harrison	6 086	67.7	48 500	198	7 356	1.0	396	5.4	307	-1	3 937	3.0	1 754	941
Hart	5 740	75.6	31 600	142	6 760	-1.3	515	7.6	227	3	2 183	19.7	796	415
Henderson	16 558	66.9	51 000	254	21 824	-0.1	1 332	6.1	1 000	-24	14 336	2.1	4 933	2 809
Henry	4 896	76.2	41 100	167	7 061	1.1	361	5.1	199	0	1 620	17.3	419	456
Hickman	2 188	79.2	32 000	120	2 624	8.6	164	6.3	88	-6	946	-19.6	0	124
Hopkins	17 760	75.2	39 600	195	19 859	0.2	1 270	6.4	1 055	-2	14 120	0.4	3 237	2 850
Jackson	4 381	77.2	26 900	106	4 350	-0.2	451	10.4	100	7	778	11.0	250	123
Jefferson	264 138	64.5	57 000	282	371 084	0.8	19 442	5.2	17 261	272	310 045	2.0	67 987	65 025
Jessamine	10 601	68.4	63 800	266	16 611	0.1	586	3.5	562	30	5 947	1.2	1 669	1 201
Johnson	8 469	73.8	40 100	195	8 445	3.3	599	7.1	482	5	4 436	5.0	0	1 521
Kenton	52 690	65.8	65 200	308	73 676	1.0	2 635	3.6	2 621	55	40 466	4.9	4 839	11 153
Knott	6 086	78.4	27 700	150	5 101	-5.8	439	8.6	255	-10	2 097	-3.8	33	439
Knox	10 718	68.8	35 300	174	10 043	0.5	707	7.0	407	9	4 351	4.5	718	1 269
Larue	4 503	79.7	39 500	164	5 337	0.1	359	6.7	214	-3	1 523	5.9	0	325
Laurel	15 585	76.4	46 900	201	18 683	2.7	1 178	6.3	809	7	13 785	17.3	2 762	2 436
Lawrence	5 007	75.1	40 500	173	4 631	2.5	449	9.7	165	-3	1 649	-2.3	50	547
Lee	2 760	75.1	28 400	125	2 941	-4.5	245	8.3	104	-7	1 365	-3.6	0	246
Leslie	4 711	77.6	24 400	120	5 327	23.8	303	5.7	126	-4	950	-0.4	0	238
Letcher	9 731	78.6	27 300	149	9 401	5.8	725	7.7	409	6	4 545	2.0	66	964
Lewis	4 713	78.8	31 400	124	6 008	5.8	594	9.9	125	4	1 234	2.9	0	291
Lincoln	7 431	76.3	37 700	157	8 087	-2.0	685	8.5	234	3	1 509	4.3	194	504
Livingston	3 593	84.8	36 500	172	3 398	-0.4	342	10.1	150	-11	1 343	-5.1	0	220
Logan	9 302	73.4	41 200	189	12 515	3.9	734	5.9	445	-1	6 574	5.7	4 083	973
Lyon	2 355	79.8	46 300	158	3 640	12.1	184	5.1	109	4	826	-7.3	0	127
McCracken	25 625	68.2	48 500	213	29 339	0.9	1 486	5.1	1 775	6	25 691	7.6	3 180	6 883
McCreary	5 479	74.7	26 300	143	4 113	2.3	581	14.1	165	1	1 262	-2.6	406	312
McLean	3 672	80.1	36 200	140	4 223	-1.7	387	9.2	127	1	868	18.1	0	168
Madison	20 012	62.1	55 500	249	28 785	0.5	1 480	5.1	1 096	37	14 700	8.5	4 036	4 347
Magoffin	4 440	78.0	35 500	130	3 726	0.9	554	14.9	139	-10	1 201	-1.7	0	345
Marion	5 688	76.9	39 500	165	8 421	2.8	692	8.2	299	6	2 908	0.3	636	660
Marshall	10 789	82.8	47 600	185	12 122	2.5	843	7.0	530	12	7 085	5.9	2 621	1 150
Martin	4 300	78.7	37 500	179	3 050	-2.3	238	7.8	197	-9	2 575	-27.1	58	412
Mason	6 537	64.9	43 800	171	7 937	2.6	406	5.1	412	16	5 713	6.4	2 188	1 327
Meade	8 080	61.3	49 700	329	7 365	4.0	575	7.8	247	14	2 281	14.5	0	590
Menifee	1 842	81.8	32 600	124	2 729	6.8	297	10.9	44	1	270	7.1	0	85
Mercer	7 413	72.8	46 600	222	9 854	2.8	570	5.8	348	-6	4 159	6.4	1 694	867
Metcalfe	3 433	77.4	31 300	126	6 615	31.2	391	5.9	115	-7	1 202	19.6	515	320
Monroe	4 505	74.9	31 500	125	6 681	5.4	419	6.3	210	15	2 354	-15.4	1 428	469
Montgomery	7 312	70.2	43 600	210	8 542	-1.5	993	11.6	493	16	5 627	-5.1	1 629	1 429
Morgan	4 089	76.5	36 600	147	3 718	10.8	368	9.9	151	-5	1 342	2.4	228	401
Muhlenberg	11 683	80.8	37 300	180	10 396	-1.7	917	8.8	579	-4	6 752	-2.1	736	1 695
Nelson	10 417	78.0	45 800	222	16 343	1.5	1 052	6.4	599	15	7 477	4.1	2 673	1 541
Nicholas	2 621	71.9	38 200	164	3 184	-2.1	247	7.8	98	2	1 113	1.2	0	126
Ohio	7 816	79.1	34 300	174	6 867	1.7	663	9.7	338	-8	3 716	-1.4	1 158	868
Oldham	10 673	83.1	86 500	277	17 234	0.7	490	2.8	542	38	5 360	6.3	758	1 496
Owen	3 412	75.6	38 200	159	4 187	2.1	219	5.2	121	1	1 131	12.5	0	249
Owsley	1 848	74.7	24 400	113	1 489	-5.0	126	8.5	48	-5	445	1.4	0	82
Pendleton	4 332	75.1	43 700	185	4 290	10.6	239	5.6	163	0	1 151	12.7	381	299

1. Percent of total civilian labor force. 2. For week including March 12. Excludes government employees, self-employed persons, farm workers, domestic service workers, railroad employees subject to the Railroad Retirement Act, and employees on oceanborne vessels or in foreign countries.

STATE County	Private nonfarm establishments, 1988 (cont'd): Employment[1] (cont'd): Finance, insurance, and real estate	Private nonfarm establishments, 1988 (cont'd): Employment[1] (cont'd): Services	Private nonfarm establishments, 1988 (cont'd): Annual payroll: Total (Mil dol)	Private nonfarm establishments, 1988 (cont'd): Annual payroll: Average per employee (Dollars)	Personal income, 1989: Total (Mil dol)	Personal income, 1989: Percent change, 1988–1989	Personal income, 1989: Wages and salaries[2] (Mil dol)	Personal income, 1989: Proprietor's income (Mil dol)	Personal income, 1989: Dividends, interest, & rent (Mil dol)	Personal income, 1989: Transfer payments (Mil dol)	Personal income, 1989: Per capita[3]: Dollars	Personal income, 1989: Per capita[3]: Rank	Earnings, 1989: Total (Mil dol)	Earnings, 1989: Percent by selected industries: Farm	Earnings, 1989: Percent by selected industries: Goods-related[4]: Total
	88	89	90	91	92	93	94	95	96	97	98	99	100	101	102
KENTUCKY—Con.															
Edmonson	0	155	6	11 059	76	6.6	22	12	9	22	8 011	3 076	34	21.0	11.6
Elliott	0	31	3	12 595	48	6.9	8	7	5	14	7 181	3 096	15	17.2	NA
Estill	65	286	24	13 846	138	6.6	42	14	17	38	9 320	2 980	56	7.4	29.5
Fayette	8 239	34 073	2 256	19 476	4 009	8.6	3 269	422	699	470	17 401	376	3 691	2.0	25.0
Fleming	105	309	25	12 418	135	7.7	48	29	20	29	11 070	2 646	78	18.3	23.2
Floyd	427	2 052	152	16 948	500	6.7	244	68	57	134	10 372	2 818	312	0.2	30.8
Franklin	848	3 648	227	15 935	702	6.4	594	63	109	125	15 649	761	657	1.2	19.1
Fulton	113	279	24	12 948	113	9.0	47	15	23	29	14 880	1 034	62	10.8	27.9
Gallatin	34	30	4	10 078	67	15.7	14	6	6	11	12 560	2 088	20	14.9	NA
Garrard	65	278	18	11 675	148	10.1	34	19	25	26	12 833	1 985	53	17.9	27.7
Grant	162	304	30	11 130	185	8.3	57	20	22	32	12 528	2 101	77	9.7	NA
Graves	426	1 560	144	15 892	468	7.5	238	50	79	90	13 825	1 521	288	5.1	51.0
Grayson	176	500	56	12 474	218	6.5	87	31	33	53	9 708	2 925	118	8.6	38.8
Green	72	219	14	11 656	119	12.1	35	26	19	25	11 233	2 589	60	21.3	NA
Greenup	249	1 297	120	25 618	485	1.4	295	26	51	86	12 988	1 909	321	1.4	50.0
Hancock	50	200	46	26 158	110	6.9	150	9	12	15	14 060	1 406	159	2.8	84.0
Hardin	728	3 923	280	14 918	1 123	5.9	897	97	122	192	13 277	1 780	995	1.6	17.2
Harlan	195	1 422	153	20 526	397	6.5	245	29	45	116	10 385	2 813	273	0.1	51.8
Harrison	150	677	66	16 650	205	10.4	107	25	35	37	12 860	1 974	131	9.5	47.9
Hart	96	319	29	13 197	158	8.2	47	29	27	36	11 055	2 651	77	21.3	27.2
Henderson	502	3 538	282	19 650	659	7.9	409	81	95	96	15 623	770	490	2.6	47.0
Henry	109	271	24	14 788	162	6.1	46	25	23	31	12 102	2 288	70	19.3	22.5
Hickman	43	182	11	11 650	72	12.3	18	13	14	14	13 851	1 504	31	17.8	NA
Hopkins	701	3 832	265	18 791	728	6.4	403	107	113	128	15 812	708	509	2.2	38.4
Jackson	0	103	11	14 177	94	7.8	25	15	10	30	7 479	3 089	40	13.3	NA
Jefferson	24 837	90 644	6 314	20 365	11 972	7.1	9 167	932	2 282	1 759	17 783	321	10 100	0.2	30.5
Jessamine	180	1 200	102	17 088	427	6.9	147	47	49	49	13 651	1 600	193	3.4	37.8
Johnson	254	866	65	14 678	261	7.1	103	41	30	66	10 840	2 703	144	0.5	24.2
Kenton	1 829	13 783	666	16 455	2 234	7.1	947	139	313	303	15 816	707	1 087	0.3	21.9
Knott	30	495	35	16 750	146	-0.4	68	12	15	48	8 216	3 060	80	0.1	49.6
Knox	211	1 189	57	13 048	274	6.7	105	28	35	79	9 195	2 990	132	1.7	29.8
Larue	104	297	18	11 540	150	8.1	32	24	23	30	12 640	2 057	56	24.3	NA
Laurel	332	3 297	246	17 827	496	6.1	298	58	57	94	11 194	2 602	356	1.8	37.0
Lawrence	42	414	26	15 740	126	4.2	45	13	14	40	8 749	3 031	58	4.3	16.4
Lee	46	753	11	8 040	61	8.5	24	8	8	23	8 204	3 061	31	1.2	25.1
Leslie	0	0	15	15 883	122	9.6	44	9	9	34	8 148	3 069	54	0.2	39.8
Letcher	168	879	92	20 165	272	9.0	141	23	32	79	9 446	2 967	164	0.2	46.9
Lewis	101	125	13	10 929	126	5.9	34	19	12	31	9 147	2 991	52	17.9	NA
Lincoln	113	439	17	11 474	192	6.6	40	24	27	45	9 898	2 894	64	17.3	17.3
Livingston	0	262	31	22 739	103	3.2	28	13	17	23	11 785	2 409	41	9.1	26.2
Logan	204	718	104	15 844	308	9.5	161	48	45	55	12 169	2 249	209	11.2	52.0
Lyon	32	193	11	13 657	73	9.0	27	8	13	17	11 431	2 530	35	11.4	NA
McCracken	1 078	8 800	430	16 749	1 017	7.7	678	114	178	175	17 054	427	791	0.6	19.6
McCreary	82	211	15	11 740	109	6.5	31	11	10	48	6 834	3 101	42	1.3	19.1
McLean	70	197	13	14 635	126	7.7	29	19	19	24	12 915	1 948	48	24.8	25.3
Madison	545	3 505	215	14 632	680	8.3	379	81	88	124	11 667	2 454	460	5.0	28.7
Magoffin	37	265	18	14 611	106	4.4	35	18	12	36	7 772	3 085	53	3.9	33.7
Marion	114	1 132	33	11 348	192	10.1	61	30	32	39	11 210	2 597	92	13.2	30.3
Marshall	320	1 451	177	24 919	385	11.2	257	45	61	69	14 238	1 308	302	1.3	NA
Martin	0	193	83	32 235	138	3.3	119	11	13	33	10 300	2 835	130	0.4	NA
Mason	267	859	94	16 478	219	9.0	150	46	40	39	12 450	2 142	196	10.3	39.3
Meade	329	298	37	16 285	261	10.8	60	18	27	39	10 183	2 858	78	7.6	NA
Menifee	0	76	4	16 622	38	7.9	9	4	3	11	7 107	3 097	13	16.4	NA
Mercer	116	862	71	16 994	283	9.7	105	36	44	43	14 029	1 422	141	8.0	39.8
Metcalfe	49	119	11	9 062	89	5.9	22	15	11	22	8 839	3 021	36	23.1	19.8
Monroe	66	198	28	11 780	131	7.7	52	25	18	31	10 973	2 672	77	14.7	NA
Montgomery	287	985	85	15 093	233	6.3	116	32	32	45	11 403	2 538	148	6.4	36.5
Morgan	73	278	19	14 230	98	7.7	34	15	12	29	8 492	3 041	49	12.6	15.7
Muhlenberg	230	1 490	130	19 226	357	5.1	204	37	62	82	11 783	2 411	242	4.7	32.0
Nelson	203	1 550	113	15 051	393	8.3	167	47	57	56	13 180	1 822	215	4.6	46.3
Nicholas	59	239	19	17 442	83	8.8	29	9	10	17	11 320	2 562	38	13.3	NA
Ohio	130	655	62	16 749	227	6.4	88	28	35	55	11 084	2 640	115	9.2	36.4
Oldham	157	1 704	80	14 913	559	8.7	143	63	80	37	15 060	963	206	13.7	23.5
Owen	88	233	16	14 027	99	9.7	28	12	13	20	10 494	2 794	40	21.6	NA
Owsley	0	302	5	11 036	40	5.4	9	6	4	18	7 334	3 092	14	14.1	NA
Pendleton	81	239	16	14 297	139	10.5	32	16	20	22	12 109	2 285	47	12.7	NA

1. For week including March 12. Excludes government employees, self-employed persons, farm workers, domestic service workers, railroad employees subject to the Railroad Retirement Act, and employees on oceanborne vessels or in foreign countries. 2. Includes other labor income. 3. Based on the resident population estimated as of July 1 of the year shown. 4. Covers mining, construction, and manufacturing.

Table A. States and Counties — **Earnings and Agriculture**

STATE County	Earnings, 1989 (cont'd)						Agriculture, 1987									
	Percent by selected industries (cont'd)						Farms			Farm operators, percent		Land in farms				
	Goods-related[1]	Service-related & other[2]						Percent with						Acres		
	Manu-facturing	Total	Retail trade	Finance, insur-ance, & real estate	Services	Govern-ment	Number	Less than 50 acres	500 acres and over	Whose principal occu-pation is farming	Residing on farm operated	Acreage (1,000)	Percent change, 1982–1987	Average size of farm	Total irrigated (1,000)	Total cropland (1,000)
	103	104	105	106	107	108	109	110	111	112	113	114	115	116	117	118
KENTUCKY—Con.																
Edmonson	4.1	NA	8.6	3.1	17.9	33.0	744	33.7	3.6	34.0	75.0	91	4.3	122	0	52
Elliott	NA	NA	11.6	3.9	12.5	32.7	534	31.1	3.2	39.5	69.5	67	-6.3	126	0	22
Estill	13.8	NA	14.8	2.5	11.2	18.9	492	30.1	4.1	36.6	64.2	69	3.8	140	0	29
Fayette	18.4	53.8	10.4	5.9	25.5	19.2	912	46.3	7.9	53.7	65.8	156	3.4	171	2	99
Fleming	15.1	39.3	9.9	2.7	14.9	19.2	1 308	27.8	4.3	55.0	66.4	205	15.3	156	0	129
Floyd	2.4	55.9	10.1	3.7	21.1	13.0	86	32.6	4.7	29.1	61.6	10	-23.2	119	0	3
Franklin	13.9	28.3	6.1	3.0	13.2	51.4	761	33.4	3.2	39.2	64.7	97	-1.4	127	0	58
Fulton	24.7	45.3	13.4	2.8	13.4	16.1	203	20.2	26.6	62.6	62.6	93	-6.9	458	D	82
Gallatin	5.5	54.7	14.7	3.2	10.8	20.4	318	24.5	6.3	40.6	66.0	52	9.8	164	0	27
Garrard	12.2	35.8	9.9	3.8	15.9	18.5	1 021	35.1	3.3	52.8	64.7	142	2.8	139	0	97
Grant	14.6	NA	17.0	4.3	15.3	16.8	1 053	29.8	2.7	35.1	71.6	133	0.7	126	0	79
Graves	45.2	33.5	9.6	2.1	14.3	10.4	1 213	33.6	8.8	46.2	69.8	221	-5.9	182	1	179
Grayson	32.1	35.7	10.6	2.8	12.6	16.9	1 520	31.1	4.4	41.3	68.8	218	2.2	143	0	130
Green	26.9	NA	7.8	2.6	16.0	15.1	1 258	33.4	2.5	52.5	64.9	148	1.0	117	0	93
Greenup	46.6	40.4	4.7	1.8	12.8	8.2	824	35.4	2.8	28.9	65.0	93	0.9	113	0	32
Hancock	80.5	NA	1.2	0.5	NA	4.1	529	38.4	4.2	32.3	65.0	70	7.7	132	0	41
Hardin	12.7	28.5	8.8	2.2	12.2	52.6	1 748	38.7	3.8	39.9	75.6	221	-7.1	126	0	153
Harlan	1.7	34.8	8.4	1.7	15.0	13.2	28	35.7	14.3	14.3	60.7	6	-2.4	226	0	1
Harrison	42.6	32.7	8.7	1.8	16.2	9.9	1 175	24.5	5.0	48.9	71.3	183	0.6	155	2	125
Hart	23.1	35.8	9.1	3.0	14.6	15.8	1 518	30.2	2.8	51.4	65.3	194	2.6	128	0	113
Henderson	32.5	42.3	8.5	1.9	21.1	8.0	638	31.2	17.2	51.1	65.5	213	-1.7	334	D	173
Henry	18.6	42.2	10.7	3.4	18.8	16.0	1 093	28.4	5.0	49.9	67.3	166	6.7	152	1	110
Hickman	16.2	48.9	7.0	3.1	18.7	14.1	283	29.0	21.2	53.4	73.5	96	-9.0	338	1	84
Hopkins	20.1	49.4	8.1	2.8	28.2	10.0	620	25.5	11.3	40.0	67.4	145	-8.7	234	0	104
Jackson	8.5	NA	8.2	1.8	11.1	22.6	789	35.9	2.0	39.4	68.9	84	-6.5	107	0	36
Jefferson	24.7	58.0	9.9	7.4	25.4	11.3	641	57.4	2.3	33.5	64.7	55	-7.3	86	0	35
Jessamine	20.4	48.3	12.1	2.3	18.1	10.6	879	47.1	2.8	44.8	62.3	102	4.8	116	0	75
Johnson	6.8	57.5	16.7	3.2	22.6	17.9	215	39.1	2.3	31.2	68.4	22	-10.2	102	D	5
Kenton	11.4	60.3	14.6	3.4	29.9	17.5	539	43.6	0.9	36.0	76.1	44	-5.5	82	0	26
Knott	0.4	31.5	7.2	1.9	12.5	18.8	29	24.1	0.0	34.5	65.5	4	63.7	130	0	1
Knox	18.7	48.4	15.3	2.9	19.4	20.1	379	33.5	5.8	35.6	71.8	51	-8.8	135	0	21
Larue	12.3	38.1	7.5	3.3	15.1	15.0	937	30.9	4.7	47.5	72.5	128	0.3	136	0	88
Laurel	21.2	50.1	11.2	2.1	19.1	11.1	1 305	50.5	1.2	34.7	69.0	102	-3.1	78	0	58
Lawrence	1.0	60.8	10.6	2.1	20.0	18.5	388	29.4	5.7	39.4	67.3	62	-6.2	160	0	21
Lee	5.1	51.2	18.6	3.4	18.1	22.5	223	38.1	0.4	33.2	70.0	23	1.0	104	0	8
Leslie	5.9	NA	8.2	1.8	20.5	21.6	29	41.4	0.0	34.5	58.6	3	-36.8	102	D	D
Letcher	0.3	39.6	8.2	2.4	17.3	13.3	36	38.9	0.0	44.4	86.1	3	-23.3	89	0	D
Lewis	29.0	29.9	7.4	3.1	10.8	18.4	927	27.3	7.4	45.0	66.0	167	2.6	180	0	58
Lincoln	9.0	44.9	12.4	3.6	20.2	20.6	1 475	41.1	3.7	46.2	70.4	184	1.9	125	0	121
Livingston	2.7	48.2	11.9	3.6	20.7	16.5	354	16.9	15.3	44.1	70.3	110	-8.5	311	0	74
Logan	47.6	27.9	7.2	1.8	12.4	9.0	1 322	26.6	8.6	54.3	67.5	267	-2.0	202	1	203
Lyon	17.2	24.9	9.0	1.3	9.6	37.3	258	22.9	5.0	37.2	72.5	45	-16.3	173	0	29
McCracken	12.9	67.5	13.1	2.9	30.7	12.2	434	40.8	8.5	40.1	73.0	70	-3.1	162	0	58
McCreary	13.8	46.4	14.9	4.0	17.8	33.2	116	47.4	0.9	22.4	67.2	12	5.8	100	D	5
McLean	20.2	34.6	7.4	3.5	14.9	15.2	527	29.8	14.4	57.7	67.0	124	-3.2	235	0	101
Madison	24.1	43.1	12.5	2.7	20.0	23.2	1 597	36.5	6.4	45.8	62.9	246	3.2	154	0	155
Magoffin	7.5	41.9	7.9	2.1	13.0	20.5	450	34.7	1.8	31.8	65.8	52	-9.5	116	D	10
Marion	21.4	42.8	11.0	2.5	21.9	13.7	1 160	28.2	4.5	47.0	67.6	181	1.5	156	0	120
Marshall	39.9	NA	7.5	2.1	11.7	8.6	578	34.4	3.5	26.6	68.3	74	-9.2	128	0	52
Martin	0.1	NA	4.9	0.8	6.7	7.8	25	24.0	4.0	44.0	64.0	4	61.2	161	D	3
Mason	35.8	41.8	9.4	2.5	16.7	8.6	895	27.7	5.9	63.5	66.0	150	11.2	168	0	108
Meade	26.6	NA	11.8	2.6	11.5	15.0	809	35.8	5.2	36.5	76.3	117	-3.9	145	0	77
Menifee	6.0	NA	12.6	0.8	10.5	39.2	385	38.2	3.1	31.9	67.8	45	3.7	117	0	16
Mercer	32.9	42.2	10.8	3.7	15.4	10.0	1 106	36.4	2.5	45.3	70.3	144	-0.9	131	0	101
Metcalfe	14.8	36.5	11.4	2.7	11.4	20.6	1 088	34.4	2.9	55.1	65.3	137	2.5	126	0	82
Monroe	39.3	28.9	9.0	1.5	10.9	14.9	1 115	28.3	5.8	46.6	64.9	173	-0.1	155	0	97
Montgomery	29.4	45.6	12.6	3.3	17.7	11.5	793	39.5	5.9	46.0	59.5	116	-4.3	146	0	81
Morgan	8.5	47.7	12.5	4.2	15.8	23.9	816	37.7	5.0	40.2	61.0	106	-8.6	130	0	38
Muhlenberg	7.1	41.7	8.0	1.9	14.3	21.6	615	29.4	9.3	39.2	69.3	118	3.8	192	0	74
Nelson	35.5	39.0	11.8	2.2	14.6	10.1	1 369	33.2	5.1	40.6	72.0	202	-0.1	148	0	132
Nicholas	39.2	30.7	7.8	3.3	15.3	13.7	733	28.0	5.0	53.3	61.0	117	-1.2	160	2	79
Ohio	21.6	38.2	9.1	2.3	14.6	16.2	1 022	30.6	5.5	39.0	65.6	161	-4.3	158	0	104
Oldham	9.9	40.6	9.5	2.3	21.4	22.2	479	43.0	9.2	47.4	71.6	81	-2.9	170	0	51
Owen	15.2	39.3	8.1	3.3	13.3	18.5	984	18.7	5.7	48.2	63.1	178	0.2	181	1	93
Owsley	NA	NA	10.5	1.9	19.9	33.2	351	47.6	3.1	38.7	61.5	35	-9.2	99	0	11
Pendleton	19.4	NA	9.6	2.6	NA	18.0	949	24.4	3.2	43.2	71.8	136	-3.1	143	1	79

1. Covers mining, construction, and manufacturing. 2. Covers private sector earnings in agricultural services, forestry, and fisheries; transportation and public utilities; wholesale trade; retail trade; finance, insurance, and real estate; and services.

STATE County	Agriculture, 1987 (cont'd): Value of land and buildings: Average per farm ($1,000)	Value of land and buildings: Average per acre (Dollars)	Value of products sold: Total (Mil dol)	Value of products sold: Average per farm (Dollars)	Value of products sold: Percent from: Crops	Value of products sold: Percent from: Livestock and poultry[1]	Percent of farms with sales of: $10,000 or more	Percent of farms with sales of: $100,000 or more	Manufactures, 1987: Establishments: Total	Establishments: Percent with 20 or more employees	All employees: Number (1,000)	All employees: Percent change, 1982–1987	All employees: Annual payroll (Mil dol)	Production workers: Number (1,000)	Production workers: Work hours (Mil)
	119	120	121	122	123	124	125	126	127	128	129	130	131	132	133
KENTUCKY—Con.															
Edmonson	74	647	10	12 820	32.6	67.4	27.0	1.7	6	33.3	0.2	0.0	2.8	0.2	0.4
Elliott	71	475	3	5 577	73.1	26.9	14.2	0.0	NA	NA	NA	NA	NA	NA	NA
Estill	75	634	4	7 995	51.0	49.0	22.8	0.4	13	30.8	D	D	D	D	D
Fayette	563	3 624	131	144 124	13.3	86.7	58.0	15.5	250	35.6	15.8	-5.4	481.2	9.0	17.8
Fleming	103	675	30	23 230	33.8	66.2	48.2	3.6	13	30.8	0.7	0.0	8.6	0.6	1.0
Floyd	83	838	1	8 213	84.6	15.4	5.8	2.3	22	22.7	D	D	D	D	D
Franklin	199	1 441	11	14 826	60.4	39.6	41.7	1.3	32	50.0	3.7	15.6	71.2	3.2	5.8
Fulton	339	772	12	60 643	89.5	10.5	58.6	18.7	9	66.7	0.7	16.7	14.2	0.5	1.0
Gallatin	146	870	5	16 250	73.1	26.9	37.4	3.1	2	50.0	D	D	D	D	D
Garrard	149	1 117	24	23 394	32.2	67.8	46.5	3.0	10	30.0	D	D	D	D	D
Grant	105	812	11	10 247	60.3	39.7	31.1	0.6	9	66.7	0.5	25.0	8.6	0.4	0.8
Graves	120	686	33	26 868	65.8	34.2	43.0	6.9	36	30.6	3.8	0.0	77.0	3.2	5.9
Grayson	99	672	25	16 128	30.7	69.3	30.7	2.7	32	40.6	1.9	18.7	25.5	1.6	3.0
Green	77	665	20	15 968	38.8	61.2	39.3	2.1	12	41.7	0.5	-16.7	7.2	0.5	0.9
Greenup	88	717	6	7 060	47.7	52.3	13.1	0.8	10	30.0	D	D	D	D	D
Hancock	105	797	8	14 669	66.8	33.2	26.3	2.1	11	18.2	D	D	D	D	D
Hardin	117	897	30	17 332	37.8	62.2	30.3	3.9	54	42.6	4.0	11.1	84.3	3.0	5.8
Harlan	127	560	D	D	NA	NA	14.3	0.0	19	15.8	0.2	0.0	2.3	0.1	0.2
Harrison	125	853	22	18 623	52.0	48.0	46.7	2.0	18	55.6	1.8	12.5	38.9	1.4	2.7
Hart	91	712	26	17 370	36.4	63.6	38.2	2.2	9	55.6	0.5	25.0	8.1	0.4	0.8
Henderson	309	914	27	42 813	82.6	17.4	51.4	12.7	61	52.5	4.6	12.2	106.9	3.7	6.6
Henry	149	961	28	25 693	44.2	55.8	52.4	3.8	9	44.4	0.4	100.0	6.5	0.3	0.6
Hickman	211	688	14	50 725	74.4	25.6	51.9	15.5	5	40.0	0.3	-25.0	4.0	0.3	0.6
Hopkins	167	720	15	23 761	75.0	25.0	35.8	5.8	48	31.2	3.1	10.7	71.2	2.3	4.6
Jackson	75	763	7	8 396	57.2	42.8	18.5	0.4	9	22.2	0.1	0.0	0.8	0.1	0.2
Jefferson	170	2 034	14	21 455	68.6	31.4	25.0	4.8	885	44.3	68.0	-11.8	1 961.6	45.0	89.9
Jessamine	232	1 996	21	23 538	39.9	60.1	43.1	3.1	31	48.4	1.7	54.5	31.9	1.2	2.4
Johnson	58	554	1	3 675	71.3	28.7	8.8	0.0	11	9.1	D	D	D	D	D
Kenton	139	1 647	5	8 764	54.7	45.3	23.2	1.5	135	39.3	4.7	17.5	102.3	2.9	5.6
Knott	99	762	0	2 851	13.3	86.7	10.3	0.0	5	0.0	0.0	0.0	0.5	0.0	0.0
Knox	83	664	2	5 961	53.7	46.3	12.7	0.5	12	41.7	0.8	0.0	12.9	0.6	1.2
Larue	107	786	20	20 959	34.3	65.7	36.7	4.7	9	33.3	0.5	0.0	6.1	0.4	0.9
Laurel	92	1 104	11	8 646	51.1	48.9	20.5	0.6	46	30.4	2.3	-4.2	39.8	1.7	3.3
Lawrence	99	708	4	9 789	23.4	76.6	10.3	1.8	7	0.0	0.0	0.0	0.6	0.0	0.0
Lee	55	462	1	4 111	82.1	17.8	9.0	0.0	4	25.0	D	D	D	D	D
Leslie	50	495	0	2 547	55.4	44.6	3.4	0.0	8	12.5	D	D	D	D	D
Letcher	85	955	D	D	NA	NA	0.0	0.0	11	9.1	0.1	0.0	0.7	0.0	0.0
Lewis	89	474	11	12 294	50.4	49.6	28.3	1.1	13	15.4	D	D	D	D	D
Lincoln	102	851	32	21 559	26.9	73.1	37.6	4.4	13	23.1	0.2	-50.0	3.0	0.1	0.3
Livingston	156	505	8	23 020	33.1	66.9	41.0	4.0	6	33.3	D	D	D	D	D
Logan	161	758	44	33 079	60.8	39.2	48.6	6.8	35	57.1	3.9	39.3	72.5	3.3	6.3
Lyon	93	565	4	16 437	46.4	53.6	28.7	2.3	3	33.3	D	D	D	D	D
McCracken	157	763	9	20 195	68.4	31.6	29.0	5.5	59	42.4	3.1	-13.9	73.6	2.1	4.1
McCreary	58	635	0	2 917	24.0	76.3	6.9	0.0	14	28.6	0.2	0.0	2.6	0.2	0.4
McLean	232	934	20	38 214	74.8	25.2	53.3	11.0	6	33.3	D	D	D	D	D
Madison	163	1 024	32	20 000	36.5	63.5	42.0	2.9	50	46.0	3.5	12.9	68.9	2.7	5.2
Magoffin	52	483	2	4 311	82.0	18.0	10.2	0.0	6	33.3	D	D	D	D	D
Marion	119	739	29	24 640	29.7	70.3	50.3	5.7	14	35.7	0.7	-12.5	8.5	0.6	1.2
Marshall	108	875	7	11 747	53.4	46.6	24.9	2.2	32	34.4	2.6	0.0	89.9	1.8	3.9
Martin	115	713	0	17 779	10.1	89.9	16.0	4.0	8	0.0	0.0	-100.0	0.6	0.0	0.1
Mason	129	817	25	27 642	45.3	54.7	59.6	4.9	17	58.8	2.4	41.2	48.4	1.8	3.4
Meade	119	840	14	17 116	39.2	60.8	35.1	3.1	7	28.6	D	D	D	D	D
Menifee	62	573	3	6 536	63.8	36.2	17.7	0.0	3	0.0	D	D	D	D	D
Mercer	163	1 179	27	24 618	33.1	66.9	43.0	5.6	18	44.4	1.4	0.0	28.9	1.0	1.9
Metcalfe	85	667	20	18 259	34.1	65.9	39.2	2.7	9	44.4	0.4	0.0	3.3	0.4	0.6
Monroe	92	637	19	16 953	28.9	71.1	35.1	3.1	25	48.0	1.9	58.3	20.9	1.6	3.0
Montgomery	165	1 010	16	20 433	45.2	54.8	48.7	4.4	21	47.6	2.1	-4.5	33.2	1.8	3.3
Morgan	68	510	6	7 315	64.3	35.7	19.7	0.2	7	42.9	0.2	0.0	2.0	0.2	0.3
Muhlenberg	136	662	15	25 181	45.8	54.2	34.3	3.4	35	34.3	0.6	20.0	9.0	0.4	0.8
Nelson	128	860	33	24 238	24.7	75.3	39.1	5.3	34	38.2	2.6	30.0	52.9	2.1	3.7
Nicholas	124	717	14	18 588	50.7	49.3	42.0	1.9	8	25.0	D	D	D	D	D
Ohio	113	795	15	14 687	72.1	27.9	28.1	2.6	29	48.3	1.1	37.5	18.3	0.9	1.7
Oldham	328	2 224	56	116 091	10.2	89.8	36.7	8.4	30	30.0	D	D	D	D	D
Owen	133	705	17	16 775	56.0	44.0	45.5	1.5	3	33.3	D	D	D	D	D
Owsley	51	544	2	5 033	85.0	15.0	12.0	0.0	1	0.0	D	D	D	D	D
Pendleton	106	767	11	11 840	53.1	46.9	31.5	0.7	6	66.7	0.3	-25.0	5.3	0.2	0.4

1. Includes livestock and poultry products.

STATE County	Manufactures, 1987 (cont'd) — Production workers (cont'd) — Wages — Total (Mil dol)	Manufactures, 1987 (cont'd) — Production workers (cont'd) — Wages — Average per worker (Dollars)	Manufactures, 1987 (cont'd) — Value added by manufacture (Mil dol)	Manufactures, 1987 (cont'd) — Value of shipments (Mil dol)	Manufactures, 1987 (cont'd) — New capital expenditures (Mil dol)	Value of construction authorized by building permits, 1990 — Total[1] ($1,000)	Nonresidential — Total ($1,000)	Nonresidential — Percent — Office	Nonresidential — Percent — Industrial	Nonresidential — Percent — Stores	Residential — New construction ($1,000)	Residential — Number of housing units	Residential — Alterations and additions ($1,000)
	134	135	136	137	138	139	140	141	142	143	144	145	146
KENTUCKY—Con.													
Edmonson	2.5	12 500	3.3	5.3	0.0	NA	NA	NA	NA	NA	NA	NA	NA
Elliott	NA	NA	NA	NA	NA	NA	NA	NA	NA	NA	NA	NA	NA
Estill	D	D	D	D	D	301	70	0.0	0.0	0.0	175	7	35
Fayette	213.1	23 678	1 284.1	2 644.6	D	202 973	52 430	19.5	26.8	34.5	113 135	1 347	8 856
Fleming	6.7	11 167	27.8	49.1	D	509	220	68.2	0.0	22.7	215	4	20
Floyd	D	D	D	D	D	1 713	249	0.0	0.0	81.6	0	0	76
Franklin	53.6	16 750	197.8	418.3	11.6	13 281	4 278	6.4	0.0	90.4	5 975	133	528
Fulton	8.5	17 000	35.1	110.9	1.9	1 479	197	0.0	0.0	17.6	902	31	61
Gallatin	D	D	D	D	D	718	572	24.9	0.0	39.4	82	2	12
Garrard	D	D	D	D	D	1 250	412	0.0	0.0	0.0	820	21	7
Grant	6.2	15 500	26.8	70.4	1.1	4 559	1 703	10.3	0.0	42.6	2 782	68	28
Graves	58.2	18 188	116.7	405.8	D	2 255	587	9.4	0.0	81.3	804	21	227
Grayson	20.2	12 625	63.8	172.1	4.1	704	657	0.0	96.2	3.8	0	0	0
Green	5.5	11 000	13.2	26.9	0.2	648	292	0.0	0.0	0.0	190	2	0
Greenup	D	D	D	D	D	7 641	1 308	0.0	0.0	2.1	5 338	64	364
Hancock	D	D	D	D	D	513	430	0.0	81.4	0.0	80	6	0
Hardin	56.9	18 967	256.4	553.9	16.4	21 236	5 340	23.2	12.9	41.8	12 012	292	1 144
Harlan	1.4	14 000	4.4	10.1	0.1	0	0	NA	NA	NA	0	0	0
Harrison	26.1	18 643	170.7	264.0	5.5	5 156	1 240	0.0	0.0	49.7	3 634	73	133
Hart	6.4	16 000	26.7	70.7	D	2 103	1 125	8.7	9.3	71.3	831	31	101
Henderson	74.9	20 243	198.9	707.9	26.5	19 298	7 592	0.0	52.5	21.0	9 641	171	634
Henry	4.5	15 000	20.8	71.3	D	628	628	0.0	0.0	68.0	0	0	0
Hickman	2.4	8 000	7.0	16.7	D	NA	NA	NA	NA	NA	NA	NA	NA
Hopkins	49.7	21 609	214.6	490.0	D	6 342	1 820	11.3	0.0	68.4	3 501	62	374
Jackson	0.6	6 000	2.8	4.0	0.0	390	0	NA	NA	NA	390	13	0
Jefferson	1 168.3	25 962	6 651.4	15 606.4	272.9	414 793	148 852	33.8	11.1	26.1	198 059	2 446	13 383
Jessamine	20.7	17 250	88.8	195.5	D	21 218	2 695	8.8	45.4	31.5	16 923	350	841
Johnson	D	D	D	D	D	3 134	1 973	27.9	64.1	3.6	435	21	96
Kenton	55.8	19 241	200.4	447.1	D	65 500	8 152	7.7	2.3	68.4	49 821	903	2 724
Knott	0.3	NA	1.8	5.4	0.1	NA	NA	NA	NA	NA	NA	NA	NA
Knox	9.3	15 500	53.0	94.4	1.3	971	98	36.2	0.0	0.0	826	31	41
Larue	4.9	12 250	5.3	12.2	0.1	615	553	0.0	51.2	45.2	0	0	0
Laurel	23.5	13 824	115.9	249.7	7.2	7 212	4 487	45.0	14.1	38.1	1 922	46	16
Lawrence	0.3	NA	2.0	4.7	0.1	0	0	NA	NA	NA	0	0	0
Lee	D	D	D	D	D	NA	NA	NA	NA	NA	NA	NA	NA
Leslie	D	D	D	D	D	NA	NA	NA	NA	NA	NA	NA	NA
Letcher	0.3	NA	2.6	5.6	D	1 166	25	0.0	0.0	0.0	226	12	153
Lewis	D	D	D	D	D	16	0	NA	NA	NA	0	0	16
Lincoln	2.0	20 000	6.3	11.8	0.3	2 259	555	21.6	28.8	34.2	1 440	35	0
Livingston	D	D	D	D	D	NA	NA	NA	NA	NA	NA	NA	NA
Logan	54.4	16 485	154.7	519.9	10.2	4 625	3 276	13.0	64.1	20.1	1 169	18	86
Lyon	D	D	D	D	D	1 320	597	33.5	0.0	0.0	646	9	23
McCracken	42.6	20 286	198.8	638.7	3.3	18 154	5 871	1.1	1.3	77.9	3 908	44	367
McCreary	1.8	9 000	8.4	15.5	0.1	36	0	NA	NA	NA	0	0	0
McLean	D	D	D	D	D	516	416	0.0	0.0	51.3	69	1	0
Madison	48.2	17 852	293.4	529.9	9.4	21 398	5 445	16.7	5.7	48.2	8 964	390	386
Magoffin	D	D	D	D	D	NA	NA	NA	NA	NA	NA	NA	NA
Marion	7.2	12 000	16.9	26.7	D	3 001	2 017	0.0	32.0	64.5	905	18	20
Marshall	59.6	33 111	328.5	813.3	54.7	4 522	4 522	2.3	77.4	0.0	0	0	0
Martin	0.4	NA	1.8	5.2	0.1	NA	NA	NA	NA	NA	NA	NA	NA
Mason	34.0	18 889	129.8	270.9	8.3	5 456	3 117	0.0	0.0	100.0	1 687	43	113
Meade	D	D	D	D	D	1 548	397	46.2	0.0	53.8	350	7	32
Menifee	D	D	D	D	D	NA	NA	NA	NA	NA	NA	NA	NA
Mercer	18.3	18 300	93.0	168.5	9.3	14 357	9 854	0.0	90.3	4.9	4 077	67	308
Metcalfe	2.8	7 000	5.1	11.8	0.2	NA	NA	NA	NA	NA	NA	NA	NA
Monroe	16.8	10 500	40.1	83.6	1.5	NA	NA	NA	NA	NA	NA	NA	NA
Montgomery	26.0	14 444	92.8	179.0	D	7 864	3 607	0.0	67.9	0.7	1 539	36	298
Morgan	1.4	7 000	3.7	8.2	D	NA	NA	NA	NA	NA	NA	NA	NA
Muhlenberg	6.2	15 500	28.4	52.0	1.6	546	0	NA	NA	NA	290	10	241
Nelson	35.9	17 095	149.8	336.4	11.3	19 864	5 121	16.2	40.9	32.7	13 408	268	528
Nicholas	D	D	D	D	D	1 436	1 301	0.0	0.0	0.0	69	1	0
Ohio	13.2	14 667	59.2	105.4	D	2 543	2 214	0.0	28.6	19.3	251	10	0
Oldham	D	D	D	D	D	47 769	4 386	47.3	6.5	8.9	41 211	416	999
Owen	D	D	D	D	D	422	192	5.2	0.0	10.4	220	7	1
Owsley	D	D	D	D	D	NA	NA	NA	NA	NA	NA	NA	NA
Pendleton	3.7	18 500	11.9	22.6	0.6	1 122	812	0.0	0.0	80.0	230	4	0

1. Includes nonresidential additions and alterations, residential nonhousekeeping buildings, and residential garages and carports not shown separately.

STATE County	Wholesale trade, 1987				Retail trade, all establishments, 1987				Retail trade, establishments with payroll, 1987					
						Sales				Sales				
											Per capita[2] (Dollars)			
	Establishments	Sales (Mil dol)	Paid employees[1]	Annual payroll (Mil dol)	Number	Total (Mil dol)	Percent change, 1982–1987	Per capita[2] (Dollars)	Number	Total (Mil dol)	General merchandise stores	Food stores	Apparel & accessory stores	Eating and drinking places
	147	148	149	150	151	152	153	154	155	156	157	158	159	160
KENTUCKY—Con.														
Edmonson	4	D	D	D	89	15.8	37.4	1 546	31	11.7	D	559	D	153
Elliott	2	D	D	D	57	13.7	110.8	2 045	21	9.2	D	552	0	D
Estill	11	19.0	70	1.1	152	49.7	16.7	3 315	71	44.8	297	673	D	178
Fayette	520	3 083.4	7 257	151.3	2 373	1 939.6	45.7	8 651	1 656	1 902.8	1 343	1 378	485	1 028
Fleming	25	41.1	144	1.5	147	62.3	46.9	5 110	63	56.2	299	942	45	206
Floyd	57	198.7	626	13.1	562	207.5	21.1	4 218	253	185.0	543	837	106	221
Franklin	43	131.5	322	5.9	485	258.5	46.6	5 821	299	251.2	617	1 325	243	564
Fulton	18	50.1	227	3.5	126	50.8	22.7	6 514	78	47.3	D	1 823	122	333
Gallatin	11	13.8	64	0.9	54	12.2	-21.3	2 389	27	10.8	D	D	D	145
Garrard	10	9.7	58	0.6	137	26.6	47.0	2 333	68	23.9	D	892	62	172
Grant	12	51.1	237	3.7	131	69.6	63.0	4 937	71	66.0	D	1 105	D	349
Graves	52	136.2	737	8.5	402	166.3	33.5	4 950	184	153.8	546	1 007	145	272
Grayson	23	63.9	245	3.8	275	75.5	25.8	3 430	122	67.0	D	872	50	149
Green	9	17.8	43	0.6	111	25.0	14.2	2 314	46	20.7	70	891	28	115
Greenup	20	17.8	156	3.2	289	89.5	22.8	2 385	124	78.8	100	786	28	159
Hancock	3	3.3	17	0.4	58	14.8	38.3	1 875	24	14.0	0	1 060	0	48
Hardin	80	115.4	712	10.3	823	539.1	62.8	6 387	499	522.4	783	1 079	207	523
Harlan	44	110.9	368	7.6	388	150.3	10.4	3 786	193	139.7	521	1 087	92	196
Harrison	20	23.0	151	1.0	174	64.0	29.8	3 997	95	59.0	D	1 148	107	436
Hart	26	43.1	291	2.4	158	45.9	37.8	3 101	65	41.8	116	949	54	111
Henderson	76	434.5	816	15.8	433	266.3	30.2	6 310	269	259.4	678	1 497	161	528
Henry	15	66.6	154	2.9	140	52.1	86.1	3 884	61	48.4	D	874	D	65
Hickman	9	19.5	59	0.8	48	10.0	28.2	1 846	25	8.6	0	D	D	45
Hopkins	73	169.4	599	11.1	482	261.8	24.5	5 642	269	253.1	795	1 328	241	354
Jackson	6	7.2	52	0.5	142	18.4	5.1	1 485	33	12.1	124	337	0	33
Jefferson	1 539	10 361.6	20 355	456.4	6 351	4 625.2	39.8	6 805	4 213	4 533.0	940	1 331	296	754
Jessamine	36	209.6	477	9.0	264	124.9	62.2	4 191	131	119.5	D	997	40	268
Johnson	32	68.4	325	5.1	276	122.6	13.2	4 964	144	115.2	497	1 038	145	385
Kenton	162	753.8	2 101	50.4	1 053	673.0	29.4	4 842	664	654.2	609	1 109	57	738
Knott	11	16.8	52	1.0	259	45.0	1.4	2 485	79	34.1	80	892	67	81
Knox	20	48.2	164	3.0	270	132.7	39.8	4 424	129	119.8	598	1 164	170	179
Larue	12	12.2	50	0.7	116	31.5	13.3	2 624	56	28.1	D	894	19	154
Laurel	76	346.4	1 325	23.0	443	195.9	20.4	4 545	237	184.2	250	1 172	89	316
Lawrence	11	32.9	156	3.0	130	47.2	27.9	3 279	58	43.3	D	1 261	41	211
Lee	9	20.7	42	0.7	90	25.5	24.4	3 316	35	22.4	D	992	D	102
Leslie	3	D	D	D	144	28.5	21.3	1 877	50	21.6	242	489	17	86
Letcher	27	61.8	214	3.6	281	95.3	23.6	3 264	112	86.1	542	1 070	99	103
Lewis	10	10.7	70	0.9	133	25.5	30.1	1 823	53	21.0	D	659	D	111
Lincoln	17	10.7	87	0.6	203	48.7	47.1	2 513	76	40.9	D	610	D	160
Livingston	12	42.1	59	0.8	122	23.6	43.0	2 625	51	16.6	0	906	D	190
Logan	39	66.8	320	3.5	232	85.9	25.0	3 408	127	79.9	D	1 142	83	223
Lyon	3	D	D	D	60	10.7	-15.7	1 693	29	9.2	0	741	D	183
McCracken	158	778.6	2 222	45.5	860	541.4	42.8	9 008	563	522.2	1 339	1 828	664	887
McCreary	7	11.7	102	1.3	161	33.3	2.5	2 069	64	27.2	D	807	D	63
McLean	8	26.5	93	1.7	82	16.4	-26.1	1 678	42	14.4	D	779	0	121
Madison	72	236.1	1 000	16.4	631	295.9	30.4	5 219	366	281.7	566	1 168	198	631
Magoffin	5	4.0	23	0.2	126	32.3	8.4	2 338	49	26.7	260	645	D	131
Marion	18	24.4	106	1.4	195	54.3	12.4	3 066	102	50.2	187	1 192	121	225
Marshall	30	37.4	164	2.6	351	129.1	40.8	4 855	146	109.4	D	768	53	316
Martin	7	12.3	31	0.8	140	53.5	13.3	3 851	62	48.4	D	1 083	37	74
Mason	46	95.8	446	4.8	238	111.6	27.5	6 378	131	106.9	806	1 706	413	500
Meade	15	9.9	58	0.7	135	63.7	88.5	2 601	79	60.4	D	441	26	224
Menifee	1	D	D	D	51	11.0	61.8	2 070	14	9.3	D	D	0	D
Mercer	23	27.3	107	1.0	206	75.6	42.1	3 782	103	67.4	D	1 112	60	248
Metcalfe	10	14.1	83	0.6	105	26.0	25.0	2 598	49	20.7	D	295	D	110
Monroe	15	17.1	93	1.2	158	41.1	28.8	3 371	71	34.7	D	1 284	97	185
Montgomery	42	175.1	535	6.9	281	122.8	27.8	6 021	150	112.8	348	1 305	316	423
Morgan	6	10.8	42	0.5	126	45.1	12.2	3 823	60	42.0	237	698	D	76
Muhlenberg	34	453.7	884	19.9	304	146.8	29.5	4 749	163	141.0	531	1 819	90	201
Nelson	29	78.9	333	4.1	339	121.5	33.8	4 145	190	114.9	D	1 295	100	415
Nicholas	4	3.1	24	0.3	64	11.5	-20.1	1 554	25	9.5	D	612	45	46
Ohio	20	27.4	91	1.1	204	78.8	13.1	3 753	108	74.6	D	924	53	179
Oldham	32	47.7	157	3.7	206	119.2	61.5	3 496	106	116.3	D	877	D	185
Owen	9	5.8	41	0.5	74	28.7	38.0	3 049	34	25.9	D	732	43	125
Owsley	3	D	D	D	64	9.1	26.4	1 619	19	5.7	D	606	0	D
Pendleton	11	6.1	36	0.6	97	29.1	54.0	2 595	48	26.4	93	862	D	104

1. For pay period including March 12. 2. Based on the estimated population as of July 1 of the year shown.

STATE County	Retail trade, establishments with payroll, 1987 (cont'd): Paid employees[1]	Retail trade, establishments with payroll, 1987 (cont'd): Annual payroll (Mil dol)	Taxable service industries–establishments with payroll, 1987: Number	Receipts (Mil dol): Total	Receipts, selected kinds of business: Hotels, motels and other lodging places	Receipts, selected kinds of business: Health services	Receipts, selected kinds of business: Legal services	Paid employees	Annual payroll (Mil dol)	Bank deposits,[2] June 1989: Total (Mil dol)	Bank deposits,[2] June 1989: Percent change, 1988–1989	Savings capital,[3] September 1989: Total (Mil dol)	Savings capital,[3] September 1989: Percent change, 1988–1989
	161	162	163	164	165	166	167	168	169	170	171	172	173
KENTUCKY—Con.													
Edmonson	151	1.2	19	7.0	4.8	D	D	186	2.0	61	11.0	0.0	NA
Elliott	91	0.8	12	0.9	0.0	0.5	D	20	0.1	26	-0.9	0.0	NA
Estill	463	3.4	40	4.9	0.5	2.7	0.2	188	1.4	68	8.6	16.6	5.3
Fayette	27 198	231.6	1 968	885.3	83.5	280.7	64.2	22 760	346.2	2 268	7.5	325.2	-3.8
Fleming	558	5.2	41	4.8	D	2.9	0.4	185	1.5	112	6.7	0.0	NA
Floyd	1 965	17.1	181	44.5	D	16.2	5.5	990	15.5	312	2.6	33.7	26.6
Franklin	3 313	27.6	256	98.4	7.8	32.4	5.3	2 481	32.2	339	6.5	138.6	7.4
Fulton	605	4.2	35	8.5	D	6.4	0.5	219	2.4	122	4.4	29.0	-9.4
Gallatin	134	1.0	10	0.6	0.0	0.0	D	19	0.2	20	-0.6	0.0	NA
Garrard	340	2.6	24	2.4	D	1.1	0.3	69	0.8	72	0.6	20.4	-1.7
Grant	742	6.6	58	9.2	1.3	4.6	0.7	288	3.3	121	11.7	5.9	-13.2
Graves	1 613	15.4	122	39.1	D	24.3	2.0	996	13.2	228	9.2	97.2	-7.8
Grayson	763	6.8	85	10.6	0.6	3.5	0.5	243	2.9	170	5.2	19.6	0.5
Green	282	2.1	32	5.9	0.0	3.8	D	173	1.6	93	12.1	13.6	-7.7
Greenup	1 051	7.8	89	D	D	D	1.9	D	D	171	6.7	39.4	4.6
Hancock	140	1.0	23	1.9	0.0	1.0	D	67	0.6	56	3.7	11.1	-6.8
Hardin	6 347	58.5	389	115.7	8.3	43.7	4.9	2 771	39.5	502	11.7	127.0	0.2
Harlan	1 693	15.0	115	33.3	D	14.4	4.0	780	11.5	128	-24.1	62.5	5.5
Harrison	922	7.0	69	10.5	D	4.5	1.1	339	3.9	136	3.2	42.1	1.9
Hart	418	3.5	50	6.6	D	2.3	0.8	210	1.8	98	5.0	19.4	4.8
Henderson	3 130	27.5	243	75.7	D	D	5.7	1 636	26.1	249	5.4	157.0	-1.9
Henry	438	4.3	33	4.4	0.0	2.5	0.9	136	1.8	146	4.2	0.0	NA
Hickman	98	1.0	20	2.9	0.0	1.8	D	118	1.0	39	6.1	11.3	15.1
Hopkins	2 824	28.4	230	83.9	1.5	47.1	3.9	2 191	28.4	393	3.2	68.8	4.5
Jackson	120	0.9	9	1.3	0.0	0.8	D	30	0.3	42	2.3	0.0	NA
Jefferson	60 926	555.6	4 903	2 355.6	103.0	875.8	187.3	57 005	857.1	8 099	4.4	1 781.0	-5.4
Jessamine	1 238	12.4	106	16.5	D	3.0	1.1	436	4.3	142	9.7	41.7	-0.8
Johnson	1 515	12.4	115	31.0	D	16.0	2.9	753	9.1	154	3.3	35.9	-4.7
Kenton	9 586	86.5	689	226.3	26.8	68.2	20.5	6 641	91.7	831	14.4	519.1	-4.5
Knott	324	2.9	30	6.7	D	D	D	221	2.2	45	8.0	6.6	-47.9
Knox	1 221	11.3	80	20.9	D	10.0	1.7	602	7.7	217	4.6	13.4	-6.8
Larue	353	3.0	40	3.1	0.0	0.7	0.8	75	1.0	96	6.3	15.0	-7.7
Laurel	1 905	18.2	166	62.6	1.8	17.3	4.9	2 106	28.8	316	8.6	10.5	-59.2
Lawrence	582	4.4	42	15.9	D	13.4	0.3	405	5.6	54	1.6	12.7	0.6
Lee	238	2.1	15	1.1	D	D	D	33	0.4	56	4.6	0.0	NA
Leslie	264	2.1	14	1.5	D	0.4	0.6	32	0.3	45	8.1	0.0	NA
Letcher	959	8.5	73	17.0	D	9.0	0.8	394	5.7	174	4.6	0.0	NA
Lewis	275	2.2	11	2.3	D	D	0.3	106	0.8	73	4.8	0.0	NA
Lincoln	531	4.1	34	6.3	D	3.9	0.7	180	2.0	76	8.9	33.4	1.3
Livingston	244	2.0	25	12.2	D	3.9	0.3	162	2.1	54	2.0	0.0	NA
Logan	1 070	8.6	90	20.2	D	13.7	0.5	463	7.0	181	2.3	34.0	-3.6
Lyon	169	0.9	23	3.5	0.3	D	0.6	147	1.2	29	10.2	1.3	-7.7
McCracken	7 006	57.0	442	157.4	14.7	70.5	9.4	3 917	67.4	758	5.2	163.2	0.1
McCreary	286	2.4	35	6.2	1.1	3.2	D	179	2.1	55	7.7	0.0	NA
McLean	169	1.4	30	4.9	D	D	0.4	203	1.8	61	4.7	22.3	-0.1
Madison	4 140	31.6	248	55.6	6.9	20.3	3.3	1 874	20.1	385	5.0	88.1	4.3
Magoffin	342	2.5	24	6.5	D	3.8	0.5	206	2.2	40	7.6	12.2	-4.6
Marion	655	4.9	57	16.6	D	9.5	1.5	526	6.0	134	4.4	5.9	1.1
Marshall	1 102	10.5	116	26.7	2.7	7.9	1.3	720	8.4	251	7.1	39.4	-6.2
Martin	409	4.6	46	9.0	0.1	2.7	1.8	164	3.0	53	0.8	11.2	-2.5
Mason	1 415	11.1	77	25.0	D	16.7	0.6	550	7.6	161	3.1	39.6	16.1
Meade	634	6.1	41	7.5	D	2.1	0.7	207	2.1	76	12.1	0.0	NA
Menifee	95	0.8	5	0.5	0.0	0.0	D	23	0.2	9	-8.1	0.0	NA
Mercer	862	7.2	73	10.5	1.8	4.5	1.0	350	3.2	98	13.2	83.8	1.9
Metcalfe	312	2.6	23	2.7	0.0	0.5	0.1	67	0.5	48	6.9	5.7	-0.6
Monroe	423	3.2	40	5.1	0.0	3.0	0.3	174	1.5	79	2.8	20.6	10.6
Montgomery	1 358	11.7	120	19.7	D	6.1	1.6	500	5.3	178	4.5	15.2	1.6
Morgan	418	4.0	29	3.3	D	1.5	0.5	120	1.0	73	-1.0	0.0	NA
Muhlenberg	1 570	13.8	142	28.2	0.9	14.5	1.7	853	10.4	175	1.4	95.9	-5.7
Nelson	1 492	12.5	119	22.3	2.4	7.3	1.4	698	7.1	169	7.6	48.6	0.8
Nicholas	127	1.0	18	1.7	0.0	1.0	D	37	0.5	45	-5.6	0.0	NA
Ohio	803	7.1	66	12.6	D	7.3	1.1	448	5.0	122	7.7	53.0	-7.6
Oldham	1 419	12.2	109	32.9	2.2	14.1	1.5	833	12.3	132	10.3	10.0	5.5
Owen	262	2.6	24	4.4	0.0	2.9	0.1	207	1.8	63	3.0	0.0	NA
Owsley	78	0.7	9	4.8	0.0	D	D	224	2.0	20	7.2	0.0	NA
Pendleton	304	2.4	34	6.1	D	3.6	0.2	183	1.7	58	4.0	26.6	4.9

1. For the period including March 12 of the year shown. 2. Includes deposits for all insured and reporting noninsured commercial and mutual savings banks. 3. Includes savings capital for all FSLIC insured savings institutions.

STATE County	Federal funds and grants, 1989: Expenditures: Total (Mil dol)	Expenditures: Percent change, 1988–1989	Per capita[1] (Dollars): Total	Per capita: Direct payments for individuals	Per capita: Procurement contract awards	Per capita: Salaries and wages	Per capita: Grant awards	Local government finances, 1981–1982: General revenue: Total (Mil dol)	Intergovernmental: Total (Mil dol)	Intergovernmental: Percent from state	Taxes: Total (Mil dol)	Taxes: Per capita[2]: Total (Dollars)	Taxes: Per capita[2]: Property (Dollars)	Direct general expenditure: Total (Mil dol)	Direct general expenditure: Percent change, 1977–1982
	174	175	176	177	178	179	180	181	182	183	184	185	186	187	188
KENTUCKY—Con.															
Edmonson	25.2	5.6	2 651	1 720	37	469	334	4.6	3.8	86.5	0.5	47	25	4.4	81.1
Elliott	12.1	-0.4	1 830	1 241	10	77	495	3.8	3.3	95.1	0.2	35	32	3.4	75.8
Estill	35.8	11.0	2 419	1 792	11	102	494	7.0	5.4	96.8	0.7	50	42	7.3	68.4
Fayette	635.5	8.6	2 758	1 382	139	694	530	163.5	60.0	68.9	82.3	395	163	160.4	64.8
Fleming	30.2	13.7	2 479	1 693	22	126	437	11.3	5.8	85.4	1.4	112	68	9.5	128.0
Floyd	134.6	15.5	2 793	1 977	290	121	395	19.9	15.8	94.2	2.1	42	32	21.6	33.2
Franklin	473.3	13.9	10 565	2 169	62	529	7 714	24.9	13.0	83.7	8.5	199	94	23.8	73.3
Fulton	32.0	2.3	4 206	2 990	103	277	607	6.5	4.2	89.2	1.4	159	99	6.5	27.9
Gallatin	12.1	-5.8	2 231	1 469	208	176	326	2.8	2.1	94.8	0.5	96	88	2.5	66.4
Garrard	22.6	4.9	1 945	1 552	11	84	251	7.2	3.4	94.1	1.1	97	87	6.9	139.7
Grant	36.3	11.3	2 451	1 640	374	101	295	9.3	5.6	85.7	1.5	111	95	8.5	66.9
Graves	93.6	5.4	2 761	2 081	40	141	258	17.0	11.5	81.8	3.5	107	64	17.8	70.4
Grayson	53.6	11.9	2 394	1 759	51	110	373	10.8	7.5	93.1	1.9	87	46	10.1	55.2
Green	22.3	-0.4	2 100	1 636	9	72	295	7.4	4.7	84.2	0.7	67	59	6.0	52.6
Greenup	80.6	10.2	2 154	1 794	46	66	237	19.0	12.2	95.2	4.5	115	108	18.2	63.8
Hancock	14.3	6.6	1 829	1 305	43	84	328	12.5	3.6	93.5	2.6	323	86	12.5	5.5
Hardin	788.0	35.1	9 314	1 746	38	7 337	159	49.5	22.7	86.4	7.7	85	46	48.5	71.9
Harlan	170.8	23.0	4 471	3 091	848	142	387	23.4	18.2	84.9	1.9	45	36	19.8	73.4
Harrison	35.7	-3.7	2 248	1 696	73	143	291	8.5	5.6	91.9	2.3	149	90	8.9	42.4
Hart	35.2	17.5	2 460	1 816	11	105	416	6.7	5.5	81.9	0.7	43	37	6.7	102.6
Henderson	85.9	5.0	2 035	1 617	45	89	174	27.1	13.7	92.7	7.4	179	124	22.8	38.6
Henry	28.6	9.7	2 137	1 591	18	150	287	6.5	4.5	96.3	1.5	116	90	6.0	67.5
Hickman	15.8	-0.9	3 046	1 915	15	151	293	3.7	2.8	77.4	0.5	85	55	3.2	11.1
Hopkins	377.5	230.9	8 190	2 085	5 656	153	250	27.3	16.7	88.8	7.6	164	106	28.7	83.2
Jackson	31.4	5.6	2 512	1 629	18	141	659	7.8	6.9	91.5	0.4	29	27	6.8	126.5
Jefferson	1 830.3	3.5	2 719	1 848	123	469	269	573.7	235.0	71.7	241.5	353	178	537.7	23.6
Jessamine	51.4	19.7	1 643	1 070	326	75	150	14.2	9.5	69.9	3.4	125	76	17.0	138.5
Johnson	68.1	12.0	2 825	1 941	171	174	533	15.4	12.0	91.9	2.1	83	62	13.3	50.6
Kenton	387.5	13.6	2 744	1 556	85	627	471	99.4	39.6	79.2	29.0	211	129	89.5	7.7
Knott	46.0	10.8	2 585	1 777	85	158	558	9.4	8.3	95.2	0.5	30	27	8.5	50.8
Knox	81.4	9.8	2 724	1 718	138	203	659	17.3	13.0	83.6	1.1	35	31	17.1	82.6
Larue	27.5	2.0	2 330	1 799	12	108	292	5.6	4.1	94.8	0.8	69	60	5.1	38.6
Laurel	109.0	13.9	2 460	1 445	543	127	330	20.1	16.6	74.3	2.0	49	40	17.1	44.2
Lawrence	38.4	7.6	2 668	1 975	52	142	491	7.5	5.9	95.2	0.9	60	54	6.8	19.9
Lee	22.6	5.3	3 009	2 043	41	272	629	4.5	3.9	92.9	0.4	56	50	4.0	29.0
Leslie	33.8	-8.3	2 256	1 537	30	129	548	8.3	7.0	94.3	0.6	38	35	7.6	56.1
Letcher	78.2	4.7	2 715	1 972	42	113	582	14.3	11.7	92.5	1.4	46	39	13.1	40.8
Lewis	29.3	4.0	2 122	1 529	13	82	467	12.3	5.8	93.0	0.7	51	40	7.4	83.3
Lincoln	44.5	5.7	2 295	1 662	11	94	475	9.3	7.4	93.9	1.2	63	57	8.6	46.6
Livingston	26.5	13.0	3 015	2 077	321	183	190	4.3	3.5	91.9	0.5	58	46	3.7	58.5
Logan	60.6	9.3	2 397	1 567	32	108	362	16.5	8.1	91.1	2.7	111	61	16.0	104.2
Lyon	16.1	7.6	2 513	2 038	11	153	182	3.7	2.8	80.9	0.5	75	54	3.0	60.7
McCracken	340.2	19.6	5 707	2 272	2 468	609	325	40.8	21.9	89.2	12.6	206	108	38.8	52.6
McCreary	51.7	-13.1	3 254	1 990	509	171	551	8.5	7.6	95.2	0.5	28	26	7.7	4.9
McLean	24.7	-3.3	2 548	1 849	14	147	217	6.5	4.4	83.0	0.9	92	58	6.4	23.8
Madison	142.1	1.4	2 437	1 553	201	358	301	25.5	15.7	84.9	6.0	112	48	25.8	58.9
Magoffin	34.4	6.0	2 529	1 587	24	175	731	7.6	7.0	96.2	0.4	31	28	6.7	20.6
Marion	38.0	9.9	2 212	1 540	15	141	407	8.8	6.3	92.4	1.7	98	71	7.6	34.4
Marshall	65.0	7.9	2 407	1 983	58	137	164	14.0	7.9	92.8	2.7	104	67	15.6	74.6
Martin	43.1	21.8	3 217	1 674	1 026	53	459	9.1	7.3	95.5	1.2	84	60	7.9	44.8
Mason	36.3	3.6	2 065	1 557	33	133	271	11.9	6.5	88.7	3.4	195	113	16.0	138.2
Meade	31.7	0.3	1 233	918	100	48	111	7.9	5.6	96.3	1.4	62	48	7.5	7.2
Menifee	20.5	5.8	3 797	1 641	19	1 634	493	2.7	2.4	93.3	0.2	29	26	2.1	65.2
Mercer	39.9	9.4	1 977	1 566	12	112	184	13.3	9.0	59.9	2.4	126	98	12.5	96.1
Metcalfe	21.3	6.2	2 107	1 487	12	96	404	4.5	3.7	94.2	0.5	54	40	4.0	43.3
Monroe	31.4	5.3	2 615	1 713	27	153	607	9.1	5.4	92.4	0.9	74	49	8.4	133.1
Montgomery	40.6	7.1	1 991	1 521	9	103	333	12.3	8.1	88.2	2.3	114	88	11.9	77.5
Morgan	28.4	-2.1	2 466	1 624	22	165	638	6.2	5.3	94.8	0.4	33	27	6.0	70.4
Muhlenberg	70.2	-40.3	2 317	2 146	-1 133	1 020	230	17.5	13.5	96.6	2.1	67	56	17.9	64.6
Nelson	53.3	9.3	1 787	1 321	39	117	221	13.7	9.6	89.4	2.7	97	90	14.7	56.0
Nicholas	15.8	-7.3	2 168	1 602	12	143	348	5.5	3.3	93.6	1.0	135	123	5.5	94.0
Ohio	50.4	5.2	2 461	1 932	16	144	263	13.7	8.2	91.3	1.7	77	46	12.7	54.0
Oldham	26.3	6.5	709	529	8	72	75	15.6	9.1	96.0	4.5	158	130	13.6	5.2
Owen	18.6	17.7	1 974	1 342	13	107	268	5.3	3.3	90.4	0.9	98	93	5.3	69.1
Owsley	18.8	16.5	3 485	2 298	21	148	1 006	3.3	3.1	90.7	0.2	31	28	2.8	51.7
Pendleton	21.8	13.0	1 913	1 457	11	88	327	6.6	4.4	96.6	0.9	82	77	5.6	23.0

1. Based on the estimated population as of July 1 of the year shown. 2. Based on the estimated population as of July 1, 1982.

STATE County	Local government finances, 1981–1982 (cont'd) — Direct general expenditure (cont'd) — Per capita[1] (Dollars)	Percent of total for— Education	Percent of total for— Health & hospitals	Percent of total for— Police protection	Percent of total for— Public welfare	Percent of total for— Highways	Debt outstanding — Total (Mil dol)	Debt outstanding — Per capita[1] (Dollars)	State and local government employment, 1989 — Total	State and local government employment, 1989 — Rate[2]	Federal government civilian employment 1989 — Total	Federal government civilian employment 1989 — Earnings ($1,000)	Elections, 1988[3] — Total vote cast for president	Elections, 1988[3] — Vote for lead party (Percent)
	189	190	191	192	193	194	195	196	197	198	199	200	201	202
KENTUCKY—Con.														
Edmonson	434	71.3	1.4	0.5	0.1	7.1	6.9	676	325	342.1	221	5 178	3 828	R–66.7
Elliott	494	72.7	6.7	0.5	0.1	12.0	0.8	119	257	389.4	18	362	2 357	D–76.2
Estill	500	75.2	3.9	1.8	0.0	5.3	6.7	456	506	341.9	33	805	4 794	R–64.2
Fayette	770	41.5	3.8	10.2	1.5	4.1	192.0	921	21 843	948.0	5 928	183 711	81 525	R–59.0
Fleming	764	46.6	37.8	1.3	0.2	3.7	7.3	580	736	603.3	51	1 227	4 522	R–53.3
Floyd	436	67.3	3.2	1.3	0.0	6.8	41.0	827	1 843	382.4	151	3 790	17 764	D–69.4
Franklin	557	50.3	2.1	6.7	0.0	4.7	33.7	789	14 093	3 145.8	394	11 912	19 271	R–50.9
Fulton	761	51.4	6.6	4.5	0.1	6.7	5.3	614	433	569.7	42	1 144	3 016	D–50.8
Gallatin	525	63.4	10.9	2.4	0.2	8.2	1.4	285	186	344.4	36	954	1 952	D–54.3
Garrard	612	46.4	35.5	2.4	0.1	3.6	3.0	269	543	468.1	32	788	4 455	R–60.2
Grant	627	52.2	16.1	1.1	0.1	7.8	8.4	621	651	439.9	46	1 150	4 801	R–59.1
Graves	537	58.1	3.0	2.8	0.1	5.1	17.4	524	1 254	369.9	151	4 150	13 545	D–52.8
Grayson	474	61.4	3.1	2.9	0.1	6.9	21.9	1 030	969	432.6	72	1 781	7 842	R–66.1
Green	549	52.2	29.5	1.2	0.0	5.7	5.4	495	490	462.3	28	689	4 751	R–66.1
Greenup	470	72.3	3.4	3.4	0.0	5.2	13.3	343	1 269	339.3	76	2 064	13 558	D–51.3
Hancock	1 560	27.6	0.0	0.7	0.0	0.4	160.1	20 008	342	438.5	20	474	3 243	R–53.4
Hardin	537	41.7	32.5	2.7	0.0	5.3	47.9	532	4 235	500.6	6 871	152 968	20 599	R–64.3
Harlan	466	69.4	0.5	3.0	0.2	6.3	10.0	235	1 715	449.0	140	4 144	12 576	D–58.4
Harrison	578	62.2	4.1	4.8	0.2	6.8	23.1	1 500	544	342.1	68	1 824	5 753	R–51.9
Hart	430	65.0	0.9	1.6	0.0	7.5	13.3	857	609	425.9	52	1 254	5 468	R–53.5
Henderson	551	58.6	1.4	4.2	0.3	6.5	175.5	4 240	1 825	432.5	112	3 010	14 620	D–52.3
Henry	464	72.6	5.8	2.9	0.0	6.9	3.9	300	501	373.9	61	1 438	4 866	D–52.3
Hickman	536	62.0	1.9	1.8	0.0	8.9	1.1	190	197	378.8	31	770	2 315	D–50.0
Hopkins	617	55.3	1.1	4.0	0.9	4.0	90.9	1 955	2 218	481.1	170	5 529	15 505	R–51.5
Jackson	549	65.2	22.1	0.8	0.1	5.5	0.6	46	396	316.8	50	1 020	4 610	R–85.2
Jefferson	785	40.7	2.1	8.0	1.5	1.7	1 034.3	1 511	33 316	494.9	9 261	321 169	268 629	R–52.0
Jessamine	628	43.0	0.9	3.7	0.1	4.6	46.5	1 716	940	300.3	66	1 888	10 116	R–69.8
Johnson	536	67.4	6.2	1.6	0.4	4.4	28.6	1 154	1 182	490.5	125	3 165	8 211	R–56.3
Kenton	652	42.9	2.7	6.8	0.2	4.9	184.9	1 348	4 757	336.9	4 022	87 453	45 793	R–67.1
Knott	469	75.5	0.3	0.9	0.1	8.7	4.1	225	666	374.2	84	2 048	6 926	D–74.9
Knox	565	58.1	17.4	1.4	0.0	5.4	11.7	386	1 225	409.7	146	4 603	7 882	R–62.2
Larue	431	72.5	2.1	3.2	0.0	6.3	3.4	283	396	335.6	45	1 102	4 423	R–58.6
Laurel	424	73.0	2.2	1.5	0.1	8.0	24.1	599	1 686	380.6	193	5 514	12 994	R–71.5
Lawrence	475	68.5	1.1	3.3	0.1	9.6	10.1	709	455	316.0	63	1 634	4 508	R–50.9
Lee	530	64.8	4.3	1.4	0.0	12.4	1.2	162	371	494.7	32	629	2 590	R–61.3
Leslie	500	72.0	0.6	0.6	0.0	12.9	1.9	122	659	439.3	51	1 228	4 409	R–74.4
Letcher	427	73.3	2.6	1.8	0.0	6.5	4.9	160	1 092	379.2	85	2 194	8 344	D–56.3
Lewis	509	68.5	1.3	1.2	0.0	6.1	127.8	8 753	462	334.8	36	746	4 696	R–66.2
Lincoln	450	73.0	3.9	1.5	0.1	7.9	8.5	448	631	325.3	58	1 365	6 232	R–56.6
Livingston	397	75.0	0.0	0.3	0.2	10.6	2.0	210	306	347.7	65	1 557	3 909	D–52.5
Logan	652	49.5	27.4	3.2	0.0	4.6	14.7	598	826	326.5	83	2 187	7 705	R–55.7
Lyon	454	59.4	11.3	2.1	0.2	7.9	1.3	200	653	1 020.3	34	1 022	2 422	D–55.2
McCracken	634	51.0	4.1	4.1	0.2	4.3	60.5	988	2 961	496.8	1 021	32 952	24 643	D–49.5
McCreary	483	79.2	7.5	0.2	0.0	3.8	5.0	310	588	369.8	139	3 150	5 193	R–67.0
McLean	650	53.1	17.0	1.2	0.0	6.3	3.2	327	338	348.5	43	1 011	4 111	D–55.2
Madison	480	50.7	4.4	3.7	1.4	5.8	60.9	1 133	4 183	717.5	612	16 432	16 766	R–59.4
Magoffin	485	68.2	7.3	0.4	0.3	7.6	4.9	357	588	432.4	48	853	5 080	D–57.0
Marion	426	76.6	1.3	3.5	0.8	2.3	5.0	283	590	343.0	54	1 352	5 673	D–55.6
Marshall	603	46.3	15.3	1.5	0.1	5.5	54.5	2 114	1 258	465.9	118	3 353	11 171	D–52.7
Martin	546	65.9	0.3	2.8	0.0	14.8	1.9	132	568	423.9	20	498	4 196	R–61.7
Mason	912	32.8	2.8	2.8	0.2	5.3	148.0	8 455	785	446.0	61	1 580	5 895	R–53.6
Meade	334	73.3	1.2	0.9	0.1	5.0	12.9	577	531	206.6	35	846	6 545	R–52.6
Menifee	401	73.2	0.0	2.5	0.0	13.2	0.6	115	202	374.1	71	1 648	1 788	D–61.3
Mercer	660	49.3	1.9	2.8	0.1	5.0	28.8	1 516	640	316.8	56	1 541	6 843	R–57.1
Metcalfe	406	74.9	4.2	1.4	0.0	8.5	2.3	239	404	400.0	30	687	3 915	R–55.7
Monroe	675	52.0	29.4	2.0	0.0	1.6	7.5	605	627	522.5	48	1 170	5 266	R–80.0
Montgomery	584	58.1	2.5	4.5	0.1	6.1	24.2	1 194	794	389.2	73	1 885	6 537	R–52.5
Morgan	493	72.0	6.7	1.3	0.0	8.8	3.2	263	602	523.5	48	877	3 817	D–61.0
Muhlenberg	561	60.9	1.5	2.2	0.1	16.1	28.7	896	1 060	349.8	1 012	31 256	12 322	D–56.1
Nelson	522	66.8	2.0	3.7	0.4	5.6	17.6	625	1 011	339.3	89	2 223	10 179	R–51.9
Nicholas	776	39.7	34.6	1.9	0.5	9.8	5.1	720	279	382.2	23	536	2 559	R–49.7
Ohio	592	54.7	23.6	1.1	0.0	4.2	10.7	501	940	458.5	87	2 269	8 545	R–57.5
Oldham	479	74.5	1.0	2.8	0.0	3.5	24.5	864	2 159	581.9	67	1 687	12 792	R–68.1
Owen	584	52.3	20.2	1.4	5.1	8.1	2.4	264	389	413.8	31	664	3 311	D–55.1
Owsley	487	66.1	12.9	1.9	0.0	4.2	2.9	512	260	481.5	20	419	1 613	R–78.5
Pendleton	521	62.4	4.1	2.0	0.1	10.0	4.5	417	440	386.0	33	792	4 091	R–60.8

1. Based on the estimated population as of July 1, 1982. 2. Per 10,000 resident population estimated as of July 1 of the year shown. 3. Data subject to copyright.

STATE–County code	MSA/CMSA/NECMA code[1]	STATE County	Land Area,[2] 1990 (Sq. Km.)	Population, 1990 Total persons	Rank	Per square kilometer	Race White	Black	Am. Indian, Eskimo, Aleut	Asian & Pacific Islander	Other race	Hispanic[3]	Age of population Percent Under 5 years	5 to 14 years	15 to 24 years
			1	2	3	4	5	6	7	8	9	10	11	12	13
		KENTUCKY—Con.													
21 193	...	Perry	886	30 283	1 279	34.2	29 660	521	29	64	9	53	6.4	16.8	16.1
21 195	...	Pike	2 040	72 583	616	35.6	72 052	282	61	173	15	184	6.3	16.2	15.5
21 197	...	Powell	467	11 686	2 236	25.0	11 574	82	10	8	12	41	7.3	17.4	15.3
21 199	...	Pulaski	1 714	49 489	849	28.9	48 671	599	103	91	25	205	6.2	14.0	14.1
21 201	...	Robertson	259	2 124	3 061	8.2	2 120	4	0	0	0	4	6.0	13.7	14.1
21 203	...	Rockcastle	822	14 803	2 000	18.0	14 760	3	17	14	9	52	6.7	14.9	15.8
21 205	...	Rowan	727	20 353	1 657	28.0	19 879	309	40	95	30	74	5.7	11.3	31.5
21 207	...	Russell	657	14 716	2 005	22.4	14 605	92	12	4	3	40	5.9	13.3	13.9
21 209	4280	Scott	739	23 867	1 496	32.3	22 201	1 510	22	102	32	100	6.8	15.8	16.5
21 211	4520	Shelby	995	24 824	1 469	24.9	22 218	2 454	26	90	36	90	6.4	14.3	13.8
21 213	...	Simpson	612	15 145	1 976	24.7	13 414	1 667	24	25	15	48	7.2	14.9	14.0
21 215	...	Spencer	482	6 801	2 677	14.1	6 671	113	3	11	3	6	6.6	15.7	13.8
21 217	...	Taylor	699	21 146	1 621	30.3	20 017	1 081	17	30	1	45	6.4	14.4	14.0
21 219	...	Todd	975	10 940	2 298	11.2	9 693	1 198	17	11	21	55	6.9	15.0	14.0
21 221	...	Trigg	1 148	10 361	2 352	9.0	9 098	1 227	15	14	7	28	5.8	12.7	12.3
21 223	...	Trimble	386	6 090	2 745	15.8	6 063	2	20	2	3	29	7.1	14.2	14.1
21 225	...	Union	894	16 557	1 884	18.5	13 902	2 545	34	47	29	122	6.0	15.2	22.4
21 227	...	Warren	1 412	76 673	589	54.3	69 566	6 250	115	644	98	429	6.4	13.8	19.7
21 229	...	Washington	779	10 441	2 344	13.4	9 483	913	8	20	17	56	6.9	15.5	14.0
21 231	...	Wayne	1 190	17 468	1 824	14.7	17 098	318	39	7	6	53	6.5	15.6	14.7
21 233	...	Webster	867	13 955	2 060	16.1	13 099	786	26	26	18	28	6.2	15.5	13.3
21 235	...	Whitley	1 140	33 326	1 180	29.2	32 997	213	60	52	4	90	6.8	15.4	17.2
21 237	...	Wolfe	577	6 503	2 711	11.3	6 486	8	5	3	1	5	6.3	16.9	14.4
21 239	4280	Woodford	494	19 955	1 680	40.4	18 558	1 294	27	28	48	98	7.2	14.8	13.8
22 000	...	LOUISIANA	112 836	4 219 973	X	37.4	2 839 138	1 299 281	18 541	41 099	21 914	93 044	7.9	16.6	15.6
22 001	...	Acadia	1 697	55 882	775	32.9	45 532	10 179	48	75	48	372	8.5	18.6	14.4
22 003	...	Allen	1 980	21 226	1 618	10.7	16 308	4 496	297	39	86	671	7.5	16.4	13.9
22 005	0760	Ascension	755	58 214	745	77.1	44 480	13 268	90	161	215	923	8.5	18.6	15.5
22 007	...	Assumption	877	22 753	1 545	25.9	15 273	7 349	44	72	15	292	8.2	18.7	15.5
22 009	...	Avoyelles	2 156	39 159	1 020	18.2	28 324	10 585	105	45	100	621	7.7	17.0	14.1
22 011	...	Beauregard	3 005	30 083	1 292	10.0	25 242	4 489	121	139	92	417	7.8	16.6	15.0
22 013	...	Bienville	2 100	15 979	1 924	7.6	8 986	6 949	23	12	9	81	7.4	16.4	13.2
22 015	7680	Bossier	2 172	86 088	531	39.6	67 030	17 381	308	908	461	1 799	8.4	16.3	15.0
22 017	7680	Caddo	2 285	248 253	201	108.6	146 580	99 511	557	1 115	490	2 595	7.9	16.2	14.1
22 019	3960	Calcasieu	2 774	168 134	285	60.6	128 181	38 445	387	590	531	1 847	7.8	17.0	14.6
22 021	...	Caldwell	1 371	9 810	2 401	7.2	7 970	1 760	11	12	57	160	7.2	16.5	14.2
22 023	...	Cameron	3 401	9 260	2 448	2.7	8 685	503	15	26	31	143	8.5	17.5	14.0
22 025	...	Catahoula	1 823	11 065	2 286	6.1	8 136	2 874	16	5	34	71	7.9	17.9	13.5
22 027	...	Claiborne	1 954	17 405	1 828	8.9	9 313	8 041	28	13	10	40	6.8	14.8	13.7
22 029	...	Concordia	1 804	20 828	1 638	11.5	13 164	7 596	29	24	15	130	7.5	18.2	14.0
22 031	...	De Soto	2 272	25 346	1 452	11.2	14 003	11 141	61	9	132	377	8.0	17.1	13.9
22 033	0760	East Baton Rouge	1 180	380 105	132	322.1	240 614	132 328	615	5 351	1 197	5 761	7.7	15.6	18.2
22 035	...	East Carroll	1 092	9 709	2 411	8.9	3 355	6 291	4	20	39	120	9.6	20.7	15.5
22 037	...	East Feliciana	1 174	19 211	1 720	16.4	10 022	9 083	23	22	61	186	7.9	17.0	14.8
22 039	...	Evangeline	1 721	33 274	1 182	19.3	24 405	8 701	31	38	99	270	8.6	18.1	14.4
22 041	...	Franklin	1 615	22 387	1 561	13.9	15 278	7 040	31	27	11	120	7.7	17.6	15.0
22 043	...	Grant	1 671	17 526	1 819	10.5	14 860	2 540	79	30	17	153	7.9	17.2	14.1
22 045	...	Iberia	1 490	68 297	647	45.8	46 940	20 154	135	843	225	1 320	8.8	18.7	14.9
22 047	...	Iberville	1 602	31 049	1 243	19.4	16 519	14 385	56	49	40	598	8.2	17.1	15.2
22 049	...	Jackson	1 476	15 705	1 942	10.6	11 065	4 589	24	19	8	50	6.8	16.9	13.8
22 051	5560	Jefferson	792	448 306	110	566.0	351 170	79 042	1 753	9 986	6 355	26 611	7.3	15.2	14.6
22 053	...	Jefferson Davis	1 690	30 722	1 256	18.2	24 721	5 836	65	44	56	201	8.1	18.0	14.0
22 055	3880	Lafayette	699	164 762	290	235.7	125 340	36 846	362	1 594	620	2 613	8.5	16.5	16.3
22 057	3350	Lafourche	2 810	85 860	535	30.6	72 371	10 703	1 909	678	199	1 249	8.3	17.2	16.8
22 059	...	La Salle	1 616	13 662	2 084	8.5	12 271	1 257	80	36	18	46	6.6	16.2	13.4
22 061	...	Lincoln	1 221	41 745	963	34.2	24 620	16 590	42	350	143	381	6.2	13.1	31.4
22 063	0760	Livingston	1 678	70 526	629	42.0	66 269	3 920	160	120	57	642	8.0	18.5	14.9
22 065	...	Madison	1 617	12 463	2 184	7.7	4 961	7 415	15	9	63	126	8.7	19.7	15.5
22 067	...	Morehouse	2 057	31 938	1 213	15.5	18 584	13 263	30	44	17	136	7.7	17.8	14.7
22 069	...	Natchitoches	3 254	36 689	1 082	11.3	22 357	13 779	175	148	230	487	7.6	16.9	20.0
22 071	5560	Orleans	468	496 938	98	1 061.8	173 554	307 728	759	9 678	5 219	17 238	7.8	15.2	15.9
22 073	5200	Ouachita	1 582	142 191	334	89.9	96 870	44 096	239	740	246	1 194	8.0	16.5	17.5
22 075	...	Plaquemines	2 188	25 575	1 439	11.7	18 522	5 944	475	518	116	590	8.4	18.3	15.4
22 077	...	Pointe Coupee	1 444	22 540	1 553	15.6	13 196	9 275	29	14	26	166	7.8	17.9	14.0
22 079	0220	Rapides	3 426	131 556	352	38.4	92 989	36 805	564	908	290	1 526	7.7	16.9	14.8

1. MSA = Metropolitan Statistical Area. CMSA = Consolidated MSA. NECMA = New England county metropolitan area. PMSA = Primary MSA. See Appendix A for explanation of these concepts. See Appendix B for list of metropolitan areas identified by type, with component counties. 2. Dry land or land partially or temporarily covered by water. 3. Hispanic persons may be of any race.

STATE County	Population, 1990 (cont'd) – Age of population (cont'd) Percent – 25 to 34 years	35 to 44 years	45 to 54 years	55 to 64 years	65 to 74 years	75 years and over	Percent female	Population–Change and components of change – Change 1980–1990 – Number	Percent	Components of change, 1980–1986 – Total persons, 1986	Total persons, 1980	Net change – Number	Percent	Natural increase – Births	Deaths
	14	15	16	17	18	19	20	21	22	23	24	25	26	27	28
KENTUCKY—Con.															
Perry	16.2	15.6	10.2	8.1	6.1	4.4	51.2	-3 480	-10.3	34 900	33 763	1 100	3.4	3 700	1 900
Pike	16.4	15.7	10.4	8.7	6.5	4.1	51.1	-8 540	-10.5	83 600	81 123	2 500	3.0	7 500	4 000
Powell	15.9	14.8	10.9	7.9	6.0	4.5	50.9	585	5.3	12 100	11 101	1 000	9.1	1 200	600
Pulaski	15.5	14.5	11.3	10.2	8.3	5.9	51.4	3 686	8.0	48 900	45 803	3 100	6.8	4 000	3 000
Robertson	14.2	13.4	11.3	9.8	10.0	7.5	51.1	-146	-6.4	2 200	2 270	-100	-3.1	200	200
Rockcastle	15.5	13.8	10.8	9.1	7.3	6.0	50.7	830	5.9	14 800	13 973	800	5.6	1 200	900
Rowan	13.6	11.8	8.9	7.2	5.6	4.4	52.0	1 304	6.8	19 200	19 049	100	0.5	1 500	900
Russell	15.2	13.8	11.2	10.6	9.4	6.7	51.9	1 008	7.4	14 800	13 708	1 100	8.0	1 100	900
Scott	16.3	15.5	10.4	7.9	6.1	4.8	51.6	2 054	9.4	22 200	21 813	400	1.8	2 000	1 100
Shelby	15.6	16.0	11.7	9.0	7.2	5.9	52.2	1 496	6.4	24 000	23 328	700	3.0	2 000	1 400
Simpson	15.7	14.7	10.6	8.5	8.0	6.4	51.7	472	3.2	14 900	14 673	200	1.2	1 300	900
Spencer	16.8	14.7	10.9	9.3	7.0	5.1	50.0	872	14.7	6 300	5 929	300	5.7	500	300
Taylor	16.0	14.2	11.1	9.9	8.0	6.1	51.7	-32	-0.2	21 800	21 178	600	2.8	1 800	1 100
Todd	15.6	12.9	10.2	9.5	9.0	7.0	51.7	-934	-7.9	10 900	11 874	-1 000	-8.2	1 000	900
Trigg	12.9	13.3	11.9	11.8	11.8	7.6	51.3	977	10.4	9 700	9 384	400	3.8	700	700
Trimble	15.2	15.2	11.5	8.8	7.8	6.1	51.0	-163	-2.6	6 200	6 253	-100	-1.2	500	300
Union	13.6	13.7	8.9	7.9	7.0	5.3	48.7	-1 264	-7.1	17 600	17 821	-200	-1.3	1 600	1 000
Warren	16.1	14.7	10.4	7.8	6.3	4.8	52.1	4 845	6.7	83 900	71 828	12 100	16.8	7 000	3 500
Washington	15.7	13.3	10.2	8.8	8.7	6.8	52.1	-323	-3.0	10 200	10 764	-600	-5.4	1 000	700
Wayne	14.7	14.2	10.5	9.7	8.2	5.8	50.8	446	2.6	17 700	17 022	700	4.2	1 600	1 000
Webster	14.5	13.9	10.3	9.7	8.6	8.0	51.9	-877	-5.9	14 600	14 832	-200	-1.5	1 400	1 100
Whitley	14.5	13.9	10.9	8.4	7.3	5.6	52.2	-70	-0.2	35 800	33 396	2 400	7.2	3 100	2 100
Wolfe	16.4	14.6	10.6	8.9	6.9	4.9	50.3	-195	-2.9	6 900	6 698	200	3.6	800	400
Woodford	16.6	17.3	11.9	7.8	6.1	4.5	52.2	2 177	12.2	19 000	17 778	1 300	7.1	1 600	900
LOUISIANA	16.7	14.4	9.6	8.1	6.5	4.6	51.9	13 973	0.3	4 501 000	4 206 000	295 000	7.0	514 000	227 000
Acadia	15.7	12.9	9.7	8.3	6.8	5.1	52.4	-545	-1.0	59 600	56 427	3 200	5.6	7 500	3 400
Allen	16.1	14.0	10.0	9.1	7.2	5.7	49.4	-182	-0.9	21 500	21 408	100	0.6	2 300	1 400
Ascension	17.8	15.2	9.8	6.7	4.8	3.2	51.0	8 146	16.3	58 900	50 068	8 900	17.7	7 200	2 200
Assumption	16.2	13.4	9.6	7.6	6.3	4.5	51.5	669	3.0	23 500	22 084	1 400	6.2	2 900	1 100
Avoyelles	14.7	13.0	9.6	9.0	8.3	6.7	51.8	-2 234	-5.4	43 100	41 393	1 700	4.2	4 600	2 800
Beauregard	16.2	14.6	10.2	8.6	6.3	4.6	49.6	391	1.3	32 700	29 692	3 000	10.2	3 200	1 600
Bienville	13.5	11.9	9.6	9.7	8.9	9.4	52.3	-408	-2.5	16 900	16 387	500	3.1	1 800	1 200
Bossier	18.1	14.6	10.4	8.2	5.6	3.5	51.4	5 367	6.6	91 800	80 721	11 100	13.8	10 200	3 300
Caddo	15.7	14.3	9.8	8.8	7.5	5.8	53.3	-4 184	-1.7	272 800	252 437	20 300	8.0	31 200	15 600
Calcasieu	16.5	14.5	10.0	8.9	6.6	4.3	51.4	911	0.5	173 100	167 223	5 900	3.5	21 100	8 400
Caldwell	14.3	13.1	10.5	9.1	8.0	7.1	51.2	-951	-8.8	11 500	10 761	700	6.7	1 000	700
Cameron	17.8	13.1	9.8	9.4	6.0	4.0	50.2	-76	-0.8	9 800	9 336	400	4.7	1 100	400
Catahoula	14.9	13.1	9.8	9.5	7.4	6.0	51.6	-1 222	-9.9	12 600	12 287	400	2.9	1 400	700
Claiborne	15.1	13.0	9.3	9.5	8.9	8.7	49.3	310	1.8	18 500	17 095	1 400	8.0	1 700	1 400
Concordia	14.4	13.2	10.1	10.1	7.5	5.0	52.6	-2 153	-9.4	23 700	22 981	800	3.3	2 600	1 300
De Soto	14.8	13.2	9.6	8.8	7.8	6.7	52.6	-381	-1.5	28 000	25 727	2 300	8.9	3 100	1 800
East Baton Rouge	17.5	15.3	9.4	7.2	5.7	3.5	52.0	13 914	3.8	392 600	366 191	26 400	7.2	44 400	15 300
East Carroll	13.3	10.6	8.1	8.6	7.3	6.4	53.0	-2 063	-17.5	11 100	11 772	-700	-6.1	1 600	800
East Feliciana	17.4	14.8	9.7	7.6	6.1	4.7	47.9	196	1.0	20 800	19 015	1 800	9.3	2 500	900
Evangeline	14.7	12.3	9.6	9.1	7.6	5.8	52.1	-69	-0.2	35 300	33 343	2 000	6.0	4 000	2 200
Franklin	13.5	12.4	9.6	9.1	8.1	7.2	52.7	-1 754	-7.3	24 300	24 141	200	0.7	2 500	1 600
Grant	15.5	12.9	10.2	8.6	7.6	6.1	51.8	823	4.9	18 200	16 703	1 500	9.1	1 600	1 100
Iberia	16.6	13.3	9.2	7.8	6.2	4.4	51.8	4 545	7.1	69 000	63 752	5 200	8.2	9 300	3 300
Iberville	17.4	14.2	9.3	7.7	6.4	4.5	51.6	-1 110	-3.5	33 700	32 159	1 500	4.7	4 200	2 000
Jackson	13.2	12.9	10.4	9.3	8.9	8.0	52.3	-1 616	-9.3	18 000	17 321	700	3.9	1 800	1 200
Jefferson	17.9	15.8	10.6	8.4	6.4	3.8	51.9	-6 286	-1.4	479 300	454 592	24 700	5.4	50 300	19 500
Jefferson Davis	15.4	12.8	9.7	9.2	7.4	5.4	51.8	-1 446	-4.5	33 400	32 168	1 300	3.9	3 900	1 900
Lafayette	19.0	15.1	8.9	7.5	4.9	3.4	51.5	14 745	9.8	171 900	150 017	21 900	14.6	21 000	5 900
Lafourche	17.3	13.7	9.6	7.8	5.8	3.6	51.1	3 377	4.1	87 500	82 483	5 000	6.1	10 600	3 600
La Salle	14.2	14.0	10.3	9.8	8.6	7.0	52.6	-3 342	-19.7	17 200	17 004	200	1.4	1 600	1 100
Lincoln	13.4	10.8	7.7	6.6	5.9	4.9	51.5	1 982	5.0	42 600	39 763	2 800	7.1	3 700	1 900
Livingston	17.2	15.7	10.2	7.3	5.2	3.0	50.5	11 720	19.9	73 000	58 806	14 200	24.2	8 000	2 500
Madison	13.0	12.2	8.8	8.2	7.4	6.5	53.8	-3 227	-20.6	15 400	15 690	-300	-1.6	1 800	1 100
Morehouse	14.1	12.7	8.8	9.5	8.2	6.4	53.0	-2 865	-8.2	36 900	34 803	2 100	6.1	4 000	2 100
Natchitoches	13.4	12.2	8.8	8.0	7.2	5.9	52.7	-3 174	-8.0	39 900	39 863	100	0.2	4 200	2 500
Orleans	16.9	14.3	8.9	8.0	7.4	5.6	53.5	-60 989	-10.9	554 500	557 927	-3 400	-0.6	65 300	37 700
Ouachita	15.7	13.6	9.4	8.1	6.4	4.8	52.8	2 950	2.1	145 900	139 241	6 600	4.8	15 800	7 200
Plaquemines	18.2	13.8	9.7	8.3	5.1	2.8	49.4	-474	-1.8	26 600	26 049	500	2.1	3 500	1 200
Pointe Coupee	15.7	13.6	9.6	8.7	7.2	5.6	51.9	-1 505	-6.3	24 900	24 045	900	3.7	3 000	1 400
Rapides	16.5	13.8	9.9	8.4	7.0	5.0	52.1	-3 726	-2.8	139 600	135 282	4 300	3.2	15 300	7 700

STATE County	Population–(cont'd): Components of change, 1980-1986 (cont'd): Net migration	Households, 1990: Number	Households, 1990: Percent change, 1980–1990	Households, 1990: Persons per household	Households, 1990: Percent: Female family householder[1]	Households, 1990: Percent: One-person	Births, 1988: Total	Births, 1988: Rate[2]	Births, 1988: Low birth weight[3] (Number)	Deaths, 1987: Number: Total	Deaths, 1987: Number: Infant[4]	Deaths, 1987: Rate: Total[2]	Deaths, 1987: Rate: Infant[5]	Marriages, 1984: Number	Marriages, 1984: Rate[2]
	29	30	31	32	33	34	35	36	37	38	39	40	41	42	43
KENTUCKY—Con.															
Perry	-600	10 598	0.2	2.83	12.4	19.0	478	14.1	46	311	2	9.1	4.0	376	10.9
Pike	-1 000	26 148	-0.9	2.75	11.0	18.6	1 004	12.6	78	649	7	8.1	6.9	774	9.4
Powell	400	4 057	15.3	2.86	12.1	17.8	189	15.5	15	102	5	8.5	29.9	168	14.2
Pulaski	2 100	18 866	17.0	2.57	9.8	21.7	627	13.1	37	440	5	9.3	8.8	484	10.0
Robertson	-100	820	1.5	2.57	6.3	27.7	28	12.7	2	25	0	11.4	0.0	NA	NA
Rockcastle	500	5 464	15.5	2.68	10.7	20.7	180	12.3	11	144	1	9.9	5.2	181	12.5
Rowan	-600	6 755	13.5	2.49	10.9	24.2	236	12.4	22	170	4	8.9	17.7	219	11.3
Russell	900	5 896	19.5	2.48	10.1	23.8	196	12.9	5	179	1	12.1	5.7	173	11.5
Scott	-500	8 501	17.0	2.69	10.9	19.9	301	13.2	21	178	3	7.9	9.0	251	11.6
Shelby	100	9 048	15.1	2.65	10.7	20.1	284	11.4	14	246	1	10.0	3.3	257	10.8
Simpson	-200	5 767	10.4	2.59	11.9	22.7	219	15.0	10	164	3	11.2	13.3	201	13.7
Spencer	200	2 451	21.0	2.75	7.5	18.5	79	12.2	6	51	0	7.8	0.0	65	10.8
Taylor	-100	8 216	8.7	2.52	9.6	22.4	274	12.5	16	223	1	10.1	3.8	237	10.8
Todd	-1 200	4 104	-0.7	2.64	10.5	22.3	140	12.7	12	132	4	12.0	29.6	97	8.8
Trigg	400	4 104	22.1	2.49	8.5	22.8	100	10.4	6	109	0	11.4	0.0	91	9.6
Trimble	-300	2 246	5.7	2.68	6.9	18.3	101	16.3	8	43	0	6.9	0.0	84	13.5
Union	-900	5 580	3.4	2.65	11.2	23.1	186	11.0	13	142	2	8.3	9.4	253	14.3
Warren	8 700	28 819	16.1	2.52	10.8	24.6	1 062	13.2	64	580	14	7.2	13.7	749	9.1
Washington	-900	3 709	6.5	2.76	10.2	19.9	124	11.9	3	114	2	10.9	14.3	96	9.3
Wayne	100	6 517	12.0	2.66	10.3	19.8	212	11.9	9	166	5	9.4	18.9	160	9.1
Webster	-500	5 372	-0.8	2.56	10.1	23.5	216	15.5	21	169	1	12.1	6.0	167	11.3
Whitley	1 300	12 153	7.2	2.65	13.8	21.8	516	14.6	44	319	3	9.1	5.8	638	18.1
Wolfe	-100	2 451	7.4	2.63	12.4	22.9	91	13.4	6	82	2	12.1	16.9	97	13.7
Woodford	500	7 223	21.5	2.71	9.2	18.1	276	13.9	19	133	1	6.9	3.7	235	12.7
LOUISIANA	8 000	1 499 269	6.2	2.74	15.6	23.7	73 902	16.8	6 504	36 443	872	8.2	11.8	41 087	9.2
Acadia	-900	19 285	6.4	2.86	14.5	20.9	1 037	17.9	95	564	9	9.6	8.8	578	9.8
Allen	-700	7 080	-2.6	2.79	13.5	21.3	358	16.1	30	230	2	10.2	5.8	222	10.3
Ascension	3 900	19 337	24.8	2.99	13.1	16.8	999	17.0	88	384	15	6.5	13.7	564	9.8
Assumption	-400	7 397	14.2	3.05	13.2	18.3	366	16.1	31	192	1	8.4	2.7	172	7.4
Avoyelles	-100	13 480	-0.5	2.77	14.4	22.5	661	15.6	62	453	5	10.6	7.6	381	8.8
Beauregard	1 400	10 362	9.0	2.79	9.9	20.5	569	17.6	50	280	5	8.5	9.4	307	9.5
Bienville	-100	5 852	0.1	2.65	15.5	26.2	260	15.7	21	242	4	14.3	15.6	56	3.4
Bossier	4 200	30 718	15.1	2.73	12.8	21.2	1 552	17.2	122	604	16	6.6	10.0	1 012	11.4
Caddo	4 800	93 248	2.8	2.61	18.3	27.1	4 575	17.0	432	2 491	65	9.2	13.8	1 954	7.2
Calcasieu	-6 800	60 328	7.0	2.74	13.2	22.2	2 864	16.6	238	1 406	25	8.2	9.0	1 740	9.9
Caldwell	400	3 575	-7.9	2.68	13.2	22.6	145	12.8	7	108	4	9.5	29.2	111	9.9
Cameron	-300	3 153	4.4	2.92	7.9	17.0	164	17.6	19	56	0	5.9	0.0	120	12.0
Catahoula	-300	3 927	-3.9	2.77	12.8	22.8	159	13.1	17	115	2	9.2	12.8	125	9.8
Claiborne	1 000	6 065	-0.7	2.64	15.0	27.2	287	15.7	40	204	3	11.0	12.0	108	5.9
Concordia	-500	7 341	-3.1	2.80	18.5	21.8	359	16.0	31	214	1	9.4	2.9	222	9.3
De Soto	1 100	9 129	1.9	2.75	18.0	23.7	428	15.9	31	277	8	10.1	16.4	193	7.0
East Baton Rouge	-2 800	138 620	11.5	2.65	15.3	24.9	6 472	16.8	594	2 539	96	6.6	15.1	3 883	9.9
East Carroll	-1 500	3 129	-13.4	3.00	27.5	24.3	221	20.3	17	143	6	12.9	34.7	74	6.5
East Feliciana	200	5 589	10.1	3.04	18.8	19.6	343	16.8	31	196	8	9.6	26.2	164	8.1
Evangeline	100	11 795	4.9	2.78	13.4	23.3	620	18.1	61	348	4	10.1	6.9	343	9.8
Franklin	-800	7 776	-3.7	2.81	15.8	22.6	386	16.3	32	251	5	10.4	14.9	203	8.4
Grant	1 000	6 261	8.5	2.76	12.2	21.2	260	14.2	31	161	2	8.8	8.1	168	9.3
Iberia	-700	22 847	14.7	2.96	15.5	19.3	1 278	19.2	112	511	11	7.6	8.5	639	9.3
Iberville	-700	9 875	2.5	2.97	19.4	20.7	585	17.6	62	303	6	9.0	10.1	255	7.7
Jackson	100	5 817	-4.7	2.65	13.1	25.2	234	13.4	22	193	4	10.8	16.5	167	9.6
Jefferson	-6 200	166 398	6.9	2.68	13.5	24.9	7 254	15.4	536	3 263	67	6.9	9.1	4 406	9.3
Jefferson Davis	-800	10 669	2.7	2.84	12.3	20.9	581	17.9	32	300	1	9.1	1.8	268	8.0
Lafayette	6 900	60 411	20.0	2.66	12.7	24.6	3 023	18.4	236	960	25	5.7	8.7	1 711	10.1
Lafourche	-2 000	28 835	13.6	2.93	11.8	17.3	1 410	16.6	101	545	10	6.3	7.0	796	9.1
La Salle	-200	5 086	-16.2	2.64	9.7	23.6	187	11.3	7	172	1	10.2	5.2	173	9.9
Lincoln	1 000	13 669	11.3	2.57	13.7	26.1	553	13.0	50	322	9	7.5	16.3	283	6.6
Livingston	8 800	23 814	29.0	2.94	9.7	16.5	1 148	15.8	62	422	14	5.8	11.8	783	11.2
Madison	-1 000	4 252	-18.1	2.87	24.1	25.4	243	16.5	29	147	5	9.7	18.4	77	4.9
Morehouse	300	10 961	-5.6	2.85	18.1	22.3	558	15.7	60	344	4	9.5	7.5	249	7.0
Natchitoches	-1 700	12 644	-4.6	2.71	18.1	25.3	601	15.4	45	368	1	9.3	1.6	48	1.2
Orleans	-31 000	188 235	-8.8	2.55	24.1	32.2	9 618	18.1	1 136	5 760	149	10.6	15.8	5 170	9.2
Ouachita	-2 000	50 518	6.8	2.72	17.0	24.1	2 470	17.2	200	1 173	31	8.1	12.6	1 327	9.3
Plaquemines	-1 800	8 213	6.0	3.04	12.4	17.1	433	16.6	27	174	4	6.7	8.7	246	9.2
Pointe Coupee	-700	7 736	0.4	2.88	15.2	21.5	337	13.9	22	234	3	9.5	7.8	196	7.8
Rapides	-3 400	45 941	2.6	2.73	15.3	23.0	2 176	15.8	208	1 222	21	8.8	9.4	1 423	10.2

1. No spouse present. 2. Per 1,000 resident population estimated as of July 1 of the year shown. 3. Under 2,500 grams. 4. Deaths of infants under 1 year old. 5. Deaths of infants under 1 year old per 1,000 live births.

STATE County	Divorces, 1984		Physicians, active non–Federal, 1989		Hospitals, 1989			Nursing homes,[4] 1986		Serious crimes known to police, 1988			Education			
						Beds				Number			Public school enrollment[7]		Attainment,[8] 1980	
	Number	Rate[1]	Number[2]	Rate[3]	Number	Number	Rate[3]	Number	Beds	Total[5]	Violent[6]	Rate[3]	1986–1987	1980	Percent 12 yrs. or more	Percent 16 yrs. or more
	44	45	46	47	48	49	50	51	52	53	54	55	56	57	58	59
KENTUCKY—Con.																
Perry	244	7.1	48	142	1	143	423	1	150	NA	NA	NA	7 459	7 793	37.3	6.0
Pike	613	7.4	72	92	2	307	391	4	359	NA	NA	NA	16 654	18 298	38.3	6.2
Powell	53	4.5	3	24	0	0	0	1	90	NA	NA	NA	2 586	2 649	34.0	5.5
Pulaski	37	0.8	59	124	1	244	514	12	361	NA	NA	NA	8 980	9 182	44.5	7.1
Robertson	1	0.4	1	45	0	0	0	3	9	NA	NA	NA	392	463	40.7	6.6
Rockcastle	104	7.2	8	55	1	60	411	3	127	NA	NA	NA	3 016	3 201	34.4	6.2
Rowan	104	5.4	37	195	1	133	700	10	139	NA	NA	NA	3 146	3 116	51.0	16.9
Russell	70	4.7	6	39	1	45	296	3	100	NA	NA	NA	2 578	2 866	37.4	6.0
Scott	100	4.6	14	61	1	75	326	5	154	NA	NA	NA	4 278	4 291	55.2	11.6
Shelby	131	5.5	17	67	1	76	300	5	421	NA	NA	NA	4 441	4 716	55.1	11.3
Simpson	98	6.7	7	48	1	50	345	5	147	NA	NA	NA	2 911	2 914	49.8	7.6
Spencer	26	4.3	2	30	0	0	0	0	0	NA	NA	NA	1 313	1 271	39.7	5.4
Taylor	143	6.5	18	82	1	90	409	10	162	NA	NA	NA	3 740	4 227	44.1	8.2
Todd	46	4.2	5	45	0	0	0	1	94	NA	NA	NA	2 038	2 439	41.3	5.8
Trigg	75	7.9	3	31	1	29	302	2	118	NA	NA	NA	1 840	1 918	49.0	9.4
Trimble	27	4.4	2	32	0	0	0	2	63	NA	NA	NA	1 164	1 351	49.2	5.3
Union	50	2.8	10	60	1	54	323	2	87	NA	NA	NA	3 086	3 507	56.4	6.7
Warren	125	1.5	142	178	2	561	702	9	671	NA	NA	NA	13 138	12 185	61.3	16.6
Washington	32	3.1	4	38	0	0	0	2	134	NA	NA	NA	1 822	2 241	45.9	8.6
Wayne	71	4.0	10	56	1	30	169	4	115	NA	NA	NA	3 608	3 668	29.6	5.3
Webster	40	2.7	4	29	0	0	0	3	175	NA	NA	NA	2 943	2 922	47.3	5.2
Whitley	34	1.0	50	142	1	210	595	4	273	NA	NA	NA	7 591	6 993	40.5	8.7
Wolfe	36	5.1	2	30	0	0	0	0	0	NA	NA	NA	1 430	1 348	26.8	6.7
Woodford	52	2.8	27	133	1	73	360	1	82	NA	NA	NA	3 496	3 681	60.8	15.6
LOUISIANA	13 894	3.1	8 198	187	178	24 265	554	286	35 674	219 393	27 759	5 909	795 921	794 072	57.7	13.9
Acadia	NA	NA	35	61	3	153	267	6	562	633	123	1 289	10 593	11 370	40.1	7.4
Allen	111	5.1	15	67	2	86	382	2	177	320	46	2 223	4 740	5 175	45.6	7.4
Ascension	168	2.9	17	29	3	149	253	4	449	470	23	804	12 380	11 060	58.0	7.7
Assumption	46	2.0	5	22	1	26	116	1	170	NA	NA	NA	5 111	5 100	38.2	6.5
Avoyelles	NA	NA	18	43	2	104	248	9	1 048	396	172	1 238	8 388	9 004	38.9	6.5
Beauregard	70	2.2	25	77	2	180	557	3	292	391	14	1 841	7 082	6 927	58.0	11.4
Bienville	NA	NA	6	36	1	30	181	2	205	NA	NA	NA	3 496	3 466	45.3	8.7
Bossier	426	4.8	83	92	2	277	306	11	1 310	5 226	376	5 726	18 305	17 792	69.1	12.8
Caddo	1 322	4.9	911	340	13	2 600	972	14	1 669	25 067	2 402	9 311	52 986	47 103	61.6	16.1
Calcasieu	890	5.1	254	148	7	868	506	11	1 539	11 388	1 226	6 690	32 819	33 968	58.5	13.6
Caldwell	63	5.6	6	54	1	49	438	1	135	188	30	1 636	2 288	2 169	45.2	7.5
Cameron	51	5.1	3	33	1	27	297	0	0	NA	NA	NA	2 085	2 017	44.4	6.9
Catahoula	NA	NA	6	50	0	0	0	2	158	NA	NA	NA	2 739	2 612	42.1	6.1
Claiborne	58	3.2	14	77	2	84	462	3	252	284	36	2 087	3 332	3 423	42.0	9.8
Concordia	100	4.2	13	59	1	42	190	2	180	130	14	708	5 214	4 855	48.7	9.1
De Soto	73	2.7	8	30	1	35	131	1	135	NA	NA	NA	5 703	5 580	46.3	8.4
East Baton Rouge	NA	NA	841	220	9	2 021	529	21	2 352	38 469	4 581	10 432	62 286	67 418	72.3	23.7
East Carroll	35	3.1	5	47	1	29	271	2	116	NA	NA	NA	2 403	2 650	39.0	9.8
East Feliciana	62	3.1	23	113	3	940	4 608	4	934	NA	NA	NA	3 597	3 671	47.3	8.0
Evangeline	131	3.8	29	86	2	346	1 021	3	353	825	86	2 359	7 300	7 057	37.3	6.6
Franklin	141	5.8	6	25	1	59	250	5	472	289	43	1 594	5 459	4 942	41.3	8.2
Grant	61	3.4	5	27	0	0	0	2	233	286	44	1 535	3 838	3 683	47.2	7.4
Iberia	282	4.1	72	110	2	163	248	5	541	1 446	56	2 149	15 897	13 664	49.6	9.7
Iberville	88	2.7	25	75	2	326	982	2	203	608	112	1 832	6 001	6 885	47.6	7.7
Jackson	66	3.8	6	34	1	66	379	4	276	150	26	850	3 420	3 362	49.7	8.8
Jefferson	1 662	3.5	1 198	255	7	1 534	327	12	1 975	31 225	2 969	7 889	57 494	65 282	68.4	16.2
Jefferson Davis	18	0.5	23	72	2	130	405	3	343	590	135	3 655	7 250	7 033	47.3	8.7
Lafayette	510	3.0	364	224	9	1 120	689	10	1 185	9 974	998	6 046	28 193	26 780	64.2	20.5
Lafourche	318	3.6	76	90	3	272	323	5	515	650	94	971	16 437	17 406	46.1	9.7
La Salle	84	4.8	14	86	2	114	704	3	294	233	25	1 383	3 208	3 459	52.1	10.0
Lincoln	NA	NA	42	99	1	129	304	3	334	1 280	114	3 454	6 782	5 740	64.7	23.7
Livingston	NA	NA	14	19	0	0	0	2	353	1 714	299	2 383	16 354	13 646	56.5	8.1
Madison	58	3.7	5	35	1	47	326	2	189	229	38	1 511	3 620	3 686	44.3	9.1
Morehouse	110	3.1	30	85	1	122	346	5	564	315	18	1 659	7 050	7 178	46.6	7.6
Natchitoches	191	4.8	23	60	1	194	503	3	370	296	34	758	8 206	8 542	54.0	16.0
Orleans	2 120	3.8	2 510	480	23	5 234	1 001	24	4 791	52 460	8 923	9 750	84 204	85 659	59.2	17.7
Ouachita	797	5.6	261	181	7	1 115	775	12	1 448	8 230	1 173	5 677	28 690	27 636	61.1	15.3
Plaquemines	106	4.0	11	42	1	39	151	0	0	677	73	2 588	5 350	5 052	50.4	5.7
Pointe Coupee	68	2.7	8	33	1	28	117	2	240	NA	NA	NA	3 897	4 552	43.6	8.0
Rapides	659	4.7	248	180	7	1 424	1 036	15	1 745	4 101	377	2 963	25 060	27 149	56.5	11.9

1. Per 1,000 resident population estimated as of July 1 of the year shown. 2. As of end of year. 3. Per 100,000 resident population as of July 1 of the year shown. 4. Preliminary. Covers nursing homes with 3 or more beds. 5. Data for serious crimes have not been adjusted for underreporting, this may affect comparability between geographic areas or over time. 6. Includes murder and nonnegligent manslaughter, forcible rape, robbery, and aggravated assault. 7. The 1986–1987 data are based on administrative reports obtained by the U.S. National Center for Education Statistics. The 1980 data are based on the 1980 Census of Population and Housing. 8. Persons 25 years old or older.

STATE County	Education (cont'd): Local government expenditures for education,[1] 1982: Total (Mil dol)	Education (cont'd): Local government expenditures for education,[1] 1982: Per capita (Dollars)	Social Security Program December 1988: Beneficiaries: Total	Social Security Program December 1988: Beneficiaries: Rate[2]	Social Security Program December 1988: Payments ($1,000)	Supplemental Security Income Program recipients June 1986	Money income: Per capita[3]: 1987 Income, (Dollars)	Money income: Per capita[3]: 1979: Current dollars	Money income: Per capita[3]: 1979: Constant 1987 dollars	Money income: Median household income 1979 (Dollars)	Money income: Percent below poverty level, 1979: Persons	Money income: Percent below poverty level, 1979: Families	Housing units, 1990: Total	Housing units, 1990: Percent change, 1980–1990
	60	61	62	63	64	65	66	67	68	69	70	71	72	73
KENTUCKY—Con.														
Perry	11.7	340	5 895	173.4	2 228	1 314	7 012	4 917	7 694	12 032	24.3	21.4	11 565	2.6
Pike	28.9	353	14 020	175.9	5 693	1 968	7 517	5 437	8 507	13 519	19.4	16.7	28 760	2.0
Powell	3.7	325	1 840	150.8	693	478	6 364	4 218	6 600	11 136	25.6	22.5	4 458	16.6
Pulaski	15.3	323	9 525	199.3	3 663	2 228	7 952	5 064	7 924	10 497	22.3	18.6	22 328	14.3
Robertson	0.9	403	435	197.7	153	108	6 841	4 392	6 872	10 976	24.5	18.8	955	5.6
Rockcastle	4.8	342	2 485	170.2	826	794	6 178	3 889	6 085	8 860	33.1	28.9	5 958	18.3
Rowan	4.7	250	2 765	145.5	1 086	654	7 075	4 563	7 140	10 566	21.8	18.5	7 375	10.9
Russell	4.4	303	3 100	203.9	1 081	868	7 717	4 350	6 806	8 650	32.4	28.1	7 375	16.2
Scott	6.4	293	3 310	145.2	1 385	442	10 004	5 951	9 312	15 240	14.1	11.5	9 173	17.9
Shelby	7.2	304	3 870	154.8	1 699	552	10 235	6 331	9 906	15 993	14.8	11.5	9 617	11.5
Simpson	5.5	381	2 745	188.0	1 108	394	9 281	5 799	9 074	13 496	16.5	14.5	6 172	8.0
Spencer	2.1	351	1 100	169.2	443	156	8 361	5 303	8 298	14 186	18.2	15.7	2 640	21.1
Taylor	6.2	292	4 210	191.4	1 683	666	8 905	5 456	8 537	13 130	18.8	15.4	8 798	7.1
Todd	3.4	299	2 180	198.2	805	478	7 381	4 995	7 816	11 021	19.8	15.7	4 415	-3.5
Trigg	3.7	392	2 470	257.3	1 022	342	8 753	5 564	8 706	12 582	17.3	15.2	5 284	20.7
Trimble	2.4	374	1 100	177.4	426	128	8 980	5 310	8 309	13 421	13.2	11.9	2 510	3.4
Union	5.0	281	2 820	166.9	1 327	256	8 607	5 914	9 254	16 595	22.2	9.5	6 091	7.4
Warren	20.4	255	11 880	147.8	5 086	1 770	9 467	6 062	9 485	14 077	15.3	12.0	31 065	16.4
Washington	3.3	314	2 070	199.0	789	352	7 980	5 024	7 861	12 299	23.2	19.7	4 009	6.7
Wayne	6.4	365	3 325	186.8	1 092	1 298	5 642	3 670	5 742	8 355	35.1	31.1	7 791	8.7
Webster	5.0	335	3 230	232.4	1 404	298	8 996	5 996	9 382	12 917	17.9	14.4	5 914	2.1
Whitley	10.6	311	7 175	203.3	2 759	1 432	6 965	4 673	7 312	9 826	26.6	23.1	13 399	8.2
Wolfe	2.6	379	1 410	207.4	456	662	5 569	3 773	5 904	7 846	34.9	30.1	2 779	8.1
Woodford	5.9	328	2 550	128.1	1 196	216	11 830	6 866	10 743	17 333	11.6	9.1	7 689	20.0
LOUISIANA	1 980.2	452	631 776	143.3	271 963	128 206	8 961	6 425	10 053	15 227	18.6	15.1	1 716 241	10.8
Acadia	22.8	388	9 715	167.8	3 622	2 930	7 032	5 603	8 767	13 507	22.2	18.6	21 441	11.3
Allen	10.6	487	3 895	174.7	1 540	912	6 581	5 163	8 079	12 202	21.4	19.0	8 275	5.5
Ascension	27.3	515	6 840	116.5	2 970	1 132	8 540	6 311	9 875	19 192	15.6	12.4	21 165	27.3
Assumption	13.6	579	3 495	154.0	1 403	890	6 336	5 169	8 088	14 883	22.0	17.7	8 644	14.4
Avoyelles	20.7	486	7 485	177.0	2 569	2 858	5 952	4 479	7 008	9 971	30.4	25.6	15 428	4.8
Beauregard	16.8	539	4 750	147.1	1 905	864	8 153	5 921	9 265	14 827	17.2	14.0	12 666	10.8
Bienville	10.4	635	3 610	217.5	1 343	904	7 537	4 983	7 797	10 367	25.4	20.9	7 085	1.9
Bossier	39.3	452	9 085	100.5	3 869	1 552	9 516	6 416	10 039	16 520	12.6	10.2	34 994	21.2
Caddo	115.8	444	41 815	155.6	18 882	6 984	10 465	7 206	11 275	15 381	16.8	13.1	107 615	10.3
Calcasieu	86.4	494	26 405	153.2	12 245	3 640	9 635	7 127	11 152	18 719	12.4	10.0	66 426	9.2
Caldwell	5.4	495	1 960	173.5	719	518	7 073	5 405	8 457	10 205	23.0	21.4	4 533	-2.0
Cameron	11.8	1 202	935	100.5	393	82	9 282	7 166	11 213	18 434	13.7	11.0	5 031	12.1
Catahoula	7.6	612	2 055	169.8	720	666	6 037	4 825	7 550	9 825	30.3	25.8	5 138	5.3
Claiborne	8.0	440	3 370	184.2	1 331	938	7 316	5 165	8 082	10 928	26.8	20.9	7 513	6.7
Concordia	11.4	483	3 590	159.6	1 463	1 104	6 491	5 306	8 302	12 175	27.9	21.7	9 043	1.4
De Soto	13.4	499	4 705	174.9	1 842	1 218	7 783	5 589	8 745	11 464	23.8	20.3	10 919	9.5
East Baton Rouge	162.4	423	45 270	117.8	21 207	6 720	10 738	7 476	11 698	18 041	14.9	11.7	156 767	17.3
East Carroll	6.1	536	1 935	177.5	632	858	5 000	4 011	6 276	7 780	41.8	34.5	3 563	-13.3
East Feliciana	7.6	384	2 785	136.5	1 075	882	6 089	4 476	7 004	14 012	22.6	17.7	6 476	10.5
Evangeline	15.6	455	6 590	192.7	2 293	2 826	6 387	4 814	7 532	10 049	28.9	25.8	13 311	8.1
Franklin	13.3	541	3 825	161.4	1 345	1 498	5 314	4 302	6 731	9 585	30.0	25.3	8 719	-1.9
Grant	8.3	476	2 965	162.0	1 103	722	6 820	5 065	7 925	11 295	21.9	18.3	7 494	10.5
Iberia	35.3	516	10 850	163.4	4 519	2 280	8 139	6 472	10 127	17 225	15.4	11.8	25 472	19.7
Iberville	18.6	562	4 820	145.2	1 976	1 392	7 366	5 479	8 573	14 026	23.2	18.7	11 352	3.4
Jackson	9.2	535	3 320	189.7	1 411	670	7 217	5 010	7 839	11 032	21.3	18.9	7 041	2.3
Jefferson	185.0	393	59 600	126.4	29 284	5 780	10 943	7 698	12 045	19 757	9.5	7.8	185 072	11.4
Jefferson Davis	16.7	508	5 635	173.9	2 275	1 094	7 414	5 782	9 047	15 042	18.9	15.3	11 963	8.4
Lafayette	84.2	511	18 220	110.6	7 773	3 382	10 645	7 830	12 252	18 602	12.9	10.0	67 431	26.9
Lafourche	40.0	456	11 460	134.7	5 061	1 684	8 391	6 492	10 158	17 891	13.6	11.0	31 332	15.9
La Salle	12.6	725	2 935	177.9	1 231	506	7 506	5 626	8 803	12 194	20.0	17.2	5 969	-9.7
Lincoln	13.0	311	5 430	127.8	2 157	1 208	7 630	5 357	8 382	12 676	21.6	14.7	15 286	14.5
Livingston	28.2	437	8 175	112.3	3 571	1 154	7 796	5 951	9 312	17 291	13.4	11.3	26 848	26.7
Madison	7.8	486	2 350	159.9	817	948	5 505	4 535	7 096	8 360	42.7	32.9	4 823	-19.9
Morehouse	15.8	448	6 215	174.6	2 559	1 958	6 676	4 834	7 564	9 646	31.9	25.8	12 314	-4.0
Natchitoches	21.5	533	6 200	159.0	2 246	2 030	7 004	5 011	7 841	10 872	26.2	21.8	15 210	2.1
Orleans	214.5	379	85 275	160.4	38 256	17 476	9 340	6 463	10 113	11 814	26.4	21.8	225 573	-0.4
Ouachita	56.7	402	20 470	142.2	8 935	4 144	8 830	6 168	9 651	13 883	20.6	16.2	56 300	9.4
Plaquemines	14.0	526	3 025	115.9	1 345	690	7 514	5 863	9 174	17 630	15.4	12.2	9 432	-1.2
Pointe Coupee	12.6	508	3 510	145.0	1 342	1 180	7 233	5 233	8 188	12 529	27.0	23.1	9 695	10.8
Rapides	56.6	413	20 545	149.1	8 144	5 558	8 669	5 924	9 269	13 398	18.7	15.4	51 239	6.2

1. Elementary and secondary. 2. Per 1,000 resident population estimated as of July 1 of the year shown. 3. Based on the resident population estimated as of July 1, 1988 for 1987 data and enumerated as of April 1, 1980 for 1979 data.

Table A. States and Counties — **Housing, Labor Force, and Employment**

STATE County	Housing units, 1990 (cont'd): Occupied units: Total	Owner occupied: Percent	Owner occupied: Median value (Dollars)	Median rent (Dollars)	Civilian labor force, 1990: Total	Percent change, 1989–1990	Unemployment: Total	Unemployment: Rate[1]	Private nonfarm establishments, 1988: Number	Net change, 1987–1988	Employment[2]: Total	Percent change, 1987–1988	Manufacturing	Retail trade
	74	75	76	77	78	79	80	81	82	83	84	85	86	87
KENTUCKY—Con.														
Perry	10 598	75.0	34 800	178	10 858	0.4	787	7.2	607	20	7 005	4.1	353	1 827
Pike	26 148	76.9	41 300	219	25 080	-0.1	1 806	7.2	1 411	-31	16 131	-4.4	340	3 964
Powell	4 057	76.8	37 400	180	5 820	4.2	530	9.1	144	13	1 608	32.3	677	587
Pulaski	18 866	75.7	44 600	191	23 081	3.8	1 888	8.2	1 224	46	14 445	10.9	4 577	3 715
Robertson	820	72.7	33 700	99	887	-3.9	64	7.2	27	-4	50	-35.1	0	12
Rockcastle	5 464	78.2	31 100	120	8 553	11.8	600	7.0	191	-11	1 678	11.3	407	381
Rowan	6 755	66.7	44 400	205	9 041	2.0	532	5.9	349	13	4 196	9.3	835	1 358
Russell	5 896	80.6	38 900	162	12 050	9.6	707	5.9	220	-9	4 302	36.0	0	633
Scott	8 501	66.2	68 500	274	12 058	-0.9	521	4.3	419	-5	6 452	4.2	2 844	1 234
Shelby	9 048	71.1	58 600	239	13 009	0.6	390	3.0	509	25	6 813	8.5	2 399	1 339
Simpson	5 767	70.4	46 300	230	7 906	1.0	532	6.7	295	-15	5 539	-1.4	3 206	952
Spencer	2 451	74.4	49 300	177	3 650	15.9	187	5.1	100	5	461	23.6	22	191
Taylor	8 216	72.3	41 500	197	11 769	4.9	665	5.7	522	11	8 426	0.5	4 826	1 377
Todd	4 104	75.8	34 100	148	6 056	11.1	360	5.9	160	-1	1 396	-3.0	820	237
Trigg	4 104	79.4	44 300	176	4 191	-1.2	298	7.1	200	2	1 674	-3.0	851	359
Trimble	2 246	81.5	43 800	166	5 881	6.1	189	3.2	54	3	0	0.0	0	47
Union	5 580	76.5	38 700	186	6 070	-0.2	345	5.7	319	-12	5 466	-2.1	526	777
Warren	28 819	65.0	57 600	265	42 890	0.7	2 650	6.2	1 945	26	27 026	1.7	6 955	7 747
Washington	3 709	78.9	40 700	158	5 257	5.5	375	7.1	210	5	1 823	13.6	425	297
Wayne	6 517	76.0	30 200	144	7 415	-2.0	614	8.3	247	3	3 291	11.4	1 708	472
Webster	5 372	78.0	29 000	156	6 132	1.3	412	6.7	264	-6	2 984	3.0	618	408
Whitley	12 153	70.8	36 600	191	11 428	0.7	820	7.2	783	-6	11 587	8.7	3 106	2 519
Wolfe	2 451	74.4	28 200	100	1 807	-5.6	277	15.3	79	-4	645	-4.2	0	131
Woodford	7 223	71.1	73 800	305	10 877	0.5	321	3.0	441	19	5 992	1.6	2 704	1 297
LOUISIANA	1 499 269	65.9	58 500	260	1 874 000	-1.4	117 000	6.2	X	X	1 182 795	0.3	163 435	278 257
Acadia	19 285	71.3	40 600	148	21 238	-0.2	1 472	6.9	888	-34	8 864	-4.8	1 580	2 182
Allen	7 080	77.7	35 400	138	9 269	-1.8	834	9.0	327	-32	2 646	-1.7	698	734
Ascension	19 337	78.3	61 000	218	26 535	-0.3	1 832	6.9	984	-9	14 386	3.0	4 430	3 025
Assumption	7 397	82.5	45 200	168	6 221	1.6	606	9.7	209	-12	1 681	-1.6	386	507
Avoyelles	13 480	74.8	34 900	118	15 847	7.7	1 498	9.5	606	-21	5 119	-0.3	563	1 438
Beauregard	10 362	76.9	45 100	221	13 448	3.6	858	6.4	514	5	4 702	4.6	1 303	1 487
Bienville	5 852	78.6	33 600	111	6 576	-0.6	472	7.2	265	7	3 124	16.2	1 704	386
Bossier	30 718	66.7	61 000	289	36 129	-3.0	2 586	7.2	1 610	-52	17 641	6.5	2 132	5 662
Caddo	93 248	64.4	55 500	264	117 511	-3.0	7 674	6.5	6 545	-158	91 271	0.2	17 228	18 636
Calcasieu	60 328	70.4	54 700	248	77 844	1.8	5 048	6.5	3 610	-40	46 818	-0.1	10 082	11 209
Caldwell	3 575	80.2	34 900	135	4 164	8.4	323	7.8	167	-4	1 091	3.4	175	256
Cameron	3 153	85.1	44 500	199	4 472	-0.4	209	4.7	180	3	2 051	11.3	237	284
Catahoula	3 927	81.5	31 600	112	3 424	-7.3	355	10.4	172	1	975	-9.0	38	323
Claiborne	6 065	75.4	35 800	100	7 305	-4.2	454	6.2	302	-22	2 919	10.8	846	606
Concordia	7 341	74.7	39 600	125	8 859	-4.3	885	10.0	352	-19	3 121	15.9	250	840
De Soto	9 129	76.3	39 400	134	10 967	-7.4	823	7.5	346	-27	3 611	-4.8	1 256	737
East Baton Rouge	138 620	60.0	69 200	287	201 402	0.2	9 639	4.8	9 685	-176	140 162	0.9	12 546	32 578
East Carroll	3 129	61.5	30 700	99	3 197	-8.1	412	12.9	170	-7	1 091	-6.5	105	348
East Feliciana	5 589	79.9	46 700	149	6 974	-2.9	452	6.5	176	-7	1 183	-10.2	264	241
Evangeline	11 795	69.5	32 700	122	13 443	5.3	921	6.9	494	-8	4 348	12.8	676	1 059
Franklin	7 776	75.6	34 100	131	8 392	2.8	741	8.8	319	0	3 135	15.4	566	855
Grant	6 261	80.7	39 400	165	7 025	1.0	517	7.4	150	-2	1 298	-0.8	496	170
Iberia	22 847	71.0	49 700	189	26 227	0.8	1 563	6.0	1 420	-39	16 764	7.4	3 121	3 493
Iberville	9 875	74.8	50 800	155	11 045	-0.9	984	8.9	491	-8	8 258	-3.0	4 071	1 176
Jackson	5 817	77.7	37 900	126	6 042	-6.4	347	5.7	256	-12	2 893	-4.6	0	674
Jefferson	166 398	62.9	71 500	334	225 730	-2.1	11 648	5.2	11 542	-45	167 088	2.0	17 686	46 286
Jefferson Davis	10 669	74.7	40 700	162	11 118	-2.4	850	7.6	571	-16	4 812	-2.9	436	1 531
Lafayette	60 411	61.3	62 700	245	85 196	2.8	3 730	4.4	5 121	-139	62 558	4.4	3 801	15 413
Lafourche	28 835	75.7	52 300	202	31 696	-0.9	1 755	5.5	1 611	-4	16 131	8.3	1 659	3 926
La Salle	5 086	82.1	34 300	148	5 677	-6.7	316	5.6	294	2	2 586	-15.2	819	582
Lincoln	13 669	62.1	56 200	243	17 623	1.2	604	3.4	795	-10	10 713	9.8	1 135	2 377
Livingston	23 814	82.2	56 900	228	32 332	-0.6	2 460	7.6	749	-43	5 420	-2.0	772	1 883
Madison	4 252	64.3	30 100	99	5 254	-3.5	529	10.1	189	-17	1 929	13.5	143	580
Morehouse	10 961	73.8	36 100	156	12 452	-1.9	1 090	8.8	479	-19	5 436	4.5	0	1 000
Natchitoches	12 644	67.0	46 600	194	14 960	-5.0	1 041	7.0	672	4	6 503	-12.9	1 405	1 790
Orleans	188 235	43.7	69 600	277	222 249	-2.5	13 365	6.0	11 288	-247	194 278	-4.0	15 933	40 191
Ouachita	50 518	64.8	52 800	235	68 722	-1.4	4 007	5.8	3 712	-107	47 655	-6.7	7 241	11 269
Plaquemines	8 213	75.9	62 200	298	8 452	0.2	543	6.4	719	-23	11 255	8.7	1 820	1 407
Pointe Coupee	7 736	74.1	48 300	130	6 790	-3.4	788	11.6	296	-6	2 074	3.2	130	641
Rapides	45 941	66.5	52 600	244	57 675	-4.1	3 670	6.4	2 846	-114	34 150	0.8	3 346	9 217

1. Percent of total civilian labor force. 2. For week including March 12. Excludes government employees, self-employed persons, farm workers, domestic service workers, railroad employees subject to the Railroad Retirement Act, and employees on oceanborne vessels or in foreign countries.

STATE County	Private nonfarm establishments, 1988 (cont'd)				Personal income, 1989								Earnings, 1989		
	Employment[1] (cont'd)		Annual payroll								Per capita[3]			Percent by selected industries	
	Finance, insurance, and real estate	Services	Total (Mil dol)	Average per employee (Dollars)	Total (Mil dol)	Percent change, 1988–1989	Wages and salaries[2] (Mil dol)	Proprietor's income (Mil dol)	Dividends, interest, & rent (Mil dol)	Transfer payments (Mil dol)	Dollars	Rank	Total (Mil dol)	Farm	Goods-related[4] Total
	88	89	90	91	92	93	94	95	96	97	98	99	100	101	102
KENTUCKY—Con.															
Perry	218	1 490	143	20 374	363	5.7	239	48	39	90	10 734	2 732	287	0.1	41.1
Pike	764	3 196	327	20 261	863	5.6	498	107	110	194	10 969	2 673	605	0.0	45.1
Powell	49	141	18	11 150	111	8.5	35	11	9	26	9 042	3 004	46	4.8	25.4
Pulaski	718	2 646	214	14 826	592	7.0	321	97	82	130	12 465	2 133	418	4.4	30.1
Robertson	0	7	1	16 420	21	10.8	4	4	3	5	9 601	2 943	7	42.0	NA
Rockcastle	79	492	19	11 372	142	8.0	41	15	13	38	9 719	2 923	57	6.5	NA
Rowan	168	1 184	56	13 403	195	7.5	121	19	22	45	10 289	2 839	140	1.7	17.7
Russell	108	302	55	12 749	173	12.3	98	30	18	40	11 400	2 540	128	9.9	NA
Scott	195	1 503	131	20 257	380	13.0	267	46	46	44	16 508	527	313	9.7	60.8
Shelby	223	1 403	105	15 428	382	8.3	164	40	56	51	15 059	964	204	7.4	41.9
Simpson	167	461	98	17 701	195	5.1	145	20	30	32	13 419	1 725	165	4.0	61.5
Spencer	0	148	5	10 475	79	13.0	12	11	10	13	11 929	2 350	24	31.6	NA
Taylor	234	1 077	128	15 221	265	7.3	181	38	35	49	12 043	2 315	218	3.6	52.7
Todd	65	121	22	15 569	122	9.1	41	22	19	25	11 061	2 649	63	22.1	35.2
Trigg	89	208	25	14 732	132	8.8	49	19	22	29	13 776	1 546	68	16.7	34.5
Trimble	40	92	D	D	84	14.3	44	9	8	13	13 511	1 674	53	10.5	NA
Union	127	1 370	134	24 450	239	6.8	175	43	36	38	14 348	1 270	218	9.0	56.1
Warren	1 255	6 406	454	16 797	1 045	8.2	711	105	165	175	13 076	1 876	816	2.1	32.5
Washington	75	542	21	11 400	127	8.5	33	24	23	23	12 087	2 295	57	25.6	28.3
Wayne	94	601	36	10 854	157	9.5	63	21	21	44	8 819	3 024	85	8.4	NA
Webster	130	412	65	21 902	220	9.0	110	25	34	39	16 209	591	135	7.3	51.8
Whitley	420	2 896	175	15 069	384	7.9	195	43	52	113	10 898	2 687	238	1.4	24.4
Wolfe	0	67	7	10 865	55	4.8	15	8	6	20	8 253	3 058	23	11.8	17.6
Woodford	173	845	118	19 653	443	6.8	182	157	51	33	21 819	98	339	40.6	32.3
LOUISIANA	81 879	332 066	22 344	X	56 636	4.9	35 108	5 189	9 079	10 256	12 923	X	40 297	1.4	26.3
Acadia	530	1 991	119	13 416	575	2.3	208	78	120	136	10 028	2 878	286	5.9	22.3
Allen	173	613	34	12 824	191	4.4	80	21	24	56	8 498	3 038	101	3.9	25.0
Ascension	651	2 288	322	22 412	720	6.7	539	62	75	107	12 224	2 219	601	0.8	60.1
Assumption	139	341	24	14 299	237	9.1	92	21	36	46	10 561	2 776	114	10.1	45.0
Avoyelles	410	1 563	56	10 958	354	1.8	107	36	56	112	8 442	3 046	143	5.3	19.4
Beauregard	273	823	90	19 107	343	0.1	155	34	46	74	10 637	2 758	189	3.2	38.4
Bienville	121	477	47	14 992	175	4.0	69	17	25	47	10 593	2 772	86	5.8	46.4
Bossier	1 283	4 321	249	14 140	1 117	3.3	561	80	128	221	12 362	2 177	640	0.8	15.0
Caddo	6 025	28 109	1 762	19 305	3 803	4.7	2 529	382	787	660	14 211	1 335	2 911	0.5	26.4
Calcasieu	2 891	12 388	922	19 700	2 267	5.8	1 523	184	355	396	13 202	1 812	1 707	0.6	39.2
Caldwell	81	355	16	14 321	103	-0.5	35	14	15	32	9 123	2 994	49	8.4	NA
Cameron	72	514	39	19 135	113	2.9	98	16	20	14	12 426	2 153	114	6.4	40.1
Catahoula	79	258	11	11 085	100	-11.0	32	18	17	30	8 428	3 049	50	17.5	9.1
Claiborne	158	396	43	14 679	187	2.7	79	19	44	45	10 270	2 843	99	6.8	29.9
Concordia	161	527	43	13 928	225	-2.5	78	29	33	53	10 195	2 857	107	3.0	17.9
De Soto	276	439	68	18 704	278	1.0	121	23	41	63	10 404	2 808	144	5.2	44.1
East Baton Rouge	11 565	43 137	2 832	20 205	6 197	7.2	4 398	480	934	844	16 236	585	4 878	0.1	25.6
East Carroll	67	295	13	11 514	94	-12.9	34	19	15	29	8 748	3 032	53	34.4	6.4
East Feliciana	112	293	17	14 719	208	2.1	83	14	27	57	10 196	2 856	97	7.8	18.0
Evangeline	324	1 559	58	13 290	334	3.5	102	38	54	101	9 868	2 898	139	7.7	14.4
Franklin	194	810	37	11 737	196	3.2	70	32	28	62	8 306	3 053	102	21.2	9.7
Grant	0	303	15	11 739	166	5.9	48	10	18	47	9 039	3 005	58	2.4	NA
Iberia	1 045	3 512	298	17 794	775	7.5	470	80	143	146	11 787	2 408	549	2.5	36.7
Iberville	274	1 230	231	27 944	361	4.8	390	24	53	75	10 888	2 688	413	1.2	63.3
Jackson	180	399	60	20 608	177	3.5	90	14	27	45	10 175	2 860	104	3.3	52.3
Jefferson	11 490	48 727	3 048	18 243	7 146	5.0	3 976	519	1 133	939	15 235	893	4 495	0.0	20.7
Jefferson Davis	317	1 002	67	13 888	323	-0.1	122	39	62	74	10 077	2 873	161	11.0	19.5
Lafayette	3 294	18 187	1 188	18 987	2 506	5.8	1 876	289	424	307	15 411	833	2 165	0.3	27.8
Lafourche	1 359	2 920	251	15 556	1 020	5.8	447	92	169	167	12 091	2 293	538	2.9	22.7
La Salle	149	301	44	16 959	149	0.8	75	17	21	42	9 220	2 988	92	1.3	41.4
Lincoln	794	2 230	174	16 211	477	7.5	273	46	81	106	11 229	2 592	319	2.8	21.3
Livingston	323	1 133	75	13 833	725	6.0	146	53	72	125	9 902	2 893	199	3.7	19.5
Madison	125	870	19	9 760	102	-13.6	45	11	14	35	7 096	3 098	56	10.0	5.3
Morehouse	258	1 148	95	17 523	369	3.5	167	49	53	90	10 465	2 798	216	13.6	36.4
Natchitoches	528	1 682	88	13 597	368	1.5	174	54	56	98	9 524	2 958	228	6.8	23.1
Orleans	17 000	76 616	4 020	20 691	7 758	4.5	6 945	852	1 492	1 550	14 838	1 057	7 798	0.0	16.8
Ouachita	5 637	13 130	846	17 750	1 839	5.1	1 202	165	292	332	12 783	2 004	1 367	0.8	24.2
Plaquemines	292	1 738	270	23 990	349	4.6	478	26	41	72	13 481	1 696	504	0.5	47.5
Pointe Coupee	183	502	26	12 743	239	0.8	99	18	50	55	9 992	2 882	117	3.7	19.8
Rapides	2 319	11 932	532	15 582	1 768	6.3	998	184	281	415	12 865	1 971	1 181	1.6	16.2

1. For week including March 12. Excludes government employees, self-employed persons, farm workers, domestic service workers, railroad employees subject to the Railroad Retirement Act, and employees on oceanborne vessels or in foreign countries. 2. Includes other labor income. 3. Based on the resident population estimated as of July 1 of the year shown. 4. Covers mining, construction, and manufacturing.

STATE County	Earnings, 1989 (cont'd)						Agriculture, 1987									
	Percent by selected industries (cont'd)						Farms			Farm operators, percent		Land in farms				
	Goods-related[1]	Service-related & other[2]						Percent with						Acres		
	Manu-facturing	Total	Retail trade	Finance, insur-ance, & real estate	Services	Govern-ment	Number	Less than 50 acres	500 acres and over	Whose principal occu-pation is farming	Residing on farm operated	Acreage (1,000)	Percent change, 1982–1987	Average size of farm	Total irrigated (1,000)	Total cropland (1,000)
	103	104	105	106	107	108	109	110	111	112	113	114	115	116	117	118
KENTUCKY—Con.																
Perry	1.6	45.9	9.8	2.1	17.3	13.0	45	42.2	0.0	15.6	60.0	3	-28.4	73	0	1
Pike	1.1	43.7	10.1	2.8	18.6	11.2	38	18.4	0.0	18.4	63.2	5	-44.3	127	0	1
Powell	20.1	NA	12.8	2.3	11.7	22.0	313	37.4	1.9	31.6	56.2	35	-12.5	112	0	15
Pulaski	23.1	51.8	13.3	2.8	21.7	13.7	2 266	41.8	1.7	43.8	70.7	231	1.4	102	0	145
Robertson	0.0	30.7	7.2	3.5	10.9	26.5	316	23.7	5.1	57.9	65.8	51	-2.4	161	0	32
Rockcastle	24.5	NA	10.8	2.2	22.6	18.1	861	38.2	2.6	42.4	64.6	95	-2.5	111	0	47
Rowan	12.1	46.1	12.0	2.3	24.2	34.4	501	36.9	1.4	39.9	68.5	56	-2.4	112	0	21
Russell	45.7	27.6	8.2	1.5	11.9	12.6	1 136	47.2	1.1	42.0	70.3	99	-0.9	87	0	62
Scott	54.9	23.0	5.9	1.3	9.4	6.5	1 062	37.6	6.1	48.7	66.9	164	-1.6	155	2	107
Shelby	36.9	40.3	9.9	3.1	17.4	10.4	1 581	36.1	5.0	45.7	69.5	224	-0.3	142	1	158
Simpson	58.7	27.0	11.0	2.4	8.1	7.6	590	27.5	11.5	60.8	66.4	130	0.6	221	0	108
Spencer	1.1	40.2	9.1	4.0	19.2	21.5	659	28.5	3.5	47.3	60.2	100	-1.0	152	0	62
Taylor	48.2	33.7	9.5	2.5	12.7	9.9	1 056	36.1	3.6	44.4	66.4	131	1.9	124	0	84
Todd	32.5	30.6	8.3	2.1	9.1	12.1	682	25.7	16.0	57.0	64.4	174	-1.5	255	1	132
Trigg	29.4	26.7	8.3	1.8	9.5	22.2	470	27.9	11.7	46.8	63.4	111	-7.7	237	0	76
Trimble	NA	NA	2.4	2.0	5.6	7.7	591	34.2	1.7	40.9	62.1	69	-2.6	117	0	33
Union	10.9	28.9	6.2	1.2	15.5	6.0	434	24.2	27.4	60.1	68.4	205	0.5	472	D	169
Warren	25.7	50.0	13.7	3.5	22.5	15.4	1 866	37.5	3.9	40.9	71.0	239	-2.4	128	0	168
Washington	20.2	32.7	8.0	3.2	13.1	13.4	1 182	24.5	2.2	49.3	67.1	169	4.7	143	0	122
Wayne	33.7	NA	12.4	2.8	16.1	16.5	979	39.8	4.7	48.3	70.3	137	-2.2	140	0	59
Webster	10.2	32.0	7.1	2.1	8.4	8.9	492	25.6	16.1	49.2	70.5	137	-12.2	278	0	109
Whitley	9.1	61.0	13.9	2.8	27.0	13.2	403	34.2	2.7	28.3	72.2	50	0.4	125	0	24
Wolfe	13.5	43.7	12.5	1.6	11.1	26.9	453	34.0	3.8	35.1	64.7	60	-10.7	132	0	19
Woodford	27.8	22.8	4.1	1.5	9.9	4.3	717	36.4	7.5	55.2	65.0	125	6.4	175	1	85
LOUISIANA	14.4	55.2	9.6	5.1	25.6	17.1	27 350	36.1	16.2	49.3	63.8	8 007	-10.3	293	647	5 563
Acadia	10.3	55.0	9.4	4.2	25.7	16.8	765	34.2	24.6	62.7	56.1	260	-5.3	341	70	229
Allen	20.4	NA	9.1	NA	19.1	29.4	370	38.6	19.2	45.4	69.5	106	-19.6	288	24	73
Ascension	39.0	31.4	6.9	2.3	13.7	7.7	263	49.8	11.4	30.8	71.1	58	-4.6	221	0	39
Assumption	37.7	30.3	6.6	2.7	11.4	14.6	118	24.6	32.2	71.2	39.8	72	-2.0	608	1	55
Avoyelles	7.0	52.8	13.3	5.0	24.9	22.4	1 080	43.8	14.4	48.8	66.9	272	-10.9	252	6	233
Beauregard	29.2	40.7	9.4	3.5	18.4	17.6	846	41.6	9.2	36.1	75.4	160	3.4	189	4	77
Bienville	38.7	31.7	6.3	3.2	13.8	16.1	301	19.3	6.6	32.9	69.1	61	-11.1	201	0	23
Bossier	6.2	39.0	10.3	2.8	17.7	45.2	399	34.3	17.3	39.8	61.4	120	-7.6	300	0	69
Caddo	18.2	58.2	9.4	4.7	28.1	14.9	559	33.6	17.7	45.8	57.6	176	-20.0	314	3	104
Calcasieu	28.9	48.6	9.3	3.7	22.9	11.6	772	45.3	19.3	38.9	65.5	326	-5.5	422	28	168
Caldwell	4.8	NA	10.1	3.6	27.8	25.1	264	32.2	9.5	52.3	65.2	58	-14.9	221	4	39
Cameron	6.5	40.4	3.0	2.3	9.6	13.1	442	27.4	20.1	42.5	68.8	255	-1.8	578	13	63
Catahoula	1.3	48.8	9.3	4.2	19.5	24.5	433	22.4	32.3	60.3	55.4	245	-15.0	567	7	198
Claiborne	18.0	38.9	10.8	2.8	12.9	24.4	291	19.6	10.0	45.0	61.2	64	-27.3	218	D	28
Concordia	7.2	55.5	12.3	3.9	16.1	23.6	357	16.0	44.5	73.9	60.5	231	-12.9	646	5	206
De Soto	28.1	36.1	7.9	4.5	11.1	14.6	585	28.4	16.8	35.4	64.8	155	-7.0	264	0	66
East Baton Rouge	13.1	55.4	9.3	6.5	27.4	18.9	582	48.3	7.6	37.6	67.9	84	-5.7	145	0	43
East Carroll	2.7	41.9	7.8	3.4	11.0	17.3	277	12.3	45.5	88.4	48.4	196	-8.5	709	32	180
East Feliciana	6.6	22.0	3.7	2.4	10.8	52.2	435	29.0	15.2	30.6	67.8	134	-29.7	308	0	51
Evangeline	9.1	57.8	12.1	4.3	30.8	20.1	582	35.9	18.9	50.0	54.1	160	-21.4	275	39	133
Franklin	6.2	46.4	11.9	4.4	15.2	22.8	929	28.1	19.2	63.3	59.0	262	-0.3	282	34	220
Grant	31.9	NA	5.5	2.0	14.5	25.3	216	37.5	13.9	37.5	69.0	43	-10.0	201	0	26
Iberia	15.3	48.9	9.1	3.7	20.8	11.9	365	41.4	16.4	56.2	57.0	103	-6.8	283	1	82
Iberville	56.3	22.1	4.0	1.5	10.1	13.5	174	20.7	28.7	57.5	50.6	81	-16.8	467	0	63
Jackson	47.8	29.4	7.7	2.8	12.8	15.0	207	39.6	1.9	34.3	69.6	22	-20.7	105	0	6
Jefferson	10.6	69.3	14.1	7.0	28.3	10.0	102	63.7	4.9	26.5	41.2	16	83.3	154	0	5
Jefferson Davis	7.6	52.0	11.8	4.1	21.0	17.5	523	23.1	41.3	68.8	61.0	290	-7.9	555	83	257
Lafayette	5.0	61.4	10.1	4.1	31.4	10.5	674	67.4	7.9	45.4	62.9	89	2.8	133	7	74
Lafourche	9.1	55.8	9.1	4.4	22.3	18.6	366	30.1	16.9	47.3	42.1	123	-33.6	336	1	70
La Salle	22.3	39.3	9.1	2.6	18.4	17.9	205	53.2	4.4	22.9	73.2	27	16.7	132	D	13
Lincoln	13.4	46.4	8.9	5.8	19.5	29.5	345	29.0	5.5	33.9	66.7	58	-11.2	168	0	25
Livingston	8.1	53.9	13.9	2.5	22.1	22.9	429	62.7	1.2	36.8	79.7	36	-18.1	84	0	15
Madison	3.3	59.3	15.6	2.8	24.6	25.4	325	13.2	44.3	72.6	51.4	259	2.5	798	12	233
Morehouse	30.7	38.2	8.5	2.0	18.4	11.7	434	15.4	38.0	71.9	44.5	266	-4.4	612	79	238
Natchitoches	16.3	43.2	9.2	3.7	19.1	26.8	622	26.8	18.0	49.4	60.9	210	-14.6	337	4	130
Orleans	6.9	66.1	7.9	7.4	33.6	17.1	7	100.0	0.0	42.9	57.1	0	-15.4	2	0	D
Ouachita	18.3	60.3	10.5	7.6	27.7	14.7	429	43.6	10.7	38.5	67.1	87	-6.8	204	5	59
Plaquemines	12.0	31.0	3.3	0.9	9.6	21.0	117	59.8	9.4	37.6	55.6	43	13.6	364	0	6
Pointe Coupee	4.1	NA	10.1	4.1	NA	18.2	439	24.8	27.1	56.5	52.4	196	-1.7	446	1	160
Rapides	8.6	53.6	10.0	4.6	28.0	28.7	875	45.3	11.9	46.3	71.7	196	-6.8	224	5	136

1. Covers mining, construction, and manufacturing. 2. Covers private sector earnings in agricultural services, forestry, and fisheries; transportation and public utilities; wholesale trade; retail trade; finance, insurance, and real estate; and services.

STATE County	Agriculture, 1987 (cont'd) — Value of land and buildings — Average per farm ($1,000)	Value of land and buildings — Average per acre (Dollars)	Value of products sold — Total (Mil dol)	Value of products sold — Average per farm (Dollars)	Value of products sold — Percent from — Crops	Value of products sold — Percent from — Livestock and poultry[1]	Percent of farms with sales of — $10,000 or more	Percent of farms with sales of — $100,000 or more	Manufactures, 1987 — Establishments — Total	Establishments — Percent with 20 or more em-ployees	All employees — Number (1,000)	All employees — Percent change, 1982–1987	All employees — Annual payroll (Mil dol)	Production workers — Number (1,000)	Production workers — Work hours (Mil)
	119	120	121	122	123	124	125	126	127	128	129	130	131	132	133
KENTUCKY—Con.															
Perry	61	846	0	1 938	63.2	36.8	0.0	0.0	12	50.0	0.3	0.0	6.1	0.2	0.4
Pike	95	747	0	3 035	44.3	55.7	5.3	0.0	27	11.1	0.3	0.0	7.0	0.2	0.3
Powell	106	814	2	7 153	58.6	41.4	17.9	0.0	12	41.7	D	D	D	D	D
Pulaski	82	834	29	12 841	31.8	68.2	29.7	1.6	67	34.3	4.3	19.4	76.2	3.4	6.6
Robertson	85	526	4	13 589	60.7	39.3	37.7	1.3	1	0.0	D	D	D	D	D
Rockcastle	76	610	9	10 014	41.3	58.7	25.0	0.7	7	42.9	0.5	150.0	6.6	0.4	0.8
Rowan	85	638	3	6 100	60.5	39.5	16.8	0.2	14	57.1	0.7	16.7	9.3	0.6	1.1
Russell	89	982	17	14 754	30.3	69.7	31.3	2.5	13	46.2	D	D	D	D	D
Scott	303	1 937	40	38 075	36.6	63.4	51.1	5.5	37	51.4	2.4	20.0	55.0	1.5	2.9
Shelby	190	1 395	47	29 515	40.1	59.9	48.1	6.6	38	47.4	D	D	D	D	D
Simpson	188	802	22	37 092	69.7	30.3	53.4	9.7	31	51.6	3.3	37.5	73.4	2.8	5.8
Spencer	128	809	16	24 354	41.3	58.7	48.3	5.5	5	0.0	0.0	0.0	0.2	0.0	0.0
Taylor	88	747	23	21 863	29.6	70.4	37.9	2.7	31	35.5	4.7	-2.1	81.2	4.4	8.1
Todd	199	785	33	48 669	52.4	47.6	52.9	13.6	16	56.2	0.9	50.0	11.9	0.7	1.4
Trigg	148	643	15	31 031	53.4	46.6	49.1	6.0	23	47.8	0.9	50.0	15.3	0.7	1.4
Trimble	102	858	8	13 966	70.4	29.6	39.8	1.4	3	0.0	0.0	0.0	0.1	0.0	0.0
Union	383	819	42	97 066	60.6	39.4	67.1	26.0	8	37.5	0.6	20.0	9.1	0.5	0.9
Warren	120	949	32	17 358	41.5	58.5	34.6	3.5	76	39.5	7.6	-3.8	176.5	5.6	10.4
Washington	90	653	26	21 717	37.8	62.2	45.9	3.6	9	44.4	0.3	-40.0	5.6	0.2	0.4
Wayne	83	585	16	16 117	32.9	67.1	30.6	2.5	30	36.7	1.8	28.6	19.7	1.6	2.9
Webster	202	714	17	35 313	79.7	20.3	47.0	9.8	19	31.6	0.5	25.0	5.8	0.4	0.7
Whitley	108	798	3	6 548	31.4	68.6	14.9	0.7	33	39.4	2.7	-3.6	45.8	2.1	3.7
Wolfe	79	529	2	5 449	76.1	23.9	15.5	0.2	4	25.0	D	D	D	D	D
Woodford	525	2 935	77	107 830	18.2	81.8	59.3	12.6	14	57.1	2.8	7.7	68.6	2.0	3.6
LOUISIANA	269	940	1 340	49 000	69.4	30.6	38.7	13.6	3 816	29.1	161.4	-20.1	4 175.9	110.8	224.9
Acadia	335	928	40	52 392	93.3	6.7	53.3	17.3	46	39.1	1.5	-6.3	17.1	1.3	2.5
Allen	214	774	11	29 137	80.7	19.3	31.4	9.5	22	18.2	0.7	75.0	13.6	0.6	1.3
Ascension	386	1 612	12	46 992	88.3	11.7	25.9	9.9	57	43.9	4.3	-24.6	162.3	2.5	5.7
Assumption	686	1 147	22	183 496	99.3	0.7	74.6	45.8	10	50.0	0.4	-42.9	8.7	0.4	0.8
Avoyelles	204	818	38	34 744	87.9	12.1	38.8	9.4	38	18.4	0.6	-25.0	7.1	0.5	1.0
Beauregard	152	809	10	12 089	33.7	66.3	17.8	2.7	40	25.0	1.3	-7.1	45.8	0.9	1.9
Bienville	136	771	7	22 970	21.1	78.9	16.3	5.3	41	22.0	1.4	16.7	24.5	1.2	2.4
Bossier	314	1 196	11	26 681	50.7	49.3	31.3	7.5	92	26.1	2.0	0.0	36.4	1.5	3.1
Caddo	283	982	22	39 613	69.4	30.6	35.8	9.8	252	32.9	17.3	-22.1	453.8	12.4	23.6
Calcasieu	337	847	16	21 064	72.2	27.8	29.3	5.8	121	34.7	9.5	-12.0	311.5	6.6	13.6
Caldwell	178	753	9	34 497	87.2	12.8	37.1	11.7	24	8.3	0.2	-33.3	2.7	0.2	0.4
Cameron	443	789	8	16 987	55.3	44.7	21.9	4.8	10	30.0	0.2	0.0	3.4	0.2	0.3
Catahoula	375	709	33	75 569	89.3	10.7	59.4	22.6	6	16.7	0.0	0.0	0.3	0.0	0.0
Claiborne	209	879	7	24 409	8.1	91.9	28.5	6.5	29	17.2	0.7	40.0	14.0	0.6	1.2
Concordia	500	809	34	95 506	97.2	2.8	73.9	31.1	15	46.7	D	D	D	D	D
De Soto	193	796	19	31 821	5.7	94.3	30.6	8.2	29	27.6	D	D	D	D	D
East Baton Rouge	293	1 914	8	13 120	15.9	84.1	22.2	3.4	323	27.9	13.0	-29.0	426.5	6.7	14.2
East Carroll	494	725	41	148 474	99.3	0.7	81.9	42.6	8	37.5	0.2	0.0	2.5	0.2	0.4
East Feliciana	308	953	8	19 020	11.5	88.5	25.5	4.6	13	38.5	D	D	D	D	D
Evangeline	235	897	22	38 389	90.6	9.4	42.1	12.9	22	22.7	0.6	20.0	13.6	0.5	1.2
Franklin	204	722	52	55 695	87.3	12.7	60.1	17.7	11	27.3	0.5	25.0	6.5	0.4	1.0
Grant	214	905	4	19 572	62.6	37.4	22.7	5.6	25	4.0	0.6	-33.3	6.9	0.5	1.1
Iberia	409	1 477	35	94 798	95.2	4.8	47.9	24.4	80	40.0	3.0	-41.2	54.1	2.3	4.6
Iberville	571	1 195	19	110 354	93.9	6.1	60.9	28.2	31	51.6	4.1	-14.6	162.4	2.6	5.4
Jackson	94	937	7	35 462	2.0	98.0	14.5	6.3	19	15.8	D	D	D	D	D
Jefferson	167	1 146	1	10 602	62.1	38.0	15.7	2.0	382	27.2	16.3	-9.9	385.1	10.6	22.8
Jefferson Davis	493	913	35	67 796	96.4	3.6	66.7	24.9	16	31.2	0.6	-40.0	10.3	0.5	1.0
Lafayette	248	1 809	13	19 970	79.5	20.5	19.4	4.3	175	20.0	3.4	-35.8	68.4	1.8	3.7
Lafourche	376	1 069	22	60 422	88.8	11.2	39.3	14.8	63	28.6	1.5	-51.6	29.2	1.1	2.3
La Salle	119	724	1	6 757	37.7	62.3	11.2	1.5	29	17.2	0.8	0.0	18.9	0.7	1.7
Lincoln	137	805	24	68 650	3.6	96.4	30.7	9.9	52	23.1	1.2	-29.4	23.3	0.9	1.6
Livingston	139	1 909	7	17 108	10.9	89.1	17.9	3.7	42	26.2	D	D	D	D	D
Madison	449	579	44	134 787	98.6	1.4	75.4	32.6	7	57.1	0.1	-75.0	2.2	0.1	0.2
Morehouse	427	741	59	135 535	97.2	2.8	71.0	37.8	21	38.1	D	D	D	D	D
Natchitoches	220	732	44	70 654	38.3	61.7	42.6	16.4	34	26.5	D	D	D	D	D
Orleans	250	159 091	D	D	NA	NA	42.9	14.3	371	31.0	16.8	-23.6	431.0	10.2	19.1
Ouachita	206	1 234	17	39 097	73.0	27.0	30.8	10.0	161	31.1	7.1	-4.1	190.7	4.8	9.6
Plaquemines	455	1 275	2	20 567	26.8	73.2	25.6	2.6	43	48.8	D	D	D	D	D
Pointe Coupee	350	830	31	71 203	88.3	11.7	56.0	19.8	10	20.0	0.2	0.0	1.7	0.1	0.3
Rapides	255	1 077	38	43 484	82.4	17.6	35.1	11.5	106	24.5	4.1	10.8	88.3	2.6	5.2

1. Includes livestock and poultry products.

STATE County	Manufactures, 1987 (cont'd): Production workers (cont'd): Wages: Total (Mil dol)	Manufactures, 1987 (cont'd): Production workers (cont'd): Wages: Average per worker (Dollars)	Manufactures, 1987 (cont'd): Value added by manufacture (Mil dol)	Manufactures, 1987 (cont'd): Value of shipments (Mil dol)	Manufactures, 1987 (cont'd): New capital expenditures (Mil dol)	Value of construction authorized by building permits, 1990: Total[1] ($1,000)	Nonresidential: Total ($1,000)	Nonresidential: Percent: Office	Nonresidential: Percent: Industrial	Nonresidential: Percent: Stores	Residential: New construction ($1,000)	Residential: Number of housing units	Residential: Alterations and additions ($1,000)
	134	135	136	137	138	139	140	141	142	143	144	145	146
KENTUCKY—Con.													
Perry	3.3	16 500	9.8	20.2	0.4	3 409	1 102	5.4	5.4	55.2	1 987	39	13
Pike	3.3	16 500	16.2	34.2	2.4	2 083	348	66.6	0.0	0.0	1 032	12	376
Powell	D	D	D	D	D	170	75	0.0	0.0	100.0	95	4	0
Pulaski	59.0	17 353	195.3	442.9	D	16 240	13 439	6.5	46.2	29.9	2 317	98	242
Robertson	D	D	D	D	D	NA	NA	NA	NA	NA	NA	NA	NA
Rockcastle	4.1	10 250	13.2	29.2	D	0	0	NA	NA	NA	0	0	0
Rowan	8.1	13 500	73.1	90.1	0.8	3 179	841	0.0	0.0	76.1	427	13	97
Russell	D	D	D	D	D	NA	NA	NA	NA	NA	NA	NA	NA
Scott	24.1	16 067	153.4	362.5	D	20 733	6 826	3.5	12.4	63.5	11 173	152	553
Shelby	D	D	D	D	D	30 787	5 220	36.1	32.2	5.7	17 703	235	444
Simpson	57.3	20 464	230.9	505.7	D	15 499	3 220	6.5	7.5	57.1	4 830	87	305
Spencer	0.1	NA	0.5	1.4	0.0	1 755	402	0.0	0.0	53.1	974	26	16
Taylor	72.4	16 455	178.5	388.6	D	4 283	2 028	26.1	0.0	38.3	2 169	49	86
Todd	8.3	11 857	38.2	81.4	0.9	0	0	NA	NA	NA	0	0	0
Trigg	11.9	17 000	32.7	56.7	3.4	758	10	0.0	0.0	100.0	701	16	20
Trimble	0.1	NA	0.3	0.4	0.0	NA	NA	NA	NA	NA	NA	NA	NA
Union	6.9	13 800	24.7	48.5	0.3	402	61	0.0	0.0	0.0	212	4	32
Warren	119.4	21 321	610.8	1 371.8	13.9	81 289	31 850	7.8	36.1	46.1	30 104	466	1 936
Washington	3.3	16 500	14.9	60.4	D	1 092	1 002	0.0	74.5	24.7	0	0	68
Wayne	16.8	10 500	55.1	106.6	D	125	125	100.0	0.0	0.0	0	0	0
Webster	4.3	10 750	17.5	29.6	0.6	481	285	0.0	70.2	29.8	95	1	59
Whitley	31.6	15 048	70.6	181.9	6.2	5 223	2 256	22.9	1.7	65.2	1 700	56	109
Wolfe	D	D	D	D	D	NA	NA	NA	NA	NA	NA	NA	NA
Woodford	40.9	20 450	217.6	341.5	D	11 204	1 221	35.2	31.2	0.0	8 884	137	534
LOUISIANA	2 587.8	23 356	16 425.8	50 699.7	1 419.8	1 170 687	375 495	17.8	21.7	32.0	440 227	6 451	81 369
Acadia	12.2	9 385	62.3	175.2	D	4 765	1 704	0.0	37.1	0.0	2 142	54	602
Allen	10.9	18 167	26.5	97.2	D	2 372	1 125	0.0	0.0	88.4	1 205	42	42
Ascension	88.5	35 400	1 367.7	3 274.7	170.4	5 443	1 371	11.4	2.8	66.8	3 151	31	196
Assumption	6.9	17 250	23.8	101.4	1.3	NA	NA	NA	NA	NA	NA	NA	NA
Avoyelles	5.1	10 200	16.3	35.7	D	7 359	2 414	13.4	0.0	28.2	4 263	85	430
Beauregard	31.2	34 667	182.5	426.4	D	1 503	192	0.0	0.0	13.0	1 014	18	151
Bienville	19.3	16 083	71.9	166.2	3.4	668	430	0.0	70.7	29.3	130	4	80
Bossier	25.1	16 733	67.5	205.4	6.6	17 801	4 925	0.3	44.0	42.7	9 297	132	978
Caddo	312.9	25 234	1 893.7	4 351.2	66.6	69 029	27 937	30.1	6.2	51.6	20 546	164	4 662
Calcasieu	202.9	30 742	1 425.3	5 679.3	193.8	135 753	72 841	2.3	86.1	3.7	36 735	592	4 856
Caldwell	2.3	11 500	6.2	12.5	0.5	3	2	0.0	0.0	0.0	0	0	0
Cameron	2.5	12 500	9.2	27.7	0.6	NA	NA	NA	NA	NA	NA	NA	NA
Catahoula	0.3	NA	1.0	2.8	D	447	47	0.0	0.0	0.0	400	5	0
Claiborne	10.5	17 500	41.0	124.8	6.2	564	184	100.0	0.0	0.0	179	7	88
Concordia	D	D	D	D	D	4 509	2 764	3.6	0.0	35.8	1 099	25	46
De Soto	D	D	D	D	D	1 924	1 406	0.0	0.0	0.0	455	17	35
East Baton Rouge	185.2	27 642	1 635.5	6 629.0	137.7	196 615	59 283	35.6	3.2	11.1	74 241	902	13 458
East Carroll	1.8	9 000	5.3	16.0	0.3	988	0	NA	NA	NA	988	32	0
East Feliciana	D	D	D	D	D	326	35	0.0	0.0	0.0	271	3	14
Evangeline	10.0	20 000	35.4	89.5	D	1 702	1 069	34.3	0.0	59.9	567	16	24
Franklin	5.2	13 000	14.2	23.0	0.5	3 620	1 137	20.6	0.0	60.6	1 890	37	532
Grant	5.5	11 000	9.3	22.4	0.9	NA	NA	NA	NA	NA	NA	NA	NA
Iberia	38.2	16 609	192.2	440.5	6.1	18 125	9 326	1.4	3.1	87.2	4 893	71	876
Iberville	93.2	35 846	916.3	2 239.8	D	2 153	373	0.0	8.6	2.1	836	26	392
Jackson	D	D	D	D	D	314	99	0.0	0.0	0.0	79	2	3
Jefferson	256.4	24 189	791.3	1 776.8	45.1	138 309	22 431	20.2	0.2	55.2	44 071	705	13 217
Jefferson Davis	7.0	14 000	28.3	57.8	D	4 352	646	0.0	0.0	86.6	1 505	54	1 087
Lafayette	33.4	18 556	194.3	395.5	7.6	95 229	29 452	9.8	1.5	52.1	33 050	335	5 613
Lafourche	19.9	18 091	114.5	232.8	D	18 989	4 751	23.4	0.7	33.5	11 437	227	1 136
La Salle	16.4	23 429	37.7	87.9	2.8	0	0	NA	NA	NA	0	0	0
Lincoln	15.9	17 667	60.1	135.6	2.2	6 608	1 649	0.6	0.0	69.4	2 968	47	624
Livingston	D	D	D	D	D	3 668	1 098	5.5	0.0	93.2	871	15	257
Madison	1.5	15 000	6.9	18.9	0.4	1 259	580	0.0	0.0	36.8	300	5	209
Morehouse	D	D	D	D	D	1 671	470	3.4	0.0	3.2	470	9	113
Natchitoches	D	D	D	D	D	3 028	876	41.9	0.0	48.7	627	11	756
Orleans	228.0	22 353	1 133.9	2 307.7	72.9	101 533	27 036	40.6	0.3	12.3	16 537	204	16 215
Ouachita	121.5	25 312	527.5	1 234.0	66.3	52 400	10 486	27.9	20.9	21.6	22 383	254	2 871
Plaquemines	D	D	D	D	D	NA	NA	NA	NA	NA	NA	NA	NA
Pointe Coupee	1.2	12 000	11.0	16.6	D	750	140	0.0	0.0	14.3	503	6	63
Rapides	48.1	18 500	425.1	731.6	17.2	22 217	14 267	10.0	4.0	75.2	4 545	60	1 107

1. Includes nonresidential additions and alterations, residential nonhousekeeping buildings, and residential garages and carports not shown separately.

STATE County	Wholesale trade, 1987				Retail trade, all establishments, 1987				Retail trade, establishments with payroll, 1987					
						Sales				Sales				
											Per capita[2] (Dollars)			
	Establishments	Sales (Mil dol)	Paid employees[1]	Annual payroll (Mil dol)	Number	Total (Mil dol)	Percent change, 1982–1987	Per capita[2] (Dollars)	Number	Total (Mil dol)	General merchandise stores	Food stores	Apparel & accessory stores	Eating and drinking places
	147	148	149	150	151	152	153	154	155	156	157	158	159	160
KENTUCKY—Con.														
Perry	49	150.2	384	9.2	380	164.4	20.4	4 807	193	154.4	699	1 253	286	304
Pike	81	277.9	724	15.9	859	400.7	21.8	4 972	377	371.4	737	1 284	215	331
Powell	7	3.5	19	0.3	133	30.4	48.3	2 537	49	25.6	D	906	D	211
Pulaski	97	180.2	958	12.3	639	307.2	42.7	6 508	364	287.0	1 043	1 302	334	493
Robertson	3	D	D	D	21	2.6	18.2	1 199	9	1.1	D	195	0	D
Rockcastle	12	10.8	68	0.6	146	33.4	18.9	2 286	70	30.4	130	815	0	174
Rowan	27	34.7	202	2.9	248	99.1	33.4	5 217	137	93.8	661	1 201	292	445
Russell	12	11.7	79	0.8	193	61.9	54.4	4 184	91	53.8	269	1 486	110	278
Scott	19	72.1	150	2.8	202	83.4	53.0	3 721	105	79.3	555	1 090	76	469
Shelby	54	111.8	717	10.6	240	108.5	37.2	4 391	134	104.4	D	1 079	82	286
Simpson	29	81.1	233	3.5	167	80.8	28.5	5 497	90	76.4	D	1 310	87	577
Spencer	3	2.7	12	0.1	56	12.8	18.5	1 963	23	10.8	0	948	D	D
Taylor	37	53.6	303	3.7	273	109.5	31.9	4 979	152	104.2	D	1 045	230	559
Todd	17	28.3	77	0.9	103	20.3	16.7	1 848	41	17.0	D	773	0	77
Trigg	9	5.9	37	0.5	125	31.4	36.5	3 266	60	27.9	D	1 119	52	220
Trimble	0	0.0	0	0.0	42	5.0	6.4	803	17	4.3	0	207	0	72
Union	30	38.8	168	2.5	181	74.7	33.9	4 371	109	70.8	D	1 154	97	188
Warren	161	1 099.4	1 658	31.4	953	601.8	47.2	7 439	596	585.4	1 202	1 287	321	592
Washington	19	43.0	146	1.6	94	24.6	50.9	2 339	49	22.1	D	890	60	153
Wayne	24	20.4	111	1.4	168	49.9	15.0	2 818	77	43.6	168	882	92	166
Webster	14	D	D	D	168	57.4	24.8	4 101	74	52.1	D	1 177	D	63
Whitley	48	136.6	565	13.2	475	206.1	12.1	5 873	255	192.3	538	810	248	545
Wolfe	5	1.4	13	0.1	71	14.7	-2.6	2 155	24	11.2	130	756	0	48
Woodford	18	54.0	248	4.2	207	79.3	39.4	4 111	120	76.6	D	1 084	147	364
LOUISIANA	7 643	31 477.3	80 533	1 652.5	40 465	22 445.8	12.3	5 046	24 262	21 627.1	681	1 220	242	455
Acadia	97	340.5	1 169	19.7	548	179.8	-12.2	3 052	291	171.1	D	1 248	99	179
Allen	20	28.3	73	1.4	228	66.3	-4.3	2 947	115	58.5	452	736	102	165
Ascension	78	131.4	584	11.7	572	276.9	26.2	4 718	296	264.2	493	1 172	82	261
Assumption	14	D	D	D	191	50.4	-2.7	2 200	84	43.8	D	691	D	D
Avoyelles	44	D	D	D	431	125.9	7.4	2 934	213	108.5	319	869	39	132
Beauregard	31	D	D	D	312	128.1	11.1	3 881	166	118.6	640	633	104	258
Bienville	18	110.1	79	1.3	143	42.7	6.0	2 527	65	37.2	75	912	43	120
Bossier	134	540.7	1 321	23.4	804	438.9	21.6	4 792	492	425.6	770	999	262	515
Caddo	625	1 821.7	7 036	142.4	2 429	1 613.4	16.1	5 940	1 613	1 572.0	836	1 086	310	491
Calcasieu	295	1 585.6	2 461	50.6	1 647	930.9	3.1	5 403	966	896.6	830	1 441	246	428
Caldwell	6	D	D	D	109	36.0	39.0	3 154	54	32.5	D	1 065	D	80
Cameron	23	D	D	D	84	23.6	-6.7	2 488	45	21.4	126	1 404	D	65
Catahoula	14	D	D	D	109	31.2	-8.2	2 492	57	27.2	209	611	D	51
Claiborne	22	D	D	D	159	54.2	8.6	2 927	95	50.5	D	928	67	144
Concordia	30	D	D	D	203	62.5	-18.9	2 741	123	58.5	303	589	110	261
De Soto	23	28.2	148	1.8	206	75.2	-11.9	2 745	114	69.9	395	769	82	119
East Baton Rouge	829	2 545.3	9 308	200.4	3 591	2 616.6	18.8	6 770	2 331	2 566.5	1 092	1 589	348	600
East Carroll	13	52.7	127	2.6	81	29.3	17.7	2 640	53	26.2	163	983	39	62
East Feliciana	11	13.3	103	1.4	116	31.6	15.3	1 551	57	27.7	65	464	D	46
Evangeline	31	37.8	198	2.8	356	104.2	-3.7	3 011	178	94.0	330	873	78	84
Franklin	29	89.8	187	3.9	194	89.0	-14.6	3 693	111	81.8	532	1 108	D	132
Grant	9	21.8	51	0.9	98	24.3	19.7	1 329	37	21.5	D	439	0	10
Iberia	132	195.1	1 030	20.2	688	321.9	-9.1	4 762	368	307.3	D	1 424	246	374
Iberville	28	76.4	389	5.8	289	116.6	-0.8	3 459	166	112.3	333	1 111	63	202
Jackson	10	8.4	42	0.7	163	58.3	34.3	3 276	89	55.1	D	1 266	107	126
Jefferson	1 314	D	D	D	4 518	3 486.3	18.3	7 360	2 844	3 405.1	993	1 636	397	723
Jefferson Davis	46	80.7	399	6.4	342	140.0	-1.7	4 269	191	134.8	452	988	107	344
Lafayette	513	1 226.5	4 953	104.4	1 823	1 186.2	-4.9	7 095	1 181	1 157.0	D	1 595	465	746
Lafourche	101	168.7	888	14.4	889	358.3	-3.5	4 171	461	341.6	501	1 407	97	224
La Salle	18	166.9	202	4.1	170	52.6	1.7	3 131	89	47.3	D	913	30	172
Lincoln	58	141.5	629	13.1	353	195.8	20.5	4 563	225	187.3	D	1 012	302	345
Livingston	54	47.8	253	3.9	508	194.9	25.3	2 677	236	182.5	D	873	D	120
Madison	14	31.7	138	1.5	122	51.8	51.9	3 432	79	50.4	197	1 080	42	438
Morehouse	27	59.4	228	4.3	278	127.2	16.1	3 523	147	116.8	D	672	110	159
Natchitoches	38	98.0	392	5.4	350	159.1	16.3	4 018	193	152.5	D	1 208	149	269
Orleans	793	4 180.7	10 501	239.8	4 264	2 674.1	10.1	4 932	2 920	2 611.6	452	1 015	347	744
Ouachita	333	1 101.1	3 959	74.3	1 601	935.2	36.3	6 454	1 012	901.3	920	1 304	393	592
Plaquemines	94	951.7	918	21.4	254	132.0	55.5	5 057	158	126.6	D	1 409	28	477
Pointe Coupee	20	32.8	164	2.0	207	66.7	-18.7	2 711	117	62.1	166	945	36	89
Rapides	228	425.8	2 277	39.0	1 292	775.8	25.1	5 557	832	746.2	1 010	1 112	345	404

1. For pay period including March 12. 2. Based on the estimated population as of July 1 of the year shown.

STATE County	Retail trade, establishments with payroll, 1987 (cont'd): Paid employees[1]	Retail trade, establishments with payroll, 1987 (cont'd): Annual payroll (Mil dol)	Taxable service industries–establishments with payroll, 1987: Number	Receipts (Mil dol): Total	Receipts, selected kinds of business: Hotels, motels and other lodging places	Receipts, selected kinds of business: Health services	Receipts, selected kinds of business: Legal services	Paid employees	Annual payroll (Mil dol)	Bank deposits,[2] June 1989: Total (Mil dol)	Bank deposits, June 1989: Percent change, 1988–1989	Savings capital,[3] September 1989: Total (Mil dol)	Savings capital, September 1989: Percent change, 1988–1989
	161	162	163	164	165	166	167	168	169	170	171	172	173
KENTUCKY—Con.													
Perry	1 774	16.5	118	28.3	2.2	11.7	3.8	671	10.3	180	9.7	75.6	3.1
Pike	4 227	37.0	274	76.3	3.8	35.5	10.7	1 745	26.5	710	4.5	3.6	29.1
Powell	310	2.9	22	3.6	D	2.1	D	121	1.2	54	5.7	3.5	13.0
Pulaski	3 409	31.5	256	77.1	2.5	49.1	2.6	1 892	26.0	366	10.8	86.0	-2.6
Robertson	21	0.1	3	0.1	0.0	D	D	2	0.0	12	-9.6	0.0	NA
Rockcastle	401	3.2	38	6.0	0.7	2.4	0.6	200	1.8	77	14.5	0.0	NA
Rowan	1 275	10.2	75	20.5	D	13.3	0.7	555	8.4	76	2.5	25.6	-2.5
Russell	583	5.1	41	7.7	D	3.3	0.6	226	2.2	86	4.7	22.9	1.5
Scott	1 148	8.8	113	23.2	2.3	11.2	0.8	710	7.5	178	16.7	15.3	-3.9
Shelby	1 383	11.5	85	30.5	0.8	13.9	1.1	784	10.5	250	11.3	22.4	-4.8
Simpson	980	8.3	50	10.6	D	4.0	1.1	376	3.5	121	6.0	33.1	4.0
Spencer	146	1.3	20	3.4	0.0	D	0.4	78	1.0	33	6.8	0.0	NA
Taylor	1 520	11.4	132	22.8	0.6	10.1	0.8	646	8.1	90	6.9	71.6	0.8
Todd	211	1.8	29	2.2	0.0	1.0	0.3	60	0.5	54	10.6	23.7	0.1
Trigg	336	2.5	29	4.4	D	1.8	0.7	125	1.2	84	2.7	16.4	-2.1
Trimble	59	0.4	10	1.8	0.0	1.5	0.2	82	0.6	54	8.8	0.0	NA
Union	745	6.6	62	38.3	0.0	8.3	1.0	1 221	16.5	156	2.9	3.6	1.9
Warren	7 116	62.8	468	221.1	12.2	134.4	12.3	5 547	83.1	463	8.1	213.9	1.3
Washington	278	1.8	28	5.1	D	2.5	0.4	148	1.2	95	-4.3	12.1	23.6
Wayne	528	4.2	53	10.6	D	2.6	0.6	294	3.4	108	8.6	12.5	-3.2
Webster	470	4.8	50	10.8	0.0	3.7	0.9	361	3.3	164	8.3	3.5	-1.9
Whitley	2 408	21.0	195	45.9	6.4	20.5	2.9	1 189	14.5	224	4.8	13.3	-18.7
Wolfe	137	1.2	9	1.4	0.0	D	D	38	0.5	13	5.9	0.0	NA
Woodford	1 053	8.4	84	15.5	0.0	2.8	2.2	339	5.0	176	7.5	0.0	NA
LOUISIANA	277 708	2 569.8	25 513	10 243.3	663.1	3 365.4	1 268.2	240 551	3 788.2	30 085	-0.3	12 887.7	-1.4
Acadia	2 256	18.9	205	43.5	D	16.0	5.0	1 530	14.8	326	0.2	194.3	-4.3
Allen	769	6.0	79	18.0	D	11.3	3.0	517	6.7	84	3.8	37.8	3.1
Ascension	2 936	27.2	229	74.6	2.2	28.1	4.8	1 981	26.0	286	-5.3	78.5	1.9
Assumption	551	4.9	43	8.9	0.0	3.5	1.4	251	2.7	100	4.4	16.6	16.4
Avoyelles	1 373	10.9	126	29.4	0.6	18.3	3.5	1 118	10.0	216	-4.2	44.0	27.6
Beauregard	1 374	12.3	102	18.8	1.0	9.9	1.5	791	6.6	163	3.7	41.0	-17.2
Bienville	368	3.3	32	6.3	D	3.3	1.1	231	2.0	100	5.8	0.0	NA
Bossier	5 647	50.9	408	147.7	11.6	38.7	3.5	3 387	46.5	467	-3.8	42.5	0.4
Caddo	18 772	179.1	1 882	740.8	19.1	312.3	66.9	19 210	286.4	2 524	-6.0	380.9	-2.5
Calcasieu	11 491	104.2	1 038	366.5	17.1	134.7	44.9	8 728	143.2	1 006	6.6	514.9	-6.4
Caldwell	264	2.7	29	13.3	0.0	10.3	1.7	307	4.9	56	6.7	14.7	12.6
Cameron	224	2.1	33	15.8	D	D	D	518	8.2	82	2.4	21.1	178.0
Catahoula	286	2.6	31	4.4	0.0	2.1	0.8	289	1.6	74	2.7	0.0	NA
Claiborne	614	4.9	58	6.9	D	2.6	0.6	178	1.8	137	-5.3	0.0	NA
Concordia	851	6.6	77	11.0	0.3	3.3	1.8	299	3.0	198	3.3	36.9	-3.7
De Soto	870	7.0	63	7.3	D	2.4	1.1	182	2.2	138	3.1	36.1	-5.2
East Baton Rouge	31 948	307.9	3 099	1 281.9	38.6	364.6	138.8	29 387	503.0	3 927	6.3	875.0	-4.5
East Carroll	334	2.8	30	5.7	D	3.4	0.8	249	2.5	59	13.6	9.4	-7.6
East Feliciana	266	2.1	38	12.4	D	5.3	0.6	282	4.8	98	-3.7	0.0	NA
Evangeline	1 151	9.5	127	31.6	D	20.9	4.1	850	11.1	212	-0.2	63.1	13.8
Franklin	839	8.0	58	12.4	D	7.3	1.3	462	5.0	119	-1.3	32.2	1.4
Grant	215	1.6	20	5.3	D	2.9	D	217	1.7	34	4.5	0.0	NA
Iberia	3 654	35.3	428	123.0	3.1	43.3	9.4	2 624	43.2	355	0.8	334.7	-1.7
Iberville	1 201	11.1	113	34.5	D	16.9	2.4	1 049	11.7	222	-2.8	24.3	-1.7
Jackson	665	5.7	49	8.7	D	3.1	1.8	280	3.0	68	0.0	63.1	3.4
Jefferson	44 169	414.1	3 623	1 756.9	64.7	600.3	97.2	40 011	632.2	1 699	-7.0	2 649.2	-1.2
Jefferson Davis	1 651	14.6	136	24.3	D	11.9	2.0	720	8.3	225	0.9	63.8	-6.8
Lafayette	16 116	145.8	1 750	695.5	D	201.4	106.7	13 552	261.1	1 258	-3.4	673.2	-4.1
Lafourche	3 933	37.1	378	87.6	2.9	35.6	8.9	2 202	34.4	683	3.3	221.9	-0.5
La Salle	563	4.4	55	8.8	0.0	3.1	0.8	617	3.5	112	1.2	6.2	24.8
Lincoln	2 507	21.1	191	49.7	2.7	23.4	3.7	1 290	15.2	306	-0.8	69.7	-2.7
Livingston	1 890	17.6	193	45.7	1.2	11.2	5.4	903	14.5	195	0.2	40.7	-0.6
Madison	720	6.1	49	14.1	D	3.5	0.9	429	5.3	73	5.0	5.3	-15.6
Morehouse	1 094	11.6	113	25.6	D	13.6	1.9	762	9.4	164	9.4	33.3	-5.3
Natchitoches	1 873	16.1	163	37.4	4.0	9.3	7.6	857	11.1	187	-1.2	89.3	-9.8
Orleans	40 794	394.4	3 920	2 318.1	400.1	511.2	546.3	53 756	887.3	6 170	-2.9	2 895.2	-0.2
Ouachita	11 912	104.4	973	380.9	13.3	143.6	29.8	8 202	140.3	1 166	7.7	394.3	-28.1
Plaquemines	1 226	13.0	150	73.5	D	7.6	2.0	1 688	27.2	142	10.9	11.5	-4.1
Pointe Coupee	662	6.0	58	9.1	0.0	3.9	1.2	269	2.9	176	-3.8	0.0	NA
Rapides	9 178	86.2	788	289.4	12.8	133.0	29.4	7 476	99.9	1 022	6.4	231.2	51.7

1. For the period including March 12 of the year shown. 2. Includes deposits for all insured and reporting noninsured commercial and mutual savings banks. 3. Includes savings capital for all FSLIC insured savings institutions.

STATE County	Federal funds and grants, 1989: Expenditures: Total (Mil dol)	Expenditures: Percent change, 1988–1989	Per capita[1] (Dollars): Total	Per capita: Direct payments for individuals	Per capita: Procurement contract awards	Per capita: Salaries and wages	Per capita: Grant awards	Local government finances, 1981–1982: General revenue: Total (Mil dol)	Intergovernmental: Total (Mil dol)	Intergovernmental: Percent from state	Taxes: Total (Mil dol)	Taxes: Per capita[2]: Total (Dollars)	Taxes: Per capita[2]: Property (Dollars)	Direct general expenditure: Total (Mil dol)	Direct general expenditure: Percent change, 1977–1982
	174	175	176	177	178	179	180	181	182	183	184	185	186	187	188
KENTUCKY—Con.															
Perry	90.0	10.7	2 661	1 911	120	189	431	17.5	13.2	96.7	2.4	70	47	16.2	31.8
Pike	202.5	2.4	2 577	1 829	263	165	314	42.8	31.9	89.9	6.4	78	45	42.1	86.5
Powell	23.4	3.5	1 903	1 363	13	93	418	5.9	4.8	91.3	0.6	53	43	6.0	50.9
Pulaski	115.9	6.1	2 439	1 738	35	148	471	25.0	18.5	87.0	4.0	84	46	21.5	58.8
Robertson	5.3	17.4	2 414	1 674	10	80	537	1.5	1.2	95.5	0.2	79	74	1.3	59.2
Rockcastle	35.2	-17.7	2 410	1 730	12	106	521	6.9	5.9	91.1	0.5	37	33	6.7	52.9
Rowan	41.5	11.1	2 185	1 610	23	154	388	8.7	6.2	90.3	1.7	88	55	8.6	69.5
Russell	41.3	-31.5	2 715	1 853	104	134	539	6.4	5.1	91.5	0.7	49	41	6.8	68.2
Scott	38.7	-3.7	1 683	1 325	13	93	198	13.2	6.9	92.8	3.1	144	89	12.0	29.8
Shelby	46.3	-2.4	1 832	1 375	66	102	203	12.0	8.3	83.6	2.6	109	90	11.6	88.6
Simpson	37.7	25.3	2 602	1 550	140	90	483	9.1	6.0	86.1	2.0	138	94	8.8	57.0
Spencer	13.5	5.4	2 011	1 351	100	121	251	3.3	2.5	95.9	0.5	91	68	3.2	88.0
Taylor	47.5	10.9	2 160	1 608	20	127	312	17.3	7.4	92.7	1.8	84	63	16.3	120.5
Todd	29.2	3.1	2 653	1 669	13	110	353	8.6	7.3	54.7	0.5	46	40	6.4	85.7
Trigg	33.9	3.3	3 529	2 447	14	574	277	5.9	4.5	85.9	0.8	86	68	5.3	27.2
Trimble	11.5	10.4	1 852	1 436	13	92	238	3.3	2.4	94.9	0.7	113	95	2.9	56.5
Union	88.8	123.3	5 320	1 649	3 074	127	175	10.8	6.8	91.7	2.8	158	110	8.8	63.7
Warren	160.6	1.2	2 010	1 494	35	192	242	46.8	23.5	85.6	15.2	190	77	45.3	65.8
Washington	21.9	8.5	2 088	1 506	14	141	330	5.5	3.8	93.4	1.0	98	59	4.8	40.5
Wayne	41.7	3.5	2 344	1 585	11	94	599	10.9	8.2	88.7	0.9	50	43	8.4	39.0
Webster	159.8	318.1	11 750	2 191	8 969	114	213	8.8	5.9	94.8	1.8	121	82	11.9	130.8
Whitley	102.7	5.6	2 909	2 283	23	178	408	23.5	14.7	79.9	2.5	73	50	19.4	73.2
Wolfe	21.0	7.5	3 138	1 978	69	203	857	4.1	3.8	89.4	0.1	19	17	3.4	18.6
Woodford	30.0	14.0	1 478	1 175	17	62	125	11.7	5.7	89.9	4.5	252	105	10.3	66.2
LOUISIANA	14 544.2	14.7	X	1 628	567	432	585	4 788.4	2 049.7	81.7	1 511.5	345	131	4 422.7	87.5
Acadia	148.6	22.2	2 593	1 509	195	83	483	47.7	25.0	87.7	12.5	213	90	43.2	43.9
Allen	83.3	16.3	3 703	1 756	569	492	586	19.9	12.4	88.9	3.6	163	84	19.0	66.7
Ascension	87.5	7.1	1 486	1 161	27	66	227	64.8	25.9	79.5	23.0	433	139	58.6	72.1
Assumption	42.5	10.0	1 899	1 384	10	58	440	21.8	11.8	89.6	5.4	230	108	22.5	170.6
Avoyelles	110.3	5.7	2 632	1 692	77	106	629	31.6	20.2	93.8	6.7	157	62	31.5	69.7
Beauregard	72.2	10.1	2 237	1 648	12	159	344	41.9	15.4	95.7	8.8	282	181	33.7	79.0
Bienville	47.5	15.1	2 861	2 014	194	111	509	17.1	10.0	91.4	4.5	276	189	16.8	36.1
Bossier	511.5	3.2	5 658	1 815	1 372	2 126	313	100.4	50.3	82.5	19.9	229	82	88.2	113.4
Caddo	797.4	19.3	2 980	1 690	505	304	447	281.4	131.0	69.9	97.9	375	180	245.8	91.1
Calcasieu	510.9	5.0	2 975	1 607	866	147	280	213.9	79.6	78.3	65.9	376	183	205.1	71.8
Caldwell	31.3	11.4	2 792	1 778	12	126	499	10.6	6.2	93.7	2.5	228	148	10.4	50.1
Cameron	20.7	-45.9	2 274	973	597	118	260	24.8	9.4	93.8	5.9	604	591	23.5	201.8
Catahoula	38.9	11.9	3 267	1 708	50	139	670	14.4	8.1	96.1	3.0	244	105	14.2	61.6
Claiborne	43.7	9.8	2 400	1 693	22	115	521	18.2	9.7	94.5	3.5	194	88	18.4	126.9
Concordia	66.0	13.9	2 986	1 584	481	130	551	22.2	12.9	87.9	4.3	182	66	20.8	52.6
De Soto	63.7	9.3	2 385	1 652	14	74	608	21.2	13.1	95.1	5.9	221	64	20.6	112.6
East Baton Rouge	1 213.5	10.2	3 179	1 352	313	221	1 279	410.4	168.6	77.2	147.6	384	116	389.5	87.7
East Carroll	44.2	17.1	4 127	1 646	-44	108	977	12.1	7.4	91.8	2.2	194	85	11.4	72.3
East Feliciana	42.6	11.7	2 090	1 480	9	66	505	11.9	8.4	93.6	2.4	119	34	10.7	85.5
Evangeline	105.4	14.0	3 108	1 912	10	73	777	26.9	18.7	88.8	5.3	156	76	25.1	53.0
Franklin	76.1	18.6	3 225	1 521	19	138	803	23.5	13.4	94.1	4.4	179	78	23.0	50.6
Grant	82.6	10.2	4 488	1 703	2 194	132	386	12.4	9.2	93.1	2.0	116	82	12.3	84.3
Iberia	134.0	9.9	2 040	1 556	38	91	344	82.5	40.3	86.7	22.0	321	101	80.2	99.3
Iberville	86.8	7.1	2 616	1 506	256	336	506	63.9	17.4	88.3	14.9	451	180	40.6	-8.2
Jackson	43.8	11.4	2 519	1 931	45	128	405	18.6	9.5	90.8	3.2	184	132	17.7	91.7
Jefferson	1 071.8	22.6	2 285	1 343	614	159	166	529.0	139.6	82.9	209.1	444	160	489.5	81.8
Jefferson Davis	84.6	12.9	2 635	1 541	22	80	411	31.3	15.9	88.7	10.6	323	152	29.7	111.5
Lafayette	296.6	14.7	1 824	1 233	43	217	312	160.1	63.5	81.2	59.6	361	88	166.9	131.6
Lafourche	144.2	12.9	1 710	1 294	105	77	229	96.9	40.5	94.8	23.5	268	154	90.8	93.7
La Salle	37.7	7.4	2 326	1 842	17	101	341	22.7	8.5	95.2	4.2	239	175	26.5	177.4
Lincoln	89.5	13.2	2 106	1 478	19	99	500	28.4	15.7	85.9	7.6	183	72	25.5	83.7
Livingston	97.9	6.6	1 336	1 084	7	56	186	46.5	26.4	95.7	11.1	172	60	43.8	122.7
Madison	46.9	25.7	3 254	1 541	168	106	772	14.4	10.0	84.0	3.5	220	113	14.6	83.0
Morehouse	109.1	20.6	3 092	1 680	12	79	583	40.5	16.4	87.3	7.6	215	128	39.6	113.2
Natchitoches	99.1	-3.6	2 567	1 764	88	179	360	44.7	21.7	91.4	9.2	228	89	41.8	90.5
Orleans	3 183.6	7.7	6 088	1 938	2 345	948	676	732.9	304.9	63.7	261.4	462	148	657.9	83.9
Ouachita	317.5	16.1	2 206	1 550	47	160	348	129.0	65.9	77.6	37.4	265	131	110.9	63.9
Plaquemines	115.7	17.2	4 469	1 281	1 723	1 232	227	65.4	22.0	94.9	16.0	600	238	48.4	100.2
Pointe Coupee	52.9	8.9	2 214	1 415	58	121	543	34.6	12.8	90.4	10.6	425	85	31.7	204.3
Rapides	497.1	-2.7	3 618	1 729	239	1 046	558	118.9	66.5	76.1	34.6	253	109	107.1	78.7

1. Based on the estimated population as of July 1 of the year shown. 2. Based on the estimated population as of July 1, 1982.

STATE County	Local government finances, 1981–1982 (cont'd) — Direct general expenditure (cont'd) — Per capita[1] (Dollars)	Percent of total for– Education	Health & hospitals	Police protection	Public welfare	Highways	Debt outstanding — Total (Mil dol)	Per capita[1] (Dollars)	State and local government employment, 1989 — Total	Rate[2]	Federal government civilian employment 1989 — Total	Earnings ($1,000)	Elections, 1988[3] — Total vote cast for president	Vote for lead party (Percent)
	189	190	191	192	193	194	195	196	197	198	199	200	201	202
KENTUCKY—Con.														
Perry	473	71.8	2.2	2.6	0.0	6.8	13.7	400	1 768	523.1	173	4 536	10 772	D–51.6
Pike	514	68.6	1.1	2.0	0.1	6.2	61.1	745	3 054	388.5	364	10 915	26 416	D–61.9
Powell	527	61.8	6.0	1.8	0.2	4.7	6.1	533	523	425.2	48	1 059	4 258	R–50.0
Pulaski	453	71.3	0.3	4.5	0.0	8.2	18.1	381	2 780	585.3	216	5 586	18 342	R–73.5
Robertson	547	73.7	2.1	0.4	0.0	9.1	0.0	11	124	563.6	NA	168	1 035	D–49.8
Rockcastle	480	71.3	6.1	0.8	0.0	8.3	5.1	362	568	389.0	34	749	4 948	R–78.4
Rowan	459	54.6	0.3	4.5	0.1	8.0	14.7	783	2 257	1 187.9	106	2 373	6 077	R–50.9
Russell	467	64.8	2.8	1.9	0.0	8.5	18.1	1 243	808	531.6	69	2 009	5 777	R–74.3
Scott	551	53.2	18.4	4.4	0.7	2.2	11.2	513	1 032	448.7	56	1 496	7 908	R–56.7
Shelby	490	62.0	1.9	2.0	0.4	4.7	19.0	801	977	386.2	76	2 081	8 871	R–56.3
Simpson	608	62.6	1.9	2.8	0.0	5.5	13.3	915	631	435.2	47	1 197	4 859	R–55.5
Spencer	540	65.0	4.0	1.7	3.9	9.1	5.0	848	243	362.7	31	728	2 505	R–54.6
Taylor	770	38.0	44.4	1.9	0.0	2.7	15.3	720	1 054	479.1	92	2 326	8 280	R–64.8
Todd	558	53.7	1.6	2.6	0.0	7.1	6.0	528	406	369.1	46	1 075	3 958	R–57.7
Trigg	561	69.9	4.8	2.2	0.0	7.6	4.1	434	533	555.2	216	5 951	4 434	R–54.7
Trimble	454	82.5	2.8	0.4	0.0	2.5	31.5	4 914	190	306.5	18	429	2 440	D–55.0
Union	496	56.7	5.2	5.0	0.1	6.2	9.7	546	575	344.3	58	1 683	5 628	D–58.9
Warren	564	45.1	7.9	5.9	0.7	4.6	293.0	3 653	5 292	662.3	411	12 533	26 484	R–63.1
Washington	458	68.6	3.2	2.8	0.1	8.8	1.9	181	419	399.0	44	990	4 454	R–54.9
Wayne	480	76.0	4.4	2.4	0.0	8.8	4.4	251	710	398.9	44	1 021	5 747	R–63.9
Webster	806	41.5	3.6	1.5	0.1	6.9	128.1	8 658	622	457.4	48	1 155	5 202	D–58.0
Whitley	571	54.5	4.7	1.7	0.2	6.5	37.5	1 102	1 368	387.5	190	5 998	11 188	R–65.6
Wolfe	505	75.0	4.6	1.0	0.0	8.5	0.9	130	313	467.2	37	956	2 480	D–61.1
Woodford	571	57.4	0.6	6.5	0.7	9.4	12.7	705	667	328.6	42	1 222	7 204	R–62.6
LOUISIANA	1 009	44.8	10.4	5.6	0.4	6.5	5 398.9	1 232	273 618	624.3	37 187	1 147 865	1 628 202	R–54.3
Acadia	736	52.7	12.7	5.7	0.3	9.4	35.1	599	2 790	486.9	143	4 035	23 110	D–49.8
Allen	873	55.8	11.4	5.7	0.0	8.7	6.4	293	1 264	561.8	394	12 088	8 989	D–57.9
Ascension	1 104	46.6	10.1	5.4	0.3	6.5	90.1	1 697	2 511	426.3	102	2 835	23 240	D–52.3
Assumption	958	60.5	12.4	4.1	0.4	8.5	16.4	697	951	424.6	34	868	9 995	D–56.1
Avoyelles	740	65.7	8.8	4.7	0.0	5.8	23.2	546	2 023	482.8	121	3 084	15 600	R–49.1
Beauregard	1 084	49.8	15.1	4.5	0.1	4.9	86.8	2 792	1 728	535.0	125	4 146	11 284	R–57.3
Bienville	1 026	61.9	9.0	3.7	0.2	10.5	12.5	761	741	446.4	55	1 404	7 537	D–49.2
Bossier	1 014	47.2	18.8	4.2	0.8	3.7	98.7	1 136	4 844	535.8	2 224	55 641	30 085	R–69.2
Caddo	943	47.1	1.9	5.9	0.0	11.3	289.4	1 110	15 539	580.7	2 700	88 326	94 402	R–57.7
Calcasieu	1 171	42.1	6.7	4.7	0.0	7.8	377.1	2 154	9 034	526.2	616	19 875	64 100	D–52.9
Caldwell	944	52.4	21.9	4.1	0.0	5.7	7.6	690	754	673.2	46	1 057	4 559	R–65.7
Cameron	2 400	50.1	8.0	6.5	0.5	22.0	10.7	1 095	817	897.8	32	879	4 070	D–55.5
Catahoula	1 141	53.6	23.8	3.5	0.0	7.6	3.9	318	680	571.4	70	1 704	4 950	R–57.8
Claiborne	1 013	43.4	17.4	3.9	0.1	9.0	9.6	527	1 322	726.4	45	1 170	7 007	R–53.6
Concordia	878	55.0	13.4	5.1	0.2	6.0	3.9	165	1 326	600.0	110	2 820	8 761	R–57.5
De Soto	768	65.0	2.3	4.2	0.3	7.7	5.4	199	1 110	415.7	56	1 461	10 516	D–51.0
East Baton Rouge	1 014	41.7	4.9	6.5	0.5	3.8	600.7	1 564	42 746	1 119.9	2 049	68 943	147 584	R–58.8
East Carroll	1 002	53.5	12.4	4.8	0.6	9.3	0.9	77	592	553.3	44	1 051	3 460	D–52.3
East Feliciana	541	71.1	4.9	3.3	0.0	7.2	9.3	467	2 664	1 305.9	37	929	7 349	D–49.8
Evangeline	735	61.9	3.9	5.6	1.3	9.2	7.8	229	1 787	527.1	75	1 944	15 400	D–50.0
Franklin	937	57.8	16.7	3.4	0.1	8.0	5.0	202	1 261	534.3	82	2 037	8 876	R–62.2
Grant	701	67.9	2.9	5.7	0.2	9.3	5.1	292	871	473.4	96	2 346	7 245	R–60.8
Iberia	1 173	44.0	15.6	4.3	0.2	13.3	59.2	865	3 645	554.8	136	4 102	28 331	R–54.5
Iberville	1 228	45.8	1.4	9.4	0.0	14.3	92.4	2 791	2 410	725.9	377	11 880	14 836	D–58.5
Jackson	1 037	51.6	22.6	4.6	0.0	7.4	8.7	510	905	520.1	49	1 189	7 249	R–58.6
Jefferson	1 040	37.8	19.0	7.3	0.0	6.1	605.3	1 286	19 519	416.2	1 676	57 111	166 370	R–66.7
Jefferson Davis	902	56.3	7.6	6.5	0.0	7.3	10.4	316	1 665	518.7	85	2 241	12 791	D–53.2
Lafayette	1 013	50.5	0.5	5.3	0.4	10.7	516.3	3 133	9 408	578.6	837	28 583	61 658	R–59.4
Lafourche	1 036	44.0	23.2	3.9	0.1	4.7	82.3	939	5 203	617.2	151	4 413	32 179	R–50.2
La Salle	1 521	47.7	33.1	2.5	0.1	5.8	15.0	859	981	605.6	44	1 137	6 359	R–71.7
Lincoln	611	50.9	2.7	5.7	0.6	9.0	25.2	604	5 357	1 260.5	109	2 994	14 657	R–60.4
Livingston	680	64.4	9.1	5.4	0.2	6.9	17.3	268	2 913	397.4	110	3 001	25 743	R–61.3
Madison	913	53.2	5.3	4.1	0.3	5.2	3.0	184	713	495.1	58	1 620	4 911	D–49.2
Morehouse	1 125	39.8	29.2	4.1	0.1	5.7	83.4	2 370	1 406	398.3	93	2 482	12 140	R–60.4
Natchitoches	1 034	51.6	20.3	4.9	0.3	5.2	33.1	818	3 286	851.3	211	5 318	13 733	R–52.6
Orleans	1 163	32.6	1.0	6.4	1.3	3.6	592.1	1 047	38 453	735.4	13 424	444 666	183 800	D–63.6
Ouachita	786	51.1	3.3	6.3	0.0	4.4	194.8	1 382	10 375	721.0	613	19 587	50 292	R–67.3
Plaquemines	1 812	29.0	6.2	4.2	0.0	23.9	5.7	214	2 778	1 072.6	988	32 246	10 293	R–59.1
Pointe Coupee	1 274	39.9	14.0	3.5	4.9	3.7	87.0	3 496	1 222	511.3	93	2 311	10 930	D–57.7
Rapides	782	52.8	1.2	5.5	0.2	5.7	133.3	974	9 619	700.1	2 956	86 481	48 891	R–61.3

1. Based on the estimated population as of July 1, 1982. 2. Per 10,000 resident population estimated as of July 1 of the year shown. 3. Data subject to copyright.

STATE–County code	MSA/ CMSA/ NECMA code[1]	STATE County	Land Area,[2] 1990 (Sq. Km.)	Population, 1990												
							Race						Age of population Percent		
				Total persons	Rank	Per square kilometer	White	Black	Am. Indian, Eskimo, Aleut	Asian & Pacific Islander	Other race	Hispanic[3]	Under 5 years	5 to 14 years	15 to 24 years
			1	2	3	4	5	6	7	8	9	10	11	12	13
		LOUISIANA—Con.													
22 081	...	Red River	1 006	9 387	2 441	9.3	5 752	3 589	18	6	22	61	8.4	18.2	13.8
22 083	...	Richland	1 447	20 629	1 648	14.3	13 020	7 539	15	13	42	199	7.7	18.0	14.1
22 085	...	Sabine	2 241	22 646	1 551	10.1	17 939	3 984	639	24	60	1 031	7.7	16.5	13.0
22 087	5560	St. Bernard	1 205	66 631	660	55.3	62 199	3 111	356	626	339	4 183	7.4	15.5	14.4
22 089	5560	St. Charles	735	42 437	948	57.7	31 638	10 253	113	177	256	1 070	9.2	18.1	13.2
22 091	...	St. Helena	1 058	9 874	2 399	9.3	4 725	5 127	12	2	8	46	8.8	17.9	15.0
22 093	...	St. James	638	20 879	1 634	32.7	10 484	10 357	5	19	14	107	8.7	18.6	15.3
22 095	5560	St. John the Baptist	567	39 996	998	70.5	25 039	14 419	100	158	280	954	9.6	20.0	13.7
22 097	...	St. Landry	2 405	80 331	569	33.4	47 532	32 392	68	174	165	639	8.4	18.5	14.4
22 099	3880	St. Martin	1 916	43 978	924	23.0	28 806	14 532	78	321	241	502	8.9	18.6	15.4
22 101	...	St. Mary	1 588	58 086	747	36.6	37 688	18 337	838	998	225	1 128	8.8	18.5	15.0
22 103	5560	St. Tammany	2 213	144 508	328	65.3	126 806	15 917	534	755	496	3 170	8.0	17.7	12.7
22 105	...	Tangipahoa	2 047	85 709	536	41.9	60 601	24 527	180	242	159	951	7.8	17.7	17.0
22 107	...	Tensas	1 561	7 103	2 645	4.6	3 292	3 785	12	4	10	43	8.0	18.8	13.4
22 109	3350	Terrebonne	3 251	96 982	474	29.8	75 082	16 032	4 905	692	271	1 376	8.7	18.8	15.3
22 111	...	Union	2 273	20 690	1 646	9.1	14 850	5 767	18	25	30	133	7.2	16.2	13.5
22 113	...	Vermilion	3 040	50 055	841	16.5	42 237	6 956	82	679	101	592	8.0	18.1	13.7
22 115	...	Vernon	3 441	61 961	703	18.0	45 828	12 867	445	1 502	1 319	3 405	10.6	15.0	25.4
22 117	...	Washington	1 734	43 185	935	24.9	29 669	13 376	59	53	28	239	7.0	16.9	13.9
22 119	...	Webster	1 543	41 989	956	27.2	28 550	13 277	79	52	31	229	7.1	15.8	13.2
22 121	0760	West Baton Rouge	495	19 419	1 709	39.2	12 329	6 993	37	25	35	206	8.1	17.4	15.1
22 123	...	West Carroll	931	12 093	2 209	13.0	9 997	2 020	35	6	35	115	7.2	17.0	13.5
22 125	...	West Feliciana	1 052	12 915	2 146	12.3	5 672	7 149	51	12	31	203	5.2	11.4	12.1
22 127	...	Winn	2 462	16 269	1 907	6.6	11 343	4 798	67	23	38	139	7.3	16.2	14.2
23 000	...	MAINE	79 939	1 227 928	X	15.4	1 208 360	5 138	5 998	6 683	1 749	6 829	7.0	14.1	14.2
23 001	4243	Androscoggin	1 218	105 259	438	86.4	103 687	485	233	557	297	780	7.4	14.3	15.0
23 003	...	Aroostook	17 280	86 936	525	5.0	84 601	932	793	405	205	554	7.0	14.4	14.6
23 005	6403	Cumberland	2 164	243 135	206	112.4	238 403	1 565	628	2 147	392	1 560	7.0	12.8	14.5
23 007	...	Franklin	4 398	29 008	1 329	6.6	28 785	30	86	81	26	110	6.9	15.0	16.2
23 009	...	Hancock	4 116	46 948	891	11.4	46 471	98	171	138	70	266	6.8	13.6	12.6
23 011	...	Kennebec	2 247	115 904	397	51.6	114 624	266	379	501	134	516	6.7	14.4	14.3
23 013	...	Knox	947	36 310	1 095	38.3	36 039	56	111	79	25	142	6.7	13.8	11.4
23 015	...	Lincoln	1 180	30 357	1 275	25.7	30 185	23	89	39	21	126	6.6	14.2	11.2
23 017	...	Oxford	5 383	52 602	806	9.8	52 267	67	98	136	34	206	7.2	14.9	11.9
23 019	0733	Penobscot	8 796	146 601	321	16.7	143 678	536	1 273	932	182	701	6.5	13.6	17.5
23 021	...	Piscataquis	10 273	18 653	1 756	1.8	18 493	20	75	58	7	69	6.1	15.5	12.0
23 023	...	Sagadahoc	658	33 535	1 175	51.0	32 783	336	78	249	89	337	8.1	14.5	13.0
23 025	...	Somerset	10 171	49 767	844	4.9	49 393	64	159	111	40	172	7.0	15.5	13.8
23 027	...	Waldo	1 890	33 018	1 188	17.5	32 797	39	82	74	26	170	7.1	15.5	12.8
23 029	...	Washington	6 653	35 308	1 120	5.3	33 734	66	1 414	81	13	127	6.4	15.1	13.1
23 031	...	York	2 567	164 587	291	64.1	162 420	555	329	1 095	188	993	7.4	14.6	12.9
24 000	...	MARYLAND	25 316	4 781 468	X	188.9	3 393 964	1 189 899	12 972	139 719	44 914	125 102	7.5	13.2	14.2
24 001	1900	Allegany	1 102	74 946	600	68.0	72 955	1 535	59	321	76	319	5.8	12.2	15.7
24 003	0720	Anne Arundel	1 077	427 239	117	396.7	365 953	50 525	1 292	7 675	1 794	6 815	7.4	13.3	14.8
24 005	0720	Baltimore	1 550	692 134	60	446.5	587 898	85 451	1 468	15 544	1 773	8 131	6.8	11.7	13.2
24 009	8840	Calvert	557	51 372	822	92.2	42 825	8 046	127	292	82	502	7.9	16.1	13.0
24 011	...	Caroline	829	27 035	1 388	32.6	22 355	4 459	58	79	84	231	7.6	14.6	12.9
24 013	0720	Carroll	1 163	123 372	373	106.1	119 336	2 933	192	747	164	903	7.8	14.7	13.4
24 015	6162	Cecil	902	71 347	621	79.1	67 450	3 240	150	310	197	635	7.9	14.9	14.7
24 017	8840	Charles	1 194	101 154	453	84.7	80 234	18 419	761	1 338	402	1 705	8.5	16.3	15.2
24 019	...	Dorchester	1 444	30 236	1 282	20.9	21 548	8 423	51	138	76	177	6.7	12.8	12.0
24 021	8840	Frederick	1 717	150 208	311	87.5	139 909	8 010	284	1 510	495	1 713	7.9	14.6	14.3
24 023	...	Garrett	1 679	28 138	1 347	16.8	27 963	105	22	40	8	110	6.9	15.4	14.1
24 025	0720	Harford	1 141	182 132	265	159.6	162 559	15 530	490	2 503	1 050	2 821	8.1	14.7	14.1
24 027	0720	Howard	653	187 328	258	286.9	155 899	22 019	402	8 098	910	3 699	8.1	14.0	12.7
24 029	...	Kent	724	17 842	1 796	24.6	14 085	3 534	29	68	126	467	6.2	11.7	15.5
24 031	8840	Montgomery	1 281	757 027	51	591.0	580 635	92 267	1 841	61 981	20 303	55 684	7.5	12.5	12.4
24 033	8840	Prince George's	1 260	729 268	54	578.8	314 616	369 791	2 339	28 255	14 267	29 983	7.6	13.1	16.7
24 035	0720	Queen Anne's	964	33 953	1 162	35.2	29 911	3 839	45	125	33	189	7.3	13.9	11.3
24 037	...	St. Mary's	936	75 974	592	81.2	64 129	10 275	268	928	374	1 230	8.9	15.3	16.0
24 039	...	Somerset	848	23 440	1 518	27.6	14 282	8 943	47	96	72	229	5.3	11.5	17.0
24 041	...	Talbot	697	30 549	1 263	43.8	24 833	5 502	42	102	70	167	6.3	11.8	10.4
24 043	3180	Washington	1 187	121 393	379	102.3	112 828	7 245	241	793	286	905	6.7	12.4	14.2
24 045	...	Wicomico	977	74 339	605	76.1	56 755	16 573	137	671	203	610	7.0	13.6	15.9

1. MSA = Metropolitan Statistical Area. CMSA = Consolidated MSA. NECMA = New England county metropolitan area. PMSA = Primary MSA. See Appendix A for explanation of these concepts. See Appendix B for list of metropolitan areas identified by type, with component counties. 2. Dry land or land partially or temporarily covered by water. 3. Hispanic persons may be of any race.

STATE County	Population, 1990 (cont'd): Age of population (cont'd) Percent: 25 to 34 years	35 to 44 years	45 to 54 years	55 to 64 years	65 to 74 years	75 years and over	Percent female	Population–Change and components of change: Change 1980–1990: Number	Percent	Components of change, 1980–1986: Total persons, 1986	Total persons, 1980	Net change: Number	Percent	Natural increase: Births	Deaths
	14	15	16	17	18	19	20	21	22	23	24	25	26	27	28
LOUISIANA—Con.															
Red River	14.3	11.8	9.3	8.7	8.7	6.8	52.7	-1 046	-10.0	10 900	10 433	500	4.3	1 200	800
Richland	14.5	12.1	9.1	8.9	8.3	7.3	53.1	-1 558	-7.0	23 400	22 187	1 200	5.2	2 600	1 500
Sabine	13.5	12.1	10.3	10.4	9.7	6.8	51.4	-2 634	-10.4	27 400	25 280	2 100	8.4	2 500	1 600
St. Bernard	16.8	14.9	9.9	9.7	7.5	3.8	52.0	2 534	4.0	68 700	64 097	4 600	7.2	6 900	3 300
St. Charles	19.3	15.6	9.5	7.7	4.6	2.8	51.1	5 178	13.9	43 500	37 259	6 200	16.7	5 300	1 500
St. Helena	14.8	13.2	9.5	8.5	6.5	5.7	52.1	47	0.5	10 300	9 827	500	5.1	1 000	500
St. James	16.8	13.6	9.4	7.8	5.6	4.2	52.1	-616	-2.9	22 400	21 495	900	4.3	2 900	1 100
St. John the Baptist	19.2	15.4	9.0	6.0	4.2	2.9	51.1	8 072	25.3	41 300	31 924	9 300	29.3	5 500	1 400
St. Landry	14.9	12.7	9.7	9.0	7.0	5.3	52.4	-3 797	-4.5	88 400	84 128	4 300	5.1	11 000	5 200
St. Martin	17.0	13.7	9.6	7.3	5.7	3.6	51.4	3 764	9.4	46 100	40 214	5 900	14.6	5 700	2 000
St. Mary	17.1	13.4	9.9	7.7	5.6	3.9	51.2	-6 167	-9.6	64 300	64 253	100	0.1	8 700	3 000
St. Tammany	16.3	17.7	11.0	7.8	5.7	3.2	50.7	33 639	30.3	147 200	110 869	36 300	32.8	14 200	5 200
Tangipahoa	15.3	14.0	9.3	7.9	6.3	4.8	52.2	5 011	6.2	92 100	80 698	11 400	14.2	11 100	4 800
Tensas	13.3	12.8	8.2	8.7	9.3	7.6	54.4	-1 422	-16.7	8 400	8 525	-100	-0.9	1 000	700
Terrebonne	17.4	14.2	9.9	7.5	5.2	3.2	51.0	2 589	2.7	101 600	94 393	7 200	7.6	14 000	4 000
Union	13.8	13.4	10.5	9.7	8.8	6.7	52.0	-477	-2.3	23 100	21 167	2 000	9.2	2 100	1 500
Vermilion	16.0	13.0	9.4	8.6	7.3	5.8	51.5	1 597	3.3	53 500	48 458	5 100	10.4	6 300	2 700
Vernon	20.3	11.4	6.5	5.1	3.5	2.4	45.0	8 486	15.9	60 400	53 475	7 000	13.0	9 300	2 000
Washington	14.9	13.7	10.0	9.3	8.5	5.9	51.7	-1 022	-2.3	47 700	44 207	3 500	7.8	5 000	3 100
Webster	14.4	13.0	10.4	10.0	9.1	7.1	52.7	-1 642	-3.8	46 100	43 631	2 400	5.5	4 500	3 200
West Baton Rouge	17.8	14.4	10.3	7.8	5.7	3.5	51.5	333	1.7	21 200	19 086	2 100	11.0	2 700	900
West Carroll	13.6	12.8	10.7	9.4	8.8	7.1	52.2	-829	-6.4	13 100	12 922	200	1.4	1 400	900
West Feliciana	26.9	22.1	9.3	6.2	4.0	2.9	32.1	729	6.0	13 500	12 186	1 400	11.1	1 000	400
Winn	14.6	13.3	10.1	9.1	8.7	6.5	50.5	-984	-5.7	17 100	17 253	-100	-0.8	1 700	1 300
MAINE	16.7	15.7	10.2	8.8	7.5	5.8	51.3	102 928	9.1	1 173 000	1 125 000	49 000	4.3	104 000	68 000
Androscoggin	17.0	14.5	9.8	8.6	7.4	6.0	51.6	5 750	5.8	101 100	99 509	1 600	1.6	9 300	6 100
Aroostook	17.0	15.2	9.9	9.2	7.3	5.5	49.5	-4 408	-4.8	87 900	91 344	-3 400	-3.8	8 400	4 800
Cumberland	18.2	16.3	9.9	8.3	7.2	5.8	51.9	27 346	12.7	228 100	215 789	12 300	5.7	20 300	13 200
Franklin	15.2	14.9	10.6	8.8	6.8	5.5	51.8	1 561	5.7	29 100	27 447	1 700	6.0	2 500	1 500
Hancock	15.7	16.0	10.4	9.6	8.2	7.1	51.0	5 167	12.4	44 000	41 781	2 300	5.4	3 900	2 900
Kennebec	15.9	16.0	10.4	8.9	7.5	5.9	51.8	6 015	5.5	112 000	109 889	2 100	1.9	9 800	6 600
Knox	14.6	16.6	10.3	9.6	9.4	7.6	51.5	3 369	10.2	35 100	32 941	2 200	6.6	3 000	2 300
Lincoln	14.1	16.3	10.9	10.2	9.2	7.3	51.3	4 666	18.2	28 300	25 691	2 600	10.3	2 400	1 900
Oxford	15.9	15.0	10.4	9.6	8.5	6.5	51.3	3 559	7.3	50 200	49 043	1 200	2.4	4 200	3 400
Penobscot	16.6	15.2	10.1	8.8	6.5	5.0	51.1	9 586	7.0	138 200	137 015	1 200	0.9	12 100	7 100
Piscataquis	14.0	15.4	10.9	10.0	9.0	7.1	51.2	1 019	5.8	18 000	17 634	400	2.1	1 600	1 200
Sagadahoc	18.8	16.6	10.5	7.3	6.2	4.9	50.6	4 740	16.5	31 700	28 795	2 900	10.2	3 300	1 600
Somerset	15.7	15.3	10.6	9.1	7.3	5.7	51.1	4 718	10.5	47 100	45 049	2 000	4.5	4 300	2 900
Waldo	15.0	16.8	10.4	9.3	7.5	5.6	50.9	4 604	16.2	30 100	28 414	1 700	6.0	2 800	1 800
Washington	14.4	14.3	10.4	10.1	9.0	7.2	51.0	345	1.0	33 900	34 963	-1 000	-3.0	3 100	2 400
York	17.6	16.4	10.0	8.5	7.2	5.4	51.3	24 848	17.8	158 800	139 739	19 000	13.6	13 300	8 200
MARYLAND	18.8	16.3	10.9	8.3	6.6	4.2	51.5	564 468	13.4	4 463 000	4 217 000	246 000	5.8	401 000	219 000
Allegany	13.0	13.1	10.7	11.0	10.6	8.0	52.9	-5 602	-7.0	74 500	80 548	-6 100	-7.5	5 800	6 100
Anne Arundel	18.7	16.8	11.9	8.2	5.7	3.1	49.7	56 464	15.2	406 000	370 775	35 300	9.5	36 000	15 300
Baltimore	18.0	15.8	10.7	9.8	8.6	5.4	52.3	36 519	5.6	670 300	655 615	14 700	2.2	52 100	35 300
Calvert	17.4	18.0	11.4	7.2	5.6	3.3	50.4	16 734	48.3	43 700	34 638	9 000	26.1	3 800	1 600
Caroline	16.1	14.6	10.5	9.2	8.3	6.1	51.5	3 892	16.8	24 000	23 143	900	3.8	2 200	1 600
Carroll	17.2	17.4	11.7	7.6	5.8	4.4	50.8	27 016	28.0	111 600	96 356	15 300	15.9	9 200	4 600
Cecil	16.7	16.2	10.9	8.5	6.5	3.8	50.1	10 917	18.1	67 500	60 430	7 100	11.7	5 500	2 900
Charles	19.2	16.7	11.3	6.3	4.1	2.4	50.3	28 403	39.0	89 000	72 751	16 200	22.3	8 200	2 700
Dorchester	15.6	14.1	10.8	10.8	10.1	7.2	52.6	-387	-1.3	29 900	30 623	-700	-2.3	2 400	2 400
Frederick	18.3	17.4	10.7	7.3	5.6	3.8	50.8	35 416	30.9	131 500	114 792	16 700	14.5	11 800	5 500
Garrett	15.7	14.1	10.8	9.2	8.0	5.8	51.2	1 648	6.2	26 500	26 490	0	-0.1	2 500	1 500
Harford	18.7	16.9	11.5	7.8	5.4	2.9	50.1	36 202	24.8	158 400	145 930	12 400	8.5	13 300	6 000
Howard	20.9	19.3	12.3	6.5	3.8	2.3	50.2	68 756	58.0	151 200	118 572	32 700	27.6	12 200	3 900
Kent	14.5	13.2	11.1	10.9	10.2	6.7	51.6	1 147	6.9	16 900	16 695	200	1.4	1 300	1 300
Montgomery	19.7	17.7	11.7	8.2	6.1	4.1	51.8	177 974	30.7	665 200	579 053	86 200	14.9	52 300	24 500
Prince George's	20.7	16.6	11.1	7.2	4.5	2.4	51.5	64 197	9.7	681 400	665 071	16 300	2.4	68 100	23 400
Queen Anne's	16.8	16.1	11.7	10.1	8.1	4.7	50.6	8 445	33.1	29 600	25 508	4 100	16.1	2 300	1 500
St. Mary's	20.3	14.9	9.7	6.5	5.1	3.2	49.1	16 079	26.8	67 300	59 895	7 400	12.4	7 000	2 300
Somerset	18.3	13.6	9.4	9.9	8.6	6.3	47.0	4 252	22.2	19 300	19 188	200	0.8	1 600	1 500
Talbot	14.8	14.2	11.1	11.3	11.7	8.4	52.6	4 945	19.3	27 200	25 604	1 600	6.1	2 100	2 200
Washington	17.8	15.0	10.6	9.5	8.1	5.7	49.5	8 307	7.3	114 100	113 086	1 000	0.9	8 900	6 600
Wicomico	16.5	15.1	10.2	8.8	7.6	5.3	52.1	9 799	15.2	69 300	64 540	4 700	7.3	5 900	4 300

STATE County	Population—(cont'd) Components of change, 1980-1986 (cont'd) Net migration	Households, 1990 Number	Households, 1990 Percent change, 1980–1990	Households, 1990 Persons per household	Households, 1990 Percent Female family householder[1]	Households, 1990 Percent One-person	Births, 1988 Total	Births, 1988 Rate[2]	Births, 1988 Low birth weight[3] (Number)	Deaths, 1987 Number Total	Deaths, 1987 Number Infant[4]	Deaths, 1987 Rate Total[2]	Deaths, 1987 Rate Infant[5]	Marriages, 1984 Number	Marriages, 1984 Rate[2]
	29	30	31	32	33	34	35	36	37	38	39	40	41	42	43
LOUISIANA—Con.															
Red River	0	3 321	-5.5	2.77	16.6	23.6	158	14.5	13	113	4	10.4	25.3	97	8.9
Richland	100	7 079	-2.0	2.84	16.8	22.2	357	15.7	23	262	5	11.4	13.6	204	8.9
Sabine	1 200	8 361	-6.2	2.64	12.0	24.1	353	13.0	21	268	3	9.8	8.3	186	6.9
St. Bernard	1 100	23 156	12.5	2.85	13.1	18.3	1 000	14.6	79	548	10	8.0	9.8	941	14.0
St. Charles	2 400	14 333	24.8	2.94	12.6	17.6	833	19.1	63	278	10	6.4	12.6	376	9.0
St. Helena	0	3 328	8.3	2.94	16.1	22.9	130	12.7	6	112	3	10.8	21.0	115	11.3
St. James	-900	6 432	6.4	3.22	18.2	15.6	386	17.5	32	156	4	7.1	9.1	201	9.1
St. John the Baptist	5 200	12 710	36.6	3.13	15.1	16.2	828	20.1	77	238	8	5.8	9.3	300	7.5
St. Landry	-1 500	27 477	2.4	2.88	16.5	21.8	1 514	17.7	144	806	20	9.3	12.7	803	9.1
St. Martin	2 100	14 634	20.2	2.98	14.7	18.4	808	18.0	79	315	7	7.0	8.5	347	7.6
St. Mary	-5 600	19 456	-2.9	2.95	15.4	20.5	1 074	17.9	78	442	11	7.2	9.5	701	10.8
St. Tammany	27 400	50 346	41.0	2.84	10.4	18.5	2 320	15.4	169	924	25	6.2	10.8	1 337	9.9
Tangipahoa	5 100	29 663	14.3	2.79	16.4	23.1	1 540	17.0	141	776	24	8.5	16.0	791	8.8
Tensas	-400	2 515	-14.4	2.77	20.6	25.2	136	16.8	14	110	2	13.4	16.4	34	4.1
Terrebonne	-2 700	31 837	8.7	3.02	12.8	17.4	1 796	18.3	151	630	22	6.4	11.9	1 047	10.3
Union	1 400	7 528	4.1	2.71	12.9	21.4	299	13.2	28	228	9	10.0	27.2	48	2.2
Vermilion	1 500	17 762	9.8	2.79	12.4	21.8	821	15.7	65	449	9	8.5	10.1	515	9.8
Vernon	-400	19 111	23.6	2.87	8.1	17.4	1 575	26.2	105	357	16	5.9	10.6	717	11.8
Washington	1 700	15 475	0.5	2.70	16.5	23.9	619	13.1	53	475	10	10.0	15.6	491	10.5
Webster	1 100	15 849	1.0	2.60	15.0	25.2	680	15.0	56	544	7	11.9	10.9	329	7.2
West Baton Rouge	300	6 606	13.9	2.91	17.3	19.1	356	17.2	38	152	2	7.4	5.3	196	9.7
West Carroll	-400	4 394	-2.3	2.72	10.2	23.8	188	14.6	11	163	3	12.6	18.5	117	8.9
West Feliciana	800	2 741	18.5	2.87	17.9	22.4	137	10.1	11	60	2	4.5	13.2	87	6.4
Winn	-600	5 787	-4.5	2.69	13.8	24.6	220	13.0	20	166	4	9.7	15.6	147	8.4
MAINE	13 000	465 312	17.7	2.56	9.5	23.3	17 172	14.2	832	11 282	139	9.5	8.3	12 525	10.8
Androscoggin	-1 600	40 017	13.6	2.55	10.9	24.4	1 564	15.1	90	1 035	13	10.2	8.6	1 019	10.1
Aroostook	-7 100	31 366	6.9	2.62	8.6	21.7	1 209	14.1	68	767	8	8.8	6.2	872	9.8
Cumberland	5 200	94 512	20.1	2.49	9.8	25.2	3 534	15.0	169	2 108	29	9.1	8.2	2 476	11.1
Franklin	700	10 778	14.4	2.60	9.0	22.3	393	13.4	18	223	2	7.8	5.1	298	10.3
Hancock	1 300	18 342	18.8	2.48	8.2	24.0	634	13.8	30	505	4	11.2	6.3	608	13.9
Kennebec	-1 100	43 889	13.8	2.55	9.9	24.2	1 430	12.3	56	1 077	8	9.5	5.2	1 147	10.3
Knox	1 500	14 344	17.9	2.45	9.2	26.0	503	14.1	20	401	4	11.4	8.3	461	13.4
Lincoln	2 100	11 968	26.1	2.52	7.5	23.6	408	13.8	16	307	3	10.7	7.8	284	10.3
Oxford	300	20 064	15.0	2.58	9.8	22.4	715	13.9	33	577	5	11.4	7.2	555	11.1
Penobscot	-3 700	54 063	17.6	2.57	9.9	22.6	1 920	13.6	103	1 227	16	8.8	8.7	1 386	10.0
Piscataquis	0	7 194	14.4	2.56	8.3	23.3	214	11.6	7	225	3	12.4	14.1	187	10.4
Sagadahoc	1 200	12 581	25.4	2.63	9.3	21.6	535	16.2	19	295	7	9.2	13.3	328	11.0
Somerset	600	18 513	20.6	2.65	10.0	21.2	636	13.3	40	436	2	9.3	3.3	537	11.5
Waldo	700	12 415	26.3	2.63	9.3	21.7	465	14.9	23	286	6	9.3	14.3	335	11.4
Washington	-1 700	13 418	9.8	2.55	10.0	23.6	470	13.5	23	425	4	12.3	9.0	351	10.3
York	14 000	61 848	24.6	2.63	8.9	21.4	2 542	15.3	117	1 388	25	8.6	10.7	1 680	11.2
MARYLAND	65 000	1 748 991	19.7	2.67	13.3	22.6	75 768	16.4	6 136	38 034	831	8.4	11.5	47 193	10.9
Allegany	-5 800	29 634	-0.1	2.43	11.0	27.7	901	12.0	53	1 021	7	13.5	8.3	1 087	14.1
Anne Arundel	14 500	149 114	23.2	2.76	10.0	18.2	6 605	15.8	423	2 733	45	6.6	7.1	4 063	10.4
Baltimore	-2 100	268 280	13.0	2.53	11.1	23.4	9 635	14.0	659	6 145	89	9.0	9.7	6 069	9.0
Calvert	6 900	16 986	58.3	3.01	9.4	14.2	761	15.9	51	285	6	6.3	8.3	294	7.5
Caroline	300	9 983	21.5	2.66	11.6	21.7	397	15.7	31	273	4	11.1	11.4	313	13.3
Carroll	10 600	42 248	37.9	2.85	7.7	16.0	1 849	15.6	84	917	20	8.0	11.1	1 078	10.3
Cecil	4 500	24 725	27.7	2.81	10.2	17.9	1 103	15.4	64	542	6	7.8	5.5	3 321	51.1
Charles	10 700	32 950	54.1	3.03	11.9	14.2	1 526	16.1	105	546	17	6.0	10.9	769	9.4
Dorchester	-700	12 117	7.0	2.46	14.7	25.8	425	14.0	43	397	3	13.1	7.6	267	8.8
Frederick	10 400	52 570	40.2	2.78	8.7	18.0	2 209	15.8	128	940	13	6.9	5.9	1 207	9.7
Garrett	-1 100	10 110	15.4	2.74	8.8	20.4	364	13.5	23	250	3	9.4	8.1	850	31.8
Harford	5 100	63 193	35.8	2.83	9.2	16.9	2 734	16.0	168	1 017	25	6.2	10.3	1 597	10.6
Howard	24 300	68 337	70.9	2.71	8.4	19.2	2 939	18.0	160	733	16	4.7	6.1	1 449	10.7
Kent	200	6 702	9.3	2.49	10.7	24.8	243	14.3	10	202	3	11.9	15.4	193	11.6
Montgomery	58 300	282 228	36.2	2.65	9.4	22.3	12 337	17.5	809	4 489	104	6.6	9.0	7 100	11.4
Prince George's	-28 400	258 011	14.8	2.76	16.3	21.6	12 715	18.1	1 213	4 326	143	6.3	12.0	6 396	9.5
Queen Anne's	3 300	12 489	41.1	2.69	8.5	17.8	468	14.6	32	274	2	8.9	4.6	191	6.8
St. Mary's	2 700	25 500	35.7	2.87	9.1	18.1	1 283	18.3	83	460	20	6.8	15.7	579	9.1
Somerset	0	7 977	18.2	2.48	14.8	25.7	265	13.7	25	265	0	13.7	0.0	185	9.7
Talbot	1 700	12 677	27.6	2.38	9.9	25.3	373	13.3	31	371	4	13.5	11.8	336	12.4
Washington	-1 300	44 762	12.0	2.53	9.7	23.6	1 547	13.1	122	1 073	18	9.2	11.8	1 831	16.2
Wicomico	3 100	27 772	21.4	2.56	13.2	23.5	1 038	14.4	89	698	15	9.9	15.4	821	12.2

1. No spouse present. 2. Per 1,000 resident population estimated as of July 1 of the year shown. 3. Under 2,500 grams. 4. Deaths of infants under 1 year old. 5. Deaths of infants under 1 year old per 1,000 live births.

STATE County	Divorces, 1984		Physicians, active non–Federal, 1989		Hospitals, 1989			Nursing homes,[4] 1986		Serious crimes known to police, 1988			Education			
						Beds				Number			Public school enrollment[7]		Attainment,[8] 1980	
	Number	Rate[1]	Number[2]	Rate[3]	Number	Number	Rate[3]	Number	Beds	Total[5]	Violent[6]	Rate[3]	1986–1987	1980	Percent 12 yrs. or more	Percent 16 yrs. or more
	44	45	46	47	48	49	50	51	52	53	54	55	56	57	58	59
LOUISIANA—Con.																
Red River	34	3.1	6	56	1	74	685	2	157	19	9	176	1 923	2 112	41.7	6.8
Richland	107	4.7	20	89	2	116	516	4	431	NA	NA	NA	4 985	4 594	42.3	7.6
Sabine	58	2.1	13	48	1	63	233	3	280	NA	NA	NA	4 981	5 225	48.9	7.1
St. Bernard	374	5.6	48	70	2	232	339	5	326	NA	NA	NA	9 627	10 918	57.6	5.7
St. Charles	141	3.4	20	45	1	50	113	0	0	2 194	655	5 067	8 286	8 106	58.9	10.3
St. Helena	13	1.3	2	20	1	35	343	1	17	NA	NA	NA	2 173	2 353	44.9	8.6
St. James	25	1.1	11	50	2	64	291	1	74	157	37	720	4 434	4 856	51.1	8.2
St. John the Baptist	NA	NA	19	46	1	102	246	1	152	677	66	1 646	6 349	5 293	57.7	9.8
St. Landry	NA	NA	100	118	4	351	414	4	569	1 203	118	1 623	18 106	18 555	41.1	8.3
St. Martin	138	3.0	13	29	1	30	67	3	390	650	90	1 727	9 185	9 435	39.3	6.7
St. Mary	299	4.6	44	75	2	107	183	3	338	2 125	245	4 099	12 773	13 699	50.0	9.2
St. Tammany	NA	NA	264	172	9	1 046	680	5	778	4 177	363	4 087	25 665	23 007	67.8	20.0
Tangipahoa	NA	NA	95	105	5	394	437	7	944	735	43	8 098	17 647	15 319	50.9	11.9
Tensas	24	2.9	3	38	0	0	0	1	59	23	6	283	1 691	1 822	42.3	9.1
Terrebonne	765	7.6	110	114	3	489	505	4	627	4 171	656	4 261	21 302	20 632	52.6	9.8
Union	63	2.8	9	40	2	60	265	4	456	185	57	4 684	4 517	4 199	45.8	8.0
Vermilion	159	3.0	41	79	2	123	237	4	428	214	24	546	9 764	9 945	43.6	8.0
Vernon	122	2.0	24	40	2	205	341	2	182	1 791	290	3 018	12 412	9 964	63.2	8.4
Washington	214	4.6	44	93	3	220	467	2	325	1 483	174	3 138	9 672	9 185	49.3	8.6
Webster	164	3.6	24	53	2	194	428	4	473	515	105	1 140	8 911	8 673	50.9	8.9
West Baton Rouge	99	4.9	4	19	0	0	0	1	125	484	130	3 389	3 793	4 104	50.4	6.7
West Carroll	50	3.8	4	31	1	52	406	1	106	NA	NA	NA	2 878	2 966	42.3	8.6
West Feliciana	26	1.9	12	89	1	23	170	1	128	NA	NA	NA	1 878	1 774	45.8	9.0
Winn	62	3.6	10	60	1	73	435	2	202	50	11	672	3 712	3 583	48.5	8.1
MAINE	5 809	5.0	2 147	176	46	6 014	492	367	11 860	43 149	1 896	3 578	207 838	232 141	68.7	14.4
Androscoggin	611	6.1	191	183	3	547	524	34	1 416	5 008	195	4 876	17 151	19 857	58.5	10.5
Aroostook	351	3.9	114	134	4	358	420	32	1 130	1 640	100	1 868	17 936	21 493	61.7	11.0
Cumberland	1 097	4.9	710	297	10	1 612	674	49	2 138	14 517	821	6 128	34 545	41 498	75.0	19.0
Franklin	133	4.6	32	109	1	70	239	8	203	835	16	2 874	5 344	6 102	70.3	14.0
Hancock	259	5.9	84	180	3	129	277	9	492	1 214	50	2 667	7 697	8 115	73.6	16.8
Kennebec	609	5.4	240	204	5	1 270	1 078	52	1 374	3 508	111	3 037	18 220	22 670	68.2	15.0
Knox	215	6.3	72	198	1	144	397	23	513	992	29	2 774	5 736	6 572	71.5	15.4
Lincoln	114	4.1	42	140	2	120	399	11	242	500	25	1 709	6 269	5 114	75.2	20.3
Oxford	212	4.2	55	106	2	113	217	16	625	1 000	45	1 945	10 457	10 621	67.9	10.8
Penobscot	709	5.1	285	199	5	880	616	49	1 189	4 756	128	3 356	22 743	27 831	71.9	14.2
Piscataquis	92	5.1	23	123	1	52	278	5	171	312	5	1 678	3 569	3 900	65.4	8.3
Sagadahoc	150	5.1	39	115	1	55	162	7	228	1 024	25	3 160	7 209	6 251	69.4	15.1
Somerset	237	5.1	36	75	2	96	199	18	541	1 311	49	2 751	12 380	10 549	63.8	9.1
Waldo	158	5.4	33	103	1	49	154	11	128	429	23	1 375	5 149	6 468	67.2	13.9
Washington	172	5.0	25	71	2	115	327	13	387	751	71	2 155	6 271	6 987	61.4	10.3
York	690	4.6	166	98	3	404	237	30	1 083	5 352	203	3 230	28 397	28 113	67.9	14.4
MARYLAND	16 134	3.7	15 167	323	83	20 713	442	228	25 714	264 919	37 464	5 706	675 731	788 752	67.4	20.4
Allegany	216	2.8	160	214	4	612	817	6	633	2 134	162	2 790	11 383	14 131	59.3	9.3
Anne Arundel	1 461	3.7	615	145	4	1 004	237	12	1 241	19 069	1 515	4 512	64 006	72 666	70.5	19.0
Baltimore	2 523	3.8	1 221	175	4	1 790	257	33	3 595	43 960	6 593	6 346	80 259	104 570	68.3	18.8
Calvert	144	3.7	51	101	1	121	241	1	100	1 112	162	2 335	8 499	8 073	64.6	11.8
Caroline	83	3.5	9	35	0	0	0	3	223	621	112	2 455	4 392	4 761	47.0	9.1
Carroll	339	3.2	141	115	2	969	793	7	680	2 967	293	2 495	20 048	20 758	61.8	14.3
Cecil	212	3.3	65	88	2	905	1 228	3	267	2 338	306	3 299	12 169	13 305	58.4	11.0
Charles	258	3.2	69	71	1	104	106	2	249	4 158	489	4 338	17 186	18 069	69.0	12.4
Dorchester	81	2.7	54	176	3	335	1 095	3	231	1 433	208	4 680	4 970	5 604	44.9	8.2
Frederick	510	4.1	173	121	2	323	225	6	623	4 486	706	3 197	24 777	23 927	63.4	16.9
Garrett	74	2.8	21	78	1	76	281	3	343	610	73	2 256	5 270	5 794	53.9	7.9
Harford	519	3.5	231	131	3	409	232	3	395	5 875	725	3 504	28 121	32 559	69.1	17.1
Howard	452	3.3	633	373	3	596	351	2	412	8 165	520	5 072	25 629	25 494	83.1	38.5
Kent	74	4.4	32	188	1	64	376	1	74	384	40	2 206	2 297	2 718	53.9	12.6
Montgomery	2 014	3.2	4 491	620	9	2 670	368	29	4 072	30 623	1 989	4 359	94 457	102 902	87.3	42.8
Prince George's	2 405	3.6	1 217	172	7	1 613	228	17	2 059	49 680	6 908	7 080	103 301	128 043	77.4	21.1
Queen Anne's	70	2.5	19	57	0	0	0	3	202	846	116	2 665	4 883	5 056	55.7	12.4
St. Mary's	223	3.5	65	91	2	123	171	3	320	2 633	391	3 689	11 604	12 607	67.2	14.0
Somerset	63	3.3	21	108	1	41	211	2	138	696	116	3 485	3 401	3 703	44.7	8.2
Talbot	102	3.8	99	350	1	201	710	4	322	988	147	3 470	3 784	4 018	59.7	18.1
Washington	424	3.7	166	140	3	519	437	11	1 032	2 925	264	2 466	17 296	21 724	59.8	9.5
Wicomico	350	5.2	171	234	2	490	669	4	602	4 365	614	6 012	11 622	12 180	56.3	14.2

1. Per 1,000 resident population estimated as of July 1 of the year shown. 2. As of end of year. 3. Per 100,000 resident population as of July 1 of the year shown. 4. Preliminary. Covers nursing homes with 3 or more beds. 5. Data for serious crimes have not been adjusted for underreporting, this may affect comparability between geographic areas or over time. 6. Includes murder and nonnegligent manslaughter, forcible rape, robbery, and aggravated assault. 7. The 1986–1987 data are based on administrative reports obtained by the U.S. National Center for Education Statistics. The 1980 data are based on the 1980 Census of Population and Housing. 8. Persons 25 years old or older.

STATE County	Education (cont'd): Local government expenditures for education,[1] 1982: Total (Mil dol)	Education (cont'd): Local government expenditures for education,[1] 1982: Per capita (Dollars)	Social Security Program December 1988: Beneficiaries: Total	Social Security Program December 1988: Beneficiaries: Rate[2]	Social Security Program December 1988: Payments ($1,000)	Supplemental Security Income Program recipients June 1986	Money income: Per capita[3]: 1987 Income, (Dollars)	Money income: Per capita[3]: 1979: Current dollars	Money income: Per capita[3]: 1979: Constant 1987 dollars	Money income: Median household income 1979 (Dollars)	Money income: Percent below poverty level, 1979: Persons	Money income: Percent below poverty level, 1979: Families	Housing units, 1990: Total	Housing units, 1990: Percent change, 1980–1990
	60	61	62	63	64	65	66	67	68	69	70	71	72	73
LOUISIANA—Con.														
Red River	4.7	422	1 655	151.8	615	592	5 944	4 391	6 871	10 185	28.2	22.8	3 839	-5.1
Richland	11.5	507	4 120	181.5	1 509	1 396	5 986	4 761	7 450	9 544	35.0	28.6	8 031	1.8
Sabine	13.2	500	4 675	172.5	1 857	1 164	7 131	5 096	7 974	11 339	23.1	18.9	12 789	5.7
St. Bernard	25.7	390	10 710	156.4	5 096	870	8 739	6 510	10 186	18 882	8.9	7.4	25 147	16.5
St. Charles	29.4	738	4 810	110.1	2 256	616	9 924	6 976	10 915	21 063	13.3	11.9	16 016	29.1
St. Helena	5.7	572	1 140	111.8	381	480	6 257	4 322	6 763	9 653	32.0	28.2	3 840	7.2
St. James	12.8	591	2 820	127.6	1 286	590	7 707	5 727	8 961	18 417	17.3	14.5	6 934	7.5
St. John the Baptist	17.9	496	3 850	93.4	1 719	582	8 580	6 372	9 970	20 158	14.4	12.1	14 255	35.5
St. Landry	45.8	521	15 690	183.1	5 619	5 808	6 322	4 744	7 423	11 300	27.7	23.1	31 137	5.6
St. Martin	25.0	575	5 875	130.6	2 167	1 846	6 772	5 234	8 190	15 093	19.8	16.9	17 592	28.4
St. Mary	35.2	529	8 530	141.9	3 741	1 476	6 789	6 789	10 623	18 430	15.6	12.6	21 884	1.6
St. Tammany	48.5	393	16 990	113.0	7 868	1 752	11 088	7 389	11 562	19 806	12.4	10.3	57 993	40.4
Tangipahoa	35.1	407	14 610	161.6	5 604	4 424	7 273	5 256	8 224	11 799	26.0	21.4	33 640	15.0
Tensas	4.1	490	1 490	184.0	556	586	5 942	4 623	7 234	8 233	41.2	34.0	3 334	-14.3
Terrebonne	50.6	503	13 980	142.7	6 057	2 074	8 235	6 710	10 499	19 176	14.4	11.4	35 416	14.9
Union	8.9	412	4 215	186.5	1 645	976	7 045	5 002	7 827	11 137	22.2	17.5	9 304	7.9
Vermilion	30.5	593	8 950	171.5	3 463	1 642	7 944	6 106	9 554	14 312	17.3	14.1	20 361	13.9
Vernon	22.1	376	4 850	80.6	1 767	1 026	6 939	4 848	7 586	11 324	18.3	15.8	21 622	19.2
Washington	22.0	490	8 990	190.5	3 731	2 150	6 820	5 093	7 969	11 096	24.9	21.0	17 617	5.1
Webster	20.8	467	9 160	201.8	3 935	1 832	8 095	5 749	8 995	12 389	20.0	15.6	18 365	3.1
West Baton Rouge	10.5	540	2 590	125.1	1 112	544	8 381	5 952	9 313	17 082	17.7	15.6	7 298	13.4
West Carroll	6.7	516	2 600	201.6	899	874	5 661	4 308	6 741	7 951	32.1	29.5	4 831	-4.8
West Feliciana	7.2	554	985	73.0	393	328	5 457	3 924	6 140	12 008	33.4	27.7	3 392	17.0
Winn	9.5	538	2 985	176.6	1 161	752	6 348	4 707	7 365	10 100	25.8	21.6	7 006	-1.1
MAINE	451.8	398	209 307	173.6	94 961	22 525	10 478	5 766	9 022	13 816	13.0	9.8	587 045	17.2
Androscoggin	32.6	327	18 975	183.7	8 691	2 224	10 115	5 631	8 811	13 524	12.6	9.7	43 815	14.2
Aroostook	42.1	468	15 035	174.8	6 165	2 812	8 577	4 809	7 525	12 357	16.2	13.3	38 421	7.0
Cumberland	81.2	372	39 170	166.3	18 964	3 468	12 738	6 694	10 474	15 359	10.5	7.5	109 890	19.7
Franklin	13.5	479	4 755	162.3	2 121	526	9 606	5 621	8 795	13 500	12.8	8.8	17 280	24.2
Hancock	16.6	391	9 035	197.3	4 177	668	9 965	5 411	8 467	12 146	14.6	11.2	30 396	21.3
Kennebec	37.7	341	19 800	170.5	8 653	2 468	10 482	5 966	9 335	14 690	11.8	8.5	51 648	13.6
Knox	13.5	403	7 565	211.3	3 495	794	9 724	5 659	8 855	12 113	14.4	10.6	19 009	16.4
Lincoln	13.3	506	6 225	211.0	2 891	460	10 288	5 600	8 762	12 831	16.7	12.4	17 538	17.1
Oxford	24.3	496	10 170	197.5	4 667	1 044	9 424	5 562	8 703	13 029	12.7	9.2	29 689	24.8
Penobscot	52.8	383	22 600	159.8	10 316	2 538	9 876	5 593	8 751	14 181	13.0	9.6	61 359	14.9
Piscataquis	8.6	483	3 515	190.0	1 518	390	8 348	4 990	7 808	12 260	14.1	10.2	13 194	23.0
Sagadahoc	14.2	484	4 230	127.8	2 014	290	10 784	5 924	9 269	14 855	11.2	8.7	14 633	21.7
Somerset	25.0	551	8 725	182.5	3 785	1 292	8 670	4 842	7 576	11 830	16.3	13.1	24 927	19.3
Waldo	9.5	332	5 660	180.8	2 394	742	8 269	4 689	7 337	11 614	20.0	16.1	16 181	20.2
Washington	14.2	413	7 315	209.6	2 961	1 092	8 126	4 581	7 168	10 443	21.6	17.5	19 124	5.4
York	52.8	364	26 210	157.9	11 997	1 706	11 430	6 210	9 717	15 377	9.8	7.2	79 941	19.7
MARYLAND	2 036.9	477	591 304	127.9	292 569	53 209	14 697	8 293	12 976	20 281	9.8	7.5	1 891 917	20.4
Allegany	38.2	486	16 495	219.3	7 954	1 398	9 669	6 049	9 465	13 885	12.2	9.0	32 513	1.9
Anne Arundel	171.7	451	44 185	105.8	22 161	3 158	15 266	8 402	13 147	22 676	6.3	5.0	157 194	21.8
Baltimore	280.3	421	104 760	152.0	56 677	4 716	15 661	9 044	14 151	21 640	5.3	4.1	281 553	15.4
Calvert	21.4	585	4 990	104.0	2 236	430	13 564	7 354	11 507	22 106	10.3	7.7	18 974	48.4
Caroline	11.1	476	4 830	190.9	2 224	520	10 612	5 946	9 304	14 452	13.5	10.1	10 745	21.9
Carroll	41.9	420	16 010	134.9	8 096	798	13 195	7 483	11 709	21 358	5.3	4.0	43 553	35.6
Cecil	31.3	499	8 850	123.3	4 180	578	11 678	6 598	10 324	18 319	9.4	6.9	27 656	20.4
Charles	47.1	604	7 330	77.3	3 161	774	13 192	7 460	11 673	24 229	8.9	6.2	34 487	51.8
Dorchester	14.5	479	6 420	211.2	2 994	784	10 912	6 200	9 701	13 766	14.5	10.7	14 269	11.9
Frederick	54.6	457	15 620	111.8	7 432	782	13 171	7 479	11 702	20 619	6.7	4.9	54 872	38.3
Garrett	13.4	502	4 425	164.5	1 887	514	8 555	5 212	8 155	13 071	15.8	12.7	14 119	15.4
Harford	73.5	497	17 195	100.9	7 984	1 010	13 550	7 628	11 936	21 587	7.5	6.2	66 446	34.4
Howard	75.0	590	10 270	63.0	5 370	498	18 276	10 065	15 749	27 612	3.6	2.9	72 583	70.8
Kent	7.7	466	4 225	248.5	2 043	294	11 830	6 502	10 174	13 979	13.2	10.2	8 181	11.4
Montgomery	342.2	572	72 250	102.5	36 938	4 072	21 576	12 335	19 301	28 987	4.3	3.0	295 723	36.8
Prince George's	331.3	496	55 190	78.7	24 942	4 714	14 865	8 616	13 481	22 395	6.7	4.9	270 090	14.2
Queen Anne's	12.9	487	4 370	136.6	2 103	296	13 260	7 027	10 995	17 327	9.6	7.5	13 944	39.0
St. Mary's	30.0	485	6 585	93.7	2 784	762	11 815	6 601	10 329	18 743	10.9	8.3	27 863	30.9
Somerset	9.3	501	4 260	219.6	1 819	606	9 464	5 284	8 268	11 975	15.7	11.0	9 393	20.3
Talbot	10.2	389	6 655	237.7	3 351	382	15 120	8 217	12 857	16 539	10.2	7.1	14 697	30.9
Washington	48.6	440	19 325	164.0	9 605	1 404	11 035	6 765	10 585	16 623	10.8	8.0	47 448	11.9
Wicomico	29.9	460	12 055	167.4	5 808	1 282	11 949	6 664	10 427	15 818	12.5	9.0	30 108	22.0

1. Elementary and secondary. 2. Per 1,000 resident population estimated as of July 1 of the year shown. 3. Based on the resident population estimated as of July 1, 1988 for 1987 data and enumerated as of April 1, 1980 for 1979 data.

STATE County	Housing units, 1990 (cont'd)				Civilian labor force, 1990				Private nonfarm establishments, 1988					
	Occupied units						Unemployment				Employment[2]			
		Owner occupied												
	Total	Percent	Median value (Dollars)	Median rent (Dollars)	Total	Percent change, 1989–1990	Total	Rate[1]	Number	Net change, 1987–1988	Total	Percent change, 1987–1988	Manufacturing	Retail trade
	74	75	76	77	78	79	80	81	82	83	84	85	86	87
LOUISIANA—Con.														
Red River	3 321	75.6	35 500	144	3 866	-8.4	327	8.5	133	-6	1 732	4.9	855	239
Richland	7 079	73.7	36 800	125	7 890	-7.7	777	9.8	387	-1	3 579	12.5	920	910
Sabine	8 361	80.1	37 800	139	9 695	-1.6	483	5.0	392	-1	3 861	-0.9	1 407	786
St. Bernard	23 156	75.8	63 300	294	30 720	-2.5	2 249	7.3	1 039	-40	10 562	-2.1	1 680	3 861
St. Charles	14 333	78.9	68 000	294	18 914	-1.7	1 092	5.8	589	-14	12 659	2.3	4 370	1 805
St. Helena	3 328	84.3	40 000	130	2 550	-2.8	225	8.8	65	4	391	21.4	0	95
St. James	6 432	82.4	57 100	114	9 318	12.9	717	7.7	320	4	5 100	-10.5	2 368	683
St. John the Baptist	12 710	79.7	62 200	276	17 120	-1.2	1 291	7.5	509	3	7 853	8.8	2 463	1 756
St. Landry	27 477	71.8	40 500	147	29 992	-2.7	2 627	8.8	1 438	-16	13 458	3.4	2 618	3 468
St. Martin	14 634	79.9	44 400	160	19 260	2.2	1 185	6.2	455	-26	6 626	16.8	3 064	1 431
St. Mary	19 456	68.6	49 200	193	23 757	-2.0	1 654	7.0	1 379	-46	17 627	8.8	3 425	2 973
St. Tammany	50 346	75.8	74 900	327	62 738	-2.1	3 483	5.6	2 814	-84	25 972	-0.6	1 661	9 515
Tangipahoa	29 663	72.7	52 200	214	36 755	-3.5	3 085	8.4	1 547	-68	15 372	-0.5	1 856	6 303
Tensas	2 515	71.7	34 100	99	2 265	-16.2	197	8.7	122	0	854	8.4	200	117
Terrebonne	31 837	73.2	52 900	250	37 414	-0.3	2 091	5.6	2 245	-98	26 613	6.8	2 236	7 458
Union	7 528	82.3	39 600	144	8 071	-3.7	559	6.9	296	-21	2 732	3.0	954	438
Vermilion	17 762	75.7	43 800	169	17 570	-5.6	1 218	6.9	927	-23	7 866	1.9	1 114	1 995
Vernon	19 111	50.4	47 800	268	18 446	3.5	1 094	5.9	535	-12	4 349	-3.9	214	1 735
Washington	15 475	76.4	37 900	155	17 337	-3.3	1 358	7.8	714	-20	6 947	3.0	2 041	1 720
Webster	15 849	74.1	40 600	171	18 288	-2.0	1 572	8.6	791	-33	7 997	-0.1	1 510	2 046
West Baton Rouge	6 606	75.9	58 400	220	9 404	-0.3	610	6.5	315	-8	4 999	3.6	1 198	538
West Carroll	4 394	77.7	30 400	125	4 314	-2.6	621	14.4	170	-6	1 303	-0.5	424	338
West Feliciana	2 741	68.2	61 300	164	4 016	-3.7	263	6.5	127	1	2 517	1.4	0	267
Winn	5 787	76.2	34 000	128	5 822	0.3	324	5.6	331	-17	4 456	40.8	1 445	779
MAINE	465 312	70.5	87 400	358	635 000	3.1	33 000	5.1	X	X	414 820	6.5	105 734	100 557
Androscoggin	40 017	62.2	86 800	334	50 499	2.1	3 519	7.0	2 741	38	39 707	6.7	11 811	8 438
Aroostook	31 366	69.5	45 900	267	39 716	4.3	2 727	6.9	2 205	55	22 058	3.5	6 093	5 379
Cumberland	94 512	64.3	118 300	458	143 802	2.6	5 207	3.6	8 680	313	118 933	6.7	17 442	31 379
Franklin	10 778	75.6	66 200	278	13 767	3.3	831	6.0	822	40	11 239	5.6	5 086	2 181
Hancock	18 342	75.7	85 200	325	27 186	8.9	1 331	4.9	1 845	37	13 369	8.5	2 846	3 276
Kennebec	43 889	70.9	79 300	330	61 557	3.6	2 660	4.3	2 962	110	39 720	7.3	7 570	9 864
Knox	14 344	73.6	92 500	333	17 607	4.2	1 029	5.8	1 258	27	11 180	6.0	2 818	2 655
Lincoln	11 968	83.2	103 000	356	19 793	8.6	632	3.2	1 059	28	6 251	3.8	880	1 989
Oxford	20 064	76.1	69 900	281	23 798	2.0	1 807	7.6	1 284	61	13 187	4.8	4 885	2 522
Penobscot	54 063	69.7	69 100	335	69 543	3.5	3 737	5.4	3 780	143	51 551	7.5	13 668	12 462
Piscataquis	7 194	78.6	46 800	250	8 594	3.7	568	6.6	489	21	5 122	11.5	2 655	1 010
Sagadahoc	12 581	70.8	95 900	416	16 438	3.5	580	3.5	706	54	14 170	11.4	0	1 714
Somerset	18 513	77.3	56 400	275	23 887	5.5	1 695	7.1	1 126	4	13 846	6.6	5 358	2 493
Waldo	12 415	80.8	71 500	283	14 078	4.5	1 188	8.4	733	35	4 763	-3.0	1 232	1 377
Washington	13 418	78.8	53 100	227	15 102	0.6	1 246	8.3	851	42	7 166	8.8	1 959	1 956
York	61 848	71.6	115 200	429	90 636	2.2	4 244	4.7	4 509	95	42 200	5.1	12 337	11 862
MARYLAND	1 748 991	65.0	116 500	473	2 535 000	0.5	118 000	4.6	X	X	1 719 047	2.7	231 375	401 333
Allegany	29 634	69.9	46 700	216	33 102	1.7	2 925	8.8	1 856	-23	22 273	-3.2	4 033	6 913
Anne Arundel	149 114	72.9	127 900	534	215 742	0.2	7 485	3.5	9 572	343	131 220	4.4	21 765	38 661
Baltimore	268 280	66.3	99 900	458	394 101	0.4	17 604	4.5	17 839	418	294 962	6.1	55 675	75 263
Calvert	16 986	85.0	136 100	519	23 425	0.4	1 055	4.5	922	85	8 592	8.6	509	2 164
Caroline	9 983	73.5	75 000	256	14 185	0.5	687	4.8	510	49	5 655	10.2	1 315	1 150
Carroll	42 248	78.5	126 700	397	63 499	0.5	2 396	3.8	3 113	251	31 930	7.6	7 176	7 919
Cecil	24 725	75.0	97 000	364	36 273	1.4	2 646	7.3	1 302	51	13 605	6.0	2 905	3 969
Charles	32 950	75.7	122 300	603	47 442	0.2	1 545	3.3	1 757	789	18 280	80.2	1 231	6 518
Dorchester	12 117	67.6	68 600	228	17 439	2.0	1 337	7.7	711	11	10 394	6.1	4 451	1 896
Frederick	52 570	70.8	129 500	487	77 808	1.2	3 664	4.7	3 422	190	44 161	9.4	7 890	11 243
Garrett	10 110	79.1	60 200	230	13 926	1.8	1 246	8.9	707	49	6 560	4.0	1 625	1 709
Harford	63 193	73.9	114 700	403	84 256	0.5	4 177	5.0	3 427	127	34 597	8.2	4 053	11 933
Howard	68 337	72.2	166 500	614	94 301	0.1	2 601	2.8	4 738	267	85 303	7.0	8 793	14 731
Kent	6 702	71.6	87 700	313	9 380	0.4	517	5.5	621	-3	5 671	10.6	1 226	1 366
Montgomery	282 228	67.9	200 800	698	427 461	-0.1	11 509	2.7	20 722	1 279	327 148	3.9	21 327	70 678
Prince George's	258 011	58.9	122 600	607	421 642	0.3	16 596	3.9	13 138	-288	236 833	1.0	14 219	68 546
Queen Anne's	12 489	81.0	118 000	350	16 000	0.3	586	3.7	726	41	5 883	17.8	911	1 875
St. Mary's	25 500	69.7	109 100	447	43 715	0.3	2 011	4.6	1 290	42	13 462	8.8	462	4 034
Somerset	7 977	72.2	55 600	230	13 288	5.1	1 457	11.0	383	19	2 744	0.8	765	735
Talbot	12 677	68.1	118 100	340	17 906	0.1	862	4.8	1 204	40	14 176	7.1	3 359	3 432
Washington	44 762	63.8	83 000	297	60 964	1.8	4 078	6.7	2 737	60	40 582	1.6	10 445	8 957
Wicomico	27 772	66.7	71 100	349	39 947	0.6	2 482	6.2	2 079	55	30 030	3.2	6 395	7 372

1. Percent of total civilian labor force. 2. For week including March 12. Excludes government employees, self-employed persons, farm workers, domestic service workers, railroad employees subject to the Railroad Retirement Act, and employees on oceanborne vessels or in foreign countries.

STATE County	Private nonfarm establishments, 1988 (cont'd): Employment[1] (cont'd): Finance, insurance, and real estate	Employment[1] (cont'd): Services	Annual payroll: Total (Mil dol)	Annual payroll: Average per employee (Dollars)	Personal income, 1989: Total (Mil dol)	Per-cent change, 1988–1989	Wages and salaries[2] (Mil dol)	Propri-etor's income (Mil dol)	Dividends, interest, & rent (Mil dol)	Transfer payments (Mil dol)	Per capita[3]: Dollars	Per capita[3]: Rank	Earnings, 1989: Total (Mil dol)	Percent by selected industries: Farm	Goods-related[4]: Total
	88	89	90	91	92	93	94	95	96	97	98	99	100	101	102
LOUISIANA—Con.															
Red River	75	419	23	13 099	98	-2.1	39	11	13	27	9 020	3 006	51	7.4	40.2
Richland	208	666	49	13 605	238	2.5	104	29	38	61	10 596	2 771	133	9.9	27.3
Sabine	120	770	57	14 813	242	4.5	93	44	36	65	8 972	3 009	137	12.7	34.3
St. Bernard	540	2 641	182	17 187	868	3.0	283	63	117	157	12 665	2 050	347	0.6	36.0
St. Charles	306	2 533	341	26 944	639	6.8	542	38	69	75	14 484	1 222	580	0.7	58.2
St. Helena	51	58	6	14 107	79	4.0	21	10	11	20	7 777	3 084	31	20.5	12.2
St. James	246	593	121	23 700	283	8.9	233	17	35	43	12 873	1 967	250	2.7	66.2
St. John the Baptist	394	1 802	169	21 525	494	6.2	268	21	48	64	11 918	2 354	289	1.4	47.8
St. Landry	944	2 962	189	14 055	820	2.8	339	77	133	229	9 667	2 933	416	2.1	22.8
St. Martin	277	608	95	14 344	429	6.2	177	38	51	80	9 585	2 946	214	3.1	43.4
St. Mary	738	3 449	327	18 532	675	8.0	614	64	113	123	11 509	2 494	679	1.5	44.7
St. Tammany	1 935	7 938	379	14 584	2 261	6.3	586	150	311	268	14 702	1 128	736	1.8	14.5
Tangipahoa	932	3 584	184	11 971	929	5.4	368	84	129	261	10 300	2 836	452	4.9	12.3
Tensas	67	225	10	11 899	72	-13.0	26	11	14	21	9 113	2 997	37	29.9	7.0
Terrebonne	1 416	5 356	481	18 091	1 127	4.3	753	105	175	187	11 641	2 461	858	0.6	32.5
Union	135	442	45	16 582	235	4.0	61	32	33	56	10 421	2 806	94	19.6	23.3
Vermilion	430	1 861	118	15 063	550	5.3	236	60	114	115	10 612	2 768	296	5.1	26.5
Vernon	326	1 224	52	11 856	562	1.9	449	34	45	100	9 328	2 978	483	1.3	4.7
Washington	603	1 429	102	14 669	464	2.5	195	47	72	130	9 852	2 901	242	6.0	30.5
Webster	367	1 867	114	14 256	519	3.3	237	42	83	131	11 461	2 519	279	0.8	48.7
West Baton Rouge	84	654	103	20 511	245	7.8	179	10	25	40	11 869	2 370	189	1.5	NA
West Carroll	35	310	16	12 019	102	-0.5	33	17	16	33	7 998	3 078	51	20.4	18.0
West Feliciana	81	419	77	30 399	114	-1.2	178	8	15	21	8 451	3 045	185	2.4	39.9
Winn	111	540	74	16 544	153	2.1	82	16	19	45	9 118	2 996	98	2.1	46.1
MAINE	25 825	103 193	7 503	X	20 066	9.5	12 107	2 008	3 504	3 213	16 422	X	14 115	1.0	30.3
Androscoggin	2 308	10 385	655	16 502	1 642	8.8	897	122	240	279	15 731	728	1 019	1.1	32.3
Aroostook	992	5 627	339	15 354	1 161	10.4	671	152	145	239	13 613	1 624	823	6.6	26.4
Cumberland	12 135	31 409	2 311	19 435	4 873	9.4	3 591	450	921	621	20 383	151	4 041	0.2	21.9
Franklin	660	2 311	193	17 132	420	10.1	270	50	68	70	14 335	1 273	321	0.6	53.0
Hancock	600	3 682	234	17 536	824	10.2	379	126	213	129	17 665	341	505	1.9	30.8
Kennebec	2 610	11 017	707	17 791	1 894	10.4	1 315	131	290	324	16 086	623	1 446	0.4	23.1
Knox	398	3 343	174	15 573	592	10.1	268	82	170	99	16 320	563	350	0.6	29.0
Lincoln	321	1 260	105	16 846	568	9.8	180	87	158	83	18 841	228	267	0.5	24.0
Oxford	435	3 492	229	17 328	745	9.0	366	93	127	143	14 310	1 281	458	1.9	47.2
Penobscot	2 114	13 021	950	18 420	2 177	9.2	1 462	186	309	373	15 239	889	1 649	0.7	29.3
Piscataquis	103	804	75	14 659	241	7.3	111	32	41	51	12 886	1 960	143	1.7	42.9
Sagadahoc	258	1 988	336	23 700	607	12.6	515	37	89	72	17 920	305	552	0.2	70.7
Somerset	359	2 567	272	19 637	625	10.8	346	73	87	130	12 943	1 932	419	1.4	46.1
Waldo	126	1 058	69	14 474	401	9.8	121	48	78	82	12 565	2 084	169	2.2	34.9
Washington	246	1 724	115	15 982	460	8.4	227	74	66	116	13 077	1 875	300	1.4	33.5
York	1 925	9 475	733	17 368	2 836	8.6	1 387	266	503	401	16 663	492	1 652	0.3	31.4
MARYLAND	132 989	567 052	36 288	X	98 159	8.3	58 391	6 022	15 839	12 347	20 929	X	64 413	0.7	19.6
Allegany	1 067	6 280	377	16 936	1 063	7.8	647	69	195	272	14 184	1 352	716	0.5	NA
Anne Arundel	6 634	33 611	2 787	21 238	9 216	8.1	5 458	450	1 140	976	21 772	101	5 908	0.1	23.8
Baltimore	24 303	84 042	6 070	20 577	15 115	7.1	8 229	807	2 865	1 708	21 725	105	9 036	0.3	28.0
Calvert	356	2 385	157	18 215	1 020	12.1	202	54	120	118	20 277	154	256	1.3	28.6
Caroline	201	1 308	121	21 473	367	6.9	164	52	64	63	14 239	1 306	216	13.8	22.7
Carroll	1 217	6 829	534	16 738	2 484	7.7	754	183	347	248	20 323	152	938	2.2	34.2
Cecil	448	2 972	228	16 744	1 236	9.3	437	87	153	154	16 768	476	524	3.8	NA
Charles	796	4 720	321	17 545	1 810	11.2	653	65	169	206	18 500	251	718	0.8	NA
Dorchester	244	1 795	165	15 906	498	7.1	243	66	95	91	16 307	568	309	6.3	40.0
Frederick	3 317	11 043	803	18 187	2 760	9.6	1 195	206	390	285	19 230	209	1 401	2.1	28.0
Garrett	361	1 591	90	13 753	350	7.7	169	52	54	69	12 932	1 935	221	4.2	32.4
Harford	1 583	9 101	563	16 265	3 524	7.7	1 268	204	415	369	20 023	170	1 472	1.0	19.0
Howard	5 706	30 930	2 044	23 958	4 797	10.6	2 227	285	543	265	28 252	20	2 512	0.6	21.1
Kent	291	1 622	82	14 378	324	8.0	121	51	94	54	19 006	220	173	13.9	23.6
Montgomery	30 802	134 015	7 879	24 084	21 476	9.5	12 386	1 448	4 519	1 974	29 639	17	13 834	0.2	13.4
Prince George's	11 756	76 876	4 841	20 442	13 419	7.5	8 058	554	1 406	1 700	18 960	223	8 612	0.2	16.0
Queen Anne's	273	1 191	89	15 067	659	8.0	156	80	123	69	19 897	174	236	9.1	25.9
St. Mary's	653	4 989	230	17 056	1 184	10.0	648	78	133	163	16 504	528	726	1.0	9.7
Somerset	124	591	39	14 084	265	8.4	114	55	41	62	13 623	1 618	169	14.8	15.3
Talbot	741	3 969	225	15 892	718	9.4	311	79	256	91	25 339	35	390	3.8	27.6
Washington	1 768	9 362	747	18 399	1 881	7.5	1 221	105	312	299	15 828	703	1 326	0.9	29.3
Wicomico	1 854	7 059	531	17 675	1 160	8.5	749	131	200	184	15 855	694	880	5.0	26.9

1. For week including March 12. Excludes government employees, self-employed persons, farm workers, domestic service workers, railroad employees subject to the Railroad Retirement Act, and employees on oceanborne vessels or in foreign countries. 2. Includes other labor income. 3. Based on the resident population estimated as of July 1 of the year shown. 4. Covers mining, construction, and manufacturing.

STATE County	Earnings, 1989 (cont'd)						Agriculture, 1987									
	Percent by selected industries (cont'd)						Farms			Farm operators, percent		Land in farms				
	Goods-related[1]	Service-related & other[2]						Percent with						Acres		
	Manu-facturing	Total	Retail trade	Finance, insur-ance, & real estate	Services	Govern-ment	Number	Less than 50 acres	500 acres and over	Whose principal occu-pation is farming	Residing on farm operated	Acreage (1,000)	Percent change, 1982–1987	Average size of farm	Total irrigated (1,000)	Total cropland (1,000)
	103	104	105	106	107	108	109	110	111	112	113	114	115	116	117	118
LOUISIANA—Con.																
Red River	32.9	35.7	7.0	2.8	20.9	16.8	251	21.1	20.7	43.4	66.5	113	-12.5	450	0	69
Richland	20.4	45.3	8.0	3.1	19.7	17.6	622	24.3	26.4	69.9	58.2	245	-7.4	394	39	197
Sabine	27.1	38.6	9.9	2.5	15.8	14.5	468	35.3	3.2	37.4	70.3	58	-10.7	124	0	26
St. Bernard	28.2	50.1	12.3	3.0	23.3	13.2	22	63.6	4.5	31.8	50.0	6	-27.8	267	0	D
St. Charles	40.2	32.8	4.6	0.8	9.4	8.3	72	41.7	15.3	45.8	29.2	38	-2.0	523	D	10
St. Helena	8.6	36.7	6.0	2.6	14.2	30.6	359	30.1	3.1	47.9	77.4	51	-30.1	142	0	30
St. James	58.1	20.0	3.6	1.6	6.0	11.1	75	26.7	42.7	73.3	45.3	48	-0.3	645	D	36
St. John the Baptist	37.8	39.6	6.8	2.1	16.7	11.2	39	46.2	23.1	51.3	46.2	19	-9.8	483	D	12
St. Landry	14.2	54.3	11.7	4.6	26.8	20.8	1 159	48.7	16.4	49.4	63.2	269	-15.9	232	18	234
St. Martin	31.8	37.9	11.1	3.2	18.1	15.6	299	45.2	18.4	54.2	54.8	73	-18.5	245	7	64
St. Mary	20.3	44.8	5.7	2.4	16.4	9.0	88	13.6	55.7	80.7	36.4	76	-13.4	859	D	60
St. Tammany	5.2	62.8	15.3	3.8	31.6	20.9	491	64.0	3.1	36.5	70.3	58	-19.3	118	1	21
Tangipahoa	7.9	54.6	17.8	4.7	22.7	28.2	1 061	43.2	3.0	52.3	77.2	131	-15.4	123	1	76
Tensas	1.7	43.7	6.2	4.5	15.6	19.3	268	10.4	53.7	85.8	53.7	263	-4.4	982	11	210
Terrebonne	8.2	55.4	12.2	2.6	23.6	11.5	145	44.1	19.3	38.6	60.0	40	-29.3	277	0	25
Union	14.0	41.0	7.4	3.0	18.9	16.0	457	32.6	3.9	38.1	72.4	65	-16.9	143	0	26
Vermilion	6.9	51.9	10.0	3.2	22.3	16.5	1 189	36.0	18.0	64.2	54.8	333	-2.7	280	83	254
Vernon	2.0	16.9	5.1	1.0	6.7	77.1	516	45.2	2.7	32.4	79.8	52	-17.8	101	0	23
Washington	22.3	42.5	10.7	3.6	18.3	20.9	839	34.4	3.0	47.7	74.5	109	-13.4	130	2	66
Webster	36.8	37.5	9.8	3.1	17.8	13.0	417	31.2	7.7	33.1	68.8	68	-12.2	164	0	29
West Baton Rouge	22.4	NA	5.0	NA	10.6	12.2	95	38.9	18.9	42.1	55.8	42	-1.1	447	0	28
West Carroll	4.3	38.7	8.3	2.1	16.0	22.9	555	24.3	13.3	65.0	65.9	137	-19.2	246	16	121
West Feliciana	29.8	NA	1.2	0.7	NA	23.5	171	19.3	22.8	39.8	66.1	89	-18.0	519	0	41
Winn	41.1	35.0	8.4	2.2	16.5	16.9	188	29.8	4.8	34.6	73.9	24	-16.4	130	D	9
MAINE	21.4	51.8	11.7	4.9	23.0	16.9	6 269	23.1	9.7	51.4	84.2	1 343	-8.6	214	6	592
Androscoggin	23.4	56.5	11.8	5.3	27.8	10.1	343	24.2	9.6	54.8	85.1	70	-6.3	203	0	31
Aroostook	21.3	41.0	9.9	2.2	17.8	26.0	1 012	12.3	17.3	70.3	76.9	330	-14.5	326	2	188
Cumberland	13.1	65.7	12.8	10.3	27.4	12.2	456	35.5	4.2	45.0	86.8	58	-7.0	127	1	27
Franklin	44.6	35.4	9.3	3.0	17.2	11.0	229	19.2	4.4	51.1	87.8	44	-13.4	193	0	17
Hancock	18.4	55.5	14.1	2.2	27.5	11.7	290	30.0	6.9	28.3	69.0	50	-2.5	173	0	14
Kennebec	14.3	49.3	10.2	3.1	21.9	27.2	576	21.9	8.3	51.9	89.4	112	-4.5	195	0	52
Knox	18.0	57.1	13.2	1.8	28.4	13.4	221	34.4	5.4	46.2	81.9	34	8.5	156	0	14
Lincoln	8.7	65.3	14.4	1.7	24.9	10.1	228	29.8	3.1	37.3	85.1	29	-9.6	128	0	12
Oxford	34.3	39.7	11.4	1.8	20.2	11.2	334	20.4	10.8	50.6	89.5	71	-9.5	212	0	24
Penobscot	22.5	51.5	12.0	3.3	22.3	18.6	572	21.5	11.4	50.3	87.8	133	-9.1	232	1	54
Piscataquis	38.3	42.0	11.9	1.6	17.6	13.4	138	22.5	21.0	46.4	89.9	38	5.9	278	D	13
Sagadahoc	66.1	20.7	5.6	1.1	11.0	8.4	124	29.0	4.8	42.7	94.4	18	2.8	148	0	7
Somerset	35.3	40.8	10.0	2.5	19.2	11.8	462	18.0	11.5	55.8	89.8	112	-8.7	243	D	47
Waldo	18.6	48.7	14.8	0.7	22.8	14.2	426	20.7	8.2	58.9	86.2	85	-5.9	200	0	33
Washington	22.2	47.1	10.2	1.5	15.8	18.0	337	23.1	11.3	32.0	68.2	86	-1.9	254	0	32
York	21.3	40.3	12.7	2.2	19.7	28.0	521	32.8	4.6	46.1	89.3	72	-13.9	138	1	26
MARYLAND	10.7	58.5	11.2	6.6	28.2	21.2	14 776	42.2	7.2	53.3	77.1	2 397	-6.3	162	51	1 745
Allegany	21.7	NA	12.8	3.3	23.2	15.2	240	19.6	7.5	47.9	72.1	49	-6.9	204	0	21
Anne Arundel	15.6	42.2	9.4	3.1	19.2	33.9	567	60.8	2.1	47.4	77.8	42	-5.2	75	0	26
Baltimore	18.9	56.1	12.4	6.3	25.7	15.6	917	56.2	3.4	43.9	82.1	93	-6.3	101	1	70
Calvert	3.8	51.6	13.3	2.9	27.5	18.5	464	53.0	2.4	52.2	80.2	41	-16.2	89	0	22
Caroline	16.1	53.0	10.9	2.3	11.9	10.5	636	34.1	12.4	62.4	74.5	133	1.3	209	13	110
Carroll	15.5	48.7	11.7	3.3	21.1	15.0	1 238	44.5	4.6	48.5	81.8	167	-5.0	135	0	130
Cecil	18.6	NA	11.6	2.8	19.3	21.0	501	40.7	7.8	50.5	84.2	87	-8.4	173	0	67
Charles	3.9	NA	16.9	3.2	20.3	29.7	601	46.3	3.2	48.1	76.9	68	-19.1	113	1	36
Dorchester	33.0	41.0	8.8	1.7	18.3	12.8	392	26.0	20.9	63.8	62.2	125	-10.3	319	11	98
Frederick	11.9	51.7	12.8	4.4	24.9	18.2	1 439	33.5	5.5	56.8	81.9	236	-3.1	164	1	183
Garrett	11.9	51.1	15.4	3.9	20.4	12.3	670	17.9	5.1	56.6	84.2	122	-4.3	181	0	58
Harford	7.0	43.2	12.6	3.2	20.4	36.8	758	42.0	5.3	47.6	82.3	100	-15.7	132	0	73
Howard	9.8	67.6	9.9	6.0	33.0	10.8	432	62.0	6.9	40.3	84.0	54	-2.0	125	1	42
Kent	13.2	53.0	12.4	3.6	25.2	9.5	361	18.0	19.7	66.8	67.0	134	-0.7	370	3	110
Montgomery	4.8	66.5	11.0	7.1	38.4	19.9	669	51.6	7.9	41.3	77.7	103	-2.6	155	0	77
Prince George's	4.7	55.7	14.8	4.4	22.4	28.1	683	60.2	2.8	46.0	71.7	62	-17.4	91	1	35
Queen Anne's	7.2	51.2	13.7	2.5	22.3	13.7	457	22.1	24.1	61.5	72.4	171	1.7	373	5	142
St. Mary's	1.4	49.7	8.6	1.5	30.9	39.7	754	42.8	2.9	54.4	73.7	80	-19.7	107	1	46
Somerset	9.2	39.7	7.0	1.4	11.9	30.1	406	48.0	8.4	61.3	72.9	64	4.3	158	3	45
Talbot	15.2	60.8	15.0	3.1	32.8	7.7	280	31.1	22.5	61.1	60.7	109	-8.9	389	1	92
Washington	21.0	52.1	13.9	3.0	20.6	17.7	906	32.6	5.0	56.0	80.7	138	-5.8	152	1	103
Wicomico	18.2	55.2	11.5	3.9	24.6	12.9	774	54.5	5.7	58.0	72.4	96	-14.0	123	5	70

1. Covers mining, construction, and manufacturing. 2. Covers private sector earnings in agricultural services, forestry, and fisheries; transportation and public utilities; wholesale trade; retail trade; finance, insurance, and real estate; and services.

STATE County	Agriculture, 1987 (cont'd): Value of land and buildings: Average per farm ($1,000)	Average per acre (Dollars)	Value of products sold: Total (Mil dol)	Average per farm (Dollars)	Percent from: Crops	Livestock and poultry[1]	Percent of farms with sales of: $10,000 or more	$100,000 or more	Manufactures, 1987: Establishments: Total	Percent with 20 or more employees	All employees: Number (1,000)	Percent change, 1982–1987	Annual payroll (Mil dol)	Production workers: Number (1,000)	Work hours (Mil)
	119	120	121	122	123	124	125	126	127	128	129	130	131	132	133
LOUISIANA—Con.															
Red River	236	580	11	42 259	57.2	42.8	40.2	8.8	7	57.1	0.7	0.0	11.3	0.6	1.4
Richland	264	669	49	78 479	93.4	6.6	61.1	28.6	17	23.5	0.9	80.0	12.8	0.8	1.6
Sabine	126	1 113	36	76 649	0.6	99.4	32.7	18.8	51	19.6	1.3	30.0	26.5	1.1	2.5
St. Bernard	160	598	1	23 189	D	D	27.3	4.5	50	14.0	1.7	-62.2	61.2	1.2	2.4
St. Charles	258	494	D	D	NA	NA	43.1	2.8	28	53.6	4.3	-27.1	165.9	2.6	5.6
St. Helena	191	1 151	13	34 969	3.1	96.9	34.8	13.9	4	50.0	D	D	D	D	D
St. James	1 177	1 824	16	210 979	97.6	2.4	73.3	49.3	28	60.7	2.8	3.7	87.5	2.0	3.7
St. John the Baptist	1 071	2 218	5	125 897	98.1	1.9	38.5	23.1	22	50.0	2.4	-17.2	77.6	1.6	3.6
St. Landry	195	889	36	30 792	87.1	12.9	34.4	10.0	44	40.9	2.2	-31.2	38.9	1.7	3.2
St. Martin	321	1 368	19	62 435	94.3	5.7	45.5	17.1	33	24.2	2.6	4.0	43.5	2.4	4.6
St. Mary	962	1 092	24	277 441	99.4	0.6	75.0	51.1	66	37.9	3.4	-57.5	79.5	2.5	5.5
St. Tammany	254	2 450	11	21 577	61.3	38.7	22.4	5.1	84	25.0	1.5	-11.8	24.6	1.1	2.0
Tangipahoa	202	1 688	56	52 692	7.4	92.6	40.8	19.3	91	20.9	1.8	-18.2	28.4	1.3	2.5
Tensas	651	679	57	212 400	98.6	1.4	84.0	52.6	6	33.3	0.1	0.0	1.7	0.1	0.2
Terrebonne	331	1 245	5	34 332	83.7	16.3	34.5	11.7	115	27.8	2.2	-48.8	44.8	1.5	3.0
Union	176	1 174	44	95 448	0.7	99.3	35.9	21.9	40	15.0	0.9	28.6	21.2	0.6	1.2
Vermilion	287	1 072	39	32 544	88.4	11.6	42.9	9.2	33	30.3	1.0	0.0	14.0	0.7	1.5
Vernon	118	1 189	9	18 206	3.8	96.2	16.3	3.9	18	16.7	0.2	0.0	4.2	0.2	0.3
Washington	162	1 324	35	41 152	12.8	87.2	34.0	14.9	33	30.3	1.9	-20.8	37.7	1.5	2.8
Webster	132	836	3	8 294	14.6	85.4	17.3	1.4	64	26.6	1.9	26.7	41.2	1.4	3.0
West Baton Rouge	539	1 205	8	87 701	83.8	16.2	35.8	15.8	34	50.0	D	D	D	D	D
West Carroll	136	527	22	39 290	86.5	13.5	45.2	10.1	10	30.0	0.3	0.0	5.1	0.3	0.6
West Feliciana	411	817	6	32 168	58.9	41.1	29.2	5.3	3	33.3	D	D	D	D	D
Winn	98	623	3	15 353	7.5	92.5	12.2	1.1	59	22.0	1.3	-7.1	25.1	1.1	2.3
MAINE	211	962	405	64 681	38.9	61.1	41.8	14.4	2 172	27.8	101.6	-7.8	2 192.1	77.4	151.3
Androscoggin	318	1 563	71	207 239	8.2	91.8	44.3	20.7	200	43.0	11.3	-10.3	193.4	8.7	17.0
Aroostook	175	552	99	97 657	94.4	5.6	69.3	30.4	178	25.3	5.7	-14.9	116.0	4.9	9.6
Cumberland	316	2 300	13	28 678	42.7	57.3	30.7	9.0	381	26.0	16.2	-6.9	372.6	10.9	21.0
Franklin	151	709	7	31 930	17.4	82.6	37.1	9.2	84	32.1	4.8	-11.1	106.9	3.3	6.1
Hancock	225	1 570	16	54 125	D	D	26.6	3.1	125	17.6	2.8	3.7	72.0	2.2	4.2
Kennebec	226	1 020	42	73 374	12.3	87.7	43.2	17.5	123	32.5	7.7	-13.5	164.2	5.4	11.1
Knox	244	1 517	9	42 196	23.2	76.8	37.6	8.6	111	27.9	2.8	3.7	49.0	2.1	4.0
Lincoln	137	1 315	5	21 127	34.0	66.0	22.4	4.8	69	15.9	D	D	D	D	D
Oxford	199	926	15	43 481	53.2	46.8	31.1	11.4	145	22.8	4.7	-23.0	101.4	3.7	7.5
Penobscot	161	723	26	46 045	31.0	69.0	37.6	13.8	234	27.8	13.4	-10.7	307.8	10.2	20.9
Piscataquis	135	534	5	35 492	21.8	78.2	31.9	9.4	54	24.1	2.2	4.8	33.3	1.8	4.2
Sagadahoc	230	1 415	3	26 212	29.1	71.0	25.0	8.1	33	24.2	D	D	D	D	D
Somerset	180	636	20	43 438	9.0	91.0	44.4	13.9	109	25.7	4.9	16.7	105.7	3.8	7.4
Waldo	187	886	32	75 446	5.9	94.1	46.9	16.7	58	15.5	1.5	-16.7	24.7	1.3	2.7
Washington	222	765	12	34 669	D	D	37.4	4.2	67	28.4	1.8	0.0	40.2	1.5	2.9
York	254	1 873	30	57 928	22.0	78.0	30.3	6.1	201	33.3	12.8	-3.0	274.3	9.6	19.0
MARYLAND	367	2 261	989	66 937	25.6	74.4	45.9	17.5	4 244	34.7	230.4	-1.7	5 955.7	139.6	273.5
Allegany	152	886	3	13 724	39.4	60.6	18.8	2.5	69	33.3	4.3	-34.8	114.3	3.0	6.1
Anne Arundel	332	3 961	8	14 909	78.2	21.8	31.4	1.9	299	21.4	20.3	10.9	685.9	10.6	17.4
Baltimore	358	3 290	40	43 348	49.6	50.4	35.8	9.5	587	37.5	56.0	0.9	1 608.3	31.4	62.5
Calvert	238	2 933	4	9 437	89.4	10.6	24.6	0.4	22	40.9	0.5	150.0	7.0	0.4	0.7
Caroline	348	1 646	72	113 746	22.5	77.5	62.9	31.3	32	40.6	1.5	15.4	22.8	1.3	2.3
Carroll	329	2 449	56	45 153	28.9	71.1	37.6	11.9	126	34.1	6.1	-24.7	138.4	3.0	5.8
Cecil	485	2 705	40	80 660	24.1	75.9	41.3	13.4	65	35.4	2.9	-25.6	61.5	1.9	3.7
Charles	233	2 334	8	13 774	72.3	27.7	31.4	1.7	30	20.0	0.5	0.0	9.6	0.4	0.7
Dorchester	457	1 410	52	131 402	29.2	70.8	64.8	30.4	65	44.6	4.5	0.0	71.4	3.6	6.4
Frederick	420	2 534	95	65 773	9.5	90.5	46.1	20.7	140	35.7	7.5	11.9	158.1	5.4	10.9
Garrett	180	978	19	28 921	8.5	91.5	41.5	6.7	45	22.2	1.6	60.0	24.1	1.3	2.3
Harford	345	2 907	24	32 322	35.4	64.6	36.1	10.0	108	28.7	3.8	-19.1	81.4	2.8	5.7
Howard	446	4 017	18	42 372	49.5	50.5	27.5	10.6	196	34.7	7.9	0.0	195.6	4.6	8.9
Kent	923	2 458	44	120 577	46.4	53.6	71.2	20.8	28	28.6	1.0	11.1	18.7	0.7	1.4
Montgomery	587	3 379	26	38 937	61.8	38.2	31.4	10.2	591	25.4	21.4	13.2	622.5	8.5	16.8
Prince George's	221	3 239	16	23 594	88.0	12.0	24.6	3.4	440	32.5	14.2	29.1	365.5	8.0	16.3
Queen Anne's	680	1 959	31	68 449	45.6	54.4	63.0	22.3	32	28.1	0.8	33.3	13.0	0.6	1.1
St. Mary's	217	2 085	13	17 601	59.3	40.7	39.5	2.7	26	19.2	0.4	33.3	6.4	0.3	0.7
Somerset	257	1 302	81	199 243	10.1	89.9	79.6	52.0	32	37.5	0.8	14.3	12.4	0.7	1.3
Talbot	920	2 364	27	94 926	46.3	53.7	59.3	26.1	67	32.8	4.1	51.9	70.8	2.6	4.7
Washington	282	1 811	54	59 703	11.9	88.1	50.7	22.7	146	45.2	11.5	-6.5	259.3	8.6	17.8
Wicomico	245	1 885	134	173 205	10.8	89.2	76.6	47.3	87	35.6	6.3	-7.4	122.6	4.7	9.0

1. Includes livestock and poultry products.

STATE County	Manufactures, 1987 (cont'd): Production workers (cont'd): Wages: Total (Mil dol)	Manufactures, 1987 (cont'd): Production workers (cont'd): Wages: Average per worker (Dollars)	Manufactures, 1987 (cont'd): Value added by manufacture (Mil dol)	Manufactures, 1987 (cont'd): Value of shipments (Mil dol)	Manufactures, 1987 (cont'd): New capital expenditures (Mil dol)	Value of construction authorized by building permits, 1990: Total[1] ($1,000)	Nonresidential: Total ($1,000)	Nonresidential: Percent: Office	Nonresidential: Percent: Industrial	Nonresidential: Percent: Stores	Residential: New construction ($1,000)	Residential: Number of housing units	Residential: Alterations and additions ($1,000)
	134	135	136	137	138	139	140	141	142	143	144	145	146
LOUISIANA—Con.													
Red River	8.5	14 167	33.9	66.9	D	4	0	NA	NA	NA	0	0	0
Richland	9.9	12 375	21.3	70.1	D	437	274	0.0	0.0	0.0	15	3	42
Sabine	21.7	19 727	52.0	191.5	6.4	624	471	0.0	0.0	100.0	105	3	17
St. Bernard	38.4	32 000	278.0	2 127.9	D	17 758	4 703	0.0	37.2	52.4	9 278	272	304
St. Charles	88.1	33 885	1 697.3	4 805.5	83.6	12 948	3 189	50.5	15.6	5.0	9 230	162	31
St. Helena	D	D	D	D	D	691	0	NA	NA	NA	691	24	0
St. James	58.6	29 300	297.4	2 498.1	45.7	1 115	25	0.0	0.0	0.0	880	9	132
St. John the Baptist	49.2	30 750	354.0	2 299.5	43.2	NA	NA	NA	NA	NA	NA	NA	NA
St. Landry	27.1	15 941	112.5	723.6	7.2	6 219	2 986	7.8	0.0	0.0	622	14	677
St. Martin	39.4	16 417	122.3	240.3	3.7	5 261	717	7.7	0.0	21.6	3 178	67	64
St. Mary	52.0	20 800	137.2	370.5	25.7	4 342	2 470	0.0	0.0	16.3	1 163	28	304
St. Tammany	16.0	14 545	60.2	148.7	D	120 442	36 872	18.4	1.6	55.6	73 797	930	3 369
Tangipahoa	16.2	12 462	62.3	172.8	3.5	15 852	2 312	0.3	24.8	19.8	10 932	223	287
Tensas	1.2	12 000	4.6	7.1	0.0	509	214	0.0	0.0	100.0	226	4	69
Terrebonne	25.4	16 933	101.2	208.7	D	24 365	6 192	7.6	0.8	73.1	11 719	228	3 549
Union	12.1	20 167	108.3	225.6	2.6	743	196	93.7	0.0	0.0	420	8	0
Vermilion	9.2	13 143	56.3	97.7	1.2	10 073	4 188	7.7	80.1	6.1	4 717	111	302
Vernon	3.0	15 000	13.9	27.1	0.4	2 313	1 332	0.0	0.0	5.3	436	11	34
Washington	26.7	17 800	210.0	362.0	D	2 752	609	13.4	0.0	70.1	576	14	375
Webster	28.9	20 643	94.8	253.6	6.2	6 095	3 978	0.0	3.1	41.3	1 427	19	557
West Baton Rouge	D	D	D	D	D	6 606	1 428	0.0	87.9	10.0	3 377	76	347
West Carroll	4.1	13 667	9.4	24.9	0.3	316	305	100.0	0.0	0.0	0	0	9
West Feliciana	D	D	D	D	D	4 179	488	0.0	0.0	87.4	3 538	42	8
Winn	19.5	17 727	74.9	179.5	4.9	1 049	0	NA	NA	NA	252	6	161
MAINE	1 457.0	18 824	5 270.6	10 661.5	539.4	680 713	169 400	19.7	17.7	26.8	329 551	4 816	76 107
Androscoggin	130.4	14 989	434.2	821.1	33.1	56 543	24 015	4.5	20.1	42.1	18 564	250	5 126
Aroostook	88.5	18 061	300.2	762.3	12.4	24 788	10 904	10.8	38.5	18.9	6 895	128	2 038
Cumberland	201.7	18 505	1 015.2	1 813.7	103.8	188 111	50 103	36.8	3.4	29.7	89 237	1 070	20 845
Franklin	69.2	20 970	320.0	591.0	D	6 540	736	0.0	1.8	19.7	3 597	59	1 384
Hancock	54.6	24 818	178.5	413.3	D	45 121	16 189	3.4	51.3	20.4	16 012	232	4 291
Kennebec	104.9	19 426	360.3	850.2	24.7	75 830	16 804	40.7	1.1	28.7	38 331	538	7 426
Knox	30.5	14 524	133.0	276.4	8.2	22 030	3 890	22.5	30.7	13.6	9 954	143	3 743
Lincoln	D	D	D	D	D	11 621	251	0.0	0.0	0.0	7 436	110	2 069
Oxford	74.2	20 054	217.4	488.9	24.1	23 776	5 487	6.4	12.3	22.0	12 391	209	1 742
Penobscot	209.9	20 578	721.2	1 447.3	174.9	63 840	14 971	10.1	39.0	18.1	30 759	559	6 860
Piscataquis	23.1	12 833	67.7	158.4	5.4	2 166	326	0.0	0.0	0.0	1 500	46	275
Sagadahoc	D	D	D	D	D	13 269	1 909	9.4	18.3	10.5	9 117	178	779
Somerset	73.0	19 211	349.9	744.7	34.9	6 607	672	0.0	14.9	0.0	4 955	97	447
Waldo	19.2	14 769	50.4	122.5	D	12 325	4 160	4.4	30.4	0.0	5 865	104	996
Washington	31.6	21 067	85.2	288.5	5.8	7 743	2 872	11.7	4.5	73.3	3 041	60	356
York	185.5	19 323	637.2	1 210.7	52.4	120 401	16 110	11.7	7.6	20.6	71 897	1 033	17 730
MARYLAND	2 994.3	21 449	14 020.0	28 009.4	875.2	4 347 338	892 215	29.3	12.9	32.8	2 185 336	32 111	545 655
Allegany	81.4	27 133	354.3	617.5	D	19 222	3 749	15.4	5.9	36.7	10 748	187	1 358
Anne Arundel	310.1	29 255	1 211.0	2 035.3	82.0	505 583	94 660	33.9	20.4	35.3	249 543	3 911	80 151
Baltimore	749.5	23 869	3 431.7	6 242.9	184.9	596 148	96 108	40.6	32.5	16.9	284 341	4 324	63 122
Calvert	4.9	12 250	14.8	29.3	1.0	104 303	15 932	1.8	4.5	48.9	74 258	954	5 733
Caroline	16.0	12 308	51.9	111.0	3.4	19 168	3 912	4.0	16.2	57.5	13 139	213	1 984
Carroll	54.7	18 233	256.1	484.0	D	133 628	20 242	7.7	0.0	81.8	79 388	1 028	15 878
Cecil	32.6	17 158	171.6	292.3	13.3	73 422	20 676	0.6	26.0	55.0	44 092	715	4 256
Charles	6.3	15 750	17.2	40.4	0.7	90 522	28 720	41.6	17.2	35.0	52 262	703	1 651
Dorchester	47.6	13 222	150.3	464.5	7.0	20 164	5 993	0.0	1.3	54.0	11 483	174	1 261
Frederick	95.4	17 667	496.0	933.8	25.7	253 071	38 324	9.7	0.0	20.0	174 002	2 127	14 311
Garrett	15.9	12 231	44.9	109.0	2.7	31 435	3 063	8.6	0.0	5.4	25 346	384	1 211
Harford	47.5	16 964	186.3	387.1	9.4	258 701	67 516	13.9	19.0	56.3	150 575	2 546	18 164
Howard	90.4	19 652	488.1	1 060.9	23.0	258 195	61 184	30.7	30.4	30.0	107 258	1 303	32 684
Kent	12.9	18 429	65.9	136.8	2.4	25 420	5 339	0.0	9.4	44.9	16 538	192	2 094
Montgomery	184.4	21 694	1 012.1	1 672.8	45.7	598 666	95 186	33.9	3.6	26.5	286 752	5 077	197 338
Prince George's	173.1	21 638	837.1	1 759.3	79.3	595 403	162 298	32.5	2.2	37.2	342 781	4 752	30 466
Queen Anne's	8.5	14 167	38.1	111.9	D	38 241	9 080	5.0	0.4	29.2	22 156	209	4 468
St. Mary's	4.9	16 333	14.8	24.5	2.1	70 463	6 367	18.4	0.0	32.0	58 387	754	3 578
Somerset	9.6	13 714	27.4	96.6	D	10 691	2 063	0.0	30.7	41.4	6 730	144	401
Talbot	34.9	13 423	174.3	366.5	11.9	43 776	6 622	57.9	10.9	7.2	23 069	249	1 966
Washington	181.3	21 081	471.4	1 112.9	63.3	100 253	20 847	21.2	7.2	48.6	56 624	678	8 716
Wicomico	75.8	16 128	311.0	718.9	25.0	91 285	22 979	10.6	1.0	58.8	38 595	628	4 471

1. Includes nonresidential additions and alterations, residential nonhousekeeping buildings, and residential garages and carports not shown separately.

STATE County	Wholesale trade, 1987				Retail trade, all establishments, 1987				Retail trade, establishments with payroll, 1987					
						Sales				Sales				
											Per capita[2] (Dollars)			
	Estab-lishments	Sales (Mil dol)	Paid employees[1]	Annual payroll (Mil dol)	Number	Total (Mil dol)	Percent change, 1982–1987	Per capita[2] (Dollars)	Number	Total (Mil dol)	General merchan-dise stores	Food stores	Apparel & acces-sory stores	Eating and drinking places
	147	148	149	150	151	152	153	154	155	156	157	158	159	160
LOUISIANA—Con.														
Red River	5	D	D	D	75	33.5	2.4	3 074	45	31.9	242	629	D	D
Richland	27	86.4	211	2.9	231	81.6	-11.5	3 546	126	76.1	364	748	55	339
Sabine	35	86.2	223	4.2	230	88.4	-2.0	3 237	106	78.9	452	909	104	121
St. Bernard	63	338.7	370	6.4	587	307.7	26.6	4 498	325	292.9	527	1 747	153	353
St. Charles	53	1 326.3	928	26.4	280	99.7	15.4	2 287	155	94.5	D	905	30	172
St. Helena	1	D	D	D	39	6.6	-14.3	634	18	4.6	D	206	0	D
St. James	19	D	D	D	173	55.8	-1.8	2 526	92	52.1	96	1 130	18	129
St. John the Baptist	43	D	D	D	281	147.0	27.3	3 577	146	142.1	D	1 092	96	294
St. Landry	133	213.2	985	14.6	845	302.7	-11.7	3 476	442	281.4	452	1 011	141	194
St. Martin	42	130.8	347	6.5	362	113.9	-0.3	2 514	164	100.8	D	852	15	220
St. Mary	117	306.7	1 177	22.9	628	238.7	-30.0	3 888	361	226.7	D	1 310	141	316
St. Tammany	195	382.5	1 371	24.1	1 440	822.3	61.9	5 530	830	796.0	703	1 517	189	426
Tangipahoa	129	262.3	1 380	19.7	898	503.3	18.6	5 531	530	486.4	613	1 468	175	381
Tensas	15	130.0	155	2.8	75	15.8	-24.8	1 932	36	14.2	102	894	D	31
Terrebonne	239	410.3	2 105	37.8	1 051	578.9	-7.0	5 895	643	558.3	908	1 350	256	701
Union	26	26.2	139	2.6	182	51.4	11.0	2 263	78	43.3	D	596	35	75
Vermilion	95	108.9	552	9.1	556	179.2	-8.6	3 387	298	165.6	315	1 042	145	165
Vernon	22	39.4	213	3.3	373	162.4	26.5	2 693	211	153.2	D	654	56	309
Washington	45	44.4	295	3.8	464	155.8	14.4	3 274	253	143.1	353	921	158	193
Webster	52	96.9	644	8.0	453	201.9	4.9	4 418	249	190.2	447	1 009	179	234
West Baton Rouge	33	523.6	415	9.8	158	61.3	27.4	2 975	76	58.2	D	1 102	D	40
West Carroll	13	18.1	95	0.9	115	84.7	151.3	6 565	58	81.2	D	742	D	D
West Feliciana	3	9.4	15	0.4	84	22.9	10.6	1 706	50	21.3	127	669	D	135
Winn	21	23.5	111	1.9	163	66.6	21.5	3 894	106	62.5	D	1 154	68	178
MAINE	1 865	6 525.0	22 665	461.8	15 242	8 939.7	67.7	7 537	9 204	8 651.0	689	1 525	284	581
Androscoggin	184	444.3	2 361	46.7	1 084	723.1	58.0	7 145	700	702.7	891	1 630	224	522
Aroostook	138	319.4	1 358	19.1	1 011	481.1	45.6	5 543	611	460.3	588	1 253	174	321
Cumberland	572	3 010.0	8 927	202.2	2 848	2 676.8	78.2	11 528	1 953	2 634.3	1 100	1 866	560	894
Franklin	28	130.3	236	8.1	407	174.6	90.4	6 103	220	167.1	D	1 456	148	458
Hancock	75	99.0	501	7.4	881	345.7	66.0	7 700	539	330.1	501	2 008	281	737
Kennebec	157	795.9	2 704	54.0	1 307	883.6	60.5	7 764	790	860.8	858	1 575	215	524
Knox	68	108.4	462	7.4	604	252.1	69.4	7 142	332	238.8	598	1 680	380	483
Lincoln	41	39.2	232	3.2	611	197.5	71.7	6 857	310	186.0	D	1 467	207	602
Oxford	52	167.8	431	7.4	645	227.4	28.5	4 485	330	209.1	393	846	86	253
Penobscot	243	884.4	3 040	64.9	1 651	1 146.6	69.2	8 225	1 054	1 116.3	971	1 638	372	534
Piscataquis	17	14.7	96	1.3	235	90.3	36.4	4 959	143	85.1	732	1 282	21	263
Sagadahoc	20	22.2	125	2.6	335	174.1	90.5	5 406	162	165.4	280	1 680	85	379
Somerset	49	72.8	335	5.6	574	243.9	53.7	5 189	310	231.8	269	1 392	86	232
Waldo	25	126.0	521	8.2	445	124.2	92.9	4 058	196	114.9	467	943	86	352
Washington	47	71.7	430	6.1	491	175.4	70.3	5 084	278	164.1	333	1 593	68	298
York	149	218.7	906	17.5	2 113	1 023.5	73.9	6 322	1 276	984.3	282	1 180	249	768
MARYLAND	6 667	41 128.0	99 512	2 495.8	39 495	32 680.2	55.7	7 205	26 538	32 009.4	826	1 348	389	662
Allegany	102	512.2	1 107	21.3	921	512.1	37.1	6 792	619	496.3	D	1 374	271	599
Anne Arundel	578	4 437.2	7 814	200.5	3 570	3 339.6	77.6	8 126	2 466	3 282.6	1 153	1 464	354	735
Baltimore	1 164	5 574.1	15 632	394.6	6 568	6 167.1	58.2	9 060	4 539	6 059.4	1 219	1 565	569	791
Calvert	14	28.3	91	2.5	317	177.2	100.9	3 912	180	169.6	D	976	33	437
Caroline	29	66.1	224	4.0	215	125.2	131.9	5 070	123	119.4	174	992	32	198
Carroll	141	373.5	1 571	30.3	1 099	634.0	66.7	5 508	623	609.9	429	1 140	134	412
Cecil	67	98.8	490	9.3	531	410.4	62.3	5 896	324	395.7	253	946	122	394
Charles	50	154.2	646	13.5	454	534.5	115.7	5 842	307	529.1	D	1 124	178	471
Dorchester	48	70.2	352	5.8	322	162.9	18.8	5 376	196	156.9	288	1 157	234	451
Frederick	173	513.3	2 275	47.0	1 325	949.3	72.3	7 006	859	929.3	891	1 417	220	623
Garrett	48	85.6	401	5.2	354	157.9	50.2	5 915	182	149.1	256	1 498	130	281
Harford	151	727.5	1 121	24.4	1 227	1 016.0	71.9	6 237	813	994.6	601	1 307	187	441
Howard	524	5 071.8	9 567	250.9	1 338	1 072.4	105.5	6 932	834	1 044.7	740	1 374	375	623
Kent	39	62.1	283	4.7	285	110.3	57.3	6 490	174	105.7	403	1 650	197	716
Montgomery	1 012	7 031.4	14 693	443.7	6 058	5 872.8	58.2	8 609	3 785	5 761.0	997	1 620	601	701
Prince George's	842	7 102.0	17 236	439.6	4 948	5 577.0	49.0	8 093	3 501	5 500.0	1 057	1 433	410	661
Queen Anne's	52	110.8	468	7.6	309	137.6	71.6	4 469	171	130.1	75	1 246	107	574
St. Mary's	36	72.6	386	7.3	573	332.5	82.3	4 904	335	318.8	429	1 230	173	459
Somerset	23	27.2	208	2.6	223	62.6	48.0	3 227	123	57.4	96	1 187	20	304
Talbot	82	285.0	714	15.7	462	290.3	64.9	10 556	310	283.8	97	1 806	635	1 166
Washington	212	724.4	2 850	58.2	1 179	788.7	38.9	6 764	774	769.6	884	1 240	230	452
Wicomico	167	708.7	2 110	43.6	749	625.5	50.3	8 860	511	613.5	1 243	1 551	507	704

1. For pay period including March 12. 2. Based on the estimated population as of July 1 of the year shown.

STATE County	Retail trade, establishments with payroll, 1987 (cont'd): Paid employees[1]	Retail trade, establishments with payroll, 1987 (cont'd): Annual payroll (Mil dol)	Taxable service industries–establishments with payroll, 1987: Number	Receipts (Mil dol): Total	Receipts, selected kinds of business: Hotels, motels and other lodging places	Receipts, selected kinds of business: Health services	Receipts, selected kinds of business: Legal services	Paid employees	Annual payroll (Mil dol)	Bank deposits,[2] June 1989: Total (Mil dol)	Bank deposits: Percent change, 1988–1989	Savings capital,[3] September 1989: Total (Mil dol)	Savings capital: Percent change, 1988–1989
	161	162	163	164	165	166	167	168	169	170	171	172	173
LOUISIANA—Con.													
Red River	255	2.3	25	11.7	D	7.9	0.6	281	3.4	58	-5.6	7.7	-4.4
Richland	875	7.6	92	18.7	D	11.7	1.8	470	6.7	163	2.8	27.1	0.5
Sabine	899	7.6	71	21.7	2.9	13.3	0.6	738	7.7	115	6.1	33.5	0.4
St. Bernard	4 067	32.9	316	95.3	D	60.7	5.3	2 159	31.3	278	5.4	293.5	4.0
St. Charles	1 286	11.3	146	47.5	D	8.4	2.6	2 010	23.8	184	0.9	23.1	-2.3
St. Helena	58	0.5	6	0.9	0.0	D	D	14	0.2	35	-0.7	0.0	NA
St. James	617	5.9	53	13.3	D	6.2	0.8	365	5.9	191	6.1	12.2	10.0
St. John the Baptist	1 772	14.8	149	74.9	D	40.0	3.0	1 675	25.8	152	0.9	919.6	17.0
St. Landry	3 486	29.8	397	103.5	0.8	49.2	17.1	2 050	33.9	511	-4.7	140.2	-6.4
St. Martin	1 249	10.8	99	15.0	D	6.7	2.1	447	4.7	200	0.8	32.7	-4.1
St. Mary	2 921	26.1	374	162.1	4.8	16.0	12.5	2 984	49.0	405	-2.1	158.4	4.7
St. Tammany	9 899	84.8	884	280.9	7.6	154.5	18.6	6 203	90.5	578	-6.6	374.7	-4.3
Tangipahoa	5 699	50.7	408	86.5	3.6	40.4	7.7	2 267	26.7	442	-4.5	128.2	-1.2
Tensas	113	1.0	25	2.1	0.0	1.2	0.3	104	0.8	71	8.5	0.0	NA
Terrebonne	7 097	73.3	620	229.1	4.9	59.8	30.7	4 311	91.2	637	-1.8	171.0	0.7
Union	371	4.0	39	8.3	0.0	5.0	0.4	398	3.0	121	1.9	23.0	-6.9
Vermilion	2 097	17.3	254	60.7	0.5	22.0	6.3	1 551	23.0	427	-1.1	69.2	3.6
Vernon	1 813	16.1	128	37.3	3.6	17.0	1.0	1 142	11.8	118	4.2	27.3	-78.0
Washington	1 761	14.7	158	25.0	D	10.4	4.3	669	7.6	249	2.4	42.7	-1.0
Webster	2 140	19.5	151	51.0	0.8	34.6	2.5	1 499	18.0	289	0.4	72.8	57.8
West Baton Rouge	515	5.0	59	15.0	6.1	2.3	0.5	567	4.7	66	0.3	26.9	0.1
West Carroll	447	4.6	31	6.1	0.0	2.6	0.7	177	1.8	54	10.1	10.5	-16.5
West Feliciana	285	2.1	32	11.6	D	2.7	0.8	380	6.2	53	-3.0	0.0	NA
Winn	779	6.7	59	19.4	D	14.4	0.7	439	5.9	62	3.9	47.3	-12.1
MAINE	91 991	958.5	8 164	2 321.0	269.4	668.2	233.6	57 526	842.2	12 224	11.8	998.5	-3.5
Androscoggin	7 716	75.9	659	199.9	9.6	73.4	20.7	5 456	80.9	708	9.1	247.2	6.2
Aroostook	5 150	47.5	423	89.0	6.1	34.3	7.0	2 738	34.5	599	7.6	25.9	-2.4
Cumberland	27 550	311.2	2 285	905.5	58.8	219.8	107.1	19 654	340.3	4 173	17.5	378.6	-10.3
Franklin	2 038	17.4	163	41.6	10.0	15.9	1.3	1 552	12.4	251	6.7	0.0	NA
Hancock	3 239	36.0	377	74.9	23.8	22.2	5.3	1 845	24.5	477	7.2	8.5	0.1
Kennebec	8 878	92.8	723	197.0	19.9	67.3	21.1	5 408	66.7	1 028	6.8	119.0	1.0
Knox	2 447	25.9	288	66.6	17.4	16.8	4.2	1 550	21.8	455	8.2	31.5	0.1
Lincoln	2 176	20.4	211	34.4	12.6	8.4	3.1	717	9.8	279	8.5	66.8	-4.5
Oxford	2 437	21.7	255	62.5	10.5	19.2	5.0	2 051	22.7	448	7.4	0.0	NA
Penobscot	11 597	120.7	891	260.6	21.6	90.3	24.9	6 504	101.0	1 508	17.8	0.0	NA
Piscataquis	886	8.2	92	15.7	3.3	6.0	1.2	537	5.7	129	-0.3	0.0	NA
Sagadahoc	1 828	17.6	167	46.7	5.3	11.2	8.6	1 032	16.7	189	4.8	26.7	-8.0
Somerset	2 278	23.0	256	49.0	3.9	16.8	3.9	1 456	18.1	343	8.4	0.0	NA
Waldo	1 225	12.1	146	20.3	2.6	7.4	1.7	602	6.2	175	9.3	0.0	NA
Washington	1 701	15.6	160	26.6	3.8	9.5	1.6	830	8.9	240	7.3	26.3	2.7
York	10 845	112.4	1 068	230.7	60.2	49.8	16.8	5 594	71.9	1 222	6.6	68.0	-4.9
MARYLAND	377 862	3 945.2	31 178	17 466.8	683.3	3 397.7	997.2	368 662	7 108.4	37 494	7.7	19 329.1	4.1
Allegany	6 699	56.9	444	98.4	D	D	3.7	2 370	37.7	468	6.9	294.6	0.3
Anne Arundel	38 763	392.4	2 625	1 184.1	63.8	235.5	43.4	24 643	461.7	2 200	6.2	1 352.5	2.6
Baltimore	72 484	746.4	5 283	2 365.0	72.0	672.6	87.9	57 329	953.3	5 746	9.5	3 879.5	-1.5
Calvert	1 950	19.4	207	52.8	3.0	22.2	2.2	1 369	21.1	240	9.7	71.6	0.1
Caroline	894	10.6	93	23.1	D	2.1	D	735	7.8	195	9.7	0.0	NA
Carroll	7 215	69.5	629	139.8	D	46.1	7.8	3 615	50.9	950	11.3	231.7	-5.8
Cecil	3 647	38.4	289	72.0	1.3	19.0	6.2	1 573	21.7	323	6.2	68.2	-5.4
Charles	5 165	61.3	236	72.2	4.5	21.3	4.1	1 625	26.7	436	7.0	263.4	9.4
Dorchester	1 769	16.8	151	32.2	D	14.3	D	885	11.8	262	7.3	74.0	-0.5
Frederick	10 896	110.2	789	268.5	16.4	74.6	11.1	6 257	98.3	1 163	7.1	205.9	9.7
Garrett	1 484	15.2	123	34.6	5.7	9.4	1.3	1 145	13.1	294	10.0	16.7	-11.9
Harford	10 990	112.5	921	251.2	34.7	66.7	10.4	6 638	97.7	880	7.1	364.1	5.5
Howard	13 426	129.1	1 260	1 186.2	19.1	135.6	32.7	21 146	521.4	918	12.6	374.7	0.9
Kent	1 336	11.7	127	19.5	1.5	5.6	2.5	426	5.3	225	1.8	52.1	8.8
Montgomery	63 085	743.8	7 260	5 541.8	134.0	772.2	200.2	97 641	2 307.6	6 489	8.2	5 869.1	11.5
Prince George's	63 120	662.8	4 014	2 835.2	61.3	513.5	84.1	60 323	1 130.0	3 243	4.8	2 613.2	7.6
Queen Anne's	1 716	17.2	136	29.1	D	6.5	2.1	669	8.8	266	13.2	14.0	-13.1
St. Mary's	3 843	37.1	304	149.7	3.6	20.5	3.8	3 192	63.1	362	10.7	57.6	4.2
Somerset	739	6.3	56	11.6	D	5.6	0.6	248	3.3	113	5.2	0.0	NA
Talbot	3 474	35.0	275	81.2	9.6	26.6	6.7	2 040	31.4	367	6.2	184.4	8.9
Washington	8 419	87.1	610	188.7	D	D	9.1	5 050	71.6	858	3.9	364.0	8.2
Wicomico	7 129	67.4	509	189.0	10.8	85.7	11.5	4 413	83.5	556	7.3	340.4	4.6

1. For the period including March 12 of the year shown. 2. Includes deposits for all insured and reporting noninsured commercial and mutual savings banks. 3. Includes savings capital for all FSLIC insured savings institutions.

STATE County	Federal funds and grants, 1989: Expenditures: Total (Mil dol)	Federal funds and grants, 1989: Expenditures: Percent change, 1988–1989	Federal funds and grants, 1989: Per capita[1] (Dollars): Total	Per capita[1] (Dollars): Direct payments for individuals	Per capita[1] (Dollars): Procurement contract awards	Per capita[1] (Dollars): Salaries and wages	Per capita[1] (Dollars): Grant awards	Local government finances, 1981–1982: General revenue: Total (Mil dol)	General revenue: Intergovernmental: Total (Mil dol)	General revenue: Intergovernmental: Percent from state	General revenue: Taxes: Total (Mil dol)	Taxes: Per capita[2]: Total (Dollars)	Taxes: Per capita[2]: Property (Dollars)	Direct general expenditure: Total (Mil dol)	Direct general expenditure: Percent change, 1977–1982
	174	175	176	177	178	179	180	181	182	183	184	185	186	187	188
LOUISIANA—Con.															
Red River	31.9	-26.9	2 952	1 577	314	123	646	8.0	5.5	96.2	2.1	192	67	7.2	44.3
Richland	75.2	20.3	3 343	1 655	18	107	732	25.2	15.6	70.0	5.3	235	133	25.4	86.3
Sabine	62.0	11.3	2 298	1 678	9	78	524	17.4	11.4	95.6	4.5	172	104	18.2	66.4
St. Bernard	148.0	12.6	2 160	1 699	217	73	166	57.0	27.8	91.3	20.1	305	121	51.5	80.7
St. Charles	125.7	106.9	2 850	1 149	156	121	1 419	67.4	21.6	86.0	28.1	706	286	58.6	103.9
St. Helena	26.8	39.5	2 625	1 074	8	62	1 447	9.5	6.6	95.8	1.3	130	88	9.4	62.1
St. James	43.2	163.3	1 963	1 300	86	183	389	34.6	12.5	87.4	13.1	605	371	25.7	41.7
St. John the Baptist	51.7	5.2	1 249	963	41	56	185	28.4	12.4	95.6	10.7	296	126	27.6	84.8
St. Landry	223.8	12.4	2 639	1 813	24	83	649	95.0	48.9	90.9	17.7	201	60	89.0	75.3
St. Martin	77.3	11.6	1 726	1 206	11	68	421	36.8	22.0	88.2	8.7	199	101	39.3	115.2
St. Mary	209.5	63.1	3 575	1 472	1 548	121	429	109.8	30.1	89.5	51.1	767	190	86.7	120.3
St. Tammany	243.7	11.0	1 585	1 206	106	131	135	103.2	39.6	96.2	26.2	212	67	108.1	117.0
Tangipahoa	212.8	10.8	2 359	1 650	15	111	573	70.1	37.6	89.9	13.2	153	53	68.8	93.9
Tensas	83.1	3.4	10 391	1 827	5 889	86	916	8.6	6.5	80.4	1.6	195	97	7.3	38.6
Terrebonne	200.8	30.6	2 074	1 318	28	104	619	146.6	49.9	88.5	56.7	563	189	143.0	200.6
Union	53.5	15.8	2 366	1 782	15	91	458	16.6	10.1	95.8	2.7	126	61	15.4	59.9
Vermilion	119.1	12.3	2 295	1 511	39	106	307	69.0	26.5	90.5	19.6	382	145	67.5	179.8
Vernon	610.6	41.5	10 142	1 212	362	8 197	364	30.7	22.6	90.2	5.3	91	42	30.5	83.8
Washington	119.9	10.3	2 546	1 924	9	115	485	43.9	24.2	88.4	10.7	239	100	42.2	60.4
Webster	118.2	10.9	2 610	2 035	16	93	448	33.9	20.6	94.0	9.1	203	100	33.1	58.4
West Baton Rouge	49.9	51.8	2 423	1 247	9	135	1 022	27.4	10.0	92.6	11.3	580	245	23.7	5.8
West Carroll	42.8	20.8	3 340	1 684	25	130	681	10.7	7.6	89.4	2.1	165	92	10.2	25.3
West Feliciana	26.5	4.6	1 965	756	863	51	262	13.8	5.3	93.6	4.2	328	99	12.7	79.7
Winn	45.1	4.7	2 685	1 874	85	157	556	15.2	10.8	98.3	2.7	153	94	14.2	68.3
MAINE	4 060.9	0.4	X	1 902	339	439	614	905.8	351.2	75.8	424.9	374	372	897.1	45.0
Androscoggin	247.2	6.2	2 368	1 788	33	158	380	68.7	30.3	67.4	30.5	305	303	68.1	46.5
Aroostook	368.1	13.1	4 315	1 866	462	1 221	724	93.1	39.1	80.7	27.3	303	301	93.6	54.2
Cumberland	768.6	8.1	3 214	1 812	242	748	396	185.7	62.1	66.2	98.9	453	449	190.0	36.3
Franklin	63.3	3.8	2 160	1 585	15	125	420	21.8	7.9	85.5	10.8	383	381	21.8	31.6
Hancock	145.9	2.0	3 131	2 012	92	433	578	30.3	7.1	80.2	20.5	482	481	30.0	59.9
Kennebec	444.9	-3.6	3 777	1 792	74	530	1 370	80.3	40.5	65.2	33.0	298	296	78.4	39.6
Knox	103.4	6.7	2 850	1 955	133	193	558	23.2	6.6	79.3	14.1	421	419	24.2	60.5
Lincoln	79.3	7.2	2 634	2 054	53	161	357	23.0	5.3	86.4	15.9	603	601	21.8	39.6
Oxford	127.1	4.1	2 440	1 902	19	139	368	42.0	17.3	85.1	19.8	404	403	39.7	48.4
Penobscot	404.3	7.5	2 829	1 728	142	392	551	114.8	44.2	77.3	50.7	368	365	109.6	46.8
Piscataquis	49.6	10.2	2 655	1 979	25	126	508	19.6	6.5	92.5	5.4	305	303	17.5	45.2
Sagadahoc	290.6	-49.4	8 571	1 444	6 070	822	227	23.1	8.8	83.5	12.2	418	416	22.9	45.6
Somerset	120.7	8.2	2 499	1 781	53	123	521	40.4	18.2	89.7	17.0	374	372	39.8	52.1
Waldo	76.5	2.0	2 399	1 681	71	154	477	16.7	7.8	91.6	7.7	272	271	14.9	36.1
Washington	125.1	-4.5	3 554	2 178	182	395	790	23.7	11.3	86.1	10.6	309	307	23.4	26.4
York	403.1	9.7	2 368	1 681	319	122	240	99.4	38.3	75.5	50.6	349	346	101.6	55.9
MARYLAND	25 041.1	4.7	X	1 921	1 327	1 227	563	5 198.2	2 086.8	80.3	2 168.6	508	309	4 935.3	28.4
Allegany	254.8	-15.3	3 402	2 629	243	177	338	69.6	32.5	85.2	24.2	309	194	67.4	13.4
Anne Arundel	1 934.9	-10.9	4 571	1 609	632	1 434	891	363.9	124.5	85.0	178.4	468	249	342.8	29.4
Baltimore	2 178.8	-2.1	3 131	1 697	450	846	134	642.0	187.3	77.9	344.1	517	283	617.0	38.5
Calvert	116.3	0.7	2 313	1 544	276	225	260	43.0	11.1	88.5	23.5	644	582	42.2	62.2
Caroline	59.0	-4.3	2 295	1 766	19	118	326	19.4	11.0	84.1	5.9	254	152	19.1	22.1
Carroll	231.3	-3.4	1 893	1 444	181	130	119	77.3	30.1	87.1	36.6	367	216	74.1	48.3
Cecil	191.1	6.3	2 592	1 471	383	568	142	42.7	23.9	84.6	12.7	202	189	47.6	36.5
Charles	289.5	-0.8	2 960	1 284	155	1 289	221	69.6	32.3	91.2	27.9	358	229	73.1	25.3
Dorchester	102.8	14.6	3 359	2 067	228	155	496	28.6	14.8	81.1	10.6	351	244	26.2	12.3
Frederick	390.6	3.2	2 722	1 388	370	740	200	113.7	49.7	84.9	49.5	414	254	105.1	43.3
Garrett	60.3	9.1	2 232	1 645	21	116	408	27.2	14.4	87.9	11.4	428	298	26.4	9.9
Harford	934.7	6.4	5 311	1 491	866	2 811	115	131.1	57.0	83.9	57.0	385	236	130.0	32.8
Howard	470.4	12.4	2 770	842	1 729	107	87	145.7	48.0	81.1	79.6	627	378	134.3	61.2
Kent	60.2	7.8	3 542	2 362	121	214	536	13.1	5.8	75.6	6.0	363	221	12.1	17.5
Montgomery	5 360.7	-1.2	7 398	2 090	2 482	2 339	480	808.6	178.4	80.8	495.5	828	502	753.7	38.7
Prince George's	4 577.5	21.4	6 467	1 731	2 789	1 643	289	886.7	262.7	79.7	315.8	473	292	857.5	30.3
Queen Anne's	67.2	-2.2	2 031	1 492	53	108	242	22.9	11.3	92.2	8.7	330	216	22.7	40.9
St. Mary's	548.9	-2.1	7 644	1 615	2 904	2 898	218	42.3	19.9	93.4	17.7	285	169	37.6	7.8
Somerset	58.8	-1.2	3 031	2 102	40	169	652	13.3	8.1	83.5	4.0	217	141	17.1	12.5
Talbot	94.6	0.6	3 344	2 498	73	349	295	20.4	7.4	65.5	9.8	373	252	18.4	18.8
Washington	370.9	12.0	3 122	1 747	458	672	227	99.5	48.2	66.1	37.4	339	206	102.1	48.6
Wicomico	195.5	26.2	2 671	1 570	67	199	817	56.2	24.3	88.5	22.4	344	221	53.7	28.8

1. Based on the estimated population as of July 1 of the year shown. 2. Based on the estimated population as of July 1, 1982.

STATE County	Local government finances, 1981–1982 (cont'd)								State and local government employment, 1989		Federal government civilian employment 1989		Elections, 1988[3]	
	Direct general expenditure (cont'd)						Debt outstanding							
	Per capita[1] (Dollars)	Percent of total for– Education	Health & hospitals	Police protection	Public welfare	Highways	Total (Mil dol)	Per capita[1] (Dollars)	Total	Rate[2]	Total	Earnings ($1,000)	Total vote cast for president	Vote for lead party (Percent)
	189	190	191	192	193	194	195	196	197	198	199	200	201	202
LOUISIANA—Con.														
Red River	645	65.4	5.1	6.9	0.9	7.2	1.3	121	507	469.4	39	942	4 586	R—49.4
Richland	1 120	45.2	12.0	2.7	0.2	7.8	12.4	546	1 326	589.3	106	2 509	8 315	R—62.9
Sabine	689	72.6	1.7	4.9	0.1	7.4	13.1	498	1 128	417.8	50	1 355	8 541	R—55.8
St. Bernard	783	50.6	2.7	7.3	0.6	7.0	88.0	1 337	2 471	360.7	133	3 964	31 736	R—61.8
St. Charles	1 472	50.1	8.1	6.4	0.1	5.2	149.6	3 759	2 306	522.9	160	5 151	17 995	R—53.8
St. Helena	952	60.1	20.7	3.1	0.7	5.4	0.8	81	684	670.6	18	437	5 153	D—58.5
St. James	1 183	49.9	13.9	5.2	0.5	6.6	63.8	2 942	1 225	556.8	134	4 962	10 719	D—62.6
St. John the Baptist	764	64.9	1.9	5.8	0.6	3.6	69.4	1 923	1 587	383.3	66	1 834	16 219	D—51.6
St. Landry	1 012	51.5	23.9	4.5	0.1	4.5	35.4	402	4 676	551.4	212	5 849	35 457	D—53.8
St. Martin	904	63.6	5.0	4.7	0.2	6.3	25.1	578	1 902	424.6	66	1 818	18 129	D—56.0
St. Mary	1 302	40.6	22.0	5.4	0.1	7.7	75.2	1 130	3 144	536.5	142	4 059	22 318	R—51.7
St. Tammany	877	44.8	23.6	5.3	0.0	5.3	152.4	1 236	7 473	485.9	433	14 361	54 823	R—69.9
Tangipahoa	798	51.0	19.6	6.3	0.1	5.3	33.1	384	7 198	798.0	263	7 611	30 688	R—54.3
Tensas	868	56.4	6.2	5.2	1.2	8.6	3.8	451	435	543.8	32	741	3 290	R—50.0
Terrebonne	1 420	35.4	33.1	3.9	0.2	3.1	179.4	1 781	4 862	502.3	309	9 359	32 212	R—58.2
Union	715	57.7	18.1	4.3	0.0	7.7	9.0	418	937	414.6	58	1 333	9 369	R—63.0
Vermilion	1 313	45.2	18.4	3.7	0.1	10.3	50.6	984	2 549	491.1	158	4 350	21 966	D—55.4
Vernon	519	72.6	2.1	5.4	0.1	6.7	9.3	159	2 546	422.9	3 045	73 584	12 761	R—58.4
Washington	937	52.3	17.4	4.7	0.3	4.3	24.3	540	2 651	562.8	123	3 414	18 094	R—51.8
Webster	742	62.9	3.0	4.7	0.2	7.4	27.0	606	1 867	412.1	111	3 282	17 805	R—57.3
West Baton Rouge	1 218	44.4	1.3	6.1	0.1	5.5	79.8	4 090	1 158	562.1	102	2 919	8 801	D—53.2
West Carroll	781	66.0	2.8	4.4	0.3	8.3	3.0	229	657	513.3	52	1 202	4 797	R—64.1
West Feliciana	986	56.2	20.4	5.9	0.4	3.3	17.4	1 351	2 221	1 645.2	20	545	4 089	D—52.5
Winn	807	66.6	2.0	3.4	0.1	8.7	5.7	322	895	532.7	89	2 279	7 057	R—59.0
MAINE	790	50.4	3.5	3.9	0.8	8.0	710.3	625	74 669	611.1	19 193	600 220	555 035	R—55.3
Androscoggin	683	47.9	0.2	5.1	0.8	9.7	59.1	593	4 323	414.1	342	9 829	44 585	R—51.7
Aroostook	1 040	45.0	19.7	2.2	0.9	7.3	51.8	575	4 946	579.8	1 631	37 061	32 246	R—53.4
Cumberland	871	42.8	1.9	5.0	0.7	6.2	200.8	921	14 904	623.3	2 820	81 472	119 075	R—52.9
Franklin	771	62.0	0.3	3.0	0.2	9.8	28.5	1 010	1 553	530.0	103	2 736	13 256	R—54.2
Hancock	706	55.3	0.5	3.6	0.5	10.7	17.1	402	2 170	465.7	310	6 623	23 107	R—56.1
Kennebec	707	48.2	0.3	3.5	0.9	7.5	62.0	560	14 384	1 221.1	1 891	63 313	51 745	R—53.6
Knox	721	55.9	0.2	3.7	0.5	8.6	10.1	302	1 934	532.8	146	4 184	17 650	R—57.5
Lincoln	830	61.0	0.2	3.6	0.2	13.5	7.0	266	1 224	406.6	111	2 757	15 920	R—61.8
Oxford	812	61.2	0.4	2.9	0.7	10.2	17.4	357	2 319	445.1	187	4 579	24 266	R—55.9
Penobscot	796	48.1	3.1	3.8	1.8	7.7	111.8	812	12 821	897.2	1 302	40 168	63 754	R—54.8
Piscataquis	982	49.1	23.8	1.9	0.4	8.9	7.3	410	955	510.7	65	1 732	8 217	R—58.3
Sagadahoc	783	61.8	0.3	4.6	0.3	6.6	16.3	555	1 348	397.6	396	14 757	15 158	R—58.2
Somerset	876	63.0	1.1	2.1	0.4	8.6	16.2	358	2 361	488.8	169	4 634	20 201	R—56.6
Waldo	524	63.4	0.0	3.2	0.2	10.4	4.8	169	1 156	362.4	120	3 204	14 778	R—55.7
Washington	681	60.6	0.2	4.3	0.4	10.1	22.9	667	2 101	596.9	366	10 678	13 828	R—56.9
York	700	52.0	0.6	4.9	0.7	7.4	77.1	531	6 170	362.5	9 234	312 493	77 249	R—60.0
MARYLAND	1 155	45.2	4.7	5.5	0.2	8.5	5 162.7	1 208	271 486	578.8	158 896	5 380 306	1 714 358	R—51.1
Allegany	859	64.7	2.8	3.6	0.0	5.3	47.8	609	4 458	595.2	239	7 524	29 503	R—59.2
Anne Arundel	899	53.9	0.0	5.4	0.0	5.5	591.1	1 551	21 607	510.4	35 526	1 025 736	155 101	R—63.5
Baltimore	926	53.0	1.7	6.6	0.2	6.6	463.8	696	34 685	498.5	13 003	456 439	287 295	R—57.0
Calvert	1 157	50.6	0.0	2.9	0.0	0.3	78.3	2 145	1 650	328.0	66	2 076	17 397	R—63.0
Caroline	821	57.9	0.1	2.8	0.0	9.6	9.5	407	906	352.5	58	1 461	7 123	R—65.4
Carroll	742	56.5	0.2	2.2	0.0	14.7	31.2	312	5 142	420.8	315	8 765	43 747	R—71.4
Cecil	760	72.0	0.0	3.2	0.0	1.9	32.9	525	2 432	330.0	1 528	49 531	21 155	R—62.5
Charles	937	73.9	0.2	4.8	0.0	1.4	31.4	403	3 824	391.0	3 389	110 764	32 764	R—63.6
Dorchester	867	55.3	0.6	4.8	0.0	11.1	18.9	626	1 529	499.7	77	2 324	10 140	R—62.6
Frederick	879	56.4	0.1	3.6	0.5	12.5	49.2	412	6 249	435.5	2 367	71 011	49 867	R—65.3
Garrett	991	63.6	0.0	1.8	0.0	22.1	8.3	311	1 252	463.7	58	1 556	9 282	R—71.8
Harford	879	63.8	0.0	3.8	0.0	8.3	77.6	525	6 017	341.9	10 560	290 402	58 566	R—65.7
Howard	1 057	60.6	0.0	5.8	0.0	4.8	136.3	1 073	9 163	539.6	398	13 011	78 530	R—56.2
Kent	735	63.5	0.0	4.4	0.0	2.4	4.1	248	636	374.1	55	1 539	6 732	R—55.9
Montgomery	1 259	51.1	3.3	4.7	0.0	3.3	868.1	1 451	31 884	440.0	42 631	1 674 338	320 896	D—51.5
Prince George's	1 283	41.2	10.4	5.1	0.2	2.0	1 423.1	2 130	49 863	704.5	24 713	879 918	222 881	D—60.0
Queen Anne's	860	73.3	0.0	1.7	0.0	9.6	8.1	306	1 313	396.7	79	2 092	11 703	R—66.7
St. Mary's	607	80.0	0.0	3.6	0.0	0.1	4.9	79	2 884	401.7	4 154	135 959	20 290	R—62.9
Somerset	922	54.3	0.2	2.2	0.0	8.1	8.1	437	2 202	1 135.1	38	1 021	7 165	R—58.9
Talbot	703	55.3	0.7	4.6	0.0	3.2	11.6	441	1 031	364.3	190	5 815	12 199	R—67.0
Washington	924	53.0	0.0	3.9	0.0	11.0	67.4	610	6 177	519.9	1 591	43 650	40 638	R—63.8
Wicomico	826	59.3	0.1	3.8	0.0	8.4	33.2	511	4 664	637.2	293	9 362	25 755	R—63.2

1. Based on the estimated population as of July 1, 1982. 2. Per 10,000 resident population estimated as of July 1 of the year shown. 3. Data subject to copyright.

STATE–County code	MSA/ CMSA/ NECMA code[1]	STATE County	Land Area,[2] 1990 (Sq. Km.)	Population, 1990										Age of population Percent		
							Race									
				Total persons	Rank	Per square kilometer	White	Black	Am. Indian, Eskimo, Aleut	Asian & Pacific Islander	Other race	Hispanic[3]	Under 5 years	5 to 14 years	15 to 24 years
			1	2	3	4	5	6	7	8	9	10	11	12	13
		MARYLAND—Con.													
24 047	...	Worcester	1 226	35 028	1 130	28.6	27 253	7 467	72	163	73	275	6.5	12.1	11.4
24 510	0720	Baltimore city	209	736 014	53	3 521.6	287 753	435 768	2 555	7 942	1 996	7 602	7.7	13.3	14.7
25 000	...	MASSACHUSETTS	20 300	6 016 425	X	296.4	5 405 374	300 130	12 241	143 392	155 288	287 549	6.9	12.1	15.4
25 001	...	Barnstable	1 025	186 605	259	182.1	179 551	2 827	1 180	968	2 079	2 287	6.4	11.6	10.5
25 003	6323	Berkshire	2 412	139 352	342	57.8	135 122	2 534	242	1 001	453	1 407	6.3	12.6	14.8
25 005	5403	Bristol	1 440	506 325	94	351.6	482 426	8 054	937	4 478	10 430	13 578	7.1	13.3	14.9
25 007	...	Dukes	269	11 639	2 243	43.3	10 979	332	253	44	31	121	7.1	12.8	9.2
25 009	1123	Essex	1 290	670 080	65	519.4	616 427	15 809	1 226	9 909	26 709	48 440	7.3	12.7	13.5
25 011	...	Franklin	1 819	70 092	632	38.5	68 617	476	206	484	309	842	7.2	13.7	12.8
25 013	8003	Hampden	1 602	456 310	108	284.8	387 805	34 289	784	3 886	29 546	45 785	7.4	13.7	14.9
25 015	8003	Hampshire	1 370	146 568	322	107.0	137 485	2 552	267	4 477	1 787	3 887	5.4	10.7	25.5
25 017	1123	Middlesex	2 133	1 398 468	18	655.6	1 287 412	40 236	1 933	51 826	17 061	47 383	6.5	11.0	15.4
25 019	...	Nantucket	124	6 012	2 755	48.5	5 787	151	5	18	51	50	7.0	10.8	10.8
25 021	1123	Norfolk	1 035	616 087	75	595.3	582 746	12 089	787	17 889	2 576	8 414	6.5	11.1	14.1
25 023	1123	Plymouth	1 711	435 276	114	254.4	406 699	16 520	888	3 452	7 717	9 571	7.6	14.4	14.6
25 025	1123	Suffolk	152	663 906	70	4 367.8	438 550	149 165	2 087	33 521	40 583	72 844	6.4	10.0	19.5
25 027	9243	Worcester	3 919	709 705	59	181.1	665 768	15 096	1 446	11 439	15 956	32 940	7.5	13.2	15.0
26 000	...	MICHIGAN	147 136	9 295 297	X	63.2	7 756 086	1 291 706	55 638	104 983	86 884	201 596	7.6	14.6	15.1
26 001	...	Alcona	1 747	10 145	2 374	5.8	10 026	27	56	26	10	55	5.1	12.1	10.1
26 003	...	Alger	2 377	8 972	2 472	3.8	8 422	213	304	24	9	43	6.1	14.7	12.2
26 005	...	Allegan	2 143	90 509	505	42.2	86 760	1 448	543	411	1 347	2 895	8.3	16.9	13.4
26 007	...	Alpena	1 487	30 605	1 260	20.6	30 372	35	93	85	20	145	6.6	15.3	12.6
26 009	...	Antrim	1 235	18 185	1 779	14.7	17 895	23	211	24	32	96	6.9	14.4	11.8
26 011	...	Arenac	950	14 931	1 992	15.7	14 695	10	139	38	49	167	6.7	15.5	12.3
26 013	...	Baraga	2 342	7 954	2 578	3.4	6 971	49	918	10	6	34	6.7	15.2	13.1
26 015	...	Barry	1 440	50 057	840	34.8	49 429	104	188	144	192	521	7.4	16.1	12.9
26 017	6960	Bay	1 151	111 723	411	97.1	107 747	1 242	726	428	1 580	3 494	7.1	14.8	13.9
26 019	...	Benzie	832	12 200	2 201	14.7	11 863	30	237	35	35	129	7.0	13.5	11.2
26 021	0870	Berrien	1 479	161 378	294	109.1	133 259	24 872	685	1 487	1 075	2 683	7.4	15.1	14.2
26 023	...	Branch	1 314	41 502	970	31.6	40 278	705	221	156	142	468	7.7	15.8	13.0
26 025	0780	Calhoun	1 836	135 982	345	74.1	118 737	14 383	696	1 068	1 098	2 583	7.4	14.8	14.2
26 027	...	Cass	1 275	49 477	850	38.8	44 827	3 725	469	191	265	651	7.1	15.4	13.4
26 029	...	Charlevoix	1 080	21 468	1 604	19.9	20 993	17	378	41	39	112	7.6	15.3	12.0
26 031	...	Cheboygan	1 853	21 398	1 610	11.5	20 837	15	478	57	11	80	6.7	15.0	11.9
26 033	...	Chippewa	4 043	34 604	1 146	8.6	28 353	2 184	3 820	152	95	278	6.1	13.5	17.4
26 035	...	Clare	1 468	24 952	1 465	17.0	24 665	40	160	53	34	132	7.3	14.8	12.3
26 037	4040	Clinton	1 480	57 883	749	39.1	56 639	218	276	199	551	1 286	7.5	16.5	14.2
26 039	...	Crawford	1 446	12 260	2 199	8.5	11 802	264	145	42	7	79	7.3	14.7	12.3
26 041	...	Delta	3 031	37 780	1 054	12.5	36 819	16	809	99	37	136	6.7	15.6	12.9
26 043	...	Dickinson	1 985	26 831	1 395	13.5	26 532	23	135	106	35	116	6.8	15.1	11.2
26 045	4040	Eaton	1 493	92 879	499	62.2	87 549	3 310	438	559	1 023	2 199	7.1	15.8	14.6
26 047	...	Emmet	1 212	25 040	1 461	20.7	24 122	133	683	69	33	118	7.5	15.1	12.0
26 049	2640	Genesee	1 657	430 459	116	259.8	336 651	84 257	3 132	2 902	3 517	8 877	7.8	15.6	15.0
26 051	...	Gladwin	1 313	21 896	1 582	16.7	21 694	19	114	40	29	136	7.2	14.8	12.4
26 053	...	Gogebic	2 854	18 052	1 788	6.3	17 486	243	283	26	14	67	5.7	12.7	12.5
26 055	...	Grand Traverse	1 205	64 273	682	53.3	63 019	259	555	318	122	503	7.6	15.5	13.2
26 057	...	Gratiot	1 477	38 982	1 023	26.4	37 827	328	144	98	585	1 467	6.9	15.7	15.9
26 059	...	Hillsdale	1 551	43 431	933	28.0	42 919	113	143	112	144	395	7.7	16.0	15.1
26 061	...	Houghton	2 620	35 446	1 112	13.5	34 469	158	153	610	56	164	6.0	12.8	23.2
26 063	...	Huron	2 167	34 951	1 133	16.1	34 627	22	89	60	153	372	7.0	15.4	12.4
26 065	4040	Ingham	1 448	281 912	175	194.7	237 183	27 837	1 941	7 562	7 389	13 478	7.4	13.3	23.1
26 067	...	Ionia	1 485	57 024	764	38.4	53 141	3 003	221	120	539	1 176	7.7	15.9	17.8
26 069	...	Iosco	1 422	30 209	1 287	21.2	28 966	632	228	269	114	357	8.3	14.4	13.9
26 071	...	Iron	3 021	13 175	2 126	4.4	13 028	4	102	32	9	67	5.4	13.1	8.8
26 073	...	Isabella	1 487	54 624	790	36.7	52 212	635	1 020	456	301	714	6.5	13.0	32.1
26 075	3520	Jackson	1 830	149 756	316	81.8	135 557	11 983	655	653	908	2 303	7.3	14.3	13.7
26 077	3720	Kalamazoo	1 455	223 411	223	153.5	197 427	19 879	1 017	3 168	1 920	3 950	7.3	13.4	19.2
26 079	...	Kalkaska	1 453	13 497	2 102	9.3	13 321	10	114	23	29	87	7.7	17.1	12.4
26 081	3000	Kent	2 218	500 631	97	225.7	444 112	40 314	2 756	5 380	8 069	14 684	8.7	15.6	14.8
26 083	...	Keweenaw	1 402	1 701	3 084	1.2	1 688	1	4	6	2	6	4.9	11.8	7.9
26 085	...	Lake	1 470	8 583	2 507	5.8	7 337	1 146	81	9	10	60	6.7	14.4	10.2
26 087	2162	Lapeer	1 695	74 768	602	44.1	73 049	483	319	282	635	1 493	7.3	17.2	14.8
26 089	...	Leelanau	903	16 527	1 888	18.3	15 958	16	451	45	57	188	7.5	14.6	10.7
26 091	...	Lenawee	1 944	91 476	503	47.1	86 323	1 431	303	486	2 933	5 515	7.3	15.8	15.5

1. MSA = Metropolitan Statistical Area. CMSA = Consolidated MSA. NECMA = New England county metropolitan area. PMSA = Primary MSA. See Appendix A for explanation of these concepts. See Appendix B for list of metropolitan areas identified by type, with component counties. 2. Dry land or land partially or temporarily covered by water. 3. Hispanic persons may be of any race.

STATE County	Population, 1990 (cont'd): Age of population (cont'd) Percent: 25 to 34 years	35 to 44 years	45 to 54 years	55 to 64 years	65 to 74 years	75 years and over	Percent female	Population–Change and components of change: Change 1980–1990: Number	Percent	Components of change, 1980–1986: Total persons, 1986	Total persons, 1980	Net change: Number	Percent	Natural increase: Births	Deaths
	14	15	16	17	18	19	20	21	22	23	24	25	26	27	28
MARYLAND—Con.															
Worcester	16.1	14.4	10.5	11.7	10.8	6.5	51.9	4 139	13.4	36 100	30 889	5 200	16.7	2 700	2 100
Baltimore city	18.7	14.3	9.1	8.5	7.9	5.8	53.3	-50 727	-6.4	752 800	786 741	-33 900	-4.3	80 100	59 600
MASSACHUSETTS	18.3	15.3	10.0	8.6	7.6	6.0	52.0	279 425	4.9	5 832 000	5 737 000	95 000	1.7	480 000	340 000
Barnstable	14.6	14.9	9.4	10.6	12.5	9.5	52.8	38 680	26.1	170 600	147 925	22 600	15.3	11 900	12 100
Berkshire	15.1	14.7	10.1	9.6	9.3	7.6	52.1	-5 758	-4.0	141 300	145 110	-3 800	-2.6	11 000	9 400
Bristol	16.8	14.8	10.0	8.7	8.3	6.1	52.2	31 684	6.7	484 900	474 641	10 300	2.2	40 400	28 900
Dukes	16.4	20.1	9.5	9.0	9.1	6.6	51.5	2 697	30.2	10 900	8 942	2 000	22.4	1 000	600
Essex	17.4	15.7	10.3	8.8	7.9	6.2	52.3	36 392	5.7	649 400	633 688	15 700	2.5	56 200	39 600
Franklin	16.5	17.8	9.7	7.9	8.2	6.4	51.6	5 775	9.0	66 000	64 317	1 600	2.5	5 500	3 800
Hampden	16.7	14.2	9.5	8.8	8.5	6.3	52.5	13 292	3.0	444 900	443 018	1 900	0.4	39 200	27 700
Hampshire	15.7	15.4	8.6	7.0	6.8	4.8	52.8	7 755	5.6	141 500	138 813	2 700	1.9	9 100	6 300
Middlesex	19.7	15.7	10.4	8.8	7.0	5.5	51.9	31 434	2.3	1 367 000	1 367 034	0	0.0	108 600	74 200
Nantucket	20.4	18.6	9.7	9.1	7.1	6.6	50.0	925	18.2	6 000	5 087	900	18.4	500	400
Norfolk	18.1	15.8	10.9	9.5	7.8	6.3	52.5	9 500	1.6	602 500	606 587	-4 000	-0.7	43 900	34 600
Plymouth	16.8	16.5	10.9	7.8	6.6	5.0	51.2	29 839	7.4	424 400	405 437	18 900	4.7	38 300	21 100
Suffolk	22.6	13.6	8.4	7.4	6.6	5.5	51.9	13 764	2.1	661 400	650 142	11 300	1.7	59 200	42 400
Worcester	17.9	15.1	9.5	8.1	7.7	6.0	51.3	63 353	9.8	661 100	646 352	14 700	2.3	56 300	38 400
MICHIGAN	16.9	15.1	10.2	8.5	7.1	4.9	51.5	33 297	0.4	9 145 000	9 262 000	-117 000	-1.3	863 000	477 000
Alcona	11.4	11.4	11.3	14.5	14.4	9.7	50.2	405	4.2	10 100	9 740	400	4.0	700	800
Alger	13.9	15.1	10.6	10.0	10.1	7.1	48.6	-253	-2.7	8 600	9 225	-600	-6.8	800	600
Allegan	17.1	15.2	9.9	7.8	6.6	4.9	50.5	8 954	11.0	86 600	81 555	5 100	6.2	8 600	3 900
Alpena	15.1	13.9	11.2	10.4	8.6	6.4	51.5	-1 710	-5.3	30 900	32 315	-1 400	-4.4	2 800	1 800
Antrim	14.3	13.6	10.4	11.2	10.4	7.0	51.1	1 991	12.3	16 800	16 194	700	4.0	1 500	1 200
Arenac	14.5	13.2	10.4	11.2	9.7	6.5	51.1	225	1.5	15 000	14 706	300	2.0	1 400	1 000
Baraga	12.3	14.6	10.5	8.1	10.8	8.8	49.7	-530	-6.2	8 200	8 484	-300	-3.8	700	700
Barry	15.7	15.8	11.5	9.0	6.8	4.8	50.0	4 276	9.3	47 800	45 781	2 000	4.4	4 300	2 300
Bay	15.9	15.1	10.9	8.9	7.9	5.5	51.6	-8 158	-6.8	114 800	119 881	-5 100	-4.2	10 900	6 000
Benzie	14.5	14.2	11.2	11.2	10.3	6.9	50.7	995	8.9	11 300	11 205	100	0.5	1 100	800
Berrien	15.5	14.4	10.4	9.3	8.0	5.7	52.1	-9 898	-5.8	163 600	171 276	-7 700	-4.5	15 700	9 400
Branch	16.1	14.5	10.6	9.1	7.7	5.6	51.1	1 314	3.3	39 500	40 188	-700	-1.8	4 100	2 300
Calhoun	15.3	15.0	10.4	9.4	7.7	5.6	51.6	-5 597	-4.0	136 900	141 579	-4 700	-3.3	12 900	7 800
Cass	15.1	15.1	11.1	9.7	7.9	5.2	50.9	-22	0.0	48 500	49 499	-1 000	-2.1	4 000	2 500
Charlevoix	15.7	15.1	10.4	9.6	8.4	6.0	51.0	1 561	7.8	20 200	19 907	300	1.6	2 100	1 300
Cheboygan	13.3	13.9	10.7	11.1	10.3	7.1	51.7	749	3.6	20 700	20 649	100	0.4	2 000	1 400
Chippewa	18.3	14.8	8.9	8.6	7.2	5.4	44.5	5 575	19.2	29 300	29 029	300	0.9	2 500	1 800
Clare	14.0	12.3	10.1	11.6	10.9	6.8	51.6	1 130	4.7	25 000	23 822	1 100	4.8	2 200	1 700
Clinton	16.4	16.2	11.9	8.0	5.4	3.9	50.2	1 990	3.6	55 700	55 893	-100	-0.3	5 300	2 000
Crawford	16.1	13.5	10.3	10.8	8.9	6.0	48.8	2 795	29.5	10 100	9 465	600	6.9	1 100	600
Delta	14.5	14.8	10.4	9.7	8.7	6.6	51.3	-1 167	-3.0	38 600	38 947	-300	-0.8	3 700	2 300
Dickinson	14.9	14.7	9.6	9.5	9.9	8.4	50.9	1 490	5.9	26 700	25 341	1 400	5.6	2 300	1 900
Eaton	16.1	17.0	11.5	7.9	5.7	4.2	51.4	4 542	5.1	91 200	88 337	2 900	3.3	7 900	3 500
Emmet	16.2	16.3	10.0	8.7	7.8	6.3	51.5	2 048	8.9	24 100	22 992	1 100	4.7	2 300	1 400
Genesee	16.9	15.0	10.8	8.7	6.1	4.1	52.1	-19 990	-4.4	434 900	450 449	-15 600	-3.5	44 000	20 900
Gladwin	13.3	12.3	10.4	12.3	10.9	6.5	50.8	1 939	9.7	21 600	19 957	1 600	8.1	1 800	1 300
Gogebic	12.2	12.6	9.7	10.7	12.7	11.2	50.9	-1 634	-8.3	18 800	19 686	-900	-4.7	1 400	1 700
Grand Traverse	17.1	17.1	9.6	7.8	6.8	5.4	51.3	9 374	17.1	59 200	54 899	4 300	7.8	5 800	2 800
Gratiot	15.0	14.1	10.2	8.4	7.3	6.4	51.4	-1 466	-3.6	39 300	40 448	-1 100	-2.7	3 700	2 500
Hillsdale	15.1	13.8	10.3	8.9	7.4	5.8	50.9	1 360	3.2	42 600	42 071	500	1.2	4 000	2 400
Houghton	12.2	11.7	8.7	7.7	9.1	8.8	47.3	-2 426	-6.4	37 300	37 872	-500	-1.4	3 100	2 700
Huron	14.1	13.3	9.4	10.1	10.5	7.8	51.0	-1 508	-4.1	36 600	36 459	100	0.3	3 500	2 400
Ingham	17.9	14.8	8.6	6.3	5.0	3.7	52.0	6 392	2.3	277 800	275 520	2 300	0.8	27 400	10 400
Ionia	17.6	14.5	9.3	7.2	5.7	4.4	46.7	5 209	10.1	53 700	51 815	1 900	3.6	5 700	2 500
Iosco	17.0	12.2	8.5	10.5	8.9	6.2	50.0	1 860	6.6	30 400	28 349	2 000	7.2	3 600	1 800
Iron	11.5	12.7	9.4	12.0	14.9	12.1	52.1	-460	-3.4	14 000	13 635	400	2.9	1 000	1 200
Isabella	14.3	12.0	7.5	6.3	5.0	3.4	52.2	514	0.9	54 200	54 110	0	0.1	4 500	1 900
Jackson	17.6	15.7	10.3	8.8	7.2	5.1	49.2	-1 739	-1.1	144 400	151 495	-7 100	-4.7	13 300	7 800
Kalamazoo	16.9	15.1	9.8	7.6	6.0	4.6	51.9	11 033	5.2	217 700	212 378	5 300	2.5	20 000	9 400
Kalkaska	16.0	13.9	10.0	9.5	8.2	5.1	49.9	2 545	23.2	11 900	10 952	1 000	8.9	1 400	600
Kent	18.8	14.9	9.0	7.4	6.1	4.7	51.6	56 125	12.6	477 500	444 506	33 000	7.4	53 600	21 600
Keweenaw	10.5	13.6	10.2	11.7	14.9	14.5	51.1	-262	-13.3	2 000	1 963	100	3.9	100	200
Lake	11.7	11.4	10.4	13.7	12.9	8.4	51.0	872	11.3	8 600	7 711	900	11.7	700	700
Lapeer	16.3	16.6	11.6	7.6	5.2	3.5	49.9	4 730	6.8	70 400	70 038	300	0.4	6 700	2 900
Leelanau	14.3	17.2	10.4	10.4	8.8	6.1	50.2	2 520	18.0	15 000	14 007	1 000	6.8	1 300	800
Lenawee	15.3	15.2	10.4	8.4	7.1	5.0	50.7	1 528	1.7	88 800	89 948	-1 200	-1.3	8 200	4 400

STATE County	Population–(cont'd) Components of change, 1980-1986 (cont'd) Net migration	Households, 1990 Number	Households, 1990 Percent change, 1980–1990	Households, 1990 Persons per household	Households, 1990 Percent Female family householder[1]	Households, 1990 Percent One-person	Births, 1988 Total	Births, 1988 Rate[2]	Births, 1988 Low birth weight[3] (Number)	Deaths, 1987 Number Total	Deaths, 1987 Number Infant[4]	Deaths, 1987 Rate Total[2]	Deaths, 1987 Rate Infant[5]	Marriages, 1984 Number	Marriages, 1984 Rate[2]
	29	30	31	32	33	34	35	36	37	38	39	40	41	42	43
MARYLAND—Con.															
Worcester	4 600	14 142	21.3	2.44	11.5	24.7	495	13.4	37	369	7	10.2	13.4	515	15.4
Baltimore city	-54 500	276 484	-1.8	2.59	24.6	30.5	13 556	18.0	1 693	9 708	261	12.8	19.2	6 682	8.8
MASSACHUSETTS	-45 000	2 247 110	10.5	2.58	12.1	25.8	88 194	15.0	5 286	55 599	611	9.5	7.2	50 306	8.7
Barnstable	22 800	77 586	32.5	2.35	9.8	27.2	2 372	13.3	113	2 198	14	12.6	6.2	1 867	11.6
Berkshire	-5 400	54 315	3.7	2.45	10.8	27.5	1 723	12.4	100	1 553	11	11.1	6.4	1 325	9.3
Bristol	-1 300	187 668	12.4	2.64	12.5	23.8	7 375	15.3	496	4 714	48	9.9	7.0	4 210	8.8
Dukes	1 700	5 003	29.2	2.31	8.7	31.5	184	15.7	12	122	0	10.8	0.0	250	24.3
Essex	-900	251 285	10.0	2.61	12.4	25.2	10 414	15.9	576	6 450	76	9.9	7.6	5 917	9.2
Franklin	-100	27 640	14.1	2.49	10.5	26.1	990	14.7	47	683	6	10.3	6.3	584	9.1
Hampden	-9 600	169 906	7.5	2.60	15.4	25.6	7 019	15.6	510	4 642	52	10.4	7.7	3 713	8.4
Hampshire	-200	50 052	13.1	2.54	9.9	24.8	1 449	10.2	60	1 084	10	7.7	6.7	1 024	7.3
Middlesex	-34 400	519 527	9.1	2.59	10.5	25.2	19 680	14.3	1 059	12 016	104	8.8	5.5	11 965	8.7
Nantucket	800	2 597	20.5	2.29	7.4	31.4	100	15.2	5	66	0	10.3	0.0	182	31.4
Norfolk	-13 400	227 798	9.6	2.63	10.0	24.5	8 094	13.3	371	5 617	42	9.2	5.4	5 180	8.6
Plymouth	1 800	149 519	12.8	2.84	11.9	20.1	6 733	15.6	349	3 576	39	8.4	5.8	3 392	8.2
Suffolk	-5 500	264 061	4.8	2.38	16.6	34.8	11 220	16.8	1 025	6 543	127	9.8	11.9	4 968	7.5
Worcester	-3 100	260 153	15.5	2.62	11.2	23.9	10 841	16.1	563	6 335	82	9.5	8.1	5 729	8.8
MICHIGAN	-503 000	3 419 331	7.0	2.66	12.9	23.7	139 714	15.1	10 192	79 622	1 508	8.7	10.7	80 810	8.9
Alcona	500	4 261	14.7	2.35	7.5	24.6	93	8.8	5	144	2	13.8	17.9	95	9.6
Alger	-800	3 337	1.8	2.52	8.5	24.3	98	11.3	5	108	0	12.4	0.0	86	9.7
Allegan	400	31 709	16.4	2.81	8.6	19.3	1 414	15.7	73	647	10	7.3	7.4	754	9.0
Alpena	-2 500	11 838	6.2	2.56	9.1	24.6	345	11.0	20	297	3	9.4	7.6	296	9.4
Antrim	300	6 980	22.0	2.58	8.5	21.5	243	13.7	16	182	2	10.6	8.4	161	9.6
Arenac	-100	5 642	10.6	2.61	9.4	22.7	204	12.9	15	139	1	9.0	4.9	134	8.9
Baraga	-400	3 065	4.6	2.51	10.2	28.0	101	12.2	2	102	3	12.4	26.8	126	15.2
Barry	-100	17 763	15.1	2.78	7.7	17.7	695	14.0	28	405	4	8.3	5.7	372	8.0
Bay	-10 000	42 188	2.0	2.62	11.0	24.1	1 602	13.9	110	949	6	8.2	3.8	994	8.5
Benzie	-200	4 772	19.1	2.52	7.3	22.6	163	14.1	12	126	2	11.1	12.1	115	10.4
Berrien	-14 000	61 025	1.2	2.60	13.3	24.4	2 530	15.2	203	1 562	35	9.4	13.7	1 685	10.3
Branch	-2 500	14 921	6.5	2.67	9.9	22.3	619	15.2	31	370	4	9.2	6.4	400	10.3
Calhoun	-9 800	51 812	1.3	2.54	13.1	25.3	2 017	14.5	146	1 360	25	9.8	12.6	1 367	10.0
Cass	-2 500	18 239	5.8	2.70	10.4	20.3	634	12.8	40	468	7	9.6	10.7	412	8.5
Charlevoix	-500	8 243	16.8	2.59	8.7	23.0	318	15.0	21	221	3	10.7	9.5	224	11.4
Cheboygan	-600	8 201	12.7	2.58	9.6	22.1	282	13.2	21	236	2	11.3	7.2	235	11.3
Chippewa	-400	11 541	16.2	2.56	10.0	25.4	356	11.8	14	264	2	8.9	6.0	244	8.5
Clare	600	9 698	11.7	2.54	10.5	22.5	342	13.0	20	291	1	11.3	2.8	239	9.7
Clinton	-3 400	20 212	13.8	2.85	7.8	17.2	745	12.8	30	295	3	5.2	3.4	438	7.9
Crawford	200	4 441	34.0	2.62	9.6	21.0	185	17.1	12	112	4	10.7	23.0	130	13.1
Delta	-1 700	14 531	7.1	2.57	8.9	25.7	463	12.1	19	364	5	9.5	10.0	375	9.6
Dickinson	900	10 633	11.5	2.49	8.3	26.2	302	11.5	14	272	2	10.4	6.3	281	10.9
Eaton	-1 500	34 027	12.9	2.69	9.4	21.2	1 161	12.4	86	599	13	6.5	10.7	743	8.4
Emmet	200	9 516	17.4	2.58	9.0	24.2	401	16.2	20	242	4	10.0	10.9	268	11.5
Genesee	-38 700	161 296	4.3	2.64	16.7	23.9	6 705	15.6	553	3 601	83	8.3	12.4	4 372	10.1
Gladwin	1 100	8 357	16.7	2.59	8.6	21.7	305	13.4	18	237	3	10.6	10.0	174	8.2
Gogebic	-600	7 449	-1.7	2.33	9.2	31.8	185	10.2	12	291	1	15.8	5.1	149	7.8
Grand Traverse	1 300	23 965	25.0	2.62	9.2	22.5	931	14.7	53	491	9	8.0	9.6	667	11.8
Gratiot	-2 400	13 659	2.6	2.68	9.5	21.5	532	13.5	34	414	4	10.5	7.4	374	9.5
Hillsdale	-1 100	15 637	8.7	2.70	8.7	21.1	644	14.9	41	356	3	8.3	4.9	366	8.8
Houghton	-1 000	13 172	1.5	2.44	8.4	31.5	411	11.5	20	383	4	10.6	9.3	271	7.2
Huron	-1 000	13 268	3.9	2.60	8.1	24.2	477	13.0	19	365	3	9.9	5.8	316	8.8
Ingham	-14 700	102 648	7.8	2.55	12.3	26.3	4 464	16.2	288	1 767	44	6.4	9.8	2 911	10.7
Ionia	-1 300	18 447	13.7	2.81	9.7	20.6	864	15.4	53	396	7	7.2	8.5	466	8.9
Iosco	200	11 588	14.0	2.52	7.7	23.7	532	17.5	23	326	5	10.8	9.1	316	10.6
Iron	600	5 655	4.1	2.27	7.5	31.0	129	9.6	9	193	1	14.1	7.2	107	7.6
Isabella	-2 500	17 591	9.6	2.74	9.4	20.6	655	12.1	23	302	3	5.6	4.6	422	7.8
Jackson	-12 500	53 660	5.3	2.62	11.5	23.2	2 124	14.2	145	1 287	15	8.7	7.0	1 362	9.4
Kalamazoo	-5 300	83 702	11.0	2.54	10.9	24.7	3 359	15.4	215	1 594	35	7.4	10.5	2 087	9.8
Kalkaska	200	4 934	30.0	2.71	8.8	20.3	202	16.0	8	101	3	8.2	15.5	128	11.2
Kent	1 000	181 740	16.8	2.69	11.5	23.0	9 068	18.7	548	3 774	87	7.9	9.8	5 081	11.1
Keweenaw	200	777	-6.7	2.19	6.3	34.5	12	6.0	1	31	0	15.5	0.0	11	5.5
Lake	900	3 536	15.9	2.39	9.8	27.9	127	14.1	3	122	1	14.0	9.9	71	8.5
Lapeer	-3 400	24 659	16.3	2.97	8.9	15.7	1 030	13.8	48	488	10	6.7	9.9	626	9.1
Leelanau	500	6 274	24.9	2.62	7.2	20.1	238	15.4	10	130	5	8.5	23.9	108	7.6
Lenawee	-5 000	31 635	5.3	2.77	9.9	20.2	1 288	14.2	55	757	8	8.4	6.4	746	8.5

1. No spouse present. 2. Per 1,000 resident population estimated as of July 1 of the year shown. 3. Under 2,500 grams. 4. Deaths of infants under 1 year old. 5. Deaths of infants under 1 year old per 1,000 live births.

Table A. States and Counties — **Vital Statistics, Health Resources, Crime, and Education**

STATE County	Divorces, 1984		Physicians, active non–Federal, 1989		Hospitals, 1989			Nursing homes,[4] 1986		Serious crimes known to police, 1988			Education			
						Beds				Number			Public school enrollment[7]		Attainment,[8] 1980	
	Number	Rate[1]	Number[2]	Rate[3]	Number	Number	Rate[3]	Number	Beds	Total[5]	Violent[6]	Rate[3]	1986–1987	1980	Percent 12 yrs. or more	Percent 16 yrs. or more
	44	45	46	47	48	49	50	51	52	53	54	55	56	57	58	59
MARYLAND—Con.																
Worcester	114	3.4	24	64	0	0	0	2	108	3 011	209	8 033	5 134	5 508	52.8	11.5
Baltimore city	3 423	4.5	5 419	724	27	7 748	1 036	68	7 793	71 840	14 806	9 405	111 243	140 582	48.4	11.3
MASSACHUSETTS	17 123	3.0	19 517	330	167	35 520	601	774	54 621	251 542	32 623	4 895	846 430	1 037 104	72.2	20.0
Barnstable	506	3.1	337	184	3	425	232	19	1 571	8 540	877	5 913	25 450	25 894	85.8	23.7
Berkshire	485	3.4	371	269	5	656	476	21	1 508	2 515	303	2 181	21 162	26 884	69.7	16.3
Bristol	1 502	3.2	549	113	8	1 839	380	63	4 143	27 633	2 590	5 943	81 082	90 289	52.6	10.8
Dukes	49	4.8	22	183	1	80	667	1	41	497	44	6 540	1 540	1 306	85.1	23.7
Essex	1 885	2.9	1 205	184	18	2 911	444	96	6 734	31 136	3 157	5 037	96 129	116 066	73.0	18.3
Franklin	303	4.7	97	142	1	128	188	11	729	818	93	2 113	10 726	11 856	73.6	19.1
Hampden	1 402	3.2	897	199	11	2 490	551	51	4 524	19 310	3 269	5 647	65 676	82 188	66.5	14.1
Hampshire	364	2.6	329	230	6	1 050	735	16	913	2 627	211	1 964	18 188	21 433	74.0	24.9
Middlesex	4 038	2.9	5 060	368	33	7 767	566	163	10 801	34 793	3 469	3 033	189 155	247 489	77.4	26.3
Nantucket	19	3.3	10	145	1	39	565	1	45	660	64	10 616	776	813	81.9	18.7
Norfolk	1 457	2.4	2 688	439	19	2 823	461	71	5 285	15 043	1 353	2 737	86 162	114 212	82.0	25.7
Plymouth	1 455	3.5	568	131	10	2 593	596	60	4 019	13 194	1 512	4 481	75 047	93 284	77.1	17.6
Suffolk	1 378	2.1	5 510	827	31	8 760	1 315	82	6 799	72 718	13 148	11 314	70 942	83 651	67.8	18.8
Worcester	2 280	3.5	1 874	275	20	3 959	580	119	7 509	22 058	2 533	3 480	104 395	121 739	66.7	15.4
MICHIGAN	37 584	4.1	16 836	182	208	41 672	449	2 189	67 994	552 586	67 848	6 051	1 605 617	1 875 899	68.0	14.3
Alcona	45	4.5	4	37	0	0	0	6	116	330	29	3 169	1 013	1 978	59.2	7.0
Alger	21	2.4	3	34	1	40	460	3	151	271	23	3 117	1 723	2 091	63.2	9.5
Allegan	320	3.8	41	45	2	118	129	11	607	2 765	266	3 112	15 988	17 541	64.8	10.2
Alpena	89	2.8	48	152	1	176	557	16	241	1 263	54	4 017	5 859	7 229	63.9	8.8
Antrim	78	4.7	8	45	0	0	0	9	183	297	10	1 770	3 397	3 486	68.3	11.9
Arenac	1	0.1	6	37	1	81	503	6	178	464	29	3 270	3 087	3 472	53.4	6.2
Baraga	32	3.9	5	60	1	61	735	6	153	238	22	2 871	1 690	1 879	65.9	8.2
Barry	173	3.7	30	59	1	92	182	18	366	1 445	105	2 947	7 262	10 735	69.4	10.4
Bay	465	4.0	99	86	1	397	344	31	642	4 885	348	4 209	19 144	22 008	64.4	8.9
Benzie	45	4.1	10	85	1	48	410	9	112	433	26	3 757	2 191	2 396	67.4	12.3
Berrien	814	5.0	193	115	5	818	488	60	1 310	11 328	1 461	6 800	30 962	34 385	64.8	13.3
Branch	194	5.0	37	90	1	130	315	17	371	1 472	121	3 875	6 305	8 301	65.3	8.7
Calhoun	765	5.6	161	115	6	1 670	1 194	74	1 385	8 535	918	6 136	25 564	29 333	67.8	11.9
Cass	224	4.6	11	22	1	63	127	16	306	2 023	188	4 143	7 341	11 032	63.4	8.1
Charlevoix	102	5.2	19	88	1	40	184	14	168	457	36	2 194	4 006	4 403	69.3	13.1
Cheboygan	112	5.4	13	60	1	129	597	11	246	589	42	2 801	3 685	4 476	64.4	9.1
Chippewa	116	4.0	21	69	1	144	474	15	319	1 124	122	3 795	5 481	5 953	64.7	11.1
Clare	125	5.1	10	37	1	64	239	10	271	1 303	60	5 055	4 791	5 205	57.8	6.5
Clinton	211	3.8	22	37	1	48	82	14	278	1 041	75	1 910	9 426	13 501	73.0	11.3
Crawford	53	5.4	11	100	1	98	891	4	188	547	49	5 203	1 803	2 035	70.9	9.6
Delta	149	3.8	32	84	1	82	215	16	378	1 319	47	3 434	8 087	8 840	68.7	10.5
Dickinson	110	4.3	35	134	2	317	1 215	6	222	635	21	2 397	4 802	4 657	69.4	10.4
Eaton	417	4.7	26	27	2	81	85	24	573	4 043	321	4 352	15 749	20 432	78.1	15.8
Emmet	117	5.0	99	394	1	261	1 040	17	380	1 091	37	4 497	4 219	4 699	75.4	17.6
Genesee	2 285	5.3	695	162	6	1 771	413	79	2 404	35 186	5 354	8 080	88 556	103 701	67.8	10.9
Gladwin	0	0.0	9	39	1	42	181	9	100	693	37	3 088	3 668	4 301	57.4	6.1
Gogebic	48	2.5	14	78	1	53	296	6	306	481	19	2 723	2 988	3 315	65.6	9.6
Grand Traverse	306	5.4	161	248	2	409	629	50	853	2 605	182	4 224	11 048	10 540	77.2	19.1
Gratiot	137	3.5	33	84	1	94	238	16	835	1 145	43	2 912	8 581	9 296	69.4	11.1
Hillsdale	194	4.7	18	41	1	68	155	12	298	1 130	114	2 612	7 798	9 160	68.7	9.8
Houghton	112	3.0	36	102	2	120	340	15	492	691	56	1 893	5 912	6 256	63.2	14.4
Huron	110	3.1	29	79	3	207	566	22	339	932	52	2 540	6 521	7 248	57.3	8.0
Ingham	1 033	3.8	694	251	4	1 457	526	51	1 478	17 305	1 921	6 964	50 442	50 195	78.0	26.0
Ionia	206	3.9	21	37	1	77	134	22	379	1 458	118	2 637	11 461	11 239	67.2	8.0
Iosco	150	5.0	27	89	2	83	272	3	187	1 000	87	3 275	6 897	5 810	67.9	11.2
Iron	44	3.1	7	52	2	71	530	4	269	360	19	2 619	2 936	2 353	63.4	10.1
Isabella	176	3.2	47	87	1	118	218	16	315	2 171	106	4 007	6 222	9 095	70.8	20.6
Jackson	645	4.5	127	84	2	491	325	59	1 299	7 415	1 226	4 993	24 355	30 208	69.2	12.2
Kalamazoo	818	3.8	607	278	4	1 512	691	75	2 044	15 354	1 901	6 951	32 858	38 583	75.8	23.0
Kalkaska	52	4.6	2	16	1	47	364	7	74	605	39	4 866	2 871	2 566	62.7	7.9
Kent	2 153	4.7	1 021	209	9	2 300	470	127	5 497	28 143	2 915	5 776	78 208	80 681	70.9	16.3
Keweenaw	4	2.0	0	0	0	0	0	0	0	81	23	4 217	7	292	49.8	7.1
Lake	0	0.0	3	33	0	0	0	4	167	569	47	6 470	908	1 582	49.1	6.9
Lapeer	312	4.5	30	39	1	184	242	18	382	1 745	160	2 388	13 971	18 339	67.5	8.6
Leelanau	33	2.3	13	82	1	90	570	4	102	250	10	1 627	1 906	2 736	76.8	19.4
Lenawee	397	4.5	83	91	4	332	362	31	726	2 973	163	3 293	18 506	19 855	67.8	11.9

1. Per 1,000 resident population estimated as of July 1 of the year shown. 2. As of end of year. 3. Per 100,000 resident population as of July 1 of the year shown. 4. Preliminary. Covers nursing homes with 3 or more beds. 5. Data for serious crimes have not been adjusted for underreporting, this may affect comparability between geographic areas or over time. 6. Includes murder and nonnegligent manslaughter, forcible rape, robbery, and aggravated assault. 7. The 1986–1987 data are based on administrative reports obtained by the U.S. National Center for Education Statistics. The 1980 data are based on the 1980 Census of Population and Housing. 8. Persons 25 years old or older.

STATE County	Education (cont'd) Local government expenditures for education,[1] 1982 Total (Mil dol)	Per capita (Dollars)	Social Security Program December 1988 Beneficiaries Total	Rate[2]	Payments ($1,000)	Supplemental Security Income Program recipients June 1986	Money income Per capita[3] 1987 Income, (Dollars)	1979 Current dollars	1979 Constant 1987 dollars	Median household income 1979 (Dollars)	Percent below poverty level, 1979 Persons	Families	Housing units, 1990 Total	Percent change, 1980–1990
	60	61	62	63	64	65	66	67	68	69	70	71	72	73
MARYLAND—Con.														
Worcester	15.5	492	7 535	204.2	3 591	508	11 860	6 566	10 274	14 149	13.2	9.7	41 800	40.0
Baltimore city	325.7	423	134 575	179.1	65 926	22 890	9 989	5 877	9 196	12 811	22.9	18.9	303 706	0.3
MASSACHUSETTS	2 609.2	454	950 589	161.4	477 182	112 985	14 389	7 457	11 668	17 575	9.6	7.6	2 472 711	12.0
Barnstable	70.8	460	48 630	272.0	24 769	2 456	14 103	7 428	11 623	15 553	8.9	7.2	135 192	35.3
Berkshire	62.7	441	28 560	205.9	14 520	2 886	12 544	6 842	10 706	15 876	9.5	7.4	64 324	8.6
Bristol	210.1	441	89 655	185.6	41 325	14 552	11 559	6 249	9 778	15 473	10.1	8.8	201 235	13.9
Dukes	5.1	529	2 090	178.6	1 067	154	13 685	7 322	11 457	13 570	9.7	6.8	11 604	31.6
Essex	288.0	450	109 125	166.8	55 189	12 002	14 708	7 673	12 006	18 077	9.1	7.6	271 977	11.3
Franklin	28.2	443	11 845	175.7	5 814	1 162	11 971	6 647	10 401	15 254	10.8	7.7	30 394	13.3
Hampden	183.5	415	80 355	178.6	39 687	10 230	12 138	6 731	10 532	16 166	11.7	9.9	180 025	7.7
Hampshire	53.4	380	19 810	139.1	9 741	1 666	11 938	6 411	10 031	16 675	11.4	6.6	53 068	13.8
Middlesex	656.2	482	193 425	140.8	100 497	17 956	16 819	8 439	13 205	20 433	7.0	5.2	543 796	10.3
Nantucket	3.1	574	960	145.5	515	50	20 405	9 987	15 627	19 012	5.6	3.6	7 021	46.8
Norfolk	296.8	493	93 340	153.0	49 655	6 486	17 405	8 828	13 813	21 894	5.5	4.2	236 816	11.3
Plymouth	195.2	477	59 370	137.8	29 436	6 366	13 636	6 978	10 918	18 749	8.0	6.8	168 555	11.4
Suffolk	269.7	411	98 065	147.1	46 905	24 598	12 875	6 557	10 260	12 798	19.1	15.8	289 276	4.5
Worcester	286.4	443	114 735	169.9	57 758	12 364	13 075	6 908	10 809	17 182	9.1	7.1	279 428	16.5
MICHIGAN	4 790.5	525	1 452 883	157.2	752 619	127 046	11 973	7 688	12 029	19 223	10.4	8.2	3 847 926	7.2
Alcona	3.1	312	3 335	314.6	1 606	466	8 108	5 111	7 997	10 730	16.5	13.7	10 414	11.1
Alger	4.3	473	2 220	255.2	1 038	198	8 468	5 470	8 559	14 224	12.9	10.1	5 775	14.0
Allegan	33.9	409	12 320	136.6	6 144	890	10 440	6 744	10 552	17 906	8.5	6.7	36 395	14.2
Alpena	14.2	445	7 145	226.8	3 585	504	8 510	5 887	9 211	15 166	10.6	8.6	14 431	3.2
Antrim	9.7	585	4 115	232.5	2 041	282	8 783	5 884	9 207	14 026	10.9	8.7	13 145	21.9
Arenac	6.8	456	3 725	235.8	1 798	260	8 310	5 497	8 601	13 184	15.3	12.3	8 891	15.5
Baraga	6.8	812	2 005	241.6	947	214	7 513	5 186	8 115	12 007	12.0	11.4	4 684	9.7
Barry	15.7	341	6 565	132.4	3 296	462	10 708	6 965	10 898	18 684	8.7	6.6	20 887	9.1
Bay	49.8	422	19 325	167.3	9 924	1 442	10 594	7 182	11 238	19 043	9.4	8.0	44 234	1.9
Benzie	5.3	477	2 660	229.3	1 295	226	8 365	5 632	8 812	13 410	12.3	9.7	8 557	14.0
Berrien	86.9	525	30 625	183.8	15 500	3 304	10 455	6 723	10 519	16 274	13.5	11.1	69 532	1.1
Branch	15.4	394	7 200	176.9	3 592	492	9 502	6 449	10 091	16 150	10.7	8.2	18 449	2.5
Calhoun	66.4	476	24 015	172.5	12 247	2 392	10 827	7 211	11 283	17 603	10.6	8.5	55 619	2.6
Cass	16.0	328	6 985	141.1	3 496	608	9 887	6 481	10 141	16 488	11.0	8.6	22 644	4.9
Charlevoix	10.2	517	4 260	200.9	2 122	282	9 211	6 005	9 396	14 028	11.1	8.7	13 119	18.0
Cheboygan	8.5	409	4 645	217.1	2 231	324	8 211	5 449	8 526	13 012	14.8	11.6	14 090	12.8
Chippewa	15.7	538	5 860	194.7	2 703	600	7 927	5 345	8 363	12 499	14.6	11.6	18 023	9.8
Clare	11.3	468	6 740	255.3	3 243	538	7 834	5 298	8 290	11 349	16.0	12.2	19 135	3.2
Clinton	22.5	408	6 040	104.1	3 040	256	11 457	7 362	11 519	21 573	5.7	4.4	20 959	13.5
Crawford	3.7	381	2 110	195.4	1 049	138	8 648	5 621	8 795	11 832	14.0	11.7	8 727	16.5
Delta	18.9	478	7 740	201.6	3 652	694	8 991	5 894	9 222	15 076	11.6	9.4	17 928	6.1
Dickinson	10.9	432	6 070	231.7	2 919	336	9 137	6 257	9 790	14 293	8.7	6.2	12 902	14.7
Eaton	36.0	409	9 385	99.8	4 808	536	12 312	8 076	12 637	21 778	5.9	4.9	35 517	12.7
Emmet	11.3	486	4 935	199.0	2 421	314	9 870	6 389	9 997	15 099	10.2	7.8	14 731	17.8
Genesee	277.1	629	64 155	149.0	33 408	6 300	11 909	7 951	12 441	20 996	10.6	9.3	170 808	4.8
Gladwin	8.1	397	5 220	228.9	2 571	346	8 322	5 499	8 604	12 255	14.7	12.0	14 885	10.2
Gogebic	8.1	412	5 565	305.8	2 634	448	7 996	5 184	8 111	10 973	12.1	8.7	10 997	8.8
Grand Traverse	26.7	475	11 030	174.2	5 573	890	10 498	6 930	10 843	16 686	8.3	6.2	28 740	21.7
Gratiot	21.0	533	7 015	177.6	3 402	710	9 027	6 042	9 454	15 796	11.7	9.6	14 699	2.9
Hillsdale	17.3	417	7 195	166.2	3 514	606	9 190	6 121	9 578	15 398	10.8	8.3	18 547	8.5
Houghton	13.2	347	7 980	222.9	3 740	742	7 702	4 970	7 777	11 456	17.0	9.9	17 296	5.0
Huron	15.6	430	8 500	232.2	4 015	548	9 193	5 753	9 002	13 860	12.4	9.9	19 755	10.7
Ingham	153.2	564	35 860	129.8	18 784	3 404	11 747	7 509	11 749	18 090	13.2	8.4	108 542	9.1
Ionia	23.8	460	7 650	136.1	3 752	598	9 243	6 100	9 545	17 439	9.2	7.4	19 674	11.7
Iosco	16.1	555	6 500	213.8	3 149	322	8 155	5 367	8 398	11 724	11.8	10.1	19 517	8.4
Iron	5.5	407	4 460	330.4	2 092	296	8 017	5 586	8 740	11 331	11.9	8.4	9 039	16.8
Isabella	16.4	307	5 910	109.4	2 920	896	8 699	5 591	8 748	15 002	18.9	9.4	19 950	9.8
Jackson	65.9	444	24 225	162.0	12 725	1 922	10 686	7 003	10 958	18 530	9.3	7.4	57 979	4.0
Kalamazoo	96.7	452	30 105	138.2	15 939	2 838	12 367	7 769	12 156	18 634	10.7	7.4	88 955	11.5
Kalkaska	4.9	441	2 215	175.8	1 062	200	8 047	5 576	8 725	13 714	14.4	11.7	9 151	20.5
Kent	225.1	498	69 105	142.6	36 086	5 758	11 883	7 522	11 770	18 554	8.7	6.7	192 698	16.6
Keweenaw	0.0	23	715	357.5	334	42	7 290	4 782	7 482	9 076	13.2	9.8	2 257	5.0
Lake	3.3	402	2 675	297.2	1 249	274	7 196	4 640	7 260	9 134	24.3	18.9	12 114	15.2
Lapeer	30.5	439	8 090	108.6	4 091	760	10 787	7 089	11 092	21 403	7.1	6.1	26 445	14.8
Leelanau	5.2	360	2 685	173.2	1 337	80	10 209	6 815	10 663	15 938	8.3	6.6	11 171	23.1
Lenawee	45.2	511	15 365	168.8	7 790	1 058	10 663	6 957	10 886	18 537	8.5	6.5	35 104	4.0

1. Elementary and secondary. 2. Per 1,000 resident population estimated as of July 1 of the year shown. 3. Based on the resident population estimated as of July 1, 1988 for 1987 data and enumerated as of April 1, 1980 for 1979 data.

STATE County	Housing units, 1990 (cont'd): Occupied units: Total	Occupied units: Owner occupied: Percent	Owner occupied: Median value (Dollars)	Median rent (Dollars)	Civilian labor force, 1990: Total	Percent change, 1989–1990	Unemployment: Total	Unemployment: Rate[1]	Private nonfarm establishments, 1988: Number	Net change, 1987–1988	Employment[2]: Total	Percent change, 1987–1988	Manu-facturing	Retail trade
	74	75	76	77	78	79	80	81	82	83	84	85	86	87
MARYLAND—Con.														
Worcester	14 142	69.3	83 500	296	22 598	1.4	1 766	7.8	1 759	21	14 559	4.9	2 041	5 097
Baltimore city	276 484	48.6	54 700	321	346 599	0.9	26 767	7.7	15 014	-883	319 371	-6.7	48 790	45 134
MASSACHUSETTS	2 247 110	59.3	162 800	506	3 166 000	-0.4	189 000	6.0	X	X	2 810 243	2.2	600 730	579 009
Barnstable	77 586	72.4	162 800	547	95 035	0.8	7 266	7.6	7 474	153	62 872	3.9	4 308	23 045
Berkshire	54 315	65.2	114 900	365	74 040	1.1	4 591	6.2	4 113	99	59 738	2.5	16 076	14 285
Bristol	187 668	59.1	141 700	345	252 045	-0.3	21 880	8.7	11 914	255	189 101	1.5	65 257	45 850
Dukes	5 003	71.3	195 800	521	7 761	3.5	424	5.5	762	17	4 110	0.0	171	1 433
Essex	251 285	61.2	176 200	522	357 011	-0.6	22 268	6.2	17 037	147	266 368	1.3	81 430	61 548
Franklin	27 640	65.6	114 100	402	38 448	3.2	2 088	5.4	1 703	33	21 593	5.1	5 502	5 068
Hampden	169 906	60.2	123 200	415	218 523	0.4	13 119	6.0	11 053	211	194 640	3.9	46 558	43 002
Hampshire	50 052	62.3	134 700	461	78 681	0.9	3 864	4.9	3 240	83	42 642	4.9	7 844	11 190
Middlesex	519 527	59.6	192 800	598	787 561	-1.1	38 256	4.9	38 903	558	762 647	2.2	183 199	133 930
Nantucket	2 597	62.7	299 400	670	5 615	-8.4	181	3.2	543	24	2 997	1.2	55	1 180
Norfolk	227 798	67.7	182 900	612	340 462	-0.6	16 421	4.8	17 797	218	288 431	0.7	51 056	67 935
Plymouth	149 519	73.0	156 400	534	221 850	0.0	15 366	6.9	10 405	220	134 125	2.4	20 656	43 256
Suffolk	264 061	32.5	162 100	546	348 785	-0.5	19 837	5.7	19 170	-35	499 023	0.2	41 883	66 907
Worcester	260 153	61.4	140 000	448	340 284	-0.8	23 657	7.0	17 036	316	281 565	6.3	76 735	60 380
MICHIGAN	3 419 331	71.0	60 600	343	4 578 000	-0.3	344 000	7.5	X	X	3 208 214	0.5	948 943	705 473
Alcona	4 261	86.4	48 200	244	4 385	0.1	519	11.8	191	9	960	0.5	335	336
Alger	3 337	80.0	39 200	206	4 892	10.4	381	7.8	234	3	1 740	-15.6	0	338
Allegan	31 709	80.7	59 300	305	60 478	3.2	3 445	5.7	1 508	9	24 307	1.2	12 217	4 093
Alpena	11 838	78.1	41 600	245	13 652	2.8	1 406	10.3	863	18	8 788	3.6	2 392	2 294
Antrim	6 980	80.9	53 000	274	7 613	-0.5	891	11.7	468	11	3 435	3.2	1 330	762
Arenac	5 642	81.4	41 800	252	7 758	10.4	601	7.7	336	4	3 171	4.9	555	990
Baraga	3 065	73.9	37 900	181	3 422	9.1	349	10.2	202	-4	1 501	4.1	571	403
Barry	17 763	84.0	54 700	287	23 412	2.1	1 685	7.2	665	6	7 783	-1.0	3 106	1 743
Bay	42 188	76.9	44 100	287	53 668	-0.3	4 414	8.2	2 277	-31	28 303	0.7	7 201	8 314
Benzie	4 772	81.9	50 200	250	5 421	2.1	686	12.7	325	12	1 868	7.0	565	602
Berrien	61 025	69.6	52 800	294	78 014	-1.3	5 747	7.4	3 621	31	57 333	3.0	22 033	11 351
Branch	14 921	76.1	40 800	265	17 307	-0.2	1 484	8.6	796	5	8 755	0.3	3 878	1 732
Calhoun	51 812	71.0	42 700	303	64 725	-1.2	4 951	7.6	2 817	11	47 807	1.4	15 409	11 162
Cass	18 239	78.9	48 600	266	22 679	-1.7	1 745	7.7	697	22	8 495	3.1	4 033	1 566
Charlevoix	8 243	77.1	53 600	288	10 646	-0.1	979	9.2	669	50	6 685	15.2	2 768	1 583
Cheboygan	8 201	79.5	47 400	250	9 726	-0.5	1 732	17.8	900	38	5 041	0.0	800	1 792
Chippewa	11 541	73.4	37 500	259	16 498	5.5	1 541	9.3	793	3	5 789	-1.9	712	2 003
Clare	9 698	78.4	36 800	243	11 066	1.7	1 034	9.3	525	-1	4 388	0.5	801	1 581
Clinton	20 212	83.0	68 000	326	31 001	0.1	2 063	6.7	857	31	8 648	1.6	1 912	2 539
Crawford	4 441	80.3	44 500	273	6 530	-0.3	381	5.8	244	26	2 342	9.0	204	1 002
Delta	14 531	76.2	43 200	233	17 194	1.9	1 588	9.2	1 020	32	9 953	3.2	2 843	2 910
Dickinson	10 633	79.4	42 900	276	13 403	4.5	998	7.4	818	17	9 184	3.6	2 415	2 360
Eaton	34 027	72.9	68 200	376	53 409	-0.2	3 117	5.8	1 667	2	24 915	1.9	3 144	9 910
Emmet	9 516	74.2	64 700	324	14 923	2.6	1 328	8.9	1 012	17	9 920	6.8	1 506	2 559
Genesee	161 296	70.4	50 500	328	184 094	-1.1	17 951	9.8	8 226	95	144 932	-7.0	0	33 651
Gladwin	8 357	81.6	42 700	226	8 773	2.7	806	9.2	324	25	2 849	11.6	828	978
Gogebic	7 449	78.2	23 300	187	6 938	2.4	561	8.1	488	6	4 063	4.7	612	1 188
Grand Traverse	23 965	74.8	66 700	377	36 350	1.0	2 545	7.0	2 542	81	28 818	1.5	5 302	7 598
Gratiot	13 659	76.2	38 800	253	19 982	1.0	1 587	7.9	782	1	9 920	7.2	2 722	2 455
Hillsdale	15 637	77.2	41 400	251	20 151	-0.9	1 690	8.4	782	21	9 889	0.0	4 627	1 764
Houghton	13 172	69.5	28 300	230	14 469	1.6	997	6.9	823	8	7 330	2.4	1 025	2 410
Huron	13 268	79.4	44 500	229	16 763	0.1	1 682	10.0	904	13	8 317	-0.3	2 814	1 935
Ingham	102 648	58.4	61 800	374	156 737	-0.4	9 414	6.0	6 329	79	111 183	0.4	27 127	25 904
Ionia	18 447	77.3	47 700	272	20 244	3.5	2 418	11.9	828	-3	8 644	-7.7	3 333	2 465
Iosco	11 588	68.4	47 400	278	11 155	-0.1	962	8.6	671	-1	4 984	6.2	1 232	1 799
Iron	5 655	80.1	30 100	191	5 352	3.0	462	8.6	353	-6	2 278	-2.5	438	898
Isabella	17 591	65.0	53 200	326	30 914	2.8	1 561	5.0	1 109	7	13 944	9.3	2 028	4 520
Jackson	53 660	73.7	47 900	309	65 723	-0.8	5 159	7.8	2 953	67	44 890	-0.3	13 183	10 753
Kalamazoo	83 702	64.4	62 800	372	120 051	-0.4	6 161	5.1	5 131	93	92 096	0.2	29 212	19 754
Kalkaska	4 934	80.5	44 500	269	6 001	3.1	648	10.8	283	5	3 215	4.6	894	802
Kent	181 740	69.7	68 200	381	275 361	0.8	16 891	6.1	12 555	294	245 262	1.9	72 287	49 085
Keweenaw	777	86.5	19 200	146	664	1.7	88	13.3	56	2	231	14.4	28	34
Lake	3 536	80.8	29 800	204	3 321	0.3	341	10.3	129	-2	849	7.6	148	302
Lapeer	24 659	81.0	62 300	335	34 292	-0.7	3 471	10.1	1 201	23	10 810	3.4	3 693	3 330
Leelanau	6 274	81.5	73 100	322	8 290	0.8	569	6.9	432	27	2 424	0.3	234	587
Lenawee	31 635	75.9	54 000	316	43 425	-0.3	3 488	8.0	1 885	47	26 051	1.4	9 918	6 055

1. Percent of total civilian labor force. 2. For week including March 12. Excludes government employees, self-employed persons, farm workers, domestic service workers, railroad employees subject to the Railroad Retirement Act, and employees on oceanborne vessels or in foreign countries.

STATE County	Private nonfarm establishments, 1988 (cont'd): Employment[1] (cont'd): Finance, insurance, and real estate	Employment[1] (cont'd): Services	Annual payroll: Total (Mil dol)	Annual payroll: Average per employee (Dollars)	Personal income, 1989: Total (Mil dol)	Percent change, 1988–1989	Wages and salaries[2] (Mil dol)	Proprietor's income (Mil dol)	Dividends, interest, & rent (Mil dol)	Transfer payments (Mil dol)	Per capita[3]: Dollars	Per capita[3]: Rank	Earnings, 1989: Total (Mil dol)	Percent by selected industries: Farm	Percent by selected industries: Goods-related[4]: Total
	88	89	90	91	92	93	94	95	96	97	98	99	100	101	102
MARYLAND—Con.															
Worcester	1 634	3 139	227	15 571	632	10.3	346	89	172	109	16 938	448	436	7.8	19.0
Baltimore city	36 715	127 456	7 114	22 276	12 201	7.1	12 633	772	2 034	2 817	16 311	567	13 404	0.0	15.8
MASSACHUSETTS	232 319	924 728	64 713	X	131 473	6.5	87 645	10 181	23 296	18 394	22 236	X	97 826	0.2	26.5
Barnstable	4 537	19 200	1 131	17 984	4 246	6.1	1 618	473	1 225	689	23 147	71	2 091	0.2	18.9
Berkshire	3 158	18 810	1 210	20 248	2 724	7.8	1 584	212	549	475	19 783	180	1 796	0.7	38.2
Bristol	8 300	40 299	3 512	18 571	9 117	6.7	4 666	590	1 263	1 576	18 845	227	5 256	0.5	36.9
Dukes	360	985	82	19 919	272	7.5	113	44	90	35	22 552	81	157	1.1	24.0
Essex	12 778	70 169	5 708	21 431	14 953	6.3	7 646	1 088	2 660	2 052	22 793	75	8 734	0.1	36.5
Franklin	1 233	6 537	393	18 191	1 244	6.2	547	116	212	231	18 228	269	663	2.9	30.8
Hampden	22 790	53 435	3 937	20 225	8 493	7.0	5 136	556	1 365	1 679	18 804	233	5 692	0.2	30.4
Hampshire	1 778	16 114	722	16 927	2 517	6.3	1 280	198	456	344	17 619	352	1 478	1.3	22.4
Middlesex	37 375	276 638	19 421	25 465	34 228	6.2	25 298	2 632	6 560	3 694	24 923	41	27 930	0.1	31.8
Nantucket	270	641	66	22 176	183	9.6	98	29	51	16	26 652	25	127	0.0	23.9
Norfolk	26 182	85 199	6 773	23 482	16 164	6.0	8 724	1 311	3 309	1 714	26 379	28	10 035	0.1	26.0
Plymouth	8 628	34 490	2 486	18 537	9 103	6.6	3 767	662	1 235	1 184	20 929	126	4 429	0.7	20.8
Suffolk	85 694	226 645	13 452	26 957	14 440	7.7	19 433	1 387	2 284	2 716	21 676	106	20 820	0.0	9.0
Worcester	19 102	75 553	5 811	20 637	13 788	6.3	7 735	882	2 037	1 989	20 200	159	8 618	0.4	35.9
MICHIGAN	184 565	864 263	75 684	X	162 610	7.0	109 417	9 623	26 304	24 918	17 535	X	119 040	0.8	39.4
Alcona	20	198	12	12 370	125	8.0	22	10	33	43	11 629	2 466	32	5.9	NA
Alger	64	361	35	19 943	96	6.1	49	9	17	27	11 045	2 654	57	2.0	47.3
Allegan	656	5 400	499	20 524	1 352	8.6	629	113	201	179	14 729	1 112	742	6.1	58.9
Alpena	430	1 718	162	18 389	429	7.0	252	35	73	103	13 574	1 648	288	1.0	35.8
Antrim	115	801	56	16 377	249	11.6	86	19	66	54	13 911	1 466	105	3.9	39.1
Arenac	150	1 062	46	14 437	194	7.3	62	19	38	53	12 064	2 306	80	8.1	23.5
Baraga	63	271	22	14 957	97	8.1	47	7	16	28	11 761	2 418	54	1.3	33.6
Barry	444	1 620	147	18 915	759	8.3	197	56	112	100	15 028	980	254	6.3	38.4
Bay	1 512	7 234	574	20 282	1 762	6.3	863	113	309	316	15 268	883	976	2.0	35.4
Benzie	104	319	29	15 791	155	7.8	54	12	39	39	13 236	1 800	66	3.6	30.7
Berrien	2 585	14 575	1 112	19 395	2 507	6.5	1 544	167	426	449	14 966	1 004	1 711	1.5	43.0
Branch	401	1 530	154	17 571	540	9.3	283	41	88	110	13 084	1 872	325	3.8	39.0
Calhoun	3 884	13 012	1 042	21 789	2 096	6.5	1 572	94	337	410	14 981	994	1 666	0.6	41.4
Cass	277	1 659	168	19 779	744	7.5	211	54	104	111	14 938	1 014	265	6.1	44.3
Charlevoix	222	1 138	117	17 553	309	9.6	164	23	66	59	14 204	1 343	187	0.8	NA
Cheboygan	229	1 370	83	16 460	263	7.6	118	19	58	68	12 144	2 262	137	1.4	30.4
Chippewa	329	1 748	81	14 007	349	8.4	178	23	60	97	11 469	2 513	201	1.5	11.7
Clare	189	1 240	61	13 887	291	7.7	104	22	52	93	10 828	2 708	126	1.7	24.3
Clinton	334	1 686	163	18 894	849	6.3	203	62	127	96	14 439	1 238	265	6.4	27.5
Crawford	95	808	29	12 251	120	9.5	64	9	27	32	10 848	2 700	73	0.0	29.2
Delta	509	2 377	185	18 635	511	8.4	294	43	84	117	13 372	1 747	337	1.8	37.4
Dickinson	308	1 594	171	18 594	435	9.4	268	41	79	80	16 638	496	309	1.4	35.9
Eaton	3 332	5 090	439	17 604	1 529	6.9	402	70	229	179	16 004	644	472	1.4	23.1
Emmet	456	3 803	170	17 117	419	10.6	242	44	101	71	16 717	481	287	0.6	22.8
Genesee	5 900	37 535	3 746	25 845	6 993	6.2	5 279	312	1 042	1 261	16 315	565	5 591	0.2	52.6
Gladwin	171	546	43	15 198	261	8.4	71	12	45	72	11 259	2 575	83	1.1	37.0
Gogebic	258	1 517	44	10 747	224	5.6	88	17	48	71	12 494	2 120	105	0.3	21.7
Grand Traverse	1 429	9 069	518	17 961	1 008	7.3	730	97	205	162	15 514	796	827	0.4	26.4
Gratiot	398	2 768	162	16 350	531	5.8	255	49	86	102	13 438	1 718	304	5.2	29.0
Hillsdale	319	2 008	169	17 121	596	7.2	274	68	91	108	13 613	1 623	342	5.5	48.1
Houghton	621	2 221	101	13 823	432	6.8	210	26	87	120	12 238	2 215	236	0.7	12.3
Huron	432	1 769	153	18 434	576	7.9	229	89	131	113	15 721	732	318	17.8	32.6
Ingham	7 829	31 993	2 604	23 422	4 808	7.8	4 724	257	686	740	17 357	386	4 981	0.3	30.9
Ionia	411	1 395	145	16 771	673	5.9	286	46	103	117	11 748	2 422	332	4.6	35.4
Iosco	403	848	71	14 290	381	8.6	228	22	71	92	12 485	2 124	250	0.7	NA
Iron	159	511	28	12 392	181	10.5	63	14	37	57	13 507	1 678	78	2.6	26.7
Isabella	763	4 047	204	14 644	739	9.0	430	56	103	145	13 631	1 610	486	1.6	22.7
Jackson	1 868	11 046	928	20 676	2 261	6.8	1 344	117	384	376	14 950	1 010	1 461	1.0	35.1
Kalamazoo	4 888	26 855	2 079	22 575	3 895	7.6	2 979	231	673	531	17 807	319	3 211	0.6	43.2
Kalkaska	47	264	67	20 791	137	6.8	79	10	26	33	10 615	2 767	89	1.5	50.9
Kent	13 089	65 330	5 381	21 942	8 803	8.1	7 014	644	1 445	1 064	17 981	298	7 658	0.4	39.7
Keweenaw	19	17	4	15 913	21	6.1	4	1	5	8	10 352	2 825	5	0.0	NA
Lake	58	275	9	10 392	90	8.7	20	9	18	36	9 836	2 906	28	4.3	12.7
Lapeer	636	1 845	186	17 164	1 193	9.2	388	65	146	191	15 687	740	453	3.4	36.2
Leelanau	98	1 036	34	13 965	265	9.9	52	26	74	39	16 732	480	78	4.4	21.7
Lenawee	1 101	6 628	487	18 705	1 434	6.0	705	94	238	222	15 649	760	799	2.3	47.1

1. For week including March 12. Excludes government employees, self-employed persons, farm workers, domestic service workers, railroad employees subject to the Railroad Retirement Act, and employees on oceanborne vessels or in foreign countries. 2. Includes other labor income. 3. Based on the resident population estimated as of July 1 of the year shown. 4. Covers mining, construction, and manufacturing.

STATE County	Earnings, 1989 (cont'd): Percent by selected industries (cont'd): Goods-related[1]: Manufacturing	Service-related & other[2]: Total	Service-related & other[2]: Retail trade	Service-related & other[2]: Finance, insurance, & real estate	Service-related & other[2]: Services	Government	Agriculture, 1987: Farms: Number	Farms: Percent with: Less than 50 acres	Farms: Percent with: 500 acres and over	Farm operators, percent: Whose principal occupation is farming	Farm operators, percent: Residing on farm operated	Land in farms: Acreage (1,000)	Land in farms: Percent change, 1982–1987	Land in farms: Acres: Average size of farm	Acres: Total irrigated (1,000)	Acres: Total cropland (1,000)
	103	104	105	106	107	108	109	110	111	112	113	114	115	116	117	118
MARYLAND—Con.																
Worcester	10.0	61.4	24.1	6.1	22.8	11.8	631	47.7	11.1	68.9	65.3	123	2.5	196	1	88
Baltimore city	11.0	65.8	7.7	11.9	30.7	18.4	NA	NA	NA	NA	NA	NA	NA	NA	NA	NA
MASSACHUSETTS	20.2	61.3	9.6	7.9	31.4	11.9	6 216	52.0	2.5	51.1	79.1	615	0.4	99	20	273
Barnstable	5.6	66.8	19.3	3.9	33.2	14.1	158	85.4	0.6	53.8	65.2	D	D	D	1	2
Berkshire	28.8	51.8	11.9	3.9	29.0	9.2	392	33.2	9.9	49.7	82.4	71	-3.6	181	0	32
Bristol	29.3	50.0	12.4	3.6	20.5	12.7	675	59.0	0.7	53.0	80.7	43	1.6	63	2	21
Dukes	2.4	62.6	20.2	4.7	25.9	12.4	58	60.3	8.6	51.7	75.9	7	-0.6	126	D	2
Essex	30.0	51.9	10.8	3.8	26.2	11.5	439	64.9	1.6	51.7	79.5	31	2.2	70	1	17
Franklin	21.9	55.3	11.9	3.8	26.7	11.0	616	35.1	2.6	50.8	89.1	83	4.3	135	1	34
Hampden	23.6	55.5	10.7	7.8	25.4	13.8	490	47.8	2.2	50.6	81.8	47	6.6	95	1	19
Hampshire	14.1	49.1	10.6	2.7	29.7	27.2	624	48.7	3.0	49.2	80.1	65	1.5	103	0	34
Middlesex	26.0	59.4	8.5	3.9	34.2	8.7	569	60.6	0.9	51.0	77.7	39	-3.6	68	1	20
Nantucket	1.5	65.7	21.8	3.9	29.4	10.4	12	66.7	0.0	58.3	83.3	1	NA	68	0	1
Norfolk	17.6	65.0	12.1	8.0	29.9	8.9	212	66.0	1.4	50.5	79.7	13	-2.0	62	0	7
Plymouth	11.7	62.6	15.4	4.7	26.2	15.9	775	64.5	2.5	56.8	63.5	77	-4.0	100	11	23
Suffolk	5.9	75.3	5.6	18.8	39.1	15.7	5	100.0	0.0	20.0	20.0	D	NA	D	D	0
Worcester	28.6	52.6	10.0	5.6	24.6	11.1	1 191	41.6	2.3	47.5	83.1	135	0.8	113	1	62
MICHIGAN	34.1	46.7	8.9	4.4	22.1	13.1	51 172	29.4	9.8	51.0	82.0	10 317	-5.7	202	315	8 181
Alcona	15.2	NA	18.4	NA	23.5	22.6	229	12.7	7.0	48.5	84.7	43	-18.3	190	D	29
Alger	44.3	31.5	8.3	1.8	13.4	19.2	63	14.3	17.5	36.5	90.5	16	-8.8	256	0	9
Allegan	54.0	24.3	7.3	1.0	11.0	10.7	1 634	35.3	5.9	48.4	81.8	254	-5.0	155	10	205
Alpena	29.9	42.8	9.4	3.1	16.3	20.4	424	15.8	6.4	45.0	84.9	82	1.8	194	0	55
Antrim	30.9	37.8	10.2	2.4	20.2	19.2	248	21.4	10.5	56.0	79.4	55	-12.7	222	4	34
Arenac	17.1	51.9	17.3	3.6	20.4	16.5	332	16.3	14.2	60.5	78.9	89	-1.1	269	1	70
Baraga	28.9	36.1	8.9	2.2	16.8	29.1	57	12.3	10.5	49.1	93.0	14	-17.4	244	D	7
Barry	31.4	41.0	8.1	4.0	22.6	14.4	908	25.2	8.6	48.2	86.7	168	-10.4	186	3	129
Bay	29.7	48.5	11.5	3.4	22.3	14.1	922	27.9	9.3	55.6	77.4	177	-1.6	192	7	161
Benzie	18.2	44.8	13.7	3.0	22.0	20.9	149	27.5	7.4	52.3	80.5	24	-8.2	161	1	13
Berrien	38.7	43.8	9.3	3.8	19.9	11.7	1 479	50.4	4.7	54.5	81.9	180	-5.4	121	9	150
Branch	34.4	31.3	9.0	2.5	13.4	25.9	1 034	26.1	12.5	48.4	79.3	227	-6.5	220	23	179
Calhoun	36.9	39.3	8.0	4.7	17.3	18.6	1 166	22.7	11.3	47.0	83.3	253	-5.0	217	8	194
Cass	39.1	34.1	7.6	1.9	16.5	15.5	839	29.2	12.6	54.4	83.8	194	-2.1	232	12	152
Charlevoix	37.1	NA	8.0	2.1	15.5	16.0	232	26.3	7.3	42.7	85.8	42	-11.1	180	0	25
Cheboygan	17.9	51.7	17.6	4.9	21.7	16.5	171	18.7	14.6	45.6	83.0	42	-8.1	248	0	26
Chippewa	4.9	47.8	14.0	2.5	19.3	38.9	338	7.7	13.6	49.1	82.8	89	-10.1	264	0	65
Clare	16.5	53.6	19.9	2.4	23.7	20.4	298	20.5	10.4	45.3	84.2	68	-11.2	228	D	48
Clinton	17.6	44.6	12.9	2.6	17.8	21.5	1 333	25.3	7.9	47.3	81.7	257	-3.7	193	4	220
Crawford	24.1	47.0	15.5	2.7	24.6	23.8	20	45.0	0.0	45.0	85.0	1	-9.6	73	0	D
Delta	31.4	43.4	10.9	3.0	18.5	17.5	271	14.0	14.8	52.4	87.5	74	-9.0	273	0	38
Dickinson	24.4	44.0	8.9	3.6	16.1	18.7	109	22.9	13.8	63.3	88.1	29	-11.1	266	1	15
Eaton	16.9	45.8	13.7	6.9	19.6	29.7	1 219	30.0	8.9	43.7	84.2	234	-4.5	192	1	188
Emmet	12.3	63.9	13.2	2.7	41.3	12.7	211	20.9	8.5	52.1	80.6	45	-6.3	213	0	26
Genesee	48.8	36.3	8.8	2.4	17.4	10.9	851	43.7	7.6	42.8	81.4	145	-9.7	171	2	127
Gladwin	26.9	42.1	13.7	3.2	19.3	19.8	411	18.7	5.6	50.1	82.7	68	-7.7	166	0	49
Gogebic	16.5	46.8	13.1	5.5	19.6	31.3	58	24.1	0.0	39.7	91.4	6	-45.5	102	0	3
Grand Traverse	15.9	56.9	13.5	4.1	29.4	16.3	447	35.3	6.3	53.9	75.2	70	-5.7	156	3	50
Gratiot	25.6	51.0	11.6	2.6	24.3	14.8	1 011	21.7	15.6	60.5	80.3	282	-2.2	279	2	250
Hillsdale	42.0	32.5	6.7	1.4	16.7	13.9	1 142	25.8	10.5	49.0	79.8	242	-8.4	212	4	196
Houghton	5.9	49.1	12.1	7.2	22.5	37.9	147	15.0	8.2	43.5	86.4	32	-10.7	216	0	16
Huron	27.3	37.0	9.2	2.6	15.7	12.6	1 390	16.6	18.0	75.8	78.1	424	-2.4	305	2	384
Ingham	26.6	40.6	7.9	5.6	18.7	28.2	960	37.1	10.8	44.1	84.2	208	-6.7	216	2	172
Ionia	31.4	32.1	10.1	2.7	13.0	27.9	1 089	22.5	11.7	52.0	84.4	254	4.4	233	4	208
Iosco	14.5	NA	9.2	2.7	12.9	49.6	215	16.7	8.4	48.4	80.5	48	-16.5	223	D	27
Iron	11.4	41.6	14.5	3.0	16.8	29.0	95	10.5	15.8	46.3	82.1	27	-8.0	281	0	11
Isabella	9.9	43.1	10.2	2.5	21.6	32.6	912	21.2	10.3	52.9	80.7	195	-3.0	214	1	159
Jackson	30.0	NA	10.0	2.6	NA	14.7	1 103	30.6	9.2	44.0	83.4	218	-7.1	198	5	161
Kalamazoo	38.1	43.5	7.9	4.7	23.1	12.6	842	41.8	10.5	46.6	81.4	168	-5.0	200	15	133
Kalkaska	20.3	35.1	8.2	0.2	10.6	12.5	89	21.3	5.6	40.4	88.8	16	-7.7	183	1	11
Kent	33.0	52.0	11.0	4.8	22.3	8.0	1 368	40.6	6.5	45.7	84.2	204	-8.7	149	7	163
Keweenaw	8.8	NA	21.0	NA	28.7	32.0	2	100.0	0.0	0.0	0.0	D	D	D	0	D
Lake	7.0	NA	15.1	3.5	21.7	30.0	111	25.2	5.4	42.3	87.4	19	-15.2	167	0	11
Lapeer	29.5	34.2	10.3	2.2	15.3	26.2	1 228	38.3	7.8	48.3	84.6	219	-3.2	178	4	175
Leelanau	3.9	58.9	15.9	0.5	36.4	15.0	394	20.8	5.1	56.9	72.6	65	-9.6	166	2	39
Lenawee	42.3	37.9	9.3	3.1	18.9	12.7	1 387	25.8	16.1	51.8	78.9	345	-8.4	249	3	310

1. Covers mining, construction, and manufacturing. 2. Covers private sector earnings in agricultural services, forestry, and fisheries; transportation and public utilities; wholesale trade; retail trade; finance, insurance, and real estate; and services.

STATE County	Agriculture, 1987 (cont'd)								Manufactures, 1987						
	Value of land and buildings		Value of products sold				Percent of farms with sales of		Establishments		All employees			Production workers	
					Percent from										
	Average per farm ($1,000)	Average per acre (Dollars)	Total (Mil dol)	Average per farm (Dollars)	Crops	Livestock and poultry[1]	$10,000 or more	$100,000 or more	Total	Percent with 20 or more em-ployees	Number (1,000)	Percent change, 1982–1987	Annual payroll (Mil dol)	Number (1,000)	Work hours (Mil)
	119	120	121	122	123	124	125	126	127	128	129	130	131	132	133
MARYLAND—Con.															
Worcester	362	1 793	122	193 420	13.0	87.0	80.0	52.1	48	20.8	2.1	10.5	33.4	1.7	3.4
Baltimore city	NA	NA	NA	NA	NA	NA	NA	NA	963	44.5	50.4	-15.0	1 252.7	33.6	67.6
MASSACHUSETTS	347	3 553	340	54 772	63.4	36.6	40.2	11.6	11 006	38.0	591.3	-8.1	15 211.3	348.3	690.5
Barnstable	319	13 288	7	43 041	93.8	6.2	55.1	7.6	220	20.9	D	D	D	D	D
Berkshire	387	2 009	18	44 805	25.2	74.8	35.2	13.5	217	35.9	16.4	-14.6	470.4	8.0	16.6
Bristol	267	4 451	30	44 401	64.0	36.0	42.1	9.5	1 072	43.3	66.8	-6.6	1 347.0	46.6	89.4
Dukes	460	3 650	D	D	NA	NA	27.6	1.7	17	17.6	0.2	0.0	3.3	0.1	0.2
Essex	463	6 754	17	38 803	71.9	28.1	39.2	10.0	1 305	37.8	82.4	1.5	2 181.1	50.2	99.6
Franklin	244	2 090	25	39 895	45.1	54.9	36.9	10.4	138	36.2	5.5	3.8	129.3	3.7	7.8
Hampden	284	2 919	19	38 889	70.1	29.9	32.2	10.4	868	41.0	44.1	-12.5	1 028.9	30.0	60.8
Hampshire	259	2 601	28	44 122	58.0	42.0	36.5	9.9	198	33.8	7.3	-8.8	167.6	4.8	10.0
Middlesex	314	4 960	50	87 628	58.1	41.9	42.2	11.6	2 793	39.5	176.6	-8.4	5 021.2	90.5	181.2
Nantucket	D	D	2	178 456	D	D	66.7	16.7	11	9.1	D	D	D	D	D
Norfolk	287	5 100	13	62 454	68.3	31.7	35.8	8.5	1 054	36.5	53.0	-7.8	1 438.1	29.9	61.3
Plymouth	397	3 963	77	99 837	94.6	5.4	56.5	20.3	682	30.8	20.9	-5.9	465.3	14.4	27.6
Suffolk	D	D	D	D	NA	NA	60.0	20.0	962	35.9	44.8	-10.8	1 207.6	22.5	41.8
Worcester	444	3 761	54	45 599	35.1	64.9	35.6	10.5	1 469	39.8	69.4	-14.6	1 668.0	44.6	88.7
MICHIGAN	196	971	2 545	49 736	50.0	50.0	47.3	12.5	16 010	35.9	980.1	10.9	30 627.8	635.5	1 300.7
Alcona	91	558	4	16 856	16.2	83.8	28.8	3.1	32	9.4	0.3	0.0	4.8	0.2	0.5
Alger	104	406	2	25 918	8.5	91.5	39.7	11.1	30	6.7	D	D	D	D	D
Allegan	184	1 162	120	73 735	36.8	63.2	50.2	17.3	155	49.0	11.7	17.0	289.6	8.1	16.6
Alpena	131	645	10	23 431	31.5	68.5	30.9	6.4	61	29.5	2.4	0.0	60.5	1.7	3.7
Antrim	183	799	11	46 335	48.5	51.5	48.4	13.3	47	31.9	1.3	18.2	24.0	1.1	1.9
Arenac	204	779	16	49 435	60.9	39.1	56.0	15.7	26	38.5	0.6	50.0	11.1	0.5	0.9
Baraga	95	390	1	13 771	D	D	35.1	1.8	36	11.1	0.6	20.0	11.4	0.4	0.8
Barry	167	909	30	33 529	26.4	73.6	36.3	9.6	47	40.4	3.2	28.0	76.0	2.3	4.8
Bay	233	1 184	44	47 472	91.7	8.3	61.3	13.3	133	34.6	D	D	D	D	D
Benzie	134	821	4	25 728	74.4	25.6	35.6	6.0	25	32.0	D	D	D	D	D
Berrien	148	1 167	63	42 881	83.2	16.8	46.8	11.4	390	39.0	22.3	12.1	559.9	13.9	28.0
Branch	172	786	49	47 638	48.8	51.2	50.1	9.7	83	47.0	4.2	16.7	84.5	3.1	6.2
Calhoun	151	717	42	36 282	45.3	54.7	41.0	8.9	211	42.7	15.3	-5.6	490.6	10.8	23.7
Cass	225	948	59	70 703	32.1	67.9	52.0	17.9	82	45.1	4.1	32.3	92.6	3.0	6.1
Charlevoix	131	739	4	18 189	24.1	75.9	26.3	4.3	61	29.5	2.2	10.0	44.8	1.7	3.5
Cheboygan	140	597	5	26 714	15.0	85.0	30.4	7.6	40	22.5	0.8	-20.0	18.9	0.7	1.3
Chippewa	92	387	7	19 897	21.1	78.9	37.0	3.8	37	27.0	0.8	60.0	10.9	0.6	1.1
Clare	155	674	9	29 138	8.0	92.0	38.3	7.4	36	27.8	0.9	80.0	15.9	0.8	1.4
Clinton	183	937	62	46 654	35.2	64.8	52.2	12.5	48	31.2	2.3	0.0	59.7	1.7	3.7
Crawford	90	1 247	D	D	NA	NA	20.0	0.0	11	27.3	0.2	-50.0	2.9	0.2	0.4
Delta	117	420	8	30 739	21.6	78.4	42.4	8.5	93	19.4	2.8	-6.7	76.4	2.1	4.0
Dickinson	153	548	4	40 606	42.5	57.5	45.9	13.8	56	35.7	2.6	36.8	58.0	1.9	3.8
Eaton	162	867	39	31 713	58.2	41.8	43.6	7.9	92	34.8	D	D	D	D	D
Emmet	156	754	5	22 061	31.7	68.3	29.4	6.6	48	33.3	1.5	36.4	26.0	1.1	2.0
Genesee	198	1 225	29	34 643	52.6	47.4	34.7	7.1	323	30.0	D	D	D	D	D
Gladwin	112	723	7	16 859	26.1	73.9	33.8	2.9	27	33.3	0.8	33.3	16.7	0.6	1.3
Gogebic	D	D	1	16 136	11.9	88.1	15.5	3.4	45	20.0	0.6	-25.0	9.2	0.5	1.0
Grand Traverse	198	1 391	13	29 009	70.6	29.4	48.8	6.0	139	36.7	5.4	31.7	107.6	4.1	8.1
Gratiot	249	825	66	65 552	56.3	43.7	61.3	17.8	46	45.7	2.1	-8.7	47.4	1.6	3.1
Hillsdale	184	835	53	46 592	39.2	60.8	47.7	10.9	87	46.0	4.7	27.0	100.3	3.7	7.4
Houghton	104	467	2	15 319	30.8	69.2	25.9	4.8	54	22.2	0.8	14.3	13.1	0.6	1.2
Huron	315	1 003	146	104 750	36.9	63.1	76.3	26.5	73	41.1	3.1	72.2	70.4	2.5	5.0
Ingham	243	1 107	46	48 105	43.6	56.4	42.0	13.3	259	34.0	29.9	0.0	1 050.2	23.1	47.1
Ionia	197	857	70	64 144	29.4	70.6	50.1	16.7	72	47.2	3.7	12.1	77.2	2.9	5.7
Iosco	136	644	7	30 680	11.4	88.6	34.9	5.1	38	28.9	0.9	12.5	18.4	0.6	1.3
Iron	121	430	2	17 186	36.5	63.5	26.3	5.3	40	10.0	0.4	-42.9	6.4	0.3	0.7
Isabella	157	680	39	43 276	25.5	74.5	49.8	12.2	39	15.4	1.4	27.3	30.1	1.0	1.9
Jackson	175	871	46	41 690	29.0	71.0	36.5	9.1	324	41.4	13.3	9.0	327.7	9.0	18.2
Kalamazoo	235	1 235	65	76 616	55.8	44.2	46.6	17.5	393	38.4	27.9	-2.4	916.7	18.1	37.7
Kalkaska	127	694	2	25 909	51.3	48.7	25.8	5.6	22	40.9	0.9	200.0	18.5	0.7	1.5
Kent	203	1 274	83	60 660	60.7	39.3	44.7	15.4	1 130	42.7	73.8	20.0	1 994.8	52.6	105.0
Keweenaw	D	D	0	0	NA	NA	0.0	0.0	6	16.7	0.0	0.0	0.3	0.0	0.1
Lake	118	607	1	11 560	11.5	88.5	22.5	2.7	9	44.4	0.1	0.0	1.9	0.1	0.2
Lapeer	212	1 121	56	45 262	54.2	45.8	36.7	10.7	103	35.9	3.5	75.0	68.0	2.6	5.3
Leelanau	275	1 617	15	38 454	76.7	23.3	51.5	10.2	24	8.3	0.2	0.0	4.3	0.2	0.4
Lenawee	297	1 190	79	56 793	59.0	41.0	59.0	16.9	168	41.7	10.0	13.6	266.1	7.3	14.7

1. Includes livestock and poultry products.

STATE County	Manufactures, 1987 (cont'd): Production workers (cont'd): Wages: Total (Mil dol)	Manufactures, 1987 (cont'd): Production workers (cont'd): Wages: Average per worker (Dollars)	Manufactures, 1987 (cont'd): Value added by manufacture (Mil dol)	Manufactures, 1987 (cont'd): Value of shipments (Mil dol)	Manufactures, 1987 (cont'd): New capital expenditures (Mil dol)	Value of construction authorized by building permits, 1990: Total[1] ($1,000)	Nonresidential: Total ($1,000)	Nonresidential: Percent: Office	Nonresidential: Percent: Industrial	Nonresidential: Percent: Stores	Residential: New construction ($1,000)	Residential: Number of housing units	Residential: Alterations and additions ($1,000)
	134	135	136	137	138	139	140	141	142	143	144	145	146
MARYLAND—Con.													
Worcester	22.9	13 471	129.4	307.9	5.3	72 368	10 043	8.3	11.0	14.6	46 503	619	5 588
Baltimore city	733.7	21 836	4 064.2	8 893.1	193.4	337 214	91 310	49.6	10.2	7.6	10 764	240	44 807
MASSACHUSETTS	7 018.9	20 152	35 769.7	62 793.7	2 169.0	3 392 541	708 453	25.5	9.1	23.0	1 321 152	14 290	607 973
Barnstable	D	D	D	D	D	240 352	37 253	8.2	0.4	12.9	129 895	1 303	55 126
Berkshire	178.3	22 288	832.0	1 442.6	53.9	104 126	30 172	29.8	6.1	5.5	35 935	377	15 229
Bristol	741.6	15 914	2 882.9	5 497.1	196.1	306 618	85 267	13.8	2.7	63.5	140 812	1 528	37 461
Dukes	2.4	24 000	7.5	13.1	0.8	47 914	3 106	0.0	0.0	41.2	34 488	236	5 214
Essex	1 055.6	21 028	6 470.9	11 107.7	310.9	351 510	47 035	7.6	6.1	48.6	123 433	1 249	85 442
Franklin	78.1	21 108	272.7	531.7	21.8	50 890	13 928	5.0	38.9	25.8	21 508	256	6 750
Hampden	596.1	19 870	3 239.3	5 622.3	143.4	245 257	49 152	12.5	31.9	22.6	80 768	998	33 202
Hampshire	92.9	19 354	347.2	753.3	20.9	109 522	17 617	5.0	6.2	21.0	68 624	716	15 149
Middlesex	1 980.6	21 885	10 839.9	19 123.8	791.8	721 212	157 006	34.1	9.0	10.2	232 347	2 314	166 346
Nantucket	D	D	D	D	D	29 337	3 217	28.4	6.2	28.6	18 194	118	6 935
Norfolk	690.8	23 104	3 065.3	5 310.5	186.3	356 716	59 893	15.9	7.3	6.3	113 854	1 174	79 180
Plymouth	263.0	18 264	1 066.0	1 826.0	61.2	252 820	52 566	10.6	6.8	32.7	120 099	1 243	46 086
Suffolk	435.3	19 347	2 634.3	4 487.0	129.3	191 017	81 818	77.4	0.8	5.9	18 497	325	8 345
Worcester	858.0	19 238	3 908.1	6 736.0	237.0	385 250	70 424	17.9	17.3	24.5	182 698	2 453	47 508
MICHIGAN	17 393.0	27 369	60 258.6	146 338.8	4 793.5	5 655 995	1 475 330	29.1	20.5	25.0	2 751 708	38 945	439 947
Alcona	3.3	16 500	9.8	18.3	0.5	7 431	987	0.0	0.0	10.9	5 132	93	740
Alger	D	D	D	D	D	3 827	1 297	0.0	0.0	65.8	2 104	78	56
Allegan	173.6	21 432	870.5	1 632.5	65.2	53 052	10 709	5.4	14.1	27.3	32 616	449	4 146
Alpena	42.1	24 765	136.5	259.9	23.6	9 632	1 855	0.0	0.0	88.1	3 657	62	1 082
Antrim	18.1	16 455	53.4	97.8	D	20 588	796	3.7	55.6	18.0	14 329	193	3 347
Arenac	7.8	15 600	26.5	51.1	0.9	225	0	NA	NA	NA	225	6	0
Baraga	7.7	19 250	23.8	65.0	0.9	2 764	1 097	0.0	8.2	35.5	1 051	32	321
Barry	47.3	20 565	165.7	368.2	6.8	25 992	3 825	19.2	0.0	14.9	16 048	307	1 847
Bay	D	D	D	D	D	42 016	21 695	4.5	17.3	68.0	12 355	178	3 500
Benzie	D	D	D	D	D	15 365	1 871	6.7	0.0	13.2	11 150	183	1 061
Berrien	282.5	20 324	970.9	2 545.7	66.6	78 493	16 241	10.0	16.4	10.7	45 889	554	10 112
Branch	54.7	17 645	162.6	426.7	11.7	16 702	5 235	4.4	7.2	54.3	6 504	132	2 512
Calhoun	308.6	28 574	1 632.4	2 544.3	236.4	60 106	33 474	73.1	9.0	7.2	14 239	229	2 291
Cass	57.1	19 033	218.8	470.3	10.4	15 663	4 388	0.0	49.9	6.0	8 872	177	1 497
Charlevoix	32.1	18 882	139.4	233.7	6.8	16 744	2 220	0.0	0.0	69.5	12 218	225	997
Cheboygan	14.4	20 571	76.6	142.8	4.0	16 282	2 685	20.5	0.0	30.3	8 530	136	1 734
Chippewa	7.0	11 667	21.4	41.0	0.9	17 131	2 452	1.9	0.0	23.4	10 864	144	1 015
Clare	11.2	14 000	43.2	93.6	1.9	6 920	745	0.0	0.0	15.1	3 080	72	738
Clinton	41.6	24 471	131.8	322.3	D	34 870	5 091	5.6	7.3	41.7	26 394	434	2 109
Crawford	2.2	11 000	6.8	14.8	D	11 498	2 372	0.0	0.0	4.8	6 556	116	1 182
Delta	53.2	25 333	266.5	505.0	D	16 824	8 022	0.5	34.7	9.0	6 146	116	961
Dickinson	37.8	19 895	176.9	305.5	D	21 544	9 350	55.8	13.4	24.4	7 177	148	561
Eaton	D	D	D	D	D	56 072	17 888	37.6	7.0	32.6	33 924	530	2 704
Emmet	15.7	14 273	58.1	115.8	3.6	21 384	3 999	0.0	5.7	63.3	10 453	180	3 011
Genesee	D	D	D	D	D	159 762	41 785	37.7	0.9	31.3	84 190	1 281	10 494
Gladwin	11.4	19 000	35.9	79.9	2.5	18 537	1 160	38.1	54.5	0.0	12 511	200	1 760
Gogebic	7.3	14 600	21.2	36.0	1.9	9 964	4 595	0.5	0.0	90.8	2 717	48	885
Grand Traverse	71.8	17 512	228.7	467.8	10.5	83 152	29 620	21.3	4.2	66.6	42 634	585	3 785
Gratiot	29.5	18 438	117.8	530.5	D	24 864	2 968	1.0	31.0	2.0	3 607	61	691
Hillsdale	70.7	19 108	300.9	598.9	18.1	15 710	1 610	1.5	32.2	25.2	10 762	208	1 122
Houghton	8.1	13 500	31.4	64.0	2.0	6 743	921	0.0	2.8	3.3	4 120	76	401
Huron	54.6	21 840	137.3	228.8	D	16 760	5 368	25.3	0.0	31.0	7 973	167	1 520
Ingham	774.3	33 519	1 641.6	6 716.7	132.4	144 879	38 815	52.6	21.1	7.5	55 397	670	10 506
Ionia	53.4	18 414	198.6	388.9	10.3	17 011	2 564	12.6	27.6	9.5	11 372	194	1 767
Iosco	13.2	22 000	49.9	87.0	1.3	19 101	2 569	0.0	1.5	17.4	11 128	230	2 100
Iron	4.6	15 333	14.2	29.9	1.4	4 429	919	10.9	21.8	0.0	3 035	65	294
Isabella	20.3	20 300	80.6	144.6	2.7	19 725	1 916	6.8	37.5	23.8	12 201	438	2 115
Jackson	184.2	20 467	627.9	1 406.8	37.4	75 688	21 497	7.3	14.6	57.4	39 826	584	4 428
Kalamazoo	515.9	28 503	2 307.7	3 970.6	206.7	161 670	36 513	46.0	10.2	18.5	79 217	728	8 469
Kalkaska	12.8	18 286	53.2	110.9	5.6	6 774	1 051	6.3	4.8	30.7	3 822	84	989
Kent	1 284.9	24 428	4 379.0	8 056.8	509.0	464 057	111 309	19.7	30.0	19.4	217 564	3 075	26 061
Keweenaw	0.3	NA	0.7	1.2	0.0	2 629	16	0.0	0.0	100.0	2 375	42	85
Lake	1.5	15 000	3.8	7.4	0.1	3 468	173	0.0	0.0	99.5	2 316	38	562
Lapeer	43.0	16 538	223.1	434.2	D	51 059	8 915	8.8	13.1	29.8	35 677	464	2 653
Leelanau	3.1	15 500	10.6	21.8	0.4	22 911	2 507	8.3	6.6	15.6	15 239	229	3 405
Lenawee	176.5	24 178	603.0	1 294.5	37.5	42 690	9 682	24.7	29.9	19.1	22 689	397	3 467

1. Includes nonresidential additions and alterations, residential nonhousekeeping buildings, and residential garages and carports not shown separately.

STATE County	Wholesale trade, 1987				Retail trade, all establishments, 1987				Retail trade, establishments with payroll, 1987					
						Sales				Sales				
											Per capita[2] (Dollars)			
	Estab-lishments	Sales (Mil dol)	Paid employees[1]	Annual payroll (Mil dol)	Number	Total (Mil dol)	Percent change, 1982–1987	Per capita[2] (Dollars)	Number	Total (Mil dol)	General merchan-dise stores	Food stores	Apparel & acces-sory stores	Eating and drinking places
	147	148	149	150	151	152	153	154	155	156	157	158	159	160
MARYLAND—Con.														
Worcester	66	178.8	641	13.8	898	457.1	70.9	12 592	693	441.2	767	2 348	877	2 825
Baltimore city	1 047	7 112.2	18 632	449.6	5 570	3 167.2	19.8	4 192	4 096	3 091.6	279	830	288	615
MASSACHUSETTS	11 087	74 697.6	160 791	4 389.9	58 623	45 997.2	59.6	7 855	38 905	44 818.5	841	1 379	474	804
Barnstable	232	372.4	1 604	35.3	3 334	2 079.3	75.2	11 957	2 300	2 024.3	886	2 177	791	1 562
Berkshire	152	277.9	1 416	28.3	1 764	1 087.1	52.9	7 799	1 165	1 054.2	808	1 495	373	749
Bristol	683	3 959.4	10 065	225.0	4 988	3 680.0	60.4	7 710	3 234	3 582.9	841	1 531	463	681
Dukes	20	22.3	86	1.8	344	140.5	72.2	12 433	240	133.9	D	2 879	986	1 739
Essex	1 098	4 971.6	14 685	407.7	6 745	5 241.9	50.9	8 047	4 262	5 081.6	970	1 240	480	856
Franklin	83	204.0	689	17.2	817	407.8	58.7	6 169	455	393.9	D	1 212	123	528
Hampden	773	2 733.8	9 844	234.9	4 526	3 282.0	53.3	7 342	2 990	3 195.1	1 001	1 273	402	661
Hampshire	128	235.3	1 029	21.0	1 503	792.4	62.2	5 627	956	765.6	402	1 215	223	642
Middlesex	3 219	27 569.3	50 562	1 536.3	12 304	10 971.2	58.9	7 991	8 223	10 713.7	897	1 434	502	705
Nantucket	4	1.7	12	0.2	244	115.6	62.6	18 063	184	112.0	D	3 282	1 353	3 612
Norfolk	1 667	15 863.3	24 920	733.5	5 546	5 457.1	65.0	8 971	3 710	5 342.1	939	1 603	595	706
Plymouth	685	3 119.6	9 100	212.9	4 243	3 505.6	84.2	8 225	2 686	3 418.5	673	1 329	428	725
Suffolk	1 268	10 551.7	20 227	548.5	5 552	4 360.9	39.0	6 520	4 234	4 268.2	648	1 120	540	1 288
Worcester	1 075	4 815.2	16 552	387.4	6 713	4 875.9	70.6	7 322	4 266	4 732.4	843	1 226	332	627
MICHIGAN	14 811	86 064.5	179 452	4 571.5	80 743	58 025.6	48.0	6 304	53 399	56 697.3	874	1 078	319	603
Alcona	3	D	D	D	128	34.9	67.8	3 360	70	32.0	167	613	D	319
Alger	10	D	D	D	123	27.8	17.8	3 201	80	25.9	D	1 623	D	404
Allegan	95	186.7	725	14.7	782	398.0	73.0	4 487	464	386.5	98	1 140	99	351
Alpena	65	115.2	582	10.3	382	194.3	41.8	6 168	256	187.6	738	1 288	257	472
Antrim	25	28.6	123	1.9	202	66.8	66.6	3 885	125	63.3	D	1 292	33	441
Arenac	17	51.7	127	2.4	195	79.5	43.0	5 132	112	75.0	D	1 133	56	634
Baraga	7	6.4	29	0.5	93	32.4	17.8	3 950	61	31.6	D	1 475	D	296
Barry	42	60.7	262	5.3	347	148.7	61.5	3 041	193	143.6	D	830	83	298
Bay	144	694.8	1 771	38.7	1 065	708.4	47.5	6 096	722	697.1	996	1 027	236	534
Benzie	5	D	D	D	183	51.9	42.2	4 549	109	48.9	108	1 348	85	494
Berrien	231	1 451.5	2 451	63.8	1 566	982.4	46.6	5 922	1 012	957.7	808	1 067	208	620
Branch	57	339.0	659	13.2	397	167.3	24.3	4 152	219	159.0	D	752	203	313
Calhoun	165	539.0	1 476	30.3	1 272	883.9	58.9	6 373	878	866.3	1 099	1 126	216	606
Cass	42	145.6	350	7.3	384	145.9	56.7	2 984	206	139.3	114	641	50	250
Charlevoix	17	11.4	51	0.8	299	107.5	42.6	5 192	189	103.0	D	1 614	208	648
Cheboygan	30	77.1	134	2.6	380	146.3	35.5	7 000	302	142.3	422	1 570	320	900
Chippewa	41	42.5	255	4.5	381	176.5	68.4	5 983	259	168.8	675	1 520	240	581
Clare	22	30.8	136	1.8	318	143.1	53.0	5 547	196	137.9	D	1 397	149	466
Clinton	67	364.3	798	18.4	410	230.3	52.2	4 026	234	222.8	99	841	121	250
Crawford	9	38.1	82	1.4	117	62.2	57.1	5 925	76	60.1	969	866	64	786
Delta	67	120.0	483	7.8	495	237.6	36.9	6 186	318	229.7	671	1 645	307	530
Dickinson	69	168.7	652	12.3	347	173.1	52.6	6 607	215	167.6	987	1 705	269	519
Eaton	96	505.2	2 398	51.9	855	692.3	49.3	7 484	567	679.6	1 558	1 257	484	664
Emmet	41	90.9	445	10.3	449	231.1	54.7	9 550	315	225.4	634	1 935	911	935
Genesee	476	1 982.7	5 549	122.6	3 707	2 977.5	45.7	6 857	2 559	2 935.2	1 106	1 100	287	617
Gladwin	11	7.5	37	0.6	207	81.4	42.1	3 649	108	76.7	119	1 202	33	284
Gogebic	21	26.0	149	2.0	241	93.9	26.4	5 102	160	90.2	771	1 046	296	389
Grand Traverse	189	444.4	1 675	35.0	969	649.1	69.3	10 588	632	633.3	1 806	1 564	623	958
Gratiot	67	198.4	654	9.8	399	176.7	21.1	4 495	240	169.4	449	1 029	122	428
Hillsdale	59	171.8	529	8.2	414	179.8	54.5	4 191	221	170.5	D	1 309	110	268
Houghton	29	43.5	220	3.3	365	176.2	42.0	4 895	267	172.1	471	1 198	233	401
Huron	56	157.9	615	11.7	462	183.7	36.5	5 006	269	172.8	339	1 160	183	365
Ingham	411	1 703.4	5 550	137.0	2 297	1 955.7	53.4	7 093	1 583	1 925.6	1 396	970	279	706
Ionia	51	94.8	299	5.1	451	211.9	30.9	3 839	257	203.8	D	941	74	264
Iosco	30	25.2	129	1.6	394	154.5	52.4	5 117	245	147.0	578	1 159	144	518
Iron	12	17.3	78	1.3	189	77.8	85.7	5 680	108	74.3	222	2 604	166	348
Isabella	84	150.0	667	12.8	466	282.1	44.6	5 263	318	269.0	D	1 052	333	675
Jackson	180	707.8	2 013	45.6	1 214	843.6	42.1	5 685	801	824.1	1 402	835	136	506
Kalamazoo	394	1 270.2	4 788	108.7	1 943	1 539.0	38.7	7 125	1 343	1 514.4	1 374	993	399	718
Kalkaska	34	40.7	178	4.4	112	67.0	45.0	5 449	70	64.9	0	925	D	486
Kent	1 268	7 993.3	20 480	544.8	4 162	3 722.6	59.5	7 808	2 796	3 658.3	D	1 051	451	668
Keweenaw	0	0.0	0	0.0	38	5.9	63.9	2 929	22	4.7	0	554	0	682
Lake	6	4.5	37	0.5	99	26.3	60.4	3 024	61	24.0	D	940	D	415
Lapeer	68	82.2	378	6.5	598	362.1	83.0	4 947	331	351.2	342	968	130	295
Leelanau	13	17.7	51	0.6	221	58.2	58.2	3 801	131	55.4	D	1 400	172	611
Lenawee	114	212.8	762	15.5	874	467.5	43.3	5 195	538	449.2	877	980	158	489

1. For pay period including March 12. 2. Based on the estimated population as of July 1 of the year shown.

STATE County	Retail trade, establishments with payroll, 1987 (cont'd)		Taxable service industries–establishments with payroll, 1987							Bank deposits,[2] June 1989		Savings capital,[3] September 1989	
				Receipts (Mil dol)									
					Selected kinds of business								
	Paid employees[1]	Annual payroll (Mil dol)	Number	Total	Hotels, motels and other lodging places	Health services	Legal services	Paid employees	Annual payroll (Mil dol)	Total (Mil dol)	Percent change, 1988–1989	Total (Mil dol)	Percent change, 1988–1989
	161	162	163	164	165	166	167	168	169	170	171	172	173
MARYLAND—Con.													
Worcester	5 334	61.1	423	141.3	73.5	11.5	5.2	2 985	37.3	369	3.7	158.3	3.5
Baltimore city	44 285	437.0	4 414	2 499.7	137.1	511.9	458.3	62 345	1 043.3	10 573	7.3	2 479.1	-4.5
MASSACHUSETTS	529 891	5 492.7	44 387	27 016.0	1 326.1	4 680.6	2 137.4	523 188	10 434.4	112 012	3.1	7 410.6	-0.7
Barnstable	23 442	263.8	1 884	573.2	144.2	155.1	34.0	14 138	200.7	2 856	8.4	581.6	4.7
Berkshire	13 326	129.3	1 021	347.5	48.9	108.4	20.5	8 965	138.1	1 884	0.5	153.2	41.2
Bristol	42 101	422.1	2 775	825.6	41.6	263.2	66.2	22 867	322.2	5 007	5.6	448.0	-0.6
Dukes	1 685	18.2	135	31.2	9.9	5.0	4.0	583	8.4	321	3.5	0.0	NA
Essex	59 821	610.1	4 620	1 830.2	69.8	574.0	107.0	39 985	720.5	9 733	4.4	228.0	7.0
Franklin	4 755	47.7	380	97.9	2.8	34.6	6.0	3 258	40.1	849	20.7	0.0	NA
Hampden	38 866	381.3	2 809	1 102.5	46.6	348.4	82.9	28 458	449.3	6 532	9.9	293.6	-5.6
Hampshire	11 525	97.1	709	201.6	6.8	65.0	13.0	4 964	79.4	1 672	-0.1	0.0	NA
Middlesex	121 565	1 303.1	11 686	9 788.4	281.3	1 041.8	186.2	160 990	3 672.3	19 771	7.7	1 924.3	-16.8
Nantucket	1 074	16.8	98	26.2	10.3	1.3	2.5	692	7.9	176	-1.3	0.0	NA
Norfolk	57 915	635.5	5 380	2 837.0	79.0	760.1	101.6	56 499	1 157.1	9 062	7.1	1 035.7	4.4
Plymouth	39 626	404.6	2 597	1 008.9	24.3	313.9	55.4	23 137	386.1	3 955	10.6	334.6	-6.4
Suffolk	61 795	637.2	6 132	6 507.1	500.2	549.6	1 342.4	118 622	2 587.7	42 386	-2.3	1 731.5	19.0
Worcester	52 395	525.8	4 161	1 838.7	60.4	460.0	115.5	40 030	664.5	7 807	5.1	680.1	-3.6
MICHIGAN	673 265	6 583.5	55 367	23 859.8	893.7	6 219.9	1 769.9	533 061	9 469.9	70 366	6.9	21 939.9	-0.8
Alcona	362	3.0	24	3.0	D	1.6	D	123	1.1	32	-7.9	0.0	NA
Alger	350	2.9	40	7.6	1.8	3.5	D	246	1.9	57	18.3	0.0	NA
Allegan	4 354	38.3	302	77.5	6.1	29.0	2.4	2 365	26.6	393	10.5	71.3	-2.2
Alpena	2 245	20.4	188	49.1	5.1	16.4	2.0	1 161	12.9	192	-2.1	84.1	2.9
Antrim	730	6.7	98	23.1	D	2.5	1.1	619	7.1	143	3.0	0.0	NA
Arenac	970	8.0	68	12.3	0.7	6.8	0.4	352	4.0	134	23.7	14.7	-13.3
Baraga	413	3.1	38	6.2	0.3	3.0	D	229	2.4	56	5.3	0.0	NA
Barry	1 987	15.8	154	37.0	0.3	13.5	1.0	914	13.6	156	8.6	79.6	-9.1
Bay	8 152	76.9	582	169.4	7.7	66.4	16.6	3 897	67.7	611	4.5	351.9	-12.7
Benzie	519	5.5	66	8.9	1.9	2.7	0.4	209	2.4	101	5.2	0.0	NA
Berrien	11 223	103.9	867	258.8	14.2	83.9	16.6	7 347	107.2	1 039	10.4	480.9	-8.5
Branch	1 800	16.2	183	45.9	1.7	15.9	D	1 181	14.3	242	2.6	66.4	0.4
Calhoun	11 039	97.3	757	221.1	14.4	81.3	9.2	6 868	84.0	656	1.7	371.4	-2.8
Cass	1 574	13.2	136	27.7	D	4.9	1.9	778	9.1	186	11.0	57.4	-12.9
Charlevoix	1 347	12.8	133	25.0	D	5.2	1.5	743	7.7	168	4.1	5.3	3.6
Cheboygan	1 675	17.4	220	31.9	12.1	8.4	2.5	847	9.3	157	4.4	10.0	2.3
Chippewa	2 086	18.1	187	26.9	4.1	9.5	1.4	802	9.6	207	8.5	34.3	-3.5
Clare	1 673	14.4	101	23.1	D	11.1	1.4	770	7.6	154	0.6	23.8	-9.7
Clinton	2 187	22.5	187	35.8	D	10.8	1.8	1 106	13.3	204	2.5	78.3	1.2
Crawford	835	6.4	68	14.4	5.2	5.3	0.3	421	3.6	65	11.6	17.1	-1.0
Delta	2 906	24.4	205	46.1	3.4	16.6	6.1	1 207	17.0	220	3.8	82.1	2.5
Dickinson	2 279	18.4	205	39.0	2.9	15.6	3.0	1 137	14.3	195	4.3	99.9	6.2
Eaton	8 271	75.9	379	107.2	D	27.1	3.3	3 144	38.7	383	3.3	250.6	-1.3
Emmet	2 600	26.6	232	83.8	17.5	37.8	3.7	1 977	32.6	308	3.3	10.4	-12.9
Genesee	32 635	326.5	2 486	886.5	23.2	342.6	45.4	21 393	372.9	2 423	4.3	373.7	1.1
Gladwin	834	7.6	59	11.1	D	4.8	0.5	298	3.1	106	0.4	12.5	-17.0
Gogebic	1 167	9.3	111	26.2	6.0	7.0	1.9	1 219	8.9	161	9.0	48.9	9.1
Grand Traverse	7 079	74.9	722	230.8	39.6	64.5	18.8	5 030	84.4	546	2.3	58.5	12.9
Gratiot	2 249	18.7	181	37.1	0.2	18.9	1.4	989	13.5	279	0.3	39.3	-3.1
Hillsdale	2 063	18.0	150	27.3	D	9.8	1.6	689	9.7	235	2.1	21.6	-1.9
Houghton	2 356	18.5	184	33.8	4.0	11.6	3.7	964	12.6	196	3.6	280.8	3.8
Huron	1 957	17.3	188	32.1	1.9	14.1	1.6	752	11.4	325	2.3	96.5	-2.4
Ingham	24 844	224.6	1 936	750.5	28.7	231.6	82.1	17 675	307.6	1 824	4.6	431.9	-4.6
Ionia	2 352	21.8	187	35.3	D	14.8	1.7	1 027	11.1	280	10.4	41.7	-6.9
Iosco	2 026	15.4	156	27.1	4.3	11.3	1.4	719	9.5	130	6.8	52.4	-6.3
Iron	868	6.6	84	11.1	0.8	4.6	1.1	342	3.4	115	6.9	11.3	16.6
Isabella	4 051	31.4	302	70.2	D	22.6	4.3	2 096	26.1	249	2.5	69.8	45.9
Jackson	9 668	96.1	738	262.6	9.1	78.2	11.5	6 691	109.0	717	2.0	310.6	2.8
Kalamazoo	19 791	178.5	1 426	730.3	19.0	317.1	51.0	17 888	310.9	1 327	9.2	500.0	-16.7
Kalkaska	686	6.3	54	8.3	1.1	1.8	D	286	2.8	47	-6.1	9.2	-19.8
Kent	44 384	435.7	3 237	1 482.8	69.3	364.6	140.4	34 879	572.2	4 852	15.8	470.2	-12.7
Keweenaw	59	0.4	7	0.9	D	0.0	D	23	0.2	8	8.9	0.0	NA
Lake	296	2.5	15	3.7	D	D	D	153	1.2	22	-2.4	0.0	NA
Lapeer	3 242	32.5	273	52.9	1.4	23.6	4.1	1 270	18.8	326	4.1	53.7	-6.6
Leelanau	729	6.9	82	24.6	D	1.9	0.5	684	6.6	85	8.0	0.0	NA
Lenawee	5 403	48.2	469	121.5	0.9	38.7	4.7	3 326	38.1	677	2.0	178.9	-0.1

1. For the period including March 12 of the year shown. 2. Includes deposits for all insured and reporting noninsured commercial and mutual savings banks. 3. Includes savings capital for all FSLIC insured savings institutions.

STATE County	Federal funds and grants, 1989: Expenditures: Total (Mil dol)	Federal funds and grants, 1989: Expenditures: Percent change, 1988–1989	Federal funds and grants, 1989: Per capita[1] (Dollars): Total	Per capita[1] (Dollars): Direct payments for individuals	Per capita[1] (Dollars): Procurement contract awards	Per capita[1] (Dollars): Salaries and wages	Per capita[1] (Dollars): Grant awards	Local government finances, 1981–1982: General revenue: Total (Mil dol)	General revenue: Intergovernmental: Total (Mil dol)	General revenue: Intergovernmental: Percent from state	General revenue: Taxes: Total (Mil dol)	Taxes: Per capita[2]: Total (Dollars)	Taxes: Per capita[2]: Property (Dollars)	Direct general expenditure: Total (Mil dol)	Direct general expenditure: Percent change, 1977–1982
	174	175	176	177	178	179	180	181	182	183	184	185	186	187	188
MARYLAND—Con.															
Worcester	118.8	4.3	3 186	2 310	88	509	228	43.3	11.9	75.1	23.9	758	581	40.3	42.2
Baltimore city	4 344.7	2.5	5 808	2 494	1 322	695	1 278	1 418.0	872.4	78.7	365.9	475	306	1 315.0	13.8
MASSACHUSETTS	28 474.4	12.9	X	1 995	1 608	431	743	6 776.3	2 916.8	71.0	2 949.5	513	507	5 839.0	21.1
Barnstable	751.2	9.8	4 096	2 775	274	557	475	174.0	37.3	81.1	108.7	706	688	159.4	45.7
Berkshire	904.9	14.0	6 572	2 111	3 836	177	438	126.9	50.8	86.9	63.6	447	442	122.1	7.6
Bristol	3 259.6	172.6	6 738	1 713	4 402	125	491	455.6	234.4	72.0	178.3	374	370	417.5	17.2
Dukes	29.4	4.9	2 454	2 021	27	213	181	14.1	3.3	76.8	8.8	915	893	13.7	48.9
Essex	3 876.9	8.2	5 910	1 821	3 479	263	340	677.5	231.8	75.8	321.5	502	497	682.3	31.4
Franklin	161.8	10.4	2 373	1 699	169	134	353	62.7	26.2	72.9	30.3	476	472	57.9	39.7
Hampden	1 322.3	3.7	2 927	1 832	154	447	474	457.4	192.1	79.6	162.8	368	365	414.1	22.8
Hampshire	408.9	3.3	2 862	1 527	292	587	427	110.7	52.5	84.1	43.1	306	303	106.9	23.5
Middlesex	7 272.9	-3.3	5 296	1 509	2 691	552	540	1 412.0	470.9	74.7	772.6	567	562	1 383.2	24.0
Nantucket	17.0	18.0	2 463	1 556	62	345	488	10.2	2.1	51.7	6.0	1 116	1 089	11.1	133.0
Norfolk	1 458.7	-6.1	2 380	1 442	429	127	380	625.7	160.2	84.7	348.5	578	574	618.0	28.1
Plymouth	954.4	6.1	2 195	1 489	115	269	312	385.0	146.3	83.0	203.9	499	495	376.2	17.4
Suffolk	4 310.2	-0.7	6 470	2 696	358	1 239	2 139	1 628.3	1 010.8	58.0	457.0	697	684	846.5	0.5
Worcester	1 754.0	4.4	2 570	1 767	211	161	423	636.2	298.2	79.9	244.5	378	374	630.0	30.6
MICHIGAN	26 109.2	9.3	X	1 815	183	248	513	11 956.8	4 137.4	74.4	5 108.6	560	516	11 394.6	47.5
Alcona	40.9	5.9	3 792	2 982	34	165	542	8.0	2.6	80.1	4.2	426	422	7.0	32.6
Alger	28.5	16.7	3 273	2 254	51	245	690	10.1	5.1	82.9	3.9	430	427	10.2	62.6
Allegan	156.8	10.8	1 708	1 187	21	77	274	64.8	26.1	86.5	29.8	360	356	62.9	41.5
Alpena	90.9	-23.5	2 877	2 198	62	125	441	54.1	14.2	85.3	17.0	534	530	50.2	44.7
Antrim	51.0	5.4	2 851	2 137	133	123	412	21.8	6.2	90.1	12.0	725	717	21.4	84.9
Arenac	57.1	7.3	3 549	2 200	617	107	445	12.3	4.2	92.3	6.4	425	421	12.5	55.1
Baraga	32.0	24.4	3 854	2 211	449	136	1 035	15.2	4.6	88.9	3.0	362	345	16.0	103.4
Barry	83.2	2.2	1 647	1 243	30	76	180	33.2	15.7	79.3	13.1	285	282	35.0	39.0
Bay	257.1	2.0	2 228	1 747	26	100	300	142.1	42.4	82.1	67.4	571	566	138.8	14.6
Benzie	34.3	7.9	2 928	2 318	74	123	352	12.3	3.8	90.3	6.1	549	544	11.9	44.9
Berrien	559.8	-5.1	3 342	1 791	888	103	481	172.3	56.6	91.3	76.9	465	461	163.4	34.8
Branch	93.1	3.6	2 255	1 614	28	86	282	45.1	12.7	88.3	15.6	398	391	47.3	45.5
Calhoun	473.5	-0.6	3 384	1 968	93	850	405	173.6	71.8	69.4	60.6	435	397	176.2	75.3
Cass	99.9	7.3	2 006	1 430	22	92	282	38.6	14.7	91.1	16.2	333	329	37.5	37.4
Charlevoix	53.1	3.4	2 449	1 909	81	167	268	24.1	5.6	88.7	14.0	712	689	22.2	72.7
Cheboygan	59.3	9.5	2 746	2 085	36	181	427	18.9	6.5	83.3	10.0	482	478	18.7	64.9
Chippewa	104.3	1.6	3 431	2 105	21	503	756	38.9	13.4	83.4	11.1	381	379	40.3	41.9
Clare	79.8	6.5	2 977	2 373	19	78	443	25.5	10.0	90.7	11.8	488	484	24.1	84.5
Clinton	145.1	13.1	2 467	942	101	908	312	43.5	15.6	92.7	21.0	380	372	40.1	46.2
Crawford	37.2	26.9	3 378	1 997	297	557	520	10.3	3.4	78.3	5.1	530	519	9.7	53.2
Delta	105.4	4.6	2 759	2 081	125	199	329	42.2	16.3	90.1	16.1	408	404	42.9	45.7
Dickinson	134.2	51.9	5 142	2 241	1 881	693	301	41.9	10.2	91.9	12.0	474	444	35.1	83.9
Eaton	383.1	60.7	4 012	992	10	222	2 672	69.7	25.1	92.2	31.3	355	352	64.8	39.6
Emmet	60.8	6.6	2 424	1 971	15	136	283	31.4	8.9	91.4	14.1	609	603	32.9	71.5
Genesee	982.8	5.9	2 293	1 702	27	130	415	649.3	257.6	67.9	236.2	537	491	635.0	39.6
Gladwin	62.7	6.8	2 702	2 175	10	69	389	17.1	5.6	85.2	7.9	387	383	17.0	66.7
Gogebic	70.4	7.0	3 932	2 831	199	258	635	27.2	12.8	90.2	7.0	356	349	27.8	91.8
Grand Traverse	147.0	6.5	2 261	1 673	46	242	273	65.4	17.8	91.0	32.2	573	564	62.4	67.7
Gratiot	96.8	-2.2	2 451	1 643	30	113	417	40.3	14.6	88.9	17.9	454	444	37.9	32.8
Hillsdale	97.2	3.7	2 219	1 565	19	101	278	46.6	11.3	92.0	15.3	369	367	41.2	56.6
Houghton	112.5	7.4	3 188	2 254	232	198	486	37.0	20.7	85.6	9.6	255	253	35.2	66.1
Huron	109.8	-4.5	3 000	2 130	30	117	312	37.6	10.8	81.2	19.8	546	542	37.2	49.6
Ingham	1 022.4	-1.4	3 691	1 469	81	159	1 953	382.8	114.9	82.1	157.1	579	521	397.1	48.3
Ionia	99.9	5.6	1 743	1 266	23	81	206	46.3	18.7	89.5	16.1	311	307	49.9	76.2
Iosco	181.4	15.4	5 949	2 239	646	2 695	337	26.6	10.6	84.2	13.0	448	444	26.6	47.6
Iron	49.1	6.2	3 665	3 050	62	160	374	20.0	4.6	77.4	6.3	466	462	20.0	72.4
Isabella	103.0	12.2	1 901	1 281	39	100	345	43.3	17.2	72.8	14.3	268	265	39.9	55.2
Jackson	342.9	4.7	2 268	1 627	157	128	295	146.9	53.6	87.1	61.6	415	386	148.7	23.6
Kalamazoo	487.7	4.4	2 230	1 514	164	211	305	230.8	71.6	65.6	112.2	524	511	235.4	73.8
Kalkaska	27.5	6.3	2 132	1 620	18	79	373	12.5	3.0	87.2	6.3	559	551	11.9	48.6
Kent	1 152.4	7.9	2 354	1 421	408	215	284	510.5	175.9	85.4	205.2	454	411	468.4	41.9
Keweenaw	7.8	-13.7	3 909	3 084	10	82	720	2.2	0.8	70.9	0.4	218	212	2.1	52.6
Lake	31.4	4.1	3 454	2 711	16	140	556	7.7	3.0	86.5	4.2	514	507	7.6	66.3
Lapeer	116.6	7.3	1 532	1 118	15	73	242	71.9	23.1	87.2	25.6	368	356	69.6	82.7
Leelanau	35.0	9.3	2 217	1 611	94	211	261	12.2	3.2	89.3	7.2	501	492	11.9	60.0
Lenawee	202.1	4.2	2 204	1 611	52	95	273	95.8	26.6	84.0	42.3	478	473	95.5	68.2

1. Based on the estimated population as of July 1 of the year shown. 2. Based on the estimated population as of July 1, 1982.

STATE County	Local government finances, 1981–1982 (cont'd) — Direct general expenditure (cont'd): Per capita[1] (Dollars)	Percent of total for– Education	Percent of total for– Health & hospitals	Percent of total for– Police protection	Percent of total for– Public welfare	Percent of total for– Highways	Debt outstanding: Total (Mil dol)	Debt outstanding: Per capita[1] (Dollars)	State and local government employment, 1989: Total	State and local government employment, 1989: Rate[2]	Federal government civilian employment 1989: Total	Federal government civilian employment 1989: Earnings ($1,000)	Elections, 1988[3]: Total vote cast for president	Elections, 1988[3]: Vote for lead party (Percent)
	189	190	191	192	193	194	195	196	197	198	199	200	201	202
MARYLAND—Con.														
Worcester	1 279	38.4	0.1	8.0	0.0	9.7	12.3	392	2 162	579.6	170	4 730	13 262	R–63.6
Baltimore city	1 708	26.2	7.8	6.8	0.3	18.1	1 145.6	1 488	69 756	932.6	17 398	581 282	232 367	D–73.5
MASSACHUSETTS	1 016	44.8	5.3	6.1	0.8	4.5	4 726.2	822	347 005	586.9	62 497	1 989 125	2 632 774	D–53.2
Barnstable	1 036	44.4	2.4	7.8	0.9	5.6	79.8	518	8 713	475.1	1 747	55 143	99 872	R–49.7
Berkshire	858	51.4	0.8	4.8	0.5	8.1	56.1	394	6 009	436.4	636	18 798	62 859	D–60.8
Bristol	877	50.3	0.8	6.1	0.7	3.6	318.1	668	25 002	516.8	1 376	42 532	193 530	D–55.7
Dukes	1 425	37.1	1.0	8.7	0.5	9.3	1.7	174	887	739.2	59	1 592	7 025	D–64.0
Essex	1 066	42.8	9.8	5.4	0.9	4.1	341.1	533	31 504	480.2	5 917	157 135	305 485	D–49.7
Franklin	909	48.8	0.4	3.8	1.0	9.8	20.6	323	3 593	526.8	200	5 527	33 123	D–58.3
Hampden	937	44.3	2.9	6.3	1.6	3.8	1 089.2	2 464	25 944	574.4	5 530	176 735	173 420	D–56.1
Hampshire	761	49.9	2.5	4.3	0.6	6.2	50.3	358	15 308	1 071.2	1 466	42 149	64 915	D–61.4
Middlesex	1 015	47.4	2.8	6.0	0.6	5.2	646.2	474	63 605	463.1	15 216	449 002	662 618	D–54.6
Nantucket	2 053	28.0	0.2	6.2	8.2	14.2	4.2	781	465	673.9	52	1 747	3 731	D–59.2
Norfolk	1 026	48.7	8.2	6.7	0.4	4.5	244.2	405	30 087	491.0	1 307	37 331	315 054	D–50.9
Plymouth	920	51.9	1.5	6.8	0.6	5.2	176.6	432	19 552	449.6	4 568	159 095	193 480	R–54.6
Suffolk	1 291	31.9	11.1	7.2	0.9	2.4	1 402.4	2 138	82 817	1 243.1	21 672	758 373	224 406	D–64.0
Worcester	974	45.5	5.3	4.8	1.4	5.1	295.9	458	33 519	491.0	2 751	83 966	293 256	R–50.6
MICHIGAN	1 250	45.8	9.3	5.8	1.3	5.4	9 265.8	1 016	538 929	581.2	60 557	1 895 263	3 669 163	R–53.6
Alcona	717	43.6	1.4	5.4	3.3	20.5	1.3	133	278	257.4	61	1 390	4 905	R–60.5
Alger	1 121	42.2	2.8	2.9	0.6	17.4	8.4	926	441	506.9	60	1 329	4 059	D–54.4
Allegan	759	53.9	3.4	3.6	4.2	12.0	44.3	535	3 485	379.6	199	5 703	33 188	R–66.8
Alpena	1 575	37.2	36.7	2.4	1.1	2.6	52.0	1 631	2 525	799.1	111	3 151	13 054	R–51.0
Antrim	1 294	45.2	16.3	3.2	1.1	9.1	15.8	958	923	515.6	69	1 674	8 444	R–61.9
Arenac	835	54.6	4.0	2.3	0.4	14.6	7.9	524	601	373.3	58	1 299	6 300	D–51.0
Baraga	1 905	42.6	21.3	1.4	1.3	12.0	9.0	1 068	610	734.9	24	550	3 404	D–51.5
Barry	761	44.9	2.7	3.5	7.9	9.0	28.0	608	1 483	293.7	113	2 817	20 681	R–60.7
Bay	1 175	54.2	6.2	5.1	1.5	5.2	183.0	1 549	5 451	472.4	282	8 533	49 152	D–57.4
Benzie	1 068	44.7	5.6	3.8	2.9	14.8	2.3	211	615	525.6	36	908	5 732	R–56.5
Berrien	987	56.7	7.7	5.4	1.4	4.7	128.0	773	8 117	484.6	482	13 623	60 183	R–62.8
Branch	1 206	32.7	34.2	2.9	1.4	7.5	27.4	698	3 573	865.1	106	2 881	14 531	R–63.5
Calhoun	1 264	43.1	7.1	6.9	1.7	7.2	119.5	857	6 444	460.6	4 328	152 628	49 787	R–53.8
Cass	772	55.5	9.4	4.5	2.6	8.3	32.6	671	1 867	374.9	100	2 593	17 756	R–57.6
Charlevoix	1 128	45.8	10.5	3.5	1.2	10.3	20.1	1 019	1 227	565.4	59	1 638	9 762	R–59.4
Cheboygan	899	45.5	1.6	5.6	2.1	14.8	9.6	462	924	427.8	58	1 521	9 380	R–57.5
Chippewa	1 383	38.9	31.4	3.0	1.6	8.4	15.7	539	2 997	985.9	379	10 317	12 068	R–56.2
Clare	997	61.4	1.4	5.4	2.5	9.8	9.8	403	1 163	434.0	62	1 529	10 448	R–54.2
Clinton	727	56.1	0.7	5.0	2.0	11.6	43.0	779	1 659	282.1	206	7 457	24 837	R–62.4
Crawford	1 011	37.7	5.8	4.7	3.0	16.8	4.0	420	620	563.6	133	3 873	4 973	R–62.3
Delta	1 085	53.0	5.2	4.9	2.0	7.5	77.5	1 962	2 183	571.5	241	6 455	16 065	D–55.3
Dickinson	1 388	31.1	31.2	2.8	1.1	7.3	10.0	394	1 768	677.4	629	18 483	12 343	R–49.9
Eaton	736	55.5	5.0	6.5	1.1	8.5	47.9	544	5 025	526.2	156	4 069	39 806	R–60.8
Emmet	1 419	45.5	8.3	3.2	6.7	8.2	52.4	2 260	1 497	596.4	102	3 061	11 386	R–62.4
Genesee	1 442	47.3	17.9	4.9	1.3	2.9	637.4	1 448	21 498	501.5	1 480	47 940	176 859	D–59.3
Gladwin	832	47.7	2.1	3.6	2.2	16.6	12.0	589	750	323.3	50	1 270	8 986	R–52.8
Gogebic	1 421	41.0	23.6	3.8	2.1	13.3	3.9	201	1 407	786.0	180	4 631	8 691	D–59.3
Grand Traverse	1 111	55.7	9.3	4.1	1.3	5.9	38.3	682	4 771	734.0	354	10 996	27 525	R–62.5
Gratiot	961	55.4	3.5	4.1	1.8	9.7	21.1	535	1 853	469.1	130	3 275	14 230	R–59.4
Hillsdale	992	42.0	24.9	3.8	2.1	9.8	105.9	2 553	2 032	463.9	131	3 185	15 479	R–68.3
Houghton	928	37.4	16.1	3.0	2.0	15.4	9.3	246	3 670	1 039.7	136	3 642	13 694	R–51.8
Huron	1 025	42.0	9.9	4.4	1.4	16.1	23.4	644	1 694	462.8	116	2 947	15 214	R–61.9
Ingham	1 462	47.0	12.0	5.3	1.5	3.3	275.5	1 014	46 833	1 690.7	2 963	94 129	115 435	R–50.6
Ionia	962	47.8	13.8	3.0	2.1	10.3	24.4	470	3 375	589.0	128	3 327	20 369	R–59.1
Iosco	918	60.5	4.8	2.0	5.7	10.7	18.2	627	1 487	487.5	945	18 207	12 225	R–59.2
Iron	1 474	27.6	37.1	1.7	1.3	12.2	5.8	426	1 103	823.1	66	1 703	6 674	D–56.5
Isabella	746	41.1	10.7	3.6	6.4	7.9	15.2	284	6 230	1 149.4	158	4 418	18 482	R–56.1
Jackson	1 002	52.5	6.0	4.6	1.6	5.3	103.9	699	7 643	505.5	466	14 248	56 127	R–60.4
Kalamazoo	1 100	46.5	2.4	6.7	2.1	4.5	196.0	916	15 137	692.1	1 157	38 695	90 235	R–55.6
Kalkaska	1 059	41.6	12.2	3.8	2.4	12.4	10.8	963	528	409.3	28	684	5 504	R–61.2
Kent	1 036	51.6	8.2	5.6	1.8	5.6	289.1	640	20 714	423.1	2 488	85 636	206 842	R–63.8
Keweenaw	1 050	2.2	0.0	3.1	2.9	39.0	0.0	0	80	400.0	NA	99	1 170	D–53.9
Lake	937	42.8	3.3	3.6	3.1	17.2	3.4	414	371	407.7	55	1 157	3 698	D–52.9
Lapeer	1 002	43.8	22.9	3.4	2.2	8.0	55.4	798	4 724	620.8	142	3 882	27 697	R–60.2
Leelanau	826	43.6	0.9	4.6	1.7	15.3	12.2	844	469	296.8	58	1 752	8 619	R–60.5
Lenawee	1 079	47.3	13.8	3.9	3.5	6.8	52.9	598	4 427	482.8	235	6 293	33 048	R–57.8

1. Based on the estimated population as of July 1, 1982. 2. Per 10,000 resident population estimated as of July 1 of the year shown. 3. Data subject to copyright.

STATE–County code	MSA/ CMSA/ NECMA code[1]	STATE County	Land Area,[2] 1990 (Sq. Km.)	Population, 1990									Age of population Percent		
							Race								
				Total persons	Rank	Per square kilometer	White	Black	Am. Indian, Eskimo, Aleut	Asian & Pacific Islander	Other race	Hispanic[3]	Under 5 years	5 to 14 years	15 to 24 years
			1	2	3	4	5	6	7	8	9	10	11	12	13
		MICHIGAN—Con.													
26 093	2162	Livingston	1 472	115 645	398	78.6	113 566	673	705	480	221	974	7.5	16.1	13.8
26 095	...	Luce	2 339	5 763	2 784	2.5	5 418	2	331	6	6	27	6.5	15.9	11.5
26 097	...	Mackinac	2 646	10 674	2 319	4.0	8 955	5	1 691	11	12	33	6.8	14.6	11.5
26 099	2162	Macomb	1 244	717 400	57	576.7	693 686	10 400	2 639	9 112	1 563	7 978	6.8	13.1	14.2
26 101	...	Manistee	1 409	21 265	1 616	15.1	20 851	54	189	54	117	323	6.2	13.7	11.4
26 103	...	Marquette	4 717	70 887	624	15.0	68 027	1 170	943	538	209	566	7.1	14.9	18.3
26 105	...	Mason	1 283	25 537	1 443	19.9	24 957	155	188	75	162	399	7.0	15.1	12.1
26 107	...	Mecosta	1 439	37 308	1 065	25.9	35 739	978	258	187	146	389	6.1	12.3	30.8
26 109	...	Menominee	2 703	24 920	1 467	9.2	24 464	7	382	60	7	59	6.3	15.7	11.8
26 111	6960	Midland	1 350	75 651	595	56.0	73 466	719	334	804	328	1 035	7.5	15.4	14.7
26 113	...	Missaukee	1 468	12 147	2 203	8.3	12 015	3	74	25	30	67	7.7	17.6	11.8
26 115	2162	Monroe	1 427	133 600	348	93.6	129 421	2 339	481	574	785	2 077	7.7	16.1	14.7
26 117	...	Montcalm	1 834	53 059	802	28.9	51 216	960	384	157	342	888	7.7	16.1	14.1
26 119	...	Montmorency	1 418	8 936	2 476	6.3	8 861	1	48	10	16	60	5.8	13.8	10.2
26 121	5320	Muskegon	1 319	158 983	298	120.5	133 931	21 617	1 338	555	1 542	3 623	8.1	15.7	13.6
26 123	...	Newaygo	2 182	38 202	1 049	17.5	36 758	468	248	103	625	968	8.4	16.6	12.3
26 125	2162	Oakland	2 260	1 083 592	28	479.5	970 674	77 488	3 948	25 103	6 379	19 630	7.2	13.5	13.3
26 127	...	Oceana	1 400	22 454	1 556	16.0	21 211	58	242	50	893	1 390	7.9	17.0	12.4
26 129	...	Ogemaw	1 462	18 681	1 751	12.8	18 489	18	140	19	15	104	6.7	15.3	11.7
26 131	...	Ontonagon	3 397	8 854	2 484	2.6	8 723	4	109	15	3	35	6.1	12.9	11.1
26 133	...	Osceola	1 466	20 146	1 667	13.7	19 899	57	117	43	30	143	7.6	17.0	13.5
26 135	...	Oscoda	1 463	7 842	2 590	5.4	7 781	2	41	5	13	50	6.8	13.6	10.3
26 137	...	Otsego	1 333	17 957	1 791	13.5	17 737	18	103	82	17	67	7.7	16.5	12.6
26 139	3000	Ottawa	1 465	187 768	257	128.2	179 675	997	638	2 451	4 007	7 947	8.5	16.5	16.1
26 141	...	Presque Isle	1 710	13 743	2 078	8.0	13 648	11	43	30	11	37	6.2	14.9	11.4
26 143	...	Roscommon	1 350	19 776	1 685	14.6	19 597	37	101	23	18	94	5.4	12.3	9.4
26 145	6960	Saginaw	2 095	211 946	236	101.2	165 430	36 849	915	1 272	7 480	13 186	7.8	15.5	14.9
26 147	2162	St. Clair	1 876	145 607	325	77.6	140 294	2 987	745	475	1 106	2 558	7.6	15.6	14.3
26 149	...	St. Joseph	1 305	58 913	738	45.1	56 661	1 600	226	258	168	546	7.8	16.4	13.4
26 151	...	Sanilac	2 496	39 928	1 004	16.0	39 232	39	195	71	391	905	7.4	16.2	12.9
26 153	...	Schoolcraft	3 051	8 302	2 535	2.7	7 755	7	519	13	8	32	6.1	14.9	11.2
26 155	...	Shiawassee	1 396	69 770	636	50.0	68 686	93	397	223	371	1 053	7.4	16.2	14.7
26 157	...	Tuscola	2 105	55 498	781	26.4	54 051	478	345	206	418	1 150	7.1	16.4	14.2
26 159	...	Van Buren	1 583	70 060	633	44.3	63 189	4 690	646	217	1 318	2 254	7.7	16.8	13.1
26 161	2162	Washtenaw	1 839	282 937	173	153.9	236 390	31 720	1 076	11 724	2 027	5 731	6.8	11.6	22.8
26 163	2162	Wayne	1 591	2 111 687	8	1 327.3	1 212 007	849 109	8 048	21 704	20 819	50 506	8.1	14.5	14.9
26 165	...	Wexford	1 465	26 360	1 410	18.0	26 040	34	178	87	21	153	7.8	16.4	12.8
27 000	...	MINNESOTA	206 207	4 375 099	X	21.2	4 130 395	94 944	49 909	77 886	21 965	53 884	7.7	15.1	14.0
27 001	...	Aitkin	4 712	12 425	2 188	2.6	12 194	13	175	30	13	35	5.4	14.4	8.8
27 003	5120	Anoka	1 098	243 641	205	221.9	236 791	1 289	1 865	2 934	762	2 269	8.8	17.2	14.3
27 005	...	Becker	3 394	27 881	1 355	8.2	25 849	20	1 861	101	50	120	7.4	17.0	11.7
27 007	...	Beltrami	6 489	34 384	1 153	5.3	28 409	100	5 641	194	40	146	8.4	17.0	18.6
27 009	6980	Benton	1 057	30 185	1 288	28.6	29 837	61	123	129	35	139	8.7	17.2	15.7
27 011	...	Big Stone	1 287	6 285	2 724	4.9	6 237	4	26	15	3	23	7.0	14.8	9.3
27 013	...	Blue Earth	1 949	54 044	797	27.7	52 648	251	132	804	209	480	6.3	13.3	26.3
27 015	...	Brown	1 582	26 984	1 392	17.1	26 791	12	15	102	64	151	7.3	16.1	12.5
27 017	...	Carlton	2 228	29 259	1 320	13.1	27 825	43	1 297	75	19	99	7.0	16.4	12.0
27 019	5120	Carver	925	47 915	874	51.8	47 167	103	112	444	89	252	9.5	16.7	12.8
27 021	...	Cass	5 226	21 791	1 589	4.2	19 309	39	2 373	54	16	94	7.0	15.9	10.0
27 023	...	Chippewa	1 510	13 228	2 119	8.8	13 114	6	29	44	35	94	6.7	16.3	10.2
27 025	5120	Chisago	1 082	30 521	1 266	28.2	30 188	65	125	90	53	137	8.1	18.2	12.2
27 027	2520	Clay	2 707	50 422	837	18.6	48 562	166	553	410	731	1 179	7.0	14.4	23.4
27 029	...	Clearwater	2 576	8 309	2 534	3.2	7 663	2	633	10	1	16	7.0	17.2	11.3
27 031	...	Cook	3 757	3 868	2 928	1.0	3 570	5	271	20	2	14	6.7	13.8	8.8
27 033	...	Cottonwood	1 658	12 694	2 165	7.7	12 563	12	10	88	21	63	6.4	15.1	10.5
27 035	...	Crow Wing	2 581	44 249	921	17.1	43 637	95	313	136	68	174	7.2	15.8	11.8
27 037	5120	Dakota	1 476	275 227	180	186.5	264 854	3 411	893	4 643	1 426	4 025	9.3	16.5	13.3
27 039	...	Dodge	1 138	15 731	1 939	13.8	15 530	12	29	57	103	164	8.5	18.5	12.4
27 041	...	Douglas	1 643	28 674	1 339	17.5	28 465	14	74	100	21	78	7.0	16.1	12.4
27 043	...	Faribault	1 848	16 937	1 852	9.2	16 670	10	23	55	179	322	6.2	15.9	10.1
27 045	...	Fillmore	2 231	20 777	1 641	9.3	20 657	7	40	49	24	71	7.2	16.2	11.4
27 047	...	Freeborn	1 833	33 060	1 187	18.0	32 217	11	64	132	636	1 076	6.8	14.9	11.3
27 049	...	Goodhue	1 965	40 690	983	20.7	40 101	82	276	178	53	173	7.4	16.4	11.7
27 051	...	Grant	1 415	6 246	2 730	4.4	6 215	3	15	12	1	7	6.4	15.5	8.6
27 053	5120	Hennepin	1 442	1 032 431	30	716.0	922 321	60 114	14 912	29 588	5 496	13 978	7.5	12.5	13.8

1. MSA = Metropolitan Statistical Area. CMSA = Consolidated MSA. NECMA = New England county metropolitan area. PMSA = Primary MSA. See Appendix A for explanation of these concepts. See Appendix B for list of metropolitan areas identified by type, with component counties. 2. Dry land or land partially or temporarily covered by water. 3. Hispanic persons may be of any race.

STATE County	Population, 1990 (cont'd)							Population–Change and components of change							
	Age of population (cont'd) Percent							Change		Components of change, 1980–1986					
								1980–1990				Net change		Natural increase	
	25 to 34 years	35 to 44 years	45 to 54 years	55 to 64 years	65 to 74 years	75 years and over	Percent female	Number	Percent	Total persons, 1986	Total persons, 1980	Number	Percent	Births	Deaths
	14	15	16	17	18	19	20	21	22	23	24	25	26	27	28
MICHIGAN—Con.															
Livingston	16.4	18.1	12.5	7.3	5.1	3.1	49.5	15 356	15.3	104 600	100 289	4 300	4.3	8 800	3 800
Luce	12.8	14.4	10.8	10.9	9.9	7.3	50.9	-896	-13.5	5 900	6 659	-800	-11.7	600	500
Mackinac	14.0	13.5	10.6	11.9	9.9	7.1	50.5	496	4.9	10 500	10 178	300	2.7	900	700
Macomb	17.9	15.0	11.1	9.5	7.7	4.6	51.4	22 800	3.3	697 200	694 600	2 600	0.4	58 500	31 300
Manistee	13.9	14.4	10.9	11.2	10.2	8.1	51.6	-1 754	-7.6	22 200	23 019	-800	-3.5	1 700	1 600
Marquette	17.1	15.5	8.8	7.1	6.2	5.0	49.2	-3 214	-4.3	71 300	74 101	-2 800	-3.7	7 800	3 100
Mason	13.9	14.4	10.3	10.1	9.6	7.5	51.3	-828	-3.1	26 400	26 365	0	0.0	2 400	1 800
Mecosta	12.3	11.2	8.2	7.8	6.8	4.5	48.4	347	0.9	38 200	36 961	1 200	3.3	2 800	1 500
Menominee	14.8	14.7	9.8	9.6	9.4	7.8	50.7	-1 281	-4.9	25 800	26 201	-400	-1.4	2 400	1 700
Midland	16.8	15.8	11.3	8.4	5.9	4.0	50.6	2 073	2.8	72 400	73 578	-1 200	-1.6	7 000	2 800
Missaukee	15.2	13.0	10.2	9.5	9.0	5.9	50.7	2 138	21.4	11 000	10 009	1 000	9.5	1 200	600
Monroe	16.3	15.5	10.8	8.5	6.1	4.3	50.7	-1 059	-0.8	132 000	134 659	-2 700	-2.0	11 500	5 700
Montcalm	16.8	14.3	10.0	8.5	7.3	5.1	49.0	5 504	11.6	50 800	47 555	3 300	6.9	5 000	2 700
Montmorency	11.6	11.9	9.5	14.3	13.9	9.0	51.0	1 444	19.3	7 900	7 492	400	5.8	700	700
Muskegon	16.4	14.7	9.7	8.7	7.7	5.3	51.2	1 394	0.9	158 500	157 589	1 000	0.6	16 100	8 600
Newaygo	15.4	13.8	10.5	9.4	8.1	5.5	50.8	3 285	9.4	37 700	34 917	2 700	7.9	3 600	2 000
Oakland	18.4	16.8	11.4	8.6	6.5	4.4	51.4	71 799	7.1	1 025 800	1 011 793	14 000	1.4	87 300	46 500
Oceana	14.9	13.9	10.7	9.5	8.2	5.5	50.9	452	2.1	22 700	22 002	700	3.0	2 400	1 200
Ogemaw	13.5	12.5	10.1	12.0	11.3	6.9	50.8	2 245	13.7	17 400	16 436	1 000	5.9	1 600	1 200
Ontonagon	12.7	13.9	12.3	11.5	10.6	8.9	49.1	-1 007	-10.2	8 900	9 861	-1 000	-9.7	700	700
Osceola	14.2	13.4	10.6	9.9	8.5	5.5	50.5	1 218	6.4	20 400	18 928	1 500	7.9	2 000	1 100
Oscoda	13.2	11.0	10.5	14.0	13.0	7.6	50.7	984	14.3	6 900	6 858	100	1.0	700	600
Otsego	15.4	14.8	9.9	9.6	8.1	5.4	50.9	2 964	19.8	15 800	14 993	800	5.4	1 600	900
Ottawa	17.1	15.1	9.8	7.1	5.6	4.2	50.7	30 594	19.5	171 300	157 174	14 100	9.0	17 300	6 200
Presque Isle	12.6	12.8	9.9	12.5	11.9	7.9	50.6	-524	-3.7	13 900	14 267	-300	-2.4	1 200	900
Roscommon	11.8	11.2	9.7	15.3	16.1	8.8	51.1	3 402	20.8	18 700	16 374	2 400	14.4	1 400	1 400
Saginaw	15.5	14.9	10.8	8.6	6.9	5.1	52.4	-16 113	-7.1	216 400	228 059	-11 700	-5.1	21 900	10 700
St. Clair	16.2	15.0	10.5	8.5	7.2	5.1	51.3	6 805	4.9	140 500	138 802	1 700	1.2	12 900	7 700
St. Joseph	15.8	14.6	10.1	8.8	7.3	5.8	51.1	2 830	5.0	59 600	56 083	3 500	6.2	5 900	3 200
Sanilac	15.0	13.4	10.0	9.5	9.0	6.6	51.0	-861	-2.1	40 300	40 789	-500	-1.2	3 900	2 500
Schoolcraft	14.0	13.7	10.4	11.2	10.5	8.0	52.0	-273	-3.2	8 300	8 575	-200	-2.9	700	600
Shiawassee	16.0	15.4	11.1	8.1	6.6	4.6	51.2	-1 370	-1.9	69 000	71 140	-2 200	-3.1	6 600	3 100
Tuscola	15.6	15.2	11.1	8.2	7.0	5.0	50.4	-1 463	-2.6	55 100	56 961	-1 900	-3.3	5 200	2 800
Van Buren	15.3	15.4	10.3	8.8	7.1	5.5	51.1	3 246	4.9	67 300	66 814	500	0.8	6 700	3 800
Washtenaw	19.9	16.1	9.3	6.1	4.4	3.1	50.5	18 197	6.9	266 000	264 740	1 200	0.5	24 200	9 000
Wayne	17.1	14.7	9.5	8.7	7.6	4.9	52.6	-226 156	-9.7	2 164 300	2 337 843	-173 500	-7.4	211 200	141 100
Wexford	15.8	14.4	9.8	9.2	8.1	5.7	51.3	1 258	5.0	26 700	25 102	1 600	6.4	2 600	1 600
MINNESOTA	17.8	15.2	9.8	7.9	6.7	5.8	51.0	299 099	7.3	4 214 000	4 076 000	138 000	3.4	421 000	211 000
Aitkin	11.4	12.6	11.1	12.7	13.9	9.6	50.4	-979	-7.3	13 600	13 404	200	1.8	1 100	1 100
Anoka	20.0	16.9	10.8	6.3	3.5	2.0	49.9	47 643	24.3	221 200	195 998	25 200	12.8	22 900	5 100
Becker	13.9	14.1	10.0	9.4	8.6	7.8	50.4	-1 455	-5.0	29 500	29 336	100	0.5	3 100	1 800
Beltrami	14.9	13.7	8.5	7.3	6.2	5.4	50.5	3 402	11.0	33 000	30 982	2 000	6.5	3 900	1 600
Benton	18.8	13.3	8.1	6.4	5.7	5.9	50.8	4 998	19.8	27 100	25 187	1 900	7.6	3 500	1 400
Big Stone	11.9	12.1	10.0	11.1	11.3	12.4	52.1	-1 431	-18.5	7 300	7 716	-400	-5.1	700	600
Blue Earth	14.9	12.4	7.8	6.8	6.3	5.8	50.5	1 730	3.3	51 000	52 314	-1 300	-2.6	5 200	2 600
Brown	14.9	13.1	9.3	9.2	8.9	8.7	51.6	-1 661	-5.8	28 000	28 645	-700	-2.4	3 000	1 800
Carlton	14.7	14.8	10.3	9.4	8.6	6.8	50.6	-677	-2.3	29 900	29 936	0	-0.2	2 800	1 700
Carver	20.3	16.1	9.6	6.6	4.5	3.9	49.7	10 869	29.3	40 900	37 046	3 900	10.4	4 400	1 500
Cass	12.6	13.1	10.7	11.6	11.0	8.2	49.7	741	3.5	21 500	21 050	400	2.1	2 100	1 700
Chippewa	13.3	13.5	9.6	9.6	10.3	10.6	51.9	-1 713	-11.5	14 200	14 941	-700	-4.9	1 400	1 000
Chisago	16.2	15.6	10.3	7.3	6.4	5.7	49.7	4 804	18.7	28 100	25 717	2 400	9.4	2 800	1 400
Clay	14.1	13.0	8.5	7.7	6.3	5.6	52.0	1 095	2.2	47 800	49 327	-1 500	-3.1	4 500	2 200
Clearwater	12.5	12.9	10.6	9.0	9.2	10.3	49.7	-452	-5.2	8 700	8 761	0	-0.3	900	600
Cook	14.3	17.7	11.7	10.4	9.4	7.1	50.2	-224	-5.5	4 100	4 092	0	0.1	400	300
Cottonwood	12.3	12.9	10.1	10.2	10.7	11.8	51.5	-2 160	-14.5	13 900	14 854	-1 000	-6.4	1 200	1 000
Crow Wing	14.0	13.9	10.0	10.0	9.6	7.7	51.6	2 527	6.1	44 600	41 722	2 900	7.0	4 200	2 700
Dakota	21.4	17.2	10.1	6.0	3.8	2.6	50.6	80 948	41.7	228 300	194 279	34 100	17.5	22 900	6 000
Dodge	16.7	14.0	9.5	7.2	7.1	6.2	50.6	958	6.5	15 300	14 773	500	3.4	1 800	800
Douglas	14.1	13.4	9.7	9.0	9.3	8.8	50.9	835	3.0	29 100	27 839	1 300	4.7	2 800	1 800
Faribault	12.5	12.8	10.1	10.7	10.7	11.0	52.1	-2 777	-14.1	18 400	19 714	-1 300	-6.8	1 800	1 500
Fillmore	13.3	12.7	9.4	9.6	10.0	10.2	50.6	-1 153	-5.3	21 400	21 930	-600	-2.6	2 100	1 600
Freeborn	14.0	13.7	10.8	9.9	9.9	8.7	51.1	-3 269	-9.0	34 500	36 329	-1 800	-5.1	3 200	2 300
Goodhue	15.7	14.6	9.8	8.4	7.6	8.2	50.8	1 941	5.0	39 400	38 749	700	1.7	3 900	2 600
Grant	12.3	12.3	9.9	11.0	11.6	12.4	51.7	-925	-12.9	6 700	7 171	-500	-6.7	700	600
Hennepin	21.0	16.5	9.9	7.6	6.2	5.1	51.6	91 020	9.7	987 900	941 411	46 500	4.9	93 700	46 800

STATE County	Population—(cont'd)	Households, 1990					Births, 1988			Deaths, 1987				Marriages, 1984	
	Components of change, 1980-1986 (cont'd)				Percent					Number		Rate			
	Net migration	Number	Percent change, 1980–1990	Persons per house-hold	Female family house-holder[1]	One-person	Total	Rate[2]	Low birth weight[3] (Number)	Total	Infant[4]	Total[2]	Infant[5]	Number	Rate[2]
	29	30	31	32	33	34	35	36	37	38	39	40	41	42	43
MICHIGAN—Con.															
Livingston	-700	38 887	24.1	2.94	6.9	15.1	1 501	13.2	65	753	11	6.9	7.0	862	8.6
Luce	-800	2 154	-1.7	2.57	8.5	25.1	69	11.9	4	73	0	12.6	0.0	56	9.5
Mackinac	100	4 240	15.2	2.49	8.3	25.2	157	14.8	10	130	4	12.5	27.8	132	12.8
Macomb	-24 500	264 991	15.3	2.68	10.1	22.2	9 627	13.6	571	5 373	73	7.6	7.6	6 473	9.4
Manistee	-1 000	8 580	1.1	2.45	8.3	26.2	213	9.5	9	252	3	11.4	10.5	201	9.0
Marquette	-7 400	25 435	3.8	2.61	8.6	23.5	975	13.9	62	512	8	7.3	7.5	630	8.8
Mason	-600	9 984	3.0	2.51	9.1	24.6	353	13.4	20	269	1	10.3	2.9	221	8.4
Mecosta	-100	12 260	10.1	2.66	8.7	20.8	440	11.5	31	257	3	6.8	6.9	287	7.7
Menominee	-1 000	9 766	5.2	2.52	8.5	26.5	311	12.0	20	309	1	11.9	3.2	229	8.9
Midland	-5 400	27 791	13.4	2.67	7.9	20.4	1 055	14.0	54	465	12	6.3	11.4	715	9.5
Missaukee	300	4 389	28.1	2.74	6.9	19.3	150	12.9	7	119	1	10.5	5.6	101	9.5
Monroe	-8 500	46 508	7.9	2.84	10.3	18.9	1 908	14.0	120	1 003	14	7.4	7.2	1 042	7.9
Montcalm	1 000	18 563	12.2	2.75	9.9	20.1	795	14.9	53	479	5	9.2	6.2	509	10.2
Montmorency	400	3 600	27.9	2.45	7.9	23.6	86	10.2	5	105	0	12.8	0.0	50	6.5
Muskegon	-6 600	57 798	6.0	2.66	13.9	23.1	2 579	16.0	191	1 486	26	9.3	10.7	1 508	9.7
Newaygo	1 100	13 776	13.5	2.74	9.0	19.4	647	16.4	33	361	8	9.3	12.7	344	9.5
Oakland	-26 900	410 488	15.6	2.61	9.6	23.6	15 638	14.9	1 001	7 897	135	7.6	8.8	9 573	9.5
Oceana	-500	8 071	8.8	2.75	8.7	19.8	355	15.2	19	216	3	9.5	8.6	209	9.5
Ogemaw	600	7 190	21.0	2.56	8.9	22.1	257	13.7	16	222	1	12.3	3.9	171	9.8
Ontonagon	-900	3 641	3.3	2.39	6.9	27.9	92	10.1	7	107	3	11.6	26.5	119	12.4
Osceola	600	7 347	12.0	2.71	9.2	21.6	293	13.9	16	184	1	8.9	3.4	166	8.3
Oscoda	-100	3 160	25.5	2.45	6.8	24.3	108	14.6	6	95	2	13.4	18.2	58	8.3
Otsego	100	6 522	32.5	2.72	7.9	20.1	244	14.4	9	149	2	9.1	7.6	135	8.8
Ottawa	3 000	62 664	24.2	2.90	6.9	16.7	3 004	16.6	122	1 110	33	6.3	11.0	1 461	8.9
Presque Isle	-600	5 376	7.3	2.53	7.3	24.3	130	9.2	10	174	4	12.3	24.8	97	7.0
Roscommon	2 400	8 516	30.6	2.30	7.2	25.9	210	10.2	10	269	1	13.6	5.2	123	6.8
Saginaw	-22 900	78 256	2.8	2.67	15.3	23.2	3 353	15.6	300	1 842	33	8.5	9.8	1 871	8.5
St. Clair	-3 500	52 882	11.8	2.73	10.9	21.3	1 968	13.5	113	1 271	19	8.8	9.0	1 236	9.0
St. Joseph	800	21 579	9.0	2.70	10.1	21.6	901	15.0	55	541	11	9.1	11.8	606	10.6
Sanilac	-1 800	14 658	5.0	2.70	8.4	22.0	534	12.9	28	416	5	10.1	8.4	313	7.8
Schoolcraft	-400	3 294	8.2	2.50	8.4	24.8	108	13.0	7	87	1	10.5	11.4	92	10.8
Shiawassee	-5 700	24 864	6.4	2.78	10.1	19.4	970	13.7	55	549	7	7.8	6.8	647	9.4
Tuscola	-4 400	19 469	6.4	2.79	9.2	19.1	784	13.9	44	484	9	8.6	12.6	473	8.6
Van Buren	-2 300	25 402	9.9	2.73	11.3	20.9	1 087	15.7	74	671	7	9.8	6.6	585	8.9
Washtenaw	-14 000	104 528	12.5	2.50	9.3	26.3	3 639	13.6	231	1 517	41	5.7	10.1	2 487	9.5
Wayne	-243 600	780 535	-5.3	2.67	20.8	26.7	35 121	16.5	3 647	22 476	540	10.5	15.1	15 437	7.1
Wexford	600	9 923	10.5	2.63	10.5	22.9	457	16.8	25	238	3	8.8	8.3	286	11.0
MINNESOTA	-72 000	1 647 853	14.0	2.58	8.6	25.1	66 748	15.5	3 322	34 524	564	8.1	8.7	36 223	8.7
Aitkin	200	5 126	2.4	2.39	5.2	26.8	131	10.1	10	171	2	13.2	12.8	86	6.4
Anoka	7 300	82 437	35.8	2.93	9.7	15.6	4 004	17.0	208	907	33	4.0	8.3	1 563	7.4
Becker	-1 200	10 477	3.6	2.62	8.3	24.6	448	15.0	24	296	5	10.0	11.9	224	7.6
Beltrami	-400	11 870	18.4	2.74	11.6	22.9	627	18.9	33	274	2	8.3	3.5	354	10.7
Benton	-200	10 935	32.1	2.71	8.2	23.9	516	18.3	21	218	2	7.9	4.1	72	2.7
Big Stone	-500	2 463	-14.3	2.43	4.6	29.0	89	12.5	6	94	1	13.1	12.0	53	6.9
Blue Earth	-4 000	19 277	7.0	2.59	7.4	24.3	696	13.7	32	396	5	7.8	7.0	569	11.0
Brown	-1 800	10 321	3.3	2.54	5.9	28.0	392	14.2	19	295	3	10.6	7.3	234	8.2
Carlton	-1 200	10 842	7.3	2.62	8.3	24.6	364	12.2	24	297	5	10.0	12.6	273	9.1
Carver	1 000	16 601	38.2	2.84	6.8	17.9	832	18.8	44	236	4	5.6	5.4	280	7.2
Cass	0	8 302	11.5	2.56	7.7	23.6	310	14.2	27	253	1	11.7	3.3	105	4.8
Chippewa	-1 100	5 245	-6.1	2.48	5.4	27.8	187	13.6	5	166	2	11.9	11.3	90	6.1
Chisago	1 000	10 551	26.4	2.84	6.9	18.7	461	15.6	25	244	1	8.5	2.2	224	8.1
Clay	-3 800	17 490	8.0	2.64	8.9	23.4	670	13.9	30	350	6	7.3	9.4	539	11.1
Clearwater	-300	3 064	2.8	2.65	8.0	25.1	113	12.8	7	96	5	10.9	42.4	74	8.3
Cook	-100	1 632	3.1	2.33	5.3	29.2	51	12.8	4	40	0	10.0	0.0	42	10.2
Cottonwood	-1 200	5 060	-7.6	2.45	5.3	27.8	131	9.6	4	177	0	12.9	0.0	99	6.9
Crow Wing	1 500	17 204	13.4	2.52	8.1	25.3	601	13.2	35	451	7	10.1	11.3	420	9.7
Dakota	17 100	98 293	53.4	2.78	8.9	18.8	4 677	18.5	216	1 043	35	4.3	7.9	805	3.8
Dodge	-500	5 538	10.9	2.81	5.6	19.9	209	13.4	7	123	2	8.0	7.5	107	6.9
Douglas	300	10 988	10.0	2.56	6.3	24.5	401	13.6	13	303	5	10.4	13.1	257	8.9
Faribault	-1 700	6 772	-8.2	2.45	6.2	28.7	215	12.1	13	207	3	11.5	12.4	115	6.1
Fillmore	-1 100	7 822	-0.1	2.59	5.4	25.2	296	14.0	9	255	1	12.0	3.5	119	5.5
Freeborn	-2 700	13 029	-1.5	2.49	6.7	25.9	476	13.9	24	357	3	10.4	7.0	299	8.5
Goodhue	-700	15 198	11.5	2.60	6.5	24.9	526	13.1	24	423	3	10.7	5.3	272	6.9
Grant	-600	2 454	-7.5	2.47	5.3	27.3	77	12.0	3	94	0	14.2	0.0	35	5.1
Hennepin	-500	419 060	14.6	2.41	10.0	29.0	16 599	16.5	937	7 901	159	7.9	10.0	11 116	11.5

1. No spouse present. 2. Per 1,000 resident population estimated as of July 1 of the year shown. 3. Under 2,500 grams. 4. Deaths of infants under 1 year old. 5. Deaths of infants under 1 year old per 1,000 live births.

STATE County	Divorces, 1984 Number	Divorces, 1984 Rate[1]	Physicians, active non-Federal, 1989 Number[2]	Physicians Rate[3]	Hospitals, 1989 Number	Hospitals Beds Number	Hospitals Beds Rate[3]	Nursing homes,[4] 1986 Number	Nursing homes Beds	Serious crimes known to police, 1988 Number Total[5]	Serious crimes Number Violent[6]	Serious crimes Rate[3]	Education Public school enrollment[7] 1986–1987	Public school enrollment 1980	Attainment,[8] 1980 Percent 12 yrs. or more	Attainment Percent 16 yrs. or more
	44	45	46	47	48	49	50	51	52	53	54	55	56	57	58	59
MICHIGAN—Con.																
Livingston	476	4.7	64	55	2	156	133	21	509	3 064	212	2 793	18 879	26 246	77.3	16.3
Luce	22	3.7	9	155	2	233	4 017	14	110	200	11	3 471	1 316	1 367	58.5	11.2
Mackinac	7	0.7	6	56	1	75	701	7	84	857	33	8 151	1 875	2 305	63.0	9.3
Macomb	3 071	4.5	715	101	7	1 155	163	45	3 678	34 754	2 231	5 474	118 285	148 770	69.2	10.8
Manistee	92	4.1	18	80	1	54	241	10	280	677	38	3 044	3 564	4 567	62.2	9.7
Marquette	319	4.4	142	204	3	394	567	13	455	2 201	125	3 101	12 955	13 852	75.6	17.5
Mason	109	4.2	29	110	1	85	323	12	281	1 186	36	4 530	4 748	5 273	66.1	10.0
Mecosta	117	3.1	25	65	1	74	192	10	190	1 774	68	4 594	5 802	5 906	69.6	14.9
Menominee	40	1.6	12	47	0	0	0	8	303	859	37	3 306	4 445	5 185	67.1	8.1
Midland	338	4.5	140	184	1	307	404	24	536	2 267	102	3 059	13 432	17 362	76.9	22.7
Missaukee	45	4.2	2	17	0	0	0	9	68	265	7	2 341	1 929	2 067	59.5	7.1
Monroe	484	3.7	76	55	1	182	132	11	659	5 063	459	3 735	24 002	30 183	63.4	8.9
Montcalm	248	5.0	20	37	5	366	673	31	364	1 610	131	3 329	12 815	10 884	63.8	8.8
Montmorency	25	3.2	3	35	0	0	0	3	114	318	25	3 884	1 145	1 514	60.1	6.4
Muskegon	768	4.9	177	109	3	693	426	48	1 435	10 499	1 533	6 544	30 710	33 474	65.3	10.6
Newaygo	168	4.7	20	50	1	82	203	8	291	1 124	105	2 895	7 864	7 920	60.6	8.9
Oakland	5 019	5.0	3 913	368	16	4 166	392	131	5 477	61 901	6 347	5 863	170 124	200 560	77.8	24.1
Oceana	84	3.8	8	34	2	71	301	9	182	557	65	2 505	3 652	5 254	63.6	9.2
Ogemaw	42	2.4	13	68	1	92	479	6	257	796	71	4 399	2 414	3 391	57.5	6.8
Ontonagon	26	2.7	4	44	1	87	967	5	137	176	15	1 934	1 771	2 389	64.6	8.9
Osceola	0	0.0	2	9	1	110	516	12	153	517	45	2 585	5 135	4 316	61.7	8.4
Oscoda	6	0.9	3	39	0	0	0	3	102	285	3	3 971	1 035	1 304	59.3	7.7
Otsego	64	4.2	21	121	1	111	642	7	201	544	29	3 322	3 717	3 161	70.9	14.1
Ottawa	0	0.0	150	81	3	337	182	39	1 657	5 278	273	2 983	28 484	30 033	69.1	14.7
Presque Isle	43	3.1	8	56	1	89	622	11	128	301	19	2 142	2 273	2 728	56.9	7.6
Roscommon	68	3.7	9	42	0	0	0	8	105	1 243	57	6 242	3 347	2 874	62.9	8.1
Saginaw	928	4.2	328	153	5	1 310	611	60	1 707	14 719	2 346	6 731	41 079	50 126	65.8	11.3
St. Clair	667	4.8	145	98	4	473	320	39	882	5 341	347	3 710	25 820	32 276	65.0	9.3
St. Joseph	261	4.6	41	68	2	117	194	26	458	2 215	216	3 777	12 299	11 824	65.7	9.3
Sanilac	139	3.5	22	53	3	129	309	22	271	958	89	2 421	8 423	9 572	60.8	7.6
Schoolcraft	29	3.4	6	73	1	47	573	8	128	216	12	2 606	1 244	1 676	58.7	9.1
Shiawassee	354	5.2	54	76	1	166	232	7	388	2 061	162	2 949	15 753	17 058	67.6	9.2
Tuscola	233	4.2	26	46	3	570	1 000	17	371	1 075	95	1 913	13 088	13 518	62.6	7.9
Van Buren	400	6.1	43	61	2	256	364	44	715	3 703	312	5 403	15 987	15 033	62.1	10.1
Washtenaw	1 266	4.9	2 082	773	7	2 726	1 013	57	1 448	18 802	2 030	6 945	39 065	44 030	80.9	36.1
Wayne	7 502	3.4	3 847	183	41	12 321	587	349	15 868	193 682	31 103	9 033	361 819	445 072	61.4	11.2
Wexford	131	5.1	32	117	1	154	562	11	298	1 308	57	4 828	5 127	5 411	62.6	10.3
MINNESOTA	14 758	3.5	9 344	215	168	24 893	572	481	48 556	X	12 490	4 315	692 274	780 003	73.1	17.4
Aitkin	39	2.9	7	54	1	84	651	1	106	466	30	3 403	2 219	2 738	61.5	8.4
Anoka	902	4.3	164	67	1	337	139	6	603	11 067	301	4 769	49 596	48 784	80.1	13.8
Becker	88	3.0	29	96	1	166	551	5	511	1 145	17	3 801	4 818	6 547	60.1	10.4
Beltrami	183	5.5	36	108	2	112	336	5	395	1 882	121	5 640	6 814	5 961	65.6	17.3
Benton	53	2.0	6	21	0	0	0	3	478	713	30	2 538	4 026	4 769	66.4	12.7
Big Stone	13	1.7	6	86	2	137	1 957	3	188	76	1	1 041	1 425	1 598	62.0	9.2
Blue Earth	145	2.8	75	149	1	177	350	6	529	2 238	57	4 378	9 021	7 820	75.0	18.3
Brown	74	2.6	24	87	4	141	513	4	371	469	12	1 675	4 172	4 242	61.5	9.9
Carlton	138	4.6	23	77	3	810	2 709	4	329	990	58	3 298	6 287	6 839	66.7	10.6
Carver	132	3.4	45	98	1	97	211	4	218	1 090	47	2 523	6 555	6 859	73.0	15.6
Cass	69	3.2	9	41	1	13	59	3	515	968	60	4 460	3 869	4 371	63.0	10.1
Chippewa	39	2.7	10	74	1	35	259	2	215	139	6	986	2 515	2 975	62.2	9.7
Chisago	89	3.2	19	63	2	118	392	4	341	1 072	33	3 696	5 681	6 100	68.3	10.8
Clay	146	3.0	22	46	1	95	197	4	426	1 852	47	3 828	8 153	8 597	73.0	18.0
Clearwater	25	2.8	5	57	1	24	273	2	166	235	24	2 663	1 981	1 995	52.5	8.4
Cook	11	2.7	6	150	1	63	1 575	1	47	184	12	4 535	625	814	76.4	18.6
Cottonwood	31	2.2	6	45	3	72	537	5	302	154	4	1 116	3 145	3 096	63.8	9.9
Crow Wing	193	4.5	60	130	3	719	1 560	4	438	2 036	125	4 422	8 285	8 753	65.0	11.1
Dakota	885	4.2	186	70	3	313	118	11	1 353	8 996	306	3 693	45 650	44 426	83.6	21.6
Dodge	37	2.4	7	45	0	0	0	2	156	456	20	2 920	3 578	3 376	68.6	9.7
Douglas	95	3.3	43	145	1	106	358	4	524	771	14	2 612	5 360	5 382	62.8	11.2
Faribault	52	2.8	12	69	2	132	759	3	329	415	22	2 299	3 283	3 853	64.2	11.2
Fillmore	31	1.4	8	38	2	135	646	7	494	141	10	653	3 678	4 698	61.3	9.4
Freeborn	130	3.7	33	97	1	115	339	7	509	759	27	2 188	5 785	7 589	65.1	9.5
Goodhue	125	3.2	47	116	3	124	307	8	865	1 079	32	2 693	7 777	8 176	65.7	11.9
Grant	22	3.2	0	0	1	32	508	3	190	162	10	2 420	1 371	1 479	59.1	8.8
Hennepin	4 206	4.3	3 638	357	13	6 573	645	89	12 687	68 227	6 535	6 757	132 102	152 746	81.7	25.1

1. Per 1,000 resident population estimated as of July 1 of the year shown. 2. As of end of year. 3. Per 100,000 resident population as of July 1 of the year shown. 4. Preliminary. Covers nursing homes with 3 or more beds. 5. Data for serious crimes have not been adjusted for underreporting, this may affect comparability between geographic areas or over time. 6. Includes murder and nonnegligent manslaughter, forcible rape, robbery, and aggravated assault. 7. The 1986–1987 data are based on administrative reports obtained by the U.S. National Center for Education Statistics. The 1980 data are based on the 1980 Census of Population and Housing. 8. Persons 25 years old or older.

STATE County	Education (cont'd): Local government expenditures for education,[1] 1982: Total (Mil dol)	Education (cont'd): Local government expenditures for education,[1] 1982: Per capita (Dollars)	Social Security Program December 1988: Beneficiaries: Total	Social Security Program December 1988: Beneficiaries: Rate[2]	Social Security Program December 1988: Payments ($1,000)	Supplemental Security Income Program recipients June 1986	Money income: Per capita[3]: 1987 Income, (Dollars)	Money income: Per capita[3]: 1979: Current dollars	Money income: Per capita[3]: 1979: Constant 1987 dollars	Money income: Median household income 1979 (Dollars)	Money income: Percent below poverty level, 1979: Persons	Money income: Percent below poverty level, 1979: Families	Housing units, 1990: Total	Housing units, 1990: Percent change, 1980–1990
	60	61	62	63	64	65	66	67	68	69	70	71	72	73
MICHIGAN—Con.														
Livingston	53.5	534	10 510	92.6	5 529	462	13 367	8 323	13 023	24 544	4.8	4.3	41 863	19.8
Luce	3.1	497	1 555	268.1	734	254	8 174	5 301	8 294	13 261	12.6	9.7	3 594	0.6
Mackinac	5.0	488	2 510	236.8	1 186	196	8 357	5 274	8 252	12 454	13.0	9.7	9 254	21.4
Macomb	377.2	549	109 115	154.4	59 365	4 580	13 558	8 655	13 542	24 222	4.6	3.9	274 843	16.2
Manistee	8.7	389	5 285	235.9	2 590	286	9 374	6 182	9 673	14 351	10.7	8.2	13 330	8.9
Marquette	35.0	480	10 270	146.7	5 030	722	8 921	6 187	9 681	16 517	9.8	6.5	31 049	1.7
Mason	13.0	490	5 245	199.4	2 529	344	9 143	6 192	9 689	14 410	12.1	9.5	14 119	6.7
Mecosta	13.3	359	5 650	147.5	2 751	448	8 338	5 230	8 183	13 081	18.2	10.5	17 274	11.3
Menominee	9.8	376	5 380	207.7	2 480	386	8 503	5 585	8 739	14 195	9.8	7.8	12 509	8.3
Midland	38.4	520	9 680	128.7	5 015	644	12 678	8 052	12 599	21 527	8.0	6.4	29 343	11.3
Missaukee	4.0	380	2 225	191.8	1 025	164	7 968	5 151	8 060	12 321	14.3	11.7	7 112	16.3
Monroe	63.4	480	18 140	133.0	9 369	1 094	11 464	7 356	11 510	21 356	7.3	6.2	48 312	6.5
Montcalm	25.7	528	9 610	179.6	4 631	832	9 011	5 905	9 240	14 792	12.0	9.4	22 817	9.2
Montmorency	3.2	427	3 225	383.9	1 571	166	7 777	4 838	7 570	10 254	20.2	16.9	8 791	11.5
Muskegon	81.4	524	29 090	180.3	14 735	2 820	9 752	6 358	9 948	16 167	12.3	10.0	61 962	6.4
Newaygo	16.6	464	6 655	168.5	3 234	556	8 716	5 696	8 913	14 082	13.6	10.7	20 105	9.8
Oakland	593.5	594	143 320	136.2	80 774	7 434	17 215	10 657	16 675	25 323	5.3	4.1	432 684	15.9
Oceana	8.7	399	4 525	193.4	2 152	346	8 433	5 627	8 805	14 157	13.3	11.1	12 857	12.8
Ogemaw	5.5	330	4 515	241.4	2 170	368	7 326	5 001	7 825	10 506	18.4	16.0	13 977	7.7
Ontonagon	6.0	593	2 290	251.6	1 081	214	8 904	5 599	8 761	13 153	12.6	9.5	5 332	5.8
Osceola	11.1	568	4 515	214.0	2 129	470	8 074	5 252	8 218	12 970	14.1	10.8	11 444	15.3
Oscoda	2.9	410	1 685	227.7	805	94	7 601	5 109	7 994	11 175	15.4	11.7	8 112	11.0
Otsego	11.8	778	3 340	197.6	1 652	232	9 285	5 933	9 283	15 341	9.4	7.6	10 669	17.5
Ottawa	71.1	445	23 000	127.4	11 985	898	11 471	7 198	11 263	20 231	6.0	4.3	66 624	23.5
Presque Isle	5.2	375	3 580	252.1	1 703	306	7 755	5 522	8 640	12 491	16.5	14.4	8 917	6.6
Roscommon	8.3	478	7 085	343.9	3 519	266	8 316	5 411	8 467	10 865	12.9	9.4	19 881	10.9
Saginaw	122.7	550	35 270	163.7	17 904	3 326	10 862	7 263	11 364	19 725	11.7	10.0	81 931	3.0
St. Clair	64.9	471	22 705	155.7	11 633	1 616	11 080	7 080	11 078	18 476	9.7	8.0	57 494	10.8
St. Joseph	26.6	465	9 865	164.4	5 058	632	9 887	6 473	10 128	16 091	9.7	7.6	24 242	7.8
Sanilac	17.5	439	8 195	197.9	3 950	526	8 945	5 932	9 282	14 586	11.6	9.3	19 465	5.3
Schoolcraft	3.3	383	2 105	253.6	1 021	192	7 870	5 283	8 266	12 450	13.8	10.1	5 487	10.3
Shiawassee	34.7	498	10 265	144.8	5 194	762	10 230	6 948	10 872	19 722	7.9	6.9	25 833	5.6
Tuscola	29.8	534	9 200	162.5	4 518	828	9 544	6 500	10 171	18 332	9.7	7.9	21 231	5.9
Van Buren	34.0	512	12 185	175.6	5 908	1 312	9 377	6 108	9 557	15 394	13.5	10.7	31 530	9.5
Washtenaw	125.1	480	27 040	101.0	14 965	2 434	14 245	8 703	13 618	20 696	11.0	5.7	111 256	13.3
Wayne	1 283.7	573	355 870	167.6	184 982	45 468	11 766	7 608	11 904	18 629	14.3	11.8	832 710	-4.8
Wexford	10.8	421	5 120	188.2	2 461	450	8 904	5 874	9 191	13 394	12.4	9.9	12 862	11.1
MINNESOTA	2 287.7	554	653 661	151.8	313 141	34 158	12 281	7 450	11 657	17 761	9.5	7.0	1 848 445	14.6
Aitkin	8.2	619	3 755	288.8	1 659	250	7 405	4 773	7 468	10 663	18.2	14.3	12 934	16.3
Anoka	133.4	655	13 400	56.9	6 900	634	12 479	7 636	11 948	23 392	4.6	3.8	85 519	36.0
Becker	16.8	571	5 675	189.8	2 374	408	8 686	5 464	8 550	12 678	16.0	13.1	15 563	0.9
Beltrami	32.0	974	5 190	156.3	2 164	562	8 049	5 161	8 075	12 244	19.6	14.7	14 670	12.0
Benton	10.3	397	3 255	115.4	1 381	206	9 608	5 736	8 975	15 517	11.3	9.1	11 521	30.7
Big Stone	4.8	622	1 895	266.9	791	74	8 464	5 490	8 590	12 318	15.5	11.2	3 192	-8.6
Blue Earth	29.0	555	8 195	161.6	3 841	388	10 382	6 608	10 340	15 609	13.0	7.5	20 358	5.0
Brown	12.9	450	5 785	208.8	2 658	176	10 329	6 299	9 856	15 403	10.5	8.4	10 814	3.3
Carlton	21.9	731	5 845	196.1	2 784	356	9 356	6 012	9 407	16 420	8.8	6.8	12 342	4.8
Carver	17.2	450	4 365	98.5	2 034	106	12 892	7 712	12 067	20 466	6.0	4.7	17 449	38.6
Cass	11.8	559	5 060	231.1	2 190	488	7 610	4 804	7 517	10 926	19.8	15.9	18 863	7.3
Chippewa	7.8	532	2 955	215.7	1 277	112	9 340	6 040	9 451	13 369	13.5	10.3	5 755	-6.0
Chisago	15.4	578	4 665	158.1	2 204	136	10 625	6 506	10 180	18 497	7.3	5.9	11 946	24.9
Clay	24.9	509	6 825	141.6	3 230	322	9 927	6 513	10 191	16 578	11.0	5.8	18 546	4.1
Clearwater	6.2	707	1 985	225.6	740	224	7 016	4 437	6 943	10 099	22.1	19.0	4 008	4.8
Cook	2.6	633	810	202.5	387	28	9 419	6 743	10 551	14 641	11.4	7.0	4 312	24.8
Cottonwood	7.7	529	3 270	240.4	1 464	152	10 246	6 448	10 089	14 121	13.6	11.3	5 495	-5.3
Crow Wing	26.8	632	9 865	216.8	4 537	578	8 921	5 632	8 812	12 685	15.5	12.9	29 916	16.5
Dakota	128.2	627	17 835	70.4	9 175	554	14 410	8 578	13 422	23 587	4.3	3.6	102 707	53.6
Dodge	8.7	573	2 505	160.6	1 079	90	9 998	6 313	9 878	16 800	10.4	8.5	5 771	4.3
Douglas	19.3	679	6 335	214.7	2 665	286	9 130	5 636	8 819	13 075	15.6	10.6	14 590	10.7
Faribault	10.4	538	4 400	248.6	1 986	158	9 807	6 484	10 146	14 417	11.9	8.7	7 416	-6.7
Fillmore	10.5	482	5 110	242.2	2 140	230	9 448	5 655	8 848	13 133	16.5	12.8	8 356	-1.1
Freeborn	17.2	481	7 085	207.2	3 376	264	10 332	6 754	10 568	16 475	9.1	6.8	13 783	-0.2
Goodhue	24.1	616	7 320	182.5	3 444	264	11 260	6 839	10 701	17 036	8.1	5.9	15 936	10.9
Grant	4.4	627	1 830	285.9	764	68	9 308	5 628	8 806	12 034	14.6	12.0	3 178	-0.4
Hennepin	473.7	494	142 905	141.7	75 720	8 192	15 804	9 403	14 713	20 077	7.5	5.0	443 583	16.9

1. Elementary and secondary. 2. Per 1,000 resident population estimated as of July 1 of the year shown. 3. Based on the resident population estimated as of July 1, 1988 for 1987 data and enumerated as of April 1, 1980 for 1979 data.

STATE County	Housing units, 1990 (cont'd)				Civilian labor force, 1990				Private nonfarm establishments, 1988					
	Occupied units						Unemployment				Employment[2]			
		Owner occupied												
	Total	Percent	Median value (Dollars)	Median rent (Dollars)	Total	Percent change, 1989–1990	Total	Rate[1]	Number	Net change, 1987–1988	Total	Percent change, 1987–1988	Manu-facturing	Retail trade
	74	75	76	77	78	79	80	81	82	83	84	85	86	87
MICHIGAN—Con.														
Livingston	38 887	84.5	97 300	448	55 511	-0.8	3 278	5.9	2 121	117	24 855	4.2	6 734	5 963
Luce	2 154	79.1	30 800	233	2 621	-0.2	237	9.0	172	5	1 006	-0.6	299	351
Mackinac	4 240	76.0	43 900	221	7 272	0.3	1 257	17.3	432	13	2 032	14.3	127	616
Macomb	264 991	77.2	76 800	437	375 866	-0.5	28 265	7.5	15 949	388	267 518	-0.1	109 249	61 243
Manistee	8 580	78.2	40 400	224	8 682	-1.5	977	11.3	585	-6	4 862	4.6	1 603	1 312
Marquette	25 435	64.2	44 800	273	29 875	1.1	2 530	8.5	1 551	32	17 632	2.5	930	5 408
Mason	9 984	75.9	43 300	243	11 144	-0.6	1 022	9.2	686	7	6 297	4.6	1 876	1 751
Mecosta	12 260	69.9	49 100	280	16 165	1.3	1 229	7.6	706	2	6 937	7.4	1 720	2 400
Menominee	9 766	78.9	37 900	222	12 079	0.7	844	7.0	530	-2	6 316	-1.1	2 837	1 093
Midland	27 791	76.9	63 300	344	36 075	0.0	2 079	5.8	1 430	31	27 906	6.6	0	4 304
Missaukee	4 389	83.0	40 500	250	5 320	2.6	568	10.7	226	1	1 680	7.8	344	397
Monroe	46 508	77.8	67 200	344	64 309	-0.4	5 127	8.0	2 006	101	26 420	2.4	7 970	6 046
Montcalm	18 563	79.4	42 600	262	25 355	2.3	3 236	12.8	923	-19	13 132	-1.2	6 274	2 714
Montmorency	3 600	81.5	41 700	223	3 088	2.1	475	15.4	204	2	1 291	17.4	329	421
Muskegon	57 798	74.4	46 300	294	68 359	-0.3	6 350	9.3	3 190	50	48 938	-0.7	17 376	10 995
Newaygo	13 776	82.2	44 300	266	18 321	2.3	1 764	9.6	605	30	6 455	6.7	2 737	1 549
Oakland	410 488	72.7	95 400	495	577 674	-1.4	33 268	5.8	35 783	1 164	560 431	0.5	109 202	116 416
Oceana	8 071	80.3	43 300	240	11 282	1.7	1 179	10.5	462	9	3 009	12.2	969	881
Ogemaw	7 190	81.4	39 500	241	6 825	2.9	705	10.3	455	22	3 631	0.6	980	1 223
Ontonagon	3 641	81.0	28 100	192	3 621	3.0	254	7.0	223	2	2 418	6.4	443	547
Osceola	7 347	79.9	37 500	228	9 309	2.1	1 027	11.0	343	7	3 186	3.1	1 620	747
Oscoda	3 160	81.9	37 400	230	4 492	-1.8	250	5.6	178	11	1 403	19.1	650	377
Otsego	6 522	79.1	56 000	292	8 521	5.3	648	7.6	591	31	5 913	9.0	1 220	1 528
Ottawa	62 664	80.7	74 600	402	102 152	1.1	5 977	5.9	4 074	199	64 148	5.0	28 362	12 718
Presque Isle	5 376	83.7	44 000	207	5 371	1.0	695	12.9	330	6	1 860	8.0	207	564
Roscommon	8 516	81.9	44 500	248	8 236	4.8	638	7.7	569	30	2 994	-0.1	329	1 581
Saginaw	78 256	70.7	48 100	301	96 234	0.5	7 672	8.0	4 583	105	74 775	-1.5	22 767	18 985
St. Clair	52 882	75.7	59 400	329	67 129	-1.2	6 272	9.3	2 651	32	32 492	0.0	9 653	7 904
St. Joseph	21 579	74.8	44 800	278	26 868	-1.2	2 523	9.4	1 186	17	17 506	0.6	8 602	3 194
Sanilac	14 658	79.4	42 400	254	19 963	-1.7	2 097	10.5	802	-3	8 508	3.5	3 894	1 809
Schoolcraft	3 294	77.0	32 300	206	3 646	-0.6	589	16.2	253	-6	1 512	4.9	359	451
Shiawassee	24 864	77.7	47 200	292	34 905	-0.9	3 268	9.4	1 143	-22	12 651	2.5	4 275	3 422
Tuscola	19 469	81.2	46 000	268	24 348	2.3	2 481	10.2	958	4	8 210	2.2	2 721	2 266
Van Buren	25 402	76.7	48 000	266	33 260	2.9	3 086	9.3	1 237	18	12 076	-2.3	3 924	3 140
Washtenaw	104 528	55.3	96 000	490	163 414	1.8	7 396	4.5	6 590	150	116 427	3.5	39 001	25 692
Wayne	780 535	63.9	48 500	297	975 905	-1.6	81 050	8.3	35 342	-311	725 634	-0.6	207 662	141 076
Wexford	9 923	74.7	41 200	279	13 761	2.9	1 536	11.2	690	11	10 060	10.6	3 673	2 196
MINNESOTA	1 647 853	71.8	74 000	384	2 404 000	2.6	116 000	4.8	X	X	1 701 452	2.9	387 642	368 205
Aitkin	5 126	83.9	48 600	186	5 654	7.4	547	9.7	285	8	1 828	3.4	315	614
Anoka	82 437	81.2	83 500	460	136 942	1.7	6 604	4.8	4 137	149	64 173	6.0	20 497	16 689
Becker	10 477	77.8	49 000	224	14 564	4.8	1 010	6.9	671	0	6 594	-2.9	1 288	1 604
Beltrami	11 870	73.1	49 200	264	17 242	5.3	1 036	6.0	843	30	8 296	10.3	864	2 890
Benton	10 935	67.0	60 800	367	16 053	1.8	1 021	6.4	498	23	7 148	5.1	1 872	1 621
Big Stone	2 463	80.9	27 000	169	2 976	3.2	144	4.8	195	3	1 208	-17.1	0	414
Blue Earth	19 277	64.0	59 500	332	29 176	2.5	937	3.2	1 521	-2	21 583	3.2	3 495	5 871
Brown	10 321	77.3	48 900	219	14 548	4.5	625	4.3	739	4	10 080	0.8	3 464	2 173
Carlton	10 842	81.1	45 200	230	13 317	7.2	951	7.1	593	10	6 380	-2.6	2 204	1 662
Carver	16 601	79.0	95 700	409	25 329	1.3	1 043	4.1	947	38	13 826	14.2	5 764	2 421
Cass	8 302	82.9	50 500	202	9 317	5.7	905	9.7	522	16	2 956	18.8	378	996
Chippewa	5 245	75.4	34 200	192	7 296	7.8	349	4.8	393	-18	3 228	-3.9	555	842
Chisago	10 551	85.0	72 600	313	15 103	2.2	1 091	7.2	605	31	6 434	4.3	1 722	1 521
Clay	17 490	68.3	58 600	296	26 039	2.8	1 081	4.2	1 007	0	12 009	2.2	1 040	3 601
Clearwater	3 064	81.6	29 400	172	3 812	7.2	558	14.6	172	0	1 084	1.9	148	299
Cook	1 632	76.6	55 600	218	2 854	4.4	192	6.7	171	7	1 174	14.1	0	394
Cottonwood	5 060	77.6	29 600	176	6 538	4.9	418	6.4	378	-16	3 345	1.3	971	734
Crow Wing	17 204	76.7	54 200	269	22 947	2.1	1 428	6.2	1 307	13	12 313	4.7	2 057	3 862
Dakota	98 293	73.9	95 900	503	148 754	1.4	6 022	4.0	5 417	223	82 303	2.8	15 322	22 835
Dodge	5 538	80.9	53 000	234	8 664	2.5	477	5.5	309	9	2 159	7.6	462	583
Douglas	10 988	74.2	56 400	253	15 979	3.1	792	5.0	874	2	8 046	3.4	1 386	2 594
Faribault	6 772	78.8	32 200	185	8 150	2.5	444	5.4	514	-9	4 683	3.7	1 778	911
Fillmore	7 822	78.1	38 000	189	10 289	4.0	551	5.4	561	4	4 297	-0.7	911	924
Freeborn	13 029	76.7	42 800	232	17 247	0.5	1 841	10.7	820	0	11 792	3.8	4 340	2 888
Goodhue	15 198	76.5	63 300	272	22 304	4.6	897	4.0	1 033	-7	13 432	4.1	4 210	2 884
Grant	2 454	79.5	29 100	161	3 155	8.2	212	6.7	200	20	1 102	10.9	75	263
Hennepin	419 060	63.4	91 000	452	625 152	1.6	25 509	4.1	32 163	572	663 359	1.9	129 419	119 396

1. Percent of total civilian labor force. 2. For week including March 12. Excludes government employees, self-employed persons, farm workers, domestic service workers, railroad employees subject to the Railroad Retirement Act, and employees on oceanborne vessels or in foreign countries.

STATE County	Private nonfarm establishments, 1988 (cont'd): Employment[1] (cont'd): Finance, insurance, and real estate	Private nonfarm establishments, 1988 (cont'd): Employment[1] (cont'd): Services	Private nonfarm establishments, 1988 (cont'd): Annual payroll: Total (Mil dol)	Private nonfarm establishments, 1988 (cont'd): Annual payroll: Average per employee (Dollars)	Personal income, 1989: Total (Mil dol)	Personal income, 1989: Percent change, 1988–1989	Personal income, 1989: Wages and salaries[2] (Mil dol)	Personal income, 1989: Proprietor's income (Mil dol)	Personal income, 1989: Dividends, interest, & rent (Mil dol)	Personal income, 1989: Transfer payments (Mil dol)	Personal income, 1989: Per capita[3]: Dollars	Personal income, 1989: Per capita[3]: Rank	Earnings, 1989: Total (Mil dol)	Earnings, 1989: Percent by selected industries: Farm	Earnings, 1989: Percent by selected industries: Goods-related[4]: Total
	88	89	90	91	92	93	94	95	96	97	98	99	100	101	102
MICHIGAN—Con.															
Livingston	2 088	5 962	479	19 257	2 292	9.5	669	129	303	176	19 555	193	799	1.4	35.3
Luce	41	170	13	12 974	98	6.6	51	7	11	35	16 816	469	58	1.0	NA
Mackinac	75	452	38	18 926	137	8.9	62	12	32	37	12 886	1 961	74	1.9	11.5
Macomb	8 455	53 598	6 945	25 962	14 188	7.6	9 212	696	2 186	1 636	19 984	171	9 908	0.2	55.9
Manistee	240	1 017	83	16 977	296	7.8	131	24	72	76	13 227	1 803	155	3.4	36.9
Marquette	978	5 136	326	18 494	930	5.0	633	52	132	182	13 394	1 730	685	0.4	NA
Mason	387	1 416	113	17 946	347	8.3	177	32	71	80	13 185	1 819	209	4.3	39.0
Mecosta	337	1 690	94	13 523	434	9.4	199	39	70	98	11 266	2 572	238	4.1	18.2
Menominee	266	1 002	101	16 055	323	7.9	158	28	61	65	12 499	2 116	186	4.0	45.2
Midland	916	6 968	815	29 194	1 394	6.6	1 070	69	291	151	18 358	259	1 139	0.7	64.0
Missaukee	151	566	22	12 912	131	8.6	31	19	25	30	11 075	2 645	50	18.7	21.3
Monroe	1 091	6 089	637	24 104	2 220	7.3	949	146	317	286	16 076	626	1 095	2.5	NA
Montcalm	410	2 660	248	18 884	692	8.9	352	65	101	135	12 714	2 030	417	6.4	47.2
Montmorency	66	341	16	12 700	101	10.6	28	7	28	38	11 765	2 417	36	2.9	18.8
Muskegon	1 743	11 702	1 013	20 703	2 258	6.6	1 403	143	353	473	13 895	1 477	1 546	1.0	43.7
Newaygo	267	1 155	124	19 157	499	7.9	167	35	86	97	12 359	2 179	202	5.4	38.1
Oakland	47 322	184 537	14 342	25 592	27 671	8.4	18 098	1 824	5 183	2 449	26 052	30	19 921	0.1	28.8
Oceana	133	547	51	16 816	314	10.0	90	33	59	66	13 272	1 784	123	15.3	28.2
Ogemaw	139	653	52	14 210	201	8.5	84	21	42	65	10 495	2 792	105	3.9	20.6
Ontonagon	70	278	47	19 251	120	9.5	83	9	18	32	13 288	1 777	92	2.0	NA
Osceola	106	258	62	19 524	224	6.7	112	23	43	60	10 543	2 782	135	5.1	NA
Oscoda	38	220	16	11 063	82	9.7	19	6	18	24	10 854	2 698	26	2.6	24.0
Otsego	206	1 871	100	16 975	244	10.0	161	22	48	46	14 100	1 389	183	1.1	36.3
Ottawa	1 927	12 659	1 304	20 327	3 180	9.0	1 901	272	510	319	17 196	410	2 173	2.7	51.1
Presque Isle	130	357	29	15 483	173	6.2	67	17	36	46	12 129	2 271	84	7.2	35.8
Roscommon	209	513	37	12 415	249	8.2	78	17	69	86	11 712	2 437	95	0.3	16.8
Saginaw	3 494	18 184	1 779	23 790	3 432	6.2	2 543	176	549	603	16 009	643	2 719	1.1	46.8
St. Clair	1 755	7 756	661	20 342	2 380	7.2	985	135	368	357	16 087	622	1 120	1.1	33.0
St. Joseph	450	2 723	359	20 532	869	7.6	513	74	149	143	14 371	1 258	587	3.5	55.0
Sanilac	481	1 379	136	16 040	580	10.2	214	67	115	117	13 885	1 488	282	9.7	40.1
Schoolcraft	93	307	27	17 935	102	7.1	49	8	20	30	12 366	2 176	57	1.2	NA
Shiawassee	559	2 821	219	17 283	1 069	6.3	381	56	146	166	14 951	1 009	437	2.0	34.9
Tuscola	395	1 623	126	15 379	777	7.4	244	61	124	159	13 629	1 613	304	8.2	25.9
Van Buren	475	2 328	212	17 527	909	6.4	371	76	137	192	12 923	1 943	447	7.0	31.9
Washtenaw	4 790	34 127	2 940	25 248	6 061	7.2	4 937	414	912	611	22 512	82	5 351	0.3	35.6
Wayne	46 192	208 074	19 169	26 417	35 612	4.6	29 589	1 416	5 071	7 099	16 955	444	31 005	0.0	39.9
Wexford	352	2 798	169	16 812	338	7.6	246	25	58	78	12 329	2 189	271	0.8	39.3
MINNESOTA	122 995	500 883	35 729	X	76 802	8.2	51 421	6 900	12 659	10 507	17 649	X	58 321	3.5	29.2
Aitkin	102	540	23	12 364	149	8.4	44	15	34	47	11 498	2 497	60	4.7	NA
Anoka	1 786	14 724	1 316	20 505	4 031	7.1	1 841	207	324	328	16 578	509	2 048	0.4	41.6
Becker	275	2 282	84	12 756	372	10.1	152	64	65	84	12 368	2 174	216	14.4	NA
Beltrami	367	2 866	114	13 733	402	7.6	230	38	57	101	12 076	2 297	268	1.3	17.2
Benton	301	1 408	129	18 061	400	7.1	198	43	55	72	13 916	1 461	241	8.4	NA
Big Stone	70	425	13	11 064	86	7.0	27	18	22	22	12 403	2 158	45	22.9	13.3
Blue Earth	1 069	7 443	317	14 665	778	8.4	496	101	170	130	15 402	837	597	7.0	18.7
Brown	441	2 488	160	15 892	425	10.2	230	70	100	69	15 461	813	300	11.3	36.9
Carlton	293	1 262	126	19 782	390	8.4	219	20	48	85	13 052	1 889	238	1.4	39.3
Carver	480	3 478	285	20 640	868	10.3	368	67	113	67	18 902	225	435	3.7	49.0
Cass	156	1 051	33	11 168	248	7.5	89	27	57	73	11 240	2 583	117	4.7	10.2
Chippewa	170	774	45	13 920	196	9.7	80	40	47	38	14 548	1 190	119	15.6	23.0
Chisago	252	2 102	97	15 073	451	7.7	160	38	62	67	14 994	989	198	3.3	34.8
Clay	605	4 982	149	12 395	691	8.1	281	93	106	126	14 343	1 271	373	11.8	15.8
Clearwater	50	334	13	11 717	90	8.1	31	12	14	30	10 245	2 847	44	12.2	NA
Cook	69	491	12	10 468	60	8.7	28	7	13	12	15 211	904	35	0.0	15.4
Cottonwood	194	919	40	11 999	206	12.1	70	56	49	37	15 438	818	126	32.2	16.6
Crow Wing	666	3 826	187	15 207	615	8.9	331	56	122	144	13 358	1 752	386	0.8	23.4
Dakota	4 549	20 197	1 681	20 420	5 337	9.6	2 361	247	589	385	20 082	163	2 608	0.9	30.6
Dodge	122	372	36	16 597	241	13.0	68	45	39	33	15 322	866	113	30.0	23.7
Douglas	348	2 385	112	13 873	385	8.3	197	46	83	78	13 007	1 902	243	3.5	26.0
Faribault	271	920	67	14 206	286	14.4	92	84	69	52	16 410	542	176	34.0	22.5
Fillmore	222	1 324	56	13 081	294	7.7	99	55	67	61	14 017	1 430	154	19.7	18.7
Freeborn	380	2 663	194	16 413	524	10.1	263	97	101	87	15 437	820	360	16.9	32.6
Goodhue	546	3 541	228	16 959	641	8.9	339	91	122	97	15 865	689	430	8.8	30.1
Grant	68	323	13	11 715	98	11.4	27	24	27	21	15 540	790	51	33.3	8.8
Hennepin	66 259	204 529	16 184	24 397	23 027	7.5	21 570	1 484	3 901	2 667	22 584	80	23 054	0.0	24.6

1. For week including March 12. Excludes government employees, self-employed persons, farm workers, domestic service workers, railroad employees subject to the Railroad Retirement Act, and employees on oceanborne vessels or in foreign countries. 2. Includes other labor income. 3. Based on the resident population estimated as of July 1 of the year shown. 4. Covers mining, construction, and manufacturing.

STATE County	Earnings, 1989 (cont'd): Percent by selected industries (cont'd): Goods-related[1]: Manu-facturing	Service-related & other[2]: Total	Retail trade	Finance, insur-ance, & real estate	Services	Govern-ment	Agriculture, 1987: Farms: Number	Percent with: Less than 50 acres	500 acres and over	Farm operators, percent: Whose principal occu-pation is farming	Residing on farm operated	Land in farms: Acreage (1,000)	Percent change, 1982–1987	Acres: Average size of farm	Total irrigated (1,000)	Total cropland (1,000)
	103	104	105	106	107	108	109	110	111	112	113	114	115	116	117	118
MICHIGAN—Con.																
Livingston	25.0	49.5	11.0	8.0	24.2	13.9	789	42.1	8.6	41.6	85.8	129	-6.8	163	2	100
Luce	16.8	26.9	9.0	1.2	9.4	52.6	34	14.7	17.6	52.9	88.2	11	-1.6	313	D	6
Mackinac	3.3	60.1	20.5	3.5	24.9	26.5	80	8.8	17.5	51.2	87.5	25	-21.0	307	D	15
Macomb	50.2	33.4	8.1	2.0	16.1	10.5	667	47.1	4.6	53.8	78.6	80	-12.6	119	2	68
Manistee	30.9	41.8	11.2	2.6	16.1	17.9	280	28.6	4.6	47.5	77.5	47	-5.3	167	4	29
Marquette	2.6	NA	8.6	3.0	NA	34.9	101	21.8	11.9	32.7	82.2	24	-17.4	242	0	11
Mason	30.4	39.5	9.2	2.2	17.3	17.2	426	28.2	8.9	49.3	83.3	76	-11.2	179	2	57
Mecosta	13.8	34.3	9.7	2.3	14.6	43.4	639	16.9	8.3	52.9	85.3	127	-6.8	199	4	90
Menominee	41.2	36.1	8.0	2.2	13.5	14.6	374	11.2	19.8	61.5	90.1	118	-14.3	316	D	64
Midland	55.4	28.1	4.6	1.3	18.6	7.2	459	30.9	12.0	38.6	78.9	94	1.2	206	1	75
Missaukee	12.8	41.1	12.6	3.6	16.2	18.9	304	13.8	15.1	67.4	82.6	87	-7.0	287	2	62
Monroe	34.3	NA	8.0	1.8	16.0	11.9	1 258	41.7	8.3	44.8	78.1	220	-8.9	175	2	204
Montcalm	43.7	32.8	10.1	1.6	15.2	13.5	980	22.0	14.6	56.1	81.8	238	-0.9	243	29	186
Montmorency	6.4	NA	16.2	2.7	35.0	19.2	108	14.8	10.2	50.0	87.0	24	-1.5	223	D	15
Muskegon	37.9	41.4	10.0	2.2	19.9	14.0	460	35.9	7.8	45.9	79.3	82	-3.6	179	6	57
Newaygo	33.0	38.4	8.9	3.3	17.6	18.2	687	26.8	7.0	50.1	84.1	116	-9.8	169	5	85
Oakland	22.7	64.4	10.2	6.5	34.1	6.7	596	65.6	3.9	37.6	82.2	60	-12.6	101	1	48
Oceana	19.2	33.8	9.7	2.1	13.7	22.7	686	28.0	9.3	51.3	80.2	133	2.2	194	4	86
Ogemaw	10.8	54.3	21.2	1.5	16.6	21.2	288	15.6	13.2	56.6	83.7	78	16.1	272	0	54
Ontonagon	21.4	NA	6.8	1.7	NA	16.1	117	7.7	12.8	58.1	87.2	37	-5.6	312	D	17
Osceola	43.5	NA	8.1	0.8	9.7	15.3	503	14.7	11.1	53.7	85.1	112	-5.1	222	1	75
Oscoda	17.0	42.6	13.1	0.9	20.6	30.8	84	17.9	7.1	71.4	89.3	17	1.8	204	D	11
Otsego	24.2	45.9	12.1	2.1	22.9	16.7	133	10.5	12.0	50.4	73.7	40	-4.1	299	1	18
Ottawa	43.1	36.4	8.0	2.4	16.1	9.8	1 471	43.2	3.6	50.4	80.2	178	-2.9	121	11	146
Presque Isle	4.1	39.0	10.0	2.2	17.9	18.0	293	9.6	14.7	54.3	79.5	82	-7.2	279	1	52
Roscommon	6.5	51.3	20.0	1.7	19.7	31.6	31	22.6	3.2	25.8	90.3	4	-22.9	134	D	2
Saginaw	41.6	41.5	9.4	2.9	18.8	10.7	1 424	28.9	10.3	53.0	79.1	308	-4.5	216	2	277
St. Clair	27.0	51.6	10.2	2.6	20.8	14.3	1 092	30.0	6.0	44.9	86.4	177	-13.9	162	0	149
St. Joseph	51.6	30.2	7.6	1.5	11.6	11.3	880	24.4	13.5	54.0	81.4	214	-3.1	243	59	180
Sanilac	33.3	36.0	9.3	3.0	17.3	14.2	1 559	18.5	14.9	69.7	83.6	431	-2.9	277	2	391
Schoolcraft	18.8	NA	12.2	3.2	NA	26.3	52	23.1	15.4	46.2	88.5	D	D	D	D	9
Shiawassee	29.5	44.0	10.9	2.5	19.7	19.2	1 160	26.2	11.2	50.3	82.6	240	-1.6	207	1	203
Tuscola	20.7	39.9	9.4	1.8	16.8	26.0	1 207	22.9	16.0	55.8	82.4	329	-4.4	272	3	294
Van Buren	24.1	40.7	10.5	1.5	14.9	20.4	1 278	38.4	5.0	49.4	79.5	190	-3.5	149	24	148
Washtenaw	31.7	39.5	7.0	2.4	22.7	24.6	1 222	36.8	7.7	46.6	84.1	204	-8.7	167	4	171
Wayne	36.6	48.1	7.4	5.6	21.0	11.9	334	66.5	1.8	49.7	79.6	22	-40.5	66	1	19
Wexford	36.6	44.5	10.6	3.5	21.3	15.4	178	20.2	5.6	51.7	88.2	31	-22.0	175	0	19
MINNESOTA	22.7	53.7	9.4	6.5	22.9	13.7	85 079	16.6	17.7	68.8	80.0	26 574	-4.1	312	354	21 876
Aitkin	9.0	NA	15.2	3.9	22.3	22.5	640	9.7	12.5	51.2	84.7	178	-2.7	278	6	82
Anoka	31.8	44.5	14.6	2.8	18.6	13.5	579	43.2	4.3	36.8	83.2	74	-11.2	129	3	48
Becker	12.9	NA	11.4	3.0	21.5	18.3	1 220	12.5	18.1	67.4	87.0	397	-6.7	326	2	270
Beltrami	8.2	49.0	12.5	3.2	21.1	32.5	742	9.8	20.4	54.4	85.4	244	-1.1	328	6	135
Benton	29.6	NA	10.9	2.9	14.3	10.4	954	18.3	5.1	64.3	84.3	184	-7.2	193	8	133
Big Stone	2.8	42.4	11.1	5.0	17.5	21.4	504	10.5	43.3	83.9	74.4	277	1.0	550	3	250
Blue Earth	12.3	53.1	11.0	3.9	23.5	21.2	1 280	14.7	19.4	75.8	78.4	402	-2.9	314	1	367
Brown	31.6	41.8	8.2	4.3	16.8	10.0	1 317	15.6	10.1	79.3	77.4	336	-1.0	255	3	308
Carlton	32.2	36.7	8.7	2.6	14.7	22.6	649	13.6	6.6	45.3	88.0	133	-7.2	205	0	66
Carver	41.1	35.1	6.7	2.9	16.7	12.3	1 038	23.6	4.0	64.5	85.1	168	-4.3	161	0	138
Cass	2.4	53.0	13.3	2.9	28.4	32.1	685	12.0	13.4	53.0	86.0	196	-6.4	286	3	90
Chippewa	13.2	46.5	10.6	3.0	18.5	14.9	820	13.4	28.7	79.6	76.3	328	-2.2	400	2	307
Chisago	22.4	46.0	9.6	2.9	25.6	15.9	885	27.3	5.6	44.0	87.6	153	-10.9	173	2	100
Clay	8.4	49.7	11.1	3.2	23.7	22.7	1 017	14.5	40.9	75.5	78.6	589	-3.8	579	4	535
Clearwater	5.8	39.2	9.4	2.9	14.5	29.5	699	8.3	19.6	59.4	83.3	230	7.7	328	7	124
Cook	6.3	54.6	15.6	1.2	27.9	30.0	9	22.2	0.0	11.1	100.0	1	-23.0	143	0	D
Cottonwood	12.2	36.9	7.3	4.1	15.9	14.3	970	12.1	27.2	83.5	74.8	378	-0.3	389	1	344
Crow Wing	14.6	53.2	13.4	4.0	22.6	22.6	585	14.2	9.9	43.9	83.8	132	-8.9	226	1	62
Dakota	22.0	55.6	11.4	5.7	18.3	12.9	986	30.3	11.8	54.3	76.9	220	-8.1	223	39	194
Dodge	16.9	30.9	7.7	2.5	10.6	15.4	830	24.5	16.3	68.0	80.2	239	-11.1	288	D	217
Douglas	18.6	51.5	15.3	3.6	20.7	19.0	1 091	14.8	8.6	70.5	80.7	260	-14.6	239	1	195
Faribault	15.7	32.0	6.4	3.2	12.2	11.4	1 160	12.3	24.7	80.8	76.9	428	0.4	369	D	401
Fillmore	13.1	46.0	10.2	4.1	18.0	15.7	1 695	16.3	14.5	72.4	79.8	451	-7.5	266	D	341
Freeborn	28.6	40.4	11.0	2.9	15.6	10.1	1 358	23.2	18.0	67.9	79.6	384	-6.9	283	2	358
Goodhue	25.6	48.7	9.0	3.4	16.9	12.3	1 686	20.5	11.0	62.2	80.8	390	-4.3	231	2	319
Grant	2.9	42.3	8.2	4.3	15.9	15.6	555	9.9	36.4	82.5	73.3	287	-4.7	517	2	264
Hennepin	19.5	64.8	8.9	9.7	26.6	10.6	852	52.9	4.0	44.5	82.3	91	-17.9	107	2	71

1. Covers mining, construction, and manufacturing. 2. Covers private sector earnings in agricultural services, forestry, and fisheries; transportation and public utilities; wholesale trade; retail trade; finance, insurance, and real estate; and services.

STATE County	Agriculture, 1987 (cont'd): Value of land and buildings: Average per farm ($1,000)	Value of land and buildings: Average per acre (Dollars)	Value of products sold: Total (Mil dol)	Value of products sold: Average per farm (Dollars)	Value of products sold: Percent from: Crops	Value of products sold: Percent from: Livestock and poultry[1]	Percent of farms with sales of: $10,000 or more	Percent of farms with sales of: $100,000 or more	Manufactures, 1987: Establishments: Total	Establishments: Percent with 20 or more employees	All employees: Number (1,000)	All employees: Percent change, 1982–1987	All employees: Annual payroll (Mil dol)	Production workers: Number (1,000)	Production workers: Work hours (Mil)
	119	120	121	122	123	124	125	126	127	128	129	130	131	132	133
MICHIGAN—Con.															
Livingston	222	1 329	30	38 552	45.7	54.3	35.6	10.3	183	35.0	5.6	43.6	123.9	4.0	8.2
Luce	139	443	1	25 311	42.0	58.0	44.1	8.8	23	17.4	0.3	200.0	5.0	0.2	0.5
Mackinac	119	389	3	33 163	8.1	92.0	41.2	8.8	16	12.5	0.1	0.0	1.7	0.1	0.2
Macomb	233	2 017	30	45 683	83.6	16.4	48.9	13.0	2 061	34.0	110.8	25.5	3 680.4	69.7	149.1
Manistee	134	799	9	33 465	87.7	12.3	31.1	8.6	39	25.6	1.7	6.2	40.0	1.3	2.5
Marquette	114	504	2	17 651	49.2	50.8	19.8	5.9	54	16.7	0.9	28.6	16.2	0.6	1.1
Mason	136	713	16	36 889	53.5	46.5	45.8	9.9	47	42.6	1.9	0.0	43.4	1.4	2.7
Mecosta	114	677	19	29 794	24.5	75.4	38.7	9.4	40	30.0	1.5	7.1	29.1	1.2	2.5
Menominee	143	474	18	47 779	6.3	93.7	47.3	13.6	78	33.3	2.8	3.7	49.8	2.3	4.3
Midland	184	953	15	33 394	64.3	35.7	43.1	7.2	52	42.3	D	D	D	D	D
Missaukee	181	630	23	74 840	6.9	93.1	59.5	29.9	29	10.3	0.3	50.0	5.2	0.2	0.4
Monroe	232	1 363	59	46 816	77.7	22.3	49.5	9.8	118	36.4	8.3	9.2	283.0	5.5	11.5
Montcalm	175	743	49	49 698	58.2	41.8	47.8	13.5	71	32.4	6.5	16.1	159.6	5.3	10.7
Montmorency	141	635	3	23 559	24.5	75.5	34.3	4.6	16	25.0	0.3	50.0	4.2	0.2	0.4
Muskegon	186	1 001	27	57 621	57.0	43.0	42.6	14.3	275	36.7	17.7	6.0	481.7	12.0	24.1
Newaygo	143	802	32	46 138	40.6	59.4	45.0	12.8	41	24.4	2.4	26.3	62.2	1.3	2.7
Oakland	212	2 405	22	37 171	84.2	15.8	28.5	5.7	2 529	34.4	111.3	19.3	3 507.3	69.1	141.1
Oceana	200	991	35	51 665	66.0	34.0	48.8	13.1	45	26.7	1.0	25.0	15.1	0.8	1.5
Ogemaw	193	747	12	41 704	16.0	84.0	44.8	13.2	42	31.0	0.9	28.6	16.7	0.7	1.4
Ontonagon	112	370	2	17 888	25.5	74.5	33.3	3.4	20	5.0	D	D	D	D	D
Osceola	157	720	16	31 654	9.2	90.8	34.6	9.9	31	35.5	1.5	-16.7	32.1	1.3	2.5
Oscoda	145	710	3	30 935	4.1	95.9	53.6	8.3	26	23.1	0.6	100.0	8.6	0.5	1.1
Otsego	164	525	3	22 070	35.5	64.5	45.9	6.0	38	26.3	1.2	71.4	27.0	0.9	1.8
Ottawa	207	1 754	183	124 378	43.0	57.0	53.9	21.9	463	39.7	27.7	31.9	653.1	19.5	39.6
Presque Isle	139	510	12	39 462	53.4	46.6	45.1	11.9	27	7.4	0.2	0.0	2.7	0.2	0.3
Roscommon	111	824	0	6 090	41.8	58.2	12.9	0.0	29	17.2	0.3	50.0	5.7	0.3	0.5
Saginaw	230	1 050	63	44 496	78.8	21.2	58.5	11.8	227	37.4	24.8	10.2	911.8	18.8	39.7
St. Clair	175	1 099	36	33 420	51.4	48.6	38.8	6.3	235	37.0	9.6	18.5	222.2	6.9	14.3
St. Joseph	248	1 039	46	52 321	59.3	40.7	57.3	14.9	150	46.7	9.0	-2.2	228.0	6.8	13.2
Sanilac	214	764	98	62 561	41.9	58.1	62.3	18.8	76	39.5	3.9	50.0	72.1	3.2	6.9
Schoolcraft	110	376	1	17 995	25.0	75.0	44.2	1.9	25	8.0	0.4	33.3	8.4	0.3	0.6
Shiawassee	178	873	38	33 125	51.9	48.1	49.3	9.2	81	55.6	4.1	5.1	91.2	2.9	5.7
Tuscola	279	1 000	75	62 230	69.8	30.2	58.1	18.3	62	32.3	2.4	9.1	53.3	1.7	3.5
Van Buren	165	1 121	70	54 479	76.2	23.8	45.5	10.3	123	38.2	3.9	-9.3	76.7	3.0	5.8
Washtenaw	253	1 523	48	39 032	41.5	58.5	41.4	11.0	428	39.3	39.5	31.7	1 322.8	27.4	55.0
Wayne	211	3 560	17	50 292	97.1	2.9	38.0	9.0	2 843	36.2	229.7	1.0	8 379.0	116.2	239.3
Wexford	97	599	3	17 733	22.8	77.2	30.9	5.1	66	31.8	3.4	47.8	69.9	2.6	5.6
MINNESOTA	219	700	5 676	66 719	44.1	55.9	68.6	19.3	7 112	34.1	374.2	6.4	10 141.7	214.9	428.0
Aitkin	155	550	18	27 456	26.6	73.4	32.8	5.0	27	11.1	0.3	-25.0	3.9	0.2	0.3
Anoka	210	1 564	21	36 095	57.3	42.7	30.2	7.1	404	31.4	19.3	0.0	569.6	11.4	22.5
Becker	180	521	75	61 092	22.0	78.0	57.5	11.5	37	24.3	1.4	75.0	20.5	1.2	2.3
Beltrami	125	404	18	24 446	34.4	65.6	42.0	5.1	53	13.2	0.8	-11.1	13.8	0.7	1.3
Benton	132	702	65	68 259	10.7	89.3	60.3	16.6	34	35.3	1.9	-5.0	46.6	1.5	3.4
Big Stone	279	497	38	74 743	59.9	40.1	83.9	21.8	2	0.0	D	D	D	D	D
Blue Earth	299	948	111	86 750	55.3	44.7	82.9	27.4	83	39.8	3.3	0.0	73.4	2.0	3.8
Brown	242	953	105	79 993	41.1	58.9	86.0	26.9	47	53.2	3.6	5.9	73.3	2.6	5.0
Carlton	84	434	10	16 162	15.0	85.0	31.6	2.2	42	23.8	D	D	D	D	D
Carver	190	1 216	58	56 341	21.6	78.4	67.2	19.9	91	46.2	5.0	78.6	128.2	3.2	6.7
Cass	108	360	14	19 987	10.8	89.2	42.3	3.4	33	9.1	0.3	0.0	4.7	0.3	0.4
Chippewa	248	649	69	84 292	75.8	24.2	85.0	24.6	24	29.2	0.6	50.0	9.7	0.4	0.8
Chisago	164	962	26	28 955	40.8	59.2	34.7	6.9	49	36.7	1.7	21.4	28.8	1.4	2.6
Clay	381	629	103	101 342	77.7	22.3	77.4	29.0	33	21.2	0.9	-18.2	22.3	0.6	1.1
Clearwater	151	407	25	35 210	24.3	75.7	48.6	4.6	13	15.4	0.1	0.0	1.3	0.1	0.2
Cook	109	765	0	2 990	D	D	0.0	0.0	11	9.1	0.1	0.0	1.8	0.1	0.2
Cottonwood	312	822	109	112 318	47.3	52.7	87.7	33.3	15	33.3	D	D	D	D	D
Crow Wing	96	455	12	19 663	19.2	80.8	30.8	5.3	59	22.0	1.8	20.0	43.4	1.3	2.4
Dakota	291	1 219	64	65 364	51.6	48.4	63.0	19.6	339	36.6	15.2	-9.0	420.0	8.2	16.4
Dodge	239	801	72	87 107	43.6	56.4	74.7	26.4	18	22.2	D	D	D	D	D
Douglas	138	581	44	40 571	22.6	77.4	63.8	12.1	42	26.2	1.3	0.0	26.6	1.0	1.9
Faribault	345	949	113	97 458	61.2	38.8	90.3	31.4	36	33.3	1.9	18.7	30.4	1.6	3.2
Fillmore	163	630	110	65 186	27.8	72.2	74.5	20.8	28	25.0	1.0	66.7	14.7	0.9	1.5
Freeborn	242	861	112	82 785	55.5	44.5	78.0	25.6	62	41.9	4.2	2.4	86.6	3.3	7.0
Goodhue	207	897	111	65 801	32.1	67.9	69.2	23.8	59	44.1	4.1	10.8	83.3	3.0	5.9
Grant	284	556	43	77 400	69.4	30.6	82.3	24.5	8	0.0	0.0	0.0	0.6	0.0	0.1
Hennepin	238	2 339	34	40 425	53.6	46.4	39.3	10.3	2 357	37.3	122.0	1.2	3 566.9	61.0	120.3

1. Includes livestock and poultry products.

STATE County	Manufactures, 1987 (cont'd): Production workers (cont'd): Wages: Total (Mil dol)	Manufactures, 1987 (cont'd): Production workers (cont'd): Wages: Average per worker (Dollars)	Manufactures, 1987 (cont'd): Value added by manufacture (Mil dol)	Manufactures, 1987 (cont'd): Value of shipments (Mil dol)	Manufactures, 1987 (cont'd): New capital expenditures (Mil dol)	Value of construction authorized by building permits, 1990: Total[1] ($1,000)	Nonresidential: Total ($1,000)	Nonresidential: Percent: Office	Nonresidential: Percent: Industrial	Nonresidential: Percent: Stores	Residential: New construction ($1,000)	Residential: Number of housing units	Residential: Alterations and additions ($1,000)
	134	135	136	137	138	139	140	141	142	143	144	145	146
MICHIGAN—Con.													
Livingston	76.6	19 150	268.4	587.2	26.0	141 186	16 604	14.5	59.6	16.1	94 004	1 442	5 832
Luce	3.6	18 000	12.9	28.6	1.0	2 017	1 223	0.0	0.0	53.7	665	31	57
Mackinac	1.2	12 000	5.2	9.4	0.1	8 088	1 167	0.0	65.2	0.0	4 728	70	802
Macomb	1 999.8	28 692	5 753.9	15 626.6	351.1	436 472	122 775	7.1	40.6	35.3	254 740	3 525	22 908
Manistee	30.9	23 769	134.5	233.4	6.7	8 401	896	0.0	0.0	26.8	4 739	82	1 186
Marquette	11.4	19 000	36.4	68.2	2.0	44 275	7 542	23.2	7.1	8.9	11 965	244	1 753
Mason	26.8	19 143	130.1	227.9	5.1	18 112	7 920	0.8	14.4	56.9	6 135	130	1 762
Mecosta	20.4	17 000	55.8	129.1	3.7	8 475	1 842	0.0	0.0	98.9	5 835	206	276
Menominee	37.0	16 087	136.4	287.4	5.3	14 946	9 125	6.0	60.9	18.3	3 473	93	509
Midland	D	D	D	D	D	77 429	23 977	17.6	7.2	61.0	38 560	457	3 453
Missaukee	3.6	18 000	19.0	38.6	0.7	6 032	1 625	0.0	1.0	21.8	2 736	53	892
Monroe	178.3	32 418	635.1	1 400.4	D	87 828	13 030	3.4	26.4	12.2	43 511	677	15 401
Montcalm	121.1	22 849	345.4	786.8	17.9	21 191	5 511	13.8	11.9	10.4	11 086	188	2 267
Montmorency	3.2	16 000	9.1	14.5	0.6	5 666	431	0.0	17.4	0.0	3 923	103	716
Muskegon	291.4	24 283	1 151.6	1 999.1	121.4	86 146	17 710	13.9	24.0	33.9	47 449	691	9 433
Newaygo	27.0	20 769	162.8	314.7	10.3	12 251	1 276	0.0	7.1	18.7	5 945	142	1 785
Oakland	1 901.0	27 511	8 437.0	22 001.9	408.9	1 004 713	207 478	42.2	23.3	20.3	517 357	6 001	83 821
Oceana	10.3	12 875	53.4	103.5	9.1	12 849	3 041	0.5	29.6	19.7	6 665	105	1 455
Ogemaw	11.9	17 000	50.1	97.9	2.3	8 526	2 889	8.1	0.0	86.5	3 903	99	1 062
Ontonagon	D	D	D	D	D	3 989	1 270	5.9	23.6	4.7	854	22	280
Osceola	22.3	17 154	39.6	175.9	14.1	5 164	1 365	5.5	30.6	33.9	2 310	73	848
Oscoda	6.6	13 200	17.2	44.7	D	7 768	858	0.0	0.0	0.0	3 060	49	674
Otsego	18.9	21 000	66.9	129.7	2.5	13 964	0	NA	NA	NA	12 012	213	48
Ottawa	393.5	20 179	1 588.7	3 078.7	100.8	217 288	39 538	26.9	27.0	14.5	131 180	1 801	11 547
Presque Isle	2.1	10 500	6.9	18.8	0.5	9 719	2 450	6.1	2.2	17.4	4 977	98	1 040
Roscommon	4.0	13 333	9.5	26.9	1.0	18 017	1 385	2.5	2.2	4.2	12 430	306	2 807
Saginaw	674.6	35 883	1 789.1	3 507.4	193.5	70 135	19 368	10.1	14.4	57.6	29 949	404	5 794
St. Clair	133.7	19 377	490.1	1 069.5	39.2	115 402	31 604	20.2	5.1	42.3	66 241	922	6 556
St. Joseph	156.6	23 029	768.0	1 373.2	30.1	22 692	6 205	13.5	40.4	16.7	10 178	150	2 109
Sanilac	52.2	16 312	161.0	342.2	6.8	19 731	3 682	8.8	0.0	3.3	12 240	197	2 465
Schoolcraft	6.7	22 333	26.2	42.7	1.3	2 646	75	0.0	0.0	9.3	1 542	73	352
Shiawassee	55.0	18 966	181.9	346.7	15.9	23 596	2 721	0.0	0.0	35.6	14 750	186	2 185
Tuscola	31.8	18 706	108.4	258.3	11.9	12 709	2 986	14.8	0.3	11.9	6 836	123	2 090
Van Buren	53.6	17 867	248.1	517.2	17.5	22 576	6 909	3.6	46.9	27.9	11 824	277	1 859
Washtenaw	866.9	31 639	2 901.2	7 348.1	227.1	246 672	54 311	36.5	32.3	19.9	136 665	1 809	19 569
Wayne	3 559.7	30 634	12 335.3	33 860.8	1 147.2	879 834	365 221	40.2	15.7	17.2	239 993	3 131	87 764
Wexford	46.9	18 038	148.4	327.5	9.5	13 430	4 290	54.1	1.7	4.1	5 369	97	914
MINNESOTA	4 512.7	20 999	23 322.1	47 774.1	1 765.5	4 206 793	1 120 736	40.6	12.6	25.5	1 881 458	23 713	303 688
Aitkin	2.5	12 500	9.0	18.8	0.4	15 340	5 200	0.0	0.0	27.2	8 704	142	13
Anoka	298.1	26 149	1 051.9	1 878.6	83.3	251 998	45 086	14.2	22.4	33.0	167 617	2 102	10 745
Becker	15.4	12 833	52.5	155.6	3.8	21 593	12 302	1.2	3.2	86.4	5 243	106	2 004
Beltrami	10.3	14 714	39.2	75.6	1.4	8 287	3 044	3.1	19.1	7.0	2 548	68	478
Benton	29.5	19 667	163.0	300.0	D	20 417	2 537	0.4	34.8	3.5	15 633	347	1 152
Big Stone	D	D	D	D	D	2 212	835	0.0	0.0	51.2	180	4	115
Blue Earth	38.4	19 200	219.2	629.4	15.6	34 735	17 778	0.0	13.4	74.1	9 161	180	2 403
Brown	46.1	17 731	374.5	934.9	19.5	16 163	2 234	0.0	10.1	27.8	4 036	55	1 374
Carlton	D	D	D	D	D	10 567	2 679	0.0	82.1	2.6	3 259	49	1 107
Carver	67.2	21 000	362.0	751.0	30.1	85 212	15 922	34.3	53.2	1.3	56 393	491	4 127
Cass	3.5	11 667	9.9	25.4	0.6	6 451	853	45.0	0.0	26.2	2 969	47	849
Chippewa	6.2	15 500	19.4	35.5	D	2 807	1 598	0.0	42.6	0.0	982	15	119
Chisago	20.0	14 286	74.0	147.7	D	33 551	3 485	0.0	17.4	11.2	26 473	346	1 704
Clay	11.1	18 500	27.2	104.4	D	28 408	7 723	0.2	7.7	77.4	9 362	171	1 791
Clearwater	1.0	10 000	2.2	6.0	0.2	1 574	927	11.9	0.0	80.3	125	2	0
Cook	1.3	13 000	3.2	6.2	0.1	4 472	457	0.0	0.0	72.2	2 515	64	533
Cottonwood	D	D	D	D	D	2 073	1 016	0.0	5.7	0.0	594	13	201
Crow Wing	30.7	23 615	136.0	260.0	5.0	114 366	18 853	2.7	0.0	65.3	56 156	892	24 768
Dakota	173.0	21 098	1 200.9	3 143.8	51.5	402 833	74 474	43.5	11.4	38.0	270 790	2 857	15 025
Dodge	D	D	D	D	D	7 991	436	0.0	11.5	27.7	5 653	90	276
Douglas	18.2	18 200	90.7	208.8	3.3	22 345	4 475	9.9	5.6	47.4	13 098	165	1 835
Faribault	21.2	13 250	101.3	256.7	3.3	3 232	1 375	11.0	30.2	0.0	797	12	398
Fillmore	10.8	12 000	29.0	79.6	2.8	4 278	181	0.0	0.0	24.8	3 383	68	129
Freeborn	62.2	18 848	194.5	637.0	D	9 523	356	0.0	4.2	9.8	3 444	48	1 867
Goodhue	49.6	16 533	213.7	567.2	10.0	23 765	4 184	5.9	5.3	5.5	14 571	268	2 364
Grant	0.4	NA	1.4	2.6	0.1	384	8	0.0	0.0	0.0	138	2	63
Hennepin	1 345.5	22 057	7 034.6	11 865.2	484.6	1 325 851	516 563	65.2	4.5	14.0	387 663	4 290	112 886

1. Includes nonresidential additions and alterations, residential nonhousekeeping buildings, and residential garages and carports not shown separately.

STATE County	Wholesale trade, 1987: Estab-lishments	Wholesale trade, 1987: Sales (Mil dol)	Wholesale trade, 1987: Paid employees[1]	Wholesale trade, 1987: Annual payroll (Mil dol)	Retail trade, all establishments, 1987: Number	Retail trade, all establishments, 1987: Sales: Total (Mil dol)	Retail trade, all establishments, 1987: Sales: Percent change, 1982–1987	Retail trade, all establishments, 1987: Sales: Per capita[2] (Dollars)	Retail trade, establishments with payroll, 1987: Number	Retail trade, establishments with payroll, 1987: Sales: Total (Mil dol)	Per capita[2] (Dollars): General merchan-dise stores	Per capita[2] (Dollars): Food stores	Per capita[2] (Dollars): Apparel & acces-sory stores	Per capita[2] (Dollars): Eating and drinking places
	147	148	149	150	151	152	153	154	155	156	157	158	159	160
MICHIGAN—Con.														
Livingston	130	290.4	1 297	28.8	760	468.2	51.6	4 268	447	454.2	743	767	58	394
Luce	13	8.3	47	0.7	84	34.4	42.1	5 927	48	31.8	D	1 733	D	387
Mackinac	19	22.0	51	0.9	248	69.7	41.7	6 705	183	67.7	D	1 948	280	1 107
Macomb	984	3 470.1	11 629	290.4	6 028	5 536.4	54.7	7 842	3 934	5 419.9	1 077	1 275	366	724
Manistee	28	57.3	287	4.5	300	115.9	42.0	5 221	197	110.6	D	1 316	267	455
Marquette	102	207.4	865	18.8	658	394.1	55.0	5 614	464	385.2	710	1 120	221	546
Mason	30	36.0	175	3.7	323	131.6	40.7	5 060	216	126.9	D	1 232	211	517
Mecosta	32	34.3	164	2.6	371	180.2	41.9	4 743	243	175.7	313	1 008	263	442
Menominee	39	82.9	354	6.7	279	80.6	29.0	3 101	147	73.7	D	480	57	436
Midland	68	124.1	488	10.9	589	329.2	13.7	4 448	389	322.4	358	990	197	491
Missaukee	20	21.4	95	1.3	102	44.8	74.3	3 966	54	42.7	389	733	0	244
Monroe	106	421.4	979	23.1	911	531.5	37.8	3 919	528	511.7	272	900	79	367
Montcalm	52	85.4	337	5.7	490	260.5	41.7	5 000	294	250.4	D	1 068	66	283
Montmorency	8	1.1	12	0.2	122	32.7	31.9	3 984	71	30.0	D	1 529	D	520
Muskegon	179	776.3	1 966	41.5	1 339	860.4	46.0	5 384	912	837.6	1 079	977	159	553
Newaygo	35	53.8	338	5.8	321	139.3	54.6	3 600	198	132.6	215	930	90	246
Oakland	3 521	33 116.9	44 224	1 336.6	10 673	9 452.1	58.2	9 049	7 057	9 245.7	1 187	1 238	710	866
Oceana	21	32.6	102	2.4	273	84.7	57.4	3 715	155	77.8	70	1 346	123	273
Ogemaw	28	41.8	199	4.3	227	100.1	26.1	5 563	139	95.3	D	1 344	134	598
Ontonagon	8	13.2	28	0.4	132	44.9	34.4	4 884	82	41.4	D	967	73	350
Osceola	21	21.9	91	1.2	223	70.3	24.0	3 394	123	65.3	D	1 128	26	255
Oscoda	2	D	D	D	112	28.5	19.2	4 016	62	26.1	D	1 418	41	345
Otsego	39	112.6	346	6.2	225	123.6	47.5	7 534	154	119.3	D	897	233	736
Ottawa	273	746.9	2 459	54.5	1 562	977.9	59.4	5 578	922	946.4	D	764	207	460
Presque Isle	14	8.4	75	0.8	168	58.2	49.2	4 130	99	53.8	141	1 181	27	254
Roscommon	22	15.4	78	1.2	340	133.8	55.2	6 759	206	126.7	D	1 601	119	811
Saginaw	342	1 383.9	3 939	91.9	1 924	1 529.6	41.5	7 085	1 344	1 505.6	1 292	1 076	424	671
St. Clair	155	323.0	1 341	28.5	1 144	702.1	46.4	4 883	728	682.2	482	1 038	197	433
St. Joseph	78	538.9	1 046	24.8	572	274.8	33.4	4 610	364	265.6	403	1 134	152	404
Sanilac	58	96.9	286	4.3	459	180.4	55.9	4 379	249	166.7	173	1 050	86	240
Schoolcraft	14	12.3	67	0.9	146	43.9	43.9	5 287	95	42.0	D	1 424	240	451
Shiawassee	86	191.0	565	10.6	582	333.2	51.5	4 733	356	325.5	372	1 087	105	351
Tuscola	63	211.3	430	7.2	521	215.5	32.0	3 835	318	207.1	184	1 081	95	234
Van Buren	74	143.4	813	11.5	663	303.7	46.3	4 439	377	292.9	194	1 172	62	395
Washtenaw	376	986.0	3 813	84.0	2 231	2 017.9	52.8	7 635	1 565	1 988.7	1 118	1 130	392	806
Wayne	2 782	21 813.6	41 073	1 065.6	14 311	11 525.4	36.2	5 362	10 221	11 320.0	696	955	291	574
Wexford	49	112.4	479	10.4	338	200.7	63.4	7 459	220	193.3	D	1 610	341	584
MINNESOTA	9 478	55 276.7	114 343	2 822.7	42 874	28 007.7	42.9	6 599	27 005	27 279.8	806	1 152	286	609
Aitkin	14	14.8	84	0.9	183	52.8	13.8	4 063	82	46.7	96	734	81	478
Anoka	238	936.5	2 658	70.2	1 629	1 345.2	73.9	5 916	943	1 315.2	951	1 073	166	494
Becker	43	59.1	385	4.9	341	142.7	43.4	4 837	190	135.6	D	906	312	386
Beltrami	51	75.6	392	7.8	421	220.2	40.5	6 694	285	210.9	614	1 270	466	578
Benton	42	226.1	1 032	18.1	210	90.3	19.6	3 273	122	86.4	D	791	93	360
Big Stone	23	67.2	250	3.4	123	32.6	8.7	4 527	71	30.3	D	885	231	346
Blue Earth	155	491.3	1 696	34.2	590	420.2	43.7	8 305	404	410.5	995	1 917	430	762
Brown	61	147.6	487	8.5	327	140.6	19.6	5 075	218	136.5	429	1 367	295	491
Carlton	27	78.9	247	4.8	319	149.7	22.5	5 057	198	143.4	D	1 095	123	496
Carver	58	48.3	246	3.8	308	151.0	53.5	3 571	180	145.2	D	906	23	571
Cass	14	47.8	146	1.6	309	93.0	36.8	4 284	183	86.7	19	927	112	430
Chippewa	51	136.0	372	6.5	184	74.1	37.2	5 328	117	71.7	D	928	228	415
Chisago	27	75.5	302	7.3	292	126.9	43.1	4 436	161	121.5	24	1 192	51	370
Clay	78	241.3	557	10.5	446	245.6	30.7	5 128	284	240.1	D	1 082	120	512
Clearwater	14	13.8	57	0.8	103	26.6	16.7	3 025	62	24.7	D	936	D	166
Cook	3	1.5	7	0.1	94	27.1	23.7	6 773	58	25.4	D	1 426	D	1 158
Cottonwood	41	138.3	295	5.2	154	54.0	-4.1	3 944	98	51.3	D	641	102	319
Crow Wing	72	106.8	499	7.5	697	341.6	55.8	7 676	445	328.9	1 631	1 254	206	683
Dakota	478	3 444.8	7 578	202.4	1 983	1 709.3	72.0	7 128	1 252	1 680.8	1 132	1 354	354	587
Dodge	25	106.1	265	5.5	153	40.0	24.6	2 615	80	37.6	90	734	D	231
Douglas	56	76.7	359	5.5	411	188.6	44.4	6 481	280	181.1	621	1 252	387	587
Faribault	53	148.7	295	4.9	244	62.6	-14.1	3 477	144	58.2	D	765	98	221
Fillmore	65	196.2	458	7.5	292	86.1	4.1	4 061	158	79.3	43	909	33	209
Freeborn	90	779.4	824	15.2	418	218.8	30.3	6 396	237	207.4	680	1 120	327	440
Goodhue	76	152.9	719	13.3	479	216.3	30.7	5 447	313	210.3	325	1 311	438	436
Grant	26	72.7	218	3.7	107	25.1	32.8	3 805	49	22.5	0	578	D	180
Hennepin	3 569	33 624.6	53 970	1 520.1	9 430	8 436.4	43.9	8 464	6 187	8 300.9	1 233	1 295	458	899

1. For pay period including March 12. 2. Based on the estimated population as of July 1 of the year shown.

STATE County	Retail trade, establishments with payroll, 1987 (cont'd)		Taxable service industries–establishments with payroll, 1987							Bank deposits,[2] June 1989		Savings capital,[3] September 1989	
				Receipts (Mil dol)									
					Selected kinds of business								
	Paid employees[1]	Annual payroll (Mil dol)	Number	Total	Hotels, motels and other lodging places	Health services	Legal services	Paid employees	Annual payroll (Mil dol)	Total (Mil dol)	Percent change, 1988–1989	Total (Mil dol)	Percent change, 1988–1989
	161	162	163	164	165	166	167	168	169	170	171	172	173
MICHIGAN—Con.													
Livingston	5 682	52.1	558	170.6	6.2	37.5	6.0	5 737	70.5	506	9.4	189.0	0.6
Luce	368	3.3	43	4.4	0.8	D	0.2	142	1.2	43	4.1	0.0	NA
Mackinac	691	7.8	91	19.7	11.6	D	D	426	6.4	74	2.6	0.0	NA
Macomb	61 861	615.3	4 385	1 904.2	23.3	519.3	65.1	41 823	791.8	5 628	8.7	2 474.7	5.1
Manistee	1 238	11.6	137	24.7	7.8	6.9	1.1	721	7.5	172	-6.1	17.3	-6.6
Marquette	5 183	41.9	386	110.7	7.1	51.8	7.0	2 668	48.2	426	-1.0	77.1	1.1
Mason	1 594	13.8	174	31.0	4.4	11.8	1.6	813	10.4	162	3.9	58.3	4.9
Mecosta	2 351	18.3	144	29.5	D	12.0	1.9	920	11.2	165	3.3	26.5	-22.4
Menominee	1 268	8.3	87	17.6	D	4.9	0.9	494	6.5	161	13.6	21.2	6.8
Midland	4 245	38.7	376	128.7	6.6	48.3	4.4	3 377	54.7	456	-2.0	117.3	-5.6
Missaukee	375	3.8	33	8.7	D	2.7	D	469	4.1	64	1.2	0.0	NA
Monroe	5 547	55.8	468	135.8	6.6	49.0	6.7	4 393	53.0	831	9.9	271.0	-2.8
Montcalm	2 621	25.0	216	39.9	0.9	14.4	1.6	1 279	13.1	316	6.6	20.5	-9.2
Montmorency	419	3.2	32	6.7	0.6	1.9	D	223	2.6	68	6.1	0.0	NA
Muskegon	10 831	96.4	807	236.1	12.0	94.1	17.6	6 281	95.9	884	5.2	144.7	-9.8
Newaygo	1 460	14.0	108	21.1	D	10.7	1.4	784	7.4	188	7.0	13.5	-10.0
Oakland	106 084	1 138.8	11 583	6 865.7	124.5	1 332.9	520.8	131 175	2 821.8	9 801	8.1	4 837.5	5.3
Oceana	827	8.0	84	18.4	1.6	3.8	1.0	385	5.4	119	5.9	17.6	1.6
Ogemaw	1 359	9.9	90	18.2	1.9	10.0	1.0	646	6.9	101	-7.7	18.6	-13.4
Ontonagon	484	3.8	41	6.2	0.6	3.3	D	179	2.0	71	22.1	0.0	NA
Osceola	788	6.7	57	8.2	D	2.6	0.5	207	2.5	115	2.0	5.9	-24.9
Oscoda	364	2.8	29	3.9	0.2	1.6	D	106	1.0	34	10.4	3.9	-11.6
Otsego	1 381	12.5	141	41.3	9.8	12.8	4.5	1 101	14.5	148	4.4	18.9	-7.9
Ottawa	11 856	109.0	921	275.0	8.1	77.4	11.5	9 097	111.2	1 440	12.0	230.1	-3.6
Presque Isle	545	5.2	65	7.9	0.6	3.2	0.5	265	2.6	88	6.0	11.9	-4.1
Roscommon	1 646	14.4	118	19.2	3.1	6.2	0.8	485	5.0	137	2.8	13.0	-2.2
Saginaw	18 412	174.0	1 249	429.0	22.2	165.2	31.5	10 161	178.7	1 186	6.2	534.3	-8.5
St. Clair	8 362	80.9	653	161.3	3.9	68.3	10.5	3 487	61.2	890	4.4	225.9	3.0
St. Joseph	3 279	28.3	267	70.2	5.1	17.2	3.4	1 907	22.2	363	-0.7	116.7	-7.9
Sanilac	1 813	16.7	154	24.4	1.3	8.9	2.6	618	6.9	260	-1.2	75.9	6.4
Schoolcraft	445	4.3	47	12.1	6.7	2.1	D	350	2.9	74	5.9	0.0	NA
Shiawassee	3 509	33.8	298	68.5	D	23.8	3.6	1 573	24.5	396	3.0	95.8	-6.9
Tuscola	2 445	20.6	182	29.0	0.5	13.5	0.8	897	9.6	319	1.2	61.8	-2.7
Van Buren	3 221	30.2	271	62.8	3.0	14.9	2.7	1 651	20.3	332	10.5	120.8	-4.1
Washtenaw	24 301	249.6	2 143	941.3	36.1	209.3	43.6	22 266	386.1	1 832	7.0	855.5	-3.6
Wayne	133 969	1 358.3	10 296	5 607.7	197.9	1 292.3	553.3	117 739	2 139.0	21 302	6.4	6 003.3	-1.7
Wexford	2 125	20.5	166	52.8	7.3	17.8	4.4	1 380	18.8	227	7.6	10.4	-22.3
MINNESOTA	347 038	3 085.8	26 458	11 621.0	653.9	2 853.5	986.9	294 807	4 591.6	39 049	1.9	10 247.0	-1.4
Aitkin	577	4.7	44	7.8	0.6	3.3	0.5	263	2.5	70	3.9	17.0	-7.9
Anoka	15 412	139.2	1 034	325.2	1.8	125.6	14.9	8 458	124.9	669	8.0	385.2	5.1
Becker	1 639	14.6	157	45.5	4.0	22.4	2.0	1 373	15.0	164	1.8	67.0	15.9
Beltrami	2 780	23.3	171	42.4	6.5	14.7	3.4	1 039	14.5	246	5.4	50.4	0.6
Benton	1 305	10.1	96	21.7	D	6.7	D	719	7.7	176	2.9	23.0	6.9
Big Stone	463	3.3	36	4.6	D	1.7	0.6	136	1.2	81	1.9	0.0	-100.0
Blue Earth	5 921	47.5	364	126.0	4.1	46.8	9.5	3 501	51.9	485	-1.4	163.9	-2.4
Brown	2 286	16.1	144	32.1	3.3	9.8	6.0	917	12.1	382	6.7	60.4	-6.8
Carlton	1 769	14.9	113	19.9	1.0	8.6	1.6	559	6.8	125	8.6	19.5	-6.5
Carver	2 383	17.9	209	89.2	D	22.2	1.8	2 287	37.0	311	4.2	68.8	0.3
Cass	976	8.5	105	18.4	9.8	3.8	0.9	476	5.6	108	1.3	20.7	2.1
Chippewa	907	7.0	60	13.2	0.5	3.8	D	339	4.6	180	1.1	22.4	-23.9
Chisago	1 359	11.1	108	19.9	0.6	7.5	1.4	826	7.5	159	9.3	27.3	-5.8
Clay	3 417	27.3	229	50.7	D	16.1	8.4	1 561	18.1	300	6.7	43.4	-5.3
Clearwater	322	2.4	33	5.0	0.2	2.7	D	167	1.5	57	6.1	13.9	5.7
Cook	389	3.3	45	9.4	6.7	D	0.2	282	2.4	20	4.3	0.0	NA
Cottonwood	764	4.9	74	12.9	0.2	4.7	0.5	437	4.9	136	-5.2	65.8	2.5
Crow Wing	3 738	33.2	285	86.6	26.3	22.7	2.6	2 382	27.9	341	7.3	82.8	-6.9
Dakota	20 799	185.2	1 388	705.0	8.9	144.5	18.5	15 678	262.6	1 042	7.5	428.2	0.7
Dodge	574	4.1	55	24.7	D	1.4	0.3	269	3.6	104	-0.9	0.0	-100.0
Douglas	2 297	19.5	203	48.4	12.8	18.3	2.4	1 164	17.3	260	1.7	70.0	-12.5
Faribault	913	6.5	76	10.8	D	4.1	1.3	277	3.8	207	0.2	98.0	5.1
Fillmore	1 027	7.9	96	15.2	D	5.8	1.8	539	4.8	221	-4.1	71.9	3.3
Freeborn	2 457	21.9	156	36.9	3.7	15.1	2.5	1 087	13.8	257	-0.2	129.5	-3.4
Goodhue	3 006	22.7	220	63.2	5.0	30.8	2.7	1 956	20.4	372	2.6	57.3	-3.5
Grant	255	2.0	30	5.5	D	3.2	0.4	218	2.2	76	-3.9	13.7	1.3
Hennepin	106 929	1 033.8	9 494	6 043.9	312.0	1 145.0	609.9	139 567	2 478.4	15 271	4.0	3 459.2	-3.7

1. For the period including March 12 of the year shown. 2. Includes deposits for all insured and reporting noninsured commercial and mutual savings banks. 3. Includes savings capital for all FSLIC insured savings institutions.

STATE County	Federal funds and grants, 1989: Expenditures: Total (Mil dol)	Expenditures: Percent change, 1988–1989	Per capita[1] (Dollars): Total	Per capita: Direct payments for individuals	Per capita: Procurement contract awards	Per capita: Salaries and wages	Per capita: Grant awards	Local government finances, 1981–1982: General revenue: Total (Mil dol)	Intergovernmental: Total (Mil dol)	Intergovernmental: Percent from state	Taxes: Total (Mil dol)	Taxes: Per capita[2]: Total (Dollars)	Taxes: Per capita[2]: Property (Dollars)	Direct general expenditure: Total (Mil dol)	Direct general expenditure: Percent change, 1977–1982
	174	175	176	177	178	179	180	181	182	183	184	185	186	187	188
MICHIGAN—Con.															
Livingston	134.8	5.6	1 150	897	16	66	130	87.1	26.5	86.1	47.1	470	467	88.7	71.2
Luce	20.1	5.5	3 472	2 693	13	90	657	8.4	4.8	81.7	2.6	412	406	8.7	50.3
Mackinac	32.8	-10.0	3 063	2 219	49	290	486	13.9	5.0	92.8	5.6	553	540	11.9	40.0
Macomb	2 091.5	16.0	2 946	1 633	670	452	184	798.9	225.8	76.2	432.1	628	624	770.0	45.0
Manistee	66.7	13.5	2 977	2 272	72	133	416	28.3	7.1	89.1	10.2	457	452	28.7	66.2
Marquette	277.3	19.8	3 990	1 753	448	1 381	392	74.8	27.6	79.3	33.8	464	425	79.8	67.7
Mason	78.5	7.5	2 986	2 068	81	133	583	31.9	8.8	84.1	16.7	631	626	31.5	43.9
Mecosta	79.5	6.8	2 066	1 572	20	98	277	35.1	7.9	86.3	12.9	349	328	34.1	89.0
Menominee	59.6	4.9	2 311	1 796	38	102	307	28.9	11.6	75.9	8.9	342	334	25.8	27.7
Midland	122.5	0.6	1 612	1 231	61	83	206	78.8	18.8	79.0	46.2	625	615	88.6	56.4
Missaukee	28.0	13.1	2 377	1 676	30	98	318	9.1	3.7	92.3	4.4	419	411	8.9	87.8
Monroe	256.7	6.5	1 859	1 355	14	71	359	133.6	33.5	85.9	76.3	578	569	129.5	36.2
Montcalm	126.6	8.3	2 326	1 646	102	90	309	48.4	19.6	94.1	19.3	396	394	44.3	43.7
Montmorency	34.9	9.0	4 062	3 364	58	68	526	7.2	2.7	67.2	3.5	476	470	7.0	69.6
Muskegon	441.2	8.5	2 715	1 786	417	111	378	169.8	70.2	81.1	62.2	400	396	166.4	26.4
Newaygo	83.3	4.3	2 068	1 554	38	86	296	37.8	19.0	69.0	13.4	377	374	37.0	99.9
Oakland	2 206.6	-0.2	2 078	1 570	123	180	195	1 304.9	282.5	79.9	713.0	713	699	1 257.8	46.2
Oceana	59.0	12.6	2 499	1 796	116	97	304	20.5	8.2	90.0	7.0	319	317	20.8	89.4
Ogemaw	53.4	8.2	2 780	2 270	12	85	358	14.0	3.4	82.1	7.4	442	435	14.3	63.0
Ontonagon	30.0	2.7	3 336	2 522	72	198	479	15.9	6.3	88.3	4.8	469	466	17.3	64.3
Osceola	56.8	12.5	2 669	1 982	25	95	448	24.3	6.0	91.0	9.9	503	499	24.0	112.7
Oscoda	19.2	10.2	2 531	2 061	13	145	294	6.6	2.5	64.3	3.4	491	486	4.9	33.1
Otsego	42.1	7.4	2 436	1 789	42	259	302	18.2	4.5	68.8	10.5	690	683	20.4	132.1
Ottawa	307.1	-3.8	1 661	1 182	187	103	132	177.8	36.5	84.1	76.0	475	471	195.7	114.5
Presque Isle	40.3	7.6	2 816	2 237	16	124	338	14.4	3.3	78.0	6.4	458	451	14.5	78.4
Roscommon	73.9	8.1	3 486	3 125	11	57	285	22.7	5.8	84.5	11.5	662	656	21.9	47.0
Saginaw	545.3	5.5	2 543	1 730	72	238	460	254.9	89.2	85.7	107.9	484	451	258.1	39.4
St. Clair	302.1	4.3	2 041	1 536	62	112	300	169.6	53.8	87.5	71.0	515	491	172.8	27.9
St. Joseph	129.5	5.2	2 144	1 590	38	85	245	65.1	17.3	91.9	24.5	429	425	68.5	74.9
Sanilac	107.2	-19.9	2 563	1 803	11	96	356	35.5	13.2	89.0	17.3	432	424	36.3	53.1
Schoolcraft	26.7	1.9	3 259	2 467	22	232	512	13.5	4.8	86.1	3.5	413	411	13.7	12.9
Shiawassee	127.5	0.1	1 783	1 460	39	83	116	69.4	28.3	91.7	26.5	380	377	65.1	54.2
Tuscola	118.7	0.1	2 083	1 534	11	86	290	59.4	23.6	85.5	23.7	425	422	55.1	62.1
Van Buren	173.5	5.0	2 467	1 707	44	90	441	70.3	25.9	91.2	25.9	390	387	71.1	46.9
Washtenaw	758.4	4.2	2 817	1 219	354	349	868	297.8	74.4	72.5	167.6	642	635	274.5	54.2
Wayne	6 525.2	1.6	3 107	2 062	91	311	632	4 004.7	1 671.8	65.0	1 487.5	663	536	3 602.3	45.3
Wexford	75.9	-11.8	2 772	1 832	328	226	348	25.6	10.1	87.5	11.5	447	444	24.9	65.2
MINNESOTA	14 436.8	4.4	X	1 579	455	283	538	6 247.6	3 185.3	87.6	1 465.5	355	338	6 121.1	62.7
Aitkin	44.0	5.8	3 409	2 501	67	151	583	16.6	11.0	92.3	3.5	261	254	17.5	67.7
Anoka	358.0	41.6	1 472	665	43	43	122	267.8	146.2	89.3	53.6	263	253	262.3	79.4
Becker	85.2	4.5	2 831	1 734	66	205	635	34.0	21.9	92.1	6.1	207	203	32.8	76.6
Beltrami	104.1	8.1	3 126	1 655	100	329	939	49.3	34.1	87.3	7.0	213	205	55.9	131.3
Benton	71.3	7.0	2 483	1 718	24	133	321	22.0	14.4	93.3	4.4	171	168	20.4	80.4
Big Stone	62.7	2.5	8 954	2 223	23	223	351	23.1	7.1	80.4	2.6	338	334	15.6	135.1
Blue Earth	139.0	-3.1	2 752	1 681	119	272	305	73.9	39.9	87.7	20.0	382	376	73.9	76.5
Brown	85.0	-7.5	3 092	1 732	67	135	197	34.2	17.4	84.8	7.7	269	263	32.9	62.6
Carlton	78.4	8.2	2 624	1 799	127	121	520	47.1	25.2	94.5	9.6	321	315	48.1	90.0
Carver	68.1	-30.9	1 483	812	80	94	165	57.4	23.5	87.9	12.2	318	308	62.5	99.5
Cass	79.3	2.0	3 586	2 088	69	350	916	26.6	16.8	88.0	6.6	314	309	27.6	59.5
Chippewa	46.2	0.6	3 420	1 822	17	179	304	21.0	10.4	88.5	4.6	311	306	20.1	38.6
Chisago	60.9	16.9	2 024	1 419	14	290	166	32.8	17.1	94.1	6.1	229	223	35.1	16.5
Clay	119.1	1.3	2 470	1 642	19	131	337	68.3	41.4	71.3	12.2	250	244	69.8	100.5
Clearwater	26.8	2.2	3 048	1 869	17	147	851	15.3	9.8	82.9	2.4	271	270	14.1	52.0
Cook	13.1	7.7	3 264	1 947	266	574	468	9.5	5.0	90.0	1.5	364	356	9.2	85.2
Cottonwood	48.3	-7.9	3 601	1 897	31	259	250	20.1	10.2	90.7	5.6	380	379	19.7	62.1
Crow Wing	126.9	7.2	2 752	2 103	19	132	454	60.3	37.8	92.3	10.2	241	236	60.6	91.9
Dakota	367.2	6.8	1 382	800	124	299	100	292.1	140.7	89.5	68.7	336	324	268.1	95.6
Dodge	37.8	-9.5	2 406	1 295	16	86	247	19.2	10.7	95.1	4.2	280	278	18.5	43.6
Douglas	76.4	2.3	2 582	1 762	17	168	339	47.6	22.9	94.3	6.8	240	234	44.6	9.0
Faribault	61.5	-7.2	3 533	2 054	30	156	244	24.9	10.9	90.0	6.8	351	345	25.6	55.4
Fillmore	74.3	-1.9	3 555	1 992	25	143	433	24.0	14.4	94.8	5.7	261	259	23.8	49.2
Freeborn	95.8	-11.8	2 827	1 778	102	138	230	44.0	23.9	95.2	10.8	302	278	40.8	52.7
Goodhue	123.4	-16.8	3 056	1 596	197	680	197	57.5	26.9	86.8	17.7	454	448	56.6	81.3
Grant	28.6	0.5	4 541	2 342	36	173	433	11.5	4.8	94.2	2.4	339	335	11.2	59.6
Hennepin	3 716.9	-3.6	3 645	1 537	1 099	424	520	1 481.8	697.7	87.5	445.4	464	438	1 408.3	50.1

1. Based on the estimated population as of July 1 of the year shown. 2. Based on the estimated population as of July 1, 1982.

STATE County	Local government finances, 1981–1982 (cont'd) — Direct general expenditure (cont'd) — Per capita[1] (Dollars)	Percent of total for– Education	Health & hospitals	Police protection	Public welfare	Highways	Debt outstanding — Total (Mil dol)	Per capita[1] (Dollars)	State and local government employment, 1989 — Total	Rate[2]	Federal government civilian employment 1989 — Total	Earnings ($1,000)	Elections, 1988[3] — Total vote cast for president	Vote for lead party (Percent)
	189	190	191	192	193	194	195	196	197	198	199	200	201	202
MICHIGAN—Con.														
Livingston	886	60.3	2.2	3.8	1.2	6.4	116.2	1 160	3 927	335.1	207	5 593	45 546	R–68.8
Luce	1 404	35.4	7.3	5.0	3.8	17.4	2.7	436	1 202	2 072.4	14	421	2 417	R–63.2
Mackinac	1 165	41.9	15.1	3.9	1.2	11.6	5.0	494	743	694.4	72	1 701	5 242	R–59.7
Macomb	1 120	55.3	2.6	6.6	0.7	5.4	611.9	890	26 390	371.7	10 422	293 172	291 116	R–60.3
Manistee	1 282	30.4	27.9	3.9	2.1	9.5	2.2	98	1 205	537.9	90	2 336	10 209	R–52.6
Marquette	1 095	43.9	9.1	3.3	1.9	8.6	104.4	1 432	5 960	857.6	1 124	23 505	27 267	D–56.5
Mason	1 190	51.3	8.0	3.8	1.7	9.3	12.4	469	1 444	549.0	79	2 095	11 413	R–59.6
Mecosta	922	38.9	24.3	2.7	1.5	8.1	28.4	768	4 339	1 127.0	92	2 323	12 981	R–63.0
Menominee	994	37.8	24.9	2.6	1.2	3.0	14.4	554	1 314	509.3	72	1 842	10 406	R–52.3
Midland	1 199	43.3	4.1	4.3	1.0	6.4	140.2	1 897	2 964	390.0	155	4 626	33 817	R–59.1
Missaukee	859	44.2	11.9	3.5	2.6	17.8	3.2	311	417	353.4	39	896	5 224	R–68.3
Monroe	981	54.0	3.2	4.6	2.4	7.8	253.5	1 920	5 466	395.8	264	7 518	48 324	R–54.2
Montcalm	911	63.5	2.8	3.1	1.3	9.0	28.3	582	2 420	444.9	138	3 452	18 754	R–58.5
Montmorency	943	45.3	0.8	8.4	2.8	7.4	3.5	474	343	398.8	14	369	4 100	R–61.3
Muskegon	1 070	54.8	4.9	4.4	2.9	2.8	149.1	960	8 156	501.9	428	13 661	62 907	R–53.4
Newaygo	1 035	44.8	9.9	2.1	1.4	10.3	19.5	546	1 599	396.8	114	2 941	15 385	R–64.3
Oakland	1 258	50.7	6.3	6.0	0.6	5.7	1 235.8	1 236	44 356	417.6	3 486	110 992	462 488	R–61.3
Oceana	950	42.0	22.1	3.4	2.3	14.7	11.0	502	1 252	530.5	67	1 719	9 114	R–62.5
Ogemaw	853	38.6	6.4	4.2	3.2	14.6	12.4	737	1 049	546.4	52	1 302	8 150	R–50.2
Ontonagon	1 694	35.0	23.8	1.9	1.5	17.2	14.6	1 434	664	737.8	72	1 617	4 562	D–55.2
Osceola	1 224	46.4	24.5	2.0	2.4	8.2	10.5	536	944	443.2	59	1 500	8 121	R–64.3
Oscoda	706	58.1	1.6	5.1	2.4	0.6	3.1	448	348	457.9	43	975	3 167	R–62.3
Otsego	1 340	58.0	0.2	2.7	1.0	8.9	14.1	928	1 079	623.7	104	2 938	7 298	R–63.3
Ottawa	1 224	36.3	15.2	2.8	1.1	6.4	265.8	1 662	8 683	469.6	426	12 283	80 729	R–76.2
Presque Isle	1 034	36.2	23.7	3.8	1.3	12.8	3.9	275	763	533.6	47	1 190	6 679	R–54.1
Roscommon	1 258	56.7	0.4	2.8	1.2	8.5	28.3	1 626	1 364	643.4	32	1 013	10 303	R–56.9
Saginaw	1 157	47.5	8.7	5.3	2.5	4.5	244.0	1 094	10 033	468.0	1 377	47 691	88 566	D–51.5
St. Clair	1 255	43.8	9.0	4.2	1.6	6.9	278.9	2 025	5 825	393.6	402	12 696	53 658	R–60.3
St. Joseph	1 200	42.5	27.3	2.9	1.6	6.8	43.6	764	3 141	520.0	133	3 541	20 196	R–64.8
Sanilac	908	48.3	8.7	4.1	2.2	12.6	26.0	649	1 806	432.1	121	3 151	16 207	R–65.7
Schoolcraft	1 609	23.8	37.8	2.0	0.1	14.3	11.6	1 368	635	774.4	58	1 278	3 886	D–53.3
Shiawassee	936	53.2	8.3	4.0	1.4	7.3	53.6	770	3 471	485.5	157	4 289	28 748	R–53.9
Tuscola	988	54.1	7.7	3.7	4.4	8.0	34.6	620	3 162	554.7	151	3 893	21 254	R–56.9
Van Buren	1 071	47.8	17.2	3.2	2.8	10.3	71.3	1 074	4 001	569.1	175	4 511	25 400	R–57.2
Washtenaw	1 053	52.8	1.4	5.8	1.5	5.9	236.8	908	56 896	2 113.5	2 781	93 133	117 920	D–52.4
Wayne	1 607	38.5	9.6	7.4	0.8	3.5	2 291.9	1 022	113 802	541.8	17 805	605 035	748 156	D–60.2
Wexford	971	43.4	5.3	4.7	1.7	10.5	15.7	611	1 494	545.3	161	4 467	10 406	R–58.1
MINNESOTA	1 481	37.4	7.5	3.7	10.6	8.7	6 730.0	1 628	285 770	656.7	34 234	1 092 967	2 096 790	D–52.9
Aitkin	1 316	47.1	1.1	3.0	13.2	12.8	9.1	686	579	448.8	56	1 279	6 955	D–55.5
Anoka	1 288	50.9	0.6	4.1	8.6	6.8	258.4	1 269	9 957	409.4	155	4 459	105 931	D–54.7
Becker	1 113	51.3	0.2	3.1	15.0	12.0	11.7	398	1 605	533.2	180	4 952	12 672	R–53.2
Beltrami	1 698	57.3	0.6	2.3	15.6	6.7	30.8	936	3 330	1 000.0	457	11 864	14 402	D–52.5
Benton	784	50.6	0.5	3.1	14.3	14.3	8.4	323	991	345.3	54	1 432	12 070	R–50.2
Big Stone	1 997	31.1	16.3	2.3	6.0	8.5	172.3	22 085	509	727.1	43	1 033	3 526	D–57.5
Blue Earth	1 416	39.2	0.6	3.7	9.5	13.2	45.4	869	5 108	1 011.5	354	10 806	24 570	D–50.4
Brown	1 146	39.2	6.1	3.8	8.0	12.4	17.7	618	1 323	481.1	85	2 219	12 200	R–56.5
Carlton	1 602	45.6	7.6	2.8	12.5	7.4	78.9	2 631	2 406	804.7	77	1 907	13 579	D–64.7
Carver	1 633	27.5	17.2	2.5	4.5	18.4	59.5	1 553	2 221	483.9	118	3 024	21 262	R–59.1
Cass	1 307	42.7	0.8	3.0	20.5	12.8	10.9	517	1 536	695.0	241	6 095	11 141	R–52.9
Chippewa	1 368	38.9	9.5	2.9	13.0	11.0	14.6	994	832	616.3	64	1 560	6 514	D–49.7
Chisago	1 319	43.8	12.0	3.4	13.4	8.9	21.5	807	1 345	446.8	96	2 397	14 196	D–55.5
Clay	1 428	35.6	1.5	3.1	7.1	6.6	52.7	1 078	3 750	778.0	135	3 532	21 715	D–51.5
Clearwater	1 597	44.3	17.9	2.7	14.7	9.1	2.9	334	593	673.9	41	975	3 569	D–49.6
Cook	2 248	28.2	20.2	2.8	6.7	17.6	2.1	522	392	980.0	116	2 709	2 189	D–49.3
Cottonwood	1 348	39.3	12.2	2.9	8.3	17.9	12.0	824	779	581.3	94	2 467	6 560	R–51.7
Crow Wing	1 431	44.2	5.3	2.9	10.8	9.6	31.1	736	3 526	764.9	160	4 412	20 929	R–52.6
Dakota	1 312	47.8	0.6	4.0	5.4	8.3	424.1	2 076	10 523	395.9	1 537	62 727	124 773	D–49.6
Dodge	1 226	46.8	6.3	4.4	14.2	12.7	13.4	890	923	587.9	43	1 043	6 854	R–56.1
Douglas	1 571	43.3	20.2	1.8	7.7	8.9	29.8	1 049	2 087	705.1	137	3 783	13 858	R–57.0
Faribault	1 325	40.6	13.7	2.7	0.0	17.8	8.6	446	944	542.5	79	1 848	8 816	R–55.0
Fillmore	1 092	44.1	0.8	3.4	9.6	23.7	12.6	578	1 166	557.9	92	2 201	9 201	R–54.4
Freeborn	1 142	42.1	0.8	4.4	11.1	10.4	45.5	1 274	1 352	398.8	133	3 669	16 219	D–54.5
Goodhue	1 447	42.6	2.9	4.2	7.7	11.9	70.0	1 791	2 242	555.0	135	3 561	19 126	R–49.4
Grant	1 580	39.7	20.2	2.8	5.1	12.5	4.0	563	411	652.4	39	845	3 687	D–52.9
Hennepin	1 468	33.6	8.3	4.6	12.1	7.0	1 660.0	1 730	75 185	737.4	14 106	480 579	539 788	D–54.3

1. Based on the estimated population as of July 1, 1982. 2. Per 10,000 resident population estimated as of July 1 of the year shown. 3. Data subject to copyright.

STATE–County code	MSA/ CMSA/ NECMA code[1]	STATE County	Land Area,[2] 1990 (Sq. Km.)	Population, 1990											
							Race						Age of population Percent		
				Total persons	Rank	Per square kilometer	White	Black	Am. Indian, Eskimo, Aleut	Asian & Pacific Islander	Other race	Hispanic[3]	Under 5 years	5 to 14 years	15 to 24 years
			1	2	3	4	5	6	7	8	9	10	11	12	13
		MINNESOTA–Con.													
27 055	...	Houston	1 446	18 497	1 761	12.8	18 364	25	48	54	6	37	7.9	16.6	11.3
27 057	...	Hubbard	2 389	14 939	1 991	6.3	14 637	4	278	15	5	37	6.9	15.9	10.4
27 059	5120	Isanti	1 137	25 921	1 426	22.8	25 583	68	137	106	27	119	7.9	18.4	12.6
27 061	...	Itasca	6 903	40 863	980	5.9	39 358	39	1 343	87	36	143	6.6	16.6	12.0
27 063	...	Jackson	1 818	11 677	2 240	6.4	11 414	2	15	165	81	113	6.8	15.8	10.9
27 065	...	Kanabec	1 360	12 802	2 156	9.4	12 656	20	60	45	21	61	7.6	17.7	12.0
27 067	...	Kandiyohi	2 062	38 761	1 032	18.8	37 837	85	164	114	561	1 363	7.7	16.5	13.8
27 069	...	Kittson	2 841	5 767	2 783	2.0	5 732	0	5	10	20	46	7.1	15.0	9.4
27 071	...	Koochiching	8 035	16 299	1 903	2.0	15 633	45	451	50	120	185	6.3	14.4	13.1
27 073	...	Lac qui Parle	1 981	8 924	2 477	4.5	8 867	11	12	28	6	23	6.8	15.4	8.8
27 075	...	Lake	5 437	10 415	2 348	1.9	10 332	3	61	16	3	32	6.0	14.0	9.9
27 077	...	Lake of the Woods	3 358	4 076	2 911	1.2	4 042	1	19	10	4	25	8.3	15.4	10.4
27 079	...	Le Sueur	1 162	23 239	1 529	20.0	23 077	13	50	63	36	123	7.7	17.4	12.1
27 081	...	Lincoln	1 391	6 890	2 674	5.0	6 857	2	9	9	13	26	5.3	16.3	9.6
27 083	...	Lyon	1 850	24 789	1 473	13.4	24 424	66	63	122	114	214	7.0	16.0	17.4
27 085	...	McLeod	1 274	32 030	1 209	25.1	31 691	32	52	130	125	284	8.1	16.5	12.8
27 087	...	Mahnomen	1 440	5 044	2 840	3.5	3 833	1	1 193	5	12	27	6.8	18.9	11.6
27 089	...	Marshall	4 590	10 993	2 296	2.4	10 889	2	50	14	38	113	6.3	17.2	11.4
27 091	...	Martin	1 837	22 914	1 537	12.5	22 714	9	35	85	71	137	6.9	15.7	10.1
27 093	...	Meeker	1 576	20 846	1 636	13.2	20 583	23	29	92	119	231	7.6	17.2	11.4
27 095	...	Mille Lacs	1 488	18 670	1 753	12.5	17 969	27	620	36	18	87	7.6	17.1	11.6
27 097	...	Morrison	2 913	29 604	1 311	10.2	29 408	33	77	45	41	98	7.9	18.6	12.3
27 099	...	Mower	1 843	37 385	1 062	20.3	36 893	71	51	295	75	248	6.5	15.0	11.4
27 101	...	Murray	1 825	9 660	2 418	5.3	9 630	0	3	17	10	21	6.6	16.2	10.4
27 103	...	Nicollet	1 172	28 076	1 348	24.0	27 636	89	57	203	91	203	7.2	15.2	19.8
27 105	...	Nobles	1 853	20 098	1 670	10.8	19 407	49	77	406	159	262	6.7	15.5	12.4
27 107	...	Norman	2 270	7 975	2 573	3.5	7 866	4	71	16	18	72	6.1	16.1	9.9
27 109	6820	Olmsted	1 691	106 470	435	63.0	101 880	788	295	3 237	270	970	8.6	15.3	13.0
27 111	...	Otter Tail	5 128	50 714	831	9.9	50 191	31	232	189	71	224	6.8	15.7	10.8
27 113	...	Pennington	1 597	13 306	2 114	8.3	13 100	11	101	48	46	106	6.8	15.5	14.8
27 115	...	Pine	3 655	21 264	1 617	5.8	20 374	352	360	82	96	348	6.8	16.9	11.7
27 117	...	Pipestone	1 207	10 491	2 336	8.7	10 245	6	153	78	9	42	7.6	16.2	11.4
27 119	...	Polk	5 104	32 498	1 200	6.4	31 501	73	418	96	410	1 146	7.2	16.8	12.5
27 121	...	Pope	1 736	10 745	2 314	6.2	10 698	5	23	12	7	7	6.9	16.7	9.3
27 123	5120	Ramsey	404	485 765	100	1 202.4	427 677	22 674	4 509	24 792	6 113	13 890	8.0	13.4	14.9
27 125	...	Red Lake	1 120	4 525	2 873	4.0	4 475	0	7	3	40	46	7.2	17.3	11.2
27 127	...	Redwood	2 279	17 254	1 839	7.6	16 875	27	280	31	41	91	7.4	16.2	10.7
27 129	...	Renville	2 546	17 673	1 807	6.9	17 422	7	58	46	140	216	7.3	16.5	10.1
27 131	...	Rice	1 289	49 183	855	38.2	48 081	174	113	607	208	530	6.9	15.3	20.5
27 133	...	Rock	1 250	9 806	2 405	7.8	9 731	12	33	19	11	29	6.9	17.0	10.8
27 135	...	Roseau	4 306	15 026	1 985	3.5	14 774	4	146	94	8	26	9.6	17.3	12.9
27 137	2240	St. Louis	16 124	198 213	245	12.3	192 053	1 106	3 682	1 076	296	952	6.1	14.2	14.2
27 139	5120	Scott	924	57 846	752	62.6	56 583	267	362	534	100	407	9.5	17.3	13.0
27 141	6980	Sherburne	1 131	41 945	957	37.1	41 182	263	208	204	88	259	8.7	18.4	16.4
27 143	...	Sibley	1 525	14 366	2 025	9.4	14 259	5	16	34	52	127	7.4	16.6	11.1
27 145	6980	Stearns	3 482	118 791	390	34.1	117 061	414	306	838	172	512	7.6	16.1	21.5
27 147	...	Steele	1 113	30 729	1 254	27.6	30 258	51	49	153	218	544	7.8	16.5	13.1
27 149	...	Stevens	1 456	10 634	2 323	7.3	10 366	58	50	119	41	56	5.8	14.2	24.6
27 151	...	Swift	1 926	10 724	2 317	5.6	10 623	4	38	38	21	79	6.3	16.4	9.8
27 153	...	Todd	2 440	23 363	1 522	9.6	23 233	8	51	53	18	58	7.0	18.5	11.9
27 155	...	Traverse	1 487	4 463	2 878	3.0	4 321	0	126	16	0	8	6.9	15.4	8.7
27 157	...	Wabasha	1 360	19 744	1 687	14.5	19 581	12	47	89	15	79	7.8	17.0	11.5
27 159	...	Wadena	1 387	13 154	2 127	9.5	13 016	8	77	36	17	47	7.3	16.5	11.6
27 161	...	Waseca	1 096	18 079	1 787	16.5	17 884	26	46	76	47	129	7.5	16.9	13.4
27 163	5120	Washington	1 015	145 896	324	143.7	141 266	1 601	687	1 648	694	1 895	8.3	17.4	12.7
27 165	...	Watonwan	1 125	11 682	2 238	10.4	11 120	9	24	57	472	593	7.5	16.6	10.8
27 167	...	Wilkin	1 946	7 516	2 616	3.9	7 426	2	41	23	24	43	7.8	16.1	11.8
27 169	...	Winona	1 622	47 828	878	29.5	46 892	195	113	526	102	350	6.7	14.1	21.9
27 171	5120	Wright	1 712	68 710	644	40.1	68 035	74	233	277	91	284	9.0	18.8	13.4
27 173	...	Yellow Medicine	1 963	11 684	2 237	6.0	11 496	3	115	23	47	82	6.7	16.2	10.4
28 000	...	MISSISSIPPI	121 506	2 573 216	X	21.2	1 633 461	915 057	8 525	13 016	3 157	15 931	7.6	16.5	16.3
28 001	...	Adams	1 192	35 356	1 118	29.7	18 028	17 212	40	63	13	152	7.5	16.7	13.3
28 003	...	Alcorn	1 036	31 722	1 219	30.6	28 085	3 540	22	53	22	127	6.3	14.6	14.0
28 005	...	Amite	1 890	13 328	2 112	7.1	7 272	6 038	11	6	1	33	7.2	17.0	14.3
28 007	...	Attala	1 904	18 481	1 764	9.7	11 114	7 299	32	28	8	58	6.9	15.6	14.3

1. MSA = Metropolitan Statistical Area. CMSA = Consolidated MSA. NECMA = New England county metropolitan area. PMSA = Primary MSA. See Appendix A for explanation of these concepts. See Appendix B for list of metropolitan areas identified by type, with component counties. 2. Dry land or land partially or temporarily covered by water. 3. Hispanic persons may be of any race.

STATE County	Population, 1990 (cont'd)							Population–Change and components of change							
	Age of population (cont'd) Percent							Change		Components of change, 1980–1986					
								1980–1990				Net change		Natural increase	
	25 to 34 years	35 to 44 years	45 to 54 years	55 to 64 years	65 to 74 years	75 years and over	Percent female	Number	Percent	Total persons, 1986	Total persons, 1980	Number	Percent	Births	Deaths
	14	15	16	17	18	19	20	21	22	23	24	25	26	27	28
MINNESOTA—Con.															
Houston	15.4	14.7	9.2	9.0	8.2	7.7	50.5	115	0.6	19 000	18 382	600	3.4	1 800	1 100
Hubbard	13.0	13.9	11.2	10.9	9.9	7.9	50.7	841	6.0	14 900	14 098	800	5.8	1 400	900
Isanti	16.3	15.8	11.0	6.9	5.5	5.6	50.0	2 321	9.8	25 300	23 600	1 700	7.3	2 500	1 100
Itasca	13.2	15.5	10.6	9.6	9.1	6.8	50.6	-2 206	-5.1	42 500	43 069	-500	-1.3	4 300	2 400
Jackson	13.7	13.2	9.2	10.4	10.1	9.8	50.5	-2 013	-14.7	13 200	13 690	-500	-3.5	1 200	800
Kanabec	15.1	13.7	10.3	8.8	8.2	6.4	50.2	641	5.3	12 600	12 161	400	3.5	1 300	700
Kandiyohi	15.3	14.1	9.5	8.1	7.9	7.1	50.8	1 998	5.4	38 100	36 763	1 300	3.6	3 900	2 000
Kittson	13.1	13.7	9.7	10.3	10.8	10.9	50.9	-905	-13.6	6 200	6 672	-500	-6.8	600	600
Koochiching	15.2	15.0	11.0	9.9	8.5	6.5	48.2	-1 272	-7.2	15 400	17 571	-2 200	-12.6	1 400	1 000
Lac qui Parle	12.7	12.7	9.6	10.9	11.6	11.5	50.6	-1 668	-15.7	10 000	10 592	-600	-5.3	1 000	800
Lake	13.5	14.2	11.6	13.3	10.0	7.5	50.2	-2 628	-20.1	11 500	13 043	-1 500	-11.9	1 000	600
Lake of the Woods	15.2	13.9	10.6	9.2	9.8	7.2	50.0	312	8.3	3 800	3 764	0	1.0	400	300
Le Sueur	15.1	14.0	10.1	8.5	8.0	7.1	50.3	-195	-0.8	23 400	23 434	-100	-0.2	2 500	1 400
Lincoln	11.0	11.5	10.4	10.8	12.3	12.9	51.2	-1 317	-16.0	7 600	8 207	-600	-7.3	700	600
Lyon	14.7	12.9	8.8	7.6	7.9	7.6	51.0	-418	-1.7	25 000	25 207	-200	-0.9	2 700	1 400
McLeod	16.1	14.2	9.7	7.9	7.5	7.3	50.5	2 373	8.0	31 200	29 657	1 600	5.2	3 000	1 700
Mahnomen	12.6	11.7	10.3	9.7	9.7	8.6	49.6	-491	-8.9	5 300	5 535	-200	-3.9	600	400
Marshall	12.9	13.4	10.5	10.0	9.9	8.4	49.4	-2 034	-15.6	12 200	13 027	-800	-6.3	1 200	800
Martin	14.2	13.9	9.9	9.4	10.0	9.8	51.3	-1 773	-7.2	24 500	24 687	-200	-0.6	2 400	1 600
Meeker	13.9	13.7	9.7	9.3	9.1	8.0	50.7	252	1.2	21 100	20 594	500	2.5	2 200	1 400
Mille Lacs	13.9	13.5	10.0	9.1	8.6	8.5	50.9	240	1.3	18 900	18 430	500	2.8	1 900	1 300
Morrison	14.7	13.0	8.9	8.9	8.5	7.1	50.1	293	1.0	30 200	29 311	900	3.2	3 300	1 800
Mower	13.8	12.9	9.5	10.8	10.8	9.4	51.5	-3 005	-7.4	38 900	40 390	-1 500	-3.7	3 500	2 500
Murray	12.0	13.2	9.6	11.3	11.3	9.3	50.6	-1 847	-16.1	10 600	11 507	-900	-8.1	1 000	700
Nicollet	15.7	14.8	8.9	7.3	5.7	5.3	50.5	1 147	4.3	27 600	26 929	600	2.3	2 700	1 100
Nobles	14.2	12.8	9.9	9.9	9.3	9.2	51.0	-1 742	-8.0	20 600	21 840	-1 200	-5.5	2 000	1 300
Norman	12.6	12.5	9.8	10.7	10.6	11.7	50.4	-1 404	-15.0	8 500	9 379	-800	-8.9	700	800
Olmsted	20.1	15.4	10.5	7.1	5.3	4.7	51.5	14 464	15.7	98 000	92 006	5 900	6.5	10 900	3 700
Otter Tail	13.4	13.4	10.1	10.5	9.9	9.5	50.5	-1 223	-2.4	52 200	51 937	300	0.5	4 900	3 600
Pennington	14.1	13.7	9.9	8.3	8.0	8.9	50.4	-1 952	-12.8	13 800	15 258	-1 500	-9.6	1 400	900
Pine	15.4	13.4	10.2	9.8	8.7	7.1	47.8	1 393	7.0	20 700	19 871	800	4.0	2 100	1 300
Pipestone	13.5	12.0	8.6	9.7	10.7	10.2	52.2	-1 199	-10.3	11 000	11 690	-700	-6.2	1 100	900
Polk	13.8	13.5	9.5	8.9	9.0	8.8	50.8	-2 346	-6.7	33 400	34 844	-1 500	-4.2	3 600	2 300
Pope	12.3	12.9	9.4	10.2	11.5	10.7	50.9	-912	-7.8	11 400	11 657	-200	-2.0	1 100	900
Ramsey	19.4	15.1	9.2	7.7	6.6	5.6	52.2	25 981	5.7	474 000	459 784	14 200	3.1	49 800	24 100
Red Lake	13.6	13.1	9.7	9.4	9.6	8.9	49.5	-946	-17.3	5 000	5 471	-500	-9.0	600	300
Redwood	13.5	12.5	9.8	9.3	10.5	10.1	50.8	-2 087	-10.8	18 500	19 341	-900	-4.5	1 900	1 400
Renville	13.7	12.6	9.1	10.4	10.4	9.9	50.6	-2 728	-13.4	19 600	20 401	-900	-4.2	2 000	1 400
Rice	15.2	13.6	9.5	7.1	6.1	5.7	50.9	3 096	6.7	47 500	46 087	1 400	3.0	4 400	2 300
Rock	13.1	13.2	9.4	9.8	10.4	9.4	51.5	-897	-8.4	10 400	10 703	-300	-2.8	1 000	600
Roseau	17.7	12.8	9.2	7.0	6.9	6.6	48.8	2 452	19.5	13 200	12 574	700	5.4	1 400	800
St. Louis	14.2	15.3	9.9	9.2	9.1	7.8	51.3	-24 016	-10.8	201 900	222 229	-20 300	-9.2	18 800	13 600
Scott	20.7	16.3	10.0	5.9	4.0	3.3	49.4	14 062	32.1	50 200	43 784	6 400	14.7	5 300	1 600
Sherburne	18.3	16.1	9.5	5.6	3.9	3.2	48.9	12 037	40.2	34 200	29 908	4 300	14.2	3 700	1 300
Sibley	14.2	12.9	9.8	10.3	9.0	8.7	50.2	-1 082	-7.0	15 000	15 448	-400	-2.7	1 500	900
Stearns	16.2	12.9	8.1	7.1	5.8	4.7	49.9	10 630	9.8	113 800	108 161	5 700	5.2	12 200	4 100
Steele	16.3	14.5	9.7	8.2	7.4	6.6	51.1	401	1.3	30 000	30 328	-400	-1.2	3 200	1 500
Stevens	11.3	11.7	7.6	8.9	8.2	7.8	51.7	-688	-6.1	10 600	11 322	-700	-6.1	1 000	700
Swift	13.4	12.4	9.5	10.0	11.3	10.8	50.8	-2 196	-17.0	12 100	12 920	-800	-6.1	1 200	900
Todd	13.0	13.2	9.9	9.3	9.0	8.0	50.3	-1 628	-6.5	25 400	24 991	500	1.8	2 800	1 500
Traverse	11.6	11.2	9.6	12.2	11.6	12.8	51.5	-1 079	-19.5	5 100	5 542	-400	-7.6	500	400
Wabasha	14.9	14.3	10.1	8.5	8.5	7.5	50.4	409	2.1	19 500	19 335	100	0.7	2 000	1 200
Wadena	13.3	12.2	10.2	9.7	9.6	9.6	51.2	-1 038	-7.3	13 900	14 192	-300	-2.3	1 400	1 100
Waseca	15.1	14.5	8.7	8.2	8.2	7.4	50.6	-369	-2.0	18 100	18 448	-300	-1.7	1 900	1 000
Washington	18.4	18.4	11.6	6.7	3.9	2.7	49.8	32 325	28.5	128 300	113 571	14 800	13.0	12 300	3 600
Watonwan	14.1	12.5	9.7	10.5	9.2	9.1	50.9	-679	-5.5	11 900	12 361	-500	-3.6	1 300	800
Wilkin	15.2	12.8	9.1	10.0	8.6	8.6	50.5	-938	-11.1	7 900	8 454	-500	-6.3	800	500
Winona	14.3	13.3	8.6	7.4	6.8	6.9	51.3	1 572	3.4	46 300	46 256	100	0.2	4 500	2 500
Wright	17.8	15.1	9.7	6.3	5.2	4.5	49.6	10 029	17.1	64 500	58 681	5 800	9.9	7 200	2 600
Yellow Medicine	13.2	11.9	10.0	10.2	10.5	10.9	50.5	-1 969	-14.4	13 000	13 653	-700	-5.0	1 300	1 000
MISSISSIPPI	15.5	13.6	9.6	8.3	7.0	5.5	52.2	52 216	2.1	2 625 000	2 521 000	104 000	4.1	281 000	149 000
Adams	14.6	13.8	9.8	9.9	8.3	6.1	54.0	-2 715	-7.1	39 000	38 071	900	2.3	4 300	2 600
Alcorn	14.5	14.5	11.5	9.2	8.4	7.0	52.1	-1 314	-4.0	32 600	33 036	-400	-1.2	2 800	2 000
Amite	14.1	12.3	10.2	9.4	8.8	6.6	51.7	-41	-0.3	13 300	13 369	-100	-0.6	1 300	900
Attala	13.1	12.1	9.8	9.8	9.8	8.6	53.1	-1 384	-7.0	19 600	19 865	-300	-1.5	1 800	1 500

STATE County	Population–(cont'd)	Households, 1990					Births, 1988			Deaths, 1987				Marriages, 1984	
	Components of change, 1980-1986 (cont'd)				Percent					Number		Rate			
	Net migration	Number	Percent change, 1980–1990	Persons per household	Female family householder[1]	One-person	Total	Rate[2]	Low birth weight[3] (Number)	Total	Infant[4]	Total[2]	Infant[5]	Number	Rate[2]
	29	30	31	32	33	34	35	36	37	38	39	40	41	42	43
MINNESOTA—Con.															
Houston	-100	6 844	8.0	2.65	7.2	23.4	303	15.9	11	174	2	9.2	6.8	152	8.1
Hubbard	300	5 781	15.0	2.55	6.0	23.5	177	11.8	11	148	1	10.0	5.0	105	7.3
Isanti	300	8 810	17.4	2.86	7.1	19.0	387	14.8	18	221	2	8.7	5.5	193	7.8
Itasca	-2 500	15 461	3.3	2.60	7.9	23.1	528	12.6	26	353	7	8.4	13.9	342	8.0
Jackson	-900	4 560	-8.6	2.51	5.3	25.7	170	13.5	4	126	2	9.8	13.3	84	6.2
Kanabec	-200	4 753	11.8	2.67	7.4	24.0	155	12.0	7	112	2	8.9	11.1	85	6.9
Kandiyohi	-600	14 298	11.1	2.64	6.8	23.9	603	15.5	26	347	4	9.1	7.2	355	9.3
Kittson	-500	2 274	-8.5	2.46	5.3	28.7	70	11.3	1	98	0	15.6	0.0	39	6.0
Koochiching	-2 600	6 025	-1.7	2.58	8.5	24.8	163	11.0	11	143	1	9.6	6.1	135	8.2
Lac qui Parle	-700	3 505	-9.8	2.48	3.6	27.7	112	11.7	5	121	0	12.5	0.0	52	5.0
Lake	-1 900	4 242	-7.3	2.42	6.2	25.4	114	10.3	4	130	0	11.5	0.0	88	7.5
Lake of the Woods	-100	1 576	13.5	2.55	5.9	23.4	65	16.7	3	33	0	8.7	0.0	50	13.5
Le Sueur	-1 100	8 468	5.4	2.71	6.2	23.1	335	14.3	16	233	3	10.0	9.0	118	5.0
Lincoln	-700	2 704	-7.7	2.47	4.3	28.0	76	10.6	4	108	0	14.6	0.0	44	5.6
Lyon	-1 500	9 073	4.5	2.56	6.3	26.1	341	13.6	17	217	1	8.8	2.4	268	10.5
McLeod	300	11 815	13.9	2.67	6.2	23.4	472	14.7	21	288	6	9.1	13.2	251	8.2
Mahnomen	-400	1 805	1.3	2.75	8.2	24.3	62	11.7	2	68	1	12.8	13.2	38	7.0
Marshall	-1 200	4 194	-6.0	2.59	4.9	26.3	131	11.1	5	128	1	10.8	6.9	64	5.2
Martin	-900	9 129	-2.1	2.46	6.4	27.8	263	11.2	14	251	1	10.5	3.4	200	8.0
Meeker	-300	7 651	6.6	2.67	5.4	24.0	319	14.9	11	223	6	10.6	19.7	136	6.4
Mille Lacs	-100	6 911	7.5	2.65	7.7	23.9	270	14.1	12	241	3	12.6	11.7	141	7.5
Morrison	-600	10 399	9.4	2.79	7.1	23.2	464	15.1	23	312	3	10.3	5.9	215	7.1
Mower	-2 400	15 028	0.4	2.44	7.2	27.8	453	11.8	23	377	3	9.8	6.1	300	7.6
Murray	-1 300	3 758	-6.9	2.53	4.1	26.2	126	12.1	4	99	0	9.5	0.0	74	6.7
Nicollet	-1 000	9 478	10.5	2.69	7.1	22.1	392	14.1	17	180	1	6.5	2.5	169	6.2
Nobles	-1 900	7 683	-1.7	2.55	5.9	25.1	270	13.3	8	183	0	9.0	0.0	188	8.8
Norman	-800	3 118	-9.1	2.48	4.5	29.3	110	13.3	3	133	0	15.6	0.0	46	5.2
Olmsted	-1 300	40 058	22.6	2.59	7.5	24.6	1 886	18.7	79	635	20	6.4	11.2	1 094	11.4
Otter Tail	-1 000	19 510	5.2	2.53	5.8	25.8	686	13.1	23	544	3	10.5	4.6	292	5.6
Pennington	-2 000	5 173	-4.9	2.50	8.1	28.1	171	12.8	8	132	2	9.8	11.6	143	10.1
Pine	0	7 577	10.6	2.64	7.2	24.2	261	12.1	13	206	2	9.7	6.9	156	7.5
Pipestone	-900	4 078	-6.4	2.51	5.6	28.7	186	17.1	10	123	0	11.3	0.0	100	8.8
Polk	-2 700	11 984	-1.4	2.61	7.9	26.0	503	15.3	24	404	10	12.2	20.7	300	8.8
Pope	-400	4 135	-2.5	2.54	4.9	26.3	133	11.8	11	139	1	12.4	7.6	70	6.0
Ramsey	-11 500	190 500	11.7	2.47	11.3	29.3	8 277	17.3	445	3 956	62	8.3	7.8	4 370	9.3
Red Lake	-700	1 730	-4.8	2.58	5.1	30.5	55	11.2	1	61	2	12.4	26.3	38	7.3
Redwood	-1 400	6 554	-4.2	2.57	5.2	27.0	206	11.4	11	179	3	9.8	10.4	161	8.5
Renville	-1 500	6 790	-7.2	2.55	4.7	26.6	216	11.4	10	212	1	11.1	3.7	98	4.9
Rice	-800	16 347	14.5	2.66	7.8	24.1	625	12.9	27	408	10	8.5	15.7	344	7.3
Rock	-700	3 754	-2.6	2.57	5.1	25.6	120	11.9	4	82	0	8.1	0.0	103	9.6
Roseau	100	5 415	25.0	2.73	6.2	22.0	266	18.6	7	138	2	10.0	8.1	110	8.7
St. Louis	-25 500	78 901	-3.2	2.43	9.2	28.8	2 298	11.5	117	2 134	34	10.7	14.4	1 620	7.7
Scott	2 800	19 367	43.4	2.95	7.2	15.5	1 046	19.2	52	270	8	5.2	8.0	559	11.9
Sherburne	1 900	13 643	52.1	2.98	6.8	15.2	624	17.2	19	215	6	6.1	10.9	230	7.1
Sibley	-1 000	5 323	-0.3	2.66	4.6	23.8	201	13.4	8	146	1	9.7	4.8	87	5.7
Stearns	-2 400	39 776	23.9	2.81	7.3	21.5	1 741	14.9	70	642	10	5.6	5.6	1 194	10.6
Steele	-2 000	11 342	7.0	2.65	6.3	23.1	466	15.5	13	245	3	8.2	6.8	220	7.4
Stevens	-1 100	3 823	-1.5	2.57	5.4	25.5	118	11.3	3	107	0	10.3	0.0	85	7.8
Swift	-1 000	4 268	-9.1	2.46	5.3	29.5	136	11.8	6	161	0	13.8	0.0	80	6.3
Todd	-800	8 589	0.9	2.69	5.4	24.7	331	13.0	16	232	4	9.2	11.9	138	5.4
Traverse	-500	1 778	-12.8	2.44	5.1	28.2	62	12.9	3	66	0	13.2	0.0	36	6.5
Wabasha	-700	7 286	8.0	2.67	5.7	23.0	300	15.4	9	184	0	9.6	0.0	110	5.7
Wadena	-600	4 978	3.2	2.56	7.3	27.3	176	12.6	15	171	3	12.1	13.8	190	13.6
Waseca	-1 200	6 649	2.8	2.64	6.9	24.6	239	13.1	8	147	1	8.1	4.0	154	8.4
Washington	6 100	49 246	40.3	2.91	8.5	16.1	2 127	15.4	80	662	19	5.0	9.6	751	6.1
Watonwan	-900	4 530	-2.3	2.54	5.5	27.9	164	14.1	9	159	1	13.7	6.9	92	7.4
Wilkin	-800	2 805	-4.4	2.63	6.0	25.3	102	13.1	10	70	0	8.9	0.0	55	6.7
Winona	-1 900	16 930	8.5	2.61	7.1	25.5	628	13.5	30	399	2	8.6	3.3	400	8.6
Wright	1 200	23 013	24.9	2.95	6.9	17.5	1 214	17.7	66	442	9	6.7	7.7	410	6.6
Yellow Medicine	-1 000	4 607	-7.7	2.48	4.4	28.6	154	12.3	4	139	0	11.0	0.0	75	5.6
MISSISSIPPI	-27 000	911 374	10.2	2.75	15.9	23.4	42 074	16.1	3 668	24 634	566	9.4	13.7	26 025	10.0
Adams	-900	13 262	3.6	2.64	19.8	25.1	595	16.0	56	431	4	11.5	7.0	452	11.5
Alcorn	-1 200	12 449	4.3	2.52	10.5	25.0	379	11.7	24	334	3	10.2	7.0	396	12.0
Amite	-500	4 830	10.7	2.76	14.4	24.3	170	12.9	16	118	2	8.9	12.5	149	11.1
Attala	-500	6 945	1.2	2.63	13.7	26.3	275	14.8	19	259	1	13.7	3.6	180	9.3

1. No spouse present. 2. Per 1,000 resident population estimated as of July 1 of the year shown. 3. Under 2,500 grams. 4. Deaths of infants under 1 year old. 5. Deaths of infants under 1 year old per 1,000 live births.

STATE County	Divorces, 1984 Number	Divorces, 1984 Rate[1]	Physicians, active non–Federal, 1989 Number[2]	Physicians, active non–Federal, 1989 Rate[3]	Hospitals, 1989 Number	Hospitals, 1989 Beds Number	Hospitals, 1989 Beds Rate[3]	Nursing homes,[4] 1986 Number	Nursing homes,[4] 1986 Beds	Serious crimes known to police, 1988 Number Total[5]	Serious crimes known to police, 1988 Number Violent[6]	Serious crimes known to police, 1988 Rate[3]	Education Public school enrollment[7] 1986–1987	Education Public school enrollment[7] 1980	Education Attainment,[8] 1980 Percent 12 yrs. or more	Education Attainment,[8] 1980 Percent 16 yrs. or more
	44	45	46	47	48	49	50	51	52	53	54	55	56	57	58	59
MINNESOTA—Con.																
Houston	46	2.4	10	52	1	89	464	4	298	291	16	1 510	3 070	3 557	64.3	12.4
Hubbard	45	3.1	13	86	1	38	250	1	130	566	28	3 720	2 770	3 106	64.1	12.4
Isanti	75	3.0	30	114	1	86	326	2	335	580	13	2 260	4 770	5 823	65.1	9.9
Itasca	158	3.7	44	106	3	245	588	5	367	945	20	2 213	8 520	9 330	70.0	12.4
Jackson	21	1.5	4	32	3	113	911	4	211	257	9	1 995	2 134	2 701	64.4	10.0
Kanabec	45	3.6	10	77	1	51	392	1	87	343	31	2 684	2 339	2 788	58.7	8.6
Kandiyohi	107	2.8	73	187	2	761	1 946	5	496	1 391	64	3 562	6 470	7 093	65.6	12.4
Kittson	9	1.4	5	82	2	150	2 459	2	166	42	4	668	1 223	1 299	61.9	9.6
Koochiching	83	5.0	12	84	1	64	448	3	198	529	35	3 454	2 884	3 995	65.5	10.2
Lac qui Parle	18	1.7	6	65	2	115	1 237	2	247	139	3	1 398	1 670	2 107	58.6	9.2
Lake	28	2.4	12	110	1	80	734	2	105	127	3	1 118	2 374	2 736	72.9	10.9
Lake of the Woods	8	2.2	2	50	1	34	850	1	52	95	0	2 465	616	839	60.1	11.5
Le Sueur	41	1.7	14	60	2	165	708	4	263	239	6	1 016	4 051	5 105	66.5	12.2
Lincoln	15	1.9	4	56	3	238	3 352	2	94	107	5	1 426	1 375	1 805	56.8	8.6
Lyon	75	2.9	22	88	2	135	542	5	366	501	26	2 000	4 628	4 589	64.9	12.4
McLeod	82	2.7	28	86	2	226	691	3	339	948	49	2 948	5 568	5 523	63.3	8.5
Mahnomen	8	1.5	3	58	1	66	1 269	0	0	128	1	2 427	1 477	1 381	51.5	8.0
Marshall	21	1.7	3	26	1	41	353	1	102	161	6	1 323	2 736	2 941	56.5	8.5
Martin	66	2.6	20	87	2	138	600	4	324	559	8	2 306	4 211	4 477	64.6	9.7
Meeker	47	2.2	13	60	1	41	190	5	411	288	5	1 346	5 272	4 253	62.0	8.8
Mille Lacs	55	2.9	20	104	3	184	953	3	339	482	32	2 488	5 542	3 981	57.6	8.7
Morrison	70	2.3	17	55	1	213	687	3	378	623	20	2 021	6 063	6 504	54.5	8.2
Mower	131	3.3	41	108	1	108	285	6	523	1 299	46	3 344	5 783	7 526	66.6	10.3
Murray	18	1.6	4	39	1	35	340	2	126	105	1	995	1 636	2 482	59.8	8.0
Nicollet	59	2.2	24	85	2	761	2 708	3	201	697	25	2 454	2 052	4 672	73.6	19.1
Nobles	53	2.5	22	109	2	157	781	5	258	417	5	2 015	3 474	4 372	60.8	9.0
Norman	19	2.2	2	24	1	79	963	4	269	159	6	1 844	1 679	1 983	56.1	8.0
Olmsted	382	4.0	1 790	1 750	3	1 661	1 624	9	852	3 736	100	3 747	17 211	17 997	81.7	24.8
Otter Tail	144	2.7	56	107	5	713	1 363	8	557	1 228	38	2 328	7 968	10 321	58.9	10.4
Pennington	60	4.3	20	150	1	190	1 429	4	314	557	22	4 068	2 606	3 051	66.4	12.0
Pine	48	2.3	8	37	1	23	106	2	211	945	30	4 501	4 118	4 432	59.3	8.9
Pipestone	17	1.5	7	64	1	87	798	3	230	70	1	639	2 065	2 183	56.9	9.2
Polk	119	3.5	24	73	2	237	725	11	747	1 125	73	3 341	6 197	6 991	62.8	11.7
Pope	42	3.6	7	62	2	53	473	3	242	178	7	1 567	1 875	2 421	61.4	9.3
Ramsey	1 899	4.1	1 435	298	7	1 213	252	45	5 563	29 187	2 710	6 060	66 583	70 306	77.2	22.3
Red Lake	15	2.9	1	21	0	0	0	1	74	20	2	402	1 073	1 290	54.6	7.0
Redwood	41	2.2	6	34	1	35	196	7	415	283	17	1 542	3 322	3 916	60.3	9.4
Renville	38	1.9	7	38	1	30	161	6	383	200	8	1 032	3 275	4 063	60.3	8.4
Rice	143	3.0	50	102	4	833	1 700	6	585	1 688	64	3 489	7 381	8 298	68.2	16.1
Rock	12	1.1	8	80	1	38	380	2	118	109	3	1 043	1 843	2 256	59.5	7.6
Roseau	35	2.8	10	68	2	196	1 333	4	199	300	17	2 143	2 921	2 766	55.6	9.0
St. Louis	825	3.9	391	198	9	1 397	707	21	2 483	7 131	325	3 514	34 831	42 293	72.0	14.8
Scott	147	3.1	32	56	1	69	121	3	338	2 071	72	3 889	9 131	10 305	74.1	13.5
Sherburne	109	3.4	5	13	0	0	0	4	476	1 153	46	3 276	7 424	6 979	72.9	14.2
Sibley	18	1.2	8	54	1	17	114	3	173	107	5	703	2 480	3 110	54.6	8.2
Stearns	243	2.2	196	166	6	1 322	1 119	8	499	3 502	88	3 000	21 706	21 257	67.0	14.5
Steele	86	2.9	26	86	1	55	183	5	360	977	26	3 190	5 974	6 137	69.1	13.6
Stevens	21	1.9	11	108	1	42	412	1	144	191	3	1 811	1 423	2 040	66.2	13.5
Swift	17	1.3	6	53	2	135	1 195	2	120	201	6	1 694	1 796	2 746	58.6	8.7
Todd	54	2.1	9	35	1	157	616	3	301	430	16	1 656	4 606	5 466	56.2	8.4
Traverse	2	0.4	3	65	1	35	761	2	127	97	3	1 952	801	1 205	57.7	7.9
Wabasha	35	1.8	14	72	2	112	574	4	272	414	14	2 104	4 029	4 128	64.0	10.0
Wadena	34	2.4	11	79	2	202	1 443	2	206	375	26	2 660	3 072	3 207	57.8	10.9
Waseca	41	2.2	9	49	1	19	104	3	199	177	4	975	3 819	3 526	68.2	11.6
Washington	442	3.6	108	75	2	103	72	8	751	5 167	218	3 839	25 693	27 889	82.9	20.4
Watonwan	39	3.1	5	44	2	56	491	2	168	215	12	1 827	2 070	2 301	60.2	9.1
Wilkin	15	1.8	8	104	1	174	2 260	1	124	227	10	2 833	1 443	1 821	62.1	9.8
Winona	105	2.2	39	84	1	203	438	7	638	1 871	28	4 010	6 453	7 269	66.1	16.4
Wright	145	2.3	42	59	2	151	214	7	556	1 807	51	2 691	13 517	13 859	69.1	10.1
Yellow Medicine	29	2.2	8	65	2	192	1 561	2	161	128	6	1 002	2 384	2 623	60.2	8.4
MISSISSIPPI	12 911	5.0	3 352	128	128	18 025	688	163	14 123	66 135	5 900	3 892	498 644	517 163	54.8	12.3
Adams	75	1.9	62	170	2	306	838	3	274	1 920	160	8 971	6 809	7 677	56.1	12.5
Alcorn	NA	NA	29	90	1	130	401	3	259	375	9	2 991	6 211	6 907	49.6	8.7
Amite	61	4.6	2	15	0	0	0	0	0	NA	NA	NA	2 139	2 693	45.1	7.8
Attala	80	4.1	14	77	1	76	415	1	119	237	15	3 377	3 410	4 057	44.5	8.6

1. Per 1,000 resident population estimated as of July 1 of the year shown. 2. As of end of year. 3. Per 100,000 resident population as of July 1 of the year shown. 4. Preliminary. Covers nursing homes with 3 or more beds. 5. Data for serious crimes have not been adjusted for underreporting, this may affect comparability between geographic areas or over time. 6. Includes murder and nonnegligent manslaughter, forcible rape, robbery, and aggravated assault. 7. The 1986–1987 data are based on administrative reports obtained by the U.S. National Center for Education Statistics. The 1980 data are based on the 1980 Census of Population and Housing. 8. Persons 25 years old or older.

STATE County	Education (cont'd): Local government expenditures for education,[1] 1982: Total (Mil dol)	Education (cont'd): Local government expenditures for education,[1] 1982: Per capita (Dollars)	Social Security Program December 1988: Beneficiaries: Total	Social Security Program December 1988: Beneficiaries: Rate[2]	Social Security Program December 1988: Payments ($1,000)	Supplemental Security Income Program recipients June 1986	Money income: Per capita[3]: 1987 Income, (Dollars)	Money income: Per capita[3]: 1979: Current dollars	Money income: Per capita[3]: 1979: Constant 1987 dollars	Money income: Median household income 1979 (Dollars)	Money income: Percent below poverty level, 1979: Persons	Money income: Percent below poverty level, 1979: Families	Housing units, 1990: Total	Housing units, 1990: Percent change, 1980–1990
	60	61	62	63	64	65	66	67	68	69	70	71	72	73
MINNESOTA—Con.														
Houston	9.2	494	3 565	186.6	1 557	148	9 973	5 945	9 302	15 005	11.2	8.5	7 257	8.8
Hubbard	9.7	681	3 510	234.0	1 483	202	8 171	5 168	8 086	11 647	19.0	15.7	10 042	10.3
Isanti	12.2	507	3 265	125.1	1 508	296	9 773	6 089	9 527	17 550	7.8	6.4	9 693	15.8
Itasca	26.1	607	8 215	196.1	3 905	470	8 758	6 148	9 620	16 157	10.6	8.5	22 494	6.0
Jackson	9.6	702	2 555	202.8	1 137	90	9 534	6 112	9 563	14 246	16.3	12.5	5 121	-7.3
Kanabec	5.7	454	2 260	175.2	952	132	9 040	5 645	8 833	13 374	14.8	11.0	6 098	11.2
Kandiyohi	24.2	640	6 625	170.7	2 935	470	10 059	6 410	10 030	14 877	11.1	7.6	16 669	10.4
Kittson	5.9	883	1 490	240.3	632	92	8 912	5 864	9 175	13 193	12.9	11.0	2 865	-5.1
Koochiching	10.8	637	3 245	219.3	1 589	168	9 043	6 062	9 485	16 015	12.2	9.2	7 825	8.1
Lac qui Parle	4.9	462	2 325	242.2	994	68	8 727	5 727	8 961	12 676	16.0	13.3	3 955	-7.4
Lake	7.7	612	1 895	170.7	871	80	9 652	7 900	12 361	20 382	4.4	3.7	6 776	10.9
Lake of the Woods	1.9	516	885	226.9	368	50	8 602	5 175	8 097	11 754	17.0	13.4	3 050	12.6
Le Sueur	12.4	528	4 425	189.1	1 963	162	10 397	6 407	10 025	16 246	9.2	7.0	9 785	2.9
Lincoln	4.1	509	1 990	276.4	765	80	8 520	4 772	7 467	10 358	22.1	17.6	3 050	-7.5
Lyon	12.5	493	4 720	188.8	2 088	226	9 929	6 113	9 565	14 830	12.1	9.2	9 675	5.2
McLeod	18.2	604	5 440	168.9	2 428	150	10 562	6 545	10 241	16 885	8.8	6.7	12 391	13.5
Mahnomen	5.3	971	1 150	217.0	444	94	7 454	4 176	6 534	10 485	24.0	18.4	2 505	3.9
Marshall	8.8	692	2 575	218.2	1 065	134	8 543	5 225	8 176	12 913	16.2	13.7	5 049	-3.9
Martin	11.9	479	5 315	227.1	2 477	144	10 892	6 908	10 809	15 302	9.6	7.7	9 847	0.6
Meeker	13.2	631	4 090	191.1	1 750	170	9 710	5 922	9 266	14 035	13.6	11.0	9 139	7.0
Mille Lacs	15.2	814	4 420	230.2	1 933	232	8 831	5 497	8 601	13 187	12.6	10.0	9 065	9.3
Morrison	18.1	613	5 770	187.3	2 266	344	7 926	4 797	7 506	12 073	20.5	16.6	12 434	7.0
Mower	23.3	593	9 295	242.7	4 542	342	10 630	7 027	10 995	16 214	10.0	7.7	15 831	1.0
Murray	5.1	454	2 315	222.6	973	88	9 211	5 623	8 798	13 241	17.7	14.3	4 611	-1.5
Nicollet	6.4	234	3 495	125.3	1 674	156	10 407	6 487	10 150	17 063	9.8	7.0	9 963	11.2
Nobles	13.4	622	4 580	225.6	2 018	194	10 256	6 314	9 880	14 529	12.7	10.4	8 094	-1.4
Norman	5.4	590	2 045	246.4	846	104	9 899	5 736	8 975	12 410	16.0	11.7	3 648	-9.2
Olmsted	49.2	525	12 320	122.0	6 145	562	13 527	8 078	12 640	20 066	6.6	4.2	41 603	21.1
Otter Tail	23.4	449	11 455	219.0	4 832	710	9 175	5 628	8 806	12 575	15.5	12.2	29 295	8.7
Pennington	11.2	770	2 690	200.7	1 131	180	9 212	6 206	9 711	14 622	11.2	8.1	5 682	-5.0
Pine	16.0	788	4 345	202.1	1 844	246	7 885	5 093	7 969	12 252	15.3	11.3	12 738	23.7
Pipestone	9.1	792	2 630	241.3	1 103	116	9 320	5 529	8 651	11 681	19.7	15.5	4 387	-5.4
Polk	20.8	606	6 870	208.8	2 931	420	9 424	5 985	9 365	14 200	13.3	9.9	14 275	-3.3
Pope	5.2	444	2 620	231.9	1 088	98	8 636	5 287	8 273	11 878	17.8	14.9	5 836	3.1
Ramsey	236.7	507	72 380	151.1	37 625	4 594	13 678	8 298	12 984	18 939	8.1	5.9	201 016	13.6
Red Lake	3.3	604	1 095	223.5	431	54	7 196	4 674	7 313	11 653	19.6	16.7	1 899	-7.0
Redwood	10.2	531	4 135	228.5	1 806	182	9 777	5 938	9 291	13 571	15.4	12.0	7 144	-3.3
Renville	10.9	546	4 110	217.5	1 771	168	9 812	6 026	9 429	14 789	12.6	9.8	7 442	-5.9
Rice	22.6	480	6 825	140.7	3 284	524	10 508	6 236	9 757	16 945	9.9	6.1	17 520	11.8
Rock	5.0	472	2 175	215.3	976	56	9 500	6 134	9 598	14 220	14.3	11.2	3 963	-3.2
Roseau	7.6	616	2 510	175.5	1 020	142	9 407	5 293	8 282	13 324	15.3	12.2	6 236	23.9
St. Louis	124.5	571	39 980	200.5	19 552	2 186	10 105	7 063	11 051	17 264	9.2	6.2	95 403	0.1
Scott	22.9	502	4 790	87.7	2 271	168	13 032	7 742	12 114	22 464	5.4	4.2	20 302	43.1
Sherburne	18.4	584	3 695	101.8	1 724	166	10 338	6 338	9 917	19 437	8.8	6.9	14 964	44.7
Sibley	6.7	436	3 060	204.0	1 294	90	9 629	5 980	9 357	14 735	12.5	10.0	5 625	-0.1
Stearns	66.3	601	16 050	137.5	6 924	804	9 512	5 750	8 997	16 020	12.4	8.5	43 806	21.8
Steele	15.6	518	5 180	172.7	2 422	138	10 792	6 688	10 465	16 866	7.9	6.5	11 840	5.2
Stevens	5.1	456	2 055	197.6	889	98	9 130	5 619	8 792	12 552	19.2	11.7	4 108	-2.7
Swift	7.5	591	2 925	254.3	1 222	130	8 425	5 252	8 218	11 899	17.3	14.8	4 795	-7.5
Todd	17.9	704	4 675	183.3	1 767	294	7 653	4 706	7 363	11 151	20.9	16.5	11 234	5.1
Traverse	2.7	493	1 255	261.5	540	52	9 221	5 796	9 069	12 135	17.0	13.8	2 220	-7.8
Wabasha	10.8	562	4 220	216.4	1 872	182	9 727	6 165	9 646	15 101	11.1	9.2	8 205	7.9
Wadena	11.2	791	3 205	228.9	1 255	292	7 898	4 820	7 542	11 148	18.4	15.1	5 801	6.7
Waseca	9.2	497	3 315	181.1	1 509	94	10 359	6 534	10 224	16 252	9.2	7.4	7 011	1.8
Washington	76.5	643	9 760	70.6	4 989	286	14 142	8 176	12 793	24 257	4.3	3.4	51 648	38.9
Watonwan	6.1	499	2 505	215.9	1 148	48	9 467	6 289	9 840	14 758	11.5	9.1	4 886	-1.3
Wilkin	4.7	565	1 475	189.1	645	58	9 434	6 188	9 682	15 463	10.7	8.3	3 140	-4.4
Winona	18.5	399	7 765	167.3	3 662	338	10 066	6 159	9 637	15 142	11.2	6.3	17 630	6.8
Wright	32.5	537	8 400	122.4	3 789	330	10 644	6 526	10 211	18 662	6.9	5.5	26 353	20.9
Yellow Medicine	11.9	882	3 075	246.0	1 327	136	8 587	5 595	8 754	12 867	17.2	12.9	4 983	-7.5
MISSISSIPPI	854.2	333	442 033	168.7	176 343	112 080	8 088	5 182	8 108	12 096	23.9	18.7	1 010 423	10.8
Adams	13.4	337	7 055	189.7	3 064	1 836	7 455	5 276	8 255	11 346	27.8	22.4	14 715	8.4
Alcorn	10.3	317	6 450	198.5	2 579	1 658	8 757	5 778	9 041	12 043	18.5	14.7	13 704	7.0
Amite	4.4	332	2 585	195.8	955	722	6 700	4 327	6 770	9 545	31.1	27.1	5 695	7.9
Attala	6.3	318	4 595	247.0	1 753	1 310	6 437	4 214	6 594	9 311	31.3	24.0	7 674	0.7

1. Elementary and secondary. 2. Per 1,000 resident population estimated as of July 1 of the year shown. 3. Based on the resident population estimated as of July 1, 1988 for 1987 data and enumerated as of April 1, 1980 for 1979 data.

STATE County	Housing units, 1990 (cont'd): Occupied units: Total	Owner occupied: Percent	Owner occupied: Median value (Dollars)	Median rent (Dollars)	Civilian labor force, 1990: Total	Percent change, 1989–1990	Unemployment: Total	Unemployment: Rate[1]	Private nonfarm establishments, 1988: Number	Net change, 1987–1988	Employment[2]: Total	Per-cent change, 1987–1988	Manu-facturing	Retail trade
	74	75	76	77	78	79	80	81	82	83	84	85	86	87
MINNESOTA—Con.														
Houston	6 844	79.6	52 400	233	9 934	6.1	394	4.0	359	0	2 746	6.8	438	570
Hubbard	5 781	83.1	48 700	208	7 522	4.5	621	8.3	416	1	2 446	8.7	336	740
Isanti	8 810	83.1	64 400	302	12 654	1.6	790	6.2	449	11	4 785	1.4	1 137	1 276
Itasca	15 461	83.1	44 300	234	18 345	4.5	1 671	9.1	870	-10	8 908	-0.7	2 179	2 253
Jackson	4 560	76.2	32 100	174	5 839	7.0	285	4.9	252	-2	1 806	7.4	340	485
Kanabec	4 753	82.6	49 200	256	5 950	0.9	641	10.8	247	-4	2 899	-1.9	972	736
Kandiyohi	14 298	72.9	56 800	269	21 002	5.4	851	4.1	1 051	24	11 901	6.1	2 663	3 039
Kittson	2 274	81.8	28 000	167	2 678	7.2	227	8.5	182	4	919	-0.8	40	245
Koochiching	6 025	77.9	41 800	252	10 721	28.5	585	5.5	422	18	3 708	9.1	1 214	846
Lac qui Parle	3 505	78.9	26 000	164	4 261	4.4	170	4.0	230	-3	1 744	8.5	343	398
Lake	4 242	82.9	39 400	217	4 667	13.7	329	7.0	220	-14	1 916	8.4	438	565
Lake of the Woods	1 576	84.5	40 900	185	2 047	7.1	75	3.7	121	2	634	-0.9	85	0
Le Sueur	8 468	82.0	57 800	256	11 658	2.4	752	6.5	500	1	4 984	-2.0	1 926	1 053
Lincoln	2 704	79.9	22 900	142	3 439	5.5	191	5.6	185	-5	1 030	-10.1	23	270
Lyon	9 073	68.4	48 200	246	13 037	3.8	559	4.3	699	-3	7 950	2.1	1 198	2 335
McLeod	11 815	77.0	62 100	283	17 746	1.4	841	4.7	806	12	12 916	7.4	7 025	2 485
Mahnomen	1 805	79.4	33 900	132	2 553	6.6	216	8.5	105	8	586	4.1	0	206
Marshall	4 194	82.1	34 600	161	5 249	5.8	683	13.0	268	-1	1 353	5.7	149	368
Martin	9 129	74.9	40 500	205	12 238	6.0	606	5.0	682	16	7 040	-5.7	2 078	1 717
Meeker	7 651	79.6	49 100	234	9 262	4.7	712	7.7	476	8	4 882	5.8	1 606	1 039
Mille Lacs	6 911	79.7	50 800	254	10 700	8.0	655	6.1	529	29	5 345	11.4	1 966	1 078
Morrison	10 399	81.8	47 100	223	15 132	4.5	1 352	8.9	613	-6	5 850	4.3	1 669	1 399
Mower	15 028	77.3	42 600	228	18 469	7.6	775	4.2	854	29	10 153	-0.3	0	2 661
Murray	3 758	79.4	30 400	156	5 070	5.3	269	5.3	238	4	1 559	6.9	52	428
Nicollet	9 478	72.9	65 200	324	15 952	2.8	537	3.4	522	10	9 071	4.5	3 810	1 310
Nobles	7 683	75.4	39 600	237	12 314	7.7	411	3.3	597	-5	7 250	8.8	2 264	1 692
Norman	3 118	80.1	30 200	161	3 776	4.6	246	6.5	219	5	1 223	-3.1	0	291
Olmsted	40 058	72.4	72 300	379	64 983	4.3	2 095	3.2	2 221	33	52 741	1.3	10 384	10 809
Otter Tail	19 510	78.1	46 600	227	26 611	6.0	1 564	5.9	1 261	38	11 644	5.1	2 682	2 926
Pennington	5 173	74.0	41 400	212	7 233	6.3	603	8.3	375	-1	4 117	8.3	663	1 389
Pine	7 577	82.5	44 900	227	10 722	4.7	945	8.8	416	9	2 969	6.9	316	1 373
Pipestone	4 078	76.7	31 700	180	5 363	-0.1	316	5.9	296	10	2 610	11.8	0	687
Polk	11 984	74.7	47 200	243	15 258	3.5	1 111	7.3	811	-15	7 746	-1.3	1 412	1 982
Pope	4 135	78.7	39 200	188	5 035	6.5	322	6.4	287	24	1 882	0.1	491	496
Ramsey	190 500	62.2	83 600	418	279 450	1.5	11 298	4.0	11 788	91	255 980	2.8	72 427	49 068
Red Lake	1 730	78.8	28 200	160	1 750	11.0	286	16.3	112	7	626	16.8	76	190
Redwood	6 554	77.1	32 800	179	7 901	2.4	328	4.2	491	-1	3 885	6.9	894	967
Renville	6 790	79.2	31 600	183	9 490	3.1	572	6.0	513	7	3 724	-4.7	775	803
Rice	16 347	75.5	67 800	316	28 703	2.8	1 127	3.9	1 070	44	15 514	5.9	3 460	3 819
Rock	3 754	75.3	36 600	178	4 975	7.7	161	3.2	257	6	1 995	0.1	374	502
Roseau	5 415	82.6	49 400	256	9 333	7.2	428	4.6	308	29	2 816	-39.6	0	739
St. Louis	78 901	74.2	42 200	256	93 812	3.1	5 586	6.0	4 889	85	59 222	6.7	5 991	15 914
Scott	19 367	81.9	90 900	431	30 224	1.3	1 510	5.0	1 317	64	16 101	6.3	3 472	3 594
Sherburne	13 643	80.5	74 800	406	19 803	1.6	1 329	6.7	626	32	6 580	6.4	1 056	1 741
Sibley	5 323	81.5	44 400	191	7 250	4.7	392	5.4	309	-9	2 280	2.4	605	483
Stearns	39 776	71.4	61 400	352	65 246	1.1	3 436	5.3	3 032	79	45 776	4.4	8 731	14 671
Steele	11 342	77.1	61 200	272	16 732	4.4	627	3.7	731	-5	12 728	5.4	4 748	2 250
Stevens	3 823	67.2	37 700	240	5 322	2.9	182	3.4	289	14	2 259	0.9	82	770
Swift	4 268	77.5	27 500	178	5 016	2.0	266	5.3	319	10	2 071	5.3	451	615
Todd	8 589	80.8	35 000	184	11 507	6.1	882	7.7	463	3	3 831	1.7	1 396	789
Traverse	1 778	79.0	23 400	152	2 221	6.1	118	5.3	146	6	666	2.0	16	238
Wabasha	7 286	81.7	51 900	245	8 988	1.4	492	5.5	481	-1	3 978	4.7	1 209	924
Wadena	4 978	76.4	36 200	181	5 178	2.6	424	8.2	361	9	3 639	5.8	493	834
Waseca	6 649	77.3	53 500	251	10 173	7.9	371	3.6	411	17	5 562	10.0	2 863	903
Washington	49 246	83.9	94 200	450	76 574	1.6	3 120	4.1	2 394	90	29 688	1.0	8 017	8 251
Watonwan	4 530	74.8	35 500	195	6 358	3.9	232	3.6	319	-2	3 119	3.6	1 184	585
Wilkin	2 805	77.6	38 400	197	3 510	2.0	164	4.7	177	-8	1 448	8.5	0	558
Winona	16 930	72.1	54 400	282	27 121	1.4	1 217	4.5	1 122	42	17 716	5.7	7 233	3 545
Wright	23 013	82.0	75 000	326	34 564	1.8	2 112	6.1	1 393	25	12 968	4.8	2 115	3 968
Yellow Medicine	4 607	77.9	31 100	174	5 983	4.9	256	4.3	348	2	2 751	33.0	516	650
MISSISSIPPI	911 374	71.5	45 600	215	1 184 000	1.5	88 000	7.5	X	X	675 321	2.5	224 900	144 947
Adams	13 262	71.5	43 900	174	13 615	0.8	1 221	9.0	1 045	-49	11 147	5.3	1 933	2 874
Alcorn	12 449	75.7	38 800	157	14 905	-2.4	1 506	10.1	767	-12	10 855	-4.0	5 859	1 957
Amite	4 830	86.0	36 800	125	4 500	7.5	289	6.4	176	-3	1 326	-5.6	665	258
Attala	6 945	78.2	36 500	128	8 152	0.5	844	10.4	371	12	4 394	-5.0	1 731	777

1. Percent of total civilian labor force. 2. For week including March 12. Excludes government employees, self-employed persons, farm workers, domestic service workers, railroad employees subject to the Railroad Retirement Act, and employees on oceanborne vessels or in foreign countries.

Table A. States and Counties — **Employment, Personal Income, and Earnings**

STATE County	Private nonfarm establishments, 1988 (cont'd): Employment[1] (cont'd): Finance, insurance, and real estate	Employment[1] (cont'd): Services	Annual payroll: Total (Mil dol)	Annual payroll: Average per employee (Dollars)	Personal income, 1989: Total (Mil dol)	Percent change, 1988–1989	Wages and salaries[2] (Mil dol)	Proprietor's income (Mil dol)	Dividends, interest, & rent (Mil dol)	Transfer payments (Mil dol)	Per capita[3]: Dollars	Per capita[3]: Rank	Earnings, 1989: Total (Mil dol)	Percent by selected industries: Farm	Goods-related[4]: Total
	88	89	90	91	92	93	94	95	96	97	98	99	100	101	102
MINNESOTA—Con.															
Houston	143	874	34	12 428	257	8.3	66	32	50	42	13 395	1 729	98	13.5	21.0
Hubbard	99	612	34	13 701	174	7.8	56	24	37	47	11 476	2 509	81	10.1	18.3
Isanti	157	1 609	70	14 587	365	7.9	133	29	45	52	13 812	1 529	163	3.7	24.3
Itasca	359	2 292	164	18 377	518	8.2	284	36	91	124	12 436	2 147	320	0.3	NA
Jackson	111	439	25	13 720	202	22.2	52	69	46	33	16 387	548	121	45.0	13.1
Kanabec	122	705	45	15 458	158	6.0	68	15	26	31	12 203	2 232	83	4.0	34.7
Kandiyohi	439	2 916	184	15 462	572	10.2	301	91	111	100	14 644	1 151	392	10.7	19.5
Kittson	67	303	11	12 213	89	-0.8	28	19	21	20	14 628	1 156	47	33.2	4.3
Koochiching	122	1 083	66	17 820	199	14.5	135	16	25	49	13 882	1 489	150	0.3	50.4
Lac qui Parle	90	596	22	12 624	125	5.8	38	29	32	26	13 364	1 749	67	28.4	14.3
Lake	196	470	29	15 072	118	11.3	60	9	24	31	10 809	2 714	69	0.1	NA
Lake of the Woods	0	235	7	10 355	51	10.5	20	7	10	11	12 764	2 009	27	18.1	NA
Le Sueur	172	1 075	78	15 635	354	7.1	126	44	70	56	15 170	918	170	11.8	38.1
Lincoln	48	462	11	10 751	96	9.0	22	26	24	21	13 571	1 649	48	31.4	5.5
Lyon	549	1 807	112	14 084	385	9.4	215	64	80	62	15 431	823	279	10.9	30.8
McLeod	343	1 550	245	18 932	509	8.0	330	53	98	68	15 570	781	384	5.1	53.2
Mahnomen	0	133	7	12 776	65	13.0	18	19	12	17	12 471	2 130	37	36.5	NA
Marshall	127	338	17	12 860	155	5.1	41	44	33	33	13 359	1 751	85	44.0	8.9
Martin	309	1 754	113	16 049	403	14.6	165	93	92	63	17 529	365	258	25.2	24.4
Meeker	194	901	77	15 794	299	7.5	116	44	55	51	13 863	1 498	159	15.9	29.9
Mille Lacs	179	1 474	76	14 155	265	7.6	121	34	42	57	13 718	1 573	154	4.5	NA
Morrison	210	1 700	89	15 170	357	9.0	154	50	65	77	11 519	2 491	204	9.8	25.7
Mower	385	2 946	182	17 953	593	10.7	252	94	125	117	15 664	752	346	14.1	28.9
Murray	125	413	20	12 782	163	17.8	38	56	37	27	15 853	695	94	44.0	12.4
Nicollet	187	3 086	116	12 773	388	8.9	195	56	74	42	13 825	1 520	251	11.0	37.8
Nobles	275	1 423	109	15 093	347	15.2	155	96	73	53	17 272	401	250	23.0	19.9
Norman	88	392	16	13 241	143	14.0	34	52	28	26	17 345	388	86	51.3	4.5
Olmsted	1 745	24 686	1 211	22 952	1 996	9.0	1 680	136	288	199	19 517	194	1 816	1.4	31.8
Otter Tail	502	3 013	166	14 214	685	9.1	289	101	150	151	13 096	1 865	390	9.6	18.9
Pennington	193	1 171	62	15 031	193	7.7	108	28	32	39	14 559	1 185	137	10.0	16.4
Pine	125	729	37	12 570	232	6.8	85	24	39	62	10 676	2 744	108	7.5	14.6
Pipestone	94	625	34	13 001	154	8.4	56	39	37	31	14 107	1 386	94	17.2	21.4
Polk	451	2 671	102	13 166	504	9.3	191	104	88	106	15 405	835	295	25.7	12.8
Pope	102	415	25	13 357	138	8.3	44	24	35	32	12 353	2 183	68	21.2	14.8
Ramsey	21 445	75 568	5 795	22 637	9 317	6.6	8 551	505	1 607	1 354	19 337	204	9 057	0.0	39.6
Red Lake	50	173	7	11 781	61	6.1	17	18	11	14	12 796	1 999	35	38.2	9.6
Redwood	334	931	52	13 367	258	12.2	90	64	71	48	14 462	1 227	154	28.0	18.8
Renville	242	828	50	13 309	285	13.0	91	72	69	48	15 323	865	162	30.7	17.3
Rice	415	5 797	248	15 989	730	7.9	395	69	125	102	14 889	1 029	465	4.4	26.9
Rock	276	468	26	13 011	162	15.8	49	51	40	24	16 274	576	100	40.6	11.8
Roseau	107	604	41	14 562	215	4.5	145	37	34	32	14 590	1 172	181	13.6	55.4
St. Louis	2 604	20 643	1 052	17 770	2 867	9.0	1 791	154	501	649	14 502	1 210	1 945	0.2	25.9
Scott	473	4 368	320	19 892	1 032	8.4	422	72	118	81	18 180	275	494	2.0	36.9
Sherburne	375	1 563	119	18 121	533	9.1	217	51	56	60	14 217	1 329	269	6.0	25.5
Sibley	132	635	27	11 926	218	11.5	49	52	50	35	14 634	1 153	101	31.9	19.2
Stearns	1 597	12 854	734	16 044	1 635	8.1	1 147	191	269	236	13 838	1 511	1 338	3.9	24.9
Steele	1 951	2 160	252	19 783	507	9.9	327	62	94	63	16 838	465	389	7.8	43.6
Stevens	153	772	31	13 786	150	7.8	70	31	35	28	14 705	1 124	101	18.0	11.5
Swift	102	439	25	11 949	155	11.5	50	40	35	33	13 705	1 576	90	30.0	11.4
Todd	210	806	58	15 174	274	7.3	108	48	53	65	10 755	2 728	156	17.2	29.5
Traverse	47	181	7	11 111	79	9.4	18	26	22	15	17 000	437	44	38.4	4.4
Wabasha	144	834	57	14 345	280	10.0	97	40	64	53	14 357	1 265	137	13.9	26.5
Wadena	129	1 540	44	12 125	152	7.9	78	26	26	41	10 904	2 685	105	7.3	17.7
Waseca	216	857	103	18 527	290	11.4	150	60	53	41	15 897	676	210	18.8	43.9
Washington	2 033	6 034	811	27 330	2 846	6.1	1 087	128	398	193	19 886	176	1 215	0.9	41.4
Watonwan	186	680	39	12 550	188	15.3	74	50	41	31	16 553	515	125	30.3	29.2
Wilkin	76	434	16	10 881	126	14.2	36	36	25	22	16 419	540	73	39.4	5.0
Winona	438	4 419	274	15 481	685	8.1	412	73	134	111	14 770	1 097	485	4.1	39.8
Wright	544	3 718	187	14 428	1 044	7.2	322	102	132	122	14 788	1 085	424	4.4	24.0
Yellow Medicine	134	978	35	12 888	167	8.0	61	38	41	37	13 578	1 645	99	21.2	16.2
MISSISSIPPI	39 046	137 796	10 728	X	30 942	6.4	18 080	3 300	4 069	6 176	11 806	X	21 380	3.7	30.5
Adams	577	2 504	185	16 561	444	6.0	269	54	75	97	12 181	2 246	322	0.8	NA
Alcorn	536	1 185	184	16 918	384	5.0	246	41	52	76	11 865	2 372	288	0.4	49.7
Amite	65	157	20	15 029	116	2.4	37	17	17	31	8 785	3 026	54	9.8	44.7
Attala	178	673	59	13 465	185	7.6	83	20	27	53	10 097	2 869	104	5.3	35.1

1. For week including March 12. Excludes government employees, self-employed persons, farm workers, domestic service workers, railroad employees subject to the Railroad Retirement Act, and employees on oceanborne vessels or in foreign countries. 2. Includes other labor income. 3. Based on the resident population estimated as of July 1 of the year shown. 4. Covers mining, construction, and manufacturing.

Table A. States and Counties — **Earnings and Agriculture**

STATE County	Earnings, 1989 (cont'd): Percent by selected industries (cont'd): Goods-related[1]: Manufacturing	Service-related & other[2]: Total	Service-related & other[2]: Retail trade	Service-related & other[2]: Finance, insurance, & real estate	Service-related & other[2]: Services	Government	Agriculture, 1987: Farms: Number	Farms: Percent with: Less than 50 acres	Farms: Percent with: 500 acres and over	Farm operators, percent: Whose principal occupation is farming	Farm operators, percent: Residing on farm operated	Land in farms: Acreage (1,000)	Land in farms: Percent change, 1982–1987	Acres: Average size of farm	Acres: Total irrigated (1,000)	Acres: Total cropland (1,000)
	103	104	105	106	107	108	109	110	111	112	113	114	115	116	117	118
MINNESOTA—Con.																
Houston	11.0	49.0	7.5	4.1	20.3	16.5	1 073	10.5	13.9	70.9	83.1	285	-0.5	266	0	164
Hubbard	9.0	50.3	13.8	3.1	25.7	21.4	460	11.5	12.6	42.2	88.3	124	-3.9	269	15	70
Isanti	15.2	46.1	9.6	2.7	25.8	25.9	817	27.1	7.6	40.9	85.9	143	-6.5	175	2	102
Itasca	21.2	NA	9.7	2.5	NA	23.6	541	14.2	9.2	37.5	85.2	124	1.7	228	1	59
Jackson	8.7	28.1	6.4	2.5	9.7	13.9	1 074	12.7	26.4	80.1	72.5	394	-4.2	367	0	367
Kanabec	17.9	43.6	19.8	3.2	15.5	17.8	771	16.7	7.5	53.0	87.4	164	-9.4	213	0	79
Kandiyohi	11.7	47.2	10.5	3.7	19.7	22.6	1 219	17.7	18.8	73.9	80.1	377	-5.0	310	7	329
Kittson	0.5	40.0	8.1	2.8	14.3	22.6	576	5.2	61.5	81.6	74.7	498	-2.8	865	1	425
Koochiching	36.8	33.0	9.2	1.8	15.5	16.3	248	8.9	17.7	44.4	83.9	81	-9.4	328	1	41
Lac qui Parle	11.3	40.1	9.0	4.0	13.6	17.2	972	11.4	32.9	81.3	75.3	411	-1.8	423	3	374
Lake	17.0	NA	11.9	2.4	NA	25.1	47	25.5	6.4	40.4	83.0	6	-21.9	136	D	D
Lake of the Woods	15.9	39.6	8.4	2.2	17.0	23.1	222	6.8	34.7	58.1	80.2	119	-0.3	536	D	84
Le Sueur	30.2	37.9	8.3	3.3	16.3	12.2	932	23.4	11.6	66.3	80.0	223	-3.1	239	1	193
Lincoln	0.9	48.0	8.8	2.1	20.6	15.1	748	10.7	20.1	82.2	77.8	253	-5.2	338	1	218
Lyon	22.3	39.4	9.5	5.0	15.4	18.9	1 036	17.9	25.2	76.7	74.2	368	-9.7	355	0	337
McLeod	46.2	30.0	7.5	2.4	10.2	11.7	1 303	20.1	7.4	69.8	79.5	258	-5.9	198	1	230
Mahnomen	2.3	36.2	8.7	3.0	10.9	22.2	393	7.1	33.1	77.9	81.7	197	1.8	501	D	157
Marshall	3.1	29.5	6.9	2.9	10.0	17.6	1 299	6.0	45.3	78.3	73.4	820	-4.8	631	0	735
Martin	20.2	40.0	8.0	4.5	15.4	10.4	1 269	13.1	22.1	80.5	75.7	433	0.6	341	1	406
Meeker	20.4	40.2	9.6	3.5	12.4	13.9	1 153	18.0	13.1	69.8	82.0	299	-8.1	259	4	256
Mille Lacs	25.4	NA	9.9	3.4	19.9	18.1	833	16.9	4.8	56.1	88.2	153	-5.9	184	0	90
Morrison	17.8	42.9	9.6	2.8	18.3	21.6	1 911	13.3	5.3	66.4	84.7	430	-0.6	225	9	254
Mower	24.1	42.7	10.3	2.6	19.3	14.3	1 341	18.4	17.4	71.9	78.4	386	-5.1	288	4	357
Murray	4.0	32.7	5.2	2.3	12.5	10.9	995	11.9	25.1	84.1	78.6	372	0.2	374	D	341
Nicollet	34.1	33.8	4.9	3.1	17.2	17.4	892	15.5	14.2	74.8	77.0	250	-1.0	280	D	230
Nobles	16.4	44.3	10.6	4.0	12.9	12.8	1 269	13.4	20.0	81.8	76.5	414	-1.5	326	D	387
Norman	1.1	31.1	5.4	4.0	10.6	13.2	718	13.2	46.0	83.7	77.7	472	-10.7	658	D	428
Olmsted	26.3	57.7	7.7	2.3	42.2	9.0	1 446	23.1	10.4	55.4	78.4	319	-3.5	220	D	258
Otter Tail	11.2	52.5	11.4	3.8	19.7	19.0	2 925	12.0	15.8	73.2	83.7	876	-5.2	300	34	631
Pennington	13.8	54.1	10.0	2.9	20.2	19.4	585	13.0	33.3	68.0	80.7	306	-2.4	523	D	268
Pine	6.6	45.4	16.9	2.9	14.3	32.5	1 085	10.8	9.1	52.9	85.8	259	-7.2	239	0	136
Pipestone	16.4	45.7	10.8	3.3	16.0	15.6	785	20.1	17.5	77.1	79.7	247	-1.7	314	2	216
Polk	8.9	43.7	7.5	3.2	19.1	17.8	1 556	9.4	46.7	80.3	74.2	1 076	-1.7	691	5	961
Pope	7.6	45.9	10.1	3.2	18.2	18.1	961	13.8	21.2	71.5	75.8	328	-4.3	341	28	265
Ramsey	34.6	45.3	7.3	6.8	21.0	15.0	61	77.0	0.0	37.7	39.3	2	-36.4	35	0	1
Red Lake	4.4	34.4	9.6	3.0	9.2	17.8	404	9.4	36.6	69.1	75.7	210	-5.2	521	0	183
Redwood	14.0	38.9	8.3	3.9	13.5	14.3	1 435	13.3	25.3	85.4	74.1	514	0.6	359	2	481
Renville	10.4	40.1	6.5	4.1	12.6	11.9	1 455	12.8	24.9	83.8	74.7	564	-3.3	388	0	531
Rice	20.3	50.2	9.6	2.1	28.4	18.5	1 186	22.0	6.7	61.5	80.0	226	-10.0	190	1	193
Rock	8.9	35.5	7.4	7.8	11.6	12.1	843	19.3	17.2	79.4	77.7	260	-5.1	309	D	235
Roseau	53.8	20.9	5.3	1.7	7.6	10.1	1 124	8.2	35.1	66.0	78.6	614	-3.1	546	0	500
St. Louis	9.1	51.8	10.7	3.2	24.6	22.0	921	17.0	6.7	37.1	86.6	180	-6.9	195	1	93
Scott	22.8	48.8	11.6	2.4	21.8	12.3	924	33.0	4.0	51.0	80.2	134	-8.1	145	0	112
Sherburne	15.7	50.2	11.0	1.9	13.0	18.3	604	28.8	10.1	43.5	81.0	124	-7.9	206	24	89
Sibley	9.9	34.7	6.4	3.7	14.8	14.2	1 252	13.6	12.5	77.0	79.4	337	0.3	269	1	302
Stearns	18.1	54.1	16.3	3.4	22.2	17.1	3 185	15.4	5.1	72.7	82.4	672	-0.3	211	35	522
Steele	38.2	39.9	7.2	11.5	13.1	8.7	951	21.7	11.5	69.7	81.0	234	-1.2	246	0	216
Stevens	5.6	42.8	8.3	4.2	18.0	27.7	619	16.6	35.2	81.1	75.1	295	-6.9	477	11	276
Swift	7.7	39.5	9.2	3.5	12.5	19.1	884	13.5	34.6	78.1	73.1	395	-5.4	447	19	360
Todd	24.6	33.6	7.7	2.3	13.2	19.7	1 946	13.5	6.7	67.8	84.7	418	-3.5	215	11	265
Traverse	0.7	40.8	8.9	3.8	13.2	16.4	457	7.2	48.4	86.9	75.1	312	-5.5	683	0	299
Wabasha	20.4	44.3	7.7	2.7	16.2	15.3	1 034	15.5	10.5	72.1	78.1	256	-4.0	247	0	196
Wadena	11.7	54.6	13.1	3.3	17.5	20.5	689	10.9	11.2	63.4	83.2	178	-4.2	259	8	101
Waseca	39.7	24.8	6.6	2.1	9.3	12.5	813	18.8	18.3	73.6	77.1	232	-6.4	285	0	212
Washington	33.2	43.9	9.7	6.3	16.9	13.8	736	40.8	6.2	45.1	83.6	109	-13.6	149	3	87
Watonwan	24.2	30.3	6.3	2.7	11.0	10.1	748	12.8	20.1	81.8	76.2	253	-2.9	338	2	235
Wilkin	0.2	43.6	7.2	3.6	17.4	12.1	505	9.3	56.4	84.6	77.0	427	0.9	846	2	411
Winona	34.9	41.2	9.4	2.2	20.0	14.9	1 174	14.3	12.9	74.4	81.6	310	-1.1	264	0	204
Wright	12.2	55.7	13.3	3.0	21.0	15.9	1 841	31.1	4.7	54.3	82.6	288	-6.6	157	3	225
Yellow Medicine	9.4	41.7	8.9	3.2	16.2	20.9	1 027	9.8	29.3	81.8	76.9	413	-6.4	402	1	379
MISSISSIPPI	24.9	45.8	9.9	4.6	18.8	20.0	34 074	22.4	15.1	44.3	67.3	10 746	-13.5	315	637	6 748
Adams	24.3	NA	12.0	3.8	23.6	13.4	159	26.4	22.0	39.6	51.6	93	-22.8	587	0	50
Alcorn	46.5	38.0	11.0	3.6	15.1	11.9	434	27.2	7.6	32.3	70.0	78	-20.3	180	D	43
Amite	39.4	29.4	7.2	3.6	11.6	16.0	528	18.6	10.8	46.6	69.1	153	-16.5	289	0	64
Attala	27.5	42.8	12.2	4.5	16.1	16.9	427	11.7	11.0	44.7	71.7	113	-20.2	264	0	46

1. Covers mining, construction, and manufacturing. 2. Covers private sector earnings in agricultural services, forestry, and fisheries; transportation and public utilities; wholesale trade; retail trade; finance, insurance, and real estate; and services.

STATE County	Agriculture, 1987 (cont'd): Value of land and buildings: Average per farm ($1,000)	Value of land and buildings: Average per acre (Dollars)	Value of products sold: Total (Mil dol)	Value of products sold: Average per farm (Dollars)	Value of products sold: Percent from: Crops	Value of products sold: Percent from: Livestock and poultry[1]	Percent of farms with sales of: $10,000 or more	Percent of farms with sales of: $100,000 or more	Manufactures, 1987: Establishments: Total	Establishments: Percent with 20 or more employees	All employees: Number (1,000)	All employees: Percent change, 1982–1987	All employees: Annual payroll (Mil dol)	Production workers: Number (1,000)	Production workers: Work hours (Mil)
	119	120	121	122	123	124	125	126	127	128	129	130	131	132	133
MINNESOTA—Con.															
Houston	177	648	67	62 668	15.5	84.5	74.3	20.9	21	14.3	0.4	0.0	5.9	0.3	0.6
Hubbard	123	456	19	40 644	60.4	39.6	28.5	5.2	37	16.2	0.5	0.0	9.3	0.4	0.8
Isanti	140	812	19	23 664	43.0	57.0	36.2	5.0	40	47.5	1.1	22.2	20.2	0.9	1.7
Itasca	101	428	7	13 720	28.7	71.3	23.1	1.7	82	14.6	2.3	9.5	61.4	1.8	3.3
Jackson	359	921	107	99 563	56.4	43.6	88.0	32.1	9	22.2	D	D	D	D	D
Kanabec	109	536	21	27 141	9.7	90.3	39.7	6.2	15	40.0	1.1	120.0	19.3	0.5	1.1
Kandiyohi	217	762	155	127 237	26.3	73.7	72.3	22.0	50	32.0	2.8	21.7	36.0	2.2	4.0
Kittson	442	486	50	86 181	90.6	9.4	78.6	28.3	6	0.0	0.0	0.0	0.4	0.0	0.0
Koochiching	111	366	5	20 964	25.8	74.2	31.0	2.4	47	12.8	1.1	0.0	32.3	0.9	1.7
Lac qui Parle	245	557	66	67 926	62.2	37.8	85.8	21.1	14	21.4	D	D	D	D	D
Lake	93	682	0	6 346	D	D	10.6	2.1	22	27.3	0.4	33.3	9.2	0.3	0.7
Lake of the Woods	203	361	6	27 958	68.4	31.6	48.2	5.9	9	11.1	D	D	D	D	D
Le Sueur	206	904	60	64 190	41.8	58.2	66.4	18.9	39	38.5	2.4	26.3	45.5	1.9	3.5
Lincoln	176	509	48	63 935	36.7	63.3	82.5	19.7	7	0.0	0.0	0.0	0.3	0.0	0.0
Lyon	249	695	93	90 136	43.8	56.2	81.9	28.7	26	42.3	1.3	-40.9	21.5	1.1	2.0
McLeod	169	826	68	52 304	41.1	58.9	73.3	16.7	53	54.7	7.1	36.5	159.6	5.2	10.9
Mahnomen	220	463	17	43 454	59.9	40.1	69.0	12.5	3	66.7	0.1	0.0	0.6	0.0	0.1
Marshall	293	466	71	55 035	89.2	10.8	72.4	17.0	10	10.0	0.1	0.0	1.9	0.1	0.2
Martin	347	1 038	135	106 334	52.6	47.4	90.0	31.0	35	34.3	2.4	4.3	46.1	1.8	3.4
Meeker	197	740	85	73 831	33.4	66.6	73.2	19.8	43	41.9	1.4	27.3	25.9	1.1	2.0
Mille Lacs	112	592	29	34 298	11.8	88.2	51.0	9.0	44	36.4	1.5	114.3	25.5	1.2	2.2
Morrison	140	628	113	59 256	8.4	91.6	61.3	13.4	36	36.1	1.5	66.7	26.8	1.2	2.3
Mower	233	793	103	76 456	52.4	47.6	80.7	24.7	28	39.3	D	D	D	D	D
Murray	246	643	87	87 671	50.7	49.3	88.6	32.1	8	12.5	0.0	0.0	0.4	0.0	0.0
Nicollet	274	948	83	93 234	43.1	56.9	85.8	31.4	39	41.0	3.5	-5.4	50.5	2.5	4.4
Nobles	240	769	115	90 629	45.5	54.5	87.7	25.8	28	32.1	1.6	33.3	29.3	1.2	2.5
Norman	370	588	58	80 484	85.1	14.9	76.6	25.9	3	33.3	D	D	D	D	D
Olmsted	191	878	86	59 514	29.6	70.4	64.1	16.2	66	36.4	10.3	4.0	378.2	3.4	12.5
Otter Tail	167	557	159	54 474	24.5	75.5	65.5	14.0	77	22.1	2.3	21.1	37.3	1.7	3.0
Pennington	171	362	22	38 284	60.7	39.3	63.9	8.9	21	38.1	0.8	60.0	12.3	0.6	1.0
Pine	133	551	32	29 536	9.0	91.0	42.7	5.2	26	11.5	0.3	-25.0	5.7	0.2	0.4
Pipestone	168	539	53	67 370	42.7	57.3	82.8	22.2	18	16.7	D	D	D	D	D
Polk	443	654	163	104 678	87.0	13.0	76.3	32.3	39	25.6	1.3	-23.5	26.8	0.9	2.0
Pope	178	535	53	55 028	40.4	59.6	69.5	15.9	21	28.6	0.4	100.0	7.7	0.3	0.6
Ramsey	203	5 767	6	93 177	80.9	19.1	50.8	23.0	792	39.8	68.9	2.2	2 248.4	29.9	58.8
Red Lake	201	378	19	47 807	57.6	42.4	67.6	12.9	10	10.0	0.1	0.0	1.3	0.1	0.1
Redwood	304	837	136	94 500	53.6	46.4	89.3	32.5	33	18.2	0.8	0.0	14.1	0.6	1.0
Renville	340	860	154	105 531	65.5	34.5	88.9	32.2	34	26.5	0.9	12.5	13.1	0.7	1.3
Rice	184	957	73	61 287	28.5	71.5	63.6	15.0	60	40.0	3.5	20.7	72.2	2.5	5.2
Rock	233	795	88	104 139	33.6	66.4	85.4	28.7	10	30.0	D	D	D	D	D
Roseau	182	349	50	44 861	55.7	44.3	62.9	11.0	14	21.4	D	D	D	D	D
St. Louis	94	523	12	13 445	22.3	77.7	21.1	2.1	231	21.6	6.6	13.8	138.5	3.3	6.0
Scott	194	1 346	40	42 808	29.3	70.7	52.7	11.9	92	31.5	3.5	12.9	88.0	2.3	4.8
Sherburne	224	1 016	33	55 019	43.8	56.2	39.1	13.1	59	23.7	1.2	20.0	28.6	0.8	1.8
Sibley	236	900	103	82 276	40.5	59.5	82.3	24.3	20	30.0	0.5	0.0	7.6	0.5	0.9
Stearns	154	696	224	70 484	11.0	89.0	72.6	21.4	157	34.4	8.0	19.4	157.9	5.9	11.3
Steele	199	830	66	69 543	48.6	51.4	77.6	21.0	56	48.2	4.2	13.5	90.1	2.8	5.5
Stevens	289	605	70	113 547	41.1	58.9	84.2	27.6	13	15.4	0.1	-50.0	2.9	0.1	0.2
Swift	248	529	69	77 884	61.4	38.6	81.2	20.5	18	22.2	0.3	0.0	4.9	0.3	0.6
Todd	113	535	96	49 485	12.8	87.2	60.1	10.5	32	37.5	1.3	8.3	26.2	1.1	2.2
Traverse	376	543	45	98 112	73.2	26.8	88.4	29.1	5	0.0	0.0	0.0	0.2	0.0	0.0
Wabasha	169	644	72	69 539	22.0	78.0	75.2	24.2	33	27.3	1.2	0.0	22.4	1.1	2.2
Wadena	100	426	27	39 863	11.1	88.9	52.2	5.5	21	14.3	0.4	0.0	6.7	0.3	0.6
Waseca	259	889	58	71 145	58.2	41.8	80.1	24.6	21	42.9	2.9	-9.4	69.0	2.1	4.6
Washington	289	2 025	27	36 146	61.7	38.3	39.7	8.6	130	30.0	8.1	39.7	315.2	5.9	12.0
Watonwan	343	976	70	94 152	58.2	41.8	89.2	29.3	16	50.0	1.1	0.0	16.0	1.0	1.8
Wilkin	574	669	61	120 818	91.5	8.5	85.0	35.2	5	0.0	0.0	0.0	0.2	0.0	0.0
Winona	187	750	87	74 449	16.7	83.3	72.3	25.1	95	50.5	7.1	31.5	129.4	5.2	10.4
Wright	177	1 110	74	40 196	26.8	73.2	54.8	12.1	109	24.8	2.2	29.4	36.6	1.6	3.1
Yellow Medicine	269	660	78	75 506	64.4	35.6	85.7	23.2	18	22.2	0.5	0.0	8.7	0.3	0.7
MISSISSIPPI	215	697	1 863	54 672	49.1	50.9	35.1	13.0	3 318	37.6	218.9	8.5	3 827.3	171.4	337.4
Adams	394	675	8	52 428	87.3	12.7	28.9	8.8	52	25.0	1.8	-45.5	50.8	1.5	3.3
Alcorn	115	664	6	13 297	57.5	42.5	22.4	2.1	68	39.7	6.1	1.7	113.5	4.9	9.9
Amite	265	800	13	25 343	5.1	94.9	27.8	7.2	25	16.0	0.6	-64.7	12.3	0.5	1.1
Attala	118	474	9	21 941	70.9	29.1	26.0	4.9	40	30.0	1.5	25.0	18.4	1.3	2.4

1. Includes livestock and poultry products.

STATE County	Manufactures, 1987 (cont'd): Production workers (cont'd): Wages: Total (Mil dol)	Manufactures, 1987 (cont'd): Production workers (cont'd): Wages: Average per worker (Dollars)	Manufactures, 1987 (cont'd): Value added by manufacture (Mil dol)	Manufactures, 1987 (cont'd): Value of shipments (Mil dol)	Manufactures, 1987 (cont'd): New capital expenditures (Mil dol)	Value of construction authorized by building permits, 1990: Total[1] ($1,000)	Nonresidential: Total ($1,000)	Nonresidential: Percent: Office	Nonresidential: Percent: Industrial	Nonresidential: Percent: Stores	Residential: New construction ($1,000)	Residential: Number of housing units	Residential: Alterations and additions ($1,000)
	134	135	136	137	138	139	140	141	142	143	144	145	146
MINNESOTA—Con.													
Houston	4.3	14 333	8.8	23.1	D	6 165	826	0.0	9.5	51.0	4 596	75	363
Hubbard	7.3	18 250	30.8	55.4	1.7	4 014	858	0.0	10.1	41.7	761	20	35
Isanti	14.3	15 889	46.2	118.8	D	16 920	2 308	73.3	13.5	6.9	12 426	183	375
Itasca	45.1	25 056	153.1	321.1	D	47 107	9 852	0.0	0.0	61.1	17 960	310	3 399
Jackson	D	D	D	D	D	4 005	2 388	0.0	21.6	0.0	525	15	574
Kanabec	8.8	17 600	30.1	67.1	1.7	1 943	280	0.0	16.1	33.9	1 114	20	121
Kandiyohi	25.3	11 500	75.0	309.2	8.1	31 429	9 655	0.1	6.5	45.6	13 133	210	1 713
Kittson	0.2	NA	1.0	3.6	0.0	1 975	940	0.0	0.0	0.0	271	4	390
Koochiching	25.2	28 000	76.5	177.9	D	7 877	1 668	0.0	7.8	11.1	4 016	65	902
Lac qui Parle	D	D	D	D	D	1 557	948	0.0	59.7	12.5	305	11	126
Lake	6.5	21 667	25.2	49.8	1.5	5 114	639	17.4	14.1	0.0	2 414	70	870
Lake of the Woods	D	D	D	D	D	7 399	109	0.0	0.0	0.0	90	2	70
Le Sueur	31.5	16 579	182.6	381.7	6.1	11 762	2 510	0.0	39.4	0.0	6 896	141	1 091
Lincoln	0.2	NA	1.0	1.7	D	422	91	54.9	0.0	0.0	63	1	22
Lyon	16.2	14 727	88.2	213.3	1.5	9 992	2 119	3.5	4.0	9.4	3 493	52	804
McLeod	98.4	18 923	703.8	1 239.9	47.9	22 640	8 158	0.0	68.5	11.7	10 245	125	1 098
Mahnomen	0.4	NA	1.2	1.7	D	186	115	0.0	0.0	0.0	27	1	18
Marshall	1.2	12 000	4.9	9.6	0.1	598	29	0.0	0.0	0.0	184	2	204
Martin	29.2	16 222	112.6	213.2	8.6	14 655	6 136	23.8	0.0	24.4	2 752	28	620
Meeker	16.5	15 000	60.5	195.8	7.5	8 965	3 860	1.3	36.7	11.4	3 277	52	703
Mille Lacs	19.9	16 583	62.3	121.4	3.4	12 277	3 793	4.8	10.5	44.6	6 252	121	783
Morrison	17.8	14 833	58.3	149.2	13.1	17 097	10 136	0.1	24.1	47.5	4 728	133	1 280
Mower	D	D	D	D	D	12 348	4 422	0.0	1.0	64.9	4 360	48	1 276
Murray	0.2	NA	1.2	2.5	0.1	2 380	698	0.0	11.5	0.0	1 081	17	68
Nicollet	25.5	10 200	136.1	433.7	27.9	26 270	6 551	0.0	1.1	5.3	10 963	226	1 975
Nobles	21.4	17 833	72.3	438.1	6.7	9 645	3 300	10.2	0.0	12.9	3 738	56	346
Norman	D	D	D	D	D	813	187	0.0	0.0	0.0	362	5	109
Olmsted	75.3	22 147	1 037.6	1 762.1	47.0	185 989	7 733	18.3	9.1	36.8	99 098	1 107	5 025
Otter Tail	23.6	13 882	105.5	343.4	8.4	16 081	5 063	9.4	14.1	31.5	6 159	118	1 248
Pennington	7.3	12 167	32.5	108.5	1.3	3 005	586	11.6	0.0	0.0	363	8	599
Pine	3.7	18 500	21.0	32.3	0.5	5 906	1 640	15.4	0.0	52.1	2 693	49	166
Pipestone	D	D	D	D	D	7 760	6 313	0.0	43.8	0.0	1 010	19	104
Polk	19.5	21 667	107.0	271.8	D	6 758	1 287	29.7	0.6	31.9	2 771	56	1 042
Pope	4.5	15 000	15.3	31.4	0.3	3 993	2 940	0.0	64.5	0.0	512	8	193
Ramsey	737.6	24 669	4 606.0	9 144.9	246.1	442 400	107 542	54.0	5.4	34.1	112 491	1 156	39 340
Red Lake	0.8	8 000	3.0	6.1	0.0	406	0	NA	NA	NA	242	4	107
Redwood	7.9	13 167	27.1	63.9	0.6	5 657	2 890	1.0	8.6	2.0	1 204	19	271
Renville	8.9	12 714	30.4	76.4	1.7	3 866	2 233	0.0	62.2	1.3	680	12	262
Rice	49.5	19 800	212.0	409.2	13.5	57 855	11 040	9.3	29.6	37.5	22 379	254	2 968
Rock	D	D	D	D	D	1 418	852	0.0	0.0	40.0	107	2	171
Roseau	D	D	D	D	D	4 942	1 814	0.0	25.0	70.3	1 579	38	529
St. Louis	62.4	18 909	271.3	493.7	D	69 825	9 700	7.2	2.1	54.2	27 828	467	9 407
Scott	56.4	24 522	261.2	592.4	D	93 836	20 851	0.0	59.6	22.2	62 893	671	4 152
Sherburne	17.4	21 750	66.6	103.0	D	50 787	6 031	7.3	30.4	10.2	38 940	597	1 901
Sibley	6.1	12 200	18.7	61.3	0.9	6 836	3 660	0.0	19.7	11.9	2 363	35	596
Stearns	105.0	17 797	378.5	887.9	25.5	90 952	22 374	6.1	33.3	47.8	49 813	1 023	4 080
Steele	48.4	17 286	221.8	477.6	22.6	35 498	18 127	1.9	54.5	31.5	11 663	169	1 327
Stevens	1.8	18 000	7.5	13.1	0.2	3 092	2 078	0.0	59.8	0.0	647	9	199
Swift	3.0	10 000	9.7	17.5	D	4 046	1 771	0.0	4.1	60.3	1 260	19	255
Todd	21.3	19 364	59.7	270.8	4.2	12 397	1 655	0.0	1.2	1.2	6 419	107	721
Traverse	0.1	NA	0.7	1.3	D	1 020	661	0.0	0.0	32.3	172	3	83
Wabasha	18.2	16 545	44.8	163.8	D	5 829	2 122	0.0	13.2	48.5	2 090	38	325
Wadena	4.4	14 667	17.6	27.0	D	4 483	2 367	0.0	53.4	17.6	1 258	29	326
Waseca	42.2	20 095	181.9	301.1	13.5	8 605	3 580	5.1	55.4	6.3	3 247	52	585
Washington	215.3	36 492	838.6	2 138.3	58.6	227 630	22 455	13.0	25.7	41.2	177 037	1 892	13 628
Watonwan	12.3	12 300	38.9	71.4	2.4	2 536	1 084	0.0	0.0	0.0	681	10	426
Wilkin	0.1	NA	0.6	2.1	0.0	1 889	25	0.0	0.0	0.0	1 125	20	0
Winona	79.6	15 308	268.9	616.1	20.1	26 923	6 870	3.3	63.2	12.7	14 649	256	1 502
Wright	23.2	14 500	88.1	218.8	D	65 914	15 459	1.4	16.6	43.7	39 594	563	4 111
Yellow Medicine	6.0	20 000	20.1	38.6	0.2	2 677	775	0.0	11.0	6.2	969	16	379
MISSISSIPPI	2 620.6	15 289	10 502.6	24 380.6	647.7	693 374	194 456	15.3	13.6	40.5	298 514	5 950	39 302
Adams	41.8	27 867	221.5	400.8	14.3	3 820	1 865	0.0	0.0	0.0	401	6	442
Alcorn	80.3	16 388	241.6	503.8	18.3	7 252	1 348	27.3	1.6	39.1	4 775	60	512
Amite	9.3	18 600	30.9	61.6	1.3	1 207	1 029	8.7	0.0	0.0	116	3	9
Attala	12.4	9 538	42.6	90.7	1.7	3 809	813	47.7	0.0	0.0	1 996	68	53

1. Includes nonresidential additions and alterations, residential nonhousekeeping buildings, and residential garages and carports not shown separately.

STATE County	Wholesale trade, 1987				Retail trade, all establishments, 1987				Retail trade, establishments with payroll, 1987					
						Sales				Sales				
											Per capita[2] (Dollars)			
	Establishments	Sales (Mil dol)	Paid employees[1]	Annual payroll (Mil dol)	Number	Total (Mil dol)	Percent change, 1982–1987	Per capita[2] (Dollars)	Number	Total (Mil dol)	General merchandise stores	Food stores	Apparel & accessory stores	Eating and drinking places
	147	148	149	150	151	152	153	154	155	156	157	158	159	160
MINNESOTA—Con.														
Houston	29	39.0	196	2.3	198	49.0	13.4	2 591	95	43.7	D	573	18	180
Hubbard	16	24.2	163	2.7	229	75.7	43.4	5 112	131	70.2	D	1 201	115	298
Isanti	26	16.7	130	1.7	214	102.1	69.3	4 021	121	98.5	D	1 019	80	280
Itasca	45	57.8	287	5.0	478	214.6	28.0	5 109	262	204.0	D	956	248	348
Jackson	26	49.1	167	2.7	117	58.5	53.9	4 570	65	56.4	D	266	71	264
Kanabec	17	11.1	79	0.9	134	56.7	45.8	4 497	77	54.9	D	858	88	405
Kandiyohi	94	365.7	1 193	23.2	487	224.2	24.8	5 854	308	214.9	878	947	344	569
Kittson	27	55.4	159	2.6	89	27.0	26.8	4 280	53	24.5	D	961	D	185
Koochiching	16	10.9	72	1.3	195	79.9	13.0	5 362	128	77.0	D	1 075	205	435
Lac qui Parle	29	100.0	267	4.4	138	27.9	-9.4	2 873	77	24.7	D	574	D	167
Lake	6	5.3	30	0.3	136	58.8	22.0	5 204	84	57.1	D	994	71	321
Lake of the Woods	9	6.3	34	0.4	55	18.7	23.8	4 926	36	17.4	D	1 176	D	372
Le Sueur	44	113.6	263	4.4	236	68.9	1.8	2 944	140	63.9	D	550	36	339
Lincoln	24	39.5	118	1.6	102	22.3	28.9	3 010	60	20.5	33	561	D	219
Lyon	79	233.1	638	11.5	299	148.6	36.1	5 993	195	145.3	510	1 323	403	622
McLeod	66	155.9	497	9.4	358	202.7	48.5	6 395	228	195.9	540	2 148	326	448
Mahnomen	10	8.9	41	0.7	64	17.3	30.1	3 266	31	14.1	D	681	D	218
Marshall	32	80.4	196	3.3	138	38.6	60.8	3 247	80	34.7	D	587	D	227
Martin	72	204.2	508	8.1	310	114.5	4.7	4 790	189	108.7	662	1 065	274	382
Meeker	44	66.4	296	5.0	221	79.5	22.5	3 787	122	76.0	D	672	97	328
Mille Lacs	32	32.7	158	2.4	249	75.4	8.3	3 947	131	70.7	123	1 188	92	326
Morrison	48	103.0	330	4.4	337	115.5	22.6	3 799	200	105.3	D	808	139	336
Mower	59	106.5	349	5.9	418	194.5	15.5	5 066	266	189.3	589	1 097	185	439
Murray	28	91.6	285	4.8	124	31.2	-6.3	3 004	70	28.4	93	477	77	271
Nicollet	44	257.4	331	5.7	218	92.2	28.2	3 330	138	88.8	D	607	176	457
Nobles	67	187.0	1 103	16.6	280	115.7	9.3	5 674	182	111.1	755	983	463	477
Norman	33	79.8	249	4.2	115	27.7	31.3	3 260	71	26.0	D	704	34	156
Olmsted	140	357.9	1 304	26.7	985	838.7	46.3	8 498	648	823.3	1 500	1 381	397	706
Otter Tail	91	135.5	602	7.6	639	243.1	31.8	4 676	371	228.2	523	958	170	343
Pennington	41	169.2	471	10.0	157	79.6	11.2	5 894	116	77.8	D	1 406	396	690
Pine	28	57.1	121	2.1	225	98.0	38.4	4 620	146	95.0	112	738	63	822
Pipestone	31	98.0	196	2.8	156	48.0	6.9	4 407	89	43.5	D	932	119	384
Polk	93	214.5	701	14.0	353	143.0	15.2	4 335	217	136.2	164	1 425	82	395
Pope	24	49.7	179	3.1	146	39.9	35.7	3 563	80	36.1	D	853	78	379
Ramsey	914	4 855.1	13 046	346.6	4 232	3 763.3	43.7	7 896	2 988	3 716.2	1 210	1 294	393	805
Red Lake	10	31.3	41	0.7	56	13.2	0.0	2 704	35	11.9	D	D	0	253
Redwood	70	149.7	363	6.8	232	72.6	8.7	3 988	129	67.0	D	953	82	287
Renville	69	212.0	560	10.6	230	63.0	10.7	3 296	123	57.4	61	744	D	221
Rice	58	328.1	720	15.2	475	243.4	35.8	5 092	306	237.1	258	1 036	268	610
Rock	32	75.6	219	3.4	104	34.5	-16.3	3 413	65	32.6	D	777	276	436
Roseau	28	42.4	199	3.2	154	59.2	47.6	4 288	94	54.8	181	1 005	157	291
St. Louis	321	962.7	3 161	67.4	2 245	1 199.1	20.2	5 999	1 486	1 163.3	D	1 187	246	491
Scott	99	1 108.4	1 190	27.1	476	231.8	50.0	4 433	257	221.1	D	771	38	485
Sherburne	26	48.0	183	3.0	290	163.0	113.1	4 606	153	157.1	D	1 106	40	253
Sibley	27	124.8	314	6.3	171	36.7	-0.5	2 447	96	34.0	D	583	35	205
Stearns	219	623.2	2 977	64.2	1 276	1 676.4	89.4	14 616	861	1 650.5	D	1 065	319	649
Steele	59	104.3	495	9.0	322	177.3	39.8	5 910	196	172.8	527	1 094	185	439
Stevens	33	102.1	255	5.5	138	54.7	29.9	5 257	79	51.3	D	1 041	213	487
Swift	39	103.5	218	3.1	148	38.6	-11.3	3 300	85	36.0	235	871	96	185
Todd	45	59.2	323	4.4	258	71.3	14.4	2 820	149	64.6	60	679	57	199
Traverse	13	46.3	94	1.5	84	17.4	3.0	3 484	48	16.2	D	742	D	153
Wabasha	44	49.0	269	4.2	254	78.6	30.8	4 096	132	73.4	64	824	46	283
Wadena	40	88.3	336	7.0	179	77.2	21.8	5 472	107	73.8	D	1 105	192	296
Waseca	39	73.3	289	4.6	200	69.6	37.0	3 846	116	65.6	D	799	D	266
Washington	102	287.8	750	15.1	1 007	637.3	55.0	4 839	577	618.2	D	1 076	161	522
Watonwan	31	77.1	215	3.5	153	41.8	-0.2	3 606	92	40.0	D	859	177	279
Wilkin	22	81.1	198	3.9	82	30.7	7.0	3 892	57	29.3	D	D	D	592
Winona	97	234.6	815	12.6	473	237.0	20.6	5 129	302	227.4	554	1 110	183	564
Wright	83	213.8	726	13.0	634	327.9	47.4	4 984	366	313.4	133	885	71	408
Yellow Medicine	38	103.3	276	4.5	154	46.3	26.8	3 677	98	44.2	D	775	102	206
MISSISSIPPI	3 850	12 249.8	39 936	733.1	26 522	11 990.5	32.6	4 569	15 729	11 357.7	624	1 052	182	337
Adams	100	132.5	751	12.7	445	237.9	9.1	6 361	322	232.4	959	1 518	383	374
Alcorn	45	115.6	598	10.2	539	181.7	38.7	5 555	267	164.8	624	1 183	411	450
Amite	13	9.6	49	0.8	113	28.3	21.5	2 143	61	25.4	170	683	D	D
Attala	23	24.5	155	2.0	215	74.4	32.6	3 934	117	67.4	D	901	181	229

1. For pay period including March 12. 2. Based on the estimated population as of July 1 of the year shown.

STATE County	Retail trade, establishments with payroll, 1987 (cont'd)		Taxable service industries–establishments with payroll, 1987							Bank deposits,[2] June 1989		Savings capital,[3] September 1989	
				Receipts (Mil dol)									
					Selected kinds of business								
	Paid employees[1]	Annual payroll (Mil dol)	Number	Total	Hotels, motels and other lodging places	Health services	Legal services	Paid employees	Annual payroll (Mil dol)	Total (Mil dol)	Percent change, 1988–1989	Total (Mil dol)	Percent change, 1988–1989
	161	162	163	164	165	166	167	168	169	170	171	172	173
MINNESOTA—Con.													
Houston	548	3.9	74	12.4	0.6	4.6	1.3	355	3.6	137	1.9	11.9	-34.2
Hubbard	773	6.8	99	14.2	3.8	5.0	0.5	385	3.8	100	3.4	18.1	-0.9
Isanti	1 333	10.4	90	26.0	D	13.9	1.3	690	9.4	148	3.9	23.8	15.6
Itasca	2 292	19.9	180	48.0	8.4	18.1	1.7	1 577	17.6	275	-0.8	81.7	-16.3
Jackson	522	4.4	53	9.1	D	1.6	1.4	225	2.4	111	-5.1	28.8	-6.6
Kanabec	743	6.0	49	9.4	0.5	5.5	0.4	276	3.1	95	4.4	12.3	13.1
Kandiyohi	2 962	22.7	216	70.2	4.2	34.1	3.4	1 610	25.7	352	3.4	67.0	6.4
Kittson	247	2.1	25	4.0	0.1	1.2	D	76	1.4	58	-1.3	21.2	-2.3
Koochiching	894	8.5	96	21.4	6.0	8.2	1.3	619	7.1	111	3.9	8.9	-18.9
Lac qui Parle	409	3.1	41	7.7	D	1.4	0.5	176	1.7	87	-2.6	13.9	-5.4
Lake	533	5.3	47	10.0	1.5	6.1	0.4	200	2.6	48	-0.6	0.0	NA
Lake of the Woods	190	1.5	33	5.2	3.7	0.0	0.0	99	0.8	33	6.0	6.1	0.8
Le Sueur	1 027	6.8	97	16.1	0.3	7.6	2.0	513	5.9	231	4.6	21.7	14.3
Lincoln	307	2.1	36	4.4	0.0	2.1	D	121	1.1	48	-7.2	0.0	NA
Lyon	2 167	16.9	130	27.6	D	10.8	2.2	954	9.8	280	-10.6	62.4	17.7
McLeod	2 438	20.2	171	31.1	1.8	11.4	2.3	939	10.4	327	4.9	77.4	-1.6
Mahnomen	207	1.5	20	3.5	D	0.8	0.4	73	0.8	32	-2.5	0.0	NA
Marshall	340	3.1	31	2.8	D	D	D	66	0.8	118	3.2	11.7	-1.0
Martin	1 692	12.9	120	22.0	D	6.5	3.4	633	8.0	283	4.3	67.6	-5.7
Meeker	1 034	7.5	72	12.0	0.3	6.4	1.0	415	4.4	149	-2.3	14.0	-17.6
Mille Lacs	1 068	8.3	112	14.2	0.9	5.1	0.6	444	4.7	143	3.0	17.1	14.0
Morrison	1 394	10.9	100	16.7	1.7	7.7	0.8	425	5.8	170	2.1	56.9	-7.9
Mower	2 698	21.7	177	47.8	D	18.4	4.1	1 388	19.0	310	0.2	134.3	-3.9
Murray	440	3.0	37	9.3	D	3.3	D	250	3.8	104	-3.2	24.6	12.9
Nicollet	1 239	9.3	106	23.9	D	6.9	1.1	793	7.9	194	3.6	0.0	NA
Nobles	1 713	12.9	113	25.0	2.3	11.9	2.1	837	9.5	229	19.0	30.6	-18.3
Norman	283	2.2	30	4.9	D	1.2	D	121	1.8	99	0.9	18.4	3.7
Olmsted	10 416	90.2	524	184.0	44.2	40.1	13.0	5 790	66.8	662	2.5	238.4	17.0
Otter Tail	2 934	24.6	217	43.3	2.5	22.3	2.1	1 167	16.5	398	0.8	118.0	2.6
Pennington	1 278	9.9	75	13.3	D	3.9	1.2	355	5.0	124	2.4	38.3	-8.8
Pine	1 264	11.0	69	10.1	1.2	4.6	D	381	3.4	97	2.8	25.6	-8.7
Pipestone	605	4.3	51	8.1	0.8	4.3	D	252	1.8	102	-4.8	59.9	1.6
Polk	1 979	15.4	147	27.9	3.5	7.2	3.2	865	9.9	261	-3.3	128.8	5.8
Pope	517	3.6	44	6.9	0.5	3.0	0.7	236	2.6	96	-2.9	6.8	-63.9
Ramsey	48 345	447.1	3 340	1 652.0	63.9	452.1	154.1	48 929	678.9	4 369	-5.9	1 813.3	-1.8
Red Lake	189	1.2	15	2.7	0.0	D	0.4	66	0.9	43	3.1	5.1	-11.3
Redwood	904	7.2	78	16.9	0.8	9.5	1.9	635	7.2	230	-1.0	22.8	-2.4
Renville	816	5.9	67	14.2	D	7.8	1.7	635	5.0	199	-1.9	26.4	21.5
Rice	3 601	27.7	227	75.5	2.0	28.8	3.7	1 827	28.8	350	7.8	78.7	-2.7
Rock	545	3.8	44	7.9	0.4	2.6	0.6	206	2.1	104	-2.5	56.2	1.5
Roseau	696	5.6	52	9.1	1.3	2.8	0.7	312	2.6	130	4.2	14.2	-4.6
St. Louis	14 856	130.5	1 135	352.1	D	111.2	25.5	9 654	144.0	1 341	1.9	474.4	0.1
Scott	2 978	26.1	275	126.1	5.5	20.8	2.6	3 267	39.3	246	0.3	24.7	12.6
Sherburne	1 620	14.3	113	20.2	D	7.3	D	660	7.2	155	6.3	9.2	11.5
Sibley	510	3.2	51	9.2	D	2.8	0.6	399	3.2	122	-1.3	16.9	3.8
Stearns	14 576	133.3	697	221.5	12.6	79.7	18.5	6 010	89.3	983	-3.5	237.6	17.4
Steele	2 291	18.9	162	41.8	2.0	13.1	2.9	1 129	13.6	270	17.8	92.5	-4.6
Stevens	684	4.9	44	11.3	D	3.8	D	328	4.2	96	-6.1	31.0	0.0
Swift	549	3.8	49	9.1	D	3.2	1.4	285	3.2	133	-1.1	12.4	1.0
Todd	834	6.4	68	10.8	0.9	5.0	0.8	254	3.7	150	0.5	17.8	4.7
Traverse	233	1.7	28	4.1	D	3.1	0.4	143	1.3	74	2.8	14.8	8.1
Wabasha	1 010	8.1	111	16.8	2.5	5.5	1.2	453	4.8	188	1.8	27.8	-40.3
Wadena	916	7.4	62	14.0	0.6	4.7	1.0	306	4.5	116	5.5	31.9	-1.5
Waseca	903	6.5	73	12.8	0.3	4.9	1.4	519	4.8	145	2.9	33.0	5.3
Washington	8 026	66.4	600	152.2	3.3	64.8	4.5	4 338	58.0	599	5.2	168.5	8.9
Watonwan	579	4.2	51	9.7	0.0	3.1	0.8	227	2.9	140	-1.4	12.5	-3.9
Wilkin	448	3.4	27	3.0	D	0.9	D	80	0.8	73	1.6	7.6	-12.3
Winona	3 195	25.2	230	68.7	1.6	14.9	4.4	1 831	22.0	479	0.8	56.3	9.6
Wright	3 959	33.2	295	75.5	4.2	20.3	3.1	2 344	25.1	378	3.7	27.5	6.8
Yellow Medicine	625	4.2	57	6.9	D	3.7	0.3	187	2.1	105	-5.3	28.7	-0.1
MISSISSIPPI	140 361	1 264.6	11 663	3 331.6	205.3	1 239.0	305.1	84 293	1 208.4	16 934	3.7	3 991.8	-3.1
Adams	2 857	26.4	256	61.4	9.9	27.7	4.4	1 608	21.0	248	2.4	64.9	-1.6
Alcorn	1 998	18.6	175	37.1	D	16.7	2.5	983	12.4	241	3.4	186.8	9.6
Amite	289	2.5	24	2.8	0.0	1.3	0.2	78	0.9	60	7.0	0.0	NA
Attala	781	7.1	81	19.3	D	5.3	2.9	420	5.5	130	7.8	41.3	1.5

1. For the period including March 12 of the year shown. 2. Includes deposits for all insured and reporting noninsured commercial and mutual savings banks. 3. Includes savings capital for all FSLIC insured savings institutions.

STATE County	Federal funds and grants, 1989: Expenditures: Total (Mil dol)	Expenditures: Percent change, 1988–1989	Per capita[1] (Dollars): Total	Per capita: Direct payments for individuals	Per capita: Procurement contract awards	Per capita: Salaries and wages	Per capita: Grant awards	Local government finances, 1981–1982: General revenue: Total (Mil dol)	Intergovernmental: Total (Mil dol)	Intergovernmental: Percent from state	Taxes: Total (Mil dol)	Taxes: Per capita[2]: Total (Dollars)	Taxes: Per capita[2]: Property (Dollars)	Direct general expenditure: Total (Mil dol)	Direct general expenditure: Percent change, 1977–1982
	174	175	176	177	178	179	180	181	182	183	184	185	186	187	188
MINNESOTA—Con.															
Houston	46.2	7.4	2 406	1 513	19	123	299	17.1	11.4	94.0	3.5	188	182	17.6	53.2
Hubbard	42.4	7.5	2 789	2 069	12	103	495	19.3	13.3	87.7	3.9	278	273	18.1	88.8
Isanti	41.5	2.7	1 572	1 093	14	93	226	23.2	15.8	96.4	4.6	189	186	23.5	72.2
Itasca	104.2	6.6	2 500	1 825	24	166	467	74.9	39.9	94.8	15.7	364	360	76.2	78.1
Jackson	45.9	-12.0	3 700	1 804	13	113	492	26.2	13.2	95.0	5.3	384	381	26.2	126.8
Kanabec	27.5	5.2	2 115	1 422	12	96	385	15.6	9.2	95.4	2.3	185	182	15.6	61.6
Kandiyohi	100.9	2.7	2 582	1 567	20	186	288	64.8	28.0	89.6	9.3	245	237	66.4	113.0
Kittson	40.0	8.0	6 552	2 145	66	276	746	12.9	4.7	93.5	3.7	556	549	13.9	77.7
Koochiching	45.2	-6.0	3 158	2 209	74	278	551	27.0	16.1	91.8	4.9	289	284	27.3	63.2
Lac qui Parle	45.1	6.0	4 850	1 903	23	217	221	14.4	6.9	83.4	3.4	320	317	14.6	28.8
Lake	26.3	4.3	2 415	1 894	59	120	335	35.3	15.2	92.3	2.1	165	161	32.9	173.7
Lake of the Woods	12.0	-0.5	3 001	1 908	89	263	463	6.8	3.7	96.2	1.3	361	355	6.0	47.3
Le Sueur	55.9	-8.7	2 398	1 530	23	108	240	24.3	14.4	93.6	6.4	272	261	25.2	79.3
Lincoln	30.6	-1.3	4 308	2 048	20	167	331	8.3	5.0	93.6	2.3	281	279	9.0	59.1
Lyon	76.9	2.6	3 090	1 635	31	211	380	35.9	17.1	91.3	7.0	277	273	35.1	16.9
McLeod	64.5	3.2	1 973	1 378	31	111	156	45.6	20.2	94.7	8.1	268	260	45.3	89.9
Mahnomen	18.9	-9.1	3 640	1 787	95	157	1 113	9.9	6.4	88.3	1.7	306	304	9.8	50.1
Marshall	60.0	-0.8	5 176	1 932	116	223	384	18.9	10.2	88.2	5.6	441	436	18.3	48.6
Martin	74.8	-9.7	3 251	1 880	106	144	272	28.7	13.0	93.8	8.4	339	336	26.3	39.2
Meeker	58.0	-30.0	2 684	1 484	14	152	263	29.7	15.5	94.2	5.6	270	267	29.1	60.2
Mille Lacs	56.2	8.0	2 911	1 941	19	245	526	29.2	18.2	88.0	5.4	290	286	31.3	74.5
Morrison	101.5	15.1	3 274	1 553	59	512	698	33.3	23.9	81.6	5.7	192	188	34.3	39.7
Mower	120.2	-9.5	3 171	2 223	27	151	305	52.9	29.1	94.3	10.8	275	272	50.4	44.0
Murray	37.5	-9.4	3 645	1 734	21	166	267	13.2	7.1	87.9	3.3	292	288	12.9	58.4
Nicollet	46.5	3.9	1 656	881	32	68	137	23.3	9.7	94.2	5.3	193	188	22.9	60.7
Nobles	62.8	-14.2	3 126	1 809	17	180	348	36.5	16.0	87.4	7.3	340	335	39.0	96.6
Norman	31.1	-25.5	3 799	1 991	40	221	378	15.0	6.7	83.2	3.9	428	423	14.1	54.0
Olmsted	235.1	1.6	2 298	1 199	79	282	579	145.8	79.1	68.8	30.5	325	309	139.1	109.9
Otter Tail	145.9	1.7	2 789	1 868	37	158	341	58.7	32.5	91.8	11.2	216	212	56.0	66.0
Pennington	43.8	-4.3	3 296	1 973	25	202	550	20.8	12.0	94.6	3.7	257	251	22.0	35.7
Pine	64.3	6.7	2 964	1 744	88	436	468	28.8	18.8	93.7	4.6	227	224	31.4	99.0
Pipestone	36.3	-7.6	3 327	1 936	21	211	308	19.8	9.4	91.7	3.8	326	323	20.1	99.8
Polk	108.7	-8.0	3 324	1 975	63	179	469	50.5	28.5	87.1	11.8	345	336	48.9	58.6
Pope	69.1	83.3	6 165	1 984	2 544	127	292	13.6	6.7	95.2	3.4	297	292	12.9	71.0
Ramsey	2 314.8	-2.2	4 805	1 716	1 320	486	1 268	961.2	443.3	80.1	242.9	520	477	976.6	61.5
Red Lake	18.2	-4.2	3 793	1 798	21	152	651	8.5	4.4	94.2	1.8	328	325	8.0	39.0
Redwood	65.3	-1.9	3 646	1 806	33	174	311	28.8	12.6	94.6	6.5	339	334	27.7	70.2
Renville	65.4	-0.1	3 516	1 677	17	150	284	28.0	14.5	80.5	6.7	336	333	25.1	46.7
Rice	94.3	4.3	1 924	1 250	34	118	300	60.8	29.0	92.5	10.7	228	222	60.0	76.5
Rock	33.8	0.9	3 381	1 630	19	192	384	12.6	5.9	94.0	3.2	304	302	12.5	81.2
Roseau	44.2	3.7	3 006	1 385	17	163	441	17.4	9.1	95.9	3.0	241	239	18.5	55.8
St. Louis	631.0	3.2	3 192	2 091	93	340	655	384.5	216.0	89.3	64.2	294	267	396.8	45.0
Scott	68.2	3.4	1 201	749	99	157	92	57.7	28.2	91.1	15.4	337	326	55.4	64.7
Sherburne	49.7	11.5	1 324	904	13	84	181	38.6	22.6	80.7	10.3	326	322	39.4	50.6
Sibley	43.3	-12.2	2 904	1 519	38	118	265	17.3	8.8	95.4	4.2	270	265	17.3	57.8
Stearns	260.1	13.4	2 202	1 198	51	374	272	141.8	85.1	90.2	26.7	242	226	133.5	66.4
Steele	65.3	-4.9	2 170	1 444	52	112	161	42.9	19.5	95.4	8.3	274	270	37.2	71.9
Stevens	42.4	3.8	4 156	1 869	101	291	388	14.5	6.9	88.6	3.4	303	300	14.2	31.9
Swift	45.3	-12.1	4 010	2 000	22	209	353	20.2	10.2	93.7	4.7	369	366	19.7	48.5
Todd	68.5	7.6	2 685	1 590	13	119	466	40.6	24.1	94.5	4.2	164	162	41.1	101.2
Traverse	22.5	-4.5	4 890	2 303	22	178	252	10.2	3.9	85.6	2.2	404	400	11.0	97.3
Wabasha	86.0	46.0	4 413	1 897	1 689	144	261	26.0	13.2	96.5	5.2	269	265	25.7	39.8
Wadena	41.9	12.1	2 993	1 873	17	158	687	21.1	13.6	93.4	2.4	167	166	20.8	78.1
Waseca	46.9	-10.6	2 579	1 494	17	128	249	22.7	10.9	94.1	5.9	318	309	22.5	60.1
Washington	132.3	9.1	924	682	15	79	110	152.8	85.2	96.4	34.0	286	278	142.1	70.9
Watonwan	40.8	-15.9	3 580	1 863	379	188	117	14.6	7.9	91.5	4.1	333	328	15.8	83.7
Wilkin	26.5	-11.4	3 444	1 782	21	159	305	12.0	6.3	88.8	3.3	403	398	10.9	21.5
Winona	102.3	1.6	2 206	1 632	20	130	221	47.1	28.2	88.7	11.2	242	233	41.5	43.1
Wright	102.4	8.6	1 450	1 011	13	87	162	76.5	43.8	79.8	16.7	275	269	72.9	68.9
Yellow Medicine	54.7	5.7	4 450	1 975	21	154	331	27.1	12.9	87.4	4.4	329	325	27.9	82.2
MISSISSIPPI	9 343.2	-6.5	X	1 882	505	473	563	2 356.2	1 136.1	84.3	431.5	168	158	2 241.4	71.6
Adams	91.9	7.7	2 519	1 918	46	129	398	39.6	14.6	92.4	7.8	197	179	38.9	55.8
Alcorn	79.0	-13.7	2 437	1 902	116	115	267	31.8	12.4	84.9	4.0	122	117	31.7	86.8
Amite	31.1	1.4	2 357	1 728	74	140	348	8.5	6.4	93.0	1.3	97	94	9.3	87.4
Attala	58.5	0.7	3 197	2 343	108	174	455	15.0	7.8	90.7	2.6	133	132	13.9	30.7

1. Based on the estimated population as of July 1 of the year shown. 2. Based on the estimated population as of July 1, 1982.

STATE County	Local government finances, 1981–1982 (cont'd): Direct general expenditure (cont'd): Per capita[1] (Dollars)	Percent of total for– Education	Health & hospitals	Police protection	Public welfare	Highways	Debt outstanding: Total (Mil dol)	Per capita[1] (Dollars)	State and local government employment, 1989: Total	Rate[2]	Federal government civilian employment 1989: Total	Earnings ($1,000)	Elections, 1988[3]: Total vote cast for president	Vote for lead party (Percent)
	189	190	191	192	193	194	195	196	197	198	199	200	201	202
MINNESOTA—Con.														
Houston	944	52.3	0.6	3.0	7.9	18.4	7.0	378	701	365.1	84	2 169	8 848	R–54.0
Hubbard	1 275	53.4	0.2	3.1	11.5	10.2	10.0	705	809	532.2	42	1 023	7 749	R–56.3
Isanti	975	52.0	0.1	3.3	15.7	9.6	17.1	709	1 795	679.9	65	1 606	11 477	D–52.9
Itasca	1 768	34.3	13.9	2.7	15.3	15.4	19.2	445	3 150	755.4	228	5 680	19 076	D–55.1
Jackson	1 913	36.7	16.4	2.1	14.5	14.1	13.1	953	927	747.6	41	976	5 979	D–54.8
Kanabec	1 251	36.3	16.9	2.9	11.4	10.0	7.7	612	690	530.8	46	1 100	5 604	D–53.0
Kandiyohi	1 756	36.4	26.2	2.1	6.7	10.1	63.4	1 676	3 583	916.4	189	5 345	17 878	D–50.1
Kittson	2 069	42.7	14.9	1.9	3.7	15.0	12.6	1 887	498	816.4	63	1 680	3 060	D–53.9
Koochiching	1 608	39.6	8.1	4.0	13.6	12.8	16.7	980	935	653.8	145	4 095	6 795	D–56.9
Lac qui Parle	1 388	33.3	12.6	2.3	5.5	15.6	10.6	1 011	620	666.7	65	1 303	4 995	D–56.2
Lake	2 609	23.5	0.3	2.7	7.5	11.4	107.3	8 516	709	650.5	60	1 321	5 785	D–67.2
Lake of the Woods	1 620	31.8	0.8	3.7	17.7	22.8	270.9	73 223	296	740.0	33	795	1 814	R–54.2
Le Sueur	1 079	48.9	1.0	3.5	8.2	13.1	13.5	576	1 033	443.3	76	1 915	10 948	R–49.5
Lincoln	1 107	45.9	0.0	3.2	0.0	27.7	4.0	491	335	471.8	44	922	3 436	D–55.0
Lyon	1 381	35.7	15.3	3.3	14.2	12.5	22.2	874	2 463	989.2	153	4 001	11 762	R–50.7
McLeod	1 505	40.1	16.2	3.0	7.6	11.2	51.8	1 722	2 166	662.4	104	2 550	13 885	R–57.4
Mahnomen	1 788	54.3	11.4	2.2	10.9	9.6	1.1	206	399	767.3	32	705	2 360	D–54.1
Marshall	1 439	48.1	0.2	2.2	6.0	14.9	14.1	1 110	658	567.2	92	2 076	5 826	D–51.5
Martin	1 057	45.3	2.4	4.6	0.0	19.6	35.0	1 404	1 269	551.7	98	2 365	10 734	R–53.3
Meeker	1 393	45.3	14.3	3.0	8.3	10.5	12.2	585	1 057	489.4	100	2 549	9 728	R–51.4
Mille Lacs	1 673	48.6	6.2	2.5	11.3	9.6	15.6	833	1 082	560.6	132	4 621	8 308	D–52.1
Morrison	1 162	52.7	1.0	2.4	14.2	9.8	20.5	695	1 461	471.3	436	11 750	13 246	R–49.8
Mower	1 283	46.2	0.7	4.0	13.4	11.2	42.7	1 085	1 968	519.3	155	4 322	19 050	D–62.4
Murray	1 139	39.9	12.5	3.5	0.0	21.7	2.4	217	492	477.7	61	1 214	5 225	D–54.4
Nicollet	840	27.9	15.4	4.0	9.1	20.5	19.5	714	1 881	669.4	54	1 529	13 822	R–49.8
Nobles	1 813	34.3	20.4	1.9	6.2	9.9	25.1	1 166	1 581	786.6	114	2 892	9 394	D–52.7
Norman	1 550	38.1	11.3	1.9	6.3	15.2	9.2	1 013	563	686.6	59	1 347	3 964	D–54.2
Olmsted	1 483	35.4	3.7	3.3	8.1	7.2	127.3	1 357	5 623	549.7	858	27 928	47 609	R–58.1
Otter Tail	1 077	41.7	11.2	3.2	9.6	13.5	42.1	810	3 152	602.7	251	6 738	24 655	R–56.8
Pennington	1 520	50.7	0.0	2.8	11.9	10.7	15.5	1 068	1 147	862.4	82	2 178	6 073	D–51.1
Pine	1 548	50.9	8.1	2.2	13.4	13.1	11.2	550	1 207	556.2	306	9 621	9 543	D–58.1
Pipestone	1 747	45.3	13.9	2.4	5.3	9.6	5.7	495	700	642.2	69	1 750	5 197	R–53.1
Polk	1 427	42.5	0.9	3.2	11.4	10.0	37.3	1 088	2 368	724.2	179	4 560	14 665	D–51.3
Pope	1 114	39.9	19.0	2.7	8.0	14.0	3.6	312	622	555.4	52	1 221	5 783	D–53.2
Ramsey	2 091	24.2	8.5	3.6	10.8	3.6	1 592.8	3 411	41 868	869.0	5 339	180 294	235 333	D–61.1
Red Lake	1 488	40.6	0.3	3.2	19.5	19.7	4.2	784	321	668.8	27	610	2 182	D–56.3
Redwood	1 445	36.8	8.5	4.7	16.3	13.5	15.9	830	1 134	633.5	99	2 321	8 379	R–60.6
Renville	1 253	43.6	7.0	2.6	7.4	13.0	18.2	910	1 009	542.5	85	1 866	8 932	D–49.9
Rice	1 273	37.7	24.2	3.4	7.9	7.9	50.6	1 074	3 733	761.8	141	3 760	21 297	D–54.3
Rock	1 176	40.1	14.4	2.8	4.9	16.9	4.4	419	621	621.0	55	1 406	5 223	R–52.4
Roseau	1 504	41.0	17.1	3.1	6.6	14.0	10.9	885	831	565.3	83	2 169	6 214	R–56.3
St. Louis	1 820	31.4	5.0	3.2	16.4	9.1	233.2	1 070	17 126	866.3	1 778	54 423	103 308	D–68.1
Scott	1 213	41.4	0.3	6.2	11.3	10.3	82.3	1 801	2 114	372.2	230	6 218	24 747	R–52.7
Sherburne	1 250	46.7	0.4	3.0	9.9	7.6	54.2	1 722	1 648	439.5	91	2 528	16 550	R–50.5
Sibley	1 123	38.9	15.5	3.2	5.3	15.0	10.1	655	750	503.4	49	1 141	6 952	R–52.6
Stearns	1 212	49.6	7.6	3.0	7.2	10.1	86.5	785	8 018	678.9	1 559	49 222	52 166	R–52.8
Steele	1 231	42.0	12.3	3.7	11.0	9.4	32.9	1 088	1 360	451.8	96	2 699	13 620	R–58.6
Stevens	1 277	35.7	20.0	3.3	6.0	13.4	6.8	616	1 320	1 294.1	107	2 844	5 468	D–49.8
Swift	1 553	38.1	18.7	2.6	8.2	16.3	9.8	774	926	819.5	67	1 526	5 806	D–61.6
Todd	1 617	43.5	20.1	1.6	10.1	10.0	18.7	735	1 558	611.0	87	2 184	10 776	R–52.3
Traverse	1 992	24.7	20.3	2.2	11.5	15.9	4.3	778	397	863.0	33	711	2 478	D–56.5
Wabasha	1 329	42.2	12.2	3.9	6.5	16.2	21.4	1 108	960	492.3	71	1 810	9 237	R–50.7
Wadena	1 476	53.6	1.8	2.7	20.3	4.3	7.2	508	1 052	751.4	57	1 377	6 309	R–59.2
Waseca	1 216	40.9	8.4	3.0	14.0	11.1	8.9	481	1 307	718.1	72	1 869	8 294	R–53.9
Washington	1 194	53.8	2.9	4.5	8.8	8.0	129.3	1 087	6 206	433.7	216	5 936	66 513	D–52.5
Watonwan	1 282	38.9	0.5	2.9	6.4	18.9	9.7	789	612	536.8	64	1 650	5 430	R–52.0
Wilkin	1 317	42.9	1.0	4.5	9.0	18.2	9.8	1 180	398	516.9	42	967	3 450	R–56.0
Winona	896	44.5	0.9	6.0	10.0	12.2	39.5	854	3 003	647.2	157	4 460	21 652	R–50.9
Wright	1 202	44.6	9.5	3.4	10.6	10.0	60.4	996	2 842	402.5	172	4 366	29 601	R–50.6
Yellow Medicine	2 063	42.7	20.7	1.6	4.9	14.1	12.6	934	1 101	895.1	62	1 385	6 298	D–52.1
MISSISSIPPI	873	43.9	18.5	3.4	0.5	10.7	1 540.3	600	168 065	641.2	27 844	823 164	931 527	R–59.9
Adams	983	34.3	32.7	4.2	0.1	7.5	34.6	873	2 135	584.9	99	2 831	15 994	R–50.7
Alcorn	972	32.6	42.7	2.2	0.4	5.6	28.0	858	1 837	567.0	106	2 904	12 102	R–54.9
Amite	705	47.1	1.2	2.9	0.8	34.8	1.8	138	391	296.2	75	1 695	6 186	R–53.9
Attala	705	45.1	25.1	2.8	0.2	13.8	4.9	249	905	494.5	86	2 436	7 556	R–59.9

1. Based on the estimated population as of July 1, 1982. 2. Per 10,000 resident population estimated as of July 1 of the year shown. 3. Data subject to copyright.

STATE–County code	MSA/CMSA/NECMA code[1]	STATE County	Land Area,[2] 1990 (Sq. Km.)	Population, 1990											
							Race						Age of population Percent		
				Total persons	Rank	Per square kilometer	White	Black	Am. Indian, Eskimo, Aleut	Asian & Pacific Islander	Other race	Hispanic[3]	Under 5 years	5 to 14 years	15 to 24 years
			1	2	3	4	5	6	7	8	9	10	11	12	13
		MISSISSIPPI—Con.													
28 009	...	Benton	1 054	8 046	2 560	7.6	4 869	3 168	5	4	0	37	7.4	17.8	14.7
28 011	...	Bolivar	2 270	41 875	958	18.4	15 259	26 326	26	138	126	377	8.7	19.3	20.2
28 013	...	Calhoun	1 519	14 908	1 994	9.8	10 829	4 027	12	4	36	78	6.8	14.7	15.1
28 015	...	Carroll	1 626	9 237	2 451	5.7	5 560	3 654	11	10	2	42	7.1	16.5	14.1
28 017	...	Chickasaw	1 299	18 085	1 786	13.9	11 060	6 981	21	19	4	85	8.1	17.0	15.1
28 019	...	Choctaw	1 086	9 071	2 462	8.4	6 319	2 731	9	10	2	31	7.0	17.7	14.4
28 021	...	Claiborne	1 261	11 370	2 263	9.0	1 994	9 340	20	16	0	56	7.0	16.2	28.9
28 023	...	Clarke	1 791	17 313	1 833	9.7	11 312	5 977	6	8	10	64	6.9	17.1	14.7
28 025	...	Clay	1 058	21 120	1 623	20.0	9 789	11 266	19	32	14	80	7.8	17.9	16.4
28 027	...	Coahoma	1 435	31 665	1 224	22.1	11 001	20 454	20	112	78	271	9.0	19.5	16.2
28 029	...	Copiah	2 012	27 592	1 370	13.7	13 602	13 920	21	27	22	108	7.7	16.8	17.9
28 031	...	Covington	1 072	16 527	1 889	15.4	10 699	5 795	9	19	5	49	7.9	17.8	15.6
28 033	4920	De Soto	1 239	67 910	652	54.8	58 860	8 675	119	157	99	306	7.9	16.2	14.9
28 035	...	Forrest	1 209	68 314	646	56.5	46 672	21 001	91	459	91	499	7.3	14.4	21.7
28 037	...	Franklin	1 462	8 377	2 525	5.7	5 290	3 079	1	4	3	21	7.5	17.0	13.4
28 039	...	George	1 239	16 673	1 870	13.5	15 025	1 587	38	18	5	48	7.6	17.1	16.3
28 041	...	Greene	1 847	10 220	2 370	5.5	7 999	2 194	11	6	10	65	7.1	17.6	15.7
28 043	...	Grenada	1 093	21 555	1 599	19.7	12 563	8 916	31	31	14	86	7.9	16.3	14.8
28 045	0920	Hancock	1 235	31 760	1 218	25.7	28 625	2 774	129	164	68	549	7.2	15.5	13.4
28 047	0920	Harrison	1 505	165 365	287	109.9	127 630	32 281	466	4 331	657	2 939	8.0	15.3	16.4
28 049	3560	Hinds	2 251	254 441	197	113.0	123 177	129 558	232	1 251	223	1 148	7.7	15.8	16.6
28 051	...	Holmes	1 958	21 604	1 597	11.0	5 176	16 375	14	32	7	62	8.9	20.3	17.4
28 053	...	Humphreys	1 083	12 134	2 204	11.2	3 856	8 222	9	43	4	69	9.0	20.9	16.3
28 055	...	Issaquena	1 070	1 909	3 075	1.8	833	1 072	1	3	0	6	8.9	17.5	16.1
28 057	...	Itawamba	1 379	20 017	1 676	14.5	18 596	1 359	19	33	10	99	6.1	13.5	16.5
28 059	6025	Jackson	1 882	115 243	400	61.2	90 114	23 581	254	1 115	179	1 060	7.6	16.8	15.0
28 061	...	Jasper	1 751	17 114	1 844	9.8	8 410	8 687	8	7	2	41	7.0	18.0	15.5
28 063	...	Jefferson	1 345	8 653	2 497	6.4	1 185	7 462	2	4	0	43	8.8	20.6	16.4
28 065	...	Jefferson Davis	1 058	14 051	2 053	13.3	6 330	7 675	22	22	2	44	7.3	18.2	16.2
28 067	...	Jones	1 797	62 031	701	34.5	46 193	15 489	213	102	34	205	6.9	15.7	14.7
28 069	...	Kemper	1 984	10 356	2 354	5.2	4 407	5 739	200	8	2	32	7.3	16.9	16.8
28 071	...	Lafayette	1 635	31 826	1 216	19.5	23 151	7 980	28	645	22	203	5.4	11.7	31.6
28 073	...	Lamar	1 288	30 424	1 271	23.6	26 599	3 637	38	113	37	168	7.9	17.1	15.6
28 075	...	Lauderdale	1 822	75 555	596	41.5	48 706	26 280	96	352	121	501	7.5	15.8	15.4
28 077	...	Lawrence	1 115	12 458	2 185	11.2	8 300	4 132	7	15	4	51	7.0	17.9	14.6
28 079	...	Leake	1 509	18 436	1 766	12.2	11 086	6 558	777	8	7	49	7.0	16.6	14.4
28 081	...	Lee	1 165	65 581	668	56.3	51 260	14 049	59	137	76	360	8.0	15.7	14.3
28 083	...	Leflore	1 533	37 341	1 064	24.4	14 516	22 642	23	130	30	146	8.3	18.7	17.1
28 085	...	Lincoln	1 517	30 278	1 280	20.0	21 162	9 038	19	49	10	60	6.4	16.5	14.7
28 087	...	Lowndes	1 301	59 308	732	45.6	36 736	22 041	76	302	153	491	8.5	16.3	17.0
28 089	3560	Madison	1 863	53 794	799	28.9	29 789	23 731	42	189	43	276	8.8	16.4	15.3
28 091	...	Marion	1 405	25 544	1 442	18.2	17 733	7 721	23	46	21	137	7.1	17.9	14.9
28 093	...	Marshall	1 830	30 361	1 274	16.6	14 842	15 378	64	37	40	133	8.1	17.0	17.2
28 095	...	Monroe	1 979	36 582	1 087	18.5	25 394	11 097	26	28	37	186	7.3	16.3	15.2
28 097	...	Montgomery	1 054	12 388	2 190	11.8	6 916	5 440	11	16	5	50	6.9	16.6	14.8
28 099	...	Neshoba	1 476	24 800	1 471	16.8	16 945	4 611	3 194	37	13	104	7.3	17.1	15.0
28 101	...	Newton	1 497	20 291	1 660	13.6	13 697	5 831	737	7	19	85	7.0	15.4	16.7
28 103	...	Noxubee	1 800	12 604	2 177	7.0	3 959	8 588	44	10	3	27	9.2	19.4	15.5
28 105	...	Oktibbeha	1 186	38 375	1 044	32.4	24 064	13 171	29	1 020	91	330	6.3	12.7	32.3
28 107	...	Panola	1 772	29 996	1 296	16.9	15 376	14 533	32	34	21	153	8.2	18.2	16.3
28 109	...	Pearl River	2 102	38 714	1 035	18.4	32 888	5 545	142	80	59	300	7.4	16.7	15.2
28 111	...	Perry	1 676	10 865	2 307	6.5	8 333	2 447	72	5	8	46	7.7	18.0	15.9
28 113	...	Pike	1 059	36 882	1 077	34.8	19 931	16 843	26	52	30	173	7.0	17.7	15.4
28 115	...	Pontotoc	1 288	22 237	1 568	17.3	18 917	3 246	32	32	10	65	7.2	15.2	14.9
28 117	...	Prentiss	1 075	23 278	1 525	21.7	20 477	2 741	24	24	12	94	7.0	14.2	17.2
28 119	...	Quitman	1 049	10 490	2 337	10.0	4 250	6 193	16	18	13	48	8.6	18.4	16.5
28 121	3560	Rankin	2 006	87 161	523	43.5	72 033	14 610	72	314	132	520	6.9	16.0	14.1
28 123	...	Scott	1 578	24 137	1 489	15.3	14 829	9 171	59	24	54	141	8.2	16.7	15.5
28 125	...	Sharkey	1 108	7 066	2 651	6.4	2 339	4 686	7	24	10	48	8.6	21.7	17.5
28 127	...	Simpson	1 525	23 953	1 495	15.7	16 124	7 737	47	26	19	67	7.5	17.0	14.5
28 129	...	Smith	1 647	14 798	2 001	9.0	11 516	3 244	21	7	10	81	7.2	16.1	14.9
28 131	...	Stone	1 154	10 750	2 312	9.3	8 362	2 344	20	14	10	54	7.6	16.0	18.0
28 133	...	Sunflower	1 797	32 867	1 192	18.3	11 604	21 092	28	97	46	184	7.8	18.7	17.5
28 135	...	Tallahatchie	1 668	15 210	1 975	9.1	6 257	8 881	14	51	7	82	8.7	18.7	16.4
28 137	...	Tate	1 048	21 432	1 606	20.5	13 945	7 417	37	27	6	121	7.6	16.6	17.6
28 139	...	Tippah	1 186	19 523	1 699	16.5	16 251	3 233	17	18	4	64	6.9	15.2	15.6

1. MSA = Metropolitan Statistical Area. CMSA = Consolidated MSA. NECMA = New England county metropolitan area. PMSA = Primary MSA. See Appendix A for explanation of these concepts. See Appendix B for list of metropolitan areas identified by type, with component counties. 2. Dry land or land partially or temporarily covered by water. 3. Hispanic persons may be of any race.

STATE County	Population, 1990 (cont'd): Age of population (cont'd) Percent: 25 to 34 years	35 to 44 years	45 to 54 years	55 to 64 years	65 to 74 years	75 years and over	Percent female	Population–Change: 1980–1990 Number	1980–1990 Percent	Total persons, 1986	Total persons, 1980	Components of change, 1980–1986: Net change Number	Net change Percent	Natural increase Births	Natural increase Deaths
	14	15	16	17	18	19	20	21	22	23	24	25	26	27	28
MISSISSIPPI—Con.															
Benton	15.1	11.4	9.3	9.5	8.4	6.3	51.8	-107	-1.3	8 500	8 153	300	4.2	800	400
Bolivar	12.9	12.0	8.0	6.5	6.6	5.8	54.0	-4 090	-8.9	44 100	45 965	-1 900	-4.1	6 300	3 100
Calhoun	13.7	13.0	10.4	9.4	8.8	8.1	52.2	-756	-4.8	15 400	15 664	-300	-1.7	1 400	1 000
Carroll	13.9	12.9	11.3	9.1	8.5	6.7	52.1	-539	-5.5	9 700	9 776	-100	-1.1	800	500
Chickasaw	15.1	12.7	9.6	8.5	7.4	6.4	52.3	234	1.3	18 000	17 851	100	0.6	2 000	1 100
Choctaw	14.2	12.7	10.4	9.0	7.5	7.2	52.6	75	0.8	8 900	8 996	-100	-1.1	900	600
Claiborne	12.3	10.6	7.0	6.3	6.3	5.4	53.7	-909	-7.4	12 000	12 279	-200	-1.9	1 400	700
Clarke	14.0	13.5	9.7	9.1	7.8	7.1	52.6	368	2.2	17 000	16 945	100	0.4	1 800	1 200
Clay	14.5	13.3	8.7	8.0	7.2	6.1	52.7	38	0.2	21 900	21 082	800	3.7	2 600	1 200
Coahoma	13.5	11.4	8.3	7.9	7.4	6.8	54.5	-5 253	-14.2	35 600	36 918	-1 400	-3.7	4 800	2 400
Copiah	14.5	12.4	9.1	8.1	7.2	6.2	52.3	1 089	4.1	26 600	26 503	100	0.5	2 900	1 700
Covington	14.5	12.8	10.3	8.3	7.2	5.7	51.7	600	3.8	16 400	15 927	500	3.1	1 900	1 000
De Soto	17.0	15.8	12.2	7.8	5.3	3.0	50.8	13 980	25.9	63 600	53 930	9 700	18.0	5 000	2 200
Forrest	16.1	12.4	8.5	7.5	6.8	5.3	53.4	2 296	3.5	68 300	66 018	2 200	3.4	6 900	4 100
Franklin	14.3	12.8	8.8	10.0	8.9	7.3	52.4	169	2.1	8 800	8 208	600	6.7	900	600
George	15.2	13.5	10.9	8.2	6.4	4.9	50.8	1 376	9.0	16 400	15 297	1 100	7.1	1 800	900
Greene	16.6	13.5	10.2	7.7	6.7	5.0	48.5	393	4.0	9 700	9 827	-200	-1.8	1 000	600
Grenada	14.9	13.9	9.6	8.5	7.9	6.2	53.4	440	2.1	20 500	21 115	-700	-3.1	2 200	1 500
Hancock	14.6	13.7	10.8	10.5	9.4	4.8	50.2	7 264	29.7	31 600	24 496	7 100	29.0	2 600	1 500
Harrison	17.9	13.8	9.4	8.4	6.7	4.1	50.2	7 700	4.9	172 600	157 665	14 900	9.4	19 000	8 100
Hinds	17.3	14.5	9.1	7.8	6.4	4.8	53.2	3 443	1.4	259 900	250 998	8 900	3.5	28 800	12 900
Holmes	13.1	10.9	7.6	7.4	7.4	6.9	53.8	-1 366	-5.9	22 900	22 970	-100	-0.4	3 200	1 600
Humphreys	14.4	11.0	8.1	7.4	6.4	6.3	53.4	-1 797	-12.9	13 800	13 931	-200	-1.2	2 000	900
Issaquena	15.0	10.5	11.5	7.6	7.1	5.9	51.4	-604	-24.0	2 300	2 513	-300	-10.3	300	100
Itawamba	13.9	13.5	11.4	9.8	8.5	6.9	51.1	-501	-2.4	20 500	20 518	0	0.0	1 600	1 200
Jackson	16.1	15.1	11.4	8.7	5.9	3.5	50.9	-2 772	-2.3	128 200	118 015	10 200	8.6	12 700	4 500
Jasper	14.3	12.6	9.3	8.5	7.8	7.0	52.3	-151	-0.9	16 900	17 265	-400	-2.3	1 900	1 100
Jefferson	14.7	11.8	8.5	7.5	6.4	5.5	52.9	-528	-5.8	8 800	9 181	-400	-4.3	1 200	600
Jefferson Davis	13.6	12.5	9.6	8.2	8.1	6.3	52.7	205	1.5	14 400	13 846	600	4.3	1 500	900
Jones	14.8	13.9	10.1	9.6	8.0	6.3	52.3	119	0.2	63 000	61 912	1 100	1.8	6 500	4 000
Kemper	13.3	12.0	9.2	8.7	8.0	7.8	52.0	208	2.0	10 100	10 148	-100	-0.9	1 000	700
Lafayette	15.1	11.5	8.2	6.5	5.4	4.7	51.3	796	2.6	30 500	31 030	-500	-1.8	2 400	1 300
Lamar	17.6	15.1	9.8	7.5	5.5	3.9	51.3	6 603	27.7	27 300	23 821	3 500	14.7	2 800	1 100
Lauderdale	15.8	13.9	9.5	8.5	7.5	6.0	52.6	-1 730	-2.2	77 500	77 285	200	0.3	8 400	5 000
Lawrence	14.8	12.7	10.2	9.3	7.6	5.9	52.0	-60	-0.5	13 100	12 518	600	4.4	1 400	800
Leake	13.8	12.8	9.5	9.8	8.2	7.9	52.2	-354	-1.9	18 900	18 790	100	0.3	2 000	1 400
Lee	17.1	14.7	10.4	8.2	6.5	5.1	52.3	8 520	14.9	62 100	57 061	5 000	8.8	6 500	3 300
Leflore	14.0	12.0	8.3	7.7	7.5	6.4	53.7	-4 184	-10.1	41 300	41 525	-300	-0.7	5 200	2 900
Lincoln	14.3	14.1	9.9	9.2	8.1	6.6	52.5	104	0.3	31 400	30 174	1 200	4.1	3 100	2 000
Lowndes	17.4	14.0	9.2	7.5	5.7	4.4	52.3	2 004	3.5	60 200	57 304	2 900	5.0	6 900	2 700
Madison	20.1	14.7	8.3	6.9	5.1	4.4	52.6	12 181	29.3	50 000	41 613	8 400	20.2	5 300	2 100
Marion	14.5	13.0	9.2	9.0	8.1	6.3	51.8	-164	-0.6	26 900	25 708	1 200	4.6	2 900	1 700
Marshall	15.4	12.9	9.7	8.3	6.7	4.8	52.2	1 065	3.6	33 200	29 296	3 900	13.3	3 400	1 600
Monroe	14.5	13.5	10.2	8.7	7.8	6.5	52.9	178	0.5	36 700	36 404	300	0.8	3 800	2 400
Montgomery	13.2	12.3	10.0	9.5	8.8	8.0	53.4	-978	-7.3	12 600	13 366	-700	-5.4	1 300	1 000
Neshoba	14.0	13.6	9.5	9.1	7.7	6.6	52.1	1 011	4.2	24 300	23 789	500	2.3	2 600	1 500
Newton	13.5	12.7	9.6	9.4	8.3	7.3	52.1	324	1.6	20 200	19 967	300	1.3	1 900	1 500
Noxubee	15.1	11.3	8.2	8.0	6.9	6.5	53.0	-608	-4.6	12 800	13 212	-400	-2.8	1 800	800
Oktibbeha	14.9	11.2	7.7	6.0	4.8	4.1	50.1	2 357	6.5	37 000	36 018	900	2.6	3 700	1 500
Panola	14.7	12.3	8.8	8.4	7.2	6.0	52.6	1 832	6.5	29 400	28 164	1 300	4.5	3 500	1 900
Pearl River	14.3	14.0	11.2	9.6	7.2	4.4	51.6	4 919	14.6	39 300	33 795	5 500	16.4	3 700	2 000
Perry	15.4	13.4	10.2	8.1	6.5	4.9	51.6	1 001	10.1	10 100	9 864	300	2.9	1 100	600
Pike	13.8	13.4	9.2	8.8	8.1	6.5	53.3	709	2.0	37 500	36 173	1 300	3.6	3 900	2 700
Pontotoc	15.6	13.9	9.9	9.0	8.0	6.3	51.6	1 319	6.3	22 300	20 918	1 400	6.8	1 900	1 300
Prentiss	14.3	13.2	10.7	9.1	8.1	6.2	52.0	-747	-3.1	24 800	24 025	700	3.0	2 000	1 400
Quitman	13.3	11.4	8.1	7.9	8.5	7.2	53.5	-2 146	-17.0	11 200	12 636	-1 400	-11.3	1 500	900
Rankin	17.1	17.0	11.3	8.4	5.5	3.7	51.3	17 734	25.5	82 100	69 427	12 700	18.3	7 400	3 300
Scott	14.8	13.0	9.6	8.9	7.1	6.2	52.0	-419	-1.7	26 000	24 556	1 400	5.7	2 700	1 600
Sharkey	13.1	12.5	7.6	6.9	6.5	5.6	53.8	-898	-11.3	7 700	7 964	-300	-3.9	1 200	600
Simpson	15.5	13.7	9.9	9.0	6.9	5.9	51.2	512	2.2	24 400	23 441	900	4.0	2 500	1 600
Smith	14.5	13.0	10.4	9.5	7.8	6.6	51.1	-279	-1.9	15 600	15 077	500	3.3	1 400	900
Stone	14.7	13.5	9.8	8.3	7.3	4.9	50.7	1 034	10.6	10 200	9 716	500	5.1	1 000	600
Sunflower	16.3	12.5	7.7	6.9	6.5	6.0	49.9	-1 977	-5.7	36 600	34 844	1 700	4.9	4 600	2 200
Tallahatchie	13.8	11.5	8.6	8.0	7.9	6.5	52.9	-1 947	-11.3	16 300	17 157	-900	-5.3	2 200	1 200
Tate	14.8	13.4	10.0	7.8	6.6	5.5	51.8	1 313	6.5	21 600	20 119	1 500	7.4	2 100	1 200
Tippah	14.6	12.9	10.3	9.1	7.9	7.5	52.0	784	4.2	18 800	18 739	100	0.5	1 800	1 300

STATE County	Population–(cont'd): Components of change, 1980-1986 (cont'd): Net migration	Households, 1990: Number	Households, 1990: Percent change, 1980–1990	Households, 1990: Persons per household	Households, 1990: Percent: Female family householder[1]	Households, 1990: Percent: One-person	Births, 1988: Total	Births, 1988: Rate[2]	Births, 1988: Low birth weight[3] (Number)	Deaths, 1987: Number: Total	Deaths, 1987: Number: Infant[4]	Deaths, 1987: Rate: Total[2]	Deaths, 1987: Rate: Infant[5]	Marriages, 1984: Number	Marriages, 1984: Rate[2]
	29	30	31	32	33	34	35	36	37	38	39	40	41	42	43
MISSISSIPPI—Con.															
Benton	0	2 842	10.3	2.82	13.9	21.7	137	16.1	13	83	3	9.7	21.7	81	9.5
Bolivar	-5 100	13 292	-2.1	3.02	26.3	24.0	875	20.6	98	493	19	11.5	22.8	348	7.7
Calhoun	-700	5 662	4.5	2.60	12.7	24.9	215	14.1	29	168	1	11.0	4.7	136	8.8
Carroll	-300	3 352	4.7	2.75	14.6	22.3	116	12.0	14	91	1	9.2	9.5	75	7.8
Chickasaw	-800	6 480	10.4	2.77	15.3	22.7	309	16.9	25	170	6	9.3	18.9	188	10.4
Choctaw	-400	3 217	7.3	2.76	13.6	23.1	111	12.3	7	81	0	9.1	0.0	69	7.8
Claiborne	-900	3 342	-6.5	2.82	25.1	27.6	157	12.9	21	103	3	8.3	15.5	63	5.2
Clarke	-500	6 334	9.9	2.71	15.5	23.2	240	14.4	32	189	2	11.3	8.8	155	9.1
Clay	-600	7 251	7.0	2.83	19.4	23.0	384	17.7	34	200	8	9.2	24.5	182	8.3
Coahoma	-3 700	10 530	-9.9	2.93	25.1	26.4	657	19.3	60	370	12	10.7	18.5	264	7.4
Copiah	-1 000	9 304	9.2	2.83	18.6	23.1	437	16.1	40	292	9	10.8	19.1	219	8.3
Covington	-400	5 786	11.9	2.84	14.4	22.1	286	17.2	26	157	6	9.5	20.5	168	10.4
De Soto	6 900	23 273	42.5	2.91	11.1	14.8	1 029	14.7	82	383	9	5.7	9.4	635	10.9
Forrest	-600	25 150	9.5	2.54	16.8	27.6	1 092	16.2	99	720	11	10.8	10.9	791	11.5
Franklin	200	3 086	5.8	2.69	14.2	24.7	139	16.4	10	98	1	11.5	7.4	72	8.4
George	100	5 779	19.7	2.86	10.4	18.9	256	15.7	12	147	0	9.0	0.0	259	16.1
Greene	-600	3 327	8.5	2.90	12.9	19.6	139	14.6	7	100	1	10.4	6.6	109	11.4
Grenada	-1 400	7 701	8.3	2.75	17.0	23.6	356	17.1	38	230	5	11.1	14.1	209	9.7
Hancock	6 000	11 817	44.4	2.64	11.3	23.3	448	13.4	19	283	4	8.6	8.8	350	12.1
Harrison	4 000	59 557	14.1	2.65	13.9	24.2	2 804	16.4	197	1 412	26	8.1	8.9	2 409	14.3
Hinds	-7 000	91 023	6.0	2.70	19.2	25.6	4 298	17.0	448	2 131	61	8.3	14.2	2 616	10.2
Holmes	-1 700	7 139	1.5	2.97	28.3	25.5	450	19.9	50	249	7	11.0	15.1	161	6.9
Humphreys	-1 200	3 926	-8.0	3.07	24.2	23.7	266	19.9	29	143	11	10.6	43.7	89	6.3
Issaquena	-400	633	-17.1	3.02	14.8	23.2	32	14.5	3	9	0	4.1	0.0	10	4.3
Itawamba	-400	7 497	6.3	2.59	8.1	21.9	242	11.9	22	207	4	10.1	17.2	185	9.0
Jackson	2 000	40 454	7.6	2.82	13.5	19.3	1 880	14.7	136	798	21	6.2	11.1	1 291	10.3
Jasper	-1 200	5 956	6.5	2.86	16.0	21.6	238	14.2	17	178	8	10.5	29.3	133	7.6
Jefferson	-1 000	2 814	1.4	3.07	27.9	23.1	153	18.2	17	89	2	10.5	12.1	80	8.9
Jefferson Davis	0	4 787	9.8	2.91	18.2	22.0	212	14.6	24	128	2	8.8	9.4	122	8.5
Jones	-1 400	22 506	4.4	2.69	13.7	22.9	927	15.0	77	613	12	9.9	12.9	679	10.7
Kemper	-400	3 626	11.7	2.77	17.1	25.7	150	13.6	11	122	1	11.0	6.8	71	6.9
Lafayette	-1 600	11 090	15.2	2.47	11.2	26.8	346	11.2	29	230	4	7.4	11.1	242	7.7
Lamar	1 800	10 883	38.6	2.78	11.6	19.1	454	16.4	49	214	12	7.6	24.8	262	9.9
Lauderdale	-3 100	28 232	4.9	2.59	17.1	26.4	1 247	16.4	75	804	12	10.5	9.6	775	9.9
Lawrence	-100	4 506	8.4	2.74	13.6	23.4	181	14.3	11	174	2	13.8	11.4	127	9.8
Leake	-500	6 788	6.4	2.69	13.3	24.3	320	17.4	22	251	3	13.6	11.8	150	7.9
Lee	1 800	24 450	22.4	2.65	13.1	23.4	1 121	17.5	88	592	22	9.3	20.4	707	11.8
Leflore	-2 600	12 749	-2.0	2.82	23.6	27.1	676	17.7	71	421	12	10.9	17.4	361	8.5
Lincoln	100	11 089	9.5	2.69	14.1	23.8	392	12.6	29	336	1	10.8	2.6	319	10.3
Lowndes	-1 300	21 402	14.7	2.71	16.7	23.5	1 087	18.5	102	447	22	7.5	21.7	546	9.2
Madison	5 200	19 276	51.6	2.74	16.7	25.1	1 039	18.6	84	363	8	6.9	8.5	360	7.9
Marion	0	9 110	6.4	2.75	13.7	23.0	378	14.6	28	271	9	10.4	23.6	307	11.4
Marshall	2 100	10 077	18.3	2.93	17.9	20.8	557	16.5	58	286	8	8.5	14.8	255	7.9
Monroe	-1 100	13 348	8.9	2.72	15.1	22.9	543	14.8	40	392	8	10.6	14.2	341	9.2
Montgomery	-1 000	4 532	-0.2	2.70	17.1	25.0	181	14.5	14	172	6	13.8	31.7	122	9.4
Neshoba	-500	8 848	10.0	2.77	13.7	21.9	407	16.4	24	289	4	11.7	10.9	243	10.0
Newton	-200	7 358	6.1	2.68	13.5	23.0	312	16.1	24	263	4	13.4	14.7	187	9.3
Noxubee	-1 300	4 140	3.0	3.04	22.6	24.2	262	21.3	22	131	4	10.4	16.4	66	5.1
Oktibbeha	-1 300	12 916	17.6	2.58	14.3	25.7	565	15.5	43	247	8	6.8	15.9	285	7.7
Panola	-300	10 130	14.1	2.91	18.0	22.6	582	19.1	63	338	13	11.2	24.3	286	9.8
Pearl River	3 800	13 760	25.0	2.77	12.2	20.3	575	14.4	37	357	11	9.0	18.8	466	12.3
Perry	-300	3 802	20.3	2.84	13.1	21.2	177	17.9	10	68	0	6.7	0.0	113	10.9
Pike	200	13 408	8.6	2.70	18.4	25.7	570	15.7	53	436	9	11.8	18.0	410	11.2
Pontotoc	900	8 346	13.1	2.65	10.6	22.3	341	14.9	20	214	1	9.4	3.1	242	11.1
Prentiss	200	8 647	4.2	2.63	11.6	22.4	347	13.7	35	244	4	9.6	13.4	199	8.1
Quitman	-2 100	3 521	-10.4	2.95	19.7	25.1	214	19.6	18	137	4	12.2	18.3	131	11.5
Rankin	8 600	29 858	37.3	2.82	11.2	17.7	1 277	14.6	93	542	8	6.3	6.8	799	10.5
Scott	300	8 511	6.2	2.82	15.9	22.0	436	16.6	41	257	5	9.9	12.3	257	10.2
Sharkey	-1 000	2 084	-7.9	3.36	23.3	20.3	149	20.7	22	93	3	12.7	21.4	63	7.9
Simpson	0	8 357	8.9	2.78	13.4	22.6	379	15.7	32	244	3	10.0	8.5	251	10.4
Smith	0	5 276	5.2	2.78	9.4	21.2	198	13.1	23	162	0	10.7	0.0	141	9.4
Stone	100	3 685	23.0	2.76	12.4	22.0	152	14.5	6	110	1	10.5	6.5	122	12.2
Sunflower	-800	9 650	-0.4	3.06	23.4	25.3	642	18.0	66	358	9	9.9	15.0	228	6.2
Tallahatchie	-1 900	5 034	-4.8	3.01	20.2	24.4	342	20.4	34	177	4	10.5	13.3	117	7.1
Tate	500	7 024	16.4	2.92	14.0	18.7	331	15.0	39	188	1	8.5	3.0	190	9.0
Tippah	-300	7 158	11.7	2.68	10.5	21.9	261	13.4	33	258	5	13.2	16.2	238	12.6

1. No spouse present. 2. Per 1,000 resident population estimated as of July 1 of the year shown. 3. Under 2,500 grams. 4. Deaths of infants under 1 year old. 5. Deaths of infants under 1 year old per 1,000 live births.

STATE County	Divorces, 1984		Physicians, active non-Federal, 1989		Hospitals, 1989			Nursing homes,[4] 1986		Serious crimes known to police, 1988			Education			
						Beds				Number			Public school enrollment[7]		Attainment,[8] 1980	
	Number	Rate[1]	Number[2]	Rate[3]	Number	Number	Rate[3]	Number	Beds	Total[5]	Violent[6]	Rate[3]	1986–1987	1980	Percent 12 yrs. or more	Percent 16 yrs. or more
	44	45	46	47	48	49	50	51	52	53	54	55	56	57	58	59
MISSISSIPPI—Con.																
Benton	32	3.8	0	0	0	0	0	0	0	NA	NA	NA	1 436	1 642	38.9	6.1
Bolivar	135	3.0	27	65	2	211	505	5	407	NA	NA	NA	10 169	12 456	45.8	14.1
Calhoun	69	4.5	3	20	2	79	523	1	120	9	3	224	2 908	3 140	45.3	7.3
Carroll	9	0.9	2	21	0	0	0	0	0	NA	NA	NA	1 235	1 832	40.3	7.3
Chickasaw	92	5.1	8	43	2	160	865	2	109	NA	NA	NA	3 839	3 930	47.2	8.1
Choctaw	32	3.6	3	33	1	88	978	1	32	19	2	1 249	1 857	2 056	44.7	7.0
Claiborne	73	6.0	5	41	1	32	262	0	0	251	28	2 565	2 109	2 295	49.2	17.0
Clarke	100	5.9	7	42	1	40	240	1	120	88	11	623	3 423	3 704	46.6	6.5
Clay	85	3.9	13	60	1	60	278	2	180	33	4	257	4 262	4 188	50.0	10.6
Coahoma	127	3.5	44	131	1	194	579	1	66	1 180	69	3 388	7 627	8 025	43.8	12.1
Copiah	134	5.1	15	55	1	49	179	1	120	130	14	2 908	5 071	5 080	47.1	8.4
Covington	71	4.4	6	36	1	82	491	1	60	15	0	578	3 538	3 586	44.4	7.4
De Soto	414	7.1	24	33	2	185	252	1	120	58	1	1 660	12 425	12 689	58.0	7.6
Forrest	473	6.9	192	287	2	645	964	6	649	2 862	273	6 033	11 968	12 119	63.4	17.7
Franklin	34	4.0	4	48	1	53	631	1	60	34	13	405	1 939	1 845	48.4	6.1
George	81	5.0	6	37	1	49	299	1	60	8	5	49	3 728	3 534	54.1	6.5
Greene	NA	NA	3	32	1	40	421	2	84	29	8	332	2 313	2 352	50.0	7.1
Grenada	92	4.3	17	83	1	86	420	2	257	797	170	7 325	4 138	4 211	49.2	10.0
Hancock	180	6.2	28	81	1	60	173	1	88	574	31	3 481	4 657	4 535	58.6	10.8
Harrison	1 318	7.8	289	168	8	1 984	1 156	6	669	8 245	734	6 576	28 764	29 257	67.7	13.9
Hinds	1 385	5.4	1 039	414	12	3 103	1 237	19	1 257	17 682	1 731	6 899	42 945	43 917	70.0	23.3
Holmes	64	2.7	8	36	2	109	487	0	0	32	10	207	5 059	5 883	39.6	10.3
Humphreys	51	3.6	6	45	1	29	220	1	60	179	32	1 325	2 635	3 458	38.7	9.1
Issaquena	NA	NA	0	0	0	0	0	0	0	NA	NA	NA	401	649	37.9	5.7
Itawamba	118	5.7	4	20	1	62	305	1	120	180	6	873	3 529	4 147	39.3	5.7
Jackson	873	7.0	160	125	2	536	417	4	284	4 736	646	3 685	24 871	26 579	67.5	11.3
Jasper	78	4.5	7	42	1	116	703	2	61	NA	NA	NA	3 392	3 687	50.4	8.5
Jefferson	NA	NA	6	73	1	30	366	0	0	5	3	254	2 125	2 249	36.3	8.2
Jefferson Davis	52	3.6	5	34	1	101	697	1	60	186	39	1 282	3 051	3 318	44.2	7.9
Jones	417	6.6	76	123	1	275	446	5	698	2 330	84	4 044	11 629	11 711	55.3	10.1
Kemper	22	2.1	3	26	1	35	307	1	60	NA	NA	NA	1 904	2 154	45.4	7.4
Lafayette	140	4.5	45	146	1	147	477	2	172	794	39	8 384	4 711	5 128	60.5	23.1
Lamar	149	5.6	5	18	1	23	82	1	120	98	8	352	5 883	5 185	61.5	13.7
Lauderdale	468	6.0	164	217	7	1 500	1 984	7	572	3 285	173	4 279	14 716	14 919	60.7	10.9
Lawrence	69	5.3	7	56	1	53	421	1	60	NA	NA	NA	3 004	2 838	49.2	7.7
Leake	89	4.7	7	38	2	94	516	2	127	7	5	203	3 253	3 713	44.4	6.6
Lee	327	5.5	129	199	2	706	1 088	3	360	1 670	95	2 715	12 538	11 861	58.7	12.5
Leflore	154	3.6	43	116	1	260	701	3	410	1 607	61	8 261	8 512	9 257	44.7	13.2
Lincoln	108	3.5	24	77	1	125	403	4	298	65	0	599	6 448	6 237	54.8	10.1
Lowndes	329	5.6	79	135	3	357	610	2	180	2 023	115	3 380	10 877	11 380	57.9	15.1
Madison	168	3.7	82	141	1	127	218	2	120	138	13	4 207	7 966	7 778	55.0	16.6
Marion	186	6.9	15	59	1	90	352	3	214	46	3	175	5 367	4 944	49.1	8.3
Marshall	166	5.2	8	23	1	40	117	1	120	NA	NA	NA	5 485	6 345	43.4	9.3
Monroe	213	5.8	29	79	2	152	414	2	132	498	115	3 411	6 734	7 897	46.3	6.8
Montgomery	61	4.7	7	56	2	68	548	0	0	40	15	320	2 421	2 646	42.8	6.8
Neshoba	128	5.2	17	68	2	194	776	2	140	336	66	1 354	4 217	4 907	47.8	8.9
Newton	76	3.8	9	47	2	84	440	1	120	83	20	447	4 121	3 753	53.0	8.6
Noxubee	29	2.2	4	33	1	49	405	0	0	NA	NA	NA	2 380	2 824	39.6	8.8
Oktibbeha	140	3.8	36	99	1	96	264	1	119	1 476	126	4 029	5 548	5 905	64.4	28.3
Panola	129	4.4	15	49	2	184	595	2	180	33	8	480	6 630	6 412	40.9	7.7
Pearl River	232	6.1	19	47	2	185	459	2	160	679	50	5 881	7 721	7 379	58.2	9.5
Perry	53	5.1	6	61	1	44	444	0	0	7	4	69	2 551	2 428	54.7	6.8
Pike	NA	NA	50	139	2	194	539	2	265	1 045	176	8 583	7 930	7 469	53.9	11.6
Pontotoc	130	5.9	10	43	1	102	442	3	131	NA	NA	NA	4 177	4 296	46.6	7.0
Prentiss	144	5.8	11	43	1	78	307	2	100	141	8	2 063	4 918	5 095	43.9	6.9
Quitman	13	1.1	6	56	1	96	889	1	60	NA	NA	NA	2 499	2 994	36.5	8.2
Rankin	473	6.2	96	107	3	1 643	1 834	3	662	615	47	2 309	15 345	13 377	64.4	14.1
Scott	160	6.3	8	30	2	104	395	2	130	115	11	445	5 679	5 684	45.4	8.2
Sharkey	16	2.0	2	29	1	29	414	1	60	39	1	1 578	2 424	2 028	42.2	13.3
Simpson	115	4.8	10	41	2	112	463	2	180	104	17	422	4 543	4 650	50.0	7.4
Smith	71	4.7	3	20	1	29	193	1	120	NA	NA	NA	3 114	3 215	50.4	7.4
Stone	51	5.1	6	57	1	49	462	1	127	141	10	4 110	2 321	2 007	58.7	11.4
Sunflower	71	1.9	19	54	2	148	418	2	165	905	35	2 658	7 248	7 586	41.1	11.3
Tallahatchie	72	4.4	2	12	1	75	444	1	40	NA	NA	NA	3 629	4 209	36.9	8.6
Tate	111	5.3	10	45	1	52	233	1	120	78	10	383	4 864	4 290	49.7	9.2
Tippah	142	7.5	11	56	1	99	503	2	180	3	1	69	4 203	4 000	45.5	6.5

1. Per 1,000 resident population estimated as of July 1 of the year shown. 2. As of end of year. 3. Per 100,000 resident population as of July 1 of the year shown. 4. Preliminary. Covers nursing homes with 3 or more beds. 5. Data for serious crimes have not been adjusted for underreporting, this may affect comparability between geographic areas or over time. 6. Includes murder and nonnegligent manslaughter, forcible rape, robbery, and aggravated assault. 7. The 1986–1987 data are based on administrative reports obtained by the U.S. National Center for Education Statistics. The 1980 data are based on the 1980 Census of Population and Housing. 8. Persons 25 years old or older.

STATE County	Education (cont'd) Local government expenditures for education,[1] 1982: Total (Mil dol)	Per capita (Dollars)	Social Security Program December 1988 Beneficiaries: Total	Rate[2]	Payments ($1,000)	Supplemental Security Income Program recipients June 1986	Money income Per capita[3]: 1987 Income, (Dollars)	1979 Current dollars	1979 Constant 1987 dollars	Median household income 1979 (Dollars)	Percent below poverty level, 1979: Persons	Families	Housing units, 1990: Total	Percent change, 1980–1990
	60	61	62	63	64	65	66	67	68	69	70	71	72	73
MISSISSIPPI—Con.														
Benton	2.7	329	1 605	188.8	569	528	6 487	4 153	6 498	11 239	24.4	19.0	3 379	10.5
Bolivar	18.3	407	7 740	182.5	2 812	3 158	6 269	4 004	6 265	9 128	40.5	31.8	14 514	-0.3
Calhoun	5.2	332	3 240	213.2	1 187	872	7 108	4 353	6 811	10 027	23.5	18.8	6 260	3.7
Carroll	2.4	256	1 580	162.9	558	554	6 452	4 040	6 321	9 647	30.1	25.0	3 948	10.2
Chickasaw	6.0	338	3 660	200.0	1 373	1 114	7 347	4 547	7 115	11 503	21.4	17.3	6 997	10.3
Choctaw	3.5	407	1 570	174.4	565	496	6 386	4 117	6 442	9 479	28.5	24.1	3 539	3.6
Claiborne	5.5	432	1 825	149.6	682	714	5 424	4 220	6 603	9 805	32.9	26.1	4 099	-6.8
Clarke	5.5	319	3 330	199.4	1 283	914	7 315	4 896	7 661	11 760	21.0	17.3	7 065	9.3
Clay	6.5	300	3 480	160.4	1 402	1 020	7 606	4 868	7 617	12 398	24.4	18.7	7 737	5.9
Coahoma	13.8	383	6 315	185.7	2 347	2 676	6 431	4 129	6 461	8 931	40.6	30.6	11 495	-11.1
Copiah	8.3	320	5 435	200.6	2 086	1 598	6 664	4 514	7 063	10 061	29.2	23.1	10 260	7.2
Covington	5.6	345	3 425	206.3	1 248	988	6 721	4 460	6 979	9 780	28.7	23.9	6 535	13.3
De Soto	18.0	323	7 200	102.7	3 125	1 318	9 672	5 889	9 215	18 434	15.5	12.1	24 472	42.7
Forrest	20.3	300	12 390	184.4	5 392	2 048	8 576	5 365	8 395	11 570	22.0	16.8	27 740	10.9
Franklin	3.5	425	1 755	206.5	684	410	6 286	4 374	6 844	9 403	31.3	23.6	3 555	4.3
George	4.9	315	3 030	185.9	1 247	416	7 283	4 890	7 651	13 551	17.2	14.8	6 663	16.4
Greene	4.0	431	1 580	166.3	559	420	5 837	3 855	6 032	10 315	24.0	20.3	3 864	13.0
Grenada	6.4	304	4 200	201.9	1 695	1 082	8 231	5 034	7 877	12 186	24.1	18.6	8 712	13.4
Hancock	7.3	280	4 860	145.1	2 176	470	8 752	5 705	8 927	13 139	19.9	15.6	16 561	32.1
Harrison	48.7	295	24 705	144.1	10 293	3 470	9 168	5 807	9 086	13 402	17.0	13.9	67 813	17.0
Hinds	79.8	316	38 700	152.8	17 401	7 842	10 340	6 728	10 527	14 976	18.9	14.4	99 860	9.0
Holmes	8.5	370	4 565	202.0	1 542	2 290	5 133	3 375	5 281	7 030	46.9	39.1	7 972	2.3
Humphreys	5.4	384	2 380	177.6	782	1 090	5 764	3 950	6 181	7 913	44.7	35.1	4 231	-10.7
Issaquena	0.0	0	205	93.2	71	96	5 928	4 538	7 101	9 167	36.6	27.8	698	-23.0
Itawamba	5.7	276	3 595	176.2	1 390	802	7 973	4 854	7 595	12 214	15.4	12.7	8 116	6.2
Jackson	45.1	367	14 435	112.7	6 739	1 342	9 604	6 122	9 579	16 986	12.1	10.0	45 542	6.8
Jasper	6.0	341	3 595	214.0	1 296	1 118	6 210	4 093	6 404	10 197	27.0	21.2	6 700	8.3
Jefferson	3.9	428	1 605	191.1	526	738	4 413	3 262	5 104	7 352	41.1	36.1	3 167	1.1
Jefferson Davis	5.4	382	2 665	183.8	956	914	6 374	4 401	6 886	10 512	27.8	22.6	5 336	8.8
Jones	19.2	300	12 995	209.6	5 514	2 628	8 204	5 484	8 581	12 430	17.4	13.6	25 044	4.7
Kemper	3.7	358	1 995	181.4	663	704	5 615	3 751	5 869	8 951	37.2	30.5	4 151	16.7
Lafayette	8.8	278	3 740	121.4	1 530	926	8 593	5 169	8 088	11 534	22.1	15.5	12 478	14.3
Lamar	8.0	312	3 625	130.9	1 441	688	8 188	5 541	8 670	14 043	17.7	14.2	11 849	37.8
Lauderdale	22.5	291	14 025	184.1	5 858	2 978	9 317	5 804	9 082	12 257	21.0	16.2	31 232	7.5
Lawrence	4.8	375	3 005	236.6	1 142	716	7 283	5 266	8 240	12 377	19.4	15.4	5 160	11.6
Leake	5.2	275	4 140	225.0	1 475	1 306	6 256	4 012	6 278	9 122	29.5	24.2	7 614	7.4
Lee	22.0	379	11 280	176.2	4 712	2 028	9 481	5 770	9 028	13 651	15.8	12.7	25 971	21.5
Leflore	17.0	406	7 330	191.9	2 810	2 634	6 585	4 378	6 850	9 550	34.9	27.0	13 799	0.4
Lincoln	10.6	341	5 775	185.7	2 381	1 212	7 200	5 085	7 956	12 078	22.1	16.8	12 133	10.0
Lowndes	18.6	309	8 395	142.5	3 421	2 088	8 593	5 299	8 291	12 683	22.1	17.2	23 117	16.3
Madison	13.2	303	6 290	112.7	2 458	1 876	8 794	4 995	7 816	12 157	29.4	23.9	20 761	48.4
Marion	10.3	384	5 660	218.5	2 197	1 436	6 876	4 756	7 442	10 761	24.8	20.2	10 132	7.0
Marshall	8.7	290	5 030	148.8	1 825	1 866	6 315	4 010	6 274	11 008	31.9	24.7	10 984	16.4
Monroe	11.1	299	6 575	178.7	2 598	1 602	7 621	4 752	7 435	11 718	21.3	16.5	14 285	7.8
Montgomery	4.2	319	2 935	234.8	1 074	986	6 380	4 101	6 417	9 524	30.7	24.9	4 987	0.0
Neshoba	6.0	252	4 320	174.2	1 602	1 210	7 224	4 666	7 301	10 880	23.8	19.0	9 770	9.9
Newton	6.5	327	5 010	258.2	1 898	1 178	7 426	4 734	7 407	10 564	24.0	19.2	8 095	4.3
Noxubee	4.6	352	2 430	197.6	824	1 138	5 544	3 656	5 721	8 662	39.5	30.8	4 645	6.1
Oktibbeha	9.8	264	4 700	128.8	1 889	1 402	7 277	4 776	7 473	10 956	28.2	19.9	13 861	17.6
Panola	10.3	360	5 680	186.2	2 069	1 802	6 402	4 196	6 565	9 654	34.3	27.6	11 482	11.5
Pearl River	12.2	343	6 565	164.5	2 793	1 048	7 528	5 137	8 038	12 085	22.6	19.2	15 793	24.0
Perry	4.5	460	1 745	176.3	627	464	6 801	4 400	6 885	11 015	26.4	25.1	4 292	22.1
Pike	12.5	343	7 640	210.5	3 005	1 858	6 965	4 741	7 418	10 524	27.3	21.5	14 995	12.2
Pontotoc	5.9	283	4 125	180.1	1 529	994	8 382	4 983	7 797	11 335	19.1	15.9	9 001	10.5
Prentiss	9.0	367	4 615	182.4	1 703	1 194	7 339	4 839	7 572	11 150	17.4	14.4	9 155	2.3
Quitman	5.7	468	2 400	220.2	818	1 114	5 996	3 838	6 005	8 157	41.4	30.9	3 880	-9.6
Rankin	21.5	285	9 435	108.2	4 088	1 570	10 165	6 447	10 088	18 348	11.9	9.3	31 872	32.8
Scott	9.5	383	4 990	190.5	1 821	1 314	7 252	4 614	7 220	10 752	27.3	21.8	9 488	6.3
Sharkey	4.3	522	1 315	182.6	475	524	6 142	4 032	6 309	8 250	44.0	37.0	2 290	-8.8
Simpson	8.1	337	4 455	184.1	1 714	1 130	7 002	4 667	7 302	11 718	20.5	17.2	9 374	7.4
Smith	5.4	365	2 740	181.5	982	932	7 206	4 577	7 162	10 383	24.1	20.7	5 850	2.4
Stone	3.4	328	2 165	206.2	862	306	6 944	4 833	7 562	13 104	20.0	14.7	4 148	19.6
Sunflower	11.7	324	5 350	149.9	1 888	2 080	5 939	3 958	6 193	9 622	39.4	30.0	10 167	-1.0
Tallahatchie	6.8	412	2 880	171.4	973	1 342	5 491	3 692	5 777	7 900	43.5	34.4	5 492	-5.5
Tate	6.9	337	3 605	163.1	1 376	1 064	7 800	4 753	7 437	12 109	25.8	20.8	7 474	16.9
Tippah	6.9	361	4 290	220.0	1 526	1 230	7 344	4 327	6 770	10 346	24.3	20.4	7 846	10.1

1. Elementary and secondary. 2. Per 1,000 resident population estimated as of July 1 of the year shown. 3. Based on the resident population estimated as of July 1, 1988 for 1987 data and enumerated as of April 1, 1980 for 1979 data.

STATE County	Housing units, 1990 (cont'd): Occupied units: Total	Owner occupied: Percent	Owner occupied: Median value (Dollars)	Median rent (Dollars)	Civilian labor force, 1990: Total	Percent change, 1989–1990	Unemployment: Total	Unemployment: Rate[1]	Private nonfarm establishments, 1988: Number	Net change, 1987–1988	Employment[2]: Total	Per-cent change, 1987–1988	Manu-facturing	Retail trade
	74	75	76	77	78	79	80	81	82	83	84	85	86	87
MISSISSIPPI—Con.														
Benton	2 842	86.0	35 100	122	3 064	0.4	342	11.2	74	13	567	-9.1	337	65
Bolivar	13 292	59.4	39 200	160	15 163	-1.3	1 345	8.9	743	10	7 531	-6.3	2 344	1 697
Calhoun	5 662	80.8	33 900	145	7 225	-0.5	655	9.1	300	-3	3 263	5.9	2 187	457
Carroll	3 352	80.5	34 400	124	3 064	-0.3	298	9.7	88	4	411	9.3	104	133
Chickasaw	6 480	78.5	37 800	144	9 115	-0.6	1 285	14.1	389	8	7 391	2.1	5 486	730
Choctaw	3 217	85.6	36 000	133	3 019	-1.6	328	10.9	129	6	1 372	-12.6	821	206
Claiborne	3 342	74.2	39 000	123	4 879	-7.7	508	10.4	139	0	2 287	0.3	605	258
Clarke	6 334	83.6	36 000	142	7 127	1.4	561	7.9	240	-8	4 163	9.7	2 754	359
Clay	7 251	74.4	41 500	171	10 171	1.9	1 003	9.9	389	13	6 816	3.1	4 139	916
Coahoma	10 530	56.7	36 700	145	11 662	-0.6	1 310	11.2	669	6	6 519	0.3	1 332	1 896
Copiah	9 304	79.7	35 600	141	10 389	1.8	910	8.8	426	4	4 768	-0.4	2 509	938
Covington	5 786	85.4	37 300	138	5 688	-1.9	625	11.0	240	-5	2 395	-9.9	1 153	384
De Soto	23 273	81.3	62 400	311	37 136	1.8	1 831	4.9	1 061	30	15 850	1.8	6 609	2 979
Forrest	25 150	60.9	45 200	244	33 369	1.3	1 962	5.9	2 016	52	24 104	3.3	4 194	6 981
Franklin	3 086	85.0	35 900	102	3 031	-3.7	229	7.6	136	10	1 135	-7.5	469	165
George	5 779	86.2	37 500	178	5 844	2.8	745	12.7	228	-7	1 674	-5.7	326	503
Greene	3 327	86.4	33 800	142	2 775	0.9	435	15.7	135	-3	926	5.7	487	189
Grenada	7 701	70.1	44 300	174	11 632	-6.0	1 154	9.9	542	26	7 677	2.8	3 754	1 320
Hancock	11 817	79.0	52 800	254	14 199	2.7	871	6.1	463	0	5 857	0.6	2 149	1 305
Harrison	59 557	61.4	55 100	280	75 295	1.6	4 646	6.2	3 700	-54	40 851	-1.4	6 329	13 488
Hinds	91 023	61.6	57 500	292	132 151	1.2	7 276	5.5	7 180	-31	109 847	4.6	13 820	21 855
Holmes	7 139	70.7	30 200	99	6 377	-2.2	861	13.5	274	-13	2 608	0.2	1 004	564
Humphreys	3 926	58.7	36 600	126	4 654	-3.8	406	8.7	191	0	1 438	-1.6	0	329
Issaquena	633	67.5	35 600	99	783	-0.3	103	13.2	14	-1	62	44.2	0	0
Itawamba	7 497	85.3	35 500	151	10 426	-0.2	708	6.8	291	2	4 098	2.2	2 338	436
Jackson	40 454	73.5	50 900	272	54 895	2.5	4 224	7.7	2 039	-25	35 432	-2.1	16 732	6 811
Jasper	5 956	88.3	36 000	121	6 192	1.2	640	10.3	227	-4	1 962	9.7	601	587
Jefferson	2 814	77.7	34 500	99	3 247	2.0	621	19.1	66	-4	660	-9.0	344	87
Jefferson Davis	4 787	84.6	36 700	136	6 001	-2.0	743	12.4	200	1	1 739	0.4	785	431
Jones	22 506	76.4	41 500	177	25 989	-0.6	1 741	6.7	1 367	4	15 333	0.4	4 984	3 680
Kemper	3 626	80.4	36 600	99	4 001	0.7	430	10.7	113	-9	775	-42.8	244	171
Lafayette	11 090	61.7	51 100	272	15 765	2.0	518	3.3	629	3	6 042	6.7	1 534	2 007
Lamar	10 883	75.3	55 400	254	18 563	6.2	832	4.5	297	20	3 013	-5.2	1 104	574
Lauderdale	28 232	66.4	47 300	222	36 339	1.8	2 332	6.4	1 911	10	25 620	2.4	6 170	5 901
Lawrence	4 506	86.4	40 200	141	5 022	-3.1	471	9.4	189	-19	2 125	-5.1	1 203	343
Leake	6 788	84.8	34 700	130	8 127	4.8	623	7.7	314	0	3 287	-5.1	1 541	604
Lee	24 450	69.0	54 000	242	37 974	4.0	2 467	6.5	1 891	56	34 471	7.4	16 094	5 529
Leflore	12 749	52.3	42 700	141	15 681	-0.3	1 652	10.5	885	-15	9 755	-0.8	2 698	2 753
Lincoln	11 089	78.6	43 800	175	13 868	3.2	1 047	7.5	631	8	6 681	13.7	1 369	2 292
Lowndes	21 402	63.6	49 500	236	29 440	4.2	1 858	6.3	1 444	-3	19 518	4.1	7 381	4 274
Madison	19 276	64.1	66 300	355	24 667	0.6	1 399	5.7	940	25	11 380	8.5	1 886	4 029
Marion	9 110	79.5	38 800	163	12 238	0.7	1 003	8.2	501	-8	5 841	6.0	1 855	1 623
Marshall	10 077	79.5	41 900	145	11 824	-0.1	1 410	11.9	332	8	4 322	6.6	1 681	727
Monroe	13 348	78.0	39 200	156	17 926	2.8	1 449	8.1	712	22	10 517	5.5	5 955	1 576
Montgomery	4 532	74.2	35 400	131	5 040	-0.8	466	9.2	229	0	2 314	13.9	738	565
Neshoba	8 848	80.1	38 000	130	11 803	4.4	831	7.0	524	21	6 531	4.1	2 841	1 164
Newton	7 358	81.5	37 600	133	11 382	3.7	598	5.3	275	2	3 649	-1.5	2 135	687
Noxubee	4 140	78.2	31 700	99	4 913	6.4	630	12.8	206	11	1 638	17.5	816	278
Oktibbeha	12 916	59.0	51 200	255	16 813	1.1	808	4.8	694	-13	7 058	-1.0	2 407	2 176
Panola	10 130	76.1	39 300	147	13 892	4.2	1 144	8.2	519	7	6 704	9.5	3 366	1 239
Pearl River	13 760	79.1	45 100	204	14 679	3.8	1 326	9.0	581	-20	4 631	6.3	905	1 674
Perry	3 802	82.5	34 300	136	3 923	4.8	376	9.6	128	-5	1 751	4.4	0	268
Pike	13 408	74.8	41 000	166	15 506	0.9	1 190	7.7	865	-20	9 125	0.0	3 104	2 572
Pontotoc	8 346	80.5	41 200	173	13 656	-0.5	756	5.5	362	4	6 749	9.2	5 058	659
Prentiss	8 647	78.9	36 700	155	14 457	6.5	1 119	7.7	419	10	6 378	3.5	3 945	875
Quitman	3 521	68.4	27 900	100	3 671	0.5	442	12.0	149	2	1 119	4.7	477	292
Rankin	29 858	79.4	64 400	314	44 813	1.5	1 922	4.3	1 591	-46	23 591	7.6	4 166	4 484
Scott	8 511	80.7	34 900	168	12 085	3.6	708	5.9	479	8	7 777	13.1	5 106	1 194
Sharkey	2 084	61.2	40 800	102	2 489	-2.5	370	14.9	132	3	814	5.2	0	194
Simpson	8 357	81.0	38 900	170	9 276	2.5	596	6.4	425	-3	5 114	8.3	0	1 113
Smith	5 276	85.7	36 900	135	6 772	0.4	446	6.6	178	-11	2 794	8.4	1 719	269
Stone	3 685	79.8	39 100	176	3 737	4.2	277	7.4	225	10	1 959	4.4	507	456
Sunflower	9 650	60.1	37 800	146	15 052	4.5	1 456	9.7	494	25	9 584	8.1	5 219	1 540
Tallahatchie	5 034	69.5	31 500	99	5 254	-1.9	686	13.1	191	-2	1 405	3.3	516	366
Tate	7 024	75.6	49 500	185	9 560	2.4	665	7.0	309	8	4 447	12.5	1 900	1 090
Tippah	7 158	79.4	35 200	140	9 723	-0.2	776	8.0	362	-10	4 625	-3.9	2 267	746

1. Percent of total civilian labor force. 2. For week including March 12. Excludes government employees, self-employed persons, farm workers, domestic service workers, railroad employees subject to the Railroad Retirement Act, and employees on oceanborne vessels or in foreign countries.

STATE County	Private nonfarm establishments, 1988 (cont'd)				Personal income, 1989								Earnings, 1989		
	Employment[1] (cont'd)		Annual payroll								Per capita[3]			Percent by selected industries	
	Finance, insurance, and real estate	Services	Total (Mil dol)	Average per employee (Dollars)	Total (Mil dol)	Percent change, 1988–1989	Wages and salaries[2] (Mil dol)	Proprietor's income (Mil dol)	Dividends, interest, & rent (Mil dol)	Transfer payments (Mil dol)	Dollars	Rank	Total (Mil dol)	Farm	Goods-related[4] Total
	88	89	90	91	92	93	94	95	96	97	98	99	100	101	102
MISSISSIPPI—Con.															
Benton	0	78	9	15 039	80	4.5	18	7	7	20	9 337	2 975	25	9.5	NA
Bolivar	394	1 638	111	14 735	438	1.3	208	59	59	120	10 478	2 796	267	13.6	24.8
Calhoun	73	280	40	12 200	160	5.2	67	21	20	37	10 531	2 783	88	4.0	49.0
Carroll	0	54	4	10 073	92	6.9	15	14	10	20	9 436	2 968	28	34.1	NA
Chickasaw	101	493	99	13 413	201	6.2	136	22	23	41	10 907	2 683	158	2.5	62.0
Choctaw	36	167	18	12 788	85	6.5	34	16	11	20	9 454	2 964	50	8.3	45.5
Claiborne	51	261	54	23 558	102	4.1	119	11	13	28	8 354	3 052	130	4.7	23.5
Clarke	93	585	53	12 798	172	5.9	81	18	19	41	10 313	2 833	99	2.1	53.1
Clay	157	1 022	126	18 487	245	8.2	177	18	29	47	11 331	2 558	194	1.6	63.2
Coahoma	415	1 672	91	13 986	373	3.5	175	50	65	99	11 129	2 630	226	15.2	17.5
Copiah	166	561	59	12 384	272	6.2	106	37	33	70	9 980	2 883	143	13.8	35.3
Covington	91	331	32	13 257	161	4.9	62	24	19	44	9 629	2 940	86	14.3	33.8
De Soto	418	2 654	257	16 197	1 000	10.4	389	75	77	102	13 633	1 609	465	1.4	45.6
Forrest	1 594	6 456	367	15 226	866	6.8	621	98	148	183	12 941	1 934	719	0.4	20.3
Franklin	0	264	16	14 463	89	2.9	30	9	10	23	10 543	2 781	40	2.9	NA
George	138	297	22	12 970	159	5.9	43	13	19	38	9 719	2 922	55	6.1	16.1
Greene	0	130	10	10 503	77	1.7	18	11	7	22	8 176	3 065	28	17.9	20.7
Grenada	415	1 060	125	16 245	270	8.9	222	36	36	54	13 204	1 810	259	3.1	53.5
Hancock	181	1 523	103	17 529	372	8.9	273	26	58	71	10 779	2 720	299	0.5	31.4
Harrison	3 129	9 938	591	14 478	2 145	6.5	1 415	187	291	433	12 497	2 117	1 602	0.2	15.1
Hinds	12 254	35 737	1 991	18 123	3 869	6.8	3 063	370	610	612	15 418	828	3 433	0.5	15.0
Holmes	144	442	33	12 707	185	4.1	65	23	26	75	8 268	3 057	88	13.8	NA
Humphreys	100	417	20	13 675	153	-3.0	54	52	17	33	11 561	2 483	106	44.4	18.2
Issaquena	0	0	1	10 742	22	-10.3	6	5	3	4	10 052	2 875	10	54.4	NA
Itawamba	63	328	58	14 053	217	6.0	93	29	19	38	10 668	2 747	121	10.4	48.6
Jackson	2 007	5 827	729	20 585	1 457	4.1	1 075	100	169	254	11 342	2 556	1 175	0.3	53.4
Jasper	69	272	30	15 371	162	4.2	61	18	22	43	9 764	2 915	78	7.9	34.2
Jefferson	0	63	8	12 794	64	0.2	21	5	6	29	7 813	3 082	26	5.3	21.2
Jefferson Davis	49	261	19	10 970	120	6.1	42	16	17	35	8 291	3 055	58	14.6	28.2
Jones	643	2 719	240	15 636	727	7.1	413	91	108	158	11 789	2 407	504	5.3	34.8
Kemper	0	186	7	9 572	90	4.5	26	7	13	26	7 913	3 079	33	5.0	NA
Lafayette	267	1 367	81	13 405	343	7.6	209	35	44	57	11 132	2 627	245	0.9	18.3
Lamar	129	380	50	16 536	280	4.9	115	29	28	51	10 046	2 876	144	5.5	29.9
Lauderdale	1 993	6 338	438	17 083	1 084	5.7	705	103	153	205	14 334	1 274	808	0.4	22.1
Lawrence	48	245	40	18 973	124	0.9	67	9	14	36	9 884	2 895	77	1.2	59.6
Leake	130	530	37	11 277	196	8.5	66	34	25	47	10 768	2 724	101	20.3	31.0
Lee	1 635	6 427	581	16 848	894	7.7	812	93	119	130	13 792	1 538	905	0.7	41.3
Leflore	443	1 734	128	13 150	453	4.7	254	74	75	109	12 184	2 244	328	6.1	23.5
Lincoln	270	1 297	94	14 049	330	7.9	179	33	52	70	10 646	2 753	212	0.5	30.3
Lowndes	760	3 430	350	17 915	778	10.4	608	63	93	125	13 306	1 770	671	0.5	42.3
Madison	449	2 437	159	13 940	712	11.5	280	52	79	99	12 204	2 230	332	1.4	23.3
Marion	212	765	70	11 979	251	6.6	112	30	46	70	9 801	2 909	142	2.9	30.0
Marshall	183	1 269	52	11 961	318	6.8	92	24	24	71	9 323	2 979	116	3.0	35.5
Monroe	359	1 342	157	14 907	429	5.9	234	49	50	78	11 677	2 450	284	2.7	54.1
Montgomery	113	605	23	9 875	129	6.7	40	17	18	37	10 355	2 822	57	5.7	NA
Neshoba	193	806	89	13 668	247	4.8	139	42	32	55	9 864	2 899	181	8.2	NA
Newton	77	474	45	12 305	241	8.8	115	31	30	59	12 620	2 066	146	10.7	38.5
Noxubee	90	213	18	11 128	105	-1.3	40	10	16	35	8 618	3 036	49	3.5	35.2
Oktibbeha	400	1 419	88	12 532	403	8.6	261	28	52	82	11 049	2 653	288	0.5	20.9
Panola	228	784	94	13 955	314	7.3	173	28	37	73	10 163	2 861	201	4.2	38.8
Pearl River	229	1 113	59	12 746	408	7.6	110	48	49	89	10 118	2 863	158	5.7	22.2
Perry	0	95	36	20 472	103	4.3	52	14	9	25	10 476	2 797	66	7.4	59.1
Pike	545	1 535	123	13 450	391	5.9	211	39	55	106	10 875	2 692	251	1.0	29.1
Pontotoc	119	337	96	14 253	269	7.2	144	25	25	44	11 619	2 467	170	3.1	65.0
Prentiss	120	640	79	12 458	249	7.8	125	24	27	51	9 784	2 913	149	2.5	48.4
Quitman	59	155	14	12 302	103	1.5	34	11	14	32	9 561	2 950	45	18.5	17.3
Rankin	1 694	4 950	426	18 047	1 195	9.4	638	96	120	127	13 330	1 764	733	2.1	24.0
Scott	271	518	96	12 408	296	10.5	153	53	31	56	11 247	2 579	206	14.9	44.6
Sharkey	45	257	10	12 397	74	-5.9	32	17	11	21	10 643	2 756	49	36.3	8.6
Simpson	167	1 114	62	12 181	244	8.0	95	37	28	53	10 092	2 871	132	14.5	34.1
Smith	0	239	42	15 093	163	8.7	74	39	17	32	10 864	2 694	113	22.7	44.4
Stone	75	397	28	14 148	112	6.7	50	18	12	31	10 569	2 775	68	7.4	NA
Sunflower	256	925	119	12 388	366	2.6	200	64	41	81	10 353	2 823	264	20.1	24.1
Tallahatchie	73	211	15	10 678	149	2.1	41	22	18	44	8 786	3 025	62	18.2	13.0
Tate	127	915	64	14 367	268	6.9	101	21	25	53	12 003	2 325	121	3.6	38.1
Tippah	140	581	67	14 421	219	7.6	125	27	26	45	11 098	2 635	153	1.1	54.9

1. For week including March 12. Excludes government employees, self-employed persons, farm workers, domestic service workers, railroad employees subject to the Railroad Retirement Act, and employees on oceanborne vessels or in foreign countries. 2. Includes other labor income. 3. Based on the resident population estimated as of July 1 of the year shown. 4. Covers mining, construction, and manufacturing.

STATE County	Earnings, 1989 (cont'd): Percent by selected industries (cont'd): Goods-related[1]: Manufacturing	Service-related & other[2]: Total	Service-related & other[2]: Retail trade	Service-related & other[2]: Finance, insurance, & real estate	Service-related & other[2]: Services	Government	Agriculture, 1987: Farms: Number	Farms: Percent with: Less than 50 acres	Farms: Percent with: 500 acres and over	Farm operators, percent: Whose principal occupation is farming	Farm operators, percent: Residing on farm operated	Land in farms: Acreage (1,000)	Land in farms: Percent change, 1982–1987	Land in farms: Acres: Average size of farm	Acres: Total irrigated (1,000)	Acres: Total cropland (1,000)
	103	104	105	106	107	108	109	110	111	112	113	114	115	116	117	118
MISSISSIPPI—Con.																
Benton	27.5	34.3	8.9	3.4	15.1	21.8	232	18.5	17.2	47.4	59.1	85	-7.8	364	D	45
Bolivar	22.1	40.8	9.7	3.5	15.3	20.7	478	16.7	51.7	75.3	46.4	403	-12.0	843	137	378
Calhoun	46.3	33.4	8.4	3.1	10.3	13.6	419	15.3	16.5	49.9	65.4	135	-13.6	322	1	91
Carroll	13.8	NA	8.0	2.6	10.2	18.1	431	14.4	20.4	45.5	60.3	173	-8.1	402	3	76
Chickasaw	60.5	26.7	7.5	1.8	9.5	8.7	447	15.7	15.7	44.5	72.0	145	-16.7	325	D	89
Choctaw	40.2	28.4	7.2	1.4	13.8	17.8	228	14.9	8.3	28.1	72.8	47	-37.9	207	D	21
Claiborne	9.8	NA	3.1	1.0	NA	17.9	219	18.3	21.5	45.7	59.8	100	-21.7	459	1	37
Clarke	44.4	32.6	7.0	2.6	14.9	12.3	352	25.0	8.0	33.5	76.4	74	-20.4	210	0	29
Clay	60.1	25.8	6.3	1.8	12.8	9.4	393	21.4	14.0	42.7	71.2	125	-7.3	319	0	71
Coahoma	13.7	46.7	10.8	4.6	19.8	20.6	237	13.5	55.3	75.9	45.6	260	-5.0	1 097	56	247
Copiah	31.6	31.2	9.8	2.4	12.7	19.7	555	17.7	11.7	40.5	71.2	152	-17.8	274	D	66
Covington	25.3	35.8	7.7	3.2	9.7	16.1	462	27.7	5.8	38.1	71.4	80	-19.6	172	0	35
De Soto	37.5	NA	9.5	NA	16.2	9.1	503	37.2	12.9	40.0	64.0	166	-16.8	330	7	124
Forrest	14.5	53.9	12.3	5.7	24.0	25.4	279	34.8	6.8	40.5	74.2	48	-26.4	171	D	24
Franklin	26.5	NA	8.9	2.9	18.9	19.8	171	14.0	14.0	42.7	66.1	48	-19.5	280	D	18
George	13.8	NA	15.0	4.7	NA	21.4	340	32.6	5.0	32.1	80.6	51	3.0	149	1	25
Greene	17.4	NA	9.4	2.0	14.1	24.7	309	26.9	7.1	32.7	77.0	55	-15.4	179	D	18
Grenada	39.2	32.5	8.5	4.7	12.3	10.9	233	17.2	21.9	42.5	51.1	85	-20.7	367	1	44
Hancock	28.8	37.7	5.9	1.4	25.5	30.4	208	38.0	6.7	26.9	68.8	34	-10.8	165	0	13
Harrison	10.4	45.5	10.9	4.4	18.7	39.2	238	62.2	1.7	36.6	74.4	18	-45.6	76	0	8
Hinds	9.8	62.6	9.6	10.2	26.4	21.9	799	26.0	14.4	34.4	60.7	266	-14.5	332	0	127
Holmes	20.3	NA	11.2	3.3	16.2	23.3	420	14.3	28.8	56.2	53.3	236	-5.5	563	26	162
Humphreys	15.7	27.6	6.3	2.3	10.2	9.8	325	15.7	38.2	79.4	47.1	210	-0.1	647	29	162
Issaquena	9.2	NA	2.1	NA	5.0	8.5	107	16.8	48.6	78.5	60.7	121	8.9	1 131	8	104
Itawamba	35.6	27.7	6.1	1.7	11.0	13.3	452	23.5	7.3	40.7	72.3	79	-19.8	175	0	38
Jackson	47.9	30.3	6.9	2.3	15.1	16.1	206	56.8	4.4	27.2	77.7	21	-29.1	101	0	10
Jasper	21.2	NA	11.0	5.3	12.6	17.4	423	21.3	12.1	37.8	74.9	98	-17.0	231	D	38
Jefferson	19.0	39.0	7.8	2.6	11.3	34.5	234	15.0	20.9	39.7	62.0	81	-29.5	346	0	33
Jefferson Davis	20.1	36.2	12.4	2.4	11.9	21.0	408	17.6	7.6	37.7	65.9	77	-13.8	188	0	40
Jones	24.2	41.2	10.2	2.9	16.2	18.6	800	36.4	2.8	43.9	78.2	104	-19.7	130	0	48
Kemper	26.6	36.2	8.4	3.1	14.8	27.8	430	14.4	11.4	42.1	71.6	108	-22.8	251	0	43
Lafayette	13.4	42.6	11.2	2.3	23.2	38.3	447	14.5	11.6	33.8	59.3	114	-13.3	254	0	47
Lamar	22.6	52.6	10.0	2.4	25.1	12.0	336	33.3	6.8	34.5	74.7	58	-30.6	171	D	27
Lauderdale	18.6	57.9	11.5	4.1	25.9	19.6	449	26.7	7.6	23.2	70.6	86	-10.5	192	0	35
Lawrence	56.0	24.1	6.2	1.6	10.7	15.0	303	17.2	7.6	37.3	71.9	61	-20.4	202	0	31
Leake	26.6	35.8	11.9	3.3	13.3	12.9	659	26.4	4.7	45.2	73.7	96	-17.5	146	0	46
Lee	36.4	49.7	9.5	4.0	22.4	8.3	567	29.3	11.1	33.2	73.0	131	-7.3	232	0	94
Leflore	16.7	51.2	11.3	3.3	21.8	19.2	281	7.8	56.6	76.5	52.0	277	-14.3	986	51	240
Lincoln	21.9	57.8	22.3	3.5	19.6	11.5	548	16.4	5.5	43.1	77.4	104	-16.9	189	0	52
Lowndes	29.3	37.3	9.8	3.0	13.8	19.9	371	26.1	22.4	42.6	64.2	131	-16.1	353	0	83
Madison	17.9	62.8	19.0	8.6	20.4	12.5	502	23.7	20.3	41.0	59.8	217	-9.0	432	1	119
Marion	17.3	49.0	16.4	3.1	18.7	18.1	574	27.7	6.1	41.8	73.5	96	-23.6	168	0	48
Marshall	29.5	42.5	9.4	4.6	20.2	19.0	554	22.6	16.4	42.2	58.7	198	-10.5	357	0	104
Monroe	49.3	33.3	7.6	3.0	12.7	9.9	542	20.8	18.8	43.5	68.8	186	-11.5	343	1	123
Montgomery	18.5	NA	14.3	3.7	20.7	19.6	307	20.2	17.9	44.6	55.0	97	-12.0	317	0	46
Neshoba	29.8	NA	8.1	2.9	16.3	13.2	721	18.7	4.9	38.1	74.8	132	-13.3	184	0	52
Newton	36.4	30.7	9.1	2.2	14.3	20.0	599	20.0	6.5	45.9	74.8	105	-18.6	176	D	50
Noxubee	30.6	39.7	10.2	2.8	16.5	21.7	449	13.4	26.3	53.5	65.5	219	-13.0	488	2	145
Oktibbeha	17.9	29.4	9.5	3.3	12.4	49.2	355	22.3	13.2	36.6	67.6	92	-26.5	259	0	51
Panola	34.6	39.3	9.7	2.8	14.3	17.6	643	19.1	21.9	47.1	59.3	238	-21.2	370	4	151
Pearl River	15.1	51.9	13.6	2.9	25.2	20.2	584	36.8	8.9	39.9	71.1	124	-5.7	212	0	61
Perry	54.2	20.2	5.8	2.5	6.8	13.3	218	27.1	7.8	39.0	75.2	36	-25.3	165	D	16
Pike	24.1	49.3	13.4	4.2	18.6	20.5	483	18.2	7.0	43.7	74.7	87	-12.3	180	0	51
Pontotoc	61.4	23.5	6.4	2.0	9.3	8.4	604	23.8	9.1	40.1	68.5	122	-25.2	202	0	83
Prentiss	42.9	33.3	9.7	3.0	11.3	15.9	405	23.5	10.1	43.7	67.4	87	-21.7	215	D	55
Quitman	15.3	42.6	13.3	3.3	14.4	21.6	256	10.5	46.9	78.1	52.3	200	-6.1	780	34	183
Rankin	17.7	57.6	7.8	5.3	17.5	16.4	551	23.8	11.4	41.2	73.1	131	-8.5	237	D	65
Scott	42.0	29.4	7.3	2.8	10.9	11.1	688	28.9	7.3	48.7	73.3	114	-17.6	166	0	56
Sharkey	7.2	37.2	6.5	2.3	13.7	17.9	127	11.8	62.2	80.3	56.7	178	-15.5	1 401	11	166
Simpson	28.1	34.8	10.6	3.9	13.5	16.6	576	26.2	5.0	43.2	70.3	95	-26.9	165	0	42
Smith	41.6	23.3	4.2	1.0	8.3	9.7	662	26.1	3.0	47.4	74.9	87	-19.6	131	0	40
Stone	24.9	42.1	8.7	2.2	18.0	22.1	221	34.8	7.2	38.9	75.6	36	-34.7	161	D	14
Sunflower	22.8	NA	6.6	2.3	9.7	24.2	442	8.6	50.7	72.6	44.3	347	-8.6	786	90	307
Tallahatchie	10.5	46.5	7.8	2.9	23.8	22.3	404	11.1	39.9	61.9	56.7	296	-1.2	733	48	251
Tate	34.6	39.5	13.1	3.6	16.7	18.8	560	20.7	13.9	42.0	65.2	163	-2.6	291	1	99
Tippah	48.9	33.5	8.1	2.8	13.2	10.4	532	23.5	5.8	37.2	71.4	100	-15.6	188	0	50

1. Covers mining, construction, and manufacturing. 2. Covers private sector earnings in agricultural services, forestry, and fisheries; transportation and public utilities; wholesale trade; retail trade; finance, insurance, and real estate; and services.

STATE County	Agriculture, 1987 (cont'd) — Value of land and buildings — Average per farm ($1,000)	Value of land and buildings — Average per acre (Dollars)	Value of products sold — Total (Mil dol)	Value of products sold — Average per farm (Dollars)	Value of products sold — Percent from — Crops	Value of products sold — Percent from — Livestock and poultry[1]	Percent of farms with sales of — $10,000 or more	Percent of farms with sales of — $100,000 or more	Manufactures, 1987 — Establishments — Total	Establishments — Percent with 20 or more employees	All employees — Number (1,000)	All employees — Percent change, 1982–1987	All employees — Annual payroll (Mil dol)	Production workers — Number (1,000)	Production workers — Work hours (Mil)
	119	120	121	122	123	124	125	126	127	128	129	130	131	132	133
MISSISSIPPI—Con.															
Benton	156	499	8	34 509	86.1	13.9	36.2	8.6	12	33.3	0.4	100.0	5.2	0.3	0.6
Bolivar	583	720	79	166 031	90.7	9.3	73.2	44.6	29	44.8	2.7	12.5	43.1	2.0	3.8
Calhoun	153	480	16	37 780	80.8	19.2	37.5	11.5	34	47.1	1.9	26.7	25.6	1.7	3.5
Carroll	222	529	16	36 773	54.2	45.8	31.3	7.7	10	10.0	0.1	0.0	1.1	0.1	0.1
Chickasaw	166	481	15	34 655	43.0	57.0	41.4	7.2	67	53.7	5.3	32.5	69.3	4.6	8.6
Choctaw	108	489	4	16 009	16.8	83.2	20.6	1.8	16	31.2	0.9	0.0	11.0	0.7	1.5
Claiborne	305	648	6	27 467	27.2	72.8	28.8	4.6	14	35.7	0.6	20.0	8.3	0.5	1.0
Clarke	108	545	3	7 912	12.9	87.1	19.3	0.9	35	28.6	2.5	4.2	33.7	2.1	4.3
Clay	158	549	13	31 964	37.2	62.8	38.9	6.1	28	35.7	4.0	2.6	85.6	3.2	6.2
Coahoma	778	745	59	247 981	99.7	0.3	78.5	54.0	32	50.0	1.3	-23.5	25.0	1.0	2.0
Copiah	183	683	26	46 797	8.9	91.1	28.8	9.4	40	35.0	2.6	18.2	34.8	2.0	3.7
Covington	118	680	17	37 642	10.3	89.7	32.0	8.4	18	38.9	1.4	40.0	15.9	1.2	2.1
De Soto	285	945	21	41 109	77.0	23.0	28.0	8.3	97	53.6	6.2	40.9	115.8	4.3	8.1
Forrest	139	970	8	29 323	33.7	66.3	30.1	9.0	76	31.6	4.0	0.0	69.8	3.0	6.4
Franklin	164	625	3	14 917	39.9	60.0	21.6	2.3	25	16.0	0.4	-33.3	6.7	0.3	0.7
George	127	1 030	5	15 866	57.1	42.9	24.7	4.7	14	14.3	0.3	0.0	2.6	0.3	0.5
Greene	94	603	8	24 943	6.4	93.6	17.2	6.1	25	24.0	D	D	D	D	D
Grenada	186	535	12	51 759	42.4	57.6	36.1	10.3	33	45.5	4.0	21.2	76.8	3.4	7.5
Hancock	202	1 050	2	8 539	15.1	84.9	16.8	1.0	14	42.9	2.0	122.2	45.2	1.5	3.2
Harrison	113	1 438	2	6 694	50.0	50.0	14.3	1.7	150	29.3	6.0	-9.1	108.3	4.3	8.2
Hinds	261	749	33	41 045	27.8	72.2	27.9	4.4	241	35.3	13.4	-2.2	280.9	9.1	18.4
Holmes	436	839	40	94 725	92.5	7.5	47.1	20.7	16	68.8	1.1	0.0	14.6	1.0	2.0
Humphreys	537	897	86	265 860	39.0	61.0	76.9	54.2	7	28.6	D	D	D	D	D
Issaquena	781	696	21	200 196	92.1	7.9	71.0	47.7	3	0.0	0.0	0.0	0.2	0.0	0.0
Itawamba	93	560	13	28 741	21.2	78.8	31.6	8.4	53	30.2	2.4	4.3	31.8	2.2	4.3
Jackson	111	956	3	12 451	18.8	81.2	16.5	1.5	89	38.2	16.8	-9.7	463.1	10.8	21.0
Jasper	137	545	9	22 051	5.9	94.1	26.2	4.7	25	24.0	0.6	20.0	8.9	0.4	1.0
Jefferson	232	744	4	17 570	62.6	37.4	20.1	3.8	10	50.0	0.4	0.0	4.6	0.3	0.6
Jefferson Davis	95	603	7	17 944	17.9	82.1	26.2	3.9	11	36.4	0.8	166.7	7.5	0.7	1.3
Jones	136	1 115	59	73 267	1.8	98.2	39.0	22.4	81	35.8	4.8	-5.9	90.2	3.4	6.5
Kemper	123	517	4	9 982	23.8	76.2	22.8	2.1	19	26.3	0.8	166.7	5.2	0.4	0.5
Lafayette	132	491	7	15 573	57.7	42.3	26.6	3.6	24	29.2	1.2	-14.3	19.3	1.0	1.8
Lamar	143	888	13	38 814	16.6	83.4	30.4	10.1	27	40.7	1.3	-7.1	22.0	1.1	2.0
Lauderdale	129	738	5	10 350	37.8	62.2	17.8	1.6	94	41.5	6.0	27.7	114.6	4.5	9.3
Lawrence	137	660	5	16 451	22.7	77.3	26.7	2.3	19	26.3	D	D	D	D	D
Leake	103	757	50	76 230	4.1	95.9	36.1	21.4	32	25.0	1.5	-16.7	14.3	1.3	2.5
Lee	164	622	16	28 235	43.1	56.9	31.9	6.2	158	41.8	14.6	15.0	250.2	11.9	24.1
Leflore	775	825	71	252 173	80.6	19.4	81.5	56.6	44	36.4	2.7	17.4	34.9	2.2	4.1
Lincoln	134	715	13	24 278	8.4	91.6	26.8	6.6	57	26.3	1.2	-33.3	17.7	0.9	1.8
Lowndes	205	610	10	26 388	69.8	30.2	34.8	7.0	62	53.2	7.3	17.7	150.7	5.6	11.1
Madison	374	907	23	46 414	74.8	25.2	40.0	12.5	58	36.2	2.0	-4.8	33.5	1.3	2.6
Marion	140	882	10	17 266	7.4	92.6	22.6	5.2	39	28.2	1.9	26.7	21.1	1.7	2.8
Marshall	217	662	18	33 070	66.3	33.7	33.8	8.3	26	50.0	2.1	10.5	26.9	1.9	3.5
Monroe	215	606	16	29 694	64.0	36.0	36.9	8.5	51	52.9	5.7	23.9	91.9	4.9	9.3
Montgomery	174	512	8	26 713	64.3	35.7	35.2	7.8	20	45.0	0.6	0.0	7.6	0.5	0.9
Neshoba	108	556	26	36 627	1.8	98.2	26.9	8.9	48	25.0	2.6	18.2	40.8	2.2	4.7
Newton	126	693	35	58 047	4.7	95.3	35.1	16.7	24	25.0	2.4	9.1	31.4	2.1	4.1
Noxubee	248	482	22	49 073	53.3	46.7	52.8	14.0	18	38.9	0.5	0.0	6.7	0.5	1.0
Oktibbeha	149	496	8	23 905	21.0	79.0	26.5	6.2	44	40.9	2.4	9.1	39.1	1.4	2.8
Panola	191	510	24	37 626	82.7	17.3	36.1	10.9	41	46.3	2.9	70.6	39.5	2.5	4.8
Pearl River	246	1 140	14	23 630	21.0	79.0	21.9	4.8	43	27.9	0.9	-30.8	13.2	0.7	1.4
Perry	118	698	9	39 257	11.8	88.2	25.2	11.0	18	27.8	D	D	D	D	D
Pike	162	894	15	31 565	6.9	93.1	31.7	11.4	61	36.1	3.1	72.2	48.1	2.3	4.5
Pontotoc	104	528	12	20 337	62.0	38.0	30.8	5.1	66	56.1	4.9	88.5	75.7	4.2	8.1
Prentiss	131	627	9	21 704	52.2	47.8	27.9	5.9	50	38.0	3.6	44.0	41.5	3.2	6.0
Quitman	467	636	33	130 018	98.1	1.9	73.4	31.6	7	85.7	0.5	25.0	7.1	0.4	0.8
Rankin	176	825	33	59 797	14.7	85.3	39.4	14.5	95	29.5	4.1	24.2	76.3	3.2	6.6
Scott	148	763	104	150 961	1.8	98.2	43.2	27.3	43	53.5	4.3	13.2	57.3	3.9	8.0
Sharkey	1 019	739	42	330 187	89.6	10.4	85.8	59.8	7	28.6	D	D	D	D	D
Simpson	127	748	55	95 295	1.8	98.2	33.7	15.5	20	20.0	1.8	-5.3	27.5	1.7	3.1
Smith	110	781	54	81 980	1.6	98.4	44.0	23.6	26	53.8	1.6	60.0	26.8	1.4	2.9
Stone	148	911	4	18 644	18.4	81.7	18.6	5.4	31	16.1	0.6	0.0	9.8	0.5	1.0
Sunflower	543	746	87	196 382	67.8	32.2	83.5	47.1	24	75.0	4.7	135.0	58.5	3.6	6.9
Tallahatchie	480	690	53	131 611	93.3	6.7	60.1	30.4	10	50.0	0.4	0.0	4.8	0.4	0.7
Tate	170	624	21	36 782	50.5	49.5	34.3	11.4	11	36.4	1.9	18.7	37.8	1.4	2.8
Tippah	104	553	8	14 932	52.1	47.9	21.2	4.3	38	28.9	2.1	-16.0	30.5	1.8	3.5

1. Includes livestock and poultry products.

STATE County	Manufactures, 1987 (cont'd): Production workers (cont'd): Wages: Total (Mil dol)	Manufactures, 1987 (cont'd): Production workers (cont'd): Wages: Average per worker (Dollars)	Manufactures, 1987 (cont'd): Value added by manu-facture (Mil dol)	Manufactures, 1987 (cont'd): Value of shipments (Mil dol)	Manufactures, 1987 (cont'd): New capital expend-itures (Mil dol)	Value of construction authorized by building permits, 1990: Total[1] ($1,000)	Nonresidential: Total ($1,000)	Nonresidential: Percent: Office	Nonresidential: Percent: Industrial	Nonresidential: Percent: Stores	Residential: New construction ($1,000)	Residential: Number of housing units	Residential: Alterations and additions ($1,000)
	134	135	136	137	138	139	140	141	142	143	144	145	146
MISSISSIPPI—Con.													
Benton	4.0	13 333	23.2	41.4	0.8	1 530	1 148	6.1	0.0	0.0	50	1	11
Bolivar	28.5	14 250	109.9	209.8	5.6	6 993	3 003	0.8	0.0	92.2	2 303	53	620
Calhoun	21.3	12 529	56.0	123.3	2.4	8	8	0.0	0.0	0.0	0	0	0
Carroll	0.7	7 000	1.8	3.6	0.0	NA	NA	NA	NA	NA	NA	NA	NA
Chickasaw	54.4	11 826	158.7	340.8	6.3	3 817	2 736	4.8	47.8	44.1	975	34	74
Choctaw	8.5	12 143	28.5	58.8	D	759	0	NA	NA	NA	660	28	38
Claiborne	6.7	13 400	17.5	43.1	0.9	46	12	0.0	0.0	0.0	33	1	0
Clarke	25.4	12 095	100.7	195.7	2.2	526	54	92.6	0.0	0.0	236	6	60
Clay	61.3	19 156	207.7	629.0	7.2	4 635	2 072	10.6	57.9	3.0	2 188	44	276
Coahoma	16.0	16 000	84.7	224.6	3.0	4 404	1 240	5.5	24.3	35.1	1 252	20	1 448
Copiah	22.2	11 100	55.7	203.7	5.6	2 420	1 220	0.0	0.0	87.5	660	12	119
Covington	12.5	10 417	37.6	114.4	D	64	0	NA	NA	NA	39	1	0
De Soto	65.5	15 233	302.0	710.6	13.3	68 234	5 813	8.7	19.6	17.6	61 388	1 241	169
Forrest	43.7	14 567	141.2	399.5	8.3	12 739	4 517	24.4	5.1	22.2	1 729	26	1 141
Franklin	5.3	17 667	15.5	37.4	1.9	NA	NA	NA	NA	NA	NA	NA	NA
George	2.0	6 667	13.0	18.5	0.3	737	661	0.0	0.0	57.1	36	1	26
Greene	D	D	D	D	D	167	0	NA	NA	NA	0	0	42
Grenada	59.7	17 559	164.7	362.6	24.7	4 410	362	18.0	0.0	0.0	1 488	68	119
Hancock	32.3	21 533	108.3	200.5	60.7	4 542	1 042	0.0	0.0	11.7	2 811	75	622
Harrison	66.2	15 395	411.5	790.2	18.5	58 782	17 076	1.5	0.8	46.9	25 670	410	6 120
Hinds	171.8	18 879	779.4	1 744.1	40.6	126 236	31 261	14.4	1.0	61.0	42 575	675	4 262
Holmes	12.0	12 000	50.0	98.2	0.5	2 390	365	0.0	0.0	64.9	1 712	62	212
Humphreys	D	D	D	D	D	766	266	15.0	0.0	80.3	452	15	48
Issaquena	0.1	NA	0.5	1.4	0.0	285	0	NA	NA	NA	285	3	0
Itawamba	26.7	12 136	98.1	237.1	3.8	1 263	447	0.0	60.1	39.1	728	27	86
Jackson	277.8	25 722	1 332.4	3 801.2	58.8	36 065	11 046	1.0	1.7	70.8	14 140	282	6 984
Jasper	6.6	16 500	23.2	46.2	2.4	354	0	NA	NA	NA	354	9	0
Jefferson	3.5	11 667	9.7	21.1	0.5	96	0	NA	NA	NA	96	5	0
Jefferson Davis	6.7	9 571	15.8	32.4	0.1	33	16	0.0	0.0	0.0	0	0	0
Jones	55.5	16 324	188.9	463.8	7.5	5 471	2 061	1.3	0.0	20.5	515	6	864
Kemper	3.4	8 500	12.6	26.0	0.4	562	0	NA	NA	NA	562	24	0
Lafayette	13.9	13 900	24.1	89.7	4.9	25 926	1 281	46.6	0.0	32.7	5 838	206	556
Lamar	16.1	14 636	78.1	300.8	1.5	1 288	831	33.7	0.0	60.2	226	5	112
Lauderdale	79.0	17 556	351.3	673.3	12.4	17 374	6 051	13.4	0.3	72.0	3 789	39	1 909
Lawrence	D	D	D	D	D	293	167	44.9	0.0	49.1	0	0	10
Leake	11.3	8 692	50.8	105.3	6.1	3 016	60	100.0	0.0	0.0	2 417	79	54
Lee	170.5	14 328	565.0	1 335.7	30.2	50 092	19 898	25.8	4.8	52.6	14 605	323	1 123
Leflore	23.9	10 864	83.8	169.8	3.6	4 721	1 361	0.0	33.7	19.1	1 111	20	759
Lincoln	12.4	13 778	38.7	92.1	3.3	2 843	128	23.4	0.0	46.9	1 965	64	306
Lowndes	99.0	17 679	412.7	801.7	22.2	34 940	12 522	4.5	68.6	16.1	16 880	259	1 218
Madison	17.8	13 692	87.2	189.5	10.1	48 246	11 204	23.6	5.6	21.0	30 743	442	888
Marion	16.5	9 706	47.2	116.6	3.0	1 912	614	0.0	0.0	0.0	1 292	30	0
Marshall	20.1	10 579	59.7	112.7	5.7	1 574	810	0.0	51.4	0.0	474	12	39
Monroe	70.3	14 347	283.4	679.7	12.9	6 495	4 464	79.5	1.5	7.2	920	17	329
Montgomery	5.3	10 600	12.7	27.4	D	1 541	20	100.0	0.0	0.0	1 447	52	62
Neshoba	33.0	15 000	98.2	227.0	5.1	0	0	NA	NA	NA	0	0	0
Newton	26.5	12 619	80.3	118.4	D	743	285	7.0	0.0	0.0	403	10	48
Noxubee	5.1	10 200	24.3	62.6	1.0	479	174	0.0	0.0	77.0	176	7	40
Oktibbeha	18.4	13 143	128.4	293.8	5.5	14 146	2 854	3.8	0.0	82.9	7 132	228	327
Panola	31.5	12 600	77.0	232.1	6.3	6 636	3 821	7.4	62.5	15.4	2 110	59	220
Pearl River	9.3	13 286	34.8	81.4	2.6	2 552	629	1.6	2.1	11.9	623	12	189
Perry	D	D	D	D	D	510	106	0.0	0.0	100.0	377	10	2
Pike	31.4	13 652	175.3	345.4	8.3	2 851	1 667	56.1	11.5	17.6	800	15	227
Pontotoc	57.5	13 690	165.1	340.4	4.8	3 670	1 733	0.0	0.0	98.6	1 858	59	80
Prentiss	32.7	10 219	135.0	276.4	3.8	3 051	1 533	0.0	56.9	35.7	1 518	33	0
Quitman	4.6	11 500	15.1	93.2	0.6	2 658	208	0.0	0.0	68.2	1 736	49	708
Rankin	49.4	15 437	272.1	569.3	21.9	23 292	6 287	23.0	15.9	4.8	9 001	182	1 045
Scott	47.6	12 205	144.5	387.5	10.6	2 091	1 329	22.6	0.0	9.4	526	9	16
Sharkey	D	D	D	D	D	468	125	0.0	0.0	0.0	182	2	41
Simpson	25.1	14 765	53.9	140.7	1.6	1 290	672	9.1	0.0	36.0	242	7	207
Smith	20.9	14 929	87.5	201.6	D	155	15	0.0	0.0	0.0	140	2	0
Stone	7.6	15 200	27.1	78.6	1.2	637	226	0.0	0.0	94.6	352	11	16
Sunflower	40.8	11 333	149.0	476.1	18.8	4 507	728	0.0	50.4	24.0	2 037	50	579
Tallahatchie	3.4	8 500	11.1	18.8	0.2	599	104	0.0	0.0	0.0	482	13	10
Tate	22.7	16 214	71.6	128.4	D	8 903	3 404	11.2	18.6	21.3	5 038	95	234
Tippah	22.6	12 556	85.1	158.6	3.0	NA	NA	NA	NA	NA	NA	NA	NA

1. Includes nonresidential additions and alterations, residential nonhousekeeping buildings, and residential garages and carports not shown separately.

STATE County	Wholesale trade, 1987				Retail trade, all establishments, 1987				Retail trade, establishments with payroll, 1987					
						Sales				Sales				
											Per capita[2] (Dollars)			
	Estab-lishments	Sales (Mil dol)	Paid employees[1]	Annual payroll (Mil dol)	Number	Total (Mil dol)	Percent change, 1982–1987	Per capita[2] (Dollars)	Number	Total (Mil dol)	General merchan-dise stores	Food stores	Apparel & acces-sory stores	Eating and drinking places
	147	148	149	150	151	152	153	154	155	156	157	158	159	160
MISSISSIPPI—Con.														
Benton	5	4.4	27	0.3	65	D	D	D	17	D	D	418	0	D
Bolivar	44	197.1	685	13.0	437	150.0	28.0	3 512	256	141.6	290	1 086	150	170
Calhoun	20	25.5	128	1.8	198	52.2	44.2	3 415	114	39.9	216	760	143	110
Carroll	7	7.3	29	0.3	49	11.6	0.9	1 169	26	10.3	0	D	D	D
Chickasaw	36	49.8	173	2.9	221	77.1	41.2	4 214	124	71.1	D	1 237	78	97
Choctaw	7	3.5	22	0.1	74	21.0	36.4	2 356	43	18.9	130	646	D	80
Claiborne	6	D	D	D	74	21.0	-2.8	1 696	42	19.7	D	550	D	266
Clarke	15	15.0	96	1.1	156	33.7	-16.8	2 015	72	28.6	119	713	D	86
Clay	21	176.1	185	3.7	187	75.7	34.0	3 475	120	71.3	456	817	65	200
Coahoma	67	159.9	643	12.1	377	149.1	12.6	4 310	231	142.4	464	1 123	283	265
Copiah	29	68.2	117	2.1	245	95.9	41.2	3 551	147	90.3	397	926	58	139
Covington	15	238.3	63	1.5	162	48.5	19.8	2 941	77	43.3	175	791	29	79
De Soto	54	853.8	1 354	28.8	490	228.3	65.9	3 392	273	218.2	548	1 274	57	228
Forrest	159	368.8	1 752	26.7	885	513.3	30.5	7 707	572	495.3	1 243	1 569	375	779
Franklin	6	6.3	22	0.3	82	17.1	47.4	2 015	37	14.9	D	509	D	19
George	13	36.6	79	1.4	172	44.4	8.6	2 726	89	41.0	228	964	16	190
Greene	9	10.1	74	0.8	94	21.0	107.9	2 187	52	18.3	149	716	D	46
Grenada	35	105.8	363	4.9	278	141.8	31.9	6 851	169	133.4	554	1 680	217	421
Hancock	15	D	D	D	287	107.1	26.9	3 245	155	102.3	D	1 159	59	200
Harrison	245	D	D	D	1 780	944.1	30.0	5 438	1 137	913.3	D	1 139	146	653
Hinds	632	2 504.7	8 330	170.6	2 556	1 865.0	36.5	7 282	1 703	1 817.0	1 058	1 149	310	613
Holmes	16	30.1	143	1.7	197	47.2	-14.2	2 080	127	43.6	141	781	47	55
Humphreys	20	53.6	136	2.5	104	37.4	9.4	2 768	64	35.5	163	896	99	75
Issaquena	3	D	D	D	7	D	D	D	2	D	0	D	0	0
Itawamba	18	40.0	243	3.2	160	43.7	7.4	2 131	81	40.1	D	538	27	134
Jackson	107	498.4	920	15.9	1 087	504.4	21.8	3 934	671	482.5	504	1 008	138	360
Jasper	18	27.8	95	2.2	128	41.5	19.9	2 458	70	37.8	111	656	D	73
Jefferson	2	D	D	D	62	9.9	-2.0	1 161	26	8.2	D	419	D	D
Jefferson Davis	11	9.6	56	0.7	125	43.7	56.6	2 991	72	40.0	384	805	32	89
Jones	116	160.2	789	14.1	625	308.8	14.8	4 972	384	296.0	793	1 170	277	356
Kemper	4	3.4	13	0.1	92	19.6	31.5	1 768	41	15.8	D	475	10	D
Lafayette	29	44.2	217	3.8	307	131.6	44.9	4 259	212	127.8	D	1 010	397	437
Lamar	20	25.2	146	1.9	178	59.5	31.9	2 125	77	52.8	84	707	D	51
Lauderdale	146	747.4	1 886	36.6	888	493.7	29.5	6 436	574	478.5	976	1 272	248	508
Lawrence	9	8.8	35	0.5	137	32.0	4.2	2 537	79	28.8	D	809	D	106
Leake	19	15.2	130	1.6	200	70.0	43.1	3 785	100	62.1	602	817	97	160
Lee	209	651.1	2 074	38.8	902	481.4	41.9	7 594	533	453.1	1 085	1 271	345	532
Leflore	73	383.5	977	16.7	450	195.9	25.7	5 061	309	188.4	490	1 195	222	603
Lincoln	40	162.5	394	6.9	323	155.1	25.5	4 987	202	147.2	763	979	234	281
Lowndes	111	252.8	1 226	22.4	681	347.7	33.2	5 843	440	331.8	1 009	1 074	350	465
Madison	74	385.3	1 045	18.5	530	291.2	172.9	5 515	344	281.3	1 677	906	426	444
Marion	34	81.4	241	4.5	299	106.9	9.6	4 094	170	97.4	480	1 148	241	172
Marshall	17	13.8	93	1.2	226	64.2	21.6	1 905	103	56.1	314	586	22	68
Monroe	47	72.5	362	5.8	392	129.5	26.3	3 501	209	120.0	505	916	117	184
Montgomery	15	38.1	98	1.1	141	43.0	10.8	3 442	86	41.0	686	1 136	68	140
Neshoba	30	83.8	268	3.4	286	110.3	50.5	4 447	166	102.2	635	1 351	180	206
Newton	21	24.4	124	1.4	166	68.6	46.0	3 500	97	66.5	297	907	D	155
Noxubee	13	21.2	67	0.9	119	26.1	12.5	2 070	69	23.3	193	727	34	30
Oktibbeha	20	16.6	114	1.6	324	147.1	27.8	4 031	221	142.4	D	898	349	386
Panola	38	138.3	447	8.1	297	115.2	46.6	3 801	175	106.3	291	1 090	114	174
Pearl River	45	42.7	249	3.5	397	151.3	30.7	3 801	209	141.8	391	959	96	263
Perry	5	6.4	32	0.3	96	20.0	12.4	1 960	45	18.1	234	921	27	140
Pike	74	109.1	666	9.8	464	208.1	26.5	5 655	294	200.2	613	1 242	358	450
Pontotoc	26	36.0	176	2.8	231	58.2	32.6	2 565	96	47.8	D	678	162	167
Prentiss	29	77.7	328	4.7	302	112.3	70.9	4 422	130	96.6	D	1 208	47	183
Quitman	12	16.0	71	1.1	107	25.0	-9.4	2 229	55	21.9	D	618	D	20
Rankin	153	667.6	2 056	46.8	693	326.6	64.2	3 825	362	305.8	451	988	29	329
Scott	42	52.7	245	2.9	265	99.3	26.2	3 821	160	92.7	239	1 201	64	209
Sharkey	15	17.4	90	1.4	71	15.9	-8.6	2 179	41	14.0	229	848	30	D
Simpson	27	27.7	149	1.9	236	91.5	38.2	3 749	134	85.9	367	953	158	256
Smith	11	8.7	41	0.4	96	30.9	11.6	2 032	52	27.9	111	900	D	18
Stone	14	13.4	58	0.9	142	44.1	40.0	4 202	70	39.4	389	1 029	D	243
Sunflower	34	448.2	1 061	27.1	276	118.9	54.0	3 302	176	111.9	340	1 202	100	151
Tallahatchie	22	40.0	210	2.0	144	30.6	29.7	1 820	69	24.5	D	560	21	54
Tate	15	38.3	124	1.2	178	105.5	42.4	4 795	100	101.4	D	1 449	97	252
Tippah	27	32.1	179	1.8	280	79.9	37.8	4 099	127	67.9	D	1 048	65	171

1. For pay period including March 12. 2. Based on the estimated population as of July 1 of the year shown.

STATE County	Retail trade, establishments with payroll, 1987 (cont'd): Paid employees[1]	Retail trade (cont'd): Annual payroll (Mil dol)	Taxable service industries–establishments with payroll, 1987: Number	Receipts (Mil dol): Total	Selected kinds of business: Hotels, motels and other lodging places	Selected kinds of business: Health services	Selected kinds of business: Legal services	Paid employees	Annual payroll (Mil dol)	Bank deposits,[2] June 1989: Total (Mil dol)	Bank deposits: Percent change, 1988–1989	Savings capital,[3] September 1989: Total (Mil dol)	Savings capital: Percent change, 1988–1989
	161	162	163	164	165	166	167	168	169	170	171	172	173
MISSISSIPPI—Con.													
Benton	D	D	9	D	D	0.0	D	D	D	32	6.2	0.0	NA
Bolivar	1 706	15.1	155	31.6	D	15.1	2.9	851	9.8	230	6.0	32.3	0.3
Calhoun	509	3.9	46	6.0	0.0	3.1	0.4	158	1.7	121	8.3	0.0	NA
Carroll	138	1.0	8	D	0.0	D	D	D	D	21	1.6	0.0	NA
Chickasaw	766	6.8	63	18.2	D	8.4	0.6	365	4.4	120	5.1	9.7	-7.1
Choctaw	223	1.8	12	1.9	0.0	0.8	D	58	0.6	44	4.7	0.0	NA
Claiborne	274	2.2	28	4.0	D	0.9	0.3	91	1.2	62	-3.9	8.3	-7.2
Clarke	388	3.3	46	10.8	D	4.8	0.5	312	3.0	113	3.2	0.0	NA
Clay	927	7.8	77	15.2	0.7	5.9	1.2	448	4.4	118	5.7	10.7	0.9
Coahoma	2 023	17.1	142	31.5	1.1	14.7	5.8	842	12.4	275	-0.1	12.4	2.5
Copiah	997	8.9	75	16.2	0.0	4.5	2.8	454	4.7	154	3.3	7.5	0.9
Covington	426	3.6	40	8.0	D	1.6	0.5	256	2.4	78	4.7	22.0	3.2
De Soto	2 666	22.8	209	54.5	D	16.5	3.6	1 518	19.2	285	8.0	31.9	-16.2
Forrest	6 674	58.5	507	176.8	10.4	94.8	15.2	4 389	71.9	470	-1.8	338.8	6.9
Franklin	178	1.4	18	2.3	0.0	1.5	D	87	0.8	54	4.2	0.0	NA
George	604	4.5	57	7.2	D	3.8	0.5	263	3.0	77	2.6	36.0	5.0
Greene	198	1.8	16	3.0	D	D	D	99	0.9	33	6.6	4.0	-5.7
Grenada	1 428	12.9	115	28.2	5.1	7.8	1.9	714	8.2	171	-5.7	33.0	-5.3
Hancock	1 316	11.3	128	74.2	D	4.9	1.1	1 875	33.5	143	-1.7	93.6	11.3
Harrison	13 317	114.3	1 037	315.5	D	123.9	35.1	8 184	107.7	933	-1.6	257.8	-4.9
Hinds	20 565	211.7	1 936	824.0	55.8	219.5	106.8	20 741	310.8	2 743	-0.1	740.4	-27.2
Holmes	576	4.6	45	5.0	D	2.0	D	134	1.2	125	7.8	0.0	NA
Humphreys	386	3.6	38	6.2	0.0	3.2	0.3	198	2.1	86	4.4	5.0	-3.7
Issaquena	D	D	1	D	0.0	0.0	0.0	D	D	3	9.7	0.0	NA
Itawamba	540	3.9	46	6.4	D	2.9	0.2	213	1.8	113	9.6	5.5	-6.1
Jackson	6 676	59.2	579	157.0	D	46.9	17.5	4 056	65.1	456	9.6	220.0	-3.6
Jasper	455	4.4	48	10.9	D	2.3	0.5	204	3.5	113	19.6	14.3	-5.7
Jefferson	85	0.8	10	1.3	0.0	0.5	D	32	0.2	11	4.8	0.0	NA
Jefferson Davis	384	4.2	29	3.3	D	1.4	D	100	1.1	59	1.1	9.1	-0.7
Jones	3 790	34.2	310	77.8	4.2	27.9	4.5	1 924	28.6	428	4.7	178.5	-5.3
Kemper	159	1.5	16	2.4	0.0	1.2	0.2	91	0.9	51	4.1	0.0	NA
Lafayette	1 861	14.9	156	45.8	2.6	27.7	5.3	978	21.6	194	8.7	25.9	1.9
Lamar	560	5.1	44	7.3	0.0	4.9	0.6	169	3.2	69	3.7	9.0	11.8
Lauderdale	5 935	56.7	473	145.0	8.4	80.6	6.9	3 211	56.7	518	1.1	191.7	-2.9
Lawrence	379	2.9	24	3.8	0.0	1.1	D	153	1.3	71	-2.5	0.0	NA
Leake	644	6.0	55	8.9	0.0	5.5	0.8	236	2.7	138	6.9	11.4	2.8
Lee	5 144	47.1	413	138.7	7.0	57.0	9.7	2 728	55.5	564	0.8	108.3	0.6
Leflore	2 580	21.4	203	45.2	3.9	15.7	4.5	1 014	14.3	300	-0.5	37.0	-6.5
Lincoln	1 538	14.7	118	29.5	1.9	13.5	1.0	892	10.2	218	7.7	53.5	-5.3
Lowndes	4 326	37.7	346	89.0	5.8	35.7	5.3	2 096	31.2	366	6.6	100.9	1.2
Madison	3 855	33.5	188	51.7	3.0	7.1	3.4	1 498	18.3	266	19.0	93.3	23.2
Marion	1 121	9.8	105	23.9	D	6.1	0.7	535	6.5	205	4.8	41.7	4.5
Marshall	698	6.0	60	6.0	D	1.5	0.9	171	1.4	123	3.5	0.0	NA
Monroe	1 521	12.5	145	21.0	D	8.7	1.6	821	8.1	295	9.3	42.0	0.7
Montgomery	475	4.0	38	5.0	0.5	1.0	D	136	1.1	108	6.0	13.5	-9.2
Neshoba	1 080	9.6	90	18.6	D	8.6	1.7	478	6.4	171	5.6	31.8	2.1
Newton	604	5.8	54	5.5	0.0	2.5	0.5	151	1.7	68	3.9	46.5	6.6
Noxubee	295	2.3	27	3.3	D	1.6	D	89	1.1	80	1.5	0.0	NA
Oktibbeha	1 982	15.6	176	28.2	D	10.7	1.4	875	9.3	292	7.0	32.0	4.8
Panola	1 188	10.6	106	23.1	0.4	10.8	4.3	504	7.9	168	5.4	199.1	316.5
Pearl River	1 688	14.7	130	22.5	0.5	6.7	2.9	556	6.7	153	-7.3	47.4	6.8
Perry	253	1.8	18	2.9	0.0	1.3	D	70	0.6	47	0.0	2.5	1.7
Pike	2 535	23.1	203	40.9	1.8	18.2	3.6	975	14.5	331	1.9	38.3	-6.6
Pontotoc	651	5.2	64	7.8	D	3.8	0.5	226	2.5	149	6.7	8.4	1.3
Prentiss	909	8.5	63	11.2	D	3.8	1.2	277	3.0	178	9.5	14.9	-9.3
Quitman	235	2.3	25	3.0	D	1.4	D	81	0.9	64	2.2	4.9	-23.0
Rankin	4 049	34.2	352	177.6	3.3	73.7	5.7	4 002	60.2	313	11.4	40.8	-6.6
Scott	1 160	9.2	76	14.4	D	5.0	0.7	366	4.0	199	7.6	33.4	-4.3
Sharkey	174	1.7	26	2.6	0.0	1.0	D	80	1.0	44	1.7	0.0	NA
Simpson	1 009	8.8	84	17.4	0.6	8.8	0.7	749	6.0	147	5.6	6.1	-10.7
Smith	264	2.7	31	4.5	0.0	2.3	0.7	153	1.5	65	4.1	0.0	NA
Stone	469	4.3	36	7.2	D	3.2	D	232	2.4	65	1.2	9.1	0.7
Sunflower	1 281	11.2	88	17.3	D	6.2	1.2	425	5.5	197	10.6	20.7	-17.2
Tallahatchie	343	2.5	35	3.6	0.0	1.7	0.4	99	1.1	72	2.5	1.4	-17.8
Tate	1 027	9.4	66	14.9	D	9.8	0.7	434	5.1	131	7.2	13.7	17.0
Tippah	768	6.7	63	9.3	D	4.8	0.3	324	3.3	169	8.7	8.7	5.0

1. For the period including March 12 of the year shown. 2. Includes deposits for all insured and reporting noninsured commercial and mutual savings banks. 3. Includes savings capital for all FSLIC insured savings institutions.

STATE County	Federal funds and grants, 1989: Expenditures: Total (Mil dol)	Federal funds and grants, 1989: Expenditures: Percent change, 1988–1989	Per capita[1] (Dollars): Total	Per capita[1] (Dollars): Direct payments for individuals	Per capita[1] (Dollars): Procurement contract awards	Per capita[1] (Dollars): Salaries and wages	Per capita[1] (Dollars): Grant awards	Local government finances, 1981–1982: General revenue: Total (Mil dol)	General revenue: Intergovernmental: Total (Mil dol)	General revenue: Intergovernmental: Percent from state	General revenue: Taxes: Total (Mil dol)	Taxes: Per capita[2]: Total (Dollars)	Taxes: Per capita[2]: Property (Dollars)	Direct general expenditure: Total (Mil dol)	Direct general expenditure: Percent change, 1977–1982
	174	175	176	177	178	179	180	181	182	183	184	185	186	187	188
MISSISSIPPI—Con.															
Benton	28.4	16.8	3 339	1 794	86	107	1 093	4.5	3.5	94.6	0.8	103	103	4.1	42.6
Bolivar	137.8	14.4	3 297	1 828	42	99	691	44.3	23.6	76.2	8.1	180	174	42.5	54.7
Calhoun	41.8	11.4	2 766	1 966	15	143	340	11.5	6.5	92.9	2.2	144	141	10.2	41.0
Carroll	23.0	12.5	2 370	1 468	14	100	342	5.8	4.4	87.6	1.0	110	108	5.4	56.4
Chickasaw	46.0	5.8	2 488	1 813	15	127	372	13.8	9.1	85.0	2.1	115	112	12.8	54.5
Choctaw	21.2	-5.3	2 360	1 610	13	180	490	6.0	4.3	92.5	1.4	161	158	6.7	26.7
Claiborne	26.6	11.7	2 178	1 487	74	95	425	15.7	4.4	90.7	8.4	653	651	10.9	140.4
Clarke	40.5	-4.0	2 425	1 966	10	98	329	11.0	7.7	89.7	2.2	130	121	10.2	19.5
Clay	49.8	5.2	2 307	1 590	59	191	393	14.9	7.9	89.7	3.0	138	135	14.4	78.6
Coahoma	116.1	13.3	3 465	1 920	33	126	790	43.6	19.9	75.7	6.5	180	175	53.2	87.9
Copiah	74.5	16.9	2 730	1 890	303	112	386	23.9	13.6	85.2	3.7	143	139	23.7	36.0
Covington	45.5	7.9	2 726	2 058	106	136	370	15.4	7.0	94.8	2.1	127	126	14.1	56.4
De Soto	107.4	18.6	1 465	1 055	21	62	280	30.2	18.6	93.4	6.6	118	110	29.9	51.2
Forrest	206.7	19.4	3 090	2 159	87	510	323	73.3	24.4	88.6	12.5	185	169	73.2	92.7
Franklin	23.0	9.8	2 733	2 148	25	177	324	9.3	5.4	91.4	1.1	127	124	8.2	87.0
George	37.7	1.9	2 301	1 847	15	85	320	10.3	5.6	95.0	1.6	101	97	10.1	54.1
Greene	21.6	3.1	2 269	1 721	14	75	439	8.2	5.0	91.0	0.9	97	94	7.7	86.6
Grenada	57.6	3.5	2 807	1 989	43	308	332	21.6	8.3	92.7	3.0	145	136	22.1	97.1
Hancock	142.2	4.7	4 111	1 616	236	2 109	131	17.4	8.7	87.1	4.5	171	147	17.2	91.1
Harrison	939.4	10.1	5 474	2 080	710	2 419	257	135.0	55.8	77.8	36.3	220	174	129.2	42.1
Hinds	1 014.2	-11.0	4 042	1 819	289	616	1 293	288.1	135.4	67.9	73.3	291	277	293.0	88.8
Holmes	84.5	13.2	3 771	2 207	56	123	883	23.1	14.7	82.2	2.7	115	112	24.2	65.9
Humphreys	40.6	-6.7	3 079	1 624	30	111	567	9.7	6.3	90.0	1.6	112	108	9.8	44.2
Issaquena	7.6	16.1	3 445	1 000	12	85	332	1.8	1.4	63.4	0.4	157	156	1.3	35.4
Itawamba	41.2	12.8	2 031	1 551	12	90	294	18.9	10.2	90.3	3.3	162	161	19.7	53.1
Jackson	981.2	-55.7	7 642	1 447	5 667	365	140	138.0	42.4	88.7	31.8	259	235	120.5	65.7
Jasper	43.8	10.9	2 656	2 015	12	137	433	13.4	7.8	90.7	1.9	111	107	13.6	55.8
Jefferson	33.4	9.7	4 071	2 516	39	170	1 239	7.7	4.8	92.2	1.1	125	121	7.2	54.9
Jefferson Davis	38.3	8.6	2 644	1 718	192	94	544	13.0	8.5	96.1	1.2	83	78	12.4	103.0
Jones	160.7	1.6	2 604	2 047	86	147	312	68.5	30.5	83.8	11.2	175	160	66.8	74.7
Kemper	26.5	-18.9	2 324	1 700	34	123	388	12.2	8.0	94.8	1.7	165	164	12.7	88.3
Lafayette	66.1	13.2	2 145	1 330	64	275	413	25.2	10.1	94.3	4.0	126	123	24.6	77.2
Lamar	45.6	5.7	1 634	1 341	16	80	160	112.5	8.9	91.1	2.6	100	97	25.8	309.0
Lauderdale	280.6	2.7	3 711	2 117	153	1 019	415	68.6	44.8	66.8	13.4	173	160	69.5	104.4
Lawrence	37.9	9.1	3 007	2 275	17	282	394	12.8	6.7	96.8	2.0	154	150	12.6	119.0
Leake	47.5	1.9	2 610	1 985	16	148	407	10.0	6.8	92.5	1.6	86	83	9.8	28.4
Lee	151.8	6.4	2 338	1 678	78	310	222	47.4	22.0	88.8	10.3	178	173	47.2	73.7
Leflore	129.3	11.3	3 485	2 029	161	206	542	44.5	21.6	84.4	7.3	173	170	43.5	71.6
Lincoln	75.1	14.4	2 422	1 792	134	123	351	19.8	13.8	92.2	3.9	124	119	20.7	84.0
Lowndes	206.9	-3.6	3 538	1 571	543	1 078	293	48.0	20.6	91.2	8.3	138	135	47.1	77.7
Madison	155.0	84.7	2 659	1 140	933	79	350	25.2	15.6	91.0	4.4	102	98	24.9	93.3
Marion	71.9	4.3	2 809	2 118	65	107	469	22.7	13.1	90.0	2.6	98	91	20.8	90.8
Marshall	91.1	26.6	2 672	1 523	11	115	913	16.5	10.4	89.7	2.7	89	88	16.4	44.6
Monroe	80.5	1.0	2 194	1 677	13	124	276	28.6	14.0	89.7	4.3	115	112	26.9	79.3
Montgomery	40.6	8.6	3 278	2 201	51	172	711	11.9	5.9	89.3	1.5	114	109	11.6	46.3
Neshoba	77.2	15.1	3 086	1 658	242	293	857	17.6	8.1	91.6	2.1	87	85	16.7	148.1
Newton	62.1	1.8	3 253	2 507	33	256	428	16.0	9.9	86.0	2.4	119	112	14.6	41.6
Noxubee	36.3	-4.1	3 003	1 928	16	129	744	10.6	6.2	89.6	1.3	96	92	10.3	49.0
Oktibbeha	100.8	8.3	2 769	1 521	80	275	872	28.7	15.8	67.6	4.3	117	114	28.6	103.7
Panola	83.9	6.5	2 714	1 692	220	125	379	22.0	12.4	86.8	3.8	131	127	24.5	48.4
Pearl River	227.2	56.3	5 637	1 766	3 550	104	184	29.4	16.6	88.8	5.1	143	135	30.0	99.6
Perry	27.8	21.1	2 811	1 880	75	117	697	9.7	6.1	94.2	1.0	108	102	9.7	57.5
Pike	103.7	11.1	2 881	2 268	13	146	433	26.5	17.0	88.7	5.4	149	140	27.7	44.3
Pontotoc	48.5	13.7	2 099	1 518	15	93	320	13.9	7.7	92.2	2.0	95	94	14.8	46.3
Prentiss	53.2	5.0	2 094	1 596	30	85	288	26.9	14.7	87.7	2.9	117	115	29.3	114.7
Quitman	43.6	14.0	4 033	2 092	15	138	730	9.6	6.9	84.7	1.9	156	150	9.2	46.6
Rankin	143.5	-3.5	1 601	1 096	88	275	120	45.8	25.0	93.8	10.8	143	137	42.3	176.1
Scott	71.7	22.7	2 725	1 672	16	193	803	19.2	12.7	80.2	2.8	115	107	18.0	37.9
Sharkey	29.6	21.6	4 231	2 060	15	209	580	7.2	5.2	92.1	1.0	120	115	7.4	69.7
Simpson	51.6	5.1	2 132	1 692	13	104	289	15.5	9.7	93.2	1.9	81	76	15.6	86.3
Smith	34.1	8.5	2 271	1 728	28	156	307	9.1	6.7	94.6	1.3	90	87	9.1	60.6
Stone	32.4	12.0	3 056	2 588	42	201	203	25.5	13.7	88.9	3.3	321	317	28.5	88.8
Sunflower	99.3	14.3	2 804	1 483	9	92	459	31.2	17.7	92.7	4.9	135	129	31.2	58.3
Tallahatchie	60.5	15.4	3 581	1 731	124	157	599	12.8	8.1	92.1	1.8	107	103	12.6	43.3
Tate	51.5	11.2	2 308	1 643	56	144	326	21.7	13.8	86.2	2.8	137	134	21.8	68.8
Tippah	49.1	11.2	2 491	1 920	19	112	373	16.2	8.6	90.8	1.7	92	89	16.1	49.5

1. Based on the estimated population as of July 1 of the year shown. 2. Based on the estimated population as of July 1, 1982.

STATE County	Local government finances, 1981–1982 (cont'd) — Direct general expenditure (cont'd) — Per capita[1] (Dollars)	Percent of total for– Educa-tion	Health & hospitals	Police protec-tion	Public welfare	High-ways	Debt outstanding — Total (Mil dol)	Per capita[1] (Dollars)	State and local government employment, 1989 — Total	Rate[2]	Federal government civilian employment 1989 — Total	Earnings ($1,000)	Elections, 1988[3] — Total vote cast for president	Vote for lead party (Percent)
	189	190	191	192	193	194	195	196	197	198	199	200	201	202
MISSISSIPPI—Con.														
Benton	510	64.5	2.2	2.8	0.4	17.3	1.3	157	299	351.8	37	884	3 309	D–51.9
Bolivar	943	43.1	15.6	3.4	0.4	7.3	41.7	925	3 157	755.3	114	2 989	14 085	D–54.0
Calhoun	657	50.5	15.0	3.1	0.0	16.5	9.0	576	657	435.1	58	1 478	5 483	R–61.6
Carroll	570	44.9	1.8	3.3	0.9	38.3	2.4	253	234	241.2	36	855	4 204	R–62.5
Chickasaw	712	47.4	11.2	3.7	0.1	16.3	8.5	474	740	400.0	64	1 552	6 125	R–55.3
Choctaw	781	52.0	1.4	2.8	0.0	18.2	1.4	158	506	562.2	70	1 427	3 647	R–63.0
Claiborne	855	50.5	17.7	4.4	0.0	15.8	5.5	427	1 424	1 167.2	37	941	4 349	D–70.9
Clarke	592	53.9	1.5	4.0	0.2	23.7	4.0	231	675	404.2	43	1 039	7 098	R–63.7
Clay	665	45.0	20.1	4.9	0.1	9.8	8.3	382	847	392.1	116	3 485	7 553	D–51.0
Coahoma	1 474	35.8	25.4	2.2	0.1	6.0	21.1	584	2 390	713.4	106	2 926	11 278	D–54.4
Copiah	912	60.5	11.4	2.8	0.3	12.3	14.4	554	1 574	576.6	74	1 972	9 334	R–54.6
Covington	876	39.4	26.4	3.0	0.4	19.3	6.8	423	703	421.0	68	1 708	6 633	R–60.4
De Soto	538	60.1	0.9	3.6	0.1	12.5	25.5	458	2 118	288.9	120	3 343	20 250	R–72.5
Forrest	1 082	27.7	43.6	3.6	0.1	5.5	25.9	382	8 813	1 317.3	692	20 005	21 318	R–66.8
Franklin	984	43.1	26.9	1.7	0.3	14.1	1.1	128	373	444.0	68	1 380	3 962	R–60.0
George	650	48.5	24.3	2.9	0.4	14.0	2.0	130	667	406.7	39	1 060	7 782	R–58.4
Greene	815	52.8	24.4	1.8	0.3	14.4	1.1	112	411	432.6	24	600	4 970	R–57.1
Grenada	1 051	28.9	42.0	3.2	0.1	13.3	12.4	592	1 245	607.3	218	6 219	9 056	R–59.1
Hancock	661	42.4	15.4	5.1	1.0	12.7	9.6	366	1 369	395.7	1 726	64 418	11 687	R–66.4
Harrison	781	37.7	18.2	4.5	0.5	10.1	206.5	1 248	8 478	494.1	6 905	187 602	47 754	R–68.9
Hinds	1 162	37.6	10.0	3.7	1.5	8.8	224.6	890	29 396	1 171.6	4 331	141 356	95 006	R–55.5
Holmes	1 046	51.8	17.1	2.1	0.2	15.4	7.3	315	1 093	487.9	83	2 009	8 126	D–65.8
Humphreys	696	55.1	10.4	3.8	0.4	15.1	1.1	79	580	439.4	45	1 084	4 695	D–56.3
Issaquena	534	0.0	13.4	3.7	0.1	49.6	0.6	236	49	222.7	11	274	973	D–52.5
Itawamba	961	72.8	10.2	1.6	0.1	6.4	17.7	862	757	372.9	60	1 606	7 693	R–58.9
Jackson	980	37.4	28.7	4.6	0.3	6.3	191.0	1 553	7 108	553.6	816	27 591	40 364	R–73.9
Jasper	772	44.2	21.5	1.9	0.4	21.7	3.1	178	727	440.6	63	1 504	6 572	R–51.2
Jefferson	791	54.1	21.4	2.3	0.0	11.8	0.2	24	485	591.5	39	1 015	3 401	D–79.2
Jefferson Davis	880	43.4	15.2	2.0	6.2	23.3	1.4	100	737	508.3	36	890	5 728	D–51.5
Jones	1 042	41.3	27.2	3.4	1.1	9.1	30.7	479	5 177	839.1	237	6 475	24 272	R–69.1
Kemper	1 245	66.6	6.3	1.6	0.2	18.0	1.2	116	522	457.9	34	841	4 235	R–50.2
Lafayette	772	36.0	32.6	3.1	0.1	11.5	8.6	270	4 797	1 557.5	245	7 965	9 852	R–59.3
Lamar	1 011	30.8	48.5	1.6	0.3	9.5	12.2	479	979	350.9	54	1 359	11 746	R–77.9
Lauderdale	898	41.1	1.0	3.9	0.2	10.2	41.1	531	4 587	606.7	976	28 607	26 529	R–69.0
Lawrence	979	38.3	28.0	2.1	0.2	21.1	4.1	320	573	454.8	74	1 819	6 223	R–59.2
Leake	517	53.2	9.1	3.2	0.0	15.5	2.5	134	651	357.7	65	1 741	6 963	R–59.9
Lee	813	46.6	1.0	3.7	0.1	8.3	94.3	1 625	3 197	492.6	520	16 086	20 728	R–66.4
Leflore	1 039	39.1	25.6	3.1	0.1	8.3	32.1	767	3 301	889.8	232	6 297	12 579	R–50.9
Lincoln	664	51.4	1.3	2.7	0.2	24.9	8.6	276	1 234	398.1	107	3 004	13 297	R–65.5
Lowndes	783	39.4	30.8	3.1	0.2	5.4	18.6	309	3 909	668.2	898	19 726	17 331	R–65.0
Madison	574	52.9	11.8	4.2	0.2	16.2	8.8	202	2 120	363.6	129	3 561	19 825	R–57.5
Marion	774	49.6	25.7	2.6	0.2	13.3	4.3	158	1 385	541.0	72	1 815	11 344	R–61.9
Marshall	542	53.5	14.8	3.4	0.4	10.5	8.0	264	1 068	313.2	141	3 494	11 751	D–59.4
Monroe	724	41.4	25.9	3.6	0.3	11.9	16.2	436	1 364	371.7	152	4 213	11 173	R–57.7
Montgomery	884	36.1	31.9	2.5	0.5	16.8	3.7	281	649	523.4	43	1 117	4 409	R–56.8
Neshoba	696	36.2	0.9	2.3	0.2	9.4	27.1	1 129	955	382.0	322	7 724	9 347	R–68.1
Newton	728	63.2	9.5	3.4	0.9	9.7	7.2	361	1 495	782.7	98	2 697	8 003	R–70.7
Noxubee	789	44.7	27.8	1.9	0.3	14.5	1.6	126	605	500.0	51	1 349	4 631	D–58.8
Oktibbeha	770	34.4	18.5	3.3	0.6	7.2	11.6	312	6 945	1 908.0	391	13 301	12 289	R–58.0
Panola	855	42.1	28.1	3.3	0.4	8.9	16.9	588	1 824	590.3	133	3 404	10 665	R–50.5
Pearl River	844	59.5	11.0	3.6	0.2	10.7	3.9	110	1 721	427.0	101	2 712	14 333	R–71.3
Perry	1 000	46.0	18.8	1.9	0.0	22.9	1.6	168	547	552.5	29	710	4 347	R–68.6
Pike	759	55.9	1.3	3.5	0.2	7.6	19.0	521	2 754	765.0	135	4 040	14 239	R–53.6
Pontotoc	710	39.8	23.3	2.0	0.1	18.0	9.5	454	692	299.6	70	1 746	7 740	R–63.8
Prentiss	1 192	63.4	19.6	1.6	0.2	6.8	8.6	350	1 149	452.4	69	1 767	7 892	R–55.1
Quitman	756	61.8	1.5	2.8	2.5	13.5	5.7	471	570	527.8	48	1 116	4 351	D–57.4
Rankin	560	50.9	13.4	4.5	0.4	10.8	27.2	360	6 219	694.1	537	14 796	29 254	R–78.4
Scott	730	52.5	4.4	3.5	0.5	16.3	15.9	645	1 015	385.9	181	4 877	8 488	R–65.1
Sharkey	901	58.0	3.2	3.8	0.5	19.8	2.0	243	459	655.7	49	1 152	2 970	D–54.2
Simpson	647	52.1	13.4	3.1	0.3	17.7	8.8	365	1 368	565.3	62	1 476	9 223	R–66.7
Smith	612	59.7	14.0	4.0	0.2	12.0	1.9	126	597	398.0	81	1 864	6 285	R–72.8
Stone	2 739	81.5	8.0	0.9	0.0	6.7	1.8	170	681	642.5	77	1 987	4 499	R–66.8
Sunflower	864	55.0	15.8	3.8	0.2	13.1	5.9	163	3 594	1 015.3	91	2 257	9 289	D–52.7
Tallahatchie	763	54.0	18.9	3.2	0.2	13.0	0.8	46	766	453.3	95	2 366	5 547	D–51.9
Tate	1 065	77.2	1.0	2.0	0.0	11.8	12.3	599	1 030	461.9	101	2 642	7 449	R–61.1
Tippah	848	42.6	31.6	1.8	0.2	14.5	5.2	273	868	440.6	72	1 795	7 603	R–60.4

1. Based on the estimated population as of July 1, 1982. 2. Per 10,000 resident population estimated as of July 1 of the year shown. 3. Data subject to copyright.

STATE–County code	MSA/CMSA/NECMA code[1]	STATE County	Land Area,[2] 1990 (Sq. Km.)	Population, 1990: Total persons	Rank	Per square kilometer	Race: White	Black	Am. Indian, Eskimo, Aleut	Asian & Pacific Islander	Other race	Hispanic[3]	Age of population Percent: Under 5 years	5 to 14 years	15 to 24 years
			1	2	3	4	5	6	7	8	9	10	11	12	13
		MISSISSIPPI—Con.													
28 141	...	Tishomingo	1 099	17 683	1 806	16.1	17 010	631	24	13	5	56	6.3	13.2	13.9
28 143	...	Tunica	1 178	8 164	2 549	6.9	1 992	6 148	5	6	13	81	9.7	21.6	17.8
28 145	...	Union	1 076	22 085	1 571	20.5	18 804	3 213	18	25	25	103	6.7	14.8	14.9
28 147	...	Walthall	1 046	14 352	2 027	13.7	8 252	6 054	15	27	4	50	7.5	18.9	14.8
28 149	...	Warren	1 519	47 880	876	31.5	28 879	18 666	52	237	46	254	7.2	17.6	14.1
28 151	...	Washington	1 875	67 935	651	36.2	28 334	39 197	63	255	86	416	8.7	19.6	15.9
28 153	...	Wayne	2 099	19 517	1 700	9.3	12 506	6 957	19	32	3	75	7.7	18.3	15.2
28 155	...	Webster	1 095	10 222	2 369	9.3	7 953	2 254	3	10	2	57	6.5	16.1	14.0
28 157	...	Wilkinson	1 753	9 678	2 415	5.5	3 123	6 532	15	2	6	45	8.1	17.9	14.3
28 159	...	Winston	1 572	19 433	1 708	12.4	11 151	8 094	168	16	4	70	7.1	16.7	14.9
28 161	...	Yalobusha	1 210	12 033	2 215	9.9	7 479	4 526	10	14	4	53	7.0	15.8	14.1
28 163	...	Yazoo	2 382	25 506	1 447	10.7	11 958	13 443	30	52	23	103	8.3	19.1	14.3
29 000	...	MISSOURI	178 446	5 117 073	X	28.7	4 486 228	548 208	19 835	41 277	21 525	61 702	7.2	14.4	14.1
29 001	...	Adair	1 470	24 577	1 477	16.7	24 029	219	42	220	67	182	5.6	11.4	29.7
29 003	...	Andrew	1 127	14 632	2 009	13.0	14 516	30	41	23	22	103	6.7	16.0	12.4
29 005	...	Atchison	1 411	7 457	2 618	5.3	7 280	83	15	14	65	104	5.3	13.0	15.6
29 007	...	Audrain	1 796	23 599	1 509	13.1	22 037	1 419	34	83	26	81	6.7	15.2	11.7
29 009	...	Barry	2 018	27 547	1 371	13.7	27 133	25	276	80	33	152	6.6	14.5	12.0
29 011	...	Barton	1 539	11 312	2 274	7.4	11 151	11	108	28	14	57	6.8	16.0	10.9
29 013	...	Bates	2 198	15 025	1 986	6.8	14 817	107	78	10	13	82	6.5	15.5	11.1
29 015	...	Benton	1 827	13 859	2 066	7.6	13 736	13	75	17	18	78	5.1	12.1	10.6
29 017	...	Bollinger	1 608	10 619	2 325	6.6	10 545	12	31	28	3	70	7.0	15.0	12.7
29 019	1740	Boone	1 775	112 379	409	63.3	100 055	8 377	394	3 129	424	1 226	7.1	12.5	25.1
29 021	7000	Buchanan	1 061	83 083	548	78.3	79 378	2 635	273	266	531	1 709	7.2	14.6	13.8
29 023	...	Butler	1 807	38 765	1 031	21.5	36 487	1 983	134	125	36	217	6.5	14.6	13.1
29 025	...	Caldwell	1 112	8 380	2 524	7.5	8 335	14	21	2	8	50	7.0	14.8	11.6
29 027	...	Callaway	2 173	32 809	1 194	15.1	30 937	1 579	104	120	69	171	7.3	14.8	15.7
29 029	...	Camden	1 697	27 495	1 375	16.2	27 259	58	107	46	25	170	5.8	12.4	10.2
29 031	...	Cape Girardeau	1 499	61 633	707	41.1	57 964	2 985	101	475	108	313	6.7	13.2	18.8
29 033	...	Carroll	1 799	10 748	2 313	6.0	10 487	220	14	11	16	40	6.5	15.1	11.7
29 035	...	Carter	1 315	5 515	2 801	4.2	5 466	1	38	5	5	33	7.1	15.6	13.0
29 037	3760	Cass	1 811	63 808	686	35.2	62 218	684	381	269	256	829	8.0	16.4	13.2
29 039	...	Cedar	1 233	12 093	2 210	9.8	11 976	3	77	20	17	58	5.9	13.2	10.8
29 041	...	Chariton	1 958	9 202	2 453	4.7	8 835	337	17	7	6	19	6.8	14.9	10.7
29 043	7920	Christian	1 459	32 644	1 198	22.4	32 274	35	190	77	68	216	7.4	16.4	13.5
29 045	...	Clark	1 314	7 547	2 613	5.7	7 528	3	7	4	5	26	6.6	16.3	12.6
29 047	3760	Clay	1 027	153 411	302	149.4	147 721	2 693	782	1 135	1 080	3 539	7.4	14.3	13.9
29 049	...	Clinton	1 085	16 595	1 878	15.3	16 122	336	73	22	42	139	7.2	16.2	12.0
29 051	...	Cole	1 014	63 579	688	62.7	58 115	4 829	235	259	141	447	6.9	14.3	14.0
29 053	...	Cooper	1 463	14 835	1 998	10.1	13 557	1 147	55	47	29	96	6.4	14.0	17.4
29 055	...	Crawford	1 923	19 173	1 722	10.0	19 092	3	36	30	12	114	6.8	15.8	12.1
29 057	...	Dade	1 270	7 449	2 620	5.9	7 336	20	68	15	10	76	7.0	14.1	10.8
29 059	...	Dallas	1 403	12 646	2 171	9.0	12 515	16	89	18	8	65	7.1	15.1	11.9
29 061	...	Daviess	1 469	7 865	2 585	5.4	7 812	2	30	12	9	46	6.9	15.2	11.8
29 063	...	De Kalb	1 099	9 967	2 389	9.1	9 006	741	81	33	106	200	5.6	12.4	13.7
29 065	...	Dent	1 952	13 702	2 080	7.0	13 568	10	67	33	24	89	6.2	15.3	12.3
29 067	...	Douglas	2 110	11 876	2 225	5.6	11 756	3	89	15	13	90	6.9	15.4	11.7
29 069	...	Dunklin	1 413	33 112	1 185	23.4	30 280	2 629	87	77	39	169	6.7	14.8	13.4
29 071	7040	Franklin	2 388	80 603	565	33.8	79 403	750	155	192	103	441	7.8	16.3	14.0
29 073	...	Gasconade	1 345	14 006	2 056	10.4	13 947	11	22	17	9	35	6.8	14.2	11.1
29 075	...	Gentry	1 273	6 848	2 675	5.4	6 803	6	25	4	10	27	6.5	14.3	10.5
29 077	7920	Greene	1 748	207 949	240	119.0	200 912	3 749	1 281	1 523	484	1 775	6.4	12.8	18.5
29 079	...	Grundy	1 129	10 536	2 332	9.3	10 450	11	43	24	8	77	6.2	13.2	11.5
29 081	...	Harrison	1 878	8 469	2 516	4.5	8 400	8	31	23	7	37	5.8	13.4	10.2
29 083	...	Henry	1 819	20 044	1 675	11.0	19 655	227	83	49	30	144	6.4	13.9	11.9
29 085	...	Hickory	1 033	7 335	2 625	7.1	7 265	5	55	6	4	29	4.6	11.0	8.8
29 087	...	Holt	1 196	6 034	2 753	5.0	5 994	7	22	5	6	16	6.6	14.6	11.4
29 089	...	Howard	1 206	9 631	2 421	8.0	8 837	732	30	17	15	45	6.3	14.5	15.5
29 091	...	Howell	2 403	31 447	1 231	13.1	31 112	62	167	75	31	161	6.8	15.1	12.7
29 093	...	Iron	1 428	10 726	2 316	7.5	10 632	49	14	14	17	44	6.3	15.5	12.7
29 095	3760	Jackson	1 566	633 232	74	404.4	478 849	135 649	3 032	6 446	9 256	18 890	7.6	13.9	13.6
29 097	3710	Jasper	1 657	90 465	506	54.6	87 093	1 153	1 504	516	199	797	6.8	14.6	14.4
29 099	7040	Jefferson	1 701	171 380	281	100.8	168 977	1 202	425	543	233	1 151	8.4	16.9	13.9
29 101	...	Johnson	2 151	42 514	944	19.8	38 996	2 452	206	603	257	709	7.6	13.5	26.8
29 103	...	Knox	1 310	4 482	2 877	3.4	4 461	6	10	3	2	9	6.4	12.8	11.7

1. MSA = Metropolitan Statistical Area. CMSA = Consolidated MSA. NECMA = New England county metropolitan area. PMSA = Primary MSA. See Appendix A for explanation of these concepts. See Appendix B for list of metropolitan areas identified by type, with component counties. 2. Dry land or land partially or temporarily covered by water. 3. Hispanic persons may be of any race.

STATE County	Population, 1990 (cont'd) — Age of population (cont'd) Percent — 25 to 34 years	35 to 44 years	45 to 54 years	55 to 64 years	65 to 74 years	75 years and over	Percent female	Population–Change and components of change — Change 1980–1990 — Number	Percent	Components of change, 1980–1986 — Total persons, 1986	Total persons, 1980	Net change — Number	Percent	Natural increase — Births	Deaths
	14	15	16	17	18	19	20	21	22	23	24	25	26	27	28
MISSISSIPPI—Con.															
Tishomingo	13.9	13.7	11.5	10.6	9.4	7.5	52.3	-751	-4.1	17 800	18 434	-600	-3.2	1 500	1 300
Tunica	13.2	11.1	7.8	6.7	6.9	5.1	53.3	-1 488	-15.4	9 000	9 652	-600	-6.4	1 300	600
Union	14.4	14.0	10.3	9.4	8.1	7.3	51.8	344	1.6	22 200	21 741	400	2.0	1 900	1 400
Walthall	14.0	11.9	9.4	9.0	7.7	6.8	51.7	591	4.3	13 600	13 761	-100	-1.0	1 500	1 000
Warren	15.3	14.7	10.2	7.8	7.2	5.9	52.8	-3 747	-7.3	51 400	51 627	-200	-0.4	5 700	3 100
Washington	14.8	12.8	8.5	7.7	6.6	5.4	53.3	-4 409	-6.1	70 700	72 344	-1 600	-2.3	9 700	4 600
Wayne	15.9	13.2	9.8	8.2	6.6	5.1	52.1	382	2.0	20 000	19 135	900	4.7	2 400	1 100
Webster	13.7	12.7	10.1	9.4	9.3	8.3	52.1	-78	-0.8	10 400	10 300	100	0.7	1 000	800
Wilkinson	14.9	12.6	9.1	8.3	8.1	6.8	53.1	-343	-3.4	10 200	10 021	200	1.5	1 200	800
Winston	12.9	13.7	9.5	9.9	8.1	7.2	52.9	-41	-0.2	19 200	19 474	-300	-1.5	2 000	1 400
Yalobusha	13.4	13.0	9.7	9.4	9.9	7.8	53.3	-1 150	-8.7	13 200	13 183	0	0.0	1 300	1 000
Yazoo	14.1	11.8	8.8	8.9	7.8	6.9	53.2	-1 843	-6.7	27 000	27 349	-400	-1.3	3 500	2 000
MISSOURI	16.7	14.4	10.2	8.9	7.7	6.3	51.8	200 073	4.1	5 066 000	4 917 000	149 000	3.0	476 000	308 000
Adair	13.6	11.8	8.0	6.7	6.8	6.5	53.2	-293	-1.2	24 000	24 870	-900	-3.5	2 200	1 400
Andrew	14.6	14.9	10.7	8.9	8.2	7.6	51.4	652	4.7	14 900	13 980	1 000	6.8	1 200	900
Atchison	12.3	13.1	9.4	10.1	10.9	10.2	51.1	-1 148	-13.3	7 900	8 605	-700	-7.8	600	700
Audrain	13.5	13.6	10.1	9.9	10.4	8.9	51.8	-2 859	-10.8	25 400	26 458	-1 100	-4.1	2 300	1 800
Barry	14.0	12.3	11.1	10.9	10.5	8.2	51.0	3 139	12.9	26 300	24 408	1 900	7.7	2 100	1 900
Barton	14.7	12.9	9.3	9.8	9.9	9.8	51.8	20	0.2	11 400	11 292	100	1.3	1 000	1 000
Bates	13.2	12.8	10.2	10.8	10.0	9.7	51.8	-848	-5.3	15 800	15 873	0	-0.2	1 400	1 400
Benton	10.8	11.7	12.1	14.9	13.5	9.1	51.1	1 676	13.8	12 900	12 183	700	6.1	800	1 100
Bollinger	14.0	13.1	10.8	10.3	9.6	7.4	50.4	318	3.1	10 700	10 301	400	3.6	900	700
Boone	18.9	14.2	8.1	5.8	4.6	3.8	51.6	12 003	12.0	106 500	100 376	6 100	6.1	9 700	3 700
Buchanan	15.8	13.5	9.5	9.2	8.7	7.7	52.6	-4 805	-5.5	85 800	87 888	-2 100	-2.3	8 200	6 300
Butler	14.4	13.5	10.5	10.6	9.4	7.1	52.4	1 072	2.8	38 300	37 693	600	1.6	3 200	2 800
Caldwell	13.1	12.5	10.5	9.8	10.4	10.4	52.4	-280	-3.2	8 100	8 660	-500	-5.9	700	800
Callaway	16.3	14.9	10.1	8.4	6.6	5.8	51.5	557	1.7	31 800	32 252	-400	-1.3	2 900	1 600
Camden	12.8	13.3	12.3	14.8	12.4	6.0	50.1	7 478	37.4	25 200	20 017	5 100	25.7	1 800	1 400
Cape Girardeau	15.7	14.2	9.6	8.1	7.4	6.4	52.0	2 796	4.8	61 300	58 837	2 500	4.3	5 000	3 200
Carroll	12.6	12.5	10.2	10.0	10.6	10.8	52.4	-1 383	-11.4	11 400	12 131	-700	-5.8	1 000	1 000
Carter	13.3	12.9	11.2	11.0	8.7	7.1	50.6	87	1.6	5 800	5 428	300	6.4	500	400
Cass	17.1	15.1	11.3	8.1	5.7	5.0	51.3	12 779	25.0	57 300	51 029	6 300	12.2	5 200	2 600
Cedar	11.5	11.5	10.6	12.4	12.6	11.5	52.6	199	1.7	12 400	11 894	500	3.9	900	1 100
Chariton	12.9	12.2	9.9	10.9	10.8	10.9	52.1	-1 287	-12.3	10 000	10 489	-500	-4.7	900	900
Christian	17.1	15.9	10.6	8.0	6.2	4.9	51.2	10 242	45.7	27 100	22 402	4 700	21.0	2 100	1 200
Clark	13.2	13.9	10.7	9.5	8.8	8.3	50.3	-946	-11.1	8 000	8 493	-500	-5.6	600	600
Clay	18.5	16.0	11.1	8.5	6.4	4.0	51.7	16 923	12.4	144 900	136 488	8 400	6.1	13 200	6 000
Clinton	14.6	14.2	11.9	9.0	7.4	7.7	51.6	679	4.3	16 400	15 916	500	3.1	1 400	1 100
Cole	19.0	16.2	9.7	7.7	6.5	5.7	49.0	6 916	12.2	63 400	56 663	6 800	11.9	5 600	2 800
Cooper	13.5	12.7	9.3	8.6	9.6	8.4	48.4	192	1.3	15 200	14 643	500	3.6	1 300	1 100
Crawford	14.6	12.7	10.6	10.3	9.4	7.8	51.3	873	4.8	19 200	18 300	900	4.7	1 700	1 200
Dade	13.0	12.0	9.9	11.0	10.7	11.5	52.4	66	0.9	7 500	7 383	100	1.5	600	700
Dallas	13.8	12.5	10.6	10.7	9.9	8.4	51.0	550	4.5	12 800	12 096	700	5.5	1 000	900
Daviess	12.6	11.9	10.8	10.5	10.4	9.9	52.5	-1 040	-11.7	8 500	8 905	-400	-4.3	800	800
De Kalb	21.0	13.6	9.2	8.2	7.9	8.5	41.6	1 745	21.2	8 100	8 222	-100	-1.6	700	700
Dent	13.2	12.9	10.9	10.4	10.0	8.7	52.0	-815	-5.6	14 300	14 517	-300	-1.8	1 200	1 100
Douglas	13.3	12.6	11.8	11.0	9.2	8.1	51.5	282	2.4	12 200	11 594	600	5.3	1 100	700
Dunklin	13.5	12.8	11.1	9.6	9.9	8.2	53.6	-3 212	-8.8	34 400	36 324	-1 900	-5.2	3 000	2 700
Franklin	16.6	14.0	10.6	8.5	6.8	5.3	50.6	9 370	13.2	77 900	71 233	6 700	9.4	7 600	4 000
Gasconade	14.6	12.5	9.5	10.3	11.2	9.9	51.7	825	6.3	13 500	13 181	300	2.6	1 200	1 100
Gentry	12.9	10.3	10.1	10.2	11.9	13.3	52.9	-1 039	-13.2	7 400	7 887	-500	-5.7	700	800
Greene	16.3	14.5	9.9	8.3	7.3	6.0	52.1	22 647	12.2	198 200	185 302	12 900	7.0	17 000	10 300
Grundy	12.8	12.7	10.9	10.6	11.0	11.1	53.6	-1 423	-11.9	11 200	11 959	-800	-6.6	900	1 000
Harrison	13.2	11.0	10.7	11.7	11.4	12.7	52.1	-1 421	-14.4	9 400	9 890	-500	-5.3	800	900
Henry	13.4	12.9	10.7	10.2	10.4	10.1	52.1	372	1.9	20 000	19 672	400	1.8	1 600	1 800
Hickory	9.4	10.6	10.5	16.9	17.7	10.6	50.9	968	15.2	7 000	6 367	700	10.4	400	600
Holt	12.8	12.8	9.3	9.8	10.9	11.9	51.2	-848	-12.3	6 500	6 882	-400	-5.9	600	600
Howard	13.8	12.4	9.3	9.3	9.3	9.7	51.6	-377	-3.8	9 800	10 008	-200	-2.3	900	800
Howell	13.6	13.3	10.9	10.3	9.4	8.0	51.9	2 640	9.2	30 000	28 807	1 200	4.2	2 600	2 100
Iron	12.9	12.7	10.7	10.4	9.6	9.3	52.9	-358	-3.2	10 800	11 084	-200	-2.1	900	800
Jackson	18.4	14.8	10.0	8.7	7.3	5.8	52.4	3 966	0.6	636 400	629 266	7 100	1.1	65 600	38 300
Jasper	15.7	14.0	9.9	9.0	8.4	7.1	52.4	3 507	4.0	89 500	86 958	2 600	3.0	8 200	6 300
Jefferson	19.0	15.6	10.6	7.3	5.0	3.3	50.4	25 197	17.2	163 800	146 183	17 600	12.0	16 800	5 800
Johnson	16.7	11.5	8.2	6.5	5.0	4.3	49.4	3 455	8.8	38 000	39 059	-1 100	-2.8	4 200	1 700
Knox	12.9	11.6	11.2	11.8	10.8	10.9	52.0	-1 026	-18.6	4 900	5 508	-600	-11.2	400	500

STATE County	Population–(cont'd) Components of change, 1980-1986 (cont'd)	Households, 1990					Births, 1988			Deaths, 1987				Marriages, 1984	
					Percent					Number		Rate			
	Net migration	Number	Percent change, 1980–1990	Persons per house-hold	Female family house-holder[1]	One-person	Total	Rate[2]	Low birth weight[3] (Number)	Total	Infant[4]	Total[2]	Infant[5]	Number	Rate[2]
	29	30	31	32	33	34	35	36	37	38	39	40	41	42	43
MISSISSIPPI—Con.															
Tishomingo	-800	7 059	4.9	2.48	9.0	23.5	211	11.7	14	193	2	10.6	9.6	266	14.7
Tunica	-1 300	2 526	-10.2	3.22	26.4	23.0	192	21.6	21	100	2	11.1	10.8	51	5.4
Union	-100	8 367	7.6	2.62	9.7	23.0	298	13.2	30	265	6	11.7	18.2	249	11.5
Walthall	-600	4 929	11.5	2.88	14.7	22.2	228	16.6	22	122	2	8.9	9.4	120	8.8
Warren	-2 900	17 407	0.3	2.72	16.5	24.9	853	17.1	83	490	10	9.8	13.7	496	9.6
Washington	-6 700	22 593	-1.5	2.98	23.7	23.2	1 262	18.1	116	713	17	10.2	13.0	595	8.4
Wayne	-400	6 858	10.8	2.83	15.8	21.1	316	15.8	25	174	4	8.6	12.5	170	8.5
Webster	-200	3 826	6.5	2.63	13.3	25.5	132	13.2	12	137	5	13.4	37.3	93	8.9
Wilkinson	-200	3 347	4.9	2.85	24.3	23.4	149	15.1	12	144	6	14.4	37.3	140	13.6
Winston	-900	7 061	7.8	2.73	15.8	24.5	264	13.7	20	223	7	11.5	22.9	158	8.2
Yalobusha	-300	4 614	0.7	2.59	15.6	28.1	207	16.0	18	149	2	11.5	11.8	133	9.9
Yazoo	-1 900	8 813	-0.1	2.86	20.3	25.0	467	17.9	45	279	7	10.6	15.5	242	8.9
MISSOURI	-18 000	1 961 206	9.4	2.54	10.6	26.0	76 492	14.9	5 221	50 695	769	9.9	10.2	52 464	10.5
Adair	-1 700	9 060	1.3	2.35	7.5	30.2	289	12.4	19	223	3	9.4	10.1	284	11.5
Andrew	600	5 429	10.1	2.64	6.8	20.6	183	12.0	5	136	1	9.1	5.1	109	7.3
Atchison	-600	2 961	-10.2	2.35	6.8	28.0	69	8.8	7	99	1	12.7	13.7	124	14.6
Audrain	-1 600	9 205	-5.9	2.50	8.5	25.5	274	10.8	25	281	3	11.0	9.3	244	9.5
Barry	1 600	10 858	16.7	2.51	7.0	23.5	375	13.5	32	336	1	12.2	3.0	218	8.4
Barton	100	4 524	2.7	2.46	7.1	27.7	143	12.4	8	147	2	12.8	14.7	93	8.1
Bates	0	5 918	-2.9	2.49	7.3	25.4	213	13.4	21	217	3	13.8	14.6	154	9.7
Benton	1 000	5 764	18.9	2.37	6.2	24.7	121	9.1	11	196	1	15.0	9.6	94	7.5
Bollinger	200	3 946	6.2	2.65	7.2	20.6	146	13.2	9	121	0	11.0	0.0	102	9.8
Boone	200	41 937	18.8	2.42	9.5	27.5	1 632	15.4	105	668	21	6.3	12.9	1 159	11.0
Buchanan	-4 000	32 486	-1.3	2.48	11.4	27.7	1 253	14.7	70	985	9	11.5	7.5	961	11.2
Butler	200	15 334	8.1	2.48	11.3	25.6	490	12.7	35	501	4	12.9	7.8	546	14.2
Caldwell	-400	3 222	-2.4	2.54	6.7	24.8	116	14.0	2	125	1	15.2	10.2	71	8.7
Callaway	-1 700	11 552	8.4	2.63	8.8	21.8	432	13.1	36	242	4	7.4	9.2	221	6.8
Camden	4 700	11 305	41.5	2.41	5.7	20.6	336	13.0	16	235	1	9.3	3.2	283	12.1
Cape Girardeau	700	23 390	11.6	2.49	8.9	25.4	820	13.2	55	531	9	8.6	11.5	780	13.0
Carroll	-700	4 332	-9.2	2.44	7.4	28.5	135	12.2	4	160	2	14.2	14.4	85	7.3
Carter	200	2 128	8.5	2.56	8.8	26.5	85	14.4	8	70	0	12.1	0.0	63	11.1
Cass	3 600	22 892	31.4	2.75	8.2	19.1	923	15.0	54	441	10	7.4	11.4	686	12.5
Cedar	700	5 003	4.4	2.37	6.8	27.4	136	11.0	7	196	0	15.8	0.0	65	5.3
Chariton	-500	3 661	-9.5	2.47	5.8	27.6	111	11.3	9	133	1	13.6	9.8	77	7.5
Christian	3 800	11 937	49.6	2.70	8.0	17.8	480	15.8	26	225	3	7.8	7.0	180	7.3
Clark	-500	2 859	-8.1	2.61	6.9	24.5	86	10.8	5	108	1	13.3	8.2	220	26.8
Clay	1 100	58 915	18.4	2.55	9.0	23.5	2 140	14.2	129	992	16	6.7	7.5	1 417	10.1
Clinton	200	6 112	10.0	2.66	7.2	21.7	208	12.3	20	188	1	11.3	4.4	130	8.0
Cole	4 000	22 976	16.2	2.53	8.8	27.4	871	14.1	32	526	9	8.6	10.9	722	11.9
Cooper	300	5 359	-0.4	2.53	7.8	25.0	199	13.6	10	153	3	10.5	14.3	132	8.7
Crawford	400	7 299	10.8	2.59	7.4	23.0	267	13.3	20	206	1	10.5	4.0	179	9.3
Dade	200	2 976	1.6	2.43	6.1	27.7	102	13.4	7	108	0	14.6	0.0	61	8.2
Dallas	600	4 899	9.9	2.55	7.2	23.6	179	13.4	14	151	1	11.5	6.0	97	7.7
Daviess	-400	3 040	-10.0	2.55	5.7	25.5	123	14.5	5	117	3	13.9	24.4	58	6.7
De Kalb	-100	3 054	-0.7	2.55	5.8	25.0	112	13.8	5	95	1	11.9	9.0	88	10.9
Dent	-500	5 327	-1.3	2.53	8.2	23.8	187	12.9	10	185	4	12.9	22.0	138	9.3
Douglas	300	4 587	10.1	2.56	6.3	23.3	165	13.1	18	140	2	11.4	14.6	137	11.0
Dunklin	-2 300	13 128	-3.4	2.48	12.3	27.2	477	13.8	33	429	9	12.4	22.0	465	13.1
Franklin	3 100	28 856	20.2	2.76	8.4	20.0	1 325	16.8	65	696	7	8.9	5.9	852	11.4
Gasconade	300	5 543	10.2	2.48	6.2	25.8	166	11.9	6	173	6	12.4	30.5	134	9.9
Gentry	-400	2 756	-11.6	2.40	6.2	29.3	94	13.2	2	108	1	15.0	13.9	62	7.9
Greene	6 200	81 463	17.7	2.43	9.2	26.6	2 701	13.2	163	1 774	21	8.8	7.7	2 353	12.2
Grundy	-600	4 346	-10.7	2.36	7.2	29.1	107	9.8	7	175	1	15.9	8.1	111	9.7
Harrison	-300	3 574	-13.6	2.32	5.8	29.7	89	9.9	5	134	1	14.7	10.8	86	8.9
Henry	600	8 189	5.5	2.41	7.8	28.0	280	14.0	32	317	3	15.9	11.5	210	10.7
Hickory	800	3 183	21.0	2.27	5.2	24.4	68	9.2	3	91	0	12.5	0.0	58	8.3
Holt	-300	2 440	-11.9	2.42	5.2	28.8	76	12.1	9	91	0	14.2	0.0	61	9.1
Howard	-400	3 571	-2.5	2.49	8.5	26.9	120	12.6	14	125	1	13.0	8.4	70	7.1
Howell	700	12 283	14.2	2.51	8.4	24.4	388	12.5	21	377	5	12.3	13.1	361	12.0
Iron	-400	3 995	5.0	2.58	8.7	23.5	124	11.1	7	167	2	15.0	15.4	110	9.6
Jackson	-20 200	252 582	4.3	2.46	13.6	29.6	10 951	17.0	872	6 247	145	9.7	13.6	7 123	11.3
Jasper	600	36 134	7.7	2.44	9.8	27.4	1 253	13.6	66	987	6	10.8	4.8	981	11.1
Jefferson	6 600	59 199	25.5	2.87	9.2	16.7	2 802	16.3	156	1 106	25	6.6	9.2	1 315	8.4
Johnson	-3 600	14 579	16.3	2.60	6.9	21.6	635	16.3	21	274	4	7.1	6.1	449	11.8
Knox	-500	1 819	-12.5	2.40	6.3	28.1	48	10.0	0	53	0	10.8	0.0	43	8.1

1. No spouse present. 2. Per 1,000 resident population estimated as of July 1 of the year shown. 3. Under 2,500 grams. 4. Deaths of infants under 1 year old. 5. Deaths of infants under 1 year old per 1,000 live births.

STATE County	Divorces, 1984		Physicians, active non–Federal, 1989		Hospitals, 1989			Nursing homes,[4] 1986		Serious crimes known to police, 1988			Education			
						Beds				Number			Public school enrollment[7]		Attainment,[8] 1980	
	Number	Rate[1]	Number[2]	Rate[3]	Number	Number	Rate[3]	Number	Beds	Total[5]	Violent[6]	Rate[3]	1986–1987	1980	Percent 12 yrs. or more	Percent 16 yrs. or more
	44	45	46	47	48	49	50	51	52	53	54	55	56	57	58	59
MISSISSIPPI—Con.																
Tishomingo	44	2.4	15	83	1	99	547	1	120	43	16	280	3 087	3 559	45.4	5.6
Tunica	NA	NA	1	11	1	22	253	0	0	NA	NA	NA	2 093	2 260	30.8	6.5
Union	133	6.1	15	66	1	153	677	1	120	NA	NA	NA	4 598	4 519	46.4	8.8
Walthall	41	3.0	7	51	1	49	355	2	108	6	2	50	3 052	3 017	48.0	9.0
Warren	262	5.1	76	155	2	374	762	5	371	1 877	184	3 699	10 446	10 566	59.5	15.7
Washington	251	3.5	78	113	2	405	585	4	356	4 515	250	7 558	14 572	15 836	50.0	12.5
Wayne	96	4.8	9	45	1	80	400	1	60	185	14	920	4 144	4 339	45.8	7.4
Webster	56	5.4	5	51	1	55	556	1	90	47	14	452	2 030	2 065	48.6	6.8
Wilkinson	NA	NA	7	72	1	66	680	1	96	NA	NA	NA	1 611	2 109	43.7	8.6
Winston	80	4.2	9	47	1	156	808	3	142	36	5	184	4 094	4 109	46.7	8.4
Yalobusha	55	4.1	6	47	1	85	664	1	42	206	24	1 583	2 539	2 749	45.4	8.0
Yazoo	83	3.0	13	51	1	88	342	2	221	955	58	7 604	5 286	5 837	46.5	11.5
MISSOURI	24 826	5.0	9 941	193	172	30 674	594	828	54 429	234 611	27 228	5 155	800 606	871 650	63.5	13.9
Adair	121	4.9	4	17	2	300	1 304	3	504	758	24	4 781	3 256	3 661	67.5	20.0
Andrew	59	4.0	4	26	0	0	0	5	297	68	1	453	2 705	2 959	65.6	10.5
Atchison	40	4.7	5	65	1	57	740	2	195	78	5	993	1 315	1 659	66.7	11.8
Audrain	120	4.7	30	120	1	144	574	6	376	428	18	1 680	3 897	4 753	61.0	9.6
Barry	66	2.6	13	46	2	71	251	6	349	202	20	890	5 165	4 626	57.0	7.0
Barton	71	6.2	4	35	1	44	383	3	190	172	15	1 485	2 009	2 116	56.5	7.0
Bates	63	4.0	8	50	1	34	213	6	351	292	42	1 859	2 628	3 000	57.7	7.3
Benton	43	3.4	1	7	0	0	0	3	155	323	6	2 467	2 095	2 090	50.2	6.3
Bollinger	41	3.9	1	9	0	0	0	2	24	107	22	975	1 930	2 073	40.4	4.9
Boone	521	4.9	725	686	7	1 564	1 480	12	776	5 636	343	5 206	15 079	15 466	79.7	34.7
Buchanan	598	7.0	136	160	3	916	1 078	29	1 211	4 382	314	5 101	14 226	15 263	63.4	10.6
Butler	335	8.7	75	194	3	559	1 448	7	414	1 221	68	7 146	6 754	7 355	48.2	8.2
Caldwell	39	4.8	2	24	0	0	0	2	170	53	7	650	1 664	1 715	61.8	6.7
Callaway	148	4.5	19	57	2	589	1 774	7	340	378	76	3 645	4 376	6 098	59.5	11.7
Camden	95	4.1	21	80	1	99	379	3	240	486	40	1 835	3 957	3 548	61.1	8.7
Cape Girardeau	290	4.8	136	218	2	524	838	13	706	2 366	56	3 826	8 490	8 917	63.8	17.1
Carroll	45	3.9	1	9	1	40	364	2	128	93	12	825	2 104	2 393	58.0	8.1
Carter	28	4.9	1	17	0	0	0	1	60	NA	NA	NA	1 283	1 211	45.2	7.2
Cass	252	4.6	22	35	2	90	143	7	344	1 398	97	2 389	11 749	11 916	70.0	10.2
Cedar	67	5.4	3	24	1	34	274	4	376	150	18	1 211	2 195	2 075	52.1	6.3
Chariton	33	3.2	0	0	0	0	0	2	160	92	18	932	1 399	1 784	58.8	7.6
Christian	139	5.7	5	16	0	0	0	3	213	227	6	785	5 656	4 986	64.2	8.0
Clark	43	5.2	0	0	0	0	0	3	140	NA	NA	NA	1 546	1 754	59.4	5.7
Clay	779	5.6	104	68	4	675	443	14	1 120	10 068	1 361	7 717	25 340	26 922	76.7	15.5
Clinton	85	5.2	7	41	1	28	164	6	341	129	21	2 076	2 701	3 657	68.1	9.0
Cole	394	6.5	77	125	4	434	707	11	778	2 104	178	3 254	9 656	7 935	70.1	19.3
Cooper	64	4.2	10	70	1	45	315	5	304	288	13	1 869	2 303	2 690	61.1	10.6
Crawford	101	5.3	4	20	0	0	0	6	213	336	33	1 711	3 126	3 644	46.5	7.1
Dade	33	4.5	2	26	1	21	276	2	186	NA	NA	NA	1 245	1 285	58.0	7.2
Dallas	63	5.0	1	7	0	0	0	3	158	144	7	1 100	1 707	2 412	51.3	5.7
Daviess	33	3.8	1	12	0	0	0	1	97	73	9	863	1 284	1 585	59.5	7.2
De Kalb	24	3.0	1	12	0	0	0	3	223	20	3	3 241	1 304	1 656	64.2	7.9
Dent	89	6.0	5	35	1	49	340	3	162	11	3	255	2 472	2 878	44.8	6.7
Douglas	35	2.8	1	8	0	0	0	1	120	20	1	161	1 707	2 380	47.6	6.7
Dunklin	291	8.2	25	73	1	97	284	7	507	716	71	2 498	6 946	7 802	42.1	6.7
Franklin	312	4.2	53	67	1	59	75	8	632	2 264	279	2 824	14 116	13 809	52.5	7.4
Gasconade	53	3.9	6	43	1	43	307	5	240	17	2	156	2 839	2 165	47.2	7.2
Gentry	27	3.5	4	58	1	55	797	6	225	37	0	510	1 283	1 371	59.6	9.3
Greene	1 301	6.8	463	225	6	2 705	1 314	23	2 260	12 973	670	6 435	32 434	32 492	71.1	15.7
Grundy	59	5.1	4	37	1	53	495	4	296	162	8	1 476	1 888	2 112	63.5	8.8
Harrison	39	4.0	3	34	1	28	318	3	200	46	6	508	1 579	1 791	61.4	7.5
Henry	103	5.3	8	40	2	149	745	4	322	742	56	3 702	3 048	3 514	58.4	8.4
Hickory	27	3.9	0	0	0	0	0	1	120	61	1	841	1 508	1 060	53.1	5.7
Holt	19	2.8	2	32	0	0	0	2	120	61	3	946	998	1 212	65.3	7.8
Howard	27	2.8	7	74	1	49	521	4	153	64	13	2 328	1 538	1 758	57.6	11.1
Howell	190	6.3	30	96	2	158	506	5	500	321	12	3 835	6 044	5 693	51.8	7.6
Iron	65	5.7	7	62	1	50	446	7	634	97	11	876	2 619	2 454	48.2	7.8
Jackson	3 826	6.1	1 686	261	23	5 161	800	84	5 481	57 692	7 581	9 047	97 161	106 035	70.7	15.7
Jasper	583	6.6	132	143	4	672	726	17	1 022	4 426	212	4 878	17 011	16 003	61.9	10.9
Jefferson	732	4.7	64	36	1	231	131	24	1 302	2 761	178	1 647	30 201	30 934	59.4	7.3
Johnson	204	5.4	23	59	2	98	250	6	360	1 030	25	8 013	6 254	6 350	72.1	18.8
Knox	16	3.0	0	0	0	0	0	2	106	NA	NA	NA	786	942	62.1	8.0

1. Per 1,000 resident population estimated as of July 1 of the year shown. 2. As of end of year. 3. Per 100,000 resident population as of July 1 of the year shown. 4. Preliminary. Covers nursing homes with 3 or more beds. 5. Data for serious crimes have not been adjusted for underreporting, this may affect comparability between geographic areas or over time. 6. Includes murder and nonnegligent manslaughter, forcible rape, robbery, and aggravated assault. 7. The 1986–1987 data are based on administrative reports obtained by the U.S. National Center for Education Statistics. The 1980 data are based on the 1980 Census of Population and Housing. 8. Persons 25 years old or older.

STATE County	Education (cont'd) Local government expenditures for education,[1] 1982 Total (Mil dol)	Education (cont'd) Local government expenditures for education,[1] 1982 Per capita (Dollars)	Social Security Program December 1988 Beneficiaries Total	Social Security Program December 1988 Beneficiaries Rate[2]	Social Security Program December 1988 Payments ($1,000)	Supplemental Security Income Program recipients June 1986	Money income Per capita[3] 1987 Income, (Dollars)	Money income Per capita[3] 1979 Current dollars	Money income Per capita[3] 1979 Constant 1987 dollars	Money income Median household income 1979 (Dollars)	Money income Percent below poverty level, 1979 Persons	Money income Percent below poverty level, 1979 Families	Housing units, 1990 Total	Housing units, 1990 Percent change, 1980–1990
	60	61	62	63	64	65	66	67	68	69	70	71	72	73
MISSISSIPPI—Con.														
Tishomingo	6.1	322	4 335	239.5	1 693	914	7 704	5 397	8 445	12 678	13.5	11.1	8 455	7.4
Tunica	4.5	470	1 640	184.3	527	804	4 625	3 251	5 087	6 620	52.9	44.8	2 990	-2.0
Union	9.2	428	4 460	198.2	1 700	968	8 013	4 958	7 758	11 499	20.0	16.4	9 104	10.2
Walthall	4.6	347	2 750	200.7	999	938	6 538	4 598	7 194	10 251	28.2	23.4	5 643	14.4
Warren	18.5	355	7 725	155.1	3 138	1 666	9 387	6 268	9 808	15 869	18.7	13.9	19 512	1.2
Washington	25.6	351	12 085	173.4	4 767	3 794	7 017	4 670	7 307	10 603	33.2	26.3	24 567	1.6
Wayne	6.3	316	3 435	171.8	1 247	1 068	6 174	4 331	6 777	10 304	29.2	23.6	7 723	12.8
Webster	3.6	342	2 240	224.0	833	612	7 683	4 857	7 600	11 302	19.6	15.7	4 326	10.4
Wilkinson	3.5	332	2 115	213.6	746	878	5 475	3 600	5 633	9 120	35.5	27.9	4 242	12.5
Winston	6.5	336	3 950	204.7	1 495	1 128	7 413	4 607	7 209	10 686	25.0	19.8	7 613	5.9
Yalobusha	5.2	397	3 230	250.4	1 211	876	6 870	4 427	6 927	10 293	24.6	19.4	5 414	-3.8
Yazoo	10.5	383	5 170	198.1	1 967	1 808	6 759	4 562	7 138	9 830	36.3	27.6	9 549	0.2
MISSOURI	1 867.3	378	895 431	174.2	425 704	80 319	11 203	6 915	10 820	15 581	12.2	9.1	2 199 129	10.6
Adair	9.2	367	3 895	166.5	1 744	624	9 049	5 903	9 236	12 146	16.0	9.9	10 097	2.7
Andrew	5.3	367	2 215	145.7	975	118	9 696	6 266	9 804	15 322	8.7	6.8	5 841	5.9
Atchison	3.6	414	1 715	219.9	817	102	8 929	6 235	9 756	13 029	12.6	9.3	3 298	-8.8
Audrain	9.2	350	5 370	212.3	2 655	306	9 466	6 523	10 207	15 505	11.5	8.6	10 039	-4.8
Barry	9.5	378	6 930	249.3	2 925	586	8 668	5 329	8 338	11 130	15.4	11.8	12 908	15.5
Barton	3.7	331	2 575	223.9	1 106	186	8 573	5 417	8 476	11 230	14.5	10.1	5 014	3.6
Bates	5.1	334	3 655	229.9	1 613	276	8 871	5 938	9 291	11 850	15.2	11.4	6 782	-3.2
Benton	3.8	314	4 055	304.9	1 819	236	8 443	5 686	8 897	10 320	17.3	15.5	10 280	23.5
Bollinger	3.7	358	2 365	213.1	907	372	6 697	4 359	6 821	9 936	24.1	21.8	4 542	6.7
Boone	31.0	299	12 130	114.7	6 031	938	11 216	6 942	10 862	15 523	12.7	5.9	44 695	19.4
Buchanan	33.1	382	17 505	205.0	8 494	1 384	10 010	6 461	10 110	14 305	11.3	7.8	35 652	-1.5
Butler	13.7	363	8 495	219.5	3 431	1 700	7 701	5 044	7 892	9 981	24.2	19.5	17 046	7.2
Caldwell	3.5	413	2 135	257.2	897	130	8 629	5 624	8 800	11 694	14.6	11.9	3 649	-5.3
Callaway	11.2	346	5 290	160.3	2 473	360	9 751	6 290	9 842	17 043	9.2	6.8	13 003	10.9
Camden	6.9	325	5 710	221.3	2 666	310	9 294	5 891	9 218	11 755	14.4	11.8	25 662	51.4
Cape Girardeau	16.0	268	10 320	165.9	4 822	784	10 570	6 561	10 266	14 832	11.9	7.9	25 315	11.3
Carroll	5.5	462	2 790	251.4	1 256	188	8 773	6 127	9 587	11 992	16.2	12.4	5 001	-8.8
Carter	3.1	554	1 315	222.9	520	262	6 558	4 281	6 698	9 423	24.4	20.0	2 693	18.8
Cass	22.7	430	7 910	128.8	3 835	318	11 340	7 187	11 245	19 000	7.9	6.6	24 337	27.2
Cedar	4.0	333	3 750	302.4	1 558	298	8 497	5 331	8 341	9 843	16.7	12.7	6 035	7.2
Chariton	4.0	381	2 150	219.4	954	180	9 089	6 283	9 831	12 384	15.4	12.5	4 479	-6.9
Christian	7.8	342	4 475	147.2	1 905	362	9 264	5 870	9 185	14 143	11.8	9.3	12 812	48.5
Clark	3.3	391	1 500	187.5	637	98	8 366	5 708	8 931	12 297	15.2	12.0	3 398	-2.8
Clay	60.8	443	19 690	130.8	10 317	752	13 136	8 351	13 067	21 029	5.3	3.8	63 000	20.4
Clinton	5.3	334	3 105	183.7	1 430	208	9 958	6 434	10 067	16 212	8.6	6.9	6 559	7.1
Cole	16.7	283	9 050	146.9	4 494	470	11 379	7 178	11 231	18 077	6.6	4.7	24 939	18.1
Cooper	5.3	365	3 085	211.3	1 412	226	8 694	5 937	9 290	13 681	11.6	9.4	6 002	2.3
Crawford	5.1	277	4 150	207.5	1 828	344	8 425	5 273	8 251	11 802	17.1	12.7	9 030	4.2
Dade	2.5	334	1 960	257.9	789	182	8 821	5 629	8 808	11 218	14.9	11.1	3 543	1.9
Dallas	3.1	255	2 840	211.9	1 127	370	7 452	4 899	7 665	9 592	19.2	15.4	5 484	8.2
Daviess	3.4	388	1 915	225.3	809	136	8 648	5 990	9 373	11 346	17.9	12.6	3 613	-5.5
De Kalb	3.2	390	1 630	201.2	705	72	8 636	5 569	8 714	11 915	16.5	13.8	3 358	-3.6
Dent	4.8	328	3 575	246.6	1 490	474	7 538	5 059	7 916	10 798	20.2	16.2	6 115	-3.2
Douglas	2.8	229	2 295	182.1	845	412	7 100	4 375	6 846	9 134	24.9	20.7	5 105	9.5
Dunklin	13.8	380	8 380	242.9	3 214	2 226	7 535	4 846	7 583	9 775	23.6	18.7	14 102	-4.8
Franklin	24.6	339	13 700	173.9	6 506	720	10 157	6 283	9 831	16 612	9.1	7.0	32 451	17.9
Gasconade	5.8	443	3 470	249.6	1 532	182	9 513	5 901	9 233	12 633	12.3	9.6	7 158	8.1
Gentry	2.8	350	2 135	300.7	864	188	8 105	5 221	8 169	10 706	16.9	13.4	3 232	-9.6
Greene	62.4	333	32 775	160.7	15 190	3 016	10 777	6 667	10 432	14 380	12.6	8.7	87 910	17.3
Grundy	3.8	324	2 770	254.1	1 171	254	8 892	5 736	8 975	11 577	16.9	12.7	5 113	-8.1
Harrison	4.2	423	2 490	276.7	986	226	8 690	5 686	8 897	10 158	19.2	17.4	4 245	-12.5
Henry	5.9	307	5 435	271.8	2 401	426	8 894	6 206	9 711	12 122	13.7	11.2	9 317	5.2
Hickory	2.6	403	2 355	318.2	1 012	182	7 334	4 600	7 198	8 608	25.5	19.0	5 482	15.8
Holt	2.2	330	1 610	255.6	740	134	8 178	5 579	8 729	11 616	16.0	12.7	3 190	-14.0
Howard	3.5	352	2 065	217.4	896	246	8 886	5 780	9 044	12 025	13.4	8.7	4 025	-1.8
Howell	11.6	400	7 610	245.5	3 029	1 010	7 555	4 661	7 293	9 760	21.3	17.6	13 326	12.3
Iron	5.3	480	2 820	251.8	1 231	454	7 445	5 005	7 831	11 760	17.3	13.4	4 700	7.1
Jackson	226.5	360	102 400	158.8	52 167	7 686	12 067	7 610	11 907	16 887	11.0	7.9	280 729	7.0
Jasper	34.7	392	19 245	209.0	8 938	1 620	9 556	6 025	9 427	12 485	13.4	9.5	39 554	9.2
Jefferson	59.6	395	17 800	103.2	8 708	996	10 553	6 642	10 393	19 597	6.6	5.6	63 423	24.0
Johnson	12.0	312	4 830	123.8	2 200	278	8 949	5 593	8 751	13 515	13.3	9.1	16 010	15.2
Knox	2.1	392	1 210	252.1	489	124	7 861	5 525	8 645	11 210	22.9	17.2	2 254	-10.3

1. Elementary and secondary. 2. Per 1,000 resident population estimated as of July 1 of the year shown. 3. Based on the resident population estimated as of July 1, 1988 for 1987 data and enumerated as of April 1, 1980 for 1979 data.

STATE County	Housing units, 1990 (cont'd) — Occupied units — Total	Owner occupied — Percent	Owner occupied — Median value (Dollars)	Median rent (Dollars)	Civilian labor force, 1990 — Total	Percent change, 1989–1990	Unemployment — Total	Unemployment — Rate[1]	Private nonfarm establishments, 1988 — Number	Net change, 1987–1988	Employment[2] — Total	Employment[2] — Percent change, 1987–1988	Employment[2] — Manufacturing	Employment[2] — Retail trade
	74	75	76	77	78	79	80	81	82	83	84	85	86	87
MISSISSIPPI—Con.														
Tishomingo	7 059	79.4	38 700	134	7 493	-1.6	1 113	14.9	314	-11	3 541	-0.4	1 837	636
Tunica	2 526	53.8	35 400	99	2 864	2.3	388	13.5	126	-5	925	5.2	0	221
Union	8 367	78.2	39 700	160	12 208	4.1	824	6.7	395	0	6 509	-3.7	4 233	856
Walthall	4 929	84.3	39 100	150	5 081	0.4	383	7.5	168	0	1 202	-13.3	327	358
Warren	17 407	68.9	50 600	211	23 227	-0.7	1 762	7.6	1 040	-1	12 842	-3.0	3 562	3 497
Washington	22 593	59.6	41 700	196	27 707	-1.7	2 955	10.7	1 525	8	18 499	-2.9	4 678	4 121
Wayne	6 858	83.7	37 100	132	8 148	2.3	745	9.1	315	-7	3 355	-5.3	1 071	755
Webster	3 826	78.5	36 000	130	4 800	0.4	366	7.6	186	-1	2 260	-6.2	1 383	305
Wilkinson	3 347	81.4	35 700	99	3 105	2.5	300	9.7	175	-8	1 472	-9.5	666	249
Winston	7 061	81.6	39 100	155	8 590	5.6	695	8.1	386	-14	4 793	3.0	2 823	718
Yalobusha	4 614	79.2	35 500	120	4 391	-5.8	467	10.6	236	8	3 234	10.9	2 177	369
Yazoo	8 813	66.3	38 400	125	9 721	-0.5	695	7.1	438	4	4 274	4.6	1 500	941
MISSOURI	1 961 206	68.8	59 800	282	2 634 000	0.8	151 000	5.7	X	X	1 898 227	1.9	432 073	398 070
Adair	9 060	59.4	41 900	217	11 852	3.5	489	4.1	622	6	7 208	5.6	1 406	2 075
Andrew	5 429	78.6	45 900	220	7 036	-1.5	426	6.1	195	6	1 312	7.1	0	429
Atchison	2 961	65.9	28 800	153	3 358	3.0	117	3.5	229	5	1 571	1.7	200	431
Audrain	9 205	74.2	36 000	178	10 544	-0.3	608	5.8	630	17	6 671	3.7	2 451	1 479
Barry	10 858	77.2	42 300	195	13 416	4.4	611	4.6	607	9	8 451	11.2	4 852	1 274
Barton	4 524	73.8	31 800	168	5 457	1.1	200	3.7	243	11	2 966	8.1	0	543
Bates	5 918	74.6	31 400	175	5 944	-2.4	481	8.1	335	-17	2 474	-4.8	359	662
Benton	5 764	81.4	38 300	184	5 603	-1.1	469	8.4	332	17	1 758	9.9	322	524
Bollinger	3 946	81.7	29 400	159	4 170	8.8	415	10.0	161	6	1 092	1.8	306	198
Boone	41 937	55.0	65 700	299	68 555	2.2	1 934	2.8	2 814	33	36 772	-0.4	4 276	10 620
Buchanan	32 486	68.0	40 800	230	42 757	0.6	2 661	6.2	2 066	7	32 384	7.4	9 058	6 842
Butler	15 334	68.1	36 300	183	17 500	4.0	1 280	7.3	999	24	9 686	2.3	1 978	2 640
Caldwell	3 222	76.2	25 600	168	3 212	1.0	232	7.2	144	10	981	8.8	0	256
Callaway	11 552	76.9	48 900	208	16 036	-2.1	773	4.8	604	1	7 112	5.4	1 142	1 478
Camden	11 305	80.7	71 700	254	15 816	5.5	1 006	6.4	998	12	7 062	-10.0	781	2 505
Cape Girardeau	23 390	67.7	56 900	251	36 542	3.7	1 594	4.4	2 044	28	27 572	1.4	5 539	7 032
Carroll	4 332	73.4	26 900	152	4 103	0.8	382	9.3	271	2	1 640	-17.9	180	401
Carter	2 128	73.8	29 900	147	2 029	-5.4	221	10.9	108	-9	765	6.2	300	107
Cass	22 892	76.4	64 600	306	30 850	-0.7	1 639	5.3	1 117	18	8 817	10.5	1 148	2 742
Cedar	5 003	79.6	34 200	161	4 773	4.3	313	6.6	259	4	2 117	0.1	710	490
Chariton	3 661	77.9	26 100	139	4 295	3.9	219	5.1	194	-9	1 358	-3.8	423	238
Christian	11 937	79.6	58 500	249	16 174	3.0	915	5.7	630	65	5 042	17.4	2 063	1 124
Clark	2 859	75.9	26 300	150	3 772	3.9	207	5.5	155	15	775	6.6	95	245
Clay	58 915	67.5	68 500	355	85 105	0.1	3 856	4.5	3 759	81	55 790	2.1	14 674	13 434
Clinton	6 112	77.6	47 900	223	7 683	6.6	500	6.5	345	2	2 612	8.6	115	799
Cole	22 976	67.6	60 200	256	35 263	0.8	1 350	3.8	1 818	14	23 328	1.4	3 379	5 806
Cooper	5 359	75.0	39 600	184	6 472	0.7	399	6.2	339	-3	3 192	3.7	926	838
Crawford	7 299	78.4	37 900	187	10 055	-1.6	820	8.2	386	5	3 592	3.1	1 435	811
Dade	2 976	77.3	30 900	151	2 879	1.6	146	5.1	126	1	889	3.0	313	206
Dallas	4 899	78.8	33 000	165	4 239	4.7	437	10.3	188	-1	2 164	13.2	422	431
Daviess	3 040	75.3	24 600	153	3 942	10.5	216	5.5	140	0	990	17.3	0	338
De Kalb	3 054	73.1	33 200	160	4 057	11.0	220	5.4	145	3	928	-1.8	0	246
Dent	5 327	73.9	34 800	163	6 374	5.4	412	6.5	306	12	2 737	3.8	689	633
Douglas	4 587	77.6	34 000	163	4 774	-1.6	382	8.0	176	-15	2 004	0.1	983	444
Dunklin	13 128	66.8	30 000	137	13 641	0.5	1 200	8.8	785	13	6 661	1.9	1 879	1 554
Franklin	28 856	78.0	58 300	259	39 826	1.4	3 788	9.5	1 899	68	22 674	3.9	8 941	5 008
Gasconade	5 543	80.3	41 800	180	7 393	0.8	537	7.3	381	10	3 541	1.1	1 732	774
Gentry	2 756	74.5	23 000	151	2 650	-3.6	120	4.5	214	0	1 367	3.3	122	320
Greene	81 463	63.4	58 200	281	113 884	2.5	4 845	4.3	6 134	77	93 933	5.3	19 985	21 634
Grundy	4 346	72.5	24 200	162	4 881	-0.4	281	5.8	295	-10	2 371	-7.1	0	584
Harrison	3 574	73.9	20 200	125	4 358	3.8	193	4.4	247	9	1 796	7.5	117	801
Henry	8 189	73.4	36 500	179	8 498	-3.1	703	8.3	574	30	4 709	-0.7	1 120	1 351
Hickory	3 183	84.2	37 500	156	2 866	3.0	175	6.1	108	2	572	2.7	117	148
Holt	2 440	73.6	22 600	138	2 250	-1.1	136	6.0	132	-9	924	10.1	0	290
Howard	3 571	75.0	31 400	172	4 467	1.2	181	4.1	211	-2	1 977	4.1	542	362
Howell	12 283	73.8	36 800	163	14 253	0.9	971	6.8	746	12	8 769	3.6	3 248	1 776
Iron	3 995	75.9	34 900	169	2 854	4.9	399	14.0	217	13	2 232	11.0	387	382
Jackson	252 582	61.3	58 400	322	344 241	-0.3	18 601	5.4	17 491	-65	323 703	-1.0	55 568	62 366
Jasper	36 134	69.3	38 300	228	48 933	1.1	2 449	5.0	2 764	18	40 467	8.2	12 280	9 403
Jefferson	59 199	81.2	65 300	316	87 510	1.2	6 917	7.9	2 681	65	24 802	3.3	4 369	7 409
Johnson	14 579	58.6	55 300	275	20 651	-1.8	910	4.4	651	24	6 863	6.1	1 606	2 197
Knox	1 819	75.0	20 500	142	1 867	4.6	112	6.0	120	8	636	6.7	66	135

1. Percent of total civilian labor force. 2. For week including March 12. Excludes government employees, self-employed persons, farm workers, domestic service workers, railroad employees subject to the Railroad Retirement Act, and employees on oceanborne vessels or in foreign countries.

STATE County	Private nonfarm establishments, 1988 (cont'd): Employment[1] (cont'd): Finance, insurance, and real estate	Private nonfarm establishments, 1988 (cont'd): Employment[1] (cont'd): Services	Private nonfarm establishments, 1988 (cont'd): Annual payroll: Total (Mil dol)	Private nonfarm establishments, 1988 (cont'd): Annual payroll: Average per employee (Dollars)	Personal income, 1989: Total (Mil dol)	Personal income, 1989: Percent change, 1988–1989	Personal income, 1989: Wages and salaries[2] (Mil dol)	Personal income, 1989: Proprietor's income (Mil dol)	Personal income, 1989: Dividends, interest, & rent (Mil dol)	Personal income, 1989: Transfer payments (Mil dol)	Personal income, 1989: Per capita[3]: Dollars	Personal income, 1989: Per capita[3]: Rank	Earnings, 1989: Total (Mil dol)	Earnings, 1989: Percent by selected industries: Farm	Earnings, 1989: Percent by selected industries: Goods-related[4]: Total
	88	89	90	91	92	93	94	95	96	97	98	99	100	101	102
MISSISSIPPI—Con.															
Tishomingo	107	436	48	13 622	189	6.2	77	22	26	46	10 446	2 800	100	0.9	42.6
Tunica	74	98	12	12 452	82	-3.5	30	13	14	26	9 336	2 976	44	30.7	16.3
Union	185	480	102	15 630	250	5.5	132	22	34	46	11 051	2 652	154	1.7	49.5
Walthall	71	233	14	11 310	116	6.1	42	13	18	35	8 456	3 044	55	5.1	NA
Warren	581	3 364	209	16 256	691	7.2	438	51	92	128	14 060	1 407	489	1.5	24.5
Washington	874	4 707	280	15 130	794	4.9	457	100	104	181	11 472	2 512	557	7.0	23.1
Wayne	125	408	47	14 007	188	5.5	79	31	26	46	9 413	2 971	110	13.7	34.8
Webster	130	253	26	11 347	110	4.2	46	12	16	26	11 102	2 634	58	4.8	47.9
Wilkinson	38	275	19	12 638	87	1.4	31	9	10	28	8 977	3 008	40	4.0	27.9
Winston	247	348	79	16 395	215	8.7	113	20	35	50	11 152	2 621	133	1.7	54.5
Yalobusha	103	216	47	14 412	131	4.6	61	12	18	36	10 211	2 853	72	2.3	49.0
Yazoo	164	827	67	15 619	297	2.5	128	55	45	71	11 538	2 488	183	18.7	27.4
MISSOURI	128 712	544 572	37 724	X	84 864	6.8	54 760	7 998	16 303	12 580	16 447	X	62 757	1.4	28.1
Adair	325	2 591	99	13 686	310	8.9	169	43	58	61	13 460	1 709	212	3.7	NA
Andrew	65	417	16	12 049	201	6.3	32	20	39	28	13 176	1 825	52	8.4	NA
Atchison	100	494	19	12 013	101	3.4	35	18	28	21	13 189	1 818	53	11.6	13.8
Audrain	292	1 142	118	17 627	345	6.4	175	40	88	68	13 738	1 557	215	4.2	36.8
Barry	269	1 056	128	15 155	356	9.6	197	72	69	75	12 585	2 077	268	4.0	43.4
Barton	143	518	44	14 767	159	5.7	65	28	38	28	13 763	1 549	93	9.4	39.0
Bates	161	495	32	13 066	225	4.4	50	42	50	44	14 053	1 412	92	13.8	NA
Benton	148	311	21	12 173	149	9.0	42	19	40	43	11 025	2 660	60	7.2	NA
Bollinger	26	264	12	10 770	110	5.8	22	17	20	25	9 784	2 912	39	16.1	NA
Boone	5 079	10 784	587	15 968	1 781	7.4	1 173	163	299	224	16 851	461	1 336	0.7	14.3
Buchanan	1 986	7 949	590	18 209	1 278	6.8	839	96	259	235	15 041	973	935	0.7	33.5
Butler	398	2 833	124	12 842	455	6.2	223	61	75	125	11 796	2 404	284	4.9	17.6
Caldwell	66	121	12	12 434	111	4.9	24	13	26	22	13 466	1 705	37	7.3	23.3
Callaway	248	1 732	130	18 242	473	6.5	254	44	78	78	14 228	1 319	298	2.2	24.7
Camden	390	2 388	95	13 434	369	8.4	166	54	93	71	14 112	1 385	219	2.3	22.5
Cape Girardeau	1 163	8 079	450	16 328	943	6.8	612	102	187	136	15 073	956	714	1.4	26.5
Carroll	154	522	17	10 324	145	5.2	38	23	47	33	13 176	1 824	61	12.9	16.3
Carter	0	202	8	10 258	50	5.9	19	8	8	17	8 493	3 040	27	4.4	NA
Cass	500	2 334	116	13 198	999	6.4	190	90	150	117	15 827	704	280	3.6	26.1
Cedar	89	443	25	11 733	138	6.5	41	20	39	39	11 134	2 626	60	7.8	25.4
Chariton	76	293	16	11 948	129	6.1	32	26	35	27	13 464	1 707	57	20.7	18.1
Christian	245	691	70	13 981	429	9.2	107	59	62	56	13 391	1 732	166	4.9	37.9
Clark	49	118	8	10 819	89	7.9	19	12	21	18	11 332	2 557	31	17.8	NA
Clay	1 904	12 863	1 160	20 794	2 736	5.6	1 579	183	393	253	17 979	299	1 763	0.3	37.2
Clinton	192	881	28	10 837	245	7.2	50	26	47	38	14 314	1 279	76	6.4	NA
Cole	1 581	7 609	410	17 584	972	7.5	819	84	191	140	15 829	702	903	0.7	15.6
Cooper	193	657	41	12 842	197	6.2	69	29	49	39	13 727	1 566	98	11.0	NA
Crawford	140	603	44	12 346	255	6.7	75	26	41	52	12 567	2 083	100	3.4	40.1
Dade	55	76	10	11 651	95	6.8	21	19	22	22	12 508	2 111	40	24.9	15.6
Dallas	74	959	18	8 343	141	9.0	29	23	27	32	10 371	2 819	52	14.6	NA
Daviess	89	166	10	10 119	93	8.8	22	15	24	20	11 022	2 661	37	22.5	15.5
De Kalb	0	230	13	13 883	105	6.9	29	14	21	21	12 966	1 922	43	11.6	NA
Dent	140	459	40	14 754	171	4.1	62	23	28	42	11 865	2 373	85	6.8	NA
Douglas	45	226	23	11 692	107	6.5	34	18	22	26	8 497	3 039	52	7.4	37.9
Dunklin	299	1 796	88	13 150	365	5.2	149	57	59	107	10 671	2 745	206	9.0	25.5
Franklin	713	3 709	379	16 716	1 248	6.4	514	100	196	166	15 776	717	614	1.3	43.0
Gasconade	106	468	44	12 345	211	6.3	71	28	46	37	15 108	938	99	4.6	37.4
Gentry	0	566	15	10 997	93	9.5	25	17	26	23	13 491	1 687	41	16.6	NA
Greene	4 831	28 522	1 583	16 848	3 224	7.6	2 225	403	626	474	15 658	756	2 628	0.5	23.1
Grundy	151	591	35	14 627	144	7.3	59	26	36	33	13 420	1 724	85	7.2	23.7
Harrison	111	521	18	10 063	115	8.9	34	21	32	27	13 139	1 846	55	16.6	5.6
Henry	191	971	62	13 248	262	6.3	105	33	71	60	13 094	1 867	137	4.8	NA
Hickory	43	175	5	8 684	73	9.2	14	12	19	26	9 665	2 934	26	19.4	18.9
Holt	52	202	13	14 084	78	3.3	23	13	23	17	12 736	2 020	36	13.3	NA
Howard	78	673	25	12 682	127	5.1	38	19	34	28	13 500	1 681	57	10.9	20.6
Howell	262	2 157	109	12 393	357	8.0	177	64	63	86	11 443	2 522	241	3.6	30.8
Iron	102	525	48	21 397	116	6.9	68	11	21	34	10 333	2 830	78	2.8	53.7
Jackson	31 260	107 364	6 930	21 409	11 185	5.4	9 704	1 109	1 985	1 661	17 328	392	10 812	0.1	22.7
Jasper	1 180	8 235	664	16 413	1 268	5.4	879	148	235	250	13 685	1 589	1 027	1.3	32.1
Jefferson	1 023	6 444	400	16 120	2 608	7.0	661	175	249	269	14 818	1 069	836	0.4	33.4
Johnson	362	1 295	86	12 603	498	7.0	292	47	86	86	12 703	2 034	340	2.2	18.2
Knox	61	162	8	12 590	60	12.1	16	14	17	14	12 599	2 071	30	31.2	NA

1. For week including March 12. Excludes government employees, self-employed persons, farm workers, domestic service workers, railroad employees subject to the Railroad Retirement Act, and employees on oceanborne vessels or in foreign countries. 2. Includes other labor income. 3. Based on the resident population estimated as of July 1 of the year shown. 4. Covers mining, construction, and manufacturing.

STATE County	Earnings, 1989 (cont'd)						Agriculture, 1987									
	Percent by selected industries (cont'd)						Farms			Farm operators, percent		Land in farms				
	Goods-related[1]	Service-related & other[2]						Percent with						Acres		
	Manu-facturing	Total	Retail trade	Finance, insur-ance, & real estate	Services	Govern-ment	Number	Less than 50 acres	500 acres and over	Whose principal occu-pation is farming	Residing on farm operated	Acreage (1,000)	Percent change, 1982–1987	Average size of farm	Total irrigated (1,000)	Total cropland (1,000)
	103	104	105	106	107	108	109	110	111	112	113	114	115	116	117	118
MISSISSIPPI—Con.																
Tishomingo	36.9	44.0	9.9	3.9	15.4	12.4	298	23.5	4.0	36.9	70.5	43	-9.4	145	0	23
Tunica	13.5	37.1	8.4	2.7	12.5	15.8	162	5.6	65.4	86.4	56.2	245	7.2	1 514	40	221
Union	46.8	37.2	9.3	2.7	14.6	11.6	579	28.0	6.7	37.0	74.4	100	-17.8	173	0	64
Walthall	22.2	NA	11.8	4.2	17.8	20.8	611	20.9	6.5	43.4	74.3	111	-24.1	181	0	66
Warren	21.4	42.5	10.2	2.6	20.2	31.5	222	19.4	23.9	50.9	63.5	107	-19.1	482	D	61
Washington	20.3	53.9	10.8	3.3	19.8	16.0	394	13.7	55.6	75.4	50.5	356	-3.9	903	67	319
Wayne	18.3	36.9	12.4	3.0	9.8	14.6	470	28.5	6.0	39.4	69.8	80	-3.0	170	D	30
Webster	43.6	31.7	7.3	3.5	12.1	15.6	300	16.3	12.7	43.3	72.3	79	-9.9	263	0	43
Wilkinson	23.9	46.2	10.7	4.1	16.6	21.8	216	19.4	24.5	36.6	52.3	103	-32.2	475	D	35
Winston	49.6	30.3	8.2	3.4	9.2	13.5	548	21.7	7.1	33.6	73.5	100	-18.1	183	D	50
Yalobusha	44.3	31.4	9.4	3.4	10.3	17.4	299	15.7	16.1	39.1	60.9	91	-14.4	306	D	45
Yazoo	22.3	38.5	7.5	3.0	16.0	15.3	569	12.1	37.6	59.9	57.1	367	-1.3	646	10	244
MISSOURI	21.7	56.9	9.5	6.3	24.3	13.6	106 105	20.7	15.3	50.6	73.1	29 209	-0.2	275	535	19 378
Adair	14.3	NA	13.4	3.1	30.6	20.3	879	16.6	18.8	56.2	71.1	285	5.0	325	0	192
Andrew	1.8	NA	12.5	3.3	20.8	19.6	916	21.2	14.1	56.7	71.9	231	-3.1	252	1	184
Atchison	9.2	60.2	9.8	4.3	23.1	14.5	622	12.5	42.9	80.5	63.8	322	4.9	517	3	281
Audrain	32.7	42.3	9.9	3.5	14.5	16.7	1 119	17.5	25.6	60.1	73.6	399	-3.9	357	20	331
Barry	38.8	43.6	10.0	2.3	14.9	8.9	1 667	26.2	6.6	47.6	77.5	288	1.0	173	1	162
Barton	33.8	39.4	7.7	5.0	16.5	12.2	946	16.0	23.5	59.6	73.7	331	-0.2	350	10	246
Bates	4.9	NA	10.4	3.4	21.8	16.4	1 294	17.0	18.9	50.9	73.6	429	-5.0	332	2	298
Benton	10.6	NA	16.3	5.4	16.3	20.6	885	15.3	15.7	56.8	78.1	263	-3.7	297	1	136
Bollinger	11.2	45.5	9.9	2.3	18.1	18.4	860	14.5	9.8	44.0	71.7	194	-8.2	225	4	107
Boone	8.5	51.1	9.4	8.0	25.2	33.9	1 344	26.1	9.2	38.7	73.8	280	-4.5	208	4	182
Buchanan	27.2	52.6	9.5	5.3	20.8	13.2	848	28.4	12.6	53.1	71.5	189	-4.6	223	D	149
Butler	10.8	56.2	13.0	3.2	25.0	21.3	844	23.9	21.8	54.0	69.8	261	-3.7	309	74	224
Caldwell	10.4	47.2	8.1	5.6	15.6	22.1	857	15.2	15.6	54.8	70.1	233	-5.6	272	0	177
Callaway	19.2	49.5	8.2	1.9	14.1	23.7	1 323	21.4	11.3	37.6	72.9	324	-0.2	245	3	202
Camden	9.9	66.1	18.2	5.8	33.3	9.1	584	14.2	15.8	40.2	74.1	179	11.2	306	0	60
Cape Girardeau	19.0	60.0	12.0	3.7	29.3	12.1	1 365	22.7	7.8	49.2	72.4	267	-1.2	195	4	197
Carroll	9.3	52.9	8.9	4.6	19.5	17.9	1 013	14.7	27.2	66.0	67.4	404	-2.3	399	2	335
Carter	15.7	48.0	11.8	2.4	17.0	28.5	190	14.2	19.5	38.9	73.2	59	9.6	312	D	21
Cass	6.1	53.3	15.5	4.3	23.3	17.0	1 649	37.1	9.0	38.2	77.4	331	0.9	201	5	231
Cedar	18.9	49.3	12.3	3.8	18.7	17.6	910	21.2	9.3	46.8	75.4	196	4.2	215	D	109
Chariton	11.8	46.9	7.1	4.1	18.7	14.2	1 145	15.5	22.9	63.5	69.8	402	-4.4	351	1	328
Christian	25.8	45.2	12.7	4.5	18.6	12.1	1 388	30.0	5.2	36.7	80.7	230	3.7	166	1	128
Clark	4.7	47.0	9.4	4.2	14.7	27.0	702	12.4	26.2	62.3	65.7	259	-1.1	369	1	194
Clay	31.6	51.5	11.0	3.4	18.8	11.0	732	39.1	9.4	38.3	69.8	140	-6.2	191	1	98
Clinton	3.1	NA	11.2	11.6	31.0	17.5	807	25.2	14.1	46.2	74.6	211	-5.6	261	0	161
Cole	7.2	43.8	8.3	4.8	19.3	40.0	1 069	19.7	3.6	38.5	71.9	181	1.8	169	1	99
Cooper	16.8	NA	10.7	3.5	19.3	19.8	929	15.9	22.2	62.4	70.2	310	-1.9	334	0	226
Crawford	31.3	44.0	12.4	3.0	15.6	12.6	713	19.6	14.0	36.2	71.0	200	2.8	281	0	75
Dade	10.1	40.5	5.6	2.7	9.9	19.0	915	16.8	15.5	52.6	74.5	264	10.1	289	4	156
Dallas	11.6	53.1	13.0	4.2	18.1	14.5	1 102	22.5	7.7	50.2	82.0	226	0.3	205	0	115
Daviess	11.8	38.8	13.1	4.1	10.7	23.2	901	15.5	17.4	58.3	67.9	282	-5.7	313	D	208
De Kalb	0.9	45.0	10.6	2.7	14.3	35.3	772	17.1	16.3	55.4	69.9	224	-3.5	290	D	169
Dent	10.7	NA	11.6	3.4	16.3	17.2	731	11.8	18.3	41.3	75.6	221	5.4	303	D	91
Douglas	29.0	40.6	10.4	2.2	15.8	14.1	1 218	14.3	10.6	50.9	80.7	295	-0.9	243	0	124
Dunklin	20.6	51.0	11.9	4.1	20.7	14.5	684	19.0	37.6	74.7	55.0	305	5.8	446	22	294
Franklin	33.4	45.6	12.1	3.3	17.9	10.1	1 731	26.3	7.1	36.1	73.8	311	-0.5	179	1	182
Gasconade	30.5	44.2	10.7	2.3	21.5	13.7	846	12.3	10.0	41.0	68.1	209	-0.4	247	0	98
Gentry	5.7	54.6	11.3	5.4	22.6	17.5	691	14.9	23.3	64.1	60.2	245	-10.1	355	D	196
Greene	17.4	64.5	11.7	4.7	29.7	11.9	2 232	40.2	4.5	34.4	79.7	290	-3.7	130	0	187
Grundy	19.5	52.9	9.7	8.5	22.5	16.2	650	17.7	20.5	59.7	72.3	224	-8.8	344	0	176
Harrison	2.4	60.9	19.2	3.4	19.2	17.0	924	13.7	27.2	62.3	68.5	382	-1.4	413	D	266
Henry	16.6	NA	12.8	3.4	NA	16.5	1 005	18.7	18.1	54.3	73.2	311	0.2	309	1	224
Hickory	4.7	39.0	8.1	2.9	18.4	22.7	587	12.3	13.5	55.9	76.7	174	12.3	296	0	78
Holt	8.0	53.8	12.3	5.6	19.7	15.2	633	13.0	27.2	72.8	60.7	260	-0.1	410	5	228
Howard	14.9	51.7	8.6	2.6	22.7	16.9	738	12.5	21.1	52.6	70.3	244	0.5	331	1	172
Howell	24.1	52.8	13.0	3.1	24.6	12.8	1 751	25.2	8.0	41.8	77.7	380	6.4	217	0	159
Iron	14.1	NA	7.2	2.2	16.0	11.6	286	14.7	12.9	37.8	73.4	67	4.6	234	D	28
Jackson	17.2	63.2	9.0	9.2	27.9	14.0	905	44.0	7.6	36.2	69.6	146	-19.0	161	1	100
Jasper	26.8	56.2	11.1	3.2	22.0	10.4	1 418	30.7	9.1	42.8	77.4	276	0.9	194	5	191
Jefferson	19.8	51.1	12.0	3.0	23.0	15.1	724	27.6	8.0	34.5	77.3	130	-4.1	179	0	69
Johnson	12.2	31.2	7.2	2.3	12.3	48.4	1 735	21.5	11.3	47.4	77.1	396	-4.1	228	0	272
Knox	NA	NA	6.1	4.4	11.5	18.8	651	10.1	30.7	74.0	67.4	292	5.6	449	0	222

1. Covers mining, construction, and manufacturing.
2. Covers private sector earnings in agricultural services, forestry, and fisheries; transportation and public utilities; wholesale trade; retail trade; finance, insurance, and real estate; and services.

STATE County	Agriculture, 1987 (cont'd): Value of land and buildings: Average per farm ($1,000)	Value of land and buildings: Average per acre (Dollars)	Value of products sold: Total (Mil dol)	Value of products sold: Average per farm (Dollars)	Value of products sold: Percent from Crops	Value of products sold: Percent from Livestock and poultry[1]	Percent of farms with sales of $10,000 or more	Percent of farms with sales of $100,000 or more	Manufactures, 1987: Establishments: Total	Establishments: Percent with 20 or more employees	All employees: Number (1,000)	All employees: Percent change, 1982–1987	All employees: Annual payroll (Mil dol)	Production workers: Number (1,000)	Production workers: Work hours (Mil)
	119	120	121	122	123	124	125	126	127	128	129	130	131	132	133
MISSISSIPPI—Con.															
Tishomingo	91	593	3	8 972	40.1	59.8	14.8	1.7	42	33.3	2.0	-20.0	21.8	1.7	2.9
Tunica	1 049	703	47	287 441	91.8	8.2	79.6	58.0	5	20.0	D	D	D	D	D
Union	98	688	10	17 446	58.8	41.2	25.0	3.5	40	50.0	4.5	-4.3	69.1	3.4	7.1
Walthall	147	855	16	26 528	9.1	90.9	28.6	9.7	11	18.2	0.5	0.0	4.6	0.4	0.7
Warren	462	986	13	57 089	87.7	12.3	43.2	15.3	51	51.0	3.4	-19.0	71.8	2.6	5.1
Washington	778	911	93	235 566	74.7	25.3	77.9	53.6	79	44.3	4.9	-2.0	87.8	3.8	7.7
Wayne	111	674	21	44 172	3.0	97.0	31.5	14.7	24	37.5	1.2	9.1	16.0	1.0	2.0
Webster	126	504	9	28 477	77.8	22.2	32.3	8.0	19	36.8	1.2	9.1	15.7	1.1	2.2
Wilkinson	299	640	4	19 618	15.3	84.7	24.5	3.7	20	20.0	0.7	0.0	7.7	0.5	0.9
Winston	91	560	7	13 071	18.1	81.9	19.3	2.9	42	35.7	2.6	36.8	43.1	2.1	4.0
Yalobusha	142	463	8	26 513	76.4	23.6	25.1	7.4	19	36.8	1.7	-29.2	25.5	1.5	2.7
Yazoo	391	604	61	107 333	80.7	19.3	55.7	27.6	21	38.1	1.5	0.0	30.5	1.1	2.4
MISSOURI	176	640	3 645	34 353	40.1	59.9	46.9	8.4	7 290	35.4	418.8	3.2	10 390.0	264.5	519.0
Adair	141	418	21	23 852	34.3	65.7	52.2	3.9	20	30.0	1.4	-22.2	23.7	1.2	2.2
Andrew	165	664	35	38 506	53.8	46.2	57.9	10.4	3	0.0	D	D	D	D	D
Atchison	353	680	49	79 085	76.1	23.9	81.7	28.6	6	16.7	D	D	D	D	D
Audrain	256	686	67	59 827	53.3	46.7	67.1	15.7	36	50.0	2.4	-7.7	52.9	1.8	3.3
Barry	119	752	62	37 122	4.6	95.4	42.2	8.5	66	37.9	4.3	48.3	70.7	3.6	7.9
Barton	173	486	36	37 581	54.0	46.0	61.3	7.8	10	30.0	D	D	D	D	D
Bates	158	485	45	34 858	37.9	62.1	50.9	7.7	17	23.5	0.3	50.0	3.6	0.2	0.4
Benton	147	457	23	26 242	22.5	77.5	47.0	6.6	19	15.8	0.3	0.0	3.9	0.2	0.4
Bollinger	129	596	13	15 571	31.6	68.4	33.5	2.9	19	21.1	0.3	-40.0	2.7	0.3	0.4
Boone	159	794	29	21 414	41.5	58.5	34.5	4.9	87	28.7	4.0	21.2	81.7	2.4	5.0
Buchanan	169	792	26	30 845	65.9	34.1	48.6	8.6	102	42.2	8.1	-5.8	181.5	6.0	11.5
Butler	244	758	32	38 152	89.9	10.1	49.2	12.0	42	31.0	1.9	26.7	27.0	1.5	3.1
Caldwell	145	540	24	27 721	49.9	50.1	50.4	5.5	6	16.7	0.3	0.0	3.4	0.3	0.5
Callaway	155	624	31	23 760	42.4	57.6	37.1	4.5	27	37.0	1.0	0.0	18.0	0.8	1.5
Camden	141	474	12	20 016	2.1	97.9	32.4	3.6	32	25.0	0.9	50.0	14.1	0.6	1.2
Cape Girardeau	161	823	36	26 361	35.5	64.5	43.6	5.8	95	36.8	5.0	13.6	104.5	4.0	7.5
Carroll	251	648	53	51 961	64.3	35.7	66.1	15.8	13	30.8	0.4	0.0	3.9	0.3	0.6
Carter	164	463	3	14 099	3.4	96.6	22.1	1.6	20	10.0	0.3	0.0	2.8	0.2	0.4
Cass	181	903	45	27 458	54.5	45.5	37.4	5.2	61	23.0	1.2	50.0	18.5	0.9	1.7
Cedar	112	478	14	15 469	12.6	87.4	36.3	2.4	22	31.8	0.7	0.0	10.3	0.6	1.2
Chariton	200	585	67	58 569	48.1	51.9	64.1	15.4	13	30.8	0.4	0.0	4.5	0.3	0.7
Christian	150	882	28	19 980	5.4	94.6	34.2	4.3	54	31.5	1.9	18.7	28.1	1.5	2.9
Clark	190	554	25	35 454	61.5	38.5	60.8	8.8	9	11.1	0.1	0.0	0.7	0.1	0.1
Clay	195	1 050	23	31 202	27.4	72.6	33.3	6.4	239	46.0	16.1	6.6	471.2	9.6	19.9
Clinton	190	725	32	40 105	37.5	62.5	52.0	10.4	11	9.1	0.1	0.0	1.3	0.1	0.1
Cole	116	691	16	14 711	16.8	83.2	31.1	2.4	50	34.0	3.2	-3.0	69.0	2.2	4.0
Cooper	173	525	46	49 039	33.9	66.1	59.1	12.1	17	52.9	0.8	-20.0	13.2	0.6	1.2
Crawford	146	560	9	12 962	5.8	94.2	28.2	1.7	47	27.7	1.6	23.1	20.7	1.3	2.6
Dade	146	486	25	27 166	28.9	71.1	48.5	5.7	10	30.0	0.3	0.0	3.0	0.3	0.5
Dallas	126	625	27	24 661	2.9	97.1	40.3	6.7	10	20.0	D	D	D	D	D
Daviess	146	522	31	34 396	58.3	41.7	58.6	8.1	7	42.9	0.3	50.0	3.1	0.2	0.4
De Kalb	157	512	27	34 486	40.6	59.4	54.0	7.8	3	0.0	0.0	0.0	0.1	0.0	0.0
Dent	136	450	10	13 970	6.0	94.0	33.9	1.6	27	22.2	0.7	-41.7	7.9	0.6	1.0
Douglas	126	537	28	22 831	3.2	96.8	39.8	5.6	16	18.8	D	D	D	D	D
Dunklin	436	960	65	94 769	98.0	2.0	77.5	33.0	32	28.1	1.8	-10.0	30.9	1.5	3.0
Franklin	170	958	35	20 370	20.5	79.5	28.9	5.0	162	43.2	8.5	25.0	162.3	6.6	13.0
Gasconade	160	637	13	15 908	17.3	82.7	31.1	3.5	34	47.1	1.9	26.7	24.8	1.6	3.2
Gentry	174	522	29	42 190	47.2	52.8	64.8	11.0	9	11.1	0.1	-75.0	1.4	0.1	0.2
Greene	161	1 298	39	17 358	10.0	90.0	30.3	3.8	324	33.6	19.2	13.6	384.6	13.3	24.8
Grundy	178	528	28	42 956	59.1	40.9	57.2	11.1	11	27.3	D	D	D	D	D
Harrison	171	435	37	40 464	48.5	51.5	61.3	8.3	5	20.0	0.1	0.0	1.0	0.1	0.2
Henry	180	553	32	31 998	37.6	62.4	50.7	7.5	20	40.0	0.9	-30.8	10.6	0.8	1.5
Hickory	142	504	12	21 060	7.5	92.5	37.8	4.3	5	40.0	0.1	0.0	1.1	0.1	0.2
Holt	283	716	39	61 503	73.0	27.0	76.9	18.2	5	20.0	D	D	D	D	D
Howard	184	558	26	35 483	49.3	50.7	53.8	9.5	14	35.7	D	D	D	D	D
Howell	111	528	39	22 022	3.6	96.4	35.6	4.2	49	38.8	2.9	3.6	35.9	2.4	4.1
Iron	112	453	4	13 765	2.5	97.5	23.4	2.4	18	16.7	D	D	D	D	D
Jackson	236	1 396	21	23 156	62.1	37.9	30.4	5.3	977	32.8	54.7	-12.3	1 568.1	29.5	58.9
Jasper	136	684	42	29 893	36.8	63.2	36.3	5.1	198	37.9	11.2	12.0	211.7	8.5	16.4
Jefferson	175	1 022	9	12 018	34.5	65.5	20.2	2.3	158	21.5	4.5	2.3	100.3	3.4	6.9
Johnson	169	736	47	27 093	29.0	71.0	42.1	4.8	31	32.3	1.5	50.0	24.0	1.2	2.2
Knox	217	483	32	49 617	52.6	47.4	70.5	14.1	6	33.3	0.1	0.0	0.7	0.1	0.1

1. Includes livestock and poultry products.

STATE County	Manufactures, 1987 (cont'd): Production workers (cont'd): Wages: Total (Mil dol)	Manufactures, 1987 (cont'd): Production workers (cont'd): Wages: Average per worker (Dollars)	Manufactures, 1987 (cont'd): Value added by manufacture (Mil dol)	Manufactures, 1987 (cont'd): Value of shipments (Mil dol)	Manufactures, 1987 (cont'd): New capital expenditures (Mil dol)	Value of construction authorized by building permits, 1990: Total[1] ($1,000)	Nonresidential: Total ($1,000)	Nonresidential: Percent: Office	Nonresidential: Percent: Industrial	Nonresidential: Percent: Stores	Residential: New construction ($1,000)	Residential: Number of housing units	Residential: Alterations and additions ($1,000)
	134	135	136	137	138	139	140	141	142	143	144	145	146
MISSISSIPPI—Con.													
Tishomingo	16.6	9 765	47.5	128.7	1.0	6 440	4 562	57.5	32.9	6.4	994	20	70
Tunica	D	D	D	D	D	546	196	0.0	0.0	0.0	279	7	40
Union	45.7	13 441	156.5	320.8	3.0	9 769	1 432	0.0	49.3	25.9	874	16	390
Walthall	3.4	8 500	6.3	15.9	D	1 042	135	0.0	0.0	63.0	879	28	0
Warren	50.9	19 577	235.9	605.9	16.4	12 274	5 569	22.9	4.0	46.1	678	12	1 421
Washington	59.9	15 763	331.8	609.5	30.6	11 505	2 022	16.0	49.0	8.2	4 777	97	1 409
Wayne	12.4	12 400	74.0	162.6	2.0	2 419	1 749	0.0	1.4	91.5	375	11	16
Webster	13.6	12 364	38.8	73.3	0.5	2 715	1 478	0.0	85.6	14.4	1 225	35	0
Wilkinson	5.9	11 800	19.7	36.3	D	NA	NA	NA	NA	NA	NA	NA	NA
Winston	31.4	14 952	127.2	306.3	6.6	749	156	0.0	0.0	100.0	531	16	24
Yalobusha	19.8	13 200	58.2	134.4	D	611	0	NA	NA	NA	426	14	185
Yazoo	18.0	16 364	67.1	138.1	1.7	1 377	365	39.7	9.6	32.9	810	27	35
MISSOURI	5 401.6	20 422	25 916.7	59 889.3	1 620.1	2 930 996	813 779	27.4	12.2	27.5	1 090 290	15 294	147 017
Adair	18.2	15 167	93.5	162.5	4.3	9 890	2 080	15.5	0.0	80.8	628	14	111
Andrew	D	D	D	D	D	1 431	360	51.1	0.0	0.0	906	19	80
Atchison	D	D	D	D	D	889	201	91.5	0.0	0.0	527	35	16
Audrain	34.9	19 389	111.5	287.8	3.3	13 161	7 156	1.9	85.1	7.0	1 766	24	1 162
Barry	52.1	14 472	234.3	656.9	8.6	5 646	3 363	21.9	9.5	32.7	1 757	39	326
Barton	D	D	D	D	D	1 778	366	0.0	15.0	79.8	733	13	111
Bates	2.6	13 000	10.6	29.7	0.2	8 163	7 577	0.0	35.6	63.8	467	11	29
Benton	3.1	15 500	6.6	14.3	0.2	1 278	59	0.0	0.0	0.0	1 055	21	109
Bollinger	2.1	7 000	3.5	7.9	0.1	1 169	686	33.5	62.0	0.0	399	16	50
Boone	44.6	18 583	244.7	439.7	14.4	125 396	49 544	68.6	0.2	20.0	57 232	787	4 267
Buchanan	123.5	20 583	645.1	1 632.1	35.2	30 281	6 352	12.0	41.2	15.1	15 177	206	2 309
Butler	20.0	13 333	64.7	115.2	D	7 636	3 184	3.5	0.0	64.6	1 630	42	2 132
Caldwell	3.0	10 000	5.6	12.0	0.0	87	0	NA	NA	NA	0	0	5
Callaway	12.1	15 125	38.1	77.8	1.0	4 379	2 782	0.0	0.0	90.1	1 163	18	320
Camden	9.3	15 500	42.0	78.3	1.1	1 151	553	0.0	9.5	67.1	286	12	30
Cape Girardeau	78.7	19 675	544.4	987.0	D	32 843	15 276	17.8	46.6	11.9	11 272	233	440
Carroll	2.9	9 667	13.4	30.3	0.2	NA	NA	NA	NA	NA	NA	NA	NA
Carter	2.5	12 500	7.5	14.1	0.4	147	12	0.0	0.0	0.0	126	2	8
Cass	12.7	14 111	47.5	99.6	D	51 774	7 809	0.1	33.0	12.6	39 482	590	1 060
Cedar	7.8	13 000	24.9	67.1	1.2	2 301	1 594	11.5	39.7	26.8	585	32	27
Chariton	3.9	13 000	16.3	24.2	0.2	NA	NA	NA	NA	NA	NA	NA	NA
Christian	20.7	13 800	62.9	113.1	3.8	5 739	1 899	36.7	1.1	0.0	1 460	44	174
Clark	0.6	6 000	0.5	5.5	0.1	172	140	100.0	0.0	0.0	0	0	32
Clay	269.7	28 094	1 685.2	5 268.7	75.2	73 091	9 835	38.5	14.5	14.1	36 320	561	1 724
Clinton	0.8	8 000	3.9	8.7	0.3	6 077	1 289	0.0	0.0	16.6	4 357	86	248
Cole	42.8	19 455	283.3	489.6	10.8	27 341	9 855	77.4	4.5	11.2	11 953	141	1 010
Cooper	8.2	13 667	34.2	72.9	D	1 449	0	NA	NA	NA	1 186	25	103
Crawford	14.4	11 077	69.9	107.0	2.7	4 488	3 060	0.0	75.2	24.8	750	17	172
Dade	2.7	9 000	9.5	19.4	0.2	125	64	46.9	0.0	21.9	0	0	11
Dallas	D	D	D	D	D	NA	NA	NA	NA	NA	NA	NA	NA
Daviess	2.4	12 000	3.9	10.8	D	NA	NA	NA	NA	NA	NA	NA	NA
De Kalb	0.1	NA	0.2	0.5	0.0	402	0	NA	NA	NA	391	21	11
Dent	5.0	8 333	12.3	46.1	0.3	1 896	1 187	0.0	84.3	15.0	435	7	112
Douglas	D	D	D	D	D	385	0	NA	NA	NA	300	10	65
Dunklin	23.7	15 800	88.7	188.6	5.1	3 636	100	0.0	0.0	23.1	1 288	24	366
Franklin	113.1	17 136	392.6	826.7	D	48 140	11 100	23.3	41.5	8.8	28 930	502	2 711
Gasconade	19.1	11 938	59.2	110.8	4.0	2 705	2 254	3.7	14.9	74.5	420	6	12
Gentry	1.1	11 000	4.8	18.4	0.2	531	400	0.0	0.0	100.0	30	1	15
Greene	237.6	17 865	890.5	2 838.8	51.1	161 224	51 175	21.2	3.9	43.2	62 049	1 345	3 796
Grundy	D	D	D	D	D	1 087	193	0.0	0.0	0.0	457	11	153
Harrison	0.8	8 000	1.9	3.4	0.0	438	0	NA	NA	NA	190	4	24
Henry	8.5	10 625	37.8	77.2	1.4	6 555	3 415	3.5	0.0	83.8	1 410	21	1 518
Hickory	0.8	8 000	3.1	5.7	0.1	NA	NA	NA	NA	NA	NA	NA	NA
Holt	D	D	D	D	D	137	11	0.0	0.0	0.0	50	1	16
Howard	D	D	D	D	D	3 095	945	0.0	12.7	0.0	211	5	15
Howell	27.1	11 292	115.5	255.8	6.3	5 634	986	6.1	0.0	92.9	3 081	72	320
Iron	D	D	D	D	D	148	30	0.0	0.0	0.0	100	2	8
Jackson	693.6	23 512	4 019.2	7 164.2	184.0	656 378	191 750	21.9	2.0	33.9	204 371	2 518	32 839
Jasper	144.5	17 000	561.7	1 362.7	25.4	45 983	7 907	6.4	0.4	35.0	14 995	261	1 945
Jefferson	70.3	20 676	263.9	559.8	13.9	67 290	20 091	31.2	1.0	38.2	38 481	877	1 647
Johnson	17.9	14 917	46.6	90.9	6.2	10 179	2 361	10.6	22.0	25.6	6 113	101	512
Knox	0.5	5 000	2.6	4.6	0.0	80	80	0.0	0.0	100.0	0	0	0

1. Includes nonresidential additions and alterations, residential nonhousekeeping buildings, and residential garages and carports not shown separately.

STATE County	Wholesale trade, 1987				Retail trade, all establishments, 1987				Retail trade, establishments with payroll, 1987					
						Sales				Sales				
											Per capita[2] (Dollars)			
	Establishments	Sales (Mil dol)	Paid employees[1]	Annual payroll (Mil dol)	Number	Total (Mil dol)	Percent change, 1982–1987	Per capita[2] (Dollars)	Number	Total (Mil dol)	General merchandise stores	Food stores	Apparel & accessory stores	Eating and drinking places
	147	148	149	150	151	152	153	154	155	156	157	158	159	160
MISSISSIPPI—Con.														
Tishomingo	22	33.5	121	1.1	234	59.7	18.7	3 278	101	50.2	D	1 045	55	136
Tunica	19	40.6	132	2.2	85	25.4	13.9	2 823	46	23.4	D	729	73	158
Union	30	46.6	221	3.1	217	83.8	50.4	3 706	115	74.5	543	906	175	228
Walthall	10	11.4	76	1.0	107	44.7	41.9	3 261	59	42.0	438	642	72	81
Warren	68	299.5	1 242	26.2	538	304.7	38.1	6 070	351	297.2	1 002	1 452	281	444
Washington	121	322.4	1 246	24.7	724	362.5	27.7	5 170	445	345.3	782	1 122	294	317
Wayne	25	105.4	252	4.0	201	68.8	19.2	3 404	122	65.3	582	828	203	172
Webster	8	8.1	48	0.6	125	29.9	26.2	2 930	68	27.2	355	874	56	126
Wilkinson	20	28.2	112	1.4	104	25.3	18.2	2 530	48	23.3	221	903	D	149
Winston	21	25.3	95	1.5	195	67.3	42.3	3 470	116	61.6	D	704	126	139
Yalobusha	12	57.4	54	1.3	146	44.6	0.2	3 427	75	39.1	256	1 380	65	78
Yazoo	42	80.6	304	5.9	254	80.9	7.2	3 077	136	76.0	439	627	163	114
MISSOURI	10 696	53 546.4	125 247	2 820.9	52 540	31 142.2	43.8	6 097	32 524	30 175.6	816	1 140	248	595
Adair	42	87.1	294	3.9	275	161.9	35.9	6 860	186	157.5	950	1 461	322	697
Andrew	20	52.4	135	1.3	102	37.8	15.2	2 519	40	33.7	D	531	D	152
Atchison	31	49.4	164	2.8	95	26.3	-8.7	3 367	57	22.8	D	838	59	327
Audrain	64	259.3	521	9.8	279	120.3	25.3	4 716	181	115.3	D	1 080	232	364
Barry	48	113.8	356	6.3	364	109.0	22.2	3 963	186	99.7	645	1 085	117	249
Barton	24	41.8	172	2.3	133	40.0	30.3	3 477	68	36.5	D	723	45	260
Bates	27	42.1	214	2.7	205	57.0	29.8	3 628	109	52.0	D	1 009	46	246
Benton	22	36.6	151	1.4	225	51.2	46.7	3 912	93	44.6	D	496	D	253
Bollinger	16	21.6	102	1.0	95	27.8	57.1	2 531	42	25.6	D	531	D	69
Boone	143	392.8	1 615	28.7	1 055	742.6	65.3	7 026	737	730.9	993	1 163	338	671
Buchanan	163	576.3	1 961	35.2	847	549.6	26.0	6 399	545	537.1	1 215	1 262	147	613
Butler	85	156.0	718	10.0	575	248.5	29.3	6 405	323	233.2	D	1 336	293	392
Caldwell	13	51.9	75	0.9	98	16.1	-14.4	1 962	38	13.3	0	771	0	126
Callaway	49	79.8	346	5.8	280	138.2	44.3	4 214	164	133.7	D	1 006	79	376
Camden	38	32.2	181	2.7	491	205.5	90.3	8 154	304	193.8	D	1 624	250	848
Cape Girardeau	190	514.7	2 275	39.8	746	519.4	59.8	8 445	538	511.4	1 568	1 301	405	703
Carroll	34	84.2	200	2.8	152	34.6	7.5	3 060	76	30.7	231	822	102	154
Carter	9	5.6	45	0.5	74	12.8	26.7	2 211	33	10.2	D	666	D	86
Cass	60	75.2	341	5.6	518	264.0	58.3	4 423	262	255.2	D	998	10	330
Cedar	17	16.8	71	0.7	184	46.6	-0.2	3 760	79	38.0	D	1 068	D	154
Chariton	29	94.8	204	3.3	106	23.1	-17.2	2 352	59	20.8	D	738	62	154
Christian	44	73.6	283	3.2	282	116.2	74.0	4 022	132	110.4	D	1 001	19	220
Clark	25	55.2	177	2.7	81	26.6	19.3	3 285	41	25.0	D	D	0	105
Clay	340	3 159.2	5 280	130.6	1 460	1 164.5	44.4	7 858	967	1 142.4	D	1 300	289	665
Clinton	21	31.7	153	1.9	191	65.1	46.6	3 896	89	62.5	D	855	24	363
Cole	113	262.1	1 310	27.4	645	605.4	77.4	9 875	435	594.2	1 227	1 232	304	622
Cooper	39	56.2	203	2.7	180	64.8	31.2	4 441	97	59.9	D	1 018	53	392
Crawford	19	29.5	124	1.6	209	83.8	28.7	4 274	114	79.0	D	729	31	180
Dade	12	39.5	112	2.3	85	15.8	17.0	2 129	36	13.9	0	583	D	141
Dallas	16	25.3	132	1.5	159	44.5	24.3	3 397	60	39.1	D	877	D	137
Daviess	14	32.2	95	1.4	133	26.2	81.9	3 113	55	22.0	D	511	D	124
De Kalb	14	24.6	94	1.5	88	19.8	34.7	2 479	45	18.1	D	566	0	D
Dent	16	D	D	D	150	54.5	16.7	3 810	75	51.1	D	927	25	235
Douglas	16	17.7	123	1.2	107	45.2	89.9	3 673	56	42.9	795	645	24	132
Dunklin	75	96.3	416	6.1	441	158.4	17.2	4 592	246	143.7	641	1 010	109	271
Franklin	96	166.0	749	13.2	839	425.8	43.5	5 445	504	414.8	500	1 187	139	392
Gasconade	26	26.3	141	1.8	207	62.4	36.8	4 491	128	59.5	D	933	77	301
Gentry	24	46.2	112	1.7	108	27.9	18.2	3 876	62	26.0	D	1 224	44	148
Greene	560	3 199.7	7 367	150.2	2 381	1 643.1	61.2	8 134	1 516	1 605.7	D	1 266	306	764
Grundy	25	71.3	139	2.0	148	46.8	10.4	4 257	83	44.1	499	1 307	212	295
Harrison	24	91.6	163	2.4	135	72.3	49.1	7 942	73	68.8	1 067	855	116	230
Henry	43	148.7	499	8.8	294	106.8	43.4	5 366	182	102.4	621	1 261	229	463
Hickory	6	3.5	13	0.1	90	12.5	56.2	1 715	34	8.7	0	D	0	311
Holt	11	44.4	85	1.2	88	23.9	7.2	3 742	42	22.2	D	615	0	97
Howard	20	31.9	113	1.8	101	22.8	8.6	2 375	63	21.6	D	502	50	236
Howell	62	148.8	491	6.9	432	167.5	35.2	5 474	239	157.2	D	1 541	104	306
Iron	10	4.1	29	0.3	118	39.0	25.0	3 512	69	36.0	113	1 088	D	101
Jackson	1 449	8 921.2	21 063	510.1	5 979	4 723.9	37.9	7 352	4 170	4 625.8	1 029	1 223	379	830
Jasper	240	682.9	2 503	44.1	1 174	717.6	47.1	7 834	722	694.7	D	1 445	374	695
Jefferson	147	200.6	907	17.2	1 159	695.4	62.1	4 139	636	674.0	581	1 095	52	297
Johnson	38	88.0	389	5.7	337	149.9	43.6	3 894	187	144.3	D	827	71	480
Knox	16	25.5	108	1.8	48	10.0	-11.5	2 039	30	9.3	245	D	D	94

1. For pay period including March 12. 2. Based on the estimated population as of July 1 of the year shown.

STATE County	Retail trade, establishments with payroll, 1987 (cont'd)		Taxable service industries–establishments with payroll, 1987							Bank deposits,[2] June 1989		Savings capital,[3] September 1989	
				Receipts (Mil dol)									
					Selected kinds of business								
	Paid employees[1]	Annual payroll (Mil dol)	Number	Total	Hotels, motels and other lodging places	Health services	Legal services	Paid employees	Annual payroll (Mil dol)	Total (Mil dol)	Percent change, 1988–1989	Total (Mil dol)	Percent change, 1988–1989
	161	162	163	164	165	166	167	168	169	170	171	172	173
MISSISSIPPI—Con.													
Tishomingo	618	4.9	50	8.6	0.2	4.5	0.2	235	2.5	156	12.7	9.1	-32.8
Tunica	213	2.0	17	1.9	D	0.6	0.4	49	0.5	55	2.4	0.0	NA
Union	883	6.9	77	13.3	D	6.6	1.3	341	4.9	188	6.4	57.2	-13.9
Walthall	360	3.7	37	6.6	0.0	3.8	0.3	230	2.4	96	4.4	3.6	8.1
Warren	3 688	33.2	233	81.4	10.1	40.2	4.3	1 928	28.3	389	6.4	43.2	-6.3
Washington	4 190	39.0	374	94.4	3.6	35.6	9.5	2 643	33.9	432	8.2	84.3	-3.0
Wayne	774	6.5	52	7.7	0.2	4.8	0.7	217	2.5	101	2.7	42.2	-4.8
Webster	343	2.7	29	5.0	0.0	2.6	0.4	150	1.5	100	11.4	7.0	-2.3
Wilkinson	283	2.2	34	6.4	D	3.6	0.5	181	1.9	47	-2.8	17.7	-4.0
Winston	753	6.4	71	10.5	D	5.6	0.7	343	3.2	126	1.6	43.3	17.5
Yalobusha	412	3.9	35	3.6	0.0	1.2	0.4	108	0.9	109	-3.7	0.0	NA
Yazoo	875	8.6	91	12.8	D	4.9	1.1	284	3.4	195	7.8	32.6	-6.1
MISSOURI	375 917	3 538.2	32 930	13 707.2	863.0	3 452.6	992.1	323 658	5 238.0	45 944	5.3	18 669.7	-3.8
Adair	2 054	16.8	175	56.1	3.3	38.8	1.8	1 746	22.4	170	-0.1	149.6	12.1
Andrew	332	3.0	30	3.6	D	2.0	0.2	164	1.2	52	5.7	22.3	-6.0
Atchison	327	2.4	36	4.6	D	2.4	D	163	1.2	104	-0.8	0.0	NA
Audrain	1 438	12.7	133	26.4	1.3	12.4	2.3	750	10.2	211	5.3	199.2	27.7
Barry	1 217	10.5	139	29.2	1.6	5.7	1.2	644	8.2	295	6.0	68.4	4.4
Barton	570	4.3	47	11.9	D	3.5	0.5	376	4.5	116	-2.3	21.7	13.2
Bates	721	5.5	73	8.7	D	4.4	0.6	269	2.9	137	-2.1	21.8	6.1
Benton	535	4.0	57	6.7	0.9	2.0	0.4	157	1.9	124	9.0	0.0	NA
Bollinger	192	1.8	23	4.0	0.0	1.8	D	160	1.5	37	83.0	9.2	-14.0
Boone	10 365	86.7	778	293.5	D	135.4	D	8 093	113.1	756	7.9	287.9	-0.9
Buchanan	6 699	60.4	541	146.0	8.7	54.6	D	4 144	56.0	822	5.0	367.0	-2.5
Butler	2 625	23.7	229	95.8	3.3	66.1	3.6	2 438	31.2	260	8.1	120.7	-7.1
Caldwell	222	1.4	24	2.9	0.0	1.5	D	102	1.0	61	0.6	5.1	-9.9
Callaway	1 643	14.1	126	20.7	1.1	5.2	1.0	564	5.5	158	1.5	80.5	4.5
Camden	2 586	22.8	273	70.1	32.0	11.3	2.4	2 770	22.8	265	2.5	49.0	6.7
Cape Girardeau	7 025	57.2	501	164.9	9.8	68.1	7.2	3 870	67.5	746	13.1	314.8	-11.9
Carroll	402	3.0	58	6.8	D	2.7	0.4	253	1.9	99	3.3	76.3	-2.9
Carter	115	0.8	18	3.0	D	D	D	155	1.3	33	3.6	5.8	-5.8
Cass	2 716	25.5	233	34.3	1.3	7.6	1.8	909	10.3	305	4.4	98.9	0.9
Cedar	477	3.7	55	6.3	D	4.1	0.3	240	2.1	120	-0.8	22.5	15.0
Chariton	277	2.0	37	6.2	0.0	1.6	0.3	223	1.7	110	-1.3	0.0	NA
Christian	1 103	10.1	98	14.8	D	4.5	0.4	431	4.2	199	11.9	6.7	21.9
Clark	257	2.0	27	2.2	D	1.0	0.2	91	0.5	56	0.6	10.5	-1.3
Clay	13 044	128.5	1 021	379.8	D	104.5	13.0	10 190	133.4	1 236	10.0	690.5	-7.5
Clinton	814	6.3	100	15.0	0.5	6.5	0.5	528	5.0	88	6.4	114.2	2.1
Cole	5 825	53.0	448	132.6	D	46.8	10.5	3 347	52.8	705	1.4	218.5	-2.6
Cooper	908	6.6	68	10.7	0.5	2.6	0.6	410	3.4	131	6.4	62.4	-13.3
Crawford	893	7.5	82	11.3	2.2	3.5	0.9	321	2.9	107	2.3	0.0	NA
Dade	200	1.4	19	1.3	0.0	0.4	D	38	0.4	58	6.9	2.9	14.6
Dallas	402	3.6	39	4.9	D	2.7	0.4	194	1.8	115	0.3	12.0	-0.5
Daviess	283	2.2	24	2.3	D	0.7	D	59	0.5	85	4.4	3.1	-5.6
De Kalb	257	2.0	25	2.2	D	1.0	D	77	0.7	52	-5.6	0.0	NA
Dent	640	5.6	69	10.4	1.3	4.9	0.8	347	3.2	101	6.1	25.2	0.2
Douglas	434	4.1	39	5.1	D	2.1	0.3	181	1.6	49	1.9	23.7	8.5
Dunklin	1 661	14.8	159	36.9	0.4	22.2	2.4	1 054	10.8	311	3.0	34.9	-3.9
Franklin	4 714	44.1	412	78.4	6.1	29.8	4.1	2 160	26.3	596	5.0	204.4	4.2
Gasconade	829	7.1	63	14.6	D	4.4	D	323	3.1	91	-0.7	33.1	-27.6
Gentry	297	2.2	40	5.3	D	3.2	0.2	215	1.7	100	-2.4	0.0	NA
Greene	20 412	192.6	1 684	623.3	D	220.5	39.9	15 609	243.3	1 591	7.9	913.2	-2.5
Grundy	562	4.8	58	8.5	D	3.7	0.8	266	2.4	134	2.5	42.0	-3.5
Harrison	673	5.6	51	6.2	0.9	2.3	0.4	236	1.8	117	2.7	23.6	0.2
Henry	1 241	10.6	118	24.1	1.8	12.7	1.5	769	9.0	182	1.8	143.8	0.0
Hickory	177	1.0	18	2.7	D	D	0.0	146	0.8	32	-1.3	0.0	NA
Holt	276	2.3	27	4.6	D	D	D	147	1.7	63	-5.7	4.7	16.8
Howard	395	2.4	43	4.7	D	2.2	D	229	1.6	116	1.0	17.9	-7.9
Howell	1 805	15.7	165	28.8	D	14.0	1.4	800	9.9	262	4.9	52.9	0.0
Iron	370	3.1	40	7.3	0.9	3.6	0.2	254	2.2	68	-1.2	13.7	7.9
Jackson	57 769	579.1	5 125	2 866.2	D	637.7	345.7	64 701	1 202.9	8 785	8.5	2 705.8	-4.2
Jasper	8 738	77.6	715	188.0	D	76.0	8.7	4 877	67.3	677	6.4	360.4	2.3
Jefferson	7 441	68.7	626	131.8	1.9	45.0	5.5	4 013	44.3	588	2.5	215.8	-3.4
Johnson	2 512	15.2	150	29.5	D	14.2	2.0	991	9.8	214	-1.2	43.2	-9.3
Knox	125	0.9	22	2.9	D	D	D	130	1.1	40	-1.7	0.0	NA

1. For the period including March 12 of the year shown. 2. Includes deposits for all insured and reporting noninsured commercial and mutual savings banks. 3. Includes savings capital for all FSLIC insured savings institutions.

STATE County	Federal funds and grants, 1989: Expenditures: Total (Mil dol)	Federal funds and grants, 1989: Expenditures: Percent change, 1988–1989	Per capita[1] (Dollars): Total	Per capita[1] (Dollars): Direct payments for individuals	Per capita[1] (Dollars): Procurement contract awards	Per capita[1] (Dollars): Salaries and wages	Per capita[1] (Dollars): Grant awards	Local government finances, 1981–1982: General revenue: Total (Mil dol)	Intergovernmental: Total (Mil dol)	Intergovernmental: Percent from state	Taxes: Total (Mil dol)	Taxes: Per capita[2]: Total (Dollars)	Taxes: Per capita[2]: Property (Dollars)	Direct general expenditure: Total (Mil dol)	Direct general expenditure: Percent change, 1977–1982
	174	175	176	177	178	179	180	181	182	183	184	185	186	187	188
MISSISSIPPI—Con.															
Tishomingo	52.4	-1.4	2 895	2 207	223	151	270	15.4	7.3	89.6	2.1	114	112	15.1	77.9
Tunica	32.7	10.0	3 763	1 769	103	95	678	8.2	5.4	92.8	1.5	151	148	8.7	65.9
Union	49.2	-5.1	2 178	1 677	12	119	264	17.2	8.2	93.0	2.5	117	115	18.5	62.6
Walthall	34.5	6.1	2 497	1 891	8	88	412	11.3	5.8	94.5	1.2	94	91	10.2	96.1
Warren	254.9	-1.3	5 192	2 002	814	2 059	244	34.7	18.4	89.5	11.2	215	208	33.3	37.1
Washington	197.0	-16.1	2 847	1 724	61	265	477	73.4	33.5	75.5	14.6	200	191	71.6	57.3
Wayne	41.9	7.7	2 093	1 636	10	90	342	17.0	9.3	89.0	1.7	83	78	16.6	74.7
Webster	29.5	9.5	2 978	2 228	16	170	338	9.5	4.6	89.8	1.1	100	97	9.3	110.0
Wilkinson	30.3	28.1	3 128	1 974	9	51	999	12.1	6.0	76.5	1.0	91	88	11.2	81.2
Winston	49.5	5.9	2 567	1 918	53	114	442	14.4	8.3	93.3	2.1	108	106	16.3	80.9
Yalobusha	44.4	5.7	3 470	2 252	273	220	562	10.9	5.4	92.0	1.8	139	135	11.0	39.8
Yazoo	84.4	4.2	3 284	1 985	20	103	505	18.3	12.3	89.3	3.6	133	131	19.3	31.6
MISSOURI	23 564.4	9.6	X	1 908	1 400	543	457	4 475.4	1 550.1	72.6	1 848.7	374	231	4 240.1	52.2
Adair	58.8	6.5	2 556	1 844	22	229	272	16.3	6.4	69.0	6.0	240	144	17.2	65.4
Andrew	30.7	-5.1	2 018	1 394	11	164	136	7.8	3.7	88.0	2.8	197	185	7.4	61.9
Atchison	32.0	-7.8	4 151	2 209	18	179	391	5.9	1.6	92.2	2.6	292	271	6.7	67.6
Audrain	70.7	4.9	2 819	2 136	15	141	265	35.0	8.5	63.8	6.9	263	188	36.9	93.1
Barry	76.9	8.0	2 718	2 122	48	136	308	15.8	7.8	94.3	3.8	153	123	14.7	9.3
Barton	32.2	9.3	2 800	1 980	16	144	281	7.4	2.2	92.3	2.0	184	156	7.5	61.8
Bates	46.5	5.2	2 906	2 097	16	141	265	11.7	3.5	92.7	2.9	186	182	12.0	111.8
Benton	45.5	6.0	3 371	2 673	131	264	204	6.9	2.8	85.9	2.2	181	143	6.9	20.0
Bollinger	29.1	19.3	2 602	1 662	20	111	669	4.4	2.9	95.6	1.0	101	81	4.8	59.9
Boone	282.0	10.9	2 668	1 361	75	587	536	108.5	42.0	49.9	32.9	317	203	117.7	113.2
Buchanan	226.4	-3.7	2 663	2 105	66	231	213	63.6	25.5	73.7	26.7	308	201	65.1	35.5
Butler	147.3	11.8	3 815	2 372	70	454	534	26.6	13.9	84.7	8.0	211	123	25.6	53.7
Caldwell	26.2	13.9	3 155	2 118	20	177	344	5.8	2.6	93.2	2.0	236	223	5.6	43.0
Callaway	93.0	-1.6	2 800	1 678	34	589	396	22.9	6.8	77.8	10.2	316	271	22.4	78.3
Camden	67.2	2.9	2 573	2 259	38	84	164	12.1	5.2	91.8	5.0	237	154	12.3	90.9
Cape Girardeau	137.1	5.5	2 194	1 617	40	217	260	32.9	9.9	86.8	17.5	293	176	31.8	23.1
Carroll	38.9	0.9	3 532	2 312	23	187	206	7.2	2.9	86.8	3.2	269	226	8.5	69.4
Carter	17.3	6.7	2 934	2 110	107	312	368	4.0	3.0	80.5	0.6	105	88	4.1	62.5
Cass	125.9	11.4	1 995	1 385	282	150	123	45.6	18.7	91.8	14.2	270	215	42.8	67.6
Cedar	37.7	9.3	3 042	2 502	14	139	285	9.7	3.1	88.2	2.0	163	121	11.1	121.0
Chariton	33.6	4.7	3 498	2 185	25	224	221	5.7	1.9	85.3	2.6	246	216	6.7	43.7
Christian	52.0	10.8	1 626	1 303	12	77	174	11.6	7.4	82.9	2.8	124	119	11.8	92.1
Clark	24.2	8.0	3 068	1 674	25	181	165	7.4	2.7	72.4	2.1	247	240	6.3	73.3
Clay	286.2	16.1	1 880	1 067	80	195	215	152.6	27.9	91.4	54.2	395	291	154.0	68.6
Clinton	39.5	13.8	2 310	1 684	22	122	255	11.9	6.0	62.8	4.1	257	196	11.6	69.9
Cole	419.5	1.7	6 832	1 509	31	196	5 081	40.7	14.5	64.8	17.5	297	203	39.1	86.0
Cooper	44.2	-4.1	3 093	2 161	22	149	454	18.3	4.9	72.7	3.8	265	214	17.4	128.3
Crawford	47.3	12.5	2 332	1 882	30	73	318	7.3	4.0	90.2	2.3	125	103	7.7	62.3
Dade	23.8	14.3	3 126	2 271	19	156	351	5.7	2.1	74.8	1.4	188	174	5.5	63.3
Dallas	31.5	11.0	2 315	1 779	13	102	244	4.5	2.7	95.7	1.1	94	74	4.5	37.7
Daviess	29.8	13.3	3 501	1 844	237	193	407	5.3	2.0	94.6	2.2	254	238	4.9	48.7
De Kalb	23.6	6.4	2 914	1 864	47	187	172	4.3	1.8	93.8	1.8	228	204	4.3	34.9
Dent	41.2	4.4	2 865	2 261	12	181	340	11.0	3.8	92.9	2.5	169	138	10.4	69.1
Douglas	25.5	5.4	2 025	1 482	13	95	288	4.3	2.6	94.2	0.9	76	75	4.0	23.0
Dunklin	119.6	10.9	3 498	2 225	17	113	701	28.8	11.6	90.0	5.9	163	119	28.6	57.7
Franklin	153.7	-0.8	1 943	1 615	45	108	141	44.0	16.8	92.1	14.4	198	148	44.5	59.2
Gasconade	38.3	17.8	2 737	2 127	14	124	396	11.9	4.4	76.0	3.2	242	190	12.2	63.2
Gentry	31.2	15.7	4 515	2 655	31	267	501	5.7	1.9	79.3	1.9	241	220	4.8	41.6
Greene	526.4	0.9	2 557	1 768	50	352	204	133.6	45.4	78.9	52.2	279	200	126.1	32.5
Grundy	36.0	9.6	3 364	2 436	19	174	318	10.0	3.9	74.5	3.3	279	197	10.2	68.3
Harrison	36.3	17.1	4 124	2 384	65	225	402	7.2	2.6	78.8	2.8	280	269	6.5	54.6
Henry	67.5	15.3	3 375	2 404	45	166	209	21.3	7.0	50.9	4.7	245	181	21.5	68.0
Hickory	25.7	11.3	3 385	2 775	21	158	312	3.4	1.9	93.8	1.1	174	158	3.3	39.3
Holt	25.3	-2.3	4 080	2 240	22	465	209	4.2	1.2	86.7	2.2	333	305	4.1	51.6
Howard	31.2	6.0	3 318	2 344	31	160	417	10.7	2.4	87.9	2.3	231	194	10.6	107.9
Howell	115.1	5.9	3 689	2 064	1 054	122	385	17.3	10.3	87.4	4.2	146	96	18.0	71.6
Iron	34.0	13.9	3 031	2 360	10	95	548	7.9	3.4	87.9	3.7	338	308	7.8	45.7
Jackson	3 071.3	-1.6	4 758	1 934	1 525	1 020	262	798.9	253.1	56.2	378.8	603	271	711.5	35.9
Jasper	240.3	3.1	2 595	2 015	86	175	281	63.4	25.6	79.9	25.6	289	183	62.0	46.6
Jefferson	226.1	5.4	1 285	1 058	13	64	144	86.4	43.9	89.3	29.6	196	149	87.5	68.9
Johnson	260.2	24.9	6 638	1 516	2 600	2 203	186	33.0	8.6	85.3	7.9	204	150	30.9	98.0
Knox	22.1	20.2	4 605	2 198	63	294	221	4.2	2.3	64.9	1.2	226	199	3.7	90.5

1. Based on the estimated population as of July 1 of the year shown. 2. Based on the estimated population as of July 1, 1982.

STATE County	Local government finances, 1981–1982 (cont'd): Direct general expenditure (cont'd): Per capita[1] (Dollars)	Percent of total for– Education	Percent of total for– Health & hospitals	Percent of total for– Police protection	Percent of total for– Public welfare	Percent of total for– Highways	Debt outstanding: Total (Mil dol)	Debt outstanding: Per capita[1] (Dollars)	State and local government employment, 1989: Total	State and local government employment, 1989: Rate[2]	Federal government civilian employment 1989: Total	Federal government civilian employment 1989: Earnings ($1,000)	Elections, 1988[3]: Total vote cast for president	Elections, 1988[3]: Vote for lead party (Percent)
	189	190	191	192	193	194	195	196	197	198	199	200	201	202
MISSISSIPPI—Con.														
Tishomingo	805	40.0	36.0	1.6	0.6	12.2	4.3	227	602	332.6	92	2 403	7 052	R—51.7
Tunica	909	51.7	10.8	3.3	0.4	21.8	1.2	124	396	455.2	28	705	2 430	D—62.1
Union	859	49.8	24.9	2.0	0.2	10.3	11.3	526	942	416.8	86	2 308	8 591	R—64.1
Walthall	769	45.2	35.9	2.2	0.4	8.8	2.6	193	636	460.9	33	810	5 502	R—56.4
Warren	641	55.4	1.3	5.3	0.1	10.1	22.1	424	2 385	485.7	3 326	110 738	20 170	R—62.0
Washington	981	35.8	19.5	4.6	0.6	7.9	39.1	536	3 887	561.7	685	20 147	20 687	R—49.4
Wayne	832	38.0	26.2	2.4	0.3	17.7	9.1	456	939	469.5	40	1 018	7 414	R—60.6
Webster	881	38.9	35.1	2.5	0.4	14.8	3.3	316	486	490.9	54	1 320	4 632	R—66.1
Wilkinson	1 052	31.5	36.6	3.3	0.0	9.9	1.2	114	484	499.0	20	506	4 223	D—63.4
Winston	844	39.8	33.2	2.2	0.1	12.0	13.5	702	932	482.9	63	1 800	9 229	R—57.6
Yalobusha	836	47.5	20.3	3.1	0.5	11.7	8.1	612	708	553.1	99	2 351	5 093	R—52.2
Yazoo	706	54.3	2.3	4.2	0.4	14.6	10.7	392	1 421	552.9	81	2 082	11 530	R—48.0
MISSOURI	858	46.4	10.9	6.5	0.3	6.5	3 076.7	623	280 955	544.5	72 266	2 197 522	2 093 713	R—51.8
Adair	687	53.4	8.6	3.4	0.0	9.8	14.2	567	2 093	910.0	113	3 356	9 336	R—61.3
Andrew	518	70.8	1.2	2.6	0.0	9.6	4.0	281	525	345.4	44	1 032	6 537	R—52.1
Atchison	759	54.5	2.5	2.5	12.6	13.3	2.6	296	395	513.0	55	1 290	3 239	R—54.4
Audrain	1 408	24.9	45.5	2.0	0.0	4.1	12.7	486	1 856	739.4	112	2 720	10 327	D—50.6
Barry	589	64.2	8.3	3.7	0.0	7.9	6.1	243	1 128	398.6	129	3 443	11 477	R—63.0
Barton	680	48.7	25.9	3.6	0.0	9.1	4.9	441	698	607.0	48	1 177	4 958	R—67.3
Bates	779	42.9	36.3	3.1	0.0	7.5	4.1	265	784	490.0	77	1 810	6 930	R—51.6
Benton	573	54.9	17.4	3.5	0.0	6.3	3.0	249	531	393.3	118	3 399	6 145	R—56.4
Bollinger	470	76.1	3.8	4.0	0.0	5.9	0.5	46	348	310.7	42	923	4 599	R—58.9
Boone	1 134	26.3	28.0	3.2	1.4	4.2	120.4	1 160	19 303	1 826.2	2 299	72 879	47 458	D—51.4
Buchanan	751	50.9	2.0	5.2	0.5	8.5	24.8	286	4 948	582.1	562	18 462	34 089	D—54.6
Butler	680	67.9	0.1	4.8	0.3	9.2	15.2	404	2 167	561.4	618	19 669	13 738	R—58.0
Caldwell	671	61.5	15.2	2.1	0.0	9.6	2.3	272	492	592.8	51	1 114	3 815	R—54.4
Callaway	691	50.1	14.9	4.1	0.1	8.7	20.0	618	3 441	1 036.4	200	5 353	11 938	R—56.0
Camden	582	55.9	11.2	6.7	0.0	13.3	4.0	188	1 021	391.2	59	1 401	11 759	R—66.1
Cape Girardeau	534	50.3	0.3	7.5	0.2	9.1	13.3	224	4 211	673.8	300	9 378	24 556	R—67.5
Carroll	722	64.0	1.5	4.8	0.1	13.1	3.6	308	560	509.1	65	1 547	5 150	R—54.6
Carter	734	75.4	1.2	1.6	0.0	4.7	0.8	134	306	518.6	83	2 163	2 528	R—56.5
Cass	811	63.2	13.6	4.2	0.1	5.8	23.8	450	2 148	340.4	168	4 774	22 961	R—55.7
Cedar	929	35.8	46.1	2.6	0.0	4.8	1.8	147	536	432.3	64	1 620	4 744	R—62.5
Chariton	646	58.9	3.0	3.7	0.0	14.3	0.8	79	422	439.6	70	1 651	4 555	D—51.5
Christian	518	65.9	1.1	2.2	0.0	5.4	5.5	242	1 013	316.6	68	1 631	12 441	R—61.7
Clark	753	51.9	19.2	2.5	0.1	10.4	2.4	283	499	631.6	51	1 115	3 431	D—56.1
Clay	1 123	39.4	33.9	3.4	0.2	4.4	61.7	450	6 957	457.1	470	16 476	60 287	R—50.2
Clinton	725	46.1	0.7	4.1	0.0	11.9	8.8	548	595	348.0	62	1 510	6 961	D—52.5
Cole	664	42.7	1.2	5.8	0.1	6.6	27.4	465	15 249	2 483.6	542	16 183	26 441	R—68.2
Cooper	1 208	30.2	45.9	2.7	0.5	5.5	6.4	446	976	682.5	54	1 400	6 266	R—59.6
Crawford	420	65.9	2.6	7.2	1.0	9.1	3.6	197	636	313.3	66	1 439	6 987	R—55.2
Dade	744	44.9	35.0	3.2	0.0	7.3	2.0	269	518	681.6	38	866	3 476	R—62.0
Dallas	371	68.7	4.9	4.5	0.0	9.5	0.6	54	385	283.1	40	958	5 223	R—55.5
Daviess	551	70.4	3.3	2.8	0.0	8.8	3.3	372	445	523.5	73	1 934	3 518	R—50.2
De Kalb	531	73.5	1.7	2.0	0.0	9.7	1.9	239	816	1 007.4	47	1 137	3 843	D—51.3
Dent	704	46.6	32.7	2.6	0.0	6.1	3.5	239	697	484.0	99	2 405	5 417	R—54.9
Douglas	334	68.7	0.7	4.3	0.0	12.6	0.4	36	327	259.5	54	1 198	4 976	R—64.8
Dunklin	791	48.0	28.0	3.8	0.1	4.7	19.8	546	1 415	413.7	122	3 058	10 320	D—51.2
Franklin	614	55.2	8.3	5.7	0.0	7.5	32.6	450	2 807	354.9	226	6 077	28 621	R—58.0
Gasconade	922	48.1	26.5	2.8	0.1	6.3	4.5	341	786	561.4	54	1 347	5 856	R—72.0
Gentry	603	58.0	0.2	3.0	0.1	12.0	3.0	384	355	514.5	53	1 234	3 433	D—54.5
Greene	673	49.5	1.6	5.5	1.8	5.5	187.5	1 000	10 892	529.0	1 940	64 781	87 959	R—59.4
Grundy	872	53.5	13.4	3.6	0.0	9.0	8.3	712	816	762.6	62	1 548	4 733	R—56.4
Harrison	654	64.7	4.3	2.8	0.5	9.0	4.9	489	526	597.7	65	1 440	4 064	R—55.9
Henry	1 114	27.6	41.2	3.0	0.0	4.6	6.5	339	1 183	591.5	99	2 482	8 328	R—50.0
Hickory	508	79.4	1.7	1.7	0.0	6.2	0.9	144	283	372.4	47	1 053	3 732	R—54.7
Holt	611	54.0	3.4	3.9	0.1	18.2	2.9	439	251	404.8	42	1 088	2 855	R—55.4
Howard	1 074	32.7	49.0	2.9	0.1	4.8	2.4	240	537	571.3	54	1 358	4 322	D—56.6
Howell	620	64.5	1.0	4.9	0.3	7.8	11.0	379	1 460	467.9	119	3 066	11 645	R—62.5
Iron	708	67.8	2.5	4.3	0.5	8.7	1.6	149	494	441.1	27	630	4 170	D—54.7
Jackson	1 132	34.7	4.3	8.8	0.3	7.1	663.1	1 055	37 790	585.4	20 607	642 013	256 621	D—57.7
Jasper	701	55.9	7.7	5.5	0.1	6.3	13.5	153	4 961	535.7	355	10 479	31 187	R—63.9
Jefferson	580	75.3	1.8	4.6	0.1	4.3	46.9	311	5 084	288.9	264	6 993	57 255	R—51.1
Johnson	804	38.8	42.6	2.8	0.0	5.4	5.4	141	3 675	937.5	1 067	24 651	12 921	R—58.1
Knox	685	57.2	21.6	2.6	0.0	9.1	0.2	43	340	708.3	51	1 110	2 472	D—50.8

1. Based on the estimated population as of July 1, 1982. 2. Per 10,000 resident population estimated as of July 1 of the year shown. 3. Data subject to copyright.

STATE–County code	MSA/CMSA/NECMA code[1]	STATE County	Land Area,[2] 1990 (Sq. Km.)	Population, 1990											
				Total persons	Rank	Per square kilometer	Race					Hispanic[3]	Age of population Percent		
							White	Black	Am. Indian, Eskimo, Aleut	Asian & Pacific Islander	Other race		Under 5 years	5 to 14 years	15 to 24 years
			1	2	3	4	5	6	7	8	9	10	11	12	13
		MISSOURI—Con.													
29 105	...	Laclede	1 984	27 158	1 384	13.7	26 816	96	144	79	23	141	7.2	15.5	13.0
29 107	3760	Lafayette	1 630	31 107	1 240	19.1	29 976	880	106	69	76	219	7.0	15.3	12.8
29 109	...	Lawrence	1 588	30 236	1 283	19.0	29 820	24	280	56	56	211	7.1	15.1	12.7
29 111	...	Lewis	1 308	10 233	2 365	7.8	9 846	342	19	16	10	26	6.0	13.7	18.3
29 113	...	Lincoln	1 633	28 892	1 333	17.7	28 080	590	102	54	66	219	8.5	17.3	12.3
29 115	...	Linn	1 607	13 885	2 065	8.6	13 714	113	22	14	22	94	6.3	14.6	10.4
29 117	...	Livingston	1 385	14 592	2 013	10.5	14 193	317	40	27	15	63	6.5	14.9	11.6
29 119	...	McDonald	1 397	16 938	1 851	12.1	16 313	4	546	41	34	121	7.8	15.7	13.0
29 121	...	Macon	2 082	15 345	1 968	7.4	14 905	363	50	19	8	59	5.8	14.5	12.0
29 123	...	Madison	1 287	11 127	2 283	8.6	11 033	10	32	34	18	62	6.7	14.8	12.3
29 125	...	Maries	1 367	7 976	2 571	5.8	7 909	27	19	10	11	40	6.8	14.5	13.0
29 127	...	Marion	1 135	27 682	1 363	24.4	26 213	1 249	75	109	36	118	7.1	15.9	12.6
29 129	...	Mercer	1 177	3 723	2 938	3.2	3 713	3	6	1	0	7	4.9	13.7	9.5
29 131	...	Miller	1 534	20 700	1 643	13.5	20 547	23	89	23	18	101	7.4	16.0	12.9
29 133	...	Mississippi	1 070	14 442	2 020	13.5	11 590	2 804	26	15	7	40	7.3	16.7	13.4
29 135	...	Moniteau	1 079	12 298	2 195	11.4	12 044	157	54	36	7	46	6.9	16.0	13.2
29 137	...	Monroe	1 673	9 104	2 460	5.4	8 713	357	18	14	2	48	7.2	16.3	11.2
29 139	...	Montgomery	1 395	11 355	2 267	8.1	11 015	289	12	20	19	45	6.9	15.1	11.4
29 141	...	Morgan	1 547	15 574	1 949	10.1	15 364	94	70	26	20	69	6.6	12.9	10.8
29 143	...	New Madrid	1 756	20 928	1 632	11.9	17 558	3 279	34	36	21	93	7.2	17.1	14.0
29 145	3710	Newton	1 623	44 445	920	27.4	43 000	174	948	235	88	353	7.2	14.8	13.7
29 147	...	Nodaway	2 271	21 709	1 591	9.6	21 278	166	43	165	57	135	5.7	13.4	26.6
29 149	...	Oregon	2 050	9 470	2 437	4.6	9 402	3	41	14	10	32	5.6	13.6	12.2
29 151	...	Osage	1 570	12 018	2 218	7.7	11 940	38	21	2	17	56	7.1	16.2	15.3
29 153	...	Ozark	1 934	8 598	2 504	4.4	8 528	2	39	12	17	56	5.0	13.6	10.7
29 155	...	Pemiscot	1 277	21 921	1 581	17.2	16 222	5 596	34	51	18	89	8.3	17.3	14.3
29 157	...	Perry	1 229	16 648	1 874	13.5	16 525	15	29	69	10	72	7.2	16.4	12.9
29 159	...	Pettis	1 774	35 437	1 113	20.0	33 963	1 167	103	123	81	268	7.2	14.8	12.9
29 161	...	Phelps	1 743	35 248	1 122	20.2	33 815	397	148	783	105	303	6.5	13.4	19.6
29 163	...	Pike	1 743	15 969	1 926	9.2	15 033	845	52	24	15	119	7.1	15.8	12.1
29 165	3760	Platte	1 089	57 867	750	53.1	55 127	1 217	307	799	417	1 161	7.3	14.7	13.7
29 167	...	Polk	1 650	21 826	1 587	13.2	21 508	70	134	76	38	173	6.5	13.8	18.4
29 169	...	Pulaski	1 417	41 307	975	29.2	33 139	5 608	261	1 209	1 090	1 953	8.8	16.0	21.2
29 171	...	Putnam	1 342	5 079	2 834	3.8	5 059	1	9	4	6	24	5.5	13.0	11.0
29 173	...	Ralls	1 220	8 476	2 515	6.9	8 312	138	18	6	2	14	6.3	15.7	11.8
29 175	...	Randolph	1 249	24 370	1 482	19.5	22 332	1 837	80	79	42	179	6.4	14.9	13.4
29 177	3760	Ray	1 475	21 971	1 576	14.9	21 477	302	112	35	45	119	7.4	16.4	12.5
29 179	...	Reynolds	2 101	6 661	2 689	3.2	6 633	3	15	5	5	28	6.3	15.0	12.5
29 181	...	Ripley	1 630	12 303	2 194	7.5	12 211	6	49	22	15	78	6.8	15.3	12.6
29 183	7040	St. Charles	1 454	212 907	234	146.4	205 424	4 963	528	1 431	561	2 308	8.9	16.9	13.2
29 185	...	St. Clair	1 753	8 457	2 517	4.8	8 379	22	41	11	4	33	6.1	13.0	10.9
29 186	...	Ste. Genevieve	1 301	16 037	1 920	12.3	15 925	45	31	24	12	49	7.2	16.3	12.6
29 187	...	St. Francois	1 164	48 904	858	42.0	47 642	962	107	123	70	239	6.5	14.6	13.7
29 189	7040	St. Louis	1 315	993 529	31	755.5	836 232	139 318	1 477	14 167	2 335	9 811	7.0	13.8	12.9
29 195	...	Saline	1 957	23 523	1 512	12.0	21 974	1 352	45	61	91	208	6.2	14.6	14.6
29 197	...	Schuyler	797	4 236	2 898	5.3	4 217	0	8	4	7	18	7.1	13.6	11.2
29 199	...	Scotland	1 136	4 822	2 855	4.2	4 808	3	10	0	1	12	7.3	13.9	11.3
29 201	...	Scott	1 091	39 376	1 015	36.1	35 660	3 497	86	68	65	206	7.7	16.1	13.8
29 203	...	Shannon	2 600	7 613	2 610	2.9	7 573	3	27	4	6	22	7.3	15.1	12.1
29 205	...	Shelby	1 297	6 942	2 667	5.4	6 858	56	18	3	7	23	6.8	14.7	10.4
29 207	...	Stoddard	2 142	28 895	1 332	13.5	28 347	409	58	47	34	132	6.1	14.2	13.4
29 209	...	Stone	1 200	19 078	1 729	15.9	18 883	6	138	37	14	114	5.3	12.2	11.0
29 211	...	Sullivan	1 686	6 326	2 720	3.8	6 304	1	14	2	5	28	5.3	12.6	11.8
29 213	...	Taney	1 638	25 561	1 440	15.6	25 251	16	152	83	59	194	5.3	11.9	13.6
29 215	...	Texas	3 053	21 476	1 603	7.0	21 294	16	84	60	22	113	6.8	15.8	11.9
29 217	...	Vernon	2 160	19 041	1 732	8.8	18 787	59	113	65	17	102	6.7	15.2	13.5
29 219	...	Warren	1 118	19 534	1 697	17.5	18 903	513	46	33	39	152	8.2	15.9	12.0
29 221	...	Washington	1 968	20 380	1 656	10.4	19 914	378	47	23	18	83	7.6	17.1	14.8
29 223	...	Wayne	1 971	11 543	2 252	5.9	11 471	7	45	9	11	44	6.0	13.5	12.3
29 225	...	Webster	1 537	23 753	1 501	15.5	23 322	190	148	45	48	140	7.6	16.5	13.9
29 227	...	Worth	690	2 440	3 027	3.5	2 425	1	1	5	8	9	6.6	14.4	9.2
29 229	...	Wright	1 767	16 758	1 864	9.5	16 575	36	119	12	16	61	7.2	16.4	12.4
29 510	7040	St. Louis city	160	396 685	126	2 479.3	202 085	188 408	950	3 733	1 509	5 124	7.9	13.6	14.2

1. MSA = Metropolitan Statistical Area. CMSA = Consolidated MSA. NECMA = New England county metropolitan area. PMSA = Primary MSA. See Appendix A for explanation of these concepts. See Appendix B for list of metropolitan areas identified by type, with component counties. 2. Dry land or land partially or temporarily covered by water. 3. Hispanic persons may be of any race.

STATE County	Population, 1990 (cont'd): Age of population (cont'd), Percent: 25 to 34 years	35 to 44 years	45 to 54 years	55 to 64 years	65 to 74 years	75 years and over	Percent female	Population–Change and components of change: Change, 1980–1990: Number	Percent	Components of change, 1980–1986: Total persons, 1986	Total persons, 1980	Net change: Number	Percent	Natural increase: Births	Deaths
	14	15	16	17	18	19	20	21	22	23	24	25	26	27	28
MISSOURI—Con.															
Laclede	15.5	13.5	10.8	9.2	8.4	6.9	51.3	2 835	11.7	26 300	24 323	2 000	8.2	2 400	1 600
Lafayette	14.5	13.8	10.7	9.3	8.2	8.4	51.1	1 176	3.9	30 500	29 931	600	2.0	2 600	2 300
Lawrence	14.2	12.9	10.8	9.3	9.4	8.4	51.6	1 263	4.4	30 400	28 973	1 400	5.0	2 500	2 100
Lewis	13.1	11.6	10.5	9.0	8.7	9.0	52.2	-668	-6.1	10 600	10 901	-300	-2.6	700	700
Lincoln	17.5	14.2	10.5	8.2	6.3	5.2	50.1	6 699	30.2	26 100	22 193	3 900	17.7	2 400	1 600
Linn	13.1	12.3	9.5	10.4	11.6	11.8	53.4	-1 610	-10.4	14 700	15 495	-800	-5.2	1 500	1 400
Livingston	14.3	13.3	10.2	9.8	9.8	9.7	54.2	-1 147	-7.3	15 000	15 739	-700	-4.4	1 400	1 300
McDonald	15.0	12.9	11.2	10.1	8.1	6.3	50.4	2 021	13.5	15 900	14 917	1 000	6.5	1 300	1 000
Macon	13.1	13.2	10.2	9.8	10.9	10.6	52.5	-968	-5.9	16 700	16 313	400	2.6	1 300	1 400
Madison	14.2	12.5	10.0	10.6	10.1	9.0	51.7	402	3.7	11 400	10 725	700	6.1	900	900
Maries	13.8	12.1	12.0	10.8	9.4	7.5	50.5	425	5.6	8 000	7 551	400	5.4	600	500
Marion	14.9	13.7	9.0	8.9	8.9	9.0	52.9	-956	-3.3	28 500	28 638	-100	-0.3	2 800	2 200
Mercer	12.0	11.8	9.4	13.2	12.7	13.0	51.4	-962	-20.5	4 100	4 685	-500	-11.7	300	400
Miller	15.2	13.3	10.0	9.6	8.2	7.3	51.3	2 161	11.7	21 100	18 539	2 500	13.5	2 000	1 300
Mississippi	14.1	12.5	10.4	9.1	8.9	7.5	53.3	-1 284	-8.2	15 500	15 726	-200	-1.6	1 700	1 200
Moniteau	15.1	13.8	9.6	8.4	8.8	8.1	50.8	230	1.9	12 800	12 068	800	6.4	1 200	1 000
Monroe	14.0	12.7	10.5	9.3	9.1	9.8	51.1	-612	-6.3	9 500	9 716	-200	-2.4	900	700
Montgomery	13.9	12.4	10.7	9.8	9.5	10.3	51.7	-182	-1.6	11 400	11 537	-100	-0.8	1 000	900
Morgan	12.0	11.7	11.7	13.8	11.9	8.8	51.1	1 767	12.8	15 600	13 807	1 800	13.3	1 200	1 200
New Madrid	14.4	13.0	10.2	9.1	8.5	6.4	52.4	-2 017	-8.8	21 800	22 945	-1 100	-5.0	2 300	1 600
Newton	14.8	14.1	11.3	9.5	8.1	6.4	51.3	3 890	9.6	43 400	40 555	2 900	7.1	3 500	2 400
Nodaway	13.0	10.7	8.0	7.4	7.4	7.7	51.7	-287	-1.3	21 100	21 996	-900	-4.1	2 000	1 400
Oregon	11.9	13.3	11.7	11.8	10.7	9.2	51.8	-768	-7.5	9 900	10 238	-300	-3.0	600	800
Osage	15.2	12.6	9.8	8.7	8.4	6.7	48.5	4	0.0	12 100	12 014	0	0.4	1 200	700
Ozark	11.8	12.7	11.5	13.5	12.5	8.6	50.5	637	8.0	8 700	7 961	700	9.2	600	600
Pemiscot	13.4	12.1	9.1	9.0	8.9	7.6	53.3	-3 066	-12.3	23 600	24 987	-1 400	-5.6	2 600	1 900
Perry	14.4	13.3	9.2	8.9	8.9	8.8	50.5	-136	-0.8	17 100	16 784	300	1.8	1 600	1 100
Pettis	15.7	13.3	10.0	9.8	8.8	7.5	51.9	-941	-2.6	36 000	36 378	-400	-1.1	3 200	2 700
Phelps	15.0	12.9	10.2	8.6	7.7	6.0	48.7	1 615	4.8	34 400	33 633	800	2.3	2 900	2 100
Pike	13.7	12.9	11.0	10.2	9.3	8.0	51.7	-1 599	-9.1	16 700	17 568	-900	-5.0	1 600	1 300
Platte	18.6	17.7	12.4	7.3	5.0	3.3	50.4	11 526	24.9	51 000	46 341	4 600	10.0	4 500	1 600
Polk	13.5	12.0	9.7	9.2	9.0	7.9	51.2	3 004	16.0	20 400	18 822	1 600	8.5	1 600	1 400
Pulaski	20.9	13.8	7.0	5.6	3.9	2.9	44.6	-704	-1.7	44 500	42 011	2 500	5.9	4 800	1 300
Putnam	12.0	12.1	10.3	12.0	12.2	11.8	51.8	-1 013	-16.6	5 500	6 092	-600	-9.8	400	600
Ralls	13.8	15.0	11.0	9.6	9.3	7.4	51.3	-508	-5.7	8 900	8 984	-100	-1.4	800	500
Randolph	16.4	14.5	9.7	8.4	8.0	8.4	49.6	-1 090	-4.3	26 200	25 460	800	3.0	2 400	1 900
Ray	15.2	14.2	11.9	9.2	7.2	6.1	51.0	593	2.8	22 100	21 378	700	3.4	1 900	1 400
Reynolds	13.7	12.8	11.8	11.4	9.4	7.2	50.8	-569	-7.9	6 600	7 230	-600	-8.5	600	500
Ripley	12.7	11.8	10.9	11.4	10.1	8.4	52.6	-155	-1.2	12 800	12 458	400	2.9	1 000	1 000
St. Charles	20.0	17.0	10.4	6.6	4.2	2.7	50.5	68 800	47.7	181 900	144 107	37 800	26.2	17 900	4 900
St. Clair	11.7	11.6	10.4	13.1	12.1	11.1	52.4	-165	-1.9	8 400	8 622	-300	-3.1	700	800
Ste. Genevieve	15.6	14.0	10.3	9.8	7.8	6.4	50.3	857	5.6	16 000	15 180	800	5.2	1 400	800
St. Francois	16.2	13.6	10.1	9.6	9.0	6.8	50.1	6 304	14.8	44 300	42 600	1 700	3.9	4 100	3 200
St. Louis	17.1	15.7	11.1	9.5	7.5	5.6	52.3	19 352	2.0	993 200	974 177	19 000	2.0	88 100	49 800
Saline	14.3	13.3	9.7	9.0	9.4	8.9	51.8	-1 390	-5.6	24 500	24 913	-400	-1.8	2 200	2 000
Schuyler	13.0	12.1	10.4	9.7	11.2	11.7	52.1	-743	-14.9	4 500	4 979	-500	-9.8	400	400
Scotland	13.0	11.6	10.3	9.8	11.1	11.6	51.9	-593	-11.0	5 100	5 415	-300	-5.4	500	500
Scott	15.3	14.2	10.4	8.2	8.0	6.3	52.7	-271	-0.7	40 200	39 647	600	1.4	3 900	2 300
Shannon	14.7	13.0	11.3	10.2	9.3	6.9	51.2	-272	-3.4	7 800	7 885	-100	-0.8	800	500
Shelby	13.5	11.7	10.0	9.6	10.6	12.7	53.1	-884	-11.3	7 300	7 826	-500	-6.6	700	700
Stoddard	13.9	13.5	11.3	10.0	9.5	8.1	52.2	-114	-0.4	28 700	29 009	-300	-1.1	2 400	2 100
Stone	11.9	12.2	12.0	14.3	13.2	7.8	51.3	3 491	22.4	18 000	15 587	2 400	15.5	1 100	1 100
Sullivan	11.7	12.1	10.9	10.8	12.3	12.6	52.1	-1 108	-14.9	6 800	7 434	-600	-8.1	500	600
Taney	12.5	12.1	10.8	12.5	12.4	8.9	51.8	5 094	24.9	24 700	20 467	4 300	20.8	1 600	1 700
Texas	13.6	13.3	11.0	10.8	9.3	7.6	51.8	406	1.9	21 500	21 070	400	2.0	2 000	1 500
Vernon	13.7	13.8	10.1	9.8	9.3	7.9	53.0	-765	-3.9	19 800	19 806	0	0.1	1 700	1 500
Warren	16.2	14.1	10.9	8.9	8.0	5.9	50.4	4 634	31.1	18 200	14 900	3 300	22.2	1 600	1 000
Washington	16.0	13.7	10.5	8.7	6.7	4.9	49.2	2 397	13.3	19 000	17 983	1 000	5.4	1 900	1 100
Wayne	12.6	11.3	11.8	12.8	11.0	8.9	51.1	266	2.4	11 700	11 277	400	3.6	900	1 000
Webster	15.6	14.0	11.1	8.4	7.0	6.0	49.6	3 339	16.4	22 600	20 414	2 200	10.9	2 000	1 200
Worth	11.9	10.0	10.4	11.8	11.4	14.2	52.4	-568	-18.9	2 700	3 008	-300	-9.6	200	300
Wright	14.0	12.3	10.3	10.4	9.1	8.0	51.7	570	3.5	16 400	16 188	300	1.6	1 600	1 300
St. Louis city	18.3	12.8	8.0	8.5	8.4	8.2	54.5	-56 119	-12.4	426 300	452 804	-26 500	-5.9	50 900	40 000

STATE County	Population–(cont'd) Components of change, 1980-1986 (cont'd) Net migration	Households, 1990 Number	Households, 1990 Percent change, 1980–1990	Households, 1990 Persons per household	Households, 1990 Percent Female family householder[1]	Households, 1990 Percent One-person	Births, 1988 Total	Births, 1988 Rate[2]	Births, 1988 Low birth weight[3] (Number)	Deaths, 1987 Number Total	Deaths, 1987 Number Infant[4]	Deaths, 1987 Rate Total[2]	Deaths, 1987 Rate Infant[5]	Marriages, 1984 Number	Marriages, 1984 Rate[2]
	29	30	31	32	33	34	35	36	37	38	39	40	41	42	43
MISSOURI—Con.															
Laclede	1 200	10 420	15.5	2.56	8.0	23.2	419	15.9	28	276	6	10.5	16.8	331	12.7
Lafayette	300	11 732	7.4	2.57	7.9	24.8	413	13.2	18	329	3	10.6	7.7	250	8.3
Lawrence	1 000	11 724	9.2	2.53	7.9	25.2	402	13.0	31	347	2	11.4	4.8	286	9.6
Lewis	-400	3 745	-5.3	2.49	7.0	26.4	100	9.8	7	141	0	13.4	0.0	58	5.3
Lincoln	3 100	10 316	35.1	2.77	7.3	20.7	467	16.5	33	255	5	9.3	10.6	251	10.5
Linn	-800	5 704	-9.6	2.37	6.5	30.6	161	11.2	7	205	1	14.2	5.7	98	6.4
Livingston	-800	5 645	-6.2	2.44	7.7	28.7	216	14.1	11	185	1	12.2	5.3	172	11.2
McDonald	700	6 386	15.6	2.61	7.9	22.5	272	16.6	20	188	4	11.6	14.3	160	10.3
Macon	500	6 160	-3.5	2.44	6.6	27.0	158	9.7	7	207	0	12.6	0.0	124	7.4
Madison	600	4 344	5.8	2.52	8.9	24.0	162	14.1	11	145	5	12.7	37.3	132	12.0
Maries	300	3 028	9.7	2.60	6.8	23.5	94	11.9	6	95	4	12.0	39.2	65	8.2
Marion	-700	10 728	0.3	2.50	9.4	28.4	400	14.0	35	350	6	12.2	15.9	411	14.3
Mercer	-500	1 577	-17.4	2.32	4.2	29.8	35	8.8	3	59	0	14.4	0.0	48	10.7
Miller	1 800	7 977	16.1	2.56	8.5	25.1	297	14.9	21	224	3	11.3	10.2	183	9.1
Mississippi	-700	5 411	-1.8	2.63	16.1	24.7	206	13.3	18	182	0	11.9	0.0	201	12.7
Moniteau	600	4 583	4.8	2.59	7.1	25.5	166	13.6	3	140	3	11.4	20.8	118	9.2
Monroe	-400	3 471	-4.1	2.56	6.3	26.9	116	12.3	3	97	2	10.3	22.0	56	5.8
Montgomery	-200	4 341	1.8	2.54	7.5	26.1	159	13.7	7	177	1	15.4	6.2	89	7.7
Morgan	1 900	6 269	18.1	2.44	6.0	23.6	208	13.6	8	210	1	13.8	5.0	148	9.7
New Madrid	-1 900	7 795	-2.1	2.65	13.7	24.3	318	14.7	26	232	2	10.6	7.0	241	10.7
Newton	1 800	16 886	13.5	2.59	7.5	22.1	622	14.2	29	424	6	9.8	9.8	358	8.3
Nodaway	-1 600	7 620	-0.9	2.48	6.5	27.1	228	11.0	14	222	1	10.6	3.7	212	9.8
Oregon	-100	3 851	-0.9	2.43	7.4	25.2	106	10.8	2	150	3	15.2	32.3	98	9.7
Osage	-400	4 262	7.1	2.78	5.9	22.3	161	13.6	8	118	2	9.9	11.0	69	5.7
Ozark	700	3 486	15.2	2.44	6.0	22.9	80	8.9	3	99	0	11.0	0.0	71	8.2
Pemiscot	-2 000	8 210	-7.6	2.62	17.2	27.6	399	16.8	40	296	3	12.5	7.4	324	13.3
Perry	-200	6 111	5.7	2.67	7.0	23.5	201	11.8	8	197	0	11.5	0.0	148	8.8
Pettis	-1 000	14 056	1.6	2.50	9.0	25.9	489	13.4	28	423	2	11.7	4.0	447	12.4
Phelps	0	13 277	15.4	2.46	8.3	26.1	448	12.9	36	382	5	11.1	10.5	450	12.9
Pike	-1 200	6 083	-3.4	2.57	8.4	25.7	233	13.8	20	241	3	14.3	13.2	195	11.5
Platte	1 700	22 142	35.0	2.58	7.9	22.9	786	14.0	45	289	9	5.3	12.1	480	9.7
Polk	1 400	8 031	18.4	2.55	6.5	22.9	284	13.4	13	226	4	10.8	14.4	192	9.6
Pulaski	-1 000	12 397	17.8	2.84	9.0	18.0	710	17.4	54	265	13	6.4	17.8	614	14.1
Putnam	-400	2 166	-9.8	2.31	6.1	30.3	45	8.3	6	92	0	17.0	0.0	56	9.7
Ralls	-400	3 226	1.4	2.60	6.1	21.5	101	11.3	9	100	1	11.2	9.4	115	12.8
Randolph	300	8 943	-3.2	2.50	8.8	26.9	313	12.0	20	257	0	9.8	0.0	282	10.9
Ray	200	8 020	6.8	2.71	7.4	20.4	294	13.0	12	213	1	9.6	3.4	191	8.8
Reynolds	-700	2 542	-3.7	2.58	7.5	21.0	79	11.8	8	82	0	12.2	0.0	87	12.1
Ripley	300	4 788	4.7	2.54	9.6	24.7	177	13.5	8	191	5	14.7	31.4	154	12.1
St. Charles	24 800	74 331	60.0	2.83	8.0	18.0	3 680	18.0	198	967	31	4.9	8.9	1 673	10.1
St. Clair	-100	3 499	2.7	2.36	6.3	28.2	102	12.1	8	112	1	13.3	11.1	75	8.7
Ste. Genevieve	200	5 707	15.5	2.77	6.6	20.2	214	13.0	9	153	1	9.6	4.4	109	7.1
St. Francois	700	17 670	16.3	2.59	10.1	23.1	631	13.3	42	556	1	12.0	1.7	503	11.6
St. Louis	-19 300	380 110	10.3	2.57	10.7	24.6	14 179	14.1	872	8 486	137	8.5	9.8	8 479	8.6
Saline	-700	8 903	-4.9	2.46	9.5	28.1	305	12.5	23	296	4	12.1	12.9	238	9.6
Schuyler	-500	1 729	-10.6	2.42	6.8	27.0	48	10.9	2	74	1	16.4	20.8	50	10.6
Scotland	-200	1 956	-4.9	2.40	6.3	30.0	69	13.8	1	74	1	14.8	15.4	91	17.5
Scott	-1 000	14 761	5.7	2.63	12.3	23.6	612	15.0	51	374	4	9.2	6.3	481	12.0
Shannon	-300	2 917	3.1	2.58	7.0	22.8	117	14.6	9	82	1	10.4	8.7	73	9.1
Shelby	-500	2 809	-9.1	2.39	6.6	29.8	112	15.6	7	113	0	15.7	0.0	68	8.9
Stoddard	-600	11 383	6.4	2.48	9.2	24.6	345	12.0	25	358	3	12.5	9.1	359	12.6
Stone	2 400	7 885	29.1	2.40	5.8	21.5	212	11.0	11	200	1	10.6	5.0	148	8.5
Sullivan	-500	2 615	-11.4	2.33	6.2	28.8	74	11.0	2	118	0	17.6	0.0	37	5.2
Taney	4 400	10 321	28.4	2.36	6.8	24.2	265	10.4	8	312	3	12.4	10.9	251	10.8
Texas	-100	8 441	7.4	2.52	7.9	24.7	270	12.4	15	249	1	11.6	3.7	242	11.3
Vernon	-200	7 301	-2.6	2.46	9.0	28.0	257	13.0	16	263	0	13.3	0.0	204	10.3
Warren	2 700	7 070	37.5	2.73	6.6	20.1	314	16.0	20	154	2	8.1	6.8	178	10.8
Washington	200	6 982	17.3	2.83	10.4	19.7	300	15.4	25	190	2	9.8	6.8	206	11.1
Wayne	500	4 607	7.7	2.47	8.9	23.2	157	12.7	8	160	0	13.2	0.0	123	10.4
Webster	1 400	8 391	21.1	2.74	7.5	19.9	329	13.8	7	237	6	10.2	16.6	211	9.7
Worth	-200	1 037	-14.8	2.28	5.2	32.4	19	7.3	0	66	0	24.4	0.0	35	12.1
Wright	-100	6 510	7.9	2.54	8.0	25.8	233	13.7	19	172	0	10.2	0.0	156	9.4
St. Louis city	-37 500	164 931	-7.4	2.34	20.5	39.2	8 018	19.9	856	6 057	103	14.7	12.9	5 687	13.3

1. No spouse present. 2. Per 1,000 resident population estimated as of July 1 of the year shown. 3. Under 2,500 grams. 4. Deaths of infants under 1 year old. 5. Deaths of infants under 1 year old per 1,000 live births.

STATE County	Divorces, 1984		Physicians, active non–Federal, 1989		Hospitals, 1989			Nursing homes,[4] 1986		Serious crimes known to police, 1988			Education			
						Beds				Number			Public school enrollment[7]		Attainment,[8] 1980	
	Number	Rate[1]	Number[2]	Rate[3]	Number	Number	Rate[3]	Number	Beds	Total[5]	Violent[6]	Rate[3]	1986–1987	1980	Percent 12 yrs. or more	Percent 16 yrs. or more
	44	45	46	47	48	49	50	51	52	53	54	55	56	57	58	59
MISSOURI—Con.																
Laclede	162	6.2	10	38	1	53	202	7	400	791	26	2 931	4 726	5 138	55.2	7.7
Lafayette	94	3.1	17	54	1	35	111	8	581	475	44	1 541	5 276	5 714	60.9	9.4
Lawrence	121	4.1	14	45	2	138	444	5	401	NA	NA	NA	5 313	5 908	58.8	8.1
Lewis	35	3.2	0	0	0	0	0	4	271	42	2	1 801	1 789	2 172	64.1	9.2
Lincoln	82	3.4	5	17	1	64	218	8	363	NA	NA	NA	4 576	4 509	52.7	5.7
Linn	90	5.9	9	63	2	141	993	7	349	159	13	1 885	2 606	2 666	62.0	7.8
Livingston	66	4.3	12	78	1	63	409	9	394	90	6	1 467	2 480	2 993	64.0	8.8
McDonald	5	0.3	2	12	0	0	0	5	234	142	18	870	2 511	3 159	55.6	6.9
Macon	69	4.1	6	37	1	22	137	4	363	106	8	1 822	2 779	2 863	58.4	8.7
Madison	66	6.0	7	60	1	163	1 405	3	160	61	1	536	2 104	2 133	42.2	6.2
Maries	28	3.5	0	0	0	0	0	1	90	94	4	1 125	1 386	1 544	46.9	5.5
Marion	154	5.3	36	127	1	128	451	9	463	1 027	59	3 604	5 270	4 798	61.5	10.9
Mercer	17	3.8	0	0	0	0	0	2	72	NA	NA	NA	596	792	59.7	7.7
Miller	103	5.1	5	26	0	0	0	3	180	23	2	138	4 315	3 735	53.8	7.3
Mississippi	82	5.2	2	13	0	0	0	3	192	135	35	1 315	3 222	3 632	41.5	7.0
Moniteau	56	4.4	3	25	0	0	0	3	180	NA	NA	NA	2 220	2 245	55.6	8.3
Monroe	31	3.2	2	21	0	0	0	7	243	60	2	634	1 779	1 836	60.1	6.7
Montgomery	48	4.2	2	17	0	0	0	6	289	NA	NA	NA	1 962	2 346	50.9	6.0
Morgan	59	3.9	3	20	0	0	0	4	257	NA	NA	NA	1 788	2 438	52.9	6.6
New Madrid	134	5.9	5	23	0	0	0	3	314	106	34	568	4 251	5 455	41.8	6.9
Newton	178	4.1	21	48	1	67	152	8	380	774	96	6 156	6 908	8 404	63.3	9.5
Nodaway	60	2.8	12	58	1	81	393	4	270	557	10	2 646	3 251	3 613	71.6	16.3
Oregon	40	4.0	1	10	0	0	0	1	35	29	9	294	1 987	2 180	49.4	6.0
Osage	12	1.0	1	9	0	0	0	1	41	46	2	374	1 652	2 049	48.7	6.7
Ozark	42	4.8	0	0	0	0	0	0	0	146	6	1 629	1 678	1 529	51.1	7.3
Pemiscot	131	5.4	11	47	1	165	702	2	210	NA	NA	NA	5 122	5 816	39.3	6.6
Perry	39	2.3	12	70	2	85	497	3	339	132	19	776	2 228	2 490	42.9	5.6
Pettis	264	7.3	40	109	1	185	505	12	365	1 017	39	5 015	5 794	6 597	61.5	9.4
Phelps	170	4.9	39	112	1	222	636	9	692	618	18	4 663	5 742	5 963	60.9	14.9
Pike	69	4.1	9	53	1	44	260	6	257	116	11	838	2 936	3 629	57.4	9.3
Platte	342	6.9	10	17	1	55	95	6	286	3 069	416	5 750	9 396	9 603	79.8	18.9
Polk	49	2.5	14	65	1	60	279	8	221	177	8	845	3 932	3 533	57.9	9.8
Pulaski	217	5.0	17	43	1	143	360	4	272	440	129	1 004	7 936	6 916	67.2	10.3
Putnam	13	2.2	0	0	0	0	0	2	81	NA	NA	NA	884	1 193	52.2	5.6
Ralls	38	4.2	0	0	0	0	0	2	72	11	1	123	1 026	1 761	59.0	7.4
Randolph	148	5.7	18	70	1	112	434	9	567	824	63	3 135	4 334	4 460	61.4	9.1
Ray	113	5.2	7	31	1	54	238	5	247	298	47	5 091	3 678	4 898	61.1	7.5
Reynolds	32	4.4	1	15	1	29	446	2	80	109	2	1 640	1 433	1 487	42.3	4.8
Ripley	94	7.4	4	30	1	26	197	3	122	51	3	396	2 337	2 366	37.2	4.8
St. Charles	848	5.1	164	76	5	718	333	14	951	6 476	440	3 330	30 914	27 129	71.3	13.7
St. Clair	42	4.9	5	60	2	69	821	2	180	213	11	2 518	1 486	1 705	52.3	7.7
Ste. Genevieve	50	3.2	9	54	1	51	307	4	192	243	8	1 489	1 768	2 432	51.3	6.2
St. Francois	302	6.9	38	78	4	479	986	24	794	788	92	1 735	8 912	8 120	52.8	7.8
St. Louis	4 127	4.2	1 150	114	4	1 095	108	62	7 075	38 532	2 812	3 878	136 843	158 640	73.9	22.9
Saline	122	4.9	16	66	2	74	305	6	357	654	33	2 661	3 887	4 425	56.3	9.9
Schuyler	15	3.2	0	0	0	0	0	1	60	35	2	790	787	976	59.9	7.1
Scotland	12	2.3	0	0	1	26	531	2	144	36	0	715	712	1 009	59.9	7.3
Scott	253	6.3	40	98	2	179	439	7	405	1 120	66	2 753	8 089	8 422	51.4	7.7
Shannon	39	4.9	2	25	0	0	0	2	97	NA	NA	NA	810	1 696	45.5	5.9
Shelby	31	4.1	2	28	0	0	0	2	180	89	0	1 227	1 317	1 490	60.7	6.8
Stoddard	220	7.7	11	38	1	40	140	11	374	NA	NA	NA	5 701	6 098	46.2	6.7
Stone	71	4.1	3	15	0	0	0	2	240	NA	NA	NA	2 960	2 886	62.0	11.3
Sullivan	20	2.8	0	0	1	45	692	4	225	38	1	572	1 050	1 364	54.6	6.3
Taney	133	5.7	18	70	1	99	384	3	191	726	88	2 884	3 740	3 231	65.4	12.6
Texas	107	5.0	6	28	1	53	245	6	197	NA	NA	NA	4 345	4 274	50.1	6.6
Vernon	127	6.4	23	117	3	269	1 365	3	198	580	44	2 924	3 138	3 616	62.5	10.0
Warren	56	3.4	5	25	0	0	0	3	215	224	28	1 171	2 609	2 899	53.6	7.7
Washington	69	3.7	4	20	1	42	213	4	164	98	8	3 746	3 829	4 326	38.9	4.2
Wayne	50	4.2	3	24	0	0	0	3	119	146	8	1 218	1 904	2 204	35.9	4.0
Webster	74	3.4	10	41	0	0	0	4	141	65	6	281	3 900	4 499	55.6	6.7
Worth	9	3.1	0	0	0	0	0	2	75	35	2	1 287	435	589	60.9	10.6
Wright	90	5.4	6	35	1	51	300	3	190	NA	NA	NA	3 482	3 391	47.1	6.0
St. Louis city	1 575	3.7	4 123	1 047	26	9 324	2 368	68	5 431	57 215	10 481	13 456	48 209	65 707	48.2	10.0

1. Per 1,000 resident population estimated as of July 1 of the year shown. 2. As of end of year. 3. Per 100,000 resident population as of July 1 of the year shown. 4. Preliminary. Covers nursing homes with 3 or more beds. 5. Data for serious crimes have not been adjusted for underreporting, this may affect comparability between geographic areas or over time. 6. Includes murder and nonnegligent manslaughter, forcible rape, robbery, and aggravated assault. 7. The 1986–1987 data are based on administrative reports obtained by the U.S. National Center for Education Statistics. The 1980 data are based on the 1980 Census of Population and Housing. 8. Persons 25 years old or older.

STATE County	Education (cont'd)		Social Security Program December 1988				Money income						Housing units, 1990	
	Local government expenditures for education,[1] 1982		Beneficiaries				Per capita[3]				Percent below poverty level, 1979			
								1979						
	Total (Mil dol)	Per capita (Dollars)	Total	Rate[2]	Payments ($1,000)	Supplemental Security Income Program recipients June 1986	1987 Income, (Dollars)	Current dollars	Constant 1987 dollars	Median household income 1979 (Dollars)	Persons	Families	Total	Percent change, 1980–1990
	60	61	62	63	64	65	66	67	68	69	70	71	72	73
MISSOURI—Con.														
Laclede	7.9	321	5 400	204.5	2 185	744	8 378	5 287	8 273	11 123	17.3	13.9	11 564	17.5
Lafayette	10.6	355	6 385	204.0	3 018	336	9 864	6 558	10 261	15 638	10.5	7.6	12 820	8.0
Lawrence	9.0	313	6 455	208.9	2 745	542	8 249	5 187	8 116	11 532	14.9	12.1	12 788	8.8
Lewis	3.8	342	2 235	219.1	980	184	8 314	5 648	8 837	13 703	13.5	10.2	4 244	-3.1
Lincoln	7.4	328	4 165	147.2	1 966	304	9 672	6 124	9 582	15 561	10.7	7.9	12 284	27.2
Linn	6.1	391	3 825	265.6	1 580	304	9 437	6 103	9 549	11 265	13.4	10.1	6 566	-8.0
Livingston	5.8	371	3 405	222.5	1 504	334	9 573	6 561	10 266	13 311	14.8	11.8	6 294	-6.1
McDonald	3.9	262	3 010	183.5	1 211	456	7 659	4 769	7 462	10 347	22.1	18.4	7 327	14.4
Macon	5.8	348	3 895	239.0	1 657	276	9 042	6 095	9 537	12 606	12.8	9.9	6 955	-3.6
Madison	3.7	343	2 855	248.3	1 227	328	7 362	4 853	7 593	9 616	21.7	17.1	5 282	5.3
Maries	2.7	352	1 435	181.6	589	144	7 763	5 077	7 944	11 605	15.8	12.2	3 715	8.7
Marion	11.6	400	6 080	213.3	2 777	628	9 096	6 174	9 660	13 928	12.0	8.2	12 026	1.9
Mercer	1.5	315	1 040	260.0	415	94	7 525	5 163	8 079	9 856	20.1	15.8	2 225	-9.6
Miller	8.0	422	4 240	213.1	1 801	394	8 093	5 315	8 316	11 859	14.4	11.6	9 766	23.2
Mississippi	7.2	456	3 400	219.4	1 374	866	7 020	4 766	7 457	10 373	25.7	19.7	5 757	-4.6
Moniteau	4.4	358	2 480	203.3	1 091	140	8 793	5 572	8 719	12 952	12.1	8.8	5 043	8.8
Monroe	4.0	417	2 115	225.0	920	184	8 545	5 573	8 720	12 400	16.5	12.9	4 114	0.5
Montgomery	4.1	355	2 790	240.5	1 258	178	8 859	5 648	8 837	12 277	13.4	9.6	5 241	1.4
Morgan	3.2	224	4 065	265.7	1 818	288	8 133	5 125	8 019	10 383	17.9	15.0	12 642	21.4
New Madrid	11.7	513	4 170	192.2	1 598	1 232	7 321	4 742	7 420	10 044	27.4	21.9	8 557	-5.2
Newton	12.1	296	7 035	160.6	3 077	566	9 139	5 666	8 866	12 528	14.4	11.6	18 384	14.6
Nodaway	8.2	370	3 985	191.6	1 713	316	8 340	5 714	8 941	12 616	16.8	12.1	8 349	-1.9
Oregon	4.4	437	2 535	258.7	944	476	6 559	4 120	6 447	7 937	28.6	22.6	4 484	-0.3
Osage	3.4	282	2 130	180.5	887	170	8 925	5 454	8 534	14 212	12.6	9.4	5 414	7.2
Ozark	3.2	386	2 105	233.9	846	338	7 454	4 520	7 072	9 152	25.4	21.2	4 451	18.8
Pemiscot	12.1	489	5 220	220.3	1 901	1 888	6 787	4 431	6 933	9 142	33.1	25.1	8 806	-10.3
Perry	4.4	260	3 410	199.4	1 498	242	8 227	5 194	8 127	12 734	12.5	10.3	6 867	6.4
Pettis	11.9	330	7 155	195.5	3 203	712	9 698	6 395	10 006	13 399	11.9	8.9	15 443	1.2
Phelps	11.7	337	6 405	184.1	2 729	656	9 357	5 726	8 959	12 367	15.9	10.6	14 715	13.9
Pike	7.6	441	3 370	199.4	1 532	326	8 963	6 055	9 474	12 933	17.4	12.8	7 128	-3.5
Platte	21.5	447	5 095	90.7	2 640	180	13 702	8 687	13 593	22 499	5.3	4.5	24 362	35.8
Polk	6.8	351	4 680	220.8	1 918	486	8 090	5 110	7 996	10 731	16.7	13.0	8 979	15.9
Pulaski	13.9	317	4 020	98.8	1 574	462	8 099	4 935	7 722	12 181	15.2	11.7	13 838	16.6
Putnam	2.3	369	1 480	274.1	560	134	7 952	5 235	8 191	9 752	20.8	17.3	2 590	-10.3
Ralls	1.9	214	1 405	157.9	609	110	9 273	6 257	9 790	15 316	11.1	8.8	3 766	10.4
Randolph	8.6	339	4 720	181.5	2 076	458	8 780	5 982	9 360	13 252	13.5	9.5	10 131	0.0
Ray	6.7	312	3 335	147.6	1 564	180	10 224	6 676	10 446	16 714	9.2	8.0	8 611	4.6
Reynolds	3.7	527	1 485	221.6	594	264	6 603	4 654	7 282	10 279	24.3	20.3	3 537	2.6
Ripley	4.4	353	3 150	240.5	1 245	646	6 191	3 917	6 129	8 004	29.8	24.8	5 597	4.9
St. Charles	61.2	399	18 610	91.0	9 552	768	13 034	7 679	12 015	22 408	4.4	3.4	79 113	58.1
St. Clair	2.9	332	2 220	264.3	915	220	7 395	4 991	7 809	9 394	22.9	19.1	4 645	11.6
Ste. Genevieve	3.5	233	2 760	168.3	1 277	164	9 027	5 863	9 174	16 093	10.4	7.7	6 766	14.1
St. Francois	17.0	400	10 645	224.1	4 949	1 162	8 550	5 534	8 659	13 182	14.0	10.5	20 321	16.7
St. Louis	416.8	425	154 740	153.4	84 720	5 982	15 654	9 214	14 417	22 127	4.9	3.5	401 839	12.2
Saline	8.2	330	5 480	224.6	2 510	522	9 051	5 995	9 380	13 154	12.1	9.2	10 033	-2.6
Schuyler	1.9	379	1 325	301.1	520	122	8 318	5 255	8 222	10 645	19.4	15.4	1 986	-5.7
Scotland	2.0	371	1 285	257.0	517	106	8 221	5 411	8 467	9 957	20.3	15.3	2 302	-2.3
Scott	15.9	399	7 905	193.8	3 358	1 288	8 508	5 565	8 708	12 886	16.7	13.3	15 881	4.4
Shannon	1.8	226	1 485	185.6	558	284	6 115	4 097	6 411	8 985	25.5	22.3	3 312	2.2
Shelby	3.5	453	1 925	267.4	825	118	8 294	5 475	8 567	11 030	16.9	12.3	3 277	-9.5
Stoddard	11.4	398	6 710	233.8	2 720	1 138	8 057	5 096	7 974	10 885	17.6	13.3	12 288	2.5
Stone	5.4	336	4 530	235.9	2 031	270	8 800	5 510	8 621	11 461	18.2	13.9	11 294	27.7
Sullivan	2.0	275	1 910	285.1	714	286	8 054	5 211	8 154	9 652	20.6	15.9	3 093	-11.7
Taney	6.0	277	6 745	265.6	3 100	386	9 243	5 805	9 083	11 849	13.8	10.1	13 273	29.2
Texas	9.0	423	4 790	220.7	1 850	566	7 321	4 699	7 353	9 810	20.8	16.4	9 525	9.4
Vernon	6.7	342	4 340	220.3	1 821	604	8 932	5 893	9 221	11 993	13.5	9.9	8 181	-1.9
Warren	4.4	280	3 000	153.1	1 448	178	10 494	6 793	10 629	16 105	9.2	6.5	8 841	35.2
Washington	6.9	379	3 200	164.1	1 340	602	6 999	4 539	7 102	11 421	20.8	17.2	8 075	13.6
Wayne	4.1	353	3 530	284.7	1 442	552	7 190	4 484	7 016	8 464	25.6	21.2	6 406	13.1
Webster	6.0	290	4 410	185.3	1 777	510	8 197	5 304	8 299	12 012	17.3	13.9	9 067	17.7
Worth	1.2	388	755	290.4	294	54	8 278	5 108	7 992	9 342	20.3	15.5	1 269	-13.0
Wright	6.0	367	4 110	241.8	1 507	710	7 247	4 836	7 567	9 728	23.3	18.5	7 214	7.6
St. Louis city	177.9	408	87 510	216.9	42 258	13 386	9 718	5 877	9 196	11 511	21.8	16.6	194 919	-3.6

1. Elementary and secondary. 2. Per 1,000 resident population estimated as of July 1 of the year shown. 3. Based on the resident population estimated as of July 1, 1988 for 1987 data and enumerated as of April 1, 1980 for 1979 data.

STATE County	Housing units, 1990 (cont'd)				Civilian labor force, 1990				Private nonfarm establishments, 1988					
	Occupied units						Unemployment				Employment[2]			
	Total	Owner occupied: Percent	Owner occupied: Median value (Dollars)	Median rent (Dollars)	Total	Percent change, 1989–1990	Total	Rate[1]	Number	Net change, 1987–1988	Total	Percent change, 1987–1988	Manufacturing	Retail trade
	74	75	76	77	78	79	80	81	82	83	84	85	86	87
MISSOURI—Con.														
Laclede	10 420	73.5	42 100	193	13 703	-0.2	1 448	10.6	691	27	8 529	13.2	4 077	1 938
Lafayette	11 732	74.1	45 300	212	15 437	0.0	982	6.4	668	7	6 095	10.5	1 532	1 573
Lawrence	11 724	74.4	37 900	188	12 844	-8.4	788	6.1	539	8	5 335	-3.8	2 032	1 204
Lewis	3 745	74.0	28 000	157	4 828	1.5	226	4.7	206	2	1 540	6.8	0	290
Lincoln	10 316	80.0	55 200	236	13 118	2.5	1 003	7.6	528	-12	4 233	-2.1	755	1 176
Linn	5 704	77.6	22 400	150	6 520	1.0	522	8.0	391	1	4 196	11.0	1 878	737
Livingston	5 645	70.9	35 800	185	6 531	-1.3	306	4.7	443	-8	4 550	7.9	825	1 113
McDonald	6 386	75.6	31 800	171	9 359	3.0	443	4.7	272	13	3 429	8.3	1 964	675
Macon	6 160	76.5	32 700	168	8 284	-1.7	617	7.4	347	26	3 253	13.3	1 132	895
Madison	4 344	76.7	33 100	181	4 845	7.6	432	8.9	249	20	2 313	0.2	857	598
Maries	3 028	82.2	35 000	160	3 901	1.9	277	7.1	127	3	832	6.4	279	168
Marion	10 728	69.1	36 000	189	14 045	2.4	763	5.4	789	11	8 338	1.1	1 965	2 048
Mercer	1 577	75.0	18 900	130	1 405	2.2	91	6.5	80	-5	404	10.1	0	131
Miller	7 977	76.2	43 700	195	9 423	4.1	969	10.3	594	-26	5 392	9.4	1 614	1 249
Mississippi	5 411	64.9	32 300	136	6 667	0.8	644	9.7	317	-13	3 169	6.4	1 160	655
Moniteau	4 583	78.8	38 700	178	6 764	9.3	441	6.5	295	5	2 773	10.9	1 231	501
Monroe	3 471	77.5	31 800	167	4 855	1.1	223	4.6	234	0	2 088	0.2	0	438
Montgomery	4 341	78.9	33 000	176	5 143	4.1	374	7.3	315	-10	2 304	-5.6	676	532
Morgan	6 269	80.7	45 300	184	7 514	-1.6	575	7.7	417	-22	2 624	12.1	624	915
New Madrid	7 795	64.0	32 800	143	9 767	0.9	844	8.6	358	3	4 711	4.5	0	720
Newton	16 886	76.9	42 900	210	22 814	1.8	1 472	6.5	782	4	11 544	3.3	5 139	1 874
Nodaway	7 620	65.4	37 100	214	11 101	2.0	334	3.0	462	-6	5 011	2.0	1 264	1 434
Oregon	3 851	79.0	26 000	132	3 565	5.7	242	6.8	185	-2	1 081	-2.8	153	450
Osage	4 262	82.9	43 700	163	6 120	0.8	306	5.0	222	-11	1 737	-2.7	734	315
Ozark	3 486	82.0	36 500	149	3 521	-3.7	248	7.0	154	13	682	4.8	151	226
Pemiscot	8 210	56.9	28 800	120	8 949	0.2	767	8.6	367	-2	3 624	-7.2	1 112	844
Perry	6 111	81.1	43 500	188	9 624	7.9	475	4.9	385	10	4 020	-5.5	1 054	1 086
Pettis	14 056	74.5	40 100	223	18 448	0.7	1 264	6.9	1 002	9	11 551	5.9	3 899	2 701
Phelps	13 277	65.6	47 200	216	16 848	-1.8	830	4.9	919	46	7 504	0.6	870	2 770
Pike	6 083	74.7	32 600	169	7 499	0.8	559	7.5	398	6	3 413	1.2	1 262	781
Platte	22 142	65.1	81 200	371	30 885	-0.3	1 296	4.2	1 185	91	19 882	2.0	1 198	3 237
Polk	8 031	73.5	39 600	185	11 347	4.7	559	4.9	447	-8	3 629	-0.2	539	997
Pulaski	12 397	55.6	51 400	278	12 969	1.0	934	7.2	583	23	4 867	-1.6	1 017	1 579
Putnam	2 166	77.0	21 300	134	2 234	2.4	106	4.7	144	8	599	-8.1	64	151
Ralls	3 226	80.3	37 900	177	4 092	3.1	270	6.6	154	7	1 354	1.5	622	150
Randolph	8 943	73.0	33 200	185	11 141	-1.4	635	5.7	517	-30	6 430	-1.6	1 258	1 368
Ray	8 020	79.0	46 400	224	10 612	0.9	810	7.6	362	-10	2 575	-4.2	546	656
Reynolds	2 542	76.5	29 300	147	2 286	8.9	201	8.8	158	0	1 265	25.2	525	142
Ripley	4 788	75.7	29 200	143	4 458	7.6	309	6.9	194	10	1 203	20.2	465	382
St. Charles	74 331	76.4	83 600	395	111 123	0.1	5 380	4.8	4 240	217	53 058	-0.7	10 119	16 723
St. Clair	3 499	75.2	28 400	141	3 915	4.8	307	7.8	168	-6	1 018	-25.3	102	318
Ste. Genevieve	5 707	82.7	53 800	192	6 554	3.7	450	6.9	311	15	4 375	4.4	2 080	653
St. Francois	17 670	74.0	40 200	224	21 663	-1.1	1 946	9.0	1 036	34	11 092	3.1	3 068	2 623
St. Louis	380 110	73.9	83 500	397	566 279	0.0	23 952	4.2	28 423	506	488 814	4.9	85 522	103 241
Saline	8 903	70.6	37 600	197	11 025	-2.1	781	7.1	574	0	6 768	2.4	2 705	1 335
Schuyler	1 729	75.4	20 400	136	2 037	2.8	98	4.8	80	3	320	0.3	0	118
Scotland	1 956	73.6	24 300	140	2 089	-1.5	96	4.6	138	-10	796	4.5	245	222
Scott	14 761	69.1	41 700	201	18 633	-1.2	1 374	7.4	1 103	39	12 065	-3.1	3 023	3 031
Shannon	2 917	78.7	25 900	125	3 418	2.8	362	10.6	123	0	1 079	-13.7	597	141
Shelby	2 809	75.7	22 900	138	3 493	0.3	152	4.4	183	6	1 072	-1.3	0	265
Stoddard	11 383	71.9	34 100	160	13 542	2.8	1 076	7.9	691	-13	6 579	2.5	2 582	1 354
Stone	7 885	81.6	58 800	217	8 764	3.4	883	10.1	450	27	2 555	-8.4	521	621
Sullivan	2 615	75.6	16 100	144	3 582	8.2	132	3.7	121	-1	1 149	-8.6	0	154
Taney	10 321	74.7	55 400	225	17 591	9.2	1 419	8.1	963	39	6 469	3.8	418	1 956
Texas	8 441	75.3	33 700	149	9 194	3.8	830	9.0	480	13	4 542	6.5	2 363	896
Vernon	7 301	72.5	32 100	179	8 908	0.0	418	4.7	419	-9	4 411	4.0	1 219	1 061
Warren	7 070	80.8	63 600	259	9 489	-3.6	744	7.8	373	24	4 343	2.2	1 909	991
Washington	6 982	78.5	34 200	180	7 081	8.2	1 055	14.9	263	0	1 667	-5.7	297	483
Wayne	4 607	76.5	29 000	156	5 536	11.8	501	9.0	195	6	1 947	30.1	1 093	440
Webster	8 391	77.8	41 200	190	10 991	9.5	945	8.6	406	7	3 164	2.4	1 181	827
Worth	1 037	75.9	14 999	118	1 237	9.6	60	4.9	68	-4	292	4.7	0	72
Wright	6 510	73.7	31 100	156	7 397	7.3	668	9.0	315	9	3 569	12.8	1 662	649
St. Louis city	164 931	45.1	50 700	252	187 334	-0.4	15 337	8.2	10 167	-116	286 102	-3.2	86 732	36 381

1. Percent of total civilian labor force. 2. For week including March 12. Excludes government employees, self-employed persons, farm workers, domestic service workers, railroad employees subject to the Railroad Retirement Act, and employees on oceanborne vessels or in foreign countries.

STATE County	Private nonfarm establishments, 1988 (cont'd): Employment[1] (cont'd): Finance, insurance, and real estate	Private nonfarm establishments, 1988 (cont'd): Employment[1] (cont'd): Services	Annual payroll: Total (Mil dol)	Annual payroll: Average per employee (Dollars)	Personal income, 1989: Total (Mil dol)	Percent change, 1988–1989	Wages and salaries[2] (Mil dol)	Proprietor's income (Mil dol)	Dividends, interest, & rent (Mil dol)	Transfer payments (Mil dol)	Per capita[3]: Dollars	Per capita[3]: Rank	Earnings, 1989: Total (Mil dol)	Percent by selected industries: Farm	Goods-related[4]: Total
	88	89	90	91	92	93	94	95	96	97	98	99	100	101	102
MISSOURI—Con.															
Laclede	432	1 172	116	13 609	347	6.3	169	55	65	67	13 185	1 820	224	3.6	42.5
Lafayette	335	1 554	72	11 815	484	5.0	130	61	101	88	15 385	841	190	8.6	21.5
Lawrence	205	779	72	13 561	383	6.4	125	50	74	77	12 333	2 186	174	6.8	27.0
Lewis	88	504	24	15 486	128	5.3	39	18	29	26	12 685	2 041	56	10.7	NA
Lincoln	180	763	62	14 652	411	7.8	98	32	66	56	13 985	1 440	129	5.3	23.5
Linn	173	968	53	12 602	187	5.8	85	25	45	45	13 199	1 815	111	7.9	29.3
Livingston	228	1 174	65	14 280	217	6.0	103	28	64	37	14 125	1 382	131	4.8	23.4
McDonald	142	314	44	12 698	183	10.0	66	26	27	38	10 990	2 667	92	11.7	42.1
Macon	153	477	39	12 093	220	8.7	74	30	56	46	13 624	1 616	104	7.5	24.9
Madison	0	219	25	10 634	133	5.4	42	20	22	34	11 466	2 516	61	6.4	27.0
Maries	0	162	11	13 125	95	6.5	20	15	18	20	11 998	2 328	36	13.6	21.6
Marion	324	2 375	120	14 437	393	6.6	213	53	81	77	13 851	1 505	265	2.9	31.9
Mercer	20	93	5	12 238	46	7.0	10	10	13	11	11 635	2 462	20	27.3	NA
Miller	181	1 163	85	15 687	260	8.5	111	36	49	54	13 257	1 790	147	4.8	33.2
Mississippi	89	601	42	13 302	166	4.8	65	26	28	43	10 838	2 704	92	12.6	19.2
Moniteau	100	435	37	13 336	174	7.2	56	25	38	30	14 469	1 225	81	6.7	32.9
Monroe	78	360	29	13 698	137	10.0	56	23	34	24	14 581	1 175	78	12.8	39.5
Montgomery	138	416	27	11 735	165	7.3	47	20	40	32	14 173	1 358	68	7.4	34.6
Morgan	145	426	31	11 646	190	8.2	50	36	45	45	12 463	2 135	86	11.2	27.3
New Madrid	160	526	103	21 775	228	2.8	171	39	33	55	10 609	2 769	210	11.6	47.5
Newton	397	2 940	172	14 914	549	7.0	240	79	94	87	12 443	2 143	319	3.3	41.4
Nodaway	219	1 302	66	13 111	274	9.2	143	37	62	47	13 307	1 767	179	5.1	36.7
Oregon	58	175	10	9 388	87	4.2	27	15	17	28	8 895	3 013	42	9.6	13.8
Osage	88	222	25	14 333	174	7.7	42	27	35	26	14 956	1 007	69	17.4	28.2
Ozark	58	117	8	11 471	97	7.5	18	18	20	25	10 638	2 757	37	27.1	13.1
Pemiscot	207	877	42	11 607	239	3.9	92	24	37	74	10 152	2 862	116	7.9	19.3
Perry	176	1 013	52	12 981	239	10.6	106	31	50	38	13 984	1 442	136	7.2	NA
Pettis	550	2 482	178	15 392	527	6.8	274	61	111	98	14 390	1 253	335	2.9	32.8
Phelps	364	2 344	93	12 329	465	6.5	236	47	82	102	13 351	1 756	284	0.8	11.3
Pike	114	703	56	16 356	207	6.0	87	23	45	43	12 219	2 222	111	6.2	33.4
Platte	537	4 666	435	21 897	1 066	9.1	754	64	139	69	18 329	263	817	1.3	9.7
Polk	195	947	47	12 930	274	8.9	79	48	53	56	12 750	2 017	127	10.5	16.1
Pulaski	250	1 166	55	11 384	438	9.9	346	33	39	78	11 022	2 662	379	1.0	6.0
Putnam	50	101	6	10 618	64	9.5	15	14	18	15	11 932	2 347	28	20.3	NA
Ralls	52	287	24	18 081	120	5.4	26	19	25	20	13 445	1 715	45	21.4	23.0
Randolph	385	1 541	113	17 640	320	6.3	194	35	70	71	12 428	2 151	228	3.5	28.3
Ray	183	411	31	12 186	330	5.3	61	28	55	44	14 540	1 194	90	8.6	20.3
Reynolds	0	145	18	14 614	69	13.0	33	8	10	18	10 514	2 787	41	5.4	54.5
Ripley	82	131	13	10 962	110	6.5	30	15	22	40	8 294	3 054	45	8.1	21.4
St. Charles	1 829	15 102	1 024	19 294	3 738	9.5	1 511	218	405	282	17 361	385	1 729	0.8	39.0
St. Clair	51	343	9	9 061	100	6.4	26	20	30	25	11 931	2 348	47	15.4	7.3
Ste. Genevieve	148	657	75	17 241	224	8.3	97	20	41	39	13 535	1 665	117	4.1	NA
St. Francois	555	3 276	149	13 475	611	5.6	251	58	99	132	12 588	2 076	309	2.8	26.1
St. Louis	36 357	154 702	11 007	22 518	22 837	7.0	16 173	1 526	5 054	2 230	22 598	79	17 700	0.0	34.5
Saline	216	1 546	95	14 021	346	5.0	157	47	80	77	14 264	1 300	204	6.9	26.3
Schuyler	0	32	3	10 447	53	7.2	10	10	14	14	12 412	2 157	19	20.0	NA
Scotland	45	134	8	9 648	64	8.8	17	12	20	14	13 139	1 845	29	11.5	NA
Scott	520	2 837	179	14 830	528	6.9	264	76	87	105	12 950	1 927	339	3.9	NA
Shannon	46	204	13	11 956	64	10.4	20	10	11	19	8 001	3 077	30	6.1	36.1
Shelby	99	144	16	15 005	98	7.5	31	16	30	21	13 894	1 478	47	12.6	NA
Stoddard	295	1 115	92	13 930	371	4.9	159	65	63	79	12 978	1 914	224	11.5	34.7
Stone	176	814	38	14 722	240	6.9	58	29	67	53	12 188	2 240	87	3.4	22.4
Sullivan	59	223	15	13 177	82	10.3	28	14	21	21	12 626	2 065	42	17.8	29.1
Taney	329	2 612	98	15 074	351	8.5	142	51	93	79	13 625	1 615	193	1.8	13.4
Texas	143	512	53	11 684	227	5.2	84	38	41	57	10 496	2 790	122	4.2	32.5
Vernon	495	1 115	66	15 054	266	5.7	126	36	50	71	13 510	1 675	162	5.3	23.6
Warren	332	594	67	15 400	296	7.4	95	26	49	38	14 579	1 176	121	4.0	43.7
Washington	96	425	23	13 502	211	9.6	62	19	23	47	10 688	2 743	81	3.5	25.9
Wayne	58	224	19	9 619	108	6.5	37	12	18	40	8 619	3 035	49	2.9	36.3
Webster	152	330	41	12 917	265	7.4	74	39	42	48	10 962	2 674	113	8.3	35.3
Worth	0	33	3	8 908	33	9.0	8	7	10	7	12 684	2 042	15	26.8	NA
Wright	159	668	41	11 497	168	7.5	69	28	32	45	9 841	2 903	97	11.6	NA
St. Louis city	21 386	85 927	7 009	24 500	6 896	6.3	8 363	542	1 513	1 481	17 513	367	8 906	0.0	23.8

1. For week including March 12. Excludes government employees, self-employed persons, farm workers, domestic service workers, railroad employees subject to the Railroad Retirement Act, and employees on oceanborne vessels or in foreign countries. 2. Includes other labor income. 3. Based on the resident population estimated as of July 1 of the year shown. 4. Covers mining, construction, and manufacturing.

STATE County	Earnings, 1989 (cont'd): Percent by selected industries (cont'd): Goods-related[1]: Manu-facturing	Service-related & other[2]: Total	Service-related & other[2]: Retail trade	Service-related & other[2]: Finance, insur-ance, & real estate	Service-related & other[2]: Services	Govern-ment	Agriculture, 1987: Farms: Number	Farms: Percent with: Less than 50 acres	Farms: Percent with: 500 acres and over	Farm operators, percent: Whose principal occu-pation is farming	Farm operators, percent: Residing on farm operated	Land in farms: Acreage (1,000)	Land in farms: Percent change, 1982–1987	Land in farms: Acres: Average size of farm	Acres: Total irrigated (1,000)	Acres: Total cropland (1,000)
	103	104	105	106	107	108	109	110	111	112	113	114	115	116	117	118
MISSOURI—Con.																
Laclede	37.2	44.6	12.3	3.2	18.1	9.3	1 271	19.6	13.1	46.8	79.2	316	5.5	249	0	162
Lafayette	14.0	51.2	11.5	4.6	23.2	18.7	1 465	25.8	13.8	55.3	72.0	352	-1.4	240	2	279
Lawrence	19.7	47.6	12.3	2.8	15.9	18.6	1 757	27.6	6.8	47.8	79.2	317	-1.9	181	1	208
Lewis	14.7	NA	9.3	3.7	23.4	19.0	721	16.2	20.4	56.9	71.0	256	-4.8	355	1	182
Lincoln	11.4	51.9	12.0	3.8	19.5	19.2	1 155	27.1	13.7	46.1	72.6	275	-1.0	238	2	203
Linn	27.1	50.1	8.9	3.0	18.4	12.7	959	17.4	21.8	63.0	71.9	334	1.9	348	0	255
Livingston	15.6	56.7	11.4	5.6	20.2	15.1	801	17.0	19.4	56.6	69.7	272	1.1	339	1	212
McDonald	36.8	34.9	8.5	2.3	11.4	11.3	1 152	27.0	6.1	46.4	79.2	201	2.7	174	0	87
Macon	20.0	42.7	11.2	4.1	14.9	24.8	1 172	13.5	19.7	51.8	71.9	393	1.9	336	0	264
Madison	20.1	48.4	12.0	3.6	20.8	18.3	410	15.4	12.4	38.8	75.1	111	0.0	271	D	42
Maries	15.9	50.1	8.2	3.8	19.5	14.7	834	15.9	16.7	41.4	72.8	233	2.7	279	0	95
Marion	22.6	52.5	11.0	2.9	23.2	12.8	770	18.4	20.1	60.1	73.1	234	-0.4	304	2	172
Mercer	NA	46.6	6.8	3.6	14.1	20.2	547	10.1	23.6	64.9	61.2	198	-9.3	363	D	133
Miller	22.9	49.8	13.4	2.4	17.8	12.2	1 091	15.2	9.2	44.2	76.1	233	-2.3	214	0	101
Mississippi	17.1	52.8	10.0	2.6	13.7	15.4	340	11.8	50.9	81.2	50.9	259	2.4	762	37	251
Moniteau	24.2	46.3	11.2	3.7	18.4	14.1	1 046	20.8	10.7	43.5	71.8	233	5.8	223	0	146
Monroe	36.5	32.6	5.5	3.1	9.2	15.1	953	12.7	21.8	58.8	71.7	330	5.2	346	2	245
Montgomery	24.3	43.9	10.2	5.0	14.9	14.0	832	16.8	16.7	51.9	67.1	235	-7.3	282	2	163
Morgan	13.3	48.5	16.2	3.3	19.1	13.0	889	18.9	11.5	48.3	71.9	207	1.1	233	0	107
New Madrid	45.4	31.2	7.5	1.6	7.0	9.7	532	7.7	53.4	82.5	53.6	369	0.7	694	81	360
Newton	34.8	45.6	11.0	2.5	22.8	9.6	1 768	32.3	5.8	39.7	79.3	267	11.1	151	1	153
Nodaway	31.0	38.1	8.8	2.9	15.1	20.1	1 475	16.4	25.0	68.5	72.4	529	3.4	359	D	426
Oregon	8.2	58.4	14.4	3.2	15.8	18.1	837	15.9	13.0	45.9	76.1	252	2.6	301	0	87
Osage	21.0	41.8	9.7	3.7	14.9	12.5	1 160	14.3	13.0	45.0	70.4	301	-4.5	259	1	131
Ozark	7.3	42.0	10.3	4.6	17.8	17.8	856	11.2	16.0	50.9	75.9	278	10.3	325	0	92
Pemiscot	17.0	48.7	10.1	3.3	17.5	24.1	453	13.9	50.1	77.9	59.8	296	3.6	653	26	285
Perry	30.6	NA	9.0	3.0	17.9	9.9	959	23.7	10.6	49.2	71.4	222	-1.8	231	0	149
Pettis	24.7	49.4	12.4	4.4	20.4	15.0	1 323	24.6	16.3	52.0	75.4	372	0.3	281	0	268
Phelps	5.9	47.9	13.7	3.2	21.9	39.9	773	22.5	12.4	37.9	75.0	202	-6.0	262	0	79
Pike	23.7	43.6	9.1	3.3	18.2	16.8	1 037	18.8	18.5	55.4	69.7	337	-2.4	325	1	229
Platte	4.7	81.7	5.0	2.3	13.6	7.3	794	31.0	15.2	50.0	67.9	194	-2.5	245	1	147
Polk	9.2	58.3	11.4	3.4	27.4	15.1	1 613	22.8	9.3	48.5	77.8	338	3.0	210	1	196
Pulaski	3.3	23.9	7.4	1.6	11.1	69.1	528	16.1	13.6	38.4	72.7	140	-7.6	265	0	59
Putnam	3.7	NA	9.2	4.9	NA	22.3	661	11.6	27.2	59.8	69.6	272	8.2	411	0	167
Ralls	17.4	40.1	5.4	3.8	17.8	15.5	650	15.5	24.9	60.2	74.8	246	4.5	379	0	183
Randolph	14.4	53.7	9.0	4.6	17.4	14.5	791	20.2	15.5	52.6	74.3	235	9.4	298	0	151
Ray	9.7	49.5	9.6	4.1	18.3	21.6	1 136	23.2	12.6	43.7	72.8	285	-6.6	251	1	218
Reynolds	39.7	25.9	5.6	1.1	10.8	14.2	307	9.8	14.0	32.9	71.0	87	-23.9	284	0	34
Ripley	19.4	48.2	12.3	3.2	21.0	22.4	511	18.4	15.3	47.9	73.2	144	7.4	281	4	71
St. Charles	29.0	50.7	14.7	3.0	22.9	9.4	901	30.2	14.3	50.8	68.9	218	-7.3	242	2	171
St. Clair	1.3	58.0	10.7	3.9	20.4	19.3	782	14.8	20.8	53.3	73.7	259	-1.8	331	1	151
Ste. Genevieve	39.4	NA	7.4	2.8	11.9	10.4	666	18.3	13.2	36.9	73.1	179	1.3	268	0	95
St. Francois	17.9	49.8	12.0	3.3	24.3	21.4	681	24.4	6.8	34.9	76.8	122	-0.3	179	0	65
St. Louis	27.7	58.5	9.5	7.1	25.6	7.0	357	50.4	9.2	42.9	50.4	57	2.4	160	1	39
Saline	22.2	45.7	8.7	3.3	20.2	21.2	1 083	17.2	26.4	65.7	65.9	436	9.4	402	1	352
Schuyler	NA	51.0	10.9	3.1	16.4	24.4	498	12.4	18.5	60.8	73.1	156	-2.6	314	0	111
Scotland	10.1	NA	11.0	4.6	15.6	23.5	585	11.3	25.1	65.6	67.7	214	-5.9	365	D	166
Scott	13.0	NA	11.1	3.5	23.0	13.9	642	23.7	25.1	59.0	61.8	241	5.2	376	30	221
Shannon	32.0	37.8	7.8	3.0	15.0	20.1	445	15.7	13.3	46.1	80.7	118	2.6	265	D	49
Shelby	14.3	NA	8.4	3.6	14.7	18.3	755	15.5	28.1	71.8	67.5	295	6.6	391	2	226
Stoddard	28.5	43.0	9.5	3.5	16.3	10.8	1 159	19.0	26.1	64.3	65.7	434	2.5	375	139	403
Stone	5.7	61.2	13.3	4.0	36.0	13.0	782	21.5	6.0	46.3	77.4	148	-7.5	190	0	71
Sullivan	25.8	36.3	6.0	2.4	15.5	16.9	828	10.7	21.7	58.8	67.5	321	-6.9	387	0	210
Taney	5.3	75.4	18.6	4.4	39.7	9.4	566	20.0	17.3	43.6	75.1	178	2.9	315	D	55
Texas	24.6	46.7	10.1	2.8	17.3	16.6	1 527	13.6	13.0	48.5	80.3	423	2.1	277	1	188
Vernon	19.5	44.7	8.1	7.3	18.3	26.4	1 251	17.6	20.1	53.8	71.9	397	-1.0	317	4	277
Warren	35.4	43.0	11.9	4.4	14.6	9.3	550	29.1	12.9	47.6	75.8	127	-14.1	231	1	82
Washington	5.6	44.6	10.1	2.7	19.9	26.0	508	19.3	11.8	30.1	69.3	122	5.5	240	0	49
Wayne	28.8	NA	10.5	2.9	15.8	20.9	360	16.9	11.7	40.3	71.7	94	-12.8	261	D	37
Webster	23.5	40.2	9.5	3.6	12.4	16.3	1 646	27.9	6.9	46.9	82.9	291	3.3	177	1	156
Worth	6.5	39.0	9.5	4.2	11.7	21.5	367	9.8	27.8	66.2	64.0	145	-6.9	394	D	106
Wright	28.1	NA	12.8	3.0	12.9	14.2	1 407	17.1	10.0	57.4	81.8	327	6.8	232	1	167
St. Louis city	19.7	60.4	6.2	8.2	26.0	15.8	NA	NA	NA	NA	NA	NA	NA	NA	NA	NA

1. Covers mining, construction, and manufacturing. 2. Covers private sector earnings in agricultural services, forestry, and fisheries; transportation and public utilities; wholesale trade; retail trade; finance, insurance, and real estate; and services.

STATE County	Agriculture, 1987 (cont'd)								Manufactures, 1987						
	Value of land and buildings		Value of products sold				Percent of farms with sales of		Establishments		All employees			Production workers	
					Percent from										
	Average per farm ($1,000)	Average per acre (Dollars)	Total (Mil dol)	Average per farm (Dollars)	Crops	Livestock and poultry[1]	$10,000 or more	$100,000 or more	Total	Percent with 20 or more employees	Number (1,000)	Percent change, 1982–1987	Annual payroll (Mil dol)	Number (1,000)	Work hours (Mil)
	119	120	121	122	123	124	125	126	127	128	129	130	131	132	133
MISSOURI—Con.															
Laclede	151	558	31	24 482	3.2	96.8	39.6	6.8	35	51.4	3.3	22.2	55.9	2.6	4.6
Lafayette	203	835	71	48 695	43.5	56.5	55.5	11.7	39	28.2	1.3	44.4	17.6	1.0	1.9
Lawrence	132	763	58	33 204	8.3	91.7	42.2	6.3	42	42.9	1.7	6.2	24.9	1.3	2.5
Lewis	175	496	30	41 801	59.8	40.2	60.5	9.7	9	11.1	0.2	-33.3	5.3	0.1	0.3
Lincoln	220	962	53	46 208	42.0	58.0	47.3	10.6	30	23.3	0.7	16.7	9.6	0.5	1.1
Linn	151	455	38	39 247	39.5	60.5	60.5	9.5	21	52.4	1.6	33.3	25.7	1.3	2.0
Livingston	177	516	31	38 962	68.7	31.3	58.4	9.7	20	65.0	0.8	33.3	15.2	0.6	0.8
McDonald	133	757	70	60 790	0.9	99.1	40.3	12.7	32	28.1	1.8	50.0	22.7	1.5	3.3
Macon	164	466	38	32 194	45.6	54.4	52.0	6.8	9	66.7	D	D	D	D	D
Madison	131	455	11	27 481	2.2	97.8	24.1	3.4	16	37.5	0.8	33.3	8.8	0.7	1.5
Maries	132	418	14	17 187	7.1	92.9	37.3	3.2	12	25.0	0.3	50.0	4.4	0.2	0.4
Marion	190	606	31	40 629	50.3	49.7	58.1	11.6	44	31.8	1.7	21.4	30.4	1.2	2.1
Mercer	158	430	16	28 523	40.5	59.5	60.0	3.8	1	0.0	D	D	D	D	D
Miller	102	523	38	34 777	3.7	96.3	40.1	8.2	25	44.0	1.3	0.0	19.7	1.2	2.6
Mississippi	752	1 020	44	128 831	94.6	5.4	85.3	39.7	10	70.0	1.0	25.0	14.3	0.9	1.8
Moniteau	119	546	28	27 094	19.2	80.8	45.2	5.1	17	41.2	1.0	-9.1	13.5	0.9	1.7
Monroe	207	567	42	44 396	42.1	57.9	59.9	12.5	8	37.5	0.9	50.0	18.3	0.6	0.8
Montgomery	207	699	30	35 597	49.0	51.0	52.8	10.1	25	28.0	0.7	-12.5	9.0	0.5	1.0
Morgan	117	535	36	40 571	8.9	91.1	43.9	8.4	26	23.1	0.5	-16.7	7.3	0.4	0.7
New Madrid	680	942	66	124 823	98.7	1.3	85.7	43.6	13	38.5	D	D	D	D	D
Newton	111	730	69	39 018	4.8	95.2	32.7	5.8	67	32.8	4.8	29.7	88.5	4.1	8.3
Nodaway	205	562	74	50 123	48.1	51.9	68.9	13.9	24	33.3	1.2	0.0	24.5	1.1	2.0
Oregon	120	413	24	28 602	3.1	96.9	44.1	5.5	19	10.5	0.2	0.0	1.6	0.1	0.3
Osage	138	480	42	36 564	7.5	92.5	47.5	9.8	22	36.4	0.8	33.3	10.2	0.6	1.1
Ozark	163	567	26	30 561	1.2	98.8	42.1	6.8	12	16.7	0.1	0.0	1.6	0.1	0.2
Pemiscot	655	937	49	108 930	98.4	1.6	81.9	40.2	15	53.3	1.0	-9.1	13.4	0.9	1.8
Perry	152	705	32	33 421	33.3	66.7	48.9	8.4	25	40.0	1.1	0.0	16.8	0.8	1.4
Pettis	181	610	53	39 901	36.0	64.0	52.2	9.8	52	42.3	3.3	6.5	60.7	2.6	4.6
Phelps	142	546	10	12 526	9.2	90.8	27.9	1.8	45	22.2	0.7	-30.0	11.8	0.6	1.0
Pike	185	626	52	49 794	41.7	58.3	55.0	11.7	24	45.8	1.1	22.2	25.0	0.8	1.7
Platte	229	902	25	31 565	73.0	27.0	51.9	8.8	49	32.7	1.2	100.0	26.7	0.7	1.4
Polk	136	640	42	26 229	7.1	92.9	43.5	6.9	25	20.0	0.5	-28.6	6.2	0.3	0.5
Pulaski	125	462	8	14 381	5.9	94.1	29.4	2.3	27	25.9	1.0	42.9	12.4	0.9	1.6
Putnam	146	367	25	37 555	20.2	79.8	60.5	8.8	5	20.0	0.1	0.0	0.6	0.0	0.1
Ralls	221	634	30	45 908	54.8	45.2	61.1	12.2	12	50.0	0.7	16.7	11.3	0.6	1.1
Randolph	163	554	24	30 549	47.5	52.5	47.2	5.9	33	33.3	1.3	-18.8	25.0	1.0	2.0
Ray	189	713	36	31 657	50.3	49.7	42.4	6.6	12	33.3	0.4	100.0	5.7	0.3	0.6
Reynolds	97	369	3	10 504	7.6	92.4	30.0	0.7	40	17.5	0.5	66.7	5.3	0.4	0.8
Ripley	122	568	8	16 100	37.8	62.2	36.0	2.9	32	9.4	0.4	0.0	4.9	0.3	0.6
St. Charles	372	1 542	35	38 674	63.3	36.7	49.1	10.5	167	30.5	11.3	85.2	330.0	8.6	16.1
St. Clair	161	442	19	23 667	29.5	70.5	46.4	4.2	5	40.0	0.1	0.0	0.9	0.1	0.1
Ste. Genevieve	166	717	20	29 829	19.9	80.1	41.6	7.8	22	36.4	1.9	26.7	37.1	1.6	3.0
St. Francois	129	805	15	22 301	28.5	71.5	27.9	3.1	56	33.9	2.8	27.3	40.3	2.2	4.0
St. Louis	295	2 259	18	49 843	91.3	8.7	40.6	9.2	1 402	36.7	86.4	-15.2	2 641.6	42.4	83.4
Saline	322	815	68	63 233	60.7	39.3	67.3	19.5	27	48.1	2.7	-3.6	45.2	2.3	4.4
Schuyler	112	367	14	28 358	32.6	67.4	55.8	5.6	3	0.0	D	D	D	D	D
Scotland	183	470	24	40 546	44.4	55.6	63.9	10.4	8	25.0	0.2	0.0	2.0	0.1	0.2
Scott	305	834	45	69 806	71.8	28.2	60.1	18.2	55	36.4	2.9	26.1	43.0	2.3	4.3
Shannon	116	411	5	12 235	2.6	97.4	32.8	1.8	18	33.3	0.7	0.0	7.2	0.6	1.0
Shelby	217	543	48	63 967	45.0	55.0	75.0	18.4	6	33.3	D	D	D	D	D
Stoddard	341	940	77	66 697	79.8	20.2	61.0	19.8	46	32.6	2.5	-7.4	35.5	2.2	4.3
Stone	114	578	16	20 904	2.1	97.9	37.7	5.6	25	12.0	0.5	-37.5	5.5	0.4	0.8
Sullivan	133	354	23	28 116	26.3	73.7	57.9	6.0	3	33.3	D	D	D	D	D
Taney	149	471	7	12 477	3.5	96.5	30.7	1.4	40	17.5	0.5	0.0	6.1	0.4	0.8
Texas	131	443	33	21 771	4.0	96.0	39.2	5.1	48	18.8	2.3	9.5	28.1	2.1	3.9
Vernon	154	474	33	26 627	48.9	51.1	44.2	6.0	18	50.0	1.2	33.3	24.0	0.9	1.9
Warren	213	973	18	32 422	41.1	58.9	40.4	8.4	26	50.0	1.9	46.2	36.1	1.5	3.0
Washington	103	525	10	18 869	2.6	97.4	28.9	1.2	16	31.2	0.3	-50.0	4.0	0.3	0.4
Wayne	139	453	4	11 539	20.6	79.4	23.9	1.4	21	42.9	0.8	33.3	9.2	0.7	1.4
Webster	119	656	43	26 198	2.0	98.0	39.8	6.6	27	37.0	1.2	0.0	18.3	1.1	2.0
Worth	182	448	13	36 529	40.9	59.1	63.5	7.9	3	33.3	D	D	D	D	D
Wright	111	510	46	32 499	2.1	97.9	48.0	10.7	21	47.6	1.6	14.3	24.7	1.4	2.8
St. Louis city	NA	NA	NA	NA	NA	NA	NA	NA	980	43.0	82.6	19.9	2 422.0	43.7	88.9

1. Includes livestock and poultry products.

STATE County	Manufactures, 1987 (cont'd): Production workers (cont'd): Wages: Total (Mil dol)	Manufactures, 1987 (cont'd): Production workers (cont'd): Wages: Average per worker (Dollars)	Manufactures, 1987 (cont'd): Value added by manufacture (Mil dol)	Manufactures, 1987 (cont'd): Value of shipments (Mil dol)	Manufactures, 1987 (cont'd): New capital expenditures (Mil dol)	Value of construction authorized by building permits, 1990: Total[1] ($1,000)	Nonresidential: Total ($1,000)	Nonresidential: Percent: Office	Nonresidential: Percent: Industrial	Nonresidential: Percent: Stores	Residential: New construction ($1,000)	Residential: Number of housing units	Residential: Alterations and additions ($1,000)
	134	135	136	137	138	139	140	141	142	143	144	145	146
MISSOURI—Con.													
Laclede	38.5	14 808	116.2	240.8	7.1	4 826	1 060	0.0	0.0	100.0	1 574	30	80
Lafayette	10.8	10 800	45.8	102.2	1.9	1 918	101	0.0	69.3	0.0	1 381	37	32
Lawrence	16.2	12 462	45.2	120.5	D	3 775	1 504	15.0	4.7	0.0	949	24	371
Lewis	3.9	39 000	7.2	12.2	0.2	460	218	0.0	0.0	0.0	148	2	76
Lincoln	6.1	12 200	21.5	47.6	D	5 412	2 991	35.4	22.9	0.0	2 268	37	0
Linn	16.7	12 846	63.0	84.8	2.0	2 373	1 776	6.9	0.0	83.1	263	5	79
Livingston	11.2	18 667	33.3	83.0	0.9	3 371	1 058	4.7	30.1	13.9	1 686	26	77
McDonald	16.3	10 867	42.0	200.8	2.6	1 306	316	58.1	3.2	5.7	923	31	22
Macon	D	D	D	D	D	2 154	965	0.0	0.0	88.5	821	13	169
Madison	7.2	10 286	17.0	34.2	0.8	373	82	0.0	73.4	0.0	240	5	0
Maries	3.4	17 000	13.5	24.2	D	NA	NA	NA	NA	NA	NA	NA	NA
Marion	19.1	15 917	349.0	515.9	17.9	9 067	2 784	0.0	32.9	28.6	5 113	106	287
Mercer	D	D	D	D	D	NA	NA	NA	NA	NA	NA	NA	NA
Miller	15.4	12 833	39.0	76.9	D	2 516	964	0.0	0.0	79.9	1 111	42	67
Mississippi	11.0	12 222	45.7	71.5	1.7	2 186	322	0.0	0.0	93.0	1 450	45	164
Moniteau	10.8	12 000	26.3	71.8	1.9	225	0	NA	NA	NA	70	1	25
Monroe	7.4	12 333	33.8	53.7	D	81	10	0.0	0.0	0.0	0	0	44
Montgomery	6.2	12 400	20.8	52.8	0.5	3 024	1 908	0.0	0.0	85.2	911	15	52
Morgan	4.7	11 750	22.5	36.1	0.9	NA	NA	NA	NA	NA	NA	NA	NA
New Madrid	D	D	D	D	D	2 006	785	80.2	0.0	0.0	1 116	21	39
Newton	66.6	16 244	217.9	495.0	11.1	8 719	3 626	6.9	80.0	0.0	2 751	57	185
Nodaway	19.8	18 000	189.0	313.1	4.6	4 529	1 059	0.0	59.7	40.3	2 450	28	0
Oregon	1.3	13 000	3.0	9.8	0.2	3 255	3 031	0.0	0.0	35.2	152	4	48
Osage	6.7	11 167	27.0	61.0	0.9	0	0	NA	NA	NA	0	3	0
Ozark	1.1	11 000	3.0	7.8	0.1	55	50	0.0	100.0	0.0	0	0	1
Pemiscot	10.3	11 444	31.7	63.1	0.8	1 309	737	0.0	0.0	57.9	277	10	102
Perry	10.4	13 000	31.0	101.8	3.2	5 629	3 357	0.0	87.6	8.8	1 713	51	135
Pettis	39.0	15 000	182.6	391.5	11.7	6 909	2 250	9.6	58.7	12.2	3 278	96	652
Phelps	8.4	14 000	26.3	62.2	1.0	17 463	9 646	13.0	3.4	75.3	5 329	119	524
Pike	16.8	21 000	99.1	189.9	8.3	768	246	0.0	0.0	0.0	300	19	176
Platte	12.3	17 571	53.9	113.1	D	25 392	2 707	4.8	22.2	9.8	20 959	204	628
Polk	3.1	10 333	15.1	28.2	0.5	5 622	159	56.5	6.3	0.0	2 992	68	127
Pulaski	10.0	11 111	27.0	43.3	0.8	1 752	635	2.4	0.0	0.0	961	13	76
Putnam	0.4	NA	1.5	2.8	D	NA	NA	NA	NA	NA	NA	NA	NA
Ralls	8.7	14 500	72.4	151.8	D	379	312	0.0	0.0	68.5	0	0	18
Randolph	17.0	17 000	127.9	228.3	2.6	3 287	2 035	13.5	28.0	19.2	470	8	60
Ray	3.6	12 000	10.7	24.0	D	4 284	117	0.0	0.0	0.0	3 736	49	204
Reynolds	4.9	12 250	12.7	24.4	0.8	NA	NA	NA	NA	NA	NA	NA	NA
Ripley	4.0	13 333	13.1	23.9	0.4	771	37	0.0	0.0	0.0	252	4	88
St. Charles	231.3	26 895	1 435.2	3 571.5	22.7	252 902	67 552	5.6	30.3	39.0	149 640	1 867	5 548
St. Clair	0.5	5 000	2.2	3.0	D	NA	NA	NA	NA	NA	NA	NA	NA
Ste. Genevieve	27.0	16 875	92.7	157.3	D	3 442	1 321	0.0	60.5	1.4	343	6	173
St. Francois	27.2	12 364	92.7	170.1	2.5	8 684	1 604	29.9	9.7	45.3	5 088	136	434
St. Louis	1 032.4	24 349	4 879.6	12 311.4	515.6	865 968	192 524	36.4	7.1	19.5	300 625	2 977	58 678
Saline	34.8	15 130	113.6	512.6	3.3	13 756	12 348	1.0	2.8	0.0	686	22	168
Schuyler	D	D	D	D	D	NA	NA	NA	NA	NA	NA	NA	NA
Scotland	1.1	11 000	5.9	12.7	0.3	128	1	0.0	0.0	0.0	50	1	31
Scott	29.2	12 696	137.5	279.6	8.1	6 912	2 278	12.2	22.3	19.6	2 697	86	377
Shannon	5.3	8 833	15.7	30.6	1.0	32	9	0.0	0.0	100.0	0	0	22
Shelby	D	D	D	D	D	NA	NA	NA	NA	NA	NA	NA	NA
Stoddard	29.5	13 409	85.6	169.2	6.7	4 366	3 288	3.0	3.2	17.3	479	11	38
Stone	4.1	10 250	9.8	18.9	0.2	4 366	1 617	55.7	0.0	44.3	2 497	41	46
Sullivan	D	D	D	D	D	145	0	NA	NA	NA	0	0	145
Taney	4.6	11 500	22.5	42.4	D	11 865	2 080	15.6	4.8	74.9	1 275	17	222
Texas	23.3	11 095	77.2	183.2	5.2	740	370	0.0	0.0	29.8	74	2	41
Vernon	16.8	18 667	151.6	235.6	3.3	4 523	3 401	10.8	37.2	31.4	697	14	177
Warren	26.3	17 533	74.3	223.2	4.7	1 932	194	21.2	0.0	0.0	1 419	65	32
Washington	2.6	8 667	10.0	17.1	0.5	1 326	615	0.0	0.0	81.3	570	25	25
Wayne	6.8	9 714	14.5	40.0	0.3	NA	NA	NA	NA	NA	NA	NA	NA
Webster	15.3	13 909	39.9	82.6	2.3	1 049	192	0.0	0.0	55.9	478	15	99
Worth	D	D	D	D	D	NA	NA	NA	NA	NA	NA	NA	NA
Wright	16.7	11 929	50.5	96.1	1.0	1 597	309	59.4	0.0	0.0	898	20	30
St. Louis city	1 132.8	25 922	5 232.2	11 964.0	318.3	178 263	48 152	56.6	23.1	0.0	2 608	39	13 972

1. Includes nonresidential additions and alterations, residential nonhousekeeping buildings, and residential garages and carports not shown separately.

STATE County	Wholesale trade, 1987				Retail trade, all establishments, 1987				Retail trade, establishments with payroll, 1987					
						Sales				Sales				
											Per capita[2] (Dollars)			
	Estab-lishments	Sales (Mil dol)	Paid employees[1]	Annual payroll (Mil dol)	Number	Total (Mil dol)	Percent change, 1982–1987	Per capita[2] (Dollars)	Number	Total (Mil dol)	General merchan-dise stores	Food stores	Apparel & acces-sory stores	Eating and drinking places
	147	148	149	150	151	152	153	154	155	156	157	158	159	160
MISSOURI—Con.														
Laclede	56	61.5	366	4.6	420	170.9	52.2	6 498	211	145.4	D	1 029	565	437
Lafayette	59	115.9	413	6.2	343	104.4	21.3	3 378	186	98.3	309	900	32	329
Lawrence	37	233.6	252	3.9	326	109.9	36.9	3 617	163	101.7	308	965	50	279
Lewis	24	36.4	152	2.3	131	32.4	-3.3	3 089	59	28.5	D	668	27	140
Lincoln	45	91.8	240	4.5	273	106.9	68.1	3 916	131	102.1	D	1 061	13	329
Linn	31	58.9	224	3.1	213	67.5	15.4	4 685	123	63.2	D	1 131	53	291
Livingston	40	115.1	503	7.8	204	90.1	19.5	5 929	130	86.9	D	1 032	238	449
McDonald	17	23.4	122	1.4	188	54.1	34.6	3 339	87	49.1	53	627	D	289
Macon	35	68.5	230	2.5	179	67.6	49.6	4 121	102	64.0	529	800	53	302
Madison	11	9.1	74	0.8	134	44.0	44.3	3 857	80	41.1	D	829	D	249
Maries	12	D	D	D	80	17.6	47.9	2 230	36	14.9	D	405	D	53
Marion	57	109.0	396	6.3	334	172.4	25.9	6 027	220	167.9	890	1 119	156	551
Mercer	13	15.3	69	0.9	55	6.9	-30.3	1 673	26	6.2	0	939	D	69
Miller	35	54.1	223	2.8	365	126.9	63.5	6 408	197	118.6	D	1 022	85	626
Mississippi	31	76.8	154	2.6	171	71.9	44.7	4 696	103	69.0	D	1 025	24	130
Moniteau	15	55.6	181	3.7	151	49.0	28.3	3 983	84	45.9	D	892	98	173
Monroe	28	46.0	119	2.0	122	29.7	35.6	3 158	80	26.8	D	943	25	291
Montgomery	25	32.5	113	1.7	172	65.6	98.2	5 706	90	61.8	107	1 124	D	215
Morgan	24	27.7	117	1.7	258	81.8	63.3	5 381	150	75.0	D	1 414	119	307
New Madrid	35	147.7	267	4.8	239	72.8	0.0	3 323	132	68.3	D	361	201	128
Newton	54	64.3	456	5.6	428	174.4	30.3	4 018	224	162.4	D	814	93	342
Nodaway	48	124.7	308	4.2	230	87.9	22.1	4 206	135	83.5	738	977	188	468
Oregon	15	19.0	105	1.0	131	41.8	41.7	4 227	65	36.8	D	845	D	234
Osage	22	38.7	153	1.8	113	49.1	73.5	4 129	61	46.6	D	439	D	105
Ozark	7	14.8	71	0.2	116	25.9	47.2	2 878	48	21.8	D	822	D	88
Pemiscot	37	74.6	227	3.5	271	79.8	40.7	3 382	134	73.4	D	927	48	281
Perry	26	30.6	178	2.7	193	86.7	55.9	5 069	108	81.6	1 733	446	D	432
Pettis	82	131.6	647	10.5	434	218.5	31.8	6 019	259	211.2	D	1 153	288	541
Phelps	50	73.3	365	5.6	432	224.5	31.9	6 508	270	217.4	846	1 111	186	579
Pike	41	126.3	239	3.8	203	60.3	8.1	3 587	113	56.3	467	738	74	220
Platte	75	558.6	816	19.5	450	260.9	99.9	4 822	258	254.1	D	1 732	67	845
Polk	41	97.6	361	5.6	246	85.9	35.5	4 108	127	79.3	D	1 064	139	348
Pulaski	22	29.1	136	1.6	389	137.1	47.4	3 337	210	125.6	D	499	84	283
Putnam	18	25.9	105	0.9	77	12.8	-17.4	2 379	37	11.0	94	991	60	142
Ralls	14	34.9	88	1.5	84	16.0	37.9	1 796	39	14.9	D	479	0	73
Randolph	41	136.6	350	5.7	257	126.0	16.3	4 811	160	119.8	D	1 055	204	367
Ray	28	50.7	167	2.3	176	68.0	28.1	3 051	98	65.5	D	546	27	192
Reynolds	8	6.4	28	0.1	86	15.7	-8.2	2 344	44	13.4	D	807	0	104
Ripley	9	11.3	50	0.6	152	53.0	68.3	4 077	56	46.6	D	1 983	D	92
St. Charles	242	368.0	1 610	31.8	1 689	1 223.3	84.0	6 254	1 065	1 198.2	785	1 252	237	537
St. Clair	16	22.9	123	1.0	136	30.5	22.0	3 635	62	26.0	D	846	D	243
Ste. Genevieve	17	21.2	95	1.6	156	49.2	17.4	3 074	93	47.2	103	581	D	396
St. Francois	56	143.9	679	12.5	478	228.5	32.2	4 915	288	218.4	D	1 037	186	317
St. Louis	2 793	19 666.2	36 220	980.3	9 121	7 935.2	45.6	7 907	6 263	7 806.9	1 154	1 295	450	769
Saline	57	136.2	401	7.2	279	106.2	15.7	4 337	169	102.6	D	1 015	254	290
Schuyler	8	7.9	25	0.3	71	14.8	16.5	3 298	25	12.5	0	476	D	D
Scotland	15	16.9	73	0.9	76	19.4	16.2	3 881	46	17.6	397	1 040	153	238
Scott	87	415.1	1 123	20.4	470	244.7	49.5	6 012	286	233.9	555	1 611	135	456
Shannon	6	3.4	21	0.2	83	12.9	31.6	1 629	39	10.0	0	492	D	95
Shelby	25	44.9	138	1.7	109	24.2	51.2	3 354	55	21.4	136	846	68	175
Stoddard	55	100.5	362	5.3	392	146.7	52.5	5 111	219	139.5	D	1 133	77	282
Stone	16	28.5	196	3.1	323	58.5	87.5	3 112	128	50.6	69	710	15	227
Sullivan	11	20.1	49	0.6	86	14.4	27.4	2 150	42	11.7	D	624	31	65
Taney	38	66.1	295	3.9	544	157.3	55.3	6 242	291	146.4	D	1 138	88	1 094
Texas	25	49.5	145	2.0	306	92.8	28.9	4 335	156	85.6	D	876	48	248
Vernon	50	70.9	269	3.9	205	83.3	51.2	4 207	128	78.2	D	771	192	430
Warren	24	32.5	134	2.4	179	63.3	72.0	3 331	87	59.9	D	745	D	398
Washington	14	13.8	77	0.8	190	54.9	28.0	2 843	85	49.0	D	660	D	77
Wayne	13	11.4	27	0.4	143	36.3	52.5	3 002	68	32.1	D	861	22	180
Webster	20	17.6	105	1.4	255	80.0	72.0	3 447	108	71.9	397	679	46	172
Worth	9	16.0	58	0.3	53	7.9	12.9	2 918	33	7.1	0	1 021	0	D
Wright	23	51.4	195	2.1	200	61.5	83.0	3 662	112	53.3	D	1 390	35	265
St. Louis city	1 123	8 385.2	19 748	466.0	3 422	2 159.1	27.1	5 242	2 532	2 124.0	522	1 074	216	974

1. For pay period including March 12. 2. Based on the estimated population as of July 1 of the year shown.

STATE County	Retail trade, establishments with payroll, 1987 (cont'd)		Taxable service industries–establishments with payroll, 1987							Bank deposits,[2] June 1989		Savings capital,[3] September 1989	
				Receipts (Mil dol)									
					Selected kinds of business								
	Paid employees[1]	Annual payroll (Mil dol)	Number	Total	Hotels, motels and other lodging places	Health services	Legal services	Paid employees	Annual payroll (Mil dol)	Total (Mil dol)	Percent change, 1988–1989	Total (Mil dol)	Percent change, 1988–1989
	161	162	163	164	165	166	167	168	169	170	171	172	173
MISSOURI—Con.													
Laclede	1 704	15.4	153	29.3	3.1	7.1	1.4	883	8.5	201	5.6	96.7	-4.7
Lafayette	1 396	10.6	141	21.7	2.0	9.1	1.3	783	7.2	315	4.8	85.7	1.3
Lawrence	1 263	10.8	106	17.2	1.1	9.7	0.8	517	6.6	185	3.6	70.8	-1.4
Lewis	301	3.1	31	3.7	0.0	1.7	0.4	148	1.2	96	-3.4	9.2	1.2
Lincoln	1 163	11.0	112	16.6	D	7.3	0.8	590	5.7	197	2.2	45.2	-7.0
Linn	770	6.0	103	13.5	D	5.8	0.5	455	4.4	161	0.8	35.7	1.7
Livingston	1 124	10.2	119	23.2	1.5	7.0	1.2	694	7.3	228	5.1	32.8	-5.5
McDonald	717	4.8	53	6.0	0.3	3.2	D	218	1.7	98	5.0	3.6	-15.4
Macon	931	7.7	59	7.9	D	3.0	0.5	266	3.1	158	10.5	90.7	1.4
Madison	572	4.8	53	5.2	0.3	2.1	D	145	1.7	110	9.4	9.4	3.2
Maries	169	1.3	20	3.7	D	D	D	125	1.1	58	10.4	0.0	NA
Marion	2 080	17.8	195	41.5	6.4	15.2	3.2	1 323	14.2	186	0.2	147.1	-0.1
Mercer	90	0.5	13	2.0	D	D	D	84	0.7	30	10.1	0.0	NA
Miller	1 358	12.8	136	54.2	36.7	6.3	0.8	1 094	16.2	170	10.5	16.2	-0.5
Mississippi	668	5.4	58	9.6	D	3.5	0.3	367	3.6	110	3.5	10.9	-4.9
Moniteau	471	4.2	58	7.9	D	3.0	0.9	292	2.6	107	8.1	50.1	-0.6
Monroe	413	3.0	36	6.1	1.1	1.8	D	210	1.4	95	3.4	32.5	-4.9
Montgomery	587	4.7	49	7.7	0.4	3.3	0.3	302	2.5	120	3.7	0.0	-100.0
Morgan	888	8.3	68	12.2	1.8	1.9	1.0	240	3.0	122	3.3	9.7	-23.3
New Madrid	745	6.2	50	8.2	D	5.5	0.3	346	2.7	116	26.7	12.8	-3.6
Newton	1 916	17.6	164	49.1	D	24.8	1.1	1 326	19.2	157	-0.5	72.6	-7.9
Nodaway	1 483	9.3	83	15.5	0.4	7.5	0.9	577	6.1	272	5.6	40.2	-2.3
Oregon	444	3.6	26	4.0	D	2.3	D	160	1.6	52	5.6	8.2	-1.0
Osage	356	3.3	31	3.4	D	1.8	D	95	1.1	87	5.4	0.0	NA
Ozark	202	1.8	23	2.0	0.2	D	0.0	97	0.7	45	-1.1	3.9	16.8
Pemiscot	990	7.4	62	12.3	1.3	6.8	0.5	372	3.5	138	9.5	37.3	-7.8
Perry	1 164	8.9	79	11.1	0.8	3.8	D	273	3.3	157	8.7	91.8	-3.8
Pettis	2 592	24.6	269	66.3	3.7	23.6	2.3	1 883	23.7	336	7.9	169.4	-4.9
Phelps	2 927	24.4	233	51.0	4.1	23.1	2.9	1 772	18.6	215	2.7	141.9	-3.5
Pike	688	5.9	81	18.6	0.5	7.7	1.1	630	6.5	185	3.3	22.3	49.6
Platte	3 263	30.5	292	128.1	28.9	18.0	3.5	3 396	35.6	242	2.5	72.4	18.7
Polk	862	7.9	108	17.0	D	6.1	0.7	583	5.8	204	7.5	33.4	-0.1
Pulaski	1 590	13.1	130	24.3	4.0	5.7	1.1	850	8.3	152	5.9	8.7	11.1
Putnam	169	1.2	27	1.8	D	0.7	D	67	0.5	64	9.7	18.8	13.3
Ralls	116	1.3	20	7.0	D	0.8	D	255	3.4	48	-0.7	0.0	NA
Randolph	1 490	12.8	119	26.4	0.8	10.5	1.6	771	8.5	227	5.0	81.5	20.2
Ray	738	6.1	79	9.9	0.0	4.1	1.1	280	3.5	146	0.0	96.9	1.4
Reynolds	149	1.2	26	2.3	1.3	D	D	90	0.6	22	8.0	6.4	9.4
Ripley	491	3.7	39	3.6	D	1.3	0.3	88	0.9	69	11.4	13.8	-4.4
St. Charles	14 591	140.8	1 109	365.3	12.7	130.6	11.4	9 843	128.3	910	13.8	574.0	1.3
St. Clair	326	2.2	23	5.9	D	4.6	0.3	154	2.3	49	1.1	0.0	NA
Ste. Genevieve	642	5.4	62	11.5	0.6	2.6	D	249	2.6	149	12.9	23.7	-21.1
St. Francois	2 569	22.2	260	53.7	2.5	19.5	2.7	1 793	19.1	289	12.2	133.6	-5.3
St. Louis	94 217	964.1	8 645	4 451.6	164.9	977.6	162.7	94 330	1 713.0	7 607	11.4	6 096.4	-5.9
Saline	1 257	10.6	122	16.5	1.8	7.1	0.9	620	5.5	201	-2.4	94.5	-4.1
Schuyler	115	0.9	11	1.1	0.0	D	D	57	0.4	37	-13.9	0.0	NA
Scotland	229	1.9	29	2.7	D	0.4	D	111	0.6	46	1.3	19.2	-0.4
Scott	2 805	23.7	256	76.2	5.5	31.7	4.0	2 190	24.2	290	5.2	86.5	-9.7
Shannon	155	0.9	26	3.6	D	1.4	D	129	1.0	37	5.2	0.0	NA
Shelby	297	2.1	26	2.7	0.0	0.4	0.5	74	0.7	92	-5.9	14.4	-7.5
Stoddard	1 360	12.1	141	22.0	D	11.3	1.3	733	7.7	196	-3.2	60.1	4.0
Stone	606	5.6	85	42.8	3.1	3.4	D	813	11.4	118	0.3	6.5	-4.3
Sullivan	166	1.1	25	5.8	D	3.3	D	230	2.1	48	1.9	13.7	1.9
Taney	1 990	19.0	332	83.0	38.8	10.0	1.1	1 910	24.8	203	-0.3	45.3	1.6
Texas	927	7.2	69	14.4	D	3.9	0.3	281	3.3	121	4.4	51.3	2.0
Vernon	1 090	8.8	93	30.0	0.9	20.1	1.9	681	10.0	120	1.3	330.0	-1.9
Warren	898	7.1	74	11.9	1.0	4.2	D	393	3.8	84	2.9	80.4	-5.9
Washington	515	4.3	46	17.1	D	3.9	D	313	4.4	94	6.3	9.1	-0.1
Wayne	410	3.1	33	4.6	0.5	1.8	0.8	147	1.3	43	3.8	8.2	0.9
Webster	815	6.6	66	7.1	D	1.6	0.4	212	1.9	120	2.7	29.7	-2.9
Worth	75	0.7	7	0.6	0.0	D	D	22	0.1	27	-1.3	0.0	NA
Wright	691	5.6	52	7.6	D	4.3	0.5	254	2.4	108	7.4	45.5	-0.6
St. Louis city	32 536	305.9	2 673	2 060.3	139.8	249.3	281.7	44 148	801.8	7 345	-3.8	1 369.1	-7.4

1. For the period including March 12 of the year shown. 2. Includes deposits for all insured and reporting noninsured commercial and mutual savings banks. 3. Includes savings capital for all FSLIC insured savings institutions.

STATE County	Federal funds and grants, 1989: Expenditures: Total (Mil dol)	Federal funds and grants, 1989: Expenditures: Percent change, 1988–1989	Per capita[1] (Dollars): Total	Per capita[1] (Dollars): Direct payments for individuals	Per capita[1] (Dollars): Procurement contract awards	Per capita[1] (Dollars): Salaries and wages	Per capita[1] (Dollars): Grant awards	Local government finances, 1981–1982: General revenue: Total (Mil dol)	Intergovernmental: Total (Mil dol)	Intergovernmental: Percent from state	Taxes: Total (Mil dol)	Taxes: Per capita[2]: Total (Dollars)	Taxes: Per capita[2]: Property (Dollars)	Direct general expenditure: Total (Mil dol)	Direct general expenditure: Percent change, 1977–1982
	174	175	176	177	178	179	180	181	182	183	184	185	186	187	188
MISSOURI—Con.															
Laclede	65.9	15.0	2 508	1 929	11	108	373	14.4	7.1	80.8	4.4	176	127	13.7	61.2
Lafayette	81.0	-3.2	2 572	1 871	47	164	282	23.2	7.6	82.0	6.2	208	162	20.2	76.9
Lawrence	72.3	13.9	2 326	1 828	15	109	262	17.3	8.3	89.2	4.3	150	100	16.9	74.3
Lewis	44.9	31.4	4 449	2 047	1 123	225	242	6.5	2.7	94.4	2.2	195	157	6.3	64.5
Lincoln	53.4	3.5	1 816	1 422	15	112	111	16.8	5.0	93.9	4.4	194	149	16.4	60.8
Linn	51.2	10.1	3 607	2 580	40	178	364	11.0	4.5	82.3	3.9	249	187	11.4	67.3
Livingston	40.0	3.6	2 600	1 798	30	269	234	15.1	4.1	80.2	4.2	271	207	16.0	60.1
McDonald	38.3	9.7	2 309	1 727	16	169	305	6.0	3.8	84.5	1.3	88	57	5.5	72.1
Macon	48.2	8.0	2 993	2 198	22	199	186	14.6	5.4	87.0	4.0	242	190	13.8	72.6
Madison	30.1	5.9	2 594	2 204	14	89	252	10.5	3.0	89.5	1.5	143	116	10.3	67.1
Maries	16.6	12.3	2 099	1 617	19	68	308	3.3	1.9	95.8	1.1	138	113	3.4	35.9
Marion	73.4	8.0	2 584	2 027	7	84	284	22.5	8.6	68.8	8.7	300	196	22.4	101.8
Mercer	15.4	6.6	3 961	2 166	17	161	215	3.5	1.1	89.2	1.3	273	264	3.2	42.3
Miller	48.2	11.1	2 461	2 077	18	98	207	12.4	5.5	87.4	4.2	222	160	13.7	92.7
Mississippi	46.4	-1.0	3 033	1 945	40	104	571	11.5	6.7	79.5	3.4	215	169	11.3	25.8
Moniteau	29.5	4.8	2 462	1 866	15	141	253	6.6	3.2	93.7	2.4	196	152	6.7	60.4
Monroe	33.2	11.2	3 536	2 078	68	258	404	8.4	3.3	87.5	2.4	245	209	7.2	38.2
Montgomery	38.1	14.1	3 282	2 164	385	165	253	6.6	2.7	93.7	2.6	229	185	6.1	41.0
Morgan	42.0	5.8	2 760	2 395	13	108	177	6.3	2.6	83.5	2.4	172	139	6.1	52.2
New Madrid	73.0	1.2	3 395	1 737	55	130	759	32.4	8.1	89.9	6.4	280	229	27.5	152.5
Newton	102.9	5.0	2 333	1 471	414	151	232	20.3	10.7	93.1	5.3	130	101	19.7	58.1
Nodaway	64.1	14.9	3 110	1 841	148	214	268	13.4	4.8	78.9	6.4	286	229	13.1	53.9
Oregon	29.7	2.8	3 026	2 210	22	243	431	5.3	3.5	92.3	1.1	109	101	5.7	72.5
Osage	23.9	6.4	2 057	1 647	21	117	161	4.5	2.2	95.1	1.7	145	118	4.8	45.8
Ozark	26.0	19.7	2 861	2 197	22	131	375	4.1	2.6	92.5	1.0	122	119	4.1	61.3
Pemiscot	76.6	-3.2	3 260	1 949	107	138	742	23.3	10.5	92.9	4.7	189	131	22.6	41.6
Perry	38.5	-4.0	2 254	1 734	49	133	178	12.4	3.2	79.3	3.9	231	176	12.8	73.0
Pettis	100.4	10.6	2 742	2 029	133	232	219	37.2	11.1	78.7	10.9	303	196	36.5	47.2
Phelps	118.3	7.9	3 390	2 162	65	806	333	35.9	10.0	84.5	6.3	181	130	34.5	103.3
Pike	44.9	2.0	2 656	1 935	52	164	221	18.1	5.9	69.1	4.9	283	213	16.7	75.6
Platte	99.8	-1.6	1 718	964	9	392	253	30.0	9.4	91.9	16.0	333	293	30.4	84.3
Polk	57.5	14.0	2 677	2 066	16	121	253	9.3	5.4	95.3	2.6	134	111	9.5	60.8
Pulaski	514.2	22.2	12 953	1 495	1 145	9 931	363	23.8	15.1	67.2	2.5	57	42	22.1	60.5
Putnam	19.2	8.0	3 629	2 292	25	221	252	4.8	1.6	90.0	1.7	271	252	4.3	49.7
Ralls	36.0	27.6	4 049	1 867	859	372	475	3.1	1.6	80.7	1.1	122	105	3.1	69.6
Randolph	66.7	-1.8	2 586	2 075	14	125	208	19.3	7.7	71.2	8.1	319	220	16.8	45.5
Ray	43.7	9.1	1 923	1 419	24	115	215	16.8	6.0	80.2	4.2	193	146	16.8	77.6
Reynolds	19.7	19.3	3 027	2 067	26	130	755	7.3	2.5	88.1	2.4	342	326	7.2	92.8
Ripley	41.9	14.9	3 178	2 273	14	131	650	8.3	4.3	87.0	1.2	93	72	7.9	100.9
St. Charles	328.3	-15.1	1 525	930	430	93	53	96.2	32.9	89.5	49.0	319	238	106.7	96.1
St. Clair	26.5	4.6	3 157	2 318	22	132	412	10.6	2.9	73.6	1.4	164	153	9.1	95.4
Ste. Genevieve	38.6	17.8	2 324	1 690	9	75	110	11.5	2.0	86.2	3.2	216	168	11.2	60.9
St. Francois	143.2	17.5	2 947	2 499	15	121	297	26.4	13.5	89.4	8.8	207	153	27.1	45.1
St. Louis	2 270.6	8.8	2 247	1 722	152	227	142	788.8	189.6	79.0	484.9	495	343	770.2	49.5
Saline	70.4	-15.0	2 898	2 127	18	153	212	17.1	6.6	67.0	6.8	274	186	17.1	59.4
Schuyler	17.8	11.0	4 144	2 726	36	272	420	3.7	1.5	91.0	1.2	246	236	3.9	79.6
Scotland	20.9	4.8	4 265	2 242	24	190	211	6.6	1.9	80.5	1.9	358	319	5.8	44.7
Scott	100.5	1.8	2 463	1 806	25	127	338	29.8	12.4	90.1	8.3	208	131	25.9	64.8
Shannon	19.6	5.2	2 450	1 652	14	190	533	3.1	2.1	86.7	0.5	63	50	2.9	35.3
Shelby	26.4	14.2	3 714	2 289	63	241	193	6.5	2.0	81.6	2.1	268	236	6.6	117.3
Stoddard	98.3	-2.2	3 436	2 008	53	190	529	16.5	8.6	90.0	5.1	180	137	16.6	44.6
Stone	50.4	4.5	2 561	2 221	17	64	167	7.0	4.0	93.3	2.2	138	124	7.0	73.0
Sullivan	27.2	15.5	4 186	2 403	60	250	371	6.2	1.7	78.2	1.3	186	169	5.5	35.0
Taney	79.9	12.1	3 098	2 608	28	114	328	11.9	5.3	73.2	4.8	223	148	11.2	124.6
Texas	55.3	1.5	2 561	2 002	18	136	293	17.7	7.3	91.1	2.9	137	114	19.2	108.2
Vernon	55.3	3.0	2 806	2 008	17	199	223	19.2	5.7	73.2	4.6	233	162	17.9	38.0
Warren	36.6	4.7	1 805	1 445	16	104	120	6.5	2.8	93.5	2.8	182	146	6.6	29.3
Washington	40.6	7.5	2 063	1 583	16	101	346	14.2	6.9	76.6	2.9	160	139	13.1	83.3
Wayne	43.6	-2.1	3 458	2 542	312	177	372	6.1	3.7	87.6	1.2	106	82	6.1	76.3
Webster	56.3	17.1	2 327	1 569	230	102	309	10.0	5.4	92.8	2.6	125	108	9.2	27.6
Worth	11.1	12.1	4 267	2 142	43	323	306	2.2	0.7	94.4	0.8	264	261	2.7	335.4
Wright	48.4	20.3	2 849	2 031	20	128	430	9.3	5.2	94.2	2.3	143	96	8.9	50.3
St. Louis city	8 112.1	13.8	20 599	2 768	14 308	2 126	1 337	770.0	308.7	57.7	293.1	671	274	659.1	38.3

1. Based on the estimated population as of July 1 of the year shown. 2. Based on the estimated population as of July 1, 1982.

STATE County	Local government finances, 1981–1982 (cont'd): Direct general expenditure (cont'd): Per capita[1] (Dollars)	Percent of total for– Education	Percent of total for– Health & hospitals	Percent of total for– Police protection	Percent of total for– Public welfare	Percent of total for– Highways	Debt outstanding: Total (Mil dol)	Debt outstanding: Per capita[1] (Dollars)	State and local government employment, 1989: Total	State and local government employment, 1989: Rate[2]	Federal government civilian employment 1989: Total	Federal government civilian employment 1989: Earnings ($1,000)	Elections, 1988[3]: Total vote cast for president	Elections, 1988[3]: Vote for lead party (Percent)
	189	190	191	192	193	194	195	196	197	198	199	200	201	202
MISSOURI—Con.														
Laclede	555	57.9	0.8	7.0	0.0	9.2	4.0	162	978	371.9	78	2 099	9 536	R—63.7
Lafayette	676	52.4	15.1	5.6	0.1	7.6	11.8	396	1 759	558.4	122	3 292	12 514	R—54.5
Lawrence	587	53.4	19.5	2.7	0.5	6.1	4.2	146	1 778	571.7	84	2 103	11 379	R—60.7
Lewis	564	60.6	12.9	3.4	0.1	10.2	4.2	372	562	556.4	75	1 967	4 273	D—57.6
Lincoln	724	45.3	36.8	3.3	0.0	5.0	5.1	226	1 170	398.0	106	2 667	9 938	R—53.4
Linn	738	53.0	0.0	12.2	0.0	15.9	9.7	627	687	483.8	78	1 841	6 230	D—50.6
Livingston	1 026	36.1	37.5	3.6	0.0	6.6	8.4	537	891	578.6	118	3 282	6 548	R—52.9
McDonald	371	70.6	0.0	4.1	0.0	5.6	5.9	395	460	277.1	87	2 240	6 153	R—62.0
Macon	833	41.8	36.3	2.3	0.1	8.0	4.5	269	1 365	847.8	95	2 402	6 639	R—51.3
Madison	963	35.6	45.3	1.9	0.0	4.4	6.5	609	578	498.3	39	949	4 703	R—53.8
Maries	448	78.6	0.2	2.7	0.0	8.6	0.8	109	302	382.3	14	351	3 480	R—55.1
Marion	776	51.6	0.0	4.3	0.9	6.6	16.9	585	1 652	581.7	107	3 369	10 677	D—52.6
Mercer	674	46.8	16.4	1.7	0.0	15.3	0.9	190	232	594.9	31	700	1 756	D—49.9
Miller	719	58.7	5.3	3.9	0.0	8.6	4.1	218	903	460.7	60	1 403	8 228	R—68.8
Mississippi	713	64.0	0.7	4.9	1.7	6.5	11.1	701	672	439.2	51	1 276	5 042	D—55.8
Moniteau	542	66.0	0.8	5.3	0.8	10.4	1.9	151	597	497.5	53	1 327	5 446	R—64.3
Monroe	747	55.8	18.2	3.7	0.0	8.4	4.7	487	640	680.9	97	2 294	4 014	D—61.3
Montgomery	537	66.2	1.8	4.7	1.1	10.7	1.4	127	458	394.8	61	1 401	4 794	R—56.6
Morgan	431	52.0	9.8	5.8	0.0	13.3	2.2	153	671	441.4	51	1 248	6 586	R—60.1
New Madrid	1 201	42.7	2.0	2.4	0.1	5.0	210.3	9 182	1 021	474.9	76	1 819	7 208	D—52.9
Newton	482	74.1	2.1	4.0	0.1	4.6	6.9	168	1 527	346.3	145	3 578	16 497	R—64.4
Nodaway	588	62.8	1.7	4.5	0.0	12.8	5.9	266	1 944	943.7	110	2 530	8 387	D—50.6
Oregon	567	77.0	0.4	3.3	0.0	8.0	1.6	164	389	396.9	34	791	3 766	D—54.2
Osage	404	69.9	1.2	3.4	0.9	10.4	2.2	183	408	351.7	50	1 061	5 665	R—68.6
Ozark	503	76.7	6.4	3.2	0.0	5.7	0.4	55	355	390.1	27	505	3 744	R—64.2
Pemiscot	911	53.6	25.3	2.8	0.0	5.1	4.4	179	1 475	627.7	97	2 584	6 364	D—51.7
Perry	762	34.2	34.6	3.1	0.0	6.9	3.8	227	667	390.1	59	1 470	5 986	R—64.1
Pettis	1 018	43.9	28.9	3.9	0.0	5.6	10.3	288	2 392	653.6	161	4 614	15 200	R—63.5
Phelps	995	33.9	43.8	2.3	0.1	3.9	20.2	582	4 392	1 258.5	852	25 638	14 253	R—58.4
Pike	963	45.8	27.8	2.8	3.6	6.7	5.1	295	989	585.2	88	2 312	7 101	D—53.7
Platte	632	70.8	1.1	4.5	0.7	7.2	16.6	345	1 703	293.1	613	22 110	23 134	R—51.2
Polk	493	71.1	1.6	2.9	0.0	9.7	2.1	107	975	453.5	81	1 834	8 471	R—59.4
Pulaski	504	62.9	19.0	3.9	0.0	3.6	6.1	139	1 315	331.2	3 043	72 676	8 114	R—57.2
Putnam	704	52.4	24.6	2.4	0.2	11.2	1.0	166	365	688.7	37	887	2 176	R—62.7
Ralls	350	61.0	5.9	4.0	0.0	10.2	1.5	174	291	327.0	58	1 539	3 990	D—62.4
Randolph	659	58.0	1.9	5.3	0.4	10.5	10.2	401	1 621	628.3	95	2 464	9 695	D—54.6
Ray	778	40.2	30.1	2.6	0.0	8.5	9.9	458	1 043	459.5	68	1 775	8 662	D—56.3
Reynolds	1 016	51.8	33.1	2.1	0.0	5.7	2.0	275	321	493.8	32	647	3 035	D—61.4
Ripley	641	55.1	25.5	2.5	0.0	4.4	0.5	36	478	362.1	66	1 536	4 620	R—57.3
St. Charles	695	57.4	1.5	5.5	0.2	12.0	88.6	577	5 947	276.2	526	16 102	79 548	R—62.9
St. Clair	1 054	31.5	46.7	1.6	0.0	4.2	4.0	467	495	589.3	38	865	4 183	R—55.3
Ste. Genevieve	746	31.3	36.0	3.5	9.8	6.6	4.4	291	679	409.0	35	889	6 164	D—58.6
St. Francois	638	74.5	2.0	4.9	0.0	6.1	8.2	193	3 222	663.0	149	4 310	16 127	D—50.6
St. Louis	786	54.1	3.7	7.9	0.2	8.2	343.1	350	40 109	396.9	8 090	246 547	480 897	R—54.6
Saline	687	48.0	2.1	5.5	0.0	10.6	17.1	688	2 351	967.5	116	3 125	9 696	D—52.0
Schuyler	801	47.4	20.5	3.0	0.0	7.7	17.5	3 570	270	627.9	33	681	2 080	R—51.1
Scotland	1 083	34.3	43.6	1.7	0.0	7.8	5.5	1 019	448	914.3	34	780	2 372	R—52.6
Scott	652	61.1	2.2	6.0	0.4	4.6	261.8	6 578	2 006	491.7	151	4 262	13 948	R—57.4
Shannon	364	61.9	7.5	4.4	0.0	10.6	0.6	74	259	323.8	75	1 557	3 500	D—51.3
Shelby	856	52.9	25.2	3.3	0.0	8.7	4.3	552	553	778.9	52	1 110	3 408	D—53.3
Stoddard	582	68.4	1.3	5.0	0.0	7.9	5.1	179	1 094	382.5	179	4 462	10 538	R—55.2
Stone	439	76.4	1.4	3.8	0.0	7.6	3.2	199	540	274.1	35	805	8 004	R—63.5
Sullivan	766	36.0	37.3	3.7	0.0	9.9	2.2	309	379	583.1	55	1 279	3 467	R—54.7
Taney	522	53.1	3.8	4.5	0.0	8.0	5.0	232	817	316.7	94	2 637	10 978	R—64.2
Texas	906	46.8	36.5	2.3	0.0	6.9	3.4	159	988	457.4	99	2 151	8 506	R—53.9
Vernon	919	37.3	27.6	3.4	0.0	6.9	18.3	937	2 285	1 159.9	105	2 632	7 572	R—54.8
Warren	425	66.0	1.2	5.8	0.0	8.2	3.3	209	511	251.7	53	1 284	7 411	R—60.1
Washington	724	52.4	22.4	4.2	0.0	4.8	8.9	490	1 060	538.1	70	1 588	7 000	D—53.5
Wayne	531	66.5	9.0	3.6	0.0	6.4	1.7	145	429	340.5	103	2 112	5 112	R—51.8
Webster	444	65.4	11.4	3.5	0.0	7.1	4.0	194	921	380.6	72	1 707	9 035	R—56.7
Worth	887	43.8	28.2	1.7	0.0	12.9	1.2	384	178	684.6	28	581	1 411	D—51.9
Wright	546	67.2	10.2	2.9	0.0	5.5	3.0	183	688	404.7	60	1 448	6 394	R—64.9
St. Louis city	1 510	35.2	11.4	9.8	0.1	2.6	407.5	934	24 019	609.9	22 620	724 206	151 758	D—72.5

1. Based on the estimated population as of July 1, 1982. 2. Per 10,000 resident population estimated as of July 1 of the year shown. 3. Data subject to copyright.

STATE–County code	MSA/CMSA/NECMA code[1]	STATE County	Land Area,[2] 1990 (Sq. Km.)	Population, 1990												
							Race						Age of population Percent		
				Total persons	Rank	Per square kilometer	White	Black	Am. Indian, Eskimo, Aleut	Asian & Pacific Islander	Other race	Hispanic[3]	Under 5 years	5 to 14 years	15 to 24 years
			1	2	3	4	5	6	7	8	9	10	11	12	13
30 000	...	MONTANA	376 991	799 065	X	2.1	741 111	2 381	47 679	4 259	3 635	12 174	7.4	16.1	13.1
30 001	...	Beaverhead	14 355	8 424	2 519	0.6	8 194	8	121	29	72	133	7.3	16.6	15.2
30 003	...	Big Horn	12 937	11 337	2 270	0.9	4 916	18	6 289	46	68	294	10.7	20.5	14.2
30 005	...	Blaine	10 946	6 728	2 684	0.6	4 040	6	2 664	6	12	54	9.5	18.7	12.7
30 007	...	Broadwater	3 086	3 318	2 972	1.1	3 254	1	45	5	13	33	6.7	17.3	10.0
30 009	...	Carbon	5 304	8 080	2 557	1.5	7 977	3	42	17	41	90	5.8	16.4	9.1
30 011	...	Carter	8 650	1 503	3 097	0.2	1 487	0	9	2	5	12	7.0	14.2	10.1
30 013	3040	Cascade	6 988	77 691	584	11.1	72 345	1 061	3 072	792	421	1 398	8.2	15.7	13.0
30 015	...	Chouteau	10 291	5 452	2 804	0.5	5 221	4	212	10	5	25	7.1	16.6	9.7
30 017	...	Custer	9 799	11 697	2 234	1.2	11 398	12	196	27	64	160	6.5	15.7	13.0
30 019	...	Daniels	3 694	2 266	3 045	0.6	2 242	0	6	18	0	12	4.5	15.9	9.3
30 021	...	Dawson	6 147	9 505	2 433	1.5	9 376	0	83	28	18	64	6.7	16.4	11.8
30 023	...	Deer Lodge	1 909	10 278	2 361	5.4	9 905	29	260	22	62	157	5.6	12.6	13.9
30 025	...	Fallon	4 197	3 103	2 993	0.7	3 078	0	9	13	3	6	7.6	17.9	9.6
30 027	...	Fergus	11 239	12 083	2 211	1.1	11 922	10	121	13	17	72	6.5	16.1	10.0
30 029	...	Flathead	13 205	59 218	735	4.5	57 897	56	880	240	145	616	7.1	16.8	10.9
30 031	...	Gallatin	6 493	50 463	836	7.8	49 180	80	608	449	146	593	7.0	13.9	21.1
30 033	...	Garfield	12 091	1 589	3 091	0.1	1 583	0	4	2	0	0	6.8	18.4	10.2
30 035	...	Glacier	7 756	12 121	2 207	1.6	5 258	11	6 823	10	19	78	11.0	20.9	13.4
30 037	...	Golden Valley	3 044	912	3 116	0.3	895	0	10	4	3	8	7.0	15.1	12.2
30 039	...	Granite	4 474	2 548	3 021	0.6	2 521	0	21	4	2	9	6.6	15.0	10.6
30 041	...	Hill	7 502	17 654	1 808	2.4	14 729	19	2 769	92	45	176	8.5	17.8	13.6
30 043	...	Jefferson	4 291	7 939	2 579	1.9	7 780	5	118	15	21	83	7.1	17.4	10.6
30 045	...	Judith Basin	4 843	2 282	3 042	0.5	2 269	0	7	6	0	8	6.1	14.8	9.7
30 047	...	Lake	3 869	21 041	1 627	5.4	16 411	15	4 498	32	85	402	8.0	17.3	12.6
30 049	...	Lewis and Clark	8 964	47 495	884	5.3	45 991	69	1 059	242	134	576	7.3	16.0	12.5
30 051	...	Liberty	3 703	2 295	3 041	0.6	2 278	3	11	3	0	4	8.2	19.3	9.2
30 053	...	Lincoln	9 357	17 481	1 822	1.9	17 103	11	282	54	31	197	7.2	17.9	11.2
30 055	...	McCone	6 844	2 276	3 044	0.3	2 256	1	17	2	0	10	6.5	17.0	11.3
30 057	...	Madison	9 289	5 989	2 759	0.6	5 908	0	43	14	24	88	6.0	14.9	10.8
30 059	...	Meagher	6 195	1 819	3 078	0.3	1 785	0	18	2	14	26	6.5	15.0	10.5
30 061	...	Mineral	3 159	3 315	2 975	1.0	3 204	3	79	22	7	41	6.8	17.9	10.3
30 063	...	Missoula	6 729	78 687	575	11.7	75 650	185	1 818	836	198	962	7.3	14.7	16.8
30 065	...	Musselshell	4 836	4 106	2 909	0.8	4 056	2	26	8	14	36	4.8	15.3	11.2
30 067	...	Park	6 879	14 562	2 017	2.1	14 227	69	113	69	84	232	7.0	14.7	9.0
30 069	...	Petroleum	4 284	519	3 134	0.1	516	0	3	0	0	0	8.3	13.9	11.0
30 071	...	Phillips	13 312	5 163	2 830	0.4	4 741	2	390	14	16	44	7.5	17.7	11.4
30 073	...	Pondera	4 208	6 433	2 715	1.5	5 691	5	704	20	13	31	8.2	18.0	10.8
30 075	...	Powder River	8 540	2 090	3 064	0.2	2 044	0	37	3	6	20	7.5	15.2	11.4
30 077	...	Powell	6 024	6 620	2 696	1.1	6 271	22	253	25	49	77	6.0	12.8	11.1
30 079	...	Prairie	4 498	1 383	3 103	0.3	1 361	0	15	4	3	16	5.0	13.6	9.7
30 081	...	Ravalli	6 201	25 010	1 462	4.0	24 528	36	287	72	87	369	6.6	16.2	10.8
30 083	...	Richland	5 398	10 716	2 318	2.0	10 445	4	140	25	102	240	8.1	18.4	11.4
30 085	...	Roosevelt	6 101	10 999	2 294	1.8	5 569	17	5 355	40	18	103	10.8	19.3	12.8
30 087	...	Rosebud	12 982	10 505	2 335	0.8	7 544	33	2 807	52	69	225	9.3	21.3	13.3
30 089	...	Sanders	7 154	8 669	2 496	1.2	8 135	12	471	37	14	104	6.9	16.8	10.5
30 091	...	Sheridan	4 343	4 732	2 861	1.1	4 650	0	50	12	20	38	5.9	16.2	8.2
30 093	...	Silver Bow	1 860	33 941	1 164	18.2	33 026	33	520	138	224	810	6.8	14.0	13.3
30 095	...	Stillwater	4 648	6 536	2 704	1.4	6 434	5	52	10	35	92	7.3	16.2	10.1
30 097	...	Sweet Grass	4 805	3 154	2 989	0.7	3 126	2	16	5	5	7	6.6	15.2	9.4
30 099	...	Teton	5 886	6 271	2 728	1.1	6 154	3	93	9	12	37	6.6	17.8	10.7
30 101	...	Toole	4 949	5 046	2 839	1.0	4 900	5	118	16	7	36	7.3	17.4	10.1
30 103	...	Treasure	2 535	874	3 119	0.3	854	0	9	2	9	26	6.5	15.6	12.8
30 105	...	Valley	12 745	8 239	2 545	0.6	7 423	9	770	19	18	62	6.6	15.9	10.9
30 107	...	Wheatland	3 686	2 246	3 052	0.6	2 203	1	19	8	15	22	6.7	15.8	11.1
30 109	...	Wibaux	2 303	1 191	3 108	0.5	1 187	0	2	2	0	2	6.1	16.6	9.9
30 111	0880	Yellowstone	6 825	113 419	404	16.6	107 921	511	3 235	612	1 140	3 158	7.4	15.6	13.0
30 113	...	Yellowstone National Park (part)	636	52	3 141	0.1	52	0	0	0	0	0	9.6	7.7	7.7
31 000	...	NEBRASKA	199 113	1 578 385	X	7.9	1 480 558	57 404	12 410	12 422	15 591	36 969	7.6	15.4	14.0
31 001	...	Adams	1 459	29 625	1 310	20.3	29 084	181	105	113	142	303	7.1	14.0	14.4
31 003	...	Antelope	2 220	7 965	2 577	3.6	7 930	2	20	9	4	5	8.2	17.6	10.0
31 005	...	Arthur	1 853	462	3 136	0.2	459	0	2	0	1	0	7.8	13.4	9.5
31 007	...	Banner	1 933	852	3 120	0.4	832	1	3	0	16	19	7.7	16.8	10.6
31 009	...	Blaine	1 841	675	3 131	0.4	671	1	1	0	2	0	6.1	16.1	10.8
31 011	...	Boone	1 779	6 667	2 688	3.7	6 648	2	11	1	5	17	8.0	17.0	9.5
31 013	...	Box Butte	2 785	13 130	2 129	4.7	12 501	49	302	57	221	722	8.1	19.3	10.9
31 015	...	Boyd	1 399	2 835	3 010	2.0	2 810	0	22	1	2	6	6.2	16.4	7.9
31 017	...	Brown	3 163	3 657	2 944	1.2	3 636	1	11	7	2	21	7.0	15.1	9.8

1. MSA = Metropolitan Statistical Area. CMSA = Consolidated MSA. NECMA = New England county metropolitan area. PMSA = Primary MSA. See Appendix A for explanation of these concepts. See Appendix B for list of metropolitan areas identified by type, with component counties. 2. Dry land or land partially or temporarily covered by water. 3. Hispanic persons may be of any race.

Table A. States and Counties — **Population**

STATE County	Population, 1990 (cont'd)							Population–Change and components of change							
	Age of population (cont'd) Percent							Change		Components of change, 1980–1986					
								1980–1990				Net change		Natural increase	
	25 to 34 years	35 to 44 years	45 to 54 years	55 to 64 years	65 to 74 years	75 years and over	Percent female	Number	Percent	Total persons, 1986	Total persons, 1980	Number	Percent	Births	Deaths
	14	15	16	17	18	19	20	21	22	23	24	25	26	27	28
MONTANA	15.4	15.9	10.3	8.6	7.6	5.7	50.5	12 065	1.5	819 000	787 000	32 000	4.1	88 000	42 000
Beaverhead	14.9	14.6	10.5	8.0	6.8	6.1	49.4	238	2.9	8 500	8 186	300	3.3	900	500
Big Horn	15.2	14.1	9.7	6.7	5.2	3.8	50.7	241	2.2	11 700	11 096	600	5.6	1 900	600
Blaine	14.1	13.9	9.3	8.6	7.0	6.2	50.1	-271	-3.9	6 900	6 999	-100	-1.3	900	400
Broadwater	13.8	14.6	11.4	9.8	10.1	6.3	49.1	51	1.6	3 500	3 267	200	6.9	300	200
Carbon	12.5	16.4	10.0	10.2	10.8	8.9	51.8	-19	-0.2	8 500	8 099	400	4.5	800	600
Carter	14.0	13.4	12.0	10.5	10.2	8.6	48.8	-296	-16.5	1 700	1 799	-100	-3.4	200	100
Cascade	17.0	14.6	10.3	8.6	7.2	5.4	50.7	-3 005	-3.7	79 400	80 696	-1 300	-1.6	9 200	3 900
Chouteau	13.6	15.1	9.8	10.6	10.2	7.3	49.0	-640	-10.5	5 900	6 092	-200	-3.0	600	400
Custer	14.1	14.6	9.7	9.5	9.5	7.5	51.1	-1 412	-10.8	13 200	13 109	0	0.3	1 300	900
Daniels	10.6	14.8	10.8	11.9	12.6	9.6	50.8	-569	-20.1	2 600	2 835	-200	-6.7	300	200
Dawson	14.2	15.3	10.5	10.0	8.3	6.8	50.4	-2 300	-19.5	11 400	11 805	-400	-3.4	1 400	500
Deer Lodge	12.6	14.6	10.2	10.6	11.7	8.2	50.6	-2 240	-17.9	10 700	12 518	-1 800	-14.1	800	900
Fallon	14.6	14.1	10.0	11.3	8.1	6.8	50.3	-660	-17.5	3 600	3 763	-100	-3.3	500	200
Fergus	13.1	14.1	10.0	10.4	10.4	9.5	51.0	-993	-7.6	12 500	13 076	-500	-4.0	1 300	1 000
Flathead	14.7	17.9	11.0	8.6	7.7	5.3	50.5	7 252	14.0	57 800	51 966	5 800	11.2	5 800	2 700
Gallatin	17.7	16.4	8.8	6.2	5.3	3.5	48.9	7 598	17.7	47 800	42 865	4 900	11.5	4 600	1 500
Garfield	13.7	14.2	9.9	9.9	9.6	7.2	48.6	-67	-4.0	1 700	1 656	0	0.7	200	100
Glacier	15.9	13.0	9.2	7.0	5.5	4.1	50.6	1 493	14.0	11 200	10 628	600	5.4	2 000	700
Golden Valley	12.4	13.5	9.6	12.0	10.1	8.1	48.8	-114	-11.1	1 100	1 026	100	7.5	100	100
Granite	12.7	15.0	12.3	9.3	10.9	7.5	48.0	-152	-5.6	2 700	2 700	0	-0.8	300	200
Hill	16.0	14.9	9.0	8.2	7.0	5.1	50.2	-331	-1.8	18 000	17 985	0	0.0	2 200	900
Jefferson	14.6	19.5	12.7	7.5	6.2	4.3	49.3	910	12.9	8 100	7 029	1 100	15.5	700	400
Judith Basin	14.0	15.4	11.7	10.6	10.3	7.5	48.9	-364	-13.8	2 600	2 646	-100	-2.9	200	100
Lake	12.7	14.3	10.1	9.4	8.8	6.9	50.1	1 985	10.4	20 600	19 056	1 500	7.8	2 300	1 200
Lewis and Clark	15.7	17.9	11.0	8.0	6.7	4.9	51.2	4 456	10.4	46 400	43 039	3 400	7.8	5 000	2 200
Liberty	15.0	14.2	9.1	9.5	8.5	7.0	51.2	-34	-1.5	2 400	2 329	100	4.3	300	100
Lincoln	14.2	16.4	11.9	9.1	7.7	4.6	49.8	-271	-1.5	18 600	17 752	800	4.6	2 000	800
McCone	13.6	14.9	9.4	10.9	10.2	6.3	48.9	-426	-15.8	2 500	2 702	-200	-5.9	300	100
Madison	13.6	16.0	11.1	10.7	9.0	7.8	48.5	541	9.9	5 700	5 448	200	4.6	600	400
Meagher	14.0	15.2	10.3	11.1	10.8	6.5	48.2	-335	-15.6	2 200	2 154	0	1.7	200	100
Mineral	14.3	15.6	11.9	10.6	8.1	4.5	49.7	-360	-9.8	3 700	3 675	0	-0.6	400	200
Missoula	17.1	17.1	9.8	6.9	5.8	4.5	50.8	2 671	3.5	77 700	76 016	1 700	2.2	8 000	3 000
Musselshell	10.9	15.9	10.6	11.3	11.2	8.8	50.1	-322	-7.3	4 600	4 428	200	4.9	500	300
Park	15.1	18.8	10.4	9.1	9.0	6.8	51.2	1 693	13.2	13 200	12 869	300	2.3	1 200	900
Petroleum	15.6	15.0	11.8	10.8	9.4	4.2	46.8	-136	-20.8	600	655	0	-2.4	100	0
Phillips	14.9	13.6	10.4	9.0	8.5	6.9	50.9	-204	-3.8	5 500	5 367	100	2.6	600	400
Pondera	14.4	13.2	9.7	9.6	8.6	7.6	50.3	-298	-4.4	6 700	6 731	-100	-0.8	800	400
Powder River	13.1	15.3	10.5	11.3	9.3	6.4	49.2	-430	-17.1	2 400	2 520	-100	-5.3	300	100
Powell	18.5	17.3	11.7	8.5	7.9	6.1	41.7	-338	-4.9	6 900	6 958	-100	-1.0	600	400
Prairie	9.5	14.8	10.6	11.6	13.9	11.4	48.3	-453	-24.7	1 700	1 836	-100	-5.2	100	100
Ravalli	11.8	16.0	12.0	10.1	9.6	7.0	50.7	2 517	11.2	25 000	22 493	2 500	11.0	2 100	1 400
Richland	15.8	14.9	9.5	8.5	7.7	5.7	50.4	-1 527	-12.5	13 400	12 243	1 100	9.2	2 000	600
Roosevelt	16.2	13.9	8.7	7.3	6.1	4.8	51.1	532	5.1	11 700	10 467	1 200	11.4	1 800	700
Rosebud	15.9	17.4	9.5	6.3	4.4	2.7	48.7	606	6.1	12 300	9 899	2 400	24.7	1 800	400
Sanders	12.4	15.9	11.2	10.1	9.1	7.0	49.5	-6	-0.1	8 900	8 675	200	2.3	900	500
Sheridan	12.7	14.4	9.9	11.1	11.7	9.9	50.7	-682	-12.6	5 700	5 414	300	4.7	600	300
Silver Bow	14.6	14.4	10.5	9.5	9.3	7.7	50.9	-4 151	-10.9	34 000	38 092	-4 100	-10.6	3 100	2 900
Stillwater	13.8	16.2	10.6	9.1	9.1	7.5	50.1	938	16.8	6 200	5 598	600	10.0	500	400
Sweet Grass	11.4	15.7	10.7	9.9	11.0	10.1	51.1	-62	-1.9	3 300	3 216	100	2.0	300	300
Teton	12.8	13.8	11.1	9.4	9.4	8.4	50.4	-220	-3.4	6 400	6 491	-100	-0.9	700	400
Toole	14.6	14.9	10.5	8.9	9.9	6.3	50.7	-513	-9.2	5 500	5 559	0	-0.5	700	300
Treasure	13.2	14.0	12.0	10.3	8.1	7.6	50.2	-107	-10.9	1 000	981	0	1.3	100	100
Valley	13.4	15.0	10.7	10.6	9.3	7.5	50.1	-2 011	-19.6	9 300	10 250	-900	-8.8	1 000	600
Wheatland	11.9	13.4	10.0	10.5	11.8	8.7	49.6	-113	-4.8	2 200	2 359	-200	-8.2	200	200
Wibaux	13.8	13.5	9.4	10.7	10.2	9.7	49.5	-285	-19.3	1 300	1 476	-100	-9.6	200	100
Yellowstone	16.7	16.0	10.3	8.6	7.2	5.2	51.5	5 384	5.0	120 100	108 035	12 100	11.2	12 200	4 800
Yellowstone National Park (part)	15.4	19.2	9.6	28.8	1.9	0.0	51.9	-14	-21.2	100	66	0	-1.5	0	0
NEBRASKA	16.3	14.5	9.5	8.6	7.5	6.7	51.3	8 385	0.5	1 598 000	1 570 000	28 000	1.8	165 000	92 000
Adams	15.6	14.1	9.4	8.7	8.4	8.3	51.7	-1 031	-3.4	30 900	30 656	300	0.8	2 900	2 000
Antelope	13.5	12.7	9.0	9.5	9.7	9.7	50.9	-710	-8.2	8 400	8 675	-200	-2.8	1 000	600
Arthur	15.2	11.5	14.1	10.2	10.8	7.6	49.6	-51	-9.9	500	513	0	-4.1	0	0
Banner	12.8	14.4	12.0	10.7	8.9	6.1	49.6	-66	-7.2	1 000	918	100	13.5	100	0
Blaine	14.1	12.0	12.9	11.3	8.0	8.7	51.3	-192	-22.1	700	867	-200	-17.6	100	100
Boone	13.9	11.9	9.1	10.6	10.3	9.7	50.1	-724	-9.8	7 100	7 391	-300	-4.5	800	500
Box Butte	16.2	16.0	8.7	7.5	6.7	6.6	50.7	-566	-4.1	14 600	13 696	900	6.6	1 800	800
Boyd	11.5	12.6	9.2	11.1	11.8	13.3	50.6	-496	-14.9	3 100	3 331	-200	-6.6	300	300
Brown	12.7	12.6	10.8	10.5	10.7	10.8	51.8	-720	-16.4	4 100	4 377	-300	-7.0	400	300

STATE County	Population—(cont'd): Components of change, 1980-1986 (cont'd)	Households, 1990					Births, 1988			Deaths, 1987				Marriages, 1984	
					Percent					Number		Rate			
	Net migration	Number	Percent change, 1980–1990	Persons per household	Female family householder[1]	One-person	Total	Rate[2]	Low birth weight[3] (Number)	Total	Infant[4]	Total[2]	Infant[5]	Number	Rate[2]
	29	30	31	32	33	34	35	36	37	38	39	40	41	42	43
MONTANA	-14 000	306 163	7.9	2.53	8.6	26.3	11 692	14.5	696	6 613	122	8.2	10.0	7 659	9.3
Beaverhead	-200	3 211	7.5	2.51	7.7	27.6	128	15.4	6	66	2	8.0	16.8	82	9.6
Big Horn	-600	3 448	4.7	3.25	15.5	18.4	295	27.1	12	88	3	8.0	9.6	91	7.9
Blaine	-600	2 379	5.4	2.76	12.7	26.4	137	19.6	8	60	2	8.6	13.4	33	4.6
Broadwater	100	1 280	12.3	2.56	7.0	24.6	45	12.9	2	21	1	6.0	20.0	37	10.9
Carbon	200	3 269	5.6	2.44	7.0	27.4	88	10.6	7	102	3	12.3	30.0	77	8.9
Carter	-100	589	-9.5	2.52	4.4	28.7	29	18.1	2	22	0	12.9	0.0	12	7.1
Cascade	-6 600	30 133	2.5	2.51	9.3	26.2	1 333	17.0	91	616	13	7.9	9.7	821	10.1
Chouteau	-400	2 064	-4.8	2.57	5.9	24.7	73	12.6	2	61	2	10.5	24.4	40	6.6
Custer	-400	4 631	-5.5	2.44	9.1	29.3	142	11.2	15	130	1	9.9	6.5	146	10.8
Daniels	-200	919	-12.1	2.42	5.1	29.2	16	6.2	0	31	0	11.9	0.0	15	5.4
Dawson	-1 300	3 691	-11.7	2.54	6.5	26.6	140	13.9	2	70	0	6.7	0.0	87	7.1
Deer Lodge	-1 700	4 060	-8.2	2.32	9.3	32.5	156	15.6	17	149	1	14.8	7.2	100	9.0
Fallon	-400	1 166	-11.5	2.64	4.9	23.8	54	16.4	3	28	1	8.0	22.2	25	6.8
Fergus	-800	4 603	-2.4	2.49	6.2	27.6	126	10.4	2	131	2	10.7	12.7	107	8.4
Flathead	2 800	22 834	21.5	2.56	8.0	24.1	780	13.3	37	443	5	7.6	5.6	618	11.2
Gallatin	1 900	19 015	27.4	2.50	6.8	24.2	679	14.0	33	261	3	5.4	4.3	514	10.9
Garfield	-100	577	-2.0	2.73	4.3	24.1	30	18.8	1	16	0	10.0	0.0	7	4.1
Glacier	-700	3 816	11.1	3.03	15.7	21.7	278	25.0	13	111	3	10.0	9.4	74	6.5
Golden Valley	0	330	-9.3	2.45	3.6	27.9	8	7.3	0	10	0	9.1	0.0	6	5.5
Granite	-100	1 051	5.3	2.40	5.8	29.7	44	16.9	3	23	0	8.8	0.0	14	5.2
Hill	-1 400	6 426	1.9	2.64	9.9	26.2	307	17.4	18	148	6	8.4	19.1	160	8.6
Jefferson	700	2 867	21.4	2.68	6.5	21.4	101	12.2	8	56	0	6.9	0.0	39	4.9
Judith Basin	-200	908	-4.9	2.44	3.6	26.5	32	12.8	0	20	0	8.0	0.0	19	7.0
Lake	400	7 814	17.9	2.62	11.0	24.1	324	15.4	16	197	3	9.4	8.6	158	7.8
Lewis and Clark	500	18 649	16.1	2.47	9.8	28.0	685	14.6	45	372	11	7.9	15.4	498	11.0
Liberty	-100	788	-5.6	2.58	5.8	28.2	46	20.0	5	31	3	13.5	103.4	17	6.5
Lincoln	-400	6 668	10.0	2.60	7.2	23.3	251	13.4	16	135	3	7.1	11.3	136	7.3
McCone	-300	844	-5.8	2.65	3.3	22.6	31	12.4	2	22	0	8.8	0.0	15	5.8
Madison	100	2 387	13.9	2.43	5.1	28.2	60	10.7	2	53	1	9.3	13.0	44	7.5
Meagher	0	709	-8.0	2.39	4.4	29.2	20	10.0	1	15	0	7.1	0.0	18	8.2
Mineral	-300	1 282	-3.5	2.55	7.6	25.5	38	11.2	1	26	0	7.4	0.0	38	10.3
Missoula	-3 300	30 782	9.9	2.47	9.5	27.3	1 127	14.4	69	502	14	6.4	13.0	830	10.9
Musselshell	100	1 661	-2.2	2.41	5.2	30.8	40	9.3	2	52	0	11.6	0.0	39	8.1
Park	-100	5 619	14.1	2.46	7.2	28.0	171	13.9	13	116	0	9.5	0.0	128	9.6
Petroleum	0	209	-9.9	2.48	4.3	23.0	3	5.0	0	2	0	3.3	0.0	7	10.0
Phillips	-100	1 931	0.8	2.59	7.6	26.8	64	11.9	2	56	0	10.4	0.0	39	6.8
Pondera	-500	2 246	-3.8	2.63	6.6	25.4	90	13.4	6	59	2	8.9	17.1	43	6.1
Powder River	-300	805	-9.4	2.55	4.7	25.8	45	20.5	3	27	0	11.7	0.0	16	6.4
Powell	-300	2 234	-3.6	2.44	6.5	28.6	34	5.0	1	71	0	10.3	0.0	63	9.3
Prairie	-100	568	-14.8	2.40	3.2	26.9	17	10.6	1	14	0	8.8	0.0	17	9.4
Ravalli	1 700	9 698	21.1	2.53	6.5	23.9	287	11.2	14	221	4	8.7	12.6	163	6.6
Richland	-200	3 956	-7.8	2.68	6.8	24.3	168	14.2	11	114	3	9.3	16.9	127	8.9
Roosevelt	100	3 694	9.0	2.94	15.3	22.8	271	24.4	11	104	2	9.3	7.1	133	11.5
Rosebud	1 100	3 479	9.1	2.98	10.6	21.4	191	15.7	8	78	5	6.3	19.8	88	6.5
Sanders	-200	3 397	6.8	2.53	5.5	27.1	110	12.8	5	96	1	11.0	8.6	55	6.0
Sheridan	0	1 899	-5.8	2.44	5.6	27.4	50	9.6	2	72	0	13.3	0.0	46	7.8
Silver Bow	-4 300	13 899	-4.8	2.39	9.5	31.9	493	14.8	37	423	6	12.6	14.5	334	9.5
Stillwater	500	2 523	21.8	2.56	5.8	24.1	71	11.3	7	41	1	6.6	13.7	48	7.9
Sweet Grass	0	1 281	3.6	2.42	4.1	29.7	38	11.9	1	55	1	17.2	23.8	34	10.0
Teton	-400	2 329	0.6	2.54	4.7	26.6	80	13.1	10	57	0	9.3	0.0	48	7.3
Toole	-400	1 922	-6.2	2.46	6.7	29.4	68	13.3	3	52	0	10.0	0.0	52	9.0
Treasure	0	339	-5.0	2.58	5.3	23.6	11	12.2	0	9	0	9.0	0.0	3	3.0
Valley	-1 300	3 268	-11.0	2.49	7.4	27.9	102	12.1	9	73	1	8.5	8.7	62	6.4
Wheatland	-200	849	-3.9	2.33	4.8	32.9	30	13.6	3	35	1	15.9	45.5	20	8.7
Wibaux	-200	454	-11.0	2.54	6.4	28.4	18	13.8	3	12	0	9.2	0.0	9	6.0
Yellowstone	4 800	44 689	12.0	2.49	9.7	26.5	1 637	14.1	105	757	12	6.4	7.0	1 207	10.1
Yellowstone National Park (part)	0	24	-80.6	2.17	0.0	29.2	0	NA	0	1	0	NA	0.0	0	0.0
NEBRASKA	-45 000	602 363	5.4	2.54	8.3	26.5	23 907	14.9	1 319	14 827	204	9.3	8.6	13 274	8.3
Adams	-600	11 593	-1.3	2.41	7.6	28.8	360	11.8	21	343	3	11.3	7.1	294	9.4
Antelope	-600	3 045	-4.9	2.59	5.1	26.8	133	15.8	9	90	1	10.7	7.6	74	8.5
Arthur	0	187	-5.6	2.47	5.3	24.1	5	10.0	0	5	0	10.0	0.0	1	2.0
Banner	100	305	-3.2	2.79	4.3	13.8	18	18.0	0	5	0	5.0	0.0	3	3.0
Blaine	-200	268	-12.7	2.52	2.6	28.0	5	7.1	0	4	0	5.7	0.0	0	0.0
Boone	-600	2 560	-4.5	2.56	3.9	27.7	106	15.1	1	78	1	11.1	10.6	50	6.8
Box Butte	-200	4 898	-2.8	2.64	7.6	26.4	192	13.7	8	123	0	8.6	0.0	94	6.6
Boyd	-200	1 148	-9.4	2.41	4.2	30.7	36	11.6	4	43	0	13.9	0.0	29	8.8
Brown	-400	1 499	-11.7	2.40	5.9	29.4	53	13.6	0	59	0	14.8	0.0	34	7.9

1. No spouse present. 2. Per 1,000 resident population estimated as of July 1 of the year shown. 3. Under 2,500 grams. 4. Deaths of infants under 1 year old. 5. Deaths of infants under 1 year old per 1,000 live births.

Table A. States and Counties — **Vital Statistics, Health Resources, Crime, and Education**

STATE County	Divorces, 1984		Physicians, active non–Federal, 1989		Hospitals, 1989			Nursing homes,[4] 1986		Serious crimes known to police, 1988			Education			
						Beds				Number			Public school enrollment[7]		Attainment,[8] 1980	
	Number	Rate[1]	Number[2]	Rate[3]	Number	Number	Rate[3]	Number	Beds	Total[5]	Violent[6]	Rate[3]	1986–1987	1980	Percent 12 yrs. or more	Percent 16 yrs. or more
	44	45	46	47	48	49	50	51	52	53	54	55	56	57	58	59
MONTANA	4 355	5.3	1 244	154	63	4 977	618	93	6 114	28 830	855	3 769	153 327	157 809	74.4	17.5
Beaverhead	55	6.5	10	119	1	31	369	1	100	NA	NA	NA	1 639	1 582	75.8	18.5
Big Horn	47	4.1	12	112	2	84	785	2	70	67	10	613	2 362	2 731	65.1	12.8
Blaine	34	4.8	3	43	1	18	257	2	94	43	0	628	1 547	1 726	68.5	13.9
Broadwater	31	9.1	4	114	1	42	1 200	1	18	149	9	4 056	723	651	72.6	11.9
Carbon	26	3.0	8	96	1	52	627	2	104	162	4	1 965	1 639	1 504	69.6	13.1
Carter	2	1.2	0	0	0	0	0	1	28	NA	NA	NA	250	384	70.4	12.5
Cascade	425	5.2	154	197	2	610	782	3	578	4 890	164	6 305	13 865	15 966	75.2	17.4
Chouteau	23	3.8	2	35	2	69	1 211	2	51	55	2	955	1 157	1 234	76.7	16.3
Custer	85	6.3	20	159	2	169	1 341	2	188	317	11	2 513	2 451	2 404	69.2	15.3
Daniels	8	2.9	2	80	1	53	2 120	1	45	15	0	581	510	570	66.1	12.9
Dawson	52	4.3	8	83	1	121	1 260	1	75	87	1	1 689	2 077	2 322	71.3	13.1
Deer Lodge	52	4.7	12	124	2	266	2 742	1	68	523	6	5 266	1 794	2 655	66.9	11.1
Fallon	5	1.4	1	31	1	44	1 375	1	32	22	0	633	757	775	63.7	9.1
Fergus	67	5.2	8	67	1	117	975	3	364	276	5	2 260	2 275	2 461	72.5	14.0
Flathead	367	6.6	110	185	3	240	403	5	411	2 447	78	4 234	11 631	10 706	76.9	15.4
Gallatin	218	4.6	83	169	1	86	175	4	228	1 083	21	2 239	7 449	6 731	84.4	30.5
Garfield	3	1.8	0	0	0	0	0	1	12	NA	NA	NA	321	333	72.9	11.2
Glacier	50	4.4	9	81	2	86	775	2	88	NA	NA	NA	2 973	2 431	67.9	13.2
Golden Valley	1	0.9	0	0	0	0	0	0	0	8	1	733	175	255	72.1	13.6
Granite	12	4.4	1	38	1	26	1 000	1	13	78	3	2 909	507	571	71.1	14.5
Hill	92	5.0	18	102	1	120	682	1	102	563	16	3 185	3 278	3 572	71.4	16.9
Jefferson	35	4.4	8	94	0	0	0	1	67	86	5	1 043	1 575	1 657	72.8	17.8
Judith Basin	10	3.7	0	0	0	0	0	0	0	2	0	81	443	573	74.4	16.1
Lake	106	5.2	21	98	2	107	500	3	178	370	7	1 774	4 190	4 281	71.6	14.5
Lewis and Clark	294	6.5	92	193	3	242	507	3	231	1 703	68	3 664	9 366	8 932	82.3	23.9
Liberty	3	1.2	3	130	1	51	2 217	1	40	25	1	1 095	486	428	68.7	14.2
Lincoln	120	6.4	14	74	1	29	153	2	103	758	21	4 017	3 971	4 248	68.9	11.4
McCone	3	1.2	3	125	1	60	2 500	1	40	3	0	121	1 031	645	69.5	12.4
Madison	29	4.9	8	143	2	25	446	2	79	84	2	1 484	492	1 049	71.6	15.5
Meagher	14	6.4	0	0	1	37	1 850	1	31	NA	NA	NA	361	452	66.4	13.2
Mineral	13	3.5	3	88	1	30	882	1	20	NA	NA	NA	838	815	71.8	12.0
Missoula	526	6.9	195	246	2	338	426	4	305	4 343	131	5 578	13 042	13 518	81.3	24.0
Musselshell	29	6.0	3	71	1	54	1 286	1	16	81	0	1 812	928	857	66.2	10.3
Park	76	5.7	15	124	1	38	314	1	120	392	17	3 209	2 182	2 493	74.7	13.7
Petroleum	0	0.0	0	0	0	0	0	0	0	NA	NA	NA	113	131	71.9	17.7
Phillips	20	3.5	0	0	1	28	519	1	60	102	3	1 902	1 082	1 052	66.0	7.9
Pondera	22	3.1	6	90	1	112	1 672	1	78	90	1	1 373	1 305	1 485	68.7	15.4
Powder River	6	2.4	0	0	0	0	0	1	39	24	0	1 051	467	528	73.8	14.1
Powell	34	5.0	9	132	1	35	515	1	60	NA	NA	NA	1 171	1 375	69.0	14.6
Prairie	2	1.1	2	133	1	20	1 333	1	14	NA	NA	NA	327	367	59.5	8.0
Ravalli	133	5.4	21	80	1	48	183	2	155	485	14	1 938	4 838	4 912	74.5	18.0
Richland	75	5.2	12	106	1	49	434	2	125	252	8	2 097	2 636	2 391	66.6	11.9
Roosevelt	76	6.6	8	72	3	140	1 261	2	82	251	10	2 257	2 738	2 283	68.4	11.9
Rosebud	63	4.6	6	49	1	75	615	1	55	107	0	876	2 863	2 253	72.5	12.8
Sanders	38	4.1	5	59	1	44	518	3	116	97	18	1 110	1 779	1 973	67.8	13.3
Sheridan	22	3.7	2	39	1	85	1 667	1	65	78	2	1 482	1 041	1 036	67.7	12.8
Silver Bow	105	3.0	66	200	1	274	830	3	395	1 540	38	4 602	5 946	7 570	69.1	14.2
Stillwater	30	4.9	3	47	1	27	422	1	81	70	7	1 137	1 317	1 191	70.9	12.3
Sweet Grass	5	1.5	2	62	1	15	469	1	48	61	1	1 981	668	628	67.3	14.0
Teton	16	2.4	3	50	1	46	767	2	64	43	3	710	1 272	1 320	67.4	14.9
Toole	41	7.1	1	20	1	73	1 460	1	43	83	1	1 607	965	1 179	71.6	14.1
Treasure	1	1.0	0	0	0	0	0	0	0	NA	NA	NA	192	213	70.7	11.0
Valley	35	3.6	9	111	1	54	667	2	98	188	6	2 201	1 879	2 326	72.8	12.9
Wheatland	5	2.2	3	136	1	56	2 545	1	33	25	1	1 144	432	485	70.1	14.4
Wibaux	2	1.3	0	0	0	0	0	1	40	8	0	620	287	343	60.1	8.4
Yellowstone	711	6.0	256	220	2	551	475	7	564	6 694	159	5 703	21 724	21 191	76.6	19.9
Yellowstone National Park (part)	0	0.0	0	NA	0	0	NA	0	0	NA	NA	NA	NA	65	75.1	33.1
NEBRASKA	6 403	4.0	2 715	169	103	10 973	682	270	20 681	64 198	4 309	4 258	266 705	288 576	73.4	15.5
Adams	135	4.3	57	188	2	427	1 409	6	513	937	24	3 069	4 345	4 865	75.5	15.0
Antelope	14	1.6	4	48	2	69	831	1	97	53	3	788	1 278	1 674	69.9	7.6
Arthur	0	0.0	0	0	0	0	0	0	0	NA	NA	NA	88	96	76.7	8.3
Banner	1	1.0	0	0	0	0	0	0	0	1	0	NA	205	184	77.7	10.1
Blaine	1	1.3	0	0	0	0	0	0	0	NA	NA	NA	187	198	72.3	10.9
Boone	10	1.4	6	87	1	34	493	2	126	1	0	NA	1 000	1 332	65.9	9.2
Box Butte	62	4.3	8	58	1	44	317	2	179	356	17	2 479	2 892	2 457	76.1	12.6
Boyd	1	0.3	5	161	1	29	935	1	62	NA	NA	NA	597	582	59.8	8.6
Brown	17	4.0	2	53	1	23	605	1	47	69	0	1 718	756	849	66.5	9.5

1. Per 1,000 resident population estimated as of July 1 of the year shown. 2. As of end of year. 3. Per 100,000 resident population as of July 1 of the year shown. 4. Preliminary. Covers nursing homes with 3 or more beds. 5. Data for serious crimes have not been adjusted for underreporting, this may affect comparability between geographic areas or over time. 6. Includes murder and nonnegligent manslaughter, forcible rape, robbery, and aggravated assault. 7. The 1986–1987 data are based on administrative reports obtained by the U.S. National Center for Education Statistics. The 1980 data are based on the 1980 Census of Population and Housing. 8. Persons 25 years old or older.

STATE County	Education (cont'd)		Social Security Program December 1988				Money income						Housing units, 1990	
	Local government expenditures for education,[1] 1982		Beneficiaries			Supplemental Security Income Program recipients June 1986	Per capita[3]			Median household income 1979 (Dollars)	Percent below poverty level, 1979			
								1979						
	Total (Mil dol)	Per capita (Dollars)	Total	Rate[2]	Payments ($1,000)		1987 Income, (Dollars)	Current dollars	Constant 1987 dollars		Persons	Families	Total	Percent change, 1980–1990
	60	61	62	63	64	65	66	67	68	69	70	71	72	73
MONTANA	459.1	570	132 986	165.3	62 765	7 976	9 322	6 589	10 310	15 420	12.3	9.2	361 155	10.0
Beaverhead	4.3	500	1 375	165.7	639	108	7 951	5 913	9 252	12 807	11.8	7.2	4 128	10.3
Big Horn	8.4	736	1 355	124.3	543	130	6 716	4 857	7 600	13 909	21.0	17.5	4 304	11.3
Blaine	6.4	927	1 090	155.7	459	134	6 935	5 035	7 878	12 987	24.1	17.8	2 930	13.4
Broadwater	1.6	475	665	190.0	294	34	7 461	5 593	8 751	13 614	15.1	12.6	1 593	9.9
Carbon	5.5	662	1 875	225.9	816	90	8 430	5 728	8 963	12 230	12.4	9.1	4 828	10.7
Carter	1.1	650	350	218.8	152	18	7 041	5 102	7 983	11 230	25.0	20.5	816	2.6
Cascade	40.6	507	12 690	162.3	6 177	1 006	10 114	6 959	10 889	16 050	10.3	8.1	33 063	2.7
Chouteau	4.5	743	1 075	185.3	553	32	9 058	6 684	10 458	15 128	12.1	8.6	2 668	-0.8
Custer	5.8	435	2 315	182.3	1 048	152	9 117	6 514	10 192	13 839	13.0	10.0	5 405	-1.2
Daniels	2.2	794	585	225.0	288	8	7 704	6 006	9 398	13 511	13.6	10.6	1 220	-6.4
Dawson	8.0	624	1 615	159.9	773	78	8 918	6 649	10 404	17 230	7.5	6.8	4 487	-3.2
Deer Lodge	6.4	549	2 570	257.0	1 314	162	8 742	6 220	9 732	15 893	11.6	7.7	4 830	-7.1
Fallon	3.2	844	585	177.3	273	14	9 453	6 589	10 310	16 175	16.4	13.4	1 525	0.4
Fergus	7.3	560	2 745	226.9	1 248	152	8 076	5 639	8 823	12 241	17.9	14.2	5 732	6.3
Flathead	26.4	504	10 120	172.7	4 726	454	9 216	6 695	10 476	16 099	9.4	6.9	26 979	20.0
Gallatin	19.0	418	5 590	115.3	2 722	230	9 125	6 459	10 106	15 325	13.2	7.7	21 350	24.3
Garfield	1.2	716	325	203.1	143	6	7 701	5 499	8 604	11 912	22.7	19.3	924	6.5
Glacier	10.2	926	1 525	137.4	666	194	7 234	5 362	8 390	13 404	23.5	16.7	4 797	19.9
Golden Valley	0.8	767	215	195.5	96	4	5 624	4 475	7 002	11 277	22.4	19.4	432	-8.5
Granite	1.7	666	545	209.6	251	16	7 749	5 845	9 146	12 719	16.7	13.4	1 924	17.7
Hill	11.6	630	2 360	134.1	1 134	202	10 064	6 972	10 909	16 561	12.1	9.8	7 345	2.1
Jefferson	4.1	561	1 175	141.6	520	148	9 558	6 324	9 895	16 777	7.2	4.8	3 302	15.2
Judith Basin	2.2	803	465	186.0	216	22	7 523	5 870	9 185	12 985	18.9	14.6	1 346	-1.0
Lake	11.0	566	4 055	192.2	1 731	300	7 848	5 410	8 465	12 270	19.1	14.2	10 972	21.4
Lewis and Clark	25.6	577	7 285	155.0	3 524	468	10 208	7 264	11 366	16 960	9.0	6.2	21 412	15.3
Liberty	2.0	829	365	158.7	202	2	9 241	6 897	10 792	14 339	16.3	14.1	1 007	-12.7
Lincoln	10.5	583	2 920	156.1	1 383	162	7 633	5 761	9 014	15 650	11.0	9.5	8 002	14.0
McCone	1.8	650	480	192.0	220	18	6 381	4 746	7 426	11 987	22.1	19.3	1 161	3.6
Madison	3.5	598	1 165	208.0	518	44	7 584	5 585	8 739	12 135	14.6	10.6	3 902	42.4
Meagher	1.2	542	385	192.5	170	22	8 239	5 854	9 160	13 011	16.0	10.5	1 259	4.8
Mineral	2.7	769	640	188.2	296	28	7 948	5 953	9 315	16 065	13.0	10.5	1 635	-0.7
Missoula	36.3	482	10 150	129.6	4 892	710	10 031	7 256	11 353	16 269	11.6	7.5	33 466	9.6
Musselshell	2.8	598	945	219.8	418	50	6 984	5 347	8 366	11 432	17.4	15.1	2 183	7.1
Park	6.7	510	2 400	195.1	1 041	138	9 102	6 597	10 322	14 612	9.7	7.3	6 926	16.1
Petroleum	0.6	809	85	141.7	34	2	5 282	5 502	8 609	10 848	32.8	25.6	293	-4.2
Phillips	3.7	677	1 000	185.2	439	86	7 036	5 159	8 072	11 921	17.4	15.0	2 765	10.0
Pondera	5.6	808	1 205	179.9	592	78	9 038	6 661	10 422	16 126	13.9	10.8	2 618	-3.1
Powder River	2.1	854	335	152.3	151	6	8 014	6 523	10 207	15 065	10.5	9.1	1 096	-2.4
Powell	3.7	556	1 135	166.9	542	48	7 661	5 662	8 859	14 697	11.2	8.7	2 835	0.2
Prairie	1.0	546	405	253.1	180	14	6 031	4 288	6 709	9 450	31.4	27.7	749	-7.3
Ravalli	11.0	469	5 265	204.9	2 323	210	8 043	5 678	8 884	13 254	16.1	12.9	11 099	21.5
Richland	8.8	588	1 785	151.3	823	88	9 067	6 897	10 792	17 615	10.0	7.5	4 825	2.9
Roosevelt	10.7	944	1 710	154.1	745	124	7 729	5 741	8 983	14 812	16.3	11.2	4 265	12.0
Rosebud	15.1	1 241	1 100	90.2	469	112	8 748	6 180	9 670	16 750	18.0	13.1	4 251	12.3
Sanders	5.5	607	1 845	214.5	804	122	7 818	5 522	8 640	12 615	12.2	10.2	4 335	12.8
Sheridan	4.2	706	1 200	230.8	587	44	8 994	6 779	10 607	14 953	13.5	11.2	2 417	0.0
Silver Bow	22.5	614	7 715	232.4	3 956	480	9 272	6 547	10 244	14 591	10.3	7.7	15 474	-3.7
Stillwater	3.6	627	1 365	216.7	600	54	8 180	5 582	8 734	13 240	14.5	12.1	3 291	22.8
Sweet Grass	1.8	536	750	234.4	335	20	8 101	5 689	8 902	11 421	13.9	9.4	1 639	10.8
Teton	3.9	611	1 355	222.1	641	58	8 826	6 070	9 498	14 012	14.8	11.4	2 725	-0.8
Toole	3.8	670	905	177.5	452	48	9 305	6 659	10 419	14 143	15.0	9.4	2 354	-3.2
Treasure	0.8	762	180	200.0	79	2	7 031	5 208	8 149	12 122	19.5	16.3	448	-3.0
Valley	7.6	765	1 675	199.4	769	100	9 202	6 187	9 681	14 550	13.7	11.4	5 304	-5.5
Wheatland	1.5	658	455	206.8	205	18	7 448	5 636	8 819	12 549	13.3	9.7	1 129	-1.0
Wibaux	1.0	621	265	203.8	116	8	6 990	4 908	7 680	11 173	20.6	18.0	563	-17.2
Yellowstone	54.2	478	17 120	147.1	8 434	912	10 519	7 600	11 892	17 460	9.3	7.1	48 781	14.1
Yellowstone National Park (part)	NA	NA	0	0.0	0	0	11 766	8 414	13 165	12 292	8.7	6.1	46	-70.1
NEBRASKA	763.6	480	263 820	164.7	127 353	14 103	11 139	6 934	10 850	15 925	10.7	8.0	660 621	5.7
Adams	14.3	454	5 695	187.3	2 864	376	10 300	6 908	10 809	15 307	9.8	6.5	12 491	-1.3
Antelope	5.1	589	1 735	206.5	747	80	8 705	4 882	7 639	10 604	23.1	19.6	3 478	-5.7
Arthur	0.5	948	85	170.0	40	0	8 931	6 598	10 324	12 065	16.2	15.7	242	3.9
Banner	0.8	796	105	105.0	52	2	8 056	5 573	8 720	11 893	19.9	17.9	366	-10.7
Blaine	1.1	1 413	125	178.6	54	6	8 227	4 691	7 340	10 469	28.1	20.9	381	3.5
Boone	3.9	536	1 560	222.9	687	62	9 597	5 673	8 877	10 900	19.9	16.7	2 878	-6.1
Box Butte	5.5	389	1 900	135.7	912	64	11 344	7 625	11 931	18 326	7.1	5.2	5 534	-0.3
Boyd	1.8	531	885	285.5	356	38	7 314	4 542	7 107	9 351	23.8	21.6	1 538	5.6
Brown	2.5	575	955	244.9	410	40	8 139	5 484	8 581	10 899	19.5	17.1	1 950	-2.3

1. Elementary and secondary. 2. Per 1,000 resident population estimated as of July 1 of the year shown. 3. Based on the resident population estimated as of July 1, 1988 for 1987 data and enumerated as of April 1, 1980 for 1979 data.

STATE County	Housing units, 1990 (cont'd): Occupied units: Total	Occupied units: Owner occupied: Percent	Owner occupied: Median value (Dollars)	Occupied units: Median rent (Dollars)	Civilian labor force, 1990: Total	Civilian labor force: Percent change, 1989–1990	Unemployment: Total	Unemployment: Rate[1]	Private nonfarm establishments, 1988: Number	Net change, 1987–1988	Employment[2]: Total	Employment: Percent change, 1987–1988	Employment: Manufacturing	Employment: Retail trade
	74	75	76	77	78	79	80	81	82	83	84	85	86	87
MONTANA	306 163	67.3	56 600	251	402 000	-0.7	23 000	5.8	X	X	203 741	-0.2	20 544	56 624
Beaverhead	3 211	61.5	55 500	195	4 356	-3.1	187	4.3	285	2	1 586	10.2	171	494
Big Horn	3 448	62.6	41 600	178	4 292	-1.6	558	13.0	192	-10	1 588	-12.2	27	364
Blaine	2 379	62.2	40 800	159	3 164	-4.2	256	8.1	163	6	874	-2.8	13	256
Broadwater	1 280	74.9	46 800	216	1 333	-5.2	82	6.2	88	-2	543	-5.7	0	141
Carbon	3 269	73.1	45 700	211	3 856	-2.9	165	4.3	198	0	1 120	4.4	67	305
Carter	589	77.4	22 500	144	856	-9.0	24	2.8	34	-2	132	-5.7	9	34
Cascade	30 133	63.7	60 100	275	39 658	0.5	1 982	5.0	2 305	-17	22 313	-4.5	906	6 614
Chouteau	2 064	69.3	41 900	189	2 548	-5.2	82	3.2	150	10	537	3.1	15	166
Custer	4 631	66.9	37 400	225	5 910	-2.0	246	4.2	366	-41	2 987	-7.9	116	1 004
Daniels	919	79.4	30 800	173	1 102	-6.4	39	3.5	75	-6	397	-14.6	0	86
Dawson	3 691	72.7	37 100	205	4 838	-4.6	192	4.0	317	-19	2 334	-5.5	62	684
Deer Lodge	4 060	72.9	34 000	148	4 317	0.5	349	8.1	234	-4	1 523	-26.9	128	503
Fallon	1 166	77.0	36 700	174	1 317	-7.7	40	3.0	110	-9	552	-16.2	9	126
Fergus	4 603	71.5	40 800	199	5 847	-3.7	360	6.2	419	3	2 355	2.9	145	685
Flathead	22 834	70.6	64 200	272	30 988	1.4	2 339	7.5	2 149	8	16 345	4.4	3 315	4 618
Gallatin	19 015	58.5	70 200	292	27 121	1.3	926	3.4	1 859	-34	13 726	-0.8	1 219	4 606
Garfield	577	70.9	32 000	173	781	-8.9	19	2.4	23	1	125	0.0	0	45
Glacier	3 816	60.9	43 800	147	5 135	-5.1	583	11.4	298	3	1 794	-9.0	146	571
Golden Valley	330	79.1	30 800	168	468	-7.1	19	4.1	21	4	66	100.0	0	13
Granite	1 051	75.4	37 700	177	1 318	-0.8	100	7.6	74	-4	412	9.3	177	105
Hill	6 426	63.1	53 200	228	7 652	-0.4	458	6.0	514	-5	3 774	3.2	168	1 274
Jefferson	2 867	80.7	63 700	215	5 818	-2.1	207	3.6	137	4	652	10.7	0	215
Judith Basin	908	72.9	30 600	153	1 293	-4.2	54	4.2	59	1	175	-7.4	0	33
Lake	7 814	70.2	61 300	207	10 579	-2.7	834	7.9	509	-2	3 424	11.9	697	1 030
Lewis and Clark	18 649	68.5	61 800	279	25 607	-0.7	1 144	4.5	1 584	-29	14 433	0.3	749	3 890
Liberty	788	71.7	41 300	202	809	-11.0	21	2.6	65	-2	233	-25.3	0	72
Lincoln	6 668	73.3	48 900	205	8 786	4.2	1 007	11.5	506	-3	3 994	11.4	1 409	784
McCone	844	78.2	32 300	181	1 114	-8.5	43	3.9	53	-1	394	2.9	0	77
Madison	2 387	68.8	56 800	224	2 967	-4.8	109	3.7	182	-3	928	7.8	0	207
Meagher	709	67.4	36 500	192	929	-7.9	34	3.7	59	-7	229	-8.0	28	87
Mineral	1 282	72.9	43 700	187	1 392	0.4	144	10.3	82	-15	656	-7.6	227	196
Missoula	30 782	60.1	66 200	273	41 796	1.1	2 076	5.0	2 626	-15	26 294	3.0	4 099	7 492
Musselshell	1 661	78.1	29 600	175	1 696	-3.9	132	7.8	105	-7	574	0.2	20	153
Park	5 619	66.3	48 100	224	5 941	-0.5	453	7.6	454	15	2 657	18.6	247	718
Petroleum	209	76.1	15 500	175	245	-10.9	9	3.7	8	-1	9	-30.8	0	0
Phillips	1 931	69.8	41 500	195	2 807	-3.5	125	4.5	148	-9	891	-7.4	35	238
Pondera	2 246	69.5	42 100	194	2 803	-6.4	124	4.4	199	5	1 107	2.9	75	263
Powder River	805	73.4	43 800	217	1 095	-9.1	26	2.4	57	3	203	-25.6	0	68
Powell	2 234	71.8	41 900	188	2 918	-1.5	153	5.2	154	-3	978	4.7	203	238
Prairie	568	78.9	19 100	158	658	-10.4	32	4.9	28	-4	93	-1.1	0	31
Ravalli	9 698	75.1	61 500	232	11 694	-0.6	980	8.4	678	17	3 690	1.4	739	887
Richland	3 956	70.7	44 200	210	5 086	-5.1	311	6.1	364	8	2 674	7.4	287	666
Roosevelt	3 694	63.9	40 400	173	5 116	-2.3	487	9.5	244	6	1 994	3.7	0	540
Rosebud	3 479	68.8	51 800	206	5 010	-2.1	338	6.7	190	7	2 573	-3.8	79	445
Sanders	3 397	75.1	42 000	173	3 079	-1.6	383	12.4	229	2	1 312	-2.4	423	281
Sheridan	1 899	77.0	39 500	193	2 151	-7.0	64	3.0	188	-1	941	0.0	0	374
Silver Bow	13 899	70.8	44 300	189	13 561	1.4	1 002	7.4	1 059	1	9 671	1.0	423	2 414
Stillwater	2 523	73.6	56 200	235	3 347	0.5	118	3.5	161	8	1 088	45.5	0	228
Sweet Grass	1 281	72.1	48 000	195	1 409	-4.9	43	3.1	100	-3	378	-2.8	14	161
Teton	2 329	73.4	44 900	202	2 728	-6.0	95	3.5	154	7	701	-0.3	52	129
Toole	1 922	71.9	39 100	189	2 117	-4.3	83	3.9	214	2	1 020	-0.5	27	306
Treasure	339	64.6	35 200	179	435	-1.4	12	2.8	21	0	94	-4.1	0	13
Valley	3 268	71.4	36 800	206	4 240	-3.2	198	4.7	262	-20	1 667	4.3	85	474
Wheatland	849	75.3	27 600	140	956	-7.0	52	5.4	62	-1	253	-7.3	0	85
Wibaux	454	72.5	28 900	175	482	-9.7	21	4.4	23	0	101	7.4	0	20
Yellowstone	44 689	65.7	62 800	289	64 473	0.1	3 078	4.8	3 981	-19	41 371	-1.8	2 991	11 109
Yellowstone National Park (part)	24	12.5	0	207	NA	NA	NA	NA	0	0	0	NA	0	0
NEBRASKA	602 363	66.5	50 400	282	839 000	3.3	18 000	2.2	X	X	539 000	5.0	94 558	128 452
Adams	11 593	64.5	44 800	250	16 462	2.5	305	1.9	881	-7	10 868	2.2	2 709	2 483
Antelope	3 045	74.0	26 100	137	3 371	2.8	70	2.1	239	-8	1 221	-3.8	80	342
Arthur	187	60.4	23 200	132	251	-1.2	12	4.8	11	2	35	84.2	0	0
Banner	305	63.0	32 500	125	460	-0.4	6	1.3	5	1	15	25.0	0	0
Blaine	268	64.6	22 300	99	350	2.0	10	2.9	11	0	35	-5.4	0	20
Boone	2 560	73.1	30 500	155	3 581	4.4	41	1.1	202	2	1 030	1.4	31	360
Box Butte	4 898	67.9	44 000	223	6 029	3.1	180	3.0	359	-22	2 672	0.4	424	807
Boyd	1 148	79.3	16 800	126	1 179	-0.4	19	1.6	78	-3	267	-8.9	6	77
Brown	1 499	73.6	29 400	180	1 713	4.2	30	1.8	130	1	547	-2.1	0	239

1. Percent of total civilian labor force. 2. For week including March 12. Excludes government employees, self-employed persons, farm workers, domestic service workers, railroad employees subject to the Railroad Retirement Act, and employees on oceanborne vessels or in foreign countries.

STATE County	Private nonfarm establishments, 1988 (cont'd): Employment[1] (cont'd): Finance, insurance, and real estate	Employment[1] (cont'd): Services	Annual payroll: Total (Mil dol)	Annual payroll: Average per employee (Dollars)	Personal income, 1989: Total (Mil dol)	Percent change, 1988–1989	Wages and salaries[2] (Mil dol)	Proprietor's income (Mil dol)	Dividends, interest, & rent (Mil dol)	Transfer payments (Mil dol)	Per capita[3]: Dollars	Per capita[3]: Rank	Earnings, 1989: Total (Mil dol)	Percent by selected industries: Farm	Goods-related[4]: Total
	88	89	90	91	92	93	94	95	96	97	98	99	100	101	102
MONTANA	12 936	64 138	3 222	X	11 392	9.3	5 830	1 537	2 433	2 128	14 149	X	7 367	6.4	17.3
Beaverhead	83	392	21	13 294	113	9.5	51	21	26	23	13 500	1 680	72	20.7	NA
Big Horn	99	333	36	22 372	131	11.4	77	22	18	26	12 215	2 225	98	15.9	33.2
Blaine	60	362	9	10 698	80	12.9	27	15	18	18	11 436	2 526	42	24.7	5.6
Broadwater	0	121	7	13 274	43	19.2	14	9	10	9	12 497	2 118	23	31.7	NA
Carbon	56	511	11	9 650	107	11.9	25	18	31	24	12 880	1 965	43	27.4	8.9
Carter	0	0	2	11 621	22	-2.4	4	7	7	4	13 888	1 483	12	47.7	NA
Cascade	1 834	7 884	355	15 889	1 245	7.8	674	151	238	227	15 962	656	825	2.9	9.1
Chouteau	69	146	6	10 631	87	14.2	20	18	32	14	15 198	909	39	42.7	5.0
Custer	170	1 048	38	12 662	176	6.9	81	25	40	35	13 957	1 451	106	7.8	6.9
Daniels	34	117	4	11 280	34	5.6	11	6	12	7	13 333	1 762	17	19.3	NA
Dawson	182	730	32	13 764	131	2.4	64	16	29	25	13 585	1 639	80	6.1	11.2
Deer Lodge	111	605	21	13 525	116	7.7	49	9	25	39	11 967	2 336	58	2.1	9.7
Fallon	42	125	9	16 618	49	7.2	20	13	10	8	15 238	890	33	10.8	19.7
Fergus	179	837	29	12 470	175	19.6	64	32	51	35	14 604	1 165	96	17.4	17.4
Flathead	1 023	4 671	274	16 769	847	8.4	442	121	173	148	14 225	1 322	563	2.2	30.0
Gallatin	710	4 343	181	13 211	668	10.9	349	97	152	102	13 604	1 627	446	5.3	16.2
Garfield	0	0	1	10 344	25	4.4	5	10	7	3	15 870	686	15	59.9	NA
Glacier	136	481	26	14 536	140	12.2	71	29	23	31	12 629	2 061	100	16.1	13.0
Golden Valley	0	9	0	4 455	14	13.3	2	4	4	3	12 993	1 908	7	55.8	NA
Granite	0	10	6	13 614	35	6.1	12	5	8	8	13 168	1 830	17	20.7	32.8
Hill	164	1 564	47	12 488	235	14.3	112	33	55	48	13 388	1 733	145	9.3	6.0
Jefferson	27	182	10	15 595	131	8.6	51	10	25	18	15 360	855	61	4.0	48.6
Judith Basin	0	18	2	9 960	31	20.9	7	7	10	6	12 765	2 008	14	33.5	NA
Lake	179	1 075	45	13 048	253	11.2	98	33	63	60	11 826	2 386	131	7.8	20.0
Lewis and Clark	1 271	5 920	212	14 718	719	7.3	465	70	126	139	15 078	950	535	1.0	9.2
Liberty	0	58	3	12 815	37	14.8	10	10	11	5	15 894	681	20	40.5	4.6
Lincoln	107	703	61	15 368	205	8.7	118	27	28	45	10 859	2 695	145	0.8	46.8
McCone	0	94	6	15 812	31	10.3	10	8	8	5	12 754	2 014	18	36.6	NA
Madison	63	134	18	19 170	73	15.0	28	10	21	15	12 963	1 923	38	16.6	NA
Meagher	0	72	2	10 694	26	14.3	8	6	8	5	12 916	1 947	14	31.3	NA
Mineral	0	158	9	13 364	36	7.9	19	3	6	10	10 778	2 722	22	2.5	NA
Missoula	1 371	7 765	435	16 533	1 117	8.7	686	134	201	194	14 079	1 398	821	0.5	21.1
Musselshell	0	154	7	12 174	58	9.5	16	14	15	13	13 740	1 556	29	18.8	14.8
Park	123	1 211	29	10 942	[5]180	[5]10.6	[5]77	[5]22	[5]49	[5]41	[5]14 969	[5]1 001	([5])	[5]6.2	[5]14.6
Petroleum	0	0	0	9 222	8	16.5	1	4	2	1	14 966	1 003	5	64.9	NA
Phillips	59	259	12	13 971	76	18.0	34	16	18	13	14 224	1 324	50	21.9	NA
Pondera	86	393	15	13 867	91	19.5	31	15	27	17	13 575	1 647	46	23.1	14.7
Powder River	0	44	2	10 335	31	-0.1	8	11	8	4	14 186	1 351	18	43.7	NA
Powell	58	259	15	15 444	82	10.9	41	9	17	19	12 111	2 282	50	8.3	NA
Prairie	0	15	1	10 699	21	3.6	5	5	6	4	14 037	1 419	11	45.2	NA
Ravalli	209	1 053	49	13 162	301	9.1	90	40	82	73	11 479	2 506	130	5.2	21.2
Richland	142	649	41	15 316	153	7.5	71	28	35	26	13 565	1 654	99	12.7	29.7
Roosevelt	99	577	24	12 257	123	7.4	59	17	25	28	11 165	2 615	77	6.4	17.0
Rosebud	114	518	63	24 632	142	10.4	118	16	18	21	11 611	2 469	134	7.5	29.2
Sanders	0	359	18	13 710	88	7.2	37	12	19	26	10 379	2 816	49	8.3	27.8
Sheridan	66	270	10	10 739	78	11.4	22	17	29	13	15 360	854	39	19.2	9.7
Silver Bow	520	3 334	186	19 204	496	6.6	278	33	94	124	15 064	959	312	0.2	NA
Stillwater	49	161	23	20 920	102	11.8	39	13	24	18	15 944	662	52	14.0	NA
Sweet Grass	30	102	4	11 571	50	12.8	12	9	20	9	15 782	716	21	27.2	11.4
Teton	76	189	10	14 569	102	27.2	26	33	27	17	16 832	467	58	45.9	5.6
Toole	88	177	14	14 076	79	13.1	33	17	18	14	15 739	726	50	15.3	10.6
Treasure	0	0	1	12 617	16	7.5	4	6	4	2	17 645	346	9	50.0	NA
Valley	150	589	20	12 250	123	10.7	48	23	32	24	15 290	876	71	13.4	9.3
Wheatland	24	80	3	9 897	33	13.9	9	8	11	7	15 109	937	17	36.5	7.4
Wibaux	0	8	1	10 851	15	-0.3	4	2	4	4	12 458	2 139	6	17.0	NA
Yellowstone	2 785	13 181	710	17 167	1 811	8.0	1 090	185	373	273	15 595	774	1 275	2.0	14.4
Yellowstone National Park (part)	0	0	0	NA	([5])	([5])	([5])	([5])	([5])	([5])	([5])	([5])	([5])	([5])	([5])
NEBRASKA	50 572	157 660	8 998	X	25 272	7.2	14 900	3 884	4 629	3 581	15 697	X	18 785	9.8	18.4
Adams	375	3 375	166	15 309	492	5.8	271	82	100	73	16 256	577	353	12.4	21.0
Antelope	103	372	14	11 462	104	2.7	32	32	27	18	12 502	2 115	64	35.1	8.5
Arthur	0	0	0	10 743	8	21.3	2	4	1	1	18 140	280	6	64.7	NA
Banner	0	0	0	13 133	15	0.9	3	7	3	1	15 601	772	10	76.5	NA
Blaine	0	0	0	9 800	11	17.1	3	4	3	2	15 040	975	7	66.4	NA
Boone	76	243	13	12 529	96	5.2	28	28	25	16	13 902	1 474	56	37.7	5.9
Box Butte	183	775	34	12 579	227	6.0	141	52	31	27	16 295	571	193	20.0	7.2
Boyd	29	65	3	10 592	39	10.7	8	13	10	8	12 436	2 146	21	36.6	NA
Brown	47	118	5	9 845	60	7.8	16	22	13	10	15 665	751	38	44.1	6.8

1. For week including March 12. Excludes government employees, self-employed persons, farm workers, domestic service workers, railroad employees subject to the Railroad Retirement Act, and employees on oceanborne vessels or in foreign countries. 2. Includes other labor income. 3. Based on the resident population estimated as of July 1 of the year shown. 4. Covers mining, construction, and manufacturing. 5. Yellowstone Park included with Park County.

STATE County	Earnings, 1989 (cont'd) — Percent by selected industries (cont'd) — Goods-related[1] — Manu-facturing	Service-related & other[2] — Total	Retail trade	Finance, insur-ance, & real estate	Services	Govern-ment	Agriculture, 1987 — Farms — Number	Percent with — Less than 50 acres	500 acres and over	Farm operators, percent — Whose principal occu-pation is farming	Residing on farm operated	Land in farms — Acreage (1,000)	Percent change, 1982–1987	Acres — Average size of farm	Total irrigated (1,000)	Total cropland (1,000)
	103	104	105	106	107	108	109	110	111	112	113	114	115	116	117	118
MONTANA	8.4	55.7	11.5	4.3	24.1	20.6	24 568	19.1	55.1	70.8	74.3	60 204	-0.6	2 451	1 997	17 830
Beaverhead	2.9	NA	9.3	2.4	14.3	24.6	373	18.5	60.1	72.7	79.4	1 526	-1.4	4 090	248	236
Big Horn	0.5	26.0	5.0	1.5	13.9	24.8	501	16.6	59.5	76.6	71.1	2 759	2.1	5 508	58	386
Blaine	0.9	39.7	8.7	1.9	18.7	30.0	529	12.7	69.4	80.9	71.5	2 434	1.8	4 601	48	589
Broadwater	13.0	30.8	7.8	1.6	11.3	14.7	213	11.7	56.8	77.0	77.9	459	-7.6	2 154	46	140
Carbon	1.7	43.0	11.4	1.7	18.7	20.7	635	17.3	37.8	71.8	77.2	537	-14.7	845	79	180
Carter	NA	35.1	6.1	3.7	8.3	14.0	353	11.6	81.3	84.4	73.9	1 630	-3.9	4 616	9	203
Cascade	3.2	61.5	12.8	5.3	28.8	26.5	805	18.4	50.2	66.8	76.1	1 461	4.9	1 815	32	485
Chouteau	1.4	32.0	7.2	3.2	11.9	20.3	795	6.4	84.9	88.6	71.2	2 228	4.1	2 803	10	1 308
Custer	2.0	56.0	11.4	4.6	24.3	29.3	397	23.7	54.9	70.5	70.5	2 184	-6.1	5 500	35	182
Daniels	NA	55.3	9.2	3.8	17.8	22.1	381	4.2	77.7	82.4	58.8	780	-4.7	2 047	1	512
Dawson	1.7	63.1	11.1	4.1	18.8	19.6	499	12.4	73.5	79.2	64.3	1 327	-2.0	2 659	14	465
Deer Lodge	5.3	49.0	12.7	3.1	22.0	39.2	72	26.4	38.9	48.6	65.3	152	-20.6	2 113	19	22
Fallon	1.1	52.7	6.8	2.6	10.9	16.7	324	11.1	73.1	75.6	75.3	920	3.8	2 838	2	260
Fergus	2.7	46.0	11.6	2.9	21.9	19.2	838	13.0	70.4	79.4	75.8	2 143	2.5	2 558	12	658
Flathead	22.9	53.8	12.2	4.4	24.6	14.0	825	39.3	12.1	44.5	83.6	259	-9.5	313	34	105
Gallatin	7.6	53.1	14.2	3.7	23.8	25.4	850	27.5	33.8	62.2	80.4	732	-5.5	861	100	305
Garfield	NA	NA	5.2	NA	6.0	14.2	297	11.4	82.8	85.9	70.4	2 063	-1.6	6 947	2	335
Glacier	2.3	45.0	8.9	3.3	20.5	26.0	405	9.1	69.6	69.4	64.9	1 646	-0.2	4 065	28	484
Golden Valley	NA	NA	4.3	NA	5.2	19.0	135	9.6	77.0	85.2	71.1	626	-0.5	4 635	14	112
Granite	23.8	23.1	7.1	2.4	7.9	23.4	149	14.8	66.4	75.2	77.9	348	2.4	2 336	43	53
Hill	2.1	63.7	12.0	3.6	24.7	21.0	713	5.3	76.9	79.7	69.0	1 722	-0.7	2 415	7	1 137
Jefferson	5.9	22.2	5.4	0.7	10.4	25.2	256	25.4	43.0	49.2	77.3	379	-8.1	1 480	29	74
Judith Basin	NA	36.5	7.5	2.7	10.6	25.0	351	11.4	76.6	80.9	72.4	871	7.0	2 481	8	306
Lake	12.0	53.5	13.9	3.2	27.6	18.7	1 079	38.4	15.2	55.8	80.4	656	-1.7	608	90	159
Lewis and Clark	4.3	55.3	10.9	6.0	27.9	34.6	480	38.3	30.4	46.5	79.0	889	-4.7	1 852	40	110
Liberty	1.0	32.7	8.4	1.6	8.7	22.3	295	4.1	83.7	87.5	67.5	934	2.9	3 167	6	D
Lincoln	32.4	32.5	8.6	1.2	12.1	19.9	245	28.2	11.8	41.6	84.1	61	10.8	251	6	19
McCone	0.0	NA	6.5	NA	9.9	16.3	441	6.8	78.9	82.8	65.8	1 277	-0.7	2 896	8	544
Madison	2.2	NA	10.5	2.6	15.9	19.5	453	17.4	52.8	74.8	79.0	1 196	-0.1	2 640	125	166
Meagher	1.5	NA	9.3	NA	22.6	18.8	144	20.8	63.9	72.9	68.8	1 013	2.3	7 033	48	108
Mineral	29.3	NA	12.6	1.2	15.3	28.0	58	22.4	12.1	34.5	81.0	15	-18.8	250	2	4
Missoula	14.9	59.3	12.7	3.8	27.5	19.1	473	49.0	15.4	35.3	85.8	253	1.2	535	19	46
Musselshell	1.1	52.7	9.5	2.3	16.4	13.7	249	14.1	64.3	69.5	74.7	1 042	-7.6	4 186	10	159
Park	[3]5.4	[3]66.7	[3]11.3	[3]3.1	[3]26.6	[3]12.6	404	23.5	52.2	70.0	81.2	790	1.2	1 956	53	147
Petroleum	0.0	NA	2.2	NA	7.0	15.6	111	8.1	82.0	82.9	77.5	664	-5.3	5 980	8	83
Phillips	0.9	NA	8.3	2.5	NA	15.3	492	9.6	69.7	81.3	69.9	1 938	-2.5	3 940	47	581
Pondera	3.1	43.0	10.2	4.3	17.4	19.2	491	10.2	72.3	83.9	72.3	907	5.4	1 847	61	580
Powder River	NA	30.3	5.8	2.2	8.7	18.8	351	14.8	71.8	78.1	81.2	1 669	0.9	4 754	10	176
Powell	12.9	NA	8.2	2.3	11.9	38.8	237	20.3	55.7	69.2	81.4	671	-9.7	2 829	61	90
Prairie	NA	NA	6.5	NA	7.7	20.8	191	9.4	72.3	82.7	69.6	705	-1.5	3 690	10	141
Ravalli	13.6	52.2	12.1	3.5	23.0	21.3	1 010	50.6	9.9	51.6	85.8	255	-6.3	252	77	100
Richland	8.5	44.8	9.5	3.3	18.8	12.8	620	14.8	61.6	76.1	71.0	1 195	10.3	1 927	38	550
Roosevelt	12.3	51.4	10.6	5.2	21.9	25.3	598	5.9	74.9	81.4	64.5	1 364	-0.5	2 281	6	752
Rosebud	1.7	49.4	4.4	1.4	13.9	13.9	363	15.7	64.2	75.2	74.4	2 908	-3.7	8 012	26	230
Sanders	22.3	39.8	7.4	1.8	16.6	24.1	382	21.5	27.2	52.4	83.8	375	-12.6	981	20	55
Sheridan	0.7	52.6	9.5	4.4	21.4	18.6	600	5.5	79.8	84.7	72.2	1 025	-2.4	1 708	4	688
Silver Bow	4.5	65.5	12.6	4.6	28.8	17.3	114	14.9	42.1	44.7	79.8	115	-9.8	1 012	7	13
Stillwater	9.0	NA	8.1	0.5	NA	12.5	447	17.4	57.7	71.8	74.9	843	-2.4	1 885	24	248
Sweet Grass	1.1	41.7	14.8	2.3	16.2	19.6	308	13.6	65.3	75.0	73.7	873	-4.0	2 835	49	93
Teton	1.3	35.2	4.7	2.7	9.4	13.3	622	12.4	61.6	81.8	72.0	1 049	-4.8	1 686	100	613
Toole	0.8	51.9	10.7	5.7	14.2	22.3	393	6.6	83.0	85.2	69.7	1 132	7.1	2 879	4	672
Treasure	0.0	NA	6.1	NA	8.0	12.8	121	19.8	61.2	75.2	59.5	616	1.3	5 092	19	49
Valley	2.6	55.9	9.8	3.9	23.1	21.5	720	9.6	71.0	81.1	66.5	1 856	4.4	2 578	48	849
Wheatland	4.4	39.5	9.1	1.8	14.4	16.6	145	9.0	72.4	80.0	64.8	823	-2.4	5 677	24	135
Wibaux	NA	NA	6.8	5.4	16.6	29.7	192	14.6	71.4	67.7	62.0	516	9.7	2 689	0	D
Yellowstone	7.7	70.2	13.1	6.1	28.7	13.4	1 043	33.3	32.2	59.9	73.3	1 398	8.5	1 340	70	376
Yellowstone National Park (part)	(3)	(3)	(3)	(3)	(3)	(3)	NA	NA	NA	NA	NA	NA	NA	NA	NA	NA
NEBRASKA	13.2	54.4	9.1	6.7	21.4	17.4	60 502	15.5	37.4	75.0	67.9	45 305	0.8	749	5 682	23 320
Adams	16.6	52.4	10.1	1.9	26.1	14.2	780	13.8	36.9	75.5	64.7	367	4.7	470	141	310
Antelope	4.5	42.8	12.6	3.7	13.4	13.6	1 009	12.4	36.6	83.8	67.1	509	1.0	504	141	388
Arthur	0.0	NA	5.5	NA	4.1	8.5	90	23.3	68.9	85.6	65.6	418	0.2	4 644	7	42
Banner	0.0	NA	NA	NA	2.2	12.4	212	5.7	73.6	75.5	65.6	412	1.3	1 942	15	D
Blaine	0.0	NA	5.1	NA	2.5	14.8	129	17.1	70.5	79.8	76.7	427	4.4	3 307	8	55
Boone	1.3	40.7	9.4	4.3	12.7	15.7	936	13.2	27.9	81.3	65.2	443	2.2	473	94	327
Box Butte	5.2	64.6	5.6	2.6	9.2	8.2	556	10.6	55.2	75.0	65.1	639	0.9	1 149	118	372
Boyd	1.4	39.7	8.5	5.0	8.8	17.4	443	12.9	44.5	76.3	70.9	294	3.8	663	3	153
Brown	1.2	32.2	8.7	3.0	9.7	16.9	344	15.4	52.6	69.5	64.2	563	-6.8	1 636	39	137

1. Covers mining, construction, and manufacturing. 2. Covers private sector earnings in agricultural services, forestry, and fisheries; transportation and public utilities; wholesale trade; retail trade; finance, insurance, and real estate; and services. 3. Yellowstone Park included with Park County.

STATE County	Agriculture, 1987 (cont'd): Value of land and buildings: Average per farm ($1,000)	Value of land and buildings: Average per acre (Dollars)	Value of products sold: Total (Mil dol)	Value of products sold: Average per farm (Dollars)	Value of products sold: Percent from: Crops	Value of products sold: Percent from: Livestock and poultry[1]	Percent of farms with sales of: $10,000 or more	Percent of farms with sales of: $100,000 or more	Manufactures, 1987: Establishments: Total	Establishments: Percent with 20 or more employees	All employees: Number (1,000)	All employees: Percent change, 1982–1987	All employees: Annual payroll (Mil dol)	Production workers: Number (1,000)	Production workers: Work hours (Mil)
	119	120	121	122	123	124	125	126	127	128	129	130	131	132	133
MONTANA	506	205	1 547	62 980	41.3	58.7	64.6	17.1	1 239	14.9	20.1	-0.5	425.8	14.8	28.8
Beaverhead	1 011	250	49	131 979	12.9	87.1	70.2	32.2	16	6.2	0.2	100.0	2.8	0.1	0.2
Big Horn	911	162	62	123 365	28.2	71.8	70.1	23.4	6	0.0	0.0	0.0	0.5	0.0	0.0
Blaine	722	157	39	73 534	50.3	49.7	75.2	21.7	4	0.0	D	D	D	D	D
Broadwater	611	271	15	69 566	45.3	54.7	71.8	21.6	10	10.0	0.1	0.0	2.2	0.1	0.2
Carbon	333	390	37	57 793	31.6	68.4	68.3	12.1	7	14.3	D	D	D	D	D
Carter	348	77	24	68 586	12.9	87.1	78.2	25.2	4	0.0	D	D	D	D	D
Cascade	430	234	51	63 062	32.8	67.2	59.0	14.9	60	20.0	1.0	-16.7	19.6	0.6	1.1
Chouteau	690	256	67	84 644	79.5	20.5	87.5	29.4	6	0.0	D	D	D	D	D
Custer	467	85	32	79 752	16.0	84.0	62.5	18.4	15	13.3	0.1	0.0	1.7	0.1	0.1
Daniels	395	182	17	45 738	74.9	25.1	74.5	9.2	2	0.0	D	D	D	D	D
Dawson	347	128	27	53 623	60.0	40.0	74.9	16.4	9	11.1	0.1	0.0	1.0	0.0	0.1
Deer Lodge	595	282	4	54 021	27.0	73.1	50.0	11.1	9	22.2	0.1	0.0	2.0	0.1	0.2
Fallon	326	106	15	47 102	30.6	69.4	72.2	13.3	5	0.0	0.0	0.0	0.5	0.0	0.0
Fergus	430	167	50	59 847	42.8	57.2	71.6	18.5	15	20.0	D	D	D	D	D
Flathead	313	1 024	20	24 714	42.6	57.4	32.2	5.6	163	17.2	3.3	13.8	81.1	2.6	5.1
Gallatin	433	527	53	62 162	40.1	59.9	59.4	18.5	101	12.9	1.1	-8.3	21.2	0.8	1.5
Garfield	588	84	25	82 921	33.0	67.0	79.5	25.3	1	0.0	D	D	D	D	D
Glacier	818	201	35	85 215	61.3	38.7	74.1	25.4	6	16.7	D	D	D	D	D
Golden Valley	768	164	10	71 697	20.3	79.7	72.6	18.5	1	0.0	D	D	D	D	D
Granite	633	273	9	57 663	5.1	94.9	75.8	19.5	16	18.8	0.1	0.0	1.9	0.1	0.2
Hill	616	254	55	76 698	81.1	18.9	80.2	24.4	16	12.5	0.2	-33.3	2.5	0.1	0.2
Jefferson	346	216	8	32 274	27.1	72.9	43.4	9.0	9	11.1	D	D	D	D	D
Judith Basin	464	193	28	80 598	40.8	59.2	79.5	25.1	2	0.0	D	D	D	D	D
Lake	337	543	33	30 754	26.8	73.2	48.4	7.7	33	15.2	0.5	0.0	9.0	0.5	0.9
Lewis and Clark	363	187	18	37 037	27.5	72.5	37.9	9.0	51	11.8	0.8	-11.1	15.4	0.5	1.0
Liberty	684	221	29	97 342	74.4	25.6	93.2	30.8	2	0.0	D	D	D	D	D
Lincoln	202	526	2	9 346	16.8	83.2	20.4	0.4	97	8.2	1.3	30.0	28.2	1.2	2.4
McCone	454	156	24	55 178	65.8	34.2	79.1	17.5	1	0.0	D	D	D	D	D
Madison	858	329	34	75 775	14.0	86.0	67.5	23.2	4	0.0	D	D	D	D	D
Meagher	1 247	176	16	111 251	14.9	85.1	68.8	29.9	11	0.0	D	D	D	D	D
Mineral	251	1 001	1	14 722	14.2	85.8	25.9	1.7	14	21.4	0.2	0.0	4.3	0.2	0.4
Missoula	333	509	6	12 954	24.9	75.1	24.7	2.3	143	19.6	3.9	2.6	92.0	3.0	5.7
Musselshell	704	158	13	53 948	26.4	73.6	50.2	15.3	4	0.0	D	D	D	D	D
Park	552	301	20	48 595	14.5	85.5	57.4	12.9	22	13.6	0.2	0.0	4.5	0.2	0.4
Petroleum	869	145	9	79 085	16.6	83.4	78.4	24.3	NA	NA	NA	NA	NA	NA	NA
Phillips	536	147	37	75 915	41.2	58.8	74.0	22.2	5	0.0	0.0	0.0	0.5	0.0	0.1
Pondera	621	316	41	82 655	75.6	24.4	83.5	26.7	11	9.1	0.1	0.0	0.9	0.0	0.1
Powder River	464	93	23	64 378	12.9	87.1	69.5	22.8	1	0.0	D	D	D	D	D
Powell	758	281	14	60 843	11.9	88.1	61.6	16.9	15	13.3	0.2	100.0	4.0	0.2	0.2
Prairie	446	117	19	97 363	30.8	69.2	78.0	32.5	1	0.0	D	D	D	D	D
Ravalli	240	1 054	22	22 133	12.8	87.2	31.9	5.2	69	11.6	0.8	60.0	12.6	0.6	1.1
Richland	396	198	48	78 027	61.4	38.6	74.0	27.1	12	25.0	0.4	0.0	7.3	0.3	0.6
Roosevelt	441	188	28	46 054	76.5	23.5	74.1	11.4	6	66.7	0.5	-16.7	7.6	0.4	0.9
Rosebud	885	108	33	90 906	25.5	74.5	70.8	23.4	8	0.0	0.0	0.0	0.5	0.0	0.1
Sanders	407	461	10	24 970	19.5	80.5	38.5	3.7	34	14.7	0.5	66.7	7.7	0.4	0.7
Sheridan	368	230	25	41 185	78.9	21.1	78.2	8.3	3	0.0	D	D	D	D	D
Silver Bow	372	364	2	19 312	3.3	96.7	40.4	6.1	26	15.4	0.5	-16.7	11.6	0.3	0.5
Stillwater	466	211	26	58 637	22.3	77.7	65.5	14.1	6	33.3	D	D	D	D	D
Sweet Grass	764	254	15	49 033	8.3	91.7	69.2	13.3	6	0.0	D	D	D	D	D
Teton	564	337	61	98 624	51.8	48.2	79.4	26.4	5	20.0	0.1	0.0	0.6	0.0	0.1
Toole	668	238	29	74 509	75.9	24.1	81.4	24.4	6	0.0	0.0	-100.0	0.6	0.0	0.0
Treasure	619	118	13	108 188	32.9	67.1	76.0	25.6	NA	NA	NA	NA	NA	NA	NA
Valley	480	183	40	55 392	57.1	42.9	74.0	15.0	9	22.2	0.1	0.0	1.6	0.1	0.1
Wheatland	940	165	16	108 143	21.1	78.9	81.4	23.4	3	33.3	D	D	D	D	D
Wibaux	348	130	10	50 267	42.0	58.0	76.0	13.0	1	0.0	D	D	D	D	D
Yellowstone	394	299	100	95 458	19.7	80.3	52.1	15.5	147	18.4	3.0	-25.0	70.0	1.8	3.6
Yellowstone National Park (part)	NA	NA	NA	NA	NA	NA	NA	NA	NA	NA	NA	NA	NA	NA	NA
NEBRASKA	344	457	6 667	110 197	32.1	67.9	77.5	23.1	1 876	33.6	90.7	-0.4	1 937.6	64.2	128.8
Adams	374	793	103	132 537	42.4	57.6	80.6	25.5	64	32.8	2.5	13.6	48.5	1.7	3.4
Antelope	287	554	102	100 864	36.2	63.8	84.2	29.0	12	16.7	D	D	D	D	D
Arthur	1 045	225	9	100 724	10.7	89.3	78.9	32.2	1	0.0	D	D	D	D	D
Banner	582	263	16	76 962	53.7	46.3	73.1	18.4	NA	NA	NA	NA	NA	NA	NA
Blaine	648	197	19	145 535	4.0	96.0	86.0	38.0	NA	NA	NA	NA	NA	NA	NA
Boone	307	647	97	103 888	30.4	69.6	83.7	22.2	7	0.0	0.0	0.0	0.5	0.0	0.0
Box Butte	405	315	90	162 003	48.5	51.5	71.0	29.7	12	33.3	0.4	33.3	5.9	0.3	0.6
Boyd	161	252	23	52 436	20.8	79.2	75.8	13.1	2	0.0	D	D	D	D	D
Brown	539	329	57	164 932	13.8	86.2	71.2	25.0	4	0.0	0.0	0.0	0.3	0.0	0.0

1. Includes livestock and poultry products.

STATE County	Manufactures, 1987 (cont'd)					Value of construction authorized by building permits, 1990							
	Production workers (cont'd)						Nonresidential				Residential		
	Wages							Percent					
	Total (Mil dol)	Average per worker (Dollars)	Value added by manufacture (Mil dol)	Value of shipments (Mil dol)	New capital expenditures (Mil dol)	Total[1] ($1,000)	Total ($1,000)	Office	Industrial	Stores	New construction ($1,000)	Number of housing units	Alterations and additions ($1,000)
	134	135	136	137	138	139	140	141	142	143	144	145	146
MONTANA	296.2	20 014	1 112.0	3 497.9	97.0	248 947	65 791	13.4	14.0	39.4	87 980	1 223	16 194
Beaverhead	2.3	23 000	5.7	13.8	0.2	1 434	838	0.0	79.8	15.5	414	5	56
Big Horn	0.2	NA	1.5	3.1	0.1	420	180	0.0	0.0	60.8	0	0	148
Blaine	D	D	D	D	D	205	104	0.0	0.0	65.6	65	1	12
Broadwater	1.9	19 000	4.8	11.6	0.0	29	29	0.0	0.0	0.0	0	0	0
Carbon	D	D	D	D	D	5 845	1 213	0.0	4.9	64.7	60	1	110
Carter	D	D	D	D	D	42	0	NA	NA	NA	0	0	21
Cascade	10.6	17 667	45.6	137.6	4.0	18 352	3 992	3.9	2.4	63.5	5 900	55	3 115
Chouteau	D	D	D	D	D	2 109	380	0.0	0.0	40.3	166	2	16
Custer	0.9	9 000	3.8	7.1	0.2	2 347	790	0.0	2.2	7.6	207	2	203
Daniels	D	D	D	D	D	18	1	0.0	0.0	0.0	0	0	6
Dawson	0.5	NA	2.6	7.2	0.1	864	193	58.0	0.0	0.0	190	3	18
Deer Lodge	1.6	16 000	4.6	8.1	D	372	29	0.0	0.0	0.0	73	2	18
Fallon	0.2	NA	1.3	4.2	0.0	618	176	0.0	0.0	28.5	0	0	40
Fergus	D	D	D	D	D	992	159	0.0	0.0	0.0	39	5	71
Flathead	59.6	22 923	213.8	485.4	8.2	37 746	4 323	4.4	0.0	65.4	13 125	190	1 580
Gallatin	13.8	17 250	60.4	119.5	5.7	22 513	4 962	25.3	0.5	45.2	10 208	114	1 013
Garfield	D	D	D	D	D	235	186	0.0	0.0	10.8	0	0	0
Glacier	D	D	D	D	D	531	0	NA	NA	NA	289	8	78
Golden Valley	D	D	D	D	D	13	0	NA	NA	NA	0	0	0
Granite	1.6	16 000	3.8	10.5	0.2	299	229	17.5	65.5	0.0	0	0	0
Hill	1.5	15 000	10.8	22.0	0.1	3 177	1 988	0.0	0.0	22.3	305	3	279
Jefferson	D	D	D	D	D	748	422	0.0	0.0	64.7	193	4	1
Judith Basin	D	D	D	D	D	77	20	0.0	0.0	0.0	0	0	0
Lake	7.4	14 800	21.8	42.7	0.8	6 107	2 697	21.2	0.0	55.2	1 730	47	203
Lewis and Clark	9.8	19 600	17.9	271.8	1.3	15 920	5 345	55.6	0.0	3.2	9 181	139	956
Liberty	D	D	D	D	D	1 420	1 415	0.0	0.0	0.0	0	0	0
Lincoln	24.5	20 417	64.8	151.2	7.4	4 189	3 740	0.0	0.0	56.8	72	3	58
McCone	D	D	D	D	D	68	2	0.0	0.0	0.0	0	0	18
Madison	D	D	D	D	D	1 294	700	0.0	0.0	43.3	479	7	0
Meagher	D	D	D	D	D	30	0	NA	NA	NA	0	0	0
Mineral	3.6	18 000	11.9	27.6	0.4	1 385	489	0.0	81.4	18.6	0	0	0
Missoula	67.4	22 467	316.8	651.9	32.4	35 032	5 171	23.6	5.4	43.0	19 621	316	1 769
Musselshell	D	D	D	D	D	487	76	0.0	0.0	0.0	65	1	225
Park	3.3	16 500	17.7	35.4	0.2	2 681	909	10.6	2.3	36.4	395	4	79
Petroleum	NA	NA	NA	NA	NA	10	0	NA	NA	NA	0	0	0
Phillips	0.3	NA	1.4	6.0	0.1	548	101	19.9	0.0	0.0	104	3	25
Pondera	0.6	NA	2.0	4.3	0.0	751	0	NA	NA	NA	150	6	349
Powder River	D	D	D	D	D	165	73	0.0	0.0	0.0	0	0	0
Powell	3.7	18 500	6.1	18.9	D	116	29	0.0	0.0	0.0	45	1	0
Prairie	D	D	D	D	D	36	0	NA	NA	NA	0	0	5
Ravalli	9.1	15 167	26.3	57.8	2.1	6 564	3 084	33.5	8.4	5.3	2 017	67	174
Richland	5.2	17 333	26.0	77.5	0.6	1 567	237	0.0	0.0	0.0	782	12	115
Roosevelt	5.7	14 250	12.6	28.5	0.6	1 179	225	0.0	0.0	94.9	83	1	41
Rosebud	0.4	NA	1.1	2.8	0.1	700	432	48.0	0.0	39.3	66	1	20
Sanders	6.3	15 750	15.9	42.2	1.3	366	207	28.3	0.0	0.0	0	0	88
Sheridan	D	D	D	D	D	1 470	1 309	0.0	0.0	0.0	95	1	3
Silver Bow	5.8	19 333	26.8	67.4	3.7	13 356	2 785	0.0	0.0	85.7	4 961	51	805
Stillwater	D	D	D	D	D	8 486	7 430	0.0	88.8	1.9	83	1	0
Sweet Grass	D	D	D	D	D	805	632	21.2	0.0	0.6	0	0	32
Teton	0.4	NA	1.3	5.0	0.1	857	542	0.0	0.0	68.0	100	1	50
Toole	0.2	NA	1.7	4.3	0.1	762	158	0.0	0.0	25.3	247	2	21
Treasure	NA	NA	NA	NA	NA	173	112	58.1	0.0	32.7	0	0	28
Valley	1.0	10 000	3.5	10.0	0.1	1 344	99	0.0	0.0	0.0	444	4	245
Wheatland	D	D	D	D	D	98	0	NA	NA	NA	0	0	0
Wibaux	D	D	D	D	D	29	25	0.0	0.0	0.0	0	0	0
Yellowstone	40.7	22 611	159.9	1 109.6	25.3	41 964	7 557	9.3	8.8	79.2	16 028	160	4 096
Yellowstone National Park (part)	NA	NA	NA	NA	NA	NA	NA	NA	NA	NA	NA	NA	NA
NEBRASKA	1 211.9	18 877	5 819.2	16 076.2	317.9	765 321	225 424	30.3	15.9	22.5	355 401	6 756	34 874
Adams	28.2	16 588	123.7	296.1	5.2	8 471	4 826	0.0	30.2	0.0	2 310	46	289
Antelope	D	D	D	D	D	2 103	1 334	0.0	7.0	0.0	516	8	163
Arthur	D	D	D	D	D	NA	NA	NA	NA	NA	NA	NA	NA
Banner	NA	NA	NA	NA	NA	NA	NA	NA	NA	NA	NA	NA	NA
Blaine	NA	NA	NA	NA	NA	NA	NA	NA	NA	NA	NA	NA	NA
Boone	0.2	NA	1.6	4.6	D	443	27	0.0	0.0	50.4	232	3	170
Box Butte	3.8	12 667	12.4	28.5	D	1 686	235	0.0	0.0	3.6	133	2	175
Boyd	D	D	D	D	D	25	0	NA	NA	NA	0	0	14
Brown	0.2	NA	0.9	1.6	0.0	317	85	100.0	0.0	0.0	140	2	39

1. Includes nonresidential additions and alterations, residential nonhousekeeping buildings, and residential garages and carports not shown separately.

STATE County	Wholesale trade, 1987				Retail trade, all establishments, 1987				Retail trade, establishments with payroll, 1987					
						Sales				Sales				
											Per capita[2] (Dollars)			
	Estab-lishments	Sales (Mil dol)	Paid employees[1]	Annual payroll (Mil dol)	Number	Total (Mil dol)	Percent change, 1982–1987	Per capita[2] (Dollars)	Number	Total (Mil dol)	General merchan-dise stores	Food stores	Apparel & acces-sory stores	Eating and drinking places
	147	148	149	150	151	152	153	154	155	156	157	158	159	160
MONTANA	1 804	4 392.1	14 824	264.2	10 720	4 510.6	14.0	5 574	6 790	4 344.4	524	1 267	211	584
Beaverhead	24	27.9	134	1.7	130	36.3	0.0	4 371	77	34.2	D	1 278	229	435
Big Horn	11	16.3	48	0.7	106	37.7	-3.8	3 431	65	35.9	114	1 047	D	283
Blaine	8	12.6	41	0.5	82	21.9	11.2	3 127	50	20.0	0	923	125	221
Broadwater	11	18.4	41	0.8	36	9.2	-12.4	2 642	24	8.9	D	1 088	0	389
Carbon	10	4.8	33	0.5	128	22.8	-8.1	2 753	70	19.7	D	641	75	391
Carter	0	0.0	0	0.0	20	3.0	-25.0	1 755	10	2.4	D	D	0	132
Cascade	203	690.1	1 907	34.5	928	515.9	13.9	6 589	599	503.4	999	1 252	D	688
Chouteau	26	67.6	104	1.7	78	15.3	11.7	2 639	41	14.0	D	704	D	168
Custer	30	82.0	418	6.2	149	78.7	4.5	6 008	105	76.3	D	2 089	325	688
Daniels	12	18.7	63	0.9	41	6.6	-21.4	2 537	24	5.8	D	D	D	270
Dawson	29	35.4	231	3.3	133	52.2	-32.9	5 022	87	51.0	D	D	230	483
Deer Lodge	5	D	D	D	132	40.9	9.4	4 054	86	38.9	D	1 270	164	489
Fallon	11	9.5	44	0.6	54	12.3	-37.9	3 522	28	11.4	D	D	133	270
Fergus	41	81.6	212	2.9	209	51.2	2.6	4 161	121	48.2	242	876	276	364
Flathead	85	135.8	624	10.0	939	377.4	39.2	6 507	593	359.0	707	1 465	196	704
Gallatin	111	229.5	903	14.4	747	344.7	26.4	7 108	512	334.8	500	1 299	289	780
Garfield	1	D	D	D	21	4.3	59.3	2 693	9	4.0	D	D	0	239
Glacier	23	37.8	101	1.8	130	49.2	-0.6	4 435	95	47.1	218	1 067	283	402
Golden Valley	2	D	D	D	10	D	D	D	5	D	0	D	0	246
Granite	1	D	D	D	47	7.7	5.5	2 978	24	6.5	0	586	D	285
Hill	41	136.8	298	4.8	208	92.3	-1.4	5 217	145	89.9	554	D	321	529
Jefferson	5	D	D	D	85	14.7	75.0	1 817	41	13.2	D	686	0	343
Judith Basin	8	22.7	22	0.3	38	3.4	-24.4	1 357	19	2.7	D	D	0	307
Lake	28	14.1	117	1.3	268	82.6	30.1	3 932	171	78.6	95	1 076	92	400
Lewis and Clark	106	211.5	916	16.5	631	297.3	19.9	6 298	402	288.5	672	1 634	155	712
Liberty	9	40.3	67	1.2	34	7.1	-2.7	3 107	17	6.4	0	1 196	D	246
Lincoln	15	11.5	71	1.2	261	71.2	30.9	3 769	134	67.0	145	1 241	108	338
McCone	8	25.1	68	1.1	28	7.2	-32.7	2 880	12	6.0	D	D	0	136
Madison	7	4.4	15	0.3	113	16.0	6.7	2 815	65	14.1	D	720	D	456
Meagher	2	D	D	D	39	5.7	-19.7	2 711	23	5.3	0	1 044	0	481
Mineral	1	D	D	D	64	13.2	24.5	3 782	33	11.5	0	D	0	575
Missoula	177	442.0	1 673	30.1	945	557.6	29.4	7 121	649	543.2	818	1 356	300	716
Musselshell	9	5.8	54	0.6	60	13.9	8.6	3 083	33	12.6	D	D	D	296
Park	18	11.1	79	1.2	209	D	D	D	144	59.3	D	1 413	201	531
Petroleum	1	D	D	D	11	0.8	0.0	1 317	4	0.5	0	D	0	D
Phillips	15	18.0	95	1.3	85	20.9	-5.0	3 870	55	19.7	D	1 028	171	387
Pondera	25	55.1	144	2.6	83	25.8	-7.2	3 907	52	25.1	D	D	178	322
Powder River	4	1.9	24	0.2	32	3.8	-30.9	1 664	13	3.1	0	0	D	187
Powell	6	9.1	43	0.3	74	23.6	0.9	3 421	48	22.9	97	1 015	D	394
Prairie	5	3.2	18	0.3	20	D	D	D	10	1.5	0	D	0	232
Ravalli	30	43.2	137	2.9	317	75.3	40.0	2 975	161	69.4	71	940	121	294
Richland	30	49.4	198	2.8	157	54.4	-38.5	4 457	98	52.2	D	637	256	479
Roosevelt	26	45.8	108	1.8	115	51.5	-10.0	4 595	90	50.2	D	1 277	203	280
Rosebud	5	2.0	21	0.3	112	36.7	-9.8	2 963	64	35.7	D	1 003	D	227
Sanders	11	10.7	39	0.4	117	21.8	26.7	2 510	58	18.8	D	910	D	258
Sheridan	20	20.7	76	1.2	96	23.7	-4.0	4 391	73	22.6	D	1 153	334	655
Silver Bow	63	164.0	485	7.7	453	206.9	13.4	6 177	303	201.7	430	1 291	169	767
Stillwater	8	9.5	43	0.7	101	27.7	45.0	4 469	52	25.2	D	804	D	322
Sweet Grass	5	2.7	13	0.3	54	14.0	22.8	4 369	35	12.9	0	D	D	487
Teton	22	29.5	125	1.9	82	16.0	-3.0	2 625	41	14.8	D	611	50	154
Toole	22	40.1	110	2.0	96	19.0	-12.0	3 660	64	18.3	0	D	238	591
Treasure	3	5.2	34	0.5	8	D	D	D	6	0.7	0	D	0	D
Valley	29	43.7	165	2.1	148	41.0	-15.8	4 771	94	38.7	303	1 136	205	445
Wheatland	4	D	D	D	37	5.7	-12.3	2 580	21	4.9	0	1 043	D	181
Wibaux	1	D	D	D	13	D	D	D	3	D	0	0	0	D
Yellowstone	391	1 393.7	4 581	94.7	1 406	906.2	15.8	7 679	932	884.1	1 005	1 632	313	788
Yellowstone National Park (part)	0	0.0	0	0.0	0	0.0	0.0	0	0	0.0	0	0	0	0
NEBRASKA	3 973	21 358.9	43 148	836.1	17 896	8 776.4	25.5	5 506	11 485	8 486.3	680	1 049	229	544
Adams	82	205.9	909	17.0	380	179.5	18.6	5 903	238	171.9	762	1 384	280	570
Antelope	35	70.9	224	3.2	110	29.2	1.0	3 478	65	27.7	D	421	D	213
Arthur	1	D	D	D	6	D	D	D	3	D	0	0	0	D
Banner	0	0.0	0	0.0	5	0.0	0.0	36	0	0.0	0	0	0	0
Blaine	1	D	D	D	8	D	D	D	6	1.3	0	0	0	D
Boone	24	99.4	168	2.7	103	32.9	16.3	4 698	72	30.5	D	803	117	312
Box Butte	33	51.4	309	4.9	161	55.3	4.1	3 864	104	51.4	521	1 070	149	329
Boyd	7	6.6	38	0.5	63	7.1	20.3	2 285	33	5.4	D	634	0	156
Brown	10	12.2	64	0.8	69	13.8	-16.4	3 452	45	12.8	D	755	D	317

1. For pay period including March 12. 2. Based on the estimated population as of July 1 of the year shown.

STATE County	Retail trade, establishments with payroll, 1987 (cont'd): Paid employees[1]	Retail trade, establishments with payroll, 1987 (cont'd): Annual payroll (Mil dol)	Taxable service industries–establishments with payroll, 1987: Number	Receipts (Mil dol): Total	Receipts, selected kinds of business: Hotels, motels and other lodging places	Receipts, selected kinds of business: Health services	Receipts, selected kinds of business: Legal services	Paid employees	Annual payroll (Mil dol)	Bank deposits,[2] June 1989: Total (Mil dol)	Bank deposits: Percent change, 1988–1989	Savings capital,[3] September 1989: Total (Mil dol)	Savings capital: Percent change, 1988–1989
	161	162	163	164	165	166	167	168	169	170	171	172	173
MONTANA	56 985	503.4	6 248	1 402.1	174.5	422.5	148.9	36 499	479.2	5 874	-3.0	1 099.5	-7.6
Beaverhead	429	3.8	70	9.5	2.3	3.8	1.2	308	2.8	70	0.5	15.1	-22.6
Big Horn	421	3.7	47	5.6	0.6	1.1	0.5	174	1.7	66	9.8	6.9	-6.9
Blaine	238	2.1	27	3.5	D	1.0	D	139	1.0	49	-8.5	0.0	NA
Broadwater	152	1.1	13	1.7	D	0.3	D	27	0.2	16	4.2	3.6	-6.3
Carbon	307	2.2	38	7.5	1.2	2.6	0.4	350	2.1	51	2.6	0.0	NA
Carter	33	0.3	5	0.2	0.0	0.0	D	7	0.0	17	2.4	0.0	NA
Cascade	6 528	60.3	635	167.8	16.4	46.7	24.7	4 275	59.1	528	-0.4	119.9	-11.8
Chouteau	161	1.2	25	1.9	D	0.8	D	87	0.6	61	-0.7	0.0	NA
Custer	969	8.7	98	17.9	1.3	6.8	1.9	471	5.8	181	-14.9	13.9	-12.2
Daniels	103	0.8	13	1.2	D	0.5	D	44	0.3	21	-2.7	0.0	NA
Dawson	717	5.6	82	12.2	2.0	3.4	0.7	364	3.7	108	-3.1	6.4	-0.9
Deer Lodge	501	4.6	49	12.3	D	1.5	1.8	321	3.6	78	-0.6	0.0	NA
Fallon	138	1.2	21	5.6	D	D	D	94	1.4	38	-10.0	0.0	NA
Fergus	631	5.3	90	14.1	2.2	6.5	0.7	417	4.4	129	6.0	12.8	-23.7
Flathead	4 663	43.1	557	109.2	15.5	31.9	9.3	2 904	36.4	368	-1.5	64.8	16.2
Gallatin	4 787	40.2	504	114.6	26.8	25.0	11.2	3 361	38.5	349	-6.3	33.8	-8.5
Garfield	45	0.4	1	D	0.0	0.0	D	D	D	16	0.1	0.0	NA
Glacier	623	5.4	61	17.8	10.5	1.3	0.8	246	4.3	81	-0.5	3.3	-46.3
Golden Valley	D	D	1	D	0.0	0.0	D	D	D	NA	NA	0.0	NA
Granite	91	0.6	8	0.4	D	D	0.0	5	0.1	17	-14.0	0.0	NA
Hill	1 195	10.4	124	25.0	3.3	8.1	2.3	710	7.9	135	-18.5	40.9	1.4
Jefferson	218	1.4	27	4.2	0.7	1.9	D	189	1.9	19	-4.2	0.0	NA
Judith Basin	60	0.3	7	0.4	D	D	D	11	0.1	19	6.9	0.0	NA
Lake	1 015	8.7	110	15.2	1.4	5.6	1.9	416	5.2	116	3.9	17.2	12.1
Lewis and Clark	3 970	33.6	463	109.7	11.5	28.6	10.8	2 854	36.3	284	3.8	93.7	-8.3
Liberty	73	0.6	14	1.5	0.3	D	0.3	34	0.4	17	-6.7	0.0	NA
Lincoln	766	6.4	113	12.5	1.7	4.7	0.7	395	3.5	61	-3.7	10.9	-32.9
McCone	82	0.7	6	0.2	D	D	D	8	0.0	17	-11.0	0.0	NA
Madison	206	1.6	34	3.2	0.9	1.1	D	105	0.8	39	5.9	0.0	NA
Meagher	84	0.6	14	1.6	0.6	D	D	46	0.5	16	-1.9	0.0	NA
Mineral	200	1.6	15	1.4	0.5	0.6	0.0	47	0.3	15	6.6	0.0	NA
Missoula	6 951	63.1	767	186.1	15.8	65.5	19.2	5 014	65.3	436	-4.2	154.6	-6.4
Musselshell	177	1.4	16	1.3	D	D	D	50	0.3	39	-4.8	0.0	NA
Park	721	6.7	120	19.5	5.8	5.1	1.4	589	5.9	97	0.4	35.7	1.9
Petroleum	8	0.0	1	D	0.0	0.0	0.0	D	D	NA	NA	0.0	NA
Phillips	267	2.1	23	4.0	1.0	0.5	D	108	1.0	62	3.7	5.2	-0.3
Pondera	259	2.6	34	3.1	D	1.1	0.3	102	1.0	75	0.2	6.9	-16.9
Powder River	68	0.4	9	0.8	D	0.0	0.0	33	0.2	21	1.1	0.0	NA
Powell	291	2.7	29	3.0	0.5	1.6	D	145	1.0	30	-1.7	25.3	-2.4
Prairie	32	0.2	8	0.4	0.0	D	D	15	0.1	28	-1.0	0.0	NA
Ravalli	907	7.2	149	21.2	2.0	8.1	1.4	656	7.2	150	0.6	31.3	-4.1
Richland	751	6.0	70	12.1	0.3	4.0	D	305	3.7	108	-4.7	14.1	-0.3
Roosevelt	507	4.6	35	3.8	1.0	1.3	0.2	162	1.1	109	-3.1	0.0	NA
Rosebud	444	3.5	41	4.0	0.7	1.1	0.2	140	0.9	54	6.5	0.0	NA
Sanders	290	2.0	42	5.8	0.4	3.6	0.5	186	2.2	45	0.0	0.0	NA
Sheridan	389	2.6	29	3.6	0.5	0.9	D	93	1.0	85	-2.3	18.4	6.3
Silver Bow	2 489	25.2	308	84.4	10.1	27.3	8.9	2 034	32.4	239	-8.9	160.9	-9.2
Stillwater	243	2.1	30	3.0	D	1.3	0.2	96	0.7	47	5.3	0.0	NA
Sweet Grass	151	1.2	24	2.8	1.1	0.3	D	77	0.8	39	0.9	3.7	-3.5
Teton	151	1.1	24	1.7	D	0.7	0.2	56	0.5	55	5.6	0.0	NA
Toole	323	2.4	34	4.8	D	1.0	D	108	1.3	95	0.2	10.5	-13.8
Treasure	20	0.1	3	0.1	0.0	D	D	2	0.0	8	-7.5	0.0	NA
Valley	491	4.0	57	6.3	1.1	1.7	1.1	210	2.2	104	0.4	9.2	-3.1
Wheatland	83	0.6	7	0.7	D	D	0.0	38	0.2	22	1.6	0.0	NA
Wibaux	D	D	6	0.3	D	0.0	D	9	0.1	9	-17.3	0.0	NA
Yellowstone	11 540	104.9	1 110	351.0	24.0	111.8	38.7	7 857	127.1	938	-5.7	180.5	-11.6
Yellowstone National Park (part)	0	0.0	0	0.0	0.0	0.0	0.0	0	0.0	NA	NA	0.0	NA
NEBRASKA	117 936	970.4	10 148	3 547.0	173.6	984.5	245.0	89 254	1 336.9	15 191	5.3	5 800.1	-6.0
Adams	2 486	20.5	206	57.5	2.1	22.4	1.9	1 183	19.7	326	3.8	157.2	-3.3
Antelope	352	2.9	48	4.6	D	2.5	0.3	195	1.6	90	0.4	16.9	-3.0
Arthur	D	D	0	0.0	0.0	0.0	0.0	0	0.0	1	-23.3	0.0	NA
Banner	0	0.0	0	0.0	0.0	0.0	0.0	0	0.0	9	-3.9	0.0	NA
Blaine	19	0.1	0	0.0	0.0	0.0	0.0	0	0.0	12	14.0	0.0	NA
Boone	398	3.3	32	2.7	D	0.8	D	90	0.8	86	1.3	31.0	12.2
Box Butte	799	6.2	95	10.4	1.1	3.4	0.7	332	3.3	131	7.4	25.3	-1.9
Boyd	94	0.6	9	0.6	0.0	D	D	17	0.1	36	-6.3	0.0	NA
Brown	209	1.5	18	2.3	D	0.8	D	75	0.6	66	4.1	13.4	-0.9

1. For the period including March 12 of the year shown. 2. Includes deposits for all insured and reporting noninsured commercial and mutual savings banks. 3. Includes savings capital for all FSLIC insured savings institutions.

STATE County	Federal funds and grants, 1989							Local government finances, 1981–1982							
	Expenditures		Per capita[1] (Dollars)					General revenue						Direct general expenditure	
									Intergovernmental		Taxes				
												Per capita[2]			
	Total (Mil dol)	Percent change, 1988–1989	Total	Direct pay-ments for indi-viduals	Procure-ment contract awards	Salaries and wages	Grant awards	Total (Mil dol)	Total (Mil dol)	Percent from state	Total (Mil dol)	Total (Dollars)	Property (Dollars)	Total (Mil dol)	Percent change, 1977–1982
	174	175	176	177	178	179	180	181	182	183	184	185	186	187	188
MONTANA	3 303.0	11.3	X	1 869	211	604	732	935.4	292.4	77.0	438.6	545	529	875.7	60.0
Beaverhead	38.5	34.9	4 583	2 027	480	843	1 008	8.7	3.2	74.2	3.8	451	440	8.0	67.0
Big Horn	46.7	3.3	4 368	1 305	117	914	1 556	22.5	8.2	41.4	11.3	994	973	17.1	106.2
Blaine	41.5	15.5	5 926	1 584	21	665	1 259	13.3	3.6	63.3	5.8	836	819	22.2	289.4
Broadwater	11.8	-4.0	3 384	1 807	115	215	309	3.4	1.2	75.9	1.5	462	448	3.4	113.8
Carbon	24.8	1.7	2 985	2 041	20	200	387	9.0	2.8	85.0	4.9	594	582	8.6	68.7
Carter	13.7	82.0	8 581	1 690	78	269	980	2.8	0.7	79.7	1.9	1 127	1 113	2.1	52.8
Cascade	528.4	19.2	6 775	2 098	655	1 764	428	82.4	31.5	74.5	33.7	420	403	75.8	15.6
Chouteau	47.6	10.3	8 354	1 749	49	211	132	9.3	1.7	81.5	5.9	960	945	8.4	54.2
Custer	49.8	14.9	3 950	1 931	100	972	366	13.9	5.0	87.4	6.3	472	458	13.1	35.5
Daniels	21.6	24.5	8 638	2 252	400	329	112	6.2	1.6	62.5	2.6	939	918	5.5	98.5
Dawson	36.7	17.4	3 821	1 807	49	218	755	14.5	3.8	92.1	8.2	643	628	14.1	61.1
Deer Lodge	36.0	5.3	3 716	2 834	28	250	557	18.4	5.1	79.5	7.6	656	621	13.3	14.6
Fallon	15.9	58.2	4 963	1 488	15	166	690	9.7	0.8	75.1	6.9	1 822	1 806	7.4	88.9
Fergus	50.6	9.7	4 217	2 079	33	428	683	11.8	4.1	91.4	6.0	462	445	10.9	-9.0
Flathead	154.5	7.5	2 592	1 731	95	348	407	52.6	20.1	84.9	23.5	449	434	48.6	56.4
Gallatin	111.1	8.0	2 262	1 373	77	341	415	36.6	11.5	78.7	17.0	375	353	36.3	61.5
Garfield	13.2	-4.7	8 252	1 565	124	368	1 191	3.3	0.7	76.0	2.0	1 204	1 092	2.4	50.5
Glacier	47.8	-3.0	4 309	1 549	60	771	1 118	14.1	6.1	64.9	7.0	634	620	14.2	47.6
Golden Valley	9.5	89.3	8 618	1 728	29	204	3 082	1.4	0.5	93.8	0.8	739	728	1.3	86.3
Granite	7.7	4.9	2 978	2 000	279	314	266	3.6	1.2	77.8	1.4	526	512	3.8	120.1
Hill	83.5	19.8	4 743	1 758	584	407	580	20.9	6.5	75.9	9.8	529	508	18.7	49.8
Jefferson	19.6	18.0	2 304	1 303	26	667	181	6.8	2.8	84.7	3.2	442	425	6.1	76.0
Judith Basin	11.6	-10.7	4 838	1 795	135	382	198	3.5	1.1	80.2	2.1	774	760	3.5	86.5
Lake	81.2	-4.3	3 794	1 863	978	262	633	21.8	8.6	78.8	6.1	312	302	21.9	134.1
Lewis and Clark	245.5	-1.1	5 146	1 874	77	900	2 250	46.8	16.7	84.6	19.8	447	433	48.2	41.5
Liberty	18.2	8.8	7 906	1 630	20	337	72	5.0	0.4	71.9	2.8	1 152	1 137	4.7	59.5
Lincoln	54.6	-5.6	2 888	1 526	89	612	654	19.0	8.2	89.1	8.1	451	441	17.3	83.6
McCone	19.7	16.8	8 223	1 567	22	229	529	3.5	0.9	75.2	2.4	846	782	3.4	0.1
Madison	17.2	11.9	3 070	1 945	64	324	381	8.3	2.3	77.0	5.0	854	840	6.7	39.8
Meagher	7.6	28.2	3 782	1 791	59	295	292	2.8	0.6	81.4	1.2	564	541	2.9	47.3
Mineral	9.6	-23.6	2 835	1 970	155	399	292	4.9	1.8	90.9	1.7	477	467	5.0	85.0
Missoula	198.8	3.2	2 506	1 511	73	540	371	75.5	19.6	85.0	41.0	545	533	73.9	79.0
Musselshell	14.5	1.4	3 448	2 201	17	161	234	6.4	0.9	61.0	4.2	915	899	4.9	94.2
Park	39.6	2.3	3 273	2 465	85	215	379	12.1	4.8	82.4	5.1	387	371	12.3	89.3
Petroleum	2.9	57.7	5 774	1 180	68	150	112	1.0	0.3	62.6	0.5	761	747	0.9	78.1
Phillips	32.7	34.2	6 064	1 782	76	388	648	8.9	2.0	65.1	5.7	1 062	1 050	7.7	91.6
Pondera	29.4	-8.3	4 387	1 744	142	345	686	10.4	3.1	70.6	4.4	640	627	10.5	64.1
Powder River	9.8	35.4	4 463	1 198	35	266	70	6.9	0.6	83.8	5.6	2 242	2 226	5.1	44.6
Powell	16.5	-9.8	2 422	1 726	36	331	198	6.7	2.6	80.5	3.4	506	493	6.6	85.6
Prairie	8.9	36.2	5 913	2 190	21	187	234	2.7	0.7	85.2	1.2	633	619	2.3	-0.5
Ravalli	81.8	11.4	3 121	2 102	361	402	236	17.6	9.6	80.9	6.3	270	259	16.8	82.4
Richland	34.8	18.9	3 082	1 495	16	170	207	17.6	2.1	67.0	11.5	769	754	17.2	123.3
Roosevelt	57.2	10.1	5 151	1 515	226	506	1 220	16.6	4.7	75.5	7.0	618	607	16.3	90.5
Rosebud	31.6	11.3	2 592	899	68	447	657	27.8	4.6	69.4	13.9	1 138	1 129	26.7	146.1
Sanders	28.6	10.5	3 361	2 264	48	429	543	10.0	4.8	66.1	4.4	489	480	9.9	66.4
Sheridan	33.3	22.0	6 521	2 008	30	376	365	11.1	1.2	84.2	7.5	1 247	1 230	8.2	119.3
Silver Bow	136.9	8.9	4 147	2 632	536	397	567	47.8	13.4	84.0	23.1	632	619	36.7	20.9
Stillwater	18.5	11.1	2 895	1 811	19	149	191	5.6	2.2	85.6	2.8	477	463	6.2	83.3
Sweet Grass	9.1	5.9	2 839	1 993	17	258	140	4.0	1.4	63.2	1.8	536	523	3.7	71.9
Teton	25.6	-18.8	4 263	2 067	24	286	342	9.6	2.2	81.9	4.0	623	608	10.7	69.7
Toole	30.8	11.5	6 151	1 880	73	505	755	10.8	1.4	50.1	6.6	1 151	1 133	10.6	91.6
Treasure	3.3	11.9	3 662	1 710	74	276	254	1.6	0.6	94.4	0.8	799	782	1.5	77.2
Valley	58.4	38.7	7 211	2 198	258	660	1 088	12.4	4.2	78.3	5.6	564	543	11.8	39.6
Wheatland	11.1	19.3	5 067	2 344	140	419	542	2.8	0.8	84.4	1.6	686	673	2.5	34.9
Wibaux	8.2	42.6	6 811	1 996	30	176	340	2.3	0.3	75.1	1.8	1 108	1 096	2.0	29.0
Yellowstone	303.7	7.8	2 615	1 581	141	554	267	126.5	40.9	69.5	48.6	428	413	116.0	65.8
Yellowstone National Park (part)	0.0	0.0	0	0	0	0	0	NA	NA	NA	0.0	NA	0	NA	NA
NEBRASKA	5 771.3	-2.1	X	1 806	252	559	412	1 851.8	491.2	76.7	786.0	494	442	1 758.8	48.7
Adams	85.0	-12.3	2 804	1 823	26	203	196	41.9	11.9	86.5	17.8	568	552	40.6	14.4
Antelope	36.4	-18.5	4 388	1 715	33	163	418	7.0	2.2	86.1	3.9	452	436	8.1	56.5
Arthur	1.5	-12.7	3 008	1 206	22	150	66	1.0	0.2	93.5	0.6	1 262	1 242	1.0	41.0
Banner	4.7	-27.2	4 727	807	11	106	40	1.7	0.4	94.3	1.1	1 078	1 066	1.4	32.5
Blaine	2.0	-5.3	2 820	1 480	46	320	184	1.7	0.4	90.2	0.9	1 156	1 144	1.4	37.3
Boone	30.3	-17.8	4 392	1 819	23	200	175	7.6	1.9	89.2	3.2	432	415	7.9	27.0
Box Butte	31.9	-7.1	2 295	1 485	31	158	124	14.7	4.0	76.4	5.1	365	352	13.9	52.0
Boyd	10.3	-3.2	3 313	2 235	29	225	158	3.3	1.1	89.6	1.5	461	452	3.1	-11.2
Brown	16.4	-3.9	4 325	2 139	19	164	694	6.4	1.3	89.2	1.9	441	424	6.3	46.4

1. Based on the estimated population as of July 1 of the year shown. 2. Based on the estimated population as of July 1, 1982.

STATE County	Local government finances, 1981–1982 (cont'd)								State and local government employment, 1989		Federal government civilian employment 1989		Elections, 1988[3]	
	Direct general expenditure (cont'd)						Debt outstanding							
	Per capita[1] (Dollars)	Percent of total for– Education	Health & hospitals	Police protection	Public welfare	Highways	Total (Mil dol)	Per capita[1] (Dollars)	Total	Rate[2]	Total	Earnings ($1,000)	Total vote cast for president	Vote for lead party (Percent)
	189	190	191	192	193	194	195	196	197	198	199	200	201	202
MONTANA	1 088	53.1	3.4	4.2	2.2	8.3	618.0	768	54 197	673.1	13 797	394 156	365 674	R–52.1
Beaverhead	945	52.9	12.2	4.4	0.7	7.5	0.5	60	715	851.2	231	5 845	3 998	R–66.7
Big Horn	1 500	49.1	0.9	5.1	0.8	12.4	2.5	223	692	646.7	425	11 006	3 984	D–56.0
Blaine	3 213	28.9	0.3	1.5	0.1	24.4	17.3	2 513	435	621.4	176	4 595	2 912	D–50.1
Broadwater	1 026	46.3	1.2	5.8	7.5	11.5	1.3	404	157	448.6	40	778	1 683	R–62.6
Carbon	1 041	63.6	2.0	4.4	1.5	13.8	2.9	348	410	494.0	74	1 591	4 470	R–52.8
Carter	1 251	52.0	2.1	3.5	1.6	12.4	1.2	708	100	625.0	19	310	942	R–72.8
Cascade	946	53.5	1.7	4.3	7.4	5.1	31.4	391	3 669	470.4	1 756	47 568	32 124	R–49.6
Chouteau	1 381	53.8	14.0	3.7	0.5	11.9	1.3	208	442	775.4	43	957	3 219	R–61.5
Custer	982	58.9	2.3	3.3	6.1	5.4	8.4	632	917	727.8	426	13 747	5 462	R–55.1
Daniels	1 954	40.7	19.6	2.5	0.0	5.3	12.0	4 298	168	672.0	34	891	1 395	R–57.5
Dawson	1 105	66.2	1.0	3.3	0.4	7.1	5.0	389	795	828.1	57	1 268	4 886	R–54.4
Deer Lodge	1 149	47.8	1.2	5.2	1.7	5.5	39.0	3 362	1 038	1 070.1	89	2 388	4 406	D–72.3
Fallon	1 945	43.4	21.8	2.0	0.1	10.4	1.0	258	281	878.1	26	552	1 636	R–61.2
Fergus	837	66.9	0.6	4.2	0.8	7.1	6.2	474	797	664.2	168	4 693	6 116	R–64.6
Flathead	927	60.5	1.0	4.7	3.0	6.1	11.8	226	2 697	452.5	866	23 397	25 225	R–57.3
Gallatin	802	52.2	1.7	5.4	3.3	4.9	28.7	634	6 013	1 224.6	608	18 033	23 205	R–56.9
Garfield	1 419	50.5	17.2	1.9	0.6	11.7	0.2	142	112	700.0	28	582	851	R–74.1
Glacier	1 287	71.9	2.6	3.8	0.9	6.7	4.6	416	794	715.3	408	10 818	4 004	D–53.7
Golden Valley	1 201	63.9	2.9	1.7	0.3	11.1	0.1	110	73	663.6	13	213	543	R–61.7
Granite	1 448	46.0	20.0	5.1	1.9	8.9	0.4	156	205	788.5	48	978	1 326	R–59.5
Hill	1 013	62.2	0.7	3.4	0.7	7.1	20.2	1 091	1 333	757.4	199	5 447	7 791	D–54.2
Jefferson	837	67.1	1.0	6.3	1.0	8.5	1.5	207	818	962.4	46	1 022	3 837	R–52.3
Judith Basin	1 279	62.8	2.7	2.9	0.0	13.8	0.3	95	158	658.3	43	842	1 516	R–59.5
Lake	1 127	50.2	0.9	2.5	0.4	5.9	4.8	249	863	403.3	302	7 742	9 150	R–53.4
Lewis and Clark	1 085	53.1	1.2	4.5	2.8	6.1	77.6	1 748	6 266	1 313.6	1 394	45 553	23 334	D–51.1
Liberty	1 944	42.7	29.6	2.7	0.0	10.4	1.3	536	238	1 034.8	34	800	1 208	R–63.8
Lincoln	963	60.6	3.3	5.1	1.5	9.0	3.5	196	779	412.2	512	13 316	7 294	D–49.4
McCone	1 211	53.7	1.7	2.5	3.3	18.6	0.8	290	166	691.7	28	551	1 399	R–58.2
Madison	1 157	51.7	4.9	5.1	14.2	6.4	2.4	414	364	650.0	86	1 823	2 980	R–68.6
Meagher	1 295	41.9	22.9	2.0	0.1	13.6	0.7	301	120	600.0	24	542	1 009	R–65.0
Mineral	1 424	54.0	21.4	3.3	0.3	6.0	0.8	234	221	650.0	82	1 843	1 428	D–55.3
Missoula	982	49.1	2.5	4.7	1.0	10.1	99.2	1 319	6 206	782.6	1 370	43 979	35 669	D–53.8
Musselshell	1 069	56.0	2.2	6.2	1.6	9.5	1.0	212	196	466.7	21	562	2 204	R–58.1
Park	928	54.9	0.5	4.2	0.7	5.7	2.9	217	547	452.1	89	2 104	6 465	R–59.1
Petroleum	1 336	60.5	0.3	1.3	0.4	19.1	0.3	439	50	1 000.0	NA	NA	302	R–67.5
Phillips	1 427	47.5	0.6	3.3	0.2	15.9	3.7	684	320	592.6	74	1 979	2 426	R–60.3
Pondera	1 517	53.3	18.9	2.8	0.8	7.2	4.8	701	392	585.1	54	1 288	3 114	R–57.6
Powder River	2 036	41.9	2.4	2.9	11.3	15.8	0.1	43	191	868.2	20	397	1 232	R–66.2
Powell	985	56.5	1.4	3.9	1.2	14.1	1.8	269	895	1 316.2	81	2 242	2 795	R–56.3
Prairie	1 213	45.0	23.0	3.8	0.4	8.1	0.3	157	165	1 100.0	15	264	900	R–60.1
Ravalli	716	65.5	1.5	4.7	0.4	8.0	4.3	184	827	315.6	452	11 971	12 490	R–59.4
Richland	1 157	50.8	1.4	4.1	0.6	18.8	11.7	782	607	537.2	68	1 698	4 546	R–57.8
Roosevelt	1 442	65.5	7.4	3.5	0.3	6.7	3.3	294	702	632.4	223	5 659	4 118	D–50.6
Rosebud	2 188	56.7	0.6	3.2	0.6	5.1	70.3	5 759	635	520.5	179	4 217	3 792	D–49.3
Sanders	1 099	55.3	0.4	2.7	0.4	15.6	2.7	305	429	504.7	171	4 257	4 200	R–51.2
Sheridan	1 372	51.5	0.7	4.0	0.3	19.3	0.4	64	280	549.0	74	1 929	2 763	R–50.0
Silver Bow	1 003	61.2	3.0	5.6	1.2	6.1	10.3	282	1 894	573.9	366	11 425	16 687	D–68.4
Stillwater	1 062	59.0	0.8	4.5	0.9	7.3	1.0	175	294	459.4	39	839	3 379	R–56.8
Sweet Grass	1 124	47.7	2.8	5.9	16.7	8.0	3.1	948	219	684.4	42	947	1 733	R–71.7
Teton	1 671	36.6	10.7	2.8	5.2	6.5	12.0	1 879	390	650.0	70	1 494	3 244	R–57.8
Toole	1 856	36.1	33.0	4.9	0.2	6.9	4.0	693	516	1 032.0	92	2 479	2 634	R–57.1
Treasure	1 451	52.5	0.6	3.3	0.5	22.1	0.1	126	69	766.7	NA	106	536	R–54.3
Valley	1 179	64.8	1.9	4.3	0.2	8.8	2.6	262	588	725.9	156	4 199	4 706	R–52.4
Wheatland	1 107	59.5	2.0	7.8	1.9	7.6	0.1	55	137	622.7	34	710	1 130	R–59.0
Wibaux	1 225	50.7	4.0	4.8	0.4	16.1	0.5	314	91	758.3	NA	181	629	R–56.9
Yellowstone	1 022	46.7	1.1	4.5	1.5	6.3	87.6	772	5 721	492.8	1 805	59 500	50 647	R–55.4
Yellowstone National Park (part)	NA	0.0	NA	0.0	NA	NA	NA	NA	0	0.0	0	0	NA	NA
NEBRASKA	1 106	46.5	9.9	3.6	1.9	10.1	4 893.7	3 078	118 973	739.0	17 694	507 458	661 465	R–60.2
Adams	1 292	66.4	0.7	2.5	0.9	7.9	147.3	4 692	2 607	860.4	133	3 965	12 287	R–65.6
Antelope	927	63.5	0.0	2.9	0.7	19.1	1.8	205	496	597.6	58	1 172	3 559	R–73.8
Arthur	2 092	45.3	0.0	1.1	0.2	12.2	0.0	0	37	740.0	NA	NA	269	R–78.1
Banner	1 354	58.8	0.0	1.0	0.1	24.7	0.0	0	72	720.0	NA	190	477	R–75.7
Blaine	1 790	78.9	0.5	0.8	0.6	8.7	0.3	356	66	942.9	NA	86	411	R–82.2
Boone	1 077	49.8	16.1	2.4	1.0	16.4	2.3	312	509	737.7	49	1 146	3 150	R–68.6
Box Butte	986	39.4	20.4	5.5	0.9	5.3	8.3	592	806	579.9	73	2 030	5 764	R–56.4
Boyd	944	56.3	0.0	2.2	1.4	17.2	0.6	192	267	861.3	24	549	1 467	R–65.9
Brown	1 430	40.2	19.4	3.3	0.5	13.9	12.8	2 900	365	960.5	31	715	1 782	R–74.9

1. Based on the estimated population as of July 1, 1982. 2. Per 10,000 resident population estimated as of July 1 of the year shown. 3. Data subject to copyright.

STATE–County code	MSA/CMSA/NECMA code[1]	STATE County	Land Area,[2] 1990 (Sq. Km.)	Population, 1990: Total persons	Rank	Per square kilometer	Race: White	Black	Am. Indian, Eskimo, Aleut	Asian & Pacific Islander	Other race	Hispanic[3]	Age of population Percent: Under 5 years	5 to 14 years	15 to 24 years
			1	2	3	4	5	6	7	8	9	10	11	12	13
		NEBRASKA—Con.													
31 019	...	Buffalo	2 507	37 447	1 061	14.9	36 430	166	118	162	571	1 023	7.2	14.4	23.1
31 021	...	Burt	1 276	7 868	2 584	6.2	7 749	8	70	14	27	74	6.6	15.9	9.6
31 023	...	Butler	1 512	8 601	2 503	5.7	8 560	10	17	13	1	20	7.0	16.6	10.5
31 025	...	Cass	1 449	21 318	1 615	14.7	21 033	42	109	71	63	195	7.9	16.4	12.3
31 027	...	Cedar	1 917	10 131	2 375	5.3	10 099	6	14	9	3	17	8.3	17.9	11.2
31 029	...	Chase	2 317	4 381	2 885	1.9	4 349	1	6	2	23	88	7.5	17.0	9.2
31 031	...	Cherry	15 438	6 307	2 721	0.4	6 107	3	177	14	6	24	8.2	15.9	9.9
31 033	...	Cheyenne	3 099	9 494	2 434	3.1	9 250	8	73	15	148	317	7.3	16.1	10.9
31 035	...	Clay	1 484	7 123	2 642	4.8	7 067	1	17	13	25	43	6.6	15.9	10.6
31 037	...	Colfax	1 070	9 139	2 456	8.5	9 002	3	32	9	93	224	7.7	16.2	10.8
31 039	...	Cuming	1 482	10 117	2 376	6.8	10 076	8	10	20	3	15	7.2	16.2	10.9
31 041	...	Custer	6 671	12 270	2 198	1.8	12 152	3	68	12	35	84	6.9	15.7	9.7
31 043	7720	Dakota	684	16 742	1 866	24.5	15 481	76	302	358	525	1 016	8.6	17.2	13.6
31 045	...	Dawes	3 616	9 021	2 467	2.5	8 492	55	355	75	44	142	6.6	14.4	22.4
31 047	...	Dawson	2 624	19 940	1 682	7.6	19 529	15	65	41	290	663	7.1	16.3	11.3
31 049	...	Deuel	1 139	2 237	3 053	2.0	2 185	1	10	7	34	102	6.1	15.9	9.7
31 051	...	Dixon	1 234	6 143	2 740	5.0	6 124	4	11	3	1	4	7.5	16.0	11.1
31 053	...	Dodge	1 384	34 500	1 148	24.9	34 132	73	111	119	65	223	6.9	15.1	13.1
31 055	5920	Douglas	857	416 444	121	485.9	359 438	45 541	2 481	4 086	4 898	11 368	8.0	14.8	14.5
31 057	...	Dundy	2 383	2 582	3 018	1.1	2 568	0	5	4	5	15	5.0	15.8	10.2
31 059	...	Fillmore	1 493	7 103	2 646	4.8	7 042	14	33	4	10	35	6.9	14.8	10.4
31 061	...	Franklin	1 492	3 938	2 923	2.6	3 915	6	10	6	1	8	6.6	12.8	8.7
31 063	...	Frontier	2 524	3 101	2 994	1.2	3 074	1	4	8	14	19	6.3	17.2	10.0
31 065	...	Furnas	1 860	5 553	2 796	3.0	5 515	4	18	6	10	37	5.2	14.5	9.0
31 067	...	Gage	2 215	22 794	1 544	10.3	22 530	45	102	77	40	110	6.7	13.9	11.2
31 069	...	Garden	4 415	2 460	3 025	0.6	2 455	0	0	1	4	15	6.5	13.8	8.4
31 071	...	Garfield	1 476	2 141	3 059	1.5	2 133	0	3	5	0	3	6.3	14.1	10.4
31 073	...	Gosper	1 187	1 928	3 071	1.6	1 927	0	0	1	0	9	5.4	14.7	9.0
31 075	...	Grant	2 011	769	3 125	0.4	760	0	5	3	1	2	8.3	16.9	8.5
31 077	...	Greeley	1 476	3 006	3 000	2.0	2 999	0	4	3	0	2	7.0	18.7	9.8
31 079	...	Hall	1 415	48 925	857	34.6	47 263	145	150	540	827	2 116	7.8	16.0	13.0
31 081	...	Hamilton	1 408	8 862	2 483	6.3	8 811	9	9	24	9	57	7.7	17.0	10.4
31 083	...	Harlan	1 432	3 810	2 931	2.7	3 804	2	2	1	1	5	6.4	14.5	8.1
31 085	...	Hayes	1 847	1 222	3 107	0.7	1 218	0	2	2	0	6	7.4	15.1	9.4
31 087	...	Hitchcock	1 839	3 750	2 936	2.0	3 733	0	8	3	6	23	6.7	17.0	9.9
31 089	...	Holt	6 249	12 599	2 178	2.0	12 537	3	30	17	12	23	8.4	17.6	10.4
31 091	...	Hooker	1 868	793	3 124	0.4	792	0	0	0	1	14	6.2	14.6	9.3
31 093	...	Howard	1 475	6 055	2 751	4.1	6 020	1	12	3	19	42	7.1	16.4	11.3
31 095	...	Jefferson	1 484	8 759	2 490	5.9	8 710	4	23	8	14	81	6.5	14.1	10.1
31 097	...	Johnson	974	4 673	2 864	4.8	4 541	1	0	107	24	47	5.7	14.8	9.0
31 099	...	Kearney	1 337	6 629	2 693	5.0	6 579	0	3	4	43	114	7.6	14.9	11.2
31 101	...	Keith	2 749	8 584	2 506	3.1	8 403	10	49	15	107	336	7.0	16.4	10.2
31 103	...	Keya Paha	2 003	1 029	3 111	0.5	1 028	0	1	0	0	1	4.9	16.2	9.3
31 105	...	Kimball	2 465	4 108	2 908	1.7	4 074	2	9	6	17	146	6.9	15.6	8.8
31 107	...	Knox	2 870	9 534	2 429	3.3	9 031	0	482	17	4	9	6.4	15.5	9.2
31 109	4360	Lancaster	2 173	213 641	233	98.3	202 663	4 659	1 207	3 367	1 745	3 938	7.1	13.3	19.1
31 111	...	Lincoln	6 641	32 508	1 199	4.9	31 354	95	120	115	824	1 623	7.3	16.9	12.2
31 113	...	Logan	1 478	878	3 118	0.6	873	3	0	0	2	3	8.1	20.6	9.5
31 115	...	Loup	1 476	683	3 130	0.5	682	0	0	1	0	1	7.2	16.3	7.8
31 117	...	McPherson	2 225	546	3 133	0.2	545	1	0	0	0	0	7.3	16.5	9.0
31 119	...	Madison	1 483	32 655	1 196	22.0	31 734	238	238	99	346	569	8.2	16.4	13.3
31 121	...	Merrick	1 255	8 042	2 561	6.4	7 996	3	13	21	9	71	7.2	15.8	11.5
31 123	...	Morrill	3 688	5 423	2 805	1.5	5 202	1	33	7	180	434	7.4	15.8	10.2
31 125	...	Nance	1 143	4 275	2 892	3.7	4 250	1	5	8	11	38	7.8	16.6	9.5
31 127	...	Nemaha	1 060	7 980	2 570	7.5	7 876	72	13	14	5	20	6.4	14.3	16.1
31 129	...	Nuckolls	1 490	5 786	2 781	3.9	5 774	1	8	0	3	17	5.9	15.8	8.5
31 131	...	Otoe	1 595	14 252	2 034	8.9	14 138	25	31	25	33	106	6.7	15.2	10.5
31 133	...	Pawnee	1 118	3 317	2 973	3.0	3 304	3	1	4	5	17	6.4	13.2	9.0
31 135	...	Perkins	2 287	3 367	2 966	1.5	3 320	0	8	8	31	53	6.7	18.1	9.8
31 137	...	Phelps	1 399	9 715	2 409	6.9	9 653	5	15	16	26	91	7.3	15.8	11.0
31 139	...	Pierce	1 487	7 827	2 594	5.3	7 782	0	25	9	11	14	7.9	17.5	10.0
31 141	...	Platte	1 756	29 820	1 302	17.0	29 523	54	61	74	108	255	8.6	17.9	12.3
31 143	...	Polk	1 137	5 675	2 788	5.0	5 632	1	13	11	18	30	6.1	16.0	9.6
31 145	...	Red Willow	1 856	11 705	2 232	6.3	11 568	13	28	25	71	210	7.2	15.9	12.4
31 147	...	Richardson	1 434	9 937	2 392	6.9	9 738	5	176	11	7	44	7.0	13.8	10.2
31 149	...	Rock	2 612	2 019	3 066	0.8	2 017	0	1	0	1	6	7.1	16.6	10.3

1. MSA = Metropolitan Statistical Area. CMSA = Consolidated MSA. NECMA = New England county metropolitan area. PMSA = Primary MSA. See Appendix A for explanation of these concepts. See Appendix B for list of metropolitan areas identified by type, with component counties. 2. Dry land or land partially or temporarily covered by water. 3. Hispanic persons may be of any race.

STATE County	Population, 1990 (cont'd): Age of population (cont'd) Percent: 25 to 34 years	35 to 44 years	45 to 54 years	55 to 64 years	65 to 74 years	75 years and over	Percent female	Population–Change and components of change: Change 1980–1990: Number	Percent	Total persons, 1986	Total persons, 1980	Components of change, 1980–1986: Net change: Number	Percent	Natural increase: Births	Deaths
	14	15	16	17	18	19	20	21	22	23	24	25	26	27	28
NEBRASKA—Con.															
Buffalo	15.2	13.2	7.7	7.0	6.1	6.0	51.3	2 650	7.6	36 800	34 797	2 000	5.7	3 800	1 800
Burt	12.3	13.3	9.6	11.2	10.1	11.5	51.5	-945	-10.7	8 400	8 813	-400	-5.0	800	800
Butler	13.3	12.7	9.5	10.1	9.9	10.5	50.3	-729	-7.8	9 100	9 330	-200	-2.2	900	700
Cass	16.0	14.9	10.5	8.9	7.1	5.9	50.1	1 021	5.0	21 900	20 297	1 600	7.8	2 200	1 200
Cedar	13.4	11.9	8.6	9.8	9.2	9.7	50.1	-1 244	-10.9	10 900	11 375	-400	-3.9	1 300	800
Chase	13.4	14.0	9.9	10.4	9.6	9.1	51.1	-377	-7.9	4 600	4 758	-100	-2.4	500	400
Cherry	14.5	13.5	11.1	10.1	8.4	8.6	50.4	-451	-6.7	6 800	6 758	100	0.8	700	400
Cheyenne	14.3	13.6	9.4	10.5	9.6	8.3	51.7	-563	-5.6	10 100	10 057	100	0.7	1 000	700
Clay	13.6	13.3	10.6	9.8	10.1	9.5	51.5	-983	-12.1	7 600	8 106	-500	-5.8	800	600
Colfax	15.0	11.6	8.8	9.4	9.4	11.2	50.6	-751	-7.6	9 500	9 890	-400	-3.6	900	700
Cuming	13.3	12.1	9.5	10.4	10.2	10.1	50.5	-1 547	-13.3	11 100	11 664	-600	-4.8	1 100	700
Custer	12.2	12.9	9.9	10.8	10.6	11.3	51.7	-1 607	-11.6	13 100	13 877	-800	-5.7	1 200	1 100
Dakota	17.1	14.4	9.7	7.7	6.3	5.4	50.5	169	1.0	17 300	16 573	700	4.2	2 000	900
Dawes	12.2	12.0	8.5	8.1	7.9	7.7	50.9	-588	-6.1	9 300	9 609	-300	-3.4	900	600
Dawson	13.7	14.5	10.3	9.5	9.1	8.2	51.4	-2 364	-10.6	21 000	22 304	-1 300	-5.8	2 200	1 400
Deuel	13.9	11.4	9.9	10.2	11.5	11.4	50.4	-225	-9.1	2 400	2 462	-100	-4.3	200	200
Dixon	12.7	13.4	9.3	9.9	9.5	10.7	50.9	-994	-13.9	6 700	7 137	-400	-5.9	600	500
Dodge	14.2	13.4	10.0	10.0	8.8	8.5	52.2	-1 347	-3.8	35 200	35 847	-700	-1.8	3 300	2 300
Douglas	18.5	15.3	9.5	8.0	6.5	4.9	51.8	19 406	4.9	414 900	397 038	17 800	4.5	44 400	21 200
Dundy	12.7	13.6	9.1	10.5	12.1	11.0	51.7	-279	-9.8	2 800	2 861	-100	-2.5	300	300
Fillmore	13.1	13.3	9.6	10.2	10.3	11.4	51.5	-817	-10.3	7 400	7 920	-500	-6.7	700	700
Franklin	12.2	12.2	10.2	10.8	12.6	13.9	51.8	-439	-10.0	4 100	4 377	-300	-7.4	300	400
Frontier	13.0	14.0	11.1	10.7	8.8	8.9	50.4	-546	-15.0	3 500	3 647	-200	-4.9	400	200
Furnas	11.8	12.8	9.1	10.4	11.9	15.5	51.9	-933	-14.4	6 200	6 486	-300	-5.0	500	600
Gage	14.8	13.7	9.8	10.3	9.8	9.9	52.1	-1 662	-6.8	23 500	24 456	-1 000	-4.0	2 100	1 800
Garden	12.3	12.3	11.1	11.7	11.9	12.1	51.9	-342	-12.2	2 800	2 802	0	-0.5	300	300
Garfield	11.3	12.2	11.9	9.8	11.3	12.8	52.1	-222	-9.4	2 200	2 363	-200	-7.2	200	200
Gosper	12.6	13.4	11.6	12.1	11.5	9.8	49.3	-212	-9.9	2 100	2 140	0	-1.0	200	100
Grant	16.1	14.3	10.3	10.3	9.5	5.9	49.2	-108	-12.3	900	877	0	-0.8	100	0
Greeley	12.3	12.3	8.9	10.1	9.8	11.0	50.8	-456	-13.2	3 300	3 462	-200	-4.8	400	300
Hall	16.0	14.8	9.4	8.7	7.7	6.6	51.5	1 235	2.6	48 900	47 690	1 200	2.5	5 300	2 900
Hamilton	14.6	14.7	9.8	9.7	8.0	8.1	51.1	-439	-4.7	9 100	9 301	-200	-2.2	1 000	500
Harlan	12.5	13.8	9.6	11.2	12.7	11.3	52.0	-482	-11.2	4 100	4 292	-200	-4.8	400	300
Hayes	13.6	13.0	11.3	12.2	10.8	7.2	48.8	-134	-9.9	1 400	1 356	0	-0.3	100	100
Hitchcock	12.7	13.2	8.7	10.3	10.5	10.9	50.9	-329	-8.1	3 900	4 079	-200	-4.3	400	300
Holt	14.6	13.0	8.9	9.8	9.0	8.4	50.2	-953	-7.0	13 500	13 552	-100	-0.4	1 600	900
Hooker	10.2	12.9	9.5	9.6	12.9	14.9	51.1	-197	-19.9	1 000	990	0	-3.9	100	100
Howard	12.6	12.7	10.0	11.0	9.6	9.3	51.1	-718	-10.6	6 500	6 773	-300	-4.7	600	500
Jefferson	12.6	13.0	9.4	10.6	11.8	11.8	51.7	-1 058	-10.8	9 300	9 817	-500	-4.8	800	700
Johnson	13.6	11.6	10.8	10.8	11.4	12.2	51.8	-612	-11.6	4 900	5 285	-400	-6.9	400	400
Kearney	15.2	14.0	10.2	9.4	8.7	8.8	50.5	-424	-6.0	6 700	7 053	-400	-5.6	700	400
Keith	14.2	13.2	11.1	11.0	9.4	7.5	51.4	-780	-8.3	8 900	9 364	-400	-4.8	1 000	600
Keya Paha	13.2	13.5	10.5	11.3	11.8	9.3	47.7	-272	-20.9	1 200	1 301	-100	-7.0	100	100
Kimball	14.2	13.0	11.4	11.0	10.6	8.4	50.9	-774	-15.9	4 800	4 882	-100	-2.5	600	300
Knox	11.6	12.5	9.6	11.3	11.9	11.9	51.2	-1 923	-16.8	10 900	11 457	-600	-5.1	1 000	900
Lancaster	18.3	15.3	8.8	7.2	5.9	4.9	51.1	20 757	10.8	206 100	192 884	13 200	6.8	19 600	8 600
Lincoln	14.2	14.9	10.0	9.3	8.2	7.1	51.5	-3 947	-10.8	33 700	36 455	-2 700	-7.4	3 800	1 900
Logan	14.1	14.0	7.7	10.7	8.2	7.1	49.8	-105	-10.7	900	983	0	-4.7	100	0
Loup	13.5	13.6	12.4	10.5	10.5	8.2	50.7	-176	-20.5	800	859	0	-1.4	100	100
McPherson	14.8	11.7	9.9	11.0	10.3	9.5	49.5	-47	-7.9	600	593	0	-3.5	100	0
Madison	17.1	13.9	8.5	8.0	7.4	7.4	51.1	1 273	4.1	32 200	31 382	800	2.7	3 700	2 000
Merrick	13.8	13.1	11.0	9.9	8.8	8.9	50.5	-903	-10.1	8 600	8 945	-400	-4.0	800	600
Morrill	13.0	13.6	10.8	10.4	9.2	9.6	50.5	-662	-10.9	5 800	6 085	-300	-4.2	600	400
Nance	14.2	12.6	8.7	10.9	9.6	10.0	50.6	-465	-9.8	4 500	4 740	-300	-5.8	400	400
Nemaha	13.2	13.2	9.3	8.9	9.4	9.6	50.4	-387	-4.6	8 300	8 367	0	-0.3	800	600
Nuckolls	12.7	12.3	9.9	11.4	11.5	12.0	51.9	-940	-14.0	6 500	6 726	-200	-2.9	600	500
Otoe	13.3	13.3	10.1	10.2	10.3	10.4	52.1	-931	-6.1	14 700	15 183	-400	-2.9	1 400	1 200
Pawnee	10.2	12.2	9.0	11.4	14.8	13.8	51.9	-620	-15.7	3 700	3 937	-200	-6.2	300	400
Perkins	11.4	14.0	10.3	9.1	10.3	10.2	50.4	-270	-7.4	3 700	3 637	0	0.5	400	300
Phelps	14.5	14.1	9.9	9.6	8.3	9.5	51.8	-54	-0.6	10 000	9 769	300	2.8	1 100	700
Pierce	14.0	12.2	9.6	9.5	9.7	9.5	51.0	-654	-7.7	8 400	8 481	-100	-0.7	900	600
Platte	15.9	14.1	9.3	8.5	7.3	6.0	50.9	968	3.4	29 500	28 852	600	2.1	3 500	1 400
Polk	11.9	13.5	9.7	10.3	10.9	12.1	50.9	-645	-10.2	6 000	6 320	-400	-5.7	500	500
Red Willow	14.5	13.2	9.3	10.3	9.1	8.1	52.5	-910	-7.2	12 800	12 615	200	1.3	1 300	800
Richardson	13.0	12.2	10.0	10.0	11.8	12.0	52.0	-1 378	-12.2	10 400	11 315	-900	-8.1	1 000	1 100
Rock	13.1	14.6	9.5	10.6	8.6	9.6	50.7	-364	-15.3	2 300	2 383	-100	-4.6	200	200

STATE County	Population–(cont'd) Components of change, 1980-1986 (cont'd)	Households, 1990					Births, 1988			Deaths, 1987				Marriages, 1984	
					Percent					Number		Rate			
	Net migration	Number	Percent change, 1980–1990	Persons per household	Female family householder[1]	One-person	Total	Rate[2]	Low birth weight[3] (Number)	Total	Infant[4]	Total[2]	Infant[5]	Number	Rate[2]
	29	30	31	32	33	34	35	36	37	38	39	40	41	42	43
NEBRASKA—Con.															
Buffalo	100	13 736	11.8	2.53	7.2	26.0	537	14.5	30	301	3	8.2	5.5	347	9.3
Burt	-400	3 139	-6.9	2.44	5.5	29.1	71	8.6	2	126	0	15.0	0.0	54	6.2
Butler	-400	3 253	-3.7	2.59	4.9	27.4	129	14.2	6	109	1	12.1	8.1	64	7.0
Cass	500	7 797	9.0	2.70	6.5	21.0	337	15.2	18	215	1	9.7	3.3	128	6.0
Cedar	-900	3 652	-4.4	2.71	3.9	26.4	193	18.0	9	144	2	13.3	11.6	93	8.3
Chase	-300	1 704	-1.0	2.52	5.5	26.8	54	11.7	2	49	1	10.7	16.9	29	5.9
Cherry	-300	2 438	-2.6	2.56	5.3	25.8	106	16.3	4	80	2	11.9	25.3	55	8.0
Cheyenne	-300	3 851	-2.1	2.44	7.5	28.7	138	13.8	9	117	0	11.5	0.0	84	8.4
Clay	-700	2 741	-9.0	2.54	4.5	24.8	97	12.8	5	101	0	13.1	0.0	56	7.1
Colfax	-600	3 562	-3.3	2.52	5.3	28.9	153	16.6	6	120	3	12.6	22.9	79	8.2
Cuming	-900	3 851	-5.0	2.56	3.5	27.0	135	12.3	8	120	1	11.0	7.5	94	8.2
Custer	-900	4 953	-6.0	2.43	5.2	28.9	168	13.1	11	144	0	11.1	0.0	83	6.0
Dakota	-500	6 035	5.6	2.73	10.5	22.9	295	17.2	18	175	2	10.3	7.5	121	7.0
Dawes	-600	3 327	-4.9	2.43	8.5	29.8	138	15.0	8	80	1	8.6	6.9	74	7.8
Dawson	-2 200	7 829	-4.3	2.51	6.3	25.6	242	11.7	16	228	2	11.0	7.4	196	8.6
Deuel	-100	915	-5.0	2.41	4.8	29.3	36	15.7	1	31	0	12.9	0.0	13	5.4
Dixon	-600	2 338	-8.3	2.58	5.8	26.3	83	12.6	4	81	1	12.1	11.8	54	7.7
Dodge	-1 600	13 445	1.2	2.48	6.8	26.8	490	13.8	23	367	2	10.4	4.2	333	9.4
Douglas	-5 400	161 113	10.3	2.53	12.2	28.1	7 044	16.8	451	3 429	62	8.3	8.9	3 576	8.7
Dundy	-100	1 085	-5.5	2.32	5.0	31.5	24	8.9	0	30	0	10.7	0.0	15	5.2
Fillmore	-500	2 829	-6.0	2.41	4.2	29.3	92	12.4	1	118	0	15.9	0.0	70	9.0
Franklin	-200	1 655	-5.0	2.32	3.7	30.3	58	14.5	1	59	0	14.8	0.0	27	6.3
Frontier	-300	1 206	-10.3	2.53	3.6	27.1	43	12.6	1	42	0	12.4	0.0	28	7.6
Furnas	-200	2 334	-10.7	2.28	4.4	33.8	57	9.7	2	109	0	18.2	0.0	34	5.2
Gage	-1 300	9 019	-2.4	2.40	6.7	28.2	306	13.2	18	298	4	12.8	12.5	176	7.3
Garden	0	1 040	-8.0	2.30	4.9	30.3	41	15.2	3	53	0	19.6	0.0	26	9.3
Garfield	-200	864	-5.5	2.40	4.7	28.7	35	16.7	0	39	0	17.7	0.0	36	15.0
Gosper	0	764	-1.3	2.45	3.7	21.2	24	11.4	0	23	0	11.0	0.0	24	10.9
Grant	-100	303	-5.9	2.54	6.6	24.1	13	16.2	0	9	0	11.2	0.0	14	15.6
Greeley	-200	1 133	-6.6	2.59	6.4	30.1	45	14.1	5	58	0	17.6	0.0	22	6.7
Hall	-1 200	18 678	7.0	2.56	8.5	26.0	786	16.2	47	410	5	8.4	6.6	499	10.1
Hamilton	-600	3 235	-1.1	2.67	4.3	21.7	137	15.1	3	88	1	9.8	8.5	64	6.9
Harlan	-300	1 585	-6.1	2.37	3.7	29.2	45	11.2	3	54	0	13.5	0.0	32	7.4
Hayes	-100	480	0.0	2.55	3.3	22.7	15	12.5	0	7	0	5.8	0.0	4	3.1
Hitchcock	-300	1 467	-4.5	2.48	4.3	28.6	50	12.8	0	54	1	13.8	21.7	28	7.0
Holt	-800	4 744	-1.0	2.62	5.1	27.3	212	16.2	6	132	1	9.9	4.5	111	8.0
Hooker	0	332	-12.2	2.29	4.5	33.7	12	12.0	0	10	0	10.0	0.0	8	8.0
Howard	-400	2 309	-2.3	2.59	4.8	25.2	79	12.3	7	68	0	10.5	0.0	38	5.6
Jefferson	-500	3 634	-7.7	2.37	5.1	28.8	107	11.8	6	114	3	12.3	31.9	87	9.1
Johnson	-300	1 940	-4.9	2.36	5.2	30.8	60	12.5	4	67	1	13.7	21.7	37	7.1
Kearney	-600	2 523	-0.8	2.54	4.8	24.1	94	14.0	3	55	1	8.3	12.8	55	8.1
Keith	-800	3 430	-1.7	2.47	6.7	27.3	113	13.0	7	99	0	11.1	0.0	74	8.0
Keya Paha	-100	419	-12.5	2.46	2.1	24.8	12	10.9	0	7	0	5.8	0.0	8	6.7
Kimball	-400	1 650	-8.3	2.45	6.8	26.7	43	9.6	4	45	0	10.0	0.0	49	10.0
Knox	-700	3 817	-8.6	2.44	5.1	29.7	146	13.8	15	153	1	14.2	9.0	80	7.1
Lancaster	2 200	82 759	15.3	2.44	8.7	27.5	2 966	14.0	149	1 399	38	6.7	12.6	1 852	9.1
Lincoln	-4 600	12 676	-4.3	2.53	8.0	27.0	467	13.9	34	322	1	9.6	2.1	265	7.7
Logan	-100	320	-8.3	2.74	4.4	21.9	10	10.0	0	11	0	11.0	0.0	4	4.0
Loup	0	276	-13.5	2.47	4.0	27.2	8	10.0	0	3	0	3.8	0.0	5	5.6
McPherson	0	212	-4.1	2.58	2.8	23.6	6	10.0	0	4	0	8.0	0.0	1	1.7
Madison	-800	12 283	6.0	2.57	7.0	26.7	531	16.4	31	309	5	9.7	9.7	296	9.2
Merrick	-600	3 061	-2.2	2.57	4.3	25.3	103	12.1	5	83	0	9.8	0.0	55	6.3
Morrill	-400	2 083	-6.6	2.55	3.8	25.7	77	13.5	4	73	2	12.6	28.2	37	6.1
Nance	-300	1 585	-7.4	2.58	4.3	27.3	53	12.0	4	66	0	15.0	0.0	39	8.5
Nemaha	-100	3 079	-3.8	2.41	5.7	28.9	106	12.8	2	88	0	10.5	0.0	89	10.3
Nuckolls	-300	2 359	-8.9	2.40	4.3	29.0	70	11.3	6	95	1	14.8	13.0	54	8.1
Otoe	-600	5 657	-2.5	2.46	6.5	28.0	180	12.4	10	218	0	14.9	0.0	121	8.0
Pawnee	-100	1 408	-10.8	2.31	3.9	31.0	42	12.0	2	45	0	12.5	0.0	23	6.1
Perkins	-100	1 283	-5.7	2.58	4.8	25.8	41	11.4	0	44	0	12.2	0.0	23	6.2
Phelps	-100	3 769	1.9	2.51	5.3	26.2	124	12.7	7	132	1	13.3	7.8	80	7.9
Pierce	-400	2 929	-3.8	2.62	4.5	25.2	113	13.5	3	93	1	11.1	8.5	63	7.4
Platte	-1 400	10 954	8.6	2.69	6.1	24.7	521	17.1	30	233	3	7.9	6.3	277	9.4
Polk	-400	2 223	-4.3	2.48	4.7	27.1	61	10.3	4	90	0	15.3	0.0	41	6.7
Red Willow	-300	4 723	-1.5	2.44	7.1	28.5	180	14.3	9	122	3	9.6	18.6	116	9.0
Richardson	-800	4 120	-8.0	2.35	6.0	31.1	136	13.3	6	158	1	15.3	8.4	94	8.5
Rock	-200	798	-9.6	2.52	5.8	26.9	30	13.6	2	23	0	10.5	0.0	12	5.0

1. No spouse present. 2. Per 1,000 resident population estimated as of July 1 of the year shown. 3. Under 2,500 grams. 4. Deaths of infants under 1 year old. 5. Deaths of infants under 1 year old per 1,000 live births.

STATE County	Divorces, 1984: Number	Divorces, 1984: Rate[1]	Physicians, active non–Federal, 1989: Number[2]	Physicians, active non–Federal, 1989: Rate[3]	Hospitals, 1989: Number	Hospitals, 1989: Beds: Number	Hospitals, 1989: Beds: Rate[3]	Nursing homes,[4] 1986: Number	Nursing homes,[4] 1986: Beds	Serious crimes known to police, 1988: Number: Total[5]	Serious crimes known to police, 1988: Number: Violent[6]	Serious crimes known to police, 1988: Rate[3]	Education: Public school enrollment[7]: 1986–1987	Education: Public school enrollment[7]: 1980	Education: Attainment,[8] 1980: Percent 12 yrs. or more	Education: Attainment,[8] 1980: Percent 16 yrs. or more
	44	45	46	47	48	49	50	51	52	53	54	55	56	57	58	59
NEBRASKA—Con.																
Buffalo	184	4.9	62	167	2	252	679	6	388	1 498	27	4 065	6 462	6 032	76.9	19.1
Burt	22	2.5	5	60	1	23	277	3	215	58	0	3 320	1 587	1 711	66.1	9.5
Butler	10	1.1	5	56	1	34	378	2	158	48	3	2 054	1 181	1 457	61.3	7.6
Cass	73	3.4	8	36	0	0	0	4	299	569	17	2 552	3 391	4 375	72.7	10.3
Cedar	6	0.5	3	28	0	0	0	4	256	17	2	186	1 690	2 148	61.5	7.8
Chase	21	4.3	3	67	1	26	578	2	122	8	0	295	1 012	1 022	72.2	12.9
Cherry	24	3.5	4	62	1	29	453	1	63	112	4	1 665	1 102	1 353	73.8	13.2
Cheyenne	43	4.3	10	100	1	117	1 170	2	107	264	15	2 603	1 846	1 921	73.3	12.9
Clay	14	1.8	0	0	0	0	0	3	164	49	1	642	1 604	1 700	68.8	10.6
Colfax	24	2.5	4	44	1	49	538	3	152	143	1	1 531	1 781	1 902	58.4	7.6
Cuming	25	2.2	4	37	1	49	450	4	224	52	1	471	1 692	1 888	61.3	7.9
Custer	41	2.9	8	63	3	162	1 286	4	255	179	0	1 371	2 448	2 671	69.6	9.8
Dakota	64	3.7	5	29	0	0	0	2	164	836	12	4 897	3 004	3 520	67.8	9.1
Dawes	42	4.4	6	66	2	58	637	2	125	320	7	3 426	1 807	1 596	76.4	18.1
Dawson	108	4.8	14	69	3	117	574	5	308	660	18	3 190	4 309	4 609	70.6	12.4
Deuel	5	2.1	0	0	0	0	0	1	24	15	0	622	463	496	71.0	13.1
Dixon	17	2.4	2	30	0	0	0	3	202	88	4	1 308	1 221	1 590	66.0	9.4
Dodge	150	4.2	34	96	1	245	688	7	642	1 129	26	3 203	6 267	6 825	68.5	10.9
Douglas	1 939	4.7	1 576	372	12	3 964	935	34	3 947	25 639	2 806	6 145	67 870	69 431	76.8	20.2
Dundy	10	3.4	2	77	1	28	1 077	1	58	31	0	1 102	427	501	60.6	10.1
Fillmore	30	3.8	4	55	1	59	808	4	208	66	4	888	1 306	1 580	69.1	9.9
Franklin	14	3.3	3	77	1	20	513	2	121	33	2	843	618	803	60.9	9.7
Frontier	7	1.9	0	0	0	0	0	1	49	NA	NA	NA	597	675	70.6	12.7
Furnas	23	3.5	4	69	1	67	1 155	4	201	22	1	371	1 232	1 155	68.3	11.1
Gage	81	3.4	22	95	1	182	788	8	578	603	6	2 588	3 166	4 285	61.8	10.0
Garden	5	1.8	2	74	1	56	2 074	2	80	22	2	812	462	517	70.0	10.4
Garfield	7	2.9	2	95	0	0	0	1	58	NA	NA	NA	432	487	61.4	10.0
Gosper	3	1.4	0	0	0	0	0	1	51	NA	NA	NA	226	418	67.9	8.6
Grant	6	6.7	0	0	0	0	0	0	0	NA	NA	NA	172	191	79.9	11.0
Greeley	6	1.8	0	0	0	0	0	2	54	1	0	NA	635	603	70.7	8.7
Hall	269	5.4	61	126	2	417	860	8	845	3 153	55	6 447	9 123	9 536	74.8	12.9
Hamilton	17	1.8	8	89	1	78	867	4	248	105	3	1 162	1 673	2 034	74.3	13.3
Harlan	8	1.9	3	75	1	25	625	1	61	NA	NA	NA	522	842	73.3	10.8
Hayes	2	1.5	0	0	0	0	0	0	0	NA	NA	NA	174	275	77.8	7.8
Hitchcock	8	2.0	0	0	0	0	0	2	58	26	0	664	788	776	69.4	9.1
Holt	32	2.3	7	54	2	45	349	4	256	54	1	401	2 244	2 644	67.9	8.7
Hooker	2	2.0	0	0	0	0	0	1	30	NA	NA	NA	225	197	70.5	11.8
Howard	17	2.5	2	31	1	36	562	1	74	80	0	1 226	1 540	1 446	68.6	9.9
Jefferson	25	2.6	4	44	1	91	1 000	1	96	65	1	1 374	1 906	1 624	64.1	8.7
Johnson	13	2.5	3	62	1	30	625	2	99	34	1	691	879	976	61.3	8.9
Kearney	27	4.0	4	60	1	80	1 194	2	111	133	3	2 007	1 296	1 390	73.3	13.7
Keith	42	4.6	5	58	1	41	477	1	82	324	6	3 585	1 631	1 797	72.9	11.4
Keya Paha	1	0.8	0	0	0	0	0	0	0	NA	NA	NA	214	279	67.8	8.1
Kimball	24	4.9	2	45	1	30	682	1	72	147	6	3 253	832	1 047	68.8	10.1
Knox	23	2.0	5	48	1	30	286	4	241	95	6	884	1 984	2 216	61.4	7.8
Lancaster	957	4.7	375	174	6	1 471	685	19	1 622	14 612	878	7 006	29 320	30 003	81.5	23.9
Lincoln	163	4.8	44	131	1	113	335	5	407	1 712	54	5 120	6 094	7 094	75.6	12.1
Logan	0	0.0	0	0	0	0	0	0	0	NA	NA	NA	212	204	74.4	10.5
Loup	1	1.1	0	0	0	0	0	0	0	NA	NA	NA	135	191	71.6	11.4
McPherson	1	1.7	0	0	0	0	0	0	0	NA	NA	NA	103	104	61.9	11.1
Madison	111	3.5	36	111	3	298	917	8	617	1 420	54	4 392	5 543	5 040	68.9	11.9
Merrick	24	2.7	2	24	1	79	929	4	188	147	3	1 722	1 556	1 867	68.9	9.6
Morrill	15	2.5	5	88	1	20	351	1	61	3	0	70	1 151	1 184	62.7	8.7
Nance	4	0.9	3	70	2	40	930	3	150	27	0	597	852	979	64.4	8.1
Nemaha	25	2.9	4	48	1	42	506	1	114	42	0	847	1 293	1 405	67.7	14.1
Nuckolls	19	2.8	4	66	1	49	803	3	180	7	0	107	1 086	1 240	68.0	9.3
Otoe	41	2.7	9	62	2	68	469	4	378	352	7	2 401	2 743	2 830	65.8	7.6
Pawnee	6	1.6	2	57	1	17	486	1	66	31	1	858	632	655	65.4	7.4
Perkins	10	2.7	3	86	1	76	2 171	1	56	NA	NA	NA	690	697	69.7	13.9
Phelps	34	3.4	9	92	1	55	561	4	287	142	4	2 472	1 862	1 900	74.0	13.6
Pierce	24	2.8	8	94	2	59	694	2	145	4	0	NA	1 273	1 474	64.2	7.9
Platte	100	3.4	24	78	1	81	264	2	191	900	10	3 018	4 227	4 872	72.7	13.3
Polk	17	2.8	4	68	1	35	593	2	165	66	4	1 114	1 103	1 346	72.0	9.4
Red Willow	56	4.3	13	103	1	56	444	1	95	163	4	1 288	2 225	2 488	75.4	12.3
Richardson	43	3.9	8	79	2	84	832	4	327	196	3	1 914	1 607	1 839	63.3	10.9
Rock	9	3.8	1	48	1	20	952	1	30	24	1	1 039	458	482	68.7	10.7

1. Per 1,000 resident population estimated as of July 1 of the year shown. 2. As of end of year. 3. Per 100,000 resident population as of July 1 of the year shown. 4. Preliminary. Covers nursing homes with 3 or more beds. 5. Data for serious crimes have not been adjusted for underreporting, this may affect comparability between geographic areas or over time. 6. Includes murder and nonnegligent manslaughter, forcible rape, robbery, and aggravated assault. 7. The 1986–1987 data are based on administrative reports obtained by the U.S. National Center for Education Statistics. The 1980 data are based on the 1980 Census of Population and Housing. 8. Persons 25 years old or older.

STATE County	Education (cont'd): Local government expenditures for education,[1] 1982: Total (Mil dol)	Education (cont'd): Local government expenditures for education,[1] 1982: Per capita (Dollars)	Social Security Program December 1988: Beneficiaries: Total	Social Security Program December 1988: Beneficiaries: Rate[2]	Social Security Program December 1988: Payments ($1,000)	Supplemental Security Income Program recipients June 1986	Money income: Per capita[3]: 1987 Income, (Dollars)	Money income: Per capita[3]: 1979: Current dollars	Money income: Per capita[3]: 1979: Constant 1987 dollars	Money income: Median household income 1979 (Dollars)	Money income: Percent below poverty level, 1979: Persons	Money income: Percent below poverty level, 1979: Families	Housing units, 1990: Total	Housing units, 1990: Percent change, 1980–1990
	60	61	62	63	64	65	66	67	68	69	70	71	72	73
NEBRASKA—Con.														
Buffalo	16.4	449	5 515	149.1	2 656	224	9 879	6 446	10 086	15 202	10.9	6.6	14 538	8.2
Burt	4.6	536	2 025	244.0	952	100	9 347	6 085	9 521	12 577	15.7	11.7	3 740	-1.7
Butler	3.6	384	2 050	225.3	911	78	9 537	5 895	9 224	13 612	12.5	10.3	3 801	-0.2
Cass	9.2	438	3 250	147.1	1 592	112	10 752	6 596	10 321	16 985	7.2	6.0	8 951	7.6
Cedar	5.0	451	2 220	207.5	927	86	8 644	5 274	8 252	11 557	19.7	14.7	4 149	1.3
Chase	3.5	718	985	214.1	474	54	8 265	5 452	8 531	12 278	17.0	14.6	2 011	-4.2
Cherry	3.3	485	1 305	200.8	578	64	9 326	6 797	10 635	13 863	13.6	9.6	3 023	2.0
Cheyenne	6.7	665	1 980	198.0	1 002	88	11 385	6 805	10 648	15 071	12.2	8.6	4 345	-2.9
Clay	5.4	685	1 745	229.6	844	66	10 027	5 997	9 384	13 836	12.1	9.0	3 173	-5.4
Colfax	5.2	534	2 375	258.2	1 049	74	9 336	6 005	9 396	12 991	13.6	11.7	3 971	-1.8
Cuming	5.0	429	2 220	201.8	1 012	68	8 857	6 118	9 573	14 472	13.4	10.6	4 132	-4.4
Custer	7.3	520	3 130	244.5	1 403	156	9 347	6 025	9 427	12 338	15.3	12.3	5 728	-7.3
Dakota	6.7	396	2 635	153.2	1 237	206	9 118	6 476	10 133	16 967	9.6	7.1	6 486	5.8
Dawes	3.4	357	1 655	179.9	756	66	8 981	6 031	9 437	12 888	15.4	9.4	3 909	-1.4
Dawson	11.7	522	4 125	199.3	2 020	198	9 957	6 685	10 460	16 401	8.6	6.4	9 021	-3.7
Deuel	1.9	783	585	254.3	312	14	10 472	6 573	10 285	13 775	11.0	8.1	1 075	-3.8
Dixon	5.2	736	1 475	223.5	640	62	8 807	5 312	8 312	11 964	19.0	15.9	2 613	-8.3
Dodge	17.4	486	7 210	203.7	3 568	256	10 297	7 070	11 062	16 123	8.8	7.1	14 601	2.5
Douglas	188.0	469	59 470	141.8	30 353	4 302	12 615	7 809	12 219	17 720	9.9	7.2	172 335	10.7
Dundy	3.0	1 019	665	246.3	309	32	9 788	6 061	9 484	11 698	17.3	13.3	1 326	-7.8
Fillmore	5.1	641	1 700	229.7	824	68	10 627	6 340	9 920	13 881	11.0	9.0	3 102	-5.3
Franklin	2.5	575	1 185	296.2	527	48	9 590	5 872	9 188	11 538	15.9	13.3	1 950	-5.1
Frontier	2.8	759	690	202.9	324	24	8 313	6 116	9 570	12 837	15.5	11.2	1 565	-12.6
Furnas	4.4	694	1 810	306.8	821	110	8 914	5 426	8 490	10 897	18.3	13.5	2 905	-5.7
Gage	10.2	422	5 510	237.5	2 583	510	10 282	6 389	9 997	13 915	10.4	7.9	9 735	-1.8
Garden	1.8	637	700	259.3	327	28	8 853	6 571	10 282	12 755	11.1	8.7	1 343	-4.1
Garfield	1.2	537	605	288.1	257	30	7 749	5 116	8 005	10 821	17.6	12.0	1 021	-5.0
Gosper	0.7	338	470	223.8	229	8	8 304	5 786	9 053	13 136	15.4	13.0	1 212	-3.0
Grant	1.1	1 168	170	212.5	84	6	7 216	5 519	8 636	12 358	15.1	13.0	425	-1.2
Greeley	2.9	841	750	234.4	318	32	7 955	4 547	7 115	9 323	29.1	24.3	1 284	-9.8
Hall	23.2	471	8 345	171.7	4 002	458	10 718	7 158	11 200	16 703	6.8	4.6	19 528	4.0
Hamilton	5.8	614	1 565	172.0	769	68	10 512	6 528	10 214	15 764	10.5	7.9	3 589	-0.4
Harlan	2.2	510	985	246.2	468	32	9 413	5 736	8 975	11 628	18.4	15.6	2 409	13.2
Hayes	0.8	623	155	129.2	71	8	8 234	5 237	8 194	11 060	19.8	17.2	583	-13.1
Hitchcock	3.3	794	900	230.8	421	32	8 536	5 608	8 775	12 409	15.5	12.5	1 873	7.6
Holt	5.8	416	2 615	199.6	1 103	158	8 207	5 108	7 992	11 563	18.2	15.2	5 472	1.1
Hooker	0.9	871	260	260.0	122	10	6 616	4 969	7 775	10 944	18.4	13.6	433	-3.6
Howard	5.9	875	1 325	207.0	578	52	9 056	5 664	8 862	13 530	11.1	8.4	2 598	-2.4
Jefferson	6.5	675	2 395	263.2	1 076	110	10 488	6 319	9 887	12 704	15.3	11.4	4 082	-4.4
Johnson	3.1	598	1 265	263.5	550	52	9 342	5 552	8 687	11 521	17.9	15.0	2 153	-2.2
Kearney	4.4	625	1 360	203.0	687	108	10 890	6 729	10 529	15 368	9.3	7.3	2 756	-2.5
Keith	8.3	890	1 775	204.0	866	52	10 159	6 723	10 519	15 846	9.5	7.7	4 938	3.2
Keya Paha	0.7	548	215	195.5	87	10	10 270	5 972	9 344	11 089	16.5	14.2	584	3.2
Kimball	3.5	666	910	202.2	470	24	10 294	6 544	10 239	15 054	12.6	10.7	1 967	-3.2
Knox	6.7	595	2 625	247.6	1 077	122	8 145	5 015	7 847	10 818	20.2	15.9	4 799	-0.1
Lancaster	75.1	378	27 295	129.0	14 081	1 564	11 735	7 645	11 962	17 428	8.6	5.4	86 734	13.6
Lincoln	14.8	427	5 220	154.9	2 383	330	11 820	7 724	12 086	18 378	7.3	5.3	14 210	-3.7
Logan	0.8	787	200	200.0	89	10	6 428	4 416	6 910	10 625	25.5	21.1	387	-3.7
Loup	0.9	1 106	115	143.8	48	4	7 121	5 440	8 512	12 375	13.3	11.6	399	8.7
McPherson	0.4	673	110	183.3	47	2	9 345	6 609	10 341	12 857	19.7	15.8	257	-2.7
Madison	12.3	386	6 075	188.1	2 803	338	10 173	6 940	10 859	16 007	9.3	6.7	13 069	6.0
Merrick	4.8	534	1 700	200.0	778	64	10 181	6 018	9 416	15 251	11.5	9.1	3 533	-2.0
Morrill	2.9	481	1 210	212.3	551	52	7 398	5 051	7 903	11 002	22.3	17.7	2 530	-2.4
Nance	2.3	497	925	210.2	413	66	8 205	4 901	7 669	11 103	20.8	15.8	1 807	-8.6
Nemaha	4.3	518	1 685	203.0	788	84	10 207	6 423	10 050	13 429	15.5	10.8	3 432	-1.9
Nuckolls	3.2	478	1 545	249.2	714	68	9 406	5 960	9 326	13 041	11.3	8.0	2 699	-6.9
Otoe	9.6	636	3 305	227.9	1 562	128	10 670	6 668	10 433	14 452	11.2	8.6	6 137	-2.9
Pawnee	2.1	549	1 075	307.1	444	46	8 399	5 009	7 838	9 934	19.3	15.1	1 674	-6.9
Perkins	3.5	948	810	225.0	410	18	9 747	5 979	9 355	13 640	16.2	12.9	1 537	-1.4
Phelps	6.8	667	1 930	196.9	997	66	11 270	7 192	11 253	15 300	9.8	7.3	4 084	0.0
Pierce	3.9	454	1 700	202.4	728	56	9 216	5 449	8 526	12 972	13.6	11.1	3 177	-1.9
Platte	11.7	402	4 660	153.3	2 271	154	10 360	6 796	10 634	17 302	8.1	6.2	11 716	7.1
Polk	3.8	611	1 330	225.4	658	36	9 043	6 021	9 421	13 756	14.1	12.9	2 742	6.5
Red Willow	6.5	509	2 350	186.5	1 104	92	10 305	7 040	11 015	15 280	9.6	6.5	5 279	-0.6
Richardson	4.9	432	2 725	267.2	1 231	126	9 695	5 813	9 096	11 621	16.0	11.8	4 704	-4.4
Rock	1.3	517	480	218.2	208	22	8 256	5 899	9 230	12 460	13.9	10.2	1 001	-3.8

1. Elementary and secondary. 2. Per 1,000 resident population estimated as of July 1 of the year shown. 3. Based on the resident population estimated as of July 1, 1988 for 1987 data and enumerated as of April 1, 1980 for 1979 data.

STATE County	Housing units, 1990 (cont'd): Occupied units: Total	Owner occupied: Percent	Owner occupied: Median value (Dollars)	Median rent (Dollars)	Civilian labor force, 1990: Total	Percent change, 1989–1990	Unemployment: Total	Unemployment: Rate[1]	Private nonfarm establishments, 1988: Number	Net change, 1987–1988	Employment[2]: Total	Per-cent change, 1987–1988	Manu-facturing	Retail trade
	74	75	76	77	78	79	80	81	82	83	84	85	86	87
NEBRASKA—Con.														
Buffalo	13 736	61.8	49 500	255	20 981	4.0	401	1.9	1 100	-2	12 589	7.9	3 028	3 708
Burt	3 139	71.1	29 600	161	3 469	0.6	97	2.8	228	-2	1 209	10.5	102	284
Butler	3 253	75.2	30 200	188	4 077	1.6	107	2.6	176	10	1 210	5.4	337	307
Cass	7 797	76.7	48 200	245	9 013	3.3	279	3.1	372	-8	2 304	-4.1	0	632
Cedar	3 652	76.9	31 100	145	4 486	7.1	79	1.8	267	4	1 316	10.1	142	283
Chase	1 704	74.9	38 000	180	1 863	5.1	32	1.7	129	9	773	-2.2	51	239
Cherry	2 438	63.5	35 500	193	3 201	0.9	61	1.9	206	4	982	8.3	0	414
Cheyenne	3 851	70.4	35 700	199	5 320	1.3	90	1.7	334	13	2 763	22.8	320	1 256
Clay	2 741	75.8	28 100	167	3 525	0.0	72	2.0	195	-7	991	1.0	62	239
Colfax	3 562	75.9	34 300	189	4 424	4.2	89	2.0	243	-6	2 738	1.2	0	491
Cuming	3 851	71.7	38 500	179	5 347	1.7	73	1.4	352	7	2 617	10.5	665	586
Custer	4 953	71.0	27 900	154	5 789	1.6	94	1.6	353	-13	2 338	7.0	0	683
Dakota	6 035	68.3	43 700	267	8 981	4.0	220	2.4	380	5	10 125	46.2	0	920
Dawes	3 327	63.1	33 400	204	5 357	1.8	119	2.2	288	-7	1 693	-4.8	44	723
Dawson	7 829	69.7	40 800	199	9 358	2.9	284	3.0	647	5	5 287	-0.4	1 379	1 482
Deuel	915	74.0	28 800	157	878	0.2	24	2.7	66	-1	329	-2.7	0	154
Dixon	2 338	74.2	27 100	162	3 423	6.1	69	2.0	117	-1	1 169	2.2	0	120
Dodge	13 445	67.6	42 800	236	16 835	2.4	465	2.8	1 024	-16	10 900	5.2	3 134	2 911
Douglas	161 113	62.7	59 900	333	239 477	3.6	5 570	2.3	12 167	228	221 843	4.0	28 235	44 878
Dundy	1 085	69.5	23 600	144	1 281	2.4	12	0.9	70	-2	320	-13.7	0	93
Fillmore	2 829	74.6	30 900	169	3 520	4.3	58	1.6	230	2	1 256	6.1	52	321
Franklin	1 655	78.9	19 300	139	1 781	-0.1	29	1.6	101	3	437	-0.9	0	122
Frontier	1 206	71.8	25 500	155	1 694	3.5	20	1.2	78	-2	341	-22.9	0	77
Furnas	2 334	75.9	19 900	135	2 606	2.4	51	2.0	186	5	940	1.0	93	255
Gage	9 019	70.7	36 600	205	11 602	2.2	202	1.7	614	-2	6 200	12.1	1 331	1 590
Garden	1 040	68.7	30 700	154	1 690	0.5	21	1.2	79	-1	358	8.5	0	84
Garfield	864	71.6	24 000	140	1 016	3.3	26	2.6	86	4	565	16.0	0	240
Gosper	764	77.2	40 300	168	1 153	9.6	21	1.8	42	4	132	3.9	0	27
Grant	303	63.4	25 900	168	458	7.0	4	0.9	23	-4	87	-11.2	0	41
Greeley	1 133	78.5	19 200	136	1 202	-1.2	32	2.7	67	-1	363	-17.3	0	77
Hall	18 678	63.6	48 200	253	26 797	1.3	636	2.4	1 608	43	19 650	1.1	4 480	5 862
Hamilton	3 235	69.4	41 400	196	4 644	4.1	79	1.7	243	-3	2 000	8.8	509	338
Harlan	1 585	77.7	28 400	158	1 704	-1.7	32	1.9	113	-1	628	8.8	20	208
Hayes	480	70.4	19 600	142	679	2.6	7	1.0	22	-1	81	2.5	0	28
Hitchcock	1 467	75.5	22 700	158	1 243	-2.2	36	2.9	72	-3	273	27.0	0	99
Holt	4 744	69.9	35 200	169	5 398	1.5	108	2.0	399	-6	2 307	8.1	54	825
Hooker	332	76.8	26 300	158	487	4.1	8	1.6	26	1	88	7.3	0	48
Howard	2 309	74.4	31 600	165	2 439	1.6	61	2.5	126	-5	650	1.9	0	231
Jefferson	3 634	76.2	19 400	153	4 354	4.6	84	1.9	264	-6	2 507	-2.7	772	598
Johnson	1 940	76.4	25 900	159	2 300	0.9	87	3.8	134	6	1 096	3.5	0	208
Kearney	2 523	72.2	42 500	213	2 833	-2.8	45	1.6	177	4	1 499	1.8	227	235
Keith	3 430	69.7	41 500	198	4 464	-0.4	120	2.7	338	-4	2 614	6.4	439	869
Keya Paha	419	70.9	17 500	117	518	-2.4	10	1.9	20	2	52	8.3	0	30
Kimball	1 650	74.5	35 300	197	2 176	5.5	40	1.8	178	1	958	-9.7	169	251
Knox	3 817	73.4	24 900	132	4 713	2.2	110	2.3	256	-13	1 388	8.9	0	476
Lancaster	82 759	60.5	62 200	322	130 100	4.4	2 160	1.7	5 466	111	86 332	5.6	14 675	21 278
Lincoln	12 676	67.9	42 900	213	15 083	3.5	413	2.7	923	-9	7 559	2.6	310	2 675
Logan	320	66.6	29 200	176	397	1.0	10	2.5	16	-2	43	22.9	0	10
Loup	276	72.8	14 999	121	362	-2.2	12	3.3	7	0	20	-4.8	0	17
McPherson	212	63.7	30 600	117	424	7.3	3	0.7	4	0	19	-9.5	0	17
Madison	12 283	65.4	48 000	249	17 219	5.0	375	2.2	1 127	15	13 833	12.0	3 838	3 298
Merrick	3 061	73.0	33 200	176	3 861	-0.5	79	2.0	202	5	1 161	1.8	165	367
Morrill	2 083	68.4	28 400	175	2 535	-2.9	79	3.1	128	13	483	2.5	0	163
Nance	1 585	76.3	24 300	149	1 999	3.5	38	1.9	108	-6	670	11.7	0	91
Nemaha	3 079	69.3	33 500	183	5 410	19.8	117	2.2	201	9	1 448	2.2	0	330
Nuckolls	2 359	78.7	22 200	139	2 794	2.4	39	1.4	202	3	1 369	4.7	0	363
Otoe	5 657	71.5	38 800	208	7 057	0.1	203	2.9	394	6	3 668	2.1	895	993
Pawnee	1 408	80.8	14 999	127	1 512	7.3	43	2.8	79	2	338	4.3	0	94
Perkins	1 283	77.5	36 600	177	1 700	2.0	23	1.4	106	6	476	9.9	0	90
Phelps	3 769	71.9	39 700	198	5 296	4.2	72	1.4	325	8	3 089	4.3	782	609
Pierce	2 929	76.6	34 200	162	3 933	0.4	75	1.9	215	8	1 209	2.0	80	346
Platte	10 954	73.4	51 900	250	16 160	4.9	338	2.1	792	22	11 743	16.7	5 317	2 500
Polk	2 223	76.3	30 700	160	2 804	3.9	52	1.9	150	4	879	4.6	22	214
Red Willow	4 723	69.7	39 000	215	6 017	3.8	123	2.0	437	-3	3 555	4.3	526	1 188
Richardson	4 120	71.7	24 800	145	4 604	3.7	130	2.8	298	6	1 989	6.0	296	526
Rock	798	70.1	26 600	147	1 068	-2.0	21	2.0	55	-11	316	-16.0	0	44

1. Percent of total civilian labor force. 2. For week including March 12. Excludes government employees, self-employed persons, farm workers, domestic service workers, railroad employees subject to the Railroad Retirement Act, and employees on oceanborne vessels or in foreign countries.

STATE County	Private nonfarm establishments, 1988 (cont'd): Employment[1] (cont'd): Finance, insurance, and real estate	Employment[1] (cont'd): Services	Annual payroll: Total (Mil dol)	Annual payroll: Average per employee (Dollars)	Personal income, 1989: Total (Mil dol)	Per-cent change, 1988–1989	Wages and salaries[2] (Mil dol)	Propri-etor's income (Mil dol)	Dividends, interest, & rent (Mil dol)	Transfer payments (Mil dol)	Per capita[3]: Dollars	Per capita[3]: Rank	Earnings, 1989: Total (Mil dol)	Percent by selected industries: Farm	Goods-related[4]: Total
	88	89	90	91	92	93	94	95	96	97	98	99	100	101	102
NEBRASKA—Con.															
Buffalo	461	3 389	189	14 975	514	7.4	309	73	92	74	13 856	1 501	382	7.9	26.4
Burt	91	371	14	11 329	124	4.4	30	41	27	23	14 974	998	71	42.7	NA
Butler	50	299	14	11 349	131	1.3	30	36	33	20	14 495	1 215	66	38.2	NA
Cass	157	574	34	14 576	310	7.6	63	37	49	49	13 781	1 543	100	16.7	NA
Cedar	101	373	15	11 699	131	9.6	35	41	29	22	12 338	2 185	76	31.4	11.8
Chase	49	148	10	12 859	72	-0.7	24	25	16	11	15 860	691	48	45.3	NA
Cherry	67	265	11	10 932	92	12.9	26	29	25	13	14 378	1 256	55	40.7	4.3
Cheyenne	155	562	34	12 410	165	8.1	70	43	31	25	16 376	553	113	22.8	11.8
Clay	64	163	13	13 280	121	1.0	45	37	25	19	16 060	631	83	38.1	NA
Colfax	105	437	37	13 420	127	7.7	60	24	34	22	13 983	1 443	84	14.6	38.5
Cuming	120	658	35	13 235	160	9.3	54	48	40	22	14 631	1 154	101	21.3	20.6
Custer	158	663	27	11 473	199	8.1	58	64	47	33	15 718	735	123	35.7	13.6
Dakota	380	1 944	186	18 376	239	10.1	191	29	29	33	13 880	1 492	219	3.0	56.6
Dawes	90	557	15	9 058	126	10.0	51	27	25	24	13 728	1 565	78	15.7	6.4
Dawson	289	990	75	14 208	300	6.5	132	78	62	46	14 689	1 137	210	21.1	23.1
Deuel	27	46	4	11 456	39	6.3	11	12	11	7	17 127	417	24	40.7	NA
Dixon	44	113	13	11 478	85	13.0	29	20	18	15	12 887	1 959	48	26.6	NA
Dodge	550	2 536	158	14 487	512	6.7	240	79	102	87	14 394	1 249	319	9.4	24.1
Douglas	28 866	73 453	4 284	19 311	7 493	7.4	6 238	556	1 269	998	17 674	340	6 794	0.1	18.8
Dundy	0	107	4	11 744	56	-0.2	12	24	14	7	21 196	121	36	57.8	1.7
Fillmore	111	250	17	13 287	140	3.7	37	46	43	18	19 081	215	83	40.7	8.4
Franklin	48	160	6	13 506	58	3.0	12	17	17	12	14 810	1 073	29	46.8	NA
Frontier	0	95	4	11 663	48	5.0	12	15	13	7	14 674	1 142	27	43.3	NA
Furnas	76	259	11	11 309	92	6.7	25	22	25	19	16 028	639	46	32.2	8.5
Gage	287	1 910	80	12 892	340	6.3	140	67	77	59	14 703	1 126	207	15.7	19.5
Garden	32	42	4	10 721	54	9.2	12	25	10	7	20 054	165	37	62.1	NA
Garfield	0	131	5	9 050	28	7.0	9	9	8	5	13 282	1 779	18	29.8	NA
Gosper	27	19	2	12 076	36	-0.2	7	14	8	5	17 417	375	22	60.8	NA
Grant	0	0	1	8 149	13	14.1	4	4	4	2	15 794	712	7	44.6	NA
Greeley	31	112	3	8 129	45	1.8	9	18	11	7	14 473	1 223	27	55.2	NA
Hall	953	4 387	303	15 439	720	5.7	459	106	134	112	14 847	1 054	564	5.8	25.6
Hamilton	91	541	31	15 359	135	-0.3	47	39	31	17	14 972	999	86	33.3	NA
Harlan	41	132	7	10 565	53	0.6	14	14	15	11	13 455	1 711	28	40.5	3.2
Hayes	0	0	1	13 136	25	3.6	3	16	4	2	20 692	138	19	82.0	NA
Hitchcock	28	37	4	13 037	61	10.0	13	18	19	9	15 630	768	31	48.9	8.3
Holt	162	638	24	10 473	189	7.8	49	78	39	28	14 592	1 170	127	40.8	4.9
Hooker	0	10	1	7 420	12	13.8	3	4	3	3	12 190	2 239	7	34.8	NA
Howard	43	217	7	10 442	80	3.2	17	20	20	14	12 635	2 058	36	35.8	NA
Jefferson	103	492	30	11 996	138	7.7	52	31	35	25	15 266	884	83	22.6	20.9
Johnson	62	216	13	12 060	66	7.1	22	18	17	12	13 752	1 552	40	25.0	NA
Kearney	88	677	17	11 195	108	2.8	32	34	27	15	16 107	617	66	44.0	6.8
Keith	207	724	32	12 173	137	5.6	53	38	29	20	15 860	692	91	27.7	13.0
Keya Paha	0	0	0	9 462	20	19.4	2	13	3	2	17 830	318	14	80.3	NA
Kimball	59	138	14	14 279	78	3.8	24	28	18	11	17 600	357	52	37.0	18.9
Knox	98	346	14	9 916	116	6.0	31	27	32	28	11 037	2 658	57	21.5	7.9
Lancaster	9 416	25 541	1 468	17 009	3 452	8.6	2 442	323	541	427	16 067	629	2 765	1.0	20.0
Lincoln	454	2 750	99	13 043	508	7.6	282	86	86	83	15 069	957	368	12.1	6.5
Logan	0	0	1	13 186	16	8.6	3	8	3	2	16 590	507	11	68.8	NA
Loup	0	0	0	5 200	11	13.4	1	5	2	1	13 725	1 568	6	78.5	NA
McPherson	0	0	0	6 158	10	19.5	1	5	2	1	18 082	285	6	86.2	NA
Madison	798	2 862	213	15 402	471	8.6	305	74	90	70	14 492	1 219	380	6.5	28.1
Merrick	98	265	16	13 648	110	1.7	32	26	25	18	12 983	1 910	58	29.7	NA
Morrill	40	74	5	11 356	85	2.6	22	32	14	13	14 906	1 024	54	46.7	NA
Nance	48	173	8	12 330	60	5.3	15	18	13	10	13 781	1 542	33	35.8	NA
Nemaha	83	552	16	11 090	122	9.9	56	25	24	21	14 661	1 147	81	18.1	17.9
Nuckolls	82	426	15	11 178	85	7.9	27	20	23	17	13 832	1 517	47	26.7	NA
Otoe	219	942	47	12 776	211	10.6	91	40	51	38	14 572	1 178	131	16.3	24.3
Pawnee	31	117	3	8 482	48	11.8	9	13	15	10	13 688	1 586	21	40.9	NA
Perkins	33	82	7	15 576	84	-0.5	17	43	15	9	23 700	60	60	64.8	NA
Phelps	163	814	48	15 407	182	5.3	77	49	40	24	18 574	247	127	29.6	17.9
Pierce	72	395	15	12 017	123	8.7	27	42	24	16	14 563	1 183	69	42.9	8.9
Platte	467	2 119	186	15 818	451	8.2	288	67	92	55	14 665	1 146	355	10.0	NA
Polk	75	294	9	10 597	94	4.3	22	31	25	14	15 966	655	53	47.9	7.8
Red Willow	168	784	46	13 009	178	6.0	88	35	38	30	14 159	1 366	123	12.3	15.2
Richardson	135	614	22	11 156	144	7.6	44	32	37	31	14 225	1 321	76	22.7	13.4
Rock	0	84	3	10 269	32	10.6	10	13	8	5	15 162	921	22	49.9	NA

1. For week including March 12. Excludes government employees, self-employed persons, farm workers, domestic service workers, railroad employees subject to the Railroad Retirement Act, and employees on oceanborne vessels or in foreign countries. 2. Includes other labor income. 3. Based on the resident population estimated as of July 1 of the year shown. 4. Covers mining, construction, and manufacturing.

STATE County	Earnings, 1989 (cont'd)						Agriculture, 1987									
	Percent by selected industries (cont'd)						Farms			Farm operators, percent		Land in farms				
	Goods-related[1]	Service-related & other[2]						Percent with						Acres		
	Manu-facturing	Total	Retail trade	Finance, insur-ance, & real estate	Services	Govern-ment	Number	Less than 50 acres	500 acres and over	Whose principal occu-pation is farming	Residing on farm operated	Acreage (1,000)	Percent change, 1982–1987	Average size of farm	Total irrigated (1,000)	Total cropland (1,000)
	103	104	105	106	107	108	109	110	111	112	113	114	115	116	117	118
NEBRASKA—Con.																
Buffalo	21.4	50.1	11.7	3.1	23.6	15.5	1 175	16.1	34.8	71.8	68.3	582	2.5	495	175	385
Burt	2.8	36.4	6.5	2.8	11.3	13.9	729	15.1	30.3	79.8	72.0	291	-1.5	399	33	267
Butler	9.0	NA	7.2	2.3	13.0	15.1	961	12.5	28.5	77.6	66.6	362	8.0	376	80	316
Cass	8.3	NA	7.7	3.9	14.8	17.7	913	24.0	27.1	64.3	71.4	338	6.9	371	4	292
Cedar	5.2	42.8	7.2	3.6	14.1	14.0	1 106	15.4	26.9	80.0	76.0	419	-0.6	379	48	351
Chase	1.1	34.0	7.8	3.7	8.4	15.8	468	15.8	58.1	78.6	62.2	534	0.9	1 142	142	324
Cherry	0.3	40.8	12.7	3.3	15.5	14.2	745	18.0	70.9	81.6	72.3	3 963	-1.5	5 319	30	406
Cheyenne	6.2	51.7	18.8	2.7	14.2	13.7	740	7.8	60.4	73.8	57.2	766	1.8	1 035	34	579
Clay	1.3	NA	4.1	2.0	8.6	21.9	710	14.2	38.6	79.4	60.8	365	1.2	514	158	303
Colfax	35.3	36.5	7.0	3.6	14.7	10.4	778	19.9	18.3	75.8	72.9	232	0.0	298	40	208
Cuming	14.1	47.7	9.2	3.5	14.9	10.4	1 185	17.5	15.8	80.3	72.7	359	4.2	303	29	310
Custer	8.5	37.5	8.2	2.0	15.2	13.2	1 457	13.7	55.5	74.4	68.1	1 489	-0.9	1 022	150	524
Dakota	50.1	33.6	6.4	5.7	10.2	6.8	345	20.0	29.0	67.5	69.6	150	-0.1	436	11	129
Dawes	0.5	52.5	12.1	1.7	15.9	25.4	498	15.9	58.4	67.3	75.5	751	5.0	1 509	14	194
Dawson	16.3	42.3	8.8	3.1	14.7	13.5	974	17.2	45.0	76.7	61.4	710	4.9	729	195	381
Deuel	NA	NA	10.2	4.3	12.1	13.7	262	8.8	58.4	71.4	52.7	268	-12.6	1 024	16	207
Dixon	22.9	24.4	4.9	2.4	9.3	21.2	704	16.6	28.3	72.9	75.1	266	5.1	378	12	219
Dodge	20.2	51.5	12.7	4.0	18.1	15.1	962	21.0	23.2	73.6	71.0	322	3.7	335	70	294
Douglas	13.4	68.1	9.1	10.9	28.0	13.0	475	40.2	17.9	52.8	66.7	121	0.6	254	16	107
Dundy	0.0	29.9	5.5	1.1	13.9	10.6	389	9.3	65.3	78.9	60.7	536	-3.8	1 379	83	232
Fillmore	2.1	37.1	5.2	3.3	12.9	13.8	779	13.1	36.5	83.7	58.7	360	0.9	462	146	332
Franklin	NA	30.9	7.4	3.8	11.2	17.4	523	14.7	43.4	79.9	62.7	355	10.2	678	68	209
Frontier	NA	NA	7.0	5.1	10.7	19.3	496	9.1	64.5	79.6	67.1	537	6.1	1 083	54	254
Furnas	0.8	40.8	9.9	2.2	17.2	18.5	539	13.7	54.2	77.7	61.2	461	6.3	855	42	297
Gage	14.5	46.1	9.9	2.9	19.3	18.7	1 347	17.8	30.2	71.9	71.4	530	2.7	394	37	434
Garden	7.1	15.2	4.0	2.8	4.7	12.3	335	7.2	65.4	76.7	62.4	1 075	3.4	3 208	36	221
Garfield	9.3	42.0	9.5	2.0	14.3	13.5	248	15.7	49.6	68.1	74.6	326	3.5	1 314	13	92
Gosper	0.3	20.4	3.2	2.3	5.3	13.7	345	10.4	51.3	78.6	61.4	256	3.4	741	54	152
Grant	NA	37.1	12.2	2.5	4.8	15.2	92	18.5	68.5	73.9	66.3	687	-0.5	7 463	3	114
Greeley	0.8	25.1	6.3	3.1	8.3	13.5	461	10.0	49.7	83.1	67.7	309	2.8	670	54	176
Hall	20.8	53.6	11.2	5.5	20.0	14.9	788	20.3	27.7	75.6	61.2	307	0.6	389	153	257
Hamilton	13.6	38.5	5.6	2.7	14.6	11.0	770	10.8	36.5	82.9	70.5	341	1.3	443	197	314
Harlan	0.5	38.1	8.6	3.5	11.6	18.3	465	13.3	49.2	76.6	57.2	319	-1.2	686	61	212
Hayes	NA	NA	1.5	2.9	1.6	7.7	317	10.4	65.0	77.3	67.5	404	-3.2	1 273	33	198
Hitchcock	0.9	23.2	5.5	2.6	6.3	19.7	426	8.5	61.5	79.1	67.1	429	5.1	1 008	29	252
Holt	1.0	44.7	9.2	3.0	14.7	9.6	1 393	15.6	51.7	74.4	62.8	1 416	5.1	1 016	173	648
Hooker	NA	NA	10.9	4.2	17.7	18.7	78	14.1	73.1	76.9	76.9	333	3.5	4 273	2	14
Howard	NA	35.2	8.8	2.6	13.1	17.5	696	14.1	31.3	74.9	68.8	308	-2.4	442	83	210
Jefferson	15.2	42.1	9.5	3.8	13.5	14.4	770	13.5	31.4	74.5	70.0	338	3.0	439	43	258
Johnson	16.6	33.0	8.7	2.9	10.6	17.9	599	13.2	24.9	69.9	66.8	210	7.1	351	7	165
Kearney	1.9	36.0	6.6	2.8	17.0	13.2	608	11.3	42.1	85.4	61.5	336	5.5	553	152	284
Keith	9.1	46.7	14.8	4.7	18.0	12.6	405	11.6	54.6	76.8	56.5	667	5.8	1 647	67	265
Keya Paha	0.0	NA	4.1	NA	2.7	6.2	259	7.7	75.7	83.0	75.7	475	4.0	1 833	12	120
Kimball	5.3	31.3	8.2	1.9	11.9	12.9	348	6.0	70.4	74.7	57.2	533	2.0	1 531	19	360
Knox	0.8	48.4	10.8	3.2	17.0	22.1	1 212	11.6	35.5	81.4	75.7	615	-4.1	507	30	374
Lancaster	14.6	55.7	10.0	8.1	23.8	23.3	1 508	27.8	20.0	53.6	71.6	448	-0.2	297	11	379
Lincoln	2.2	65.6	9.6	2.7	18.9	15.8	1 127	17.8	50.1	65.3	65.9	1 462	-0.8	1 297	144	443
Logan	NA	NA	6.3	1.4	2.9	16.0	147	15.0	55.8	72.8	68.0	362	6.6	2 460	13	62
Loup	0.0	NA	5.3	2.0	4.1	4.2	142	9.2	66.9	79.6	75.4	293	1.9	2 065	10	49
McPherson	0.0	NA	NA	NA	3.2	6.5	146	14.4	72.6	75.3	65.8	426	-16.1	2 915	10	D
Madison	21.8	51.8	10.7	3.7	17.9	13.6	958	20.8	23.7	73.3	69.3	326	-3.1	340	56	276
Merrick	1.2	38.6	8.5	5.5	12.5	17.6	664	16.6	30.9	75.8	67.9	276	-0.6	415	133	230
Morrill	7.0	27.9	5.3	2.5	8.1	13.0	535	14.2	44.1	73.8	66.2	725	-2.5	1 355	100	257
Nance	1.0	46.0	4.7	5.3	11.1	13.8	508	16.9	32.9	78.3	70.3	249	1.1	489	43	180
Nemaha	9.9	28.3	7.2	2.5	11.2	35.7	591	13.2	30.1	77.0	64.1	241	0.7	408	2	200
Nuckolls	8.2	47.5	10.2	4.5	19.1	13.9	621	14.5	40.4	76.7	68.3	336	-3.4	541	45	252
Otoe	18.0	42.3	9.3	3.2	18.2	17.2	1 005	16.8	26.1	72.1	67.6	361	4.1	360	4	301
Pawnee	2.4	31.2	5.5	2.1	15.0	21.2	520	11.0	32.5	70.8	66.9	228	4.5	438	3	161
Perkins	0.3	22.3	2.9	1.5	6.2	9.4	591	7.8	60.4	77.5	61.1	570	4.1	965	107	474
Phelps	14.3	41.4	7.8	2.9	17.0	11.1	616	13.1	46.6	84.7	66.1	371	-3.5	603	187	298
Pierce	2.1	37.9	7.9	2.8	11.8	10.3	857	13.9	27.5	77.4	71.4	333	4.1	388	81	282
Platte	32.9	NA	8.3	3.3	13.7	16.9	1 245	19.4	21.4	75.2	71.3	403	4.0	323	118	360
Polk	2.2	29.4	4.8	3.4	10.0	14.9	736	16.6	26.5	81.5	64.5	265	0.6	360	106	238
Red Willow	8.8	58.2	12.8	3.4	15.3	14.3	489	16.8	56.9	72.0	65.8	452	2.2	924	47	269
Richardson	9.3	50.3	11.5	3.2	17.8	13.6	826	15.0	24.7	70.8	62.6	310	6.5	375	1	245
Rock	2.1	32.2	5.2	1.7	8.4	12.1	313	12.5	67.1	78.9	64.5	583	-2.6	1 862	37	183

1. Covers mining, construction, and manufacturing. 2. Covers private sector earnings in agricultural services, forestry, and fisheries; transportation and public utilities; wholesale trade; retail trade; finance, insurance, and real estate; and services.

STATE County	Agriculture, 1987 (cont'd)								Manufactures, 1987						
	Value of land and buildings		Value of products sold				Percent of farms with sales of		Establishments		All employees			Production workers	
					Percent from										
	Average per farm ($1,000)	Average per acre (Dollars)	Total (Mil dol)	Average per farm (Dollars)	Crops	Livestock and poultry[1]	$10,000 or more	$100,000 or more	Total	Percent with 20 or more em-ployees	Number (1,000)	Percent change, 1982–1987	Annual payroll (Mil dol)	Number (1,000)	Work hours (Mil)
	119	120	121	122	123	124	125	126	127	128	129	130	131	132	133
NEBRASKA—Con.															
Buffalo	298	605	122	104 165	39.1	60.9	75.8	22.4	45	26.7	2.7	-12.9	54.9	2.2	4.5
Burt	332	834	81	111 485	44.7	55.3	81.9	29.8	7	14.3	0.1	0.0	1.2	0.0	0.1
Butler	300	774	69	72 158	53.3	46.7	77.5	17.2	9	33.3	0.3	0.0	4.2	0.3	0.6
Cass	368	952	55	60 634	64.6	35.4	68.1	18.2	9	33.3	D	D	D	D	D
Cedar	236	620	106	96 229	24.0	76.0	86.9	29.4	12	16.7	D	D	D	D	D
Chase	504	455	67	143 865	59.2	40.8	83.8	39.1	5	20.0	0.0	-100.0	0.5	0.0	0.0
Cherry	1 302	248	87	117 039	3.1	96.9	78.9	31.9	3	0.0	0.0	0.0	0.1	0.0	0.0
Cheyenne	374	366	94	127 575	30.8	69.2	78.6	18.2	10	40.0	D	D	D	D	D
Clay	458	916	123	173 312	35.4	64.6	84.2	30.1	4	25.0	0.0	0.0	0.8	0.0	0.0
Colfax	270	884	128	164 231	17.4	82.6	77.4	24.7	9	22.2	D	D	D	D	D
Cuming	256	858	338	285 425	9.7	90.3	86.5	32.9	21	23.8	D	D	D	D	D
Custer	280	265	154	105 814	27.0	73.0	78.9	23.0	11	9.1	D	D	D	D	D
Dakota	312	711	23	67 018	67.9	32.1	74.8	19.4	18	44.4	D	D	D	D	D
Dawes	375	260	22	43 496	26.1	73.9	64.7	10.2	5	20.0	0.0	0.0	0.3	0.0	0.0
Dawson	429	588	300	307 603	16.1	83.9	81.0	35.5	31	41.9	1.5	-40.0	27.2	1.2	2.7
Deuel	389	383	19	74 221	63.0	37.0	82.1	22.1	5	0.0	D	D	D	D	D
Dixon	211	580	91	128 756	18.7	81.3	78.8	18.9	5	20.0	D	D	D	D	D
Dodge	307	946	105	108 641	39.5	60.5	82.6	28.2	69	39.1	3.0	3.4	58.9	2.3	4.2
Douglas	304	1 305	39	81 192	42.5	57.5	55.6	18.7	561	38.7	28.8	-2.0	698.5	19.7	38.0
Dundy	527	378	56	143 416	41.9	58.1	79.7	36.2	1	0.0	D	D	D	D	D
Fillmore	371	837	90	115 013	51.0	49.0	85.0	28.4	9	0.0	0.0	0.0	0.6	0.0	0.1
Franklin	424	544	39	75 086	55.5	44.5	76.1	21.6	2	0.0	D	D	D	D	D
Frontier	327	312	36	72 313	50.6	49.4	81.7	23.0	2	0.0	D	D	D	D	D
Furnas	341	400	51	94 130	41.7	58.3	77.7	24.3	7	28.6	D	D	D	D	D
Gage	237	598	88	65 564	38.5	61.5	73.3	17.7	23	52.2	1.3	18.2	26.9	1.0	1.9
Garden	711	216	45	134 969	23.3	76.7	78.5	24.2	4	25.0	D	D	D	D	D
Garfield	327	223	19	75 818	9.8	90.2	72.6	17.3	4	0.0	D	D	D	D	D
Gosper	338	435	31	89 024	53.3	46.7	79.4	26.1	1	0.0	D	D	D	D	D
Grant	1 279	171	11	115 950	6.0	94.0	75.0	32.6	2	0.0	D	D	D	D	D
Greeley	223	334	33	71 760	39.0	61.0	82.6	23.9	1	0.0	D	D	D	D	D
Hall	352	911	134	170 370	31.6	68.4	76.8	26.0	79	40.5	4.7	9.3	90.6	3.5	7.0
Hamilton	442	981	104	135 058	52.4	47.6	87.5	36.6	18	22.2	0.4	33.3	6.7	0.3	0.5
Harlan	381	532	56	119 434	35.8	64.2	78.9	24.7	4	0.0	0.0	-100.0	0.1	0.0	0.0
Hayes	373	322	53	167 273	22.9	77.1	79.5	21.5	3	33.3	D	D	D	D	D
Hitchcock	413	356	32	74 408	45.0	55.0	80.8	20.7	1	0.0	D	D	D	D	D
Holt	333	329	144	103 131	28.2	71.8	79.0	24.5	12	0.0	0.0	0.0	0.7	0.0	0.0
Hooker	1 164	273	6	72 041	D	D	75.6	25.6	1	0.0	D	D	D	D	D
Howard	193	442	48	68 267	41.2	58.8	79.2	20.1	1	0.0	D	D	D	D	D
Jefferson	248	519	54	70 338	37.1	62.9	73.2	16.5	13	46.2	0.8	33.3	9.5	0.7	1.4
Johnson	163	519	26	43 388	36.8	63.2	68.4	9.7	3	33.3	D	D	D	D	D
Kearney	499	885	128	209 906	35.1	64.9	85.2	34.5	11	9.1	D	D	D	D	D
Keith	604	387	65	161 665	31.3	68.7	72.6	26.2	11	18.2	0.4	0.0	7.5	0.3	0.5
Keya Paha	439	255	19	71 772	12.1	87.9	82.2	20.8	NA	NA	NA	NA	NA	NA	NA
Kimball	330	221	17	49 626	60.2	39.8	74.1	15.2	8	12.5	0.1	-50.0	1.9	0.0	0.1
Knox	211	432	99	81 879	14.7	85.3	81.5	21.6	8	0.0	0.0	0.0	0.5	0.0	0.0
Lancaster	220	727	56	36 914	55.7	44.3	53.1	9.5	237	40.1	13.9	12.1	324.1	9.3	18.6
Lincoln	519	385	96	85 311	40.3	59.7	69.2	22.8	20	20.0	0.4	33.3	5.5	0.2	0.4
Logan	726	280	16	108 956	21.7	78.3	80.3	23.1	2	0.0	D	D	D	D	D
Loup	406	187	11	78 804	12.9	87.1	80.3	24.6	NA	NA	NA	NA	NA	NA	NA
McPherson	338	117	10	70 629	D	D	78.8	21.2	NA	NA	NA	NA	NA	NA	NA
Madison	258	764	83	86 190	32.1	67.9	76.9	19.6	41	43.9	2.9	0.0	58.9	2.1	4.3
Merrick	299	697	73	110 443	43.0	57.0	78.5	27.1	9	22.2	0.2	0.0	2.7	0.1	0.3
Morrill	496	337	88	164 601	29.1	70.9	74.4	25.4	3	0.0	D	D	D	D	D
Nance	232	525	41	81 131	37.8	62.2	77.0	22.2	3	0.0	0.0	0.0	0.1	0.0	0.0
Nemaha	290	705	41	68 694	54.3	45.7	78.3	19.3	7	42.9	0.3	0.0	4.9	0.2	0.7
Nuckolls	249	491	45	73 019	44.6	55.4	82.6	21.4	5	20.0	D	D	D	D	D
Otoe	258	684	54	54 214	49.3	50.7	74.4	13.7	12	50.0	0.9	12.5	15.5	0.7	1.4
Pawnee	202	481	25	48 453	39.3	60.7	68.3	13.7	2	0.0	D	D	D	D	D
Perkins	424	433	48	81 781	80.6	19.4	80.0	24.7	2	50.0	D	D	D	D	D
Phelps	557	866	192	311 507	27.0	73.0	87.2	41.1	14	35.7	D	D	D	D	D
Pierce	239	612	83	96 646	31.9	68.1	84.5	27.3	8	12.5	D	D	D	D	D
Platte	360	1 092	131	104 852	30.7	69.3	82.4	28.2	61	39.3	4.4	-6.4	89.1	3.0	6.5
Polk	340	910	99	135 005	31.8	68.2	81.9	25.0	4	0.0	D	D	D	D	D
Red Willow	330	379	70	142 872	27.9	72.1	78.1	28.0	20	20.0	0.5	-28.6	9.0	0.5	0.9
Richardson	215	597	48	58 147	51.5	48.5	72.2	14.4	9	22.2	0.3	50.0	4.8	0.2	0.5
Rock	455	266	36	115 780	17.0	83.0	80.8	23.0	3	33.3	D	D	D	D	D

1. Includes livestock and poultry products.

STATE County	Manufactures, 1987 (cont'd): Production workers (cont'd): Wages: Total (Mil dol)	Manufactures, 1987 (cont'd): Production workers (cont'd): Wages: Average per worker (Dollars)	Manufactures, 1987 (cont'd): Value added by manufacture (Mil dol)	Manufactures, 1987 (cont'd): Value of shipments (Mil dol)	Manufactures, 1987 (cont'd): New capital expenditures (Mil dol)	Value of construction authorized by building permits, 1990: Total[1] ($1,000)	Nonresidential: Total ($1,000)	Nonresidential: Percent: Office	Nonresidential: Percent: Industrial	Nonresidential: Percent: Stores	Residential: New construction ($1,000)	Residential: Number of housing units	Residential: Alterations and additions ($1,000)
	134	135	136	137	138	139	140	141	142	143	144	145	146
NEBRASKA—Con.													
Buffalo	41.9	19 045	202.5	486.0	7.9	16 007	4 189	38.5	0.7	16.6	7 944	98	490
Burt	0.6	NA	2.8	6.4	0.1	94	7	0.0	0.0	0.0	40	1	22
Butler	3.3	11 000	3.3	25.5	D	685	207	0.0	98.1	0.0	185	2	29
Cass	D	D	D	D	D	9 683	2 088	0.0	8.1	30.4	6 194	106	698
Cedar	D	D	D	D	D	1 612	1 289	0.0	0.0	0.0	268	8	48
Chase	0.3	NA	1.1	2.0	0.0	871	386	27.4	33.9	1.8	336	4	77
Cherry	0.0	NA	0.2	0.3	0.0	1 195	821	0.0	0.0	14.9	240	5	48
Cheyenne	D	D	D	D	D	5 732	4 910	0.0	0.0	92.6	55	1	290
Clay	0.3	NA	1.8	2.7	0.1	3 137	1 248	0.0	0.0	3.0	1 287	16	116
Colfax	D	D	D	D	D	1 197	491	0.0	0.0	35.8	502	9	101
Cuming	D	D	D	D	D	721	178	0.0	0.0	99.4	285	6	20
Custer	D	D	D	D	D	1 984	130	0.0	23.0	15.3	75	2	150
Dakota	D	D	D	D	D	7 939	3 299	0.0	0.0	30.8	4 025	55	170
Dawes	0.1	NA	0.7	1.1	0.0	587	153	11.6	0.0	86.4	0	0	89
Dawson	20.2	16 833	122.4	418.2	D	8 150	3 671	2.2	52.0	22.1	3 388	71	830
Deuel	D	D	D	D	D	10	0	NA	NA	NA	0	0	3
Dixon	D	D	D	D	D	1 917	546	0.0	97.1	2.7	1 090	13	76
Dodge	40.4	17 565	309.9	695.4	5.2	9 265	2 927	26.8	0.0	60.8	3 262	61	863
Douglas	431.6	21 909	2 118.2	4 795.6	107.0	296 133	84 453	54.8	2.0	14.1	123 867	2 422	13 441
Dundy	D	D	D	D	D	41	35	0.0	0.0	71.4	0	0	0
Fillmore	0.3	NA	1.7	7.3	0.1	1 595	765	13.1	21.4	31.4	664	8	51
Franklin	D	D	D	D	D	105	52	0.0	0.0	0.0	0	0	45
Frontier	D	D	D	D	D	205	4	0.0	0.0	0.0	155	2	4
Furnas	D	D	D	D	D	281	90	0.0	0.0	42.7	120	3	33
Gage	17.9	17 900	62.0	160.6	6.0	4 946	1 773	23.9	55.6	8.7	2 247	35	225
Garden	D	D	D	D	D	223	150	0.0	0.0	100.0	30	1	0
Garfield	D	D	D	D	D	90	64	0.0	97.0	0.0	0	0	8
Gosper	D	D	D	D	D	126	0	NA	NA	NA	0	0	6
Grant	D	D	D	D	D	NA	NA	NA	NA	NA	NA	NA	NA
Greeley	D	D	D	D	D	10	0	NA	NA	NA	0	0	0
Hall	62.7	17 914	403.0	1 431.2	20.7	19 962	3 996	8.5	4.4	61.3	8 296	96	1 830
Hamilton	3.5	11 667	17.7	38.3	0.4	2 143	938	4.3	0.0	7.5	882	19	100
Harlan	0.1	NA	0.3	0.7	D	165	0	NA	NA	NA	74	3	29
Hayes	D	D	D	D	D	8	0	0.0	0.0	0.0	0	0	8
Hitchcock	D	D	D	D	D	535	214	0.0	0.0	0.0	87	1	36
Holt	0.3	NA	1.6	2.5	0.1	1 464	680	17.7	0.0	23.2	322	7	81
Hooker	D	D	D	D	D	20	10	0.0	0.0	0.0	0	0	8
Howard	D	D	D	D	D	1 172	627	0.4	0.0	12.8	401	11	76
Jefferson	7.3	10 429	36.0	58.9	0.6	1 707	1 210	0.0	0.0	99.2	298	3	50
Johnson	D	D	D	D	D	681	215	93.0	0.0	0.0	0	0	16
Kearney	D	D	D	D	D	990	552	19.6	0.0	2.9	300	3	16
Keith	3.4	11 333	17.1	28.1	D	2 889	571	0.0	1.8	70.9	1 298	23	453
Keya Paha	NA	NA	NA	NA	NA	NA	NA	NA	NA	NA	NA	NA	NA
Kimball	0.5	NA	6.1	9.3	0.1	62	17	0.0	69.8	0.0	0	0	6
Knox	0.3	NA	1.3	6.3	0.0	8 188	321	0.0	0.0	0.0	1 942	44	889
Lancaster	187.8	20 194	867.0	1 805.2	62.4	169 127	26 873	20.4	13.1	33.9	107 567	2 070	5 141
Lincoln	2.9	14 500	13.0	47.1	1.3	34 172	29 274	18.9	68.8	7.8	2 742	40	553
Logan	D	D	D	D	D	NA	NA	NA	NA	NA	NA	NA	NA
Loup	NA	NA	NA	NA	NA	NA	NA	NA	NA	NA	NA	NA	NA
McPherson	NA	NA	NA	NA	NA	NA	NA	NA	NA	NA	NA	NA	NA
Madison	37.7	17 952	169.8	638.5	6.4	14 812	2 939	15.2	3.8	32.7	7 588	149	737
Merrick	2.1	21 000	5.8	13.5	0.0	2 939	988	4.0	5.1	6.5	1 258	20	510
Morrill	D	D	D	D	D	89	23	0.0	0.0	65.2	0	0	37
Nance	0.1	NA	0.3	0.8	0.0	776	254	0.0	0.0	0.0	200	3	61
Nemaha	3.6	18 000	11.8	22.9	D	1 026	85	0.0	0.0	40.0	687	10	144
Nuckolls	D	D	D	D	D	1 637	1 223	0.0	51.7	34.9	12	1	56
Otoe	8.9	12 714	52.2	91.7	2.2	2 397	424	0.0	33.0	0.0	1 071	13	139
Pawnee	D	D	D	D	D	6	0	NA	NA	NA	0	0	0
Perkins	D	D	D	D	D	387	251	0.0	0.0	0.0	90	1	26
Phelps	D	D	D	D	D	3 513	2 853	0.0	1.8	0.0	385	5	131
Pierce	D	D	D	D	D	2 230	861	64.0	1.7	2.3	817	13	123
Platte	51.8	17 267	286.5	490.8	16.5	15 532	4 593	6.5	19.6	69.0	8 807	192	434
Polk	D	D	D	D	D	808	11	0.0	0.0	0.0	617	7	42
Red Willow	6.6	13 200	10.6	44.6	D	2 023	904	67.5	20.8	0.0	847	10	148
Richardson	3.1	15 500	14.5	34.3	0.1	887	342	14.5	0.0	7.3	267	3	98
Rock	D	D	D	D	D	178	0	NA	NA	NA	0	0	16

1. Includes nonresidential additions and alterations, residential nonhousekeeping buildings, and residential garages and carports not shown separately.

STATE County	Wholesale trade, 1987				Retail trade, all establishments, 1987				Retail trade, establishments with payroll, 1987					
						Sales				Sales				
											Per capita[2] (Dollars)			
	Establishments	Sales (Mil dol)	Paid employees[1]	Annual payroll (Mil dol)	Number	Total (Mil dol)	Percent change, 1982–1987	Per capita[2] (Dollars)	Number	Total (Mil dol)	General merchandise stores	Food stores	Apparel & accessory stores	Eating and drinking places
	147	148	149	150	151	152	153	154	155	156	157	158	159	160
NEBRASKA–Con.														
Buffalo	78	354.7	777	14.4	484	231.4	21.6	6 288	329	223.5	821	1 170	359	763
Burt	29	72.9	219	3.5	112	26.0	-1.9	3 094	64	23.7	D	713	75	236
Butler	17	53.3	124	2.2	115	23.7	31.7	2 636	56	20.1	D	554	D	108
Cass	32	48.5	167	2.7	207	48.6	6.6	2 191	104	43.8	D	423	22	275
Cedar	40	52.3	201	2.9	137	25.7	7.1	2 379	73	21.9	D	493	0	169
Chase	19	78.2	243	4.1	66	20.2	-5.6	4 381	38	19.3	D	1 044	146	220
Cherry	27	46.3	103	1.4	103	33.2	6.4	4 963	62	31.3	D	1 136	232	543
Cheyenne	30	54.3	154	2.8	142	169.9	110.8	16 652	104	167.4	D	1 083	D	D
Clay	26	92.9	215	3.5	104	22.3	27.4	2 892	65	20.3	D	820	D	297
Colfax	27	61.6	207	3.2	143	32.1	10.7	3 375	76	29.0	183	763	49	410
Cuming	39	130.0	301	4.7	146	44.5	12.1	4 083	96	43.1	43	765	86	278
Custer	33	48.4	207	3.0	203	53.1	1.3	4 084	119	47.4	D	1 067	90	233
Dakota	27	D	D	D	176	58.9	10.3	3 466	102	56.1	D	895	D	578
Dawes	19	29.7	100	1.2	161	51.1	17.2	5 490	110	48.7	D	952	139	573
Dawson	66	232.6	478	7.2	287	105.1	-2.5	5 079	176	100.8	D	1 248	149	335
Deuel	5	34.1	35	0.8	31	16.6	-18.2	6 898	21	16.3	D	D	D	969
Dixon	17	18.8	82	1.3	86	12.1	36.0	1 799	34	9.7	D	567	D	79
Dodge	90	310.2	922	17.3	442	230.8	28.9	6 519	295	222.4	847	1 017	144	556
Douglas	1 159	7 575.9	18 054	404.8	3 806	2 965.3	34.7	7 152	2 715	2 914.4	948	1 333	340	796
Dundy	10	9.7	43	0.7	43	6.2	-17.3	2 199	20	5.6	0	D	D	222
Fillmore	32	60.0	214	3.3	102	19.3	-19.2	2 611	62	17.0	D	575	106	365
Franklin	7	8.5	26	0.4	68	11.9	1.7	2 975	35	10.1	0	807	D	220
Frontier	10	33.9	88	1.2	33	6.4	-16.9	1 886	24	6.3	0	370	D	203
Furnas	18	30.4	107	1.9	94	21.7	4.8	3 620	58	19.7	D	876	D	168
Gage	60	120.1	428	6.4	302	112.5	11.1	4 847	183	109.2	487	1 074	282	365
Garden	8	13.4	28	0.4	48	6.5	8.3	2 422	24	6.1	D	D	0	201
Garfield	8	D	D	D	45	11.7	13.6	5 326	29	11.2	0	D	D	310
Gosper	2	D	D	D	23	1.9	-32.1	882	7	0.9	0	D	0	137
Grant	3	3.4	6	0.1	19	1.9	-26.9	2 435	10	1.8	0	D	D	D
Greeley	13	14.6	86	0.7	46	6.4	-34.0	1 930	23	5.3	0	585	0	123
Hall	138	461.3	1 684	32.8	666	374.1	26.1	7 665	453	363.6	1 719	831	456	765
Hamilton	32	117.9	319	4.7	103	27.0	1.9	2 998	51	25.6	166	D	D	162
Harlan	14	58.5	131	1.8	76	13.0	-12.2	3 262	48	12.4	D	626	122	308
Hayes	0	0.0	0	0.0	13	D	D	D	9	2.1	0	D	0	D
Hitchcock	11	19.4	53	0.9	41	7.6	40.7	1 944	22	6.5	0	D	0	141
Holt	47	79.9	307	4.0	183	62.2	22.7	4 644	118	57.1	D	909	161	292
Hooker	4	3.3	12	0.1	18	3.5	25.0	3 528	11	3.0	D	D	0	D
Howard	16	28.3	94	1.4	77	16.4	1.2	2 530	44	14.0	0	532	D	207
Jefferson	31	79.1	249	3.4	113	42.3	7.1	4 552	75	40.5	D	908	135	405
Johnson	13	39.3	117	1.5	81	14.3	-1.4	2 926	43	11.6	D	D	45	322
Kearney	22	90.7	148	2.9	79	19.6	3.2	2 969	46	18.7	D	633	D	332
Keith	29	133.7	252	3.3	170	72.5	7.1	8 148	115	70.5	531	1 506	150	684
Keya Paha	2	D	D	D	16	2.5	19.0	2 075	10	2.3	0	D	0	160
Kimball	19	49.2	92	2.0	78	21.8	-10.3	4 854	46	20.5	D	1 062	D	428
Knox	33	86.1	214	2.9	182	30.2	12.3	2 794	97	25.3	D	575	23	241
Lancaster	353	1 808.4	5 041	104.0	1 998	1 283.5	39.0	6 168	1 318	1 262.7	D	1 151	D	657
Lincoln	83	140.1	645	9.9	414	193.4	2.0	5 774	272	189.5	863	1 044	234	606
Logan	1	D	D	D	11	1.5	87.5	1 549	7	1.3	D	D	D	D
Loup	0	0.0	0	0.0	10	D	D	D	6	0.8	0	D	0	264
McPherson	1	D	D	D	5	D	D	D	3	D	0	D	0	D
Madison	108	761.6	1 356	22.8	449	218.7	26.3	6 835	291	212.3	1 393	1 462	410	555
Merrick	24	72.8	176	2.8	114	30.7	16.3	3 608	62	28.0	D	766	D	233
Morrill	18	22.6	143	1.8	67	11.6	-18.3	1 999	33	10.8	D	374	D	194
Nance	16	45.6	149	2.3	56	7.3	2.8	1 651	29	6.3	D	556	D	122
Nemaha	19	56.4	119	1.9	118	26.4	-0.8	3 148	58	23.0	D	334	49	373
Nuckolls	27	122.2	151	1.9	80	27.4	11.8	4 288	54	26.2	D	D	171	288
Otoe	37	102.3	238	3.3	216	70.7	4.6	4 841	131	66.3	451	1 065	201	493
Pawnee	6	3.3	16	0.1	48	8.1	-22.1	2 251	24	6.6	0	D	D	198
Perkins	19	59.3	128	2.3	52	8.8	4.8	2 448	24	7.2	D	D	D	65
Phelps	37	107.8	297	5.4	136	48.7	-5.8	4 920	82	46.1	D	707	206	267
Pierce	22	84.0	206	2.2	99	26.0	6.6	3 097	64	22.9	D	698	20	171
Platte	67	187.2	505	8.4	341	168.1	31.3	5 679	225	161.0	805	1 217	331	521
Polk	20	59.9	124	2.6	71	11.4	-24.5	1 935	40	10.2	D	551	D	207
Red Willow	38	198.2	363	7.0	173	90.6	15.7	7 134	131	88.8	1 099	1 478	462	457
Richardson	34	55.6	183	2.4	167	44.0	8.1	4 269	97	41.2	491	788	92	300
Rock	9	48.6	109	1.3	33	6.2	-17.3	2 815	17	5.9	D	D	D	D

1. For pay period including March 12. 2. Based on the estimated population as of July 1 of the year shown.

Table A. States and Counties — **Retail Trade, Services, and Banking**

STATE County	Retail trade, establishments with payroll, 1987 (cont'd)		Taxable service industries–establishments with payroll, 1987							Bank deposits,[2] June 1989		Savings capital,[3] September 1989	
				Receipts (Mil dol)									
					Selected kinds of business								
	Paid employees[1]	Annual payroll (Mil dol)	Number	Total	Hotels, motels and other lodging places	Health services	Legal services	Paid employees	Annual payroll (Mil dol)	Total (Mil dol)	Percent change, 1988–1989	Total (Mil dol)	Percent change, 1988–1989
	161	162	163	164	165	166	167	168	169	170	171	172	173
NEBRASKA—Con.													
Buffalo	3 706	28.1	263	59.9	8.9	22.5	4.3	1 640	22.6	306	7.1	112.2	0.4
Burt	283	2.2	45	5.9	0.0	3.5	0.7	196	2.0	85	-7.0	15.1	-14.9
Butler	302	2.1	29	4.6	D	D	0.4	150	1.8	125	5.7	16.6	-0.1
Cass	652	4.5	71	8.1	D	3.1	0.7	327	2.8	135	4.8	24.4	-7.5
Cedar	256	1.9	38	5.3	D	2.5	0.5	191	1.9	101	-1.3	16.2	5.5
Chase	239	2.0	23	2.5	0.0	1.3	D	86	0.8	82	6.0	4.5	-16.2
Cherry	429	3.5	50	6.1	1.0	1.4	0.5	152	1.4	96	5.7	16.2	-1.5
Cheyenne	1 022	10.3	65	9.8	1.9	3.5	0.9	313	2.7	115	0.3	37.7	4.3
Clay	260	1.8	32	3.2	D	1.2	0.6	130	1.0	75	1.8	0.0	NA
Colfax	459	3.2	53	8.6	D	4.2	0.7	259	2.5	117	1.1	28.6	3.5
Cuming	496	4.1	65	10.6	D	2.7	0.9	310	2.6	169	1.7	36.5	-5.9
Custer	664	4.4	75	9.0	0.3	4.1	0.9	310	2.9	131	4.0	73.1	-9.4
Dakota	847	6.7	91	30.5	D	5.6	1.2	1 059	9.4	73	-1.5	46.5	-4.4
Dawes	842	5.4	65	7.7	0.7	3.5	0.5	242	2.3	82	5.3	32.3	-7.5
Dawson	1 344	11.3	146	26.4	1.1	10.9	2.8	787	8.4	238	3.7	84.6	0.6
Deuel	195	1.5	12	1.0	D	D	D	28	0.2	30	0.0	0.0	NA
Dixon	121	0.8	22	2.1	0.0	0.9	0.1	91	0.6	59	-1.4	0.0	NA
Dodge	2 825	23.8	238	46.1	1.6	21.1	4.0	1 461	18.0	320	5.9	194.6	-5.4
Douglas	40 633	355.3	3 386	1 883.9	66.8	463.9	135.7	45 035	752.1	3 913	9.4	1 868.1	-12.3
Dundy	101	0.7	14	1.6	0.0	D	0.3	28	0.3	19	-8.2	9.0	14.5
Fillmore	307	1.8	31	4.9	0.0	1.9	D	148	1.3	105	-7.0	9.2	-3.0
Franklin	128	1.0	14	2.5	0.0	1.2	D	88	0.8	58	2.2	10.9	-4.6
Frontier	89	0.6	14	1.4	D	0.0	D	46	0.4	42	0.5	0.0	NA
Furnas	232	1.8	31	2.7	D	D	0.7	69	0.6	105	3.0	4.3	9.1
Gage	1 406	10.5	124	18.7	0.5	8.8	1.3	555	5.9	218	0.9	152.3	-0.7
Garden	77	0.6	15	0.8	0.2	D	0.1	30	0.3	39	-0.8	0.0	NA
Garfield	178	1.2	13	0.6	D	D	D	20	0.1	22	-1.3	0.0	NA
Gosper	26	0.1	4	0.4	D	0.0	D	12	0.1	20	-2.8	0.0	NA
Grant	61	0.3	3	D	0.0	0.0	0.0	D	D	15	4.6	0.0	NA
Greeley	81	0.4	7	0.9	0.0	D	D	56	0.3	41	6.3	0.0	NA
Hall	5 273	41.0	397	109.9	7.9	33.9	4.8	2 933	40.6	459	9.5	237.9	-3.2
Hamilton	331	2.6	44	7.5	1.3	2.2	0.6	260	2.6	113	2.9	18.0	0.5
Harlan	187	1.3	12	1.9	D	0.7	D	44	0.6	62	2.6	0.0	NA
Hayes	27	0.2	1	D	D	0.0	0.0	D	D	14	0.6	0.0	NA
Hitchcock	65	0.7	7	0.2	D	0.0	0.0	8	0.1	27	-2.1	0.0	NA
Holt	660	5.0	67	8.1	0.6	3.5	0.5	262	2.5	154	1.4	39.9	-2.0
Hooker	45	0.3	1	D	0.0	0.0	0.0	D	D	15	5.9	0.0	NA
Howard	225	1.6	26	2.9	D	1.6	D	128	1.1	63	2.4	13.9	3.3
Jefferson	581	4.4	52	7.6	D	4.9	0.4	324	2.9	131	1.4	47.7	0.6
Johnson	183	1.1	19	2.7	D	D	D	92	0.9	40	-2.6	37.6	5.2
Kearney	276	2.4	30	4.5	D	0.8	D	113	1.3	110	4.1	10.5	15.9
Keith	809	7.6	89	15.5	4.6	4.0	1.6	474	4.9	130	2.8	24.5	-6.4
Keya Paha	28	0.2	1	D	0.0	0.0	0.0	D	D	12	6.0	0.0	NA
Kimball	301	2.2	33	3.3	0.5	D	0.3	99	0.8	63	-3.2	4.7	-3.1
Knox	421	2.7	35	3.9	D	2.5	0.3	169	1.3	118	2.2	19.9	3.0
Lancaster	18 493	153.5	1 426	619.2	29.1	160.2	38.9	14 176	216.7	1 740	8.1	693.7	-4.2
Lincoln	2 602	22.6	242	54.3	10.9	18.2	5.1	1 555	19.3	217	2.1	148.9	0.3
Logan	12	0.1	1	D	0.0	0.0	0.0	D	D	6	4.1	0.0	NA
Loup	18	0.1	1	D	0.0	D	0.0	D	D	16	1.9	0.0	NA
McPherson	D	D	0	0.0	0.0	0.0	0.0	0	0.0	NA	NA	0.0	NA
Madison	3 031	24.0	260	56.3	5.6	20.6	5.3	1 561	20.3	364	6.0	172.9	1.5
Merrick	328	2.6	31	5.3	D	1.7	0.4	143	1.7	67	0.7	7.1	-3.4
Morrill	148	1.1	16	2.5	D	0.7	0.2	46	0.3	38	14.2	0.0	NA
Nance	96	0.7	21	D	0.0	D	D	D	D	62	5.3	0.0	NA
Nemaha	407	2.3	37	6.3	D	1.7	0.3	222	1.8	93	3.9	21.5	-8.0
Nuckolls	340	2.6	36	3.7	D	1.7	0.2	113	1.2	96	5.5	27.3	2.6
Otoe	985	7.2	83	14.1	0.8	6.0	1.2	515	4.6	131	3.6	93.5	-3.6
Pawnee	76	0.5	13	2.6	0.0	1.4	D	83	0.8	26	2.4	0.0	NA
Perkins	76	0.6	17	2.8	D	0.9	D	53	0.6	54	16.5	8.7	7.7
Phelps	545	5.2	64	12.3	0.5	5.5	0.8	266	4.8	186	4.4	28.5	5.8
Pierce	317	2.2	38	5.6	D	2.6	D	204	1.9	73	2.6	8.5	5.1
Platte	2 203	17.4	177	46.6	3.2	11.3	1.8	1 327	17.1	322	3.3	148.7	0.2
Polk	215	1.3	22	2.6	D	0.7	0.4	56	0.5	74	3.9	10.8	8.7
Red Willow	1 133	9.7	100	13.4	1.2	4.6	1.1	358	3.9	171	-4.9	81.4	6.5
Richardson	548	4.2	59	8.6	D	4.6	0.7	349	3.4	128	-2.1	48.2	-2.4
Rock	64	0.6	16	1.1	D	D	D	57	0.3	18	4.4	0.0	NA

1. For the period including March 12 of the year shown. 2. Includes deposits for all insured and reporting noninsured commercial and mutual savings banks. 3. Includes savings capital for all FSLIC insured savings institutions.

STATE County	Federal funds and grants, 1989							Local government finances, 1981–1982							
	Expenditures		Per capita[1] (Dollars)					General revenue						Direct general expenditure	
									Intergovernmental		Taxes				
												Per capita[2]			
	Total (Mil dol)	Percent change, 1988–1989	Total	Direct payments for individuals	Procurement contract awards	Salaries and wages	Grant awards	Total (Mil dol)	Total (Mil dol)	Percent from state	Total (Mil dol)	Total (Dollars)	Property (Dollars)	Total (Mil dol)	Percent change, 1977–1982
	174	175	176	177	178	179	180	181	182	183	184	185	186	187	188
NEBRASKA—Con.															
Buffalo	87.2	-12.2	2 350	1 520	29	171	167	28.0	7.2	89.7	14.1	386	369	31.6	57.7
Burt	31.6	-13.5	3 809	2 174	26	164	178	9.3	2.3	89.0	5.1	588	571	8.7	24.5
Butler	35.0	-12.8	3 886	1 802	23	210	245	10.0	2.5	71.9	4.1	435	411	9.2	25.7
Cass	52.8	-0.6	2 346	1 651	16	131	187	15.3	5.4	81.1	8.1	390	374	15.7	27.4
Cedar	35.1	-5.6	3 313	1 607	290	182	167	10.8	3.9	90.5	4.8	435	423	8.0	15.1
Chase	23.1	-20.6	5 133	1 863	23	222	108	8.4	1.8	91.1	4.0	825	812	7.6	28.7
Cherry	16.0	-15.9	2 495	1 632	26	265	250	9.0	2.4	81.9	4.2	616	602	8.4	52.0
Cheyenne	31.7	-13.8	3 167	1 926	113	161	292	11.6	3.1	90.6	6.0	597	550	11.7	62.6
Clay	39.2	-14.3	5 224	2 022	152	586	126	10.1	3.0	65.9	5.2	660	642	10.2	43.7
Colfax	36.9	5.7	4 060	2 023	762	229	163	9.2	2.3	88.0	5.2	531	514	8.7	41.5
Cuming	31.2	-5.7	2 863	1 592	51	174	193	9.6	2.7	86.0	3.8	326	310	10.5	60.9
Custer	49.3	-12.7	3 915	1 994	48	189	268	15.5	4.1	85.1	7.7	552	537	15.8	37.6
Dakota	40.0	2.8	2 325	1 454	213	166	207	12.7	4.0	90.8	5.1	301	291	11.6	49.7
Dawes	27.5	-1.1	3 027	2 042	95	372	243	7.0	2.0	89.2	3.3	345	308	6.7	16.5
Dawson	66.6	-17.1	3 266	1 742	83	152	420	27.4	6.7	74.8	10.4	468	455	28.5	88.8
Deuel	9.3	-49.3	4 062	2 331	16	137	156	3.5	0.8	93.6	1.8	768	749	3.5	52.2
Dixon	33.3	-0.7	5 039	1 755	1 462	229	217	8.5	2.7	71.2	4.0	559	546	9.2	40.4
Dodge	89.6	-2.4	2 517	1 901	20	159	133	47.9	8.7	92.5	16.4	456	444	43.4	62.0
Douglas	1 276.5	0.5	3 011	1 743	364	534	315	542.5	141.7	65.8	229.3	571	456	503.7	48.3
Dundy	15.5	-25.8	5 946	2 162	24	190	193	4.1	0.8	92.4	1.8	610	595	5.4	152.5
Fillmore	36.3	-20.7	4 971	1 977	27	197	157	11.1	2.2	91.8	5.0	634	616	9.7	34.2
Franklin	21.7	-12.4	5 569	2 519	34	253	385	5.9	1.3	77.4	2.6	600	577	5.2	43.3
Frontier	14.9	-27.7	4 509	1 735	25	198	142	5.7	1.5	70.2	3.1	833	794	5.3	81.4
Furnas	28.3	-16.8	4 873	2 745	30	233	290	8.3	1.8	87.5	4.3	667	648	8.3	17.4
Gage	70.2	-6.2	3 039	1 976	16	167	197	20.3	5.9	80.0	10.1	417	396	20.0	23.6
Garden	10.1	-16.8	3 726	2 122	54	196	143	5.0	0.9	88.4	2.0	709	691	4.3	44.5
Garfield	6.6	-7.1	3 165	2 146	18	154	150	2.5	0.9	62.6	1.2	504	467	2.2	145.8
Gosper	12.3	-22.0	6 171	2 003	18	158	261	2.0	0.6	86.2	1.2	558	540	1.9	25.7
Grant	1.8	2.0	2 245	1 802	40	280	24	1.3	0.3	92.2	0.8	932	876	1.4	36.5
Greeley	14.4	-13.1	4 647	1 874	27	435	147	3.8	1.1	90.3	2.0	599	576	4.1	41.8
Hall	146.7	-11.1	3 024	1 765	84	481	288	50.5	13.4	83.6	21.9	446	411	49.0	78.5
Hamilton	39.4	-23.8	4 376	1 478	22	135	135	10.7	2.4	90.5	5.6	597	575	10.7	54.0
Harlan	19.2	-22.9	4 799	2 167	25	269	226	5.1	1.5	70.4	2.3	538	502	5.0	40.2
Hayes	6.4	-34.7	5 364	1 173	18	191	83	1.4	0.4	91.0	0.8	651	594	1.5	30.3
Hitchcock	14.8	-24.9	3 788	2 018	20	175	162	5.8	1.6	73.6	3.0	722	707	5.0	6.6
Holt	46.4	-19.5	3 601	1 647	15	135	236	11.8	4.0	81.0	5.7	410	393	11.5	39.4
Hooker	2.5	5.6	2 453	2 056	16	186	105	2.0	0.3	89.5	0.9	862	856	1.8	45.4
Howard	23.2	-15.3	3 620	1 795	22	173	126	8.0	2.2	88.8	3.9	586	570	10.2	87.9
Jefferson	34.9	-6.8	3 834	2 236	22	225	309	10.5	2.7	88.6	6.1	630	616	10.5	67.4
Johnson	18.5	-4.1	3 844	2 031	25	279	244	6.9	1.4	87.3	3.2	609	591	6.8	38.9
Kearney	31.5	-22.7	4 706	1 803	69	158	127	8.7	1.8	91.6	4.6	659	641	8.4	41.4
Keith	28.8	0.5	3 345	1 906	18	188	478	10.4	2.4	90.5	5.7	611	555	12.2	94.5
Keya Paha	3.1	-10.4	2 809	1 572	19	135	195	1.4	0.5	91.7	0.8	598	552	1.3	49.2
Kimball	18.5	-10.9	4 212	2 010	112	140	87	10.8	2.1	63.7	3.8	734	714	7.8	36.5
Knox	39.6	-0.5	3 776	1 954	315	190	382	10.8	4.1	77.1	5.0	443	424	10.8	31.9
Lancaster	693.6	3.8	3 228	1 771	126	467	797	231.7	59.1	75.2	94.8	477	399	227.0	66.4
Lincoln	103.0	2.5	3 057	1 853	79	242	425	37.4	13.2	83.3	17.1	493	428	41.9	49.3
Logan	3.6	-12.0	3 586	1 524	11	75	207	1.1	0.4	92.1	0.6	606	586	1.1	22.4
Loup	1.9	-15.7	2 326	1 289	14	94	26	1.1	0.3	93.1	0.7	828	813	1.3	65.4
McPherson	1.6	-11.9	3 144	1 720	22	158	356	0.7	0.2	91.7	0.4	622	615	0.6	19.8
Madison	80.7	-10.6	2 484	1 673	26	252	155	35.1	12.9	72.0	13.3	416	397	35.2	69.5
Merrick	32.0	-14.1	3 761	1 678	20	256	205	9.5	2.3	88.6	4.8	529	513	9.7	33.3
Morrill	18.5	-8.8	3 239	1 794	75	143	160	6.5	1.9	88.5	3.0	484	473	6.7	58.6
Nance	18.2	-17.9	4 224	1 863	15	123	246	4.5	1.3	84.6	2.1	459	413	4.7	54.2
Nemaha	25.8	-2.1	3 108	1 924	20	201	190	8.3	1.9	91.2	3.6	438	420	8.3	32.9
Nuckolls	24.8	-13.5	4 061	2 242	24	190	160	6.6	2.0	89.6	3.0	444	430	6.1	36.5
Otoe	46.5	-6.7	3 207	2 032	19	187	326	13.8	3.9	83.9	7.3	481	465	17.7	58.6
Pawnee	16.6	-2.0	4 742	2 397	68	290	192	5.1	1.8	56.8	1.9	500	483	5.6	98.7
Perkins	22.7	-29.2	6 492	2 061	19	147	39	6.3	1.1	93.6	2.9	778	771	7.0	72.4
Phelps	44.1	-17.6	4 497	1 912	79	169	121	11.0	3.0	89.9	5.7	559	533	11.9	63.9
Pierce	25.8	-13.6	3 036	1 472	17	128	86	7.4	2.0	90.8	3.3	387	369	7.2	28.2
Platte	71.2	-5.0	2 319	1 403	49	197	135	54.8	6.3	86.3	11.3	387	361	21.6	44.6
Polk	27.4	-18.0	4 649	1 989	20	137	83	8.2	1.6	87.3	4.0	638	607	8.0	57.0
Red Willow	36.4	-10.4	2 885	1 876	40	206	127	13.2	4.2	65.9	6.1	479	458	12.6	53.9
Richardson	38.2	-0.5	3 786	2 456	92	205	228	11.0	3.4	72.5	5.1	455	428	9.8	37.6
Rock	8.8	-23.6	4 190	1 793	12	143	132	2.9	0.8	89.0	1.3	538	530	3.1	86.1

1. Based on the estimated population as of July 1 of the year shown. 2. Based on the estimated population as of July 1, 1982.

STATE County	Local government finances, 1981–1982 (cont'd): Direct general expenditure (cont'd): Per capita[1] (Dollars)	Percent of total for– Education	Health & hospitals	Police protection	Public welfare	Highways	Debt outstanding: Total (Mil dol)	Per capita[1] (Dollars)	State and local government employment, 1989: Total	Rate[2]	Federal government civilian employment 1989: Total	Earnings ($1,000)	Elections, 1988[3]: Total vote cast for president	Vote for lead party (Percent)
	189	190	191	192	193	194	195	196	197	198	199	200	201	202
NEBRASKA—Con.														
Buffalo	865	51.9	0.0	3.9	1.0	16.8	32.0	876	2 703	728.6	161	4 394	14 825	R—67.3
Burt	1 013	52.9	0.0	3.4	0.8	23.2	5.9	691	601	724.1	48	1 130	3 531	R—58.1
Butler	980	39.1	18.1	1.6	0.8	18.4	8.8	937	513	570.0	70	1 611	3 816	R—54.6
Cass	750	58.4	0.1	3.1	0.6	15.6	13.0	621	875	388.9	86	2 057	8 378	R—55.6
Cedar	716	63.0	0.0	2.9	0.8	8.9	4.8	433	651	614.2	65	1 392	4 238	R—58.1
Chase	1 541	46.6	14.6	1.6	1.3	12.6	4.1	834	487	1 082.2	35	831	2 082	R—69.5
Cherry	1 234	39.3	15.3	2.4	0.7	21.4	6.5	960	468	731.2	46	1 034	2 896	R—77.3
Cheyenne	1 154	57.6	0.4	6.0	1.5	13.6	15.4	1 523	798	798.0	49	1 216	4 223	R—67.8
Clay	1 297	52.8	0.7	2.6	4.8	12.9	7.2	911	780	1 040.0	127	4 138	3 470	R—67.8
Colfax	891	60.0	0.1	2.8	0.8	15.1	6.5	668	477	524.2	78	2 115	3 898	R—59.7
Cuming	907	47.4	0.0	2.5	4.4	20.9	9.4	808	612	561.5	70	1 785	4 463	R—71.7
Custer	1 128	46.1	9.3	2.2	1.3	22.3	17.8	1 273	884	701.6	76	1 747	5 725	R—73.4
Dakota	681	58.1	0.2	5.3	1.2	7.8	18.3	1 077	704	409.3	87	2 564	5 696	D—51.6
Dawes	710	50.3	0.0	6.3	7.0	10.3	4.4	462	877	963.7	138	3 526	3 767	R—69.5
Dawson	1 279	40.9	22.5	3.0	0.9	14.1	22.1	991	1 473	722.1	96	2 417	7 755	R—71.3
Deuel	1 462	53.5	0.0	2.2	9.3	13.2	0.7	294	190	826.1	14	342	1 080	R—71.2
Dixon	1 301	56.6	9.2	2.0	0.8	14.8	2.1	293	554	839.4	53	1 317	2 977	R—60.5
Dodge	1 208	40.2	30.8	2.7	0.9	8.8	48.1	1 340	2 307	648.0	146	4 037	14 592	R—57.6
Douglas	1 255	39.9	14.1	4.5	0.4	5.4	1 420.6	3 540	28 897	681.5	6 300	192 580	177 355	R—56.3
Dundy	1 870	54.5	20.0	0.8	0.8	10.6	2.5	846	223	857.7	22	464	1 178	R—70.3
Fillmore	1 231	52.1	16.1	2.0	0.5	15.2	4.3	541	721	987.7	51	1 149	3 413	R—57.2
Franklin	1 177	48.8	8.6	1.2	0.9	22.5	5.2	1 181	293	751.3	43	920	2 085	R—62.1
Frontier	1 425	53.3	0.0	3.8	0.6	17.4	2.1	567	307	930.3	25	491	1 459	R—72.4
Furnas	1 294	53.6	0.1	1.9	0.7	11.0	15.8	2 470	550	948.3	45	971	2 645	R—69.2
Gage	826	51.1	0.7	3.7	1.0	13.8	25.3	1 047	2 087	903.5	120	3 038	9 185	R—55.7
Garden	1 519	41.9	32.9	2.6	1.3	9.8	0.8	298	294	1 088.9	22	514	1 362	R—72.4
Garfield	978	54.9	0.0	2.4	0.9	12.2	1.1	489	131	623.8	15	372	1 057	R—76.0
Gosper	860	39.3	0.0	3.9	1.7	30.2	0.6	288	171	855.0	15	341	1 034	R—67.1
Grant	1 604	72.8	0.0	2.1	1.2	9.1	0.5	544	75	937.5	NA	128	392	R—76.8
Greeley	1 212	69.4	0.0	1.4	1.4	12.0	0.8	231	246	793.5	28	582	1 438	R—53.1
Hall	997	47.2	0.4	3.0	1.7	11.4	171.3	3 481	3 046	628.0	738	24 153	18 950	R—63.4
Hamilton	1 144	53.7	0.4	2.9	8.6	14.4	8.0	846	503	558.9	46	1 076	4 331	R—69.7
Harlan	1 160	43.9	13.9	1.9	1.6	17.5	1.3	304	293	732.5	50	1 253	2 154	R—65.1
Hayes	1 142	54.6	0.0	2.1	0.7	23.0	0.3	210	89	741.7	15	293	682	R—75.1
Hitchcock	1 222	65.0	0.6	2.0	1.1	15.4	8.6	2 093	349	894.9	27	648	1 630	R—69.4
Holt	826	50.4	0.1	2.8	0.9	22.9	5.7	408	714	553.5	55	1 255	5 466	R—74.7
Hooker	1 836	47.4	29.6	1.7	1.3	7.2	0.3	346	87	870.0	NA	155	471	R—80.3
Howard	1 517	57.7	8.1	1.2	0.8	16.4	16.5	2 469	378	590.6	39	844	2 743	R—55.6
Jefferson	1 097	61.5	0.0	2.8	0.8	17.4	4.2	442	596	654.9	63	1 532	4 322	R—57.1
Johnson	1 304	45.9	21.0	1.7	1.3	12.6	2.3	438	407	847.9	49	1 231	2 354	R—50.2
Kearney	1 199	52.1	15.5	3.2	1.0	15.0	1.6	229	506	755.2	41	938	3 213	R—66.0
Keith	1 312	67.8	0.1	3.5	1.3	8.3	5.1	548	570	662.8	52	1 292	3 976	R—72.4
Keya Paha	996	55.1	0.0	0.9	1.3	21.0	0.0	36	65	590.9	NA	63	595	R—75.0
Kimball	1 505	44.3	15.7	2.7	10.6	7.3	3.3	629	396	900.0	25	597	1 890	R—69.9
Knox	953	62.4	0.1	2.1	0.8	16.5	10.8	952	818	779.0	57	1 225	4 147	R—63.8
Lancaster	1 142	39.1	13.1	4.1	6.1	8.1	501.9	2 525	25 188	1 172.1	2 665	88 207	89 447	R—49.9
Lincoln	1 206	48.4	0.4	4.0	0.9	8.3	18.9	544	2 374	704.5	209	6 517	14 556	R—57.7
Logan	1 116	70.5	0.0	2.9	1.2	12.1	0.1	90	109	1 090.0	NA	152	468	R—79.7
Loup	1 615	68.5	0.0	1.5	1.1	12.4	0.6	800	27	337.5	NA	NA	399	R—73.9
McPherson	960	70.1	0.0	1.7	1.0	13.2	0.1	217	35	700.0	NA	NA	292	R—78.4
Madison	1 102	53.7	0.2	3.2	0.8	7.9	32.2	1 009	2 551	784.9	216	6 448	11 973	R—76.3
Merrick	1 080	49.5	12.4	2.1	0.8	13.9	2.6	290	552	649.4	46	1 125	3 592	R—66.1
Morrill	1 099	43.8	7.9	3.0	7.1	13.6	7.4	1 217	408	715.8	27	611	2 328	R—66.8
Nance	1 014	49.0	10.2	3.1	2.2	17.4	2.0	440	298	693.0	25	567	1 990	R—59.5
Nemaha	998	51.9	17.3	2.9	1.0	12.4	4.1	490	1 061	1 278.3	55	1 231	3 785	R—60.6
Nuckolls	911	52.5	0.1	2.3	1.1	25.0	2.5	373	368	603.3	44	1 030	2 891	R—60.5
Otoe	1 170	54.3	3.7	2.4	0.9	13.4	14.2	943	1 016	700.7	83	2 051	6 366	R—58.5
Pawnee	1 482	37.1	18.5	1.2	0.6	17.2	1.5	398	243	694.3	37	846	1 758	R—55.5
Perkins	1 891	50.1	18.9	2.1	0.9	11.0	3.4	930	345	985.7	24	532	1 602	R—69.7
Phelps	1 166	57.2	0.2	2.5	1.3	18.1	3.7	364	730	744.9	53	1 279	4 387	R—75.6
Pierce	850	53.4	11.0	2.5	1.5	15.2	2.0	230	397	467.1	40	892	3 399	R—72.8
Platte	741	54.2	0.0	4.3	0.9	14.9	1 890.8	64 752	2 318	755.0	175	5 401	12 385	R—72.9
Polk	1 296	47.1	18.2	1.9	0.5	16.7	3.7	603	491	832.2	34	692	2 723	R—64.9
Red Willow	983	51.8	2.0	3.6	0.6	11.1	24.5	1 912	916	727.0	70	1 842	4 873	R—68.2
Richardson	867	49.8	0.2	3.9	1.5	15.8	11.0	973	530	524.8	71	1 615	4 658	R—58.0
Rock	1 232	41.9	24.7	3.1	1.2	15.8	0.4	170	172	819.0	10	235	956	R—79.1

1. Based on the estimated population as of July 1, 1982. 2. Per 10,000 resident population estimated as of July 1 of the year shown. 3. Data subject to copyright.

STATE–County code	MSA/CMSA/NECMA code[1]	STATE County	Land Area,[2] 1990 (Sq. Km.)	Population, 1990											
				Total persons	Rank	Per square kilometer	Race					Hispanic[3]	Age of population Percent		
							White	Black	Am. Indian, Eskimo, Aleut	Asian & Pacific Islander	Other race		Under 5 years	5 to 14 years	15 to 24 years
			1	2	3	4	5	6	7	8	9	10	11	12	13
		NEBRASKA—Con.													
31 151	...	Saline	1 490	12 715	2 164	8.5	12 537	16	24	111	27	74	6.5	14.5	14.7
31 153	5920	Sarpy	623	102 583	449	164.7	93 712	5 336	399	1 970	1 166	3 383	9.3	18.1	15.1
31 155	...	Saunders	1 953	18 285	1 774	9.4	18 157	15	46	29	38	104	7.5	16.6	10.9
31 157	...	Scotts Bluff	1 915	36 025	1 099	18.8	32 822	70	662	180	2 291	5 237	7.1	16.3	12.4
31 159	...	Seward	1 489	15 450	1 957	10.4	15 334	20	31	36	29	80	6.9	15.8	16.8
31 161	...	Sheridan	6 323	6 750	2 681	1.1	6 200	3	524	16	7	68	6.0	17.2	10.6
31 163	...	Sherman	1 466	3 718	2 940	2.5	3 700	0	3	10	5	8	6.5	16.2	11.7
31 165	...	Sioux	5 353	1 549	3 093	0.3	1 510	0	1	2	36	44	6.5	15.7	9.3
31 167	...	Stanton	1 113	6 244	2 731	5.6	6 167	23	37	5	12	23	9.2	18.8	11.7
31 169	...	Thayer	1 488	6 635	2 692	4.5	6 595	4	18	7	11	59	5.8	14.7	9.5
31 171	...	Thomas	1 846	851	3 121	0.5	847	0	4	0	0	11	6.1	19.3	11.2
31 173	...	Thurston	1 020	6 936	2 668	6.8	3 861	8	3 046	7	14	62	10.9	20.0	12.5
31 175	...	Valley	1 471	5 169	2 828	3.5	5 127	6	11	10	15	17	6.2	15.2	10.1
31 177	5920	Washington	1 011	16 607	1 877	16.4	16 403	85	39	34	46	104	6.4	16.4	13.4
31 179	...	Wayne	1 149	9 364	2 442	8.1	9 257	40	28	34	5	22	6.9	13.6	24.8
31 181	...	Webster	1 489	4 279	2 891	2.9	4 256	1	6	13	3	11	6.1	13.5	8.6
31 183	...	Wheeler	1 490	948	3 115	0.6	945	0	0	3	0	0	9.4	18.7	9.3
31 185	...	York	1 491	14 428	2 023	9.7	14 216	89	48	44	31	112	7.9	15.4	12.5
32 000	...	NEVADA	284 397	1 201 833	X	4.2	1 012 695	78 771	19 637	38 127	52 603	124 419	7.7	13.4	13.5
32 001	...	Churchill	12 767	17 938	1 792	1.4	16 028	203	895	466	346	1 008	8.4	15.8	13.0
32 003	4120	Clark	20 489	741 459	52	36.2	602 658	70 738	6 416	26 043	35 604	82 904	7.7	13.3	13.8
32 005	...	Douglas	1 839	27 637	1 366	15.0	26 130	86	570	361	490	1 652	7.4	14.7	9.7
32 007	...	Elko	44 500	33 530	1 176	0.8	28 970	266	2 128	277	1 889	4 339	9.6	17.9	14.3
32 009	...	Esmeralda	9 295	1 344	3 104	0.1	1 171	7	74	8	84	125	6.3	13.5	12.1
32 011	...	Eureka	10 816	1 547	3 094	0.1	1 442	5	41	11	48	138	8.8	15.3	11.1
32 013	...	Humboldt	24 989	12 844	2 153	0.5	10 761	81	714	63	1 225	2 335	8.6	17.5	13.7
32 015	...	Lander	14 229	6 266	2 729	0.4	5 663	9	295	16	283	789	9.8	19.2	14.5
32 017	...	Lincoln	27 544	3 775	2 934	0.1	3 555	81	58	16	65	156	8.1	17.8	13.7
32 019	...	Lyon	5 164	20 001	1 678	3.9	18 387	66	623	159	766	1 511	7.9	15.4	10.2
32 021	...	Mineral	9 730	6 475	2 713	0.7	5 142	351	748	70	164	546	8.8	15.1	12.8
32 023	...	Nye	47 001	17 781	1 799	0.4	16 393	291	499	155	443	1 237	7.3	13.9	10.4
32 027	...	Pershing	15 564	4 336	2 890	0.3	3 763	13	204	25	331	662	9.9	17.0	12.2
32 029	...	Storey	682	2 526	3 022	3.7	2 390	8	51	29	48	96	6.6	13.9	8.8
32 031	6720	Washoe	16 427	254 667	196	15.5	225 095	5 680	4 921	9 824	9 147	22 959	7.4	12.5	13.8
32 033	...	White Pine	22 990	9 264	2 447	0.4	8 454	188	294	35	293	852	7.6	16.0	11.9
32 510	...	Carson City city	372	40 443	987	108.7	36 693	698	1 106	569	1 377	3 110	6.7	12.1	12.0
33 000	...	NEW HAMPSHIRE	23 231	1 109 252	X	47.7	1 087 433	7 198	2 134	9 343	3 144	11 333	7.6	13.7	14.4
33 001	...	Belknap	1 039	49 216	853	47.4	48 788	67	108	216	37	245	7.0	14.6	11.9
33 003	...	Carroll	2 419	35 410	1 117	14.6	35 150	66	60	106	28	132	6.9	13.6	10.2
33 005	...	Cheshire	1 832	70 121	631	38.3	69 404	207	147	300	63	334	7.1	13.6	16.4
33 007	...	Coos	4 664	34 828	1 137	7.5	34 563	37	62	130	36	150	6.4	13.8	12.5
33 009	...	Grafton	4 438	74 929	601	16.9	73 395	404	186	831	113	599	6.6	12.9	19.2
33 011	4763	Hillsborough	2 270	336 073	152	148.0	326 821	3 001	612	3 816	1 823	5 696	8.1	13.7	14.1
33 013	...	Merrimack	2 420	120 005	385	49.6	118 580	451	224	595	155	780	7.5	14.1	13.1
33 015	6453	Rockingham	1 801	245 845	204	136.5	240 203	2 326	395	2 266	655	2 395	8.1	14.1	12.8
33 017	6453	Strafford	955	104 233	442	109.1	102 308	575	212	937	201	837	7.4	12.8	19.5
33 019	...	Sullivan	1 392	38 592	1 037	27.7	38 221	64	128	146	33	165	7.4	14.0	12.5
34 000	...	NEW JERSEY	19 215	7 730 188	X	402.3	6 130 465	1 036 825	14 970	272 521	275 407	739 861	6.9	12.6	13.9
34 001	0560	Atlantic	1 453	224 327	222	154.4	172 088	39 064	565	4 782	7 828	16 117	7.2	12.1	14.1
34 003	5602	Bergen	607	825 380	44	1 359.8	717 907	40 031	1 060	54 775	11 607	49 776	5.9	11.0	12.4
34 005	6162	Burlington	2 084	395 066	127	189.6	324 731	56 545	949	8 105	4 736	12 819	7.2	13.7	14.7
34 007	6162	Camden	576	502 824	96	873.0	385 350	81 665	1 055	11 579	23 175	36 022	7.9	14.5	13.8
34 009	0560	Cape May	661	95 089	488	143.9	88 097	5 334	213	607	838	1 855	6.7	12.2	11.8
34 011	6162	Cumberland	1 267	138 053	343	109.0	101 467	23 318	1 311	1 134	10 823	18 348	7.3	14.4	14.5
34 013	5602	Essex	327	778 206	50	2 379.8	398 024	316 262	1 639	21 191	41 090	97 777	7.0	13.1	15.0
34 015	6162	Gloucester	841	230 082	213	273.6	205 509	19 935	440	2 876	1 322	4 131	7.6	15.1	14.4
34 017	5602	Hudson	121	553 099	85	4 571.1	380 612	79 770	1 460	36 777	54 480	183 465	6.7	11.8	14.8
34 019	5602	Hunterdon	1 114	107 776	427	96.7	103 768	2 217	111	1 387	293	1 732	7.1	13.2	12.3
34 021	6162	Mercer	585	325 824	157	557.0	244 656	61 481	533	9 992	9 162	19 665	6.7	12.2	15.5
34 023	5602	Middlesex	805	671 780	64	834.5	550 006	53 629	1 066	44 869	22 210	59 776	6.7	11.4	15.5
34 025	5602	Monmouth	1 222	553 124	84	452.6	483 277	47 229	712	15 224	6 682	22 407	7.0	13.3	13.1
34 027	5602	Morris	1 215	421 353	120	346.8	386 681	12 491	429	16 759	4 993	19 814	6.6	12.3	13.7

1. MSA = Metropolitan Statistical Area. CMSA = Consolidated MSA. NECMA = New England county metropolitan area. PMSA = Primary MSA. See Appendix A for explanation of these concepts. See Appendix B for list of metropolitan areas identified by type, with component counties. 2. Dry land or land partially or temporarily covered by water. 3. Hispanic persons may be of any race.

STATE County	Population, 1990 (cont'd)							Population–Change and components of change							
	Age of population (cont'd) Percent							Change		Components of change, 1980–1986					
								1980–1990				Net change		Natural increase	
	25 to 34 years	35 to 44 years	45 to 54 years	55 to 64 years	65 to 74 years	75 years and over	Percent female	Number	Percent	Total persons, 1986	Total persons, 1980	Number	Percent	Births	Deaths
	14	15	16	17	18	19	20	21	22	23	24	25	26	27	28
NEBRASKA—Con.															
Saline	13.3	12.7	8.8	9.0	9.6	10.9	51.7	-416	-3.2	13 000	13 131	-100	-0.8	1 200	1 000
Sarpy	20.1	17.1	9.6	5.8	3.0	1.8	49.6	16 568	19.3	95 600	86 015	9 600	11.2	11 100	2 000
Saunders	14.8	14.1	10.0	10.1	7.9	8.0	49.9	-431	-2.3	18 600	18 716	-100	-0.4	1 800	1 200
Scotts Bluff	14.1	14.6	9.6	9.9	8.7	7.4	52.0	-2 319	-6.0	37 900	38 344	-500	-1.2	4 000	2 300
Seward	13.3	13.4	9.2	8.6	8.0	7.9	49.8	-339	-2.1	15 700	15 789	-100	-0.8	1 500	900
Sheridan	11.8	13.6	9.3	10.8	10.9	9.9	51.3	-794	-10.5	7 300	7 544	-200	-2.8	900	600
Sherman	11.0	12.3	10.0	11.0	11.0	10.3	49.3	-508	-12.0	4 000	4 226	-200	-5.4	400	400
Sioux	13.0	14.2	12.9	12.2	9.0	7.2	49.8	-296	-16.0	1 700	1 845	-100	-7.9	100	100
Stanton	16.3	13.4	10.0	8.5	6.0	6.2	50.3	-305	-4.7	6 500	6 549	-100	-1.3	700	300
Thayer	11.6	12.3	9.7	10.4	12.4	13.6	51.6	-947	-12.5	7 200	7 582	-300	-4.4	700	600
Thomas	11.9	15.5	10.7	10.6	8.6	6.2	51.7	-122	-12.5	900	973	0	-3.5	100	100
Thurston	13.7	11.2	8.8	9.2	7.7	6.0	50.6	-250	-3.5	7 100	7 186	-100	-0.8	1 100	500
Valley	11.9	13.0	9.9	10.5	11.0	12.0	52.0	-464	-8.2	5 800	5 633	200	3.7	600	500
Washington	14.1	16.0	10.9	9.2	7.0	6.6	51.0	1 099	7.1	15 800	15 508	300	2.1	1 400	900
Wayne	13.4	11.0	7.9	8.4	6.7	7.3	51.7	-494	-5.0	9 600	9 858	-200	-2.5	900	500
Webster	11.9	11.3	10.2	11.7	12.9	13.8	51.8	-579	-11.9	4 700	4 858	-200	-4.3	400	500
Wheeler	15.4	12.1	9.9	10.4	7.9	6.9	49.8	-112	-10.6	1 000	1 060	0	-3.5	100	0
York	14.5	14.0	9.7	9.1	8.7	8.3	51.7	-370	-2.5	14 900	14 798	100	0.4	1 600	900
NEVADA	18.5	16.0	11.3	9.0	7.1	3.5	49.1	401 833	50.2	963 000	800 000	163 000	20.3	90 000	40 000
Churchill	16.0	15.1	10.1	8.9	7.9	4.9	49.6	4 021	28.9	15 300	13 917	1 400	10.1	1 700	900
Clark	18.8	15.6	11.3	9.1	7.2	3.3	49.3	278 372	60.1	569 500	463 087	106 400	23.0	53 300	22 800
Douglas	15.9	18.9	11.7	9.6	8.6	3.5	49.7	8 216	42.3	23 200	19 421	3 800	19.6	1 900	700
Elko	19.4	16.2	10.6	6.0	3.7	2.4	46.8	16 261	94.2	21 900	17 269	4 700	26.9	2 500	900
Esmeralda	16.8	16.7	13.2	10.3	7.2	3.8	44.3	567	73.0	1 300	777	500	65.1	100	100
Eureka	17.7	16.1	13.1	9.7	5.8	2.5	45.4	349	29.1	1 200	1 198	0	2.6	200	0
Humboldt	19.1	16.1	10.4	7.4	4.9	2.4	46.3	3 395	35.9	10 600	9 449	1 100	11.8	1 200	500
Lander	18.3	15.8	10.7	5.7	3.8	2.1	48.1	2 190	53.7	4 200	4 076	200	4.2	600	200
Lincoln	12.6	11.7	10.6	9.8	9.4	6.5	48.0	43	1.2	3 400	3 732	-300	-9.1	400	200
Lyon	14.3	14.7	11.6	10.8	10.3	4.8	49.0	6 407	47.1	17 200	13 594	3 600	26.7	1 600	900
Mineral	15.1	13.8	10.4	10.9	8.6	4.5	49.0	258	4.1	6 100	6 217	-100	-2.1	600	400
Nye	16.2	14.5	13.4	12.1	9.0	3.3	46.6	8 733	96.5	14 600	9 048	5 500	61.1	1 300	600
Pershing	16.8	12.8	10.8	8.8	7.1	4.5	48.7	928	27.2	3 700	3 408	300	9.1	400	200
Storey	15.5	19.3	15.5	10.1	6.4	4.0	50.5	1 023	68.1	1 900	1 503	400	25.7	100	100
Washoe	19.0	17.3	11.2	8.5	6.7	3.6	49.3	61 044	31.5	224 600	193 623	31 000	16.0	20 500	9 400
White Pine	16.5	15.5	11.2	9.5	7.3	4.5	45.5	1 097	13.4	7 600	8 167	-500	-6.4	900	600
Carson City city	16.5	16.5	11.4	9.7	9.6	5.4	48.9	8 421	26.3	36 900	32 022	4 900	15.2	3 100	1 900
NEW HAMPSHIRE	18.5	16.5	10.1	8.0	6.4	4.8	51.0	188 252	20.4	1 027 000	921 000	106 000	11.5	89 000	50 000
Belknap	16.5	16.6	10.5	9.2	8.1	5.6	51.1	6 332	14.8	47 100	42 884	4 200	9.7	4 000	2 800
Carroll	16.0	16.8	10.3	10.2	9.5	6.6	51.3	7 479	26.8	31 700	27 931	3 800	13.6	2 400	1 900
Cheshire	15.6	15.5	10.2	8.5	7.4	5.7	51.7	8 005	12.9	66 900	62 116	4 800	7.8	5 700	3 500
Coos	15.2	14.7	10.3	10.5	9.4	7.1	51.5	-319	-0.9	34 000	35 147	-1 100	-3.2	2 800	2 400
Grafton	15.8	15.4	9.5	8.2	6.9	5.5	50.7	9 123	13.9	69 600	65 806	3 800	5.7	5 600	3 600
Hillsborough	19.7	16.5	10.1	7.5	5.9	4.4	51.1	59 465	21.5	314 300	276 608	37 700	13.6	28 000	14 200
Merrimack	18.4	16.9	10.0	8.0	6.4	5.7	51.0	21 703	22.1	109 700	98 302	11 400	11.6	9 000	5 700
Rockingham	20.0	17.9	10.6	7.2	5.4	3.8	50.4	55 500	29.2	221 800	190 345	31 500	16.5	19 500	8 800
Strafford	18.6	14.3	9.1	7.7	6.2	4.5	51.6	18 825	22.0	94 000	85 408	8 500	10.0	8 300	4 300
Sullivan	15.6	16.1	10.4	9.3	8.6	6.1	51.0	2 529	7.0	37 800	36 063	1 800	4.9	3 200	2 200
NEW JERSEY	17.6	15.5	10.9	9.3	7.9	5.5	51.7	365 188	5.0	7 619 000	7 365 000	255 000	3.5	624 000	431 000
Atlantic	18.5	14.6	9.8	9.1	8.3	6.2	51.9	30 208	15.6	205 500	194 119	11 300	5.8	18 100	15 000
Bergen	16.5	15.7	12.1	11.1	9.1	6.2	52.0	-20 005	-2.4	836 900	845 385	-8 500	-1.0	55 400	48 400
Burlington	18.1	15.8	10.9	9.0	6.7	4.0	50.6	32 524	9.0	384 700	362 542	22 100	6.1	32 800	16 300
Camden	17.8	15.1	10.1	8.6	7.4	4.8	51.9	31 174	6.6	492 800	471 650	21 200	4.5	48 100	27 000
Cape May	15.5	13.5	9.5	10.7	11.6	8.5	52.0	12 823	15.6	91 900	82 266	9 700	11.7	7 300	7 400
Cumberland	16.6	14.5	10.3	8.9	7.9	5.6	51.2	5 187	3.9	135 300	132 866	2 500	1.9	13 000	8 100
Essex	17.6	15.0	10.6	9.0	7.3	5.4	52.7	-73 098	-8.6	841 900	851 304	-9 400	-1.1	74 500	51 400
Gloucester	17.7	16.0	10.2	8.4	6.8	4.0	51.3	30 165	15.1	211 500	199 917	11 600	5.8	19 200	10 100
Hudson	20.4	14.4	10.1	9.1	7.5	5.2	51.5	-3 873	-0.7	553 100	556 972	-3 900	-0.7	51 300	36 500
Hunterdon	17.1	19.1	13.3	8.4	5.6	3.9	50.1	20 415	23.4	96 200	87 361	8 900	10.1	7 200	4 000
Mercer	17.3	15.7	10.7	9.0	7.8	5.2	51.6	17 961	5.8	320 800	307 863	13 000	4.2	26 300	17 900
Middlesex	19.6	15.5	10.5	9.1	7.6	4.2	50.8	75 887	12.7	638 200	595 893	42 300	7.1	48 700	29 300
Monmouth	16.5	16.7	11.5	9.1	7.3	5.4	51.5	49 951	9.9	542 600	503 173	39 500	7.8	41 400	30 500
Morris	17.0	17.1	13.3	9.5	6.2	4.4	51.2	13 723	3.4	419 100	407 630	11 500	2.8	31 100	18 000

STATE County	Population—(cont'd): Components of change, 1980–1986 (cont'd): Net migration	Households, 1990: Number	Households, 1990: Percent change, 1980–1990	Households, 1990: Persons per household	Households, 1990: Percent: Female family householder[1]	Households, 1990: Percent: One-person	Births, 1988: Total	Births, 1988: Rate[2]	Births, 1988: Low birth weight[3] (Number)	Deaths, 1987: Number: Total	Deaths, 1987: Number: Infant[4]	Deaths, 1987: Rate: Total[2]	Deaths, 1987: Rate: Infant[5]	Marriages, 1984: Number	Marriages, 1984: Rate[2]
	29	30	31	32	33	34	35	36	37	38	39	40	41	42	43
NEBRASKA—Con.															
Saline	-300	4 829	-1.9	2.45	4.9	28.8	153	11.9	5	174	0	13.4	0.0	82	6.3
Sarpy	600	33 960	29.1	2.97	8.4	15.1	1 785	18.2	80	403	15	4.2	8.3	680	7.2
Saunders	-600	6 809	3.1	2.65	5.6	23.6	245	13.1	10	228	4	12.3	16.1	163	8.8
Scotts Bluff	-2 200	14 056	1.8	2.52	9.0	27.1	541	14.6	41	377	8	10.1	13.7	311	8.2
Seward	-700	5 432	3.3	2.63	5.0	22.5	193	12.1	12	153	1	9.7	4.8	130	8.2
Sheridan	-500	2 618	-6.9	2.52	6.6	27.8	86	11.8	9	90	2	12.3	18.2	40	5.2
Sherman	-300	1 431	-6.5	2.55	3.9	28.0	45	11.5	0	54	1	13.5	25.6	32	7.8
Sioux	-200	612	-7.7	2.53	5.6	22.7	18	11.2	0	21	0	13.1	0.0	6	3.5
Stanton	-500	2 167	0.7	2.85	5.9	19.5	96	14.5	9	63	0	9.5	0.0	27	4.2
Thayer	-300	2 669	-8.7	2.40	4.1	28.3	68	9.7	4	114	0	16.1	0.0	55	7.3
Thomas	-100	316	-11.7	2.69	5.7	21.2	6	6.7	0	7	0	7.8	0.0	10	10.0
Thurston	-700	2 288	-2.5	2.98	16.3	23.3	180	25.4	6	98	2	14.0	10.7	51	7.1
Valley	100	2 141	-1.3	2.37	4.1	31.2	66	11.8	1	59	3	10.4	51.7	39	6.6
Washington	-100	6 017	14.5	2.68	5.5	21.3	184	11.5	10	119	0	7.5	0.0	116	7.5
Wayne	-700	3 232	-3.0	2.53	4.9	25.6	118	12.0	2	80	2	8.2	14.6	55	5.5
Webster	-100	1 755	-8.4	2.35	4.0	29.8	53	11.8	1	67	0	14.9	0.0	35	7.3
Wheeler	-100	350	-4.9	2.71	4.6	23.7	25	25.0	4	6	0	6.0	0.0	1	0.9
York	-600	5 467	0.7	2.53	5.1	26.1	217	14.6	7	135	3	9.2	13.3	136	9.1
NEVADA	113 000	466 297	53.2	2.53	10.2	25.7	18 008	17.1	1 358	7 884	160	7.8	9.6	109 020	118.9
Churchill	700	6 666	31.4	2.62	7.9	23.0	310	18.8	12	159	1	10.0	3.1	205	14.9
Clark	75 900	287 025	65.1	2.54	11.2	25.5	10 997	17.4	851	4 633	101	7.7	10.0	58 078	106.9
Douglas	2 600	10 571	43.1	2.59	7.4	18.2	399	16.0	33	156	2	6.5	5.2	7 348	346.6
Elko	3 000	11 777	85.5	2.79	7.7	22.4	463	17.5	35	176	3	7.4	7.0	2 193	108.6
Esmeralda	400	588	89.1	2.28	4.8	34.0	13	10.8	1	13	0	10.8	0.0	31	25.8
Eureka	-100	617	38.3	2.49	3.2	30.6	22	15.7	1	11	0	8.5	0.0	18	15.0
Humboldt	400	4 538	37.6	2.76	7.4	23.2	195	16.5	11	66	2	6.2	10.5	424	39.3
Lander	-300	2 212	55.1	2.82	6.2	21.6	128	26.7	16	40	1	9.3	12.0	49	11.1
Lincoln	-600	1 325	4.3	2.63	8.1	29.3	57	16.3	6	44	0	12.6	0.0	40	11.4
Lyon	2 900	7 680	52.4	2.58	7.2	22.1	277	15.1	17	192	1	11.0	4.0	128	8.3
Mineral	-400	2 529	11.4	2.50	9.1	26.7	114	18.7	11	74	3	12.3	30.0	104	17.6
Nye	4 800	6 664	94.1	2.50	5.1	25.0	213	13.7	11	100	0	6.9	0.0	120	8.8
Pershing	100	1 614	28.5	2.65	5.8	25.2	74	17.2	3	33	0	8.0	0.0	78	23.6
Storey	300	1 006	69.6	2.44	6.8	25.0	25	13.2	3	13	0	6.8	0.0	721	450.6
Washoe	20 000	102 294	32.5	2.43	9.4	27.6	4 020	16.8	303	1 729	37	7.4	9.8	35 394	165.2
White Pine	-800	3 296	9.8	2.59	7.0	26.6	129	16.3	10	79	0	10.3	0.0	173	21.1
Carson City city	3 700	15 895	31.6	2.39	9.6	27.2	572	14.9	34	366	9	9.8	18.4	3 916	111.6
NEW HAMPSHIRE	67 000	411 186	27.1	2.62	8.5	22.0	17 364	16.0	837	8 417	132	8.0	7.8	11 325	11.6
Belknap	2 900	18 839	21.0	2.58	8.5	22.8	731	14.8	44	483	8	10.0	11.4	531	11.7
Carroll	3 300	14 253	28.7	2.45	7.6	24.3	476	13.6	26	343	3	10.3	6.7	411	13.7
Cheshire	2 600	25 856	18.4	2.57	8.7	22.8	1 003	14.3	46	565	8	8.2	7.7	792	12.3
Coos	-1 500	13 799	6.7	2.48	8.2	25.6	414	11.9	23	403	8	11.7	18.0	356	10.5
Grafton	1 800	27 542	18.6	2.51	8.2	24.4	1 055	14.5	54	605	6	8.5	6.3	726	10.6
Hillsborough	23 900	124 567	30.0	2.64	8.9	22.1	5 805	17.5	284	2 455	40	7.6	7.2	3 364	11.4
Merrimack	8 000	44 595	28.6	2.59	8.6	22.5	1 784	15.3	92	1 007	15	9.0	8.4	1 081	10.4
Rockingham	20 700	89 118	35.1	2.72	7.7	19.3	3 930	16.7	160	1 517	28	6.6	7.1	2 707	13.1
Strafford	4 500	37 744	29.7	2.59	9.1	21.9	1 574	15.9	69	677	12	7.0	7.4	973	10.7
Sullivan	700	14 873	11.8	2.56	8.6	22.9	592	14.9	39	362	4	9.3	7.3	384	10.3
NEW JERSEY	62 000	2 794 711	9.7	2.70	12.1	23.1	117 764	15.3	8 285	72 181	1 063	9.4	9.4	62 654	8.3
Atlantic	8 300	85 123	18.5	2.56	13.7	26.6	3 743	17.6	272	2 421	32	11.6	9.1	1 918	9.6
Bergen	-15 500	308 880	2.8	2.64	9.4	23.2	9 994	12.0	524	7 859	59	9.4	6.1	6 917	8.2
Burlington	5 500	136 554	18.9	2.79	10.3	19.6	5 815	14.6	408	2 864	40	7.4	7.1	3 065	8.1
Camden	0	178 758	10.0	2.76	14.7	23.1	8 522	17.0	617	4 455	90	9.0	10.6	3 537	7.3
Cape May	9 800	37 856	17.0	2.44	10.3	27.5	1 387	14.4	67	1 188	15	12.6	11.6	852	9.6
Cumberland	-2 300	47 118	6.4	2.79	15.8	21.6	2 291	16.6	176	1 294	29	9.4	13.3	1 034	7.7
Essex	-32 500	278 752	-7.2	2.72	19.2	27.1	13 825	16.5	1 455	8 643	175	10.2	13.2	7 591	9.0
Gloucester	2 400	78 845	21.1	2.87	10.7	18.9	3 424	15.6	186	1 739	32	8.1	10.0	1 594	7.7
Hudson	-18 700	208 739	0.4	2.62	16.5	28.7	9 207	17.0	811	5 920	88	10.8	10.0	5 184	9.2
Hunterdon	5 700	37 906	32.9	2.76	6.3	17.9	1 465	14.6	61	626	7	6.3	4.8	760	8.3
Mercer	4 600	116 941	10.5	2.65	13.2	24.2	5 080	15.3	400	3 101	73	9.5	15.3	2 590	8.2
Middlesex	22 900	238 833	21.4	2.71	10.0	21.3	9 847	15.1	603	5 145	78	8.0	8.2	4 932	8.0
Monmouth	28 600	197 570	16.1	2.74	9.8	22.0	8 052	14.4	492	5 176	73	9.4	9.1	4 407	8.4
Morris	-1 700	148 751	12.8	2.78	8.0	19.0	5 711	13.6	288	2 973	40	7.1	7.1	3 453	8.3

1. No spouse present. 2. Per 1,000 resident population estimated as of July 1 of the year shown. 3. Under 2,500 grams. 4. Deaths of infants under 1 year old. 5. Deaths of infants under 1 year old per 1,000 live births.

STATE County	Divorces, 1984: Number	Divorces, 1984: Rate[1]	Physicians, active non-Federal, 1989: Number[2]	Physicians: Rate[3]	Hospitals, 1989: Number	Hospitals, 1989: Beds: Number	Hospitals, 1989: Beds: Rate[3]	Nursing homes,[4] 1986: Number	Nursing homes: Beds	Serious crimes known to police, 1988: Number: Total[5]	Serious crimes: Number: Violent[6]	Serious crimes: Rate[3]	Education: Public school enrollment[7]: 1986–1987	Public school enrollment: 1980	Attainment,[8] 1980: Percent 12 yrs. or more	Attainment, 1980: Percent 16 yrs. or more
	44	45	46	47	48	49	50	51	52	53	54	55	56	57	58	59
NEBRASKA–Con.																
Saline	44	3.4	8	62	2	130	1 008	4	310	259	19	1 999	2 404	2 257	66.7	10.6
Sarpy	424	4.5	44	44	2	277	277	4	358	2 618	48	2 693	16 533	20 378	85.8	21.4
Saunders	58	3.1	5	27	1	105	559	3	249	215	8	1 145	2 846	3 608	67.5	9.1
Scotts Bluff	206	5.4	73	197	1	246	663	6	478	1 654	77	4 392	7 507	8 143	66.4	12.5
Seward	35	2.2	6	37	1	55	342	5	309	303	3	1 934	2 429	2 416	68.4	12.3
Sheridan	26	3.4	4	55	1	40	548	4	165	172	19	2 379	1 536	1 478	66.8	12.0
Sherman	12	2.9	1	26	0	0	0	1	85	43	1	1 070	767	935	60.9	6.4
Sioux	2	1.2	0	0	0	0	0	0	0	3	0	NA	173	346	76.9	10.9
Stanton	8	1.2	0	0	0	0	0	1	69	11	0	726	508	1 371	66.4	9.6
Thayer	15	2.0	3	43	1	16	229	3	238	55	2	782	1 183	1 299	62.3	9.2
Thomas	2	2.0	0	0	0	0	0	0	0	7	0	697	168	214	76.6	11.0
Thurston	18	2.5	5	70	2	69	972	1	62	NA	NA	NA	1 346	1 581	59.5	7.7
Valley	16	2.7	5	91	1	99	1 800	2	103	106	5	1 852	874	1 039	66.9	10.2
Washington	48	3.1	11	68	1	46	284	2	195	249	8	1 569	3 135	3 383	72.2	13.8
Wayne	26	2.6	5	51	1	31	316	1	94	141	2	1 447	1 610	1 642	72.3	18.2
Webster	5	1.0	1	22	1	22	489	2	106	59	4	1 306	756	929	67.8	9.2
Wheeler	1	0.9	0	0	0	0	0	0	0	NA	NA	NA	192	245	69.9	10.8
York	42	2.8	12	81	2	108	725	2	211	360	5	2 439	2 184	2 640	73.8	13.6
NEVADA	13 822	15.1	1 657	149	33	4 132	372	57	3 329	63 339	7 417	6 362	160 964	147 055	75.5	14.4
Churchill	189	13.7	17	98	1	40	230	3	178	416	63	2 471	3 033	2 810	71.6	11.3
Clark	7 844	14.4	903	135	12	2 171	325	28	1 478	42 896	4 917	6 796	95 416	87 481	74.0	12.6
Douglas	160	7.5	19	72	0	0	0	2	105	NA	NA	NA	4 394	3 614	85.1	17.2
Elko	202	10.0	24	83	2	65	226	1	97	133	16	7 769	4 794	3 734	69.4	12.7
Esmeralda	2	1.7	0	0	0	0	0	0	0	27	4	2 138	160	122	67.6	13.0
Eureka	1	0.8	1	67	0	0	0	0	0	35	11	2 558	205	265	61.9	10.3
Humboldt	87	8.1	9	73	1	32	258	1	14	559	68	4 965	2 204	1 999	69.4	12.5
Lander	41	9.3	2	39	1	15	294	0	0	112	4	2 475	1 033	784	66.6	9.8
Lincoln	18	5.1	2	56	0	0	0	1	12	43	9	1 202	874	883	68.6	13.3
Lyon	7	0.5	4	21	1	48	249	1	30	435	105	2 349	3 351	2 643	70.4	8.5
Mineral	41	6.9	3	48	2	67	1 081	1	20	143	39	2 228	1 171	1 195	62.4	7.3
Nye	85	6.2	9	56	1	45	281	1	24	NA	NA	NA	2 632	1 861	69.5	9.5
Pershing	27	8.2	3	65	1	47	1 022	1	25	144	28	3 259	709	587	64.8	6.3
Storey	1	0.6	0	0	0	0	0	0	0	74	8	3 517	280	259	81.8	15.6
Washoe	4 496	21.0	582	233	9	1 457	583	13	1 017	16 451	1 985	6 736	33 712	31 465	80.1	19.7
White Pine	55	6.7	5	62	1	40	494	1	99	122	2	1 526	1 428	1 668	70.7	14.4
Carson City city	566	16.1	74	186	1	105	264	3	230	1 749	158	4 351	5 568	5 685	78.5	15.8
NEW HAMPSHIRE	4 949	5.1	2 101	190	43	5 068	458	175	8 567	34 708	1 549	3 268	153 954	173 562	72.3	18.2
Belknap	255	5.6	94	186	1	157	311	21	629	2 064	124	4 075	7 725	7 973	70.2	16.2
Carroll	166	5.5	46	126	2	120	330	8	255	1 166	25	3 415	6 055	5 104	77.5	20.7
Cheshire	309	4.8	107	150	4	497	696	14	550	1 523	112	2 155	7 781	11 637	71.9	18.0
Coos	94	2.8	49	141	3	182	524	9	385	574	47	1 608	4 845	6 849	58.7	8.2
Grafton	343	5.0	509	688	6	611	826	14	555	1 756	70	2 724	11 616	11 871	73.1	21.9
Hillsborough	1 343	4.5	556	164	9	1 548	457	41	2 575	13 144	385	3 975	52 072	52 549	71.1	18.5
Merrimack	526	5.1	226	190	4	688	579	22	1 336	3 196	150	2 814	13 681	17 930	74.0	19.8
Rockingham	1 149	5.5	324	134	8	757	313	19	1 320	7 457	444	3 146	28 902	37 604	77.3	19.1
Strafford	473	5.2	138	138	3	338	337	18	610	2 797	145	3 291	13 607	15 062	70.0	17.6
Sullivan	291	7.8	52	129	3	170	422	9	352	1 031	47	2 574	8 014	6 983	65.5	12.5
NEW JERSEY	28 470	3.8	18 515	239	124	38 641	499	599	44 937	408 255	44 951	5 297	1 107 328	1 314 835	67.4	18.3
Atlantic	910	4.5	368	171	6	1 890	877	28	2 255	24 931	1 874	11 883	31 025	34 425	61.4	12.5
Bergen	2 956	3.5	3 158	384	8	3 573	435	40	3 454	29 567	1 333	3 538	102 094	132 778	73.7	23.8
Burlington	1 429	3.8	703	175	7	1 367	340	25	2 257	12 671	1 047	3 245	61 537	72 618	74.3	18.4
Camden	1 762	3.6	1 200	238	7	2 333	462	45	2 927	28 697	3 484	5 746	79 839	89 230	65.5	16.2
Cape May	422	4.8	100	102	1	217	222	9	673	6 782	386	7 155	12 296	12 465	62.5	13.0
Cumberland	571	4.3	179	129	3	645	464	7	844	8 056	1 002	6 196	25 007	27 165	53.3	8.7
Essex	2 611	3.1	2 774	333	17	5 900	708	83	4 904	76 842	14 295	9 043	124 033	158 287	62.8	18.0
Gloucester	728	3.5	179	81	1	339	153	20	1 077	8 198	542	3 825	36 367	39 230	66.2	13.1
Hudson	2 001	3.6	1 041	195	10	3 050	570	11	1 849	41 310	5 432	7 503	68 286	81 864	51.5	11.2
Hunterdon	407	4.4	167	163	1	182	178	12	502	1 583	86	1 661	16 819	19 360	76.1	24.1
Mercer	1 074	3.4	905	271	8	2 186	654	26	1 608	22 003	2 765	6 685	44 052	48 487	67.8	21.8
Middlesex	2 497	4.0	1 602	244	10	2 683	408	27	2 985	27 101	1 926	4 171	84 485	103 132	70.0	18.1
Monmouth	2 158	4.1	1 283	227	7	2 817	498	89	5 071	20 051	1 743	3 599	83 013	97 808	74.0	21.6
Morris	1 780	4.3	1 149	274	6	2 456	585	37	2 876	12 654	627	2 998	64 197	82 239	80.2	28.6

1. Per 1,000 resident population estimated as of July 1 of the year shown. 2. As of end of year. 3. Per 100,000 resident population as of July 1 of the year shown. 4. Preliminary. Covers nursing homes with 3 or more beds. 5. Data for serious crimes have not been adjusted for underreporting, this may affect comparability between geographic areas or over time. 6. Includes murder and nonnegligent manslaughter, forcible rape, robbery, and aggravated assault. 7. The 1986–1987 data are based on administrative reports obtained by the U.S. National Center for Education Statistics. The 1980 data are based on the 1980 Census of Population and Housing. 8. Persons 25 years old or older.

STATE County	Education (cont'd): Local government expenditures for education,[1] 1982: Total (Mil dol)	Education (cont'd): Local government expenditures for education,[1] 1982: Per capita (Dollars)	Social Security Program December 1988: Beneficiaries: Total	Social Security Program December 1988: Beneficiaries: Rate[2]	Social Security Program December 1988: Payments ($1,000)	Supple-mental Security Income Program recipients June 1986	Money income: Per capita[3]: 1987 Income, (Dollars)	Money income: Per capita[3]: 1979: Current dollars	Money income: Per capita[3]: 1979: Constant 1987 dollars	Money income: Median household income 1979 (Dollars)	Money income: Percent below poverty level, 1979: Persons	Money income: Percent below poverty level, 1979: Families	Housing units, 1990: Total	Housing units, 1990: Percent change, 1980–1990
	60	61	62	63	64	65	66	67	68	69	70	71	72	73
NEBRASKA—Con.														
Saline	7.0	524	2 985	231.4	1 376	80	10 194	6 821	10 673	15 223	12.0	8.7	5 299	-1.7
Sarpy	41.7	458	4 205	42.8	2 079	174	11 555	6 968	10 903	20 446	4.9	4.2	35 994	30.0
Saunders	7.6	407	3 515	188.0	1 672	94	10 578	6 422	10 049	15 587	9.6	7.5	7 594	0.1
Scotts Bluff	17.7	460	7 365	198.5	3 617	478	9 616	6 288	9 839	14 472	11.8	8.5	15 514	1.3
Seward	7.6	488	2 640	166.0	1 266	66	10 463	6 332	9 908	15 847	10.3	7.8	5 908	3.8
Sheridan	4.0	515	1 690	231.5	776	60	8 530	6 605	10 335	13 412	13.5	11.7	3 211	1.1
Sherman	2.5	603	965	247.4	403	52	7 462	4 467	6 990	10 613	20.0	15.2	1 874	3.3
Sioux	0.7	403	145	90.6	72	6	8 024	6 488	10 152	14 174	13.5	11.0	869	5.8
Stanton	1.5	235	720	109.1	320	30	9 148	5 940	9 294	15 788	14.8	11.7	2 355	2.9
Thayer	5.0	658	1 920	274.3	887	80	9 616	6 153	9 628	13 502	11.3	8.9	3 017	-5.2
Thomas	0.7	668	190	211.1	84	10	7 397	6 017	9 415	13 415	10.4	11.3	404	-5.2
Thurston	4.8	655	1 260	177.5	515	180	7 641	4 908	7 680	12 393	24.3	20.0	2 548	-0.9
Valley	2.8	491	1 360	242.9	597	66	8 874	5 598	8 759	11 295	17.6	13.2	2 469	-2.9
Washington	7.4	469	2 415	150.9	1 204	68	11 601	6 955	10 882	17 960	8.0	6.4	6 378	12.1
Wayne	4.1	422	1 495	152.6	685	66	9 104	5 917	9 258	13 813	16.8	11.8	3 517	-1.5
Webster	2.9	608	1 355	301.1	580	50	8 892	5 758	9 010	11 559	15.3	11.5	2 048	-7.1
Wheeler	0.9	803	185	185.0	73	4	8 137	4 811	7 528	11 127	20.9	16.7	561	3.5
York	7.5	502	2 855	191.6	1 414	74	10 533	6 961	10 892	15 761	10.1	8.0	5 861	1.2
NEVADA	391.2	446	145 790	138.3	72 767	8 568	12 603	8 453	13 226	18 211	8.7	6.3	518 858	52.6
Churchill	6.6	471	2 750	166.7	1 222	216	10 336	6 447	10 088	14 128	11.2	8.6	7 290	26.3
Clark	210.5	413	87 590	138.7	44 298	5 672	12 535	8 259	12 923	18 102	9.1	6.7	317 188	66.4
Douglas	10.2	505	3 235	129.4	1 643	56	15 679	10 717	16 769	21 133	5.6	3.5	14 121	50.2
Elko	10.4	535	2 320	87.9	1 038	206	11 031	7 263	11 364	16 217	11.0	8.5	13 461	75.6
Esmeralda	0.7	601	150	125.0	67	10	11 704	7 410	11 594	17 371	9.9	2.5	966	162.5
Eureka	1.3	934	155	110.7	71	10	8 764	5 813	9 096	13 187	24.2	22.8	817	35.0
Humboldt	6.5	584	1 170	99.2	532	84	9 476	6 876	10 759	14 591	13.8	7.7	5 044	31.8
Lander	3.1	656	435	90.6	196	46	11 154	7 254	11 350	18 008	14.5	11.3	2 586	55.4
Lincoln	3.3	879	600	171.4	262	16	8 294	5 582	8 734	14 252	10.8	9.0	1 800	6.8
Lyon	8.5	574	3 865	210.1	1 823	160	10 679	7 061	11 048	16 132	9.8	6.5	8 722	50.0
Mineral	3.2	549	930	152.5	364	72	9 755	6 153	9 628	14 674	12.7	10.0	2 994	-0.8
Nye	12.0	916	1 965	126.8	954	70	10 951	7 169	11 217	16 548	11.8	9.2	8 073	88.1
Pershing	1.9	502	535	124.4	246	30	10 547	6 591	10 313	14 185	14.1	12.4	1 908	34.9
Storey	1.3	766	185	97.4	90	4	12 921	8 167	12 779	17 411	10.1	6.4	1 085	49.4
Washoe	91.2	439	30 830	128.6	15 549	1 552	13 510	9 491	14 851	19 560	7.0	4.5	112 193	30.4
White Pine	4.8	559	1 445	182.9	711	78	10 450	7 079	11 077	16 050	10.2	8.9	3 982	8.7
Carson City city	15.7	453	7 330	190.9	3 556	248	12 355	8 148	12 749	18 676	7.0	5.3	16 628	24.4
NEW HAMPSHIRE	375.9	396	155 145	143.0	77 763	6 470	13 529	6 966	10 900	17 013	8.5	6.1	503 904	30.4
Belknap	19.2	435	9 310	188.1	4 754	474	12 362	6 553	10 253	15 225	9.9	7.7	30 306	26.3
Carroll	13.4	465	7 175	205.0	3 517	246	12 636	6 659	10 419	13 561	11.8	8.7	32 146	40.7
Cheshire	29.2	460	11 350	161.5	5 876	514	12 104	6 576	10 289	16 037	10.0	7.0	30 350	19.6
Coos	14.3	417	7 555	217.7	3 669	400	10 249	5 746	8 991	13 699	11.7	9.2	18 712	16.9
Grafton	31.7	473	11 785	161.4	5 769	474	11 925	6 403	10 019	14 523	11.1	6.9	42 206	30.9
Hillsborough	109.6	384	42 535	128.0	21 739	1 726	14 746	7 390	11 563	18 689	7.2	5.5	135 622	34.0
Merrimack	37.8	375	17 650	151.8	8 962	812	13 226	6 920	10 828	16 717	8.0	5.5	50 870	28.3
Rockingham	82.5	416	27 070	114.8	13 373	846	14 919	7 445	11 649	18 993	6.6	5.1	101 773	33.7
Strafford	27.5	309	13 580	137.6	6 487	630	11 767	6 309	9 872	16 118	10.4	6.6	42 387	30.6
Sullivan	10.7	286	6 755	169.7	3 426	334	10 985	6 486	10 149	15 304	10.5	7.8	19 532	18.5
NEW JERSEY	3 917.4	527	1 205 439	156.1	652 100	95 203	15 028	8 127	12 716	19 800	9.5	7.6	3 075 310	10.9
Atlantic	107.4	550	38 180	179.1	19 332	3 854	13 337	7 194	11 256	15 752	12.6	9.0	106 877	19.6
Bergen	457.3	543	139 105	167.7	81 010	4 884	19 248	10 188	15 941	24 053	4.1	3.1	324 817	5.9
Burlington	197.4	531	48 590	122.2	25 619	3 106	14 045	7 671	12 003	21 197	6.3	5.1	143 236	18.2
Camden	250.1	523	76 325	152.0	39 880	7 008	12 859	7 278	11 388	18 056	11.8	9.6	190 145	9.5
Cape May	40.8	476	22 720	236.7	11 719	1 090	12 621	7 079	11 077	14 048	9.1	6.2	85 537	18.6
Cumberland	75.1	562	25 310	182.9	12 580	3 138	10 314	6 032	9 438	15 378	14.5	12.0	50 294	6.2
Essex	456.6	543	118 235	140.9	63 068	17 540	13 718	7 538	11 795	16 186	17.9	15.2	298 710	-5.8
Gloucester	98.2	480	30 065	137.2	15 470	2 026	12 167	6 939	10 857	19 837	8.6	6.4	82 459	19.3
Hudson	228.5	408	80 945	149.3	41 754	13 560	11 465	6 476	10 133	14 384	16.9	14.7	229 682	3.8
Hunterdon	55.2	620	11 640	116.1	6 406	742	18 483	9 168	14 345	24 115	4.4	3.3	39 987	33.2
Mercer	165.0	534	52 310	158.0	28 219	4 514	14 996	8 095	12 666	19 659	9.4	7.4	123 666	10.8
Middlesex	324.7	538	90 390	138.7	50 179	5 122	15 513	8 357	13 076	22 826	6.3	4.7	250 174	23.0
Monmouth	280.1	548	84 460	151.1	45 232	5 804	16 428	8 539	13 361	21 061	7.5	6.0	218 408	17.6
Morris	257.5	626	48 815	116.0	27 361	2 026	19 438	9 909	15 505	26 626	3.5	2.7	155 745	12.9

1. Elementary and secondary. 2. Per 1,000 resident population estimated as of July 1 of the year shown. 3. Based on the resident population estimated as of July 1, 1988 for 1987 data and enumerated as of April 1, 1980 for 1979 data.

Table A. States and Counties — **Housing, Labor Force, and Employment**

STATE County	Housing units, 1990 (cont'd): Occupied units: Total	Owner occupied: Percent	Owner occupied: Median value (Dollars)	Median rent (Dollars)	Civilian labor force, 1990: Total	Percent change, 1989–1990	Unemployment: Total	Unemployment: Rate[1]	Private nonfarm establishments, 1988: Number	Net change, 1987–1988	Employment[2]: Total	Per-cent change, 1987–1988	Manu-facturing	Retail trade
	74	75	76	77	78	79	80	81	82	83	84	85	86	87
NEBRASKA—Con.														
Saline	4 829	73.3	37 500	229	6 138	5.5	102	1.7	310	4	4 021	7.4	1 881	762
Sarpy	33 960	63.0	66 900	411	44 358	4.2	874	2.0	1 381	27	14 609	4.2	1 140	5 501
Saunders	6 809	79.7	43 600	217	9 335	3.0	209	2.2	379	2	2 206	-7.4	241	773
Scotts Bluff	14 056	64.3	40 400	231	17 344	2.5	569	3.3	1 152	24	10 637	-0.2	1 740	3 023
Seward	5 432	70.4	48 900	234	7 953	1.1	131	1.6	361	14	3 597	4.0	0	900
Sheridan	2 618	69.3	28 800	178	3 290	-0.5	70	2.1	190	-18	1 028	-3.0	143	358
Sherman	1 431	75.6	16 400	142	1 470	1.1	52	3.5	99	-2	419	8.5	0	97
Sioux	612	64.2	27 000	171	839	1.5	8	1.0	30	-4	152	-23.6	0	21
Stanton	2 167	76.1	41 700	198	2 859	0.7	63	2.2	83	0	959	4.4	0	84
Thayer	2 669	78.1	24 200	162	3 285	5.8	42	1.3	218	-8	1 328	3.6	194	313
Thomas	316	71.2	24 800	172	437	-11.4	15	3.4	32	-3	130	68.8	0	33
Thurston	2 288	60.7	30 700	127	2 797	2.8	142	5.1	114	-6	959	5.2	210	308
Valley	2 141	71.8	23 800	160	2 578	0.6	57	2.2	178	10	881	10.3	39	308
Washington	6 017	74.9	58 200	240	8 710	3.7	190	2.2	376	-10	3 179	-1.7	389	801
Wayne	3 232	64.8	44 100	209	5 223	2.9	79	1.5	221	1	2 080	10.3	710	651
Webster	1 755	78.4	22 600	138	1 885	1.5	27	1.4	107	8	519	-7.0	19	123
Wheeler	350	66.0	18 800	125	600	7.0	8	1.3	15	1	110	7.8	0	0
York	5 467	68.6	45 200	227	7 615	-3.7	125	1.6	498	8	4 806	5.2	844	1 299
NEVADA	466 297	54.8	95 700	445	626 000	4.0	31 000	4.9	X	X	462 446	7.3	26 243	88 534
Churchill	6 666	63.1	84 500	377	8 116	-2.4	491	6.0	400	4	3 179	15.0	147	1 084
Clark	287 025	51.9	93 300	461	385 330	7.1	19 043	4.9	14 470	812	270 247	6.6	8 604	52 958
Douglas	10 571	68.9	121 000	539	12 447	-1.8	657	5.3	738	28	17 749	11.2	0	1 693
Elko	11 777	64.5	81 600	359	15 613	1.6	771	4.9	686	65	9 292	9.4	173	1 817
Esmeralda	588	60.4	41 400	248	607	-10.7	34	5.6	19	1	157	-18.2	0	44
Eureka	617	68.2	54 600	293	3 333	2.5	57	1.7	36	-2	0	X	0	28
Humboldt	4 538	67.3	74 000	361	6 866	-2.4	344	5.0	302	1	3 325	23.1	217	896
Lander	2 212	70.3	58 300	277	3 063	-5.9	188	6.1	92	8	1 315	29.0	0	181
Lincoln	1 325	73.5	50 900	180	2 068	-2.8	101	4.9	62	-3	326	18.5	5	143
Lyon	7 680	72.4	74 900	313	12 100	2.8	671	5.5	371	20	3 165	10.4	881	674
Mineral	2 529	66.5	56 900	328	2 974	-2.7	159	5.3	109	6	1 655	5.5	0	230
Nye	6 664	70.2	70 800	304	7 534	-2.6	358	4.8	257	4	8 377	3.1	76	636
Pershing	1 614	60.7	66 500	299	2 662	0.4	106	4.0	90	0	1 118	24.5	0	295
Storey	1 006	73.0	99 500	343	964	0.1	39	4.0	59	5	250	20.8	0	112
Washoe	102 294	54.1	111 200	429	135 849	-0.7	6 519	4.8	8 042	198	122 909	6.1	9 321	23 917
White Pine	3 296	72.6	53 000	285	4 681	5.7	296	6.3	207	0	1 696	-5.8	47	507
Carson City city	15 895	60.3	99 300	406	21 794	-0.7	1 166	5.4	1 369	39	14 887	9.1	4 819	3 319
NEW HAMPSHIRE	411 186	68.2	129 400	479	630 000	3.1	36 000	5.6	X	X	455 663	4.2	110 611	108 094
Belknap	18 839	71.5	114 000	438	29 346	4.8	1 845	6.3	1 939	34	19 740	4.7	4 421	5 293
Carroll	14 253	75.3	119 000	417	20 740	4.1	1 110	5.4	1 822	59	13 364	2.9	1 175	4 802
Cheshire	25 856	70.4	110 600	449	39 570	5.4	1 599	4.0	1 958	49	26 211	5.5	7 432	5 852
Coos	13 799	70.3	71 600	289	21 873	4.9	1 305	6.0	1 077	31	12 929	5.3	4 602	2 858
Grafton	27 542	67.2	105 700	418	45 443	5.1	2 111	4.6	2 788	95	35 933	5.6	6 465	7 893
Hillsborough	124 567	63.7	137 500	513	189 253	2.2	11 542	6.1	10 304	271	164 160	1.8	45 168	34 564
Merrimack	44 595	69.7	117 800	461	66 165	5.2	3 446	5.2	3 610	115	46 878	4.3	10 558	10 348
Rockingham	89 118	72.2	149 800	541	131 168	2.3	8 343	6.4	7 738	182	92 470	7.4	16 240	26 225
Strafford	37 744	64.8	116 400	453	63 996	3.0	3 355	5.2	2 337	17	32 198	7.0	10 106	7 603
Sullivan	14 873	70.7	90 900	390	23 446	6.6	1 345	5.7	1 075	-9	11 538	-0.6	4 444	2 656
NEW JERSEY	2 794 711	64.9	162 300	521	4 048 000	1.5	202 000	5.0	X	X	3 155 697	1.7	684 408	602 564
Atlantic	85 123	64.5	105 900	503	137 023	5.1	8 027	5.9	5 981	176	109 414	-2.1	7 329	20 976
Bergen	308 880	67.9	227 700	627	466 379	-0.4	17 153	3.7	31 296	479	434 607	0.1	95 125	79 832
Burlington	136 554	75.4	122 500	526	189 583	2.6	7 691	4.1	8 679	271	128 725	4.7	25 792	31 803
Camden	178 758	69.8	99 300	440	239 167	2.5	12 078	5.1	12 354	246	182 901	2.3	33 411	39 449
Cape May	37 856	72.0	112 800	474	50 855	4.8	3 627	7.1	3 767	9	23 163	2.0	982	7 714
Cumberland	47 118	68.5	73 900	396	61 665	5.3	4 938	8.0	3 168	30	48 422	-1.2	14 652	8 694
Essex	278 752	45.3	196 100	461	396 832	0.4	25 332	6.4	20 448	42	344 269	1.2	63 967	50 798
Gloucester	78 845	78.3	99 300	437	105 893	2.5	5 386	5.1	4 683	187	59 008	4.5	13 089	16 812
Hudson	208 739	32.5	157 000	464	275 844	0.7	20 497	7.4	12 499	-20	208 827	2.1	45 157	36 183
Hunterdon	37 906	80.5	209 900	630	57 198	3.2	1 540	2.7	3 146	107	31 872	-1.7	8 245	7 617
Mercer	116 941	66.5	137 900	507	175 319	2.2	7 163	4.1	8 520	127	152 853	3.0	34 618	25 442
Middlesex	238 833	67.4	164 700	608	393 571	3.4	16 448	4.2	16 533	506	310 763	3.0	77 502	58 977
Monmouth	197 570	72.6	180 400	567	305 542	1.1	13 196	4.3	15 693	399	179 570	2.4	29 289	47 576
Morris	148 751	74.0	217 300	659	226 254	0.0	7 931	3.5	14 434	487	232 808	3.0	50 715	37 183

1. Percent of total civilian labor force. 2. For week including March 12. Excludes government employees, self-employed persons, farm workers, domestic service workers, railroad employees subject to the Railroad Retirement Act, and employees on oceanborne vessels or in foreign countries.

STATE County	Private nonfarm establishments, 1988 (cont'd): Employment[1] (cont'd): Finance, insurance, and real estate	Employment[1] (cont'd): Services	Annual payroll: Total (Mil dol)	Annual payroll: Average per employee (Dollars)	Personal income, 1989: Total (Mil dol)	Percent change, 1988–1989	Wages and salaries[2] (Mil dol)	Proprietor's income (Mil dol)	Dividends, interest, & rent (Mil dol)	Transfer payments (Mil dol)	Per capita[3]: Dollars	Per capita[3]: Rank	Earnings, 1989: Total (Mil dol)	Percent by selected industries: Farm	Goods-related[4]: Total
	88	89	90	91	92	93	94	95	96	97	98	99	100	101	102
NEBRASKA—Con.															
Saline	139	833	65	16 131	192	7.8	103	36	48	30	14 842	1 056	139	14.6	41.5
Sarpy	0	4 805	207	14 181	1 500	7.6	774	70	132	149	15 009	986	843	0.4	6.0
Saunders	153	398	26	11 722	258	7.9	62	47	50	39	13 703	1 577	109	26.7	14.6
Scotts Bluff	580	3 140	159	14 979	536	6.3	272	99	96	92	14 431	1 242	372	12.3	14.9
Seward	159	1 017	52	14 487	217	8.5	95	40	43	30	13 522	1 668	135	11.3	24.0
Sheridan	90	181	11	10 577	113	9.7	28	44	25	18	15 554	786	72	43.8	4.5
Sherman	49	134	4	9 107	50	3.7	11	20	11	10	13 196	1 816	31	53.4	NA
Sioux	0	23	3	21 645	28	5.3	5	13	6	2	17 299	397	17	71.4	3.7
Stanton	40	141	28	29 170	85	7.9	39	15	15	9	12 796	2 000	54	19.8	NA
Thayer	114	337	15	11 270	105	6.8	33	27	28	20	15 035	977	60	30.1	17.9
Thomas	0	26	1	6 115	13	14.9	4	5	3	2	13 972	1 447	9	32.6	NA
Thurston	53	205	12	12 787	68	13.7	33	10	12	20	9 673	2 931	43	6.4	NA
Valley	72	217	10	11 449	80	3.9	26	24	18	14	14 523	1 201	50	34.3	3.8
Washington	141	1 203	42	13 204	254	10.7	92	32	44	30	15 686	741	125	14.2	NA
Wayne	115	350	20	9 743	124	13.6	42	24	25	18	12 620	2 067	67	19.8	16.8
Webster	44	198	5	10 387	69	6.4	13	26	17	13	15 421	827	39	54.4	5.2
Wheeler	0	0	1	10 082	31	6.8	6	21	3	2	32 706	7	27	87.7	NA
York	285	1 398	63	13 124	232	2.3	107	55	51	32	15 598	773	161	17.5	18.0
NEVADA	21 064	226 650	8 771	X	21 087	13.6	14 601	1 254	3 644	2 737	18 989	X	15 856	0.5	18.0
Churchill	165	1 095	46	14 362	274	9.7	146	22	48	50	15 788	714	168	3.7	13.4
Clark	13 012	143 088	5 065	18 743	12 378	15.0	8 651	633	1 881	1 678	18 508	248	9 284	0.1	14.5
Douglas	460	13 420	286	16 099	578	14.5	400	38	168	55	22 014	91	438	0.9	16.2
Elko	290	4 337	167	17 997	461	15.0	328	40	74	47	16 003	645	368	3.4	27.1
Esmeralda	0	0	3	21 127	26	16.3	11	3	2	8	22 419	84	14	19.1	60.0
Eureka	0	13	D	D	39	24.7	151	3	4	3	26 148	29	154	1.0	NA
Humboldt	50	739	69	20 648	217	20.3	165	21	29	21	17 503	368	186	5.8	48.3
Lander	0	264	31	23 465	103	23.3	92	8	11	8	20 432	148	100	4.5	71.1
Lincoln	0	54	3	9 613	57	9.1	55	2	7	12	15 845	696	57	1.6	NA
Lyon	135	583	53	16 727	311	14.0	106	24	59	54	16 097	621	130	8.7	37.1
Mineral	47	391	33	20 111	99	10.2	68	5	11	22	16 072	628	73	2.0	38.3
Nye	83	729	249	29 753	255	14.9	391	14	29	35	15 967	654	406	0.5	24.2
Pershing	21	125	27	24 002	70	9.9	44	7	8	10	15 093	946	51	9.9	NA
Storey	0	105	3	13 280	40	14.6	16	2	6	4	20 127	162	18	0.0	36.0
Washoe	6 218	57 088	2 370	19 284	5 225	10.2	3 404	340	1 127	589	20 920	127	3 744	0.2	16.0
White Pine	76	422	28	16 738	145	20.9	92	12	22	23	17 935	303	104	2.3	43.2
Carson City city	444	4 175	257	17 286	809	10.7	481	80	157	119	20 396	150	561	0.0	24.5
NEW HAMPSHIRE	32 921	115 346	9 241	X	22 486	6.6	12 887	2 132	3 936	2 249	20 312	X	15 018	0.4	34.0
Belknap	953	4 577	395	20 025	1 012	5.8	530	115	206	122	20 050	166	644	0.3	34.2
Carroll	811	4 151	197	14 726	752	7.7	296	104	234	92	20 669	140	400	0.7	24.8
Cheshire	2 164	6 447	495	18 902	1 285	8.5	697	119	266	147	17 989	295	815	0.9	36.6
Coos	594	3 194	217	16 794	575	6.8	316	60	104	102	16 557	513	376	0.8	40.5
Grafton	1 806	14 863	655	18 216	1 393	8.1	978	161	330	166	18 820	230	1 139	0.2	25.9
Hillsborough	12 795	37 285	3 729	22 713	7 452	5.9	4 870	584	1 143	636	22 010	92	5 454	0.2	38.6
Merrimack	4 102	12 648	917	19 558	2 367	6.3	1 407	241	451	248	19 916	172	1 648	0.5	27.2
Rockingham	6 506	22 536	1 840	19 902	5 223	6.7	2 578	535	788	425	21 586	107	3 113	0.3	30.5
Strafford	2 439	7 406	583	18 105	1 743	6.6	912	137	271	217	17 375	381	1 049	0.7	36.0
Sullivan	612	2 191	207	17 911	684	6.4	303	77	144	92	16 971	443	380	1.1	40.8
NEW JERSEY	240 052	885 302	77 351	X	183 622	6.9	109 917	11 849	34 348	20 781	23 726	X	121 767	0.2	26.2
Atlantic	5 769	60 715	2 328	21 277	5 112	7.2	3 731	358	798	662	23 723	59	4 089	0.3	NA
Bergen	28 404	114 012	11 481	26 417	25 456	6.8	14 854	1 854	6 073	2 081	30 967	13	16 709	0.0	26.4
Burlington	9 438	33 951	2 805	21 794	8 544	7.3	4 358	464	1 207	926	21 270	118	4 822	0.5	24.8
Camden	12 998	55 956	3 945	21 567	9 684	7.0	5 745	639	1 520	1 484	19 180	211	6 384	0.1	25.6
Cape May	1 791	6 710	432	18 629	2 089	8.5	757	139	497	327	21 406	115	896	0.3	NA
Cumberland	3 335	11 117	949	19 602	2 206	7.7	1 356	148	359	437	15 869	687	1 504	1.5	36.5
Essex	36 618	111 231	8 661	25 158	18 224	7.0	12 653	1 187	3 510	2 753	21 873	97	13 839	0.0	19.3
Gloucester	2 051	12 930	1 188	20 125	4 033	7.7	1 836	248	509	519	18 187	274	2 084	1.1	32.7
Hudson	13 412	41 890	4 754	22 765	9 861	7.2	7 183	458	1 630	1 630	18 440	256	7 641	0.0	20.5
Hunterdon	1 439	8 159	751	23 569	3 096	8.6	1 142	262	517	182	30 301	14	1 404	1.9	31.2
Mercer	10 772	62 202	3 804	24 887	7 988	7.6	5 782	454	1 516	960	23 913	54	6 236	0.2	22.6
Middlesex	21 642	70 596	8 059	25 933	15 861	6.5	11 311	822	2 356	1 460	24 139	49	12 133	0.2	31.2
Monmouth	12 727	53 601	3 948	21 988	14 357	6.6	6 229	829	2 586	1 437	25 393	34	7 057	0.4	17.5
Morris	25 978	63 136	6 676	28 677	12 583	6.5	8 659	889	2 303	815	29 981	15	9 548	0.2	29.7

1. For week including March 12. Excludes government employees, self-employed persons, farm workers, domestic service workers, railroad employees subject to the Railroad Retirement Act, and employees on oceanborne vessels or in foreign countries. 2. Includes other labor income. 3. Based on the resident population estimated as of July 1 of the year shown. 4. Covers mining, construction, and manufacturing.

STATE County	Earnings, 1989 (cont'd): Percent by selected industries (cont'd): Goods-related[1]: Manufacturing	Service-related & other[2]: Total	Service-related & other[2]: Retail trade	Service-related & other[2]: Finance, insurance, & real estate	Service-related & other[2]: Services	Government	Agriculture, 1987: Farms: Number	Farms: Percent with: Less than 50 acres	Farms: Percent with: 500 acres and over	Farm operators, percent: Whose principal occupation is farming	Farm operators, percent: Residing on farm operated	Land in farms: Acreage (1,000)	Land in farms: Percent change, 1982–1987	Land in farms: Acres: Average size of farm	Land in farms: Acres: Total irrigated (1,000)	Land in farms: Acres: Total cropland (1,000)
	103	104	105	106	107	108	109	110	111	112	113	114	115	116	117	118
NEBRASKA—Con.																
Saline	38.8	31.7	7.7	3.0	11.9	12.2	881	10.9	29.1	75.4	64.4	343	3.4	389	64	291
Sarpy	2.6	35.7	6.1	2.0	12.1	57.9	437	27.9	15.8	60.0	69.6	110	-6.1	252	4	98
Saunders	4.1	41.9	10.5	5.0	14.1	16.9	1 417	20.5	19.5	70.5	70.4	445	-0.6	314	52	394
Scotts Bluff	11.0	58.9	11.2	3.4	25.4	13.9	898	17.6	20.8	71.9	74.4	406	-12.0	453	153	231
Seward	19.0	50.6	8.0	6.6	20.9	14.1	974	18.9	26.5	69.5	69.1	339	0.1	348	86	297
Sheridan	1.2	37.2	10.9	2.7	12.5	14.4	721	11.9	59.9	75.2	72.3	1 439	-0.5	1 996	68	368
Sherman	1.0	26.7	5.6	2.4	10.3	16.5	576	14.2	36.3	70.3	61.6	320	11.3	555	49	188
Sioux	0.0	NA	4.2	NA	5.0	7.6	353	7.4	63.2	80.5	74.5	1 122	-4.6	3 180	35	105
Stanton	50.9	NA	2.7	1.9	5.7	7.5	695	12.2	21.6	77.7	74.4	242	0.0	348	19	199
Thayer	12.6	37.4	8.8	5.7	11.4	14.7	744	11.7	39.5	80.2	62.5	380	4.9	511	87	303
Thomas	NA	NA	7.0	NA	9.9	18.0	94	13.8	74.5	80.9	75.5	362	10.9	3 853	3	14
Thurston	9.8	52.9	10.9	4.3	27.3	27.1	462	15.8	31.0	82.0	73.6	193	-5.4	419	3	174
Valley	1.3	40.3	8.6	4.3	12.7	21.5	541	12.9	42.5	76.9	68.4	337	5.5	622	60	181
Washington	6.9	NA	8.7	2.4	21.3	28.1	826	25.3	17.3	65.3	78.2	232	4.6	280	11	207
Wayne	11.4	37.5	9.7	4.0	14.4	25.9	744	12.9	23.0	79.8	76.2	264	-2.2	355	17	236
Webster	0.5	26.7	7.4	2.0	10.9	13.6	508	14.2	40.9	74.0	62.6	300	0.9	591	23	193
Wheeler	0.0	NA	0.7	0.8	0.6	7.1	213	12.2	58.2	77.5	62.9	283	-7.4	1 330	35	109
York	13.8	51.4	9.9	4.4	18.6	13.0	899	14.7	30.8	80.9	66.9	349	-1.3	388	176	320
NEVADA	4.4	67.6	10.0	4.5	41.7	14.0	3 027	41.1	24.9	55.3	75.8	9 989	0.1	3 300	779	803
Churchill	4.3	50.9	11.7	2.5	22.5	32.0	542	44.1	9.4	58.1	81.9	366	2.8	676	63	63
Clark	3.0	71.6	10.4	5.0	45.3	13.8	267	75.3	5.2	32.2	70.8	68	3.2	254	8	11
Douglas	8.0	75.7	5.4	4.0	62.8	7.2	202	51.5	15.8	53.0	78.2	115	1.6	567	41	29
Elko	1.0	54.2	9.7	2.1	30.4	15.3	386	25.4	51.0	58.8	75.1	3 376	16.4	8 745	235	D
Esmeralda	0.0	NA	4.0	NA	2.3	12.8	28	10.7	42.9	89.3	78.6	1 799	-15.7	64 244	9	25
Eureka	NA	NA	0.5	0.1	0.6	2.1	85	5.9	43.5	82.4	89.4	202	-13.8	2 381	29	D
Humboldt	1.2	34.2	8.5	1.3	13.8	11.7	191	26.2	54.5	68.6	78.0	834	-13.9	4 366	101	136
Lander	0.2	14.1	4.5	0.6	4.4	10.2	64	21.9	43.8	78.1	79.7	D	D	D	36	37
Lincoln	NA	75.8	3.7	0.8	67.8	19.8	102	28.4	23.5	46.1	52.9	46	-9.9	455	14	17
Lyon	20.6	39.8	9.0	2.6	16.9	14.4	346	39.3	22.8	65.6	74.3	210	-7.5	606	93	75
Mineral	0.8	NA	6.7	1.1	31.0	17.2	38	63.2	7.9	47.4	68.4	D	NA	D	D	4
Nye	0.4	NA	2.6	NA	62.2	6.5	136	34.6	24.3	46.3	72.1	370	-3.9	2 724	29	D
Pershing	NA	NA	9.1	NA	5.3	13.1	120	20.8	33.3	64.2	63.3	661	2.1	5 506	43	D
Storey	8.0	NA	16.1	NA	21.5	13.9	10	60.0	10.0	30.0	90.0	1	NA	111	D	1
Washoe	6.6	71.1	11.1	5.2	38.8	12.7	346	57.5	14.7	38.2	75.1	881	0.8	2 546	32	42
White Pine	1.0	35.8	10.2	1.8	13.6	18.7	127	33.1	33.9	66.9	82.7	217	-7.4	1 706	32	28
Carson City city	16.4	43.2	11.0	2.6	24.4	32.3	37	62.2	16.2	32.4	78.4	18	-4.9	483	2	D
NEW HAMPSHIRE	24.2	54.3	12.1	6.1	25.4	11.4	2 515	32.7	7.6	45.8	87.5	426	-9.2	169	3	148
Belknap	15.7	52.0	15.3	3.6	23.4	13.5	153	32.7	3.9	42.5	88.2	21	-1.4	140	0	6
Carroll	7.3	64.4	23.0	3.9	29.8	10.1	136	33.8	10.3	41.9	80.9	27	4.3	195	0	6
Cheshire	26.1	53.6	12.4	7.6	23.8	9.0	231	29.4	7.8	50.6	89.6	38	-5.4	165	0	14
Coos	33.3	46.9	11.6	2.3	22.6	11.7	154	16.9	18.8	55.2	85.1	48	-15.3	311	0	19
Grafton	16.4	63.7	11.9	3.5	40.5	10.2	356	18.8	11.5	55.9	88.5	81	-10.5	227	0	30
Hillsborough	31.0	53.0	10.5	6.5	24.2	8.2	338	42.3	4.1	43.5	85.5	43	-20.0	128	1	17
Merrimack	16.8	54.1	9.9	7.7	25.9	18.2	370	31.1	8.4	44.9	88.4	60	-5.7	161	1	20
Rockingham	18.9	58.1	14.0	6.8	24.9	11.2	382	48.7	1.8	40.3	88.5	37	-15.4	96	0	14
Strafford	28.7	43.5	11.8	5.0	19.6	19.8	189	31.2	3.7	39.7	87.8	27	-15.8	141	0	9
Sullivan	30.5	44.8	12.2	3.5	21.1	13.2	206	30.1	11.7	42.7	88.8	45	5.4	218	0	13
NEW JERSEY	19.5	60.1	9.1	7.1	26.8	13.5	9 032	59.9	4.1	46.3	79.4	894	-2.4	99	91	643
Atlantic	5.3	NA	9.4	3.2	50.8	13.3	384	65.4	1.6	55.5	72.7	29	7.0	77	11	19
Bergen	19.8	65.6	10.0	6.2	27.2	7.9	126	91.3	0.0	51.6	65.9	3	-4.8	21	0	1
Burlington	17.3	55.4	10.9	5.8	25.9	19.2	834	58.8	5.3	50.6	73.6	103	-8.4	124	9	68
Camden	17.8	60.9	10.7	5.9	29.2	13.4	177	72.3	1.7	45.2	76.3	10	-14.2	57	4	8
Cape May	2.6	NA	20.4	3.9	NA	23.9	124	62.9	4.8	51.6	79.8	14	-3.1	109	2	10
Cumberland	29.0	45.0	9.4	6.1	18.8	17.0	612	54.7	5.6	56.2	77.9	72	-3.7	118	19	57
Essex	14.5	64.1	6.7	10.5	29.2	16.6	25	84.0	0.0	52.0	60.0	1	-51.8	23	0	0
Gloucester	23.3	50.6	13.0	2.5	21.1	15.6	681	58.0	3.4	56.4	80.3	62	-6.1	91	14	48
Hudson	16.7	63.0	9.0	8.7	19.6	16.5	0	NA	NA	NA	NA	0	NA	NA	0	0
Hunterdon	19.1	53.8	10.8	5.5	27.2	13.1	1 398	60.4	3.3	36.1	85.3	124	2.9	88	1	87
Mercer	18.7	51.5	6.9	5.7	30.2	25.7	309	57.3	8.4	49.5	76.1	41	3.2	134	1	34
Middlesex	26.1	57.3	8.3	7.0	21.7	11.3	252	65.9	6.0	58.3	77.0	25	-22.2	100	2	21
Monmouth	9.1	63.2	11.0	5.6	33.2	18.9	840	73.6	3.5	44.5	75.8	66	-3.6	78	8	50
Morris	22.8	60.8	7.7	9.8	26.9	9.3	430	69.1	1.6	36.0	82.3	27	5.9	63	0	14

1. Covers mining, construction, and manufacturing. 2. Covers private sector earnings in agricultural services, forestry, and fisheries; transportation and public utilities; wholesale trade; retail trade; finance, insurance, and real estate; and services.

STATE County	Agriculture, 1987 (cont'd): Value of land and buildings: Average per farm ($1,000)	Average per acre (Dollars)	Value of products sold: Total (Mil dol)	Average per farm (Dollars)	Percent from: Crops	Livestock and poultry[1]	Percent of farms with sales of: $10,000 or more	$100,000 or more	Manufactures, 1987: Establishments: Total	Percent with 20 or more employees	All employees: Number (1,000)	Percent change, 1982–1987	Annual payroll (Mil dol)	Production workers: Number (1,000)	Work hours (Mil)
	119	120	121	122	123	124	125	126	127	128	129	130	131	132	133
NEBRASKA—Con.															
Saline	243	614	50	57 267	55.8	44.2	74.6	14.9	16	43.8	1.8	-5.3	39.1	1.5	3.0
Sarpy	296	1 156	60	136 262	23.5	76.5	70.0	16.9	47	29.8	D	D	D	D	D
Saunders	282	905	146	102 933	31.2	68.8	72.5	13.8	17	23.5	0.2	-33.3	3.4	0.2	0.4
Scotts Bluff	275	592	130	145 016	25.9	74.1	72.6	21.4	49	36.7	2.1	0.0	40.4	1.4	3.1
Seward	310	906	89	91 460	39.4	60.6	73.5	18.6	10	40.0	D	D	D	D	D
Sheridan	560	278	60	82 548	23.5	76.5	71.6	20.0	7	14.3	D	D	D	D	D
Sherman	169	365	30	52 442	39.4	60.6	76.4	13.5	3	0.0	0.0	0.0	0.2	0.0	0.0
Sioux	741	226	40	112 318	15.0	85.0	80.2	26.6	1	0.0	D	D	D	D	D
Stanton	232	662	95	136 685	16.1	83.9	81.7	23.3	4	25.0	D	D	D	D	D
Thayer	326	657	81	108 802	41.5	58.5	77.4	22.6	15	13.3	0.2	-33.3	2.6	0.1	0.3
Thomas	840	218	9	93 375	3.7	96.3	87.2	27.7	NA	NA	NA	NA	NA	NA	NA
Thurston	271	646	40	87 201	42.7	57.3	81.6	25.1	9	44.4	0.2	0.0	3.3	0.1	0.2
Valley	280	464	51	93 578	27.8	72.2	80.6	23.5	4	25.0	0.1	0.0	0.5	0.0	0.1
Washington	291	1 079	76	91 985	36.4	63.6	71.8	21.1	19	26.3	0.3	-25.0	6.2	0.2	0.4
Wayne	221	646	80	107 584	24.5	75.5	84.9	27.4	12	25.0	D	D	D	D	D
Webster	271	394	33	64 482	37.6	62.4	74.0	15.0	5	0.0	0.0	0.0	0.1	0.0	0.0
Wheeler	446	319	119	559 008	5.6	94.4	80.3	32.9	1	0.0	D	D	D	D	D
York	389	1 000	109	121 372	47.1	52.9	84.6	32.5	25	32.0	0.8	0.0	16.3	0.6	1.1
NEVADA	750	227	250	82 741	30.2	69.8	48.8	16.7	975	24.7	23.7	16.2	521.4	15.8	30.9
Churchill	353	507	32	59 461	23.8	76.2	50.0	13.1	7	28.6	0.2	0.0	4.1	0.1	0.2
Clark	339	1 152	15	55 136	7.3	92.7	21.0	5.6	408	21.3	8.1	19.1	178.7	5.6	11.0
Douglas	712	1 318	9	44 707	12.1	87.9	42.6	12.4	28	14.3	1.1	-8.3	28.4	0.5	1.1
Elko	1 249	142	39	101 154	3.8	96.2	57.3	25.4	14	14.3	0.1	0.0	2.3	0.1	0.2
Esmeralda	4 576	71	4	143 551	D	D	82.1	32.1	1	100.0	D	D	D	D	D
Eureka	456	191	9	101 210	47.6	52.4	83.5	30.6	1	0.0	D	D	D	D	D
Humboldt	1 077	244	40	209 279	58.6	41.4	70.7	31.9	7	42.9	0.2	0.0	3.0	0.2	0.4
Lander	D	D	7	112 970	20.5	79.5	82.8	31.2	1	0.0	D	D	D	D	D
Lincoln	334	734	3	31 677	33.4	66.6	38.2	7.8	3	0.0	0.0	0.0	0.0	0.0	0.0
Lyon	576	1 068	46	132 615	32.1	67.9	53.8	18.2	24	33.3	0.8	60.0	17.9	0.5	1.1
Mineral	D	D	1	24 018	21.4	78.6	31.6	5.3	5	20.0	D	D	D	D	D
Nye	861	313	6	42 411	34.6	65.4	44.9	10.3	9	22.2	D	D	D	D	D
Pershing	1 037	186	18	150 895	60.3	39.8	74.2	25.8	3	33.3	D	D	D	D	D
Storey	D	D	0	16 065	D	D	30.0	0.0	4	0.0	D	D	D	D	D
Washoe	506	202	12	34 149	28.0	72.0	25.7	8.7	357	27.2	9.1	8.3	203.8	6.0	11.9
White Pine	531	308	9	67 986	11.7	88.3	56.7	22.0	5	0.0	0.0	0.0	0.9	0.0	0.1
Carson City city	384	795	1	29 563	20.7	79.2	27.0	8.1	98	33.7	3.1	63.2	65.2	2.1	3.9
NEW HAMPSHIRE	358	2 112	107	42 585	33.0	67.0	32.0	10.5	2 328	31.6	107.9	0.5	2 508.7	71.5	141.6
Belknap	316	2 099	3	17 175	22.9	77.1	20.3	4.6	152	26.3	4.8	-2.0	91.0	3.6	7.4
Carroll	301	1 329	2	16 725	49.1	50.9	27.2	5.9	94	18.1	1.3	-13.3	21.5	1.0	2.0
Cheshire	435	2 628	19	81 086	6.3	93.7	33.3	10.8	198	29.3	7.1	-7.8	157.7	4.8	9.5
Coos	297	1 066	8	50 580	6.7	93.3	41.6	18.2	97	23.7	4.0	-9.1	86.2	3.1	6.0
Grafton	308	1 290	16	44 395	7.9	92.1	43.0	15.4	164	29.9	6.3	10.5	122.5	4.7	9.3
Hillsborough	423	3 629	15	45 178	60.8	39.2	32.0	10.4	697	37.3	43.9	-1.1	1 151.3	27.0	54.8
Merrimack	317	2 002	14	37 174	48.9	51.1	30.5	10.0	236	36.0	10.9	26.7	229.8	7.5	13.7
Rockingham	381	4 271	12	32 260	49.3	50.7	28.0	7.9	425	27.8	14.8	0.7	339.8	8.9	17.0
Strafford	382	2 681	9	47 232	71.9	28.1	26.5	6.9	151	32.5	9.9	-10.0	217.5	7.1	14.0
Sullivan	378	1 622	10	46 602	22.3	77.7	31.1	12.6	114	31.6	4.9	11.4	91.4	3.9	7.9
NEW JERSEY	396	3 969	496	54 916	74.7	25.3	38.7	12.0	14 442	37.9	690.8	-8.4	18 549.9	394.4	780.9
Atlantic	250	3 421	37	97 038	99.3	0.7	52.6	21.4	190	34.2	7.4	-5.1	155.4	5.5	10.7
Bergen	462	29 697	6	48 054	91.2	8.8	50.8	12.7	2 330	36.9	101.3	-1.5	2 710.1	51.5	103.0
Burlington	419	3 441	56	66 570	79.1	20.9	42.7	13.7	531	38.4	25.3	19.9	715.1	17.1	33.0
Camden	235	4 465	8	44 761	95.1	4.9	37.3	11.9	733	40.4	35.0	5.7	879.9	22.3	43.5
Cape May	301	2 395	5	37 113	89.4	10.6	31.5	5.6	59	18.6	0.9	28.6	14.5	0.7	1.2
Cumberland	266	2 213	58	95 155	89.6	10.4	52.0	22.9	235	40.9	15.2	-12.1	308.4	11.6	22.5
Essex	276	11 917	D	D	NA	NA	52.0	12.0	1 587	38.9	66.0	-21.2	1 838.3	39.7	77.9
Gloucester	305	3 222	46	68 122	91.2	8.8	48.6	17.9	276	34.4	12.7	-11.8	328.8	7.9	15.8
Hudson	NA	NA	0	NA	NA	NA	NA	NA	1 385	37.0	46.0	-23.1	977.8	32.1	61.4
Hunterdon	392	4 796	28	19 710	46.5	53.5	26.5	3.9	179	35.2	7.8	13.0	197.2	4.6	9.6
Mercer	459	4 093	14	45 164	80.6	19.4	41.1	12.0	468	37.2	39.8	36.8	1 058.1	15.9	32.7
Middlesex	465	4 427	29	116 696	94.5	5.5	52.8	16.3	1 192	44.6	76.3	-8.7	2 172.4	42.8	87.1
Monmouth	473	5 069	57	67 378	87.8	12.2	37.5	11.3	667	30.3	27.6	-5.8	737.2	14.0	27.9
Morris	336	5 183	13	30 270	87.4	12.6	27.7	8.4	890	33.8	46.7	-14.6	1 401.1	22.0	44.8

1. Includes livestock and poultry products.

STATE County	Manufactures, 1987 (cont'd): Production workers (cont'd): Wages: Total (Mil dol)	Manufactures, 1987 (cont'd): Production workers (cont'd): Wages: Average per worker (Dollars)	Manufactures, 1987 (cont'd): Value added by manufacture (Mil dol)	Manufactures, 1987 (cont'd): Value of shipments (Mil dol)	Manufactures, 1987 (cont'd): New capital expenditures (Mil dol)	Value of construction authorized by building permits, 1990: Total[1] ($1,000)	Nonresidential: Total ($1,000)	Nonresidential: Percent: Office	Nonresidential: Percent: Industrial	Nonresidential: Percent: Stores	Residential: New construction ($1,000)	Residential: Number of housing units	Residential: Alterations and additions ($1,000)
	134	135	136	137	138	139	140	141	142	143	144	145	146
NEBRASKA—Con.													
Saline	31.5	21 000	156.4	490.8	8.1	3 330	2 191	5.0	53.9	16.2	878	15	38
Sarpy	D	D	D	D	D	44 896	11 360	2.1	8.3	58.7	29 033	685	1 401
Saunders	2.7	13 500	6.8	26.1	0.3	2 894	571	6.1	24.9	0.0	1 259	25	251
Scotts Bluff	27.4	19 571	92.5	294.8	6.5	7 083	616	19.8	6.9	15.3	4 974	84	689
Seward	D	D	D	D	D	5 570	862	0.0	3.5	2.7	3 611	67	400
Sheridan	D	D	D	D	D	478	372	0.0	0.0	12.1	0	0	41
Sherman	0.1	NA	0.6	0.9	0.0	128	33	0.0	0.0	0.0	0	0	45
Sioux	D	D	D	D	D	NA	NA	NA	NA	NA	NA	NA	NA
Stanton	D	D	D	D	D	1 785	294	28.9	0.0	0.0	1 348	32	101
Thayer	1.6	16 000	7.9	16.6	0.2	2 494	2 193	0.0	0.0	1.0	238	3	12
Thomas	NA	NA	NA	NA	NA	NA	NA	NA	NA	NA	NA	NA	NA
Thurston	1.8	18 000	8.7	14.4	0.7	544	7	0.0	0.0	0.0	470	1	14
Valley	0.3	NA	1.7	3.0	D	415	267	0.0	4.5	80.0	0	0	54
Washington	3.9	19 500	15.1	31.6	0.6	13 722	4 778	93.1	0.0	0.5	6 511	94	695
Wayne	D	D	D	D	D	1 149	154	0.0	16.2	68.0	300	5	166
Webster	0.1	NA	0,3	0.5	0.0	225	31	0.0	0.0	95.4	85	1	15
Wheeler	D	D	D	D	D	NA	NA	NA	NA	NA	NA	NA	NA
York	10.4	17 333	32.2	70.9	D	497	12	0.0	0.0	0.0	249	7	176
NEVADA	299.6	18 962	1 279.3	2 470.4	114.0	2 428 627	483 494	10.0	13.3	52.6	1 427 079	25 096	47 368
Churchill	2.3	23 000	12.3	22.7	0.4	16 089	8 163	3.7	40.4	51.8	6 717	94	605
Clark	112.0	20 000	442.0	839.8	34.2	1 833 693	367 907	7.4	9.7	58.0	1 055 766	20 703	21 083
Douglas	9.3	18 600	23.1	63.9	D	77 652	0	NA	NA	NA	71 120	617	4 979
Elko	2.0	20 000	7.6	24.6	D	33 072	7 758	9.7	15.8	33.1	17 858	312	997
Esmeralda	D	D	D	D	D	NA	NA	NA	NA	NA	NA	NA	NA
Eureka	D	D	D	D	D	NA	NA	NA	NA	NA	NA	NA	NA
Humboldt	2.5	12 500	6.7	10.8	D	12 318	3 801	4.0	36.3	20.0	4 603	75	696
Lander	D	D	D	D	D	3 617	2 135	0.7	73.8	24.2	100	2	28
Lincoln	0.0	NA	0.1	0.2	0.0	166	0	NA	NA	NA	82	2	62
Lyon	10.3	20 600	49.0	90.9	2.0	9 094	4 307	0.3	0.0	42.7	2 899	76	682
Mineral	D	D	D	D	D	1 157	19	0.0	0.0	0.0	487	20	0
Nye	D	D	D	D	D	22	0	0.0	0.0	0.0	0	0	1
Pershing	D	D	D	D	D	1 975	776	5.2	0.0	83.8	197	4	20
Storey	D	D	D	D	D	2 918	354	0.0	2.5	0.0	1 491	20	113
Washoe	114.7	19 117	564.5	1 075.4	55.1	384 093	78 249	21.6	25.1	33.8	228 013	2 602	16 292
White Pine	0.8	NA	2.1	3.0	0.1	2 774	1 692	88.7	0.0	0.0	1 012	78	67
Carson City city	36.4	17 333	128.5	273.6	18.0	49 985	8 335	17.8	17.6	49.9	36 733	491	1 742
NEW HAMPSHIRE	1 426.8	19 955	8 188.6	12 214.2	339.8	769 406	179 959	14.1	11.3	43.3	367 943	4 201	93 499
Belknap	58.8	16 333	172.8	284.5	9.5	38 101	4 887	1.0	9.6	39.9	24 347	227	6 411
Carroll	13.9	13 900	60.7	118.5	2.5	44 839	3 751	46.7	11.7	13.9	34 882	200	4 217
Cheshire	89.6	18 667	324.0	525.9	19.9	44 956	7 664	8.6	26.7	37.8	23 137	358	6 540
Coos	61.3	19 774	227.0	528.8	24.6	10 554	1 388	0.0	45.5	18.0	2 906	64	2 755
Grafton	82.2	17 489	324.1	511.8	20.6	57 438	21 709	77.0	0.0	17.7	19 799	226	5 045
Hillsborough	632.9	23 441	3 112.8	4 690.2	146.3	227 525	39 529	10.4	4.9	47.4	104 956	1 202	33 305
Merrimack	126.9	16 920	462.9	891.0	31.2	72 812	20 043	2.1	17.6	6.1	31 569	433	5 635
Rockingham	161.8	18 180	2 692.9	3 433.4	47.2	197 476	59 664	2.1	6.8	70.4	91 085	1 055	22 744
Strafford	133.9	18 859	578.3	846.0	32.4	51 703	14 584	0.2	30.1	41.0	22 622	295	5 022
Sullivan	65.6	16 821	233.2	384.2	5.5	24 004	6 739	5.3	41.7	8.9	12 640	141	1 826
NEW JERSEY	8 389.3	21 271	42 526.6	82 451.0	2 312.5	4 520 015	1 190 179	31.4	10.5	32.1	1 397 723	17 524	802 442
Atlantic	104.4	18 982	636.6	876.2	23.3	175 177	24 598	46.9	4.1	16.1	79 203	1 026	26 746
Bergen	1 016.5	19 738	5 251.2	9 578.8	236.5	397 154	72 108	70.6	4.7	6.8	90 674	817	124 454
Burlington	477.7	27 936	1 718.7	3 211.6	88.3	219 246	43 108	14.9	12.7	36.0	104 108	1 600	31 521
Camden	472.8	21 202	2 127.1	4 012.6	97.9	188 631	26 158	25.0	17.2	19.8	65 936	1 125	30 410
Cape May	9.4	13 429	31.7	70.5	2.3	119 422	15 823	6.6	25.2	54.7	53 773	621	34 828
Cumberland	211.2	18 207	820.4	1 537.9	47.8	56 724	13 914	3.4	39.4	27.3	18 810	294	8 992
Essex	889.0	22 393	3 802.5	6 904.5	246.8	361 347	95 316	4.6	4.2	3.0	48 214	540	76 626
Gloucester	171.8	21 747	1 052.3	3 463.8	72.8	197 863	73 684	12.5	23.6	48.8	73 769	1 183	20 757
Hudson	536.7	16 720	2 635.9	5 372.9	212.7	210 067	110 479	88.6	2.2	1.2	30 070	486	21 424
Hunterdon	98.2	21 348	626.6	1 362.6	34.1	106 824	6 666	29.7	0.0	25.5	45 237	281	15 763
Mercer	377.8	23 761	1 359.2	2 593.0	84.0	232 653	54 698	24.1	45.5	7.6	63 078	1 004	23 036
Middlesex	982.0	22 944	6 172.4	12 153.0	410.1	535 868	255 474	9.5	3.1	72.9	109 800	1 486	51 832
Monmouth	265.6	18 971	1 442.6	2 560.6	63.1	295 122	41 042	15.7	12.9	39.5	141 570	1 529	64 412
Morris	478.9	21 768	2 977.2	5 007.0	119.7	433 006	158 352	38.0	18.9	26.6	97 667	798	72 474

1. Includes nonresidential additions and alterations, residential nonhousekeeping buildings, and residential garages and carports not shown separately.

STATE County	Wholesale trade, 1987: Establishments	Wholesale trade, 1987: Sales (Mil dol)	Wholesale trade, 1987: Paid employees[1]	Wholesale trade, 1987: Annual payroll (Mil dol)	Retail trade, all establishments, 1987: Number	Retail trade, all establishments, 1987: Sales: Total (Mil dol)	Retail trade, all establishments, 1987: Sales: Percent change, 1982–1987	Retail trade, all establishments, 1987: Sales: Per capita[2] (Dollars)	Retail trade, establishments with payroll, 1987: Number	Retail trade, establishments with payroll, 1987: Sales: Total (Mil dol)	Sales: Per capita[2] (Dollars): General merchandise stores	Sales: Per capita[2] (Dollars): Food stores	Sales: Per capita[2] (Dollars): Apparel & accessory stores	Sales: Per capita[2] (Dollars): Eating and drinking places
	147	148	149	150	151	152	153	154	155	156	157	158	159	160
NEBRASKA—Con.														
Saline	20	49.6	154	2.6	159	67.7	56.0	5 211	102	65.9	D	794	59	360
Sarpy	51	D	D	D	592	357.2	40.4	3 729	362	348.6	D	869	90	372
Saunders	28	43.9	163	2.0	195	63.4	26.8	3 408	120	59.0	D	556	23	214
Scotts Bluff	119	355.7	1 009	16.9	465	237.9	15.5	6 344	307	232.3	952	1 635	291	503
Seward	36	68.5	275	4.7	168	55.2	8.9	3 514	106	53.0	D	765	39	429
Sheridan	23	53.2	207	2.1	129	26.7	-20.5	3 657	76	23.4	D	682	98	335
Sherman	10	24.1	77	0.8	57	8.1	8.0	2 012	33	6.7	0	293	D	203
Sioux	10	6.3	45	0.4	15	2.7	12.5	1 658	9	2.4	D	D	D	D
Stanton	10	21.0	85	1.4	26	4.6	-14.8	704	18	4.5	D	D	0	142
Thayer	32	72.2	190	2.7	130	29.6	-2.3	4 170	70	26.4	D	684	D	313
Thomas	1	D	D	D	17	D	D	D	11	2.4	0	1 120	0	D
Thurston	17	36.8	122	1.7	56	13.6	-30.6	1 948	31	12.6	0	580	0	95
Valley	18	55.1	151	2.3	76	21.4	11.5	3 749	58	19.5	D	844	113	301
Washington	29	51.4	165	2.4	178	59.9	29.1	3 793	111	56.8	D	397	86	413
Wayne	18	37.1	123	1.6	112	39.7	16.1	4 095	73	37.7	452	575	88	478
Webster	8	15.4	68	0.9	76	10.7	2.9	2 386	33	8.3	0	292	D	181
Wheeler	3	D	D	D	7	0.6	-33.3	552	3	0.4	0	0	0	D
York	46	107.1	371	6.2	205	83.5	24.1	5 682	126	80.8	782	1 224	234	738
NEVADA	1 589	5 506.9	17 627	379.1	10 054	7 494.7	40.3	7 448	6 442	7 321.0	834	1 527	320	755
Churchill	19	29.4	143	2.3	184	90.1	34.1	5 664	119	87.8	D	1 386	218	708
Clark	805	3 079.7	10 005	209.6	5 413	4 460.0	45.6	7 445	3 524	4 370.3	823	1 570	368	832
Douglas	18	15.6	73	1.5	292	113.3	33.0	4 701	159	106.9	D	1 149	239	750
Elko	44	113.1	349	7.5	295	135.1	16.6	5 701	178	131.4	D	1 295	D	529
Esmeralda	1	D	D	D	18	3.2	-3.0	2 687	10	2.9	D	D	0	D
Eureka	2	D	D	D	21	3.3	17.9	2 532	9	2.7	0	D	0	578
Humboldt	23	32.5	125	2.1	129	74.6	-1.1	6 971	83	73.3	D	D	304	576
Lander	3	D	D	D	53	14.6	-5.2	3 398	27	12.6	0	1 231	D	305
Lincoln	2	D	D	D	47	7.3	-14.1	2 081	22	6.5	518	616	0	D
Lyon	26	32.6	124	1.7	192	60.3	32.5	3 464	93	56.8	D	1 119	D	287
Mineral	2	D	D	D	73	27.3	25.2	4 548	46	25.7	D	1 547	112	255
Nye	11	19.4	66	1.3	177	50.8	25.7	3 503	85	47.3	35	1 191	D	360
Pershing	4	7.2	24	0.4	48	22.2	-20.1	5 420	34	21.8	324	D	0	534
Storey	1	D	D	D	50	6.5	47.7	3 441	26	5.4	0	D	0	1 480
Washoe	555	2 066.6	6 340	144.2	2 454	2 027.0	34.6	8 696	1 660	1 983.5	1 251	1 545	332	694
White Pine	17	16.5	65	1.1	111	46.6	10.7	6 051	66	44.6	D	718	221	527
Carson City city	56	80.8	276	6.7	497	352.5	62.5	9 399	301	341.4	1 064	2 013	119	732
NEW HAMPSHIRE	1 966	6 771.3	22 548	560.6	12 928	10 211.7	90.7	9 667	8 403	9 961.3	1 118	1 802	412	715
Belknap	72	146.2	638	15.1	760	553.2	86.8	11 477	498	535.6	670	2 255	380	737
Carroll	66	109.2	363	7.7	817	420.9	107.3	12 641	549	404.6	737	2 266	796	1 385
Cheshire	109	262.5	1 068	21.0	790	615.2	118.5	8 941	460	598.0	624	1 798	220	507
Coos	51	185.1	811	20.4	525	269.4	66.5	7 853	341	258.9	579	1 587	232	524
Grafton	102	178.0	789	15.6	1 103	701.7	66.8	9 841	753	681.9	759	1 930	457	860
Hillsborough	742	3 301.0	10 323	278.6	3 356	3 165.0	88.0	9 753	2 265	3 100.7	1 592	1 681	518	706
Merrimack	177	623.3	2 463	60.2	1 241	1 032.7	98.6	9 229	749	1 007.1	621	1 913	242	603
Rockingham	485	1 665.0	4 631	112.6	2 960	2 494.9	101.3	10 909	1 928	2 439.4	1 446	1 888	507	852
Strafford	104	230.0	1 018	20.7	890	701.5	79.7	7 293	569	686.6	690	1 676	162	574
Sullivan	58	71.1	444	8.5	486	257.2	63.2	6 594	291	248.5	616	1 301	209	332
NEW JERSEY	17 643	144 620.7	270 976	7 528.6	74 524	56 326.2	55.1	7 339	48 395	54 778.6	745	1 449	481	608
Atlantic	308	1 014.2	3 263	79.4	2 584	1 887.4	61.1	9 031	1 764	1 840.8	863	1 624	576	1 063
Bergen	3 718	50 935.5	61 051	1 814.0	9 391	7 904.5	53.2	9 503	6 016	7 686.9	978	1 756	735	746
Burlington	671	4 286.6	10 137	259.0	3 304	2 943.4	72.1	7 565	2 045	2 871.9	889	1 310	270	585
Camden	1 122	8 599.7	14 665	370.1	4 532	3 353.9	45.7	6 744	2 950	3 273.4	783	1 436	447	540
Cape May	97	165.2	902	15.2	1 751	876.1	51.5	9 271	1 313	852.1	616	2 000	404	1 588
Cumberland	225	767.9	2 899	60.4	1 347	932.3	54.9	6 781	837	900.2	672	1 496	287	386
Essex	1 765	11 308.6	27 436	775.5	6 606	4 361.5	30.0	5 171	4 506	4 235.4	569	1 098	498	529
Gloucester	358	1 943.2	4 642	116.3	1 921	1 626.4	61.2	7 611	1 197	1 587.9	1 157	1 402	372	472
Hudson	1 164	10 911.0	27 088	712.3	5 376	2 805.7	46.6	5 133	3 365	2 683.7	288	1 119	632	394
Hunterdon	158	324.5	935	23.8	1 206	816.4	73.4	8 246	743	786.9	255	1 680	635	578
Mercer	521	2 621.2	7 376	203.8	3 026	2 399.6	57.7	7 340	2 015	2 341.7	865	1 364	478	649
Middlesex	1 550	16 786.8	31 356	942.6	5 658	4 719.6	55.4	7 309	3 622	4 602.5	1 093	1 428	571	570
Monmouth	1 026	3 244.4	9 335	224.8	5 773	4 455.0	66.2	8 050	3 779	4 342.2	832	1 580	461	699
Morris	1 146	7 671.0	14 662	445.0	4 306	3 686.9	62.7	8 797	2 902	3 591.6	876	1 973	417	695

1. For pay period including March 12. 2. Based on the estimated population as of July 1 of the year shown.

STATE County	Retail trade, establishments with payroll, 1987 (cont'd)		Taxable service industries–establishments with payroll, 1987							Bank deposits,[2] June 1989		Savings capital,[3] September 1989	
				Receipts (Mil dol)									
					Selected kinds of business								
	Paid employees[1]	Annual payroll (Mil dol)	Number	Total	Hotels, motels and other lodg-ing places	Health services	Legal services	Paid employees	Annual payroll (Mil dol)	Total (Mil dol)	Percent change, 1988–1989	Total (Mil dol)	Percent change, 1988–1989
	161	162	163	164	165	166	167	168	169	170	171	172	173
NEBRASKA–Con.													
Saline	711	6.4	58	8.9	D	4.2	0.7	305	3.0	177	2.4	42.2	-2.6
Sarpy	4 906	39.3	374	121.6	D	19.4	D	2 988	47.3	270	-1.2	121.5	3.9
Saunders	700	5.6	54	5.4	0.0	1.8	0.9	208	1.8	158	5.1	54.2	-1.7
Scotts Bluff	3 067	25.6	274	63.5	2.2	29.8	6.3	1 706	27.0	351	4.5	402.9	-8.6
Seward	787	5.5	54	15.1	D	8.3	0.5	438	5.3	173	2.0	32.3	-6.5
Sheridan	306	2.4	38	4.5	D	1.7	0.5	128	1.5	122	3.1	0.0	NA
Sherman	94	0.6	17	1.6	D	D	0.2	44	0.4	34	10.6	0.0	NA
Sioux	23	0.2	5	0.6	D	D	D	23	0.1	12	-5.5	0.0	NA
Stanton	95	0.5	13	0.7	0.0	D	D	17	0.1	45	2.3	0.0	NA
Thayer	325	2.3	27	2.1	0.2	D	0.5	68	0.7	126	3.3	12.9	-5.0
Thomas	31	0.2	6	0.5	D	0.0	0.0	17	0.1	8	2.0	0.0	NA
Thurston	151	1.1	15	1.7	0.0	D	D	36	0.6	43	-4.1	3.0	-3.8
Valley	290	2.0	39	4.7	D	2.1	0.7	127	1.4	83	-0.6	28.6	-2.8
Washington	794	5.9	86	14.4	D	2.5	D	391	6.3	128	14.1	33.9	-10.5
Wayne	582	3.9	38	6.5	D	2.6	D	245	2.1	105	1.9	25.7	-1.4
Webster	109	0.7	21	3.5	D	1.6	0.2	114	1.2	51	-0.5	0.0	NA
Wheeler	12	0.1	0	0.0	0.0	0.0	0.0	0	0.0	9	7.4	0.0	NA
York	1 257	9.3	108	18.0	4.7	4.4	1.1	533	5.7	215	14.1	52.0	-8.6
NEVADA	81 491	923.8	8 308	10 192.2	5 417.5	1 186.5	261.9	205 709	3 405.7	6 719	12.7	3 201.2	-3.1
Churchill	954	10.4	89	25.4	4.6	6.6	1.0	725	9.3	102	5.5	55.2	3.4
Clark	49 889	556.6	4 450	6 999.6	3 874.1	828.9	156.8	135 439	2 344.4	3 928	23.5	2 003.2	-1.5
Douglas	1 450	14.7	201	545.0	345.1	7.5	D	11 636	190.1	219	5.5	58.3	-4.2
Elko	1 422	14.6	169	144.9	98.3	10.4	3.8	3 678	46.6	181	1.1	29.0	-6.8
Esmeralda	49	0.3	1	D	0.0	0.0	0.0	D	D	NA	NA	0.0	NA
Eureka	32	0.3	9	D	0.4	0.0	D	D	D	13	16.1	0.0	NA
Humboldt	683	8.6	82	33.7	18.1	1.7	0.3	1 074	7.2	73	9.0	23.1	-3.2
Lander	197	1.2	14	7.9	4.9	D	0.0	205	1.8	21	-4.8	7.4	-3.3
Lincoln	112	0.9	12	1.2	0.3	0.5	0.0	39	0.2	19	5.8	0.0	NA
Lyon	675	6.3	63	20.0	D	3.5	D	491	6.9	69	3.6	23.1	8.1
Mineral	235	2.7	14	10.9	D	D	0.0	589	4.0	20	-2.8	0.0	NA
Nye	588	5.6	53	40.3	6.8	1.7	0.0	583	9.7	83	49.7	0.0	NA
Pershing	270	2.3	17	5.6	2.8	D	0.0	110	1.0	20	4.2	6.8	-15.7
Storey	96	1.0	13	3.1	D	0.0	0.0	93	1.0	2	14.6	0.0	NA
Washoe	20 800	254.6	2 629	2 178.4	992.2	288.1	85.9	46 735	722.9	1 553	-5.6	804.5	-8.5
White Pine	601	5.5	54	12.6	3.1	3.7	D	354	4.4	71	7.6	12.5	-7.3
Carson City city	3 438	38.4	438	162.9	52.6	32.7	9.8	3 935	55.8	343	12.5	178.1	3.8
NEW HAMPSHIRE	102 082	1 121.6	8 439	3 031.2	249.3	756.1	234.4	68 191	1 136.3	15 659	7.4	1 408.9	-13.7
Belknap	4 740	60.5	429	125.3	15.8	30.6	11.6	2 986	45.8	1 817	11.2	120.1	28.3
Carroll	4 579	47.8	379	99.2	38.2	8.3	5.7	2 721	29.0	530	-2.1	18.1	25.3
Cheshire	5 426	63.9	433	138.1	5.1	48.9	7.7	3 198	48.9	843	5.1	81.8	-18.3
Coos	2 775	25.7	208	65.6	25.4	14.5	3.3	1 869	22.4	412	4.7	81.5	9.5
Grafton	7 758	81.9	667	241.3	40.4	62.6	8.5	5 740	88.4	1 420	5.0	9.5	64.4
Hillsborough	32 882	360.9	2 694	1 154.4	71.8	247.7	105.5	24 753	458.3	4 868	9.6	447.2	-32.4
Merrimack	9 667	107.0	869	309.9	11.0	75.7	39.8	6 632	118.8	1 855	7.4	47.0	-14.3
Rockingham	24 571	266.8	1 937	701.1	36.3	193.0	37.3	15 113	250.6	2 308	6.1	412.2	-6.8
Strafford	7 229	78.7	604	152.1	3.1	56.1	12.1	4 153	59.1	1 115	7.4	109.3	0.9
Sullivan	2 455	28.5	219	44.1	2.2	18.6	2.9	1 026	15.2	491	5.0	82.1	6.6
NEW JERSEY	566 214	6 467.2	59 624	32 175.1	4 059.5	5 833.2	2 252.1	595 807	11 940.6	84 178	5.9	42 862.1	2.1
Atlantic	19 402	232.5	1 599	3 559.7	3 037.2	136.7	61.2	54 123	1 070.0	1 420	5.6	1 212.8	1.7
Bergen	73 285	921.6	9 301	4 958.6	156.5	950.6	251.4	84 041	1 816.3	13 319	7.2	6 065.7	1.1
Burlington	29 071	317.8	2 374	1 146.9	41.5	231.0	46.8	23 012	439.8	2 690	11.6	1 399.7	0.1
Camden	37 402	392.9	3 560	1 884.4	76.6	417.0	156.8	37 437	730.1	3 839	5.8	1 707.1	0.7
Cape May	8 951	109.4	1 051	260.6	109.1	38.0	13.8	4 769	80.2	759	-4.6	738.8	5.7
Cumberland	8 662	94.1	761	244.2	4.9	77.0	22.6	6 746	95.5	701	5.1	895.6	2.1
Essex	48 542	540.9	6 195	3 873.0	113.0	652.0	572.1	67 150	1 391.7	12 115	-2.1	4 001.6	1.8
Gloucester	16 759	165.6	1 156	373.5	10.4	110.0	18.9	9 164	150.9	1 294	4.8	685.1	3.4
Hudson	28 538	318.5	2 858	1 224.5	44.3	212.6	90.4	24 524	455.8	5 849	1.6	2 187.2	-2.9
Hunterdon	7 688	94.1	760	362.1	7.1	45.8	24.3	5 309	127.4	1 095	4.2	270.0	-8.1
Mercer	25 324	281.4	2 590	1 484.4	64.5	293.0	95.4	29 629	600.2	3 422	5.1	1 718.2	0.6
Middlesex	49 664	530.9	4 504	2 722.4	86.9	426.8	177.7	47 958	1 076.7	6 892	18.2	3 344.5	-1.2
Monmouth	47 630	519.4	4 784	1 919.5	42.6	466.0	131.8	36 900	748.7	5 286	10.0	2 542.1	4.8
Morris	36 159	431.2	4 351	2 385.4	80.2	397.6	200.7	47 016	945.8	5 354	9.7	2 182.7	18.3

1. For the period including March 12 of the year shown. 2. Includes deposits for all insured and reporting noninsured commercial and mutual savings banks. 3. Includes savings capital for all FSLIC insured savings institutions.

STATE County	Federal funds and grants, 1989: Expenditures: Total (Mil dol)	Federal funds and grants, 1989: Expenditures: Percent change, 1988–1989	Per capita[1] (Dollars): Total	Per capita[1] (Dollars): Direct payments for individuals	Per capita[1] (Dollars): Procurement contract awards	Per capita[1] (Dollars): Salaries and wages	Per capita[1] (Dollars): Grant awards	Local government finances, 1981–1982: General revenue: Total (Mil dol)	General revenue: Intergovernmental: Total (Mil dol)	General revenue: Intergovernmental: Percent from state	General revenue: Taxes: Total (Mil dol)	Taxes: Per capita[2]: Total (Dollars)	Taxes: Per capita[2]: Property (Dollars)	Direct general expenditure: Total (Mil dol)	Direct general expenditure: Percent change, 1977–1982
	174	175	176	177	178	179	180	181	182	183	184	185	186	187	188
NEBRASKA—Con.															
Saline	82.9	5.9	6 430	1 963	3 199	209	143	17.0	3.4	89.9	6.7	505	477	14.5	15.4
Sarpy	632.7	10.6	6 327	1 068	1 136	3 854	238	91.9	28.1	74.7	25.3	278	252	86.0	53.0
Saunders	52.7	-7.1	2 802	1 695	31	267	106	16.8	4.9	80.4	8.5	455	437	15.9	30.7
Scotts Bluff	105.8	8.8	2 851	1 809	325	214	341	39.6	13.1	86.1	16.5	428	414	36.9	41.7
Seward	43.6	-10.1	2 711	1 438	22	143	185	14.2	3.8	83.6	8.2	528	515	13.5	42.0
Sheridan	21.4	-12.8	2 926	1 909	17	170	115	10.4	2.7	71.5	3.3	433	419	10.8	79.1
Sherman	17.2	-14.7	4 519	2 016	64	209	524	4.1	1.4	86.7	2.1	518	500	4.1	43.3
Sioux	4.7	28.2	2 954	892	10	157	576	1.6	0.6	74.7	0.8	453	437	1.4	42.7
Stanton	15.0	-12.1	2 233	904	9	80	139	4.1	1.2	87.1	1.4	222	210	4.2	79.3
Thayer	32.4	-15.3	4 634	2 224	30	232	201	9.5	2.2	91.3	6.0	784	725	8.9	24.3
Thomas	2.4	5.8	2 718	1 987	43	463	24	1.1	0.3	77.4	0.6	613	599	1.2	89.4
Thurston	38.2	-2.8	5 379	1 549	74	618	2 020	7.9	4.2	64.0	2.8	384	372	7.3	17.2
Valley	21.0	-18.7	3 818	1 877	108	353	281	7.8	1.5	90.2	2.8	493	479	8.3	65.2
Washington	36.3	4.7	2 243	1 426	12	112	276	12.9	4.0	92.8	6.5	414	405	12.2	20.5
Wayne	24.5	-6.6	2 500	1 382	15	190	103	7.3	2.1	90.3	3.7	376	354	7.5	48.6
Webster	19.7	-11.8	4 370	2 354	29	249	174	6.8	1.4	86.1	2.8	578	556	6.0	39.2
Wheeler	7.0	-15.2	7 005	1 382	32	224	271	1.6	0.5	70.0	0.9	851	841	1.8	22.7
York	51.3	-23.2	3 442	1 648	20	150	86	14.6	3.3	90.1	8.8	590	564	14.4	3.2
NEVADA	3 955.0	13.4	X	1 738	849	537	412	1 206.4	544.4	88.4	271.6	309	186	1 156.2	101.1
Churchill	121.2	26.9	6 968	1 964	3 076	1 641	265	20.0	8.8	90.4	1.7	124	88	19.4	110.1
Clark	2 544.6	13.4	3 805	1 716	1 231	616	235	676.3	299.0	89.1	157.9	310	178	615.1	99.1
Douglas	39.6	1.5	1 507	1 306	41	82	73	34.2	11.5	94.7	13.7	677	475	31.9	153.3
Elko	51.8	-8.0	1 800	858	120	360	343	25.0	16.7	81.1	4.3	222	148	25.3	114.5
Esmeralda	3.0	47.7	2 490	2 031	67	192	185	2.2	1.5	84.3	0.4	353	337	1.8	90.8
Eureka	1.9	-1.9	1 249	857	61	83	-185	3.0	2.1	78.0	0.6	419	403	3.4	86.0
Humboldt	21.0	17.0	1 690	938	52	295	224	14.5	7.3	90.2	3.0	268	159	14.8	78.8
Lander	7.9	3.7	1 543	737	44	481	228	6.9	4.1	91.0	1.3	285	236	7.0	93.6
Lincoln	10.7	24.6	2 978	2 095	23	423	409	6.9	4.3	92.6	0.7	184	176	6.3	110.5
Lyon	48.1	-10.6	2 492	2 057	169	94	137	16.2	10.4	94.5	2.7	179	148	17.2	126.2
Mineral	52.4	19.8	8 459	2 528	4 759	782	379	8.9	4.9	83.7	1.3	212	180	9.9	96.8
Nye	40.9	36.4	2 554	1 477	580	322	170	16.9	9.5	85.5	4.0	308	248	21.2	156.0
Pershing	7.5	-8.1	1 630	1 165	20	98	317	5.3	2.8	87.7	0.9	234	209	5.2	63.8
Storey	2.8	-6.4	1 382	1 026	8	63	281	2.7	1.9	82.4	0.6	354	246	3.2	198.0
Washoe	567.2	0.8	2 271	1 528	50	408	275	319.3	134.5	85.9	71.7	345	203	323.4	97.8
White Pine	21.8	8.0	2 689	1 840	66	497	251	11.0	6.8	91.2	1.1	134	115	11.2	67.5
Carson City city	176.0	12.3	4 432	1 702	133	422	2 170	37.1	18.4	96.0	5.6	163	108	40.0	108.5
NEW HAMPSHIRE	3 402.3	6.1	X	1 577	472	603	392	809.8	179.1	69.2	533.7	563	555	821.6	65.0
Belknap	120.3	8.7	2 382	1 860	117	186	212	40.7	6.4	76.4	29.8	678	668	40.4	73.5
Carroll	88.6	13.2	2 433	1 984	16	130	293	29.3	4.6	77.9	21.8	756	749	27.5	97.3
Cheshire	143.0	4.7	2 003	1 589	41	115	250	55.0	12.0	77.3	37.9	597	590	54.8	62.2
Coos	93.9	0.2	2 707	2 132	48	146	362	36.4	12.4	68.8	20.7	601	595	30.5	46.2
Grafton	205.8	-2.3	2 782	1 659	220	330	563	61.9	12.8	72.1	42.1	628	620	60.0	70.0
Hillsborough	1 093.0	6.8	3 228	1 372	1 192	435	215	241.7	51.1	68.9	156.6	549	541	258.5	55.4
Merrimack	316.9	2.2	2 668	1 563	35	237	825	96.7	31.8	47.4	53.1	527	519	100.2	79.2
Rockingham	857.7	3.1	3 546	1 303	327	1 737	168	160.5	26.5	76.6	116.3	587	580	161.9	78.8
Strafford	227.2	11.3	2 265	1 654	68	162	374	59.7	14.6	86.2	37.6	422	415	60.4	41.7
Sullivan	86.6	-0.6	2 149	1 740	47	104	245	28.0	6.9	75.0	17.8	476	470	27.4	79.5
NEW JERSEY	26 044.1	7.8	X	1 900	535	429	473	9 550.1	3 888.1	88.8	4 390.6	591	578	9 407.0	46.3
Atlantic	614.3	3.1	2 850	1 989	64	476	297	314.2	116.8	88.6	149.9	767	716	310.0	72.7
Bergen	2 278.6	3.9	2 772	1 903	549	193	117	980.7	228.9	91.4	622.5	739	730	939.3	37.5
Burlington	2 023.9	-1.5	5 038	1 555	1 732	1 418	322	378.5	169.2	91.0	157.2	423	416	378.6	50.5
Camden	1 414.1	0.2	2 801	1 827	374	277	308	671.2	298.8	89.3	244.8	512	505	670.5	48.0
Cape May	308.0	6.6	3 155	2 427	44	386	292	131.1	38.1	73.2	70.6	824	786	130.5	57.6
Cumberland	354.3	-0.6	2 549	1 863	106	125	429	163.5	95.2	93.5	49.9	374	367	163.8	50.2
Essex	3 027.0	4.2	3 633	1 802	754	433	631	1 351.1	711.0	89.4	509.4	606	575	1 313.8	32.0
Gloucester	468.8	-5.6	2 113	1 457	364	99	173	211.5	87.8	95.9	88.5	433	424	201.1	53.6
Hudson	1 600.8	5.0	2 993	1 743	295	451	489	800.9	430.3	87.7	258.9	462	456	781.6	54.9
Hunterdon	153.7	5.9	1 504	1 207	70	126	83	110.2	33.3	89.8	63.5	712	701	98.3	58.2
Mercer	1 852.2	23.7	5 546	1 788	1 087	415	2 242	443.9	201.4	84.4	183.3	593	584	460.1	65.1
Middlesex	1 709.5	17.5	2 602	1 488	613	240	250	727.6	265.8	93.3	363.0	601	593	749.2	43.8
Monmouth	1 964.0	2.6	3 474	1 763	628	881	191	638.5	246.6	90.1	298.6	584	572	610.2	41.4
Morris	1 094.6	-9.5	2 608	1 368	507	598	127	505.3	137.7	88.8	299.4	728	711	505.3	48.1

1. Based on the estimated population as of July 1 of the year shown. 2. Based on the estimated population as of July 1, 1982.

STATE County	Local government finances, 1981–1982 (cont'd)								State and local government employment, 1989		Federal government civilian employment 1989		Elections, 1988[3]	
	Direct general expenditure (cont'd)						Debt outstanding							
		Percent of total for–												
	Per capita[1] (Dollars)	Education	Health & hospitals	Police protection	Public welfare	Highways	Total (Mil dol)	Per capita[1] (Dollars)	Total	Rate[2]	Total	Earnings ($1,000)	Total vote cast for president	Vote for lead party (Percent)
	189	190	191	192	193	194	195	196	197	198	199	200	201	202
NEBRASKA—Con.														
Saline	1 092	48.0	13.9	3.6	7.2	9.3	11.1	832	973	754.3	87	2 266	5 500	D—56.7
Sarpy	945	48.4	14.1	3.1	0.9	5.3	121.6	1 336	3 135	313.5	2 791	70 209	31 261	R—64.6
Saunders	854	47.6	7.7	3.0	5.3	17.1	9.9	532	979	520.7	120	2 963	8 033	R—55.4
Scotts Bluff	960	56.9	0.3	4.4	3.1	7.9	21.7	565	2 464	664.2	184	5 599	13 142	R—65.4
Seward	870	56.1	0.0	4.0	0.6	16.7	11.4	737	891	553.4	70	1 626	6 199	R—55.9
Sheridan	1 400	36.8	26.7	3.4	1.2	11.8	10.4	1 347	645	883.6	34	810	2 898	R—77.7
Sherman	1 011	59.6	0.2	2.1	1.7	19.3	1.6	395	337	886.8	28	647	1 770	R—51.6
Sioux	796	50.6	0.0	2.7	1.4	24.7	0.1	80	90	562.5	NA	139	767	R—74.1
Stanton	639	36.7	0.0	2.6	12.3	20.9	4.2	648	259	386.6	28	599	2 356	R—72.5
Thayer	1 173	56.1	0.6	3.5	0.8	14.8	7.1	931	565	807.1	54	1 145	3 326	R—59.6
Thomas	1 227	54.4	0.0	2.0	1.1	14.7	0.2	242	76	844.4	38	636	466	R—82.2
Thurston	999	65.5	0.0	4.3	3.6	13.4	1.4	190	474	667.6	167	4 305	2 340	D—52.4
Valley	1 461	33.6	15.2	2.0	1.2	19.9	8.8	1 548	548	996.4	160	3 276	2 502	R—64.1
Washington	777	60.3	0.3	4.3	1.4	14.1	12.2	777	1 189	734.0	46	1 282	7 155	R—63.8
Wayne	764	55.3	0.0	3.4	0.5	20.7	4.7	476	843	860.2	54	1 349	3 614	R—68.4
Webster	1 256	48.4	15.5	2.1	0.9	14.7	6.9	1 442	312	693.3	45	1 008	2 226	R—59.0
Wheeler	1 643	48.9	0.0	2.3	0.6	16.5	0.6	548	78	780.0	29	892	455	R—67.9
York	968	51.8	0.8	3.3	0.7	16.6	12.6	847	995	667.8	70	1 707	6 522	R—72.7
NEVADA	1 317	33.8	12.5	5.8	1.2	5.4	940.0	1 071	59 591	536.6	11 807	384 732	350 067	R—58.9
Churchill	1 389	33.9	13.3	5.1	0.9	4.2	4.3	306	964	554.0	454	10 061	6 283	R—72.9
Clark	1 207	34.2	10.9	4.3	1.3	4.8	563.9	1 106	30 079	449.7	6 672	219 139	191 779	R—56.4
Douglas	1 571	32.1	0.6	7.9	0.3	5.1	37.4	1 841	1 161	441.4	70	2 086	10 555	R—67.0
Elko	1 297	41.3	0.8	6.9	1.0	5.8	7.4	381	1 984	688.9	359	9 923	8 372	R—68.3
Esmeralda	1 533	39.2	1.3	11.5	0.1	10.0	0.5	383	102	850.0	NA	119	552	R—68.8
Eureka	2 405	38.8	2.6	6.4	0.1	16.5	0.5	366	150	1 000.0	NA	159	582	R—71.0
Humboldt	1 333	43.8	12.8	5.9	0.2	6.8	7.9	713	787	634.7	139	3 956	3 576	R—66.5
Lander	1 480	44.3	11.2	7.2	1.6	9.3	3.7	782	353	692.2	87	2 665	1 714	R—70.8
Lincoln	1 691	52.0	14.4	7.1	0.7	7.3	4.6	1 234	464	1 288.9	44	1 111	1 564	R—66.2
Lyon	1 163	49.3	9.0	6.7	0.4	6.7	14.1	954	818	423.8	44	1 310	6 987	R—62.8
Mineral	1 681	32.7	14.2	4.6	0.7	7.6	5.0	846	409	659.7	113	3 683	2 602	R—56.9
Nye	1 619	56.6	7.5	7.0	0.5	6.0	9.4	717	866	541.2	188	6 395	5 603	R—64.6
Pershing	1 415	35.4	18.5	7.0	1.5	6.6	4.9	1 325	301	654.3	12	341	1 396	R—62.1
Storey	1 853	41.3	5.0	9.0	0.0	7.3	0.9	532	120	600.0	NA	71	1 155	R—56.4
Washoe	1 556	28.2	17.3	8.0	1.4	6.1	241.2	1 161	13 877	555.5	2 975	104 034	88 728	R—59.3
White Pine	1 299	43.0	15.9	7.8	1.0	5.9	0.2	24	718	886.4	155	4 302	3 328	R—53.3
Carson City city	1 156	39.2	19.1	5.3	0.1	4.3	34.2	987	6 438	1 621.7	484	15 377	15 291	R—63.4
NEW HAMPSHIRE	867	45.7	0.5	4.9	5.5	7.8	463.4	489	61 528	555.8	8 639	275 760	451 074	R—62.4
Belknap	918	47.5	0.5	6.2	6.4	9.1	15.0	340	3 377	668.7	254	7 616	21 280	R—67.9
Carroll	954	48.7	0.9	5.7	6.6	10.8	11.5	398	1 755	482.1	174	4 385	18 344	R—70.8
Cheshire	863	53.3	0.4	3.7	6.6	8.7	22.6	357	3 482	487.7	201	5 784	27 512	R—54.5
Coos	888	46.9	0.7	4.3	12.2	9.1	16.5	480	2 173	626.2	144	3 902	13 900	R—63.0
Grafton	894	52.9	0.4	4.5	4.2	9.0	24.8	370	4 947	668.5	762	22 907	30 699	R—62.0
Hillsborough	907	42.4	0.5	5.1	3.3	8.1	159.2	559	12 407	366.4	3 706	135 018	135 778	R—65.0
Merrimack	994	37.7	0.3	4.0	7.0	5.7	73.7	731	11 945	1 005.5	729	22 293	48 686	R—60.7
Rockingham	818	50.9	0.4	5.2	4.3	6.8	66.9	338	8 962	370.5	2 160	58 265	101 747	R—62.9
Strafford	678	45.5	0.4	5.2	7.9	6.9	54.4	611	9 874	984.4	403	12 730	37 845	R—54.5
Sullivan	734	38.9	0.6	4.9	11.8	9.9	18.8	504	2 606	646.7	106	2 860	15 283	R—57.8
NEW JERSEY	1 266	43.9	3.4	5.7	8.0	4.5	7 305.8	983	468 025	604.7	79 566	2 698 269	3 099 553	R—56.2
Atlantic	1 586	39.5	1.2	6.6	8.1	4.2	382.5	1 958	16 056	745.1	2 565	99 721	79 442	R—56.3
Bergen	1 114	51.1	4.6	6.9	2.3	4.3	611.0	725	38 169	464.3	3 976	130 146	389 933	R—58.2
Burlington	1 018	55.7	2.0	4.4	6.0	7.3	242.6	652	19 671	489.7	6 287	176 014	149 949	R—58.3
Camden	1 401	38.9	3.2	4.4	10.5	6.7	689.6	1 441	27 874	552.1	3 420	116 146	192 515	R—52.0
Cape May	1 522	31.3	1.5	7.0	2.5	8.2	194.6	2 271	7 751	794.2	347	10 870	44 117	R—65.1
Cumberland	1 225	48.7	1.2	4.2	16.9	4.0	122.7	918	9 642	693.7	491	15 732	48 349	R—53.8
Essex	1 562	36.3	4.4	6.3	14.4	2.2	644.8	767	62 732	752.9	10 981	385 972	276 967	D—56.4
Gloucester	984	52.1	0.9	5.3	6.3	4.7	186.8	914	13 242	597.0	530	16 435	88 117	R—58.7
Hudson	1 395	29.8	10.2	6.8	11.9	1.5	443.4	792	30 993	579.5	11 676	382 692	184 463	D—53.4
Hunterdon	1 103	56.2	1.2	3.8	2.2	10.0	50.5	566	6 293	615.8	309	8 874	46 182	R—69.1
Mercer	1 489	39.9	1.7	4.9	9.8	4.3	414.0	1 339	46 580	1 394.6	3 594	120 546	135 345	D—50.8
Middlesex	1 241	46.3	3.8	5.8	5.4	4.5	702.1	1 163	45 155	687.2	3 364	109 737	264 119	R—54.3
Monmouth	1 194	49.2	1.3	5.5	8.0	4.7	498.7	976	27 844	492.5	11 998	474 539	240 957	R—61.1
Morris	1 229	54.3	1.6	5.7	3.4	5.7	450.5	1 095	22 466	535.3	7 488	236 463	187 249	R—68.0

1. Based on the estimated population as of July 1, 1982. 2. Per 10,000 resident population estimated as of July 1 of the year shown. 3. Data subject to copyright.

STATE–County code	MSA/ CMSA/ NECMA code[1]	STATE County	Land Area,[2] 1990 (Sq. Km.)	Population, 1990											
							Race						Age of population Percent		
				Total persons	Rank	Per square kilometer	White	Black	Am. Indian, Eskimo, Aleut	Asian & Pacific Islander	Other race	Hispanic[3]	Under 5 years	5 to 14 years	15 to 24 years
			1	2	3	4	5	6	7	8	9	10	11	12	13
		NEW JERSEY—Con.													
34 029	5602	Ocean	1 648	433 203	115	262.9	412 709	12 035	615	3 874	3 970	13 950	6.7	12.4	11.5
34 031	5602	Passaic	479	453 060	109	945.8	325 530	66 077	1 161	11 968	48 324	98 092	7.3	12.8	15.1
34 033	6162	Salem	875	65 294	672	74.6	54 394	9 567	218	379	736	1 436	6.6	14.6	13.4
34 035	5602	Somerset	789	240 279	207	304.5	211 384	14 824	243	10 548	3 280	10 187	7.0	11.5	12.0
34 037	5602	Sussex	1 350	130 943	354	97.0	127 831	1 242	196	1 222	452	2 911	8.3	15.2	12.6
34 039	5602	Union	268	493 819	99	1 842.6	367 416	92 807	880	13 726	18 990	67 797	6.6	11.8	13.2
34 041	0240	Warren	927	91 607	501	98.8	89 028	1 302	114	747	416	1 784	7.6	13.4	12.7
35 000	...	NEW MEXICO	314 334	1 515 069	X	4.8	1 146 028	30 210	134 355	14 124	190 352	579 224	8.3	16.7	14.5
35 001	0200	Bernalillo	3 020	480 577	102	159.1	369 445	13 199	16 296	7 386	74 251	178 310	7.7	14.5	14.3
35 003	...	Catron	17 944	2 563	3 020	0.1	2 508	7	21	2	25	728	6.2	15.3	11.0
35 005	...	Chaves	15 725	57 849	751	3.7	47 790	1 197	375	282	8 205	21 271	8.2	17.5	14.5
35 006	...	Cibola	11 757	23 794	1 499	2.0	13 899	191	9 155	81	468	8 109	8.9	19.8	14.6
35 007	...	Colfax	9 730	12 925	2 144	1.3	10 697	44	95	23	2 066	6 190	7.0	15.7	13.1
35 009	...	Curry	3 642	42 207	954	11.6	31 904	2 909	279	815	6 300	10 015	9.1	17.1	16.0
35 011	...	De Baca	6 022	2 252	3 048	0.4	2 107	2	42	0	101	736	6.3	15.1	9.5
35 013	4100	Dona Ana	9 861	135 510	346	13.7	123 434	2 172	1 009	1 164	7 731	76 448	8.6	17.0	19.2
35 015	...	Eddy	10 832	48 605	861	4.5	39 597	826	249	201	7 732	17 145	7.8	17.7	12.6
35 017	...	Grant	10 272	27 676	1 364	2.7	25 745	137	229	69	1 496	14 061	7.5	17.8	14.3
35 019	...	Guadalupe	7 849	4 156	2 901	0.5	3 076	12	21	28	1 019	3 505	7.6	18.1	13.0
35 021	...	Harding	5 505	987	3 114	0.2	787	2	5	1	192	461	6.7	16.1	11.8
35 023	...	Hidalgo	8 925	5 958	2 764	0.7	5 457	11	20	37	433	2 984	8.0	19.2	14.7
35 025	...	Lea	11 379	55 765	777	4.9	45 817	2 611	355	197	6 785	16 598	8.7	19.4	14.0
35 027	...	Lincoln	12 513	12 219	2 200	1.0	11 175	65	132	28	819	3 427	6.6	14.7	10.8
35 028	7490	Los Alamos	283	18 115	1 783	64.0	17 064	96	126	428	401	2 008	6.2	15.1	9.7
35 029	...	Luna	7 680	18 110	1 784	2.4	16 297	253	107	53	1 400	8 628	7.2	16.9	12.3
35 031	...	McKinley	14 113	60 686	716	4.3	13 295	295	43 570	245	3 281	7 764	11.7	21.3	16.3
35 033	...	Mora	5 002	4 264	2 894	0.9	2 423	2	21	3	1 815	3 623	6.9	17.6	13.3
35 035	...	Otero	17 164	51 928	814	3.0	41 313	2 755	2 984	966	3 910	12 380	9.5	16.7	15.6
35 037	...	Quay	7 447	10 823	2 309	1.5	8 031	151	109	39	2 493	4 060	6.8	15.6	12.1
35 039	...	Rio Arriba	15 172	34 365	1 156	2.3	24 323	138	5 225	58	4 621	24 955	9.2	18.0	14.8
35 041	...	Roosevelt	6 342	16 702	1 868	2.6	13 317	221	140	99	2 925	4 548	7.4	15.4	21.7
35 043	...	Sandoval	9 608	63 319	689	6.6	43 440	939	12 491	503	5 946	17 372	9.9	17.9	11.9
35 045	...	San Juan	14 282	91 605	502	6.4	51 806	429	33 646	215	5 509	12 009	9.7	21.4	14.0
35 047	...	San Miguel	12 218	25 743	1 430	2.1	16 392	170	222	151	8 808	20 491	8.1	17.3	15.9
35 049	7490	Santa Fe	4 945	98 928	465	20.0	79 390	615	2 822	513	15 588	48 939	7.3	14.7	12.7
35 051	...	Sierra	10 828	9 912	2 395	0.9	9 254	39	77	12	530	2 379	5.6	11.0	8.5
35 053	...	Socorro	17 216	14 764	2 002	0.9	11 423	114	1 491	212	1 524	7 057	8.2	17.3	16.4
35 055	...	Taos	5 707	23 118	1 532	4.1	16 868	63	1 571	86	4 530	15 008	7.6	16.8	12.7
35 057	...	Torrance	8 664	10 285	2 360	1.2	8 951	43	128	23	1 140	3 892	7.8	18.9	12.0
35 059	...	Union	9 920	4 124	2 905	0.4	3 966	2	13	4	139	1 390	7.5	16.1	10.6
35 061	...	Valencia	2 765	45 235	910	16.4	35 037	500	1 329	200	8 169	22 733	8.4	17.7	13.1
36 000	...	NEW YORK	122 310	17 990 455	X	147.1	13 385 255	2 859 055	62 651	693 760	989 734	2 214 026	7.0	12.9	14.7
36 001	0160	Albany	1 357	292 594	166	215.6	260 596	24 702	531	4 974	1 791	5 311	6.3	11.7	16.9
36 003	...	Allegany	2 668	50 470	835	18.9	49 670	305	103	304	88	313	6.9	14.5	21.0
36 005	5602	Bronx	109	1 203 789	24	11 043.9	430 077	449 399	6 069	35 562	282 682	523 111	8.5	14.8	15.9
36 007	0960	Broome	1 831	212 160	235	115.9	202 949	4 333	355	3 677	846	2 478	6.8	12.5	15.4
36 009	...	Cattaraugus	3 393	84 234	542	24.8	81 091	757	1 866	327	193	534	7.5	15.6	15.3
36 011	...	Cayuga	1 796	82 313	551	45.8	78 320	2 995	275	331	392	1 202	7.4	14.8	14.0
36 013	3610	Chautauqua	2 751	141 895	336	51.6	136 311	2 405	558	545	2 076	4 055	6.9	14.3	15.1
36 015	2335	Chemung	1 057	95 195	486	90.1	88 370	5 245	211	690	679	1 441	7.1	14.2	14.2
36 017	...	Chenango	2 317	51 768	816	22.3	50 976	384	145	165	98	476	7.5	15.8	12.8
36 019	...	Clinton	2 692	85 969	533	31.9	80 595	3 744	209	682	739	2 105	7.5	13.6	18.9
36 021	...	Columbia	1 647	62 982	692	38.2	59 889	2 441	109	251	292	1 021	7.0	13.3	12.5
36 023	...	Cortland	1 294	48 963	856	37.8	48 132	348	135	222	126	447	7.1	13.7	21.0
36 025	...	Delaware	3 746	47 225	888	12.6	46 307	476	116	184	142	536	6.8	14.2	14.9
36 027	6460	Dutchess	2 076	259 462	194	125.0	229 194	21 788	374	5 826	2 280	9 765	7.1	13.0	14.9
36 029	1282	Erie	2 706	968 532	32	357.9	831 903	109 852	5 600	10 220	10 957	22 249	6.9	12.7	14.4
36 031	...	Essex	4 654	37 152	1 069	8.0	35 682	1 051	94	146	179	748	6.9	13.5	12.8
36 033	...	Franklin	4 226	46 540	896	11.0	41 897	1 741	2 348	127	427	1 123	6.9	14.6	14.8
36 035	...	Fulton	1 285	54 191	793	42.2	53 121	647	100	228	95	411	6.7	14.7	13.5
36 037	...	Genesee	1 280	60 060	723	46.9	57 937	1 065	683	211	164	451	7.5	14.9	13.9
36 039	0160	Greene	1 678	44 739	915	26.7	41 603	2 170	133	184	649	1 522	6.5	12.8	13.6
36 041	...	Hamilton	4 457	5 279	2 823	1.2	5 247	12	10	6	4	31	4.8	12.8	11.3
36 043	8680	Herkimer	3 657	65 797	666	18.0	65 285	188	109	139	76	370	6.8	14.4	13.9

1. MSA = Metropolitan Statistical Area. CMSA = Consolidated MSA. NECMA = New England county metropolitan area. PMSA = Primary MSA. See Appendix A for explanation of these concepts. See Appendix B for list of metropolitan areas identified by type, with component counties. 2. Dry land or land partially or temporarily covered by water. 3. Hispanic persons may be of any race.

STATE County	Population, 1990 (cont'd): Age of population (cont'd) Percent: 25 to 34 years	35 to 44 years	45 to 54 years	55 to 64 years	65 to 74 years	75 years and over	Percent female	Population–Change and components of change: Change 1980–1990: Number	Percent	Components of change, 1980–1986: Total persons, 1986	Total persons, 1980	Net change: Number	Percent	Natural increase: Births	Deaths
	14	15	16	17	18	19	20	21	22	23	24	25	26	27	28
NEW JERSEY—Con.															
Ocean	14.5	13.6	9.0	9.1	12.9	10.3	52.9	87 165	25.2	392 600	346 038	46 600	13.5	29 700	29 600
Passaic	17.7	14.7	10.6	9.0	7.4	5.5	51.8	5 475	1.2	460 900	447 585	13 300	3.0	42 000	26 400
Salem	15.2	15.2	10.9	9.4	8.6	6.0	51.8	618	1.0	65 400	64 676	700	1.1	5 700	3 900
Somerset	20.0	17.0	12.0	9.7	6.6	4.2	50.9	37 150	18.3	215 700	203 129	12 500	6.2	15 500	9 400
Sussex	17.9	18.6	11.6	6.7	5.0	3.9	50.4	14 824	12.8	123 700	116 119	7 600	6.5	11 300	5 100
Union	17.2	14.9	11.1	10.2	8.9	6.1	52.1	-10 275	-2.0	504 000	504 094	-100	0.0	38 600	30 600
Warren	17.4	16.1	10.8	8.8	7.7	5.6	51.7	7 178	8.5	86 800	84 429	2 300	2.8	7 200	5 000
NEW MEXICO	16.9	15.0	9.7	8.0	6.4	4.3	50.8	212 069	16.3	1 479 000	1 303 000	176 000	13.5	170 000	58 000
Bernalillo	18.7	16.2	10.1	7.9	6.4	4.1	51.2	60 315	14.4	474 400	420 262	54 100	12.9	48 100	17 500
Catron	12.5	16.0	12.4	11.3	9.4	5.9	47.4	-157	-5.8	2 700	2 720	0	-0.8	200	200
Chaves	14.6	13.1	8.9	8.7	8.2	6.4	50.8	6 746	13.2	56 700	51 103	5 600	10.9	6 600	3 200
Cibola	16.2	13.9	9.8	8.3	5.2	3.2	51.0	-6 553	-21.6	24 800	30 347	-5 600	-18.3	3 800	800
Colfax	13.5	14.2	10.4	9.9	9.1	7.2	49.9	-742	-5.4	14 300	13 667	600	4.4	1 500	700
Curry	18.3	12.8	8.5	7.3	6.0	4.8	50.9	188	0.4	43 400	42 019	1 300	3.2	5 800	1 900
De Baca	12.4	11.4	10.8	12.0	11.4	11.1	51.0	-202	-8.2	2 400	2 454	-100	-3.0	200	200
Dona Ana	16.9	13.3	8.6	7.5	5.5	3.3	50.3	39 170	40.7	123 000	96 340	26 600	27.6	12 900	3 500
Eddy	14.4	13.9	9.2	9.1	8.4	6.8	51.0	750	1.6	52 400	47 855	4 600	9.6	6 100	2 700
Grant	12.8	13.8	10.2	9.4	8.4	5.7	50.9	1 472	5.6	27 400	26 204	1 200	4.5	3 300	1 100
Guadalupe	15.8	12.3	10.4	9.1	6.8	6.9	49.8	-340	-7.6	4 400	4 496	-100	-2.6	500	200
Harding	10.5	13.8	9.1	11.1	11.1	9.7	48.5	-103	-9.4	1 000	1 090	-100	-5.0	100	100
Hidalgo	14.9	13.3	9.9	8.5	6.5	5.0	49.3	-91	-1.5	6 100	6 049	0	0.3	800	300
Lea	16.0	13.6	9.0	8.7	6.4	4.2	50.6	-228	-0.4	64 900	55 993	8 900	15.9	9 100	2 600
Lincoln	14.3	15.4	11.4	11.1	9.8	5.8	50.7	1 222	11.1	13 600	10 997	2 600	23.5	1 500	600
Los Alamos	14.1	18.1	16.7	10.9	6.8	2.4	49.3	516	2.9	18 600	17 599	1 000	5.8	1 300	400
Luna	11.7	11.2	9.4	11.2	12.2	8.0	51.9	2 525	16.2	17 800	15 585	2 200	14.0	1 900	1 200
McKinley	16.8	13.1	8.3	6.0	3.7	2.6	51.7	4 150	7.3	65 800	56 536	9 200	16.3	10 500	2 200
Mora	14.0	13.8	9.7	10.0	8.0	6.7	50.0	59	1.4	4 600	4 205	400	8.3	500	200
Otero	18.5	13.5	8.9	8.0	5.8	3.3	49.4	7 263	16.3	50 200	44 665	5 600	12.5	6 700	1 700
Quay	12.7	14.1	11.5	10.4	9.3	7.4	51.8	246	2.3	11 600	10 577	1 100	10.0	1 100	800
Rio Arriba	16.3	14.5	9.6	7.8	5.7	4.0	50.4	5 083	17.4	33 200	29 282	3 900	13.4	4 400	1 500
Roosevelt	14.0	11.5	8.6	7.9	7.5	6.1	51.3	1 007	6.4	16 500	15 695	800	5.0	1 800	800
Sandoval	18.8	16.1	8.6	6.7	6.4	3.7	50.9	28 919	84.1	47 700	34 400	13 300	38.7	5 100	1 600
San Juan	16.7	14.6	9.0	7.0	4.8	2.9	50.9	10 172	12.5	92 000	81 433	10 500	12.9	14 500	2 800
San Miguel	16.0	13.9	9.7	7.5	6.4	5.2	50.4	2 992	13.2	25 300	22 751	2 500	11.2	3 000	1 200
Santa Fe	16.5	19.1	11.5	8.0	6.1	4.0	51.0	23 409	31.0	87 600	75 519	12 000	15.9	8 400	3 100
Sierra	9.7	9.4	9.8	14.5	17.4	14.1	50.9	1 458	17.2	9 600	8 454	1 200	13.7	600	1 000
Socorro	16.1	13.9	9.9	7.7	6.2	4.2	49.2	2 198	17.5	14 000	12 566	1 400	11.1	1 600	500
Taos	14.6	17.3	11.2	8.6	6.3	4.7	51.0	3 662	18.8	22 000	19 456	2 500	12.8	2 800	900
Torrance	15.0	15.9	10.5	8.5	6.8	4.6	49.8	2 794	37.3	9 000	7 491	1 500	20.6	800	400
Union	13.1	12.9	11.1	10.7	9.5	8.5	51.2	-601	-12.7	5 100	4 725	400	7.5	500	300
Valencia	17.1	15.5	10.0	8.1	6.3	3.8	49.8	14 467	47.0	37 700	30 768	7 000	22.6	3 900	1 500
NEW YORK	17.4	15.1	10.6	9.1	7.5	5.6	52.1	432 455	2.5	17 772 000	17 558 000	214 000	1.2	1 554 000	1 059 000
Albany	16.9	15.3	9.5	8.8	8.1	6.6	52.6	6 685	2.3	283 400	285 909	-2 500	-0.9	22 600	18 300
Allegany	12.9	13.0	9.5	8.9	7.2	6.2	50.4	-1 272	-2.5	50 500	51 742	-1 200	-2.4	4 400	2 700
Bronx	17.7	13.7	9.8	7.9	6.2	5.4	53.9	34 817	3.0	1 193 600	1 168 972	24 700	2.1	127 900	78 600
Broome	16.7	14.0	10.1	9.4	8.5	6.5	51.8	-1 488	-0.7	210 800	213 648	-2 900	-1.3	18 000	12 800
Cattaraugus	14.4	14.2	9.7	9.3	8.1	6.0	51.5	-1 463	-1.7	85 300	85 697	-400	-0.4	8 400	5 500
Cayuga	17.1	14.7	9.4	8.4	8.0	6.0	50.0	2 419	3.0	79 900	79 894	0	0.1	7 300	4 800
Chautauqua	14.7	13.9	9.8	9.5	8.5	7.2	51.8	-5 030	-3.4	143 100	146 925	-3 800	-2.6	12 900	9 600
Chemung	15.6	14.5	10.0	9.3	8.8	6.3	51.4	-2 461	-2.5	90 500	97 656	-7 100	-7.3	8 500	6 000
Chenango	15.7	14.8	10.7	8.7	7.8	6.1	51.0	2 424	4.9	50 000	49 344	600	1.3	4 600	3 000
Clinton	19.6	14.1	9.1	7.6	5.4	4.2	48.8	5 219	6.5	81 200	80 750	500	0.6	8 300	3 600
Columbia	14.8	15.6	11.1	9.4	9.0	7.4	50.8	3 495	5.9	60 700	59 487	1 200	2.0	4 700	4 200
Cortland	15.2	13.7	9.4	7.7	6.7	5.4	52.4	143	0.3	47 400	48 820	-1 400	-2.9	4 200	2 600
Delaware	13.3	13.9	10.7	10.0	9.3	7.1	50.8	401	0.9	47 100	46 824	200	0.5	3 800	3 300
Dutchess	17.9	16.1	11.1	8.5	6.4	5.0	49.7	14 407	5.9	256 800	245 055	11 700	4.8	19 100	12 200
Erie	16.5	14.3	10.0	9.9	9.0	6.2	52.4	-46 940	-4.6	964 700	1 015 472	-50 700	-5.0	83 100	64 800
Essex	16.8	15.1	10.7	9.5	8.3	6.4	48.7	976	2.7	36 300	36 176	100	0.4	3 000	2 500
Franklin	17.9	14.6	9.8	8.7	7.4	5.5	48.4	1 611	3.6	43 800	44 929	-1 100	-2.5	4 100	3 000
Fulton	14.8	14.4	10.1	9.3	9.2	7.3	51.9	-962	-1.7	54 600	55 153	-600	-1.0	4 600	3 700
Genesee	16.5	14.3	10.3	8.9	7.7	5.9	51.3	660	1.1	58 800	59 400	-600	-1.0	5 800	3 300
Greene	16.2	14.7	10.5	9.7	8.7	7.2	49.2	3 878	9.5	42 100	40 861	1 300	3.1	3 100	3 100
Hamilton	13.4	14.7	12.5	13.4	10.7	6.4	49.7	245	4.9	5 000	5 034	-100	-1.3	400	400
Herkimer	14.4	14.2	10.3	9.1	9.8	7.1	51.7	-917	-1.4	66 900	66 714	200	0.3	5 700	4 500

STATE County	Population–(cont'd) Components of change, 1980-1986 (cont'd) Net migration	Households, 1990 Number	Households, 1990 Percent change, 1980–1990	Households, 1990 Persons per house-hold	Households, 1990 Percent Female family house-holder[1]	Households, 1990 Percent One-person	Births, 1988 Total	Births, 1988 Rate[2]	Births, 1988 Low birth weight[3] (Number)	Deaths, 1987 Number Total	Deaths, 1987 Number Infant[4]	Deaths, 1987 Rate Total[2]	Deaths, 1987 Rate Infant[5]	Marriages, 1984 Number	Marriages, 1984 Rate[2]
	29	30	31	32	33	34	35	36	37	38	39	40	41	42	43
NEW JERSEY—Con.															
Ocean	46 400	168 147	31.1	2.54	8.6	24.9	5 959	14.5	331	5 395	38	13.4	6.8	2 532	6.8
Passaic	-2 300	155 269	1.2	2.85	14.7	21.7	8 006	17.3	636	4 314	74	9.3	9.7	4 126	9.0
Salem	-1 100	23 794	6.6	2.68	12.7	22.4	952	14.3	69	661	4	10.1	4.8	426	6.5
Somerset	6 500	88 346	31.1	2.67	8.2	20.6	3 514	15.5	173	1 629	27	7.4	8.4	1 749	8.4
Sussex	1 300	44 456	19.4	2.91	7.6	16.2	2 178	17.2	103	902	11	7.2	5.2	873	7.3
Union	-8 200	180 076	1.2	2.71	12.7	23.0	7 307	14.6	554	5 093	66	10.1	9.3	4 277	8.5
Warren	100	33 997	15.6	2.66	9.1	22.2	1 485	16.7	59	783	12	8.9	8.6	657	7.7
NEW MEXICO	64 000	542 709	22.9	2.74	11.9	23.0	27 015	17.9	1 950	10 344	221	6.9	8.1	14 204	10.0
Bernalillo	23 500	185 582	22.9	2.55	11.9	26.1	8 157	16.5	636	3 102	71	6.4	8.4	4 996	10.9
Catron	-100	1 010	5.2	2.54	5.8	27.1	38	13.6	2	21	1	7.5	32.3	1	0.4
Chaves	2 100	20 589	13.2	2.74	11.7	23.3	907	16.3	59	505	9	9.1	10.1	575	10.2
Cibola	-8 500	7 292	NA	3.17	16.0	17.8	([6])	([6])	([6])	([6])	([6])	([6])	([6])	172	7.0
Colfax	-200	4 959	1.2	2.53	10.9	25.3	190	14.0	15	121	2	8.8	9.7	220	15.5
Curry	-2 600	15 113	4.8	2.72	11.1	21.2	880	20.7	59	292	6	6.7	6.6	590	13.7
De Baca	-100	913	-7.7	2.41	7.9	28.5	33	15.0	4	36	0	15.7	0.0	16	6.7
Dona Ana	17 200	NA	NA	NA	NA	NA	2 552	19.3	167	656	17	5.1	7.1	1 209	10.6
Eddy	1 200	17 472	4.8	2.74	9.9	21.8	740	15.2	45	477	5	9.6	6.8	538	10.3
Grant	-900	9 773	13.8	2.77	11.3	21.2	420	15.4	26	227	2	8.5	4.4	235	8.6
Guadalupe	-400	1 520	1.5	2.72	16.2	23.2	83	20.2	7	45	1	10.7	15.4	34	7.6
Harding	-100	396	-3.9	2.49	7.1	29.5	9	9.0	0	15	1	15.0	55.6	8	8.0
Hidalgo	-500	2 004	5.2	2.92	10.5	20.5	94	15.9	4	39	1	6.5	9.3	39	6.2
Lea	2 400	19 306	1.9	2.86	10.5	20.3	1 023	17.5	88	437	8	7.3	7.8	657	10.1
Lincoln	1 800	4 789	16.6	2.48	9.6	24.9	166	12.4	14	91	2	6.7	9.8	152	11.1
Los Alamos	200	7 213	14.8	2.50	5.0	22.9	185	9.7	15	95	3	4.9	15.5	147	8.2
Luna	1 500	6 797	22.3	2.63	11.8	25.4	288	15.9	17	224	4	12.4	13.1	167	9.5
McKinley	800	16 588	10.0	3.61	20.1	17.0	1 861	28.1	140	406	19	6.3	10.5	273	4.4
Mora	100	1 519	9.3	2.79	12.4	22.8	54	12.6	4	39	0	8.9	0.0	0	0.0
Otero	600	18 155	24.3	2.77	9.8	20.1	1 129	22.2	90	348	14	6.8	12.6	610	12.5
Quay	700	4 238	7.7	2.53	10.1	25.6	153	13.4	7	101	3	8.7	20.3	118	10.2
Rio Arriba	1 000	11 461	26.3	2.97	14.3	19.9	688	21.1	49	259	7	8.0	9.6	58	1.8
Roosevelt	-200	5 991	6.1	2.58	10.5	25.5	260	15.9	14	149	3	9.0	11.2	175	10.6
Sandoval	9 800	20 867	99.4	3.02	11.5	16.8	1 182	19.6	85	338	6	6.0	5.0	290	7.3
San Juan	-1 200	28 740	14.9	3.16	13.0	17.7	1 878	21.7	87	485	10	5.5	5.2	691	7.5
San Miguel	700	8 701	18.1	2.81	16.2	22.8	472	18.9	43	199	4	8.0	8.8	186	7.6
Santa Fe	6 700	37 840	43.9	2.54	11.5	26.9	1 485	15.9	118	600	5	6.5	3.4	1 057	12.8
Sierra	1 500	4 428	18.2	2.16	7.6	33.0	115	11.9	13	172	1	17.7	10.1	76	8.2
Socorro	400	5 217	29.6	2.75	10.6	24.0	261	18.0	11	118	2	8.2	7.6	118	8.7
Taos	600	8 752	35.3	2.64	13.2	25.6	354	16.3	26	148	2	6.8	6.7	270	12.4
Torrance	1 100	3 670	38.8	2.80	9.0	21.0	125	12.4	6	70	1	7.0	6.8	78	9.4
Union	200	1 615	-6.3	2.52	9.0	27.2	66	14.3	7	58	0	12.3	0.0	112	21.5
Valencia	4 600	15 170	-20.6	2.89	11.1	17.3	[6]1 167	[6]18.9	[6]92	[6]471	[6]11	[6]7.8	[6]9.3	336	9.8
NEW YORK	-281 000	6 639 322	4.7	2.63	13.8	27.2	280 650	15.7	21 774	173 567	2 906	9.7	10.7	167 607	9.4
Albany	-6 800	115 824	8.7	2.40	11.5	30.3	3 712	13.1	246	3 011	34	10.6	9.2	2 106	7.4
Allegany	-2 900	17 011	3.1	2.68	8.6	23.2	620	12.3	38	464	4	9.3	6.2	392	7.7
Bronx	-24 600	424 112	-1.2	2.74	28.0	28.1	25 394	20.8	2 857	13 028	333	10.7	13.7	11 708	9.9
Broome	-8 100	81 843	6.6	2.50	10.0	26.9	3 039	14.6	168	2 096	39	10.1	13.3	1 586	7.5
Cattaraugus	-3 300	30 456	4.0	2.65	10.6	24.8	1 235	14.7	59	883	7	10.5	5.7	823	9.6
Cayuga	-2 500	29 075	8.1	2.68	10.8	23.6	1 198	15.0	67	765	13	9.6	11.3	680	8.5
Chautauqua	-7 000	53 696	1.7	2.54	10.3	26.1	1 943	13.8	102	1 639	13	11.6	6.8	1 364	9.4
Chemung	-9 600	35 275	2.2	2.56	11.5	25.5	1 349	14.7	91	1 000	3	11.0	2.3	871	9.4
Chenango	-1 000	19 141	13.5	2.66	8.7	23.3	764	14.9	40	515	11	10.2	14.6	463	9.3
Clinton	-4 300	29 123	17.0	2.68	8.9	22.1	1 347	16.4	88	575	16	7.0	12.1	786	9.7
Columbia	600	23 696	11.1	2.57	9.9	24.0	815	13.3	40	655	10	10.8	12.3	506	8.3
Cortland	-3 000	17 247	5.7	2.65	9.7	23.6	654	13.7	38	456	5	9.5	7.4	430	9.1
Delaware	-300	17 646	7.1	2.56	8.8	25.3	629	13.2	49	519	4	11.0	6.1	404	8.7
Dutchess	4 900	89 567	11.1	2.69	9.3	22.2	3 852	14.7	238	2 267	32	8.8	8.6	2 031	8.0
Erie	-69 000	376 994	3.2	2.50	13.3	27.9	13 572	14.2	957	10 380	137	10.9	10.1	8 006	8.2
Essex	-300	13 721	6.5	2.54	8.8	25.7	504	13.8	37	403	7	11.1	14.0	402	11.1
Franklin	-2 200	16 284	7.6	2.61	10.3	25.8	585	13.4	43	486	3	11.2	4.9	398	9.1
Fulton	-1 500	20 995	3.6	2.54	10.7	25.8	765	14.2	49	575	4	10.7	6.0	412	7.4
Genesee	-3 100	21 614	7.5	2.72	9.5	21.6	897	15.3	48	550	4	9.5	4.5	534	9.1
Greene	1 300	16 596	11.2	2.54	9.7	25.6	542	12.6	23	462	8	10.9	14.5	390	9.5
Hamilton	0	2 153	12.0	2.41	7.9	25.5	53	10.8	2	70	0	14.3	0.0	74	15.4
Herkimer	-1 000	24 936	5.3	2.59	9.5	25.0	855	12.8	60	680	14	10.2	15.9	541	8.1

1. No spouse present. 2. Per 1,000 resident population estimated as of July 1 of the year shown. 3. Under 2,500 grams. 4. Deaths of infants under 1 year old. 5. Deaths of infants under 1 year old per 1,000 live births. 6. Cibola County included with Valencia County

STATE County	Divorces, 1984		Physicians, active non–Federal, 1989		Hospitals, 1989			Nursing homes,[4] 1986		Serious crimes known to police, 1988			Education			
						Beds				Number			Public school enrollment[7]		Attainment,[8] 1980	
	Number	Rate[1]	Number[2]	Rate[3]	Number	Number	Rate[3]	Number	Beds	Total[5]	Violent[6]	Rate[3]	1986–1987	1980	Percent 12 yrs. or more	Percent 16 yrs. or more
	44	45	46	47	48	49	50	51	52	53	54	55	56	57	58	59
NEW JERSEY—Con.																
Ocean	1 613	4.3	499	119	6	1 477	352	26	2 736	16 695	931	4 117	60 714	61 835	65.2	12.4
Passaic	1 742	3.8	820	178	6	1 877	407	30	2 697	29 423	3 914	6 306	66 139	78 703	58.3	13.8
Salem	224	3.4	71	107	2	243	366	12	699	2 079	249	3 159	11 978	13 596	62.5	9.0
Somerset	888	4.2	745	323	4	2 034	882	21	1 607	7 059	327	3 166	30 432	38 138	77.0	26.6
Sussex	554	4.6	133	104	2	264	206	12	1 014	2 726	158	2 179	23 973	24 922	75.5	18.9
Union	1 792	3.5	1 335	269	10	2 788	563	27	2 218	27 839	2 712	5 506	66 131	81 730	68.6	19.1
Warren	351	4.1	104	116	2	320	358	10	646	1 988	118	2 266	14 911	16 823	66.6	12.6
NEW MEXICO	11 216	7.9	2 665	175	68	7 108	466	128	6 093	X	8 251	6 310	281 943	270 555	68.9	17.6
Bernalillo	3 972	8.7	1 503	300	21	2 863	571	34	1 562	40 185	4 364	8 215	79 919	79 654	76.5	22.8
Catron	9	3.2	3	111	0	0	0	0	0	42	10	1 439	594	566	61.6	13.5
Chaves	465	8.2	65	118	4	378	687	9	237	2 916	257	6 641	11 078	10 614	63.5	13.5
Cibola	130	5.3	([9])	([9])	([9])	([9])	([9])			719	70	3 403	4 309	0	0.0	0.0
Colfax	83	5.8	22	165	1	70	526	2	62	467	64	5 604	2 836	2 816	64.2	13.0
Curry	423	9.8	40	94	2	131	309	4	244	1 947	122	4 438	8 993	9 155	70.3	11.5
De Baca	8	3.3	3	136	1	25	1 136	1	44	44	4	1 901	423	481	56.0	9.3
Dona Ana	859	7.5	164	120	2	357	261	9	379	8 290	406	6 547	26 355	21 759	65.1	19.3
Eddy	386	7.4	56	118	2	176	371	5	361	2 746	166	5 362	10 663	10 267	62.8	11.0
Grant	172	6.3	38	140	2	299	1 103	4	357	1 349	179	5 326	6 004	6 004	63.2	12.6
Guadalupe	14	3.1	2	50	1	18	450	2	14	214	68	4 947	1 040	1 063	49.0	7.3
Harding	2	2.0	0	0	0	0	0	0	0	5	0	497	170	206	59.4	8.4
Hidalgo	36	5.7	2	34	0	0	0	1	83	NA	NA	NA	1 461	1 454	59.9	9.1
Lea	658	10.1	41	73	2	278	496	3	225	2 842	255	4 669	14 003	12 391	60.0	10.0
Lincoln	501	36.6	21	159	2	200	1 515	1	86	476	33	7 312	2 945	2 252	69.8	15.7
Los Alamos	137	7.6	45	233	1	53	275	1	60	287	14	1 486	3 761	4 413	94.2	47.8
Luna	114	6.5	11	60	1	119	650	1	70	1 157	90	6 353	3 964	3 246	57.0	10.7
McKinley	159	2.6	85	126	5	317	472	2	162	2 772	238	4 879	14 017	13 454	51.2	10.7
Mora	19	4.2	4	95	0	0	0	1	5	6	0	146	972	1 050	44.1	9.9
Otero	177	3.6	44	86	3	110	215	1	90	1 761	125	5 488	9 453	9 974	77.1	14.7
Quay	88	7.6	7	62	1	37	327	2	66	NA	NA	NA	2 465	2 397	59.7	12.3
Rio Arriba	161	5.0	27	83	1	80	245	4	174	NA	NA	NA	6 999	6 526	56.4	10.1
Roosevelt	106	6.4	8	49	1	100	613	1	49	879	82	5 139	3 128	2 772	64.6	16.2
Sandoval	124	3.1	46	69	0	0	0	3	240	1 013	80	1 938	4 309	7 348	67.0	14.9
San Juan	630	6.9	89	105	2	171	201	2	142	3 859	343	4 271	21 810	18 426	65.1	11.4
San Miguel	142	5.8	30	120	2	443	1 765	19	466	1 499	207	5 889	5 313	4 937	55.9	15.3
Santa Fe	814	9.8	220	229	3	295	307	8	436	NA	NA	NA	13 322	14 172	75.8	27.2
Sierra	82	8.8	7	72	1	34	351	1	110	462	124	4 686	1 287	1 362	54.3	6.9
Socorro	108	7.9	8	54	1	32	216	1	62	61	2	954	2 338	2 836	63.6	15.7
Taos	130	6.0	29	135	1	33	153	0	0	990	111	4 493	5 210	4 308	62.8	13.4
Torrance	284	34.2	2	19	0	0	0	0	0	77	19	1 021	3 249	1 649	58.4	9.5
Union	29	5.6	3	67	1	28	622	2	74	154	12	4 769	982	1 033	62.2	10.7
Valencia	194	5.6	[9]40	[9]65	[9]4	[9]461	[9]744	4	233	1 663	291	4 810	8 571	11 970	64.3	10.2
NEW YORK	64 634	3.6	55 730	310	309	107 414	598	1 059	125 715	1 113 318	195 181	6 252	2 607 469	3 025 316	66.3	17.9
Albany	937	3.3	1 252	445	6	2 048	727	18	1 658	12 499	1 157	4 393	35 501	41 723	71.7	22.3
Allegany	117	2.3	32	63	2	208	412	10	374	1 045	101	2 172	9 259	10 480	68.0	13.6
Bronx	4 580	3.9	2 754	223	14	6 923	561	50	11 342	X	0	0	NA	205 310	50.8	9.1
Broome	817	3.9	462	223	3	1 507	727	15	1 951	6 898	212	3 287	33 905	39 460	69.4	15.6
Cattaraugus	258	3.0	110	132	4	348	418	7	451	2 278	116	2 750	17 673	17 628	64.8	10.7
Cayuga	206	2.6	76	95	1	266	332	11	918	2 314	138	2 881	13 007	16 438	62.3	10.9
Chautauqua	566	3.9	163	116	4	567	404	19	1 458	4 956	206	3 486	25 829	28 812	65.8	11.8
Chemung	367	4.0	190	207	3	717	781	17	828	4 005	253	4 412	14 855	18 931	69.5	13.3
Chenango	209	4.2	47	91	1	113	219	9	594	1 011	80	1 990	10 659	11 483	64.5	12.0
Clinton	274	3.4	111	135	2	435	529	7	468	2 087	199	2 544	13 840	15 297	63.7	14.1
Columbia	201	3.3	75	122	0	0	0	8	776	1 816	246	2 960	9 729	12 280	63.0	13.8
Cortland	216	4.5	48	100	1	177	369	7	428	2 177	74	4 517	7 985	9 754	66.2	15.1
Delaware	151	3.2	44	92	3	170	356	10	411	1 059	79	2 244	8 538	9 843	64.4	11.8
Dutchess	859	3.4	525	198	7	2 888	1 091	20	1 800	8 831	999	3 404	39 756	48 061	70.6	18.9
Erie	3 390	3.5	2 714	284	18	6 539	685	62	7 662	45 677	6 164	4 841	136 448	173 760	65.4	15.1
Essex	115	3.2	32	87	3	87	238	6	317	762	71	2 068	4 975	7 523	65.1	14.1
Franklin	111	2.5	70	161	2	247	568	6	199	985	119	2 260	9 014	10 185	59.8	11.6
Fulton	213	3.8	56	104	1	124	231	9	414	2 082	86	3 847	10 056	11 594	59.5	9.3
Genesee	217	3.7	60	102	3	386	659	5	555	1 727	61	2 935	10 947	13 112	69.2	11.8
Greene	106	2.6	28	64	1	342	786	5	343	1 136	198	2 675	6 575	8 090	62.7	9.8
Hamilton	11	2.3	3	61	0	0	0	0	0	89	5	1 809	792	1 093	67.3	11.2
Herkimer	178	2.7	41	61	2	200	299	9	634	1 260	58	1 965	12 079	14 147	62.8	10.4

1. Per 1,000 resident population estimated as of July 1 of the year shown. 2. As of end of year. 3. Per 100,000 resident population as of July 1 of the year shown. 4. Preliminary. Covers nursing homes with 3 or more beds. 5. Data for serious crimes have not been adjusted for underreporting, this may affect comparability between geographic areas or over time. 6. Includes murder and nonnegligent manslaughter, forcible rape, robbery, and aggravated assault. 7. The 1986–1987 data are based on administrative reports obtained by the U.S. National Center for Education Statistics. The 1980 data are based on the 1980 Census of Population and Housing. 8. Persons 25 years old or older. 9. Cibola County included with Valencia County

STATE County	Education (cont'd) Local government expenditures for education,[1] 1982 Total (Mil dol)	Per capita (Dollars)	Social Security Program December 1988 Beneficiaries Total	Rate[2]	Payments ($1,000)	Supplemental Security Income Program recipients June 1986	Money income Per capita[3] 1987 Income, (Dollars)	1979 Current dollars	1979 Constant 1987 dollars	Median household income 1979 (Dollars)	Percent below poverty level, 1979 Persons	Families	Housing units, 1990 Total	Percent change, 1980–1990
	60	61	62	63	64	65	66	67	68	69	70	71	72	73
NEW JERSEY—Con.														
Ocean	185.0	516	110 625	269.4	59 644	3 074	13 046	7 009	10 967	16 224	8.1	6.1	219 863	26.7
Passaic	199.9	441	72 060	155.7	38 615	7 944	12 989	7 214	11 288	17 907	12.8	10.5	162 512	1.8
Salem	41.0	629	11 120	167.5	5 747	900	11 454	6 714	10 505	18 017	11.7	9.2	25 349	4.9
Somerset	127.8	623	27 565	121.8	15 610	1 312	20 171	10 123	15 839	26 235	3.8	2.7	92 653	32.8
Sussex	78.1	659	14 475	114.2	7 670	732	14 825	7 755	12 134	21 870	5.5	4.1	51 574	17.6
Union	247.4	490	86 265	172.6	48 351	5 982	16 140	9 031	14 131	21 625	7.5	5.8	187 033	2.3
Warren	44.2	521	15 425	173.9	8 215	760	13 788	7 463	11 677	18 969	6.5	5.0	36 589	16.2
NEW MEXICO	771.8	564	206 295	136.9	90 866	27 455	9 434	6 120	9 576	14 654	17.6	14.0	632 058	24.5
Bernalillo	225.9	521	62 110	126.0	28 953	6 080	11 463	7 137	11 167	16 239	13.2	10.1	201 235	24.1
Catron	2.2	798	500	178.6	209	40	7 260	4 695	7 346	10 265	23.0	17.4	1 552	11.2
Chaves	28.5	534	10 485	188.9	4 794	1 134	8 639	5 828	9 119	12 376	19.2	14.3	23 386	12.3
Cibola	11.9	399	1 585	74.1	707	NA	5 694	6 091	9 531	0	0.0	0.0	9 692	NA
Colfax	8.5	626	2 495	183.5	1 119	228	7 984	5 515	8 629	12 381	17.0	13.5	8 265	19.9
Curry	23.8	555	5 490	129.2	2 383	764	9 033	5 962	9 329	13 077	15.1	11.7	16 906	4.3
De Baca	1.4	599	615	279.5	254	80	7 289	5 187	8 116	9 699	20.1	14.5	1 329	-1.6
Dona Ana	58.3	564	15 325	116.1	6 353	2 092	8 532	5 284	8 268	12 362	22.7	18.3	NA	NA
Eddy	25.8	501	9 305	190.7	4 509	916	8 928	6 057	9 477	14 725	13.5	10.1	20 134	10.9
Grant	18.0	637	4 925	181.1	2 323	494	7 860	5 703	8 923	15 903	14.4	12.4	11 349	17.8
Guadalupe	4.1	940	745	181.7	259	248	5 804	3 850	6 024	8 798	30.5	27.0	2 149	0.3
Harding	1.6	1 638	250	250.0	103	18	9 010	5 267	8 241	10 991	19.0	16.9	614	11.0
Hidalgo	4.6	733	850	144.1	357	110	7 539	5 242	8 202	13 449	17.0	14.7	2 413	3.7
Lea	39.0	619	8 040	137.9	3 915	784	9 510	6 921	10 829	18 381	12.2	9.0	23 333	10.7
Lincoln	9.7	825	2 575	192.2	1 127	240	9 275	6 388	9 995	13 425	17.0	13.2	12 622	29.6
Los Alamos	13.4	755	1 540	80.6	720	34	18 758	10 442	16 339	27 901	4.1	3.5	7 565	14.9
Luna	8.4	518	4 665	257.7	2 009	438	6 944	4 790	7 495	9 849	23.3	19.2	7 766	23.5
McKinley	38.6	645	5 845	88.2	1 914	2 082	5 238	4 196	6 565	12 124	36.8	33.2	20 933	15.5
Mora	3.8	857	880	204.7	292	290	5 112	3 404	5 326	7 600	38.3	36.9	2 486	18.1
Otero	22.6	488	5 760	113.4	2 402	510	8 430	5 379	8 417	13 416	14.5	11.6	23 177	29.0
Quay	7.1	666	2 135	187.3	900	276	8 888	5 561	8 701	12 392	18.2	15.3	5 576	13.5
Rio Arriba	26.7	863	5 325	163.3	1 913	1 516	6 202	3 937	6 160	10 461	28.3	25.1	14 357	29.3
Roosevelt	8.8	543	2 800	170.7	1 215	390	7 834	5 180	8 105	10 095	27.2	21.1	6 902	6.0
Sandoval	15.7	433	7 220	119.9	3 202	824	9 195	5 108	7 992	14 535	18.6	14.4	23 667	92.6
San Juan	54.0	601	10 300	118.8	4 296	1 780	7 668	5 812	9 094	16 691	20.9	16.1	34 248	15.2
San Miguel	19.5	833	4 040	161.6	1 488	1 414	5 977	3 904	6 109	9 062	30.8	26.9	11 066	11.7
Santa Fe	32.7	419	11 795	126.3	5 471	1 318	11 153	6 848	10 715	15 852	13.7	11.2	41 464	46.4
Sierra	3.5	390	3 540	364.9	1 516	296	7 585	4 637	7 256	7 959	22.4	18.9	6 457	19.8
Socorro	6.6	477	1 825	125.9	681	418	7 063	4 469	6 993	10 910	29.6	22.2	6 289	35.7
Taos	16.9	835	3 555	163.8	1 343	926	6 545	4 613	7 218	10 717	27.5	24.1	12 020	28.7
Torrance	8.2	1 035	1 545	153.0	625	240	6 954	4 691	7 340	10 830	23.3	19.7	4 878	47.4
Union	3.8	733	900	195.7	389	108	8 689	5 957	9 321	11 170	21.3	19.1	2 299	1.2
Valencia	18.1	547	6 865	170.8	2 934	938	8 827	5 615	8 786	16 178	14.9	12.4	16 781	-24.9
NEW YORK	9 822.0	558	2 799 788	156.3	1 475 184	366 751	13 167	7 496	11 729	16 647	13.4	10.8	7 226 891	5.2
Albany	132.1	464	48 065	170.3	25 192	4 088	13 248	7 598	11 889	17 006	10.2	6.4	124 255	7.4
Allegany	31.5	610	8 325	164.9	4 099	732	8 175	5 181	8 107	13 617	15.0	10.5	21 951	5.9
Bronx	NA	NA	166 505	136.1	82 125	49 036	9 065	5 343	8 360	10 947	27.6	24.8	440 955	-2.3
Broome	135.3	635	41 215	197.7	21 124	2 996	11 689	6 871	10 751	16 263	8.8	6.0	87 969	7.3
Cattaraugus	58.3	678	15 780	188.1	7 702	1 546	8 659	5 612	8 781	14 140	13.5	10.5	36 839	5.7
Cayuga	43.7	547	14 300	178.8	7 240	1 184	9 630	5 936	9 288	15 603	11.3	8.5	33 280	7.5
Chautauqua	85.7	586	29 320	207.5	14 803	2 330	9 738	6 181	9 671	14 902	11.2	8.1	62 682	2.9
Chemung	53.2	558	18 695	203.9	9 476	1 734	10 124	6 253	9 784	15 213	11.0	8.8	37 290	1.6
Chenango	37.3	748	9 150	178.4	4 462	854	9 741	5 717	8 945	14 269	12.3	9.2	22 164	17.5
Clinton	49.5	614	10 705	130.5	5 011	1 376	9 348	5 343	8 360	14 186	13.3	9.3	32 190	14.6
Columbia	35.4	591	11 860	194.1	6 050	1 170	11 252	6 395	10 006	14 989	10.5	7.8	29 139	12.3
Cortland	30.1	623	7 525	157.1	3 704	686	9 356	5 625	8 801	14 248	14.7	9.4	18 681	5.6
Delaware	29.6	634	9 230	194.3	4 461	884	9 512	5 677	8 883	13 565	14.1	10.1	27 361	20.3
Dutchess	150.5	605	37 940	144.7	20 015	4 264	13 454	7 559	11 828	20 267	7.3	5.6	97 632	12.4
Erie	559.4	560	183 360	191.3	96 354	15 408	11 290	7 094	11 100	17 119	10.6	8.3	402 131	3.4
Essex	20.4	561	7 430	203.0	3 563	716	9 926	5 798	9 072	13 711	13.4	9.7	21 493	12.4
Franklin	33.3	757	8 930	205.3	4 012	1 174	8 791	5 283	8 266	12 265	16.7	12.7	21 962	8.0
Fulton	31.5	572	11 295	209.6	5 569	972	10 012	5 973	9 346	13 898	11.8	8.5	26 260	3.0
Genesee	36.1	608	10 515	179.4	5 356	704	10 560	6 677	10 448	17 612	9.1	6.7	22 596	6.3
Greene	23.2	568	9 050	210.0	4 443	652	10 488	6 010	9 404	13 679	11.7	9.4	25 000	17.1
Hamilton	4.1	830	1 205	245.9	584	86	10 306	5 469	8 557	12 282	13.0	9.5	8 234	16.6
Herkimer	39.3	591	13 915	207.7	6 792	1 090	9 132	5 651	8 842	14 030	12.9	9.0	30 799	8.0

1. Elementary and secondary. 2. Per 1,000 resident population estimated as of July 1 of the year shown. 3. Based on the resident population estimated as of July 1, 1988 for 1987 data and enumerated as of April 1, 1980 for 1979 data.

STATE County	Housing units, 1990 (cont'd): Occupied units: Total	Owner occupied: Percent	Owner occupied: Median value (Dollars)	Median rent (Dollars)	Civilian labor force, 1990: Total	Percent change, 1989–1990	Unemployment: Total	Unemployment: Rate[1]	Private nonfarm establishments, 1988: Number	Net change, 1987–1988	Employment[2]: Total	Per-cent change, 1987–1988	Manu-facturing	Retail trade
	74	75	76	77	78	79	80	81	82	83	84	85	86	87
NEW JERSEY—Con.														
Ocean	168 147	82.9	126 000	578	185 349	1.7	10 450	5.6	9 371	180	89 119	3.4	8 385	28 537
Passaic	155 269	55.8	185 500	499	240 284	-0.3	14 976	6.2	12 168	-20	182 218	-0.8	55 669	34 647
Salem	23 794	72.3	82 700	361	31 452	1.9	1 420	4.5	1 194	54	17 813	1.6	5 960	3 317
Somerset	88 346	75.3	196 300	639	139 553	3.1	3 992	2.9	7 279	295	122 815	4.3	26 773	20 646
Sussex	44 456	82.3	156 300	594	62 273	0.5	2 987	4.8	3 207	159	25 404	5.0	3 274	6 526
Union	180 076	62.5	180 500	530	267 174	0.4	14 868	5.6	15 212	124	241 693	0.9	74 725	33 529
Warren	33 997	69.5	143 900	488	40 993	3.6	2 019	4.9	2 431	51	28 971	0.7	9 749	6 288
NEW MEXICO	542 709	67.4	70 100	312	700 000	0.3	44 000	6.3	X	X	387 410	0.9	35 841	103 135
Bernalillo	185 582	60.7	85 300	351	264 817	-0.3	13 225	5.0	13 300	15	181 695	0.1	19 601	41 845
Catron	1 010	76.3	39 700	197	1 285	4.9	173	13.5	42	-1	171	-16.2	80	39
Chaves	20 589	69.9	44 600	267	23 670	-1.3	1 235	5.2	1 333	-80	14 328	3.2	2 909	3 344
Cibola	7 292	73.8	37 500	158	8 731	-6.4	1 028	11.8	328	-13	2 911	0.0	276	980
Colfax	4 959	70.6	46 700	192	6 332	-2.6	487	7.7	417	-19	2 884	1.0	254	1 049
Curry	15 113	61.6	51 300	290	16 418	-2.4	1 043	6.4	1 025	-16	8 961	-0.7	491	3 578
De Baca	913	74.5	33 000	162	976	4.9	67	6.9	65	5	305	-18.2	0	118
Dona Ana	NA	NA	67 300	290	59 168	1.5	3 961	6.7	2 460	127	24 754	5.1	2 585	7 181
Eddy	17 472	72.9	44 800	238	19 991	-2.2	1 381	6.9	1 191	-56	12 589	2.1	574	3 238
Grant	9 773	70.3	50 900	201	10 478	0.7	886	8.5	553	1	5 824	-2.5	503	1 694
Guadalupe	1 520	70.9	33 100	167	1 683	0.6	194	11.5	99	3	724	0.8	0	431
Harding	396	77.8	16 000	125	367	-2.7	55	15.0	17	-3	62	-17.3	0	14
Hidalgo	2 004	61.2	36 700	99	2 744	-1.5	162	5.9	107	-2	1 342	3.0	0	472
Lea	19 306	71.5	39 600	241	21 330	-2.8	1 114	5.2	1 511	-46	15 105	-1.2	796	3 323
Lincoln	4 789	72.4	67 400	268	6 508	-2.2	363	5.6	497	-45	2 620	-7.8	101	1 133
Los Alamos	7 213	74.4	126 100	403	13 644	4.7	205	1.5	399	-10	5 376	-5.3	93	1 088
Luna	6 797	71.1	47 200	206	6 074	1.3	785	12.9	341	10	2 487	-1.7	92	975
McKinley	16 588	71.1	42 800	221	18 359	2.4	1 738	9.5	952	-20	9 762	0.4	841	4 128
Mora	1 519	81.2	30 200	161	1 219	2.6	287	23.5	33	-5	141	0.0	0	56
Otero	18 155	62.3	58 000	291	18 557	0.8	1 322	7.1	943	18	9 289	0.5	733	2 722
Quay	4 238	72.2	37 600	196	4 713	2.5	343	7.3	291	-7	2 379	2.5	45	909
Rio Arriba	11 461	80.4	58 800	191	13 431	-0.5	1 804	13.4	481	-17	3 499	2.4	152	1 296
Roosevelt	5 991	64.4	41 000	217	7 553	1.5	303	4.0	340	-2	2 383	-5.7	357	753
Sandoval	20 867	82.8	69 600	376	29 191	3.0	1 803	6.2	659	30	6 336	12.1	1 620	2 018
San Juan	28 740	72.0	58 400	272	34 429	0.1	3 034	8.8	1 859	-62	21 095	1.2	958	5 560
San Miguel	8 701	72.0	47 500	193	9 781	0.0	932	9.5	410	4	3 170	-2.2	281	1 304
Santa Fe	37 840	67.7	103 300	425	57 032	4.1	2 252	3.9	3 076	33	28 457	5.3	1 342	8 928
Sierra	4 428	73.3	49 500	186	2 764	-1.1	146	5.3	211	-7	1 152	-5.5	0	479
Socorro	5 217	68.7	52 500	221	6 118	0.0	420	6.9	261	2	2 141	2.1	180	634
Taos	8 752	74.8	71 700	281	10 600	4.8	1 538	14.5	718	5	5 206	-1.8	282	1 636
Torrance	3 670	82.0	46 500	233	3 785	1.6	301	8.0	149	-10	759	-1.0	25	347
Union	1 615	72.4	36 200	197	2 009	1.0	96	4.8	118	-4	621	-4.5	18	212
Valencia	15 170	83.4	72 100	270	16 244	1.3	1 319	8.1	635	-2	4 278	0.0	91	1 651
NEW YORK	6 639 322	52.2	131 600	428	8 673 000	-0.1	451 000	5.2	X	X	6 884 681	1.5	1 249 626	1 206 312
Albany	115 824	57.0	110 900	402	155 330	0.8	4 272	2.8	8 541	30	148 322	4.0	14 461	32 147
Allegany	17 011	73.1	37 600	232	20 922	1.1	1 227	5.9	827	-35	10 856	-3.1	3 304	1 995
Bronx	424 112	17.9	173 900	392	470 980	1.5	38 718	8.2	13 386	119	178 571	0.6	22 657	29 694
Broome	81 843	65.4	79 000	333	99 307	-2.8	4 063	4.1	4 598	7	84 945	2.4	29 356	19 167
Cattaraugus	30 456	73.2	42 100	227	36 804	0.8	2 279	6.2	1 722	-1	24 611	4.0	7 851	5 220
Cayuga	29 075	70.9	59 800	308	37 432	0.5	2 332	6.2	1 540	12	18 227	2.2	5 267	4 263
Chautauqua	53 696	68.6	47 800	251	65 040	-0.8	3 508	5.4	3 272	36	43 750	-0.5	15 020	9 310
Chemung	35 275	68.3	53 600	291	44 163	0.3	1 963	4.4	2 030	32	32 637	7.3	7 791	7 465
Chenango	19 141	74.4	55 900	273	21 936	-1.4	1 342	6.1	1 053	12	13 705	4.1	6 136	2 794
Clinton	29 123	63.9	65 000	317	36 588	1.8	2 060	5.6	1 805	87	20 257	7.6	3 878	6 513
Columbia	23 696	69.5	103 100	350	30 683	2.2	1 060	3.5	1 536	60	14 426	3.9	2 768	3 107
Cortland	17 247	64.4	66 200	321	23 943	-0.9	1 328	5.5	981	-3	16 042	3.3	5 583	3 886
Delaware	17 646	74.1	67 000	279	20 116	0.4	1 070	5.3	1 317	36	13 273	4.8	5 293	2 846
Dutchess	89 567	69.1	149 200	530	129 091	-1.0	3 874	3.0	6 273	193	92 789	-1.3	29 109	20 286
Erie	376 994	63.7	74 000	292	461 287	-0.8	22 100	4.8	22 254	447	366 032	3.5	79 999	83 900
Essex	13 721	72.1	62 200	294	18 007	1.7	1 357	7.5	1 143	43	8 924	4.2	1 523	2 487
Franklin	16 284	68.9	48 900	253	21 878	-0.6	1 617	7.4	1 000	32	8 893	2.5	1 316	2 204
Fulton	20 995	71.4	56 000	256	25 076	-2.3	2 051	8.2	1 097	1	13 986	7.9	5 859	2 596
Genesee	21 614	72.8	65 800	322	28 236	-1.6	1 627	5.8	1 296	48	15 969	8.1	4 815	3 975
Greene	16 596	72.9	91 700	336	19 670	0.9	1 018	5.2	1 191	32	9 415	4.9	1 120	2 668
Hamilton	2 153	77.5	71 800	253	3 081	5.8	242	7.9	208	2	676	-5.8	114	195
Herkimer	24 936	71.4	54 400	250	30 600	-0.9	1 707	5.6	1 198	51	13 110	5.3	5 042	3 639

1. Percent of total civilian labor force. 2. For week including March 12. Excludes government employees, self-employed persons, farm workers, domestic service workers, railroad employees subject to the Railroad Retirement Act, and employees on oceanborne vessels or in foreign countries.

STATE County	Private nonfarm establishments, 1988 (cont'd): Employment[1] (cont'd): Finance, insurance, and real estate	Employment[1] (cont'd): Services	Annual payroll: Total (Mil dol)	Annual payroll: Average per employee (Dollars)	Personal income, 1989: Total (Mil dol)	Percent change, 1988–1989	Wages and salaries[2] (Mil dol)	Proprietor's income (Mil dol)	Dividends, interest, & rent (Mil dol)	Transfer payments (Mil dol)	Per capita[3]: Dollars	Per capita[3]: Rank	Earnings, 1989: Total (Mil dol)	Percent by selected industries: Farm	Goods-related[4]: Total
	88	89	90	91	92	93	94	95	96	97	98	99	100	101	102
NEW JERSEY—Con.															
Ocean	6 430	28 610	1 655	18 568	8 736	7.5	2 657	501	2 225	1 396	20 844	134	3 158	0.1	18.9
Passaic	13 561	44 398	4 316	23 688	9 684	6.4	5 953	891	1 692	1 241	20 977	124	6 844	0.1	36.6
Salem	679	3 521	472	26 515	1 124	7.6	750	64	207	180	16 933	450	814	2.0	41.6
Somerset	14 276	29 479	3 660	29 799	7 486	6.7	4 549	571	1 311	451	32 469	8	5 119	0.7	26.3
Sussex	2 526	7 517	468	18 432	3 044	6.5	764	218	403	233	23 782	57	982	1.2	23.1
Union	15 181	58 983	6 341	26 236	12 552	6.5	8 732	708	2 783	1 379	25 328	36	9 440	0.1	34.5
Warren	926	6 582	645	22 278	1 904	5.7	917	146	347	228	21 327	117	1 063	1.5	44.2
NEW MEXICO	25 337	123 410	6 668	X	20 165	7.3	12 477	1 659	3 509	3 485	13 221	X	14 136	2.3	18.0
Bernalillo	13 411	65 042	3 402	18 724	7 929	7.0	5 724	497	1 396	1 178	15 806	709	6 221	0.3	16.0
Catron	0	28	3	20 322	32	4.9	12	6	8	7	11 531	2 490	17	24.9	NA
Chaves	1 018	3 358	222	15 493	758	8.7	392	90	158	146	13 778	1 545	483	5.9	27.0
Cibola	120	661	41	14 112	200	4.8	83	14	16	44	9 869	2 897	97	4.4	25.3
Colfax	625	577	31	10 795	176	4.2	79	21	37	46	13 220	1 804	101	4.9	21.0
Curry	694	2 307	113	12 644	550	5.8	304	66	93	105	12 982	1 911	370	8.0	9.4
De Baca	22	82	2	7 475	27	4.5	7	6	7	7	12 668	2 049	13	26.5	NA
Dona Ana	1 759	7 623	346	13 968	1 419	9.1	826	118	237	291	10 389	2 812	944	4.3	15.2
Eddy	547	3 192	219	17 400	641	9.7	364	64	128	121	13 496	1 684	428	2.0	36.4
Grant	240	911	107	18 395	331	5.7	197	28	60	67	12 227	2 217	226	2.1	46.1
Guadalupe	0	221	7	9 271	40	7.2	18	6	6	12	9 929	2 892	24	15.2	NA
Harding	0	0	1	14 806	12	2.0	4	3	3	3	12 647	2 056	7	37.6	NA
Hidalgo	0	204	24	17 636	75	9.9	49	9	7	12	12 946	1 931	58	11.0	47.6
Lea	592	3 344	265	17 568	720	2.9	441	85	119	111	12 851	1 979	526	2.4	35.0
Lincoln	246	724	33	12 550	165	8.2	73	22	47	33	12 482	2 125	95	4.0	13.4
Los Alamos	328	3 317	109	20 339	460	6.7	540	19	84	51	23 828	56	559	0.0	1.4
Luna	222	760	29	11 482	182	9.5	69	21	40	56	9 962	2 886	90	11.4	12.0
McKinley	372	2 359	140	14 322	548	7.2	350	45	50	124	8 156	3 068	395	1.4	21.4
Mora	0	41	2	12 823	35	4.4	9	6	6	12	8 194	3 062	14	20.8	NA
Otero	480	3 729	131	14 152	600	2.2	428	42	84	121	11 727	2 430	470	1.1	11.3
Quay	120	586	36	15 113	140	6.5	64	24	29	29	12 421	2 156	88	16.5	5.1
Rio Arriba	138	1 152	45	12 821	292	5.7	119	25	34	82	8 948	3 011	144	5.1	12.9
Roosevelt	109	609	31	13 063	193	8.9	73	43	41	43	11 816	2 393	116	22.7	10.1
Sandoval	393	1 099	103	16 196	749	9.9	177	41	93	111	11 189	2 606	218	2.9	44.0
San Juan	853	3 962	441	20 917	996	8.8	708	86	128	161	11 708	2 438	794	2.5	25.8
San Miguel	232	858	40	12 488	226	8.0	117	20	29	67	9 020	3 007	137	3.9	11.3
Santa Fe	1 751	11 609	441	15 509	1 519	9.2	830	138	353	196	15 795	711	968	0.2	12.9
Sierra	87	341	13	11 040	118	9.2	36	11	35	41	12 137	2 267	46	7.7	NA
Socorro	111	887	29	13 333	145	8.2	82	12	23	33	9 747	2 918	95	5.0	10.3
Taos	345	2 268	55	10 602	218	10.0	113	23	45	52	10 113	2 864	135	1.5	17.8
Torrance	44	89	8	10 576	99	7.5	28	10	14	22	9 299	2 982	39	17.1	9.5
Union	69	186	8	12 593	69	1.4	21	20	18	11	15 382	843	41	37.2	10.6
Valencia	304	1 274	51	11 936	502	8.5	138	42	80	93	12 053	2 311	180	4.6	10.5
NEW YORK	816 431	2 312 452	174 486	X	373 682	7.4	251 046	30 700	70 212	60 318	20 817	X	281 747	0.3	20.1
Albany	17 309	53 397	3 085	20 801	5 885	8.4	6 045	357	1 087	1 047	20 897	129	6 402	0.2	12.4
Allegany	377	3 928	182	16 801	611	8.3	302	49	99	141	12 101	2 289	351	3.5	NA
Bronx	9 089	79 885	3 725	20 857	17 558	7.9	5 470	522	2 435	4 817	14 234	1 313	5 992	0.0	17.5
Broome	3 197	20 459	1 797	21 158	3 717	7.5	2 634	269	672	639	17 930	304	2 903	0.4	42.2
Cattaraugus	823	6 738	395	16 051	1 089	7.4	620	88	181	242	13 072	1 878	708	1.9	34.4
Cayuga	648	5 137	318	17 467	1 151	7.8	517	74	186	223	14 359	1 264	591	2.6	28.2
Chautauqua	1 381	11 480	756	17 270	2 075	7.5	1 177	164	378	441	14 778	1 091	1 341	1.5	39.3
Chemung	1 942	9 826	576	17 654	1 452	8.6	869	93	244	306	15 825	705	962	0.8	30.9
Chenango	813	2 341	251	18 315	743	8.1	386	62	127	132	14 367	1 261	447	2.3	37.9
Clinton	740	5 130	339	16 714	1 103	7.7	749	79	137	214	13 419	1 726	828	1.7	20.2
Columbia	707	4 429	232	16 062	1 164	7.6	369	93	229	190	19 008	219	461	3.9	21.4
Cortland	413	4 932	255	15 898	657	8.7	406	61	107	122	13 677	1 593	467	3.0	40.7
Delaware	567	2 984	227	17 122	648	10.1	363	75	153	136	13 581	1 643	439	4.2	40.9
Dutchess	3 824	26 524	2 211	23 824	5 435	7.0	3 433	324	909	689	20 533	146	3 756	0.5	43.6
Erie	29 152	110 851	7 202	19 676	16 922	7.4	10 772	1 099	3 168	3 131	17 724	332	11 871	0.3	27.3
Essex	333	3 208	145	16 208	533	9.4	284	37	111	124	14 545	1 192	321	1.3	24.5
Franklin	383	3 879	129	14 493	603	11.4	295	47	86	148	13 871	1 496	341	2.4	11.9
Fulton	438	2 941	225	16 065	812	7.8	344	54	147	174	15 145	930	397	1.0	33.6
Genesee	656	3 910	282	17 644	986	7.8	479	68	154	159	16 829	468	547	3.5	33.4
Greene	506	3 267	135	14 301	685	7.4	255	47	127	138	15 755	719	303	3.0	20.3
Hamilton	26	219	10	15 186	82	9.9	28	6	20	18	16 486	530	35	0.0	20.2
Herkimer	475	2 590	207	15 800	910	8.1	374	65	159	194	13 588	1 638	440	3.0	40.1

1. For week including March 12. Excludes government employees, self-employed persons, farm workers, domestic service workers, railroad employees subject to the Railroad Retirement Act, and employees on oceanborne vessels or in foreign countries. 2. Includes other labor income. 3. Based on the resident population estimated as of July 1 of the year shown. 4. Covers mining, construction, and manufacturing.

STATE County	Earnings, 1989 (cont'd): Percent by selected industries (cont'd): Goods-related[1]: Manu-facturing	Service-related & other[2]: Total	Service-related & other[2]: Retail trade	Service-related & other[2]: Finance, insur-ance, & real estate	Service-related & other[2]: Services	Govern-ment	Agriculture, 1987: Farms: Number	Farms: Percent with: Less than 50 acres	Farms: Percent with: 500 acres and over	Farm operators, percent: Whose principal occu-pation is farming	Farm operators, percent: Residing on farm operated	Land in farms: Acreage (1,000)	Land in farms: Percent change, 1982–1987	Acres: Average size of farm	Acres: Total irrigated (1,000)	Acres: Total cropland (1,000)
	103	104	105	106	107	108	109	110	111	112	113	114	115	116	117	118
NEW JERSEY—Con.																
Ocean	6.7	60.5	15.5	4.7	29.8	20.4	206	85.0	1.0	44.2	78.6	9	-11.4	43	0	5
Passaic	29.5	52.7	9.0	9.5	21.6	10.6	57	86.0	0.0	33.3	78.9	1	-7.9	24	0	1
Salem	31.9	NA	6.8	1.6	NA	12.1	697	42.3	6.9	50.5	80.1	95	-1.4	137	17	79
Somerset	19.7	64.7	7.6	10.5	23.7	8.4	407	60.7	5.2	44.2	83.0	45	-8.7	111	0	34
Sussex	9.7	57.9	12.0	6.6	29.9	17.9	776	53.9	3.4	36.2	83.5	79	7.5	101	1	45
Union	28.1	56.7	7.6	5.1	24.9	8.7	31	90.3	0.0	64.5	64.5	0	-22.5	14	0	0
Warren	33.3	42.8	10.5	3.5	19.4	11.5	666	42.5	4.5	47.7	81.4	88	0.3	132	2	61
NEW MEXICO	7.8	53.1	10.6	4.3	26.1	26.6	14 249	36.0	35.8	50.8	64.8	46 018	-2.3	3 230	718	2 279
Bernalillo	9.4	62.5	10.2	5.8	32.7	21.2	434	74.9	9.9	33.6	69.1	D	D	D	7	17
Catron	13.2	NA	4.9	NA	7.5	40.4	260	11.5	56.2	61.2	65.0	1 670	-9.0	6 425	2	11
Chaves	16.9	48.1	11.1	4.2	21.0	19.0	622	28.9	40.8	60.6	65.6	2 992	-2.3	4 810	65	113
Cibola	9.8	37.2	12.9	2.1	15.2	33.1	210	38.1	46.2	43.8	56.7	2 088	-4.8	9 942	7	26
Colfax	6.0	49.8	12.0	4.4	23.6	24.3	303	12.9	57.4	55.4	60.7	1 878	-9.2	6 198	21	36
Curry	4.4	45.2	11.0	3.4	15.1	37.4	659	13.8	55.8	66.9	56.6	990	8.4	1 503	85	475
De Baca	1.3	41.3	10.6	3.6	13.9	25.1	191	27.7	50.8	60.7	64.9	1 297	11.2	6 789	7	D
Dona Ana	8.8	40.8	10.4	3.5	18.2	39.7	1 104	68.4	8.3	44.5	71.3	573	42.5	519	78	92
Eddy	6.3	48.1	9.7	3.0	19.7	13.5	503	35.8	30.8	55.1	68.4	968	1.1	1 924	47	64
Grant	10.4	30.6	8.6	2.4	12.5	21.2	282	25.2	50.4	59.9	71.3	1 203	4.9	4 265	4	11
Guadalupe	NA	NA	20.1	4.5	16.6	25.2	258	14.7	70.9	58.1	45.7	1 560	-3.9	6 046	2	12
Harding	NA	NA	4.0	NA	3.6	30.1	181	6.6	78.5	64.6	54.1	1 130	-10.8	6 241	1	D
Hidalgo	43.6	28.3	8.9	1.2	9.7	13.1	157	7.6	59.2	70.7	66.2	1 226	-7.6	7 809	10	22
Lea	3.1	51.2	9.5	2.6	21.1	11.4	561	24.8	47.4	46.3	59.4	2 220	1.9	3 958	26	115
Lincoln	1.6	57.0	18.3	3.7	27.5	25.7	349	25.2	48.4	55.9	65.9	1 894	-5.6	5 428	5	15
Los Alamos	0.2	26.4	2.8	1.1	21.3	72.2	2	100.0	0.0	50.0	100.0	D	NA	D	0	0
Luna	5.4	45.4	13.9	3.2	16.4	31.2	207	15.0	53.1	67.1	64.3	930	NA	4 495	27	D
McKinley	5.9	46.6	16.4	1.8	16.6	30.7	240	37.1	41.7	40.4	52.9	2 959	-7.1	12 328	3	22
Mora	0.7	NA	6.3	NA	8.6	39.7	401	17.2	30.9	48.1	61.3	951	5.1	2 371	12	37
Otero	6.4	33.8	8.4	1.9	18.7	53.8	439	47.8	23.0	43.1	73.1	1 131	-17.1	2 576	7	D
Quay	1.6	NA	14.2	3.4	14.6	18.4	589	15.4	59.4	65.5	69.8	1 636	-6.2	2 777	24	237
Rio Arriba	1.9	53.1	11.4	3.4	27.2	28.9	936	51.7	20.2	38.0	64.5	1 491	0.0	1 593	24	D
Roosevelt	5.7	42.8	8.6	2.8	18.6	24.4	810	17.0	51.1	65.1	65.6	1 535	-1.2	1 895	72	389
Sandoval	33.4	37.6	10.0	3.8	18.1	15.5	379	49.1	22.7	41.2	60.7	788	-15.5	2 080	10	29
San Juan	3.1	55.0	10.1	2.6	19.8	16.6	650	59.8	6.8	36.6	75.8	1 857	-0.8	2 857	63	87
San Miguel	4.6	37.9	10.5	2.9	19.2	46.9	634	14.0	46.4	47.6	51.6	1 949	2.7	3 074	9	51
Santa Fe	4.1	57.6	14.6	4.7	32.9	29.3	324	55.6	20.1	32.7	71.6	510	-3.2	1 573	7	17
Sierra	NA	NA	15.4	3.8	20.6	27.7	192	27.6	42.7	60.9	58.9	1 227	-6.1	6 388	7	D
Socorro	4.7	40.3	10.4	1.9	21.9	44.3	396	43.4	30.6	56.3	68.9	1 965	-4.2	4 961	16	22
Taos	3.8	59.2	16.5	4.0	29.9	21.5	497	57.9	9.7	38.6	69.0	291	-12.5	585	16	30
Torrance	2.1	40.5	17.0	1.3	9.8	32.9	460	13.5	48.9	49.1	60.7	1 805	8.4	3 924	11	37
Union	1.6	36.9	7.3	4.1	14.6	15.3	438	10.7	71.2	72.4	53.2	2 604	9.8	5 945	31	97
Valencia	2.5	53.8	13.4	3.9	21.0	31.1	581	78.8	3.8	36.0	76.6	318	-24.4	547	13	D
NEW YORK	14.8	64.4	7.5	14.3	29.5	15.2	37 743	22.9	10.3	60.9	84.5	8 416	-8.4	223	51	5 382
Albany	7.7	51.1	7.6	7.5	23.4	36.3	460	33.7	3.5	43.7	86.3	68	-18.2	147	0	41
Allegany	27.2	NA	8.9	1.4	NA	23.7	798	11.4	9.5	54.1	84.0	193	-10.3	242	0	102
Bronx	7.8	69.0	9.2	4.6	42.2	13.6	1	100.0	0.0	0.0	0.0	D	NA	D	D	D
Broome	36.1	42.2	8.5	3.2	20.1	15.1	590	16.9	7.8	49.2	87.3	117	-11.7	198	0	62
Cattaraugus	30.0	44.4	9.0	2.1	25.0	19.3	1 102	15.9	7.1	61.7	87.8	235	-7.0	213	0	128
Cayuga	21.7	46.3	10.5	2.3	21.8	23.0	995	20.0	15.2	62.8	86.7	262	-5.0	264	0	200
Chautauqua	33.3	43.4	10.1	2.8	20.5	15.8	1 972	33.8	4.5	56.3	83.4	290	-5.6	147	1	169
Chemung	24.5	50.3	10.6	3.3	24.9	18.0	327	21.1	7.3	48.6	86.5	64	-9.4	196	0	37
Chenango	33.7	41.7	13.6	4.4	16.8	18.0	933	13.6	10.7	63.5	85.7	224	-2.7	240	0	116
Clinton	14.3	40.6	12.0	2.1	16.7	37.5	591	12.7	15.4	66.3	82.2	173	-16.3	292	1	90
Columbia	12.2	55.0	12.2	2.7	29.0	19.7	567	25.6	12.5	67.0	79.4	134	-12.3	236	1	88
Cortland	35.6	40.7	11.2	1.7	22.6	15.6	535	19.1	16.6	66.9	88.8	148	-15.3	277	D	81
Delaware	33.7	34.6	9.8	3.1	15.7	20.4	883	15.2	12.0	68.0	84.8	226	-24.0	256	0	107
Dutchess	36.0	38.1	8.2	3.2	20.8	17.8	613	33.8	10.6	54.8	83.0	124	-9.8	203	1	70
Erie	21.8	54.3	9.5	6.7	25.2	18.1	1 201	36.3	5.0	52.2	83.4	166	-12.7	138	2	120
Essex	14.4	46.8	13.0	2.0	24.9	27.4	219	15.5	15.1	48.4	83.6	60	-16.2	273	0	29
Franklin	7.4	46.3	11.2	1.7	26.7	39.4	557	8.3	11.8	78.8	88.2	157	-8.7	282	1	91
Fulton	28.5	46.2	10.5	2.2	21.4	19.2	195	16.4	6.2	61.5	88.2	39	-13.4	199	0	24
Genesee	26.6	42.8	9.4	2.6	18.4	20.3	660	26.1	15.8	60.0	82.4	185	0.1	280	1	151
Greene	10.2	49.4	12.8	3.9	24.5	27.3	279	24.0	8.6	51.6	84.2	56	-11.3	202	0	26
Hamilton	5.0	NA	15.0	NA	19.7	42.5	2	100.0	0.0	0.0	100.0	D	NA	D	0	D
Herkimer	34.9	36.0	11.5	2.2	16.7	20.9	708	12.9	9.9	72.7	86.9	176	-9.5	248	0	110

1. Covers mining, construction, and manufacturing. 2. Covers private sector earnings in agricultural services, forestry, and fisheries; transportation and public utilities; wholesale trade; retail trade; finance, insurance, and real estate; and services.

STATE County	Agriculture, 1987 (cont'd)								Manufactures, 1987						
	Value of land and buildings		Value of products sold				Percent of farms with sales of		Establishments		All employees			Production workers	
					Percent from										
	Average per farm ($1,000)	Average per acre (Dollars)	Total (Mil dol)	Average per farm (Dollars)	Crops	Livestock and poultry[1]	$10,000 or more	$100,000 or more	Total	Percent with 20 or more em-ployees	Number (1,000)	Percent change, 1982–1987	Annual payroll (Mil dol)	Number (1,000)	Work hours (Mil)
	119	120	121	122	123	124	125	126	127	128	129	130	131	132	133
NEW JERSEY—Con.															
Ocean	233	3 956	5	23 864	60.4	39.6	28.6	6.8	329	18.2	7.2	28.6	150.9	4.8	8.9
Passaic	184	7 590	D	D	NA	NA	40.4	5.3	1 391	40.6	61.4	-5.1	1 535.3	39.8	78.9
Salem	261	2 021	50	71 626	59.5	40.6	47.5	15.6	53	34.0	6.0	-26.8	211.6	4.2	8.1
Somerset	1 020	6 728	17	42 856	43.3	56.7	33.9	7.9	382	40.1	26.1	2.0	880.8	9.8	19.2
Sussex	355	3 671	20	25 673	32.1	67.9	26.2	8.5	132	22.7	3.0	-6.3	59.1	2.0	3.8
Union	276	19 051	8	260 507	99.0	1.0	51.6	19.4	1 278	42.4	69.7	-23.3	1 947.8	40.1	80.1
Warren	496	3 923	35	52 954	23.4	76.6	41.4	13.5	155	45.8	9.4	-18.3	270.1	5.8	10.9
NEW MEXICO	582	180	1 060	74 399	24.7	75.3	39.6	11.3	1 322	21.5	34.7	5.2	713.3	23.7	47.3
Bernalillo	D	D	27	61 505	11.1	88.9	15.0	4.4	592	23.3	19.2	9.7	421.4	12.8	25.2
Catron	651	102	11	40 661	D	D	49.6	8.8	8	12.5	0.1	0.0	1.8	0.1	0.2
Chaves	613	129	85	137 458	25.2	74.8	56.8	25.7	42	26.2	2.5	8.7	43.4	1.9	3.6
Cibola	1 180	118	9	42 878	6.2	93.8	36.7	5.2	18	38.9	0.3	200.0	3.1	0.2	0.3
Colfax	1 027	169	25	82 035	4.2	95.8	51.5	14.2	21	38.1	0.4	0.0	4.2	0.3	0.4
Curry	522	365	153	232 867	16.5	83.5	68.1	25.2	28	35.7	0.5	-37.5	8.9	0.3	0.6
De Baca	772	118	15	76 521	9.9	90.1	55.0	24.1	2	0.0	D	D	D	D	D
Dona Ana	780	1 485	156	141 498	52.4	47.6	39.0	14.6	74	28.4	2.5	25.0	43.3	2.0	4.8
Eddy	451	233	47	93 557	34.5	65.5	54.1	14.1	31	12.9	D	D	D	D	D
Grant	598	131	8	26 895	2.1	97.9	37.6	6.7	16	18.8	D	D	D	D	D
Guadalupe	543	92	17	64 672	0.7	99.3	39.5	14.7	1	0.0	D	D	D	D	D
Harding	862	137	12	67 139	D	D	56.4	12.2	2	0.0	D	D	D	D	D
Hidalgo	D	D	20	128 735	25.1	74.9	74.5	18.5	3	66.7	D	D	D	D	D
Lea	505	117	31	55 429	23.3	76.7	44.9	12.7	51	13.7	0.7	-46.2	15.1	0.3	0.6
Lincoln	796	151	12	34 889	1.9	98.1	43.8	10.9	17	5.9	D	D	D	D	D
Los Alamos	D	D	D	D	NA	NA	0.0	0.0	12	8.3	0.1	0.0	1.6	0.0	0.1
Luna	633	139	32	155 099	51.7	48.3	73.9	27.5	9	22.2	0.1	-50.0	2.0	0.1	0.1
McKinley	1 854	151	9	37 892	2.9	97.1	25.8	5.4	33	39.4	0.9	12.5	17.2	0.7	1.3
Mora	415	176	10	24 348	3.8	96.2	21.7	6.2	1	0.0	D	D	D	D	D
Otero	673	245	10	23 526	15.4	84.6	26.7	4.6	32	18.8	0.6	0.0	9.6	0.5	1.0
Quay	331	127	29	49 075	19.5	80.5	57.2	11.0	4	25.0	D	D	D	D	D
Rio Arriba	391	233	11	12 041	11.7	88.3	20.1	1.2	22	4.5	0.2	0.0	2.9	0.1	0.3
Roosevelt	379	203	96	118 937	31.5	68.5	61.6	20.2	14	50.0	0.4	0.0	7.7	0.2	0.4
Sandoval	456	229	12	30 810	39.0	61.0	19.8	3.7	35	17.1	D	D	D	D	D
San Juan	942	327	23	35 903	67.5	32.5	20.5	3.5	48	20.8	0.8	-42.9	16.0	0.5	0.9
San Miguel	518	170	17	26 363	1.5	98.5	19.2	4.3	14	14.3	0.3	200.0	5.2	0.2	0.4
Santa Fe	366	257	7	22 536	27.9	72.1	19.4	3.4	118	12.7	1.4	7.7	23.7	0.9	1.8
Sierra	727	115	12	62 823	20.1	79.9	49.5	8.3	4	0.0	D	D	D	D	D
Socorro	622	126	21	53 455	18.9	81.1	47.0	13.9	10	20.0	D	D	D	D	D
Taos	239	432	D	D	NA	NA	11.3	0.6	26	15.4	D	D	D	D	D
Torrance	481	119	22	46 744	22.7	77.3	37.2	8.9	10	0.0	D	D	D	D	D
Union	764	129	106	241 543	4.0	96.0	71.7	29.9	4	0.0	D	D	D	D	D
Valencia	246	474	12	21 154	21.9	78.1	20.0	3.8	20	5.0	0.1	0.0	1.9	0.1	0.1
NEW YORK	219	993	2 442	64 697	28.7	71.3	54.6	19.3	29 608	32.1	1 278.7	-9.9	33 915.8	723.3	1 403.5
Albany	212	1 356	16	35 342	34.4	65.6	36.5	6.3	312	36.5	15.2	0.7	419.3	8.4	17.3
Allegany	133	586	30	37 579	5.9	94.1	45.1	11.3	59	22.0	2.8	-9.7	71.4	1.8	3.3
Bronx	D	D	D	D	NA	NA	0.0	0.0	766	36.9	24.1	-11.7	477.4	17.5	33.8
Broome	155	788	24	40 155	11.0	89.0	37.1	13.6	267	41.6	29.3	-12.3	820.4	12.3	24.3
Cattaraugus	129	604	53	47 961	16.1	83.9	57.1	13.7	120	35.8	7.6	-6.2	161.2	5.2	10.3
Cayuga	227	889	77	77 803	26.6	73.4	58.6	21.6	99	34.3	5.2	-1.9	117.4	3.5	7.1
Chautauqua	119	804	79	40 126	34.5	65.5	51.8	11.4	255	37.6	14.7	-7.0	331.0	10.5	20.9
Chemung	151	766	13	39 582	29.1	70.9	40.1	10.7	102	42.2	7.4	-20.4	156.7	5.0	9.7
Chenango	151	647	55	59 295	4.5	95.5	54.2	18.8	97	36.1	6.0	0.0	138.4	3.5	6.7
Clinton	190	664	49	82 494	22.1	77.9	60.9	28.1	82	35.4	4.4	12.8	101.8	3.0	5.9
Columbia	595	2 647	56	97 953	22.5	77.5	62.1	25.2	89	34.8	2.7	0.0	50.6	2.0	4.1
Cortland	189	642	43	79 790	4.7	95.3	60.6	31.2	61	42.6	5.7	7.5	108.4	4.0	8.2
Delaware	225	993	55	62 622	6.9	93.1	60.7	22.4	77	29.9	5.2	-13.3	119.3	3.8	7.7
Dutchess	645	3 122	38	61 249	36.7	63.3	51.5	17.9	207	38.6	30.9	-5.8	1 102.8	10.0	19.5
Erie	170	1 175	73	60 475	40.6	59.4	44.4	16.7	1 310	36.3	80.4	-8.1	2 218.4	53.9	107.6
Essex	237	812	9	42 000	24.0	76.0	38.8	15.1	56	14.3	1.5	0.0	38.4	1.2	2.3
Franklin	179	660	44	78 653	12.6	87.4	73.1	26.8	52	19.2	1.4	-6.7	22.8	1.1	2.4
Fulton	174	876	9	44 185	8.9	91.1	48.2	15.9	133	36.1	4.7	-26.6	75.0	3.7	7.3
Genesee	249	895	67	101 608	38.6	61.4	56.2	23.3	86	44.2	4.4	0.0	97.9	3.2	6.4
Greene	313	1 743	9	32 153	23.7	76.3	41.9	8.6	51	29.4	1.2	-20.0	24.9	0.9	1.9
Hamilton	D	D	D	D	NA	NA	0.0	0.0	15	6.7	0.1	0.0	1.6	0.1	0.2
Herkimer	173	699	47	66 906	4.5	95.5	65.3	26.1	77	42.9	4.6	-41.0	93.6	3.6	6.7

1. Includes livestock and poultry products.

STATE County	Manufactures, 1987 (cont'd): Production workers (cont'd): Wages: Total (Mil dol)	Manufactures, 1987 (cont'd): Production workers (cont'd): Wages: Average per worker (Dollars)	Manufactures, 1987 (cont'd): Value added by manufacture (Mil dol)	Manufactures, 1987 (cont'd): Value of shipments (Mil dol)	Manufactures, 1987 (cont'd): New capital expenditures (Mil dol)	Value of construction authorized by building permits, 1990: Total[1] ($1,000)	Nonresidential: Total ($1,000)	Nonresidential: Percent: Office	Nonresidential: Percent: Industrial	Nonresidential: Percent: Stores	Residential: New construction ($1,000)	Residential: Number of housing units	Residential: Alterations and additions ($1,000)
	134	135	136	137	138	139	140	141	142	143	144	145	146
NEW JERSEY—Con.													
Ocean	83.4	17 375	351.7	722.3	34.4	266 407	48 205	18.3	8.5	15.9	134 198	1 824	59 655
Passaic	783.8	19 693	2 985.9	5 420.0	144.3	111 335	16 460	32.9	1.7	46.8	36 611	728	28 223
Salem	128.5	30 595	802.9	1 455.0	19.6	46 775	13 168	0.0	11.5	5.9	19 285	207	4 217
Somerset	235.2	24 000	2 000.1	3 198.6	85.7	265 459	59 673	78.7	1.8	7.9	119 570	1 273	40 686
Sussex	31.7	15 850	131.4	245.9	4.8	61 689	7 390	27.9	11.5	20.5	34 232	337	14 132
Union	892.5	22 257	4 781.6	11 178.8	234.1	192 636	44 774	31.8	2.9	57.0	11 341	138	44 355
Warren	142.3	24 534	818.7	1 525.2	50.2	46 612	9 087	20.1	0.2	15.6	20 574	227	7 901
NEW MEXICO	432.5	18 249	1 652.9	4 226.4	196.4	786 563	121 568	17.0	13.3	22.0	463 625	5 988	66 047
Bernalillo	251.7	19 664	648.1	1 646.1	98.1	269 703	49 993	15.0	14.8	15.1	151 742	1 890	10 106
Catron	1.4	14 000	3.7	10.5	0.3	NA	NA	NA	NA	NA	NA	NA	NA
Chaves	32.4	17 053	133.8	240.7	11.9	10 632	1 977	43.6	1.8	35.5	5 134	67	1 275
Cibola	2.1	10 500	6.8	17.0	0.1	NA	NA	NA	NA	NA	NA	NA	NA
Colfax	2.8	9 333	9.1	16.4	0.8	1 185	87	0.0	0.0	0.0	453	6	285
Curry	5.2	17 333	18.0	96.9	D	30 416	3 103	9.3	51.4	5.1	22 249	236	2 121
De Baca	D	D	D	D	D	NA	NA	NA	NA	NA	NA	NA	NA
Dona Ana	29.9	14 950	127.3	262.5	5.5	53 443	13 822	14.5	9.1	35.7	33 369	553	3 098
Eddy	D	D	D	D	D	10 250	2 086	37.8	3.2	10.7	3 168	41	1 527
Grant	D	D	D	D	D	NA	NA	NA	NA	NA	NA	NA	NA
Guadalupe	D	D	D	D	D	NA	NA	NA	NA	NA	NA	NA	NA
Harding	D	D	D	D	D	NA	NA	NA	NA	NA	NA	NA	NA
Hidalgo	D	D	D	D	D	NA	NA	NA	NA	NA	NA	NA	NA
Lea	5.2	17 333	18.9	38.4	D	3 762	1 636	7.8	0.8	39.7	0	0	498
Lincoln	D	D	D	D	D	9 505	1 021	18.7	0.0	17.3	6 454	63	1 202
Los Alamos	0.7	NA	4.2	6.9	0.5	6 542	647	78.9	12.4	0.0	3 832	27	1 361
Luna	1.4	14 000	7.9	11.3	D	1 985	123	0.0	0.0	97.1	1 062	21	438
McKinley	10.7	15 286	48.5	219.9	D	8 264	1 356	0.0	0.0	83.0	2 942	79	269
Mora	D	D	D	D	D	NA	NA	NA	NA	NA	NA	NA	NA
Otero	6.7	13 400	22.9	53.5	D	6 428	1 527	29.6	0.0	30.8	3 860	52	497
Quay	D	D	D	D	D	1 589	147	0.0	44.7	0.0	0	0	248
Rio Arriba	2.4	24 000	4.6	11.6	D	1 817	506	0.0	0.0	76.6	637	11	462
Roosevelt	2.8	14 000	26.3	111.3	2.4	2 090	125	28.0	0.0	0.0	1 405	37	446
Sandoval	D	D	D	D	D	26 448	2 396	3.3	3.0	73.7	20 857	428	1 227
San Juan	7.8	15 600	42.2	158.2	3.0	17 610	5 493	22.1	20.2	12.4	5 376	95	1 700
San Miguel	3.7	18 500	6.8	27.0	0.5	NA	NA	NA	NA	NA	NA	NA	NA
Santa Fe	13.0	14 444	55.2	89.0	3.0	99 954	7 448	52.5	15.0	21.5	52 281	483	16 128
Sierra	D	D	D	D	D	1 817	268	6.7	0.0	0.0	940	27	31
Socorro	D	D	D	D	D	551	0	NA	NA	NA	296	9	255
Taos	D	D	D	D	D	10 280	3 299	20.6	1.1	33.2	4 316	76	1 205
Torrance	D	D	D	D	D	285	0	NA	NA	NA	74	1	8
Union	D	D	D	D	D	NA	NA	NA	NA	NA	NA	NA	NA
Valencia	1.1	11 000	5.6	10.4	0.4	13 794	2 273	12.8	16.0	3.6	10 178	154	888
NEW YORK	14 408.2	19 920	80 033.3	145 656.5	4 296.5	6 825 322	1 687 133	22.6	15.9	28.9	2 892 990	36 637	872 327
Albany	203.8	24 262	1 236.1	2 232.7	77.4	192 457	59 356	36.4	1.2	32.1	68 145	698	33 460
Allegany	36.1	20 056	128.2	297.0	14.1	15 834	7 128	2.5	52.1	12.2	5 309	105	1 614
Bronx	272.4	15 566	966.9	1 771.2	46.1	113 871	28 149	0.9	8.6	31.6	65 668	1 182	7 103
Broome	241.3	19 618	1 856.7	2 898.1	D	106 409	27 280	17.6	43.9	19.5	36 744	410	9 205
Cattaraugus	89.0	17 115	410.7	679.0	11.9	27 368	5 518	0.0	23.4	11.6	14 921	276	2 839
Cayuga	68.3	19 514	268.0	539.1	17.8	29 857	7 182	16.6	0.2	50.4	17 042	261	2 086
Chautauqua	222.0	21 143	859.5	1 887.7	55.8	46 325	17 121	1.3	6.8	52.7	16 141	237	6 625
Chemung	93.1	18 620	349.0	623.1	19.7	47 724	9 571	47.2	6.4	29.4	10 267	113	13 599
Chenango	55.5	15 857	312.8	489.2	9.1	21 686	5 536	7.2	34.7	18.9	8 773	191	902
Clinton	64.9	21 633	356.8	662.2	16.7	34 874	8 741	4.1	9.6	9.2	18 146	295	1 812
Columbia	31.9	15 950	132.6	295.7	5.7	39 325	20 246	32.2	7.4	10.6	11 562	148	6 460
Cortland	64.9	16 225	362.6	637.6	20.9	18 291	3 556	8.4	23.1	12.3	8 451	140	1 085
Delaware	78.6	20 684	235.0	475.6	16.9	24 479	3 419	0.8	2.6	27.4	14 476	224	2 206
Dutchess	198.1	19 810	2 063.3	5 464.8	D	172 262	46 346	21.0	0.3	33.6	67 457	647	18 975
Erie	1 366.5	25 353	5 255.8	10 907.1	280.8	504 172	109 421	28.6	7.3	39.6	263 530	2 743	33 927
Essex	30.4	25 333	133.0	242.6	12.3	23 751	522	0.0	12.4	16.3	16 777	264	4 130
Franklin	14.3	13 000	43.0	102.9	4.2	20 319	7 883	7.0	0.0	83.0	8 241	168	1 478
Fulton	51.4	13 892	186.9	409.0	7.3	18 426	6 426	1.6	59.1	17.4	5 014	74	4 675
Genesee	62.7	19 594	232.7	530.9	12.4	26 498	7 785	0.0	16.2	21.1	11 176	159	2 586
Greene	16.8	18 667	71.3	139.1	4.1	30 897	2 286	31.9	0.0	9.8	23 438	319	2 999
Hamilton	1.4	14 000	2.8	5.7	0.3	7 175	637	0.0	0.0	9.4	4 942	81	1 004
Herkimer	65.1	18 083	207.1	395.6	11.2	32 887	8 985	17.9	1.0	45.2	15 578	214	2 453

1. Includes nonresidential additions and alterations, residential nonhousekeeping buildings, and residential garages and carports not shown separately.

STATE County	Wholesale trade, 1987: Establishments	Wholesale trade, 1987: Sales (Mil dol)	Wholesale trade, 1987: Paid employees[1]	Wholesale trade, 1987: Annual payroll (Mil dol)	Retail trade, all establishments, 1987: Number	Retail trade, all establishments, 1987: Sales: Total (Mil dol)	Retail trade, all establishments, 1987: Sales: Percent change, 1982–1987	Retail trade, all establishments, 1987: Sales: Per capita[2] (Dollars)	Retail trade, establishments with payroll, 1987: Number	Retail trade, establishments with payroll, 1987: Sales: Total (Mil dol)	Per capita[2] (Dollars): General merchandise stores	Per capita[2] (Dollars): Food stores	Per capita[2] (Dollars): Apparel & accessory stores	Per capita[2] (Dollars): Eating and drinking places
	147	148	149	150	151	152	153	154	155	156	157	158	159	160
NEW JERSEY—Con.														
Ocean	386	812.0	3 055	67.4	3 752	3 075.9	69.6	7 640	2 390	3 008.8	733	1 622	312	561
Passaic	1 110	6 761.3	15 787	419.7	4 255	3 325.5	58.1	7 178	2 691	3 224.0	927	1 129	554	545
Salem	64	194.1	693	11.0	514	327.5	64.1	4 985	298	313.7	D	811	116	434
Somerset	525	3 574.0	7 520	223.1	2 221	1 970.0	65.0	8 902	1 420	1 922.3	702	1 874	324	758
Sussex	132	221.2	1 012	23.0	1 267	726.5	70.6	5 830	737	694.6	252	1 545	162	389
Union	1 462	11 838.5	25 194	673.9	4 795	3 487.7	46.4	6 945	3 224	3 390.6	284	1 300	382	562
Warren	135	639.7	1 968	68.5	939	644.6	57.0	7 359	581	627.7	413	1 559	204	463
NEW MEXICO	2 398	5 102.4	22 137	421.8	15 168	8 202.1	29.8	5 482	9 032	7 919.6	626	1 114	227	572
Bernalillo	1 149	3 032.1	12 616	271.6	4 490	3 373.9	47.0	6 924	2 868	3 296.9	922	1 155	316	766
Catron	0	0.0	0	0.0	38	3.6	-2.7	1 281	11	2.5	D	D	0	0
Chaves	101	359.2	1 534	19.8	584	277.5	-4.0	5 027	349	266.1	616	1 201	200	516
Cibola	21	21.2	104	1.4	208	82.7	7.8	3 865	114	76.5	337	704	D	472
Colfax	18	14.8	58	0.9	222	75.0	3.6	5 434	140	71.6	D	1 089	202	895
Curry	72	115.5	557	7.1	515	263.2	32.1	6 078	334	256.1	773	1 304	262	561
De Baca	0	0.0	0	0.0	46	8.1	19.1	3 507	23	7.0	0	1 096	D	333
Dona Ana	129	229.8	1 141	17.9	1 004	532.3	32.2	4 146	606	515.6	561	810	175	424
Eddy	78	79.0	446	7.6	519	252.0	-1.1	5 050	316	244.3	624	1 016	200	422
Grant	29	25.3	190	2.2	273	133.2	41.1	4 970	164	129.3	299	1 444	226	486
Guadalupe	4	D	D	D	72	27.1	-14.5	6 457	41	25.3	D	D	70	903
Harding	3	D	D	D	24	3.5	25.0	3 488	8	2.6	0	D	0	D
Hidalgo	3	2.3	16	0.1	83	26.4	-7.7	4 393	49	25.7	D	952	D	320
Lea	170	326.2	1 039	20.3	673	284.1	-18.1	4 767	385	272.3	431	1 460	282	349
Lincoln	16	15.1	68	0.8	313	89.4	11.6	6 620	158	83.4	D	1 340	380	846
Los Alamos	13	80.6	212	5.6	180	71.9	33.9	3 709	103	68.1	D	1 594	161	399
Luna	21	31.7	147	1.9	202	86.6	34.9	4 784	110	80.6	D	1 282	101	278
McKinley	73	136.6	667	10.2	520	332.0	18.3	5 132	373	323.3	472	1 019	173	542
Mora	0	0.0	0	0.0	45	5.0	4.2	1 133	12	2.6	0	172	0	D
Otero	41	27.9	200	2.9	522	232.4	25.6	4 531	289	225.0	429	1 040	144	354
Quay	16	27.5	172	2.0	182	58.5	0.5	5 044	98	55.6	D	1 224	144	737
Rio Arriba	17	12.5	161	1.4	304	109.3	39.4	3 385	136	99.6	168	960	D	263
Roosevelt	25	24.2	182	1.9	163	77.0	36.0	4 665	97	74.6	211	1 479	179	378
Sandoval	11	6.0	33	0.7	348	87.0	71.3	1 535	152	79.2	51	401	D	223
San Juan	170	283.2	1 186	22.4	843	497.5	13.9	5 603	517	481.7	750	1 288	193	447
San Miguel	10	11.6	74	0.7	245	90.3	25.1	3 611	139	85.6	307	1 136	116	427
Santa Fe	122	155.9	974	17.7	1 284	666.8	44.0	7 240	787	640.0	D	985	385	888
Sierra	10	3.3	25	0.3	165	41.7	51.1	4 296	83	37.8	314	1 169	29	779
Socorro	10	13.5	45	0.4	145	44.5	1.8	3 089	80	41.7	280	730	D	476
Taos	20	D	D	D	438	131.9	45.6	6 080	231	121.4	617	1 658	338	666
Torrance	5	2.6	12	0.1	93	34.7	26.6	3 467	48	32.7	0	626	D	205
Union	6	4.4	20	0.2	75	16.3	-2.4	3 463	41	14.6	188	857	D	493
Valencia	35	34.3	133	1.7	350	186.8	52.0	4 778	170	180.1	193	1 793	59	315
NEW YORK	41 765	283 745.4	466 027	12 644.1	171 579	106 452.7	47.3	5 969	110 562	103 212.2	644	1 194	420	588
Albany	778	3 645.9	11 503	281.5	3 100	2 649.7	55.5	9 366	2 173	2 596.3	1 403	1 607	649	858
Allegany	55	D	D	D	520	163.2	26.4	3 271	270	152.9	239	1 000	44	355
Bronx	981	5 178.6	13 918	327.1	6 074	2 783.7	30.5	2 277	3 996	2 665.0	219	561	181	190
Broome	304	985.8	4 034	83.8	2 171	1 490.5	43.5	7 155	1 367	1 453.8	1 045	1 410	342	638
Cattaraugus	100	D	D	D	978	390.5	34.0	4 660	594	376.2	640	1 054	214	502
Cayuga	118	202.5	956	17.6	747	369.6	32.0	4 649	415	356.1	497	1 236	285	328
Chautauqua	207	647.0	2 666	49.1	1 629	744.1	33.4	5 259	1 004	719.8	627	1 262	182	440
Chemung	147	549.1	2 432	48.9	935	600.7	37.5	6 623	620	583.7	1 267	1 170	367	540
Chenango	48	D	D	D	574	236.2	47.8	4 659	279	226.4	252	1 223	128	260
Clinton	135	D	D	D	862	509.9	50.6	6 249	553	492.9	916	1 160	393	436
Columbia	102	167.8	943	15.5	726	307.3	48.5	5 063	359	290.1	281	1 320	59	336
Cortland	59	199.4	529	12.6	536	298.1	61.6	6 236	329	288.7	479	1 344	269	667
Delaware	56	44.4	271	4.5	712	293.1	63.3	6 222	364	276.1	573	1 582	71	328
Dutchess	294	653.5	2 715	65.5	2 718	1 793.1	60.9	6 926	1 688	1 740.2	903	1 505	424	497
Erie	1 860	10 282.7	23 362	522.9	9 023	5 772.0	39.2	6 035	6 006	5 648.3	713	1 362	309	596
Essex	39	49.7	265	5.5	574	219.2	70.2	6 038	359	208.9	D	1 634	225	703
Franklin	44	141.3	431	9.3	565	231.7	42.7	5 351	304	218.4	441	1 253	115	341
Fulton	85	242.0	902	15.4	581	281.9	49.2	5 240	294	266.7	450	1 274	152	252
Genesee	114	190.1	1 011	18.3	619	314.5	50.8	5 405	364	306.1	540	1 196	178	526
Greene	46	85.5	351	7.4	618	261.7	49.0	6 188	346	251.1	447	1 683	133	399
Hamilton	2	D	D	D	128	21.0	48.9	4 292	71	19.0	D	1 291	D	598
Herkimer	63	86.2	424	7.5	771	319.8	54.0	4 802	381	300.7	578	1 168	140	447

1. For pay period including March 12. 2. Based on the estimated population as of July 1 of the year shown.

STATE County	Retail trade, establishments with payroll, 1987 (cont'd)		Taxable service industries–establishments with payroll, 1987							Bank deposits,[2] June 1989		Savings capital,[3] September 1989	
				Receipts (Mil dol)									
					Selected kinds of business								
	Paid employees[1]	Annual payroll (Mil dol)	Number	Total	Hotels, motels and other lodging places	Health services	Legal services	Paid employees	Annual payroll (Mil dol)	Total (Mil dol)	Percent change, 1988–1989	Total (Mil dol)	Percent change, 1988–1989
	161	162	163	164	165	166	167	168	169	170	171	172	173
NEW JERSEY—Con.													
Ocean	28 260	326.1	2 530	810.2	27.7	267.4	70.6	17 255	306.2	4 390	3.3	2 926.6	1.4
Passaic	33 870	389.6	3 214	1 371.5	23.4	273.1	89.8	28 834	513.3	4 675	7.3	2 577.1	0.0
Salem	3 186	32.8	312	73.4	7.4	22.3	4.3	1 803	29.6	428	8.9	256.4	0.2
Somerset	18 346	232.0	2 145	1 058.9	39.0	235.5	58.7	21 180	416.9	3 033	7.5	887.5	-4.7
Sussex	6 300	73.5	785	211.3	15.9	58.8	15.5	5 150	80.0	947	4.0	309.6	1.8
Union	32 998	393.9	4 223	2 104.0	65.8	474.6	139.8	40 778	815.1	5 761	5.3	6 522.4	4.6
Warren	6 177	69.1	571	146.7	5.3	47.5	9.8	3 029	50.6	907	8.0	431.4	5.6
NEW MEXICO	104 620	941.2	9 471	4 223.2	306.1	970.3	261.6	88 313	1 602.5	8 598	2.4	4 438.3	-4.9
Bernalillo	42 368	397.4	4 082	2 615.3	105.7	505.0	155.9	48 102	1 031.2	3 298	0.6	2 462.5	6.5
Catron	28	0.2	9	0.9	0.5	D	0.0	38	0.2	NA	NA	0.0	NA
Chaves	3 460	31.8	349	84.2	8.0	29.5	11.5	2 178	30.9	337	4.7	263.0	-11.4
Cibola	1 131	8.5	76	12.2	2.8	4.6	0.3	348	2.7	31	NA	X	X
Colfax	1 150	9.6	108	18.2	5.6	3.9	1.5	491	4.8	149	-2.2	6.9	-94.8
Curry	4 967	30.5	252	46.0	4.4	19.1	2.8	1 208	15.4	358	2.9	133.2	-20.8
De Baca	125	0.8	9	D	D	D	0.0	D	D	19	1.6	0.0	NA
Dona Ana	7 063	60.9	633	235.6	15.2	64.0	8.0	5 903	90.2	560	5.3	220.3	-13.7
Eddy	3 297	27.8	292	78.7	9.0	40.4	4.1	1 896	26.8	406	1.2	144.9	-10.7
Grant	1 650	14.3	133	22.2	3.5	9.1	1.2	777	7.6	168	12.2	59.1	-0.1
Guadalupe	420	3.3	27	6.5	3.3	2.0	0.0	169	1.7	18	-5.9	0.0	NA
Harding	24	0.2	0	0.0	0.0	0.0	0.0	0	0.0	5	5.7	0.0	NA
Hidalgo	411	3.6	16	3.4	2.0	D	0.0	178	0.9	30	4.8	0.0	NA
Lea	3 385	32.1	346	124.6	3.0	55.0	4.6	2 476	38.1	339	-1.4	103.6	-15.7
Lincoln	1 268	9.7	132	27.6	6.7	3.4	1.8	500	7.0	119	-6.4	16.9	-6.5
Los Alamos	1 056	8.4	126	164.2	D	14.0	D	2 794	72.0	240	8.2	14.6	-24.5
Luna	1 021	8.6	85	13.2	5.0	3.1	0.8	413	3.8	90	2.8	54.1	-18.4
McKinley	4 369	39.1	228	46.6	12.8	9.9	1.6	1 402	13.2	215	5.9	48.4	-16.7
Mora	42	0.4	2	D	0.0	D	0.0	D	D	8	6.6	0.0	NA
Otero	2 746	25.0	199	100.7	15.6	8.8	2.7	2 582	38.6	207	1.1	115.2	2.1
Quay	931	7.0	78	13.8	6.0	2.5	0.4	407	3.6	93	4.1	18.2	-10.0
Rio Arriba	1 165	10.5	117	16.2	3.5	6.1	0.5	602	5.3	138	3.3	15.5	-14.3
Roosevelt	957	7.5	71	14.3	D	9.7	D	424	5.4	81	4.6	73.2	-6.8
Sandoval	1 206	9.6	138	19.9	D	8.2	0.6	707	7.7	96	8.5	90.8	-8.5
San Juan	5 496	54.5	470	113.5	8.2	27.9	5.8	3 043	35.8	428	14.2	92.0	-18.0
San Miguel	1 235	9.4	107	17.5	2.4	6.5	0.8	489	5.1	110	10.3	31.5	-2.6
Santa Fe	8 366	83.2	910	340.7	D	115.6	D	8 171	128.7	537	-3.0	250.9	-12.6
Sierra	619	4.7	45	5.1	1.6	1.3	D	156	1.2	61	0.2	28.4	2.2
Socorro	632	4.4	60	10.6	2.5	3.4	0.4	313	3.4	57	2.3	20.3	-13.1
Taos	1 738	15.2	170	44.7	18.6	5.8	1.5	1 693	13.3	102	7.8	120.3	-0.2
Torrance	364	2.9	26	1.5	D	D	D	58	0.4	33	3.5	0.0	NA
Union	212	1.8	26	3.7	0.8	1.5	D	120	1.0	57	-2.1	5.0	-1.6
Valencia	1 718	18.2	149	20.9	0.6	9.1	1.7	630	6.3	206	-7.4	X	X
NEW YORK	1 150 448	12 774.2	126 684	74 289.4	3 384.9	12 344.6	9 948.4	1 292 626	27 386.7	360 267	3.1	43 198.1	-2.2
Albany	30 272	304.1	2 279	1 227.5	70.6	231.4	123.5	25 513	454.7	4 648	1.8	1 008.9	2.9
Allegany	2 141	16.5	153	32.2	1.1	16.1	1.9	1 086	11.7	283	6.0	47.8	-0.2
Bronx	28 429	328.4	2 959	1 097.2	15.0	458.5	41.0	24 200	414.8	8 000	2.1	1 634.0	0.9
Broome	17 668	164.1	1 176	426.7	D	160.4	31.7	10 980	172.9	1 879	3.5	138.6	9.9
Cattaraugus	5 323	42.4	337	84.7	3.4	39.1	6.4	2 565	28.0	635	6.4	115.2	-3.9
Cayuga	4 197	39.0	367	94.4	5.2	28.6	5.8	2 373	32.8	677	1.4	0.0	NA
Chautauqua	9 312	79.6	732	198.9	23.9	67.7	12.4	5 551	69.5	1 058	2.1	206.0	-0.6
Chemung	7 482	67.1	480	152.0	6.2	61.8	10.1	3 750	58.5	710	5.2	199.6	1.6
Chenango	2 112	22.0	232	48.2	1.8	12.6	5.2	1 479	15.4	379	3.2	33.0	15.9
Clinton	5 676	56.2	384	94.7	10.9	34.6	6.0	2 555	35.0	538	11.6	191.9	1.7
Columbia	3 032	31.1	315	86.7	3.4	24.1	5.5	2 315	33.6	656	2.9	3.7	14.6
Cortland	3 709	35.0	228	64.4	4.5	17.0	2.8	1 608	21.4	402	2.6	40.5	-2.5
Delaware	2 647	27.1	267	49.2	15.4	8.3	4.6	1 301	12.9	373	-1.2	63.2	-1.8
Dutchess	18 543	202.9	1 621	550.2	31.1	184.8	42.6	12 256	202.1	1 963	6.2	992.0	-2.6
Erie	81 128	678.6	5 819	2 325.0	83.0	640.5	223.7	62 147	926.3	11 881	3.7	3 194.7	1.6
Essex	2 405	23.8	240	49.3	29.3	5.0	2.8	1 143	15.2	212	7.9	43.7	-2.4
Franklin	2 314	22.0	202	42.5	3.9	13.8	4.2	1 108	12.6	316	8.7	61.4	-3.9
Fulton	2 507	25.2	228	44.4	D	14.8	4.6	972	12.0	411	14.0	247.3	-1.1
Genesee	3 905	34.1	285	100.3	9.3	19.8	4.5	2 104	28.4	414	6.9	130.3	5.4
Greene	2 557	26.2	305	91.6	26.9	12.6	3.9	2 595	26.0	463	0.2	0.0	NA
Hamilton	194	2.2	47	5.9	2.5	D	0.0	156	1.2	31	10.4	0.0	NA
Herkimer	3 367	32.7	246	45.3	5.0	12.3	3.3	1 177	13.6	563	9.2	25.6	-10.9

1. For the period including March 12 of the year shown. 2. Includes deposits for all insured and reporting noninsured commercial and mutual savings banks. 3. Includes savings capital for all FSLIC insured savings institutions.

STATE County	Federal funds and grants, 1989							Local government finances, 1981–1982							
	Expenditures		Per capita[1] (Dollars)					General revenue						Direct general expenditure	
									Intergovernmental		Taxes				
												Per capita[2]			
	Total (Mil dol)	Percent change, 1988–1989	Total	Direct pay-ments for indi-viduals	Procure-ment contract awards	Salaries and wages	Grant awards	Total (Mil dol)	Total (Mil dol)	Percent from state	Total (Mil dol)	Total (Dollars)	Property (Dollars)	Total (Mil dol)	Percent change, 1977–1982
	174	175	176	177	178	179	180	181	182	183	184	185	186	187	188
NEW JERSEY—Con.															
Ocean	1 381.9	8.9	3 297	2 639	142	347	163	453.5	166.8	80.2	207.6	579	569	450.4	41.9
Passaic	1 306.3	-1.9	2 829	1 657	637	177	347	490.7	229.1	86.8	219.8	485	480	515.4	46.9
Salem	303.1	4.2	4 565	1 704	308	2 122	260	91.0	48.6	95.3	28.7	440	436	85.1	63.9
Somerset	500.5	12.3	2 171	1 443	214	390	115	257.3	66.8	89.9	154.0	751	740	243.9	50.4
Sussex	208.8	0.2	1 631	1 243	67	146	165	128.6	43.1	94.2	71.8	606	597	123.8	52.7
Union	1 323.2	2.5	2 670	1 936	248	255	219	610.0	235.8	85.0	308.6	612	606	586.9	50.6
Warren	202.0	1.6	2 262	1 812	87	142	195	90.7	37.0	92.6	40.7	479	474	89.2	67.0
NEW MEXICO	8 183.7	-6.8	X	1 746	2 053	840	653	1 465.9	931.6	88.7	261.4	191	137	1 426.8	97.1
Bernalillo	3 368.2	4.0	6 715	1 795	3 455	1 140	317	506.0	297.9	89.2	103.8	239	203	449.1	86.0
Catron	14.3	78.2	5 311	1 899	346	1 023	2 003	3.7	3.0	93.1	0.3	127	121	3.7	119.4
Chaves	153.1	3.4	2 784	2 030	82	261	302	64.9	38.5	87.6	7.8	145	78	56.0	83.4
Cibola	46.5	-4.6	2 291	378	762	328	815	22.1	16.7	87.4	2.8	94	61	20.6	0.0
Colfax	46.7	-7.5	3 513	2 700	41	184	560	14.4	10.3	95.3	2.5	184	132	13.6	94.1
Curry	208.2	3.9	4 911	1 735	330	2 147	266	36.4	28.5	89.1	4.2	97	56	36.1	70.0
De Baca	11.4	52.5	5 176	2 639	265	278	1 640	2.9	2.2	96.7	0.4	169	139	2.9	101.4
Dona Ana	649.4	17.1	4 754	1 566	1 472	1 332	365	123.9	66.3	91.4	10.5	102	66	124.0	130.5
Eddy	151.5	-31.0	3 190	2 006	626	248	259	54.1	35.2	81.3	12.7	246	139	49.6	86.1
Grant	66.0	10.7	2 435	1 854	16	202	358	32.5	19.9	88.3	4.5	160	114	31.6	120.4
Guadalupe	13.4	-46.9	3 345	1 942	102	206	964	6.5	5.4	91.2	0.8	171	102	5.8	71.7
Harding	3.5	12.9	3 526	1 921	58	458	302	1.6	1.3	94.4	0.1	144	127	2.1	115.3
Hidalgo	15.7	35.3	2 715	1 382	12	199	862	7.8	5.2	91.0	1.8	291	275	6.9	17.4
Lea	107.3	13.5	1 915	1 479	17	86	272	75.2	44.2	91.3	20.5	325	185	66.0	113.3
Lincoln	33.6	0.4	2 548	1 958	83	272	189	23.7	15.7	78.4	4.8	408	299	19.8	86.9
Los Alamos	1 036.5	-47.3	53 702	987	51 770	383	557	21.9	15.8	63.7	2.1	121	100	22.5	75.9
Luna	64.9	3.2	3 547	2 372	52	233	745	20.0	13.7	81.2	1.8	111	94	19.5	145.3
McKinley	219.7	9.6	3 270	1 008	253	958	1 038	46.3	34.5	89.8	7.5	125	85	52.6	101.6
Mora	15.3	-5.7	3 645	1 815	57	267	1 474	4.6	4.3	89.2	0.2	38	37	4.6	28.3
Otero	328.9	-5.9	6 436	1 824	1 222	3 123	258	35.5	27.3	88.8	4.0	85	63	32.6	71.3
Quay	37.3	-8.6	3 305	2 012	19	272	385	16.5	10.8	78.1	1.4	134	72	13.7	69.2
Rio Arriba	103.2	17.7	3 167	1 666	278	276	933	33.1	23.5	92.1	6.9	223	103	34.2	84.7
Roosevelt	53.6	0.9	3 288	1 950	15	152	394	15.6	10.7	93.8	2.0	124	68	14.1	55.6
Sandoval	115.4	17.0	1 723	1 219	33	117	351	20.5	15.8	87.1	3.1	84	74	20.7	71.0
San Juan	187.0	-6.7	2 197	1 159	89	480	438	101.4	52.5	90.0	30.8	342	220	150.3	186.9
San Miguel	84.2	21.3	3 356	1 615	138	186	1 406	25.2	19.6	90.0	3.0	129	86	25.1	75.7
Santa Fe	352.9	0.6	3 668	1 431	78	535	1 614	63.9	44.0	91.0	10.8	139	81	66.3	99.1
Sierra	46.7	13.3	4 813	3 656	376	340	424	6.6	4.8	90.8	0.8	94	59	6.0	42.6
Socorro	52.8	23.0	3 566	1 480	705	477	885	10.7	8.2	89.8	1.4	97	68	10.7	66.2
Taos	56.2	3.5	2 612	1 637	69	317	574	25.6	21.3	87.5	2.9	140	78	24.9	81.9
Torrance	19.8	-38.9	1 849	1 416	41	153	130	11.2	9.3	94.2	1.2	149	136	10.9	120.1
Union	19.5	27.7	4 325	1 967	49	379	1 346	6.4	4.9	93.6	0.9	169	108	5.9	61.1
Valencia	108.9	9.6	2 612	2 012	34	123	430	25.3	20.2	91.2	3.3	99	86	24.5	1.5
NEW YORK	66 655.7	9.4	X	1 900	493	351	924	35 526.1	14 351.9	88.3	16 005.3	910	575	32 638.0	33.6
Albany	2 754.4	5.1	9 781	2 195	776	1 128	5 658	455.6	218.6	97.1	191.7	674	479	408.3	21.8
Allegany	115.5	6.6	2 287	1 650	53	113	441	73.4	39.4	90.2	23.2	449	354	75.0	68.7
Bronx	X	NA	X	X	X	X	X	NA	NA	NA	NA	NA	NA	NA	NA
Broome	708.8	-6.2	3 419	1 959	838	195	415	320.6	147.6	90.5	122.6	576	414	321.3	30.4
Cattaraugus	216.1	1.8	2 594	1 810	130	135	467	128.1	65.9	90.2	43.7	508	374	130.1	47.5
Cayuga	189.5	10.2	2 363	1 688	100	104	414	111.4	57.0	90.8	39.2	491	386	108.8	36.4
Chautauqua	418.0	12.5	2 977	1 980	226	141	607	219.2	103.3	90.3	82.8	566	425	220.7	26.9
Chemung	272.0	3.6	2 963	2 137	63	227	523	121.8	54.6	91.6	53.7	562	408	124.6	13.0
Chenango	126.0	10.0	2 437	1 629	247	110	432	70.1	38.8	93.1	24.5	491	419	70.2	36.6
Clinton	289.2	8.4	3 518	1 438	294	1 316	444	110.6	65.7	89.7	35.3	437	312	110.8	48.2
Columbia	157.4	8.4	2 567	1 836	109	122	478	69.7	31.2	94.8	31.2	521	442	71.8	52.7
Cortland	99.8	10.4	2 079	1 503	40	117	398	68.3	35.7	93.9	25.0	518	380	68.3	23.8
Delaware	117.4	7.3	2 462	1 790	100	131	415	78.7	33.7	77.0	28.2	606	598	82.9	87.8
Dutchess	578.7	2.9	2 186	1 492	57	282	343	313.8	130.6	93.1	142.6	573	503	309.9	35.3
Erie	3 091.6	4.6	3 238	2 129	148	332	617	1 720.2	874.9	82.6	644.9	646	454	1 684.8	28.1
Essex	114.7	9.6	3 133	2 006	35	335	742	59.6	26.2	85.6	25.3	694	553	62.2	61.6
Franklin	127.6	10.6	2 934	1 923	87	171	736	73.9	43.9	90.2	22.9	520	408	77.8	62.0
Fulton	133.3	-11.8	2 487	1 925	66	92	393	73.3	41.4	92.9	25.0	454	339	69.7	43.3
Genesee	149.6	9.3	2 552	1 730	16	282	456	83.5	39.2	92.0	31.0	521	369	85.7	28.4
Greene	106.0	4.6	2 437	1 928	28	125	339	63.4	20.6	92.1	27.6	677	537	64.2	47.3
Hamilton	13.7	9.8	2 787	2 284	29	212	248	11.1	2.1	91.2	8.2	1 639	1 497	11.6	41.4
Herkimer	159.4	5.0	2 380	1 872	56	93	345	101.6	48.9	93.3	30.2	454	443	101.0	61.0

1. Based on the estimated population as of July 1 of the year shown. 2. Based on the estimated population as of July 1, 1982.

STATE County	Local government finances, 1981–1982 (cont'd) — Direct general expenditure (cont'd) — Per capita[1] (Dollars)	Percent of total for– Education	Percent of total for– Health & hospitals	Percent of total for– Police protection	Percent of total for– Public welfare	Percent of total for– Highways	Debt outstanding — Total (Mil dol)	Debt outstanding — Per capita[1] (Dollars)	State and local government employment, 1989 — Total	State and local government employment, 1989 — Rate[2]	Federal government civilian employment 1989 — Total	Federal government civilian employment 1989 — Earnings ($1,000)	Elections, 1988[3] — Total vote cast for president	Elections, 1988[3] — Vote for lead party (Percent)
	189	190	191	192	193	194	195	196	197	198	199	200	201	202
NEW JERSEY—Con.														
Ocean	1 256	43.8	1.2	5.7	5.7	5.4	557.7	1 556	18 775	448.0	3 784	127 882	190 558	R–65.4
Passaic	1 138	40.2	2.4	5.5	10.4	4.1	387.7	856	22 948	497.0	2 090	67 690	157 513	R–55.9
Salem	1 305	51.4	2.9	4.0	3.5	9.7	82.1	1 259	3 806	573.2	233	6 524	25 606	R–59.5
Somerset	1 190	55.4	1.3	5.1	3.4	7.5	221.8	1 082	11 784	511.2	3 120	102 227	106 193	R–63.7
Sussex	1 045	63.0	1.7	3.3	2.2	9.3	73.9	623	6 275	490.2	307	9 149	50 160	R–71.9
Union	1 164	43.1	2.6	5.9	5.9	3.0	298.0	591	25 387	512.2	2 683	91 322	208 153	R–54.3
Warren	1 051	49.5	2.3	3.3	5.8	8.1	50.9	599	4 582	513.1	323	9 588	33 666	R–64.5
NEW MEXICO	1 043	54.1	4.9	5.3	0.3	5.7	2 197.1	1 606	114 769	752.5	31 574	941 895	521 287	R–51.9
Bernalillo	1 036	50.3	2.6	6.3	0.1	4.1	503.7	1 162	37 826	754.1	13 851	442 193	173 135	R–53.6
Catron	1 381	57.8	1.2	5.3	0.0	15.6	0.4	159	193	714.8	158	3 399	1 486	R–62.2
Chaves	1 047	50.9	12.3	5.3	0.2	10.6	63.6	1 188	3 986	724.7	388	12 662	20 303	R–65.8
Cibola	694	57.5	0.2	6.8	0.0	12.0	6.9	231	1 403	691.1	350	8 963	6 137	D–56.3
Colfax	1 001	62.5	0.1	5.5	0.0	5.0	2.9	213	1 151	865.4	51	1 348	5 085	D–54.8
Curry	841	66.1	0.1	4.9	0.0	5.1	5.6	129	1 808	426.4	921	18 961	12 138	R–66.2
De Baca	1 208	49.6	0.2	3.3	0.2	10.9	2.9	1 198	178	809.1	17	418	1 136	R–56.6
Dona Ana	1 200	47.0	31.0	3.5	0.0	4.2	51.2	496	11 559	846.2	4 598	155 286	41 747	R–51.7
Eddy	965	51.9	0.3	5.9	0.0	10.2	18.4	358	2 282	480.4	413	12 273	18 535	R–52.9
Grant	1 116	57.1	14.0	4.3	0.3	5.1	10.1	356	2 238	825.8	221	5 837	9 735	D–55.9
Guadalupe	1 322	71.1	0.2	5.6	0.1	5.4	1.4	323	307	767.5	27	658	2 119	D–58.7
Harding	2 116	77.4	0.4	1.7	0.0	8.5	0.2	241	86	860.0	15	272	672	R–56.1
Hidalgo	1 094	67.0	1.7	10.3	0.0	4.9	3.2	510	362	624.1	32	1 084	2 020	R–54.5
Lea	1 049	59.0	0.4	7.2	0.0	6.7	45.0	715	2 644	472.1	138	4 099	17 303	R–65.4
Lincoln	1 676	49.2	1.5	6.1	0.0	8.1	14.3	1 208	984	745.5	134	3 394	5 288	R–66.4
Los Alamos	1 274	59.3	0.5	6.2	0.0	10.1	7.5	424	9 864	5 110.9	235	7 805	10 153	R–65.2
Luna	1 194	43.4	13.1	4.4	0.2	13.2	5.1	311	1 154	630.6	150	5 371	6 636	R–51.5
McKinley	879	73.4	0.1	3.9	0.6	4.9	19.6	327	2 691	400.4	2 411	63 379	15 467	D–62.0
Mora	1 037	82.7	0.0	1.5	0.0	2.1	0.6	140	240	571.4	36	721	2 545	D–62.9
Otero	702	69.5	0.1	5.3	0.1	4.2	16.4	353	2 341	458.1	2 578	62 890	15 478	R–64.5
Quay	1 292	51.5	15.4	4.9	0.0	6.5	8.1	761	758	670.8	86	2 431	4 412	R–55.6
Rio Arriba	1 106	78.0	0.1	3.4	1.0	3.7	8.4	272	2 084	639.3	379	8 422	10 626	D–70.6
Roosevelt	872	62.3	9.8	3.9	0.0	7.8	2.5	155	1 481	908.6	68	1 689	5 681	R–63.2
Sandoval	571	75.9	0.0	5.5	0.0	5.9	6.6	182	1 203	179.6	357	8 545	19 011	R–49.5
San Juan	1 672	35.9	0.2	3.6	0.4	6.1	1 282.7	14 268	4 452	523.1	1 436	38 961	27 750	R–58.4
San Miguel	1 075	77.5	0.1	4.3	1.0	3.0	4.6	199	3 427	1 365.3	166	4 100	9 023	D–67.9
Santa Fe	850	49.3	0.3	5.9	2.5	5.3	86.6	1 110	10 664	1 108.5	1 468	43 243	36 927	D–63.9
Sierra	669	58.3	0.6	6.9	0.2	6.7	1.5	163	542	558.8	113	3 363	4 165	R–60.2
Socorro	771	61.9	0.3	4.2	0.2	8.8	2.5	180	1 962	1 325.7	220	6 569	6 217	R–50.1
Taos	1 226	68.1	0.0	4.4	2.1	4.4	3.6	176	1 099	511.2	305	7 458	9 259	D–67.7
Torrance	1 378	75.1	0.0	3.2	3.2	4.5	2.3	289	581	543.0	68	1 398	3 938	R–57.2
Union	1 130	64.9	2.1	4.6	0.8	8.5	1.7	323	281	624.4	53	1 203	1 960	R–65.9
Valencia	738	74.0	0.8	4.4	0.0	7.4	7.4	223	2 938	704.6	131	3 500	15 200	R–51.8
NEW YORK	1 856	33.5	7.0	5.0	16.7	4.5	23 547.8	1 339	1 245 839	694.0	163 477	5 260 775	6 485 683	D–51.6
Albany	1 435	32.4	1.5	4.3	15.1	5.8	906.7	3 187	68 366	2 427.8	7 692	252 258	147 461	D–58.7
Allegany	1 453	42.0	10.1	1.3	18.1	12.7	22.5	437	3 470	687.1	121	3 381	17 626	R–67.4
Bronx	NA	NA	NA	NA	NA	NA	NA	NA	16 626	134.8	9 810	314 271	298 081	D–73.2
Broome	1 509	45.6	3.3	2.8	14.6	6.6	193.2	907	16 774	809.2	901	28 572	96 365	D–49.9
Cattaraugus	1 515	44.8	4.9	2.0	16.8	11.2	40.3	469	5 683	682.2	243	7 198	32 428	R–60.7
Cayuga	1 364	45.9	4.0	2.4	14.6	9.9	34.4	431	5 125	639.0	176	5 211	32 285	R–52.5
Chautauqua	1 509	42.9	5.8	2.9	16.5	9.1	111.5	762	8 919	635.3	427	13 008	57 867	R–54.7
Chemung	1 305	42.7	2.3	3.0	16.2	6.5	75.1	786	6 293	685.5	436	14 914	37 139	R–56.4
Chenango	1 409	53.1	1.8	1.5	10.7	12.0	43.6	876	3 584	693.2	116	3 415	19 902	R–58.9
Clinton	1 374	48.2	5.7	1.2	14.6	7.9	43.7	542	6 911	840.8	1 416	35 841	28 563	R–55.0
Columbia	1 199	49.3	2.1	1.7	14.3	12.0	25.2	420	3 613	589.4	166	4 768	26 924	R–56.1
Cortland	1 415	44.1	2.2	2.2	15.1	9.5	28.6	593	3 594	748.8	95	2 924	18 769	R–58.3
Delaware	1 778	35.7	13.4	0.9	14.8	13.3	30.5	655	3 895	816.6	134	3 845	19 010	R–59.9
Dutchess	1 246	53.8	3.7	2.4	11.3	6.3	175.3	705	21 608	816.3	2 239	73 006	101 959	R–61.0
Erie	1 688	35.0	5.8	3.5	15.3	4.8	1 101.8	1 104	64 483	675.4	9 105	284 065	430 792	D–55.4
Essex	1 709	32.8	2.8	1.0	20.6	13.2	24.7	679	3 448	942.1	340	10 864	17 113	R–60.5
Franklin	1 769	47.6	1.7	1.1	19.4	9.6	24.1	547	5 441	1 250.8	155	5 095	17 192	R–53.1
Fulton	1 266	45.2	1.5	2.8	18.7	7.6	25.4	461	3 127	583.4	118	3 544	20 931	R–56.2
Genesee	1 443	50.1	2.0	2.5	14.6	10.3	46.1	775	4 117	702.6	633	18 680	24 332	R–58.3
Greene	1 573	41.7	12.2	1.3	15.2	13.0	23.9	586	3 197	734.9	106	2 941	19 319	R–61.5
Hamilton	2 324	35.7	3.7	1.4	6.5	22.9	2.4	484	710	1 449.0	18	405	3 317	R–69.9
Herkimer	1 516	43.8	14.2	1.6	11.3	9.2	40.8	613	4 436	662.1	134	3 904	28 022	R–53.9

1. Based on the estimated population as of July 1, 1982. 2. Per 10,000 resident population estimated as of July 1 of the year shown. 3. Data subject to copyright.

STATE-County code	MSA/CMSA/NECMA code[1]	STATE County	Land Area,[2] 1990 (Sq. Km.)	Population, 1990: Total persons	Rank	Per square kilometer	Race: White	Race: Black	Race: Am. Indian, Eskimo, Aleut	Race: Asian & Pacific Islander	Race: Other race	Hispanic[3]	Age of population, Percent: Under 5 years	5 to 14 years	15 to 24 years
			1	2	3	4	5	6	7	8	9	10	11	12	13
		NEW YORK—Con.													
36 045	...	Jefferson	3 295	110 943	416	33.7	101 157	6 501	436	959	1 890	3 136	8.6	15.0	18.0
36 047	5602	Kings	183	2 300 664	6	12 571.9	1 078 549	872 305	7 969	111 251	230 590	462 411	7.8	14.4	15.0
36 049	...	Lewis	3 304	26 796	1 396	8.1	26 470	113	61	93	59	128	8.4	17.4	13.6
36 051	6840	Livingston	1 637	62 372	698	38.1	59 983	1 513	188	323	365	975	6.8	13.8	19.2
36 053	8160	Madison	1 699	69 120	641	40.7	67 481	752	260	421	206	572	7.1	14.2	19.9
36 055	6840	Monroe	1 708	713 968	58	418.0	600 328	85 041	2 020	12 667	13 912	26 450	7.6	13.3	15.0
36 057	0160	Montgomery	1 048	51 981	813	49.6	50 173	444	94	217	1 053	2 703	6.9	13.8	12.5
36 059	5602	Nassau	743	1 287 348	21	1 732.6	1 115 119	111 057	1 642	39 299	20 231	77 386	6.1	11.9	13.7
36 061	5602	New York	73	1 487 536	15	20 377.2	867 227	326 967	5 728	110 629	176 985	386 630	5.3	8.7	12.7
36 063	1282	Niagara	1 354	220 756	225	163.0	205 308	12 104	2 011	806	527	2 098	7.1	13.9	13.6
36 065	8680	Oneida	3 141	250 836	199	79.9	232 461	13 661	504	2 175	2 035	5 804	7.0	13.4	15.2
36 067	8160	Onondaga	2 021	468 973	104	232.0	418 533	37 724	3 259	6 842	2 615	7 195	7.5	13.4	15.7
36 069	6840	Ontario	1 669	95 101	487	57.0	92 273	1 718	228	500	382	1 266	7.3	13.9	14.2
36 071	5602	Orange	2 114	307 647	162	145.5	273 600	22 223	824	3 549	7 451	21 535	8.3	15.2	14.8
36 073	6840	Orleans	1 014	41 846	959	41.3	38 288	2 754	194	147	463	1 029	7.4	15.3	14.4
36 075	8160	Oswego	2 469	121 771	378	49.3	119 910	619	429	477	336	1 159	7.8	15.7	17.5
36 077	...	Otsego	2 598	60 517	717	23.3	59 111	810	116	316	164	720	6.3	13.1	20.1
36 079	5602	Putnam	600	83 941	545	139.9	81 827	851	121	758	384	2 246	7.7	13.8	13.5
36 081	5602	Queens	283	1 951 598	9	6 896.1	1 129 192	423 211	7 050	238 336	153 809	381 120	6.2	11.2	13.7
36 083	0160	Rensselaer	1 694	154 429	301	91.2	146 197	5 170	277	2 204	581	1 864	7.0	13.0	16.8
36 085	5602	Richmond	152	378 977	133	2 493.3	322 043	30 630	715	16 941	8 648	30 239	7.4	13.3	14.7
36 087	5602	Rockland	451	265 475	185	588.6	222 858	26 468	654	10 753	4 742	17 711	7.2	14.3	14.7
36 089	...	St. Lawrence	6 956	111 974	410	16.1	108 270	1 621	830	805	448	1 275	6.6	14.3	20.6
36 091	0160	Saratoga	2 103	181 276	270	86.2	176 903	2 278	264	1 388	443	1 951	7.4	14.1	14.7
36 093	0160	Schenectady	534	149 285	317	279.6	139 843	6 348	261	1 822	1 011	2 489	7.0	12.3	13.5
36 095	...	Schoharie	1 611	31 859	1 215	19.8	31 096	428	69	105	161	538	6.3	13.8	18.1
36 097	...	Schuyler	851	18 662	1 754	21.9	18 353	157	50	39	63	165	7.1	15.5	12.9
36 099	...	Seneca	842	33 683	1 172	40.0	32 731	538	84	215	115	363	7.4	14.1	13.3
36 101	...	Steuben	3 607	99 088	463	27.5	97 039	1 153	205	551	140	518	7.4	15.4	13.0
36 103	5602	Suffolk	2 360	1 321 864	20	560.1	1 190 315	82 910	2 994	23 100	22 545	87 852	7.0	13.3	15.1
36 105	...	Sullivan	2 512	69 277	640	27.6	61 248	5 884	140	547	1 458	4 747	7.2	13.8	13.0
36 107	0960	Tioga	1 343	52 337	809	39.0	51 498	314	95	313	117	367	7.9	16.0	12.7
36 109	...	Tompkins	1 233	94 097	491	76.3	84 874	3 132	281	5 144	666	2 117	5.6	10.8	29.6
36 111	...	Ulster	2 918	165 304	288	56.6	153 130	8 055	470	1 969	1 680	6 832	6.9	12.8	13.9
36 113	2975	Warren	2 253	59 209	736	26.3	58 452	301	110	270	76	476	6.8	13.8	14.4
36 115	2975	Washington	2 164	59 330	731	27.4	56 705	2 051	104	122	348	1 313	7.3	14.2	14.6
36 117	6840	Wayne	1 565	89 123	515	56.9	85 014	2 793	240	341	735	1 518	8.1	15.7	13.0
36 119	5602	Westchester	1 121	874 866	35	780.4	694 308	120 195	1 405	32 169	26 789	86 194	6.6	11.6	13.1
36 121	...	Wyoming	1 536	42 507	945	27.7	39 735	2 065	89	127	491	1 004	7.0	15.2	14.0
36 123	...	Yates	876	22 810	1 542	26.0	22 501	148	47	69	45	230	7.4	15.0	13.4
37 000	...	NORTH CAROLINA	126 180	6 628 637	X	52.5	5 008 491	1 456 323	80 155	52 166	31 502	76 726	6.9	13.2	15.9
37 001	1300	Alamance	1 115	108 213	425	97.1	86 373	20 822	303	487	228	736	6.3	11.8	15.2
37 003	3290	Alexander	674	27 544	1 372	40.9	25 667	1 673	52	49	103	184	6.3	13.9	14.9
37 005	...	Alleghany	608	9 590	2 424	15.8	9 338	177	8	5	62	85	4.9	12.5	12.1
37 007	...	Anson	1 377	23 474	1 515	17.0	12 264	11 106	69	27	8	67	6.7	15.0	15.0
37 009	...	Ashe	1 104	22 209	1 570	20.1	21 960	144	21	31	53	102	5.1	12.4	13.0
37 011	...	Avery	640	14 867	1 997	23.2	14 596	158	23	23	67	118	5.7	12.6	17.7
37 013	...	Beaufort	2 144	42 283	953	19.7	28 949	13 194	28	48	64	197	6.5	14.7	13.3
37 015	...	Bertie	1 811	20 388	1 655	11.3	7 790	12 531	46	14	7	32	7.4	16.2	13.8
37 017	...	Bladen	2 266	28 663	1 341	12.6	16 926	11 199	464	30	44	150	6.3	15.3	14.3
37 019	...	Brunswick	2 214	50 985	828	23.0	41 336	9 211	242	81	115	376	6.5	12.8	12.8
37 021	0480	Buncombe	1 700	174 821	276	102.8	158 979	14 336	486	765	255	1 173	6.3	12.1	13.3
37 023	3290	Burke	1 312	75 744	593	57.7	69 521	5 178	133	794	118	344	6.3	12.5	15.0
37 025	1520	Cabarrus	944	98 935	464	104.8	85 286	12 853	313	375	108	483	6.9	13.1	14.3
37 027	...	Caldwell	1 222	70 709	627	57.9	66 506	3 881	105	111	106	315	6.4	12.8	14.9
37 029	...	Camden	623	5 904	2 772	9.5	4 388	1 481	21	9	5	24	6.5	13.4	13.0
37 031	...	Carteret	1 376	52 556	807	38.2	47 445	4 385	269	293	164	450	6.3	12.5	13.0
37 033	...	Caswell	1 103	20 693	1 645	18.8	12 155	8 436	26	20	56	136	6.0	13.2	13.8
37 035	3290	Catawba	1 036	118 412	393	114.3	106 370	10 689	232	830	291	921	6.5	13.1	14.8
37 037	...	Chatham	1 769	38 759	1 033	21.9	29 423	8 845	125	69	297	564	6.9	12.0	12.1
37 039	...	Cherokee	1 179	20 170	1 665	17.1	19 313	361	405	42	49	131	5.3	13.0	13.2
37 041	...	Chowan	447	13 506	2 101	30.2	8 349	5 087	24	29	17	95	6.9	15.0	12.0
37 043	...	Clay	556	7 155	2 638	12.9	7 061	41	39	7	7	40	4.8	13.1	12.2
37 045	...	Cleveland	1 203	84 714	541	70.4	66 362	17 741	114	394	103	376	6.8	13.3	15.0
37 047	...	Columbus	2 426	49 587	847	20.4	32 897	15 181	1 370	53	86	242	6.8	15.6	14.0

1. MSA = Metropolitan Statistical Area. CMSA = Consolidated MSA. NECMA = New England county metropolitan area. PMSA = Primary MSA. See Appendix A for explanation of these concepts. See Appendix B for list of metropolitan areas identified by type, with component counties. 2. Dry land or land partially or temporarily covered by water. 3. Hispanic persons may be of any race.

STATE County	Population, 1990 (cont'd): Age of population (cont'd), Percent: 25 to 34 years	35 to 44 years	45 to 54 years	55 to 64 years	65 to 74 years	75 years and over	Percent female	Population–Change and components of change: Change, 1980–1990: Number	Percent	Components of change, 1980–1986: Total persons, 1986	Total persons, 1980	Net change: Number	Net change: Percent	Natural increase: Births	Natural increase: Deaths
	14	15	16	17	18	19	20	21	22	23	24	25	26	27	28
NEW YORK—Con.															
Jefferson	18.6	13.4	8.2	7.1	6.1	4.8	48.7	22 792	25.9	90 600	88 151	2 500	2.8	9 000	5 900
Kings	17.6	14.7	9.9	8.3	7.0	5.4	53.4	69 636	3.1	2 293 200	2 231 028	62 200	2.8	248 900	139 500
Lewis	16.6	13.8	9.5	8.8	6.8	5.2	50.1	1 761	7.0	25 300	25 035	300	1.2	2 600	1 400
Livingston	16.6	14.6	9.7	8.2	6.3	4.9	51.8	5 366	9.4	58 600	57 006	1 600	2.8	5 100	2 800
Madison	15.1	14.1	10.2	7.9	6.7	4.8	50.8	3 970	6.1	66 600	65 150	1 400	2.2	6 100	3 200
Monroe	17.7	15.4	10.3	8.2	7.1	5.4	52.0	11 730	1.7	702 600	702 238	400	0.1	66 200	36 900
Montgomery	14.4	13.9	9.3	9.6	10.8	8.6	52.4	-1 458	-2.7	52 100	53 439	-1 400	-2.6	4 300	4 100
Nassau	15.7	15.3	11.5	11.4	9.0	5.2	51.7	-34 234	-2.6	1 323 000	1 321 582	1 500	0.1	90 800	73 300
New York	21.6	17.6	11.7	9.1	7.2	6.1	52.9	59 251	4.1	1 478 000	1 428 285	49 700	3.5	112 500	99 200
Niagara	16.1	14.4	10.0	9.7	9.0	6.1	52.1	-6 598	-2.9	216 900	227 354	-10 500	-4.6	19 600	13 900
Oneida	16.4	13.8	9.8	9.0	8.9	6.6	50.5	-2 630	-1.0	248 500	253 466	-5 000	-2.0	22 800	16 300
Onondaga	17.4	14.7	9.7	8.7	7.5	5.5	52.1	5 053	1.1	463 200	463 920	-800	-0.2	43 700	25 500
Ontario	16.1	16.1	10.5	8.6	7.5	5.6	50.9	6 192	7.0	92 200	88 909	3 300	3.7	7 900	4 800
Orange	17.3	16.1	10.3	7.4	5.9	4.5	49.7	48 044	18.5	281 700	259 603	22 100	8.5	25 600	14 600
Orleans	17.4	14.8	10.0	8.1	7.2	5.4	49.9	3 350	8.7	38 900	38 496	400	1.1	3 800	2 400
Oswego	16.6	14.4	9.6	7.7	6.3	4.4	50.9	7 870	6.9	119 600	113 901	5 700	5.0	11 200	5 800
Otsego	13.1	13.7	10.0	8.7	8.2	6.9	52.3	1 442	2.4	59 200	59 075	100	0.1	4 600	3 700
Putnam	17.4	18.0	12.7	7.8	5.0	4.0	50.1	6 748	8.7	81 600	77 193	4 400	5.7	6 600	3 400
Queens	18.6	14.9	10.9	9.7	8.3	6.4	52.5	60 273	3.2	1 923 300	1 891 325	32 000	1.7	158 600	123 600
Rensselaer	16.8	14.8	9.7	8.6	7.5	5.7	50.9	2 463	1.6	151 700	151 966	-200	-0.1	13 000	9 400
Richmond	17.5	16.1	11.3	8.5	6.6	4.6	51.7	26 948	7.7	374 600	352 029	22 500	6.4	30 300	19 100
Rockland	15.3	15.5	12.9	10.0	5.7	4.4	51.4	5 945	2.3	265 900	259 530	6 400	2.5	21 800	12 000
St. Lawrence	14.7	13.4	9.5	8.6	6.9	5.2	49.7	-2 373	-2.1	112 800	114 347	-1 600	-1.4	9 800	6 300
Saratoga	17.9	16.6	11.0	8.0	6.2	4.1	50.6	27 517	17.9	164 100	153 759	10 300	6.7	14 100	7 400
Schenectady	16.3	14.8	9.9	9.6	9.2	7.3	52.3	-661	-0.4	150 200	149 946	200	0.2	12 200	10 000
Schoharie	14.0	14.4	10.1	9.1	8.1	6.1	51.2	2 149	7.2	29 800	29 710	100	0.4	2 300	1 900
Schuyler	14.8	15.3	11.0	9.0	8.1	6.1	50.4	976	5.5	17 400	17 686	-200	-1.4	1 600	1 100
Seneca	15.7	15.1	10.2	9.4	8.4	6.4	50.8	-50	-0.1	32 100	33 733	-1 600	-4.8	2 900	1 900
Steuben	15.0	14.4	10.5	9.6	8.4	6.1	50.9	-129	-0.1	96 900	99 217	-2 300	-2.3	9 100	6 200
Suffolk	17.2	15.7	11.9	9.1	6.3	4.5	51.1	37 633	2.9	1 312 000	1 284 231	27 800	2.2	105 600	61 900
Sullivan	16.4	15.4	10.4	9.2	8.6	6.1	48.7	4 122	6.3	68 600	65 155	3 500	5.3	5 600	4 700
Tioga	17.0	15.0	11.3	9.1	6.4	4.5	50.7	2 525	5.1	51 000	49 812	1 200	2.4	4 700	2 300
Tompkins	16.9	13.9	8.1	6.1	5.0	4.0	50.4	7 012	8.1	87 600	87 085	600	0.6	7 000	3 400
Ulster	17.5	16.1	10.7	9.0	7.3	5.7	50.4	7 146	4.5	164 200	158 158	6 000	3.8	12 900	9 600
Warren	16.0	15.2	10.4	9.0	8.1	6.3	51.8	4 355	7.9	55 500	54 854	700	1.2	4 800	3 500
Washington	17.4	14.6	10.1	8.8	7.6	5.5	48.7	4 535	8.3	56 900	54 795	2 100	3.8	4 700	3 500
Wayne	17.1	15.7	10.7	8.3	6.5	5.0	50.7	4 542	5.4	88 000	84 581	3 400	4.0	8 900	4 600
Westchester	16.7	15.5	11.7	10.3	8.0	6.4	52.5	8 267	1.0	863 200	866 599	-3 400	-0.4	63 500	50 200
Wyoming	18.8	15.3	10.1	7.6	6.9	5.2	46.7	2 612	6.5	40 800	39 895	900	2.2	3 800	2 200
Yates	14.6	14.6	10.1	9.7	8.3	7.0	51.6	1 351	6.3	21 200	21 459	-300	-1.2	1 900	1 400
NORTH CAROLINA	17.3	15.2	10.5	8.9	7.3	4.8	51.5	746 637	12.7	6 333 000	5 882 000	451 000	7.7	536 000	316 000
Alamance	15.8	14.8	11.1	10.1	8.9	5.9	52.6	8 894	9.0	102 400	99 319	3 100	3.1	7 500	5 800
Alexander	16.9	15.6	12.3	9.2	6.6	4.5	50.2	2 545	10.2	26 900	24 999	1 900	7.5	2 100	1 200
Alleghany	14.2	13.9	12.1	11.8	10.4	8.2	51.8	3	0.0	9 700	9 587	100	1.3	700	600
Anson	14.5	14.4	9.6	9.1	9.0	6.7	53.2	-2 175	-8.5	26 300	25 649	600	2.4	2 300	1 600
Ashe	14.4	14.7	12.3	11.1	9.5	7.7	51.6	-116	-0.5	23 400	22 325	1 100	4.9	1 600	1 400
Avery	14.0	14.7	11.1	9.6	8.6	6.0	49.9	458	3.2	15 000	14 409	600	4.3	1 200	800
Beaufort	14.3	14.9	10.9	10.3	8.7	6.2	52.8	1 928	4.8	43 900	40 355	3 600	8.9	3 600	2 700
Bertie	15.2	13.1	9.6	10.1	8.7	5.9	53.9	-636	-3.0	21 300	21 024	300	1.3	2 000	1 500
Bladen	14.3	15.0	11.0	9.6	8.5	5.7	53.0	-1 828	-6.0	30 800	30 491	300	0.9	2 400	1 800
Brunswick	14.8	14.1	11.8	12.5	10.3	4.4	51.1	15 208	42.5	47 500	35 777	11 700	32.6	3 600	2 100
Buncombe	15.4	15.7	11.2	9.9	9.2	6.9	52.5	13 887	8.6	170 000	160 934	9 000	5.6	12 500	10 300
Burke	16.0	15.3	12.1	9.8	7.8	5.2	51.1	3 240	4.5	76 300	72 504	3 800	5.2	5 400	3 500
Cabarrus	16.4	15.5	11.3	9.3	7.8	5.4	51.6	13 040	15.2	92 300	85 895	6 400	7.4	7 300	5 000
Caldwell	16.5	15.4	12.2	9.7	7.3	4.8	51.0	2 963	4.4	70 300	67 746	2 600	3.8	5 400	3 200
Camden	15.9	14.5	12.0	10.7	8.8	5.3	49.9	75	1.3	5 800	5 829	0	-0.2	400	400
Carteret	16.8	15.0	11.1	11.0	9.2	5.1	50.6	11 464	27.9	50 900	41 092	9 800	23.8	4 400	2 500
Caswell	15.7	15.6	11.9	9.4	8.5	5.8	51.2	-12	-0.1	22 200	20 705	1 500	7.4	1 600	1 100
Catawba	16.8	15.9	11.5	9.4	7.3	4.6	51.4	13 204	12.6	114 500	105 208	9 200	8.8	8 800	5 300
Chatham	16.8	17.1	10.8	9.8	8.7	5.7	51.5	5 344	16.0	35 700	33 415	2 300	6.9	3 100	1 900
Cherokee	12.8	14.1	11.5	11.2	11.3	7.6	52.0	1 237	6.5	20 400	18 933	1 400	7.5	1 400	1 100
Chowan	14.0	14.1	10.0	10.5	10.3	7.3	53.5	948	7.5	13 400	12 558	800	6.7	1 100	900
Clay	12.5	14.5	11.3	11.3	12.5	7.8	51.3	536	8.1	7 300	6 619	600	9.6	500	500
Cleveland	15.4	15.0	11.4	9.5	8.1	5.5	52.0	1 279	1.5	86 500	83 435	3 100	3.7	6 900	4 700
Columbus	14.7	14.5	11.1	9.8	8.2	5.2	52.9	-1 450	-2.8	52 400	51 037	1 300	2.6	5 000	3 200

STATE County	Population—(cont'd) Components of change, 1980-1986 (cont'd)	Households, 1990					Births, 1988			Deaths, 1987				Marriages, 1984	
					Percent					Number		Rate			
	Net migration	Number	Percent change, 1980–1990	Persons per house-hold	Female family house-holder[1]	One-person	Total	Rate[2]	Low birth weight[3] (Number)	Total	Infant[4]	Total[2]	Infant[5]	Number	Rate[2]
	29	30	31	32	33	34	35	36	37	38	39	40	41	42	43
NEW YORK—Con.															
Jefferson	-600	37 851	22.9	2.74	9.7	21.1	1 933	19.1	114	935	15	9.8	9.2	938	10.6
Kings	-47 100	828 199	0.0	2.74	21.5	28.6	44 769	19.3	4 438	23 255	604	10.1	13.9	15 161	6.6
Lewis	-800	9 253	14.9	2.86	8.0	20.4	455	17.2	11	239	2	9.3	4.8	210	8.4
Livingston	-800	21 197	16.1	2.68	8.9	21.9	791	13.3	26	453	7	7.7	8.3	497	8.6
Madison	-1 400	23 567	13.3	2.72	9.2	21.4	919	13.7	59	543	10	8.2	10.3	578	8.7
Monroe	-29 000	271 944	7.8	2.54	12.5	26.2	11 281	16.1	709	5 911	98	8.5	8.9	5 857	8.3
Montgomery	-1 500	20 185	1.7	2.52	10.9	26.9	711	13.8	47	620	4	12.1	6.3	456	8.6
Nassau	-16 000	431 515	1.9	2.94	10.2	17.1	17 093	13.0	1 063	11 781	170	8.9	10.3	11 275	8.5
New York	36 500	716 422	1.7	1.99	12.8	48.6	21 507	14.2	2 311	16 601	256	11.1	12.3	31 379	21.3
Niagara	-16 200	84 809	5.7	2.56	11.6	26.1	3 112	14.3	186	2 191	19	10.2	6.2	2 208	10.2
Oneida	-11 400	92 562	5.2	2.55	11.2	27.0	3 487	14.2	216	2 714	37	11.0	10.2	2 204	8.8
Onondaga	-19 000	177 898	7.4	2.55	11.9	26.4	7 173	15.5	503	4 123	85	9.0	11.9	4 012	8.7
Ontario	200	34 929	15.3	2.64	9.2	22.1	1 313	14.3	55	761	14	8.3	10.4	868	9.5
Orange	11 100	101 506	20.5	2.89	10.2	19.7	5 052	17.2	290	2 513	42	8.7	8.7	2 259	8.3
Orleans	-1 000	14 428	11.2	2.74	10.3	21.6	593	14.9	31	338	4	8.6	6.7	358	9.3
Oswego	300	42 434	14.0	2.76	10.0	21.6	1 911	15.7	112	1 037	27	8.7	14.7	1 035	8.8
Otsego	-800	21 725	7.4	2.56	8.3	24.9	733	12.2	42	609	5	10.2	6.7	486	8.2
Putnam	1 200	28 094	15.3	2.95	7.2	15.7	1 368	16.4	79	586	9	7.1	7.3	647	8.1
Queens	-3 000	720 149	1.2	2.67	14.3	27.2	29 646	15.4	2 399	20 075	325	10.4	11.4	17 131	8.9
Rensselaer	-3 800	57 612	9.2	2.58	11.2	25.5	2 090	13.8	133	1 522	24	10.1	10.7	1 205	8.0
Richmond	11 300	130 519	13.9	2.85	12.4	20.9	6 132	16.1	400	3 290	46	8.7	8.2	3 572	9.7
Rockland	-3 400	84 874	8.9	3.03	9.8	17.8	3 948	14.9	232	2 043	16	7.7	4.0	2 001	7.6
St. Lawrence	-5 100	37 964	6.0	2.67	9.6	23.5	1 498	13.5	96	1 052	20	9.5	13.8	965	8.5
Saratoga	3 700	66 425	27.9	2.67	8.4	21.4	2 593	15.0	129	1 204	13	7.2	5.3	1 438	9.1
Schenectady	-2 000	59 181	5.4	2.45	11.1	28.1	2 134	14.2	131	1 603	11	10.8	5.3	1 285	8.6
Schoharie	-300	11 257	16.3	2.64	9.0	22.4	371	12.3	22	305	5	10.2	13.7	235	7.9
Schuyler	-800	6 818	12.9	2.67	9.1	21.6	235	13.6	11	155	0	9.0	0.0	175	9.9
Seneca	-2 700	12 285	7.7	2.64	9.4	22.0	450	14.0	20	268	5	8.3	10.7	284	8.7
Steuben	-5 200	37 299	6.1	2.60	9.7	24.6	1 378	14.0	80	957	14	9.9	10.2	924	9.4
Suffolk	-15 900	424 719	10.1	3.04	10.4	16.0	19 903	15.1	1 148	10 449	147	8.0	7.8	10 482	8.0
Sullivan	2 600	24 576	6.8	2.60	9.5	25.3	1 061	14.8	69	823	8	11.7	7.8	598	9.0
Tioga	-1 200	18 838	14.0	2.76	8.7	19.5	840	16.2	47	382	3	7.5	3.9	449	9.0
Tompkins	-3 100	33 338	12.8	2.46	8.0	27.2	1 027	11.6	53	565	15	6.4	14.0	731	8.3
Ulster	2 700	60 807	8.9	2.58	10.2	24.3	2 410	14.4	133	1 585	12	9.6	5.2	1 427	8.8
Warren	-600	22 559	16.2	2.58	10.0	24.5	770	13.5	52	555	6	9.9	7.2	620	11.3
Washington	800	20 256	13.2	2.75	10.0	21.2	863	14.6	41	568	5	9.8	5.8	515	9.2
Wayne	-900	31 977	12.4	2.75	9.5	20.1	1 457	16.4	74	710	10	8.1	7.2	819	9.4
Westchester	-16 800	320 030	4.1	2.64	11.6	24.8	12 424	14.4	821	8 181	108	9.5	9.2	6 730	7.8
Wyoming	-700	13 897	8.8	2.79	8.5	20.5	565	13.5	36	349	1	8.4	1.7	475	11.7
Yates	-800	8 419	9.2	2.63	8.3	22.7	330	15.3	15	237	3	11.1	8.8	211	9.9
NORTH CAROLINA	230 000	2 517 026	23.2	2.54	12.3	23.7	97 579	15.0	7 823	55 316	1 112	8.6	11.9	52 170	8.5
Alamance	1 400	42 652	18.6	2.47	12.0	24.5	1 522	14.4	121	958	11	9.1	7.7	993	9.8
Alexander	900	10 331	21.1	2.64	9.2	19.6	321	11.6	28	179	4	6.6	11.6	203	7.7
Alleghany	100	3 894	8.3	2.41	7.8	25.4	83	8.5	3	106	4	10.8	52.6	267	27.2
Anson	0	8 531	1.7	2.71	17.3	23.9	399	15.2	37	244	2	9.3	5.8	109	4.2
Ashe	900	8 848	10.2	2.48	9.2	21.9	220	9.4	14	221	2	9.4	8.7	235	10.1
Avery	200	5 520	14.4	2.52	8.7	22.3	201	13.2	11	131	2	8.6	10.5	180	12.0
Beaufort	2 700	16 157	13.4	2.58	13.5	24.2	590	13.9	54	479	8	11.4	13.9	428	10.1
Bertie	-300	7 412	7.5	2.74	19.1	24.2	316	15.0	27	244	4	11.6	12.2	145	6.8
Bladen	-400	10 760	6.4	2.62	16.4	24.0	399	12.9	38	305	10	9.9	27.4	136	4.4
Brunswick	10 200	20 069	61.7	2.52	10.1	21.1	687	13.5	59	429	3	8.6	4.5	266	6.1
Buncombe	6 800	70 802	17.5	2.40	10.9	26.6	2 358	13.6	145	1 755	23	10.2	10.0	1 634	9.8
Burke	2 000	29 184	15.2	2.51	10.8	22.6	960	12.4	73	576	5	7.5	5.0	525	7.0
Cabarrus	4 100	37 515	22.6	2.59	10.6	21.4	1 397	14.6	140	863	18	9.1	14.5	754	8.2
Caldwell	400	27 172	16.5	2.57	10.8	20.8	1 010	14.1	86	566	5	8.0	5.4	618	9.0
Camden	-100	2 180	12.9	2.69	10.3	20.0	64	10.5	5	49	1	8.2	17.5	46	7.8
Carteret	8 000	21 238	40.4	2.43	9.5	23.9	687	13.5	47	465	8	9.2	11.0	544	11.6
Caswell	1 100	7 468	14.6	2.69	13.7	21.3	271	12.2	25	198	1	8.9	4.0	154	7.0
Catawba	5 800	45 700	22.5	2.55	10.6	22.5	1 681	14.3	115	950	24	8.2	14.9	937	8.5
Chatham	1 100	15 293	26.8	2.51	10.5	22.5	584	15.9	41	321	5	8.8	9.4	257	7.3
Cherokee	1 100	7 966	16.3	2.50	9.6	22.1	215	10.1	5	200	3	9.6	13.4	222	11.1
Chowan	600	5 113	17.5	2.59	15.0	24.2	188	13.7	11	163	0	12.0	0.0	85	6.5
Clay	600	2 928	17.6	2.44	6.9	23.9	74	10.1	5	74	1	10.3	14.3	56	8.0
Cleveland	900	32 037	12.6	2.59	13.0	21.9	1 296	14.9	115	787	17	9.1	13.9	464	5.5
Columbus	-500	18 459	6.9	2.65	14.9	23.6	692	13.2	58	502	6	9.5	8.3	238	4.6

1. No spouse present. 2. Per 1,000 resident population estimated as of July 1 of the year shown. 3. Under 2,500 grams. 4. Deaths of infants under 1 year old. 5. Deaths of infants under 1 year old per 1,000 live births.

STATE County	Divorces, 1984		Physicians, active non–Federal, 1989		Hospitals, 1989			Nursing homes,[4] 1986		Serious crimes known to police, 1988			Education			
						Beds				Number			Public school enrollment[7]		Attainment,[8] 1980	
	Number	Rate[1]	Number[2]	Rate[3]	Number	Number	Rate[3]	Number	Beds	Total[5]	Violent[6]	Rate[3]	1986–1987	1980	Percent 12 yrs. or more	Percent 16 yrs. or more
	44	45	46	47	48	49	50	51	52	53	54	55	56	57	58	59
NEW YORK—Con.																
Jefferson	275	3.1	120	114	4	708	670	11	720	2 943	134	3 126	17 731	18 299	64.0	10.3
Kings	4 738	2.1	4 906	211	18	10 618	458	55	11 824	X	162 978	9 793	938 606	362 702	54.9	11.6
Lewis	46	1.8	16	59	1	189	703	3	111	296	25	1 192	5 182	6 112	62.4	9.7
Livingston	172	3.0	41	69	1	72	120	8	493	1 852	127	3 126	9 810	11 931	67.3	14.8
Madison	228	3.4	67	99	2	293	435	6	390	1 745	86	2 610	12 617	14 346	68.2	15.4
Monroe	2 553	3.6	2 376	340	9	3 825	547	50	6 625	40 193	2 381	5 723	105 116	123 993	71.7	21.3
Montgomery	145	2.7	65	126	2	360	699	12	505	1 052	40	2 027	8 288	10 097	60.6	8.4
Nassau	3 574	2.7	5 990	456	15	4 959	377	49	8 047	43 257	3 455	3 273	180 716	234 424	77.7	23.6
New York	16 632	11.3	13 941	917	31	17 403	1 145	29	8 924	X	0	0	NA	135 535	68.0	33.2
Niagara	720	3.3	241	111	5	867	400	23	1 960	9 718	826	4 477	34 651	43 464	65.7	11.5
Oneida	826	3.3	452	185	7	2 640	1 082	30	3 022	7 707	360	3 108	40 249	48 715	65.0	13.2
Onondaga	1 598	3.5	1 486	323	7	2 254	490	26	2 888	21 582	1 659	4 671	74 401	87 286	72.7	19.4
Ontario	365	4.0	147	160	4	1 346	1 461	13	506	2 632	119	2 819	17 015	18 494	71.0	15.4
Orange	851	3.1	465	155	8	1 905	636	12	2 294	12 041	1 434	4 305	51 303	55 103	67.5	14.9
Orleans	96	2.5	33	82	1	101	251	4	312	842	93	2 172	8 944	8 925	61.8	9.9
Oswego	331	2.8	83	68	2	269	220	13	654	3 043	122	2 519	24 951	24 979	63.4	10.9
Otsego	197	3.3	195	323	2	424	703	10	579	1 467	70	2 456	9 072	10 914	67.7	16.2
Putnam	137	1.7	119	141	3	309	365	3	181	1 916	109	2 324	12 853	17 855	77.4	19.5
Queens	4 432	2.3	4 624	241	16	7 624	397	70	12 382	X	0	0	NA	240 266	63.1	15.5
Rensselaer	388	2.6	201	133	3	630	417	14	1 292	4 935	374	3 246	23 212	27 545	66.0	13.9
Richmond	1 082	2.9	1 215	317	5	1 798	470	17	3 918	X	0	0	NA	56 818	68.5	14.8
Rockland	721	2.7	912	343	6	2 750	1 034	24	2 222	7 450	608	2 796	39 386	53 219	76.6	25.8
St. Lawrence	245	2.2	130	118	6	914	831	10	680	3 437	178	3 065	20 383	24 057	64.4	13.3
Saratoga	557	3.5	201	114	2	255	144	9	783	4 508	394	2 738	31 296	34 435	73.2	18.6
Schenectady	567	3.8	397	265	5	1 012	676	10	1 276	5 479	296	3 648	17 313	26 537	71.5	18.3
Schoharie	99	3.3	20	66	1	70	230	5	226	670	57	2 232	8 424	6 200	64.2	11.5
Schuyler	55	3.1	18	104	1	169	977	4	170	549	7	3 161	2 605	4 005	63.8	11.3
Seneca	110	3.4	38	119	2	617	1 928	4	200	966	55	2 997	5 313	6 664	65.7	12.2
Steuben	350	3.6	108	110	4	780	793	12	581	2 871	207	2 986	20 018	21 793	66.6	12.6
Suffolk	4 050	3.1	2 937	222	22	10 950	826	87	7 573	48 155	3 626	3 648	238 356	298 234	73.7	17.8
Sullivan	221	3.3	75	103	1	280	384	9	580	2 458	337	3 477	10 370	12 634	61.8	12.0
Tioga	162	3.2	32	62	0	0	0	4	217	817	75	1 628	9 717	12 123	71.9	14.8
Tompkins	347	3.9	151	169	1	191	214	6	613	4 579	182	5 200	12 627	13 266	80.8	36.3
Ulster	592	3.6	254	151	3	429	255	13	876	4 660	533	2 890	25 507	30 932	66.8	16.0
Warren	211	3.8	145	251	1	440	763	7	432	2 064	46	3 833	10 477	11 834	68.8	16.3
Washington	163	2.9	33	55	1	113	189	6	368	1 338	168	2 306	10 882	12 976	62.5	10.3
Wayne	337	3.9	65	73	2	258	289	12	438	2 550	161	3 128	17 682	19 361	63.8	11.5
Westchester	2 166	2.5	4 476	518	22	4 993	578	63	6 885	37 957	3 046	4 545	111 766	140 904	75.2	28.0
Wyoming	117	2.9	38	90	1	174	410	3	252	971	174	2 325	6 091	8 847	63.2	8.6
Yates	79	3.7	24	110	1	133	610	3	135	523	17	2 492	3 117	4 488	64.6	13.1
NORTH CAROLINA	29 601	4.8	11 847	180	164	30 338	462	901	38 954	X	31 584	4 775	1 084 470	1 182 045	54.8	13.2
Alamance	577	5.7	139	130	2	340	317	28	651	4 066	349	3 884	17 014	19 752	54.0	11.8
Alexander	96	3.7	9	32	1	51	183	2	66	483	28	1 751	4 818	5 370	43.9	6.8
Alleghany	37	3.8	7	71	1	46	465	1	98	164	57	1 661	1 660	1 921	38.5	5.1
Anson	93	3.5	16	61	1	95	363	3	175	849	200	3 466	4 997	5 726	46.9	6.9
Ashe	105	4.5	16	68	1	57	243	2	81	299	30	1 261	3 852	4 421	41.0	6.0
Avery	69	4.6	22	144	2	117	765	2	134	216	43	1 406	2 742	2 967	49.6	9.5
Beaufort	185	4.4	54	128	2	159	378	8	284	1 341	165	3 187	8 295	8 434	50.5	8.6
Bertie	50	2.3	6	29	1	24	115	3	35	309	60	1 439	4 250	4 832	37.9	6.5
Bladen	86	2.8	14	45	1	49	158	8	247	987	185	3 219	6 044	6 885	43.9	7.0
Brunswick	130	3.0	39	74	2	100	189	1	106	783	50	1 600	8 593	8 099	51.5	8.0
Buncombe	937	5.6	452	259	7	1 569	898	48	1 619	7 633	455	4 415	26 606	29 574	59.4	14.6
Burke	320	4.3	111	142	3	1 139	1 462	16	540	2 091	150	2 696	12 494	14 875	46.0	8.8
Cabarrus	390	4.3	103	106	1	360	370	13	736	3 462	205	3 630	16 739	17 613	49.0	8.6
Caldwell	352	5.1	65	91	1	94	131	6	324	2 487	232	3 461	12 315	14 541	44.4	7.7
Camden	9	1.5	3	49	0	0	0	0	0	103	24	1 687	1 089	1 273	44.6	4.9
Carteret	226	4.8	52	100	2	193	373	7	461	2 355	139	4 582	7 694	7 548	57.1	12.1
Caswell	51	2.3	7	32	0	0	0	6	87	464	61	2 026	3 824	4 632	41.0	5.1
Catawba	686	6.2	165	139	3	543	457	10	602	5 140	699	4 361	20 068	21 617	51.8	11.3
Chatham	109	3.1	43	116	1	68	183	7	262	899	56	2 433	5 736	6 505	51.5	13.0
Cherokee	62	3.1	18	84	2	220	1 023	3	144	314	23	1 476	3 765	3 963	43.6	6.2
Chowan	53	4.1	19	137	1	110	791	3	276	404	59	2 940	2 494	2 624	45.1	7.8
Clay	16	2.3	6	81	0	0	0	0	0	74	0	1 010	1 192	1 224	46.4	9.8
Cleveland	360	4.3	101	116	3	401	459	22	640	3 426	311	4 075	15 766	18 511	47.4	9.2
Columbus	183	3.5	32	61	1	136	258	4	273	1 825	181	3 594	10 767	11 546	44.2	8.1

1. Per 1,000 resident population estimated as of July 1 of the year shown. 2. As of end of year. 3. Per 100,000 resident population as of July 1 of the year shown. 4. Preliminary. Covers nursing homes with 3 or more beds. 5. Data for serious crimes have not been adjusted for underreporting, this may affect comparability between geographic areas or over time. 6. Includes murder and nonnegligent manslaughter, forcible rape, robbery, and aggravated assault. 7. The 1986–1987 data are based on administrative reports obtained by the U.S. National Center for Education Statistics. The 1980 data are based on the 1980 Census of Population and Housing. 8. Persons 25 years old or older.

STATE County	Education (cont'd)		Social Security Program December 1988				Money income						Housing units, 1990	
	Local government expenditures for education,[1] 1982		Beneficiaries			Supple-mental Security Income Program recipients June 1986	Per capita[3]			Median household income 1979 (Dollars)	Percent below poverty level, 1979			
								1979						
	Total (Mil dol)	Per capita (Dollars)	Total	Rate[2]	Payments ($1,000)		1987 Income, (Dollars)	Current dollars	Constant 1987 dollars		Persons	Families	Total	Percent change, 1980–1990
	60	61	62	63	64	65	66	67	68	69	70	71	72	73
NEW YORK—Con.														
Jefferson	58.5	671	16 825	166.4	7 994	1 660	9 277	5 602	8 765	13 547	13.7	10.9	50 519	20.2
Kings	2 725.2	384	327 065	141.3	164 738	75 956	9 806	5 754	9 003	11 919	24.0	21.0	873 671	-0.9
Lewis	21.1	849	4 125	156.2	1 928	450	9 170	5 315	8 316	14 472	13.2	10.6	13 182	13.6
Livingston	32.4	565	8 975	151.1	4 539	658	10 276	6 204	9 707	16 987	10.1	6.8	23 084	13.7
Madison	41.6	638	10 210	151.9	5 029	862	10 055	5 961	9 327	16 091	12.4	8.9	26 641	11.4
Monroe	442.8	625	113 220	161.7	61 174	9 134	13 299	8 294	12 978	20 194	8.8	6.5	285 524	8.0
Montgomery	28.0	529	13 310	257.4	6 564	936	9 886	6 022	9 423	14 030	10.5	7.7	21 851	3.1
Nassau	1 017.6	772	213 170	161.7	123 476	11 114	18 036	9 969	15 598	26 090	4.8	3.6	446 292	2.8
New York	NA	NA	205 845	136.3	115 553	50 522	20 904	10 776	16 861	13 904	21.8	18.7	785 127	4.0
Niagara	132.2	596	43 155	199.0	22 708	2 740	10 679	6 975	10 914	17 834	8.8	7.1	90 385	6.1
Oneida	134.3	533	49 750	202.6	24 341	5 164	10 338	6 148	9 620	15 261	11.0	8.6	101 251	5.7
Onondaga	280.8	610	74 640	161.7	39 426	5 972	12 285	7 286	11 400	17 574	9.6	6.6	190 878	7.8
Ontario	55.5	620	14 870	161.6	7 545	984	11 274	6 880	10 765	18 033	7.9	5.7	38 947	14.3
Orange	175.8	662	40 970	139.6	20 568	3 876	11 949	6 707	10 494	18 012	10.0	7.9	110 814	18.8
Orleans	26.5	686	6 655	167.2	3 348	480	10 073	6 534	10 224	17 246	9.8	7.6	16 345	8.7
Oswego	75.5	661	18 340	150.8	9 237	1 608	9 725	5 898	9 229	16 156	12.3	8.9	48 548	13.2
Otsego	30.6	518	11 140	185.7	5 353	1 066	9 377	5 552	8 687	13 081	15.3	9.3	26 385	10.5
Putnam	66.3	844	8 845	105.8	4 791	480	15 318	8 159	12 766	24 103	4.1	3.2	31 898	14.5
Queens	NA	NA	301 140	156.4	163 875	42 300	12 677	7 549	11 812	17 028	11.4	9.1	752 690	1.7
Rensselaer	81.9	541	25 250	166.9	12 901	2 034	10 998	6 327	9 900	15 970	11.2	8.0	62 591	9.1
Richmond	NA	NA	53 155	139.9	28 135	5 590	13 945	7 576	11 854	21 204	8.2	7.0	139 726	17.4
Rockland	211.0	811	32 895	123.8	17 745	4 146	15 917	8 628	13 500	25 648	6.2	4.8	88 264	10.1
St. Lawrence	75.1	667	18 815	169.8	8 899	2 476	8 787	5 272	8 249	13 673	17.2	12.9	47 521	8.8
Saratoga	100.5	648	23 385	135.5	11 904	1 536	12 223	6 884	10 771	18 325	8.0	6.2	75 105	24.4
Schenectady	78.5	525	32 300	215.5	16 822	2 260	12 623	7 470	11 688	16 928	8.7	6.0	62 769	5.4
Schoharie	19.0	642	5 460	180.8	2 580	512	9 197	5 353	8 376	13 750	13.3	10.2	14 431	14.1
Schuyler	12.2	695	3 005	173.7	1 485	310	9 358	5 580	8 731	14 477	10.6	8.3	8 472	12.1
Seneca	18.6	565	5 755	178.7	2 824	590	10 315	6 391	10 000	16 396	8.5	6.5	14 314	7.2
Steuben	66.7	680	18 240	185.9	8 892	1 550	9 756	6 247	9 775	14 988	12.2	9.1	43 019	6.2
Suffolk	1 140.8	886	179 670	136.0	95 127	15 258	14 469	7 576	11 854	22 359	6.6	5.3	481 317	11.5
Sullivan	39.7	615	14 405	200.9	7 051	1 864	10 292	5 860	9 169	12 988	15.1	10.2	41 814	-8.8
Tioga	34.0	682	7 070	136.8	3 447	456	10 931	6 605	10 335	17 322	8.7	6.9	20 254	12.6
Tompkins	46.8	532	10 475	118.0	5 529	768	10 850	6 262	9 798	14 400	17.0	7.8	35 338	14.0
Ulster	101.2	636	26 815	160.7	13 748	2 640	11 656	6 629	10 372	15 691	11.2	7.9	71 716	3.5
Warren	37.3	680	11 160	195.4	5 597	912	11 043	6 186	9 679	14 617	12.7	9.4	31 737	18.3
Washington	35.6	647	9 815	166.1	4 850	866	9 294	5 433	8 501	14 759	12.5	9.5	24 216	10.5
Wayne	66.5	773	14 220	160.3	7 100	1 510	10 822	6 666	10 430	17 723	8.8	6.8	35 188	9.6
Westchester	661.8	767	137 805	159.3	79 594	10 848	19 567	10 603	16 591	22 725	7.1	5.6	336 727	6.3
Wyoming	19.4	479	6 380	152.3	3 135	444	9 200	5 746	8 991	16 019	9.4	7.1	15 848	5.1
Yates	11.2	528	4 610	213.4	2 265	318	9 532	5 976	9 351	13 610	14.4	10.3	11 629	8.1
NORTH CAROLINA	2 345.0	390	1 023 303	157.7	457 338	140 303	10 856	6 132	9 595	14 481	14.8	11.6	2 818 193	23.9
Alamance	38.1	377	20 680	195.5	9 944	2 092	11 408	6 534	10 224	15 672	10.4	7.4	45 312	18.7
Alexander	9.0	349	3 900	141.3	1 653	378	10 343	5 731	8 967	15 004	8.8	6.9	11 197	19.3
Alleghany	3.8	384	2 275	232.1	862	396	8 351	4 934	7 720	10 698	19.6	16.2	5 344	14.4
Anson	10.5	406	4 730	180.5	1 915	924	8 129	4 826	7 551	12 289	16.1	13.4	9 255	2.0
Ashe	9.2	404	4 540	193.2	1 664	926	8 148	4 652	7 279	10 372	22.8	19.6	11 119	16.7
Avery	6.4	434	2 930	192.8	1 167	496	7 761	4 575	7 159	11 135	18.0	14.5	8 923	26.1
Beaufort	16.8	404	8 250	194.6	3 324	1 524	8 783	5 193	8 125	11 984	21.0	17.3	19 598	14.1
Bertie	9.9	467	4 140	197.1	1 538	1 142	7 736	4 376	6 847	9 818	29.4	22.9	8 331	5.4
Bladen	13.6	443	5 195	168.1	1 969	1 392	7 873	4 514	7 063	10 821	25.6	21.3	12 685	11.0
Brunswick	16.9	433	9 040	177.6	4 026	1 064	9 137	5 321	8 326	12 883	19.8	17.1	37 114	72.2
Buncombe	59.9	366	33 570	193.9	15 367	3 524	11 022	6 360	9 951	14 030	12.9	10.1	77 951	17.9
Burke	24.8	335	12 690	164.2	5 806	1 540	9 991	5 881	9 202	14 328	10.1	7.6	31 575	14.7
Cabarrus	34.0	382	18 600	194.0	9 153	1 352	11 404	6 457	10 103	15 887	9.3	7.2	39 713	22.3
Caldwell	25.8	379	10 770	150.8	4 883	1 058	9 868	5 653	8 845	14 552	10.4	8.1	29 454	15.2
Camden	2.7	462	1 055	173.0	429	118	9 166	5 539	8 667	15 007	16.1	13.2	2 466	14.8
Carteret	13.5	310	8 235	161.5	3 573	696	10 213	6 146	9 617	14 012	14.0	11.5	34 576	45.6
Caswell	8.4	392	3 220	145.0	1 242	774	8 449	4 918	7 695	12 683	19.5	16.8	8 254	7.8
Catawba	41.0	381	18 775	160.1	9 010	1 240	11 775	6 672	10 440	16 233	8.2	6.2	49 192	20.8
Chatham	12.9	377	5 760	156.9	2 540	646	11 071	6 203	9 706	15 388	9.1	6.4	16 642	29.0
Cherokee	7.2	368	4 830	227.8	1 969	794	7 988	4 445	6 955	9 715	22.2	18.7	10 319	20.9
Chowan	5.4	425	2 975	217.2	1 203	432	9 112	5 202	8 140	11 480	24.0	19.7	5 910	12.3
Clay	2.5	373	1 830	250.7	716	300	8 572	4 737	7 412	10 252	22.8	19.4	4 158	23.4
Cleveland	35.8	427	15 105	173.4	6 850	1 984	10 293	5 904	9 238	15 155	13.2	10.5	34 232	12.6
Columbus	23.4	457	9 720	185.1	3 638	2 694	8 124	4 751	7 434	10 898	26.5	21.6	20 513	7.6

1. Elementary and secondary. 2. Per 1,000 resident population estimated as of July 1 of the year shown. 3. Based on the resident population estimated as of July 1, 1988 for 1987 data and enumerated as of April 1, 1980 for 1979 data.

STATE County	Housing units, 1990 (cont'd) — Occupied units — Total	Owner occupied — Percent	Owner occupied — Median value (Dollars)	Median rent (Dollars)	Civilian labor force, 1990 — Total	Percent change, 1989–1990	Unemployment — Total	Unemployment — Rate[1]	Private nonfarm establishments, 1988 — Number	Net change, 1987–1988	Employment[2] — Total	Per-cent change, 1987–1988	Manu-facturing	Retail trade
	74	75	76	77	78	79	80	81	82	83	84	85	86	87
NEW YORK—Con.														
Jefferson	37 851	59.3	59 400	334	46 278	-3.2	3 625	7.8	2 288	49	26 286	8.4	5 061	7 373
Kings	828 199	25.9	196 100	428	947 697	1.5	74 712	7.9	33 840	294	384 026	1.3	73 636	65 600
Lewis	9 253	76.3	49 800	275	10 696	3.3	838	7.8	482	-5	4 016	-5.2	1 860	806
Livingston	21 197	73.3	72 800	322	29 244	-0.9	1 287	4.4	1 078	33	11 722	6.4	3 256	3 227
Madison	23 567	74.3	69 300	322	31 766	0.4	1 511	4.8	1 310	17	12 683	0.3	2 596	3 830
Monroe	271 944	65.1	90 700	418	370 510	-0.7	12 150	3.3	16 159	280	349 922	4.6	112 504	62 894
Montgomery	20 185	66.3	61 600	245	26 555	-0.8	1 648	6.2	1 120	9	15 773	-3.5	6 430	2 759
Nassau	431 515	80.4	209 500	678	739 100	-2.1	24 527	3.3	47 437	405	575 235	2.4	86 899	121 139
New York	716 422	17.9	487 300	478	804 018	1.1	46 665	5.8	100 270	-942	2 025 539	-1.9	226 509	204 499
Niagara	84 809	68.1	62 700	288	97 397	-0.2	5 670	5.8	4 507	139	66 520	2.2	22 504	15 952
Oneida	92 562	65.2	72 300	297	107 333	-0.6	4 608	4.3	5 374	27	76 112	0.5	19 008	18 103
Onondaga	177 898	63.5	81 000	376	239 680	0.7	8 260	3.4	12 016	270	222 834	6.3	43 610	45 815
Ontario	34 929	73.3	78 300	364	47 093	-1.1	2 081	4.4	2 259	101	28 540	3.4	7 063	7 868
Orange	101 506	67.5	141 700	513	135 587	-2.3	6 263	4.6	7 188	256	81 160	4.5	14 305	21 631
Orleans	14 428	74.4	56 900	291	19 790	-1.6	1 247	6.3	644	43	6 980	12.1	2 768	1 885
Oswego	42 434	73.0	65 100	311	54 078	-0.2	3 551	6.6	1 951	84	24 037	7.2	8 104	6 378
Otsego	21 725	73.0	67 800	304	30 978	1.2	1 235	4.0	1 345	25	15 898	9.5	2 134	4 499
Putnam	28 094	81.9	195 000	672	53 063	-3.4	1 774	3.3	2 077	56	16 246	6.2	2 015	4 200
Queens	720 149	42.4	191 000	513	944 406	1.3	57 017	6.0	33 635	251	436 716	0.9	71 721	73 613
Rensselaer	57 612	63.9	93 200	344	76 285	0.9	3 060	4.0	2 757	64	38 405	6.0	6 280	8 569
Richmond	130 519	63.7	186 300	509	171 899	1.9	10 971	6.4	6 581	210	68 377	0.9	3 809	17 176
Rockland	84 874	72.1	217 100	633	149 775	-0.8	4 805	3.2	7 337	161	82 799	3.2	17 362	15 590
St. Lawrence	37 964	68.8	44 100	261	46 265	2.3	3 412	7.4	2 024	27	25 187	2.4	5 267	6 198
Saratoga	66 425	72.3	107 500	418	85 945	0.7	3 238	3.8	3 401	180	36 821	7.8	6 467	12 302
Schenectady	59 181	65.7	94 000	365	76 805	1.1	2 760	3.6	3 420	163	49 356	-19.1	7 560	11 989
Schoharie	11 257	74.1	73 600	299	14 586	1.2	733	5.0	532	-3	4 679	-0.1	740	1 251
Schuyler	6 818	77.3	48 500	265	8 485	3.7	486	5.7	335	16	3 264	-0.2	1 057	792
Seneca	12 285	74.3	57 500	308	13 215	-0.9	702	5.3	568	24	8 970	38.4	0	1 545
Steuben	37 299	73.1	46 200	262	42 007	0.1	2 305	5.5	1 911	55	28 749	7.2	13 305	5 942
Suffolk	424 719	80.1	165 900	696	663 700	-2.2	29 029	4.4	37 625	807	439 025	2.9	100 989	93 339
Sullivan	24 576	68.7	93 400	390	31 787	2.1	1 530	4.8	2 062	51	18 243	-0.7	934	4 040
Tioga	18 838	78.8	72 800	300	23 527	-2.6	1 042	4.4	745	18	12 836	4.5	7 723	1 742
Tompkins	33 338	55.3	94 700	426	57 173	2.1	1 271	2.2	2 070	68	37 863	2.9	3 631	6 916
Ulster	60 807	69.2	114 300	450	85 174	1.6	2 986	3.5	4 092	45	42 454	4.9	7 829	11 682
Warren	22 559	69.3	91 200	369	26 574	0.5	1 670	6.3	2 221	70	26 213	3.2	5 375	6 861
Washington	20 256	73.8	70 200	319	27 024	0.9	1 450	5.4	1 069	26	10 874	5.0	5 175	2 309
Wayne	31 977	76.7	70 700	316	43 341	-1.5	2 135	4.9	1 444	-10	18 528	1.3	7 436	3 926
Westchester	320 030	59.7	283 500	543	468 629	-1.9	15 922	3.4	28 493	523	389 633	8.3	69 507	68 952
Wyoming	13 897	75.1	52 500	266	16 983	-6.3	1 104	6.5	751	1	7 548	-7.5	3 092	1 806
Yates	8 419	76.5	55 500	262	8 540	-2.8	540	6.3	433	11	4 122	12.7	933	957
NORTH CAROLINA	2 517 026	68.0	65 800	284	3 401 000	0.3	139 000	4.1	X	X	2 507 241	4.5	X	512 021
Alamance	42 652	71.8	65 300	279	65 594	-1.0	2 159	3.3	2 964	37	51 169	3.0	24 138	9 993
Alexander	10 331	82.3	58 100	224	16 221	-0.4	611	3.8	534	15	9 132	10.0	6 391	1 073
Alleghany	3 894	80.0	48 300	175	4 994	-0.2	195	3.9	217	16	2 189	8.0	1 024	448
Anson	8 531	75.5	41 600	186	12 062	-1.1	539	4.5	464	21	6 874	-3.9	4 348	1 007
Ashe	8 848	82.7	57 600	181	11 463	0.6	667	5.8	413	-8	5 108	8.8	2 696	1 074
Avery	5 520	81.0	55 100	214	8 877	0.9	362	4.1	496	44	4 859	3.8	633	1 018
Beaufort	16 157	74.1	52 600	191	19 791	-0.1	1 070	5.4	982	24	13 020	-8.5	5 624	2 888
Bertie	7 412	74.2	39 100	135	8 659	0.1	459	5.3	368	5	5 975	5.3	4 048	528
Bladen	10 760	77.5	41 000	151	12 678	-2.0	850	6.7	520	8	5 513	8.9	2 853	1 158
Brunswick	20 069	81.5	70 600	263	18 355	0.2	1 459	7.9	1 081	-16	8 764	3.0	937	2 489
Buncombe	70 802	70.3	64 400	281	92 205	2.2	3 033	3.3	4 771	104	69 093	6.4	19 542	16 298
Burke	29 184	74.8	52 800	235	43 810	-0.2	1 702	3.9	1 333	22	28 876	2.7	18 785	4 097
Cabarrus	37 515	73.7	65 500	270	56 442	1.3	2 161	3.8	2 243	113	34 377	2.2	15 962	6 611
Caldwell	27 172	74.8	51 600	238	37 814	-2.2	1 639	4.3	1 335	13	27 554	6.0	17 002	4 254
Camden	2 180	80.9	59 400	209	2 401	-1.2	83	3.5	82	11	366	17.7	55	124
Carteret	21 238	74.2	73 100	280	23 238	0.2	1 062	4.6	1 452	41	11 433	-0.1	1 594	3 920
Caswell	7 468	78.5	47 300	162	9 548	0.4	416	4.4	195	4	1 052	12.6	149	254
Catawba	45 700	72.8	62 400	281	71 084	0.1	3 071	4.3	3 802	131	76 830	4.2	41 098	13 037
Chatham	15 293	77.1	63 600	278	19 828	1.0	653	3.3	693	8	10 216	4.7	5 995	1 492
Cherokee	7 966	81.0	52 900	181	9 342	8.4	818	8.8	436	-6	5 793	3.3	2 952	1 180
Chowan	5 113	70.6	60 700	179	5 629	-0.2	314	5.6	324	-24	3 944	-7.7	1 709	851
Clay	2 928	84.4	56 500	172	3 068	4.2	176	5.7	136	-1	1 146	22.0	539	235
Cleveland	32 037	72.8	53 400	227	43 530	-0.5	2 030	4.7	1 902	60	32 271	5.5	16 629	5 267
Columbus	18 459	75.8	45 800	168	21 837	-1.6	1 276	5.8	1 070	-3	14 030	-1.2	5 816	2 865

1. Percent of total civilian labor force. 2. For week including March 12. Excludes government employees, self-employed persons, farm workers, domestic service workers, railroad employees subject to the Railroad Retirement Act, and employees on oceanborne vessels or in foreign countries.

STATE County	Private nonfarm establishments, 1988 (cont'd): Employment[1] (cont'd): Finance, insurance, and real estate	Employment[1] (cont'd): Services	Annual payroll: Total (Mil dol)	Annual payroll: Average per employee (Dollars)	Personal income, 1989: Total (Mil dol)	Percent change, 1988–1989	Wages and salaries[2] (Mil dol)	Proprietor's income (Mil dol)	Dividends, interest, & rent (Mil dol)	Transfer payments (Mil dol)	Per capita[3]: Dollars	Per capita[3]: Rank	Earnings, 1989: Total (Mil dol)	Percent by selected industries: Farm	Goods-related[4]: Total
	88	89	90	91	92	93	94	95	96	97	98	99	100	101	102
NEW YORK—Con.															
Jefferson	1 392	6 690	509	19 350	1 645	12.4	1 173	99	206	286	15 581	778	1 272	1.2	22.1
Kings	21 888	146 202	7 250	18 880	36 387	7.6	10 476	1 536	6 168	8 783	15 683	744	12 013	0.0	21.4
Lewis	128	581	75	18 774	317	9.6	132	30	58	69	11 773	2 415	162	8.6	41.3
Livingston	365	2 704	192	16 399	943	8.9	381	63	135	150	15 772	718	444	4.0	NA
Madison	504	3 878	202	15 926	1 027	8.8	365	94	168	158	15 232	898	458	3.6	20.6
Monroe	21 197	102 976	8 256	23 594	14 822	8.3	11 280	1 053	2 773	2 004	21 192	122	12 333	0.2	45.6
Montgomery	608	3 720	247	15 657	785	7.0	366	51	153	184	15 250	887	416	2.5	34.1
Nassau	60 799	195 451	13 532	23 524	37 711	6.6	18 056	3 274	8 737	4 052	28 678	18	21 330	0.0	18.1
New York	492 258	775 613	71 018	35 061	53 479	7.6	98 715	11 013	11 781	6 522	35 193	3	109 728	0.0	9.4
Niagara	1 988	17 734	1 331	20 011	3 508	7.3	2 016	174	580	666	16 183	599	2 190	0.9	46.5
Oneida	6 127	21 315	1 401	18 410	3 957	7.3	2 454	265	713	826	16 214	589	2 719	0.6	25.1
Onondaga	19 108	68 195	4 734	21 245	8 650	8.3	6 614	640	1 373	1 307	18 794	234	7 254	0.2	28.0
Ontario	995	8 082	481	16 857	1 646	8.6	805	122	274	242	17 869	313	927	1.9	30.6
Orange	4 838	21 965	1 511	18 622	5 741	7.0	2 578	350	801	801	19 178	212	2 929	1.2	20.0
Orleans	172	1 373	106	15 187	612	8.1	227	41	96	107	15 213	903	268	7.4	27.1
Oswego	740	4 312	506	21 059	1 695	7.6	909	119	200	300	13 836	1 513	1 028	1.6	37.5
Otsego	1 038	6 060	246	15 495	900	9.2	411	71	213	167	14 917	1 020	482	3.2	13.7
Putnam	727	5 038	321	19 766	2 096	6.4	456	125	284	184	24 760	43	580	0.6	26.1
Queens	22 974	125 010	9 929	22 737	38 117	7.4	13 769	1 767	7 523	7 510	19 835	178	15 536	0.0	22.8
Rensselaer	1 384	15 670	689	17 939	2 607	8.7	1 084	143	415	482	17 239	406	1 226	1.0	27.5
Richmond	3 988	29 398	1 293	18 910	8 325	7.0	1 733	314	1 138	1 312	21 746	102	2 046	0.0	16.4
Rockland	4 907	28 237	1 815	21 915	6 675	7.1	2 794	435	1 073	775	25 094	38	3 229	0.0	23.3
St. Lawrence	830	9 012	450	17 873	1 353	10.2	815	99	211	323	12 295	2 199	914	1.8	29.5
Saratoga	1 925	10 147	674	18 315	3 188	8.5	1 186	168	439	403	18 050	290	1 354	0.7	31.5
Schenectady	3 071	19 391	1 117	22 629	2 912	7.7	1 796	177	639	521	19 435	197	1 972	0.1	33.8
Schoharie	282	1 670	68	14 613	420	8.1	146	31	73	83	13 772	1 548	177	6.0	NA
Schuyler	90	888	57	17 519	233	6.9	86	16	37	52	13 466	1 706	102	4.1	35.5
Seneca	224	1 238	189	21 117	520	7.6	270	39	84	95	16 245	580	309	2.9	35.5
Steuben	1 062	6 225	635	22 075	1 401	8.4	994	93	239	292	14 237	1 310	1 088	1.2	53.4
Suffolk	25 619	118 868	9 766	22 244	29 945	6.3	14 419	1 936	4 623	3 602	22 601	78	16 356	0.5	27.0
Sullivan	1 157	7 822	317	17 370	1 186	7.2	539	100	230	239	16 236	586	639	1.5	15.1
Tioga	272	1 858	330	25 719	774	6.0	412	54	107	112	14 880	1 035	465	2.6	62.2
Tompkins	1 572	21 955	609	16 092	1 351	10.5	933	125	281	183	15 154	924	1 057	1.4	17.9
Ulster	3 127	12 570	715	16 852	2 953	7.0	1 516	206	523	463	17 554	363	1 722	1.0	37.1
Warren	1 828	7 565	526	20 070	975	7.4	695	77	213	170	16 891	456	772	0.2	27.3
Washington	275	1 641	201	18 455	774	8.7	376	71	137	156	12 913	1 949	447	5.3	41.1
Wayne	512	3 876	323	17 409	1 455	8.4	591	93	223	220	16 296	570	684	4.0	42.3
Westchester	32 016	126 906	9 970	25 589	26 934	6.4	12 950	1 834	6 199	2 929	31 188	11	14 784	0.1	26.8
Wyoming	359	1 092	116	15 397	555	9.1	273	48	105	100	13 101	1 863	321	5.3	32.6
Yates	139	1 395	53	12 821	287	8.2	86	22	70	63	13 165	1 831	108	6.0	21.3
NORTH CAROLINA	136 308	510 927	45 232	X	100 418	8.1	68 617	8 848	14 363	13 902	15 287	X	77 465	2.3	34.4
Alamance	1 253	9 216	806	15 755	1 775	6.9	1 055	138	266	237	16 576	510	1 193	0.9	43.8
Alexander	132	760	134	14 700	386	8.8	174	47	40	45	13 842	1 509	221	8.2	55.8
Alleghany	48	360	30	13 491	118	8.3	50	23	20	24	11 930	2 349	73	17.3	NA
Anson	134	430	107	15 593	306	8.5	157	40	38	59	11 681	2 447	197	10.6	NA
Ashe	104	617	71	13 905	263	7.8	117	41	44	53	11 176	2 613	158	10.1	45.0
Avery	260	1 912	63	12 984	174	8.4	90	29	22	36	11 325	2 560	119	4.8	21.0
Beaufort	401	2 264	200	15 332	555	6.8	341	80	82	102	13 161	1 832	421	6.4	NA
Bertie	120	330	67	11 147	247	5.5	111	42	30	51	11 800	2 400	153	18.7	42.3
Bladen	206	623	74	13 453	342	6.7	156	52	35	71	11 041	2 656	208	13.9	40.8
Brunswick	696	1 587	148	16 855	598	8.7	328	66	86	124	11 303	2 567	395	3.0	32.9
Buncombe	2 766	18 620	1 187	17 177	2 730	9.1	1 796	201	508	440	15 627	769	1 997	0.8	31.0
Burke	536	3 608	465	16 098	1 064	6.3	712	91	131	153	13 661	1 597	803	2.0	51.0
Cabarrus	1 078	4 904	571	16 611	1 513	7.8	862	116	179	217	15 571	780	978	1.3	48.8
Caldwell	414	3 030	433	15 699	983	7.2	570	82	109	133	13 688	1 587	653	1.0	57.0
Camden	0	68	4	9 801	81	7.4	15	6	11	15	13 237	1 799	20	14.5	NA
Carteret	779	2 916	150	13 083	698	9.0	258	73	124	141	13 484	1 693	331	1.4	18.9
Caswell	34	359	12	11 580	216	7.2	47	13	21	41	9 796	2 911	60	10.2	29.3
Catawba	1 599	9 314	1 314	17 103	1 927	7.4	1 738	152	286	224	16 210	590	1 889	0.6	53.4
Chatham	161	1 027	160	15 650	595	8.6	236	87	86	76	16 012	642	323	14.0	47.2
Cherokee	176	643	75	12 997	234	9.2	121	33	37	58	10 850	2 699	154	5.6	40.6
Chowan	125	577	61	15 552	175	6.4	91	17	31	37	12 596	2 072	108	6.2	33.9
Clay	28	200	13	11 717	80	9.3	19	8	16	20	10 832	2 705	26	6.1	32.3
Cleveland	758	5 064	551	17 063	1 255	8.1	770	88	149	177	14 355	1 267	858	1.7	52.1
Columbus	1 256	2 503	239	17 039	584	8.9	330	73	71	132	11 085	2 639	403	6.3	43.2

1. For week including March 12. Excludes government employees, self-employed persons, farm workers, domestic service workers, railroad employees subject to the Railroad Retirement Act, and employees on oceanborne vessels or in foreign countries. 2. Includes other labor income. 3. Based on the resident population estimated as of July 1 of the year shown. 4. Covers mining, construction, and manufacturing.

Table A. States and Counties — **Earnings and Agriculture**

STATE County	Earnings, 1989 (cont'd): Percent by selected industries (cont'd): Goods-related[1]: Manufacturing	Service-related & other[2]: Total	Service-related & other[2]: Retail trade	Service-related & other[2]: Finance, insurance, & real estate	Service-related & other[2]: Services	Government	Agriculture, 1987: Farms: Number	Farms: Percent with: Less than 50 acres	Farms: Percent with: 500 acres and over	Farm operators, percent: Whose principal occupation is farming	Farm operators, percent: Residing on farm operated	Land in farms: Acreage (1,000)	Land in farms: Percent change, 1982–1987	Land in farms: Acres: Average size of farm	Acres: Total irrigated (1,000)	Acres: Total cropland (1,000)
	103	104	105	106	107	108	109	110	111	112	113	114	115	116	117	118
NEW YORK—Con.																
Jefferson	12.7	35.7	9.4	2.8	15.2	41.1	1 058	9.5	16.4	71.2	89.3	338	-8.1	320	D	225
Kings	14.2	67.9	10.3	5.0	37.4	10.7	4	100.0	0.0	25.0	50.0	0	-20.0	1	D	0
Lewis	34.3	26.7	9.0	1.5	10.0	23.4	707	10.0	11.9	79.8	89.4	193	-6.2	273	0	113
Livingston	17.9	34.8	10.4	1.3	15.7	33.8	737	20.6	19.5	60.0	83.3	234	-3.9	318	0	183
Madison	12.5	52.6	12.3	2.5	27.3	23.1	785	15.5	14.9	69.0	86.0	213	-8.7	271	D	140
Monroe	40.5	44.7	7.4	4.8	23.6	9.6	682	42.2	10.3	51.3	78.2	135	-7.3	197	2	114
Montgomery	29.5	46.9	10.1	3.1	24.0	16.5	616	13.3	9.4	74.4	87.8	156	-4.7	254	0	120
Nassau	12.2	69.4	10.3	9.5	34.3	12.5	67	80.6	0.0	44.8	50.7	1	-22.5	22	0	1
New York	7.3	76.3	4.3	27.9	32.0	14.4	0	NA	NA	NA	NA	0	NA	0	0	0
Niagara	40.5	37.6	9.4	2.1	17.6	15.0	923	38.4	6.8	47.0	85.5	147	-2.6	159	1	125
Oneida	19.9	46.9	9.7	6.3	21.5	27.5	1 251	18.5	9.0	67.1	88.6	286	-5.7	228	1	180
Onondaga	21.2	57.7	8.9	7.4	24.7	14.1	772	30.8	10.9	59.7	83.3	158	-11.6	205	1	120
Ontario	21.1	48.5	11.8	5.4	21.3	18.9	837	31.5	14.8	58.1	85.9	202	-7.7	241	0	163
Orange	12.8	54.5	12.8	3.9	23.3	24.2	789	39.9	4.7	67.3	74.1	115	-11.5	146	3	79
Orleans	21.6	33.5	8.7	3.3	14.0	32.0	581	28.7	12.7	58.3	81.8	152	-0.6	262	1	126
Oswego	29.2	NA	8.7	1.3	NA	22.4	749	24.6	4.5	51.0	86.9	123	-12.0	164	2	77
Otsego	8.3	64.6	12.1	5.2	34.0	18.5	1 029	11.2	11.2	69.1	86.8	264	-4.6	257	0	140
Putnam	10.8	55.4	11.7	3.4	29.2	17.9	51	49.0	2.0	33.3	84.3	6	-39.2	119	0	2
Queens	11.5	69.9	9.0	4.5	28.2	7.3	6	100.0	0.0	33.3	50.0	0	-30.8	2	0	0
Rensselaer	17.7	54.7	10.1	2.9	32.9	16.7	526	22.6	7.0	54.9	84.4	107	-9.4	203	0	65
Richmond	5.5	73.6	12.5	6.3	42.8	10.0	7	100.0	0.0	57.1	57.1	0	NA	2	0	D
Rockland	16.3	56.9	8.9	5.7	28.3	19.7	27	74.1	0.0	63.0	70.4	1	18.6	41	0	1
St. Lawrence	22.9	40.2	10.2	2.0	21.3	28.5	1 602	7.6	13.5	66.2	87.7	456	-7.4	285	0	243
Saratoga	20.7	45.3	14.3	3.2	21.0	22.5	528	31.1	5.9	52.1	87.5	83	-9.4	157	0	52
Schenectady	25.0	54.6	9.3	3.8	31.8	11.5	182	26.9	0.0	41.8	83.0	22	-8.7	122	0	12
Schoharie	7.4	NA	12.8	3.1	19.9	33.8	572	18.4	9.4	59.6	83.6	132	-15.9	230	1	86
Schuyler	28.4	37.7	12.3	1.3	19.1	22.7	371	18.3	8.4	50.4	85.2	76	-8.4	205	D	44
Seneca	29.6	26.4	6.9	1.4	10.6	35.2	432	16.7	19.2	62.3	86.3	126	1.6	292	0	104
Steuben	49.7	29.6	7.6	2.2	14.4	15.8	1 407	12.5	14.2	57.9	84.2	389	-5.8	276	1	230
Suffolk	18.2	53.5	10.4	5.3	24.6	19.0	696	69.1	1.3	69.0	61.2	42	-16.2	60	19	36
Sullivan	4.8	60.7	11.9	4.9	31.8	22.7	373	21.7	5.4	57.1	85.3	63	-16.8	169	0	32
Tioga	57.2	24.1	6.1	0.8	13.5	11.2	579	16.6	9.8	56.3	90.3	126	-10.3	217	0	71
Tompkins	12.1	69.4	9.9	3.5	47.1	11.3	532	25.2	9.8	53.4	83.6	111	-8.6	208	0	76
Ulster	30.7	43.7	10.0	4.5	21.3	18.1	539	41.4	5.0	51.4	81.6	78	-7.9	146	3	44
Warren	19.6	60.9	14.7	4.8	29.6	11.6	61	41.0	3.3	26.2	67.2	8	-18.8	139	0	3
Washington	33.6	27.1	8.5	0.8	11.6	26.5	861	13.6	16.1	68.2	84.9	241	-6.2	280	0	147
Wayne	36.3	32.2	9.0	1.5	15.6	21.5	1 064	30.5	8.3	58.2	84.7	191	-9.0	180	1	142
Westchester	18.9	61.6	8.5	7.9	31.3	11.6	121	66.9	2.5	37.2	65.3	9	-18.3	70	0	4
Wyoming	26.6	32.5	11.7	2.8	10.8	29.6	812	16.3	13.8	71.2	88.4	220	-5.5	271	1	154
Yates	13.4	54.3	13.0	2.4	24.2	18.4	619	22.1	8.6	60.4	81.9	114	1.4	184	0	85
NORTH CAROLINA	27.7	46.9	10.1	4.6	18.6	16.4	59 284	39.4	6.6	51.8	68.7	9 448	-8.5	159	138	5 716
Alamance	37.6	46.6	11.6	4.3	20.9	8.8	821	35.9	3.4	40.4	73.1	100	-13.2	122	2	54
Alexander	51.5	26.8	7.2	1.2	11.2	9.2	594	44.4	2.4	45.8	75.1	57	-2.8	97	0	30
Alleghany	23.8	NA	10.1	2.3	15.2	14.3	514	32.1	5.3	52.3	71.0	75	-3.6	146	0	36
Anson	38.9	NA	7.2	1.2	11.1	15.5	316	24.1	12.0	53.8	67.7	85	-18.2	269	0	37
Ashe	35.9	33.9	11.0	1.3	13.1	11.0	1 182	46.5	1.9	42.2	68.4	114	-11.8	96	0	48
Avery	10.4	61.3	13.0	4.3	31.5	12.9	280	56.1	1.8	49.3	70.7	21	2.6	74	0	8
Beaufort	26.4	NA	9.7	1.8	NA	11.9	630	31.4	13.5	61.0	64.1	156	-1.2	248	0	132
Bertie	39.8	25.6	6.0	1.8	8.0	13.5	564	31.2	14.7	69.7	49.8	172	-4.3	305	7	95
Bladen	36.0	28.3	7.4	1.8	9.4	17.1	719	37.1	9.5	54.8	68.0	131	-12.0	182	1	80
Brunswick	26.4	NA	7.8	3.3	NA	14.8	313	39.9	7.3	49.2	77.6	48	-21.2	154	0	27
Buncombe	24.0	53.7	11.5	3.4	26.6	14.4	1 200	61.8	2.1	37.2	73.2	104	-7.0	87	0	40
Burke	47.3	28.2	6.8	1.3	14.1	18.8	366	48.1	2.7	36.6	73.2	35	-2.6	95	0	16
Cabarrus	40.4	37.2	11.3	3.0	15.2	12.7	488	31.6	7.0	41.2	70.9	77	-6.4	158	0	49
Caldwell	51.6	32.6	8.9	1.7	13.1	9.4	368	45.9	1.9	33.7	74.2	35	-19.0	96	0	15
Camden	9.4	NA	10.0	NA	19.0	27.2	102	31.4	32.4	71.6	53.9	50	-1.5	487	0	45
Carteret	8.7	58.8	18.9	5.3	22.0	20.9	122	43.4	9.8	55.7	66.4	66	-3.1	537	0	D
Caswell	23.0	28.4	8.0	2.1	14.4	32.1	707	28.6	8.1	53.0	65.1	130	-7.9	184	2	52
Catawba	48.5	38.4	10.6	2.1	13.0	7.6	567	42.5	3.9	38.4	74.6	67	-17.2	119	0	41
Chatham	39.7	29.6	6.8	0.9	11.8	9.1	961	39.3	2.3	49.4	76.0	113	-4.9	117	1	49
Cherokee	32.5	36.5	12.8	2.1	15.2	17.3	267	46.4	3.4	43.8	74.5	27	-9.9	101	0	10
Chowan	27.3	47.1	10.7	1.8	17.5	12.8	220	35.9	11.4	66.4	70.0	50	-7.9	229	2	37
Clay	16.9	39.8	16.0	1.8	17.0	21.8	184	43.5	2.2	46.2	74.5	D	D	D	0	9
Cleveland	46.1	36.1	8.9	1.8	15.2	10.2	830	38.3	5.2	37.6	73.0	107	-12.0	129	0	69
Columbus	37.7	37.1	10.6	4.7	15.5	13.4	1 334	39.9	5.6	55.2	66.0	180	-4.8	135	0	118

1. Covers mining, construction, and manufacturing. 2. Covers private sector earnings in agricultural services, forestry, and fisheries; transportation and public utilities; wholesale trade; retail trade; finance, insurance, and real estate; and services.

STATE County	Agriculture, 1987 (cont'd): Value of land and buildings: Average per farm ($1,000)	Value of land and buildings: Average per acre (Dollars)	Value of products sold: Total (Mil dol)	Value of products sold: Average per farm (Dollars)	Value of products sold: Percent from: Crops	Value of products sold: Percent from: Livestock and poultry[1]	Percent of farms with sales of: $10,000 or more	Percent of farms with sales of: $100,000 or more	Manufactures, 1987: Establishments: Total	Establishments: Percent with 20 or more employees	All employees: Number (1,000)	All employees: Percent change, 1982–1987	All employees: Annual payroll (Mil dol)	Production workers: Number (1,000)	Production workers: Work hours (Mil)
	119	120	121	122	123	124	125	126	127	128	129	130	131	132	133
NEW YORK—Con.															
Jefferson	223	661	77	73 104	5.0	95.0	64.5	25.2	77	36.4	4.8	-11.1	115.6	3.4	6.5
Kings	D	D	0	54 883	100.0	0.0	75.0	25.0	3 002	32.7	77.9	-15.5	1 383.0	60.6	114.0
Lewis	191	673	59	82 977	3.2	96.8	76.2	34.9	41	31.7	2.0	0.0	45.8	1.5	3.0
Livingston	261	867	55	75 184	34.1	65.9	50.1	21.7	50	48.0	3.3	-19.5	67.7	2.6	5.3
Madison	196	746	66	83 784	9.1	90.9	68.3	31.8	74	32.4	2.7	22.7	54.7	2.0	4.2
Monroe	319	1 529	44	63 826	71.2	28.8	50.7	16.1	1 029	36.7	109.6	-16.7	3 633.0	52.9	106.6
Montgomery	207	779	42	67 529	9.7	90.3	66.2	24.5	72	55.6	6.0	-7.7	103.8	4.0	8.0
Nassau	D	D	3	51 160	55.9	44.1	53.7	14.9	2 176	28.6	88.8	0.6	2 532.7	48.0	92.4
New York	0	0	0	0	NA	NA	NA	NA	8 271	28.6	255.4	-20.5	7 052.1	110.0	198.6
Niagara	148	970	42	45 854	62.1	37.9	43.4	13.0	294	42.5	22.7	-10.3	678.3	15.5	31.3
Oneida	181	799	74	59 477	18.0	82.0	60.2	20.0	290	30.3	19.0	-14.8	459.1	12.3	24.3
Onondaga	251	1 272	54	69 733	22.8	77.2	51.7	21.2	580	39.0	41.3	-11.8	1 192.8	23.3	45.8
Ontario	264	1 147	52	61 704	43.7	56.3	52.4	18.4	140	45.7	7.3	37.7	153.4	5.0	9.9
Orange	429	2 805	74	93 438	59.2	40.8	67.4	25.7	362	38.7	13.6	3.8	269.5	9.7	18.6
Orleans	221	823	51	87 527	72.2	27.8	52.5	21.7	44	43.2	2.7	28.6	49.6	2.2	4.2
Oswego	147	915	34	45 251	47.2	52.8	39.9	12.7	105	34.3	8.0	5.3	233.3	5.8	11.7
Otsego	195	730	61	59 219	5.7	94.3	60.5	21.0	71	32.4	1.9	18.7	30.7	1.4	2.5
Putnam	338	2 848	1	15 609	D	D	21.6	3.9	80	18.8	2.0	42.9	50.1	1.3	2.5
Queens	D	D	D	D	NA	NA	33.3	0.0	2 415	34.5	74.6	-11.3	1 523.5	54.6	103.3
Rensselaer	268	1 316	26	50 238	25.2	74.8	47.1	15.0	122	36.1	6.1	3.4	148.7	3.0	5.7
Richmond	D	D	1	75 251	100.0	0.0	100.0	14.3	141	30.5	4.0	0.0	94.0	2.9	5.6
Rockland	505	12 311	1	54 458	D	D	59.3	22.2	342	28.4	17.7	12.7	474.0	10.3	19.5
St. Lawrence	135	478	81	50 590	5.2	94.8	59.4	15.2	90	32.2	5.5	-17.9	162.4	4.0	8.0
Saratoga	173	1 329	23	43 255	23.2	76.8	36.9	13.4	134	35.1	6.2	-1.6	171.8	4.3	8.7
Schenectady	163	1 115	3	18 149	44.0	56.0	28.0	3.3	137	26.3	13.2	-27.9	365.4	5.2	11.9
Schoharie	238	1 055	31	54 484	13.2	86.8	50.9	18.9	29	31.0	0.7	16.7	11.3	0.6	1.1
Schuyler	142	697	13	35 968	27.5	72.5	38.3	11.9	24	25.0	1.1	-8.3	26.0	0.7	1.3
Seneca	235	836	25	58 275	49.5	50.5	61.1	19.7	38	31.6	2.8	-26.3	75.2	1.3	2.5
Steuben	151	560	74	52 312	26.2	73.8	48.8	14.4	99	40.4	12.4	-1.6	343.9	6.8	13.8
Suffolk	421	7 008	115	165 445	84.7	15.3	71.3	30.0	2 772	30.1	98.3	17.9	2 435.2	59.3	117.7
Sullivan	286	1 940	23	60 793	7.3	92.7	44.8	15.3	74	13.5	1.0	0.0	18.6	0.7	1.5
Tioga	141	652	30	51 149	7.7	92.3	45.9	19.5	45	37.8	7.3	-6.4	245.0	2.4	4.9
Tompkins	186	1 022	42	79 052	11.0	89.0	47.7	16.2	109	21.1	2.9	-34.1	70.5	1.9	3.7
Ulster	453	3 149	50	91 871	53.5	46.5	44.7	15.4	231	28.6	7.8	-33.9	148.9	5.6	10.6
Warren	187	1 345	1	21 969	60.1	39.9	34.4	6.6	117	31.6	5.9	31.1	140.1	4.0	8.0
Washington	282	1 006	73	85 095	6.4	93.6	61.6	29.5	96	35.4	5.0	-10.7	114.4	3.8	7.7
Wayne	187	1 063	76	71 092	61.6	38.4	52.9	18.5	128	38.3	7.2	-1.4	153.3	5.1	10.4
Westchester	520	6 519	7	57 773	61.5	38.5	60.3	18.2	1 260	31.7	66.5	1.2	2 268.9	24.8	49.4
Wyoming	201	751	84	103 254	14.2	85.8	66.1	32.6	48	43.8	3.2	-11.1	61.2	2.2	4.6
Yates	185	1 037	29	47 383	51.6	48.4	58.6	12.4	27	25.9	0.6	-14.3	12.9	0.4	0.8
NORTH CAROLINA	200	1 263	3 541	59 737	40.6	59.4	43.4	13.7	10 995	43.4	842.4	5.4	16 293.4	637.3	1 258.8
Alamance	177	1 446	28	34 310	22.5	77.5	31.7	9.1	303	53.8	24.3	14.6	425.6	19.1	37.1
Alexander	141	1 427	31	51 890	7.3	92.7	40.7	18.4	104	35.6	6.0	-6.3	93.3	5.2	10.1
Alleghany	186	1 315	16	30 886	5.9	94.1	36.4	10.9	18	50.0	1.0	-28.6	14.1	0.8	1.5
Anson	227	898	45	141 183	7.4	92.6	43.7	21.8	60	40.0	4.8	20.0	67.4	3.9	7.8
Ashe	109	1 144	18	15 057	19.6	80.4	23.0	3.3	46	26.1	2.5	-7.4	35.9	2.1	4.2
Avery	105	1 333	4	16 054	90.0	10.0	30.7	3.6	19	36.8	0.7	0.0	9.0	0.6	1.2
Beaufort	247	1 016	49	78 330	66.6	33.4	62.9	20.3	73	43.8	5.5	-12.7	92.1	4.4	8.9
Bertie	306	1 004	50	89 534	57.1	42.9	70.6	21.5	37	29.7	3.9	21.9	44.7	3.6	6.3
Bladen	160	1 006	37	50 811	62.6	37.4	48.8	12.2	66	28.8	2.7	0.0	38.9	2.3	4.5
Brunswick	175	1 150	10	32 698	67.9	32.1	39.3	7.7	37	21.6	0.8	-11.1	14.5	0.7	1.3
Buncombe	171	2 117	19	16 090	35.1	64.9	16.8	3.5	285	44.6	18.7	-2.1	353.5	13.7	26.6
Burke	156	1 358	17	45 780	20.8	79.2	24.0	8.7	157	50.3	19.1	15.1	328.8	16.0	31.1
Cabarrus	234	1 338	30	60 950	10.5	89.5	25.8	4.3	136	47.1	15.8	-27.9	286.0	12.6	26.1
Caldwell	160	1 252	9	25 656	27.8	72.2	28.0	6.5	157	53.5	16.0	3.2	254.6	13.5	27.4
Camden	513	D	10	99 741	83.6	16.4	68.6	28.4	7	0.0	0.0	0.0	0.4	0.0	0.1
Carteret	894	1 669	11	90 989	83.5	16.5	45.1	18.0	63	20.6	1.5	-16.7	22.9	1.2	2.3
Caswell	173	953	15	20 555	77.2	22.8	41.3	3.4	10	20.0	0.1	0.0	2.1	0.1	0.3
Catawba	176	1 588	13	23 093	19.5	80.5	21.0	5.6	591	56.0	40.8	19.6	705.9	33.1	63.8
Chatham	161	1 275	88	91 886	4.6	95.4	47.1	25.8	77	46.8	5.7	3.6	96.6	4.8	9.4
Cherokee	147	1 533	11	40 425	8.4	91.6	19.1	4.5	30	43.3	3.0	20.0	40.5	2.6	4.7
Chowan	256	1 140	16	73 388	68.9	31.1	70.5	23.6	32	43.8	1.7	30.8	30.4	1.4	3.0
Clay	175	1 886	6	32 911	5.3	94.6	21.7	6.5	10	20.0	0.3	0.0	3.7	0.3	0.4
Cleveland	146	1 164	32	38 965	22.1	77.9	23.6	8.3	181	50.3	15.6	13.9	296.5	13.2	26.9
Columbus	164	1 085	51	38 018	83.8	16.2	55.5	9.4	79	41.8	6.2	6.9	123.7	5.3	10.9

1. Includes livestock and poultry products.

STATE County	Manufactures, 1987 (cont'd)					Value of construction authorized by building permits, 1990							
	Production workers (cont'd)						Nonresidential				Residential		
	Wages							Percent					
	Total (Mil dol)	Average per worker (Dollars)	Value added by manufacture (Mil dol)	Value of shipments (Mil dol)	New capital expenditures (Mil dol)	Total[1] ($1,000)	Total ($1,000)	Office	Industrial	Stores	New construction ($1,000)	Number of housing units	Alterations and additions ($1,000)
	134	135	136	137	138	139	140	141	142	143	144	145	146
NEW YORK—Con.													
Jefferson	58.5	17 206	303.8	677.5	27.2	37 673	9 748	9.6	22.3	25.5	16 819	246	4 126
Kings	900.8	14 865	3 295.3	6 727.5	112.4	256 488	52 289	0.5	4.1	16.2	104 073	1 634	38 487
Lewis	33.0	22 000	125.5	331.3	6.7	11 993	2 916	0.0	0.0	34.4	6 761	199	1 224
Livingston	44.5	17 115	268.7	396.5	11.8	27 589	8 312	7.6	11.6	14.1	13 365	187	2 974
Madison	30.6	15 300	109.3	272.9	10.5	33 588	11 566	3.9	1.9	7.7	15 898	248	3 006
Monroe	1 413.2	26 715	11 173.7	16 626.7	625.4	587 890	204 725	34.4	13.3	32.6	241 525	2 330	32 944
Montgomery	62.7	15 675	250.1	487.6	16.4	12 101	2 900	7.2	56.3	3.2	5 444	76	1 258
Nassau	1 028.2	21 421	5 356.2	8 740.0	263.8	459 064	78 427	16.1	21.9	36.6	79 675	651	145 161
New York	1 855.0	16 864	16 406.8	28 685.2	391.3	483 470	48 090	67.9	0.0	30.5	246 005	2 398	69 752
Niagara	431.6	27 845	1 769.7	3 282.5	87.9	143 542	44 836	6.5	46.2	18.9	66 871	897	12 296
Oneida	246.7	20 057	967.8	2 053.5	52.5	87 005	24 448	12.5	9.0	15.0	43 786	728	6 469
Onondaga	557.7	23 936	2 529.3	4 763.6	183.2	351 940	122 674	13.6	1.8	48.5	115 523	1 415	26 754
Ontario	86.5	17 300	393.2	811.4	31.5	68 127	15 083	10.3	12.8	13.9	43 830	495	2 972
Orange	161.3	16 629	675.9	1 344.3	48.8	167 500	46 134	14.6	1.1	56.1	80 290	1 075	16 426
Orleans	37.0	16 818	169.3	301.4	6.2	15 161	3 018	0.0	33.1	7.2	9 367	149	1 372
Oswego	159.8	27 552	793.0	2 442.6	63.2	39 839	7 744	23.8	13.3	26.2	26 097	362	2 126
Otsego	19.2	13 714	77.3	152.2	8.9	40 696	17 961	3.1	31.7	2.8	17 174	299	2 396
Putnam	28.5	21 923	125.5	187.1	9.5	79 926	12 821	49.2	5.1	9.7	54 103	527	8 638
Queens	906.5	16 603	3 452.9	6 619.5	130.7	115 210	19 027	5.6	26.3	41.9	41 951	704	20 321
Rensselaer	59.9	19 967	407.0	680.1	16.9	76 384	18 069	31.5	40.0	14.0	41 827	638	8 169
Richmond	59.2	20 414	420.9	890.1	17.1	97 520	21 814	18.4	0.0	59.9	62 231	940	7 568
Rockland	214.7	20 845	2 287.1	3 056.0	136.5	143 495	32 717	62.7	0.1	14.0	59 107	691	22 160
St. Lawrence	111.6	27 900	366.6	1 097.0	46.3	44 449	17 041	2.2	2.0	71.5	12 296	303	3 721
Saratoga	100.5	23 372	518.8	950.5	69.7	244 270	127 364	31.5	55.6	9.2	91 169	934	9 552
Schenectady	131.5	25 288	625.8	1 022.4	17.2	70 550	6 623	42.4	0.0	5.4	36 354	485	8 700
Schoharie	7.8	13 000	28.2	52.4	5.2	12 178	1 103	0.0	0.0	44.1	7 735	98	1 416
Schuyler	14.4	20 571	56.2	94.4	2.3	3 674	1 123	0.0	0.0	66.6	1 981	31	248
Seneca	29.1	22 385	150.2	285.0	D	39 507	2 101	3.1	1.0	36.5	5 497	89	1 949
Steuben	147.0	21 618	573.7	1 075.4	39.9	32 374	7 188	8.0	42.8	12.8	13 216	225	6 110
Suffolk	1 153.6	19 454	5 558.8	9 209.1	295.7	610 624	155 748	12.2	17.3	34.5	251 465	4 373	95 444
Sullivan	13.8	19 714	38.0	91.6	2.2	72 064	21 192	60.8	10.3	11.3	40 931	632	6 366
Tioga	48.9	20 375	627.0	922.4	D	23 708	7 984	31.3	27.4	23.1	12 955	186	1 537
Tompkins	37.4	19 684	128.3	288.4	7.9	77 003	33 857	9.1	26.8	3.3	25 018	291	8 253
Ulster	86.7	15 482	325.4	636.2	17.4	101 214	16 871	36.7	21.0	7.3	57 756	644	16 823
Warren	82.0	20 500	300.7	687.8	54.0	77 175	13 293	24.6	21.4	21.2	43 132	427	5 124
Washington	79.3	20 868	317.6	605.5	17.6	27 215	5 075	10.7	36.2	28.7	15 792	313	2 539
Wayne	87.8	17 216	404.2	826.9	21.9	48 494	9 389	14.6	9.3	27.5	28 480	355	3 998
Westchester	507.9	20 480	2 789.8	6 201.3	258.0	416 845	54 257	26.2	4.9	14.4	130 507	1 014	99 432
Wyoming	38.7	17 591	161.0	315.4	7.5	17 568	5 574	3.0	6.3	7.5	7 812	141	1 742
Yates	6.3	15 750	34.0	79.0	D	15 319	2 937	0.0	21.5	23.4	7 375	258	1 546
NORTH CAROLINA	10 293.0	16 151	47 007.4	95 317.3	2 958.7	5 625 670	1 674 605	21.9	23.9	22.4	2 805 340	41 504	271 475
Alamance	283.5	14 843	942.5	2 262.3	72.7	83 685	33 127	30.5	39.3	20.4	24 756	370	6 212
Alexander	71.2	13 692	231.1	543.4	5.9	10 955	4 473	18.3	51.3	8.8	5 571	96	272
Alleghany	10.5	13 125	29.9	61.3	4.0	8 430	1 799	11.1	0.0	5.0	5 849	81	624
Anson	48.5	12 436	138.0	280.3	22.1	7 329	3 839	7.3	10.1	78.4	1 835	31	761
Ashe	28.0	13 333	167.5	270.3	2.7	14 816	2 858	25.4	7.7	16.5	10 881	162	240
Avery	7.1	11 833	22.2	55.6	0.6	22 822	4 931	3.7	0.0	34.6	16 401	212	499
Beaufort	67.1	15 250	284.0	613.1	24.9	14 085	1 464	6.5	13.0	9.7	10 788	158	1 200
Bertie	39.4	10 944	93.3	257.0	4.9	6 676	4 082	3.3	0.0	4.5	2 050	50	338
Bladen	29.4	12 783	77.7	200.3	5.9	6 584	1 926	62.9	18.4	0.1	4 504	81	144
Brunswick	9.4	13 429	57.7	115.2	D	72 509	17 440	7.8	26.0	14.9	48 221	667	5 858
Buncombe	220.7	16 109	927.0	1 773.0	D	172 291	57 295	6.7	0.2	16.3	72 764	816	11 570
Burke	231.7	14 481	566.5	1 163.0	49.6	33 626	11 086	7.3	48.1	20.3	14 924	253	1 780
Cabarrus	214.2	17 000	1 610.1	2 507.5	47.5	80 130	23 343	2.3	26.8	19.5	48 608	928	3 116
Caldwell	192.7	14 274	488.5	987.1	18.5	28 370	2 511	2.4	48.4	20.2	18 947	336	2 103
Camden	0.3	NA	1.0	2.7	D	3 945	238	0.0	0.0	89.7	3 584	56	56
Carteret	15.6	13 000	76.9	188.5	D	50 591	5 411	0.0	17.8	38.6	34 758	385	2 672
Caswell	1.3	13 000	4.6	8.9	D	8 274	422	25.5	11.3	0.0	6 268	65	1 093
Catawba	487.4	14 725	1 433.2	3 114.7	77.3	90 494	24 560	3.4	35.9	34.7	48 130	734	5 138
Chatham	73.3	15 271	258.8	564.5	15.1	16 893	5 350	10.2	72.0	0.0	9 612	142	1 113
Cherokee	32.6	12 538	115.8	215.3	3.5	2 006	1 305	0.0	0.0	65.4	292	5	8
Chowan	20.8	14 857	65.1	165.5	3.9	8 252	2 717	6.9	12.9	0.7	4 333	45	882
Clay	2.1	7 000	5.5	12.2	D	5 664	1 110	0.0	0.0	100.0	4 160	64	350
Cleveland	217.8	16 500	712.8	1 500.4	116.5	55 698	17 206	29.6	27.2	8.9	33 582	507	3 098
Columbus	94.9	17 906	394.8	766.0	31.4	10 557	1 717	30.6	16.0	23.1	6 011	133	1 960

1. Includes nonresidential additions and alterations, residential nonhousekeeping buildings, and residential garages and carports not shown separately.

STATE County	Wholesale trade, 1987 Estab-lishments	Wholesale trade, 1987 Sales (Mil dol)	Wholesale trade, 1987 Paid employees[1]	Wholesale trade, 1987 Annual payroll (Mil dol)	Retail trade, all establishments, 1987 Number	Retail trade, all establishments, 1987 Sales Total (Mil dol)	Retail trade, all establishments, 1987 Sales Percent change, 1982–1987	Retail trade, all establishments, 1987 Sales Per capita[2] (Dollars)	Retail trade, establishments with payroll, 1987 Number	Retail trade, establishments with payroll, 1987 Sales Total (Mil dol)	Retail trade, establishments with payroll, 1987 Sales Per capita[2] (Dollars) General merchan-dise stores	Retail trade, establishments with payroll, 1987 Sales Per capita[2] (Dollars) Food stores	Retail trade, establishments with payroll, 1987 Sales Per capita[2] (Dollars) Apparel & acces-sory stores	Retail trade, establishments with payroll, 1987 Sales Per capita[2] (Dollars) Eating and drinking places
	147	148	149	150	151	152	153	154	155	156	157	158	159	160
NEW YORK—Con.														
Jefferson	142	252.1	1 325	25.1	1 167	691.6	83.4	7 264	750	674.6	797	1 283	360	651
Kings	2 716	8 918.5	27 614	591.3	14 712	6 584.7	32.0	2 846	9 212	6 284.8	274	718	239	189
Lewis	23	70.9	176	2.7	266	76.6	40.8	2 993	144	71.8	D	894	D	257
Livingston	74	146.3	609	9.6	622	286.1	49.0	4 865	331	272.7	D	1 184	56	394
Madison	83	256.7	692	12.8	752	306.8	50.8	4 613	397	292.5	289	1 162	108	512
Monroe	1 310	6 851.6	15 564	382.6	6 219	4 966.5	49.0	7 123	3 988	4 851.3	760	1 478	352	657
Montgomery	82	185.2	939	15.5	674	264.4	37.8	5 143	342	247.3	553	1 351	151	289
Nassau	4 967	21 018.7	48 365	1 361.9	15 387	12 383.3	50.5	9 394	10 411	12 082.1	957	1 578	674	746
New York	13 163	161 797.3	147 836	4 915.6	21 829	15 628.2	44.0	10 406	17 076	15 324.3	1 315	1 130	1 525	1 965
Niagara	232	513.1	2 323	43.3	2 233	1 213.0	42.0	5 634	1 451	1 181.4	720	1 251	304	523
Oneida	399	933.5	4 273	89.2	2 796	1 468.3	36.4	5 961	1 603	1 412.1	715	1 204	335	499
Onondaga	1 243	7 502.0	15 487	376.3	4 597	3 268.6	49.2	7 121	3 009	3 198.8	723	1 507	482	673
Ontario	144	274.6	1 098	21.5	1 046	708.0	60.0	7 754	651	690.9	1 073	1 445	429	617
Orange	448	2 789.6	6 838	148.1	2 893	2 022.0	63.2	7 026	1 854	1 962.5	845	1 603	369	505
Orleans	34	54.1	300	4.8	343	140.6	32.9	3 586	191	135.1	D	1 151	104	308
Oswego	96	167.6	801	11.8	1 131	541.3	45.7	4 522	601	520.0	339	1 062	75	440
Otsego	79	176.6	690	12.2	760	395.1	76.4	6 640	401	378.7	584	1 266	102	637
Putnam	101	224.0	859	21.9	765	427.2	56.6	5 203	454	409.0	331	1 217	73	355
Queens	2 836	9 513.9	31 990	824.0	15 053	7 038.5	37.7	3 647	8 497	6 674.8	284	905	222	426
Rensselaer	147	682.8	1 690	37.8	1 311	717.1	57.6	4 762	724	689.4	335	1 354	81	394
Richmond	366	1 032.6	2 335	49.4	2 785	1 699.8	56.8	4 508	1 672	1 627.3	560	1 329	277	302
Rockland	601	3 571.1	5 230	135.5	2 603	1 600.3	43.6	6 034	1 608	1 545.3	603	1 289	277	479
St. Lawrence	111	298.6	1 119	23.0	1 272	572.2	61.0	5 183	671	546.9	433	1 259	99	412
Saratoga	183	326.6	1 200	24.9	1 692	1 061.7	83.3	6 358	991	1 019.6	575	1 328	195	605
Schenectady	172	776.0	2 469	58.0	1 493	1 022.2	45.0	6 860	946	992.9	830	1 550	337	450
Schoharie	29	36.0	161	2.6	368	130.9	45.0	4 380	156	121.7	D	1 254	105	219
Schuyler	13	13.5	95	1.3	232	80.3	89.8	4 642	107	75.0	D	734	79	456
Seneca	35	97.6	504	9.3	340	152.3	49.3	4 730	173	145.4	D	1 108	49	326
Steuben	94	102.0	594	9.4	1 050	497.5	43.6	5 124	627	479.8	501	1 387	165	417
Suffolk	3 227	12 509.2	37 923	950.5	13 426	9 775.3	65.5	7 462	8 890	9 504.2	716	1 606	383	500
Sullivan	117	306.7	1 228	24.5	943	436.7	52.7	6 212	528	414.9	422	1 650	208	403
Tioga	54	98.4	533	8.0	450	198.1	57.3	3 884	214	189.3	158	981	24	198
Tompkins	77	128.4	642	13.1	914	537.5	50.5	6 135	622	522.8	702	1 383	275	585
Ulster	199	428.9	2 207	43.7	2 053	1 093.4	60.4	6 607	1 132	1 048.5	712	1 485	223	513
Warren	105	335.5	1 535	36.3	985	625.6	66.3	11 152	668	611.2	D	2 210	588	1 055
Washington	72	106.6	465	7.7	650	231.6	57.8	3 987	333	219.6	D	1 199	45	265
Wayne	90	272.2	820	15.6	841	366.9	44.6	4 184	404	351.1	D	1 160	82	233
Westchester	2 173	16 780.8	27 118	768.5	9 018	6 936.5	45.1	8 025	6 224	6 764.5	951	1 419	554	621
Wyoming	58	83.4	284	4.7	462	170.0	48.7	4 078	244	161.6	223	1 172	59	274
Yates	33	34.2	217	4.0	285	84.1	40.9	3 951	129	79.2	D	1 049	67	349
NORTH CAROLINA	12 109	57 027.6	140 158	3 064.1	69 125	40 651.5	62.6	6 344	42 991	39 051.8	630	1 225	295	559
Alamance	185	545.1	1 782	32.7	1 332	823.9	59.1	7 869	847	799.6	681	1 404	531	636
Alexander	29	29.0	201	3.2	242	94.2	75.1	3 463	140	89.2	63	623	80	259
Alleghany	6	1.5	35	0.4	150	43.9	68.8	4 476	74	38.4	102	777	52	283
Anson	23	D	D	D	217	87.5	37.6	3 340	115	81.4	94	986	99	192
Ashe	18	D	D	D	297	117.4	60.6	5 017	134	109.1	338	929	171	289
Avery	16	D	D	D	226	75.8	53.1	4 986	135	71.3	614	1 143	154	531
Beaufort	69	D	D	D	523	227.4	34.6	5 402	303	217.5	519	1 015	174	528
Bertie	23	56.5	210	3.2	201	53.9	36.8	2 554	109	51.0	59	717	33	57
Bladen	31	D	D	D	250	100.8	39.0	3 272	150	96.0	198	759	139	181
Brunswick	43	D	D	D	639	207.2	76.8	4 177	364	196.3	305	1 207	93	488
Buncombe	325	872.1	3 486	69.0	1 977	1 215.8	43.3	7 098	1 254	1 176.7	899	1 406	382	704
Burke	55	86.4	363	6.7	733	366.6	87.8	4 799	384	343.8	246	1 205	183	377
Cabarrus	135	330.9	1 391	23.1	992	617.2	56.4	6 531	588	598.8	730	1 244	310	451
Caldwell	64	D	D	D	759	377.6	60.3	5 348	455	363.0	441	1 172	140	359
Camden	5	D	D	D	46	8.4	-21.5	1 394	19	7.2	D	D	0	D
Carteret	89	135.3	859	11.2	693	341.7	73.1	6 767	467	331.6	648	1 688	246	736
Caswell	6	3.2	30	0.5	118	26.0	30.7	1 165	56	23.6	62	319	D	23
Catawba	300	1 640.6	5 581	115.4	1 475	966.1	63.2	8 358	1 011	936.5	956	1 453	406	786
Chatham	49	191.2	524	8.0	328	131.9	49.2	3 635	192	124.9	110	980	96	317
Cherokee	26	33.9	174	2.3	255	124.8	82.5	5 972	147	118.2	850	1 796	212	475
Chowan	27	77.5	328	5.3	141	67.6	44.1	4 967	96	66.1	417	1 389	148	410
Clay	4	D	D	D	80	25.3	18.2	3 513	37	22.7	D	717	D	49
Cleveland	129	382.2	1 449	28.6	866	491.2	72.7	5 692	524	471.4	562	1 314	250	438
Columbus	98	149.7	587	6.9	584	253.7	36.4	4 804	344	241.7	375	1 104	279	267

1. For pay period including March 12. 2. Based on the estimated population as of July 1 of the year shown.

STATE County	Retail trade, establishments with payroll, 1987 (cont'd)		Taxable service industries–establishments with payroll, 1987							Bank deposits,[2] June 1989		Savings capital,[3] September 1989	
				Receipts (Mil dol)									
					Selected kinds of business								
	Paid employees[1]	Annual payroll (Mil dol)	Number	Total	Hotels, motels and other lodging places	Health services	Legal services	Paid employees	Annual payroll (Mil dol)	Total (Mil dol)	Percent change, 1988–1989	Total (Mil dol)	Percent change, 1988–1989
	161	162	163	164	165	166	167	168	169	170	171	172	173
NEW YORK—Con.													
Jefferson	7 222	75.3	428	113.7	18.7	38.5	8.9	2 185	42.0	927	8.1	132.8	1.2
Kings	64 863	764.3	7 607	2 343.9	22.3	884.8	141.3	48 866	848.4	23 547	4.0	3 341.0	-0.4
Lewis	811	7.2	65	9.6	0.7	2.8	1.0	240	2.1	154	5.5	27.0	19.1
Livingston	3 141	27.2	218	65.1	1.5	33.2	3.3	1 413	18.9	396	8.3	67.4	-2.4
Madison	3 751	32.9	276	57.5	2.2	17.0	4.4	1 655	19.9	456	2.3	19.1	-10.2
Monroe	58 802	562.3	4 484	1 920.7	80.8	419.1	169.4	49 375	751.0	10 809	6.5	1 954.5	5.9
Montgomery	2 743	25.8	245	48.9	2.8	20.0	5.1	1 050	15.6	520	7.7	209.2	10.1
Nassau	118 522	1 446.1	15 245	7 700.5	157.4	1 890.7	571.1	137 498	2 713.5	28 791	10.1	6 465.9	1.5
New York	185 719	2 445.6	31 944	36 908.7	1 787.0	1 901.0	7 454.1	507 499	13 833.7	174 248	0.8	2 160.8	-36.6
Niagara	15 938	133.4	1 055	290.4	32.6	96.7	17.2	8 512	106.0	2 255	5.8	14.8	-33.1
Oneida	17 552	159.8	1 319	446.1	26.4	138.3	28.1	11 957	174.8	2 637	6.2	168.7	2.7
Onondaga	40 074	380.1	3 137	1 422.1	72.0	308.8	120.6	33 334	557.5	5 671	6.5	295.9	0.9
Ontario	8 243	76.8	513	137.2	7.4	36.1	6.8	3 859	43.9	588	6.3	228.0	-0.4
Orange	20 027	222.2	1 788	554.7	31.3	172.0	55.2	12 338	201.3	2 607	5.1	815.5	4.0
Orleans	1 780	14.5	123	19.4	D	10.1	1.9	470	7.0	234	-3.7	45.2	8.9
Oswego	5 890	62.3	368	84.5	4.7	31.6	5.8	2 368	30.0	706	9.1	246.0	-1.0
Otsego	4 564	42.1	310	60.7	10.1	18.0	6.4	1 419	19.9	560	10.1	0.0	NA
Putnam	3 858	47.6	554	143.2	5.1	56.1	10.0	2 987	52.1	579	5.0	135.5	-4.5
Queens	74 088	872.2	8 246	3 385.0	127.3	1 072.9	111.0	68 333	1 204.9	19 390	2.9	7 744.3	2.0
Rensselaer	8 218	79.5	680	188.5	6.2	62.0	15.2	4 834	72.6	1 386	5.3	95.3	-0.6
Richmond	17 184	176.0	1 870	608.6	9.2	266.9	39.1	14 255	240.4	3 568	7.2	1 159.1	-3.9
Rockland	16 185	183.9	2 268	835.5	25.9	235.9	61.1	14 889	284.5	3 095	6.3	1 013.7	-6.0
St. Lawrence	6 142	56.2	404	89.4	5.3	36.4	6.5	2 798	32.1	683	8.7	138.5	-1.2
Saratoga	11 655	114.0	812	255.8	19.6	40.9	10.4	4 745	63.1	993	11.9	260.0	3.0
Schenectady	11 266	113.0	912	570.3	4.8	135.0	20.9	9 681	226.1	965	3.3	1 336.2	-0.5
Schoharie	1 145	12.6	117	26.4	2.1	6.3	0.9	697	8.4	241	7.6	0.0	NA
Schuyler	784	8.4	69	11.2	1.7	5.0	0.5	351	3.5	81	2.3	18.8	-1.2
Seneca	1 502	14.5	113	20.1	D	7.2	1.6	520	6.0	218	-2.1	38.6	7.0
Steuben	5 567	53.3	428	104.2	11.5	39.9	6.5	2 613	35.7	634	3.1	123.6	-1.7
Suffolk	90 954	1 094.0	10 076	3 852.2	95.9	1 128.4	201.4	76 610	1 413.5	15 117	8.0	3 693.2	-1.9
Sullivan	3 961	46.3	529	252.7	130.1	35.2	15.8	6 158	74.4	583	5.3	208.8	-5.7
Tioga	1 741	19.3	143	31.9	D	8.8	2.7	943	11.2	263	8.9	34.6	-1.3
Tompkins	6 452	62.2	499	140.5	11.0	39.2	8.6	3 216	47.3	494	7.3	378.5	-0.3
Ulster	11 109	115.6	1 038	359.8	66.6	80.8	20.9	8 840	127.4	1 199	5.0	423.1	-0.2
Warren	6 431	69.6	618	247.7	65.1	48.9	13.5	4 704	82.2	671	5.8	85.4	16.3
Washington	2 158	23.0	181	26.9	0.9	9.0	2.3	620	7.0	339	7.7	0.0	NA
Wayne	3 793	34.6	316	58.4	D	17.9	5.6	2 190	21.4	488	7.2	235.5	-0.8
Westchester	64 947	815.3	8 563	3 953.3	161.2	915.9	243.7	68 617	1 377.2	17 216	2.6	1 442.6	0.9
Wyoming	1 882	16.1	135	23.5	0.8	10.9	1.9	802	8.6	333	4.6	0.0	NA
Yates	864	8.6	86	9.3	0.6	D	1.2	251	3.0	134	10.4	63.5	-2.2
NORTH CAROLINA	464 862	4 422.8	36 016	12 829.8	929.7	3 580.9	754.1	331 402	4 928.3	48 996	15.3	17 334.6	1.4
Alamance	9 288	88.2	602	175.3	12.0	72.3	7.9	5 539	68.8	789	12.4	441.5	-3.6
Alexander	949	8.9	89	14.7	D	4.9	0.6	491	4.7	126	24.3	77.3	3.8
Alleghany	432	3.8	37	6.8	D	4.1	0.4	202	3.1	88	27.9	27.7	-1.2
Anson	864	8.4	74	10.1	D	4.0	0.9	288	3.9	126	9.6	36.6	-0.7
Ashe	1 044	10.1	72	11.6	0.5	2.7	0.7	250	3.2	194	16.9	39.3	-3.6
Avery	957	8.3	94	35.4	11.5	5.6	0.7	1 390	12.0	97	17.5	22.7	14.6
Beaufort	2 767	24.9	204	67.4	2.1	16.6	2.5	1 350	17.5	269	12.0	90.7	-1.4
Bertie	547	5.0	54	5.9	0.0	0.9	1.1	222	2.1	118	9.4	5.5	19.4
Bladen	1 175	10.9	95	18.6	1.1	6.4	1.5	427	5.5	112	10.1	36.5	0.1
Brunswick	2 454	20.9	229	51.0	3.1	14.5	3.4	1 339	17.4	221	16.8	129.8	5.4
Buncombe	14 596	139.6	1 280	440.7	52.5	176.7	23.7	10 426	184.4	1 270	16.7	474.5	-0.8
Burke	3 788	36.1	297	73.1	D	35.0	5.5	2 085	30.0	333	19.9	221.7	6.0
Cabarrus	6 622	65.2	479	134.9	3.7	47.4	5.8	3 249	54.4	433	11.8	446.7	9.1
Caldwell	3 722	37.6	233	68.3	3.4	29.0	3.5	1 699	27.6	270	16.0	290.7	5.2
Camden	104	0.8	9	1.2	0.0	D	D	30	0.4	5	12.1	0.0	NA
Carteret	4 079	37.2	321	64.1	16.4	16.6	4.9	1 789	21.2	304	7.6	85.3	-0.4
Caswell	252	2.3	43	5.1	0.0	1.4	0.9	145	1.9	58	10.0	0.0	NA
Catawba	11 242	112.6	776	280.5	8.6	121.1	10.3	6 919	100.9	918	20.0	491.6	-1.8
Chatham	1 486	13.0	125	21.7	D	9.7	1.9	608	7.6	203	19.7	77.1	6.4
Cherokee	1 348	12.3	90	12.7	D	5.8	1.2	328	4.4	156	12.2	35.3	-2.6
Chowan	828	7.3	68	15.0	0.7	7.7	0.5	502	6.0	84	26.1	37.8	2.4
Clay	204	1.9	24	2.4	0.0	1.3	0.4	57	1.0	51	18.1	0.0	NA
Cleveland	5 138	50.9	408	96.4	4.3	42.8	3.6	2 455	39.6	352	11.5	342.6	-3.2
Columbus	2 720	25.0	209	44.6	D	22.3	3.1	1 363	17.0	463	4.7	94.6	-0.6

1. For the period including March 12 of the year shown. 2. Includes deposits for all insured and reporting noninsured commercial and mutual savings banks. 3. Includes savings capital for all FSLIC insured savings institutions.

STATE County	Federal funds and grants, 1989							Local government finances, 1981–1982							
	Expenditures		Per capita[1] (Dollars)					General revenue						Direct general expenditure	
									Intergovernmental		Taxes				
												Per capita[2]			
	Total (Mil dol)	Percent change, 1988–1989	Total	Direct payments for individuals	Procurement contract awards	Salaries and wages	Grant awards	Total (Mil dol)	Total (Mil dol)	Percent from state	Total (Mil dol)	Total (Dollars)	Property (Dollars)	Total (Mil dol)	Percent change, 1977–1982
	174	175	176	177	178	179	180	181	182	183	184	185	186	187	188
NEW YORK—Con.															
Jefferson	589.5	-29.0	5 583	1 632	324	3 151	447	139.8	76.2	85.4	47.6	546	397	139.5	43.7
Kings	X	X	X	X	X	X	X	18 508.5	7 332.6	86.4	8 080.8	1 138	512	15 680.2	30.4
Lewis	68.8	-12.0	2 558	1 451	398	112	565	41.9	19.7	91.8	12.0	486	481	44.8	65.3
Livingston	116.3	7.4	1 944	1 403	19	111	330	65.7	28.4	96.1	27.4	478	372	67.2	47.5
Madison	128.6	-14.8	1 908	1 459	18	108	303	105.9	55.7	95.2	31.1	477	406	99.1	42.2
Monroe	1 896.5	5.0	2 712	1 690	172	218	618	1 154.4	489.2	84.8	512.6	724	524	1 169.0	44.9
Montgomery	157.9	-10.5	3 067	2 379	182	116	350	71.7	32.8	83.7	26.8	506	390	70.6	41.2
Nassau	6 070.3	-7.4	4 616	1 888	2 153	281	277	2 544.2	692.2	92.7	1 532.5	1 162	967	2 507.5	36.0
New York	X	NA	X	X	X	X	X	NA	NA	NA	NA	NA	NA	NA	NA
Niagara	612.4	11.4	2 825	1 917	234	231	418	370.4	168.1	89.4	131.6	593	429	382.2	24.4
Oneida	1 037.2	9.3	4 249	2 151	696	910	470	328.4	174.4	88.7	103.2	410	384	334.5	36.1
Onondaga	1 882.8	2.4	4 090	1 716	1 575	332	454	732.0	343.3	87.5	303.8	660	494	775.5	55.1
Ontario	247.9	9.1	2 692	1 686	181	447	329	118.3	50.5	93.4	48.0	537	366	119.6	40.8
Orange	921.5	17.7	3 078	1 461	237	1 003	357	355.1	171.5	93.5	145.1	546	529	363.4	42.9
Orleans	89.2	15.4	2 220	1 566	21	121	390	52.8	27.3	95.3	18.7	482	375	55.3	46.9
Oswego	232.0	10.0	1 894	1 398	18	99	361	171.9	86.1	91.8	69.7	611	557	164.9	38.1
Otsego	150.4	5.3	2 494	1 810	119	137	407	71.6	35.1	91.1	28.2	477	398	70.5	32.8
Putnam	118.6	6.9	1 402	1 149	26	105	116	111.4	35.1	96.3	67.6	860	799	107.7	49.3
Queens	X	NA	X	X	X	X	X	NA	NA	NA	NA	NA	NA	NA	NA
Rensselaer	389.9	5.8	2 579	1 854	103	136	473	205.3	102.6	93.5	66.9	443	363	218.8	44.0
Richmond	X	NA	X	X	X	X	X	NA	NA	NA	NA	NA	NA	NA	NA
Rockland	653.9	30.7	2 458	1 404	575	105	369	445.8	143.8	91.5	234.2	900	887	447.8	38.5
St. Lawrence	276.9	8.1	2 517	1 651	43	190	610	164.0	91.4	92.8	52.4	465	345	170.4	55.1
Saratoga	331.9	7.0	1 879	1 323	69	309	169	184.2	86.7	94.5	73.5	474	419	178.6	21.5
Schenectady	1 051.0	-4.1	7 016	2 156	4 245	259	348	189.2	78.3	94.2	84.2	563	532	193.7	40.4
Schoharie	68.8	9.8	2 256	1 580	17	126	495	35.8	18.1	92.7	15.2	513	506	35.6	38.0
Schuyler	42.4	-0.4	2 453	1 762	33	120	498	19.9	9.3	94.9	9.0	510	406	22.9	38.8
Seneca	125.6	2.5	3 924	1 880	228	1 377	358	39.9	16.6	92.4	14.7	448	436	42.1	52.1
Steuben	287.4	11.1	2 921	1 962	174	304	439	129.1	65.8	88.5	50.4	513	382	133.5	39.8
Suffolk	4 016.7	23.7	3 031	1 426	955	272	372	2 347.2	942.0	93.5	1 215.7	944	801	2 297.0	38.5
Sullivan	207.6	6.6	2 844	2 015	64	158	592	107.4	34.4	89.4	59.1	915	730	109.1	36.4
Tioga	422.5	64.3	8 125	1 292	6 388	144	281	59.7	33.8	94.6	20.5	411	336	60.2	43.6
Tompkins	319.4	7.9	3 585	1 327	341	175	1 718	104.0	44.2	92.6	46.1	524	378	105.3	14.3
Ulster	371.0	7.7	2 206	1 563	110	122	402	231.7	93.1	91.7	115.2	723	575	222.5	42.0
Warren	150.6	11.9	2 609	1 885	108	232	374	86.5	35.8	91.9	40.6	739	527	84.6	49.1
Washington	126.3	9.7	2 109	1 656	14	105	311	74.5	37.2	92.9	25.1	457	374	74.5	44.1
Wayne	191.8	8.0	2 148	1 479	122	100	383	122.2	57.2	94.8	49.2	571	452	120.8	46.0
Westchester	2 401.2	7.0	2 780	1 874	145	270	479	1 631.2	492.8	91.2	957.7	1 110	967	1 632.5	29.1
Wyoming	73.7	6.4	1 739	1 353	25	104	186	53.4	21.4	92.7	19.1	473	403	52.8	45.5
Yates	56.8	3.7	2 606	1 971	43	161	347	23.4	10.1	82.1	11.2	528	428	24.0	34.3
NORTH CAROLINA	19 105.6	6.6	X	1 594	228	596	455	5 292.3	2 741.3	83.0	1 414.9	235	192	5 010.1	49.3
Alamance	257.7	17.2	2 406	1 703	311	100	279	91.8	51.1	74.0	25.1	249	203	83.5	51.3
Alexander	39.2	10.0	1 404	1 126	7	61	175	12.8	8.4	92.5	2.7	105	86	12.2	59.4
Alleghany	26.7	7.4	2 696	1 883	55	145	512	6.1	4.4	94.1	1.2	120	93	5.4	52.5
Anson	63.6	14.4	2 429	1 578	165	97	534	31.8	20.1	65.0	4.5	173	148	29.4	113.1
Ashe	50.5	9.1	2 148	1 608	12	131	381	12.9	8.8	90.1	2.8	125	98	12.3	47.5
Avery	34.5	8.7	2 258	1 745	24	99	382	8.8	5.7	91.4	2.3	155	122	8.6	59.9
Beaufort	94.7	2.7	2 249	1 727	14	111	335	27.3	14.7	81.0	7.5	180	133	32.5	48.5
Bertie	53.1	-9.8	2 539	1 673	41	133	567	17.6	11.1	91.0	3.1	145	125	16.3	54.9
Bladen	68.9	6.4	2 223	1 547	35	92	482	28.0	16.8	92.0	5.2	170	147	25.3	43.7
Brunswick	145.2	18.4	2 745	1 764	274	207	447	36.0	16.8	88.7	12.3	317	280	32.9	55.1
Buncombe	491.4	2.8	2 813	1 955	192	435	219	134.4	71.5	77.7	41.1	251	193	131.6	46.9
Burke	137.0	8.6	1 758	1 379	83	63	228	56.2	35.9	76.5	11.6	157	154	46.4	50.1
Cabarrus	189.2	5.8	1 947	1 692	10	84	152	82.9	32.7	92.5	14.6	163	126	83.6	45.3
Caldwell	122.4	2.8	1 705	1 338	124	66	171	48.7	30.3	88.8	12.3	181	150	46.8	56.3
Camden	14.1	-6.3	2 312	1 817	9	92	269	3.8	2.7	95.5	0.9	157	136	3.4	47.7
Carteret	141.0	8.6	2 721	2 049	82	308	271	30.4	17.4	87.3	10.5	239	183	28.7	71.8
Caswell	36.7	5.9	1 662	1 220	8	66	341	12.7	9.4	88.4	2.3	105	92	12.9	52.5
Catawba	209.8	10.0	1 764	1 421	55	144	134	97.2	46.0	89.9	25.3	234	179	90.4	48.9
Chatham	61.9	-4.2	1 664	1 342	13	105	181	19.4	11.3	82.7	6.1	178	153	20.0	40.7
Cherokee	70.1	7.2	3 261	2 641	28	183	399	21.6	11.7	67.6	2.5	130	92	18.0	147.9
Chowan	38.8	14.8	2 791	2 190	8	108	372	10.6	6.1	85.1	2.8	219	181	9.1	26.4
Clay	19.6	9.6	2 642	2 145	13	103	353	3.5	2.6	81.7	0.7	103	82	3.5	61.5
Cleveland	167.4	8.2	1 915	1 463	59	76	278	59.6	38.2	88.8	14.6	174	138	61.0	44.9
Columbus	120.3	3.5	2 283	1 656	14	98	464	38.4	25.0	87.9	9.7	190	150	39.2	26.0

1. Based on the estimated population as of July 1 of the year shown. 2. Based on the estimated population as of July 1, 1982.

STATE County	Local government finances, 1981–1982 (cont'd): Direct general expenditure (cont'd): Per capita[1] (Dollars)	Percent of total for– Education	Percent of total for– Health & hospitals	Percent of total for– Police protection	Percent of total for– Public welfare	Percent of total for– Highways	Debt outstanding: Total (Mil dol)	Debt outstanding: Per capita[1] (Dollars)	State and local government employment, 1989: Total	State and local government employment, 1989: Rate[2]	Federal government civilian employment 1989: Total	Federal government civilian employment 1989: Earnings ($1,000)	Elections, 1988[3]: Total vote cast for president	Elections, 1988[3]: Vote for lead party (Percent)
	189	190	191	192	193	194	195	196	197	198	199	200	201	202
NEW YORK—Con.														
Jefferson	1 600	44.9	1.2	1.8	16.2	10.9	78.2	897	6 976	660.6	3 399	77 466	33 622	R–57.4
Kings	2 209	22.0	9.9	5.4	21.2	2.9	12 513.1	1 762	26 906	116.0	11 853	385 655	549 019	D–66.3
Lewis	1 808	47.0	13.6	0.7	14.8	9.7	17.9	723	1 777	660.6	65	1 611	10 138	R–57.1
Livingston	1 170	48.3	2.0	2.4	16.4	11.4	27.5	480	5 732	958.5	132	4 057	23 697	R–59.1
Madison	1 521	41.9	10.1	1.3	10.6	8.7	43.5	667	4 453	660.7	150	4 364	25 754	R–57.9
Monroe	1 650	40.1	3.7	3.8	13.8	5.4	797.4	1 125	37 712	539.2	3 194	107 931	311 466	R–49.9
Montgomery	1 331	45.9	1.6	2.6	18.0	8.6	30.5	575	2 860	555.3	121	3 650	22 685	D–50.1
Nassau	1 902	42.5	5.9	9.3	4.4	4.0	1 838.8	1 395	69 950	531.9	10 607	354 557	592 418	R–57.0
New York	NA	NA	NA	NA	NA	NA	NA	NA	447 076	2 942.1	42 995	1 475 165	506 551	D–76.1
Niagara	1 723	37.7	5.0	2.6	13.6	7.6	269.3	1 214	11 128	513.3	1 361	40 726	86 868	D–50.4
Oneida	1 328	44.1	5.3	2.4	16.1	5.8	207.6	824	20 352	833.8	4 394	139 526	103 461	R–53.2
Onondaga	1 685	38.5	2.7	3.1	16.4	6.3	639.9	1 390	33 263	722.6	3 852	131 600	200 485	R–51.9
Ontario	1 337	52.3	1.2	2.4	8.5	9.7	90.9	1 015	5 413	587.7	1 553	48 750	39 435	R–55.2
Orange	1 368	52.0	2.2	2.5	14.9	5.9	201.0	756	17 438	582.4	5 082	137 649	104 810	R–62.4
Orleans	1 428	48.0	1.7	2.0	19.6	7.7	27.6	712	3 389	843.0	85	2 481	15 055	R–60.0
Oswego	1 444	45.8	2.1	2.5	13.0	11.9	80.6	706	8 676	708.2	218	7 032	44 211	R–57.4
Otsego	1 195	43.4	1.4	1.2	18.6	15.2	24.3	413	4 066	674.3	184	5 242	24 334	R–53.5
Putnam	1 371	61.6	2.2	3.0	5.3	8.0	45.2	575	3 292	389.1	167	5 323	36 501	R–66.0
Queens	NA	NA	NA	NA	NA	NA	NA	NA	21 968	114.3	13 369	436 004	546 729	D–59.5
Rensselaer	1 447	47.1	5.3	3.4	15.0	5.9	98.0	648	7 974	527.4	359	10 972	69 197	R–51.2
Richmond	NA	NA	NA	NA	NA	NA	NA	NA	5 287	138.1	1 018	33 308	125 975	R–61.5
Rockland	1 721	51.0	8.1	3.7	10.8	3.2	256.8	987	20 052	753.8	951	31 424	112 301	R–56.8
St. Lawrence	1 514	44.0	6.0	1.8	17.0	9.4	90.8	807	9 581	871.0	488	15 753	39 481	R–51.4
Saratoga	1 151	56.3	2.8	1.9	12.2	6.9	86.4	557	10 259	580.9	296	8 927	75 788	R–57.4
Schenectady	1 297	43.6	1.6	4.2	17.0	3.9	75.4	505	8 079	539.3	761	24 962	70 386	D–51.8
Schoharie	1 201	53.5	2.0	0.9	12.1	14.8	7.4	250	2 277	746.6	79	2 141	12 536	R–55.9
Schuyler	1 303	53.4	1.6	2.2	8.1	15.6	16.5	935	977	564.7	40	1 223	7 242	R–59.3
Seneca	1 280	44.2	14.6	2.3	5.9	8.5	23.0	699	2 507	783.4	1 157	30 674	13 571	R–53.2
Steuben	1 361	50.0	1.5	1.7	11.0	13.9	48.7	497	6 367	647.1	1 021	28 989	38 466	R–65.9
Suffolk	1 783	51.3	1.7	7.1	12.6	4.7	1 762.9	1 369	85 998	649.0	11 459	337 248	514 350	R–60.5
Sullivan	1 689	42.7	3.4	2.8	12.1	16.0	50.1	775	5 345	732.2	261	7 874	27 568	R–57.0
Tioga	1 208	56.5	1.4	2.1	13.3	9.6	24.8	498	2 274	437.3	78	2 350	20 946	R–60.5
Tompkins	1 196	50.3	3.0	2.5	12.9	8.9	67.4	765	4 864	545.9	339	10 872	36 699	D–58.5
Ulster	1 397	49.5	5.3	2.3	13.0	8.3	78.6	494	11 349	674.7	419	11 998	72 557	R–56.7
Warren	1 541	44.1	4.7	2.9	11.6	10.8	27.7	505	3 639	630.7	287	9 113	24 622	R–64.4
Washington	1 354	56.0	1.5	1.7	9.7	11.6	67.2	1 222	4 507	752.4	126	3 810	22 515	R–62.6
Wayne	1 403	55.1	1.7	1.6	8.6	11.2	69.5	807	6 022	674.4	171	5 072	33 902	R–60.8
Westchester	1 892	42.0	5.8	5.0	13.5	3.0	702.9	815	48 107	557.1	6 641	218 442	371 008	R–53.4
Wyoming	1 308	36.6	20.6	1.8	9.1	13.8	28.1	695	3 696	871.7	99	2 858	14 863	R–63.6
Yates	1 132	46.7	1.5	2.9	5.1	16.1	12.6	593	831	381.2	65	1 866	9 074	R–60.5
NORTH CAROLINA	833	52.2	10.9	4.7	3.2	2.2	4 397.6	731	426 790	649.7	55 919	1 665 106	2 134 370	R–58.0
Alamance	828	51.1	2.2	5.3	2.6	1.4	54.2	537	5 132	479.2	287	9 157	36 851	R–65.5
Alexander	473	73.6	2.0	2.9	4.0	0.5	5.7	220	950	340.5	44	1 122	12 154	R–65.6
Alleghany	547	70.3	1.1	4.6	5.5	0.5	0.0	0	520	525.3	64	1 133	4 264	R–51.0
Anson	1 132	41.6	16.3	2.5	2.2	0.7	6.7	259	1 559	595.0	65	1 703	7 633	D–63.3
Ashe	540	74.9	1.1	3.4	5.1	1.1	7.6	335	793	337.4	66	1 589	10 083	R–59.7
Avery	587	73.9	1.5	4.4	3.9	0.8	1.6	110	769	502.6	46	1 068	5 678	R–75.3
Beaufort	780	60.7	1.7	3.1	3.3	1.7	26.3	631	2 586	614.3	122	3 326	13 570	R–60.4
Bertie	767	60.9	17.9	2.7	4.4	1.3	4.2	199	950	454.5	108	2 731	5 919	D–63.6
Bladen	826	60.3	16.9	2.9	3.3	1.7	5.3	171	1 879	606.1	83	2 028	8 814	D–57.1
Brunswick	844	55.6	13.4	4.5	2.4	1.5	33.5	859	2 467	466.4	395	10 676	17 939	R–55.8
Buncombe	804	50.1	2.6	5.3	2.1	1.8	76.4	467	10 155	581.3	2 507	78 688	63 992	R–57.6
Burke	626	62.8	2.3	5.4	3.4	2.3	31.4	424	6 937	890.5	154	4 353	26 819	R–59.4
Cabarrus	937	40.7	36.0	3.7	1.9	0.3	32.2	361	5 245	539.6	197	5 966	33 284	R–67.7
Caldwell	686	66.9	2.5	4.1	2.6	1.8	39.2	574	3 048	424.5	119	3 368	23 071	R–65.8
Camden	592	78.2	0.0	2.0	5.2	0.0	0.3	50	292	478.7	17	389	2 249	R–50.9
Carteret	658	57.8	1.6	7.1	2.7	2.4	15.1	347	2 954	570.3	241	6 708	17 994	R–61.6
Caswell	599	65.5	3.4	2.2	4.5	0.0	7.9	365	1 004	454.3	52	1 214	7 509	D–55.8
Catawba	839	51.0	15.6	4.7	2.8	2.9	58.4	542	6 175	519.3	433	14 783	41 838	R–69.0
Chatham	584	64.5	1.2	11.6	4.2	1.6	10.5	306	1 229	330.4	110	3 239	14 639	D–51.9
Cherokee	923	50.5	27.0	1.6	2.7	0.9	11.0	565	1 377	640.5	160	3 766	7 145	R–63.8
Chowan	722	58.9	0.5	6.9	5.8	1.2	6.9	551	602	433.1	38	1 089	3 654	R–51.6
Clay	521	71.6	4.7	2.9	5.5	0.3	0.0	0	280	378.4	24	612	3 480	R–62.5
Cleveland	728	65.8	2.8	4.0	3.3	1.7	41.7	497	4 013	459.2	186	5 269	24 397	R–57.5
Columbus	763	72.4	2.1	3.2	3.3	1.5	13.4	261	2 633	499.6	168	4 293	15 882	D–57.8

1. Based on the estimated population as of July 1, 1982. 2. Per 10,000 resident population estimated as of July 1 of the year shown. 3. Data subject to copyright.

STATE–County code	MSA/CMSA/NECMA code[1]	STATE County	Land Area,[2] 1990 (Sq. Km.)	Population, 1990											
				Total persons	Rank	Per square kilometer	Race					Hispanic[3]	Age of population Percent		
							White	Black	Am. Indian, Eskimo, Aleut	Asian & Pacific Islander	Other race		Under 5 years	5 to 14 years	15 to 24 years
			1	2	3	4	5	6	7	8	9	10	11	12	13
		NORTH CAROLINA—Con.													
37 049	...	Craven	1 801	81 613	556	45.3	58 660	21 116	319	765	753	1 821	8.5	14.6	17.1
37 051	2560	Cumberland	1 692	274 566	181	162.3	170 069	87 496	4 425	5 769	6 807	13 298	9.1	14.9	21.1
37 053	...	Currituck	678	13 736	2 079	20.3	12 051	1 545	66	51	23	110	7.3	14.2	12.2
37 055	...	Dare	989	22 746	1 547	23.0	21 766	811	37	79	53	199	6.8	12.2	11.4
37 057	3120	Davidson	1 430	126 677	366	88.6	113 296	12 314	395	477	195	602	6.5	13.1	14.4
37 059	3120	Davie	687	27 859	1 356	40.6	25 194	2 482	86	53	44	129	5.8	13.3	13.5
37 061	...	Duplin	2 118	39 995	999	18.9	25 927	13 259	104	47	658	1 015	6.9	14.7	14.3
37 063	6640	Durham	753	181 835	268	241.5	109 886	67 654	425	3 233	637	2 054	7.1	12.1	17.0
37 065	...	Edgecombe	1 308	56 558	769	43.2	24 665	31 661	73	68	91	255	7.5	16.0	14.5
37 067	3120	Forsyth	1 061	265 878	184	250.6	196 918	66 102	551	1 662	645	2 102	6.8	12.1	14.9
37 069	6640	Franklin	1 273	36 414	1 092	28.6	23 288	12 843	74	63	146	290	6.7	13.4	15.2
37 071	1520	Gaston	923	175 093	274	189.7	150 868	22 676	397	915	237	864	7.1	13.5	15.4
37 073	...	Gates	882	9 305	2 443	10.5	5 101	4 180	8	13	3	21	7.3	14.1	13.2
37 075	...	Graham	756	7 196	2 633	9.5	6 731	1	454	6	4	29	5.7	13.7	14.4
37 077	...	Granville	1 376	38 345	1 045	27.9	23 069	14 909	99	100	168	356	6.6	13.1	14.1
37 079	...	Greene	688	15 384	1 965	22.4	8 747	6 521	16	6	94	169	6.5	14.8	13.8
37 081	3120	Guilford	1 684	347 420	148	206.3	249 584	91 655	1 637	3 726	818	2 887	6.5	12.1	16.6
37 083	...	Halifax	1 879	55 516	780	29.5	26 009	27 586	1 711	145	65	237	7.2	15.6	14.0
37 085	...	Harnett	1 541	67 822	653	44.0	51 117	15 315	601	299	490	1 159	7.7	13.5	17.7
37 087	...	Haywood	1 435	46 942	892	32.7	46 011	648	180	67	36	240	5.5	11.2	12.8
37 089	...	Henderson	968	69 285	639	71.6	66 158	2 361	197	286	283	846	5.5	11.8	11.3
37 091	...	Hertford	916	22 523	1 554	24.6	9 214	12 970	228	94	17	81	7.1	15.4	15.3
37 093	...	Hoke	1 013	22 856	1 539	22.6	9 635	9 878	3 176	85	82	218	8.3	16.9	16.9
37 095	...	Hyde	1 587	5 411	2 807	3.4	3 596	1 781	4	3	27	43	6.3	14.2	13.5
37 097	...	Iredell	1 488	92 931	498	62.5	77 207	14 869	193	356	306	672	6.7	13.1	14.2
37 099	...	Jackson	1 271	26 846	1 394	21.1	23 609	425	2 667	109	36	155	5.0	11.3	23.6
37 101	...	Johnston	2 051	81 306	560	39.6	65 773	14 389	178	159	807	1 262	6.8	13.5	14.1
37 103	...	Jones	1 226	9 414	2 440	7.7	5 687	3 677	8	19	23	53	7.7	14.5	13.1
37 105	...	Lee	666	41 374	973	62.1	31 216	9 401	169	191	397	800	7.2	14.6	13.4
37 107	...	Lenoir	1 036	57 274	762	55.3	34 322	22 539	70	151	192	463	6.4	14.5	14.3
37 109	1520	Lincoln	774	50 319	838	65.0	45 710	4 108	120	172	209	570	7.0	13.5	14.6
37 111	...	McDowell	1 144	35 681	1 107	31.2	33 901	1 479	72	200	29	114	6.2	12.9	14.6
37 113	...	Macon	1 338	23 499	1 513	17.6	22 919	385	76	60	59	165	5.1	11.1	11.1
37 115	...	Madison	1 164	16 953	1 850	14.6	16 744	136	19	32	22	86	5.5	12.0	16.6
37 117	...	Martin	1 198	25 078	1 458	20.9	13 788	11 186	20	40	44	99	7.0	14.7	14.2
37 119	1520	Mecklenburg	1 366	511 433	92	374.4	364 651	134 468	1 936	8 461	1 917	6 693	7.5	12.9	15.1
37 121	...	Mitchell	574	14 433	2 021	25.1	14 354	23	19	19	18	50	5.7	12.2	12.0
37 123	...	Montgomery	1 272	23 346	1 523	18.4	16 773	6 001	92	150	330	556	6.7	14.3	15.1
37 125	...	Moore	1 810	59 013	737	32.6	47 464	10 882	309	150	208	470	6.1	12.7	11.9
37 127	...	Nash	1 399	76 677	588	54.8	51 874	24 142	218	223	220	606	6.9	14.2	14.3
37 129	9200	New Hanover	515	120 284	384	233.6	94 895	24 097	435	616	241	924	6.2	12.6	16.5
37 131	...	Northampton	1 389	20 798	1 639	15.0	8 397	12 328	42	11	20	116	6.3	14.4	12.9
37 133	3605	Onslow	1 986	149 838	315	75.4	111 939	29 808	939	2 994	4 158	8 035	9.1	12.4	30.2
37 135	6640	Orange	1 035	93 851	493	90.7	75 871	14 893	286	2 361	440	1 279	5.7	10.4	25.6
37 137	...	Pamlico	873	11 372	2 262	13.0	8 362	2 951	33	20	6	61	6.3	13.4	11.8
37 139	...	Pasquotank	588	31 298	1 235	53.2	19 403	11 583	59	184	69	246	7.9	15.2	15.4
37 141	...	Pender	2 255	28 855	1 334	12.8	19 828	8 770	76	44	137	273	6.8	13.5	13.2
37 143	...	Perquimans	640	10 447	2 341	16.3	6 979	3 426	18	20	4	28	6.6	14.2	11.7
37 145	...	Person	1 016	30 180	1 289	29.7	20 740	9 106	181	15	138	249	6.8	13.4	13.4
37 147	...	Pitt	1 688	107 924	426	63.9	70 643	35 921	214	709	437	977	7.1	13.2	21.7
37 149	...	Polk	616	14 416	2 024	23.4	13 276	1 053	17	25	45	115	5.3	10.7	10.6
37 151	3120	Randolph	2 040	106 546	434	52.2	99 042	6 367	453	358	326	734	6.9	13.1	14.1
37 153	...	Richmond	1 228	44 518	918	36.3	30 816	12 869	502	195	136	293	6.7	14.6	15.4
37 155	...	Robeson	2 458	105 179	439	42.8	37 986	26 185	40 511	239	258	704	8.1	17.1	16.8
37 157	...	Rockingham	1 467	86 064	532	58.7	67 893	17 548	149	190	284	620	6.5	12.9	14.0
37 159	1520	Rowan	1 325	110 605	418	83.5	91 851	17 773	262	444	275	651	6.7	13.2	13.8
37 161	...	Rutherford	1 461	56 918	766	39.0	50 133	6 514	95	98	78	342	6.5	13.5	14.4
37 163	...	Sampson	2 449	47 297	886	19.3	30 273	15 686	876	75	387	727	6.5	14.9	14.2
37 165	...	Scotland	827	33 754	1 170	40.8	19 025	12 176	2 430	83	40	318	7.2	16.7	16.9
37 167	...	Stanly	1 023	51 765	817	50.6	45 269	5 972	155	249	120	309	7.1	13.2	14.6
37 169	3120	Stokes	1 170	37 223	1 066	31.8	34 917	2 069	52	79	106	254	6.4	13.5	14.6
37 171	...	Surry	1 390	61 704	706	44.4	58 383	2 780	66	84	391	602	6.0	12.6	14.2
37 173	...	Swain	1 368	11 268	2 277	8.2	7 950	196	3 075	31	16	78	6.6	13.8	14.7
37 175	...	Transylvania	980	25 520	1 445	26.0	24 121	1 189	79	99	32	154	5.6	11.9	14.9
37 177	...	Tyrrell	1 010	3 856	2 929	3.8	2 297	1 543	4	5	7	11	6.5	16.5	12.1
37 179	1520	Union	1 651	84 211	543	51.0	70 023	13 427	294	257	210	675	7.7	15.0	15.7

1. MSA = Metropolitan Statistical Area. CMSA = Consolidated MSA. NECMA = New England county metropolitan area. PMSA = Primary MSA. See Appendix A for explanation of these concepts. See Appendix B for list of metropolitan areas identified by type, with component counties. 2. Dry land or land partially or temporarily covered by water. 3. Hispanic persons may be of any race.

STATE County	Population, 1990 (cont'd) — Age of population (cont'd) Percent — 25 to 34 years	35 to 44 years	45 to 54 years	55 to 64 years	65 to 74 years	75 years and over	Percent female	Population–Change and components of change — Change 1980–1990 — Number	Percent	Components of change, 1980–1986 — Total persons, 1986	Total persons, 1980	Net change — Number	Percent	Natural increase — Births	Deaths
	14	15	16	17	18	19	20	21	22	23	24	25	26	27	28
NORTH CAROLINA—Con.															
Craven	17.9	13.6	8.7	8.4	7.3	3.9	50.2	10 570	14.9	81 100	71 043	10 100	14.2	9 700	3 200
Cumberland	20.3	13.6	8.4	6.5	4.1	2.1	48.3	27 406	11.1	258 500	247 160	11 400	4.6	33 300	8 300
Currituck	17.6	14.9	11.2	10.1	7.8	4.7	49.6	2 647	23.9	13 200	11 089	2 100	19.2	1 100	700
Dare	19.2	17.0	10.5	10.3	8.3	4.1	50.3	9 369	70.0	18 800	13 377	5 400	40.2	1 400	800
Davidson	16.8	15.6	12.0	9.6	7.3	4.7	51.0	13 515	11.9	118 200	113 162	5 000	4.5	9 300	5 500
Davie	15.2	16.5	12.0	9.9	8.3	5.5	50.9	3 260	13.3	29 100	24 599	4 500	18.4	1 800	1 200
Duplin	15.2	14.5	10.7	9.7	8.3	5.7	52.0	-957	-2.3	41 800	40 952	900	2.2	3 500	2 600
Durham	20.2	16.5	9.2	7.1	6.1	4.6	52.8	29 599	19.4	166 500	152 236	14 300	9.4	13 600	8 300
Edgecombe	16.1	15.1	9.8	8.7	7.5	4.8	54.3	570	1.0	58 800	55 988	2 800	5.1	5 400	3 400
Forsyth	18.1	15.8	10.9	9.2	7.1	5.2	52.8	22 174	9.1	260 100	243 704	16 400	6.7	20 300	13 000
Franklin	16.9	15.1	10.6	8.8	7.8	5.6	52.0	6 359	21.2	34 100	30 055	4 000	13.4	2 400	1 900
Gaston	16.5	15.2	10.9	9.3	7.2	4.9	52.0	12 525	7.7	170 800	162 568	8 200	5.1	14 600	8 600
Gates	16.6	13.9	10.3	9.9	8.7	5.9	50.6	430	4.8	9 500	8 875	600	6.7	800	600
Graham	13.4	14.3	12.0	10.5	9.7	6.4	50.3	-21	-0.3	7 100	7 217	-100	-1.6	600	400
Granville	18.0	15.4	11.3	9.2	7.3	5.1	50.5	4 302	12.6	37 400	34 043	3 300	9.7	2 800	2 100
Greene	17.6	15.2	10.3	9.5	7.5	4.8	50.2	-733	-4.5	16 500	16 117	400	2.4	1 500	900
Guilford	17.5	15.6	10.7	9.0	7.0	4.9	52.7	30 266	9.5	328 100	317 154	11 000	3.5	26 000	16 600
Halifax	15.3	14.0	9.9	9.6	8.4	5.8	52.5	440	0.8	55 800	55 076	700	1.3	5 500	3 700
Harnett	16.8	13.8	10.0	8.7	7.0	4.7	51.4	8 252	13.9	64 400	59 570	4 800	8.1	6 200	3 400
Haywood	13.7	14.3	12.7	11.7	10.7	7.5	52.3	447	1.0	48 400	46 495	1 900	4.1	3 200	2 900
Henderson	13.4	14.0	10.8	11.2	12.9	9.0	52.2	10 705	18.3	67 300	58 580	8 700	14.8	4 700	4 100
Hertford	14.3	13.6	10.1	9.6	8.4	6.2	53.6	-845	-3.6	24 100	23 368	800	3.2	2 300	1 500
Hoke	17.5	14.2	9.2	7.8	5.8	3.5	49.9	2 473	12.1	23 300	20 383	2 900	14.1	2 100	900
Hyde	14.6	14.2	10.5	10.1	9.1	7.5	51.0	-462	-7.9	5 900	5 873	0	0.6	500	400
Iredell	16.3	14.9	11.6	9.9	7.8	5.4	51.7	10 393	12.6	88 600	82 538	6 100	7.4	6 800	4 600
Jackson	12.6	13.7	11.1	9.0	7.9	5.9	51.8	1 035	4.0	26 800	25 811	1 000	4.0	1 800	1 300
Johnston	16.7	15.6	11.5	9.1	7.8	4.9	51.7	10 707	15.2	78 100	70 599	7 500	10.6	6 100	4 300
Jones	16.1	13.8	10.6	9.9	9.0	5.3	53.0	-291	-3.0	9 700	9 705	0	0.2	900	500
Lee	16.2	15.1	10.7	9.7	8.3	4.8	51.8	4 656	12.7	41 400	36 718	4 600	12.7	3 800	2 300
Lenoir	15.3	15.0	11.0	9.8	8.4	5.3	53.3	-2 545	-4.3	60 100	59 819	300	0.4	5 100	3 700
Lincoln	16.7	15.6	11.8	9.1	7.2	4.4	50.8	7 947	18.8	46 100	42 372	3 700	8.7	3 600	2 100
McDowell	15.2	14.9	11.6	10.1	8.5	6.0	51.3	546	1.6	36 300	35 135	1 100	3.2	2 700	1 800
Macon	12.2	13.7	11.6	12.7	12.9	9.6	52.0	3 321	16.5	23 000	20 178	2 800	14.0	1 500	1 400
Madison	13.2	14.5	11.5	10.0	9.2	7.5	50.9	126	0.7	17 400	16 827	600	3.6	1 100	1 100
Martin	14.6	14.6	10.7	9.8	8.8	5.7	53.0	-870	-3.4	26 500	25 948	600	2.3	2 300	1 600
Mecklenburg	20.5	16.6	10.3	7.7	5.7	3.7	52.0	107 163	26.5	450 800	404 270	46 600	11.5	39 800	18 900
Mitchell	14.1	14.5	11.9	11.8	9.8	7.9	52.0	5	0.0	14 500	14 428	100	0.4	1 200	1 000
Montgomery	16.0	14.7	10.4	9.0	8.3	5.3	49.6	877	3.9	24 000	22 469	1 500	6.8	2 000	1 400
Moore	14.4	13.1	9.6	11.5	13.3	7.5	52.3	8 508	16.8	55 800	50 505	5 300	10.5	4 400	3 500
Nash	16.7	16.1	10.6	8.9	7.6	4.8	52.6	9 524	14.2	71 400	67 153	4 200	6.3	6 400	4 100
New Hanover	16.5	16.0	10.7	9.0	7.8	4.7	52.6	16 813	16.2	114 100	103 471	10 700	10.3	8 800	5 800
Northampton	14.6	13.6	10.5	10.9	10.4	6.5	51.6	-1 397	-6.3	22 400	22 195	200	1.1	2 000	1 600
Onslow	22.3	11.3	5.8	4.5	2.9	1.5	40.2	37 054	32.9	126 600	112 784	13 800	12.2	19 400	3 000
Orange	19.4	15.3	8.7	6.3	5.1	3.6	52.6	16 796	21.8	84 600	77 055	7 500	9.7	5 800	2 900
Pamlico	13.8	14.2	11.3	12.5	10.2	6.6	52.0	974	9.4	11 200	10 398	800	7.3	800	700
Pasquotank	16.3	13.5	9.2	8.7	8.2	5.7	53.1	2 836	10.0	29 700	28 462	1 200	4.2	2 800	1 700
Pender	15.1	14.9	11.6	10.7	9.3	5.0	51.4	6 593	29.6	25 100	22 262	2 800	12.6	2 000	1 400
Perquimans	14.0	12.8	10.7	11.7	10.9	7.3	52.1	961	10.1	10 600	9 486	1 200	12.2	800	600
Person	16.7	15.0	10.9	9.6	8.3	5.9	52.2	1 016	3.5	30 700	29 164	1 500	5.2	2 200	1 600
Pitt	17.4	14.5	8.8	7.4	6.0	3.9	52.5	17 778	19.7	98 000	90 146	7 800	8.7	8 500	4 600
Polk	12.4	13.2	10.9	12.2	13.7	10.9	53.1	1 432	11.0	14 200	12 984	1 200	9.5	800	1 100
Randolph	17.1	15.6	11.7	9.3	7.4	4.8	51.1	15 246	16.7	98 600	91 300	7 300	8.0	7 500	4 400
Richmond	14.6	14.2	10.6	9.6	8.8	5.4	52.2	-963	-2.1	46 600	45 481	1 100	2.5	3 800	2 800
Robeson	15.5	14.4	9.6	7.8	6.6	4.1	52.7	3 569	3.5	106 000	101 610	4 400	4.4	11 200	5 600
Rockingham	15.8	15.2	11.4	9.8	8.4	5.9	52.4	2 638	3.2	85 500	83 426	2 100	2.5	6 800	4 800
Rowan	16.0	14.5	10.7	9.9	8.9	6.3	51.5	11 419	11.5	104 900	99 186	5 700	5.7	8 100	6 200
Rutherford	14.7	14.2	11.1	10.1	8.9	6.6	51.9	3 131	5.8	57 000	53 787	3 200	6.0	4 400	3 300
Sampson	14.8	14.5	11.0	9.8	8.5	5.8	52.5	-2 390	-4.8	50 200	49 687	500	1.1	4 100	3 100
Scotland	14.4	15.5	10.3	7.8	6.8	4.3	53.3	1 481	4.6	33 800	32 273	1 500	4.6	3 200	1 800
Stanly	15.2	14.5	10.8	9.8	8.7	5.9	51.8	3 248	6.7	50 300	48 517	1 800	3.7	3 900	2 700
Stokes	16.8	16.2	12.3	8.7	6.7	4.8	50.9	4 137	12.5	35 700	33 086	2 600	8.0	2 600	1 600
Surry	15.2	14.8	12.0	10.4	8.6	6.2	52.1	2 255	3.8	61 900	59 449	2 400	4.1	4 500	3 500
Swain	14.4	13.8	11.0	10.3	8.6	6.7	50.2	985	9.6	10 900	10 283	600	6.1	1 100	800
Transylvania	13.6	13.0	11.2	11.3	11.4	7.1	51.1	2 103	9.0	26 300	23 417	2 900	12.2	1 800	1 200
Tyrrell	14.3	13.0	10.0	9.9	9.8	7.8	52.2	-119	-3.0	4 200	3 975	200	4.5	400	300
Union	16.7	15.6	11.5	8.0	5.9	3.7	51.0	13 775	19.6	79 700	70 436	9 300	13.2	6 700	3 200

STATE County	Population–(cont'd) Components of change, 1980-1986 (cont'd)	Households, 1990					Births, 1988			Deaths, 1987				Marriages, 1984	
					Percent					Number		Rate			
	Net migration	Number	Percent change, 1980–1990	Persons per house-hold	Female family house-holder[1]	One-person	Total	Rate[2]	Low birth weight[3] (Number)	Total	Infant[4]	Total[2]	Infant[5]	Number	Rate[2]
	29	30	31	32	33	34	35	36	37	38	39	40	41	42	43
NORTH CAROLINA—Con.															
Craven	3 600	29 542	25.7	2.64	11.9	20.7	1 624	20.0	118	513	12	6.4	7.7	872	11.4
Cumberland	-13 600	91 500	22.1	2.77	14.1	19.4	5 663	22.1	442	1 598	73	6.2	13.7	2 004	7.8
Currituck	1 800	5 038	29.3	2.68	8.1	19.5	200	14.3	18	147	5	10.7	27.6	73	5.7
Dare	4 800	9 349	74.5	2.41	7.3	24.2	328	15.3	18	160	1	8.0	3.2	256	15.8
Davidson	1 300	48 944	22.3	2.56	10.5	21.0	1 640	13.2	144	1 029	22	8.4	13.3	981	8.4
Davie	4 000	10 785	26.3	2.55	8.8	20.8	327	11.8	23	221	2	8.0	6.4	235	8.8
Duplin	0	14 925	6.7	2.64	14.1	23.8	601	14.4	52	448	7	10.7	12.2	314	7.6
Durham	9 000	72 297	30.0	2.40	14.3	28.9	2 717	15.9	215	1 404	35	8.3	13.1	1 446	9.1
Edgecombe	800	20 319	10.4	2.75	21.1	23.1	915	15.3	98	556	12	9.3	13.1	404	7.0
Forsyth	9 100	107 419	19.2	2.40	13.1	27.8	3 858	14.5	352	2 397	37	9.1	10.1	2 500	9.8
Franklin	3 500	13 503	35.3	2.61	13.8	23.1	499	14.1	33	325	3	9.3	6.2	251	7.9
Gaston	2 200	65 347	15.9	2.64	12.9	20.8	2 678	15.4	220	1 539	34	8.9	13.6	969	5.7
Gates	400	3 352	16.0	2.75	12.1	21.0	125	12.8	13	105	2	10.8	16.1	44	4.8
Graham	-300	2 772	11.7	2.59	8.9	20.3	98	14.0	4	83	1	11.7	11.1	84	11.7
Granville	2 700	13 134	25.7	2.68	14.1	22.0	521	13.4	52	387	6	10.1	11.5	250	6.9
Greene	-200	5 395	6.6	2.72	16.2	22.0	181	11.0	22	123	2	7.5	10.7	136	8.2
Guilford	1 600	137 706	20.7	2.44	12.8	26.6	4 915	14.6	400	2 901	59	8.7	12.8	3 250	10.0
Halifax	-1 000	20 335	11.2	2.66	19.8	24.6	889	15.7	90	617	9	10.9	11.2	418	7.5
Harnett	2 000	25 150	24.8	2.60	12.5	23.0	1 182	17.8	97	554	9	8.5	7.7	353	5.7
Haywood	1 600	19 211	13.0	2.40	9.2	23.9	532	11.0	35	528	5	11.0	9.2	473	10.0
Henderson	8 100	28 709	28.2	2.38	8.2	23.8	748	10.8	61	749	12	11.0	14.6	462	7.1
Hertford	0	8 150	8.7	2.65	18.1	25.3	357	15.1	32	266	5	11.2	15.6	162	6.8
Hoke	1 700	7 405	22.9	2.92	21.7	19.2	392	16.3	30	152	3	6.4	7.8	96	4.3
Hyde	-100	2 094	3.2	2.57	15.3	24.6	61	10.7	8	78	1	13.4	15.6	65	11.0
Iredell	4 000	35 573	22.1	2.59	11.3	21.5	1 225	13.4	73	806	17	9.0	14.1	776	9.0
Jackson	400	9 683	13.9	2.46	10.1	23.2	293	10.8	12	220	4	8.2	15.2	208	7.7
Johnston	5 700	31 566	25.5	2.55	11.5	23.6	1 161	14.4	105	767	14	9.7	12.7	640	8.5
Jones	-300	3 492	9.0	2.70	13.8	22.2	140	14.3	11	108	4	11.0	30.3	63	6.4
Lee	3 100	15 689	21.5	2.59	13.6	22.2	634	15.1	55	355	5	8.6	8.3	344	8.8
Lenoir	-1 200	21 938	6.1	2.54	17.3	26.0	792	13.1	79	639	12	10.6	15.5	533	8.8
Lincoln	2 300	18 764	27.9	2.65	9.7	19.1	726	15.0	43	396	6	8.4	9.0	334	7.5
McDowell	200	13 680	11.9	2.56	10.0	21.9	464	12.8	32	317	4	8.7	8.7	319	8.8
Macon	2 800	9 834	27.7	2.34	7.9	24.3	239	10.2	19	274	4	11.8	18.4	209	9.2
Madison	500	6 488	11.0	2.48	8.0	23.3	185	10.8	6	189	2	10.9	10.5	123	7.2
Martin	-100	9 317	8.1	2.66	16.3	23.8	348	13.2	26	286	5	10.8	13.2	223	8.4
Mecklenburg	25 600	200 219	36.2	2.50	12.5	26.0	8 251	17.3	765	3 462	98	7.4	12.7	3 040	7.0
Mitchell	-200	5 779	9.8	2.47	8.3	21.9	200	13.6	4	164	1	11.3	6.5	136	9.4
Montgomery	1 000	8 290	6.8	2.69	13.5	22.2	326	13.5	18	199	3	8.2	9.6	166	7.0
Moore	4 400	23 827	28.2	2.43	10.4	23.8	718	12.1	60	662	3	11.5	3.8	359	6.6
Nash	1 900	29 041	23.7	2.60	13.7	23.8	1 139	15.7	96	721	14	10.0	12.4	618	8.8
New Hanover	7 600	48 139	27.7	2.43	13.3	25.8	1 642	14.0	135	1 060	17	9.1	11.3	996	9.0
Northampton	-200	7 591	7.0	2.64	18.9	23.9	281	12.7	21	275	8	12.3	28.2	118	5.3
Onslow	-2 600	40 658	34.2	2.84	9.5	15.4	3 322	26.3	241	557	36	4.4	10.8	1 553	12.9
Orange	4 600	36 104	33.5	2.34	9.4	28.0	1 129	12.8	87	485	10	5.6	9.1	630	7.8
Pamlico	600	4 523	23.0	2.49	12.1	23.3	146	13.3	13	106	2	9.7	14.3	100	9.3
Pasquotank	0	11 384	17.1	2.63	14.8	23.9	512	16.7	39	282	3	9.3	6.3	1 414	48.6
Pender	2 200	11 112	47.9	2.56	12.3	21.5	371	13.7	30	222	3	8.4	9.6	198	8.3
Perquimans	900	3 988	21.5	2.58	11.7	21.6	141	12.8	7	120	3	11.2	19.9	70	7.1
Person	900	11 423	15.9	2.61	13.5	22.8	411	13.1	35	290	5	9.4	11.8	258	8.6
Pitt	4 000	40 491	34.1	2.53	14.5	25.7	1 611	15.8	123	850	19	8.5	12.3	801	8.4
Polk	1 500	6 110	21.6	2.32	8.4	26.2	152	10.3	9	189	3	12.9	21.4	94	6.5
Randolph	4 200	41 096	24.8	2.57	9.6	20.9	1 469	14.3	112	776	16	7.7	11.5	757	7.9
Richmond	200	16 793	6.2	2.59	15.2	24.9	657	14.3	56	462	10	10.1	16.7	207	4.6
Robeson	-1 200	36 154	15.2	2.85	20.3	21.8	1 850	17.1	187	959	19	8.9	10.5	324	3.1
Rockingham	100	33 446	12.9	2.55	12.5	23.8	1 179	13.6	99	808	14	9.4	12.3	850	10.0
Rowan	3 700	42 512	18.3	2.52	10.9	24.1	1 456	13.7	118	1 074	17	10.2	11.7	901	8.9
Rutherford	2 100	22 198	15.5	2.53	11.5	23.7	771	13.3	67	619	6	10.8	8.4	356	6.3
Sampson	-400	17 526	5.3	2.67	14.4	22.7	644	12.7	42	509	6	10.1	9.9	303	6.0
Scotland	100	11 837	14.4	2.76	19.8	22.1	534	15.4	59	327	5	9.5	9.7	137	4.1
Stanly	700	19 747	13.6	2.57	10.0	22.3	735	14.4	65	502	11	9.9	16.4	364	7.3
Stokes	1 700	14 123	25.5	2.61	9.0	20.0	454	12.4	37	281	4	7.8	9.5	291	8.3
Surry	1 400	24 252	13.9	2.51	9.7	22.6	772	12.4	55	587	10	9.5	13.8	605	10.0
Swain	400	4 173	17.1	2.55	13.2	23.6	200	19.0	15	106	2	9.9	12.2	209	19.4
Transylvania	2 300	9 924	21.0	2.45	8.0	22.4	305	11.6	15	222	3	8.5	10.6	194	7.8
Tyrrell	100	1 471	6.5	2.62	14.5	24.4	53	12.9	3	41	3	10.0	42.3	28	6.8
Union	5 800	29 307	27.9	2.82	10.5	17.1	1 280	15.2	95	587	15	7.2	12.5	450	5.9

1. No spouse present. 2. Per 1,000 resident population estimated as of July 1 of the year shown. 3. Under 2,500 grams. 4. Deaths of infants under 1 year old. 5. Deaths of infants under 1 year old per 1,000 live births.

STATE County	Divorces, 1984		Physicians, active non–Federal, 1989		Hospitals, 1989			Nursing homes,[4] 1986		Serious crimes known to police, 1988			Education			
						Beds				Number			Public school enrollment[7]		Attainment,[8] 1980	
	Number	Rate[1]	Number[2]	Rate[3]	Number	Number	Rate[3]	Number	Beds	Total[5]	Violent[6]	Rate[3]	1986–1987	1980	Percent 12 yrs. or more	Percent 16 yrs. or more
	44	45	46	47	48	49	50	51	52	53	54	55	56	57	58	59
NORTH CAROLINA–Con.																
Craven	384	5.0	133	162	2	319	388	5	445	3 310	359	4 135	13 904	13 276	60.9	11.7
Cumberland	1 611	6.3	281	110	5	1 369	535	19	868	20 902	1 942	7 945	43 783	51 467	69.6	14.2
Currituck	26	2.0	5	35	0	0	0	3	13	218	9	1 564	2 237	2 210	50.4	4.9
Dare	33	2.0	13	56	0	0	0	2	124	1 500	59	7 369	2 683	2 236	64.7	15.4
Davidson	389	3.3	77	61	2	215	170	11	761	3 931	262	3 130	21 720	23 643	47.2	8.3
Davie	70	2.6	17	61	1	46	165	5	158	605	45	2 169	4 808	5 421	50.5	9.9
Duplin	140	3.4	20	48	1	80	192	8	278	1 032	143	2 516	8 069	9 001	43.7	6.9
Durham	884	5.5	1 805	1 033	4	1 754	1 003	45	1 376	11 790	814	6 851	25 935	26 451	65.1	24.1
Edgecombe	201	3.5	123	204	1	127	210	7	525	3 196	348	5 462	8 488	12 610	45.6	7.5
Forsyth	1 846	7.3	1 166	434	6	1 683	626	34	1 889	16 243	2 399	6 027	38 857	45 074	62.7	18.3
Franklin	96	3.0	16	44	1	80	220	10	315	754	95	2 145	5 934	6 371	43.2	7.0
Gaston	988	5.8	145	83	1	372	213	14	842	9 147	946	5 315	31 497	34 204	46.1	8.7
Gates	19	2.1	1	10	0	0	0	0	0	173	12	1 752	1 647	1 811	42.9	7.1
Graham	25	3.5	4	57	0	0	0	0	0	29	3	401	1 386	1 571	40.0	6.0
Granville	113	3.1	48	121	3	876	2 212	11	402	1 715	239	4 400	6 745	7 378	44.4	7.1
Greene	40	2.4	4	25	0	0	0	2	88	253	43	1 507	2 811	3 494	42.5	6.1
Guilford	2 096	6.5	664	195	7	1 399	411	48	2 474	21 202	1 981	6 245	53 463	61 160	63.3	19.7
Halifax	160	2.9	54	94	2	191	334	7	369	2 361	170	4 164	10 719	11 883	42.6	7.8
Harnett	247	4.0	30	45	2	144	214	11	491	2 643	338	3 995	11 769	12 227	47.4	8.8
Haywood	194	4.1	63	130	1	152	314	17	493	1 408	80	2 948	7 717	9 321	51.6	9.2
Henderson	281	4.3	108	154	2	298	424	12	485	1 983	163	2 870	10 097	10 601	61.5	15.2
Hertford	94	4.0	27	114	1	100	424	10	273	793	81	3 260	4 202	4 931	45.5	10.4
Hoke	35	1.6	4	16	1	81	331	1	75	862	114	3 544	5 041	5 030	47.5	8.9
Hyde	17	2.9	2	36	0	0	0	0	0	20	0	339	995	1 198	42.5	8.6
Iredell	335	3.9	115	124	3	457	491	12	412	2 115	151	2 357	15 952	17 759	50.1	9.2
Jackson	93	3.4	43	159	1	116	428	2	149	485	17	1 771	3 850	4 420	52.7	15.5
Johnston	320	4.3	45	55	1	114	139	10	568	3 373	249	4 274	14 536	15 469	46.6	7.1
Jones	19	1.9	8	81	0	0	0	1	5	120	24	1 203	1 640	2 097	41.8	5.8
Lee	236	6.0	64	151	1	100	236	5	269	2 430	218	5 767	7 503	7 923	56.9	11.5
Lenoir	346	5.7	79	131	2	1 154	1 914	8	387	2 902	373	4 721	11 273	12 530	52.2	10.3
Lincoln	197	4.4	27	55	1	75	152	2	96	1 164	85	2 408	8 796	9 241	46.9	8.3
McDowell	156	4.3	25	69	1	65	179	6	394	1 005	55	2 720	6 646	7 394	46.2	7.9
Macon	83	3.6	24	102	2	86	366	1	52	240	2	1 161	3 436	3 756	52.4	10.4
Madison	56	3.3	12	69	0	0	0	2	106	3	0	138	2 771	3 100	41.6	9.4
Martin	97	3.6	14	53	1	49	186	4	164	724	70	2 654	5 228	6 009	44.8	8.3
Mecklenburg	3 017	7.0	1 047	215	10	2 244	460	33	2 635	49 781	7 256	10 494	73 360	76 503	69.3	21.2
Mitchell	46	3.2	17	116	1	57	388	3	25	27	0	1 084	2 435	2 686	43.1	8.1
Montgomery	84	3.5	11	45	1	71	292	6	141	620	48	2 685	4 347	4 632	42.3	7.1
Moore	243	4.5	123	202	1	307	504	9	500	1 852	131	3 220	8 828	9 757	58.3	15.4
Nash	334	4.8	10	14	2	332	452	6	271	4 020	383	5 523	16 657	13 850	50.3	11.1
New Hanover	676	6.1	292	245	3	549	461	17	994	9 885	668	8 427	19 457	20 953	64.9	16.3
Northampton	62	2.8	4	18	0	0	0	3	99	411	53	2 039	4 117	4 847	36.0	6.1
Onslow	683	5.7	109	85	3	379	297	12	423	5 786	649	4 516	16 511	18 659	66.4	11.4
Orange	202	2.5	1 162	1 283	1	578	638	10	331	4 992	218	5 684	10 570	11 018	73.6	41.3
Pamlico	31	2.9	7	64	0	0	0	0	0	143	10	1 396	2 090	2 343	48.0	8.1
Pasquotank	139	4.8	47	151	1	137	441	3	301	1 182	216	3 820	5 225	5 575	51.1	12.9
Pender	81	3.4	13	46	1	66	236	2	82	889	170	3 321	4 724	4 943	47.4	7.2
Perquimans	26	2.6	2	18	0	0	0	6	73	196	30	1 800	1 804	1 764	41.5	6.1
Person	136	4.5	15	47	1	86	270	3	149	1 042	229	3 303	5 468	6 219	45.4	7.2
Pitt	357	3.8	445	427	2	619	595	15	509	5 700	527	5 649	16 809	16 217	56.8	17.7
Polk	48	3.3	24	162	1	52	351	7	157	220	27	1 598	2 031	2 341	58.5	17.1
Randolph	316	3.3	71	68	1	145	139	11	426	2 692	157	2 632	16 933	18 796	46.6	7.6
Richmond	162	3.6	26	57	2	151	328	6	178	1 632	229	3 494	8 831	10 004	46.4	8.0
Robeson	385	3.7	81	75	1	281	259	17	496	3 921	378	3 594	24 270	25 161	44.4	8.7
Rockingham	407	4.8	68	78	2	278	320	19	443	2 392	296	2 736	15 146	17 235	44.6	8.0
Rowan	403	4.0	111	103	2	1 101	1 024	13	647	3 609	303	3 566	16 056	18 460	49.4	10.5
Rutherford	224	4.0	44	76	1	145	250	25	657	1 482	138	2 581	10 141	11 218	44.9	8.2
Sampson	132	2.6	41	80	1	146	286	7	274	1 276	157	2 503	9 361	10 816	45.7	7.0
Scotland	58	1.7	30	86	1	165	471	9	216	1 845	99	5 357	7 512	7 950	47.8	11.2
Stanly	181	3.6	35	68	1	124	242	4	230	1 443	132	2 808	8 612	9 807	46.4	8.2
Stokes	56	1.6	11	30	1	91	247	4	117	538	62	1 460	6 591	7 517	44.9	5.4
Surry	215	3.6	51	82	2	266	426	10	604	1 204	120	1 905	10 987	12 125	41.0	6.3
Swain	32	3.0	12	114	2	83	790	2	170	100	26	2 051	1 674	2 114	44.5	8.8
Transylvania	114	4.6	32	121	1	89	337	1	137	271	15	1 024	4 015	4 667	59.3	14.1
Tyrrell	4	1.0	1	24	0	0	0	0	0	66	6	1 582	771	830	35.8	6.3
Union	267	3.5	60	70	1	176	204	7	217	2 590	224	3 221	15 130	16 261	52.8	9.1

1. Per 1,000 resident population estimated as of July 1 of the year shown. 2. As of end of year. 3. Per 100,000 resident population as of July 1 of the year shown. 4. Preliminary. Covers nursing homes with 3 or more beds. 5. Data for serious crimes have not been adjusted for underreporting, this may affect comparability between geographic areas or over time. 6. Includes murder and nonnegligent manslaughter, forcible rape, robbery, and aggravated assault. 7. The 1986–1987 data are based on administrative reports obtained by the U.S. National Center for Education Statistics. The 1980 data are based on the 1980 Census of Population and Housing. 8. Persons 25 years old or older.

STATE County	Education (cont'd): Local government expenditures for education,[1] 1982: Total (Mil dol)	Education (cont'd): Local government expenditures for education,[1] 1982: Per capita (Dollars)	Social Security Program December 1988: Beneficiaries: Total	Social Security Program December 1988: Beneficiaries: Rate[2]	Social Security Program December 1988: Payments ($1,000)	Supplemental Security Income Program recipients June 1986	Money income: Per capita[3]: 1987 Income, (Dollars)	Money income: Per capita[3]: 1979: Current dollars	Money income: Per capita[3]: 1979: Constant 1987 dollars	Money income: Median household income 1979 (Dollars)	Money income: Percent below poverty level, 1979: Persons	Money income: Percent below poverty level, 1979: Families	Housing units, 1990: Total	Housing units, 1990: Percent change, 1980–1990
	60	61	62	63	64	65	66	67	68	69	70	71	72	73
NORTH CAROLINA—Con.														
Craven	27.3	370	11 625	142.8	4 872	1 796	9 604	5 650	8 841	13 060	18.5	15.5	32 293	26.4
Cumberland	91.1	365	23 855	93.3	9 875	4 250	9 454	5 425	8 488	13 433	17.2	14.8	98 360	20.9
Currituck	5.1	437	2 225	158.9	927	208	9 218	5 266	8 240	12 785	18.3	15.5	7 367	36.3
Dare	7.8	531	3 155	146.7	1 455	140	12 099	7 022	10 987	13 555	11.3	8.9	21 567	96.0
Davidson	43.0	373	18 005	144.9	8 383	1 410	10 581	6 227	9 743	15 238	10.6	8.2	53 266	20.3
Davie	9.3	357	4 505	162.1	2 035	436	11 400	6 343	9 925	15 749	10.9	9.5	11 496	21.3
Duplin	17.3	422	7 255	174.4	2 634	1 746	8 302	4 653	7 281	11 133	23.1	20.1	16 395	5.2
Durham	62.9	403	24 320	141.9	11 805	3 164	12 510	6 828	10 684	15 395	14.0	9.5	77 710	33.2
Edgecombe	17.9	315	10 625	177.4	4 331	2 186	8 425	5 068	7 930	13 057	20.2	15.9	21 827	7.6
Forsyth	92.1	368	42 135	158.2	20 875	4 092	13 311	7 454	11 663	16 600	11.6	8.4	115 715	20.7
Franklin	12.2	397	5 470	154.5	2 183	1 200	8 632	4 836	7 567	11 758	20.3	16.3	14 957	34.1
Gaston	65.3	393	28 625	164.3	13 592	2 660	11 089	6 309	9 872	15 898	10.5	8.2	69 133	16.8
Gates	4.3	478	1 790	182.7	706	328	8 868	5 143	8 047	13 050	19.7	16.8	3 696	14.6
Graham	3.2	439	1 625	232.1	627	270	7 686	4 615	7 221	11 250	19.6	17.8	4 132	15.5
Granville	13.9	394	6 375	163.9	2 532	1 360	9 004	4 989	7 806	13 575	17.3	13.4	14 164	22.5
Greene	7.7	478	2 115	129.0	792	422	8 443	4 976	7 786	12 127	25.3	19.2	5 944	6.4
Guilford	136.6	426	52 550	156.0	26 215	4 480	13 324	7 426	11 619	16 473	11.1	8.3	146 812	21.9
Halifax	28.9	521	11 670	205.5	4 735	3 042	8 018	4 513	7 061	10 461	29.5	25.0	22 480	10.8
Harnett	22.5	369	9 310	140.4	3 729	1 764	8 648	5 063	7 922	12 112	19.3	14.5	27 896	25.8
Haywood	17.2	365	10 310	213.5	4 725	1 220	10 090	5 735	8 974	12 978	15.6	12.7	23 975	17.7
Henderson	21.9	353	18 030	260.5	8 787	1 048	11 443	6 412	10 033	14 177	12.3	9.3	34 131	25.5
Hertford	9.4	400	4 515	191.3	1 802	1 016	8 246	4 787	7 490	11 961	24.3	19.9	8 870	7.4
Hoke	9.5	441	2 290	95.4	900	632	7 649	4 484	7 016	12 805	20.9	18.0	7 999	23.5
Hyde	2.8	478	1 195	209.6	434	268	6 691	4 295	6 720	9 736	28.3	24.7	2 905	2.4
Iredell	33.3	394	15 445	168.6	7 228	1 300	10 866	6 125	9 584	15 119	10.1	8.0	39 191	21.1
Jackson	7.9	299	4 545	167.7	1 899	678	8 469	4 987	7 803	11 387	19.3	14.8	14 052	17.5
Johnston	29.4	406	13 290	164.9	5 123	2 866	9 308	5 303	8 298	12 320	17.9	14.9	34 172	22.2
Jones	4.2	436	1 750	178.6	631	378	7 422	4 461	6 980	11 183	21.8	17.9	3 829	4.8
Lee	17.7	468	7 525	179.6	3 387	962	10 825	6 320	9 889	14 782	13.5	10.5	16 954	21.1
Lenoir	26.0	432	11 605	192.5	4 619	2 586	9 134	5 421	8 482	12 869	19.9	15.7	23 739	5.2
Lincoln	16.7	386	7 195	148.4	3 283	608	10 658	6 058	9 479	15 861	9.7	7.3	20 189	24.9
McDowell	13.3	368	6 840	188.4	3 028	858	8 820	5 274	8 252	13 452	11.8	9.3	15 091	8.2
Macon	7.4	339	6 295	269.0	2 693	628	10 378	5 671	8 873	11 148	17.2	14.4	17 174	28.6
Madison	6.3	372	3 425	199.1	1 219	884	7 949	4 670	7 307	9 519	25.8	22.1	7 667	7.0
Martin	13.4	512	4 960	187.9	1 936	1 084	8 614	4 781	7 481	11 787	24.1	19.3	10 104	8.4
Mecklenburg	169.5	404	59 670	125.4	30 447	5 544	14 192	7 872	12 317	17 837	10.9	8.3	216 416	38.6
Mitchell	5.5	379	3 145	213.9	1 257	630	8 362	5 018	7 852	12 018	16.8	14.2	6 983	15.3
Montgomery	8.7	382	4 130	170.7	1 709	672	8 776	5 128	8 024	12 824	14.2	11.2	10 421	9.5
Moore	20.0	386	13 830	233.2	6 692	1 132	11 940	6 545	10 241	14 475	13.7	10.8	27 358	30.0
Nash	35.7	521	10 650	146.5	4 259	2 208	10 948	6 043	9 455	13 628	19.9	15.6	31 024	20.6
New Hanover	40.8	380	19 180	163.5	9 144	2 220	11 596	6 747	10 557	15 341	15.2	11.7	57 076	31.8
Northampton	10.8	478	4 620	209.0	1 771	1 192	8 378	4 610	7 213	10 347	28.1	22.3	8 974	2.9
Onslow	27.3	236	8 795	69.5	3 495	1 246	8 598	5 114	8 002	12 336	16.9	14.8	47 526	34.1
Orange	24.4	312	9 190	103.8	4 614	782	12 929	6 927	10 839	14 939	15.1	8.2	38 683	34.7
Pamlico	4.3	405	2 010	182.7	798	314	8 692	5 076	7 942	11 765	20.6	17.5	6 050	20.7
Pasquotank	10.7	373	5 555	181.5	2 327	734	8 561	5 276	8 255	12 288	17.7	14.1	12 298	17.1
Pender	10.8	473	4 860	179.3	1 978	830	8 745	5 000	7 824	11 879	21.3	16.6	15 437	50.0
Perquimans	4.2	433	2 260	205.5	907	344	7 245	4 523	7 077	10 914	24.4	20.7	4 972	19.2
Person	11.9	400	5 310	169.1	2 207	926	9 541	5 424	8 487	13 652	16.6	13.4	12 548	17.4
Pitt	35.5	381	14 475	141.9	5 878	3 346	9 759	5 577	8 726	12 913	23.5	17.3	43 070	30.6
Polk	5.4	381	4 030	274.1	1 941	222	11 328	6 472	10 127	13 428	13.7	10.2	7 273	22.7
Randolph	31.3	334	16 015	155.9	7 376	1 230	10 555	6 275	9 818	15 527	8.9	6.7	43 634	23.8
Richmond	17.7	395	7 855	170.8	3 275	1 442	8 984	5 492	8 593	13 419	15.2	11.9	18 218	6.9
Robeson	53.1	513	16 930	156.8	6 278	4 948	7 603	4 502	7 044	11 494	24.9	20.9	39 045	17.2
Rockingham	33.0	391	16 705	193.1	7 528	2 102	10 331	6 045	9 459	14 606	12.8	10.1	35 657	10.5
Rowan	32.2	319	17 830	167.4	8 400	1 400	10 538	6 315	9 881	15 282	9.7	7.3	46 264	18.5
Rutherford	20.7	371	10 980	190.0	4 904	1 446	9 418	5 519	8 636	13 308	13.7	10.7	25 220	15.7
Sampson	22.0	440	8 630	169.5	3 236	1 906	8 237	4 732	7 404	11 498	21.2	17.5	19 183	5.2
Scotland	15.9	482	5 080	146.8	2 110	1 320	9 385	5 435	8 504	13 902	17.3	15.4	12 759	14.8
Stanly	18.0	370	9 670	189.6	4 499	664	10 266	5 966	9 335	14 510	10.5	8.4	21 808	13.7
Stokes	14.4	422	4 445	121.8	1 775	574	10 024	5 610	8 778	15 287	12.6	10.5	15 160	19.3
Surry	23.9	401	12 735	205.1	5 284	1 680	9 919	5 691	8 905	13 295	13.7	11.0	26 022	11.8
Swain	3.8	362	2 370	225.7	889	476	6 635	4 123	6 451	9 866	25.9	23.3	5 664	16.7
Transylvania	9.0	372	5 595	213.5	2 690	418	10 642	6 292	9 845	16 048	12.9	9.9	12 893	26.0
Tyrrell	2.0	479	845	206.1	316	200	6 515	4 139	6 476	10 654	25.2	20.2	1 907	8.0
Union	28.5	387	9 420	112.1	4 240	892	11 598	6 341	9 922	16 628	10.3	8.2	30 760	27.8

1. Elementary and secondary. 2. Per 1,000 resident population estimated as of July 1 of the year shown. 3. Based on the resident population estimated as of July 1, 1988 for 1987 data and enumerated as of April 1, 1980 for 1979 data.

STATE County	Housing units, 1990 (cont'd)				Civilian labor force, 1990				Private nonfarm establishments, 1988					
	Occupied units						Unemployment				Employment[2]			
		Owner occupied												
	Total	Percent	Median value (Dollars)	Median rent (Dollars)	Total	Percent change, 1989–1990	Total	Rate[1]	Number	Net change, 1987–1988	Total	Percent change, 1987–1988	Manufacturing	Retail trade
	74	75	76	77	78	79	80	81	82	83	84	85	86	87
NORTH CAROLINA–Con.														
Craven	29 542	63.3	65 900	302	32 287	0.9	1 513	4.7	1 719	-1	18 878	5.3	4 348	5 779
Cumberland	91 500	57.7	63 500	318	93 797	-1.9	4 414	4.7	4 670	106	59 912	-0.1	12 053	19 063
Currituck	5 038	80.3	79 200	304	9 877	-3.2	235	2.4	237	28	1 279	11.6	91	613
Dare	9 349	71.1	108 100	416	17 218	2.5	696	4.0	1 234	65	7 918	10.3	370	3 038
Davidson	48 944	73.6	60 800	246	71 127	0.4	2 791	3.9	2 221	72	39 557	6.0	23 291	6 194
Davie	10 785	82.1	68 000	249	14 847	0.7	686	4.6	531	12	7 093	9.5	3 673	1 396
Duplin	14 925	75.9	42 600	156	22 526	2.9	1 093	4.9	781	8	9 853	9.1	5 048	1 917
Durham	72 297	53.0	85 500	355	102 746	0.6	2 461	2.4	4 450	93	107 510	12.9	30 565	16 557
Edgecombe	20 319	61.8	47 100	191	29 776	-1.0	1 476	5.0	781	16	14 924	7.1	6 489	2 443
Forsyth	107 419	63.5	75 700	302	147 049	-0.2	5 706	3.9	7 092	163	149 100	2.9	45 142	28 262
Franklin	13 503	75.5	55 500	188	18 762	0.8	897	4.8	556	26	6 838	14.8	3 343	1 319
Gaston	65 347	69.3	57 700	253	101 422	1.5	4 180	4.1	3 654	89	71 209	2.0	36 430	11 933
Gates	3 352	81.1	49 700	135	3 822	0.8	115	3.0	126	3	854	-3.3	272	256
Graham	2 772	81.7	47 400	145	2 320	4.6	444	19.1	145	1	1 625	-0.2	793	198
Granville	13 134	73.4	59 100	207	20 278	-0.7	900	4.4	620	4	8 935	8.6	5 075	1 610
Greene	5 395	70.3	48 600	160	8 885	1.1	310	3.5	217	5	2 144	-1.2	710	540
Guilford	137 706	61.3	79 400	340	191 639	-0.1	6 820	3.6	11 357	263	206 343	5.5	57 851	41 118
Halifax	20 335	65.3	44 800	178	23 479	-1.1	1 397	5.9	1 182	10	14 997	6.0	5 867	3 837
Harnett	25 150	68.4	50 800	214	29 418	1.5	1 263	4.3	1 189	68	14 986	10.2	4 520	3 052
Haywood	19 211	77.1	59 600	214	21 325	-1.2	1 108	5.2	1 186	20	11 666	3.1	4 267	3 102
Henderson	28 709	76.7	78 400	288	34 592	0.0	1 084	3.1	1 796	32	21 305	3.2	7 435	5 120
Hertford	8 150	68.6	44 900	176	9 017	-2.0	490	5.4	560	-7	6 917	5.4	1 835	1 829
Hoke	7 405	75.3	44 800	217	10 316	-0.4	595	5.8	227	-6	5 541	17.1	4 238	686
Hyde	2 094	77.0	43 700	158	2 212	-1.1	204	9.2	162	4	853	-0.8	88	199
Iredell	35 573	75.1	63 300	265	52 557	0.5	2 312	4.4	2 280	101	37 180	5.6	17 620	6 941
Jackson	9 683	75.6	63 000	224	12 460	-5.5	521	4.2	638	16	4 910	-10.5	1 038	1 414
Johnston	31 566	69.9	59 400	208	38 480	-0.1	1 751	4.6	1 895	67	20 441	5.2	8 538	4 713
Jones	3 492	78.1	43 700	164	4 644	-1.0	220	4.7	176	14	1 587	5.0	777	193
Lee	15 689	72.6	61 100	242	20 129	-1.8	1 065	5.3	1 251	26	17 548	2.6	6 959	4 098
Lenoir	21 938	63.1	52 400	175	29 191	1.1	1 472	5.0	1 421	12	21 887	0.7	7 644	4 742
Lincoln	18 764	78.9	60 500	244	27 719	1.2	1 249	4.5	1 076	36	14 307	3.4	8 024	2 463
McDowell	13 680	77.1	45 100	202	16 917	0.7	1 092	6.5	668	5	13 074	-1.3	8 623	2 033
Macon	9 834	82.8	62 500	240	11 832	1.8	435	3.7	766	14	5 091	4.1	1 208	1 454
Madison	6 488	77.8	47 800	161	7 513	-1.6	333	4.4	227	18	2 048	2.7	349	372
Martin	9 317	68.8	46 600	160	11 419	-0.3	630	5.5	550	3	6 409	1.9	2 809	1 606
Mecklenburg	200 219	59.7	86 900	383	282 679	0.6	8 411	3.0	17 303	632	332 964	4.8	55 991	58 350
Mitchell	5 779	82.5	48 700	196	6 994	0.5	447	6.4	322	20	4 363	5.3	2 027	924
Montgomery	8 290	77.1	43 900	196	12 375	0.6	732	5.9	494	8	8 768	-1.0	5 949	1 096
Moore	23 827	77.6	80 300	260	31 193	0.4	1 124	3.6	1 596	51	19 720	0.6	6 730	4 118
Nash	29 041	64.4	63 200	228	37 294	-0.9	1 759	4.7	2 180	51	36 989	2.3	13 863	8 600
New Hanover	48 139	62.7	72 000	324	64 990	0.1	2 756	4.2	3 912	92	51 418	5.3	11 260	12 545
Northampton	7 591	76.6	38 100	129	7 515	-1.6	387	5.1	327	3	2 773	1.5	844	533
Onslow	40 658	53.7	62 200	316	39 146	1.9	1 543	3.9	2 135	63	20 418	0.9	2 842	8 628
Orange	36 104	55.3	101 500	389	52 627	0.6	980	1.9	2 018	54	21 503	11.7	2 405	7 582
Pamlico	4 523	81.1	54 300	219	4 704	0.3	205	4.4	177	10	1 430	3.6	298	422
Pasquotank	11 384	65.2	59 300	242	13 124	-0.1	555	4.2	787	16	7 737	3.2	1 206	2 908
Pender	11 112	82.6	60 200	242	15 390	2.5	686	4.5	449	25	3 209	12.7	674	764
Perquimans	3 988	76.8	53 200	193	4 018	-0.5	147	3.7	164	-10	1 211	-2.7	438	295
Person	11 423	72.5	55 700	203	15 504	4.6	1 013	6.5	585	4	8 375	-4.8	4 235	1 562
Pitt	40 491	58.1	65 300	250	58 906	1.0	2 084	3.5	2 383	109	31 953	9.1	8 877	9 454
Polk	6 110	79.9	68 200	234	5 795	0.1	181	3.1	368	10	2 690	-5.0	1 041	554
Randolph	41 096	77.0	60 200	248	61 346	0.0	1 833	3.0	2 031	88	36 994	7.8	23 129	4 927
Richmond	16 793	72.3	40 000	191	22 591	-0.1	1 273	5.6	985	6	13 638	4.0	6 601	3 114
Robeson	36 154	70.1	44 200	165	46 005	-1.7	3 363	7.3	1 873	7	28 163	-1.2	14 874	5 763
Rockingham	33 446	74.3	48 800	209	40 668	-0.2	2 331	5.7	1 641	27	27 943	6.0	15 067	5 192
Rowan	42 512	73.6	54 600	252	59 805	1.2	2 490	4.2	2 114	83	33 868	3.2	14 759	7 725
Rutherford	22 198	73.0	46 300	216	30 542	0.0	1 622	5.3	1 177	9	20 526	11.0	11 677	3 413
Sampson	17 526	72.9	46 500	172	23 386	-0.9	1 090	4.7	873	29	10 783	5.2	4 658	2 075
Scotland	11 837	69.4	48 000	202	15 490	0.5	1 242	8.0	646	-2	14 708	8.9	8 439	2 414
Stanly	19 747	76.6	52 800	227	27 008	-0.8	1 272	4.7	1 218	16	17 788	2.2	9 292	3 208
Stokes	14 123	81.0	59 100	238	18 735	-0.9	827	4.4	503	34	3 911	7.6	1 295	1 005
Surry	24 252	76.6	48 600	206	32 602	-0.6	1 542	4.7	1 488	-2	30 964	9.3	16 448	4 987
Swain	4 173	76.3	49 100	160	5 759	1.6	593	10.3	338	6	3 384	4.9	950	749
Transylvania	9 924	78.9	72 200	257	10 603	-1.0	327	3.1	610	11	8 066	-17.4	0	1 330
Tyrrell	1 471	76.4	37 400	155	1 478	1.9	208	14.1	79	-4	478	12.5	223	119
Union	29 307	75.9	70 600	308	46 441	0.6	1 334	2.9	1 910	98	28 243	6.0	12 546	4 971

1. Percent of total civilian labor force. 2. For week including March 12. Excludes government employees, self-employed persons, farm workers, domestic service workers, railroad employees subject to the Railroad Retirement Act, and employees on oceanborne vessels or in foreign countries.

STATE County	Private nonfarm establishments, 1988 (cont'd): Employment[1] (cont'd): Finance, insurance, and real estate	Employment[1] (cont'd): Services	Annual payroll: Total (Mil dol)	Annual payroll: Average per employee (Dollars)	Personal income, 1989: Total (Mil dol)	Percent change, 1988–1989	Wages and salaries[2] (Mil dol)	Proprietor's income (Mil dol)	Dividends, interest, & rent (Mil dol)	Transfer payments (Mil dol)	Per capita[3]: Dollars	Per capita[3]: Rank	Earnings, 1989: Total (Mil dol)	Percent by selected industries: Farm	Goods-related[4]: Total
	88	89	90	91	92	93	94	95	96	97	98	99	100	101	102
NORTH CAROLINA—Con.															
Craven	1 070	4 271	300	15 900	1 126	7.8	849	84	142	199	13 698	1 583	933	1.5	17.3
Cumberland	3 211	14 743	931	15 547	3 473	7.4	2 679	196	337	570	13 576	1 646	2 874	0.6	15.5
Currituck	46	274	15	11 702	181	9.5	39	12	22	35	12 570	2 082	51	3.0	17.7
Dare	678	1 878	121	15 262	332	10.2	198	61	62	50	14 392	1 250	258	0.0	25.5
Davidson	1 033	4 309	637	16 112	1 792	6.6	912	145	233	211	14 191	1 349	1 056	1.2	54.1
Davie	130	877	115	16 168	468	9.4	171	50	83	54	16 770	475	221	2.4	49.0
Duplin	233	1 010	142	14 421	454	9.3	244	73	55	92	10 907	2 684	317	14.7	39.9
Durham	4 768	41 873	2 444	22 734	3 208	9.6	3 445	260	466	374	18 346	262	3 705	0.8	40.1
Edgecombe	248	2 136	264	17 697	722	8.0	459	60	96	122	11 958	2 337	519	4.1	38.5
Forsyth	11 021	39 188	3 162	21 210	5 285	7.6	4 272	361	939	556	19 655	187	4 634	0.1	38.4
Franklin	167	1 016	90	13 090	421	8.7	112	39	45	69	11 563	2 482	151	9.7	31.3
Gaston	1 628	10 778	1 276	17 921	2 659	6.2	1 721	151	286	343	15 194	910	1 872	0.4	50.3
Gates	71	120	10	12 028	122	4.5	22	14	17	23	12 264	2 209	35	20.4	NA
Graham	0	232	22	13 413	64	4.0	27	9	10	19	9 140	2 992	35	3.9	NA
Granville	208	1 165	136	15 235	500	8.8	310	60	59	75	12 631	2 060	370	8.7	38.0
Greene	56	458	29	13 354	181	9.7	55	31	24	30	11 090	2 637	86	27.5	NA
Guilford	17 827	41 814	3 934	19 065	6 547	6.8	5 633	546	1 101	734	19 239	208	6 180	0.3	35.9
Halifax	522	2 416	225	14 990	665	7.3	372	73	84	154	11 633	2 464	445	7.1	35.4
Harnett	605	4 387	208	13 856	749	9.8	306	70	80	143	11 120	2 632	376	4.1	NA
Haywood	555	2 157	226	19 334	642	4.1	336	61	111	124	13 272	1 785	397	2.9	46.8
Henderson	719	4 440	388	18 197	1 173	7.3	533	132	313	198	16 691	485	665	6.7	40.1
Hertford	169	2 002	86	12 473	276	6.7	145	37	35	61	11 723	2 431	183	9.3	29.3
Hoke	68	326	80	14 351	222	8.3	120	22	18	42	9 091	2 999	142	9.0	53.6
Hyde	0	114	10	11 948	67	8.4	21	21	9	15	12 075	2 301	42	27.7	NA
Iredell	801	5 976	625	16 797	1 474	7.3	811	129	194	187	15 841	698	940	1.9	46.1
Jackson	161	1 379	69	13 978	327	8.5	167	35	52	64	12 072	2 303	202	2.4	21.2
Johnston	545	2 912	294	14 361	1 082	9.7	454	120	129	173	13 201	1 814	575	5.7	42.8
Jones	22	175	24	14 859	107	9.6	27	12	12	26	10 816	2 712	39	19.8	NA
Lee	733	2 530	286	16 324	637	8.6	405	55	107	102	15 021	983	459	1.4	47.5
Lenoir	865	4 184	347	15 853	799	8.6	547	79	117	152	13 264	1 787	626	4.8	37.7
Lincoln	348	1 548	249	17 424	713	6.8	291	59	84	85	14 397	1 248	351	3.3	49.1
McDowell	157	1 260	205	15 659	423	6.5	285	43	47	78	11 635	2 463	329	1.6	65.4
Macon	230	1 061	72	14 200	309	9.4	125	39	75	69	13 159	1 835	164	2.1	31.2
Madison	124	937	22	10 814	188	8.5	58	20	24	40	10 904	2 686	78	10.3	23.7
Martin	171	669	85	13 330	339	7.4	230	46	48	61	12 890	1 957	276	8.2	50.7
Mecklenburg	32 925	76 847	7 533	22 624	9 769	8.2	9 917	686	1 429	879	20 040	167	10 603	0.2	22.7
Mitchell	118	611	63	14 449	166	5.7	87	17	25	38	11 255	2 577	104	1.8	44.4
Montgomery	165	627	127	14 464	290	6.5	188	39	32	49	11 952	2 339	227	6.5	58.8
Moore	744	5 721	294	14 925	1 054	10.3	468	115	300	175	17 306	395	583	7.3	29.6
Nash	2 271	5 454	647	17 491	1 166	9.0	875	147	143	175	15 900	674	1 021	5.1	37.0
New Hanover	2 088	14 130	936	18 206	1 894	9.6	1 263	188	345	295	15 896	678	1 451	0.2	28.1
Northampton	69	487	34	12 426	257	5.5	85	41	31	58	11 658	2 459	126	24.9	19.9
Onslow	1 044	4 188	242	11 832	1 554	7.9	1 264	116	102	214	12 157	2 257	1 380	2.4	7.8
Orange	2 575	5 969	320	14 896	1 658	9.4	982	131	304	165	18 295	265	1 113	0.8	11.1
Pamlico	70	164	16	11 240	141	6.9	36	19	22	31	12 859	1 976	55	7.5	22.5
Pasquotank	490	1 533	118	15 256	395	8.0	234	28	63	80	12 723	2 026	262	0.6	15.0
Pender	154	647	39	12 064	359	11.7	95	50	51	68	12 820	1 992	145	13.8	29.0
Perquimans	40	221	11	9 242	127	5.3	26	16	18	29	11 236	2 587	42	21.8	NA
Person	155	792	137	16 375	383	9.9	211	32	47	65	12 028	2 320	244	4.0	48.5
Pitt	1 511	6 144	524	16 414	1 543	11.7	1 007	141	194	219	14 824	1 067	1 147	4.2	29.0
Polk	121	660	33	12 449	262	9.6	56	24	95	43	17 690	338	80	6.9	29.2
Randolph	665	3 772	601	16 236	1 488	7.4	766	155	176	170	14 224	1 325	921	4.7	54.8
Richmond	368	1 786	189	13 892	549	9.2	352	47	57	111	11 950	2 341	399	4.5	NA
Robeson	984	2 971	407	14 452	1 062	6.5	633	90	112	231	9 769	2 914	723	3.5	43.2
Rockingham	639	4 109	498	17 810	1 235	5.9	695	100	163	198	14 228	1 320	794	2.3	56.5
Rowan	954	5 576	563	16 633	1 614	8.3	874	122	229	231	15 011	985	996	1.3	42.6
Rutherford	364	2 430	329	16 052	771	10.1	461	59	91	128	13 275	1 781	520	1.4	52.6
Sampson	257	2 277	151	14 003	593	9.0	259	95	66	114	11 608	2 470	354	18.1	31.8
Scotland	309	2 384	241	16 395	413	4.6	320	35	40	73	11 812	2 396	355	3.6	54.5
Stanly	417	2 171	276	15 540	730	6.9	414	71	103	108	14 221	1 327	485	2.9	55.6
Stokes	70	568	54	13 884	503	6.8	107	43	56	57	13 642	1 607	150	8.3	31.5
Surry	648	2 645	469	15 142	886	7.1	599	84	119	138	14 176	1 356	683	2.4	52.5
Swain	0	1 385	39	11 489	104	7.8	72	13	14	29	9 933	2 891	85	2.7	22.9
Transylvania	592	1 566	179	22 147	365	6.4	235	26	90	65	13 856	1 502	262	1.4	59.2
Tyrrell	16	40	5	10 381	43	10.5	20	8	5	11	10 460	2 799	28	23.3	NA
Union	1 076	3 740	467	16 541	1 424	9.5	718	170	139	124	16 535	521	888	8.5	49.6

1. For week including March 12. Excludes government employees, self-employed persons, farm workers, domestic service workers, railroad employees subject to the Railroad Retirement Act, and employees on oceanborne vessels or in foreign countries. 2. Includes other labor income. 3. Based on the resident population estimated as of July 1 of the year shown. 4. Covers mining, construction, and manufacturing.

STATE County	Earnings, 1989 (cont'd) — Percent by selected industries (cont'd) — Goods-related[1] — Manu-facturing	Service-related & other[2] — Total	Retail trade	Finance, insur-ance, & real estate	Services	Govern-ment	Agriculture, 1987 — Farms — Number	Percent with — Less than 50 acres	500 acres and over	Farm operators, percent — Whose principal occu-pation is farming	Residing on farm operated	Land in farms — Acreage (1,000)	Percent change, 1982–1987	Acres — Average size of farm	Total irrigated (1,000)	Total cropland (1,000)
	103	104	105	106	107	108	109	110	111	112	113	114	115	116	117	118
NORTH CAROLINA—Con.																
Craven	12.3	32.1	7.9	2.4	14.5	49.2	406	30.5	10.1	64.3	65.8	89	-3.1	220	0	66
Cumberland	11.7	33.6	9.5	2.8	11.4	50.3	524	38.2	10.3	42.2	70.8	100	-16.0	191	3	67
Currituck	2.3	50.2	18.6	2.6	17.1	29.0	106	28.3	27.4	66.0	65.1	47	-12.1	447	1	39
Dare	3.8	60.2	22.2	5.6	19.0	14.3	4	50.0	50.0	100.0	75.0	D	NA	D	D	D
Davidson	47.1	34.7	9.5	1.9	13.2	10.0	1 042	46.6	1.7	39.7	77.9	96	-15.7	92	1	57
Davie	40.3	36.7	7.8	2.2	18.3	11.9	623	36.8	3.4	40.4	71.3	79	1.6	127	1	46
Duplin	34.4	30.5	7.4	1.9	9.5	14.9	1 531	41.2	5.8	62.0	65.6	235	-5.5	153	1	151
Durham	35.8	47.5	6.4	3.6	31.1	11.6	234	47.9	3.4	46.6	68.8	24	-41.4	103	0	12
Edgecombe	28.6	40.7	6.2	1.2	12.7	16.8	449	26.1	24.1	75.7	55.9	182	-16.8	406	8	126
Forsyth	33.3	54.4	9.6	5.8	24.7	7.2	735	49.1	0.8	42.9	72.0	55	-7.6	75	1	29
Franklin	25.2	40.6	11.3	2.3	19.8	18.5	666	33.0	6.6	56.9	67.7	125	-8.8	187	4	62
Gaston	45.8	40.8	9.2	2.5	14.9	8.5	336	37.8	3.3	38.4	80.4	41	-14.9	122	0	25
Gates	11.9	40.5	10.2	3.1	10.1	25.5	251	26.3	15.1	66.9	70.9	69	1.5	275	2	49
Graham	26.8	27.2	8.5	0.9	9.9	23.3	147	68.7	0.7	34.7	68.0	8	-28.3	51	D	3
Granville	34.4	20.6	6.0	1.0	8.6	32.7	847	30.0	8.5	53.1	59.1	160	-7.4	189	4	62
Greene	15.3	27.8	6.2	2.2	15.8	23.6	510	19.2	12.7	76.5	56.7	117	9.0	230	1	89
Guilford	27.7	54.2	10.3	5.9	19.9	9.6	1 141	46.9	3.6	46.1	72.5	126	-7.1	111	3	71
Halifax	30.9	38.7	11.3	2.1	13.7	18.8	428	26.9	28.7	73.4	60.7	208	-3.6	487	3	131
Harnett	25.0	NA	12.0	2.4	19.5	16.6	875	34.7	5.7	51.1	68.1	139	-13.8	159	4	79
Haywood	40.3	35.3	12.0	2.2	16.0	15.0	912	53.9	1.8	36.5	71.2	80	-1.7	87	0	28
Henderson	30.8	42.4	12.3	2.0	18.7	10.8	592	53.2	3.5	53.4	76.0	59	-3.1	100	1	34
Hertford	23.5	45.0	10.4	1.6	20.4	16.4	271	21.8	22.9	70.1	50.6	92	1.2	339	2	58
Hoke	50.0	16.0	5.5	1.3	7.2	21.3	193	40.9	19.2	61.1	61.1	66	-8.5	343	0	49
Hyde	4.0	43.3	8.6	6.7	5.5	20.3	163	17.2	39.9	75.5	69.3	102	-8.3	628	0	87
Iredell	37.6	40.7	11.5	1.8	16.9	11.3	1 206	35.0	4.6	48.3	76.3	162	-0.9	134	1	97
Jackson	11.3	43.0	10.6	4.7	21.4	33.4	234	50.0	1.3	33.8	73.5	18	-2.7	77	0	7
Johnston	31.4	36.9	12.4	2.0	13.5	14.6	1 713	40.9	5.0	56.8	68.4	234	-11.9	137	5	154
Jones	10.1	43.7	9.5	1.2	18.5	21.4	248	22.6	17.3	65.3	65.7	72	-2.2	291	0	50
Lee	38.9	40.6	12.6	3.1	15.1	10.5	345	38.3	2.9	54.2	69.6	43	-19.0	124	1	17
Lenoir	30.9	36.6	10.1	3.0	15.6	20.9	667	28.8	12.4	68.2	64.9	146	3.0	219	1	106
Lincoln	42.1	35.2	10.8	2.3	11.8	12.3	480	35.4	3.8	41.7	73.8	59	-14.3	124	0	40
McDowell	60.1	22.7	8.3	0.9	9.9	10.3	232	40.1	2.2	44.4	74.6	23	-4.8	100	0	9
Macon	14.6	52.0	15.9	3.7	23.9	14.8	318	42.5	0.0	41.5	68.6	26	-13.5	81	0	11
Madison	19.2	45.5	10.0	1.3	21.2	20.5	1 305	50.5	0.9	44.0	69.2	101	-4.8	78	0	32
Martin	46.3	28.6	7.4	1.1	9.0	12.6	591	22.8	12.5	71.7	55.2	140	-3.6	237	1	94
Mecklenburg	15.8	68.8	9.6	10.4	21.4	8.3	348	44.0	1.7	40.8	76.7	36	-22.0	103	0	20
Mitchell	31.0	38.1	10.4	2.4	18.6	15.7	351	58.4	2.0	34.5	75.8	26	-10.4	73	0	9
Montgomery	50.8	22.1	6.7	1.3	9.3	12.6	241	38.6	8.3	45.2	73.0	42	-15.3	174	1	16
Moore	21.9	52.5	11.0	1.8	32.1	10.6	759	40.4	3.0	52.8	71.5	84	-13.9	111	3	33
Nash	32.4	49.6	14.0	7.8	15.2	8.3	692	36.1	14.0	65.8	67.5	184	-14.2	266	11	111
New Hanover	20.0	53.5	12.8	3.9	23.1	18.2	65	69.2	1.5	40.0	44.6	9	-29.0	136	0	4
Northampton	15.8	34.4	6.6	0.9	16.4	20.8	452	23.9	25.4	68.4	56.9	169	0.1	375	2	109
Onslow	3.8	19.8	7.2	1.4	7.1	70.0	436	37.8	6.9	55.0	67.9	69	-9.1	158	0	43
Orange	6.3	38.6	8.2	6.8	19.1	49.6	522	30.1	6.1	51.0	74.7	81	-10.5	155	1	44
Pamlico	14.3	50.9	11.5	1.1	15.3	19.1	86	31.4	29.1	77.9	68.6	38	-13.1	445	1	35
Pasquotank	8.3	46.6	15.4	4.1	16.6	37.9	225	21.8	18.2	67.1	60.4	82	10.7	363	0	73
Pender	13.8	39.0	13.7	2.3	12.3	18.2	393	33.6	9.2	60.8	64.6	70	-23.7	179	0	41
Perquimans	10.3	37.3	8.6	2.2	14.2	25.6	272	25.7	17.6	70.6	75.4	76	-12.2	279	D	66
Person	38.9	NA	9.2	1.6	NA	12.4	555	25.8	8.8	61.4	68.5	117	-8.6	212	2	55
Pitt	23.0	38.1	11.3	3.3	16.1	28.7	757	26.3	14.3	70.8	60.0	214	-8.6	282	2	162
Polk	20.5	50.0	9.6	1.3	33.6	13.8	192	39.6	3.1	35.9	72.4	26	-4.8	136	0	10
Randolph	47.5	31.6	8.8	1.9	13.0	8.9	1 350	37.2	3.1	46.8	73.0	154	-5.9	114	1	76
Richmond	38.5	39.2	9.1	1.6	11.6	12.6	214	30.8	9.3	50.9	65.9	55	-4.1	256	2	28
Robeson	36.9	36.1	10.6	3.2	14.9	17.2	1 476	37.5	10.3	60.5	59.4	305	-1.7	207	1	219
Rockingham	50.2	31.1	8.2	1.6	14.0	10.2	1 056	33.2	3.7	51.1	65.2	137	-7.2	130	5	61
Rowan	35.2	40.8	14.8	2.1	14.6	15.3	823	35.8	4.7	37.9	75.9	108	-15.9	131	1	69
Rutherford	47.2	35.5	9.6	2.5	12.4	10.5	503	31.0	2.6	33.8	75.0	58	-13.9	115	0	28
Sampson	26.6	32.8	9.0	1.9	13.2	17.3	1 477	36.9	8.9	61.1	63.8	264	0.2	178	8	182
Scotland	51.6	32.2	9.1	1.6	16.5	9.7	123	31.7	24.4	61.8	59.3	60	-32.9	488	0	45
Stanly	48.1	30.9	10.1	1.8	12.3	10.7	572	36.0	8.6	41.1	68.9	97	-16.3	169	0	70
Stokes	18.2	38.8	10.5	2.0	15.8	21.4	1 153	43.5	1.6	46.2	67.4	102	-15.8	89	1	43
Surry	40.7	34.8	10.8	2.0	11.4	10.3	1 314	42.5	2.4	51.1	69.7	133	-8.1	101	2	68
Swain	19.0	52.3	14.3	1.1	31.7	22.1	79	55.7	5.1	39.2	69.6	7	NA	92	0	2
Transylvania	52.1	30.8	9.5	2.5	14.2	8.6	196	50.5	1.0	36.7	73.0	14	-19.3	73	0	8
Tyrrell	39.5	NA	9.7	NA	4.0	15.8	120	18.3	24.2	65.8	57.5	62	-9.3	517	D	54
Union	35.1	32.6	9.1	2.7	11.2	9.3	1 086	46.6	6.5	50.2	74.2	170	-15.9	157	1	125

1. Covers mining, construction, and manufacturing. 2. Covers private sector earnings in agricultural services, forestry, and fisheries; transportation and public utilities; wholesale trade; retail trade; finance, insurance, and real estate; and services.

STATE County	Agriculture, 1987 (cont'd)								Manufactures, 1987						
	Value of land and buildings		Value of products sold				Percent of farms with sales of		Establishments		All employees			Production workers	
					Percent from										
	Average per farm ($1,000)	Average per acre (Dollars)	Total (Mil dol)	Average per farm (Dollars)	Crops	Livestock and poultry[1]	$10,000 or more	$100,000 or more	Total	Percent with 20 or more employees	Number (1,000)	Percent change, 1982–1987	Annual payroll (Mil dol)	Number (1,000)	Work hours (Mil)
	119	120	121	122	123	124	125	126	127	128	129	130	131	132	133
NORTH CAROLINA—Con.															
Craven	236	1 082	38	92 624	54.6	45.4	59.9	21.9	82	36.6	D	D	D	D	D
Cumberland	182	964	24	45 200	62.6	37.4	42.6	9.9	146	43.8	11.6	12.6	274.8	8.8	17.0
Currituck	582	1 300	12	117 912	56.1	43.9	60.4	23.6	8	12.5	0.1	0.0	0.7	0.1	0.1
Dare	960	D	D	D	NA	NA	100.0	50.0	29	20.7	0.5	150.0	7.2	0.4	0.6
Davidson	165	1 776	17	15 904	29.5	70.5	22.7	3.4	294	45.2	21.4	0.0	354.9	18.1	35.9
Davie	192	1 413	18	28 349	15.8	84.2	28.9	9.6	47	55.3	D	D	D	D	D
Duplin	162	1 037	215	140 343	19.2	80.8	64.6	29.7	63	38.1	4.5	21.6	68.1	3.8	8.2
Durham	206	2 000	4	15 956	84.3	15.7	32.5	3.0	185	36.2	27.7	25.9	807.0	9.8	16.0
Edgecombe	385	994	56	125 250	63.9	36.1	75.9	33.2	43	69.8	6.0	0.0	102.6	4.7	9.5
Forsyth	177	2 579	8	11 073	64.8	35.2	24.1	2.4	365	40.0	45.4	-5.6	1 212.9	26.8	47.4
Franklin	253	1 406	39	58 635	50.8	49.2	52.1	12.9	52	46.2	D	D	D	D	D
Gaston	230	1 943	7	21 699	21.2	78.7	17.6	6.2	477	44.4	38.4	4.3	700.4	31.4	64.1
Gates	306	1 051	21	82 113	48.7	51.3	63.3	25.5	13	30.8	0.2	0.0	3.1	0.2	0.4
Graham	79	1 670	D	D	NA	NA	12.2	1.4	11	27.3	0.8	0.0	9.2	0.7	1.3
Granville	198	1 041	25	29 277	68.1	31.9	50.6	6.3	51	49.0	4.5	15.4	82.7	3.6	7.2
Greene	293	1 369	81	159 069	35.0	65.0	83.1	27.8	14	71.4	0.9	28.6	10.3	0.7	1.4
Guilford	231	2 106	28	24 277	57.3	42.7	30.6	6.5	917	46.5	56.9	0.2	1 211.2	39.6	78.9
Halifax	409	849	70	162 700	48.8	51.2	69.4	36.4	90	43.3	6.0	3.4	107.4	5.1	10.4
Harnett	204	1 434	38	43 566	78.6	21.4	51.2	12.5	77	39.0	4.5	-4.3	75.1	3.7	7.4
Haywood	146	1 908	12	13 217	37.7	62.3	21.8	2.7	34	38.2	D	D	D	D	D
Henderson	249	2 045	35	58 457	75.1	24.9	44.1	10.8	122	32.8	7.3	-16.1	166.1	5.4	11.4
Hertford	297	1 020	25	90 973	63.6	36.4	76.0	24.7	42	45.2	1.8	-30.8	28.0	1.3	2.5
Hoke	278	781	25	127 252	42.6	57.4	49.7	17.6	17	35.3	4.1	5.1	65.7	3.7	8.5
Hyde	595	930	19	118 919	78.8	21.2	82.8	36.8	7	42.9	0.1	0.0	1.0	0.1	0.1
Iredell	182	1 441	57	46 986	6.6	93.4	36.0	15.3	213	51.2	17.6	20.5	310.8	13.6	27.5
Jackson	156	2 534	2	7 910	59.6	40.4	9.4	2.1	31	25.8	1.1	-21.4	14.7	0.9	1.6
Johnston	197	1 436	82	48 043	72.5	27.5	52.9	13.3	123	43.9	8.4	2.4	135.5	6.1	11.0
Jones	289	1 016	16	62 550	81.8	18.2	60.1	19.4	20	20.0	0.8	0.0	10.4	0.6	1.3
Lee	185	1 320	13	37 814	53.1	46.9	47.0	5.8	95	44.2	7.0	-5.4	120.7	5.5	10.7
Lenoir	276	1 224	65	97 696	51.5	48.5	67.3	25.0	71	56.3	7.7	-8.3	148.2	5.7	11.4
Lincoln	139	1 247	13	27 930	22.9	77.1	26.0	7.9	110	43.6	7.8	30.0	128.9	6.4	12.5
McDowell	114	1 264	4	18 801	29.0	71.0	19.0	5.6	68	44.1	9.1	-4.2	148.9	7.3	14.8
Macon	167	2 231	4	14 017	33.5	66.6	19.2	2.8	40	20.0	1.1	10.0	13.4	0.9	1.8
Madison	96	1 319	8	6 025	65.4	34.6	12.5	0.4	19	26.3	0.3	-70.0	3.7	0.3	0.5
Martin	247	1 080	47	79 527	73.7	26.3	75.5	23.0	33	36.4	2.9	61.1	37.7	2.5	4.6
Mecklenburg	295	2 752	25	72 491	73.9	26.1	23.6	7.2	1 048	35.9	53.6	15.8	1 315.2	29.6	59.8
Mitchell	80	1 178	2	5 592	71.6	28.4	12.3	0.3	20	25.0	2.0	25.0	28.5	1.9	3.8
Montgomery	193	1 076	22	89 212	15.6	84.4	42.3	19.5	88	42.0	6.2	31.9	86.2	5.5	10.2
Moore	144	1 294	63	82 817	18.7	81.3	50.5	24.6	103	37.9	6.7	4.7	99.6	5.7	11.3
Nash	356	1 300	113	162 871	50.1	49.9	64.7	29.6	120	57.5	13.8	19.0	229.2	11.6	23.4
New Hanover	224	1 643	D	D	NA	NA	43.1	4.6	154	35.1	11.1	-5.1	285.0	7.5	15.7
Northampton	270	768	54	119 411	50.3	49.7	74.6	31.9	26	42.3	0.9	-18.2	13.5	0.8	1.5
Onslow	183	1 201	30	69 752	43.7	56.3	49.5	16.1	48	29.2	3.0	25.0	40.1	2.6	4.9
Orange	316	1 739	20	38 920	26.8	73.2	37.0	11.5	76	23.7	D	D	D	D	D
Pamlico	390	869	12	139 496	87.5	12.5	66.3	32.6	16	37.5	0.3	-25.0	2.8	0.3	0.4
Pasquotank	514	1 298	22	99 121	94.2	5.8	72.9	21.8	34	29.4	1.1	22.2	22.2	0.8	2.0
Pender	162	891	27	68 007	59.5	40.5	48.6	15.0	22	36.4	0.6	0.0	7.7	0.5	0.9
Perquimans	319	1 077	20	72 975	56.7	43.3	72.4	21.0	14	14.3	0.5	400.0	4.2	0.5	0.8
Person	216	1 080	19	33 894	72.7	27.3	48.8	9.2	37	54.1	4.6	27.8	74.5	3.7	7.8
Pitt	364	1 332	100	131 563	57.6	42.4	73.1	30.6	103	37.9	8.0	19.4	178.9	6.1	11.4
Polk	160	1 263	4	20 214	23.3	76.7	21.9	3.6	33	33.3	1.0	11.1	14.8	0.8	1.6
Randolph	146	1 406	88	64 991	9.4	90.6	40.4	19.9	286	46.2	19.5	-10.1	298.3	16.1	30.9
Richmond	164	729	22	103 351	25.4	74.6	57.0	26.2	70	55.7	6.8	19.3	104.6	5.9	12.6
Robeson	181	869	73	49 207	81.8	18.2	56.4	12.8	128	50.8	14.7	16.7	208.1	12.7	24.5
Rockingham	157	1 156	23	21 836	82.4	17.6	40.0	4.6	111	55.0	14.6	-8.8	328.9	11.6	24.0
Rowan	152	1 292	29	34 860	21.2	78.8	22.7	8.0	156	53.8	14.3	2.1	284.8	11.4	23.1
Rutherford	129	982	5	10 603	16.7	83.3	14.7	2.0	90	47.8	10.4	5.1	181.9	9.0	19.0
Sampson	182	1 043	187	126 833	31.5	68.5	61.9	21.5	58	51.7	4.9	4.3	70.8	4.0	7.5
Scotland	357	723	25	204 301	33.4	66.6	53.7	21.1	51	62.7	8.2	17.1	163.0	7.1	15.5
Stanly	179	1 121	37	64 659	18.5	81.5	33.6	11.4	103	53.4	9.7	-4.0	168.5	8.2	16.8
Stokes	103	1 253	16	14 194	74.1	25.9	36.9	1.0	34	26.5	1.2	0.0	20.6	1.0	2.0
Surry	140	1 303	45	34 172	37.6	62.4	39.0	7.8	127	47.2	15.5	0.6	224.2	13.6	25.6
Swain	153	1 663	2	25 928	22.3	77.7	17.7	3.8	9	55.6	0.9	12.5	9.2	0.8	1.3
Transylvania	151	1 985	4	21 899	54.3	45.7	28.6	3.6	20	30.0	D	D	D	D	D
Tyrrell	520	1 000	20	163 971	59.5	40.5	66.7	31.7	9	44.4	0.2	0.0	2.3	0.2	0.3
Union	266	1 587	171	157 171	8.4	91.6	48.3	30.8	147	49.7	12.5	19.0	210.2	10.2	19.8

1. Includes livestock and poultry products.

STATE County	Manufactures, 1987 (cont'd): Production workers (cont'd): Wages: Total (Mil dol)	Manufactures, 1987 (cont'd): Production workers (cont'd): Wages: Average per worker (Dollars)	Manufactures, 1987 (cont'd): Value added by manufacture (Mil dol)	Manufactures, 1987 (cont'd): Value of shipments (Mil dol)	Manufactures, 1987 (cont'd): New capital expenditures (Mil dol)	Value of construction authorized by building permits, 1990: Total[1] ($1,000)	Nonresidential: Total ($1,000)	Nonresidential: Percent: Office	Nonresidential: Percent: Industrial	Nonresidential: Percent: Stores	Residential: New construction ($1,000)	Residential: Number of housing units	Residential: Alterations and additions ($1,000)
	134	135	136	137	138	139	140	141	142	143	144	145	146
NORTH CAROLINA—Con.													
Craven	D	D	D	D	D	63 818	13 532	10.5	0.7	50.9	42 409	417	2 501
Cumberland	196.8	22 364	1 002.8	2 051.4	66.6	118 470	28 912	24.3	2.3	26.3	61 805	1 218	7 710
Currituck	0.6	6 000	1.2	2.9	0.0	22 959	1 674	19.8	0.0	3.0	20 693	190	371
Dare	5.0	12 500	11.9	28.0	0.4	31 672	3 766	25.1	0.0	23.9	24 292	377	1 832
Davidson	265.2	14 652	800.0	1 486.7	47.6	70 656	16 355	10.9	18.5	33.3	42 639	812	3 260
Davie	D	D	D	D	D	15 948	3 278	0.0	6.1	0.0	10 452	129	882
Duplin	53.0	13 947	127.9	361.6	16.7	16 744	12 116	4.5	41.7	21.1	4 135	92	378
Durham	215.2	21 959	2 094.2	4 907.4	122.2	278 082	98 373	47.8	8.1	21.4	122 860	1 686	7 635
Edgecombe	68.9	14 660	339.8	729.7	10.8	17 494	9 964	29.6	43.3	21.5	4 549	109	1 309
Forsyth	621.6	23 194	5 469.7	8 676.8	340.5	206 237	54 262	15.7	4.8	4.1	93 662	1 309	11 532
Franklin	D	D	D	D	D	15 640	2 373	12.1	6.5	6.1	10 499	233	2 588
Gaston	499.0	15 892	1 548.1	3 849.9	102.4	133 935	32 643	9.1	20.8	41.3	67 352	1 013	6 547
Gates	2.8	14 000	4.6	15.2	0.4	NA	NA	NA	NA	NA	NA	NA	NA
Graham	7.9	11 286	23.2	38.8	0.2	0	0	NA	NA	NA	0	0	0
Granville	58.2	16 167	367.1	634.7	15.6	15 531	5 388	0.0	0.0	91.5	7 458	102	1 250
Greene	7.7	11 000	24.7	38.6	1.0	7 214	4 838	0.0	100.0	0.0	1 932	30	411
Guilford	685.9	17 321	3 559.1	6 147.8	142.5	360 488	117 746	25.9	9.8	46.1	155 573	2 162	15 148
Halifax	85.5	16 765	316.2	743.0	21.3	18 013	4 243	3.3	7.9	56.3	8 626	206	2 143
Harnett	53.3	14 405	201.6	405.4	18.7	22 893	4 732	17.6	3.2	43.7	15 412	356	1 823
Haywood	D	D	D	D	D	128 515	103 922	0.2	96.3	3.1	17 191	262	2 102
Henderson	109.5	20 278	545.3	1 007.5	31.8	63 918	8 743	14.6	38.0	15.3	46 019	504	2 992
Hertford	18.5	14 231	65.1	255.9	2.7	4 822	273	0.0	0.0	40.0	3 856	113	520
Hoke	56.3	15 216	247.0	515.5	6.8	6 042	1 949	5.3	32.4	35.6	3 617	58	257
Hyde	0.6	6 000	3.6	8.0	D	3 825	1 615	7.7	0.0	0.0	1 892	29	240
Iredell	207.5	15 257	826.4	1 631.8	37.2	103 625	38 230	4.9	40.8	36.7	49 965	629	4 649
Jackson	12.2	13 556	33.6	70.7	D	21 755	937	45.6	1.6	16.4	17 569	233	2 982
Johnston	79.8	13 082	396.5	965.2	34.5	53 475	7 105	13.8	32.3	16.0	37 998	698	2 596
Jones	7.5	12 500	20.4	81.9	D	4 710	0	NA	NA	NA	4 680	76	0
Lee	82.5	15 000	379.7	739.8	18.7	37 018	6 591	17.2	66.1	9.8	10 313	139	1 101
Lenoir	89.0	15 614	448.6	923.1	32.7	34 176	12 362	9.1	29.1	42.2	9 603	157	3 700
Lincoln	90.8	14 187	285.8	628.6	13.2	44 291	22 189	57.0	11.2	8.8	20 760	300	420
McDowell	105.0	14 384	468.5	790.1	24.3	9 961	1 588	30.2	6.3	32.6	6 678	124	1 069
Macon	10.6	11 778	36.5	61.4	3.5	29 324	2 418	41.1	6.6	15.6	18 289	245	1 842
Madison	2.8	9 333	10.2	22.5	D	7 775	514	0.0	0.0	0.0	5 117	127	264
Martin	30.6	12 240	112.4	290.3	D	11 167	6 343	0.7	7.9	73.1	3 065	49	1 190
Mecklenburg	551.3	18 625	2 579.5	6 154.0	196.8	925 122	275 043	25.0	13.4	16.1	395 820	6 093	30 704
Mitchell	24.0	12 632	62.8	99.4	6.1	8 756	3 519	0.0	53.9	36.4	4 335	64	290
Montgomery	67.7	12 309	187.3	346.9	15.3	14 902	6 272	7.7	39.8	44.0	4 227	70	2 787
Moore	74.0	12 982	250.6	600.8	15.5	66 504	10 460	8.9	6.6	10.2	46 993	485	4 731
Nash	171.0	14 741	716.9	1 411.8	42.4	70 264	22 920	45.5	4.0	8.6	33 632	483	2 990
New Hanover	172.7	23 027	1 009.1	2 004.5	81.0	133 920	27 400	35.6	2.7	35.4	92 626	1 406	4 512
Northampton	10.1	12 625	50.1	134.7	1.8	7 472	2 051	0.0	3.9	0.0	4 246	52	816
Onslow	31.2	12 000	116.2	251.5	D	38 780	9 596	8.2	6.7	32.6	24 020	532	2 032
Orange	D	D	D	D	D	67 916	1 907	25.7	1.0	0.0	49 879	523	8 308
Pamlico	2.1	7 000	8.3	23.6	0.6	8 638	3 425	0.0	0.0	12.5	3 737	56	861
Pasquotank	10.5	13 125	42.4	126.9	1.7	25 959	3 760	22.8	17.4	8.0	6 767	148	1 355
Pender	5.2	10 400	17.8	42.3	1.4	19 224	4 460	0.0	38.1	49.9	13 692	207	327
Perquimans	3.8	7 600	5.4	10.9	0.1	3 962	84	0.0	0.0	0.0	3 403	50	290
Person	52.8	14 270	163.0	402.6	20.1	22 559	4 589	2.2	35.6	29.7	16 532	146	996
Pitt	104.2	17 082	985.0	1 529.2	86.1	128 971	49 667	7.6	60.8	11.1	61 868	1 161	3 250
Polk	10.5	13 125	25.3	73.7	2.5	10 048	3 692	5.0	0.0	23.1	5 742	110	451
Randolph	219.4	13 627	863.2	1 824.5	D	66 894	27 321	5.0	16.5	25.2	29 979	471	3 108
Richmond	85.0	14 407	286.2	598.4	19.6	8 948	2 042	3.1	50.4	10.6	5 631	132	530
Robeson	157.4	12 394	693.4	1 366.6	30.0	40 132	17 219	4.8	64.6	9.6	12 466	162	3 467
Rockingham	237.3	20 457	1 453.3	2 834.3	72.4	45 794	16 748	7.0	38.9	37.3	19 300	299	2 235
Rowan	203.0	17 807	710.3	1 561.7	60.0	86 782	26 636	7.1	31.9	44.5	41 815	439	3 655
Rutherford	144.3	16 033	452.7	1 008.8	33.1	33 587	4 278	4.5	3.0	3.8	15 641	243	2 233
Sampson	49.3	12 325	141.6	553.5	8.2	18 271	3 665	25.3	27.0	30.6	7 735	144	2 524
Scotland	133.7	18 831	366.6	986.0	34.9	15 097	4 762	3.7	77.6	7.5	6 488	83	895
Stanly	127.8	15 585	386.0	942.7	43.3	25 180	5 129	0.4	1.6	75.8	11 888	198	1 856
Stokes	14.4	14 400	36.0	104.2	D	16 560	3 437	5.8	3.5	5.9	10 895	145	1 001
Surry	175.7	12 919	476.0	1 023.6	47.5	41 941	16 008	18.3	52.5	15.2	11 311	187	2 463
Swain	6.8	8 500	21.6	48.3	0.3	3 466	487	0.0	0.0	5.1	2 574	88	297
Transylvania	D	D	D	D	D	26 112	2 730	5.1	11.7	32.8	20 491	186	1 665
Tyrrell	1.8	9 000	4.5	11.1	1.2	889	0	NA	NA	NA	808	10	75
Union	143.5	14 069	693.3	1 410.4	41.4	83 005	17 835	11.0	11.4	52.2	52 127	992	3 493

1. Includes nonresidential additions and alterations, residential nonhousekeeping buildings, and residential garages and carports not shown separately.

STATE County	Wholesale trade, 1987				Retail trade, all establishments, 1987				Retail trade, establishments with payroll, 1987					
						Sales				Sales				
											Per capita[2] (Dollars)			
	Estab-lishments	Sales (Mil dol)	Paid employees[1]	Annual payroll (Mil dol)	Number	Total (Mil dol)	Percent change, 1982–1987	Per capita[2] (Dollars)	Number	Total (Mil dol)	General merchan-dise stores	Food stores	Apparel & acces-sory stores	Eating and drinking places
	147	148	149	150	151	152	153	154	155	156	157	158	159	160
NORTH CAROLINA—Con.														
Craven	96	204.0	925	18.2	851	485.8	52.2	6 050	556	474.3	720	1 220	181	468
Cumberland	268	564.5	2 722	48.3	2 123	1 544.6	58.6	6 017	1 468	1 519.7	869	993	236	546
Currituck	9	7.2	39	0.5	126	62.3	174.4	4 549	66	60.5	D	637	D	147
Dare	34	74.9	275	4.1	571	247.1	115.1	12 356	445	242.3	1 004	3 289	553	2 197
Davidson	144	542.5	1 601	29.8	1 147	550.7	57.0	4 478	625	519.7	263	987	157	384
Davie	33	53.9	239	3.5	273	95.8	60.5	3 483	129	88.6	D	884	52	238
Duplin	63	369.9	706	12.3	466	164.5	40.8	3 945	269	152.1	244	1 120	128	244
Durham	231	1 006.3	3 073	69.3	1 612	1 225.2	63.9	7 241	1 199	1 207.8	951	1 340	394	729
Edgecombe	52	108.1	417	7.6	399	195.6	20.6	3 288	261	189.0	254	949	65	208
Forsyth	560	2 011.1	7 335	152.3	2 967	2 174.0	60.9	8 222	1 910	2 123.4	888	1 286	507	788
Franklin	37	84.7	409	6.8	270	106.5	69.9	3 035	167	100.3	131	751	101	244
Gaston	268	950.7	2 176	48.4	1 600	1 028.6	62.4	5 959	968	996.5	728	1 297	216	478
Gates	13	18.2	80	1.5	72	25.7	83.6	2 653	42	24.1	81	893	0	79
Graham	5	D	D	D	90	20.8	56.4	2 932	42	16.8	D	774	53	240
Granville	32	144.1	255	5.6	320	146.1	72.3	3 824	187	136.0	208	1 036	165	267
Greene	20	22.3	156	1.8	114	33.2	79.5	2 014	67	30.0	D	393	D	143
Guilford	1 289	6 423.1	16 575	411.4	3 736	2 978.1	68.8	8 938	2 576	2 911.8	1 052	1 344	469	887
Halifax	76	124.5	816	12.9	609	290.1	32.6	5 126	414	281.4	673	1 157	227	382
Harnett	72	158.4	640	10.3	600	251.3	44.3	3 854	323	239.5	410	910	97	251
Haywood	47	50.9	262	3.7	594	308.8	51.5	6 433	356	299.8	410	1 301	194	487
Henderson	91	208.6	1 035	17.3	837	505.4	66.0	7 454	483	490.2	577	1 261	336	535
Hertford	47	90.0	404	6.0	267	134.7	52.7	5 660	186	130.3	520	1 559	156	409
Hoke	6	7.5	30	0.5	130	49.0	65.0	2 048	84	46.8	169	1 002	33	111
Hyde	24	40.2	202	2.4	99	22.5	125.0	3 877	57	20.3	439	1 250	D	520
Iredell	161	600.1	1 543	30.2	965	522.7	66.0	5 814	613	507.4	470	1 187	268	540
Jackson	17	16.1	79	1.0	361	120.7	44.6	4 486	208	114.4	D	1 430	178	417
Johnston	130	851.6	922	15.2	907	455.7	63.6	5 740	543	430.0	270	1 099	257	431
Jones	15	18.0	119	1.8	96	20.6	21.9	2 099	43	18.2	D	604	0	D
Lee	78	260.5	857	17.8	570	349.7	86.0	8 488	372	341.3	662	1 740	376	603
Lenoir	96	452.5	1 399	19.2	733	382.5	50.0	6 333	448	369.7	726	1 375	316	464
Lincoln	62	204.9	665	9.9	540	226.5	79.6	4 799	295	214.7	237	969	165	370
McDowell	27	74.3	251	3.5	374	166.3	46.8	4 581	217	158.1	346	1 158	121	409
Macon	23	15.0	107	1.6	426	137.2	44.1	5 913	235	129.6	461	1 529	306	600
Madison	4	3.7	38	0.6	145	38.5	41.5	2 228	66	33.4	146	569	D	132
Martin	59	226.8	427	7.5	284	123.1	53.3	4 646	177	119.3	483	982	145	457
Mecklenburg	2 438	23 121.7	33 845	905.3	4 958	4 218.7	68.6	9 074	3 413	4 144.7	881	1 486	546	933
Mitchell	10	40.1	134	1.6	165	71.4	53.9	4 924	92	66.6	D	1 208	180	387
Montgomery	21	10.7	87	1.1	247	91.5	62.2	3 783	133	85.9	141	931	74	311
Moore	89	130.4	517	7.6	717	359.7	82.4	6 256	433	345.0	360	1 366	286	454
Nash	159	769.2	2 173	41.9	1 039	581.2	61.8	8 039	654	560.6	1 068	1 301	331	751
New Hanover	282	820.8	3 110	60.7	1 607	972.1	57.9	8 359	1 088	947.9	1 100	1 516	468	910
Northampton	36	68.2	303	4.0	163	50.4	44.4	2 249	87	48.1	D	635	D	58
Onslow	85	101.5	523	8.0	1 101	663.7	59.8	5 272	761	651.7	629	888	181	546
Orange	72	171.1	629	14.1	815	525.7	78.0	6 092	547	514.0	301	1 606	208	704
Pamlico	18	41.9	287	3.1	96	30.7	14.6	2 814	50	29.0	D	1 112	D	223
Pasquotank	67	141.1	675	10.7	316	253.6	64.4	8 343	232	251.2	774	1 685	362	513
Pender	25	55.6	200	3.8	246	68.0	38.2	2 586	128	62.3	111	882	49	112
Perquimans	18	32.8	114	1.5	98	28.4	42.0	2 655	62	26.7	D	549	50	370
Person	33	58.0	300	5.2	293	149.8	53.5	4 831	188	145.0	262	1 290	231	357
Pitt	172	752.2	1 942	41.5	1 055	743.2	73.2	7 432	703	727.3	677	1 327	317	649
Polk	14	19.3	39	0.7	185	48.7	42.8	3 337	95	45.6	136	944	43	262
Randolph	132	230.4	1 074	19.4	980	443.7	65.9	4 402	502	412.5	357	893	238	316
Richmond	78	80.4	444	6.7	513	232.3	44.2	5 072	322	226.0	726	1 200	244	406
Robeson	114	311.3	1 126	18.2	985	520.7	51.3	4 853	595	502.6	296	986	541	364
Rockingham	76	310.8	557	10.4	905	430.3	47.0	5 009	521	410.9	359	1 257	286	388
Rowan	126	376.7	1 415	26.0	947	509.8	24.9	4 860	569	493.5	393	1 189	229	426
Rutherford	73	92.1	464	6.8	711	331.7	61.0	5 789	368	292.2	550	1 094	183	371
Sampson	74	150.7	539	8.3	479	195.2	38.0	3 859	270	185.0	447	827	103	267
Scotland	37	68.4	368	5.9	291	166.8	32.8	4 862	209	162.1	608	1 164	96	510
Stanly	73	142.0	575	10.6	602	274.0	69.3	5 416	373	263.5	474	1 265	151	357
Stokes	19	9.8	68	1.1	322	92.2	59.2	2 548	128	78.9	84	707	56	183
Surry	95	220.1	747	10.9	912	447.3	55.2	7 238	479	415.3	595	1 444	350	402
Swain	9	8.9	53	1.0	207	58.7	32.5	5 484	141	55.7	D	1 490	89	945
Transylvania	16	8.6	76	0.9	263	114.9	43.3	4 420	158	109.7	299	1 239	138	305
Tyrrell	10	9.9	36	0.4	53	11.1	60.9	2 697	29	10.2	D	D	52	131
Union	137	288.1	1 347	30.1	694	390.7	67.2	4 776	415	376.6	522	970	200	330

1. For pay period including March 12. 2. Based on the estimated population as of July 1 of the year shown.

STATE County	Retail trade, establishments with payroll, 1987 (cont'd)		Taxable service industries–establishments with payroll, 1987							Bank deposits,[2] June 1989		Savings capital,[3] September 1989	
				Receipts (Mil dol)									
					Selected kinds of business								
	Paid employees[1]	Annual payroll (Mil dol)	Number	Total	Hotels, motels and other lodging places	Health services	Legal services	Paid employees	Annual payroll (Mil dol)	Total (Mil dol)	Percent change, 1988–1989	Total (Mil dol)	Percent change, 1988–1989
	161	162	163	164	165	166	167	168	169	170	171	172	173
NORTH CAROLINA—Con.													
Craven	5 736	52.6	412	123.2	5.9	52.4	11.0	3 269	50.0	476	17.0	69.6	24.7
Cumberland	18 196	175.7	1 108	418.0	35.9	140.8	22.5	11 860	149.7	940	13.9	241.8	-2.3
Currituck	490	5.0	36	6.6	2.4	2.2	0.3	144	1.5	38	-3.3	0.0	NA
Dare	3 137	31.1	256	66.7	30.9	6.8	6.1	1 585	19.8	253	26.8	136.3	5.0
Davidson	5 933	56.4	403	89.2	D	31.0	6.5	2 385	32.9	713	8.1	324.3	3.0
Davie	954	9.0	109	25.9	D	7.3	0.9	730	8.5	143	25.4	79.0	5.6
Duplin	1 890	16.0	151	21.8	D	9.2	1.7	836	7.5	183	15.9	73.2	1.0
Durham	15 779	149.5	1 215	529.6	38.6	94.7	25.4	14 564	215.4	1 420	8.7	489.3	0.9
Edgecombe	2 316	20.8	147	67.3	D	27.0	2.2	1 625	19.8	167	12.7	56.6	-1.1
Forsyth	25 619	250.7	1 818	862.5	65.2	225.3	74.8	22 071	339.4	5 817	33.6	1 089.3	5.9
Franklin	1 283	9.9	105	28.3	D	12.1	1.3	686	9.2	89	12.5	68.6	6.9
Gaston	11 320	107.2	783	213.0	3.7	72.0	11.4	10 507	84.6	1 019	14.5	342.2	0.0
Gates	320	2.5	17	3.9	0.0	D	D	78	1.1	63	5.8	0.0	NA
Graham	192	1.7	26	8.4	0.9	D	0.4	208	2.5	59	20.8	0.0	NA
Granville	1 566	14.0	136	24.0	D	7.0	2.0	962	8.1	203	12.5	48.5	4.2
Greene	357	3.2	41	7.4	0.0	3.7	D	298	2.9	42	4.3	24.8	2.8
Guilford	35 149	356.6	2 774	1 130.5	64.3	274.2	63.0	28 534	433.3	2 798	10.9	1 513.6	-2.5
Halifax	3 509	31.5	241	49.3	5.3	18.6	2.3	1 319	17.0	242	10.3	179.7	8.0
Harnett	2 839	25.6	240	56.8	1.9	12.4	4.7	2 098	24.3	299	12.2	126.0	13.3
Haywood	3 052	31.0	316	66.2	8.6	26.5	3.0	1 759	25.0	247	19.9	192.9	-2.5
Henderson	4 914	50.2	435	112.2	15.9	39.9	5.3	3 376	44.2	455	21.5	398.4	15.0
Hertford	1 648	14.2	116	28.4	1.6	12.0	2.0	588	8.0	178	12.3	27.9	0.6
Hoke	583	5.3	51	7.4	0.0	1.6	0.7	230	2.4	54	8.9	28.8	-8.7
Hyde	254	2.2	21	3.3	1.5	0.6	D	88	0.8	44	15.1	0.0	NA
Iredell	6 391	56.5	472	159.3	13.8	69.6	6.0	3 769	59.8	650	18.2	305.6	1.7
Jackson	1 327	12.8	143	26.1	5.5	10.5	1.8	681	10.2	166	12.8	41.0	1.6
Johnston	4 451	42.7	343	71.9	8.9	17.1	5.5	2 947	27.6	361	13.1	137.4	6.8
Jones	174	1.7	27	5.6	0.0	D	D	108	1.8	40	6.7	0.0	NA
Lee	3 731	36.1	251	68.8	D	35.2	2.9	1 787	25.3	293	9.8	168.5	0.2
Lenoir	4 470	39.1	340	105.0	4.1	41.2	4.8	3 282	45.1	311	11.5	184.3	0.6
Lincoln	2 369	22.6	209	38.5	1.0	11.3	2.5	1 058	12.8	235	19.2	135.7	1.9
McDowell	1 955	17.1	120	27.2	2.3	10.2	1.6	851	10.8	150	21.0	76.9	2.9
Macon	1 552	14.2	155	23.7	3.3	6.0	2.2	608	8.4	192	47.8	127.8	3.3
Madison	418	3.3	40	5.9	D	3.4	0.3	222	2.1	93	9.7	15.0	-5.1
Martin	1 577	13.9	91	14.1	2.0	6.2	0.5	454	4.7	147	10.9	41.9	-8.6
Mecklenburg	47 914	484.4	4 406	2 487.4	167.1	481.2	143.8	56 918	970.5	7 943	8.2	1 335.0	-0.2
Mitchell	735	6.6	65	12.8	0.3	6.6	0.6	213	4.8	134	20.1	19.7	-0.9
Montgomery	1 113	9.2	91	14.7	D	4.5	0.7	456	4.8	123	1.2	49.0	3.8
Moore	3 603	36.6	332	154.7	39.3	64.4	5.5	4 304	65.0	459	12.2	269.7	5.9
Nash	6 781	62.1	457	176.9	17.1	51.3	12.5	3 923	60.4	698	10.9	337.4	-3.8
New Hanover	12 350	113.2	983	399.6	25.0	89.8	17.4	9 838	174.5	937	16.9	340.7	-1.0
Northampton	555	4.9	49	9.7	D	3.1	0.5	277	2.7	79	9.6	0.0	NA
Onslow	8 422	75.8	451	116.9	10.5	40.6	7.9	3 517	39.5	343	13.4	50.8	-3.6
Orange	7 512	64.5	538	156.3	D	55.0	8.8	3 564	52.0	561	12.1	159.5	-2.7
Pamlico	347	3.2	25	3.5	D	D	D	89	1.2	75	11.1	0.0	NA
Pasquotank	2 783	27.2	191	41.3	3.2	17.1	4.5	1 055	15.3	254	11.5	188.0	12.6
Pender	706	6.2	78	13.2	D	3.7	1.1	307	2.9	108	20.8	17.6	-0.1
Perquimans	387	3.6	27	3.0	0.0	1.0	0.7	94	1.1	51	14.0	7.1	-7.1
Person	1 578	14.4	119	16.6	0.6	5.9	1.5	461	5.0	171	21.1	94.4	4.6
Pitt	9 084	79.3	554	166.6	8.5	70.5	9.5	4 561	70.9	648	14.0	206.1	3.4
Polk	540	4.9	83	13.1	2.0	5.7	0.8	544	5.5	121	10.0	76.6	7.0
Randolph	4 739	44.2	392	87.0	D	25.7	3.9	2 456	32.7	541	16.7	312.9	-6.6
Richmond	2 791	25.7	197	39.1	2.1	14.1	2.4	1 032	12.8	174	14.7	107.8	-7.4
Robeson	5 496	53.4	384	86.0	8.3	34.1	5.7	2 126	28.8	496	7.4	139.8	3.4
Rockingham	4 867	44.7	348	81.8	3.4	29.1	3.5	2 260	31.0	594	18.5	221.5	-0.4
Rowan	6 124	55.5	447	100.1	5.1	39.7	4.6	2 712	38.8	566	8.7	328.9	2.3
Rutherford	3 288	31.2	215	48.6	1.4	18.7	1.8	1 350	17.3	361	17.9	156.0	-3.1
Sampson	2 112	19.1	178	47.2	D	10.8	2.4	1 605	19.8	218	16.9	88.3	-1.1
Scotland	2 034	19.0	148	35.8	D	9.8	2.3	1 364	15.5	144	11.1	42.7	-0.1
Stanly	3 095	27.5	218	37.7	1.2	14.4	2.4	1 144	13.9	334	16.4	204.0	-5.7
Stokes	892	8.8	102	16.9	D	3.9	1.0	393	5.2	128	28.7	26.4	10.0
Surry	4 401	43.3	312	60.0	D	24.5	3.8	1 486	21.6	484	23.8	294.7	2.6
Swain	756	7.0	91	19.9	10.3	3.6	D	384	5.8	73	18.3	0.0	NA
Transylvania	1 366	11.7	153	29.5	4.6	9.2	1.8	809	10.0	143	17.9	133.7	4.2
Tyrrell	132	1.1	9	1.0	D	0.5	D	25	0.3	13	9.3	7.8	23.0
Union	4 086	39.8	325	78.6	2.4	24.8	3.9	1 745	29.4	433	19.2	294.7	16.7

1. For the period including March 12 of the year shown. 2. Includes deposits for all insured and reporting noninsured commercial and mutual savings banks. 3. Includes savings capital for all FSLIC insured savings institutions.

STATE County	Federal funds and grants, 1989							Local government finances, 1981–1982							
	Expenditures		Per capita[1] (Dollars)					General revenue						Direct general expenditure	
									Intergovernmental		Taxes				
												Per capita[2]			
	Total (Mil dol)	Percent change, 1988–1989	Total	Direct payments for individuals	Procurement contract awards	Salaries and wages	Grant awards	Total (Mil dol)	Total (Mil dol)	Percent from state	Total (Mil dol)	Total (Dollars)	Property (Dollars)	Total (Mil dol)	Percent change, 1977–1982
	174	175	176	177	178	179	180	181	182	183	184	185	186	187	188
NORTH CAROLINA—Con.															
Craven	574.8	-4.1	6 993	1 832	907	3 972	260	74.7	32.3	88.6	11.8	161	120	74.4	120.7
Cumberland	1 998.0	3.8	7 808	1 597	573	5 348	276	177.8	109.6	80.4	46.3	185	150	170.9	25.6
Currituck	36.2	3.6	2 514	1 881	37	117	423	7.0	4.4	95.3	2.2	186	161	6.8	33.9
Dare	57.0	9.3	2 468	1 680	120	338	226	15.0	5.7	86.9	7.9	539	414	16.4	183.9
Davidson	194.2	7.7	1 538	1 204	125	54	147	61.9	34.1	91.6	19.4	168	139	71.1	45.8
Davie	48.0	-4.9	1 720	1 450	34	68	148	18.5	8.0	89.9	4.6	177	157	17.8	130.9
Duplin	98.0	-14.3	2 350	1 513	184	110	452	34.4	24.5	83.7	6.7	163	135	28.9	30.3
Durham	755.7	4.1	4 323	1 464	839	787	1 228	154.4	71.7	78.6	55.6	356	302	138.2	23.9
Edgecombe	124.9	0.7	2 068	1 265	53	265	406	40.9	26.3	81.5	8.6	151	125	35.9	32.8
Forsyth	668.7	20.9	2 487	1 515	150	148	668	307.9	114.7	79.0	80.6	323	265	285.6	41.2
Franklin	62.0	8.4	1 704	1 238	8	85	351	22.4	12.4	93.8	4.3	139	118	21.1	42.0
Gaston	313.7	0.9	1 793	1 434	36	77	240	116.2	69.9	91.6	33.1	199	163	119.3	32.3
Gates	22.7	2.8	2 290	1 724	20	106	328	5.5	3.9	91.0	1.2	137	124	5.3	32.0
Graham	18.0	-4.7	2 576	1 888	37	246	396	5.1	3.8	79.3	0.9	131	101	4.9	46.2
Granville	81.5	11.9	2 057	1 290	130	343	279	23.9	11.9	82.3	5.9	168	140	23.8	52.1
Greene	28.7	-9.4	1 762	1 108	70	75	345	11.1	7.3	91.0	2.8	174	158	10.0	37.6
Guilford	1 178.1	7.0	3 462	1 587	1 165	398	294	324.1	147.3	85.6	110.6	345	283	326.4	48.7
Halifax	148.9	-7.9	2 602	1 819	52	81	575	49.9	33.8	87.4	11.2	202	164	55.4	71.3
Harnett	127.5	7.0	1 892	1 411	70	66	318	47.9	26.2	90.9	9.9	163	136	42.0	57.6
Haywood	123.4	1.5	2 549	1 915	279	86	261	45.2	20.2	93.1	9.4	200	161	44.0	29.2
Henderson	206.7	13.7	2 940	2 352	38	252	229	50.7	23.2	89.3	11.1	179	133	51.2	78.9
Hertford	62.1	13.5	2 630	1 827	19	123	603	19.4	13.2	88.6	4.6	196	153	18.2	41.2
Hoke	37.7	4.3	1 539	1 041	41	84	319	12.7	8.5	79.0	3.1	146	127	13.5	32.9
Hyde	18.5	-1.0	3 295	1 861	27	295	634	5.1	3.1	88.9	1.6	265	238	4.2	53.5
Iredell	164.1	6.9	1 763	1 463	46	81	159	62.4	38.6	85.6	15.2	181	143	60.1	44.7
Jackson	57.6	8.6	2 124	1 680	13	93	332	18.2	12.5	81.7	4.1	155	121	18.0	40.8
Johnston	164.9	-12.9	2 011	1 422	72	72	399	64.5	38.1	82.1	12.2	169	138	62.4	60.9
Jones	24.6	-2.2	2 484	1 842	13	83	401	5.8	4.2	91.9	1.2	127	114	5.8	33.6
Lee	90.5	6.8	2 135	1 748	23	104	251	43.0	21.0	81.5	9.6	255	207	43.6	77.9
Lenoir	145.0	5.8	2 404	1 737	77	179	355	68.6	32.0	80.3	11.9	197	154	71.8	119.9
Lincoln	80.4	15.4	1 624	1 219	15	66	296	29.2	19.5	77.7	7.7	178	152	23.2	54.8
McDowell	84.9	7.6	2 332	1 666	104	73	476	22.1	14.7	91.1	5.4	151	119	21.1	70.1
Macon	74.4	14.4	3 167	2 524	58	245	330	12.3	7.6	89.1	3.4	158	104	11.5	41.4
Madison	43.9	15.9	2 536	1 583	13	109	816	10.6	8.1	84.5	1.9	112	94	10.7	65.6
Martin	60.2	-2.3	2 290	1 647	21	105	438	28.6	16.3	79.0	7.0	266	231	30.4	71.8
Mecklenburg	994.2	2.1	2 039	1 236	216	300	275	579.7	229.9	64.9	186.9	445	373	550.6	57.3
Mitchell	36.9	-0.2	2 512	1 904	14	103	472	12.2	8.1	92.2	2.5	176	144	11.2	23.3
Montgomery	60.6	-0.8	2 493	1 439	697	76	265	16.1	10.8	90.7	3.6	159	132	14.8	54.7
Moore	165.2	9.4	2 712	2 396	23	83	202	42.8	25.4	91.7	11.9	230	184	40.2	16.2
Nash	167.2	-2.9	2 277	1 713	208	39	294	67.3	44.0	83.8	15.0	219	165	71.9	77.1
New Hanover	309.4	1.1	2 597	1 796	250	318	229	99.5	52.5	82.3	34.3	319	252	94.6	35.5
Northampton	58.1	3.8	2 642	1 783	14	113	578	16.3	11.7	91.8	3.4	152	135	17.8	63.0
Onslow	1 133.9	1.4	8 872	1 201	675	6 794	194	70.0	36.0	86.5	14.0	121	92	62.1	45.5
Orange	268.4	9.9	2 962	1 156	173	125	1 493	59.7	29.1	64.2	22.7	290	243	56.8	85.8
Pamlico	32.8	8.8	2 980	2 448	21	119	291	7.9	5.7	91.0	1.6	155	137	7.2	34.2
Pasquotank	105.0	0.2	3 378	1 908	66	1 082	281	35.7	15.0	88.5	5.4	188	135	32.1	52.3
Pender	63.5	12.5	2 267	1 714	22	73	423	16.2	8.8	85.4	3.9	170	148	17.1	75.1
Perquimans	30.1	-13.4	2 664	2 031	13	87	354	6.4	4.2	88.2	1.6	165	147	5.8	57.1
Person	56.5	-25.0	1 777	1 328	7	71	344	28.9	14.5	88.9	7.2	243	207	28.1	56.0
Pitt	206.9	6.6	1 987	1 275	104	153	419	91.1	47.2	83.5	20.5	220	176	78.4	30.6
Polk	41.7	1.6	2 816	2 459	14	92	206	7.9	5.5	92.8	1.8	131	109	8.1	49.4
Randolph	148.3	3.2	1 418	1 192	26	69	119	58.0	36.7	91.9	14.1	151	124	52.2	57.7
Richmond	102.6	6.9	2 230	1 776	19	91	326	32.6	22.3	87.1	7.4	164	125	31.6	45.8
Robeson	225.4	6.9	2 073	1 362	42	88	527	94.2	67.6	80.7	16.2	156	123	87.1	51.9
Rockingham	186.1	-4.2	2 144	1 672	160	75	230	65.3	37.1	92.6	20.1	238	206	61.9	38.0
Rowan	239.8	5.0	2 231	1 619	64	388	150	60.6	35.1	85.0	16.8	166	133	57.8	46.5
Rutherford	115.7	6.7	1 992	1 644	14	67	251	36.2	22.1	94.2	10.3	185	152	35.2	48.1
Sampson	117.9	7.4	2 307	1 470	12	102	578	37.6	25.6	89.9	8.8	175	150	35.4	54.3
Scotland	69.0	8.4	1 972	1 319	21	66	477	27.5	17.7	67.6	6.2	186	149	27.1	58.2
Stanly	110.6	12.8	2 156	1 588	275	98	175	34.4	20.2	90.8	9.6	197	165	32.1	50.6
Stokes	46.4	6.3	1 256	1 026	9	57	155	25.1	13.0	93.9	6.0	174	157	25.6	85.5
Surry	125.5	7.2	2 008	1 653	10	90	235	53.0	26.6	89.7	12.2	204	165	49.5	92.2
Swain	55.7	6.9	5 301	2 158	1 040	981	1 117	7.7	5.5	62.0	1.2	110	73	7.1	-38.1
Transylvania	61.4	5.8	2 327	1 980	30	163	146	16.3	9.2	92.5	5.2	213	177	14.3	38.2
Tyrrell	11.5	-10.4	2 802	1 803	32	100	448	4.0	2.7	95.4	1.0	237	214	3.1	35.3
Union	130.6	5.7	1 517	1 129	87	134	141	50.0	28.3	83.1	13.6	185	152	46.1	54.1

1. Based on the estimated population as of July 1 of the year shown. 2. Based on the estimated population as of July 1, 1982.

STATE County	Local government finances, 1981–1982 (cont'd)								State and local government employment, 1989		Federal government civilian employment 1989		Elections, 1988[3]	
	Direct general expenditure (cont'd)						Debt outstanding							
		Percent of total for–												
	Per capita[1] (Dollars)	Education	Health & hospitals	Police protection	Public welfare	Highways	Total (Mil dol)	Per capita[1] (Dollars)	Total	Rate[2]	Total	Earnings ($1,000)	Total vote cast for president	Vote for lead party (Percent)
	189	190	191	192	193	194	195	196	197	198	199	200	201	202
NORTH CAROLINA—Con.														
Craven	1 010	41.6	35.8	3.1	3.5	0.9	28.1	381	5 388	655.5	5 887	178 671	19 417	R–62.1
Cumberland	685	61.1	3.0	5.3	4.3	1.3	72.5	291	14 568	569.3	9 370	256 118	50 979	R–53.1
Currituck	583	75.0	2.4	3.3	3.0	0.0	2.7	233	659	457.6	56	1 412	4 006	R–61.0
Dare	1 116	47.5	3.2	7.6	2.1	3.1	15.3	1 044	1 469	635.9	186	3 387	8 071	R–64.8
Davidson	617	67.7	3.0	4.8	2.4	1.9	31.2	271	5 136	406.7	183	5 300	41 662	R–68.1
Davie	689	51.9	26.8	3.3	2.6	0.4	12.1	469	1 278	458.1	55	1 431	11 192	R–71.4
Duplin	705	69.2	2.8	4.5	3.2	1.7	11.0	269	2 387	572.4	125	3 320	11 726	D–50.7
Durham	886	50.6	5.5	7.8	3.4	3.6	79.1	507	12 297	703.5	4 404	153 860	65 883	D–53.8
Edgecombe	629	59.4	3.4	3.6	5.5	1.5	20.4	358	3 814	631.5	339	10 740	15 916	D–56.8
Forsyth	1 143	34.7	25.6	5.9	3.1	3.5	191.2	765	13 080	486.4	1 096	35 299	97 735	R–59.0
Franklin	686	57.9	22.8	3.2	2.5	1.0	3.9	126	1 376	378.0	71	1 850	10 960	R–50.2
Gaston	717	60.9	1.9	6.1	3.2	3.2	65.0	391	7 170	409.7	346	10 826	49 451	R–70.3
Gates	584	82.0	1.6	1.0	5.6	0.5	2.6	288	436	440.4	33	771	3 485	D–58.1
Graham	682	64.4	2.5	3.4	4.5	2.2	0.3	42	348	497.1	107	1 989	3 419	R–61.2
Granville	675	58.3	13.7	3.5	3.0	2.1	19.7	557	4 952	1 250.5	412	12 648	10 439	D–50.6
Greene	620	77.0	0.0	3.7	5.0	0.1	2.9	178	884	542.3	44	1 002	5 238	D–52.1
Guilford	1 017	45.2	4.2	6.2	3.4	2.8	266.3	830	22 404	658.4	3 357	115 363	117 232	R–56.3
Halifax	1 000	57.2	4.4	3.6	4.8	2.2	25.1	453	4 185	731.6	140	3 983	16 211	D–53.8
Harnett	689	53.6	22.1	4.6	2.8	2.1	9.2	150	2 715	402.8	119	3 259	17 029	R–57.2
Haywood	934	49.1	27.0	3.4	2.3	2.0	20.2	429	2 905	600.2	116	3 293	18 028	D–50.0
Henderson	826	48.1	30.0	3.0	2.4	1.0	21.2	341	3 418	486.2	184	5 185	29 125	R–67.7
Hertford	776	69.8	1.2	4.5	3.3	2.0	4.7	200	1 555	658.9	76	1 970	7 930	D–62.3
Hoke	623	70.8	2.4	4.0	4.5	1.4	2.2	103	1 419	579.2	46	1 390	5 333	D–61.5
Hyde	714	67.0	4.3	4.6	5.8	0.0	1.0	167	419	748.2	21	508	2 264	D–58.1
Iredell	712	61.0	1.8	4.5	2.5	2.4	58.8	696	4 886	524.8	201	5 861	32 135	R–67.0
Jackson	680	63.3	4.1	2.5	4.6	0.6	5.3	200	3 308	1 220.7	52	1 474	10 123	R–51.0
Johnston	861	53.6	19.5	3.2	2.4	1.6	15.6	216	4 026	491.0	183	5 369	24 329	R–64.0
Jones	599	72.7	3.3	3.2	6.7	1.2	1.8	188	417	421.2	33	829	3 602	D–54.0
Lee	1 153	53.9	18.8	4.0	2.7	2.0	17.2	456	2 319	546.9	121	3 411	11 371	R–62.5
Lenoir	1 194	42.8	26.1	3.3	2.3	0.9	32.4	540	6 343	1 051.9	239	7 282	18 353	R–58.1
Lincoln	537	71.9	2.0	4.9	2.6	0.9	22.1	511	2 076	419.4	89	2 474	18 130	R–64.3
McDowell	586	71.2	1.5	3.9	5.3	1.0	9.9	276	1 671	459.1	106	2 406	10 997	R–59.3
Macon	528	64.2	3.2	4.7	3.0	1.4	2.2	103	946	402.6	257	5 955	9 816	R–61.4
Madison	628	59.2	2.9	2.1	11.4	1.0	0.7	39	837	483.8	87	1 844	6 506	R–53.1
Martin	1 160	51.5	10.6	2.5	2.3	1.4	21.0	803	1 720	654.0	96	2 515	6 756	D–53.3
Mecklenburg	1 311	35.2	23.8	4.6	2.6	3.1	489.5	1 166	32 438	665.4	4 056	137 597	178 796	R–59.4
Mitchell	780	68.6	0.7	3.3	2.3	1.8	12.8	886	963	655.1	59	1 160	6 014	R–76.8
Montgomery	650	71.1	2.6	4.5	3.0	2.7	6.2	274	1 367	562.6	79	1 682	8 530	R–52.8
Moore	776	64.7	1.7	4.3	2.7	1.8	27.2	526	3 141	515.8	152	4 238	22 248	R–65.4
Nash	1 050	54.2	1.9	4.8	2.9	3.3	28.9	422	4 060	553.1	192	5 989	24 722	R–64.3
New Hanover	880	50.6	2.3	6.3	3.6	1.9	63.0	586	10 132	850.7	1 085	37 587	39 313	R–60.6
Northampton	789	60.6	3.6	2.4	6.7	1.8	10.9	484	1 319	599.5	73	1 794	7 033	D–65.4
Onslow	537	56.1	19.2	4.3	3.6	1.0	28.2	243	5 321	416.4	5 111	109 081	19 488	R–62.9
Orange	726	43.0	2.0	5.6	2.8	2.5	30.0	383	20 602	2 274.0	243	7 069	37 067	D–60.2
Pamlico	678	72.7	2.9	2.6	2.9	1.6	3.6	340	592	538.2	29	649	4 506	R–51.0
Pasquotank	1 121	45.5	32.7	3.1	1.8	1.4	13.0	454	3 248	1 044.4	602	17 476	7 892	R–50.8
Pender	748	63.3	18.0	3.4	2.7	0.6	0.7	29	1 384	494.3	75	1 614	9 323	R–52.8
Perquimans	604	71.6	0.0	3.8	4.9	1.8	3.4	350	580	513.3	34	788	3 340	R–53.3
Person	945	52.3	1.0	2.7	3.7	1.3	79.1	2 664	1 639	515.4	71	1 825	8 628	R–56.0
Pitt	843	52.4	1.7	4.1	3.4	2.0	68.9	741	14 130	1 357.3	409	13 225	33 127	R–55.1
Polk	572	66.7	2.5	4.9	4.3	2.2	1.4	97	539	364.2	42	1 095	6 423	R–60.3
Randolph	559	66.1	3.8	4.4	2.0	2.2	41.3	442	4 240	405.4	174	4 924	32 571	R–73.3
Richmond	703	66.5	1.2	4.0	2.8	1.7	18.8	418	2 498	543.0	119	3 359	12 257	D–58.3
Robeson	841	65.2	1.9	3.2	4.4	2.2	61.8	597	6 222	572.4	264	7 391	27 000	D–62.9
Rockingham	733	59.7	4.0	6.0	3.2	2.7	53.4	632	3 975	457.9	189	5 258	26 164	R–55.8
Rowan	573	64.3	1.5	4.7	3.7	2.9	20.3	202	4 792	445.8	1 697	56 672	35 416	R–65.5
Rutherford	631	69.7	1.2	4.7	3.3	1.9	8.4	151	2 782	478.8	120	3 120	17 306	R–59.7
Sampson	709	69.6	2.0	3.6	3.3	1.4	8.6	172	3 079	602.5	140	3 714	16 555	R–51.5
Scotland	819	58.8	2.8	3.6	4.3	1.1	19.6	591	1 754	501.1	63	1 759	7 084	D–54.6
Stanly	659	66.0	1.8	4.6	3.6	1.9	19.4	398	2 556	498.2	103	2 991	18 532	R–64.1
Stokes	748	56.4	20.0	2.9	2.4	0.1	8.7	253	1 539	417.1	72	1 828	14 012	R–61.8
Surry	830	56.5	17.0	3.4	2.6	1.3	24.7	413	3 360	537.6	170	4 677	18 660	R–61.1
Swain	674	53.7	3.8	3.0	4.2	1.1	14.0	1 332	635	604.8	323	6 837	3 625	D–50.2
Transylvania	591	62.9	1.8	6.0	4.6	1.3	6.6	273	938	355.3	195	4 196	11 330	R–61.9
Tyrrell	767	62.4	1.6	3.8	5.6	1.0	0.7	181	249	607.3	20	519	1 425	D–55.1
Union	625	61.9	2.3	6.7	4.7	2.0	52.9	718	3 638	422.5	178	4 997	25 896	R–65.7

1. Based on the estimated population as of July 1, 1982. 2. Per 10,000 resident population estimated as of July 1 of the year shown. 3. Data subject to copyright.

STATE–County code	MSA/ CMSA/ NECMA code[1]	STATE County	Land Area,[2] 1990 (Sq. Km.)	Population, 1990											
							Race						Age of population Percent		
				Total persons	Rank	Per square kilometer	White	Black	Am. Indian, Eskimo, Aleut	Asian & Pacific Islander	Other race	Hispanic[3]	Under 5 years	5 to 14 years	15 to 24 years
			1	2	3	4	5	6	7	8	9	10	11	12	13
		NORTH CAROLINA—Con.													
37 181	...	Vance	657	38 892	1 024	59.2	21 146	17 512	69	60	105	271	7.4	14.5	15.5
37 183	6640	Wake	2 160	423 380	118	196.0	324 011	88 057	1 148	8 177	1 987	5 396	7.1	12.5	16.5
37 185	...	Warren	1 110	17 265	1 838	15.6	6 593	9 847	763	14	48	98	6.6	14.1	12.7
37 187	...	Washington	901	13 997	2 058	15.5	7 556	6 366	13	35	27	65	7.4	15.6	14.4
37 189	...	Watauga	810	36 952	1 073	45.6	35 930	768	59	152	43	249	4.6	9.7	32.0
37 191	...	Wayne	1 431	104 666	441	73.1	69 172	33 793	265	839	597	1 356	7.6	14.3	15.1
37 193	...	Wilkes	1 961	59 393	728	30.3	56 237	2 824	69	100	163	362	5.9	13.1	14.3
37 195	...	Wilson	961	66 061	662	68.7	40 623	24 896	70	177	295	537	6.6	14.8	15.2
37 197	3120	Yadkin	869	30 488	1 268	35.1	28 884	1 295	22	26	261	388	6.0	12.3	13.5
37 199	...	Yancey	809	15 419	1 962	19.1	15 221	151	27	11	9	49	5.8	12.1	13.4
38 000	...	NORTH DAKOTA	178 695	638 800	X	3.6	604 142	3 524	25 917	3 462	1 755	4 665	7.5	15.8	14.8
38 001	...	Adams	2 559	3 174	2 987	1.2	3 161	3	10	0	0	1	6.7	14.8	9.7
38 003	...	Barnes	3 864	12 545	2 179	3.2	12 409	27	57	40	12	34	6.4	14.2	14.4
38 005	...	Benson	3 596	7 198	2 632	2.0	4 417	0	2 772	3	6	24	9.9	19.9	12.8
38 007	...	Billings	2 982	1 108	3 110	0.4	1 105	0	3	0	0	0	7.6	19.8	10.8
38 009	...	Bottineau	4 322	8 011	2 565	1.9	7 928	6	58	15	4	16	6.1	15.1	12.4
38 011	...	Bowman	3 010	3 596	2 951	1.2	3 585	0	4	4	3	6	6.5	16.5	10.4
38 013	...	Burke	2 858	3 002	3 001	1.1	2 981	1	11	6	3	14	4.6	15.3	9.0
38 015	1010	Burleigh	4 230	60 131	722	14.2	58 106	66	1 596	239	124	361	7.5	16.1	14.1
38 017	2520	Cass	4 573	102 874	447	22.5	100 442	280	944	986	222	700	7.4	14.0	18.9
38 019	...	Cavalier	3 857	6 064	2 750	1.6	6 011	4	45	4	0	8	7.0	15.6	9.5
38 021	...	Dickey	2 930	6 107	2 743	2.1	6 055	8	21	13	10	33	5.8	14.8	14.2
38 023	...	Divide	3 262	2 899	3 007	0.9	2 880	1	9	6	3	7	5.5	14.7	7.5
38 025	...	Dunn	5 206	4 005	2 919	0.8	3 605	0	382	6	12	26	8.2	18.3	9.9
38 027	...	Eddy	1 637	2 951	3 004	1.8	2 900	0	49	1	1	4	5.8	15.1	9.0
38 029	...	Emmons	3 911	4 830	2 854	1.2	4 821	0	5	4	0	7	6.5	14.5	10.4
38 031	...	Foster	1 645	3 983	2 920	2.4	3 956	0	22	2	3	10	6.9	15.9	10.3
38 033	...	Golden Valley	2 595	2 108	3 063	0.8	2 087	0	12	8	1	1	6.4	18.5	11.9
38 035	2985	Grand Forks	3 724	70 683	628	19.0	66 766	1 446	1 244	881	346	1 053	8.4	14.3	22.4
38 037	...	Grant	4 298	3 549	2 954	0.8	3 510	1	32	5	1	10	6.4	15.6	9.7
38 039	...	Griggs	1 835	3 303	2 977	1.8	3 289	0	8	5	1	4	6.1	15.4	9.3
38 041	...	Hettinger	2 933	3 445	2 960	1.2	3 431	0	7	6	1	3	7.1	14.9	9.1
38 043	...	Kidder	3 501	3 332	2 968	1.0	3 328	0	0	4	0	7	6.1	16.7	10.2
38 045	...	La Moure	2 971	5 383	2 811	1.8	5 371	0	5	2	5	8	6.2	16.0	10.0
38 047	...	Logan	2 571	2 847	3 009	1.1	2 838	1	5	1	2	9	6.1	13.7	9.7
38 049	...	McHenry	4 854	6 528	2 706	1.3	6 498	4	13	11	2	13	6.0	16.4	9.8
38 051	...	McIntosh	2 526	4 021	2 917	1.6	4 007	1	6	6	1	6	5.6	12.8	7.1
38 053	...	McKenzie	7 102	6 383	2 719	0.9	5 442	3	922	3	13	54	9.0	18.8	10.9
38 055	...	McLean	5 466	10 457	2 340	1.9	9 870	3	561	9	14	38	6.5	17.6	9.9
38 057	...	Mercer	2 708	9 808	2 403	3.6	9 519	12	226	37	14	42	8.8	19.0	9.4
38 059	1010	Morton	4 989	23 700	1 503	4.8	23 200	13	420	47	20	74	7.2	17.7	12.8
38 061	...	Mountrail	4 724	7 021	2 655	1.5	5 606	4	1 395	14	2	25	7.2	17.6	11.3
38 063	...	Nelson	2 543	4 410	2 880	1.7	4 396	2	7	3	2	8	5.4	14.2	7.6
38 065	...	Oliver	1 874	2 381	3 034	1.3	2 340	0	40	0	1	4	7.9	20.4	10.6
38 067	...	Pembina	2 898	9 238	2 450	3.2	8 997	14	148	12	67	87	6.7	16.6	10.3
38 069	...	Pierce	2 636	5 052	2 836	1.9	5 011	2	23	15	1	1	5.4	15.6	10.2
38 071	...	Ramsey	3 072	12 681	2 167	4.1	12 022	21	591	30	17	49	7.0	15.4	12.3
38 073	...	Ransom	2 235	5 921	2 768	2.6	5 889	4	13	7	8	24	6.2	15.1	9.7
38 075	...	Renville	2 266	3 160	2 988	1.4	3 107	14	23	11	5	6	5.6	16.8	10.6
38 077	...	Richland	3 722	18 148	1 780	4.9	17 614	21	414	82	17	46	7.2	16.2	16.0
38 079	...	Rolette	2 338	12 772	2 159	5.5	4 211	28	8 497	13	23	65	11.1	21.8	14.6
38 081	...	Sargent	2 224	4 549	2 869	2.0	4 528	1	10	5	5	10	6.5	15.6	11.0
38 083	...	Sheridan	2 517	2 148	3 058	0.9	2 138	0	9	1	0	1	6.3	13.6	8.5
38 085	...	Sioux	2 834	3 761	2 935	1.3	906	3	2 836	12	4	29	12.2	24.7	15.7
38 087	...	Slope	3 155	907	3 117	0.3	903	0	3	0	1	1	6.9	18.2	11.7
38 089	...	Stark	3 466	22 832	1 540	6.6	22 555	17	144	79	37	126	7.8	17.3	14.0
38 091	...	Steele	1 845	2 420	3 029	1.3	2 415	0	2	2	1	5	6.6	15.6	8.5
38 093	...	Stutsman	5 754	22 241	1 567	3.9	21 930	51	141	96	23	84	6.7	15.3	12.7
38 095	...	Towner	2 656	3 627	2 949	1.4	3 566	2	53	5	1	5	7.9	15.1	9.6
38 097	...	Traill	2 232	8 752	2 491	3.9	8 618	12	44	22	56	101	6.3	15.2	14.1
38 099	...	Walsh	3 320	13 840	2 070	4.2	13 453	17	97	59	214	441	7.0	16.3	10.6
38 101	...	Ward	5 214	57 921	748	11.1	54 545	1 411	962	594	409	857	8.7	15.4	17.5
38 103	...	Wells	3 293	5 864	2 775	1.8	5 849	2	6	3	4	7	6.3	14.0	8.8
38 105	...	Williams	5 363	21 129	1 622	3.9	20 025	18	1 010	43	33	110	7.5	18.1	11.1

1. MSA = Metropolitan Statistical Area. CMSA = Consolidated MSA. NECMA = New England county metropolitan area. PMSA = Primary MSA. See Appendix A for explanation of these concepts. See Appendix B for list of metropolitan areas identified by type, with component counties. 2. Dry land or land partially or temporarily covered by water. 3. Hispanic persons may be of any race.

STATE County	Population, 1990 (cont'd) — Age of population (cont'd) Percent — 25 to 34 years	35 to 44 years	45 to 54 years	55 to 64 years	65 to 74 years	75 years and over	Percent female	Population–Change and components of change — Change 1980–1990 — Number	Percent	Components of change, 1980–1986 — Total persons, 1986	Total persons, 1980	Net change — Number	Percent	Natural increase — Births	Deaths
	14	15	16	17	18	19	20	21	22	23	24	25	26	27	28
NORTH CAROLINA—Con.															
Vance	15.7	14.9	9.9	9.0	7.7	5.3	52.8	2 144	5.8	38 700	36 748	1 900	5.3	3 500	2 500
Wake	21.5	17.4	10.4	6.8	4.7	3.1	51.1	121 951	40.5	365 500	301 429	64 000	21.2	28 100	12 700
Warren	13.4	13.7	9.9	11.7	10.6	7.3	52.1	1 033	6.4	16 700	16 232	400	2.6	1 500	1 200
Washington	14.3	14.8	10.3	9.4	8.3	5.5	52.5	-804	-5.4	14 400	14 801	-400	-2.7	1 400	800
Watauga	13.4	12.6	9.5	7.6	6.3	4.3	51.1	5 286	16.7	34 500	31 666	2 800	8.9	2 300	1 200
Wayne	18.9	15.0	10.3	8.7	6.4	3.8	50.2	7 612	7.8	97 900	97 054	800	0.9	10 100	5 200
Wilkes	16.2	15.5	12.1	9.5	7.8	5.4	51.1	736	1.3	60 700	58 657	2 000	3.4	4 600	3 000
Wilson	15.3	15.5	10.7	9.2	7.8	5.0	53.3	2 929	4.6	64 500	63 132	1 400	2.1	5 800	3 800
Yadkin	15.8	15.0	12.3	10.3	8.6	6.3	51.5	2 049	7.2	29 600	28 439	1 200	4.1	2 000	1 600
Yancey	14.2	15.2	11.4	10.7	9.9	7.3	51.6	485	3.2	15 800	14 934	900	6.1	1 100	800
NORTH DAKOTA	16.3	14.1	8.9	8.4	7.4	6.8	50.2	-14 200	-2.2	679 000	653 000	26 000	4.1	76 000	35 000
Adams	12.3	15.0	9.6	10.3	10.9	10.6	50.6	-410	-11.4	3 600	3 584	0	-0.7	400	200
Barnes	12.7	12.9	9.3	9.0	10.6	10.5	51.2	-1 415	-10.1	13 200	13 960	-800	-5.6	1 200	1 000
Benson	12.7	12.0	8.6	8.5	8.0	7.6	49.6	-746	-9.4	7 800	7 944	-200	-2.2	1 100	500
Billings	15.2	14.9	9.9	10.5	6.4	5.0	47.7	-30	-2.6	1 300	1 138	100	11.6	200	0
Bottineau	12.4	13.8	9.5	9.8	10.0	10.9	49.7	-1 228	-13.3	9 200	9 239	-100	-0.6	800	600
Bowman	13.1	14.5	9.8	10.8	9.7	8.8	51.0	-633	-15.0	4 300	4 229	100	1.4	500	300
Burke	11.3	12.9	10.0	13.4	11.5	12.0	49.8	-820	-21.5	3 600	3 822	-200	-5.7	300	300
Burleigh	17.8	16.1	9.7	8.0	5.9	4.8	51.5	5 320	9.7	60 300	54 811	5 500	10.0	6 500	2 100
Cass	19.1	15.5	8.5	6.8	5.2	4.6	50.2	14 627	16.6	97 500	88 247	9 200	10.5	9 700	3 800
Cavalier	12.3	13.3	10.7	11.9	9.9	9.7	50.0	-1 572	-20.6	6 900	7 636	-800	-9.8	700	500
Dickey	12.1	12.1	9.4	10.0	10.5	11.1	50.5	-1 100	-15.3	7 000	7 207	-200	-3.1	700	500
Divide	11.2	12.7	10.9	10.8	13.6	13.2	50.1	-595	-17.0	3 300	3 494	-200	-6.6	300	300
Dunn	13.3	14.5	9.6	9.5	9.8	6.8	48.4	-622	-13.4	4 900	4 627	300	5.7	600	200
Eddy	12.7	12.3	8.4	12.1	12.0	12.5	50.6	-603	-17.0	3 200	3 554	-400	-10.9	300	300
Emmons	11.8	11.8	10.7	12.9	11.4	10.0	49.0	-1 047	-17.8	5 600	5 877	-200	-3.9	500	400
Foster	13.6	12.0	9.4	11.3	9.7	11.0	51.1	-628	-13.6	4 500	4 611	-100	-1.8	500	300
Golden Valley	12.0	12.3	8.5	9.8	10.8	9.8	49.1	-283	-11.8	2 400	2 391	100	2.4	300	100
Grand Forks	20.0	13.3	7.1	5.7	4.7	4.1	48.9	4 583	6.9	69 400	66 100	3 300	5.0	8 700	2 400
Grant	11.2	13.6	10.3	11.9	10.5	10.8	49.3	-725	-17.0	4 200	4 274	0	-1.1	400	200
Griggs	10.1	14.8	9.2	11.0	12.0	12.1	50.3	-411	-11.1	3 600	3 714	-100	-3.4	300	300
Hettinger	11.8	12.2	10.4	12.0	12.2	10.2	50.4	-830	-19.4	4 000	4 275	-300	-7.0	400	200
Kidder	12.0	12.4	10.4	12.2	10.7	9.2	48.5	-501	-13.1	3 800	3 833	-100	-2.0	300	200
La Moure	12.3	11.9	10.0	11.4	11.4	10.9	49.4	-1 090	-16.8	6 100	6 473	-400	-6.1	600	400
Logan	12.6	10.6	10.7	13.8	12.2	10.7	49.5	-646	-18.5	3 200	3 493	-300	-9.1	300	200
McHenry	11.4	13.7	10.7	11.2	10.3	10.5	49.3	-1 330	-16.9	7 500	7 858	-300	-4.4	700	500
McIntosh	11.3	9.8	9.8	14.2	13.9	15.4	51.7	-779	-16.2	4 500	4 800	-300	-6.7	400	400
McKenzie	14.6	14.8	9.7	8.4	8.2	5.6	49.4	-749	-10.5	8 500	7 132	1 400	19.0	1 100	400
McLean	12.3	15.2	9.7	9.6	10.4	8.9	49.5	-1 926	-15.6	12 200	12 383	-200	-1.3	1 300	700
Mercer	18.2	16.0	9.1	6.8	7.0	5.7	49.6	404	4.3	13 800	9 404	4 400	47.0	1 400	400
Morton	15.4	14.8	9.4	9.1	7.4	6.1	50.5	-1 477	-5.9	25 600	25 177	400	1.8	3 000	1 200
Mountrail	12.6	13.7	10.0	9.2	9.8	8.6	50.6	-658	-8.6	8 100	7 679	400	5.2	1 000	600
Nelson	11.4	12.2	10.4	12.2	12.7	13.9	50.5	-823	-15.7	4 900	5 233	-300	-6.3	400	500
Oliver	14.1	17.4	9.4	8.9	6.7	4.7	48.0	-114	-4.6	2 600	2 495	100	5.7	300	100
Pembina	13.6	14.8	9.4	10.1	9.4	9.1	50.5	-1 161	-11.2	10 300	10 399	-100	-1.0	1 000	800
Pierce	12.1	11.8	9.8	10.8	10.9	13.3	50.6	-1 114	-18.1	5 800	6 166	-400	-6.0	500	400
Ramsey	15.1	13.3	9.4	9.3	8.9	9.4	50.9	-367	-2.8	12 800	13 048	-300	-2.0	1 300	900
Ransom	13.4	13.7	9.1	11.0	10.2	11.5	48.9	-777	-11.6	6 400	6 698	-300	-3.9	600	500
Renville	13.6	13.6	9.9	10.3	9.1	10.5	50.6	-448	-12.4	3 500	3 608	-100	-1.7	300	200
Richland	14.9	12.9	8.2	8.5	8.0	8.1	48.7	-1 059	-5.5	19 000	19 207	-200	-1.1	2 000	1 100
Rolette	15.0	11.7	8.5	6.9	5.8	4.6	51.0	595	4.9	13 000	12 177	900	7.1	2 100	700
Sargent	12.9	14.6	11.7	9.8	10.0	7.9	48.7	-963	-17.5	5 200	5 512	-300	-6.1	500	400
Sheridan	11.5	12.7	11.0	13.2	13.0	10.2	48.1	-671	-23.8	2 600	2 819	-200	-7.8	200	200
Sioux	14.7	12.3	8.1	6.0	4.5	1.7	48.3	141	3.9	3 800	3 620	200	5.3	700	200
Slope	13.7	14.9	9.2	13.0	8.8	3.6	47.3	-250	-21.6	1 200	1 157	0	0.9	100	0
Stark	17.1	13.9	8.7	8.0	7.2	6.0	50.8	-865	-3.7	25 600	23 697	1 900	8.0	3 600	1 000
Steele	12.9	12.3	11.5	12.3	11.9	8.4	49.8	-686	-22.1	2 800	3 106	-300	-8.3	300	200
Stutsman	15.4	14.4	9.5	9.9	8.5	7.7	51.2	-1 913	-7.9	23 300	24 154	-800	-3.4	2 300	1 400
Towner	13.6	12.3	8.5	10.4	10.9	11.7	49.9	-425	-10.5	4 100	4 052	0	0.4	400	300
Traill	13.3	12.4	9.3	9.0	9.7	10.6	51.0	-872	-9.1	9 500	9 624	-200	-1.7	800	800
Walsh	14.4	13.7	9.6	9.6	9.9	8.9	50.2	-1 531	-10.0	15 400	15 371	0	-0.1	1 500	1 100
Ward	18.6	13.6	8.0	7.0	5.9	5.3	50.2	-471	-0.8	61 300	58 392	2 900	4.9	8 100	2 400
Wells	12.6	11.6	10.7	11.9	11.1	13.0	51.7	-1 115	-16.0	6 800	6 979	-200	-2.5	600	500
Williams	16.2	15.0	9.4	8.5	7.6	6.6	50.8	-1 108	-5.0	26 300	22 237	4 100	18.4	3 700	1 100

STATE County	Population—(cont'd): Components of change, 1980-1986 (cont'd): Net migration	Households, 1990: Number	Households, 1990: Percent change, 1980–1990	Households, 1990: Persons per household	Households, 1990: Percent: Female family householder[1]	Households, 1990: Percent: One-person	Births, 1988: Total	Births, 1988: Rate[2]	Births, 1988: Low birth weight[3] (Number)	Deaths, 1987: Number: Total	Deaths, 1987: Number: Infant[4]	Deaths, 1987: Rate: Total[2]	Deaths, 1987: Rate: Infant[5]	Marriages, 1984: Number	Marriages, 1984: Rate[2]
	29	30	31	32	33	34	35	36	37	38	39	40	41	42	43
NORTH CAROLINA—Con.															
Vance	900	14 166	15.7	2.69	18.2	22.9	631	16.1	71	390	7	9.9	12.5	357	9.4
Wake	48 600	165 743	55.6	2.46	10.0	25.7	6 161	15.9	390	2 269	88	6.1	15.5	2 838	8.4
Warren	200	6 305	19.9	2.68	17.9	22.6	237	14.3	18	229	4	13.8	16.7	127	7.7
Washington	-900	5 052	6.8	2.72	16.5	22.8	237	16.2	20	125	3	8.6	15.7	95	6.6
Watauga	1 800	13 693	27.4	2.37	7.1	25.1	367	10.6	22	232	4	6.7	11.6	346	10.1
Wayne	-4 100	36 889	14.2	2.65	14.4	22.4	1 604	16.3	119	949	17	9.7	11.0	884	9.0
Wilkes	300	23 021	12.2	2.55	9.9	21.1	687	11.2	56	549	8	9.0	10.3	553	9.2
Wilson	-600	25 093	16.4	2.57	16.7	25.0	927	14.1	78	651	9	10.0	9.8	601	9.3
Yadkin	700	12 068	18.2	2.49	9.3	22.1	343	11.3	28	284	2	9.5	4.9	265	9.0
Yancey	700	6 124	16.1	2.49	8.3	22.1	201	12.6	12	132	0	8.2	0.0	211	13.7
NORTH DAKOTA	-15 000	240 878	5.8	2.55	7.3	26.5	10 103	15.1	485	5 483	90	8.2	8.7	5 793	8.4
Adams	-100	1 266	-5.0	2.44	4.0	29.9	44	13.3	2	44	0	12.6	0.0	27	7.7
Barnes	-1 000	4 975	-2.3	2.40	6.2	29.6	174	13.3	6	154	0	11.7	0.0	92	6.7
Benson	-800	2 415	-4.5	2.97	13.9	22.7	180	24.3	13	73	3	9.7	19.4	64	8.2
Billings	0	387	5.4	2.86	1.8	19.1	17	13.1	0	4	1	3.1	71.4	7	5.4
Bottineau	-300	3 105	-5.0	2.46	5.4	28.3	107	12.4	5	110	0	12.6	0.0	61	6.6
Bowman	-100	1 420	-5.6	2.48	5.3	29.0	49	12.3	0	43	0	10.5	0.0	48	11.2
Burke	-300	1 252	-13.3	2.38	4.3	29.5	26	7.9	0	45	0	13.2	0.0	29	7.8
Burleigh	1 100	22 684	16.8	2.57	8.8	25.4	869	14.4	47	360	12	6.0	14.1	581	9.8
Cass	3 300	40 281	23.5	2.45	7.4	28.2	1 494	14.9	73	601	13	6.1	8.5	848	9.0
Cavalier	-900	2 375	-11.6	2.51	3.3	27.9	83	12.8	2	85	0	13.1	0.0	40	5.6
Dickey	-400	2 299	-6.3	2.46	4.8	28.3	72	10.9	4	79	1	11.8	11.9	48	6.9
Divide	-200	1 193	-8.9	2.34	5.0	29.2	36	11.6	1	40	0	12.5	0.0	20	5.9
Dunn	-100	1 433	-7.1	2.76	5.9	23.2	63	14.0	3	34	0	7.4	0.0	27	5.2
Eddy	-400	1 194	-11.0	2.40	4.8	31.7	38	11.9	0	44	0	13.8	0.0	21	6.4
Emmons	-300	1 849	-3.9	2.58	3.9	24.3	58	10.7	0	57	0	10.4	0.0	31	5.3
Foster	-200	1 541	-5.1	2.52	4.7	26.9	59	14.0	5	52	0	12.1	0.0	39	8.5
Golden Valley	-100	811	-4.6	2.50	4.2	30.9	26	11.3	2	18	0	7.5	0.0	16	6.2
Grand Forks	-2 900	25 340	14.6	2.56	8.0	25.6	1 304	18.5	60	469	9	6.7	6.8	654	9.5
Grant	-200	1 374	-8.3	2.55	3.6	26.4	43	10.8	3	30	0	7.3	0.0	24	5.6
Griggs	-200	1 294	-7.0	2.51	4.8	25.4	47	13.4	2	44	0	12.2	0.0	34	9.2
Hettinger	-500	1 341	-10.4	2.53	3.3	25.8	60	16.2	3	42	1	11.1	16.1	25	6.1
Kidder	-200	1 247	-7.8	2.64	3.4	22.0	39	10.5	3	35	1	9.5	17.9	10	2.6
La Moure	-600	2 075	-8.4	2.55	3.3	27.5	65	11.2	2	57	0	9.7	0.0	46	7.4
Logan	-400	1 096	-9.0	2.53	2.4	24.5	29	9.4	1	26	0	8.4	0.0	13	3.9
McHenry	-500	2 551	-9.9	2.54	5.3	26.4	76	10.6	2	74	1	10.1	13.2	40	5.2
McIntosh	-300	1 687	-9.0	2.30	3.1	28.4	52	12.1	3	60	1	14.0	18.9	31	6.7
McKenzie	600	2 301	-3.4	2.75	7.3	25.2	135	17.5	3	61	3	7.7	22.4	44	5.1
McLean	-700	3 933	-8.0	2.61	5.1	25.4	136	11.5	6	101	1	8.4	6.8	79	6.1
Mercer	3 400	3 560	9.3	2.72	4.6	22.2	172	12.7	5	50	2	3.7	9.6	108	7.1
Morton	-1 400	8 677	1.7	2.68	7.5	23.6	407	16.0	19	192	4	7.5	10.9	203	7.7
Mountrail	100	2 587	-3.3	2.64	9.9	26.6	102	13.4	1	79	1	10.1	9.9	65	7.9
Nelson	-200	1 831	-7.7	2.31	5.2	31.9	51	10.9	2	64	1	13.6	18.5	29	5.7
Oliver	-100	809	1.4	2.94	3.0	18.7	38	14.6	3	15	0	5.8	0.0	13	4.8
Pembina	-400	3 555	-5.3	2.54	5.7	27.6	122	11.8	8	101	0	9.8	0.0	80	7.8
Pierce	-500	1 974	-6.6	2.45	5.3	29.7	71	13.1	8	99	1	18.0	15.6	42	7.0
Ramsey	-700	4 977	7.8	2.44	9.0	29.4	190	14.6	8	158	1	12.1	5.0	106	8.2
Ransom	-300	2 284	-5.0	2.47	4.6	27.8	73	11.8	3	98	0	15.3	0.0	34	5.2
Renville	-200	1 209	-6.1	2.56	6.1	24.8	32	9.4	2	30	1	8.8	28.6	21	5.7
Richland	-1 200	6 518	1.6	2.55	5.9	27.0	247	12.8	8	198	3	10.2	11.8	147	7.5
Rolette	-600	4 150	21.2	3.04	21.3	22.3	343	27.9	19	107	5	8.7	16.6	60	4.4
Sargent	-400	1 763	-9.9	2.55	4.0	26.5	62	12.4	2	57	0	11.4	0.0	40	7.4
Sheridan	-300	858	-14.8	2.47	2.8	23.5	19	7.3	1	18	0	6.9	0.0	16	5.9
Sioux	-300	1 022	11.1	3.68	23.5	16.8	97	23.1	9	26	2	6.5	14.7	54	15.0
Slope	-100	333	-14.2	2.72	4.2	24.0	11	10.0	1	3	0	2.7	0.0	7	5.8
Stark	-700	8 479	8.3	2.62	7.9	26.1	372	15.1	13	146	1	5.8	2.6	270	10.0
Steele	-300	991	-13.2	2.44	2.1	27.9	34	12.1	3	31	1	11.1	27.8	24	8.0
Stutsman	-1 800	8 661	0.1	2.44	7.1	29.3	317	13.6	14	203	3	8.7	9.0	220	9.2
Towner	-100	1 433	-4.2	2.47	5.7	30.6	52	13.7	1	35	0	9.0	0.0	40	9.5
Traill	-200	3 327	-2.9	2.50	5.2	27.1	115	12.8	8	113	2	12.4	18.2	61	6.4
Walsh	-400	5 229	-0.3	2.56	6.4	27.4	211	14.5	10	176	0	11.9	0.0	141	8.9
Ward	-2 900	21 485	8.0	2.59	8.0	24.9	1 149	19.0	64	377	11	6.2	9.1	687	11.2
Wells	-200	2 406	-5.6	2.39	5.0	29.1	78	12.4	4	84	0	12.9	0.0	60	8.7
Williams	1 500	8 041	1.3	2.58	7.4	26.8	357	15.3	18	181	4	7.5	11.4	266	9.8

1. No spouse present. 2. Per 1,000 resident population estimated as of July 1 of the year shown. 3. Under 2,500 grams. 4. Deaths of infants under 1 year old. 5. Deaths of infants under 1 year old per 1,000 live births.

STATE County	Divorces, 1984 Number	Divorces, 1984 Rate[1]	Physicians, active non-Federal, 1989 Number[2]	Physicians Rate[3]	Hospitals, 1989 Number	Hospitals Beds Number	Hospitals Beds Rate[3]	Nursing homes,[4] 1986 Number	Nursing homes Beds	Serious crimes known to police, 1988 Number Total[5]	Serious crimes Number Violent[6]	Serious crimes Rate[3]	Education Public school enrollment[7] 1986–1987	Public school enrollment 1980	Attainment,[8] 1980 Percent 12 yrs. or more	Attainment Percent 16 yrs. or more
	44	45	46	47	48	49	50	51	52	53	54	55	56	57	58	59
NORTH CAROLINA—Con.																
Vance	173	4.6	34	86	1	78	197	10	517	2 905	329	7 300	7 626	8 197	43.3	7.8
Wake	1 773	5.2	719	180	12	2 364	591	47	1 487	19 737	1 602	5 205	58 202	55 702	72.5	26.6
Warren	56	3.4	7	42	0	0	0	6	223	250	6	1 480	3 032	3 217	37.4	6.3
Washington	35	2.4	6	41	1	49	333	1	4	517	149	3 638	2 972	3 351	47.5	8.5
Watauga	116	3.4	61	175	2	241	693	5	277	1 229	64	3 490	4 586	4 874	60.1	20.9
Wayne	483	4.9	111	112	3	1 077	1 091	6	375	5 179	498	5 320	18 001	20 163	56.8	10.8
Wilkes	234	3.9	38	62	1	111	180	5	425	1 597	135	2 581	10 770	12 487	43.4	7.4
Wilson	361	5.6	86	130	1	277	420	9	636	825	94	2 779	12 354	13 417	48.0	11.3
Yadkin	98	3.3	13	42	1	50	163	3	292	376	19	1 262	4 832	5 600	42.4	5.0
Yancey	42	2.7	5	31	0	0	0	1	29	3	1	21	2 680	3 049	43.0	6.6
NORTH DAKOTA	2 249	3.3	1 102	167	59	5 616	851	104	8 192	18 014	390	2 733	120 007	124 113	66.4	14.8
Adams	10	2.9	14	438	1	46	1 438	1	88	18	0	521	630	694	67.9	10.6
Barnes	52	3.8	9	70	1	50	388	1	157	200	2	1 524	2 160	2 598	65.8	14.8
Benson	10	1.3	0	0	0	0	0	1	26	100	0	1 351	1 591	2 062	55.2	8.9
Billings	2	1.5	0	0	0	0	0	0	0	24	0	2 027	102	212	61.3	10.5
Bottineau	26	2.8	4	48	1	67	807	3	166	126	1	1 468	1 740	1 813	59.9	11.0
Bowman	7	1.6	4	103	1	39	1 000	0	0	37	4	893	947	905	67.0	11.2
Burke	6	1.6	0	0	0	0	0	1	15	25	0	724	711	728	60.1	9.2
Burleigh	251	4.3	190	315	2	506	838	3	382	2 749	41	4 605	10 562	9 920	76.7	22.3
Cass	386	4.1	344	340	4	849	839	7	782	4 283	107	4 389	15 408	14 418	78.3	22.2
Cavalier	15	2.1	2	32	1	28	444	2	104	116	3	1 809	1 059	1 596	61.8	11.0
Dickey	11	1.6	2	31	2	51	797	3	242	78	1	1 162	1 303	1 429	60.6	11.0
Divide	10	2.9	2	67	1	25	833	2	115	52	0	1 700	473	635	58.3	9.2
Dunn	3	0.6	0	0	0	0	0	0	0	21	1	463	736	1 028	58.1	7.3
Eddy	6	1.8	3	97	1	26	839	1	86	42	1	1 330	550	622	55.9	10.3
Emmons	6	1.0	2	38	1	25	472	1	80	69	1	1 249	1 003	1 368	43.9	8.6
Foster	7	1.5	5	122	1	70	1 707	2	98	44	2	1 037	914	1 046	60.2	11.4
Golden Valley	4	1.5	2	87	0	0	0	0	0	40	2	1 689	561	567	68.2	15.2
Grand Forks	284	4.1	171	242	5	582	823	6	678	2 974	43	4 318	11 120	11 248	76.2	22.6
Grant	5	1.2	2	51	1	50	1 282	2	45	48	0	1 186	692	938	48.5	7.6
Griggs	5	1.4	3	88	1	69	2 029	1	50	16	2	450	634	674	60.6	8.9
Hettinger	4	1.0	0	0	0	0	0	1	60	6	0	160	683	660	54.1	9.8
Kidder	8	2.1	0	0	0	0	0	1	42	32	0	853	742	846	50.8	9.1
La Moure	6	1.0	0	0	0	0	0	2	100	15	0	267	1 259	1 340	57.1	10.0
Logan	4	1.2	0	0	0	0	0	2	74	1	0	33	573	802	39.3	4.9
McHenry	8	1.0	3	42	0	0	0	1	48	67	2	930	1 515	1 714	54.3	8.1
McIntosh	5	1.1	3	71	2	82	1 952	2	125	28	1	645	725	921	36.7	6.4
McKenzie	17	2.0	2	27	1	26	351	1	47	127	7	1 589	1 463	1 568	62.6	9.9
McLean	30	2.3	4	35	2	75	652	3	159	221	6	1 866	2 788	2 613	60.6	11.2
Mercer	41	2.7	4	30	1	37	280	2	122	56	1	424	2 277	1 955	57.4	10.7
Morton	55	2.1	9	36	2	139	552	4	275	785	16	3 084	4 644	4 832	60.2	11.5
Mountrail	15	1.8	4	54	1	28	378	3	184	54	2	711	1 758	1 661	61.7	9.7
Nelson	5	1.0	2	44	1	14	311	5	209	26	0	561	963	1 040	61.5	8.9
Oliver	5	1.9	0	0	0	0	0	0	0	20	0	811	475	596	54.4	6.1
Pembina	30	2.9	5	49	1	113	1 108	4	228	129	4	1 282	2 092	2 127	60.7	11.7
Pierce	12	2.0	7	135	1	233	4 481	2	284	112	3	2 064	998	1 454	52.7	8.2
Ramsey	52	4.0	18	138	1	55	423	4	304	492	3	3 806	2 483	2 505	66.4	13.1
Ransom	19	2.9	6	98	1	70	1 148	4	306	35	0	554	1 283	1 349	62.4	10.6
Renville	1	0.3	3	91	1	26	788	1	59	31	0	873	814	791	65.8	10.2
Richland	34	1.7	18	93	1	55	285	3	285	322	24	1 665	3 324	3 221	63.3	10.8
Rolette	6	0.4	12	100	2	148	1 233	2	108	178	8	1 467	2 957	3 148	48.6	9.6
Sargent	10	1.9	0	0	0	0	0	1	62	59	1	1 220	937	1 244	63.0	7.7
Sheridan	3	1.1	0	0	0	0	0	1	34	16	0	649	309	571	44.6	6.9
Sioux	1	0.3	5	116	1	16	372	0	0	NA	NA	NA	1 049	997	54.4	8.9
Slope	0	0.0	0	0	0	0	0	0	0	9	0	829	65	251	63.6	11.3
Stark	107	3.9	30	124	2	124	515	2	268	650	21	2 635	4 275	4 034	63.2	14.5
Steele	1	0.3	1	37	0	0	0	0	0	NA	NA	NA	405	668	65.2	12.6
Stutsman	104	4.4	38	165	2	661	2 861	3	269	710	10	3 062	3 966	4 232	63.9	13.8
Towner	6	1.4	2	54	1	32	865	1	74	24	0	624	690	829	62.8	10.4
Traill	36	3.8	7	80	2	52	591	3	209	113	4	1 272	1 828	1 815	64.7	14.3
Walsh	44	2.8	11	77	2	49	343	2	199	232	5	1 578	2 606	3 121	53.6	8.6
Ward	329	5.4	112	187	4	806	1 348	4	608	1 674	46	2 745	11 073	11 057	74.8	16.2
Wells	11	1.6	5	82	1	164	2 689	1	116	68	1	1 060	1 201	1 461	54.7	9.0
Williams	134	4.9	32	145	2	128	582	2	220	660	14	2 822	4 891	4 189	71.1	12.7

1. Per 1,000 resident population estimated as of July 1 of the year shown. 2. As of end of year. 3. Per 100,000 resident population as of July 1 of the year shown. 4. Preliminary. Covers nursing homes with 3 or more beds. 5. Data for serious crimes have not been adjusted for underreporting, this may affect comparability between geographic areas or over time. 6. Includes murder and nonnegligent manslaughter, forcible rape, robbery, and aggravated assault. 7. The 1986–1987 data are based on administrative reports obtained by the U.S. National Center for Education Statistics. The 1980 data are based on the 1980 Census of Population and Housing. 8. Persons 25 years old or older.

STATE County	Education (cont'd): Local government expenditures for education,[1] 1982: Total (Mil dol)	Education (cont'd): Local government expenditures for education,[1] 1982: Per capita (Dollars)	Social Security Program December 1988: Beneficiaries: Total	Social Security Program December 1988: Beneficiaries: Rate[2]	Social Security Program December 1988: Payments ($1,000)	Supplemental Security Income Program recipients June 1986	Money income: Per capita[3]: 1987 Income, (Dollars)	Money income: Per capita[3]: 1979: Current dollars	Money income: Per capita[3]: 1979: Constant 1987 dollars	Money income: Median household income 1979 (Dollars)	Money income: Percent below poverty level, 1979: Persons	Money income: Percent below poverty level, 1979: Families	Housing units, 1990: Total	Housing units, 1990: Percent change, 1980–1990
	60	61	62	63	64	65	66	67	68	69	70	71	72	73
NORTH CAROLINA—Con.														
Vance	15.0	402	7 175	182.6	2 943	1 466	8 556	4 988	7 805	11 931	21.0	17.8	15 743	14.0
Wake	116.3	369	43 845	113.0	21 047	5 110	14 290	7 708	12 061	18 643	10.0	7.1	177 146	56.3
Warren	7.4	460	3 320	200.0	1 233	910	7 926	4 375	6 846	10 121	30.5	24.9	8 714	24.3
Washington	6.6	450	2 635	180.5	1 144	480	9 025	5 199	8 135	13 322	21.7	18.1	5 644	3.9
Watauga	10.4	312	4 510	130.0	1 895	584	8 925	5 097	7 975	11 039	22.7	14.1	19 538	33.3
Wayne	37.5	384	15 395	156.0	6 153	3 700	9 400	5 320	8 324	12 931	17.9	14.6	39 483	12.7
Wilkes	21.0	353	9 910	161.4	4 008	1 752	10 036	5 767	9 024	13 554	13.8	11.5	24 960	12.9
Wilson	27.4	430	11 170	170.3	4 594	2 398	9 973	5 754	9 003	13 537	20.0	14.7	26 662	13.7
Yadkin	10.5	363	5 505	181.7	2 237	702	10 011	5 645	8 833	13 636	14.3	11.9	12 921	16.4
Yancey	5.5	359	3 335	208.4	1 236	676	7 732	4 530	7 088	10 788	23.4	19.2	7 994	16.2
NORTH DAKOTA	351.0	522	110 538	165.7	49 935	6 930	9 641	6 417	10 041	15 293	12.6	9.8	276 340	6.8
Adams	2.2	630	740	224.2	340	62	8 416	5 864	9 175	13 933	17.1	13.4	1 504	-3.8
Barnes	6.5	470	3 080	235.1	1 390	124	8 800	6 220	9 732	13 998	13.4	10.1	5 801	-2.9
Benson	4.6	592	1 510	204.1	633	146	7 296	4 958	7 758	12 827	23.2	17.9	3 163	2.6
Billings	0.8	639	100	76.9	37	2	10 572	8 094	12 665	20 257	19.0	14.8	533	3.1
Bottineau	5.8	627	1 975	229.7	890	90	9 101	5 765	9 020	13 169	12.5	10.2	4 661	-0.4
Bowman	3.4	786	855	213.8	388	28	8 943	6 195	9 693	13 807	13.4	10.5	1 691	-1.8
Burke	2.7	714	910	275.8	400	38	7 939	5 351	8 373	12 039	18.0	14.4	1 691	-6.9
Burleigh	24.5	432	8 035	133.0	3 798	528	11 503	7 767	12 153	19 090	7.9	5.4	23 803	14.2
Cass	41.9	463	12 355	123.3	6 147	776	11 294	7 686	12 026	17 620	9.1	5.4	42 407	20.4
Cavalier	4.4	608	1 415	217.7	635	56	10 346	6 107	9 556	14 570	13.3	11.2	3 038	-2.7
Dickey	3.9	553	1 525	231.1	639	98	7 942	5 243	8 204	11 932	18.6	13.8	2 763	-2.6
Divide	1.9	553	755	243.5	363	38	10 138	6 235	9 756	14 060	10.7	9.2	1 667	-6.5
Dunn	2.9	577	715	158.9	280	36	7 724	5 650	8 841	12 676	21.1	16.1	2 057	11.2
Eddy	2.0	565	855	267.2	375	54	9 313	5 830	9 122	12 724	13.1	8.7	1 470	-4.6
Emmons	3.5	597	1 260	233.3	479	74	8 044	4 692	7 342	10 983	24.6	21.3	2 200	-5.3
Foster	3.0	651	980	233.3	436	28	8 752	6 357	9 947	14 230	11.7	9.1	1 876	2.7
Golden Valley	1.7	614	545	237.0	260	14	9 498	6 239	9 762	14 219	14.4	11.1	1 035	0.2
Grand Forks	29.2	434	7 425	105.3	3 615	490	9 957	6 519	10 200	15 478	11.0	7.9	27 085	10.3
Grant	2.4	566	920	230.0	338	60	7 172	4 262	6 669	9 400	32.4	27.4	2 011	2.1
Griggs	1.8	492	900	257.1	404	44	8 435	5 782	9 047	13 278	12.3	10.5	1 660	-4.5
Hettinger	2.6	627	950	256.8	410	48	8 099	5 104	7 986	11 775	20.9	17.1	1 637	-1.9
Kidder	2.3	605	785	212.2	299	42	6 595	4 543	7 108	10 455	28.5	25.0	1 672	-3.9
La Moure	4.0	645	1 430	246.6	612	74	8 431	5 218	8 165	12 209	16.9	13.0	2 434	-3.7
Logan	1.8	535	830	267.7	317	52	7 020	4 639	7 259	10 423	22.8	19.7	1 335	-6.1
McHenry	5.3	695	1 800	250.0	748	86	7 199	4 949	7 744	11 478	18.4	17.2	3 320	-3.4
McIntosh	2.9	636	1 375	319.8	516	88	8 318	5 145	8 050	10 132	24.3	18.7	2 031	-7.6
McKenzie	5.9	658	1 000	129.9	440	34	8 440	6 142	9 610	15 428	14.6	11.7	3 178	7.9
McLean	7.9	633	2 450	207.6	1 094	180	8 815	6 068	9 495	15 178	13.0	9.7	5 515	-4.2
Mercer	5.6	531	1 490	110.4	629	94	10 310	7 071	11 064	18 680	10.5	8.1	4 496	13.0
Morton	14.8	572	3 970	156.3	1 669	254	8 919	6 249	9 778	16 438	10.7	8.6	9 467	0.9
Mountrail	5.4	676	1 585	208.6	698	128	8 290	5 476	8 568	12 871	16.3	13.2	3 675	14.8
Nelson	4.1	815	1 385	294.7	619	66	8 089	5 529	8 651	11 755	15.7	13.7	2 261	-7.4
Oliver	1.5	567	285	109.6	117	10	9 155	5 984	9 363	16 792	14.9	13.1	968	0.8
Pembina	6.4	629	2 195	213.1	988	120	9 690	6 104	9 551	13 985	12.1	9.9	4 294	-3.2
Pierce	3.5	576	1 310	242.6	567	78	8 472	5 279	8 260	12 141	14.6	12.5	2 355	-0.9
Ramsey	8.3	637	2 830	217.7	1 323	184	9 649	6 347	9 931	15 243	9.4	7.0	5 616	6.8
Ransom	3.5	541	1 390	224.2	574	76	8 737	5 636	8 819	13 654	11.9	9.7	2 569	-5.3
Renville	3.6	1 013	740	217.6	351	18	8 218	5 730	8 966	13 497	16.7	13.6	1 558	1.8
Richland	8.4	427	3 225	167.1	1 416	194	10 096	6 267	9 806	15 589	11.2	7.5	7 394	3.0
Rolette	8.9	714	1 770	143.9	685	388	6 117	4 147	6 489	11 188	30.2	25.7	4 742	20.9
Sargent	2.8	524	1 060	212.0	464	50	9 156	5 761	9 014	14 190	10.6	8.7	2 057	-6.9
Sheridan	1.2	384	570	219.2	220	52	7 425	4 936	7 723	11 590	23.1	19.2	1 061	-10.1
Sioux	2.4	660	375	89.3	115	82	5 341	3 642	5 699	11 468	32.5	27.6	1 175	10.6
Slope	0.2	158	120	109.1	54	6	6 167	4 936	7 723	12 147	22.9	19.3	481	-6.2
Stark	13.1	461	3 915	158.5	1 621	300	8 933	6 442	10 080	16 650	11.8	9.0	9 585	12.9
Steele	2.3	778	575	205.4	283	18	11 130	6 919	10 826	16 115	12.0	9.7	1 311	-9.4
Stutsman	11.0	461	4 440	190.6	1 999	368	9 422	6 494	10 161	15 064	11.5	9.3	9 770	1.1
Towner	2.2	546	920	242.1	433	36	9 082	6 212	9 720	14 462	15.6	12.4	1 770	4.6
Traill	5.6	592	2 105	233.9	993	60	9 525	6 508	10 183	15 397	8.9	6.6	3 770	-4.0
Walsh	8.0	521	3 335	228.4	1 495	270	8 682	5 211	8 154	12 544	15.4	13.2	6 093	-1.0
Ward	28.8	481	7 700	127.5	3 638	430	9 196	6 389	9 997	15 517	10.1	8.6	23 585	9.6
Wells	4.3	637	1 690	268.3	733	84	8 622	5 520	8 637	12 178	17.2	14.3	2 869	-0.6
Williams	13.3	478	3 795	162.9	1 856	170	10 081	7 565	11 837	18 768	8.8	6.6	10 180	13.7

1. Elementary and secondary. 2. Per 1,000 resident population estimated as of July 1 of the year shown. 3. Based on the resident population estimated as of July 1, 1988 for 1987 data and enumerated as of April 1, 1980 for 1979 data.

STATE County	Housing units, 1990 (cont'd): Occupied units: Total	Owner occupied: Percent	Owner occupied: Median value (Dollars)	Median rent (Dollars)	Civilian labor force, 1990: Total	Percent change, 1989–1990	Unemployment: Total	Unemployment: Rate[1]	Private nonfarm establishments, 1988: Number	Net change, 1987–1988	Employment[2]: Total	Per-cent change, 1987–1988	Manu-facturing	Retail trade
	74	75	76	77	78	79	80	81	82	83	84	85	86	87
NORTH CAROLINA—Con.														
Vance	14 166	65.3	53 100	181	18 916	-1.1	1 556	8.2	853	-3	15 229	-0.7	6 518	4 490
Wake	165 743	60.9	97 200	392	244 397	0.9	5 950	2.4	12 501	533	188 429	4.6	27 041	42 055
Warren	6 305	76.4	48 200	130	7 846	0.7	416	5.3	267	-2	2 890	11.1	1 550	388
Washington	5 052	73.6	45 500	171	5 583	-1.2	261	4.7	262	1	4 447	5.8	0	893
Watauga	13 693	64.2	73 200	312	18 514	0.1	518	2.8	1 109	47	9 691	4.3	1 481	3 593
Wayne	36 889	62.7	58 000	213	45 981	1.6	2 208	4.8	2 069	-29	29 851	5.6	10 504	6 655
Wilkes	23 021	79.4	52 800	213	32 304	0.4	1 276	3.9	1 160	8	21 163	-0.5	10 595	4 979
Wilson	25 093	59.3	59 600	205	35 268	4.5	2 462	7.0	1 631	33	26 175	3.9	8 059	5 609
Yadkin	12 068	81.2	52 900	199	16 284	0.2	739	4.5	486	-9	4 923	6.7	2 065	1 101
Yancey	6 124	80.8	51 300	179	11 265	1.3	534	4.7	270	-3	3 548	3.6	2 109	680
NORTH DAKOTA	240 878	65.6	50 800	266	325 000	-1.8	13 000	3.9	X	X	184 257	2.2	16 269	48 519
Adams	1 266	70.4	34 000	189	1 679	3.3	36	2.1	117	-1	879	4.5	12	210
Barnes	4 975	68.5	38 400	198	5 664	-0.9	188	3.3	395	9	3 310	2.1	163	930
Benson	2 415	68.2	18 900	132	2 847	-15.4	282	9.9	122	-7	1 057	29.9	0	103
Billings	387	77.5	50 800	222	877	-3.5	27	3.1	23	-6	63	-45.7	0	10
Bottineau	3 105	78.3	37 400	193	3 215	-7.8	157	4.9	292	9	1 640	7.0	111	425
Bowman	1 420	78.9	44 000	171	2 061	-4.4	40	1.9	165	4	927	-3.2	19	256
Burke	1 252	81.8	19 900	160	1 279	-4.1	55	4.3	119	4	423	6.5	0	124
Burleigh	22 684	64.8	67 500	315	34 518	0.3	1 242	3.6	1 903	-9	22 828	3.3	1 191	5 978
Cass	40 281	54.8	67 900	315	62 460	0.6	1 381	2.2	3 345	89	47 700	2.2	3 863	11 708
Cavalier	2 375	79.7	39 300	193	2 516	-4.8	132	5.2	217	11	1 083	4.0	68	353
Dickey	2 299	70.1	32 900	180	2 994	-3.7	75	2.5	192	-16	1 388	-2.8	65	376
Divide	1 193	79.6	27 600	172	1 332	-7.4	26	2.0	102	2	510	-1.4	0	133
Dunn	1 433	78.4	27 300	145	1 621	1.1	92	5.7	98	0	350	-5.4	0	91
Eddy	1 194	71.5	27 400	207	1 366	-5.1	111	8.1	74	-6	491	9.4	0	114
Emmons	1 849	82.2	31 500	143	2 115	-3.3	94	4.4	148	8	691	1.2	40	168
Foster	1 541	74.0	36 500	189	2 140	-0.1	91	4.3	174	-2	1 008	2.6	37	246
Golden Valley	811	75.6	31 800	191	1 012	-4.0	22	2.2	82	-3	420	3.4	0	136
Grand Forks	25 340	48.7	62 700	320	35 804	-1.0	1 304	3.6	1 687	27	20 908	2.3	1 766	6 630
Grant	1 374	81.4	24 100	139	1 698	-4.8	60	3.5	92	-5	369	-5.6	0	113
Griggs	1 294	75.9	29 500	163	1 481	-4.3	52	3.5	104	-4	539	10.7	50	101
Hettinger	1 341	82.0	24 900	140	1 725	-5.6	76	4.4	110	-5	465	-1.7	0	130
Kidder	1 247	83.8	22 600	139	1 493	-2.2	126	8.4	81	8	286	9.2	0	49
La Moure	2 075	79.1	22 300	147	2 252	-4.6	74	3.3	150	-4	647	1.1	42	165
Logan	1 096	86.6	20 900	143	1 405	-6.0	43	3.1	84	0	429	-2.3	0	79
McHenry	2 551	80.6	22 600	143	2 516	-3.7	274	10.9	151	3	660	0.3	80	187
McIntosh	1 687	81.9	20 300	141	2 186	-1.8	39	1.8	149	2	713	-3.0	65	214
McKenzie	2 301	74.3	43 900	155	2 668	-8.3	82	3.1	179	7	1 182	14.1	20	189
McLean	3 933	79.0	40 100	178	4 342	-3.9	244	5.6	270	0	1 636	-11.6	58	372
Mercer	3 560	80.4	52 200	215	5 579	-3.9	323	5.8	246	-12	2 912	-3.7	25	454
Morton	8 677	73.1	51 100	265	12 661	0.0	591	4.7	603	8	5 315	1.5	825	1 281
Mountrail	2 587	75.4	31 400	143	3 212	-1.4	197	6.1	196	-11	1 248	3.0	0	357
Nelson	1 831	76.0	23 900	151	1 831	-4.7	76	4.2	169	1	819	-6.0	0	201
Oliver	809	85.4	47 300	176	1 084	-3.1	49	4.5	41	2	494	-2.8	0	45
Pembina	3 555	77.4	41 700	191	5 192	-3.0	424	8.2	347	17	2 236	6.1	0	553
Pierce	1 974	73.9	35 400	204	2 411	-6.6	75	3.1	153	-6	1 237	7.4	0	312
Ramsey	4 977	64.1	45 700	241	6 594	0.7	228	3.5	435	1	3 572	3.8	79	1 258
Ransom	2 284	74.9	32 200	171	2 634	-3.4	68	2.6	175	-10	1 039	-1.1	37	348
Renville	1 209	78.5	35 000	198	1 146	-4.4	40	3.5	89	0	378	-4.5	0	98
Richland	6 518	68.9	43 800	235	8 584	-2.3	304	3.5	490	-3	4 646	8.5	1 644	1 030
Rolette	4 150	64.9	39 400	108	4 428	3.6	664	15.0	228	19	1 681	-5.8	382	355
Sargent	1 763	79.4	25 000	157	2 727	1.8	44	1.6	139	0	1 362	7.9	0	127
Sheridan	858	85.1	14 999	140	1 115	-4.5	61	5.5	49	0	149	-2.0	0	37
Sioux	1 022	43.6	20 700	122	1 121	3.6	196	17.5	33	1	118	4.4	0	52
Slope	333	82.0	14 999	99	435	-7.8	29	6.7	14	-3	56	-16.4	0	0
Stark	8 479	68.7	42 800	226	11 403	-3.2	480	4.2	813	-8	6 888	-0.2	537	1 928
Steele	991	75.6	24 800	162	1 047	-8.2	35	3.3	80	1	287	-3.4	37	50
Stutsman	8 661	65.7	45 400	246	11 455	-4.5	422	3.7	624	-14	6 473	1.9	967	1 796
Towner	1 433	70.8	30 900	206	1 723	-1.0	53	3.1	121	-9	876	-3.5	0	194
Traill	3 327	71.0	40 200	213	4 201	-3.9	160	3.8	309	7	2 150	5.8	355	502
Walsh	5 229	75.0	41 900	218	7 672	-7.9	343	4.5	475	4	3 416	5.4	512	962
Ward	21 485	59.7	54 200	278	25 768	-1.0	1 120	4.3	1 545	1	15 700	1.8	767	5 080
Wells	2 406	74.7	29 100	168	2 736	-4.1	179	6.5	205	-5	1 155	-4.4	28	342
Williams	8 041	70.7	43 100	212	10 975	-4.0	415	3.8	848	-31	6 281	-0.5	191	1 564

1. Percent of total civilian labor force. 2. For week including March 12. Excludes government employees, self-employed persons, farm workers, domestic service workers, railroad employees subject to the Railroad Retirement Act, and employees on oceanborne vessels or in foreign countries.

STATE County	Private nonfarm establishments, 1988 (cont'd): Employment[1] (cont'd): Finance, insurance, and real estate	Employment[1] (cont'd): Services	Annual payroll: Total (Mil dol)	Annual payroll: Average per employee (Dollars)	Personal income, 1989: Total (Mil dol)	Per-cent change, 1988–1989	Wages and salaries[2] (Mil dol)	Propri-etor's income (Mil dol)	Dividends, interest, & rent (Mil dol)	Transfer payments (Mil dol)	Per capita[3]: Dollars	Per capita[3]: Rank	Earnings, 1989: Total (Mil dol)	Percent by selected industries: Farm	Goods-related[4]: Total
	88	89	90	91	92	93	94	95	96	97	98	99	100	101	102
NORTH CAROLINA—Con.															
Vance	327	2 275	236	15 517	483	9.2	346	37	76	89	12 205	2 229	383	1.9	NA
Wake	16 723	54 079	3 699	19 628	8 016	9.8	5 867	587	1 104	712	20 025	169	6 454	0.3	19.6
Warren	53	556	32	11 050	193	9.9	64	27	25	43	11 589	2 476	91	16.7	35.0
Washington	93	248	116	26 173	173	5.8	54	22	22	36	11 785	2 410	76	20.1	NA
Watauga	490	2 718	129	13 290	422	8.3	258	56	73	66	12 118	2 278	314	2.6	16.3
Wayne	1 214	5 632	453	15 186	1 291	7.8	826	120	147	228	13 089	1 870	946	4.4	25.5
Wilkes	1 006	2 114	333	15 726	828	7.1	453	122	98	115	13 436	1 719	575	10.5	37.3
Wilson	1 596	4 864	472	18 038	971	8.2	678	113	134	154	14 707	1 122	791	6.8	35.7
Yadkin	169	881	71	14 329	430	8.2	134	41	55	59	14 042	1 417	175	6.4	41.9
Yancey	50	280	50	14 139	184	7.8	91	16	25	36	11 367	2 550	107	2.9	61.5
NORTH DAKOTA	12 778	60 884	2 915	X	9 037	8.5	5 021	1 307	1 753	1 621	13 693	X	6 327	9.2	13.7
Adams	49	451	11	12 461	45	5.5	16	9	11	9	13 972	1 448	25	17.5	NA
Barnes	112	1 224	39	11 710	169	9.9	64	25	44	38	13 061	1 884	89	12.7	11.0
Benson	56	214	16	14 869	76	16.7	28	14	19	21	10 390	2 810	42	23.4	NA
Billings	0	8	1	17 810	15	17.1	9	5	3	1	12 462	2 137	14	27.5	28.1
Bottineau	106	528	19	11 329	121	17.9	35	31	32	26	14 611	1 161	66	35.5	9.4
Bowman	78	265	11	12 201	55	-0.8	20	9	19	9	14 011	1 433	29	9.0	20.7
Burke	55	41	6	13 253	47	17.3	14	11	14	10	14 715	1 119	25	23.7	16.9
Burleigh	1 496	9 330	391	17 139	935	6.9	639	96	142	134	15 477	811	735	1.5	11.3
Cass	4 403	15 120	852	17 872	1 560	8.0	1 209	145	254	209	15 416	831	1 354	1.2	13.6
Cavalier	100	317	14	12 691	102	27.3	25	35	27	16	16 247	579	59	44.7	6.7
Dickey	73	616	14	10 336	78	8.8	26	15	20	19	12 155	2 259	42	19.6	NA
Divide	60	222	5	10 433	47	14.7	10	14	15	9	15 497	804	24	36.9	4.9
Dunn	17	60	5	13 763	41	-0.8	11	8	12	9	9 476	2 962	19	20.6	12.8
Eddy	108	204	5	11 059	42	13.9	12	6	10	13	13 293	1 776	18	20.9	NA
Emmons	47	219	8	10 913	62	6.7	16	18	17	13	11 584	2 478	34	36.5	8.8
Foster	90	348	12	12 369	55	12.9	21	11	14	12	13 579	1 644	32	13.1	5.2
Golden Valley	33	118	5	12 133	33	-2.0	11	6	10	6	14 457	1 232	18	18.4	14.7
Grand Forks	1 137	7 333	330	15 776	956	8.0	683	93	135	138	13 521	1 669	777	4.7	9.4
Grant	59	120	4	10 873	41	8.5	9	12	11	10	10 390	2 811	20	36.0	NA
Griggs	0	202	7	13 083	50	21.1	13	15	13	10	14 526	1 200	28	42.9	8.9
Hettinger	50	144	5	11 656	45	6.2	12	11	12	11	12 565	2 085	24	28.0	9.1
Kidder	0	110	3	10 266	33	5.4	9	7	11	8	8 886	3 015	16	24.3	NA
La Moure	75	134	7	11 201	64	15.9	17	15	19	15	11 222	2 595	33	25.7	4.9
Logan	39	75	4	8 734	33	8.0	8	6	11	8	10 646	2 754	15	28.3	NA
McHenry	65	94	8	12 098	78	14.4	19	16	23	20	11 043	2 655	35	29.2	11.7
McIntosh	0	244	7	9 764	52	2.1	15	11	14	14	12 548	2 096	26	22.9	NA
McKenzie	63	358	18	14 841	85	5.3	36	18	21	13	11 375	2 547	55	17.8	20.5
McLean	118	454	30	18 185	136	8.1	61	21	32	31	11 815	2 394	82	12.7	NA
Mercer	99	544	76	26 073	151	2.7	130	14	21	20	11 477	2 508	144	2.0	27.3
Morton	238	1 896	79	14 779	301	4.6	145	34	49	58	11 976	2 332	178	5.2	22.7
Mountrail	114	444	15	12 315	91	9.8	32	14	24	22	12 356	2 181	46	15.4	10.1
Nelson	67	331	10	11 783	69	18.8	17	20	18	16	15 204	907	37	39.9	NA
Oliver	0	25	14	29 267	29	0.9	20	7	6	3	11 348	2 553	27	18.9	NA
Pembina	203	645	33	14 968	155	17.2	67	38	33	28	15 147	927	105	28.1	19.8
Pierce	74	510	14	11 539	65	11.2	24	10	19	15	12 650	2 054	34	15.6	NA
Ramsey	221	1 390	42	11 892	196	14.3	81	40	44	38	15 089	947	121	18.4	6.4
Ransom	72	417	10	9 313	75	2.2	27	10	20	18	12 198	2 234	37	9.4	NA
Renville	34	138	4	11 190	46	21.2	11	14	12	9	14 057	1 409	26	40.4	NA
Richland	186	876	68	14 666	240	7.0	114	34	52	44	12 399	2 161	148	11.4	29.9
Rolette	76	489	23	13 440	126	10.0	54	19	15	47	10 520	2 785	73	14.0	17.8
Sargent	46	152	34	24 854	67	2.3	41	11	15	13	13 628	1 614	52	7.8	NA
Sheridan	0	30	2	15 322	32	25.3	5	10	10	6	12 546	2 097	16	43.5	NA
Sioux	0	18	1	10 373	30	3.9	16	6	2	10	7 052	3 100	21	21.9	NA
Slope	0	0	1	19 589	11	-0.4	1	4	4	1	10 287	2 840	6	56.8	NA
Stark	363	2 375	99	14 357	296	1.4	162	37	54	54	12 300	2 197	198	1.7	20.0
Steele	44	43	4	14 230	41	24.3	9	14	12	7	15 148	926	23	58.0	NA
Stutsman	370	2 278	93	14 413	313	7.7	167	37	62	64	13 559	1 656	204	6.7	18.9
Towner	79	178	11	12 345	60	23.3	17	17	16	11	16 110	615	34	37.9	12.6
Traill	133	694	27	12 715	132	15.1	48	29	33	25	15 031	979	77	28.4	13.5
Walsh	220	899	42	12 291	241	15.1	82	53	45	68	16 912	452	135	31.4	6.6
Ward	964	5 431	228	14 538	802	6.5	506	76	129	135	13 418	1 727	582	3.0	8.1
Wells	80	431	12	10 401	87	13.6	24	20	25	21	14 142	1 374	45	28.8	7.4
Williams	414	2 090	100	15 859	328	4.5	171	54	69	54	14 899	1 027	224	7.1	21.9

1. For week including March 12. Excludes government employees, self-employed persons, farm workers, domestic service workers, railroad employees subject to the Railroad Retirement Act, and employees on oceanborne vessels or in foreign countries. 2. Includes other labor income. 3. Based on the resident population estimated as of July 1 of the year shown. 4. Covers mining, construction, and manufacturing.

Table A. States and Counties — **Earnings and Agriculture**

STATE County	Earnings, 1989 (cont'd)						Agriculture, 1987									
	Percent by selected industries (cont'd)						Farms			Farm operators, percent		Land in farms				
	Goods-related[1]	Service-related & other[2]						Percent with						Acres		
	Manu-facturing	Total	Retail trade	Finance, insur-ance, & real estate	Services	Govern-ment	Number	Less than 50 acres	500 acres and over	Whose principal occu-pation is farming	Residing on farm operated	Acreage (1,000)	Percent change, 1982–1987	Average size of farm	Total irrigated (1,000)	Total cropland (1,000)
	103	104	105	106	107	108	109	110	111	112	113	114	115	116	117	118
NORTH CAROLINA—Con.																
Vance	33.7	NA	23.3	1.8	15.5	12.6	352	29.5	10.2	59.7	66.8	71	-1.5	203	3	31
Wake	12.3	59.3	10.5	7.1	25.0	20.9	1 003	43.1	4.8	52.6	70.1	129	-20.1	128	6	69
Warren	28.5	29.0	8.0	1.5	13.9	19.4	336	26.8	11.6	63.4	65.5	86	-6.9	257	2	38
Washington	11.0	38.7	11.8	2.2	12.1	26.9	269	33.8	24.5	60.2	63.6	115	-9.3	429	2	98
Watauga	8.7	51.5	15.2	5.2	23.5	29.6	747	56.6	1.1	42.3	71.1	54	-2.3	72	0	22
Wayne	18.3	38.7	10.9	3.4	13.3	31.4	1 076	37.6	8.6	67.2	62.4	186	-6.3	173	2	142
Wilkes	32.5	39.7	15.5	3.5	12.2	12.6	1 204	48.5	2.2	48.9	70.3	112	-12.5	93	0	47
Wilson	27.3	43.1	9.2	5.3	16.8	14.4	666	33.3	12.2	67.6	62.0	145	0.9	217	3	103
Yadkin	33.1	36.3	10.2	2.0	14.0	15.4	1 045	42.9	2.6	49.4	73.3	106	-8.3	102	1	67
Yancey	55.1	22.6	8.1	1.0	8.2	12.9	724	64.8	0.6	35.8	68.1	41	-24.8	57	0	15
NORTH DAKOTA	6.2	55.8	9.7	4.8	22.6	21.3	35 289	7.0	67.0	82.3	70.7	40 337	0.3	1 143	168	28 208
Adams	0.6	65.2	9.9	3.4	31.7	12.1	410	7.8	72.7	79.3	67.8	627	6.7	1 528	0	380
Barnes	3.7	55.7	11.7	4.9	23.3	20.6	917	8.1	61.6	85.8	77.0	859	-4.9	937	2	760
Benson	20.8	33.8	3.7	3.8	14.8	19.6	717	4.5	71.0	88.0	72.8	816	-0.9	1 138	2	653
Billings	0.0	NA	2.9	NA	12.4	19.0	267	7.1	68.2	82.4	72.3	799	7.1	2 994	0	146
Bottineau	1.8	38.2	7.3	3.2	14.2	16.9	929	4.3	66.5	78.0	65.9	1 002	3.1	1 078	1	874
Bowman	1.7	56.5	12.6	6.0	21.8	13.8	390	11.0	68.2	80.0	69.0	721	1.6	1 849	2	345
Burke	0.8	39.3	7.7	2.8	6.3	20.1	525	2.3	73.5	79.0	57.9	610	-4.9	1 162	D	470
Burleigh	5.1	64.9	10.5	4.7	32.6	22.3	803	13.4	58.3	68.0	69.2	883	1.2	1 099	4	500
Cass	7.1	70.2	9.9	8.1	29.4	15.0	1 183	10.5	62.7	81.7	73.3	1 059	0.0	895	12	1 001
Cavalier	0.6	37.6	6.4	4.6	11.4	11.0	922	3.3	72.2	89.5	65.9	917	5.1	995	D	840
Dickey	4.8	55.1	10.3	3.6	20.3	14.8	597	6.9	63.5	83.2	74.0	626	1.7	1 049	12	508
Divide	0.3	43.0	8.5	6.5	16.7	15.2	599	3.5	79.5	86.5	65.8	735	-0.3	1 228	2	558
Dunn	1.4	44.6	9.6	2.6	11.6	22.0	733	6.4	72.3	83.2	75.0	1 359	-2.7	1 854	2	429
Eddy	NA	NA	7.0	4.8	26.0	18.7	326	5.5	68.1	84.7	76.4	352	-6.6	1 079	2	258
Emmons	1.7	40.0	6.4	4.0	15.1	14.6	868	4.7	69.2	80.5	66.4	866	6.4	998	5	570
Foster	0.8	67.8	9.0	5.5	25.6	14.0	377	5.6	65.3	83.0	69.0	394	2.2	1 045	3	343
Golden Valley	1.7	51.2	10.0	4.4	18.2	15.6	261	5.4	72.4	87.4	63.6	532	-3.4	2 039	1	267
Grand Forks	4.1	48.3	11.0	3.5	20.0	37.7	893	7.6	59.9	80.3	72.3	808	-5.5	904	5	740
Grant	NA	44.6	6.4	3.9	14.3	16.1	688	4.1	76.5	87.4	70.9	1 020	10.2	1 483	2	509
Griggs	4.2	36.7	7.7	3.9	11.2	11.4	444	6.8	64.2	86.0	75.9	421	0.0	948	4	348
Hettinger	1.4	45.7	8.2	5.3	10.4	17.2	525	9.3	76.6	84.8	67.6	725	-5.6	1 381	0	599
Kidder	NA	48.7	7.0	5.1	12.8	23.2	557	3.6	79.4	89.6	75.9	758	5.0	1 362	6	422
La Moure	1.2	50.6	7.4	6.3	13.4	18.8	738	6.8	61.9	84.1	73.8	648	-6.5	878	4	556
Logan	0.6	48.6	10.7	5.1	12.3	19.2	531	5.8	75.5	88.9	71.4	597	4.7	1 123	1	349
McHenry	5.8	38.7	6.7	3.3	9.5	20.5	964	8.3	64.7	80.2	70.7	1 048	-2.7	1 087	7	716
McIntosh	1.0	57.7	11.6	5.2	25.3	15.3	556	3.2	75.4	85.6	69.4	568	1.1	1 021	D	408
McKenzie	0.7	44.3	6.4	3.0	15.0	17.3	752	8.5	66.0	80.1	73.8	1 123	-4.1	1 493	22	495
McLean	0.6	NA	6.2	3.3	NA	17.0	1 058	6.2	70.1	79.6	68.4	1 151	-1.0	1 088	5	900
Mercer	-0.3	63.3	4.9	1.5	8.5	7.4	575	9.0	55.8	69.0	67.0	558	-1.1	970	3	293
Morton	14.3	58.0	11.4	3.3	21.0	14.2	988	10.8	65.2	80.2	73.3	1 227	10.0	1 242	4	588
Mountrail	5.8	52.8	9.9	6.2	17.9	21.8	873	4.8	71.7	78.6	68.7	1 049	3.8	1 202	1	692
Nelson	1.0	42.3	7.9	6.6	13.5	13.7	564	5.3	73.4	86.3	68.3	599	-1.5	1 062	D	503
Oliver	NA	NA	1.8	NA	5.1	8.4	367	9.5	61.9	74.1	77.1	386	2.8	1 052	1	195
Pembina	15.2	39.2	7.6	3.0	14.5	12.9	763	6.3	58.6	85.6	63.2	640	-5.0	839	D	591
Pierce	2.8	64.2	11.5	5.2	27.4	13.8	578	4.5	72.7	86.9	73.2	593	-1.2	1 026	D	480
Ramsey	1.5	55.4	14.4	4.2	23.1	19.9	633	6.5	71.7	85.5	73.5	723	-3.4	1 143	D	656
Ransom	8.9	59.1	8.2	5.4	20.6	16.6	498	12.0	55.0	78.9	76.3	487	0.1	978	15	354
Renville	NA	36.9	6.3	1.7	15.3	13.4	454	4.0	69.6	82.4	67.0	505	-0.8	1 111	0	446
Richland	25.4	40.7	9.2	3.1	14.9	18.0	1 126	10.2	52.4	83.7	75.8	860	-2.9	763	3	795
Rolette	11.1	39.6	8.3	3.9	19.2	28.6	536	6.5	59.9	74.1	74.6	506	4.9	945	D	361
Sargent	54.1	27.4	6.0	2.1	4.9	8.3	541	7.9	61.4	81.9	78.2	478	-7.1	883	7	403
Sheridan	0.4	36.0	5.2	4.4	9.5	16.5	470	5.3	76.6	87.9	72.6	523	0.4	1 112	D	367
Sioux	NA	NA	3.9	NA	NA	42.7	229	3.9	80.3	83.8	69.4	808	6.3	3 527	D	178
Slope	0.0	NA	1.7	NA	16.2	9.9	299	5.7	80.9	87.3	76.3	809	6.0	2 705	1	283
Stark	6.9	62.0	12.5	3.9	26.1	16.3	822	12.7	62.8	74.6	72.1	804	0.0	978	0	556
Steele	2.2	NA	3.5	3.7	5.4	12.0	396	3.8	77.0	90.9	75.5	445	-1.8	1 125	3	401
Stutsman	14.9	54.1	9.9	5.3	22.8	20.3	1 113	7.7	67.9	86.1	74.8	1 301	-2.0	1 168	5	999
Towner	9.2	38.6	6.6	4.6	12.3	10.9	557	5.6	77.0	90.3	68.0	631	4.9	1 132	D	560
Traill	10.0	43.3	8.1	3.7	14.6	14.8	603	5.5	65.3	86.4	73.1	508	-2.0	843	D	486
Walsh	2.5	38.4	7.5	3.8	13.2	23.7	928	6.0	57.2	83.5	69.2	759	-1.0	818	0	684
Ward	2.8	52.7	11.2	3.9	21.6	36.3	1 215	10.8	60.1	74.8	67.0	1 187	-1.3	977	1	932
Wells	0.6	48.9	11.3	6.1	17.7	14.9	683	5.6	69.5	88.6	68.1	738	-3.2	1 080	1	629
Williams	1.6	58.4	9.4	3.7	25.1	12.6	948	5.7	70.0	75.6	61.3	1 190	2.5	1 255	15	834

1. Covers mining, construction, and manufacturing. 2. Covers private sector earnings in agricultural services, forestry, and fisheries; transportation and public utilities; wholesale trade; retail trade; finance, insurance, and real estate; and services.

STATE County	Agriculture, 1987 (cont'd)								Manufactures, 1987						
	Value of land and buildings		Value of products sold				Percent of farms with sales of		Establishments		All employees			Production workers	
					Percent from										
	Average per farm ($1,000)	Average per acre (Dollars)	Total (Mil dol)	Average per farm (Dollars)	Crops	Livestock and poultry[1]	$10,000 or more	$100,000 or more	Total	Percent with 20 or more em-ployees	Number (1,000)	Percent change, 1982–1987	Annual payroll (Mil dol)	Number (1,000)	Work hours (Mil)
	119	120	121	122	123	124	125	126	127	128	129	130	131	132	133
NORTH CAROLINA—Con.															
Vance	182	943	15	41 396	86.7	13.3	55.1	12.5	52	61.5	6.6	6.5	100.5	5.6	11.2
Wake	320	2 391	48	48 230	80.1	19.9	48.8	14.0	521	32.6	27.5	14.6	623.0	17.4	35.9
Warren	182	717	17	50 070	49.5	50.5	53.3	15.5	33	42.4	1.4	75.0	16.8	1.3	2.4
Washington	375	939	55	203 364	37.1	62.9	65.4	31.2	22	36.4	D	D	D	D	D
Watauga	136	2 034	8	11 374	34.3	65.7	22.9	1.5	51	25.5	1.5	-25.0	23.1	1.1	2.1
Wayne	230	1 387	134	124 541	26.7	73.3	65.2	25.7	110	44.5	9.7	22.8	161.9	7.6	15.1
Wilkes	144	1 603	132	109 915	2.7	97.3	45.3	27.4	114	36.0	11.2	20.4	173.6	8.6	16.5
Wilson	304	1 345	70	104 441	65.0	35.0	68.8	21.6	99	47.5	8.7	1.2	179.1	6.9	13.9
Yadkin	148	1 383	33	31 173	35.3	64.7	37.3	9.4	34	38.2	2.0	0.0	33.1	1.7	3.3
Yancey	82	1 442	4	6 134	62.4	37.6	10.4	1.0	31	35.5	1.9	171.4	29.3	1.6	3.2
NORTH DAKOTA	366	319	2 188	62 007	68.4	31.6	80.2	16.9	627	22.2	15.4	4.1	310.4	10.4	20.4
Adams	314	193	23	55 447	45.2	54.8	80.0	15.1	5	0.0	0.0	0.0	0.2	0.0	0.0
Barnes	369	392	58	63 036	80.4	19.6	83.3	20.2	14	28.6	D	D	D	D	D
Benson	342	308	37	52 213	70.6	29.4	82.6	13.7	7	42.9	D	D	D	D	D
Billings	437	144	11	40 533	23.1	76.9	78.3	7.9	NA	NA	NA	NA	NA	NA	NA
Bottineau	356	334	40	42 628	83.9	16.1	74.6	9.4	8	25.0	0.1	0.0	1.1	0.0	0.1
Bowman	429	231	24	62 457	38.4	61.6	76.9	13.1	6	0.0	D	D	D	D	D
Burke	329	298	18	33 372	81.8	18.2	71.6	6.3	2	0.0	D	D	D	D	D
Burleigh	274	255	37	46 075	41.1	58.9	66.6	10.1	58	24.1	D	D	D	D	D
Cass	570	661	131	110 689	82.0	18.0	87.1	36.4	122	33.6	4.0	14.3	75.1	2.7	5.1
Cavalier	395	415	59	64 501	96.2	3.8	88.4	19.2	6	0.0	0.0	0.0	0.3	0.0	0.0
Dickey	323	285	45	75 236	58.1	41.9	82.7	23.6	9	22.2	D	D	D	D	D
Divide	310	265	24	39 837	81.2	18.8	82.0	7.0	2	0.0	D	D	D	D	D
Dunn	352	186	35	47 413	23.8	76.2	79.0	9.7	3	0.0	0.0	0.0	0.1	0.0	0.0
Eddy	284	260	17	52 474	63.7	36.3	81.3	12.6	2	0.0	D	D	D	D	D
Emmons	221	222	46	52 447	35.2	64.8	81.6	12.7	6	16.7	D	D	D	D	D
Foster	364	363	30	78 923	66.8	33.2	81.4	20.4	5	0.0	0.0	-100.0	0.4	0.0	0.0
Golden Valley	476	231	19	71 438	40.0	60.0	77.4	14.6	3	0.0	D	D	D	D	D
Grand Forks	479	530	91	102 110	90.9	9.1	83.4	31.5	48	22.9	1.5	36.4	27.6	1.1	2.2
Grant	322	219	38	54 986	32.5	67.5	85.8	13.4	1	0.0	D	D	D	D	D
Griggs	302	337	26	58 535	75.4	24.6	82.0	17.6	6	0.0	0.0	-100.0	0.6	0.0	0.1
Hettinger	386	269	32	60 920	65.5	34.5	82.9	17.5	4	0.0	0.0	0.0	0.1	0.0	0.0
Kidder	280	198	29	52 061	30.7	69.3	85.8	12.2	2	0.0	D	D	D	D	D
La Moure	277	298	46	62 817	64.6	35.4	82.8	18.4	6	0.0	D	D	D	D	D
Logan	266	229	33	62 812	29.1	70.9	85.7	16.9	2	0.0	D	D	D	D	D
McHenry	267	242	39	40 930	48.5	51.5	74.9	9.1	4	25.0	D	D	D	D	D
McIntosh	209	221	31	54 943	35.8	64.2	84.2	14.2	7	14.3	0.1	0.0	0.7	0.0	0.1
McKenzie	450	291	39	51 442	50.1	49.9	74.6	13.7	4	0.0	D	D	D	D	D
McLean	356	331	47	44 457	69.9	30.1	78.1	9.5	8	0.0	0.1	0.0	0.6	0.0	0.1
Mercer	217	237	21	36 084	36.7	63.3	67.3	8.0	5	0.0	0.0	0.0	0.4	0.0	0.0
Morton	314	236	56	56 358	27.7	72.3	77.4	16.8	25	36.0	D	D	D	D	D
Mountrail	315	255	30	34 535	64.0	36.0	73.1	4.9	7	14.3	D	D	D	D	D
Nelson	354	328	34	60 843	81.2	18.8	84.6	18.8	4	0.0	D	D	D	D	D
Oliver	218	206	17	45 601	31.0	69.0	75.2	10.6	2	0.0	D	D	D	D	D
Pembina	612	747	99	129 205	93.1	6.9	86.4	37.9	12	8.3	D	D	D	D	D
Pierce	288	282	24	42 365	62.7	37.3	83.0	7.3	4	25.0	D	D	D	D	D
Ramsey	369	331	38	60 529	92.3	7.7	82.1	18.3	10	10.0	0.1	0.0	1.1	0.1	0.1
Ransom	369	368	37	74 817	64.9	35.1	78.3	22.3	5	0.0	D	D	D	D	D
Renville	403	370	20	43 184	86.1	13.9	79.7	9.5	1	0.0	D	D	D	D	D
Richland	520	687	113	100 041	83.4	16.6	85.6	30.6	26	26.9	1.5	15.4	31.7	1.2	2.5
Rolette	284	307	20	37 279	64.7	35.3	69.4	7.6	4	75.0	0.4	33.3	6.0	0.3	0.7
Sargent	306	339	38	70 404	67.9	32.1	81.9	24.4	6	33.3	D	D	D	D	D
Sheridan	295	269	21	44 092	62.0	38.0	78.5	9.6	2	0.0	D	D	D	D	D
Sioux	581	159	14	62 883	19.3	80.7	80.3	19.2	1	0.0	D	D	D	D	D
Slope	601	205	18	61 067	42.6	57.4	85.3	15.1	NA	NA	NA	NA	NA	NA	NA
Stark	288	289	39	47 885	38.4	61.6	75.1	11.3	32	18.8	0.5	-16.7	8.7	0.3	0.6
Steele	524	462	34	84 857	93.9	6.1	90.7	30.8	5	20.0	0.0	0.0	0.5	0.0	0.1
Stutsman	366	327	76	68 563	64.6	35.4	82.4	22.6	22	31.8	1.0	0.0	20.5	0.6	1.0
Towner	380	348	33	60 094	92.1	7.9	86.4	17.1	6	16.7	D	D	D	D	D
Traill	593	702	65	107 286	95.3	4.7	91.0	36.7	11	18.2	D	D	D	D	D
Walsh	500	605	110	118 354	94.6	5.4	84.1	27.2	16	25.0	D	D	D	D	D
Ward	323	337	47	38 669	71.5	28.5	69.3	9.0	37	29.7	0.8	0.0	17.2	0.4	0.9
Wells	373	330	44	64 928	71.4	28.6	83.9	18.0	5	0.0	0.0	0.0	0.3	0.0	0.0
Williams	320	252	36	37 872	76.8	23.2	73.3	7.7	28	7.1	0.2	-60.0	3.5	0.1	0.2

1. Includes livestock and poultry products.

STATE County	Manufactures, 1987 (cont'd)					Value of construction authorized by building permits, 1990							
	Production workers (cont'd)						Nonresidential				Residential		
	Wages							Percent					
	Total (Mil dol)	Average per worker (Dollars)	Value added by manu-facture (Mil dol)	Value of shipments (Mil dol)	New capital expend-itures (Mil dol)	Total[1] ($1,000)	Total ($1,000)	Office	Industrial	Stores	New construction ($1,000)	Number of housing units	Alterations and additions ($1,000)
	134	135	136	137	138	139	140	141	142	143	144	145	146
NORTH CAROLINA—Con.													
Vance	73.3	13 089	228.4	566.8	D	6 924	3 765	18.8	0.8	64.1	1 681	43	572
Wake	307.0	17 644	2 483.6	4 176.1	126.8	600 016	194 015	50.6	16.7	17.1	307 259	4 160	21 457
Warren	13.6	10 462	36.1	99.2	6.4	6 649	586	21.3	8.5	22.0	4 958	62	443
Washington	D	D	D	D	D	3 691	1 260	4.8	44.3	41.0	1 556	22	272
Watauga	15.0	13 636	39.4	73.7	1.7	34 218	5 394	20.4	0.0	45.0	23 609	348	3 043
Wayne	109.2	14 368	353.4	784.0	34.5	37 234	10 984	24.5	24.6	9.1	23 419	366	1 587
Wilkes	108.0	12 558	336.1	879.8	15.2	28 865	8 815	0.0	38.8	17.9	12 267	175	1 058
Wilson	122.8	17 797	673.4	1 761.1	27.3	29 687	6 731	4.2	9.3	36.4	17 741	292	2 540
Yadkin	24.7	14 529	88.8	331.7	5.6	14 090	3 329	2.3	0.0	22.0	8 113	106	1 931
Yancey	21.8	13 625	70.5	263.7	D	3 770	3 400	5.9	0.0	94.1	280	4	50
NORTH DAKOTA	180.1	17 317	979.0	2 574.0	47.0	211 578	55 028	15.6	12.6	52.9	88 505	1 512	13 248
Adams	0.1	NA	0.4	1.6	0.0	847	627	0.0	20.1	8.0	0	0	62
Barnes	D	D	D	D	D	1 435	865	22.6	7.9	0.0	279	5	130
Benson	D	D	D	D	D	17	12	0.0	0.0	0.0	0	0	0
Billings	NA	NA	NA	NA	NA	0	0	NA	NA	NA	0	0	0
Bottineau	0.6	NA	4.1	15.4	D	192	20	100.0	0.0	0.0	0	0	92
Bowman	D	D	D	D	D	53	46	0.0	0.0	0.0	0	0	0
Burke	D	D	D	D	D	140	50	0.0	0.0	0.0	0	0	72
Burleigh	D	D	D	D	D	40 395	6 483	28.7	3.1	62.3	22 774	338	2 090
Cass	44.7	16 556	228.7	562.1	D	76 563	13 675	29.2	9.0	48.3	40 486	819	4 466
Cavalier	0.1	NA	0.7	1.2	0.0	653	307	0.0	0.0	0.0	174	3	72
Dickey	D	D	D	D	D	387	173	0.0	86.9	13.1	60	1	75
Divide	D	D	D	D	D	10	10	0.0	0.0	0.0	0	0	0
Dunn	0.0	NA	0.2	0.3	0.0	38	15	0.0	0.0	0.0	0	0	12
Eddy	D	D	D	D	D	337	20	0.0	0.0	0.0	25	1	36
Emmons	D	D	D	D	D	205	13	0.0	0.0	0.0	0	0	173
Foster	0.2	NA	1.1	2.2	0.0	470	97	0.0	0.0	0.0	244	3	55
Golden Valley	D	D	D	D	D	47	4	0.0	0.0	0.0	0	0	12
Grand Forks	17.5	15 909	97.6	199.5	D	24 230	8 695	2.8	8.6	71.0	6 624	77	1 830
Grant	D	D	D	D	D	64	29	87.4	0.0	0.0	0	0	20
Griggs	0.4	NA	1.3	3.5	0.0	102	0	NA	NA	NA	44	2	15
Hettinger	0.1	NA	0.3	0.4	0.0	872	90	0.0	0.0	0.0	55	1	28
Kidder	D	D	D	D	D	212	33	0.0	0.0	0.0	105	2	56
La Moure	D	D	D	D	D	590	422	23.7	0.0	0.0	75	1	41
Logan	D	D	D	D	D	557	384	0.0	0.0	0.0	142	5	8
McHenry	D	D	D	D	D	177	111	94.6	0.0	0.0	0	0	32
McIntosh	0.3	NA	1.1	2.5	0.1	331	61	0.0	0.0	0.0	244	4	0
McKenzie	D	D	D	D	D	108	16	0.0	0.0	0.0	20	1	51
McLean	0.5	NA	1.0	2.7	0.0	350	90	0.0	0.0	36.8	143	3	19
Mercer	0.3	NA	0.7	1.4	0.0	5 358	1 431	0.0	0.0	85.8	3 321	44	217
Morton	D	D	D	D	D	7 906	1 350	16.7	11.5	4.3	4 500	54	515
Mountrail	D	D	D	D	D	574	25	0.0	0.0	0.0	428	6	14
Nelson	D	D	D	D	D	417	249	97.8	0.0	0.0	133	2	0
Oliver	D	D	D	D	D	348	49	0.0	0.0	0.0	186	2	97
Pembina	D	D	D	D	D	1 355	739	0.0	31.1	1.6	369	6	46
Pierce	D	D	D	D	D	510	111	26.9	0.0	0.0	262	4	64
Ramsey	0.6	6 000	2.6	3.9	D	4 739	1 902	0.0	64.7	9.5	887	17	276
Ransom	D	D	D	D	D	1 483	348	35.9	0.0	0.0	526	7	94
Renville	D	D	D	D	D	2 436	2 100	0.0	90.3	0.0	125	3	72
Richland	21.3	17 750	131.4	263.4	3.1	2 951	972	72.6	10.3	1.0	820	12	244
Rolette	4.6	15 333	10.2	22.7	D	371	14	0.0	0.0	0.0	300	6	0
Sargent	D	D	D	D	D	439	30	0.0	0.0	72.3	362	8	16
Sheridan	D	D	D	D	D	35	31	0.0	0.0	96.2	0	0	1
Sioux	D	D	D	D	D	0	0	NA	NA	NA	0	0	0
Slope	NA	NA	NA	NA	NA	0	0	NA	NA	NA	0	0	0
Stark	5.1	17 000	18.1	40.4	2.0	5 037	2 745	0.0	0.5	96.5	229	3	52
Steele	0.3	NA	1.7	4.9	0.1	90	77	0.0	0.0	0.0	0	0	8
Stutsman	9.3	15 500	58.8	133.8	5.0	5 255	3 009	0.0	19.7	75.4	699	10	248
Towner	D	D	D	D	D	114	55	0.0	0.0	0.0	39	1	0
Traill	D	D	D	D	D	1 113	345	29.0	50.8	0.0	248	6	220
Walsh	D	D	D	D	D	477	51	39.2	0.0	0.0	100	1	178
Ward	7.9	19 750	38.0	84.1	1.1	15 740	3 581	14.0	0.0	75.9	2 718	41	858
Wells	0.2	NA	0.7	1.3	0.0	219	130	76.9	0.0	0.0	0	0	14
Williams	2.1	21 000	6.3	11.7	0.1	5 232	3 336	0.0	0.0	90.9	757	13	568

1. Includes nonresidential additions and alterations, residential nonhousekeeping buildings, and residential garages and carports not shown separately.

STATE / County	Wholesale trade, 1987				Retail trade, all establishments, 1987				Retail trade, establishments with payroll, 1987					
						Sales				Sales				
											Per capita[2] (Dollars)			
	Establishments	Sales (Mil dol)	Paid employees[1]	Annual payroll (Mil dol)	Number	Total (Mil dol)	Percent change, 1982–1987	Per capita[2] (Dollars)	Number	Total (Mil dol)	General merchandise stores	Food stores	Apparel & accessory stores	Eating and drinking places
	147	148	149	150	151	152	153	154	155	156	157	158	159	160
NORTH CAROLINA—Con.														
Vance	58	210.5	760	11.7	432	270.1	83.1	6 890	281	257.3	688	1 339	222	456
Wake	973	5 284.5	13 855	341.6	4 427	3 424.7	103.0	9 150	2 686	3 092.7	995	1 441	436	817
Warren	16	16.2	64	0.8	116	32.4	6.6	1 951	71	29.4	77	702	D	87
Washington	16	30.0	158	2.6	170	56.0	55.6	3 836	96	52.1	116	1 145	186	354
Watauga	46	77.9	379	6.5	518	265.7	54.9	7 701	313	253.7	853	1 461	292	852
Wayne	192	568.7	2 341	39.1	1 094	551.0	44.1	5 617	665	526.8	677	997	206	385
Wilkes	75	270.5	869	15.6	649	301.5	52.5	4 926	348	281.1	406	1 029	198	336
Wilson	144	446.3	1 718	32.7	754	445.2	53.2	6 828	496	434.2	771	1 177	255	562
Yadkin	30	25.0	170	2.1	395	121.2	44.5	4 040	162	101.6	D	889	45	256
Yancey	7	4.4	70	0.8	207	71.6	92.0	4 474	86	63.5	236	1 072	63	302
NORTH DAKOTA	2 049	6 011.0	17 525	324.7	7 803	3 848.8	14.3	5 732	5 235	3 729.6	743	1 015	247	505
Adams	16	53.4	103	1.7	50	17.7	18.0	5 050	34	16.0	D	D	282	420
Barnes	48	D	D	D	174	68.0	8.3	5 155	112	65.6	D	1 212	311	529
Benson	19	41.2	99	1.6	62	9.2	35.3	1 223	29	6.9	D	439	0	97
Billings	2	D	D	D	16	D	D	D	12	1.0	0	0	0	412
Bottineau	26	65.9	171	2.9	139	38.8	13.5	4 455	88	36.4	D	784	279	440
Bowman	10	D	D	D	73	18.9	-4.5	4 598	50	17.8	D	1 042	D	594
Burke	16	D	D	D	53	8.1	-32.5	2 390	37	7.0	D	608	D	428
Burleigh	148	413.6	1 365	27.2	664	464.7	22.5	7 745	473	457.2	1 647	1 170	326	659
Cass	396	1 901.5	5 551	122.2	1 003	841.4	28.2	8 481	694	829.1	D	1 363	D	843
Cavalier	32	D	D	D	120	31.0	30.8	4 771	66	28.5	D	1 027	196	345
Dickey	26	39.3	192	2.6	88	24.3	5.2	3 621	60	23.3	D	770	105	453
Divide	10	17.3	41	0.8	54	10.4	-3.7	3 238	38	9.8	D	D	156	383
Dunn	12	10.5	56	0.9	49	13.0	25.0	2 821	28	11.7	D	686	0	86
Eddy	8	D	D	D	42	9.7	-19.2	3 025	31	9.2	D	D	0	189
Emmons	16	27.6	104	1.1	72	15.9	-4.2	2 896	42	13.7	D	711	D	153
Foster	23	52.6	162	2.4	73	23.2	-5.3	5 397	54	22.7	D	1 103	D	330
Golden Valley	9	22.8	70	1.3	40	14.9	-14.4	6 210	23	14.2	D	D	D	532
Grand Forks	140	332.9	1 262	23.9	648	526.4	36.4	7 531	494	518.9	1 473	1 108	399	624
Grant	12	13.3	30	0.4	48	9.7	-1.0	2 354	32	7.8	0	608	D	146
Griggs	20	35.9	112	1.9	49	10.1	32.9	2 792	29	9.3	D	811	D	236
Hettinger	15	23.0	84	1.3	56	10.7	-16.4	2 809	35	9.6	0	815	D	216
Kidder	12	9.5	33	0.4	38	5.4	17.4	1 458	21	4.9	D	406	0	D
La Moure	25	46.7	171	2.4	85	12.3	0.8	2 078	45	10.6	D	653	0	195
Logan	13	99.5	168	1.2	33	9.6	-10.3	3 101	24	8.8	0	D	D	175
McHenry	18	41.2	87	1.6	86	14.7	-3.9	2 015	47	12.2	0	537	D	184
McIntosh	14	21.9	61	0.9	75	17.3	20.1	4 017	46	15.9	D	451	D	308
McKenzie	17	32.4	125	2.1	73	16.3	-36.1	2 066	48	14.7	0	629	46	225
McLean	29	60.5	191	2.8	133	31.9	-10.1	2 661	85	29.0	42	697	35	223
Mercer	19	21.0	118	1.4	128	41.3	14.7	3 057	74	39.9	D	1 208	64	205
Morton	60	120.3	388	5.6	246	125.4	18.5	4 899	167	123.4	45	1 014	81	416
Mountrail	13	25.2	74	1.4	122	32.3	19.6	4 141	84	30.8	40	987	61	275
Nelson	22	59.1	130	2.2	81	20.3	-14.0	4 315	50	18.3	D	800	D	219
Oliver	2	D	D	D	20	1.8	20.0	685	9	1.7	0	D	0	188
Pembina	50	119.3	290	4.4	160	48.9	39.3	4 752	101	46.0	63	710	41	451
Pierce	18	35.4	143	1.7	67	26.0	-16.1	4 721	45	25.2	D	D	D	302
Ramsey	50	91.5	311	5.6	205	98.7	20.1	7 536	146	94.9	D	1 183	487	686
Ransom	16	32.4	93	1.7	94	19.5	-1.0	3 042	61	16.9	D	716	148	503
Renville	12	26.7	62	1.1	59	12.3	32.3	3 613	31	10.9	0	D	D	143
Richland	55	148.9	364	5.9	197	87.8	30.3	4 501	140	83.7	D	972	175	310
Rolette	17	42.5	129	2.0	95	34.9	7.4	2 837	65	32.7	D	815	D	214
Sargent	25	54.7	149	2.3	78	10.4	6.1	2 087	40	8.7	0	654	D	211
Sheridan	7	7.7	24	0.4	23	3.0	-18.9	1 171	10	2.8	0	D	0	168
Sioux	3	3.1	16	0.2	22	D	D	D	16	4.6	D	D	D	124
Slope	2	D	D	D	8	0.4	-60.0	349	3	0.1	0	0	0	D
Stark	76	170.6	522	8.0	325	170.9	-17.0	6 807	236	165.9	736	1 120	335	568
Steele	13	35.0	52	1.1	31	5.5	-15.4	1 970	17	5.3	D	D	0	181
Stutsman	52	213.8	531	8.7	286	145.1	14.4	6 200	186	141.1	471	973	386	515
Towner	28	53.9	112	1.8	57	10.2	-23.3	2 628	34	9.6	D	701	D	293
Traill	37	105.5	297	4.3	134	39.0	31.8	4 281	91	36.5	D	673	D	486
Walsh	64	142.6	409	6.8	207	73.0	9.9	4 933	132	68.5	560	1 088	162	359
Ward	147	590.3	1 565	27.9	643	403.7	14.2	6 586	444	398.0	1 116	1 076	293	572
Wells	24	46.0	149	2.1	99	31.4	18.5	4 824	61	30.1	D	1 145	225	361
Williams	105	254.4	667	12.8	320	127.5	-32.4	5 290	215	122.6	469	978	334	454

1. For pay period including March 12. 2. Based on the estimated population as of July 1 of the year shown.

STATE County	Retail trade, establishments with payroll, 1987 (cont'd): Paid employees[1]	Retail trade, establishments with payroll, 1987 (cont'd): Annual payroll (Mil dol)	Taxable service industries–establishments with payroll, 1987: Number	Receipts (Mil dol): Total	Receipts (Mil dol), Selected kinds of business: Hotels, motels and other lodging places	Receipts (Mil dol), Selected kinds of business: Health services	Receipts (Mil dol), Selected kinds of business: Legal services	Paid employees	Annual payroll (Mil dol)	Bank deposits,[2] June 1989: Total (Mil dol)	Bank deposits,[2] June 1989: Percent change, 1988–1989	Savings capital,[3] September 1989: Total (Mil dol)	Savings capital,[3] September 1989: Percent change, 1988–1989
	161	162	163	164	165	166	167	168	169	170	171	172	173
NORTH CAROLINA—Con.													
Vance	2 942	27.9	187	42.1	3.1	14.0	1.9	1 527	16.3	265	13.0	48.8	0.5
Wake	38 112	360.8	3 275	1 677.0	93.3	332.4	113.0	39 631	660.2	3 183	10.7	979.6	10.7
Warren	358	3.3	51	8.1	0.0	2.9	0.7	272	2.9	74	6.8	12.5	0.9
Washington	746	6.1	51	6.9	D	1.4	0.5	177	2.0	72	14.1	35.0	-0.1
Watauga	3 204	28.3	263	61.7	11.3	19.5	2.8	1 593	21.3	215	21.9	106.9	-9.2
Wayne	6 375	59.7	437	115.1	4.1	36.1	5.9	3 220	44.6	474	15.1	224.0	2.2
Wilkes	3 398	31.6	242	52.1	3.6	18.4	3.8	1 630	18.6	461	51.5	40.4	-67.3
Wilson	5 344	48.8	325	127.1	6.4	41.6	5.5	2 803	42.9	926	17.4	64.9	-7.4
Yadkin	1 114	9.8	112	24.4	D	7.7	1.4	670	8.2	198	31.4	50.3	5.8
Yancey	623	5.5	45	6.2	0.3	2.2	0.8	147	1.9	97	21.6	11.3	1.7
NORTH DAKOTA	48 163	407.7	3 881	1 090.4	96.5	453.1	76.2	27 753	419.4	5 910	-0.1	2 284.3	-3.4
Adams	254	1.6	21	6.1	D	5.4	0.3	198	3.0	39	4.4	7.9	-8.4
Barnes	910	7.6	64	11.4	1.3	4.4	0.6	282	3.7	151	3.8	67.3	-5.8
Benson	95	0.5	15	1.1	0.0	D	D	34	0.3	36	-4.2	0.0	NA
Billings	11	0.1	3	0.2	D	0.0	0.0	9	0.0	7	-41.1	0.0	NA
Bottineau	498	3.9	45	5.4	D	1.7	0.3	177	1.8	121	-3.8	16.1	-6.6
Bowman	277	1.8	29	4.3	0.3	1.6	0.2	70	0.9	74	-5.4	6.4	-4.8
Burke	123	0.7	11	0.8	D	D	D	17	0.2	38	-6.2	0.0	NA
Burleigh	5 996	51.6	464	183.5	D	86.1	17.5	4 229	83.8	455	7.2	219.3	-10.6
Cass	11 243	93.6	788	357.5	D	152.7	19.1	8 338	131.4	812	-6.2	464.7	-7.7
Cavalier	336	2.8	33	4.3	0.2	2.5	0.4	156	1.8	88	-0.7	42.2	2.6
Dickey	357	2.3	39	4.9	0.3	2.8	0.2	191	1.6	57	-4.3	12.5	10.0
Divide	141	1.1	17	1.7	D	0.6	D	58	0.4	47	-9.0	16.6	7.2
Dunn	109	0.8	14	1.1	D	0.0	D	44	0.2	25	5.6	8.1	16.8
Eddy	129	0.9	11	1.1	0.0	D	D	26	0.4	16	-6.6	0.0	NA
Emmons	153	1.2	28	1.7	0.2	D	D	59	0.5	71	-2.4	0.0	NA
Foster	252	2.1	25	4.8	D	2.5	D	177	1.5	63	6.4	19.1	-6.8
Golden Valley	158	1.2	18	1.1	D	D	0.2	37	0.2	34	1.2	11.8	7.8
Grand Forks	6 611	59.3	355	133.4	13.5	52.4	9.0	3 498	57.4	469	3.2	218.6	-3.1
Grant	113	0.9	19	1.5	D	D	0.2	32	0.4	33	-1.3	0.0	NA
Griggs	99	0.9	16	2.5	D	0.8	D	66	0.6	57	-0.8	0.0	NA
Hettinger	123	1.0	14	1.9	D	D	D	54	0.4	43	-5.3	0.0	NA
Kidder	46	0.3	9	1.3	D	D	D	86	0.5	38	-0.7	0.0	NA
La Moure	160	1.0	21	2.2	D	D	D	94	0.7	55	1.0	0.0	NA
Logan	99	0.6	10	0.7	D	D	D	20	0.1	55	1.9	0.0	NA
McHenry	178	1.2	21	1.3	D	0.4	D	37	0.2	56	0.1	0.0	NA
McIntosh	205	1.3	28	2.2	D	0.9	D	64	0.7	60	0.3	0.0	NA
McKenzie	222	1.6	27	3.6	0.4	D	0.4	94	0.9	59	-6.3	17.9	15.7
McLean	358	2.6	50	6.3	0.3	3.7	D	252	2.4	107	-2.6	16.1	0.6
Mercer	474	3.9	62	6.5	0.4	2.3	D	230	2.6	82	-6.3	12.8	31.7
Morton	1 303	12.4	114	29.2	D	7.3	1.8	829	10.2	187	3.4	25.2	-3.9
Mountrail	344	3.0	39	3.2	0.3	0.8	0.3	113	0.8	86	2.2	16.7	-3.3
Nelson	195	1.6	20	3.1	D	1.3	D	143	1.1	86	-3.6	0.0	NA
Oliver	41	0.2	7	0.3	0.0	D	D	6	0.1	11	7.7	0.0	NA
Pembina	576	4.4	45	10.0	D	2.0	0.7	163	4.0	124	0.0	22.9	-1.3
Pierce	260	2.3	26	5.0	0.5	D	D	117	2.0	62	-4.3	33.2	-5.0
Ramsey	1 296	11.0	81	16.0	1.4	7.4	1.0	408	5.5	130	-1.7	99.2	-1.7
Ransom	330	2.1	29	2.9	D	1.3	D	95	0.7	70	-2.8	35.4	2.8
Renville	94	0.9	13	0.9	D	D	D	25	0.2	17	-8.5	15.1	1.7
Richland	984	8.7	91	18.4	D	9.7	1.7	616	6.0	161	2.4	125.5	1.9
Rolette	360	3.2	30	3.5	0.2	2.1	D	94	1.3	65	-2.0	15.1	-0.3
Sargent	143	0.8	15	1.8	D	D	D	71	0.7	50	2.0	0.0	NA
Sheridan	42	0.3	8	0.5	D	0.0	D	15	0.1	26	-1.1	0.0	NA
Sioux	60	0.4	2	D	D	0.0	0.0	D	D	1	-14.4	0.0	NA
Slope	5	0.0	4	D	0.0	0.0	0.0	D	D	NA	NA	0.0	NA
Stark	2 054	18.0	201	45.3	4.5	17.4	3.7	1 268	16.0	170	-1.2	118.0	1.1
Steele	43	0.5	12	0.3	0.0	D	0.0	15	0.1	39	-3.1	0.0	NA
Stutsman	1 797	14.9	132	35.7	4.9	13.0	1.4	1 027	11.4	217	2.6	109.0	0.2
Towner	163	1.0	17	3.2	0.0	2.4	D	139	1.3	51	0.3	20.1	-2.7
Traill	504	3.7	55	6.1	D	2.3	0.9	142	2.2	119	-0.4	32.8	-0.4
Walsh	879	7.2	80	12.0	1.0	2.3	1.5	291	2.7	186	3.3	87.8	-2.3
Ward	4 910	44.5	362	91.8	10.4	37.1	6.3	2 426	36.5	476	8.6	248.7	-4.7
Wells	369	3.0	43	4.3	D	1.5	0.3	128	1.0	92	-1.8	32.4	-0.9
Williams	1 681	15.0	198	41.6	3.8	15.2	3.7	977	16.9	234	-5.6	89.6	5.8

1. For the period including March 12 of the year shown. 2. Includes deposits for all insured and reporting noninsured commercial and mutual savings banks. 3. Includes savings capital for all FSLIC insured savings institutions.

STATE County	Federal funds and grants, 1989: Expenditures: Total (Mil dol)	Federal funds and grants, 1989: Expenditures: Percent change, 1988–1989	Federal funds and grants, 1989: Per capita[1] (Dollars): Total	Per capita[1]: Direct payments for individuals	Per capita[1]: Procurement contract awards	Per capita[1]: Salaries and wages	Per capita[1]: Grant awards	Local government finances, 1981–1982: General revenue: Total (Mil dol)	General revenue: Intergovernmental: Total (Mil dol)	General revenue: Intergovernmental: Percent from state	General revenue: Taxes: Total (Mil dol)	General revenue: Taxes: Per capita[2]: Total (Dollars)	General revenue: Taxes: Per capita[2]: Property (Dollars)	Direct general expenditure: Total (Mil dol)	Direct general expenditure: Percent change, 1977–1982
	174	175	176	177	178	179	180	181	182	183	184	185	186	187	188
NORTH CAROLINA–Con.															
Vance	99.1	21.1	2 502	1 591	136	88	678	33.3	22.2	83.7	6.8	183	144	27.9	60.0
Wake	1 237.0	6.3	3 090	1 302	152	365	1 257	340.6	126.3	85.7	109.7	348	282	265.6	43.0
Warren	42.0	7.7	2 516	1 761	26	90	606	14.1	9.5	82.3	2.5	156	137	13.0	49.5
Washington	33.4	1.5	2 271	1 667	10	92	397	10.9	7.2	91.6	2.8	192	162	11.9	50.8
Watauga	62.6	16.6	1 800	1 314	128	110	243	20.7	12.4	79.8	6.4	192	141	17.9	43.4
Wayne	366.2	15.2	3 710	1 584	445	1 273	376	88.6	44.5	77.5	16.1	165	129	88.0	53.0
Wilkes	105.6	4.9	1 714	1 291	29	103	278	45.5	25.5	90.5	9.3	155	123	42.2	70.1
Wilson	145.2	7.5	2 200	1 563	141	95	364	62.3	32.3	88.1	15.8	248	201	59.0	52.4
Yadkin	67.5	19.6	2 206	1 539	10	180	434	18.5	9.8	96.2	4.1	142	117	17.4	-5.0
Yancey	34.1	5.0	2 102	1 586	15	102	389	8.1	6.1	91.9	1.5	100	78	7.2	30.2
NORTH DAKOTA	3 089.8	7.6	X	1 766	266	767	747	738.2	355.4	86.4	206.6	307	295	684.0	65.1
Adams	19.5	35.0	6 101	2 122	21	325	691	4.0	1.7	95.5	1.5	419	411	3.9	73.1
Barnes	58.9	3.3	4 566	2 258	24	353	608	13.4	5.9	93.9	4.4	319	309	12.0	46.8
Benson	73.9	71.3	10 129	1 981	3 980	461	1 232	7.9	4.6	83.2	2.3	299	291	7.7	56.7
Billings	5.4	21.5	4 473	788	238	642	228	4.2	2.3	98.5	0.5	367	214	3.3	312.5
Bottineau	39.3	-6.7	4 740	2 367	36	289	291	10.8	5.8	95.1	3.2	344	341	9.0	55.0
Bowman	17.0	24.1	4 371	1 798	17	166	221	5.7	3.2	97.6	1.6	365	358	5.4	40.1
Burke	16.3	-15.7	5 087	2 589	31	501	249	5.0	2.8	95.7	1.4	378	311	4.8	56.5
Burleigh	266.2	12.8	4 407	1 429	111	625	1 974	63.9	27.4	84.9	20.2	356	347	58.5	46.3
Cass	345.1	14.1	3 410	1 429	106	697	438	102.4	43.9	75.6	28.5	315	294	102.3	80.0
Cavalier	33.3	-19.6	5 293	1 907	163	305	493	9.4	4.0	91.8	2.8	382	369	9.6	82.7
Dickey	36.1	18.6	5 634	2 302	65	290	387	7.9	4.6	74.9	2.1	306	300	6.9	56.6
Divide	21.1	-1.3	7 038	2 356	51	326	436	3.9	1.8	94.0	1.5	424	406	3.6	48.2
Dunn	21.4	25.7	4 863	1 332	238	185	328	5.7	3.5	91.4	1.5	291	284	5.2	93.2
Eddy	17.4	4.0	5 608	2 872	46	263	499	3.6	1.6	90.9	1.3	376	370	3.3	22.0
Emmons	32.6	39.9	6 160	1 812	21	219	687	5.8	3.5	91.5	1.7	289	282	6.4	83.8
Foster	19.0	6.1	4 638	2 215	32	315	775	5.0	2.6	93.8	1.6	357	351	4.1	40.1
Golden Valley	14.3	21.7	6 236	2 285	27	230	357	2.8	1.4	95.1	0.8	287	284	2.7	25.6
Grand Forks	325.8	1.7	4 608	1 284	543	1 978	592	66.3	33.0	73.1	16.7	248	233	60.0	52.9
Grant	22.2	27.4	5 691	1 949	23	228	501	4.4	2.3	93.9	1.4	317	314	3.9	55.5
Griggs	15.8	-17.2	4 658	2 374	28	245	371	3.9	1.8	92.2	1.4	400	394	3.5	64.4
Hettinger	26.3	15.5	7 309	2 465	22	280	575	4.8	2.5	95.1	1.7	410	406	3.9	34.4
Kidder	21.8	35.0	5 879	1 701	212	242	388	4.1	2.2	94.3	1.3	352	345	3.4	35.0
La Moure	32.3	12.7	5 664	2 139	35	382	391	7.7	3.8	88.8	2.7	440	436	7.1	60.7
Logan	19.5	20.4	6 290	2 096	25	224	466	3.5	1.8	94.4	1.1	331	325	3.1	31.4
McHenry	39.3	-3.4	5 536	2 319	32	302	367	8.3	4.7	94.7	2.6	348	342	8.2	70.8
McIntosh	26.3	35.0	6 258	2 600	21	274	395	4.7	2.7	95.6	1.4	309	303	4.1	41.6
McKenzie	26.4	5.0	3 571	1 179	20	272	604	16.9	11.6	73.0	1.9	211	206	12.7	200.6
McLean	64.1	25.9	5 577	1 970	113	433	804	13.6	7.8	91.0	3.6	293	287	12.7	78.0
Mercer	23.0	11.0	1 743	960	33	106	169	23.4	7.3	96.9	2.7	259	251	16.2	137.5
Morton	72.9	-10.7	2 893	1 548	19	194	502	28.1	13.1	90.6	7.7	296	284	26.7	108.3
Mountrail	38.5	5.4	5 208	2 012	171	485	807	9.7	5.8	79.0	2.2	270	261	9.1	53.0
Nelson	23.6	-21.0	5 242	2 728	38	238	431	7.3	3.3	91.9	2.6	527	514	7.1	57.9
Oliver	9.2	19.0	3 673	933	8	80	320	10.4	2.1	97.4	0.8	293	286	8.0	246.2
Pembina	56.7	-6.2	5 558	2 054	1 024	493	483	11.8	5.9	92.7	4.2	409	388	10.1	39.7
Pierce	28.8	22.2	5 534	2 163	21	225	467	5.7	3.2	94.8	1.9	311	308	5.2	7.0
Ramsey	56.7	1.9	4 358	2 209	40	439	782	18.9	8.6	90.9	4.9	377	368	16.8	63.3
Ransom	31.9	3.6	5 232	2 250	21	206	487	6.8	3.4	93.8	2.3	360	354	6.1	47.6
Renville	15.6	-27.9	4 728	2 220	30	252	235	4.7	2.4	93.9	1.4	389	367	5.1	65.2
Richland	67.9	-3.4	3 516	1 706	25	256	234	18.7	7.9	87.5	7.6	386	363	16.6	58.1
Rolette	70.1	-19.7	5 846	1 675	977	872	1 596	13.3	10.1	81.5	1.8	145	142	12.4	74.8
Sargent	26.8	6.3	5 477	2 083	40	271	317	5.3	2.7	94.1	1.7	312	304	6.0	96.7
Sheridan	18.6	25.8	7 454	1 952	128	352	645	2.5	1.3	92.1	0.8	276	271	2.3	44.2
Sioux	23.7	16.3	5 521	1 017	330	1 512	1 755	3.2	2.6	81.5	0.5	127	126	3.0	53.4
Slope	7.0	-3.3	6 364	933	10	68	396	1.4	0.8	48.7	0.3	287	284	1.1	142.2
Stark	65.0	13.2	2 695	1 525	22	294	269	25.4	11.3	93.0	7.3	255	248	24.1	130.7
Steele	14.7	-25.6	5 444	1 974	281	358	617	3.8	1.7	84.2	1.6	546	533	3.9	55.5
Stutsman	105.3	2.5	4 556	1 886	590	336	595	23.0	10.9	91.7	7.0	294	288	20.7	61.3
Towner	23.4	-18.2	6 320	2 142	954	264	358	4.4	2.1	92.0	1.7	410	405	4.0	45.4
Traill	31.9	-15.8	3 622	2 208	72	206	566	10.5	4.6	93.1	4.0	418	408	9.7	56.4
Walsh	60.5	3.1	4 232	2 140	25	194	334	15.8	7.0	90.8	6.1	394	382	14.7	45.4
Ward	308.6	6.8	5 161	1 556	533	2 354	342	52.0	27.1	91.1	13.2	221	212	50.0	59.5
Wells	38.1	10.8	6 247	2 605	37	408	390	7.3	3.6	95.6	2.7	396	389	6.6	12.5
Williams	77.9	18.6	3 540	1 717	192	175	442	25.9	12.0	95.2	6.9	249	231	27.5	127.6

1. Based on the estimated population as of July 1 of the year shown.   2. Based on the estimated population as of July 1, 1982.

STATE County	Local government finances, 1981–1982 (cont'd): Direct general expenditure (cont'd): Per capita[1] (Dollars)	Percent of total for– Education	Percent of total for– Health & hospitals	Percent of total for– Police protection	Percent of total for– Public welfare	Percent of total for– Highways	Debt outstanding: Total (Mil dol)	Debt outstanding: Per capita[1] (Dollars)	State and local government employment, 1989: Total	State and local government employment, 1989: Rate[2]	Federal government civilian employment 1989: Total	Federal government civilian employment 1989: Earnings ($1,000)	Elections, 1988[3]: Total vote cast for president	Elections, 1988[3]: Vote for lead party (Percent)
	189	190	191	192	193	194	195	196	197	198	199	200	201	202
NORTH CAROLINA—Con.														
Vance	747	67.7	1.1	4.4	4.1	2.0	13.1	351	2 596	655.6	102	2 941	11 276	D–49.9
Wake	843	46.7	5.1	5.7	2.8	2.8	1 458.7	4 631	49 411	1 234.3	3 709	135 869	143 504	R–56.9
Warren	807	57.0	13.5	2.5	3.4	0.6	3.9	245	847	507.2	45	1 073	6 429	D–66.1
Washington	814	55.3	1.1	2.8	5.7	3.0	6.7	456	1 113	757.1	43	1 034	5 004	D–56.1
Watauga	538	58.0	1.0	5.9	3.7	2.7	14.2	426	4 140	1 189.7	88	2 345	14 785	R–58.6
Wayne	900	49.9	22.3	3.1	2.4	1.9	36.0	369	7 833	793.6	1 297	30 165	24 474	R–62.5
Wilkes	709	60.1	18.8	2.6	3.6	1.1	20.1	338	3 382	549.0	192	5 307	22 514	R–67.7
Wilson	925	54.5	0.9	4.2	4.0	1.9	29.8	468	5 450	825.8	217	6 489	19 257	R–57.1
Yadkin	601	60.4	19.2	3.3	3.8	1.2	2.9	99	1 344	439.2	72	1 798	11 137	R–71.1
Yancey	474	75.7	0.0	3.3	4.4	0.7	1.8	116	602	371.6	92	1 709	8 000	R–52.0
NORTH DAKOTA	1 018	52.4	0.9	3.7	2.0	12.2	610.3	908	45 561	690.3	10 349	268 496	297 261	R–56.0
Adams	1 113	56.6	0.6	2.5	1.8	17.0	0.4	106	139	434.4	29	653	1 737	R–58.6
Barnes	868	54.2	0.6	3.3	2.0	14.4	7.9	576	861	667.4	114	2 891	6 546	R–55.5
Benson	988	59.9	1.6	1.9	7.4	15.7	1.5	188	341	467.1	131	2 991	3 031	D–55.8
Billings	2 535	25.2	0.4	4.5	1.3	51.8	0.0	0	91	758.3	43	1 045	659	R–66.3
Bottineau	967	64.8	2.0	1.9	2.7	11.3	7.0	755	539	649.4	83	2 056	4 251	R–59.5
Bowman	1 245	63.1	0.5	2.8	1.1	15.5	1.8	412	229	587.2	29	642	1 867	R–59.5
Burke	1 273	56.1	0.4	2.4	2.9	24.2	0.6	148	184	575.0	72	1 935	1 690	R–57.5
Burleigh	1 034	51.6	0.6	4.5	2.0	11.3	66.7	1 179	6 175	1 022.4	1 016	32 694	29 084	R–61.9
Cass	1 130	41.0	1.7	4.7	1.2	5.6	109.9	1 214	7 226	714.0	2 148	66 525	49 137	R–54.3
Cavalier	1 315	46.2	13.0	2.7	3.2	15.9	0.8	106	299	474.6	70	1 649	3 457	R–60.6
Dickey	983	56.3	0.1	2.4	1.2	10.5	1.6	233	319	498.4	60	1 376	3 336	R–61.9
Divide	1 035	53.4	0.0	3.6	1.2	22.1	0.6	163	146	486.7	51	1 196	1 768	D–49.5
Dunn	1 034	55.8	0.4	2.7	3.3	20.4	1.0	202	211	479.5	42	823	2 178	R–58.0
Eddy	934	60.5	0.2	4.6	3.7	11.3	0.4	115	184	593.5	32	773	1 658	R–53.7
Emmons	1 107	53.9	1.0	1.5	2.6	12.3	2.2	383	282	532.1	43	917	2 596	R–62.9
Foster	886	73.5	0.5	3.6	1.8	8.6	0.3	72	219	534.1	42	972	2 070	R–58.8
Golden Valley	1 016	60.5	0.0	6.3	3.1	11.4	0.5	189	148	643.5	21	441	1 183	R–66.0
Grand Forks	893	48.6	0.7	3.9	1.0	7.3	45.0	669	7 132	1 008.8	1 505	34 578	27 531	R–53.8
Grant	896	63.1	0.0	2.4	2.3	15.6	2.3	525	166	425.6	42	851	2 043	R–66.1
Griggs	968	50.8	1.7	3.1	2.8	25.5	0.2	68	156	458.8	32	702	1 885	R–54.1
Hettinger	962	65.2	0.1	2.0	4.3	17.1	0.7	160	192	533.3	44	919	2 111	R–66.1
Kidder	894	67.7	0.0	2.5	2.5	13.4	0.7	181	177	478.4	42	854	1 761	R–59.0
La Moure	1 153	56.0	0.1	1.1	0.0	19.1	0.9	140	286	501.8	63	1 371	2 901	R–56.6
Logan	898	59.6	0.5	2.6	2.1	14.1	0.9	260	141	454.8	35	688	1 671	R–66.5
McHenry	1 079	64.4	0.5	2.3	2.4	10.6	1.3	171	349	491.5	88	1 793	3 583	R–52.7
McIntosh	921	69.1	0.3	3.0	2.8	9.3	2.0	441	207	492.9	45	970	2 347	R–73.5
McKenzie	1 415	46.5	0.4	2.6	1.6	34.4	2.0	221	379	512.2	89	2 113	3 253	R–59.9
McLean	1 022	62.0	0.3	4.9	2.7	11.8	6.4	516	577	501.7	175	4 187	5 396	R–53.9
Mercer	1 539	34.5	0.3	3.3	2.1	10.7	67.4	6 418	535	405.3	52	1 149	4 902	R–61.5
Morton	1 031	55.5	0.9	4.3	2.6	12.2	32.9	1 272	1 197	475.0	150	4 253	10 447	R–53.5
Mountrail	1 132	59.7	0.1	4.3	1.8	10.3	2.1	260	374	505.4	154	3 520	3 458	D–57.2
Nelson	1 415	57.6	0.8	1.9	1.3	21.9	3.9	788	243	540.0	48	1 012	2 243	D–51.3
Oliver	3 068	18.5	0.2	1.0	0.8	10.5	84.5	32 501	130	520.0	14	270	1 237	R–56.3
Pembina	987	63.7	0.6	3.1	3.7	11.1	3.9	378	489	479.4	146	4 187	4 149	R–59.6
Pierce	859	67.1	0.0	3.4	3.1	10.0	2.0	321	220	423.1	46	977	2 477	R–57.4
Ramsey	1 292	60.2	0.2	2.8	2.5	9.1	13.0	999	1 142	878.5	181	4 867	5 841	R–53.1
Ransom	932	58.1	0.5	3.2	2.6	12.5	1.8	274	348	570.5	45	966	2 858	D–51.0
Renville	1 418	71.5	0.4	2.2	1.1	12.5	1.7	476	179	542.4	30	723	1 750	R–51.0
Richland	847	50.4	0.3	3.1	1.8	21.9	9.7	493	1 379	714.5	160	3 759	8 274	R–56.4
Rolette	993	71.9	0.2	2.2	4.8	6.5	2.3	186	583	485.8	407	10 130	3 606	D–67.3
Sargent	1 109	47.3	0.3	1.7	1.6	33.5	1.8	337	215	438.8	52	1 193	2 436	D–53.6
Sheridan	750	51.2	0.8	2.5	4.8	17.3	0.4	117	111	444.0	47	1 073	1 318	R–67.1
Sioux	825	80.0	0.3	0.9	4.6	5.2	0.2	50	165	383.7	255	6 490	1 042	D–67.3
Slope	937	16.8	1.1	3.6	3.5	60.8	0.2	193	49	445.5	10	176	530	R–59.4
Stark	846	54.5	0.7	4.8	1.6	11.4	28.1	987	1 417	588.0	196	5 418	10 003	R–61.4
Steele	1 334	58.3	0.4	1.4	3.4	19.2	1.9	661	126	466.7	32	890	1 595	D–56.1
Stutsman	864	53.4	0.9	4.1	3.6	14.9	13.6	568	1 813	784.8	239	6 910	9 669	R–55.6
Towner	978	55.9	0.0	2.8	1.2	19.3	1.4	330	172	464.9	42	913	1 934	D–50.2
Traill	1 021	58.0	0.3	3.0	2.3	19.3	3.3	352	601	683.0	58	1 266	4 559	R–56.2
Walsh	953	54.7	0.5	3.8	1.9	17.4	14.5	940	2 076	1 451.7	92	2 191	5 966	R–54.5
Ward	834	57.7	0.5	4.3	1.8	6.6	30.0	501	2 933	490.5	1 492	32 336	23 228	R–56.7
Wells	975	65.3	0.0	2.1	2.4	16.4	2.5	361	263	431.1	81	1 906	3 241	R–58.7
Williams	987	48.4	0.6	5.2	2.0	14.4	21.9	785	1 446	657.3	134	3 316	9 768	R–57.9

1. Based on the estimated population as of July 1, 1982. 2. Per 10,000 resident population estimated as of July 1 of the year shown. 3. Data subject to copyright.

STATE–County code	MSA/CMSA/NECMA code[1]	STATE County	Land Area,[2] 1990 (Sq. Km.)	Population, 1990												
							Race						Age of population Percent		
				Total persons	Rank	Per square kilometer	White	Black	Am. Indian, Eskimo, Aleut	Asian & Pacific Islander	Other race	Hispanic[3]	Under 5 years	5 to 14 years	15 to 24 years
			1	2	3	4	5	6	7	8	9	10	11	12	13
39 000	...	OHIO	106 067	10 847 115	X	102.3	9 521 756	1 154 826	20 358	91 179	58 996	139 696	7.2	14.4	14.6
39 001	...	Adams	1 512	25 371	1 451	16.8	25 212	47	67	30	15	90	7.3	16.4	14.9
39 003	4320	Allen	1 048	109 755	420	104.7	96 177	12 313	202	572	491	1 240	7.6	15.4	14.4
39 005	...	Ashland	1 099	47 507	883	43.2	46 686	460	49	271	41	191	7.0	15.6	15.6
39 007	...	Ashtabula	1 820	99 821	460	54.8	95 465	3 138	196	350	672	1 538	7.3	15.4	13.4
39 009	...	Athens	1 313	59 549	727	45.4	56 163	1 678	167	1 374	167	438	5.4	11.8	32.2
39 011	4320	Auglaize	1 039	44 585	916	42.9	44 225	66	50	177	67	243	8.0	16.7	13.2
39 013	9000	Belmont	1 392	71 074	623	51.1	69 520	1 308	81	129	36	194	5.9	13.6	12.3
39 015	...	Brown	1 274	34 966	1 132	27.4	34 487	406	28	30	15	49	7.5	16.4	13.9
39 017	1642	Butler	1 210	291 479	167	240.9	274 892	13 134	379	2 659	415	1 467	7.4	14.7	17.3
39 019	1320	Carroll	1 022	26 521	1 408	26.0	26 254	135	65	29	38	99	7.0	15.8	12.8
39 021	...	Champaign	1 110	36 019	1 100	32.4	34 698	992	68	113	148	246	6.8	15.1	14.1
39 023	2000	Clark	1 036	147 548	319	142.4	133 242	13 031	294	653	328	970	6.9	14.4	15.0
39 025	1642	Clermont	1 171	150 187	312	128.3	148 084	1 291	218	453	141	721	8.2	16.6	14.3
39 027	...	Clinton	1 064	35 415	1 116	33.3	34 471	716	59	138	31	122	7.2	15.7	15.1
39 029	...	Columbiana	1 379	108 276	424	78.5	106 369	1 409	174	219	105	405	7.0	15.0	13.2
39 031	...	Coshocton	1 461	35 427	1 115	24.2	34 819	415	68	112	13	106	7.2	15.8	12.5
39 033	...	Crawford	1 042	47 870	877	45.9	47 361	253	67	116	73	246	7.2	15.1	13.5
39 035	1692	Cuyahoga	1 187	1 412 140	17	1 189.7	1 025 756	350 185	2 533	18 085	15 581	31 447	7.1	13.1	13.1
39 037	...	Darke	1 554	53 619	800	34.5	53 067	184	96	114	158	343	7.2	15.8	13.5
39 039	...	Defiance	1 065	39 350	1 016	36.9	36 962	493	80	121	1 694	2 673	7.3	16.4	14.9
39 041	1840	Delaware	1 146	66 929	659	58.4	64 888	1 424	104	385	128	336	7.4	15.4	14.7
39 043	...	Erie	659	76 779	587	116.5	69 613	6 312	150	265	439	1 180	7.0	14.7	13.0
39 045	1840	Fairfield	1 310	103 461	445	79.0	101 610	1 153	193	378	127	489	6.9	15.5	14.6
39 047	...	Fayette	1 053	27 466	1 376	26.1	26 593	662	50	102	59	89	6.9	15.0	13.5
39 049	1840	Franklin	1 399	961 437	33	687.2	783 714	152 840	2 056	19 437	3 390	9 236	7.6	13.3	17.1
39 051	8400	Fulton	1 054	38 498	1 040	36.5	37 097	93	62	137	1 109	1 842	7.7	16.7	13.8
39 053	...	Gallia	1 214	30 954	1 246	25.5	29 831	871	79	136	37	156	6.8	15.5	14.5
39 055	1692	Geauga	1 047	81 129	562	77.5	79 629	1 056	83	312	49	294	7.9	16.1	12.9
39 057	2000	Greene	1 075	136 731	344	127.2	124 081	9 611	398	2 133	508	1 379	6.7	14.6	17.6
39 059	...	Guernsey	1 352	39 024	1 021	28.9	38 166	616	70	141	31	130	7.0	15.4	13.1
39 061	1642	Hamilton	1 055	866 228	36	821.1	672 972	181 145	1 204	9 198	1 709	5 198	7.8	14.3	14.4
39 063	...	Hancock	1 376	65 536	670	47.6	63 572	591	91	401	881	1 680	7.4	15.1	14.3
39 065	...	Hardin	1 218	31 111	1 239	25.5	30 661	236	66	115	33	145	6.7	14.4	19.3
39 067	...	Harrison	1 045	16 085	1 916	15.4	15 645	393	22	15	10	43	5.8	14.6	13.0
39 069	...	Henry	1 079	29 108	1 325	27.0	27 951	147	53	95	862	1 332	7.7	16.5	13.6
39 071	...	Highland	1 433	35 728	1 104	24.9	34 876	692	73	71	16	108	7.3	15.3	13.8
39 073	...	Hocking	1 095	25 533	1 444	23.3	25 199	234	55	25	20	93	7.0	15.1	13.8
39 075	...	Holmes	1 096	32 849	1 193	30.0	32 706	52	24	43	24	123	10.8	19.7	15.4
39 077	...	Huron	1 277	56 240	772	44.0	54 982	597	85	153	423	1 006	8.1	16.2	14.4
39 079	...	Jackson	1 089	30 230	1 284	27.8	29 895	218	53	39	25	89	7.0	15.6	14.1
39 081	8080	Jefferson	1 061	80 298	571	75.7	75 270	4 488	167	266	107	426	5.7	13.4	13.4
39 083	...	Knox	1 365	47 473	885	34.8	46 747	381	93	195	57	171	6.4	14.4	16.1
39 085	1692	Lake	591	215 499	232	364.6	209 879	3 528	250	1 447	395	1 469	6.9	13.9	13.2
39 087	3400	Lawrence	1 180	61 834	705	52.4	60 115	1 559	57	75	28	139	6.7	15.4	14.6
39 089	1840	Licking	1 778	128 300	362	72.2	125 181	2 217	247	475	180	604	7.2	14.8	14.6
39 091	...	Logan	1 187	42 310	951	35.6	41 156	804	58	240	52	159	7.4	15.6	13.9
39 093	1692	Lorain	1 276	271 126	183	212.5	241 549	21 230	738	1 479	6 130	15 261	7.4	15.3	14.9
39 095	8400	Lucas	882	462 361	107	524.2	380 155	68 456	1 164	4 981	7 605	15 658	7.8	14.4	15.2
39 097	1840	Madison	1 205	37 068	1 070	30.8	33 947	2 764	96	157	104	216	6.8	13.8	14.9
39 099	9320	Mahoning	1 076	264 806	187	246.1	221 109	39 681	444	985	2 587	5 946	6.5	13.8	13.1
39 101	...	Marion	1 046	64 274	681	61.4	60 948	2 707	148	285	186	485	7.5	14.8	13.6
39 103	1692	Medina	1 092	122 354	376	112.0	120 504	850	172	684	144	711	7.3	16.4	13.5
39 105	...	Meigs	1 112	22 987	1 535	20.7	22 734	177	44	20	12	59	6.6	15.6	13.6
39 107	...	Mercer	1 200	39 443	1 013	32.9	39 131	14	85	100	113	280	8.7	17.5	13.5
39 109	2000	Miami	1 054	93 182	496	88.4	90 519	1 779	158	606	120	366	7.0	15.3	13.5
39 111	...	Monroe	1 180	15 497	1 954	13.1	15 437	19	26	12	3	24	6.2	14.9	13.1
39 113	2000	Montgomery	1 196	573 809	83	479.8	463 551	101 817	1 065	5 886	1 490	4 539	7.4	13.7	14.4
39 115	...	Morgan	1 082	14 194	2 038	13.1	13 524	570	64	12	24	36	7.2	16.8	12.8
39 117	...	Morrow	1 050	27 749	1 362	26.4	27 579	64	49	38	19	92	7.3	16.6	14.2
39 119	...	Muskingum	1 721	82 068	553	47.7	78 125	3 468	214	152	109	247	7.2	15.2	14.7
39 121	...	Noble	1 033	11 336	2 271	11.0	11 301	7	15	9	4	23	7.5	17.1	12.4
39 123	...	Ottawa	661	40 029	997	60.6	39 029	265	51	94	590	1 491	6.2	14.4	12.4
39 125	...	Paulding	1 078	20 488	1 654	19.0	19 920	236	54	20	258	628	7.7	17.2	14.3
39 127	...	Perry	1 062	31 557	1 228	29.7	31 408	57	46	21	25	81	7.5	16.8	14.2
39 129	1840	Pickaway	1 301	48 255	865	37.1	44 867	3 036	127	95	130	323	6.6	13.5	14.8
39 131	...	Pike	1 144	24 249	1 486	21.2	23 807	327	72	41	2	74	7.2	16.4	14.5
39 133	1692	Portage	1 275	142 585	333	111.8	136 998	3 906	292	1 191	198	798	6.6	13.9	21.5
39 135	...	Preble	1 100	40 113	996	36.5	39 819	147	53	65	29	105	7.1	16.0	13.4

1. MSA = Metropolitan Statistical Area. CMSA = Consolidated MSA. NECMA = New England county metropolitan area. PMSA = Primary MSA. See Appendix A for explanation of these concepts. See Appendix B for list of metropolitan areas identified by type, with component counties. 2. Dry land or land partially or temporarily covered by water. 3. Hispanic persons may be of any race.

STATE County	Population, 1990 (cont'd) — Age of population (cont'd) Percent — 25 to 34 years	35 to 44 years	45 to 54 years	55 to 64 years	65 to 74 years	75 years and over	Percent female	Population–Change and components of change — Change 1980–1990 — Number	Percent	Total persons, 1986	Total persons, 1980	Components of change, 1980–1986 — Net change — Number	Percent	Natural increase — Births	Deaths
	14	15	16	17	18	19	20	21	22	23	24	25	26	27	28
OHIO	16.5	14.9	10.3	9.0	7.6	5.3	51.8	49 115	0.5	10 752 000	10 798 000	-45 000	-0.4	1 015 000	609 000
Adams	14.4	13.8	10.5	9.1	7.8	5.8	50.9	1 043	4.3	24 700	24 328	400	1.5	2 300	1 600
Allen	16.1	14.5	9.8	8.9	7.7	5.7	50.5	-2 486	-2.2	110 500	112 241	-1 800	-1.6	11 100	6 100
Ashland	14.6	14.1	10.5	8.9	7.7	6.0	51.2	1 329	2.9	46 300	46 178	100	0.3	4 500	2 500
Ashtabula	14.8	14.6	10.3	9.5	8.5	6.2	51.7	-4 394	-4.2	101 200	104 215	-3 000	-2.9	9 400	6 100
Athens	14.3	12.0	8.0	6.5	5.6	4.2	50.9	3 150	5.6	57 600	56 399	1 200	2.2	4 700	2 700
Auglaize	15.7	14.7	9.5	8.7	7.6	5.9	51.3	2 031	4.8	43 700	42 554	1 100	2.6	4 700	2 500
Belmont	13.8	14.7	10.3	10.7	10.7	8.0	53.0	-11 495	-13.9	78 200	82 569	-4 300	-5.3	6 500	5 800
Brown	16.0	14.1	10.4	8.9	7.2	5.6	50.9	3 046	9.5	34 700	31 920	2 800	8.7	3 300	1 900
Butler	16.7	15.2	10.1	8.5	6.1	4.1	51.6	32 692	12.6	271 500	258 787	12 700	4.9	25 200	12 400
Carroll	15.5	15.0	10.9	9.4	8.3	5.4	50.9	923	3.6	26 800	25 598	1 200	4.9	2 300	1 400
Champaign	15.0	14.9	12.6	8.5	7.3	5.5	50.8	2 370	7.0	33 900	33 649	300	0.8	3 100	1 900
Clark	14.6	14.6	11.4	9.2	8.0	5.8	52.1	-2 688	-1.8	147 400	150 236	-2 800	-1.9	13 800	9 300
Clermont	18.3	16.0	10.4	7.5	5.3	3.4	51.0	21 704	16.9	140 600	128 483	12 100	9.4	14 900	5 500
Clinton	15.8	14.6	10.0	8.5	7.5	5.6	51.4	812	2.3	34 800	34 603	200	0.4	3 400	2 100
Columbiana	14.8	14.8	10.5	9.9	9.0	5.9	51.8	-5 296	-4.7	110 100	113 572	-3 400	-3.0	10 000	7 200
Coshocton	14.9	14.6	10.8	9.8	8.3	6.1	51.7	-597	-1.7	35 900	36 024	-100	-0.4	3 400	2 200
Crawford	15.1	14.2	11.2	9.4	8.2	6.3	51.7	-2 205	-4.4	49 000	50 075	-1 100	-2.2	4 600	3 100
Cuyahoga	16.9	14.4	10.0	9.8	9.2	6.4	53.0	-86 260	-5.8	1 445 400	1 498 400	-53 000	-3.5	133 200	98 100
Darke	15.1	14.0	10.8	8.8	8.1	6.6	51.6	-1 477	-2.7	54 000	55 096	-1 100	-2.0	5 000	3 200
Defiance	15.3	15.2	10.8	8.3	6.8	4.9	50.7	-637	-1.6	39 200	39 987	-800	-2.0	4 000	1 900
Delaware	15.4	18.0	11.7	8.2	5.3	3.8	50.5	13 089	24.3	59 000	53 840	5 200	9.6	5 000	2 500
Erie	15.3	15.2	11.3	9.8	8.4	5.2	51.4	-2 876	-3.6	77 100	79 655	-2 500	-3.2	7 200	4 300
Fairfield	15.3	16.3	11.6	8.6	6.5	4.8	50.4	9 783	10.4	97 400	93 678	3 700	3.9	8 300	4 600
Fayette	14.8	14.7	10.8	9.5	8.2	6.6	51.5	-1	0.0	27 700	27 467	200	0.7	2 500	1 800
Franklin	20.1	15.3	9.3	7.6	5.7	3.9	51.8	92 311	10.6	907 000	869 126	37 900	4.4	89 800	42 400
Fulton	16.1	15.0	10.0	8.1	7.1	5.6	51.1	747	2.0	38 800	37 751	1 100	2.9	3 800	1 900
Gallia	15.8	14.1	11.2	9.3	7.2	5.6	51.1	856	2.8	29 800	30 098	-300	-1.0	2 900	1 800
Geauga	13.9	16.9	12.7	8.9	6.5	4.1	50.5	6 655	8.9	75 500	74 474	1 000	1.4	7 000	3 000
Greene	15.3	15.9	11.3	8.8	6.2	3.6	51.0	6 962	5.4	130 200	129 769	500	0.4	11 400	5 100
Guernsey	15.0	14.5	10.6	9.5	8.5	6.4	52.3	-3 000	-7.1	40 200	42 024	-1 800	-4.2	4 100	2 900
Hamilton	17.4	14.3	9.6	8.9	7.4	5.9	52.7	-6 976	-0.8	865 100	873 204	-8 100	-0.9	88 000	52 800
Hancock	16.6	14.9	10.4	8.3	7.4	5.6	51.6	955	1.5	65 900	64 581	1 300	2.0	6 300	3 300
Hardin	14.6	13.1	9.9	8.5	7.5	6.1	51.0	-1 608	-4.9	31 700	32 719	-1 000	-3.2	2 900	1 900
Harrison	13.8	14.5	10.5	10.4	9.9	7.5	51.7	-2 067	-11.4	16 400	18 152	-1 800	-9.8	1 400	1 200
Henry	15.6	13.9	10.1	9.0	7.5	6.1	50.8	725	2.6	28 500	28 383	100	0.3	2 900	1 600
Highland	14.8	13.7	10.5	9.6	8.5	6.5	51.4	2 251	6.7	34 600	33 477	1 200	3.5	3 200	2 300
Hocking	15.2	14.4	11.7	9.5	7.7	5.7	50.0	1 229	5.1	24 700	24 304	400	1.4	2 300	1 500
Holmes	14.7	12.4	8.7	7.5	5.8	4.9	50.8	3 433	11.7	30 000	29 416	600	2.1	4 200	1 300
Huron	16.1	14.6	10.0	8.6	7.0	4.9	51.3	1 632	3.0	55 100	54 608	500	0.9	5 600	2 900
Jackson	15.1	14.5	10.1	9.6	8.0	6.0	52.3	-362	-1.2	30 000	30 592	-600	-1.9	2 900	2 200
Jefferson	13.4	14.6	11.0	11.3	10.4	6.8	52.7	-11 266	-12.3	85 700	91 564	-5 800	-6.4	6 800	6 000
Knox	14.4	14.3	10.5	9.3	8.4	6.4	51.8	1 169	2.5	47 600	46 304	1 300	2.8	4 100	2 800
Lake	17.3	15.9	11.4	9.4	7.5	4.5	51.4	2 698	1.3	212 500	212 801	-300	-0.2	18 300	9 600
Lawrence	14.6	14.2	11.4	9.9	8.0	5.3	52.4	-2 015	-3.2	62 200	63 849	-1 600	-2.6	5 900	4 000
Licking	16.0	15.1	11.5	9.1	6.9	4.9	51.6	7 319	6.0	125 400	120 981	4 400	3.6	11 500	6 600
Logan	15.2	14.2	10.0	9.3	8.4	6.0	51.6	3 155	8.1	40 200	39 155	1 000	2.7	3 800	2 500
Lorain	16.2	15.5	10.4	8.7	7.1	4.5	51.3	-3 783	-1.4	270 600	274 909	-4 300	-1.6	25 500	12 400
Lucas	16.9	14.6	9.5	8.6	7.5	5.5	52.3	-9 380	-2.0	462 100	471 741	-9 600	-2.0	47 000	29 100
Madison	20.0	16.2	10.6	7.6	6.1	4.0	45.8	4 064	12.3	34 800	33 004	1 800	5.5	3 100	1 800
Mahoning	14.6	14.4	9.9	10.6	10.5	6.6	52.8	-24 681	-8.5	276 600	289 487	-12 900	-4.5	23 900	18 900
Marion	16.7	15.4	10.5	8.9	7.5	5.2	50.2	-3 700	-5.4	65 300	67 974	-2 700	-3.9	6 400	3 700
Medina	15.8	17.5	11.9	7.9	5.8	3.9	50.8	9 204	8.1	116 900	113 150	3 700	3.3	10 700	4 500
Meigs	14.1	14.6	10.9	9.6	8.7	6.3	51.6	-654	-2.8	23 900	23 641	200	1.0	2 100	1 500
Mercer	15.4	13.6	8.9	8.9	7.8	5.7	50.1	1 109	2.9	39 000	38 334	600	1.6	4 500	2 000
Miami	15.4	15.3	11.8	9.1	7.5	5.1	51.4	2 801	3.1	89 600	90 381	-800	-0.9	8 300	4 900
Monroe	13.6	14.5	12.0	10.0	8.5	7.1	50.9	-1 885	-10.8	16 200	17 382	-1 200	-6.8	1 300	1 000
Montgomery	17.5	14.8	10.5	9.3	7.6	5.0	52.1	2 112	0.4	566 300	571 697	-5 400	-0.9	55 500	30 400
Morgan	14.5	13.6	10.4	9.6	8.5	6.5	51.5	-47	-0.3	14 200	14 241	0	0.0	1 400	1 000
Morrow	15.2	15.3	11.7	8.6	6.3	4.7	50.4	1 269	4.8	27 000	26 480	500	1.8	2 500	1 300
Muskingum	15.4	14.0	10.3	9.4	7.8	6.0	52.4	-1 272	-1.5	84 100	83 340	800	0.9	8 200	5 400
Noble	15.2	13.4	9.7	9.7	8.0	7.0	51.1	26	0.2	11 500	11 310	200	2.0	1 200	800
Ottawa	14.9	15.0	11.1	10.5	9.5	6.0	51.1	-47	-0.1	39 900	40 076	-100	-0.4	3 400	2 400
Paulding	15.5	14.5	10.7	8.2	7.0	4.9	50.8	-814	-3.8	20 900	21 302	-400	-1.7	2 100	1 000
Perry	15.9	14.1	10.0	8.6	7.4	5.5	51.2	525	1.7	31 800	31 032	700	2.3	3 200	1 900
Pickaway	19.1	16.2	11.4	8.4	6.1	3.9	45.2	4 593	10.5	44 700	43 662	1 000	2.4	3 800	2 100
Pike	15.2	13.8	10.3	9.0	7.5	6.0	51.3	1 447	6.3	25 000	22 802	2 200	9.8	2 200	1 400
Portage	16.1	14.5	9.9	8.1	5.8	3.6	51.3	6 729	5.0	137 000	135 856	1 100	0.8	12 300	5 500
Preble	15.6	15.3	11.1	9.2	7.5	4.8	50.7	1 890	4.9	39 300	38 223	1 100	2.8	3 500	2 000

STATE County	Population– (cont'd) Components of change, 1980-1986 (cont'd) Net migration	Households, 1990 Number	Households, 1990 Percent change, 1980–1990	Households, 1990 Persons per household	Households, 1990 Percent Female family householder[1]	Households, 1990 Percent One-person	Births, 1988 Total	Births, 1988 Rate[2]	Births, 1988 Low birth weight[3] (Number)	Deaths, 1987 Number Total	Deaths, 1987 Number Infant[4]	Deaths, 1987 Rate Total[2]	Deaths, 1987 Rate Infant[5]	Marriages, 1984 Number	Marriages, 1984 Rate[2]
	29	30	31	32	33	34	35	36	37	38	39	40	41	42	43
OHIO	-452 000	4 087 546	6.6	2.59	11.7	25.0	160 529	14.8	11 017	99 240	1 461	9.2	9.3	98 646	9.2
Adams	-400	9 192	11.2	2.72	11.2	21.4	358	13.9	30	260	1	10.2	2.7	237	9.6
Allen	-6 700	39 408	0.6	2.66	11.7	23.6	1 693	15.1	105	1 025	14	9.2	8.0	1 058	9.7
Ashland	-1 800	17 101	7.5	2.66	8.0	22.6	667	14.3	31	441	7	9.5	11.3	436	9.4
Ashtabula	-6 300	36 760	2.6	2.66	11.0	22.8	1 433	14.3	88	985	13	9.8	8.5	1 093	10.8
Athens	-800	20 139	9.7	2.53	9.8	25.8	663	11.2	45	463	4	7.8	5.8	523	9.1
Auglaize	-1 100	15 976	9.9	2.76	7.6	21.0	760	17.0	38	378	7	8.6	9.7	388	9.0
Belmont	-5 100	28 161	-6.9	2.49	10.8	26.1	890	11.7	46	916	2	12.0	2.2	739	9.1
Brown	1 400	12 379	15.9	2.79	9.6	19.1	563	15.7	35	328	3	9.3	6.5	281	8.3
Butler	-100	104 535	18.6	2.68	10.4	20.8	4 103	14.7	263	2 128	37	7.7	9.2	2 944	11.1
Carroll	300	9 667	12.7	2.70	7.6	20.6	347	12.9	28	233	2	8.7	5.3	255	9.6
Champaign	-900	13 253	12.4	2.67	8.3	21.2	444	12.5	24	292	1	8.4	2.0	333	9.9
Clark	-7 300	55 198	3.4	2.60	11.9	23.3	2 025	13.7	135	1 446	15	9.8	7.2	1 331	9.1
Clermont	2 700	52 726	26.1	2.82	10.0	18.2	2 389	16.2	134	1 022	14	7.1	5.9	1 499	11.0
Clinton	-1 200	13 038	7.3	2.65	9.5	22.3	474	13.2	29	364	5	10.3	9.5	370	10.7
Columbiana	-6 200	40 775	1.9	2.63	10.3	22.9	1 417	13.0	96	1 115	14	10.3	9.8	1 087	9.7
Coshocton	-1 400	13 433	2.8	2.60	8.7	23.7	513	14.2	31	350	6	9.8	12.1	352	9.7
Crawford	-2 600	18 383	1.2	2.57	9.9	23.8	674	13.8	49	454	7	9.3	10.5	428	8.7
Cuyahoga	-88 100	563 243	0.0	2.46	14.9	30.2	21 836	15.3	1 879	15 514	243	10.7	11.3	12 858	8.8
Darke	-3 000	19 459	3.2	2.71	7.9	21.0	813	14.9	50	528	4	9.8	5.1	684	12.7
Defiance	-3 000	14 070	5.7	2.74	8.1	21.5	562	14.1	23	334	11	8.4	18.9	406	10.6
Delaware	2 700	23 116	31.2	2.78	7.2	17.0	910	14.5	43	470	7	7.7	8.6	461	8.3
Erie	-5 400	28 932	4.3	2.61	10.4	24.1	1 086	14.0	75	714	9	9.2	8.1	706	9.1
Fairfield	-100	36 813	15.9	2.74	8.8	19.0	1 315	12.9	75	810	10	8.1	7.3	897	9.4
Fayette	-500	10 221	5.5	2.64	10.5	21.8	403	14.7	28	291	5	10.6	13.9	290	10.5
Franklin	-9 500	378 723	17.3	2.47	12.6	28.0	15 831	16.9	1 197	7 185	131	7.8	8.8	10 196	11.4
Fulton	-900	13 504	7.7	2.82	7.2	19.5	609	15.7	23	329	6	8.6	10.4	376	9.8
Gallia	-1 400	11 367	10.6	2.63	10.2	22.4	430	14.2	37	288	2	9.5	4.9	302	10.1
Geauga	-3 000	26 906	17.6	2.98	7.1	14.9	1 223	15.4	65	474	7	6.1	6.0	586	7.9
Greene	-5 800	48 351	12.2	2.70	9.2	19.3	1 725	12.9	90	904	10	6.8	5.8	1 341	10.4
Guernsey	-3 000	14 894	-1.0	2.57	11.4	25.1	528	13.2	31	434	3	10.9	5.3	411	9.9
Hamilton	-43 300	338 881	5.2	2.50	14.0	29.9	14 263	16.3	1 044	8 252	144	9.4	10.2	7 629	8.8
Hancock	-1 700	24 642	6.9	2.61	8.0	23.5	1 030	15.7	58	535	10	8.2	10.2	661	10.1
Hardin	-2 000	11 250	1.1	2.60	8.6	24.7	397	12.6	17	299	4	9.4	10.1	304	9.6
Harrison	-2 000	6 111	-2.8	2.59	9.0	23.4	161	10.2	11	192	1	12.2	5.7	147	8.8
Henry	-1 300	10 401	6.9	2.75	7.2	21.3	446	15.7	23	256	2	9.0	4.7	242	8.7
Highland	300	13 230	11.0	2.67	10.0	22.4	511	14.3	30	378	4	10.7	8.1	335	9.8
Hocking	-400	9 351	8.8	2.66	9.1	21.2	338	13.4	24	288	1	11.5	3.0	239	9.7
Holmes	-2 400	9 315	14.1	3.42	6.1	15.8	742	23.8	33	217	6	7.0	8.3	283	9.3
Huron	-2 300	20 239	8.3	2.75	9.2	21.2	845	15.0	43	452	4	8.1	4.4	561	10.2
Jackson	-1 300	11 260	5.2	2.65	12.0	22.6	412	13.7	26	338	3	11.1	7.1	386	12.7
Jefferson	-6 600	31 311	-4.3	2.51	11.7	25.5	973	11.8	75	1 026	15	12.4	16.2	750	8.6
Knox	100	17 230	8.4	2.57	8.7	22.8	584	12.2	26	469	5	9.9	9.1	417	8.8
Lake	-9 100	80 421	11.6	2.65	9.6	22.0	2 957	13.8	152	1 679	26	7.8	9.2	1 915	9.0
Lawrence	-3 500	22 899	3.9	2.67	12.2	21.6	836	13.3	56	629	5	10.1	5.8	526	8.3
Licking	-500	47 254	11.9	2.65	9.5	21.3	1 816	14.4	117	1 080	16	8.6	9.3	1 261	10.2
Logan	-200	15 952	11.9	2.62	8.7	23.0	626	15.2	40	428	7	10.5	11.5	446	11.3
Lorain	-17 400	96 064	5.8	2.76	11.7	20.8	3 842	14.2	239	2 122	35	7.9	9.1	2 393	8.8
Lucas	-27 500	177 500	3.1	2.56	13.9	27.3	7 894	16.9	618	4 534	68	9.7	8.9	NA	NA
Madison	500	11 990	12.5	2.74	9.2	19.8	484	13.6	21	293	4	8.2	8.4	281	8.2
Mahoning	-17 900	101 136	-1.4	2.57	13.9	25.5	3 300	12.1	271	3 031	36	11.1	11.2	2 325	8.3
Marion	-5 300	23 484	-1.3	2.62	10.7	22.8	965	14.9	51	600	6	9.2	6.6	724	10.9
Medina	-2 500	41 792	16.2	2.90	7.7	16.3	1 693	14.1	89	767	15	6.5	9.0	1 038	9.0
Meigs	-400	8 662	3.0	2.62	10.1	22.7	294	12.5	17	253	1	10.7	3.3	251	10.6
Mercer	-1 900	13 398	10.1	2.91	6.7	20.4	688	17.6	29	310	6	8.0	9.1	397	10.3
Miami	-4 100	34 559	8.1	2.67	8.7	21.0	1 279	14.0	71	803	12	8.9	9.8	982	11.0
Monroe	-1 600	5 754	-3.5	2.66	8.1	21.7	193	12.5	11	176	1	11.2	5.2	163	9.8
Montgomery	-30 500	226 192	6.8	2.49	13.2	27.0	9 028	15.7	690	5 162	83	9.0	9.2	5 947	10.5
Morgan	-400	5 170	5.3	2.70	9.4	21.9	199	13.9	14	164	1	11.5	4.5	129	9.1
Morrow	-700	9 656	10.1	2.85	8.1	16.7	404	14.6	31	232	4	8.5	10.7	226	8.5
Muskingum	-2 000	30 753	4.5	2.61	11.5	23.8	1 150	13.7	80	814	9	9.7	7.2	878	10.4
Noble	-200	4 137	4.8	2.70	7.6	22.7	141	12.7	9	114	0	10.2	0.0	90	8.0
Ottawa	-1 200	15 170	6.8	2.60	7.7	21.9	520	13.0	33	412	6	10.4	12.6	347	8.7
Paulding	-1 500	7 252	3.5	2.81	7.5	19.8	276	13.1	12	176	1	8.4	3.3	169	8.2
Perry	-500	11 264	7.0	2.77	10.2	20.8	465	14.5	25	304	3	9.5	6.8	279	8.8
Pickaway	-600	15 602	10.2	2.72	9.3	18.8	625	13.4	36	350	8	7.5	13.3	478	11.3
Pike	1 500	8 805	14.3	2.70	12.4	21.5	371	14.7	28	244	4	9.8	11.3	250	10.5
Portage	-5 700	49 229	11.3	2.72	9.5	20.3	1 873	13.4	109	889	16	6.4	8.8	1 257	9.2
Preble	-400	14 347	9.3	2.77	8.1	18.1	555	14.0	41	350	8	8.9	14.2	291	7.5

1. No spouse present. 2. Per 1,000 resident population estimated as of July 1 of the year shown. 3. Under 2,500 grams. 4. Deaths of infants under 1 year old. 5. Deaths of infants under 1 year old per 1,000 live births.

STATE County	Divorces, 1984		Physicians, active non–Federal, 1989		Hospitals, 1989			Nursing homes,[4] 1986		Serious crimes known to police, 1988			Education			
						Beds				Number			Public school enrollment[7]		Attainment,[8] 1980	
	Number	Rate[1]	Number[2]	Rate[3]	Number	Number	Rate[3]	Number	Beds	Total[5]	Violent[6]	Rate[3]	1986–1987	1980	Percent 12 yrs. or more	Percent 16 yrs. or more
	44	45	46	47	48	49	50	51	52	53	54	55	56	57	58	59
OHIO	53 433	5.0	21 066	193	228	54 454	500	1 011	85 719	434 887	43 336	4 628	1 830 301	2 029 858	67.0	13.7
Adams	150	6.1	14	54	1	68	261	4	206	NA	NA	NA	5 833	5 738	47.9	5.4
Allen	533	4.9	169	150	4	758	673	12	1 173	7 128	1 169	7 048	21 221	22 151	67.5	10.0
Ashland	215	4.6	39	83	2	88	188	8	514	687	45	1 465	8 286	9 123	69.3	12.4
Ashtabula	560	5.5	68	68	4	377	376	14	1 343	3 247	161	3 338	19 461	22 069	65.6	8.1
Athens	305	5.3	31	52	3	300	504	6	383	761	61	3 565	10 068	9 484	67.9	20.3
Auglaize	158	3.6	33	73	1	95	211	6	548	697	43	1 964	8 557	8 976	67.3	8.4
Belmont	325	4.0	79	106	3	336	450	11	602	647	19	1 004	12 135	15 488	62.7	7.5
Brown	205	6.1	19	52	1	58	160	5	313	NA	NA	NA	6 841	7 281	53.4	7.0
Butler	1 869	7.1	307	108	4	891	314	25	2 115	12 859	1 093	6 058	47 765	49 729	64.7	14.1
Carroll	136	5.1	5	19	0	0	0	3	143	74	1	3 348	4 084	5 723	62.7	6.2
Champaign	172	5.1	18	50	1	61	169	3	281	779	78	2 340	7 299	7 258	64.1	8.7
Clark	894	6.1	172	116	2	626	420	20	1 802	8 183	1 229	5 515	27 763	30 373	65.3	10.6
Clermont	836	6.1	79	53	1	151	101	7	650	4 687	368	3 296	27 525	27 961	61.3	10.4
Clinton	194	5.6	35	97	1	94	260	7	357	528	18	3 704	7 810	7 397	64.1	10.8
Columbiana	446	4.0	76	71	3	516	479	13	789	1 067	108	1 141	20 362	23 899	63.1	8.5
Coshocton	162	4.5	20	55	1	151	418	5	356	456	8	1 260	6 711	7 481	63.9	8.9
Crawford	265	5.4	44	91	3	198	407	9	441	1 137	44	2 311	9 503	10 039	65.6	7.6
Cuyahoga	6 409	4.4	5 533	389	33	10 222	718	85	9 523	72 700	8 988	5 285	190 833	231 229	66.7	15.7
Darke	273	5.1	26	48	1	88	161	8	585	1 263	87	2 333	10 069	12 478	63.7	7.8
Defiance	172	4.5	46	115	2	126	315	6	414	1 612	164	4 058	7 977	9 018	67.0	11.0
Delaware	265	4.8	89	138	1	117	181	7	354	1 806	68	2 981	10 050	11 392	74.8	18.6
Erie	375	4.8	109	140	4	733	941	13	1 011	3 661	301	4 710	15 506	15 920	68.0	11.4
Fairfield	560	5.9	82	79	1	184	178	10	848	3 166	312	3 156	18 858	20 897	69.8	11.5
Fayette	144	5.2	17	62	1	63	230	6	469	777	26	2 792	5 657	5 882	57.3	7.3
Franklin	5 377	6.0	2 580	271	10	4 680	491	49	5 212	74 019	7 099	8 252	143 852	152 529	73.0	21.2
Fulton	143	3.7	20	52	1	86	222	5	282	931	122	2 455	8 626	8 552	69.1	9.3
Gallia	195	6.5	70	231	1	269	888	2	216	791	72	2 589	6 704	6 116	55.2	8.8
Geauga	323	4.3	71	88	1	125	155	6	463	812	74	1 160	12 044	14 949	76.7	20.5
Greene	734	5.7	135	100	1	216	160	14	1 313	4 561	280	3 425	24 533	26 367	75.7	21.1
Guernsey	226	5.5	48	121	2	476	1 196	4	402	608	4	4 839	6 766	8 260	61.2	8.2
Hamilton	4 091	4.7	3 058	349	19	6 549	746	88	7 858	46 881	3 984	5 474	125 837	139 978	65.0	18.7
Hancock	275	4.2	80	122	1	181	275	9	706	NA	NA	NA	11 414	13 317	75.8	14.7
Hardin	114	3.6	20	63	1	51	162	3	284	381	10	1 746	6 765	6 485	66.2	10.4
Harrison	60	3.6	12	77	1	48	310	2	108	243	39	1 535	3 582	3 947	60.5	5.5
Henry	88	3.2	14	49	1	42	148	3	216	515	18	1 920	6 374	5 674	65.2	7.8
Highland	196	5.7	19	52	2	70	193	3	264	994	132	2 793	7 377	7 297	57.4	6.8
Hocking	129	5.2	10	39	1	91	358	3	227	495	14	1 956	3 835	5 262	60.6	7.2
Holmes	91	3.0	21	67	1	55	175	7	647	205	3	755	4 506	5 178	42.7	6.7
Huron	235	4.3	51	90	2	216	380	4	386	1 109	55	1 971	11 900	11 433	67.5	8.9
Jackson	184	6.1	6	20	1	68	227	5	241	235	2	1 773	6 341	6 671	53.9	7.8
Jefferson	353	4.0	92	114	2	423	523	9	539	2 380	155	2 855	14 427	16 786	62.3	7.6
Knox	246	5.2	41	86	1	153	319	11	668	105	15	314	8 769	8 685	67.4	10.7
Lake	1 020	4.8	231	107	1	359	167	16	1 339	5 246	192	2 983	34 187	41 372	73.9	14.2
Lawrence	369	5.8	30	48	1	117	186	7	543	361	74	2 695	13 641	13 883	57.9	6.5
Licking	703	5.7	100	79	1	192	151	10	1 121	2 686	245	5 450	23 796	26 176	68.0	11.2
Logan	253	6.4	29	70	1	105	253	4	400	433	18	1 521	8 099	8 160	65.4	8.7
Lorain	1 246	4.6	286	106	6	996	368	27	2 178	7 620	738	2 978	50 084	58 430	67.0	10.9
Lucas	1 836	4.0	1 359	291	10	3 567	763	32	2 890	19 818	1 784	4 412	72 073	79 628	66.8	14.0
Madison	165	4.8	26	72	1	109	302	2	150	426	52	2 463	7 293	6 991	60.7	7.4
Mahoning	NA	NA	603	224	6	1 582	587	29	2 583	10 842	2 197	5 982	44 550	48 841	65.5	10.8
Marion	471	7.1	109	169	2	278	432	8	691	3 125	163	4 899	13 055	14 394	65.4	9.9
Medina	549	4.7	120	99	3	233	191	13	1 224	776	54	1 531	25 540	26 315	75.9	15.4
Meigs	138	5.8	8	34	1	69	294	2	115	NA	NA	NA	4 438	5 038	55.4	6.0
Mercer	90	2.3	28	71	1	93	236	6	433	591	41	1 696	8 852	8 808	63.4	8.3
Miami	455	5.1	99	107	3	399	432	9	817	2 924	213	3 212	18 496	19 359	66.9	10.6
Monroe	70	4.2	3	20	0	0	0	2	149	182	20	1 205	3 934	3 879	61.1	5.4
Montgomery	3 823	6.8	1 304	226	10	5 148	891	40	3 493	35 382	3 860	6 862	91 057	106 584	69.4	16.0
Morgan	62	4.4	4	28	0	0	0	3	230	118	3	824	2 651	3 180	61.3	6.0
Morrow	114	4.3	7	25	1	62	223	4	200	392	15	1 601	5 600	6 340	63.6	6.5
Muskingum	511	6.1	119	141	2	586	697	9	704	2 942	271	3 540	17 605	17 161	62.6	8.5
Noble	26	2.3	1	9	0	0	0	1	150	NA	NA	NA	2 371	2 491	63.2	5.9
Ottawa	182	4.6	26	65	1	71	178	2	266	970	21	2 424	6 765	8 468	66.8	9.2
Paulding	97	4.7	6	28	1	45	212	2	100	NA	NA	NA	4 660	5 066	63.3	5.4
Perry	140	4.4	6	19	0	0	0	3	180	749	78	2 659	6 358	6 969	60.9	6.3
Pickaway	257	6.1	27	57	1	44	93	4	336	NA	NA	NA	9 393	9 764	60.2	8.5
Pike	125	5.2	17	67	1	44	173	5	327	491	35	1 948	5 928	5 283	52.3	8.6
Portage	712	5.2	101	72	1	285	203	5	545	2 587	92	5 099	24 986	27 432	71.0	15.1
Preble	215	5.6	4	10	0	0	0	5	244	967	40	2 571	8 006	8 611	64.5	7.6

1. Per 1,000 resident population estimated as of July 1 of the year shown. 2. As of end of year. 3. Per 100,000 resident population as of July 1 of the year shown. 4. Preliminary. Covers nursing homes with 3 or more beds. 5. Data for serious crimes have not been adjusted for underreporting, this may affect comparability between geographic areas or over time. 6. Includes murder and nonnegligent manslaughter, forcible rape, robbery, and aggravated assault. 7. The 1986–1987 data are based on administrative reports obtained by the U.S. National Center for Education Statistics. The 1980 data are based on the 1980 Census of Population and Housing. 8. Persons 25 years old or older.

STATE County	Education (cont'd): Local government expenditures for education,[1] 1982: Total (Mil dol)	Education (cont'd): Local government expenditures for education,[1] 1982: Per capita (Dollars)	Social Security Program December 1988: Beneficiaries: Total	Social Security Program December 1988: Beneficiaries: Rate[2]	Social Security Program December 1988: Payments ($1,000)	Supplemental Security Income Program recipients June 1986	Money income: Per capita[3]: 1987 Income, (Dollars)	Money income: Per capita[3]: 1979: Current dollars	Money income: Per capita[3]: 1979: Constant 1987 dollars	Money income: Median household income 1979 (Dollars)	Money income: Percent below poverty level, 1979: Persons	Money income: Percent below poverty level, 1979: Families	Housing units, 1990: Total	Housing units, 1990: Percent change, 1980–1990
	60	61	62	63	64	65	66	67	68	69	70	71	72	73
OHIO	4 797.0	445	1 763 600	162.5	877 065	133 867	11 323	7 284	11 397	17 754	10.3	8.0	4 371 945	6.4
Adams	11.6	467	4 815	187.4	1 779	1 464	7 128	4 598	7 194	10 596	24.7	20.7	10 237	12.3
Allen	52.0	473	18 670	166.7	9 242	1 186	10 651	6 902	10 800	17 396	10.5	8.3	42 758	2.1
Ashland	18.8	404	7 665	164.1	3 755	288	9 998	6 516	10 196	16 678	8.8	6.4	18 139	6.2
Ashtabula	47.1	458	18 045	179.6	8 676	1 192	9 324	6 523	10 207	17 127	9.1	7.1	41 214	1.7
Athens	22.8	397	8 010	135.8	3 281	1 228	7 802	5 091	7 966	11 839	21.6	14.2	21 737	9.4
Auglaize	16.3	380	7 685	171.9	3 772	226	10 217	6 620	10 358	17 469	6.5	5.3	16 907	9.1
Belmont	28.0	342	16 665	219.9	8 167	956	9 185	6 647	10 401	16 547	9.3	7.3	30 575	-4.0
Brown	12.5	377	5 545	154.9	2 349	594	8 444	5 641	8 826	14 996	15.0	12.3	13 720	15.8
Butler	111.1	423	39 250	140.3	19 583	2 974	11 457	7 344	11 491	19 584	9.8	7.1	110 353	19.3
Carroll	7.0	271	3 460	129.1	1 661	272	8 394	6 018	9 416	16 441	9.9	8.4	11 536	11.8
Champaign	14.4	429	5 610	158.5	2 651	368	10 478	6 500	10 171	16 488	9.9	7.7	14 030	12.2
Clark	62.3	420	25 770	173.8	12 318	2 220	10 925	6 804	10 646	16 842	11.6	9.2	58 377	3.5
Clermont	57.1	428	15 720	106.9	7 561	1 228	10 957	7 001	10 954	20 093	8.1	6.7	55 315	23.6
Clinton	17.1	494	5 775	161.3	2 626	470	9 731	6 280	9 826	15 464	11.2	8.8	13 740	6.8
Columbiana	43.1	380	21 390	197.0	10 614	1 266	9 012	6 532	10 221	16 721	9.6	7.5	44 035	2.3
Coshocton	16.9	466	6 355	176.5	3 037	422	9 593	6 534	10 224	15 847	10.2	7.7	14 964	5.2
Crawford	20.8	420	8 760	179.9	4 286	416	9 672	6 579	10 294	16 145	10.4	8.2	19 514	-0.1
Cuyahoga	711.4	484	270 670	189.2	141 998	20 914	12 528	8 098	12 671	18 009	11.5	9.1	604 538	1.3
Darke	19.6	365	9 085	167.0	4 343	412	10 194	6 303	9 862	16 234	9.0	6.8	20 338	1.6
Defiance	16.5	422	5 925	148.9	2 965	316	10 807	7 147	11 183	19 513	7.1	5.4	14 737	3.4
Delaware	19.8	356	6 550	104.3	3 184	324	12 732	7 366	11 526	19 984	6.7	5.1	24 377	29.6
Erie	42.0	535	12 820	165.0	6 520	644	11 629	7 523	11 771	19 130	8.0	6.1	32 827	4.8
Fairfield	39.9	418	14 220	140.0	6 778	870	11 228	7 067	11 058	18 374	7.2	5.7	39 014	15.1
Fayette	10.6	387	4 680	170.8	2 091	506	8 862	5 766	9 022	13 978	14.4	11.8	10 816	4.2
Franklin	382.2	433	117 905	125.7	57 588	12 310	12 417	7 590	11 876	17 081	12.3	8.9	405 418	16.8
Fulton	19.4	513	6 450	166.7	3 268	164	10 636	6 873	10 754	18 648	8.1	6.8	14 095	5.7
Gallia	17.7	593	5 395	178.6	2 176	956	8 575	5 954	9 316	14 422	14.9	12.3	12 564	9.8
Geauga	34.1	457	6 825	86.1	3 554	188	13 594	8 770	13 722	24 351	4.7	3.6	27 922	15.0
Greene	59.3	453	13 705	102.7	6 127	972	12 077	7 501	11 737	20 306	7.9	6.2	50 238	11.5
Guernsey	13.2	316	8 030	200.8	3 451	794	8 772	5 986	9 366	14 260	12.6	8.9	17 262	3.7
Hamilton	381.0	438	144 495	165.3	72 892	12 902	12 770	7 871	12 316	17 446	11.3	8.7	361 421	5.3
Hancock	26.5	408	9 955	151.3	5 006	418	11 706	7 411	11 596	18 305	6.5	5.0	26 107	6.1
Hardin	14.5	448	5 215	165.0	2 405	302	9 108	6 159	9 637	15 882	12.9	9.2	11 976	-0.2
Harrison	7.9	449	3 655	231.3	1 688	194	8 575	5 998	9 385	15 335	11.0	9.3	7 301	3.3
Henry	16.1	576	4 760	167.6	2 334	180	10 789	6 959	10 889	18 346	5.7	4.5	11 000	1.8
Highland	13.1	388	6 845	191.7	2 889	766	8 632	5 533	8 657	13 042	15.0	11.9	14 842	6.8
Hocking	6.7	277	4 065	161.3	1 810	438	8 568	5 665	8 864	14 255	12.4	9.8	10 481	9.4
Holmes	8.2	272	2 900	92.9	1 315	228	7 347	4 961	7 762	14 986	18.2	14.4	10 007	13.9
Huron	24.0	440	9 395	166.9	4 526	458	10 492	6 759	10 576	17 584	7.5	6.1	21 382	5.9
Jackson	12.6	419	5 790	192.4	2 398	960	8 115	5 309	8 307	12 482	16.6	13.8	12 452	6.8
Jefferson	40.4	448	17 990	218.6	9 098	1 254	9 809	7 191	11 252	18 173	10.2	8.4	33 911	-4.9
Knox	18.6	395	8 660	181.2	4 080	692	9 335	5 957	9 321	14 803	11.6	9.2	18 508	7.2
Lake	101.1	471	32 805	152.8	17 664	968	12 589	8 239	12 892	22 369	4.0	3.1	83 194	10.7
Lawrence	28.0	444	11 390	181.7	4 988	1 740	8 535	5 776	9 038	14 972	15.2	12.3	24 788	5.2
Licking	56.2	454	18 020	142.5	8 598	1 276	10 910	7 010	10 969	17 709	8.1	6.3	50 032	11.2
Logan	17.6	450	7 625	185.5	3 578	444	9 986	6 209	9 715	14 800	11.1	8.7	19 473	5.0
Lorain	124.3	454	40 180	148.5	20 717	2 442	10 812	7 209	11 280	20 371	8.4	7.0	99 937	4.2
Lucas	195.5	418	75 420	161.7	38 548	6 638	11 857	7 588	11 873	17 726	11.5	9.0	191 388	3.5
Madison	15.9	467	5 055	141.6	2 341	386	10 012	6 318	9 886	17 469	9.7	7.5	12 621	11.1
Mahoning	116.9	412	58 150	213.9	29 098	4 456	9 965	6 928	10 840	17 489	11.0	8.7	107 915	-0.6
Marion	29.9	444	10 510	162.2	4 996	802	9 975	6 672	10 440	16 958	10.7	8.3	25 149	-0.6
Medina	60.9	530	14 475	120.4	7 472	514	12 156	7 862	12 302	22 804	4.4	3.6	43 330	14.0
Meigs	9.2	390	4 265	180.7	1 765	560	7 811	5 359	8 385	12 750	16.7	14.1	9 795	5.4
Mercer	18.0	466	6 475	165.2	3 165	200	10 323	6 611	10 344	18 311	7.4	6.0	14 969	5.2
Miami	41.5	461	15 275	166.9	7 655	706	11 106	7 102	11 112	17 861	7.5	5.7	35 985	6.8
Monroe	10.1	594	2 885	186.1	1 194	390	8 551	5 968	9 338	15 864	13.5	11.0	6 567	1.2
Montgomery	279.3	493	93 720	163.1	46 308	7 574	12 207	7 641	11 956	17 632	11.0	8.8	240 820	5.8
Morgan	5.5	384	2 415	168.9	1 040	258	8 279	5 413	8 470	13 687	14.8	11.3	6 681	8.9
Morrow	12.2	455	3 350	121.4	1 551	232	9 158	5 974	9 348	16 336	10.2	8.1	10 312	8.6
Muskingum	38.5	457	15 680	186.4	7 410	1 306	9 475	6 134	9 598	14 719	12.0	9.2	33 029	3.5
Noble	7.5	667	1 845	166.2	768	158	8 173	5 721	8 952	14 442	13.0	10.2	4 998	4.3
Ottawa	19.1	479	7 815	195.4	3 902	196	11 663	7 329	11 468	18 570	6.1	5.2	23 340	1.2
Paulding	8.7	417	3 120	147.9	1 507	162	10 350	6 519	10 200	18 869	7.2	5.8	7 951	4.2
Perry	14.7	469	5 740	178.8	2 549	512	8 219	5 436	8 506	14 112	12.5	10.0	12 260	6.9
Pickaway	17.1	397	6 090	130.7	2 735	596	9 723	6 267	9 806	16 981	10.9	9.1	16 385	8.3
Pike	12.7	541	4 090	161.7	1 661	844	7 682	5 015	7 847	11 802	20.6	16.4	9 722	11.6
Portage	60.6	440	16 880	121.0	8 499	976	10 587	6 894	10 787	18 788	9.4	6.3	52 299	10.0
Preble	18.1	477	5 885	148.2	2 804	302	10 030	6 545	10 241	17 187	9.2	7.7	15 174	8.7

1. Elementary and secondary. 2. Per 1,000 resident population estimated as of July 1 of the year shown. 3. Based on the resident population estimated as of July 1, 1988 for 1987 data and enumerated as of April 1, 1980 for 1979 data.

Table A. States and Counties — **Housing, Labor Force, and Employment**

STATE County	Housing units, 1990 (cont'd) — Occupied units — Total	Owner occupied — Percent	Owner occupied — Median value (Dollars)	Median rent (Dollars)	Civilian labor force, 1990 — Total	Percent change, 1989–1990	Unemployment — Total	Unemployment — Rate[1]	Private nonfarm establishments, 1988 — Number	Net change, 1987–1988	Employment[2] — Total	Percent change, 1987–1988	Manu-facturing	Retail trade
	74	75	76	77	78	79	80	81	82	83	84	85	86	87
OHIO	4 087 546	67.5	63 500	296	5 433 000	0.3	307 000	5.7	X	X	4 020 528	3.0	1 119 170	857 555
Adams	9 192	73.2	36 900	176	8 420	1.5	1 010	12.0	325	23	1 978	8.0	308	801
Allen	39 408	71.7	52 100	264	55 014	-0.9	3 916	7.1	2 706	-1	46 162	-0.1	14 838	10 333
Ashland	17 101	74.0	53 600	243	23 033	1.0	1 301	5.6	954	-5	14 973	7.9	7 437	2 599
Ashtabula	36 760	71.9	45 800	243	41 216	-3.1	3 588	8.7	1 986	10	25 449	0.4	8 866	5 853
Athens	20 139	62.0	47 600	285	25 039	0.7	1 468	5.9	1 045	23	9 854	5.2	1 338	3 869
Auglaize	15 976	76.9	58 500	256	22 709	-0.7	1 343	5.9	962	19	14 502	6.4	6 713	2 886
Belmont	28 161	73.8	42 100	195	31 310	-1.5	1 772	5.7	1 466	-55	15 814	-2.5	1 940	5 852
Brown	12 379	76.0	49 200	212	14 373	-2.5	1 136	7.9	474	15	5 741	4.4	1 834	1 232
Butler	104 535	69.2	73 000	325	132 315	0.0	7 679	5.8	5 055	79	80 776	4.0	22 324	17 667
Carroll	9 667	78.5	46 600	205	11 723	-1.0	730	6.2	410	13	4 362	10.1	1 809	1 027
Champaign	13 253	73.9	55 400	248	17 215	0.3	1 179	6.8	581	20	7 946	-0.6	3 760	1 618
Clark	55 198	69.1	54 900	256	72 143	-0.1	4 332	6.0	2 736	19	45 112	5.1	13 400	10 876
Clermont	52 726	72.1	71 200	340	79 496	1.1	3 946	5.0	2 318	78	28 899	7.1	7 146	8 395
Clinton	13 038	67.7	52 200	261	20 361	3.9	1 075	5.3	717	8	11 968	5.9	4 384	2 105
Columbiana	40 775	75.0	42 600	209	49 874	0.9	2 962	5.9	2 315	55	25 842	6.2	8 680	6 206
Coshocton	13 433	75.7	44 500	208	16 293	0.0	1 057	6.5	670	-4	10 879	-0.4	4 853	1 911
Crawford	18 383	71.1	43 100	205	21 572	-0.9	2 269	10.5	990	20	16 002	3.2	7 665	3 007
Cuyahoga	563 243	62.0	72 100	321	732 415	0.1	35 095	4.8	36 428	167	662 296	-0.2	161 522	119 943
Darke	19 459	76.4	52 300	230	27 512	1.4	1 913	7.0	1 173	37	14 096	6.1	4 870	3 151
Defiance	14 070	78.4	53 300	252	19 084	0.7	1 563	8.2	831	12	14 803	6.8	6 948	2 806
Delaware	23 116	78.1	95 900	330	34 163	1.1	1 439	4.2	1 188	10	15 915	2.5	5 168	3 488
Erie	28 932	71.3	65 100	286	41 329	0.4	2 572	6.2	1 904	10	27 408	-2.9	9 281	6 894
Fairfield	36 813	74.7	68 900	284	52 826	0.8	3 208	6.1	1 896	136	20 542	1.4	6 570	5 660
Fayette	10 221	64.9	43 800	214	12 506	-0.9	915	7.3	534	14	6 896	-7.2	2 821	1 968
Franklin	378 723	54.9	73 800	355	528 834	0.7	20 769	3.9	24 196	772	458 927	3.4	66 953	105 998
Fulton	13 504	78.5	59 700	263	20 212	-0.8	1 500	7.4	967	26	13 942	9.3	6 931	2 574
Gallia	11 367	73.8	48 400	208	12 252	1.4	940	7.7	568	2	7 397	0.3	907	1 986
Geauga	26 906	85.7	107 700	368	41 323	0.2	1 664	4.0	1 824	54	20 341	2.2	7 747	3 464
Greene	48 351	69.4	78 200	352	65 168	-0.5	3 051	4.7	2 305	81	29 236	7.2	4 479	8 323
Guernsey	14 894	73.0	38 600	211	16 531	-2.7	1 432	8.7	911	20	10 907	4.4	3 490	2 517
Hamilton	338 881	58.3	72 200	304	483 245	1.1	19 034	3.9	23 995	300	492 504	4.0	126 858	91 823
Hancock	24 642	74.2	63 300	286	39 085	0.3	1 847	4.7	1 588	19	29 078	0.1	9 931	5 604
Hardin	11 250	71.7	42 100	201	12 987	-0.9	1 015	7.8	524	-4	6 995	0.4	2 629	1 389
Harrison	6 111	75.7	33 300	180	4 271	-4.5	473	11.1	318	-19	2 420	-17.5	203	455
Henry	10 401	78.4	55 200	238	14 410	1.2	1 135	7.9	612	19	7 667	1.0	3 608	1 185
Highland	13 230	72.9	42 200	199	14 423	-2.7	1 151	8.0	658	-8	7 210	4.0	2 574	1 768
Hocking	9 351	75.8	43 400	219	10 315	0.4	970	9.4	451	1	4 888	9.7	2 163	1 118
Holmes	9 315	77.2	63 400	219	17 842	4.5	847	4.7	590	-5	8 433	9.7	4 321	1 364
Huron	20 239	71.6	56 700	264	30 084	2.5	2 846	9.5	1 207	1	21 288	10.3	10 846	3 708
Jackson	11 260	73.4	39 400	192	12 340	0.6	1 046	8.5	601	5	6 486	1.2	2 432	1 539
Jefferson	31 311	73.5	42 900	191	30 907	0.3	1 891	6.1	1 647	21	21 210	0.9	4 911	5 589
Knox	17 230	72.2	49 100	235	21 326	0.1	1 268	5.9	910	-24	11 892	4.9	3 311	2 682
Lake	80 421	75.8	74 200	406	119 434	0.0	5 920	5.0	5 297	176	74 819	3.4	23 176	19 291
Lawrence	22 899	72.2	43 700	210	24 508	1.9	1 529	6.2	790	-8	7 264	1.3	1 074	2 477
Licking	47 254	72.0	61 600	271	66 505	1.0	4 266	6.4	2 428	58	34 492	4.8	8 819	8 548
Logan	15 952	73.3	53 000	249	19 894	5.8	1 268	6.4	891	31	12 250	23.5	4 309	2 658
Lorain	96 064	71.9	66 100	296	119 630	0.1	9 242	7.7	4 892	44	80 315	6.0	30 096	16 966
Lucas	177 500	65.0	57 300	297	235 115	-0.7	17 185	7.3	11 115	108	196 287	1.7	45 454	43 604
Madison	11 990	70.2	62 300	254	17 497	1.3	880	5.0	619	12	6 418	11.0	1 442	1 954
Mahoning	101 136	71.7	47 900	260	116 816	-0.6	8 033	6.9	6 397	116	86 565	5.8	13 433	22 769
Marion	23 484	70.9	42 500	235	28 884	0.5	2 339	8.1	1 299	1	20 658	4.4	6 765	4 893
Medina	41 792	79.3	83 700	357	61 647	0.3	2 994	4.9	2 549	65	29 819	4.1	8 084	7 657
Meigs	8 662	78.7	35 700	174	7 923	-2.5	597	7.5	346	-2	3 524	-2.8	222	937
Mercer	13 398	79.8	61 100	235	18 475	2.1	1 151	6.2	872	19	10 992	1.7	4 362	2 305
Miami	34 559	72.7	65 000	291	48 779	0.6	2 973	6.1	1 961	25	31 276	2.1	14 835	6 244
Monroe	5 754	79.9	39 600	166	4 457	-3.0	483	10.8	275	10	4 223	10.8	0	438
Montgomery	226 192	62.9	65 000	316	290 718	-0.4	14 995	5.2	13 319	194	257 738	1.7	70 695	52 792
Morgan	5 170	77.2	39 900	190	5 954	1.4	518	8.7	175	-20	2 960	12.2	1 180	376
Morrow	9 656	81.0	47 600	217	11 436	-1.9	802	7.0	397	-8	4 334	-9.5	1 608	862
Muskingum	30 753	73.0	47 100	229	41 003	2.2	3 495	8.5	1 881	8	26 309	1.5	7 383	6 051
Noble	4 137	80.0	37 200	187	4 138	-1.5	353	8.5	184	-2	1 708	11.0	603	369
Ottawa	15 170	78.3	68 600	282	24 231	3.2	1 718	7.1	1 075	46	11 570	3.1	3 872	2 353
Paulding	7 252	83.2	42 500	201	9 331	-0.6	630	6.8	330	-7	3 462	4.8	1 724	634
Perry	11 264	78.1	36 900	207	13 797	2.4	1 642	11.9	468	16	5 189	7.5	2 114	961
Pickaway	15 602	71.7	62 200	263	22 600	0.7	1 301	5.8	712	11	10 352	5.9	5 163	2 204
Pike	8 805	69.4	42 300	210	8 805	-1.4	852	9.7	370	-2	5 713	6.5	2 961	1 060
Portage	49 229	70.1	69 200	331	72 206	0.5	3 821	5.3	2 382	8	29 119	3.7	9 526	8 509
Preble	14 347	77.1	52 700	231	21 785	4.7	1 231	5.7	634	-13	7 265	13.1	2 948	1 624

1. Percent of total civilian labor force. 2. For week including March 12. Excludes government employees, self-employed persons, farm workers, domestic service workers, railroad employees subject to the Railroad Retirement Act, and employees on oceanborne vessels or in foreign countries.

STATE County	Private nonfarm establishments, 1988 (cont'd): Employment[1] (cont'd): Finance, insurance, and real estate	Private nonfarm establishments, 1988 (cont'd): Employment[1] (cont'd): Services	Private nonfarm establishments, 1988 (cont'd): Annual payroll: Total (Mil dol)	Private nonfarm establishments, 1988 (cont'd): Annual payroll: Average per employee (Dollars)	Personal income, 1989: Total (Mil dol)	Personal income, 1989: Percent change, 1988–1989	Personal income, 1989: Wages and salaries[2] (Mil dol)	Personal income, 1989: Proprietor's income (Mil dol)	Personal income, 1989: Dividends, interest, & rent (Mil dol)	Personal income, 1989: Transfer payments (Mil dol)	Personal income, 1989: Per capita[3]: Dollars	Personal income, 1989: Per capita[3]: Rank	Earnings, 1989: Total (Mil dol)	Earnings, 1989: Percent by selected industries: Farm	Earnings, 1989: Percent by selected industries: Goods-related[4]: Total
	88	89	90	91	92	93	94	95	96	97	98	99	100	101	102
OHIO	249 559	1 091 724	85 608	X	179 381	6.6	118 327	12 002	29 377	30 259	16 462	X	130 329	0.7	35.9
Adams	128	439	24	12 013	236	7.4	107	29	31	77	9 044	3 003	137	7.7	NA
Allen	1 723	12 088	941	20 386	1 731	5.0	1 320	108	268	359	15 363	852	1 428	0.8	47.3
Ashland	470	3 179	265	17 711	680	6.1	367	53	116	111	14 529	1 199	420	1.2	51.1
Ashtabula	1 448	5 883	454	17 823	1 291	5.3	642	70	199	311	12 886	1 962	712	0.7	40.8
Athens	509	2 583	128	12 996	644	6.9	344	37	80	166	10 831	2 707	381	0.6	9.2
Auglaize	543	2 775	270	18 594	683	8.1	375	64	129	102	15 145	929	439	5.2	52.8
Belmont	811	3 983	242	15 292	977	6.0	404	63	194	253	13 095	1 866	467	0.2	28.2
Brown	211	1 178	87	15 216	438	6.7	108	34	66	81	12 062	2 308	142	7.0	29.3
Butler	6 548	17 842	1 723	21 336	4 550	6.2	2 292	236	652	657	16 029	638	2 529	0.3	42.1
Carroll	105	787	68	15 483	330	6.6	106	32	54	58	12 270	2 205	138	3.8	36.6
Champaign	306	1 331	152	19 075	486	8.1	215	36	68	87	13 492	1 686	251	3.8	48.4
Clark	2 567	12 195	896	19 869	2 327	5.7	1 239	131	295	475	15 633	767	1 370	1.7	41.3
Clermont	1 264	7 059	592	20 472	2 255	7.5	812	118	259	279	15 023	981	930	0.4	35.5
Clinton	403	2 060	217	18 120	523	7.5	305	51	81	94	14 438	1 239	355	5.6	NA
Columbiana	1 131	6 546	409	15 840	1 313	6.8	587	97	215	291	12 182	2 245	684	1.7	39.0
Coshocton	401	1 930	220	20 233	466	5.4	282	32	84	91	12 918	1 946	314	1.2	50.2
Crawford	584	3 094	299	18 685	644	5.8	344	44	125	126	13 255	1 791	388	2.0	49.5
Cuyahoga	51 373	207 735	15 624	23 591	28 081	6.9	21 581	2 195	5 390	4 918	19 722	182	23 777	0.0	30.8
Darke	606	2 800	249	17 677	821	7.9	322	101	148	119	15 075	953	423	10.4	NA
Defiance	468	3 041	348	23 511	580	7.1	487	42	95	88	14 511	1 207	529	1.9	60.3
Delaware	540	4 378	305	19 165	1 142	7.6	440	72	150	122	17 664	342	511	1.2	39.2
Erie	830	7 008	609	22 214	1 245	5.7	851	67	206	202	15 981	650	919	0.5	48.3
Fairfield	1 012	4 462	338	16 431	1 551	6.4	561	108	224	229	14 980	996	668	1.4	36.8
Fayette	223	1 090	115	16 635	354	6.9	160	36	57	75	12 913	1 950	196	7.9	37.8
Franklin	51 727	136 855	9 637	20 999	17 063	7.1	13 934	1 076	2 359	2 539	17 917	306	15 010	0.1	20.1
Fulton	419	2 057	263	18 892	620	5.8	350	60	114	88	15 977	651	410	1.8	51.9
Gallia	317	2 272	134	18 116	373	7.5	199	28	54	110	12 317	2 191	228	1.1	14.8
Geauga	579	5 018	387	19 032	1 571	7.8	540	116	283	120	19 421	198	655	0.8	44.8
Greene	885	11 575	462	15 818	2 272	5.9	1 089	120	291	362	16 839	464	1 209	1.4	15.5
Guernsey	419	2 610	184	16 896	481	3.5	262	40	69	126	12 090	2 294	302	0.6	36.0
Hamilton	34 286	140 844	11 516	23 382	16 710	6.6	14 492	1 045	3 499	2 601	19 046	217	15 537	0.0	33.7
Hancock	1 414	6 019	644	22 142	1 165	4.4	777	78	208	133	17 703	336	855	2.3	48.5
Hardin	216	1 987	119	17 006	388	6.5	175	40	63	67	12 306	2 196	216	6.8	42.1
Harrison	125	635	47	19 335	171	4.9	76	16	38	52	11 007	2 665	93	1.8	42.8
Henry	240	1 317	160	20 807	446	7.6	244	43	82	66	15 675	746	287	4.7	NA
Highland	409	1 431	112	15 582	454	8.3	169	36	78	97	12 555	2 093	205	3.7	39.2
Hocking	128	776	82	16 708	303	7.6	129	22	44	67	11 926	2 351	151	0.7	47.8
Holmes	244	1 290	136	16 108	330	8.3	189	57	55	47	10 525	2 784	246	9.2	50.2
Huron	574	2 951	416	19 528	878	7.4	541	73	124	147	15 439	817	615	4.1	47.9
Jackson	328	1 299	91	14 074	323	5.7	158	25	46	92	10 779	2 721	183	2.8	40.7
Jefferson	1 097	5 867	373	17 580	1 108	6.7	579	68	207	280	13 698	1 582	646	0.4	37.3
Knox	495	4 109	190	15 945	658	6.8	301	57	105	141	13 726	1 567	358	3.7	37.5
Lake	2 435	17 359	1 496	19 992	3 910	7.2	1 960	196	548	500	18 141	279	2 156	1.0	45.1
Lawrence	357	1 790	114	15 742	675	5.7	221	40	77	189	10 752	2 729	260	0.5	25.3
Licking	3 334	8 967	639	18 536	1 961	7.2	1 011	153	273	309	15 417	830	1 164	2.6	33.6
Logan	414	2 608	205	16 739	593	7.8	279	57	86	114	14 297	1 290	336	3.0	34.2
Lorain	3 093	20 413	1 768	22 014	4 137	5.6	2 330	193	560	671	15 286	877	2 523	0.9	49.1
Lucas	11 231	66 015	4 403	22 433	7 953	5.3	5 893	534	1 282	1 447	17 005	436	6 427	0.3	34.4
Madison	177	1 281	91	14 117	533	9.9	176	57	58	81	14 764	1 103	233	9.5	25.2
Mahoning	6 800	27 891	1 517	17 526	4 104	6.8	2 265	273	731	931	15 216	901	2 539	0.4	26.3
Marion	580	4 878	395	19 125	830	5.4	568	62	132	176	12 885	1 963	630	1.4	38.0
Medina	1 869	7 078	538	18 041	2 163	7.3	774	137	268	239	17 773	322	910	0.5	34.7
Meigs	125	594	82	23 292	256	7.8	126	20	30	72	10 878	2 691	146	3.3	55.8
Mercer	750	1 778	197	17 939	619	7.6	311	100	123	68	15 719	734	410	13.9	39.3
Miami	1 237	5 957	607	19 397	1 504	6.7	827	93	246	228	16 278	575	921	1.6	54.2
Monroe	92	297	111	26 314	193	4.5	154	23	30	41	12 699	2 036	177	0.6	70.7
Montgomery	13 304	79 922	5 887	22 839	10 043	6.1	8 305	522	1 626	1 702	17 372	383	8 827	0.1	36.6
Morgan	82	352	67	22 790	175	5.3	120	12	24	38	12 122	2 276	132	1.8	60.6
Morrow	80	742	88	20 272	346	8.1	99	32	47	56	12 467	2 132	131	7.6	42.2
Muskingum	918	7 034	451	17 124	1 147	6.6	655	92	175	224	13 645	1 605	747	0.6	36.9
Noble	65	340	31	18 025	134	8.1	49	11	25	28	12 143	2 264	60	1.0	43.7
Ottawa	421	2 122	245	21 150	705	5.4	339	47	122	119	17 612	353	386	1.7	33.0
Paulding	115	466	67	19 384	289	6.9	82	31	44	37	13 646	1 603	112	15.7	NA
Perry	168	979	84	16 250	354	6.0	134	19	43	87	10 974	2 671	154	0.8	NA
Pickaway	257	1 547	214	20 666	632	9.4	326	54	86	102	13 393	1 731	381	4.6	49.3
Pike	153	951	140	24 498	275	7.9	199	20	36	75	10 819	2 710	219	0.8	61.4
Portage	716	6 453	526	18 062	2 118	6.2	919	121	259	311	15 076	952	1 040	0.4	37.2
Preble	276	1 074	120	16 557	558	6.2	181	40	82	88	13 971	1 449	221	2.0	44.6

1. For week including March 12. Excludes government employees, self-employed persons, farm workers, domestic service workers, railroad employees subject to the Railroad Retirement Act, and employees on oceanborne vessels or in foreign countries. 2. Includes other labor income. 3. Based on the resident population estimated as of July 1 of the year shown. 4. Covers mining, construction, and manufacturing.

STATE County	Earnings, 1989 (cont'd) — Percent by selected industries (cont'd) — Goods-related[1] — Manufacturing	Service-related & other[2] — Total	Retail trade	Finance, insurance, & real estate	Services	Government	Agriculture, 1987 — Farms — Number	Percent with — Less than 50 acres	500 acres and over	Farm operators, percent — Whose principal occupation is farming	Residing on farm operated	Land in farms — Acreage (1,000)	Percent change, 1982–1987	Acres — Average size of farm	Total irrigated (1,000)	Total cropland (1,000)
	103	104	105	106	107	108	109	110	111	112	113	114	115	116	117	118
OHIO	30.0	50.4	9.3	5.2	23.3	13.0	79 277	28.6	8.6	49.9	76.4	14 997	-2.6	189	32	11 920
Adams	5.4	NA	9.3	2.7	NA	19.6	1 412	27.5	5.2	48.8	70.3	215	1.7	152	0	121
Allen	40.9	41.2	9.0	2.3	18.8	10.8	1 148	30.5	8.7	44.8	73.4	201	2.0	175	0	182
Ashland	45.5	NA	8.6	1.8	19.2	12.4	1 078	24.4	7.1	51.2	76.3	179	-5.0	166	0	139
Ashtabula	35.3	45.1	10.9	2.4	18.2	13.3	1 188	27.4	4.7	51.3	84.6	182	-1.9	153	1	123
Athens	6.1	41.3	10.8	2.7	18.3	49.0	564	20.0	5.1	39.0	84.9	93	-10.7	164	0	39
Auglaize	47.4	30.7	9.1	2.1	12.9	11.4	1 119	26.8	8.4	51.9	74.6	217	-0.9	194	D	195
Belmont	11.2	57.6	16.4	5.3	21.4	14.0	668	17.5	5.5	48.7	80.7	127	-6.2	189	0	64
Brown	22.6	42.0	11.2	2.2	21.2	21.6	1 605	31.7	3.6	45.2	66.0	216	-3.6	134	0	153
Butler	34.1	43.6	8.9	4.3	18.6	14.0	1 014	34.7	5.9	47.0	75.5	160	-4.3	157	0	126
Carroll	28.9	47.6	11.7	1.6	15.7	12.0	703	21.1	5.3	50.2	83.2	117	-7.7	167	0	71
Champaign	43.7	34.0	9.1	3.2	14.3	13.8	948	30.6	12.2	53.3	73.8	222	-4.2	234	2	194
Clark	36.9	45.9	10.2	4.0	22.0	11.2	812	36.3	14.5	50.5	75.0	194	-0.3	239	2	171
Clermont	25.1	51.1	14.9	3.7	19.7	13.1	951	43.4	4.7	36.4	73.1	116	0.3	122	0	88
Clinton	30.1	NA	7.8	2.6	14.6	13.0	870	24.8	16.0	62.0	75.7	226	1.0	259	0	197
Columbiana	32.2	46.7	11.4	3.6	21.7	12.6	1 093	31.2	4.4	46.6	87.5	155	1.3	142	0	110
Coshocton	43.6	38.6	6.4	1.7	16.0	9.9	884	18.7	6.2	50.2	80.3	176	-8.8	199	0	104
Crawford	44.7	37.5	8.8	2.9	17.4	11.0	877	25.1	13.6	56.3	77.0	222	-0.6	253	0	201
Cuyahoga	26.3	58.3	7.6	6.8	29.2	10.9	150	80.0	0.7	48.7	68.7	6	-37.2	37	0	3
Darke	30.8	NA	9.8	3.1	17.8	9.3	2 067	31.8	7.3	50.7	76.6	345	1.5	167	0	311
Defiance	56.5	30.7	7.6	2.3	12.5	7.1	987	21.7	9.9	42.9	75.1	207	-1.8	210	0	183
Delaware	31.9	45.6	10.7	3.2	22.7	14.0	799	38.5	12.0	46.8	79.2	176	-6.4	220	0	157
Erie	43.3	40.6	10.1	1.8	20.8	10.6	480	37.7	11.5	50.4	72.7	90	-9.1	188	0	80
Fairfield	29.5	45.4	10.9	5.9	20.5	16.4	1 217	35.6	7.8	48.2	76.3	214	-3.4	176	0	178
Fayette	33.8	40.5	12.7	1.9	15.6	13.8	628	23.9	28.2	69.3	72.6	244	3.4	389	D	224
Franklin	14.4	62.5	12.0	10.6	26.0	17.3	581	44.2	11.2	48.7	64.9	122	-11.6	210	1	107
Fulton	45.0	34.6	8.6	2.2	14.1	11.7	1 043	31.7	11.6	54.9	74.2	220	-0.8	211	1	204
Gallia	10.2	65.9	11.9	2.3	30.0	18.2	885	26.9	2.6	35.6	76.5	117	-7.7	132	0	47
Geauga	34.6	44.3	8.4	1.8	22.7	10.1	702	36.6	2.4	54.4	86.2	73	-2.1	104	0	45
Greene	10.3	39.9	8.0	2.2	24.1	43.2	903	35.8	12.1	54.9	78.3	195	2.9	216	1	170
Guernsey	29.3	44.7	9.9	2.6	20.0	18.8	860	17.4	4.5	42.2	79.8	138	-6.6	160	0	68
Hamilton	28.4	56.1	8.8	6.9	24.9	10.1	350	62.3	2.9	45.4	72.9	28	-15.9	81	1	19
Hancock	38.6	41.9	8.7	2.9	17.7	7.4	1 203	23.7	14.0	53.2	72.7	288	-1.4	240	0	265
Hardin	37.2	38.2	7.8	1.8	20.3	12.8	1 034	21.1	13.7	60.8	74.8	264	-0.3	255	0	239
Harrison	14.7	38.4	8.0	1.8	15.7	17.0	465	16.3	7.3	46.7	75.5	119	0.3	256	D	50
Henry	48.2	NA	7.5	1.8	11.1	10.0	1 125	21.5	9.8	58.0	70.8	246	2.1	218	0	229
Highland	32.8	40.5	13.3	4.6	13.9	16.6	1 323	27.8	8.4	54.6	74.8	252	-2.5	190	0	201
Hocking	41.3	32.7	10.8	1.5	13.0	18.9	414	22.5	4.1	31.9	79.7	63	5.2	153	0	29
Holmes	40.1	31.1	8.9	1.7	12.6	9.5	1 518	21.5	2.3	69.1	79.4	186	-4.6	123	0	123
Huron	38.9	39.6	7.4	2.1	12.8	8.4	934	24.0	12.8	55.4	75.1	234	-4.4	251	3	202
Jackson	30.4	41.3	12.6	4.0	14.6	15.3	422	20.1	5.9	36.7	78.2	79	-2.2	188	0	43
Jefferson	28.7	51.6	10.4	3.3	19.7	10.7	440	15.5	5.5	38.6	87.3	76	-0.4	173	D	39
Knox	30.3	43.4	9.5	2.5	23.8	15.3	1 185	25.7	8.1	49.5	78.3	222	0.0	187	0	164
Lake	36.5	43.2	10.2	2.8	20.2	10.7	268	61.6	1.1	56.3	78.7	18	-12.4	68	2	13
Lawrence	17.8	52.0	12.3	3.2	18.9	22.3	545	29.5	2.8	31.9	76.3	64	-16.7	117	0	23
Licking	28.4	44.7	10.2	5.5	20.5	19.1	1 402	31.5	6.8	47.1	77.5	243	-6.1	174	0	183
Logan	25.3	50.5	10.2	2.6	22.5	12.2	979	27.5	13.5	52.4	75.4	228	1.2	233	0	198
Lorain	43.3	37.6	8.1	2.5	19.1	12.4	985	42.0	6.4	50.5	81.2	144	-2.8	146	0	120
Lucas	28.4	53.7	9.3	4.4	26.0	11.6	492	47.0	9.3	53.5	71.7	83	-5.3	169	2	79
Madison	18.5	39.5	10.9	2.1	17.9	25.7	735	24.6	21.8	62.7	72.9	267	-2.1	364	0	243
Mahoning	17.7	60.4	11.1	5.1	29.3	12.9	668	37.4	2.1	49.6	86.1	81	-6.9	121	0	61
Marion	34.7	45.5	9.3	1.9	19.7	15.1	650	23.8	20.0	58.3	71.8	224	2.2	345	0	210
Medina	25.0	52.5	11.4	7.1	21.1	12.2	1 012	43.5	3.4	46.5	84.6	116	-9.6	115	0	89
Meigs	4.0	26.7	9.2	1.6	11.5	14.2	528	19.5	4.9	37.9	82.8	85	-16.1	161	0	35
Mercer	33.1	35.4	7.1	4.6	11.7	11.5	1 562	27.2	7.6	54.2	74.1	276	1.7	177	0	250
Miami	47.8	34.5	9.4	2.3	16.5	9.7	1 133	36.2	10.8	48.5	73.9	210	6.7	185	2	189
Monroe	58.6	18.4	3.0	1.3	10.2	10.3	716	13.5	3.1	45.3	81.7	116	-10.8	163	0	49
Montgomery	31.8	47.6	8.0	3.8	24.8	15.8	940	48.0	4.8	43.3	72.2	119	-1.9	126	1	100
Morgan	27.2	NA	4.6	1.2	NA	8.3	590	15.3	5.6	44.9	82.7	112	-3.7	190	D	45
Morrow	34.9	32.2	8.7	1.1	14.4	18.0	864	28.8	8.2	49.4	78.5	166	-2.9	192	0	137
Muskingum	27.1	50.6	11.2	2.6	25.1	11.9	1 094	19.4	6.0	41.1	82.3	194	-7.4	178	0	106
Noble	31.2	38.4	10.4	3.0	14.2	16.9	567	13.4	5.3	37.0	81.3	104	-11.5	184	0	51
Ottawa	27.7	NA	10.2	2.3	NA	12.1	573	30.0	9.6	46.4	73.3	105	-11.5	184	0	97
Paulding	31.2	NA	8.0	1.9	11.7	17.0	718	23.5	22.6	56.1	65.3	228	2.2	317	D	211
Perry	25.3	NA	8.4	2.3	13.6	16.7	641	22.0	3.7	40.6	78.9	103	1.8	161	0	66
Pickaway	44.4	26.3	8.1	1.3	11.0	19.8	783	25.9	22.2	61.7	68.1	261	-8.4	333	1	236
Pike	57.5	26.0	7.3	1.4	11.6	11.7	454	16.5	9.9	41.4	77.5	101	-7.9	222	0	61
Portage	30.2	35.8	9.2	1.4	17.9	26.5	820	42.4	4.0	41.5	83.8	102	-9.4	125	0	73
Preble	37.5	38.3	11.2	2.1	14.0	15.0	1 183	31.1	7.9	53.3	81.0	211	1.2	179	0	184

1. Covers mining, construction, and manufacturing. 2. Covers private sector earnings in agricultural services, forestry, and fisheries; transportation and public utilities; wholesale trade; retail trade; finance, insurance, and real estate; and services.

STATE County	Agriculture, 1987 (cont'd)								Manufactures, 1987						
	Value of land and buildings		Value of products sold				Percent of farms with sales of		Establishments		All employees			Production workers	
	Average per farm ($1,000)	Average per acre (Dollars)	Total (Mil dol)	Average per farm (Dollars)	Percent from: Crops	Percent from: Livestock and poultry[1]	$10,000 or more	$100,000 or more	Total	Percent with 20 or more employees	Number (1,000)	Percent change, 1982–1987	Annual payroll (Mil dol)	Number (1,000)	Work hours (Mil)
	119	120	121	122	123	124	125	126	127	128	129	130	131	132	133
OHIO	227	1 199	3 434	43 317	51.0	49.0	50.3	10.8	17 544	39.2	1 100.2	-0.7	30 765.2	713.4	1 447.9
Adams	114	717	23	16 252	35.8	64.2	31.5	3.2	17	11.8	0.3	-40.0	5.2	0.2	0.4
Allen	268	1 504	48	42 065	64.6	35.4	62.4	11.3	152	40.1	15.0	7.1	451.1	11.0	23.0
Ashland	180	1 092	43	39 740	28.8	71.2	52.3	11.9	90	43.3	6.5	6.6	146.4	4.9	10.2
Ashtabula	159	1 070	37	31 395	31.6	68.4	40.3	8.2	150	50.7	8.8	-9.3	214.1	6.7	13.3
Athens	109	659	5	8 701	21.9	78.2	15.6	1.4	49	20.4	1.1	0.0	19.1	0.8	1.5
Auglaize	252	1 318	63	56 463	46.2	53.8	69.0	17.1	95	38.9	6.3	5.0	149.9	4.4	8.8
Belmont	116	623	10	15 002	17.3	82.7	28.9	2.2	54	25.9	2.0	-39.4	42.9	1.4	2.9
Brown	141	1 036	26	16 093	67.0	33.0	38.0	2.1	28	50.0	1.8	125.0	32.0	1.4	2.7
Butler	282	1 911	31	30 695	48.9	51.1	42.9	8.1	288	38.5	22.5	-11.4	693.7	15.3	31.7
Carroll	124	761	18	25 225	26.1	73.9	37.7	4.8	39	48.7	1.8	28.6	33.4	1.4	3.0
Champaign	263	1 151	49	51 679	60.4	39.6	59.9	15.5	52	38.5	4.0	14.3	94.9	2.9	6.0
Clark	286	1 233	77	95 017	48.4	51.6	56.0	15.6	230	35.7	12.6	12.5	351.5	9.7	18.3
Clermont	203	1 497	17	17 670	75.8	24.2	28.1	4.2	113	28.3	6.3	31.2	200.3	4.3	8.8
Clinton	284	1 092	51	59 066	63.6	36.4	67.8	19.8	48	58.3	4.1	-2.4	81.5	3.3	6.6
Columbiana	160	1 197	43	39 578	33.9	66.1	43.0	11.1	205	39.5	7.7	-6.1	160.6	5.8	11.6
Coshocton	164	788	26	29 572	28.1	71.9	42.4	7.5	55	45.5	4.8	0.0	122.0	3.3	6.7
Crawford	271	1 059	50	56 728	68.7	31.3	68.2	15.7	86	51.2	7.7	0.0	177.1	5.7	11.4
Cuyahoga	191	6 110	15	96 680	97.3	2.7	44.7	18.7	3 079	37.8	163.8	-12.8	4 844.9	95.6	196.4
Darke	268	1 566	157	75 831	31.1	68.9	64.1	16.6	80	36.2	4.6	35.3	99.3	3.5	7.1
Defiance	241	1 143	34	34 306	56.1	43.9	55.7	6.1	43	53.5	6.7	17.5	221.5	5.4	11.0
Delaware	337	1 496	33	41 670	67.5	32.5	44.8	12.6	71	36.6	5.3	3.9	134.1	3.5	6.6
Erie	300	1 384	26	53 810	67.8	32.2	55.2	17.3	127	46.5	9.9	6.5	323.1	7.2	15.5
Fairfield	223	1 232	39	32 200	55.0	45.0	44.0	8.8	122	33.6	D	D	D	D	D
Fayette	404	1 095	52	82 613	70.7	29.3	72.9	27.2	40	55.0	2.7	28.6	64.4	2.0	3.8
Franklin	380	1 779	32	54 786	82.5	17.5	49.1	11.9	1 135	38.0	64.6	-1.8	1 794.4	38.8	77.8
Fulton	317	1 460	80	76 303	46.3	53.7	73.3	21.2	98	54.1	6.6	24.5	153.9	5.2	10.3
Gallia	89	652	9	10 600	24.9	75.0	16.9	2.6	28	32.1	0.9	-10.0	20.6	0.7	1.3
Geauga	190	1 841	15	21 984	27.0	73.0	41.6	5.1	184	37.5	8.0	45.5	173.0	5.5	11.0
Greene	316	1 446	49	53 803	65.5	34.5	55.4	12.7	112	34.8	D	D	D	D	D
Guernsey	115	635	9	10 395	18.3	81.7	24.4	0.9	52	48.1	3.4	6.2	78.8	2.3	4.2
Hamilton	223	3 329	14	39 777	75.0	25.0	34.3	12.9	1 675	40.3	124.8	-2.0	3 758.0	63.5	128.2
Hancock	329	1 374	56	46 295	75.3	24.7	68.5	12.2	89	40.4	9.8	16.7	253.4	7.2	14.1
Hardin	239	953	49	47 593	73.4	26.6	68.0	12.5	39	48.7	2.7	8.0	62.6	2.2	4.1
Harrison	146	567	8	18 191	14.4	85.6	23.9	3.4	12	25.0	0.2	-75.0	3.5	0.1	0.3
Henry	347	1 611	52	46 041	70.2	29.8	70.4	10.5	57	35.1	3.7	0.0	89.3	3.0	5.9
Highland	160	879	35	26 695	59.5	40.5	48.3	5.8	43	46.5	2.5	-7.4	47.4	2.0	3.9
Hocking	100	630	3	7 026	45.0	55.0	15.2	0.0	29	37.9	2.0	0.0	41.5	1.7	3.1
Holmes	143	1 220	62	40 537	6.6	93.4	69.6	8.8	97	44.3	3.5	52.2	60.1	2.8	5.7
Huron	293	1 152	63	67 667	78.6	21.4	64.8	13.7	109	54.1	9.3	36.8	194.1	7.3	14.6
Jackson	128	768	13	30 886	70.5	29.5	24.2	3.1	45	31.1	2.5	25.0	44.3	2.1	3.9
Jefferson	116	737	6	12 955	24.9	75.1	23.6	2.5	54	29.6	D	D	D	D	D
Knox	175	875	55	46 719	25.6	74.4	48.4	11.1	54	40.7	3.1	-13.9	76.4	2.1	4.4
Lake	242	3 295	33	121 525	97.6	2.4	43.7	13.1	657	36.1	23.7	-3.7	605.0	14.2	28.4
Lawrence	84	879	5	9 596	28.3	71.7	13.2	1.7	46	23.9	D	D	D	D	D
Licking	257	1 488	88	62 821	26.3	73.7	38.0	7.5	128	39.1	8.7	-13.9	247.9	6.2	13.1
Logan	236	962	56	57 354	50.6	49.4	58.5	15.3	51	41.2	2.9	7.4	57.2	2.2	4.1
Lorain	205	1 444	60	61 130	75.0	25.0	47.8	11.3	382	37.2	28.5	-4.7	876.7	20.3	41.7
Lucas	294	1 839	35	70 618	83.1	16.9	57.9	16.1	719	36.9	45.4	-2.2	1 547.2	29.6	65.1
Madison	433	1 192	56	76 697	67.8	32.2	71.3	22.3	30	50.0	1.0	-16.7	18.9	0.8	1.7
Mahoning	153	1 296	24	36 620	42.1	57.9	41.6	9.7	376	36.4	13.3	-24.4	298.4	9.3	18.1
Marion	327	976	43	65 969	74.7	25.3	68.2	18.0	76	42.1	6.7	-19.3	174.9	4.6	9.2
Medina	192	1 753	29	28 351	39.1	60.9	37.7	7.5	235	39.1	7.9	31.7	164.9	5.8	11.5
Meigs	127	732	7	13 873	38.8	61.2	23.7	3.4	19	21.1	D	D	D	D	D
Mercer	302	1 670	143	91 596	23.5	76.5	76.8	25.9	57	33.3	4.4	12.8	99.8	3.4	7.3
Miami	290	1 488	55	48 664	67.0	33.0	56.8	12.5	223	40.4	D	D	D	D	D
Monroe	92	559	7	9 182	8.8	91.2	17.3	1.0	17	17.6	D	D	D	D	D
Montgomery	238	1 889	28	30 293	68.6	31.4	40.0	6.9	1 023	40.7	75.4	10.6	2 270.2	41.8	85.7
Morgan	107	573	9	15 829	12.5	87.5	20.8	3.7	14	28.6	1.2	33.3	22.8	1.0	1.8
Morrow	183	989	32	37 398	55.0	45.0	48.4	9.6	33	27.3	1.6	33.3	26.1	1.0	2.0
Muskingum	131	726	24	21 654	20.6	79.4	32.9	4.8	100	37.0	7.3	4.3	147.3	6.0	11.7
Noble	101	548	4	7 068	14.4	85.6	15.5	0.7	14	50.0	0.8	0.0	20.8	0.6	1.2
Ottawa	272	1 371	19	33 595	85.1	14.9	56.4	7.9	83	28.9	3.8	58.3	102.8	2.9	6.3
Paulding	352	1 141	46	63 620	59.8	40.2	61.6	14.6	38	36.8	1.8	38.5	40.1	1.5	3.0
Perry	113	681	11	17 239	44.9	55.1	29.2	4.7	35	37.1	1.6	6.7	32.7	1.3	2.7
Pickaway	347	1 039	47	59 517	67.1	32.9	66.8	17.6	43	41.9	5.1	10.9	138.9	3.9	8.1
Pike	169	806	10	21 007	38.4	61.6	29.1	4.6	37	32.4	2.9	0.0	88.2	1.6	3.1
Portage	203	1 734	25	30 680	38.8	61.2	34.3	7.3	247	40.1	9.4	13.3	217.1	6.6	13.8
Preble	239	1 333	54	45 611	50.5	49.5	55.9	14.0	51	39.2	2.7	35.0	55.3	2.0	3.8

1. Includes livestock and poultry products.

STATE County	Manufactures, 1987 (cont'd)					Value of construction authorized by building permits, 1990							
	Production workers (cont'd)						Nonresidential				Residential		
	Wages							Percent					
	Total (Mil dol)	Average per worker (Dollars)	Value added by manufacture (Mil dol)	Value of shipments (Mil dol)	New capital expenditures (Mil dol)	Total[1] ($1,000)	Total ($1,000)	Office	Industrial	Stores	New construction ($1,000)	Number of housing units	Alterations and additions ($1,000)
	134	135	136	137	138	139	140	141	142	143	144	145	146
OHIO	17 490.4	24 517	71 707.4	158 559.9	4 742.2	6 575 203	1 676 680	26.4	14.9	29.2	3 039 006	38 491	381 754
Adams	4.3	21 500	4.8	15.0	1.6	3 135	1 876	16.2	33.7	28.7	541	17	13
Allen	310.2	28 200	1 309.6	4 917.2	76.4	44 410	12 018	10.1	39.8	33.6	20 284	272	2 789
Ashland	101.7	20 755	333.8	651.1	18.0	20 595	3 704	3.5	0.3	91.0	9 060	139	548
Ashtabula	146.3	21 836	640.0	1 228.6	31.3	31 397	4 977	13.1	37.3	17.4	12 218	168	2 771
Athens	12.3	15 375	39.5	79.4	1.6	11 412	6 397	5.9	0.0	23.7	2 626	25	729
Auglaize	93.5	21 250	403.4	875.2	21.5	25 768	4 615	0.0	28.6	47.3	16 117	230	764
Belmont	29.4	21 000	204.8	539.3	2.1	13 929	8 404	23.7	0.0	51.4	1 526	22	1 728
Brown	22.8	16 286	114.7	211.9	9.3	4 712	1 312	1.3	0.0	27.8	1 771	40	0
Butler	457.4	29 895	1 496.7	3 202.3	69.7	200 757	50 248	2.5	58.3	26.2	94 582	1 535	5 495
Carroll	23.1	16 500	82.8	192.6	5.9	2 974	1 902	3.4	0.0	88.2	404	4	47
Champaign	67.1	23 138	320.9	551.5	16.0	14 130	1 622	20.0	0.0	53.9	10 210	174	393
Clark	256.5	26 443	1 135.0	2 939.6	81.2	55 415	19 135	45.2	0.7	39.3	28 056	443	2 905
Clermont	126.6	29 442	439.9	806.1	40.0	135 407	32 363	6.6	6.9	64.4	81 577	1 489	2 694
Clinton	60.2	18 242	191.1	357.6	11.0	22 830	3 221	5.7	0.9	81.4	11 101	170	840
Columbiana	109.3	18 845	356.9	632.8	19.6	18 633	5 781	20.1	11.2	40.8	8 013	113	1 062
Coshocton	75.5	22 879	314.5	744.8	14.7	2 108	1 070	0.0	1.4	78.9	182	4	214
Crawford	122.1	21 421	502.9	866.5	29.8	4 016	1 065	15.0	59.4	24.8	1 666	29	626
Cuyahoga	2 483.5	25 978	8 881.5	18 354.5	728.1	1 035 282	258 185	41.8	9.2	18.5	340 437	3 346	86 918
Darke	66.9	19 114	298.6	573.6	11.5	17 811	2 335	7.6	26.3	43.6	13 099	135	603
Defiance	176.9	32 759	408.3	737.2	24.9	12 158	2 783	50.3	11.9	31.4	6 946	105	863
Delaware	80.5	23 000	364.8	861.1	26.2	108 773	15 218	24.9	7.7	39.5	85 246	632	4 249
Erie	234.1	32 514	702.5	1 643.2	70.7	71 750	29 964	2.2	29.6	29.1	34 394	566	2 999
Fairfield	D	D	D	D	D	79 521	10 006	16.3	5.9	60.4	63 026	837	2 622
Fayette	39.1	19 550	147.1	274.3	14.5	6 127	1 786	13.3	35.4	42.7	3 251	53	165
Franklin	911.1	23 482	4 419.1	8 202.2	221.2	1 039 993	332 576	43.0	11.2	15.1	457 954	6 934	59 431
Fulton	103.9	19 981	381.7	841.5	25.1	18 593	7 305	0.0	0.0	98.6	5 918	94	485
Gallia	13.9	19 857	59.6	112.6	D	4 290	1 776	0.0	0.0	61.2	275	5	108
Geauga	98.6	17 927	417.6	762.7	24.0	78 119	8 756	7.6	0.0	32.3	52 530	390	6 399
Greene	D	D	D	D	D	85 856	14 993	14.5	8.2	41.0	59 413	564	3 530
Guernsey	39.7	17 261	158.0	375.8	13.6	6 279	2 831	9.9	17.0	47.1	2 167	43	10
Hamilton	1 556.5	24 512	9 807.3	19 348.3	582.7	619 430	203 793	26.0	5.9	32.4	227 522	2 658	35 748
Hancock	168.4	23 389	739.3	1 637.1	80.2	22 353	5 427	0.0	72.8	0.5	14 094	199	2 518
Hardin	46.7	21 227	164.0	365.9	8.3	4 087	1 495	25.3	0.0	58.8	1 827	40	264
Harrison	2.2	22 000	6.6	12.6	0.8	449	320	0.0	78.2	11.6	0	0	4
Henry	66.3	22 100	430.4	852.2	21.3	9 336	1 821	0.0	4.0	15.7	5 061	68	596
Highland	33.1	16 550	177.6	291.4	4.6	3 927	1 559	0.5	20.3	46.8	1 361	33	264
Hocking	32.3	19 000	95.7	249.7	7.3	2 705	1 364	0.6	46.4	14.4	655	16	111
Holmes	43.0	15 357	182.5	395.6	10.7	5 682	4 415	2.3	15.1	61.8	428	9	59
Huron	138.6	18 986	576.1	1 165.0	47.3	10 540	0	NA	NA	NA	9 106	172	1 434
Jackson	33.2	15 810	90.5	221.8	14.5	5 966	1 601	3.8	0.0	51.9	3 536	61	110
Jefferson	D	D	D	D	D	22 417	13 241	26.4	1.9	55.8	1 134	18	1 753
Knox	45.3	21 571	165.5	358.4	12.7	25 443	4 454	13.7	26.7	37.9	9 946	180	548
Lake	288.4	20 310	1 161.8	2 034.8	59.4	144 598	47 586	0.0	24.3	7.4	62 988	902	8 000
Lawrence	D	D	D	D	D	6 133	4 070	14.8	0.0	35.5	623	18	195
Licking	157.4	25 387	699.0	1 388.6	32.3	84 133	9 839	5.1	6.0	67.9	44 544	570	3 254
Logan	41.2	18 727	127.1	277.1	D	23 744	6 692	12.9	61.0	19.4	12 220	229	375
Lorain	602.6	29 685	3 435.0	9 549.2	119.6	162 564	20 110	18.0	22.0	28.3	104 353	1 033	9 387
Lucas	902.9	30 503	3 788.3	10 121.9	217.4	225 996	51 515	16.8	8.0	39.0	87 696	996	27 481
Madison	13.4	16 750	29.6	94.9	3.8	15 407	1 739	13.8	0.9	66.4	12 260	144	699
Mahoning	173.6	18 667	592.9	1 316.6	26.7	115 906	43 234	14.8	28.6	35.7	55 716	688	6 368
Marion	107.2	23 304	560.9	1 145.0	24.3	10 042	2 279	15.8	27.7	33.6	3 727	57	415
Medina	106.4	18 345	465.4	904.6	30.1	125 896	16 087	9.6	41.0	34.7	98 873	955	3 600
Meigs	D	D	D	D	D	1 265	842	0.0	6.9	71.3	322	8	83
Mercer	70.5	20 735	234.8	499.1	12.8	11 298	1 547	17.0	18.7	59.4	8 310	103	323
Miami	D	D	D	D	D	43 324	4 020	18.5	0.0	67.9	29 641	397	1 223
Monroe	D	D	D	D	D	1 296	392	0.0	38.3	35.2	80	2	264
Montgomery	1 161.7	27 792	4 190.7	8 688.7	251.3	273 878	73 820	22.4	9.8	54.0	103 735	1 280	11 204
Morgan	17.3	17 300	68.2	133.5	D	689	379	0.0	0.0	90.2	87	3	34
Morrow	16.6	16 600	55.5	122.3	3.4	3 377	680	43.1	0.0	46.9	2 353	57	84
Muskingum	111.1	18 517	399.6	706.8	10.9	19 888	5 790	30.7	5.2	9.6	5 784	176	461
Noble	14.6	24 333	49.8	168.4	4.0	827	244	0.0	0.0	100.0	583	15	0
Ottawa	74.8	25 793	276.0	528.4	24.0	17 158	52	0.0	0.0	100.0	10 726	153	289
Paulding	32.2	21 467	97.5	181.6	9.1	4 209	789	0.0	0.0	96.8	2 537	58	556
Perry	23.5	18 077	68.3	143.1	2.5	4 578	816	0.0	0.0	96.8	2 840	76	454
Pickaway	93.1	23 872	479.1	912.8	63.3	52 840	8 056	5.2	58.4	25.2	12 966	165	807
Pike	42.2	26 375	227.9	479.5	4.1	2 268	1 190	0.0	53.1	36.2	404	6	362
Portage	135.4	20 515	559.3	1 109.5	34.1	68 803	7 861	5.9	27.3	32.2	54 897	884	2 543
Preble	35.0	17 500	131.2	273.3	14.4	13 594	2 636	0.0	19.2	41.9	8 357	137	861

1. Includes nonresidential additions and alterations, residential nonhousekeeping buildings, and residential garages and carports not shown separately.

Table A. States and Counties — **Wholesale and Retail Trade**

STATE County	Wholesale trade, 1987				Retail trade, all establishments, 1987				Retail trade, establishments with payroll, 1987					
						Sales				Sales				
											Per capita[2] (Dollars)			
	Establishments	Sales (Mil dol)	Paid employees[1]	Annual payroll (Mil dol)	Number	Total (Mil dol)	Percent change, 1982–1987	Per capita[2] (Dollars)	Number	Total (Mil dol)	General merchandise stores	Food stores	Apparel & accessory stores	Eating and drinking places
	147	148	149	150	151	152	153	154	155	156	157	158	159	160
OHIO	18 748	104 110.7	248 661	5 774.1	96 973	64 705.2	39.7	5 983	63 025	63 190.8	772	1 200	240	604
Adams	17	18.1	71	0.9	270	97.0	50.4	3 820	113	85.6	237	738	13	98
Allen	227	1 095.2	3 182	63.6	1 183	819.2	46.4	7 327	788	800.8	1 300	1 280	306	650
Ashland	67	107.7	437	8.4	425	209.8	31.7	4 531	240	200.5	297	1 039	112	426
Ashtabula	105	172.7	833	13.0	988	506.6	29.9	5 061	579	488.1	609	1 081	121	382
Athens	43	81.8	430	7.9	543	241.6	26.6	4 095	333	233.4	311	1 003	109	476
Auglaize	66	153.9	414	7.0	484	222.7	40.5	5 038	286	215.3	244	1 142	117	504
Belmont	72	101.6	559	9.9	830	458.4	22.0	6 001	545	446.8	1 338	1 379	307	476
Brown	28	43.1	188	2.0	304	87.0	35.3	2 479	160	80.1	194	774	14	265
Butler	328	1 182.7	3 955	92.5	2 061	1 380.2	49.3	4 981	1 332	1 348.0	468	1 139	82	519
Carroll	25	35.3	157	3.0	219	95.9	40.6	3 579	115	92.1	D	713	72	190
Champaign	46	144.7	475	8.2	302	136.4	42.4	3 909	164	130.9	D	1 082	65	310
Clark	161	626.9	2 046	43.6	1 193	840.9	46.6	5 693	749	822.9	948	1 180	160	506
Clermont	141	348.9	1 032	25.0	983	770.4	55.0	5 324	642	758.6	555	1 423	171	420
Clinton	67	163.3	517	9.0	360	205.9	48.1	5 800	219	199.4	304	1 637	135	413
Columbiana	123	241.6	944	15.6	1 138	492.2	20.8	4 541	666	475.6	388	1 185	109	388
Coshocton	44	47.5	236	3.8	326	137.4	30.5	3 837	196	133.3	296	1 213	179	329
Crawford	60	118.4	424	7.6	488	213.3	34.7	4 379	286	201.7	294	939	116	410
Cuyahoga	3 621	23 992.7	54 884	1 390.9	12 479	9 051.3	31.1	6 249	8 755	8 879.7	813	1 180	359	679
Darke	89	292.5	1 057	21.2	558	301.0	77.1	5 574	306	290.0	353	1 168	169	393
Defiance	67	138.0	544	10.8	409	231.1	48.6	5 836	269	225.8	689	1 435	187	469
Delaware	77	173.3	518	13.1	494	271.7	58.1	4 462	296	263.5	188	871	100	528
Erie	108	330.7	1 188	23.9	842	522.6	35.1	6 760	562	510.0	1 367	1 105	289	768
Fairfield	85	193.6	535	11.7	891	441.8	38.5	4 409	492	426.6	448	1 049	212	407
Fayette	42	136.8	313	6.1	231	163.0	44.9	5 948	156	159.0	453	1 293	219	590
Franklin	2 040	14 891.9	33 884	837.6	7 874	7 239.9	54.3	7 829	5 412	7 134.4	1 051	1 271	364	850
Fulton	72	395.4	794	15.7	451	216.9	45.1	5 679	273	206.9	178	1 238	84	526
Gallia	39	93.5	400	6.3	333	175.2	35.9	5 783	206	168.4	620	1 324	198	487
Geauga	134	404.2	1 265	28.7	705	314.3	39.7	4 066	382	300.1	238	957	34	374
Greene	101	738.7	1 312	30.4	1 006	669.6	44.7	5 050	608	656.2	398	1 056	96	482
Guernsey	63	118.3	435	8.6	420	201.7	31.1	5 056	248	194.4	554	1 090	151	597
Hamilton	2 360	23 178.9	40 256	933.4	7 631	6 287.8	42.5	7 172	5 456	6 187.1	1 044	1 376	358	853
Hancock	107	277.3	924	18.5	716	467.4	51.7	7 125	454	457.5	1 372	946	158	731
Hardin	45	117.6	268	4.5	308	118.2	41.6	3 717	167	112.6	220	1 257	84	319
Harrison	25	66.2	246	4.7	174	43.2	16.1	2 749	87	39.5	D	891	D	96
Henry	56	160.6	378	6.8	278	125.4	23.2	4 399	165	120.0	D	989	67	262
Highland	50	131.3	360	5.2	361	146.6	47.8	4 142	208	139.3	299	1 091	87	397
Hocking	21	29.2	176	2.5	223	108.4	44.0	4 320	125	103.0	392	841	105	338
Holmes	45	62.7	317	4.3	292	115.3	53.1	3 719	133	105.4	177	671	D	433
Huron	90	221.6	931	17.6	573	315.9	57.0	5 641	369	307.3	371	1 290	86	414
Jackson	36	33.7	251	4.2	320	135.6	37.5	4 460	202	129.7	426	1 271	76	326
Jefferson	89	250.6	899	19.3	840	444.6	27.8	5 376	534	431.1	D	1 101	218	398
Knox	48	89.3	330	5.0	418	197.8	28.7	4 164	245	131.5	467	996	126	465
Lake	346	1 177.5	4 868	119.5	2 005	1 605.0	43.9	7 486	1 294	1 569.0	1 224	1 430	280	609
Lawrence	46	123.9	404	8.2	475	215.6	33.2	3 449	260	204.7	271	965	D	278
Licking	148	330.5	1 259	24.1	1 138	676.0	50.7	5 387	683	658.2	821	959	200	504
Logan	63	479.5	1 055	24.6	485	183.8	51.5	4 517	265	172.1	251	1 111	230	549
Lorain	230	780.3	2 068	41.0	2 085	1 433.1	38.0	5 318	1 346	1 406.1	650	1 079	142	453
Lucas	877	4 121.3	11 180	272.3	3 999	3 256.2	35.0	6 998	2 931	3 215.8	1 218	1 327	299	779
Madison	47	109.4	340	5.7	290	165.2	54.8	4 640	164	159.2	D	944	26	437
Mahoning	456	1 970.0	6 196	124.3	2 673	1 667.6	33.8	6 118	1 766	1 616.5	798	1 200	266	548
Marion	76	190.9	894	17.4	596	373.8	36.1	5 742	382	364.1	1 014	1 114	211	533
Medina	210	680.2	2 006	43.1	1 040	661.6	49.7	5 626	562	641.9	388	1 493	113	369
Meigs	18	18.3	114	1.3	222	78.0	23.6	3 305	121	72.8	237	923	57	204
Mercer	69	191.8	674	11.3	407	190.6	59.6	4 899	257	181.4	537	999	99	465
Miami	122	327.5	1 060	21.4	867	548.0	50.1	6 055	525	535.6	650	1 128	210	526
Monroe	16	17.4	106	1.7	172	45.1	15.9	2 872	72	38.7	0	962	D	136
Montgomery	1 088	6 062.9	14 254	348.0	4 769	3 918.3	41.1	6 859	3 347	3 862.2	1 033	1 292	296	750
Morgan	11	18.4	69	1.2	125	29.4	2.4	2 055	62	26.3	77	D	D	158
Morrow	18	20.7	114	1.7	192	80.0	55.3	2 918	100	76.6	177	733	9	112
Muskingum	122	422.6	1 620	34.3	929	501.0	45.9	5 986	563	482.6	783	1 232	238	576
Noble	11	14.2	85	1.4	113	36.2	8.7	3 234	52	33.6	D	814	D	129
Ottawa	45	73.7	252	5.6	472	213.8	23.6	5 385	292	205.1	D	1 364	59	722
Paulding	38	86.5	206	3.8	200	50.4	22.0	2 400	100	46.7	D	729	D	230
Perry	19	13.3	63	1.0	264	81.0	32.8	2 531	141	75.4	D	686	22	170
Pickaway	46	86.0	249	4.5	377	173.3	24.1	3 726	216	163.8	D	845	93	391
Pike	25	27.0	172	2.4	223	94.9	33.1	3 798	125	87.4	D	998	59	289
Portage	135	305.2	737	15.2	1 025	637.2	43.8	4 614	614	618.2	338	988	31	422
Preble	48	183.1	526	11.2	359	129.7	52.6	3 293	189	121.5	D	831	55	293

1. For pay period including March 12. 2. Based on the estimated population as of July 1 of the year shown.

STATE County	Retail trade, establishments with payroll, 1987 (cont'd)		Taxable service industries–establishments with payroll, 1987							Bank deposits,[2] June 1989		Savings capital,[3] September 1989	
				Receipts (Mil dol)									
					Selected kinds of business								
	Paid employees[1]	Annual payroll (Mil dol)	Number	Total	Hotels, motels and other lodging places	Health services	Legal services	Paid employees	Annual payroll (Mil dol)	Total (Mil dol)	Percent change, 1988–1989	Total (Mil dol)	Percent change, 1988–1989
	161	162	163	164	165	166	167	168	169	170	171	172	173
OHIO	804 182	7 434.2	63 858	26 449.4	1 024.3	7 324.4	1 897.6	648 361	10 473.2	81 135	8.5	44 211.1	-2.1
Adams	768	6.8	65	10.7	D	5.2	1.1	328	3.1	138	4.5	18.5	-2.2
Allen	9 930	87.2	639	204.2	D	91.1	7.9	5 466	87.7	858	4.8	445.3	-1.1
Ashland	2 422	22.3	239	50.9	3.3	18.1	3.4	1 379	19.5	311	13.2	132.7	-5.5
Ashtabula	5 905	49.5	458	108.4	5.6	54.6	5.4	3 154	40.2	497	7.2	321.4	-4.6
Athens	3 408	26.9	225	45.4	1.3	23.2	3.2	1 241	16.6	306	4.2	38.5	1.7
Auglaize	2 707	23.7	201	49.3	D	17.8	2.6	1 504	16.4	397	4.2	116.2	3.5
Belmont	5 816	48.0	306	62.3	5.5	D	4.9	1 977	21.4	530	2.7	372.5	-5.0
Brown	1 145	8.0	102	19.9	1.0	9.7	1.5	678	7.8	214	5.8	34.4	-5.6
Butler	17 315	153.1	1 266	400.9	13.8	148.9	18.4	15 110	158.2	1 392	12.3	846.1	-6.0
Carroll	1 010	9.3	84	16.3	1.0	8.5	0.6	499	6.5	158	14.6	0.0	-100.0
Champaign	1 603	12.3	114	18.2	D	8.2	1.0	488	6.0	200	11.6	152.8	-4.5
Clark	10 686	91.7	706	192.4	7.7	79.1	10.9	6 022	78.1	791	11.9	366.1	-5.9
Clermont	8 323	81.9	560	254.4	D	43.6	6.2	5 221	95.8	500	9.3	315.1	1.2
Clinton	2 081	20.5	162	37.8	1.1	15.5	2.9	1 007	13.1	224	8.6	108.8	-0.1
Columbiana	6 119	50.4	504	124.6	3.0	54.0	5.3	3 622	46.7	619	4.7	359.1	-3.0
Coshocton	1 880	14.6	142	26.9	0.7	15.2	1.6	1 082	10.1	255	8.0	63.0	-0.9
Crawford	2 795	25.1	207	61.3	2.3	19.0	2.8	1 765	21.5	312	-9.8	231.5	0.1
Cuyahoga	116 112	1 113.3	10 704	5 585.2	162.8	1 238.8	625.6	117 084	2 269.7	14 677	9.3	10 597.0	-1.7
Darke	3 037	30.4	231	53.0	2.0	15.2	3.4	1 393	17.0	453	7.6	178.9	-5.1
Defiance	2 677	22.8	181	62.1	D	24.8	3.2	1 455	23.9	211	2.6	247.1	-1.8
Delaware	3 261	29.3	264	89.6	2.2	17.5	3.0	5 284	43.5	273	15.8	130.5	-2.6
Erie	6 694	59.9	483	253.0	30.6	51.9	11.4	4 144	84.0	586	5.4	45.4	-1.8
Fairfield	5 292	48.5	468	123.1	D	44.0	5.1	4 361	47.6	463	7.1	297.9	-7.4
Fayette	1 952	17.1	120	23.6	2.8	12.3	0.9	717	8.3	150	10.5	82.0	-1.1
Franklin	92 720	890.5	6 850	3 888.3	160.0	839.5	338.3	90 402	1 517.9	9 480	6.7	3 993.8	-1.5
Fulton	2 291	22.8	180	45.6	D	10.7	3.0	1 057	13.5	388	8.6	123.4	-2.2
Gallia	1 890	17.4	118	41.2	2.1	29.5	1.8	936	18.7	259	6.9	23.8	-3.3
Geauga	3 700	35.0	445	108.5	0.8	31.4	5.6	2 620	39.3	373	13.3	237.5	-0.3
Greene	7 992	71.4	624	275.5	11.2	54.5	6.0	6 279	99.7	519	16.5	384.8	-0.8
Guernsey	2 344	21.0	219	51.8	7.4	17.0	1.6	1 529	16.9	219	1.2	181.9	4.4
Hamilton	81 245	784.6	6 835	3 805.6	198.0	861.4	253.9	89 403	1 553.9	9 787	15.3	5 117.6	-0.2
Hancock	5 544	50.9	398	133.5	3.2	37.9	6.2	3 155	51.4	416	3.9	229.2	-1.9
Hardin	1 456	11.9	107	17.6	0.2	10.0	1.8	581	6.2	195	6.6	91.1	1.5
Harrison	433	3.6	67	10.5	0.0	4.9	D	385	3.7	116	-0.7	10.0	-2.2
Henry	1 216	11.7	98	19.8	D	7.1	2.2	668	6.5	185	4.1	106.8	-3.4
Highland	1 798	15.0	137	27.4	0.4	9.7	1.6	1 209	9.0	291	7.3	84.1	2.3
Hocking	1 107	11.0	94	16.8	0.4	8.2	1.2	516	5.7	134	10.3	41.1	-3.3
Holmes	1 382	13.1	91	30.8	D	17.4	0.8	980	10.6	238	5.4	27.7	-9.7
Huron	3 347	31.0	250	62.3	0.9	27.0	3.8	1 459	22.5	447	2.0	146.2	-4.7
Jackson	1 474	13.4	120	22.5	D	10.8	1.4	740	7.0	211	3.4	13.9	37.4
Jefferson	5 438	47.2	382	93.0	D	41.0	5.0	2 516	33.1	678	0.4	156.0	-9.9
Knox	2 569	21.3	210	42.5	1.3	22.3	2.2	1 312	16.0	316	11.2	104.4	-6.7
Lake	17 819	168.3	1 365	446.8	20.0	121.4	13.6	11 585	167.6	1 486	11.3	754.5	1.3
Lawrence	2 514	22.6	166	36.8	D	D	3.1	1 093	12.6	233	13.3	118.6	-8.7
Licking	8 584	76.1	565	151.6	6.5	58.5	7.0	4 701	60.6	767	8.4	316.6	-7.0
Logan	2 519	18.3	208	45.7	2.4	16.6	2.4	1 498	16.6	214	6.5	187.8	4.6
Lorain	16 678	156.6	1 285	367.5	19.7	155.7	22.0	9 358	144.7	1 409	3.9	765.5	-1.8
Lucas	40 780	391.4	3 271	1 440.1	D	460.9	102.2	39 334	617.9	3 540	16.4	2 041.3	-2.9
Madison	1 958	16.2	134	22.0	D	6.9	1.5	508	6.2	155	8.4	97.4	53.5
Mahoning	20 633	176.0	1 719	554.5	11.5	241.9	30.4	13 748	224.1	1 813	4.9	1 139.9	-2.2
Marion	4 734	42.2	344	90.5	2.6	43.1	3.7	2 439	36.9	363	9.9	231.7	-2.9
Medina	7 083	67.8	661	169.9	6.8	59.4	6.2	4 963	64.5	610	10.7	398.5	3.9
Meigs	838	8.0	59	8.5	D	5.1	1.0	280	2.7	144	4.0	0.0	NA
Mercer	2 279	18.3	165	55.2	D	16.2	1.1	1 175	17.7	443	4.7	82.6	-1.4
Miami	6 216	57.4	424	105.3	4.4	43.5	7.8	3 042	40.9	512	17.8	450.3	-3.8
Monroe	434	3.9	43	7.5	D	2.8	0.6	264	2.4	63	3.1	11.0	-4.1
Montgomery	49 626	463.3	3 838	2 117.2	60.2	528.9	98.5	48 360	853.7	3 844	8.4	2 733.5	-4.0
Morgan	370	2.7	26	2.4	0.0	1.2	0.5	46	0.8	84	5.6	18.1	-1.7
Morrow	827	6.8	82	15.9	0.6	7.9	0.6	632	5.7	63	-20.2	23.3	-1.3
Muskingum	6 320	54.2	461	123.3	5.7	48.7	7.4	2 700	46.3	433	6.9	320.7	-1.6
Noble	379	3.6	35	6.9	D	3.9	0.3	228	2.3	65	9.6	27.5	0.9
Ottawa	2 305	23.6	230	45.3	7.1	10.6	2.4	1 126	13.6	331	5.1	78.3	0.3
Paulding	635	5.3	56	10.3	D	3.9	1.3	268	2.9	110	4.3	33.1	-9.3
Perry	823	7.9	81	17.0	D	8.5	1.0	545	5.9	164	6.0	13.9	4.6
Pickaway	2 028	18.7	153	32.5	1.4	14.2	2.5	930	11.7	295	7.9	34.0	-16.5
Pike	984	9.2	72	12.1	0.7	7.9	0.4	462	4.8	115	-2.5	13.5	-9.5
Portage	6 917	65.7	572	182.3	11.9	48.9	4.6	4 243	59.9	582	8.2	302.4	-1.4
Preble	1 461	12.2	146	26.3	D	10.7	1.6	811	7.8	236	5.9	41.5	0.2

1. For the period including March 12 of the year shown. 2. Includes deposits for all insured and reporting noninsured commercial and mutual savings banks. 3. Includes savings capital for all FSLIC insured savings institutions.

STATE County	Federal funds and grants, 1989							Local government finances, 1981–1982							
	Expenditures		Per capita[1] (Dollars)					General revenue						Direct general expenditure	
									Intergovernmental		Taxes				
												Per capita[2]			
	Total (Mil dol)	Percent change, 1988–1989	Total	Direct payments for individuals	Procurement contract awards	Salaries and wages	Grant awards	Total (Mil dol)	Total (Mil dol)	Percent from state	Total (Mil dol)	Total (Dollars)	Property (Dollars)	Total (Mil dol)	Percent change, 1977–1982
	174	175	176	177	178	179	180	181	182	183	184	185	186	187	188
OHIO	36 313.4	7.7	X	1 829	629	338	483	11 644.2	4 690.2	78.2	4 656.2	432	312	11 315.7	44.1
Adams	82.0	14.3	3 142	1 777	36	118	1 045	24.9	10.2	93.9	7.8	312	306	25.5	51.6
Allen	1 159.0	1.9	10 293	2 334	7 450	186	270	102.1	42.3	83.5	39.2	356	276	95.3	17.9
Ashland	87.9	-2.6	1 878	1 536	46	96	132	38.4	13.7	92.1	16.0	345	270	36.2	62.5
Ashtabula	246.4	-5.8	2 459	1 951	28	104	350	89.5	40.0	91.3	38.7	376	315	87.7	54.1
Athens	138.1	5.9	2 321	1 602	33	172	495	44.3	25.8	82.0	12.1	211	177	43.2	40.3
Auglaize	120.8	-10.2	2 678	1 481	817	89	165	45.4	16.0	80.1	12.6	294	229	44.2	73.0
Belmont	228.2	2.5	3 060	2 474	67	110	395	56.1	26.9	82.0	18.5	226	207	55.5	47.3
Brown	70.2	10.4	1 933	1 327	10	80	404	29.4	13.0	89.2	7.3	219	202	29.0	74.5
Butler	516.6	8.3	1 820	1 389	65	87	260	242.3	98.1	76.0	92.8	353	251	240.5	32.6
Carroll	46.6	8.5	1 732	1 278	34	73	297	14.9	8.0	83.5	4.6	178	171	14.7	65.2
Champaign	93.5	6.8	2 597	1 537	487	84	252	32.4	14.8	95.6	9.8	291	247	29.8	84.3
Clark	413.9	-0.5	2 780	2 063	196	166	319	139.0	66.4	84.1	53.9	364	260	132.4	38.4
Clermont	202.5	5.9	1 349	1 041	22	78	195	114.8	59.7	70.2	38.7	290	264	116.4	105.5
Clinton	84.1	-6.3	2 323	1 656	30	107	324	38.1	12.7	90.8	9.9	288	244	39.2	68.8
Columbiana	257.8	7.9	2 392	1 928	61	85	294	75.2	38.8	91.2	25.3	223	180	74.4	53.6
Coshocton	86.3	-12.1	2 391	1 610	325	126	257	32.7	10.5	92.0	15.8	437	373	37.0	89.7
Crawford	114.9	0.3	2 364	1 767	135	80	242	41.6	15.9	86.6	19.0	384	315	39.4	31.0
Cuyahoga	5 199.9	5.7	3 652	2 207	446	483	505	2 348.5	936.9	67.2	1 014.2	690	442	2 195.3	42.5
Darke	110.3	5.6	2 024	1 448	23	86	254	38.6	17.9	89.7	14.6	271	220	35.3	41.1
Defiance	78.8	7.9	1 970	1 446	44	104	195	34.8	13.9	88.2	13.3	340	283	36.1	79.3
Delaware	98.2	2.4	1 518	1 043	61	201	135	41.1	14.2	95.5	17.3	311	256	37.8	48.0
Erie	174.8	6.6	2 244	1 754	95	112	238	91.3	33.4	87.0	38.7	494	400	87.0	51.3
Fairfield	178.4	-10.3	1 723	1 300	19	90	257	79.4	27.4	91.7	27.2	285	240	82.5	67.4
Fayette	63.0	0.2	2 298	1 517	18	83	411	29.2	10.4	84.5	8.4	308	271	27.1	84.0
Franklin	3 155.0	4.4	3 313	1 489	213	456	1 143	1 005.3	381.6	76.5	394.6	447	312	1 001.1	52.0
Fulton	86.0	-4.1	2 216	1 536	54	329	122	38.3	13.9	95.0	16.0	425	341	35.5	42.7
Gallia	79.4	2.4	2 622	1 805	18	93	674	28.0	12.3	92.6	11.5	387	362	28.4	78.5
Geauga	97.1	28.3	1 200	834	25	62	268	64.6	23.0	90.7	28.6	384	351	61.9	47.7
Greene	1 378.5	-7.2	10 219	1 658	2 640	5 639	239	125.8	57.9	77.4	40.6	310	253	122.2	44.3
Guernsey	96.5	1.0	2 423	1 891	18	124	365	29.0	13.2	83.4	11.0	262	205	27.2	60.2
Hamilton	4 729.3	2.5	5 391	1 843	2 647	449	438	1 062.4	386.1	70.9	492.9	566	372	987.4	3.7
Hancock	136.0	-20.7	2 067	1 286	96	107	413	54.0	18.9	92.1	25.2	387	292	53.6	52.7
Hardin	59.8	4.2	1 897	1 214	47	108	237	26.0	11.6	93.6	10.1	312	263	25.9	51.4
Harrison	47.5	7.9	3 061	2 350	20	191	419	16.6	7.9	95.1	5.3	303	278	15.4	73.6
Henry	57.2	-2.3	2 016	1 491	16	110	191	29.5	12.1	88.5	12.8	458	391	33.6	98.8
Highland	90.3	-1.1	2 495	1 720	21	97	434	29.7	11.9	94.8	7.4	218	189	30.5	74.6
Hocking	50.1	2.1	1 974	1 533	15	87	312	20.8	9.2	77.0	5.5	229	184	20.3	68.6
Holmes	32.5	-0.7	1 034	744	35	78	131	20.8	8.0	92.4	6.9	230	206	18.4	51.3
Huron	131.7	-2.6	2 314	1 748	134	98	209	47.2	20.0	88.2	19.0	348	278	48.7	56.0
Jackson	88.3	15.1	2 944	1 911	24	89	874	22.1	14.6	92.2	4.3	144	140	22.1	53.4
Jefferson	284.6	-5.0	3 518	2 643	29	167	658	84.3	31.0	80.8	37.7	418	351	80.4	53.4
Knox	103.4	5.3	2 159	1 657	18	89	303	37.0	14.4	93.6	14.7	312	256	36.1	59.3
Lake	408.5	7.6	1 896	1 537	57	98	196	253.9	66.2	92.7	108.6	506	390	248.6	54.4
Lawrence	166.8	7.8	2 656	1 914	23	74	635	52.3	27.4	92.1	10.0	158	136	53.9	98.9
Licking	357.2	1.6	2 808	1 514	259	729	267	105.2	52.2	80.4	39.0	315	239	102.0	66.4
Logan	103.7	2.1	2 499	1 875	88	147	228	34.4	15.7	95.7	12.5	319	262	33.6	29.7
Lorain	594.4	5.8	2 197	1 558	104	220	296	250.3	106.7	84.6	99.2	362	293	243.2	32.3
Lucas	1 186.4	4.0	2 537	1 876	84	179	385	564.7	232.6	63.9	217.4	464	305	569.6	51.3
Madison	69.6	-3.6	1 929	1 367	30	102	247	28.4	12.3	95.0	11.0	322	287	28.0	61.8
Mahoning	787.3	4.8	2 919	2 261	49	181	415	254.8	119.3	84.8	94.7	334	240	237.9	33.0
Marion	143.6	4.1	2 230	1 720	19	110	285	76.6	22.9	90.9	23.9	355	298	74.7	45.9
Medina	174.5	11.2	1 433	1 154	20	84	152	102.5	39.1	96.1	44.5	387	335	101.1	65.3
Meigs	60.7	7.6	2 582	1 812	14	114	566	19.8	14.3	93.6	4.1	172	171	19.2	107.4
Mercer	54.4	12.5	1 382	763	20	78	224	40.8	14.8	96.1	12.7	329	278	39.7	66.8
Miami	249.5	29.3	2 700	1 616	731	103	185	84.2	33.8	89.0	31.9	354	278	85.7	67.2
Monroe	39.4	10.0	2 590	1 694	22	198	649	15.9	6.0	94.7	8.9	524	509	15.6	36.8
Montgomery	2 420.2	16.0	4 187	1 950	1 187	671	364	700.1	268.8	74.9	298.6	527	347	707.4	53.5
Morgan	33.0	13.4	2 291	1 558	27	114	548	10.8	6.3	89.3	3.5	247	222	10.4	46.4
Morrow	45.4	-21.9	1 633	1 150	21	72	218	21.6	10.7	89.6	5.6	210	188	23.4	90.3
Muskingum	202.2	8.1	2 404	1 768	22	143	447	74.5	35.7	89.7	25.7	305	225	69.7	47.7
Noble	26.6	1.8	2 416	1 490	19	119	789	11.9	7.3	97.6	3.2	281	265	11.8	97.0
Ottawa	107.4	-14.1	2 685	1 952	260	209	132	38.4	13.2	87.5	17.6	442	383	36.2	72.5
Paulding	40.9	6.5	1 930	1 099	54	90	293	20.0	7.5	94.0	6.3	300	282	22.7	72.8
Perry	71.5	-1.4	2 213	1 691	16	94	369	25.4	15.7	89.0	5.7	183	152	26.0	100.4
Pickaway	90.5	1.9	1 918	1 275	62	79	291	38.8	16.5	83.0	12.9	299	265	37.1	102.4
Pike	670.2	101.2	26 387	1 599	23 951	83	678	28.7	18.2	76.0	4.7	201	197	25.9	95.3
Portage	246.4	7.5	1 754	1 338	99	90	209	142.0	54.0	83.0	42.8	311	258	142.4	59.5
Preble	76.3	2.5	1 908	1 342	18	95	247	29.8	14.5	92.7	10.1	265	230	30.5	68.4

1. Based on the estimated population as of July 1 of the year shown. 2. Based on the estimated population as of July 1, 1982.

STATE County	Local government finances, 1981–1982 (cont'd): Direct general expenditure (cont'd): Per capita[1] (Dollars)	Percent of total for– Education	Percent of total for– Health & hospitals	Percent of total for– Police protection	Percent of total for– Public welfare	Percent of total for– Highways	Debt outstanding: Total (Mil dol)	Debt outstanding: Per capita[1] (Dollars)	State and local government employment, 1989: Total	State and local government employment, 1989: Rate[2]	Federal government civilian employment 1989: Total	Federal government civilian employment 1989: Earnings ($1,000)	Elections, 1988[3]: Total vote cast for president	Elections, 1988[3]: Vote for lead party (Percent)
	189	190	191	192	193	194	195	196	197	198	199	200	201	202
OHIO	1 050	43.2	7.2	5.3	5.7	5.6	7 301.3	678	605 826	556.0	96 126	3 001 372	4 393 585	R–55.0
Adams	1 026	45.5	25.6	2.2	5.6	6.8	1.6	64	1 399	536.0	80	2 007	9 744	R–60.7
Allen	866	54.6	1.6	4.9	3.6	5.7	67.9	617	6 329	562.1	564	17 638	44 975	R–69.0
Ashland	778	51.9	2.6	4.6	5.5	8.9	34.2	735	2 320	495.7	114	3 144	18 939	R–67.2
Ashtabula	852	53.8	2.6	4.1	8.1	10.0	19.5	189	4 380	437.1	275	7 712	38 556	D–53.3
Athens	752	52.8	11.3	2.9	5.2	7.3	16.5	287	8 707	1 463.4	242	6 650	20 281	D–53.2
Auglaize	1 031	36.9	23.6	3.8	4.1	7.5	13.1	306	2 356	522.4	124	3 433	18 479	R–73.4
Belmont	677	50.5	4.1	3.5	5.9	8.5	33.5	409	3 169	424.8	185	5 256	31 973	D–61.0
Brown	874	43.1	24.7	2.4	4.0	5.8	3.6	108	1 508	415.4	86	2 138	12 698	R–59.4
Butler	916	46.2	3.2	4.9	3.8	6.9	309.0	1 177	15 141	533.3	559	17 035	110 208	R–68.7
Carroll	568	47.7	3.2	3.0	5.3	14.6	3.2	124	825	306.7	59	1 455	10 994	R–56.2
Champaign	888	48.4	3.6	3.7	9.2	8.9	9.1	269	1 761	489.2	78	2 070	13 368	R–67.3
Clark	893	47.1	7.0	5.0	7.6	3.7	62.1	419	6 152	413.2	655	20 467	56 503	R–57.9
Clermont	873	49.0	3.5	2.9	4.2	4.1	59.6	447	5 258	350.3	277	8 120	53 085	R–70.5
Clinton	1 136	43.5	27.6	3.2	3.1	5.3	23.1	670	2 318	640.3	99	2 673	12 699	R–69.7
Columbiana	656	57.9	3.1	4.4	3.0	9.1	30.6	270	3 953	366.7	240	6 819	43 140	D–50.0
Coshocton	1 021	45.6	3.1	4.0	6.4	7.0	17.2	475	1 414	391.7	119	3 405	14 506	R–57.1
Crawford	795	52.8	2.2	5.2	5.6	8.8	13.5	273	1 842	379.0	102	2 824	18 700	R–66.7
Cuyahoga	1 493	34.6	10.2	7.0	7.3	3.8	1 509.9	1 027	79 111	555.6	19 845	697 351	601 117	D–58.8
Darke	658	55.5	0.6	3.5	5.4	10.7	8.6	161	1 871	343.3	130	3 264	21 954	R–67.9
Defiance	923	45.7	4.5	3.6	5.1	9.7	10.9	280	1 784	446.0	127	3 495	15 153	R–63.1
Delaware	680	52.3	4.8	5.0	4.6	7.6	21.8	392	2 925	452.1	207	5 929	28 498	R–72.6
Erie	1 110	48.2	3.4	4.4	3.6	6.2	47.5	606	4 254	546.1	198	6 049	32 198	R–51.8
Fairfield	864	48.4	19.6	3.4	2.7	6.0	26.6	278	5 021	485.1	228	6 305	42 051	R–69.5
Fayette	990	39.1	22.4	3.2	4.7	8.1	3.0	109	1 291	471.2	57	1 589	8 873	R–69.7
Franklin	1 134	38.2	3.9	6.8	7.1	3.7	1 315.4	1 491	89 993	945.0	12 292	398 856	377 357	R–60.0
Fulton	938	54.7	1.8	3.5	4.6	10.4	17.8	471	2 123	547.2	150	4 741	15 428	R–66.3
Gallia	954	62.2	3.3	3.1	4.4	8.1	2.2	74	1 876	619.1	84	2 164	12 349	R–59.9
Geauga	830	55.1	4.6	3.8	4.4	8.8	26.2	352	2 842	351.3	126	3 587	34 608	R–64.5
Greene	934	48.5	4.6	5.0	5.5	4.8	58.1	444	9 927	735.9	275	8 420	52 856	R–65.1
Guernsey	651	48.6	1.9	4.5	4.4	11.5	15.5	371	2 535	636.9	126	3 271	14 563	R–58.4
Hamilton	1 135	38.6	6.1	6.8	4.6	4.6	538.1	618	51 613	588.3	9 981	335 085	370 384	R–61.3
Hancock	825	49.5	2.3	5.1	3.5	10.0	36.1	556	2 801	425.7	190	5 702	27 643	R–72.0
Hardin	802	55.8	1.5	3.3	8.9	9.6	8.4	260	1 481	470.2	88	2 331	11 606	R–62.8
Harrison	872	51.5	12.0	2.6	5.0	14.5	2.0	113	798	514.8	63	1 569	7 252	D–53.5
Henry	1 199	48.0	15.4	3.0	3.1	7.6	17.6	629	1 388	488.7	80	2 021	12 468	R–69.1
Highland	899	43.1	26.0	2.8	3.7	9.4	6.5	191	1 697	468.8	101	2 644	13 178	R–66.6
Hocking	842	32.9	25.4	3.3	5.4	11.9	2.5	106	1 300	511.8	54	1 369	9 243	R–58.7
Holmes	614	44.4	18.9	2.9	5.1	13.2	2.6	86	1 139	362.7	75	1 875	7 316	R–69.2
Huron	894	49.2	3.1	4.7	4.1	9.7	14.7	270	2 238	393.3	153	4 182	20 642	R–61.2
Jackson	733	57.1	3.6	3.9	6.8	9.5	5.7	188	1 270	423.3	67	1 829	11 267	R–59.2
Jefferson	892	50.3	4.4	3.8	3.9	7.3	41.5	460	2 839	350.9	308	8 962	36 509	D–60.5
Knox	767	51.5	4.4	3.7	5.9	9.2	23.1	490	2 576	537.8	116	2 973	19 200	R–63.4
Lake	1 158	45.4	15.0	5.5	1.9	5.4	136.0	633	9 321	432.5	509	16 374	93 524	R–56.6
Lawrence	854	52.1	18.9	4.0	5.6	4.5	17.3	275	2 810	447.5	141	3 525	24 768	R–52.2
Licking	824	55.1	3.5	3.7	3.3	8.0	35.2	284	5 649	444.1	3 097	103 520	51 767	R–66.7
Logan	857	52.5	2.3	4.0	8.0	11.9	4.4	113	1 845	444.6	142	4 233	15 697	R–70.7
Lorain	888	55.5	3.7	4.1	5.0	5.1	214.7	784	12 034	444.7	1 286	57 363	106 926	D–52.0
Lucas	1 217	34.3	3.9	5.9	7.1	5.0	476.6	1 018	27 317	584.1	2 243	74 447	185 095	D–53.9
Madison	820	56.9	3.2	3.7	4.8	8.8	13.5	396	2 668	739.1	96	2 771	11 817	R–70.3
Mahoning	838	49.1	3.1	4.4	11.0	4.8	88.0	310	13 792	511.4	1 178	37 667	120 126	D–62.9
Marion	1 110	40.0	24.4	3.4	6.9	4.9	14.6	217	4 326	671.7	189	5 397	24 718	R–60.1
Medina	879	60.3	2.5	4.2	2.6	6.3	60.6	527	4 682	384.7	265	7 641	49 874	R–60.1
Meigs	812	48.0	20.0	1.9	3.9	8.5	6.7	285	1 074	457.0	84	2 210	9 276	R–59.1
Mercer	1 030	45.2	25.3	2.7	3.6	6.6	15.4	398	2 372	602.0	97	2 662	16 286	R–68.5
Miami	951	48.4	2.3	4.3	2.2	7.2	61.9	687	3 716	402.2	236	6 970	36 434	R–68.4
Monroe	919	64.6	1.6	1.3	2.4	11.8	2.2	131	935	615.1	79	1 898	6 874	D–62.1
Montgomery	1 248	42.9	4.6	5.3	5.1	4.6	396.8	700	26 428	457.2	27 168	732 049	228 943	R–57.5
Morgan	728	52.8	4.2	2.6	7.2	15.8	1.6	110	489	339.6	49	1 334	5 859	R–63.4
Morrow	873	52.1	15.0	2.0	5.1	9.3	6.9	257	1 220	438.8	65	1 571	10 760	R–66.3
Muskingum	826	55.3	6.2	3.5	7.1	7.5	26.0	308	4 003	476.0	310	9 186	31 674	R–62.3
Noble	1 045	63.8	1.6	1.1	2.8	13.1	2.9	253	547	497.3	35	841	5 308	R–59.4
Ottawa	910	52.6	2.2	4.2	9.3	9.2	34.4	864	1 883	470.7	185	4 933	17 517	R–53.4
Paulding	1 087	38.4	32.1	2.6	3.8	8.5	10.0	478	1 009	475.9	59	1 331	8 571	R–62.8
Perry	830	56.5	5.0	2.7	7.2	9.4	5.0	159	1 399	433.1	72	1 849	11 731	R–56.3
Pickaway	862	46.1	15.4	3.8	2.9	8.2	8.4	196	3 104	657.6	97	2 497	15 794	R–68.4
Pike	1 102	49.1	14.1	2.1	5.8	6.2	4.3	184	1 350	531.5	55	1 446	10 919	R–51.4
Portage	1 035	42.5	22.0	3.6	4.3	6.2	54.7	397	12 666	901.5	288	8 212	52 480	R–50.2
Preble	805	59.3	2.7	2.7	3.9	8.0	11.4	301	1 678	419.5	100	2 515	15 381	R–66.9

1. Based on the estimated population as of July 1, 1982. 2. Per 10,000 resident population estimated as of July 1 of the year shown. 3. Data subject to copyright.

STATE–County code	MSA/CMSA/NECMA code[1]	STATE County	Land Area,[2] 1990 (Sq. Km.)	Population, 1990											
							Race						Age of population Percent		
				Total persons	Rank	Per square kilometer	White	Black	Am. Indian, Eskimo, Aleut	Asian & Pacific Islander	Other race	Hispanic[3]	Under 5 years	5 to 14 years	15 to 24 years
			1	2	3	4	5	6	7	8	9	10	11	12	13
		OHIO—Con.													
39 137	...	Putnam	1 253	33 819	1 167	27.0	33 197	26	44	25	527	1 418	8.7	18.2	13.8
39 139	4800	Richland	1 287	126 137	367	98.0	115 078	9 981	223	578	277	903	6.9	14.7	13.9
39 141	...	Ross	1 783	69 330	638	38.9	64 362	4 467	155	266	80	346	6.4	14.4	13.6
39 143	...	Sandusky	1 060	61 963	702	58.5	58 282	1 553	94	142	1 892	3 544	7.3	16.1	13.7
39 145	...	Scioto	1 586	80 327	570	50.6	77 253	2 458	409	126	81	261	6.6	15.4	13.9
39 147	...	Seneca	1 426	59 733	725	41.9	57 474	1 172	90	234	763	1 676	7.2	16.6	15.1
39 149	...	Shelby	1 060	44 915	914	42.4	43 789	615	49	393	69	185	8.0	17.1	14.1
39 151	1320	Stark	1 492	367 585	140	246.4	339 421	25 052	950	1 529	633	2 755	6.9	14.1	13.6
39 153	1692	Summit	1 069	514 990	91	481.7	446 902	61 185	1 065	4 989	849	3 017	7.0	13.5	14.1
39 155	9320	Trumbull	1 595	227 813	216	142.8	210 915	15 221	341	973	363	1 454	6.7	14.0	13.6
39 157	...	Tuscarawas	1 470	84 090	544	57.2	83 107	623	138	187	35	228	7.0	15.0	12.6
39 159	1840	Union	1 131	31 969	1 212	28.3	30 563	1 168	57	132	49	159	7.3	14.8	13.8
39 161	...	Van Wert	1 062	30 464	1 269	28.7	29 900	193	31	78	262	482	7.2	15.9	12.9
39 163	...	Vinton	1 073	11 098	2 284	10.3	11 071	4	16	3	4	33	7.1	15.2	14.9
39 165	1642	Warren	1 036	113 909	402	110.0	110 526	2 415	231	627	110	524	7.7	14.9	13.2
39 167	6020	Washington	1 645	62 254	699	37.8	61 129	774	111	185	55	225	6.5	14.7	14.2
39 169	...	Wayne	1 438	101 461	452	70.6	99 131	1 557	130	535	108	429	7.9	16.0	14.9
39 171	...	Williams	1 092	36 956	1 072	33.8	36 366	23	46	127	394	826	7.5	16.2	13.2
39 173	8400	Wood	1 599	113 269	406	70.8	109 303	1 168	197	1 028	1 573	2 882	6.4	13.9	23.2
39 175	...	Wyandot	1 051	22 254	1 565	21.2	22 087	20	20	65	62	162	7.2	15.7	13.1
40 000	...	OKLAHOMA	177 878	3 145 585	X	17.7	2 583 512	233 801	252 420	33 563	42 289	86 160	7.2	15.1	14.5
40 001	...	Adair	1 491	18 421	1 768	12.4	10 235	4	8 065	12	105	245	7.8	17.4	15.2
40 003	...	Alfalfa	2 245	6 416	2 716	2.9	5 971	203	165	6	71	102	5.2	12.4	10.9
40 005	...	Atoka	2 534	12 778	2 157	5.0	10 365	760	1 587	16	50	118	6.3	14.8	13.5
40 007	...	Beaver	4 699	6 023	2 754	1.3	5 741	1	62	3	216	300	6.2	16.5	11.1
40 009	...	Beckham	2 336	18 812	1 746	8.1	17 565	382	351	43	471	788	7.4	16.4	11.9
40 011	...	Blaine	2 405	11 470	2 257	4.8	9 778	499	995	20	178	287	7.2	16.1	11.8
40 013	...	Bryan	2 354	32 089	1 208	13.6	26 790	422	4 557	143	177	465	6.7	14.1	16.3
40 015	...	Caddo	3 311	29 550	1 313	8.9	21 270	750	6 667	68	795	1 430	7.5	16.4	13.0
40 017	5880	Canadian	2 331	74 409	603	31.9	67 453	1 816	3 152	1 226	762	1 921	7.7	17.6	12.7
40 019	...	Carter	2 134	42 919	939	20.1	35 199	3 580	3 632	164	344	781	7.0	15.6	12.2
40 021	...	Cherokee	1 945	34 049	1 160	17.5	22 068	384	11 380	68	149	470	7.2	15.4	17.3
40 023	...	Choctaw	2 005	15 302	1 973	7.6	10 933	1 958	2 319	25	67	195	7.2	15.9	12.9
40 025	...	Cimarron	4 753	3 301	2 978	0.7	3 057	0	32	12	200	412	6.7	15.9	11.8
40 027	5880	Cleveland	1 389	174 253	277	125.5	154 153	5 271	8 959	4 012	1 858	4 655	7.1	15.1	19.0
40 029	...	Coal	1 342	5 780	2 782	4.3	4 757	48	955	2	18	39	6.2	15.3	13.1
40 031	4200	Comanche	2 770	111 486	412	40.2	79 666	19 908	5 153	3 065	3 694	6 923	8.5	15.7	19.6
40 033	...	Cotton	1 649	6 651	2 690	4.0	5 813	142	523	6	167	231	6.1	15.0	12.4
40 035	...	Craig	1 971	14 104	2 047	7.2	10 864	483	2 695	34	28	101	5.9	13.2	12.1
40 037	8560	Creek	2 475	60 915	715	24.6	53 522	1 918	5 128	142	205	660	7.3	15.9	13.5
40 039	...	Custer	2 555	26 897	1 393	10.5	22 896	930	1 660	169	1 242	1 625	7.2	15.5	20.1
40 041	...	Delaware	1 919	28 070	1 350	14.6	20 848	20	7 096	43	63	227	6.2	13.7	12.1
40 043	...	Dewey	2 591	5 551	2 797	2.1	5 182	5	315	6	43	73	6.3	15.8	10.1
40 045	...	Ellis	3 184	4 497	2 876	1.4	4 351	3	66	11	66	138	5.5	15.2	10.3
40 047	2340	Garfield	2 742	56 735	768	20.7	52 403	2 020	1 234	587	491	1 086	6.9	15.4	12.7
40 049	...	Garvin	2 096	26 605	1 403	12.7	23 780	726	1 882	59	158	331	6.1	14.9	12.3
40 051	...	Grady	2 852	41 747	962	14.6	37 602	1 537	2 152	121	335	728	7.1	16.6	13.2
40 053	...	Grant	2 592	5 689	2 786	2.2	5 564	3	72	14	36	58	6.8	14.4	9.4
40 055	...	Greer	1 656	6 559	2 703	4.0	5 710	452	144	16	237	336	5.0	11.4	12.3
40 057	...	Harmon	1 393	3 793	2 932	2.7	2 854	288	38	6	607	656	6.8	16.2	12.0
40 059	...	Harper	2 691	4 063	2 912	1.5	3 972	3	30	6	52	72	5.6	15.1	9.5
40 061	...	Haskell	1 495	10 940	2 299	7.3	9 216	98	1 592	8	26	74	6.1	15.1	12.5
40 063	...	Hughes	2 090	13 023	2 141	6.2	10 354	384	2 232	13	40	136	5.6	14.2	11.8
40 065	...	Jackson	2 079	28 764	1 337	13.8	23 060	2 696	510	392	2 106	3 325	9.1	16.2	16.2
40 067	...	Jefferson	1 965	7 010	2 657	3.6	6 340	40	342	18	270	310	5.9	14.2	12.1
40 069	...	Johnston	1 669	10 032	2 384	6.0	8 173	215	1 583	14	47	120	6.2	15.7	14.8
40 071	...	Kay	2 380	48 056	869	20.2	42 978	856	3 650	240	332	851	7.1	15.3	12.1
40 073	...	Kingfisher	2 339	13 212	2 121	5.6	12 201	305	358	14	334	407	7.2	17.1	11.2
40 075	...	Kiowa	2 628	11 347	2 269	4.3	9 526	615	757	37	412	604	6.9	15.1	11.7
40 077	...	Latimer	1 871	10 333	2 355	5.5	8 524	154	1 574	20	61	115	6.7	16.2	15.2
40 079	...	Le Flore	4 108	43 270	934	10.5	36 907	1 030	5 112	94	127	419	7.1	15.6	13.9
40 081	...	Lincoln	2 483	29 216	1 322	11.8	26 392	789	1 849	56	130	307	6.8	16.5	12.6
40 083	5880	Logan	1 929	29 011	1 328	15.0	23 636	4 029	935	98	313	556	6.7	15.5	17.1
40 085	...	Love	1 335	8 157	2 550	6.1	6 992	360	559	12	234	335	5.9	14.4	13.6
40 087	5880	McClain	1 475	22 795	1 543	15.5	20 759	233	1 513	36	254	578	6.4	16.1	13.5

1. MSA = Metropolitan Statistical Area. CMSA = Consolidated MSA. NECMA = New England county metropolitan area. PMSA = Primary MSA. See Appendix A for explanation of these concepts. See Appendix B for list of metropolitan areas identified by type, with component counties. 2. Dry land or land partially or temporarily covered by water. 3. Hispanic persons may be of any race.

STATE County	Population, 1990 (cont'd): Age of population (cont'd) Percent: 25 to 34 years	35 to 44 years	45 to 54 years	55 to 64 years	65 to 74 years	75 years and over	Percent female	Population–Change and components of change: Change 1980–1990: Number	Percent	Components of change, 1980–1986: Total persons, 1986	Total persons, 1980	Net change: Number	Percent	Natural increase: Births	Deaths
	14	15	16	17	18	19	20	21	22	23	24	25	26	27	28
OHIO—Con.															
Putnam	16.3	13.5	9.1	8.2	6.7	5.5	50.2	828	2.5	33 400	32 991	400	1.3	4 000	1 600
Richland	15.5	14.8	11.3	9.8	7.7	5.2	51.0	-5 068	-3.9	128 800	131 205	-2 400	-1.8	11 700	6 900
Ross	17.9	15.5	11.0	8.9	7.4	5.0	47.9	4 326	6.7	67 300	65 004	2 300	3.5	5 800	3 900
Sandusky	16.0	14.5	9.8	9.2	7.7	5.7	51.0	-1 304	-2.1	62 200	63 267	-1 000	-1.6	6 200	3 300
Scioto	15.3	13.8	10.3	9.8	8.3	6.6	51.5	-4 218	-5.0	82 300	84 545	-2 300	-2.7	7 800	5 900
Seneca	15.3	14.3	9.4	8.9	7.6	5.8	51.3	-2 168	-3.5	61 600	61 901	-300	-0.6	6 100	3 200
Shelby	16.6	14.5	9.9	8.3	6.6	5.0	50.1	1 826	4.2	44 000	43 089	900	2.1	4 700	2 100
Stark	15.5	15.2	10.7	9.6	8.6	5.8	52.1	-11 238	-3.0	373 500	378 823	-5 300	-1.4	33 400	21 700
Summit	16.6	15.4	10.1	9.5	8.3	5.5	52.1	-9 482	-1.8	507 800	524 472	-16 700	-3.2	45 500	30 700
Trumbull	14.7	15.2	11.2	10.1	9.0	5.4	52.1	-14 050	-5.8	233 500	241 863	-8 400	-3.5	20 700	13 000
Tuscarawas	15.4	14.8	10.5	9.7	8.5	6.4	52.2	-524	-0.6	85 500	84 614	900	1.0	8 100	5 600
Union	18.2	16.1	10.6	8.1	6.3	4.8	53.4	2 433	8.2	31 100	29 536	1 600	5.4	3 000	1 500
Van Wert	15.6	14.4	9.8	9.2	8.2	6.8	51.4	6	0.0	30 000	30 458	-500	-1.6	2 800	1 800
Vinton	15.0	14.1	10.5	9.3	7.8	6.0	50.9	-486	-4.2	11 400	11 584	-200	-1.8	1 000	700
Warren	18.7	16.9	11.2	8.3	5.4	3.6	49.5	14 633	14.7	104 500	99 276	5 200	5.3	9 500	4 300
Washington	15.2	15.0	11.1	9.6	7.8	5.9	51.8	-2 012	-3.1	64 200	64 266	-100	-0.1	5 800	3 600
Wayne	15.9	15.0	10.3	8.4	6.6	5.0	51.0	4 053	4.2	101 200	97 408	3 800	3.9	10 300	4 500
Williams	16.3	14.4	10.3	8.4	7.7	6.0	50.9	587	1.6	36 800	36 369	400	1.1	3 700	1 900
Wood	15.3	14.4	9.2	7.5	5.9	4.3	52.0	5 897	5.5	110 300	107 372	2 900	2.7	9 600	4 700
Wyandot	15.4	13.8	10.4	9.6	7.8	6.9	51.9	-397	-1.8	22 600	22 651	-100	-0.4	2 400	1 400
OKLAHOMA	16.2	14.4	10.3	8.9	7.5	6.0	51.3	120 585	4.0	3 305 000	3 025 000	280 000	9.2	342 000	182 000
Adair	14.4	12.9	10.2	8.6	7.7	5.9	50.9	-154	-0.8	19 800	18 575	1 200	6.7	2 100	1 200
Alfalfa	14.9	12.0	11.0	10.9	10.8	12.0	47.4	-661	-9.3	6 900	7 077	-200	-2.8	600	700
Atoka	15.7	13.7	10.5	10.0	8.6	6.8	47.5	30	0.2	13 700	12 748	1 000	7.5	1 100	900
Beaver	13.8	14.0	11.1	10.3	9.0	7.9	50.8	-783	-11.5	7 400	6 806	600	8.5	600	400
Beckham	15.2	12.9	9.2	9.0	8.6	9.4	52.2	-431	-2.2	21 900	19 243	2 700	13.8	2 900	1 600
Blaine	13.7	12.3	10.0	9.5	9.6	9.7	52.0	-1 973	-14.7	13 600	13 443	100	1.0	1 700	1 200
Bryan	13.4	12.8	10.2	9.4	9.1	8.0	52.0	1 554	5.1	33 300	30 535	2 800	9.2	2 800	2 300
Caddo	14.1	12.8	10.2	9.5	8.4	8.3	51.6	-1 355	-4.4	33 400	30 905	2 500	8.2	3 900	2 400
Canadian	17.7	17.5	11.2	7.2	4.6	3.7	49.9	17 957	31.8	73 000	56 452	16 500	29.3	7 400	2 500
Carter	14.8	14.1	10.0	9.8	8.6	7.9	52.1	-691	-1.6	47 500	43 610	3 900	9.0	4 600	3 200
Cherokee	14.6	12.9	9.9	9.0	7.8	5.9	51.5	3 365	11.0	34 800	30 684	4 100	13.4	3 100	1 800
Choctaw	12.9	12.4	10.0	10.2	10.0	8.6	52.5	-1 901	-11.1	16 600	17 203	-600	-3.6	1 500	1 300
Cimarron	12.2	14.0	10.1	10.1	10.4	8.8	50.3	-347	-9.5	3 900	3 648	300	7.5	400	200
Cleveland	19.1	16.3	10.2	6.5	4.1	2.6	49.7	41 080	30.8	161 800	133 173	28 600	21.5	14 400	4 300
Coal	13.5	13.0	10.0	10.2	9.3	9.5	52.1	-261	-4.3	6 000	6 041	-100	-1.5	500	600
Comanche	19.0	13.1	8.4	7.1	5.2	3.5	48.1	-970	-0.9	120 700	112 456	8 200	7.3	16 400	4 400
Cotton	13.8	12.1	10.8	9.8	10.0	10.0	52.7	-687	-9.4	7 000	7 338	-300	-4.4	600	600
Craig	14.4	14.1	12.1	10.5	9.5	8.1	51.3	-910	-6.1	15 100	15 014	100	0.8	1 200	1 200
Creek	14.6	15.0	11.6	9.1	7.2	5.7	51.4	1 899	3.2	69 300	59 016	10 200	17.4	6 300	3 500
Custer	15.3	12.4	8.7	7.5	6.7	6.6	51.2	902	3.5	30 100	25 995	4 100	15.7	3 700	1 700
Delaware	12.0	12.0	11.4	12.5	12.2	7.9	51.4	4 124	17.2	28 000	23 946	4 100	17.0	2 200	1 800
Dewey	14.0	12.2	10.4	9.6	10.2	11.5	51.6	-371	-6.3	6 300	5 922	400	5.9	600	500
Ellis	11.5	14.8	10.4	9.6	11.2	11.6	51.2	-1 099	-19.6	5 600	5 596	0	0.5	500	400
Garfield	16.3	13.9	10.1	9.3	8.1	7.3	52.0	-6 085	-9.7	62 900	62 820	0	0.1	7 400	3 900
Garvin	14.1	12.5	10.1	10.3	9.9	9.9	52.5	-1 251	-4.5	29 800	27 856	1 900	6.9	2 900	2 300
Grady	15.6	14.2	11.1	8.6	7.0	6.5	51.9	2 257	5.7	44 500	39 490	5 100	12.8	4 500	2 500
Grant	13.5	12.7	9.3	11.1	11.0	11.8	52.5	-829	-12.7	6 500	6 518	0	0.2	600	600
Greer	14.9	12.0	9.8	10.2	11.4	13.0	47.8	-469	-6.7	6 900	7 028	-100	-1.9	500	700
Harmon	11.9	10.6	8.7	9.9	11.3	12.6	52.3	-726	-16.1	4 400	4 519	-100	-2.7	400	400
Harper	13.2	13.5	10.5	11.9	9.9	10.8	50.8	-652	-13.8	4 700	4 715	-100	-1.1	400	400
Haskell	12.5	13.0	10.9	10.9	10.6	8.3	51.7	-70	-0.6	11 800	11 010	800	7.2	1 000	800
Hughes	11.7	12.2	10.6	11.2	11.1	11.6	53.0	-1 315	-9.2	14 500	14 338	100	0.9	1 200	1 300
Jackson	17.6	12.9	8.7	7.2	6.4	5.7	50.4	-1 592	-5.2	30 800	30 356	500	1.5	4 100	1 500
Jefferson	12.8	12.9	9.7	10.4	10.4	11.5	52.5	-1 284	-15.5	7 900	8 294	-400	-5.0	700	700
Johnston	13.0	13.0	10.5	9.5	9.2	8.2	51.3	-324	-3.1	10 900	10 356	600	5.7	900	800
Kay	14.5	14.0	10.0	9.4	9.2	8.3	51.8	-1 796	-3.6	52 200	49 852	2 300	4.6	5 300	3 600
Kingfisher	16.1	13.2	10.2	9.2	8.1	7.8	51.5	-975	-6.9	15 700	14 187	1 600	11.0	2 000	900
Kiowa	12.9	11.5	9.4	10.1	10.3	12.0	52.9	-1 364	-10.7	12 400	12 711	-300	-2.4	1 300	1 200
Latimer	13.5	12.1	9.7	9.4	9.7	7.6	50.2	493	5.0	10 600	9 840	800	8.0	800	700
Le Flore	14.5	13.5	11.2	9.0	8.0	7.1	50.9	2 572	6.3	44 500	40 698	3 800	9.3	3 600	2 900
Lincoln	14.4	13.9	11.3	9.7	8.0	6.9	51.0	2 615	9.8	29 900	26 601	3 300	12.5	2 800	1 800
Logan	14.2	14.2	10.4	8.5	6.8	6.6	51.1	2 130	7.9	31 100	26 881	4 200	15.7	3 000	1 800
Love	14.4	14.4	11.1	9.7	8.9	7.5	48.7	688	9.2	7 900	7 469	500	6.4	700	500
McClain	15.1	14.7	12.6	9.5	6.7	5.4	50.1	2 504	12.3	24 900	20 291	4 600	22.7	2 200	1 100

STATE County	Population–(cont'd) Components of change, 1980-1986 (cont'd) Net migration	Households, 1990 Number	Households, 1990 Percent change, 1980–1990	Households, 1990 Persons per household	Households, 1990 Percent Female family householder[1]	Households, 1990 Percent One-person	Births, 1988 Total	Births, 1988 Rate[2]	Births, 1988 Low birth weight[3] (Number)	Deaths, 1987 Number Total	Deaths, 1987 Number Infant[4]	Deaths, 1987 Rate Total[2]	Deaths, 1987 Rate Infant[5]	Marriages, 1984 Number	Marriages, 1984 Rate[2]
	29	30	31	32	33	34	35	36	37	38	39	40	41	42	43
OHIO–Con.															
Putnam	-2 000	11 082	9.6	3.02	6.7	18.2	589	17.3	29	278	5	8.2	8.8	282	8.4
Richland	-7 300	47 573	2.5	2.57	10.4	24.1	1 773	13.7	118	1 144	23	8.9	12.9	1 285	9.9
Ross	300	24 325	10.4	2.62	11.2	22.6	875	12.8	60	612	10	9.0	11.6	678	10.0
Sandusky	-4 000	22 464	4.2	2.71	9.9	21.7	863	13.9	39	558	13	9.0	14.4	644	10.3
Scioto	-4 200	29 786	0.9	2.58	12.9	25.2	1 040	12.7	64	926	5	11.3	4.4	698	8.3
Seneca	-3 200	21 277	2.2	2.71	9.4	22.9	882	14.3	46	531	6	8.6	6.7	592	9.6
Shelby	-1 700	15 626	10.2	2.83	8.0	19.7	671	15.1	32	350	5	7.9	7.2	414	9.5
Stark	-16 900	139 573	4.1	2.58	10.9	23.9	5 172	13.8	368	3 489	51	9.4	10.3	3 406	9.1
Summit	-31 500	199 998	5.3	2.54	12.3	25.7	7 155	13.9	485	4 896	72	9.6	10.3	4 932	9.6
Trumbull	-16 100	86 056	2.3	2.62	11.6	23.5	3 017	13.1	192	2 228	31	9.7	10.2	2 234	9.5
Tuscarawas	-1 700	31 971	4.9	2.60	8.6	23.4	1 199	14.1	62	819	10	9.7	8.8	792	9.2
Union	100	11 037	10.2	2.73	8.2	19.6	469	14.3	19	254	2	7.9	4.4	312	10.2
Van Wert	-1 600	11 266	3.0	2.67	7.4	21.6	425	14.2	20	324	0	10.8	0.0	328	11.0
Vinton	-600	4 069	3.7	2.70	9.2	20.9	171	14.7	10	119	0	10.2	0.0	106	9.1
Warren	0	39 150	23.8	2.80	8.7	16.3	1 632	14.7	91	776	14	7.2	8.4	1 107	10.8
Washington	-2 300	23 636	5.7	2.57	9.2	23.4	779	12.3	34	578	6	9.1	7.5	558	8.6
Wayne	-2 000	35 619	10.5	2.76	8.4	21.0	1 670	16.0	103	855	15	8.4	9.3	977	9.8
Williams	-1 400	13 807	7.1	2.65	7.7	22.4	538	14.5	25	347	4	9.5	7.3	408	11.2
Wood	-2 000	39 677	11.8	2.64	7.9	22.8	1 445	13.0	82	800	7	7.3	4.7	805	7.4
Wyandot	-1 100	8 168	4.2	2.67	8.7	22.2	304	13.8	15	263	2	11.8	6.9	223	9.9
OKLAHOMA	120 000	1 206 135	7.8	2.53	10.4	25.6	47 408	14.6	3 102	29 290	458	9.0	9.6	39 219	11.8
Adair	400	6 386	4.5	2.85	12.3	21.1	365	17.8	17	216	6	10.6	17.5	176	9.1
Alfalfa	-100	2 469	-13.9	2.33	5.2	28.5	73	11.4	5	94	1	14.2	15.9	40	5.8
Atoka	700	4 495	4.7	2.60	10.0	23.8	168	12.4	10	134	0	10.0	0.0	121	8.8
Beaver	300	2 327	-8.0	2.56	5.0	22.7	79	11.4	4	56	2	8.0	26.3	47	6.3
Beckham	1 300	7 351	-1.7	2.51	9.4	27.2	284	14.4	15	268	1	13.5	3.7	208	8.7
Blaine	-300	4 418	-13.0	2.53	7.5	27.3	167	12.9	7	183	4	13.9	21.2	122	8.6
Bryan	2 300	12 524	7.8	2.49	10.5	26.1	464	14.0	34	386	4	11.7	8.8	807	24.8
Caddo	900	10 879	-1.7	2.66	11.8	24.0	493	15.4	31	359	4	11.0	7.4	281	8.2
Canadian	11 600	25 597	37.3	2.81	8.8	18.1	1 078	14.6	55	416	7	5.7	6.2	500	7.2
Carter	2 500	16 601	1.9	2.52	11.1	25.3	609	13.4	39	513	4	11.1	6.4	702	14.8
Cherokee	2 700	12 657	19.5	2.59	11.7	23.2	484	13.5	25	274	2	7.7	4.6	351	10.4
Choctaw	-800	5 952	-6.5	2.53	13.1	27.2	247	14.9	21	223	1	13.4	4.1	326	19.6
Cimarron	200	1 300	-5.7	2.51	5.8	26.3	45	11.0	5	43	0	10.2	0.0	37	9.3
Cleveland	18 500	63 991	39.8	2.60	9.2	23.2	2 216	13.6	119	792	26	4.9	11.5	1 258	8.0
Coal	0	2 279	1.3	2.51	10.3	28.5	74	12.3	5	68	2	11.3	26.3	56	9.3
Comanche	-3 800	37 569	6.9	2.72	12.1	20.4	2 267	19.0	163	724	13	6.0	5.6	1 566	13.1
Cotton	-300	2 609	-7.8	2.51	9.2	25.3	79	11.4	2	103	0	14.7	0.0	47	6.5
Craig	100	5 272	-3.9	2.45	8.6	27.5	200	13.3	17	217	1	14.6	5.4	93	6.0
Creek	7 400	22 470	7.5	2.68	9.4	20.7	855	13.3	51	536	4	8.3	4.4	705	10.3
Custer	2 100	9 918	4.6	2.55	8.9	25.4	383	13.6	16	223	6	7.8	15.2	266	8.6
Delaware	3 600	11 003	24.9	2.51	8.0	22.4	369	12.8	23	332	2	11.6	5.4	160	5.8
Dewey	200	2 221	-3.6	2.46	5.9	27.6	70	11.9	4	78	0	12.8	0.0	2	0.3
Ellis	-100	1 826	-17.8	2.43	6.4	27.1	36	7.2	2	59	1	11.1	19.6	33	5.3
Garfield	-3 500	22 460	-5.8	2.45	9.1	26.9	824	14.1	54	632	7	10.6	8.3	772	11.7
Garvin	1 300	10 417	-0.9	2.47	9.6	26.0	354	12.5	29	335	3	11.6	8.5	252	8.3
Grady	3 100	15 544	8.7	2.64	9.5	21.6	580	13.7	36	355	5	8.3	8.2	375	8.4
Grant	0	2 327	-12.4	2.40	5.5	27.8	59	9.8	2	103	0	16.6	0.0	53	[illegible]
Greer	100	2 551	-11.1	2.24	8.4	33.5	77	11.7	7	125	0	18.4	0.0	44	6.1
Harmon	-100	1 486	-15.5	2.45	8.1	31.0	52	12.7	2	62	0	14.8	0.0	30	6.5
Harper	-100	1 645	-13.6	2.42	5.4	27.5	43	9.8	5	64	0	14.2	0.0	24	4.9
Haskell	700	4 319	3.1	2.51	8.5	25.4	143	12.2	9	129	0	10.8	0.0	147	12.5
Hughes	300	5 224	-6.5	2.43	11.5	27.2	143	9.9	10	179	0	12.2	0.0	95	6.3
Jackson	-2 100	10 455	-0.8	2.65	10.3	22.4	615	20.8	35	241	4	7.9	6.6	304	9.7
Jefferson	-400	2 843	-10.4	2.40	8.1	29.7	83	11.2	5	108	1	14.2	14.5	81	9.8
Johnston	500	3 783	-1.3	2.55	11.3	25.2	129	11.8	7	173	0	15.7	0.0	69	6.3
Kay	600	19 083	-1.8	2.46	7.8	27.2	655	12.8	33	587	8	11.4	10.6	584	10.9
Kingfisher	500	4 932	-4.4	2.64	7.0	23.8	186	12.7	13	146	0	9.7	0.0	176	10.7
Kiowa	-400	4 551	-9.7	2.43	11.0	28.8	166	13.7	20	183	1	15.0	5.6	63	4.8
Latimer	700	3 693	8.7	2.64	10.0	22.8	126	11.6	7	102	0	9.5	0.0	67	6.6
Le Flore	3 000	15 938	10.0	2.65	10.3	22.4	604	13.0	32	448	9	9.8	14.7	556	12.8
Lincoln	2 300	10 839	12.3	2.67	7.8	21.4	360	12.2	22	270	4	9.2	10.2	256	8.6
Logan	3 000	10 180	8.1	2.65	10.0	22.6	363	12.2	30	281	4	9.4	10.0	274	8.8
Love	300	2 992	5.6	2.57	8.4	23.3	115	14.2	11	87	4	10.7	38.8	153	19.1
McClain	3 500	8 332	17.9	2.71	7.2	18.5	303	12.6	19	196	1	8.1	3.4	231	9.5

1. No spouse present. 2. Per 1,000 resident population estimated as of July 1 of the year shown. 3. Under 2,500 grams. 4. Deaths of infants under 1 year old. 5. Deaths of infants under 1 year old per 1,000 live births.

STATE County	Divorces, 1984		Physicians, active non–Federal, 1989		Hospitals, 1989			Nursing homes,[4] 1986		Serious crimes known to police, 1988			Education			
						Beds				Number			Public school enrollment[7]		Attainment,[8] 1980	
	Number	Rate[1]	Number[2]	Rate[3]	Number	Number	Rate[3]	Number	Beds	Total[5]	Violent[6]	Rate[3]	1986–1987	1980	Percent 12 yrs. or more	Percent 16 yrs. or more
	44	45	46	47	48	49	50	51	52	53	54	55	56	57	58	59
OHIO—Con.																
Putnam	59	1.8	10	29	0	0	0	6	393	256	21	756	6 879	7 265	66.7	7.3
Richland	743	5.7	155	120	4	590	457	16	1 038	2 162	165	2 799	24 311	26 296	66.1	10.1
Ross	335	5.0	70	102	2	876	1 277	8	521	2 676	202	3 921	12 884	13 547	57.3	8.7
Sandusky	336	5.4	51	82	3	341	548	9	696	1 397	113	2 239	12 875	12 769	67.2	9.2
Scioto	401	4.8	73	90	1	379	465	16	1 051	2 940	200	3 565	16 977	18 143	54.2	7.1
Seneca	287	4.7	66	107	2	165	267	10	738	722	72	3 666	10 377	12 195	66.4	9.2
Shelby	235	5.4	26	58	1	112	251	4	351	240	15	911	8 938	9 340	63.8	8.5
Stark	1 850	4.9	596	159	7	2 123	567	48	3 808	16 520	1 721	4 444	66 789	73 538	67.4	11.3
Summit	2 623	5.1	1 181	229	10	3 022	586	30	2 619	24 386	2 600	6 063	81 375	98 543	69.2	15.5
Trumbull	1 241	5.3	228	100	4	911	399	17	1 770	6 842	767	3 140	41 082	48 129	68.2	10.0
Tuscarawas	420	4.9	75	88	2	231	272	13	976	1 351	96	1 588	16 088	16 500	62.3	7.8
Union	172	5.6	17	50	1	71	211	3	262	266	11	3 413	5 172	6 312	69.0	10.3
Van Wert	138	4.6	18	60	1	100	333	6	325	146	18	488	5 056	5 671	70.3	7.5
Vinton	65	5.6	0	0	0	0	0	2	119	154	1	1 328	2 534	2 642	50.8	5.5
Warren	677	6.6	73	64	0	0	0	12	1 037	3 404	263	3 138	19 765	21 891	62.7	11.3
Washington	305	4.7	56	89	2	280	443	7	633	1 428	53	2 295	12 396	13 487	68.3	11.4
Wayne	469	4.7	86	82	3	493	467	12	893	2 003	92	1 957	19 153	19 216	65.8	12.6
Williams	179	4.9	37	100	1	115	310	5	433	882	91	2 397	7 300	7 704	68.6	8.3
Wood	433	4.0	126	112	1	125	111	10	781	3 787	133	3 452	18 882	18 844	75.0	18.6
Wyandot	153	6.8	11	50	1	36	165	7	615	510	27	2 268	4 224	4 731	66.8	8.7
OKLAHOMA	24 130	7.3	4 696	145	144	15 461	478	405	31 445	182 361	14 178	5 589	593 838	587 364	66.0	15.1
Adair	112	5.8	8	38	0	0	0	1	79	392	18	1 946	4 352	4 505	45.1	8.7
Alfalfa	28	4.1	1	16	1	20	317	3	169	135	20	2 021	1 011	1 366	66.4	14.8
Atoka	136	9.9	2	15	1	37	276	3	261	249	23	1 850	2 427	2 524	44.1	6.8
Beaver	41	5.5	2	29	1	24	353	1	62	130	3	1 836	1 442	1 451	70.4	14.4
Beckham	177	7.4	20	106	2	124	656	4	311	773	52	3 876	3 785	3 492	55.6	10.9
Blaine	84	5.9	7	56	2	104	825	3	256	386	45	2 955	2 522	2 682	59.7	11.3
Bryan	235	7.2	18	54	1	100	300	6	420	1 585	128	4 788	6 259	5 900	55.0	12.6
Caddo	206	6.0	10	32	2	83	262	5	354	733	68	2 248	6 772	6 745	53.2	9.3
Canadian	535	7.7	50	67	2	67	89	11	1 011	3 321	239	4 525	15 741	13 154	75.5	15.2
Carter	344	7.3	57	126	3	228	506	9	663	2 242	202	4 814	9 253	8 880	60.1	11.2
Cherokee	204	6.0	33	90	2	133	363	5	342	1 393	87	3 924	5 718	6 214	56.2	17.8
Choctaw	132	8.0	8	48	1	66	395	3	210	632	42	3 818	3 251	3 763	46.6	7.2
Cimarron	13	3.3	2	49	1	64	1 561	1	44	42	3	1 053	720	716	67.6	12.7
Cleveland	1 082	6.9	216	130	4	690	417	8	930	10 726	567	6 583	31 059	26 346	78.8	25.7
Coal	29	4.8	3	50	1	20	333	1	75	73	3	1 200	1 240	1 272	42.6	7.4
Comanche	936	7.8	121	102	4	546	458	8	632	6 426	555	5 397	22 307	22 417	73.3	15.1
Cotton	52	7.2	1	14	0	0	0	2	102	234	4	3 352	1 295	1 470	55.4	8.4
Craig	107	6.9	20	134	2	437	2 933	8	378	255	17	1 705	2 817	2 952	56.5	8.1
Creek	462	6.7	29	46	3	186	296	7	564	1 986	129	2 977	13 073	13 296	58.4	8.7
Custer	203	6.5	29	106	4	193	704	7	561	1 271	92	4 441	5 137	4 594	66.1	17.8
Delaware	122	4.4	14	48	1	41	140	6	391	678	49	2 420	6 221	4 863	52.8	7.3
Dewey	15	2.3	5	86	1	19	328	2	92	107	9	1 759	1 283	1 113	60.9	10.5
Ellis	27	4.4	6	125	1	72	1 500	1	60	50	4	946	971	1 061	63.5	12.0
Garfield	479	7.3	96	170	3	450	795	8	592	3 679	279	6 170	10 865	11 235	71.6	16.1
Garvin	207	6.8	15	54	2	95	339	7	600	1 075	79	3 667	5 847	5 422	51.3	8.6
Grady	281	6.3	43	103	1	156	375	5	352	1 981	121	4 577	8 229	8 292	58.1	11.8
Grant	18	2.6	1	17	0	0	0	2	131	76	1	1 229	1 041	1 231	72.0	13.7
Greer	49	6.8	8	123	1	40	615	1	112	118	9	1 766	1 076	1 210	52.0	9.7
Harmon	31	6.7	3	75	1	22	550	2	161	101	4	2 412	767	932	48.5	8.2
Harper	21	4.3	3	70	1	25	581	2	125	58	3	1 293	903	820	66.6	11.2
Haskell	86	7.3	3	26	1	31	265	1	74	258	6	2 174	2 086	2 282	46.3	8.1
Hughes	95	6.3	4	28	2	83	576	4	276	342	9	2 365	2 647	2 839	47.0	8.0
Jackson	221	7.0	34	116	2	153	524	3	273	1 720	98	5 582	6 069	6 708	66.7	13.6
Jefferson	40	4.8	4	56	1	32	444	3	202	149	16	1 916	1 520	1 608	50.1	7.5
Johnston	54	5.0	4	36	1	42	382	2	85	251	25	2 288	2 107	2 148	47.7	7.6
Kay	372	7.0	58	115	2	211	418	8	609	1 950	115	3 790	8 998	9 034	68.0	15.7
Kingfisher	116	7.0	4	28	2	63	444	3	149	275	6	1 814	3 171	2 703	65.4	11.3
Kiowa	75	5.7	6	50	1	50	420	4	229	330	26	2 781	2 119	2 268	54.7	8.5
Latimer	79	7.7	4	36	1	33	297	3	135	214	27	2 006	1 739	2 134	54.4	10.2
Le Flore	374	8.6	17	36	2	141	298	7	537	1 113	82	2 458	9 062	8 936	47.9	8.0
Lincoln	190	6.4	7	24	2	61	208	6	306	578	40	1 965	5 322	5 766	57.7	7.7
Logan	187	6.0	14	48	1	50	171	8	579	1 190	100	3 978	4 741	5 326	61.4	11.7
Love	55	6.9	2	24	1	30	366	1	62	285	16	3 572	1 518	1 573	51.2	7.0
McClain	118	4.9	8	33	1	42	176	3	224	710	52	2 883	5 152	4 878	57.9	9.7

1. Per 1,000 resident population estimated as of July 1 of the year shown. 2. As of end of year. 3. Per 100,000 resident population as of July 1 of the year shown. 4. Preliminary. Covers nursing homes with 3 or more beds. 5. Data for serious crimes have not been adjusted for underreporting, this may affect comparability between geographic areas or over time. 6. Includes murder and nonnegligent manslaughter, forcible rape, robbery, and aggravated assault. 7. The 1986–1987 data are based on administrative reports obtained by the U.S. National Center for Education Statistics. The 1980 data are based on the 1980 Census of Population and Housing. 8. Persons 25 years old or older.

STATE County	Education (cont'd): Local government expenditures for education,[1] 1982: Total (Mil dol)	Education (cont'd): Local government expenditures for education,[1] 1982: Per capita (Dollars)	Social Security Program December 1988: Beneficiaries: Total	Social Security Program December 1988: Beneficiaries: Rate[2]	Social Security Program December 1988: Payments ($1,000)	Supplemental Security Income Program recipients June 1986	Money income: Per capita[3]: 1987 Income, (Dollars)	Money income: Per capita[3]: 1979: Current dollars	Money income: Per capita[3]: 1979: Constant 1987 dollars	Money income: Median household income 1979 (Dollars)	Money income: Percent below poverty level, 1979: Persons	Money income: Percent below poverty level, 1979: Families	Housing units, 1990: Total	Housing units, 1990: Percent change, 1980–1990
	60	61	62	63	64	65	66	67	68	69	70	71	72	73
OHIO—Con.														
Putnam	14.2	427	5 095	149.9	2 427	200	10 183	6 381	9 984	19 019	6.7	5.4	11 600	5.5
Richland	62.2	479	21 690	168.1	10 796	1 438	10 771	6 803	10 645	17 162	9.4	7.4	50 350	2.4
Ross	27.5	418	10 585	154.8	4 672	1 352	9 593	6 251	9 781	15 954	11.7	8.7	26 173	10.2
Sandusky	26.5	426	9 400	151.1	4 731	406	11 114	6 968	10 903	18 392	7.5	5.7	23 753	2.4
Scioto	35.3	420	16 275	198.7	6 997	2 906	8 303	5 442	8 515	12 448	17.9	14.1	32 408	2.3
Seneca	22.5	367	11 365	183.9	5 615	624	9 595	6 379	9 981	17 524	8.5	6.6	22 473	1.0
Shelby	18.6	428	6 360	143.2	3 128	306	10 530	6 532	10 221	17 492	8.2	7.2	16 509	7.9
Stark	160.4	424	69 645	186.0	35 647	4 010	10 794	7 288	11 404	18 620	8.5	6.6	146 910	2.6
Summit	237.6	459	88 410	172.0	46 102	5 700	12 156	7 666	11 995	18 381	9.4	7.1	211 477	5.5
Trumbull	111.2	463	40 640	176.8	20 912	2 060	10 841	7 581	11 862	19 536	8.1	6.7	90 533	2.6
Tuscarawas	34.1	400	15 680	184.3	7 655	844	9 424	6 436	10 070	16 062	9.0	6.9	33 982	5.4
Union	11.2	368	3 895	118.4	1 833	220	11 132	6 733	10 535	17 458	8.4	6.5	11 599	9.2
Van Wert	12.1	403	4 990	166.3	2 489	178	10 425	6 947	10 870	17 932	6.7	4.9	11 998	3.2
Vinton	4.3	379	1 955	168.5	790	312	7 543	4 804	7 517	11 861	17.6	15.1	4 856	10.3
Warren	43.0	426	12 705	114.4	6 243	858	11 721	7 159	11 202	20 769	7.3	6.2	40 636	22.1
Washington	27.2	420	11 345	178.7	5 258	884	9 755	6 402	10 017	16 187	9.8	7.5	25 752	7.5
Wayne	42.1	426	14 735	141.5	7 340	950	10 212	6 768	10 590	18 013	8.9	6.5	37 036	7.9
Williams	17.0	471	6 235	168.5	3 029	224	10 590	6 839	10 701	17 566	7.9	6.0	14 745	5.7
Wood	47.6	437	13 365	119.9	6 740	550	11 353	7 235	11 321	18 855	10.0	5.3	41 760	10.7
Wyandot	9.1	404	4 050	184.1	1 933	230	9 953	6 295	9 850	16 259	10.2	8.2	8 596	3.6
OKLAHOMA	1 387.7	430	517 832	159.7	237 998	59 213	9 927	6 854	10 724	14 750	13.4	10.3	1 406 499	13.7
Adair	10.5	551	3 290	160.5	1 208	1 232	6 108	3 908	6 115	9 114	27.6	22.1	7 124	7.5
Alfalfa	4.4	610	1 700	265.6	821	80	9 637	7 175	11 227	14 052	11.6	7.6	3 357	3.2
Atoka	4.8	373	2 395	177.4	884	632	6 371	4 356	6 816	8 924	26.5	21.1	5 110	10.5
Beaver	5.6	758	1 160	168.1	566	28	9 811	7 259	11 358	16 519	14.6	12.6	2 923	5.5
Beckham	9.9	393	4 180	212.2	1 768	500	8 609	6 608	10 340	13 055	15.5	12.2	9 117	11.0
Blaine	7.4	495	2 595	201.2	1 139	234	9 297	6 690	10 468	13 662	17.3	14.0	5 729	-2.4
Bryan	10.5	338	7 055	213.1	2 875	1 242	7 516	5 067	7 928	10 143	20.4	15.4	14 875	11.6
Caddo	20.1	598	6 515	203.0	2 715	926	7 895	5 570	8 715	12 164	21.6	17.0	13 191	6.2
Canadian	34.2	533	6 040	82.0	2 740	366	10 987	7 581	11 862	20 753	7.4	6.2	28 560	38.1
Carter	21.3	460	8 880	194.7	4 050	1 150	9 322	6 472	10 127	13 649	15.4	12.0	19 201	7.6
Cherokee	11.8	375	5 415	150.8	2 254	1 006	7 089	4 794	7 501	10 503	22.2	18.3	15 935	24.9
Choctaw	7.0	418	3 745	225.6	1 422	1 104	6 625	4 696	7 348	8 956	26.0	21.6	6 844	-5.2
Cimarron	2.7	735	715	174.4	341	48	8 594	6 138	9 604	12 778	14.0	10.4	1 690	6.2
Cleveland	64.3	437	12 550	76.8	5 887	988	10 895	7 372	11 535	18 208	9.3	6.0	71 038	43.4
Coal	3.0	512	1 415	235.8	549	310	6 752	4 495	7 033	8 806	25.1	19.6	2 725	8.2
Comanche	46.6	388	11 905	99.8	5 063	1 270	8 818	5 665	8 864	13 789	14.6	12.0	43 589	9.1
Cotton	2.7	387	1 545	223.9	666	196	7 776	5 216	8 161	11 142	17.8	14.6	3 152	-0.3
Craig	6.5	423	3 495	233.0	1 504	540	8 380	5 530	8 653	12 199	13.8	10.8	6 041	-0.5
Creek	29.1	453	7 285	113.5	3 339	894	8 862	6 225	9 740	15 340	12.4	9.7	25 143	11.0
Custer	13.5	433	4 210	149.8	1 888	336	9 584	6 705	10 491	14 262	16.1	11.7	11 636	11.5
Delaware	11.4	433	5 525	191.2	2 364	774	7 546	4 760	7 448	10 126	21.4	16.7	16 808	57.8
Dewey	8.3	1 279	1 525	258.5	627	86	9 144	6 718	10 512	13 324	15.3	12.1	2 733	1.9
Ellis	3.4	516	1 155	231.0	512	46	9 182	6 817	10 667	13 364	10.4	8.7	2 449	-0.6
Garfield	27.2	402	10 480	179.8	5 197	906	10 904	7 744	12 117	16 579	8.5	6.3	26 502	3.6
Garvin	13.9	461	6 750	237.7	2 968	1 152	7 852	5 891	9 218	12 355	14.9	11.3	11 932	4.9
Grady	19.3	442	6 585	155.7	2 853	826	9 064	6 267	9 806	13 829	14.2	11.4	17 788	12.9
Grant	3.9	584	1 470	245.0	736	66	9 268	7 092	11 097	14 024	12.9	10.4	2 955	-0.9
Greer	2.4	325	1 940	293.9	813	286	7 947	5 568	8 712	9 712	22.0	15.0	3 126	-5.4
Harmon	2.0	432	1 045	254.9	436	152	7 511	5 463	8 548	9 281	27.2	20.1	1 793	-8.2
Harper	3.7	737	1 025	233.0	491	58	10 558	7 646	11 964	16 580	10.0	7.7	2 077	-2.9
Haskell	4.8	420	2 730	233.3	1 067	534	6 872	4 929	7 712	9 690	20.7	17.5	5 138	8.2
Hughes	6.3	423	3 625	250.0	1 463	690	6 778	4 671	7 309	8 940	24.4	18.1	6 021	-4.5
Jackson	13.8	456	4 255	143.8	1 863	666	8 417	5 431	8 498	11 908	17.0	13.7	12 125	3.3
Jefferson	3.1	374	1 970	266.2	808	308	7 707	5 452	8 531	10 185	19.7	16.3	3 522	-4.4
Johnston	4.2	393	2 105	193.1	818	480	6 348	4 227	6 614	8 085	30.6	25.1	4 478	3.3
Kay	21.0	398	10 545	206.8	5 298	532	10 458	7 333	11 474	15 493	9.1	6.3	22 456	5.6
Kingfisher	11.4	705	2 395	164.0	1 130	140	9 525	7 113	11 130	16 905	10.4	8.8	5 791	2.2
Kiowa	5.7	440	3 165	261.6	1 361	424	7 609	5 466	8 553	9 686	23.1	19.6	5 645	-3.3
Latimer	9.7	956	1 700	156.0	688	292	6 437	4 492	7 029	9 498	25.4	23.3	4 303	8.0
Le Flore	18.1	431	8 725	188.4	3 426	1 844	7 377	4 827	7 553	10 785	20.1	16.4	18 029	15.1
Lincoln	10.2	359	5 065	172.3	2 104	532	7 999	5 616	8 787	13 030	14.6	11.9	12 302	15.7
Logan	8.4	289	4 125	138.9	1 833	390	8 553	6 125	9 584	14 113	14.8	10.5	12 277	16.2
Love	3.2	404	1 540	190.1	652	216	9 554	5 980	9 357	13 073	17.0	13.4	3 583	11.8
McClain	12.7	574	3 270	135.7	1 384	342	8 924	6 153	9 628	15 933	11.5	10.0	9 300	20.6

1. Elementary and secondary. 2. Per 1,000 resident population estimated as of July 1 of the year shown. 3. Based on the resident population estimated as of July 1, 1988 for 1987 data and enumerated as of April 1, 1980 for 1979 data.

STATE County	Housing units, 1990 (cont'd) — Occupied units — Total	Owner occupied — Percent	Owner occupied — Median value (Dollars)	Median rent (Dollars)	Civilian labor force, 1990 — Total	Percent change, 1989–1990	Unemployment — Total	Unemployment — Rate[1]	Private nonfarm establishments, 1988 — Number	Net change, 1987–1988	Employment[2] — Total	Per-cent change, 1987–1988	Manu-facturing	Retail trade
	74	75	76	77	78	79	80	81	82	83	84	85	86	87
OHIO—Con.														
Putnam	11 082	84.3	58 000	222	15 930	3.0	1 162	7.3	631	5	7 774	3.0	3 021	1 655
Richland	47 573	70.8	52 200	260	64 953	-1.7	4 733	7.3	2 866	9	49 839	1.8	18 422	10 693
Ross	24 325	70.5	49 200	223	28 155	-0.6	2 284	8.1	1 211	8	15 416	5.2	4 858	4 210
Sandusky	22 464	74.5	57 200	266	34 192	1.6	2 454	7.2	1 332	18	19 788	2.5	9 172	3 624
Scioto	29 786	69.7	37 100	199	29 341	0.8	2 540	8.7	1 453	1	15 899	2.0	2 052	5 241
Seneca	21 277	74.0	47 700	225	25 337	1.1	2 070	8.2	1 279	16	18 041	2.6	7 100	3 893
Shelby	15 626	74.3	59 900	260	25 343	0.3	1 397	5.5	843	21	17 148	9.9	10 041	2 496
Stark	139 573	70.1	57 700	272	182 059	-0.2	11 298	6.2	8 716	79	140 364	2.2	44 315	30 271
Summit	199 998	68.7	61 900	311	260 048	0.1	13 499	5.2	12 522	166	212 696	6.6	59 525	44 850
Trumbull	86 056	73.1	53 300	269	104 963	-0.7	7 889	7.5	4 419	22	84 219	0.8	36 671	19 028
Tuscarawas	31 971	75.0	49 900	236	41 689	-1.6	2 671	6.4	2 166	62	25 393	4.6	8 255	6 253
Union	11 037	74.4	67 400	286	17 107	1.3	767	4.5	567	2	12 221	8.8	7 940	1 570
Van Wert	11 266	80.6	46 000	228	15 489	-0.4	1 018	6.6	637	14	10 105	2.6	5 023	1 632
Vinton	4 069	80.4	34 900	176	4 214	3.1	385	9.1	155	-1	1 858	0.3	451	250
Warren	39 150	74.7	77 600	340	58 703	1.5	2 943	5.0	1 905	75	25 246	11.3	5 814	7 858
Washington	23 636	74.5	51 900	227	29 859	0.3	1 786	6.0	1 513	-23	18 411	4.2	5 105	3 903
Wayne	35 619	71.2	65 700	283	51 981	2.3	2 660	5.1	2 121	34	32 747	1.7	14 489	6 017
Williams	13 807	77.0	48 200	245	20 837	1.8	1 262	6.1	846	2	14 720	-1.2	8 091	2 317
Wood	39 677	69.9	72 200	320	58 593	-0.8	3 119	5.3	2 289	40	35 236	8.5	11 749	8 774
Wyandot	8 168	75.7	46 600	213	11 668	0.8	784	6.7	520	-7	7 302	0.0	3 854	1 211
OKLAHOMA	1 206 135	68.1	48 100	259	1 540 000	1.1	86 000	5.6	X	X	876 083	1.2	154 804	207 818
Adair	6 386	73.0	30 200	143	8 451	0.4	439	5.2	182	11	2 499	3.5	1 440	399
Alfalfa	2 469	81.1	23 900	143	3 177	6.2	86	2.7	135	-14	735	-7.0	0	234
Atoka	4 495	75.0	30 300	150	8 078	-1.0	405	5.0	179	-10	1 573	17.9	170	568
Beaver	2 327	77.7	47 800	214	3 018	1.8	103	3.4	144	11	630	-8.3	0	162
Beckham	7 351	69.8	31 200	178	7 712	-3.8	466	6.0	569	-11	3 810	2.4	165	1 241
Blaine	4 418	76.1	34 000	160	6 048	3.5	278	4.6	306	-8	2 328	5.1	0	517
Bryan	12 524	69.7	36 000	189	15 609	4.9	639	4.1	542	-50	6 180	8.3	831	1 428
Caddo	10 879	72.6	31 400	158	12 218	3.7	882	7.2	541	-6	4 258	0.9	520	975
Canadian	25 597	76.5	58 100	296	36 498	-0.3	1 686	4.6	1 147	-52	9 391	3.6	659	3 221
Carter	16 601	72.4	38 100	214	19 992	1.0	1 307	6.5	1 246	-45	12 053	-1.6	2 814	3 012
Cherokee	12 657	68.2	43 300	221	16 725	5.5	1 011	6.0	555	11	4 288	11.7	282	1 596
Choctaw	5 952	72.3	30 900	126	6 264	6.2	533	8.5	257	8	1 908	9.3	98	482
Cimarron	1 300	74.5	29 000	138	1 603	5.3	54	3.4	98	-1	344	4.2	0	120
Cleveland	63 991	63.1	61 800	303	86 748	-0.4	3 895	4.5	2 786	-51	26 040	1.1	2 987	10 299
Coal	2 279	73.7	25 100	131	2 367	-2.5	272	11.5	72	1	710	2.0	0	114
Comanche	37 569	60.2	54 000	299	48 298	-0.6	2 625	5.4	2 026	-47	21 588	1.8	3 260	7 126
Cotton	2 609	77.0	32 800	161	3 422	10.9	336	9.8	113	6	1 000	12.6	0	238
Craig	5 272	75.5	33 000	180	6 662	2.0	271	4.1	305	-6	3 216	11.8	699	800
Creek	22 470	77.6	44 500	223	27 219	1.7	1 846	6.8	1 066	-43	9 894	1.3	3 143	2 255
Custer	9 918	63.5	46 900	219	14 694	-0.4	733	5.0	811	-15	7 191	6.1	1 898	1 892
Delaware	11 003	79.1	44 500	194	11 981	6.2	676	5.6	413	-32	2 681	-8.8	420	901
Dewey	2 221	80.9	27 900	133	2 570	5.3	98	3.8	141	-10	847	10.9	21	162
Ellis	1 826	80.3	29 800	172	2 544	6.3	90	3.5	116	2	497	17.5	19	169
Garfield	22 460	69.1	38 000	240	27 328	-1.4	1 191	4.4	1 630	-28	16 717	-3.7	1 344	4 277
Garvin	10 417	74.4	32 800	187	11 833	4.8	806	6.8	635	-30	4 907	-0.5	940	1 398
Grady	15 544	75.8	42 000	218	17 570	2.5	1 178	6.7	866	-28	7 723	3.0	1 953	1 795
Grant	2 327	80.2	26 100	165	2 994	7.2	98	3.3	152	0	947	6.5	47	150
Greer	2 551	75.6	21 800	137	2 808	6.1	103	3.7	127	-3	657	0.8	25	177
Harmon	1 486	75.2	22 800	102	1 674	4.6	80	4.8	80	-1	533	2.3	0	115
Harper	1 645	79.0	29 100	166	2 496	1.8	81	3.2	111	-3	572	6.7	0	149
Haskell	4 319	78.0	31 300	153	4 834	3.8	580	12.0	166	-4	1 289	2.6	142	336
Hughes	5 224	77.1	21 000	135	4 958	-3.1	544	11.0	226	-17	1 361	-5.2	251	424
Jackson	10 455	60.8	43 800	278	11 040	0.9	757	6.9	589	-23	4 308	-3.1	518	1 791
Jefferson	2 843	73.4	22 800	117	3 488	-3.5	246	7.1	156	5	821	2.2	153	207
Johnston	3 783	73.1	28 600	154	4 150	7.8	227	5.5	132	2	1 106	2.4	127	265
Kay	19 083	72.9	42 600	230	25 889	1.1	1 167	4.5	1 256	-51	17 762	9.3	3 357	3 288
Kingfisher	4 932	79.2	47 900	213	6 621	2.7	264	4.0	397	-15	3 520	8.1	184	591
Kiowa	4 551	74.2	27 000	143	5 284	-0.1	205	3.9	264	3	1 649	-2.1	0	429
Latimer	3 693	74.9	33 900	173	5 205	8.4	336	6.5	146	6	1 179	11.4	0	266
Le Flore	15 938	75.3	34 900	182	25 304	1.1	1 693	6.7	553	-5	4 155	7.7	825	1 106
Lincoln	10 839	80.5	35 100	194	13 557	6.2	831	6.1	440	2	3 407	6.6	699	1 019
Logan	10 180	77.4	46 200	196	13 480	-1.4	510	3.8	439	0	3 054	-7.3	239	857
Love	2 992	78.7	35 900	189	4 781	13.0	207	4.3	107	-5	1 228	-4.9	0	231
McClain	8 332	80.2	46 500	229	11 082	-0.3	592	5.3	319	-5	2 637	12.7	518	1 016

1. Percent of total civilian labor force. 2. For week including March 12. Excludes government employees, self-employed persons, farm workers, domestic service workers, railroad employees subject to the Railroad Retirement Act, and employees on oceanborne vessels or in foreign countries.

STATE County	Private nonfarm establishments, 1988 (cont'd): Employment[1] (cont'd): Finance, insurance, and real estate	Private nonfarm establishments, 1988 (cont'd): Employment[1] (cont'd): Services	Private nonfarm establishments, 1988 (cont'd): Annual payroll: Total (Mil dol)	Private nonfarm establishments, 1988 (cont'd): Annual payroll: Average per employee (Dollars)	Personal income, 1989: Total (Mil dol)	Personal income, 1989: Percent change, 1988–1989	Personal income, 1989: Wages and salaries[2] (Mil dol)	Personal income, 1989: Proprietor's income (Mil dol)	Personal income, 1989: Dividends, interest, & rent (Mil dol)	Personal income, 1989: Transfer payments (Mil dol)	Personal income, 1989: Per capita[3]: Dollars	Personal income, 1989: Per capita[3]: Rank	Earnings, 1989: Total (Mil dol)	Earnings, 1989: Percent by selected industries: Farm	Earnings, 1989: Percent by selected industries: Goods-related[4]: Total
	88	89	90	91	92	93	94	95	96	97	98	99	100	101	102
OHIO—Con.															
Putnam	227	1 843	123	15 762	515	7.9	184	65	91	61	15 068	958	249	7.6	47.6
Richland	2 756	11 067	1 015	20 367	1 982	5.6	1 426	139	304	329	15 366	849	1 564	0.7	47.0
Ross	633	3 638	312	20 225	886	5.9	544	57	123	180	12 921	1 944	601	1.8	38.6
Sandusky	590	3 752	394	19 908	1 009	4.8	553	82	157	158	16 220	588	636	2.8	52.1
Scioto	772	5 357	233	14 639	955	6.0	432	62	137	288	11 716	2 433	493	1.0	18.6
Seneca	682	4 228	336	18 618	841	6.7	487	58	154	176	13 603	1 629	545	1.8	49.6
Shelby	353	2 457	371	21 607	724	8.9	540	49	112	91	16 207	592	589	2.6	67.1
Stark	6 774	37 171	2 724	19 410	5 841	5.9	3 593	358	960	1 053	15 587	776	3 951	0.2	43.2
Summit	9 650	54 575	4 837	22 740	8 915	6.2	6 032	436	1 418	1 459	17 276	400	6 468	0.1	37.5
Trumbull	2 850	16 404	2 054	24 390	3 520	7.3	2 682	186	532	650	15 418	829	2 868	0.2	60.4
Tuscarawas	796	5 477	441	17 361	1 196	6.2	623	102	203	222	14 074	1 400	725	1.5	42.1
Union	248	1 290	353	28 875	561	12.2	622	42	70	66	16 655	493	665	2.5	72.4
Van Wert	845	1 624	203	20 105	446	4.7	238	52	92	64	14 884	1 032	290	5.6	46.7
Vinton	99	180	43	23 112	116	5.7	55	9	15	30	10 003	2 880	64	1.0	49.6
Warren	612	7 553	379	15 032	1 783	8.2	582	107	209	213	15 639	764	689	1.2	33.2
Washington	846	4 683	345	18 715	860	5.2	469	65	139	165	13 600	1 631	534	0.4	41.4
Wayne	1 500	5 713	674	20 592	1 561	5.9	926	121	267	231	14 792	1 080	1 047	1.7	50.3
Williams	352	2 414	282	19 143	592	6.7	380	49	101	88	15 950	660	430	1.0	55.8
Wood	1 314	7 771	705	19 996	1 880	7.4	1 043	133	308	242	16 742	478	1 176	1.8	42.2
Wyandot	210	1 177	121	16 562	325	4.6	158	34	65	55	14 947	1 011	193	4.6	NA
OKLAHOMA	61 123	234 855	16 426	X	45 614	6.0	26 279	5 361	7 668	8 115	14 111	X	31 640	3.7	25.6
Adair	71	496	32	12 917	185	9.4	61	29	19	48	8 900	3 012	89	22.0	NA
Alfalfa	73	149	9	12 080	127	4.3	31	56	23	21	20 274	155	87	55.9	13.6
Atoka	62	344	17	10 713	109	2.8	45	15	17	36	8 133	3 070	59	9.4	15.2
Beaver	56	80	9	15 000	112	5.8	33	38	28	14	16 394	546	70	38.8	12.3
Beckham	286	1 205	49	12 747	229	5.1	83	38	67	53	12 144	2 263	121	9.7	17.5
Blaine	185	632	32	13 559	175	5.8	57	44	42	32	13 907	1 470	102	29.0	21.3
Bryan	556	2 308	71	11 447	357	8.2	129	49	59	97	10 713	2 738	178	10.7	11.5
Caddo	277	937	64	15 096	362	4.3	120	54	80	104	11 428	2 532	174	14.4	11.0
Canadian	573	2 117	138	14 685	1 085	8.2	340	99	122	135	14 491	1 220	439	3.3	30.6
Carter	804	2 551	221	18 306	636	5.8	354	92	137	121	14 105	1 387	446	1.0	39.4
Cherokee	286	1 461	43	10 090	364	8.0	137	63	48	93	9 950	2 889	200	17.3	7.5
Choctaw	83	772	21	10 855	160	5.8	59	23	25	52	9 571	2 948	82	8.8	NA
Cimarron	0	51	5	13 131	78	2.9	15	41	14	9	18 969	221	56	65.2	NA
Cleveland	1 408	7 160	361	13 874	2 369	6.4	765	174	249	311	14 307	1 284	939	0.8	15.6
Coal	0	194	7	10 473	58	5.8	17	8	10	19	9 726	2 921	26	16.2	22.0
Comanche	1 742	5 383	326	15 094	1 424	3.9	968	116	147	285	11 945	2 344	1 084	1.8	13.9
Cotton	35	212	13	12 558	89	0.3	22	24	15	21	13 017	1 901	46	38.1	13.5
Craig	201	620	49	15 083	190	5.5	95	23	36	44	12 760	2 011	118	6.8	16.9
Creek	479	1 977	159	16 035	847	6.1	254	81	116	131	13 484	1 694	335	2.0	37.0
Custer	463	1 580	109	15 117	364	4.5	195	56	87	54	13 261	1 788	250	9.2	28.5
Delaware	99	917	29	10 799	291	9.2	65	50	56	73	9 936	2 890	114	18.6	12.7
Dewey	72	267	12	13 691	88	6.4	23	22	29	16	15 046	971	45	30.4	17.5
Ellis	50	97	7	13 618	72	6.5	21	19	18	14	15 162	922	41	31.9	5.2
Garfield	1 014	4 538	284	17 005	896	4.0	467	121	178	171	15 840	699	589	5.4	16.7
Garvin	271	943	65	13 286	368	4.8	132	50	74	111	13 145	1 843	182	6.4	28.0
Grady	462	1 645	117	15 189	517	3.7	191	70	93	98	12 424	2 154	261	7.4	27.7
Grant	74	178	18	19 309	107	-3.4	27	34	28	18	18 166	277	61	43.6	7.6
Greer	40	190	7	11 085	77	3.4	26	14	17	26	11 895	2 361	40	21.4	8.0
Harmon	0	222	5	9 983	50	-2.5	13	13	10	14	12 628	2 064	27	36.9	7.4
Harper	0	138	9	15 297	76	10.1	21	26	20	13	17 621	351	47	41.2	8.2
Haskell	0	326	16	12 397	122	8.3	39	18	21	34	10 443	2 803	57	12.5	21.2
Hughes	87	260	15	11 124	141	6.4	37	22	29	49	9 750	2 917	58	9.1	12.4
Jackson	315	888	53	12 225	361	1.9	214	49	49	80	12 361	2 178	262	7.3	6.5
Jefferson	76	213	9	10 390	87	4.0	23	18	17	23	12 205	2 228	41	23.0	17.6
Johnston	0	291	13	11 972	96	3.7	31	11	13	31	8 752	3 030	42	9.9	19.1
Kay	1 220	3 225	385	21 656	777	-2.6	467	97	158	128	15 383	842	564	3.0	NA
Kingfisher	276	507	59	16 673	218	3.6	92	38	69	31	15 365	850	131	13.9	27.7
Kiowa	112	470	20	11 834	164	5.7	42	42	39	42	13 812	1 530	84	33.5	12.2
Latimer	53	237	17	14 531	104	9.6	50	10	15	31	9 314	2 981	59	4.8	24.3
Le Flore	273	1 036	54	13 051	493	10.2	166	58	62	125	10 420	2 807	224	6.4	31.9
Lincoln	323	663	45	13 312	339	8.3	85	34	49	71	11 552	2 485	119	6.8	20.9
Logan	195	1 218	37	12 266	368	5.9	90	43	53	72	12 555	2 094	133	9.9	13.8
Love	76	141	16	13 070	100	7.8	31	16	16	20	12 203	2 233	47	16.1	21.1
McClain	155	345	37	13 921	305	7.9	69	32	39	50	12 763	2 010	101	10.7	23.4

1. For week including March 12. Excludes government employees, self-employed persons, farm workers, domestic service workers, railroad employees subject to the Railroad Retirement Act, and employees on oceanborne vessels or in foreign countries. 2. Includes other labor income. 3. Based on the resident population estimated as of July 1 of the year shown. 4. Covers mining, construction, and manufacturing.

STATE County	Earnings, 1989 (cont'd)						Agriculture, 1987									
	Percent by selected industries (cont'd)						Farms			Farm operators, percent		Land in farms				
	Goods-related[1]	Service-related & other[2]						Percent with						Acres		
	Manu-facturing	Total	Retail trade	Finance, insur-ance, & real estate	Services	Govern-ment	Number	Less than 50 acres	500 acres and over	Whose principal occu-pation is farming	Residing on farm operated	Acreage (1,000)	Percent change, 1982–1987	Average size of farm	Total irrigated (1,000)	Total cropland (1,000)
	103	104	105	106	107	108	109	110	111	112	113	114	115	116	117	118
OHIO—Con.																
Putnam	39.5	33.6	7.8	1.8	16.7	11.2	1 584	24.6	7.1	48.7	69.7	290	2.7	183	0	269
Richland	41.9	41.7	9.1	4.0	17.4	10.6	1 022	26.6	6.4	47.5	80.7	169	-10.8	165	0	131
Ross	34.4	36.5	10.2	1.8	15.6	23.2	815	21.3	17.4	48.5	71.8	253	-1.9	310	0	183
Sandusky	45.1	35.1	7.7	2.1	17.7	10.0	936	26.0	11.3	56.1	74.9	207	0.1	221	1	191
Scioto	11.3	59.0	12.6	3.6	26.4	21.4	658	24.5	5.6	35.9	78.4	104	2.3	158	0	57
Seneca	42.6	38.4	8.0	2.1	18.2	10.2	1 398	21.7	10.7	52.0	69.7	299	-1.4	214	0	265
Shelby	60.3	22.0	5.6	1.4	9.7	8.2	1 113	24.3	9.5	52.3	71.2	216	-3.3	194	0	194
Stark	36.1	46.5	9.9	3.9	21.9	10.1	1 306	43.3	3.4	44.3	80.8	153	-4.6	117	1	124
Summit	32.6	51.2	9.6	4.0	23.4	11.2	297	66.3	1.0	37.7	77.8	20	-9.6	67	0	15
Trumbull	57.2	31.7	7.8	2.0	14.9	7.7	951	30.8	2.8	46.1	86.4	122	3.4	129	0	87
Tuscarawas	31.7	44.9	11.8	2.5	18.7	11.5	1 022	25.4	4.5	50.3	78.8	153	-5.7	150	0	94
Union	69.3	18.6	3.4	0.6	8.0	6.5	907	26.8	15.3	55.3	77.0	233	-3.7	256	0	208
Van Wert	41.5	38.8	7.4	7.7	17.0	8.9	922	24.3	17.2	56.0	70.6	246	-0.4	266	D	232
Vinton	21.0	30.1	7.1	3.1	8.2	19.3	217	20.3	7.8	26.7	73.7	43	-14.3	200	0	21
Warren	25.1	49.0	14.6	1.9	25.2	16.6	920	40.8	6.1	44.0	75.5	137	-11.7	149	0	106
Washington	33.1	46.1	9.7	2.9	22.1	12.1	955	19.1	3.5	40.5	82.5	146	-8.4	153	1	69
Wayne	42.3	35.2	8.8	2.8	15.1	12.8	1 734	30.9	5.0	63.1	82.8	263	-1.9	152	1	216
Williams	51.3	34.6	6.4	1.8	15.5	8.6	963	23.7	12.5	48.8	74.7	224	5.0	233	D	198
Wood	35.9	36.4	9.6	1.8	16.5	19.6	1 279	25.8	15.4	53.3	65.1	318	1.9	249	0	300
Wyandot	42.3	NA	8.1	2.2	15.5	11.3	727	23.8	18.4	58.2	69.1	217	-4.0	298	0	197
OKLAHOMA	15.3	50.9	9.8	4.9	22.3	19.8	70 228	19.7	22.9	47.1	66.1	31 542	-2.6	449	478	14 443
Adair	29.1	NA	7.4	1.8	11.7	20.8	997	24.1	8.2	45.2	81.1	207	-1.6	208	1	93
Alfalfa	0.4	19.8	3.9	1.5	6.5	10.7	785	12.5	40.3	66.1	45.5	480	-6.8	612	1	356
Atoka	9.8	38.2	13.4	2.1	11.7	37.2	942	16.0	16.5	39.0	73.5	386	-11.2	410	2	96
Beaver	0.8	34.7	3.6	1.9	9.0	14.3	824	8.5	57.9	62.6	59.7	1 012	-1.4	1 228	22	461
Beckham	3.2	57.8	16.7	3.8	26.0	15.0	815	12.5	34.0	57.4	51.5	495	-0.6	608	3	237
Blaine	14.2	33.3	7.4	3.7	12.8	16.4	919	10.8	38.2	62.5	52.0	521	-0.8	566	1	305
Bryan	7.0	53.8	11.5	3.1	26.9	24.0	1 388	20.1	15.1	45.2	66.4	414	1.7	299	10	172
Caddo	4.8	49.9	9.1	4.6	17.0	24.6	1 530	12.9	29.5	60.3	61.6	718	1.8	469	44	421
Canadian	19.8	45.4	12.8	3.2	19.1	20.7	1 085	22.9	28.3	55.0	63.0	475	1.7	438	4	293
Carter	24.9	47.7	9.6	3.9	23.7	11.9	1 056	24.5	16.8	29.6	64.9	402	4.1	381	1	109
Cherokee	1.6	40.7	10.4	2.4	22.4	34.5	1 045	25.5	7.3	39.0	78.7	230	-6.5	220	1	81
Choctaw	3.1	NA	10.3	3.6	21.9	19.9	929	18.7	17.5	45.3	67.5	319	-0.4	343	1	121
Cimarron	NA	NA	4.3	1.7	8.4	9.5	458	4.8	67.7	80.3	53.1	1 006	-6.8	2 197	47	D
Cleveland	7.8	45.9	12.9	3.6	23.7	37.7	894	35.3	7.4	32.2	71.1	149	-2.7	167	0	71
Coal	16.7	35.3	6.8	2.7	16.8	26.4	580	12.6	21.2	47.6	69.1	269	-4.0	465	0	68
Comanche	9.9	33.0	8.8	3.1	13.4	51.4	959	18.1	22.6	49.8	68.2	374	-9.1	390	2	175
Cotton	8.5	33.2	6.1	2.8	11.6	15.1	513	7.0	41.9	59.1	53.2	348	-4.0	678	0	225
Craig	9.1	44.0	9.7	3.3	13.3	32.3	1 070	20.5	17.9	46.2	74.4	414	2.7	386	2	163
Creek	24.4	45.6	10.5	3.7	18.8	15.4	1 130	28.1	11.0	29.2	76.2	280	-14.1	248	0	77
Custer	20.3	39.8	10.6	4.6	15.2	22.6	859	12.9	42.0	63.7	51.0	574	0.6	669	4	328
Delaware	5.5	49.9	12.0	2.1	27.3	18.8	1 198	24.4	8.2	47.2	78.6	255	6.3	213	0	121
Dewey	2.9	34.5	6.4	4.3	12.2	17.6	725	10.6	45.2	60.4	54.1	581	-0.3	801	1	212
Ellis	1.2	42.1	6.5	3.7	14.8	20.7	622	8.4	50.3	60.8	56.6	667	0.7	1 072	13	224
Garfield	6.8	58.3	10.9	4.3	24.3	19.7	1 182	12.9	35.3	64.1	57.3	633	-3.9	536	0	467
Garvin	12.0	41.1	11.8	3.8	15.6	24.5	1 324	20.2	16.4	42.6	67.5	404	0.5	305	3	168
Grady	18.6	47.4	12.9	3.7	21.8	17.5	1 509	18.8	21.8	49.0	70.8	547	-0.1	363	6	257
Grant	0.6	37.4	4.3	3.8	9.5	11.5	866	7.9	46.4	66.5	48.6	583	2.3	673	D	465
Greer	1.6	32.6	8.6	3.2	10.9	38.0	476	8.4	41.2	63.4	46.8	326	-9.3	684	6	181
Harmon	1.7	37.4	8.9	3.7	14.5	18.3	380	7.9	47.4	58.9	39.7	285	-3.0	749	16	181
Harper	0.2	33.0	5.5	3.5	10.3	17.6	504	8.5	56.7	64.1	55.0	554	-7.4	1 100	4	224
Haskell	1.6	46.3	11.4	3.0	19.3	20.0	771	17.8	16.2	41.1	69.0	269	0.5	348	0	102
Hughes	5.8	51.0	11.0	3.1	26.7	27.5	880	12.5	20.0	38.4	65.9	328	-3.0	373	6	105
Jackson	4.4	33.5	8.0	2.5	15.3	52.7	700	14.9	40.1	58.1	40.6	461	4.0	659	37	336
Jefferson	13.0	40.0	9.5	4.5	14.5	19.5	521	12.3	37.4	58.9	56.4	394	0.7	757	0	114
Johnston	2.8	37.0	8.8	2.0	17.9	34.0	539	16.1	20.4	43.0	67.2	323	0.4	600	1	63
Kay	19.5	NA	8.3	3.4	NA	9.0	971	19.9	28.1	56.0	62.8	455	-9.3	468	1	315
Kingfisher	5.1	47.2	7.9	5.2	14.9	11.2	942	10.9	33.5	61.0	58.9	478	-7.0	507	5	327
Kiowa	7.1	37.9	6.9	3.4	14.4	16.4	760	10.3	46.8	63.4	48.4	565	-4.0	744	1	365
Latimer	7.9	29.9	6.1	2.0	12.1	41.0	617	22.0	12.2	38.2	72.6	191	15.4	310	0	50
Le Flore	9.7	39.7	9.6	2.9	17.6	22.1	1 541	24.3	9.5	40.3	73.6	366	-2.1	237	4	159
Lincoln	11.1	52.7	10.2	10.5	18.2	19.6	1 617	16.3	10.7	36.2	73.8	387	-4.2	239	1	145
Logan	5.0	51.4	10.0	2.9	28.1	24.9	925	18.8	22.1	44.2	61.3	350	7.7	379	1	166
Love	16.7	46.5	11.1	3.3	24.4	16.3	589	17.3	17.7	41.1	67.7	216	-1.7	366	4	84
McClain	8.8	43.2	12.6	4.5	14.3	22.8	900	26.4	14.9	39.9	73.9	271	-3.3	301	1	113

1. Covers mining, construction, and manufacturing. 2. Covers private sector earnings in agricultural services, forestry, and fisheries; transportation and public utilities; wholesale trade; retail trade; finance, insurance, and real estate; and services.

STATE County	Agriculture, 1987 (cont'd): Value of land and buildings: Average per farm ($1,000)	Agriculture, 1987 (cont'd): Value of land and buildings: Average per acre (Dollars)	Agriculture, 1987 (cont'd): Value of products sold: Total (Mil dol)	Agriculture, 1987 (cont'd): Value of products sold: Average per farm (Dollars)	Agriculture, 1987 (cont'd): Value of products sold: Percent from: Crops	Agriculture, 1987 (cont'd): Value of products sold: Percent from: Livestock and poultry[1]	Agriculture, 1987 (cont'd): Percent of farms with sales of: $10,000 or more	Agriculture, 1987 (cont'd): Percent of farms with sales of: $100,000 or more	Manufactures, 1987: Establishments: Total	Manufactures, 1987: Establishments: Percent with 20 or more employees	Manufactures, 1987: All employees: Number (1,000)	Manufactures, 1987: All employees: Percent change, 1982–1987	Manufactures, 1987: All employees: Annual payroll (Mil dol)	Manufactures, 1987: Production workers: Number (1,000)	Manufactures, 1987: Production workers: Work hours (Mil)
	119	120	121	122	123	124	125	126	127	128	129	130	131	132	133
OHIO—Con.															
Putnam	283	1 453	73	46 152	57.7	42.3	70.8	11.8	37	43.2	3.1	10.7	70.5	2.5	5.1
Richland	178	1 061	37	35 899	47.4	52.6	48.7	10.1	219	43.4	18.1	2.8	511.0	13.6	28.5
Ross	244	761	29	35 631	61.6	38.4	45.8	11.3	59	28.8	4.6	-6.1	146.8	3.5	7.6
Sandusky	289	1 371	53	56 440	81.0	19.0	67.4	17.3	108	48.1	9.7	12.8	239.2	7.9	15.6
Scioto	120	750	14	20 552	30.8	69.2	21.4	3.3	62	24.2	1.9	-9.5	41.5	1.4	2.6
Seneca	265	1 214	68	48 747	64.4	35.6	69.5	12.3	72	45.8	7.0	-16.7	201.7	5.4	10.9
Shelby	263	1 403	60	53 909	44.0	56.0	70.5	16.2	103	56.3	9.9	37.5	231.6	6.9	14.3
Stark	191	1 588	50	38 332	41.1	58.9	42.3	10.3	604	36.1	41.8	-10.9	1 099.0	29.3	59.1
Summit	257	3 087	7	22 528	75.3	24.6	26.9	5.4	978	39.1	55.2	-12.2	1 762.2	28.7	56.6
Trumbull	149	1 173	24	25 518	33.8	66.2	38.8	6.4	261	41.0	36.2	5.8	1 203.9	28.5	55.9
Tuscarawas	158	956	39	38 548	18.2	81.8	41.5	9.6	200	39.5	8.4	-1.2	186.7	5.9	12.3
Union	253	1 022	68	75 439	43.5	56.5	62.0	15.3	44	59.1	D	D	D	D	D
Van Wert	439	1 543	53	57 865	76.8	23.2	75.7	17.8	60	41.7	5.2	52.9	132.7	3.7	7.5
Vinton	109	515	2	7 440	28.9	71.1	14.7	0.9	23	30.4	D	D	D	D	D
Warren	278	1 830	26	28 470	65.7	34.3	37.3	7.0	133	45.1	5.5	52.8	116.9	3.8	8.1
Washington	116	749	16	17 016	23.0	77.0	24.1	3.6	106	30.2	5.1	8.5	131.4	3.4	6.9
Wayne	233	1 604	126	72 444	15.2	84.8	64.3	20.2	195	45.6	14.0	12.9	361.9	10.0	21.4
Williams	233	1 001	48	50 128	48.4	51.6	58.9	11.5	108	54.6	8.3	31.7	180.0	6.0	11.9
Wood	348	1 454	63	49 469	77.4	22.6	65.0	12.2	171	45.6	11.3	29.9	301.1	8.1	16.7
Wyandot	313	1 111	44	60 417	71.1	28.9	70.0	17.6	42	47.6	3.9	44.4	73.5	3.3	6.1
OKLAHOMA	215	480	2 715	38 658	22.5	77.5	40.8	7.2	3 728	27.3	151.2	-23.4	3 629.3	104.8	207.0
Adair	141	645	66	65 720	1.7	98.3	38.4	15.3	14	28.6	1.4	40.0	22.0	1.0	2.1
Alfalfa	362	585	71	90 897	25.2	74.8	73.1	21.0	2	0.0	D	D	D	D	D
Atoka	132	314	16	17 122	9.6	90.4	31.3	2.3	9	11.1	0.2	0.0	2.2	0.1	0.2
Beaver	379	305	43	52 047	29.4	70.6	61.7	10.4	5	0.0	D	D	D	D	D
Beckham	210	338	26	31 477	39.1	60.9	52.5	6.1	19	15.8	0.2	-33.3	2.5	0.1	0.2
Blaine	313	560	53	57 186	20.5	79.5	60.4	7.2	10	40.0	0.6	0.0	11.8	0.5	1.1
Bryan	146	495	27	19 338	26.6	73.4	36.5	3.6	30	43.3	0.8	-20.0	10.6	0.7	1.2
Caddo	238	521	72	46 741	54.2	45.8	57.5	12.0	16	12.5	0.4	0.0	8.6	0.3	0.6
Canadian	375	793	53	48 540	24.1	75.9	54.4	12.4	40	25.0	0.5	-72.2	7.9	0.3	0.6
Carter	174	480	17	15 755	9.7	90.3	24.8	2.9	41	22.0	D	D	D	D	D
Cherokee	151	687	54	51 766	53.0	47.0	27.6	6.9	21	9.5	0.2	-33.3	2.3	0.2	0.4
Choctaw	150	429	21	22 894	7.4	92.6	34.6	4.0	13	15.4	0.1	-66.7	0.9	0.1	0.1
Cimarron	517	240	70	152 526	19.1	80.9	76.2	22.9	2	0.0	D	D	D	D	D
Cleveland	186	1 317	11	11 763	17.9	82.1	20.5	2.5	107	26.2	2.8	-26.3	55.4	1.9	3.7
Coal	163	340	14	24 388	3.2	96.8	42.1	4.0	5	20.0	D	D	D	D	D
Comanche	238	585	24	25 195	22.1	77.9	41.6	4.8	52	26.9	3.3	22.2	83.8	2.5	5.2
Cotton	277	431	27	51 785	37.4	62.6	60.2	11.7	5	20.0	D	D	D	D	D
Craig	148	398	44	40 788	8.7	91.3	40.4	5.0	13	38.5	0.6	20.0	9.2	0.4	1.1
Creek	143	596	9	8 121	9.7	90.3	16.5	1.0	76	21.1	2.7	-25.0	55.7	2.2	4.3
Custer	395	561	48	56 208	29.4	70.6	64.8	16.1	28	35.7	1.7	6.2	36.8	1.2	2.7
Delaware	151	711	61	50 702	3.4	96.6	40.2	13.1	18	16.7	0.4	0.0	5.2	0.3	0.6
Dewey	295	362	28	38 806	25.7	74.3	57.8	8.7	7	0.0	0.0	0.0	0.2	0.0	0.0
Ellis	311	286	39	62 269	17.1	82.9	57.9	9.8	6	0.0	0.0	0.0	0.3	0.0	0.0
Garfield	302	602	57	48 541	35.7	64.3	65.1	13.1	56	16.1	1.3	-43.5	28.4	0.8	1.7
Garvin	180	554	28	20 960	20.9	79.1	32.2	3.0	24	29.2	D	D	D	D	D
Grady	212	584	57	38 069	16.0	84.0	44.8	7.3	55	29.1	1.8	-25.0	33.9	1.6	3.1
Grant	354	525	47	54 667	43.1	56.9	70.1	12.4	7	0.0	0.0	-100.0	0.8	0.0	0.1
Greer	200	326	18	37 521	45.4	54.6	57.6	6.7	4	25.0	D	D	D	D	D
Harmon	252	333	20	53 310	49.7	50.3	64.5	15.3	2	0.0	D	D	D	D	D
Harper	325	286	42	82 916	15.6	84.4	65.7	14.9	1	0.0	D	D	D	D	D
Haskell	145	410	15	19 298	7.0	93.0	33.5	3.0	4	25.0	D	D	D	D	D
Hughes	141	391	15	16 716	28.9	71.1	31.8	3.1	9	11.1	0.1	0.0	0.9	0.1	0.1
Jackson	315	506	50	71 496	52.9	47.1	60.7	20.0	13	30.8	0.5	25.0	8.6	0.4	0.9
Jefferson	281	392	32	62 001	13.0	87.0	60.5	13.4	5	40.0	0.2	-33.3	2.5	0.2	0.3
Johnston	209	343	18	33 809	6.2	93.8	36.4	6.1	6	16.7	0.1	-50.0	1.3	0.1	0.2
Kay	292	597	33	34 495	42.6	57.4	50.5	7.7	78	30.8	3.0	-65.9	71.4	2.2	4.3
Kingfisher	307	631	68	71 856	16.8	83.2	63.4	15.6	13	15.4	0.2	0.0	3.8	0.1	0.2
Kiowa	353	480	43	56 511	43.6	56.4	66.1	14.7	7	14.3	D	D	D	D	D
Latimer	146	475	6	10 364	3.8	96.2	23.0	1.3	7	28.6	D	D	D	D	D
Le Flore	150	622	52	33 610	9.3	90.7	28.6	8.6	27	22.2	0.7	40.0	11.9	0.5	1.1
Lincoln	133	542	21	13 072	10.3	89.7	22.5	2.5	20	25.0	0.5	0.0	5.5	0.4	0.8
Logan	209	551	31	32 999	20.5	79.5	39.1	3.7	14	21.4	0.3	-50.0	5.0	0.2	0.3
Love	179	479	13	22 341	28.9	71.1	39.9	4.1	6	33.3	D	D	D	D	D
McClain	203	663	33	36 805	15.9	84.1	35.8	7.3	14	42.9	0.4	33.3	6.1	0.3	0.6

1. Includes livestock and poultry products.

STATE County	Manufactures, 1987 (cont'd): Production workers (cont'd): Wages: Total (Mil dol)	Manufactures, 1987 (cont'd): Production workers (cont'd): Wages: Average per worker (Dollars)	Manufactures, 1987 (cont'd): Value added by manufacture (Mil dol)	Manufactures, 1987 (cont'd): Value of shipments (Mil dol)	Manufactures, 1987 (cont'd): New capital expenditures (Mil dol)	Value of construction authorized by building permits, 1990: Total[1] ($1,000)	Nonresidential: Total ($1,000)	Nonresidential: Percent: Office	Nonresidential: Percent: Industrial	Nonresidential: Percent: Stores	Residential: New construction ($1,000)	Residential: Number of housing units	Residential: Alterations and additions ($1,000)
	134	135	136	137	138	139	140	141	142	143	144	145	146
OHIO—Con.													
Putnam	52.1	20 840	143.2	383.9	13.0	8 346	2 996	8.8	3.2	72.6	4 155	58	497
Richland	362.2	26 632	775.7	1 896.4	239.9	47 941	6 770	10.6	0.0	50.3	22 040	299	3 640
Ross	105.6	30 171	363.6	963.6	D	13 497	3 774	0.8	2.6	77.3	2 936	31	410
Sandusky	184.3	23 329	972.1	1 890.3	62.4	12 731	1 527	1.3	0.0	93.6	7 371	120	1 100
Scioto	27.4	19 571	241.8	495.1	11.2	12 861	8 102	5.8	17.9	68.1	653	12	1 490
Seneca	146.6	27 148	395.7	693.2	32.5	13 104	3 539	0.0	0.3	95.7	7 250	116	1 350
Shelby	136.4	19 768	558.9	1 361.0	34.3	36 097	5 029	1.0	35.3	62.7	23 277	341	893
Stark	701.8	23 952	2 887.5	5 929.7	139.0	180 881	21 381	24.1	6.8	32.6	114 613	1 252	12 682
Summit	637.1	22 199	2 341.6	4 381.9	160.0	440 037	84 579	28.4	13.5	30.7	212 627	2 448	23 279
Trumbull	919.4	32 260	2 296.4	6 790.6	124.9	80 551	26 897	55.2	0.4	7.1	39 155	443	2 411
Tuscarawas	120.3	20 390	465.2	958.5	23.2	26 449	5 848	6.6	14.7	66.1	15 107	179	651
Union	D	D	D	D	D	27 383	3 895	16.7	4.5	61.3	13 496	164	5 336
Van Wert	87.0	23 514	263.7	676.7	12.9	4 536	619	11.3	0.0	88.7	3 021	48	253
Vinton	D	D	D	D	D	1 442	394	0.0	0.0	59.3	900	33	0
Warren	67.8	17 842	233.2	557.3	16.2	136 707	44 527	6.5	45.1	15.0	80 525	935	4 142
Washington	78.2	23 000	400.1	1 040.8	D	25 269	14 902	24.4	46.3	7.5	1 586	21	707
Wayne	225.9	22 590	971.5	1 839.2	63.5	47 738	7 324	0.1	42.3	15.2	26 053	334	3 257
Williams	111.7	18 617	466.0	1 089.1	22.4	7 602	1 510	0.0	23.2	41.9	2 658	45	721
Wood	197.8	24 420	755.1	1 482.8	52.5	105 817	32 869	22.6	17.8	40.6	33 257	422	3 934
Wyandot	57.5	17 424	166.4	387.4	8.9	3 990	220	0.0	0.0	54.5	2 444	46	271
OKLAHOMA	2 195.6	20 950	9 856.9	24 073.9	538.4	909 433	287 939	15.6	15.6	22.7	400 621	5 284	46 786
Adair	13.6	13 600	85.2	169.0	1.5	2 683	803	15.6	0.0	6.4	1 870	66	10
Alfalfa	D	D	D	D	D	204	29	0.0	0.0	0.0	55	1	8
Atoka	1.3	13 000	4.3	8.7	D	400	170	0.0	0.0	38.3	176	4	17
Beaver	D	D	D	D	D	94	0	NA	NA	NA	83	1	0
Beckham	1.1	11 000	6.6	11.5	0.2	5 303	4 519	0.3	0.0	77.3	111	2	160
Blaine	9.3	18 600	32.8	71.4	D	282	1	0.0	0.0	0.0	206	4	28
Bryan	8.3	11 857	23.4	79.1	1.0	2 698	982	0.0	0.0	52.1	772	15	512
Caddo	5.8	19 333	25.2	76.2	D	1 567	221	0.0	0.0	96.7	1 042	35	124
Canadian	5.1	17 000	20.6	52.6	0.9	9 496	1 308	0.0	0.0	88.5	5 280	63	726
Carter	D	D	D	D	D	7 961	5 838	24.3	9.1	53.5	1 425	33	423
Cherokee	1.9	9 500	4.6	6.8	0.1	2 975	1 311	18.2	0.0	67.2	1 346	30	133
Choctaw	0.7	7 000	3.2	6.6	0.0	882	381	0.0	0.0	0.0	394	13	16
Cimarron	D	D	D	D	D	82	82	0.0	0.0	0.0	0	0	0
Cleveland	31.2	16 421	271.8	467.8	9.6	41 543	7 748	14.7	10.9	63.2	25 711	351	2 888
Coal	D	D	D	D	D	157	140	71.4	0.0	28.6	0	0	15
Comanche	61.5	24 600	337.3	583.4	7.9	18 870	7 072	46.9	34.9	17.7	6 377	61	2 458
Cotton	D	D	D	D	D	212	162	0.0	0.0	0.0	35	1	6
Craig	6.8	17 000	27.9	48.1	1.2	NA	NA	NA	NA	NA	NA	NA	NA
Creek	42.4	19 273	135.7	276.6	5.7	3 470	622	8.0	64.3	22.0	2 297	37	98
Custer	22.9	19 083	182.7	391.5	18.4	5 136	302	0.0	14.9	22.3	2 153	29	390
Delaware	4.2	14 000	12.1	30.3	0.7	8 189	3 837	0.0	33.0	55.6	3 005	69	121
Dewey	0.1	NA	0.4	1.1	0.0	29	0	NA	NA	NA	0	0	14
Ellis	0.1	NA	0.4	1.5	0.0	NA	NA	NA	NA	NA	NA	NA	NA
Garfield	16.6	20 750	92.4	278.5	1.4	10 791	1 096	16.4	4.6	28.3	3 567	31	788
Garvin	D	D	D	D	D	671	38	0.0	54.5	39.0	160	3	151
Grady	27.1	16 938	202.8	274.1	4.4	4 450	2 609	0.0	52.6	0.0	948	17	477
Grant	0.5	NA	1.9	5.0	0.1	88	0	NA	NA	NA	75	1	0
Greer	D	D	D	D	D	0	0	NA	NA	NA	0	0	0
Harmon	D	D	D	D	D	NA	NA	NA	NA	NA	NA	NA	NA
Harper	D	D	D	D	D	167	62	0.0	0.0	35.9	70	2	22
Haskell	D	D	D	D	D	896	714	0.0	0.0	0.0	146	4	33
Hughes	0.7	7 000	1.8	2.4	0.1	220	2	0.0	0.0	0.0	55	1	0
Jackson	6.6	16 500	37.7	64.3	D	3 431	1 053	24.7	0.0	42.5	1 843	22	250
Jefferson	1.6	8 000	5.5	12.9	D	0	0	NA	NA	NA	0	0	0
Johnston	0.9	9 000	2.2	3.9	0.1	492	21	0.0	0.0	0.0	82	3	46
Kay	46.3	21 045	175.7	1 241.3	21.0	11 085	238	38.6	0.0	10.5	8 296	85	814
Kingfisher	2.4	24 000	13.1	20.1	0.2	1 009	308	2.6	0.0	0.0	449	5	63
Kiowa	D	D	D	D	D	183	10	0.0	0.0	0.0	161	5	12
Latimer	D	D	D	D	D	380	115	21.7	0.0	47.8	0	0	265
Le Flore	8.3	16 600	25.8	53.7	D	5 628	1 834	0.8	0.0	44.4	2 923	75	355
Lincoln	4.4	11 000	8.4	17.4	1.4	2 088	893	8.1	0.0	17.8	876	13	193
Logan	2.7	13 500	9.0	25.9	0.4	1 373	362	0.0	5.1	26.7	538	8	184
Love	D	D	D	D	D	NA	NA	NA	NA	NA	NA	NA	NA
McClain	3.3	11 000	17.3	30.9	0.2	6 266	2 724	0.0	0.0	14.9	2 893	38	52

1. Includes nonresidential additions and alterations, residential nonhousekeeping buildings, and residential garages and carports not shown separately.

STATE County	Wholesale trade, 1987: Establishments	Wholesale trade, 1987: Sales (Mil dol)	Wholesale trade, 1987: Paid employees[1]	Wholesale trade, 1987: Annual payroll (Mil dol)	Retail trade, all establishments, 1987: Number	Retail trade, all establishments, 1987: Sales: Total (Mil dol)	Retail trade, all establishments, 1987: Sales: Percent change, 1982–1987	Retail trade, all establishments, 1987: Sales: Per capita[2] (Dollars)	Retail trade, establishments with payroll, 1987: Number	Retail trade, establishments with payroll, 1987: Sales: Total (Mil dol)	Per capita[2] (Dollars): General merchandise stores	Per capita[2] (Dollars): Food stores	Per capita[2] (Dollars): Apparel & accessory stores	Per capita[2] (Dollars): Eating and drinking places
	147	148	149	150	151	152	153	154	155	156	157	158	159	160
OHIO—Con.														
Putnam	52	101.0	373	5.6	303	142.4	67.1	4 224	188	133.9	D	785	65	342
Richland	211	541.3	2 179	45.4	1 245	851.6	41.6	6 622	800	830.9	1 126	1 200	223	592
Ross	65	92.9	446	7.7	567	337.9	42.8	4 976	367	331.2	984	1 034	123	445
Sandusky	77	214.4	887	13.9	577	302.6	29.4	4 889	360	292.6	305	1 170	143	396
Scioto	92	199.4	859	13.8	799	408.7	23.1	4 990	496	392.7	555	1 117	165	565
Seneca	78	364.4	805	13.9	592	285.5	39.5	4 597	377	276.2	401	1 005	204	373
Shelby	57	145.2	437	7.7	358	170.3	37.4	3 844	236	164.9	151	900	126	513
Stark	534	2 782.7	8 447	183.5	3 704	2 267.1	31.4	6 099	2 330	2 210.4	D	1 346	263	596
Summit	999	6 855.6	13 509	347.9	4 646	3 267.4	34.4	6 399	3 181	3 203.1	880	1 371	279	726
Trumbull	239	889.9	2 790	53.3	2 114	1 385.3	39.3	6 028	1 339	1 347.3	812	1 032	275	536
Tuscarawas	137	308.7	1 404	26.5	1 014	485.0	38.2	5 740	577	464.7	615	1 297	143	452
Union	33	165.7	495	11.4	247	121.9	49.4	3 774	147	116.7	353	822	107	291
Van Wert	49	107.9	450	7.6	262	134.1	33.6	4 484	164	130.6	262	1 030	145	365
Vinton	11	10.8	56	0.8	98	21.9	36.9	1 873	51	18.9	D	D	0	89
Warren	110	723.8	1 239	30.8	901	539.4	69.4	4 980	564	526.4	758	1 315	166	542
Washington	100	318.8	961	16.8	591	325.6	21.0	5 103	354	313.9	468	1 265	140	436
Wayne	162	406.5	1 589	31.2	926	506.0	42.6	4 985	499	486.3	371	1 168	80	378
Williams	58	152.6	682	12.1	387	182.0	41.5	4 974	242	174.9	D	1 120	179	531
Wood	181	609.3	1 829	39.8	954	607.9	23.4	5 516	643	595.3	756	1 088	211	477
Wyandot	43	85.3	288	5.7	262	96.4	35.2	4 342	158	92.1	D	895	90	427
OKLAHOMA	5 974	20 212.6	54 918	1 117.8	35 949	16 912.5	5.2	5 189	20 235	16 073.5	639	1 119	272	491
Adair	10	9.9	50	0.6	154	36.4	5.5	1 783	61	31.0	D	681	D	79
Alfalfa	17	D	D	D	102	19.1	-28.5	2 893	50	16.9	D	837	D	100
Atoka	15	D	D	D	128	51.7	16.4	3 859	70	46.3	D	958	65	159
Beaver	13	D	D	D	86	14.5	16.0	2 070	35	12.4	0	654	D	101
Beckham	51	D	D	D	330	115.4	-38.6	5 799	176	106.4	D	1 428	363	520
Blaine	19	D	D	D	194	40.4	-34.4	3 057	95	33.0	D	970	82	186
Bryan	57	D	D	D	438	130.8	15.2	3 950	178	112.8	529	869	161	298
Caddo	46	D	D	D	394	103.0	-23.4	3 159	196	92.9	325	869	69	165
Canadian	80	D	D	D	616	308.5	-1.7	4 220	307	293.4	D	1 012	139	384
Carter	102	D	D	D	670	248.3	5.7	5 363	368	226.7	661	1 148	385	448
Cherokee	21	42.1	214	1.9	341	125.3	27.7	3 531	198	117.0	D	1 031	168	299
Choctaw	22	15.2	96	1.2	188	52.4	10.3	3 137	87	46.9	D	772	90	161
Cimarron	12	12.7	53	0.8	61	14.2	3.6	3 388	30	13.3	0	772	D	213
Cleveland	135	276.4	1 040	20.8	1 420	822.7	2.4	5 041	841	793.7	600	891	282	514
Coal	3	D	D	D	56	11.9	26.6	1 988	23	10.0	D	856	0	81
Comanche	100	184.0	958	15.5	1 049	565.8	13.6	4 715	669	547.7	931	866	205	447
Cotton	13	36.3	99	1.4	80	18.6	-19.5	2 656	31	15.7	142	731	D	179
Craig	20	D	D	D	198	69.3	-0.4	4 648	103	65.8	D	1 035	141	442
Creek	73	87.7	402	7.6	561	187.6	-15.9	2 908	301	172.6	D	1 057	96	293
Custer	69	126.6	409	7.8	396	164.0	-24.9	5 755	260	157.2	D	1 389	383	487
Delaware	18	26.2	82	0.8	310	93.1	45.2	3 266	158	84.8	D	873	82	249
Dewey	10	18.9	58	1.0	99	14.4	-12.2	2 365	43	11.5	0	813	D	90
Ellis	8	20.5	57	0.8	78	15.8	-29.5	2 983	37	13.0	D	611	D	137
Garfield	146	D	D	D	719	351.8	-8.0	5 903	478	339.6	1 003	1 171	361	525
Garvin	40	40.3	202	3.7	416	111.5	-10.0	3 845	212	100.4	333	1 107	140	296
Grady	73	130.1	593	10.8	531	174.6	3.7	4 080	241	157.8	D	943	179	323
Grant	23	44.7	128	2.2	81	14.5	-29.3	2 335	44	13.1	0	445	D	81
Greer	8	18.0	114	1.2	86	14.0	-13.0	2 053	38	12.3	D	1 007	22	124
Harmon	5	9.7	63	1.0	62	10.5	4.0	2 511	27	8.6	D	774	D	95
Harper	7	10.0	30	0.5	67	11.3	-15.0	2 502	35	10.2	D	D	D	125
Haskell	5	D	D	D	134	41.2	4.6	3 461	58	37.4	D	777	63	96
Hughes	9	17.9	61	0.5	174	40.3	-7.6	2 742	79	35.3	D	798	D	104
Jackson	61	68.5	371	5.2	359	157.8	7.9	5 191	217	150.4	D	840	312	482
Jefferson	9	15.4	14	0.3	136	21.7	4.3	2 856	46	17.0	55	822	30	178
Johnston	10	17.3	114	1.1	107	19.7	45.9	1 795	47	16.1	0	519	44	196
Kay	93	188.6	670	11.9	638	272.9	1.4	5 279	373	258.8	707	1 209	231	415
Kingfisher	46	124.3	344	6.9	161	60.6	-22.6	4 041	92	56.2	D	1 051	59	265
Kiowa	22	56.2	159	2.2	169	41.3	-13.2	3 383	84	36.7	D	1 118	95	117
Latimer	7	17.0	52	0.7	98	23.4	9.3	2 191	44	20.7	117	1 054	D	133
Le Flore	27	31.2	181	2.1	466	126.3	15.8	2 764	179	109.4	D	829	63	141
Lincoln	29	55.9	150	2.6	318	76.8	-9.8	2 613	137	66.4	D	638	58	264
Logan	17	D	D	D	254	81.5	-0.9	2 734	132	75.6	D	631	58	260
Love	5	12.8	89	0.2	115	26.7	80.4	3 297	42	23.2	D	1 167	D	208
McClain	23	22.7	130	1.6	235	92.2	8.7	3 808	111	83.7	D	813	40	285

1. For pay period including March 12. 2. Based on the estimated population as of July 1 of the year shown.

STATE County	Retail trade, establishments with payroll, 1987 (cont'd)		Taxable service industries–establishments with payroll, 1987							Bank deposits,[2] June 1989		Savings capital,[3] September 1989	
				Receipts (Mil dol)									
					Selected kinds of business								
	Paid employees[1]	Annual payroll (Mil dol)	Number	Total	Hotels, motels and other lodging places	Health services	Legal services	Paid employees	Annual payroll (Mil dol)	Total (Mil dol)	Percent change, 1988–1989	Total (Mil dol)	Percent change, 1988–1989
	161	162	163	164	165	166	167	168	169	170	171	172	173
OHIO—Con.													
Putnam	1 602	12.7	121	22.4	D	9.9	1.3	706	7.5	292	4.7	78.7	1.4
Richland	10 291	96.8	707	212.9	4.6	83.1	9.3	7 777	86.1	763	2.7	417.6	-3.5
Ross	4 202	37.0	311	68.8	4.8	32.4	3.3	2 104	25.6	332	6.0	114.8	-16.5
Sandusky	3 328	31.3	306	68.1	5.6	26.3	3.2	1 633	22.9	514	3.8	101.0	-1.6
Scioto	5 231	45.8	347	91.1	2.9	56.1	4.0	2 546	38.8	395	7.5	217.9	-3.2
Seneca	3 327	31.1	289	58.3	1.3	24.4	2.9	1 735	22.8	478	-1.0	204.8	-1.7
Shelby	2 093	19.1	170	43.1	4.6	13.1	3.6	1 087	16.9	342	11.5	157.9	-4.0
Stark	29 564	258.3	2 315	751.1	20.8	273.0	41.3	23 238	293.7	2 233	6.8	1 661.7	-7.6
Summit	42 685	388.9	3 601	1 269.4	47.2	370.7	82.7	31 418	528.6	3 420	5.1	1 967.3	-1.4
Trumbull	18 006	160.5	1 160	378.6	24.9	155.8	14.5	9 537	140.6	1 469	3.0	863.9	-0.5
Tuscarawas	5 813	51.8	458	124.6	4.1	41.4	6.1	3 187	42.9	688	8.4	204.2	-2.5
Union	1 376	11.8	125	29.5	D	9.6	2.2	873	12.5	155	10.8	86.8	-8.1
Van Wert	1 623	14.0	139	36.3	D	18.6	2.0	910	13.4	194	0.2	118.0	1.7
Vinton	243	2.0	15	3.9	0.0	2.7	D	143	1.6	67	9.8	18.2	4.2
Warren	7 026	61.2	436	200.2	D	31.7	5.7	4 075	59.3	533	9.1	195.7	14.3
Washington	3 910	35.4	338	81.8	5.6	30.9	4.1	2 177	29.4	514	4.8	120.9	1.7
Wayne	5 891	55.6	429	114.9	3.5	46.0	8.0	3 356	41.2	596	7.5	457.9	-1.9
Williams	2 291	19.7	153	46.7	3.1	21.0	2.4	1 431	19.9	364	4.4	100.6	-1.4
Wood	7 780	69.0	516	169.9	25.4	42.5	6.8	4 714	58.3	720	4.9	247.7	-0.4
Wyandot	1 272	10.9	105	18.0	D	5.9	1.3	647	6.6	227	5.7	65.7	1.4
OKLAHOMA	206 897	1 859.3	19 456	6 347.9	308.5	2 049.5	670.9	149 370	2 416.2	22 520	-2.0	7 592.8	-9.5
Adair	417	3.1	38	7.2	0.0	3.9	0.5	316	3.0	58	-4.9	7.6	3.7
Alfalfa	202	1.7	24	2.9	0.0	2.0	0.4	134	1.0	74	-5.7	11.8	-3.7
Atoka	515	4.2	33	5.5	0.7	2.4	0.5	189	2.0	65	2.4	10.2	36.6
Beaver	143	1.2	19	2.6	D	1.1	0.5	45	0.6	61	-7.5	11.4	45.6
Beckham	1 295	11.1	124	25.8	4.0	6.9	0.7	555	7.2	208	-1.4	134.9	-23.3
Blaine	483	3.7	52	7.5	D	2.6	D	269	2.6	157	0.8	0.0	-100.0
Bryan	1 731	12.7	147	46.6	D	22.6	1.5	1 338	15.6	285	10.7	27.1	-2.2
Caddo	1 088	8.7	93	15.5	0.1	10.1	0.8	651	5.8	227	-4.9	83.2	5.4
Canadian	3 472	30.8	307	60.1	1.7	15.0	4.3	1 589	20.0	287	-4.0	181.4	1.9
Carter	3 052	26.8	304	79.0	5.5	32.1	5.5	1 895	28.2	431	2.5	68.0	-11.7
Cherokee	1 801	12.5	122	21.1	1.8	8.4	1.2	672	6.4	177	4.2	35.9	-20.1
Choctaw	526	4.2	57	14.1	D	3.0	1.1	325	3.6	74	2.8	24.6	16.7
Cimarron	150	1.3	22	1.4	D	0.4	D	48	0.3	28	0.3	0.0	NA
Cleveland	10 269	86.4	838	214.8	5.0	72.4	19.0	5 106	77.3	655	0.9	125.3	NA
Coal	122	1.1	15	1.4	0.0	D	0.2	36	0.4	34	1.4	0.0	-100.0
Comanche	7 107	63.5	568	164.7	9.0	61.6	8.8	4 092	62.0	427	1.4	193.3	-6.0
Cotton	164	1.5	28	3.6	D	1.0	0.3	89	0.9	61	1.1	0.0	NA
Craig	742	7.3	57	16.7	D	4.3	2.0	483	5.7	138	2.9	36.0	-10.0
Creek	2 512	20.6	222	39.0	D	13.1	7.6	1 080	12.9	316	3.6	74.4	-8.7
Custer	1 990	16.8	189	33.1	3.2	11.8	3.0	982	11.5	314	1.1	149.3	0.3
Delaware	979	8.5	101	18.1	4.4	7.9	0.5	540	5.0	102	1.0	41.5	0.5
Dewey	162	1.1	16	2.3	D	D	D	92	0.9	105	0.7	5.8	NA
Ellis	151	1.4	19	4.0	D	3.3	D	82	1.9	54	-4.5	9.1	44.1
Garfield	4 702	40.5	403	133.1	3.8	78.3	10.5	3 132	53.1	366	-7.5	227.3	-24.2
Garvin	1 413	10.8	134	23.5	D	9.4	1.9	727	7.8	235	-3.1	49.8	-11.7
Grady	1 906	17.3	190	43.8	D	18.8	5.9	1 169	16.1	271	-1.3	111.4	-42.5
Grant	140	1.2	18	2.1	D	0.9	D	41	0.6	105	-3.3	0.0	-100.0
Greer	157	1.3	27	3.9	D	2.2	0.1	134	1.0	57	-5.7	0.0	NA
Harmon	107	0.8	11	2.5	D	1.9	D	97	0.8	26	-3.3	0.0	NA
Harper	135	1.1	29	4.1	0.0	2.4	D	118	1.1	52	3.4	0.0	NA
Haskell	398	3.5	26	2.5	D	0.8	0.1	67	0.8	54	3.2	0.0	NA
Hughes	445	3.7	45	7.6	D	5.3	0.8	295	2.4	90	-1.6	10.6	-9.9
Jackson	1 825	15.6	143	33.3	2.5	18.5	1.6	739	11.9	181	-6.8	31.5	-11.1
Jefferson	216	1.7	31	3.8	D	2.2	0.3	169	1.4	87	1.2	0.0	NA
Johnston	254	1.8	18	3.8	D	2.1	D	128	1.4	50	-0.7	0.0	NA
Kay	3 303	28.7	325	82.8	3.1	28.1	8.4	2 074	27.1	407	1.4	250.7	0.5
Kingfisher	601	5.8	74	11.6	0.3	4.9	1.7	289	3.6	190	-2.4	157.5	157.9
Kiowa	445	3.4	49	6.9	D	4.0	0.6	251	2.2	141	-7.0	15.7	-0.5
Latimer	277	2.4	30	3.7	D	2.0	D	120	1.4	56	0.4	0.0	NA
Le Flore	1 333	10.5	123	24.6	D	10.2	1.7	717	7.0	229	4.5	19.1	-11.3
Lincoln	926	7.9	69	15.9	D	4.1	1.7	459	5.3	228	-1.3	37.3	1.5
Logan	909	7.8	98	25.0	D	8.6	1.1	941	8.7	121	-1.3	63.2	-5.7
Love	240	2.5	21	2.5	D	1.1	0.2	105	0.9	59	-2.1	0.0	NA
McClain	890	8.3	67	8.4	0.3	3.4	0.9	230	2.4	162	-9.3	14.1	11.8

1. For the period including March 12 of the year shown. 2. Includes deposits for all insured and reporting noninsured commercial and mutual savings banks. 3. Includes savings capital for all FSLIC insured savings institutions.

STATE County	Federal funds and grants, 1989: Expenditures: Total (Mil dol)	Federal funds and grants, 1989: Expenditures: Percent change, 1988–1989	Per capita[1] (Dollars): Total	Per capita[1] (Dollars): Direct payments for individuals	Per capita[1] (Dollars): Procurement contract awards	Per capita[1] (Dollars): Salaries and wages	Per capita[1] (Dollars): Grant awards	Local government finances, 1981–1982: General revenue: Total (Mil dol)	Intergovernmental: Total (Mil dol)	Intergovernmental: Percent from state	Taxes: Total (Mil dol)	Taxes: Per capita[2]: Total (Dollars)	Taxes: Per capita[2]: Property (Dollars)	Direct general expenditure: Total (Mil dol)	Direct general expenditure: Percent change, 1977–1982
	174	175	176	177	178	179	180	181	182	183	184	185	186	187	188
OHIO—Con.															
Putnam	47.9	8.8	1 402	947	14	85	167	26.8	12.5	93.0	10.2	307	255	25.2	49.2
Richland	283.1	5.2	2 195	1 616	61	222	257	118.6	52.5	88.3	46.4	358	278	118.0	43.2
Ross	197.9	4.9	2 885	1 644	122	632	401	57.9	29.8	76.8	20.4	309	245	55.6	66.4
Sandusky	130.5	7.3	2 098	1 556	95	84	230	56.6	23.0	87.4	22.4	360	291	52.6	41.2
Scioto	244.6	6.4	3 001	2 184	13	104	679	70.7	43.9	79.1	17.6	210	165	67.6	74.1
Seneca	148.3	10.5	2 399	1 820	79	99	218	47.9	17.7	93.2	22.1	362	289	45.7	43.3
Shelby	78.2	-3.4	1 753	1 253	77	79	209	36.1	15.0	92.9	15.3	352	268	35.8	72.9
Stark	913.3	5.2	2 437	1 849	197	145	234	336.5	131.3	87.3	134.1	355	265	327.3	48.1
Summit	1 417.7	7.1	2 747	1 784	469	182	304	575.1	232.5	76.9	235.7	456	317	587.2	43.0
Trumbull	515.7	5.5	2 259	1 831	41	141	234	198.9	84.8	88.0	75.4	314	255	197.5	42.6
Tuscarawas	180.4	-2.4	2 122	1 722	50	102	216	78.0	33.6	83.4	28.6	335	270	75.0	56.7
Union	347.3	-22.2	10 304	1 079	8 731	106	192	31.8	9.3	94.6	9.7	321	287	31.0	89.3
Van Wert	58.8	0.5	1 959	1 322	56	102	258	23.7	8.8	90.0	11.1	369	301	23.3	30.7
Vinton	25.5	-1.1	2 199	1 537	19	99	498	8.8	5.2	94.6	2.3	206	204	8.6	68.9
Warren	173.4	-31.1	1 521	1 081	132	78	192	80.5	35.9	85.8	28.4	281	229	80.5	72.2
Washington	237.8	78.5	3 763	1 727	1 474	130	396	50.7	21.4	91.1	22.5	348	302	49.9	73.2
Wayne	177.5	3.0	1 683	1 276	44	91	221	100.5	36.3	75.7	36.5	369	285	95.9	46.0
Williams	75.0	4.2	2 022	1 559	28	100	151	33.9	10.4	91.8	13.8	382	303	32.0	55.1
Wood	181.7	4.2	1 618	1 208	15	107	190	97.4	33.2	90.0	41.0	376	278	99.1	47.1
Wyandot	50.3	5.0	2 308	1 654	21	110	192	22.4	7.8	94.1	7.5	333	285	21.4	66.3
OKLAHOMA	11 272.0	3.6	X	1 864	254	712	521	3 317.4	1 323.6	85.2	974.2	302	170	3 172.0	106.0
Adair	58.2	9.7	2 799	1 600	47	82	991	21.4	17.8	57.2	1.3	70	43	36.1	409.2
Alfalfa	26.4	-17.0	4 187	2 698	116	290	438	9.7	4.6	95.7	2.7	368	331	8.9	72.2
Atoka	37.5	-7.7	2 798	1 791	19	214	603	11.0	6.9	83.5	1.8	143	90	17.7	256.4
Beaver	20.4	-22.9	3 002	1 499	58	177	86	11.8	6.6	98.6	3.3	448	410	11.0	67.1
Beckham	54.1	-0.9	2 864	2 001	14	118	436	21.8	11.3	93.9	6.9	274	143	21.3	167.1
Blaine	34.5	-43.9	2 742	1 901	49	215	314	15.1	8.1	95.1	4.2	277	206	13.9	80.1
Bryan	128.7	20.5	3 866	2 149	295	186	1 090	25.7	12.1	94.5	5.9	190	101	23.5	94.6
Caddo	109.8	4.5	3 465	2 063	239	405	527	34.9	19.4	92.1	8.4	251	184	32.7	78.4
Canadian	172.5	-22.8	2 303	1 186	49	453	577	57.0	26.6	93.0	20.6	322	230	58.3	150.5
Carter	116.8	8.8	2 590	1 934	18	161	457	53.2	26.8	77.8	13.8	298	149	44.3	121.6
Cherokee	138.3	23.3	3 778	1 741	567	318	1 125	27.4	12.2	92.8	3.2	101	53	26.4	146.5
Choctaw	58.3	9.1	3 493	2 221	16	143	909	12.2	8.0	93.3	2.6	153	77	11.3	32.3
Cimarron	19.2	-32.5	4 693	1 681	41	160	129	6.3	3.3	97.4	1.7	454	417	5.3	31.3
Cleveland	388.0	40.8	2 343	1 234	649	171	282	165.2	48.9	92.5	41.4	281	164	166.4	203.6
Coal	20.7	2.9	3 444	2 278	25	210	745	5.4	3.3	82.8	1.5	258	226	5.0	93.1
Comanche	898.4	0.7	7 537	1 787	794	4 597	327	131.9	50.4	80.5	21.1	176	95	130.1	108.1
Cotton	23.2	-17.5	3 362	2 260	19	179	428	5.0	3.2	95.6	1.3	179	122	4.6	58.5
Craig	44.1	9.0	2 963	2 161	16	136	496	13.1	7.2	78.0	3.0	199	135	11.5	81.3
Creek	124.8	5.4	1 988	1 468	109	84	316	47.5	26.6	93.3	12.4	193	130	55.0	137.1
Custer	158.6	33.4	5 787	1 261	1 418	253	272	33.2	13.7	93.3	10.5	336	167	25.5	150.1
Delaware	69.9	9.0	2 384	1 795	13	72	456	16.8	11.7	92.6	3.8	145	100	15.2	77.1
Dewey	19.9	-13.3	3 439	2 259	42	256	354	11.2	6.6	98.1	2.9	442	391	12.2	196.9
Ellis	16.5	-10.8	3 441	2 240	43	214	183	7.0	4.1	98.1	2.3	342	287	6.1	81.7
Garfield	227.1	2.7	4 012	1 978	865	842	238	56.9	23.1	95.9	22.3	329	173	50.0	77.1
Garvin	78.6	4.8	2 809	2 246	14	127	353	28.4	14.0	95.9	6.1	202	113	27.1	99.1
Grady	91.3	-2.2	2 195	1 675	28	128	272	51.9	22.1	78.3	9.0	207	131	56.8	109.1
Grant	23.6	-64.8	4 000	2 472	27	222	474	7.6	3.7	96.3	2.8	424	367	7.4	64.1
Greer	29.1	1.4	4 480	3 050	20	195	490	9.8	2.6	91.6	1.7	232	180	8.1	127.5
Harmon	18.9	-1.5	4 718	2 471	20	212	564	3.6	2.2	96.1	1.1	232	181	3.5	22.9
Harper	13.9	-18.2	3 241	2 193	22	193	87	6.8	3.8	97.7	1.9	385	325	6.5	96.9
Haskell	38.1	4.2	3 257	2 151	23	199	756	8.0	5.4	94.0	1.9	165	116	7.7	90.1
Hughes	49.0	4.9	3 401	2 466	18	139	676	13.1	7.8	81.0	2.6	178	124	11.3	109.3
Jackson	181.9	-17.7	6 230	2 004	371	3 121	392	37.7	13.3	89.8	5.6	186	85	34.9	101.7
Jefferson	27.5	3.4	3 820	2 444	24	192	819	9.5	5.5	61.0	1.7	205	141	8.1	118.7
Johnston	33.5	13.3	3 049	2 050	54	192	669	9.6	4.7	86.2	1.6	150	109	9.1	78.0
Kay	178.2	13.2	3 530	2 013	1 099	148	192	51.2	16.6	91.4	15.6	296	196	52.5	121.8
Kingfisher	45.6	-36.3	3 213	1 650	906	182	221	20.0	10.8	98.2	6.4	397	277	18.2	106.8
Kiowa	46.6	-7.7	3 915	2 579	27	183	450	13.0	8.1	88.5	3.1	242	177	13.6	78.0
Latimer	36.6	36.5	3 298	1 834	631	102	684	13.2	8.1	94.1	3.0	293	258	11.6	99.7
Le Flore	126.4	8.5	2 672	1 892	17	148	584	32.6	20.8	91.4	4.9	118	73	30.5	98.2
Lincoln	64.4	6.2	2 197	1 755	17	122	275	18.5	10.8	90.2	5.2	185	115	18.4	112.6
Logan	74.2	-6.4	2 531	1 651	237	160	430	22.8	9.7	88.7	5.4	187	114	20.3	102.7
Love	20.2	8.8	2 463	1 819	119	89	355	6.2	4.2	87.4	1.3	163	124	5.2	55.5
McClain	42.7	1.9	1 788	1 338	14	98	266	21.0	11.4	97.0	5.4	245	172	19.1	107.1

1. Based on the estimated population as of July 1 of the year shown. 2. Based on the estimated population as of July 1, 1982.

STATE County	Local government finances, 1981–1982 (cont'd) — Direct general expenditure (cont'd) — Per capita[1] (Dollars)	Percent of total for– Education	Percent of total for– Health & hospitals	Percent of total for– Police protection	Percent of total for– Public welfare	Percent of total for– Highways	Debt outstanding — Total (Mil dol)	Debt outstanding — Per capita[1] (Dollars)	State and local government employment, 1989 — Total	State and local government employment, 1989 — Rate[2]	Federal government civilian employment 1989 — Total	Federal government civilian employment 1989 — Earnings ($1,000)	Elections, 1988[3] — Total vote cast for president	Elections, 1988[3] — Vote for lead party (Percent)
	189	190	191	192	193	194	195	196	197	198	199	200	201	202
OHIO—Con.														
Putnam	756	56.5	3.2	3.4	4.0	11.3	6.7	200	1 533	448.2	83	2 129	15 301	R–73.1
Richland	909	52.7	5.7	4.0	4.5	5.8	50.2	387	6 781	525.7	748	23 298	50 047	R–60.0
Ross	845	49.5	3.6	3.1	5.8	6.8	29.0	441	4 069	593.1	1 627	51 535	24 113	R–60.4
Sandusky	844	50.5	1.3	4.6	9.4	7.3	22.6	363	2 855	459.0	143	4 163	24 118	R–58.9
Scioto	803	52.3	4.1	2.8	6.6	6.9	32.2	382	4 727	580.0	206	5 988	30 760	R–52.1
Seneca	747	49.2	5.6	4.9	4.3	9.0	11.5	188	2 544	411.7	163	4 380	23 430	R–58.5
Shelby	822	52.0	2.0	4.6	7.0	9.2	12.8	294	2 145	480.9	107	2 844	17 425	R–70.0
Stark	866	49.0	5.6	4.4	4.7	6.2	256.7	679	16 489	440.1	1 311	41 738	158 096	R–55.1
Summit	1 135	40.5	5.6	5.1	5.8	5.9	374.4	724	26 743	518.3	2 114	69 759	215 589	D–52.2
Trumbull	822	56.3	5.5	4.2	5.7	5.1	89.5	373	8 939	391.5	901	28 007	98 250	D–59.7
Tuscarawas	879	45.5	3.1	3.6	4.0	8.4	20.5	241	3 784	445.2	233	6 442	31 589	R–54.3
Union	1 023	36.0	30.4	2.4	8.0	6.1	8.5	281	1 857	551.0	77	1 947	12 071	R–73.3
Van Wert	778	51.8	2.6	4.5	6.8	12.1	7.7	258	1 227	409.0	85	2 175	13 336	R–70.6
Vinton	755	50.2	4.1	3.6	6.4	19.1	3.2	282	703	606.0	30	730	5 081	R–52.2
Warren	796	53.4	3.5	4.4	3.6	6.0	55.6	550	4 511	395.7	249	7 298	42 818	R–73.4
Washington	772	54.5	7.6	3.1	5.5	8.4	17.7	274	2 769	438.1	256	7 027	24 916	R–59.3
Wayne	969	44.0	14.1	3.8	3.1	6.0	36.2	366	6 300	597.2	263	7 660	36 208	R–61.6
Williams	886	53.2	8.1	4.7	3.3	11.7	27.8	771	1 809	487.6	97	2 432	15 585	R–69.2
Wood	910	48.0	3.6	4.6	4.7	5.8	47.6	436	11 053	984.2	259	7 164	44 933	R–57.9
Wyandot	950	42.5	18.7	3.3	6.5	9.9	1.8	81	1 146	525.7	70	1 805	9 239	R–66.9
OKLAHOMA	982	43.7	10.6	4.1	0.1	6.9	4 080.7	1 263	203 326	629.0	51 935	1 570 037	1 171 036	R–57.9
Adair	1 891	29.2	0.5	0.6	0.0	2.6	52.6	2 756	981	471.6	49	1 142	6 240	R–57.0
Alfalfa	1 233	49.5	15.5	2.7	0.1	15.8	4.5	628	458	727.0	52	1 230	3 132	R–62.6
Atoka	1 381	27.0	4.8	2.0	0.1	7.5	39.8	3 107	1 098	819.4	89	2 407	4 570	D–56.1
Beaver	1 485	51.0	10.0	1.9	0.2	26.3	0.8	109	479	704.4	47	1 090	2 834	R–71.0
Beckham	849	46.3	0.5	4.0	0.0	11.9	25.7	1 024	815	431.2	68	1 874	6 915	R–50.1
Blaine	924	53.6	9.6	3.8	0.0	16.6	3.8	251	905	718.3	84	2 034	4 734	R–61.0
Bryan	754	44.7	18.0	3.9	0.0	7.6	21.3	684	2 285	686.2	178	5 006	11 501	D–59.6
Caddo	973	61.5	10.3	2.7	0.0	9.3	19.8	588	1 710	539.4	453	11 685	10 177	D–52.9
Canadian	909	58.6	3.0	3.0	0.1	6.0	72.5	1 132	3 000	400.5	632	20 338	25 530	R–70.0
Carter	959	48.0	21.9	2.7	0.2	11.5	18.3	396	2 595	575.4	172	5 091	16 535	R–51.0
Cherokee	838	44.7	23.2	2.3	0.1	4.6	5.6	178	3 232	883.1	417	11 308	12 424	D–52.2
Choctaw	671	62.3	1.4	4.5	0.0	8.9	5.7	338	831	497.6	80	2 159	5 599	D–60.0
Cimarron	1 441	51.0	14.4	2.8	0.0	16.9	1.8	475	311	758.5	26	608	1 647	R–70.0
Cleveland	1 130	38.7	24.7	3.7	0.2	2.6	313.8	2 131	15 683	947.0	656	21 940	58 933	R–61.6
Coal	845	60.5	0.9	2.8	0.1	14.4	1.7	288	344	573.3	36	964	2 270	D–60.1
Comanche	1 084	35.8	30.8	3.9	0.0	6.8	109.3	911	6 306	529.0	5 495	132 432	29 099	R–60.0
Cotton	655	59.1	1.1	3.8	0.1	14.3	2.6	378	370	536.2	38	854	2 775	D–53.4
Craig	749	56.5	17.3	3.0	0.2	10.0	4.5	292	1 755	1 177.9	61	1 562	5 446	D–54.0
Creek	855	53.0	0.3	2.4	0.0	6.0	50.6	786	2 375	378.2	127	3 605	20 982	R–53.9
Custer	816	53.1	8.6	4.2	0.1	10.0	13.7	439	2 770	1 010.9	207	5 798	10 527	R–64.0
Delaware	581	74.5	0.4	3.1	0.0	10.5	2.0	76	1 051	358.7	62	1 538	10 212	R–51.4
Dewey	1 870	68.4	0.0	1.0	0.0	14.9	3.8	588	401	691.4	47	1 028	2 551	R–60.5
Ellis	930	55.5	0.0	3.8	0.0	23.5	2.5	376	442	920.8	34	797	2 244	R–63.4
Garfield	738	54.4	0.9	4.7	0.0	12.4	18.6	275	3 361	593.8	394	9 918	23 538	R–64.8
Garvin	902	51.1	18.2	3.6	0.2	10.8	8.2	272	2 232	797.1	91	2 366	10 656	D–51.0
Grady	1 302	33.9	19.4	2.3	0.0	6.8	105.3	2 416	2 249	540.6	128	3 499	14 848	R–53.8
Grant	1 109	52.7	0.3	3.4	0.4	19.6	1.6	239	331	561.0	41	920	2 980	R–56.7
Greer	1 112	29.2	20.0	3.0	0.0	6.7	1.4	188	736	1 132.3	35	919	2 503	D–50.2
Harmon	734	58.8	0.4	5.7	0.0	16.2	0.2	43	227	567.5	29	723	1 504	D–59.2
Harper	1 307	56.4	0.0	3.5	0.0	27.1	0.2	43	429	997.7	26	620	1 900	R–67.4
Haskell	678	62.0	2.0	3.3	0.0	13.5	3.7	326	562	480.3	60	1 560	4 829	D–61.4
Hughes	760	55.6	13.3	3.0	0.0	11.6	6.4	426	822	570.8	50	1 274	5 327	D–61.2
Jackson	1 150	39.6	33.3	3.5	0.0	6.4	7.9	262	1 839	629.8	1 043	21 471	8 001	R–55.3
Jefferson	959	39.0	8.2	3.2	0.1	8.3	31.6	3 767	396	550.0	50	1 287	2 846	D–62.1
Johnston	854	46.0	21.2	3.1	3.8	8.3	3.0	280	775	704.5	59	1 507	3 581	D–57.0
Kay	996	39.9	0.5	4.9	0.1	7.3	113.2	2 148	2 539	502.8	195	5 605	20 564	R–61.5
Kingfisher	1 129	62.5	0.6	4.0	0.0	16.8	6.0	372	670	471.8	76	1 892	5 852	R–68.5
Kiowa	1 044	42.1	0.4	3.0	0.0	8.2	8.3	642	707	594.1	66	1 583	4 358	D–52.7
Latimer	1 153	82.9	0.4	1.8	0.0	6.3	3.3	330	1 423	1 282.0	32	872	4 233	D–55.9
Le Flore	726	59.3	10.3	3.1	0.1	10.5	9.5	225	2 347	496.2	227	5 791	13 641	R–51.1
Lincoln	650	55.3	1.2	4.2	0.0	11.5	21.1	747	1 120	382.3	81	2 091	10 740	R–59.7
Logan	700	41.2	19.2	3.9	0.0	9.6	19.1	658	1 765	602.4	79	2 037	11 704	R–59.4
Love	664	60.8	0.7	3.8	0.1	16.2	2.1	269	383	467.1	26	656	3 267	D–57.8
McClain	864	66.4	0.4	3.4	0.0	7.0	6.0	270	1 058	442.7	59	1 529	8 453	R–56.4

1. Based on the estimated population as of July 1, 1982. 2. Per 10,000 resident population estimated as of July 1 of the year shown. 3. Data subject to copyright.

STATE–County code	MSA/CMSA/NECMA code[1]	STATE County	Land Area,[2] 1990 (Sq. Km.)	Population, 1990: Total persons	Rank	Per square kilometer	Race: White	Black	Am. Indian, Eskimo, Aleut	Asian & Pacific Islander	Other race	Hispanic[3]	Age of population Percent: Under 5 years	5 to 14 years	15 to 24 years
			1	2	3	4	5	6	7	8	9	10	11	12	13
		OKLAHOMA—Con.													
40 089	...	McCurtain	4 798	33 433	1 177	7.0	24 821	3 452	4 873	89	198	459	7.7	16.9	14.1
40 091	...	McIntosh	1 606	16 779	1 861	10.4	12 757	885	3 072	27	38	150	5.6	13.5	11.4
40 093	...	Major	2 478	8 055	2 558	3.3	7 834	3	137	10	71	132	6.3	16.3	10.8
40 095	...	Marshall	961	10 829	2 308	11.3	9 412	186	1 088	13	130	275	5.8	12.4	12.1
40 097	...	Mayes	1 700	33 366	1 178	19.6	27 119	68	6 020	74	85	308	7.0	15.7	12.7
40 099	...	Murray	1 083	12 042	2 213	11.1	10 421	207	1 331	16	67	169	6.0	15.2	11.7
40 101	...	Muskogee	2 108	68 078	649	32.3	48 865	9 527	9 049	258	379	873	7.0	15.9	13.3
40 103	...	Noble	1 896	11 045	2 288	5.8	9 828	200	935	24	58	126	7.0	15.8	11.8
40 105	...	Nowata	1 463	9 992	2 386	6.8	7 973	364	1 634	6	15	73	6.3	14.5	11.8
40 107	...	Okfuskee	1 618	11 551	2 251	7.1	7 833	1 332	2 333	17	36	140	6.5	14.9	13.1
40 109	5880	Oklahoma	1 837	599 611	77	326.4	461 657	88 407	24 313	12 033	13 201	25 452	7.6	14.5	14.3
40 111	...	Okmulgee	1 805	36 490	1 089	20.2	27 372	4 422	4 454	80	162	458	7.1	15.2	13.8
40 113	8560	Osage	5 830	41 645	965	7.1	30 994	4 210	6 161	83	197	660	7.0	16.1	12.2
40 115	...	Ottawa	1 221	30 561	1 262	25.0	24 495	188	5 568	102	208	375	6.2	13.6	15.0
40 117	...	Pawnee	1 475	15 575	1 948	10.6	13 770	119	1 631	25	30	113	6.8	15.5	12.1
40 119	...	Payne	1 778	61 507	709	34.6	54 991	1 782	2 652	1 750	332	917	5.8	12.2	28.5
40 121	...	Pittsburg	3 383	40 581	984	12.0	33 765	1 505	5 005	111	195	479	5.9	14.4	12.2
40 123	...	Pontotoc	1 864	34 119	1 159	18.3	28 246	862	4 741	113	157	411	6.4	14.4	16.5
40 125	5880	Pottawatomie	2 041	58 760	739	28.8	49 931	1 326	6 848	337	318	990	6.7	15.6	15.7
40 127	...	Pushmataha	3 619	10 997	2 295	3.0	9 164	112	1 669	9	43	136	6.3	14.6	12.2
40 129	...	Roger Mills	2 958	4 147	2 902	1.4	3 948	3	167	4	25	73	6.4	16.7	11.6
40 131	8560	Rogers	1 748	55 170	782	31.6	47 242	456	7 117	188	167	618	7.3	16.3	13.2
40 133	...	Seminole	1 638	25 412	1 450	15.5	19 033	1 936	4 304	40	99	340	6.5	15.5	13.0
40 135	2720	Sequoyah	1 745	33 828	1 166	19.4	25 887	791	7 000	75	75	299	7.3	16.1	14.5
40 137	...	Stephens	2 272	42 299	952	18.6	38 829	945	1 720	158	647	943	6.4	15.1	11.5
40 139	...	Texas	5 277	16 419	1 896	3.1	15 131	71	186	39	992	1 634	6.9	16.4	15.1
40 141	...	Tillman	2 259	10 384	2 349	4.6	7 857	1 043	348	28	1 108	1 461	7.0	16.2	13.1
40 143	8560	Tulsa	1 477	503 341	95	340.8	417 737	49 618	25 401	5 976	4 609	11 958	7.7	14.5	13.9
40 145	8560	Wagoner	1 458	47 883	875	32.8	41 117	1 984	4 389	174	219	638	7.2	17.2	13.8
40 147	...	Washington	1 080	48 066	868	44.5	42 324	1 276	3 783	411	272	788	6.8	15.1	11.4
40 149	...	Washita	2 599	11 441	2 259	4.4	10 948	20	260	28	185	406	6.7	15.8	11.2
40 151	...	Woods	3 332	9 103	2 461	2.7	8 811	49	134	28	81	141	5.6	12.6	16.5
40 153	...	Woodward	3 218	18 976	1 736	5.9	17 980	132	465	80	319	575	6.9	16.8	12.6
41 000	...	OREGON	248 647	2 842 321	X	11.4	2 636 787	46 178	38 496	69 269	51 591	112 707	7.1	14.5	13.3
41 001	...	Baker	7 947	15 317	1 972	1.9	15 024	30	147	52	64	276	6.7	15.3	10.1
41 003	...	Benton	1 752	70 811	626	40.4	65 116	606	553	3 891	645	1 735	6.2	12.7	24.5
41 005	6442	Clackamas	4 839	278 850	177	57.6	268 479	1 134	1 971	4 827	2 439	7 129	7.0	15.4	12.4
41 007	...	Clatsop	2 143	33 301	1 181	15.5	32 118	114	373	443	253	648	6.9	14.7	12.3
41 009	...	Columbia	1 701	37 557	1 059	22.1	36 539	42	511	284	181	684	7.4	16.5	12.1
41 011	...	Coos	4 145	60 273	719	14.5	57 787	144	1 401	577	364	1 353	6.4	14.6	11.2
41 013	...	Crook	7 717	14 111	2 045	1.8	13 637	11	221	47	195	388	7.3	15.6	12.2
41 015	...	Curry	4 215	19 327	1 713	4.6	18 626	31	462	122	86	354	5.6	12.0	8.3
41 017	...	Deschutes	7 817	74 958	599	9.6	73 343	85	648	444	438	1 526	6.9	14.9	11.4
41 019	...	Douglas	13 045	94 649	490	7.3	91 718	143	1 479	673	636	2 225	7.1	15.4	12.1
41 021	...	Gilliam	3 119	1 717	3 083	0.6	1 693	0	10	9	5	30	6.6	17.0	8.1
41 023	...	Grant	11 730	7 853	2 588	0.7	7 691	6	87	16	53	152	6.9	15.8	10.8
41 025	...	Harney	26 249	7 060	2 653	0.3	6 695	2	259	40	64	221	7.7	15.9	10.8
41 027	...	Hood River	1 353	16 903	1 856	12.5	15 346	46	201	305	1 005	2 752	7.6	15.5	12.1
41 029	4890	Jackson	7 214	146 389	323	20.3	140 188	340	1 863	1 429	2 569	5 949	6.7	14.4	12.5
41 031	...	Jefferson	4 613	13 676	2 083	3.0	10 144	24	2 674	62	772	1 448	10.2	16.8	12.9
41 033	...	Josephine	4 247	62 649	694	14.8	60 764	127	874	460	424	1 749	6.3	13.9	10.5
41 035	...	Klamath	15 397	57 702	754	3.7	53 191	381	2 370	461	1 299	2 984	7.1	15.1	13.9
41 037	...	Lake	21 073	7 186	2 634	0.3	6 825	5	198	46	112	270	7.4	16.3	10.6
41 039	2400	Lane	11 795	282 912	174	24.0	269 798	2 107	3 207	5 557	2 243	6 852	6.7	14.1	15.5
41 041	...	Lincoln	2 537	38 889	1 025	15.3	37 380	68	952	346	143	598	6.1	13.8	9.3
41 043	...	Linn	5 935	91 227	504	15.4	88 364	182	1 056	799	826	2 177	7.2	15.2	13.1
41 045	...	Malheur	25 609	26 038	1 419	1.0	21 243	65	224	813	3 693	5 155	8.2	17.4	13.4
41 047	7080	Marion	3 069	228 483	215	74.4	209 006	2 132	3 292	4 075	9 978	18 225	7.4	14.9	13.7
41 049	...	Morrow	5 265	7 625	2 608	1.4	6 829	8	75	30	683	825	7.8	17.8	12.3
41 051	6442	Multnomah	1 127	583 887	81	518.1	507 890	35 133	6 734	27 326	6 804	18 390	7.1	12.7	13.3
41 053	7080	Polk	1 919	49 541	848	25.8	46 206	200	749	671	1 715	2 802	6.9	15.6	15.5
41 055	...	Sherman	2 132	1 918	3 073	0.9	1 864	0	24	13	17	28	8.0	15.6	8.0
41 057	...	Tillamook	2 855	21 570	1 598	7.6	21 001	39	239	163	128	374	6.1	13.9	9.5
41 059	...	Umatilla	8 328	59 249	734	7.1	52 743	371	1 850	533	3 752	5 307	7.5	15.8	14.0
41 061	...	Union	5 275	23 598	1 510	4.5	22 830	100	248	281	139	381	6.9	16.1	15.2

1. MSA = Metropolitan Statistical Area. CMSA = Consolidated MSA. NECMA = New England county metropolitan area. PMSA = Primary MSA. See Appendix A for explanation of these concepts. See Appendix B for list of metropolitan areas identified by type, with component counties. 2. Dry land or land partially or temporarily covered by water. 3. Hispanic persons may be of any race.

STATE County	Population, 1990 (cont'd) — Age of population (cont'd) Percent — 25 to 34 years	35 to 44 years	45 to 54 years	55 to 64 years	65 to 74 years	75 years and over	Percent female	Population–Change and components of change — Change 1980–1990 — Number	Percent	Components of change, 1980–1986 — Total persons, 1986	Total persons, 1980	Net change — Number	Percent	Natural increase — Births	Deaths
	14	15	16	17	18	19	20	21	22	23	24	25	26	27	28
OKLAHOMA—Con.															
McCurtain	14.0	13.3	10.7	9.2	7.7	6.5	52.1	-2 718	-7.5	36 300	36 151	100	0.3	3 600	2 500
McIntosh	11.3	11.4	11.6	13.7	12.7	8.9	51.8	1 217	7.8	17 700	15 562	2 200	14.0	1 300	1 400
Major	13.4	13.4	10.8	9.8	9.5	9.8	51.5	-717	-8.2	9 100	8 772	300	3.2	900	600
Marshall	12.9	11.6	10.8	11.5	13.0	9.9	52.0	279	2.6	11 800	10 550	1 200	11.5	800	900
Mayes	13.8	13.4	11.5	10.3	9.2	6.4	51.0	1 105	3.4	35 000	32 261	2 700	8.3	3 100	2 200
Murray	12.7	14.0	10.4	10.8	10.2	9.1	51.3	-105	-0.9	13 100	12 147	1 000	7.9	1 200	1 000
Muskogee	14.9	13.9	9.9	9.3	8.7	7.1	52.1	1 045	1.6	70 300	67 033	3 200	4.8	7 500	4 900
Noble	15.2	13.5	11.1	9.3	7.9	8.4	51.4	-528	-4.6	11 800	11 573	200	1.6	1 200	900
Nowata	12.8	13.1	11.1	11.2	9.9	9.3	51.2	-1 494	-13.0	11 000	11 486	-500	-4.7	1 000	900
Okfuskee	14.1	12.7	11.0	9.9	9.3	8.6	49.2	426	3.8	11 600	11 125	500	4.2	1 100	900
Oklahoma	18.1	14.8	9.9	8.6	7.0	5.1	52.0	30 678	5.4	630 300	568 933	61 400	10.8	73 100	31 600
Okmulgee	13.2	13.1	10.8	9.5	9.2	8.0	51.7	-2 679	-6.8	40 000	39 169	800	2.1	4 000	3 100
Osage	14.9	15.3	11.4	9.4	7.9	5.8	50.3	2 318	5.9	41 100	39 327	1 800	4.5	3 800	2 000
Ottawa	12.5	12.8	10.5	10.8	10.9	7.6	52.6	-2 309	-7.0	33 900	32 870	1 100	3.2	2 900	2 300
Pawnee	13.8	14.4	11.4	9.7	9.1	7.1	50.5	265	1.7	17 300	15 310	2 000	12.8	1 600	1 100
Payne	16.7	11.7	7.8	6.3	5.7	5.2	50.0	-928	-1.5	64 900	62 435	2 400	3.9	6 000	2 700
Pittsburg	14.0	13.5	11.0	10.8	9.9	8.3	51.0	57	0.1	43 900	40 524	3 300	8.2	3 500	2 900
Pontotoc	13.9	13.1	9.8	9.2	8.7	8.1	52.7	1 521	4.7	34 800	32 598	2 200	6.9	3 200	2 400
Pottawatomie	14.3	13.7	10.5	9.1	7.6	6.8	52.2	3 521	6.4	61 900	55 239	6 700	12.0	6 000	3 900
Pushmataha	12.1	12.6	11.8	11.6	10.0	8.8	50.9	-776	-6.6	12 100	11 773	300	2.4	1 100	900
Roger Mills	13.6	13.6	10.5	9.3	9.6	8.6	50.7	-652	-13.6	5 600	4 799	800	16.5	500	300
Rogers	14.8	16.1	12.7	9.2	6.1	4.1	50.6	8 734	18.8	55 700	46 436	9 300	20.0	5 100	2 000
Seminole	13.2	12.7	10.4	10.0	9.8	8.8	52.4	-2 053	-7.5	29 000	27 465	1 500	5.6	2 900	2 200
Sequoyah	14.4	13.7	11.4	9.4	7.4	5.8	51.2	3 079	10.0	34 900	30 749	4 100	13.4	3 100	1 900
Stephens	14.0	14.1	9.8	10.8	9.8	8.4	52.3	-1 120	-2.6	44 600	43 419	1 100	2.6	4 500	3 000
Texas	14.9	14.0	10.3	9.4	7.3	5.7	50.4	-1 308	-7.4	18 000	17 727	300	1.7	2 100	900
Tillman	12.5	11.5	10.0	9.4	10.1	10.2	52.1	-2 014	-16.2	11 300	12 398	-1 100	-8.9	1 200	900
Tulsa	18.1	15.7	10.1	8.4	6.7	4.8	51.8	32 748	7.0	517 000	470 593	46 400	9.9	55 300	24 700
Wagoner	15.2	16.5	12.2	8.1	5.8	3.9	50.7	6 082	14.5	50 400	41 801	8 600	20.7	4 200	1 700
Washington	14.1	14.9	11.3	10.3	9.4	6.8	52.2	-47	-0.1	44 900	48 113	-3 200	-6.7	5 100	2 900
Washita	13.9	12.5	10.1	10.0	10.2	9.6	51.7	-2 357	-17.1	13 600	13 798	-200	-1.1	1 800	1 000
Woods	12.4	11.3	9.7	9.6	10.8	11.5	52.1	-1 820	-16.7	10 400	10 923	-600	-5.0	900	900
Woodward	16.8	14.2	10.4	9.1	7.1	6.2	50.0	-2 196	-10.4	21 800	21 172	600	2.8	2 900	1 100
OREGON	15.9	16.7	10.4	8.3	7.9	5.9	50.8	209 321	7.9	2 698 000	2 633 000	65 000	2.5	255 000	141 000
Baker	13.3	14.0	11.2	10.5	10.2	8.6	50.2	-817	-5.1	15 500	16 134	-600	-3.7	1 500	1 100
Benton	16.0	15.7	8.8	6.5	5.7	4.0	49.4	2 600	3.8	64 600	68 211	-3 600	-5.3	5 600	2 300
Clackamas	15.1	18.4	12.2	8.1	6.7	4.8	50.9	36 939	15.3	256 900	241 911	15 000	6.2	21 200	11 100
Clatsop	14.5	16.0	10.2	9.2	9.2	7.0	50.3	812	2.5	32 600	32 489	100	0.4	3 100	2 100
Columbia	14.3	17.0	11.7	8.4	7.5	5.1	50.0	1 911	5.4	36 900	35 646	1 200	3.4	3 200	1 800
Coos	13.7	14.9	11.3	10.6	10.3	7.0	50.6	-3 774	-5.9	59 900	64 047	-4 200	-6.5	5 700	3 700
Crook	13.7	15.1	10.5	9.7	9.5	6.4	49.9	1 020	7.8	13 200	13 091	100	0.7	1 300	800
Curry	11.4	14.0	10.8	13.5	15.7	8.7	50.6	2 335	13.7	16 900	16 992	-100	-0.8	1 300	1 100
Deschutes	15.1	17.9	10.8	9.1	8.7	5.2	50.2	12 816	20.6	68 700	62 142	6 500	10.5	6 300	3 000
Douglas	13.8	15.2	10.9	10.2	9.2	6.2	50.5	901	1.0	93 200	93 748	-600	-0.6	8 800	4 900
Gilliam	14.2	14.0	9.5	11.2	11.3	8.0	50.1	-340	-16.5	1 800	2 057	-200	-11.8	200	100
Grant	14.2	15.9	11.6	10.3	8.3	6.2	49.7	-357	-4.3	8 400	8 210	200	1.8	800	500
Harney	14.6	15.0	12.1	10.1	8.0	5.9	49.7	-1 254	-15.1	7 300	8 314	-1 000	-11.9	700	400
Hood River	16.4	15.9	10.2	8.4	8.0	6.0	49.0	1 068	6.7	16 200	15 835	400	2.6	1 700	900
Jackson	13.7	16.3	10.9	9.4	9.5	6.7	51.2	13 933	10.5	140 000	132 456	7 500	5.7	12 200	7 100
Jefferson	15.5	13.7	9.5	9.0	7.7	4.8	49.8	2 077	17.9	12 300	11 599	700	6.1	1 500	600
Josephine	12.1	14.8	11.1	10.7	12.2	8.3	51.4	3 794	6.4	68 200	58 855	9 300	15.8	5 100	3 900
Klamath	14.1	15.4	10.5	9.6	8.6	5.7	49.6	-1 415	-2.4	57 500	59 117	-1 600	-2.7	5 700	3 100
Lake	13.6	15.3	11.5	10.8	8.6	5.8	49.7	-346	-4.6	7 400	7 532	-200	-2.1	800	400
Lane	15.6	16.9	10.3	7.9	7.6	5.5	51.3	7 686	2.8	263 200	275 226	-12 000	-4.4	24 900	12 300
Lincoln	12.9	16.0	10.3	11.5	12.7	7.3	51.8	3 625	10.3	36 700	35 264	1 400	4.0	3 200	2 600
Linn	14.8	15.3	10.9	8.7	8.7	6.2	50.8	1 732	1.9	89 000	89 495	-500	-0.5	8 500	4 500
Malheur	12.8	13.0	10.0	9.6	8.9	6.7	51.0	-858	-3.2	28 300	26 896	1 400	5.4	3 100	1 400
Marion	16.1	15.6	10.0	7.9	7.8	6.5	50.4	23 791	11.6	215 400	204 692	10 700	5.2	21 500	11 400
Morrow	14.4	15.6	10.6	9.9	6.6	5.2	49.4	106	1.4	8 100	7 519	600	7.6	900	300
Multnomah	18.4	17.6	9.6	7.6	7.4	6.2	51.4	21 240	3.8	567 000	562 647	4 300	0.8	55 100	35 000
Polk	13.2	15.7	9.9	8.3	8.4	6.6	51.8	4 338	9.6	46 700	45 203	1 500	3.4	4 200	2 400
Sherman	14.1	15.5	9.2	12.7	11.0	5.8	48.7	-254	-11.7	2 100	2 172	-100	-2.7	200	100
Tillamook	12.5	14.3	10.3	12.6	13.0	7.9	50.8	406	1.9	21 100	21 164	-100	-0.3	1 900	1 400
Umatilla	15.5	15.0	10.0	8.4	8.0	5.9	49.4	388	0.7	60 200	58 861	1 400	2.4	6 400	3 200
Union	13.2	15.8	10.2	8.4	7.5	6.6	50.7	-323	-1.4	23 700	23 921	-200	-0.9	2 400	1 200

STATE County	Population–(cont'd) Components of change, 1980-1986 (cont'd) Net migration	Households, 1990 Number	Households, 1990 Percent change, 1980–1990	Households, 1990 Persons per household	Households, 1990 Percent Female family householder[1]	Households, 1990 Percent One-person	Births, 1988 Total	Births, 1988 Rate[2]	Births, 1988 Low birth weight[3] (Number)	Deaths, 1987 Number Total	Deaths, 1987 Number Infant[4]	Deaths, 1987 Rate Total[2]	Deaths, 1987 Rate Infant[5]	Marriages, 1984 Number	Marriages, 1984 Rate[2]
	29	30	31	32	33	34	35	36	37	38	39	40	41	42	43
OKLAHOMA—Con.															
McCurtain	-1 000	12 234	-1.1	2.69	13.4	23.0	609	16.6	44	367	5	10.1	9.0	418	11.6
McIntosh	2 300	6 786	14.3	2.43	9.4	24.3	171	9.9	12	255	1	14.6	4.7	123	7.2
Major	-100	3 121	-4.6	2.54	6.0	23.6	110	12.5	7	87	2	9.8	21.5	52	5.5
Marshall	1 400	4 350	4.6	2.41	8.2	25.2	121	10.3	10	132	1	11.3	8.3	116	10.1
Mayes	1 700	12 672	9.0	2.61	8.4	21.7	508	14.6	29	374	5	10.7	10.8	270	7.5
Murray	700	4 651	2.5	2.49	9.2	26.3	137	11.0	13	146	0	11.5	0.0	84	6.3
Muskogee	700	25 174	1.8	2.59	12.5	25.5	1 019	14.7	69	757	9	10.9	9.1	699	9.9
Noble	-200	4 225	-2.8	2.55	7.7	26.0	163	14.3	6	138	1	11.9	6.4	109	9.2
Nowata	-700	3 994	-7.7	2.45	8.6	26.4	110	10.5	5	122	2	11.5	17.1	75	6.5
Okfuskee	300	4 164	0.9	2.58	10.8	25.8	142	12.6	10	158	3	13.7	17.6	75	6.4
Oklahoma	19 800	237 879	7.8	2.46	12.6	28.6	10 148	16.5	760	5 184	112	8.4	11.1	8 545	13.6
Okmulgee	-100	14 044	-1.9	2.52	12.4	26.5	533	13.7	34	466	7	11.7	12.3	380	9.4
Osage	0	15 383	7.0	2.63	9.2	23.3	488	12.4	38	295	1	7.4	2.1	96	2.3
Ottawa	500	12 124	-1.0	2.42	9.7	27.3	458	14.0	22	379	6	11.6	15.1	4 573	134.9
Pawnee	1 500	6 006	4.5	2.57	7.2	23.1	212	12.8	9	164	2	9.7	8.6	124	7.3
Payne	-800	23 834	7.8	2.34	7.6	29.1	757	11.9	40	464	5	7.3	6.6	647	9.7
Pittsburg	2 700	15 911	5.8	2.44	10.2	26.4	503	11.7	31	467	5	10.8	10.3	431	10.0
Pontotoc	1 400	13 310	8.5	2.46	10.3	27.1	459	13.3	24	386	5	11.1	10.7	383	11.0
Pottawatomie	4 500	21 796	8.6	2.60	10.2	24.0	798	13.5	53	599	11	10.0	13.3	640	10.3
Pushmataha	100	4 370	0.3	2.48	8.4	26.5	149	12.5	7	130	1	11.0	6.7	83	6.8
Roger Mills	600	1 586	-10.3	2.59	6.3	23.8	51	10.0	1	48	1	9.1	18.5	23	3.8
Rogers	6 200	19 866	26.9	2.75	7.7	17.8	764	13.7	39	376	9	6.7	11.6	388	7.2
Seminole	800	9 665	-4.9	2.57	11.9	25.7	364	13.4	23	321	4	11.5	10.8	263	9.0
Sequoyah	2 900	12 335	17.8	2.71	11.3	20.8	479	13.3	24	333	7	9.4	13.4	289	8.6
Stephens	-400	16 764	1.5	2.49	8.2	24.5	534	12.4	36	467	5	10.9	10.0	370	8.1
Texas	-900	6 214	-1.9	2.57	7.4	23.4	222	13.2	16	144	5	8.3	20.0	179	9.8
Tillman	-1 400	3 933	-16.0	2.57	10.2	26.4	181	16.3	21	172	2	15.1	11.7	76	6.4
Tulsa	15 800	202 537	11.5	2.43	11.0	28.8	8 396	16.2	557	4 007	76	7.7	9.0	5 925	11.5
Wagoner	6 000	16 946	23.1	2.81	8.6	17.2	640	12.6	40	314	9	6.2	14.5	279	5.6
Washington	-5 400	19 242	2.6	2.46	7.9	24.8	603	13.4	37	514	9	11.4	14.7	517	10.8
Washita	-900	4 421	-14.0	2.53	6.4	24.1	140	11.6	13	132	1	10.6	7.0	93	6.2
Woods	-500	3 803	-14.1	2.26	6.2	32.4	98	9.9	3	119	2	11.8	15.4	117	10.6
Woodward	-1 200	7 087	-6.5	2.57	8.1	24.2	256	12.9	11	170	2	8.5	7.1	267	11.6
OREGON	-49 000	1 103 313	11.3	2.52	9.2	25.3	40 052	14.5	2 101	24 265	403	8.9	10.4	23 074	8.6
Baker	-1 000	6 118	-0.8	2.45	7.2	26.0	185	12.3	12	170	0	11.2	0.0	128	8.0
Benton	-6 900	26 126	9.0	2.47	7.1	25.2	864	13.3	23	402	5	6.2	5.7	524	7.9
Clackamas	4 900	103 530	22.2	2.67	8.2	20.5	3 575	13.2	182	2 001	33	7.6	10.0	1 939	7.7
Clatsop	-800	13 374	4.5	2.43	8.3	28.0	431	13.1	12	310	4	9.5	9.0	320	9.8
Columbia	-200	13 910	9.2	2.68	7.6	21.3	520	13.6	25	323	6	8.6	12.8	275	7.5
Coos	-6 200	24 134	1.1	2.45	9.1	24.6	778	12.8	39	608	7	10.1	9.3	572	9.3
Crook	-400	5 455	11.5	2.56	6.4	22.7	216	15.9	8	135	3	10.2	17.1	144	11.1
Curry	-300	8 311	22.9	2.30	5.9	24.4	227	12.1	7	203	5	11.5	21.4	171	10.2
Deschutes	3 300	29 217	27.2	2.54	7.6	21.0	980	14.1	43	545	11	7.9	11.6	583	9.0
Douglas	-4 400	35 872	7.5	2.60	8.8	21.5	1 278	13.3	72	891	11	9.4	8.1	948	10.2
Gilliam	-300	696	-10.5	2.47	5.0	25.3	16	9.4	0	14	0	8.2	0.0	16	8.4
Grant	-100	3 092	2.9	2.51	5.9	24.6	97	11.5	3	53	2	6.3	18.0	74	9.0
Harney	-1 300	2 760	-6.2	2.54	7.2	24.6	118	15.7	8	74	2	10.1	19.6	62	8.5
Hood River	-400	6 425	7.8	2.59	7.5	24.2	291	17.9	20	154	0	9.6	0.0	202	12.2
Jackson	2 500	57 238	16.8	2.50	9.1	24.0	1 913	13.1	99	1 344	12	9.4	6.4	1 297	9.5
Jefferson	-200	4 744	20.6	2.84	9.8	18.8	297	23.6	21	113	6	9.1	22.1	126	10.1
Josephine	8 100	25 081	14.6	2.46	9.3	23.7	840	11.8	34	707	10	10.3	12.5	549	8.7
Klamath	-4 200	22 341	3.0	2.54	8.4	24.2	822	14.3	50	497	9	8.7	10.6	459	7.9
Lake	-600	2 765	-0.9	2.57	6.3	22.5	107	14.3	8	68	1	8.9	9.1	61	7.8
Lane	-24 600	110 799	7.0	2.49	9.4	25.1	3 817	14.1	172	2 256	36	8.5	9.6	2 354	8.9
Lincoln	800	16 455	12.6	2.34	7.7	26.5	478	12.4	19	429	3	11.4	6.4	414	11.2
Linn	-4 500	34 716	5.9	2.60	9.0	22.2	1 313	14.4	69	816	20	9.1	16.0	794	8.8
Malheur	-200	9 457	1.9	2.71	8.8	24.1	467	17.4	19	243	5	8.9	11.4	199	6.9
Marion	700	83 494	12.5	2.60	10.3	24.6	3 430	15.5	170	1 995	39	9.2	11.8	1 995	9.4
Morrow	0	2 803	6.1	2.71	7.5	21.5	108	14.4	5	64	1	8.1	7.9	63	8.0
Multnomah	-15 800	242 140	3.9	2.36	10.9	31.9	8 923	15.8	600	5 762	88	10.3	10.4	5 117	9.1
Polk	-200	18 167	10.7	2.64	9.1	21.9	625	12.9	35	407	6	8.6	9.2	279	6.1
Sherman	-100	784	-4.4	2.44	5.6	26.1	24	12.0	0	7	0	3.5	0.0	9	4.1
Tillamook	-500	8 846	5.3	2.39	7.1	25.7	247	11.3	13	261	6	12.1	29.6	210	9.7
Umatilla	-1 800	22 020	4.5	2.60	9.5	24.3	901	15.0	46	540	12	8.9	12.7	498	8.2
Union	-1 400	9 035	3.8	2.55	7.6	24.0	318	13.6	13	193	3	8.3	9.7	208	8.4

1. No spouse present. 2. Per 1,000 resident population estimated as of July 1 of the year shown. 3. Under 2,500 grams. 4. Deaths of infants under 1 year old. 5. Deaths of infants under 1 year old per 1,000 live births.

STATE County	Divorces, 1984: Number	Divorces, 1984: Rate[1]	Physicians, active non–Federal, 1989: Number[2]	Physicians: Rate[3]	Hospitals, 1989: Number	Hospitals, 1989: Beds: Number	Hospitals, 1989: Beds: Rate[3]	Nursing homes,[4] 1986: Number	Nursing homes, 1986: Beds	Serious crimes known to police, 1988: Number: Total[5]	Serious crimes: Number: Violent[6]	Serious crimes: Rate[3]	Education: Public school enrollment[7]: 1986–1987	Education: Public school enrollment: 1980	Education: Attainment,[8] 1980: Percent 12 yrs. or more	Education: Attainment, 1980: Percent 16 yrs. or more
	44	45	46	47	48	49	50	51	52	53	54	55	56	57	58	59
OKLAHOMA—Con.																
McCurtain	177	4.9	8	22	1	89	243	6	466	1 280	113	3 507	7 950	8 537	47.6	7.9
McIntosh	86	5.0	9	52	1	33	191	6	391	668	68	3 828	3 062	2 947	48.4	8.1
Major	34	3.6	1	12	1	24	279	1	100	188	5	2 142	1 570	1 684	60.7	10.4
Marshall	57	5.0	4	34	1	40	336	2	200	314	0	2 691	1 620	1 992	52.1	8.1
Mayes	225	6.3	9	26	2	75	215	8	441	915	50	2 614	6 421	6 686	58.2	9.0
Murray	75	5.6	10	81	2	234	1 902	4	220	413	28	3 261	2 304	2 430	53.5	10.1
Muskogee	596	8.4	97	141	2	388	562	14	1 058	3 569	277	5 098	13 741	13 248	59.1	12.0
Noble	71	6.0	4	35	1	28	248	1	82	216	28	1 851	2 225	2 171	62.3	8.8
Nowata	74	6.4	3	29	1	24	233	2	93	323	31	2 972	1 948	2 376	53.0	7.5
Okfuskee	77	6.5	2	18	0	0	0	2	101	174	15	1 517	2 276	2 430	46.4	7.1
Oklahoma	4 383	7.0	1 885	309	17	3 983	653	38	3 719	58 535	4 200	9 425	105 034	99 842	73.7	19.2
Okmulgee	323	8.0	23	60	2	118	306	5	470	1 849	170	4 647	6 934	8 022	54.8	8.8
Osage	235	5.6	7	18	3	80	205	12	864	1 337	112	3 319	5 113	8 031	63.6	10.8
Ottawa	236	7.0	19	59	2	178	549	8	432	1 164	50	3 548	5 563	6 476	58.7	8.9
Pawnee	98	5.8	6	36	2	58	352	2	102	293	12	1 749	2 841	3 122	61.5	9.8
Payne	362	5.4	69	109	3	242	382	7	514	2 715	182	4 247	9 152	8 657	74.6	27.4
Pittsburg	217	5.0	49	114	1	176	410	10	532	1 663	103	3 834	7 850	8 179	54.9	9.3
Pontotoc	233	6.7	51	148	3	227	658	6	399	1 285	127	3 703	6 468	5 932	58.8	15.3
Pottawatomie	470	7.6	55	94	3	202	346	9	742	3 651	308	6 042	12 195	11 587	61.8	10.8
Pushmataha	75	6.1	5	42	1	47	398	1	133	344	51	2 875	2 255	2 613	49.0	8.3
Roger Mills	33	5.5	1	20	1	15	300	1	36	97	5	1 801	995	985	58.8	10.4
Rogers	393	7.3	33	59	2	123	219	5	360	1 704	178	3 057	10 585	11 063	64.9	10.4
Seminole	198	6.8	15	56	2	71	266	3	250	1 340	92	4 799	5 629	5 778	54.7	9.3
Sequoyah	202	6.0	7	19	1	50	137	4	335	518	8	1 467	7 388	7 298	48.2	8.3
Stephens	393	8.6	29	68	1	100	236	10	824	1 787	95	4 207	8 537	8 277	61.2	11.7
Texas	96	5.3	10	61	1	53	323	1	77	479	22	2 729	3 629	3 538	68.2	15.5
Tillman	67	5.7	4	36	1	48	436	2	150	338	48	3 026	2 288	2 535	52.4	11.7
Tulsa	5 123	10.0	1 167	224	11	2 758	530	30	3 300	40 736	4 053	7 880	92 364	85 008	75.7	19.7
Wagoner	413	8.3	6	12	1	100	195	3	241	962	66	1 881	5 698	10 106	63.3	12.0
Washington	374	7.8	83	186	1	312	698	5	471	2 133	114	5 021	8 773	9 065	75.1	24.2
Washita	79	5.3	2	17	1	28	241	3	196	145	5	1 154	2 264	2 675	60.8	8.3
Woods	47	4.3	3	31	1	120	1 237	3	184	218	33	2 143	1 604	1 748	66.8	20.8
Woodward	178	7.7	20	104	2	373	1 943	3	182	736	56	3 654	3 927	4 205	66.7	10.9
OREGON	15 631	5.8	5 564	197	80	10 287	365	268	18 390	192 933	14 919	7 049	444 879	472 611	75.6	17.9
Baker	98	6.1	13	87	1	122	813	2	149	629	31	4 112	2 608	3 192	69.7	13.0
Benton	302	4.6	129	196	1	164	250	4	300	3 952	76	6 051	8 091	10 728	86.1	36.6
Clackamas	1 120	4.5	425	152	4	682	244	39	2 298	13 176	531	4 958	44 968	49 930	79.4	19.2
Clatsop	171	5.3	40	120	2	92	276	6	273	1 811	92	5 537	4 698	6 043	74.4	14.3
Columbia	460	12.6	15	38	1	38	97	2	133	1 226	70	3 266	8 121	7 784	69.3	10.0
Coos	378	6.2	98	160	3	177	288	6	419	3 456	190	5 733	10 695	12 825	68.0	11.2
Crook	112	8.6	10	72	1	25	180	2	105	472	7	3 527	2 369	2 574	69.6	9.4
Curry	103	6.1	13	66	1	24	122	1	71	855	41	4 827	2 771	3 015	68.1	11.3
Deschutes	408	6.3	138	194	2	231	324	4	292	3 712	75	5 292	11 982	11 505	78.3	16.6
Douglas	626	6.8	122	125	6	658	673	5	502	4 701	178	4 964	16 713	18 877	67.9	10.5
Gilliam	4	2.1	0	0	0	0	0	0	0	32	0	3 062	341	400	79.0	17.1
Grant	60	7.3	6	71	1	39	459	1	52	171	18	1 976	1 544	1 656	70.5	11.2
Harney	36	4.9	5	66	1	38	500	1	49	195	13	2 691	1 458	1 749	72.0	12.7
Hood River	302	18.3	23	140	1	32	195	1	131	627	27	3 846	2 927	2 753	69.5	11.3
Jackson	981	7.2	256	171	3	517	345	13	727	7 151	548	4 969	23 905	24 990	73.9	15.3
Jefferson	62	5.0	6	47	1	104	819	1	68	513	11	4 111	2 525	2 601	70.2	13.6
Josephine	470	7.5	80	109	2	144	197	6	485	3 648	135	5 277	9 881	10 868	68.1	10.9
Klamath	398	6.8	65	112	1	262	453	3	326	3 307	174	5 775	10 135	11 479	74.3	12.4
Lake	40	5.1	5	66	1	68	895	1	47	83	6	1 085	1 446	1 577	67.4	13.1
Lane	1 825	6.9	467	170	5	669	244	19	1 493	16 607	882	6 234	43 038	48 143	77.6	20.4
Lincoln	203	5.5	40	102	2	74	188	4	206	2 261	133	6 023	5 301	5 184	72.4	14.4
Linn	493	5.5	93	101	2	139	150	8	510	5 133	302	5 693	16 260	17 908	69.5	10.6
Malheur	123	4.3	37	139	2	146	549	3	230	1 188	48	4 277	5 585	5 923	67.7	12.0
Marion	940	4.4	376	166	4	1 208	535	21	1 603	16 089	777	7 407	37 882	35 448	73.5	16.7
Morrow	39	4.9	5	68	1	44	595	1	28	259	16	3 217	1 809	1 655	71.8	11.7
Multnomah	3 107	5.5	2 479	436	17	3 589	631	67	4 572	77 398	9 446	13 632	78 730	82 144	76.4	19.8
Polk	489	10.7	17	34	1	44	88	8	447	2 679	148	5 523	5 214	8 195	73.7	20.0
Sherman	3	1.4	0	0	0	0	0	0	0	51	0	2 534	380	448	75.4	14.3
Tillamook	206	9.5	23	104	2	112	505	1	101	572	45	2 607	3 227	3 540	68.2	11.2
Umatilla	319	5.2	77	128	3	192	318	5	419	2 793	157	4 610	11 431	11 518	71.3	12.2
Union	103	4.2	41	175	1	69	295	3	196	729	104	3 136	4 423	4 797	75.0	15.5

1. Per 1,000 resident population estimated as of July 1 of the year shown. 2. As of end of year. 3. Per 100,000 resident population as of July 1 of the year shown. 4. Preliminary. Covers nursing homes with 3 or more beds. 5. Data for serious crimes have not been adjusted for underreporting, this may affect comparability between geographic areas or over time. 6. Includes murder and nonnegligent manslaughter, forcible rape, robbery, and aggravated assault. 7. The 1986–1987 data are based on administrative reports obtained by the U.S. National Center for Education Statistics. The 1980 data are based on the 1980 Census of Population and Housing. 8. Persons 25 years old or older.

STATE County	Education (cont'd): Local government expenditures for education,[1] 1982: Total (Mil dol)	Education (cont'd): Local government expenditures for education,[1] 1982: Per capita (Dollars)	Social Security Program December 1988: Beneficiaries: Total	Social Security Program December 1988: Beneficiaries: Rate[2]	Social Security Program December 1988: Payments ($1,000)	Supplemental Security Income Program recipients June 1986	Money income: Per capita[3]: 1987 Income, (Dollars)	Money income: Per capita[3]: 1979: Current dollars	Money income: Per capita[3]: 1979: Constant 1987 dollars	Money income: Median household income 1979 (Dollars)	Money income: Percent below poverty level, 1979: Persons	Money income: Percent below poverty level, 1979: Families	Housing units, 1990: Total	Housing units, 1990: Percent change, 1980–1990
	60	61	62	63	64	65	66	67	68	69	70	71	72	73
OKLAHOMA—Con.														
McCurtain	18.6	519	6 520	178.1	2 490	1 870	6 457	4 532	7 091	10 243	24.1	19.8	13 828	0.7
McIntosh	6.3	385	4 430	256.1	1 846	726	7 026	4 832	7 561	9 864	23.7	19.3	10 708	28.6
Major	5.6	580	1 670	189.8	730	54	9 578	7 120	11 141	15 215	10.9	9.6	3 855	8.1
Marshall	3.9	358	2 895	245.3	1 222	334	8 954	5 673	8 877	9 970	19.4	14.2	7 389	43.2
Mayes	13.2	390	5 165	148.0	2 287	710	7 833	5 576	8 725	12 623	15.5	12.7	15 470	11.4
Murray	5.9	452	2 590	207.2	1 138	382	8 149	5 683	8 892	12 669	14.1	12.2	5 742	11.5
Muskogee	32.2	470	13 450	194.4	5 861	2 294	8 488	5 872	9 188	12 376	18.7	14.9	28 882	5.1
Noble	5.8	487	2 110	185.1	959	172	8 981	6 476	10 133	13 956	11.0	7.7	4 894	0.5
Nowata	4.5	373	2 335	222.4	1 062	234	8 708	6 130	9 592	13 293	13.1	9.7	4 534	-6.6
Okfuskee	6.6	573	2 610	231.0	1 042	546	6 357	4 468	6 991	9 123	24.3	20.5	4 894	2.5
Oklahoma	231.5	383	89 100	145.2	42 802	7 526	11 580	7 985	12 494	16 456	10.7	8.1	279 340	15.5
Okmulgee	15.5	381	8 000	205.7	3 588	1 284	7 570	5 291	8 279	10 976	19.5	15.4	16 431	5.2
Osage	13.3	319	4 335	109.7	1 964	446	9 298	6 778	10 606	15 760	10.8	9.1	18 196	11.6
Ottawa	15.5	464	8 020	244.5	3 642	800	7 349	5 554	8 690	11 965	15.8	11.8	14 064	0.8
Pawnee	5.7	355	2 910	176.4	1 296	276	8 950	6 522	10 205	14 014	12.0	8.9	7 407	15.1
Payne	20.8	317	8 350	131.3	3 967	624	9 185	6 061	9 484	11 939	16.6	9.2	27 381	12.9
Pittsburg	17.2	416	8 810	204.9	3 593	1 336	8 080	5 351	8 373	11 386	16.5	13.2	19 433	8.2
Pontotoc	13.4	395	7 080	204.6	3 189	978	8 318	5 825	9 114	12 056	17.0	12.8	15 094	13.5
Pottawatomie	27.0	458	10 435	176.3	4 438	1 266	8 598	6 008	9 401	13 397	14.2	10.9	24 528	11.5
Pushmataha	5.2	444	2 775	233.2	1 050	624	6 352	4 490	7 026	8 785	26.7	22.9	5 190	3.8
Roger Mills	3.1	505	915	179.4	346	74	9 447	6 736	10 540	12 865	15.0	12.9	2 048	2.1
Rogers	25.6	500	4 900	88.0	2 266	570	9 843	6 953	10 879	18 540	8.3	6.5	21 455	26.5
Seminole	13.6	473	5 825	214.2	2 528	1 034	7 298	5 502	8 609	11 429	18.8	13.5	11 404	1.3
Sequoyah	15.0	475	5 980	166.6	2 387	1 354	7 050	4 727	7 396	11 131	20.1	16.3	14 314	20.4
Stephens	19.0	406	9 495	220.8	4 493	876	9 169	6 840	10 703	14 966	11.3	8.5	19 675	9.5
Texas	10.3	576	2 610	155.4	1 304	126	10 378	7 027	10 995	16 585	8.9	7.0	7 328	3.5
Tillman	5.3	438	2 490	224.3	1 095	374	7 895	5 934	9 285	10 879	22.8	18.1	4 704	-10.5
Tulsa	226.9	452	80 750	156.1	41 853	5 940	12 084	8 444	13 212	17 443	9.9	7.1	227 834	16.6
Wagoner	10.6	230	4 455	87.5	1 977	624	9 256	6 484	10 146	17 465	11.0	9.0	19 262	22.7
Washington	21.7	417	10 100	224.4	5 327	456	12 861	8 921	13 959	19 076	7.3	5.1	21 707	7.2
Washita	7.4	422	2 525	208.7	1 099	164	9 040	6 776	10 602	15 033	10.9	9.2	6 101	2.7
Woods	7.4	667	2 140	216.2	1 028	94	10 973	7 441	11 643	13 550	11.6	7.1	4 782	-2.8
Woodward	10.2	409	2 940	147.7	1 414	200	9 975	7 601	11 893	18 188	9.2	6.8	8 512	4.2
OREGON	1 539.0	577	473 000	171.0	238 001	26 822	11 045	7 556	11 823	16 780	10.7	7.7	1 193 567	10.2
Baker	9.2	558	3 620	239.7	1 692	280	8 674	6 196	9 695	13 326	12.8	9.7	7 525	3.0
Benton	33.1	484	7 530	115.7	3 858	326	11 521	7 162	11 206	16 191	13.6	7.4	27 024	7.3
Clackamas	161.4	648	34 455	127.2	17 976	1 408	12 874	8 600	13 456	21 177	6.0	4.6	109 003	20.8
Clatsop	18.5	565	6 680	203.0	3 390	296	10 503	7 555	11 821	15 262	11.6	7.8	17 367	4.5
Columbia	36.8	1 007	5 995	156.9	3 039	224	10 532	7 281	11 393	18 562	9.3	7.5	14 576	6.9
Coos	40.3	648	13 225	217.5	6 589	700	9 818	6 930	10 843	16 094	10.5	8.2	26 668	3.8
Crook	7.1	554	2 800	205.9	1 379	106	9 823	6 961	10 892	15 515	10.0	8.0	6 066	7.7
Curry	10.5	605	5 305	282.2	2 605	146	10 600	7 188	11 247	14 643	12.2	9.3	9 885	32.0
Deschutes	31.3	492	13 735	197.1	6 771	446	10 481	7 290	11 407	16 587	9.3	7.7	35 928	27.8
Douglas	56.1	608	17 945	187.1	8 766	868	9 605	6 680	10 452	16 683	11.1	8.6	38 298	7.4
Gilliam	2.2	1 055	420	247.1	215	10	10 682	7 002	10 956	15 323	7.3	7.2	932	-11.2
Grant	5.1	631	1 520	181.0	713	88	9 315	6 378	9 980	15 204	12.3	9.0	3 774	-1.0
Harney	5.8	779	1 235	164.7	610	58	9 591	6 922	10 831	16 928	8.9	7.7	3 305	-2.1
Hood River	10.0	621	2 910	178.5	1 445	124	10 380	7 521	11 768	16 124	9.5	6.9	7 569	5.8
Jackson	73.2	543	28 210	193.4	13 745	1 214	10 439	6 944	10 865	15 465	12.0	8.8	60 376	15.5
Jefferson	9.8	801	2 065	163.9	980	114	9 054	6 091	9 531	15 468	13.3	10.1	6 311	21.4
Josephine	31.3	522	16 215	228.1	7 689	728	8 670	5 875	9 193	13 075	15.6	12.6	26 912	15.4
Klamath	29.4	496	10 245	178.2	5 023	512	9 115	6 561	10 266	15 408	12.6	9.9	25 954	2.3
Lake	5.6	714	1 360	181.3	673	40	8 649	6 287	9 837	15 493	13.3	10.7	3 434	3.2
Lane	153.1	563	44 615	165.2	22 543	2 606	10 627	7 302	11 425	16 272	12.8	8.5	116 676	5.0
Lincoln	20.7	567	9 210	239.8	4 592	318	10 380	7 501	11 737	14 664	11.5	8.1	22 389	6.9
Linn	56.5	625	16 900	185.5	8 265	988	9 816	6 641	10 391	16 042	12.4	10.2	36 482	3.8
Malheur	15.5	560	5 185	192.8	2 360	304	8 134	5 478	8 571	12 994	17.4	13.9	10 649	0.1
Marion	110.8	531	43 460	196.3	21 448	3 250	10 290	7 080	11 078	16 099	10.8	8.1	86 869	9.1
Morrow	6.3	842	980	130.7	480	28	9 424	7 148	11 184	17 803	10.5	8.1	3 412	6.2
Multnomah	294.5	522	102 790	182.3	53 796	8 006	11 787	8 129	12 719	16 078	11.4	7.6	255 751	3.9
Polk	17.2	375	6 250	129.1	3 017	488	10 094	6 994	10 944	16 713	12.0	8.2	18 978	8.1
Sherman	2.2	963	450	225.0	221	12	8 948	6 232	9 751	14 028	14.4	11.1	900	-8.4
Tillamook	15.7	725	5 240	240.4	2 602	164	10 103	7 016	10 978	14 266	10.1	7.6	13 324	4.6
Umatilla	41.8	693	10 240	170.7	4 905	650	9 273	6 651	10 407	15 742	10.8	7.9	24 333	3.5
Union	17.1	693	3 975	169.9	1 897	204	9 269	6 416	10 039	14 961	12.7	9.8	9 974	2.9

1. Elementary and secondary. 2. Per 1,000 resident population estimated as of July 1 of the year shown. 3. Based on the resident population estimated as of July 1, 1988 for 1987 data and enumerated as of April 1, 1980 for 1979 data.

STATE County	Housing units, 1990 (cont'd): Occupied units: Total	Owner occupied: Percent	Owner occupied: Median value (Dollars)	Median rent (Dollars)	Civilian labor force, 1990: Total	Percent change, 1989–1990	Unemployment: Total	Unemployment: Rate[1]	Private nonfarm establishments, 1988: Number	Net change, 1987–1988	Employment[2]: Total	Per-cent change, 1987–1988	Manu-facturing	Retail trade
	74	75	76	77	78	79	80	81	82	83	84	85	86	87
OKLAHOMA—Con.														
McCurtain	12 234	73.1	29 200	146	14 945	-0.3	1 152	7.7	526	-11	6 103	-2.1	2 984	1 303
McIntosh	6 786	77.8	38 700	159	7 150	1.0	394	5.5	308	6	2 147	4.3	377	774
Major	3 121	80.8	37 700	165	3 697	-0.4	162	4.4	224	-13	1 518	5.9	0	414
Marshall	4 350	78.5	37 000	181	4 874	5.7	274	5.6	228	0	1 856	5.4	648	432
Mayes	12 672	76.8	42 400	219	15 362	1.6	1 013	6.6	616	-11	7 096	9.6	3 530	1 419
Murray	4 651	72.5	33 700	177	5 769	-0.4	435	7.5	228	-8	1 866	-3.2	207	606
Muskogee	25 174	69.9	40 900	217	31 146	1.0	2 022	6.5	1 515	-38	18 005	-1.2	4 765	4 473
Noble	4 225	75.0	33 500	176	4 991	0.6	204	4.1	239	-10	2 939	10.8	0	636
Nowata	3 994	78.1	27 900	155	4 201	8.9	289	6.9	173	6	1 253	2.1	173	310
Okfuskee	4 164	76.5	25 700	135	5 882	3.7	307	5.2	149	-16	1 312	-9.2	335	265
Oklahoma	237 879	61.3	53 300	285	325 873	0.2	18 511	5.7	18 231	-247	255 811	0.1	40 222	58 417
Okmulgee	14 044	72.6	30 900	173	14 773	-1.3	1 205	8.2	678	-10	6 017	3.3	1 357	1 663
Osage	15 383	78.6	43 300	168	16 902	1.3	942	5.6	438	-11	3 499	-6.0	1 016	672
Ottawa	12 124	73.9	30 200	179	12 066	1.0	1 016	8.4	663	23	5 882	3.6	1 716	1 568
Pawnee	6 006	79.0	39 200	195	8 836	6.7	477	5.4	301	-24	2 077	-0.4	205	685
Payne	23 834	54.5	50 700	295	32 304	0.4	1 474	4.6	1 377	-63	13 228	0.8	2 599	4 435
Pittsburg	15 911	75.4	34 700	191	17 524	-0.1	1 379	7.9	787	0	7 073	4.7	1 683	1 985
Pontotoc	13 310	69.0	39 900	201	17 195	1.2	945	5.5	867	-16	8 732	3.9	2 141	2 099
Pottawatomie	21 796	73.9	42 400	230	26 305	-0.3	1 615	6.1	1 221	-1	13 023	1.3	2 478	4 313
Pushmataha	4 370	76.6	27 700	127	5 223	5.1	375	7.2	170	0	974	-2.6	180	368
Roger Mills	1 586	79.1	25 900	118	1 914	7.8	116	6.1	78	-8	342	3.6	0	89
Rogers	19 866	79.4	63 700	268	25 059	1.0	1 770	7.1	862	2	7 858	3.4	2 567	1 946
Seminole	9 665	73.0	27 300	163	9 535	-1.5	883	9.3	538	-31	5 005	-4.7	1 291	994
Sequoyah	12 335	73.8	37 800	196	17 464	1.5	1 368	7.8	466	21	3 879	5.6	598	1 255
Stephens	16 764	74.7	39 000	204	17 694	-3.0	909	5.1	989	11	10 342	-0.7	1 661	2 388
Texas	6 214	71.6	44 500	218	8 090	2.3	298	3.7	464	-10	3 123	-7.2	271	919
Tillman	3 933	75.0	22 700	153	4 430	1.7	274	6.2	214	-10	1 751	-1.7	699	331
Tulsa	202 537	60.7	60 700	296	256 757	1.4	12 814	5.0	16 058	-94	238 989	1.0	41 620	48 136
Wagoner	16 946	79.0	58 300	244	21 257	1.8	1 156	5.4	425	-25	4 381	7.0	1 767	939
Washington	19 242	74.5	51 900	263	23 827	5.8	875	3.7	1 175	-12	17 132	-0.4	3 022	3 939
Washita	4 421	76.5	28 400	181	5 495	7.0	334	6.1	220	-14	1 395	-5.6	195	274
Woods	3 803	73.0	32 700	173	5 469	5.9	117	2.1	297	6	1 642	-5.8	50	625
Woodward	7 087	72.5	40 300	210	9 715	3.2	468	4.8	679	-26	5 260	9.2	330	1 348
OREGON	1 103 313	63.1	67 100	344	1 492 000	1.2	82 000	5.5	X	X	929 517	5.2	208 623	217 575
Baker	6 118	68.8	42 100	209	6 955	1.1	572	8.2	455	13	4 864	74.8	2 258	858
Benton	26 126	55.1	72 900	330	38 655	2.5	1 456	3.8	1 728	8	19 347	4.8	5 971	4 813
Clackamas	103 530	71.7	85 100	404	148 230	1.5	5 224	3.5	6 403	224	73 472	4.8	16 765	20 038
Clatsop	13 374	63.2	62 500	288	18 538	1.0	1 194	6.4	1 130	25	8 951	2.8	2 035	2 942
Columbia	13 910	74.1	62 800	280	17 438	0.4	1 292	7.4	691	-12	7 522	8.0	3 302	1 447
Coos	24 134	66.5	49 800	265	27 468	0.2	2 455	8.9	1 719	11	16 035	5.5	4 735	4 095
Crook	5 455	71.4	50 300	263	7 325	1.2	482	6.6	310	-7	3 806	3.4	1 733	716
Curry	8 311	72.5	83 400	316	9 798	1.0	570	5.8	591	35	3 985	10.9	1 387	1 230
Deschutes	29 217	71.0	74 500	364	41 980	5.0	2 462	5.9	2 565	53	22 916	4.9	4 596	6 209
Douglas	35 872	68.9	56 000	281	45 859	0.3	3 847	8.4	2 528	49	25 428	0.7	9 270	5 824
Gilliam	696	66.7	31 600	221	994	2.6	34	3.4	47	3	309	6.6	0	78
Grant	3 092	70.8	46 900	240	4 633	1.9	394	8.5	248	11	1 641	8.2	719	347
Harney	2 760	70.3	37 800	205	4 103	-2.1	373	9.1	206	4	1 620	12.7	623	401
Hood River	6 425	62.1	77 200	316	10 043	3.9	780	7.8	487	2	4 946	-5.8	966	1 041
Jackson	57 238	66.2	74 900	346	72 670	-0.7	4 954	6.8	3 977	72	42 578	6.4	8 580	12 827
Jefferson	4 744	64.9	53 700	264	7 197	3.0	456	6.3	250	-1	2 875	14.9	1 227	718
Josephine	25 081	70.4	74 700	319	26 393	-2.9	2 102	8.0	1 575	22	15 336	12.6	4 238	4 027
Klamath	22 341	65.2	52 700	260	25 914	-0.9	2 404	9.3	1 466	45	14 542	8.1	4 330	4 052
Lake	2 765	67.8	41 900	238	3 954	-5.9	365	9.2	199	2	1 309	-3.0	445	467
Lane	110 799	60.8	65 800	360	149 171	1.1	8 748	5.9	7 954	25	87 564	6.2	21 213	22 560
Lincoln	16 455	66.0	69 400	317	19 732	2.0	1 174	5.9	1 271	16	9 688	5.2	1 482	3 454
Linn	34 716	65.6	51 300	293	44 000	0.6	3 452	7.8	2 215	116	24 239	4.6	9 487	5 424
Malheur	9 457	64.1	46 300	227	13 638	1.9	721	5.3	695	8	6 846	-2.1	1 366	1 958
Marion	83 494	62.9	59 900	335	116 269	2.1	6 267	5.4	5 698	155	64 407	6.3	9 498	17 182
Morrow	2 803	68.0	43 500	247	3 408	-0.6	302	8.9	139	-16	1 753	-12.1	953	189
Multnomah	242 140	55.3	61 800	347	327 180	0.8	15 884	4.9	19 583	83	300 097	4.4	44 296	55 015
Polk	18 167	66.4	63 600	300	24 418	1.8	1 354	5.5	905	24	7 870	5.1	2 579	1 714
Sherman	784	66.1	30 600	214	892	-0.6	51	5.7	45	5	184	-15.6	0	106
Tillamook	8 846	71.3	61 300	277	9 318	2.1	572	6.1	591	7	4 036	6.1	1 042	1 196
Umatilla	22 020	62.0	47 800	252	30 034	-0.9	2 504	8.3	1 396	-35	14 433	0.1	4 793	3 706
Union	9 035	64.4	43 900	243	11 420	-1.1	779	6.8	660	-13	5 399	0.9	1 377	1 528

1. Percent of total civilian labor force. 2. For week including March 12. Excludes government employees, self-employed persons, farm workers, domestic service workers, railroad employees subject to the Railroad Retirement Act, and employees on oceanborne vessels or in foreign countries.

STATE County	Private nonfarm establishments, 1988 (cont'd)				Personal income, 1989								Earnings, 1989		
	Employment[1] (cont'd)		Annual payroll								Per capita[3]			Percent by selected industries	
															Goods-related[4]
	Finance, insurance, and real estate	Services	Total (Mil dol)	Average per employee (Dollars)	Total (Mil dol)	Percent change, 1988–1989	Wages and salaries[2] (Mil dol)	Proprietor's income (Mil dol)	Dividends, interest, & rent (Mil dol)	Transfer payments (Mil dol)	Dollars	Rank	Total (Mil dol)	Farm	Total
	88	89	90	91	92	93	94	95	96	97	98	99	100	101	102
OKLAHOMA—Con.															
McCurtain	228	838	102	16 740	356	5.3	184	53	38	96	9 696	2 927	237	7.0	46.2
McIntosh	118	550	23	10 700	177	8.9	53	21	33	60	10 225	2 850	74	7.2	16.5
Major	64	313	22	14 369	117	5.1	38	33	29	19	13 653	1 598	71	29.1	27.9
Marshall	49	392	25	13 404	137	6.4	47	15	30	38	11 488	2 503	61	4.7	29.2
Mayes	302	1 102	119	16 831	392	6.4	182	43	61	81	11 239	2 586	225	3.2	43.1
Murray	89	318	24	12 969	133	3.8	56	16	23	38	10 802	2 716	72	5.2	NA
Muskogee	1 118	3 094	307	17 062	861	6.0	508	103	123	203	12 471	2 131	610	5.0	29.6
Noble	109	799	48	16 403	152	5.1	80	23	32	29	13 381	1 740	103	12.8	36.3
Nowata	87	420	17	13 283	120	4.1	27	15	24	29	11 575	2 480	42	11.6	17.9
Okfuskee	67	433	14	10 717	115	8.5	33	19	16	38	10 177	2 859	52	14.9	20.0
Oklahoma	21 968	78 000	5 110	19 977	10 057	6.4	8 463	979	1 631	1 629	16 490	529	9 443	0.2	22.1
Okmulgee	337	1 816	93	15 502	418	4.7	160	45	65	122	10 817	2 711	206	3.0	28.0
Osage	358	861	62	17 616	448	2.8	145	35	66	73	11 469	2 514	180	4.1	42.3
Ottawa	341	1 610	79	13 478	351	7.0	140	47	69	102	10 831	2 706	187	10.1	24.8
Pawnee	127	429	28	13 695	209	6.8	55	29	36	39	12 728	2 023	84	3.7	26.5
Payne	647	3 051	187	14 127	782	7.5	446	85	135	146	12 367	2 175	530	1.5	20.0
Pittsburg	499	1 583	97	13 682	472	5.9	215	60	85	133	10 999	2 666	275	3.1	18.4
Pontotoc	517	2 409	119	13 606	434	5.4	210	54	81	99	12 574	2 079	265	2.1	23.6
Pottawatomie	658	3 414	183	14 052	761	5.3	307	90	111	164	13 021	1 899	397	2.7	28.6
Pushmataha	73	166	10	10 618	104	8.3	29	18	15	37	8 775	3 028	47	12.9	11.7
Roger Mills	0	119	4	10 655	67	5.7	14	15	30	11	13 488	1 688	28	29.2	NA
Rogers	429	1 380	140	17 798	750	7.6	231	66	93	88	13 380	1 741	297	2.2	35.3
Seminole	237	962	72	14 313	300	3.9	116	39	60	86	11 230	2 591	155	3.6	31.8
Sequoyah	171	1 192	47	12 008	343	5.4	98	28	43	85	9 356	2 973	127	2.9	20.8
Stephens	539	2 358	176	17 001	552	4.0	270	69	116	120	13 007	1 903	338	2.0	41.2
Texas	253	581	48	15 419	285	-0.4	86	109	48	35	17 385	379	195	44.8	10.1
Tillman	72	240	25	14 356	132	0.8	45	32	24	34	11 990	2 330	77	28.5	18.2
Tulsa	16 836	70 599	5 178	21 666	9 003	7.5	7 008	942	1 664	1 169	17 289	399	7 950	0.4	30.6
Wagoner	142	753	75	17 083	643	6.8	98	50	61	73	12 527	2 102	147	8.5	33.2
Washington	788	4 005	435	25 406	837	4.5	514	71	197	117	18 708	237	585	1.1	45.8
Washita	98	396	19	13 277	151	0.9	38	41	43	32	13 111	1 859	79	35.1	14.2
Woods	167	358	19	11 339	159	7.0	49	41	39	30	16 327	561	90	32.3	10.8
Woodward	290	1 087	82	15 514	257	2.9	136	45	52	42	13 429	1 721	180	3.8	26.7
OREGON	61 391	255 097	17 604	X	45 129	9.6	27 778	4 774	8 198	7 136	16 009	X	32 552	3.1	26.4
Baker	288	892	79	16 248	211	9.8	84	36	50	49	14 056	1 410	120	16.0	18.4
Benton	863	5 059	359	18 581	1 097	8.8	651	101	208	144	16 687	486	752	4.5	28.4
Clackamas	3 003	17 839	1 449	19 715	5 086	10.6	1 982	472	797	502	18 191	273	2 454	3.1	27.7
Clatsop	357	2 292	128	14 294	549	12.2	314	74	101	95	16 484	531	388	2.0	37.1
Columbia	209	1 266	174	23 076	542	9.7	234	45	80	85	13 891	1 481	279	4.0	38.6
Coos	671	3 278	266	16 579	835	6.2	421	104	156	186	13 608	1 626	524	3.5	24.7
Crook	82	900	67	17 680	197	10.0	116	23	35	35	14 120	1 384	138	6.6	44.7
Curry	188	616	59	14 825	272	11.0	102	35	78	66	13 799	1 536	136	7.8	31.9
Deschutes	1 648	6 776	367	16 006	1 130	13.4	598	151	240	189	15 836	701	749	3.2	27.1
Douglas	740	5 409	455	17 911	1 305	6.2	734	164	220	262	13 353	1 755	898	4.6	38.6
Gilliam	0	31	4	13 608	31	-13.2	11	9	7	5	18 965	222	20	44.1	NA
Grant	60	221	27	16 494	116	5.2	53	24	22	21	13 589	1 637	77	20.1	24.2
Harney	63	258	28	17 061	102	2.1	48	20	21	18	13 510	1 676	68	20.6	NA
Hood River	127	1 498	79	15 895	253	6.9	141	21	49	40	15 438	819	162	6.0	22.1
Jackson	2 106	11 128	719	16 885	2 103	8.4	1 094	256	437	398	14 046	1 414	1 350	1.7	25.7
Jefferson	83	453	49	17 052	177	5.2	101	25	31	31	13 880	1 493	126	14.2	34.9
Josephine	503	4 554	239	15 574	837	9.9	345	90	214	205	11 438	2 525	435	1.3	30.9
Klamath	693	3 172	247	16 956	784	8.2	434	95	138	155	13 540	1 664	529	5.0	30.1
Lake	44	168	20	15 503	109	4.8	53	23	19	19	14 443	1 236	76	21.2	NA
Lane	4 380	24 343	1 547	17 670	4 132	9.2	2 463	453	724	682	15 049	970	2 916	1.7	27.4
Lincoln	429	2 784	132	13 594	579	9.6	255	81	133	128	14 722	1 115	336	2.7	20.7
Linn	733	4 760	473	19 499	1 208	7.9	761	151	196	234	13 059	1 886	912	4.9	44.0
Malheur	302	1 526	101	14 688	345	7.8	178	59	69	68	12 969	1 921	238	15.3	17.5
Marion	5 884	21 397	1 006	15 623	3 379	9.9	1 990	317	615	627	14 957	1 006	2 307	4.0	19.9
Morrow	50	155	27	15 502	126	4.9	57	47	15	15	17 015	433	104	44.2	NA
Multnomah	29 834	95 328	6 349	21 158	10 407	9.8	9 770	952	1 988	1 760	18 308	264	10 722	0.2	20.4
Polk	236	1 692	122	15 467	679	8.1	205	60	133	97	13 582	1 642	265	8.9	34.7
Sherman	0	0	2	12 967	47	-0.9	11	22	8	6	24 474	45	34	62.9	NA
Tillamook	163	1 022	57	14 032	297	9.1	107	50	72	70	13 360	1 750	157	14.3	22.5
Umatilla	762	2 823	210	14 557	832	8.0	403	136	128	161	13 805	1 533	539	13.4	21.7
Union	165	1 533	86	15 891	328	7.6	178	45	55	66	14 026	1 425	224	8.6	25.1

1. For week including March 12. Excludes government employees, self-employed persons, farm workers, domestic service workers, railroad employees subject to the Railroad Retirement Act, and employees on oceanborne vessels or in foreign countries. 2. Includes other labor income. 3. Based on the resident population estimated as of July 1 of the year shown. 4. Covers mining, construction, and manufacturing.

Table A. States and Counties — **Earnings and Agriculture**

STATE County	Earnings, 1989 (cont'd): Percent by selected industries (cont'd): Goods-related[1]: Manufacturing	Service-related & other[2]: Total	Service-related & other[2]: Retail trade	Service-related & other[2]: Finance, insurance, & real estate	Service-related & other[2]: Services	Government	Agriculture, 1987: Farms: Number	Farms: Percent with: Less than 50 acres	Farms: Percent with: 500 acres and over	Farm operators, percent: Whose principal occupation is farming	Farm operators, percent: Residing on farm operated	Land in farms: Acreage (1,000)	Land in farms: Percent change, 1982–1987	Land in farms: Acres: Average size of farm	Land in farms: Acres: Total irrigated (1,000)	Land in farms: Acres: Total cropland (1,000)
	103	104	105	106	107	108	109	110	111	112	113	114	115	116	117	118
OKLAHOMA—Con.																
McCurtain	35.4	30.3	8.1	2.3	12.5	16.5	1 446	29.7	8.6	42.2	75.0	323	-4.8	223	0	133
McIntosh	9.1	55.6	17.3	4.5	23.0	20.7	857	18.9	12.0	43.3	69.3	235	-1.7	274	0	91
Major	5.0	31.1	6.6	3.2	11.4	12.0	897	12.4	35.2	55.5	58.2	503	1.5	560	7	257
Marshall	21.6	47.3	11.8	3.5	16.2	18.8	398	23.6	18.3	36.9	66.3	173	0.7	434	3	42
Mayes	35.1	34.6	9.8	2.7	16.2	19.1	1 258	24.6	9.1	42.7	80.0	260	-2.9	207	0	126
Murray	14.0	38.5	10.9	2.7	14.9	29.0	418	24.2	19.6	45.5	67.2	171	-1.2	409	1	48
Muskogee	23.4	42.7	9.0	4.1	16.4	22.7	1 357	29.7	9.3	37.5	73.2	372	4.1	274	5	172
Noble	30.9	NA	7.0	2.8	NA	15.5	727	11.1	31.6	54.5	60.7	388	-2.8	534	0	205
Nowata	9.3	50.4	8.7	5.2	24.6	20.1	679	16.9	17.8	45.7	77.3	231	-15.7	341	0	88
Okfuskee	5.6	37.2	9.0	3.4	16.6	28.0	736	15.5	20.5	41.0	69.0	275	2.5	374	1	94
Oklahoma	13.8	54.6	9.7	6.4	25.2	23.1	986	41.9	7.1	36.1	65.5	154	-17.5	156	1	68
Okmulgee	19.1	45.1	10.0	4.1	22.2	23.9	1 009	27.2	11.5	31.7	72.5	250	-9.8	248	1	99
Osage	6.5	35.6	11.8	2.4	13.3	17.9	1 026	20.3	29.4	43.2	69.7	982	-12.1	957	D	142
Ottawa	20.1	44.9	11.1	3.6	22.2	20.3	953	31.3	11.9	43.8	77.6	216	2.3	227	0	129
Pawnee	1.9	50.4	10.9	3.3	25.7	19.4	629	14.6	22.6	45.8	70.1	285	1.4	453	0	84
Payne	13.8	39.0	10.9	2.9	18.7	39.6	1 110	19.4	15.9	37.7	72.7	314	3.0	283	1	119
Pittsburg	11.7	47.2	11.4	3.5	21.0	31.2	1 411	19.6	16.4	38.2	69.8	497	-6.5	352	2	134
Pontotoc	15.2	53.2	11.0	3.8	27.1	21.1	1 030	23.9	14.5	36.4	67.9	364	-7.8	353	3	104
Pottawatomie	20.0	52.2	17.1	3.5	22.5	16.6	1 284	23.7	11.4	37.1	74.9	323	-1.0	252	2	122
Pushmataha	6.5	44.6	9.6	4.3	20.1	30.8	715	18.6	13.1	44.3	74.7	245	-17.8	343	1	60
Roger Mills	NA	NA	5.7	5.2	16.7	20.5	716	7.8	47.3	66.8	66.2	640	5.8	894	2	176
Rogers	24.6	43.4	9.2	3.9	18.5	19.0	1 178	35.4	10.6	33.0	76.8	267	-1.8	227	0	111
Seminole	17.6	44.6	8.3	2.7	19.5	20.0	990	20.0	9.5	34.8	71.0	256	0.1	259	2	86
Sequoyah	15.0	50.3	17.3	4.9	20.5	26.0	976	30.4	9.2	34.5	76.0	206	0.7	211	1	84
Stephens	28.1	44.7	12.1	3.6	20.5	12.1	1 067	18.8	19.9	42.5	70.3	436	0.8	408	1	174
Texas	2.8	32.8	6.0	3.0	11.5	12.3	804	7.8	64.8	67.9	52.9	1 177	2.5	1 464	158	D
Tillman	14.7	36.8	6.7	2.9	14.3	16.5	662	7.9	45.5	65.4	41.4	484	-1.8	730	9	353
Tulsa	19.6	60.7	8.7	5.9	25.5	8.3	913	47.1	5.1	32.1	67.9	140	-13.8	153	2	66
Wagoner	20.4	41.1	9.9	2.4	20.7	17.2	898	32.3	11.2	36.1	67.5	224	-11.4	250	1	125
Washington	12.5	46.0	16.6	3.6	19.9	7.2	669	30.0	10.3	37.4	76.2	216	-0.2	323	1	65
Washita	4.9	32.0	6.0	2.3	14.9	18.7	1 089	11.6	39.3	67.9	51.1	589	0.5	541	5	416
Woods	1.4	36.7	8.2	2.9	11.5	20.3	752	9.2	47.6	62.2	44.0	698	-5.1	928	2	318
Woodward	7.2	50.7	10.5	3.0	22.1	18.8	751	12.9	45.4	51.3	57.5	685	-4.2	912	4	213
OREGON	20.6	54.8	10.6	5.2	23.5	15.6	32 014	52.9	13.3	48.0	83.3	17 809	0.4	556	1 648	5 236
Baker	12.4	43.3	11.6	3.2	17.1	22.3	621	26.1	33.7	64.9	80.4	919	-2.7	1 480	109	152
Benton	25.4	37.9	8.1	1.8	21.3	29.1	645	60.2	9.6	39.1	82.9	125	1.2	193	19	81
Clackamas	19.0	57.3	14.1	3.7	23.0	11.9	3 175	75.4	0.8	36.3	87.0	161	-8.6	51	19	99
Clatsop	31.6	47.1	13.1	1.4	18.6	13.9	237	46.4	4.2	44.3	78.9	26	8.6	109	1	14
Columbia	29.9	43.1	7.9	1.5	13.6	14.3	695	60.1	2.6	34.2	89.2	74	-4.2	106	3	31
Coos	20.3	52.0	11.6	2.7	18.7	19.8	736	36.3	9.4	53.5	83.7	163	-2.8	222	9	42
Crook	41.8	32.9	5.4	1.1	10.5	15.9	415	41.2	27.0	45.1	83.9	861	0.0	2 074	49	84
Curry	23.6	42.2	14.4	2.0	14.8	18.1	160	23.1	29.4	61.9	71.2	80	5.8	497	2	9
Deschutes	17.8	55.3	12.8	5.1	26.7	14.3	884	64.8	3.7	38.3	87.1	152	-2.7	172	30	41
Douglas	34.1	39.3	9.2	1.6	18.4	17.5	1 753	44.7	10.2	41.5	85.6	438	5.9	250	14	115
Gilliam	NA	35.4	5.5	1.3	7.7	16.1	154	7.1	85.7	82.5	67.5	764	2.3	4 959	6	288
Grant	20.8	27.1	7.7	1.4	8.0	28.6	402	20.4	51.2	59.7	77.4	1 021	0.9	2 539	43	86
Harney	21.9	29.3	8.4	1.2	10.0	24.0	412	17.2	54.1	60.9	77.7	1 520	1.9	3 689	137	172
Hood River	18.3	58.1	10.7	2.4	21.0	13.8	573	70.3	0.5	57.4	84.5	29	6.1	50	19	21
Jackson	19.4	56.9	13.9	4.0	24.5	15.7	1 588	65.9	4.5	40.1	86.8	298	-1.1	188	53	73
Jefferson	32.7	34.5	8.4	1.4	15.8	16.4	341	22.9	25.5	63.6	79.5	507	-1.3	1 486	47	100
Josephine	24.1	52.2	15.5	2.8	24.3	15.6	580	72.4	1.4	49.0	89.1	37	-3.2	63	12	18
Klamath	26.2	46.7	11.1	3.2	18.3	18.2	1 006	32.9	21.2	56.0	76.7	718	-8.4	714	212	227
Lake	18.4	NA	9.5	0.5	9.1	27.5	373	18.0	38.9	61.7	79.1	853	2.9	2 286	155	170
Lane	21.7	53.7	12.0	3.6	25.2	17.2	2 039	62.0	4.9	37.0	86.9	277	1.6	136	24	122
Lincoln	14.1	56.4	15.2	2.1	21.4	20.2	274	46.0	4.7	45.6	88.0	35	-0.1	129	1	12
Linn	39.6	38.9	8.6	2.0	16.6	12.2	1 924	53.7	10.4	46.0	84.5	392	4.6	204	28	309
Malheur	13.6	50.8	11.1	2.7	18.1	16.5	1 243	27.0	21.6	72.3	81.7	1 382	-8.2	1 112	193	253
Marion	14.0	46.8	10.5	4.7	21.7	29.4	2 586	62.8	5.8	50.1	82.6	307	-1.4	119	87	236
Morrow	19.0	22.6	3.7	2.3	3.8	12.9	363	25.1	56.7	70.2	74.4	1 116	1.5	3 074	75	443
Multnomah	15.3	65.3	9.0	8.7	27.0	14.0	552	77.7	2.4	39.1	80.8	34	-3.6	62	7	23
Polk	27.8	38.4	10.1	2.0	17.0	17.9	1 072	53.2	8.7	43.8	83.5	176	-1.9	164	11	127
Sherman	0.0	NA	4.6	NA	4.1	18.6	187	11.2	77.5	82.9	72.2	462	7.2	2 473	3	289
Tillamook	16.2	42.5	11.4	1.5	18.1	20.6	360	31.1	0.8	71.9	86.4	40	2.2	111	4	23
Umatilla	17.5	45.2	10.1	2.6	18.3	19.8	1 453	50.4	28.3	58.5	75.6	1 451	3.1	999	112	738
Union	21.1	45.9	10.1	2.0	16.3	20.4	767	36.2	27.6	48.0	81.2	443	3.3	578	46	172

1. Covers mining, construction, and manufacturing. 2. Covers private sector earnings in agricultural services, forestry, and fisheries; transportation and public utilities; wholesale trade; retail trade; finance, insurance, and real estate; and services.

STATE County	Agriculture, 1987 (cont'd)								Manufactures, 1987						
	Value of land and buildings		Value of products sold				Percent of farms with sales of		Establishments		All employees			Production workers	
					Percent from										
	Average per farm ($1,000)	Average per acre (Dollars)	Total (Mil dol)	Average per farm (Dollars)	Crops	Livestock and poultry[1]	$10,000 or more	$100,000 or more	Total	Percent with 20 or more employees	Number (1,000)	Percent change, 1982–1987	Annual payroll (Mil dol)	Number (1,000)	Work hours (Mil)
	119	120	121	122	123	124	125	126	127	128	129	130	131	132	133
OKLAHOMA—Con.															
McCurtain	133	573	71	49 162	3.2	96.8	35.6	13.8	46	30.4	D	D	D	D	D
McIntosh	115	468	11	12 572	16.1	83.9	31.3	1.5	12	33.3	0.4	0.0	4.3	0.3	0.6
Major	272	462	30	33 863	31.6	68.4	53.0	8.8	9	11.1	0.1	-50.0	2.0	0.1	0.1
Marshall	176	405	8	20 572	25.0	75.0	31.7	4.8	17	35.3	0.6	20.0	9.9	0.5	1.0
Mayes	140	700	23	18 200	7.3	92.7	31.5	4.3	49	59.2	2.9	3.6	64.9	2.3	4.5
Murray	195	438	15	35 627	4.5	95.5	33.7	5.3	14	14.3	0.2	0.0	4.0	0.2	0.4
Muskogee	162	595	30	22 238	33.1	66.9	27.9	4.2	82	36.6	5.0	-3.8	114.0	3.7	7.3
Noble	263	471	23	32 233	26.6	73.4	49.1	7.7	7	28.6	D	D	D	D	D
Nowata	154	459	15	22 268	9.2	90.8	36.1	3.2	9	33.3	0.1	0.0	3.4	0.1	0.2
Okfuskee	177	478	13	18 303	9.4	90.6	30.4	2.4	9	55.6	0.4	0.0	4.5	0.3	0.6
Oklahoma	158	977	12	11 933	48.1	51.8	20.1	1.8	841	25.4	41.3	-9.6	1 031.3	28.1	52.7
Okmulgee	144	681	13	12 929	17.9	82.1	23.3	2.2	34	29.4	1.3	-13.3	31.7	1.1	1.9
Osage	296	302	55	53 901	4.8	95.2	39.1	8.7	26	26.9	1.0	-33.3	24.1	0.6	1.2
Ottawa	142	637	31	32 687	44.9	55.1	35.6	5.5	53	35.8	1.6	-60.0	27.0	1.2	2.7
Pawnee	197	436	18	28 814	9.5	90.5	37.0	5.2	14	14.3	0.2	100.0	3.0	0.1	0.3
Payne	163	588	22	20 142	11.2	88.8	28.3	3.8	55	18.2	2.5	8.7	56.0	2.1	4.2
Pittsburg	149	387	22	15 634	12.0	88.0	31.3	2.6	20	40.0	1.3	8.3	23.7	0.9	1.8
Pontotoc	177	485	19	18 917	3.8	96.2	29.1	3.2	35	34.3	2.1	23.5	37.0	1.8	3.5
Pottawatomie	170	689	16	12 356	23.8	76.2	23.4	2.4	55	45.5	2.9	26.1	62.3	2.1	3.9
Pushmataha	122	353	9	12 663	3.7	96.3	25.9	2.1	11	27.3	0.2	0.0	1.9	0.2	0.3
Roger Mills	281	322	29	40 581	10.9	89.1	58.4	9.8	2	0.0	D	D	D	D	D
Rogers	183	861	17	14 278	17.4	82.6	23.7	2.1	66	33.3	2.4	-29.4	54.8	1.5	3.0
Seminole	130	504	13	12 921	13.1	86.9	17.2	1.4	28	21.4	1.2	-29.4	18.1	0.9	1.5
Sequoyah	125	625	11	10 911	26.1	73.9	23.6	1.9	21	14.3	D	D	D	D	D
Stephens	166	420	20	18 313	17.9	82.1	36.0	3.6	42	16.7	1.5	0.0	38.6	1.1	2.4
Texas	529	368	357	444 265	10.1	89.9	69.8	19.4	12	41.7	0.3	0.0	6.3	0.2	0.4
Tillman	349	470	46	69 860	66.7	33.3	71.9	21.0	14	28.6	0.7	16.7	11.4	0.5	1.1
Tulsa	214	1 487	15	16 100	58.2	41.8	23.1	3.3	1 116	27.9	40.9	-29.1	1 157.2	24.8	52.3
Wagoner	201	833	16	18 323	41.8	58.2	28.3	3.7	38	34.2	1.6	60.0	32.4	1.1	2.0
Washington	186	599	14	20 450	19.3	80.7	27.1	2.4	41	29.3	2.7	-75.9	85.2	1.1	2.1
Washita	275	538	55	50 229	41.7	58.3	65.1	14.0	8	37.5	0.2	-33.3	3.1	0.2	0.3
Woods	388	422	45	60 018	29.5	70.5	67.0	13.7	8	0.0	0.1	0.0	0.7	0.0	0.1
Woodward	286	300	28	37 266	24.9	75.1	58.2	8.8	22	22.7	0.3	-25.0	6.8	0.2	0.5
OREGON	300	542	1 846	57 664	56.8	43.2	36.6	12.0	6 353	25.9	202.9	9.6	4 767.2	144.3	280.0
Baker	410	285	41	65 631	9.5	90.5	59.7	15.6	39	12.8	0.5	25.0	10.3	0.4	0.8
Benton	245	1 509	31	48 786	75.1	24.9	26.2	9.6	153	26.8	5.7	11.8	155.7	3.8	7.2
Clackamas	180	3 754	120	37 654	66.7	33.3	24.6	6.6	511	25.6	16.4	14.7	409.3	10.9	21.0
Clatsop	207	1 641	8	35 695	12.0	88.0	26.2	8.4	77	23.4	2.7	50.0	65.3	2.2	4.1
Columbia	181	1 527	9	12 603	28.1	71.9	12.8	1.6	89	23.6	-2.5	-10.7	69.5	2.2	4.3
Coos	210	897	22	30 422	29.3	70.7	39.5	9.4	192	19.8	4.5	15.4	93.2	3.9	7.3
Crook	588	251	23	55 906	25.9	74.1	43.1	15.2	45	22.2	1.9	58.3	37.9	1.7	3.2
Curry	379	794	7	44 237	54.3	45.7	52.5	8.8	50	20.0	1.3	44.4	24.5	1.1	2.2
Deschutes	188	1 213	15	16 805	22.7	77.3	22.5	2.8	177	17.5	4.7	67.9	95.5	3.5	6.8
Douglas	201	911	26	15 115	19.5	80.5	23.8	3.0	313	19.5	9.1	19.7	227.1	7.2	15.3
Gilliam	775	155	20	132 408	66.6	33.4	78.6	46.1	1	0.0	D	D	D	D	D
Grant	508	216	17	42 323	8.5	91.5	49.8	11.2	46	17.4	0.7	40.0	16.3	0.6	1.2
Harney	704	191	29	69 469	7.9	92.1	57.0	17.0	16	25.0	0.5	150.0	14.6	0.5	1.0
Hood River	224	4 763	41	71 682	96.1	3.9	51.1	21.6	47	17.0	1.0	-9.1	18.3	0.9	1.7
Jackson	213	1 260	41	25 531	59.3	40.7	20.1	3.8	326	22.7	8.1	42.1	179.4	6.4	12.6
Jefferson	394	274	32	92 905	80.1	19.9	65.1	24.0	32	18.8	1.1	37.5	25.1	1.0	2.0
Josephine	174	3 625	13	21 812	20.7	79.3	18.6	4.0	139	18.7	3.8	35.7	76.9	3.1	6.1
Klamath	486	640	68	68 043	43.0	57.0	53.3	15.7	102	36.3	4.0	5.3	93.1	3.2	6.6
Lake	677	301	31	83 609	22.4	77.6	56.8	20.1	18	33.3	0.5	25.0	9.9	0.4	0.9
Lane	194	1 444	60	29 314	50.5	49.5	20.7	5.8	769	23.3	20.3	20.8	444.2	15.5	29.6
Lincoln	152	1 451	3	11 459	41.3	58.7	20.1	1.5	74	18.9	1.4	-6.7	34.1	1.1	2.0
Linn	255	1 280	114	59 379	69.8	30.2	31.4	13.2	245	35.1	9.5	3.3	236.5	7.3	14.6
Malheur	412	381	145	116 374	53.9	46.1	66.0	26.9	26	19.2	1.5	-11.8	26.9	1.2	2.1
Marion	284	2 148	208	80 317	73.6	26.4	43.0	16.4	367	29.4	10.8	12.5	195.4	8.2	15.4
Morrow	810	257	120	331 323	53.8	46.2	63.4	35.0	17	29.4	D	D	D	D	D
Multnomah	202	3 840	29	52 012	89.6	10.4	29.9	9.8	1 308	27.3	41.8	-1.6	1 038.0	28.5	54.5
Polk	254	1 525	47	44 112	59.2	40.8	33.5	9.6	96	28.1	2.8	-6.7	60.7	2.2	4.1
Sherman	630	257	16	83 023	87.4	12.6	78.1	30.5	NA	NA	NA	NA	NA	NA	NA
Tillamook	266	2 448	50	140 225	0.6	99.4	61.4	46.9	50	28.0	1.2	20.0	20.4	0.9	1.7
Umatilla	468	447	169	116 048	62.8	37.2	50.7	20.6	86	30.2	5.0	22.0	77.5	4.3	7.5
Union	248	466	46	59 796	38.5	61.5	44.7	10.4	65	24.6	1.5	15.4	34.1	1.3	2.4

1. Includes livestock and poultry products.

STATE County	Manufactures, 1987 (cont'd): Production workers (cont'd): Wages: Total (Mil dol)	Manufactures, 1987 (cont'd): Production workers (cont'd): Wages: Average per worker (Dollars)	Manufactures, 1987 (cont'd): Value added by manufacture (Mil dol)	Manufactures, 1987 (cont'd): Value of shipments (Mil dol)	Manufactures, 1987 (cont'd): New capital expenditures (Mil dol)	Value of construction authorized by building permits, 1990: Total[1] ($1,000)	Nonresidential: Total ($1,000)	Nonresidential: Percent: Office	Nonresidential: Percent: Industrial	Nonresidential: Percent: Stores	Residential: New construction ($1,000)	Residential: Number of housing units	Residential: Alterations and additions ($1,000)
	134	135	136	137	138	139	140	141	142	143	144	145	146
OKLAHOMA—Con.													
McCurtain	D	D	D	D	D	2 526	623	0.0	0.0	92.0	1 737	65	75
McIntosh	3.0	10 000	12.2	18.2	D	2 325	1 458	0.0	31.4	0.0	779	19	0
Major	1.1	11 000	4.8	11.1	0.0	719	55	0.0	0.0	0.0	510	9	100
Marshall	7.5	15 000	18.5	48.2	0.4	420	208	88.2	0.0	0.0	138	4	32
Mayes	44.5	19 348	178.3	386.8	7.5	2 223	496	10.1	0.0	23.0	1 330	20	157
Murray	3.2	16 000	14.7	17.0	0.0	440	102	0.0	0.0	0.0	298	9	40
Muskogee	84.4	22 811	349.5	735.8	33.5	11 406	791	8.7	84.4	1.5	4 516	105	1 337
Noble	D	D	D	D	D	653	550	0.0	0.0	45.5	70	1	15
Nowata	2.3	23 000	5.6	10.4	D	398	119	0.0	0.0	0.0	244	8	16
Okfuskee	3.5	11 667	8.6	11.8	0.2	0	0	NA	NA	NA	0	0	0
Oklahoma	636.1	22 637	3 168.0	8 408.9	118.8	277 801	49 833	28.4	4.1	36.1	140 657	1 532	16 346
Okmulgee	23.3	21 182	109.7	175.9	8.0	3 668	285	0.0	8.5	0.0	598	11	1 460
Osage	10.7	17 833	56.4	113.9	D	1 210	561	0.0	0.0	0.0	460	13	40
Ottawa	19.1	15 917	57.0	136.4	D	4 661	2 974	6.2	0.0	76.4	1 407	29	114
Pawnee	2.3	23 000	6.5	13.7	D	1 136	964	0.0	0.0	0.0	60	1	8
Payne	42.4	20 190	262.5	683.7	20.6	15 377	5 018	62.3	2.3	32.0	4 345	50	1 099
Pittsburg	13.5	15 000	56.1	109.6	3.3	4 827	1 803	22.8	0.0	29.6	1 901	31	174
Pontotoc	29.4	16 333	78.2	185.7	6.6	1 519	470	0.0	0.0	62.8	535	6	72
Pottawatomie	42.5	20 238	166.8	362.2	11.0	8 069	2 376	4.2	30.3	26.1	3 459	75	498
Pushmataha	1.6	8 000	4.5	11.2	0.1	25	0	NA	NA	NA	25	1	0
Roger Mills	D	D	D	D	D	0	0	NA	NA	NA	0	0	0
Rogers	29.9	19 933	136.7	314.4	D	19 470	4 485	13.1	44.0	6.6	13 631	175	583
Seminole	11.9	13 222	68.3	149.7	1.6	1 793	448	0.0	82.1	0.0	120	4	52
Sequoyah	D	D	D	D	D	6 912	4 652	70.3	0.0	0.5	950	16	292
Stephens	27.3	24 818	33.9	93.4	0.5	3 301	303	24.7	0.0	0.0	1 929	27	623
Texas	4.7	23 500	12.5	131.6	0.6	2 237	488	0.0	0.0	0.0	1 210	37	150
Tillman	7.5	15 000	22.7	43.7	D	641	320	0.0	100.0	0.0	288	4	4
Tulsa	590.7	23 819	2 310.7	5 008.1	144.8	347 277	155 531	10.1	18.7	12.9	126 728	1 756	9 327
Wagoner	18.9	17 182	96.4	219.8	4.3	6 344	1 627	0.0	8.0	3.4	3 827	62	307
Washington	24.2	22 000	96.1	177.1	6.4	17 716	2 885	0.0	68.9	9.6	13 309	84	1 416
Washita	2.2	11 000	6.5	14.2	0.1	83	0	NA	NA	NA	0	0	45
Woods	0.4	NA	1.6	6.7	0.1	689	390	0.0	0.0	2.3	0	0	157
Woodward	4.3	21 500	30.4	85.1	D	2 117	514	0.0	0.0	0.0	137	2	394
OREGON	2 948.6	20 434	11 610.3	25 351.7	735.4	2 721 037	536 000	19.5	29.5	20.1	1 657 464	22 858	121 703
Baker	8.0	20 000	33.7	69.9	1.6	6 789	3 385	32.5	25.9	2.8	2 101	22	806
Benton	87.7	23 079	320.6	666.2	63.7	103 552	65 346	3.8	85.8	7.3	28 899	401	3 430
Clackamas	236.4	21 688	948.6	1 874.5	52.9	382 112	53 965	12.8	8.3	44.6	276 157	3 386	13 854
Clatsop	52.6	23 909	311.1	555.6	7.5	29 968	4 255	15.7	25.3	7.0	20 474	259	2 485
Columbia	58.0	26 364	249.4	492.5	20.5	18 232	5 029	1.3	55.6	9.2	10 899	140	1 175
Coos	75.7	19 410	234.9	621.6	D	28 047	6 085	0.0	53.0	8.6	15 630	187	3 076
Crook	31.7	18 647	69.5	252.1	5.2	10 712	3 898	18.4	5.0	53.9	5 527	89	513
Curry	20.5	18 636	52.8	126.7	2.0	24 796	3 211	23.7	13.4	0.0	17 414	191	1 575
Deschutes	65.2	18 629	194.1	439.7	8.7	185 935	24 994	7.2	23.2	13.2	146 917	1 720	6 313
Douglas	169.9	23 597	526.9	1 301.9	27.2	47 701	10 249	8.3	17.7	13.4	30 754	398	1 663
Gilliam	D	D	D	D	D	273	150	33.4	0.0	0.0	61	1	56
Grant	13.6	22 667	35.2	106.8	2.5	1 915	594	0.0	0.0	7.7	503	6	397
Harney	12.4	24 800	34.9	86.5	0.5	866	256	45.7	0.0	0.0	457	3	64
Hood River	14.7	16 333	38.6	94.0	1.1	8 971	1 451	0.0	83.4	0.0	4 996	75	859
Jackson	134.9	21 078	451.5	1 163.2	25.7	157 843	24 352	42.5	8.9	14.9	111 423	1 511	8 279
Jefferson	19.7	19 700	72.2	173.1	2.9	7 772	1 258	33.8	47.4	1.7	5 046	144	332
Josephine	57.7	18 613	211.7	414.7	8.9	58 386	11 414	6.1	23.9	5.8	40 842	614	2 472
Klamath	71.3	22 281	228.3	598.3	D	19 610	231	0.0	0.0	0.0	12 250	123	2 253
Lake	8.8	22 000	30.1	62.1	D	1 398	67	0.0	0.0	0.0	913	12	342
Lane	310.1	20 006	1 060.3	2 617.9	56.8	197 006	34 789	10.6	15.5	49.5	120 861	1 872	11 196
Lincoln	25.6	23 273	150.5	303.0	12.9	42 873	12 836	1.7	4.6	4.9	23 249	334	2 983
Linn	166.2	22 767	656.2	1 404.4	32.6	34 395	12 694	1.1	23.0	37.3	13 427	157	2 462
Malheur	19.4	16 167	99.8	204.9	D	9 705	3 863	23.8	28.0	35.4	1 825	23	520
Marion	125.2	15 268	509.5	1 094.1	28.8	149 400	31 651	21.4	37.9	16.3	95 232	2 028	5 265
Morrow	D	D	D	D	D	1 787	1 187	16.9	17.3	36.6	311	4	148
Multnomah	612.7	21 498	2 318.8	5 151.4	119.8	481 341	101 726	20.1	30.2	15.9	161 411	2 620	33 232
Polk	41.9	19 045	153.9	406.5	14.5	16 124	1 648	24.9	24.0	19.7	10 833	128	1 212
Sherman	NA	NA	NA	NA	NA	303	161	0.0	0.0	72.9	0	0	121
Tillamook	14.9	16 556	59.0	168.5	4.4	17 971	3 358	1.6	57.1	3.3	12 825	204	799
Umatilla	60.7	14 116	268.1	550.3	13.9	16 502	10 010	14.7	37.4	19.9	3 204	37	1 212
Union	26.3	20 231	88.4	250.5	3.6	8 850	1 689	14.8	40.2	18.4	2 215	25	901

1. Includes nonresidential additions and alterations, residential nonhousekeeping buildings, and residential garages and carports not shown separately.

STATE County	Wholesale trade, 1987				Retail trade, all establishments, 1987				Retail trade, establishments with payroll, 1987					
						Sales				Sales				
											Per capita² (Dollars)			
	Establishments	Sales (Mil dol)	Paid employees¹	Annual payroll (Mil dol)	Number	Total (Mil dol)	Percent change, 1982–1987	Per capita² (Dollars)	Number	Total (Mil dol)	General merchandise stores	Food stores	Apparel & accessory stores	Eating and drinking places
	147	148	149	150	151	152	153	154	155	156	157	158	159	160
OKLAHOMA—Con.														
McCurtain	34	56.0	218	2.8	433	147.4	29.3	4 050	183	128.7	D	997	86	273
McIntosh	15	13.4	72	0.7	215	72.7	10.8	4 152	115	66.1	D	987	98	273
Major	17	25.7	80	1.3	124	40.0	-16.7	4 494	74	38.4	D	964	150	182
Marshall	14	25.8	96	1.5	167	43.7	7.4	3 731	73	38.1	159	1 200	D	230
Mayes	35	39.5	203	3.5	446	147.4	30.1	4 224	217	133.5	475	1 088	93	231
Murray	11	9.1	74	0.9	156	57.4	0.2	4 521	78	54.6	D	1 101	49	296
Muskogee	123	245.5	1 371	23.8	828	347.4	10.1	4 991	445	326.4	656	1 148	312	462
Noble	22	39.0	130	1.9	149	40.7	-13.6	3 511	88	38.7	146	1 012	30	370
Nowata	11	12.9	85	1.1	101	25.9	-10.7	2 444	46	24.4	D	825	D	177
Okfuskee	12	13.3	64	1.6	125	30.8	28.9	2 675	57	24.8	58	929	D	54
Oklahoma	1 661	7 289.1	19 028	425.8	6 859	4 509.1	6.5	7 307	4 321	4 382.6	901	1 270	452	794
Okmulgee	30	38.4	143	2.5	390	139.7	-3.1	3 518	204	128.1	D	833	166	305
Osage	31	28.9	103	1.8	279	76.0	6.0	1 894	144	68.2	D	864	28	86
Ottawa	38	61.7	321	5.2	429	149.0	12.5	4 542	204	137.2	D	983	230	285
Pawnee	21	D	D	D	196	70.6	40.4	4 175	99	66.3	D	1 220	76	324
Payne	94	136.1	599	9.3	666	282.6	0.6	4 423	425	269.7	587	1 134	276	542
Pittsburg	60	162.8	593	8.8	496	189.5	23.2	4 387	249	171.6	731	990	146	332
Pontotoc	67	73.2	423	6.7	438	161.6	-2.4	4 631	233	150.4	654	961	339	399
Pottawatomie	65	109.9	621	9.9	625	283.3	2.5	4 721	346	268.6	D	1 530	214	579
Pushmataha	9	6.7	55	0.6	176	41.8	52.6	3 538	62	35.3	281	1 110	D	150
Roger Mills	3	D	D	D	56	10.1	-43.6	1 898	29	8.6	D	D	D	91
Rogers	49	136.2	262	6.1	523	174.8	11.8	3 133	236	160.9	D	850	103	280
Seminole	46	52.2	211	4.0	284	89.0	-13.7	3 201	156	82.1	D	952	134	289
Sequoyah	19	75.0	155	1.9	362	119.3	40.7	3 352	173	106.5	D	892	103	283
Stephens	70	91.5	451	7.0	544	235.9	3.6	5 486	269	216.8	692	1 468	225	338
Texas	45	90.8	372	5.6	230	74.3	-6.4	4 270	132	68.9	D	1 075	213	321
Tillman	21	33.7	152	2.4	121	26.5	-18.0	2 323	69	24.3	347	579	117	163
Tulsa	1 562	6 486.1	15 671	356.8	5 837	3 760.5	14.4	7 271	3 665	3 660.5	D	1 440	462	750
Wagoner	29	50.3	152	3.1	274	71.0	10.4	1 400	133	64.9	D	500	19	121
Washington	49	58.6	330	6.4	582	297.2	11.0	6 590	352	286.9	996	1 706	396	564
Washita	23	28.6	135	1.9	135	25.9	-54.2	2 072	67	22.3	89	765	28	89
Woods	25	37.8	192	2.6	144	48.6	-17.8	4 811	85	46.5	D	990	238	400
Woodward	84	129.1	449	7.7	284	129.3	-28.2	6 467	173	122.6	D	1 582	356	549
OREGON	5 952	29 884.8	64 115	1 465.5	29 488	17 339.8	37.2	6 367	18 712	16 821.0	927	1 222	280	630
Baker	34	30.9	206	2.8	231	63.4	5.7	4 168	132	59.7	D	1 261	142	392
Benton	87	138.9	566	10.7	588	301.5	20.4	4 631	406	295.5	517	1 091	189	616
Clackamas	569	3 485.5	7 752	182.4	2 314	1 521.7	56.7	5 757	1 324	1 475.2	D	1 302	298	455
Clatsop	48	70.4	315	5.4	547	210.4	39.2	6 454	372	199.8	156	1 840	351	1 054
Columbia	30	22.7	141	1.6	352	114.2	27.5	3 045	205	108.8	20	1 025	88	313
Coos	87	153.3	697	12.6	723	355.5	32.6	5 896	464	343.9	866	1 193	204	493
Crook	10	11.0	51	1.0	139	44.4	30.2	3 341	83	41.6	D	1 243	140	216
Curry	16	14.4	66	1.1	300	100.4	49.2	5 673	177	95.9	D	1 836	D	583
Deschutes	160	219.5	885	16.1	968	505.8	60.5	7 352	628	492.5	657	1 587	396	703
Douglas	109	142.1	851	14.3	1 055	488.9	39.3	5 168	645	469.2	724	1 141	128	496
Gilliam	6	24.4	17	0.4	28	5.5	14.6	3 229	18	5.2	0	D	0	447
Grant	13	13.8	98	1.4	112	31.5	50.0	3 749	63	28.7	D	1 281	D	185
Harney	12	12.9	76	1.3	99	37.1	41.6	5 080	64	35.5	155	D	84	419
Hood River	24	68.3	200	4.4	202	91.5	28.9	5 684	132	88.2	D	1 783	D	667
Jackson	263	579.4	1 991	40.7	1 604	1 080.2	63.4	7 549	1 022	1 048.6	1 015	1 205	239	575
Jefferson	22	59.7	274	3.5	119	53.6	12.1	4 326	75	52.0	223	1 425	146	437
Josephine	66	104.2	417	6.9	726	354.4	24.0	5 151	446	340.1	D	1 016	173	425
Klamath	98	179.3	918	14.3	638	318.9	21.5	5 605	421	308.8	830	1 273	D	459
Lake	7	D	D	D	131	37.2	25.7	4 901	79	34.6	90	1 529	D	433
Lane	532	1 803.1	5 400	116.3	2 870	1 719.9	38.9	6 459	1 863	1 678.0	897	1 275	256	609
Lincoln	40	41.8	255	4.0	711	256.5	56.1	6 840	431	241.0	D	1 942	169	1 023
Linn	131	315.2	1 159	21.3	873	452.6	25.1	5 045	527	437.0	784	994	129	466
Malheur	74	136.4	756	12.4	343	168.5	22.4	6 172	209	159.7	695	1 335	359	574
Marion	348	1 388.1	3 587	81.8	2 071	1 309.9	38.5	6 031	1 321	1 273.7	1 004	1 127	258	579
Morrow	24	32.3	123	2.0	68	17.4	-2.8	2 197	47	16.5	0	818	38	163
Multnomah	2 005	15 039.9	26 727	658.0	6 118	4 161.3	24.8	7 431	4 166	4 055.6	1 215	1 129	366	928
Polk	55	43.7	298	3.7	388	121.5	36.7	2 564	214	115.9	72	1 036	11	303
Sherman	13	30.6	43	0.9	40	8.9	7.2	4 450	19	8.3	D	D	D	1 255
Tillamook	30	21.9	146	2.1	344	91.2	13.4	4 220	189	83.4	142	1 353	D	518
Umatilla	106	225.9	881	16.7	733	329.5	13.3	5 456	456	316.6	333	1 280	D	490
Union	45	55.3	269	4.2	314	105.8	15.4	4 562	201	101.7	D	1 103	300	577

1. For pay period including March 12. 2. Based on the estimated population as of July 1 of the year shown.

STATE County	Retail trade, establishments with payroll, 1987 (cont'd): Paid employees[1]	Retail trade, establishments with payroll, 1987 (cont'd): Annual payroll (Mil dol)	Taxable service industries–establishments with payroll, 1987: Number	Receipts (Mil dol): Total	Receipts (Mil dol), Selected kinds of business: Hotels, motels and other lodging places	Receipts (Mil dol), Selected kinds of business: Health services	Receipts (Mil dol), Selected kinds of business: Legal services	Paid employees	Annual payroll (Mil dol)	Bank deposits,[2] June 1989: Total (Mil dol)	Bank deposits,[2] June 1989: Percent change, 1988–1989	Savings capital,[3] September 1989: Total (Mil dol)	Savings capital,[3] September 1989: Percent change, 1988–1989
	161	162	163	164	165	166	167	168	169	170	171	172	173
OKLAHOMA—Con.													
McCurtain	1 351	12.9	125	23.8	2.2	10.9	1.2	794	7.8	177	5.4	13.1	-4.5
McIntosh	804	6.6	70	12.5	0.8	8.1	0.9	406	4.2	110	-1.8	31.1	38.9
Major	443	3.6	32	4.7	0.0	1.9	0.5	120	1.4	77	-4.8	20.2	-46.1
Marshall	446	3.8	49	8.7	1.1	3.8	1.1	211	2.7	73	-3.6	14.9	49.2
Mayes	1 539	12.6	132	21.4	0.9	10.6	1.7	776	8.2	210	3.5	46.2	-16.9
Murray	642	5.3	40	5.3	D	2.9	0.4	201	1.8	76	-3.9	17.6	-3.6
Muskogee	4 272	38.4	377	85.3	3.7	40.5	6.8	2 638	31.6	454	-3.1	176.8	-49.1
Noble	658	5.5	47	10.0	0.9	5.5	0.5	448	4.2	137	-5.5	18.0	2.2
Nowata	345	2.6	35	5.6	D	4.0	D	244	2.0	60	-3.1	12.2	0.2
Okfuskee	313	2.5	29	5.2	0.4	3.6	0.2	292	1.7	62	1.1	0.0	NA
Oklahoma	55 941	536.3	5 534	2 244.1	99.1	680.1	306.9	47 852	901.6	4 646	-4.7	1 875.2	-7.5
Okmulgee	1 691	14.3	169	35.0	4.0	15.6	2.2	1 085	12.2	239	2.7	39.2	-9.7
Osage	829	7.3	82	13.6	0.0	6.9	0.7	423	4.1	107	-3.8	35.8	2.1
Ottawa	1 612	15.1	144	35.3	2.6	18.3	2.1	896	12.0	190	-2.4	67.9	-6.5
Pawnee	761	6.2	68	40.0	0.0	4.3	D	523	15.3	95	-2.0	20.5	53.7
Payne	4 596	32.6	358	75.9	5.1	27.4	4.6	2 317	27.9	457	4.6	127.8	-25.5
Pittsburg	2 034	17.4	175	49.7	5.9	22.4	4.2	1 221	18.9	412	-2.3	75.3	1.0
Pontotoc	2 198	17.9	223	53.4	2.5	20.7	8.4	1 333	18.7	270	1.0	132.3	9.6
Pottawatomie	3 710	31.7	280	74.2	D	33.1	4.4	2 186	29.0	444	-7.4	106.1	-10.4
Pushmataha	412	3.1	37	6.2	0.3	3.3	1.2	149	1.6	57	2.8	0.0	NA
Roger Mills	90	0.7	12	1.2	0.2	0.6	D	70	0.6	58	-4.6	8.9	-25.7
Rogers	1 907	16.3	212	42.7	1.7	24.7	2.7	1 203	14.2	256	-0.3	107.1	1.3
Seminole	1 146	8.4	107	19.9	1.0	10.7	1.8	774	6.9	119	-1.7	86.2	-10.1
Sequoyah	1 341	10.9	109	26.4	1.0	8.9	1.5	990	7.9	145	7.6	16.2	-5.3
Stephens	2 440	22.4	225	47.8	1.6	19.7	4.5	1 248	17.5	383	-1.0	167.4	-7.6
Texas	1 036	8.1	104	15.5	1.8	4.2	1.8	472	4.6	173	-3.8	17.3	-3.8
Tillman	317	2.5	36	5.3	D	1.8	0.9	127	1.9	79	-0.5	20.0	-74.6
Tulsa	46 909	443.9	4 666	2 003.1	101.4	497.3	201.2	43 891	770.6	4 506	-4.9	1 690.0	-6.6
Wagoner	920	7.2	98	19.7	D	11.6	0.8	570	6.7	100	6.9	18.6	-23.0
Washington	4 021	35.5	298	84.7	5.0	35.3	3.8	2 083	33.2	354	41.6	201.4	-9.5
Washita	317	2.5	40	5.5	D	1.7	0.5	184	2.1	131	-10.6	28.0	3.9
Woods	702	5.2	66	7.8	0.3	3.3	0.6	237	2.4	163	0.9	28.2	-5.5
Woodward	1 459	13.7	151	26.1	D	8.8	3.9	796	8.8	194	-2.0	154.3	1.1
OREGON	203 847	2 027.1	20 741	6 471.3	421.8	1 930.6	552.9	157 257	2 402.4	16 218	5.7	7 999.7	-2.4
Baker	848	7.6	87	14.6	5.1	2.9	1.2	415	3.9	95	8.0	53.7	0.6
Benton	4 491	36.7	467	162.8	4.4	50.9	4.6	3 378	63.0	255	4.7	208.6	-14.2
Clackamas	16 412	165.1	1 572	407.2	21.4	140.5	16.2	10 372	151.2	1 050	6.7	572.3	-3.3
Clatsop	2 972	26.8	242	56.1	14.2	15.0	2.1	1 509	17.0	201	4.2	106.3	-6.0
Columbia	1 426	12.7	133	21.4	D	7.6	2.5	698	7.4	149	11.7	34.4	-17.9
Coos	3 984	39.5	414	97.8	8.8	48.2	5.6	2 369	33.1	354	5.1	113.3	-1.0
Crook	590	5.1	66	26.8	1.8	3.7	1.0	818	10.3	75	-2.8	17.8	10.7
Curry	1 117	11.1	131	22.8	7.8	7.1	1.3	500	5.5	116	15.2	16.6	1.0
Deschutes	6 140	58.0	631	187.6	32.3	57.7	8.3	4 798	59.8	401	7.9	132.0	6.1
Douglas	5 839	53.7	627	138.9	9.2	66.4	4.8	3 526	50.4	513	4.7	122.1	4.1
Gilliam	73	0.6	6	D	D	D	D	D	D	17	2.9	0.0	NA
Grant	305	3.2	37	5.2	1.2	1.5	0.8	155	1.5	60	7.9	11.4	-7.1
Harney	345	3.4	52	7.9	1.0	2.1	2.0	208	2.0	67	-0.8	9.7	-1.8
Hood River	1 087	11.5	117	33.0	5.8	8.3	1.2	1 213	9.8	103	8.7	40.4	-5.2
Jackson	12 041	144.5	983	257.7	22.4	99.2	14.9	6 095	97.9	645	5.9	425.8	-1.7
Jefferson	699	6.2	47	6.8	0.9	1.9	0.8	156	1.9	59	-4.9	18.6	7.2
Josephine	3 804	38.0	417	96.8	8.6	44.9	3.6	2 562	32.7	316	8.7	237.7	-2.8
Klamath	3 557	37.7	350	66.2	5.7	26.4	4.3	1 775	23.4	294	13.2	244.8	2.0
Lake	428	4.0	39	5.3	1.3	2.2	D	123	1.4	54	-4.6	22.2	-3.4
Lane	20 655	201.9	2 207	619.6	34.8	207.9	52.6	16 752	252.1	1 201	4.1	666.9	-1.3
Lincoln	3 542	31.1	307	76.4	35.6	15.1	4.1	2 266	23.4	293	6.3	102.4	-2.6
Linn	5 190	49.9	496	99.6	3.2	39.9	5.1	2 928	36.4	424	6.2	212.3	-7.6
Malheur	2 089	17.2	179	30.5	3.0	11.2	2.8	779	8.9	152	-1.9	89.5	-12.3
Marion	15 840	157.2	1 613	450.8	D	176.1	32.5	12 406	166.8	1 363	2.3	495.6	-7.5
Morrow	210	1.8	24	3.9	D	D	D	117	1.1	42	0.6	9.1	9.8
Multnomah	52 175	521.7	5 892	2 607.3	137.7	562.7	346.9	57 733	972.4	5 348	7.0	2 515.9	-0.3
Polk	1 562	13.6	173	34.9	D	23.5	1.1	832	13.2	138	6.5	78.9	-11.8
Sherman	159	1.1	3	D	D	0.0	D	D	D	8	-4.3	0.0	NA
Tillamook	1 208	9.8	126	19.8	4.8	4.3	1.2	507	5.4	137	10.0	53.9	-1.4
Umatilla	3 797	34.5	349	69.5	6.1	27.4	5.9	1 774	24.3	317	3.6	150.6	-1.4
Union	1 489	12.2	164	28.0	2.3	13.3	1.9	764	9.9	111	4.7	61.8	-1.4

1. For the period including March 12 of the year shown. 2. Includes deposits for all insured and reporting noninsured commercial and mutual savings banks. 3. Includes savings capital for all FSLIC insured savings institutions.

STATE County	Federal funds and grants, 1989: Expenditures: Total (Mil dol)	Expenditures: Percent change, 1988–1989	Per capita[1] (Dollars): Total	Per capita: Direct payments for individuals	Per capita: Procurement contract awards	Per capita: Salaries and wages	Per capita: Grant awards	Local government finances, 1981–1982: General revenue: Total (Mil dol)	Intergovernmental: Total (Mil dol)	Intergovernmental: Percent from state	Taxes: Total (Mil dol)	Taxes: Per capita[2]: Total (Dollars)	Taxes: Per capita[2]: Property (Dollars)	Direct general expenditure: Total (Mil dol)	Direct general expenditure: Percent change, 1977–1982
	174	175	176	177	178	179	180	181	182	183	184	185	186	187	188
OKLAHOMA—Con.															
McCurtain	101.0	7.8	2 752	1 769	13	144	783	32.8	18.0	92.8	6.1	170	119	31.7	116.8
McIntosh	61.7	10.4	3 564	2 723	19	112	601	11.0	7.3	84.9	2.2	135	76	10.4	78.4
Major	22.5	-18.3	2 615	1 693	194	169	191	12.5	7.7	98.5	3.3	338	258	10.9	84.0
Marshall	35.9	6.4	3 020	2 513	19	95	348	8.8	4.3	95.7	1.7	159	97	8.5	100.4
Mayes	89.0	25.5	2 549	1 605	45	106	739	40.8	13.9	90.3	6.0	176	112	29.2	181.7
Murray	39.0	5.8	3 172	2 200	113	224	524	10.1	4.9	92.8	2.8	211	141	9.3	111.7
Muskogee	229.5	3.0	3 326	2 171	74	545	494	106.1	27.9	91.3	21.2	310	178	103.1	99.9
Noble	33.5	-22.6	2 968	1 761	201	195	637	15.4	5.5	95.5	6.8	571	498	11.1	73.7
Nowata	27.0	-5.8	2 619	2 040	14	124	343	7.3	3.9	94.8	1.8	153	105	7.5	89.6
Okfuskee	41.8	12.8	3 695	2 319	18	164	1 101	9.2	6.0	93.3	2.0	172	143	8.9	77.2
Oklahoma	2 736.2	0.2	4 486	1 926	237	1 741	570	675.6	210.9	74.3	241.2	398	198	620.6	82.1
Okmulgee	137.8	13.2	3 569	2 226	352	190	770	29.2	16.0	88.7	7.7	189	93	26.8	71.1
Osage	86.3	-9.3	2 213	1 352	47	462	291	27.1	14.6	93.8	5.9	142	111	25.6	82.3
Ottawa	137.9	44.2	4 257	2 399	1 148	148	489	23.7	13.8	89.8	6.5	194	130	22.0	31.8
Pawnee	40.3	7.3	2 441	1 781	38	222	358	10.6	6.0	89.9	2.9	183	123	9.6	87.8
Payne	167.8	-8.1	2 651	1 532	203	225	672	66.8	19.8	84.2	16.8	255	127	83.5	221.8
Pittsburg	187.1	10.9	4 362	2 312	306	810	880	47.0	19.7	91.9	8.3	200	92	42.3	119.1
Pontotoc	125.8	10.7	3 645	2 086	371	379	779	43.6	18.2	68.8	7.4	217	121	47.6	255.3
Pottawatomie	160.9	7.2	2 755	2 004	71	152	498	71.3	28.9	78.4	12.1	206	116	68.8	191.5
Pushmataha	41.6	2.4	3 523	2 297	78	112	855	9.1	6.8	92.4	1.6	135	96	8.0	74.0
Roger Mills	13.1	0.8	2 627	1 564	26	235	330	8.7	6.6	98.9	1.1	172	138	7.5	267.8
Rogers	85.5	11.4	1 525	1 023	38	202	232	47.3	18.4	93.8	14.9	292	229	47.1	150.3
Seminole	85.2	11.7	3 189	2 195	77	163	709	25.2	13.4	92.0	6.9	240	160	23.6	53.0
Sequoyah	95.1	16.3	2 599	1 602	97	159	723	21.3	16.2	95.7	2.9	92	55	19.1	72.8
Stephens	114.1	4.2	2 691	2 180	23	118	333	37.9	19.7	92.3	10.7	229	121	29.5	72.5
Texas	50.5	-13.2	3 081	1 596	15	149	207	19.9	11.1	93.4	6.2	348	259	18.1	61.5
Tillman	51.0	8.9	4 640	2 296	28	159	687	11.9	6.0	88.8	2.4	200	167	23.7	295.8
Tulsa	1 271.6	5.8	2 442	1 624	204	293	251	564.5	172.3	78.8	240.7	480	244	533.4	83.9
Wagoner	65.1	9.0	1 270	906	18	69	252	17.5	10.6	96.5	3.9	84	57	16.9	136.4
Washington	116.2	0.5	2 601	2 027	41	56	465	55.5	20.6	69.6	15.4	296	161	50.7	157.1
Washita	39.1	-13.1	3 370	2 092	155	196	235	20.3	11.1	98.2	3.5	200	145	16.8	194.1
Woods	32.7	-11.9	3 371	2 476	20	199	176	16.2	6.7	97.1	4.6	413	314	14.9	123.6
Woodward	43.9	1.3	2 284	1 554	28	216	357	28.6	8.7	88.3	11.5	459	212	23.6	102.8
OREGON	8 684.9	5.3	X	1 930	133	372	577	3 451.1	1 314.6	77.6	1 379.4	517	468	3 385.9	72.9
Baker	54.9	7.7	3 658	2 391	140	646	374	18.5	9.3	85.8	6.3	382	365	18.0	75.9
Benton	180.7	2.5	2 751	1 411	109	359	860	70.3	23.5	75.7	28.8	422	391	66.1	60.4
Clackamas	596.1	14.8	2 132	1 402	69	226	416	271.5	97.3	87.6	135.4	544	528	269.9	88.6
Clatsop	100.1	-1.7	3 005	2 145	184	413	257	50.5	17.6	93.0	19.8	604	574	43.6	59.4
Columbia	73.0	7.1	1 872	1 569	10	85	200	51.7	17.9	83.7	20.8	568	551	60.3	67.6
Coos	194.2	11.1	3 163	2 182	123	335	516	100.1	38.4	72.4	27.2	437	420	100.6	58.9
Crook	39.3	0.8	2 828	1 901	102	584	206	15.1	7.7	89.2	3.8	298	284	13.3	77.0
Curry	67.8	6.9	3 443	2 743	121	327	242	24.4	12.4	68.8	4.7	270	257	27.1	105.5
Deschutes	191.2	8.1	2 681	1 999	110	332	232	79.9	28.4	84.0	33.2	522	490	80.3	121.2
Douglas	275.7	9.4	2 822	1 935	143	464	271	131.7	75.7	62.7	34.4	372	361	127.3	66.0
Gilliam	10.2	-24.2	6 028	2 342	28	182	472	3.8	0.8	90.8	2.5	1 191	1 184	4.0	84.1
Grant	26.9	-7.1	3 162	1 718	215	953	174	14.6	8.7	72.1	1.9	238	230	14.5	82.4
Harney	26.5	28.4	3 486	1 671	167	747	598	15.6	8.8	91.8	3.7	494	479	12.3	61.6
Hood River	39.1	-43.2	2 386	1 754	113	261	250	26.5	12.2	95.6	6.7	417	404	21.5	84.7
Jackson	390.7	-7.2	2 610	1 983	65	330	224	148.9	67.8	71.0	53.6	397	363	140.0	72.8
Jefferson	38.5	20.7	3 032	1 585	79	320	890	18.2	7.3	85.9	4.9	397	389	17.9	81.2
Josephine	195.5	-4.2	2 670	2 150	129	160	226	64.6	35.4	63.3	18.5	308	289	65.2	44.6
Klamath	161.2	11.4	2 785	1 945	117	353	352	60.2	31.7	81.3	17.5	295	279	57.5	55.5
Lake	25.9	4.1	3 407	1 768	183	1 012	228	17.5	10.5	90.9	2.8	365	359	14.3	111.0
Lane	676.1	7.5	2 463	1 743	70	272	369	361.0	156.8	73.0	132.9	489	449	377.1	72.1
Lincoln	125.4	3.8	3 184	2 509	90	227	352	60.0	19.4	84.3	19.7	539	479	62.3	128.1
Linn	221.2	3.1	2 391	1 832	97	194	254	111.4	53.1	86.8	40.1	444	419	108.3	69.8
Malheur	77.0	20.5	2 895	1 804	374	232	273	35.9	16.1	82.3	11.9	431	415	33.4	52.6
Marion	834.6	-1.9	3 694	1 960	48	265	1 409	218.8	85.1	77.9	96.8	464	440	223.6	55.7
Morrow	27.8	-22.1	3 753	1 458	586	237	101	18.1	2.7	91.2	8.6	1 147	1 137	17.1	154.6
Multnomah	2 136.1	-2.3	3 758	2 206	232	803	503	897.4	272.8	72.0	382.1	677	539	845.2	66.2
Polk	155.2	31.4	3 104	1 202	22	85	1 777	31.5	16.5	75.0	11.4	247	235	32.0	67.2
Sherman	14.8	-24.8	7 773	2 256	395	1 822	147	3.9	0.9	90.1	2.4	1 060	1 053	3.9	74.7
Tillamook	69.8	6.1	3 146	2 537	146	248	195	29.3	13.4	80.3	8.4	388	374	30.5	40.3
Umatilla	190.6	8.3	3 160	1 811	91	403	644	74.5	29.2	85.2	28.9	479	461	73.3	91.8
Union	63.3	-1.5	2 705	2 022	32	291	283	30.0	14.2	86.3	11.6	470	450	28.8	62.4

1. Based on the estimated population as of July 1 of the year shown. 2. Based on the estimated population as of July 1, 1982.

STATE County	Local government finances, 1981–1982 (cont'd): Direct general expenditure (cont'd): Per capita[1] (Dollars)	Percent of total for– Educa-tion	Health & hospitals	Police protec-tion	Public welfare	High-ways	Debt outstanding: Total (Mil dol)	Per capita[1] (Dollars)	State and local government employment, 1989: Total	Rate[2]	Federal government civilian employment 1989: Total	Earnings ($1,000)	Elections, 1988[3]: Total vote cast for president	Vote for lead party (Percent)
	189	190	191	192	193	194	195	196	197	198	199	200	201	202
OKLAHOMA–Con.														
McCurtain	886	58.6	15.3	2.8	0.2	8.0	13.2	369	1 853	504.9	166	4 353	9 911	D–49.7
McIntosh	632	60.8	1.3	3.0	0.1	8.5	2.7	163	797	460.7	51	1 272	6 742	D–59.9
Major	1 119	51.9	0.3	3.4	0.1	28.9	2.2	222	391	454.7	45	1 032	3 671	R–71.9
Marshall	777	46.1	22.2	4.5	0.1	10.8	2.2	196	623	523.5	36	911	4 669	D–58.5
Mayes	863	45.2	0.3	2.4	0.1	5.5	44.2	1 304	1 728	495.1	89	2 395	12 901	D–51.9
Murray	711	63.6	0.8	3.9	0.3	8.7	11.8	898	1 089	885.4	75	1 971	4 794	D–56.3
Muskogee	1 507	31.2	47.3	2.7	0.0	2.3	86.7	1 267	4 716	683.5	1 392	43 291	25 068	D–54.9
Noble	936	52.0	10.8	4.8	0.1	12.7	5.9	499	788	697.3	68	1 736	4 726	R–63.8
Nowata	627	59.6	0.0	3.8	0.2	14.0	2.5	208	420	407.8	39	898	4 234	D–52.0
Okfuskee	772	74.2	0.6	2.5	0.3	10.9	2.4	208	702	621.2	52	1 266	4 098	D–53.9
Oklahoma	1 025	37.3	4.3	5.7	0.3	5.7	1 336.6	2 208	46 844	768.1	29 652	949 619	212 891	R–63.6
Okmulgee	659	57.8	2.6	5.0	0.0	8.3	16.4	403	2 510	650.3	152	4 265	14 004	D–59.0
Osage	617	51.8	6.6	3.8	0.0	16.3	19.4	466	1 416	363.1	165	4 341	15 055	D–51.7
Ottawa	658	70.5	0.3	4.4	0.1	6.1	9.0	269	1 995	615.7	135	3 545	11 729	D–56.8
Pawnee	594	59.7	9.4	3.9	0.0	10.3	5.5	341	690	418.2	127	3 176	6 162	R–53.9
Payne	1 269	25.0	20.7	2.3	0.1	2.8	112.1	1 704	11 164	1 763.7	369	11 436	26 905	R–59.6
Pittsburg	1 023	40.7	29.3	2.3	0.0	7.6	18.9	458	2 792	650.8	1 100	31 903	16 342	D–52.8
Pontotoc	1 399	28.2	26.3	2.1	0.0	6.0	52.9	1 555	2 334	676.5	386	11 530	13 239	R–49.9
Pottawatomie	1 168	39.2	28.0	3.0	0.1	4.8	73.1	1 241	2 947	504.6	243	6 793	21 169	R–57.2
Pushmataha	676	65.7	0.7	2.5	0.8	11.0	6.2	521	799	677.1	43	1 042	4 301	D–56.5
Roger Mills	1 211	41.7	0.5	2.8	0.3	38.4	0.6	91	271	542.0	38	848	2 012	R–56.3
Rogers	921	54.3	13.3	2.0	0.0	5.6	38.0	744	2 383	424.8	383	10 360	21 851	R–59.2
Seminole	819	57.8	11.2	3.1	0.1	7.8	16.2	561	1 595	597.4	121	3 279	9 073	D–54.1
Sequoyah	606	78.5	0.3	2.3	0.1	6.0	4.2	134	1 430	390.7	137	3 810	10 729	R–53.2
Stephens	629	64.4	0.4	5.2	0.1	6.2	18.2	389	1 873	441.7	128	3 679	17 795	R–55.3
Texas	1 010	57.0	0.6	3.2	0.1	16.0	3.3	186	1 291	787.2	71	1 811	6 752	R–73.6
Tillman	1 958	22.4	8.6	2.1	0.1	5.7	18.4	1 520	667	606.4	54	1 265	3 928	D–54.7
Tulsa	1 064	42.5	1.5	5.4	0.2	5.2	927.0	1 849	24 827	476.7	4 169	139 672	197 763	R–64.5
Wagoner	368	62.5	0.4	3.5	0.0	8.2	28.1	613	1 133	220.9	94	2 565	17 718	R–57.7
Washington	972	42.9	0.2	3.9	0.0	4.7	31.3	601	1 806	404.0	147	4 767	21 713	R–67.3
Washita	956	44.1	0.1	2.9	0.0	6.7	4.3	244	740	637.9	67	1 658	4 745	R–50.6
Woods	1 342	49.7	19.5	1.7	0.0	13.2	3.8	344	965	994.8	57	1 341	4 651	R–61.0
Woodward	945	43.2	23.3	4.5	0.0	7.6	10.2	407	1 579	822.4	127	3 597	7 493	R–66.7
OREGON	1 269	50.5	4.4	4.6	0.6	7.2	2 550.3	956	181 182	642.7	32 434	1 029 301	1 201 694	D–51.3
Baker	1 097	50.9	0.8	3.2	0.0	14.5	3.7	225	784	522.7	444	11 127	6 826	R–54.1
Benton	968	50.0	2.8	4.5	0.1	10.9	49.8	729	9 972	1 517.8	742	23 494	31 610	D–53.6
Clackamas	1 084	64.3	1.5	3.1	0.5	5.5	186.2	748	11 457	409.8	1 034	28 945	123 351	R–49.8
Clatsop	1 329	52.7	2.6	4.5	0.0	4.0	28.8	879	2 013	604.5	151	4 735	14 316	D–56.4
Columbia	1 648	61.1	8.9	2.8	0.0	3.6	70.8	1 933	1 671	428.5	85	2 332	15 806	D–56.8
Coos	1 618	46.5	20.4	3.4	0.0	4.4	37.3	599	3 907	636.3	462	14 428	24 836	D–56.4
Crook	1 028	53.9	1.3	3.9	3.4	10.5	3.0	233	563	405.0	358	9 616	5 882	R–51.8
Curry	1 556	38.9	12.2	5.0	0.0	19.6	6.0	343	927	470.6	275	6 461	9 012	R–52.8
Deschutes	1 261	49.7	11.8	4.4	0.1	7.5	74.3	1 166	3 647	511.5	864	24 486	31 366	R–52.4
Douglas	1 379	49.2	3.8	3.9	1.5	10.6	34.9	378	5 070	518.9	1 720	52 917	38 415	R–52.4
Gilliam	1 892	55.8	1.5	2.0	0.0	11.0	5.5	2 597	160	941.2	14	318	897	R–52.4
Grant	1 791	35.2	15.4	2.9	0.0	14.3	4.7	580	677	796.5	446	10 504	3 844	R–58.9
Harney	1 636	47.6	16.7	2.4	0.0	16.8	0.4	56	565	743.4	240	6 381	3 330	R–55.0
Hood River	1 333	46.6	1.0	2.6	0.0	15.4	8.3	515	989	603.0	105	2 813	6 689	D–49.0
Jackson	1 038	52.3	5.7	6.9	0.6	5.4	64.3	477	7 532	503.1	1 753	53 651	61 912	R–52.5
Jefferson	1 458	54.9	18.3	1.8	0.0	5.7	16.3	1 324	865	681.1	137	3 883	4 995	R–50.2
Josephine	1 088	56.3	3.4	5.2	0.1	6.2	27.0	450	2 701	369.0	485	12 945	27 272	R–58.2
Klamath	969	51.2	2.8	3.4	3.7	10.5	14.3	241	3 401	587.4	996	26 115	22 470	R–60.0
Lake	1 834	38.9	17.3	2.0	0.0	25.3	1.4	183	587	772.4	420	10 492	3 463	R–62.4
Lane	1 386	47.5	2.3	4.4	0.3	9.4	392.8	1 444	20 018	729.3	2 435	73 760	119 702	D–58.4
Lincoln	1 708	33.2	20.7	3.7	0.1	7.8	52.2	1 431	2 843	721.6	239	6 480	17 443	D–55.0
Linn	1 199	63.7	2.2	4.2	0.0	8.1	29.3	324	4 765	515.1	541	17 127	36 122	R–50.7
Malheur	1 204	57.2	9.3	3.6	0.0	6.4	25.6	925	1 884	708.3	200	5 785	9 443	R–66.6
Marion	1 072	57.4	3.2	4.8	0.0	5.5	103.4	495	26 157	1 157.9	1 673	50 502	88 492	R–51.2
Morrow	2 276	37.0	6.8	2.2	0.9	10.4	58.4	7 793	612	827.0	73	1 656	2 970	R–51.5
Multnomah	1 497	42.1	2.6	6.2	1.2	3.8	826.6	1 464	42 209	742.6	13 466	474 446	261 843	D–61.6
Polk	697	53.8	2.6	6.0	0.0	5.7	16.9	369	2 444	488.8	106	3 962	20 621	R–51.2
Sherman	1 710	56.4	0.5	0.0	0.0	14.9	0.2	104	159	836.8	96	3 708	1 016	R–54.6
Tillamook	1 411	51.4	8.8	2.9	0.1	8.8	30.9	1 432	1 294	582.9	163	4 525	10 070	D–54.9
Umatilla	1 216	65.1	2.9	3.1	0.0	4.2	40.6	673	3 934	652.4	854	24 922	18 981	R–54.0
Union	1 171	59.2	1.9	3.5	0.0	7.7	16.2	659	2 081	889.3	277	6 864	10 090	R–50.2

1. Based on the estimated population as of July 1, 1982. 2. Per 10,000 resident population estimated as of July 1 of the year shown. 3. Data subject to copyright.

STATE–County code	MSA/CMSA/NECMA code[1]	STATE County	Land Area,[2] 1990 (Sq. Km.)	Population, 1990: Total persons	Rank	Per square kilometer	Race: White	Black	Am. Indian, Eskimo, Aleut	Asian & Pacific Islander	Other race	Hispanic[3]	Age of population Percent: Under 5 years	5 to 14 years	15 to 24 years
			1	2	3	4	5	6	7	8	9	10	11	12	13
		OREGON—Con.													
41 063	...	Wallowa	8 147	6 911	2 671	0.8	6 826	6	35	25	19	113	6.8	15.5	9.6
41 065	...	Wasco	6 167	21 683	1 593	3.5	19 907	67	896	240	573	1 065	6.9	15.8	10.9
41 067	6442	Washington	1 875	311 554	161	166.2	286 459	2 058	1 779	13 424	7 834	14 401	7.8	15.0	13.0
41 069	...	Wheeler	4 442	1 396	3 102	0.3	1 382	1	11	2	0	12	5.4	12.8	9.7
41 071	6442	Yamhill	1 853	65 551	669	35.4	62 135	370	823	783	1 440	4 129	7.5	16.6	14.3
42 000	...	PENNSYLVANIA	116 083	11 881 643	X	102.4	10 520 201	1 089 795	14 733	137 438	119 476	232 262	6.7	13.0	14.1
42 001	9280	Adams	1 347	78 274	577	58.1	76 355	926	85	368	540	1 216	7.0	14.0	15.3
42 003	6282	Allegheny	1 891	1 336 449	19	706.7	1 169 452	149 550	1 452	13 469	2 526	8 731	6.3	11.5	13.0
42 005	...	Armstrong	1 694	73 478	612	43.4	72 727	566	59	81	45	164	6.0	13.8	12.7
42 007	6282	Beaver	1 127	186 093	261	165.1	174 759	10 475	203	377	279	1 124	6.3	13.2	12.3
42 009	...	Bedford	2 628	47 919	873	18.2	47 607	150	40	78	44	118	6.4	14.2	13.6
42 011	6680	Berks	2 225	336 523	151	151.2	314 561	10 003	333	2 746	8 880	17 174	6.7	12.9	13.7
42 013	0280	Blair	1 362	130 542	357	95.8	128 840	1 073	118	380	131	431	6.3	13.9	13.4
42 015	...	Bradford	2 980	60 967	714	20.5	60 409	149	117	214	78	218	7.1	15.4	13.0
42 017	6162	Bucks	1 574	541 174	89	343.8	514 240	15 313	566	8 446	2 609	8 895	7.3	14.2	13.2
42 019	...	Butler	2 042	152 013	306	74.4	150 407	810	109	545	142	563	6.8	14.0	15.0
42 021	3680	Cambria	1 782	163 029	292	91.5	158 584	3 734	109	384	218	985	5.7	13.3	13.6
42 023	...	Cameron	1 029	5 913	2 771	5.7	5 880	7	15	6	5	3	7.2	14.0	12.0
42 025	0240	Carbon	991	56 846	767	57.4	56 403	119	45	176	103	509	6.2	12.7	12.4
42 027	8050	Centre	2 869	123 786	371	43.1	116 552	2 801	179	3 841	413	1 350	5.6	9.8	31.1
42 029	6162	Chester	1 958	376 396	135	192.2	344 931	23 995	510	4 070	2 890	8 565	7.4	13.6	14.0
42 031	...	Clarion	1 560	41 699	964	26.7	41 187	200	66	210	36	116	5.8	13.3	21.0
42 033	...	Clearfield	2 972	78 097	579	26.3	77 609	176	87	182	43	200	6.5	14.1	13.4
42 035	...	Clinton	2 307	37 182	1 067	16.1	36 857	144	49	117	15	91	5.8	13.3	17.8
42 037	7560	Columbia	1 258	63 202	691	50.2	62 588	268	38	228	80	341	5.9	12.2	19.3
42 039	...	Crawford	2 623	86 169	529	32.9	84 615	1 072	112	272	98	303	6.8	14.7	15.1
42 041	3240	Cumberland	1 425	195 257	246	137.0	189 037	3 062	254	2 495	409	1 355	5.9	12.3	16.6
42 043	3240	Dauphin	1 361	237 813	211	174.7	195 881	35 609	340	2 770	3 213	6 024	7.0	12.8	13.0
42 045	6162	Delaware	477	547 651	86	1 148.1	473 741	61 394	609	10 002	1 905	5 998	7.0	12.6	14.3
42 047	...	Elk	2 146	34 878	1 134	16.3	34 702	15	35	98	28	56	6.8	14.4	12.8
42 049	2360	Erie	2 077	275 572	179	132.7	257 879	14 304	438	1 411	1 540	3 364	7.2	14.5	16.2
42 051	6282	Fayette	2 046	145 351	326	71.0	139 773	5 116	139	219	104	452	6.1	13.7	13.2
42 053	...	Forest	1 109	4 802	2 858	4.3	4 731	43	11	3	14	23	5.4	11.4	13.9
42 055	...	Franklin	1 999	121 082	380	60.6	117 072	2 771	176	619	444	1 065	6.6	13.5	14.2
42 057	...	Fulton	1 133	13 837	2 071	12.2	13 669	125	22	17	4	31	7.1	14.9	14.2
42 059	...	Greene	1 492	39 550	1 010	26.5	38 948	377	69	112	44	209	6.4	14.6	14.7
42 061	...	Huntingdon	2 267	44 164	922	19.5	41 994	1 982	53	83	52	195	6.3	12.8	16.1
42 063	...	Indiana	2 148	89 994	511	41.9	88 033	1 175	92	574	120	370	5.8	13.5	21.4
42 065	...	Jefferson	1 698	46 083	902	27.1	45 891	49	49	70	24	98	6.5	14.6	12.8
42 067	...	Juniata	1 014	20 625	1 649	20.3	20 529	27	18	41	10	49	6.8	14.9	13.3
42 069	7560	Lackawanna	1 188	219 039	226	184.4	215 634	1 572	163	1 364	306	1 089	6.0	12.1	13.9
42 071	4000	Lancaster	2 458	422 822	119	172.0	397 815	10 038	484	4 652	9 833	15 639	7.9	14.6	14.6
42 073	...	Lawrence	934	96 246	481	103.0	92 896	2 915	61	274	100	357	6.2	13.3	13.3
42 075	3240	Lebanon	937	113 744	403	121.4	110 904	706	93	917	1 124	2 666	6.7	13.6	13.6
42 077	0240	Lehigh	898	291 130	169	324.2	271 674	6 776	320	3 661	8 699	15 001	6.6	12.5	12.9
42 079	7560	Luzerne	2 308	328 149	155	142.2	321 906	3 958	224	1 488	573	2 023	5.9	11.8	13.4
42 081	9140	Lycoming	3 198	118 710	391	37.1	115 040	2 816	219	469	166	641	6.9	14.0	14.0
42 083	...	McKean	2 542	47 131	889	18.5	46 147	520	111	161	192	511	6.5	13.9	13.5
42 085	7610	Mercer	1 740	121 003	381	69.5	114 479	5 882	115	393	134	506	6.2	13.1	14.5
42 087	...	Mifflin	1 064	46 197	899	43.4	45 939	108	31	98	21	132	7.0	13.6	13.7
42 089	7560	Monroe	1 573	95 709	483	60.8	92 766	1 727	130	666	420	2 052	7.4	13.8	14.0
42 091	6162	Montgomery	1 251	678 111	61	542.1	620 087	39 124	752	15 995	2 153	8 357	6.8	12.3	12.5
42 093	...	Montour	339	17 735	1 801	52.3	17 472	76	7	138	42	116	7.1	13.1	12.6
42 095	0240	Northampton	968	247 105	202	255.3	232 785	5 269	209	2 709	6 133	11 591	6.7	12.9	14.7
42 097	...	Northumberland	1 191	96 771	476	81.3	95 997	326	79	180	189	532	6.2	12.9	12.5
42 099	3240	Perry	1 434	41 172	976	28.7	40 916	95	50	69	42	194	7.3	15.1	13.7
42 101	6162	Philadelphia	350	1 585 577	12	4 530.2	848 586	631 936	3 454	43 522	58 079	89 193	7.3	12.9	15.3
42 103	...	Pike	1 417	27 966	1 352	19.7	27 420	256	48	133	109	651	8.1	13.8	9.9
42 105	...	Potter	2 800	16 717	1 867	6.0	16 629	20	29	31	8	72	7.1	15.5	12.6
42 107	...	Schuylkill	2 017	152 585	303	75.6	150 987	842	111	496	149	677	5.7	12.3	12.6
42 109	...	Snyder	858	36 680	1 083	42.8	36 347	146	30	95	62	148	7.3	13.9	17.1
42 111	3680	Somerset	2 784	78 218	578	28.1	77 875	102	43	143	55	231	6.4	14.2	12.7
42 113	...	Sullivan	1 165	6 104	2 744	5.2	6 001	59	30	9	5	25	5.3	12.8	14.6
42 115	...	Susquehanna	2 132	40 380	988	18.9	40 086	79	83	87	45	162	7.2	15.4	12.2
42 117	...	Tioga	2 936	41 126	977	14.0	40 648	227	108	106	37	139	6.5	14.3	16.6

1. MSA = Metropolitan Statistical Area. CMSA = Consolidated MSA. NECMA = New England county metropolitan area. PMSA = Primary MSA. See Appendix A for explanation of these concepts. See Appendix B for list of metropolitan areas identified by type, with component counties. 2. Dry land or land partially or temporarily covered by water. 3. Hispanic persons may be of any race.

STATE County	Population, 1990 (cont'd): Age of population (cont'd), Percent: 25 to 34 years	35 to 44 years	45 to 54 years	55 to 64 years	65 to 74 years	75 years and over	Percent female	Population–Change and components of change: Change 1980–1990: Number	Percent	Total persons, 1986	Total persons, 1980	Components of change, 1980–1986: Net change: Number	Percent	Natural increase: Births	Deaths
	14	15	16	17	18	19	20	21	22	23	24	25	26	27	28
OREGON—Con.															
Wallowa	12.9	15.5	10.9	10.8	10.1	7.8	50.4	-362	-5.0	7 200	7 273	0	-0.6	700	400
Wasco	13.4	15.6	10.6	9.4	9.7	7.8	51.5	-49	-0.2	21 300	21 732	-400	-1.9	2 000	1 400
Washington	18.6	18.2	10.5	6.8	5.7	4.4	51.1	65 694	26.7	271 400	245 860	25 500	10.4	26 600	9 400
Wheeler	9.2	14.0	13.3	14.0	13.0	8.4	50.2	-117	-7.7	1 500	1 513	-100	-3.8	100	100
Yamhill	15.1	15.7	9.8	7.7	7.4	5.8	49.9	10 219	18.5	57 500	55 332	2 200	3.9	5 900	3 100
PENNSYLVANIA	16.1	14.7	10.2	9.8	9.0	6.4	52.1	17 643	0.1	11 888 000	11 864 000	24 000	0.2	995 000	760 000
Adams	16.2	14.8	10.2	8.8	7.7	5.8	51.2	9 982	14.6	71 200	68 292	2 900	4.2	6 200	3 800
Allegheny	16.5	14.7	10.0	10.6	10.3	7.1	53.1	-113 746	-7.8	1 373 600	1 450 195	-76 600	-5.3	111 200	98 600
Armstrong	15.0	14.4	10.2	10.3	10.2	7.4	51.9	-4 290	-5.5	78 500	77 768	700	0.9	6 400	5 200
Beaver	15.1	14.2	10.5	11.4	10.5	6.4	52.4	-18 348	-9.0	193 200	204 441	-11 200	-5.5	15 700	12 300
Bedford	14.9	13.7	11.4	10.5	9.2	6.2	51.1	1 135	2.4	47 700	46 784	1 000	2.1	3 700	2 800
Berks	16.1	14.8	10.3	9.9	8.8	6.8	51.7	24 014	7.7	321 000	312 509	8 500	2.7	25 800	19 600
Blair	14.5	14.5	10.2	10.2	9.8	7.2	52.9	-6 079	-4.4	132 500	136 621	-4 100	-3.0	11 100	9 700
Bradford	15.0	14.5	11.0	9.3	8.4	6.3	51.4	-1 952	-3.1	64 300	62 919	1 300	2.1	5 900	3 700
Bucks	17.5	16.7	11.1	9.0	6.7	4.2	50.8	61 994	12.9	522 100	479 180	42 900	9.0	44 200	22 400
Butler	16.0	15.5	10.3	9.0	7.8	5.7	51.2	4 101	2.8	151 100	147 912	3 200	2.1	13 100	8 200
Cambria	13.7	14.4	9.7	10.8	11.2	7.5	52.1	-20 234	-11.0	173 200	183 263	-10 000	-5.5	13 600	12 200
Cameron	13.4	14.0	10.1	10.8	11.1	7.4	51.1	-761	-11.4	6 500	6 674	-200	-2.9	600	500
Carbon	15.1	14.0	10.1	11.1	11.0	7.4	51.7	3 561	6.7	54 400	53 285	1 100	2.1	3 900	4 100
Centre	16.8	12.5	8.4	6.9	5.3	3.7	48.2	11 026	9.8	114 600	112 760	1 800	1.6	8 300	4 200
Chester	17.1	16.9	11.4	8.7	6.6	4.3	51.0	59 736	18.9	339 100	316 660	22 400	7.1	29 100	15 400
Clarion	13.8	12.9	10.1	9.2	7.9	6.0	51.7	-1 663	-3.8	42 600	43 362	-700	-1.7	3 600	2 500
Clearfield	15.0	13.9	10.5	9.9	9.8	6.8	51.8	-5 481	-6.6	82 100	83 578	-1 500	-1.7	7 100	5 300
Clinton	13.4	13.3	10.1	10.3	9.5	6.4	52.1	-1 789	-4.6	38 100	38 971	-900	-2.3	3 200	2 400
Columbia	14.0	13.6	9.9	9.4	9.3	6.5	52.7	1 235	2.0	61 300	61 967	-700	-1.1	4 700	4 000
Crawford	14.0	14.3	10.3	9.3	8.8	6.6	51.5	-2 700	-3.0	87 200	88 869	-1 600	-1.9	8 000	5 500
Cumberland	15.8	15.6	10.9	9.5	7.9	5.5	51.7	15 632	8.7	189 900	179 625	10 300	5.7	13 400	9 500
Dauphin	17.4	15.9	10.3	9.5	8.3	6.0	52.2	5 496	2.4	236 700	232 317	4 400	1.9	20 700	14 500
Delaware	16.9	14.2	9.7	9.8	9.2	6.3	52.3	-7 372	-1.3	560 600	555 023	5 500	1.0	47 300	36 000
Elk	15.3	13.6	10.4	10.6	9.6	6.4	50.9	-3 460	-9.0	37 500	38 338	-900	-2.3	3 400	2 200
Erie	15.5	14.4	9.6	8.9	8.4	5.4	51.7	-4 208	-1.5	279 200	279 780	-500	-0.2	26 500	16 200
Fayette	14.1	14.4	10.0	10.6	10.7	7.3	52.5	-14 066	-8.8	155 800	159 417	-3 600	-2.3	12 700	11 300
Forest	11.8	12.9	12.1	12.3	12.3	7.9	48.5	-270	-5.3	4 800	5 072	-300	-5.0	300	400
Franklin	15.6	14.8	11.0	9.7	8.4	6.0	51.5	7 453	6.6	118 700	113 629	5 100	4.4	9 400	6 400
Fulton	15.2	14.1	11.5	10.0	7.8	5.2	50.4	995	7.7	14 000	12 842	1 100	8.7	1 100	700
Greene	14.1	15.2	9.6	9.0	9.3	7.1	52.5	-926	-2.3	40 800	40 476	300	0.8	3 400	2 700
Huntingdon	15.8	15.2	10.4	9.8	7.7	5.8	48.3	1 911	4.5	42 900	42 253	600	1.4	3 500	2 400
Indiana	13.9	13.7	9.4	8.4	8.1	5.7	51.8	-2 287	-2.5	92 400	92 281	100	0.1	7 700	4 900
Jefferson	14.9	13.9	10.0	10.0	9.7	7.6	51.7	-2 220	-4.6	48 400	48 303	100	0.1	4 300	3 200
Juniata	15.7	14.5	10.8	9.6	8.1	6.3	50.8	1 437	7.5	20 000	19 188	800	4.4	1 800	1 200
Lackawanna	14.1	13.6	9.9	10.5	11.2	8.6	53.3	-8 869	-3.9	223 000	227 908	-4 900	-2.2	16 900	17 600
Lancaster	16.6	14.7	9.9	8.6	7.4	5.7	51.4	60 476	16.7	393 500	362 346	31 200	8.6	36 800	20 000
Lawrence	13.8	14.0	10.1	10.9	11.1	7.4	52.6	-10 904	-10.2	101 900	107 150	-5 200	-4.9	8 200	6 900
Lebanon	15.8	14.9	10.6	9.8	8.5	6.5	51.2	5 162	4.8	111 900	108 582	3 300	3.1	9 200	6 600
Lehigh	16.9	15.4	10.4	9.9	8.9	6.5	51.9	18 781	6.9	281 500	272 349	9 100	3.4	22 100	16 500
Luzerne	14.4	13.8	10.2	10.9	11.2	8.5	52.7	-14 930	-4.4	331 100	343 079	-12 000	-3.5	23 600	26 500
Lycoming	15.5	14.7	10.1	9.7	8.7	6.4	51.8	294	0.2	116 300	118 416	-2 100	-1.8	10 600	7 200
McKean	14.8	14.1	10.3	10.2	9.0	7.7	50.7	-3 504	-6.9	47 300	50 635	-3 300	-6.5	4 100	3 500
Mercer	14.2	13.8	10.3	10.7	10.0	7.2	51.5	-7 296	-5.7	123 600	128 299	-4 700	-3.7	9 800	7 800
Mifflin	14.7	13.7	11.2	10.0	9.2	6.8	52.1	-711	-1.5	46 400	46 908	-500	-1.0	4 000	2 900
Monroe	16.6	16.0	10.1	9.2	8.1	5.0	50.8	26 300	37.9	82 700	69 409	13 300	19.1	5 700	4 200
Montgomery	17.2	15.5	10.9	9.9	8.6	6.4	51.9	34 734	5.4	672 100	643 377	28 700	4.5	52 700	37 600
Montour	16.8	14.2	10.4	9.3	8.6	7.9	53.2	1 060	6.4	16 700	16 675	0	0.0	1 500	1 300
Northampton	15.8	15.2	10.2	9.5	9.0	6.0	51.4	21 687	9.6	234 100	225 418	8 700	3.9	17 300	13 100
Northumberland	14.3	13.9	10.5	10.7	10.7	8.2	52.6	-3 610	-3.6	99 400	100 381	-1 000	-1.0	7 800	7 800
Perry	16.8	16.7	10.6	8.7	6.9	4.2	50.2	5 454	15.3	38 800	35 718	3 100	8.6	3 300	2 000
Philadelphia	17.5	13.5	9.3	9.0	8.7	6.5	53.5	-102 633	-6.1	1 642 900	1 688 210	-45 400	-2.7	160 200	127 200
Pike	16.8	15.0	9.8	11.1	10.1	5.4	50.4	9 695	53.1	22 300	18 271	4 100	22.2	1 400	1 400
Potter	13.7	14.0	10.6	10.1	9.6	6.9	51.4	-1 009	-5.7	18 300	17 726	600	3.3	1 700	1 100
Schuylkill	14.2	13.8	9.9	11.3	11.6	8.4	51.8	-8 045	-5.0	156 400	160 630	-4 300	-2.7	11 300	13 200
Snyder	15.5	14.4	10.3	8.9	7.5	5.1	51.2	3 096	9.2	35 600	33 584	2 000	6.0	3 000	1 800
Somerset	14.7	14.5	10.2	10.4	10.0	6.9	51.8	-3 025	-3.7	80 900	81 243	-300	-0.4	6 900	5 000
Sullivan	13.4	12.2	9.5	11.3	10.9	10.0	49.9	-245	-3.9	6 300	6 349	-100	-1.0	400	500
Susquehanna	15.3	14.2	11.1	9.2	8.8	6.5	50.6	2 504	6.6	39 900	37 876	2 000	5.4	3 500	2 300
Tioga	13.8	13.3	11.0	9.5	8.7	6.3	51.3	153	0.4	40 500	40 973	-500	-1.3	3 500	2 400

STATE County	Population—(cont'd): Components of change, 1980-1986 (cont'd): Net migration	Households, 1990: Number	Households, 1990: Percent change, 1980–1990	Households, 1990: Persons per household	Households, 1990: Percent: Female family householder[1]	Households, 1990: Percent: One-person	Births, 1988: Total	Births, 1988: Rate[2]	Births, 1988: Low birth weight[3] (Number)	Deaths, 1987: Number: Total	Deaths, 1987: Number: Infant[4]	Deaths, 1987: Rate: Total[2]	Deaths, 1987: Rate: Infant[5]	Marriages, 1984: Number	Marriages, 1984: Rate[2]
	29	30	31	32	33	34	35	36	37	38	39	40	41	42	43
OREGON—Con.															
Wallowa	-400	2 796	-0.6	2.45	6.2	25.9	89	12.7	2	51	1	7.2	13.3	69	9.0
Wasco	-1 100	8 607	4.8	2.48	9.5	25.9	284	13.8	11	248	1	12.0	3.4	193	8.7
Washington	8 400	118 997	30.9	2.59	8.7	23.3	4 537	15.5	207	1 871	46	6.6	11.0	1 760	6.7
Wheeler	-100	584	-0.3	2.37	4.1	24.5	10	7.7	0	15	0	11.5	0.0	5	3.3
Yamhill	-700	22 424	16.8	2.77	9.0	19.6	926	15.3	54	495	9	8.3	8.6	457	7.9
PENNSYLVANIA	-210 000	4 495 966	6.5	2.57	11.3	25.6	165 639	13.8	11 417	125 436	1 685	10.5	10.4	91 610	7.7
Adams	500	28 067	22.6	2.68	8.1	19.9	999	13.4	54	691	9	9.5	8.8	469	6.7
Allegheny	-89 200	541 261	0.1	2.41	12.5	29.7	17 369	12.8	1 251	15 793	201	11.6	11.4	10 541	7.5
Armstrong	-500	28 309	0.9	2.56	8.6	24.1	841	10.8	50	834	12	10.7	12.9	626	7.9
Beaver	-14 700	71 939	0.3	2.54	11.2	24.4	2 299	12.1	142	1 968	19	10.3	8.4	1 290	6.5
Bedford	100	18 038	10.7	2.64	7.7	21.6	584	12.2	29	483	2	10.1	3.5	373	7.8
Berks	2 200	127 649	11.4	2.56	9.1	23.5	4 445	13.5	240	3 371	33	10.4	7.6	2 541	8.0
Blair	-5 500	50 332	2.5	2.54	11.4	25.9	1 601	12.1	95	1 612	14	12.1	8.5	953	7.1
Bradford	-900	22 492	4.9	2.67	8.7	22.3	888	13.8	56	598	7	9.3	8.0	560	8.8
Bucks	21 100	190 507	21.6	2.80	8.4	19.2	7 794	14.3	431	4 061	61	7.6	7.9	4 068	8.0
Butler	-1 700	55 325	12.1	2.65	8.3	22.4	1 978	12.9	101	1 459	23	9.6	11.8	1 099	7.3
Cambria	-11 500	62 004	-2.2	2.53	10.4	26.9	1 827	10.7	104	2 022	14	11.8	7.6	1 209	6.8
Cameron	-300	2 395	-6.1	2.45	9.7	29.4	85	13.3	9	70	1	11.1	10.6	61	9.2
Carbon	1 300	21 989	11.9	2.55	9.2	24.1	677	12.1	46	684	3	12.4	4.8	405	7.5
Centre	-2 300	42 683	18.2	2.55	6.2	23.6	1 413	12.2	70	758	14	6.6	9.9	855	7.5
Chester	8 700	133 257	27.2	2.73	8.3	20.2	5 551	15.1	255	2 673	36	7.5	6.7	2 420	7.2
Clarion	-1 800	14 990	5.8	2.59	8.0	24.0	490	11.7	28	472	3	11.3	5.7	362	8.5
Clearfield	-3 300	29 808	2.3	2.58	9.3	24.4	1 011	12.4	75	899	12	11.0	11.1	672	8.1
Clinton	-1 700	13 844	2.3	2.54	9.6	24.8	429	11.3	28	371	3	9.8	6.9	298	7.8
Columbia	-1 400	23 478	8.3	2.53	8.6	24.1	766	12.6	36	611	4	10.0	6.0	508	8.3
Crawford	-4 100	32 185	4.0	2.60	9.3	24.6	1 103	12.8	55	920	13	10.7	11.6	743	8.3
Cumberland	6 300	73 452	17.0	2.51	7.6	24.2	2 222	11.4	137	1 612	20	8.4	9.2	1 651	8.8
Dauphin	-1 900	95 264	8.1	2.45	11.7	28.4	3 514	14.6	238	2 383	45	10.0	13.1	1 911	8.1
Delaware	-5 700	201 374	4.7	2.63	11.9	25.1	8 150	14.6	510	5 815	66	10.5	8.2	5 398	9.8
Elk	-2 100	13 131	1.8	2.63	8.4	24.2	515	14.0	31	374	1	10.1	2.0	317	8.4
Erie	-10 900	101 564	4.9	2.61	11.5	25.4	4 013	14.5	248	2 585	45	9.3	11.5	2 381	8.4
Fayette	-5 000	56 110	-0.8	2.56	12.3	25.0	1 756	11.5	126	1 758	17	11.5	9.3	1 157	7.3
Forest	-200	1 908	-0.2	2.40	7.1	26.3	51	10.9	2	59	0	12.6	0.0	46	9.4
Franklin	2 100	45 675	14.3	2.59	7.8	21.8	1 598	13.3	58	1 023	7	8.6	4.5	672	5.7
Fulton	700	5 139	15.0	2.68	8.0	20.7	174	12.1	15	136	1	9.6	5.1	77	5.7
Greene	-400	14 624	3.3	2.62	10.6	24.3	477	12.0	33	427	5	10.7	10.0	329	8.0
Huntingdon	-400	15 527	7.4	2.58	8.5	24.3	516	12.0	31	442	6	10.3	10.8	374	8.8
Indiana	-2 700	31 710	5.7	2.65	8.2	23.2	1 024	11.1	48	796	10	8.6	9.8	579	6.2
Jefferson	-1 000	17 608	2.0	2.57	9.0	24.7	600	12.6	32	535	3	11.1	5.0	497	10.2
Juniata	300	7 598	13.5	2.66	6.6	20.4	286	14.1	12	214	4	10.6	13.8	155	7.8
Lackawanna	-4 300	84 528	3.0	2.50	11.9	28.4	2 722	12.2	179	2 776	22	12.5	8.6	1 617	7.2
Lancaster	14 400	150 956	21.9	2.71	7.9	20.9	6 890	16.6	352	3 467	54	8.6	8.3	3 105	8.1
Lawrence	-6 500	36 350	-3.1	2.57	10.8	24.2	1 143	11.3	86	1 166	7	11.5	5.8	1 160	11.0
Lebanon	800	42 688	12.5	2.58	8.7	22.9	1 481	13.0	71	1 147	13	10.1	8.5	904	8.1
Lehigh	3 500	112 887	11.4	2.51	9.4	25.0	3 884	13.5	232	2 769	33	9.7	8.7	2 130	7.7
Luzerne	-9 100	128 483	2.4	2.47	11.9	28.6	3 824	11.5	212	4 502	36	13.6	10.0	2 457	7.3
Lycoming	-5 500	44 949	6.8	2.56	9.9	24.1	1 627	13.8	92	1 189	13	10.1	8.3	1 057	9.0
McKean	-3 900	17 837	-2.5	2.52	9.9	26.4	549	11.9	35	576	4	12.4	6.7	430	8.8
Mercer	-6 700	45 591	2.1	2.54	10.3	24.6	1 506	12.3	93	1 344	13	10.9	9.3	1 084	8.6
Mifflin	-1 600	17 697	5.3	2.58	8.7	24.5	642	13.7	36	494	6	10.6	8.8	374	8.1
Monroe	11 800	34 206	35.9	2.69	7.5	19.2	1 276	13.6	70	752	5	8.6	4.5	748	9.8
Montgomery	13 600	254 995	14.2	2.58	8.3	24.6	9 659	14.0	459	6 196	72	9.1	7.8	5 927	9.0
Montour	-200	6 543	17.9	2.52	7.7	26.3	284	17.2	19	209	1	12.7	4.4	142	8.4
Northampton	4 600	90 955	13.6	2.62	9.1	21.8	3 187	13.1	185	2 250	27	9.4	9.1	1 966	8.5
Northumberland	-1 000	38 736	2.4	2.46	9.5	27.4	1 178	12.0	74	1 285	9	13.1	7.8	815	8.1
Perry	1 700	14 949	21.1	2.73	7.7	18.4	578	14.2	27	325	2	8.1	3.4	271	7.2
Philadelphia	-78 400	603 075	-2.7	2.56	20.3	31.6	28 979	17.6	3 390	20 768	494	12.5	17.3	10 124	6.1
Pike	4 100	10 536	47.9	2.62	6.1	20.0	375	14.0	18	270	1	11.0	3.2	163	8.0
Potter	-100	6 246	1.7	2.63	8.1	23.1	242	13.4	12	184	3	10.3	11.0	182	9.9
Schuylkill	-2 400	60 773	1.4	2.47	10.0	28.0	1 744	11.3	107	2 081	17	13.5	10.4	1 130	7.2
Snyder	800	12 764	19.5	2.70	6.6	20.2	529	14.5	26	309	2	8.6	4.0	313	8.9
Somerset	-2 200	29 574	3.6	2.60	8.6	23.2	995	12.4	59	874	14	10.9	14.3	608	7.4
Sullivan	0	2 280	5.1	2.49	8.0	26.7	51	8.0	2	88	0	13.8	0.0	75	12.1
Susquehanna	800	14 898	14.5	2.69	8.3	21.5	593	14.5	35	437	2	10.8	3.5	327	8.4
Tioga	-1 600	14 974	8.7	2.61	8.1	22.1	507	12.6	31	362	2	9.1	4.1	402	10.0

1. No spouse present. 2. Per 1,000 resident population estimated as of July 1 of the year shown. 3. Under 2,500 grams. 4. Deaths of infants under 1 year old. 5. Deaths of infants under 1 year old per 1,000 live births.

STATE County	Divorces, 1984		Physicians, active non–Federal, 1989		Hospitals, 1989			Nursing homes,[4] 1986		Serious crimes known to police, 1988			Education			
						Beds				Number			Public school enrollment[7]		Attainment,[8] 1980	
	Number	Rate[1]	Number[2]	Rate[3]	Number	Number	Rate[3]	Number	Beds	Total[5]	Violent[6]	Rate[3]	1986–1987	1980	Percent 12 yrs. or more	Percent 16 yrs. or more
	44	45	46	47	48	49	50	51	52	53	54	55	56	57	58	59
OREGON–Con.																
Wallowa	22	2.9	6	87	1	33	478	2	59	115	5	1 587	1 194	1 380	74.5	13.2
Wasco	146	6.6	44	217	1	87	429	2	200	1 218	63	5 900	3 697	4 397	75.2	13.6
Washington	1 165	4.4	325	107	3	340	112	17	1 361	13 255	454	4 692	47 778	45 990	85.0	25.9
Wheeler	8	5.3	0	0	0	0	0	0	0	39	3	2 982	278	309	67.2	6.9
Yamhill	309	5.4	85	137	2	124	200	9	538	2 830	113	4 912	11 474	11 086	72.0	15.0
PENNSYLVANIA	40 375	3.4	27 771	231	302	68 253	567	1 398	101 183	358 958	41 288	3 023	1 630 570	1 970 925	64.7	13.6
Adams	205	2.9	57	75	1	102	135	11	895	1 149	81	1 579	11 892	12 557	59.2	11.5
Allegheny	4 339	3.1	5 133	382	39	12 178	907	174	8 906	47 454	5 609	3 650	164 004	220 027	69.0	16.5
Armstrong	176	2.2	56	72	1	200	257	15	608	882	57	1 107	13 654	15 042	58.7	6.7
Beaver	500	2.5	193	103	2	660	351	19	1 550	3 172	349	1 675	29 380	38 029	64.8	9.4
Bedford	128	2.7	22	46	1	95	198	21	407	699	47	1 448	8 457	10 029	58.0	6.5
Berks	930	2.9	566	170	6	1 800	541	24	2 817	8 863	842	2 800	47 966	53 493	58.5	11.4
Blair	373	2.8	215	163	7	909	687	29	2 070	3 137	176	2 360	20 992	23 974	65.4	8.1
Bradford	201	3.2	170	263	3	510	788	5	449	1 127	61	1 740	12 243	13 786	64.9	8.9
Bucks	1 815	3.6	836	151	10	1 727	312	45	3 786	14 502	1 673	2 712	72 656	88 065	74.7	18.6
Butler	500	3.3	122	79	2	673	436	29	1 787	2 612	174	1 701	23 322	29 669	69.1	11.7
Cambria	395	2.2	305	181	5	1 035	615	11	1 340	2 577	341	1 580	26 162	31 710	61.1	8.6
Cameron	4 524	685.5	4	63	0	0	0	2	58	129	16	2 000	1 114	1 397	64.5	7.3
Carbon	122	2.3	40	70	2	268	471	3	403	1 093	81	1 965	7 687	9 009	57.4	7.3
Centre	327	2.9	173	149	4	465	401	6	514	4 133	114	3 579	13 020	17 398	75.8	27.5
Chester	1 110	3.3	575	152	11	1 960	519	22	2 273	8 088	788	2 315	48 930	57 515	76.4	26.3
Clarion	101	2.4	11	27	1	87	210	4	414	725	33	1 775	8 811	8 235	63.7	11.0
Clearfield	222	2.7	88	108	2	325	400	7	775	1 415	76	1 844	17 157	17 144	59.6	7.6
Clinton	155	4.1	40	105	2	312	821	3	317	959	76	2 604	6 042	7 310	63.7	9.3
Columbia	195	3.2	76	125	2	424	696	9	669	1 321	41	2 156	11 045	10 959	63.5	10.2
Crawford	290	3.3	85	100	2	419	492	12	1 100	1 930	85	2 220	12 507	18 179	66.9	10.5
Cumberland	689	3.7	371	188	5	716	362	14	1 701	3 910	234	2 020	33 091	32 872	72.9	19.0
Dauphin	793	3.4	787	325	5	1 946	804	19	2 462	10 350	1 377	4 305	33 590	39 303	69.9	14.3
Delaware	1 348	2.4	1 351	243	8	2 055	369	37	5 209	15 726	2 901	2 760	57 486	76 296	72.3	18.9
Elk	115	3.1	39	107	2	315	865	5	309	650	66	1 730	4 766	6 480	64.6	8.8
Erie	960	3.4	459	166	10	1 830	663	23	2 258	9 592	853	3 416	41 151	46 792	69.9	13.2
Fayette	402	2.5	121	80	3	394	261	56	1 204	3 602	318	2 388	23 862	30 076	57.8	7.2
Forest	10	2.0	1	21	0	0	0	0	0	139	6	2 935	814	1 003	59.1	5.8
Franklin	434	3.7	136	112	3	872	720	11	1 830	2 117	277	1 758	18 645	22 356	58.6	10.3
Fulton	45	3.3	4	27	1	94	644	1	57	203	13	1 419	2 598	2 856	51.9	7.3
Greene	167	4.1	33	84	1	84	214	15	463	676	26	1 669	7 671	8 570	55.4	9.5
Huntingdon	138	3.2	43	100	1	104	241	4	253	619	39	1 435	7 034	8 910	61.5	8.6
Indiana	195	2.1	85	93	1	171	186	11	466	1 540	126	1 656	14 658	16 942	64.5	11.2
Jefferson	189	3.9	43	91	2	148	312	11	596	728	29	1 505	7 960	9 516	62.4	8.4
Juniata	50	2.5	5	25	0	0	0	5	269	216	12	1 067	3 574	3 930	55.3	6.7
Lackawanna	554	2.5	430	194	8	1 776	801	37	2 410	3 477	397	1 662	28 632	34 171	63.8	10.7
Lancaster	1 220	3.2	558	132	5	1 281	303	52	4 460	10 532	748	2 606	54 002	61 003	59.6	13.0
Lawrence	294	2.8	85	85	3	536	535	18	1 047	2 400	267	2 396	16 386	19 707	63.2	10.0
Lebanon	380	3.4	153	133	4	1 021	887	17	1 351	2 613	85	2 293	16 801	20 822	59.6	9.4
Lehigh	901	3.3	635	218	5	1 915	657	14	2 579	10 182	627	3 552	37 427	45 645	64.6	14.2
Luzerne	764	2.3	592	179	11	2 249	679	40	2 960	5 710	443	1 757	42 967	52 775	61.2	9.2
Lycoming	427	3.6	214	180	4	674	567	17	1 120	2 879	167	2 440	19 669	22 875	65.6	10.3
McKean	186	3.8	48	105	2	273	600	10	609	823	27	1 753	9 053	10 471	65.0	9.2
Mercer	395	3.1	147	121	4	620	509	20	1 327	2 907	257	2 336	19 599	23 688	66.8	11.7
Mifflin	133	2.9	59	126	1	213	455	5	460	786	34	1 678	6 608	9 279	57.6	6.8
Monroe	267	3.5	121	122	1	231	234	8	517	2 949	156	3 341	12 162	12 238	67.8	14.0
Montgomery	2 005	3.0	3 155	454	19	4 034	580	61	6 202	19 234	1 342	2 807	74 103	95 531	75.8	24.9
Montour	56	3.3	350	2 121	2	1 105	6 697	3	345	212	12	1 260	2 532	2 886	60.3	13.8
Northampton	747	3.2	435	176	3	800	323	10	1 537	5 689	401	2 361	34 189	37 552	61.8	12.3
Northumberland	322	3.2	80	82	2	230	235	13	1 156	1 763	203	1 780	14 580	17 478	57.6	6.7
Perry	101	2.7	12	29	0	0	0	5	227	517	34	1 283	7 120	7 626	61.1	7.2
Philadelphia	4 943	3.0	6 614	402	47	11 769	715	190	12 232	100 015	17 086	6 035	190 119	223 903	54.3	11.1
Pike	51	2.5	12	42	0	0	0	2	130	883	31	3 606	1 826	3 315	65.0	11.7
Potter	51	2.8	19	106	1	135	754	4	205	264	19	1 464	3 198	4 111	61.6	8.4
Schuylkill	364	2.3	154	101	4	615	401	9	950	1 866	174	1 213	20 907	25 489	56.3	6.1
Snyder	95	2.7	25	68	0	0	0	2	242	484	24	1 346	5 217	6 290	59.2	9.7
Somerset	225	2.7	79	99	4	518	647	12	701	1 087	53	1 348	13 910	15 782	58.0	7.4
Sullivan	11	1.8	1	16	0	0	0	2	190	204	5	3 163	946	1 247	61.0	8.0
Susquehanna	99	2.5	29	70	2	138	333	4	258	471	40	1 221	7 974	8 337	65.1	8.7
Tioga	132	3.3	36	90	1	127	316	8	347	649	43	1 583	6 715	8 941	63.9	10.3

1. Per 1,000 resident population estimated as of July 1 of the year shown. 2. As of end of year. 3. Per 100,000 resident population as of July 1 of the year shown. 4. Preliminary. Covers nursing homes with 3 or more beds. 5. Data for serious crimes have not been adjusted for underreporting, this may affect comparability between geographic areas or over time. 6. Includes murder and nonnegligent manslaughter, forcible rape, robbery, and aggravated assault. 7. The 1986–1987 data are based on administrative reports obtained by the U.S. National Center for Education Statistics. The 1980 data are based on the 1980 Census of Population and Housing. 8. Persons 25 years old or older.

STATE County	Education (cont'd)		Social Security Program December 1988			Supple-mental Security Income Program recipients June 1986	Money income						Housing units, 1990	
	Local government expenditures for education,[1] 1982		Beneficiaries		Payments ($1,000)		Per capita[3]			Median household income 1979 (Dollars)	Percent below poverty level, 1979		Total	Percent change, 1980–1990
	Total (Mil dol)	Per capita (Dollars)	Total	Rate[2]			1987 Income, (Dollars)	1979 Current dollars	1979 Constant 1987 dollars		Persons	Families		
	60	61	62	63	64	65	66	67	68	69	70	71	72	73
OREGON—Con.														
Wallowa	5.2	696	1 585	226.4	727	82	8 659	6 277	9 822	13 640	11.2	7.3	3 755	3.3
Wasco	15.0	669	4 405	213.8	2 190	192	9 954	7 368	11 529	17 030	10.1	8.5	10 476	5.9
Washington	152.1	588	31 085	106.2	16 325	1 282	13 407	9 192	14 383	21 572	6.1	4.3	124 716	28.5
Wheeler	1.3	895	350	269.2	169	8	8 916	5 489	8 589	10 139	18.2	14.2	782	0.9
Yamhill	37.0	651	10 185	168.1	5 008	488	9 870	6 889	10 779	16 874	10.0	7.8	23 194	14.6
PENNSYLVANIA	5 005.4	421	2 195 942	183.0	1 121 515	170 247	11 544	7 075	11 070	16 880	10.5	7.8	4 938 140	7.4
Adams	34.8	497	11 670	157.1	5 633	980	10 648	6 323	9 894	16 684	8.2	6.0	30 141	23.0
Allegheny	631.4	441	272 515	201.2	143 693	19 828	12 652	7 984	12 493	17 944	9.2	6.7	580 738	1.7
Armstrong	43.7	559	17 355	222.8	8 611	1 246	9 501	6 286	9 836	15 474	9.6	6.8	31 757	2.3
Beaver	82.1	406	38 295	201.8	20 267	2 298	10 054	7 457	11 668	20 031	7.5	5.8	76 336	1.7
Bedford	20.4	429	9 145	190.5	4 212	810	8 481	5 403	8 454	13 167	14.7	11.3	21 738	9.7
Berks	145.6	463	61 870	188.0	32 368	3 236	12 102	7 342	11 488	17 530	8.2	5.6	134 482	12.1
Blair	55.1	406	22 365	168.8	10 301	2 260	9 420	6 052	9 470	14 768	10.9	8.5	54 349	4.4
Bradford	29.6	461	11 155	172.9	5 220	1 094	9 081	5 576	8 725	14 417	13.6	10.6	27 058	7.4
Bucks	252.9	510	67 375	123.9	36 487	2 794	14 341	8 048	12 593	22 016	5.8	4.7	199 934	20.9
Butler	59.0	394	25 940	169.1	13 265	1 818	10 376	6 782	10 612	18 466	7.3	5.2	59 061	11.4
Cambria	73.3	408	38 290	225.1	18 745	2 734	8 988	6 324	9 895	15 772	9.7	7.6	67 374	0.4
Cameron	2.6	378	1 415	221.1	709	98	9 288	6 035	9 443	14 072	11.1	8.0	4 399	-0.7
Carbon	18.9	351	12 695	226.3	6 216	560	9 540	6 353	9 941	15 369	7.6	5.6	27 380	18.1
Centre	45.5	400	13 730	118.7	6 892	882	10 058	5 909	9 246	14 862	16.7	7.8	46 195	16.8
Chester	155.1	476	43 365	118.3	23 520	2 276	15 576	8 763	13 711	22 206	6.4	4.7	139 597	26.7
Clarion	22.4	519	7 455	178.3	3 614	630	8 636	6 029	9 434	15 663	11.9	7.9	18 022	4.8
Clearfield	38.6	466	15 795	193.3	7 533	1 264	8 918	6 027	9 430	14 903	10.4	7.7	34 300	3.3
Clinton	14.2	367	7 070	186.1	3 496	590	8 817	5 830	9 122	14 851	11.2	8.0	16 478	2.7
Columbia	25.0	403	12 810	210.0	6 246	782	9 384	5 722	8 953	14 148	11.4	7.4	25 598	7.2
Crawford	31.5	351	16 515	192.0	8 170	1 282	9 310	6 194	9 692	15 193	11.5	8.5	40 462	2.7
Cumberland	93.6	515	29 515	151.1	14 834	1 030	13 073	7 757	12 137	19 270	5.8	3.6	77 108	17.4
Dauphin	91.4	390	39 110	162.4	19 714	3 008	12 120	7 525	11 774	17 139	9.9	7.4	102 684	7.3
Delaware	226.3	411	95 840	172.1	52 327	4 970	14 051	8 044	12 586	19 950	7.4	5.8	211 024	4.7
Elk	11.0	291	7 100	193.5	3 744	270	10 104	6 422	10 049	16 648	6.4	5.2	17 249	5.5
Erie	114.5	407	48 430	174.8	24 839	3 472	10 397	6 654	10 412	16 760	10.0	7.4	108 585	4.7
Fayette	56.0	355	34 005	223.4	16 205	4 232	8 371	5 874	9 191	14 282	15.5	12.3	61 406	0.6
Forest	2.5	506	1 335	284.0	648	60	8 603	5 691	8 905	12 657	12.0	8.6	8 445	-2.2
Franklin	44.6	388	19 150	159.2	8 982	1 460	10 609	6 675	10 444	16 911	7.4	5.5	48 629	14.1
Fulton	6.7	507	2 140	148.6	930	246	8 470	5 402	8 453	13 573	14.4	12.4	6 184	16.7
Greene	23.0	564	8 320	209.6	3 985	998	8 630	5 991	9 374	14 966	14.0	10.5	15 982	6.1
Huntingdon	16.0	376	7 540	174.9	3 466	716	8 094	5 233	8 188	12 951	13.7	9.7	19 286	14.1
Indiana	38.2	412	16 195	176.0	7 812	1 550	8 939	6 087	9 524	15 955	13.5	8.1	34 770	7.1
Jefferson	18.5	382	9 695	203.2	4 626	714	9 323	6 247	9 775	14 961	10.2	7.9	21 242	2.8
Juniata	6.7	348	3 410	168.0	1 533	300	8 925	5 570	8 715	13 883	12.7	10.4	8 505	9.2
Lackawanna	82.7	367	51 915	233.5	24 936	3 592	10 165	6 107	9 556	14 267	9.8	7.2	91 707	2.4
Lancaster	151.8	409	63 245	152.7	33 192	3 424	11 721	7 087	11 089	17 933	8.5	6.0	156 462	20.9
Lawrence	41.3	389	23 005	228.0	11 724	1 542	9 502	6 569	10 279	16 588	9.9	7.8	38 844	-1.9
Lebanon	40.1	362	19 805	173.3	10 077	920	11 056	6 895	10 789	17 669	7.4	5.4	44 634	11.3
Lehigh	108.1	393	50 545	175.1	26 677	2 822	12 715	7 873	12 319	18 790	7.2	5.2	118 335	11.6
Luzerne	119.6	351	78 595	237.1	37 514	4 818	9 902	6 008	9 401	13 990	9.9	7.2	138 724	1.9
Lycoming	56.7	483	22 630	191.3	11 249	1 510	9 973	6 170	9 654	15 025	10.8	8.1	49 580	4.3
McKean	26.6	534	10 440	226.0	5 321	754	9 511	6 133	9 596	14 780	10.2	7.2	21 454	-0.5
Mercer	62.7	492	25 715	210.1	13 329	1 568	9 641	6 745	10 554	17 160	9.1	6.7	48 689	2.2
Mifflin	18.8	404	8 830	189.1	4 258	884	8 903	5 812	9 094	13 958	13.1	9.7	19 641	5.8
Monroe	32.5	444	15 830	169.3	8 051	666	11 478	6 771	10 595	15 999	8.6	6.3	54 823	47.3
Montgomery	301.3	463	111 870	162.7	63 840	3 844	17 122	9 727	15 220	22 508	4.7	3.3	265 856	14.3
Montour	6.2	367	3 435	208.2	1 679	368	11 270	6 336	9 914	16 052	8.7	6.1	6 885	15.2
Northampton	106.4	467	49 015	201.2	25 818	2 484	11 669	7 382	11 551	18 470	7.8	5.6	95 345	13.1
Northumberland	41.8	417	22 645	230.1	10 594	1 702	9 030	5 681	8 889	12 931	11.4	8.1	41 900	2.5
Perry	13.6	370	5 475	134.2	2 504	372	9 864	6 124	9 582	16 275	8.3	6.4	17 063	15.4
Philadelphia	643.8	387	299 305	181.7	149 439	48 772	10 002	6 053	9 471	13 169	20.6	16.6	674 899	-1.6
Pike	6.9	350	4 305	160.6	2 208	110	11 969	6 869	10 748	14 726	9.0	7.0	30 852	74.0
Potter	7.7	427	3 550	197.2	1 681	294	8 226	5 125	8 019	12 993	15.4	12.3	11 334	4.4
Schuylkill	59.5	375	38 720	251.3	18 448	2 002	9 389	5 883	9 205	13 340	10.8	7.7	66 457	2.5
Snyder	11.2	326	5 995	164.7	2 824	578	9 476	5 754	9 003	15 542	10.7	7.5	13 629	16.7
Somerset	30.1	370	16 360	203.2	7 501	1 388	8 454	6 011	9 405	14 716	11.7	9.1	35 713	6.9
Sullivan	2.8	437	1 520	237.5	698	90	8 484	5 089	7 963	12 526	16.2	9.7	5 458	12.4
Susquehanna	19.0	500	7 450	182.2	3 503	532	9 086	5 615	8 786	14 182	12.9	9.9	20 308	18.1
Tioga	17.6	430	7 870	195.3	3 763	724	8 369	5 412	8 468	13 785	15.4	12.0	18 202	7.1

1. Elementary and secondary. 2. Per 1,000 resident population estimated as of July 1 of the year shown. 3. Based on the resident population estimated as of July 1, 1988 for 1987 data and enumerated as of April 1, 1980 for 1979 data.

STATE County	Housing units, 1990 (cont'd): Occupied units: Total	Housing units, 1990 (cont'd): Occupied units: Owner occupied: Percent	Housing units, 1990 (cont'd): Occupied units: Owner occupied: Median value (Dollars)	Housing units, 1990 (cont'd): Occupied units: Median rent (Dollars)	Civilian labor force, 1990: Total	Civilian labor force, 1990: Percent change, 1989–1990	Civilian labor force, 1990: Unemployment: Total	Civilian labor force, 1990: Unemployment: Rate[1]	Private nonfarm establishments, 1988: Number	Private nonfarm establishments, 1988: Net change, 1987–1988	Private nonfarm establishments, 1988: Employment[2]: Total	Private nonfarm establishments, 1988: Employment[2]: Percent change, 1987–1988	Private nonfarm establishments, 1988: Employment[2]: Manufacturing	Private nonfarm establishments, 1988: Employment[2]: Retail trade
	74	75	76	77	78	79	80	81	82	83	84	85	86	87
OREGON—Con.														
Wallowa	2 796	69.2	47 400	220	3 865	0.3	279	7.2	244	11	1 105	1.8	274	345
Wasco	8 607	65.1	50 000	275	10 387	-1.1	805	7.8	636	27	5 049	3.9	923	1 600
Washington	118 997	60.8	85 500	429	177 088	2.0	5 955	3.4	8 102	197	108 802	6.4	30 811	26 267
Wheeler	584	70.7	30 400	167	645	6.8	69	10.7	25	-1	87	20.8	0	28
Yamhill	22 424	67.6	62 300	328	31 394	1.2	1 671	5.3	1 393	-2	15 702	2.7	5 332	3 173
PENNSYLVANIA	4 495 966	70.6	69 700	322	5 901 000	0.8	318 000	5.4	X	X	4 375 495	2.6	1 051 180	893 289
Adams	28 067	73.3	79 600	300	39 661	-0.4	1 703	4.3	1 551	7	20 821	4.9	7 360	4 283
Allegheny	541 261	66.2	57 100	315	661 838	0.9	27 819	4.2	33 672	317	596 381	0.9	82 905	120 965
Armstrong	28 309	76.4	44 300	205	28 908	-0.6	2 344	8.1	1 552	21	14 966	4.3	2 905	3 700
Beaver	71 939	73.3	50 500	230	59 982	0.0	4 655	7.8	3 283	71	40 700	2.2	9 655	11 142
Bedford	18 038	79.1	46 800	189	22 083	3.6	2 027	9.2	976	23	9 540	4.2	2 388	3 113
Berks	127 649	73.9	81 800	342	175 804	-0.2	9 070	5.2	7 389	108	133 597	2.3	48 629	27 088
Blair	50 332	72.6	41 100	224	61 796	2.4	4 472	7.2	2 958	-13	42 415	0.5	10 588	10 546
Bradford	22 492	75.3	50 900	231	32 535	4.2	1 798	5.5	1 143	31	16 903	5.0	6 878	3 264
Bucks	190 507	75.7	140 000	524	299 460	0.4	12 597	4.2	14 105	543	197 082	3.4	49 070	46 818
Butler	55 325	76.6	62 900	275	76 033	2.6	4 217	5.5	3 280	90	41 194	4.8	11 722	10 184
Cambria	62 004	73.3	39 900	191	64 849	1.1	4 989	7.7	3 448	43	46 587	0.6	8 272	10 637
Cameron	2 395	73.2	39 800	184	2 810	0.3	217	7.7	156	16	1 891	21.8	1 014	341
Carbon	21 989	77.9	62 900	255	25 714	2.0	2 003	7.8	1 054	32	12 195	11.3	4 364	2 540
Centre	42 683	59.8	74 700	401	67 569	2.9	3 590	5.3	2 669	51	35 182	3.4	8 109	10 011
Chester	133 257	74.5	155 900	496	200 266	0.1	6 504	3.2	9 395	418	144 250	5.3	31 689	23 791
Clarion	14 990	72.5	46 200	209	18 056	-1.1	1 613	8.9	938	5	9 518	7.1	2 463	2 570
Clearfield	29 808	78.5	40 000	207	34 678	-0.5	3 434	9.9	1 890	46	22 514	-1.3	5 108	5 586
Clinton	13 844	72.8	46 300	214	15 570	1.3	1 530	9.8	708	-12	9 110	1.9	3 751	2 487
Columbia	23 478	73.5	54 800	241	31 748	0.5	2 126	6.7	1 412	53	20 725	4.6	9 536	4 137
Crawford	32 185	73.4	43 200	210	40 254	3.3	2 843	7.1	1 874	27	24 655	5.2	8 144	5 144
Cumberland	73 452	71.8	85 000	378	110 468	0.4	3 972	3.6	4 541	105	91 000	4.7	17 171	20 901
Dauphin	95 264	63.7	71 300	357	136 121	0.3	6 309	4.6	5 873	75	108 390	3.1	22 804	20 495
Delaware	201 374	72.6	113 200	445	290 860	-0.1	10 992	3.8	12 816	312	193 733	3.1	36 589	41 344
Elk	13 131	79.7	49 900	209	17 464	0.3	1 092	6.3	829	50	12 283	1.0	6 965	1 677
Erie	101 564	68.6	54 000	248	134 670	1.5	7 442	5.5	6 260	130	99 820	0.3	34 083	20 604
Fayette	56 110	72.3	39 700	196	59 481	1.3	4 720	7.9	2 832	37	30 919	3.9	5 519	8 960
Forest	1 908	81.0	35 700	191	1 935	1.7	176	9.1	99	-10	664	7.6	0	133
Franklin	45 675	72.7	70 500	273	60 126	2.7	3 126	5.2	2 411	83	34 324	7.4	12 785	7 763
Fulton	5 139	78.8	50 700	210	6 372	2.4	476	7.5	242	12	2 343	12.4	884	497
Greene	14 624	72.5	38 400	187	13 166	1.0	1 197	9.1	622	10	6 763	-6.2	394	1 485
Huntingdon	15 527	76.3	43 100	197	19 089	-0.5	1 901	10.0	799	22	9 700	10.4	3 087	1 883
Indiana	31 710	73.5	50 500	254	35 064	0.5	3 072	8.8	1 883	16	22 793	-1.1	4 107	5 937
Jefferson	17 608	77.2	42 500	203	19 746	-1.0	1 488	7.5	1 085	18	12 738	4.1	4 663	2 419
Juniata	7 598	77.5	51 700	184	10 117	2.2	1 057	10.4	441	14	5 311	11.0	2 543	988
Lackawanna	84 528	67.0	68 900	253	109 991	0.7	7 388	6.7	5 112	104	85 016	3.5	24 624	18 256
Lancaster	150 956	69.4	89 400	363	227 715	0.8	9 428	4.1	9 671	333	175 369	5.1	61 042	35 892
Lawrence	36 350	76.1	41 500	211	48 564	1.0	2 745	5.7	2 048	30	27 096	6.4	6 981	5 659
Lebanon	42 688	71.0	71 000	293	64 663	0.1	3 000	4.6	2 380	21	33 834	3.8	11 442	8 159
Lehigh	112 887	69.3	97 800	400	150 436	1.6	7 789	5.2	7 581	191	137 479	1.6	38 553	27 562
Luzerne	128 483	69.4	56 000	243	160 673	0.5	11 532	7.2	7 398	188	111 277	4.9	29 341	24 470
Lycoming	44 949	69.7	54 900	256	60 262	0.1	4 362	7.2	2 772	48	45 669	2.1	16 734	8 721
McKean	17 837	74.0	37 400	219	21 246	2.5	1 470	6.9	1 103	-4	12 767	-1.2	4 865	2 482
Mercer	45 591	75.0	41 900	221	52 274	2.3	2 769	5.3	2 558	49	36 326	8.2	11 449	8 183
Mifflin	17 697	72.8	44 800	204	21 551	1.2	1 776	8.2	893	22	13 780	9.7	5 626	2 993
Monroe	34 206	75.7	116 500	432	49 772	2.0	3 398	6.8	2 815	185	31 742	7.7	5 005	7 497
Montgomery	254 995	72.3	143 400	521	388 889	0.2	14 324	3.7	23 573	556	408 866	2.9	91 525	75 303
Montour	6 543	71.6	62 200	256	8 067	-0.7	425	5.3	362	27	9 789	9.3	2 180	1 077
Northampton	90 955	73.6	105 400	381	118 438	2.2	6 685	5.6	5 173	151	74 333	2.8	24 972	14 721
Northumberland	38 736	73.3	39 500	205	48 794	0.4	4 197	8.6	1 966	-25	26 497	3.9	10 906	5 207
Perry	14 949	79.5	64 400	262	21 194	0.8	1 230	5.8	600	38	4 104	6.0	722	1 309
Philadelphia	603 075	61.9	49 400	358	732 351	0.3	44 110	6.0	29 246	-138	611 194	-0.3	93 488	101 985
Pike	10 536	83.3	117 700	445	13 272	3.7	774	5.8	616	57	5 232	19.0	484	897
Potter	6 246	75.4	40 900	216	8 032	-1.2	581	7.2	405	8	3 810	7.7	1 200	667
Schuylkill	60 773	78.1	38 200	222	73 969	1.1	5 738	7.8	3 097	56	41 823	2.7	17 459	8 718
Snyder	12 764	77.2	56 700	234	19 224	0.7	1 449	7.5	745	30	12 056	6.0	4 924	3 493
Somerset	29 574	77.4	43 400	196	32 913	0.9	2 483	7.5	1 756	22	17 657	3.5	4 848	3 779
Sullivan	2 280	78.6	47 000	179	3 264	8.9	178	5.5	174	12	1 281	2.7	544	225
Susquehanna	14 898	79.2	64 200	254	17 928	1.6	1 402	7.8	678	42	7 306	19.4	2 964	1 458
Tioga	14 974	75.5	43 900	202	19 100	3.9	1 368	7.2	801	18	8 846	10.3	2 873	2 049

1. Percent of total civilian labor force. 2. For week including March 12. Excludes government employees, self-employed persons, farm workers, domestic service workers, railroad employees subject to the Railroad Retirement Act, and employees on oceanborne vessels or in foreign countries.

STATE County	Private nonfarm establishments, 1988 (cont'd) — Employment[1] (cont'd) — Finance, insurance, and real estate	Employment[1] (cont'd) — Services	Annual payroll — Total (Mil dol)	Annual payroll — Average per employee (Dollars)	Personal income, 1989 — Total (Mil dol)	Percent change, 1988–1989	Wages and salaries[2] (Mil dol)	Proprietor's income (Mil dol)	Dividends, interest, & rent (Mil dol)	Transfer payments (Mil dol)	Per capita[3] — Dollars	Per capita[3] — Rank	Earnings, 1989 — Total (Mil dol)	Percent by selected industries — Farm	Percent by selected industries — Goods-related[4] — Total
	88	89	90	91	92	93	94	95	96	97	98	99	100	101	102
OREGON—Con.															
Wallowa	73	236	16	14 438	113	10.6	41	32	24	21	16 362	558	73	29.1	20.7
Wasco	236	1 402	79	15 664	339	9.7	165	43	67	64	16 672	490	209	9.2	25.6
Washington	5 674	25 998	2 286	21 013	5 656	11.4	3 252	432	908	486	18 596	244	3 683	1.6	35.9
Wheeler	0	0	1	16 724	25	8.7	5	10	6	4	19 560	192	15	57.6	NA
Yamhill	646	4 242	277	17 652	905	9.9	422	116	155	144	14 585	1 174	537	10.3	37.7
PENNSYLVANIA	295 453	1 321 073	89 999	X	209 393	7.6	129 357	16 939	37 794	35 767	17 387	X	146 296	0.7	30.4
Adams	944	4 855	300	14 433	1 235	7.7	511	120	197	168	16 326	562	631	3.0	38.7
Allegheny	47 235	221 773	13 173	22 088	25 853	7.2	17 904	2 148	5 095	4 508	19 249	207	20 052	0.1	23.4
Armstrong	676	3 490	253	16 933	1 146	7.3	409	109	195	234	14 750	1 107	518	5.7	31.6
Beaver	1 734	10 788	790	19 418	2 641	5.9	1 204	159	448	567	14 046	1 415	1 364	0.6	33.4
Bedford	339	1 720	144	15 112	583	7.3	226	81	97	122	12 116	2 279	307	7.9	NA
Berks	8 245	28 636	2 783	20 834	6 339	8.4	3 984	434	1 085	874	19 068	216	4 418	1.5	41.1
Blair	1 899	11 031	681	16 062	1 810	7.3	1 094	160	290	425	13 685	1 590	1 254	0.9	26.9
Bradford	531	4 284	332	19 637	892	9.3	474	108	139	157	13 789	1 540	582	4.8	39.4
Bucks	8 738	53 288	4 143	21 020	11 368	7.9	5 528	801	1 731	1 140	20 534	145	6 330	0.3	34.6
Butler	1 666	7 986	800	19 413	2 410	8.0	1 252	206	384	382	15 619	771	1 458	1.6	41.8
Cambria	3 620	13 681	828	17 767	2 246	7.3	1 224	172	405	619	13 337	1 759	1 396	0.6	29.6
Cameron	0	368	30	15 744	86	6.7	51	6	17	20	13 547	1 663	57	1.2	NA
Carbon	495	3 216	165	13 508	812	6.9	267	50	151	181	14 284	1 293	318	0.9	35.5
Centre	1 611	9 643	630	17 895	1 781	9.7	1 242	172	272	275	15 345	860	1 415	1.0	23.0
Chester	10 672	45 725	3 450	23 918	8 489	9.2	4 653	565	1 518	778	22 491	83	5 219	1.6	32.6
Clarion	358	1 988	149	15 627	559	8.1	271	76	99	116	13 485	1 692	347	2.3	32.3
Clearfield	1 089	5 304	370	16 428	1 079	6.4	554	130	186	238	13 275	1 782	684	0.9	31.3
Clinton	257	1 570	145	15 899	474	5.7	230	40	85	114	12 465	2 134	270	1.6	45.0
Columbia	661	3 618	347	16 751	866	7.8	472	80	153	174	14 230	1 318	552	2.7	42.6
Crawford	1 225	7 060	421	17 059	1 188	8.4	642	135	197	245	13 935	1 455	777	2.5	43.4
Cumberland	9 385	23 632	1 777	19 524	3 532	8.5	2 778	238	662	521	17 873	312	3 017	0.5	21.0
Dauphin	8 842	31 800	2 270	20 947	4 152	7.9	3 811	296	681	729	17 158	415	4 107	0.3	24.9
Delaware	14 390	68 452	4 143	21 388	12 246	7.7	5 701	827	2 566	1 578	21 991	93	6 528	0.1	31.6
Elk	276	2 304	260	21 153	560	6.4	335	42	94	96	15 353	859	377	0.2	62.3
Erie	5 026	28 427	1 938	19 412	4 235	7.6	2 769	329	681	735	15 332	862	3 097	0.6	40.7
Fayette	1 399	8 366	478	15 453	1 948	6.7	664	191	314	526	12 930	1 939	855	1.0	27.0
Forest	0	218	9	14 114	59	5.8	26	6	9	17	12 671	2 048	32	1.7	NA
Franklin	1 249	7 277	564	16 418	1 848	8.4	997	163	347	334	15 255	885	1 160	3.1	37.7
Fulton	90	374	39	16 790	190	11.4	71	28	28	32	13 066	1 881	100	10.3	NA
Greene	268	1 656	136	20 092	478	7.9	269	38	76	126	12 166	2 251	307	1.9	47.9
Huntingdon	480	2 696	145	14 924	513	8.0	242	47	74	114	11 872	2 369	288	3.6	NA
Indiana	968	4 507	413	18 108	1 181	6.0	669	142	209	254	12 863	1 973	811	1.7	36.4
Jefferson	401	2 712	213	16 712	653	6.7	324	86	124	141	13 747	1 554	410	1.5	43.9
Juniata	212	627	74	13 941	291	7.0	102	40	51	50	14 281	1 296	142	8.8	47.7
Lackawanna	4 465	24 222	1 420	16 701	3 549	7.6	1 979	327	649	820	16 003	646	2 306	0.3	31.9
Lancaster	7 599	37 349	3 424	19 523	7 467	8.7	4 540	744	1 324	862	17 645	347	5 285	2.3	43.8
Lawrence	1 669	8 024	462	17 058	1 373	7.2	674	119	243	320	13 716	1 574	793	1.4	35.2
Lebanon	1 106	8 051	567	16 746	1 774	8.4	895	159	305	274	15 405	836	1 054	2.7	37.5
Lehigh	6 778	38 940	3 054	22 216	5 488	7.9	3 829	437	1 053	707	18 822	229	4 266	0.3	36.5
Luzerne	6 096	31 174	1 810	16 263	5 104	7.4	2 743	458	916	1 242	15 423	825	3 201	0.3	28.9
Lycoming	2 513	10 109	829	18 160	1 795	6.9	1 116	175	299	332	15 106	939	1 291	1.6	39.7
McKean	452	3 189	213	16 704	652	6.4	340	61	122	143	14 323	1 276	401	0.6	45.6
Mercer	1 276	9 604	663	18 254	1 744	8.1	950	166	325	362	14 322	1 277	1 116	1.5	39.1
Mifflin	429	2 976	242	17 572	600	7.8	348	71	83	119	12 810	1 995	418	4.0	46.5
Monroe	1 597	10 347	520	16 389	1 568	9.3	913	135	269	222	15 874	685	1 048	0.2	23.3
Montgomery	37 787	129 618	9 397	22 982	18 067	7.8	12 409	1 433	4 191	1 764	25 989	31	13 842	0.2	34.1
Montour	144	0	211	21 605	304	8.1	297	32	46	71	18 460	254	329	1.7	12.2
Northampton	3 049	20 008	1 427	19 197	4 332	8.2	2 116	287	780	665	17 500	370	2 404	0.5	42.0
Northumberland	896	4 245	442	16 689	1 347	7.1	659	127	230	311	13 759	1 551	786	2.2	44.9
Perry	232	804	47	11 518	582	9.7	101	55	84	90	13 931	1 459	157	11.1	21.3
Philadelphia	66 341	249 440	14 302	23 400	25 474	6.4	22 567	1 853	4 024	6 410	15 479	809	24 420	NA	15.8
Pike	639	2 373	82	15 634	489	10.0	124	33	89	58	16 903	454	156	0.9	29.3
Potter	142	1 022	54	14 245	220	7.4	83	31	36	48	12 270	2 206	115	5.3	27.1
Schuylkill	1 560	7 486	656	15 691	2 315	7.0	995	191	398	535	15 115	936	1 187	1.0	44.8
Snyder	345	1 937	181	14 975	609	8.3	284	65	89	144	16 626	497	349	3.9	39.7
Somerset	1 014	3 913	275	15 580	1 053	7.8	467	148	191	240	13 146	1 842	614	3.7	34.4
Sullivan	43	263	18	13 789	82	6.4	25	11	19	19	12 693	2 037	37	9.1	33.0
Susquehanna	348	1 639	92	12 540	540	7.8	141	53	99	99	13 061	1 885	194	5.9	28.1
Tioga	341	2 178	124	14 068	505	7.8	218	70	86	106	12 559	2 091	288	3.9	28.9

1. For week including March 12. Excludes government employees, self-employed persons, farm workers, domestic service workers, railroad employees subject to the Railroad Retirement Act, and employees on oceanborne vessels or in foreign countries. 2. Includes other labor income. 3. Based on the resident population estimated as of July 1 of the year shown. 4. Covers mining, construction, and manufacturing.

STATE County	Earnings, 1989 (cont'd)						Agriculture, 1987									
	Percent by selected industries (cont'd)						Farms			Farm operators, percent		Land in farms				
	Goods-related[1]	Service-related & other[2]						Percent with						Acres		
	Manu-facturing	Total	Retail trade	Finance, insur-ance, & real estate	Services	Govern-ment	Number	Less than 50 acres	500 acres and over	Whose principal occu-pation is farming	Residing on farm operated	Acreage (1,000)	Percent change, 1982–1987	Average size of farm	Total irrigated (1,000)	Total cropland (1,000)
	103	104	105	106	107	108	109	110	111	112	113	114	115	116	117	118
OREGON—Con.																
Wallowa	17.0	30.7	8.2	1.3	10.9	19.5	455	28.8	38.7	57.8	78.0	676	-4.4	1 486	44	119
Wasco	21.7	46.4	13.1	2.4	20.4	18.8	487	32.2	37.4	62.4	78.6	1 173	18.0	2 408	25	257
Washington	28.9	54.9	11.2	4.7	25.0	7.6	1 724	66.7	3.7	43.0	85.2	150	-0.7	87	22	112
Wheeler	NA	NA	5.5	NA	5.3	14.9	130	6.9	63.8	66.2	78.5	766	-5.6	5 896	8	50
Yamhill	30.4	39.2	9.0	4.0	17.2	12.8	1 648	63.5	5.2	39.9	84.0	186	-5.3	113	19	129
PENNSYLVANIA	22.9	56.3	9.5	6.2	27.4	12.6	51 549	27.2	4.6	57.8	82.2	7 866	-5.2	153	30	5 398
Adams	28.9	45.6	11.0	2.7	19.7	12.7	1 104	32.8	6.3	57.7	77.8	187	-4.9	169	3	143
Allegheny	16.5	65.9	9.3	7.4	35.6	10.6	451	48.3	1.8	40.1	77.8	43	19.1	95	0	24
Armstrong	14.4	49.5	10.1	2.2	23.0	13.2	735	16.7	4.8	45.9	81.1	122	-3.0	167	D	76
Beaver	24.5	53.9	9.8	2.6	23.2	12.2	570	33.5	1.8	46.8	87.2	59	-0.1	104	0	37
Bedford	21.9	NA	14.1	2.5	17.6	14.3	1 043	13.9	7.1	55.5	80.0	221	-5.7	212	0	126
Berks	34.3	48.2	9.5	5.5	21.0	9.3	1 809	36.7	3.8	62.0	81.0	243	-5.1	134	1	204
Blair	20.6	59.0	12.7	3.4	23.4	13.2	489	22.9	6.3	66.5	84.3	87	-0.5	177	1	60
Bradford	36.2	45.4	9.4	1.8	25.4	10.3	1 432	14.1	10.9	69.1	87.8	339	-4.2	237	0	207
Bucks	24.5	54.8	12.2	4.2	25.9	10.3	841	54.2	3.7	50.5	84.5	85	-24.1	101	1	70
Butler	32.7	43.3	9.2	2.6	17.3	13.4	1 199	30.9	2.5	50.2	85.3	144	-4.4	120	1	96
Cambria	17.0	55.5	10.0	6.1	25.1	14.3	605	26.1	4.6	46.3	80.8	86	-0.5	142	0	55
Cameron	57.4	NA	7.9	NA	9.4	13.8	25	40.0	4.0	48.0	96.0	3	NA	104	0	1
Carbon	25.9	48.3	14.9	3.5	21.8	15.3	177	37.9	3.4	39.0	82.5	22	4.2	123	0	14
Centre	14.4	40.7	9.2	3.6	21.0	35.3	817	21.7	5.8	60.5	82.3	149	-6.4	182	0	104
Chester	24.0	57.4	8.9	7.5	26.3	8.5	1 573	44.4	4.3	65.8	79.4	190	-13.7	121	1	148
Clarion	19.5	43.9	10.9	2.3	15.6	21.5	541	13.5	7.6	47.7	81.3	103	1.9	190	0	65
Clearfield	17.6	55.0	13.6	2.7	21.2	12.7	421	23.5	3.6	49.6	81.5	62	-7.4	148	0	40
Clinton	39.5	35.3	10.9	1.6	14.9	18.2	295	20.7	4.1	64.7	83.4	47	-3.2	159	1	32
Columbia	36.1	40.0	10.9	2.7	18.1	14.7	701	24.3	4.9	51.4	83.3	110	-10.2	157	0	80
Crawford	36.6	43.5	9.7	3.9	21.8	10.6	1 281	17.3	5.9	57.8	86.0	236	-6.4	185	0	147
Cumberland	15.0	60.8	10.0	8.8	21.4	17.6	1 100	28.5	4.2	64.9	81.4	154	-5.8	140	1	129
Dauphin	18.8	48.7	7.1	5.6	21.6	26.2	675	33.8	4.7	56.3	80.3	102	-9.9	151	1	82
Delaware	22.8	59.6	10.4	6.2	30.3	8.7	95	70.5	5.3	58.9	72.6	8	13.3	85	0	5
Elk	58.2	30.3	6.1	1.3	16.3	7.2	168	28.6	1.8	35.7	85.1	19	0.9	111	0	11
Erie	35.7	48.1	9.1	4.8	22.9	10.7	1 355	29.9	3.0	56.4	84.1	185	-7.5	136	1	118
Fayette	16.5	57.2	13.2	4.1	26.0	14.8	902	27.6	3.0	40.1	81.4	116	-5.5	129	0	75
Forest	21.4	NA	10.5	1.3	23.1	26.7	34	11.8	2.9	47.1	73.5	6	-14.4	181	0	3
Franklin	31.1	36.4	9.5	2.2	17.5	22.8	1 441	23.7	5.3	66.8	78.3	254	2.0	177	2	208
Fulton	26.3	NA	9.1	NA	11.4	13.0	467	12.8	7.3	46.9	76.0	100	-4.7	214	0	57
Greene	2.2	36.3	7.7	2.0	15.7	13.9	838	15.9	5.6	37.2	82.1	146	-2.1	174	0	74
Huntingdon	24.6	NA	8.7	3.5	20.4	20.1	635	12.8	8.5	57.5	81.4	135	-3.1	212	0	82
Indiana	13.4	44.1	8.8	2.7	17.0	17.8	911	17.3	5.4	57.3	85.6	166	-1.0	182	0	108
Jefferson	32.5	44.9	9.8	2.0	16.6	9.6	495	15.8	4.2	48.5	85.3	85	-2.5	171	0	54
Juniata	37.5	34.2	9.1	2.8	10.2	9.4	566	21.2	3.7	64.8	80.2	91	-4.8	161	0	62
Lackawanna	25.4	56.8	10.2	4.5	28.9	11.1	299	25.1	4.3	54.2	86.3	42	-11.9	141	0	26
Lancaster	34.3	46.7	10.3	4.0	19.7	7.2	4 775	38.0	0.8	73.4	79.4	404	-3.2	85	4	345
Lawrence	27.4	51.0	11.1	4.8	22.3	12.4	749	24.4	2.0	56.6	85.2	96	-0.2	129	0	68
Lebanon	30.5	43.2	12.9	2.8	19.4	16.6	948	33.1	2.2	67.1	81.1	117	0.5	124	1	101
Lehigh	28.7	55.1	9.9	4.8	26.1	8.0	541	38.3	8.3	56.7	80.4	97	1.7	179	1	84
Luzerne	20.9	57.5	11.8	4.7	24.0	13.3	473	33.8	3.2	52.2	85.0	58	-13.2	124	0	39
Lycoming	32.7	46.3	10.2	4.4	21.4	12.3	847	17.6	3.4	56.0	84.3	139	-9.9	165	1	90
McKean	37.4	41.6	9.5	2.3	20.1	12.2	243	16.9	5.8	37.9	84.0	45	-8.4	185	D	19
Mercer	33.3	49.3	10.6	2.8	25.5	10.0	1 267	18.7	3.2	56.3	83.7	183	2.6	144	0	122
Mifflin	42.6	40.5	10.6	2.4	19.6	9.0	677	21.7	2.2	70.6	76.8	88	-3.7	129	0	58
Monroe	12.2	55.3	10.9	2.8	29.4	21.2	192	36.5	5.7	44.3	84.9	27	-9.1	140	0	18
Montgomery	25.5	59.8	8.7	8.1	29.4	6.0	586	51.5	2.9	52.9	81.1	57	-22.6	97	0	47
Montour	11.0	75.3	3.5	0.6	63.7	10.8	270	21.1	5.2	55.6	79.6	42	-14.2	155	0	33
Northampton	35.0	47.7	9.7	5.0	22.1	9.8	484	39.0	8.3	59.7	77.7	87	-15.2	179	0	75
Northumberland	38.6	42.3	13.3	3.0	15.7	10.6	675	29.6	6.5	60.4	82.4	126	2.7	186	1	101
Perry	7.7	47.2	13.1	2.9	17.7	20.5	628	19.3	5.9	55.7	82.8	113	-4.2	179	0	76
Philadelphia	12.6	65.7	6.9	10.6	34.5	18.5	5	100.0	0.0	0.0	100.0	0	NA	9	0	0
Pike	9.6	57.3	12.7	6.1	34.4	12.5	44	40.9	2.3	40.9	77.3	5	-11.7	124	D	2
Potter	20.2	50.3	9.5	2.5	24.2	17.3	328	11.3	18.3	61.6	84.8	96	-10.8	291	0	50
Schuylkill	35.0	42.2	11.3	2.7	18.6	12.0	647	32.6	5.7	55.2	80.7	97	-2.4	150	1	75
Snyder	35.4	40.4	12.1	1.8	17.0	16.1	702	31.5	3.0	61.4	79.3	90	-4.8	128	0	66
Somerset	18.4	49.1	9.9	3.1	23.3	12.8	1 062	14.6	8.0	62.9	84.5	228	-1.8	214	0	138
Sullivan	22.3	NA	11.6	2.7	16.0	18.7	165	13.3	7.9	50.9	84.8	30	-14.5	185	D	17
Susquehanna	19.9	48.8	13.9	3.7	18.9	17.3	814	10.0	9.3	67.0	86.0	190	-12.3	233	0	100
Tioga	22.0	47.9	11.6	3.1	18.5	19.3	876	9.6	10.6	65.1	88.1	223	-7.2	254	0	132

1. Covers mining, construction, and manufacturing. 2. Covers private sector earnings in agricultural services, forestry, and fisheries; transportation and public utilities; wholesale trade; retail trade; finance, insurance, and real estate; and services.

STATE County	Agriculture, 1987 (cont'd): Value of land and buildings: Average per farm ($1,000)	Value of land and buildings: Average per acre (Dollars)	Value of products sold: Total (Mil dol)	Value of products sold: Average per farm (Dollars)	Value of products sold: Percent from: Crops	Value of products sold: Percent from: Livestock and poultry[1]	Percent of farms with sales of: $10,000 or more	Percent of farms with sales of: $100,000 or more	Manufactures, 1987: Establishments: Total	Establishments: Percent with 20 or more employees	All employees: Number (1,000)	All employees: Percent change, 1982–1987	All employees: Annual payroll (Mil dol)	Production workers: Number (1,000)	Production workers: Work hours (Mil)
	119	120	121	122	123	124	125	126	127	128	129	130	131	132	133
OREGON—Con.															
Wallowa	449	301	23	51 140	25.6	74.4	54.7	14.1	34	14.7	0.3	0.0	7.1	0.3	0.5
Wasco	703	297	38	77 319	82.4	17.6	55.0	20.3	27	37.0	0.9	-10.0	19.8	0.6	1.3
Washington	260	2 861	96	55 607	82.8	17.2	32.1	9.5	657	31.5	30.9	-1.9	806.0	15.2	30.4
Wheeler	712	125	6	44 863	19.7	80.3	47.7	16.9	3	0.0	D	D	D	D	D
Yamhill	231	2 100	83	50 090	63.4	36.6	28.5	8.7	155	31.6	5.0	6.4	123.7	3.7	7.5
PENNSYLVANIA	239	1 579	3 078	59 701	26.9	73.1	50.3	14.8	17 844	40.5	1 037.5	-12.1	25 301.6	681.9	1 330.1
Adams	309	1 806	105	95 247	33.6	66.4	53.2	18.8	102	53.9	7.1	1.4	121.9	5.5	11.1
Allegheny	203	1 999	16	34 528	68.4	31.6	30.2	4.9	1 627	33.7	82.7	-31.8	2 574.5	39.7	77.4
Armstrong	183	1 247	55	74 165	80.4	19.6	34.1	6.0	82	34.1	2.7	-25.0	61.5	2.2	4.3
Beaver	136	1 356	12	21 294	35.5	64.5	30.4	5.4	172	36.6	9.8	-60.3	258.2	7.0	12.6
Bedford	223	1 084	46	44 136	10.5	89.5	47.1	15.1	61	31.1	2.3	4.5	40.8	1.8	3.6
Berks	351	2 595	168	92 735	45.7	54.3	60.4	23.2	624	47.3	47.3	-4.1	1 180.5	34.5	69.8
Blair	238	1 345	33	67 909	13.8	86.2	61.6	24.5	145	42.1	10.3	-11.2	204.0	7.8	14.2
Bradford	215	925	96	66 851	5.1	94.9	62.8	23.0	82	35.4	7.1	14.5	167.1	4.8	9.3
Bucks	365	3 652	54	63 677	62.5	37.5	41.4	12.5	1 205	36.9	48.5	-1.6	1 186.6	31.9	63.3
Butler	177	1 508	28	23 431	42.3	57.7	36.5	5.5	218	31.7	10.5	-1.9	308.2	7.5	15.9
Cambria	126	995	17	28 260	42.6	57.4	31.7	7.8	160	33.1	7.8	-23.5	153.1	6.2	11.5
Cameron	76	735	D	D	NA	NA	8.0	0.0	18	38.9	0.9	12.5	20.1	0.7	1.6
Carbon	263	1 909	5	25 618	69.1	30.9	36.7	4.0	84	59.5	4.6	-11.5	69.2	3.8	6.8
Centre	300	1 548	37	45 435	20.1	79.9	58.4	14.2	141	38.3	7.8	1.3	153.9	5.6	10.6
Chester	521	4 235	235	149 149	68.5	31.5	60.8	25.3	631	39.9	31.3	-11.3	835.1	18.8	37.5
Clarion	162	936	12	22 684	24.7	75.3	31.8	5.9	52	28.8	2.2	0.0	45.6	1.9	3.6
Clearfield	136	977	10	22 638	29.9	70.1	31.6	6.7	119	37.8	5.4	-3.6	97.1	4.2	7.7
Clinton	198	1 234	16	53 109	27.9	72.1	50.8	12.5	55	36.4	3.6	-25.0	74.5	2.9	5.6
Columbia	208	1 286	28	39 294	52.9	47.1	43.4	8.3	126	52.4	9.1	4.6	156.8	7.1	14.0
Crawford	144	800	47	36 578	14.1	85.9	49.6	9.4	230	35.2	8.4	-7.7	191.4	6.1	12.0
Cumberland	280	1 945	68	61 723	14.6	85.4	54.5	17.2	217	44.7	18.3	18.1	412.1	11.2	22.4
Dauphin	287	2 017	47	69 550	16.7	83.3	50.7	14.8	247	43.3	23.1	-11.2	607.8	13.6	24.9
Delaware	529	6 492	8	81 592	84.5	15.5	48.4	15.8	601	32.6	34.0	0.3	1 037.6	16.8	33.7
Elk	122	1 260	3	18 487	16.7	83.3	20.8	3.0	107	36.4	6.8	-8.1	174.6	5.1	10.4
Erie	154	1 133	59	43 783	52.6	47.4	51.3	11.7	538	42.6	34.0	-10.5	856.6	22.7	46.6
Fayette	119	931	15	16 102	31.7	68.3	24.9	3.0	127	33.1	5.2	-10.3	107.3	4.1	7.6
Forest	162	891	1	17 529	12.1	87.9	32.4	5.9	10	20.0	D	D	D	D	D
Franklin	300	1 763	136	94 300	13.1	86.9	65.8	29.5	179	40.8	12.4	-16.2	248.8	9.1	17.3
Fulton	178	875	14	30 455	10.1	89.9	37.3	10.3	23	26.1	0.8	0.0	16.0	0.6	1.0
Greene	140	728	7	8 238	19.8	80.2	14.3	1.3	21	23.8	0.4	0.0	6.7	0.3	0.6
Huntingdon	191	884	31	48 590	9.5	90.5	48.7	13.7	70	28.6	2.9	-3.3	53.2	2.4	4.4
Indiana	193	993	33	36 624	42.7	57.3	42.9	7.8	93	31.2	4.1	-6.8	88.6	2.8	5.7
Jefferson	144	803	11	22 814	18.8	81.2	35.6	5.9	86	40.7	4.4	-8.3	91.8	3.4	6.6
Juniata	197	1 189	39	68 954	9.9	90.1	60.8	19.4	61	31.1	2.8	0.0	35.4	2.3	4.6
Lackawanna	222	1 403	11	36 174	45.6	54.4	41.8	7.0	384	48.4	22.8	-8.1	432.5	17.7	34.5
Lancaster	315	3 778	601	125 816	9.7	90.3	78.1	29.3	821	45.2	60.0	4.7	1 378.0	42.5	83.3
Lawrence	120	992	24	32 707	22.8	77.2	46.9	8.4	155	41.3	7.1	-11.3	162.0	5.2	10.7
Lebanon	301	2 451	106	111 471	10.4	89.6	67.8	32.6	191	51.8	11.6	-12.1	216.6	8.8	17.2
Lehigh	580	3 189	41	75 541	55.0	45.0	51.2	13.3	468	45.5	38.2	-18.9	1 021.1	21.5	40.0
Luzerne	167	1 537	16	33 573	56.5	43.5	39.3	7.8	512	49.2	28.9	-16.7	528.0	21.7	40.4
Lycoming	217	1 313	34	40 426	29.4	70.6	46.5	9.0	231	48.5	17.2	16.2	344.7	12.5	23.5
McKean	124	704	4	16 961	14.2	85.8	29.2	2.5	73	41.1	5.0	-15.3	103.8	3.7	7.1
Mercer	122	899	40	31 177	32.0	68.0	46.4	6.9	169	36.7	10.4	-19.4	253.2	7.5	14.1
Mifflin	192	1 460	42	61 738	5.5	94.5	65.7	18.0	58	48.3	5.1	-5.6	114.4	4.0	8.2
Monroe	306	2 321	5	23 617	51.6	48.4	33.9	8.3	103	45.6	D	D	D	D	D
Montgomery	349	3 551	31	52 878	40.7	59.3	43.7	12.5	1 550	39.3	92.5	-1.8	2 573.3	48.9	95.9
Montour	229	1 273	11	41 848	36.7	63.3	51.9	12.2	16	75.0	2.0	5.3	50.0	1.6	3.1
Northampton	387	2 068	29	59 193	48.2	51.8	50.2	17.8	384	45.8	25.9	-23.4	588.1	19.3	36.3
Northumberland	255	1 357	44	65 329	29.7	70.3	53.3	18.1	128	56.2	11.0	-3.5	214.5	8.3	16.1
Perry	234	1 323	33	52 975	11.8	88.2	48.7	14.6	35	25.7	0.7	16.7	8.5	0.6	1.0
Philadelphia	149	15 894	D	D	NA	NA	60.0	0.0	1 887	38.4	95.9	-23.3	2 425.1	60.7	116.3
Pike	239	1 920	1	29 193	72.6	27.5	34.1	9.1	20	30.0	D	D	D	D	D
Potter	197	730	17	50 823	20.4	79.6	48.2	17.1	42	31.0	1.1	37.5	16.0	0.8	1.6
Schuylkill	212	1 388	40	62 427	28.8	71.2	46.2	15.5	251	55.8	17.9	1.1	305.4	14.4	27.5
Snyder	178	1 312	39	54 934	14.4	85.6	53.3	12.4	73	50.7	4.5	40.6	84.7	3.8	7.4
Somerset	198	931	49	46 160	13.2	86.8	53.3	15.4	120	32.5	4.8	20.0	79.7	3.7	7.2
Sullivan	159	839	6	38 904	6.8	93.3	38.8	11.5	22	27.3	0.5	25.0	7.2	0.4	0.9
Susquehanna	224	928	40	48 877	5.3	94.7	55.2	14.3	59	28.8	2.0	-25.9	34.7	1.5	2.8
Tioga	191	719	44	50 178	8.5	91.5	57.0	15.1	50	38.0	2.5	4.2	41.8	2.2	4.4

1. Includes livestock and poultry products.

STATE County	Manufactures, 1987 (cont'd)					Value of construction authorized by building permits, 1990							
	Production workers (cont'd)						Nonresidential				Residential		
	Wages							Percent					
	Total (Mil dol)	Average per worker (Dollars)	Value added by manu-facture (Mil dol)	Value of shipments (Mil dol)	New capital expend-itures (Mil dol)	Total[1] ($1,000)	Total ($1,000)	Office	Industrial	Stores	New construction ($1,000)	Number of housing units	Alterations and additions ($1,000)
	134	135	136	137	138	139	140	141	142	143	144	145	146
OREGON—Con.													
Wallowa	6.2	20 667	19.9	46.3	0.5	1 806	594	0.0	1.9	2.0	854	13	223
Wasco	13.6	22 667	39.8	108.5	1.5	10 918	4 211	3.6	60.5	28.5	2 109	22	1 095
Washington	291.3	19 164	1 682.8	3 010.8	164.5	584 845	85 359	49.8	12.2	19.0	444 297	5 678	8 530
Wheeler	D	D	D	D	D	410	10	0.0	0.0	0.0	344	3	26
Yamhill	78.9	21 324	398.3	810.8	19.7	51 925	10 026	3.9	19.1	3.4	33 202	428	1 835
PENNSYLVANIA	13 731.1	20 137	57 605.2	118 651.3	3 440.5	6 703 578	2 206 297	27.9	19.5	23.1	2 898 341	37 244	552 345
Adams	83.9	15 255	304.2	710.6	21.8	73 612	11 201	10.3	9.2	31.7	45 912	654	4 688
Allegheny	939.3	23 660	3 442.4	7 634.9	183.8	579 311	136 744	28.0	7.9	34.8	253 065	2 430	62 109
Armstrong	44.4	20 182	154.0	258.5	6.3	7 182	949	19.3	0.0	31.9	4 396	62	761
Beaver	167.6	23 943	562.4	1 764.9	30.8	116 259	67 154	1.4	85.8	3.6	41 149	470	4 077
Bedford	28.3	15 722	161.7	290.3	4.5	13 205	2 656	46.6	1.1	21.6	6 373	129	841
Berks	752.5	21 812	2 628.6	5 227.5	184.5	207 525	69 892	26.2	27.6	34.7	102 899	1 401	12 592
Blair	139.6	17 897	607.1	1 127.5	31.0	41 241	10 758	17.7	7.7	38.5	20 938	337	2 203
Bradford	95.2	19 833	591.3	1 060.1	32.4	28 575	18 929	1.4	33.8	11.0	5 887	101	1 268
Bucks	659.4	20 671	2 590.3	5 373.3	170.5	379 843	73 727	34.8	12.2	8.9	186 611	2 225	47 268
Butler	200.8	26 773	627.2	1 449.7	55.1	127 471	21 427	18.7	10.7	19.2	84 739	932	5 096
Cambria	106.7	17 210	244.5	660.8	12.5	104 947	82 772	4.1	0.3	5.2	15 399	253	2 561
Cameron	17.2	24 571	41.0	73.7	D	2 330	986	0.0	74.2	0.0	1 156	15	144
Carbon	50.1	13 184	128.1	273.7	11.8	56 344	34 607	0.2	85.3	1.0	13 810	167	2 440
Centre	94.2	16 821	333.0	663.5	32.1	92 279	26 842	21.1	1.0	45.5	52 353	807	3 868
Chester	411.2	21 872	1 696.8	3 693.0	112.9	370 148	88 548	32.1	14.3	30.4	202 217	1 819	30 392
Clarion	37.2	19 579	120.4	242.2	4.4	7 662	2 446	27.2	36.8	25.9	4 144	71	627
Clearfield	67.5	16 071	240.5	588.9	14.6	10 157	1 239	1.6	31.6	12.1	7 880	105	506
Clinton	51.3	17 690	160.3	398.3	8.6	9 683	1 937	9.5	32.6	30.9	4 356	100	703
Columbia	105.4	14 845	350.3	755.0	20.5	15 839	5 952	13.7	23.2	34.2	5 015	93	1 720
Crawford	128.6	21 082	466.3	880.9	17.8	34 694	17 224	1.4	7.7	17.7	9 664	212	2 754
Cumberland	220.0	19 643	1 187.6	2 375.4	72.6	203 666	74 085	11.0	14.0	46.8	93 612	1 288	12 425
Dauphin	280.1	20 596	1 307.3	2 553.5	71.0	253 236	115 825	49.3	4.5	26.1	77 218	1 097	14 584
Delaware	410.7	24 446	2 565.0	7 105.9	161.6	165 555	40 693	48.4	3.6	10.2	61 276	641	30 273
Elk	117.0	22 941	347.0	648.2	18.5	11 361	1 658	3.0	34.1	30.8	5 819	117	981
Erie	489.1	21 546	1 922.4	3 382.3	100.8	108 861	31 518	8.9	16.2	37.7	44 215	678	7 820
Fayette	78.6	19 171	229.5	466.0	15.1	50 908	30 477	9.4	1.7	19.8	13 648	300	1 548
Forest	D	D	D	D	D	3 198	650	0.0	97.3	0.0	766	15	248
Franklin	162.2	17 824	670.2	1 371.2	20.1	56 525	25 859	1.2	0.0	78.2	22 716	310	5 936
Fulton	9.5	15 833	32.0	70.3	1.8	3 440	1 081	13.9	0.0	15.0	1 933	40	271
Greene	5.0	16 667	22.8	32.8	D	1 388	462	0.0	0.0	91.0	623	14	51
Huntingdon	39.6	16 500	150.4	258.9	4.5	12 883	2 490	18.5	5.0	19.2	7 765	158	1 446
Indiana	54.2	19 357	182.5	352.7	8.2	23 401	3 558	21.5	8.9	32.6	12 397	159	2 705
Jefferson	63.9	18 794	206.7	372.4	11.5	13 629	7 150	5.2	20.5	60.0	4 005	80	1 026
Juniata	25.4	11 043	64.2	148.8	3.9	8 312	1 016	0.0	4.8	0.0	4 854	111	595
Lackawanna	299.6	16 927	924.4	1 883.0	49.4	79 177	24 850	11.2	22.9	28.5	43 095	638	3 950
Lancaster	838.2	19 722	3 883.7	7 429.1	264.7	421 148	141 063	8.5	32.6	27.9	192 580	2 692	33 967
Lawrence	107.0	20 577	468.6	930.5	29.0	28 638	6 050	38.3	10.7	21.2	17 025	351	1 746
Lebanon	140.3	15 943	684.8	1 369.3	31.5	40 744	11 034	39.1	22.8	17.8	25 844	403	609
Lehigh	464.4	21 600	2 495.1	4 896.6	181.4	165 076	48 651	8.3	5.2	53.0	72 056	782	13 537
Luzerne	346.7	15 977	1 321.3	2 475.1	77.6	161 466	51 639	9.5	8.7	35.8	79 930	1 210	10 573
Lycoming	205.9	16 472	950.4	1 814.7	45.9	61 612	11 042	39.8	0.7	36.4	17 345	315	8 413
McKean	75.5	20 405	281.5	576.2	17.8	19 513	13 305	1.4	84.7	2.2	2 956	55	1 512
Mercer	172.7	23 027	630.7	1 521.5	30.8	48 116	18 904	23.2	20.0	35.8	16 898	272	3 213
Mifflin	84.2	21 050	244.6	520.7	8.6	16 121	4 541	11.7	4.8	12.3	8 760	165	1 115
Monroe	D	D	D	D	D	187 022	27 647	29.7	8.0	31.7	136 484	1 626	10 780
Montgomery	1 050.8	21 489	6 477.9	11 362.2	353.7	846 466	424 352	67.3	15.9	7.6	206 735	2 567	85 280
Montour	36.3	22 687	195.4	285.6	8.0	21 781	10 383	81.7	0.0	4.7	7 111	113	722
Northampton	375.9	19 477	1 251.9	2 387.9	69.4	163 956	50 110	18.9	23.1	17.4	77 057	975	14 294
Northumberland	149.3	17 988	610.0	1 309.2	32.2	29 643	9 757	5.0	47.0	20.5	9 251	172	4 842
Perry	6.9	11 500	17.8	34.1	1.9	15 286	1 527	0.0	0.9	8.3	10 569	200	1 336
Philadelphia	1 210.5	19 942	5 084.5	11 567.6	213.3	248 017	53 831	24.2	8.1	36.7	46 205	747	34 382
Pike	D	D	D	D	D	106 510	2 171	8.1	0.0	38.3	94 256	1 053	6 938
Potter	11.5	14 375	36.3	68.2	2.2	5 760	4 100	1.9	82.4	0.0	1 057	42	263
Schuylkill	212.3	14 743	707.2	1 474.5	45.3	35 232	13 797	0.7	36.9	34.4	14 309	233	2 368
Snyder	60.8	16 000	163.4	332.7	9.0	10 315	2 415	50.6	0.6	14.9	6 036	85	431
Somerset	56.2	15 189	179.8	420.9	10.9	44 334	28 545	0.3	4.8	18.3	10 987	182	1 418
Sullivan	6.1	15 250	12.4	30.4	0.8	5 143	813	0.0	0.0	31.8	3 397	64	442
Susquehanna	22.4	14 933	37.5	187.5	D	15 850	2 127	11.0	29.7	10.3	11 912	159	546
Tioga	32.8	14 909	109.3	193.2	5.8	13 306	3 622	5.2	0.0	22.4	7 393	180	980

1. Includes nonresidential additions and alterations, residential nonhousekeeping buildings, and residential garages and carports not shown separately.

STATE County	Wholesale trade, 1987				Retail trade, all establishments, 1987				Retail trade, establishments with payroll, 1987					
						Sales				Sales				
											Per capita[2] (Dollars)			
	Establishments	Sales (Mil dol)	Paid employees[1]	Annual payroll (Mil dol)	Number	Total (Mil dol)	Percent change, 1982–1987	Per capita[2] (Dollars)	Number	Total (Mil dol)	General merchandise stores	Food stores	Apparel & accessory stores	Eating and drinking places
	147	148	149	150	151	152	153	154	155	156	157	158	159	160
OREGON—Con.														
Wallowa	9	10.2	47	0.7	127	30.9	15.3	4 354	77	29.1	33	1 490	85	271
Wasco	48	78.8	377	5.0	284	153.7	26.7	7 462	179	147.9	D	1 227	322	633
Washington	752	5 189.0	7 943	204.8	2 693	2 401.2	55.4	8 494	1 687	2 350.3	1 776	1 254	504	663
Wheeler	2	D	D	D	19	3.7	5.7	2 871	10	2.9	D	D	0	194
Yamhill	77	134.7	560	10.3	616	291.0	38.8	4 899	360	279.6	D	1 130	120	425
PENNSYLVANIA	19 793	104 454.3	247 599	5 832.5	118 675	73 786.7	45.3	6 178	70 823	71 216.6	734	1 208	306	522
Adams	95	405.0	1 199	20.6	834	283.9	50.3	3 889	404	263.4	191	971	51	565
Allegheny	2 991	21 822.5	37 049	948.7	12 352	8 810.0	28.8	6 472	8 405	8 606.2	941	1 211	369	661
Armstrong	73	D	D	D	819	309.6	25.0	3 974	447	291.7	370	954	105	263
Beaver	163	377.7	1 152	22.4	1 625	872.5	16.0	4 582	988	846.1	878	1 079	159	374
Bedford	46	D	D	D	579	279.7	64.4	5 877	296	261.1	D	830	D	679
Berks	484	2 463.5	7 981	186.2	3 534	2 242.5	48.6	6 896	2 081	2 171.8	842	1 259	650	577
Blair	194	1 026.9	2 596	56.3	1 432	880.9	44.3	6 638	856	850.9	1 015	1 496	303	489
Bradford	77	D	D	D	674	335.3	61.8	5 239	342	320.0	393	995	138	282
Bucks	1 181	5 928.7	13 570	334.2	5 171	4 345.8	63.3	8 156	3 032	4 214.2	892	1 475	279	581
Butler	227	D	D	D	1 442	823.3	42.9	5 417	838	794.4	723	1 095	149	448
Cambria	211	414.5	2 147	36.5	1 739	858.0	25.9	5 003	997	817.8	646	1 168	193	344
Cameron	3	D	D	D	95	26.7	34.2	4 235	50	25.0	D	1 222	58	292
Carbon	30	67.6	211	3.3	627	233.5	51.7	4 230	296	214.2	133	1 092	60	279
Centre	136	210.6	1 151	22.3	1 175	719.4	46.2	6 272	732	697.0	712	1 143	301	666
Chester	955	7 113.5	12 710	369.3	2 994	2 211.7	71.7	6 188	1 794	2 145.9	378	1 233	220	508
Clarion	65	124.0	530	8.9	513	192.2	17.3	4 598	290	180.1	378	1 108	260	420
Clearfield	109	D	D	D	922	519.0	29.7	6 344	507	498.7	561	1 438	394	350
Clinton	34	31.5	163	2.3	439	248.6	47.8	6 578	252	239.9	442	1 234	409	341
Columbia	68	79.6	431	7.2	741	350.9	58.8	5 761	391	331.7	D	1 121	157	483
Crawford	108	208.2	835	13.6	996	430.1	27.7	4 989	533	408.5	561	872	164	491
Cumberland	304	1 865.2	4 897	114.0	2 036	1 708.1	54.5	8 878	1 231	1 662.2	1 098	1 439	303	684
Dauphin	414	2 609.8	7 264	167.5	2 392	1 753.4	49.1	7 340	1 508	1 712.0	862	1 191	287	586
Delaware	909	8 977.1	9 743	256.6	4 756	3 830.5	48.3	6 897	3 053	3 733.1	798	1 364	313	549
Elk	40	51.6	283	5.2	394	145.8	27.2	3 951	206	135.7	D	1 038	88	241
Erie	402	861.1	4 069	82.5	2 763	1 621.8	36.9	5 847	1 753	1 571.9	774	1 234	235	549
Fayette	170	1 019.7	2 453	48.0	1 610	835.2	36.4	5 480	885	795.5	756	1 410	249	367
Forest	4	1.3	8	0.1	74	13.8	1.5	2 944	37	12.0	D	D	0	261
Franklin	135	264.7	1 459	23.9	1 230	657.0	47.7	5 535	679	629.8	680	1 058	259	456
Fulton	15	12.1	68	0.8	135	50.8	81.4	3 580	65	45.6	86	718	D	209
Greene	42	90.0	357	6.1	367	155.3	27.1	3 893	189	143.4	308	1 025	62	222
Huntingdon	40	151.2	505	9.3	444	166.1	37.8	3 872	224	155.0	261	1 063	112	301
Indiana	104	174.0	761	12.4	918	476.7	42.5	5 176	493	456.3	799	1 067	171	398
Jefferson	79	166.8	705	11.9	576	221.2	28.5	4 600	293	205.5	257	1 067	97	240
Juniata	22	36.4	182	3.2	215	73.8	45.8	3 672	100	68.4	D	936	D	184
Lackawanna	364	1 188.5	4 720	83.0	2 622	1 440.0	52.3	6 478	1 420	1 373.4	1 007	1 271	373	502
Lancaster	700	3 466.7	10 527	210.3	4 713	2 806.8	67.4	6 924	2 475	2 682.4	654	1 345	305	599
Lawrence	145	254.9	1 306	23.1	1 069	495.2	25.2	4 898	600	470.0	460	1 088	132	371
Lebanon	133	573.6	1 729	32.6	1 274	812.2	58.3	7 175	700	782.1	D	1 170	D	434
Lehigh	579	2 331.0	7 492	176.3	3 125	2 464.7	50.7	8 639	1 932	2 401.3	1 278	1 404	492	694
Luzerne	503	1 797.9	6 980	126.3	3 809	1 985.9	47.1	6 000	2 108	1 896.5	875	1 206	298	460
Lycoming	182	372.2	1 840	34.2	1 299	783.0	51.7	6 669	793	754.7	778	1 371	351	446
McKean	69	168.6	663	12.5	558	216.4	23.6	4 654	323	206.4	337	1 213	103	397
Mercer	168	873.2	1 938	31.7	1 232	639.1	26.2	5 205	751	615.8	719	1 038	262	437
Mifflin	63	155.3	935	18.2	478	251.4	53.7	5 406	271	239.6	541	1 204	168	381
Monroe	96	186.1	837	18.8	1 225	739.3	94.8	8 439	738	707.2	857	1 647	234	657
Montgomery	2 248	13 687.1	26 246	727.6	7 790	6 441.2	62.6	9 467	4 923	6 268.5	1 376	1 622	640	674
Montour	25	86.4	250	4.4	172	73.2	16.6	4 436	99	69.4	D	1 234	48	495
Northampton	282	974.6	2 998	66.2	2 182	1 232.0	52.4	5 148	1 273	1 181.7	401	1 267	188	435
Northumberland	119	326.0	1 137	19.4	1 061	484.4	46.3	4 933	591	456.4	418	1 203	126	291
Perry	21	41.6	116	2.0	358	161.1	63.7	4 038	152	147.7	D	889	D	153
Philadelphia	2 197	12 518.2	35 693	901.2	12 793	7 207.9	33.7	4 348	8 388	6 958.1	439	927	371	534
Pike	11	6.7	63	1.1	283	88.8	86.9	3 610	137	81.5	61	821	33	383
Potter	18	10.2	78	0.9	259	70.3	57.3	3 926	106	60.8	0	1 038	D	161
Schuylkill	189	433.6	2 179	34.2	1 847	757.0	38.3	4 916	920	708.2	693	1 186	174	315
Snyder	37	136.0	480	9.0	453	273.0	56.0	7 605	254	260.8	1 610	1 060	288	683
Somerset	127	205.7	1 057	18.6	865	343.1	34.0	4 267	429	321.6	264	896	74	317
Sullivan	12	6.3	35	0.6	104	24.9	50.0	3 897	43	22.5	D	D	0	227
Susquehanna	30	21.8	176	2.3	389	143.1	50.9	3 543	177	130.3	212	785	D	199
Tioga	45	62.2	345	4.7	500	170.7	49.1	4 278	260	159.1	349	978	46	410

1. For pay period including March 12. 2. Based on the estimated population as of July 1 of the year shown.

STATE County	Retail trade, establishments with payroll, 1987 (cont'd): Paid employees[1]	Retail trade, establishments with payroll, 1987 (cont'd): Annual payroll (Mil dol)	Taxable service industries–establishments with payroll, 1987: Number	Receipts (Mil dol): Total	Receipts, Selected kinds of business: Hotels, motels and other lodging places	Receipts, Selected kinds of business: Health services	Receipts, Selected kinds of business: Legal services	Paid employees	Annual payroll (Mil dol)	Bank deposits,[2] June 1989: Total (Mil dol)	Bank deposits,[2] June 1989: Percent change, 1988–1989	Savings capital,[3] September 1989: Total (Mil dol)	Savings capital,[3] September 1989: Percent change, 1988–1989
	161	162	163	164	165	166	167	168	169	170	171	172	173
OREGON—Con.													
Wallowa	338	3.1	50	5.1	0.6	1.9	D	139	1.5	53	10.9	21.3	5.7
Wasco	1 550	15.9	155	33.4	4.5	15.2	1.5	828	11.8	174	4.7	70.6	-8.5
Washington	24 631	259.9	2 276	708.0	23.3	207.6	16.7	16 791	277.5	1 353	4.0	905.3	-1.9
Wheeler	26	0.3	1	D	0.0	0.0	0.0	D	D	11	2.1	0.0	NA
Yamhill	3 228	30.4	308	68.5	0.8	37.3	4.6	1 916	25.2	268	5.5	177.8	-1.3
PENNSYLVANIA	847 907	8 096.8	70 071	33 232.2	1 649.2	7 998.4	2 747.9	693 760	12 407.8	129 248	5.3	35 496.6	1.9
Adams	3 938	31.4	318	69.6	10.9	21.1	4.3	1 981	20.6	726	7.5	27.5	-8.8
Allegheny	115 369	1 036.4	9 788	6 500.1	185.6	1 190.1	476.7	117 063	2 441.9	21 938	8.1	7 709.8	-1.8
Armstrong	3 516	28.6	326	69.2	1.4	30.4	2.6	1 649	22.8	626	6.0	106.4	2.1
Beaver	10 903	91.4	835	236.7	4.7	82.4	11.6	5 247	94.3	1 073	7.8	628.5	-5.8
Bedford	2 917	27.3	210	40.3	10.6	9.3	1.1	978	11.7	354	8.5	52.2	0.9
Berks	25 121	245.8	1 739	685.3	30.6	205.0	35.8	15 336	266.5	3 768	1.7	931.4	8.8
Blair	10 494	88.4	724	229.7	10.8	80.5	8.0	6 376	79.4	987	8.0	235.9	-2.7
Bradford	2 919	29.7	222	79.0	4.1	56.1	5.1	1 484	32.5	501	8.6	50.5	-3.9
Bucks	43 007	472.1	3 766	1 597.1	39.2	398.2	69.5	35 365	608.1	4 493	6.4	2 012.7	-5.9
Butler	9 810	84.5	740	198.4	11.4	54.5	5.9	4 452	64.0	1 040	9.5	383.4	0.7
Cambria	10 213	87.2	774	209.5	8.4	80.7	12.6	4 960	84.8	1 453	4.2	416.7	3.3
Cameron	327	2.6	22	2.2	D	D	0.5	78	0.6	52	8.1	0.0	NA
Carbon	2 252	22.0	201	47.4	1.2	15.2	3.9	1 343	14.5	522	6.4	69.7	-2.0
Centre	9 531	77.5	619	324.7	20.9	68.7	8.4	6 601	134.9	773	6.2	319.7	3.5
Chester	21 521	235.5	2 496	1 640.8	19.2	252.2	48.4	25 497	539.4	2 604	5.9	1 001.9	7.7
Clarion	2 504	20.6	167	35.4	5.4	13.4	2.4	998	11.6	402	4.4	38.5	3.4
Clearfield	5 193	47.1	393	93.3	10.3	37.0	5.0	2 312	29.7	707	5.7	89.6	-0.6
Clinton	2 281	20.5	143	26.2	3.2	11.1	2.4	637	9.1	244	6.0	30.5	-8.6
Columbia	3 736	32.8	286	63.7	5.0	25.8	4.8	1 696	21.8	554	5.8	73.1	-2.4
Crawford	5 336	46.1	400	98.5	5.7	36.5	5.6	2 393	32.9	604	4.5	119.3	-0.5
Cumberland	18 728	173.4	1 168	540.9	37.8	157.5	13.3	12 420	219.2	1 682	9.9	662.0	1.7
Dauphin	19 424	190.7	1 578	876.5	92.1	166.9	87.4	20 435	303.0	2 096	6.9	950.6	-1.7
Delaware	42 190	448.2	3 798	1 631.9	61.8	441.7	63.1	35 066	608.6	5 479	5.4	1 594.6	0.2
Elk	1 621	13.4	156	24.9	1.4	11.6	2.0	594	8.0	296	4.3	87.6	2.7
Erie	20 569	174.0	1 553	655.2	40.3	226.5	29.5	13 234	216.0	1 710	1.8	652.8	-2.2
Fayette	9 222	76.1	667	171.4	35.3	53.5	7.3	4 699	54.7	1 029	4.5	188.9	1.1
Forest	146	1.1	17	2.5	1.1	D	D	57	0.6	29	6.8	0.0	NA
Franklin	7 448	67.6	561	121.0	7.7	45.2	6.0	3 083	41.9	1 123	4.3	73.0	-5.3
Fulton	407	4.2	44	5.8	0.3	2.2	0.3	141	1.5	103	8.7	0.0	NA
Greene	1 483	14.1	138	29.0	1.2	12.1	1.8	794	9.6	197	4.4	142.5	3.8
Huntingdon	1 786	15.3	157	35.5	2.5	10.0	1.6	1 058	14.8	297	5.7	35.2	13.1
Indiana	6 126	45.5	438	90.8	6.0	35.8	4.4	2 293	29.7	739	6.7	185.1	1.7
Jefferson	2 393	18.9	218	42.0	5.6	18.5	2.1	1 055	12.1	506	2.6	55.1	2.1
Juniata	739	6.4	77	11.3	D	D	0.7	347	3.5	187	10.9	26.1	1.2
Lackawanna	16 873	146.7	1 213	467.8	32.1	151.2	30.4	11 387	178.2	2 929	8.0	291.1	-8.6
Lancaster	34 206	335.0	2 178	795.5	77.9	220.5	38.5	18 836	292.9	3 848	6.6	713.6	7.6
Lawrence	5 634	48.9	486	115.3	D	47.0	4.9	3 791	42.2	624	9.5	436.6	-1.9
Lebanon	7 822	78.9	521	211.8	5.3	55.8	7.5	3 961	76.7	1 045	4.3	140.4	2.4
Lehigh	26 914	277.1	2 061	920.2	27.8	258.0	39.2	23 418	355.0	2 964	0.5	932.8	7.8
Luzerne	23 663	202.4	1 709	574.7	52.5	220.8	35.5	14 661	214.8	3 486	9.9	923.9	-13.9
Lycoming	8 617	77.4	607	174.6	11.9	70.6	12.5	3 935	65.0	954	4.0	81.2	-3.5
McKean	2 576	21.8	218	34.2	2.8	13.7	2.8	1 044	11.1	300	4.4	157.5	-0.3
Mercer	7 997	66.0	642	169.3	10.2	72.6	6.8	4 031	64.1	1 103	4.5	234.1	-1.6
Mifflin	2 813	27.7	171	43.0	D	23.4	2.0	914	15.9	310	8.2	56.4	-6.0
Monroe	7 107	73.2	635	310.5	165.3	41.3	10.4	8 772	93.4	798	5.5	162.5	-4.7
Montgomery	70 340	744.7	7 037	3 945.9	131.4	982.2	136.5	87 703	1 577.0	9 631	5.3	4 597.8	25.3
Montour	1 027	7.1	63	95.8	D	D	D	1 327	48.9	157	3.5	18.0	-4.2
Northampton	13 356	129.7	1 258	404.0	16.7	121.7	25.2	9 276	148.5	2 387	2.0	429.4	2.2
Northumberland	4 975	46.4	423	102.8	1.2	36.7	6.7	2 608	34.1	761	5.7	206.4	3.4
Perry	1 262	13.2	109	11.6	1.2	4.5	1.2	317	3.0	208	3.6	30.2	-2.2
Philadelphia	93 684	954.1	8 633	6 132.5	256.0	1 043.6	1 343.7	113 123	2 327.3	25 865	1.6	3 782.9	0.1
Pike	786	8.5	136	64.2	34.6	12.3	3.4	1 491	21.7	199	7.3	0.0	NA
Potter	576	5.4	76	15.1	0.9	8.6	1.0	420	5.3	133	5.2	0.0	NA
Schuylkill	8 196	76.3	610	156.7	6.2	64.3	10.7	3 993	54.8	1 634	5.3	163.4	2.9
Snyder	3 349	29.2	141	32.9	3.1	7.1	1.8	906	11.4	310	1.1	30.9	-1.6
Somerset	3 634	31.2	332	78.3	5.8	28.1	4.3	1 828	26.3	688	6.3	106.3	-0.5
Sullivan	224	1.9	19	7.1	0.7	D	D	258	2.8	64	7.0	0.0	NA
Susquehanna	1 170	11.2	113	28.2	1.7	14.5	1.9	1 010	8.1	346	6.1	6.3	-3.9
Tioga	1 785	16.6	140	24.8	3.7	7.5	2.3	636	8.1	293	9.3	8.5	-2.7

1. For the period including March 12 of the year shown. 2. Includes deposits for all insured and reporting noninsured commercial and mutual savings banks. 3. Includes savings capital for all FSLIC insured savings institutions.

STATE County	Federal funds and grants, 1989							Local government finances, 1981–1982							
	Expenditures		Per capita[1] (Dollars)					General revenue						Direct general expenditure	
									Intergovernmental		Taxes				
												Per capita[2]			
	Total (Mil dol)	Percent change, 1988–1989	Total	Direct payments for individuals	Procurement contract awards	Salaries and wages	Grant awards	Total (Mil dol)	Total (Mil dol)	Percent from state	Total (Mil dol)	Total (Dollars)	Property (Dollars)	Total (Mil dol)	Percent change, 1977–1982
	174	175	176	177	178	179	180	181	182	183	184	185	186	187	188
OREGON—Con.															
Wallowa	23.5	-2.2	3 405	2 257	107	505	239	12.4	4.7	93.4	3.7	489	464	11.2	96.8
Wasco	67.3	-0.4	3 316	2 283	105	510	206	29.3	10.9	94.6	12.4	552	531	27.8	66.6
Washington	455.3	4.8	1 497	1 099	196	83	113	286.7	81.2	86.8	156.2	603	572	290.4	101.2
Wheeler	4.5	2.8	3 423	2 432	19	230	228	3.6	1.6	95.7	1.5	993	991	2.6	39.8
Yamhill	144.3	-32.0	2 327	1 652	169	177	221	63.6	24.7	84.3	24.3	427	404	64.9	81.6
PENNSYLVANIA	41 961.2	6.0	X	2 183	323	401	535	12 417.6	4 923.6	78.8	5 038.2	424	281	11 326.7	47.7
Adams	181.2	19.6	2 397	1 595	102	215	442	56.9	27.0	88.7	20.7	296	197	56.4	57.7
Allegheny	5 398.6	-2.5	4 019	2 421	666	437	483	1 919.6	735.3	70.6	807.4	564	417	1 676.9	59.6
Armstrong	223.1	11.6	2 871	2 232	94	140	375	63.5	28.9	92.8	22.9	293	218	63.4	76.5
Beaver	491.6	-23.8	2 615	2 179	39	105	285	215.0	73.9	92.2	73.0	361	261	202.1	58.0
Bedford	118.6	10.9	2 465	1 813	160	112	332	32.6	18.7	96.2	8.8	185	124	28.0	40.3
Berks	777.8	4.8	2 339	1 835	156	145	190	320.0	117.8	82.9	118.9	378	270	347.8	77.7
Blair	399.1	-6.8	3 016	2 283	48	253	414	112.7	48.8	87.2	38.1	281	200	101.8	47.7
Bradford	159.6	5.2	2 467	1 711	241	129	344	56.0	28.9	94.0	16.7	260	175	46.6	7.1
Bucks	1 106.6	1.0	1 999	1 372	187	304	130	498.3	140.6	78.0	241.2	487	425	443.6	46.9
Butler	383.5	7.5	2 486	1 744	176	314	239	122.7	53.7	80.0	44.1	294	213	117.4	65.7
Cambria	548.1	-0.7	3 255	2 545	178	242	276	169.3	85.0	82.0	49.5	276	206	156.8	31.6
Cameron	18.5	2.2	2 931	2 256	23	119	524	4.6	2.2	93.2	1.6	243	168	5.4	55.3
Carbon	178.9	7.6	3 144	2 392	264	104	372	42.2	18.9	75.7	16.6	308	219	38.3	46.0
Centre	352.7	8.2	3 038	1 442	607	181	787	87.2	34.6	88.0	28.6	252	159	83.4	86.2
Chester	744.0	-7.6	1 971	1 289	323	210	141	299.7	88.0	91.5	146.5	450	362	263.2	18.5
Clarion	102.6	-5.3	2 473	1 963	42	137	280	34.9	19.2	93.1	11.4	264	178	30.3	50.9
Clearfield	220.7	3.6	2 715	2 057	161	161	318	63.9	33.4	93.3	21.1	254	177	63.6	40.6
Clinton	133.1	15.1	3 502	2 086	940	159	290	26.5	12.2	87.4	8.7	224	138	24.2	12.9
Columbia	530.3	-9.7	8 707	2 355	69	121	6 118	46.9	21.5	84.7	17.1	276	177	40.3	28.7
Crawford	212.3	3.5	2 492	2 008	40	118	298	64.6	31.5	88.4	22.7	254	182	56.2	24.1
Cumberland	828.5	-6.7	4 193	1 933	246	1 879	111	177.5	65.9	83.6	68.8	378	232	177.8	63.6
Dauphin	1 599.6	12.6	6 610	2 007	110	484	3 990	259.6	90.4	79.5	86.6	370	233	267.8	72.0
Delaware	1 488.7	-6.7	2 673	2 103	229	164	171	526.3	168.1	83.6	235.6	428	388	489.2	39.1
Elk	83.6	7.9	2 297	1 947	27	120	178	24.1	11.4	82.6	8.9	235	147	20.5	40.2
Erie	681.6	5.4	2 468	1 835	111	214	296	263.3	118.8	79.0	99.2	352	274	236.1	18.1
Fayette	514.4	8.2	3 414	2 527	146	139	588	98.0	52.4	89.5	30.2	192	132	90.7	42.0
Forest	16.9	-2.1	3 596	2 838	106	312	327	5.5	2.6	88.8	2.2	444	347	3.8	42.9
Franklin	436.1	-1.9	3 601	1 846	288	1 288	152	88.3	39.0	82.0	30.6	266	191	95.5	77.3
Fulton	30.2	15.6	2 067	1 498	134	81	266	9.6	6.0	88.8	2.3	174	114	9.4	43.3
Greene	113.5	5.1	2 889	2 273	17	155	425	41.2	17.1	92.5	16.2	398	274	38.6	21.7
Huntingdon	109.0	8.3	2 524	1 845	69	131	411	32.2	16.7	87.5	8.8	207	146	30.9	52.4
Indiana	230.2	5.6	2 508	1 955	54	139	335	68.0	30.7	91.5	23.3	251	171	60.1	55.3
Jefferson	122.4	-3.4	2 576	2 141	29	132	253	37.4	20.8	94.7	11.5	237	162	34.2	66.8
Juniata	44.8	11.8	2 194	1 670	98	119	199	10.9	5.5	93.8	3.1	162	92	9.7	44.8
Lackawanna	772.5	3.8	3 483	2 707	272	190	305	184.8	77.8	77.9	69.7	309	218	169.5	45.7
Lancaster	809.5	4.7	1 913	1 446	157	141	158	275.8	102.1	85.9	116.6	314	223	259.5	55.2
Lawrence	295.0	5.5	2 947	2 344	83	201	301	95.0	36.4	74.5	32.8	309	232	90.3	65.1
Lebanon	413.7	0.7	3 594	1 726	142	1 562	154	87.6	37.1	81.5	34.7	313	228	76.8	43.3
Lehigh	649.1	4.2	2 226	1 645	141	212	215	264.3	84.2	83.6	116.9	425	318	240.5	43.0
Luzerne	1 192.0	3.9	3 601	2 765	130	347	348	270.1	118.1	74.2	103.6	305	215	252.2	33.9
Lycoming	339.8	9.0	2 860	1 975	244	216	405	133.8	59.1	73.7	42.1	358	232	118.8	42.0
McKean	126.0	-2.8	2 768	2 233	53	175	294	51.1	24.6	87.5	14.6	293	211	44.2	67.7
Mercer	315.6	5.3	2 591	2 197	22	112	244	114.9	51.4	82.4	42.6	334	244	106.9	48.7
Mifflin	109.9	3.9	2 349	1 776	144	109	293	35.8	15.8	83.4	10.2	219	129	37.2	-4.5
Monroe	365.6	20.1	3 701	1 679	754	1 184	78	55.4	15.4	79.9	31.7	433	335	52.4	69.1
Montgomery	2 180.7	5.4	3 137	1 876	847	314	90	622.1	151.0	82.3	333.7	513	445	575.1	43.5
Montour	51.7	3.7	3 134	2 233	454	89	296	20.3	5.1	86.1	5.0	300	167	28.8	282.7
Northampton	612.0	10.6	2 472	2 019	85	100	256	235.5	85.9	81.6	102.4	450	332	221.3	37.8
Northumberland	277.2	5.5	2 832	2 353	40	108	294	75.3	38.3	89.9	23.0	229	128	74.5	33.3
Perry	77.0	4.6	1 842	1 501	12	93	176	24.8	11.6	95.6	8.7	236	118	20.9	37.9
Philadelphia	8 121.1	1.7	4 935	2 506	527	1 051	827	2 765.7	1 212.9	70.8	1 142.3	686	239	2 388.8	43.6
Pike	50.0	9.0	1 730	1 525	11	113	76	12.2	2.8	85.0	7.3	371	309	12.2	90.1
Potter	42.7	9.4	2 383	1 856	24	113	352	14.7	7.6	94.9	4.5	253	190	12.0	8.5
Schuylkill	552.5	15.2	3 606	2 721	384	122	361	121.2	56.7	84.4	38.6	243	161	124.3	65.5
Snyder	66.2	8.9	1 809	1 475	17	87	187	24.2	9.3	87.9	8.1	235	128	20.4	35.8
Somerset	211.8	3.2	2 645	2 060	65	118	330	59.5	25.3	93.2	19.7	242	164	52.9	54.8
Sullivan	19.5	21.0	3 041	2 259	181	175	380	5.0	2.4	94.5	2.0	321	252	4.5	23.6
Susquehanna	91.2	5.0	2 204	1 762	69	119	214	31.2	16.6	94.5	9.7	257	216	27.5	27.2
Tioga	99.5	-5.1	2 475	1 889	79	166	290	33.7	17.8	90.5	10.9	266	184	35.4	24.0

1. Based on the estimated population as of July 1 of the year shown. 2. Based on the estimated population as of July 1, 1982.

STATE County	Local government finances, 1981–1982 (cont'd): Direct general expenditure (cont'd): Per capita[1] (Dollars)	Percent of total for– Education	Percent of total for– Health & hospitals	Percent of total for– Police protection	Percent of total for– Public welfare	Percent of total for– Highways	Debt outstanding: Total (Mil dol)	Debt outstanding: Per capita[1] (Dollars)	State and local government employment, 1989: Total	State and local government employment, 1989: Rate[2]	Federal government civilian employment 1989: Total	Federal government civilian employment 1989: Earnings ($1,000)	Elections, 1988[3]: Total vote cast for president	Elections, 1988[3]: Vote for lead party (Percent)
	189	190	191	192	193	194	195	196	197	198	199	200	201	202
OREGON—Con.														
Wallowa	1 497	46.5	20.4	3.3	5.0	11.8	1.9	255	527	763.8	226	4 954	3 503	R–56.9
Wasco	1 236	54.1	3.3	4.4	6.4	10.0	22.4	994	1 476	727.1	316	9 695	9 834	D–52.3
Washington	1 122	52.4	1.5	3.5	0.0	13.2	256.4	991	10 416	342.5	676	22 815	129 211	R–51.9
Wheeler	1 759	50.9	5.5	1.0	0.0	19.9	0.1	51	129	992.3	NA	150	673	R–54.5
Yamhill	1 140	57.1	9.8	4.0	0.0	3.8	39.6	696	2 746	442.9	357	12 307	25 388	R–52.5
PENNSYLVANIA	954	45.7	4.0	4.9	3.9	4.3	14 559.6	1 226	549 201	456.0	142 277	4 435 342	4 536 251	R–50.7
Adams	805	61.7	0.1	1.4	4.1	11.9	54.6	780	3 225	426.6	607	14 098	24 105	R–64.9
Allegheny	1 172	40.0	6.1	5.3	1.9	5.2	2 677.5	1 871	58 626	436.5	15 998	538 602	586 151	D–59.5
Armstrong	811	68.9	0.2	1.6	7.3	4.6	38.7	496	2 837	365.1	275	7 410	25 683	D–54.1
Beaver	999	43.2	4.7	2.9	6.9	4.1	734.5	3 631	7 454	396.5	466	13 525	76 469	D–65.8
Bedford	587	73.0	0.4	1.0	0.7	6.6	17.5	367	1 910	397.1	140	3 487	16 969	R–65.5
Berks	1 106	43.0	1.9	2.7	4.9	4.0	440.4	1 400	15 547	467.6	1 397	44 430	112 444	R–62.4
Blair	750	54.1	4.3	3.7	5.3	4.6	114.6	844	6 313	477.2	963	32 155	41 662	R–61.5
Bradford	726	63.4	0.2	1.5	6.7	6.5	56.7	884	2 569	397.1	216	5 701	20 337	R–66.7
Bucks	896	60.7	2.6	4.3	2.3	5.0	510.1	1 030	17 769	321.0	4 120	131 903	212 640	R–60.0
Butler	784	54.3	2.9	2.1	8.1	5.0	130.2	869	6 069	393.3	1 864	50 946	50 667	R–54.8
Cambria	874	46.7	2.3	2.6	6.9	4.9	240.8	1 342	7 965	473.0	997	30 684	64 552	D–59.7
Cameron	788	47.9	0.3	1.8	2.1	6.4	5.9	862	390	619.0	19	478	2 655	R–65.2
Carbon	710	49.4	0.4	2.8	12.5	5.7	27.3	505	2 046	359.6	139	4 077	19 547	R–52.3
Centre	733	54.6	2.1	2.9	5.0	4.5	144.2	1 268	21 827	1 880.0	430	13 243	42 527	R–56.1
Chester	808	58.9	3.7	3.5	4.3	4.0	240.9	739	13 627	361.1	2 457	82 260	139 585	R–67.0
Clarion	702	73.8	0.0	1.3	1.4	5.9	8.9	206	2 920	703.6	143	3 397	13 751	R–58.4
Clearfield	767	60.7	10.1	1.7	0.9	5.4	92.2	1 112	3 591	441.7	318	8 980	26 713	R–53.5
Clinton	626	58.6	0.3	2.6	1.7	7.3	23.6	610	2 074	545.8	138	3 679	11 613	D–49.6
Columbia	651	62.0	0.4	2.5	2.0	5.6	30.9	498	3 244	532.7	193	5 368	20 021	R–60.5
Crawford	627	56.0	2.6	2.1	4.8	8.0	26.9	300	3 549	416.5	255	6 786	30 628	R–56.3
Cumberland	977	52.7	2.3	2.2	4.3	3.2	224.4	1 233	9 059	458.5	8 436	268 147	72 433	R–65.3
Dauphin	1 144	38.5	8.4	3.2	5.7	3.4	371.5	1 587	38 503	1 591.0	2 666	89 640	84 677	R–57.8
Delaware	888	48.5	2.9	5.3	5.4	2.9	651.4	1 182	19 332	347.1	2 178	73 718	246 305	R–59.9
Elk	541	53.7	0.6	3.0	1.5	8.5	25.0	660	1 226	336.8	134	3 227	12 744	R–52.9
Erie	838	48.5	4.1	3.6	5.3	5.5	236.2	839	12 120	438.8	1 588	51 026	103 300	D–52.2
Fayette	576	61.7	0.5	2.2	0.9	5.5	50.2	319	4 782	317.3	536	14 412	50 349	D–65.7
Forest	760	66.5	0.4	0.7	2.6	8.3	0.1	16	380	808.5	69	1 419	2 065	R–56.1
Franklin	830	46.7	4.9	1.7	3.7	4.2	76.5	664	4 888	403.6	5 499	154 327	39 644	R–68.3
Fulton	710	71.4	0.1	0.7	1.1	7.1	11.4	864	619	424.0	36	822	4 646	R–66.4
Greene	949	59.4	0.4	0.7	6.6	6.7	55.2	1 356	1 757	447.1	163	4 530	14 095	D–64.7
Huntingdon	726	51.8	0.4	1.3	8.8	6.2	20.1	473	2 459	569.2	155	3 924	13 631	R–64.6
Indiana	648	63.5	0.2	1.8	3.1	5.8	106.1	1 144	5 528	602.2	313	8 406	31 739	D–52.0
Jefferson	704	54.2	0.1	2.3	12.3	8.0	41.7	859	1 638	344.8	159	4 074	16 109	R–60.5
Juniata	497	69.9	0.6	0.6	1.0	8.3	3.4	175	537	263.2	85	2 080	7 764	R–62.9
Lackawanna	752	48.8	0.4	3.6	4.4	3.2	301.4	1 338	9 232	416.2	1 096	35 796	88 741	D–51.4
Lancaster	698	58.5	2.3	3.1	3.5	4.4	260.7	702	14 284	337.5	1 522	47 091	137 029	R–70.8
Lawrence	851	45.7	1.9	2.2	2.2	4.9	160.9	1 515	3 743	373.9	492	15 082	37 904	D–57.7
Lebanon	692	52.2	1.6	2.9	9.8	5.0	73.8	665	4 070	353.6	2 996	83 143	36 608	R–66.7
Lehigh	874	47.6	2.6	3.3	8.3	4.5	452.9	1 647	11 869	407.0	1 486	47 520	100 107	R–56.3
Luzerne	741	50.2	5.5	3.2	3.3	4.9	286.5	842	14 126	426.8	3 602	104 365	118 092	R–50.0
Lycoming	1 011	59.9	2.0	1.8	3.8	4.4	116.1	988	6 160	518.5	531	16 826	38 735	R–64.0
McKean	889	60.1	0.6	1.9	5.8	4.7	47.6	957	2 146	471.6	239	6 055	14 747	R–63.2
Mercer	840	58.6	2.7	3.7	4.3	5.9	115.0	904	4 771	391.7	334	9 561	45 880	D–52.9
Mifflin	798	50.6	16.1	1.8	1.0	3.8	83.0	1 781	1 579	337.4	116	3 115	13 075	R–62.5
Monroe	716	62.0	0.5	2.6	4.5	5.8	39.8	544	4 332	438.5	4 158	118 384	27 371	R–62.8
Montgomery	884	54.6	5.0	5.7	2.7	3.9	498.2	766	23 695	340.8	4 666	146 905	282 870	R–60.2
Montour	1 714	21.4	48.6	0.9	0.7	2.6	36.3	2 162	1 484	899.4	43	1 163	5 696	R–63.5
Northampton	972	52.3	2.0	4.0	7.0	4.0	233.0	1 024	9 584	387.1	623	19 172	82 978	R–51.5
Northumberland	743	56.1	1.9	2.5	5.7	4.9	85.8	856	3 660	373.9	276	7 963	34 800	R–58.1
Perry	569	65.0	0.3	0.6	2.2	6.2	12.3	335	1 414	338.3	102	2 470	12 533	R–68.2
Philadelphia	1 435	28.1	4.7	9.5	3.4	2.5	3 142.9	1 888	84 680	514.6	57 546	1 825 030	674 977	D–66.6
Pike	622	56.3	0.7	1.3	1.2	9.1	14.5	734	891	308.3	72	1 804	9 917	R–67.1
Potter	670	63.8	0.3	1.3	2.1	7.9	10.5	584	977	545.8	57	1 328	6 592	R–67.2
Schuylkill	784	47.9	10.3	2.2	6.5	4.4	134.4	848	6 191	404.1	461	13 418	57 842	R–56.5
Snyder	594	54.8	0.2	1.3	0.7	9.4	31.6	921	2 371	647.8	84	2 207	11 779	R–76.9
Somerset	649	57.0	0.3	1.7	5.1	7.3	57.7	708	3 467	432.8	272	6 993	30 768	R–54.6
Sullivan	707	61.8	0.2	1.6	5.3	11.3	0.6	94	349	545.3	26	556	2 922	R–61.9
Susquehanna	726	68.9	0.5	1.2	2.8	6.4	17.3	457	1 406	339.6	127	3 179	14 056	R–64.6
Tioga	864	49.8	0.1	1.2	2.9	5.8	22.8	556	2 297	571.4	202	5 046	14 350	R–66.0

1. Based on the estimated population as of July 1, 1982. 2. Per 10,000 resident population estimated as of July 1 of the year shown. 3. Data subject to copyright.

STATE–County code	MSA/ CMSA/ NECMA code[1]	STATE County	Land Area,[2] 1990 (Sq. Km.)	Population, 1990												
							Race						Age of population Percent		
				Total persons	Rank	Per square kilometer	White	Black	Am. Indian, Eskimo, Aleut	Asian & Pacific Islander	Other race	Hispanic[3]	Under 5 years	5 to 14 years	15 to 24 years
			1	2	3	4	5	6	7	8	9	10	11	12	13
		PENNSYLVANIA—Con.													
42 119	...	Union	820	36 176	1 097	44.1	34 784	972	76	239	105	638	6.6	12.6	20.2
42 121	...	Venango	1 749	59 381	729	34.0	58 636	497	55	138	55	201	6.6	14.7	12.5
42 123	...	Warren	2 288	45 050	912	19.7	44 782	53	74	111	30	116	6.7	14.3	12.0
42 125	6282	Washington	2 220	204 584	243	92.2	196 810	6 786	201	543	244	1 186	5.8	12.7	13.4
42 127	...	Wayne	1 889	39 944	1 003	21.1	39 470	282	43	97	52	371	6.7	14.2	12.4
42 129	6282	Westmoreland	2 648	370 321	138	139.8	361 103	6 930	262	1 566	460	1 359	6.0	12.6	12.4
42 131	7560	Wyoming	1 029	28 076	1 349	27.3	27 798	135	25	81	37	135	7.1	15.4	15.6
42 133	9280	York	2 343	339 574	150	144.9	323 339	10 985	416	2 103	2 731	5 165	7.0	13.3	13.5
44 000	...	RHODE ISLAND	2 707	1 003 464	X	370.7	917 375	38 861	4 071	18 325	24 832	45 752	6.7	12.3	15.5
44 001	6483	Bristol	64	48 859	859	763.4	48 250	186	39	297	87	672	6.5	12.0	14.7
44 003	6483	Kent	440	161 135	296	366.2	158 122	1 050	296	1 289	378	1 737	6.3	12.5	12.9
44 005	...	Newport	269	87 194	521	324.1	81 838	3 396	352	1 061	547	1 712	6.6	12.5	15.5
44 007	6483	Providence	1 070	596 270	78	557.3	522 953	33 171	2 360	14 233	23 553	40 569	6.8	12.1	15.9
44 009	6483	Washington	862	110 006	419	127.6	106 212	1 058	1 024	1 445	267	1 062	6.6	13.0	18.0
45 000	...	SOUTH CAROLINA	77 988	3 486 703	X	44.7	2 406 974	1 039 884	8 246	22 382	9 217	30 551	7.4	14.6	16.1
45 001	...	Abbeville	1 316	23 862	1 498	18.1	16 244	7 529	17	53	19	98	7.0	14.3	15.9
45 003	0600	Aiken	2 779	120 940	382	43.5	90 684	29 241	218	545	252	867	7.5	15.4	14.3
45 005	...	Allendale	1 057	11 722	2 231	11.1	3 642	7 968	11	7	94	161	7.6	16.9	17.2
45 007	0405	Anderson	1 860	145 196	327	78.1	120 384	24 151	173	340	148	559	6.6	13.8	14.3
45 009	...	Bamberg	1 019	16 902	1 857	16.6	6 472	10 371	22	20	17	75	7.2	15.9	20.5
45 011	...	Barnwell	1 421	20 293	1 659	14.3	11 510	8 693	32	17	41	146	8.1	17.2	14.7
45 013	...	Beaufort	1 520	86 425	527	56.9	59 843	24 582	251	813	936	2 168	8.5	13.3	18.1
45 015	1440	Berkeley	2 848	128 776	360	45.2	93 900	31 111	391	2 637	737	2 599	9.8	17.9	15.7
45 017	...	Calhoun	985	12 753	2 161	12.9	6 152	6 575	12	9	5	39	7.2	15.3	13.9
45 019	1440	Charleston	2 376	295 039	165	124.2	187 553	102 988	673	2 690	1 135	3 873	8.0	13.5	18.0
45 021	...	Cherokee	1 017	44 506	919	43.8	34 981	9 171	65	193	96	259	7.0	14.2	15.7
45 023	...	Chester	1 504	32 170	1 207	21.4	19 178	12 852	71	36	33	80	7.5	15.6	14.9
45 025	...	Chesterfield	2 069	38 577	1 039	18.6	25 549	12 902	65	31	30	160	7.1	15.6	14.9
45 027	...	Clarendon	1 573	28 450	1 344	18.1	12 267	16 078	31	28	46	144	7.8	17.1	14.3
45 029	...	Colleton	2 736	34 377	1 154	12.6	18 671	15 469	165	38	34	176	7.6	16.6	14.5
45 031	...	Darlington	1 456	61 851	704	42.5	36 888	24 773	71	66	53	211	7.0	15.6	15.6
45 033	...	Dillon	1 049	29 114	1 324	27.8	15 877	12 735	426	65	11	76	8.0	17.8	15.7
45 035	1440	Dorchester	1 489	83 060	549	55.8	62 323	19 128	549	786	274	1 040	8.8	16.3	15.4
45 037	...	Edgefield	1 300	18 375	1 771	14.1	9 796	8 516	11	29	23	79	7.8	16.1	14.2
45 039	...	Fairfield	1 778	22 295	1 563	12.5	9 244	12 994	14	32	11	105	7.2	15.9	15.9
45 041	2655	Florence	2 070	114 344	401	55.2	69 501	44 276	145	307	115	508	7.3	16.1	15.6
45 043	...	Georgetown	2 110	46 302	898	21.9	26 151	19 980	49	61	61	187	7.7	17.1	14.1
45 045	3160	Greenville	2 052	320 167	158	156.0	259 160	57 646	467	2 139	755	3 028	7.1	13.5	15.0
45 047	...	Greenwood	1 180	59 567	726	50.5	41 239	17 970	51	237	70	251	6.9	14.2	15.7
45 049	...	Hampton	1 450	18 191	1 778	12.5	8 279	9 884	6	18	4	71	8.4	18.1	15.1
45 051	...	Horry	2 936	144 053	329	49.1	117 098	25 160	340	1 128	327	1 259	6.6	13.3	14.3
45 053	...	Jasper	1 695	15 487	1 955	9.1	6 529	8 889	20	32	17	69	8.8	18.0	14.5
45 055	...	Kershaw	1 881	43 599	929	23.2	31 039	12 337	70	100	53	245	6.7	15.3	13.9
45 057	...	Lancaster	1 422	54 516	791	38.3	40 536	13 820	61	64	35	212	7.4	14.7	14.9
45 059	...	Laurens	1 847	58 092	746	31.5	41 493	16 386	45	95	73	211	6.8	13.8	16.1
45 061	...	Lee	1 063	18 437	1 765	17.3	6 850	11 516	17	29	25	75	7.5	18.0	15.0
45 063	1760	Lexington	1 815	167 611	286	92.3	147 391	18 512	330	1 010	368	1 302	7.3	14.6	14.7
45 065	...	McCormick	931	8 868	2 480	9.5	3 647	5 190	6	11	14	26	5.2	14.0	17.3
45 067	...	Marion	1 267	33 899	1 165	26.8	15 152	18 505	86	128	28	110	7.4	18.2	14.7
45 069	...	Marlboro	1 242	29 361	1 319	23.6	14 308	14 249	733	26	45	79	7.3	16.1	16.0
45 071	...	Newberry	1 634	33 172	1 184	20.3	21 488	11 507	45	92	40	147	6.8	14.0	15.6
45 073	...	Oconee	1 619	57 494	758	35.5	52 038	5 060	72	172	152	528	6.2	13.9	13.7
45 075	...	Orangeburg	2 865	84 803	540	29.6	34 949	49 257	214	322	61	331	7.3	16.1	17.7
45 077	3160	Pickens	1 287	93 894	492	73.0	86 045	6 817	160	768	104	571	6.1	12.3	23.4
45 079	1760	Richland	1 959	285 720	171	145.8	160 063	119 394	683	3 810	1 770	4 647	7.0	13.0	19.2
45 081	...	Saluda	1 169	16 357	1 899	14.0	10 871	5 417	16	9	44	86	6.5	15.3	14.0
45 083	3160	Spartanburg	2 100	226 800	217	108.0	177 427	46 871	332	1 710	460	1 521	6.7	13.6	15.3
45 085	...	Sumter	1 724	102 637	448	59.5	56 779	44 340	204	933	381	1 239	8.4	16.0	16.3
45 087	...	Union	1 332	30 337	1 277	22.8	21 176	9 082	26	38	15	69	6.2	14.2	14.2
45 089	...	Williamsburg	2 419	36 815	1 079	15.2	13 092	23 643	15	28	37	129	7.8	18.8	16.1
45 091	1520	York	1 768	131 497	353	74.4	103 515	26 349	785	680	168	735	7.3	14.2	16.4

1. MSA = Metropolitan Statistical Area. CMSA = Consolidated MSA. NECMA = New England county metropolitan area. PMSA = Primary MSA. See Appendix A for explanation of these concepts. See Appendix B for list of metropolitan areas identified by type, with component counties. 2. Dry land or land partially or temporarily covered by water. 3. Hispanic persons may be of any race.

STATE County	Population, 1990 (cont'd) — Age of population (cont'd) Percent: 25 to 34 years	35 to 44 years	45 to 54 years	55 to 64 years	65 to 74 years	75 years and over	Percent female	Population–Change and components of change — Change 1980–1990: Number	Percent	Total persons, 1986	Total persons, 1980	Components of change, 1980–1986 — Net change: Number	Percent	Natural increase: Births	Deaths
	14	15	16	17	18	19	20	21	22	23	24	25	26	27	28
PENNSYLVANIA—Con.															
Union	14.6	14.8	10.2	8.4	6.8	5.7	48.4	3 306	10.1	34 600	32 870	1 800	5.4	2 700	1 800
Venango	14.9	15.1	10.5	10.7	8.8	6.2	51.5	-5 063	-7.9	62 100	64 444	-2 300	-3.6	5 400	4 200
Warren	14.9	14.7	11.3	10.4	8.9	6.7	51.3	-2 399	-5.1	46 400	47 449	-1 100	-2.3	4 100	3 100
Washington	14.3	15.0	10.7	10.7	10.6	6.9	52.1	-12 490	-5.8	212 500	217 074	-4 600	-2.1	16 100	14 300
Wayne	14.8	14.5	10.3	10.2	9.7	7.2	50.4	4 707	13.4	38 700	35 237	3 500	9.9	3 000	2 600
Westmoreland	14.7	15.2	11.0	10.9	10.4	6.7	52.2	-21 863	-5.6	381 100	392 184	-11 100	-2.8	28 500	23 900
Wyoming	14.9	15.5	10.5	8.3	7.4	5.2	50.6	1 643	6.2	27 800	26 433	1 400	5.3	2 500	1 300
York	17.1	16.0	10.9	9.1	7.7	5.4	51.1	26 611	8.5	326 600	312 963	13 600	4.3	26 300	16 600
RHODE ISLAND	17.3	14.7	9.6	8.9	8.5	6.5	52.0	56 464	6.0	975 000	947 000	28 000	2.9	79 000	58 000
Bristol	15.6	14.7	10.6	10.1	9.4	6.4	51.4	1 917	4.1	47 700	46 942	700	1.5	3 400	2 600
Kent	17.1	16.0	10.7	9.6	9.0	6.1	52.1	6 972	4.5	159 500	154 163	5 300	3.4	11 900	8 800
Newport	17.8	16.3	10.0	8.4	7.5	5.5	50.2	5 811	7.1	84 800	81 383	3 400	4.2	7 100	4 300
Providence	17.6	13.9	9.1	8.9	8.8	7.0	52.5	24 921	4.4	581 700	571 349	10 300	1.8	48 000	38 100
Washington	16.4	15.9	9.8	7.9	7.2	5.1	51.2	16 689	17.9	101 300	93 317	8 000	8.5	8 400	4 400
SOUTH CAROLINA	17.0	15.0	10.2	8.4	7.1	4.3	51.6	364 703	11.7	3 377 000	3 122 000	255 000	8.2	321 000	163 000
Abbeville	14.0	14.2	10.3	9.6	8.3	6.5	52.6	1 235	5.5	22 600	22 627	0	0.1	2 000	1 300
Aiken	16.8	15.1	10.3	9.2	7.2	4.2	51.5	15 310	14.5	118 500	105 630	12 900	12.2	11 000	5 800
Allendale	15.7	14.1	8.5	7.3	7.5	5.2	49.4	1 022	9.6	10 600	10 700	-100	-0.7	1 300	700
Anderson	15.6	15.0	11.6	9.6	8.3	5.3	52.2	11 961	9.0	140 700	133 235	7 500	5.6	11 600	7 000
Bamberg	13.3	13.3	8.8	8.2	7.8	5.0	53.1	-1 216	-6.7	18 200	18 118	100	0.5	1 800	1 000
Barnwell	15.6	14.4	9.4	8.3	7.4	4.9	52.0	425	2.1	21 000	19 868	1 100	5.5	2 000	1 200
Beaufort	18.5	12.8	7.8	8.5	8.4	3.9	49.3	21 061	32.2	83 100	65 364	17 700	27.1	8 900	2 900
Berkeley	20.3	15.4	9.1	6.0	3.9	1.9	49.5	34 031	35.9	123 700	94 745	29 000	30.6	13 100	3 300
Calhoun	14.8	15.3	10.8	8.8	7.9	5.9	52.6	547	4.5	12 200	12 206	0	-0.3	1 200	700
Charleston	19.5	14.4	9.0	7.5	6.4	3.7	50.3	18 466	6.7	286 300	276 573	9 700	3.5	33 500	12 600
Cherokee	15.1	14.8	11.0	9.2	7.8	5.2	52.1	3 523	8.6	41 100	40 983	100	0.2	3 700	2 200
Chester	15.0	14.3	10.5	9.0	7.9	5.4	52.7	2 022	6.7	30 700	30 148	500	1.8	3 300	1 900
Chesterfield	14.9	14.8	10.7	9.2	7.7	5.0	52.2	416	1.1	38 600	38 161	400	1.1	3 500	2 200
Clarendon	14.3	14.2	10.2	8.8	8.4	4.9	52.3	986	3.6	28 200	27 464	700	2.7	2 900	1 500
Colleton	14.6	14.4	10.4	9.2	7.8	5.0	52.3	2 601	8.2	34 600	31 776	2 800	8.9	3 400	2 100
Darlington	14.9	15.6	10.6	8.6	7.3	4.7	53.0	-866	-1.4	64 300	62 717	1 600	2.5	5 500	3 600
Dillon	14.5	14.0	9.6	8.1	7.6	4.7	53.6	-1 969	-6.3	32 300	31 083	1 200	4.0	3 400	1 800
Dorchester	19.7	16.3	9.8	6.3	4.7	2.7	50.1	24 032	40.7	75 600	59 028	16 600	28.1	7 400	2 600
Edgefield	16.0	15.3	9.9	8.5	7.4	4.8	51.6	847	4.8	18 000	17 528	500	2.9	1 800	900
Fairfield	15.0	14.2	9.5	8.7	8.0	5.6	52.1	1 595	7.7	21 200	20 700	500	2.5	2 000	1 400
Florence	15.6	15.5	10.5	8.3	7.0	4.2	52.9	4 181	3.8	116 000	110 163	5 900	5.3	11 400	6 200
Georgetown	14.9	14.7	9.6	9.1	8.6	4.3	52.5	3 841	9.0	47 000	42 461	4 500	10.7	4 700	2 200
Greenville	17.2	15.5	11.1	8.7	7.2	4.7	51.9	32 271	11.2	306 300	287 896	18 400	6.4	27 100	14 500
Greenwood	15.2	14.4	10.5	9.3	8.1	5.7	53.1	3 708	6.6	58 000	55 859	2 200	3.9	5 200	3 300
Hampton	14.1	14.3	9.6	8.0	7.5	4.8	53.1	32	0.2	18 800	18 159	700	3.8	2 200	1 000
Horry	17.8	14.7	10.3	10.3	8.8	3.9	51.0	42 634	42.0	130 600	101 419	29 200	28.8	11 900	5 600
Jasper	15.0	13.1	9.5	8.4	7.4	5.2	52.1	983	6.8	15 000	14 504	500	3.1	1 800	900
Kershaw	15.7	15.7	11.0	9.4	7.6	4.5	51.9	4 584	11.7	42 600	39 015	3 600	9.2	3 800	2 000
Lancaster	15.5	15.1	11.2	9.0	7.6	4.7	52.2	1 155	2.2	55 000	53 361	1 600	3.0	4 800	2 600
Laurens	14.8	14.6	11.0	9.5	7.8	5.6	52.1	5 878	11.3	53 500	52 214	1 300	2.5	4 700	3 200
Lee	16.0	14.2	8.9	8.1	7.3	5.0	53.3	-492	-2.6	18 800	18 929	-100	-0.6	1 900	900
Lexington	17.8	17.1	11.7	7.9	5.7	3.2	51.3	27 258	19.4	170 100	140 353	29 700	21.2	13 300	5 800
McCormick	17.8	14.7	9.5	8.5	7.7	5.4	46.0	1 071	13.7	7 300	7 797	-500	-6.7	800	400
Marion	14.2	14.8	9.7	8.4	7.7	4.8	54.6	-280	-0.8	34 500	34 179	400	1.1	3 600	2 000
Marlboro	15.3	14.1	9.9	8.4	7.8	5.0	52.7	-2 273	-7.2	31 700	31 634	100	0.3	3 300	1 900
Newberry	14.8	14.1	10.4	8.9	9.0	6.5	52.3	1 930	6.2	32 100	31 242	800	2.6	2 900	2 100
Oconee	15.4	14.6	11.9	10.5	8.6	5.1	50.9	8 883	18.3	53 100	48 611	4 500	9.3	4 300	2 800
Orangeburg	14.7	13.9	9.6	8.3	7.7	4.8	53.4	2 527	3.1	87 300	82 276	5 100	6.2	9 000	4 800
Pickens	15.0	13.9	10.1	8.1	6.6	4.6	50.3	14 602	18.4	87 500	79 292	8 200	10.4	6 200	3 400
Richland	19.7	15.6	8.9	7.2	5.9	3.6	51.4	16 118	6.0	274 600	269 602	5 000	1.8	26 000	13 700
Saluda	14.8	14.3	11.0	9.7	8.4	5.9	51.3	216	1.3	17 100	16 141	1 000	6.1	1 600	1 000
Spartanburg	16.0	15.4	11.2	9.0	7.6	5.0	51.8	23 777	11.7	212 600	203 023	9 600	4.7	18 700	11 400
Sumter	19.6	14.5	8.8	7.1	5.8	3.6	50.0	14 394	16.3	95 000	88 243	6 700	7.6	10 900	4 300
Union	15.0	14.5	11.1	10.0	8.7	6.1	53.5	-427	-1.4	30 300	30 764	-500	-1.6	2 500	1 900
Williamsburg	13.7	14.1	9.1	8.2	7.5	4.5	53.3	-1 411	-3.7	38 200	38 226	0	0.1	4 100	2 100
York	16.6	15.3	10.9	8.5	6.6	4.0	52.0	24 777	23.2	120 800	106 720	14 100	13.2	10 500	5 500

STATE County	Population—(cont'd): Components of change, 1980-1986 (cont'd): Net migration	Households, 1990: Number	Households, 1990: Percent change, 1980–1990	Households, 1990: Persons per household	Households, 1990: Percent: Female family householder[1]	Households, 1990: Percent: One-person	Births, 1988: Total	Births, 1988: Rate[2]	Births, 1988: Low birth weight[3] (Number)	Deaths, 1987: Number: Total	Deaths, 1987: Number: Infant[4]	Deaths, 1987: Rate: Total[2]	Deaths, 1987: Rate: Infant[5]	Marriages, 1984: Number	Marriages, 1984: Rate[2]
	29	30	31	32	33	34	35	36	37	38	39	40	41	42	43
PENNSYLVANIA—Con.															
Union	900	11 689	16.8	2.64	7.0	22.2	456	13.1	28	284	3	8.2	7.4	308	9.0
Venango	-3 600	22 408	-1.3	2.58	9.6	23.9	731	12.0	36	608	9	9.9	11.7	514	8.1
Warren	-2 100	17 244	3.1	2.54	8.2	24.5	597	13.1	33	464	11	10.2	17.7	396	8.3
Washington	-6 500	78 533	1.9	2.54	10.3	24.5	2 356	11.3	150	2 356	19	11.2	8.3	1 507	7.0
Wayne	3 000	14 638	18.2	2.65	8.3	22.1	511	12.6	30	423	4	10.7	8.2	348	9.2
Westmoreland	-15 700	144 080	3.5	2.53	9.5	24.2	4 376	11.6	275	3 861	23	10.2	5.4	2 902	7.5
Wyoming	200	10 002	12.8	2.72	9.1	22.0	350	12.3	22	222	5	8.0	13.4	241	8.8
York	3 900	128 666	14.6	2.60	8.4	21.3	4 771	14.2	265	2 889	45	8.7	10.0	2 263	7.0
RHODE ISLAND	7 000	377 977	11.6	2.55	11.7	26.2	14 224	14.3	854	9 703	118	9.8	8.4	7 971	8.3
Bristol	0	17 559	13.8	2.64	8.9	21.7	638	13.3	34	418	2	8.8	3.4	393	8.3
Kent	2 200	62 058	14.6	2.57	9.7	25.5	2 026	12.6	106	1 538	10	9.6	4.8	1 254	8.0
Newport	600	32 687	15.7	2.53	10.2	25.4	1 165	13.8	54	715	8	8.5	7.3	1 004	12.0
Providence	400	226 362	7.9	2.53	13.2	27.7	8 926	15.0	603	6 207	83	10.5	9.4	4 386	7.6
Washington	3 900	39 311	26.5	2.64	9.0	21.6	1 469	14.1	57	825	15	8.1	10.2	934	9.6
SOUTH CAROLINA	96 000	1 258 044	22.1	2.68	14.0	22.4	55 114	15.9	4 935	28 493	673	8.3	12.7	55 357	16.8
Abbeville	-800	8 780	14.0	2.64	14.2	23.6	348	15.3	27	243	3	10.7	9.8	229	10.0
Aiken	7 700	44 883	23.1	2.66	12.5	22.5	1 979	16.2	154	1 002	22	8.3	11.8	3 256	28.8
Allendale	-600	3 791	9.9	2.81	25.7	26.0	191	18.0	23	126	2	11.9	10.6	259	24.9
Anderson	3 000	55 481	18.2	2.59	11.7	22.7	1 859	13.0	166	1 253	21	8.9	11.4	1 477	10.7
Bamberg	-700	5 587	-0.7	2.84	20.8	24.3	271	15.4	25	178	7	9.9	30.0	173	9.4
Barnwell	200	7 100	9.7	2.82	17.9	22.3	370	17.6	41	188	3	9.0	8.3	185	9.1
Beaufort	11 700	30 712	52.7	2.59	11.7	20.5	1 677	19.7	118	493	15	5.9	9.4	1 000	12.3
Berkeley	19 100	42 386	46.5	3.01	10.9	15.7	2 446	19.2	160	631	24	5.1	10.4	900	8.0
Calhoun	-600	4 487	14.7	2.82	15.7	22.4	192	15.9	25	100	2	8.3	11.0	118	10.0
Charleston	-11 200	107 069	18.2	2.61	15.1	24.7	5 574	18.4	476	2 157	71	7.2	13.1	4 248	14.6
Cherokee	-1 400	16 456	20.2	2.67	14.2	22.8	656	15.7	66	421	7	10.1	10.9	2 361	57.9
Chester	-900	11 448	14.8	2.80	17.5	22.5	531	17.0	51	335	8	10.8	16.0	308	10.1
Chesterfield	-900	14 047	9.3	2.72	15.9	22.7	540	13.8	53	363	12	9.3	21.6	1 131	29.4
Clarendon	-600	9 544	14.0	2.96	19.9	20.6	491	17.2	66	277	10	9.8	21.5	235	8.4
Colleton	1 600	12 040	16.5	2.83	16.1	21.5	537	15.4	47	364	6	10.5	11.0	311	9.3
Darlington	-400	21 999	9.7	2.76	17.8	22.1	917	14.1	90	565	14	8.7	16.0	592	9.2
Dillon	-400	9 887	5.9	2.91	21.1	22.9	529	16.1	53	334	9	10.2	16.1	7 024	218.1
Dorchester	11 800	28 213	53.6	2.87	11.5	17.0	1 513	18.6	101	422	6	5.4	4.1	746	10.7
Edgefield	-400	6 424	16.0	2.82	14.4	21.9	304	16.2	24	166	3	8.9	9.6	156	8.7
Fairfield	-100	7 467	17.5	2.93	18.7	21.9	362	16.5	52	266	3	12.3	9.6	179	8.5
Florence	700	40 217	12.6	2.78	17.3	21.8	1 818	15.4	195	1 105	26	9.4	15.2	1 185	10.4
Georgetown	2 000	16 275	22.1	2.83	15.0	20.6	793	16.1	71	377	5	7.8	6.6	546	11.8
Greenville	5 800	122 878	21.0	2.54	12.1	24.7	4 764	15.1	375	2 522	52	8.2	11.7	3 738	12.5
Greenwood	200	22 730	11.9	2.55	14.0	25.3	928	15.8	91	626	9	10.7	11.4	590	9.9
Hampton	-400	6 322	6.3	2.87	17.7	22.7	351	18.4	32	166	4	8.7	13.6	175	9.4
Horry	22 800	55 764	60.3	2.52	11.2	22.3	2 111	15.3	162	1 030	17	7.6	8.0	2 256	18.7
Jasper	-500	5 298	16.1	2.87	19.4	21.7	295	19.4	37	150	5	9.9	18.3	1 187	81.3
Kershaw	1 800	15 810	20.4	2.73	12.8	20.4	682	15.2	58	339	7	7.8	10.8	454	11.0
Lancaster	-500	19 778	11.0	2.74	13.9	20.1	866	15.3	103	472	18	8.4	21.4	890	16.2
Laurens	-200	20 660	21.5	2.68	14.2	22.3	812	15.1	76	568	9	10.6	11.6	576	10.9
Lee	-1 100	6 054	8.1	3.02	22.5	21.1	267	14.4	27	178	2	9.5	7.7	144	7.7
Lexington	22 200	61 633	29.4	2.70	10.7	18.9	2 570	15.1	216	1 054	26	6.3	10.6	1 423	9.3
McCormick	-900	2 731	13.8	2.75	17.2	22.7	100	13.7	10	75	3	10.3	24.2	132	18.3
Marion	-1 200	11 766	9.4	2.86	22.4	22.6	510	14.5	49	331	4	9.5	7.7	309	8.9
Marlboro	-1 300	10 163	3.5	2.82	21.1	24.0	458	14.5	52	319	6	10.1	13.6	1 106	34.3
Newberry	0	12 314	13.0	2.63	15.0	24.9	461	14.2	46	345	8	10.7	17.4	293	9.2
Oconee	3 000	22 358	28.7	2.55	10.0	22.0	721	13.0	53	538	8	9.9	11.7	1 676	33.0
Orangeburg	900	28 909	12.7	2.81	19.3	22.7	1 371	15.4	135	931	23	10.5	16.7	771	9.1
Pickens	5 500	33 422	28.6	2.58	8.8	21.5	1 228	13.6	100	667	14	7.5	13.0	969	11.5
Richland	-7 300	101 590	18.9	2.56	15.2	26.5	4 474	15.6	448	2 228	64	7.9	15.1	3 081	11.0
Saluda	400	5 824	10.5	2.76	12.8	21.1	220	13.3	20	176	4	10.6	19.7	143	8.4
Spartanburg	2 300	84 503	20.8	2.61	13.1	22.5	3 198	14.8	307	1 955	48	9.2	15.4	2 411	11.6
Sumter	100	32 723	20.0	2.91	16.7	19.0	1 800	18.6	174	758	23	7.8	13.2	958	10.3
Union	-1 100	11 407	8.0	2.64	16.0	23.6	382	12.5	31	322	4	10.6	10.1	274	8.9
Williamsburg	-2 000	12 108	7.2	3.03	20.5	21.1	621	16.1	60	388	10	10.1	17.4	333	8.6
York	9 100	47 006	34.8	2.72	12.7	19.6	2 026	16.0	189	989	26	8.0	13.6	4 844	42.1

1. No spouse present. 2. Per 1,000 resident population estimated as of July 1 of the year shown. 3. Under 2,500 grams. 4. Deaths of infants under 1 year old. 5. Deaths of infants under 1 year old per 1,000 live births.

STATE County	Divorces, 1984		Physicians, active non-Federal, 1989		Hospitals, 1989			Nursing homes,[4] 1986		Serious crimes known to police, 1988			Education			
						Beds				Number			Public school enrollment[7]		Attainment,[8] 1980	
	Number	Rate[1]	Number[2]	Rate[3]	Number	Number	Rate[3]	Number	Beds	Total[5]	Violent[6]	Rate[3]	1986–1987	1980	Percent 12 yrs. or more	Percent 16 yrs. or more
	44	45	46	47	48	49	50	51	52	53	54	55	56	57	58	59
PENNSYLVANIA—Con.																
Union	77	2.2	57	162	2	172	490	4	414	388	23	1 110	5 078	5 621	65.5	14.3
Venango	157	2.5	105	174	2	347	575	4	456	1 535	39	2 449	11 856	12 261	64.9	9.2
Warren	107	2.3	59	130	2	712	1 572	10	609	820	38	1 797	7 412	9 723	66.8	9.1
Washington	619	2.9	240	116	3	702	338	56	1 867	4 438	439	2 108	32 964	39 345	62.4	10.7
Wayne	118	3.1	54	131	2	315	763	12	530	581	31	1 467	6 463	7 058	62.1	8.8
Westmoreland	1 059	2.7	513	136	8	1 801	478	52	2 871	6 296	495	1 656	57 305	70 922	68.6	12.4
Wyoming	107	3.9	27	94	1	89	311	4	174	376	16	1 333	4 899	5 900	68.6	10.7
York	1 265	3.9	428	126	4	977	287	28	2 311	9 893	535	3 020	47 045	59 504	61.8	11.3
RHODE ISLAND	3 642	3.8	2 468	247	19	4 547	456	130	10 339	X	3 939	5 214	135 542	156 892	61.1	15.4
Bristol	132	2.8	103	215	0	0	0	8	544	970	46	2 002	6 689	7 908	61.6	20.6
Kent	686	4.4	263	163	1	359	222	24	1 551	8 372	791	5 181	22 711	27 586	66.8	14.8
Newport	322	3.9	117	138	2	220	260	8	543	4 310	238	5 042	12 080	14 906	72.0	23.5
Providence	2 095	3.6	1 827	305	14	3 727	623	78	6 913	33 795	2 680	5 670	77 278	88 943	56.1	12.9
Washington	407	4.2	158	150	2	241	229	12	788	3 994	158	4 066	16 784	17 549	73.7	23.2
SOUTH CAROLINA	13 674	4.1	5 446	155	93	15 033	428	316	16 020	187 919	25 746	5 395	605 102	645 817	53.7	13.4
Abbeville	73	3.2	13	57	1	52	228	2	60	411	73	1 894	3 941	4 748	42.5	8.7
Aiken	516	4.6	131	105	1	190	152	16	494	5 462	686	4 465	22 564	21 711	54.9	13.3
Allendale	26	2.5	4	38	1	78	736	1	44	190	76	1 757	2 393	2 483	43.2	10.8
Anderson	673	4.9	190	132	1	473	328	14	601	6 514	825	4 548	24 972	27 005	47.3	10.1
Bamberg	49	2.7	10	57	1	81	463	2	53	192	36	1 040	3 478	4 174	43.2	9.1
Barnwell	45	2.2	11	52	1	87	410	4	171	299	43	1 395	4 667	4 846	45.3	9.2
Beaufort	209	2.6	140	161	3	216	249	5	250	5 997	669	7 022	11 015	10 663	72.0	21.9
Berkeley	506	4.5	19	15	0	0	0	2	137	5 459	441	4 116	25 635	22 821	61.4	8.9
Calhoun	56	4.7	5	42	0	0	0	0	0	342	70	2 841	1 933	2 313	47.5	10.0
Charleston	1 371	4.7	1 318	428	11	2 328	756	32	1 040	21 110	2 851	7 059	41 849	48 633	63.6	17.3
Cherokee	205	5.0	34	81	1	125	296	2	132	1 678	248	3 934	8 659	9 305	43.0	8.9
Chester	120	3.9	18	57	1	125	398	2	72	1 119	240	3 538	6 793	6 729	41.6	8.6
Chesterfield	78	2.0	18	46	1	72	184	2	206	962	135	2 467	7 911	9 062	40.6	7.6
Clarendon	49	1.8	13	45	1	52	181	2	154	661	93	2 336	5 986	6 270	41.7	8.7
Colleton	122	3.6	19	54	1	135	384	2	158	1 146	143	3 237	6 621	6 475	45.1	8.8
Darlington	174	2.7	51	78	2	142	217	5	390	3 133	515	4 731	12 968	14 205	47.0	10.5
Dillon	80	2.5	23	70	1	83	252	3	255	1 511	354	4 557	7 327	8 160	39.3	7.9
Dorchester	210	3.0	38	45	0	0	0	5	485	3 173	282	3 931	14 461	14 025	64.3	13.8
Edgefield	64	3.6	9	47	1	40	209	3	173	674	120	3 674	3 748	3 552	41.3	9.8
Fairfield	73	3.5	11	49	1	34	152	2	262	996	238	4 561	4 318	4 859	43.3	9.4
Florence	405	3.5	214	180	4	661	557	21	947	6 443	1 022	5 397	22 948	24 238	51.5	12.0
Georgetown	170	3.7	58	115	1	116	231	1	84	2 215	308	4 513	10 194	9 931	50.6	11.1
Greenville	1 615	5.4	637	200	12	1 673	524	20	1 382	19 394	2 223	6 143	50 319	53 708	56.1	15.5
Greenwood	301	5.1	125	212	1	317	538	4	248	3 391	671	5 701	11 366	12 151	49.2	13.8
Hampton	54	2.9	8	41	1	112	580	2	51	330	54	1 693	4 384	4 163	42.7	7.4
Horry	515	4.3	170	120	5	570	403	5	255	12 192	1 037	8 881	22 943	20 870	58.5	12.5
Jasper	23	1.6	9	59	1	31	203	1	88	746	113	4 810	2 827	3 262	46.2	7.8
Kershaw	181	4.4	44	96	1	183	400	1	88	1 563	169	3 641	8 865	8 692	51.6	12.1
Lancaster	231	4.2	33	58	1	166	292	5	251	2 664	369	4 704	10 887	12 431	46.2	8.2
Laurens	252	4.8	40	74	3	177	328	6	392	2 322	510	4 278	9 215	10 807	40.3	8.7
Lee	42	2.3	7	38	1	35	188	2	12	336	32	1 780	3 572	4 227	39.8	8.2
Lexington	776	5.0	151	86	2	325	186	10	709	9 152	1 013	5 307	34 956	31 848	64.2	17.4
McCormick	21	2.9	4	55	0	0	0	0	0	161	27	2 192	1 610	1 879	42.1	9.3
Marion	177	5.1	29	82	2	143	406	4	163	1 234	168	3 455	7 647	8 040	43.6	8.0
Marlboro	83	2.6	20	63	1	111	352	4	205	1 125	196	3 489	6 530	7 837	39.7	8.5
Newberry	121	3.8	28	86	1	102	312	3	170	897	193	2 739	6 366	6 036	45.8	12.0
Oconee	222	4.4	70	123	1	189	333	5	272	1 334	180	2 421	10 164	10 384	46.0	9.3
Orangeburg	310	3.7	86	96	1	286	319	12	388	5 069	1 074	5 751	15 538	17 273	49.3	12.7
Pickens	207	2.4	65	70	2	139	151	11	494	3 174	252	3 523	14 281	15 009	50.5	13.4
Richland	1 024	3.7	971	336	11	3 733	1 292	39	2 199	23 225	3 638	8 060	40 007	47 192	67.4	23.0
Saluda	58	3.4	6	37	0	0	0	3	154	224	59	1 355	2 320	3 665	42.4	7.5
Spartanburg	1 160	5.6	354	163	4	870	400	24	1 133	14 876	2 112	6 890	37 717	42 498	49.5	12.5
Sumter	465	5.0	85	87	2	254	259	14	511	4 875	853	4 941	17 579	18 871	54.4	11.5
Union	135	4.4	20	66	2	109	359	2	152	627	118	2 028	5 823	6 243	41.4	8.0
Williamsburg	56	1.5	16	42	1	48	125	2	80	783	142	2 004	7 997	9 127	43.5	8.8
York	371	3.2	121	93	2	370	285	9	455	8 538	1 075	6 721	22 388	23 396	52.6	13.2

1. Per 1,000 resident population estimated as of July 1 of the year shown. 2. As of end of year. 3. Per 100,000 resident population as of July 1 of the year shown. 4. Preliminary. Covers nursing homes with 3 or more beds. 5. Data for serious crimes have not been adjusted for underreporting, this may affect comparability between geographic areas or over time. 6. Includes murder and nonnegligent manslaughter, forcible rape, robbery, and aggravated assault. 7. The 1986–1987 data are based on administrative reports obtained by the U.S. National Center for Education Statistics. The 1980 data are based on the 1980 Census of Population and Housing. 8. Persons 25 years old or older.

STATE County	Education (cont'd): Local government expenditures for education,[1] 1982: Total (Mil dol)	Education (cont'd): Local government expenditures for education,[1] 1982: Per capita (Dollars)	Social Security Program December 1988: Beneficiaries: Total	Social Security Program December 1988: Beneficiaries: Rate[2]	Social Security Program December 1988: Payments ($1,000)	Supplemental Security Income Program recipients June 1986	Money income: Per capita[3]: 1987 Income, (Dollars)	Money income: Per capita[3]: 1979: Current dollars	Money income: Per capita[3]: 1979: Constant 1987 dollars	Money income: Median household income 1979 (Dollars)	Money income: Percent below poverty level, 1979: Persons	Money income: Percent below poverty level, 1979: Families	Housing units, 1990: Total	Housing units, 1990: Percent change, 1980–1990
	60	61	62	63	64	65	66	67	68	69	70	71	72	73
PENNSYLVANIA—Con.														
Union	20.4	612	5 490	157.3	2 662	410	9 680	5 789	9 058	15 868	9.4	6.4	12 886	15.1
Venango	28.9	442	11 740	192.5	5 913	1 238	9 580	6 684	10 458	16 796	8.7	6.7	26 961	1.2
Warren	18.9	395	8 775	192.4	4 491	506	10 024	6 563	10 269	16 455	8.5	6.1	22 236	1.6
Washington	94.1	434	44 890	214.7	23 160	3 268	10 442	7 070	11 062	17 664	8.9	6.6	84 113	3.7
Wayne	19.4	536	9 360	231.1	4 574	480	9 737	5 735	8 974	13 187	12.3	9.4	28 480	45.3
Westmoreland	164.4	420	75 560	199.5	38 592	4 718	10 799	7 105	11 117	17 795	7.4	5.7	153 554	3.7
Wyoming	12.2	456	4 430	156.0	2 100	262	10 162	5 849	9 152	15 298	10.7	8.4	11 857	11.2
York	107.8	341	53 870	160.3	27 859	3 024	11 994	7 326	11 463	18 389	7.0	5.1	134 761	14.6
RHODE ISLAND	413.9	434	178 081	179.4	89 114	16 147	12 351	6 897	10 792	16 097	10.3	7.7	414 572	11.2
Bristol	21.7	464	8 280	172.5	4 213	478	14 230	7 610	11 907	18 561	6.3	4.8	18 567	13.4
Kent	73.7	476	28 690	178.2	14 602	1 624	13 146	7 389	11 562	18 455	7.1	5.7	65 450	14.8
Newport	40.3	485	12 880	152.2	6 036	936	13 785	7 138	11 169	16 847	9.9	7.6	37 475	13.9
Providence	229.7	401	112 460	189.0	56 177	12 196	11 703	6 641	10 391	14 834	11.9	9.0	243 224	7.9
Washington	48.5	510	15 530	149.5	7 976	894	12 787	7 087	11 089	18 104	8.2	5.2	49 856	21.9
SOUTH CAROLINA	1 299.3	403	517 330	149.1	229 121	87 482	9 967	5 884	9 207	14 711	16.6	13.1	1 424 155	23.4
Abbeville	8.1	357	4 030	177.5	1 798	728	8 678	5 379	8 417	13 735	14.9	11.5	9 846	15.2
Aiken	38.8	357	18 630	152.5	8 680	2 734	10 978	6 369	9 966	16 006	13.0	10.5	49 266	23.8
Allendale	4.7	448	1 935	182.5	721	772	7 058	4 317	6 755	9 646	32.3	27.2	4 242	6.8
Anderson	49.4	360	25 970	181.5	11 913	2 792	10 280	6 148	9 620	15 435	12.5	9.7	60 745	18.3
Bamberg	6.8	376	2 645	150.3	1 074	782	7 144	4 335	6 783	10 486	27.2	21.8	6 408	0.4
Barnwell	9.8	492	3 390	161.4	1 396	1 008	9 027	5 231	8 185	12 640	19.7	15.6	7 854	7.9
Beaufort	21.1	283	11 595	136.3	5 577	1 286	12 493	6 863	10 739	15 490	17.1	13.3	45 981	68.4
Berkeley	47.1	456	9 035	71.1	3 586	1 662	9 054	5 531	8 654	16 200	14.4	12.2	45 697	43.8
Calhoun	8.6	709	1 825	150.8	744	442	8 035	4 724	7 392	12 527	22.0	17.3	5 225	20.8
Charleston	105.7	368	37 855	125.3	16 453	6 162	10 805	6 361	9 953	14 826	17.9	14.5	123 550	23.7
Cherokee	21.5	526	7 105	169.6	3 151	980	9 499	5 552	8 687	14 801	14.2	11.1	17 610	17.8
Chester	13.3	431	5 925	189.9	2 693	754	8 570	5 310	8 309	13 922	16.1	12.6	12 293	14.5
Chesterfield	17.0	446	6 660	170.8	2 650	1 850	8 459	4 987	7 803	12 277	19.5	15.9	15 101	8.4
Clarendon	12.8	458	4 780	167.1	1 798	1 648	6 884	4 175	6 533	11 108	29.3	24.6	12 101	9.2
Colleton	12.2	377	5 920	169.6	2 348	1 588	7 421	4 633	7 249	11 668	25.7	20.8	14 926	22.9
Darlington	26.6	415	9 775	150.4	4 182	2 412	8 574	5 141	8 044	12 989	23.1	18.5	23 601	9.8
Dillon	13.9	437	4 860	147.7	1 789	1 736	7 038	4 162	6 512	10 909	30.0	24.4	10 590	4.3
Dorchester	21.7	335	8 490	104.2	3 507	1 666	9 742	6 003	9 393	17 169	13.3	11.3	30 632	51.5
Edgefield	7.1	398	2 675	142.3	1 080	656	7 809	4 750	7 432	12 101	25.9	20.2	7 290	17.4
Fairfield	10.4	502	3 730	169.5	1 525	832	7 538	4 496	7 035	12 563	22.2	18.5	8 730	17.1
Florence	44.8	398	17 575	148.9	7 072	5 150	9 224	5 526	8 647	13 914	21.4	17.3	43 209	10.3
Georgetown	20.9	476	8 115	164.9	3 565	1 398	8 981	5 445	8 520	14 325	21.7	17.9	21 134	28.7
Greenville	117.3	397	51 375	163.1	24 661	5 286	11 638	6 746	10 555	15 998	11.8	9.1	131 645	21.7
Greenwood	24.1	405	11 210	191.0	5 246	1 392	9 986	6 121	9 578	14 612	13.7	10.4	24 735	13.9
Hampton	8.5	459	3 480	182.2	1 347	1 062	7 494	4 827	7 553	10 855	28.3	24.1	7 058	6.3
Horry	40.6	370	22 305	162.1	9 911	3 112	9 955	5 803	9 080	13 485	18.0	14.2	89 960	63.6
Jasper	6.4	435	2 240	147.4	873	678	7 192	4 312	6 747	10 804	29.0	25.7	6 070	14.7
Kershaw	18.1	452	7 805	174.2	3 436	1 272	9 694	6 028	9 432	15 077	16.4	13.0	17 479	14.7
Lancaster	23.9	435	8 520	150.8	3 879	1 116	9 436	5 758	9 010	15 756	11.2	8.6	20 929	8.9
Laurens	18.6	352	10 135	188.4	4 568	1 816	8 885	5 509	8 620	15 025	11.7	8.8	23 201	18.2
Lee	8.1	434	2 645	142.2	1 002	970	7 193	4 272	6 684	11 322	30.3	24.3	6 537	6.5
Lexington	74.0	503	18 930	111.0	8 655	1 770	11 681	6 919	10 826	18 253	9.5	7.6	67 556	28.3
McCormick	3.6	472	1 460	200.0	568	390	7 204	4 284	6 703	11 756	26.7	20.4	3 347	12.4
Marion	15.2	440	6 120	174.4	2 302	1 888	7 331	4 424	6 922	11 351	26.3	20.3	12 777	7.0
Marlboro	13.8	424	5 400	170.9	2 076	1 646	7 212	4 483	7 015	11 744	24.6	19.4	10 955	2.5
Newberry	11.3	357	6 895	212.2	3 078	982	9 350	5 834	9 128	14 389	12.6	9.5	14 455	17.6
Oconee	23.7	472	10 075	181.9	4 522	1 156	10 098	5 784	9 050	13 635	14.0	10.6	25 983	28.5
Orangeburg	36.2	430	14 720	165.6	6 031	3 782	7 752	4 648	7 273	11 520	26.7	22.7	32 340	11.1
Pickens	21.2	255	12 770	141.3	6 006	1 152	10 109	6 011	9 405	15 586	10.7	7.6	35 865	26.0
Richland	105.0	379	36 400	127.3	16 676	5 746	10 914	6 435	10 069	15 691	15.3	11.6	109 564	19.2
Saluda	4.3	261	2 510	152.1	1 016	544	8 130	4 723	7 390	12 103	22.2	18.1	6 792	13.6
Spartanburg	90.0	437	36 700	170.0	17 082	4 702	10 723	6 310	9 873	15 094	13.8	10.7	89 927	19.3
Sumter	40.2	442	13 020	134.2	5 326	3 310	7 960	4 774	7 470	12 191	23.5	19.3	35 016	18.4
Union	11.9	385	5 795	190.0	2 596	758	8 820	5 334	8 346	14 183	11.9	8.8	12 230	7.4
Williamsburg	16.1	420	5 825	151.3	2 091	2 120	6 809	4 094	6 406	11 758	28.0	23.0	13 265	6.1
York	44.8	404	18 200	143.3	8 733	1 784	11 048	6 371	9 969	17 075	11.0	8.4	50 438	36.4

1. Elementary and secondary. 2. Per 1,000 resident population estimated as of July 1 of the year shown. 3. Based on the resident population estimated as of July 1, 1988 for 1987 data and enumerated as of April 1, 1980 for 1979 data.

STATE County	Housing units, 1990 (cont'd) — Occupied units — Total	Owner occupied — Percent	Owner occupied — Median value (Dollars)	Median rent (Dollars)	Civilian labor force, 1990 — Total	Percent change, 1989–1990	Unemployment — Total	Unemployment — Rate[1]	Private nonfarm establishments, 1988 — Number	Net change, 1987–1988	Employment[2] — Total	Per-cent change, 1987–1988	Manu-facturing	Retail trade
	74	75	76	77	78	79	80	81	82	83	84	85	86	87
PENNSYLVANIA—Con.														
Union	11 689	74.6	66 800	276	16 925	-0.2	933	5.5	763	20	13 576	11.7	4 268	2 488
Venango	22 408	74.5	38 600	209	25 709	2.1	1 507	5.9	1 293	-1	16 115	0.7	4 280	3 459
Warren	17 244	77.2	43 900	228	22 241	0.3	1 083	4.9	969	-2	13 639	1.3	4 150	4 577
Washington	78 533	75.6	53 600	241	93 893	1.2	5 200	5.5	4 313	-31	56 105	3.3	11 867	12 155
Wayne	14 638	79.2	89 800	299	20 706	3.9	1 424	6.9	1 326	82	10 723	9.1	2 126	2 418
Westmoreland	144 080	76.3	56 800	247	176 591	0.7	10 106	5.7	7 903	58	99 327	1.5	25 497	25 330
Wyoming	10 002	76.9	67 600	267	13 397	0.3	890	6.6	537	12	7 931	6.6	0	1 330
York	128 666	74.4	79 700	329	184 280	0.1	9 255	5.0	7 543	98	139 324	2.7	53 880	27 334
RHODE ISLAND	377 977	59.5	133 500	416	516 000	-1.7	35 000	6.7	X	X	406 179	2.0	114 087	84 374
Bristol	17 559	71.3	162 100	417	25 422	-0.5	1 892	7.4	1 037	39	13 323	7.2	4 671	2 528
Kent	62 058	72.0	122 500	468	87 647	-1.2	5 539	6.3	4 611	160	62 810	9.0	15 120	18 514
Newport	32 687	59.4	160 900	551	44 971	-4.5	2 753	6.1	2 425	26	28 422	3.4	5 968	7 951
Providence	226 362	53.5	127 400	393	303 868	-1.4	22 040	7.3	16 822	54	268 568	-0.4	78 491	45 846
Washington	39 311	68.9	152 700	497	54 094	-2.3	2 777	5.1	2 955	133	32 957	6.8	9 837	9 535
SOUTH CAROLINA	1 258 044	69.8	61 100	276	1 724 000	1.7	81 000	4.7	X	X	1 159 089	3.8	374 828	247 089
Abbeville	8 780	80.1	43 600	158	10 726	1.4	675	6.3	312	1	4 295	-3.1	2 720	615
Aiken	44 883	74.6	61 700	268	67 366	4.8	2 664	4.0	2 065	68	38 668	-0.8	18 626	7 493
Allendale	3 791	68.2	39 100	123	5 119	-0.5	303	5.9	185	12	2 065	8.8	1 187	278
Anderson	55 481	75.2	53 700	224	70 699	0.3	3 794	5.4	3 086	50	47 291	8.6	20 509	9 992
Bamberg	5 587	72.5	43 100	132	6 443	-2.2	518	8.0	290	-5	3 218	-1.1	1 532	664
Barnwell	7 100	73.2	44 900	165	8 903	-0.3	864	9.7	355	8	5 606	3.5	3 207	854
Beaufort	30 712	64.9	112 100	423	37 743	4.2	1 233	3.3	2 744	128	24 506	4.3	1 257	7 316
Berkeley	42 386	69.7	68 500	357	53 967	4.4	1 762	3.3	1 221	-7	15 076	4.3	5 526	3 339
Calhoun	4 487	81.9	45 000	127	4 620	-9.1	338	7.3	175	8	1 633	4.1	662	221
Charleston	107 069	57.6	73 800	346	145 401	3.2	5 031	3.5	8 360	116	108 103	2.3	11 809	31 337
Cherokee	16 456	75.2	46 900	201	23 518	-0.4	1 345	5.7	833	30	15 892	8.1	8 467	2 554
Chester	11 448	76.4	40 700	169	14 275	-2.9	1 404	9.8	535	5	10 175	4.8	6 940	1 416
Chesterfield	14 047	75.4	42 200	167	21 259	4.3	1 007	4.7	672	22	11 485	1.9	6 788	1 788
Clarendon	9 544	77.4	45 900	119	12 197	4.0	808	6.6	447	-2	5 096	-2.9	1 675	1 256
Colleton	12 040	79.4	47 400	177	17 986	1.7	854	4.7	683	-10	7 734	7.0	2 541	2 037
Darlington	21 999	74.6	49 000	172	28 202	0.0	1 588	5.6	1 142	12	18 297	4.2	8 289	2 993
Dillon	9 887	67.0	40 800	142	14 408	-0.3	947	6.6	459	-23	6 770	1.4	3 073	1 727
Dorchester	28 213	71.0	73 600	335	37 888	4.8	1 262	3.3	1 324	16	14 602	8.2	3 249	4 313
Edgefield	6 424	76.3	52 100	161	7 109	-2.2	343	4.8	300	-13	3 807	-0.1	2 356	553
Fairfield	7 467	78.1	47 500	151	10 048	-7.6	952	9.5	328	12	5 888	31.8	3 267	946
Florence	40 217	70.5	54 900	224	57 719	1.3	2 605	4.5	2 843	25	43 710	7.2	13 385	8 970
Georgetown	16 275	79.4	63 800	232	22 881	7.3	1 698	7.4	1 183	31	13 097	1.7	4 928	3 563
Greenville	122 878	66.2	66 300	292	177 392	1.2	6 332	3.6	8 676	123	183 869	1.3	51 391	29 581
Greenwood	22 730	69.1	50 100	215	29 124	0.3	1 643	5.6	1 332	24	24 750	7.2	12 309	5 169
Hampton	6 322	74.4	43 700	138	7 356	0.0	413	5.6	397	2	4 359	8.6	1 544	944
Horry	55 764	68.5	75 600	350	73 876	3.2	4 811	6.5	4 997	115	49 897	6.3	6 318	17 613
Jasper	5 298	78.0	44 400	180	6 317	-4.4	281	4.4	314	14	2 613	3.9	256	787
Kershaw	15 810	81.4	60 200	218	19 499	-0.8	1 216	6.2	959	-13	12 751	-3.2	5 796	2 420
Lancaster	19 778	74.8	49 400	210	24 915	0.1	1 507	6.0	965	3	15 959	2.8	8 788	2 921
Laurens	20 660	75.9	44 700	197	24 726	0.9	1 367	5.5	805	23	14 018	4.5	7 511	2 677
Lee	6 054	78.7	42 000	142	8 888	0.3	448	5.0	269	2	2 577	15.7	1 325	449
Lexington	61 633	76.1	74 900	331	97 448	2.4	3 367	3.5	3 529	132	39 184	0.7	8 686	10 184
McCormick	2 731	77.3	39 200	122	3 187	6.0	277	8.7	126	1	1 435	5.9	967	147
Marion	11 766	71.3	42 600	154	14 959	-0.5	1 298	8.7	606	-9	10 066	10.3	6 316	1 543
Marlboro	10 163	68.9	37 100	162	12 916	3.8	1 164	9.0	409	-6	7 160	-3.3	4 660	929
Newberry	12 314	76.1	49 200	183	14 941	-0.6	789	5.3	621	29	8 642	-4.3	4 328	1 638
Oconee	22 358	76.9	56 900	208	30 396	3.0	1 580	5.2	1 091	38	15 174	6.5	7 373	3 095
Orangeburg	28 909	73.2	50 500	173	39 973	0.2	2 546	6.4	1 693	29	22 998	0.0	9 535	5 814
Pickens	33 422	73.2	59 800	253	49 910	1.3	2 057	4.1	1 711	43	27 382	5.8	13 728	5 660
Richland	101 590	59.2	71 200	343	145 029	1.7	5 013	3.5	7 673	63	129 011	3.1	17 999	26 343
Saluda	5 824	81.6	46 600	145	8 501	7.7	455	5.4	269	-9	3 985	1.3	2 598	430
Spartanburg	84 503	69.8	54 200	257	115 778	1.4	5 146	4.4	5 166	176	95 572	8.8	38 626	17 709
Sumter	32 723	65.2	56 900	241	36 857	1.2	2 084	5.7	1 708	19	25 732	1.7	9 829	5 735
Union	11 407	76.9	38 000	163	14 055	-2.3	1 057	7.5	502	23	8 408	0.7	5 800	1 255
Williamsburg	12 108	79.2	42 600	132	17 304	-2.3	1 420	8.2	490	-14	7 051	5.2	3 878	1 195
York	47 006	71.9	71 300	298	72 175	0.8	2 735	3.8	2 854	131	39 016	6.4	13 274	8 626

1. Percent of total civilian labor force. 2. For week including March 12. Excludes government employees, self-employed persons, farm workers, domestic service workers, railroad employees subject to the Railroad Retirement Act, and employees on oceanborne vessels or in foreign countries.

STATE County	Private nonfarm establishments, 1988 (cont'd): Employment[1] (cont'd): Finance, insurance, and real estate	Employment[1] (cont'd): Services	Annual payroll: Total (Mil dol)	Annual payroll: Average per employee (Dollars)	Personal income, 1989: Total (Mil dol)	Percent change, 1988–1989	Wages and salaries[2] (Mil dol)	Proprietor's income (Mil dol)	Dividends, interest, & rent (Mil dol)	Transfer payments (Mil dol)	Per capita[3]: Dollars	Per capita[3]: Rank	Earnings, 1989: Total (Mil dol)	Percent by selected industries: Farm	Goods-related[4]: Total
	88	89	90	91	92	93	94	95	96	97	98	99	100	101	102
PENNSYLVANIA—Con.															
Union	301	4 954	216	15 918	528	9.5	335	59	96	101	15 053	968	394	3.0	36.7
Venango	1 036	4 034	306	19 004	928	7.3	451	78	174	261	15 359	857	529	0.9	33.2
Warren	341	2 717	242	17 766	708	8.5	376	70	131	141	15 637	765	445	1.7	38.2
Washington	1 881	15 097	1 194	21 282	3 203	6.7	1 520	233	543	677	15 436	821	1 753	0.8	37.4
Wayne	912	2 773	163	15 169	609	8.9	251	70	127	117	14 765	1 101	321	2.3	28.6
Westmoreland	3 789	25 435	1 841	18 534	5 909	6.3	2 698	443	1 032	1 121	15 681	745	3 141	0.7	34.2
Wyoming	178	1 275	179	22 629	412	6.5	229	41	63	67	14 388	1 254	270	3.3	55.4
York	4 580	26 874	2 818	20 226	6 321	7.3	3 729	479	1 021	731	18 575	246	4 208	0.6	45.7
RHODE ISLAND	27 406	115 071	7 789	X	18 070	7.1	11 278	1 234	3 339	2 987	18 113	X	12 512	0.3	29.6
Bristol	298	3 878	211	15 849	993	7.5	296	69	219	117	20 663	142	366	0.4	40.5
Kent	4 928	14 787	1 133	18 042	3 116	7.1	1 552	186	509	461	19 300	205	1 737	0.1	31.0
Newport	1 083	10 089	547	19 244	1 704	6.0	1 084	123	324	250	20 162	160	1 208	1.2	22.4
Providence	19 828	78 358	5 308	19 766	10 241	7.2	7 370	689	1 916	1 883	17 117	419	8 059	0.1	29.5
Washington	1 213	7 958	586	17 793	2 016	7.3	976	166	371	276	19 142	214	1 142	1.5	32.4
SOUTH CAROLINA	62 862	247 100	20 003	X	47 905	6.6	32 876	3 424	5 807	7 500	13 624	X	36 300	1.2	34.1
Abbeville	151	533	72	16 774	267	7.3	152	19	35	50	11 744	2 423	172	2.3	NA
Aiken	1 370	6 675	888	22 957	1 929	14.7	1 620	119	236	252	15 485	807	1 739	1.5	64.8
Allendale	0	187	30	14 324	114	7.7	62	9	11	28	10 763	2 725	71	6.1	NA
Anderson	1 407	9 125	773	16 355	1 932	7.1	1 084	149	260	298	13 388	1 734	1 233	0.7	46.4
Bamberg	133	538	43	13 324	169	7.8	77	14	21	42	9 663	2 935	91	3.4	33.9
Barnwell	92	942	77	13 757	266	8.7	162	25	28	49	12 560	2 089	187	4.2	NA
Beaufort	2 495	8 351	380	15 499	1 433	9.5	864	100	384	193	16 526	523	964	0.2	11.9
Berkeley	365	1 833	262	17 379	1 463	3.6	576	45	28	197	11 244	2 580	621	1.2	43.9
Calhoun	32	260	25	15 409	147	8.2	104	13	20	23	12 210	2 227	118	5.1	64.4
Charleston	6 615	32 480	1 741	16 102	3 934	-2.3	4 011	267	308	731	12 775	2 005	4 278	0.3	11.6
Cherokee	316	2 185	264	16 616	620	6.7	381	40	69	82	14 696	1 132	421	1.3	56.6
Chester	139	605	170	16 707	361	8.1	241	24	42	70	11 496	2 498	265	1.3	58.1
Chesterfield	274	1 100	187	16 319	462	4.9	273	42	44	83	11 821	2 389	315	4.1	57.2
Clarendon	155	728	57	11 209	262	2.3	110	21	19	69	9 098	2 998	130	7.2	26.1
Colleton	320	1 361	109	14 093	370	5.5	181	40	33	85	10 495	2 793	221	2.2	31.4
Darlington	559	3 009	369	20 141	766	8.1	500	67	95	140	11 737	2 427	567	3.0	48.0
Dillon	189	1 075	88	12 967	318	7.4	164	36	27	70	9 612	2 941	201	8.9	35.0
Dorchester	485	3 404	204	13 959	1 058	6.5	373	56	71	177	12 506	2 112	429	2.1	39.5
Edgefield	56	384	49	12 900	199	4.9	83	17	29	36	10 435	2 804	100	5.1	42.7
Fairfield	87	386	116	19 640	281	11.0	189	14	26	52	12 594	2 074	203	1.3	NA
Florence	2 695	10 387	732	16 736	1 500	5.2	1 118	117	136	276	12 635	2 059	1 236	1.7	33.1
Georgetown	554	2 253	221	16 853	563	1.6	342	43	80	110	11 191	2 604	385	0.8	41.0
Greenville	10 133	40 637	3 661	19 912	5 273	8.7	4 481	355	775	618	16 523	524	4 837	0.3	37.9
Greenwood	845	3 737	405	16 383	838	7.1	605	65	115	135	14 237	1 311	670	1.1	47.9
Hampton	205	706	72	16 543	220	7.5	108	22	32	45	11 397	2 542	130	7.3	NA
Horry	4 027	14 033	686	13 745	1 858	4.1	1 160	190	301	325	13 122	1 851	1 350	1.3	16.6
Jasper	114	783	32	12 249	165	8.4	55	14	17	34	10 759	2 726	69	0.9	21.8
Kershaw	484	1 803	225	17 654	590	4.2	375	44	68	99	12 897	1 954	419	2.4	53.1
Lancaster	601	1 965	270	16 892	685	5.5	364	41	82	103	12 053	2 310	404	1.2	51.4
Laurens	468	2 107	226	16 103	749	9.7	400	43	113	156	13 890	1 482	443	0.6	NA
Lee	55	344	46	17 990	164	4.0	72	17	8	39	8 824	3 023	89	11.2	NA
Lexington	1 399	7 863	673	17 170	2 789	9.0	1 201	173	279	293	15 961	657	1 373	0.8	39.7
McCormick	22	174	21	14 316	87	8.8	36	7	9	18	11 894	2 362	43	4.1	NA
Marion	290	1 020	137	13 632	374	7.9	210	35	45	84	10 633	2 761	245	5.2	47.4
Marlboro	138	784	101	14 081	301	7.6	156	25	31	68	9 556	2 952	181	5.4	NA
Newberry	248	1 031	132	15 241	435	6.4	209	35	66	82	13 326	1 765	244	1.6	49.0
Oconee	590	2 445	231	15 196	822	8.8	570	51	123	119	14 512	1 206	621	0.5	43.6
Orangeburg	965	3 910	364	15 809	1 018	7.5	577	84	136	208	11 355	2 552	661	3.0	35.7
Pickens	939	3 821	403	14 726	1 275	8.2	648	94	154	160	13 833	1 515	742	1.5	42.2
Richland	16 844	37 023	2 356	18 262	4 525	7.6	4 302	322	624	715	15 663	753	4 623	0.1	13.6
Saluda	73	281	53	13 313	197	6.3	58	30	25	32	12 131	2 270	88	21.8	NA
Spartanburg	2 735	20 955	1 734	18 144	3 326	8.2	2 393	255	411	454	15 304	874	2 649	1.0	46.0
Sumter	1 158	4 201	391	15 177	1 118	7.5	769	82	115	224	11 420	2 536	850	1.7	31.4
Union	190	692	132	15 716	346	6.2	198	19	42	67	11 379	2 546	216	1.1	59.4
Williamsburg	258	681	108	15 380	341	0.9	204	24	16	83	8 857	3 019	228	3.7	45.9
York	1 524	8 251	678	17 385	1 994	7.2	1 057	121	216	226	15 330	863	1 178	1.7	36.2

1. For week including March 12. Excludes government employees, self-employed persons, farm workers, domestic service workers, railroad employees subject to the Railroad Retirement Act, and employees on oceanborne vessels or in foreign countries. 2. Includes other labor income. 3. Based on the resident population estimated as of July 1 of the year shown. 4. Covers mining, construction, and manufacturing.

STATE County	Earnings, 1989 (cont'd): Percent by selected industries (cont'd)						Agriculture, 1987: Farms			Farm operators, percent		Land in farms				
	Goods-related[1]	Service-related & other[2]						Percent with						Acres		
	Manu-facturing	Total	Retail trade	Finance, insur-ance, & real estate	Services	Govern-ment	Number	Less than 50 acres	500 acres and over	Whose principal occu-pation is farming	Residing on farm operated	Acreage (1,000)	Percent change, 1982–1987	Average size of farm	Total irrigated (1,000)	Total cropland (1,000)
	103	104	105	106	107	108	109	110	111	112	113	114	115	116	117	118
PENNSYLVANIA—Con.																
Union	27.3	42.2	7.9	1.5	26.9	18.1	505	23.6	2.2	66.9	83.2	65	-11.4	128	0	54
Venango	27.7	47.9	8.1	2.7	23.9	18.0	456	21.9	3.1	39.7	86.8	65	-2.2	143	0	36
Warren	33.1	44.7	17.1	2.2	16.9	15.4	472	19.7	5.7	49.8	86.7	81	-1.4	171	D	43
Washington	19.9	49.0	11.2	1.9	23.1	12.7	1 594	23.6	2.6	45.8	85.6	219	-1.3	137	1	136
Wayne	11.4	53.6	12.5	4.8	25.5	15.5	691	10.4	5.2	64.7	85.5	139	-9.8	201	0	72
Westmoreland	26.4	53.4	11.0	2.7	23.8	11.7	1 335	28.9	2.4	47.7	80.4	165	-0.8	123	0	115
Wyoming	48.9	32.9	7.1	1.4	14.5	8.4	367	13.9	7.4	56.7	76.8	73	-6.5	198	0	38
York	37.2	45.3	11.6	2.5	19.2	8.4	2 041	42.2	4.7	52.0	80.5	278	-7.2	136	1	224
RHODE ISLAND	22.9	54.8	10.4	6.5	27.2	15.3	701	54.4	1.9	49.2	77.0	59	-6.1	84	3	26
Bristol	29.3	45.9	11.7	2.4	24.6	13.2	27	63.0	0.0	66.7	74.1	2	-24.0	63	0	1
Kent	23.6	55.7	16.1	6.7	23.8	13.2	64	54.7	3.1	34.4	75.0	7	4.6	103	0	2
Newport	16.1	44.1	10.3	2.3	25.9	32.2	137	51.8	1.5	53.3	73.0	10	-6.6	76	0	7
Providence	23.2	58.0	8.8	7.8	29.3	12.4	267	62.5	0.0	49.8	76.0	16	-9.3	59	0	7
Washington	24.6	44.8	13.2	3.0	19.6	21.3	206	44.2	4.4	48.1	82.0	24	-4.7	117	3	9
SOUTH CAROLINA	27.0	44.4	10.2	4.5	18.7	20.2	20 517	33.0	10.9	43.8	69.6	4 759	-14.9	232	81	2 686
Abbeville	52.1	NA	4.9	1.6	9.6	12.8	457	23.2	7.2	35.4	72.0	88	-7.7	192	0	37
Aiken	49.5	25.5	6.5	2.0	12.2	8.2	604	31.1	9.6	39.1	71.2	137	-6.6	227	2	70
Allendale	39.5	28.9	8.8	1.5	11.1	22.6	107	18.7	36.4	58.9	70.1	119	-12.9	1 111	4	60
Anderson	40.2	39.8	11.9	2.6	17.9	13.0	1 038	33.5	5.7	37.1	75.7	157	-10.1	151	1	90
Bamberg	31.4	37.3	9.2	2.8	16.8	25.3	220	14.5	21.4	58.2	78.6	84	-19.4	383	3	61
Barnwell	33.7	NA	6.5	0.8	25.3	13.5	242	23.6	21.1	48.8	57.4	86	-19.8	355	3	59
Beaufort	2.7	54.4	13.2	8.7	25.8	33.5	125	49.6	16.8	52.8	61.6	54	-7.7	433	1	18
Berkeley	33.3	26.4	7.3	1.2	10.8	28.5	350	52.9	8.9	32.3	72.9	71	-4.7	203	D	21
Calhoun	61.7	19.9	2.8	0.9	7.2	10.5	242	26.9	23.6	50.4	67.4	93	-20.4	383	5	64
Charleston	6.2	45.5	9.4	4.5	20.4	42.7	202	49.5	11.4	41.1	62.4	42	-22.8	209	1	20
Cherokee	50.0	32.8	8.0	1.5	13.9	9.2	412	26.9	6.3	32.8	73.5	70	-18.2	171	1	37
Chester	54.2	25.9	7.4	1.2	9.3	14.7	350	18.6	12.0	40.3	77.4	96	-6.8	274	0	32
Chesterfield	53.3	27.4	8.9	2.2	10.0	11.3	429	28.0	10.3	43.6	69.9	110	-21.3	256	0	54
Clarendon	18.3	44.0	14.8	3.2	16.4	22.7	419	36.8	18.4	57.5	60.9	137	-22.6	327	4	106
Colleton	24.0	50.7	11.6	5.7	16.9	15.7	481	36.0	11.6	41.0	72.8	133	-30.4	277	1	57
Darlington	42.0	39.1	7.2	1.8	15.9	9.9	440	24.5	20.9	59.3	65.2	156	-19.9	354	1	118
Dillon	33.5	41.8	12.9	1.7	16.4	14.3	274	21.9	21.9	66.4	63.9	112	-13.0	409	0	83
Dorchester	33.1	41.3	12.5	2.2	16.8	17.1	362	42.3	9.4	42.0	60.8	67	-15.7	186	0	36
Edgefield	37.7	34.4	10.2	1.2	13.5	17.8	244	26.2	17.6	40.2	70.5	73	-16.5	297	6	38
Fairfield	35.6	NA	6.5	1.2	NA	12.6	186	18.3	20.4	35.5	67.7	57	-8.2	308	D	19
Florence	26.1	48.7	11.3	5.5	20.1	16.4	926	33.8	11.6	57.5	60.7	210	-15.3	226	1	136
Georgetown	33.3	39.8	11.1	4.2	16.9	18.4	224	42.9	8.5	40.2	67.0	38	-4.8	170	0	17
Greenville	28.8	52.4	10.7	5.5	22.3	9.4	678	43.1	2.7	37.3	77.1	75	-16.6	110	1	40
Greenwood	40.1	34.9	10.2	3.2	15.6	16.1	365	31.8	9.3	36.2	67.9	79	-3.3	217	0	23
Hampton	38.5	32.4	10.2	2.3	12.5	17.1	232	25.4	22.4	44.4	66.8	104	-33.9	450	2	65
Horry	9.0	62.7	21.0	6.8	27.1	19.3	1 177	33.6	5.3	56.5	66.5	175	-11.9	149	1	102
Jasper	7.3	53.3	14.9	2.8	21.2	24.0	150	44.0	12.7	41.3	70.7	102	-0.9	681	0	17
Kershaw	43.3	31.2	7.7	2.7	11.7	13.3	254	33.5	11.8	29.1	68.1	66	-16.4	259	1	28
Lancaster	45.6	34.6	9.6	3.5	15.2	12.7	438	29.5	4.3	31.1	76.3	58	-18.4	133	0	26
Laurens	41.0	NA	15.2	2.1	12.2	17.5	647	30.6	9.1	31.8	74.3	124	-19.5	192	1	62
Lee	35.2	30.3	9.5	1.5	10.7	20.8	262	27.1	32.1	56.9	61.5	134	-6.3	510	1	112
Lexington	28.6	46.0	11.8	3.0	16.4	13.5	702	43.6	4.6	38.5	72.9	82	-24.2	116	5	47
McCormick	34.7	25.1	4.7	3.9	9.6	31.6	86	23.3	12.8	29.1	68.6	22	-22.0	258	D	9
Marion	44.6	31.0	7.7	3.2	15.0	16.4	337	36.5	14.8	54.3	56.4	86	-22.0	255	3	56
Marlboro	43.1	NA	6.9	1.5	13.9	16.5	182	19.2	44.0	69.2	56.6	113	-12.5	624	1	82
Newberry	42.3	34.5	10.0	2.4	13.4	14.8	541	22.9	8.3	39.9	72.8	109	-5.7	201	0	56
Oconee	35.1	NA	6.7	2.5	NA	9.5	588	38.3	2.9	39.3	72.6	66	-7.8	112	0	31
Orangeburg	31.4	41.0	13.0	2.9	16.7	20.3	961	30.1	17.4	50.5	67.5	292	-14.1	304	12	201
Pickens	35.9	31.3	9.5	1.9	14.9	24.9	490	45.5	2.7	35.7	79.2	47	-8.7	96	0	21
Richland	8.8	55.7	9.0	10.1	23.8	30.6	326	46.3	9.2	40.5	71.5	62	-16.1	190	1	36
Saluda	24.6	33.1	9.0	5.8	11.2	16.3	559	19.7	9.1	46.5	72.8	116	-10.6	207	3	59
Spartanburg	39.4	42.0	10.4	2.4	17.7	10.9	1 010	43.1	3.5	35.9	73.0	118	-17.4	117	3	67
Sumter	25.6	35.7	9.2	2.7	15.9	31.1	488	38.9	16.4	56.1	66.4	152	-13.9	312	6	114
Union	56.5	23.2	8.6	2.3	8.9	16.3	257	19.5	8.9	33.9	69.3	57	-13.4	222	D	23
Williamsburg	44.1	32.8	8.4	2.3	9.8	17.6	833	37.0	13.7	52.0	63.0	201	-9.3	241	1	121
York	30.3	49.2	10.0	3.0	18.1	12.9	620	25.6	9.2	29.8	76.6	129	-9.0	208	0	58

1. Covers mining, construction, and manufacturing. 2. Covers private sector earnings in agricultural services, forestry, and fisheries; transportation and public utilities; wholesale trade; retail trade; finance, insurance, and real estate; and services.

STATE County	Agriculture, 1987 (cont'd)								Manufactures, 1987						
	Value of land and buildings		Value of products sold				Percent of farms with sales of		Establishments		All employees			Production workers	
	Average per farm ($1,000)	Average per acre (Dollars)	Total (Mil dol)	Average per farm (Dollars)	Percent from: Crops	Percent from: Livestock and poultry[1]	$10,000 or more	$100,000 or more	Total	Percent with 20 or more em-ployees	Number (1,000)	Percent change, 1982–1987	Annual payroll (Mil dol)	Number (1,000)	Work hours (Mil)
	119	120	121	122	123	124	125	126	127	128	129	130	131	132	133
PENNSYLVANIA—Con.															
Union	234	1 895	31	60 758	14.6	85.4	66.5	19.0	36	47.2	4.0	42.9	75.5	3.3	6.5
Venango	131	892	7	15 328	25.6	74.4	28.3	3.7	85	42.4	4.0	-41.2	113.6	2.5	5.1
Warren	144	817	15	31 461	9.4	90.6	39.8	9.7	81	39.5	3.9	-25.0	93.1	2.4	5.1
Washington	170	1 230	28	17 690	25.6	74.4	29.6	4.6	263	37.6	11.3	-22.1	288.3	7.9	15.9
Wayne	246	1 329	29	41 400	5.5	94.5	55.0	12.2	64	21.9	2.1	-4.5	30.6	1.6	3.0
Westmoreland	202	1 597	33	24 974	31.9	68.1	34.0	5.4	501	36.9	24.4	-25.4	620.7	16.2	30.5
Wyoming	166	936	25	68 170	7.9	92.1	49.6	11.2	41	34.1	D	D	D	D	D
York	266	2 140	114	55 759	27.8	72.2	45.9	13.1	657	51.4	52.1	-1.1	1 238.7	35.7	72.4
RHODE ISLAND	420	4 748	38	53 903	70.6	29.4	35.7	10.7	2 878	31.2	112.0	-2.3	2 292.0	76.3	149.4
Bristol	676	10 718	1	43 185	85.9	14.1	37.0	11.1	93	41.9	4.5	-8.2	83.7	3.6	6.8
Kent	333	3 223	1	23 167	51.7	48.3	26.6	6.2	388	29.1	14.3	-4.7	304.4	9.9	20.6
Newport	527	7 621	11	80 827	81.8	18.2	47.4	18.2	87	25.3	6.0	22.4	172.0	2.9	5.7
Providence	251	3 873	7	27 794	41.0	59.0	36.0	7.1	2 162	31.7	77.5	-3.7	1 505.1	52.7	102.0
Washington	562	4 290	17	80 790	77.0	23.0	30.1	11.7	148	26.4	9.7	4.3	226.9	7.2	14.4
SOUTH CAROLINA	201	871	879	42 827	51.4	48.6	32.6	9.3	4 534	41.7	365.8	-0.4	7 323.9	279.6	566.2
Abbeville	155	661	6	12 521	14.8	85.2	22.1	2.4	31	58.1	3.1	-16.2	57.1	2.6	5.4
Aiken	182	895	26	42 306	28.2	71.8	31.6	8.8	96	46.9	19.9	-1.0	571.8	11.7	24.4
Allendale	596	540	10	92 934	90.6	9.4	48.6	22.4	16	56.2	1.1	-8.3	17.7	0.9	1.8
Anderson	203	1 321	32	30 881	46.5	53.5	20.6	4.2	204	43.6	19.9	-10.0	386.7	16.5	33.0
Bamberg	256	712	11	50 056	46.3	53.7	45.5	15.0	34	35.3	1.5	7.1	20.1	1.3	2.2
Barnwell	179	553	10	42 175	74.4	25.6	46.7	10.3	24	54.2	3.1	29.2	49.8	2.7	5.4
Beaufort	363	860	8	64 251	71.4	28.6	32.0	12.0	71	22.5	1.2	-29.4	19.4	0.9	1.3
Berkeley	224	1 021	11	32 618	81.8	18.2	17.4	2.3	74	39.2	5.3	8.2	124.5	3.9	7.9
Calhoun	218	639	13	53 655	53.6	46.4	46.3	16.5	16	68.8	0.7	0.0	12.2	0.5	1.0
Charleston	390	1 815	19	94 104	97.0	3.0	35.6	15.3	236	30.5	12.1	0.0	294.9	7.7	14.8
Cherokee	173	996	10	23 425	35.1	64.9	18.7	4.4	65	53.8	8.3	16.9	156.4	7.1	14.8
Chester	191	708	5	14 384	13.7	86.4	21.4	3.1	64	50.0	6.6	-13.2	118.9	5.5	10.4
Chesterfield	169	745	47	110 258	14.4	85.6	31.0	9.8	63	52.4	7.1	1.4	114.5	5.7	11.4
Clarendon	244	721	29	68 469	70.6	29.4	49.4	20.5	33	51.5	1.6	-5.9	19.6	1.3	2.4
Colleton	214	769	11	22 791	56.4	43.6	22.9	4.8	54	38.9	2.4	9.1	42.5	1.9	4.1
Darlington	225	687	35	78 532	66.6	33.4	59.1	18.6	79	51.9	8.2	18.8	197.9	6.1	13.1
Dillon	269	649	24	85 977	83.9	16.1	67.5	24.5	36	50.0	2.4	-11.1	35.2	2.1	4.3
Dorchester	192	987	10	26 341	47.2	52.8	24.6	6.9	79	34.2	2.9	26.1	55.3	2.3	4.6
Edgefield	271	982	22	88 460	71.9	28.1	35.2	14.8	46	32.6	2.3	4.5	33.2	1.9	3.8
Fairfield	255	725	2	11 434	5.0	95.0	18.8	1.6	52	21.2	2.3	21.1	34.2	1.8	3.8
Florence	197	826	44	47 392	84.9	15.1	53.2	13.9	143	46.2	11.5	-5.7	217.3	8.7	17.8
Georgetown	208	823	6	27 257	89.0	11.0	33.0	7.6	94	33.0	4.7	6.8	102.2	3.9	8.0
Greenville	223	1 662	11	16 743	41.9	58.1	18.1	3.1	641	45.9	51.1	3.0	1 050.8	37.4	75.5
Greenwood	158	710	10	28 215	3.4	96.6	16.4	3.6	97	47.4	11.5	-17.3	224.1	9.4	19.9
Hampton	279	624	11	46 490	76.1	23.9	42.2	13.8	39	30.8	1.5	-11.8	36.6	1.2	2.8
Horry	161	1 104	53	45 335	86.1	13.9	53.0	12.7	138	27.5	6.6	-8.3	100.2	5.4	10.7
Jasper	387	595	2	12 632	42.7	57.2	18.7	1.3	18	16.7	0.3	200.0	4.9	0.2	0.5
Kershaw	241	912	18	72 643	10.2	89.8	23.2	6.3	79	35.4	6.6	-7.0	147.6	5.2	10.7
Lancaster	124	1 028	5	12 152	24.0	76.0	15.3	1.8	64	37.5	7.9	-31.3	151.3	6.0	11.4
Laurens	154	851	15	22 872	13.9	86.1	23.3	3.9	79	41.8	7.6	-8.4	136.4	6.6	13.4
Lee	369	711	23	89 040	78.9	21.1	55.7	25.2	22	40.9	1.0	11.1	20.5	0.8	1.7
Lexington	146	1 243	42	59 341	18.3	81.7	31.6	13.2	198	31.8	9.4	-19.0	207.5	6.5	12.9
McCormick	223	858	2	27 665	0.8	99.2	15.1	3.5	23	13.0	0.9	0.0	16.8	0.8	1.8
Marion	187	860	23	66 943	80.7	19.3	53.4	17.2	50	42.0	6.0	27.7	87.3	5.1	10.4
Marlboro	360	570	16	85 985	87.9	12.1	62.1	29.7	32	59.4	4.9	2.1	69.4	4.0	8.2
Newberry	169	856	41	74 978	4.5	95.5	27.2	13.3	62	41.9	4.7	-11.3	79.6	4.0	8.2
Oconee	150	1 275	20	33 774	21.2	78.8	21.9	6.3	93	36.6	7.0	20.7	110.6	5.9	11.5
Orangeburg	190	654	47	48 550	49.0	51.0	40.6	11.7	105	41.9	9.5	20.3	157.7	7.4	14.1
Pickens	153	1 586	4	8 756	37.6	62.4	10.8	1.6	124	41.9	13.3	-10.1	220.9	11.1	22.3
Richland	223	1 366	7	22 891	46.0	54.0	25.5	4.0	250	40.4	17.6	22.2	400.2	11.8	23.2
Saluda	161	779	31	56 262	20.0	80.0	34.0	12.0	33	30.3	2.7	107.7	40.1	2.3	5.1
Spartanburg	191	1 484	22	22 171	57.3	42.7	21.7	4.9	407	46.9	34.8	-10.1	739.7	25.7	52.5
Sumter	236	847	41	84 250	48.7	51.3	40.2	17.6	80	60.0	9.2	4.5	163.3	7.4	14.8
Union	120	637	2	6 625	18.0	81.9	14.4	0.8	49	49.0	5.8	7.4	101.0	4.9	10.2
Williamsburg	180	737	29	34 522	80.9	19.1	41.3	8.6	39	53.8	4.8	65.5	78.1	4.1	8.2
York	232	1 046	14	22 062	23.2	76.8	21.0	3.7	202	41.6	13.1	10.1	298.1	9.7	20.2

1. Includes livestock and poultry products.

STATE County	Manufactures, 1987 (cont'd) — Production workers (cont'd) — Wages — Total (Mil dol)	Average per worker (Dollars)	Value added by manufacture (Mil dol)	Value of shipments (Mil dol)	New capital expenditures (Mil dol)	Value of construction authorized by building permits, 1990 — Total[1] ($1,000)	Nonresidential — Total ($1,000)	Nonresidential — Percent — Office	Industrial	Stores	Residential — New construction ($1,000)	Number of housing units	Alterations and additions ($1,000)
	134	135	136	137	138	139	140	141	142	143	144	145	146
PENNSYLVANIA—Con.													
Union	54.1	16 394	191.7	379.7	21.3	21 806	10 353	3.4	1.7	1.0	9 810	160	1 136
Venango	62.4	24 960	289.6	595.4	19.0	12 974	6 145	5.5	12.0	0.7	2 983	69	1 473
Warren	48.8	20 333	180.4	719.4	23.0	17 908	11 656	0.2	76.3	5.4	3 743	75	771
Washington	192.8	24 405	722.4	1 691.8	41.4	79 949	16 956	16.0	10.3	16.6	52 308	587	5 713
Wayne	22.9	14 312	96.9	228.3	1.7	58 668	13 728	1.4	61.4	10.2	37 043	546	2 923
Westmoreland	367.0	22 654	1 366.0	2 640.5	74.1	233 869	106 115	11.6	36.9	32.7	97 937	1 100	8 240
Wyoming	D	D	D	D	D	4 783	954	0.0	0.0	83.9	2 809	52	771
York	724.6	20 297	2 671.1	5 251.4	241.8	288 724	61 602	12.7	18.3	32.1	153 650	1 983	21 137
RHODE ISLAND	1 252.3	16 413	4 787.5	9 166.4	276.4	440 818	52 754	16.6	10.5	30.6	233 137	3 042	73 702
Bristol	52.8	14 667	193.5	372.3	7.0	16 841	0	NA	NA	NA	12 507	168	3 499
Kent	177.8	17 960	723.8	1 325.7	48.9	79 903	12 057	14.3	1.4	66.3	46 141	561	12 015
Newport	66.4	22 897	362.2	555.4	13.2	40 827	2 237	14.5	0.0	44.7	23 709	295	10 890
Providence	807.0	15 313	3 045.3	6 023.7	193.0	215 887	31 089	18.9	15.1	20.8	97 542	1 405	33 674
Washington	148.2	20 583	462.7	889.3	14.3	87 358	7 372	11.4	9.3	9.2	53 238	613	13 623
SOUTH CAROLINA	4 742.2	16 961	19 111.9	41 211.7	1 586.0	2 727 709	787 959	17.0	23.9	30.2	1 445 118	21 251	153 677
Abbeville	42.9	16 500	122.0	284.8	9.4	8 562	1 032	0.0	61.3	27.7	5 003	153	411
Aiken	285.7	24 419	1 485.0	2 173.8	46.9	138 073	40 612	39.7	9.0	24.6	85 993	935	4 968
Allendale	12.2	13 556	74.3	140.6	3.9	1 645	430	0.0	23.3	75.6	812	31	244
Anderson	289.1	17 521	812.7	2 026.9	57.4	165 980	98 299	6.0	71.5	11.4	53 769	915	4 164
Bamberg	13.9	10 692	43.5	99.4	2.2	4 045	565	0.0	0.0	0.0	2 689	60	338
Barnwell	36.8	13 630	89.9	222.7	D	3 585	1 004	39.6	43.5	5.2	2 078	45	349
Beaufort	12.6	14 000	50.9	86.4	4.4	154 984	17 169	10.9	0.2	60.2	125 902	964	6 748
Berkeley	78.6	20 154	464.7	1 140.5	21.5	74 841	9 364	22.8	0.0	45.9	61 095	1 077	2 122
Calhoun	7.0	14 000	42.4	96.5	1.8	4 036	1 547	35.6	40.9	0.0	2 235	54	193
Charleston	147.0	19 091	909.6	2 109.2	87.3	342 286	88 887	33.4	9.9	23.1	159 987	1 881	34 836
Cherokee	124.2	17 493	509.9	1 042.3	45.0	20 662	10 356	2.5	30.2	51.3	8 943	183	995
Chester	87.7	15 945	353.5	721.6	14.0	22 848	11 052	1.7	51.8	35.8	8 635	193	710
Chesterfield	84.5	14 825	353.1	807.7	27.4	7 411	4 056	5.1	0.0	49.1	1 348	54	838
Clarendon	13.1	10 077	30.6	116.4	3.9	10 037	1 246	3.0	0.0	30.2	6 947	142	565
Colleton	30.5	16 053	89.8	180.0	6.3	10 577	639	31.2	0.0	32.2	7 348	108	1 873
Darlington	129.2	21 180	578.2	1 497.1	51.3	20 123	4 522	5.2	0.0	68.5	12 969	223	749
Dillon	27.0	12 857	105.2	286.7	3.7	9 465	1 724	51.7	13.8	10.4	6 368	192	944
Dorchester	38.0	16 522	124.5	258.2	16.4	69 924	19 007	5.0	53.3	15.7	42 223	584	3 700
Edgefield	24.9	13 105	68.2	221.4	2.6	7 454	1 002	0.0	3.0	8.6	5 706	73	358
Fairfield	23.2	12 889	55.3	132.0	5.6	5 530	1 045	61.0	0.0	3.1	3 462	84	495
Florence	146.0	16 782	581.6	1 205.9	54.1	75 037	16 477	0.6	1.5	76.4	42 025	710	4 434
Georgetown	76.5	19 615	315.9	695.7	33.3	65 994	10 357	16.3	5.3	6.2	41 518	408	9 942
Greenville	643.1	17 195	2 728.3	5 357.2	180.0	329 021	86 471	25.8	31.3	18.9	170 677	2 710	11 444
Greenwood	156.1	16 606	562.8	1 185.9	31.5	58 426	13 180	23.5	33.8	27.1	17 189	336	1 754
Hampton	25.9	21 583	80.6	167.1	5.0	4 296	1 010	0.1	34.6	45.0	2 245	63	414
Horry	72.3	13 389	277.4	472.6	13.6	167 135	56 079	22.6	1.2	25.2	84 233	1 394	8 613
Jasper	3.7	18 500	15.3	35.0	0.9	6 707	1 741	18.3	7.7	12.2	4 276	64	0
Kershaw	98.6	18 962	463.7	958.6	75.8	34 735	14 055	1.8	59.6	24.2	17 926	300	1 735
Lancaster	95.7	15 950	314.9	1 139.6	33.3	37 131	17 359	18.9	14.4	8.4	13 274	244	2 474
Laurens	107.4	16 273	297.1	554.3	25.9	27 602	16 306	4.9	0.5	91.1	10 390	221	534
Lee	13.3	16 625	74.3	221.7	1.7	4 758	183	27.9	0.0	0.0	4 401	103	70
Lexington	106.1	16 323	406.4	1 178.4	29.9	119 833	25 369	11.6	4.5	53.0	76 481	1 081	4 645
McCormick	12.4	15 500	48.3	170.3	D	5 227	765	24.0	0.0	6.5	3 159	74	225
Marion	68.3	13 392	246.5	463.5	11.4	12 550	6 756	20.1	51.6	3.7	3 735	91	250
Marlboro	49.9	12 475	127.1	339.1	6.6	1 409	0	NA	NA	NA	997	38	0
Newberry	64.1	16 025	189.9	485.0	12.9	17 377	6 116	4.2	61.8	22.1	7 890	125	278
Oconee	82.8	14 034	338.5	586.4	53.4	46 473	7 926	13.8	2.3	53.7	33 998	456	4 128
Orangeburg	103.7	14 014	407.4	879.6	32.8	26 964	5 569	18.1	0.8	34.9	16 811	313	1 080
Pickens	163.3	14 712	418.5	1 313.4	67.5	52 532	14 858	4.5	46.8	22.0	31 243	507	2 234
Richland	230.3	19 517	1 278.5	2 443.7	206.2	210 379	62 089	19.8	0.1	35.5	94 143	1 399	15 386
Saluda	30.2	13 130	72.0	181.7	4.9	8 789	4 625	4.3	48.5	29.2	3 673	77	431
Spartanburg	449.1	17 475	1 820.7	3 875.0	144.9	129 064	40 485	15.1	20.8	27.4	57 080	899	7 061
Sumter	111.3	15 041	449.4	1 108.8	39.3	61 961	14 422	2.6	58.7	17.9	29 079	561	4 541
Union	77.8	15 878	234.9	529.0	16.8	6 653	2 427	1.2	14.8	68.2	3 526	67	302
Williamsburg	59.0	14 390	272.2	494.3	18.0	6 554	2 818	0.0	49.1	0.0	3 352	72	342
York	186.8	19 258	726.3	1 526.0	69.2	129 032	46 957	5.7	8.2	67.1	68 284	987	5 759

1. Includes nonresidential additions and alterations, residential nonhousekeeping buildings, and residential garages and carports not shown separately.

STATE County	Wholesale trade, 1987: Estab-lishments	Wholesale trade, 1987: Sales (Mil dol)	Wholesale trade, 1987: Paid employees[1]	Wholesale trade, 1987: Annual payroll (Mil dol)	Retail trade, all establishments, 1987: Number	Retail trade, all establishments, 1987: Sales: Total (Mil dol)	Retail trade, all establishments, 1987: Sales: Percent change, 1982–1987	Retail trade, all establishments, 1987: Sales: Per capita[2] (Dollars)	Retail trade, establishments with payroll, 1987: Number	Retail trade, establishments with payroll, 1987: Sales: Total (Mil dol)	Retail trade, establishments with payroll, 1987: Sales: Per capita[2] (Dollars): General merchan-dise stores	Per capita[2] (Dollars): Food stores	Per capita[2] (Dollars): Apparel & acces-sory stores	Per capita[2] (Dollars): Eating and drinking places
	147	148	149	150	151	152	153	154	155	156	157	158	159	160
PENNSYLVANIA—Con.														
Union	48	77.0	414	7.1	374	154.7	46.2	4 485	204	143.7	209	1 088	123	725
Venango	79	136.7	538	9.2	612	301.9	33.8	4 917	358	289.6	825	1 043	150	359
Warren	43	47.4	199	3.8	465	588.6	47.7	12 880	276	578.6	499	1 119	D	387
Washington	269	973.9	2 824	64.9	2 104	1 083.9	33.4	5 174	1 208	1 040.7	493	1 182	236	394
Wayne	50	100.4	358	6.1	595	283.2	75.9	7 169	307	267.2	388	1 523	143	412
Westmoreland	458	2 343.3	6 104	131.3	3 670	2 087.7	27.7	5 516	2 186	2 019.8	742	1 071	188	442
Wyoming	28	20.9	154	2.0	326	123.7	38.4	4 434	154	114.7	D	964	110	300
York	525	2 170.8	7 024	158.8	3 456	2 375.2	70.8	7 191	2 020	2 301.5	801	1 279	253	519
RHODE ISLAND	1 724	6 056.7	22 284	490.8	10 276	6 521.0	56.6	6 612	6 682	6 314.7	784	1 195	363	651
Bristol	51	62.7	234	4.6	460	213.8	50.8	4 491	263	203.3	D	1 065	207	442
Kent	277	853.6	3 068	71.5	1 818	1 492.0	62.9	9 343	1 188	1 458.0	1 959	1 342	682	755
Newport	80	153.5	394	9.0	1 101	623.8	68.2	7 399	735	603.5	D	1 098	344	1 080
Providence	1 212	4 809.6	17 712	388.4	5 661	3 413.5	50.3	5 759	3 689	3 294.0	644	1 085	301	555
Washington	104	177.3	876	17.4	1 236	777.9	68.0	7 627	807	755.9	403	1 747	317	795
SOUTH CAROLINA	5 271	17 084.4	54 551	1 064.8	36 493	19 750.4	58.0	5 768	21 859	18 949.6	589	1 195	298	537
Abbeville	11	11.7	47	0.7	211	46.5	22.0	2 050	93	41.4	193	802	59	157
Aiken	87	200.7	536	9.0	1 113	586.3	64.6	4 886	593	559.0	588	1 202	165	416
Allendale	16	14.4	79	1.3	118	28.2	6.8	2 657	53	25.5	D	1 084	83	78
Anderson	196	551.5	1 400	24.7	1 691	862.0	59.7	6 096	940	809.8	702	1 301	263	455
Bamberg	10	19.6	50	1.0	165	52.1	23.8	2 892	97	49.3	190	829	137	240
Barnwell	13	12.7	48	0.5	233	78.7	76.1	3 749	126	72.6	D	1 426	162	225
Beaufort	111	119.7	599	11.6	1 042	591.9	69.6	7 088	739	574.3	477	1 489	503	1 100
Berkeley	53	179.3	580	11.3	734	291.3	66.4	2 351	349	277.1	D	592	47	173
Calhoun	11	14.3	91	1.1	81	20.5	20.6	1 705	41	19.3	D	464	71	13
Charleston	533	2 639.1	6 095	115.6	3 241	2 407.4	56.0	8 030	2 321	2 362.9	928	1 553	493	862
Cherokee	51	107.7	489	7.8	423	215.5	58.3	5 167	234	208.9	509	1 219	458	469
Chester	23	69.9	211	3.6	273	102.9	28.6	3 309	158	97.8	235	1 098	154	336
Chesterfield	45	78.7	309	3.8	501	148.4	48.8	3 815	225	134.8	331	1 008	152	255
Clarendon	30	42.0	208	3.4	311	107.5	45.5	3 784	159	99.9	228	941	161	208
Colleton	40	108.9	556	7.3	362	152.3	50.9	4 402	195	143.6	272	1 231	196	321
Darlington	94	582.9	1 209	15.3	675	255.0	43.7	3 935	377	231.7	209	906	192	293
Dillon	44	108.1	473	8.5	318	128.7	27.9	3 925	173	121.9	372	988	220	390
Dorchester	59	69.3	414	7.0	665	318.7	59.9	4 050	345	304.2	D	940	83	369
Edgefield	17	254.7	141	2.1	170	79.3	84.4	4 264	100	76.8	D	891	44	98
Fairfield	17	18.2	101	1.1	174	64.2	52.5	2 973	90	60.8	140	1 109	89	138
Florence	241	656.3	2 958	54.1	1 485	804.0	57.3	6 872	877	772.2	889	1 216	289	428
Georgetown	52	57.2	288	4.3	597	263.8	45.9	5 462	362	254.7	374	1 293	277	706
Greenville	832	3 399.4	10 364	236.8	3 448	2 267.6	55.1	7 329	2 200	2 202.5	987	1 373	354	633
Greenwood	73	162.1	683	9.3	696	381.2	53.0	6 516	414	364.2	696	1 173	263	460
Hampton	34	103.4	338	5.0	226	81.5	34.7	4 265	125	77.3	239	1 276	244	168
Horry	240	415.7	1 677	29.4	2 532	1 371.5	78.3	10 167	1 676	1 321.7	1 051	1 801	803	1 444
Jasper	8	27.7	133	2.4	182	63.6	16.7	4 211	101	59.8	79	788	108	505
Kershaw	36	31.0	187	2.9	472	240.5	69.0	5 502	284	230.9	504	1 202	151	373
Lancaster	37	59.0	305	6.0	578	239.0	34.2	4 268	319	223.3	325	1 158	177	318
Laurens	43	55.1	322	5.2	455	197.5	45.0	3 691	246	184.6	335	960	125	238
Lee	27	37.5	157	2.3	202	44.9	21.7	2 403	89	40.1	95	599	76	143
Lexington	281	794.8	2 958	62.5	1 608	869.3	77.0	5 212	870	822.7	342	1 332	146	502
McCormick	6	4.0	21	0.3	93	13.2	22.2	1 815	40	9.6	D	565	D	69
Marion	38	75.1	378	3.8	392	135.4	36.8	3 868	207	127.2	265	858	204	223
Marlboro	22	31.2	160	2.6	318	85.8	27.5	2 715	145	78.1	97	877	153	175
Newberry	31	79.3	455	6.9	342	146.9	38.6	4 548	180	140.2	600	1 010	172	312
Oconee	54	60.7	372	5.7	593	255.2	71.7	4 709	304	233.7	401	896	98	374
Orangeburg	115	273.6	1 030	16.1	892	430.4	56.2	4 864	530	414.2	519	900	230	338
Pickens	87	93.1	480	7.8	885	379.8	40.6	4 262	490	361.3	369	1 052	125	527
Richland	646	2 406.8	9 155	197.9	2 683	2 057.3	59.5	7 295	1 922	2 012.3	1 004	1 035	440	763
Saluda	20	103.8	318	2.9	153	48.4	48.0	2 914	88	45.4	140	836	D	108
Spartanburg	465	2 183.9	4 345	96.8	2 371	1 385.0	67.7	6 499	1 388	1 313.2	492	1 416	500	542
Sumter	120	154.1	997	16.6	882	508.2	60.4	5 250	519	492.8	512	952	254	358
Union	27	29.1	121	1.5	287	111.9	28.2	3 680	162	104.7	D	1 183	149	240
Williamsburg	47	110.9	521	7.9	357	113.3	27.7	2 934	169	100.4	96	794	164	115
York	228	476.2	2 192	41.3	1 263	717.9	69.9	5 789	744	690.9	461	1 289	237	560

1. For pay period including March 12. 2. Based on the estimated population as of July 1 of the year shown.

STATE County	Retail trade, establishments with payroll, 1987 (cont'd) — Paid employees[1]	Retail trade, establishments with payroll, 1987 (cont'd) — Annual payroll (Mil dol)	Taxable service industries–establishments with payroll, 1987 — Number	Receipts (Mil dol) — Total	Receipts — Selected kinds of business — Hotels, motels and other lodging places	Receipts — Selected kinds of business — Health services	Receipts — Selected kinds of business — Legal services	Paid employees	Annual payroll (Mil dol)	Bank deposits,[2] June 1989 — Total (Mil dol)	Bank deposits — Percent change, 1988–1989	Savings capital,[3] September 1989 — Total (Mil dol)	Savings capital — Percent change, 1988–1989
	161	162	163	164	165	166	167	168	169	170	171	172	173
PENNSYLVANIA—Con.													
Union	2 289	15.8	180	48.2	4.3	19.9	2.0	1 030	17.9	323	6.8	24.9	0.3
Venango	3 582	30.0	282	68.0	2.6	33.3	3.5	1 433	25.0	384	-6.1	128.9	-0.4
Warren	4 458	54.2	193	45.7	4.2	20.9	2.4	1 234	15.7	325	4.6	100.9	0.7
Washington	12 156	109.9	1 040	453.1	11.5	99.7	16.8	8 648	159.5	1 588	7.1	663.6	2.1
Wayne	2 353	24.5	263	69.3	31.9	14.3	4.6	1 477	19.0	558	10.0	15.7	-7.5
Westmoreland	24 912	214.1	1 976	533.5	22.9	190.4	21.6	12 692	206.7	2 810	9.1	1 318.1	-4.8
Wyoming	1 145	9.9	99	18.8	0.8	9.1	1.0	495	6.7	179	6.7	20.7	-3.1
York	25 256	231.6	1 768	593.0	29.3	179.4	32.2	15 383	226.4	3 149	8.4	762.8	0.7
RHODE ISLAND	76 449	772.4	7 133	2 603.8	96.2	679.7	248.0	60 638	1 006.6	13 442	10.5	2 101.9	-0.9
Bristol	2 426	24.5	206	75.1	D	22.6	0.7	1 888	31.9	395	12.8	91.4	0.4
Kent	16 494	167.9	1 184	388.2	5.8	127.5	13.8	9 383	141.6	1 492	16.0	414.8	4.0
Newport	7 752	79.5	603	313.9	34.7	37.4	10.0	6 559	121.1	684	7.1	43.6	0.4
Providence	41 204	408.1	4 430	1 656.3	37.2	436.2	214.7	38 536	652.1	9 922	10.0	1 434.8	-2.5
Washington	8 573	92.3	710	170.3	18.3	56.0	8.7	4 272	59.8	949	9.3	117.3	0.2
SOUTH CAROLINA	237 122	2 177.5	18 810	6 355.0	668.7	1 775.0	473.6	169 535	2 397.0	15 993	10.9	8 802.6	-1.1
Abbeville	635	5.0	67	7.6	D	3.3	D	223	2.3	111	16.3	50.9	1.7
Aiken	6 930	60.8	502	199.5	D	62.7	6.3	4 898	86.1	453	28.5	312.1	8.0
Allendale	297	2.7	36	4.2	D	1.4	0.5	134	1.3	48	6.8	0.0	NA
Anderson	9 760	90.1	714	177.4	D	70.9	9.6	4 634	72.9	636	13.9	525.6	2.7
Bamberg	706	6.1	67	9.8	0.3	3.8	0.9	292	3.8	96	9.2	27.6	4.0
Barnwell	858	7.3	77	17.9	D	9.8	1.1	510	7.1	92	15.1	31.8	8.8
Beaufort	7 527	74.4	716	233.8	72.6	29.9	21.8	6 491	86.2	563	11.8	189.9	5.6
Berkeley	3 218	28.9	244	43.9	3.9	10.5	3.5	1 443	15.0	118	5.3	86.5	3.3
Calhoun	226	2.2	35	4.6	0.0	0.6	0.6	155	1.4	48	7.1	9.1	-32.6
Charleston	31 674	280.7	2 397	926.8	113.6	305.6	74.9	24 003	322.4	1 234	8.1	965.4	1.0
Cherokee	2 532	21.1	175	45.9	1.9	20.7	1.8	1 481	18.0	193	10.3	132.1	3.9
Chester	1 312	11.2	110	17.0	D	5.1	0.8	458	6.0	77	1.0	83.8	-1.0
Chesterfield	1 639	15.0	126	26.6	D	14.0	1.4	719	8.6	175	9.4	32.2	0.6
Clarendon	1 281	11.4	88	19.2	2.8	6.3	3.2	530	5.9	101	11.9	15.5	-6.0
Colleton	1 991	15.1	166	42.2	8.8	17.7	3.8	1 160	12.3	108	16.4	78.9	9.0
Darlington	2 923	25.6	237	66.5	1.4	28.4	4.7	1 759	22.6	252	17.2	88.6	-4.6
Dillon	1 620	15.3	116	22.2	3.9	8.8	1.1	606	7.3	125	14.4	20.7	-15.7
Dorchester	3 693	32.7	327	64.0	2.6	16.8	3.4	2 258	21.8	222	4.2	89.2	-1.7
Edgefield	562	5.8	52	5.9	D	2.9	0.4	261	1.9	67	12.8	26.5	2.5
Fairfield	581	6.2	48	7.5	1.5	1.4	0.7	248	2.5	75	15.7	32.3	-0.5
Florence	8 774	81.1	666	231.6	26.9	100.8	13.2	6 062	92.2	599	15.0	305.3	-2.8
Georgetown	3 598	31.1	243	58.2	4.8	14.7	5.3	1 468	19.3	185	9.6	133.1	9.8
Greenville	26 194	254.1	2 265	1 047.4	42.1	212.7	77.8	25 067	412.0	1 938	11.3	1 316.1	0.2
Greenwood	4 517	43.3	296	82.1	11.3	28.5	3.1	2 364	33.7	329	12.1	234.5	0.2
Hampton	929	8.2	71	12.5	D	1.7	4.2	328	4.3	111	5.3	31.7	0.5
Horry	16 614	162.9	1 364	533.4	223.7	87.3	26.6	12 330	157.9	888	17.6	461.9	-6.7
Jasper	790	6.4	64	20.7	7.6	7.6	1.3	588	5.3	38	4.6	13.9	-1.0
Kershaw	2 556	21.9	213	45.5	2.1	14.0	3.3	1 321	16.5	163	9.4	136.5	-0.3
Lancaster	2 669	23.6	221	44.0	D	13.5	1.7	1 096	14.3	154	4.6	52.1	-9.7
Laurens	1 991	19.6	162	32.0	2.0	10.0	2.1	934	10.6	215	6.9	148.3	2.0
Lee	492	4.0	40	5.6	D	1.2	D	143	2.2	49	14.3	21.2	0.1
Lexington	10 111	92.3	828	255.2	17.3	84.6	8.2	6 798	89.6	706	13.1	282.0	-5.0
McCormick	118	1.0	14	2.6	0.0	0.0	D	76	1.1	17	6.5	13.2	4.2
Marion	1 476	13.5	148	31.3	0.5	13.4	1.0	946	11.9	173	5.3	42.4	0.6
Marlboro	1 019	8.1	93	24.2	0.7	17.2	1.9	606	8.1	102	3.1	28.9	-3.9
Newberry	1 622	14.7	126	21.6	0.6	7.1	1.5	561	6.8	151	12.7	147.7	-4.9
Oconee	2 805	23.8	229	51.8	D	16.5	2.6	1 450	23.6	231	17.9	171.0	-0.7
Orangeburg	5 362	47.5	385	104.3	14.0	31.0	17.2	2 566	38.6	418	11.0	130.9	-11.2
Pickens	5 190	41.9	348	80.4	6.6	28.6	3.3	2 253	27.4	336	6.6	239.5	-6.5
Richland	27 023	252.3	2 292	953.9	48.2	211.8	113.4	27 083	403.9	2 293	5.6	924.4	-1.5
Saluda	462	4.4	45	7.1	D	1.4	D	228	2.0	79	28.1	21.1	-2.3
Spartanburg	16 423	151.6	1 197	437.4	15.3	127.0	23.4	13 877	188.5	879	11.1	585.4	-4.1
Sumter	5 732	54.5	381	101.5	4.4	29.6	8.3	3 253	38.8	316	14.0	117.1	-13.3
Union	1 266	11.1	98	14.5	D	6.2	0.7	535	5.5	100	3.7	102.3	19.8
Williamsburg	1 228	10.7	110	16.8	D	4.7	1.5	464	4.9	125	1.7	20.4	-0.6
York	8 196	76.3	611	196.6	12.4	83.5	9.7	4 875	72.4	608	11.6	323.1	-7.8

1. For the period including March 12 of the year shown. 2. Includes deposits for all insured and reporting noninsured commercial and mutual savings banks. 3. Includes savings capital for all FSLIC insured savings institutions.

STATE County	Federal funds and grants, 1989							Local government finances, 1981–1982							
	Expenditures		Per capita[1] (Dollars)					General revenue						Direct general expenditure	
									Intergovernmental		Taxes				
												Per capita[2]			
	Total (Mil dol)	Percent change, 1988–1989	Total	Direct pay-ments for indi-viduals	Procure-ment contract awards	Salaries and wages	Grant awards	Total (Mil dol)	Total (Mil dol)	Percent from state	Total (Mil dol)	Total (Dollars)	Property (Dollars)	Total (Mil dol)	Percent change, 1977–1982
	174	175	176	177	178	179	180	181	182	183	184	185	186	187	188
PENNSYLVANIA—Con.															
Union	82.1	9.0	2 340	1 502	26	572	215	28.8	17.2	75.5	7.6	228	136	27.3	90.6
Venango	180.6	22.7	2 990	2 152	22	131	672	59.6	26.3	90.4	20.5	314	217	58.5	45.3
Warren	115.1	8.7	2 542	1 919	140	191	282	41.1	19.9	91.5	16.0	334	232	37.2	200.1
Washington	617.8	8.5	2 977	2 375	36	145	404	170.0	78.1	82.0	67.7	312	235	157.1	42.2
Wayne	107.9	7.1	2 614	2 237	20	133	200	32.9	11.9	91.8	14.8	407	347	37.8	55.4
Westmoreland	979.5	3.1	2 600	2 151	85	115	238	343.7	147.8	86.2	133.9	342	259	319.9	58.8
Wyoming	55.2	7.2	1 930	1 599	21	88	194	18.8	9.9	88.0	7.0	260	186	18.3	45.1
York	806.2	5.0	2 369	1 519	561	103	172	229.9	81.5	88.5	96.5	305	205	214.0	46.8
RHODE ISLAND	3 827.9	7.2	X	2 078	456	530	739	831.2	285.1	73.7	483.8	507	503	808.6	50.0
Bristol	107.1	4.9	2 232	1 766	36	144	280	41.6	15.5	65.2	24.1	515	511	42.5	38.3
Kent	390.7	4.6	2 419	1 889	73	167	286	130.3	40.1	79.5	81.9	529	525	127.1	52.7
Newport	804.9	0.8	9 525	2 057	3 800	3 212	450	73.4	26.8	74.2	40.1	483	476	70.5	28.3
Providence	1 912.5	2.4	3 197	1 953	176	314	743	499.9	176.9	72.3	283.5	495	490	486.3	51.6
Washington	321.5	19.6	3 054	1 714	143	337	853	86.0	25.7	79.3	54.3	571	565	82.2	66.2
SOUTH CAROLINA	12 311.9	12.0	X	1 602	708	720	424	2 460.7	1 107.8	82.2	679.9	211	195	2 487.5	93.8
Abbeville	48.1	10.3	2 108	1 706	13	109	257	15.7	7.3	94.1	3.1	139	130	15.5	129.2
Aiken	2 065.6	35.9	16 578	1 534	14 593	217	215	69.1	35.6	85.9	19.4	178	166	67.2	122.2
Allendale	31.4	13.1	2 963	1 784	116	118	661	9.4	4.7	85.5	1.9	179	166	8.9	123.8
Anderson	294.2	14.6	2 039	1 586	98	108	226	76.3	38.7	92.1	26.8	196	183	74.1	97.1
Bamberg	46.2	6.2	2 639	1 642	286	101	481	13.3	7.2	89.1	1.9	107	98	13.2	124.0
Barnwell	51.8	9.1	2 443	1 547	252	89	424	16.5	7.8	93.4	3.9	194	163	16.6	115.1
Beaufort	474.0	3.8	5 467	1 791	334	3 140	192	48.8	17.0	70.8	17.6	235	219	49.6	101.3
Berkeley	178.6	-14.1	1 373	932	152	71	211	67.6	35.5	84.7	17.5	170	161	71.2	162.8
Calhoun	28.6	-2.3	2 380	1 284	9	105	638	8.3	4.3	93.2	2.7	227	222	10.8	178.3
Charleston	2 130.8	7.8	6 920	1 804	932	3 700	442	220.1	90.1	74.9	75.2	262	234	234.7	108.2
Cherokee	74.5	7.8	1 766	1 418	10	80	243	54.3	15.8	83.9	8.6	211	202	60.1	334.0
Chester	69.0	6.7	2 198	1 652	11	78	434	30.0	12.7	84.2	5.5	178	166	30.3	107.0
Chesterfield	81.0	8.7	2 073	1 501	20	105	403	30.0	13.6	91.8	6.0	158	147	31.9	115.4
Clarendon	66.6	6.2	2 313	1 560	9	86	488	20.5	10.9	92.0	3.3	119	101	21.1	111.6
Colleton	78.0	-0.4	2 216	1 610	55	102	396	24.0	11.1	88.1	1.7	54	41	24.8	66.2
Darlington	127.4	5.5	1 952	1 441	32	74	345	37.0	21.2	92.8	11.8	185	166	36.8	55.0
Dillon	63.7	-11.9	1 931	1 323	15	83	433	20.7	14.4	90.1	3.6	112	95	18.4	67.9
Dorchester	147.1	11.5	1 739	1 379	13	97	235	31.8	18.8	93.9	8.9	138	131	30.2	101.0
Edgefield	38.5	19.1	2 018	1 262	20	139	400	11.0	6.1	92.7	2.1	121	112	10.9	84.3
Fairfield	48.6	6.7	2 178	1 613	65	98	387	18.5	11.6	78.8	4.1	198	192	20.3	119.4
Florence	257.9	10.1	2 172	1 506	36	175	421	71.4	40.5	86.0	20.8	185	164	70.9	78.2
Georgetown	109.7	6.1	2 181	1 627	39	76	300	33.7	19.9	73.5	9.7	222	211	37.9	91.9
Greenville	594.2	1.7	1 862	1 452	41	188	173	206.3	89.5	73.2	78.6	266	245	210.7	70.5
Greenwood	129.3	3.9	2 196	1 740	56	144	248	64.2	18.2	88.0	12.8	214	201	69.2	104.7
Hampton	47.6	3.0	2 469	1 649	54	161	499	15.3	8.7	84.2	3.0	160	149	13.4	52.5
Horry	381.3	11.7	2 693	1 694	91	653	210	98.6	50.5	55.3	30.7	280	249	96.8	99.1
Jasper	36.5	5.1	2 385	1 517	113	106	627	11.1	5.7	88.3	2.6	179	161	11.3	81.2
Kershaw	92.3	8.5	2 016	1 636	16	101	242	33.7	14.0	89.3	7.7	191	184	35.2	74.6
Lancaster	92.0	4.7	1 619	1 342	8	74	186	39.1	22.0	91.5	10.4	190	181	35.5	113.8
Laurens	104.5	2.6	1 934	1 593	11	86	225	35.5	17.0	88.2	7.7	145	138	32.8	68.3
Lee	46.4	-2.2	2 497	1 598	7	83	486	11.9	7.7	87.2	2.2	116	101	12.2	73.2
Lexington	251.9	5.1	1 442	1 121	69	108	132	132.1	50.1	91.0	42.3	287	274	127.8	77.6
McCormick	21.9	-5.8	3 007	1 726	309	437	519	5.6	4.1	84.5	0.9	113	105	5.4	54.9
Marion	114.6	48.0	3 257	1 654	1 033	119	412	38.3	15.1	88.3	6.2	179	162	36.8	102.6
Marlboro	69.9	-17.7	2 220	1 500	8	88	469	18.4	13.4	87.9	3.1	96	92	20.2	87.5
Newberry	80.7	9.9	2 468	1 909	44	180	315	27.7	11.5	78.1	5.8	185	168	24.8	89.7
Oconee	107.1	6.9	1 889	1 574	45	92	162	35.7	16.7	82.0	13.2	262	255	35.2	86.4
Orangeburg	205.5	-0.1	2 291	1 567	40	98	478	66.2	32.2	90.0	11.7	139	129	78.4	138.4
Pickens	165.1	9.1	1 791	1 330	73	109	275	35.5	19.5	89.9	12.7	153	145	32.9	63.5
Richland	1 583.4	10.6	5 481	1 782	549	1 923	1 214	257.2	92.3	73.3	73.5	265	245	256.3	81.9
Saluda	31.7	16.4	1 959	1 295	11	129	401	6.2	4.1	93.0	1.5	90	79	6.1	88.2
Spartanburg	427.1	-2.5	1 964	1 593	46	99	213	212.5	71.0	85.5	52.2	253	237	207.1	95.6
Sumter	372.3	7.2	3 803	1 566	206	1 628	357	53.2	32.3	86.8	12.7	140	124	57.2	101.1
Union	70.5	22.0	2 319	1 677	11	121	503	23.9	10.4	90.0	4.9	160	149	23.3	54.2
Williamsburg	80.8	3.0	2 103	1 374	39	104	486	28.1	17.0	88.3	4.1	107	101	28.9	85.5
York	205.7	3.1	1 582	1 284	32	99	159	76.8	39.9	77.6	23.2	210	201	74.3	55.8

1. Based on the estimated population as of July 1 of the year shown. 2. Based on the estimated population as of July 1, 1982.

STATE County	Local government finances, 1981–1982 (cont'd): Direct general expenditure (cont'd): Per capita[1] (Dollars)	Percent of total for– Educa-tion	Health & hospitals	Police protec-tion	Public welfare	High-ways	Debt outstanding: Total (Mil dol)	Per capita[1] (Dollars)	State and local government employ-ment, 1989: Total	Rate[2]	Federal government civilian employment 1989: Total	Earnings ($1,000)	Elections, 1988[3]: Total vote cast for president	Vote for lead party (Percent)
	189	190	191	192	193	194	195	196	197	198	199	200	201	202
PENNSYLVANIA—Con.														
Union	817	74.9	0.0	1.9	1.1	4.8	15.6	466	1 929	549.6	856	29 192	11 136	R–71.0
Venango	895	49.4	2.3	1.9	5.5	5.3	44.4	680	4 011	664.1	220	6 291	20 263	R–56.6
Warren	776	50.9	3.3	2.2	9.6	7.0	23.8	497	2 625	579.5	309	8 136	15 995	R–56.2
Washington	724	59.9	0.2	2.9	4.0	5.9	135.2	623	8 731	420.8	722	20 263	76 553	D–62.1
Wayne	1 040	51.5	15.2	0.9	1.8	4.6	43.8	1 207	1 985	480.6	131	3 378	13 862	R–71.6
Westmoreland	817	53.2	1.6	2.3	3.6	5.2	355.4	907	13 929	369.7	1 094	31 294	139 290	D–55.1
Wyoming	684	66.6	0.0	1.0	1.5	5.7	10.1	378	991	346.5	72	1 798	9 447	R–69.9
York	676	50.4	4.7	3.9	3.9	4.5	206.5	652	9 842	289.2	4 592	129 857	111 116	R–65.2
RHODE ISLAND	848	51.2	0.2	7.0	2.7	4.6	589.8	618	53 103	532.3	10 986	349 880	404 569	D–55.6
Bristol	908	51.1	0.2	4.8	0.8	5.9	44.0	940	1 529	318.5	116	3 474	21 883	D–51.0
Kent	821	58.0	0.3	7.2	1.4	4.6	113.9	736	8 423	521.5	1 013	32 199	71 801	D–51.8
Newport	848	57.1	0.2	7.9	1.3	5.1	38.4	463	3 023	357.8	4 149	134 071	34 664	D–50.8
Providence	848	47.2	0.1	7.1	3.6	4.3	353.1	616	29 458	492.4	5 221	164 124	231 159	D–58.8
Washington	864	59.0	0.4	6.2	1.1	5.0	40.4	425	10 670	1 013.3	487	16 012	45 062	D–51.5
SOUTH CAROLINA	771	52.2	14.6	4.4	0.5	2.2	1 906.8	591	227 708	647.6	39 369	1 244 522	986 009	R–61.5
Abbeville	687	51.9	22.1	4.0	0.1	2.3	7.0	308	1 088	477.2	53	1 483	7 401	R–50.5
Aiken	618	57.7	2.0	5.7	4.5	1.7	56.5	519	5 566	446.7	678	24 874	38 507	R–71.8
Allendale	843	53.1	17.9	4.1	0.2	1.0	6.0	569	807	761.3	34	810	3 114	D–57.7
Anderson	541	66.7	0.4	5.4	0.3	3.3	71.7	523	7 118	493.3	368	12 091	38 383	R–67.6
Bamberg	725	51.9	20.7	4.0	0.0	2.2	2.0	109	1 145	654.3	43	1 168	5 255	D–53.9
Barnwell	832	59.1	17.6	4.2	0.6	2.3	5.2	263	1 333	628.8	47	1 249	7 075	R–63.1
Beaufort	664	42.6	15.2	5.0	0.4	1.8	53.4	714	4 080	470.6	1 781	40 141	25 021	R–64.7
Berkeley	689	66.1	1.1	3.0	0.4	2.1	126.2	1 222	5 415	416.2	1 657	48 115	26 297	R–63.8
Calhoun	897	79.0	2.2	2.1	0.2	0.8	12.0	992	632	526.7	39	951	4 787	R–54.0
Charleston	816	45.1	8.4	5.6	0.2	1.7	194.2	675	24 652	800.6	18 360	648 564	82 916	R–59.3
Cherokee	1 470	35.8	43.0	2.2	0.1	1.3	8.6	210	1 648	390.5	94	2 586	12 151	R–63.9
Chester	984	43.9	22.9	3.5	0.2	1.9	32.0	1 040	1 875	597.1	68	1 916	7 748	R–51.2
Chesterfield	837	53.3	22.3	3.9	0.3	2.2	13.6	358	1 594	407.7	96	2 697	9 735	R–51.4
Clarendon	758	60.4	18.9	4.3	0.0	1.6	12.6	450	1 355	470.5	85	2 184	9 397	D–53.5
Colleton	768	49.1	26.9	4.1	1.1	3.0	14.3	442	1 599	454.3	100	2 588	9 547	R–52.0
Darlington	574	72.3	1.8	4.3	0.4	2.0	5.1	79	2 480	379.8	113	3 233	17 843	R–55.2
Dillon	580	75.3	1.3	4.1	0.2	1.4	4.4	137	1 310	397.0	85	2 385	7 069	R–53.7
Dorchester	467	71.9	1.4	4.2	0.5	2.3	18.1	279	3 308	391.0	166	4 907	22 232	R–66.4
Edgefield	612	65.0	13.7	4.4	0.2	1.2	1.2	66	804	420.9	70	1 572	6 863	R–55.6
Fairfield	978	51.3	7.0	2.9	0.1	5.6	3.8	182	1 181	529.6	54	1 456	6 583	D–58.1
Florence	629	63.2	1.4	4.8	0.3	2.9	41.8	371	9 013	759.3	568	17 465	32 214	R–60.5
Georgetown	863	55.1	1.6	4.2	0.3	2.4	101.4	2 309	3 056	607.6	91	2 665	12 506	R–56.2
Greenville	713	55.6	0.6	5.4	0.8	2.4	213.6	723	18 024	564.8	1 339	45 405	95 126	R–70.8
Greenwood	1 163	34.8	45.6	3.8	0.2	1.2	32.6	547	5 182	879.8	203	5 447	15 704	R–57.9
Hampton	719	63.8	11.6	3.2	0.0	1.0	4.9	265	1 142	591.7	57	1 363	6 306	D–54.5
Horry	881	42.0	1.0	4.9	0.5	2.9	80.9	737	6 594	465.7	1 270	27 679	38 409	R–64.7
Jasper	767	56.7	16.6	4.4	0.3	1.7	1.6	107	811	530.1	43	1 166	4 929	D–58.7
Kershaw	878	51.5	24.7	3.3	0.7	1.5	16.3	406	2 488	543.2	114	3 135	13 473	R–65.9
Lancaster	646	67.3	1.3	5.3	3.5	2.5	27.7	504	2 419	425.9	94	2 664	15 393	R–59.5
Laurens	620	56.9	14.0	4.6	0.3	2.5	27.8	525	4 005	741.7	108	3 195	15 702	R–62.0
Lee	652	66.6	11.7	3.5	0.3	1.9	1.8	95	861	462.9	50	1 259	6 359	D–53.8
Lexington	868	57.9	20.1	3.2	0.6	1.2	125.5	852	8 185	468.5	430	14 159	53 238	R–77.9
McCormick	714	66.2	0.9	4.9	0.8	2.7	0.9	114	606	830.1	105	2 988	2 914	D–59.1
Marion	1 063	41.4	36.9	2.7	0.5	2.0	10.7	308	2 112	600.0	89	2 352	9 486	D–52.8
Marlboro	623	68.1	0.5	4.8	0.2	2.0	5.7	175	1 327	421.3	84	2 272	6 870	D–57.3
Newberry	785	45.5	27.2	4.3	0.1	1.6	21.1	667	1 622	496.0	135	3 354	10 305	R–62.4
Oconee	700	67.4	0.6	3.6	0.7	5.8	24.8	493	2 685	473.5	152	3 963	14 585	R–69.8
Orangeburg	931	46.2	35.3	2.4	1.5	1.4	34.3	408	6 178	688.7	214	5 776	28 049	D–52.2
Pickens	396	64.3	0.8	6.9	0.2	4.5	20.5	247	7 819	848.0	245	7 664	23 696	R–73.6
Richland	925	41.0	22.9	5.1	0.0	1.6	180.4	651	46 423	1 606.9	7 616	226 071	83 123	R–52.7
Saluda	373	70.0	0.8	5.0	1.3	4.9	1.6	96	734	453.1	51	1 291	5 232	R–61.6
Spartanburg	1 007	43.4	31.6	3.6	0.1	2.6	167.0	812	12 302	565.9	496	15 350	64 568	R–63.2
Sumter	630	70.3	0.9	4.8	0.1	3.9	54.0	594	4 516	461.3	1 356	30 388	22 801	R–57.7
Union	755	51.0	24.5	5.3	0.6	2.8	11.7	379	1 789	588.5	94	2 196	10 465	R–57.5
Williamsburg	751	55.8	26.0	2.8	0.5	3.2	7.0	181	2 034	529.7	96	2 516	13 324	D–55.1
York	670	60.3	0.5	4.3	0.5	1.6	43.7	394	6 791	522.4	278	7 769	33 308	R–65.0

1. Based on the estimated population as of July 1, 1982. 2. Per 10,000 resident population estimated as of July 1 of the year shown. 3. Data subject to copyright.

STATE–County code	MSA/CMSA/NECMA code[1]	STATE County	Land Area,[2] 1990 (Sq. Km.)	Population, 1990 Total persons	Rank	Per square kilometer	Race White	Black	Am. Indian, Eskimo, Aleut	Asian & Pacific Islander	Other race	Hispanic[3]	Age of population Percent Under 5 years	5 to 14 years	15 to 24 years
			1	2	3	4	5	6	7	8	9	10	11	12	13
46 000	...	SOUTH DAKOTA	196 575	696 004	X	3.5	637 515	3 258	50 575	3 123	1 533	5 252	7.8	16.4	14.1
46 003	...	Aurora	1 834	3 135	2 991	1.7	3 086	0	42	3	4	7	5.8	16.6	11.9
46 005	...	Beadle	3 262	18 253	1 776	5.6	17 937	70	161	52	33	76	7.2	15.7	11.4
46 007	...	Bennett	3 070	3 206	2 984	1.0	1 709	8	1 481	2	6	35	9.5	21.2	13.4
46 009	...	Bon Homme	1 459	7 089	2 647	4.9	6 900	22	155	4	8	34	6.6	14.2	11.0
46 011	...	Brookings	2 058	25 207	1 454	12.2	24 656	77	156	300	18	76	6.0	13.5	28.5
46 013	...	Brown	4 436	35 580	1 108	8.0	34 382	45	982	140	31	111	6.9	14.9	15.8
46 015	...	Brule	2 121	5 485	2 802	2.6	5 078	6	383	12	6	31	7.6	20.6	11.2
46 017	...	Buffalo	1 219	1 759	3 081	1.4	393	0	1 365	0	1	3	12.6	26.0	15.3
46 019	...	Butte	5 824	7 914	2 581	1.4	7 629	21	117	17	130	219	8.1	16.6	11.2
46 021	...	Campbell	1 906	1 965	3 069	1.0	1 960	2	3	0	0	0	7.1	14.7	9.0
46 023	...	Charles Mix	2 845	9 131	2 458	3.2	7 122	4	1 995	4	6	34	8.8	18.0	11.9
46 025	...	Clark	2 481	4 403	2 882	1.8	4 376	6	12	7	2	13	6.6	16.7	10.0
46 027	...	Clay	1 066	13 186	2 124	12.4	12 556	58	395	146	31	100	5.8	11.5	35.8
46 029	...	Codington	1 781	22 698	1 548	12.7	22 345	16	260	72	5	55	7.4	16.9	13.5
46 031	...	Corson	6 405	4 195	2 899	0.7	2 151	1	2 034	3	6	47	10.8	21.8	13.2
46 033	...	Custer	4 035	6 179	2 735	1.5	6 000	9	155	11	4	45	6.0	17.1	10.2
46 035	...	Davison	1 128	17 503	1 821	15.5	17 162	22	243	62	14	38	7.5	16.0	13.6
46 037	...	Day	2 664	6 978	2 663	2.6	6 500	1	468	5	4	11	7.2	15.5	10.4
46 039	...	Deuel	1 615	4 522	2 874	2.8	4 498	1	10	9	4	14	7.0	14.8	10.5
46 041	...	Dewey	5 964	5 523	2 800	0.9	1 820	11	3 680	8	4	46	12.3	22.2	14.2
46 043	...	Douglas	1 123	3 746	2 937	3.3	3 721	0	22	2	1	2	8.4	17.1	10.4
46 045	...	Edmunds	2 967	4 356	2 889	1.5	4 329	1	19	4	3	5	6.8	15.2	9.6
46 047	...	Fall River	4 506	7 353	2 624	1.6	6 807	27	450	30	39	120	5.1	14.9	9.0
46 049	...	Faulk	2 591	2 744	3 014	1.1	2 737	0	6	1	0	3	7.1	15.8	9.4
46 051	...	Grant	1 768	8 372	2 526	4.7	8 314	3	33	17	5	11	7.0	17.8	10.7
46 053	...	Gregory	2 631	5 359	2 814	2.0	5 065	1	284	5	4	27	7.3	16.7	9.3
46 055	...	Haakon	4 696	2 624	3 017	0.6	2 569	4	36	12	3	11	7.5	22.8	10.4
46 057	...	Hamlin	1 324	4 974	2 843	3.8	4 944	4	10	7	9	13	6.9	17.4	10.7
46 059	...	Hand	3 721	4 272	2 893	1.1	4 251	3	5	11	2	11	6.8	15.5	10.6
46 061	...	Hanson	1 126	2 994	3 002	2.7	2 987	0	7	0	0	2	7.4	18.2	12.3
46 063	...	Harding	6 917	1 669	3 087	0.2	1 645	5	16	0	3	3	8.8	18.6	11.9
46 065	...	Hughes	1 919	14 817	1 999	7.7	13 726	19	994	43	35	112	7.8	17.5	11.2
46 067	...	Hutchinson	2 106	8 262	2 541	3.9	8 221	1	22	11	7	14	6.3	14.8	9.2
46 069	...	Hyde	2 230	1 696	3 085	0.8	1 637	1	57	1	0	7	7.0	15.7	7.6
46 071	...	Jackson	4 841	2 811	3 012	0.6	1 609	3	1 193	5	1	14	10.1	20.1	13.3
46 073	...	Jerauld	1 373	2 425	3 028	1.8	2 413	0	5	7	0	1	5.4	15.9	9.9
46 075	...	Jones	2 514	1 324	3 105	0.5	1 316	0	7	1	0	1	7.7	15.9	10.8
46 077	...	Kingsbury	2 172	5 925	2 767	2.7	5 905	0	11	7	2	5	6.6	15.5	9.1
46 079	...	Lake	1 459	10 550	2 331	7.2	10 468	12	33	22	15	27	6.7	15.9	14.5
46 081	...	Lawrence	2 072	20 655	1 647	10.0	19 950	29	535	56	85	327	6.9	15.9	16.2
46 083	...	Lincoln	1 497	15 427	1 961	10.3	15 292	21	58	42	14	23	8.0	18.3	11.0
46 085	...	Lyman	4 248	3 638	2 947	0.9	2 579	3	1 051	2	3	18	9.1	19.2	12.5
46 087	...	McCook	1 488	5 688	2 787	3.8	5 652	0	28	6	2	8	7.1	16.1	10.2
46 089	...	McPherson	2 945	3 228	2 983	1.1	3 223	1	2	2	0	0	5.2	13.4	8.4
46 091	...	Marshall	2 173	4 844	2 850	2.2	4 568	1	271	2	2	13	7.0	15.7	9.6
46 093	...	Meade	8 989	21 878	1 584	2.4	20 652	518	395	172	141	387	8.8	18.8	14.4
46 095	...	Mellette	3 384	2 137	3 060	0.6	1 133	1	999	2	2	15	9.7	20.5	13.1
46 097	...	Miner	1 477	3 272	2 979	2.2	3 267	0	4	0	1	6	6.9	16.3	9.3
46 099	7760	Minnehaha	2 096	123 809	369	59.1	120 454	754	1 680	714	207	648	7.9	15.3	14.4
46 101	...	Moody	1 346	6 507	2 710	4.8	5 951	10	527	13	6	13	8.2	17.9	11.4
46 103	6660	Pennington	7 191	81 343	558	11.3	72 769	1 288	5 835	933	518	1 777	9.2	16.0	15.0
46 105	...	Perkins	7 442	3 932	2 924	0.5	3 859	6	56	2	9	17	6.0	16.1	8.9
46 107	...	Potter	2 244	3 190	2 986	1.4	3 157	0	26	2	5	5	6.2	16.7	9.6
46 109	...	Roberts	2 852	9 914	2 394	3.5	7 615	0	2 280	10	9	28	8.0	17.0	12.1
46 111	...	Sanborn	1 474	2 833	3 011	1.9	2 830	0	0	3	0	15	7.5	17.5	9.6
46 113	...	Shannon	5 423	9 902	2 397	1.8	499	5	9 374	5	19	179	14.0	24.3	18.5
46 115	...	Spink	3 895	7 981	2 569	2.0	7 909	2	65	2	3	15	7.4	15.5	10.9
46 117	...	Stanley	3 738	2 453	3 026	0.7	2 294	1	155	0	3	10	8.2	18.0	12.9
46 119	...	Sully	2 608	1 589	3 092	0.6	1 572	1	15	0	1	3	5.8	17.4	11.0
46 121	...	Todd	3 596	8 352	2 528	2.3	1 431	10	6 883	6	22	123	13.8	25.0	16.8
46 123	...	Tripp	4 179	6 924	2 670	1.7	6 245	0	670	7	2	9	8.0	17.4	11.0
46 125	...	Turner	1 598	8 576	2 508	5.4	8 542	4	26	4	0	18	6.3	16.2	9.5
46 127	...	Union	1 192	10 189	2 372	8.5	10 091	20	34	27	17	67	7.1	17.6	11.4
46 129	...	Walworth	1 833	6 087	2 746	3.3	5 606	2	467	11	1	26	6.5	15.1	10.0
46 135	...	Yankton	1 351	19 252	1 715	14.3	18 661	114	412	53	12	89	7.4	15.3	13.0
46 137	...	Ziebach	5 083	2 220	3 054	0.4	790	3	1 420	4	3	29	11.9	24.5	14.3

1. MSA = Metropolitan Statistical Area. CMSA = Consolidated MSA. NECMA = New England county metropolitan area. PMSA = Primary MSA. See Appendix A for explanation of these concepts. See Appendix B for list of metropolitan areas identified by type, with component counties. 2. Dry land or land partially or temporarily covered by water. 3. Hispanic persons may be of any race.

STATE County	Population, 1990 (cont'd)							Population–Change and components of change							
	Age of population (cont'd) Percent						Percent female	Change		Components of change, 1980–1986					
								1980–1990		Total persons, 1986	Total persons, 1980	Net change		Natural increase	
	25 to 34 years	35 to 44 years	45 to 54 years	55 to 64 years	65 to 74 years	75 years and over		Number	Percent			Number	Percent	Births	Deaths
	14	15	16	17	18	19	20	21	22	23	24	25	26	27	28
SOUTH DAKOTA	15.7	13.7	9.0	8.6	7.8	6.9	50.8	5 004	0.7	708 000	691 000	17 000	2.5	79 000	41 000
Aurora	11.8	11.7	9.3	11.3	10.4	11.3	49.6	-493	-13.6	3 300	3 628	-300	-8.0	300	300
Beadle	15.0	13.4	9.3	9.8	9.8	8.4	51.4	-942	-4.9	18 300	19 195	-900	-4.7	1 800	1 200
Bennett	14.5	12.0	9.0	8.5	6.1	5.7	51.1	162	5.3	3 400	3 044	300	10.8	500	200
Bon Homme	14.6	12.6	8.5	10.1	10.9	11.6	48.9	-970	-12.0	6 800	8 059	-1 300	-16.0	700	600
Brookings	14.6	11.9	7.3	6.3	6.3	5.6	49.0	875	3.6	24 600	24 332	300	1.2	2 400	1 100
Brown	15.6	14.0	9.0	8.7	7.9	7.2	52.1	-1 382	-3.7	36 700	36 962	-300	-0.8	3 800	2 000
Brule	14.1	11.9	9.2	8.8	8.9	7.7	50.1	240	4.6	5 500	5 245	200	4.7	600	300
Buffalo	14.3	10.4	8.7	5.2	5.2	2.3	47.5	-36	-2.0	1 600	1 795	-200	-9.1	400	100
Butte	15.0	13.9	9.6	9.5	9.2	6.8	50.5	-458	-5.5	8 200	8 372	-100	-1.7	800	600
Campbell	14.0	11.3	11.5	12.2	11.4	8.9	49.8	-278	-12.4	2 200	2 243	0	-1.3	200	100
Charles Mix	12.8	11.8	9.5	9.6	8.7	8.9	50.9	-549	-5.7	9 400	9 680	-300	-3.0	1 300	700
Clark	11.4	12.6	9.4	11.6	11.7	9.9	50.1	-491	-10.0	4 800	4 894	-100	-1.5	500	400
Clay	12.9	10.9	6.5	6.2	5.4	4.9	51.5	-503	-3.7	12 800	13 689	-900	-6.5	1 100	600
Codington	15.6	13.6	9.0	8.0	8.2	7.7	51.5	1 813	8.7	22 500	20 885	1 600	7.5	2 400	1 300
Corson	13.7	10.7	9.7	9.2	6.4	4.4	49.2	-1 001	-19.3	5 000	5 196	-200	-3.2	800	300
Custer	13.6	16.5	11.3	10.4	8.5	6.4	49.4	179	3.0	6 900	6 000	900	15.6	600	400
Davison	15.1	13.1	8.7	8.5	8.6	8.8	52.3	-317	-1.8	17 400	17 820	-400	-2.1	2 000	1 200
Day	12.3	11.7	9.0	10.8	11.5	11.7	50.8	-1 155	-14.2	7 900	8 133	-300	-3.4	800	700
Deuel	13.0	12.1	10.6	11.3	10.6	10.1	48.9	-767	-14.5	5 000	5 289	-200	-4.7	500	400
Dewey	16.4	11.3	8.1	7.3	4.9	3.4	50.9	157	2.9	5 500	5 366	100	2.1	1 000	300
Douglas	12.0	11.3	9.5	10.4	9.7	11.2	50.8	-435	-10.4	4 000	4 181	-200	-5.2	400	300
Edmunds	12.4	11.0	10.4	11.8	12.0	10.9	50.3	-803	-15.6	5 000	5 159	-200	-3.9	500	400
Fall River	11.7	15.2	11.1	12.1	12.4	8.4	48.2	-1 086	-12.9	7 800	8 439	-700	-8.2	800	800
Faulk	12.5	11.0	10.6	12.8	11.0	9.8	50.2	-583	-17.5	3 100	3 327	-300	-7.5	400	300
Grant	14.6	13.7	8.9	9.2	9.2	8.8	50.4	-641	-7.1	8 900	9 013	-100	-1.1	1 000	600
Gregory	12.4	12.4	9.4	9.9	11.3	11.3	51.4	-656	-10.9	5 700	6 015	-300	-4.6	600	500
Haakon	14.5	14.1	8.6	7.5	7.7	6.8	51.1	-170	-6.1	2 800	2 794	0	-0.1	400	200
Hamlin	11.4	12.2	8.6	10.1	11.6	11.0	50.9	-287	-5.5	5 200	5 261	0	-0.3	500	500
Hand	13.1	11.8	9.6	12.2	11.0	9.4	50.8	-676	-13.7	4 700	4 948	-300	-6.0	400	300
Hanson	12.7	12.5	10.2	10.6	9.5	6.7	49.7	-421	-12.3	3 300	3 415	-100	-3.9	300	200
Harding	15.8	14.5	8.4	8.3	8.0	5.8	48.2	-31	-1.8	1 800	1 700	100	4.5	200	100
Hughes	16.6	16.7	10.2	8.3	6.5	5.4	52.3	597	4.2	14 900	14 220	700	4.7	1 600	700
Hutchinson	11.7	11.5	9.2	11.5	12.9	12.9	50.3	-1 088	-11.6	8 700	9 350	-700	-7.5	800	800
Hyde	13.4	12.0	8.7	12.1	10.6	12.9	52.7	-373	-18.0	1 900	2 069	-200	-7.6	200	200
Jackson	13.4	12.7	9.3	8.5	6.5	6.1	49.9	-626	-18.2	3 400	3 437	-100	-2.1	400	200
Jerauld	11.0	12.7	10.4	10.4	12.6	11.6	50.4	-504	-17.2	2 800	2 929	-100	-4.3	300	200
Jones	13.4	13.4	10.4	11.3	9.8	7.3	48.2	-139	-9.5	1 500	1 463	0	1.3	200	100
Kingsbury	12.3	12.4	9.1	11.3	11.5	12.3	51.5	-754	-11.3	6 300	6 679	-300	-5.0	600	600
Lake	14.8	12.7	8.3	9.0	9.2	9.0	51.3	-174	-1.6	10 800	10 724	100	1.0	1 100	700
Lawrence	15.4	14.6	8.5	8.2	7.8	6.5	50.8	2 316	12.6	19 400	18 339	1 100	6.0	2 000	1 100
Lincoln	15.9	15.6	9.1	7.8	7.2	7.1	50.3	1 485	10.7	14 400	13 942	400	3.0	1 500	800
Lyman	14.6	12.4	9.4	9.5	7.7	5.7	49.1	-226	-5.8	3 700	3 864	-100	-3.8	500	200
McCook	12.2	12.2	9.0	10.5	11.3	11.4	50.8	-756	-11.7	6 100	6 444	-300	-5.2	600	500
McPherson	10.0	11.1	10.4	13.9	14.3	13.2	51.2	-799	-19.8	3 600	4 027	-400	-9.5	300	300
Marshall	12.3	12.5	10.1	11.0	10.7	11.1	49.9	-560	-10.4	5 000	5 404	-400	-6.9	500	400
Meade	18.1	15.3	8.0	6.8	5.6	4.2	48.2	1 161	5.6	23 500	20 717	2 700	13.2	2 600	800
Mellette	13.4	12.4	8.8	8.8	7.1	6.0	50.3	-112	-5.0	2 300	2 249	0	2.1	300	200
Miner	12.4	11.2	8.2	11.2	11.9	12.6	50.2	-467	-12.5	3 500	3 739	-300	-7.3	300	400
Minnehaha	19.1	15.0	8.9	7.7	6.4	5.2	51.9	14 374	13.1	122 700	109 435	13 200	12.1	12 300	5 500
Moody	13.7	13.4	9.3	8.3	9.7	8.0	49.9	-185	-2.8	6 700	6 692	0	0.2	800	400
Pennington	18.6	14.7	8.9	7.5	5.7	4.3	50.5	10 982	15.6	76 900	70 361	6 500	9.3	10 100	3 200
Perkins	13.9	13.7	9.6	10.9	11.8	9.3	50.2	-768	-16.3	4 600	4 700	-100	-1.3	400	300
Potter	12.2	12.9	9.9	10.9	10.4	11.0	50.8	-484	-13.2	3 700	3 674	0	0.0	400	300
Roberts	12.2	12.1	9.8	9.8	9.1	9.7	49.9	-997	-9.1	11 000	10 911	100	0.6	1 300	800
Sanborn	14.0	12.4	8.7	11.4	10.5	8.5	49.1	-380	-11.8	3 000	3 213	-200	-5.7	300	300
Shannon	14.1	10.6	7.7	5.5	3.3	2.0	49.3	-1 421	-12.5	12 800	11 323	1 400	12.7	2 400	600
Spink	14.5	13.4	9.0	10.8	9.7	8.7	51.4	-1 220	-13.3	8 900	9 201	-300	-2.9	900	600
Stanley	15.2	14.3	11.9	8.6	6.1	4.7	50.1	-80	-3.2	2 700	2 533	100	5.4	300	100
Sully	14.9	12.9	12.5	10.3	8.1	7.1	49.2	-401	-20.2	1 900	1 990	-100	-3.4	200	100
Todd	14.5	11.6	6.8	5.9	3.7	1.9	50.5	1 024	14.0	6 800	7 328	-500	-6.6	1 600	400
Tripp	14.2	12.4	9.8	10.0	9.8	7.4	50.1	-344	-4.7	7 200	7 268	-100	-0.9	900	500
Turner	12.4	13.0	9.3	10.8	10.9	11.6	50.9	-679	-7.3	8 700	9 255	-600	-6.1	800	800
Union	13.9	14.8	9.2	9.4	9.0	7.6	50.7	-749	-6.8	10 500	10 938	-500	-4.3	1 100	700
Walworth	12.0	12.7	11.1	11.7	10.6	10.3	51.7	-924	-13.2	6 700	7 011	-300	-4.3	700	600
Yankton	16.9	14.1	9.8	8.5	7.7	7.3	51.0	300	1.6	18 800	18 952	-200	-0.8	2 000	1 000
Ziebach	15.5	10.1	8.0	7.9	5.0	2.8	50.0	-88	-3.8	2 500	2 308	200	9.2	400	100

Table A. States and Counties — **Population, Households, and Vital Statistics**

STATE County	Population–(cont'd) Components of change, 1980-1986 (cont'd) Net migration	Households, 1990 Number	Households, 1990 Percent change, 1980–1990	Households, 1990 Persons per household	Households, 1990 Percent Female family householder[1]	Households, 1990 Percent One-person	Births, 1988 Total	Births, 1988 Rate[2]	Births, 1988 Low birth weight[3] (Number)	Deaths, 1987 Number Total	Deaths, 1987 Number Infant[4]	Deaths, 1987 Rate Total[2]	Deaths, 1987 Rate Infant[5]	Marriages, 1984 Number	Marriages, 1984 Rate[2]
	29	30	31	32	33	34	35	36	37	38	39	40	41	42	43
SOUTH DAKOTA	-20 000	259 034	6.8	2.59	8.0	26.4	11 194	15.7	523	6 672	114	9.4	9.9	8 057	11.4
Aurora	-300	1 146	-7.9	2.54	4.8	27.6	36	10.6	1	58	0	17.1	0.0	21	6.0
Beadle	-1 500	7 341	0.1	2.43	6.9	29.3	262	14.3	11	194	1	10.5	3.8	172	9.3
Bennett	100	1 030	7.3	3.07	12.8	24.0	62	18.2	4	44	2	12.9	30.3	52	15.8
Bon Homme	-1 400	2 647	-7.4	2.44	4.2	28.3	95	14.0	3	87	1	12.8	11.0	74	10.7
Brookings	-1 100	8 910	10.9	2.48	5.9	27.3	322	13.3	16	151	3	6.3	9.3	208	8.3
Brown	-2 000	13 867	3.8	2.45	7.8	28.4	502	13.6	25	348	4	9.5	8.0	403	11.0
Brule	-100	1 996	6.3	2.58	5.3	30.1	75	14.4	5	65	0	12.3	0.0	51	9.4
Buffalo	-400	446	0.2	3.88	25.8	10.8	54	30.0	1	18	1	10.6	17.2	4	2.4
Butte	-400	3 033	-0.5	2.57	7.4	26.8	121	14.8	6	94	3	11.5	24.4	87	10.5
Campbell	-100	767	-4.6	2.53	3.5	23.6	25	11.4	1	21	0	9.5	0.0	16	7.0
Charles Mix	-900	3 232	0.1	2.75	8.3	27.6	152	16.3	5	123	1	13.2	6.1	77	8.1
Clark	-200	1 700	-8.4	2.56	3.4	26.8	69	14.7	3	55	1	11.5	14.5	36	7.2
Clay	-1 500	4 433	0.2	2.40	7.7	29.2	142	11.1	4	102	1	8.0	6.2	127	9.5
Codington	400	8 739	13.9	2.55	7.3	28.1	331	14.6	16	201	6	8.8	17.6	432	19.6
Corson	-700	1 303	-10.1	3.22	13.3	21.3	105	21.9	7	48	1	10.0	10.4	24	4.7
Custer	700	2 352	11.8	2.52	7.7	24.0	83	12.2	7	69	0	10.1	0.0	83	12.4
Davison	-1 200	6 948	4.4	2.44	7.3	31.6	262	15.0	11	187	2	10.7	7.6	200	11.2
Day	-400	2 732	-8.3	2.50	5.6	28.4	109	14.3	6	88	0	11.4	0.0	95	12.0
Deuel	-300	1 767	-5.6	2.52	4.9	25.1	72	14.7	6	50	0	10.2	0.0	57	11.0
Dewey	-600	1 721	12.4	3.21	21.2	21.6	150	27.8	11	54	2	9.8	13.1	31	5.6
Douglas	-400	1 352	-5.1	2.69	2.8	25.7	55	14.1	1	40	2	10.3	30.3	21	5.4
Edmunds	-300	1 669	-5.8	2.53	3.7	26.1	61	12.7	2	51	0	10.4	0.0	34	6.9
Fall River	-700	2 864	-5.3	2.34	8.3	31.6	87	11.4	6	145	1	18.8	12.5	111	14.1
Faulk	-400	1 057	-12.3	2.55	3.1	28.0	39	13.0	0	35	0	11.7	0.0	22	6.9
Grant	-500	3 154	-0.6	2.60	5.0	26.3	129	14.2	10	99	1	11.0	8.3	181	19.3
Gregory	-400	2 139	-4.3	2.47	5.4	32.3	73	13.0	1	86	0	15.1	0.0	48	8.1
Haakon	-200	926	-4.2	2.79	3.7	27.8	30	11.1	3	24	0	8.6	0.0	13	4.5
Hamlin	-100	1 854	-1.7	2.60	4.5	27.6	64	12.3	3	84	0	16.2	0.0	36	6.8
Hand	-400	1 625	-8.1	2.55	4.5	26.1	50	10.9	0	54	0	11.7	0.0	44	9.2
Hanson	-300	1 072	-6.2	2.79	3.5	23.6	38	11.5	2	19	0	5.8	0.0	10	3.0
Harding	-100	592	1.7	2.75	4.6	23.1	28	16.5	0	15	0	8.8	0.0	13	7.2
Hughes	-300	5 780	11.6	2.52	8.6	28.9	229	15.1	12	109	2	7.2	9.1	240	16.3
Hutchinson	-700	3 221	-5.7	2.47	3.6	28.2	99	11.6	1	114	0	13.3	0.0	51	5.6
Hyde	-200	680	-7.4	2.43	3.5	31.3	27	15.0	1	21	0	12.4	0.0	15	7.5
Jackson	-300	903	-8.2	3.09	10.5	22.9	59	17.9	1	24	3	7.1	39.0	18	5.3
Jerauld	-200	966	-10.5	2.47	4.0	28.5	26	9.3	1	36	0	12.9	0.0	23	8.2
Jones	-100	519	-6.3	2.55	5.0	25.0	30	21.4	0	13	0	9.3	0.0	16	10.7
Kingsbury	-300	2 357	-6.7	2.44	3.6	29.3	75	11.9	4	105	0	16.4	0.0	54	8.3
Lake	-400	4 030	2.3	2.50	5.3	28.3	107	10.3	2	120	3	11.5	20.7	87	8.2
Lawrence	200	7 926	17.6	2.48	8.1	28.1	275	14.0	21	163	4	8.3	14.4	262	13.8
Lincoln	-300	5 461	14.1	2.77	5.2	20.3	195	13.1	6	134	0	9.1	0.0	76	5.4
Lyman	-400	1 268	1.4	2.87	9.9	24.3	66	17.8	2	26	0	7.0	0.0	14	3.6
McCook	-400	2 145	-5.2	2.57	4.6	26.6	82	13.7	4	71	0	11.8	0.0	48	7.7
McPherson	-400	1 332	-12.4	2.38	3.5	26.4	32	8.9	1	47	0	13.1	0.0	41	10.8
Marshall	-400	1 919	-2.4	2.49	5.5	28.2	55	11.0	0	63	1	12.6	18.5	36	6.9
Meade	1 000	7 084	11.3	2.89	7.4	18.3	332	14.0	19	138	3	5.9	8.7	170	7.6
Mellette	-100	681	-0.6	3.06	16.2	22.2	51	22.2	4	16	0	7.3	0.0	25	10.9
Miner	-200	1 276	-7.7	2.50	4.6	28.4	48	14.1	0	37	0	10.9	0.0	32	8.9
Minnehaha	6 300	47 681	19.0	2.50	8.8	27.0	1 999	15.9	94	936	21	7.6	10.7	1 447	12.2
Moody	-300	2 398	0.5	2.68	6.3	24.3	103	15.4	1	73	0	10.9	0.0	60	8.8
Pennington	-300	30 553	21.4	2.61	10.2	23.4	1 708	20.8	90	546	16	6.8	8.8	1 202	15.9
Perkins	-200	1 586	-9.4	2.44	5.2	28.6	39	8.5	2	58	2	12.6	40.8	30	6.4
Potter	-100	1 249	-5.2	2.50	4.8	28.2	52	14.4	0	53	1	14.7	25.6	28	7.6
Roberts	-400	3 619	-2.2	2.68	9.7	26.8	171	15.8	7	110	2	10.2	11.5	215	19.7
Sanborn	-300	1 059	-8.5	2.63	3.7	25.2	48	16.6	2	32	0	11.0	0.0	22	7.1
Shannon	-300	2 205	-4.4	4.45	33.3	12.2	407	34.8	11	102	15	8.9	36.1	12	1.1
Spink	-500	3 022	-6.6	2.51	5.7	29.4	111	12.9	3	118	0	13.6	0.0	68	7.6
Stanley	-100	921	6.8	2.66	10.3	24.1	37	13.7	1	19	0	7.3	0.0	20	8.0
Sully	-200	621	-9.2	2.56	3.5	23.8	22	12.2	0	15	0	7.9	0.0	18	9.5
Todd	-1 700	2 210	17.7	3.74	28.7	16.7	243	31.6	16	56	2	7.4	7.9	5	0.7
Tripp	-400	2 573	0.4	2.65	7.0	25.8	109	15.6	4	84	2	12.0	18.2	82	11.4
Turner	-600	3 332	-4.2	2.51	4.1	26.1	86	9.9	6	122	0	13.9	0.0	69	7.6
Union	-800	3 859	-1.8	2.61	6.5	24.8	153	14.4	7	89	0	8.6	0.0	430	40.2
Walworth	-400	2 447	-4.2	2.42	7.0	27.4	76	11.5	5	96	0	14.5	0.0	68	10.1
Yankton	-1 200	7 107	7.3	2.51	7.8	28.3	303	16.0	14	201	4	10.7	13.9	273	14.3
Ziebach	-100	630	5.0	3.52	17.1	20.6	56	23.3	4	16	0	6.7	0.0	17	6.8

1. No spouse present. 2. Per 1,000 resident population estimated as of July 1 of the year shown. 3. Under 2,500 grams. 4. Deaths of infants under 1 year old. 5. Deaths of infants under 1 year old per 1,000 live births.

STATE County	Divorces, 1984		Physicians, active non–Federal, 1989		Hospitals, 1989			Nursing homes,[4] 1986		Serious crimes known to police, 1988			Education			
						Beds				Number			Public school enrollment[7]		Attainment,[8] 1980	
	Number	Rate[1]	Number[2]	Rate[3]	Number	Number	Rate[3]	Number	Beds	Total[5]	Violent[6]	Rate[3]	1986–1987	1980	Percent 12 yrs. or more	Percent 16 yrs. or more
	44	45	46	47	48	49	50	51	52	53	54	55	56	57	58	59
SOUTH DAKOTA	2 498	3.5	991	139	66	5 338	747	136	8 279	13 718	574	2 536	122 247	133 965	67.9	14.0
Aurora	10	2.9	0	0	0	0	0	2	130	14	0	421	622	838	59.5	8.7
Beadle	66	3.6	22	120	1	98	536	2	221	396	20	2 123	3 284	3 402	67.4	12.9
Bennett	9	2.7	0	0	1	68	2 000	1	50	NA	NA	NA	599	730	60.3	9.4
Bon Homme	10	1.4	4	60	2	57	851	3	142	34	0	496	1 439	1 478	55.9	11.0
Brookings	86	3.4	19	79	1	132	550	5	235	532	7	3 608	3 688	3 780	74.6	24.3
Brown	150	4.1	70	191	1	200	545	5	467	1 298	40	3 507	5 887	6 884	71.8	14.5
Brule	15	2.8	8	154	1	54	1 038	1	58	81	6	3 687	1 415	1 106	63.6	11.3
Buffalo	1	0.6	1	53	0	0	0	0	0	NA	NA	NA	NA	459	60.5	7.2
Butte	45	5.4	7	85	1	128	1 561	3	116	139	3	3 029	1 625	1 774	65.6	12.4
Campbell	3	1.3	0	0	0	0	0	1	27	NA	NA	NA	296	482	54.5	9.2
Charles Mix	14	1.5	7	75	3	112	1 204	3	177	NA	NA	NA	1 810	2 022	56.6	9.5
Clark	12	2.4	0	0	0	0	0	1	45	15	0	310	771	909	60.1	8.3
Clay	33	2.5	9	71	1	25	197	3	179	364	4	2 820	1 594	1 986	79.2	30.6
Codington	86	3.9	34	149	1	122	535	4	243	661	8	3 897	4 191	4 078	68.6	11.7
Corson	11	2.2	0	0	0	0	0	0	0	NA	NA	NA	849	1 353	51.1	7.9
Custer	26	3.9	7	103	1	11	162	1	80	163	4	2 309	1 148	1 193	68.1	13.4
Davison	53	3.0	32	184	2	133	764	7	359	862	27	6 240	2 915	3 264	68.1	14.5
Day	15	1.9	4	53	1	34	447	4	140	33	0	425	1 446	1 669	57.5	9.7
Deuel	10	1.9	2	42	1	20	417	1	85	74	3	1 529	718	1 138	55.9	8.2
Dewey	9	1.6	5	93	1	27	500	0	0	NA	NA	NA	1 322	1 344	55.6	9.9
Douglas	4	1.0	3	79	1	9	237	2	107	NA	NA	NA	652	774	47.8	7.9
Edmunds	10	2.0	3	64	1	20	426	3	137	27	5	558	862	1 033	54.2	9.8
Fall River	49	6.2	15	200	2	243	3 240	1	48	NA	NA	NA	1 470	1 496	65.3	13.4
Faulk	6	1.9	2	69	1	32	1 103	1	54	NA	NA	NA	419	693	60.8	8.8
Grant	20	2.1	3	33	1	115	1 278	2	158	16	1	176	1 668	1 885	62.7	9.8
Gregory	13	2.2	5	89	2	113	2 018	1	58	NA	NA	NA	1 111	1 173	59.7	9.2
Haakon	13	4.5	1	37	1	50	1 852	1	30	17	0	602	736	633	70.6	8.7
Hamlin	7	1.3	2	38	1	16	308	3	175	NA	NA	NA	1 174	1 065	57.3	7.4
Hand	6	1.3	3	67	1	30	667	1	78	23	1	507	694	948	64.2	10.1
Hanson	4	1.2	0	0	0	0	0	0	0	NA	NA	NA	574	708	59.2	6.5
Harding	2	1.1	0	0	0	0	0	0	0	2	0	117	343	363	63.9	11.8
Hughes	60	4.1	18	118	1	86	562	2	177	508	10	3 358	2 754	3 010	79.5	26.1
Hutchinson	6	0.7	9	107	2	178	2 119	6	300	NA	NA	NA	1 618	1 805	50.7	9.5
Hyde	4	2.0	0	0	0	0	0	1	48	9	0	525	320	476	67.1	13.0
Jackson	5	1.5	2	61	0	0	0	1	35	17	1	482	417	904	58.5	10.5
Jerauld	5	1.8	3	111	1	28	1 037	1	40	NA	NA	NA	645	599	61.0	9.1
Jones	4	2.7	0	0	0	0	0	0	0	10	1	661	263	324	66.3	11.4
Kingsbury	13	2.0	3	48	1	17	270	3	189	NA	NA	NA	1 122	1 242	62.3	9.6
Lake	26	2.5	6	59	1	49	480	2	121	249	3	2 351	1 912	1 873	66.9	13.3
Lawrence	93	4.9	23	116	2	70	354	4	145	556	17	3 092	3 229	3 231	75.1	16.3
Lincoln	29	2.0	6	40	1	28	187	4	269	80	0	681	2 978	2 735	66.7	11.1
Lyman	9	2.3	2	54	0	0	0	0	0	43	1	1 185	415	846	64.0	7.9
McCook	14	2.3	1	17	0	0	0	3	183	13	0	993	1 012	1 260	62.9	9.8
McPherson	5	1.3	2	56	1	25	694	1	62	NA	NA	NA	594	724	39.0	7.1
Marshall	13	2.5	3	61	1	38	776	1	63	77	1	1 527	906	1 233	55.3	9.1
Meade	77	3.4	14	59	3	500	2 092	5	140	122	1	2 255	2 989	4 376	74.8	15.5
Mellette	6	2.6	0	0	0	0	0	0	0	NA	NA	NA	568	528	54.7	10.7
Miner	5	1.4	0	0	0	0	0	1	76	38	0	1 142	579	670	57.8	7.3
Minnehaha	595	5.0	368	290	6	1 369	1 080	11	1 006	4 818	252	3 862	19 429	19 529	75.8	16.7
Moody	11	1.6	0	0	1	20	299	1	80	114	4	1 687	1 133	1 384	68.2	10.7
Pennington	473	6.3	165	197	3	385	459	8	470	1 444	112	1 797	16 394	13 568	78.8	18.3
Perkins	10	2.1	0	0	1	52	1 156	1	32	NA	NA	NA	691	952	63.7	10.1
Potter	5	1.4	6	167	2	58	1 611	1	70	18	1	482	626	687	60.8	10.1
Roberts	20	1.8	6	56	2	49	458	3	196	NA	NA	NA	2 016	2 552	55.1	8.2
Sanborn	3	1.0	0	0	0	0	0	1	52	NA	NA	NA	591	623	69.5	10.7
Shannon	1	0.1	9	79	1	46	404	0	0	NA	NA	NA	795	2 597	47.3	9.9
Spink	18	2.0	6	71	1	44	518	2	117	17	1	196	1 554	1 701	61.8	10.1
Stanley	10	4.0	0	0	0	0	0	0	0	11	2	629	595	614	67.9	14.6
Sully	6	3.2	0	0	0	0	0	0	0	6	0	313	449	470	71.7	13.1
Todd	14	1.9	6	74	1	29	358	0	0	NA	NA	NA	1 934	1 768	58.6	14.8
Tripp	28	3.9	5	72	1	35	507	1	81	NA	NA	NA	1 356	1 569	62.0	8.1
Turner	21	2.3	3	35	1	80	930	4	216	NA	NA	NA	1 474	1 727	61.3	9.7
Union	34	3.2	0	0	0	0	0	2	134	92	7	869	2 266	2 113	65.6	10.5
Walworth	25	3.7	6	92	1	46	708	2	191	164	0	3 958	1 163	1 448	62.2	9.9
Yankton	50	2.6	51	271	1	257	1 367	2	187	561	31	2 959	3 200	3 583	68.9	17.9
Ziebach	2	0.8	0	0	0	0	0	0	0	NA	NA	NA	565	584	57.8	8.3

1. Per 1,000 resident population estimated as of July 1 of the year shown. 2. As of end of year. 3. Per 100,000 resident population as of July 1 of the year shown. 4. Preliminary. Covers nursing homes with 3 or more beds. 5. Data for serious crimes have not been adjusted for underreporting, this may affect comparability between geographic areas or over time. 6. Includes murder and nonnegligent manslaughter, forcible rape, robbery, and aggravated assault. 7. The 1986–1987 data are based on administrative reports obtained by the U.S. National Center for Education Statistics. The 1980 data are based on the 1980 Census of Population and Housing. 8. Persons 25 years old or older.

STATE County	Education (cont'd): Local government expenditures for education,[1] 1982: Total (Mil dol)	Education (cont'd): Local government expenditures for education,[1] 1982: Per capita (Dollars)	Social Security Program December 1988: Beneficiaries: Total	Social Security Program December 1988: Beneficiaries: Rate[2]	Social Security Program December 1988: Payments ($1,000)	Supplemental Security Income Program recipients June 1986	Money income: Per capita[3]: 1987 Income, (Dollars)	Money income: Per capita[3]: 1979: Current dollars	Money income: Per capita[3]: 1979: Constant 1987 dollars	Money income: Median household income 1979 (Dollars)	Money income: Percent below poverty level, 1979: Persons	Money income: Percent below poverty level, 1979: Families	Housing units, 1990: Total	Housing units, 1990: Percent change, 1980–1990
	60	61	62	63	64	65	66	67	68	69	70	71	72	73
SOUTH DAKOTA	294.4	424	125 570	176.1	55 546	8 690	8 910	5 696	8 913	13 156	16.9	13.1	292 436	5.6
Aurora	1.8	487	705	207.4	284	34	7 379	4 373	6 842	10 372	24.0	19.6	1 342	-7.4
Beadle	7.7	404	3 935	215.0	1 776	254	9 362	6 259	9 793	13 398	14.0	10.7	8 093	-1.7
Bennett	1.8	575	490	144.1	201	72	6 336	3 965	6 204	9 904	33.5	27.1	1 292	12.7
Bon Homme	4.0	516	1 825	268.4	734	90	7 514	4 609	7 212	10 671	22.5	17.3	3 087	-4.7
Brookings	8.6	346	3 405	140.7	1 553	168	8 922	5 468	8 556	13 597	17.4	9.6	9 824	8.3
Brown	14.0	377	6 510	176.9	2 969	408	9 731	6 189	9 684	14 034	11.3	8.4	15 101	2.9
Brule	3.2	610	1 055	202.9	464	72	7 764	4 669	7 306	11 371	24.7	21.4	2 275	4.8
Buffalo	0.0	0	200	111.1	63	40	4 250	2 642	4 134	9 095	42.5	38.0	535	7.2
Butte	4.0	481	1 675	204.3	750	94	7 858	5 633	8 814	12 973	16.0	12.7	3 502	2.9
Campbell	1.0	454	530	240.9	207	40	6 889	4 042	6 325	9 037	30.9	27.1	944	-1.7
Charles Mix	4.4	450	1 945	209.1	778	196	6 698	4 128	6 459	10 119	28.8	23.3	3 751	-1.3
Clark	2.0	405	1 180	251.1	479	78	7 500	4 634	7 251	10 122	25.7	19.9	2 026	-6.9
Clay	4.0	290	1 795	140.2	836	92	8 529	5 443	8 517	11 820	19.3	10.9	4 892	-0.6
Codington	7.3	338	4 260	187.7	1 905	246	9 089	6 015	9 412	13 557	11.0	7.9	9 539	12.1
Corson	3.0	562	615	128.1	223	84	5 374	3 521	5 509	9 543	41.5	34.3	1 557	-7.5
Custer	2.2	349	1 235	181.6	537	144	8 516	5 974	9 348	15 166	13.5	10.2	3 003	7.8
Davison	7.3	415	3 775	215.7	1 690	282	8 686	5 675	8 880	12 399	14.0	9.4	7 490	3.6
Day	4.1	518	1 980	260.5	805	120	8 114	4 825	7 550	10 675	19.5	15.7	3 914	-3.0
Deuel	2.0	370	1 120	228.6	442	68	7 313	4 450	6 963	10 198	23.6	20.8	2 208	-5.2
Dewey	2.6	487	705	130.6	246	74	5 797	3 943	6 170	10 632	35.4	28.6	2 123	13.5
Douglas	1.7	433	915	234.6	363	26	6 080	3 774	5 905	9 329	29.1	25.7	1 517	-4.9
Edmunds	2.4	476	1 145	238.5	463	78	7 228	4 435	6 939	10 246	24.3	19.3	2 004	-5.1
Fall River	3.7	467	1 875	246.7	752	102	9 095	6 197	9 696	14 274	18.5	12.5	3 692	-7.6
Faulk	1.7	529	785	261.7	332	26	7 368	4 324	6 766	9 495	31.2	24.4	1 286	-9.8
Grant	4.1	443	1 870	205.5	813	92	8 302	5 200	8 136	12 613	13.2	9.9	3 549	-0.5
Gregory	2.8	483	1 505	268.8	601	86	6 355	4 417	6 911	8 898	25.8	22.9	2 595	-0.6
Haakon	1.6	555	470	174.1	221	16	7 137	4 924	7 705	12 076	20.6	18.4	1 071	-5.1
Hamlin	2.5	477	1 305	251.0	549	76	7 580	4 458	6 975	9 903	23.7	17.5	2 500	-2.1
Hand	2.2	448	920	200.0	382	36	7 763	4 892	7 655	10 352	28.4	22.6	2 053	1.7
Hanson	1.3	396	585	177.3	234	18	6 865	4 029	6 304	10 010	31.3	24.2	1 232	-1.7
Harding	1.0	598	260	152.9	118	4	6 832	5 132	8 030	12 385	23.8	19.1	776	-3.4
Hughes	6.1	424	2 275	149.7	1 058	134	10 553	7 217	11 292	17 458	7.1	4.9	6 255	11.6
Hutchinson	4.5	485	2 435	286.5	983	98	8 042	4 793	7 500	10 275	23.5	19.7	3 657	-5.4
Hyde	1.0	493	435	241.7	181	20	7 895	4 674	7 313	11 812	23.2	18.8	816	-5.4
Jackson	1.2	365	445	134.8	173	54	6 642	4 623	7 234	12 172	35.6	27.4	1 147	-11.5
Jerauld	1.9	639	700	250.0	286	36	8 573	4 794	7 501	10 600	20.3	15.6	1 182	-2.3
Jones	0.8	590	250	178.6	115	10	7 713	5 171	8 091	11 835	18.3	17.1	699	-3.6
Kingsbury	3.7	549	1 780	282.5	777	72	8 329	4 878	7 633	10 666	20.1	15.0	2 765	-9.1
Lake	4.4	401	2 320	223.1	1 042	120	8 837	5 378	8 415	12 028	15.0	11.9	5 148	1.3
Lawrence	6.8	364	3 545	179.9	1 726	192	8 579	5 821	9 108	13 590	14.3	10.3	9 092	14.3
Lincoln	6.0	438	2 210	148.3	1 002	116	9 105	6 047	9 462	15 221	11.0	9.8	5 823	8.9
Lyman	2.4	620	645	174.3	278	50	8 004	4 763	7 453	11 241	28.5	24.8	1 523	-3.5
McCook	3.1	494	1 430	238.3	582	70	8 148	4 837	7 568	11 250	19.0	16.6	2 371	-8.3
McPherson	1.8	450	1 040	288.9	400	62	6 954	4 277	6 692	8 975	27.2	20.8	1 566	-7.8
Marshall	2.7	502	1 195	239.0	502	74	8 657	4 928	7 711	10 262	22.8	18.3	2 640	-4.5
Meade	5.9	279	2 565	108.2	1 095	160	8 133	5 564	8 706	14 848	10.6	8.0	7 592	7.0
Mellette	1.6	703	290	126.1	112	74	5 684	3 581	5 603	9 672	38.9	32.8	910	4.8
Miner	1.8	499	985	289.7	397	42	7 742	4 201	6 573	8 429	32.5	27.8	1 474	-11.0
Minnehaha	42.2	376	18 405	146.7	9 027	1 196	10 838	7 206	11 275	16 891	8.7	6.5	49 780	16.6
Moody	2.6	380	1 270	189.6	554	52	8 929	5 494	8 596	12 695	15.9	13.7	2 666	-2.3
Pennington	31.8	440	10 475	127.7	4 927	796	9 689	6 594	10 318	14 890	12.2	9.5	33 741	19.6
Perkins	2.8	605	1 025	222.8	446	80	9 101	5 817	9 102	12 205	19.4	15.9	2 007	-3.6
Potter	1.7	455	835	231.9	368	32	8 104	4 759	7 446	11 266	21.0	17.2	1 664	8.5
Roberts	5.8	528	2 250	208.3	887	174	7 291	4 431	6 933	10 302	26.5	21.1	4 728	-0.8
Sanborn	1.5	473	800	275.9	309	34	6 767	3 918	6 130	7 972	35.1	32.6	1 326	-7.8
Shannon	5.0	439	915	78.2	243	502	3 943	2 637	4 126	9 948	44.7	43.3	2 699	1.2
Spink	4.5	494	2 010	233.7	881	188	8 897	5 141	8 044	12 080	20.0	15.9	3 545	-6.7
Stanley	1.5	619	365	135.2	169	20	9 056	6 111	9 562	14 807	13.0	11.2	1 056	9.1
Sully	1.6	847	280	155.6	130	6	8 537	4 731	7 403	11 875	21.8	19.8	811	-2.4
Todd	5.4	748	705	91.6	200	270	4 785	3 159	4 943	9 662	43.5	39.0	2 572	8.7
Tripp	3.1	441	1 420	202.9	618	110	7 890	5 077	7 944	11 071	23.5	18.9	3 023	-0.4
Turner	3.6	396	2 165	248.9	932	106	8 013	5 358	8 384	11 364	15.4	12.0	3 800	-5.5
Union	5.3	491	2 305	217.5	1 050	98	8 924	5 638	8 822	13 785	13.2	11.0	4 286	-3.7
Walworth	3.1	458	1 415	214.4	610	106	8 363	5 370	8 402	12 016	14.8	12.6	2 928	-1.2
Yankton	6.8	357	3 515	186.0	1 584	252	9 665	6 128	9 588	14 332	10.0	6.5	7 571	5.6
Ziebach	0.9	371	185	77.1	61	44	4 688	3 042	4 760	9 263	43.7	37.2	800	2.4

1. Elementary and secondary. 2. Per 1,000 resident population estimated as of July 1 of the year shown. 3. Based on the resident population estimated as of July 1, 1988 for 1987 data and enumerated as of April 1, 1980 for 1979 data.

STATE County	Housing units, 1990 (cont'd)				Civilian labor force, 1990				Private nonfarm establishments, 1988					
	Occupied units						Unemployment				Employment[2]			
		Owner occupied												
	Total	Percent	Median value (Dollars)	Median rent (Dollars)	Total	Percent change, 1989–1990	Total	Rate[1]	Number	Net change, 1987–1988	Total	Percent change, 1987–1988	Manufacturing	Retail trade
	74	75	76	77	78	79	80	81	82	83	84	85	86	87
SOUTH DAKOTA	259 034	66.1	45 200	242	360 000	-0.3	13 000	3.7	X	X	193 904	3.6	29 408	50 119
Aurora	1 146	76.7	15 500	128	1 469	1.4	25	1.7	81	0	342	2.1	0	101
Beadle	7 341	65.8	34 200	198	9 081	-2.7	338	3.7	604	-3	5 654	7.4	1 041	1 359
Bennett	1 030	65.0	29 500	164	1 505	-3.8	60	4.0	64	1	366	-1.9	0	150
Bon Homme	2 647	75.8	25 100	141	3 440	-0.5	42	1.2	207	1	1 259	3.2	314	267
Brookings	8 910	58.6	51 200	254	14 965	-1.6	728	4.9	604	21	6 156	11.4	1 672	1 785
Brown	13 867	62.9	46 600	243	19 920	-2.1	985	4.9	1 212	20	13 185	2.8	2 417	3 629
Brule	1 996	72.5	41 300	179	2 753	0.5	57	2.1	193	6	1 341	-1.3	55	420
Buffalo	446	42.4	14 999	99	439	-6.2	39	8.9	16	-2	61	-33.0	0	0
Butte	3 033	68.0	38 700	195	3 500	0.3	150	4.3	253	-7	1 570	-1.8	39	485
Campbell	767	82.5	16 400	135	1 097	0.9	31	2.8	52	0	264	9.5	0	78
Charles Mix	3 232	67.9	27 200	127	3 816	-1.5	141	3.7	249	5	1 570	2.4	47	411
Clark	1 700	78.4	18 700	131	1 880	-5.0	73	3.9	116	6	642	49.3	211	111
Clay	4 433	52.9	47 800	240	7 182	1.5	329	4.6	281	-2	1 990	4.1	145	827
Codington	8 739	67.6	50 600	228	12 458	0.0	497	4.0	748	1	8 166	4.9	2 272	2 313
Corson	1 303	59.2	18 100	106	1 584	2.5	210	13.3	66	6	259	8.4	0	79
Custer	2 352	71.9	45 200	220	3 912	5.6	98	2.5	173	-3	773	-8.6	50	229
Davison	6 948	60.5	38 400	215	9 212	-2.5	198	2.1	621	6	6 411	-0.4	1 065	2 049
Day	2 732	73.8	22 500	156	3 262	-4.0	152	4.7	205	3	1 381	3.4	0	320
Deuel	1 767	78.5	23 100	171	2 235	0.7	102	4.6	116	-14	662	0.0	45	132
Dewey	1 721	49.2	23 700	99	2 043	-2.2	199	9.7	93	-1	483	12.1	0	166
Douglas	1 352	78.6	19 600	133	1 624	-3.9	48	3.0	111	3	566	-2.9	11	112
Edmunds	1 669	79.4	22 700	140	1 996	-5.7	62	3.1	108	9	566	3.1	44	114
Fall River	2 864	65.6	34 100	205	3 280	-4.3	138	4.2	179	-16	1 019	4.6	102	379
Faulk	1 057	80.1	17 900	140	1 162	-1.4	26	2.2	65	1	275	-4.8	0	76
Grant	3 154	73.2	36 600	186	4 099	-4.8	155	3.8	248	7	2 363	-3.4	457	463
Gregory	2 139	73.0	26 300	136	2 365	-0.8	59	2.5	155	4	854	0.8	53	221
Haakon	926	73.2	33 800	168	1 168	-0.6	29	2.5	77	2	515	6.4	0	148
Hamlin	1 854	77.8	22 800	131	2 447	-0.2	92	3.8	117	4	441	0.0	11	97
Hand	1 625	71.1	32 600	153	1 851	-6.5	42	2.3	127	-1	847	11.6	54	200
Hanson	1 072	74.8	19 900	152	1 428	-5.1	46	3.2	56	1	235	6.8	0	89
Harding	592	73.3	33 300	150	822	5.2	23	2.8	39	0	171	-20.8	0	41
Hughes	5 780	63.2	58 700	272	8 397	-1.1	202	2.4	509	4	4 415	4.4	143	1 392
Hutchinson	3 221	79.1	25 000	141	4 035	-4.9	90	2.2	250	-5	1 710	3.1	351	436
Hyde	680	72.2	21 900	140	836	-6.9	22	2.6	51	0	311	-4.9	0	47
Jackson	903	63.7	22 100	135	1 663	0.4	66	4.0	60	5	297	38.8	0	104
Jerauld	966	72.8	18 200	140	1 130	-5.3	36	3.2	63	3	387	10.3	0	103
Jones	519	76.9	23 400	170	673	1.2	36	5.3	57	2	235	7.3	0	123
Kingsbury	2 357	73.8	22 800	146	2 662	-5.7	80	3.0	189	-18	1 175	6.1	167	355
Lake	4 030	67.5	37 600	186	5 060	-3.3	265	5.2	298	10	2 723	4.7	675	751
Lawrence	7 926	64.2	52 300	250	12 592	11.7	510	4.1	613	-22	5 592	2.8	566	1 372
Lincoln	5 461	79.3	49 100	207	7 124	-2.5	182	2.6	325	1	2 555	10.0	489	534
Lyman	1 268	73.3	30 200	135	1 461	-5.6	69	4.7	75	3	432	3.8	0	244
McCook	2 145	77.0	22 500	155	2 803	-3.4	98	3.5	180	-10	1 003	-2.3	200	225
McPherson	1 332	81.3	14 999	127	1 494	-2.4	48	3.2	101	-10	472	-4.3	33	113
Marshall	1 919	73.0	22 900	143	2 217	-4.8	90	4.1	136	5	817	8.6	289	149
Meade	7 084	66.8	50 600	246	9 614	4.9	361	3.8	366	-1	2 254	4.1	199	755
Mellette	681	65.9	14 999	128	884	4.4	46	5.2	23	2	104	7.2	0	38
Miner	1 276	74.8	19 600	138	1 495	-8.2	48	3.2	96	3	763	34.3	0	118
Minnehaha	47 681	62.3	58 400	331	75 833	0.8	2 070	2.7	3 882	89	60 739	2.3	8 626	13 526
Moody	2 398	71.2	33 100	165	3 181	-4.0	179	5.6	151	5	1 217	4.1	0	224
Pennington	30 553	61.4	56 600	320	40 347	0.9	1 440	3.6	2 590	19	26 646	2.4	3 366	7 799
Perkins	1 586	76.3	25 700	142	2 291	-2.0	58	2.5	143	-6	928	3.7	0	249
Potter	1 249	75.3	29 300	157	1 426	-4.1	42	2.9	124	-6	547	-3.5	67	125
Roberts	3 619	66.5	24 100	132	4 627	0.5	228	4.9	250	-1	1 493	0.4	0	385
Sanborn	1 059	77.2	14 999	129	1 115	1.7	43	3.9	53	-5	392	1.8	0	53
Shannon	2 205	44.9	14 999	108	2 345	2.5	238	10.1	47	5	709	20.8	0	78
Spink	3 022	70.9	20 300	160	3 601	0.5	99	2.7	190	3	915	-3.8	35	240
Stanley	921	73.6	48 300	240	1 361	-10.1	57	4.2	59	-4	424	9.0	0	125
Sully	621	72.6	28 400	174	754	-3.3	18	2.4	50	-1	213	-15.5	0	111
Todd	2 210	46.4	14 999	110	2 623	-4.1	199	7.6	57	4	637	1.9	0	119
Tripp	2 573	73.6	35 600	175	3 242	-2.8	93	2.9	210	-6	1 304	6.9	0	400
Turner	3 332	76.1	22 800	145	4 284	-2.5	108	2.5	229	13	1 053	11.2	29	304
Union	3 859	72.7	37 600	180	6 102	6.3	288	4.7	190	10	1 962	9.2	892	214
Walworth	2 447	71.5	27 600	207	2 871	-2.7	88	3.1	247	-8	1 550	1.6	0	470
Yankton	7 107	66.0	48 500	224	10 735	-1.1	262	2.4	629	40	7 386	10.4	1 985	1 943
Ziebach	630	58.3	14 999	99	1 127	-0.9	65	5.8	18	0	71	2.9	0	33

1. Percent of total civilian labor force. 2. For week including March 12. Excludes government employees, self-employed persons, farm workers, domestic service workers, railroad employees subject to the Railroad Retirement Act, and employees on oceanborne vessels or in foreign countries.

STATE County	Private nonfarm establishments, 1988 (cont'd)				Personal income, 1989								Earnings, 1989		
	Employment[1] (cont'd)		Annual payroll								Per capita[3]			Percent by selected industries	
	Finance, insurance, and real estate	Services	Total (Mil dol)	Average per employee (Dollars)	Total (Mil dol)	Percent change, 1988–1989	Wages and salaries[2] (Mil dol)	Proprietor's income (Mil dol)	Dividends, interest, & rent (Mil dol)	Transfer payments (Mil dol)	Dollars	Rank	Total (Mil dol)	Farm	Goods-related[4] Total
	88	89	90	91	92	93	94	95	96	97	98	99	100	101	102
SOUTH DAKOTA	13 913	58 570	2 890	X	9 893	8.9	4 965	1 868	1 897	1 620	13 852	X	6 833	13.4	16.6
Aurora	0	102	4	10 795	40	15.3	10	12	10	8	12 092	2 292	22	40.6	NA
Beadle	289	1 899	75	13 332	276	10.1	132	49	61	49	15 123	933	181	14.4	19.3
Bennett	0	35	4	11 199	42	28.0	12	16	6	8	12 454	2 141	28	49.9	NA
Bon Homme	60	303	14	11 487	100	10.3	27	32	24	17	14 814	1 070	59	38.1	13.2
Brookings	314	1 325	85	13 873	322	9.4	179	51	56	52	13 430	1 720	230	10.7	24.5
Brown	680	4 297	192	14 530	536	5.1	293	79	107	87	14 593	1 169	372	8.0	17.9
Brule	74	551	16	11 665	72	13.7	25	18	18	12	14 002	1 436	43	23.6	7.8
Buffalo	0	23	1	12 754	14	19.7	7	5	1	4	7 695	3 087	11	41.0	NA
Butte	96	400	19	12 187	101	9.9	35	21	24	19	12 290	2 201	56	15.2	NA
Campbell	0	33	3	9 655	28	1.7	7	11	7	4	12 870	1 968	18	51.0	NA
Charles Mix	0	808	16	10 098	115	12.1	34	36	26	23	12 463	2 136	70	30.5	4.3
Clark	43	112	6	9 685	69	12.9	14	28	16	11	14 697	1 130	42	56.8	9.2
Clay	82	750	18	8 899	162	7.3	68	36	30	29	12 729	2 022	104	18.4	4.9
Codington	411	2 054	115	14 132	308	9.8	175	45	60	50	13 487	1 690	221	7.1	31.2
Corson	0	20	3	9 954	37	-1.2	10	8	7	10	7 731	3 086	18	30.4	NA
Custer	35	236	12	15 003	91	8.2	32	14	18	22	13 383	1 739	46	9.8	16.0
Davison	249	1 851	89	13 883	257	9.7	140	37	53	47	14 796	1 079	177	5.1	22.4
Day	76	383	17	12 471	102	15.3	29	29	24	22	13 568	1 651	58	37.3	13.7
Deuel	79	188	9	13 269	59	8.7	16	16	16	11	12 187	2 242	32	28.9	NA
Dewey	0	133	6	12 236	46	3.4	25	10	7	11	8 435	3 048	35	18.5	NA
Douglas	0	199	6	10 353	44	8.8	12	13	12	8	11 347	2 554	25	29.8	NA
Edmunds	38	231	6	10 470	55	-0.1	13	13	16	12	11 702	2 439	26	30.8	5.7
Fall River	36	351	10	9 813	104	5.1	49	23	16	24	13 793	1 537	72	21.5	7.9
Faulk	0	103	3	10 044	39	3.5	8	11	13	8	13 302	1 771	19	41.6	NA
Grant	272	469	39	16 331	114	7.4	57	22	26	19	12 719	2 027	79	14.1	21.9
Gregory	110	247	10	11 610	68	11.8	18	18	18	17	12 125	2 275	35	25.2	6.4
Haakon	0	118	6	12 173	38	-1.2	12	13	10	5	14 265	1 299	25	32.2	NA
Hamlin	48	157	5	10 966	61	9.8	15	17	14	14	11 847	2 380	33	38.1	NA
Hand	69	262	9	10 908	66	12.1	17	23	17	10	14 715	1 118	40	39.2	NA
Hanson	47	6	3	10 804	36	9.9	8	11	9	5	10 924	2 680	18	44.0	NA
Harding	0	0	3	15 860	21	-1.6	6	6	8	3	12 479	2 126	12	37.6	NA
Hughes	402	1 967	55	12 556	229	9.3	141	31	39	34	14 944	1 012	172	6.7	5.9
Hutchinson	81	551	19	11 236	123	14.4	33	40	34	21	14 675	1 141	73	37.5	12.1
Hyde	0	150	4	11 904	25	9.3	6	6	9	5	14 739	1 111	12	32.9	NA
Jackson	0	145	4	12 525	24	6.8	8	5	5	6	7 303	3 094	13	26.0	NA
Jerauld	0	145	4	9 798	33	13.0	8	10	8	7	11 855	2 378	18	34.9	NA
Jones	0	46	3	12 643	21	9.4	6	8	4	3	15 285	878	14	42.4	NA
Kingsbury	82	372	13	11 466	94	13.2	24	33	21	18	15 078	951	57	40.4	10.7
Lake	91	650	37	13 547	154	9.8	60	41	28	27	15 062	961	102	26.4	16.2
Lawrence	145	1 264	103	18 416	272	8.5	176	30	51	46	13 733	1 560	206	1.5	49.8
Lincoln	209	821	33	12 885	208	8.4	55	45	33	27	13 856	1 503	100	27.1	20.5
Lyman	0	28	4	9 472	47	15.5	14	17	11	8	12 679	2 043	31	45.2	NA
McCook	55	291	12	11 674	85	9.6	21	27	19	14	14 096	1 391	48	36.5	10.4
McPherson	51	153	4	9 400	44	10.8	10	13	13	9	12 284	2 203	24	39.2	6.2
Marshall	31	162	10	12 230	67	10.4	19	19	19	13	13 745	1 555	38	40.5	NA
Meade	163	559	25	11 203	279	9.2	69	32	40	39	11 667	2 455	101	11.2	11.5
Mellette	0	0	1	8 644	22	9.7	4	7	4	6	9 717	2 924	11	43.0	NA
Miner	49	409	8	10 304	50	15.8	12	18	11	9	14 923	1 018	30	40.1	NA
Minnehaha	6 375	18 191	1 066	17 550	2 080	8.4	1 465	256	323	253	16 412	541	1 721	2.2	18.1
Moody	83	260	19	15 359	91	10.5	31	30	19	13	13 492	1 685	61	36.3	NA
Pennington	1 478	8 385	413	15 514	1 170	8.0	813	142	200	176	13 944	1 454	955	1.2	16.1
Perkins	54	237	9	9 948	63	8.9	18	18	17	11	13 874	1 495	37	26.2	NA
Potter	0	213	6	11 320	46	-4.0	14	10	15	9	12 918	1 945	24	18.9	NA
Roberts	132	568	15	10 031	115	11.0	35	30	25	26	10 704	2 739	65	30.2	6.8
Sanborn	0	123	4	11 181	39	10.3	9	12	9	8	13 894	1 479	22	43.5	NA
Shannon	0	509	9	13 152	61	11.3	32	8	2	24	5 294	3 105	40	15.6	NA
Spink	64	235	11	12 345	142	14.4	36	45	30	34	16 684	488	81	44.8	2.9
Stanley	0	40	7	16 241	35	3.8	14	8	7	5	13 139	1 847	22	18.4	NA
Sully	0	13	3	12 286	34	4.3	7	16	7	3	19 210	210	24	60.4	NA
Todd	0	424	7	11 163	57	10.9	30	10	4	16	7 053	3 099	40	20.1	NA
Tripp	111	391	17	12 873	92	11.3	31	25	22	18	13 336	1 760	56	28.1	NA
Turner	99	360	11	10 281	126	11.4	27	43	31	20	14 608	1 163	70	40.6	5.5
Union	79	401	33	16 798	158	9.5	55	38	28	25	14 813	1 071	93	27.5	23.0
Walworth	69	582	18	11 382	87	7.1	32	17	23	18	13 375	1 746	48	15.2	6.1
Yankton	336	2 177	99	13 390	274	9.7	159	48	52	45	14 565	1 181	207	11.6	25.1
Ziebach	0	6	1	10 746	22	4.4	4	7	4	5	9 127	2 993	11	62.0	NA

1. For week including March 12. Excludes government employees, self-employed persons, farm workers, domestic service workers, railroad employees subject to the Railroad Retirement Act, and employees on oceanborne vessels or in foreign countries. 2. Includes other labor income. 3. Based on the resident population estimated as of July 1 of the year shown. 4. Covers mining, construction, and manufacturing.

Table A. States and Counties — **Earnings and Agriculture**

STATE County	Earnings, 1989 (cont'd): Percent by selected industries (cont'd): Goods-related[1]: Manu-facturing	Service-related & other[2]: Total	Service-related & other[2]: Retail trade	Service-related & other[2]: Finance, insur-ance, & real estate	Service-related & other[2]: Services	Govern-ment	Agriculture, 1987: Farms: Number	Farms: Percent with: Less than 50 acres	Farms: Percent with: 500 acres and over	Farm operators, percent: Whose principal occu-pation is farming	Farm operators, percent: Residing on farm operated	Land in farms: Acreage (1,000)	Land in farms: Percent change, 1982–1987	Acres: Average size of farm	Acres: Total irrigated (1,000)	Acres: Total cropland (1,000)
	103	104	105	106	107	108	109	110	111	112	113	114	115	116	117	118
SOUTH DAKOTA	10.1	51.5	10.1	5.5	21.6	18.5	36 376	12.4	49.9	78.1	73.4	44 158	0.8	1 214	362	19 642
Aurora	1.2	NA	6.6	4.1	12.2	19.6	496	11.7	56.0	84.5	78.4	377	-0.6	760	D	260
Beadle	15.2	50.6	9.8	3.9	22.2	15.7	872	12.6	52.3	72.8	71.1	742	0.7	851	15	524
Bennett	2.7	27.5	11.6	1.4	5.8	17.3	304	13.5	64.5	77.0	74.7	702	-6.6	2 309	4	230
Bon Homme	9.8	33.2	8.0	4.1	11.9	15.4	787	10.4	27.3	81.4	75.1	306	-2.4	389	6	255
Brookings	20.2	35.3	8.3	2.6	14.0	29.5	1 004	17.9	28.8	70.7	75.9	433	-2.4	431	15	355
Brown	13.2	57.9	11.5	5.2	29.2	16.3	1 183	15.9	51.5	73.3	73.3	993	-5.2	839	7	775
Brule	1.8	53.5	13.6	3.2	23.6	15.1	437	8.0	67.7	86.3	76.4	472	5.3	1 079	4	270
Buffalo	NA	NA	1.5	NA	13.8	36.4	118	7.6	72.9	75.4	61.9	303	-1.1	2 566	9	94
Butte	1.7	NA	11.2	4.7	NA	18.7	550	16.0	47.8	66.0	71.5	1 104	-1.5	2 008	44	161
Campbell	8.8	26.8	4.2	5.1	4.3	10.9	361	8.9	73.4	83.4	74.0	426	-3.2	1 179	3	257
Charles Mix	1.0	45.6	8.3	3.1	16.7	19.6	830	11.1	53.9	85.8	78.2	646	0.5	778	12	441
Clark	5.2	24.1	5.2	2.2	5.5	9.9	688	9.6	56.1	82.7	70.1	541	-1.7	786	6	400
Clay	2.3	35.1	9.2	2.2	13.1	41.7	498	9.2	39.6	82.9	71.9	237	0.0	476	8	218
Codington	25.9	48.8	12.6	4.0	21.0	12.8	636	18.9	39.9	70.9	74.1	341	-3.1	536	1	267
Corson	NA	33.8	4.9	2.3	10.2	31.3	492	8.7	77.0	83.7	69.5	1 698	3.1	3 452	1	386
Custer	8.0	NA	10.9	1.4	18.6	34.3	303	15.5	53.1	54.1	74.6	477	14.2	1 575	5	68
Davison	17.1	60.0	14.4	3.8	29.3	12.5	464	20.3	37.3	65.9	78.4	246	-3.0	531	3	195
Day	8.6	35.4	7.0	1.6	13.4	13.6	778	7.5	54.5	84.1	75.3	571	2.3	734	3	437
Deuel	5.5	47.2	8.6	5.5	14.8	12.6	690	8.7	36.4	82.5	76.1	351	1.4	509	2	264
Dewey	0.6	NA	5.8	4.9	NA	31.8	386	11.4	66.6	75.1	68.9	1 687	-0.2	4 371	D	279
Douglas	1.4	49.7	7.9	2.2	18.8	13.8	478	11.1	46.0	83.1	79.1	254	-2.7	532	2	207
Edmunds	0.6	41.8	9.2	4.4	12.0	21.7	515	7.4	72.2	82.7	66.2	616	-3.9	1 196	1	437
Fall River	0.6	34.8	8.4	1.8	13.7	35.9	339	10.6	66.4	65.2	73.5	1 010	0.8	2 979	13	99
Faulk	0.5	38.1	8.2	1.7	15.2	15.7	363	6.3	74.4	88.4	68.6	576	-0.8	1 586	D	374
Grant	15.7	54.5	8.3	9.9	14.7	9.5	706	11.9	38.2	79.3	80.0	381	2.6	540	6	292
Gregory	1.1	53.4	9.8	5.9	19.6	15.0	670	12.8	51.8	80.0	73.0	568	-3.6	848	2	277
Haakon	11.0	39.7	11.7	3.5	11.2	13.0	344	14.0	75.3	85.5	68.9	1 249	3.4	3 632	1	363
Hamlin	4.2	33.5	8.1	3.4	9.2	20.5	501	14.8	42.5	79.2	71.5	284	1.2	566	8	243
Hand	2.0	44.3	8.0	3.2	15.8	11.0	614	12.1	69.1	85.0	73.3	1 028	18.7	1 675	3	513
Hanson	8.2	NA	7.1	4.3	6.0	13.3	413	13.8	40.9	79.9	71.9	245	-3.0	594	1	193
Harding	NA	NA	7.0	2.1	18.4	18.3	301	12.3	81.4	82.7	80.4	1 568	-1.1	5 209	2	210
Hughes	2.4	45.3	9.7	4.7	24.1	42.2	297	14.5	55.2	68.4	61.6	368	0.6	1 241	15	229
Hutchinson	6.7	39.9	9.0	3.4	17.1	10.4	995	11.5	36.7	86.9	73.7	490	-0.5	493	2	419
Hyde	NA	45.4	10.9	3.0	11.5	15.1	231	11.7	71.4	84.8	71.4	486	-10.6	2 106	D	199
Jackson	0.6	41.8	11.9	1.5	14.8	26.3	314	13.7	72.3	82.5	72.0	1 280	2.4	4 075	2	208
Jerauld	NA	47.2	8.8	3.2	16.0	15.5	305	10.8	56.7	81.3	71.1	310	2.3	1 017	2	177
Jones	NA	42.2	17.7	4.1	5.6	13.0	213	8.9	77.0	85.0	64.3	594	10.0	2 790	1	216
Kingsbury	7.2	38.0	7.6	4.2	13.1	10.8	649	12.2	48.4	78.3	71.6	466	-2.7	717	1	367
Lake	13.0	42.9	9.3	2.4	15.2	14.5	606	15.2	35.3	76.4	70.6	294	-2.6	485	2	251
Lawrence	8.5	34.3	9.5	1.7	16.8	14.3	253	18.6	28.5	58.5	79.1	207	5.5	819	3	39
Lincoln	13.4	41.8	8.2	3.4	15.6	10.6	1 064	15.9	20.7	70.7	75.4	331	-0.6	311	1	299
Lyman	0.4	33.1	9.3	2.6	10.8	17.7	437	7.3	74.4	82.8	60.4	898	-2.7	2 055	8	404
McCook	7.5	41.8	6.7	4.8	12.2	11.4	683	9.1	37.5	82.9	78.3	327	-2.9	479	0	273
McPherson	2.2	41.0	7.5	5.0	16.1	13.6	473	5.7	72.7	87.3	69.1	602	-1.3	1 272	2	345
Marshall	16.4	27.7	4.6	1.9	9.2	13.4	522	8.6	56.1	81.8	71.6	469	-4.4	898	1	342
Meade	4.7	41.6	9.8	2.7	16.7	35.7	826	15.3	65.9	74.0	76.3	2 020	-1.8	2 445	7	397
Mellette	NA	NA	3.3	1.6	9.1	23.7	233	6.4	79.4	82.0	69.1	649	0.8	2 786	1	149
Miner	2.5	44.1	6.2	2.3	21.2	9.5	488	8.6	43.9	77.9	68.4	328	-1.2	672	0	253
Minnehaha	11.8	69.7	10.9	10.8	28.6	10.0	1 382	23.2	21.6	66.4	78.2	432	1.5	313	2	373
Moody	3.4	41.8	5.6	2.8	11.3	14.7	662	10.7	30.8	80.1	75.5	281	-4.2	424	2	242
Pennington	8.4	51.3	11.7	3.9	23.3	31.3	614	16.8	52.0	60.6	75.4	1 142	6.2	1 860	9	271
Perkins	6.0	50.5	10.8	5.5	18.3	13.9	607	10.5	76.6	83.5	70.2	1 817	8.7	2 993	2	455
Potter	6.9	51.7	8.4	7.2	24.7	16.2	371	10.5	68.5	79.5	61.5	553	2.2	1 490	4	366
Roberts	3.1	45.0	9.2	4.6	17.7	18.0	994	10.1	45.6	82.0	75.6	608	-2.2	611	3	476
Sanborn	9.0	31.2	5.5	3.2	11.5	13.5	421	11.6	47.5	74.8	76.2	325	8.9	772	D	194
Shannon	0.0	NA	3.7	NA	34.0	40.6	208	13.0	58.7	65.4	64.9	1 357	-0.6	6 523	0	100
Spink	0.5	30.2	7.3	2.8	9.0	22.1	813	7.5	69.5	87.0	75.0	906	0.7	1 114	21	734
Stanley	NA	49.6	12.4	3.0	12.7	26.2	196	10.2	77.0	80.1	65.3	861	0.1	4 394	0	206
Sully	0.5	25.9	7.5	2.6	7.1	10.5	309	6.8	72.2	75.1	55.7	609	-0.7	1 971	19	454
Todd	0.2	NA	3.6	0.8	25.6	35.2	281	10.0	64.4	79.7	75.4	1 056	-0.3	3 757	8	147
Tripp	NA	53.7	12.3	5.2	19.3	13.4	770	10.1	63.9	82.7	70.4	960	2.4	1 247	3	479
Turner	0.8	42.7	6.9	6.1	13.0	11.2	1 038	12.9	23.6	76.7	78.1	371	4.0	357	15	327
Union	20.0	39.2	4.1	3.6	10.1	10.3	635	15.7	27.6	79.4	73.5	250	-4.1	393	26	228
Walworth	2.1	63.7	14.6	4.0	24.4	15.1	360	11.4	68.9	81.4	75.8	410	-2.7	1 140	3	260
Yankton	21.2	47.8	11.8	3.0	23.5	15.5	733	15.8	29.1	73.7	74.6	269	7.7	367	5	226
Ziebach	NA	NA	2.8	NA	5.0	18.0	272	10.7	75.7	83.8	68.8	1 398	4.3	5 139	D	191

1. Covers mining, construction, and manufacturing. 2. Covers private sector earnings in agricultural services, forestry, and fisheries; transportation and public utilities; wholesale trade; retail trade; finance, insurance, and real estate; and services.

STATE County	Agriculture, 1987 (cont'd)								Manufactures, 1987						
	Value of land and buildings		Value of products sold				Percent of farms with sales of		Establishments		All employees			Production workers	
					Percent from										
	Average per farm ($1,000)	Average per acre (Dollars)	Total (Mil dol)	Average per farm (Dollars)	Crops	Livestock and poultry[1]	$10,000 or more	$100,000 or more	Total	Percent with 20 or more em-ployees	Number (1,000)	Percent change, 1982–1987	Annual payroll (Mil dol)	Number (1,000)	Work hours (Mil)
	119	120	121	122	123	124	125	126	127	128	129	130	131	132	133
SOUTH DAKOTA	326	269	2 719	74 761	31.5	68.5	77.7	18.6	764	30.2	27.5	12.2	497.9	19.9	38.8
Aurora	172	254	32	65 486	21.0	79.0	83.3	17.5	3	0.0	D	D	D	D	D
Beadle	216	257	79	90 198	25.8	74.2	77.6	22.0	22	40.9	0.6	-33.3	12.9	0.4	0.9
Bennett	489	217	19	62 995	35.5	64.5	80.3	15.5	3	33.3	0.0	0.0	0.4	0.0	0.0
Bon Homme	186	480	51	64 186	26.8	73.2	81.4	16.9	6	50.0	D	D	D	D	D
Brookings	183	438	70	69 592	32.8	67.2	70.7	16.6	24	37.5	1.4	0.0	30.9	1.1	2.2
Brown	281	340	100	84 223	36.9	63.1	76.1	19.4	33	33.3	2.0	5.3	40.6	1.4	3.0
Brule	252	232	34	77 929	21.2	78.8	83.8	22.2	6	16.7	0.1	0.0	0.9	0.0	0.1
Buffalo	684	267	14	120 551	28.4	71.6	76.3	21.2	1	0.0	D	D	D	D	D
Butte	480	243	27	49 639	15.2	84.8	63.5	11.8	9	0.0	0.0	0.0	0.4	0.0	0.0
Campbell	236	211	25	68 542	25.9	74.1	85.6	18.3	4	0.0	0.0	0.0	0.3	0.0	0.0
Charles Mix	231	294	65	77 878	31.1	68.9	83.4	22.2	7	14.3	0.0	0.0	0.6	0.0	0.1
Clark	235	281	58	84 826	33.7	66.3	81.1	17.9	2	50.0	D	D	D	D	D
Clay	276	604	37	75 230	63.5	36.5	86.3	25.1	12	8.3	D	D	D	D	D
Codington	198	392	44	69 228	35.8	64.2	73.4	19.7	46	41.3	2.0	33.3	32.9	1.5	3.1
Corson	632	182	33	67 185	23.5	76.5	81.7	19.3	1	0.0	D	D	D	D	D
Custer	368	236	9	31 332	7.5	92.5	50.8	8.6	8	12.5	0.0	-100.0	0.6	0.0	0.1
Davison	148	318	25	54 371	31.6	68.4	68.1	15.7	27	44.4	1.1	120.0	19.3	0.8	1.7
Day	199	268	41	52 660	39.4	60.6	78.9	11.4	11	36.4	D	D	D	D	D
Deuel	207	385	42	60 440	32.9	67.1	81.9	14.8	6	0.0	0.1	0.0	0.7	0.0	0.1
Dewey	1 043	233	22	57 131	26.0	74.0	76.9	15.0	2	0.0	D	D	D	D	D
Douglas	202	367	36	75 166	20.1	79.9	82.6	22.4	4	0.0	0.0	0.0	0.1	0.0	0.0
Edmunds	239	192	34	66 923	32.3	67.7	81.7	16.5	6	0.0	0.0	0.0	0.3	0.0	0.0
Fall River	452	152	65	191 650	2.8	97.2	62.8	8.8	7	14.3	D	D	D	D	D
Faulk	366	218	28	77 169	36.2	63.8	85.4	22.0	1	0.0	D	D	D	D	D
Grant	222	415	51	71 594	38.1	61.9	76.2	18.3	12	41.7	0.4	0.0	9.1	0.3	0.7
Gregory	169	217	34	51 037	23.1	76.9	78.1	13.4	9	11.1	0.0	-100.0	0.5	0.0	0.1
Haakon	1 064	286	35	100 359	30.1	69.9	84.3	25.6	2	50.0	D	D	D	D	D
Hamlin	209	381	35	68 980	43.1	56.9	78.0	18.0	5	0.0	0.0	0.0	0.1	0.0	0.0
Hand	409	244	58	93 699	25.1	74.9	82.9	25.4	4	25.0	D	D	D	D	D
Hanson	208	327	27	65 939	34.7	65.3	80.1	13.6	2	0.0	D	D	D	D	D
Harding	1 010	197	22	74 586	14.7	85.3	81.7	22.3	2	0.0	D	D	D	D	D
Hughes	381	300	19	65 419	55.1	44.9	65.7	20.9	8	37.5	0.2	100.0	2.3	0.2	0.3
Hutchinson	222	441	70	70 308	35.1	64.9	82.7	20.2	18	27.8	0.3	50.0	5.2	0.2	0.5
Hyde	599	281	18	79 106	27.9	72.1	79.7	26.0	2	0.0	D	D	D	D	D
Jackson	1 002	230	21	65 944	26.8	73.2	82.2	18.2	1	0.0	D	D	D	D	D
Jerauld	239	249	29	95 186	18.4	81.6	77.0	20.7	1	0.0	D	D	D	D	D
Jones	555	203	18	83 397	38.4	61.6	81.7	27.2	1	0.0	D	D	D	D	D
Kingsbury	239	321	60	92 023	32.7	67.3	79.2	17.4	9	22.2	0.2	100.0	2.8	0.1	0.2
Lake	213	468	56	93 200	37.1	62.9	80.0	20.3	14	57.1	0.6	100.0	10.8	0.5	0.9
Lawrence	287	386	9	33 794	5.5	94.5	48.6	8.3	34	20.6	0.5	0.0	10.5	0.4	0.8
Lincoln	217	720	64	59 985	48.6	51.4	77.9	16.6	18	22.2	0.4	0.0	7.6	0.3	0.6
Lyman	537	264	35	79 664	46.1	53.9	82.8	23.8	NA	NA	NA	NA	NA	NA	NA
McCook	173	361	43	63 619	39.9	60.1	83.2	19.6	9	22.2	0.2	0.0	3.3	0.2	0.3
McPherson	222	179	33	69 186	17.7	82.3	80.8	17.3	5	0.0	0.0	0.0	0.3	0.0	0.0
Marshall	272	316	68	129 410	21.8	78.2	80.5	22.6	10	50.0	0.3	50.0	3.9	0.3	0.5
Meade	556	216	43	51 907	21.4	78.6	68.9	14.2	13	30.8	0.2	0.0	3.4	0.1	0.3
Mellette	414	160	17	72 869	22.4	77.6	84.5	21.9	NA	NA	NA	NA	NA	NA	NA
Miner	185	312	30	61 245	31.2	68.8	78.3	12.7	2	0.0	D	D	D	D	D
Minnehaha	215	698	95	69 090	38.0	62.0	71.9	17.9	138	36.2	8.9	7.2	164.8	6.3	11.5
Moody	253	581	59	88 597	42.1	57.9	86.4	24.0	4	25.0	D	D	D	D	D
Pennington	446	254	26	41 553	31.3	68.7	56.4	11.2	102	31.4	3.5	12.9	68.2	2.4	5.0
Perkins	591	198	43	70 243	19.9	80.1	78.1	19.8	5	20.0	D	D	D	D	D
Potter	394	270	33	89 060	34.7	65.3	84.9	25.3	6	16.7	D	D	D	D	D
Roberts	207	359	58	58 274	43.2	56.8	77.1	17.0	6	16.7	0.1	0.0	0.7	0.1	0.1
Sanborn	188	253	39	91 852	14.9	85.1	72.9	14.0	4	25.0	D	D	D	D	D
Shannon	920	141	9	44 143	30.0	70.0	56.2	15.4	1	0.0	D	D	D	D	D
Spink	333	308	93	114 708	36.8	63.2	84.3	28.0	5	0.0	0.0	0.0	0.3	0.0	0.0
Stanley	1 209	279	21	107 985	32.5	67.5	70.4	24.0	NA	NA	NA	NA	NA	NA	NA
Sully	861	410	50	161 687	38.0	62.0	78.6	23.9	2	0.0	D	D	D	D	D
Todd	646	175	22	78 206	14.3	85.7	76.5	18.5	1	0.0	D	D	D	D	D
Tripp	268	211	50	64 501	24.1	75.9	77.9	19.2	5	0.0	D	D	D	D	D
Turner	203	565	97	93 151	29.3	70.7	81.3	19.1	9	0.0	0.0	0.0	0.3	0.0	0.0
Union	308	757	50	79 444	48.4	51.6	81.1	22.0	17	58.8	0.9	0.0	16.2	0.7	1.3
Walworth	268	227	23	63 236	35.5	64.5	79.7	20.0	3	33.3	D	D	D	D	D
Yankton	179	496	51	68 946	34.6	65.4	76.9	17.7	24	45.8	1.5	0.0	26.3	1.0	2.2
Ziebach	834	163	18	65 707	26.4	73.6	86.4	20.2	NA	NA	NA	NA	NA	NA	NA

1. Includes livestock and poultry products.

STATE County	Manufactures, 1987 (cont'd) — Production workers (cont'd) — Wages — Total (Mil dol)	Average per worker (Dollars)	Value added by manufacture (Mil dol)	Value of shipments (Mil dol)	New capital expenditures (Mil dol)	Value of construction authorized by building permits, 1990 — Total[1] ($1,000)	Nonresidential — Total ($1,000)	Percent — Office	Industrial	Stores	Residential — New construction ($1,000)	Number of housing units	Alterations and additions ($1,000)
	134	135	136	137	138	139	140	141	142	143	144	145	146
SOUTH DAKOTA	312.6	15 709	1 476.1	3 858.7	79.3	358 436	122 240	14.2	11.9	30.7	139 723	2 830	16 953
Aurora	D	D	D	D	D	110	63	0.0	0.0	0.0	0	0	35
Beadle	8.6	21 500	32.9	225.1	1.9	5 463	852	0.0	4.7	13.4	2 558	79	540
Bennett	0.2	NA	0.8	1.7	0.0	372	112	0.0	0.0	0.0	225	10	26
Bon Homme	D	D	D	D	D	1 242	182	0.0	89.5	3.3	890	14	75
Brookings	24.6	22 364	193.8	334.3	9.0	12 110	5 515	7.6	29.8	35.5	2 751	54	540
Brown	25.9	18 500	123.5	228.2	4.5	12 198	3 661	24.9	2.4	35.7	3 557	79	1 619
Brule	0.4	NA	2.9	5.4	0.1	1 241	154	0.0	64.8	16.2	842	8	119
Buffalo	D	D	D	D	D	NA	NA	NA	NA	NA	NA	NA	NA
Butte	0.2	NA	1.0	2.0	D	623	18	0.0	0.0	100.0	46	1	234
Campbell	0.1	NA	0.7	1.3	D	0	0	NA	NA	NA	0	0	0
Charles Mix	0.3	NA	0.7	2.6	0.0	1 124	753	9.6	0.0	63.6	189	3	85
Clark	D	D	D	D	D	8 397	7 756	0.0	0.3	0.0	328	5	106
Clay	D	D	D	D	D	3 895	1 098	0.0	1.8	64.6	1 855	44	219
Codington	20.5	13 667	88.8	168.9	4.0	17 883	7 656	38.4	5.5	15.0	6 116	113	601
Corson	D	D	D	D	D	30	0	NA	NA	NA	0	0	24
Custer	0.5	NA	1.1	1.9	0.0	1 312	1	0.0	0.0	0.0	540	13	34
Davison	12.7	15 875	34.1	133.5	2.2	2 551	261	51.3	0.0	38.5	863	30	267
Day	D	D	D	D	D	247	62	0.0	0.0	13.6	118	3	27
Deuel	0.5	NA	1.3	2.6	0.1	336	109	0.0	0.0	0.0	0	0	6
Dewey	D	D	D	D	D	95	62	0.0	0.0	0.0	0	0	6
Douglas	0.1	NA	0.4	0.6	0.0	182	11	0.0	0.0	0.0	45	1	75
Edmunds	0.1	NA	0.6	1.6	0.0	352	104	0.0	91.8	0.0	65	1	43
Fall River	D	D	D	D	D	1 359	916	0.0	0.0	98.3	166	3	95
Faulk	D	D	D	D	D	174	75	0.0	0.0	0.0	68	2	14
Grant	6.4	21 333	28.0	102.1	D	2 060	712	0.0	0.0	2.8	450	8	169
Gregory	0.3	NA	1.2	4.4	0.0	361	115	0.0	0.0	0.0	120	3	94
Haakon	D	D	D	D	D	148	130	23.1	0.0	0.0	0	0	0
Hamlin	0.1	NA	0.2	0.4	0.0	2 015	1 346	0.0	3.0	0.0	323	9	137
Hand	D	D	D	D	D	1 164	780	0.0	81.1	0.0	153	3	134
Hanson	D	D	D	D	D	NA	NA	NA	NA	NA	NA	NA	NA
Harding	D	D	D	D	D	73	16	0.0	0.0	0.0	0	0	45
Hughes	1.9	9 500	10.4	22.2	0.9	6 688	978	83.8	0.0	9.7	2 615	46	769
Hutchinson	3.1	15 500	24.4	57.6	0.8	837	598	0.0	86.4	13.4	100	1	13
Hyde	D	D	D	D	D	88	25	100.0	0.0	0.0	0	0	8
Jackson	D	D	D	D	D	0	0	NA	NA	NA	0	0	0
Jerauld	D	D	D	D	D	184	12	0.0	0.0	100.0	80	1	2
Jones	D	D	D	D	D	34	0	NA	NA	NA	0	0	10
Kingsbury	1.6	16 000	4.8	11.3	0.1	1 437	711	0.0	0.0	90.1	325	5	120
Lake	6.5	13 000	33.8	63.7	0.6	5 351	2 602	10.1	0.0	30.7	1 815	36	442
Lawrence	7.2	18 000	24.5	58.1	0.9	33 468	14 534	41.9	6.6	46.4	8 085	180	704
Lincoln	4.9	16 333	16.3	28.0	1.2	5 151	1 065	0.0	9.4	35.4	3 387	40	274
Lyman	NA	NA	NA	NA	NA	360	176	0.0	0.0	0.0	120	2	64
McCook	2.5	12 500	6.8	13.0	D	1 751	1 131	8.3	0.0	18.9	424	9	94
McPherson	0.1	NA	0.6	2.9	D	637	348	0.0	0.0	0.0	29	2	35
Marshall	3.2	10 667	20.8	36.1	D	452	175	0.0	0.0	0.0	65	3	79
Meade	2.1	21 000	10.4	24.8	0.7	30 561	427	0.0	0.0	10.5	29 612	867	93
Mellette	NA	NA	NA	NA	NA	66	35	0.0	0.0	0.0	0	0	0
Miner	D	D	D	D	D	1 604	689	0.0	0.0	0.0	617	20	150
Minnehaha	100.4	15 937	463.8	1 518.2	20.7	114 573	33 837	12.9	3.1	30.3	43 290	692	5 572
Moody	D	D	D	D	D	6 335	5 607	0.9	78.9	0.2	392	6	173
Pennington	37.4	15 583	161.0	398.2	6.2	47 732	16 207	5.7	19.1	50.3	17 280	297	1 745
Perkins	D	D	D	D	D	197	174	0.0	0.0	99.5	0	0	0
Potter	D	D	D	D	D	244	111	0.0	0.0	0.0	57	1	41
Roberts	0.6	6 000	2.5	4.4	D	1 400	701	0.0	0.0	27.4	372	9	137
Sanborn	D	D	D	D	D	0	0	NA	NA	NA	0	0	0
Shannon	D	D	D	D	D	NA	NA	NA	NA	NA	NA	NA	NA
Spink	0.1	NA	0.8	2.9	0.0	1 753	685	0.0	0.0	0.0	574	13	130
Stanley	NA	NA	NA	NA	NA	1 682	349	0.0	23.5	0.0	1 170	19	102
Sully	D	D	D	D	D	66	5	0.0	0.0	0.0	39	1	5
Todd	D	D	D	D	D	540	532	43.6	0.0	56.4	0	0	2
Tripp	D	D	D	D	D	1 176	772	0.0	0.0	77.7	260	8	58
Turner	0.3	NA	1.0	1.5	0.0	46	12	0.0	0.0	0.0	0	0	24
Union	10.8	15 429	33.4	75.5	2.8	8 785	5 091	0.0	13.8	14.9	2 772	25	212
Walworth	D	D	D	D	D	2 013	1 539	0.0	15.3	65.0	119	5	183
Yankton	15.6	15 600	76.0	193.3	10.7	6 106	593	0.0	21.8	49.4	3 855	56	341
Ziebach	NA	NA	NA	NA	NA	NA	NA	NA	NA	NA	NA	NA	NA

1. Includes nonresidential additions and alterations, residential nonhousekeeping buildings, and residential garages and carports not shown separately.

STATE County	Wholesale trade, 1987				Retail trade, all establishments, 1987				Retail trade, establishments with payroll, 1987					
						Sales				Sales				
											Per capita[2] (Dollars)			
	Estab-lishments	Sales (Mil dol)	Paid employees[1]	Annual payroll (Mil dol)	Number	Total (Mil dol)	Percent change, 1982–1987	Per capita[2] (Dollars)	Number	Total (Mil dol)	General merchan-dise stores	Food stores	Apparel & acces-sory stores	Eating and drinking places
	147	148	149	150	151	152	153	154	155	156	157	158	159	160
SOUTH DAKOTA	1 793	5 194.0	15 311	255.0	8 736	3 822.3	27.9	5 388	5 514	3 683.4	549	1 035	216	476
Aurora	9	D	D	D	42	7.2	44.0	2 104	27	6.3	D	323	0	209
Beadle	48	D	D	D	244	96.2	7.1	5 230	166	93.8	D	1 010	471	498
Bennett	4	D	D	D	39	15.5	22.0	4 557	27	14.9	0	868	D	147
Bon Homme	23	D	D	D	110	23.4	4.9	3 441	70	20.8	D	631	44	259
Brookings	41	D	D	D	294	108.5	2.5	4 503	189	104.7	D	743	312	515
Brown	116	D	D	D	440	268.3	31.9	7 291	292	261.1	1 010	1 292	269	739
Brule	17	D	D	D	90	38.1	32.3	7 198	57	35.9	D	723	D	632
Buffalo	4	D	D	D	4	D	D	D	2	D	0	D	0	0
Butte	27	D	D	D	144	39.1	-0.3	4 771	89	37.3	D	1 142	131	372
Campbell	7	D	D	D	35	7.2	30.9	3 264	16	6.4	0	D	D	268
Charles Mix	27	D	D	D	126	25.3	7.2	2 718	77	23.8	D	1 015	21	237
Clark	12	D	D	D	66	10.3	1.0	2 152	27	9.1	0	D	0	217
Clay	19	D	D	D	126	48.8	37.1	3 815	93	48.0	D	1 075	109	435
Codington	71	D	D	D	319	175.8	36.2	7 709	215	171.0	1 016	2 054	490	480
Corson	10	D	D	D	46	6.2	17.0	1 298	22	4.8	0	D	D	190
Custer	6	D	D	D	104	21.8	22.5	3 205	54	20.2	D	949	D	517
Davison	48	84.1	351	5.5	250	135.7	18.6	7 799	175	132.6	D	1 547	407	797
Day	25	37.9	158	2.2	88	24.8	11.2	3 222	56	22.6	58	550	D	219
Deuel	10	10.0	40	0.6	73	13.7	59.3	2 794	43	12.3	D	391	32	232
Dewey	7	5.4	14	0.2	60	16.5	26.0	3 007	38	15.3	D	953	D	240
Douglas	14	25.3	92	1.4	52	8.9	20.3	2 276	31	8.1	D	583	0	206
Edmunds	17	34.5	97	1.5	50	12.6	-16.0	2 567	30	11.6	0	610	D	132
Fall River	4	6.1	41	0.3	130	35.3	18.5	4 587	69	33.0	D	1 249	D	431
Faulk	11	10.6	45	0.7	33	7.3	30.4	2 428	17	6.3	D	D	0	121
Grant	26	121.4	492	7.7	121	42.6	33.5	4 734	71	40.8	D	897	141	222
Gregory	17	21.7	110	1.3	95	15.3	-17.3	2 682	49	12.6	D	1 014	D	177
Haakon	10	14.5	64	0.9	48	11.9	-3.3	4 244	31	11.5	D	D	D	312
Hamlin	14	28.2	82	1.4	65	8.4	-25.7	1 613	36	7.0	0	142	0	232
Hand	15	30.6	149	2.1	76	17.2	17.0	3 731	36	15.7	D	D	D	256
Hanson	8	16.8	42	0.5	28	6.5	85.7	1 976	17	5.7	0	D	0	112
Harding	3	D	D	D	27	4.4	41.9	2 594	15	4.0	0	D	0	142
Hughes	36	50.2	207	3.3	205	106.8	33.8	7 074	149	104.8	D	1 691	571	537
Hutchinson	30	59.9	208	2.5	129	29.2	10.6	3 392	70	26.4	D	903	D	172
Hyde	6	D	D	D	29	7.2	44.0	4 222	19	6.8	0	965	D	D
Jackson	5	8.3	20	0.3	32	11.0	-9.1	3 224	22	10.7	0	643	D	324
Jerauld	7	30.4	65	1.1	33	11.0	8.9	3 944	19	10.6	D	702	D	D
Jones	5	5.4	16	0.2	34	14.7	7.3	10 512	24	14.1	D	D	0	632
Kingsbury	25	49.9	125	1.9	106	26.5	68.8	4 134	68	24.6	D	1 124	D	257
Lake	24	71.5	171	2.3	149	56.0	43.6	5 382	89	52.6	D	900	181	594
Lawrence	28	41.3	202	2.3	298	101.2	39.0	5 136	186	96.5	D	1 260	127	702
Lincoln	35	98.7	236	3.5	162	35.3	24.7	2 399	89	31.6	D	498	D	351
Lyman	9	64.0	83	0.8	41	18.4	52.1	4 969	24	15.8	0	D	0	227
McCook	25	38.5	115	1.6	99	20.2	16.1	3 363	61	18.8	D	267	D	259
McPherson	10	11.9	51	0.7	53	8.8	23.9	2 453	35	8.2	D	476	D	116
Marshall	20	59.3	127	1.6	62	9.5	-32.1	1 897	39	8.0	D	535	D	271
Meade	29	79.0	227	2.2	198	58.5	28.3	2 501	110	56.1	212	604	20	244
Mellette	2	D	D	D	16	D	D	D	6	D	D	D	0	D
Miner	14	21.9	92	1.3	50	10.6	23.3	3 107	32	9.0	D	383	D	323
Minnehaha	375	1 439.8	4 255	86.6	1 293	977.0	40.1	7 943	875	963.2	1 085	1 276	362	705
Moody	16	30.0	132	2.5	63	13.6	24.8	2 032	35	12.8	D	524	D	135
Pennington	167	388.2	1 558	29.9	1 034	668.9	41.5	8 279	678	654.9	1 134	1 413	351	733
Perkins	15	25.2	126	1.0	70	16.0	-3.6	3 478	47	15.1	D	879	109	191
Potter	14	20.1	64	1.0	50	10.8	-3.6	2 998	32	9.2	D	956	D	254
Roberts	30	124.3	179	2.6	145	28.2	6.0	2 609	79	24.3	320	193	32	294
Sanborn	4	5.2	20	0.3	37	6.2	26.5	2 143	18	4.9	0	D	0	148
Shannon	0	0.0	0	0.0	20	7.9	14.5	689	12	7.2	0	378	0	D
Spink	32	72.1	208	2.9	87	24.9	-1.2	2 862	55	23.7	D	442	D	233
Stanley	5	D	D	D	29	13.2	55.3	5 092	12	12.8	D	D	0	247
Sully	5	D	D	D	29	D	D	D	21	13.1	0	657	0	573
Todd	4	7.0	32	0.4	28	10.0	-11.5	1 322	18	9.1	D	D	0	D
Tripp	22	73.0	234	3.4	106	41.9	42.0	5 987	63	40.0	D	1 121	234	318
Turner	22	32.5	138	1.8	125	23.9	39.0	2 715	66	21.0	D	736	D	199
Union	18	42.5	110	1.8	87	16.8	-14.3	1 617	48	15.8	D	213	D	159
Walworth	23	59.1	186	2.0	119	39.0	-1.3	5 909	89	38.1	D	1 260	293	420
Yankton	59	190.3	439	6.6	276	124.3	0.2	6 646	178	119.8	993	1 457	287	508
Ziebach	2	D	D	D	17	4.3	138.9	1 788	9	3.0	0	D	0	D

1. For pay period including March 12. 2. Based on the estimated population as of July 1 of the year shown.

STATE County	Retail trade, establishments with payroll, 1987 (cont'd)		Taxable service industries–establishments with payroll, 1987							Bank deposits,[2] June 1989		Savings capital,[3] September 1989	
				Receipts (Mil dol)									
					Selected kinds of business								
	Paid employees[1]	Annual payroll (Mil dol)	Number	Total	Hotels, motels and other lodging places	Health services	Legal services	Paid employees	Annual payroll (Mil dol)	Total (Mil dol)	Percent change, 1988–1989	Total (Mil dol)	Percent change, 1988–1989
	161	162	163	164	165	166	167	168	169	170	171	172	173
SOUTH DAKOTA	49 324	407.7	4 296	1 001.5	112.0	361.2	78.5	26 538	355.6	9 172	12.9	1 356.5	2.4
Aurora	87	0.7	16	1.6	D	D	D	85	0.6	50	4.6	0.0	NA
Beadle	1 406	10.9	139	22.8	1.5	8.7	1.5	773	7.4	222	2.0	43.5	-2.6
Bennett	140	1.4	9	0.9	D	D	D	25	0.3	13	-1.9	0.0	NA
Bon Homme	258	1.7	22	2.1	D	1.2	0.3	48	0.6	62	-6.2	0.0	NA
Brookings	1 962	11.9	117	22.8	3.4	7.0	1.6	757	7.9	235	8.1	85.2	-4.3
Brown	3 674	30.4	314	76.8	13.8	26.3	6.8	1 991	25.1	412	6.7	80.5	-8.0
Brule	401	3.3	44	4.6	0.7	1.4	0.4	143	1.1	86	-2.8	1.7	13.7
Buffalo	D	D	2	D	0.0	0.0	0.0	D	D	NA	NA	0.0	NA
Butte	519	4.0	54	6.6	0.7	1.2	1.8	162	1.6	96	-1.7	13.3	-6.8
Campbell	70	0.5	2	D	0.0	D	0.0	D	D	21	-2.9	0.0	NA
Charles Mix	402	2.4	53	7.1	1.6	1.8	0.4	244	1.8	113	3.6	4.1	-10.0
Clark	112	1.0	13	2.1	0.0	D	D	75	0.6	52	2.8	0.0	NA
Clay	776	5.4	53	6.5	D	2.1	0.5	271	2.2	81	-0.1	14.1	-2.9
Codington	2 269	18.2	162	32.2	4.4	11.9	2.4	911	10.2	199	3.0	92.4	-3.3
Corson	60	0.4	4	0.1	D	0.0	D	5	0.0	21	2.8	0.0	NA
Custer	240	2.4	47	7.4	3.2	2.1	0.3	223	1.9	25	30.4	10.0	-13.3
Davison	1 956	15.3	139	34.5	3.4	12.7	1.5	865	12.9	196	1.0	29.7	-0.1
Day	293	1.9	28	5.4	1.3	1.4	0.4	114	1.0	57	-17.1	5.5	11.1
Deuel	138	1.0	15	1.4	0.0	D	D	36	0.2	42	1.1	0.4	NA
Dewey	165	1.5	11	1.3	D	D	D	30	0.3	24	-9.0	0.0	NA
Douglas	116	0.7	18	2.5	D	0.9	D	88	0.6	36	3.1	0.0	NA
Edmunds	125	1.0	12	2.2	D	1.6	D	123	1.0	46	-0.3	0.0	NA
Fall River	456	3.5	51	5.4	1.2	1.6	0.5	113	1.2	50	-1.8	8.4	-10.7
Faulk	71	0.5	11	0.6	0.0	D	D	22	0.2	24	-4.5	0.0	NA
Grant	487	4.5	45	7.1	0.4	4.1	0.5	220	2.3	94	1.1	10.9	-12.8
Gregory	212	1.4	27	3.6	0.2	1.3	D	85	0.9	91	4.7	0.0	NA
Haakon	161	1.1	8	1.1	D	D	D	27	0.2	53	8.0	0.0	NA
Hamlin	113	0.7	12	2.2	0.0	D	D	136	1.0	49	-2.5	0.0	NA
Hand	209	1.6	22	2.1	D	0.7	D	50	0.7	74	12.9	6.8	-3.9
Hanson	80	0.6	3	0.1	0.0	0.0	D	3	0.0	37	-2.0	0.0	NA
Harding	63	0.5	4	0.2	0.0	0.0	D	11	0.1	16	0.4	0.0	NA
Hughes	1 373	11.9	120	26.4	4.5	8.9	3.1	813	8.2	132	-3.7	48.5	0.5
Hutchinson	406	2.6	45	4.4	D	1.8	0.6	126	1.4	159	6.3	42.1	2.3
Hyde	79	0.7	7	1.0	D	D	0.0	67	0.4	22	5.2	0.0	NA
Jackson	98	1.1	12	0.9	D	D	D	24	0.2	11	-7.0	0.0	NA
Jerauld	100	0.7	9	0.5	0.0	0.3	0.0	15	0.1	37	1.1	0.0	NA
Jones	121	1.3	11	1.3	0.7	D	0.0	38	0.2	21	-0.2	0.0	NA
Kingsbury	378	2.5	31	4.0	D	1.6	D	139	1.1	69	-12.2	5.0	-12.8
Lake	697	5.7	57	8.7	D	3.9	0.8	274	2.8	111	2.9	33.9	-0.7
Lawrence	1 421	10.4	174	26.2	4.4	9.6	1.5	661	7.1	150	-0.8	17.4	-9.3
Lincoln	566	3.5	53	13.1	D	8.3	0.9	267	5.4	83	2.9	24.4	-1.6
Lyman	245	2.2	12	1.4	0.9	D	D	31	0.3	25	8.2	0.0	NA
McCook	221	1.8	31	4.7	D	2.7	0.2	212	1.9	62	7.2	0.0	NA
McPherson	130	0.8	15	1.4	D	0.6	D	34	0.3	32	-0.2	0.0	NA
Marshall	142	1.0	23	2.7	0.1	D	0.4	109	0.8	18	-60.2	6.3	-0.9
Meade	750	6.1	80	9.2	1.4	3.1	0.9	294	2.8	97	5.4	18.1	-2.1
Mellette	D	D	4	D	D	D	D	D	D	11	17.0	0.0	NA
Miner	135	0.9	12	2.3	D	D	D	83	0.7	26	-1.5	0.0	NA
Minnehaha	12 672	109.8	932	351.7	26.3	136.5	21.6	8 375	148.6	3 964	36.2	308.1	-0.9
Moody	234	1.4	24	8.3	0.0	2.0	0.3	210	2.1	46	3.5	11.7	13.2
Pennington	7 570	76.2	741	192.2	29.6	54.9	17.6	4 813	61.9	504	2.9	213.9	-6.2
Perkins	259	1.9	20	2.6	0.3	0.7	D	78	0.4	82	-0.6	4.6	2.1
Potter	143	1.0	25	2.5	0.0	1.0	0.4	50	0.7	83	25.0	5.1	-13.9
Roberts	436	2.8	40	5.7	0.4	2.0	D	244	1.7	88	3.3	17.6	-1.1
Sanborn	53	0.5	12	1.2	0.0	D	D	61	0.5	24	-1.4	0.0	NA
Shannon	102	0.7	3	0.0	0.0	D	D	2	0.0	NA	NA	0.0	NA
Spink	292	2.1	22	4.1	D	1.8	0.4	152	1.6	119	-0.5	4.9	-9.8
Stanley	117	1.7	11	0.8	D	0.0	D	22	0.2	14	5.2	0.0	NA
Sully	137	1.1	7	1.3	D	0.0	D	16	0.1	21	-4.8	0.0	NA
Todd	103	0.8	6	0.6	D	D	0.0	17	0.2	14	7.9	0.0	NA
Tripp	405	3.4	48	6.6	0.5	3.6	1.0	192	2.4	111	6.3	10.0	12.3
Turner	310	1.8	31	3.5	D	1.0	D	90	0.9	65	-60.2	5.7	8.1
Union	224	1.4	31	5.7	D	1.1	0.6	150	1.7	69	-21.9	97.7	330.2
Walworth	483	3.9	55	10.7	0.9	4.8	0.8	327	3.3	108	5.9	12.8	-3.2
Yankton	1 816	13.4	133	31.4	2.3	13.5	2.6	864	11.4	204	8.9	62.0	-7.8
Ziebach	43	0.3	2	D	0.0	0.0	D	D	D	14	-5.9	0.0	NA

1. For the period including March 12 of the year shown. 2. Includes deposits for all insured and reporting noninsured commercial and mutual savings banks. 3. Includes savings capital for all FSLIC insured savings institutions.

STATE County	Federal funds and grants, 1989							Local government finances, 1981–1982							
	Expenditures		Per capita[1] (Dollars)					General revenue						Direct general expenditure	
									Intergovernmental		Taxes				
												Per capita[2]			
	Total (Mil dol)	Percent change, 1988–1989	Total	Direct payments for individuals	Procurement contract awards	Salaries and wages	Grant awards	Total (Mil dol)	Total (Mil dol)	Percent from state	Total (Mil dol)	Total (Dollars)	Property (Dollars)	Total (Mil dol)	Percent change, 1977–1982
	174	175	176	177	178	179	180	181	182	183	184	185	186	187	188
SOUTH DAKOTA	2 928.3	8.8	X	1 802	216	652	685	644.3	214.6	69.6	305.2	440	385	582.2	49.7
Aurora	11.4	-5.6	3 468	1 825	21	193	149	3.2	1.2	89.5	1.5	408	393	2.8	41.5
Beadle	68.6	2.4	3 747	2 071	27	693	436	15.7	4.5	87.9	8.5	445	376	14.3	13.9
Bennett	15.0	-20.3	4 425	1 296	1 532	313	532	4.0	1.2	73.6	1.4	439	393	3.9	60.8
Bon Homme	26.3	4.4	3 925	2 086	63	211	404	6.6	2.4	86.0	3.4	445	425	5.9	30.8
Brookings	68.2	2.4	2 843	1 570	105	245	468	25.6	4.6	77.2	9.4	377	361	25.4	71.4
Brown	144.1	7.1	3 927	2 150	35	536	600	30.4	8.4	87.0	17.1	460	391	27.2	39.6
Brule	18.4	-0.2	3 533	2 011	92	285	462	7.1	3.3	60.3	2.8	526	459	6.1	74.9
Buffalo	9.2	-20.3	4 868	749	245	2 179	907	0.3	0.1	72.6	0.1	69	61	0.2	-6.1
Butte	28.8	27.6	3 516	1 771	430	414	286	8.3	2.9	67.5	4.0	477	412	9.2	103.6
Campbell	14.4	49.0	6 546	1 688	26	216	409	2.1	0.7	91.6	1.1	485	455	1.7	10.0
Charles Mix	39.1	-8.2	4 207	1 871	114	669	666	8.8	3.9	72.6	3.0	308	290	8.9	42.3
Clark	23.2	6.7	4 934	1 986	26	247	542	3.9	1.2	81.1	2.3	470	439	3.6	19.4
Clay	38.3	2.9	3 016	1 904	20	175	369	7.9	1.9	88.3	4.4	324	284	7.8	45.6
Codington	62.2	1.2	2 730	1 694	168	312	191	19.5	5.6	76.5	8.0	373	293	21.2	98.1
Corson	23.1	21.5	4 823	1 249	116	390	1 069	4.6	2.5	63.8	1.4	265	246	3.9	2.2
Custer	24.0	9.8	3 523	1 900	188	651	622	4.6	1.5	83.6	2.5	409	335	4.1	67.5
Davison	51.8	-6.0	2 979	2 078	55	303	301	16.3	4.4	84.1	8.1	459	388	14.6	50.9
Day	32.4	3.1	4 270	2 279	28	343	370	9.8	2.8	81.8	3.7	464	436	8.2	44.7
Deuel	20.5	7.5	4 265	1 746	28	258	231	4.2	1.5	81.0	2.2	415	383	3.6	20.1
Dewey	36.1	-1.0	6 692	1 283	449	1 383	2 353	4.9	3.0	64.3	1.0	184	178	5.2	122.6
Douglas	11.9	-6.5	3 130	1 706	25	262	171	4.3	1.3	84.4	2.0	506	486	3.4	42.4
Edmunds	25.6	50.4	5 457	2 020	52	143	191	6.1	1.9	72.4	3.2	635	603	4.8	3.4
Fall River	43.2	5.6	5 764	2 807	156	2 001	541	7.3	2.8	76.3	3.4	420	355	7.3	69.2
Faulk	21.8	67.7	7 502	2 377	31	250	1 731	4.2	1.1	87.3	2.3	690	668	3.8	76.6
Grant	30.9	8.0	3 438	1 677	295	184	242	12.0	3.5	49.1	5.0	539	517	11.8	51.7
Gregory	22.0	10.8	3 931	2 220	551	220	404	5.4	2.1	86.0	2.7	458	438	4.9	24.3
Haakon	14.1	32.1	5 214	1 487	14	270	57	3.1	0.9	89.5	1.7	597	525	2.9	75.3
Hamlin	18.8	-9.8	3 618	2 006	26	199	182	5.9	1.9	75.0	2.8	539	518	4.5	-10.2
Hand	19.7	7.0	4 370	1 734	12	148	206	5.7	1.6	80.2	2.4	503	480	5.1	42.6
Hanson	9.9	-7.4	3 001	1 277	19	135	174	3.3	1.3	88.8	1.6	479	461	2.8	97.5
Harding	9.4	47.4	5 546	1 336	254	414	86	2.3	0.8	87.7	1.1	625	604	2.2	30.7
Hughes	106.4	-7.5	6 956	1 466	316	615	4 105	11.2	3.0	90.8	6.3	436	359	11.0	47.3
Hutchinson	31.9	-21.0	3 794	2 009	185	237	291	7.9	2.7	87.6	4.5	488	466	7.0	21.4
Hyde	8.9	3.2	5 232	2 080	45	175	292	2.0	0.7	84.6	1.1	544	488	1.8	40.6
Jackson	11.3	11.2	3 426	1 121	223	387	500	2.3	1.0	64.9	1.0	289	258	2.0	41.6
Jerauld	10.6	11.1	3 908	2 365	20	193	437	3.5	1.2	91.2	1.9	644	593	3.0	44.3
Jones	8.5	16.8	6 037	1 581	266	304	560	1.9	0.5	83.4	1.1	813	741	1.6	23.9
Kingsbury	28.2	-3.4	4 484	2 294	34	307	639	7.7	2.1	89.3	3.9	581	545	6.6	46.4
Lake	33.6	-8.4	3 291	2 070	19	222	313	16.8	2.6	82.2	4.8	437	385	7.5	29.3
Lawrence	48.8	-0.3	2 466	1 893	50	238	253	18.5	5.4	58.3	8.6	462	398	16.7	92.9
Lincoln	36.5	-4.7	2 432	1 361	12	121	210	11.5	4.2	71.1	6.2	448	419	10.2	64.9
Lyman	22.6	-5.6	6 117	1 540	171	795	937	3.6	1.2	57.0	1.8	466	422	3.8	44.2
McCook	21.4	0.1	3 570	1 818	28	239	391	5.6	2.0	88.3	3.0	477	453	5.0	24.1
McPherson	21.4	55.6	5 940	2 067	16	146	594	3.5	1.2	87.7	2.0	509	491	3.3	35.4
Marshall	21.8	6.3	4 453	2 184	30	216	262	6.2	1.8	86.3	2.9	539	516	5.6	27.2
Meade	101.9	10.6	4 264	1 224	1 423	746	560	13.4	5.9	52.6	5.8	274	250	11.9	36.4
Mellette	8.9	22.1	4 024	1 330	262	188	1 336	2.5	1.2	71.1	1.0	419	390	2.3	46.7
Miner	13.8	-4.1	4 071	2 183	26	217	234	3.5	1.2	89.1	1.9	538	517	3.2	44.4
Minnehaha	390.0	12.9	3 076	1 728	313	507	274	101.7	32.9	52.7	53.5	476	385	92.4	67.3
Moody	25.8	-12.4	3 849	1 557	146	672	369	6.0	1.9	77.7	2.9	423	399	5.6	26.8
Pennington	372.1	11.7	4 435	1 580	170	2 282	354	64.3	22.1	67.7	32.7	452	357	58.9	31.4
Perkins	21.7	34.3	4 821	1 847	84	244	485	4.8	1.5	86.7	2.4	518	505	4.3	43.2
Potter	27.0	43.1	7 497	2 101	21	272	1 913	3.5	1.2	74.8	1.7	455	435	3.1	11.2
Roberts	43.5	3.1	4 069	1 854	23	376	720	10.0	4.6	77.1	4.4	400	365	8.8	36.4
Sanborn	13.5	-12.8	4 831	2 317	32	328	312	3.3	1.2	89.7	1.5	468	438	2.6	28.2
Shannon	50.4	16.1	4 424	1 029	445	991	1 877	5.4	4.8	37.8	0.2	15	15	5.0	83.3
Spink	39.7	5.4	4 669	2 166	34	238	582	10.8	3.2	90.6	5.4	591	559	8.9	50.7
Stanley	10.7	9.3	3 945	1 280	16	44	92	2.7	0.7	86.8	1.6	659	606	3.2	100.8
Sully	16.5	10.7	9 148	1 522	21	161	71	3.5	0.9	77.6	2.3	1 221	1 198	2.9	47.8
Todd	56.0	94.3	6 915	1 035	1 109	756	3 901	8.6	7.2	38.8	0.4	58	57	8.3	100.5
Tripp	25.0	-4.0	3 629	1 826	21	231	620	7.6	2.6	71.9	3.9	556	499	6.7	61.5
Turner	30.8	4.6	3 587	1 888	23	185	437	7.4	2.2	90.0	4.2	463	433	6.1	39.2
Union	37.0	-0.4	3 492	1 905	222	147	223	10.6	2.8	88.8	5.7	524	493	8.9	53.5
Walworth	25.7	18.7	3 952	2 101	25	206	330	5.4	1.8	90.0	2.9	432	415	5.0	21.7
Yankton	54.6	16.7	2 905	1 700	148	430	268	18.6	7.9	51.9	7.6	398	333	16.9	94.3
Ziebach	9.2	29.3	3 835	899	9	203	757	1.5	0.9	59.2	0.5	212	197	1.4	211.5

1. Based on the estimated population as of July 1 of the year shown. 2. Based on the estimated population as of July 1, 1982.

STATE County	Local government finances, 1981–1982 (cont'd) — Direct general expenditure (cont'd) — Per capita[1] (Dollars)	Percent of total for– Education	Percent of total for– Health & hospitals	Percent of total for– Police protection	Percent of total for– Public welfare	Percent of total for– Highways	Debt outstanding — Total (Mil dol)	Debt outstanding — Per capita[1] (Dollars)	State and local government employment, 1989 — Total	State and local government employment, 1989 — Rate[2]	Federal government civilian employment 1989 — Total	Federal government civilian employment 1989 — Earnings ($1,000)	Elections, 1988[3] — Total vote cast for president	Elections, 1988[3] — Vote for lead party (Percent)
	189	190	191	192	193	194	195	196	197	198	199	200	201	202
SOUTH DAKOTA	839	50.6	3.1	4.1	0.7	11.9	520.7	750	45 122	631.8	11 226	314 172	312 991	R–52.8
Aurora	789	61.6	0.5	3.2	1.0	16.3	0.1	30	255	772.7	28	641	1 854	D–53.2
Beadle	747	54.1	0.4	5.0	1.5	13.8	4.7	244	985	538.3	384	12 739	9 180	R–50.2
Bennett	1 265	45.5	25.3	5.8	0.2	8.5	0.0	0	258	758.8	55	1 176	1 262	R–52.5
Bon Homme	763	67.6	0.4	3.2	0.5	12.7	1.1	142	530	791.0	37	854	3 417	R–53.4
Brookings	1 025	33.7	21.6	4.2	0.3	7.5	14.2	572	4 016	1 673.3	161	4 063	10 305	R–52.3
Brown	731	51.5	0.9	4.3	1.0	13.7	9.3	250	2 388	650.7	607	17 871	17 302	D–50.1
Brule	1 142	53.4	1.2	4.0	0.2	19.0	1.0	195	331	636.5	48	1 134	1 974	D–50.2
Buffalo	126	0.0	0.0	10.3	1.4	40.7	0.1	52	14	73.7	152	3 879	490	D–68.2
Butte	1 105	43.5	0.5	3.6	1.1	11.4	4.6	556	430	524.4	76	2 133	3 582	R–64.0
Campbell	789	57.5	0.5	2.2	0.5	16.5	0.2	73	115	522.7	19	441	1 252	R–72.6
Charles Mix	916	49.2	0.3	3.0	0.5	13.8	8.8	902	577	620.4	200	5 208	4 184	D–52.7
Clark	729	55.5	0.9	3.1	0.9	18.7	1.0	197	219	466.0	42	966	2 424	R–51.4
Clay	568	51.1	1.7	6.1	0.2	17.5	4.1	300	2 445	1 925.2	57	1 425	5 200	D–55.0
Codington	983	34.4	0.2	3.6	0.9	8.6	32.5	1 502	1 201	526.8	188	6 417	9 714	R–52.0
Corson	734	76.6	0.0	2.3	0.0	10.5	0.3	55	249	518.8	78	1 751	1 448	D–49.9
Custer	657	53.1	0.6	4.1	7.3	15.1	2.0	317	619	910.3	224	5 389	3 036	R–59.5
Davison	823	50.4	1.0	4.8	0.5	12.7	11.4	646	1 018	585.1	138	3 997	7 786	R–51.7
Day	1 027	50.4	22.1	2.4	0.5	12.8	0.4	51	395	519.7	79	1 892	3 774	D–56.6
Deuel	670	55.3	1.0	2.5	1.2	20.3	0.6	118	227	472.9	42	915	2 528	R–49.5
Dewey	976	49.9	0.0	2.1	0.0	9.3	4.1	771	271	501.9	289	7 084	1 789	D–56.3
Douglas	855	50.6	16.0	2.5	0.1	13.9	0.7	168	188	494.7	30	744	2 139	R–67.2
Edmunds	958	49.7	9.9	2.9	0.2	18.6	1.2	244	370	787.2	31	744	2 599	R–51.1
Fall River	908	51.4	0.6	6.0	0.2	12.4	0.7	87	529	705.3	580	17 554	3 417	R–58.6
Faulk	1 154	45.9	16.4	3.0	0.5	18.0	0.2	52	167	575.9	26	579	1 561	R–53.9
Grant	1 280	34.6	0.5	1.8	0.5	10.1	47.7	5 183	393	436.7	48	1 122	4 172	R–51.5
Gregory	834	57.9	0.4	4.0	0.3	18.1	0.0	3	294	525.0	39	895	2 722	R–57.5
Haakon	1 044	53.2	0.0	2.9	1.4	10.7	1.0	348	163	603.7	24	597	1 351	R–70.9
Hamlin	856	55.7	0.7	2.4	0.7	15.8	1.5	282	428	823.1	36	804	2 651	R–52.1
Hand	1 054	42.5	21.4	3.0	0.7	15.4	0.1	24	238	528.9	27	584	2 578	R–56.7
Hanson	821	48.2	0.5	1.9	0.2	20.5	0.0	3	143	433.3	19	411	1 572	R–50.0
Harding	1 277	46.8	0.1	2.5	0.3	30.2	0.1	61	115	676.5	35	623	900	R–70.3
Hughes	761	55.7	0.7	6.3	0.3	11.1	2.0	140	2 804	1 832.7	303	9 506	7 442	R–61.1
Hutchinson	759	63.8	0.1	2.3	0.8	20.1	0.8	92	414	492.9	59	1 258	4 316	R–62.6
Hyde	904	54.5	0.6	2.6	0.2	18.5	0.0	10	118	694.1	14	295	1 019	R–53.6
Jackson	615	59.3	0.7	3.8	0.0	17.2	0.1	27	134	406.1	63	1 388	1 141	R–58.8
Jerauld	1 040	61.5	1.5	2.4	0.9	15.0	1.1	374	167	618.5	15	367	1 534	R–50.7
Jones	1 114	53.0	1.0	4.0	0.4	18.3	0.0	3	96	685.7	18	359	786	R–66.3
Kingsbury	987	55.6	8.8	2.0	0.3	15.9	0.7	103	345	547.6	59	1 253	3 087	R–51.6
Lake	684	58.7	0.4	4.7	0.3	14.0	242.2	22 223	912	894.1	65	1 617	5 122	D–52.0
Lawrence	898	40.5	0.5	5.2	0.2	8.6	13.8	740	1 530	772.7	200	4 758	9 379	R–59.4
Lincoln	741	59.1	0.3	2.5	0.6	14.0	3.6	261	621	414.0	44	1 042	6 757	R–52.3
Lyman	991	62.6	0.3	2.2	0.6	16.6	0.8	197	174	470.3	113	2 783	1 480	R–57.0
McCook	789	62.6	0.9	3.2	0.4	18.2	0.2	27	315	525.0	49	1 030	3 002	R–50.0
McPherson	835	53.9	0.2	1.7	0.1	29.4	0.6	162	184	511.1	26	579	1 936	R–70.1
Marshall	1 052	47.7	19.3	2.7	0.4	15.6	1.0	196	295	602.0	37	791	2 525	D–54.3
Meade	568	49.1	0.5	4.3	0.4	9.8	5.2	249	737	308.4	718	22 685	8 473	R–61.2
Mellette	1 001	70.2	0.1	2.6	0.2	8.0	0.0	0	162	736.4	16	327	852	R–54.0
Miner	891	56.1	0.7	3.2	0.3	24.2	0.3	94	166	488.2	23	492	1 755	D–54.4
Minnehaha	824	45.7	1.0	4.8	1.1	6.6	26.5	236	5 044	397.8	1 932	63 947	56 095	D–51.9
Moody	825	46.1	9.1	4.1	0.4	21.3	1.7	254	302	450.7	169	4 016	2 889	D–59.4
Pennington	815	54.0	0.7	6.3	1.0	8.1	15.3	212	4 497	536.0	1 991	52 406	31 757	R–61.4
Perkins	931	65.0	0.7	4.0	0.2	15.4	0.1	23	304	675.6	41	901	2 197	R–60.4
Potter	804	56.5	1.3	4.4	0.3	15.0	0.9	247	181	502.8	38	1 063	1 893	R–62.1
Roberts	798	66.2	0.2	2.9	1.4	14.1	2.1	188	515	481.3	144	3 626	4 311	D–52.6
Sanborn	806	58.6	1.2	3.1	0.3	20.7	0.2	61	168	600.0	24	562	1 595	R–51.1
Shannon	440	99.7	0.0	0.0	0.0	0.0	0.0	4	243	213.2	461	11 587	1 479	D–81.5
Spink	974	50.7	17.5	2.9	0.2	15.5	0.5	54	1 041	1 224.7	60	1 407	4 062	D–51.0
Stanley	1 341	46.1	0.8	3.9	0.5	12.6	1.2	483	313	1 159.3	NA	79	1 219	R–57.3
Sully	1 517	55.8	0.4	3.3	0.3	25.4	0.5	266	137	761.1	16	334	1 006	R–56.8
Todd	1 152	65.0	0.0	0.1	0.0	0.2	26.0	3 615	434	535.8	261	6 692	1 676	D–66.6
Tripp	954	46.3	0.9	4.4	0.2	22.7	0.2	27	394	571.0	52	1 155	3 356	R–63.0
Turner	672	59.0	0.7	3.2	0.4	19.8	1.0	106	448	520.9	47	1 132	4 239	R–57.5
Union	817	60.0	0.4	3.7	0.1	20.8	3.0	272	537	506.6	50	1 235	4 550	D–57.4
Walworth	733	62.5	0.3	5.8	0.1	12.9	0.3	41	372	572.3	48	1 144	3 060	R–63.4
Yankton	890	40.0	0.7	4.6	0.5	10.6	15.1	796	1 356	721.3	249	7 339	8 043	R–52.0
Ziebach	589	63.0	0.2	3.5	0.0	16.6	0.1	40	91	379.2	19	385	795	D–53.7

1. Based on the estimated population as of July 1, 1982. 2. Per 10,000 resident population estimated as of July 1 of the year shown. 3. Data subject to copyright.

STATE–County code	MSA/CMSA/NECMA code[1]	STATE County	Land Area,[2] 1990 (Sq. Km.)	Population, 1990												
							Race						Age of population Percent		
				Total persons	Rank	Per square kilometer	White	Black	Am. Indian, Eskimo, Aleut	Asian & Pacific Islander	Other race	Hispanic[3]	Under 5 years	5 to 14 years	15 to 24 years
			1	2	3	4	5	6	7	8	9	10	11	12	13
47 000	...	TENNESSEE	106 759	4 877 185	X	45.7	4 048 068	778 035	10 039	31 839	9 204	32 741	6.8	13.9	15.1
47 001	3840	Anderson	874	68 250	648	78.1	64 615	2 763	243	547	82	381	6.2	13.6	12.8
47 003	...	Bedford	1 227	30 411	1 272	24.8	27 097	3 068	36	147	63	172	6.7	14.2	14.1
47 005	...	Benton	1 023	14 524	2 018	14.2	14 109	345	23	31	16	72	5.6	13.1	12.9
47 007	...	Bledsoe	1 052	9 669	2 416	9.2	9 242	375	42	3	7	38	5.9	13.3	15.2
47 009	3840	Blount	1 447	85 969	534	59.4	82 503	2 783	195	409	79	368	6.1	12.6	13.8
47 011	...	Bradley	851	73 712	610	86.6	70 132	2 900	200	232	248	712	6.4	13.9	16.3
47 013	...	Campbell	1 243	35 079	1 126	28.2	34 727	130	175	41	6	117	6.3	14.3	15.0
47 015	...	Cannon	688	10 467	2 339	15.2	10 236	186	15	14	16	39	6.3	14.6	13.8
47 017	...	Carroll	1 552	27 514	1 374	17.7	24 303	3 138	35	10	28	125	6.2	13.5	13.6
47 019	3660	Carter	883	51 505	820	58.3	50 763	456	91	144	51	191	5.7	12.1	15.2
47 021	5360	Cheatham	784	27 140	1 387	34.6	26 460	534	84	36	26	139	7.7	15.8	13.4
47 023	...	Chester	747	12 819	2 155	17.2	11 355	1 412	20	22	10	53	6.4	13.1	19.9
47 025	...	Claiborne	1 125	26 137	1 417	23.2	25 701	250	56	112	18	83	6.2	14.3	16.1
47 027	...	Clay	612	7 238	2 630	11.8	7 103	116	11	3	5	27	5.4	13.4	13.8
47 029	...	Cocke	1 125	29 141	1 323	25.9	28 398	613	78	31	21	144	5.9	13.4	14.9
47 031	...	Coffee	1 111	40 339	991	36.3	38 459	1 493	84	251	52	261	6.9	14.6	13.2
47 033	...	Crockett	687	13 378	2 107	19.5	11 097	2 252	9	9	11	49	6.3	13.8	12.8
47 035	...	Cumberland	1 765	34 736	1 140	19.7	34 475	42	137	49	33	124	6.1	12.8	13.4
47 037	5360	Davidson	1 301	510 784	93	392.6	381 740	119 273	1 162	7 081	1 528	4 775	7.0	12.3	15.2
47 039	...	Decatur	865	10 472	2 338	12.1	10 000	417	23	21	11	49	5.2	13.3	13.2
47 041	...	De Kalb	789	14 360	2 026	18.2	14 074	215	19	12	40	62	6.1	13.7	13.7
47 043	5360	Dickson	1 269	35 061	1 129	27.6	33 145	1 744	68	71	33	177	7.4	15.3	14.4
47 045	...	Dyer	1 322	34 854	1 136	26.4	30 541	4 145	64	63	41	137	6.7	14.5	14.3
47 047	...	Fayette	1 825	25 559	1 441	14.0	14 204	11 295	33	15	12	130	7.8	16.7	14.5
47 049	...	Fentress	1 292	14 669	2 007	11.4	14 636	2	10	18	3	39	6.1	14.8	15.3
47 051	...	Franklin	1 433	34 725	1 142	24.2	32 425	2 095	55	95	55	187	6.3	13.7	15.4
47 053	...	Gibson	1 561	46 315	897	29.7	37 237	8 944	37	61	36	181	6.2	13.6	13.2
47 055	...	Giles	1 582	25 741	1 431	16.3	22 184	3 405	57	61	34	109	6.7	13.9	14.4
47 057	3840	Grainger	726	17 095	1 847	23.5	16 939	102	42	8	4	41	6.0	13.8	15.1
47 059	...	Greene	1 611	55 853	776	34.7	54 440	1 223	89	70	31	163	5.7	12.8	14.3
47 061	...	Grundy	934	13 362	2 109	14.3	13 294	19	28	6	15	68	6.4	16.1	15.3
47 063	...	Hamblen	417	50 480	834	121.1	47 891	2 323	85	128	53	175	6.2	13.1	15.1
47 065	1560	Hamilton	1 405	285 536	172	203.2	227 413	54 477	585	2 479	582	1 946	6.6	13.4	14.4
47 067	...	Hancock	576	6 739	2 682	11.7	6 596	122	18	1	2	35	6.1	14.9	13.9
47 069	...	Hardeman	1 729	23 377	1 521	13.5	14 536	8 748	20	62	11	175	7.6	16.1	14.2
47 071	...	Hardin	1 497	22 633	1 552	15.1	21 539	997	34	37	26	87	6.3	14.0	14.0
47 073	3660	Hawkins	1 261	44 565	917	35.3	43 664	741	78	59	23	134	6.0	13.2	14.6
47 075	...	Haywood	1 381	19 437	1 707	14.1	9 676	9 651	24	19	67	156	7.0	17.2	14.2
47 077	...	Henderson	1 347	21 844	1 585	16.2	19 982	1 816	20	19	7	100	6.2	14.5	13.3
47 079	...	Henry	1 455	27 888	1 354	19.2	24 955	2 813	50	54	16	110	5.7	13.2	12.0
47 081	...	Hickman	1 587	16 754	1 865	10.6	15 831	859	40	8	16	67	6.3	13.4	13.5
47 083	...	Houston	519	7 018	2 656	13.5	6 725	268	12	5	8	41	6.0	13.4	13.4
47 085	...	Humphreys	1 379	15 795	1 934	11.5	15 175	551	26	32	11	63	6.3	14.3	13.3
47 087	...	Jackson	800	9 297	2 444	11.6	9 247	7	19	19	5	38	5.6	12.7	13.6
47 089	3840	Jefferson	709	33 016	1 189	46.6	31 937	930	75	41	33	100	5.4	12.0	17.5
47 091	...	Johnson	773	13 766	2 075	17.8	13 668	61	14	14	9	32	5.7	12.7	14.1
47 093	3840	Knox	1 317	335 749	153	254.9	301 421	29 603	797	3 327	601	2 067	6.4	12.3	16.4
47 095	...	Lake	423	7 129	2 640	16.9	5 418	1 702	4	2	3	27	5.6	12.2	16.5
47 097	...	Lauderdale	1 219	23 491	1 514	19.3	16 007	7 303	127	20	34	178	7.2	15.8	14.1
47 099	...	Lawrence	1 599	35 303	1 121	22.1	34 666	482	59	73	23	145	7.2	14.4	14.5
47 101	...	Lewis	731	9 247	2 449	12.6	9 082	119	26	7	13	54	6.7	15.3	14.1
47 103	...	Lincoln	1 477	28 157	1 346	19.1	25 583	2 422	38	64	50	137	6.6	14.1	13.5
47 105	...	Loudon	592	31 255	1 236	52.8	30 732	400	52	50	21	83	6.2	12.8	13.6
47 107	...	McMinn	1 114	42 383	950	38.0	40 085	2 051	96	121	30	174	6.1	13.9	14.4
47 109	...	McNairy	1 451	22 422	1 559	15.5	20 918	1 432	21	40	11	95	5.9	14.2	12.8
47 111	...	Macon	796	15 906	1 930	20.0	15 810	44	35	10	7	39	6.8	14.3	14.3
47 113	3580	Madison	1 443	77 982	581	54.0	53 423	24 170	66	253	70	376	7.1	14.9	15.3
47 115	1560	Marion	1 295	24 860	1 468	19.2	23 749	1 035	36	32	8	85	6.6	14.7	14.6
47 117	...	Marshall	972	21 539	1 600	22.2	19 536	1 909	24	53	17	92	6.4	14.5	13.9
47 119	...	Maury	1 587	54 812	784	34.5	45 868	8 607	79	157	101	323	7.1	14.9	13.3
47 121	...	Meigs	505	8 033	2 562	15.9	7 884	118	28	2	1	17	5.7	14.4	15.3
47 123	...	Monroe	1 645	30 541	1 264	18.6	29 561	833	48	71	28	123	6.4	14.1	15.6
47 125	1660	Montgomery	1 396	100 498	456	72.0	79 118	17 872	394	1 831	1 283	3 228	8.6	14.0	19.7
47 127	...	Moore	335	4 721	2 862	14.1	4 536	174	8	2	1	20	5.7	14.8	14.0
47 129	...	Morgan	1 352	17 300	1 834	12.8	16 957	265	46	25	7	60	6.2	14.5	15.3
47 131	...	Obion	1 411	31 717	1 220	22.5	28 324	3 256	47	48	42	138	5.8	14.0	14.5
47 133	...	Overton	1 122	17 636	1 809	15.7	17 582	30	10	4	10	73	5.8	13.7	14.4
47 135	...	Perry	1 075	6 612	2 698	6.2	6 470	119	8	7	8	36	6.9	13.6	12.7

1. MSA = Metropolitan Statistical Area. CMSA = Consolidated MSA. NECMA = New England county metropolitan area. PMSA = Primary MSA. See Appendix A for explanation of these concepts. See Appendix B for list of metropolitan areas identified by type, with component counties. 2. Dry land or land partially or temporarily covered by water. 3. Hispanic persons may be of any race.

STATE County	Population, 1990 (cont'd): Age of population (cont'd), Percent: 25 to 34 years	35 to 44 years	45 to 54 years	55 to 64 years	65 to 74 years	75 years and over	Percent female	Population–Change and components of change: Change, 1980–1990: Number	Percent	Components of change, 1980–1986: Total persons, 1986	Total persons, 1980	Net change: Number	Percent	Natural increase: Births	Deaths
	14	15	16	17	18	19	20	21	22	23	24	25	26	27	28
TENNESSEE	16.7	15.2	10.8	8.9	7.3	5.4	51.8	286 185	6.2	4 803 000	4 591 000	212 000	4.6	416 000	261 000
Anderson	15.0	15.3	11.4	10.3	9.4	5.9	52.3	904	1.3	68 800	67 346	1 400	2.1	5 100	3 600
Bedford	15.2	14.1	11.1	9.7	8.4	6.5	51.5	2 495	8.9	29 200	27 916	1 200	4.4	2 300	1 800
Benton	13.7	13.8	11.8	11.3	10.1	7.7	52.6	-377	-2.5	15 100	14 901	200	1.2	1 100	1 100
Bledsoe	17.2	16.0	11.3	9.0	7.0	5.0	45.6	191	2.0	9 600	9 478	100	1.1	700	500
Blount	15.6	15.9	11.8	9.3	8.7	6.0	52.0	8 199	10.5	83 200	77 770	5 400	6.9	6 300	4 200
Bradley	16.5	15.1	11.8	9.0	6.5	4.5	51.8	6 165	9.1	72 300	67 547	4 700	7.0	6 000	3 100
Campbell	14.3	14.2	11.6	9.6	8.5	6.3	52.3	156	0.4	35 500	34 923	600	1.7	3 000	2 200
Cannon	14.8	13.6	11.3	10.4	8.4	6.8	51.2	233	2.3	10 800	10 234	600	5.5	800	700
Carroll	13.7	13.4	11.2	10.4	9.9	8.1	51.9	-771	-2.7	28 200	28 285	-100	-0.4	2 200	2 100
Carter	15.1	14.7	11.9	9.9	8.7	6.5	51.7	1 300	2.6	51 300	50 205	1 100	2.2	3 700	2 900
Cheatham	18.6	16.9	11.4	7.8	5.0	3.4	50.0	5 524	25.6	24 700	21 616	3 100	14.3	2 000	1 000
Chester	13.6	13.1	10.0	8.9	8.2	6.8	52.2	92	0.7	13 000	12 727	200	1.8	900	700
Claiborne	14.9	15.2	11.2	9.1	7.7	5.3	51.5	1 542	6.3	26 900	24 595	2 300	9.4	2 100	1 500
Clay	14.4	14.0	12.4	10.3	9.2	7.0	50.7	-438	-5.7	7 900	7 676	200	2.8	500	500
Cocke	15.5	15.1	12.0	10.3	7.3	5.6	51.8	349	1.2	29 300	28 792	500	1.6	2 300	1 900
Coffee	15.3	14.1	11.5	10.5	8.4	5.5	51.8	2 028	5.3	41 300	38 311	3 000	7.8	3 400	2 200
Crockett	15.2	12.9	11.1	8.8	9.9	9.1	52.4	-1 563	-10.5	14 200	14 941	-700	-4.9	1 200	1 000
Cumberland	14.4	13.4	10.9	11.5	10.8	6.8	51.6	6 060	21.1	31 700	28 676	3 000	10.6	2 400	1 700
Davidson	20.4	15.5	9.8	8.2	6.6	5.0	52.5	32 973	6.9	497 900	477 811	20 100	4.2	46 500	26 700
Decatur	13.3	13.5	11.9	10.6	10.4	8.5	51.8	-385	-3.5	11 000	10 857	200	1.6	900	700
De Kalb	14.3	14.1	11.8	10.4	9.0	6.8	52.3	771	5.7	14 400	13 589	800	5.8	1 200	1 000
Dickson	16.2	14.4	11.0	8.8	6.9	5.6	51.4	5 024	16.7	32 500	30 037	2 500	8.2	2 800	1 800
Dyer	15.5	14.6	10.9	8.6	8.0	6.9	52.6	191	0.6	34 600	34 663	-100	-0.3	3 000	2 300
Fayette	15.2	13.8	10.3	8.7	7.1	5.8	51.3	254	1.0	25 800	25 305	500	1.8	2 500	1 400
Fentress	14.3	15.1	11.7	9.2	7.9	5.6	51.1	-157	-1.1	15 700	14 826	900	6.1	1 300	900
Franklin	14.5	14.3	11.3	10.1	8.3	6.1	50.8	2 742	8.6	33 700	31 983	1 700	5.4	2 600	1 900
Gibson	14.3	13.3	10.7	10.4	10.0	8.3	53.1	-3 152	-6.4	48 700	49 467	-800	-1.5	3 900	3 700
Giles	14.3	13.8	11.7	9.2	9.0	7.1	51.7	1 116	4.5	24 800	24 625	200	0.8	2 100	1 700
Grainger	15.6	14.6	12.2	9.8	7.3	5.6	50.4	344	2.1	17 400	16 751	600	3.9	1 300	900
Greene	15.1	15.1	12.5	10.7	8.0	5.8	51.6	1 431	2.6	56 500	54 422	2 100	3.8	4 100	3 100
Grundy	14.0	13.5	11.7	8.6	8.2	6.1	51.7	-425	-3.1	14 500	13 787	700	5.0	1 300	800
Hamblen	15.5	15.1	13.0	10.1	7.4	4.6	51.8	1 180	2.4	52 900	49 300	3 600	7.4	4 000	2 700
Hamilton	16.0	15.6	10.9	9.6	7.7	5.8	52.8	-2 204	-0.8	284 300	287 740	-3 500	-1.2	25 500	16 400
Hancock	15.0	13.3	11.0	10.1	9.1	6.6	50.7	-148	-2.1	6 800	6 887	-100	-1.0	600	500
Hardeman	15.3	13.8	9.6	9.1	7.9	6.4	51.9	-496	-2.1	24 100	23 873	200	0.8	2 300	1 500
Hardin	13.8	14.3	11.5	10.6	8.7	6.9	51.7	353	1.6	22 200	22 280	0	-0.2	1 600	1 400
Hawkins	15.7	15.3	12.5	9.5	7.7	5.5	51.2	814	1.9	45 100	43 751	1 300	3.1	3 300	2 400
Haywood	14.8	13.7	8.9	8.6	8.0	7.5	53.2	-881	-4.3	20 800	20 318	500	2.3	2 000	1 300
Henderson	15.0	14.4	11.0	10.4	8.6	6.5	51.9	454	2.1	22 500	21 390	1 100	5.0	1 800	1 400
Henry	13.6	13.3	11.2	11.3	11.1	8.5	52.1	-768	-2.7	29 200	28 656	600	2.1	2 200	2 200
Hickman	16.8	15.2	11.4	9.3	8.4	5.5	48.5	1 603	10.6	16 400	15 151	1 200	8.0	1 200	900
Houston	13.4	13.6	11.6	10.9	9.9	7.9	51.5	147	2.1	7 100	6 871	200	2.6	500	400
Humphreys	14.1	14.5	12.2	10.8	8.7	5.8	50.9	-162	-1.0	16 000	15 957	0	0.2	1 200	1 000
Jackson	14.0	14.7	11.5	10.7	9.6	7.6	51.3	-101	-1.1	9 300	9 398	-100	-1.1	600	600
Jefferson	14.5	14.1	12.7	10.4	7.9	5.4	51.1	1 732	5.5	33 400	31 284	2 100	6.7	2 200	1 700
Johnson	13.8	14.6	12.5	10.1	9.1	7.4	50.4	21	0.2	14 200	13 745	400	3.2	1 000	800
Knox	17.3	15.5	10.5	8.9	7.4	5.3	52.2	16 055	5.0	329 500	319 694	9 800	3.1	26 400	17 800
Lake	17.2	14.6	10.2	9.0	7.8	7.0	46.6	-326	-4.4	7 500	7 455	100	1.0	600	600
Lauderdale	16.4	13.3	10.0	8.1	8.0	7.0	51.6	-1 064	-4.3	24 900	24 555	300	1.3	2 400	1 700
Lawrence	15.1	13.3	11.2	9.6	8.4	6.3	52.0	1 193	3.5	34 900	34 110	800	2.4	3 100	2 200
Lewis	14.5	14.2	10.5	9.6	8.4	6.7	51.1	-453	-4.7	10 400	9 700	700	7.4	800	500
Lincoln	15.1	13.8	11.4	10.1	8.9	6.6	51.8	1 674	6.3	27 100	26 483	600	2.3	2 200	1 800
Loudon	15.2	15.2	12.0	10.4	8.7	5.9	51.8	2 702	9.5	30 500	28 553	1 900	6.8	2 300	1 800
McMinn	15.2	14.4	11.9	9.8	8.3	6.1	52.3	505	1.2	43 200	41 878	1 400	3.2	3 300	2 500
McNairy	14.1	14.2	12.1	10.5	8.8	7.3	51.7	-103	-0.5	23 500	22 525	1 000	4.2	1 700	1 400
Macon	15.4	14.3	11.1	9.4	8.6	5.9	51.4	206	1.3	15 800	15 700	100	0.9	1 300	1 000
Madison	16.2	14.8	9.6	8.4	7.5	6.3	52.9	3 436	4.6	78 000	74 546	3 500	4.7	7 300	4 600
Marion	15.5	15.1	11.7	9.5	7.0	5.2	51.3	444	1.8	24 800	24 416	400	1.5	2 000	1 500
Marshall	15.4	14.7	10.8	9.1	8.8	6.4	51.7	1 841	9.3	20 900	19 698	1 200	5.9	1 600	1 300
Maury	16.4	15.3	10.4	9.3	7.5	5.7	52.1	3 717	7.3	53 900	51 095	2 800	5.5	4 500	3 200
Meigs	14.5	16.1	12.4	9.2	7.6	4.6	49.7	602	8.1	7 900	7 431	500	6.2	600	400
Monroe	14.4	14.6	11.9	9.2	8.1	5.6	51.4	1 841	6.4	30 600	28 700	1 900	6.5	2 400	1 600
Montgomery	20.0	14.2	8.6	7.0	4.7	3.2	48.8	17 156	20.6	91 100	83 342	7 800	9.3	10 500	3 400
Moore	14.1	15.0	12.9	9.9	8.2	5.4	50.2	211	4.7	4 900	4 510	400	9.6	300	200
Morgan	17.1	15.6	10.8	8.8	6.8	5.0	47.3	696	4.2	16 800	16 604	200	1.1	1 400	900
Obion	14.0	14.8	11.6	9.6	8.5	7.0	52.2	-1 064	-3.2	33 000	32 781	200	0.7	2 600	2 300
Overton	14.0	14.6	12.0	10.2	8.8	6.6	50.8	61	0.3	17 900	17 575	300	1.6	1 400	1 100
Perry	13.1	13.9	11.4	11.8	9.3	7.3	50.9	501	8.2	6 500	6 111	300	5.6	500	500

STATE County	Population–(cont'd) Components of change, 1980-1986 (cont'd) Net migration	Households, 1990 Number	Households, 1990 Percent change, 1980–1990	Households, 1990 Persons per household	Households, 1990 Percent Female family householder[1]	Households, 1990 Percent One-person	Births, 1988 Total	Births, 1988 Rate[2]	Births, 1988 Low birth weight[3] (Number)	Deaths, 1987 Number Total	Deaths, 1987 Number Infant[4]	Deaths, 1987 Rate Total[2]	Deaths, 1987 Rate Infant[5]	Marriages, 1984 Number	Marriages, 1984 Rate[2]
	29	30	31	32	33	34	35	36	37	38	39	40	41	42	43
TENNESSEE	56 000	1 853 725	14.5	2.56	12.6	23.9	70 711	14.4	5 556	44 919	795	9.3	11.7	55 203	11.7
Anderson	-100	27 384	11.2	2.47	10.8	25.2	838	11.9	73	667	4	9.5	5.1	741	10.7
Bedford	700	11 608	16.7	2.59	11.1	21.8	380	12.9	25	316	4	10.8	10.8	419	14.7
Benton	200	5 784	3.7	2.46	8.0	23.3	163	10.9	10	188	3	12.6	22.7	175	11.7
Bledsoe	-100	3 261	9.5	2.64	9.2	20.5	118	11.9	5	92	1	9.2	10.4	80	8.4
Blount	3 400	33 624	19.3	2.51	9.6	22.0	996	11.8	55	757	15	9.1	15.7	724	9.0
Bradley	1 900	27 604	19.9	2.61	10.3	20.7	963	13.0	60	593	10	8.1	11.3	555	7.9
Campbell	-200	13 150	8.8	2.65	12.9	21.2	513	14.7	40	383	6	10.9	13.0	1 747	49.2
Cannon	400	3 980	9.8	2.60	8.8	21.9	124	11.4	5	109	2	10.0	17.2	289	27.3
Carroll	-200	10 727	3.9	2.50	10.2	23.6	335	11.9	22	383	2	13.6	5.9	308	10.9
Carter	300	20 189	13.0	2.49	10.5	23.7	591	11.5	43	501	6	9.7	10.6	462	8.9
Cheatham	2 100	9 515	34.7	2.82	8.2	16.0	395	14.8	22	186	3	7.2	8.4	178	7.7
Chester	0	4 558	8.3	2.59	9.8	21.1	159	12.3	10	115	0	8.8	0.0	150	11.8
Claiborne	1 700	9 629	16.1	2.65	10.5	19.8	318	11.9	25	258	4	9.8	12.0	622	23.6
Clay	200	2 855	4.5	2.51	10.5	22.7	73	9.2	7	70	0	8.9	0.0	233	29.5
Cocke	100	11 191	10.2	2.58	13.4	22.1	365	12.4	32	317	4	10.8	12.0	384	13.2
Coffee	1 700	15 500	13.6	2.57	10.0	22.1	562	13.3	32	376	1	9.0	1.8	440	10.9
Crockett	-900	5 183	-3.7	2.53	10.9	24.3	152	10.9	9	166	1	11.8	5.9	144	10.1
Cumberland	2 300	13 426	35.8	2.55	9.4	20.0	378	11.3	21	305	4	9.3	10.1	384	12.6
Davidson	300	207 530	16.8	2.36	14.2	30.3	8 506	16.8	782	4 513	91	8.9	11.2	4 810	9.9
Decatur	0	4 216	3.3	2.45	9.3	24.5	108	9.9	7	142	0	12.8	0.0	110	10.0
De Kalb	600	5 696	14.9	2.50	10.3	22.7	167	11.6	10	149	1	10.3	5.6	206	14.7
Dickson	1 500	13 019	24.4	2.65	11.6	20.3	502	14.5	33	322	7	9.5	14.0	371	11.8
Dyer	-900	13 617	7.3	2.52	12.1	24.7	438	12.5	23	382	9	11.1	20.4	427	12.5
Fayette	-700	8 453	13.8	2.97	15.8	18.6	422	16.0	35	248	2	9.4	5.1	271	10.8
Fentress	500	5 511	9.6	2.64	12.1	21.1	204	13.0	12	168	0	10.7	0.0	301	19.3
Franklin	1 100	12 660	17.3	2.64	9.0	20.0	424	12.3	25	337	5	9.9	12.0	298	8.9
Gibson	-900	18 361	0.9	2.48	12.2	24.9	601	12.4	48	634	13	13.0	22.4	589	12.0
Giles	-300	9 832	11.4	2.58	11.4	22.6	357	14.2	17	286	4	11.4	10.8	297	11.9
Grainger	300	6 394	12.3	2.64	9.2	19.0	208	12.0	17	160	2	9.2	11.5	137	8.0
Greene	1 100	21 482	12.1	2.52	10.7	22.1	625	11.1	51	575	5	10.2	8.2	609	10.8
Grundy	200	4 784	6.1	2.75	11.2	20.4	165	11.5	11	128	4	8.8	24.1	142	10.0
Hamblen	2 300	19 429	12.6	2.56	11.9	21.3	645	12.5	46	486	3	9.5	5.0	732	13.8
Hamilton	-12 600	111 799	8.2	2.50	13.5	26.0	4 314	14.8	316	2 713	48	9.4	11.9	2 228	7.8
Hancock	-200	2 484	5.7	2.65	12.9	21.4	86	12.6	8	91	0	13.2	0.0	59	8.6
Hardeman	-500	8 276	8.6	2.73	16.4	22.8	367	15.0	32	248	2	10.2	5.6	197	8.3
Hardin	-300	8 726	9.5	2.56	10.1	22.2	308	13.8	27	233	0	10.4	0.0	184	8.3
Hawkins	400	17 167	12.3	2.58	9.5	21.2	510	11.2	33	404	8	9.0	15.7	431	9.6
Haywood	-200	7 014	7.7	2.74	18.8	24.4	301	14.3	33	239	8	11.3	28.8	205	10.0
Henderson	700	8 527	10.9	2.54	9.6	22.5	284	12.5	18	242	5	10.7	18.9	296	13.5
Henry	500	11 362	4.1	2.42	9.9	25.5	323	11.0	24	391	3	13.3	8.7	303	10.4
Hickman	1 000	5 976	17.3	2.63	8.8	20.6	208	12.5	18	179	6	10.9	29.4	137	8.7
Houston	100	2 683	11.3	2.55	9.7	22.5	87	12.1	2	76	1	10.7	12.2	55	7.9
Humphreys	-200	6 063	7.6	2.56	9.3	22.6	207	12.9	13	183	3	11.4	15.8	169	10.6
Jackson	-100	3 642	8.3	2.52	9.2	22.1	101	10.7	7	147	0	15.6	0.0	157	16.9
Jefferson	1 500	12 329	16.1	2.55	9.3	20.5	360	10.8	14	283	1	8.5	3.0	304	9.0
Johnson	300	5 406	11.7	2.52	11.1	22.8	154	11.0	13	147	2	10.4	12.6	165	11.7
Knox	1 100	133 639	13.3	2.42	11.6	27.4	4 381	13.2	321	3 026	44	9.2	10.0	3 727	11.3
Lake	100	2 418	-6.1	2.50	13.4	25.8	100	13.3	12	93	2	12.1	25.3	86	10.6
Lauderdale	-300	8 423	1.7	2.68	14.9	22.5	357	14.2	30	266	8	10.6	22.8	301	12.2
Lawrence	-100	13 338	12.4	2.62	9.7	21.6	552	15.7	26	343	2	9.8	4.1	312	9.0
Lewis	400	3 533	15.6	2.58	9.3	24.3	101	9.5	13	91	0	8.7	0.0	86	8.3
Lincoln	200	10 881	14.1	2.57	10.1	22.6	371	13.4	33	290	2	10.7	5.7	327	12.3
Loudon	1 500	12 155	18.1	2.54	10.7	21.7	402	12.9	30	331	1	10.7	2.7	330	11.0
McMinn	500	16 351	11.0	2.55	10.7	22.0	526	12.1	39	423	4	9.7	8.1	550	12.8
McNairy	600	8 834	8.0	2.51	9.3	22.8	320	13.3	17	257	3	10.8	12.0	214	9.2
Macon	-200	6 159	9.1	2.57	8.5	22.0	209	12.9	12	187	2	11.6	12.4	159	10.1
Madison	800	29 609	10.8	2.55	15.2	25.0	1 198	15.3	101	854	10	10.9	8.8	768	10.0
Marion	-200	9 215	11.4	2.67	11.2	20.3	325	12.7	27	229	4	9.0	13.6	233	9.5
Marshall	900	8 268	15.7	2.57	10.7	23.6	247	11.6	11	233	4	11.0	17.0	305	15.0
Maury	1 500	20 608	13.4	2.62	12.7	22.1	782	14.1	62	550	10	10.0	13.5	461	8.8
Meigs	200	2 996	18.9	2.64	8.7	19.8	82	9.8	8	74	0	9.0	0.0	97	12.4
Monroe	1 000	11 363	17.9	2.63	10.2	21.0	436	14.0	22	295	5	9.5	12.8	337	11.3
Montgomery	700	34 345	26.3	2.72	10.8	18.1	1 774	18.3	110	595	22	6.3	13.1	1 073	12.3
Moore	300	1 734	13.0	2.72	6.5	18.9	47	9.6	6	29	1	6.0	13.5	51	10.6
Morgan	-300	5 841	8.4	2.74	11.6	19.2	204	11.5	13	191	2	10.8	11.4	170	9.9
Obion	-100	12 412	2.8	2.53	10.3	23.8	392	12.0	14	349	6	10.5	17.4	362	10.9
Overton	0	6 734	10.0	2.59	9.6	20.3	199	11.1	10	213	1	11.9	5.1	208	11.7
Perry	400	2 512	12.1	2.57	7.4	22.6	92	14.2	9	81	2	12.7	25.6	67	10.3

1. No spouse present. 2. Per 1,000 resident population estimated as of July 1 of the year shown. 3. Under 2,500 grams. 4. Deaths of infants under 1 year old. 5. Deaths of infants under 1 year old per 1,000 live births.

STATE County	Divorces, 1984: Number	Divorces, 1984: Rate[1]	Physicians, active non–Federal, 1989: Number[2]	Physicians, active non–Federal, 1989: Rate[3]	Hospitals, 1989: Number	Hospitals, 1989: Beds: Number	Hospitals, 1989: Beds: Rate[3]	Nursing homes,[4] 1986: Number	Nursing homes,[4] 1986: Beds	Serious crimes known to police, 1988: Number: Total[5]	Serious crimes known to police, 1988: Number: Violent[6]	Serious crimes known to police, 1988: Rate[3]	Education: Public school enrollment[7]: 1986–1987	Education: Public school enrollment[7]: 1980	Education: Attainment,[8] 1980: Percent 12 yrs. or more	Education: Attainment,[8] 1980: Percent 16 yrs. or more
	44	45	46	47	48	49	50	51	52	53	54	55	56	57	58	59
TENNESSEE	29 638	6.3	9 360	190	161	29 712	602	381	30 917	201 413	24 589	4 843	855 157	880 774	56.2	12.6
Anderson	396	5.7	140	196	2	286	401	5	535	1 489	201	4 596	12 620	13 939	62.2	18.2
Bedford	246	8.6	19	64	1	182	615	3	245	520	50	3 727	5 613	5 766	48.5	7.5
Benton	95	6.3	10	67	1	76	510	2	198	NA	NA	NA	2 568	2 941	46.4	5.5
Bledsoe	60	6.3	5	50	1	32	320	1	49	NA	NA	NA	1 825	2 063	39.6	5.9
Blount	581	7.2	129	151	2	374	437	5	694	628	27	3 249	14 840	15 472	57.1	11.3
Bradley	593	8.4	93	124	2	267	355	3	360	2 102	175	2 846	13 972	14 184	53.0	10.5
Campbell	207	5.8	21	60	2	215	618	1	98	327	42	2 495	7 414	7 710	37.5	6.1
Cannon	45	4.2	8	73	1	50	455	1	84	19	0	815	1 907	1 951	44.6	6.1
Carroll	162	5.7	11	39	2	124	443	6	339	340	84	2 975	5 203	5 753	43.3	7.2
Carter	329	6.4	34	66	1	100	195	6	411	436	10	1 101	9 535	9 896	47.0	8.2
Cheatham	83	3.6	6	22	0	0	0	4	116	8	4	282	5 090	4 924	49.6	6.6
Chester	504	39.7	3	23	0	0	0	1	89	190	5	1 431	2 294	2 286	44.4	7.7
Claiborne	34	1.3	13	49	1	124	463	1	50	213	20	790	5 320	5 299	38.8	6.9
Clay	31	3.9	4	50	1	36	450	1	60	NA	NA	NA	1 400	1 507	34.3	5.3
Cocke	177	6.1	14	47	1	105	356	2	194	1 014	73	3 404	5 674	6 196	40.1	5.3
Coffee	221	5.5	43	101	3	290	681	3	294	661	23	3 928	7 639	7 967	56.1	13.3
Crockett	63	4.4	5	36	0	0	0	2	136	283	27	2 203	2 599	3 132	45.0	5.5
Cumberland	164	5.4	40	117	1	184	538	3	265	267	15	3 548	6 088	6 263	44.4	8.6
Davidson	3 245	6.6	2 265	442	16	5 489	1 071	34	2 952	38 253	5 371	7 463	68 479	73 321	66.1	19.5
Decatur	52	4.7	4	37	1	40	370	1	94	97	6	1 133	1 975	2 113	42.5	4.9
De Kalb	110	7.9	12	83	2	86	593	1	80	NA	NA	NA	2 611	2 602	40.2	6.1
Dickson	206	6.6	24	67	1	176	494	5	250	233	23	880	6 639	6 695	48.0	7.5
Dyer	259	7.6	43	123	1	240	684	2	163	1 350	146	7 044	6 765	7 293	43.0	6.6
Fayette	155	6.2	7	26	1	38	142	2	214	157	53	4 470	4 882	5 369	42.0	6.9
Fentress	128	8.2	8	51	1	84	532	1	100	171	7	1 075	2 564	3 388	33.6	6.5
Franklin	189	5.7	24	69	1	184	530	6	192	468	25	1 351	6 161	6 456	51.2	10.1
Gibson	320	6.5	31	64	4	325	676	6	491	1 377	257	2 791	8 680	10 278	46.6	6.6
Giles	138	5.5	17	67	1	95	377	5	256	659	87	2 633	4 696	4 858	48.4	7.0
Grainger	96	5.6	4	23	0	0	0	1	132	381	33	2 161	3 201	3 519	34.4	4.1
Greene	424	7.5	61	108	2	276	490	3	395	1 109	50	1 950	9 945	10 986	47.5	8.9
Grundy	60	4.2	3	21	0	0	0	3	190	NA	NA	NA	2 893	2 909	32.9	4.8
Hamblen	390	7.3	52	101	2	256	499	1	161	1 571	71	2 953	9 428	10 707	51.0	9.2
Hamilton	2 028	7.1	711	242	12	2 019	686	22	1 706	18 195	2 685	6 251	47 104	49 620	63.7	15.5
Hancock	31	4.5	3	45	1	31	463	0	0	NA	NA	NA	1 392	1 319	28.6	4.2
Hardeman	96	4.1	20	82	2	428	1 747	2	174	535	77	2 356	5 053	5 426	38.8	5.5
Hardin	111	5.0	17	76	1	132	589	4	158	535	19	2 389	4 339	4 636	43.6	5.1
Hawkins	304	6.8	20	44	1	55	121	3	289	43	0	397	8 058	9 364	47.1	6.7
Haywood	129	6.3	8	38	1	52	245	2	154	402	64	1 907	4 662	4 744	43.0	7.9
Henderson	127	5.8	8	35	1	45	197	2	154	339	43	1 510	4 339	4 447	41.9	5.3
Henry	189	6.5	25	85	1	107	364	6	299	108	6	567	4 878	5 309	47.3	6.9
Hickman	86	5.5	6	36	1	68	402	2	162	14	11	472	2 829	3 154	41.1	5.2
Houston	37	5.3	3	41	1	33	452	1	104	68	5	1 225	1 403	1 438	46.2	7.7
Humphreys	25	1.6	9	56	1	52	321	1	66	144	16	888	3 105	3 392	52.0	7.5
Jackson	40	4.3	5	53	1	41	432	1	66	NA	NA	NA	1 559	1 797	32.5	5.6
Jefferson	182	5.4	18	54	1	91	272	2	269	538	77	1 767	5 773	6 286	48.3	8.1
Johnson	83	5.9	6	43	0	0	0	2	140	NA	NA	NA	2 734	2 783	36.5	4.1
Knox	2 330	7.0	908	274	8	2 707	817	16	1 515	16 818	1 550	5 039	52 472	57 168	64.4	18.8
Lake	31	3.8	0	0	0	0	0	1	120	12	7	200	1 322	1 568	33.2	6.1
Lauderdale	169	6.9	10	40	1	70	279	3	249	469	22	1 837	5 010	5 318	40.4	5.6
Lawrence	196	5.6	23	65	1	87	246	3	277	552	38	1 569	6 413	7 116	42.9	6.1
Lewis	57	5.5	6	56	1	52	486	1	61	103	5	2 587	1 810	1 787	49.5	8.1
Lincoln	186	7.0	19	68	1	91	327	4	270	505	52	1 832	5 233	5 601	46.9	7.4
Loudon	193	6.4	23	73	1	28	89	2	288	549	31	1 759	5 726	5 885	48.7	6.7
McMinn	241	5.6	36	82	2	214	490	5	387	856	51	1 951	8 414	8 628	47.3	7.8
McNairy	147	6.3	12	50	1	86	357	1	124	249	1	1 245	4 460	4 420	43.3	5.0
Macon	77	4.9	6	37	1	43	265	2	148	56	6	1 410	2 798	3 127	34.7	4.5
Madison	462	6.0	202	258	3	861	1 098	11	600	5 416	772	6 844	13 979	14 291	57.6	12.8
Marion	133	5.4	16	62	2	102	395	1	124	55	1	721	5 423	5 161	42.1	5.6
Marshall	137	6.7	18	84	1	114	530	8	240	NA	NA	NA	3 875	3 870	49.4	7.2
Maury	286	5.5	77	138	1	275	492	7	557	1 988	124	3 607	9 628	9 918	52.3	8.8
Meigs	7	0.9	1	12	0	0	0	0	0	NA	NA	NA	1 613	1 709	43.4	5.8
Monroe	166	5.6	15	48	1	59	188	3	202	264	23	5 474	6 128	6 209	39.2	6.0
Montgomery	783	9.0	81	81	1	212	213	5	350	3 589	337	3 768	16 295	16 090	65.8	14.5
Moore	23	4.8	0	0	0	0	0	0	0	43	2	884	1 028	931	52.0	9.2
Morgan	82	4.8	2	11	0	0	0	1	124	73	11	426	3 455	3 854	40.5	3.9
Obion	215	6.5	32	98	1	130	399	3	253	818	43	5 211	6 800	6 790	51.0	7.2
Overton	53	3.0	9	50	1	74	413	1	164	201	2	1 102	3 197	3 764	35.1	5.9
Perry	52	8.0	5	76	1	53	803	1	72	11	0	170	1 116	1 261	43.3	3.9

1. Per 1,000 resident population estimated as of July 1 of the year shown. 2. As of end of year. 3. Per 100,000 resident population as of July 1 of the year shown. 4. Preliminary. Covers nursing homes with 3 or more beds. 5. Data for serious crimes have not been adjusted for underreporting, this may affect comparability between geographic areas or over time. 6. Includes murder and nonnegligent manslaughter, forcible rape, robbery, and aggravated assault. 7. The 1986–1987 data are based on administrative reports obtained by the U.S. National Center for Education Statistics. The 1980 data are based on the 1980 Census of Population and Housing. 8. Persons 25 years old or older.

STATE County	Education (cont'd): Local government expenditures for education,[1] 1982: Total (Mil dol)	Education (cont'd): Local government expenditures for education,[1] 1982: Per capita (Dollars)	Social Security Program December 1988: Beneficiaries: Total	Social Security Program December 1988: Beneficiaries: Rate[2]	Social Security Program December 1988: Payments ($1,000)	Supplemental Security Income Program recipients June 1986	Money income: Per capita[3]: 1987 Income, (Dollars)	Money income: Per capita[3]: 1979: Current dollars	Money income: Per capita[3]: 1979: Constant 1987 dollars	Money income: Median household income 1979 (Dollars)	Money income: Percent below poverty level, 1979: Persons	Money income: Percent below poverty level, 1979: Families	Housing units, 1990: Total	Housing units, 1990: Percent change, 1980–1990
	60	61	62	63	64	65	66	67	68	69	70	71	72	73
TENNESSEE	1 402.9	301	796 999	162.8	351 573	129 337	10 448	6 212	9 720	14 142	16.5	13.1	2 026 067	15.9
Anderson	33.6	493	13 380	189.3	6 466	1 714	11 177	6 987	10 933	16 088	14.6	11.3	29 323	13.4
Bedford	7.0	251	5 590	189.5	2 422	736	10 702	6 323	9 894	13 757	14.1	11.4	12 638	16.9
Benton	3.8	249	3 435	230.5	1 459	448	8 376	5 552	8 687	12 052	16.5	13.1	7 107	8.9
Bledsoe	2.5	272	1 460	147.5	551	382	7 504	4 495	7 033	10 619	24.2	21.4	3 771	10.7
Blount	24.9	314	15 940	188.4	7 592	1 538	10 505	6 544	10 239	15 058	12.7	10.4	36 532	18.5
Bradley	19.9	290	10 980	147.8	4 905	1 452	10 241	5 958	9 322	14 653	13.9	11.0	29 562	19.7
Campbell	12.5	355	7 625	217.9	2 971	1 546	7 009	4 530	7 088	10 277	24.8	21.1	14 817	11.8
Cannon	2.7	254	1 820	167.0	720	284	8 426	5 072	7 936	11 682	17.5	13.4	4 368	9.1
Carroll	8.6	306	6 780	241.3	2 737	1 098	8 737	5 306	8 302	11 764	17.1	13.8	11 783	4.2
Carter	16.0	312	8 760	170.8	3 703	1 478	8 181	4 923	7 703	11 436	18.8	14.8	21 779	12.8
Cheatham	6.1	280	2 880	107.9	1 247	304	10 340	6 243	9 768	16 290	10.9	9.1	10 297	37.6
Chester	2.7	220	2 165	167.8	828	478	8 217	4 913	7 687	11 695	20.7	18.9	4 944	10.6
Claiborne	8.0	315	5 145	192.0	1 875	1 226	6 830	4 253	6 655	9 359	29.3	24.8	10 711	14.1
Clay	3.3	428	1 310	165.8	417	494	6 994	4 176	6 534	8 876	26.8	23.4	3 340	10.8
Cocke	8.2	282	5 255	178.7	1 996	1 448	7 097	4 412	6 903	10 344	27.5	23.4	12 282	8.6
Coffee	13.0	326	7 815	185.2	3 416	1 010	10 313	6 153	9 628	14 331	14.3	11.3	16 786	12.0
Crockett	4.3	300	3 050	217.9	1 178	650	8 614	4 979	7 791	11 448	21.8	17.7	5 521	-2.4
Cumberland	9.0	307	7 095	212.4	3 146	964	8 387	4 977	7 788	11 578	21.9	17.8	15 864	44.2
Davidson	143.4	299	73 305	144.5	35 923	8 854	13 107	7 578	11 857	16 408	12.3	9.2	229 064	22.2
Decatur	2.7	242	2 315	212.4	904	456	7 969	5 049	7 900	10 832	19.0	16.5	5 346	9.6
De Kalb	3.9	290	2 925	203.1	1 125	552	9 487	5 522	8 640	10 847	22.9	18.8	6 694	10.1
Dickson	8.9	294	5 905	170.2	2 525	788	10 146	6 044	9 457	14 276	12.1	10.2	14 149	27.0
Dyer	11.3	328	6 955	198.7	2 962	1 492	9 252	5 556	8 693	12 098	16.3	12.9	14 384	7.9
Fayette	8.3	339	3 280	124.2	1 168	1 294	7 419	4 232	6 622	11 423	30.3	23.8	9 115	11.8
Fentress	3.8	253	3 030	193.0	1 058	886	5 741	3 564	5 577	8 246	33.5	29.7	6 120	9.2
Franklin	7.9	244	6 035	175.4	2 566	890	9 188	5 544	8 675	13 487	16.5	13.1	13 717	18.4
Gibson	13.4	274	11 080	229.4	4 684	1 800	8 997	5 448	8 524	12 120	18.8	14.5	19 635	0.3
Giles	7.0	286	5 210	207.6	2 114	956	8 972	5 434	8 503	12 843	16.7	13.4	10 828	13.3
Grainger	4.0	237	3 130	179.9	1 148	814	7 596	4 403	6 889	10 942	22.9	20.3	7 501	5.9
Greene	16.7	305	10 750	190.9	4 270	2 160	8 991	5 216	8 161	12 188	18.0	14.9	23 270	10.1
Grundy	4.1	287	2 570	178.5	982	524	6 880	4 716	7 379	10 533	25.5	21.2	5 155	0.4
Hamblen	16.8	328	8 365	161.8	3 587	1 450	9 477	5 607	8 773	13 343	15.6	13.0	20 514	11.1
Hamilton	88.1	308	48 965	167.8	24 147	6 024	11 911	6 888	10 778	15 694	13.5	10.2	122 588	11.1
Hancock	2.3	344	1 240	182.4	360	582	5 168	3 054	4 779	6 693	43.0	39.5	2 890	7.6
Hardeman	7.1	303	4 570	187.3	1 754	1 386	7 163	4 412	6 903	10 859	27.3	21.7	9 174	9.1
Hardin	6.5	288	4 400	196.4	1 679	1 118	7 844	5 003	7 828	11 655	20.4	18.0	10 275	14.8
Hawkins	11.9	268	7 410	163.2	3 048	1 500	8 910	5 187	8 116	12 903	18.3	15.7	18 779	10.4
Haywood	6.2	306	3 475	164.7	1 274	1 316	7 426	4 435	6 939	9 781	32.9	26.9	7 475	6.1
Henderson	6.1	284	4 635	203.3	1 813	842	8 025	5 060	7 917	12 096	17.6	14.5	9 278	11.8
Henry	8.0	274	7 050	239.8	3 076	832	8 741	5 628	8 806	11 919	15.0	11.3	13 774	2.1
Hickman	4.1	270	3 105	185.9	1 262	450	8 219	4 973	7 781	13 063	13.4	11.5	6 662	18.2
Houston	1.9	266	1 530	212.5	621	282	7 682	5 105	7 988	11 869	17.7	15.1	3 085	10.2
Humphreys	5.1	318	3 025	187.9	1 342	476	9 271	6 029	9 434	15 789	13.0	10.6	7 136	9.6
Jackson	2.5	270	1 725	183.5	609	498	8 015	4 692	7 342	9 922	24.9	22.4	4 219	13.9
Jefferson	8.6	266	6 280	188.0	2 691	848	8 449	5 042	7 889	12 138	17.1	13.5	14 170	15.9
Johnson	4.1	296	3 230	230.7	1 126	830	6 877	4 084	6 390	9 861	26.5	23.9	6 090	13.1
Knox	101.2	308	53 490	161.6	25 542	6 854	11 733	6 895	10 789	14 787	14.7	10.8	143 582	14.1
Lake	4.0	513	1 565	208.7	613	458	7 359	4 687	7 334	9 954	31.3	23.8	2 610	-13.0
Lauderdale	7.1	288	5 085	202.6	1 907	1 430	7 639	4 554	7 126	10 985	24.9	20.4	9 343	0.8
Lawrence	9.4	277	7 405	210.4	3 059	1 224	8 422	5 321	8 326	12 921	16.6	13.2	14 229	13.5
Lewis	2.1	209	1 735	163.7	700	326	7 071	4 350	6 806	10 690	21.3	17.7	3 943	21.4
Lincoln	7.8	300	5 505	199.5	2 164	1 002	9 102	5 323	8 329	12 161	16.4	13.3	11 902	15.6
Loudon	12.2	406	5 950	190.7	2 664	748	9 348	5 942	9 297	13 868	12.8	10.3	12 995	19.9
McMinn	13.6	319	7 670	175.9	3 263	1 194	9 523	5 791	9 061	13 762	16.0	13.9	17 616	11.5
McNairy	6.1	267	5 180	215.8	1 949	1 332	7 891	4 968	7 773	11 296	18.3	14.8	9 734	8.0
Macon	3.6	224	2 840	175.3	1 018	630	8 759	5 575	8 723	12 458	16.6	14.0	6 879	12.8
Madison	11.1	146	13 825	176.8	6 004	2 590	9 916	6 010	9 404	13 694	17.6	13.2	31 809	10.3
Marion	7.4	301	4 175	163.1	1 787	712	8 233	5 317	8 320	12 781	18.8	16.3	10 011	10.9
Marshall	5.3	270	3 925	184.3	1 695	582	10 487	6 092	9 532	13 523	12.8	10.1	8 909	16.5
Maury	13.3	258	9 820	177.6	4 356	1 462	10 138	6 186	9 679	14 726	15.5	13.1	22 286	14.1
Meigs	2.4	320	1 375	163.7	556	272	8 504	5 511	8 623	14 067	14.3	12.3	3 689	23.1
Monroe	9.0	307	5 775	185.7	2 307	1 212	8 215	4 970	7 777	11 783	19.4	16.2	12 803	16.4
Montgomery	23.2	262	10 115	104.3	4 270	1 546	9 218	5 727	8 961	14 110	13.0	11.0	37 233	25.3
Moore	1.3	293	550	112.2	231	62	9 184	5 531	8 654	14 654	16.3	12.5	1 912	14.6
Morgan	5.5	326	2 565	144.9	989	590	7 282	4 753	7 437	10 862	25.7	21.6	6 378	7.7
Obion	10.7	326	6 540	200.0	2 756	976	10 312	6 116	9 570	13 102	15.6	12.2	13 359	2.3
Overton	4.7	269	3 445	192.5	1 250	888	7 634	4 563	7 140	10 276	25.4	21.7	7 388	13.2
Perry	0.8	132	1 405	216.2	549	266	7 923	4 992	7 811	11 414	15.3	11.4	3 225	13.5

1. Elementary and secondary. 2. Per 1,000 resident population estimated as of July 1 of the year shown. 3. Based on the resident population estimated as of July 1, 1988 for 1987 data and enumerated as of April 1, 1980 for 1979 data.

STATE County	Housing units, 1990 (cont'd)				Civilian labor force, 1990				Private nonfarm establishments, 1988					
	Occupied units						Unemployment				Employment[2]			
		Owner occupied												
	Total	Percent	Median value (Dollars)	Median rent (Dollars)	Total	Percent change, 1989–1990	Total	Rate[1]	Number	Net change, 1987–1988	Total	Percent change, 1987–1988	Manufacturing	Retail trade
	74	75	76	77	78	79	80	81	82	83	84	85	86	87
TENNESSEE	1 853 725	68.0	58 400	273	2 397 000	1.2	125 000	5.2	X	X	1 761 394	5.1	496 633	360 954
Anderson	27 384	70.8	55 100	262	33 268	-0.3	1 496	4.5	1 501	-1	32 371	13.3	10 864	4 448
Bedford	11 608	71.8	48 400	227	14 085	2.1	891	6.3	641	25	9 844	11.3	5 167	1 474
Benton	5 784	80.2	39 700	169	7 216	2.4	530	7.3	297	16	3 009	19.7	1 017	595
Bledsoe	3 261	78.7	36 000	143	5 355	0.3	251	4.7	120	1	1 136	6.6	468	175
Blount	33 624	74.6	60 200	239	38 536	-1.6	2 033	5.3	1 666	-7	22 566	6.7	6 668	6 320
Bradley	27 604	68.8	55 000	247	39 742	5.4	1 863	4.7	1 584	66	29 856	6.5	13 410	5 015
Campbell	13 150	73.8	37 900	174	12 184	-0.1	1 312	10.8	535	-3	6 119	3.7	2 256	1 618
Cannon	3 980	79.3	41 500	174	4 283	4.3	330	7.7	143	13	1 595	6.2	890	213
Carroll	10 727	79.0	35 700	170	13 836	7.0	958	6.9	535	11	6 412	-1.9	3 171	1 137
Carter	20 189	76.3	43 800	202	24 453	0.0	1 207	4.9	699	26	8 641	0.9	3 380	1 976
Cheatham	9 515	83.1	64 000	281	13 297	0.9	482	3.6	289	14	3 578	16.2	1 789	527
Chester	4 558	77.4	40 200	164	4 843	-3.6	259	5.3	182	5	2 270	-15.2	1 190	371
Claiborne	9 629	78.3	41 400	164	12 284	11.0	778	6.3	370	-2	5 599	12.4	2 763	899
Clay	2 855	81.4	37 100	141	5 475	-0.2	217	4.0	101	2	2 284	16.1	1 519	138
Cocke	11 191	72.7	40 300	145	13 328	3.3	1 464	11.0	443	11	5 548	0.6	2 404	1 528
Coffee	15 500	70.1	52 800	234	18 236	1.3	962	5.3	1 036	46	19 732	3.0	5 452	3 743
Crockett	5 183	76.4	38 600	156	7 497	5.1	375	5.0	241	18	2 404	18.6	1 188	426
Cumberland	13 426	78.4	49 100	217	14 916	6.3	1 142	7.7	681	10	8 689	6.8	2 604	1 885
Davidson	207 530	53.8	76 000	359	286 860	0.6	10 134	3.5	16 702	385	315 345	3.8	44 854	62 698
Decatur	4 216	80.5	34 700	150	4 353	1.2	406	9.3	227	16	2 051	-20.7	780	480
De Kalb	5 696	76.4	44 200	189	7 104	7.9	430	6.1	239	-6	3 355	2.5	2 015	469
Dickson	13 019	75.7	54 100	257	16 986	0.5	989	5.8	652	57	6 996	-2.6	2 143	2 103
Dyer	13 617	65.8	44 100	212	18 208	3.2	964	5.3	811	19	11 426	7.3	4 593	2 586
Fayette	8 453	74.8	51 400	137	10 267	-0.6	796	7.8	277	13	4 679	28.8	2 986	448
Fentress	5 511	78.6	32 300	139	6 460	5.0	602	9.3	241	-4	3 203	-2.5	1 789	594
Franklin	12 660	77.7	48 700	210	16 205	3.3	801	4.9	564	19	6 044	3.9	1 670	1 487
Gibson	18 361	72.6	39 200	177	22 773	-0.8	1 745	7.7	1 013	11	15 409	2.5	8 698	2 159
Giles	9 832	73.0	44 600	195	10 293	1.9	648	6.3	485	-10	6 420	-2.2	3 504	1 199
Grainger	6 394	82.4	40 300	161	7 166	-0.5	463	6.5	182	7	1 918	18.0	1 170	294
Greene	21 482	77.0	44 500	194	27 421	-0.9	2 383	8.7	1 042	3	19 364	2.6	10 015	3 202
Grundy	4 784	81.4	29 800	155	5 426	-4.1	492	9.1	189	22	1 748	20.0	654	421
Hamblen	19 429	72.1	51 300	210	25 549	1.3	1 538	6.0	1 174	15	23 197	-0.2	12 693	4 246
Hamilton	111 799	64.1	62 000	285	143 318	-0.4	5 984	4.2	8 020	86	135 831	4.4	34 828	28 214
Hancock	2 484	78.3	32 200	99	3 166	1.0	152	4.8	49	-5	555	71.8	307	103
Hardeman	8 276	73.6	39 200	163	11 223	3.2	654	5.8	382	9	5 261	1.5	2 642	1 032
Hardin	8 726	77.4	39 100	165	9 939	1.5	757	7.6	428	6	5 927	4.2	3 538	1 187
Hawkins	17 167	77.1	48 600	211	20 479	0.7	992	4.8	508	-1	9 754	13.4	5 929	1 487
Haywood	7 014	66.4	40 400	174	8 914	3.4	767	8.6	335	11	4 306	5.6	2 047	823
Henderson	8 527	79.7	42 200	174	10 954	-1.8	890	8.1	362	-19	5 685	0.7	3 710	879
Henry	11 362	76.5	41 700	176	13 091	4.0	857	6.5	670	28	7 482	-1.5	3 045	1 665
Hickman	5 976	80.8	43 200	199	7 120	-1.1	615	8.6	220	-3	2 706	15.1	1 553	300
Houston	2 683	78.7	35 300	170	3 149	5.4	326	10.4	99	-2	979	-9.0	432	157
Humphreys	6 063	77.3	43 700	198	5 465	3.9	780	14.3	291	-3	4 209	24.2	1 977	764
Jackson	3 642	81.6	38 000	137	4 375	7.0	298	6.8	209	-8	2 032	-0.2	1 011	232
Jefferson	12 329	77.2	47 900	195	15 590	0.9	1 067	6.8	517	10	6 519	3.3	2 416	1 172
Johnson	5 406	80.7	41 300	147	5 216	-0.3	382	7.3	186	-9	2 828	9.7	1 487	344
Knox	133 639	63.9	63 900	272	163 546	-0.3	6 620	4.0	9 958	143	140 578	3.7	25 109	35 439
Lake	2 418	58.4	35 100	119	2 703	6.8	199	7.4	122	3	1 091	-8.7	547	184
Lauderdale	8 423	66.9	38 700	183	11 226	1.9	810	7.2	367	10	7 110	5.7	4 941	837
Lawrence	13 338	76.6	43 300	176	15 032	2.5	1 370	9.1	705	12	9 969	1.6	5 934	1 705
Lewis	3 533	75.8	37 200	158	4 606	6.2	368	8.0	165	-2	2 706	6.1	1 504	392
Lincoln	10 881	73.4	47 100	189	13 123	2.2	664	5.1	574	16	6 435	2.3	2 416	1 192
Loudon	12 155	77.6	51 000	190	15 896	8.7	818	5.1	507	-19	6 778	7.2	2 898	1 410
McMinn	16 351	76.1	45 600	192	21 564	1.4	1 741	8.1	785	-3	16 025	2.4	9 731	2 674
McNairy	8 834	79.2	36 400	159	10 682	-0.1	772	7.2	379	-3	6 433	7.6	3 417	645
Macon	6 159	78.8	36 600	170	7 618	2.9	553	7.3	256	5	3 075	-6.7	1 653	546
Madison	29 609	65.4	53 500	242	39 656	2.4	1 972	5.0	2 145	42	30 263	4.8	8 807	7 168
Marion	9 215	79.0	42 600	192	10 013	-1.2	703	7.0	364	11	4 449	12.2	1 387	1 283
Marshall	8 268	70.8	47 900	228	11 169	4.0	611	5.5	413	9	8 575	4.9	6 048	1 050
Maury	20 608	69.0	60 700	284	29 877	11.6	1 859	6.2	1 291	9	15 837	-0.7	5 425	3 718
Meigs	2 996	79.9	44 200	183	4 448	14.1	418	9.4	80	7	779	15.8	273	163
Monroe	11 363	79.7	40 200	180	17 920	13.1	1 458	8.1	557	33	7 162	3.6	3 680	1 559
Montgomery	34 345	61.1	58 100	298	35 215	2.5	2 219	6.3	1 751	54	20 206	7.0	5 441	7 260
Moore	1 734	83.7	50 400	214	1 813	3.5	96	5.3	44	4	723	-6.0	0	56
Morgan	5 841	82.9	37 800	165	6 533	4.9	583	8.9	135	0	1 618	9.5	938	176
Obion	12 412	70.6	43 500	194	14 901	-2.0	938	6.3	726	13	12 420	6.0	6 511	2 086
Overton	6 734	80.3	36 700	154	7 678	-0.2	707	9.2	238	-2	2 538	22.1	1 377	456
Perry	2 512	83.9	35 600	158	3 113	-1.8	215	6.9	108	8	1 584	-10.3	898	147

1. Percent of total civilian labor force. 2. For week including March 12. Excludes government employees, self-employed persons, farm workers, domestic service workers, railroad employees subject to the Railroad Retirement Act, and employees on oceanborne vessels or in foreign countries.

STATE County	Private nonfarm establishments, 1988 (cont'd)				Personal income, 1989								Earnings, 1989		
	Employment[1] (cont'd)		Annual payroll								Per capita[3]			Percent by selected industries	
	Finance, insurance, and real estate	Services	Total (Mil dol)	Average per employee (Dollars)	Total (Mil dol)	Percent change, 1988–1989	Wages and salaries[2] (Mil dol)	Proprietor's income (Mil dol)	Dividends, interest, & rent (Mil dol)	Transfer payments (Mil dol)	Dollars	Rank	Total (Mil dol)	Farm	Goods-related[4] Total
	88	89	90	91	92	93	94	95	96	97	98	99	100	101	102
TENNESSEE	113 626	447 273	32 561	X	72 757	6.7	48 199	7 025	10 455	11 426	14 736	X	55 224	1.3	30.9
Anderson	777	14 326	834	25 766	1 078	8.8	945	80	177	186	15 126	932	1 025	0.3	52.7
Bedford	458	1 389	168	17 024	432	6.7	240	57	69	64	14 567	1 179	297	5.9	54.9
Benton	93	741	41	13 703	179	7.4	73	18	26	40	12 048	2 313	91	6.5	NA
Bledsoe	0	272	16	14 357	95	5.2	34	10	12	20	9 495	2 960	44	6.1	36.1
Blount	957	4 836	425	18 828	1 214	4.4	562	77	199	203	14 192	1 347	639	1.9	37.4
Bradley	873	7 415	496	16 599	1 039	6.7	660	106	149	134	13 827	1 519	766	1.9	45.3
Campbell	216	1 050	81	13 235	360	5.7	145	34	44	106	10 325	2 831	179	1.4	36.4
Cannon	30	323	19	11 668	134	6.1	33	18	17	23	12 245	2 212	51	16.1	NA
Carroll	218	1 282	83	12 869	331	5.8	141	31	47	77	11 817	2 391	172	1.4	42.0
Carter	335	1 979	120	13 909	548	5.0	186	42	63	112	10 696	2 740	227	1.9	40.5
Cheatham	113	721	59	16 463	364	8.2	95	31	37	40	13 129	1 849	127	3.9	53.4
Chester	0	391	32	13 902	145	5.0	51	15	18	26	11 222	2 594	66	5.2	NA
Claiborne	373	590	73	13 030	315	8.8	122	42	38	63	11 772	2 416	164	7.8	43.2
Clay	0	459	31	13 545	80	10.5	40	13	9	16	10 079	2 872	52	5.7	NA
Cocke	217	971	78	14 129	290	6.1	120	29	37	72	9 841	2 904	148	2.3	41.9
Coffee	452	8 533	396	20 052	598	6.6	480	68	87	101	14 028	1 423	549	1.8	28.6
Crockett	107	270	38	15 785	164	8.9	58	25	26	33	11 819	2 390	83	8.8	40.2
Cumberland	430	1 892	125	14 389	405	7.6	178	58	72	84	11 822	2 388	236	1.8	34.1
Davidson	31 865	104 571	6 396	20 284	9 404	6.0	8 763	894	1 580	1 211	18 359	258	9 658	0.1	20.3
Decatur	104	291	33	15 876	114	6.2	53	17	16	25	10 554	2 778	70	9.6	40.9
De Kalb	124	417	44	13 198	176	0.0	75	25	28	34	12 136	2 268	99	7.1	NA
Dickson	349	1 357	114	16 357	492	7.2	172	48	56	76	13 817	1 526	220	3.1	36.3
Dyer	431	1 717	199	17 436	498	10.9	328	53	74	87	14 161	1 365	382	1.9	50.2
Fayette	124	446	53	11 328	322	8.3	103	38	28	58	12 073	2 302	141	16.7	40.5
Fentress	92	467	33	10 385	134	6.0	53	22	13	40	8 489	3 042	75	4.4	37.6
Franklin	332	1 851	79	13 122	395	6.7	133	53	67	77	11 388	2 544	186	9.8	24.1
Gibson	516	1 659	259	16 786	637	4.4	356	80	101	127	13 251	1 793	437	2.7	51.6
Giles	277	800	106	16 490	333	5.1	162	43	51	66	13 239	1 797	205	5.5	46.1
Grainger	0	241	23	11 733	167	5.9	46	23	18	35	9 534	2 956	70	11.7	42.1
Greene	445	2 954	304	15 708	686	6.7	439	54	100	118	12 195	2 235	493	2.4	51.6
Grundy	0	246	17	9 554	141	8.4	30	28	14	36	9 797	2 910	58	19.1	20.6
Hamblen	563	3 233	384	16 568	653	7.6	583	79	84	110	12 735	2 021	661	0.5	58.3
Hamilton	10 930	35 325	2 494	18 364	4 904	5.2	3 824	440	788	734	16 672	489	4 263	0.2	27.4
Hancock	0	87	6	10 440	55	6.7	13	10	5	17	8 160	3 066	24	21.2	NA
Hardeman	271	910	80	15 215	259	6.0	141	25	31	66	10 550	2 779	166	4.6	42.3
Hardin	140	551	87	14 641	250	4.9	126	27	31	53	11 135	2 625	153	4.1	46.3
Hawkins	255	1 256	204	20 877	497	5.9	246	38	62	90	10 935	2 677	284	3.0	57.3
Haywood	238	566	66	15 374	234	1.1	111	21	32	53	11 068	2 647	132	6.0	42.4
Henderson	101	519	89	15 609	262	6.6	135	39	35	49	11 433	2 528	174	6.3	53.8
Henry	297	1 052	112	15 005	348	6.9	180	41	65	80	11 850	2 379	221	1.3	NA
Hickman	122	403	35	13 117	192	2.9	52	24	25	35	11 327	2 559	75	6.0	38.2
Houston	0	256	14	14 374	81	5.8	25	7	9	19	11 189	2 605	32	8.2	NA
Humphreys	91	502	84	19 916	196	4.9	141	19	29	38	12 076	2 298	160	2.2	NA
Jackson	56	292	29	14 126	91	5.5	31	16	11	20	9 646	2 938	47	7.8	44.9
Jefferson	271	1 249	97	14 853	403	7.6	185	42	57	74	12 006	2 324	227	4.0	45.4
Johnson	85	338	36	12 669	124	3.6	46	17	18	39	8 882	3 016	63	9.7	37.2
Knox	7 375	39 773	2 515	17 890	5 481	6.0	3 847	556	854	790	16 538	520	4 402	0.2	22.1
Lake	49	188	12	11 368	70	2.9	23	9	12	20	9 528	2 957	31	12.6	NA
Lauderdale	216	575	106	14 889	277	2.8	158	28	31	65	11 035	2 659	186	3.9	53.0
Lawrence	270	1 022	154	15 449	432	5.0	214	56	59	84	12 221	2 220	271	3.1	48.5
Lewis	59	547	35	12 890	92	8.5	48	10	12	21	8 630	3 034	59	2.5	NA
Lincoln	422	700	97	15 054	368	6.3	152	49	47	66	13 272	1 786	201	6.9	42.7
Loudon	353	1 162	110	16 256	397	6.0	177	30	58	72	12 615	2 068	207	4.9	49.3
McMinn	397	2 017	292	18 202	542	8.8	391	40	74	95	12 399	2 160	432	2.0	57.4
McNairy	163	1 287	93	14 515	259	6.4	121	29	29	58	10 734	2 733	150	4.6	NA
Macon	99	373	40	13 041	172	2.2	67	27	22	32	10 632	2 763	95	8.8	NA
Madison	1 363	7 283	542	17 905	1 102	7.1	857	109	166	196	14 062	1 405	966	0.7	35.0
Marion	176	820	60	13 381	275	5.5	98	24	29	61	10 635	2 760	122	3.1	31.1
Marshall	200	717	149	17 389	297	7.2	205	32	43	48	13 809	1 531	237	3.7	63.8
Maury	1 200	3 023	272	17 194	832	16.8	583	76	126	126	14 874	1 039	659	1.2	51.2
Meigs	0	179	9	11 997	89	5.8	28	7	9	17	10 280	2 841	34	9.4	NA
Monroe	148	960	96	13 354	341	8.0	159	33	41	66	10 844	2 701	192	3.5	NA
Montgomery	1 235	3 553	287	14 199	1 253	7.1	470	106	135	201	12 595	2 073	577	1.3	33.9
Moore	0	39	12	16 824	55	6.5	32	4	7	7	11 091	2 636	36	8.2	NA
Morgan	0	215	24	14 944	172	11.9	62	14	15	38	9 543	2 954	77	4.4	49.5
Obion	343	1 878	275	22 111	449	2.5	364	55	73	74	13 791	1 539	419	2.1	56.7
Overton	88	373	32	12 741	161	5.0	66	23	22	40	8 962	3 010	89	7.1	NA
Perry	0	385	25	15 843	76	6.3	35	12	10	17	11 585	2 477	47	9.1	NA

1. For week including March 12. Excludes government employees, self-employed persons, farm workers, domestic service workers, railroad employees subject to the Railroad Retirement Act, and employees on oceanborne vessels or in foreign countries. 2. Includes other labor income. 3. Based on the resident population estimated as of July 1 of the year shown. 4. Covers mining, construction, and manufacturing.

STATE County	Earnings, 1989 (cont'd): Percent by selected industries (cont'd): Goods-related[1]: Manu-facturing	Service-related & other[2]: Total	Service-related & other[2]: Retail trade	Service-related & other[2]: Finance, insur-ance, & real estate	Service-related & other[2]: Services	Govern-ment	Agriculture, 1987: Farms: Number	Farms: Percent with: Less than 50 acres	Farms: Percent with: 500 acres and over	Farm operators, percent: Whose principal occu-pation is farming	Farm operators, percent: Residing on farm operated	Land in farms: Acreage (1,000)	Land in farms: Percent change, 1982–1987	Land in farms: Acres: Average size of farm	Land in farms: Acres: Total irrigated (1,000)	Land in farms: Acres: Total cropland (1,000)
	103	104	105	106	107	108	109	110	111	112	113	114	115	116	117	118
TENNESSEE	24.2	53.3	10.2	5.2	23.5	14.6	79 711	38.3	5.3	38.6	70.9	11 731	-6.0	147	38	7 186
Anderson	42.2	34.8	5.2	1.7	24.5	12.3	463	45.4	1.9	27.9	76.2	40	-6.4	87	0	20
Bedford	48.4	28.9	7.4	2.3	10.9	10.4	1 244	25.8	7.4	42.7	74.9	221	-1.2	178	0	131
Benton	23.7	NA	10.3	1.7	NA	19.8	392	27.0	6.1	31.9	66.8	65	-6.4	165	0	34
Bledsoe	30.1	31.5	5.9	1.7	12.1	26.3	482	26.1	8.1	45.6	78.6	89	-13.2	184	D	49
Blount	28.2	47.5	12.9	3.1	19.6	13.2	1 185	51.1	1.7	35.6	74.3	101	-8.7	86	0	69
Bradley	39.9	42.1	9.7	2.8	21.7	10.7	738	43.0	4.6	36.0	76.6	92	-2.4	125	0	49
Campbell	22.1	41.4	13.4	3.2	13.7	20.8	470	55.1	0.6	31.9	66.4	35	-1.8	74	0	20
Cannon	26.8	40.3	9.1	4.5	14.8	11.8	694	32.1	4.6	34.1	72.3	101	-7.1	145	0	49
Carroll	37.2	42.9	10.9	3.3	17.0	13.7	848	26.3	8.0	40.9	66.2	166	-12.2	196	0	111
Carter	30.8	41.3	11.4	3.3	21.0	16.3	686	68.5	0.6	26.5	69.0	38	-20.2	55	0	19
Cheatham	41.0	29.1	9.1	0.9	12.0	13.5	567	37.0	3.4	33.0	68.8	67	-10.5	118	0	35
Chester	30.4	41.7	11.9	2.2	18.3	14.8	387	22.2	7.8	40.8	67.4	73	-15.8	189	0	47
Claiborne	27.4	35.9	10.5	2.3	15.2	13.1	1 528	46.1	1.8	41.2	68.1	142	2.1	93	0	68
Clay	51.5	NA	7.2	1.8	10.1	13.5	528	29.9	3.4	39.2	68.4	76	-13.3	143	0	35
Cocke	36.9	41.0	14.9	2.7	17.9	14.8	1 081	48.8	1.4	39.5	68.5	89	-7.5	83	0	49
Coffee	24.0	57.2	7.4	2.5	41.7	12.4	887	36.9	6.0	41.3	77.6	143	-5.8	162	0	93
Crockett	32.2	39.5	10.6	2.9	13.9	11.5	506	31.4	21.9	55.1	63.6	184	26.7	364	6	157
Cumberland	25.1	53.3	12.0	8.9	25.8	10.8	622	35.2	6.4	36.3	77.2	94	-12.4	151	0	47
Davidson	14.0	67.7	11.6	8.5	30.6	12.0	561	44.7	2.9	28.5	72.7	58	-21.7	103	0	27
Decatur	30.9	35.6	10.6	2.6	11.8	13.9	474	21.3	6.3	37.3	72.4	92	-4.7	193	0	42
De Kalb	39.0	37.1	9.8	3.5	14.8	9.6	823	37.8	3.4	36.3	66.0	101	-3.1	123	0	55
Dickson	25.2	47.5	14.2	3.6	22.4	13.0	1 068	28.9	3.5	35.0	72.3	149	-7.1	139	0	76
Dyer	42.5	37.3	9.4	3.1	15.8	10.7	603	25.0	23.4	65.2	57.4	235	-13.5	390	2	215
Fayette	35.0	26.3	6.6	2.2	9.4	16.5	765	28.2	17.5	45.1	60.7	271	-13.2	354	0	182
Fentress	28.5	42.5	11.0	3.4	21.1	15.5	454	33.0	7.0	40.1	68.7	79	-11.1	173	0	36
Franklin	17.4	52.5	13.0	1.9	30.5	13.6	1 126	40.7	4.6	43.7	72.6	153	2.9	136	0	108
Gibson	45.2	35.8	9.7	2.4	13.2	9.9	1 057	30.5	15.1	53.5	64.3	280	-4.3	265	0	242
Giles	41.0	38.1	11.9	3.0	16.4	10.3	1 551	21.3	5.2	36.0	74.2	263	-6.6	170	0	143
Grainger	37.1	31.2	6.0	1.9	10.5	15.0	1 219	49.7	1.5	39.8	68.0	108	-0.9	89	0	53
Greene	47.9	33.9	8.3	2.4	16.3	12.1	3 580	56.0	1.3	40.8	71.7	264	0.6	74	1	171
Grundy	12.8	43.2	9.9	0.4	11.0	17.0	333	49.8	3.9	43.8	73.3	38	-5.0	113	1	20
Hamblen	54.5	33.1	8.3	2.0	14.0	8.1	843	59.8	0.8	33.0	73.5	58	-5.5	69	0	38
Hamilton	21.2	54.5	10.4	7.4	23.6	17.9	587	43.4	2.7	28.1	76.7	58	-11.2	98	0	30
Hancock	18.3	NA	7.2	2.5	21.4	19.9	760	38.6	1.8	49.6	67.6	77	-4.8	101	0	31
Hardeman	37.8	31.3	10.5	2.5	13.9	21.7	488	19.7	21.7	43.0	61.5	187	-5.6	384	D	94
Hardin	40.8	32.9	10.7	2.1	9.2	16.7	570	30.7	8.4	45.3	64.0	121	-13.7	212	0	70
Hawkins	53.0	23.5	6.8	1.9	8.3	16.2	1 985	49.6	1.1	34.7	68.5	168	-2.2	85	0	81
Haywood	37.9	37.6	12.6	3.5	11.9	14.0	527	27.5	23.3	60.0	54.3	222	-0.4	422	2	185
Henderson	50.1	29.1	9.8	2.0	9.6	10.8	849	22.6	9.8	36.7	68.4	164	-2.1	193	D	95
Henry	33.2	NA	11.8	2.9	18.6	15.0	805	23.5	10.2	47.7	72.2	187	-5.5	232	0	119
Hickman	25.4	33.4	8.9	2.8	14.0	22.4	650	23.1	7.5	36.6	73.5	130	-0.3	199	0	59
Houston	29.7	39.6	9.3	2.0	21.2	15.0	245	22.4	6.1	35.9	71.8	46	-3.2	186	0	20
Humphreys	41.8	NA	7.0	1.3	12.9	18.6	506	20.8	8.7	36.8	71.9	121	-2.9	238	0	50
Jackson	38.0	35.8	7.9	2.7	16.3	11.4	732	33.2	4.4	36.6	68.4	99	-3.8	135	0	34
Jefferson	31.8	38.1	8.5	1.8	14.1	12.4	1 326	50.3	1.5	37.1	71.4	110	-4.9	83	0	71
Johnson	30.8	37.3	7.2	3.1	12.5	15.9	888	59.6	1.4	36.9	72.7	62	-6.6	70	0	28
Knox	14.8	59.9	11.2	4.4	27.8	17.9	1 253	56.7	1.2	31.6	76.8	95	-12.7	76	0	59
Lake	24.8	40.0	12.9	6.4	11.4	19.4	85	12.9	47.1	78.8	43.5	92	0.0	1 082	2	87
Lauderdale	50.6	30.3	6.9	2.6	8.5	12.8	572	30.9	18.7	50.7	61.7	198	-1.4	345	D	165
Lawrence	42.7	37.7	9.8	2.1	15.3	10.8	1 428	32.9	4.3	33.3	74.0	201	-7.7	141	0	119
Lewis	46.5	NA	8.4	2.9	15.3	10.8	223	23.8	5.8	31.8	75.3	38	-1.0	171	D	13
Lincoln	32.6	35.2	11.5	2.4	14.5	15.2	1 628	26.7	5.5	38.7	73.2	279	-5.0	172	0	163
Loudon	43.7	33.1	8.2	3.0	14.0	12.7	760	46.6	2.5	32.5	72.4	78	-6.9	102	0	50
McMinn	52.2	31.2	10.2	2.1	10.1	9.4	1 076	34.7	3.7	36.6	72.4	138	-5.5	128	0	82
McNairy	41.2	NA	7.8	2.8	17.7	12.9	715	22.8	9.4	38.9	65.0	150	-4.0	209	D	83
Macon	38.6	37.5	7.6	2.9	14.2	10.5	1 242	35.9	1.4	34.1	69.6	125	-5.3	101	0	68
Madison	25.5	47.4	11.1	3.2	23.4	17.0	614	27.0	13.4	46.9	64.5	160	-14.5	261	2	110
Marion	26.5	48.8	16.1	3.3	15.3	17.1	310	30.3	8.1	31.6	67.4	56	-2.2	181	D	31
Marshall	59.4	24.1	6.8	1.6	10.2	8.4	1 013	25.0	5.9	39.1	74.5	173	-3.6	171	0	94
Maury	33.1	35.7	8.0	4.4	13.7	12.0	1 575	31.1	6.3	39.2	70.5	257	-8.9	163	0	142
Meigs	28.9	NA	6.1	3.2	8.0	14.3	322	28.0	5.3	34.2	71.4	55	-0.2	171	0	29
Monroe	41.4	NA	10.7	4.2	13.5	11.3	930	41.5	3.0	35.5	74.2	105	-12.2	113	0	65
Montgomery	25.0	46.1	15.2	4.3	18.3	18.7	998	28.9	8.8	42.9	68.7	188	3.1	188	0	119
Moore	53.6	NA	2.5	2.0	2.3	26.1	427	28.3	3.3	25.8	71.2	58	-6.4	135	0	32
Morgan	42.2	27.0	5.6	1.2	8.7	19.1	304	36.2	4.3	26.0	75.7	44	-7.6	145	0	21
Obion	52.4	34.1	8.7	1.7	14.5	7.1	761	24.6	19.6	51.5	67.7	259	-0.5	340	1	215
Overton	32.1	NA	11.4	2.7	15.4	16.7	842	38.1	4.2	37.3	72.6	110	-13.1	131	0	54
Perry	47.8	NA	4.6	2.6	16.4	10.9	220	28.2	16.4	38.2	67.7	58	-23.6	265	D	22

1. Covers mining, construction, and manufacturing. 2. Covers private sector earnings in agricultural services, forestry, and fisheries; transportation and public utilities; wholesale trade; retail trade; finance, insurance, and real estate; and services.

STATE County	Agriculture, 1987 (cont'd)								Manufactures, 1987						
	Value of land and buildings		Value of products sold				Percent of farms with sales of		Establishments		All employees			Production workers	
					Percent from										
	Average per farm ($1,000)	Average per acre (Dollars)	Total (Mil dol)	Average per farm (Dollars)	Crops	Livestock and poultry[1]	$10,000 or more	$100,000 or more	Total	Percent with 20 or more em-ployees	Number (1,000)	Percent change, 1982–1987	Annual payroll (Mil dol)	Number (1,000)	Work hours (Mil)
	119	120	121	122	123	124	125	126	127	128	129	130	131	132	133
TENNESSEE	146	1 001	1 618	20 294	43.4	56.6	27.3	4.3	6 864	40.8	484.9	5.0	9 869.2	359.2	707.4
Anderson	149	1 707	5	11 706	39.4	60.6	14.3	1.5	98	27.6	10.4	4.0	301.2	5.5	11.3
Bedford	154	901	43	34 353	7.4	92.6	35.4	9.0	52	55.8	4.6	24.3	86.3	3.7	7.6
Benton	98	607	5	12 067	32.2	67.8	27.8	1.5	19	42.1	0.8	33.3	13.4	0.7	1.3
Bledsoe	160	744	10	21 632	30.0	70.0	38.2	5.0	11	36.4	0.5	66.7	6.9	0.4	0.8
Blount	170	2 135	14	11 552	30.0	70.0	18.6	2.2	90	28.9	6.3	0.0	169.2	5.3	10.2
Bradley	154	1 292	34	46 572	1.9	98.1	29.9	15.0	138	46.4	13.1	5.6	245.8	9.7	19.3
Campbell	94	1 343	4	7 541	30.9	69.2	13.8	1.5	42	35.7	2.0	0.0	29.7	1.6	3.0
Cannon	110	779	10	14 994	19.2	80.8	24.8	3.2	17	47.1	D	D	D	D	D
Carroll	128	643	17	20 004	52.6	47.4	32.5	5.1	49	38.8	3.4	21.4	45.8	2.9	5.6
Carter	73	1 673	6	8 336	34.6	65.4	12.8	1.2	42	38.1	3.6	12.5	59.7	3.0	5.5
Cheatham	151	1 229	5	9 691	55.2	44.8	28.2	0.5	24	25.0	D	D	D	D	D
Chester	123	633	7	17 727	50.9	49.1	32.6	3.4	18	44.4	1.0	0.0	13.8	0.9	1.7
Claiborne	84	876	15	9 728	41.9	58.1	20.2	1.3	31	29.0	2.6	44.4	28.3	2.2	4.0
Clay	80	675	4	8 484	39.7	60.3	23.5	0.6	13	61.5	1.4	55.6	18.9	1.3	2.2
Cocke	91	1 083	13	11 616	39.8	60.2	19.5	1.1	33	48.5	2.5	0.0	42.4	2.1	4.5
Coffee	162	1 013	21	24 199	31.4	68.6	32.4	6.1	71	49.3	5.1	4.1	90.2	3.9	7.8
Crockett	345	976	40	79 789	94.3	5.7	61.7	23.1	17	41.2	D	D	D	D	D
Cumberland	131	942	10	16 711	26.7	73.3	25.7	4.0	54	38.9	2.8	64.7	49.8	2.2	4.4
Davidson	230	1 981	8	14 407	51.9	48.1	15.7	2.0	863	34.8	48.1	5.7	1 234.5	30.7	62.7
Decatur	93	525	7	14 423	13.9	86.1	31.6	1.9	24	33.3	1.3	-31.6	16.6	0.9	1.8
De Kalb	114	1 000	13	15 487	63.2	36.8	21.5	2.6	26	57.7	2.0	25.0	25.5	1.7	3.1
Dickson	121	898	9	8 703	29.7	70.3	23.1	0.7	38	31.6	D	D	D	D	D
Dyer	287	742	34	55 879	87.3	12.7	64.5	16.4	39	33.3	4.4	15.8	93.2	3.5	7.5
Fayette	281	768	52	67 652	45.7	54.3	42.0	15.4	26	46.2	1.8	12.5	28.3	1.5	3.0
Fentress	127	676	16	34 362	13.3	86.7	30.8	6.8	35	45.7	1.7	13.3	15.3	1.5	2.8
Franklin	152	1 134	35	30 973	34.8	65.2	34.9	6.7	34	47.1	1.6	0.0	21.2	1.4	2.7
Gibson	180	704	48	45 669	72.2	27.8	50.0	12.7	72	50.0	8.3	7.8	157.0	6.9	13.5
Giles	135	777	26	16 665	10.1	89.9	25.2	3.0	41	39.0	3.3	-19.5	63.5	2.8	5.9
Grainger	92	997	10	8 196	40.6	59.4	18.6	0.7	26	26.9	0.8	-11.1	10.1	0.7	1.3
Greene	95	1 262	42	11 797	29.3	70.7	22.1	2.1	85	49.4	9.9	17.9	174.7	7.7	15.1
Grundy	92	811	21	63 851	18.2	81.8	51.1	21.6	16	31.2	0.6	-14.3	4.5	0.5	0.8
Hamblen	112	1 636	9	11 246	31.6	68.4	17.8	1.9	117	56.4	13.2	14.8	240.4	10.2	20.9
Hamilton	156	1 577	12	20 089	19.9	80.1	18.9	4.9	465	43.9	31.0	-14.1	669.2	21.8	43.1
Hancock	83	842	6	7 588	49.2	50.8	19.1	0.3	2	100.0	D	D	D	D	D
Hardeman	185	514	16	32 457	61.8	38.2	35.5	8.6	32	37.5	2.7	35.0	47.9	2.2	4.2
Hardin	142	664	11	18 496	39.6	60.4	33.5	3.5	55	34.5	3.3	17.9	53.8	2.7	5.6
Hawkins	98	1 157	13	6 794	46.9	53.1	15.4	0.4	35	37.1	5.2	23.8	135.9	4.1	8.9
Haywood	340	777	47	88 357	89.7	10.3	63.0	24.9	20	70.0	2.1	50.0	36.0	1.7	3.5
Henderson	124	651	20	23 619	23.9	76.1	36.9	4.7	31	58.1	3.6	16.1	54.7	3.1	6.1
Henry	152	649	23	28 623	40.5	59.5	40.2	6.7	55	43.6	3.3	-10.8	57.4	2.4	4.8
Hickman	129	672	8	12 703	18.2	81.8	25.7	1.8	22	40.9	1.3	18.2	19.1	1.2	2.2
Houston	114	610	3	10 455	21.5	78.4	29.4	1.6	12	41.7	0.5	25.0	6.9	0.5	0.9
Humphreys	147	682	8	14 979	25.3	74.7	30.6	3.0	22	31.8	1.8	-10.0	49.5	1.5	2.8
Jackson	86	622	5	6 474	43.5	56.5	17.5	0.0	26	34.6	1.0	-28.6	14.6	0.8	1.4
Jefferson	116	1 572	17	12 572	23.1	76.9	21.2	2.3	51	39.2	2.6	-13.3	38.9	2.1	4.1
Johnson	73	1 134	6	6 940	46.7	53.3	15.3	0.6	21	23.8	1.6	-23.8	19.3	1.3	2.4
Knox	176	2 412	11	9 084	38.6	61.4	14.0	1.3	452	36.3	25.5	11.4	490.2	18.0	34.4
Lake	955	878	15	172 991	D	D	80.0	43.5	8	37.5	0.5	25.0	6.6	0.4	0.7
Lauderdale	242	698	31	53 989	88.0	12.0	49.8	13.6	27	70.4	4.7	30.6	76.0	4.2	8.3
Lawrence	119	854	24	16 846	22.7	77.3	26.5	3.9	57	36.8	5.6	27.3	95.4	4.7	8.8
Lewis	127	774	2	7 951	16.9	83.1	20.2	0.9	24	33.3	1.0	-23.1	16.3	0.9	1.7
Lincoln	140	849	33	20 015	21.9	78.1	30.6	4.1	33	21.2	2.5	19.0	39.9	2.1	3.8
Loudon	151	1 600	31	41 429	D	D	20.0	4.5	37	54.1	2.8	-3.4	58.9	2.3	4.6
McMinn	139	1 089	32	30 178	7.0	93.0	24.5	8.2	75	52.0	9.4	16.0	199.2	7.2	14.0
McNairy	139	659	17	23 968	38.9	61.1	30.2	4.5	51	39.2	3.3	-8.3	44.0	2.7	5.8
Macon	72	722	10	7 671	49.6	50.4	20.9	0.2	28	35.7	1.9	11.8	26.4	1.7	2.8
Madison	213	839	23	37 597	84.4	15.6	39.3	11.2	100	44.0	8.5	4.9	191.4	6.2	13.2
Marion	188	992	6	18 824	22.4	77.6	21.6	5.5	23	43.5	1.4	7.7	19.9	1.2	2.6
Marshall	164	874	21	20 727	7.4	92.6	30.5	5.8	44	59.1	5.9	31.1	106.3	4.5	9.1
Maury	200	1 206	23	14 434	23.5	76.5	27.5	2.6	77	42.9	5.0	0.0	106.5	4.2	8.3
Meigs	172	911	5	16 134	26.9	73.1	28.6	3.4	7	57.1	0.2	0.0	2.8	0.2	0.3
Monroe	136	1 177	17	18 515	16.7	83.3	20.1	5.1	56	44.6	3.6	44.0	53.8	3.1	5.5
Montgomery	161	907	22	22 443	56.3	43.7	38.5	4.8	70	32.9	5.3	-14.5	105.2	3.8	7.0
Moore	129	881	7	15 977	10.6	89.4	28.1	3.5	7	42.9	D	D	D	D	D
Morgan	106	674	4	12 811	14.0	86.0	22.4	2.3	21	28.6	0.8	0.0	10.0	0.7	1.3
Obion	253	753	41	54 026	69.4	30.6	55.2	14.8	44	47.7	6.4	23.1	166.9	5.4	11.0
Overton	98	746	10	11 531	17.5	82.5	22.0	2.3	33	24.2	0.9	-18.2	10.0	0.7	1.3
Perry	114	496	3	14 443	16.6	83.4	29.5	3.2	19	31.6	1.1	57.1	13.6	0.9	1.7

1. Includes livestock and poultry products.

STATE County	Manufactures, 1987 (cont'd): Production workers (cont'd): Wages: Total (Mil dol)	Manufactures, 1987 (cont'd): Production workers (cont'd): Wages: Average per worker (Dollars)	Manufactures, 1987 (cont'd): Value added by manufacture (Mil dol)	Manufactures, 1987 (cont'd): Value of shipments (Mil dol)	Manufactures, 1987 (cont'd): New capital expenditures (Mil dol)	Value of construction authorized by building permits, 1990: Total[1] ($1,000)	Nonresidential: Total ($1,000)	Nonresidential: Percent: Office	Nonresidential: Percent: Industrial	Nonresidential: Percent: Stores	Residential: New construction ($1,000)	Residential: Number of housing units	Residential: Alterations and additions ($1,000)
	134	135	136	137	138	139	140	141	142	143	144	145	146
TENNESSEE	6 282.6	17 491	27 049.7	57 752.9	1 904.7	3 015 402	880 640	20.4	18.4	30.5	1 430 895	21 977	138 726
Anderson	135.6	24 655	828.0	983.1	D	66 540	22 299	53.8	29.2	8.5	32 403	394	1 897
Bedford	63.6	17 189	277.5	549.1	35.4	7 917	3 385	6.6	32.2	50.9	2 660	52	263
Benton	10.5	15 000	25.9	51.6	1.1	764	128	0.0	0.0	98.8	538	12	0
Bledsoe	4.6	11 500	20.0	45.9	D	NA	NA	NA	NA	NA	NA	NA	NA
Blount	136.3	25 717	393.2	1 427.3	D	32 195	12 443	16.6	66.3	6.8	11 089	141	474
Bradley	154.0	15 876	864.9	1 768.9	66.4	33 007	7 108	0.8	0.0	60.8	25 192	388	411
Campbell	20.4	12 750	58.3	126.4	2.4	0	0	NA	NA	NA	0	0	0
Cannon	D	D	D	D	D	1 037	0	NA	NA	NA	137	3	0
Carroll	35.6	12 276	141.4	328.0	10.4	7 268	3 340	9.1	84.2	1.9	2 504	66	88
Carter	43.6	14 533	111.5	210.8	5.6	2 597	1 042	69.5	0.0	14.8	924	31	82
Cheatham	D	D	D	D	D	31 673	3 495	7.5	2.1	61.1	24 796	335	1 528
Chester	9.5	10 556	22.0	51.2	1.4	2 141	325	23.1	12.3	9.2	1 649	41	86
Claiborne	22.6	10 273	48.2	102.6	1.4	5 928	807	28.5	0.0	42.5	4 523	129	136
Clay	15.9	12 231	37.6	65.6	1.0	497	191	0.0	0.0	0.0	0	0	306
Cocke	31.1	14 810	190.7	340.8	10.8	2 226	854	0.0	0.0	100.0	1 227	45	145
Coffee	60.4	15 487	230.4	379.4	8.7	16 945	2 806	17.5	17.4	36.7	9 847	153	819
Crockett	D	D	D	D	D	0	0	NA	NA	NA	0	0	0
Cumberland	33.0	15 000	135.1	256.7	5.4	7 071	2 728	12.6	0.0	60.8	3 474	69	71
Davidson	709.2	23 101	2 881.8	6 089.8	165.5	489 393	183 501	27.8	4.6	28.1	130 788	1 692	35 807
Decatur	11.9	13 222	30.6	45.5	0.6	763	667	0.0	13.5	4.5	88	4	0
De Kalb	18.3	10 765	60.1	98.9	2.3	1 429	230	19.6	0.0	32.7	833	16	54
Dickson	D	D	D	D	D	18 375	4 896	7.8	67.6	5.4	10 935	195	613
Dyer	64.3	18 371	275.2	511.8	11.5	16 437	3 501	35.4	5.7	23.6	7 294	152	1 802
Fayette	20.0	13 333	67.0	158.1	3.0	16 750	4 197	1.5	35.6	1.4	10 264	170	1 944
Fentress	12.9	8 600	25.8	44.7	1.0	1 205	285	0.0	0.0	100.0	895	33	0
Franklin	15.8	11 286	55.1	136.9	5.1	10 122	1 325	4.7	47.7	16.1	7 442	156	146
Gibson	113.8	16 493	395.6	843.1	18.2	16 695	5 995	19.2	26.6	6.7	6 402	148	434
Giles	50.1	17 893	190.8	338.7	7.9	2 115	494	0.0	0.0	73.5	658	18	492
Grainger	7.6	10 857	23.0	51.0	D	NA	NA	NA	NA	NA	NA	NA	NA
Greene	120.0	15 584	492.5	1 225.4	27.5	17 203	10 442	1.3	71.2	25.7	6 071	116	116
Grundy	3.2	6 400	7.7	10.1	0.2	NA	NA	NA	NA	NA	NA	NA	NA
Hamblen	152.1	14 912	645.1	1 366.2	46.8	18 251	9 865	4.5	58.5	14.2	5 089	100	306
Hamilton	401.1	18 399	1 691.4	3 642.0	117.9	229 045	88 882	20.8	8.0	25.8	74 542	1 032	12 718
Hancock	D	D	D	D	D	1 384	0	NA	NA	NA	1 368	49	0
Hardeman	37.3	16 955	143.0	245.8	6.2	3 184	1 210	28.3	3.3	38.8	1 584	31	93
Hardin	40.1	14 852	198.4	411.7	7.3	1 390	736	24.9	50.8	4.4	533	13	22
Hawkins	100.2	24 439	383.4	658.2	20.8	5 482	1 585	0.0	0.0	29.0	3 086	107	41
Haywood	28.1	16 529	96.9	234.3	6.2	4 402	1 401	10.7	46.4	15.2	733	14	1 008
Henderson	42.6	13 742	164.9	482.2	7.4	2 861	1 156	19.3	2.6	30.6	1 558	30	17
Henry	38.2	15 917	122.5	293.7	6.6	2 019	782	0.0	22.8	0.0	503	8	210
Hickman	14.7	12 250	76.3	128.8	1.5	1 420	568	0.0	31.9	52.8	754	12	85
Houston	5.5	11 000	13.5	23.7	0.2	522	287	54.9	0.0	14.5	197	6	2
Humphreys	36.0	24 000	340.7	511.0	D	1 511	237	0.0	21.1	29.6	975	15	124
Jackson	11.1	13 875	28.3	52.2	1.1	0	0	NA	NA	NA	0	0	0
Jefferson	30.0	14 286	104.3	263.0	3.1	2 968	556	2.2	0.9	13.5	1 376	38	291
Johnson	15.8	12 154	57.7	140.2	2.0	6 638	685	0.0	0.0	0.0	5 383	87	12
Knox	269.8	14 989	1 160.9	2 404.9	51.6	260 397	45 741	19.4	28.2	18.9	157 373	2 401	12 143
Lake	4.8	12 000	D	33.0	0.5	482	80	0.0	0.0	49.7	350	18	50
Lauderdale	61.2	14 571	299.2	506.7	16.0	11 078	2 570	7.1	49.2	37.1	7 565	144	223
Lawrence	77.3	16 447	254.4	659.1	D	3 419	498	6.0	40.2	48.2	2 094	27	135
Lewis	12.6	14 000	36.6	72.6	D	911	296	0.0	0.0	83.8	355	6	47
Lincoln	28.4	13 524	94.4	231.6	4.5	1 844	32	0.0	0.0	100.0	1 462	49	307
Loudon	45.5	19 783	226.5	458.4	26.6	15 319	1 447	0.0	13.1	63.7	11 381	177	768
McMinn	137.3	19 069	520.9	1 110.4	55.6	16 142	12 495	3.9	11.7	44.2	2 454	150	687
McNairy	32.6	12 074	120.2	207.5	7.8	1 844	830	21.1	59.1	17.0	714	18	141
Macon	21.4	12 588	45.2	127.3	3.1	593	164	51.7	0.0	28.2	248	6	96
Madison	121.0	19 516	621.1	1 341.2	D	90 791	43 406	3.5	37.6	11.5	30 253	433	1 619
Marion	14.5	12 083	53.6	128.6	D	13 042	4 896	16.7	0.0	65.8	7 346	155	152
Marshall	67.6	15 022	339.1	714.7	39.2	14 527	8 719	0.0	72.5	24.5	5 590	169	97
Maury	82.5	19 643	217.7	639.9	19.8	60 963	6 453	22.6	21.1	43.2	42 760	815	1 936
Meigs	2.1	10 500	4.5	7.7	D	241	101	76.2	0.0	19.8	140	2	0
Monroe	41.6	13 419	154.6	301.3	7.1	4 727	1 195	0.0	5.0	23.3	3 048	88	289
Montgomery	63.3	16 658	295.5	548.8	D	61 075	13 544	30.5	10.7	42.7	40 140	833	2 353
Moore	D	D	D	D	D	765	12	0.0	0.0	0.0	753	27	0
Morgan	8.3	11 857	30.2	42.2	0.6	0	0	NA	NA	NA	0	0	0
Obion	134.0	24 815	636.2	1 130.6	32.7	7 566	1 787	10.3	45.0	24.8	4 375	86	507
Overton	8.1	11 571	17.9	35.3	0.5	671	318	0.0	0.0	94.3	220	10	127
Perry	10.7	11 889	36.0	69.0	2.9	0	0	NA	NA	NA	0	0	0

1. Includes nonresidential additions and alterations, residential nonhousekeeping buildings, and residential garages and carports not shown separately.

STATE County	Wholesale trade, 1987: Establishments	Wholesale trade, 1987: Sales (Mil dol)	Wholesale trade, 1987: Paid employees[1]	Wholesale trade, 1987: Annual payroll (Mil dol)	Retail trade, all establishments, 1987: Number	Retail trade, all establishments, 1987: Sales: Total (Mil dol)	Retail trade, all establishments, 1987: Sales: Percent change, 1982–1987	Retail trade, all establishments, 1987: Sales: Per capita[2] (Dollars)	Retail trade, establishments with payroll, 1987: Number	Retail trade, establishments with payroll, 1987: Sales: Total (Mil dol)	Sales: Per capita[2] (Dollars): General merchandise stores	Sales: Per capita[2] (Dollars): Food stores	Sales: Per capita[2] (Dollars): Apparel & accessory stores	Sales: Per capita[2] (Dollars): Eating and drinking places
	147	148	149	150	151	152	153	154	155	156	157	158	159	160
TENNESSEE	8 782	48 278.9	115 927	2 518.1	50 423	29 694.4	51.5	6 116	29 373	28 532.9	784	1 165	275	535
Anderson	56	133.2	723	15.7	660	410.0	36.3	5 848	400	400.9	732	1 316	209	444
Bedford	39	D	D	D	332	131.1	48.5	4 473	182	121.6	473	1 149	102	325
Benton	18	18.2	104	1.5	179	55.2	13.3	3 704	89	50.4	D	736	57	259
Bledsoe	2	D	D	D	92	19.9	31.8	1 990	32	15.9	90	489	0	98
Blount	85	350.8	1 258	23.5	781	619.7	63.7	7 413	472	607.2	846	1 344	138	458
Bradley	97	582.0	1 234	20.9	775	440.8	50.5	6 039	404	419.8	707	1 323	253	501
Campbell	27	D	D	D	365	149.1	22.6	4 261	188	139.9	333	1 175	143	297
Cannon	4	D	D	D	87	24.4	13.5	2 238	39	20.8	102	671	41	49
Carroll	34	D	D	D	336	110.2	38.1	3 923	175	101.4	350	938	121	140
Carter	23	D	D	D	424	165.5	44.4	3 208	210	153.4	458	788	48	303
Cheatham	7	D	D	D	176	57.3	27.9	2 213	72	52.4	40	855	D	127
Chester	14	19.8	73	1.1	131	39.6	32.0	3 046	65	34.6	103	532	100	171
Claiborne	19	D	D	D	287	58.8	14.6	2 226	129	48.6	80	733	38	124
Clay	4	D	D	D	85	13.5	35.0	1 712	35	10.2	23	527	0	93
Cocke	26	52.6	146	1.6	334	137.0	50.4	4 675	152	127.3	D	1 141	156	433
Coffee	55	D	D	D	522	266.2	47.5	6 368	325	257.2	1 012	1 206	228	618
Crockett	16	D	D	D	190	53.8	71.9	3 817	75	46.1	D	793	D	78
Cumberland	33	D	D	D	412	181.8	47.7	5 560	202	168.8	D	1 627	186	430
Davidson	1 506	8 818.4	24 329	575.2	5 521	4 763.0	63.5	9 394	3 619	4 673.2	1 513	1 376	487	1 054
Decatur	10	D	D	D	139	48.9	51.9	4 407	73	45.3	D	1 220	31	171
De Kalb	11	9.1	75	0.9	179	46.4	30.0	3 222	82	40.5	172	931	80	190
Dickson	34	D	D	D	385	187.7	65.1	5 552	204	177.5	D	1 471	163	367
Dyer	68	176.3	573	8.9	447	257.7	88.5	7 471	270	243.1	1 000	1 378	333	489
Fayette	16	41.9	204	3.2	163	48.5	37.0	1 844	83	44.2	189	550	D	88
Fentress	6	6.3	33	0.4	184	45.9	10.3	2 925	78	37.3	148	983	256	141
Franklin	24	45.6	217	3.1	311	136.7	38.2	4 009	179	130.6	421	1 096	44	260
Gibson	67	140.7	467	7.6	582	227.0	40.7	4 672	314	210.3	534	761	165	323
Giles	38	60.3	283	4.3	318	115.7	29.0	4 629	179	107.5	D	1 116	153	204
Grainger	10	11.5	68	1.1	161	31.5	71.2	1 822	51	24.9	0	415	0	72
Greene	67	170.2	718	8.5	553	261.6	27.4	4 629	315	246.5	475	1 094	145	334
Grundy	9	6.5	53	0.7	156	41.6	20.2	2 853	59	35.3	78	626	D	241
Hamblen	86	275.5	1 135	19.5	579	342.9	38.9	6 684	351	328.8	714	1 402	272	516
Hamilton	816	3 957.1	10 530	226.2	3 179	2 167.3	48.8	7 486	2 035	2 110.2	953	1 339	390	722
Hancock	5	2.6	24	0.2	63	10.5	-1.9	1 521	22	7.9	0	D	D	D
Hardeman	23	31.6	195	2.1	261	103.5	62.0	4 259	138	95.9	D	923	31	198
Hardin	21	44.2	135	2.3	267	107.3	47.2	4 789	146	99.4	D	1 156	70	310
Hawkins	20	D	D	D	318	127.2	32.9	2 820	151	116.1	192	910	36	231
Haywood	20	26.3	139	1.6	202	80.0	50.9	3 792	113	76.2	D	848	161	194
Henderson	22	59.0	252	3.1	275	100.1	54.2	4 409	134	92.5	496	862	115	231
Henry	50	99.6	547	8.0	384	152.4	44.7	5 184	210	140.8	555	1 128	239	336
Hickman	10	6.7	40	0.5	174	33.3	23.8	2 030	61	25.8	49	522	D	71
Houston	9	3.6	27	0.3	71	14.5	14.2	2 048	33	12.3	D	843	D	107
Humphreys	16	38.0	101	1.7	184	69.3	29.1	4 328	102	64.0	D	1 173	D	241
Jackson	9	D	D	D	178	31.4	122.7	3 343	52	24.8	D	1 264	0	78
Jefferson	24	22.7	169	2.3	335	121.6	66.8	3 661	146	112.2	D	1 045	D	338
Johnson	11	9.6	65	0.7	157	35.8	36.6	2 542	66	30.8	127	841	45	86
Knox	956	4 066.8	12 780	305.6	3 896	2 771.4	48.5	8 426	2 565	2 710.0	1 116	1 444	478	833
Lake	14	42.5	211	2.0	77	13.8	-0.7	1 789	39	12.4	D	748	D	133
Lauderdale	30	50.2	212	3.0	264	74.7	51.8	2 975	122	67.2	410	715	59	163
Lawrence	40	74.6	271	3.9	466	171.1	47.9	4 887	218	152.2	D	1 118	103	210
Lewis	9	19.5	109	1.3	100	26.5	11.8	2 523	51	24.1	186	786	D	161
Lincoln	43	72.2	383	4.8	336	122.8	55.6	4 513	163	112.1	D	986	115	308
Loudon	26	48.7	228	3.4	311	141.3	47.2	4 572	158	135.1	D	1 005	D	337
McMinn	51	91.9	453	6.8	484	214.7	30.8	4 914	259	198.5	513	1 101	270	404
McNairy	27	87.5	540	11.4	316	75.7	31.4	3 165	121	63.3	D	773	48	111
Macon	12	15.1	66	0.6	182	50.4	31.9	3 133	80	42.7	486	838	44	117
Madison	167	453.1	1 922	34.2	871	603.6	50.5	7 738	584	589.1	1 448	1 415	374	544
Marion	19	28.4	132	2.1	290	109.3	49.5	4 301	145	100.3	D	1 190	D	214
Marshall	14	18.1	121	1.9	213	107.4	54.3	5 066	123	104.1	D	1 471	77	213
Maury	83	135.7	636	10.5	643	316.7	63.2	5 757	383	298.4	677	1 176	306	405
Meigs	0	0.0	0	0.0	80	10.9	-20.4	1 330	29	8.1	D	464	0	97
Monroe	36	102.8	321	4.3	376	129.1	39.9	4 164	178	115.8	471	1 076	131	332
Montgomery	90	169.9	726	11.8	907	598.8	68.6	6 356	595	582.5	914	941	258	548
Moore	2	D	D	D	26	3.9	-22.0	821	10	3.0	D	D	0	D
Morgan	10	10.0	43	0.6	101	23.7	55.9	1 339	36	18.8	D	441	D	33
Obion	64	161.3	553	8.3	415	182.2	41.3	5 506	242	170.5	620	986	207	399
Overton	18	23.9	80	1.1	159	42.3	5.2	2 364	69	38.2	211	787	45	138
Perry	5	11.6	97	1.5	80	15.0	59.6	2 348	30	12.9	D	1 089	D	170

1. For pay period including March 12. 2. Based on the estimated population as of July 1 of the year shown.

STATE County	Retail trade, establishments with payroll, 1987 (cont'd)		Taxable service industries–establishments with payroll, 1987							Bank deposits,[2] June 1989		Savings capital,[3] September 1989	
				Receipts (Mil dol)									
					Selected kinds of business								
	Paid employees[1]	Annual payroll (Mil dol)	Number	Total	Hotels, motels and other lodging places	Health services	Legal services	Paid employees	Annual payroll (Mil dol)	Total (Mil dol)	Percent change, 1988–1989	Total (Mil dol)	Percent change, 1988–1989
	161	162	163	164	165	166	167	168	169	170	171	172	173
TENNESSEE	338 168	3 198.1	27 829	12 010.2	814.4	3 797.9	605.8	282 908	4 486.9	36 450	6.9	9 722.5	1.1
Anderson	4 451	42.4	447	683.1	7.2	50.8	3.8	8 439	200.8	448	11.1	147.3	-4.6
Bedford	1 525	12.9	134	34.5	D	7.2	1.6	1 093	12.2	258	5.5	45.1	-1.9
Benton	596	4.6	61	19.1	D	11.4	0.5	514	5.9	143	2.3	17.3	-1.9
Bledsoe	146	1.4	29	7.3	D	6.4	D	180	2.3	41	11.6	0.0	-100.0
Blount	5 897	63.6	442	132.2	9.3	63.5	3.9	3 139	48.4	571	10.8	237.0	-1.1
Bradley	4 705	45.1	388	179.7	6.9	53.7	4.6	5 329	64.7	432	8.7	136.6	-0.8
Campbell	1 552	13.5	108	21.3	5.3	8.1	1.5	679	6.4	213	3.2	56.9	3.2
Cannon	207	1.9	27	8.9	0.0	7.1	0.1	239	3.3	95	5.6	0.0	NA
Carroll	1 029	8.7	107	17.3	D	8.9	1.2	508	5.7	192	3.7	31.9	4.9
Carter	1 991	15.5	157	41.4	D	27.6	1.1	1 055	15.0	206	12.5	134.2	-0.2
Cheatham	473	4.3	41	4.1	0.5	0.6	0.7	95	1.0	118	6.2	9.5	11.3
Chester	386	3.5	22	3.1	0.0	1.7	D	123	1.0	90	3.9	10.0	-0.9
Claiborne	678	4.7	65	15.2	D	4.8	0.6	465	4.1	172	6.7	20.0	3.5
Clay	144	1.0	26	12.2	D	5.0	D	317	4.8	39	5.1	0.0	NA
Cocke	1 544	12.2	90	20.1	4.6	6.5	0.9	594	6.1	156	11.6	49.0	-6.1
Coffee	3 291	27.9	257	387.3	D	35.2	3.7	8 153	219.8	205	3.4	117.5	0.4
Crockett	410	3.6	35	5.9	D	2.6	D	197	2.4	121	7.6	9.9	-1.5
Cumberland	2 088	17.8	145	29.9	3.1	12.9	1.8	898	10.5	188	9.5	77.7	-2.2
Davidson	57 518	571.6	4 843	2 786.7	260.9	735.4	158.3	63 282	1 006.9	6 170	2.0	1 162.9	2.3
Decatur	466	4.5	39	9.3	D	4.3	0.5	316	3.0	72	1.2	0.0	NA
De Kalb	468	3.8	54	19.9	D	13.5	0.7	391	6.7	150	9.1	0.0	NA
Dickson	2 163	19.3	130	31.1	2.3	15.5	1.5	975	12.3	213	-0.2	75.0	3.1
Dyer	2 473	24.3	181	37.3	2.8	14.5	3.4	829	11.4	322	5.6	38.0	-0.3
Fayette	487	4.7	44	6.8	D	3.8	0.5	212	2.2	119	5.3	10.2	-4.2
Fentress	654	4.5	52	16.2	0.5	12.7	0.6	466	6.0	71	3.3	12.6	-12.6
Franklin	1 528	13.4	122	18.5	D	9.7	1.6	439	6.1	179	3.5	44.0	-3.8
Gibson	2 406	20.8	212	46.7	1.0	29.0	2.2	1 383	15.1	430	7.4	97.9	-10.0
Giles	1 214	11.5	100	35.1	0.8	22.2	1.2	910	12.6	283	3.2	46.9	19.3
Grainger	293	2.3	27	4.8	D	D	0.2	177	1.4	58	9.8	0.0	NA
Greene	3 103	25.4	249	58.0	3.4	23.1	2.7	1 517	20.2	353	6.8	158.6	6.6
Grundy	403	3.4	26	5.5	D	2.7	0.0	229	1.5	52	9.6	0.0	NA
Hamblen	3 784	33.1	275	82.8	3.8	39.9	4.0	1 869	28.0	292	5.4	160.0	5.1
Hamilton	25 566	254.9	2 147	1 005.6	D	391.0	66.0	23 946	377.7	2 338	9.5	711.6	-2.8
Hancock	101	0.7	13	2.0	0.0	1.5	0.1	89	0.7	17	17.8	0.0	NA
Hardeman	1 019	9.5	66	14.6	D	5.4	0.9	416	4.2	169	5.9	13.5	0.4
Hardin	1 136	9.7	78	13.9	D	6.6	0.7	352	4.0	144	9.0	29.2	-0.1
Hawkins	1 481	11.7	95	17.2	D	9.4	1.5	494	5.5	214	7.2	88.8	4.0
Haywood	810	7.4	65	16.0	D	9.4	0.6	361	5.0	149	5.5	8.2	-5.3
Henderson	1 001	8.8	76	9.1	D	3.8	0.7	262	2.9	172	6.9	18.0	-6.8
Henry	1 653	14.1	148	37.8	2.2	11.1	1.4	705	10.8	232	5.3	71.7	1.2
Hickman	281	2.5	46	6.9	D	3.4	0.5	212	2.1	94	6.4	13.4	-15.6
Houston	167	1.4	16	6.3	D	5.6	D	172	2.4	27	5.2	0.0	NA
Humphreys	760	6.8	61	16.0	1.7	7.3	1.0	373	4.7	105	16.2	31.5	2.4
Jackson	186	1.5	30	7.7	0.0	5.0	D	227	2.5	58	4.4	0.0	NA
Jefferson	1 423	10.9	88	15.1	D	6.8	1.0	430	4.5	196	7.3	15.5	-7.6
Johnson	347	2.9	35	7.2	0.0	4.0	0.7	196	2.3	73	5.1	19.7	4.7
Knox	33 053	311.7	2 715	1 111.2	54.9	393.8	78.3	25 018	441.5	2 287	10.8	934.2	-2.8
Lake	190	1.3	24	3.5	0.5	D	D	178	1.2	34	4.3	0.0	NA
Lauderdale	880	6.8	67	11.4	D	4.6	0.7	374	3.7	191	10.3	22.7	5.1
Lawrence	1 634	15.5	133	29.7	0.8	16.7	1.7	777	9.3	279	7.6	39.7	-3.1
Lewis	271	2.2	32	8.9	0.0	5.6	0.6	299	3.4	62	13.3	0.0	NA
Lincoln	1 291	10.7	122	18.7	0.4	5.7	1.3	563	5.5	195	9.8	68.0	5.8
Loudon	1 320	11.8	106	22.1	1.4	8.0	0.8	703	7.5	271	9.3	21.3	7.4
McMinn	2 615	20.3	172	60.6	1.3	31.0	2.0	1 597	19.3	238	4.9	145.0	8.8
McNairy	702	5.6	70	29.1	D	7.3	0.5	953	13.4	137	7.2	22.5	-5.3
Macon	481	4.1	47	8.0	D	4.2	0.7	234	2.4	131	3.9	19.3	10.8
Madison	6 882	64.3	542	208.9	9.5	113.6	10.1	5 101	96.3	684	18.5	77.4	-8.3
Marion	1 093	9.9	70	22.3	D	16.5	1.4	625	7.9	134	6.8	18.0	12.8
Marshall	1 015	10.1	88	25.4	D	16.4	0.8	972	8.7	188	13.5	33.3	-0.4
Maury	3 717	31.6	310	96.2	2.0	38.1	6.3	2 276	32.3	466	7.1	108.1	-4.8
Meigs	136	1.1	13	2.2	0.0	1.8	D	82	0.9	34	6.3	0.0	NA
Monroe	1 457	11.4	83	18.9	2.7	4.9	1.3	524	6.0	179	6.2	42.9	8.2
Montgomery	6 778	66.6	418	93.0	D	30.0	6.7	2 501	30.7	503	-1.9	174.6	5.0
Moore	39	0.3	3	D	0.0	0.0	0.0	D	D	43	11.0	0.0	NA
Morgan	177	1.4	17	3.5	D	2.2	D	146	1.3	45	7.9	22.4	7.1
Obion	2 072	18.1	161	41.3	D	14.2	1.7	901	12.8	305	5.2	73.6	0.0
Overton	443	3.4	49	16.1	0.0	11.4	0.8	378	4.8	75	0.4	28.5	14.4
Perry	134	1.2	22	8.5	0.0	7.4	D	244	2.9	52	9.5	0.0	NA

1. For the period including March 12 of the year shown. 2. Includes deposits for all insured and reporting noninsured commercial and mutual savings banks. 3. Includes savings capital for all FSLIC insured savings institutions.

STATE County	Federal funds and grants, 1989: Expenditures: Total (Mil dol)	Expenditures: Percent change, 1988–1989	Per capita[1] (Dollars): Total	Per capita: Direct payments for individuals	Per capita: Procurement contract awards	Per capita: Salaries and wages	Per capita: Grant awards	Local government finances, 1981–1982: General revenue: Total (Mil dol)	Intergovernmental: Total (Mil dol)	Intergovernmental: Percent from state	Taxes: Total (Mil dol)	Taxes: Per capita[2]: Total (Dollars)	Taxes: Per capita[2]: Property (Dollars)	Direct general expenditure: Total (Mil dol)	Direct general expenditure: Percent change, 1977–1982
	174	175	176	177	178	179	180	181	182	183	184	185	186	187	188
TENNESSEE	16 596.7	7.4	X	1 758	633	455	455	3 884.6	1 332.2	75.1	1 394.0	299	192	3 771.1	55.6
Anderson	1 823.6	10.6	25 576	2 050	22 346	802	374	46.3	21.4	80.1	18.0	264	221	50.0	55.8
Bedford	64.6	3.5	2 182	1 677	16	139	267	25.1	9.2	67.0	6.3	224	138	21.7	19.8
Benton	38.1	-18.4	2 560	2 244	16	112	118	15.7	4.1	95.2	2.5	166	88	11.4	124.3
Bledsoe	20.7	0.5	2 069	1 378	21	57	413	7.5	3.6	94.0	1.4	148	112	6.4	38.3
Blount	183.9	4.2	2 149	1 784	15	135	198	46.6	18.2	82.4	20.4	258	151	47.7	28.8
Bradley	132.5	7.4	1 761	1 374	42	121	207	58.6	16.8	82.5	15.9	231	153	57.3	87.0
Campbell	112.7	17.2	3 240	2 200	425	121	488	31.4	14.1	78.1	6.0	172	94	29.0	64.2
Cannon	25.3	2.7	2 300	1 685	39	95	409	6.4	3.6	75.8	1.5	139	95	6.9	78.0
Carroll	145.2	6.1	5 187	2 219	2 295	133	408	20.2	7.6	91.3	5.4	192	120	21.2	62.0
Carter	106.2	8.4	2 074	1 570	32	97	366	34.2	11.6	86.1	9.3	183	135	35.8	86.3
Cheatham	36.0	11.3	1 299	1 018	44	94	131	12.0	5.6	84.9	4.2	190	115	11.7	81.4
Chester	28.0	3.1	2 170	1 525	8	166	372	5.8	3.4	84.4	1.7	133	86	5.5	43.8
Claiborne	65.3	10.9	2 436	1 716	108	95	500	15.7	8.2	93.3	2.8	109	69	16.4	54.2
Clay	17.9	-11.2	2 234	1 374	25	212	567	5.5	4.2	79.6	1.1	144	99	5.1	45.6
Cocke	85.9	34.1	2 913	1 514	691	89	594	19.2	9.1	68.0	6.0	205	127	18.8	46.3
Coffee	373.2	0.9	8 760	1 830	6 109	388	371	32.7	12.2	70.2	9.0	226	120	32.4	63.4
Crockett	42.6	7.1	3 062	1 803	75	153	405	8.8	5.1	76.0	2.6	180	116	8.1	47.0
Cumberland	89.5	19.8	2 618	1 961	80	108	435	17.6	8.4	86.9	6.6	226	118	15.6	21.2
Davidson	1 334.8	5.9	2 606	1 627	100	528	301	502.7	137.5	58.4	231.7	484	265	456.2	36.1
Decatur	28.6	12.5	2 651	1 793	39	143	616	9.5	4.0	82.9	1.3	117	78	7.2	60.4
De Kalb	35.8	6.3	2 471	1 798	21	124	443	7.6	3.8	86.7	2.2	161	107	7.1	56.3
Dickson	69.3	10.4	1 946	1 555	13	96	266	17.0	8.1	79.7	6.3	206	109	18.2	44.1
Dyer	100.2	-6.2	2 854	1 823	332	144	439	38.3	9.8	80.6	8.7	252	126	33.9	131.0
Fayette	57.6	8.1	2 156	1 183	17	79	578	17.6	9.1	93.2	3.3	136	83	17.2	72.1
Fentress	43.6	18.3	2 761	1 858	168	96	573	11.6	4.9	76.3	1.6	108	61	10.2	81.5
Franklin	86.8	14.8	2 500	1 817	190	173	246	23.2	7.8	93.3	5.3	164	103	23.9	68.9
Gibson	133.3	-22.6	2 771	2 033	53	187	313	32.7	14.6	84.9	9.3	190	111	31.3	57.8
Giles	71.4	10.6	2 832	2 045	24	131	521	23.1	6.5	86.0	5.6	229	151	22.8	53.7
Grainger	40.3	18.1	2 304	1 493	259	99	429	7.0	4.8	87.0	1.7	97	79	6.4	68.2
Greene	128.8	9.5	2 287	1 556	220	113	344	30.8	13.7	82.7	11.9	217	147	30.8	69.9
Grundy	33.6	9.8	2 331	1 743	100	92	364	6.0	3.7	90.6	1.8	127	90	6.7	70.2
Hamblen	116.1	13.8	2 263	1 526	151	110	468	37.5	16.1	60.9	14.4	280	193	37.9	83.4
Hamilton	1 129.8	0.4	3 840	1 852	352	1 252	374	320.2	84.0	65.5	110.8	387	261	373.8	73.0
Hancock	17.7	9.9	2 644	1 653	8	62	899	7.9	3.2	92.3	0.4	58	40	7.7	115.9
Hardeman	81.6	3.9	3 332	1 723	806	108	543	13.3	7.6	88.1	3.8	164	103	11.4	29.5
Hardin	56.2	8.7	2 509	1 790	21	195	429	18.2	6.4	87.2	3.9	175	98	16.2	76.7
Hawkins	203.6	4.2	4 484	1 516	2 275	266	407	26.9	11.3	86.5	8.5	191	155	23.9	52.7
Haywood	57.0	11.4	2 689	1 526	18	95	576	12.3	7.2	79.8	3.6	176	123	11.8	30.6
Henderson	56.4	13.3	2 461	1 672	22	101	520	12.9	6.0	87.6	3.2	147	69	12.9	94.4
Henry	83.9	-21.8	2 854	2 226	26	176	308	23.9	7.6	82.7	5.5	189	129	23.1	63.9
Hickman	36.4	13.5	2 156	1 601	12	144	364	10.8	4.6	82.1	2.6	168	118	9.2	22.7
Houston	19.5	12.2	2 665	2 054	15	91	458	4.1	2.6	78.0	1.2	168	104	4.1	70.4
Humphreys	55.1	-5.4	3 403	1 919	209	912	326	10.3	4.8	93.4	4.3	267	190	8.9	22.9
Jackson	21.1	10.9	2 219	1 530	13	103	522	5.1	2.7	93.3	1.1	115	84	5.1	54.5
Jefferson	74.2	9.5	2 216	1 722	12	131	318	20.0	8.0	90.1	5.0	153	97	18.6	108.0
Johnson	37.4	13.1	2 694	2 021	15	101	541	7.1	4.0	85.9	2.6	185	139	6.6	33.4
Knox	1 018.2	-2.7	3 072	1 787	245	654	377	279.4	106.6	58.8	119.6	364	237	257.1	43.2
Lake	26.1	24.1	3 531	2 147	420	231	544	4.7	2.5	92.7	1.4	179	108	6.0	79.6
Lauderdale	67.8	7.7	2 702	1 736	12	98	575	14.3	8.0	81.4	3.6	147	83	13.6	14.0
Lawrence	83.0	8.9	2 352	1 827	14	121	290	17.9	8.6	91.5	5.9	173	110	17.8	47.8
Lewis	21.1	20.2	1 972	1 557	14	91	286	4.7	2.6	89.9	1.3	128	77	4.5	46.5
Lincoln	69.6	10.6	2 503	1 863	70	95	360	22.9	7.7	87.4	4.8	186	103	20.9	60.1
Loudon	76.5	-7.8	2 429	1 841	94	183	290	23.8	8.5	82.9	6.2	206	135	24.1	87.8
McMinn	91.6	8.7	2 095	1 608	21	124	300	32.3	13.2	70.8	12.0	281	197	31.3	71.3
McNairy	66.6	9.7	2 765	1 843	13	123	675	16.7	6.6	81.6	3.1	136	80	16.3	88.7
Macon	33.4	10.1	2 059	1 428	31	92	462	7.2	4.0	90.1	2.3	147	99	6.8	31.0
Madison	215.5	16.7	2 748	1 784	186	261	435	87.1	20.2	81.0	21.6	284	163	77.1	27.1
Marion	63.3	-12.3	2 453	1 739	85	139	474	19.6	7.9	84.9	4.7	189	88	18.5	131.9
Marshall	52.4	15.2	2 436	1 816	64	124	347	13.1	5.0	88.1	5.5	277	160	10.8	46.0
Maury	119.0	8.6	2 128	1 660	43	165	231	49.4	12.3	84.0	12.3	239	148	47.7	60.4
Meigs	17.7	9.6	2 052	1 481	22	110	384	4.3	2.8	83.4	1.0	131	93	4.2	66.3
Monroe	64.4	7.4	2 051	1 575	29	104	318	14.6	8.1	88.0	4.7	161	80	15.0	74.0
Montgomery	185.6	10.1	1 865	1 512	14	79	228	66.9	19.7	83.3	20.5	232	132	61.4	68.2
Moore	6.4	1.8	1 307	919	9	36	303	2.8	1.5	94.4	1.1	239	158	2.4	49.7
Morgan	35.9	-13.7	1 995	1 398	139	75	364	11.0	6.4	71.3	2.7	158	125	10.5	87.3
Obion	92.6	-3.8	2 841	1 740	455	131	347	32.8	9.0	85.4	9.2	281	196	31.9	45.2
Overton	41.2	0.7	2 304	1 617	17	107	480	8.7	4.8	89.2	3.2	181	123	8.1	10.7
Perry	18.0	13.5	2 721	2 055	12	89	504	3.6	2.3	94.6	1.0	152	113	2.5	-45.8

1. Based on the estimated population as of July 1 of the year shown. 2. Based on the estimated population as of July 1, 1982.

STATE County	Local government finances, 1981–1982 (cont'd)								State and local government employment, 1989		Federal government civilian employment 1989		Elections, 1988[3]	
	Direct general expenditure (cont'd)						Debt outstanding							
	Per capita[1] (Dollars)	Percent of total for– Education	Health & hospitals	Police protection	Public welfare	Highways	Total (Mil dol)	Per capita[1] (Dollars)	Total	Rate[2]	Total	Earnings ($1,000)	Total vote cast for president	Vote for lead party (Percent)
	189	190	191	192	193	194	195	196	197	198	199	200	201	202
TENNESSEE	808	37.2	13.7	5.6	1.0	6.0	5 195.0	1 114	276 747	560.5	61 863	2 023 411	1 636 251	R–57.9
Anderson	735	67.1	0.8	4.9	0.2	3.9	37.9	557	2 902	407.0	1 666	63 374	24 788	R–60.7
Bedford	773	32.4	29.5	3.9	0.2	10.4	18.5	659	1 562	527.7	97	3 114	8 939	R–54.3
Benton	752	33.1	41.9	3.9	0.1	7.4	8.9	589	607	407.4	238	6 875	5 009	D–56.4
Bledsoe	690	39.4	31.8	2.5	0.0	12.2	4.9	522	643	643.0	12	344	3 147	R–59.0
Blount	601	52.3	1.6	5.4	0.1	12.5	70.7	891	3 814	445.6	204	5 970	29 776	R–67.3
Bradley	834	34.8	30.0	2.9	0.5	4.3	87.0	1 267	3 518	467.8	259	8 442	22 031	R–71.8
Campbell	823	43.1	23.1	3.3	0.1	6.3	36.1	1 025	1 955	561.8	105	3 476	9 416	R–55.2
Cannon	653	38.9	2.1	2.8	0.1	9.8	15.5	1 472	328	298.2	26	737	3 348	D–51.6
Carroll	754	40.5	18.9	3.4	0.3	4.8	12.5	446	1 151	411.1	79	2 232	9 830	R–57.3
Carter	701	44.5	29.4	3.2	0.4	3.9	26.0	508	1 655	323.2	120	3 944	16 778	R–71.7
Cheatham	536	52.3	9.3	3.0	0.0	9.2	18.2	831	866	312.6	60	1 787	7 250	R–57.0
Chester	441	49.7	2.5	6.5	0.3	13.2	5.5	441	543	420.9	40	1 148	4 555	R–61.1
Claiborne	642	49.1	27.8	2.8	0.0	8.8	7.6	299	1 168	435.8	61	1 677	7 082	R–57.5
Clay	662	64.7	0.5	2.4	0.0	11.0	2.8	358	345	431.2	66	1 570	2 493	R–51.8
Cocke	649	43.5	8.4	3.4	0.4	10.1	19.5	673	1 116	378.3	53	1 502	7 579	R–71.6
Coffee	813	40.0	19.4	4.0	0.0	5.3	35.4	890	2 312	542.7	445	12 750	13 615	R–57.6
Crockett	572	52.3	6.6	4.2	0.0	11.3	5.2	367	484	348.2	47	1 149	3 970	R–55.8
Cumberland	535	57.4	1.0	3.5	0.0	9.8	30.8	1 054	1 231	359.9	83	2 694	11 594	R–65.2
Davidson	953	31.4	9.5	7.4	1.2	3.7	785.9	1 641	34 821	679.7	8 497	272 149	188 946	R–52.2
Decatur	657	36.9	30.7	3.2	0.0	8.6	5.0	458	519	480.6	37	950	4 191	R–54.5
De Kalb	521	55.7	0.6	7.2	0.0	8.8	10.4	763	490	337.9	46	1 368	4 581	D–53.5
Dickson	600	49.0	0.2	5.3	2.3	9.4	19.1	629	1 458	409.6	76	2 229	10 536	R–50.7
Dyer	982	33.4	32.1	2.0	0.2	5.8	24.3	705	1 824	519.7	128	3 895	10 243	R–63.5
Fayette	704	48.2	19.0	3.4	7.1	11.9	12.4	508	1 398	523.6	45	1 150	6 921	R–51.6
Fentress	676	37.4	32.1	2.0	5.3	9.5	7.7	510	624	394.9	40	1 107	4 992	R–62.2
Franklin	736	33.1	30.0	3.9	0.1	5.8	17.4	536	1 093	315.0	126	3 777	10 886	D–50.0
Gibson	638	43.0	16.1	4.8	0.2	8.0	32.9	671	2 061	428.5	191	5 799	16 038	R–52.5
Giles	927	30.8	25.4	3.0	0.0	7.5	32.8	1 332	996	395.2	67	2 032	7 478	D–52.4
Grainger	375	63.3	0.3	3.6	1.1	9.9	3.2	189	532	304.0	42	1 123	4 174	R–65.5
Greene	562	54.2	1.9	3.4	0.0	14.4	37.0	675	3 033	538.7	150	4 207	17 132	R–69.7
Grundy	474	60.6	0.3	5.4	0.1	12.6	6.3	448	553	384.0	33	843	3 857	D–62.6
Hamblen	739	44.4	1.1	5.0	0.4	5.7	61.4	1 197	2 438	475.2	139	4 386	15 565	R–66.9
Hamilton	1 305	23.6	26.6	3.9	4.9	3.2	295.1	1 031	18 118	615.8	8 700	346 904	109 709	R–62.1
Hancock	1 130	30.4	54.1	2.0	0.0	6.9	0.6	83	256	382.1	16	463	2 082	R–62.6
Hardeman	489	62.0	0.3	6.2	0.1	13.5	10.2	438	1 939	791.4	62	1 628	7 138	R–49.7
Hardin	720	39.9	25.2	3.7	0.4	6.8	14.3	634	1 338	597.3	133	3 656	7 089	R–60.0
Hawkins	539	49.8	14.3	4.1	0.1	7.5	25.7	580	1 817	400.2	376	11 790	14 646	R–63.9
Haywood	581	52.7	0.8	4.2	0.3	14.4	5.2	256	908	428.3	55	1 376	5 640	D–51.8
Henderson	599	47.4	16.0	3.8	0.1	10.7	13.2	615	933	407.4	53	1 544	7 819	R–69.3
Henry	794	34.5	34.7	4.3	0.1	9.4	9.4	322	1 602	544.9	112	3 230	9 975	D–51.5
Hickman	608	44.5	19.5	3.7	0.0	9.9	11.4	752	893	528.4	40	1 206	4 918	D–53.7
Houston	591	45.0	1.0	3.1	0.0	13.2	4.0	571	320	438.4	15	401	2 367	D–62.0
Humphreys	547	58.1	0.8	5.3	0.4	8.9	37.0	2 286	683	421.6	547	17 650	5 188	D–58.5
Jackson	547	49.4	1.9	4.6	0.1	11.8	22.9	2 459	275	289.5	22	591	3 144	D–62.4
Jefferson	574	46.3	24.8	3.9	0.1	6.7	12.9	399	1 451	433.1	121	3 617	10 069	R–67.9
Johnson	475	62.3	0.5	5.2	0.6	11.6	3.1	220	591	425.2	32	978	5 079	R–73.1
Knox	784	39.4	1.8	6.3	2.2	2.1	408.7	1 245	28 023	845.6	5 331	205 278	115 521	R–63.3
Lake	785	65.4	1.4	4.0	0.4	12.0	3.2	410	318	429.7	16	458	1 750	D–53.4
Lauderdale	556	51.8	0.7	5.0	5.7	12.5	11.9	484	1 319	525.5	51	1 307	6 639	R–49.8
Lawrence	523	53.0	0.2	6.3	0.1	11.6	11.4	336	1 397	395.8	99	2 835	11 183	R–56.1
Lewis	441	47.3	0.3	3.8	0.3	18.0	5.1	503	383	357.9	23	665	2 761	D–51.4
Lincoln	803	37.3	25.1	3.1	0.0	8.0	19.6	752	1 741	626.3	57	1 698	8 017	R–53.5
Loudon	800	50.7	12.8	3.5	0.3	5.3	58.3	1 936	1 080	342.9	150	4 241	10 679	R–66.7
McMinn	737	43.3	11.1	4.3	0.2	9.2	38.4	905	1 872	428.4	146	3 964	13 078	R–64.7
McNairy	711	37.5	30.0	3.4	0.1	7.5	17.2	749	1 005	417.0	80	2 339	8 191	R–56.5
Macon	427	52.3	0.4	6.1	0.1	18.4	4.1	254	553	341.4	38	1 033	4 531	R–65.4
Madison	1 017	14.4	47.5	4.4	0.5	4.4	64.4	849	7 020	895.4	531	18 751	28 039	R–60.5
Marion	750	40.2	27.1	4.8	0.0	7.4	21.8	886	862	334.1	105	3 487	8 618	R–51.1
Marshall	549	49.1	0.2	6.3	0.3	16.3	14.0	709	939	436.7	60	1 819	5 791	R–51.4
Maury	927	27.8	34.4	3.6	0.1	5.3	59.0	1 146	3 438	615.0	234	7 357	14 788	R–56.8
Meigs	558	57.3	1.1	5.5	0.0	15.5	2.3	305	280	325.6	11	337	2 568	R–58.7
Monroe	515	59.7	0.3	4.7	0.2	10.4	8.6	294	1 038	330.6	79	2 028	10 393	R–61.1
Montgomery	693	37.9	23.7	4.7	1.3	8.0	67.5	762	5 058	508.3	205	6 529	21 856	R–57.6
Moore	524	55.9	0.7	2.8	0.0	20.9	1.0	215	569	1 161.2	NA	118	1 530	R–51.4
Morgan	618	52.7	0.3	1.9	0.0	9.3	20.5	1 207	822	456.7	36	883	4 546	R–56.7
Obion	972	33.5	33.8	3.0	0.0	8.5	13.2	402	1 305	400.3	119	3 621	10 858	R–55.6
Overton	465	57.9	0.4	4.7	0.3	11.0	10.8	620	869	485.5	36	1 020	4 397	D–57.1
Perry	395	33.5	6.4	5.0	0.4	22.8	2.7	436	289	437.9	14	411	2 076	D–58.2

1. Based on the estimated population as of July 1, 1982. 2. Per 10,000 resident population estimated as of July 1 of the year shown. 3. Data subject to copyright.

STATE–County code	MSA/CMSA/NECMA code[1]	STATE County	Land Area,[2] 1990 (Sq. Km.)	Population, 1990										Age of population Percent		
							Race									
				Total persons	Rank	Per square kilometer	White	Black	Am. Indian, Eskimo, Aleut	Asian & Pacific Islander	Other race	Hispanic[3]	Under 5 years	5 to 14 years	15 to 24 years
			1	2	3	4	5	6	7	8	9	10	11	12	13
		TENNESSEE—Con.													
47 137	...	Pickett	422	4 548	2 870	10.8	4 542	0	4	2	0	13	6.5	13.7	12.6
47 139	...	Polk	1 127	13 643	2 086	12.1	13 571	0	25	42	5	36	5.8	13.1	15.3
47 141	...	Putnam	1 039	51 373	821	49.4	49 878	873	79	457	86	294	6.0	12.2	20.6
47 143	...	Rhea	818	24 344	1 483	29.8	23 571	581	62	53	77	132	6.2	14.2	15.6
47 145	...	Roane	935	47 227	887	50.5	45 444	1 456	95	191	41	212	5.6	13.4	13.3
47 147	5360	Robertson	1 234	41 494	971	33.6	36 802	4 555	63	43	31	173	7.6	15.5	13.1
47 149	5360	Rutherford	1 603	118 570	392	74.0	105 740	10 678	234	1 706	212	926	7.5	15.0	18.4
47 151	...	Scott	1 378	18 358	1 772	13.3	18 263	5	67	13	10	38	7.0	17.0	15.6
47 153	1560	Sequatchie	689	8 863	2 482	12.9	8 851	2	4	5	1	25	6.5	14.7	15.0
47 155	3840	Sevier	1 534	51 043	826	33.3	50 462	216	130	203	32	237	6.1	13.4	13.9
47 157	4920	Shelby	1 955	826 330	43	422.7	455 063	360 083	1 468	7 740	1 976	7 091	8.1	15.0	15.6
47 159	...	Smith	814	14 143	2 042	17.4	13 626	459	36	13	9	48	6.7	14.1	13.1
47 161	...	Stewart	1 185	9 479	2 435	8.0	9 294	96	56	26	7	48	5.1	12.9	12.9
47 163	3660	Sullivan	1 070	143 596	331	134.2	140 076	2 562	372	485	101	521	5.9	12.2	14.1
47 165	5360	Sumner	1 371	103 281	446	75.3	97 073	5 562	195	347	104	567	7.0	15.7	14.1
47 167	4920	Tipton	1 190	37 568	1 058	31.6	28 436	8 852	114	100	66	253	8.6	17.2	14.4
47 169	...	Trousdale	296	5 920	2 769	20.0	5 040	853	14	8	5	31	5.8	14.4	13.0
47 171	3660	Unicoi	482	16 549	1 885	34.3	16 488	3	11	14	33	97	5.3	12.1	13.2
47 173	3840	Union	579	13 694	2 081	23.7	13 658	3	23	5	5	38	7.0	15.3	15.1
47 175	...	Van Buren	708	4 846	2 849	6.8	4 823	5	16	0	2	10	6.5	15.4	14.1
47 177	...	Warren	1 121	32 992	1 190	29.4	31 511	1 131	51	119	180	276	6.4	14.4	14.0
47 179	3660	Washington	845	92 315	500	109.2	88 409	3 275	155	378	98	471	5.7	12.1	16.7
47 181	...	Wayne	1 901	13 935	2 062	7.3	13 762	137	17	10	9	52	6.6	14.5	14.5
47 183	...	Weakley	1 503	31 972	1 211	21.3	29 368	2 222	39	277	66	128	5.7	12.6	20.2
47 185	...	White	976	20 090	1 672	20.6	19 654	378	24	25	9	74	6.2	13.4	13.7
47 187	5360	Williamson	1 509	81 021	563	53.7	74 903	5 396	130	469	123	522	7.4	16.9	12.1
47 189	5360	Wilson	1 478	67 675	655	45.8	62 561	4 607	185	259	63	386	7.2	15.8	13.2
48 000	...	TEXAS	678 358	16 986 510	X	25.0	12 774 762	2 021 632	65 877	319 459	1 804 780	4 339 905	8.2	15.8	15.6
48 001	...	Anderson	2 774	48 024	871	17.3	33 354	11 143	129	125	3 273	3 953	6.2	13.4	15.9
48 003	...	Andrews	3 887	14 338	2 029	3.7	10 834	274	82	154	2 994	4 552	9.2	19.7	14.5
48 005	...	Angelina	2 076	69 884	634	33.7	54 752	10 731	153	295	3 953	6 072	7.6	16.2	15.1
48 007	...	Aransas	653	17 892	1 794	27.4	15 282	319	111	589	1 591	3 588	6.7	14.6	11.2
48 009	...	Archer	2 356	7 973	2 574	3.4	7 789	11	36	4	133	189	7.1	16.3	11.9
48 011	...	Armstrong	2 366	2 021	3 065	0.9	1 976	0	10	7	28	55	6.1	17.2	9.8
48 013	...	Atascosa	3 191	30 533	1 265	9.6	25 019	143	109	65	5 197	16 064	8.5	19.2	14.5
48 015	...	Austin	1 690	19 832	1 684	11.7	16 244	2 608	46	26	908	2 073	6.8	15.8	12.4
48 017	...	Bailey	2 141	7 064	2 652	3.3	6 537	124	10	12	381	2 740	8.0	18.4	13.8
48 019	...	Bandera	2 051	10 562	2 330	5.1	10 027	23	66	26	420	1 172	6.0	13.2	10.1
48 021	...	Bastrop	2 301	38 263	1 048	16.6	29 607	4 512	181	129	3 834	6 933	8.0	16.5	12.0
48 023	...	Baylor	2 255	4 385	2 884	1.9	3 962	180	9	13	221	334	6.3	13.0	9.6
48 025	...	Bee	2 280	25 135	1 457	11.0	19 443	727	103	231	4 631	12 909	8.7	18.0	15.6
48 027	3810	Bell	2 743	191 088	251	69.7	136 066	36 095	944	5 531	12 452	24 995	9.6	15.3	19.0
48 029	7240	Bexar	3 230	1 185 394	25	367.0	878 736	84 670	4 265	15 429	202 294	589 180	8.4	16.1	16.2
48 031	...	Blanco	1 842	5 972	2 763	3.2	5 598	56	17	22	279	840	6.8	14.2	10.7
48 033	...	Borden	2 328	799	3 123	0.3	769	2	10	0	18	120	7.1	16.8	9.9
48 035	...	Bosque	2 562	15 125	1 980	5.9	14 173	319	26	41	566	1 430	6.1	13.7	10.9
48 037	8360	Bowie	2 300	81 665	555	35.5	62 878	17 798	412	262	315	1 334	7.0	15.6	13.5
48 039	3362	Brazoria	3 592	191 707	250	53.4	154 875	15 981	812	1 961	18 078	33 797	8.1	16.8	13.9
48 041	1260	Brazos	1 517	121 862	377	80.3	94 866	13 672	274	4 313	8 737	16 713	6.8	11.8	34.9
48 043	...	Brewster	16 040	8 681	2 495	0.5	8 300	85	20	52	224	3 702	6.5	13.2	19.9
48 045	...	Briscoe	2 332	1 971	3 068	0.8	1 559	68	5	0	339	367	6.5	16.9	9.6
48 047	...	Brooks	2 443	8 204	2 547	3.4	6 748	3	13	10	1 430	7 338	9.1	18.7	14.6
48 049	...	Brown	2 445	34 371	1 155	14.1	30 267	1 552	131	88	2 333	3 799	6.9	14.9	14.8
48 051	...	Burleson	1 724	13 625	2 090	7.9	10 173	2 430	53	18	951	1 624	7.2	15.6	12.6
48 053	...	Burnet	2 578	22 677	1 549	8.8	20 793	269	109	59	1 447	2 440	6.4	14.1	10.4
48 055	...	Caldwell	1 414	26 392	1 409	18.7	18 919	2 825	65	86	4 497	9 988	7.8	16.1	17.7
48 057	...	Calhoun	1 327	19 053	1 731	14.4	14 819	556	35	556	3 087	6 893	7.5	17.3	13.4
48 059	...	Callahan	2 328	11 859	2 226	5.1	11 482	2	44	40	291	489	6.6	16.8	10.6
48 061	1240	Cameron	2 345	260 120	193	110.9	214 424	825	413	750	43 708	212 995	8.9	19.9	17.7
48 063	...	Camp	512	9 904	2 396	19.3	7 130	2 360	35	5	374	501	6.7	15.3	13.0
48 065	...	Carson	2 391	6 576	2 702	2.8	6 315	11	44	9	197	354	7.1	17.9	11.4
48 067	...	Cass	2 428	29 982	1 297	12.3	23 651	6 057	105	25	144	373	6.6	16.0	13.0
48 069	...	Castro	2 327	9 070	2 464	3.9	5 526	261	10	15	3 258	4 187	9.5	20.8	15.2
48 071	...	Chambers	1 552	20 088	1 673	12.9	16 725	2 550	53	116	644	1 195	6.9	17.7	14.0
48 073	...	Cherokee	2 726	41 049	979	15.1	32 039	6 931	108	196	1 775	2 697	7.1	14.8	13.9

1. MSA = Metropolitan Statistical Area. CMSA = Consolidated MSA. NECMA = New England county metropolitan area. PMSA = Primary MSA. See Appendix A for explanation of these concepts. See Appendix B for list of metropolitan areas identified by type, with component counties. 2. Dry land or land partially or temporarily covered by water. 3. Hispanic persons may be of any race.

STATE County	Population, 1990 (cont'd) Age of population (cont'd) Percent 25 to 34 years	35 to 44 years	45 to 54 years	55 to 64 years	65 to 74 years	75 years and over	Percent female	Population–Change and components of change Change 1980–1990 Number	Percent	Components of change, 1980–1986 Total persons, 1986	Total persons, 1980	Net change Number	Net change Percent	Natural increase Births	Deaths
	14	15	16	17	18	19	20	21	22	23	24	25	26	27	28
TENNESSEE—Con.															
Pickett	13.2	13.7	11.8	11.5	9.1	7.9	51.1	190	4.4	4 500	4 358	200	3.6	300	300
Polk	13.9	14.5	12.8	10.2	8.4	6.0	50.7	41	0.3	13 700	13 602	100	0.8	1 000	800
Putnam	15.3	13.7	10.4	8.8	7.4	5.6	51.0	3 683	7.7	51 100	47 690	3 400	7.2	3 700	2 600
Rhea	14.5	14.4	11.6	9.2	8.1	6.2	51.7	109	0.4	24 900	24 235	700	2.7	2 100	1 400
Roane	13.8	15.3	12.4	11.2	9.3	5.7	51.8	-1 198	-2.5	49 400	48 425	1 000	2.1	3 600	2 600
Robertson	17.1	15.1	10.5	8.8	6.8	5.3	51.0	4 473	12.1	40 000	37 021	3 000	8.1	3 400	2 100
Rutherford	18.9	15.5	9.6	6.6	5.0	3.4	50.8	34 512	41.1	102 700	84 058	18 700	22.2	8 500	3 600
Scott	15.2	14.1	10.8	8.3	6.9	5.1	51.3	-901	-4.7	20 700	19 259	1 400	7.4	1 800	1 100
Sequatchie	15.6	15.7	11.6	8.7	6.5	5.7	50.5	258	3.0	8 900	8 605	300	4.0	700	500
Sevier	16.0	15.8	12.4	9.9	7.7	4.8	51.3	9 625	23.2	46 700	41 418	5 300	12.8	3 600	2 200
Shelby	18.1	15.6	9.5	7.7	6.1	4.3	52.4	49 217	6.3	809 600	777 113	32 400	4.2	86 600	42 300
Smith	15.8	14.1	10.7	9.6	8.7	7.2	51.6	-792	-5.3	14 600	14 935	-300	-1.9	1 200	900
Stewart	13.7	14.3	12.1	11.6	9.9	7.5	50.7	814	9.4	9 300	8 665	600	7.4	600	600
Sullivan	14.9	15.3	12.8	10.6	8.8	5.5	52.0	-372	-0.3	146 300	143 968	2 300	1.6	10 500	7 400
Sumner	16.2	16.7	12.1	8.1	6.0	4.2	51.0	17 491	20.4	96 600	85 790	10 800	12.6	8 000	3 900
Tipton	16.6	14.5	10.1	7.8	6.1	4.7	51.2	4 638	14.1	35 900	32 930	3 000	9.1	3 500	1 800
Trousdale	14.9	14.6	11.0	9.6	9.4	7.4	51.5	-217	-3.5	5 900	6 137	-200	-3.7	500	400
Unicoi	15.0	14.5	11.7	11.0	9.9	7.3	52.2	187	1.1	16 900	16 362	500	3.0	1 200	1 100
Union	17.0	14.7	11.5	8.5	6.2	4.8	50.6	1 987	17.0	12 200	11 707	500	4.3	1 100	600
Van Buren	15.9	15.2	10.9	9.8	7.2	5.0	50.5	118	2.5	4 800	4 728	100	1.7	400	200
Warren	15.2	14.5	11.2	9.8	8.2	6.3	51.8	339	1.0	33 100	32 653	500	1.4	2 800	1 900
Washington	16.1	15.0	11.0	9.4	8.0	5.9	51.6	3 560	4.0	93 000	88 755	4 300	4.8	7 000	5 000
Wayne	14.7	13.9	11.7	9.4	8.5	6.3	51.0	-11	-0.1	14 200	13 946	200	1.5	1 200	900
Weakley	14.2	12.5	9.9	8.8	8.5	7.6	52.1	-924	-2.8	33 100	32 896	200	0.6	2 300	2 300
White	14.3	14.3	11.6	10.5	9.2	6.9	51.7	523	2.7	20 200	19 567	600	3.0	1 500	1 200
Williamson	15.1	20.0	12.6	7.6	4.8	3.4	50.9	22 913	39.4	72 100	58 108	14 000	24.1	5 400	2 600
Wilson	16.6	17.3	12.3	7.8	5.8	4.0	50.6	11 611	20.7	64 100	56 064	8 000	14.3	5 100	2 800
TEXAS	18.2	14.9	9.6	7.6	5.9	4.2	50.7	2 757 510	19.4	16 685 000	14 229 000	2 456 000	17.3	1 839 000	714 000
Anderson	21.9	13.9	8.5	7.5	6.7	6.0	42.1	9 643	25.1	47 200	38 381	8 800	22.9	4 000	2 700
Andrews	15.9	13.4	9.2	8.5	5.9	3.6	50.6	1 015	7.6	16 700	13 323	3 400	25.2	2 200	600
Angelina	15.5	13.7	10.2	8.7	7.2	5.8	51.5	5 712	8.9	69 400	64 172	5 200	8.1	7 100	3 600
Aransas	13.4	12.6	10.6	12.4	11.9	6.6	50.4	3 632	25.5	17 900	14 260	3 600	25.6	1 700	900
Archer	15.1	14.1	11.3	10.1	8.1	5.9	50.1	707	9.7	7 900	7 266	600	8.6	700	400
Armstrong	12.4	12.2	9.3	11.1	11.0	10.7	51.6	27	1.4	1 900	1 994	-100	-3.6	200	100
Atascosa	14.8	13.5	9.7	8.1	6.7	5.1	50.5	5 478	21.9	29 100	25 055	4 100	16.2	3 200	1 500
Austin	14.0	13.7	10.4	9.2	8.9	8.8	51.2	2 106	11.9	20 800	17 726	3 100	17.3	1 900	1 500
Bailey	14.1	12.7	10.0	9.3	7.5	6.2	50.5	-1 104	-13.5	8 200	8 168	0	0.0	1 000	400
Bandera	12.5	14.9	12.2	13.4	10.9	6.7	50.3	3 478	49.1	9 400	7 084	2 300	33.0	600	600
Bastrop	16.4	16.2	10.1	8.5	6.8	5.5	49.3	13 537	54.7	36 500	24 726	11 700	47.5	3 300	1 800
Baylor	11.4	12.0	10.3	11.2	12.7	13.3	52.7	-534	-10.9	4 600	4 919	-300	-5.7	400	400
Bee	16.1	13.2	8.8	8.2	6.4	5.0	50.5	-895	-3.4	26 800	26 030	800	2.9	3 400	1 200
Bell	19.6	13.3	8.1	6.5	5.1	3.7	49.1	33 268	21.1	174 500	157 820	16 700	10.6	29 600	7 000
Bexar	17.9	14.6	9.3	7.5	6.0	3.9	51.5	196 423	19.9	1 170 000	988 971	181 100	18.3	129 800	46 700
Blanco	13.0	13.8	10.7	10.6	11.8	8.4	52.3	1 291	27.6	6 000	4 681	1 300	28.0	400	400
Borden	14.6	11.6	14.0	11.8	9.0	5.1	48.7	-60	-7.0	900	859	0	2.2	100	0
Bosque	12.0	12.2	10.4	10.2	12.5	12.1	51.7	1 724	12.9	14 300	13 401	900	6.9	1 200	1 400
Bowie	15.5	14.9	10.3	8.8	8.2	6.2	51.7	6 364	8.5	80 900	75 301	5 600	7.5	7 400	4 500
Brazoria	19.2	16.3	10.3	7.6	4.8	3.0	48.1	22 120	13.0	188 700	169 587	19 200	11.3	21 400	6 400
Brazos	17.5	11.0	6.7	4.7	3.7	3.0	48.6	28 274	30.2	120 800	93 588	27 200	29.1	11 900	3 300
Brewster	14.1	13.4	9.6	9.3	8.4	5.6	49.5	1 108	14.6	8 000	7 573	400	5.5	800	400
Briscoe	11.1	13.3	11.1	10.6	11.6	9.1	50.4	-608	-23.6	2 200	2 579	-400	-14.3	200	200
Brooks	13.9	11.9	9.4	9.2	7.5	5.7	51.5	-224	-2.7	9 100	8 428	600	7.7	1 200	500
Brown	13.3	13.1	9.7	9.5	9.3	8.4	51.5	1 314	4.0	34 800	33 057	1 700	5.1	3 300	2 600
Burleson	14.0	12.8	9.4	10.9	9.7	7.7	51.2	1 312	10.7	15 000	12 313	2 700	21.8	1 500	1 100
Burnet	12.5	12.7	9.7	11.6	12.6	9.9	51.8	4 874	27.4	23 900	17 803	6 100	34.3	1 800	1 500
Caldwell	14.7	13.3	8.7	8.1	7.1	6.5	49.8	2 755	11.7	29 200	23 637	5 600	23.6	2 400	1 500
Calhoun	15.6	13.8	10.7	10.7	7.0	4.0	50.5	-521	-2.7	21 400	19 574	1 800	9.4	2 400	900
Callahan	13.4	13.9	10.7	10.7	9.0	8.2	51.6	867	7.9	12 700	10 992	1 700	15.9	1 100	900
Cameron	14.6	12.8	8.1	7.3	6.4	4.2	52.1	50 393	24.0	257 300	209 727	47 600	22.7	33 500	8 600
Camp	13.5	13.6	9.8	10.4	10.0	7.8	52.0	629	6.8	10 400	9 275	1 100	11.8	1 000	700
Carson	14.4	13.5	10.3	9.9	9.0	6.4	51.5	-96	-1.4	6 800	6 672	200	2.4	700	300
Cass	13.5	13.4	10.7	9.8	9.2	7.9	52.0	552	1.9	30 800	29 430	1 400	4.6	2 900	2 200
Castro	13.9	12.5	9.5	8.6	5.8	4.2	50.3	-1 486	-14.1	10 300	10 556	-300	-2.6	1 300	400
Chambers	15.3	17.3	11.1	8.2	6.1	3.4	49.7	1 550	8.4	19 800	18 538	1 200	6.6	2 100	800
Cherokee	14.3	12.9	10.2	9.4	9.2	8.3	50.8	2 922	7.7	40 300	38 127	2 100	5.6	3 500	3 000

STATE County	Population–(cont'd)	Households, 1990					Births, 1988			Deaths, 1987				Marriages, 1984	
	Components of change, 1980-1986 (cont'd)				Percent					Number		Rate			
	Net migration	Number	Percent change, 1980–1990	Persons per house-hold	Female family house-holder[1]	One-person	Total	Rate[2]	Low birth weight[3] (Number)	Total	Infant[4]	Total[2]	Infant[5]	Number	Rate[2]
	29	30	31	32	33	34	35	36	37	38	39	40	41	42	43
TENNESSEE—Con.															
Pickett	100	1 786	15.8	2.52	9.5	24.1	47	10.4	2	47	0	10.2	0.0	122	27.1
Polk	-100	5 092	10.5	2.66	8.9	19.4	174	12.5	17	147	4	10.6	25.6	140	10.2
Putnam	2 300	19 753	18.2	2.45	9.7	24.1	649	12.4	36	418	3	8.1	5.3	470	9.4
Rhea	0	9 185	10.9	2.57	11.8	22.0	337	13.3	27	229	4	9.2	12.0	273	11.0
Roane	0	18 453	8.1	2.53	9.9	22.4	525	10.6	42	468	2	9.5	3.8	561	11.3
Robertson	1 700	14 801	18.1	2.77	10.4	17.7	645	15.1	47	353	3	8.4	5.1	3 645	94.4
Rutherford	13 900	42 118	50.4	2.69	10.1	20.3	1 782	16.0	115	691	18	6.4	10.7	831	8.8
Scott	700	6 534	5.4	2.78	11.7	20.1	254	12.3	21	177	4	8.5	14.2	233	11.4
Sequatchie	200	3 287	13.7	2.67	10.7	20.0	92	10.2	6	65	0	7.3	0.0	77	8.9
Sevier	3 900	19 520	32.4	2.58	9.5	19.8	600	12.0	27	386	7	7.9	12.0	1 209	26.3
Shelby	-11 900	303 571	12.8	2.65	18.6	25.7	15 195	18.5	1 542	7 159	233	8.8	15.9	7 952	10.0
Smith	-500	5 358	-0.6	2.61	8.3	21.0	185	12.5	6	159	2	10.7	11.0	166	11.4
Stewart	600	3 678	18.5	2.53	6.8	21.6	100	10.6	4	99	1	10.5	10.6	84	9.2
Sullivan	-800	56 729	9.0	2.49	9.9	23.0	1 666	11.3	102	1 388	17	9.4	10.3	1 411	9.7
Sumner	6 800	36 850	29.0	2.77	9.6	17.3	1 414	13.8	81	689	15	6.9	10.8	1 309	14.3
Tipton	1 300	13 033	20.9	2.86	13.7	18.5	675	17.7	58	336	6	9.0	9.4	457	13.2
Trousdale	-300	2 261	1.5	2.56	10.7	22.6	76	12.3	9	72	2	11.8	28.2	347	60.9
Unicoi	300	6 621	11.3	2.46	9.9	23.6	199	11.9	11	168	0	10.1	0.0	189	11.2
Union	0	4 932	25.0	2.75	10.3	17.1	170	13.4	21	120	5	9.7	27.0	159	13.0
Van Buren	-100	1 799	13.1	2.69	10.6	17.9	49	10.4	6	46	0	9.6	0.0	55	11.5
Warren	-500	12 681	6.8	2.57	10.8	22.3	422	12.3	38	348	3	10.2	7.6	355	10.7
Washington	2 300	35 823	14.9	2.45	10.6	25.1	1 108	12.1	73	866	10	9.5	8.8	897	9.8
Wayne	-100	5 174	8.0	2.65	9.3	19.5	167	11.8	8	144	3	10.1	16.9	94	6.7
Weakley	100	11 992	3.7	2.47	9.0	24.4	387	11.9	32	349	0	10.7	0.0	307	9.2
White	300	7 722	10.5	2.57	9.9	21.0	269	13.1	24	186	6	9.2	23.1	212	10.7
Williamson	11 200	27 928	49.2	2.88	8.0	14.8	1 055	13.6	49	416	5	5.5	4.7	534	8.1
Wilson	5 700	24 070	27.6	2.79	9.3	16.2	967	14.1	55	505	4	7.6	4.3	655	10.8
TEXAS	1 331 000	6 070 937	23.2	2.73	11.6	23.9	303 418	18.0	20 727	120 022	2 760	7.2	9.1	210 978	13.1
Anderson	7 500	14 223	14.8	2.67	11.5	22.6	672	14.1	49	468	7	9.9	11.1	505	11.0
Andrews	1 800	4 758	7.6	2.99	8.1	18.0	311	20.1	23	92	0	5.9	0.0	271	17.2
Angelina	1 700	25 004	14.8	2.73	11.1	22.2	1 180	17.2	66	636	11	9.3	10.7	926	13.5
Aransas	2 800	6 938	34.2	2.55	8.2	23.0	270	15.4	11	143	1	8.2	3.4	295	17.1
Archer	300	2 957	11.8	2.68	6.0	20.5	84	10.5	7	61	0	7.6	0.0	104	13.2
Armstrong	-100	768	2.4	2.56	4.8	24.9	12	5.7	0	23	0	11.0	0.0	45	23.7
Atascosa	2 400	9 940	23.7	3.03	11.1	18.7	493	16.5	36	278	10	9.5	19.9	280	10.0
Austin	2 600	7 478	16.2	2.62	8.7	25.3	277	13.8	16	195	1	9.5	3.6	240	11.7
Bailey	-600	2 454	-8.5	2.86	6.2	20.6	112	14.0	7	55	1	6.8	6.5	118	14.2
Bandera	2 300	4 180	49.2	2.46	5.5	23.5	124	12.3	7	108	2	11.0	17.1	112	13.3
Bastrop	10 300	13 379	53.4	2.77	10.1	21.5	619	16.2	50	310	7	8.2	9.6	343	10.8
Baylor	-300	1 906	-6.0	2.26	5.9	31.7	57	12.7	5	93	0	20.2	0.0	59	11.6
Bee	-1 500	8 592	5.0	2.86	11.6	21.7	473	17.9	24	218	4	8.0	7.7	329	11.8
Bell	-6 000	67 240	27.7	2.70	10.6	21.4	4 694	26.3	373	1 158	37	6.5	7.5	3 521	20.5
Bexar	98 000	409 043	27.6	2.83	14.5	23.2	21 951	18.1	1 411	8 023	200	6.7	8.8	14 749	13.3
Blanco	1 300	2 338	28.1	2.48	5.9	25.1	72	11.6	4	74	0	12.1	0.0	72	13.8
Borden	0	294	-1.7	2.72	5.1	16.7	6	6.7	0	0	0	0.0	0.0	3	3.3
Bosque	1 200	5 990	8.7	2.46	6.7	25.7	195	13.4	13	248	2	17.2	9.3	142	10.1
Bowie	2 700	30 595	11.5	2.59	13.2	24.4	1 163	14.5	94	736	6	9.1	5.3	1 157	14.6
Brazoria	4 100	64 019	18.8	2.86	8.6	18.5	3 078	16.7	193	1 093	21	5.9	6.4	2 263	12.2
Brazos	18 700	43 725	34.6	2.51	9.1	25.2	1 827	15.7	115	568	12	4.8	7.0	1 175	9.9
Brewster	0	3 350	24.4	2.43	9.2	29.2	124	15.9	8	49	1	6.3	8.4	81	9.8
Briscoe	-400	789	-18.4	2.49	5.8	26.7	32	15.2	4	16	0	7.6	0.0	16	6.7
Brooks	-100	2 673	2.3	3.04	16.1	20.8	175	18.8	11	87	3	9.4	18.2	103	11.2
Brown	900	13 097	6.4	2.51	10.3	25.8	523	15.6	32	414	5	12.3	10.0	458	12.9
Burleson	2 300	5 176	16.1	2.58	10.3	26.4	199	13.7	9	166	2	11.4	6.4	167	11.2
Burnet	5 800	9 055	30.3	2.47	7.5	23.9	295	12.1	21	281	4	11.3	11.2	315	14.5
Caldwell	4 600	8 745	18.8	2.83	11.6	22.5	413	14.3	25	260	0	8.9	0.0	198	7.4
Calhoun	300	6 777	4.8	2.79	9.1	21.9	312	15.2	22	147	1	7.0	3.1	246	11.4
Callahan	1 500	4 565	10.0	2.57	8.1	23.7	149	11.6	12	130	2	10.0	11.3	119	9.4
Cameron	22 700	73 278	25.4	3.48	16.1	16.0	5 853	22.2	304	1 558	39	6.0	7.1	2 885	11.7
Camp	800	3 773	10.8	2.59	11.6	25.0	145	14.5	10	147	5	14.7	33.6	103	10.3
Carson	-200	2 402	0.3	2.70	5.6	20.5	81	11.9	10	58	0	8.3	0.0	83	11.9
Cass	700	11 320	7.7	2.61	11.1	23.5	417	13.8	46	353	2	11.7	5.0	347	11.4
Castro	-1 100	2 877	-8.3	3.13	8.0	19.1	181	17.9	13	63	2	6.2	10.8	122	11.7
Chambers	0	6 930	10.9	2.88	9.0	18.5	244	13.4	23	146	3	7.8	11.0	606	31.4
Cherokee	1 600	14 981	9.9	2.61	11.4	24.9	631	15.7	50	477	8	11.9	12.4	402	10.2

1. No spouse present. 2. Per 1,000 resident population estimated as of July 1 of the year shown. 3. Under 2,500 grams. 4. Deaths of infants under 1 year old. 5. Deaths of infants under 1 year old per 1,000 live births.

STATE County	Divorces, 1984 Number	Divorces, 1984 Rate[1]	Physicians, active non–Federal, 1989 Number[2]	Physicians Rate[3]	Hospitals, 1989 Number	Hospitals Beds Number	Hospitals Beds Rate[3]	Nursing homes,[4] 1986 Number	Nursing homes Beds	Serious crimes known to police, 1988 Number Total[5]	Serious crimes Number Violent[6]	Serious crimes Rate[3]	Education Public school enrollment[7] 1986–1987	Public school enrollment 1980	Attainment,[8] 1980 Percent 12 yrs. or more	Attainment Percent 16 yrs. or more
	44	45	46	47	48	49	50	51	52	53	54	55	56	57	58	59
TENNESSEE—Con.																
Pickett	25	5.6	1	22	0	0	0	1	48	NA	NA	NA	788	818	36.3	5.8
Polk	50	3.6	9	64	1	44	314	1	80	6	1	478	2 927	3 085	40.7	6.1
Putnam	324	6.5	60	114	2	183	347	4	419	748	43	2 404	8 605	8 169	50.0	14.1
Rhea	27	1.1	10	39	1	136	535	3	175	290	4	3 771	4 993	5 226	47.2	8.1
Roane	306	6.2	25	51	2	149	301	2	280	822	107	1 969	8 441	10 354	54.1	10.6
Robertson	183	4.7	28	64	1	115	262	7	354	1 224	224	3 140	7 830	7 627	52.4	6.8
Rutherford	624	6.6	128	110	2	841	723	7	659	4 633	431	4 262	20 285	16 052	62.8	14.8
Scott	101	4.9	7	34	1	79	385	2	139	NA	NA	NA	4 434	4 485	37.7	5.1
Sequatchie	41	4.7	3	33	1	49	544	1	60	NA	NA	NA	1 997	1 964	39.2	5.7
Sevier	342	7.5	25	49	1	112	220	2	203	1 279	56	2 641	9 022	8 392	50.9	9.3
Shelby	3 913	4.9	2 412	292	15	6 325	767	43	4 282	68 713	9 414	8 281	146 932	140 288	65.9	15.9
Smith	87	6.0	9	60	2	95	638	1	120	43	13	308	2 648	2 921	43.0	6.1
Stewart	36	4.0	2	21	0	0	0	1	88	72	5	756	1 656	1 668	40.8	5.6
Sullivan	886	6.1	369	249	4	1 040	703	5	655	5 549	385	3 718	25 951	29 688	57.0	13.2
Sumner	632	6.9	93	88	3	254	241	7	484	2 413	300	2 391	19 955	19 064	60.5	11.8
Tipton	529	15.3	19	49	1	100	256	2	210	79	8	264	7 701	7 417	47.1	5.9
Trousdale	38	6.7	3	48	1	34	540	4	101	109	9	1 763	1 131	1 193	42.3	6.8
Unicoi	86	5.1	7	42	1	94	563	2	126	193	26	1 134	2 976	3 179	45.2	7.7
Union	58	4.8	2	16	0	0	0	0	0	154	9	1 236	2 405	2 556	36.2	2.8
Van Buren	37	7.7	1	21	0	0	0	0	0	40	4	823	867	966	39.1	5.0
Warren	232	7.0	31	90	2	152	442	4	400	921	69	2 713	6 709	6 525	48.5	6.7
Washington	583	6.4	355	388	5	1 120	1 225	10	889	3 539	162	3 817	14 838	17 027	57.1	15.0
Wayne	83	5.9	4	28	1	70	493	3	149	13	4	1 199	2 843	3 101	38.5	5.0
Weakley	173	5.2	20	62	1	100	309	6	312	612	64	1 842	5 257	5 720	45.5	9.8
White	114	5.8	11	53	1	60	290	1	120	277	1	1 347	3 619	3 744	41.8	6.5
Williamson	523	7.9	160	198	1	130	160	7	438	1 667	266	2 179	14 153	11 650	68.9	23.6
Wilson	348	5.8	53	75	2	284	402	5	373	146	18	2 844	12 251	11 971	61.2	11.7
TEXAS	98 958	6.2	28 873	170	570	81 487	480	1 058	106 751	1 345 092	109 478	8 021	3 209 515	2 910 728	62.6	16.9
Anderson	69	1.5	41	85	2	179	373	6	576	2 249	296	4 726	8 203	7 049	51.4	8.4
Andrews	116	7.3	13	86	1	65	430	1	98	457	28	2 875	3 714	3 053	55.2	11.0
Angelina	430	6.3	81	118	3	331	482	5	528	3 523	225	5 078	14 559	13 862	53.6	11.1
Aransas	131	7.6	9	52	0	0	0	0	0	1 303	82	7 406	2 777	2 976	58.0	12.0
Archer	44	5.6	2	25	0	0	0	2	132	149	8	1 840	1 691	1 527	56.8	8.2
Armstrong	7	3.7	0	0	0	0	0	1	56	19	0	905	389	398	66.2	14.3
Atascosa	67	2.4	14	46	1	30	99	5	318	845	87	2 885	6 957	6 317	45.9	8.7
Austin	87	4.2	10	51	1	32	162	3	333	475	56	2 263	4 375	3 630	45.6	7.6
Bailey	41	4.9	3	38	1	78	975	1	54	261	16	3 146	1 789	2 061	48.9	9.0
Bandera	32	3.8	4	38	0	0	0	1	62	320	23	3 266	1 607	1 306	64.9	13.9
Bastrop	155	4.9	15	38	1	30	76	4	276	1 417	101	3 780	7 909	5 073	49.0	10.2
Baylor	14	2.7	3	68	1	49	1 114	1	100	136	23	2 894	772	758	50.3	7.7
Bee	121	4.3	17	65	1	59	225	3	321	859	132	3 242	5 471	5 480	50.3	10.5
Bell	2 141	12.5	502	280	6	1 529	851	15	1 296	10 727	728	6 097	37 218	28 027	67.1	15.8
Bexar	7 539	6.8	2 962	240	30	8 126	657	46	5 356	132 895	6 044	11 108	221 199	208 962	63.1	16.0
Blanco	23	4.4	3	48	0	0	0	5	242	90	3	1 501	1 139	881	54.3	13.1
Borden	8	8.9	0	0	0	0	0	0	0	21	0	2 100	217	188	51.2	11.2
Bosque	72	5.1	14	96	1	72	493	3	332	330	20	2 292	2 541	2 125	48.2	9.7
Bowie	624	7.9	159	199	3	491	616	8	920	5 677	289	6 985	16 131	16 545	59.9	11.7
Brazoria	1 278	6.9	152	83	5	335	182	10	1 101	7 548	464	4 042	39 296	37 365	65.2	13.6
Brazos	457	3.9	163	142	4	390	339	4	589	10 744	635	9 123	15 847	13 688	69.1	31.9
Brewster	36	4.3	12	156	1	34	442	1	98	360	37	4 617	1 379	1 415	67.5	23.5
Briscoe	12	5.0	0	0	0	0	0	0	0	21	3	1 000	234	555	53.0	8.0
Brooks	15	1.6	4	43	1	26	280	1	98	166	4	1 786	1 975	2 148	40.7	8.9
Brown	192	5.4	38	114	1	126	378	6	472	1 978	121	5 802	6 971	6 547	57.2	12.3
Burleson	74	5.0	3	21	1	37	259	1	152	485	50	3 323	2 913	2 496	42.3	8.1
Burnet	152	7.0	19	76	1	50	201	4	326	801	60	3 257	4 469	3 405	51.7	9.9
Caldwell	114	4.3	14	48	2	56	192	6	411	874	116	2 984	5 032	5 040	47.2	11.0
Calhoun	118	5.5	15	75	1	53	264	1	120	691	48	3 276	4 525	4 815	53.7	10.0
Callahan	88	7.0	4	31	0	0	0	3	167	138	9	1 070	2 647	2 119	54.5	9.9
Cameron	916	3.7	267	100	6	993	371	8	907	19 275	1 979	7 314	67 350	55 312	43.8	10.5
Camp	38	3.8	4	40	1	42	420	2	130	331	24	3 246	2 024	1 848	50.8	7.4
Carson	26	3.7	0	0	0	0	0	1	52	46	4	657	1 507	1 495	62.8	13.4
Cass	196	6.4	14	47	3	149	497	5	452	720	78	2 377	6 294	6 423	52.5	8.3
Castro	46	4.4	2	20	1	30	297	1	118	267	54	2 644	2 567	2 868	52.3	13.2
Chambers	109	5.6	7	40	2	93	525	1	100	603	45	3 191	4 208	4 344	57.5	10.0
Cherokee	230	5.8	49	122	3	677	1 684	7	643	1 625	159	4 074	6 962	7 432	49.6	10.3

1. Per 1,000 resident population estimated as of July 1 of the year shown. 2. As of end of year. 3. Per 100,000 resident population as of July 1 of the year shown. 4. Preliminary. Covers nursing homes with 3 or more beds. 5. Data for serious crimes have not been adjusted for underreporting, this may affect comparability between geographic areas or over time. 6. Includes murder and nonnegligent manslaughter, forcible rape, robbery, and aggravated assault. 7. The 1986–1987 data are based on administrative reports obtained by the U.S. National Center for Education Statistics. The 1980 data are based on the 1980 Census of Population and Housing. 8. Persons 25 years old or older.

STATE County	Education (cont'd): Local government expenditures for education,[1] 1982: Total (Mil dol)	Education (cont'd): Local government expenditures for education,[1] 1982: Per capita (Dollars)	Social Security Program December 1988: Beneficiaries: Total	Social Security Program December 1988: Beneficiaries: Rate[2]	Social Security Program December 1988: Payments ($1,000)	Supplemental Security Income Program recipients June 1986	Money income: Per capita[3]: 1987 Income, (Dollars)	Money income: Per capita[3]: 1979: Current dollars	Money income: Per capita[3]: 1979: Constant 1987 dollars	Money income: Median household income 1979 (Dollars)	Money income: Percent below poverty level, 1979: Persons	Money income: Percent below poverty level, 1979: Families	Housing units, 1990: Total	Housing units, 1990: Percent change, 1980–1990
	60	61	62	63	64	65	66	67	68	69	70	71	72	73
TENNESSEE—Con.														
Pickett	1.2	266	865	192.2	300	310	6 290	3 873	6 060	9 005	28.5	22.9	2 253	20.7
Polk	4.7	346	3 075	221.2	1 301	470	7 714	4 661	7 293	12 084	19.4	16.7	5 659	11.2
Putnam	12.7	257	9 450	180.7	3 913	1 516	9 406	5 558	8 697	12 279	16.7	12.8	21 417	20.3
Rhea	7.2	295	4 620	182.6	1 962	850	8 498	5 115	8 003	12 522	19.7	15.6	10 361	10.4
Roane	13.1	268	9 300	187.5	4 200	1 352	9 739	6 286	9 836	15 181	13.2	10.1	20 334	8.6
Robertson	10.0	267	5 975	139.6	2 571	884	9 599	5 846	9 147	15 181	13.4	11.5	15 823	18.9
Rutherford	26.7	298	12 335	110.4	5 378	1 508	11 091	6 346	9 930	15 928	11.5	8.8	45 755	49.8
Scott	6.8	340	3 590	174.3	1 253	1 116	7 162	4 673	7 312	9 838	28.6	23.9	7 122	7.8
Sequatchie	3.1	354	1 300	144.4	523	228	7 034	4 563	7 140	10 972	22.4	20.5	3 570	12.9
Sevier	11.5	263	7 890	158.4	3 353	998	9 212	5 641	8 826	13 078	15.1	13.0	24 166	38.1
Shelby	235.6	300	112 200	136.9	51 528	20 896	11 249	6 697	10 479	15 289	19.6	15.3	327 796	14.5
Smith	4.0	272	2 835	191.6	1 076	476	9 638	5 812	9 094	13 948	12.9	11.0	6 049	0.0
Stewart	2.6	304	2 125	226.1	814	382	7 928	4 772	7 467	11 525	18.6	16.9	4 384	22.4
Sullivan	55.2	379	27 920	189.4	13 165	3 256	10 759	6 497	10 166	15 528	12.9	10.1	60 623	10.3
Sumner	25.0	283	12 965	126.6	5 804	1 654	11 697	6 833	10 692	17 845	9.7	8.3	39 807	32.0
Tipton	19.9	589	4 945	129.8	1 921	1 366	8 405	5 287	8 273	13 158	20.1	16.0	14 071	21.6
Trousdale	1.6	279	1 095	176.6	422	204	8 924	6 226	9 742	14 930	9.3	7.1	2 537	1.6
Unicoi	4.5	269	3 170	189.8	1 233	598	8 975	5 237	8 194	12 347	15.0	11.8	7 076	10.6
Union	3.0	252	1 860	146.5	690	428	6 984	4 399	6 883	11 072	24.3	20.9	5 696	22.7
Van Buren	1.1	233	710	151.1	253	166	8 499	4 903	7 672	11 380	17.0	13.9	2 001	14.1
Warren	8.2	248	6 460	188.9	2 626	1 072	8 911	5 269	8 244	11 922	17.2	14.4	13 802	6.4
Washington	25.5	281	17 075	186.2	7 517	2 222	10 680	6 397	10 009	14 112	14.2	10.5	38 378	14.0
Wayne	4.2	300	2 465	173.6	939	606	6 874	4 630	7 245	11 716	18.5	16.5	5 741	10.9
Weakley	7.4	225	6 175	189.4	2 610	718	8 775	5 203	8 141	11 530	16.3	12.4	12 857	3.2
White	5.5	281	4 460	217.6	1 713	802	8 380	5 089	7 963	11 447	17.5	13.5	8 369	10.3
Williamson	24.1	392	7 255	93.3	3 453	726	15 444	8 489	13 283	21 734	8.4	6.8	29 875	51.5
Wilson	15.6	274	8 310	121.1	3 698	1 018	11 505	6 785	10 616	18 298	10.7	8.3	26 198	30.1
TEXAS	6 782.2	441	2 100 048	124.7	962 725	264 760	10 645	7 203	11 271	16 708	14.7	11.1	7 008 999	26.3
Anderson	22.1	521	7 710	161.6	3 308	1 362	8 484	5 889	9 215	13 606	18.5	14.6	16 909	21.4
Andrews	14.4	957	1 800	116.1	896	116	9 218	7 003	10 958	18 229	11.4	8.8	5 462	17.1
Angelina	32.6	481	12 355	179.6	5 677	1 764	9 193	6 229	9 747	15 630	13.8	10.3	28 796	16.8
Aransas	8.2	508	3 280	187.4	1 531	174	8 610	6 820	10 671	14 066	15.6	12.6	10 889	37.0
Archer	3.6	486	1 190	148.8	547	68	9 975	7 080	11 078	15 975	8.1	6.2	3 680	10.1
Armstrong	0.8	407	445	211.9	220	18	9 596	7 262	11 363	15 556	9.2	8.0	916	2.2
Atascosa	11.5	439	3 780	126.8	1 444	778	6 993	4 949	7 744	12 829	23.9	19.6	11 614	24.9
Austin	11.4	590	4 155	206.7	1 798	402	10 451	7 000	10 953	14 378	16.1	11.7	8 885	13.3
Bailey	4.0	480	1 230	153.8	559	110	8 225	5 682	8 891	12 521	20.6	16.9	3 109	-1.3
Bandera	3.0	400	1 980	196.0	855	92	9 402	6 457	10 103	13 368	12.9	10.2	6 485	36.3
Bastrop	10.1	357	5 695	149.1	2 424	736	8 961	5 864	9 175	12 437	17.8	14.4	16 301	52.5
Baylor	1.6	306	1 380	306.7	613	116	8 282	6 257	9 790	11 597	13.4	11.1	3 006	-4.3
Bee	11.4	417	3 645	138.1	1 473	748	7 782	5 392	8 437	12 694	22.7	17.7	10 208	14.0
Bell	61.0	370	19 975	112.0	8 328	2 200	9 156	5 810	9 091	13 071	16.1	13.4	75 957	27.3
Bexar	423.1	401	143 965	118.8	59 424	21 230	9 560	6 135	9 599	15 085	18.5	14.8	455 832	32.0
Blanco	1.7	356	1 505	242.7	652	64	9 523	6 375	9 975	12 431	9.7	7.2	3 135	28.3
Borden	1.5	1 546	55	61.1	25	0	10 277	7 008	10 965	14 946	17.1	14.4	478	-14.5
Bosque	4.2	312	4 215	290.7	1 861	278	9 218	5 994	9 379	11 686	15.4	11.4	8 074	8.5
Bowie	27.6	360	13 725	171.6	5 607	1 972	9 426	6 246	9 773	14 150	16.2	12.4	34 234	14.8
Brazoria	90.1	503	19 575	106.0	9 922	1 524	11 149	8 016	12 543	23 341	8.2	6.3	74 504	23.2
Brazos	32.2	287	9 470	81.2	4 358	1 172	8 819	5 903	9 236	12 305	22.3	10.4	48 799	36.7
Brewster	3.6	471	1 325	169.9	575	178	7 162	4 837	7 568	10 804	21.9	14.8	4 486	38.2
Briscoe	0.8	303	600	285.7	269	62	7 746	5 506	8 615	10 925	25.8	18.5	1 074	-6.3
Brooks	6.1	698	1 430	153.8	513	534	5 780	4 515	7 065	10 545	29.8	26.2	3 104	6.3
Brown	12.4	358	7 600	226.2	3 306	874	8 949	5 972	9 344	12 558	13.0	9.3	16 909	12.6
Burleson	6.8	456	2 840	195.9	1 163	452	7 905	5 675	8 880	12 977	18.0	13.7	7 044	12.8
Burnet	7.1	370	5 945	243.6	2 729	354	9 037	6 003	9 393	12 138	16.0	11.7	12 801	29.2
Caldwell	8.8	354	4 205	146.0	1 777	802	7 369	4 915	7 691	11 818	29.1	18.1	10 123	23.1
Calhoun	12.7	595	2 735	133.4	1 269	314	9 071	6 898	10 793	18 098	14.8	11.7	9 559	14.1
Callahan	4.3	366	2 510	196.1	1 098	212	8 119	6 105	9 552	13 833	11.8	9.7	5 503	13.3
Cameron	106.8	462	33 220	125.8	12 441	9 350	6 132	4 336	6 785	11 731	31.8	26.0	88 759	34.5
Camp	3.3	337	2 350	235.0	1 014	422	9 113	6 236	9 757	13 824	17.3	13.7	4 530	18.9
Carson	5.0	694	1 185	174.3	622	44	10 434	7 240	11 328	17 522	8.9	6.6	2 856	8.4
Cass	13.4	437	6 200	205.3	2 653	948	7 962	5 827	9 118	13 521	18.3	14.5	13 191	12.3
Castro	5.7	542	1 150	113.9	504	122	6 613	4 850	7 589	12 917	27.7	21.0	3 357	-9.0
Chambers	13.6	709	1 965	108.0	956	200	9 554	7 323	11 458	19 897	14.2	11.7	8 061	10.6
Cherokee	12.9	335	7 910	197.3	3 402	1 136	8 312	5 761	9 014	12 189	17.6	13.7	17 629	12.9

1. Elementary and secondary. 2. Per 1,000 resident population estimated as of July 1 of the year shown. 3. Based on the resident population estimated as of July 1, 1988 for 1987 data and enumerated as of April 1, 1980 for 1979 data.

STATE County	Housing units, 1990 (cont'd) — Occupied units — Total	Owner occupied — Percent	Owner occupied — Median value (Dollars)	Median rent (Dollars)	Civilian labor force, 1990 — Total	Percent change, 1989–1990	Unemployment — Total	Unemployment — Rate[1]	Private nonfarm establishments, 1988 — Number	Net change, 1987–1988	Employment[2] — Total	Per-cent change, 1987–1988	Manu-facturing	Retail trade
	74	75	76	77	78	79	80	81	82	83	84	85	86	87
TENNESSEE—Con.														
Pickett	1 786	78.8	34 200	99	1 893	5.4	142	7.5	61	-4	714	5.5	465	76
Polk	5 092	82.9	37 800	170	4 127	4.1	489	11.8	221	10	2 331	-27.9	1 015	349
Putnam	19 753	66.8	55 000	230	27 845	3.8	1 514	5.4	1 272	49	20 396	0.5	8 272	4 277
Rhea	9 185	74.5	45 300	207	10 686	2.7	783	7.3	374	15	7 145	0.8	4 636	975
Roane	18 453	76.4	48 700	194	26 381	0.6	1 782	6.8	637	7	8 133	-14.5	3 453	1 903
Robertson	14 801	74.9	61 300	240	21 682	1.3	1 148	5.3	584	4	7 464	1.5	3 453	1 648
Rutherford	42 118	66.1	71 800	333	60 850	1.0	2 680	4.4	2 248	59	40 168	10.5	16 575	7 648
Scott	6 534	75.4	33 600	156	7 729	3.0	685	8.9	283	17	3 879	15.2	1 768	621
Sequatchie	3 287	77.6	39 000	183	3 540	-0.9	191	5.4	142	1	1 615	15.6	624	284
Sevier	19 520	75.8	62 400	254	24 011	0.0	2 257	9.4	1 698	43	15 422	5.1	2 664	5 193
Shelby	303 571	59.5	66 500	302	398 099	0.4	17 405	4.4	19 825	606	356 294	9.3	50 096	73 629
Smith	5 358	78.8	45 900	175	6 987	-5.0	469	6.7	235	-1	3 857	17.2	1 759	639
Stewart	3 678	82.4	43 700	156	5 125	5.9	321	6.3	100	-4	1 094	3.0	691	197
Sullivan	56 729	75.0	55 600	231	75 336	1.2	2 721	3.6	3 192	-12	57 187	-2.3	20 323	11 574
Sumner	36 850	75.0	73 900	339	53 783	1.0	2 780	5.2	2 006	10	23 126	-1.9	9 626	5 144
Tipton	13 033	71.9	56 100	215	16 614	-0.1	843	5.1	521	11	5 456	15.6	2 273	1 218
Trousdale	2 261	74.7	41 900	187	3 864	-11.4	200	5.2	112	1	1 717	2.2	1 002	307
Unicoi	6 621	77.2	48 100	184	7 988	1.6	588	7.4	262	-9	3 339	1.2	1 968	699
Union	4 932	79.8	45 500	181	5 480	-0.3	308	5.6	110	0	894	-7.0	481	143
Van Buren	1 799	83.8	33 000	132	2 508	-4.3	233	9.3	40	3	1 006	7.2	900	4
Warren	12 681	73.2	42 200	209	14 923	5.0	1 210	8.1	664	17	10 850	11.2	5 866	1 778
Washington	35 823	67.4	57 300	244	47 490	1.0	2 012	4.2	2 296	24	34 686	5.4	10 250	7 786
Wayne	5 174	83.6	32 800	145	7 396	0.5	495	6.7	181	-5	2 976	-3.5	2 061	351
Weakley	11 992	70.5	39 800	184	16 516	6.3	823	5.0	605	-14	8 472	16.2	4 597	1 347
White	7 722	81.5	40 300	180	8 660	-1.9	837	9.7	347	-9	5 450	10.1	3 449	796
Williamson	27 928	79.5	131 100	407	42 685	0.7	1 125	2.6	2 362	103	28 131	4.6	5 381	5 509
Wilson	24 070	80.5	82 000	310	36 563	1.1	1 802	4.9	1 215	22	15 302	5.6	4 812	3 480
TEXAS	6 070 937	60.9	59 600	328	8 443 000	0.2	521 000	6.2	X	X	5 452 505	0.3	938 491	1 215 779
Anderson	14 223	72.8	42 800	275	21 930	-2.4	1 342	6.1	855	-46	8 140	7.1	1 499	2 681
Andrews	4 758	76.2	39 200	243	6 998	-1.8	281	4.0	364	13	3 478	0.3	0	646
Angelina	25 004	71.6	43 600	252	32 995	-1.2	2 089	6.3	1 641	26	23 056	3.8	7 371	5 070
Aransas	6 938	73.1	56 700	278	7 776	-2.0	344	4.4	374	-11	2 300	-6.1	174	921
Archer	2 957	80.4	45 200	213	3 247	0.3	126	3.9	166	2	776	-3.5	0	130
Armstrong	768	80.7	43 700	213	976	-2.4	52	5.3	37	-8	290	-16.9	0	45
Atascosa	9 940	75.6	37 800	199	11 392	-4.8	820	7.2	469	-12	3 744	-2.0	142	1 105
Austin	7 478	74.4	57 400	239	10 174	3.4	358	3.5	472	-50	3 773	-10.9	545	948
Bailey	2 454	69.7	35 300	201	3 131	3.7	115	3.7	189	-11	1 252	5.5	64	377
Bandera	4 180	79.6	61 900	256	4 437	3.3	118	2.7	175	-8	858	-14.7	43	277
Bastrop	13 379	77.6	53 900	253	16 960	2.2	809	4.8	532	-38	3 698	6.0	696	1 396
Baylor	1 906	70.3	34 000	144	2 305	-1.1	86	3.7	160	-6	961	5.6	34	228
Bee	8 592	63.8	39 400	233	10 967	4.7	712	6.5	507	-22	4 168	-6.4	154	1 366
Bell	67 240	52.1	59 000	301	79 601	0.1	5 355	6.7	3 388	-71	45 545	-5.6	7 188	12 920
Bexar	409 043	57.8	56 300	317	551 122	-1.6	39 196	7.1	25 394	-415	367 245	-1.8	37 029	94 535
Blanco	2 338	72.8	56 400	210	2 903	-2.3	73	2.5	163	3	1 781	12.5	87	200
Borden	294	69.0	22 800	125	396	-4.1	17	4.3	5	-1	17	-10.5	0	0
Bosque	5 990	75.8	42 000	211	6 456	0.0	402	6.2	282	-14	2 530	1.1	882	435
Bowie	30 595	70.8	48 100	263	39 344	-1.5	2 513	6.4	1 895	-12	23 254	0.3	4 988	5 926
Brazoria	64 019	69.2	61 800	313	87 156	1.1	4 819	5.5	3 171	-91	45 459	-0.7	13 917	9 983
Brazos	43 725	41.9	66 600	336	61 806	0.2	2 159	3.5	2 402	-43	27 974	3.4	3 107	8 733
Brewster	3 350	59.6	45 500	227	3 912	-1.3	159	4.1	245	1	1 452	9.6	36	515
Briscoe	789	76.4	22 400	164	1 186	3.4	29	2.4	50	-2	188	-3.1	0	37
Brooks	2 673	71.7	26 700	99	3 800	-3.5	270	7.1	156	-7	1 448	24.7	0	456
Brown	13 097	71.8	36 500	236	16 501	-1.9	1 051	6.4	860	6	9 030	0.7	2 469	2 023
Burleson	5 176	78.8	41 600	215	6 002	-3.7	335	5.6	265	-3	1 795	4.1	320	396
Burnet	9 055	75.7	58 400	246	9 531	-1.8	393	4.1	603	-26	4 334	0.3	888	1 316
Caldwell	8 745	68.4	44 200	223	10 009	-2.8	570	5.7	460	-42	4 205	3.6	530	980
Calhoun	6 777	71.0	45 000	249	9 601	0.9	559	5.8	408	-15	5 463	-2.2	2 547	1 037
Callahan	4 565	81.0	35 500	211	5 396	-1.5	246	4.6	234	-6	1 129	-0.6	90	312
Cameron	73 278	64.4	38 400	235	104 812	1.4	12 280	11.7	4 671	97	53 621	2.3	9 278	15 715
Camp	3 773	74.3	42 200	218	6 158	-6.4	360	5.8	246	-15	2 156	-1.2	577	659
Carson	2 402	81.2	40 200	237	3 959	-5.2	133	3.4	150	-1	821	2.1	50	165
Cass	11 320	77.8	38 700	177	14 727	-4.3	1 016	6.9	511	-14	4 282	7.2	761	1 340
Castro	2 877	66.6	39 900	209	4 467	-5.8	193	4.3	218	4	1 228	3.9	201	289
Chambers	6 930	80.9	57 000	266	7 897	1.3	363	4.6	322	-3	3 050	2.0	837	611
Cherokee	14 981	72.7	39 500	213	20 415	0.0	1 157	5.7	783	-1	9 333	-2.5	3 078	2 368

1. Percent of total civilian labor force. 2. For week including March 12. Excludes government employees, self-employed persons, farm workers, domestic service workers, railroad employees subject to the Railroad Retirement Act, and employees on oceanborne vessels or in foreign countries.

STATE County	Private nonfarm establishments, 1988 (cont'd): Employment[1] (cont'd): Finance, insurance, and real estate	Employment[1] (cont'd): Services	Annual payroll: Total (Mil dol)	Annual payroll: Average per employee (Dollars)	Personal income, 1989: Total (Mil dol)	Percent change, 1988–1989	Wages and salaries[2] (Mil dol)	Proprietor's income (Mil dol)	Dividends, interest, & rent (Mil dol)	Transfer payments (Mil dol)	Per capita[3]: Dollars	Per capita[3]: Rank	Earnings, 1989: Total (Mil dol)	Percent by selected industries: Farm	Goods-related[4]: Total
	88	89	90	91	92	93	94	95	96	97	98	99	100	101	102
TENNESSEE—Con.															
Pickett	0	82	7	9 957	37	7.7	16	6	6	10	8 081	3 072	22	7.3	NA
Polk	138	316	43	18 259	145	4.4	43	20	19	35	10 398	2 809	63	11.7	35.7
Putnam	559	4 024	319	15 617	706	7.9	495	86	98	119	13 379	1 742	581	1.5	37.3
Rhea	119	761	98	13 655	310	4.6	243	28	34	62	12 194	2 236	271	1.8	35.4
Roane	389	1 679	101	12 411	686	6.8	556	48	84	121	13 851	1 506	604	0.7	32.3
Robertson	266	874	108	14 527	533	5.7	184	42	71	79	12 142	2 265	226	3.8	41.7
Rutherford	2 846	6 692	807	20 103	1 728	8.3	1 182	163	189	189	14 859	1 050	1 345	0.9	47.8
Scott	127	346	64	16 419	187	1.9	94	23	19	52	9 087	3 000	117	2.3	43.9
Sequatchie	0	284	20	12 115	94	9.7	36	14	11	18	10 365	2 820	50	3.5	34.6
Sevier	945	4 934	216	14 009	644	8.0	324	83	107	100	12 663	2 052	407	1.2	21.9
Shelby	29 667	106 275	7 286	20 450	14 270	7.4	10 940	1 111	1 955	2 160	17 301	396	12 052	0.1	18.9
Smith	104	517	61	15 709	193	5.9	91	20	29	32	12 999	1 906	111	4.2	NA
Stewart	92	58	13	12 025	104	3.3	48	12	15	27	11 015	2 663	60	6.2	NA
Sullivan	1 941	12 981	1 240	21 677	2 117	7.1	1 753	188	335	332	14 303	1 287	1 942	0.5	49.2
Sumner	647	4 427	383	16 573	1 611	7.0	564	163	187	173	15 291	875	727	2.0	40.5
Tipton	292	1 035	84	15 476	466	5.4	125	38	43	85	11 919	2 353	163	4.8	37.3
Trousdale	45	205	23	13 678	73	5.9	45	10	11	12	11 729	2 428	56	5.8	NA
Unicoi	57	427	57	17 217	195	5.0	94	13	24	44	11 678	2 448	107	1.1	50.8
Union	36	127	11	12 365	124	10.0	31	11	11	24	9 675	2 930	42	7.6	44.1
Van Buren	0	14	14	13 843	45	1.6	21	6	3	8	9 655	2 936	27	12.0	NA
Warren	299	1 282	180	16 591	420	7.0	259	65	64	76	12 214	2 226	323	5.7	50.0
Washington	1 982	8 436	542	15 613	1 360	7.0	870	148	189	229	14 871	1 042	1 018	1.5	29.3
Wayne	88	295	38	12 665	145	4.1	54	17	20	29	10 243	2 848	71	7.0	45.8
Weakley	245	1 449	115	13 524	423	7.3	188	54	62	72	13 057	1 887	241	3.9	NA
White	143	453	79	14 404	251	4.9	111	41	34	46	12 159	2 255	152	6.1	50.7
Williamson	3 487	7 511	557	19 794	1 790	8.1	605	204	271	113	22 097	89	809	1.5	26.7
Wilson	499	3 488	245	16 037	1 090	7.6	353	105	133	117	15 413	832	458	2.3	39.0
TEXAS	441 510	1 481 397	112 851	X	263 610	7.3	171 800	25 655	44 235	34 316	15 512	X	197 455	1.8	26.4
Anderson	331	1 615	117	14 412	575	8.1	306	63	109	115	11 975	2 333	369	5.3	14.9
Andrews	151	510	58	16 762	204	4.4	122	26	37	27	13 496	1 683	148	2.4	44.8
Angelina	1 437	4 971	404	17 522	980	6.8	606	100	187	170	14 261	1 301	706	0.6	38.4
Aransas	177	485	31	13 506	230	6.8	72	24	70	47	13 171	1 829	96	0.2	22.2
Archer	78	137	13	16 762	121	4.4	29	28	21	16	15 074	954	56	24.0	17.9
Armstrong	13	64	5	18 728	39	-0.2	7	10	9	6	17 983	297	18	44.8	11.6
Atascosa	227	826	53	14 244	326	7.8	104	33	56	67	10 782	2 719	138	9.3	23.4
Austin	239	687	57	15 026	344	9.2	126	48	89	49	17 346	387	174	5.7	20.6
Bailey	95	194	18	14 586	130	-2.5	37	46	32	16	16 367	556	83	48.5	2.9
Bandera	82	194	10	11 255	158	11.0	28	15	39	29	15 123	934	43	6.5	20.1
Bastrop	271	695	45	12 115	471	6.9	107	44	84	86	11 872	2 368	151	5.6	17.6
Baylor	52	301	11	11 709	74	8.7	22	19	18	17	16 797	471	41	23.5	11.1
Bee	239	1 292	51	12 247	290	6.1	154	39	40	63	11 086	2 638	193	8.5	15.7
Bell	2 835	14 502	700	15 372	2 446	5.4	2 007	186	325	412	13 620	1 619	2 193	0.5	13.8
Bexar	37 710	116 929	6 487	17 665	17 368	7.2	11 776	1 175	2 840	3 126	14 053	1 413	12 950	0.2	13.8
Blanco	95	726	26	14 501	96	13.0	34	14	22	19	15 206	905	49	17.8	11.5
Borden	0	0	0	13 588	15	-6.1	4	7	2	1	18 231	268	11	57.7	NA
Bosque	146	593	36	14 087	225	8.0	62	29	65	48	15 402	838	90	12.0	28.3
Bowie	1 166	6 514	396	17 009	1 156	7.3	725	111	195	237	14 495	1 216	837	1.3	17.5
Brazoria	1 730	8 720	1 142	25 118	3 139	7.6	1 804	217	391	299	17 099	420	2 021	1.0	57.7
Brazos	1 507	9 300	412	14 742	1 467	8.6	1 012	128	234	190	12 760	2 012	1 140	1.5	14.7
Brewster	172	416	16	10 760	94	5.5	47	12	23	20	12 192	2 237	59	8.0	8.5
Briscoe	0	19	3	13 516	36	-6.4	6	13	9	7	17 855	315	20	56.7	NA
Brooks	65	474	13	8 723	77	6.7	33	13	12	22	8 217	3 059	46	11.1	18.7
Brown	446	2 469	150	16 635	454	7.0	240	43	90	103	13 646	1 604	283	2.1	33.5
Burleson	174	314	23	12 870	164	6.6	51	16	38	39	11 475	2 511	67	10.5	22.0
Burnet	295	1 009	62	14 202	353	6.1	96	47	128	80	14 167	1 362	143	6.4	30.6
Caldwell	160	1 554	55	13 120	316	7.0	93	33	65	63	10 859	2 696	126	6.2	21.6
Calhoun	188	549	142	25 949	269	7.4	266	34	43	39	13 355	1 754	300	2.5	66.2
Callahan	90	273	14	12 779	151	4.9	27	22	26	33	11 738	2 426	49	9.7	17.5
Cameron	3 870	14 893	705	13 148	2 260	9.3	1 285	197	385	513	8 435	3 047	1 483	2.8	17.1
Camp	112	338	32	14 636	167	11.9	49	37	34	30	16 692	484	86	31.4	30.1
Carson	65	160	13	16 069	106	-0.2	134	23	20	15	15 672	748	157	9.8	67.8
Cass	290	974	52	12 099	387	6.7	149	48	66	86	12 888	1 958	198	6.5	39.4
Castro	59	237	19	15 518	138	2.4	42	68	16	16	13 751	1 553	110	58.8	5.7
Chambers	145	487	64	21 136	245	3.8	152	25	37	32	13 824	1 522	177	3.2	54.5
Cherokee	387	2 277	145	15 559	515	7.1	233	63	98	112	12 824	1 989	296	4.9	26.2

1. For week including March 12. Excludes government employees, self-employed persons, farm workers, domestic service workers, railroad employees subject to the Railroad Retirement Act, and employees on oceanborne vessels or in foreign countries. 2. Includes other labor income. 3. Based on the resident population estimated as of July 1 of the year shown. 4. Covers mining, construction, and manufacturing.

STATE County	Earnings, 1989 (cont'd)						Agriculture, 1987									
	Percent by selected industries (cont'd)						Farms			Farm operators, percent		Land in farms				
	Goods-related[1]	Service-related & other[2]						Percent with						Acres		
	Manu-facturing	Total	Retail trade	Finance, insur-ance, & real estate	Services	Govern-ment	Number	Less than 50 acres	500 acres and over	Whose principal occu-pation is farming	Residing on farm operated	Acreage (1,000)	Percent change, 1982–1987	Average size of farm	Total irrigated (1,000)	Total cropland (1,000)
	103	104	105	106	107	108	109	110	111	112	113	114	115	116	117	118
TENNESSEE—Con.																
Pickett	40.1	33.5	10.9	3.2	10.5	15.8	369	37.4	1.6	33.1	71.8	37	-4.2	100	0	19
Polk	30.9	34.2	10.8	4.3	11.8	18.4	260	37.3	5.4	35.8	81.2	37	5.0	143	0	21
Putnam	31.9	43.3	9.8	2.4	18.5	17.8	1 072	46.8	2.1	37.4	73.0	105	-7.2	98	0	53
Rhea	31.3	18.5	5.9	1.5	8.2	44.2	374	27.8	4.8	38.0	75.1	56	-8.5	150	1	33
Roane	29.9	54.9	4.8	1.0	46.0	12.1	542	36.2	1.5	33.4	74.4	59	-12.9	108	0	29
Robertson	34.6	36.5	11.5	1.4	15.3	18.0	1 543	33.1	6.9	47.0	72.1	255	0.9	165	0	188
Rutherford	41.1	37.0	7.2	4.4	15.0	14.3	1 562	34.7	5.2	32.2	74.5	225	-4.1	144	0	127
Scott	32.1	36.3	7.8	2.5	12.9	17.6	239	35.6	4.2	27.6	72.4	35	5.9	145	D	13
Sequatchie	15.8	45.2	9.6	1.9	19.8	16.7	156	21.2	5.8	31.4	75.6	25	-8.2	162	D	12
Sevier	13.0	65.5	25.4	4.6	31.1	11.4	953	45.9	1.0	35.5	70.5	78	-17.0	82	0	46
Shelby	13.4	64.4	10.0	6.5	24.6	16.6	733	54.2	10.0	37.1	60.2	140	-21.1	190	2	99
Smith	28.3	NA	12.5	2.7	NA	11.4	1 123	25.3	2.6	39.2	67.7	146	-6.5	130	0	73
Stewart	19.0	23.2	8.2	2.8	9.2	49.2	371	28.3	3.8	32.6	64.4	56	-10.3	150	D	23
Sullivan	43.0	42.9	8.5	2.7	21.3	7.5	1 432	60.6	1.5	34.6	71.6	98	-2.2	68	0	58
Sumner	31.7	42.7	8.9	3.0	23.1	14.8	1 864	42.5	2.9	34.8	70.0	206	-5.6	110	0	136
Tipton	25.8	41.9	9.8	4.2	19.5	16.0	650	36.6	17.5	48.2	68.3	191	-8.8	293	1	164
Trousdale	30.6	29.2	7.6	3.0	9.5	32.2	439	34.9	3.4	46.9	71.1	59	-0.6	133	0	34
Unicoi	47.0	33.3	8.4	1.6	14.2	14.7	266	75.6	0.0	34.6	71.8	10	-28.0	39	0	4
Union	36.8	NA	7.5	2.0	12.4	17.9	612	44.9	1.3	38.7	71.7	53	-1.5	87	0	28
Van Buren	52.6	12.3	1.9	1.4	5.2	19.2	217	30.9	2.3	39.6	74.7	30	-16.3	140	0	14
Warren	44.8	35.5	7.7	2.3	14.8	8.7	1 238	38.9	4.9	42.4	73.5	165	-8.0	133	3	108
Washington	24.0	50.0	11.6	2.8	26.5	19.2	1 909	61.0	1.2	37.2	75.7	124	3.8	65	1	91
Wayne	43.1	NA	9.1	3.1	10.4	16.3	698	21.3	7.0	30.1	70.8	135	-1.2	194	0	51
Weakley	29.6	NA	10.3	3.1	15.3	22.1	926	27.9	11.9	45.6	69.0	208	-6.4	225	0	169
White	46.7	34.1	7.9	0.5	11.9	9.1	1 006	37.8	2.7	35.9	71.9	133	-7.4	132	0	72
Williamson	15.4	64.7	9.6	7.8	34.4	7.2	1 421	36.9	5.2	32.4	72.3	220	-10.1	155	0	117
Wilson	27.1	49.8	11.7	3.0	22.5	8.9	1 755	32.1	3.0	39.5	74.6	216	-8.3	123	0	122
TEXAS	16.1	55.9	9.8	6.8	24.2	15.9	188 788	26.4	22.3	44.3	54.9	130 503	-0.6	691	4 271	35 611
Anderson	6.3	46.0	12.3	3.1	16.4	33.9	1 598	30.2	8.9	33.8	58.9	351	9.6	220	1	120
Andrews	5.9	36.9	7.2	2.6	15.5	15.9	147	27.9	49.0	56.5	40.1	929	24.5	6 320	5	78
Angelina	30.4	46.5	11.2	3.4	20.0	14.5	747	41.4	4.8	25.2	70.5	104	-12.6	139	0	41
Aransas	9.3	62.0	16.3	5.0	18.3	15.6	54	42.6	22.2	25.9	48.1	23	-18.0	424	0	8
Archer	0.2	43.7	4.7	2.1	21.3	14.4	486	13.4	40.7	49.4	49.0	561	3.0	1 154	0	98
Armstrong	0.0	31.0	4.4	9.0	8.1	12.6	222	6.3	68.0	70.7	58.6	482	-12.8	2 171	8	170
Atascosa	2.2	47.6	12.4	3.3	14.5	19.7	1 341	21.9	25.1	42.9	52.6	743	-1.5	554	27	207
Austin	6.9	61.9	7.9	5.8	25.4	11.8	1 865	32.3	7.5	35.3	53.8	347	11.1	186	3	155
Bailey	0.8	37.7	6.1	2.6	8.0	10.8	443	11.3	51.5	70.4	49.0	433	-4.2	977	65	294
Bandera	2.8	56.2	10.1	4.7	24.6	17.2	540	17.2	30.0	40.9	63.3	335	-1.2	620	0	48
Bastrop	8.7	46.8	12.8	3.3	20.9	30.0	1 655	28.9	10.5	38.7	54.1	410	8.8	248	3	124
Baylor	3.8	49.0	9.6	4.3	19.1	16.4	295	11.9	45.8	57.3	41.7	356	-11.4	1 205	2	133
Bee	6.9	39.7	8.9	5.1	17.4	36.1	743	21.9	28.3	43.2	50.6	481	16.2	648	2	142
Bell	9.5	34.1	7.9	2.6	17.2	51.5	1 655	32.3	11.5	39.2	62.2	423	-5.9	256	1	232
Bexar	7.8	55.0	11.3	8.4	25.2	31.0	1 950	47.8	8.0	37.0	62.9	477	-4.7	245	12	154
Blanco	2.1	NA	13.1	11.1	NA	14.6	549	15.1	34.1	43.0	56.6	379	2.2	691	0	35
Borden	NA	NA	2.5	NA	8.7	17.5	128	5.5	72.7	78.1	68.0	594	3.1	4 640	D	63
Bosque	21.1	46.3	9.8	4.4	18.5	13.5	968	14.7	23.1	44.9	55.8	569	3.2	588	2	137
Bowie	13.0	49.3	12.0	3.7	23.8	31.9	1 129	33.1	9.8	34.6	68.6	251	-1.1	222	3	120
Brazoria	41.4	28.4	6.9	2.2	12.5	13.0	1 498	45.8	13.6	35.3	59.5	537	-14.9	359	33	196
Brazos	7.2	43.2	10.7	3.8	20.8	40.6	971	31.8	11.8	35.6	53.8	271	5.7	280	9	109
Brewster	0.6	45.2	12.6	3.3	17.4	38.2	118	11.9	83.1	56.8	46.6	2 378	-6.8	20 151	0	2
Briscoe	NA	NA	3.5	NA	7.7	9.9	224	7.6	59.4	79.9	46.4	404	1.7	1 803	28	144
Brooks	2.2	40.9	11.8	3.0	16.2	29.3	330	22.1	21.2	43.9	34.2	529	9.3	1 603	3	33
Brown	28.5	49.4	11.0	3.2	21.9	15.1	1 144	20.7	22.5	38.6	53.4	547	4.3	478	5	143
Burleson	5.6	45.4	12.2	5.8	11.1	22.1	1 360	26.1	10.7	40.2	53.2	315	-5.4	231	6	112
Burnet	15.6	46.4	13.2	5.0	19.8	16.6	889	17.8	28.7	39.8	56.9	510	-3.8	573	0	82
Caldwell	9.3	54.6	9.6	3.2	31.7	17.6	1 026	23.6	13.9	37.3	50.8	266	4.0	259	1	110
Calhoun	48.7	22.8	5.0	1.8	8.1	8.6	277	27.4	29.6	52.3	51.3	189	-4.3	682	6	76
Callahan	2.3	51.2	11.9	5.2	23.6	21.6	802	22.2	22.6	39.3	60.5	496	-7.9	618	1	106
Cameron	12.6	56.1	13.7	5.1	24.7	24.1	1 002	52.2	19.0	53.1	58.6	389	0.8	389	123	257
Camp	15.6	30.0	11.2	2.6	10.3	8.6	413	28.8	7.0	40.9	65.1	78	12.4	190	D	37
Carson	64.2	12.4	1.6	1.3	3.5	10.0	335	12.8	68.4	71.6	43.9	650	-10.8	1 940	64	289
Cass	31.2	37.6	9.8	2.8	15.6	16.5	885	25.0	7.8	35.4	63.2	191	-2.5	215	0	76
Castro	3.8	25.0	4.4	1.6	6.5	10.5	573	7.9	61.3	81.8	40.0	522	-4.9	911	180	425
Chambers	35.2	27.4	5.5	1.5	8.7	14.9	337	26.4	33.8	49.6	55.2	307	-2.0	910	25	110
Cherokee	20.2	48.8	14.1	3.4	19.7	20.0	1 463	29.5	8.5	38.5	61.4	284	14.4	194	0	120

1. Covers mining, construction, and manufacturing. 2. Covers private sector earnings in agricultural services, forestry, and fisheries; transportation and public utilities; wholesale trade; retail trade; finance, insurance, and real estate; and services.

STATE County	Agriculture, 1987 (cont'd): Value of land and buildings: Average per farm ($1,000)	Value of land and buildings: Average per acre (Dollars)	Value of products sold: Total (Mil dol)	Value of products sold: Average per farm (Dollars)	Value of products sold: Percent from: Crops	Value of products sold: Percent from: Livestock and poultry[1]	Percent of farms with sales of: $10,000 or more	Percent of farms with sales of: $100,000 or more	Manufactures, 1987: Establishments: Total	Establishments: Percent with 20 or more employees	All employees: Number (1,000)	All employees: Percent change, 1982–1987	All employees: Annual payroll (Mil dol)	Production workers: Number (1,000)	Production workers: Work hours (Mil)
	119	120	121	122	123	124	125	126	127	128	129	130	131	132	133
TENNESSEE—Con.															
Pickett	71	735	3	8 503	34.5	65.5	23.3	0.3	10	70.0	0.5	-28.6	3.8	0.4	0.6
Polk	185	1 450	15	56 776	3.4	96.6	29.6	13.5	18	38.9	D	D	D	D	D
Putnam	99	1 062	10	9 348	28.7	71.3	19.2	0.7	104	44.2	8.1	42.1	129.3	6.3	11.9
Rhea	151	1 129	9	23 226	46.5	53.5	28.3	5.3	37	54.1	4.9	32.4	73.4	4.4	8.5
Roane	128	1 226	4	8 076	22.5	77.5	15.3	1.3	33	42.4	2.9	0.0	33.3	2.5	4.3
Robertson	211	1 208	43	28 112	54.8	45.2	44.7	6.2	43	46.5	D	D	D	D	D
Rutherford	216	1 451	22	13 955	15.8	84.2	23.8	3.5	153	45.8	14.8	62.6	350.1	10.6	20.8
Scott	131	983	4	17 662	D	D	16.3	4.6	35	25.7	1.5	150.0	25.4	1.1	2.3
Sequatchie	128	875	3	19 597	16.9	83.1	28.2	5.8	10	50.0	0.4	0.0	4.2	0.4	0.7
Sevier	134	1 813	8	8 577	31.4	68.6	19.1	0.9	70	25.7	2.6	8.3	44.3	2.2	4.4
Shelby	266	1 491	25	33 782	80.2	19.8	29.3	8.3	1 005	42.9	50.3	-5.1	1 150.6	32.9	66.0
Smith	97	763	12	10 422	34.5	65.5	27.1	1.2	13	61.5	1.3	-18.8	20.1	1.1	1.9
Stewart	101	589	3	8 162	54.6	45.4	24.3	0.0	10	20.0	0.7	600.0	8.6	0.6	0.9
Sullivan	144	2 067	14	9 702	31.3	68.7	15.7	1.7	153	35.3	22.4	-7.1	640.0	14.2	29.4
Sumner	170	1 512	29	15 450	34.5	65.5	26.2	2.6	182	37.4	8.8	29.4	158.6	6.9	13.8
Tipton	282	948	33	50 742	90.6	9.4	45.4	14.3	28	60.7	1.9	46.2	32.9	1.6	3.0
Trousdale	129	951	6	14 389	51.4	48.6	39.4	1.6	11	72.7	1.1	10.0	13.2	0.9	1.6
Unicoi	62	1 829	1	4 228	81.2	18.8	9.8	0.0	27	40.7	1.9	35.7	37.9	1.5	2.7
Union	78	1 008	4	6 003	51.0	49.0	13.1	0.2	9	55.6	0.5	0.0	7.2	0.4	0.7
Van Buren	102	643	4	17 070	10.5	89.5	24.4	4.1	11	45.5	0.9	50.0	10.3	0.8	1.6
Warren	154	1 152	55	44 417	70.9	29.1	36.7	7.7	58	44.8	5.0	-7.4	95.4	4.1	8.0
Washington	141	2 094	31	16 277	38.4	61.6	22.0	3.1	126	42.9	10.2	-8.9	194.4	7.1	13.8
Wayne	103	526	7	10 190	10.7	89.3	23.2	1.1	26	46.2	2.2	22.2	26.0	1.9	3.2
Weakley	140	608	38	40 720	44.5	55.5	44.4	11.0	48	41.7	3.5	12.9	50.8	2.9	5.8
White	119	933	16	16 050	12.2	87.8	25.9	3.0	38	57.9	3.4	13.3	50.7	2.9	5.4
Williamson	288	2 028	26	18 171	31.9	68.1	27.9	3.4	110	34.5	5.0	16.3	96.1	3.2	6.6
Wilson	138	1 151	17	9 965	12.2	87.8	21.7	1.1	93	33.3	5.1	-10.5	95.1	4.0	7.2
TEXAS	375	544	10 549	55 877	28.1	71.9	36.4	8.7	20 370	30.4	914.0	-13.6	23 240.9	560.8	1 125.2
Anderson	184	930	18	11 509	15.8	84.2	21.8	1.8	39	33.3	1.0	-41.2	15.0	0.8	1.5
Andrews	950	151	11	72 392	65.3	34.7	50.3	24.5	5	40.0	D	D	D	D	D
Angelina	163	1 205	13	17 900	6.0	94.0	16.2	1.1	112	30.4	6.8	-19.0	146.8	5.4	11.0
Aransas	436	1 029	1	12 416	31.5	68.5	18.5	3.7	15	20.0	0.2	-50.0	4.8	0.2	0.3
Archer	412	385	47	96 050	5.9	94.1	56.2	20.4	4	50.0	D	D	D	D	D
Armstrong	595	258	24	107 047	22.3	77.7	77.9	25.7	1	0.0	D	D	D	D	D
Atascosa	412	727	40	29 509	40.6	59.4	38.2	6.4	7	28.6	0.1	0.0	1.8	0.1	0.1
Austin	304	1 563	22	11 593	18.0	82.0	23.5	1.9	27	18.5	0.4	-71.4	7.2	0.3	0.6
Bailey	309	325	86	193 386	34.0	66.0	73.6	35.2	7	14.3	0.1	0.0	0.9	0.0	0.1
Bandera	605	972	4	7 403	5.3	94.7	15.7	1.1	12	0.0	0.1	0.0	1.0	0.0	0.1
Bastrop	345	1 320	20	12 048	11.0	89.0	22.3	1.6	37	21.6	0.6	-14.3	7.6	0.5	0.9
Baylor	418	356	25	83 744	24.5	75.5	62.7	16.6	4	0.0	0.0	0.0	0.5	0.0	0.0
Bee	444	753	20	26 477	40.8	59.2	41.5	7.0	9	33.3	0.2	0.0	3.1	0.1	0.2
Bell	257	1 052	47	28 604	23.4	76.6	25.2	3.4	125	39.2	D	D	D	D	D
Bexar	367	1 637	42	21 683	55.1	44.9	18.3	3.0	1 054	30.1	37.6	-15.7	711.1	24.9	48.4
Blanco	670	984	14	25 568	D	D	31.0	3.8	10	0.0	0.1	0.0	0.9	0.0	0.1
Borden	890	184	18	141 666	34.4	65.6	80.5	28.1	1	0.0	D	D	D	D	D
Bosque	545	858	25	25 442	15.4	84.6	32.7	4.1	24	29.2	0.7	-22.2	12.2	0.6	1.0
Bowie	171	771	34	30 181	13.4	86.6	26.7	6.5	77	32.5	4.9	11.4	107.0	3.5	5.9
Brazoria	397	1 030	37	24 796	68.6	31.4	23.6	5.0	171	33.3	14.4	-19.1	550.6	6.6	13.5
Brazos	339	1 310	35	36 154	20.0	80.0	27.0	3.5	87	27.6	2.4	-25.0	49.4	1.6	3.4
Brewster	3 569	179	10	83 105	D	D	62.7	20.3	5	0.0	0.0	0.0	0.3	0.0	0.0
Briscoe	467	267	16	73 322	53.8	46.2	72.3	24.6	2	0.0	D	D	D	D	D
Brooks	607	384	12	35 516	13.5	86.6	24.8	8.5	4	25.0	D	D	D	D	D
Brown	282	580	24	21 097	15.5	84.5	28.0	3.6	34	32.4	2.5	-7.4	56.2	2.0	4.3
Burleson	232	1 092	19	13 838	30.8	69.2	25.4	2.7	9	33.3	0.3	-25.0	4.3	0.3	0.5
Burnet	544	884	12	13 294	2.9	97.1	26.7	1.6	35	22.9	1.0	42.9	20.1	0.7	1.6
Caldwell	331	1 259	32	31 407	12.0	88.0	29.0	4.9	19	21.1	0.5	25.0	8.0	0.4	0.8
Calhoun	444	683	10	37 413	72.2	27.8	50.2	10.1	21	47.6	2.7	0.0	93.8	1.8	3.7
Callahan	205	361	17	21 121	16.3	83.7	30.8	3.6	10	10.0	0.1	0.0	1.1	0.0	0.1
Cameron	444	1 209	87	86 932	81.0	19.0	47.3	19.5	168	33.9	8.9	-21.9	122.2	6.9	13.4
Camp	200	1 008	91	221 060	1.2	98.8	31.7	11.1	14	35.7	0.5	0.0	10.7	0.3	0.6
Carson	552	281	61	181 391	21.3	78.7	80.6	31.0	5	20.0	D	D	D	D	D
Cass	150	709	15	16 774	11.8	88.2	23.2	2.5	30	20.0	0.6	-14.3	8.2	0.5	1.0
Castro	487	507	281	491 190	17.4	82.6	89.4	50.8	11	9.1	D	D	D	D	D
Chambers	664	718	15	43 592	77.0	23.0	43.9	12.8	13	46.2	D	D	D	D	D
Cherokee	193	1 136	49	33 604	43.0	57.0	27.5	4.3	90	42.2	3.1	-6.1	45.1	2.6	5.0

1. Includes livestock and poultry products.

STATE County	Manufactures, 1987 (cont'd): Production workers (cont'd): Wages: Total (Mil dol)	Average per worker (Dollars)	Value added by manufacture (Mil dol)	Value of shipments (Mil dol)	New capital expenditures (Mil dol)	Value of construction authorized by building permits, 1990: Total[1] ($1,000)	Nonresidential: Total ($1,000)	Nonresidential: Percent: Office	Industrial	Stores	Residential: New construction ($1,000)	Number of housing units	Alterations and additions ($1,000)
	134	135	136	137	138	139	140	141	142	143	144	145	146
TENNESSEE—Con.													
Pickett	3.0	7 500	4.6	10.3	D	NA	NA	NA	NA	NA	NA	NA	NA
Polk	D	D	D	D	D	0	0	NA	NA	NA	0	0	0
Putnam	85.0	13 492	357.1	772.2	14.9	21 620	8 810	9.6	78.6	5.3	10 809	173	520
Rhea	60.2	13 682	196.3	323.5	7.9	3 164	1 620	15.6	45.2	13.2	933	28	34
Roane	24.7	9 880	89.6	154.9	3.3	12 597	4 550	35.0	46.3	6.8	6 686	103	323
Robertson	D	D	D	D	D	25 010	4 622	16.1	41.7	15.3	18 779	336	508
Rutherford	226.8	21 396	1 022.3	3 093.9	92.8	119 289	21 537	8.3	43.5	29.6	76 466	1 437	4 596
Scott	14.5	13 182	59.0	115.8	4.6	4 368	3 776	4.9	50.2	39.6	296	9	121
Sequatchie	3.3	8 250	3.5	12.5	D	NA	NA	NA	NA	NA	NA	NA	NA
Sevier	33.1	15 045	98.9	172.1	10.4	42 102	13 431	6.3	0.0	60.9	11 948	263	1 095
Shelby	631.5	19 195	3 582.5	8 089.0	D	643 841	139 225	35.9	10.0	26.6	332 167	4 217	28 653
Smith	14.9	13 545	64.5	183.7	5.1	3 532	910	40.4	35.7	23.5	2 235	62	103
Stewart	7.8	13 000	25.7	41.0	0.6	451	0	NA	NA	NA	405	6	33
Sullivan	366.5	25 810	1 532.4	3 450.2	D	99 232	38 011	2.7	12.9	64.7	40 801	539	2 180
Sumner	106.2	15 391	373.1	882.3	18.6	79 228	18 265	11.8	25.0	1.9	52 095	1 038	2 592
Tipton	24.3	15 188	152.3	297.6	D	24 532	5 853	0.0	11.3	70.4	17 320	341	941
Trousdale	7.8	8 667	31.7	47.7	0.7	2 038	0	NA	NA	NA	2 038	48	0
Unicoi	23.8	15 867	87.2	128.4	D	2 606	1 400	0.0	97.3	0.0	553	10	157
Union	5.5	13 750	13.4	35.0	0.2	2 112	608	44.4	0.0	0.0	1 426	40	10
Van Buren	7.7	9 625	13.5	35.6	0.7	NA	NA	NA	NA	NA	NA	NA	NA
Warren	72.2	17 610	289.1	533.3	9.8	3 012	515	9.7	0.0	29.1	1 868	52	413
Washington	109.8	15 465	576.9	1 071.5	25.3	51 024	20 218	11.3	51.0	11.6	14 494	220	6 511
Wayne	17.6	9 263	70.9	122.4	1.3	1 803	440	0.0	0.0	79.5	1 330	49	30
Weakley	37.0	12 759	96.1	225.7	13.9	5 123	1 796	12.0	15.4	56.4	2 101	54	119
White	39.0	13 448	106.6	193.2	12.7	2 185	224	0.0	0.0	55.7	744	9	203
Williamson	47.2	14 750	184.6	363.3	9.1	150 968	49 814	9.9	3.3	80.6	80 527	653	2 843
Wilson	64.7	16 175	224.8	566.8	29.1	59 797	15 995	20.6	8.7	33.2	35 943	575	2 421
TEXAS	11 443.9	20 406	63 899.1	162 750.9	4 548.0	8 131 845	2 316 470	29.9	13.9	23.1	3 879 086	47 195	408 348
Anderson	9.9	12 375	28.6	90.8	0.6	3 218	1 598	85.0	0.0	11.3	364	10	536
Andrews	D	D	D	D	D	1 228	404	24.0	14.8	0.0	499	5	187
Angelina	103.2	19 111	336.4	823.9	41.0	14 707	5 009	3.7	0.0	64.1	3 686	64	1 145
Aransas	3.1	15 500	9.9	31.1	1.6	3 971	1 578	7.0	0.0	11.6	1 590	16	715
Archer	D	D	D	D	D	408	12	0.0	0.0	0.0	362	6	24
Armstrong	D	D	D	D	D	NA	NA	NA	NA	NA	NA	NA	NA
Atascosa	0.9	9 000	4.5	7.6	0.2	2 924	258	16.3	0.0	12.4	1 020	24	351
Austin	4.8	16 000	18.0	34.0	0.6	6 220	4 916	0.0	91.5	1.1	795	11	353
Bailey	0.6	NA	2.1	9.2	0.2	411	0	NA	NA	NA	104	1	88
Bandera	0.6	NA	2.0	2.9	0.1	84	0	NA	NA	NA	0	0	46
Bastrop	5.3	10 600	16.5	29.0	0.5	2 897	1 062	0.0	1.6	20.1	376	8	474
Baylor	0.3	NA	1.4	2.9	0.1	220	0	NA	NA	NA	147	4	6
Bee	1.7	17 000	8.6	20.3	0.2	397	1	0.0	0.0	0.0	0	0	254
Bell	D	D	D	D	D	54 581	19 228	9.3	27.5	33.2	14 777	198	10 392
Bexar	386.6	15 526	1 761.8	3 745.5	68.7	383 604	133 805	2.6	15.1	23.5	86 554	1 487	23 161
Blanco	0.4	NA	1.4	2.9	0.0	593	260	0.0	0.0	0.0	120	2	105
Borden	D	D	D	D	D	NA	NA	NA	NA	NA	NA	NA	NA
Bosque	6.6	11 000	21.4	64.1	3.3	466	151	0.0	0.0	0.0	265	4	29
Bowie	64.8	18 514	272.0	499.9	D	15 527	3 139	57.7	1.5	34.6	6 137	124	1 607
Brazoria	239.1	36 227	2 788.8	7 732.6	271.5	130 469	45 538	1.3	80.9	5.4	74 935	940	3 511
Brazos	28.5	17 812	136.7	283.2	7.8	34 715	5 616	26.7	1.1	34.2	20 202	213	2 860
Brewster	0.2	NA	0.8	1.3	0.0	571	68	0.0	0.0	37.0	332	9	57
Briscoe	D	D	D	D	D	NA	NA	NA	NA	NA	NA	NA	NA
Brooks	D	D	D	D	D	590	388	0.0	0.0	13.0	78	3	117
Brown	41.8	20 900	233.0	400.4	12.9	5 041	1 481	2.0	0.0	59.8	1 340	52	463
Burleson	3.2	10 667	11.9	29.8	0.2	97	25	0.0	0.0	0.0	30	1	8
Burnet	14.1	20 143	41.1	81.9	2.3	4 434	1 511	1.3	2.5	66.2	2 171	25	305
Caldwell	5.0	12 500	14.8	34.4	0.4	1 850	835	21.4	6.9	51.1	375	8	475
Calhoun	57.8	32 111	323.5	1 255.7	45.4	30 353	27 555	0.7	98.0	0.8	1 788	39	670
Callahan	0.7	NA	1.6	4.9	D	0	0	NA	NA	NA	0	0	0
Cameron	85.4	12 377	348.3	730.5	34.9	75 547	25 294	17.1	7.4	56.4	27 618	665	6 836
Camp	5.4	18 000	21.1	84.6	2.9	7 898	7 236	0.0	75.5	0.0	145	4	117
Carson	D	D	D	D	D	170	34	70.6	29.4	0.0	60	1	52
Cass	6.0	12 000	20.9	46.8	0.5	460	213	0.0	0.0	0.0	196	3	0
Castro	D	D	D	D	D	481	104	0.5	0.0	0.0	314	31	49
Chambers	D	D	D	D	D	2 393	838	3.0	84.8	10.5	1 450	21	61
Cherokee	34.0	13 077	139.8	274.5	5.3	4 370	1 470	20.4	10.2	6.1	1 408	31	543

1. Includes nonresidential additions and alterations, residential nonhousekeeping buildings, and residential garages and carports not shown separately.

STATE County	Wholesale trade, 1987				Retail trade, all establishments, 1987				Retail trade, establishments with payroll, 1987					
						Sales				Sales				
											Per capita[2] (Dollars)			
	Estab- lishments	Sales (Mil dol)	Paid employees[1]	Annual payroll (Mil dol)	Number	Total (Mil dol)	Percent change, 1982–1987	Per capita[2] (Dollars)	Number	Total (Mil dol)	General merchan- dise stores	Food stores	Apparel & acces- sory stores	Eating and drinking places
	147	148	149	150	151	152	153	154	155	156	157	158	159	160
TENNESSEE—Con.														
Pickett	5	3.9	32	0.3	64	10.4	0.0	2 253	25	7.7	D	D	D	87
Polk	12	40.5	98	2.2	158	29.6	35.2	2 132	58	22.4	161	826	D	154
Putnam	101	207.0	1 033	15.5	582	344.0	65.8	6 667	375	332.1	918	1 506	313	576
Rhea	11	14.3	54	0.6	233	97.6	55.9	3 905	115	90.4	366	1 310	110	221
Roane	29	98.3	392	6.5	412	203.0	24.8	4 100	218	191.9	403	1 120	99	252
Robertson	46	105.1	471	6.2	294	174.9	62.5	4 174	167	169.0	D	1 115	D	203
Rutherford	146	432.5	1 956	40.0	968	634.1	80.6	5 910	554	609.6	542	1 167	223	531
Scott	15	21.0	115	1.2	208	55.1	6.8	2 650	76	46.2	D	650	46	242
Sequatchie	5	8.7	26	0.3	93	33.5	51.6	3 760	41	30.8	D	1 413	D	178
Sevier	42	44.4	225	3.6	988	366.0	59.5	7 516	620	348.4	493	1 392	675	1 748
Shelby	2 081	21 108.5	33 584	803.8	6 932	5 756.1	50.8	7 085	4 680	5 635.3	967	1 178	400	600
Smith	19	33.4	199	1.5	172	63.0	68.4	4 255	84	58.6	D	923	73	150
Stewart	4	D	D	D	102	23.2	40.6	2 473	44	18.4	121	1 011	D	131
Sullivan	253	D	D	D	1 466	1 000.2	33.2	6 790	859	974.3	1 262	1 066	284	572
Sumner	123	219.1	834	14.8	983	463.0	67.9	4 626	484	436.6	405	1 246	114	377
Tipton	26	60.5	204	2.4	310	115.0	32.6	3 090	171	105.3	389	720	61	174
Trousdale	12	21.9	93	0.6	62	23.6	41.3	3 862	41	22.4	D	1 360	D	D
Unicoi	5	D	D	D	152	44.6	38.5	2 668	86	41.2	150	731	4	359
Union	5	8.2	41	0.5	118	17.6	20.5	1 418	42	13.2	D	448	D	23
Van Buren	5	D	D	D	37	3.0	7.1	618	4	0.4	0	D	0	D
Warren	49	84.7	449	6.5	425	165.6	47.2	4 855	194	150.3	584	1 271	275	288
Washington	177	597.5	2 783	43.4	1 044	552.5	31.6	6 045	603	528.1	D	1 136	271	593
Wayne	11	12.8	70	0.7	161	40.8	43.2	2 877	64	34.7	122	1 073	15	35
Weakley	50	88.4	372	6.5	347	124.9	41.0	3 832	206	116.7	D	839	162	298
White	28	55.7	251	2.9	239	93.5	74.8	4 606	110	83.9	D	966	100	204
Williamson	168	839.6	1 076	24.4	832	507.0	116.6	6 751	444	488.6	D	1 398	283	499
Wilson	71	235.2	631	11.8	554	304.3	76.2	4 569	296	286.5	D	858	144	395
TEXAS	35 029	192 193.7	396 138	9 098.3	173 677	100 682.1	22.4	6 001	101 150	97 175.8	744	1 269	323	583
Anderson	66	184.6	780	12.6	463	201.6	13.2	4 263	281	191.0	458	1 015	234	340
Andrews	27	31.3	155	3.3	154	58.8	-4.2	3 767	93	56.0	255	1 018	112	273
Angelina	109	196.2	1 221	19.9	732	390.8	14.2	5 705	447	375.7	829	1 249	292	438
Aransas	18	19.2	44	1.0	233	84.4	23.8	4 824	117	78.7	D	1 687	55	454
Archer	14	23.7	80	1.9	74	15.2	-29.3	1 898	39	12.9	D	530	D	108
Armstrong	4	D	D	D	34	4.0	-38.5	1 924	15	3.0	0	D	D	232
Atascosa	42	D	D	D	321	107.2	24.8	3 645	160	100.2	D	1 220	107	238
Austin	40	D	D	D	293	93.4	12.7	4 558	151	89.5	548	888	51	332
Bailey	32	D	D	D	87	26.7	-5.7	3 295	54	24.9	D	1 048	186	244
Bandera	4	D	D	D	112	27.2	49.5	2 777	48	25.4	D	1 174	27	236
Bastrop	27	32.3	143	2.7	353	112.2	39.4	2 967	185	106.1	280	864	34	197
Baylor	20	32.6	114	1.4	76	19.1	-34.4	4 162	42	17.2	D	1 276	84	338
Bee	26	D	D	D	266	114.5	8.7	4 226	172	111.7	D	959	243	370
Bell	190	788.5	2 276	43.2	1 861	1 003.1	27.5	5 670	1 199	975.7	D	1 169	233	544
Bexar	1 959	8 967.6	26 201	550.1	10 680	6 956.5	33.8	5 771	6 665	6 800.3	684	1 255	368	706
Blanco	12	D	D	D	99	12.4	-16.8	2 039	49	10.6	D	499	D	353
Borden	0	0.0	0	0.0	2	D	D	D	1	D	0	D	0	0
Bosque	24	47.2	221	3.0	213	45.1	9.2	3 131	92	41.0	85	912	43	151
Bowie	177	406.2	1 819	33.2	945	558.0	29.6	6 932	538	523.6	D	867	332	501
Brazoria	230	388.0	1 710	40.0	1 811	914.4	14.9	4 972	953	873.6	685	1 354	193	391
Brazos	147	287.9	1 333	24.6	1 043	665.4	12.5	5 644	693	649.3	799	1 289	307	579
Brewster	18	14.5	79	0.9	139	41.7	18.5	5 349	84	38.9	369	1 287	353	548
Briscoe	5	5.9	37	0.6	32	5.1	-3.8	2 416	14	3.9	0	883	0	D
Brooks	16	15.8	78	0.9	104	37.0	6.9	3 973	61	35.1	D	1 366	D	307
Brown	73	121.4	544	9.9	468	175.7	7.1	5 214	253	162.2	781	1 291	253	455
Burleson	25	49.0	129	2.0	147	36.6	-24.4	2 526	74	34.0	D	575	38	178
Burnet	27	25.0	88	1.5	358	130.2	30.6	5 228	197	121.0	D	1 078	91	462
Caldwell	34	45.4	162	1.9	250	89.4	9.6	3 061	144	84.1	D	1 061	75	236
Calhoun	35	43.1	214	3.5	254	78.9	-15.9	3 757	138	72.2	194	1 242	191	347
Callahan	15	12.6	64	1.0	189	32.4	18.7	2 491	63	26.4	86	730	15	160
Cameron	393	838.2	3 830	57.6	2 296	1 132.8	10.5	4 350	1 462	1 095.3	642	1 046	334	400
Camp	12	32.0	75	1.2	159	56.9	51.3	5 689	80	50.1	84	1 380	198	194
Carson	19	32.0	94	1.9	81	19.1	25.7	2 732	36	17.2	0	810	0	251
Cass	31	D	D	D	356	120.8	34.8	4 000	178	106.4	D	1 312	121	236
Castro	35	D	D	D	88	26.6	-8.9	2 636	57	24.6	D	880	137	140
Chambers	28	216.8	208	4.4	194	64.3	-0.8	3 436	103	61.6	82	1 046	31	327
Cherokee	57	100.4	414	5.5	393	177.1	15.8	4 417	211	161.9	D	1 031	141	261

1. For pay period including March 12. 2. Based on the estimated population as of July 1 of the year shown.

STATE County	Retail trade, establishments with payroll, 1987 (cont'd): Paid employees[1]	Retail trade, establishments with payroll, 1987 (cont'd): Annual payroll (Mil dol)	Taxable service industries–establishments with payroll, 1987: Number	Receipts (Mil dol): Total	Receipts, Selected kinds of business: Hotels, motels and other lodging places	Receipts, Selected kinds of business: Health services	Receipts, Selected kinds of business: Legal services	Paid employees	Annual payroll (Mil dol)	Bank deposits,[2] June 1989: Total (Mil dol)	Bank deposits,[2] June 1989: Percent change, 1988–1989	Savings capital,[3] September 1989: Total (Mil dol)	Savings capital,[3] September 1989: Percent change, 1988–1989
	161	162	163	164	165	166	167	168	169	170	171	172	173
TENNESSEE—Con.													
Pickett	84	0.7	12	2.3	D	1.0	D	88	0.7	48	4.5	0.0	NA
Polk	264	2.2	44	7.4	0.0	3.5	D	201	2.3	135	4.3	0.0	NA
Putnam	4 414	36.1	320	91.2	8.4	33.5	4.1	2 968	36.1	505	7.4	86.9	-7.5
Rhea	901	8.1	73	10.1	D	4.9	0.3	235	3.1	77	-28.6	55.7	-8.0
Roane	2 028	19.6	167	32.1	2.3	14.4	2.6	791	10.4	220	5.0	76.2	1.2
Robertson	1 692	17.2	128	22.6	D	10.3	1.0	664	7.2	176	8.4	104.2	4.2
Rutherford	7 287	66.2	538	180.5	10.1	62.3	8.6	4 350	67.6	706	13.5	198.5	2.9
Scott	628	5.0	44	8.3	D	4.8	1.4	229	2.9	125	3.4	0.0	NA
Sequatchie	274	2.5	32	8.7	D	5.9	0.8	249	3.2	42	6.3	0.0	NA
Sevier	5 437	50.2	470	185.7	103.0	12.4	3.0	4 061	48.4	473	8.8	68.9	-1.5
Shelby	65 221	649.6	5 289	2 517.8	D	687.4	141.6	63 148	984.8	6 558	7.7	1 768.4	4.3
Smith	586	5.1	55	14.3	0.0	11.4	0.4	375	4.5	138	5.7	28.7	21.1
Stewart	232	1.6	14	1.7	D	D	0.2	42	0.5	78	3.5	0.0	NA
Sullivan	11 375	106.3	893	346.3	D	170.3	16.5	7 374	135.5	795	9.9	575.7	3.2
Sumner	5 270	46.9	521	163.8	D	66.4	5.9	4 305	61.3	525	10.7	175.4	6.5
Tipton	1 230	11.0	103	15.4	D	6.4	1.5	361	4.1	200	12.7	35.5	-6.6
Trousdale	232	2.1	23	5.6	0.0	4.4	D	155	2.0	46	3.6	0.0	NA
Unicoi	598	4.6	60	10.9	D	2.7	0.7	326	4.3	56	7.0	87.5	1.0
Union	140	1.3	20	4.3	0.0	D	0.1	146	1.2	47	1.6	0.0	NA
Van Buren	4	0.0	3	D	0.0	D	D	D	D	12	29.8	0.0	NA
Warren	1 721	15.4	151	40.5	1.5	26.7	1.9	996	13.1	295	0.2	58.8	1.8
Washington	6 857	61.8	588	173.6	14.7	83.6	9.3	5 117	67.3	501	7.9	361.0	2.8
Wayne	331	3.1	30	7.4	D	4.9	0.3	208	2.7	98	8.7	19.9	3.1
Weakley	1 416	11.7	111	33.0	D	19.8	0.8	1 114	11.9	267	8.4	38.2	0.0
White	849	7.0	71	12.4	0.3	6.5	0.8	323	3.7	184	5.5	13.5	0.9
Williamson	5 492	54.3	601	213.4	7.1	40.6	4.1	4 756	85.5	737	13.1	113.1	0.2
Wilson	3 221	28.9	305	103.5	D	63.8	3.0	2 606	33.3	430	10.0	77.8	-4.3
TEXAS	1 174 108	11 496.0	108 431	50 953.3	2 369.0	13 497.1	4 852.0	1 060 911	18 808.1	134 952	-4.1	75 124.6	-14.0
Anderson	2 220	21.3	201	42.2	2.4	17.8	4.8	1 080	14.0	263	10.4	64.6	0.9
Andrews	625	6.6	76	18.0	D	5.6	1.1	361	6.3	111	-1.9	26.4	-19.9
Angelina	4 766	44.9	408	122.2	6.6	57.6	11.5	2 797	46.1	492	-2.2	347.9	4.0
Aransas	1 021	9.4	100	15.3	2.5	4.4	D	475	4.3	162	5.8	38.8	78.5
Archer	144	1.2	22	5.8	0.0	4.8	D	138	1.5	44	11.0	9.4	-18.4
Armstrong	47	0.3	4	1.1	0.0	D	0.0	55	0.5	17	3.0	0.0	NA
Atascosa	1 228	11.3	91	20.5	D	9.5	1.0	631	6.7	167	2.2	63.5	-9.6
Austin	1 048	9.5	104	23.3	D	11.0	1.5	720	7.7	214	3.2	107.5	5.4
Bailey	317	2.9	45	4.6	D	0.9	D	146	1.2	66	-3.6	27.1	20.6
Bandera	299	2.7	34	6.0	0.6	D	0.1	175	1.2	53	4.1	22.4	2.0
Bastrop	1 214	11.6	118	19.1	D	7.6	1.6	532	6.5	197	1.5	110.7	-3.9
Baylor	221	1.9	41	8.2	D	2.0	0.2	197	2.1	58	3.4	27.8	-15.1
Bee	1 381	12.0	128	23.6	D	7.5	1.3	758	7.7	166	0.0	55.5	-6.1
Bell	12 560	114.2	881	349.3	D	159.6	16.5	7 290	117.0	885	-2.4	481.0	-35.1
Bexar	89 827	868.1	7 880	3 370.3	192.1	990.0	302.3	76 657	1 265.9	7 722	-3.4	6 909.3	-0.2
Blanco	175	1.4	32	14.0	D	D	D	513	5.3	69	-1.0	17.9	-82.8
Borden	D	D	0	0.0	0.0	0.0	0.0	0	0.0	NA	NA	0.0	NA
Bosque	468	3.8	51	8.4	0.6	4.1	0.8	230	3.4	164	-5.3	16.1	-33.7
Bowie	6 066	56.3	498	165.9	D	80.5	12.8	3 901	61.9	500	-2.9	379.5	4.7
Brazoria	10 147	98.0	884	256.7	5.7	70.3	16.5	6 242	100.3	893	1.8	646.3	-13.7
Brazos	9 103	78.9	724	255.5	14.4	73.4	14.4	7 090	92.0	838	20.6	289.6	-17.5
Brewster	623	4.8	48	8.6	3.6	2.0	0.3	230	2.1	48	2.3	19.4	-3.3
Briscoe	50	0.4	6	0.3	0.0	0.0	0.0	9	0.1	41	-1.7	0.0	NA
Brooks	516	4.1	29	4.2	D	1.7	0.2	178	1.2	43	-0.1	12.8	1.2
Brown	2 301	19.0	219	63.7	2.9	42.3	1.9	1 598	21.9	277	5.8	110.6	-33.2
Burleson	437	3.7	40	6.8	0.8	D	0.4	285	2.0	141	-2.1	58.1	-8.6
Burnet	1 436	13.7	163	36.0	6.3	7.4	1.4	1 069	12.7	216	-11.2	49.5	-44.8
Caldwell	1 074	9.5	94	17.3	D	10.8	1.2	548	5.5	145	0.4	76.2	-65.2
Calhoun	1 036	8.6	92	13.9	1.1	5.0	1.6	400	5.1	191	3.2	33.8	22.7
Callahan	347	2.6	44	5.5	D	2.7	D	210	1.8	83	4.7	13.3	-9.5
Cameron	15 334	132.2	1 069	353.4	34.8	144.0	29.2	10 010	114.8	1 756	-2.5	632.4	7.4
Camp	552	5.2	47	6.6	D	3.4	D	222	1.8	101	7.1	21.3	-2.7
Carson	215	1.6	18	2.4	D	D	D	56	0.7	57	4.0	16.6	-2.7
Cass	1 295	11.2	104	21.0	1.2	11.1	1.6	727	7.3	170	-1.1	118.4	-3.5
Castro	293	2.9	35	5.4	0.0	1.6	D	135	1.5	59	17.0	15.9	-1.8
Chambers	717	6.3	69	11.9	D	2.1	0.4	316	4.6	120	3.0	7.9	16.4
Cherokee	1 724	15.7	171	37.8	0.4	14.6	2.5	1 269	14.4	282	3.4	266.4	3.2

1. For the period including March 12 of the year shown. 2. Includes deposits for all insured and reporting noninsured commercial and mutual savings banks. 3. Includes savings capital for all FSLIC insured savings institutions.

STATE County	Federal funds and grants, 1989: Expenditures: Total (Mil dol)	Expenditures: Percent change, 1988–1989	Per capita[1] (Dollars): Total	Per capita: Direct payments for individuals	Per capita: Procurement contract awards	Per capita: Salaries and wages	Per capita: Grant awards	Local government finances, 1981–1982: General revenue: Total (Mil dol)	Intergovernmental: Total (Mil dol)	Intergovernmental: Percent from state	Taxes: Total (Mil dol)	Taxes: Per capita[2]: Total (Dollars)	Taxes: Per capita[2]: Property (Dollars)	Direct general expenditure: Total (Mil dol)	Direct general expenditure: Percent change, 1977–1982
	174	175	176	177	178	179	180	181	182	183	184	185	186	187	188
TENNESSEE—Con.															
Pickett	11.6	9.9	2 568	1 778	80	69	526	2.9	2.2	71.7	0.6	126	64	3.3	83.3
Polk	37.5	7.0	2 680	2 024	34	231	351	11.2	4.3	90.9	3.6	267	229	10.6	31.2
Putnam	123.9	5.1	2 347	1 763	-8	172	394	46.9	10.4	85.6	11.4	231	115	39.7	97.5
Rhea	147.3	-12.7	5 798	1 865	40	3 519	322	16.8	6.8	85.6	3.7	150	113	17.5	56.4
Roane	136.0	5.1	2 747	1 933	23	489	290	30.7	13.5	72.2	9.6	196	118	27.8	42.4
Robertson	76.7	9.5	1 746	1 311	14	71	265	28.9	9.3	89.0	7.9	211	127	25.6	98.0
Rutherford	218.0	7.6	1 874	1 144	56	440	204	62.6	21.7	81.5	23.1	257	161	52.3	68.4
Scott	62.2	16.0	3 032	1 812	447	108	657	15.0	6.8	91.1	2.4	120	87	14.7	55.2
Sequatchie	51.7	99.8	5 746	1 360	3 944	96	327	5.4	3.2	94.3	1.8	203	133	5.3	47.4
Sevier	95.4	9.1	1 874	1 468	20	171	204	36.6	11.2	78.6	13.1	299	127	35.5	70.6
Shelby	2 657.8	8.3	3 222	1 693	195	870	446	794.9	248.6	69.9	333.1	424	290	779.3	53.3
Smith	50.4	5.1	3 379	1 690	116	684	802	8.3	4.1	91.8	2.5	168	106	7.2	67.4
Stewart	50.3	-29.4	5 294	2 377	17	2 407	461	4.5	3.2	92.3	0.9	109	65	4.6	46.9
Sullivan	697.4	6.1	4 712	1 780	2 526	146	253	102.4	31.6	85.2	53.5	367	272	102.6	57.2
Sumner	171.8	7.0	1 630	1 219	36	185	169	60.4	20.9	86.0	19.9	225	157	66.3	89.0
Tipton	85.9	15.0	2 197	1 417	112	100	446	26.4	10.0	87.7	5.5	162	115	35.6	117.5
Trousdale	13.7	6.0	2 175	1 500	10	420	222	4.3	2.3	88.9	1.2	209	103	3.6	33.4
Unicoi	106.9	4.1	6 403	2 088	3 847	140	321	12.6	4.5	84.9	2.7	161	114	12.6	82.4
Union	22.8	13.9	1 785	1 281	9	71	413	5.3	3.6	89.3	1.2	98	65	5.2	21.5
Van Buren	8.1	-6.7	1 728	1 273	29	58	336	4.5	3.9	45.0	0.5	110	81	2.1	28.0
Warren	76.8	1.0	2 232	1 710	36	159	274	21.1	8.5	81.6	5.2	158	93	20.1	50.4
Washington	271.8	5.8	2 974	1 952	156	541	293	52.0	19.6	84.8	20.9	231	155	50.3	57.9
Wayne	29.8	4.3	2 097	1 513	12	108	419	11.1	4.4	93.4	2.4	173	106	10.6	32.4
Weakley	78.6	-12.7	2 425	1 732	37	224	238	25.8	7.8	81.8	5.4	166	105	21.8	76.5
White	47.1	6.6	2 276	1 759	17	99	308	10.2	5.5	83.9	2.8	145	95	9.6	28.4
Williamson	112.2	5.5	1 385	1 010	84	98	172	49.5	12.4	91.7	17.5	284	211	47.3	83.5
Wilson	115.4	21.8	1 632	1 215	10	76	315	29.9	13.1	89.4	12.1	212	156	26.9	51.7
TEXAS	55 233.1	9.9	X	1 544	668	541	382	15 660.2	5 266.8	82.4	6 286.1	409	340	15 036.5	90.3
Anderson	112.9	14.4	2 353	1 719	267	109	239	40.9	11.5	93.1	12.0	284	237	44.6	176.7
Andrews	23.7	8.5	1 572	1 215	6	63	73	26.2	2.5	88.5	15.4	1 020	969	26.3	117.0
Angelina	158.2	10.3	2 303	1 816	18	185	274	58.4	23.7	91.2	17.2	254	193	60.3	113.8
Aransas	40.6	4.6	2 335	2 164	5	41	111	12.1	3.6	91.2	5.9	366	328	12.3	176.0
Archer	24.0	-7.0	3 000	2 330	9	426	113	6.7	2.0	95.5	3.1	418	352	6.2	47.2
Armstrong	8.9	-7.9	4 027	1 977	10	109	58	1.5	0.5	95.0	0.8	413	355	1.3	49.7
Atascosa	61.4	13.6	2 033	1 517	9	71	290	18.9	9.4	93.5	6.7	257	220	17.4	90.4
Austin	45.6	7.7	2 304	1 890	15	113	195	16.1	5.4	92.4	7.6	391	351	17.0	114.8
Bailey	31.4	-2.7	3 926	1 516	14	136	164	7.4	3.1	92.6	3.0	366	315	5.8	59.2
Bandera	27.1	10.1	2 582	2 341	9	74	84	5.1	2.1	70.7	1.8	242	210	4.8	33.2
Bastrop	81.4	6.0	2 054	1 539	24	291	164	18.3	9.7	84.7	4.5	159	133	17.6	77.3
Baylor	19.7	4.1	4 468	3 075	22	190	448	5.1	1.1	95.4	1.4	264	207	5.2	31.4
Bee	97.9	3.0	3 737	1 694	169	1 334	324	28.0	14.6	85.8	7.1	258	213	26.0	60.5
Bell	1 807.6	11.4	10 065	1 791	755	7 267	229	140.3	67.3	81.0	34.7	210	166	141.2	120.0
Bexar	5 315.0	6.1	4 300	1 891	480	1 628	294	963.4	450.0	71.2	275.1	261	191	961.0	68.0
Blanco	19.8	15.6	3 150	2 575	15	314	82	3.4	1.3	96.2	1.1	216	158	3.6	74.6
Borden	5.1	129.4	6 352	669	2 031	120	64	2.9	0.2	88.4	2.5	2 493	2 438	2.4	32.4
Bosque	45.9	6.8	3 145	2 664	32	173	208	7.4	3.4	94.1	2.0	149	118	7.1	35.8
Bowie	463.4	-5.0	5 814	2 301	1 187	2 040	236	61.8	32.9	81.4	15.8	207	161	59.0	80.2
Brazoria	278.7	-9.2	1 518	1 136	82	91	125	196.3	51.9	89.7	99.0	553	503	188.3	114.1
Brazos	249.9	15.2	2 175	1 051	141	277	685	61.7	20.0	90.0	25.7	228	172	64.3	61.5
Brewster	22.5	-20.1	2 920	1 938	162	568	215	8.4	3.8	71.4	1.9	243	202	8.0	50.8
Briscoe	13.0	2.7	6 490	2 830	24	226	321	1.6	0.4	92.6	1.0	385	340	1.2	47.7
Brooks	26.9	31.2	2 889	1 504	8	190	852	13.3	3.7	73.1	7.1	803	757	12.7	99.1
Brown	97.7	6.9	2 934	2 340	91	197	231	22.0	9.7	92.5	8.4	243	191	22.2	23.2
Burleson	38.1	8.2	2 663	2 060	29	130	264	13.7	4.4	95.0	7.5	506	452	10.5	174.7
Burnet	68.9	4.8	2 766	2 495	9	104	120	15.3	4.5	87.3	6.2	325	283	14.1	107.4
Caldwell	55.9	11.4	1 920	1 476	16	77	288	16.6	7.3	89.1	4.8	192	153	16.6	64.6
Calhoun	42.3	10.7	2 106	1 358	245	105	159	28.6	5.6	85.7	13.4	625	565	27.8	131.0
Callahan	29.5	-1.1	2 290	1 910	71	86	112	7.0	3.1	96.7	2.8	237	202	6.1	64.9
Cameron	569.8	15.7	2 126	1 280	163	150	458	215.9	122.3	84.5	46.9	203	150	198.7	88.0
Camp	29.4	16.2	2 939	2 299	13	102	457	5.6	2.8	95.7	1.8	184	138	4.9	73.0
Carson	32.1	-0.8	4 722	1 721	1 394	103	130	7.2	1.4	93.3	4.9	686	653	7.0	82.1
Cass	82.9	3.7	2 763	2 136	53	101	452	23.5	8.6	95.7	6.9	224	195	23.6	104.1
Castro	40.2	-9.2	3 983	1 112	7	75	199	11.4	4.2	94.6	4.3	408	360	8.9	38.3
Chambers	40.7	-45.0	2 298	1 269	161	180	164	30.4	3.4	88.8	22.6	1 185	1 153	26.7	91.8
Cherokee	97.9	6.6	2 434	2 084	17	81	213	22.8	11.2	86.8	8.0	206	168	20.1	58.7

1. Based on the estimated population as of July 1 of the year shown. 2. Based on the estimated population as of July 1, 1982.

STATE County	Local government finances, 1981–1982 (cont'd)								State and local government employment, 1989		Federal government civilian employment 1989		Elections, 1988[3]	
	Direct general expenditure (cont'd)						Debt outstanding							
		Percent of total for–												
	Per capita[1] (Dollars)	Education	Health & hospitals	Police protection	Public welfare	Highways	Total (Mil dol)	Per capita[1] (Dollars)	Total	Rate[2]	Total	Earnings ($1,000)	Total vote cast for president	Vote for lead party (Percent)
	189	190	191	192	193	194	195	196	197	198	199	200	201	202
TENNESSEE—Con.														
Pickett	743	35.9	27.3	3.2	0.0	15.7	2.3	503	201	446.7	14	405	1 756	R–63.7
Polk	784	44.2	23.5	4.0	0.3	7.0	18.9	1 401	478	341.4	103	2 762	4 391	R–52.3
Putnam	807	31.9	39.2	4.1	0.1	5.6	56.0	1 138	6 060	1 147.7	243	7 296	16 285	R–58.6
Rhea	718	41.0	27.3	4.1	0.0	5.5	12.7	522	1 212	477.2	2 439	95 134	7 776	R–66.2
Roane	568	47.2	15.4	5.1	0.1	6.2	37.3	764	2 690	543.4	717	22 480	17 497	R–62.2
Robertson	681	39.1	24.1	4.8	0.1	8.3	34.7	925	1 980	451.0	68	2 156	11 672	D–50.4
Rutherford	582	51.1	4.4	5.3	0.1	9.4	71.4	795	5 463	469.7	1 833	62 831	32 801	R–62.2
Scott	738	46.1	32.9	2.8	0.1	5.1	8.1	405	1 159	565.4	71	1 875	4 193	R–61.1
Sequatchie	611	57.9	3.6	4.9	0.1	14.3	6.2	707	486	540.0	22	572	2 869	R–57.8
Sevier	813	32.4	15.6	5.5	0.2	7.8	45.3	1 037	2 034	399.6	259	7 294	15 631	R–76.3
Shelby	991	30.2	4.8	8.2	0.1	4.8	1 573.5	2 002	54 349	658.9	20 124	579 512	308 988	R–51.0
Smith	493	55.1	0.4	4.0	0.1	9.7	10.5	714	530	355.7	117	2 777	4 686	D–53.8
Stewart	529	57.4	1.0	6.3	0.0	16.7	3.5	397	395	415.8	742	22 321	3 296	D–60.0
Sullivan	705	53.8	0.8	5.2	0.4	7.6	118.0	810	6 178	417.4	539	17 127	50 977	R–64.7
Sumner	751	37.7	25.3	4.8	0.1	6.8	98.3	1 112	4 188	397.3	737	22 728	31 389	R–62.2
Tipton	1 054	55.9	17.7	2.3	0.0	7.1	34.4	1 019	1 308	334.5	72	2 109	9 918	R–61.0
Trousdale	609	45.8	1.2	8.8	0.1	17.0	4.6	784	635	1 007.9	29	806	2 173	D–54.9
Unicoi	757	35.5	37.2	3.6	0.3	6.2	6.9	418	768	459.9	69	1 722	5 486	R–66.8
Union	433	58.2	0.6	3.8	0.5	13.0	2.7	221	364	284.4	14	439	3 564	R–59.2
Van Buren	443	52.7	0.7	3.9	0.1	20.8	3.3	688	263	559.6	12	296	1 580	D–50.4
Warren	608	40.9	21.0	4.1	0.4	6.0	32.3	976	1 373	399.1	130	3 842	9 218	D–50.4
Washington	556	50.7	0.5	7.5	0.4	9.7	63.6	703	6 887	753.5	2 032	59 473	29 887	R–65.6
Wayne	752	39.9	35.6	3.1	0.0	7.2	8.7	619	681	479.6	32	817	4 951	R–68.8
Weakley	668	33.7	21.8	3.7	7.5	10.8	18.3	560	2 668	823.5	170	4 589	9 989	R–57.1
White	489	57.3	0.4	5.6	0.1	12.0	8.9	454	723	349.3	39	1 080	5 249	R–50.4
Williamson	769	51.0	20.2	4.4	0.0	6.8	45.7	743	2 428	299.8	152	4 791	28 823	R–72.3
Wilson	471	58.1	0.2	4.3	0.1	9.2	41.2	722	1 902	269.0	97	3 164	21 793	R–61.1
TEXAS	978	48.9	8.4	4.8	0.4	5.6	22 161.3	1 441	1 014 646	597.1	197 381	6 413 639	5 427 410	R–56.0
Anderson	1 054	49.5	18.5	2.6	0.1	4.1	54.7	1 293	5 334	1 111.2	142	4 114	14 045	R–55.9
Andrews	1 744	54.9	20.1	2.8	0.0	5.7	9.5	632	993	657.6	30	1 034	4 191	R–72.8
Angelina	889	61.5	6.4	2.8	0.0	4.1	62.5	922	4 681	681.4	413	12 088	23 852	R–53.4
Aransas	762	66.7	0.6	4.7	0.2	7.7	7.6	474	728	418.4	21	713	6 196	R–62.3
Archer	822	59.2	12.4	4.0	0.0	11.7	3.2	429	369	461.2	23	613	3 646	R–55.1
Armstrong	688	59.2	0.0	4.4	0.0	7.7	0.3	154	107	486.4	16	399	1 040	R–69.2
Atascosa	664	66.2	0.2	3.2	0.1	9.8	9.0	343	1 353	448.0	64	1 706	9 504	R–50.3
Austin	882	66.8	0.4	3.1	0.1	6.6	15.5	804	955	482.3	67	1 854	7 160	R–63.2
Bailey	704	68.2	0.4	6.7	0.1	8.0	1.1	134	437	546.2	45	1 115	2 343	R–62.3
Bandera	644	62.1	0.6	3.8	0.1	5.6	4.1	548	376	358.1	20	539	4 761	R–72.1
Bastrop	621	57.4	7.9	3.6	0.3	8.0	13.7	483	1 776	448.5	333	10 741	14 092	D–56.8
Baylor	992	30.9	38.9	2.7	0.5	5.8	0.6	111	361	820.5	30	757	2 070	D–55.7
Bee	954	74.7	0.3	2.9	0.4	3.5	12.9	474	1 748	667.2	562	13 083	9 281	R–49.8
Bell	856	65.9	4.6	4.2	0.2	3.5	104.1	631	11 314	630.0	7 559	192 569	47 551	R–61.8
Bexar	910	49.5	7.9	4.7	0.4	3.3	1 845.8	1 749	67 588	546.9	45 651	1 592 114	369 749	R–52.2
Blanco	736	48.4	26.4	3.3	0.0	4.3	1.5	304	261	414.3	79	1 917	2 719	R–61.8
Borden	2 442	63.3	0.0	2.0	0.0	20.0	0.7	680	80	1 000.0	NA	189	454	R–62.3
Bosque	520	60.0	13.2	2.9	0.3	7.0	3.4	249	613	419.9	53	1 383	6 147	R–56.3
Bowie	770	59.0	0.6	4.3	0.2	5.5	71.3	929	3 946	495.1	7 154	187 041	27 941	R–55.3
Brazoria	1 052	55.9	4.1	4.5	0.2	7.5	246.1	1 375	10 991	598.6	381	11 954	59 081	R–57.6
Brazos	572	50.1	0.5	5.9	0.1	5.6	139.4	1 240	21 464	1 868.1	888	31 913	44 690	R–65.7
Brewster	1 034	45.6	20.3	4.4	0.3	6.1	1.9	248	1 053	1 367.5	159	4 847	3 313	R–51.6
Briscoe	499	60.7	0.1	6.9	0.0	10.1	3.3	1 321	96	480.0	16	419	1 048	D–54.8
Brooks	1 438	48.5	14.3	2.8	0.3	11.6	3.5	392	552	593.5	63	2 360	3 489	D–81.9
Brown	641	55.8	0.5	4.5	0.0	4.1	30.5	882	2 085	626.1	115	3 342	11 606	R–58.7
Burleson	709	64.4	0.2	4.2	0.0	15.5	14.2	958	716	500.7	48	1 264	5 339	D–57.8
Burnet	735	50.3	14.5	4.3	0.4	4.8	29.2	1 523	1 125	451.8	51	1 456	9 508	R–53.8
Caldwell	667	53.1	17.4	2.9	0.1	6.8	4.3	172	1 100	378.0	64	1 659	8 262	D–56.3
Calhoun	1 301	45.7	15.2	2.9	0.1	6.5	33.5	1 568	1 178	586.1	43	1 213	6 524	D–50.8
Callahan	518	70.5	1.1	3.1	0.5	5.3	3.6	307	508	393.8	34	892	4 921	R–58.7
Cameron	858	58.2	3.8	3.3	0.5	3.2	197.0	851	15 862	591.9	1 233	42 197	55 552	D–55.8
Camp	502	67.1	0.1	4.4	0.3	7.1	4.5	454	343	343.0	33	862	4 042	D–52.5
Carson	976	71.1	0.2	2.4	0.3	5.9	2.2	305	403	592.6	183	7 734	3 148	R–66.7
Cass	769	56.8	18.6	2.0	0.0	5.4	30.6	996	1 551	517.0	76	1 958	11 262	D–52.8
Castro	835	64.9	13.9	4.0	0.1	5.0	3.1	288	588	582.2	40	1 032	3 049	R–52.6
Chambers	1 398	50.7	6.5	2.9	0.3	10.6	35.7	1 871	1 136	641.8	35	1 058	6 781	R–54.5
Cherokee	520	64.4	1.2	4.3	0.1	8.8	16.9	437	2 922	726.9	93	2 393	13 165	R–57.1

1. Based on the estimated population as of July 1, 1982. 2. Per 10,000 resident population estimated as of July 1 of the year shown. 3. Data subject to copyright.

STATE–County code	MSA/CMSA/NECMA code[1]	STATE County	Land Area,[2] 1990 (Sq. Km.)	Population, 1990: Total persons	Rank	Per square kilometer	Race: White	Black	Am. Indian, Eskimo, Aleut	Asian & Pacific Islander	Other race	Hispanic[3]	Age of population Percent: Under 5 years	5 to 14 years	15 to 24 years
			1	2	3	4	5	6	7	8	9	10	11	12	13
		TEXAS—Con.													
48 075	...	Childress	1 840	5 953	2 765	3.2	4 969	321	26	17	620	853	5.7	15.7	11.4
48 077	...	Clay	2 843	10 024	2 385	3.5	9 751	33	88	23	129	242	6.3	15.4	11.1
48 079	...	Cochran	2 008	4 377	2 886	2.2	2 997	234	13	1	1 132	1 857	8.4	19.4	14.6
48 081	...	Coke	2 328	3 424	2 962	1.5	3 222	6	17	2	177	422	5.3	13.7	9.6
48 083	...	Coleman	3 297	9 710	2 410	2.9	8 995	246	29	7	433	1 139	6.6	13.6	10.3
48 085	1922	Collin	2 196	264 036	188	120.2	235 290	10 925	1 112	7 480	9 229	18 158	8.5	16.0	13.5
48 087	...	Collingsworth	2 380	3 573	2 953	1.5	2 977	230	32	3	331	561	6.6	15.5	11.5
48 089	...	Colorado	2 494	18 383	1 770	7.4	13 352	3 118	30	16	1 867	2 833	7.0	15.4	11.2
48 091	7240	Comal	1 454	51 832	815	35.6	46 821	443	148	164	4 256	11 864	7.0	14.3	12.1
48 093	...	Comanche	2 429	13 381	2 106	5.5	12 297	16	51	8	1 009	2 205	6.4	12.9	11.5
48 095	...	Concho	2 568	3 044	2 997	1.2	2 718	16	5	5	300	1 194	5.4	13.8	12.5
48 097	...	Cooke	2 263	30 777	1 252	13.6	28 375	1 169	232	131	870	1 408	7.5	15.6	13.5
48 099	3810	Coryell	2 724	64 213	683	23.6	45 078	13 592	461	1 670	3 412	6 243	8.4	14.5	26.0
48 101	...	Cottle	2 334	2 247	3 051	1.0	1 853	199	4	3	188	367	5.9	15.2	10.3
48 103	...	Crane	2 035	4 652	2 865	2.3	3 097	130	11	10	1 404	1 577	8.4	20.6	14.4
48 105	...	Crockett	7 272	4 078	2 910	0.6	4 018	39	9	4	8	2 021	8.4	17.3	12.0
48 107	...	Crosby	2 330	7 304	2 627	3.1	5 784	321	13	8	1 178	3 111	8.0	18.1	13.5
48 109	...	Culberson	9 875	3 407	2 964	0.3	2 400	2	16	27	962	2 419	9.6	19.0	16.1
48 111	...	Dallam	3 897	5 461	2 803	1.4	4 600	112	43	14	692	1 151	8.4	17.4	11.8
48 113	1922	Dallas	2 279	1 852 810	11	813.0	1 241 455	369 597	9 437	52 238	180 083	315 630	8.4	14.4	15.0
48 115	...	Dawson	2 336	14 349	2 028	6.1	9 789	622	23	19	3 896	6 120	8.0	18.5	13.0
48 117	...	Deaf Smith	3 878	19 153	1 723	4.9	14 522	307	49	39	4 236	9 356	9.6	20.6	14.8
48 119	...	Delta	718	4 857	2 848	6.8	4 388	404	41	7	17	67	6.3	13.3	13.1
48 121	1922	Denton	2 301	273 525	182	118.9	241 982	13 569	1 416	6 870	9 688	19 013	8.6	14.6	17.5
48 123	...	De Witt	2 355	18 840	1 744	8.0	14 356	2 114	22	17	2 331	4 567	6.9	15.7	11.2
48 125	...	Dickens	2 342	2 571	3 019	1.1	2 193	113	13	1	251	479	5.4	13.5	12.2
48 127	...	Dimmit	3 447	10 433	2 345	3.0	7 599	60	16	12	2 746	8 688	8.8	20.9	16.9
48 129	...	Donley	2 408	3 696	2 941	1.5	3 522	127	13	2	32	139	4.9	12.6	14.4
48 131	...	Duval	4 643	12 918	2 145	2.8	10 183	12	12	17	2 694	11 267	8.7	18.3	15.7
48 133	...	Eastland	2 399	18 488	1 762	7.7	17 474	397	52	37	528	1 404	5.6	13.9	13.5
48 135	5800	Ector	2 334	118 934	389	51.0	91 309	5 557	647	662	20 759	37 315	9.1	18.0	14.2
48 137	...	Edwards	5 491	2 266	3 046	0.4	2 114	0	4	4	144	1 182	8.1	18.7	13.4
48 139	1922	Ellis	2 435	85 167	539	35.0	69 049	8 525	370	214	7 009	11 243	8.4	17.6	14.2
48 141	2320	El Paso	2 624	591 610	79	225.5	452 512	22 110	2 590	6 485	107 913	411 619	9.0	18.0	17.9
48 143	...	Erath	2 814	27 991	1 351	9.9	26 413	195	94	115	1 174	2 458	7.0	13.3	21.2
48 145	...	Falls	1 992	17 712	1 803	8.9	11 390	4 810	41	21	1 450	2 072	7.2	14.2	13.8
48 147	...	Fannin	2 309	24 804	1 470	10.7	22 722	1 633	182	54	213	485	6.3	13.6	12.1
48 149	...	Fayette	2 461	20 095	1 671	8.2	17 323	1 686	29	15	1 042	1 702	6.0	14.1	10.6
48 151	...	Fisher	2 334	4 842	2 852	2.1	4 445	190	19	0	188	997	6.0	15.4	11.0
48 153	...	Floyd	2 570	8 497	2 512	3.3	5 523	320	16	15	2 623	3 381	8.7	18.4	13.2
48 155	...	Foard	1 830	1 794	3 079	1.0	1 552	88	11	4	139	233	6.2	14.4	10.5
48 157	3362	Fort Bend	2 266	225 421	219	99.5	141 125	46 593	525	14 328	22 850	43 892	9.4	18.8	13.1
48 159	...	Franklin	740	7 802	2 597	10.5	7 139	349	47	18	249	357	6.8	14.6	11.5
48 161	...	Freestone	2 293	15 818	1 933	6.9	12 382	3 013	53	37	333	619	6.6	15.8	11.9
48 163	...	Frio	2 935	13 472	2 103	4.6	9 119	183	23	38	4 109	9 749	9.1	19.8	16.0
48 165	...	Gaines	3 891	14 123	2 044	3.6	10 378	334	38	15	3 358	4 608	10.0	21.1	14.5
48 167	3362	Galveston	1 033	217 399	228	210.5	164 210	38 154	752	3 569	10 714	30 962	7.6	15.6	13.5
48 169	...	Garza	2 320	5 143	2 831	2.2	4 588	328	9	21	197	1 454	7.9	18.7	12.7
48 171	...	Gillespie	2 748	17 204	1 843	6.3	16 325	34	60	27	758	2 426	6.0	13.5	9.6
48 173	...	Glasscock	2 333	1 447	3 098	0.6	1 156	0	2	0	289	424	9.9	20.2	14.0
48 175	...	Goliad	2 211	5 980	2 760	2.7	4 953	407	19	5	596	2 145	7.1	15.7	11.4
48 177	...	Gonzales	2 766	17 205	1 842	6.2	13 025	1 716	46	23	2 395	6 142	7.9	16.5	13.0
48 179	...	Gray	2 404	23 967	1 494	10.0	21 566	899	216	115	1 171	1 895	6.7	15.6	11.6
48 181	7640	Grayson	2 418	95 021	489	39.3	85 553	6 565	1 046	412	1 445	2 795	6.8	14.5	13.6
48 183	4420	Gregg	710	104 948	440	147.8	81 883	19 937	478	491	2 159	3 775	7.6	15.6	14.2
48 185	...	Grimes	2 056	18 828	1 745	9.2	12 879	4 614	52	30	1 253	2 657	6.8	15.3	15.0
48 187	7240	Guadalupe	1 842	64 873	675	35.2	52 948	3 665	235	465	7 560	19 246	7.9	16.1	14.2
48 189	...	Hale	2 602	34 671	1 145	13.3	23 823	1 852	148	136	8 712	14 428	9.1	18.2	15.4
48 191	...	Hall	2 339	3 905	2 925	1.7	2 908	303	15	7	672	727	5.8	13.5	11.1
48 193	...	Hamilton	2 165	7 733	2 602	3.6	7 389	2	21	24	297	403	5.9	12.8	10.2
48 195	...	Hansford	2 382	5 848	2 776	2.5	4 821	0	23	14	990	1 174	7.7	18.8	11.9
48 197	...	Hardeman	1 801	5 283	2 822	2.9	4 427	321	26	16	493	589	6.8	15.3	11.0
48 199	0840	Hardin	2 316	41 320	974	17.8	37 485	3 485	123	58	169	679	7.2	17.2	13.6
48 201	3362	Harris	4 478	2 818 199	3	629.3	1 824 137	541 180	8 044	110 848	333 990	644 935	8.6	15.6	15.3
48 203	4420	Harrison	2 328	57 483	759	24.7	40 387	16 038	192	144	722	1 278	7.1	16.9	14.3
48 205	...	Hartley	3 788	3 634	2 948	1.0	3 510	9	30	7	78	201	6.4	17.1	10.9

1. MSA = Metropolitan Statistical Area. CMSA = Consolidated MSA. NECMA = New England county metropolitan area. PMSA = Primary MSA. See Appendix A for explanation of these concepts. See Appendix B for list of metropolitan areas identified by type, with component counties. 2. Dry land or land partially or temporarily covered by water. 3. Hispanic persons may be of any race.

STATE County	Population, 1990 (cont'd): Age of population (cont'd) Percent: 25 to 34 years	35 to 44 years	45 to 54 years	55 to 64 years	65 to 74 years	75 years and over	Percent female	Population–Change and components of change: Change 1980–1990: Number	Percent	Components of change, 1980–1986: Total persons, 1986	Total persons, 1980	Net change: Number	Percent	Natural increase: Births	Deaths
	14	15	16	17	18	19	20	21	22	23	24	25	26	27	28
TEXAS—Con.															
Childress	11.4	12.1	10.0	11.0	10.1	12.5	53.5	-997	-14.3	6 400	6 950	-600	-8.4	600	600
Clay	14.0	13.3	11.9	11.0	9.1	7.9	51.3	442	4.6	9 800	9 582	200	1.8	700	700
Cochran	15.1	10.7	10.4	8.9	6.9	5.6	50.4	-448	-9.3	4 600	4 825	-200	-4.2	500	200
Coke	11.4	10.9	10.0	13.5	12.6	12.9	52.3	228	7.1	3 400	3 196	300	7.9	300	300
Coleman	11.8	11.4	9.8	10.8	12.4	13.3	52.6	-729	-7.0	10 300	10 439	-200	-1.8	900	1 100
Collin	20.8	19.1	11.6	5.3	3.1	2.2	50.3	119 460	82.6	210 600	144 576	66 000	45.7	19 200	5 300
Collingsworth	11.9	12.0	8.4	10.4	11.5	12.2	51.9	-1 075	-23.1	4 000	4 648	-700	-14.2	400	400
Colorado	13.0	12.7	10.0	10.7	10.3	9.6	52.1	-440	-2.3	20 100	18 823	1 200	6.5	2 100	1 500
Comal	13.9	15.2	11.0	10.3	9.5	6.6	51.3	15 386	42.2	49 300	36 446	12 800	35.2	3 900	2 400
Comanche	11.7	11.7	10.9	11.3	11.5	12.1	51.1	764	6.1	13 000	12 617	300	2.8	1 100	1 200
Concho	17.1	13.1	9.9	8.8	9.8	9.6	45.7	129	4.4	2 800	2 915	-100	-4.5	200	300
Cooke	14.5	13.8	9.9	9.3	9.0	6.9	51.0	3 121	11.3	29 600	27 656	1 900	6.9	2 900	1 800
Coryell	22.4	12.1	6.5	4.6	3.1	2.5	43.6	7 446	13.1	59 200	56 767	2 400	4.2	5 600	1 500
Cottle	11.7	11.2	10.0	11.6	12.7	11.5	51.3	-700	-23.8	2 600	2 947	-400	-13.1	300	300
Crane	15.2	14.8	9.7	7.1	6.1	3.8	50.1	52	1.1	4 800	4 600	200	5.2	700	200
Crockett	15.4	14.8	10.8	9.6	6.8	4.9	49.4	-530	-11.5	4 600	4 608	0	0.8	600	200
Crosby	13.5	10.6	10.6	9.7	8.0	7.9	51.6	-1 555	-17.6	8 200	8 859	-600	-7.0	900	500
Culberson	14.0	13.9	9.8	8.8	5.8	2.9	49.3	92	2.8	3 300	3 315	0	0.7	600	100
Dallam	16.0	12.7	9.7	9.5	7.7	6.8	51.3	-1 070	-16.4	6 400	6 531	-100	-1.4	800	400
Dallas	21.5	15.7	9.7	6.9	4.9	3.3	50.8	296 391	19.0	1 833 100	1 556 419	276 700	17.8	200 500	71 100
Dawson	13.7	12.4	9.3	9.5	8.4	7.1	51.6	-1 835	-11.3	16 100	16 184	-100	-0.6	2 200	900
Deaf Smith	15.0	12.6	8.8	7.8	5.9	4.9	50.5	-2 012	-9.5	19 700	21 165	-1 400	-6.8	3 000	800
Delta	12.0	11.2	10.5	10.0	11.5	12.1	52.5	18	0.4	4 700	4 839	-100	-2.7	400	500
Denton	23.1	17.2	9.2	4.7	2.9	2.1	50.6	130 399	91.1	204 300	143 126	61 200	42.7	21 400	5 100
De Witt	13.3	12.4	9.1	10.3	10.5	10.6	52.7	-63	-0.3	20 100	18 903	1 200	6.4	2 000	1 700
Dickens	10.8	11.6	10.7	10.5	12.2	13.1	52.5	-968	-27.4	2 900	3 539	-600	-17.1	300	300
Dimmit	12.3	13.3	8.7	7.5	6.6	5.0	51.2	-934	-8.2	11 700	11 367	400	3.2	1 600	500
Donley	10.6	10.7	10.0	11.1	13.1	12.5	52.2	-379	-9.3	4 100	4 075	0	-0.1	300	300
Duval	14.0	12.1	9.3	8.8	7.4	5.7	51.2	401	3.2	13 500	12 517	1 000	8.0	1 700	800
Eastland	12.1	11.9	9.5	10.5	11.9	11.0	52.0	-992	-5.1	20 500	19 480	1 000	5.3	1 900	1 900
Ector	17.5	14.3	9.3	8.4	5.8	3.5	51.1	3 560	3.1	133 100	115 374	17 800	15.4	18 700	5 000
Edwards	13.8	13.0	10.8	9.8	7.1	5.4	49.8	233	11.5	2 000	2 033	-100	-2.8	200	100
Ellis	16.8	15.1	10.5	7.3	5.4	4.7	50.7	25 424	42.6	77 900	59 743	18 100	30.4	7 100	3 700
El Paso	17.2	13.7	8.7	7.4	5.1	3.0	51.4	111 711	23.3	561 500	479 899	81 600	17.0	69 500	16 900
Erath	14.5	11.9	8.6	7.8	7.6	8.0	50.8	5 431	24.1	24 900	22 560	2 300	10.3	2 100	1 800
Falls	14.8	11.6	8.8	10.0	9.6	10.2	50.0	-234	-1.3	17 600	17 946	-300	-1.9	1 500	1 600
Fannin	13.1	12.7	10.6	10.6	10.6	10.4	51.7	519	2.1	24 800	24 285	500	2.1	1 800	2 200
Fayette	13.2	12.9	9.4	10.5	12.0	11.4	51.4	1 263	6.7	20 600	18 832	1 800	9.5	1 800	1 900
Fisher	12.1	12.1	10.6	11.4	10.3	11.2	51.7	-1 049	-17.8	5 500	5 891	-400	-6.3	500	500
Floyd	13.0	11.3	9.6	9.3	8.5	7.9	51.5	-1 337	-13.6	8 900	9 834	-900	-9.6	1 100	600
Foard	12.2	11.4	9.8	10.2	11.5	13.8	53.9	-364	-16.9	1 800	2 158	-300	-14.6	200	200
Fort Bend	18.7	20.1	9.7	5.3	3.1	1.8	49.8	94 459	72.1	194 700	130 962	63 800	48.7	22 500	4 300
Franklin	13.2	12.7	10.9	11.5	10.2	8.5	51.5	909	13.2	7 400	6 893	500	6.9	600	600
Freestone	13.5	13.4	9.8	9.7	9.5	9.8	51.8	988	6.7	17 100	14 830	2 300	15.6	1 400	1 200
Frio	15.2	12.4	8.9	7.6	6.4	4.7	50.5	-313	-2.3	14 400	13 785	600	4.6	1 800	700
Gaines	16.1	12.2	9.1	7.9	5.3	3.9	50.0	973	7.4	14 800	13 150	1 600	12.4	2 000	600
Galveston	17.7	15.7	10.5	8.8	6.5	4.0	50.8	21 661	11.1	214 800	195 738	19 100	9.8	23 900	10 500
Garza	13.7	12.4	9.9	8.6	8.5	7.7	52.0	-193	-3.6	5 400	5 336	100	1.8	700	400
Gillespie	11.9	12.5	10.1	12.0	13.3	11.1	52.1	3 672	27.1	15 800	13 532	2 300	16.8	1 300	1 200
Glasscock	17.2	12.6	11.3	8.8	3.5	2.5	48.9	143	11.0	1 200	1 304	-100	-5.5	200	0
Goliad	14.4	13.9	9.8	10.8	9.8	7.2	51.8	787	15.2	5 700	5 193	500	8.9	500	400
Gonzales	14.0	11.8	9.3	9.8	9.3	8.4	51.0	256	1.5	18 600	16 949	1 600	9.7	2 100	1 400
Gray	14.6	12.9	10.4	10.8	9.2	8.2	52.0	-2 419	-9.2	26 200	26 386	-200	-0.6	3 100	1 700
Grayson	15.1	13.9	10.3	9.5	8.8	7.5	52.3	5 225	5.8	98 300	89 796	8 500	9.4	9 000	6 600
Gregg	16.4	14.3	9.9	8.7	7.3	6.0	52.0	5 453	5.5	112 300	99 495	12 900	12.9	11 900	6 100
Grimes	17.3	14.3	9.0	8.6	7.6	6.1	45.4	5 248	38.6	19 200	13 580	5 600	41.2	1 900	1 200
Guadalupe	16.1	14.4	10.6	8.6	7.2	4.8	50.6	18 165	38.9	57 100	46 708	10 300	22.2	5 300	2 600
Hale	15.5	11.9	9.1	8.5	6.8	5.6	51.0	-2 921	-7.8	36 900	37 592	-700	-1.9	4 800	2 000
Hall	10.4	11.6	9.9	11.4	12.6	13.8	53.1	-1 689	-30.2	4 700	5 594	-900	-16.9	400	500
Hamilton	11.9	10.9	10.0	11.1	12.3	14.9	52.4	-564	-6.8	7 800	8 297	-500	-5.9	600	900
Hansford	15.0	13.8	10.8	9.2	7.1	5.7	50.2	-361	-5.8	6 400	6 209	200	3.3	800	300
Hardeman	11.9	11.5	10.1	10.3	11.3	11.8	52.6	-1 085	-17.0	6 200	6 368	-200	-2.4	700	600
Hardin	15.0	14.9	11.2	9.1	6.9	4.8	50.9	599	1.5	42 600	40 721	1 900	4.6	4 500	2 100
Harris	20.4	16.6	9.8	6.7	4.4	2.7	50.3	408 652	17.0	2 798 300	2 409 547	388 800	16.1	337 100	95 700
Harrison	15.0	14.3	10.1	8.8	7.5	6.0	51.9	5 218	10.0	58 000	52 265	5 700	11.0	5 400	3 500
Hartley	11.9	15.1	12.6	10.2	8.0	7.6	52.0	-353	-8.9	3 600	3 987	-400	-10.8	300	200

STATE County	Population–(cont'd) Components of change, 1980-1986 (cont'd) Net migration	Households, 1990 Number	Households, 1990 Percent change, 1980–1990	Households, 1990 Persons per household	Households, 1990 Percent Female family householder[1]	Households, 1990 Percent One-person	Births, 1988 Total	Births, 1988 Rate[2]	Births, 1988 Low birth weight[3] (Number)	Deaths, 1987 Number Total	Deaths, 1987 Number Infant[4]	Deaths, 1987 Rate Total[2]	Deaths, 1987 Rate Infant[5]	Marriages, 1984 Number	Marriages, 1984 Rate[2]
	29	30	31	32	33	34	35	36	37	38	39	40	41	42	43
TEXAS—Con.															
Childress	-600	2 435	-12.3	2.40	9.7	29.8	90	14.5	11	92	1	14.6	15.9	73	10.9
Clay	100	3 808	5.6	2.60	6.6	21.6	100	10.6	6	117	0	12.3	0.0	146	14.9
Cochran	-500	1 430	-5.6	2.97	7.9	19.2	99	22.5	5	35	0	7.8	0.0	55	11.7
Coke	300	1 374	9.3	2.41	6.0	25.9	31	9.4	1	61	0	18.5	0.0	36	10.0
Coleman	0	4 026	-5.1	2.36	8.0	30.3	115	11.9	6	174	3	17.8	21.4	119	11.0
Collin	52 200	95 805	106.6	2.73	7.2	20.8	4 204	18.6	238	980	33	4.5	8.3	2 121	11.6
Collingsworth	-700	1 447	-19.2	2.42	7.4	30.1	47	12.7	2	48	1	13.0	18.2	73	17.0
Colorado	700	7 024	1.2	2.57	9.5	26.3	267	14.2	15	228	2	11.9	6.5	210	10.4
Comal	11 300	19 315	49.1	2.64	7.9	21.2	793	15.6	51	457	4	9.0	5.6	574	13.0
Comanche	500	5 318	6.9	2.45	5.8	26.2	167	13.5	11	191	3	15.2	18.9	159	12.1
Concho	-100	1 063	-2.6	2.51	7.3	27.5	40	15.4	9	45	0	17.3	0.0	24	8.3
Cooke	800	11 545	14.6	2.60	8.4	23.8	440	14.6	24	294	8	9.8	16.7	1 299	45.1
Coryell	-1 700	16 687	18.4	2.95	8.2	16.3	978	16.0	56	272	9	4.5	9.7	523	9.1
Cottle	-400	915	-21.4	2.42	7.8	30.8	20	8.7	2	44	1	18.3	31.2	16	5.9
Crane	-300	1 537	-1.0	3.00	6.5	18.6	67	15.2	6	33	1	7.3	13.7	69	13.3
Crockett	-300	1 449	-7.0	2.76	8.4	22.7	63	14.7	4	30	0	6.8	0.0	56	11.4
Crosby	-1 000	2 516	-13.8	2.86	7.3	23.3	133	16.8	10	87	1	11.0	7.5	61	7.1
Culberson	-400	1 076	9.0	3.15	12.2	16.8	67	20.9	1	13	0	3.9	0.0	50	14.3
Dallam	-500	2 122	-11.1	2.56	8.6	27.3	112	20.0	4	75	2	12.9	19.0	98	14.6
Dallas	147 300	701 686	21.5	2.60	12.7	27.8	36 179	19.5	2 818	11 984	344	6.5	9.5	23 534	13.6
Dawson	-1 400	5 084	-7.3	2.80	8.3	23.7	261	17.4	18	126	1	8.2	4.1	150	9.3
Deaf Smith	-3 600	6 182	-4.7	3.06	9.8	18.7	420	21.2	31	151	7	7.6	16.2	255	12.3
Delta	0	1 901	-1.6	2.48	8.5	26.5	56	11.7	6	74	0	15.7	0.0	63	12.9
Denton	45 000	101 984	107.6	2.61	7.4	24.0	4 812	21.0	251	1 084	43	4.9	9.1	2 246	12.9
De Witt	1 000	7 195	2.0	2.55	10.3	27.7	264	14.3	24	290	2	15.4	7.5	206	10.1
Dickens	-600	1 073	-21.6	2.36	6.5	32.6	35	12.5	0	42	1	15.0	32.3	28	8.8
Dimmit	-800	3 072	-2.0	3.38	14.6	15.5	215	19.2	13	59	2	5.2	8.5	117	9.8
Donley	100	1 515	-5.8	2.32	6.0	28.0	44	11.3	3	46	1	11.8	25.6	32	7.6
Duval	100	4 159	11.3	3.10	15.4	20.0	253	19.5	26	117	2	8.9	7.7	141	10.6
Eastland	1 100	7 354	-4.9	2.39	7.3	29.2	201	10.4	10	270	6	13.7	23.4	236	11.2
Ector	4 100	42 322	4.6	2.79	11.3	22.5	2 383	19.1	183	785	19	6.2	8.4	1 932	14.4
Edwards	-200	795	14.1	2.84	7.7	23.3	31	15.5	1	24	2	12.0	58.8	30	14.3
Ellis	14 800	28 588	43.9	2.93	9.8	17.3	1 416	17.1	101	641	15	7.9	10.4	1 011	14.7
El Paso	28 900	178 366	26.7	3.25	15.8	17.0	12 981	22.2	889	2 973	122	5.2	10.0	7 996	14.9
Erath	2 000	10 877	25.0	2.44	7.0	28.4	427	16.6	18	264	4	10.3	10.8	280	11.3
Falls	-200	6 492	-6.2	2.53	13.2	29.3	261	15.4	21	277	2	16.0	8.1	173	9.5
Fannin	900	9 691	4.6	2.48	8.2	26.4	320	13.2	22	402	0	16.4	0.0	295	11.9
Fayette	1 800	8 101	8.2	2.43	7.3	28.4	212	10.7	5	278	0	13.8	0.0	193	9.7
Fisher	-400	1 892	-14.2	2.52	6.7	25.8	53	9.8	5	74	2	13.5	29.4	59	10.4
Floyd	-1 400	2 982	-9.8	2.81	6.6	22.7	167	19.4	15	76	2	8.7	12.8	78	8.5
Foard	-300	739	-14.1	2.38	8.3	31.0	26	14.4	2	27	0	15.0	0.0	18	9.5
Fort Bend	45 500	70 424	76.8	3.14	10.4	13.6	3 916	19.1	257	718	22	3.7	5.7	2 224	12.5
Franklin	500	3 017	15.3	2.54	7.4	23.6	78	10.4	3	105	1	13.8	10.8	82	11.4
Freestone	2 200	6 063	8.1	2.54	9.9	26.7	202	12.2	10	198	1	11.9	5.0	187	11.1
Frio	-500	4 129	2.2	3.20	13.9	18.1	240	17.0	12	89	0	6.2	0.0	124	8.6
Gaines	200	4 502	7.4	3.13	6.9	18.4	271	19.8	13	79	3	5.8	12.4	381	26.6
Galveston	5 700	81 451	17.6	2.64	12.6	24.3	3 493	16.6	271	1 787	30	8.5	8.5	2 689	12.6
Garza	-200	1 822	-1.1	2.79	9.6	22.4	74	14.8	3	53	2	10,2	20.6	55	9.8
Gillespie	2 200	6 711	28.6	2.46	5.6	24.2	192	11.9	7	211	3	13.1	14.0	188	12.3
Glasscock	-200	456	17.8	3.17	3.5	13.4	26	21.7	0	2	0	1.7	0.0	8	6.2
Goliad	300	2 208	24.3	2.68	7.8	22.9	78	13.2	2	65	0	11.0	0.0	59	10.4
Gonzales	900	6 231	4.7	2.71	10.9	25.8	307	16.8	28	210	3	11.3	10.2	168	9.0
Gray	-1 500	9 548	-6.6	2.48	8.1	25.8	382	15.7	23	258	5	10.4	16.1	345	12.6
Grayson	6 000	36 847	8.5	2.51	10.2	25.2	1 357	13.9	73	1 050	11	10.7	7.9	1 512	15.9
Gregg	7 000	40 027	11.5	2.56	11.7	25.9	1 723	15.8	123	957	13	8.8	7.4	1 591	14.2
Grimes	4 900	6 040	24.4	2.72	12.6	23.7	268	14.3	27	189	2	10.0	7.9	176	9.5
Guadalupe	7 600	22 663	44.0	2.80	10.0	19.2	991	16.4	61	465	5	7.8	5.2	696	13.1
Hale	-3 500	11 703	-5.5	2.90	9.2	21.6	638	17.6	48	292	11	7.9	16.5	383	10.2
Hall	-900	1 669	-23.3	2.31	7.4	33.7	54	13.2	5	80	0	18.6	0.0	62	12.4
Hamilton	-200	3 250	-5.1	2.29	7.1	30.4	83	10.5	10	156	1	19.3	10.5	101	12.3
Hansford	-300	2 112	-6.9	2.73	5.5	21.9	87	14.3	4	44	3	7.1	31.2	64	10.0
Hardeman	-200	2 101	-15.1	2.45	7.8	30.3	69	11.9	6	93	1	15.5	13.2	64	9.7
Hardin	-500	14 693	7.0	2.79	9.8	19.2	547	13.3	34	350	11	8.4	18.1	655	15.1
Harris	147 400	1 026 448	18.0	2.72	12.7	26.2	52 543	18.9	3 900	15 841	503	5.7	9.8	32 781	11.8
Harrison	3 800	20 705	14.7	2.71	13.1	23.0	787	13.7	61	602	9	10.4	11.7	1 663	28.9
Hartley	-500	1 332	-2.1	2.66	4.0	20.4	37	10.6	3	33	1	9.2	20.8	27	7.5

1. No spouse present. 2. Per 1,000 resident population estimated as of July 1 of the year shown. 3. Under 2,500 grams. 4. Deaths of infants under 1 year old. 5. Deaths of infants under 1 year old per 1,000 live births.

STATE County	Divorces, 1984 Number	Divorces, 1984 Rate[1]	Physicians, active non-Federal, 1989 Number[2]	Physicians Rate[3]	Hospitals, 1989 Number	Hospitals Beds Number	Hospitals Beds Rate[3]	Nursing homes,[4] 1986 Number	Nursing homes Beds	Serious crimes known to police, 1988 Number Total[5]	Serious crimes Number Violent[6]	Serious crimes Rate[3]	Education Public school enrollment[7] 1986–1987	Public school enrollment 1980	Attainment,[8] 1980 Percent 12 yrs. or more	Attainment Percent 16 yrs. or more
	44	45	46	47	48	49	50	51	52	53	54	55	56	57	58	59
TEXAS—Con.																
Childress	32	4.8	7	115	1	35	574	3	300	255	37	4 049	1 291	1 261	47.7	7.9
Clay	40	4.1	3	32	1	20	215	2	150	363	30	3 705	1 865	1 918	50.3	6.9
Cochran	13	2.8	1	23	1	30	698	1	30	138	9	3 001	1 096	1 372	47.8	10.2
Coke	5	1.4	0	0	0	0	0	2	93	69	8	2 092	639	594	52.7	10.5
Coleman	50	4.6	8	84	1	22	232	3	208	249	9	2 516	1 787	1 773	44.4	7.3
Collin	1 174	6.4	265	112	6	635	269	9	1 094	11 506	715	5 265	46 520	36 179	76.0	26.9
Collingsworth	17	4.0	1	28	1	23	639	1	84	157	5	4 133	735	1 013	53.3	13.6
Colorado	74	3.7	14	76	3	121	658	5	482	622	60	3 174	3 695	3 477	42.3	8.5
Comal	241	5.5	56	107	1	104	198	3	465	2 711	253	5 328	15 610	7 324	60.0	15.0
Comanche	43	3.3	8	65	2	59	480	3	326	208	15	1 613	2 209	2 288	44.7	8.4
Concho	13	4.5	0	0	1	20	800	1	82	63	4	2 334	557	609	48.6	12.3
Cooke	156	5.4	22	72	2	98	320	4	314	1 284	53	4 399	5 368	5 031	58.1	10.1
Coryell	253	4.4	21	34	1	48	77	4	470	1 600	127	2 759	8 194	10 322	72.2	12.2
Cottle	10	3.7	2	91	0	0	0	1	46	44	9	1 834	496	497	41.9	7.5
Crane	22	4.2	2	47	1	26	605	1	30	137	9	2 979	1 237	1 082	57.6	7.1
Crockett	10	2.0	2	49	1	20	488	1	42	123	14	2 796	1 000	1 035	50.3	9.4
Crosby	33	3.8	2	26	1	46	597	2	108	61	2	763	1 802	2 275	45.3	8.1
Culberson	13	3.7	1	32	1	25	806	0	0	40	8	1 212	861	883	44.3	9.8
Dallam	35	5.2	2	38	1	108	2 038	0	0	135	10	2 178	1 730	1 419	58.1	7.9
Dallas	12 594	7.3	4 586	245	44	8 909	475	66	9 153	237 776	24 602	12 843	508 313	291 523	71.2	21.8
Dawson	74	4.6	6	41	1	42	290	3	168	640	32	3 976	3 587	3 796	42.9	8.3
Deaf Smith	69	3.3	11	56	1	40	203	1	78	1 177	122	5 857	4 925	5 363	51.4	12.6
Delta	21	4.3	2	42	0	0	0	2	148	149	8	3 171	979	933	41.6	7.5
Denton	1 146	6.6	215	88	4	411	168	8	677	16 640	907	7 401	36 837	28 063	76.9	26.1
De Witt	55	2.7	7	39	1	54	300	6	532	322	25	1 695	4 532	3 422	39.5	7.4
Dickens	9	2.8	1	37	0	0	0	1	40	89	4	3 180	607	706	40.3	6.0
Dimmit	28	2.3	3	27	1	49	445	1	100	146	19	1 292	3 218	3 191	35.4	7.6
Donley	3	0.7	1	26	0	0	0	1	43	113	20	2 898	640	716	52.6	10.2
Duval	36	2.7	3	23	0	0	0	0	0	273	24	2 008	3 656	3 343	36.6	6.9
Eastland	33	1.6	10	53	4	177	932	7	498	698	66	3 509	3 305	3 096	49.9	8.6
Ector	1 202	8.9	153	126	2	455	374	4	445	12 552	482	9 863	25 579	23 143	61.1	12.0
Edwards	9	4.3	1	50	0	0	0	0	0	55	2	2 751	803	533	50.2	10.7
Ellis	409	5.9	50	58	3	176	205	7	731	4 186	205	5 215	17 211	12 801	55.7	9.8
El Paso	3 166	5.9	774	129	10	2 288	382	12	1 179	53 558	4 743	9 353	128 355	117 799	59.5	14.0
Erath	151	6.1	21	81	2	85	327	6	543	997	43	3 926	4 240	3 571	58.3	14.8
Falls	57	3.1	12	72	2	237	1 419	3	361	420	73	5 155	3 035	3 564	42.3	8.4
Fannin	149	6.0	9	37	2	468	1 942	8	688	937	48	3 810	4 359	4 637	47.0	9.1
Fayette	62	3.1	15	77	1	43	219	3	278	216	7	1 044	3 369	2 844	39.8	7.6
Fisher	19	3.3	3	57	1	30	566	2	83	35	2	637	1 000	1 232	47.0	8.5
Floyd	36	3.9	7	83	2	58	690	2	104	261	6	3 072	2 063	2 329	45.1	9.5
Foard	9	4.7	1	59	0	0	0	1	80	25	2	1 390	343	402	47.5	10.0
Fort Bend	834	4.7	227	107	6	514	243	6	564	7 560	598	4 022	42 026	29 727	71.6	25.5
Franklin	25	3.5	5	66	1	30	395	2	127	167	4	2 227	1 134	1 278	51.0	6.8
Freestone	77	4.6	6	37	1	43	262	4	374	485	34	2 837	3 343	2 863	49.3	7.8
Frio	50	3.5	4	29	2	59	421	2	156	482	102	3 395	3 448	3 770	40.7	9.6
Gaines	66	4.6	8	60	1	43	323	1	33	456	8	3 258	3 021	3 201	50.9	10.6
Galveston	722	3.4	965	463	6	1 575	755	10	1 067	15 601	1 251	7 382	103 819	39 143	65.3	15.4
Garza	21	3.8	2	42	1	15	312	2	98	151	23	2 905	1 316	1 168	44.4	9.7
Gillespie	69	4.5	26	159	1	58	354	5	384	319	3	1 994	2 416	2 241	53.3	11.3
Glasscock	2	1.5	0	0	0	0	0	0	0	18	2	1 500	378	328	51.4	10.6
Goliad	29	5.1	2	33	1	24	400	1	60	12	0	207	1 225	1 230	44.4	8.2
Gonzales	99	5.3	11	61	2	68	376	3	276	457	47	2 432	3 644	3 617	40.9	7.8
Gray	222	8.1	32	136	1	113	481	3	269	1 324	77	5 194	4 853	4 762	61.4	11.3
Grayson	722	7.6	154	157	3	595	605	11	1 222	7 463	537	7 495	17 473	16 740	60.5	12.9
Gregg	627	5.6	160	148	5	436	403	10	1 014	8 232	550	7 548	22 463	19 844	65.5	14.5
Grimes	63	3.4	9	48	1	38	203	1	172	623	63	3 263	3 555	2 898	45.6	10.1
Guadalupe	328	6.2	45	72	1	75	120	4	455	2 990	297	5 069	11 861	10 116	57.6	11.2
Hale	163	4.3	43	119	2	168	467	5	301	1 854	127	4 972	8 429	8 828	53.3	11.1
Hall	23	4.6	4	103	1	28	718	1	80	52	3	1 182	990	978	48.0	6.6
Hamilton	46	5.6	5	63	2	50	633	4	325	227	33	2 838	1 294	1 377	45.7	9.5
Hansford	27	4.2	3	50	1	112	1 867	1	39	107	3	1 726	1 425	1 339	66.5	12.4
Hardeman	33	5.0	4	70	2	44	772	3	153	113	4	1 916	1 219	1 321	47.2	10.3
Hardin	313	7.2	18	44	1	54	133	3	248	715	72	1 703	10 184	9 574	56.7	9.1
Harris	19 047	6.8	7 403	266	63	15 592	560	65	8 422	247 975	24 721	8 880	502 724	470 992	70.5	23.0
Harrison	311	5.4	44	77	1	96	167	4	583	2 443	249	4 221	12 494	10 822	56.4	12.3
Hartley	14	3.9	0	0	0	0	0	1	88	74	5	1 948	289	909	73.0	18.2

1. Per 1,000 resident population estimated as of July 1 of the year shown. 2. As of end of year. 3. Per 100,000 resident population as of July 1 of the year shown. 4. Preliminary. Covers nursing homes with 3 or more beds. 5. Data for serious crimes have not been adjusted for underreporting, this may affect comparability between geographic areas or over time. 6. Includes murder and nonnegligent manslaughter, forcible rape, robbery, and aggravated assault. 7. The 1986–1987 data are based on administrative reports obtained by the U.S. National Center for Education Statistics. The 1980 data are based on the 1980 Census of Population and Housing. 8. Persons 25 years old or older.

STATE County	Education (cont'd) — Local government expenditures for education,[1] 1982		Social Security Program December 1988 — Beneficiaries			Supplemental Security Income Program recipients June 1986	Money income — Per capita[3]						Housing units, 1990	
	Total (Mil dol)	Per capita (Dollars)	Total	Rate[2]	Payments ($1,000)		1987 Income, (Dollars)	1979 Current dollars	1979 Constant 1987 dollars	Median household income 1979 (Dollars)	Percent below poverty level, 1979 — Persons	Percent below poverty level, 1979 — Families	Total	Percent change, 1980–1990
	60	61	62	63	64	65	66	67	68	69	70	71	72	73
TEXAS—Con.														
Childress	1.8	267	1 590	256.5	698	168	7 825	5 795	9 067	10 908	14.7	10.9	3 046	-0.5
Clay	4.3	441	1 745	185.6	782	112	9 937	6 861	10 735	14 662	12.1	8.8	4 708	7.3
Cochran	4.0	826	690	156.8	303	92	8 566	5 624	8 800	12 650	26.6	20.4	1 763	-7.0
Coke	1.9	538	965	292.4	432	50	10 130	6 835	10 695	12 794	11.4	7.7	2 793	33.1
Coleman	4.3	411	2 995	308.8	1 282	304	8 414	5 501	8 607	10 859	18.3	12.8	5 382	2.7
Collin	76.6	475	15 340	68.0	7 322	1 276	14 906	8 430	13 190	24 200	6.4	4.9	103 827	102.9
Collingsworth	1.8	390	965	260.8	419	112	8 765	5 591	8 748	10 647	26.3	20.7	1 952	-9.8
Colorado	8.1	414	4 140	220.2	1 823	550	8 507	6 608	10 340	12 938	19.4	15.7	8 537	-0.4
Comal	17.6	447	9 225	181.2	4 218	514	10 803	7 164	11 210	16 452	9.5	7.6	22 987	47.4
Comanche	3.9	306	3 485	281.0	1 459	374	8 976	5 925	9 271	10 556	16.2	11.8	6 724	9.9
Concho	1.5	492	645	248.1	278	80	8 995	5 917	9 258	11 547	21.5	14.8	1 514	6.3
Cooke	10.2	357	5 445	180.3	2 562	356	9 231	6 639	10 388	15 668	11.6	9.3	13 315	15.6
Coryell	13.5	228	4 400	71.9	1 775	474	8 243	4 994	7 814	12 523	14.3	11.9	18 970	18.3
Cottle	1.2	427	660	287.0	280	90	9 271	7 263	11 364	11 259	21.8	15.2	1 286	-6.3
Crane	4.4	877	585	133.0	310	34	7 928	6 199	9 700	17 420	12.8	9.5	1 795	6.4
Crockett	2.7	524	560	130.2	263	88	9 297	6 767	10 588	16 315	11.8	10.7	1 897	-4.3
Crosby	5.4	622	1 455	184.2	630	156	7 730	5 211	8 154	11 719	28.5	22.8	3 312	-5.6
Culberson	2.2	625	360	112.5	142	52	5 331	4 290	6 713	11 379	18.2	17.3	1 286	9.2
Dallam	4.1	619	1 340	239.3	636	88	7 834	5 242	8 202	11 659	18.0	14.9	2 577	-8.1
Dallas	648.2	396	187 850	101.3	95 574	16 920	13 513	8 667	13 561	18 571	10.6	7.9	795 513	27.3
Dawson	11.3	679	2 795	186.3	1 249	392	8 193	5 983	9 362	14 230	21.4	14.7	5 969	-3.5
Deaf Smith	11.1	543	2 545	128.5	1 115	272	8 229	5 691	8 905	14 784	19.3	14.3	7 152	-2.0
Delta	1.8	373	1 355	282.3	538	256	8 245	5 233	8 188	9 856	19.7	13.5	2 305	1.3
Denton	60.0	380	15 975	69.8	7 757	1 534	12 979	8 116	12 699	20 862	7.7	4.6	112 263	104.8
De Witt	11.8	589	4 220	228.1	1 668	704	8 752	5 583	8 736	11 030	23.3	17.6	8 568	4.1
Dickens	1.8	538	855	305.4	347	118	7 119	4 758	7 445	8 917	27.0	20.1	1 564	-3.1
Dimmit	7.8	654	1 685	150.4	547	606	5 310	3 922	6 137	10 400	36.7	32.8	3 991	9.5
Donley	1.4	332	1 085	278.2	486	76	9 250	6 279	9 825	11 489	19.0	15.2	2 304	9.1
Duval	11.8	911	2 315	178.1	822	870	5 990	4 310	6 744	11 245	27.2	24.3	5 127	19.0
Eastland	6.7	321	5 350	277.2	2 319	460	7 755	5 608	8 775	10 680	16.8	12.6	9 768	4.3
Ector	65.5	485	14 715	118.0	7 394	1 234	10 484	7 754	12 133	18 764	11.2	8.5	48 789	14.5
Edwards	2.1	982	375	187.5	152	52	7 452	4 939	7 728	10 320	33.3	23.8	1 550	22.7
Ellis	25.4	406	11 515	139.4	5 226	1 250	10 125	6 467	10 119	16 966	12.6	9.7	31 314	46.9
El Paso	203.6	397	61 740	105.4	24 473	10 580	7 723	5 306	8 302	14 002	21.7	18.0	187 473	26.7
Erath	6.6	283	5 040	195.3	2 168	464	10 636	6 870	10 749	11 992	16.5	10.4	12 758	25.7
Falls	6.0	330	3 920	232.0	1 525	824	7 683	5 078	7 946	9 455	23.6	19.3	7 733	-2.6
Fannin	8.1	336	6 110	252.5	2 528	922	8 824	5 862	9 172	12 041	16.0	12.0	11 504	10.7
Fayette	6.4	310	5 445	275.0	2 157	620	9 180	6 110	9 560	11 436	16.8	13.2	10 756	12.9
Fisher	2.4	403	1 235	228.7	537	142	9 756	7 051	11 033	14 586	16.6	12.8	2 413	-8.7
Floyd	4.9	519	1 560	181.4	720	198	7 722	5 363	8 391	12 793	27.8	20.3	3 535	-8.4
Foard	0.9	462	530	294.4	241	60	8 235	6 170	9 654	11 127	18.6	14.7	890	-18.4
Fort Bend	84.5	545	9 890	48.3	4 763	1 552	12 322	8 966	14 029	25 591	8.4	6.4	77 075	78.6
Franklin	2.1	296	1 210	161.3	546	150	10 121	6 696	10 477	12 899	13.2	10.0	4 219	32.6
Freestone	6.6	420	3 095	186.4	1 304	492	9 160	6 078	9 510	11 803	17.3	12.7	7 812	14.2
Frio	8.0	561	1 685	119.5	597	546	5 545	4 108	6 428	10 785	32.3	26.1	4 879	0.4
Gaines	9.3	677	1 610	117.5	726	184	8 277	5 965	9 333	14 199	21.3	16.1	5 221	11.8
Galveston	131.9	633	28 715	136.7	14 434	2 660	11 501	7 892	12 349	19 477	10.6	8.0	99 451	19.9
Garza	4.9	861	1 000	200.0	442	112	9 114	6 420	10 045	13 432	18.4	13.9	2 184	7.1
Gillespie	5.6	395	4 465	277.3	1 997	148	9 443	6 054	9 473	12 758	14.4	10.0	8 265	32.8
Glasscock	1.8	1 468	105	87.5	48	10	8 932	6 546	10 243	15 439	23.0	17.6	600	4.3
Goliad	4.0	746	1 160	196.6	457	204	7 558	5 544	8 675	13 125	19.1	16.2	2 835	33.8
Gonzales	8.8	471	3 865	211.2	1 528	646	7 520	5 187	8 116	10 796	23.9	17.4	7 810	7.1
Gray	11.8	423	5 100	209.9	2 645	324	10 746	7 845	12 275	16 663	9.5	7.5	11 532	2.7
Grayson	34.1	369	18 650	190.5	8 390	1 758	10 512	6 934	10 850	15 254	9.7	7.3	44 223	12.0
Gregg	58.9	535	19 220	176.2	9 343	1 918	10 304	7 157	11 199	16 787	12.5	10.0	44 689	13.1
Grimes	6.3	406	3 275	174.2	1 369	624	8 346	5 825	9 114	11 378	25.4	21.8	7 744	21.3
Guadalupe	20.4	411	8 610	142.1	3 637	992	9 311	5 995	9 380	15 662	15.8	12.9	25 592	42.1
Hale	19.9	522	5 790	159.5	2 632	762	7 985	5 652	8 844	13 518	21.2	16.5	13 168	-6.2
Hall	2.6	504	1 180	287.8	523	138	7 782	5 539	8 667	10 072	28.5	21.5	2 189	-16.8
Hamilton	2.8	343	2 505	317.1	1 011	204	9 557	5 855	9 161	10 137	17.8	14.7	4 266	-2.5
Hansford	4.7	740	915	150.0	459	32	11 585	8 136	12 730	17 801	10.7	8.4	2 525	-0.4
Hardeman	2.7	423	1 430	246.6	649	164	9 612	6 626	10 368	12 625	17.9	12.2	2 678	-6.3
Hardin	21.4	506	6 615	160.9	3 218	662	8 938	6 829	10 685	19 121	11.4	8.8	16 486	7.3
Harris	1 241.3	461	248 975	89.3	126 570	27 578	12 420	9 062	14 179	20 805	10.4	8.1	1 173 808	19.2
Harrison	24.9	448	9 130	158.8	3 922	1 640	8 651	6 050	9 466	14 942	17.7	13.1	23 481	15.9
Hartley	1.4	401	185	52.9	91	2	12 912	8 172	12 787	18 975	10.2	8.7	1 541	0.1

1. Elementary and secondary. 2. Per 1,000 resident population estimated as of July 1 of the year shown. 3. Based on the resident population estimated as of July 1, 1988 for 1987 data and enumerated as of April 1, 1980 for 1979 data.

STATE County	Housing units, 1990 (cont'd)				Civilian labor force, 1990				Private nonfarm establishments, 1988					
	Occupied units						Unemployment				Employment[2]			
	Total	Owner occupied: Percent	Owner occupied: Median value (Dollars)	Median rent (Dollars)	Total	Percent change, 1989–1990	Total	Rate[1]	Number	Net change, 1987–1988	Total	Percent change, 1987–1988	Manu-facturing	Retail trade
	74	75	76	77	78	79	80	81	82	83	84	85	86	87
TEXAS—Con.														
Childress	2 435	73.9	31 100	170	2 366	2.1	145	6.1	190	-6	998	-0.1	0	344
Clay	3 808	82.7	37 500	194	4 925	3.7	193	3.9	138	-2	1 196	30.4	0	315
Cochran	1 430	72.7	22 400	161	1 912	-1.7	76	4.0	73	-2	462	-11.7	92	111
Coke	1 374	76.9	37 300	144	1 718	-3.0	31	1.8	71	1	441	13.1	0	96
Coleman	4 026	73.1	26 300	152	4 665	-13.3	360	7.7	253	4	1 555	0.0	141	378
Collin	95 805	66.6	106 600	451	121 078	-0.4	5 542	4.6	4 937	-132	75 286	5.1	18 563	19 301
Collingsworth	1 447	78.9	25 100	156	1 990	2.5	93	4.7	89	0	484	-0.4	0	142
Colorado	7 024	75.8	45 300	185	7 022	-4.4	253	3.6	519	-16	4 157	-3.7	713	1 100
Comal	19 315	74.0	76 500	338	25 177	-2.2	1 256	5.0	1 330	-6	12 575	1.4	3 181	3 563
Comanche	5 318	77.3	31 700	160	5 090	-0.7	327	6.4	277	-26	1 870	-8.0	197	588
Concho	1 063	70.6	34 300	147	1 786	12.3	69	3.9	53	-5	311	10.3	23	92
Cooke	11 545	71.4	47 700	243	12 409	-0.2	630	5.1	737	-55	7 582	2.8	2 795	1 829
Coryell	16 687	51.7	51 200	330	17 269	0.6	1 493	8.6	605	2	4 275	1.7	503	1 557
Cottle	915	72.1	25 700	120	1 101	-6.5	33	3.0	59	-8	265	-11.4	0	114
Crane	1 537	80.2	37 500	217	1 450	-4.7	62	4.3	113	-7	1 036	-5.6	0	198
Crockett	1 449	67.2	43 100	174	1 756	-4.5	102	5.8	127	-1	674	-13.3	0	247
Crosby	2 516	70.9	29 700	157	3 092	-1.1	146	4.7	148	2	1 108	5.1	146	182
Culberson	1 076	65.0	27 500	191	1 648	-0.3	112	6.8	82	-5	513	-12.5	0	213
Dallam	2 122	68.7	28 100	222	3 231	-0.2	113	3.5	222	-10	1 225	0.8	35	366
Dallas	701 686	51.7	79 200	389	1 095 660	-0.7	57 580	5.3	57 184	-998	1 061 865	-0.9	184 751	187 337
Dawson	5 084	73.4	34 200	207	7 023	-2.6	522	7.4	372	-17	2 433	-1.2	219	823
Deaf Smith	6 182	66.3	41 700	239	9 028	-0.4	515	5.7	491	-7	4 362	4.3	839	944
Delta	1 901	76.0	30 300	160	2 360	-2.1	128	5.4	81	4	502	24.3	0	110
Denton	101 984	57.4	89 100	402	131 960	-0.5	6 286	4.8	4 253	-23	49 953	1.2	12 480	14 483
De Witt	7 195	73.9	35 500	165	8 099	-4.2	433	5.3	381	-9	3 141	-0.3	925	893
Dickens	1 073	75.8	19 100	110	1 103	-4.0	49	4.4	59	-1	377	22.4	0	98
Dimmit	3 072	74.3	21 600	167	4 208	-2.9	501	11.9	158	-12	1 069	-1.1	0	418
Donley	1 515	72.9	31 000	175	1 950	-1.1	72	3.7	102	-2	580	7.4	0	201
Duval	4 159	79.9	23 400	172	5 660	-7.2	448	7.9	165	-2	1 396	-7.1	13	315
Eastland	7 354	74.3	27 800	176	8 090	-5.1	493	6.1	498	-46	4 006	-5.7	460	887
Ector	42 322	65.8	43 400	239	51 268	-2.1	3 092	6.0	3 433	-73	35 936	4.1	4 012	9 473
Edwards	795	72.2	30 900	169	865	-1.7	61	7.1	42	-7	210	-1.4	0	65
Ellis	28 588	72.5	67 900	320	41 386	-1.4	2 310	5.6	1 468	-65	18 389	2.7	7 319	3 921
El Paso	178 366	58.7	57 300	301	250 793	0.2	26 892	10.7	10 503	100	152 179	4.4	39 170	35 311
Erath	10 877	62.7	48 600	256	13 611	1.0	620	4.6	675	-12	6 318	1.6	1 384	1 834
Falls	6 492	70.2	31 400	150	7 545	7.4	329	4.4	296	-3	1 948	-15.1	360	557
Fannin	9 691	75.9	35 100	202	12 608	-1.0	783	6.2	450	-4	4 026	1.6	1 085	864
Fayette	8 101	75.1	53 100	208	9 351	-5.0	266	2.8	651	-22	4 563	1.6	524	1 468
Fisher	1 892	76.4	26 500	137	2 437	3.9	157	6.4	94	-4	707	-11.1	0	139
Floyd	2 982	69.8	29 200	172	4 241	1.2	191	4.5	199	-4	1 237	7.8	0	332
Foard	739	72.0	20 700	151	1 163	-0.5	24	2.1	37	-7	194	-10.6	0	33
Fort Bend	70 424	75.4	71 600	401	101 103	2.1	3 537	3.5	2 450	7	29 502	-1.1	5 686	6 606
Franklin	3 017	76.2	46 800	205	3 978	0.4	193	4.9	133	4	4 746	3.3	265	245
Freestone	6 063	79.5	44 700	197	5 857	-4.0	375	6.4	293	-1	3 152	0.8	122	629
Frio	4 129	67.6	26 800	167	6 409	4.8	445	6.9	233	-25	1 402	-1.6	0	493
Gaines	4 502	72.1	39 800	216	5 598	-3.2	270	4.8	307	14	2 103	-5.0	52	525
Galveston	81 451	62.0	59 700	322	109 581	-0.6	7 797	7.1	4 025	-53	52 528	-4.0	8 406	15 449
Garza	1 822	71.4	31 300	155	2 016	-6.1	101	5.0	129	2	811	2.7	0	271
Gillespie	6 711	79.3	63 900	292	7 770	1.4	188	2.4	543	-13	4 214	0.5	418	1 345
Glasscock	456	60.1	47 500	100	1 250	19.6	22	1.8	16	2	47	-2.1	0	18
Goliad	2 208	78.0	39 900	201	2 641	-2.1	152	5.8	121	3	568	12.7	0	219
Gonzales	6 231	68.2	36 800	160	6 800	-5.1	260	3.8	428	-1	4 296	4.0	1 434	896
Gray	9 548	75.6	35 500	244	11 447	-9.4	530	4.6	764	-56	6 757	-1.1	1 115	1 664
Grayson	36 847	69.3	46 600	277	47 282	-0.6	2 513	5.3	2 299	-128	30 488	0.5	10 168	6 892
Gregg	40 027	63.2	56 000	269	54 585	-0.4	3 990	7.3	3 728	-106	44 312	1.1	10 990	10 525
Grimes	6 040	74.0	39 300	199	10 634	-0.7	429	4.0	280	-3	2 660	3.3	950	550
Guadalupe	22 663	72.4	60 100	279	29 403	-2.2	1 301	4.4	1 042	-50	12 430	4.5	4 306	3 295
Hale	11 703	62.4	39 000	241	17 342	-0.8	930	5.4	860	-14	9 296	16.1	2 298	3 031
Hall	1 669	74.7	21 400	145	2 046	-5.7	142	6.9	112	-20	499	-15.4	0	155
Hamilton	3 250	77.2	33 300	182	3 870	1.0	161	4.2	223	1	1 567	-9.6	326	308
Hansford	2 112	74.1	43 800	235	3 645	-2.3	110	3.0	187	6	1 239	25.2	41	272
Hardeman	2 101	75.3	25 500	170	2 596	-3.2	163	6.3	158	-3	1 056	-3.4	0	232
Hardin	14 693	80.5	48 300	243	17 385	0.7	1 123	6.5	607	-11	5 484	-2.2	1 702	1 414
Harris	1 026 448	52.0	63 500	339	1 504 242	2.3	79 229	5.3	70 401	-207	1 177 809	1.9	151 355	224 260
Harrison	20 705	75.3	46 000	235	25 049	-2.1	1 503	6.0	990	-6	12 214	6.9	4 117	2 493
Hartley	1 332	77.3	60 600	258	1 997	-0.5	49	2.5	40	2	326	0.9	0	78

1. Percent of total civilian labor force. 2. For week including March 12. Excludes government employees, self-employed persons, farm workers, domestic service workers, railroad employees subject to the Railroad Retirement Act, and employees on oceanborne vessels or in foreign countries.

STATE County	Private nonfarm establishments, 1988 (cont'd)				Personal income, 1989								Earnings, 1989		
	Employment[1] (cont'd)		Annual payroll								Per capita[3]			Percent by selected industries	
															Goods-related[4]
	Finance, insurance, and real estate	Services	Total (Mil dol)	Average per employee (Dollars)	Total (Mil dol)	Percent change, 1988–1989	Wages and salaries[2] (Mil dol)	Proprietor's income (Mil dol)	Dividends, interest, & rent (Mil dol)	Transfer payments (Mil dol)	Dollars	Rank	Total (Mil dol)	Farm	Total
	88	89	90	91	92	93	94	95	96	97	98	99	100	101	102
TEXAS—Con.															
Childress	59	344	11	11 416	83	8.5	31	13	21	22	13 600	1 630	44	8.0	6.6
Clay	322	175	14	12 112	143	5.4	30	23	32	24	15 423	826	54	22.4	22.1
Cochran	26	119	10	22 126	64	-1.1	25	18	15	10	15 146	928	43	35.8	19.8
Coke	47	99	7	15 966	51	6.6	18	9	12	11	15 675	747	27	15.1	32.1
Coleman	114	509	18	11 314	147	11.7	52	31	32	34	15 527	794	83	20.0	27.3
Collin	6 340	19 386	1 735	23 051	5 386	12.5	2 007	306	559	272	22 777	77	2 312	0.7	29.7
Collingsworth	0	142	6	11 475	46	0.6	15	8	12	12	12 801	1 998	22	13.2	10.9
Colorado	157	866	59	14 172	284	6.7	99	49	88	53	15 485	806	149	12.3	25.1
Comal	657	2 799	188	14 986	873	8.5	288	78	193	146	16 653	494	365	0.4	34.9
Comanche	128	397	23	12 228	176	10.6	49	32	46	42	14 385	1 255	81	25.0	11.3
Concho	0	129	3	10 839	45	3.7	11	13	10	9	18 002	293	24	46.0	NA
Cooke	264	1 378	119	15 744	405	5.9	184	53	112	74	13 242	1 795	236	3.8	31.0
Coryell	301	1 147	45	10 641	740	6.7	175	45	57	115	11 906	2 358	220	3.9	16.7
Cottle	0	82	3	10 513	37	10.4	16	5	8	9	17 320	394	21	11.9	8.7
Crane	26	58	21	20 016	61	5.2	42	5	13	8	14 305	1 286	47	0.3	54.4
Crockett	0	93	9	13 135	61	6.2	25	17	14	8	14 743	1 110	42	28.8	17.4
Crosby	52	282	16	14 082	96	-1.7	34	22	20	21	12 529	2 100	55	31.1	NA
Culberson	0	144	5	10 232	35	0.7	33	6	4	6	11 240	2 584	39	7.9	NA
Dallam	128	230	17	13 978	95	-1.9	39	39	21	11	17 761	325	77	35.5	5.3
Dallas	124 577	294 607	25 995	24 480	36 744	6.4	34 962	3 479	6 369	3 124	19 602	189	38 441	0.0	24.5
Dawson	154	464	34	13 832	201	1.6	74	36	63	35	13 819	1 524	110	9.7	22.5
Deaf Smith	244	812	65	14 821	293	1.0	111	118	51	36	14 872	1 041	229	42.4	11.7
Delta	53	212	6	12 127	63	4.8	12	10	12	17	13 232	1 802	23	22.2	16.3
Denton	2 133	12 047	920	18 419	4 563	8.5	1 417	259	533	301	18 688	240	1 676	0.5	31.1
De Witt	231	563	42	13 391	253	7.2	96	40	72	54	14 070	1 402	136	11.9	23.0
Dickens	0	164	6	16 525	38	6.9	11	11	7	11	14 076	1 399	22	36.5	NA
Dimmit	67	218	12	11 404	73	0.8	38	7	10	24	6 576	3 103	45	7.6	18.3
Donley	58	173	8	13 422	64	0.6	15	24	13	13	16 796	473	39	49.1	5.3
Duval	57	174	19	13 410	139	8.5	58	30	18	37	10 816	2 713	87	26.5	25.4
Eastland	177	1 040	52	13 007	233	8.2	88	31	57	67	12 312	2 195	119	5.5	29.2
Ector	1 991	8 150	646	17 989	1 685	5.7	1 032	175	284	220	13 850	1 507	1 207	0.2	37.3
Edwards	12	19	3	11 919	29	14.0	8	7	9	5	14 369	1 260	16	33.2	NA
Ellis	870	3 320	319	17 354	1 291	8.3	488	130	168	179	15 055	966	618	4.3	42.7
El Paso	8 571	39 366	2 246	14 760	6 423	9.4	4 379	464	842	1 200	10 735	2 731	4 842	0.5	20.9
Erath	320	1 544	83	13 160	396	9.6	162	78	93	70	15 235	894	240	17.2	NA
Falls	117	562	23	12 013	204	7.0	65	19	48	54	12 242	2 213	85	10.0	16.1
Fannin	410	969	63	15 526	321	4.9	110	34	61	81	13 295	1 775	144	6.9	22.5
Fayette	263	981	58	12 647	324	6.7	118	53	103	62	16 539	519	171	9.2	19.7
Fisher	65	152	12	16 693	68	5.0	26	14	15	14	12 924	1 942	40	23.9	17.8
Floyd	67	311	16	12 714	110	-4.2	38	26	28	22	13 071	1 880	64	28.2	9.0
Foard	0	91	2	10 469	31	4.7	7	8	9	7	18 156	278	15	38.9	NA
Fort Bend	1 514	7 608	630	21 351	3 630	10.2	1 140	216	441	204	17 164	414	1 356	3.0	30.1
Franklin	89	3 955	26	5 420	104	6.8	24	17	20	17	13 698	1 584	41	22.6	14.6
Freestone	142	565	74	23 441	205	6.5	98	22	46	43	12 530	2 098	120	5.1	26.3
Frio	98	374	16	11 526	116	9.5	48	15	21	31	8 274	3 056	63	13.7	13.3
Gaines	110	292	33	15 503	148	-4.8	84	19	24	23	11 141	2 622	103	11.2	24.1
Galveston	4 507	14 031	995	18 936	3 545	8.3	1 872	199	512	474	16 995	439	2 072	0.1	32.5
Garza	0	136	10	11 737	56	3.0	26	9	13	13	11 740	2 424	35	10.6	30.8
Gillespie	225	1 037	54	12 762	291	9.9	75	55	107	51	17 757	326	130	14.7	21.9
Glasscock	0	0	1	19 872	22	-5.8	8	8	4	2	18 788	235	16	45.7	NA
Goliad	0	182	6	10 229	83	7.3	23	12	21	15	13 892	1 480	36	22.6	10.0
Gonzales	207	729	54	12 625	240	8.3	83	52	55	49	13 209	1 807	135	29.2	17.1
Gray	449	1 628	129	19 023	426	1.2	221	69	96	67	18 103	282	290	7.4	43.1
Grayson	1 855	7 167	604	19 801	1 478	5.5	866	121	281	271	15 040	976	987	0.9	44.0
Gregg	2 007	10 140	846	19 097	1 647	6.5	1 068	191	346	268	15 238	891	1 259	0.1	35.7
Grimes	172	455	44	16 618	225	7.4	107	26	52	46	12 000	2 327	133	9.4	27.2
Guadalupe	573	2 118	194	15 643	865	7.3	299	68	153	151	13 838	1 512	367	2.6	42.0
Hale	486	1 932	126	13 604	471	1.1	219	101	87	80	13 080	1 873	320	14.8	18.6
Hall	44	73	7	13 263	54	-5.9	16	11	15	14	13 813	1 528	27	25.1	NA
Hamilton	76	499	21	13 708	115	8.1	31	22	29	29	14 629	1 155	52	19.2	16.4
Hansford	110	271	19	15 353	142	1.3	46	67	23	12	23 690	62	113	50.6	17.2
Hardeman	68	289	15	13 976	84	4.8	28	21	20	19	14 888	1 030	49	26.5	NA
Hardin	214	1 280	109	19 809	514	6.1	141	42	79	98	12 691	2 039	183	1.1	21.9
Harris	98 609	345 443	29 125	24 728	50 003	8.9	40 830	4 423	7 721	4 445	17 948	301	45 253	0.1	28.3
Harrison	671	2 503	205	16 802	738	5.5	469	77	123	132	12 839	1 984	547	0.9	57.2
Hartley	0	164	4	13 267	78	3.1	14	34	12	11	22 066	90	48	65.3	NA

1. For week including March 12. Excludes government employees, self-employed persons, farm workers, domestic service workers, railroad employees subject to the Railroad Retirement Act, and employees on oceanborne vessels or in foreign countries. 2. Includes other labor income. 3. Based on the resident population estimated as of July 1 of the year shown. 4. Covers mining, construction, and manufacturing.

STATE County	Earnings, 1989 (cont'd): Percent by selected industries (cont'd): Goods-related[1]: Manu-facturing	Service-related & other[2]: Total	Service-related & other[2]: Retail trade	Service-related & other[2]: Finance, insur-ance, & real estate	Service-related & other[2]: Services	Govern-ment	Agriculture, 1987: Farms: Number	Farms: Percent with: Less than 50 acres	Farms: Percent with: 500 acres and over	Farm operators, percent: Whose principal occu-pation is farming	Farm operators, percent: Residing on farm operated	Land in farms: Acreage (1,000)	Land in farms: Percent change, 1982–1987	Land in farms: Acres: Average size of farm	Land in farms: Acres: Total irrigated (1,000)	Land in farms: Acres: Total cropland (1,000)
	103	104	105	106	107	108	109	110	111	112	113	114	115	116	117	118
TEXAS—Con.																
Childress	0.7	60.9	14.9	1.8	27.0	24.4	262	7.6	46.6	64.5	40.1	407	18.8	1 552	6	143
Clay	1.9	37.9	10.1	2.2	13.2	17.7	836	15.1	30.0	47.4	54.9	570	-2.2	681	1	122
Cochran	14.4	25.9	4.5	1.5	8.9	18.5	252	6.7	67.1	76.6	48.0	331	-11.9	1 312	40	233
Coke	2.5	32.6	7.5	4.5	10.7	20.2	344	8.4	52.3	50.0	39.8	506	1.1	1 470	1	47
Coleman	6.2	40.5	7.6	3.6	15.6	12.2	784	6.6	44.3	47.2	52.3	702	-6.3	896	1	211
Collin	20.1	57.4	11.2	6.8	30.7	12.3	1 501	43.0	9.1	32.9	63.5	305	-14.0	203	0	199
Collingsworth	4.4	50.8	10.7	3.8	15.7	25.1	365	9.9	54.5	66.8	35.6	455	-1.1	1 245	6	160
Colorado	9.9	50.6	12.6	2.9	18.6	12.0	1 589	24.8	14.3	40.7	48.0	560	-6.2	352	33	207
Comal	21.6	51.0	16.4	4.0	22.3	13.7	652	25.6	19.5	37.6	62.6	224	14.6	343	0	37
Comanche	6.0	47.5	9.6	3.6	19.7	16.2	1 335	18.4	18.5	49.1	56.0	506	2.2	379	25	191
Concho	1.3	NA	7.7	2.7	12.3	16.6	367	4.9	59.7	69.2	47.7	655	8.4	1 786	2	143
Cooke	21.5	48.8	11.6	3.1	15.3	16.3	1 289	24.7	15.6	41.2	65.7	515	25.1	400	1	167
Coryell	4.6	35.1	9.1	3.5	19.2	44.3	1 009	13.5	25.8	47.1	57.9	609	-2.0	604	0	134
Cottle	0.6	63.7	13.1	7.5	14.3	15.7	222	7.7	64.4	71.2	32.9	500	2.3	2 252	0	D
Crane	3.2	26.4	6.5	1.0	5.6	18.9	42	9.5	64.3	61.9	38.1	337	9.9	8 018	D	1
Crockett	0.3	37.4	12.7	3.7	9.8	16.5	163	3.7	87.1	74.2	48.5	1 855	6.0	11 378	1	3
Crosby	3.6	NA	4.7	2.5	13.2	16.3	380	7.1	62.9	76.8	41.1	465	-2.6	1 223	84	301
Culberson	NA	NA	9.3	1.9	NA	14.4	74	12.2	70.3	58.1	40.5	1 606	-15.9	21 704	D	12
Dallam	1.5	51.0	6.6	4.0	7.6	8.2	397	8.1	67.3	78.6	43.1	786	-6.5	1 981	135	384
Dallas	17.2	66.8	9.4	11.3	26.2	8.6	927	56.9	7.0	24.5	47.5	147	-23.2	159	2	74
Dawson	5.3	50.1	12.0	4.4	14.0	17.6	527	8.5	73.1	84.4	40.4	595	1.8	1 129	19	450
Deaf Smith	8.0	35.7	6.2	2.2	9.5	10.1	687	17.5	57.6	72.5	47.2	852	3.9	1 240	152	520
Delta	5.4	38.6	7.1	5.0	15.1	22.9	421	23.8	16.6	45.8	49.6	142	-5.1	338	D	75
Denton	24.4	48.4	11.6	3.2	22.1	19.9	1 469	43.2	10.5	36.8	66.6	391	1.6	266	1	170
De Witt	17.2	45.1	10.5	5.5	19.3	20.1	1 626	19.2	15.1	48.3	49.0	582	11.2	358	1	155
Dickens	1.7	44.1	4.9	3.6	13.5	16.6	285	9.1	48.1	57.2	40.7	439	-14.5	1 541	3	118
Dimmit	1.4	34.3	10.3	3.9	12.7	39.7	249	14.5	49.4	40.2	43.0	695	-6.4	2 793	11	36
Donley	1.4	29.7	7.9	4.1	11.3	15.9	343	12.8	39.7	52.8	35.3	588	-0.4	1 716	4	79
Duval	0.1	23.4	5.3	1.9	10.4	24.7	1 151	13.9	28.2	38.9	25.9	997	2.7	866	3	154
Eastland	11.6	47.4	9.8	4.4	18.1	17.9	1 085	13.1	20.8	46.3	53.2	434	-7.6	400	12	150
Ector	16.6	48.5	11.2	3.7	20.4	14.0	223	69.1	17.0	26.5	69.1	589	0.7	2 641	2	6
Edwards	NA	NA	8.2	NA	12.2	19.6	237	5.5	78.9	65.0	54.0	1 033	0.7	4 358	1	5
Ellis	35.4	41.5	8.3	3.1	17.7	11.4	1 612	35.9	11.2	32.5	63.5	393	-11.9	244	0	244
El Paso	16.1	50.4	10.8	4.1	21.0	28.2	422	68.7	10.9	39.8	63.5	237	-21.0	561	41	45
Erath	12.9	NA	11.5	3.1	15.9	17.0	1 599	19.3	18.4	45.3	63.9	562	1.5	351	10	185
Falls	10.0	40.9	9.1	5.5	16.4	33.0	1 086	16.2	18.9	49.7	53.8	414	7.1	381	3	235
Fannin	15.5	47.2	9.9	7.0	15.5	23.4	1 533	23.1	13.5	39.3	55.8	442	2.3	288	3	258
Fayette	9.1	49.4	11.5	4.2	17.8	21.7	2 750	26.5	6.9	41.1	51.7	530	13.4	193	3	209
Fisher	14.2	42.3	5.4	4.6	12.9	16.0	629	12.4	40.5	61.2	46.3	504	-0.7	801	2	236
Floyd	5.5	44.6	7.7	2.6	13.7	18.1	523	5.9	65.2	83.9	48.2	608	-1.6	1 162	145	451
Foard	NA	NA	5.4	4.5	13.7	15.2	231	6.1	53.2	66.2	31.6	397	16.0	1 720	2	131
Fort Bend	19.8	49.3	7.8	3.6	25.2	17.6	1 233	42.4	13.5	44.0	49.0	364	-9.4	295	13	163
Franklin	9.4	48.3	9.5	4.7	20.5	14.5	479	21.9	12.5	46.3	65.1	119	1.3	248	0	49
Freestone	4.4	NA	8.7	3.6	14.0	14.6	1 178	24.4	13.0	37.3	46.2	405	6.2	344	0	110
Frio	3.6	48.6	11.1	3.6	18.6	24.4	523	11.1	43.4	54.1	40.9	638	-4.9	1 221	46	175
Gaines	1.8	46.1	7.6	2.4	12.7	18.6	627	7.3	65.6	76.7	36.7	674	-11.9	1 076	160	526
Galveston	21.9	41.5	8.5	5.8	17.8	25.9	471	57.1	8.9	29.5	57.5	99	0.7	210	5	38
Garza	1.7	38.1	10.6	2.4	15.4	20.5	236	9.3	55.9	58.9	49.6	548	-4.0	2 323	2	96
Gillespie	8.1	52.5	12.5	4.0	26.8	11.0	1 367	17.8	27.3	45.3	57.9	662	4.3	484	2	117
Glasscock	1.1	NA	2.4	0.6	8.5	15.7	199	4.5	75.4	78.4	60.8	529	5.1	2 660	28	111
Goliad	0.2	43.5	8.1	2.6	10.0	23.8	747	17.1	23.3	38.8	41.5	492	12.1	659	1	68
Gonzales	12.2	39.3	8.4	3.1	14.4	14.4	1 712	21.4	17.3	46.7	47.5	616	-1.6	360	3	152
Gray	20.2	41.0	10.1	3.0	18.6	8.5	323	13.6	51.7	54.2	45.8	505	1.7	1 562	17	163
Grayson	36.8	45.6	9.9	4.5	21.6	9.6	1 900	37.5	8.8	32.5	63.7	414	2.0	218	2	234
Gregg	20.6	53.2	12.6	3.8	22.4	11.0	351	42.2	6.0	21.7	61.0	54	-15.8	154	0	22
Grimes	21.6	30.7	6.4	3.5	13.4	32.6	1 360	28.5	10.3	36.3	51.1	363	3.5	267	1	130
Guadalupe	33.2	38.8	11.3	3.5	17.1	16.6	1 770	36.6	7.6	39.9	64.9	331	-4.0	187	1	172
Hale	13.1	53.9	15.0	3.0	17.9	12.8	818	9.7	56.2	79.0	46.1	582	-4.6	712	241	507
Hall	NA	NA	10.9	NA	12.3	20.3	296	6.8	53.7	73.6	31.4	394	-14.2	1 331	5	173
Hamilton	8.5	51.8	11.8	2.9	21.1	12.6	919	10.6	25.5	47.0	55.7	416	-5.1	453	1	126
Hansford	0.4	23.8	4.5	2.0	5.4	8.5	343	11.7	70.0	78.4	39.7	576	-1.6	1 679	116	343
Hardeman	13.6	NA	6.2	3.4	14.1	15.1	310	6.5	52.3	62.3	39.7	331	2.5	1 067	5	188
Hardin	8.8	58.2	13.0	3.8	18.8	18.8	337	62.0	8.3	28.8	72.1	64	-8.9	190	1	12
Harris	12.9	61.7	8.2	7.4	28.1	9.9	1 936	54.4	7.7	32.0	49.9	375	-3.6	194	14	162
Harrison	50.0	32.2	7.1	2.7	12.9	9.7	1 043	33.2	9.4	31.5	62.5	194	-1.9	186	0	82
Hartley	NA	NA	3.7	NA	12.5	9.7	246	5.3	72.8	74.8	32.9	957	8.8	3 890	81	251

1. Covers mining, construction, and manufacturing. 2. Covers private sector earnings in agricultural services, forestry, and fisheries; transportation and public utilities; wholesale trade; retail trade; finance, insurance, and real estate; and services.

STATE County	Agriculture, 1987 (cont'd) — Value of land and buildings — Average per farm ($1,000)	Value of land and buildings — Average per acre (Dollars)	Value of products sold — Total (Mil dol)	Value of products sold — Average per farm (Dollars)	Value of products sold — Percent from — Crops	Value of products sold — Percent from — Livestock and poultry[1]	Percent of farms with sales of — $10,000 or more	Percent of farms with sales of — $100,000 or more	Manufactures, 1987 — Establishments — Total	Establishments — Percent with 20 or more employees	All employees — Number (1,000)	All employees — Percent change, 1982–1987	All employees — Annual payroll (Mil dol)	Production workers — Number (1,000)	Production workers — Work hours (Mil)
	119	120	121	122	123	124	125	126	127	128	129	130	131	132	133
TEXAS—Con.															
Childress	360	240	17	63 961	69.7	30.3	61.8	22.1	3	0.0	D	D	D	D	D
Clay	277	396	37	43 894	10.8	89.2	46.8	10.2	4	50.0	D	D	D	D	D
Cochran	373	271	50	198 037	D	D	78.2	36.1	4	25.0	D	D	D	D	D
Coke	441	307	9	26 114	4.9	95.1	50.0	5.2	3	0.0	D	D	D	D	D
Coleman	398	416	17	22 089	19.5	80.5	45.3	3.7	10	30.0	0.2	0.0	2.7	0.1	0.3
Collin	421	2 296	42	27 823	29.6	70.4	24.5	3.7	237	30.8	14.4	136.1	391.2	6.0	11.9
Collingsworth	270	225	22	60 337	56.8	43.2	65.8	16.2	3	33.3	D	D	D	D	D
Colorado	388	1 108	37	23 599	49.0	51.0	31.6	5.7	26	26.9	0.6	-25.0	12.9	0.4	0.9
Comal	523	1 592	4	6 722	14.4	85.6	16.0	0.3	65	30.8	2.6	-7.1	45.8	2.2	4.6
Comanche	270	652	66	49 809	33.8	66.2	45.2	11.4	18	16.7	0.2	-60.0	3.1	0.2	0.3
Concho	758	420	21	57 339	33.7	66.3	73.8	16.3	3	33.3	D	D	D	D	D
Cooke	258	703	43	33 411	11.4	88.6	39.6	7.2	63	33.3	2.3	-25.8	41.3	2.0	3.2
Coryell	288	491	22	21 528	11.7	88.3	35.8	3.4	23	26.1	D	D	D	D	D
Cottle	425	191	14	63 649	52.6	47.4	77.0	17.6	1	0.0	D	D	D	D	D
Crane	913	114	2	50 834	0.8	99.2	40.5	9.5	4	25.0	D	D	D	D	D
Crockett	1 782	157	16	101 034	D	D	87.7	30.1	3	0.0	D	D	D	D	D
Crosby	458	373	43	112 752	91.0	9.0	82.4	36.1	9	22.2	0.1	0.0	2.0	0.1	0.2
Culberson	4 176	192	8	105 101	18.6	81.4	52.7	25.7	3	0.0	D	D	D	D	D
Dallam	595	309	167	420 286	19.1	80.9	84.4	45.3	5	0.0	D	D	D	D	D
Dallas	416	2 513	15	16 397	53.8	46.2	16.4	3.0	3 616	32.7	182.5	-5.3	5 026.3	95.8	191.5
Dawson	418	368	42	80 537	94.2	5.8	80.6	30.9	16	12.5	0.2	-50.0	2.9	0.2	0.4
Deaf Smith	472	375	578	841 486	7.4	92.6	81.1	44.0	29	27.6	0.7	-36.4	13.6	0.5	1.1
Delta	230	634	11	25 821	26.5	73.5	34.9	5.5	4	25.0	0.1	0.0	0.4	0.0	0.1
Denton	411	1 621	25	17 340	32.2	67.8	30.7	2.9	234	26.5	12.2	47.0	292.9	7.6	15.6
De Witt	290	769	36	22 324	5.4	94.6	33.0	3.0	19	42.1	0.9	-18.2	15.1	0.6	1.2
Dickens	436	276	12	43 706	52.2	47.8	56.8	10.9	1	0.0	D	D	D	D	D
Dimmit	1 318	487	25	101 326	21.8	78.2	47.0	11.2	3	33.3	D	D	D	D	D
Donley	370	220	46	134 994	12.2	87.8	51.6	15.2	4	0.0	0.0	0.0	0.3	0.0	0.0
Duval	372	437	20	17 099	33.4	66.6	24.8	3.5	4	0.0	0.0	0.0	0.1	0.0	0.0
Eastland	239	586	25	22 702	45.6	54.4	35.3	4.7	33	15.2	0.4	-50.0	6.2	0.3	0.6
Ector	301	117	3	15 583	9.6	90.4	19.3	3.6	223	24.2	4.0	-55.6	107.3	2.2	4.6
Edwards	1 189	279	11	47 978	0.2	99.8	61.6	11.4	NA	NA	NA	NA	NA	NA	NA
Ellis	296	1 310	28	17 375	48.4	51.6	22.0	3.9	134	47.0	7.0	6.1	152.0	5.5	10.9
El Paso	708	1 310	66	156 552	43.0	57.0	37.4	16.6	546	38.8	35.2	-8.1	522.6	27.1	51.0
Erath	264	825	112	70 311	6.2	93.8	38.8	13.8	34	32.4	1.2	9.1	23.7	0.9	1.8
Falls	281	752	54	50 053	20.1	79.9	44.8	11.3	12	33.3	0.4	-20.0	6.7	0.4	0.7
Fannin	209	747	25	16 452	42.1	57.9	29.2	3.3	37	32.4	1.2	-20.0	21.9	1.0	2.0
Fayette	263	1 317	54	19 576	5.9	94.1	22.8	2.3	39	25.6	0.6	20.0	7.7	0.4	0.9
Fisher	307	387	30	47 382	56.5	43.6	63.0	11.9	2	50.0	D	D	D	D	D
Floyd	437	398	134	256 565	33.0	67.0	83.6	36.1	6	16.7	0.1	-50.0	1.9	0.1	0.1
Foard	391	250	12	50 630	48.9	51.1	62.8	15.2	1	0.0	D	D	D	D	D
Fort Bend	541	1 814	45	36 357	76.4	23.6	33.7	6.6	130	33.8	5.5	-54.9	159.6	3.4	6.7
Franklin	219	870	30	63 217	2.0	98.0	44.5	14.8	11	18.2	0.2	-50.0	2.7	0.1	0.3
Freestone	276	836	15	12 368	5.8	94.2	27.6	1.6	11	27.3	0.2	100.0	2.8	0.1	0.2
Frio	609	525	78	148 439	34.9	65.1	52.2	17.8	6	0.0	0.0	0.0	0.2	0.0	0.0
Gaines	422	393	84	133 512	94.2	5.8	80.9	41.6	9	0.0	0.0	-100.0	0.6	0.0	0.1
Galveston	186	1 169	6	11 906	56.8	43.2	21.2	2.5	138	26.8	8.5	-24.8	298.2	5.7	11.7
Garza	502	218	20	83 699	44.4	55.6	68.6	19.9	1	0.0	D	D	D	D	D
Gillespie	579	1 231	36	26 017	5.3	94.7	29.5	2.7	32	18.8	0.5	0.0	6.4	0.4	0.8
Glasscock	968	359	22	112 348	85.5	14.5	74.4	42.7	NA	NA	NA	NA	NA	NA	NA
Goliad	407	632	18	23 835	8.4	91.6	34.8	4.0	3	0.0	0.0	0.0	0.0	0.0	0.0
Gonzales	344	952	163	95 435	3.1	96.9	44.0	13.0	20	35.0	1.2	71.4	19.3	0.9	2.0
Gray	406	249	88	273 062	6.2	93.8	57.6	16.7	24	33.3	1.1	-50.0	35.6	0.6	1.3
Grayson	276	1 287	27	14 305	36.3	63.7	22.2	2.9	127	39.4	10.4	-6.3	273.9	7.3	15.1
Gregg	230	1 424	3	8 225	14.5	85.5	14.5	1.7	203	36.5	11.0	-2.7	288.7	7.8	15.2
Grimes	329	1 115	26	19 213	4.3	95.7	26.1	4.1	21	38.1	0.8	-42.9	16.1	0.7	1.4
Guadalupe	301	1 637	28	15 549	31.2	68.8	23.2	2.3	74	37.8	3.9	21.9	81.4	2.7	5.5
Hale	397	557	160	195 938	56.3	43.7	83.4	46.0	36	30.6	D	D	D	D	D
Hall	268	194	21	72 464	81.7	18.3	70.9	22.0	2	0.0	D	D	D	D	D
Hamilton	357	642	25	27 376	8.1	91.9	35.3	5.8	12	25.0	0.3	50.0	5.3	0.3	0.5
Hansford	565	380	311	906 248	5.6	94.4	83.7	44.0	4	0.0	D	D	D	D	D
Hardeman	351	355	13	41 028	63.9	36.1	61.6	12.6	6	33.3	D	D	D	D	D
Hardin	159	1 077	2	5 030	40.5	59.5	8.9	0.3	44	22.7	D	D	D	D	D
Harris	358	1 872	40	20 511	58.6	41.4	19.8	3.8	4 078	29.0	150.5	-33.8	4 506.3	78.6	163.4
Harrison	199	1 038	10	9 498	12.6	87.4	22.1	0.9	77	42.9	4.3	-8.5	85.8	3.0	5.9
Hartley	983	251	221	899 505	7.6	92.4	85.8	50.8	1	0.0	D	D	D	D	D

1. Includes livestock and poultry products.

STATE County	Manufactures, 1987 (cont'd): Production workers (cont'd): Wages: Total (Mil dol)	Manufactures, 1987 (cont'd): Production workers (cont'd): Wages: Average per worker (Dollars)	Manufactures, 1987 (cont'd): Value added by manufacture (Mil dol)	Manufactures, 1987 (cont'd): Value of shipments (Mil dol)	Manufactures, 1987 (cont'd): New capital expenditures (Mil dol)	Value of construction authorized by building permits, 1990: Total[1] ($1,000)	Nonresidential: Total ($1,000)	Nonresidential: Percent: Office	Nonresidential: Percent: Industrial	Nonresidential: Percent: Stores	Residential: New construction ($1,000)	Residential: Number of housing units	Residential: Alterations and additions ($1,000)
	134	135	136	137	138	139	140	141	142	143	144	145	146
TEXAS—Con.													
Childress	D	D	D	D	D	725	287	0.0	67.8	7.7	254	3	110
Clay	D	D	D	D	D	222	27	0.0	0.0	100.0	147	3	24
Cochran	D	D	D	D	D	2	0	NA	NA	NA	0	0	2
Coke	D	D	D	D	D	382	4	0.0	0.0	0.0	208	6	38
Coleman	1.5	15 000	6.2	11.6	0.1	156	120	0.0	0.0	0.0	0	0	36
Collin	121.4	20 233	658.4	1 241.9	53.7	719 650	317 077	82.8	0.1	4.5	368 971	4 338	7 513
Collingsworth	D	D	D	D	D	161	10	0.0	0.0	0.0	140	3	11
Colorado	6.7	16 750	20.2	50.3	0.7	2 536	303	88.0	0.0	9.3	1 535	55	164
Comal	33.8	15 364	101.4	212.0	9.0	19 599	2 063	14.1	0.0	71.0	15 225	209	432
Comanche	2.1	10 500	18.9	43.9	0.4	42	42	0.0	0.0	100.0	0	0	0
Concho	D	D	D	D	D	NA	NA	NA	NA	NA	NA	NA	NA
Cooke	26.4	13 200	107.0	215.0	3.2	5 914	3 314	4.6	0.0	26.4	477	5	436
Coryell	D	D	D	D	D	5 770	530	0.0	0.0	0.0	4 145	61	939
Cottle	D	D	D	D	D	35	0	NA	NA	NA	0	0	15
Crane	D	D	D	D	D	130	0	NA	NA	NA	92	3	10
Crockett	D	D	D	D	D	NA	NA	NA	NA	NA	NA	NA	NA
Crosby	1.6	16 000	4.3	7.6	0.2	473	190	99.9	0.0	0.0	204	2	68
Culberson	D	D	D	D	D	331	230	0.0	0.0	78.2	15	2	80
Dallam	D	D	D	D	D	1 514	1 289	0.0	49.1	33.1	36	2	105
Dallas	1 935.8	20 207	10 369.7	18 745.6	664.1	1 408 473	331 085	58.9	2.1	14.9	698 898	8 839	56 467
Dawson	2.0	10 000	5.2	12.6	0.1	1 524	944	0.0	0.0	0.0	339	5	107
Deaf Smith	9.0	18 000	50.2	132.6	1.0	2 405	332	0.0	25.2	0.0	1 272	31	178
Delta	0.3	NA	0.7	1.5	0.0	700	140	0.0	0.0	0.0	413	6	56
Denton	144.8	19 053	990.2	1 666.1	46.0	196 944	55 766	1.2	2.8	81.6	127 424	1 258	3 311
De Witt	9.4	15 667	27.8	59.0	0.6	896	202	0.0	0.0	0.0	244	5	344
Dickens	D	D	D	D	D	0	0	NA	NA	NA	0	0	0
Dimmit	D	D	D	D	D	302	8	0.0	0.0	0.0	87	6	116
Donley	0.2	NA	0.7	1.2	0.0	35	11	0.0	0.0	0.0	0	0	9
Duval	0.1	NA	0.2	0.3	0.0	NA	NA	NA	NA	NA	NA	NA	NA
Eastland	3.9	13 000	13.1	36.0	1.3	434	390	0.0	0.0	12.8	44	2	0
Ector	48.8	22 182	386.5	963.0	31.2	13 671	2 097	11.7	7.6	48.3	5 437	45	2 045
Edwards	NA	NA	NA	NA	NA	NA	NA	NA	NA	NA	NA	NA	NA
Ellis	106.7	19 400	522.0	1 084.0	38.6	15 629	2 383	29.3	32.9	18.5	8 679	141	1 160
El Paso	342.0	12 620	1 489.2	4 455.4	65.6	235 648	72 008	29.1	8.6	52.2	102 566	2 111	15 550
Erath	14.2	15 778	111.9	169.6	3.3	2 124	864	46.0	0.0	42.7	665	17	135
Falls	5.4	13 500	19.7	38.5	0.3	507	94	24.5	0.0	58.7	366	9	11
Fannin	15.6	15 600	48.8	144.2	1.4	2 071	296	27.1	0.0	37.2	1 689	63	67
Fayette	5.2	13 000	17.0	39.9	1.1	2 506	1 871	1.1	20.4	0.0	284	5	264
Fisher	D	D	D	D	D	0	0	0.0	0.0	0.0	0	0	0
Floyd	0.9	9 000	5.2	8.0	D	244	64	0.0	0.0	0.0	124	2	29
Foard	D	D	D	D	D	0	0	NA	NA	NA	0	0	0
Fort Bend	77.9	22 912	377.0	848.6	29.8	102 627	20 065	21.3	14.6	35.6	71 745	989	3 224
Franklin	1.8	18 000	6.0	11.5	D	798	15	0.0	0.0	0.0	318	6	12
Freestone	1.8	18 000	5.6	10.9	0.2	1 085	481	17.3	0.0	7.3	538	8	50
Frio	0.2	NA	1.0	1.7	D	678	108	0.0	0.0	96.6	241	17	39
Gaines	0.4	NA	1.7	3.0	0.0	2 309	1 817	30.3	7.4	11.8	234	3	161
Galveston	188.4	33 053	1 652.9	7 346.9	117.5	227 951	104 228	1.2	5.3	33.8	104 672	982	8 164
Garza	D	D	D	D	D	118	4	0.0	0.0	0.0	0	0	79
Gillespie	4.8	12 000	15.8	35.6	1.7	8 928	5 123	5.0	0.0	44.0	1 395	23	368
Glasscock	NA	NA	NA	NA	NA	NA	NA	NA	NA	NA	NA	NA	NA
Goliad	0.0	NA	0.1	0.1	D	241	82	0.0	0.0	0.0	0	0	32
Gonzales	12.5	13 889	40.2	130.8	3.4	1 696	238	0.0	0.0	89.5	774	9	386
Gray	18.6	31 000	25.0	181.8	D	935	60	100.0	0.0	0.0	605	6	199
Grayson	158.1	21 658	774.0	1 591.8	54.8	24 852	4 842	11.7	13.5	25.3	3 720	61	2 645
Gregg	177.7	22 782	868.4	1 965.1	76.1	29 115	4 582	23.2	3.7	45.9	7 531	99	5 343
Grimes	12.0	17 143	36.8	78.3	6.0	744	164	0.0	0.0	0.0	290	5	144
Guadalupe	44.8	16 593	264.5	543.3	18.6	7 449	2 229	9.3	0.0	21.5	4 079	53	346
Hale	D	D	D	D	D	2 811	599	4.1	0.0	1.8	878	11	728
Hall	D	D	D	D	D	3	0	NA	NA	NA	0	0	3
Hamilton	4.0	13 333	14.4	36.1	0.4	130	75	100.0	0.0	0.0	55	1	0
Hansford	D	D	D	D	D	400	0	NA	NA	NA	215	2	79
Hardeman	D	D	D	D	D	0	0	NA	NA	NA	0	0	0
Hardin	D	D	D	D	D	1 355	197	0.0	0.0	69.0	741	15	221
Harris	1 896.0	24 122	13 474.8	36 085.2	1 017.9	1 660 753	281 342	15.2	14.7	33.4	913 106	10 151	108 499
Harrison	50.6	16 867	197.3	375.4	11.5	6 513	3 009	7.1	1.7	6.0	1 130	18	1 074
Hartley	D	D	D	D	D	NA	NA	NA	NA	NA	NA	NA	NA

1. Includes nonresidential additions and alterations, residential nonhousekeeping buildings, and residential garages and carports not shown separately.

STATE County	Wholesale trade, 1987				Retail trade, all establishments, 1987				Retail trade, establishments with payroll, 1987					
						Sales				Sales				
											Per capita[2] (Dollars)			
	Estab- lishments	Sales (Mil dol)	Paid employees[1]	Annual payroll (Mil dol)	Number	Total (Mil dol)	Percent change, 1982–1987	Per capita[2] (Dollars)	Number	Total (Mil dol)	General merchan- dise stores	Food stores	Apparel & acces- sory stores	Eating and drinking places
	147	148	149	150	151	152	153	154	155	156	157	158	159	160
TEXAS—Con.														
Childress	17	30.2	76	1.0	118	31.7	16.5	5 028	70	29.4	D	1 461	206	491
Clay	12	21.3	107	1.2	94	27.3	-15.7	2 878	46	25.3	D	702	32	207
Cochran	8	7.4	40	0.6	49	9.4	-23.0	2 098	20	8.4	0	D	D	D
Coke	5	2.6	17	0.2	48	11.9	-14.4	3 616	23	11.3	D	874	D	139
Coleman	19	30.1	101	1.2	140	34.4	2.1	3 509	72	29.8	161	1 040	194	185
Collin	401	2 100.2	3 558	105.1	2 447	1 591.7	107.3	7 311	1 288	1 542.8	1 082	1 470	377	626
Collingsworth	7	11.8	60	0.8	66	11.5	-31.5	3 105	28	9.2	405	905	D	208
Colorado	44	85.4	423	6.9	341	103.2	2.2	5 377	163	96.9	D	1 385	78	650
Comal	77	98.7	458	8.5	639	309.0	81.1	6 071	316	298.4	D	1 351	180	575
Comanche	37	87.1	284	3.7	182	53.4	23.0	4 235	103	48.9	243	1 438	77	196
Concho	7	4.0	31	0.3	39	12.6	3.3	4 836	18	11.6	D	D	D	D
Cooke	81	147.3	630	9.6	386	171.9	15.5	5 730	224	162.7	D	1 346	176	484
Coryell	12	14.7	121	1.5	367	129.9	23.1	2 168	200	122.0	D	674	14	190
Cottle	6	3.3	26	0.3	37	12.6	18.9	5 248	23	11.6	D	1 832	D	254
Crane	11	7.0	29	0.6	68	17.8	-23.6	3 956	37	16.9	D	1 508	D	174
Crockett	5	3.3	13	0.2	75	20.8	-36.4	4 727	47	19.6	D	D	109	280
Crosby	20	36.4	296	3.8	81	16.1	-4.7	2 043	41	14.3	D	786	D	D
Culberson	7	4.2	28	0.3	68	27.6	4.5	8 364	42	25.8	D	1 092	89	574
Dallam	36	70.5	230	4.5	117	32.8	0.6	5 649	64	30.0	D	D	D	D
Dallas	6 782	55 434.3	97 796	2 635.4	19 653	15 169.0	36.7	8 176	12 212	14 808.1	980	1 391	505	912
Dawson	43	73.6	291	4.2	192	67.9	-6.6	4 412	114	65.1	247	1 338	262	321
Deaf Smith	68	143.2	633	9.7	205	80.0	16.4	4 040	126	76.2	224	1 178	181	343
Delta	9	6.0	55	0.8	55	11.4	18.8	2 418	20	9.2	D	660	0	D
Denton	313	641.1	2 166	41.5	2 189	1 347.2	87.0	6 047	1 152	1 292.0	641	1 426	176	466
De Witt	34	160.2	276	4.1	246	72.8	-8.4	3 873	139	68.9	D	1 281	91	267
Dickens	5	D	D	D	46	10.2	-31.5	3 643	25	9.5	D	2 035	0	271
Dimmit	7	3.8	22	0.4	117	29.6	3.9	2 623	58	27.9	536	971	43	203
Donley	5	3.2	28	0.3	64	17.7	-37.0	4 534	32	16.3	D	621	0	332
Duval	13	13.1	85	0.6	147	22.7	-15.0	1 718	56	20.3	D	608	16	106
Eastland	36	209.7	560	6.5	280	87.2	14.6	4 426	148	78.6	517	1 166	70	322
Ector	473	1 271.4	3 420	78.3	1 463	805.3	-18.9	6 391	858	775.3	903	1 504	321	599
Edwards	4	9.5	27	0.4	25	5.7	29.5	2 874	14	5.3	D	D	D	D
Ellis	100	136.5	727	13.2	820	362.8	57.4	4 474	436	340.3	D	1 100	121	348
El Paso	909	2 699.6	10 024	187.6	4 346	2 898.6	36.7	5 051	2 813	2 832.0	752	1 018	272	454
Erath	55	78.7	419	5.8	359	147.4	37.2	5 760	213	141.3	D	1 283	345	529
Falls	29	141.7	170	2.3	187	47.0	-17.3	2 718	99	43.4	375	1 010	214	159
Fannin	27	160.6	324	6.4	290	105.1	19.8	4 289	130	90.3	D	926	56	226
Fayette	62	97.5	464	8.7	387	117.7	11.0	5 854	214	109.4	541	1 726	166	654
Fisher	6	6.0	29	0.4	51	11.9	-11.2	2 170	32	10.9	D	828	D	134
Floyd	25	44.7	181	2.1	101	28.8	13.8	3 314	62	28.1	D	896	D	175
Foard	5	5.4	25	0.3	19	D	D	D	13	2.7	0	D	0	112
Fort Bend	250	1 438.4	2 346	58.1	1 356	723.7	46.1	3 713	677	694.7	330	995	148	232
Franklin	9	8.7	55	0.6	73	24.6	13.9	3 230	41	23.2	D	1 044	D	181
Freestone	16	15.1	82	1.1	173	55.2	2.8	3 308	94	50.5	93	918	38	393
Frio	28	60.1	269	4.0	142	38.0	12.1	2 658	81	35.9	D	689	45	160
Gaines	31	45.6	199	3.4	152	41.0	-10.5	2 990	86	39.4	D	1 017	D	300
Galveston	215	995.7	1 727	34.5	2 222	1 238.4	18.7	5 917	1 320	1 189.8	810	1 615	343	601
Garza	9	5.2	43	0.7	71	18.1	-8.1	3 490	43	16.3	D	D	D	236
Gillespie	34	73.8	253	3.1	296	92.0	17.0	5 717	167	88.0	219	1 627	213	470
Glasscock	0	0.0	0	0.0	12	1.4	75.0	1 153	5	0.9	0	D	0	D
Goliad	9	4.7	34	0.3	70	15.6	-0.6	2 647	35	14.2	D	827	0	270
Gonzales	37	77.2	285	2.9	217	67.3	-4.8	3 616	133	64.5	492	869	161	283
Gray	68	203.7	369	8.6	380	132.4	-17.3	5 316	219	121.0	791	916	610	460
Grayson	167	283.4	1 195	20.0	1 248	633.0	29.6	6 426	700	604.1	933	1 297	253	446
Gregg	354	1 006.7	3 329	72.4	1 802	921.4	9.9	8 446	1 124	885.0	927	1 634	473	746
Grimes	26	78.1	179	2.3	196	58.0	-2.4	3 070	84	53.3	451	592	52	156
Guadalupe	75	169.2	687	13.7	573	249.2	50.8	4 189	311	237.4	D	972	202	328
Hale	96	177.0	671	13.4	415	174.0	15.5	4 728	250	167.3	698	1 339	251	441
Hall	13	7.7	43	0.5	77	13.8	-17.4	3 217	45	11.4	D	1 139	67	296
Hamilton	17	49.4	162	1.9	139	25.9	-1.5	3 193	71	23.8	D	1 188	64	152
Hansford	30	162.7	217	4.8	81	26.6	-11.6	4 283	44	25.4	D	1 102	214	184
Hardeman	17	18.4	80	1.3	89	16.7	-3.5	2 781	49	15.6	D	1 072	170	433
Hardin	36	111.9	203	3.6	436	170.2	2.5	4 101	194	161.0	D	941	55	196
Harris	7 261	68 810.4	88 457	2 338.8	26 588	18 817.6	8.5	6 767	15 726	18 288.5	872	1 366	424	684
Harrison	70	169.4	444	7.9	523	238.8	5.5	4 132	297	223.9	407	861	192	251
Hartley	6	D	D	D	23	11.3	-8.9	3 138	12	10.9	0	D	D	D

1. For pay period including March 12. 2. Based on the estimated population as of July 1 of the year shown.

STATE County	Retail trade, establishments with payroll, 1987 (cont'd)		Taxable service industries–establishments with payroll, 1987							Bank deposits,[2] June 1989		Savings capital,[3] September 1989	
				Receipts (Mil dol)									
					Selected kinds of business								
	Paid employees[1]	Annual payroll (Mil dol)	Number	Total	Hotels, motels and other lodging places	Health services	Legal services	Paid employees	Annual payroll (Mil dol)	Total (Mil dol)	Percent change, 1988–1989	Total (Mil dol)	Percent change, 1988–1989
	161	162	163	164	165	166	167	168	169	170	171	172	173
TEXAS—Con.													
Childress	450	3.5	36	6.8	2.0	3.7	D	249	2.1	39	1.6	40.6	-25.3
Clay	310	2.4	23	2.3	0.0	1.3	D	70	0.9	62	4.6	22.7	-6.5
Cochran	112	1.1	14	1.6	0.0	D	D	42	0.7	38	7.0	7.8	15.4
Coke	92	1.0	7	0.9	D	0.0	D	25	0.1	39	0.6	6.1	-7.9
Coleman	371	3.4	48	6.4	D	2.1	0.5	232	1.9	105	-3.2	25.6	-7.6
Collin	17 511	174.2	1 501	904.1	D	214.4	25.2	15 440	318.3	1 440	-5.9	869.7	-0.4
Collingsworth	141	1.0	15	1.8	D	D	0.1	76	0.6	42	-13.5	8.5	28.9
Colorado	1 323	11.2	114	16.9	0.9	7.3	0.6	546	5.8	270	-26.3	97.0	-29.8
Comal	3 452	32.8	363	77.5	5.0	23.9	3.9	2 055	25.6	357	0.8	307.2	-7.7
Comanche	667	4.9	48	10.3	D	6.6	0.5	311	3.3	157	-2.9	36.6	-6.1
Concho	80	0.9	8	3.4	D	D	D	133	1.1	28	8.1	0.0	NA
Cooke	1 957	16.6	160	33.0	2.8	13.7	3.0	742	10.2	241	4.7	163.3	-8.7
Coryell	1 660	13.8	135	26.2	D	11.2	1.1	847	8.3	229	6.7	98.5	-85.8
Cottle	121	1.1	12	1.4	D	0.9	0.0	80	0.6	32	-1.8	2.4	-88.5
Crane	194	1.8	15	1.3	D	D	D	38	0.4	19	-5.3	14.4	10.5
Crockett	299	2.6	24	3.2	0.7	0.4	D	95	1.1	59	-0.1	0.0	NA
Crosby	188	1.4	22	4.9	0.0	3.5	D	204	1.9	60	1.5	23.9	-3.2
Culberson	298	2.3	15	3.3	2.0	D	D	124	1.0	13	1.7	0.0	-100.0
Dallam	389	3.2	43	7.4	2.0	D	0.4	160	2.0	93	-9.0	56.6	-2.1
Dallas	170 465	1 863.4	17 415	11 848.0	703.4	2 122.6	1 175.3	218 304	4 466.3	21 058	-7.5	11 319.9	-24.4
Dawson	819	7.1	70	14.1	0.3	2.3	1.0	316	3.8	174	12.7	71.3	-9.5
Deaf Smith	1 029	8.7	95	17.4	D	3.7	1.7	347	5.4	129	-2.3	44.9	-53.9
Delta	105	0.8	15	4.2	0.0	D	0.0	714	2.5	53	-4.0	0.0	NA
Denton	14 767	144.2	1 213	352.8	13.2	159.7	10.6	9 649	128.2	1 072	-2.8	557.7	-5.8
De Witt	903	7.9	73	15.7	0.3	6.7	1.0	483	4.5	284	-1.7	108.7	-23.9
Dickens	105	0.8	8	0.8	0.0	0.0	D	49	0.3	19	-9.6	0.0	NA
Dimmit	429	3.1	32	4.7	D	2.1	0.6	169	1.6	42	-11.3	10.4	-0.3
Donley	168	1.4	21	2.8	D	1.2	0.5	61	0.8	58	0.0	0.0	NA
Duval	281	1.8	26	4.2	0.6	D	0.2	147	1.2	41	-10.1	0.0	-100.0
Eastland	919	7.8	103	15.9	0.6	8.3	1.0	604	5.5	126	-4.6	68.5	-9.0
Ector	9 164	92.6	861	314.3	11.2	D	28.3	6 288	114.8	784	-3.5	510.9	-11.5
Edwards	56	0.5	6	0.4	D	D	D	11	0.1	17	3.6	0.0	NA
Ellis	3 831	34.3	301	63.6	1.4	24.6	3.9	1 846	24.5	477	-7.4	137.4	-2.4
El Paso	35 571	329.3	2 796	1 133.3	58.9	377.7	76.2	28 896	413.7	3 378	-2.7	1 224.4	7.5
Erath	1 891	15.7	154	37.5	1.8	14.0	2.7	1 191	13.5	253	-5.4	96.3	-22.2
Falls	629	5.0	55	9.8	D	4.3	D	330	3.7	130	-7.5	44.8	-9.8
Fannin	898	8.1	83	14.5	D	7.9	0.7	555	5.2	194	1.3	44.1	-34.4
Fayette	1 453	13.7	131	23.2	1.3	9.8	1.2	646	7.4	303	-2.0	132.2	22.6
Fisher	150	1.2	21	3.1	D	2.2	D	201	1.0	44	-2.0	0.0	-100.0
Floyd	323	2.8	35	3.7	0.1	1.3	D	189	1.2	75	1.7	16.5	27.9
Foard	40	0.3	8	0.9	0.0	D	D	44	0.3	17	-6.7	4.0	-3.2
Fort Bend	7 330	75.4	822	407.8	D	80.3	5.0	6 873	138.8	697	-2.9	581.8	17.0
Franklin	226	2.4	27	15.7	D	13.6	0.4	3 133	10.0	70	4.8	13.6	5.3
Freestone	636	5.2	63	11.9	D	6.5	1.1	443	4.6	106	-0.6	0.0	NA
Frio	458	3.9	40	8.5	D	5.3	0.3	277	2.6	109	-7.4	11.5	-18.2
Gaines	574	4.4	55	8.2	0.2	2.4	0.5	229	2.5	86	4.5	27.8	13.8
Galveston	14 949	144.1	1 096	341.0	44.0	96.7	33.0	9 355	133.7	1 339	7.9	707.1	-23.6
Garza	216	1.7	25	3.6	0.0	0.5	D	117	1.0	39	-2.2	27.7	198.7
Gillespie	1 189	10.7	119	25.0	1.3	11.4	1.2	763	8.6	264	4.0	103.6	-2.4
Glasscock	27	0.1	3	D	0.0	0.0	0.0	D	D	NA	NA	0.0	NA
Goliad	193	1.4	29	4.3	D	1.6	D	132	1.1	27	-5.9	27.6	60.1
Gonzales	886	7.2	88	13.2	0.6	5.5	1.2	444	4.7	149	3.8	65.4	-23.4
Gray	1 673	13.9	184	52.5	D	26.4	2.9	1 194	17.0	252	-3.1	128.9	-22.2
Grayson	7 278	68.8	622	192.8	10.3	98.1	13.9	4 356	74.5	972	-3.1	422.1	-10.6
Gregg	10 771	103.3	889	262.5	11.5	94.4	19.8	7 394	92.9	1 158	-4.8	533.5	-4.3
Grimes	568	4.9	50	16.2	1.1	9.3	D	417	5.3	129	6.7	48.7	-1.8
Guadalupe	2 911	25.6	240	50.6	3.1	20.2	2.3	1 489	18.4	370	-0.6	156.0	-23.8
Hale	2 401	20.7	204	41.4	D	19.7	2.0	1 244	13.7	246	-1.0	131.6	-7.2
Hall	203	1.3	20	1.4	D	0.6	0.0	52	0.3	52	-1.4	10.5	-58.2
Hamilton	288	2.6	47	9.4	0.0	5.8	D	410	3.8	83	-7.3	40.5	-20.7
Hansford	276	2.7	31	4.1	D	0.8	0.3	84	1.5	120	17.5	11.8	-5.4
Hardeman	261	1.9	36	5.4	D	2.8	0.3	226	1.9	65	-3.5	48.7	-2.0
Hardin	1 547	15.3	120	30.9	D	12.2	0.9	811	10.2	216	18.4	195.0	-17.2
Harris	213 977	2 193.3	22 192	14 438.9	451.4	3 232.2	1 590.3	263 259	5 396.8	24 312	-5.3	19 719.3	-8.4
Harrison	2 420	23.6	214	51.2	4.1	18.1	11.5	1 230	19.2	409	1.6	169.4	-6.5
Hartley	82	0.9	6	D	0.0	D	0.0	D	D	NA	NA	0.0	NA

1. For the period including March 12 of the year shown. 2. Includes deposits for all insured and reporting noninsured commercial and mutual savings banks. 3. Includes savings capital for all FSLIC insured savings institutions.

STATE County	Federal funds and grants, 1989: Expenditures: Total (Mil dol)	Federal funds and grants, 1989: Expenditures: Percent change, 1988–1989	Federal funds and grants, 1989: Per capita[1] (Dollars): Total	Per capita[1]: Direct payments for individuals	Per capita[1]: Procurement contract awards	Per capita[1]: Salaries and wages	Per capita[1]: Grant awards	Local government finances, 1981–1982: General revenue: Total (Mil dol)	General revenue: Intergovernmental: Total (Mil dol)	General revenue: Intergovernmental: Percent from state	General revenue: Taxes: Total (Mil dol)	Taxes: Per capita[2]: Total (Dollars)	Taxes: Per capita[2]: Property (Dollars)	Direct general expenditure: Total (Mil dol)	Direct general expenditure: Percent change, 1977–1982
	174	175	176	177	178	179	180	181	182	183	184	185	186	187	188
TEXAS—Con.															
Childress	27.3	10.3	4 480	2 868	43	206	228	4.3	2.0	62.7	1.5	217	158	4.0	9.9
Clay	21.1	-1.4	2 266	1 869	52	112	93	16.9	3.2	90.0	3.3	341	307	14.9	60.7
Cochran	20.7	5.0	4 807	1 551	17	165	233	9.3	2.0	88.6	5.7	1 169	1 135	6.9	80.0
Coke	11.0	5.9	3 442	2 750	20	151	97	5.4	1.1	85.1	2.8	791	751	4.6	78.1
Coleman	36.8	7.0	3 873	2 871	38	201	402	7.4	3.4	86.1	2.7	253	192	7.2	64.8
Collin	287.8	-6.3	1 217	789	171	93	146	151.5	49.6	93.9	56.3	349	300	156.2	160.3
Collingsworth	19.0	6.5	5 274	2 457	53	272	423	3.4	1.4	93.8	1.4	315	268	3.1	17.9
Colorado	70.7	19.7	3 844	2 215	593	129	280	14.4	5.5	79.5	6.3	319	270	13.1	95.1
Comal	141.8	-9.5	2 706	2 486	14	108	88	31.4	12.1	90.9	11.8	298	249	28.1	103.2
Comanche	44.5	17.5	3 622	2 665	29	157	256	10.5	3.5	91.3	2.6	202	157	10.5	59.9
Concho	18.9	45.1	7 550	2 797	50	228	1 514	3.7	1.2	91.8	1.0	349	316	3.7	78.8
Cooke	73.0	-13.8	2 385	1 873	277	99	83	33.3	10.2	82.6	10.2	355	303	30.2	53.5
Coryell	100.9	11.4	1 626	1 293	44	133	115	24.7	12.2	90.7	5.3	90	71	23.4	86.2
Cottle	15.1	24.5	6 862	3 229	17	222	305	3.1	0.9	87.3	1.2	437	383	4.0	62.7
Crane	6.0	7.4	1 395	1 251	9	61	65	8.8	0.6	81.8	7.3	1 470	1 413	7.3	52.4
Crockett	13.7	28.0	3 336	1 407	6	54	784	7.9	0.9	88.6	5.2	1 019	998	7.2	122.5
Crosby	34.4	16.9	4 469	1 881	12	110	245	9.0	4.0	91.7	3.5	404	370	7.5	59.0
Culberson	5.5	-18.8	1 772	1 111	34	397	175	4.9	1.0	87.0	2.7	775	704	4.7	53.0
Dallam	30.9	-13.4	5 833	2 607	35	158	149	6.8	2.6	91.7	3.0	451	370	6.8	91.6
Dallas	5 389.6	-4.6	2 875	1 199	997	489	175	1 780.0	501.1	81.3	852.3	521	410	1 773.7	83.0
Dawson	53.5	16.5	3 688	1 765	10	95	338	18.5	6.3	89.6	7.7	459	405	17.3	68.4
Deaf Smith	60.0	-11.2	3 044	1 229	108	91	264	19.5	8.3	95.1	7.1	345	303	19.0	65.2
Delta	32.2	4.4	6 712	2 658	3 093	181	430	3.1	1.7	84.8	1.0	200	168	5.5	221.5
Denton	841.5	260.0	3 446	774	2 427	109	121	114.9	41.4	79.8	43.1	273	231	114.4	109.1
De Witt	47.9	3.6	2 658	2 154	17	109	325	20.1	7.3	85.3	6.2	307	271	20.0	78.3
Dickens	16.0	11.7	5 911	3 300	23	249	303	3.1	1.5	75.1	1.2	358	317	2.8	65.4
Dimmit	25.0	7.5	2 273	1 398	7	164	605	15.9	6.4	95.4	4.5	378	336	12.8	70.7
Donley	14.9	6.8	3 918	2 755	15	157	169	5.1	2.3	97.8	1.3	320	272	5.2	137.2
Duval	41.6	14.3	3 227	1 836	27	131	795	20.3	6.9	87.9	11.0	857	817	17.1	146.9
Eastland	60.7	11.9	3 194	2 688	20	135	242	20.4	8.5	96.5	5.0	239	192	19.0	55.3
Ector	179.6	8.0	1 475	1 236	10	77	149	165.3	47.7	69.1	71.7	532	450	154.8	131.2
Edwards	12.1	48.8	6 068	1 874	13	227	1 611	3.7	1.5	95.4	1.5	704	663	2.9	41.7
Ellis	161.1	23.0	1 880	1 341	246	82	155	43.4	20.1	92.7	14.0	224	180	40.7	58.0
El Paso	2 031.9	8.4	3 396	1 516	387	1 227	260	488.5	249.6	72.4	137.8	269	219	425.7	82.7
Erath	65.0	9.0	2 498	1 993	16	156	146	16.4	5.7	86.3	5.1	216	165	12.1	86.1
Falls	62.6	-3.3	3 746	2 409	75	632	382	11.0	5.4	94.0	3.3	183	143	9.7	48.0
Fannin	98.9	14.7	4 102	2 630	250	536	498	15.2	8.6	75.2	4.7	195	155	12.5	58.8
Fayette	59.6	2.5	3 042	2 439	58	152	319	14.7	4.9	91.7	6.0	291	250	12.1	124.6
Fisher	26.7	35.6	5 046	2 038	20	178	207	6.6	1.6	95.1	3.0	511	477	5.6	33.0
Floyd	43.6	2.4	5 191	1 906	21	159	272	10.6	3.9	91.6	3.6	381	343	8.5	20.2
Foard	10.2	11.2	5 971	3 219	15	175	378	2.4	0.7	86.3	0.9	473	425	2.1	76.5
Fort Bend	223.3	27.2	1 056	580	93	102	107	135.4	37.5	95.9	74.0	477	438	130.5	145.3
Franklin	16.4	14.5	2 153	1 686	9	64	166	7.3	1.3	81.7	2.8	393	368	6.4	125.3
Freestone	41.6	6.5	2 534	1 957	39	244	207	15.6	4.0	89.4	4.8	306	264	14.9	104.7
Frio	32.6	14.4	2 330	1 449	9	63	423	27.8	7.7	82.1	4.2	294	249	25.0	185.5
Gaines	50.2	11.4	3 776	1 182	7	71	142	21.0	3.2	72.6	14.7	1 067	1 020	18.6	8.4
Galveston	530.2	-12.7	2 542	1 647	275	214	295	303.6	79.3	84.6	128.1	615	554	298.5	88.9
Garza	15.1	-9.8	3 148	1 929	15	133	251	7.6	1.5	91.6	4.7	828	737	7.3	115.6
Gillespie	51.2	6.8	3 123	2 602	78	179	93	9.7	4.2	89.0	3.9	274	229	9.7	94.8
Glasscock	7.6	32.5	6 318	905	9	78	191	3.1	0.3	90.4	2.5	2 123	2 076	3.1	245.6
Goliad	15.0	14.2	2 501	1 747	11	137	374	7.5	2.6	90.7	3.1	577	541	6.8	89.5
Gonzales	105.8	133.5	5 845	1 990	3 190	163	341	14.3	6.2	96.0	4.3	232	186	13.7	65.1
Gray	69.1	2.0	2 942	2 269	290	106	122	20.9	5.7	92.5	11.4	412	335	19.6	31.2
Grayson	257.0	9.5	2 614	2 159	118	95	208	97.2	35.4	75.8	29.6	321	263	92.0	99.8
Gregg	252.2	10.6	2 333	1 850	49	166	259	124.0	36.1	87.0	60.7	552	461	126.3	103.4
Grimes	43.3	12.3	2 315	1 783	26	83	347	11.2	5.1	94.7	3.9	248	206	10.2	93.1
Guadalupe	128.3	1.4	2 053	1 709	42	99	156	35.6	16.3	90.6	10.2	205	173	35.4	78.8
Hale	114.1	4.3	3 170	1 600	58	126	280	39.9	14.5	90.6	13.7	359	313	37.6	67.6
Hall	21.2	10.0	5 430	2 771	23	229	333	4.6	2.0	88.6	1.9	357	307	4.6	54.6
Hamilton	27.8	11.8	3 518	2 832	21	167	222	4.8	2.7	86.1	1.4	168	128	4.4	119.6
Hansford	21.0	-21.0	3 504	1 434	10	90	78	7.7	1.5	93.5	5.2	812	745	7.6	21.7
Hardeman	23.1	3.1	4 047	2 686	18	154	218	7.7	2.0	93.0	2.3	351	303	7.4	73.0
Hardin	85.3	6.2	2 107	1 828	8	52	166	32.3	14.3	96.5	12.9	306	284	28.6	91.2
Harris	6 530.7	12.9	2 344	1 100	558	333	324	3 157.5	895.8	81.9	1 539.4	572	479	3 061.8	106.0
Harrison	191.2	3.8	3 325	1 645	1 212	109	349	41.5	19.0	84.1	16.7	300	261	39.6	68.7
Hartley	11.5	-27.9	3 281	514	6	94	40	2.3	0.5	94.4	1.6	455	429	2.1	81.0

1. Based on the estimated population as of July 1 of the year shown. 2. Based on the estimated population as of July 1, 1982.

STATE County	Local government finances, 1981–1982 (cont'd) — Direct general expenditure (cont'd) — Per capita[1] (Dollars)	Percent of total for– Education	Health & hospitals	Police protection	Public welfare	Highways	Debt outstanding — Total (Mil dol)	Per capita[1] (Dollars)	State and local government employment, 1989 — Total	Rate[2]	Federal government civilian employment 1989 — Total	Earnings ($1,000)	Elections, 1988[3] — Total vote cast for president	Vote for lead party (Percent)
	189	190	191	192	193	194	195	196	197	198	199	200	201	202
TEXAS—Con.														
Childress	586	45.6	0.1	5.3	0.2	8.0	2.8	399	493	808.2	46	1 328	2 267	R–53.0
Clay	1 538	28.7	9.1	2.4	0.0	5.5	119.1	12 278	475	510.8	32	811	4 340	D–52.7
Cochran	1 411	58.6	12.8	3.5	0.1	9.8	1.3	261	383	890.7	32	852	1 462	R–52.7
Coke	1 312	41.0	31.5	1.7	0.1	6.5	1.8	525	347	1 084.4	17	414	1 542	R–56.0
Coleman	688	59.7	0.1	3.6	0.1	7.1	3.8	362	519	546.3	49	1 210	4 321	R–54.2
Collin	968	49.0	5.0	4.7	0.3	8.3	383.3	2 375	11 386	481.6	464	14 080	91 230	R–74.3
Collingsworth	680	57.4	0.0	8.3	0.1	13.0	1.3	280	276	766.7	32	797	1 683	R–51.8
Colorado	670	61.8	0.6	4.8	0.0	10.7	8.3	421	822	446.7	60	1 672	6 600	R–56.4
Comal	711	62.8	0.4	5.3	0.4	4.5	31.2	789	2 269	433.0	103	3 135	19 980	R–70.0
Comanche	814	37.6	31.8	2.9	0.1	5.2	5.9	461	678	551.2	59	1 562	4 761	D–55.1
Concho	1 248	39.4	39.5	1.9	0.0	7.3	0.6	200	211	844.0	25	563	1 263	D–50.9
Cooke	1 052	44.8	23.7	3.3	0.0	4.7	21.0	732	1 855	606.2	79	2 259	11 452	R–62.8
Coryell	396	57.5	11.6	4.2	0.2	3.7	22.8	385	3 382	544.6	904	26 664	11 627	R–64.2
Cottle	1 426	29.9	13.5	1.8	0.0	6.2	2.9	1 034	158	718.2	21	492	1 083	D–63.7
Crane	1 460	60.0	6.3	4.7	0.3	11.1	4.5	904	394	916.3	NA	256	1 818	R–67.1
Crockett	1 418	36.9	22.1	2.6	7.1	15.3	2.5	487	333	812.2	11	313	1 819	R–51.2
Crosby	861	72.3	0.3	3.4	0.1	8.8	2.9	337	467	606.5	39	929	2 562	D–56.0
Culberson	1 350	46.3	13.7	0.8	0.4	11.1	1.8	511	255	822.6	26	839	982	D–56.7
Dallam	1 009	61.3	0.0	5.8	0.2	8.0	1.3	187	273	515.1	41	1 116	1 862	R–64.7
Dallas	1 083	40.3	10.5	6.2	0.3	6.1	2 194.8	1 341	92 613	494.1	27 426	933 176	594 538	R–58.4
Dawson	1 037	65.5	12.7	3.1	0.2	5.8	85.3	5 109	888	612.4	95	2 125	5 317	R–59.3
Deaf Smith	926	58.7	14.8	5.3	0.3	4.6	3.2	154	1 084	550.3	65	1 949	5 726	R–65.4
Delta	1 148	32.5	0.0	1.7	0.0	6.6	2.1	443	249	518.8	31	718	2 101	D–59.2
Denton	725	52.5	9.1	4.6	0.1	3.8	177.8	1 127	15 427	631.7	661	21 407	84 210	R–68.2
De Witt	996	59.2	13.1	2.4	0.1	6.2	8.4	417	1 360	755.6	45	1 213	6 255	R–58.0
Dickens	849	63.4	0.8	2.7	0.2	11.4	1.0	299	166	614.8	31	680	1 141	D–61.0
Dimmit	1 079	60.6	19.1	2.1	0.1	4.2	4.3	358	939	853.6	64	2 182	3 651	D–74.9
Donley	1 247	57.8	16.6	1.8	0.0	5.4	12.6	3 004	335	881.6	25	553	1 713	R–60.9
Duval	1 327	68.7	0.3	2.4	1.5	6.6	8.6	667	1 154	894.6	63	2 054	5 097	D–82.0
Eastland	915	66.6	12.0	2.5	0.2	3.4	10.2	492	1 046	550.5	76	2 015	7 166	R–54.8
Ector	1 148	51.2	17.5	4.0	1.0	2.9	73.0	541	7 623	626.4	258	8 021	34 152	R–67.8
Edwards	1 380	71.2	10.1	1.9	0.4	4.2	0.3	139	161	805.0	17	575	930	R–59.8
Ellis	652	62.3	2.7	5.0	0.1	6.1	57.1	913	3 133	365.6	183	5 099	27 749	R–59.2
El Paso	830	52.6	5.4	5.2	0.2	2.9	423.5	826	32 621	545.2	9 421	311 677	118 781	D–52.7
Erath	516	54.8	1.1	6.3	0.0	8.2	21.8	929	2 066	794.6	130	4 015	9 570	R–56.7
Falls	534	61.8	0.0	4.8	0.2	9.8	3.9	214	788	471.9	385	12 904	5 237	D–54.9
Fannin	518	65.0	1.1	4.4	0.4	8.0	11.1	459	898	372.6	507	16 170	9 214	D–56.0
Fayette	588	52.6	1.3	4.3	0.4	15.5	7.2	348	1 393	710.7	88	2 360	7 971	R–57.1
Fisher	948	42.5	24.0	2.7	0.1	9.2	4.8	817	320	603.8	38	934	2 240	D–67.7
Floyd	898	57.8	11.9	2.6	0.1	11.1	2.2	230	581	691.7	59	1 324	3 138	R–55.5
Foard	1 049	44.0	21.0	2.1	0.0	12.8	0.2	79	117	688.2	15	382	820	D–62.6
Fort Bend	841	64.8	0.8	5.7	0.1	7.9	212.5	1 369	10 356	489.6	354	10 748	63 784	R–62.4
Franklin	905	32.7	32.4	2.5	0.0	9.9	5.2	729	281	369.7	13	377	2 896	D–50.2
Freestone	943	44.5	29.2	3.3	0.0	6.3	8.1	511	730	445.1	117	3 391	6 092	R–51.9
Frio	1 746	32.1	0.4	1.5	0.0	6.7	185.6	12 978	815	582.1	36	939	4 538	D–66.5
Gaines	1 348	50.3	11.7	3.6	0.2	11.1	6.8	489	889	668.4	47	1 214	3 606	R–62.8
Galveston	1 433	50.1	7.8	3.6	0.3	4.1	389.2	1 868	21 591	1 035.0	1 012	32 996	74 042	D–52.2
Garza	1 287	66.9	9.5	4.0	0.4	7.6	0.7	129	335	697.9	23	671	2 190	R–54.0
Gillespie	682	57.9	0.5	4.7	0.0	11.4	3.6	256	602	367.1	76	2 661	7 313	R–77.4
Glasscock	2 607	56.3	0.0	1.9	0.0	16.8	1.9	1 542	111	925.0	NA	215	528	R–72.7
Goliad	1 259	59.3	13.5	3.3	0.2	10.9	0.6	111	433	721.7	21	540	2 792	R–51.1
Gonzales	738	63.8	13.5	3.0	0.2	7.3	6.3	340	935	516.6	88	2 308	5 916	R–50.4
Gray	705	60.0	0.5	5.5	0.2	9.1	3.6	129	1 067	454.0	75	2 376	9 781	R–74.2
Grayson	995	45.8	18.2	3.3	0.1	7.6	139.5	1 510	3 986	405.5	280	7 974	33 287	R–56.6
Gregg	1 149	55.9	5.3	3.9	0.5	6.3	154.7	1 406	5 866	542.6	512	15 719	39 387	R–67.2
Grimes	654	62.1	0.0	5.2	0.1	12.3	14.5	929	1 711	915.0	47	1 270	5 582	R–50.5
Guadalupe	713	57.7	11.9	3.9	0.1	6.6	23.2	468	2 938	470.1	171	5 117	20 609	R–64.4
Hale	983	53.1	17.7	4.5	0.2	4.8	13.9	365	2 114	587.2	157	4 566	9 811	R–64.1
Hall	877	57.5	0.0	1.9	0.4	12.8	3.0	568	279	715.4	35	865	1 743	D–59.0
Hamilton	538	63.8	0.3	3.8	0.1	11.9	2.3	287	278	351.9	43	1 085	3 086	R–55.7
Hansford	1 184	62.6	0.0	4.6	0.1	8.6	1.0	158	468	780.0	24	681	2 421	R–81.2
Hardeman	1 139	37.1	35.8	2.4	0.2	8.1	3.4	525	370	649.1	32	897	2 001	D–57.1
Hardin	678	74.7	4.1	3.4	0.2	3.9	18.2	431	1 689	417.0	61	1 739	15 173	D–54.3
Harris	1 137	43.0	6.2	5.5	0.5	5.5	4 696.5	1 744	150 079	538.7	24 476	895 665	814 160	R–57.0
Harrison	713	62.8	0.5	3.7	0.4	5.0	41.6	748	2 339	406.8	125	3 613	21 285	R–56.2
Hartley	597	67.0	0.0	1.7	2.2	9.4	0.4	123	209	597.1	15	379	1 747	R–70.3

1. Based on the estimated population as of July 1, 1982. 2. Per 10,000 resident population estimated as of July 1 of the year shown. 3. Data subject to copyright.

STATE–County code	MSA/CMSA/NECMA code[1]	STATE County	Land Area,[2] 1990 (Sq. Km.)	Population, 1990											
							Race						Age of population Percent		
				Total persons	Rank	Per square kilometer	White	Black	Am. Indian, Eskimo, Aleut	Asian & Pacific Islander	Other race	Hispanic[3]	Under 5 years	5 to 14 years	15 to 24 years
			1	2	3	4	5	6	7	8	9	10	11	12	13
		TEXAS—Con.													
48 207	...	Haskell	2 339	6 820	2 676	2.9	5 481	244	17	16	1 062	1 312	6.3	14.9	10.0
48 209	0640	Hays	1 756	65 614	667	37.4	55 360	2 220	230	427	7 377	18 249	6.7	13.8	27.1
48 211	...	Hemphill	2 356	3 720	2 939	1.6	3 503	7	22	5	183	412	7.4	18.8	11.1
48 213	...	Henderson	2 265	58 543	742	25.8	52 216	4 755	181	141	1 250	2 368	6.3	13.8	12.2
48 215	4880	Hidalgo	4 064	383 545	131	94.4	286 858	806	668	1 088	94 125	326 972	9.3	20.8	18.2
48 217	...	Hill	2 493	27 146	1 386	10.9	23 669	2 520	80	38	839	2 230	6.6	14.4	12.7
48 219	...	Hockley	2 353	24 199	1 487	10.3	18 937	1 023	86	33	4 120	7 654	8.5	19.0	16.2
48 221	...	Hood	1 092	28 981	1 331	26.5	28 054	52	154	177	544	1 353	6.8	14.8	10.5
48 223	...	Hopkins	2 033	28 833	1 336	14.2	25 381	2 476	126	70	780	1 407	7.2	15.1	13.7
48 225	...	Houston	3 188	21 375	1 612	6.7	14 373	6 326	32	49	595	965	6.4	14.3	12.1
48 227	...	Howard	2 339	32 343	1 203	13.8	25 282	1 225	179	162	5 495	8 607	7.6	15.2	13.0
48 229	...	Hudspeth	11 840	2 915	3 006	0.2	2 345	15	9	2	544	1 935	7.4	19.0	15.3
48 231	...	Hunt	2 179	64 343	680	29.5	55 705	6 802	266	351	1 219	2 876	7.4	14.8	14.5
48 233	...	Hutchinson	2 298	25 689	1 434	11.2	22 661	677	362	105	1 884	2 509	7.2	17.4	12.3
48 235	...	Irion	2 724	1 629	3 089	0.6	1 609	2	1	0	17	385	8.1	15.5	13.1
48 237	...	Jack	2 376	6 981	2 662	2.9	6 748	51	18	10	154	232	7.0	15.7	10.3
48 239	...	Jackson	2 148	13 039	2 138	6.1	10 857	1 218	41	12	911	2 772	7.0	16.5	12.1
48 241	...	Jasper	2 428	31 102	1 241	12.8	24 750	5 868	76	38	370	594	6.7	16.6	13.0
48 243	...	Jeff Davis	5 865	1 946	3 070	0.3	1 671	7	12	4	252	770	5.7	15.1	12.7
48 245	0840	Jefferson	2 340	239 397	208	102.3	154 273	74 412	578	5 145	4 989	12 629	7.4	15.6	13.6
48 247	...	Jim Hogg	2 943	5 109	2 832	1.7	4 375	4	12	4	714	4 659	9.3	18.4	14.7
48 249	...	Jim Wells	2 239	37 679	1 056	16.8	28 504	218	82	103	8 772	27 201	8.7	18.5	15.0
48 251	1922	Johnson	1 889	97 165	473	51.4	90 328	2 521	419	447	3 450	7 457	7.7	16.7	14.1
48 253	...	Jones	2 411	16 490	1 894	6.8	13 786	666	47	31	1 960	2 786	6.7	16.1	11.9
48 255	...	Karnes	1 943	12 455	2 186	6.4	9 548	362	35	14	2 496	5 916	8.2	17.7	12.5
48 257	1922	Kaufman	2 036	52 220	811	25.6	42 810	7 295	198	229	1 688	3 340	7.7	16.8	13.6
48 259	...	Kendall	1 716	14 589	2 014	8.5	13 682	58	71	38	740	2 392	7.0	14.6	12.1
48 261	...	Kenedy	3 773	460	3 137	0.1	378	0	0	0	82	362	7.8	18.3	12.0
48 263	...	Kent	2 337	1 010	3 113	0.4	902	6	1	0	101	120	6.6	15.2	8.8
48 265	...	Kerr	2 865	36 304	1 096	12.7	32 842	805	128	141	2 388	5 994	6.3	13.2	11.0
48 267	...	Kimble	3 240	4 122	2 906	1.3	3 654	2	5	10	451	772	6.5	14.5	10.2
48 269	...	King	2 363	354	3 138	0.1	317	0	0	0	37	53	6.8	17.5	13.8
48 271	...	Kinney	3 532	3 119	2 992	0.9	2 746	57	26	9	281	1 570	6.3	14.4	11.8
48 273	...	Kleberg	2 256	30 274	1 281	13.4	20 650	998	81	414	8 131	18 529	8.4	16.2	20.5
48 275	...	Knox	2 212	4 837	2 853	2.2	3 765	338	7	5	722	1 088	7.4	15.6	10.8
48 277	...	Lamar	2 375	43 949	925	18.5	36 814	6 397	406	153	179	475	7.1	14.6	14.2
48 279	...	Lamb	2 632	15 072	1 984	5.7	13 036	822	88	25	1 101	5 509	7.4	18.0	12.5
48 281	...	Lampasas	1 844	13 521	2 100	7.3	12 164	268	79	136	874	1 753	7.8	15.1	13.1
48 283	...	La Salle	3 856	5 254	2 824	1.4	3 567	53	9	10	1 615	4 068	8.6	19.7	14.5
48 285	...	Lavaca	2 512	18 690	1 750	7.4	16 541	1 342	20	14	773	1 596	6.3	14.3	11.2
48 287	...	Lee	1 628	12 854	2 151	7.9	10 057	1 780	14	15	988	1 410	7.2	16.2	13.9
48 289	...	Leon	2 777	12 665	2 168	4.6	10 730	1 615	39	8	273	509	6.9	14.9	11.4
48 291	3362	Liberty	3 004	52 726	805	17.6	44 014	6 911	181	124	1 496	2 880	7.4	17.0	13.9
48 293	...	Limestone	2 354	20 946	1 631	8.9	15 695	4 156	41	50	1 004	1 459	7.2	14.9	11.8
48 295	...	Lipscomb	2 414	3 143	2 990	1.3	3 092	1	34	13	3	379	6.9	16.7	10.9
48 297	...	Live Oak	2 684	9 556	2 428	3.6	8 316	10	36	31	1 163	3 324	6.8	16.2	11.5
48 299	...	Llano	2 421	11 631	2 245	4.8	11 386	22	39	20	164	453	4.5	9.0	7.4
48 301	...	Loving	1 743	107	3 140	0.1	93	0	0	0	14	14	5.6	15.0	12.1
48 303	4600	Lubbock	2 330	222 636	224	95.6	176 037	17 154	686	2 722	26 037	51 011	7.7	14.8	20.4
48 305	...	Lynn	2 310	6 758	2 679	2.9	5 214	223	22	11	1 288	2 819	8.2	17.6	13.2
48 307	...	McCulloch	2 770	8 778	2 488	3.2	7 855	166	14	8	735	2 317	7.1	15.1	12.3
48 309	8800	McLennan	2 699	189 123	254	70.1	146 100	29 520	563	1 384	11 556	23 643	7.5	14.4	18.7
48 311	...	McMullen	2 883	817	3 122	0.3	713	0	3	0	101	320	8.0	13.5	10.9
48 313	...	Madison	1 216	10 931	2 302	9.0	7 984	2 575	67	13	292	1 178	5.7	12.2	21.6
48 315	...	Marion	987	9 984	2 387	10.1	6 792	3 100	44	7	41	147	6.4	14.0	11.2
48 317	...	Martin	2 369	4 956	2 844	2.1	3 159	89	11	8	1 689	1 960	8.9	20.0	13.6
48 319	...	Mason	2 414	3 423	2 963	1.4	3 084	6	13	4	316	671	5.9	13.7	9.8
48 321	...	Matagorda	2 887	36 928	1 074	12.8	26 622	5 106	88	842	4 270	9 088	8.6	18.3	12.9
48 323	...	Maverick	3 316	36 378	1 094	11.0	23 748	32	714	71	11 813	34 024	9.6	21.4	18.2
48 325	...	Medina	3 439	27 312	1 380	7.9	23 608	92	119	68	3 425	12 134	7.8	17.1	13.7
48 327	...	Menard	2 336	2 252	3 049	1.0	2 076	7	5	0	164	726	6.9	13.9	9.2
48 329	5040	Midland	2 332	106 611	433	45.7	86 977	8 281	414	888	10 051	22 780	9.4	17.8	12.7
48 331	...	Milam	2 633	22 946	1 536	8.7	18 603	2 940	69	37	1 297	3 456	7.1	16.4	12.5
48 333	...	Mills	1 938	4 531	2 871	2.3	4 238	10	4	1	278	484	5.7	14.0	9.8
48 335	...	Mitchell	2 357	8 016	2 564	3.4	6 317	363	14	5	1 317	2 389	6.5	16.3	11.9
48 337	...	Montague	2 411	17 274	1 837	7.2	16 834	5	72	13	350	548	6.5	13.7	11.6

1. MSA = Metropolitan Statistical Area. CMSA = Consolidated MSA. NECMA = New England county metropolitan area. PMSA = Primary MSA. See Appendix A for explanation of these concepts. See Appendix B for list of metropolitan areas identified by type, with component counties. 2. Dry land or land partially or temporarily covered by water. 3. Hispanic persons may be of any race.

STATE County	Population, 1990 (cont'd): Age of population (cont'd) Percent: 25 to 34 years	35 to 44 years	45 to 54 years	55 to 64 years	65 to 74 years	75 years and over	Percent female	Population–Change and components of change: Change 1980–1990: Number	Percent	Total persons, 1986	Total persons, 1980	Components of change, 1980–1986: Net change: Number	Percent	Natural increase: Births	Deaths
	14	15	16	17	18	19	20	21	22	23	24	25	26	27	28
TEXAS—Con.															
Haskell	12.3	11.2	9.0	11.7	12.5	12.1	51.9	-905	-11.7	7 200	7 725	-600	-7.2	700	700
Hays	15.9	14.6	8.3	5.8	4.7	3.3	49.8	25 020	61.6	60 800	40 594	20 200	49.8	4 800	1 600
Hemphill	14.7	15.1	10.9	8.7	6.4	6.8	51.2	-1 584	-29.9	4 900	5 304	-500	-8.6	800	200
Henderson	12.8	12.3	11.1	12.4	12.1	7.1	51.5	15 937	37.4	54 500	42 606	11 900	27.9	3 900	3 300
Hidalgo	14.6	12.7	7.8	6.6	6.1	4.0	51.7	100 222	35.4	365 900	283 323	82 600	29.1	47 500	10 700
Hill	12.6	12.3	10.0	10.4	11.0	9.9	52.1	2 122	8.5	27 200	25 024	2 200	8.7	2 200	2 400
Hockley	15.8	12.7	9.3	7.8	5.9	4.7	50.7	969	4.2	24 900	23 230	1 600	7.0	3 400	1 100
Hood	14.9	14.3	11.1	11.4	10.6	5.5	50.4	11 267	63.6	28 000	17 714	10 300	58.1	1 900	1 200
Hopkins	14.9	13.7	10.3	8.8	8.5	7.8	51.0	3 586	14.2	29 400	25 247	4 100	16.3	2 700	2 000
Houston	15.7	13.2	9.4	9.6	9.8	9.4	49.3	-924	-4.1	23 000	22 299	700	3.2	1 700	1 600
Howard	15.9	13.2	10.3	10.3	8.5	6.0	49.6	-799	-2.4	36 200	33 142	3 000	9.1	4 000	2 200
Hudspeth	16.1	12.8	10.2	9.2	5.6	4.5	48.4	187	6.9	2 700	2 728	0	0.3	300	100
Hunt	15.4	13.3	11.5	9.1	7.8	6.3	51.1	9 095	16.5	67 100	55 248	11 800	21.4	5 600	3 700
Hutchinson	14.7	13.9	9.3	10.2	9.0	6.0	50.6	-615	-2.3	27 200	26 304	900	3.5	3 300	1 500
Irion	14.5	13.4	11.7	10.4	7.4	5.8	50.2	243	17.5	2 000	1 386	600	42.2	200	100
Jack	14.0	13.0	10.1	11.0	9.5	9.3	51.2	-427	-5.8	7 500	7 408	100	1.3	700	700
Jackson	13.4	13.6	10.2	10.0	9.5	7.6	51.8	-313	-2.3	13 400	13 352	0	0.4	1 500	900
Jasper	13.6	13.0	10.5	10.4	9.3	6.9	52.2	321	1.0	32 100	30 781	1 300	4.3	3 300	2 100
Jeff Davis	11.5	13.4	11.8	10.9	11.1	7.9	48.6	299	18.2	1 800	1 647	100	9.0	100	100
Jefferson	16.2	14.0	9.6	9.7	8.1	5.9	52.0	-9 254	-3.7	249 800	248 651	1 200	0.5	27 600	14 700
Jim Hogg	13.4	12.4	9.5	8.7	7.3	6.3	51.1	-59	-1.1	5 500	5 168	300	6.7	700	300
Jim Wells	14.5	13.5	9.4	8.8	6.6	5.1	50.8	1 181	3.2	40 300	36 498	3 800	10.5	5 000	1 900
Johnson	16.4	15.5	11.1	8.0	5.8	4.6	50.4	29 516	43.6	92 100	67 649	24 500	36.1	7 900	4 100
Jones	13.3	12.9	10.5	9.7	9.7	9.2	52.2	-778	-4.5	18 300	17 268	1 000	5.8	1 700	1 400
Karnes	13.6	11.5	8.6	10.0	9.6	8.3	52.3	-1 138	-8.4	13 300	13 593	-300	-2.2	1 500	1 000
Kaufman	15.4	15.4	10.9	8.4	6.6	5.3	51.1	13 182	33.8	52 300	39 038	13 200	33.9	4 500	2 900
Kendall	13.7	14.8	12.2	9.4	8.7	7.5	51.3	3 954	37.2	14 700	10 635	4 000	38.0	1 000	800
Kenedy	16.1	12.4	12.0	12.6	5.4	3.5	51.1	-83	-15.3	600	543	0	6.4	0	0
Kent	12.3	12.5	11.5	11.6	11.5	10.0	52.0	-135	-11.8	1 100	1 145	-100	-4.5	100	100
Kerr	12.6	12.1	9.4	10.8	13.8	10.9	52.7	7 524	26.1	35 900	28 780	7 100	24.6	2 700	2 700
Kimble	11.1	13.0	11.3	12.2	11.4	9.9	51.0	59	1.5	4 300	4 063	200	5.6	300	300
King	16.7	17.5	12.1	9.3	5.4	0.8	48.3	-71	-16.7	400	425	0	-3.8	0	0
Kinney	11.9	11.9	8.7	12.9	15.3	6.8	49.3	840	36.9	2 500	2 279	200	8.5	200	200
Kleberg	16.2	12.4	9.0	7.6	5.6	4.2	50.2	-3 084	-9.2	33 800	33 358	400	1.2	4 800	1 300
Knox	12.8	11.6	9.2	10.3	11.4	10.8	51.9	-492	-9.2	5 300	5 329	0	0.3	600	500
Lamar	13.9	13.2	10.5	9.0	9.1	8.3	52.6	1 793	4.3	45 000	42 156	2 900	6.8	4 000	3 200
Lamb	13.4	11.4	9.7	9.8	9.3	8.6	51.7	-3 597	-19.3	16 500	18 669	-2 200	-11.5	2 200	1 200
Lampasas	13.4	13.5	11.3	10.1	8.1	7.6	51.5	1 516	12.6	14 200	12 005	2 200	17.9	1 200	900
La Salle	14.0	12.9	9.1	7.8	7.9	5.5	50.4	-260	-4.7	5 600	5 514	100	1.0	800	300
Lavaca	12.6	12.3	9.8	9.9	12.2	11.5	52.2	-314	-1.7	18 500	19 004	-500	-2.8	1 700	1 700
Lee	14.8	13.4	9.3	9.4	8.4	7.5	49.5	1 902	17.4	13 800	10 952	2 900	26.3	1 400	900
Leon	13.4	12.1	9.8	11.7	11.0	8.8	51.5	3 071	32.0	12 800	9 594	3 200	33.2	1 100	1 100
Liberty	15.7	14.7	10.6	9.0	7.1	4.6	50.1	5 638	12.0	54 700	47 088	7 600	16.2	5 900	3 100
Limestone	14.5	13.3	9.8	9.6	9.6	9.4	52.8	722	3.6	21 200	20 224	1 000	5.0	1 900	1 800
Lipscomb	14.4	13.8	11.0	9.9	8.7	7.7	49.7	-623	-16.5	3 600	3 766	-100	-3.4	500	200
Live Oak	13.4	13.2	11.2	11.2	9.4	6.9	50.9	-50	-0.5	9 500	9 606	-100	-1.1	900	500
Llano	8.8	10.3	9.5	16.5	19.5	14.5	52.7	1 487	14.7	12 500	10 144	2 400	23.5	600	1 200
Loving	16.8	11.2	12.1	14.0	10.3	2.8	44.9	16	17.6	100	91	0	-42.9	0	0
Lubbock	17.7	13.3	8.7	7.5	5.7	4.1	50.7	10 985	5.2	224 800	211 651	13 200	6.2	26 200	8 800
Lynn	14.7	10.7	10.3	9.8	8.2	7.1	50.9	-1 847	-21.5	7 600	8 605	-1 000	-11.5	900	400
McCulloch	11.7	12.4	9.4	9.8	10.5	11.7	52.3	43	0.5	9 000	8 735	200	2.8	800	900
McLennan	15.3	13.0	9.1	8.4	7.5	6.1	51.5	18 368	10.8	187 600	170 755	16 800	9.9	18 600	10 700
McMullen	13.7	13.0	13.2	12.9	8.4	6.5	49.8	28	3.5	900	789	100	18.0	100	0
Madison	17.8	10.5	8.6	7.7	7.7	8.3	41.8	282	2.6	12 100	10 649	1 400	13.4	800	700
Marion	12.4	12.5	11.7	12.2	11.3	8.3	50.8	-376	-3.6	10 000	10 360	-300	-3.3	900	800
Martin	14.0	13.4	9.8	8.6	6.0	5.7	50.4	272	5.8	5 300	4 684	600	12.1	700	300
Mason	11.4	12.6	10.4	11.7	12.2	12.3	52.4	-260	-7.1	3 600	3 683	-100	-1.6	300	300
Matagorda	16.4	14.0	9.6	8.5	6.6	5.0	50.5	-900	-2.4	41 000	37 828	3 100	8.3	5 000	2 100
Maverick	13.6	13.0	8.4	7.4	5.3	3.2	52.5	4 980	15.9	37 400	31 398	6 000	19.1	4 900	1 000
Medina	14.1	14.0	9.8	9.5	8.1	5.9	50.4	4 148	17.9	26 100	23 164	3 000	12.8	2 600	1 300
Menard	12.0	12.4	10.0	11.9	11.6	12.1	50.5	-94	-4.0	2 300	2 346	0	-0.6	200	200
Midland	18.4	15.3	9.1	8.4	5.5	3.5	51.5	23 975	29.0	111 300	82 636	28 600	34.7	14 200	3 700
Milam	12.9	12.9	9.8	9.6	9.7	9.0	51.5	214	0.9	23 700	22 732	1 000	4.3	2 300	1 800
Mills	11.0	12.3	9.6	10.9	12.9	13.8	51.4	54	1.2	4 500	4 477	0	0.8	300	500
Mitchell	12.4	12.4	8.8	10.7	10.7	10.2	52.3	-1 072	-11.8	9 100	9 088	0	-0.1	1 000	800
Montague	12.6	12.1	10.6	10.9	11.3	10.7	52.1	-136	-0.8	18 500	17 410	1 100	6.4	1 600	1 600

STATE County	Population—(cont'd): Components of change, 1980-1986 (cont'd): Net migration	Households, 1990: Number	Households, 1990: Percent change, 1980–1990	Households, 1990: Persons per household	Households, 1990: Percent: Female family householder[1]	Households, 1990: Percent: One-person	Births, 1988: Total	Births, 1988: Rate[2]	Births, 1988: Low birth weight[3] (Number)	Deaths, 1987: Number: Total	Deaths, 1987: Number: Infant[4]	Deaths, 1987: Rate: Total[2]	Deaths, 1987: Rate: Infant[5]	Marriages, 1984: Number	Marriages, 1984: Rate[2]
	29	30	31	32	33	34	35	36	37	38	39	40	41	42	43
TEXAS—Con.															
Haskell	-600	2 753	-7.6	2.43	6.8	27.7	87	13.0	10	111	0	16.1	0.0	127	16.9
Hays	17 000	22 218	76.6	2.68	7.9	22.3	977	15.3	55	292	4	4.6	4.2	564	11.0
Hemphill	-1 000	1 348	-26.6	2.72	6.2	22.0	55	13.4	5	33	0	8.0	0.0	78	13.4
Henderson	11 200	22 947	42.6	2.51	8.8	22.6	675	12.2	47	629	8	11.4	12.1	681	13.6
Hidalgo	45 800	103 479	36.5	3.67	15.0	13.4	8 906	23.0	500	1 896	72	5.0	8.6	3 715	10.7
Hill	2 400	10 268	6.0	2.55	9.0	25.7	383	14.0	24	391	5	14.3	14.2	339	12.4
Hockley	-700	7 988	6.2	2.96	8.6	18.9	449	18.7	33	164	6	6.9	14.8	272	11.0
Hood	9 600	11 137	64.8	2.57	6.3	19.2	380	12.3	17	245	2	8.4	5.0	372	15.4
Hopkins	3 500	10 965	15.1	2.59	8.5	24.2	426	14.6	19	356	4	12.2	10.4	352	12.5
Houston	600	7 792	8.2	2.51	13.6	26.4	305	13.3	20	283	2	12.3	7.3	245	10.8
Howard	1 200	11 477	-4.1	2.63	11.0	23.7	545	16.0	46	335	5	9.7	9.8	453	12.3
Hudspeth	-200	946	15.1	2.97	8.9	22.1	35	14.0	2	14	0	5.6	0.0	28	11.2
Hunt	9 900	24 075	18.4	2.61	9.7	23.9	1 004	15.0	69	625	14	9.3	13.1	748	11.7
Hutchinson	-900	9 642	-2.0	2.63	6.9	22.5	358	14.3	26	245	3	9.6	8.0	315	11.0
Irion	500	601	18.5	2.71	6.0	19.1	21	11.1	2	13	2	6.8	76.9	24	12.6
Jack	0	2 725	-5.8	2.52	6.7	26.1	95	13.4	7	89	2	12.2	20.6	99	12.9
Jackson	-600	4 833	3.2	2.67	9.7	23.7	190	15.0	12	121	2	9.3	10.2	137	10.0
Jasper	100	11 427	6.7	2.69	11.0	21.9	447	14.2	34	368	4	11.6	8.0	474	14.7
Jeff Davis	100	779	31.6	2.43	5.8	28.6	25	13.9	0	22	0	12.2	0.0	32	18.8
Jefferson	-11 700	90 520	0.3	2.60	14.1	26.1	3 699	15.4	289	2 522	41	10.4	10.9	3 103	12.0
Jim Hogg	-100	1 675	7.1	3.05	14.4	20.4	109	21.0	10	45	1	8.5	9.5	63	11.7
Jim Wells	700	11 979	7.3	3.11	12.1	18.2	672	17.5	43	298	3	7.6	4.2	381	9.5
Johnson	20 700	33 462	44.7	2.85	8.8	17.1	1 462	15.0	89	781	23	8.1	15.6	1 165	14.1
Jones	700	6 180	-2.9	2.60	8.1	24.4	221	13.1	14	233	2	13.4	8.2	196	10.7
Karnes	-900	4 337	-4.1	2.82	11.5	23.7	222	17.5	14	161	2	12.3	9.7	151	11.0
Kaufman	11 600	17 827	35.5	2.86	10.2	19.0	781	14.0	63	474	6	8.7	7.6	885	18.8
Kendall	3 800	5 342	40.5	2.66	8.5	19.7	247	15.9	14	131	0	8.7	0.0	143	10.7
Kenedy	0	145	-14.2	3.10	5.5	16.6	6	12.0	1	4	0	6.7	0.0	7	11.7
Kent	0	399	-7.4	2.47	4.5	26.6	11	10.0	1	13	0	11.8	0.0	5	4.2
Kerr	7 000	14 384	28.8	2.38	8.6	27.4	483	13.6	36	440	7	12.4	13.6	389	11.8
Kimble	200	1 624	3.8	2.50	8.1	24.4	65	15.5	4	44	1	10.5	10.8	51	11.9
King	0	124	-19.5	2.85	3.2	14.5	5	12.5	0	2	0	5.0	0.0	4	10.0
Kinney	200	1 187	54.0	2.59	6.4	26.7	37	14.2	2	34	2	13.6	39.2	37	15.4
Kleberg	-3 100	10 058	-2.2	2.89	12.7	21.8	636	20.1	28	223	5	6.9	8.0	455	13.0
Knox	-100	1 887	-7.6	2.51	7.4	28.8	78	15.3	3	70	1	13.5	12.5	52	9.1
Lamar	2 100	16 798	6.9	2.56	11.5	25.0	690	15.3	54	554	5	12.3	7.8	704	15.8
Lamb	-3 200	5 488	-14.4	2.72	8.3	24.1	265	17.0	13	179	1	11.4	3.8	147	8.4
Lampasas	1 800	5 058	14.6	2.64	8.6	23.2	236	16.6	10	136	2	9.6	9.5	227	16.9
La Salle	-400	1 701	-1.4	3.05	14.2	21.6	104	20.4	6	43	0	8.3	0.0	50	8.5
Lavaca	-500	7 349	2.8	2.49	8.0	27.5	242	13.2	10	241	0	13.0	0.0	200	10.8
Lee	2 300	4 706	22.0	2.62	8.3	24.5	193	14.4	11	114	3	8.4	16.6	173	12.9
Leon	3 100	5 006	30.8	2.51	8.2	26.2	196	16.1	18	191	1	15.5	5.0	135	11.3
Liberty	4 900	18 538	14.2	2.79	10.3	21.1	757	14.3	54	519	11	9.7	13.5	847	15.7
Limestone	1 000	7 722	4.1	2.54	12.1	27.4	305	13.8	28	256	4	11.5	12.8	291	13.9
Lipscomb	-400	1 230	-12.3	2.55	4.7	25.1	40	12.1	1	20	0	5.9	0.0	63	15.4
Live Oak	-600	3 550	7.3	2.67	7.6	22.6	115	12.8	3	84	0	9.0	0.0	106	11.0
Llano	3 000	5 278	19.9	2.15	4.6	27.7	98	7.8	12	220	2	17.6	16.7	123	10.4
Loving	0	42	23.5	2.55	0.0	33.3	2	20.0	1	0	0	0.0	0.0	6	60.0
Lubbock	-4 200	81 534	12.3	2.61	10.4	25.5	3 769	16.6	278	1 483	23	6.5	5.9	2 876	12.9
Lynn	-1 400	2 383	-15.8	2.81	8.2	21.8	111	15.9	7	87	2	12.3	18.5	96	12.2
McCulloch	300	3 409	0.3	2.52	8.4	28.0	132	14.5	6	136	2	15.5	15.7	100	11.1
McLennan	8 900	70 208	14.1	2.58	12.1	25.8	3 117	16.6	237	1 760	30	9.3	9.9	2 463	13.5
McMullen	100	319	7.4	2.54	3.8	24.1	13	13.0	1	7	0	7.8	0.0	2	2.2
Madison	1 400	3 349	7.8	2.55	11.2	26.8	129	11.1	9	133	5	11.4	36.8	135	11.3
Marion	-400	4 048	4.5	2.45	11.9	27.0	128	13.5	14	124	2	12.9	17.5	174	16.7
Martin	200	1 632	5.5	3.01	7.0	19.5	85	16.7	4	44	1	8.6	11.8	53	9.8
Mason	0	1 435	-1.8	2.35	5.6	28.7	34	10.3	0	43	0	12.6	0.0	43	11.9
Matagorda	200	13 164	0.4	2.79	11.7	22.9	741	19.0	43	325	5	8.1	6.4	545	13.7
Maverick	2 100	9 756	28.7	3.70	14.5	14.9	870	22.0	42	134	4	3.4	5.2	505	14.0
Medina	1 700	9 109	22.2	2.94	9.7	18.4	446	16.5	27	221	2	8.3	4.4	213	8.7
Menard	0	937	2.2	2.37	7.2	30.8	39	17.0	3	42	1	17.5	25.6	22	9.2
Midland	18 100	38 920	31.3	2.72	9.8	23.7	2 142	20.0	138	615	16	5.7	7.4	1 319	12.4
Milam	500	8 686	4.7	2.61	10.0	27.0	315	14.0	20	250	5	10.9	13.5	277	11.8
Mills	200	1 782	0.6	2.39	5.6	27.5	63	14.3	3	88	0	20.0	0.0	39	8.5
Mitchell	-200	3 054	-7.6	2.56	8.5	27.2	122	14.2	6	121	1	13.9	7.2	107	11.4
Montague	1 200	6 858	0.3	2.46	7.2	26.2	235	13.3	15	285	1	15.8	4.4	259	14.1

1. No spouse present. 2. Per 1,000 resident population estimated as of July 1 of the year shown. 3. Under 2,500 grams. 4. Deaths of infants under 1 year old. 5. Deaths of infants under 1 year old per 1,000 live births.

STATE County	Divorces, 1984		Physicians, active non-Federal, 1989		Hospitals, 1989			Nursing homes,[4] 1986		Serious crimes known to police, 1988			Education			
						Beds				Number			Public school enrollment[7]		Attainment,[8] 1980	
	Number	Rate[1]	Number[2]	Rate[3]	Number	Number	Rate[3]	Number	Beds	Total[5]	Violent[6]	Rate[3]	1986–1987	1980	Percent 12 yrs. or more	Percent 16 yrs. or more
	44	45	46	47	48	49	50	51	52	53	54	55	56	57	58	59
TEXAS—Con.																
Haskell	42	5.6	3	45	1	30	455	2	150	135	7	1 957	1 248	1 435	44.1	10.9
Hays	226	4.4	59	89	1	109	164	3	301	3 132	230	4 918	11 803	6 919	62.1	22.6
Hemphill	24	4.1	5	132	1	20	526	1	59	42	4	955	853	1 030	56.4	9.5
Henderson	150	3.0	32	57	1	103	182	4	400	2 362	182	4 304	8 489	7 798	50.7	8.4
Hidalgo	137	0.4	297	74	8	970	243	13	1 192	24 569	1 512	6 491	99 012	78 126	41.1	10.8
Hill	141	5.2	22	81	3	139	509	7	625	931	76	3 399	4 964	4 610	45.5	8.0
Hockley	135	5.5	10	42	1	44	186	1	89	866	54	3 550	5 648	5 158	51.6	9.9
Hood	156	6.5	13	40	1	57	173	2	229	1 015	41	3 513	4 699	3 106	62.4	13.1
Hopkins	210	7.4	23	78	1	100	341	4	379	1 113	82	3 749	5 650	4 831	51.3	10.3
Houston	62	2.7	13	57	1	72	314	4	310	667	73	2 939	4 084	4 132	48.5	7.8
Howard	58	1.6	63	189	4	759	2 272	2	292	2 202	221	6 384	5 997	6 815	54.3	10.0
Hudspeth	5	2.0	0	0	0	0	0	0	0	14	6	467	680	705	46.3	9.3
Hunt	467	7.3	48	71	2	203	301	6	542	5 112	769	7 542	12 004	10 303	56.6	13.7
Hutchinson	213	7.4	18	74	0	0	0	3	286	782	34	2 952	5 550	4 747	64.4	12.4
Irion	6	3.2	0	0	0	0	0	0	0	24	0	1 264	350	318	59.1	11.6
Jack	42	5.5	3	43	1	18	261	2	134	196	1	2 686	1 676	1 357	49.3	6.7
Jackson	50	3.6	7	56	1	31	250	2	117	324	19	2 455	3 202	2 808	45.5	8.8
Jasper	253	7.9	21	68	3	222	714	3	268	685	21	2 148	7 251	7 149	51.6	7.7
Jeff Davis	14	8.2	0	0	0	0	0	0	0	8	2	471	403	332	55.0	22.4
Jefferson	1 593	6.2	438	186	8	1 869	794	14	1 781	20 797	2 155	8 522	44 454	48 258	63.5	13.6
Jim Hogg	NA	NA	4	77	0	0	0	0	0	38	14	704	1 269	1 306	34.8	9.4
Jim Wells	193	4.8	22	58	1	105	277	4	427	2 467	124	6 263	9 101	8 841	43.1	8.8
Johnson	334	4.0	63	62	1	97	96	10	1 073	3 624	147	3 804	19 252	14 534	60.3	10.5
Jones	63	3.4	8	48	3	90	542	4	316	422	21	2 412	3 388	3 694	47.2	9.9
Karnes	2	0.1	5	40	1	39	312	4	281	90	22	687	2 827	3 222	38.8	8.6
Kaufman	239	5.1	57	98	4	723	1 242	9	1 581	2 891	216	5 336	12 550	8 294	52.0	10.7
Kendall	52	3.9	26	161	0	0	0	3	265	356	21	2 328	3 211	2 302	64.9	17.2
Kenedy	2	3.3	0	0	0	0	0	0	0	1	0	167	70	126	33.9	16.6
Kent	6	5.0	0	0	0	0	0	1	33	8	1	667	202	222	52.9	9.8
Kerr	214	6.5	87	243	5	1 100	3 073	4	518	1 276	123	3 507	5 326	4 565	64.2	16.8
Kimble	39	9.1	3	71	1	18	429	1	70	32	0	744	782	801	51.9	8.0
King	NA	NA	0	0	0	0	0	0	0	9	1	2 250	108	91	67.4	8.1
Kinney	16	6.7	1	37	0	0	0	0	0	20	2	770	557	567	40.1	7.4
Kleberg	223	6.4	28	91	1	98	318	1	194	2 268	197	6 875	6 494	6 653	58.8	18.1
Knox	15	2.6	0	0	1	20	408	2	131	42	7	793	1 076	1 062	45.7	9.5
Lamar	357	8.0	71	158	2	337	749	7	760	3 983	488	8 776	8 635	8 766	53.1	10.0
Lamb	75	4.3	8	53	1	40	263	3	152	415	55	2 578	3 702	4 324	46.5	10.1
Lampasas	53	4.0	9	63	1	22	154	2	160	408	18	2 795	2 637	2 682	56.9	13.2
La Salle	5	0.8	1	20	0	0	0	0	0	80	14	1 482	1 348	1 421	29.7	7.8
Lavaca	56	3.0	15	82	2	53	290	3	342	289	15	1 554	1 981	2 864	38.6	8.1
Lee	57	4.3	4	30	1	26	195	2	142	267	20	1 964	2 842	2 080	43.5	9.6
Leon	48	4.0	5	42	0	0	0	2	142	247	11	1 977	2 663	1 785	45.3	8.7
Liberty	390	7.2	27	51	2	127	242	4	460	2 312	159	4 267	11 801	10 638	50.1	8.1
Limestone	131	6.2	11	49	2	74	332	4	284	770	74	3 517	4 019	3 475	42.6	7.1
Lipscomb	28	6.8	1	32	0	0	0	0	0	56	3	1 600	758	785	64.2	16.2
Live Oak	61	6.4	1	11	0	0	0	1	74	130	3	1 383	2 055	1 937	47.4	10.3
Llano	26	2.2	7	56	1	25	200	3	313	281	12	2 249	1 310	1 311	56.1	12.9
Loving	NA	NA	0	0	0	0	0	0	0	3	1	3 000	NA	13	55.1	4.3
Lubbock	1 512	6.8	642	282	8	1 667	731	14	1 222	20 261	1 134	8 905	40 542	40 701	66.4	20.1
Lynn	33	4.2	4	60	1	24	358	1	46	208	19	2 930	1 533	2 320	42.6	10.0
McCulloch	69	7.7	5	55	1	27	297	3	237	375	26	4 263	1 685	1 739	45.0	11.0
McLennan	1 093	6.0	297	157	6	1 519	804	18	1 856	17 725	1 186	9 361	32 150	30 295	58.5	14.5
McMullen	8	8.9	0	0	0	0	0	0	0	14	0	1 556	155	156	51.6	15.4
Madison	45	3.8	6	52	1	52	452	2	106	510	75	4 360	1 998	2 634	48.7	11.7
Marion	63	6.1	6	64	0	0	0	1	60	357	40	3 644	1 519	2 061	48.4	6.5
Martin	21	3.9	2	40	1	26	520	1	65	86	8	1 687	1 090	1 078	47.7	6.7
Mason	17	4.7	1	31	0	0	0	1	60	27	3	794	607	670	50.5	14.5
Matagorda	298	7.5	32	83	2	141	365	3	235	2 738	193	6 762	8 947	8 087	53.6	10.9
Maverick	87	2.4	23	57	1	50	123	1	120	1 416	60	3 604	9 228	9 147	32.2	8.4
Medina	94	3.8	9	33	1	27	98	7	352	909	102	3 393	6 295	5 569	45.4	7.5
Menard	5	2.1	2	83	0	0	0	1	40	22	2	917	426	494	44.5	12.6
Midland	654	6.2	141	132	4	380	356	5	474	6 806	553	6 321	20 480	16 078	72.5	24.3
Milam	114	4.9	23	105	2	75	341	4	246	653	27	2 768	4 556	4 620	45.4	7.7
Mills	20	4.3	3	68	1	21	477	2	174	25	2	556	828	701	45.3	11.5
Mitchell	25	2.7	4	47	1	33	388	3	224	296	19	3 365	1 838	1 907	47.1	8.1
Montague	105	5.7	11	63	2	84	483	5	512	480	23	2 653	3 247	3 073	46.2	7.5

1. Per 1,000 resident population estimated as of July 1 of the year shown. 2. As of end of year. 3. Per 100,000 resident population as of July 1 of the year shown. 4. Preliminary. Covers nursing homes with 3 or more beds. 5. Data for serious crimes have not been adjusted for underreporting, this may affect comparability between geographic areas or over time. 6. Includes murder and nonnegligent manslaughter, forcible rape, robbery, and aggravated assault. 7. The 1986–1987 data are based on administrative reports obtained by the U.S. National Center for Education Statistics. The 1980 data are based on the 1980 Census of Population and Housing. 8. Persons 25 years old or older.

STATE County	Education (cont'd): Local government expenditures for education,[1] 1982: Total (Mil dol)	Education (cont'd): Local government expenditures for education,[1] 1982: Per capita (Dollars)	Social Security Program December 1988: Beneficiaries: Total	Social Security Program December 1988: Beneficiaries: Rate[2]	Social Security Program December 1988: Payments ($1,000)	Supplemental Security Income Program recipients June 1986	Money income: Per capita[3]: 1987 Income, (Dollars)	Money income: Per capita[3]: 1979: Current dollars	Money income: Per capita[3]: 1979: Constant 1987 dollars	Money income: Median household income 1979 (Dollars)	Money income: Percent below poverty level, 1979: Persons	Money income: Percent below poverty level, 1979: Families	Housing units, 1990: Total	Housing units, 1990: Percent change, 1980–1990
	60	61	62	63	64	65	66	67	68	69	70	71	72	73
TEXAS—Con.														
Haskell	2.9	386	2 000	298.5	874	198	8 649	6 427	10 056	11 841	20.9	14.5	3 843	5.0
Hays	17.0	386	6 230	97.3	2 753	848	8 535	5 438	8 509	12 969	22.2	13.1	25 247	74.5
Hemphill	3.9	610	555	135.4	286	12	9 663	7 808	12 217	19 202	7.5	6.0	1 712	-15.4
Henderson	14.6	320	9 425	170.1	4 278	1 056	9 310	6 371	9 969	13 573	13.0	10.3	31 779	35.8
Hidalgo	171.4	542	46 335	119.5	16 465	13 154	5 622	4 040	6 321	11 232	35.2	29.0	128 241	44.0
Hill	9.4	363	6 500	238.1	2 803	752	9 008	5 833	9 127	11 368	16.1	12.5	12 899	8.0
Hockley	15.9	656	3 185	132.7	1 483	362	8 281	5 825	9 114	15 604	19.9	15.6	9 279	10.3
Hood	5.4	271	5 170	167.3	2 477	224	12 422	8 112	12 693	18 105	8.9	5.8	14 958	67.7
Hopkins	9.2	348	5 585	191.3	2 399	708	9 544	6 210	9 717	12 813	14.5	11.6	12 676	18.3
Houston	8.6	365	5 170	225.8	2 151	960	7 179	4 780	7 479	9 868	25.0	20.6	10 265	10.9
Howard	21.4	584	5 965	175.4	2 743	680	9 605	6 876	10 759	15 023	15.4	12.4	13 651	-1.6
Hudspeth	1.9	641	265	106.0	98	24	6 721	4 480	7 010	10 514	30.9	25.7	1 288	12.5
Hunt	25.9	437	11 380	170.1	5 127	1 274	9 518	6 133	9 596	13 877	16.0	11.8	28 959	20.2
Hutchinson	13.8	472	4 890	194.8	2 601	228	9 891	7 735	12 103	18 893	7.3	5.4	11 419	4.8
Irion	1.5	966	270	142.1	124	12	9 263	7 015	10 976	15 194	12.2	11.5	842	19.9
Jack	3.8	483	1 540	216.9	717	90	9 563	6 645	10 397	13 617	11.7	9.4	3 497	3.7
Jackson	7.4	543	2 510	197.6	1 116	298	8 547	6 226	9 742	14 608	15.4	12.9	5 841	8.5
Jasper	13.9	444	6 410	204.1	2 901	930	8 228	5 913	9 252	14 290	15.7	12.7	13 824	7.3
Jeff Davis	0.9	561	375	208.3	158	48	8 641	5 675	8 880	10 511	24.9	19.6	1 348	40.0
Jefferson	129.0	500	43 270	180.4	22 080	4 428	10 467	7 604	11 898	18 416	13.4	10.3	101 289	3.6
Jim Hogg	4.1	738	885	170.2	303	318	6 581	4 772	7 467	11 535	22.4	21.8	2 103	19.1
Jim Wells	18.6	487	6 000	156.2	2 505	1 530	6 948	5 601	8 764	14 460	20.9	17.7	13 948	14.7
Johnson	31.2	425	12 210	125.2	5 609	1 036	10 319	6 979	10 920	18 252	8.1	6.1	37 029	49.4
Jones	7.4	420	3 560	210.7	1 573	450	8 543	6 264	9 801	12 616	16.4	12.3	7 639	2.4
Karnes	7.5	544	2 835	223.2	1 053	714	7 375	5 343	8 360	12 262	23.7	19.0	5 117	-3.1
Kaufman	20.6	487	11 070	198.4	5 189	974	9 636	6 510	10 186	15 585	14.6	11.0	20 097	40.6
Kendall	4.5	384	2 855	184.2	1 269	104	11 238	7 133	11 161	16 311	13.1	10.4	6 137	30.3
Kenedy	0.3	556	60	120.0	26	6	9 883	10 078	15 769	11 339	34.9	29.5	213	3.9
Kent	1.3	1 063	220	200.0	97	12	9 521	6 155	9 631	12 057	18.7	17.2	603	9.8
Kerr	12.6	419	9 485	267.2	4 456	342	11 043	7 336	11 479	14 694	12.3	8.0	17 161	30.6
Kimble	1.4	338	920	219.0	400	100	8 272	5 535	8 661	12 317	15.8	12.5	2 593	7.4
King	0.8	2 028	25	62.5	10	0	8 102	5 511	8 623	12 566	16.1	12.7	191	-11.2
Kinney	1.3	570	665	255.8	262	94	6 757	4 146	6 487	10 192	35.3	29.0	1 821	65.4
Kleberg	19.0	550	3 630	114.5	1 509	644	8 060	5 577	8 726	13 666	22.0	16.7	12 008	7.1
Knox	3.3	588	1 300	254.9	556	162	8 821	6 832	10 690	11 434	22.9	17.7	2 459	0.9
Lamar	15.1	351	9 330	207.3	3 919	1 752	8 575	5 577	8 726	11 974	19.6	15.1	18 964	7.6
Lamb	11.6	626	3 245	208.0	1 379	434	8 598	5 768	9 025	12 513	22.6	15.9	6 531	-6.6
Lampasas	4.1	324	2 700	190.1	1 090	252	8 724	5 731	8 967	12 235	16.7	13.4	6 193	21.6
La Salle	3.4	569	895	175.5	317	304	6 174	4 241	6 636	8 855	40.5	35.5	2 244	3.3
Lavaca	4.6	252	5 850	317.9	2 260	772	8 755	5 641	8 826	11 863	16.2	13.0	9 549	9.2
Lee	7.8	572	2 090	156.0	842	258	8 315	5 828	9 119	12 424	17.6	14.3	5 773	32.0
Leon	6.8	642	3 565	292.2	1 524	566	8 093	5 725	8 958	9 925	24.4	20.3	7 019	43.6
Liberty	25.7	500	9 060	171.3	4 224	1 086	8 601	6 677	10 448	16 801	13.6	10.7	22 243	12.3
Limestone	6.1	300	5 050	228.5	2 124	1 114	7 662	5 183	8 110	9 991	23.1	17.3	9 922	11.4
Lipscomb	4.6	1 070	665	201.5	297	18	9 956	7 017	10 979	15 309	12.5	10.9	1 683	8.0
Live Oak	4.9	496	1 420	157.8	600	204	8 830	6 661	10 422	15 674	15.9	13.2	5 519	12.7
Llano	2.1	198	4 330	346.4	2 020	188	11 626	7 550	11 813	12 345	11.6	8.5	9 773	29.1
Loving	0.0	0	10	100.0	11	0	23 500	21 673	33 912	17 625	0.0	0.0	59	18.0
Lubbock	90.3	416	27 795	122.6	13 095	3 206	10 172	6 926	10 837	15 704	14.3	9.9	91 770	14.0
Lynn	4.5	542	1 255	179.3	577	182	7 523	4 938	7 726	11 761	25.8	20.8	2 978	-6.1
McCulloch	3.2	358	2 330	256.0	986	308	8 463	5 414	8 471	9 881	20.8	16.5	4 424	8.7
McLennan	58.7	333	31 655	168.4	14 116	3 760	9 260	6 236	9 757	13 588	17.2	11.4	78 857	19.6
McMullen	0.8	968	125	125.0	49	14	11 682	8 116	12 699	16 667	9.3	5.6	565	10.8
Madison	3.4	296	1 945	167.7	869	272	7 314	5 010	7 839	10 973	21.8	16.7	4 326	10.9
Marion	3.5	329	2 030	213.7	838	424	7 418	4 917	7 694	10 638	27.1	21.9	5 729	1.7
Martin	4.2	790	650	127.5	280	82	9 463	6 930	10 843	16 266	16.0	12.4	2 039	11.1
Mason	1.9	540	1 050	318.2	444	96	8 401	5 869	9 183	11 543	20.5	13.0	2 356	17.2
Matagorda	21.7	581	5 290	135.6	2 477	652	10 503	7 142	11 175	19 082	12.5	9.8	18 540	14.4
Maverick	15.5	451	4 660	117.7	1 393	1 784	4 269	3 100	4 851	9 698	39.5	34.4	11 143	28.5
Medina	10.3	436	3 950	146.3	1 528	710	7 900	5 138	8 039	12 804	22.1	17.6	10 860	23.9
Menard	1.5	650	725	315.2	289	98	6 924	4 865	7 612	9 693	28.3	22.3	1 562	10.9
Midland	42.5	433	11 365	105.9	5 891	860	13 680	10 060	15 741	21 055	8.6	6.2	45 181	44.1
Milam	9.0	391	4 930	219.1	2 078	766	8 062	5 503	8 611	11 737	22.0	17.0	10 511	12.0
Mills	1.9	430	1 325	301.1	541	192	8 000	5 233	8 188	10 660	19.7	14.0	2 582	13.4
Mitchell	4.9	512	2 115	245.9	942	260	8 576	6 060	9 482	11 759	21.4	16.2	4 559	4.7
Montague	8.2	443	4 725	266.9	2 085	378	8 416	6 006	9 398	12 013	13.0	10.4	9 262	8.5

1. Elementary and secondary. 2. Per 1,000 resident population estimated as of July 1 of the year shown. 3. Based on the resident population estimated as of July 1, 1988 for 1987 data and enumerated as of April 1, 1980 for 1979 data.

STATE County	Housing units, 1990 (cont'd): Occupied units: Total	Owner occupied: Percent	Owner occupied: Median value (Dollars)	Median rent (Dollars)	Civilian labor force, 1990: Total	Percent change, 1989–1990	Unemployment: Total	Unemployment: Rate[1]	Private nonfarm establishments, 1988: Number	Net change, 1987–1988	Employment[2]: Total	Percent change, 1987–1988	Manufacturing	Retail trade
	74	75	76	77	78	79	80	81	82	83	84	85	86	87
TEXAS—Con.														
Haskell	2 753	76.2	28 200	152	3 350	-4.8	117	3.5	178	-7	1 101	6.8	33	327
Hays	22 218	58.2	81 300	337	32 116	0.0	1 467	4.6	1 116	-66	11 055	-1.5	1 352	3 977
Hemphill	1 348	73.5	47 500	241	1 797	-4.7	72	4.0	161	-1	973	-4.9	0	251
Henderson	22 947	79.1	53 600	245	26 461	-0.7	2 361	8.9	898	-24	8 702	2.9	2 329	2 300
Hidalgo	103 479	70.3	35 900	221	164 362	2.7	31 324	19.1	5 757	228	67 775	3.6	10 031	20 734
Hill	10 268	74.3	37 200	205	10 832	0.3	669	6.2	560	-26	4 622	-9.7	988	1 259
Hockley	7 988	72.6	41 900	233	10 477	-2.3	499	4.8	525	0	5 142	11.5	194	1 241
Hood	11 137	79.1	73 800	333	15 593	2.8	1 286	8.2	608	-25	4 038	-0.1	180	1 617
Hopkins	10 965	70.8	43 600	247	13 955	-2.0	830	5.9	642	-11	6 856	5.9	1 678	1 777
Houston	7 792	74.4	40 000	168	7 979	-2.7	411	5.2	406	-23	3 398	-9.1	932	809
Howard	11 477	70.7	34 900	250	14 396	0.6	716	5.0	836	-20	7 413	-2.3	1 071	2 059
Hudspeth	946	68.8	23 100	179	1 237	5.0	43	3.5	44	-1	215	18.8	0	135
Hunt	24 075	70.0	47 300	288	35 795	1.8	2 171	6.1	1 207	-42	17 877	0.1	8 536	3 590
Hutchinson	9 642	77.5	38 200	239	12 356	-2.9	533	4.3	635	-25	6 987	2.6	1 970	1 395
Irion	601	74.0	44 600	199	818	2.4	25	3.1	32	-4	263	-3.7	0	27
Jack	2 725	76.9	33 800	170	3 064	2.5	138	4.5	178	-22	953	-15.7	18	268
Jackson	4 833	75.2	42 000	197	5 482	-2.1	200	3.6	296	-12	2 037	-5.4	29	579
Jasper	11 427	79.1	40 300	200	14 284	-4.7	1 145	8.0	626	8	5 674	-7.7	1 226	1 545
Jeff Davis	779	67.1	43 800	213	894	-1.9	31	3.5	41	-1	195	-3.9	0	57
Jefferson	90 520	66.0	41 800	268	110 326	1.2	7 740	7.0	5 806	-107	93 628	0.9	18 527	19 821
Jim Hogg	1 675	78.1	28 300	173	2 528	-3.7	220	8.7	105	-8	535	0.0	0	263
Jim Wells	11 979	74.3	33 700	201	16 406	4.0	1 091	6.7	798	-39	7 401	-1.3	101	2 005
Johnson	33 462	76.2	61 100	311	51 264	1.8	2 630	5.1	1 630	-77	16 992	5.1	3 574	4 698
Jones	6 180	78.1	29 600	176	5 727	-4.0	338	5.9	339	-8	3 268	-0.1	74	544
Karnes	4 337	74.5	29 600	154	4 329	-4.6	204	4.7	311	-22	2 436	-3.4	367	547
Kaufman	17 827	76.3	56 600	282	27 616	-1.4	1 358	4.9	1 033	-42	9 043	4.5	2 653	2 324
Kendall	5 342	74.5	79 000	340	7 248	1.1	195	2.7	455	3	2 981	-5.4	231	923
Kenedy	145	20.0	22 500	135	357	-1.4	6	1.7	5	-1	10	11.1	0	0
Kent	399	74.4	28 100	143	540	-4.6	10	1.9	12	0	42	-10.6	0	0
Kerr	14 384	69.5	67 300	294	16 891	2.0	519	3.1	1 001	-61	8 545	-0.5	885	2 633
Kimble	1 624	73.8	38 900	191	2 210	-2.3	54	2.4	131	0	818	-2.7	131	314
King	124	35.5	17 500	150	339	3.0	5	1.5	3	-1	19	-9.5	0	0
Kinney	1 187	68.6	32 400	173	1 039	1.1	58	5.6	36	3	245	-25.1	0	52
Kleberg	10 058	59.7	40 800	273	15 061	3.7	937	6.2	619	-29	6 899	8.4	272	2 155
Knox	1 887	76.0	27 600	133	2 374	0.7	75	3.2	123	2	659	0.0	0	154
Lamar	16 798	68.9	39 000	253	21 650	-1.5	1 436	6.6	1 034	-17	13 278	-6.5	4 715	2 853
Lamb	5 488	73.5	28 900	185	6 277	-4.8	314	5.0	337	-21	2 675	28.0	0	773
Lampasas	5 058	72.7	49 600	227	6 221	1.7	374	6.0	289	-6	2 296	2.1	404	569
La Salle	1 701	67.7	18 300	149	1 950	-3.9	146	7.5	85	-2	448	-4.3	0	209
Lavaca	7 349	78.7	40 700	166	8 080	-2.8	164	2.0	512	-2	4 553	-4.1	1 234	1 113
Lee	4 706	77.5	47 800	241	4 832	-1.8	229	4.7	358	-22	3 094	0.3	510	731
Leon	5 006	81.1	43 500	223	5 817	-3.7	312	5.4	254	-5	2 413	-10.9	0	511
Liberty	18 538	75.5	42 100	245	22 311	1.2	1 543	6.9	936	-59	9 080	2.4	1 377	2 598
Limestone	7 722	73.1	36 900	209	9 350	-0.8	433	4.6	381	-10	3 048	-1.7	437	1 017
Lipscomb	1 230	77.2	35 500	198	1 541	0.7	48	3.1	96	-3	412	6.5	0	100
Live Oak	3 550	79.9	42 000	202	4 326	0.0	185	4.3	218	-8	1 407	-12.7	0	443
Llano	5 278	79.3	66 700	237	4 745	0.2	140	3.0	299	-27	1 817	-6.9	40	479
Loving	42	73.8	14 999	175	67	-2.9	0	0.0	3	0	0	0.0	0	0
Lubbock	81 534	58.2	54 500	311	115 267	1.3	5 485	4.8	5 835	-80	72 150	1.8	7 373	20 834
Lynn	2 383	71.0	31 900	161	2 550	5.7	113	4.4	126	10	649	5.4	0	119
McCulloch	3 409	71.8	33 900	186	3 706	-11.6	378	10.2	235	7	2 376	12.7	0	549
McLennan	70 208	58.9	50 300	282	92 420	-0.6	5 357	5.8	4 507	-69	66 628	-1.2	13 832	13 868
McMullen	319	75.9	40 000	150	530	3.5	3	0.6	18	-1	83	0.0	0	19
Madison	3 349	75.5	41 900	225	4 813	-2.1	176	3.7	189	-6	1 292	-0.8	25	566
Marion	4 048	81.0	34 500	176	4 914	-2.3	291	5.9	177	-2	1 154	2.7	355	318
Martin	1 632	72.4	40 500	183	2 392	1.5	35	1.5	92	6	579	9.9	0	161
Mason	1 435	77.4	35 200	134	1 681	-0.4	46	2.7	100	-11	606	-17.3	0	334
Matagorda	13 164	65.0	53 000	269	16 062	-13.9	1 676	10.4	817	11	7 581	2.3	0	2 180
Maverick	9 756	67.0	36 200	176	13 952	-2.9	3 735	26.8	494	-9	4 018	2.9	1 028	1 534
Medina	9 109	78.3	45 300	221	10 762	-3.7	625	5.8	474	-2	3 967	-1.2	491	1 208
Menard	937	73.6	25 700	163	921	-1.5	44	4.8	44	-8	167	-16.5	0	61
Midland	38 920	65.9	62 300	283	47 885	-3.6	2 611	5.5	3 505	40	38 296	0.2	2 905	7 915
Milam	8 686	72.2	40 000	190	8 829	-4.7	537	6.1	450	1	4 810	-3.9	0	891
Mills	1 782	79.3	34 100	136	2 041	-2.6	66	3.2	102	5	707	13.8	113	168
Mitchell	3 054	76.1	25 700	169	3 618	-5.5	242	6.7	194	-20	1 314	-7.9	0	396
Montague	6 858	78.1	35 000	181	6 591	-3.5	339	5.1	440	-7	3 076	-7.1	918	736

1. Percent of total civilian labor force. 2. For week including March 12. Excludes government employees, self-employed persons, farm workers, domestic service workers, railroad employees subject to the Railroad Retirement Act, and employees on oceanborne vessels or in foreign countries.

STATE County	Private nonfarm establishments, 1988 (cont'd): Employment[1] (cont'd): Finance, insurance, and real estate	Private nonfarm establishments, 1988 (cont'd): Employment[1] (cont'd): Services	Private nonfarm establishments, 1988 (cont'd): Annual payroll: Total (Mil dol)	Private nonfarm establishments, 1988 (cont'd): Annual payroll: Average per employee (Dollars)	Personal income, 1989: Total (Mil dol)	Personal income, 1989: Percent change, 1988–1989	Personal income, 1989: Wages and salaries[2] (Mil dol)	Personal income, 1989: Proprietor's income (Mil dol)	Personal income, 1989: Dividends, interest, & rent (Mil dol)	Personal income, 1989: Transfer payments (Mil dol)	Personal income, 1989: Per capita[3]: Dollars	Personal income, 1989: Per capita[3]: Rank	Earnings, 1989: Total (Mil dol)	Earnings, 1989: Percent by selected industries: Farm	Earnings, 1989: Percent by selected industries: Goods-related[4]: Total
	88	89	90	91	92	93	94	95	96	97	98	99	100	101	102
TEXAS—Con.															
Haskell	77	221	14	12 644	107	4.0	29	34	25	22	16 289	573	62	39.5	6.7
Hays	851	3 150	148	13 395	810	8.8	308	62	123	117	12 174	2 248	370	1.7	22.0
Hemphill	68	256	14	14 683	69	2.6	27	14	24	7	18 212	270	42	14.3	20.8
Henderson	593	1 847	129	14 771	708	7.2	207	85	150	128	12 519	2 106	292	6.0	28.1
Hidalgo	3 645	14 856	847	12 491	3 118	10.0	1 730	310	507	722	7 814	3 081	2 040	2.2	16.3
Hill	237	1 012	65	14 069	358	6.1	99	54	80	87	13 130	1 848	153	13.8	23.0
Hockley	193	1 617	72	14 084	293	1.1	156	44	52	51	12 385	2 166	200	7.8	32.5
Hood	238	1 283	53	13 138	523	10.2	105	40	100	71	15 894	682	145	2.2	15.2
Hopkins	348	1 108	118	17 152	413	7.3	182	88	84	69	14 094	1 392	270	15.3	23.8
Houston	187	794	47	13 699	314	6.5	176	32	60	68	13 699	1 580	208	4.1	19.5
Howard	423	1 652	120	16 164	474	4.6	240	69	94	89	14 213	1 332	309	3.8	28.2
Hudspeth	0	9	2	9 405	33	-5.9	13	12	4	5	13 029	1 896	25	46.9	NA
Hunt	783	2 748	358	20 034	953	5.7	543	78	147	158	14 150	1 370	621	1.3	51.0
Hutchinson	310	1 363	147	21 034	421	-0.2	275	49	79	58	17 400	377	323	4.0	61.7
Irion	0	0	5	20 844	31	9.9	11	7	6	3	16 935	449	18	31.7	29.4
Jack	80	196	13	13 358	93	7.7	31	18	24	19	13 510	1 677	49	8.3	24.3
Jackson	112	370	30	14 952	193	2.9	62	34	47	33	15 569	782	96	21.3	22.1
Jasper	452	1 546	78	13 742	397	4.4	181	53	69	90	12 772	2 007	234	3.3	44.3
Jeff Davis	0	87	2	10 313	24	8.5	9	3	8	5	12 932	1 936	12	11.3	6.1
Jefferson	4 036	26 029	1 959	20 921	3 854	6.1	2 702	339	753	648	16 375	554	3 041	0.3	35.8
Jim Hogg	57	70	5	9 774	60	11.0	20	8	16	13	11 682	2 446	28	16.0	12.7
Jim Wells	453	2 502	101	13 708	397	6.0	182	53	67	95	10 496	2 791	235	5.8	26.8
Johnson	727	5 082	248	14 614	1 437	7.2	416	137	197	193	14 215	1 330	553	3.1	26.5
Jones	119	1 693	38	11 482	225	3.9	68	38	46	51	13 593	1 636	106	15.2	19.0
Karnes	158	518	34	13 932	147	8.1	58	21	33	37	11 796	2 405	79	10.2	29.4
Kaufman	491	2 197	138	15 236	801	7.1	246	72	124	141	13 779	1 544	317	2.0	26.2
Kendall	256	897	37	12 391	297	7.5	51	36	82	46	18 504	250	88	4.3	22.8
Kenedy	0	0	0	4 700	10	1.9	5	2	4	1	20 548	143	7	14.9	49.6
Kent	0	0	1	16 095	15	2.5	5	2	4	3	13 723	1 571	8	27.5	NA
Kerr	574	3 077	119	13 941	628	8.8	211	74	244	125	17 550	364	285	1.5	19.8
Kimble	42	176	9	11 413	65	9.1	19	15	19	12	15 704	739	34	20.8	15.3
King	0	0	0	14 211	7	14.9	5	3	1	0	18 091	283	8	32.7	NA
Kinney	16	84	3	12 845	34	9.1	11	7	8	9	12 849	1 980	18	34.6	4.8
Kleberg	295	1 503	103	14 938	400	5.7	202	40	66	80	12 969	1 920	242	8.0	17.0
Knox	47	221	9	13 915	64	4.8	22	9	16	17	12 995	1 907	31	13.3	17.3
Lamar	471	3 258	230	17 308	624	6.5	350	76	114	127	13 858	1 500	426	2.4	43.5
Lamb	154	433	40	15 008	253	-4.1	79	85	45	43	16 625	498	164	40.2	11.0
Lampasas	127	561	30	13 130	182	8.2	44	17	46	45	12 710	2 032	61	5.4	29.1
La Salle	44	119	5	10 141	46	7.4	14	10	8	14	9 427	2 970	24	29.7	6.1
Lavaca	282	1 068	56	12 290	284	8.5	78	49	84	62	15 470	812	128	15.9	31.7
Lee	221	457	47	15 173	179	6.0	78	29	45	28	13 475	1 700	106	4.6	33.5
Leon	77	243	57	23 800	179	7.1	66	27	47	42	14 876	1 037	93	14.2	42.1
Liberty	457	2 215	130	14 294	689	7.8	234	84	96	131	13 124	1 850	318	3.0	28.1
Limestone	194	550	40	13 077	263	7.7	136	31	52	63	11 792	2 406	167	6.4	NA
Lipscomb	42	55	6	13 971	53	-0.1	14	13	19	7	17 227	407	26	31.7	NA
Live Oak	71	199	23	16 501	127	7.4	49	18	28	20	14 244	1 304	67	15.0	35.0
Llano	217	613	23	12 919	212	9.8	49	27	80	51	16 911	453	76	8.9	16.8
Loving	0	0	D	D	3	8.9	NA	1	2	0	37 122	2	1	33.2	NA
Lubbock	5 244	21 492	1 241	17 204	3 240	6.6	2 008	388	551	466	14 208	1 340	2 396	1.3	14.6
Lynn	58	158	11	17 146	93	-9.2	28	27	19	17	13 849	1 508	54	37.1	2.3
McCulloch	107	378	33	13 809	120	-0.3	40	16	37	30	13 107	1 860	57	9.9	NA
McLennan	5 192	22 258	1 054	15 812	2 697	7.1	1 574	257	551	463	14 276	1 297	1 831	1.2	26.8
McMullen	0	7	2	20 120	20	13.5	9	6	5	2	21 408	114	16	29.9	31.5
Madison	126	225	17	13 144	147	9.5	59	32	36	27	12 870	1 969	91	30.8	6.5
Marion	51	261	15	13 081	109	10.3	32	12	21	28	11 662	2 457	44	2.5	NA
Martin	45	125	10	17 041	75	-5.0	36	19	15	9	15 173	915	54	32.3	NA
Mason	47	83	6	9 117	51	10.2	12	15	14	12	15 933	664	26	38.4	6.7
Matagorda	436	1 582	170	22 363	591	-2.0	401	62	90	81	15 320	867	463	4.7	37.5
Maverick	261	621	42	10 504	250	7.7	126	33	26	72	6 155	3 104	159	15.3	14.8
Medina	200	1 026	47	11 952	335	6.6	90	36	64	69	12 121	2 277	126	12.7	18.1
Menard	29	16	2	12 575	35	6.5	7	11	9	8	14 749	1 108	17	41.7	NA
Midland	2 690	9 090	852	22 259	1 898	4.7	1 218	200	467	170	17 765	323	1 418	0.2	36.5
Milam	192	704	115	23 973	306	4.5	169	35	65	63	13 882	1 490	204	7.7	46.4
Mills	57	183	9	13 378	72	9.9	17	19	19	15	16 398	545	36	26.6	17.3
Mitchell	100	270	18	13 436	109	0.9	38	18	28	26	12 795	2 001	56	8.9	17.2
Montague	182	549	37	12 149	228	8.0	69	36	65	54	13 063	1 883	105	7.2	28.6

1. For week including March 12. Excludes government employees, self-employed persons, farm workers, domestic service workers, railroad employees subject to the Railroad Retirement Act, and employees on oceanborne vessels or in foreign countries. 2. Includes other labor income. 3. Based on the resident population estimated as of July 1 of the year shown. 4. Covers mining, construction, and manufacturing.

STATE County	Earnings, 1989 (cont'd)						Agriculture, 1987									
	Percent by selected industries (cont'd)						Farms			Farm operators, percent		Land in farms				
	Goods-related[1]	Service-related & other[2]						Percent with						Acres		
	Manufacturing	Total	Retail trade	Finance, insurance, & real estate	Services	Government	Number	Less than 50 acres	500 acres and over	Whose principal occupation is farming	Residing on farm operated	Acreage (1,000)	Percent change, 1982–1987	Average size of farm	Total irrigated (1,000)	Total cropland (1,000)
	103	104	105	106	107	108	109	110	111	112	113	114	115	116	117	118
TEXAS—Con.																
Haskell	0.6	40.3	9.8	3.2	12.9	13.5	619	9.4	48.0	72.4	38.3	454	0.1	733	14	298
Hays	13.4	45.4	13.5	3.6	21.7	30.9	701	30.1	19.1	36.5	64.6	297	41.2	424	1	48
Hemphill	1.2	49.0	8.6	5.8	18.0	16.0	228	11.0	61.8	70.2	56.6	615	-0.4	2 699	3	69
Henderson	15.0	51.2	12.7	3.9	24.1	14.7	1 577	33.5	7.5	34.7	61.2	333	2.9	211	1	132
Hidalgo	10.1	55.3	15.0	4.4	22.1	26.2	1 929	57.1	15.5	46.3	48.6	762	-8.5	395	231	448
Hill	15.3	45.2	11.9	3.7	21.0	18.0	1 501	25.5	17.3	43.6	56.4	442	-4.8	294	0	296
Hockley	1.9	42.4	8.0	3.3	16.0	17.2	563	12.6	57.5	76.4	52.8	505	-4.0	896	75	383
Hood	1.9	65.8	19.3	5.4	30.0	16.8	638	32.6	14.1	33.9	64.7	213	-10.7	333	D	58
Hopkins	11.9	49.5	10.8	3.2	15.8	11.4	1 766	20.8	9.2	54.8	64.3	374	5.2	212	0	200
Houston	12.9	55.9	7.8	6.2	21.6	20.5	1 421	23.7	12.3	41.8	49.9	422	-6.4	297	0	151
Howard	11.8	44.3	9.2	3.5	18.9	23.6	385	20.3	47.8	64.2	49.9	483	4.9	1 255	2	181
Hudspeth	NA	NA	3.6	NA	3.0	26.3	148	6.8	66.9	70.3	52.7	2 267	6.1	15 317	31	51
Hunt	47.0	32.9	8.3	2.6	12.6	14.8	1 939	36.5	7.0	31.0	59.6	348	-3.4	180	1	204
Hutchinson	34.7	24.8	5.8	1.4	9.9	9.5	173	14.5	62.4	61.8	51.4	445	-5.7	2 571	31	103
Irion	1.5	NA	6.2	NA	7.1	13.0	137	23.4	56.9	53.3	46.0	609	-23.1	4 449	1	11
Jack	1.2	49.5	9.7	4.3	13.9	17.9	653	10.6	31.5	40.4	47.2	519	2.1	795	0	56
Jackson	0.6	39.2	8.9	3.2	13.5	17.5	783	21.5	29.4	54.4	51.1	457	3.1	584	27	207
Jasper	35.7	38.2	10.0	2.9	16.5	14.2	602	54.2	4.2	33.1	74.3	102	34.0	169	0	26
Jeff Davis	0.0	NA	11.3	2.7	19.8	41.2	90	10.0	71.1	68.9	44.4	1 532	-5.5	17 023	0	1
Jefferson	26.7	52.3	9.2	3.5	25.6	11.5	532	40.4	24.2	44.7	53.9	312	-15.3	586	30	118
Jim Hogg	0.0	40.0	13.8	3.2	10.6	31.3	202	10.9	52.5	46.0	25.2	786	-7.4	3 891	D	18
Jim Wells	2.3	50.6	11.9	3.8	22.5	16.8	771	23.3	26.6	40.5	45.4	502	8.8	651	3	193
Johnson	18.1	57.0	13.1	3.4	24.1	13.4	1 867	47.5	6.7	32.5	71.8	312	-3.1	167	1	162
Jones	9.4	47.5	9.2	3.2	20.0	18.3	896	16.0	29.9	48.1	49.8	488	-8.6	545	7	306
Karnes	13.9	42.5	8.2	6.4	13.5	17.9	1 115	12.8	18.5	41.3	45.5	403	-4.2	362	1	162
Kaufman	18.2	48.4	14.2	3.5	21.9	23.5	1 704	41.0	8.3	29.2	66.4	361	-7.8	212	0	173
Kendall	4.9	57.1	14.6	5.7	30.9	15.9	659	18.8	28.5	41.4	64.5	351	1.1	533	0	50
Kenedy	0.0	NA	2.5	NA	7.4	11.0	24	12.5	66.7	62.5	45.8	622	9.2	25 912	D	3
Kent	NA	NA	4.9	3.7	6.4	35.4	179	8.4	58.7	64.8	47.5	554	-4.5	3 097	1	71
Kerr	9.0	54.8	12.0	6.6	30.4	24.0	584	17.3	33.0	40.4	56.5	539	-8.5	924	1	44
Kimble	11.2	47.1	13.7	3.9	17.6	16.7	442	8.1	58.4	52.0	50.7	781	8.5	1 767	2	26
King	0.0	NA	2.5	0.0	3.5	20.5	50	8.0	66.0	76.0	32.0	410	-2.0	8 194	D	D
Kinney	0.4	NA	3.8	5.3	10.9	26.6	110	2.7	79.1	59.1	39.1	654	-7.2	5 941	2	10
Kleberg	5.6	37.0	10.5	2.7	17.1	38.0	274	40.1	18.2	32.5	57.7	938	2.1	3 424	1	81
Knox	0.5	45.8	8.1	3.6	17.3	23.7	351	11.1	47.6	65.2	40.7	534	12.0	1 522	20	198
Lamar	37.9	42.0	10.4	2.5	21.0	12.1	1 488	25.8	13.3	37.0	60.9	407	4.7	273	1	222
Lamb	7.8	37.5	6.2	2.3	11.5	11.4	791	8.0	47.9	75.9	42.6	496	-11.1	627	178	402
Lampasas	14.3	46.0	13.5	4.9	19.3	19.5	615	15.3	33.2	49.6	59.3	405	-6.1	658	0	66
La Salle	0.0	33.4	8.9	3.5	12.4	30.8	265	6.0	57.0	53.6	28.3	767	-5.1	2 894	2	49
Lavaca	21.1	41.4	10.2	3.3	18.6	11.0	2 514	26.5	7.5	41.1	51.9	508	3.3	202	6	188
Lee	10.0	44.5	9.4	3.4	16.2	17.4	1 583	24.1	8.5	39.5	52.2	325	11.2	205	1	108
Leon	25.1	31.5	9.6	3.9	11.1	12.2	1 619	23.8	14.6	37.4	49.7	499	12.9	308	0	144
Liberty	15.5	52.6	11.3	4.0	23.5	16.3	955	44.1	13.5	31.7	68.4	363	-3.0	380	21	184
Limestone	7.6	NA	8.0	2.5	11.8	30.9	1 200	14.9	15.2	38.9	45.0	460	-0.1	383	0	173
Lipscomb	NA	NA	6.8	5.3	7.9	21.7	314	8.3	66.9	62.4	48.1	558	3.4	1 778	10	186
Live Oak	16.5	34.2	9.2	4.4	10.1	15.8	803	16.3	27.5	44.8	48.3	517	-0.7	644	3	143
Llano	1.7	57.8	10.6	9.5	24.8	16.6	530	11.1	45.3	49.1	50.8	534	0.3	1 008	1	37
Loving	0.0	NA	NA	NA	18.1	22.5	17	5.9	70.6	47.1	52.9	416	18.6	24 444	0	0
Lubbock	8.2	61.3	13.5	6.1	26.4	22.8	969	29.1	35.5	61.1	49.4	465	-15.6	480	124	411
Lynn	0.6	44.5	4.0	3.6	10.1	16.1	503	7.0	62.8	83.3	46.5	474	-8.5	943	31	389
McCulloch	12.6	NA	12.7	3.0	18.0	18.4	489	11.0	47.0	50.3	50.3	636	-6.3	1 301	1	108
McLennan	20.2	55.7	11.1	6.6	25.5	16.3	1 977	36.5	10.8	36.8	62.9	445	0.4	225	1	269
McMullen	0.0	26.7	3.0	2.3	6.6	11.9	211	4.3	67.3	56.9	47.4	543	2.3	2 575	D	31
Madison	0.4	30.4	8.4	3.0	11.3	32.3	756	23.0	12.2	38.0	52.5	223	13.4	294	0	72
Marion	20.5	47.7	12.0	3.5	19.8	18.5	207	20.8	11.6	38.6	65.7	50	1.2	240	D	18
Martin	NA	NA	5.0	1.9	6.7	13.7	366	7.7	64.8	79.5	54.1	504	-10.8	1 376	6	264
Mason	2.3	40.3	11.4	5.2	11.7	14.6	567	9.3	48.3	51.1	47.1	548	-2.1	967	5	50
Matagorda	8.1	NA	6.8	2.2	NA	10.9	721	23.2	32.5	57.8	44.1	579	1.1	803	35	222
Maverick	12.2	38.7	13.3	2.9	11.9	31.2	202	40.1	27.7	44.1	51.0	672	-6.4	3 329	16	26
Medina	9.1	47.1	13.6	4.5	18.5	22.0	1 570	24.3	23.9	45.5	54.5	685	-3.5	437	33	211
Menard	NA	37.0	6.9	3.6	16.7	17.5	261	9.2	58.2	56.3	48.3	502	8.2	1 922	1	19
Midland	5.2	51.2	8.6	5.2	23.1	12.1	343	49.0	29.4	39.1	53.6	733	-10.8	2 138	10	72
Milam	41.4	35.6	7.1	2.7	11.7	10.3	1 577	23.1	14.3	44.1	56.1	515	-0.3	326	1	237
Mills	9.9	42.8	10.1	3.2	17.7	13.4	682	10.4	32.7	50.1	58.8	403	2.8	591	2	85
Mitchell	1.6	52.5	15.4	4.8	15.7	21.4	387	16.8	48.6	57.6	47.0	531	-21.6	1 372	0	176
Montague	15.3	46.4	11.2	5.0	19.2	17.8	1 118	16.4	19.6	39.8	55.0	448	3.2	401	1	135

1. Covers mining, construction, and manufacturing. 2. Covers private sector earnings in agricultural services, forestry, and fisheries; transportation and public utilities; wholesale trade; retail trade; finance, insurance, and real estate; and services.

STATE County	Agriculture, 1987 (cont'd): Value of land and buildings: Average per farm ($1,000)	Average per acre (Dollars)	Value of products sold: Total (Mil dol)	Average per farm (Dollars)	Percent from: Crops	Percent from: Livestock and poultry[1]	Percent of farms with sales of: $10,000 or more	$100,000 or more	Manufactures, 1987: Establishments: Total	Percent with 20 or more em-ployees	All employees: Number (1,000)	Percent change, 1982–1987	Annual payroll (Mil dol)	Production workers: Number (1,000)	Work hours (Mil)
	119	120	121	122	123	124	125	126	127	128	129	130	131	132	133
TEXAS—Con.															
Haskell	312	413	33	52 643	76.2	23.8	70.3	14.5	4	0.0	0.0	0.0	0.5	0.0	0.0
Hays	622	1 724	10	14 877	18.3	81.6	19.8	2.0	49	32.7	1.3	0.0	28.5	0.8	1.6
Hemphill	533	186	50	217 232	3.1	96.9	71.9	21.9	4	0.0	0.0	0.0	0.3	0.0	0.0
Henderson	210	1 038	23	14 889	22.8	77.2	24.5	2.3	44	29.5	2.3	15.0	36.4	1.8	3.6
Hidalgo	505	1 241	233	120 837	94.3	5.7	41.1	15.1	190	33.7	10.4	46.5	138.9	8.2	15.9
Hill	237	812	36	24 002	48.4	51.6	36.9	5.0	34	32.4	0.9	-18.2	17.0	0.7	1.5
Hockley	330	369	75	132 606	65.5	34.5	80.1	36.2	15	26.7	0.2	-33.3	2.8	0.1	0.2
Hood	313	950	20	31 487	38.0	62.0	24.3	3.8	14	21.4	0.2	0.0	3.1	0.2	0.3
Hopkins	186	897	119	67 605	1.8	98.2	45.9	22.7	34	47.1	1.5	-34.8	32.5	1.0	2.1
Houston	265	833	25	17 632	10.8	89.2	26.7	2.3	32	28.1	1.1	-8.3	22.2	0.8	1.6
Howard	416	348	27	69 646	87.3	12.7	64.2	21.8	37	29.7	1.1	0.0	25.8	0.8	1.8
Hudspeth	2 539	166	23	156 787	57.0	43.0	74.3	34.5	NA	NA	NA	NA	NA	NA	NA
Hunt	161	881	19	9 638	29.3	70.7	20.1	1.7	65	44.6	8.2	13.9	212.1	6.3	12.9
Hutchinson	552	233	41	234 311	13.1	86.9	64.7	24.9	35	34.3	D	D	D	D	D
Irion	939	209	6	43 240	3.4	96.6	49.6	15.3	NA	NA	NA	NA	NA	NA	NA
Jack	387	516	15	23 327	3.7	96.3	34.3	4.1	5	0.0	0.0	0.0	0.3	0.0	0.0
Jackson	488	862	32	40 550	72.9	27.1	44.1	12.3	3	0.0	0.0	0.0	0.3	0.0	0.0
Jasper	147	1 040	4	6 665	9.8	90.2	11.5	0.7	43	18.6	1.4	-46.2	29.4	1.0	2.2
Jeff Davis	2 318	136	9	104 220	0.1	99.9	61.1	25.6	2	0.0	D	D	D	D	D
Jefferson	412	663	18	33 562	74.5	25.5	36.3	11.5	219	32.0	17.9	-33.9	596.8	11.8	23.7
Jim Hogg	1 075	288	12	58 971	5.6	94.4	39.6	8.4	2	0.0	D	D	D	D	D
Jim Wells	419	676	39	50 106	49.3	50.7	38.4	8.8	9	22.2	0.1	-66.7	1.4	0.1	0.2
Johnson	297	1 903	56	29 995	8.6	91.4	20.9	5.1	132	28.8	3.4	-15.0	66.4	2.5	5.0
Jones	238	441	37	41 294	63.6	36.4	50.1	11.7	10	10.0	0.1	0.0	0.9	0.0	0.1
Karnes	262	636	19	17 412	15.2	84.8	35.7	3.0	14	21.4	0.3	0.0	7.0	0.3	0.5
Kaufman	285	1 467	19	11 073	20.2	79.8	19.6	1.6	88	25.0	2.5	0.0	44.8	1.8	3.5
Kendall	708	1 306	9	13 149	7.8	92.2	27.3	2.4	25	16.0	0.2	0.0	3.3	0.1	0.2
Kenedy	6 563	253	6	261 441	D	D	66.7	37.5	NA	NA	NA	NA	NA	NA	NA
Kent	492	168	10	56 430	26.7	73.3	67.0	10.1	NA	NA	NA	NA	NA	NA	NA
Kerr	844	906	9	14 749	9.3	90.7	25.3	3.1	28	21.4	0.9	-18.2	13.5	0.6	1.1
Kimble	662	388	9	20 216	5.3	94.7	43.7	3.4	5	60.0	0.1	0.0	2.4	0.1	0.2
King	1 145	140	8	158 105	13.2	86.8	74.0	18.0	NA	NA	NA	NA	NA	NA	NA
Kinney	1 888	318	10	94 239	2.6	97.4	60.0	24.5	NA	NA	NA	NA	NA	NA	NA
Kleberg	1 114	329	49	178 267	25.2	74.8	31.0	9.5	15	20.0	0.2	-33.3	3.0	0.2	0.3
Knox	428	281	38	109 544	38.9	61.1	70.1	19.9	1	0.0	D	D	D	D	D
Lamar	206	693	28	18 665	26.0	74.0	35.3	3.6	57	45.6	5.1	6.2	115.6	3.9	8.0
Lamb	289	459	168	212 037	37.6	62.4	83.4	40.6	10	10.0	0.1	0.0	1.4	0.1	0.2
Lampasas	380	546	11	18 458	6.5	93.5	35.1	3.3	14	35.7	0.4	33.3	6.0	0.3	0.6
La Salle	1 111	381	26	99 547	9.2	90.8	53.6	9.8	NA	NA	NA	NA	NA	NA	NA
Lavaca	202	1 006	34	13 665	11.7	88.3	22.9	1.8	38	36.8	1.1	-31.2	16.6	0.8	1.5
Lee	242	1 225	21	13 454	22.5	77.5	29.8	1.3	18	22.2	0.4	100.0	6.7	0.3	0.7
Leon	294	992	22	13 772	9.0	91.0	27.7	1.5	15	6.7	D	D	D	D	D
Liberty	356	930	21	22 124	63.0	37.0	19.7	4.1	63	20.6	D	D	D	D	D
Limestone	243	647	26	22 059	10.5	89.5	32.2	3.5	17	23.5	0.4	-33.3	5.9	0.3	0.6
Lipscomb	415	240	32	101 648	12.2	87.8	69.1	17.2	4	25.0	D	D	D	D	D
Live Oak	452	692	16	19 674	31.9	68.1	36.6	4.0	5	20.0	D	D	D	D	D
Llano	713	778	11	20 977	5.7	94.3	43.2	3.0	8	12.5	0.1	0.0	0.8	0.1	0.1
Loving	2 606	107	1	56 007	D	D	58.8	23.5	NA	NA	NA	NA	NA	NA	NA
Lubbock	309	650	140	144 460	44.4	55.6	64.1	25.2	270	23.3	6.9	-41.0	141.2	4.2	8.0
Lynn	355	391	49	96 928	92.3	7.7	86.7	34.2	3	0.0	D	D	D	D	D
McCulloch	631	474	19	38 218	17.3	82.7	53.8	9.8	12	25.0	D	D	D	D	D
McLennan	192	889	79	39 984	28.3	71.7	26.0	4.5	249	39.8	13.8	-7.4	263.5	10.0	19.7
McMullen	1 270	467	7	33 506	4.6	95.3	55.0	9.0	NA	NA	NA	NA	NA	NA	NA
Madison	342	1 092	36	48 011	D	D	30.2	2.9	4	0.0	D	D	D	D	D
Marion	170	810	3	14 029	6.9	93.1	20.8	2.4	21	19.0	0.3	0.0	5.1	0.3	0.5
Martin	437	316	32	86 873	90.9	9.1	79.5	37.2	1	0.0	D	D	D	D	D
Mason	580	608	23	41 428	14.8	85.2	54.5	5.3	3	0.0	0.0	0.0	0.1	0.0	0.0
Matagorda	586	708	37	51 342	74.9	25.1	48.7	16.6	18	22.2	D	D	D	D	D
Maverick	1 124	342	53	263 157	6.4	93.6	37.1	13.9	21	33.3	0.9	-10.0	9.0	0.8	1.4
Medina	463	949	44	28 073	36.4	63.6	33.9	3.8	17	23.5	0.5	-16.7	7.4	0.4	0.6
Menard	720	370	19	71 347	1.3	98.7	50.6	7.3	2	0.0	D	D	D	D	D
Midland	539	254	15	42 372	44.2	55.8	38.2	11.1	111	20.7	2.5	-41.9	72.9	1.2	2.5
Milam	286	798	42	26 420	31.2	68.8	34.1	5.1	20	20.0	D	D	D	D	D
Mills	331	553	21	30 213	5.1	94.9	42.5	4.1	5	20.0	0.1	0.0	1.9	0.1	0.1
Mitchell	349	251	23	58 974	63.2	36.8	63.0	16.8	2	0.0	D	D	D	D	D
Montague	219	575	25	22 719	13.9	86.1	34.5	4.5	27	25.9	1.0	11.1	13.3	0.8	1.5

1. Includes livestock and poultry products.

STATE County	Manufactures, 1987 (cont'd) — Production workers (cont'd) — Wages — Total (Mil dol)	Manufactures, 1987 (cont'd) — Production workers (cont'd) — Wages — Average per worker (Dollars)	Manufactures, 1987 (cont'd) — Value added by manufacture (Mil dol)	Manufactures, 1987 (cont'd) — Value of shipments (Mil dol)	Manufactures, 1987 (cont'd) — New capital expenditures (Mil dol)	Value of construction authorized by building permits, 1990 — Total[1] ($1,000)	Nonresidential — Total ($1,000)	Nonresidential — Percent — Office	Nonresidential — Percent — Industrial	Nonresidential — Percent — Stores	Residential — New construction ($1,000)	Residential — Number of housing units	Residential — Alterations and additions ($1,000)
	134	135	136	137	138	139	140	141	142	143	144	145	146
TEXAS—Con.													
Haskell	0.3	NA	1.3	2.3	0.0	52	16	0.0	0.0	34.7	0	0	11
Hays	13.2	16 500	49.9	128.5	3.3	14 601	11 076	18.1	78.1	0.0	948	18	663
Hemphill	0.2	NA	0.6	1.2	0.0	105	32	0.0	0.0	0.0	0	0	3
Henderson	23.7	13 167	65.9	156.5	2.8	6 745	2 804	0.0	0.0	69.2	3 153	53	469
Hidalgo	91.6	11 171	338.4	734.1	20.5	112 771	30 682	46.1	9.1	18.5	61 155	1 402	6 396
Hill	12.1	17 286	36.6	80.4	2.3	3 941	873	0.0	11.3	13.6	1 718	15	31
Hockley	1.7	17 000	4.7	16.6	0.4	2 222	652	30.5	0.0	14.9	777	10	333
Hood	2.4	12 000	9.2	17.3	0.1	2 472	10	0.0	0.0	0.0	1 160	12	48
Hopkins	20.1	20 100	131.9	318.8	8.2	5 926	3 670	4.8	5.2	23.0	1 622	25	406
Houston	14.1	17 625	54.4	157.4	10.3	2 450	1 438	0.0	0.0	0.0	231	2	105
Howard	16.9	21 125	78.5	491.2	11.6	6 236	4 699	0.5	0.0	0.2	415	6	134
Hudspeth	NA	NA	NA	NA	NA	NA	NA	NA	NA	NA	NA	NA	NA
Hunt	163.1	25 889	441.0	798.8	43.6	4 550	1 603	36.8	5.3	1.9	1 572	22	628
Hutchinson	D	D	D	D	D	2 441	372	74.9	0.0	0.0	1 482	13	291
Irion	NA	NA	NA	NA	NA	NA	NA	NA	NA	NA	NA	NA	NA
Jack	0.1	NA	1.1	1.4	D	194	0	NA	NA	NA	151	3	8
Jackson	0.1	NA	0.6	1.0	D	551	20	0.0	0.0	0.0	31	1	457
Jasper	17.7	17 700	66.6	265.4	3.0	1 598	306	0.0	0.0	0.0	832	15	148
Jeff Davis	D	D	D	D	D	NA	NA	NA	NA	NA	NA	NA	NA
Jefferson	371.4	31 475	2 093.8	11 573.5	268.2	74 658	18 437	38.0	17.5	25.2	30 405	308	7 747
Jim Hogg	D	D	D	D	D	NA	NA	NA	NA	NA	NA	NA	NA
Jim Wells	1.0	10 000	2.7	4.3	D	3 408	1 250	33.6	0.0	52.7	264	15	207
Johnson	41.8	16 720	192.2	337.5	7.6	11 945	2 976	31.5	18.5	7.4	6 966	110	971
Jones	0.7	NA	3.0	7.7	0.1	537	221	0.0	0.0	96.5	121	4	80
Karnes	4.6	15 333	24.9	62.8	1.9	191	6	0.0	0.0	0.0	0	0	109
Kaufman	27.9	15 500	101.9	225.8	7.0	9 838	4 294	1.5	46.8	14.8	4 363	81	354
Kendall	1.5	15 000	5.7	9.6	0.1	14 395	1 057	14.2	0.0	3.8	9 461	78	183
Kenedy	NA	NA	NA	NA	NA	NA	NA	NA	NA	NA	NA	NA	NA
Kent	NA	NA	NA	NA	NA	0	0	NA	NA	NA	0	0	0
Kerr	7.9	13 167	25.1	50.4	1.5	5 495	558	17.6	0.0	10.8	3 960	43	559
Kimble	1.7	17 000	5.0	12.1	0.6	174	0	NA	NA	NA	154	4	17
King	NA	NA	NA	NA	NA	NA	NA	NA	NA	NA	NA	NA	NA
Kinney	NA	NA	NA	NA	NA	646	238	0.0	0.0	89.7	126	2	64
Kleberg	1.8	9 000	7.4	18.1	0.2	3 985	442	0.0	0.0	58.8	318	6	1 302
Knox	D	D	D	D	D	0	0	NA	NA	NA	0	0	0
Lamar	85.3	21 872	523.8	988.8	31.4	16 952	11 899	13.1	76.8	3.9	3 433	70	198
Lamb	1.3	13 000	3.8	8.2	0.1	343	55	45.5	0.0	0.0	186	3	49
Lampasas	4.5	15 000	17.2	29.9	0.5	484	167	27.0	55.1	0.0	74	2	93
La Salle	NA	NA	NA	NA	NA	185	0	NA	NA	NA	0	0	40
Lavaca	8.0	10 000	37.2	93.4	1.4	3 067	1 074	0.0	8.6	0.0	553	10	634
Lee	4.8	16 000	8.9	45.6	0.6	645	397	0.0	0.0	68.1	0	0	30
Leon	D	D	D	D	D	NA	NA	NA	NA	NA	NA	NA	NA
Liberty	D	D	D	D	D	11 256	2 641	31.5	0.0	0.0	7 208	174	536
Limestone	3.9	13 000	13.8	30.0	0.4	1 419	222	33.7	9.1	0.0	1 049	19	98
Lipscomb	D	D	D	D	D	0	0	NA	NA	NA	0	0	0
Live Oak	D	D	D	D	D	232	0	NA	NA	NA	202	6	29
Llano	0.5	5 000	1.1	4.0	0.0	1 434	47	0.0	0.0	53.4	990	15	132
Loving	NA	NA	NA	NA	NA	NA	NA	NA	NA	NA	NA	NA	NA
Lubbock	69.7	16 595	410.6	867.4	17.8	71 525	32 147	20.1	0.3	12.7	38 998	453	203
Lynn	D	D	D	D	D	107	23	0.0	0.0	0.0	77	1	3
McCulloch	D	D	D	D	D	348	34	70.6	0.0	0.0	160	3	128
McLennan	165.2	16 520	837.9	1 635.1	70.6	67 196	13 784	36.5	11.4	29.4	18 226	237	7 365
McMullen	NA	NA	NA	NA	NA	NA	NA	NA	NA	NA	NA	NA	NA
Madison	D	D	D	D	D	NA	NA	NA	NA	NA	NA	NA	NA
Marion	3.8	12 667	13.2	35.9	0.4	932	784	0.0	0.0	13.9	77	2	10
Martin	D	D	D	D	D	352	50	0.0	0.0	79.3	196	4	14
Mason	0.0	NA	0.3	0.4	0.0	NA	NA	NA	NA	NA	NA	NA	NA
Matagorda	D	D	D	D	D	3 750	617	23.5	0.0	36.0	1 242	13	970
Maverick	6.7	8 375	25.1	52.9	0.3	3 480	1 164	12.8	0.0	38.5	2 017	65	262
Medina	4.8	12 000	15.0	23.3	D	2 050	648	0.0	0.0	39.0	881	21	199
Menard	D	D	D	D	D	NA	NA	NA	NA	NA	NA	NA	NA
Midland	26.8	22 333	135.0	214.8	4.1	41 274	3 811	27.0	6.6	48.4	22 595	216	3 441
Milam	D	D	D	D	D	3 700	2 779	2.7	3.5	5.0	591	15	152
Mills	0.9	9 000	3.0	5.6	D	NA	NA	NA	NA	NA	NA	NA	NA
Mitchell	D	D	D	D	D	713	696	32.3	0.0	0.0	0	0	7
Montague	9.8	12 250	34.4	51.4	0.2	66	16	0.0	0.0	100.0	20	1	0

1. Includes nonresidential additions and alterations, residential nonhousekeeping buildings, and residential garages and carports not shown separately.

STATE County	Wholesale trade, 1987				Retail trade, all establishments, 1987				Retail trade, establishments with payroll, 1987					
						Sales				Sales				
											Per capita[2] (Dollars)			
	Establishments	Sales (Mil dol)	Paid employees[1]	Annual payroll (Mil dol)	Number	Total (Mil dol)	Percent change, 1982–1987	Per capita[2] (Dollars)	Number	Total (Mil dol)	General merchandise stores	Food stores	Apparel & accessory stores	Eating and drinking places
	147	148	149	150	151	152	153	154	155	156	157	158	159	160
TEXAS—Con.														
Haskell	11	32.3	92	0.8	110	33.4	7.4	4 840	61	30.1	278	1 199	413	197
Hays	46	50.2	351	6.2	630	280.6	67.3	4 406	347	268.9	D	984	258	544
Hemphill	13	14.7	34	0.9	64	17.3	-34.7	4 208	36	15.8	D	1 118	112	286
Henderson	42	140.5	313	5.0	524	228.7	38.4	4 158	292	213.4	D	742	179	278
Hidalgo	547	1 343.9	9 313	99.1	2 866	1 552.4	14.8	4 086	1 657	1 495.0	692	932	304	308
Hill	37	61.3	186	2.4	365	133.4	21.6	4 870	200	123.6	378	1 018	109	412
Hockley	51	68.7	217	4.7	235	99.6	10.1	4 167	124	95.5	430	1 249	110	298
Hood	33	51.6	158	3.3	403	168.6	72.7	5 792	213	158.9	D	1 336	153	428
Hopkins	58	395.7	912	16.5	362	169.0	40.6	5 807	207	149.5	D	1 235	500	430
Houston	24	33.3	157	2.3	218	80.5	8.6	3 499	125	76.2	D	905	111	147
Howard	63	69.0	403	6.8	473	185.2	-18.5	5 368	247	173.5	573	1 274	224	469
Hudspeth	3	1.8	12	0.1	47	5.3	10.4	2 132	23	4.7	D	324	0	392
Hunt	66	191.2	687	12.6	792	323.9	28.2	4 841	422	301.8	D	1 159	240	422
Hutchinson	43	181.8	390	8.0	299	111.8	-13.7	4 385	169	106.2	D	1 329	239	365
Irion	3	D	D	D	17	2.3	0.0	1 226	9	2.2	0	D	0	D
Jack	19	72.8	146	2.7	103	21.4	-13.7	2 928	58	20.1	D	1 092	69	320
Jackson	27	54.8	133	2.4	152	52.1	-0.8	4 011	94	49.9	D	1 438	45	238
Jasper	37	53.2	271	4.5	380	161.8	9.7	5 120	205	152.4	561	1 288	286	265
Jeff Davis	0	0.0	0	0.0	34	5.2	62.5	2 869	17	4.6	D	1 793	0	D
Jefferson	475	1 620.4	4 966	106.3	2 683	1 699.1	10.5	6 995	1 649	1 660.3	1 137	1 199	439	646
Jim Hogg	9	18.8	48	0.6	72	18.9	-30.3	3 574	49	18.3	D	1 472	D	293
Jim Wells	82	102.9	514	8.7	417	153.1	-19.7	3 917	242	148.7	D	1 043	163	306
Johnson	101	129.9	826	12.4	1 011	438.8	49.5	4 552	477	404.7	D	1 040	191	386
Jones	34	154.2	201	3.8	195	54.8	-13.4	3 148	98	51.8	141	908	135	158
Karnes	32	101.4	312	3.3	174	43.4	-30.2	3 316	92	41.7	D	927	D	252
Kaufman	73	136.1	389	7.6	691	292.8	58.6	5 383	313	272.7	D	1 256	D	313
Kendall	19	17.7	103	1.4	255	102.5	113.5	6 789	112	97.2	89	1 990	67	381
Kenedy	0	0.0	0	0.0	3	D	D	D	3	D	D	D	0	0
Kent	0	0.0	0	0.0	15	D	D	D	4	D	D	D	0	0
Kerr	54	55.5	271	4.8	501	198.1	25.0	5 564	289	188.9	807	1 179	281	526
Kimble	11	30.5	92	0.7	80	21.7	-18.1	5 163	42	20.5	D	1 061	0	625
King	0	0.0	0	0.0	6	D	D	D	2	D	0	0	0	D
Kinney	0	0.0	0	0.0	32	4.5	32.4	1 781	13	3.8	D	D	0	D
Kleberg	25	38.6	410	4.9	320	152.3	-1.4	4 699	215	149.1	D	1 612	288	544
Knox	16	23.3	94	1.6	77	14.0	-1.4	2 693	36	11.7	D	1 195	D	D
Lamar	86	151.6	675	10.1	574	254.2	24.5	5 623	310	236.5	687	1 087	439	483
Lamb	41	63.5	209	3.6	201	48.1	-13.6	3 065	107	45.0	212	1 252	159	217
Lampasas	22	39.5	190	1.4	172	52.2	22.5	3 678	84	48.1	D	995	68	258
La Salle	3	D	D	D	86	17.2	28.4	3 309	37	15.4	458	774	D	D
Lavaca	47	121.4	635	6.0	310	83.1	2.8	4 468	156	76.7	284	1 317	92	224
Lee	36	86.9	315	4.8	165	58.5	-12.8	4 304	89	54.9	D	1 407	70	334
Leon	21	57.7	225	3.5	197	52.1	53.7	4 239	90	45.0	D	1 351	D	246
Liberty	78	90.8	524	9.4	612	232.0	-8.8	4 353	290	217.1	D	1 343	95	345
Limestone	33	123.1	363	4.5	275	95.2	32.2	4 269	141	86.8	D	1 161	166	237
Lipscomb	12	15.5	50	1.1	54	8.7	-21.6	2 562	29	8.1	D	856	0	245
Live Oak	12	D	D	D	142	52.5	26.8	5 648	77	50.3	D	2 635	63	255
Llano	18	41.4	200	3.0	246	48.1	18.5	3 848	112	42.1	102	1 050	66	408
Loving	1	D	D	D	3	D	D	D	0	0.0	0	0	0	0
Lubbock	598	2 717.8	6 860	138.5	2 495	1 661.1	23.5	7 305	1 487	1 587.1	986	1 324	380	739
Lynn	13	15.4	57	1.3	75	13.1	-7.1	1 851	31	11.8	D	572	D	101
McCulloch	15	23.8	107	1.6	150	53.3	40.3	6 052	83	49.7	D	1 418	231	372
McLennan	398	1 061.8	4 354	81.7	2 137	1 141.7	21.0	6 054	1 236	1 096.9	943	1 255	289	606
McMullen	0	0.0	0	0.0	9	D	D	D	7	1.1	D	D	0	D
Madison	14	28.3	99	1.5	102	45.7	-1.9	3 906	60	44.5	D	1 008	D	435
Marion	8	4.0	15	0.5	134	28.0	13.8	2 912	61	24.6	D	742	63	177
Martin	7	8.2	41	1.0	47	22.3	16.8	4 376	27	22.0	D	867	D	254
Mason	13	21.9	70	0.9	73	16.7	46.5	4 919	44	15.1	D	1 327	146	1 165
Matagorda	55	128.9	461	7.8	441	183.7	7.8	4 580	265	176.4	340	1 454	181	397
Maverick	38	35.6	174	2.2	331	128.1	-10.3	3 293	199	120.8	515	774	386	188
Medina	43	122.4	386	5.3	275	140.5	54.6	5 261	143	130.3	D	1 496	41	208
Menard	6	16.8	45	0.7	37	4.4	-38.0	1 845	17	3.7	0	671	D	D
Midland	289	1 623.8	2 586	60.7	1 227	730.3	2.4	6 825	724	704.4	1 062	1 626	361	572
Milam	29	59.0	229	2.2	293	86.6	36.2	3 764	140	80.7	353	1 321	84	189
Mills	9	11.7	59	0.5	82	15.9	12.8	3 620	30	13.3	D	744	D	191
Mitchell	13	24.6	121	1.4	114	40.4	0.2	4 641	77	39.2	D	1 512	369	315
Montague	32	30.4	155	1.7	279	76.4	7.2	4 245	130	67.2	D	1 213	58	204

1. For pay period including March 12. 2. Based on the estimated population as of July 1 of the year shown.

STATE County	Retail trade, establishments with payroll, 1987 (cont'd): Paid employees[1]	Retail trade: Annual payroll (Mil dol)	Taxable service industries–establishments with payroll, 1987: Number	Receipts (Mil dol): Total	Receipts, selected kinds of business: Hotels, motels and other lodging places	Health services	Legal services	Paid employees	Annual payroll (Mil dol)	Bank deposits,[2] June 1989: Total (Mil dol)	Percent change, 1988–1989	Savings capital,[3] September 1989: Total (Mil dol)	Percent change, 1988–1989
	161	162	163	164	165	166	167	168	169	170	171	172	173
TEXAS—Con.													
Haskell	349	3.1	37	D	D	2.5	D	D	D	87	0.7	26.0	-2.8
Hays	3 713	31.3	324	89.8	4.4	43.1	3.6	2 234	26.5	267	-1.6	135.5	-14.2
Hemphill	190	2.0	27	4.7	D	1.1	0.6	127	1.4	79	-6.2	4.7	-7.1
Henderson	2 498	22.1	207	47.6	2.9	20.0	2.9	1 316	16.6	352	1.1	128.8	-19.8
Hidalgo	18 700	168.0	1 268	452.3	32.2	208.6	43.7	10 714	142.9	2 246	2.1	1 052.1	-7.9
Hill	1 394	11.8	114	27.2	1.6	14.0	1.3	785	9.6	202	-3.8	79.9	-3.5
Hockley	1 218	10.1	104	27.9	D	10.4	1.1	681	9.2	310	-4.8	23.8	-83.8
Hood	1 697	16.4	146	30.7	3.5	11.3	1.6	826	10.1	227	10.4	75.1	-6.7
Hopkins	1 790	15.9	147	32.2	4.6	11.8	3.1	947	10.7	245	5.1	85.0	7.0
Houston	816	7.7	98	23.5	1.9	8.0	1.3	692	7.3	170	-1.9	85.5	-69.0
Howard	2 145	19.2	201	51.6	2.3	25.8	3.0	1 227	18.5	338	13.0	119.8	-23.0
Hudspeth	97	0.5	4	0.3	D	D	0.0	11	0.1	8	17.5	0.0	NA
Hunt	3 800	34.0	283	69.4	3.2	30.5	4.1	1 889	23.9	533	-0.5	155.8	-28.4
Hutchinson	1 296	11.2	129	35.5	0.9	19.4	1.3	1 121	12.8	174	-6.7	76.6	-8.3
Irion	39	0.2	6	1.0	0.0	0.0	0.0	31	0.3	40	5.2	0.0	NA
Jack	302	2.4	35	4.2	D	2.0	0.2	167	1.6	98	6.9	14.1	-14.1
Jackson	603	5.2	66	12.2	D	3.6	1.4	334	4.0	117	-9.7	37.0	0.0
Jasper	1 617	14.2	139	37.7	0.6	16.0	5.9	997	11.7	167	6.9	138.4	0.7
Jeff Davis	76	0.4	5	0.9	D	D	0.0	23	0.1	11	9.8	0.0	NA
Jefferson	19 520	188.7	1 748	742.6	22.9	323.3	103.1	17 074	269.9	2 219	-2.7	1 555.7	3.7
Jim Hogg	287	2.0	14	3.3	D	D	D	66	0.7	66	20.0	3.9	-5.0
Jim Wells	1 958	17.4	219	85.1	D	25.1	4.9	2 531	27.5	280	13.8	80.8	87.9
Johnson	4 623	42.6	401	88.4	1.3	33.2	6.0	2 360	29.8	598	4.3	184.0	-1.3
Jones	562	5.1	52	12.7	D	7.3	0.6	528	4.7	94	-3.7	107.1	0.1
Karnes	592	4.6	57	8.1	0.3	3.7	0.6	272	2.5	110	1.8	38.2	-3.5
Kaufman	2 721	25.5	242	59.2	D	29.8	3.4	1 616	20.3	395	-1.9	83.2	11.7
Kendall	1 052	9.5	108	19.9	D	6.8	1.9	711	7.6	150	-3.6	36.1	-7.7
Kenedy	D	D	1	D	0.0	0.0	0.0	D	D	NA	NA	0.0	NA
Kent	D	D	3	D	0.0	0.0	0.0	D	D	7	-7.2	0.0	NA
Kerr	2 437	23.0	288	74.4	17.4	29.9	4.4	1 763	24.6	516	-2.7	178.2	-6.7
Kimble	252	2.4	36	4.8	1.9	1.4	0.2	162	1.2	32	7.7	19.4	-8.0
King	D	D	0	0.0	0.0	0.0	0.0	0	0.0	NA	NA	0.0	NA
Kinney	50	0.4	4	D	0.0	0.0	D	D	D	10	-2.6	0.0	NA
Kleberg	2 285	18.3	170	35.5	2.1	12.0	1.0	1 023	14.6	191	2.2	133.2	-4.2
Knox	163	1.3	18	7.4	0.0	1.6	D	155	1.9	48	6.0	0.0	NA
Lamar	3 047	28.5	283	64.4	3.4	38.8	2.8	1 931	25.3	319	2.3	294.4	-34.6
Lamb	604	4.9	69	9.6	D	4.3	0.5	319	3.2	101	-13.9	85.7	4.7
Lampasas	589	5.6	60	25.3	1.2	6.8	D	478	5.5	128	0.8	53.9	14.5
La Salle	205	1.7	18	1.8	D	D	0.0	77	0.6	17	7.9	7.0	-15.4
Lavaca	998	8.4	101	17.9	0.5	8.5	1.2	663	6.1	156	-1.4	105.2	8.7
Lee	746	6.8	76	17.3	1.3	7.3	1.2	411	5.3	169	-5.7	0.0	-100.0
Leon	611	4.6	43	8.0	0.6	4.5	0.5	247	2.2	83	2.0	17.2	12.3
Liberty	2 531	23.0	211	51.5	1.5	24.4	4.1	1 486	18.2	336	-3.6	172.0	19.6
Limestone	1 039	9.0	76	12.1	1.1	5.4	1.5	313	3.6	162	1.0	89.6	-12.6
Lipscomb	104	0.9	15	1.2	D	D	D	38	0.4	71	-4.7	3.2	-15.0
Live Oak	581	5.2	42	4.7	D	1.6	0.7	139	1.4	87	4.2	2.0	NA
Llano	540	4.9	70	12.0	1.2	5.2	1.1	380	4.3	187	9.2	295.2	-7.9
Loving	0	0.0	1	D	0.0	0.0	0.0	D	D	NA	NA	0.0	NA
Lubbock	19 022	186.7	1 586	597.1	19.3	238.5	45.9	13 293	210.5	2 040	-1.4	1 112.2	-17.7
Lynn	148	1.3	22	3.0	0.0	0.7	D	57	0.7	86	7.2	11.3	3.6
McCulloch	552	5.0	44	9.8	D	2.9	0.2	286	2.9	76	3.2	45.8	-58.5
McLennan	14 391	131.9	1 184	395.2	18.5	127.1	29.5	10 163	149.9	1 601	-7.8	894.1	-11.9
McMullen	22	0.1	3	0.2	D	0.0	0.0	5	0.0	18	11.7	0.0	NA
Madison	580	5.0	34	6.9	0.0	2.6	2.3	191	2.4	163	14.8	32.6	-7.0
Marion	296	2.2	32	6.0	D	3.2	D	194	1.6	46	-6.6	20.8	8.1
Martin	174	1.7	14	2.3	0.0	1.4	D	80	0.8	44	10.0	12.9	2.6
Mason	436	2.2	16	1.9	D	0.9	0.4	51	0.6	48	-2.0	12.3	-19.6
Matagorda	2 190	19.9	211	50.3	3.6	10.7	3.1	1 256	19.2	258	-4.8	245.6	-31.5
Maverick	1 668	13.6	86	18.3	1.5	6.8	5.0	410	5.9	220	4.8	34.0	0.1
Medina	1 265	11.7	105	21.1	1.1	7.2	1.5	774	8.7	129	9.2	90.5	-16.8
Menard	61	0.5	8	D	D	D	D	D	D	24	13.0	0.0	-100.0
Midland	7 521	79.8	874	319.9	13.3	73.5	36.6	7 105	120.0	1 487	5.0	493.4	-45.0
Milam	960	8.1	90	14.7	1.0	5.2	1.1	517	5.2	221	6.5	12.7	-94.6
Mills	158	1.5	17	2.9	0.0	2.2	D	120	1.2	85	-4.0	7.8	-8.8
Mitchell	470	4.1	45	5.7	D	2.7	0.7	239	1.8	84	-3.1	59.9	-42.9
Montague	824	6.8	87	12.9	D	5.5	D	506	4.1	180	1.4	75.1	-17.2

1. For the period including March 12 of the year shown. 2. Includes deposits for all insured and reporting noninsured commercial and mutual savings banks. 3. Includes savings capital for all FSLIC insured savings institutions.

STATE County	Federal funds and grants, 1989							Local government finances, 1981–1982							
	Expenditures		Per capita[1] (Dollars)					General revenue						Direct general expenditure	
									Intergovernmental		Taxes				
												Per capita[2]			
	Total (Mil dol)	Percent change, 1988–1989	Total	Direct payments for individuals	Procurement contract awards	Salaries and wages	Grant awards	Total (Mil dol)	Total (Mil dol)	Percent from state	Total (Mil dol)	Total (Dollars)	Property (Dollars)	Total (Mil dol)	Percent change, 1977–1982
	174	175	176	177	178	179	180	181	182	183	184	185	186	187	188
TEXAS—Con.															
Haskell	36.8	23.8	5 577	2 577	34	195	402	8.1	2.4	76.2	2.7	355	307	7.7	57.3
Hays	130.3	10.1	1 956	1 182	429	97	235	36.2	14.7	84.3	10.2	232	195	39.3	97.6
Hemphill	7.9	-20.7	2 076	1 401	207	107	61	9.8	0.8	86.6	5.9	929	860	8.8	105.9
Henderson	112.9	-0.1	1 995	1 680	9	82	210	39.1	14.6	89.4	12.6	276	239	34.9	114.0
Hidalgo	767.3	5.6	1 923	1 187	145	129	398	294.8	169.5	87.4	65.8	208	162	281.3	98.5
Hill	87.4	4.2	3 202	2 515	25	125	309	20.7	8.8	91.0	4.5	173	137	19.7	80.0
Hockley	65.6	14.4	2 778	1 505	10	88	243	38.8	13.2	88.8	18.7	771	720	34.0	51.2
Hood	61.8	8.6	1 878	1 732	10	78	37	14.1	4.0	92.6	5.3	264	240	12.9	114.2
Hopkins	68.2	17.5	2 327	1 779	13	116	98	22.5	7.7	83.8	7.1	270	224	21.8	32.5
Houston	61.9	5.4	2 702	2 131	30	117	341	17.8	7.1	88.2	4.5	189	153	15.8	45.1
Howard	107.2	13.8	3 209	1 987	30	577	330	41.3	14.0	90.1	17.7	484	426	40.4	89.9
Hudspeth	9.4	-25.9	3 740	1 314	48	924	906	4.5	2.2	66.3	1.4	468	443	3.2	55.0
Hunt	253.0	4.7	3 754	1 756	1 589	182	180	43.9	16.1	92.3	13.8	232	195	51.5	108.0
Hutchinson	54.6	2.8	2 258	1 921	21	102	80	29.4	7.2	94.9	13.3	455	396	28.7	103.3
Irion	6.4	76.2	3 560	1 449	12	83	1 317	2.6	0.3	89.1	1.9	1 189	1 124	2.7	131.6
Jack	18.9	2.6	2 733	2 233	18	148	244	7.4	1.9	89.0	3.9	498	417	7.5	141.9
Jackson	43.2	-3.0	3 482	1 951	26	109	217	19.1	3.7	91.5	8.3	608	563	17.5	85.2
Jasper	78.0	2.1	2 509	2 095	45	95	266	25.4	11.3	90.5	7.5	239	208	22.8	73.9
Jeff Davis	5.0	-1.2	2 774	2 046	61	293	164	1.4	0.5	94.1	0.6	366	338	1.3	53.3
Jefferson	865.1	16.4	3 675	2 019	1 053	210	329	318.4	71.4	76.1	156.4	606	535	297.5	90.9
Jim Hogg	14.0	9.8	2 698	1 673	8	269	462	5.4	1.8	89.3	2.7	490	472	6.1	152.3
Jim Wells	85.7	8.3	2 262	1 602	9	113	379	33.4	14.7	84.4	14.4	377	300	31.0	82.3
Johnson	162.3	5.7	1 606	1 430	-56	95	96	51.7	21.9	94.3	14.3	194	161	52.9	93.4
Jones	62.1	-16.2	3 741	2 223	13	203	405	17.6	5.7	91.2	4.8	273	236	16.6	74.3
Karnes	37.4	6.7	2 993	2 093	14	129	541	14.4	4.8	80.9	5.3	387	333	14.9	122.2
Kaufman	130.8	9.8	2 247	1 939	13	115	144	31.2	16.0	91.0	9.9	233	192	29.9	84.1
Kendall	41.3	13.3	2 566	2 329	20	109	44	7.4	3.4	84.2	2.8	238	206	7.2	118.4
Kenedy	1.1	26.7	2 222	1 218	284	226	158	0.9	0.1	30.4	0.7	1 412	1 398	0.8	56.9
Kent	5.4	16.5	4 895	2 040	19	274	148	2.7	0.2	84.5	2.2	1 860	1 826	2.0	31.0
Kerr	134.2	3.8	3 749	2 991	44	576	107	19.4	6.4	95.3	8.5	282	234	22.2	134.0
Kimble	13.7	17.0	3 251	2 239	14	145	191	3.0	1.2	83.6	1.3	308	254	3.1	79.8
King	2.3	-8.1	5 665	790	52	372	155	1.8	0.1	88.2	1.6	3 933	3 908	1.4	80.4
Kinney	12.7	15.6	4 709	2 790	21	539	286	2.1	0.7	90.0	1.0	447	404	2.2	41.2
Kleberg	269.1	-2.0	8 736	2 085	1 089	5 143	309	37.5	11.5	81.3	14.7	424	370	37.3	107.2
Knox	23.0	2.2	4 689	2 660	143	235	270	7.5	2.3	92.4	2.2	399	353	6.6	68.0
Lamar	123.1	5.2	2 736	2 123	36	144	308	47.4	19.3	91.4	9.0	209	150	45.2	133.4
Lamb	69.0	-0.5	4 537	2 070	13	118	279	18.8	6.3	96.0	6.0	324	285	19.0	140.8
Lampasas	44.9	11.5	3 141	2 624	78	88	196	7.2	3.5	89.0	2.1	166	134	6.7	50.8
La Salle	17.2	9.3	3 518	1 730	10	225	852	5.2	2.4	92.1	2.2	364	333	4.6	15.7
Lavaca	59.3	9.6	3 240	2 692	16	119	296	11.3	2.9	81.8	4.3	233	187	11.6	93.5
Lee	23.9	12.6	1 796	1 442	10	80	147	13.4	3.9	95.4	7.4	542	436	13.8	310.0
Leon	41.7	6.1	3 472	2 880	18	139	364	8.1	3.7	96.3	2.9	277	240	8.5	115.2
Liberty	122.5	4.9	2 333	1 781	15	77	295	43.0	18.3	81.2	18.5	361	319	44.2	141.6
Limestone	60.1	4.4	2 696	2 051	25	102	359	13.6	5.8	83.1	4.4	215	174	12.3	73.6
Lipscomb	10.3	-19.3	3 335	1 830	24	234	92	7.7	1.2	92.3	5.6	1 310	1 257	6.9	149.1
Live Oak	84.1	240.1	9 445	1 562	6 871	86	237	8.9	2.2	90.3	5.4	543	465	8.3	92.2
Llano	47.1	8.5	3 771	3 494	29	109	85	6.3	1.2	76.5	2.5	236	204	5.6	86.6
Loving	0.3	21.0	3 290	2 320	110	750	0	0.6	0.0	86.4	0.5	4 780	4 610	0.5	54.8
Lubbock	584.9	8.4	2 565	1 436	179	544	291	188.2	66.6	82.6	73.4	337	267	175.6	66.1
Lynn	34.6	20.3	5 163	1 872	14	139	277	9.0	3.3	89.1	3.9	465	433	7.4	58.2
McCulloch	30.4	13.4	3 344	2 378	16	164	418	7.6	2.7	83.4	1.9	214	168	7.6	93.9
McLennan	568.3	7.2	3 009	1 859	458	432	234	142.4	62.5	77.1	51.7	293	229	131.7	71.1
McMullen	2.3	26.9	2 561	1 248	23	227	61	1.8	0.1	64.0	1.4	1 774	1 730	2.3	201.8
Madison	23.6	14.4	2 055	1 673	9	71	218	9.9	2.3	93.3	2.9	250	206	9.0	66.2
Marion	26.9	-6.9	2 866	2 201	109	108	435	6.0	3.0	94.6	2.1	193	167	5.0	71.3
Martin	21.1	11.4	4 224	1 221	9	106	210	7.5	1.6	92.5	4.7	878	841	7.4	132.9
Mason	13.0	8.2	4 076	2 881	20	173	194	3.1	1.5	95.4	1.0	270	233	2.7	29.5
Matagorda	89.7	8.2	2 323	1 474	175	97	184	51.2	12.6	68.6	25.0	669	624	44.0	97.0
Maverick	73.9	10.2	1 821	1 123	7	195	486	32.7	15.4	93.9	7.1	207	154	31.6	137.4
Medina	68.4	6.8	2 477	1 834	121	106	230	17.6	8.9	95.3	5.4	229	198	15.9	63.3
Menard	9.1	9.6	3 804	2 613	15	142	264	3.5	1.2	90.2	1.1	489	376	3.4	102.6
Midland	171.4	11.8	1 605	1 096	44	311	114	108.1	24.2	91.5	50.1	511	397	100.7	165.8
Milam	66.5	6.6	3 020	2 207	75	117	304	20.9	7.5	84.0	6.1	265	230	17.6	119.6
Mills	17.8	17.0	4 049	2 644	31	150	204	3.0	1.4	96.9	0.9	202	169	2.9	107.4
Mitchell	31.3	10.1	3 677	2 258	14	110	402	12.4	2.4	91.8	5.7	598	546	11.4	55.2
Montague	51.7	11.0	2 972	2 462	17	132	205	15.0	4.6	95.2	5.4	294	240	15.0	102.0

1. Based on the estimated population as of July 1 of the year shown. 2. Based on the estimated population as of July 1, 1982.

STATE County	Local government finances, 1981–1982 (cont'd) — Direct general expenditure (cont'd): Per capita[1] (Dollars)	Percent of total for– Educa-tion	Health & hospitals	Police protec-tion	Public welfare	High-ways	Debt outstanding: Total (Mil dol)	Per capita[1] (Dollars)	State and local government employ-ment, 1989: Total	Rate[2]	Federal government civilian employment 1989: Total	Earnings ($1,000)	Elections, 1988[3]: Total vote cast for president	Vote for lead party (Percent)
	189	190	191	192	193	194	195	196	197	198	199	200	201	202
TEXAS—Con.														
Haskell	1 011	38.2	33.6	1.8	0.0	11.2	1.1	144	419	634.8	46	1 200	2 915	D–58.8
Hays	895	43.1	0.6	2.8	0.8	4.3	125.3	2 854	6 088	914.1	123	3 463	23 264	R–50.4
Hemphill	1 372	44.4	19.6	7.6	0.3	7.3	7.4	1 148	303	797.4	15	484	1 705	R–68.6
Henderson	766	64.7	11.8	2.7	0.1	4.6	27.2	597	2 010	355.1	92	2 501	20 918	R–52.6
Hidalgo	889	60.9	4.7	3.2	0.3	3.3	216.2	683	24 210	606.6	2 137	73 042	83 870	D–64.8
Hill	761	58.7	17.4	2.8	0.0	5.9	8.7	335	1 347	493.4	101	2 542	9 198	R–52.1
Hockley	1 404	74.6	0.2	2.4	0.1	4.5	29.3	1 211	1 673	708.9	75	2 013	7 250	R–60.2
Hood	646	41.9	30.8	4.1	0.0	5.9	9.3	467	1 125	341.9	74	2 048	11 716	R–63.2
Hopkins	825	42.2	25.3	4.3	0.0	6.2	12.7	480	1 471	502.0	90	2 435	10 142	R–50.6
Houston	668	54.6	20.5	3.0	0.1	5.6	11.5	486	1 923	839.7	112	2 605	7 764	R–50.0
Howard	1 105	69.5	0.5	3.9	0.1	5.4	92.4	2 525	2 529	757.2	700	21 577	10 517	R–57.3
Hudspeth	1 118	57.3	0.7	3.2	0.8	11.4	1.6	539	224	896.0	72	2 534	816	D–49.8
Hunt	867	50.3	11.7	3.1	0.5	7.1	77.3	1 302	4 423	656.2	229	6 977	21 238	R–58.1
Hutchinson	979	55.4	14.7	4.1	0.2	4.0	7.4	252	1 418	586.0	82	2 493	10 526	R–71.5
Irion	1 659	58.2	0.0	2.1	0.0	12.5	0.9	534	115	638.9	NA	206	867	R–62.2
Jack	967	50.0	13.0	1.9	0.1	5.1	2.7	349	393	569.6	32	824	3 074	R–50.2
Jackson	1 275	42.6	28.4	2.8	0.3	7.3	28.5	2 077	793	639.5	48	1 196	5 115	R–57.8
Jasper	730	60.9	17.8	2.7	0.1	5.0	12.2	388	1 569	504.5	63	1 865	11 629	D–56.9
Jeff Davis	782	71.7	0.0	5.0	0.2	6.2	0.0	9	214	1 188.9	27	656	870	R–60.2
Jefferson	1 153	43.4	4.9	6.5	0.4	7.2	323.5	1 253	13 698	581.9	1 214	39 620	91 693	D–60.7
Jim Hogg	1 111	66.4	0.3	3.3	0.2	12.1	3.2	585	433	832.7	48	1 568	2 143	D–76.1
Jim Wells	810	60.1	0.0	4.9	0.6	8.6	16.6	434	1 865	492.1	103	3 179	12 886	D–65.9
Johnson	721	59.0	14.4	3.6	0.3	4.0	43.0	586	3 315	327.9	219	6 299	30 171	R–58.0
Jones	941	44.7	31.6	3.1	0.2	4.2	5.7	321	958	577.1	70	1 941	5 916	R–50.7
Karnes	1 079	50.4	5.0	2.9	0.1	7.4	11.3	816	711	568.8	54	1 387	4 933	D–51.3
Kaufman	706	68.9	0.8	3.8	0.1	3.5	34.6	815	3 534	607.2	159	4 386	15 916	R–53.2
Kendall	611	62.8	1.0	4.4	0.2	6.4	4.7	402	666	413.7	38	1 157	6 398	R–76.2
Kenedy	1 594	34.9	0.8	9.2	0.0	0.0	0.0	0	57	1 140.0	NA	NA	196	D–60.7
Kent	1 702	62.4	0.0	2.3	1.0	7.5	0.7	583	142	1 290.9	12	307	674	D–59.1
Kerr	734	57.1	0.8	3.7	0.0	4.1	29.6	980	2 339	653.4	765	22 487	14 937	R–75.0
Kimble	746	45.3	22.4	3.9	0.2	6.9	1.1	267	268	638.1	21	588	1 617	R–65.6
King	3 455	58.7	0.0	1.8	0.0	26.6	0.0	0	70	1 750.0	NA	187	175	R–63.4
Kinney	942	60.5	0.3	3.7	0.4	4.6	3.0	1 307	175	648.1	52	1 870	1 450	R–53.2
Kleberg	1 078	51.0	17.2	3.9	0.9	5.7	24.7	713	2 752	893.5	540	14 461	9 946	D–54.0
Knox	1 184	49.7	31.6	2.3	0.0	4.8	6.5	1 165	345	704.1	49	1 033	1 782	D–56.8
Lamar	1 049	48.9	26.4	3.1	0.2	5.6	30.2	701	2 291	509.1	155	4 338	15 598	R–51.4
Lamb	1 028	60.9	16.4	3.3	0.0	4.3	12.8	690	887	583.6	68	1 762	5 316	R–57.6
Lampasas	524	61.7	0.0	4.2	0.1	7.7	3.2	253	564	394.4	40	1 140	4 966	R–60.4
La Salle	784	72.6	0.0	4.9	0.4	7.3	0.9	157	343	700.0	38	1 389	2 352	D–70.2
Lavaca	628	40.1	15.3	5.0	0.2	10.5	3.9	211	641	350.3	68	1 898	7 962	R–55.0
Lee	1 007	56.8	0.0	4.3	0.1	9.5	8.3	602	864	649.6	35	906	5 067	D–49.9
Leon	803	79.9	0.0	2.0	0.1	4.3	6.1	579	521	434.2	50	1 217	5 115	R–54.3
Liberty	859	58.2	8.1	3.7	0.2	9.0	28.4	553	2 543	484.4	123	3 421	16 973	R–50.2
Limestone	606	49.5	11.5	4.8	0.1	7.6	7.7	380	2 822	1 265.5	69	1 911	6 763	D–51.4
Lipscomb	1 599	66.9	2.4	1.7	0.2	11.3	4.6	1 064	271	874.2	30	717	1 499	R–74.1
Live Oak	840	59.1	0.7	5.3	0.1	14.7	0.9	90	510	573.0	33	786	3 880	R–58.7
Llano	527	37.5	25.7	5.1	0.1	10.6	2.6	247	565	452.0	40	1 199	6 202	R–57.2
Loving	5 170	0.0	0.0	4.6	0.0	23.2	0.0	0	NA	NA	NA	58	77	R–70.1
Lubbock	808	51.4	12.3	5.6	0.1	3.7	132.9	611	20 075	880.5	2 232	64 199	73 292	R–69.3
Lynn	888	61.1	12.4	3.4	0.1	8.1	2.7	326	435	649.3	43	1 068	2 367	R–54.0
McCulloch	858	41.8	22.7	3.5	0.1	7.8	4.1	457	523	574.7	41	1 006	3 293	D–50.6
McLennan	748	51.5	5.4	5.2	0.5	5.6	70.7	402	9 909	524.6	2 807	88 595	66 423	R–58.1
McMullen	2 883	33.6	0.4	1.5	0.0	53.5	0.5	569	92	1 022.2	NA	171	398	R–75.9
Madison	773	38.2	40.7	2.6	0.1	4.2	6.5	556	1 397	1 214.8	24	688	3 747	R–50.6
Marion	464	70.8	0.5	4.2	0.0	11.0	1.0	91	405	430.9	19	546	4 129	D–54.6
Martin	1 398	56.5	17.0	2.6	0.5	9.4	2.4	453	343	686.0	31	691	1 651	R–61.6
Mason	758	71.2	0.4	4.8	0.0	5.9	0.9	257	199	621.9	19	452	1 655	R–58.9
Matagorda	1 179	49.3	21.9	4.0	0.4	5.6	10.3	276	2 272	588.6	97	2 743	12 566	R–54.0
Maverick	920	49.0	19.5	2.2	0.0	3.1	11.7	341	2 130	524.6	265	9 290	6 003	D–73.2
Medina	671	65.0	0.7	4.5	0.0	10.7	12.0	506	1 438	521.0	65	1 826	10 029	R–57.1
Menard	1 488	43.7	35.2	2.3	0.0	5.6	0.4	178	183	762.5	12	334	1 171	D–52.4
Midland	1 027	49.8	18.9	5.4	0.1	3.8	93.0	949	5 908	553.2	1 015	35 294	39 326	R–77.9
Milam	762	51.4	8.5	3.3	0.7	8.1	26.7	1 156	1 033	469.5	79	1 984	8 396	D–57.9
Mills	641	67.0	0.0	2.1	0.0	6.6	1.2	265	227	515.9	25	615	1 888	R–55.2
Mitchell	1 192	42.9	30.3	2.8	0.5	8.7	3.9	408	650	764.7	35	903	3 376	D–52.5
Montague	810	54.6	21.0	4.0	0.0	5.3	9.8	528	909	522.4	71	1 973	7 186	D–51.3

1. Based on the estimated population as of July 1, 1982. 2. Per 10,000 resident population estimated as of July 1 of the year shown. 3. Data subject to copyright.

STATE–County code	MSA/CMSA/NECMA code[1]	STATE County	Land Area,[2] 1990 (Sq. Km.)	Population, 1990: Total persons	Population, 1990: Rank	Population, 1990: Per square kilometer	Race: White	Race: Black	Race: Am. Indian, Eskimo, Aleut	Race: Asian & Pacific Islander	Race: Other race	Hispanic[3]	Age of population Percent: Under 5 years	Age of population Percent: 5 to 14 years	Age of population Percent: 15 to 24 years
			1	2	3	4	5	6	7	8	9	10	11	12	13
		TEXAS—Con.													
48 339	3362	Montgomery	2 705	182 201	264	67.4	166 107	7 763	687	1 232	6 412	13 237	7.9	16.9	13.7
48 341	...	Moore	2 330	17 865	1 795	7.7	12 789	95	123	282	4 576	5 693	9.5	18.5	14.8
48 343	...	Morris	659	13 200	2 123	20.0	9 770	3 227	70	18	115	239	6.7	16.1	11.9
48 345	...	Motley	2 563	1 532	3 095	0.6	1 362	68	5	4	93	136	5.5	13.3	10.3
48 347	...	Nacogdoches	2 452	54 753	786	22.3	43 772	9 020	144	311	1 506	2 788	6.4	13.1	26.6
48 349	...	Navarro	2 774	39 926	1 005	14.4	30 322	7 574	127	271	1 632	2 891	7.5	15.1	14.2
48 351	...	Newton	2 416	13 569	2 095	5.6	10 402	3 039	44	11	73	153	7.0	17.5	13.8
48 353	...	Nolan	2 362	16 594	1 879	7.0	12 942	775	46	18	2 813	4 246	7.4	15.9	13.5
48 355	1880	Nueces	2 165	291 145	168	134.5	220 168	12 691	1 175	2 483	54 628	152 051	8.3	17.4	14.9
48 357	...	Ochiltree	2 377	9 128	2 459	3.8	8 023	2	105	8	990	1 641	8.3	18.2	12.4
48 359	...	Oldham	3 887	2 278	3 043	0.6	2 112	9	29	18	110	200	6.0	22.8	18.2
48 361	0840	Orange	923	80 509	566	87.2	72 607	6 768	189	484	461	1 933	7.2	16.7	14.0
48 363	...	Palo Pinto	2 468	25 055	1 459	10.2	22 810	792	87	171	1 195	2 301	7.3	14.8	12.6
48 365	...	Panola	2 075	22 035	1 573	10.6	17 702	4 057	57	23	196	477	6.9	16.5	13.2
48 367	1922	Parker	2 340	64 785	676	27.7	62 267	589	367	231	1 331	2 697	7.4	16.0	13.2
48 369	...	Parmer	2 284	9 863	2 400	4.3	8 980	123	29	24	707	4 096	9.1	18.7	14.2
48 371	...	Pecos	12 339	14 675	2 006	1.2	9 449	62	45	31	5 088	8 331	8.7	19.9	15.1
48 373	...	Polk	2 739	30 687	1 258	11.2	25 100	3 896	662	78	951	1 610	6.4	14.0	11.7
48 375	0320	Potter	2 355	97 874	470	41.6	73 884	8 673	901	2 570	11 846	19 246	8.9	15.7	14.4
48 377	...	Presidio	9 987	6 637	2 691	0.7	5 624	6	16	16	975	5 417	8.0	18.3	15.7
48 379	...	Rains	601	6 715	2 686	11.2	6 310	286	29	8	82	158	5.9	15.1	11.6
48 381	0320	Randall	2 368	89 673	512	37.9	84 633	1 115	454	646	2 825	6 144	7.3	15.9	14.5
48 383	...	Reagan	3 044	4 514	2 875	1.5	3 550	127	7	1	829	1 941	10.0	22.5	14.4
48 385	...	Real	1 813	2 412	3 031	1.3	2 064	0	23	0	325	574	6.1	12.9	13.8
48 387	...	Red River	2 720	14 317	2 030	5.3	11 203	2 872	75	14	153	273	5.8	13.8	12.8
48 389	...	Reeves	6 827	15 852	1 932	2.3	15 293	347	36	36	140	11 545	8.8	19.3	15.4
48 391	...	Refugio	1 995	7 976	2 572	4.0	6 201	645	25	5	1 100	3 164	6.5	16.1	13.5
48 393	...	Roberts	2 394	1 025	3 112	0.4	1 002	0	1	2	20	34	6.8	17.8	10.0
48 395	...	Robertson	2 213	15 511	1 952	7.0	10 047	4 259	36	15	1 154	1 904	8.1	16.0	13.1
48 397	1922	Rockwall	334	25 604	1 438	76.7	23 991	855	102	164	492	1 500	7.6	17.2	12.2
48 399	...	Runnels	2 731	11 294	2 276	4.1	10 438	183	16	16	641	2 740	6.9	15.8	12.2
48 401	...	Rusk	2 392	43 735	928	18.3	33 730	8 984	150	51	820	1 736	7.0	16.2	12.6
48 403	...	Sabine	1 270	9 586	2 425	7.5	8 394	1 117	10	12	53	111	5.5	11.7	10.4
48 405	...	San Augustine	1 367	7 999	2 567	5.9	5 663	2 244	15	6	71	138	6.5	14.2	11.6
48 407	...	San Jacinto	1 478	16 372	1 897	11.1	13 525	2 544	74	14	215	431	6.3	15.2	12.3
48 409	1880	San Patricio	1 792	58 749	740	32.8	44 834	968	219	163	12 565	29 809	8.2	18.8	15.1
48 411	...	San Saba	2 938	5 401	2 808	1.8	4 944	14	8	1	434	998	6.6	15.0	11.5
48 413	...	Schleicher	3 395	2 990	3 003	0.9	2 078	27	3	1	881	1 062	7.9	19.5	11.2
48 415	...	Scurry	2 338	18 634	1 758	8.0	14 113	879	62	35	3 545	4 454	7.2	16.9	13.4
48 417	...	Shackelford	2 367	3 316	2 974	1.4	3 125	12	9	2	168	272	6.3	15.8	10.7
48 419	...	Shelby	2 057	22 034	1 574	10.7	17 047	4 727	36	31	193	539	7.1	14.6	13.0
48 421	...	Sherman	2 391	2 858	3 008	1.2	2 816	4	12	7	19	538	7.5	16.6	12.7
48 423	8640	Smith	2 405	151 309	308	62.9	113 676	31 572	520	638	4 903	8 986	7.4	15.0	14.5
48 425	...	Somervell	485	5 360	2 813	11.1	4 849	10	34	22	445	749	8.4	18.7	13.2
48 427	...	Starr	3 168	40 518	986	12.8	25 067	25	31	25	15 370	39 390	9.9	22.3	19.5
48 429	...	Stephens	2 317	9 010	2 469	3.9	8 187	252	30	28	513	767	6.8	16.3	11.0
48 431	...	Sterling	2 392	1 438	3 099	0.6	1 244	0	9	0	185	366	8.8	20.4	10.9
48 433	...	Stonewall	2 380	2 013	3 067	0.8	1 898	89	2	7	17	237	6.8	14.6	10.7
48 435	...	Sutton	3 766	4 135	2 903	1.1	3 125	2	16	6	986	1 866	7.7	17.1	14.7
48 437	...	Swisher	2 332	8 133	2 553	3.5	5 702	340	26	17	2 048	2 496	8.3	17.5	12.2
48 439	1922	Tarrant	2 236	1 170 103	27	523.3	917 501	140 740	5 551	29 705	76 606	139 879	8.5	14.7	15.0
48 441	0040	Taylor	2 372	119 655	387	50.4	100 237	7 547	450	1 449	9 972	17 511	8.2	15.1	17.3
48 443	...	Terrell	6 107	1 410	3 101	0.2	1 189	1	5	2	213	751	6.4	17.9	10.8
48 445	...	Terry	2 305	13 218	2 120	5.7	10 202	449	38	28	2 501	5 194	8.6	19.4	13.6
48 447	...	Throckmorton	2 363	1 880	3 076	0.8	1 778	0	4	8	90	136	6.5	13.7	9.4
48 449	...	Titus	1 063	24 009	1 492	22.6	18 664	3 229	107	27	1 982	2 556	8.4	15.6	14.3
48 451	7200	Tom Green	3 942	98 458	466	25.0	79 533	4 136	373	998	13 418	25 501	7.8	15.3	16.8
48 453	0640	Travis	2 563	576 407	82	224.9	422 749	63 173	2 089	16 497	71 899	121 689	7.7	12.9	19.2
48 455	...	Trinity	1 795	11 445	2 258	6.4	9 619	1 645	24	21	136	272	6.2	13.3	10.9
48 457	...	Tyler	2 391	16 646	1 875	7.0	14 550	1 994	46	12	44	177	5.9	14.6	11.7
48 459	...	Upshur	1 522	31 370	1 232	20.6	27 076	3 881	121	29	263	641	7.1	16.1	13.7
48 461	...	Upton	3 216	4 447	2 879	1.4	3 487	94	20	2	844	1 666	8.7	21.4	13.3
48 463	...	Uvalde	4 032	23 340	1 524	5.8	15 078	47	49	70	8 096	14 104	8.6	18.1	16.6
48 465	...	Val Verde	8 212	38 721	1 034	4.7	26 694	757	126	244	10 900	27 299	9.2	17.9	17.9
48 467	...	Van Zandt	2 198	37 944	1 052	17.3	35 351	1 451	155	47	940	1 515	6.4	14.7	12.1
48 469	8750	Victoria	2 286	74 361	604	32.5	59 251	4 906	208	257	9 739	25 372	8.3	17.5	13.8

1. MSA = Metropolitan Statistical Area. CMSA = Consolidated MSA. NECMA = New England county metropolitan area. PMSA = Primary MSA. See Appendix A for explanation of these concepts. See Appendix B for list of metropolitan areas identified by type, with component counties. 2. Dry land or land partially or temporarily covered by water. 3. Hispanic persons may be of any race.

STATE County	Population, 1990 (cont'd) – Age of population (cont'd) Percent – 25 to 34 years	35 to 44 years	45 to 54 years	55 to 64 years	65 to 74 years	75 years and over	Percent female	Population–Change and components of change – Change 1980–1990 – Number	Percent	Components of change, 1980–1986 – Total persons, 1986	Total persons, 1980	Net change – Number	Percent	Natural increase – Births	Deaths
	14	15	16	17	18	19	20	21	22	23	24	25	26	27	28
TEXAS—Con.															
Montgomery	16.7	16.8	11.6	7.8	5.3	3.3	50.3	54 979	43.2	159 500	127 222	32 300	25.4	16 800	5 700
Moore	16.7	13.3	9.1	8.3	6.0	3.9	50.0	1 290	7.8	17 600	16 575	1 000	6.1	2 400	700
Morris	14.2	13.3	10.1	10.7	9.0	7.9	51.8	-1 429	-9.8	14 400	14 629	-200	-1.4	1 500	1 000
Motley	10.8	11.6	10.6	11.6	13.4	12.9	51.6	-418	-21.4	1 700	1 950	-200	-11.4	100	200
Nacogdoches	14.3	12.3	8.1	7.3	6.3	5.5	51.6	7 967	17.0	50 600	46 786	3 800	8.0	4 500	2 700
Navarro	14.4	12.6	9.9	9.1	8.4	8.7	51.9	4 603	13.0	39 600	35 323	4 200	12.0	3 700	2 900
Newton	13.8	13.3	11.0	10.2	7.8	5.7	51.2	315	2.4	13 300	13 254	100	0.6	1 300	800
Nolan	14.0	13.4	9.9	9.3	8.5	8.0	51.4	-765	-4.4	17 600	17 359	300	1.6	1 900	1 200
Nueces	17.4	14.8	9.3	8.0	6.1	4.0	51.1	22 930	8.5	301 600	268 215	33 400	12.4	36 200	12 100
Ochiltree	17.7	14.2	9.4	8.9	6.4	4.5	50.0	-460	-4.8	10 600	9 588	1 000	10.4	1 600	500
Oldham	12.5	12.6	9.0	8.5	6.2	4.3	43.5	-5	-0.2	2 500	2 283	200	8.4	200	100
Orange	15.7	14.6	11.4	9.6	6.9	4.0	51.1	-3 329	-4.0	83 400	83 838	-500	-0.6	9 000	3 800
Palo Pinto	14.5	13.1	10.4	10.4	9.3	7.7	51.7	993	4.1	26 600	24 062	2 500	10.5	2 500	1 900
Panola	13.9	13.9	10.3	9.5	8.6	7.2	52.2	1 311	6.3	22 200	20 724	1 500	7.3	1 900	1 400
Parker	15.7	16.1	11.8	8.8	6.5	4.4	50.0	20 176	45.2	60 200	44 609	15 600	35.0	4 300	2 500
Parmer	14.9	12.7	10.0	7.9	6.8	5.7	49.7	-1 175	-10.6	10 900	11 038	-200	-1.5	1 300	500
Pecos	14.2	13.0	10.1	9.2	5.8	4.0	50.5	57	0.4	17 200	14 618	2 600	17.5	2 400	600
Polk	12.2	11.7	10.5	13.1	12.4	8.0	51.2	6 280	25.7	30 300	24 407	5 900	24.2	2 500	2 000
Potter	17.2	13.2	8.8	8.6	7.2	5.9	51.9	-763	-0.8	106 600	98 637	8 000	8.1	13 300	6 100
Presidio	12.1	12.5	9.7	9.9	7.9	6.0	51.6	1 449	27.9	5 700	5 188	500	10.0	500	300
Rains	13.6	13.0	11.0	11.8	10.9	7.2	50.9	1 876	38.8	6 100	4 839	1 200	25.6	400	400
Randall	17.2	16.0	10.3	8.8	6.2	3.7	51.8	14 611	19.5	88 700	75 062	13 600	18.1	8 100	2 700
Reagan	16.7	14.9	7.8	6.2	4.5	3.0	49.3	379	9.2	5 100	4 135	1 000	23.9	800	100
Real	10.0	11.4	12.7	12.6	11.7	8.9	51.9	-57	-2.3	2 800	2 469	400	14.9	200	200
Red River	12.4	12.1	10.5	10.7	11.1	10.7	53.0	-1 784	-11.1	15 400	16 101	-700	-4.1	1 200	1 400
Reeves	15.8	12.6	9.4	8.4	6.1	4.2	48.5	51	0.3	15 900	15 801	100	0.7	2 400	700
Refugio	13.8	13.1	10.8	10.0	9.0	7.3	52.1	-1 313	-14.1	8 600	9 289	-700	-7.6	900	600
Roberts	15.2	15.7	12.7	10.4	5.9	5.6	51.2	-162	-13.6	1 100	1 187	-100	-11.5	100	100
Robertson	13.9	11.7	9.1	9.8	9.8	8.6	52.2	858	5.9	15 900	14 653	1 300	8.6	1 800	1 300
Rockwall	16.6	18.2	12.8	7.7	4.5	3.2	50.3	11 076	76.2	23 200	14 528	8 700	59.7	1 700	700
Runnels	12.6	12.3	9.7	9.8	10.2	10.5	51.3	-578	-4.9	12 400	11 872	500	4.4	1 300	1 000
Rusk	14.3	13.7	9.8	9.2	8.9	8.3	52.1	2 353	5.7	42 800	41 382	1 400	3.3	4 100	3 100
Sabine	10.6	9.8	11.2	15.5	15.8	9.7	51.8	884	10.2	10 100	8 702	1 400	15.5	700	800
San Augustine	12.3	10.4	10.3	12.4	11.8	10.5	52.8	-786	-8.9	8 800	8 785	0	0.1	700	700
San Jacinto	12.9	13.1	11.7	12.9	9.8	5.9	49.9	4 938	43.2	14 100	11 434	2 700	23.6	1 100	800
San Patricio	14.7	14.2	10.1	8.6	6.2	4.2	50.5	736	1.3	61 700	58 013	3 700	6.4	7 600	2 700
San Saba	11.5	12.1	9.9	10.2	10.9	12.3	51.2	-440	-7.5	5 500	5 841	-400	-6.5	500	500
Schleicher	13.7	14.0	9.0	9.2	7.9	7.5	51.6	170	6.0	3 000	2 820	200	7.8	400	200
Scurry	16.7	14.2	9.1	9.2	7.1	6.2	48.9	442	2.4	19 800	18 192	1 600	8.6	2 500	1 000
Shackelford	14.1	13.1	9.2	10.3	9.6	10.9	51.4	-599	-15.3	3 900	3 915	0	-0.1	500	300
Shelby	13.4	12.0	10.2	10.4	10.2	9.1	52.5	-1 050	-4.5	23 800	23 084	700	3.0	1 900	1 800
Sherman	14.0	13.9	11.2	10.4	7.8	5.8	50.2	-316	-10.0	3 100	3 174	-100	-1.7	300	200
Smith	16.0	14.4	10.0	9.0	7.8	5.9	51.9	22 943	17.9	152 100	128 366	23 700	18.5	15 000	7 700
Somervell	14.9	15.7	9.8	7.4	6.4	5.6	49.4	1 206	29.0	4 900	4 154	700	17.0	500	300
Starr	14.6	11.7	8.6	6.2	4.2	2.8	50.8	13 252	48.6	36 100	27 266	8 800	32.4	4 500	1 000
Stephens	13.1	12.8	10.3	10.5	10.4	8.8	52.1	-916	-9.2	10 500	9 926	600	6.2	1 200	800
Sterling	19.0	12.6	8.3	7.7	7.1	5.2	51.2	232	19.2	1 700	1 206	500	38.4	200	100
Stonewall	14.4	10.8	10.7	11.4	9.5	11.2	51.6	-393	-16.3	2 300	2 406	-100	-4.1	200	200
Sutton	14.7	15.6	10.7	9.0	6.4	4.1	51.6	-995	-19.4	5 100	5 130	0	0.3	700	300
Swisher	13.1	11.9	9.7	10.7	9.3	7.4	50.8	-1 590	-16.4	9 000	9 723	-700	-7.4	1 100	500
Tarrant	21.0	15.7	9.8	6.9	5.0	3.3	50.5	309 223	35.9	1 101 600	860 880	240 700	28.0	113 000	42 300
Taylor	17.3	13.3	8.8	7.9	6.6	5.4	51.4	8 723	7.9	125 900	110 932	14 900	13.5	15 300	6 000
Terrell	13.3	14.1	12.4	10.9	8.0	6.2	47.7	-185	-11.6	1 500	1 595	-100	-4.7	200	100
Terry	13.8	12.0	9.8	9.2	7.6	6.0	51.5	-1 363	-9.3	15 100	14 581	500	3.6	2 000	800
Throckmorton	13.7	12.1	11.2	10.9	11.1	11.4	51.8	-173	-8.4	2 100	2 053	100	3.5	200	200
Titus	15.1	13.4	9.4	8.2	8.2	7.4	51.3	2 567	12.0	23 400	21 442	1 900	8.9	2 500	1 600
Tom Green	16.4	13.9	9.0	8.1	7.0	5.7	51.5	13 674	16.1	98 100	84 784	13 400	15.8	11 000	5 000
Travis	22.2	16.4	8.4	5.9	4.3	3.0	50.0	156 834	37.4	551 000	419 573	131 400	31.3	56 000	16 500
Trinity	12.6	11.2	10.6	13.3	12.9	8.9	51.6	1 995	21.1	11 900	9 450	2 400	25.9	800	900
Tyler	12.1	11.8	11.4	12.3	12.1	8.2	51.4	423	2.6	18 700	16 223	2 400	15.1	1 500	1 300
Upshur	14.3	13.6	10.8	9.6	7.9	6.7	51.5	2 775	9.7	32 300	28 595	3 800	13.1	2 900	1 900
Upton	15.4	14.1	9.5	8.2	5.4	4.0	50.5	-172	-3.7	5 500	4 619	900	19.2	800	200
Uvalde	13.8	12.4	9.4	8.6	6.7	5.8	51.8	899	4.0	24 600	22 441	2 200	9.8	2 600	1 200
Val Verde	15.6	12.2	9.5	7.9	6.0	3.7	50.4	2 811	7.8	40 000	35 910	4 000	11.3	5 700	1 500
Van Zandt	12.8	13.4	11.4	11.2	10.0	7.9	51.2	6 518	20.7	38 600	31 426	7 100	22.7	2 600	2 600
Victoria	16.4	15.0	9.8	8.3	6.4	4.5	51.3	5 554	8.1	76 000	68 807	7 200	10.4	9 600	3 300

STATE County	Population–(cont'd) Components of change, 1980-1986 (cont'd) Net migration	Households, 1990 Number	Percent change, 1980–1990	Persons per household	Percent Female family householder[1]	Percent One-person	Births, 1988 Total	Rate[2]	Low birth weight[3] (Number)	Deaths, 1987 Number Total	Number Infant[4]	Rate Total[2]	Rate Infant[5]	Marriages, 1984 Number	Rate[2]
	29	30	31	32	33	34	35	36	37	38	39	40	41	42	43
TEXAS—Con.															
Montgomery	21 200	63 563	53.2	2.84	9.1	18.0	2 791	15.6	184	1 091	15	6.2	5.5	2 451	15.7
Moore	-700	6 101	9.1	2.90	7.1	18.8	333	19.8	18	128	7	7.5	20.7	277	16.0
Morris	-700	4 988	-3.8	2.60	13.3	23.3	175	12.4	18	148	3	10.6	15.3	126	8.5
Motley	-200	647	-20.3	2.36	7.3	29.8	17	9.4	2	17	0	9.4	0.0	20	11.1
Nacogdoches	1 900	20 124	22.3	2.49	10.9	26.6	738	14.3	46	441	6	8.5	8.1	583	11.6
Navarro	3 400	14 874	11.6	2.60	11.9	25.3	579	14.7	49	532	7	13.4	11.0	527	13.5
Newton	-400	4 910	9.8	2.75	10.8	21.8	192	14.4	6	116	0	8.7	0.0	204	15.2
Nolan	-400	6 183	-4.1	2.59	9.3	25.1	251	14.7	13	182	5	10.5	18.8	241	13.5
Nueces	9 300	99 740	14.7	2.87	13.7	21.9	5 149	17.3	301	1 991	48	6.7	9.3	3 474	11.7
Ochiltree	-100	3 328	-4.5	2.73	6.9	20.6	152	15.8	8	67	0	6.8	0.0	249	22.8
Oldham	100	681	1.0	2.76	5.3	20.0	32	11.4	0	23	0	8.2	0.0	40	16.0
Orange	-5 700	29 025	4.0	2.75	10.7	19.5	1 239	14.9	85	645	9	7.7	7.6	1 489	17.7
Palo Pinto	1 900	9 531	6.2	2.57	9.4	24.3	366	14.5	29	305	1	11.8	2.5	371	14.1
Panola	1 000	8 241	10.9	2.63	10.0	24.3	260	11.8	13	234	6	10.5	21.4	280	12.5
Parker	13 900	23 048	47.4	2.76	7.3	17.8	933	14.4	66	416	8	6.6	8.9	1 079	20.4
Parmer	-1 000	3 241	-7.1	3.01	7.0	18.6	201	19.5	4	85	0	8.0	0.0	157	14.5
Pecos	700	4 712	3.2	3.07	9.8	18.3	321	20.3	23	91	2	5.7	6.3	194	11.3
Polk	5 400	11 855	33.1	2.55	8.9	23.5	414	13.4	24	357	3	11.6	6.9	405	13.9
Potter	700	37 344	-1.1	2.57	12.8	28.3	2 083	20.3	188	953	42	9.2	19.1	1 952	18.2
Presidio	300	2 255	34.2	2.91	12.3	23.5	98	16.3	5	51	1	8.4	8.6	49	8.6
Rains	1 200	2 609	36.5	2.53	7.2	23.7	71	11.1	3	78	2	12.4	30.3	91	16.0
Randall	8 300	34 553	29.4	2.55	8.2	23.9	1 250	13.4	71	553	16	5.9	12.5	690	8.1
Reagan	300	1 358	4.1	3.29	3.8	15.7	93	19.8	7	26	1	5.5	12.0	37	7.9
Real	400	924	2.7	2.55	8.3	23.8	30	10.7	3	22	0	8.1	0.0	32	11.9
Red River	-500	5 688	-5.9	2.46	11.1	27.9	198	13.1	14	250	3	16.3	16.3	272	17.2
Reeves	-1 600	4 838	1.0	3.14	10.5	19.0	296	19.9	31	160	5	10.6	17.8	221	13.6
Refugio	-1 000	2 937	-7.3	2.69	12.6	23.8	116	13.5	7	88	2	10.0	15.0	98	11.0
Roberts	-200	391	-8.2	2.62	4.6	22.0	6	5.5	0	4	0	3.6	0.0	17	17.0
Robertson	800	5 793	5.0	2.63	14.1	26.9	250	16.3	14	198	2	12.9	7.5	177	11.1
Rockwall	7 700	8 838	81.7	2.87	7.1	15.4	368	13.4	16	135	2	5.1	5.3	1 371	72.2
Runnels	300	4 346	-3.3	2.56	8.6	26.2	147	12.7	15	163	2	13.6	13.2	147	11.6
Rusk	400	16 327	8.8	2.64	10.2	24.0	609	14.4	45	580	3	13.6	4.6	461	10.7
Sabine	1 400	3 985	19.5	2.37	7.5	24.8	97	9.8	2	133	1	13.4	10.2	202	20.8
San Augustine	0	3 073	-1.9	2.52	12.9	25.3	130	14.9	3	128	2	14.5	16.9	133	15.1
San Jacinto	2 400	6 247	52.8	2.61	9.2	21.6	191	12.7	12	154	1	10.3	5.3	189	14.0
San Patricio	-1 200	18 776	7.0	3.10	11.7	17.4	1 038	17.3	62	480	6	7.9	5.9	506	8.2
San Saba	-300	2 122	-11.0	2.46	7.8	28.0	76	13.8	5	113	0	20.5	0.0	57	9.7
Schleicher	0	1 051	6.4	2.81	6.9	21.5	33	11.8	0	31	2	10.7	37.0	34	10.3
Scurry	100	6 368	-0.1	2.73	7.7	21.9	297	16.7	17	172	4	9.3	14.6	238	11.9
Shackelford	-100	1 336	-10.5	2.43	6.7	29.6	38	11.2	1	40	1	11.1	22.2	44	10.7
Shelby	700	8 476	-0.9	2.55	12.0	25.9	348	14.6	19	310	4	13.0	11.9	225	9.4
Sherman	-200	1 053	-5.7	2.68	3.6	21.4	43	14.3	2	34	0	11.3	0.0	42	13.5
Smith	16 500	56 800	23.4	2.61	11.3	24.3	2 334	15.3	138	1 299	21	8.5	8.6	1 948	13.3
Somervell	500	1 902	24.2	2.74	8.3	22.1	99	18.7	4	38	1	7.6	11.0	112	24.3
Starr	5 400	10 331	50.6	3.90	14.2	10.3	837	21.4	41	181	2	4.7	2.8	493	14.7
Stephens	200	3 556	-9.5	2.50	8.8	27.8	152	15.5	16	161	1	15.6	5.5	139	13.1
Sterling	300	494	19.6	2.87	7.1	18.4	29	19.3	2	11	1	7.3	32.3	21	13.1
Stonewall	-100	806	-14.3	2.43	6.7	28.4	31	14.1	1	35	1	15.9	33.3	16	6.4
Sutton	-400	1 466	-12.5	2.79	6.6	22.0	70	16.3	3	32	0	7.3	0.0	43	7.8
Swisher	-1 300	2 993	-9.1	2.69	7.9	24.4	167	19.2	20	92	2	10.6	13.1	69	7.7
Tarrant	170 000	438 634	41.4	2.62	10.8	24.7	21 803	19.3	1 447	7 351	201	6.6	9.3	12 617	12.4
Taylor	5 600	43 301	12.4	2.61	9.3	24.7	2 290	18.8	173	993	15	8.0	6.5	1 840	15.0
Terrell	-100	524	-8.1	2.69	7.1	24.6	14	9.3	1	11	0	7.3	0.0	18	12.0
Terry	-700	4 478	-7.5	2.92	9.4	19.7	215	14.7	13	98	1	6.8	4.1	191	12.4
Throckmorton	100	790	-7.4	2.33	5.2	31.6	26	13.0	0	25	1	11.9	28.6	11	4.6
Titus	1 000	8 508	9.9	2.75	9.7	21.9	449	19.6	30	306	4	13.4	9.5	324	14.2
Tom Green	7 400	35 408	16.6	2.63	10.5	24.8	1 751	17.6	120	860	18	8.7	10.9	1 319	13.6
Travis	91 900	232 861	47.0	2.39	10.5	31.5	10 049	18.1	606	2 868	77	5.2	7.5	7 138	14.2
Trinity	2 500	4 647	27.4	2.43	9.4	25.2	139	11.4	8	127	4	10.4	25.0	124	10.9
Tyler	2 200	6 459	10.0	2.54	8.9	23.0	202	11.2	11	221	1	12.2	4.6	204	11.3
Upshur	2 800	11 360	12.7	2.69	9.4	21.1	404	12.7	22	323	3	10.1	6.7	331	10.3
Upton	400	1 472	-5.6	3.00	7.0	20.2	92	18.0	4	34	0	6.8	0.0	52	9.6
Uvalde	800	7 553	8.5	3.04	12.2	19.3	417	17.1	24	207	2	8.6	4.7	246	10.1
Val Verde	-100	11 840	14.3	3.21	12.5	16.6	901	22.4	51	243	2	6.0	2.4	571	14.5
Van Zandt	7 100	14 349	23.1	2.60	7.6	21.7	426	10.8	29	436	7	11.2	16.2	387	10.7
Victoria	900	26 228	14.1	2.81	11.1	21.2	1 355	18.2	99	518	16	6.9	12.7	949	12.7

1. No spouse present. 2. Per 1,000 resident population estimated as of July 1 of the year shown. 3. Under 2,500 grams. 4. Deaths of infants under 1 year old. 5. Deaths of infants under 1 year old per 1,000 live births.

STATE County	Divorces, 1984		Physicians, active non–Federal, 1989		Hospitals, 1989	Beds		Nursing homes,[4] 1986		Serious crimes known to police, 1988 Number			Education Public school enrollment[7]		Attainment,[8] 1980	
	Number	Rate[1]	Number[2]	Rate[3]	Number	Number	Rate[3]	Number	Beds	Total[5]	Violent[6]	Rate[3]	1986–1987	1980	Percent 12 yrs. or more	Percent 16 yrs. or more
	44	45	46	47	48	49	50	51	52	53	54	55	56	57	58	59
TEXAS—Con.																
Montgomery	973	6.2	117	63	5	554	296	4	471	8 966	703	5 301	73 936	31 734	65.8	15.4
Moore	106	6.1	9	54	1	115	689	1	47	431	3	2 478	4 079	3 766	59.7	11.1
Morris	92	6.2	9	65	2	75	540	3	262	462	29	3 301	3 054	2 966	54.0	9.7
Motley	1	0.6	0	0	0	0	0	0	0	32	0	1 883	285	356	51.8	10.5
Nacogdoches	166	3.3	82	158	3	320	615	7	469	2 618	208	5 105	8 561	7 403	57.9	18.3
Navarro	256	6.6	51	129	1	142	359	7	596	2 589	157	6 556	7 357	6 720	48.6	11.2
Newton	106	7.9	3	23	0	0	0	1	82	248	25	1 865	2 896	3 237	45.2	4.0
Nolan	121	6.8	5	30	1	35	208	3	208	789	70	4 589	3 770	3 700	49.4	7.3
Nueces	1 905	6.4	569	191	12	1 682	565	10	1 314	29 923	2 104	9 994	61 494	57 657	59.0	14.5
Ochiltree	75	6.9	3	33	1	45	489	1	60	311	13	3 111	2 036	1 852	66.5	13.7
Oldham	7	2.8	1	34	0	0	0	0	0	58	0	2 072	827	812	63.5	14.9
Orange	649	7.7	41	50	1	147	178	6	573	4 758	352	5 599	17 731	19 436	62.2	9.0
Palo Pinto	215	8.1	22	88	1	69	276	3	280	1 485	72	5 735	4 640	4 697	53.9	9.6
Panola	111	5.0	10	45	1	40	181	2	212	534	29	2 395	4 045	4 317	52.3	9.5
Parker	360	6.8	29	43	1	75	110	4	373	2 569	99	4 066	10 650	9 547	59.3	11.5
Parmer	40	3.7	3	30	1	26	257	2	159	221	20	2 028	2 524	2 770	51.7	9.5
Pecos	59	3.5	8	52	2	51	333	1	68	450	39	2 728	4 078	3 716	49.3	9.3
Polk	83	2.9	14	45	1	32	102	3	259	1 276	89	4 144	5 503	4 810	46.0	9.1
Potter	908	8.5	346	342	5	1 172	1 157	7	630	8 211	567	7 800	30 046	18 408	60.1	10.3
Presidio	14	2.5	2	32	0	0	0	0	0	9	5	153	1 406	1 370	41.1	12.2
Rains	40	7.0	0	0	0	0	0	1	64	158	12	2 634	1 125	843	42.7	5.0
Randall	561	6.6	10	10	1	49	51	6	517	6 042	405	6 577	5 364	14 642	81.7	24.1
Reagan	15	3.2	3	65	1	71	1 543	1	44	112	5	2 334	1 228	965	55.1	9.1
Real	18	6.7	0	0	0	0	0	0	0	22	1	786	212	633	46.9	7.9
Red River	91	5.8	24	161	1	36	242	2	286	703	54	4 627	3 207	3 339	43.6	8.9
Reeves	66	4.1	5	34	1	48	331	1	60	630	60	4 040	4 072	4 097	44.5	8.7
Refugio	37	4.2	3	35	1	20	233	1	64	192	18	2 183	2 009	2 177	43.6	9.5
Roberts	1	1.0	1	91	0	0	0	0	0	9	0	818	253	287	64.4	14.1
Robertson	61	3.8	4	27	0	0	0	3	250	573	81	3 674	3 169	3 191	40.0	7.1
Rockwall	137	7.2	16	53	1	92	307	1	192	1 294	73	4 998	5 336	3 487	70.3	18.2
Runnels	48	3.8	6	53	2	40	351	3	250	165	21	1 375	2 522	2 364	42.2	9.0
Rusk	227	5.3	27	64	1	96	229	5	615	2 234	185	5 270	7 743	8 333	53.1	9.3
Sabine	31	3.2	2	20	1	36	364	1	60	116	5	1 184	1 499	1 680	41.7	7.3
San Augustine	9	1.0	3	34	1	22	253	1	70	169	5	1 900	1 625	1 893	38.2	8.1
San Jacinto	111	8.2	1	7	0	0	0	0	0	544	23	3 652	2 963	2 532	43.9	6.3
San Patricio	313	5.1	25	42	1	75	126	4	396	2 260	161	3 718	15 669	15 395	51.6	10.9
San Saba	41	6.9	2	36	0	0	0	2	143	81	17	1 501	1 124	1 251	49.7	11.1
Schleicher	14	4.2	5	185	1	49	1 815	1	38	73	3	2 434	706	590	54.7	13.9
Scurry	136	6.8	9	53	1	91	532	2	197	473	30	2 558	3 996	3 768	55.5	10.0
Shackelford	17	4.1	1	30	1	24	727	1	80	38	0	1 027	684	706	51.7	10.8
Shelby	169	7.0	12	50	1	58	243	3	247	766	69	3 233	4 391	4 805	44.0	7.5
Sherman	14	4.5	1	34	0	0	0	1	38	48	0	1 601	711	704	64.3	9.0
Smith	802	5.5	339	221	6	930	607	13	1 450	12 456	796	8 165	28 212	25 449	65.1	16.1
Somervell	2	0.4	2	36	1	68	1 214	1	42	162	3	3 307	1 213	810	51.2	9.2
Starr	2	0.1	7	17	1	44	107	1	100	676	52	1 752	10 690	8 272	26.6	6.0
Stephens	69	6.5	5	53	1	30	316	2	164	230	11	2 212	2 042	1 910	52.0	9.3
Sterling	7	4.4	2	143	0	0	0	1	29	16	2	1 067	342	271	53.3	11.0
Stonewall	15	6.0	0	0	1	25	1 190	1	80	7	1	304	379	377	48.3	8.0
Sutton	43	7.8	2	50	1	54	1 350	1	39	109	5	2 423	1 194	1 142	58.6	10.2
Swisher	38	4.2	4	47	1	30	349	1	52	254	35	2 887	1 979	2 352	50.0	12.1
Tarrant	7 666	7.5	1 648	143	33	4 889	424	60	6 819	125 019	10 223	11 262	189 694	166 688	69.6	18.4
Taylor	954	7.8	215	177	4	663	546	8	932	6 937	701	5 642	22 061	20 021	64.5	17.4
Terrell	1	0.7	0	0	0	0	0	0	0	15	2	1 071	370	346	59.9	11.4
Terry	90	5.8	7	49	1	42	294	2	170	712	115	4 812	3 217	3 616	48.8	9.0
Throckmorton	7	2.9	1	50	1	20	1 000	1	58	21	3	1 000	403	358	50.2	11.9
Titus	73	3.2	28	123	1	140	614	5	444	1 164	63	4 997	4 302	4 381	52.9	9.7
Tom Green	712	7.3	162	162	5	880	882	5	830	6 514	467	6 582	17 462	15 960	59.8	14.7
Travis	3 391	6.8	1 200	213	15	2 868	509	30	3 020	57 625	2 887	10 439	79 148	70 981	75.4	30.2
Trinity	10	0.9	2	16	1	22	179	1	35	240	13	1 952	2 277	1 837	45.0	8.4
Tyler	93	5.1	8	45	1	48	268	2	210	313	31	1 720	3 784	3 333	49.8	9.4
Upshur	198	6.1	15	47	1	46	145	2	209	1 299	110	3 926	5 902	6 184	54.0	10.0
Upton	4	0.7	2	40	2	66	1 320	1	30	105	15	2 143	1 330	1 022	52.9	10.6
Uvalde	77	3.2	18	74	1	48	198	2	227	772	80	3 101	5 864	5 346	46.7	13.3
Val Verde	200	5.1	23	57	2	97	240	2	132	1 958	167	4 789	9 771	9 316	51.1	12.2
Van Zandt	208	5.7	14	35	1	27	67	7	564	1 272	71	3 254	7 379	6 367	49.3	8.2
Victoria	520	7.0	150	203	5	749	1 014	4	504	4 762	476	6 309	14 675	14 404	58.4	12.0

1. Per 1,000 resident population estimated as of July 1 of the year shown. 2. As of end of year. 3. Per 100,000 resident population as of July 1 of the year shown. 4. Preliminary. Covers nursing homes with 3 or more beds. 5. Data for serious crimes have not been adjusted for underreporting, this may affect comparability between geographic areas or over time. 6. Includes murder and nonnegligent manslaughter, forcible rape, robbery, and aggravated assault. 7. The 1986–1987 data are based on administrative reports obtained by the U.S. National Center for Education Statistics. The 1980 data are based on the 1980 Census of Population and Housing. 8. Persons 25 years old or older.

STATE County	Education (cont'd): Local government expenditures for education,[1] 1982: Total (Mil dol)	Education (cont'd): Local government expenditures for education,[1] 1982: Per capita (Dollars)	Social Security Program December 1988: Beneficiaries: Total	Social Security Program December 1988: Beneficiaries: Rate[2]	Social Security Program December 1988: Payments ($1,000)	Supplemental Security Income Program recipients June 1986	Money income: Per capita[3]: 1987 Income, (Dollars)	Money income: Per capita[3]: 1979: Current dollars	Money income: Per capita[3]: 1979: Constant 1987 dollars	Money income: Median household income 1979 (Dollars)	Money income: Percent below poverty level, 1979: Persons	Money income: Percent below poverty level, 1979: Families	Housing units, 1990: Total	Housing units, 1990: Percent change, 1980–1990
	60	61	62	63	64	65	66	67	68	69	70	71	72	73
TEXAS—Con.														
Montgomery	87.9	589	18 270	102.1	9 052	1 556	11 170	8 160	12 768	22 381	7.7	6.2	73 871	48.0
Moore	9.6	556	2 150	128.0	1 104	88	10 279	7 019	10 983	18 482	10.1	7.3	6 837	12.4
Morris	7.1	457	3 140	222.7	1 378	430	8 151	6 366	9 961	16 288	14.7	12.1	5 800	2.0
Motley	0.8	445	475	263.9	204	54	8 744	5 930	9 279	9 656	28.7	23.0	1 026	7.1
Nacogdoches	14.8	304	8 645	167.9	3 789	1 456	8 799	5 854	9 160	11 989	19.3	12.9	22 768	24.3
Navarro	18.5	502	8 490	215.5	3 753	1 268	8 658	6 034	9 441	11 747	17.9	13.5	17 219	15.2
Newton	6.9	522	2 230	167.7	926	426	6 644	5 113	8 000	12 967	20.6	16.3	6 378	4.4
Nolan	10.5	581	3 560	208.2	1 596	374	9 214	6 307	9 869	13 262	15.4	11.9	7 462	-0.1
Nueces	137.1	483	37 585	126.2	16 706	6 372	9 296	6 609	10 341	16 564	16.8	13.4	114 326	21.1
Ochiltree	5.8	530	1 180	122.9	601	36	11 145	8 454	13 228	20 330	8.0	5.5	3 996	3.4
Oldham	3.0	1 307	325	116.1	158	4	7 100	5 083	7 953	13 656	9.3	5.9	861	8.0
Orange	56.6	639	12 355	148.9	6 237	1 048	9 443	7 160	11 203	20 641	10.0	8.2	32 032	4.5
Palo Pinto	9.1	353	4 935	195.1	2 215	390	9 403	6 650	10 405	13 470	12.0	8.9	13 349	9.1
Panola	11.3	512	4 015	181.7	1 742	554	9 324	6 225	9 740	14 785	14.8	11.3	9 700	10.6
Parker	16.9	353	7 395	114.1	3 392	416	10 910	7 043	11 020	17 245	10.5	9.0	26 044	47.0
Parmer	6.3	571	1 375	133.5	632	112	7 564	5 252	8 218	14 026	22.0	17.2	3 685	-7.4
Pecos	15.5	916	1 820	115.2	807	242	7 320	5 708	8 931	16 316	17.2	12.1	5 841	9.7
Polk	9.2	351	7 760	251.9	3 670	806	7 777	5 527	8 648	11 115	19.3	15.5	18 662	31.6
Potter	64.0	617	18 620	181.1	9 018	1 474	9 371	6 691	10 469	14 307	13.1	9.8	42 927	4.6
Presidio	2.1	386	1 045	174.2	352	328	4 858	3 751	5 869	8 594	40.7	34.6	2 890	36.6
Rains	1.7	323	1 205	188.3	513	130	10 009	6 481	10 141	12 132	16.6	13.6	3 533	43.0
Randall	7.8	99	6 990	74.7	3 586	222	13 200	9 044	14 151	21 253	5.4	3.4	37 807	32.5
Reagan	3.5	734	425	90.4	213	24	8 653	6 466	10 117	17 039	16.3	12.4	1 685	12.4
Real	0.6	225	645	230.4	273	76	7 047	4 636	7 254	9 180	34.2	23.9	2 049	33.3
Red River	6.6	418	3 815	252.6	1 476	864	7 230	5 033	7 875	9 584	26.0	20.5	6 650	-2.2
Reeves	11.4	690	1 980	132.9	790	456	6 575	4 908	7 680	12 645	24.4	21.0	6 044	7.5
Refugio	6.4	698	1 640	190.7	778	214	9 477	6 186	9 679	14 415	18.1	13.4	3 739	3.5
Roberts	0.9	760	145	131.8	66	6	10 034	8 114	12 696	17 370	9.6	8.3	492	0.0
Robertson	6.2	405	3 315	216.7	1 330	692	8 024	5 460	8 543	10 360	26.4	20.1	7 338	5.8
Rockwall	7.8	467	1 880	68.4	932	96	14 241	9 333	14 603	23 055	8.1	6.6	9 816	77.6
Runnels	5.6	464	2 955	254.7	1 267	320	8 446	5 868	9 182	12 083	19.9	14.0	5 345	-3.2
Rusk	19.7	462	7 920	187.7	3 557	948	9 412	6 191	9 687	14 572	14.0	11.1	19 092	12.3
Sabine	3.2	351	3 325	335.9	1 514	350	7 906	5 131	8 028	9 687	21.3	17.6	6 996	10.7
San Augustine	2.9	317	2 110	242.5	863	466	7 436	5 144	8 049	10 345	24.5	19.1	4 168	-2.3
San Jacinto	5.6	469	2 550	170.0	1 151	396	7 662	5 422	8 484	11 850	23.2	18.7	9 823	51.0
San Patricio	32.2	525	8 460	140.8	3 681	1 534	7 945	6 028	9 432	17 048	18.2	14.7	22 126	13.6
San Saba	2.3	385	1 425	259.1	577	226	8 367	5 298	8 290	10 072	24.2	18.0	3 078	2.1
Schleicher	1.8	590	480	171.4	208	56	8 184	6 610	10 343	14 448	15.4	13.4	1 288	6.4
Scurry	9.7	497	3 005	168.8	1 405	256	10 094	7 063	11 051	16 324	12.0	9.0	7 702	6.4
Shackelford	1.6	393	760	223.5	366	36	9 124	7 009	10 967	13 511	12.2	8.1	1 755	-0.9
Shelby	7.8	330	5 590	233.9	2 275	1 150	8 218	5 576	8 725	10 991	21.5	17.1	10 616	1.3
Sherman	2.2	703	370	123.3	183	6	16 260	10 504	16 436	16 590	9.2	8.5	1 293	0.5
Smith	54.7	399	25 030	164.0	11 862	2 668	10 666	7 115	11 133	16 348	13.4	9.5	64 369	25.8
Somervell	2.2	526	660	124.5	285	86	9 350	6 963	10 895	16 356	11.0	8.3	2 429	29.4
Starr	21.8	723	4 090	104.3	1 091	1 656	3 464	2 668	4 175	7 619	50.6	45.0	12 209	55.9
Stephens	3.4	315	2 020	206.1	963	178	8 479	6 374	9 973	12 681	14.4	10.7	4 982	1.7
Sterling	1.3	959	190	126.7	91	18	9 290	7 138	11 169	13 720	16.6	14.4	623	12.7
Stonewall	1.6	675	535	243.2	224	46	8 033	5 972	9 344	12 137	16.6	12.9	1 085	-4.7
Sutton	3.2	552	545	126.7	237	84	10 366	8 144	12 743	17 983	17.3	15.8	1 924	-4.3
Swisher	5.6	601	1 735	199.4	805	152	7 493	5 355	8 379	12 455	25.1	19.3	3 497	-10.5
Tarrant	343.6	364	117 935	104.5	57 829	9 266	12 498	7 965	12 463	18 642	9.4	6.9	491 152	45.4
Taylor	40.0	336	17 990	147.7	8 353	2 172	9 675	6 806	10 649	15 072	12.0	8.6	49 988	20.1
Terrell	1.2	781	215	143.3	91	36	9 036	7 069	11 061	15 213	18.2	16.1	810	-14.6
Terry	9.4	617	2 175	149.0	971	314	8 066	5 799	9 074	14 332	23.1	17.3	5 296	-2.7
Throckmorton	1.1	508	510	255.0	231	38	8 629	6 397	10 009	10 712	19.4	14.5	1 106	-0.5
Titus	9.5	426	4 560	199.1	2 007	640	9 370	6 438	10 074	15 285	13.0	8.8	9 357	10.8
Tom Green	31.1	342	15 110	152.2	6 917	1 670	9 982	6 798	10 637	14 509	12.5	8.9	40 135	22.1
Travis	174.0	388	50 525	90.8	24 661	6 410	12 316	7 540	11 798	15 741	14.4	8.9	264 173	50.9
Trinity	3.4	327	3 020	247.5	1 374	442	7 705	5 403	8 454	10 486	20.4	15.2	7 200	22.8
Tyler	9.0	545	4 175	231.9	1 924	438	7 997	5 834	9 128	12 135	16.2	12.7	9 047	8.1
Upshur	10.6	340	5 670	177.7	2 534	678	8 506	6 038	9 448	15 026	13.8	10.6	12 887	12.1
Upton	6.8	1 258	605	118.6	289	52	7 544	5 927	9 274	14 663	18.6	13.6	1 868	-0.4
Uvalde	10.4	450	3 760	154.1	1 515	696	6 802	4 697	7 349	11 577	28.4	22.3	9 692	16.1
Val Verde	17.8	468	4 855	120.8	1 692	1 170	6 747	4 542	7 107	11 529	30.0	24.3	13 905	13.4
Van Zandt	11.1	335	7 845	198.6	3 528	748	8 946	6 028	9 432	12 825	12.9	10.5	17 013	24.8
Victoria	28.1	382	10 475	141.0	4 765	1 320	9 947	7 124	11 147	18 349	13.1	9.9	29 162	18.3

1. Elementary and secondary. 2. Per 1,000 resident population estimated as of July 1 of the year shown. 3. Based on the resident population estimated as of July 1, 1988 for 1987 data and enumerated as of April 1, 1980 for 1979 data.

STATE County	Housing units, 1990 (cont'd): Occupied units: Total	Housing units, 1990 (cont'd): Occupied units: Owner occupied: Percent	Housing units, 1990 (cont'd): Occupied units: Owner occupied: Median value (Dollars)	Housing units, 1990 (cont'd): Occupied units: Median rent (Dollars)	Civilian labor force, 1990: Total	Civilian labor force, 1990: Percent change, 1989–1990	Civilian labor force, 1990: Unemployment: Total	Civilian labor force, 1990: Unemployment: Rate[1]	Private nonfarm establishments, 1988: Number	Private nonfarm establishments, 1988: Net change, 1987–1988	Private nonfarm establishments, 1988: Employment[2]: Total	Private nonfarm establishments, 1988: Employment[2]: Percent change, 1987–1988	Private nonfarm establishments, 1988: Employment[2]: Manufacturing	Private nonfarm establishments, 1988: Employment[2]: Retail trade
	74	75	76	77	78	79	80	81	82	83	84	85	86	87
TEXAS—Con.														
Montgomery	63 563	71.9	69 400	325	85 775	2.2	4 372	5.1	2 643	4	28 523	5.0	3 381	7 137
Moore	6 101	69.4	46 400	251	9 061	-1.3	317	3.5	417	-12	4 228	-5.0	1 617	975
Morris	4 988	75.9	35 300	184	3 912	-12.8	533	13.6	280	3	0	0.0	2 686	484
Motley	647	76.7	23 700	119	1 035	-3.9	26	2.5	43	-4	196	-9.7	0	58
Nacogdoches	20 124	58.1	54 100	276	27 890	1.0	1 434	5.1	1 159	-5	12 799	3.8	3 602	3 713
Navarro	14 874	69.5	40 900	248	18 248	-2.2	1 264	6.9	878	-37	10 858	3.4	2 426	2 798
Newton	4 910	83.2	30 500	157	4 906	-6.4	454	9.3	157	-19	1 299	-0.7	682	234
Nolan	6 183	70.4	29 300	196	7 827	-2.0	564	7.2	395	-16	3 930	-7.3	946	1 011
Nueces	99 740	58.2	54 700	300	138 999	3.0	9 460	6.8	7 279	-209	88 101	-0.7	9 414	22 384
Ochiltree	3 328	71.4	45 400	266	4 422	-2.5	166	3.8	320	-15	2 520	-0.8	89	510
Oldham	681	64.9	42 100	242	1 284	-2.4	55	4.3	39	-1	160	9.6	0	81
Orange	29 025	75.6	44 400	254	37 355	-0.2	3 290	8.8	1 332	-5	18 217	5.5	6 448	4 419
Palo Pinto	9 531	72.5	37 400	222	11 477	0.3	732	6.4	587	-58	5 729	-4.0	1 793	1 587
Panola	8 241	80.4	43 100	228	14 076	-6.0	622	4.4	404	-11	3 724	-3.8	961	879
Parker	23 048	79.0	67 600	302	32 449	1.7	1 425	4.4	978	-22	7 735	-7.6	1 396	2 702
Parmer	3 241	69.9	39 100	223	5 908	-4.9	215	3.6	217	2	2 715	10.1	0	281
Pecos	4 712	69.8	38 100	206	5 874	-4.3	359	6.1	379	-28	2 934	6.6	57	908
Polk	11 855	80.3	39 900	218	11 013	-1.3	745	6.8	533	-46	5 624	2.4	1 359	1 423
Potter	37 344	60.2	39 100	274	48 569	-1.7	3 031	6.2	3 743	-68	47 925	-0.5	9 577	11 094
Presidio	2 255	69.1	28 200	147	2 236	6.7	372	16.6	109	-16	536	5.7	0	282
Rains	2 609	81.6	42 500	203	2 433	-9.3	141	5.8	108	-11	685	-12.6	0	208
Randall	34 553	68.4	64 800	318	47 649	-1.3	1 835	3.9	1 513	3	15 364	4.6	1 523	6 345
Reagan	1 358	73.0	44 000	236	1 862	0.6	75	4.0	108	-12	750	-2.1	18	159
Real	924	77.7	38 300	172	1 426	6.3	81	5.7	48	0	203	9.1	0	77
Red River	5 688	75.6	25 700	130	6 322	-4.6	445	7.0	235	-7	2 156	4.9	895	544
Reeves	4 838	74.5	25 800	191	6 561	-3.8	571	8.7	302	-24	2 312	-7.3	33	536
Refugio	2 937	71.4	39 300	193	3 543	-1.9	122	3.4	217	-17	1 402	-7.3	19	498
Roberts	391	71.9	42 200	191	615	3.7	37	6.0	19	-1	137	28.0	0	26
Robertson	5 793	71.1	37 400	156	5 982	-12.1	375	6.3	252	8	2 024	2.4	340	579
Rockwall	8 838	77.4	97 900	428	15 175	-1.1	499	3.3	552	12	4 498	-13.4	485	1 190
Runnels	4 346	75.7	30 300	169	5 646	0.6	232	4.1	297	-13	2 595	1.5	1 008	498
Rusk	16 327	79.0	41 800	220	17 174	-2.1	1 272	7.4	758	-39	9 066	-4.9	1 842	1 393
Sabine	3 985	84.5	36 200	147	3 494	6.6	254	7.3	155	-12	1 115	0.1	435	306
San Augustine	3 073	79.2	35 200	136	3 821	-0.9	187	4.9	162	6	1 006	-0.2	132	293
San Jacinto	6 247	84.6	40 300	217	5 897	-5.2	287	4.9	155	2	1 546	8.6	531	265
San Patricio	18 776	68.3	47 000	254	25 149	1.9	1 792	7.1	925	-41	8 141	-0.6	1 195	2 537
San Saba	2 122	73.0	33 100	169	2 925	-2.3	153	5.2	159	7	1 291	-2.6	108	229
Schleicher	1 051	71.6	33 300	181	1 443	13.0	76	5.3	58	-6	285	-32.9	0	52
Scurry	6 368	73.3	38 100	230	10 677	9.6	489	4.6	529	-37	4 557	-6.1	209	1 153
Shackelford	1 336	75.4	32 800	177	1 729	0.1	51	2.9	127	0	610	-3.5	25	103
Shelby	8 476	77.7	35 200	161	10 617	0.0	606	5.7	440	8	4 605	7.7	1 873	1 046
Sherman	1 053	70.1	36 900	215	1 572	-1.6	37	2.4	66	-18	369	-21.3	0	98
Smith	56 800	66.5	59 900	296	74 118	-1.6	4 601	6.2	4 251	-120	50 934	-3.4	10 702	11 967
Somervell	1 902	70.9	55 300	246	1 879	-36.7	352	18.7	98	-2	1 837	6.2	59	203
Starr	10 331	78.8	21 900	163	17 944	6.0	6 478	36.1	356	13	2 518	20.2	0	1 236
Stephens	3 556	74.8	35 900	199	4 112	-4.6	179	4.4	335	-22	2 188	-13.1	179	539
Sterling	494	69.2	48 100	197	802	-4.4	18	2.2	41	1	180	23.3	0	56
Stonewall	806	76.9	29 600	147	1 255	7.7	48	3.8	62	-1	359	6.5	0	58
Sutton	1 466	67.5	39 500	209	2 038	3.7	98	4.8	139	-1	1 029	-0.7	0	231
Swisher	2 993	68.4	34 200	193	3 636	-5.1	158	4.3	193	-2	1 274	-2.5	94	360
Tarrant	438 634	58.1	72 900	364	650 164	1.3	34 353	5.3	27 345	-171	426 938	2.2	109 583	98 210
Taylor	43 301	62.2	45 500	289	50 932	-3.1	3 122	6.1	3 420	-23	38 469	-4.2	4 877	10 312
Terrell	524	65.5	27 200	150	935	-3.4	18	1.9	30	-5	94	-8.7	0	43
Terry	4 478	72.6	38 600	223	5 258	-1.6	322	6.1	326	5	2 675	-4.4	0	675
Throckmorton	790	76.2	28 700	142	943	-2.7	15	1.6	70	5	273	8.8	0	46
Titus	8 508	72.3	44 400	256	14 285	5.4	797	5.6	599	3	8 492	21.5	2 798	1 542
Tom Green	35 408	62.3	49 600	300	43 827	-3.6	2 461	5.6	2 496	-39	31 425	5.7	5 066	7 902
Travis	232 861	45.7	78 300	349	333 969	1.0	15 505	4.6	15 876	-354	221 970	-3.3	34 624	54 212
Trinity	4 647	78.9	38 700	191	4 495	0.7	241	5.4	207	-2	1 214	-9.8	241	388
Tyler	6 459	83.0	37 900	210	7 426	11.5	449	6.0	278	2	1 804	-6.3	535	521
Upshur	11 360	80.4	42 100	209	18 964	-1.7	934	4.9	372	-14	3 683	7.6	607	1 001
Upton	1 472	75.2	27 600	174	1 903	-0.1	65	3.4	109	0	658	10.6	0	121
Uvalde	7 553	69.1	38 600	204	13 774	1.5	1 396	10.1	544	1	4 907	-9.3	691	1 485
Val Verde	11 840	61.1	43 400	267	13 435	-1.9	1 687	12.6	671	-2	5 266	0.2	475	2 115
Van Zandt	14 349	80.5	45 600	239	17 035	-2.5	933	5.5	628	-11	4 408	7.1	653	1 139
Victoria	26 228	64.6	54 700	276	35 896	-0.9	1 787	5.0	2 059	-51	21 305	-1.8	2 728	5 834

1. Percent of total civilian labor force. 2. For week including March 12. Excludes government employees, self-employed persons, farm workers, domestic service workers, railroad employees subject to the Railroad Retirement Act, and employees on oceanborne vessels or in foreign countries.

STATE County	Private nonfarm establishments, 1988 (cont'd): Employment[1] (cont'd): Finance, insurance, and real estate	Private nonfarm establishments, 1988 (cont'd): Employment[1] (cont'd): Services	Private nonfarm establishments, 1988 (cont'd): Annual payroll: Total (Mil dol)	Private nonfarm establishments, 1988 (cont'd): Annual payroll: Average per employee (Dollars)	Personal income, 1989: Total (Mil dol)	Personal income, 1989: Percent change, 1988–1989	Personal income, 1989: Wages and salaries[2] (Mil dol)	Personal income, 1989: Proprietor's income (Mil dol)	Personal income, 1989: Dividends, interest, & rent (Mil dol)	Personal income, 1989: Transfer payments (Mil dol)	Personal income, 1989: Per capita[3]: Dollars	Personal income, 1989: Per capita[3]: Rank	Earnings, 1989: Total (Mil dol)	Earnings, 1989: Percent by selected industries: Farm	Earnings, 1989: Percent by selected industries: Goods-related[4]: Total
	88	89	90	91	92	93	94	95	96	97	98	99	100	101	102
TEXAS—Con.															
Montgomery	2 207	7 546	538	18 877	2 751	10.1	832	184	394	290	14 705	1 125	1 016	0.2	27.3
Moore	177	565	74	17 612	281	-0.8	162	70	45	28	16 797	472	233	22.4	36.8
Morris	107	476	D	D	169	-1.0	112	12	33	44	12 155	2 260	124	3.5	49.7
Motley	0	16	2	10 668	25	2.9	8	7	5	6	13 566	1 653	15	35.4	NA
Nacogdoches	631	2 584	181	14 140	686	8.7	330	115	123	128	13 208	1 809	446	8.6	28.1
Navarro	646	2 775	171	15 778	530	5.1	232	63	124	110	13 428	1 722	295	3.6	29.4
Newton	0	185	20	15 535	129	6.2	38	15	16	32	9 699	2 926	53	5.4	43.0
Nolan	182	770	62	15 832	246	5.7	113	34	65	47	14 598	1 168	147	4.6	28.3
Nueces	5 768	28 377	1 572	17 839	4 035	5.5	2 684	406	687	670	13 561	1 655	3 090	0.6	24.0
Ochiltree	154	629	44	17 441	148	1.6	75	34	33	15	16 060	632	109	15.3	34.4
Oldham	0	10	2	11 525	54	-1.2	13	33	6	4	18 441	255	46	69.1	NA
Orange	701	3 307	406	22 307	1 132	4.4	580	81	165	181	13 687	1 588	662	0.1	55.0
Palo Pinto	312	1 018	86	14 950	335	7.4	140	35	72	71	13 428	1 723	175	3.0	31.0
Panola	191	467	53	14 155	326	8.3	173	46	62	54	14 791	1 082	219	7.6	54.4
Parker	453	1 318	113	14 564	987	8.2	207	89	143	113	14 553	1 187	297	4.6	29.6
Parmer	69	263	40	14 827	215	-6.2	78	114	33	17	21 362	116	192	57.1	19.5
Pecos	169	626	50	17 029	153	5.2	95	24	26	25	9 964	2 885	118	4.5	31.1
Polk	302	1 515	82	14 535	370	9.1	138	41	89	97	11 833	2 385	178	1.8	34.3
Potter	3 380	12 834	868	18 118	1 506	4.6	1 349	200	271	304	14 863	1 048	1 549	0.7	20.5
Presidio	54	74	6	11 858	52	8.5	25	4	9	14	8 486	3 043	29	9.5	NA
Rains	53	120	10	14 642	79	6.2	18	12	18	15	11 811	2 397	29	19.7	21.4
Randall	739	2 457	235	15 302	1 530	5.7	320	212	294	117	15 960	658	532	9.7	20.6
Reagan	0	63	13	17 459	56	-0.6	32	11	9	6	12 225	2 218	42	8.3	31.7
Real	0	31	2	11 601	33	8.5	6	6	12	8	11 840	2 381	12	31.9	13.6
Red River	86	386	24	11 263	173	7.6	51	24	34	52	11 632	2 465	75	13.8	27.7
Reeves	140	545	41	17 816	154	1.7	70	30	21	29	10 593	2 773	100	19.9	9.9
Refugio	85	186	21	15 153	143	5.6	49	19	51	22	16 592	506	68	15.5	26.0
Roberts	0	5	4	25 547	17	4.6	6	6	4	2	15 373	846	12	47.6	NA
Robertson	118	451	29	14 409	199	11.6	85	20	41	47	13 239	1 798	105	5.6	32.4
Rockwall	298	1 453	61	13 597	493	7.2	97	40	83	33	16 409	544	136	1.0	21.6
Runnels	147	353	33	12 832	181	7.2	60	42	48	36	15 930	665	102	16.5	32.0
Rusk	356	1 987	170	18 795	596	5.2	232	66	149	104	14 222	1 326	298	2.9	31.8
Sabine	64	153	17	15 143	112	7.9	35	13	33	36	11 324	2 561	48	2.6	39.7
San Augustine	79	270	13	12 483	93	5.8	26	15	19	29	10 729	2 736	42	12.7	18.1
San Jacinto	103	434	28	17 942	151	10.2	25	14	26	36	9 854	2 900	38	2.5	26.5
San Patricio	434	1 545	149	18 342	707	5.9	279	68	103	134	11 834	2 383	347	3.1	39.7
San Saba	135	421	14	10 537	82	8.8	23	15	24	18	14 993	991	39	17.4	NA
Schleicher	0	29	5	18 298	38	6.4	16	7	9	6	14 178	1 354	23	15.6	NA
Scurry	201	961	68	14 846	251	4.4	127	35	59	41	14 687	1 138	162	5.2	36.7
Shackelford	38	148	10	15 811	57	7.0	19	13	16	10	17 342	389	31	13.1	41.0
Shelby	230	651	61	13 246	284	7.0	101	38	55	72	11 883	2 364	139	12.0	33.0
Sherman	0	29	7	17 756	78	-8.8	17	45	12	5	26 900	24	63	70.1	6.8
Smith	3 729	13 650	996	19 557	2 472	6.8	1 446	339	528	347	16 139	607	1 786	1.4	28.4
Somervell	31	388	59	32 202	78	8.6	409	4	11	10	14 020	1 429	414	0.1	NA
Starr	158	645	24	9 539	186	7.8	89	23	16	65	4 549	3 106	112	14.0	5.9
Stephens	229	344	33	15 044	120	5.0	53	18	32	26	12 564	2 086	71	3.0	31.9
Sterling	0	18	2	12 444	19	2.3	8	4	6	2	13 112	1 858	12	19.9	28.1
Stonewall	0	81	5	13 596	35	6.1	13	8	8	7	16 703	482	21	24.9	NA
Sutton	58	126	19	18 225	59	9.0	30	11	15	8	14 835	1 058	40	16.0	31.2
Swisher	100	227	18	14 246	153	-0.3	40	52	41	20	17 863	314	92	51.6	6.3
Tarrant	26 748	107 547	8 880	20 799	20 371	6.9	12 903	1 536	2 855	2 014	17 686	339	14 439	0.1	33.4
Taylor	2 503	11 445	633	16 463	1 820	5.0	1 081	248	357	282	15 001	988	1 330	2.4	18.2
Terrell	0	27	1	9 840	28	15.1	12	9	5	4	19 381	200	21	38.7	NA
Terry	136	546	47	17 647	164	-9.3	81	22	34	33	11 424	2 535	103	12.1	23.5
Throckmorton	25	80	3	11 110	33	1.1	8	10	8	7	16 799	470	18	31.4	NA
Titus	341	1 317	149	17 492	338	7.7	238	34	65	65	14 809	1 074	271	1.8	41.6
Tom Green	1 792	8 028	524	16 668	1 462	5.9	810	188	304	238	14 658	1 148	998	2.1	20.1
Travis	25 237	72 222	4 468	20 130	9 639	7.5	7 836	901	1 622	1 091	17 097	421	8 737	0.1	20.5
Trinity	65	287	16	13 110	133	9.1	32	16	30	38	10 770	2 723	48	9.3	17.7
Tyler	113	374	22	12 099	234	8.0	57	24	47	53	13 074	1 877	81	3.6	30.5
Upshur	144	1 293	48	12 929	385	6.3	80	47	69	77	12 112	2 281	127	12.9	19.1
Upton	0	58	12	18 012	60	2.3	33	8	12	8	11 956	2 338	42	9.8	NA
Uvalde	318	1 018	60	12 131	279	5.5	119	43	66	58	11 486	2 504	161	10.8	15.3
Val Verde	370	1 210	60	11 465	391	8.4	234	37	57	83	9 678	2 929	271	5.9	5.1
Van Zandt	235	1 142	59	13 426	521	8.1	108	78	93	101	12 942	1 933	186	11.7	24.5
Victoria	1 472	5 838	378	17 762	1 164	6.6	597	138	244	155	15 749	722	735	1.3	29.3

1. For week including March 12. Excludes government employees, self-employed persons, farm workers, domestic service workers, railroad employees subject to the Railroad Retirement Act, and employees on oceanborne vessels or in foreign countries. 2. Includes other labor income. 3. Based on the resident population estimated as of July 1 of the year shown. 4. Covers mining, construction, and manufacturing.

STATE County	Earnings, 1989 (cont'd)						Agriculture, 1987									
	Percent by selected industries (cont'd)						Farms			Farm operators, percent		Land in farms				
	Goods-related[1]	Service-related & other[2]						Percent with						Acres		
	Manu-facturing	Total	Retail trade	Finance, insur-ance, & real estate	Services	Govern-ment	Number	Less than 50 acres	500 acres and over	Whose principal occu-pation is farming	Residing on farm operated	Acreage (1,000)	Percent change, 1982–1987	Average size of farm	Total irrigated (1,000)	Total cropland (1,000)
	103	104	105	106	107	108	109	110	111	112	113	114	115	116	117	118
TEXAS—Con.																
Montgomery	12.4	54.3	11.1	4.9	27.0	18.2	952	54.3	6.9	30.4	68.0	188	13.9	198	0	44
Moore	26.6	29.7	6.6	1.9	8.2	11.1	297	12.1	70.7	77.1	29.3	565	5.5	1 902	100	262
Morris	46.9	35.4	3.9	3.2	12.4	11.5	349	26.9	12.0	37.0	64.8	75	1.6	216	D	31
Motley	11.9	32.3	15.6	3.4	7.3	14.4	202	5.0	65.3	62.4	38.6	467	-8.8	2 313	4	105
Nacogdoches	21.3	42.6	12.5	3.2	21.0	20.8	1 243	29.6	7.2	46.1	64.4	240	2.2	193	0	90
Navarro	20.3	52.0	11.6	4.7	24.6	15.0	1 463	19.3	16.8	38.1	47.2	505	0.8	345	0	242
Newton	32.7	27.5	6.7	1.2	11.0	24.2	268	43.3	4.1	32.5	64.2	64	-38.0	239	0	12
Nolan	18.2	48.8	9.0	3.3	16.2	18.3	454	13.4	46.9	49.3	51.8	556	17.5	1 224	2	174
Nueces	12.4	52.4	10.4	4.5	26.3	22.9	656	22.6	36.0	55.3	45.9	466	1.5	710	2	342
Ochiltree	2.6	39.5	7.3	3.8	13.3	10.8	391	9.7	70.6	72.6	44.8	607	-0.9	1 553	63	363
Oldham	NA	NA	2.7	0.9	9.6	11.0	133	6.0	74.4	71.4	33.8	812	-27.2	6 108	4	115
Orange	46.7	31.9	8.3	2.4	15.0	13.0	309	63.4	7.1	24.6	70.2	54	-9.9	174	1	18
Palo Pinto	21.0	49.4	13.9	3.9	18.4	16.7	719	21.4	26.4	41.0	53.3	511	6.8	710	2	86
Panola	9.4	25.7	6.0	1.9	8.6	12.3	912	25.0	9.9	38.0	67.9	202	-2.6	221	0	74
Parker	16.3	47.6	13.7	4.1	18.7	18.2	1 943	44.4	8.9	31.5	72.1	403	7.7	208	1	121
Parmer	18.7	16.6	2.5	0.9	5.3	6.8	653	9.0	57.6	79.6	48.9	499	-8.4	764	172	431
Pecos	2.8	41.8	10.2	4.3	12.3	22.6	286	17.5	69.9	55.2	51.4	2 918	11.5	10 203	21	63
Polk	25.0	47.4	12.1	4.2	17.1	16.4	559	34.2	9.1	31.7	61.7	144	-10.7	258	0	37
Potter	11.0	62.5	11.1	5.6	26.5	16.3	177	33.3	35.0	45.2	53.1	547	11.4	3 089	8	58
Presidio	NA	42.8	10.7	4.2	14.5	43.4	139	10.1	77.7	59.7	39.6	1 891	-4.6	13 602	9	10
Rains	9.8	40.7	13.7	2.2	16.0	18.2	454	31.5	8.8	43.0	61.0	97	2.9	213	0	44
Randall	8.8	57.1	13.7	4.0	23.0	12.6	619	33.4	36.0	48.8	55.7	445	-7.6	720	31	263
Reagan	1.7	NA	6.2	2.3	10.8	15.9	127	3.9	81.9	78.0	53.5	712	11.9	5 609	18	51
Real	4.8	32.5	10.4	2.8	12.0	22.0	189	12.7	55.6	47.1	53.4	318	2.2	1 683	1	9
Red River	21.5	38.0	11.0	3.4	15.3	20.5	1 035	20.3	18.4	41.7	59.5	388	8.5	375	1	153
Reeves	1.3	48.8	9.7	2.8	18.6	21.5	174	13.2	52.9	56.9	32.2	1 432	14.8	8 232	13	48
Refugio	0.5	40.4	8.9	4.7	15.1	18.1	254	22.8	33.1	44.1	35.8	529	0.9	2 083	D	106
Roberts	NA	NA	4.0	5.4	7.6	15.2	106	12.3	72.6	68.9	37.7	524	-7.3	4 945	4	58
Robertson	10.6	47.4	8.5	2.9	12.9	14.6	1 207	22.3	15.7	44.0	46.6	395	2.5	327	11	145
Rockwall	8.8	62.3	14.3	5.0	29.7	15.1	181	38.1	11.0	31.5	63.0	41	-18.7	227	0	21
Runnels	20.8	39.7	7.0	2.9	15.5	11.8	838	10.9	42.4	56.4	50.8	577	-4.3	688	4	301
Rusk	12.2	50.9	8.4	3.2	20.4	14.4	1 327	25.5	9.0	34.7	61.8	271	-3.7	204	1	122
Sabine	32.6	40.5	9.3	3.4	15.7	17.3	224	33.9	5.4	37.5	64.3	34	-8.7	151	0	12
San Augustine	7.1	47.1	11.5	3.3	17.3	22.1	320	30.3	6.2	44.4	59.7	55	-9.3	171	0	23
San Jacinto	7.5	40.7	8.6	5.4	15.2	30.4	349	39.0	10.0	35.2	57.6	91	17.6	261	0	20
San Patricio	24.2	39.6	9.1	2.6	18.7	17.6	549	27.7	36.1	54.6	47.7	340	-11.1	619	D	259
San Saba	3.3	NA	10.4	5.7	21.2	15.2	609	8.2	40.7	49.3	52.9	742	4.6	1 218	3	80
Schleicher	NA	44.8	4.0	3.7	13.0	19.6	252	4.8	71.0	57.5	52.8	760	-5.2	3 018	1	39
Scurry	2.6	41.3	9.0	3.4	14.3	16.8	573	14.3	42.4	56.0	64.0	506	4.4	883	0	207
Shackelford	1.3	32.5	4.4	3.1	16.2	13.4	251	5.2	44.2	46.2	42.2	550	-4.0	2 193	D	60
Shelby	28.5	40.1	10.0	4.0	16.8	15.0	1 135	28.3	6.8	46.4	66.7	204	2.0	180	0	76
Sherman	1.4	16.0	3.3	1.6	3.8	7.1	297	6.4	77.4	80.5	35.4	546	-3.8	1 839	120	343
Smith	20.0	58.2	12.6	5.1	26.3	12.0	1 701	39.5	4.8	30.9	62.4	249	1.0	147	1	117
Somervell	0.3	NA	0.4	0.1	NA	1.9	234	24.8	17.5	35.9	65.4	65	3.9	278	0	21
Starr	0.5	33.6	12.8	2.9	10.6	46.5	885	15.3	25.0	40.2	29.9	599	7.8	677	9	195
Stephens	7.1	51.3	12.8	5.5	17.8	13.8	419	7.2	38.4	46.3	53.9	474	-11.2	1 131	0	50
Sterling	0.0	29.6	7.8	4.1	8.2	22.4	75	8.0	81.3	66.7	53.3	676	-7.0	9 013	0	10
Stonewall	NA	NA	4.1	2.0	9.1	15.5	312	10.3	52.2	56.4	42.3	506	-4.6	1 622	D	91
Sutton	0.6	33.1	7.1	3.8	10.7	19.7	191	8.9	81.2	66.0	57.1	851	-7.4	4 458	0	8
Swisher	2.8	30.4	5.4	2.6	8.3	11.8	546	7.7	54.8	74.9	47.3	531	-2.9	972	115	389
Tarrant	26.5	54.4	11.0	5.4	22.1	12.1	1 117	62.9	6.6	28.4	62.8	198	-1.9	177	2	71
Taylor	9.9	55.7	11.1	4.0	27.4	23.7	903	23.8	24.5	38.2	58.6	431	-1.0	478	1	190
Terrell	NA	NA	3.6	2.9	4.2	14.5	91	8.8	83.5	62.6	46.2	1 129	-9.4	12 410	D	1
Terry	4.0	45.7	9.5	2.9	16.0	18.7	517	12.2	61.1	79.7	43.1	463	-9.5	896	81	386
Throckmorton	NA	NA	5.4	4.6	13.2	16.1	303	7.3	50.5	63.4	42.6	610	20.9	2 012	D	98
Titus	20.6	42.7	9.5	2.5	14.5	13.9	738	27.9	7.0	34.0	66.5	178	-6.5	241	0	65
Tom Green	11.8	54.7	10.7	4.2	25.5	23.0	867	33.7	35.6	49.1	56.7	1 014	4.8	1 170	26	208
Travis	15.6	52.5	9.0	7.1	27.3	26.9	1 034	38.6	14.8	39.4	60.5	307	-15.4	297	1	120
Trinity	10.5	49.7	10.6	5.4	22.7	23.3	550	32.5	10.7	38.2	52.0	133	-7.6	242	0	47
Tyler	18.2	44.3	11.2	3.5	18.1	21.6	500	45.4	8.6	32.0	65.0	97	-3.7	193	0	27
Upshur	7.7	49.4	11.8	3.1	20.6	18.7	1 038	28.2	5.0	38.7	66.7	171	8.8	164	0	69
Upton	NA	NA	6.5	2.6	6.4	24.0	86	8.1	69.8	62.8	50.0	739	-1.5	8 595	8	26
Uvalde	6.7	50.5	12.2	5.1	19.6	23.5	575	16.3	45.7	53.0	52.2	850	0.0	1 479	50	143
Val Verde	2.3	37.0	10.1	3.2	15.0	52.0	242	24.4	59.9	59.5	50.0	1 762	-4.0	7 280	5	6
Van Zandt	3.9	48.6	12.2	3.6	20.9	15.2	2 395	36.1	5.8	38.5	64.3	381	1.4	159	2	191
Victoria	15.4	55.1	12.3	5.3	25.6	14.4	1 119	28.7	16.7	40.2	53.4	428	-13.2	382	7	155

1. Covers mining, construction, and manufacturing. 2. Covers private sector earnings in agricultural services, forestry, and fisheries; transportation and public utilities; wholesale trade; retail trade; finance, insurance, and real estate; and services.

STATE County	Agriculture, 1987 (cont'd): Value of land and buildings: Average per farm ($1,000)	Value of land and buildings: Average per acre (Dollars)	Value of products sold: Total (Mil dol)	Value of products sold: Average per farm (Dollars)	Value of products sold: Percent from: Crops	Value of products sold: Percent from: Livestock and poultry[1]	Percent of farms with sales of: $10,000 or more	Percent of farms with sales of: $100,000 or more	Manufactures, 1987: Establishments: Total	Establishments: Percent with 20 or more employees	All employees: Number (1,000)	All employees: Percent change, 1982–1987	All employees: Annual payroll (Mil dol)	Production workers: Number (1,000)	Production workers: Work hours (Mil)
	119	120	121	122	123	124	125	126	127	128	129	130	131	132	133
TEXAS—Con.															
Montgomery	291	1 686	9	9 159	29.9	70.1	18.4	0.8	176	22.7	2.6	-36.6	59.5	1.7	3.4
Moore	663	335	208	701 946	9.4	90.6	82.5	42.4	14	35.7	D	D	D	D	D
Morris	155	736	7	18 872	7.7	92.3	24.6	2.9	19	42.1	D	D	D	D	D
Motley	602	240	13	65 075	47.5	52.5	74.3	17.3	4	50.0	D	D	D	D	D
Nacogdoches	245	1 167	112	89 805	1.2	98.8	39.8	18.2	68	36.8	3.2	-15.8	54.6	2.4	5.0
Navarro	233	710	28	19 006	24.9	75.1	33.4	3.2	52	40.4	2.0	-25.9	40.8	1.5	2.8
Newton	204	943	2	6 774	24.6	75.4	10.4	1.1	37	13.5	0.7	0.0	12.0	0.6	1.4
Nolan	373	317	38	84 151	29.7	70.3	51.5	12.6	16	62.5	1.0	-23.1	21.5	0.7	1.5
Nueces	693	1 088	51	77 529	91.3	8.7	58.1	23.3	236	28.0	D	D	D	D	D
Ochiltree	571	360	109	278 565	14.2	85.8	79.8	27.6	10	10.0	0.1	0.0	1.4	0.0	0.1
Oldham	897	145	63	471 312	5.7	94.3	81.2	33.1	1	0.0	D	D	D	D	D
Orange	196	1 342	2	6 488	26.5	73.4	10.4	0.6	73	38.4	D	D	D	D	D
Palo Pinto	366	544	13	18 528	11.5	88.5	31.3	3.6	41	36.6	1.7	-29.2	30.0	1.2	2.3
Panola	224	1 090	31	34 362	1.5	98.5	27.4	8.1	21	19.0	D	D	D	D	D
Parker	341	1 464	32	16 256	28.8	71.2	19.6	2.8	62	35.5	D	D	D	D	D
Parmer	444	581	343	524 597	14.9	85.1	87.3	42.7	6	33.3	D	D	D	D	D
Pecos	1 242	122	35	120 877	34.8	65.2	59.4	21.0	9	0.0	0.0	-100.0	0.7	0.0	0.1
Polk	212	1 007	5	8 620	11.2	88.8	16.8	0.7	49	12.2	1.4	16.7	29.4	1.2	2.6
Potter	662	215	18	101 282	9.4	90.6	51.4	18.6	144	26.4	D	D	D	D	D
Presidio	2 115	156	15	105 397	20.2	79.8	56.8	18.0	2	0.0	D	D	D	D	D
Rains	188	857	11	24 295	13.9	86.1	29.1	7.9	6	33.3	0.2	0.0	3.0	0.2	0.4
Randall	302	467	166	268 711	7.4	92.6	53.3	18.7	40	27.5	D	D	D	D	D
Reagan	943	172	13	105 454	66.7	33.3	78.7	37.0	4	0.0	0.0	0.0	0.3	0.0	0.0
Real	1 185	662	3	16 142	3.3	96.7	34.9	2.6	3	33.3	D	D	D	D	D
Red River	227	589	29	28 185	14.3	85.7	35.4	4.4	18	38.9	0.8	-38.5	9.1	0.7	1.3
Reeves	1 022	124	66	378 306	7.4	92.6	62.1	22.4	6	16.7	0.0	0.0	0.6	0.0	0.0
Refugio	801	375	15	57 502	56.5	43.5	46.9	13.8	5	0.0	D	D	D	D	D
Roberts	864	175	23	217 001	5.4	94.6	76.4	30.2	NA	NA	NA	NA	NA	NA	NA
Robertson	302	956	32	26 278	31.4	68.6	35.2	4.4	8	62.5	0.3	-25.0	5.9	0.3	0.5
Rockwall	422	1 788	2	11 161	27.0	73.0	22.1	2.2	43	16.3	0.7	0.0	14.1	0.5	1.0
Runnels	329	487	36	43 408	44.2	55.8	57.6	8.2	15	46.7	1.0	42.9	13.6	0.7	1.4
Rusk	200	893	19	14 692	13.9	86.1	23.9	1.7	54	29.6	1.9	5.6	29.9	1.4	3.0
Sabine	147	839	4	18 544	2.9	97.1	18.8	4.0	20	10.0	D	D	D	D	D
San Augustine	171	984	14	42 999	1.7	98.3	29.1	10.9	17	17.6	0.1	-50.0	2.1	0.1	0.2
San Jacinto	232	908	3	9 413	10.1	89.9	19.2	1.4	20	15.0	D	D	D	D	D
San Patricio	655	1 065	67	122 031	63.2	36.8	57.4	27.0	22	31.8	D	D	D	D	D
San Saba	694	548	25	41 180	11.7	88.3	49.1	10.8	7	28.6	0.1	0.0	2.5	0.1	0.1
Schleicher	877	286	15	60 285	13.5	86.5	69.8	13.5	1	0.0	D	D	D	D	D
Scurry	291	325	22	38 569	69.5	30.5	58.6	12.4	16	18.8	0.2	-33.3	3.1	0.2	0.3
Shackelford	604	274	9	34 741	14.9	85.1	45.8	9.2	5	0.0	0.0	0.0	0.4	0.0	0.0
Shelby	177	1 011	89	78 655	1.0	99.0	35.9	18.9	48	16.7	1.8	0.0	28.0	1.5	3.1
Sherman	654	361	217	729 019	8.8	91.2	80.1	44.4	2	0.0	D	D	D	D	D
Smith	206	1 404	33	19 108	54.5	45.5	22.8	2.5	172	28.5	11.5	-6.5	296.8	7.8	13.8
Somervell	258	1 007	2	9 407	27.7	72.3	20.1	1.3	3	33.3	0.0	0.0	0.5	0.0	0.1
Starr	406	516	63	71 304	51.1	48.9	23.3	3.4	3	33.3	D	D	D	D	D
Stephens	444	391	9	21 144	5.0	95.0	31.7	4.3	17	17.6	0.2	-60.0	4.0	0.1	0.3
Sterling	2 076	230	7	99 126	2.3	97.7	77.3	29.3	NA	NA	NA	NA	NA	NA	NA
Stonewall	417	237	17	53 285	20.0	80.0	55.4	10.3	1	0.0	D	D	D	D	D
Sutton	1 185	268	9	49 530	0.8	99.2	71.7	13.1	1	0.0	D	D	D	D	D
Swisher	373	388	268	490 510	12.2	87.8	79.1	34.1	10	20.0	0.1	-50.0	1.4	0.1	0.1
Tarrant	442	2 698	23	20 615	26.7	73.3	18.9	4.1	1 945	34.1	D	D	D	D	D
Taylor	232	419	72	79 740	8.5	91.5	32.7	4.0	122	27.0	4.9	-18.3	93.6	2.9	5.5
Terrell	1 894	153	7	71 699	D	D	62.6	26.4	1	0.0	D	D	D	D	D
Terry	355	359	57	111 212	93.2	6.8	83.8	41.6	7	14.3	0.0	-100.0	0.4	0.0	0.0
Throckmorton	539	271	20	66 196	21.8	78.2	58.4	14.2	2	0.0	D	D	D	D	D
Titus	204	892	21	28 018	3.9	96.1	24.7	3.8	33	36.4	1.3	-13.3	20.2	1.0	2.2
Tom Green	569	456	76	87 196	24.3	75.7	48.6	14.4	102	27.5	4.1	-19.6	68.0	2.9	5.1
Travis	568	1 928	16	15 038	41.4	58.6	23.8	3.2	611	26.0	36.1	24.5	1 025.4	16.3	31.7
Trinity	223	950	6	11 436	3.9	96.1	24.7	1.1	17	23.5	0.3	50.0	3.4	0.2	0.4
Tyler	202	1 262	3	6 825	15.0	85.0	16.0	0.4	40	15.0	0.7	16.7	9.0	0.6	1.0
Upshur	176	1 067	29	28 222	2.9	97.1	24.5	6.9	30	26.7	0.6	20.0	8.5	0.5	1.0
Upton	1 502	175	7	84 601	44.0	56.0	66.3	20.9	2	0.0	D	D	D	D	D
Uvalde	773	507	47	82 400	44.2	55.8	51.7	17.4	18	22.2	D	D	D	D	D
Val Verde	1 531	212	16	64 849	0.9	99.1	51.2	17.8	24	20.8	0.4	-50.0	5.8	0.2	0.4
Van Zandt	185	1 173	44	18 404	38.1	61.9	28.9	2.8	31	25.8	0.6	-40.0	10.3	0.4	0.8
Victoria	334	866	21	19 046	46.1	53.9	30.8	3.8	58	24.1	D	D	D	D	D

1. Includes livestock and poultry products.

STATE County	Manufactures, 1987 (cont'd): Production workers (cont'd): Wages: Total (Mil dol)	Manufactures, 1987 (cont'd): Production workers (cont'd): Wages: Average per worker (Dollars)	Manufactures, 1987 (cont'd): Value added by manufacture (Mil dol)	Manufactures, 1987 (cont'd): Value of shipments (Mil dol)	Manufactures, 1987 (cont'd): New capital expenditures (Mil dol)	Value of construction authorized by building permits, 1990: Total[1] ($1,000)	Nonresidential: Total ($1,000)	Nonresidential: Percent: Office	Nonresidential: Percent: Industrial	Nonresidential: Percent: Stores	Residential: New construction ($1,000)	Residential: Number of housing units	Residential: Alterations and additions ($1,000)
	134	135	136	137	138	139	140	141	142	143	144	145	146
TEXAS—Con.													
Montgomery	30.4	17 882	201.7	433.8	12.8	11 514	1 660	5.6	19.9	52.1	4 219	49	348
Moore	D	D	D	D	D	925	293	0.0	0.0	97.2	143	2	275
Morris	D	D	D	D	D	220	20	71.8	0.0	0.0	160	3	20
Motley	D	D	D	D	D	0	0	NA	NA	NA	0	0	0
Nacogdoches	38.0	15 833	136.5	415.1	7.0	12 178	1 567	62.5	6.4	6.5	3 720	64	1 467
Navarro	25.7	17 133	171.8	270.1	5.2	5 649	3 271	24.5	0.0	13.9	936	17	200
Newton	10.3	17 167	29.2	66.6	1.2	328	191	0.0	0.0	0.0	95	1	0
Nolan	14.0	20 000	77.2	131.7	2.5	1 117	42	0.0	0.0	0.0	671	9	82
Nueces	D	D	D	D	D	85 926	14 690	22.2	9.3	21.0	33 351	486	14 415
Ochiltree	0.5	NA	2.9	5.6	0.0	1 051	292	0.0	66.8	27.4	660	3	71
Oldham	D	D	D	D	D	67	66	0.0	0.0	0.0	0	0	0
Orange	D	D	D	D	D	15 702	2 976	19.8	3.7	14.6	9 836	171	1 359
Palo Pinto	16.4	13 667	58.3	112.7	2.9	1 289	513	0.0	0.0	16.4	346	3	102
Panola	D	D	D	D	D	1 802	108	0.0	0.0	0.0	510	8	48
Parker	D	D	D	D	D	9 234	1 245	51.4	40.3	3.7	4 620	58	471
Parmer	D	D	D	D	D	457	80	0.0	0.0	0.0	170	4	150
Pecos	0.4	NA	1.9	4.7	0.0	8 279	7 980	0.0	0.0	0.0	63	4	158
Polk	24.4	20 333	67.7	167.9	5.6	1 130	556	0.0	0.0	7.4	298	6	17
Potter	D	D	D	D	D	55 441	11 399	29.0	0.1	27.9	13 383	121	5 723
Presidio	D	D	D	D	D	274	0	NA	NA	NA	10	1	137
Rains	2.5	12 500	2.5	8.4	0.2	214	25	0.0	0.0	0.0	69	1	72
Randall	D	D	D	D	D	4 717	2 016	0.0	0.0	78.2	2 251	37	249
Reagan	0.2	NA	0.6	1.7	0.0	315	9	0.0	0.0	0.0	172	5	80
Real	D	D	D	D	D	414	240	0.0	0.0	0.0	69	1	105
Red River	7.4	10 571	16.7	43.5	1.0	NA	NA	NA	NA	NA	NA	NA	NA
Reeves	0.1	NA	0.8	5.5	0.2	172	34	0.0	0.0	0.0	7	2	103
Refugio	D	D	D	D	D	99	8	0.0	0.0	0.0	30	1	46
Roberts	NA	NA	NA	NA	NA	NA	NA	NA	NA	NA	NA	NA	NA
Robertson	4.6	15 333	12.3	24.2	0.3	1 675	0	NA	NA	NA	375	10	27
Rockwall	8.2	16 400	24.8	64.5	2.2	22 049	1 432	0.0	82.4	16.2	20 132	162	309
Runnels	7.6	10 857	34.3	89.6	1.7	830	714	0.0	0.0	41.2	70	3	25
Rusk	20.9	14 929	67.9	123.3	4.0	4 161	1 226	0.0	59.4	19.9	877	14	228
Sabine	D	D	D	D	D	10	0	NA	NA	NA	10	1	0
San Augustine	1.7	17 000	4.1	10.8	0.3	82	56	0.0	0.0	49.6	25	1	0
San Jacinto	D	D	D	D	D	NA	NA	NA	NA	NA	NA	NA	NA
San Patricio	D	D	D	D	D	10 997	3 807	21.5	0.0	10.6	4 277	66	1 439
San Saba	1.0	10 000	1.9	3.7	0.1	305	2	0.0	0.0	0.0	222	4	66
Schleicher	D	D	D	D	D	24	0	NA	NA	NA	0	0	24
Scurry	2.2	11 000	7.3	20.9	0.3	690	62	0.0	0.0	67.0	266	3	194
Shackelford	0.2	NA	1.1	1.9	0.0	0	0	NA	NA	NA	0	0	0
Shelby	22.2	14 800	72.4	180.4	3.1	307	190	26.2	61.4	7.9	92	3	25
Sherman	D	D	D	D	D	178	14	0.0	0.0	0.0	150	2	8
Smith	182.0	23 333	634.6	1 521.0	32.9	31 013	4 862	3.0	1.4	38.5	13 385	119	2 442
Somervell	0.3	NA	1.6	3.5	0.0	NA	NA	NA	NA	NA	NA	NA	NA
Starr	D	D	D	D	D	1 358	858	0.0	0.0	49.8	428	16	72
Stephens	2.4	24 000	5.3	9.4	0.3	158	46	0.0	0.0	0.0	0	0	96
Sterling	NA	NA	NA	NA	NA	NA	NA	NA	NA	NA	NA	NA	NA
Stonewall	D	D	D	D	D	NA	NA	NA	NA	NA	NA	NA	NA
Sutton	D	D	D	D	D	1 155	295	0.0	0.0	0.0	753	33	33
Swisher	0.9	9 000	3.4	6.6	0.1	9 735	8 500	5.9	0.0	0.0	232	4	101
Tarrant	D	D	D	D	D	1 032 259	333 147	4.8	31.0	17.7	523 587	4 894	28 069
Taylor	44.6	15 379	330.7	900.6	11.8	41 628	8 979	30.0	3.4	50.2	10 162	118	2 657
Terrell	D	D	D	D	D	NA	NA	NA	NA	NA	NA	NA	NA
Terry	0.2	NA	1.0	1.6	0.0	736	0	0.0	0.0	0.0	411	3	133
Throckmorton	D	D	D	D	D	NA	NA	NA	NA	NA	NA	NA	NA
Titus	13.8	13 800	45.3	186.0	2.3	4 038	1 630	25.1	0.0	18.3	1 477	25	41
Tom Green	44.0	15 172	204.1	478.7	9.6	18 387	2 574	1.6	0.0	30.4	5 427	131	1 600
Travis	328.6	20 160	2 611.6	4 795.0	267.1	461 359	126 461	47.5	3.7	11.5	213 033	1 754	17 043
Trinity	2.7	13 500	7.3	21.1	0.4	907	770	0.0	0.0	100.0	111	3	1
Tyler	7.3	12 167	20.7	52.7	2.3	390	277	0.0	0.0	99.3	113	3	0
Upshur	6.3	12 600	21.1	43.4	0.8	4 611	4 116	4.5	0.0	1.8	391	11	37
Upton	D	D	D	D	D	152	13	0.0	0.0	90.9	129	2	10
Uvalde	D	D	D	D	D	922	103	0.0	0.0	0.0	475	13	301
Val Verde	2.0	10 000	33.4	82.2	1.9	3 918	1 148	0.0	0.0	27.6	2 770	58	0
Van Zandt	6.9	17 250	25.5	47.0	1.5	1 909	227	0.0	0.0	39.9	913	25	124
Victoria	D	D	D	D	D	27 121	8 369	5.2	72.9	2.6	11 641	107	2 732

1. Includes nonresidential additions and alterations, residential nonhousekeeping buildings, and residential garages and carports not shown separately.

STATE County	Wholesale trade, 1987				Retail trade, all establishments, 1987				Retail trade, establishments with payroll, 1987					
						Sales				Sales				
											Per capita[2] (Dollars)			
	Estab-lishments	Sales (Mil dol)	Paid employees[1]	Annual payroll (Mil dol)	Number	Total (Mil dol)	Percent change, 1982–1987	Per capita[2] (Dollars)	Number	Total (Mil dol)	General merchan-dise stores	Food stores	Apparel & acces-sory stores	Eating and drinking places
	147	148	149	150	151	152	153	154	155	156	157	158	159	160
TEXAS—Con.														
Montgomery	196	638.1	1 857	48.2	1 275	685.0	24.7	3 887	574	646.7	D	890	127	298
Moore	44	81.5	273	5.2	217	88.4	4.7	5 200	131	84.3	678	1 253	276	412
Morris	24	D	D	D	181	35.9	-31.5	2 561	88	33.1	D	902	88	134
Motley	3	D	D	D	30	4.6	9.5	2 567	16	3.6	0	D	D	D
Nacogdoches	81	151.2	795	11.6	645	301.0	37.0	5 834	360	284.9	496	1 281	303	556
Navarro	60	179.6	712	10.2	475	222.6	14.7	5 607	288	211.5	489	1 234	290	401
Newton	14	8.8	33	0.9	113	26.5	2.3	1 980	53	23.4	63	963	113	77
Nolan	31	58.5	229	4.0	223	82.3	-15.9	4 758	123	76.6	398	1 076	218	381
Nueces	667	1 740.1	6 372	127.1	2 940	1 767.9	9.9	5 923	1 848	1 720.1	749	1 339	281	622
Ochiltree	38	86.4	253	4.7	125	46.2	-22.7	4 712	64	43.6	D	D	332	373
Oldham	5	7.4	27	0.5	29	6.1	-12.9	2 192	15	5.7	0	491	0	240
Orange	60	57.9	330	5.2	850	383.9	-1.3	4 603	408	366.4	D	1 152	170	325
Palo Pinto	47	69.7	370	6.4	390	133.8	1.8	5 187	207	124.3	D	1 305	116	481
Panola	26	30.9	143	1.4	214	86.6	16.7	3 901	111	80.0	D	735	69	275
Parker	65	121.2	464	6.8	628	316.2	59.7	5 043	273	296.9	D	1 360	137	336
Parmer	41	88.9	220	4.3	96	27.4	39.1	2 589	56	26.2	D	944	D	95
Pecos	28	35.6	181	2.9	181	69.2	-19.6	4 298	134	67.7	D	1 320	144	275
Polk	33	56.4	251	4.0	360	144.0	33.6	4 674	174	134.3	D	1 201	107	330
Potter	355	1 109.9	4 274	85.5	1 502	955.4	11.2	9 196	977	928.6	1 424	1 778	703	920
Presidio	6	2.9	14	0.2	101	23.7	13.4	3 888	57	22.1	1 051	1 112	119	143
Rains	7	7.1	15	0.3	52	17.7	43.9	2 809	32	16.9	0	932	D	144
Randall	102	754.7	1 510	31.1	901	597.8	65.4	6 394	500	580.9	860	1 083	271	548
Reagan	10	D	D	D	47	19.8	5.3	4 221	28	18.7	D	1 000	0	635
Real	1	D	D	D	48	7.9	58.0	2 913	23	6.2	D	743	D	194
Red River	13	16.7	44	0.8	186	48.5	-26.6	3 170	90	44.4	D	1 325	37	107
Reeves	27	18.8	133	2.1	179	59.6	-17.5	3 945	104	55.3	535	1 047	190	205
Refugio	22	33.3	82	1.1	134	36.9	-17.4	4 199	79	34.8	D	1 250	140	363
Roberts	2	D	D	D	12	1.9	-26.9	1 734	6	1.8	0	D	0	D
Robertson	20	89.3	143	1.9	208	52.4	6.1	3 402	91	47.8	D	1 143	44	199
Rockwall	35	43.2	163	2.6	288	127.9	94.1	4 807	122	119.0	D	778	D	249
Runnels	23	23.1	120	1.7	160	35.3	-30.4	2 945	91	31.8	D	797	130	232
Rusk	44	67.7	374	5.4	451	137.5	-1.1	3 235	225	126.8	347	836	133	249
Sabine	7	3.4	22	0.2	134	35.7	17.4	3 607	60	30.6	D	1 190	0	205
San Augustine	11	10.2	64	0.4	104	30.1	18.0	3 417	56	26.4	148	854	96	135
San Jacinto	5	4.4	51	0.8	107	28.9	73.1	1 938	43	25.1	0	849	0	78
San Patricio	58	92.6	376	5.3	599	221.5	-5.9	3 655	323	213.5	339	1 174	104	253
San Saba	17	67.8	210	1.8	80	22.6	27.0	4 101	47	20.3	D	1 273	33	219
Schleicher	5	6.6	31	0.4	31	4.8	-20.0	1 644	14	4.2	D	D	D	109
Scurry	46	45.4	278	5.8	242	88.8	-0.3	4 827	148	84.4	324	982	253	557
Shackelford	7	2.7	22	0.4	59	10.2	-27.7	2 838	29	9.2	D	1 090	D	188
Shelby	42	109.3	316	4.5	262	93.5	1.5	3 911	134	83.4	D	1 019	104	142
Sherman	16	24.2	119	1.8	31	7.4	-5.1	2 473	21	7.3	D	489	D	221
Smith	372	953.5	3 497	67.5	1 869	1 036.4	29.3	6 774	1 012	990.6	1 047	1 269	378	608
Somervell	6	1.2	7	0.1	72	16.3	56.7	3 254	30	13.8	D	D	D	321
Starr	19	40.6	86	1.5	360	88.9	20.8	2 302	159	78.8	83	864	115	133
Stephens	25	16.8	105	1.5	164	51.8	0.4	5 030	75	47.4	D	1 298	100	303
Sterling	6	2.0	35	0.2	25	4.2	16.7	2 833	14	3.9	0	1 553	0	380
Stonewall	4	1.8	10	0.1	27	5.5	-19.1	2 489	15	4.9	0	1 118	D	D
Sutton	9	12.2	48	0.9	66	16.6	-37.8	3 784	38	15.9	D	1 101	96	470
Swisher	27	79.5	246	3.9	89	29.1	-10.5	3 348	51	26.9	117	1 227	D	208
Tarrant	2 288	12 375.9	30 128	701.0	11 363	8 017.5	42.4	7 189	6 734	7 789.8	930	1 413	320	710
Taylor	296	1 319.5	2 960	59.8	1 427	799.5	-0.6	6 468	884	769.4	988	923	315	633
Terrell	1	D	D	D	34	4.8	-28.4	3 200	19	3.9	D	D	0	297
Terry	39	173.5	316	6.6	154	60.6	-10.0	4 178	88	58.7	336	1 264	161	298
Throckmorton	3	D	D	D	32	4.1	-25.5	1 948	14	3.3	0	483	0	D
Titus	49	84.4	382	5.7	292	157.1	9.6	6 859	181	151.0	928	1 066	364	627
Tom Green	186	551.8	1 593	30.6	1 161	601.4	5.3	6 118	697	580.0	837	1 243	376	564
Travis	1 070	2 923.1	11 572	275.6	5 763	4 160.6	41.8	7 478	3 877	4 075.8	D	1 686	444	924
Trinity	12	21.0	106	2.3	158	43.4	20.2	3 561	68	38.9	D	1 179	100	140
Tyler	14	17.0	41	0.6	192	59.6	22.4	3 295	85	54.3	491	865	D	126
Upshur	23	39.5	89	1.9	276	106.1	23.8	3 307	123	95.4	D	607	40	158
Upton	14	11.0	48	1.0	79	11.4	-15.6	2 276	32	9.7	D	1 163	0	167
Uvalde	50	184.9	703	11.2	277	132.1	38.5	5 457	166	127.0	576	1 552	215	394
Val Verde	37	42.7	291	4.3	409	169.8	-0.5	4 215	230	162.5	568	1 058	213	455
Van Zandt	41	49.1	206	2.3	446	140.2	40.9	3 586	197	127.9	238	886	64	177
Victoria	186	594.3	1 850	33.1	959	495.0	0.4	6 618	576	479.9	903	1 514	385	545

1. For pay period including March 12. 2. Based on the estimated population as of July 1 of the year shown.

STATE County	Retail trade, establishments with payroll, 1987 (cont'd): Paid employees[1]	Retail trade, establishments with payroll, 1987 (cont'd): Annual payroll (Mil dol)	Taxable service industries–establishments with payroll, 1987: Number	Taxable service industries: Receipts (Mil dol): Total	Receipts: Selected kinds of business: Hotels, motels and other lodging places	Receipts: Selected kinds of business: Health services	Receipts: Selected kinds of business: Legal services	Taxable service industries: Paid employees	Taxable service industries: Annual payroll (Mil dol)	Bank deposits,[2] June 1989: Total (Mil dol)	Bank deposits: Percent change, 1988–1989	Savings capital,[3] September 1989: Total (Mil dol)	Savings capital: Percent change, 1988–1989
	161	162	163	164	165	166	167	168	169	170	171	172	173
TEXAS—Con.													
Montgomery	6 946	66.0	754	316.8	D	108.4	15.1	6 025	111.5	841	-1.0	766.1	12.4
Moore	1 017	9.1	86	15.8	1.2	6.3	1.9	425	4.8	99	-1.5	64.3	-4.1
Morris	439	3.4	53	13.5	0.0	5.3	D	323	4.2	113	3.2	23.3	-1.0
Motley	62	0.4	4	D	0.0	D	0.0	D	D	6	-6.4	0.0	-100.0
Nacogdoches	3 639	31.6	297	83.9	4.4	51.4	4.0	2 110	24.9	480	-2.6	143.4	-3.3
Navarro	2 684	24.7	181	93.0	D	57.7	5.5	2 140	30.3	473	-1.4	126.3	-8.2
Newton	282	1.9	17	4.0	0.0	2.7	0.2	101	1.4	25	8.3	11.1	-2.3
Nolan	1 051	8.5	95	21.1	2.7	6.4	3.1	655	7.5	124	-7.3	82.9	-15.6
Nueces	21 894	205.9	2 237	873.1	D	293.0	121.5	19 864	331.2	2 091	-4.7	1 193.2	6.9
Ochiltree	530	5.3	86	20.9	1.0	3.5	1.5	514	8.2	113	-4.9	44.2	-4.2
Oldham	97	0.6	7	0.4	D	0.0	D	9	0.1	18	7.7	0.0	NA
Orange	4 424	38.5	351	105.2	D	51.3	9.0	2 661	37.0	421	-0.8	213.0	-37.9
Palo Pinto	1 649	14.2	142	29.5	D	11.0	1.3	758	9.3	246	-20.5	58.8	-11.4
Panola	944	7.5	85	13.7	D	4.0	1.2	427	4.1	166	4.2	74.1	2.6
Parker	3 343	28.8	208	38.2	3.1	13.6	2.7	971	12.1	334	3.3	86.2	-14.9
Parmer	311	2.6	42	6.4	0.0	1.0	D	178	1.9	118	3.7	14.7	-34.5
Pecos	925	7.6	88	18.0	3.5	3.5	0.8	479	5.7	125	4.0	16.0	-38.7
Polk	1 619	14.1	117	37.1	1.2	10.7	1.4	940	14.0	241	8.3	60.3	0.4
Potter	11 790	111.2	1 050	442.3	24.8	142.8	53.6	8 186	150.8	1 599	0.5	364.4	-22.9
Presidio	286	2.3	16	2.2	D	D	0.4	49	0.3	41	2.6	0.0	-100.0
Rains	213	2.2	21	3.5	D	D	D	149	1.1	53	-1.2	14.3	-22.6
Randall	6 015	60.4	351	71.1	1.5	24.4	1.6	1 882	23.1	133	10.3	148.9	-1.0
Reagan	210	2.0	22	3.2	D	0.4	D	52	0.8	37	8.7	0.0	-100.0
Real	107	0.7	6	0.3	D	0.0	0.0	11	0.1	13	5.4	0.0	-100.0
Red River	562	4.6	42	8.2	D	5.4	0.4	335	3.0	66	-1.2	33.2	5.9
Reeves	730	6.2	60	11.3	1.7	2.2	D	401	4.7	107	0.9	0.0	-100.0
Refugio	490	3.7	38	5.8	D	1.4	D	158	2.1	74	-1.5	23.4	-52.7
Roberts	28	0.2	2	D	0.0	0.0	0.0	D	D	12	-16.9	0.0	NA
Robertson	566	4.5	47	12.3	D	7.2	0.5	437	4.0	117	-0.3	45.1	-3.1
Rockwall	1 230	13.2	130	28.5	D	7.5	1.3	614	8.8	77	-24.3	69.3	1.8
Runnels	469	3.5	57	8.2	0.0	4.0	0.4	292	2.6	138	-2.0	52.7	-8.0
Rusk	1 656	14.1	191	46.5	D	17.4	4.6	1 427	16.0	402	-4.8	110.8	-12.4
Sabine	336	3.0	30	5.5	1.1	2.2	D	100	1.8	74	4.5	21.2	2.5
San Augustine	273	2.5	29	7.6	D	5.5	D	261	3.0	62	-0.6	27.2	3.2
San Jacinto	231	2.1	28	7.2	D	0.9	D	199	3.2	28	8.0	5.1	4.2
San Patricio	2 590	23.3	220	45.0	D	24.5	1.5	1 265	15.3	297	3.6	58.4	-42.6
San Saba	259	2.2	25	4.6	D	1.7	D	177	1.4	46	-2.2	22.9	-64.8
Schleicher	61	0.5	12	1.1	D	0.0	0.0	27	0.3	30	0.9	0.0	NA
Scurry	1 183	10.4	111	22.1	2.6	4.5	D	613	6.9	167	-3.5	64.5	-13.5
Shackelford	113	1.0	20	4.5	0.0	0.9	D	142	2.3	58	-4.3	6.3	-5.6
Shelby	908	8.1	76	19.0	0.7	10.3	1.8	516	5.4	162	-1.4	65.1	-1.9
Sherman	96	1.0	12	1.7	0.0	D	0.0	97	0.4	49	2.6	7.2	-5.8
Smith	12 029	120.6	1 248	414.9	10.5	159.6	37.9	8 959	162.2	1 507	-2.7	532.3	-7.0
Somervell	175	1.3	26	9.5	D	0.2	D	267	5.0	36	11.4	9.4	-14.8
Starr	1 004	7.9	57	7.1	D	2.3	1.1	290	2.1	171	9.3	7.1	31.6
Stephens	593	5.4	60	7.6	D	2.4	0.8	235	2.3	137	-8.3	18.7	-6.7
Sterling	58	0.4	6	0.2	D	D	0.0	14	0.1	28	0.0	0.0	NA
Stonewall	69	0.5	7	1.5	D	D	0.0	54	0.5	21	4.6	0.0	NA
Sutton	214	1.9	25	3.0	D	0.5	0.2	122	0.8	53	4.8	12.0	24.8
Swisher	342	2.9	41	4.9	0.0	1.4	0.4	159	1.4	99	-3.1	15.7	-1.0
Tarrant	89 499	906.2	7 902	3 365.9	124.3	1 007.8	245.3	73 828	1 243.6	8 338	-7.1	3 739.6	-8.5
Taylor	10 606	96.2	938	345.4	19.4	151.1	17.9	7 241	112.8	978	-18.7	411.4	-34.2
Terrell	59	0.5	7	0.7	D	0.0	D	17	0.1	16	3.3	0.0	NA
Terry	635	5.9	66	11.5	D	3.8	0.9	355	4.1	133	9.8	12.6	-77.8
Throckmorton	53	0.4	13	2.0	0.0	D	D	59	0.5	25	-1.0	5.9	-20.8
Titus	1 684	15.4	158	38.4	2.4	18.4	1.8	1 066	14.2	289	2.9	50.1	-14.8
Tom Green	7 753	71.5	609	210.0	D	67.3	17.1	4 436	73.1	818	-7.4	294.5	-48.5
Travis	54 539	530.5	5 122	2 774.8	153.3	506.9	407.9	59 005	1 071.2	4 059	-18.9	2 746.5	-20.0
Trinity	405	3.6	39	8.5	D	2.7	D	215	2.2	55	-1.3	15.6	-13.8
Tyler	548	4.9	42	9.5	D	3.6	0.7	320	2.4	64	-2.3	40.4	0.0
Upshur	945	8.7	65	8.8	D	3.9	1.3	263	2.8	206	8.8	41.0	-21.2
Upton	139	1.1	13	1.6	D	D	D	31	0.4	43	6.8	4.2	-18.9
Uvalde	1 578	13.2	120	28.0	2.1	12.3	1.9	703	9.9	268	5.3	65.2	7.7
Val Verde	2 231	19.3	165	32.6	6.1	7.6	1.5	934	10.4	176	-2.8	24.5	-8.9
Van Zandt	1 226	12.0	137	23.7	0.5	11.5	1.5	840	8.6	180	-3.2	99.7	1.4
Victoria	6 071	58.5	583	209.1	6.4	114.8	11.7	4 382	75.1	979	-10.1	912.7	4.9

1. For the period including March 12 of the year shown. 2. Includes deposits for all insured and reporting noninsured commercial and mutual savings banks. 3. Includes savings capital for all FSLIC insured savings institutions.

STATE County	Federal funds and grants, 1989: Expenditures: Total (Mil dol)	Expenditures: Percent change, 1988–1989	Per capita[1] (Dollars): Total	Per capita: Direct payments for individuals	Per capita: Procurement contract awards	Per capita: Salaries and wages	Per capita: Grant awards	Local government finances, 1981–1982: General revenue: Total (Mil dol)	Intergovernmental: Total (Mil dol)	Intergovernmental: Percent from state	Taxes: Total (Mil dol)	Taxes: Per capita[2]: Total (Dollars)	Taxes: Per capita[2]: Property (Dollars)	Direct general expenditure: Total (Mil dol)	Direct general expenditure: Percent change, 1977–1982
	174	175	176	177	178	179	180	181	182	183	184	185	186	187	188
TEXAS—Con.															
Montgomery	286.1	15.8	1 529	1 097	58	113	219	131.9	40.0	95.1	65.1	436	413	137.8	170.0
Moore	68.3	-20.0	4 088	1 202	1 741	298	126	18.8	4.0	95.0	9.6	557	511	18.0	97.0
Morris	38.1	5.6	2 738	2 315	15	90	270	11.3	4.3	95.0	5.5	358	317	10.0	82.2
Motley	10.3	24.5	5 416	2 501	25	238	770	1.6	0.8	94.3	0.7	342	305	1.3	10.7
Nacogdoches	120.2	1.7	2 312	1 786	21	126	350	51.8	14.9	74.2	13.2	270	218	49.0	94.8
Navarro	104.8	6.8	2 653	2 075	28	114	325	34.2	15.1	86.9	10.5	286	231	37.2	91.4
Newton	29.1	7.9	2 186	1 736	10	71	341	11.4	5.4	86.6	3.7	280	264	11.2	115.1
Nolan	47.2	9.2	2 809	2 067	19	120	179	22.7	6.2	93.6	7.9	435	371	22.5	139.5
Nueces	961.7	2.8	3 233	1 565	852	499	243	358.2	126.7	77.2	124.9	440	365	344.8	87.5
Ochiltree	21.3	-23.0	2 312	1 220	11	104	45	13.9	2.2	91.9	8.1	747	649	12.3	112.2
Oldham	7.6	-4.8	2 609	1 099	13	115	132	4.3	1.6	96.5	1.7	735	684	3.8	125.1
Orange	165.0	16.7	1 996	1 591	114	79	193	91.1	26.6	87.5	42.6	480	438	96.2	87.0
Palo Pinto	63.7	-7.3	2 547	2 186	29	119	176	30.2	9.3	74.4	6.6	255	196	26.4	16.8
Panola	49.8	-1.5	2 253	1 780	11	103	316	27.9	6.6	92.9	11.9	539	503	25.4	129.1
Parker	97.5	5.5	1 435	1 258	9	78	59	36.8	14.6	91.2	11.6	241	214	33.5	87.6
Parmer	45.6	-15.5	4 516	1 211	45	155	149	8.9	3.5	96.0	4.3	384	346	8.8	56.4
Pecos	24.5	9.6	1 601	1 085	10	102	199	30.1	4.6	60.0	19.7	1 166	1 113	25.6	62.6
Polk	92.8	5.6	2 966	2 454	52	76	369	22.5	7.4	88.0	8.6	326	291	17.2	45.3
Potter	555.3	11.5	5 481	2 494	2 124	596	197	175.7	52.7	82.3	64.0	617	495	165.0	67.0
Presidio	18.7	13.5	3 010	1 591	13	781	585	4.5	2.6	82.4	1.0	175	144	3.5	37.8
Rains	14.3	21.0	2 141	1 613	12	84	220	2.5	1.1	92.7	1.1	206	170	2.5	55.4
Randall	60.7	1.2	633	490	17	29	14	17.5	5.3	93.9	7.4	93	82	15.7	87.3
Reagan	7.7	13.4	1 678	842	7	64	72	8.2	1.0	91.3	6.0	1 268	1 201	6.7	22.6
Real	8.5	7.1	3 031	2 334	13	95	281	1.1	0.5	87.5	0.5	180	123	1.0	32.1
Red River	51.3	2.4	3 443	2 546	33	121	476	14.0	5.5	92.2	3.6	225	193	12.2	87.9
Reeves	29.4	-1.3	2 031	1 317	13	132	379	23.0	6.9	78.3	10.0	605	550	21.6	71.4
Refugio	23.5	-1.3	2 733	1 925	12	131	129	13.9	1.8	87.1	9.6	1 045	958	12.6	68.6
Roberts	2.9	-5.9	2 665	1 444	32	170	65	2.0	0.1	80.0	1.6	1 323	1 262	1.8	90.5
Robertson	50.7	20.3	3 383	2 310	17	108	627	11.1	6.3	76.5	2.8	185	147	9.5	69.0
Rockwall	25.2	5.1	839	739	9	67	12	11.4	4.3	96.6	5.1	303	256	12.5	153.3
Runnels	45.0	14.7	3 951	2 494	248	162	239	10.9	3.6	92.5	4.6	377	321	9.1	83.8
Rusk	95.0	11.0	2 268	1 802	12	89	346	31.2	10.9	91.7	15.4	361	329	29.7	103.5
Sabine	35.2	7.8	3 558	3 102	21	129	295	5.1	3.3	89.2	1.0	109	84	4.6	60.9
San Augustine	26.8	15.1	3 079	2 361	23	106	562	6.2	3.1	88.2	1.1	126	93	7.6	111.7
San Jacinto	36.4	8.1	2 380	1 854	222	52	232	8.7	3.7	91.9	3.7	310	291	7.7	99.1
San Patricio	153.3	-31.0	2 568	1 549	348	60	340	60.3	23.1	92.1	24.0	392	353	54.9	88.2
San Saba	21.5	9.0	3 905	2 517	18	153	465	4.8	2.4	78.3	1.3	216	173	4.2	65.6
Schleicher	11.4	51.5	4 206	1 678	-71	1 171	162	4.4	0.9	94.1	2.5	791	732	4.5	251.7
Scurry	47.0	23.2	2 747	1 802	13	102	299	29.1	4.8	91.6	14.5	742	679	27.3	112.8
Shackelford	10.1	13.0	3 066	2 382	43	135	75	3.8	0.8	94.1	1.8	449	385	3.6	98.9
Shelby	69.6	10.9	2 911	2 257	17	120	487	13.5	8.1	92.6	3.2	136	106	11.3	41.3
Sherman	17.0	-30.2	5 877	1 180	6	82	61	4.1	0.8	90.0	2.9	899	844	3.6	54.4
Smith	344.9	4.3	2 251	1 715	161	182	181	104.5	46.9	89.9	39.0	285	225	104.7	73.1
Somervell	8.8	11.4	1 580	1 222	10	189	119	4.1	0.9	93.7	2.9	680	628	3.6	193.4
Starr	75.7	12.2	1 846	977	17	154	519	34.3	18.8	85.4	8.2	271	260	30.8	82.6
Stephens	23.6	6.2	2 482	2 093	26	116	203	7.3	2.1	93.1	3.9	358	292	5.9	28.4
Sterling	2.9	-15.4	2 080	1 190	11	134	104	3.2	0.4	93.5	1.8	1 258	1 197	2.8	150.6
Stonewall	9.5	18.5	4 518	2 450	22	228	119	4.1	0.4	88.7	2.7	1 108	1 055	3.8	156.6
Sutton	10.9	16.5	2 723	1 355	9	117	179	7.4	1.9	50.9	4.4	757	659	5.5	92.6
Swisher	39.8	-2.3	4 623	1 796	12	125	211	10.6	3.7	95.4	4.6	500	458	9.2	47.7
Tarrant	6 293.5	8.8	5 464	1 272	3 493	498	151	1 050.3	284.8	80.9	348.5	369	292	951.4	86.9
Taylor	519.0	18.1	4 275	1 754	1 086	1 255	141	86.5	33.7	81.8	37.2	312	219	74.6	83.2
Terrell	5.9	-2.5	4 245	1 972	19	455	186	1.6	0.5	90.9	0.9	607	583	1.7	86.0
Terry	51.0	14.4	3 564	1 567	10	91	248	19.9	5.3	95.1	8.4	551	501	17.9	41.6
Throckmorton	7.8	-13.1	3 890	2 894	24	202	220	3.3	0.7	94.8	1.5	689	635	2.6	76.9
Titus	56.9	4.5	2 494	2 098	20	156	198	28.5	5.6	93.1	9.2	414	363	22.3	174.9
Tom Green	340.1	8.5	3 408	1 843	185	1 077	195	66.3	27.1	81.8	25.5	280	217	60.9	68.0
Travis	2 634.0	-8.4	4 672	1 290	437	801	2 130	504.8	136.8	75.1	181.7	405	336	494.7	90.8
Trinity	39.3	17.4	3 192	2 515	12	134	505	7.2	3.7	69.6	2.5	240	202	6.2	57.9
Tyler	47.6	8.0	2 658	2 298	15	94	241	12.5	5.8	89.4	5.2	312	284	12.4	121.8
Upshur	68.7	11.4	2 161	1 781	8	61	291	17.0	8.6	91.9	6.2	199	176	14.7	98.2
Upton	8.1	12.6	1 630	1 100	17	75	119	10.5	1.3	90.9	8.2	1 518	1 462	11.0	128.3
Uvalde	59.7	8.8	2 455	1 598	38	130	304	23.3	13.0	90.7	5.2	224	175	20.6	34.6
Val Verde	182.5	15.2	4 517	1 583	406	2 051	327	27.2	18.5	87.2	5.0	131	85	23.9	86.6
Van Zandt	87.8	11.9	2 185	1 894	13	73	153	19.4	8.9	86.4	7.6	228	205	17.0	49.0
Victoria	141.6	4.8	1 916	1 478	39	132	192	76.9	21.6	93.9	29.6	403	320	70.7	96.3

1. Based on the estimated population as of July 1 of the year shown. 2. Based on the estimated population as of July 1, 1982.

STATE County	Local government finances, 1981–1982 (cont'd): Direct general expenditure (cont'd): Per capita[1] (Dollars)	Percent of total for– Education	Health & hospitals	Police protection	Public welfare	Highways	Debt outstanding: Total (Mil dol)	Per capita[1] (Dollars)	State and local government employment, 1989: Total	Rate[2]	Federal government civilian employment 1989: Total	Earnings ($1,000)	Elections, 1988[3]: Total vote cast for president	Vote for lead party (Percent)
	189	190	191	192	193	194	195	196	197	198	199	200	201	202
TEXAS—Con.														
Montgomery	924	63.8	11.3	3.0	0.2	4.5	233.2	1 563	7 803	417.0	546	17 611	59 146	R–68.2
Moore	1 043	53.3	11.9	4.9	0.7	9.4	10.2	589	991	593.4	173	5 813	5 281	R–70.3
Morris	642	71.1	0.0	6.3	0.1	7.5	5.1	331	638	459.0	35	961	5 630	D–62.6
Motley	662	67.3	0.0	1.4	0.0	11.5	0.0	25	96	505.3	20	450	692	R–62.0
Nacogdoches	1 004	30.3	40.2	3.0	0.0	5.3	35.7	732	4 898	941.9	186	5 245	18 883	R–62.3
Navarro	1 010	70.4	0.5	2.6	0.1	6.7	34.4	934	1 971	499.0	121	3 378	13 232	D–51.0
Newton	838	62.3	11.5	2.7	0.1	7.9	8.7	658	680	511.3	25	604	5 309	D–68.6
Nolan	1 242	46.8	22.8	3.1	1.0	4.0	6.7	370	1 351	804.2	62	1 703	5 609	D–50.9
Nueces	1 214	46.0	13.4	4.3	0.4	4.2	429.5	1 512	18 517	622.4	7 281	226 023	95 932	D–51.3
Ochiltree	1 129	46.9	15.4	4.7	0.3	13.2	3.6	333	588	639.1	35	931	3 517	R–83.3
Oldham	1 659	78.8	0.1	4.4	0.0	5.3	0.9	408	236	813.8	16	422	1 004	R–68.8
Orange	1 086	58.8	0.5	3.7	0.2	4.6	317.7	3 585	3 697	447.0	129	3 899	29 908	D–59.6
Palo Pinto	1 022	34.6	12.0	3.3	0.0	3.5	222.7	8 632	1 392	556.8	60	1 792	8 634	R–53.8
Panola	1 150	52.8	20.8	2.4	2.1	7.8	11.8	534	1 336	604.5	66	1 798	8 780	R–52.9
Parker	700	60.4	13.7	3.4	0.0	5.5	18.9	394	2 512	370.0	123	3 424	22 723	R–62.0
Parmer	789	72.4	1.3	3.8	0.0	5.7	5.2	473	678	671.3	67	1 787	2 839	R–72.6
Pecos	1 516	60.4	8.1	3.7	0.2	8.7	16.5	976	1 169	764.1	59	1 799	4 460	R–55.7
Polk	656	53.5	12.1	3.0	0.9	7.5	174.6	6 639	1 464	467.7	68	1 844	11 929	D–49.8
Potter	1 591	47.3	15.8	6.1	0.7	6.8	70.6	681	8 707	859.5	1 710	61 558	26 131	R–62.8
Presidio	643	60.0	0.7	5.0	0.1	6.3	1.9	347	360	580.6	167	6 257	1 771	D–66.4
Rains	479	67.3	0.0	6.1	0.1	9.1	2.2	430	268	400.0	19	521	2 736	D–52.9
Randall	198	49.8	12.5	4.9	0.5	6.5	12.1	152	3 495	364.4	43	1 390	36 666	R–76.3
Reagan	1 431	51.3	11.9	3.0	0.3	8.5	1.7	364	309	671.7	13	389	1 355	R–69.0
Real	383	58.7	0.0	3.7	2.6	12.2	0.0	2	140	500.0	NA	200	1 291	R–61.6
Red River	775	54.0	24.5	2.6	0.0	6.0	8.7	550	765	513.4	57	1 491	5 652	D–56.0
Reeves	1 301	53.0	15.6	6.5	0.4	3.9	12.6	759	1 003	691.7	66	2 027	4 554	D–61.7
Refugio	1 367	51.0	16.6	4.3	0.0	9.0	1.6	170	589	684.9	27	713	3 724	R–50.6
Roberts	1 484	51.2	0.0	3.6	0.0	16.6	0.0	35	83	754.5	15	380	581	R–75.9
Robertson	618	65.5	0.1	3.3	0.0	8.4	8.1	531	761	507.3	48	1 216	5 832	D–62.2
Rockwall	746	62.6	0.7	4.6	0.0	5.1	13.8	826	871	290.3	61	1 654	9 939	R–72.6
Runnels	750	61.8	7.0	3.3	0.5	8.2	9.7	804	615	539.5	50	1 346	4 147	R–58.3
Rusk	696	66.4	2.1	3.3	0.3	7.3	16.4	384	1 726	411.9	128	4 005	14 313	R–63.7
Sabine	510	68.7	0.0	2.3	0.0	9.3	1.6	177	380	383.8	59	1 315	3 987	D–51.5
San Augustine	843	37.6	13.9	2.9	0.0	4.5	4.9	542	444	510.3	33	829	4 084	D–51.9
San Jacinto	643	73.0	0.1	3.6	0.3	9.4	4.2	347	531	347.1	38	786	5 688	D–52.3
San Patricio	895	58.7	6.1	4.8	0.6	6.4	33.7	549	2 909	487.3	98	2 991	19 458	D–51.0
San Saba	705	54.6	16.7	2.8	0.0	4.8	1.4	231	290	527.3	30	684	2 277	D–51.2
Schleicher	1 459	40.4	28.4	2.0	0.1	6.8	1.9	617	237	877.8	14	362	1 157	R–56.4
Scurry	1 393	52.6	22.2	3.1	0.1	4.8	5.0	257	1 259	736.3	56	1 481	5 894	R–63.6
Shackelford	871	45.1	21.9	3.5	0.0	6.2	0.5	130	216	654.5	16	402	1 554	R–55.7
Shelby	477	69.1	0.0	5.0	0.0	10.1	8.4	354	947	396.2	106	2 640	8 273	D–51.5
Sherman	1 116	63.0	0.0	6.9	0.2	9.5	1.5	477	220	758.6	18	481	1 499	R–76.4
Smith	764	64.3	0.5	3.8	0.2	5.9	125.2	913	9 144	596.9	793	26 331	53 592	R–64.7
Somervell	854	61.6	1.3	4.3	0.3	8.7	4.0	951	359	641.1	17	429	2 296	R–56.8
Starr	1 019	70.9	7.1	1.4	0.1	5.6	10.2	339	2 748	670.2	230	7 807	8 211	D–84.7
Stephens	539	58.5	0.0	5.6	0.0	6.4	14.5	1 331	463	487.4	32	867	3 874	R–60.5
Sterling	2 014	47.6	21.8	2.4	0.0	4.3	0.4	318	151	1 078.6	NA	214	656	R–70.7
Stonewall	1 587	42.5	19.2	1.8	0.1	13.9	0.9	389	169	804.8	18	405	1 147	D–63.1
Sutton	945	58.4	1.3	5.7	0.1	11.6	1.8	308	403	1 007.5	13	471	1 570	R–63.4
Swisher	992	60.6	13.2	2.2	0.0	7.1	4.9	522	542	630.2	48	1 226	3 179	D–59.5
Tarrant	1 007	40.3	5.8	5.0	0.3	6.8	3 180.4	3 367	50 661	439.8	13 130	442 560	396 237	R–61.2
Taylor	627	53.6	0.7	6.4	0.3	7.5	50.9	428	7 577	624.1	1 440	34 191	42 024	R–68.0
Terrell	1 126	69.3	1.4	1.0	0.0	5.9	1.6	1 043	128	914.3	24	735	689	D–56.6
Terry	1 175	52.6	19.6	3.3	0.1	5.7	7.5	495	853	596.5	50	1 377	4 600	R–57.5
Throckmorton	1 179	43.1	31.2	2.4	0.0	8.2	0.4	194	157	785.0	14	344	998	D–53.5
Titus	999	42.6	30.4	2.3	0.0	5.6	102.6	4 600	1 778	779.8	111	3 342	8 620	D–50.5
Tom Green	669	51.1	1.2	6.2	0.7	8.6	56.3	618	5 909	592.1	1 221	32 674	34 012	R–63.1
Travis	1 102	39.3	12.6	6.6	0.8	4.3	1 603.1	3 570	80 204	1 422.6	11 373	323 460	236 084	D–54.1
Trinity	594	55.0	0.1	5.2	0.0	10.9	6.7	640	538	437.4	72	1 494	5 137	D–51.7
Tyler	749	72.8	0.0	3.5	0.6	6.0	8.1	490	880	491.6	37	1 005	7 292	D–57.6
Upshur	473	71.9	0.2	4.3	0.5	7.3	10.2	329	1 109	348.7	58	1 506	11 265	R–53.2
Upton	2 038	61.7	12.7	2.0	0.2	4.1	8.7	1 618	463	926.0	10	293	1 740	R–68.3
Uvalde	894	78.0	0.6	3.3	0.1	3.6	4.6	199	1 978	814.0	105	3 572	8 001	R–53.3
Val Verde	627	74.7	0.5	5.3	0.2	2.7	3.5	92	2 380	589.1	1 503	37 456	10 211	R–50.0
Van Zandt	512	65.3	0.5	4.0	0.1	7.1	10.2	308	1 277	317.7	89	2 282	13 559	R–54.4
Victoria	962	46.9	22.7	4.6	0.3	5.8	50.3	684	4 911	664.5	259	8 132	24 253	R–62.1

1. Based on the estimated population as of July 1, 1982. 2. Per 10,000 resident population estimated as of July 1 of the year shown. 3. Data subject to copyright.

STATE–County code	MSA/CMSA/NECMA code[1]	STATE County	Land Area,[2] 1990 (Sq. Km.)	Population, 1990											
							Race						Age of population Percent		
				Total persons	Rank	Per square kilometer	White	Black	Am. Indian, Eskimo, Aleut	Asian & Pacific Islander	Other race	Hispanic[3]	Under 5 years	5 to 14 years	15 to 24 years
			1	2	3	4	5	6	7	8	9	10	11	12	13
		TEXAS–Con.													
48 471	...	Walker	2 040	50 917	829	25.0	34 946	12 334	187	323	3 127	5 493	5.3	10.4	23.6
48 473	3362	Waller	1 330	23 390	1 519	17.6	12 987	8 796	28	69	1 510	2 592	6.7	14.8	24.2
48 475	...	Ward	2 164	13 115	2 130	6.1	9 905	457	75	25	2 653	4 830	8.0	18.9	15.2
48 477	...	Washington	1 578	26 154	1 413	16.6	19 782	5 463	46	186	677	1 158	6.9	14.6	15.1
48 479	4080	Webb	8 695	133 239	349	15.3	93 657	156	201	484	38 741	125 069	10.1	20.3	18.8
48 481	...	Wharton	2 824	39 955	1 002	14.1	29 127	6 308	38	131	4 351	10 103	7.9	17.5	13.5
48 483	...	Wheeler	2 368	5 879	2 773	2.5	5 424	154	42	23	236	378	6.0	16.4	10.2
48 485	9080	Wichita	1 626	122 378	375	75.3	102 427	11 221	903	1 851	5 976	10 555	7.6	14.6	16.1
48 487	...	Wilbarger	2 515	15 121	1 981	6.0	12 010	1 349	80	82	1 600	2 185	7.2	14.4	13.7
48 489	...	Willacy	1 545	17 705	1 805	11.5	13 820	79	29	13	3 764	14 937	8.9	21.1	16.5
48 491	0640	Williamson	2 912	139 551	340	47.9	121 914	6 861	508	1 846	8 422	20 004	8.8	17.5	14.1
48 493	...	Wilson	2 091	22 650	1 550	10.8	19 652	242	45	22	2 689	8 054	8.0	17.9	13.6
48 495	...	Winkler	2 178	8 626	2 502	4.0	6 184	167	48	9	2 218	3 172	8.2	19.6	13.2
48 497	...	Wise	2 343	34 679	1 144	14.8	32 550	390	210	83	1 446	2 663	7.6	15.9	13.2
48 499	...	Wood	1 684	29 380	1 317	17.4	26 363	2 402	109	40	466	788	5.8	14.1	12.0
48 501	...	Yoakum	2 071	8 786	2 487	4.2	6 300	86	31	11	2 358	3 217	8.6	20.9	13.5
48 503	...	Young	2 389	18 126	1 782	7.6	17 023	268	62	49	724	1 164	7.2	15.2	11.1
48 505	...	Zapata	2 582	9 279	2 446	3.6	6 680	1	9	8	2 581	7 519	9.5	19.7	15.5
48 507	...	Zavala	3 363	12 162	2 202	3.6	6 443	296	16	3	5 404	10 875	9.6	19.5	18.2
49 000	...	UTAH	212 816	1 722 850	X	8.1	1 615 845	11 576	24 283	33 371	37 775	84 597	9.8	21.3	16.8
49 001	...	Beaver	6 708	4 765	2 860	0.7	4 647	5	39	19	55	120	8.0	22.5	12.2
49 003	...	Box Elder	14 824	36 485	1 090	2.5	34 733	19	391	409	933	1 610	10.4	24.7	12.6
49 005	...	Cache	3 016	70 183	630	23.3	66 551	217	547	1 910	958	1 780	10.7	21.0	21.3
49 007	...	Carbon	3 829	20 228	1 663	5.3	19 060	62	150	116	840	2 247	7.9	21.0	14.0
49 009	...	Daggett	1 809	690	3 129	0.4	674	0	9	5	2	15	9.1	20.3	11.7
49 011	7160	Davis	789	187 941	256	238.2	178 391	2 355	1 114	3 263	2 818	7 275	10.6	23.7	16.0
49 013	...	Duchesne	8 387	12 645	2 172	1.5	11 807	10	664	39	125	350	10.7	25.6	13.7
49 015	...	Emery	11 531	10 332	2 356	0.9	10 127	4	44	36	121	219	9.5	27.2	12.7
49 017	...	Garfield	13 402	3 980	2 921	0.3	3 890	1	73	8	8	35	9.2	21.3	12.0
49 019	...	Grand	9 536	6 620	2 697	0.7	6 341	7	203	24	45	291	7.9	19.0	10.8
49 021	...	Iron	8 543	20 789	1 640	2.4	19 922	43	635	98	91	382	9.0	21.2	20.8
49 023	...	Juab	8 785	5 817	2 779	0.7	5 680	2	85	10	40	73	8.7	23.7	13.3
49 025	...	Kane	10 340	5 169	2 829	0.5	5 032	5	77	25	30	101	8.8	22.2	12.5
49 027	...	Millard	17 067	11 333	2 273	0.7	10 798	2	184	105	244	402	10.6	26.2	11.9
49 029	...	Morgan	1 578	5 528	2 799	3.5	5 462	7	8	15	36	78	9.3	25.5	13.5
49 031	...	Piute	1 963	1 277	3 106	0.7	1 267	0	9	1	0	15	6.3	20.6	12.1
49 033	...	Rich	2 664	1 725	3 082	0.6	1 704	1	1	6	13	21	10.8	26.3	10.7
49 035	7160	Salt Lake	1 910	725 956	55	380.1	675 141	5 663	6 111	20 035	19 006	43 647	9.6	20.3	15.3
49 037	...	San Juan	20 256	12 621	2 176	0.6	5 501	11	6 859	40	210	440	12.1	24.5	16.2
49 039	...	Sanpete	4 113	16 259	1 908	4.0	15 539	11	131	246	332	560	8.3	23.7	18.8
49 041	...	Sevier	4 948	15 431	1 960	3.1	14 982	6	318	27	98	289	9.0	24.2	12.6
49 043	...	Summit	4 846	15 518	1 951	3.2	15 304	18	66	78	52	326	8.9	19.9	12.6
49 045	...	Tooele	17 990	26 601	1 404	1.5	24 347	228	391	205	1 430	2 960	8.7	21.4	15.2
49 047	...	Uintah	11 596	22 211	1 569	1.9	19 537	9	2 335	82	248	691	10.3	25.2	13.1
49 049	6520	Utah	5 176	263 590	189	50.9	253 596	374	1 913	3 958	3 749	8 488	10.7	21.5	24.3
49 051	...	Wasatch	3 059	10 089	2 378	3.3	9 937	3	68	19	62	253	9.7	24.0	13.8
49 053	...	Washington	6 286	48 560	862	7.7	47 202	66	706	290	296	862	9.4	21.5	15.4
49 055	...	Wayne	6 373	2 177	3 057	0.3	2 123	1	40	2	11	25	8.3	23.2	12.0
49 057	7160	Weber	1 491	158 330	299	106.2	146 550	2 446	1 112	2 300	5 922	11 042	9.0	19.6	15.5
50 000	...	VERMONT	23 956	562 758	X	23.5	555 088	1 951	1 696	3 215	808	3 661	7.3	14.2	15.1
50 001	...	Addison	1 994	32 953	1 191	16.5	32 506	133	77	193	44	208	7.5	14.4	18.0
50 003	...	Bennington	1 752	35 845	1 103	20.5	35 464	116	54	184	27	220	7.3	13.9	13.6
50 005	...	Caledonia	1 686	27 846	1 357	16.5	27 607	54	100	70	15	90	7.5	15.5	14.4
50 007	1303	Chittenden	1 396	131 761	351	94.4	128 897	819	294	1 466	285	1 179	7.3	12.6	20.0
50 009	...	Essex	1 723	6 405	2 718	3.7	6 356	13	18	11	7	30	6.9	15.3	11.2
50 011	...	Franklin	1 650	39 980	1 001	24.2	39 201	58	585	99	37	136	8.4	16.5	13.4
50 013	1303	Grand Isle	214	5 318	2 817	24.9	5 268	15	23	11	1	20	7.9	15.0	11.2
50 015	...	Lamoille	1 193	19 735	1 689	16.5	19 557	27	48	71	32	89	7.5	14.5	15.8
50 017	...	Orange	1 784	26 149	1 414	14.7	25 935	46	67	71	30	103	7.7	15.8	13.3
50 019	...	Orleans	1 805	24 053	1 491	13.3	23 873	49	56	50	25	92	7.3	16.5	12.9
50 021	...	Rutland	2 414	62 142	700	25.7	61 639	152	70	214	67	273	7.0	13.4	14.4
50 023	...	Washington	1 786	54 928	783	30.8	54 334	177	106	236	75	663	7.1	14.4	14.0
50 025	...	Windham	2 043	41 588	968	20.4	41 012	157	74	259	86	303	7.3	14.4	12.3

1. MSA = Metropolitan Statistical Area. CMSA = Consolidated MSA. NECMA = New England county metropolitan area. PMSA = Primary MSA. See Appendix A for explanation of these concepts. See Appendix B for list of metropolitan areas identified by type, with component counties. 2. Dry land or land partially or temporarily covered by water. 3. Hispanic persons may be of any race.

STATE County	Population, 1990 (cont'd) — Age of population (cont'd) Percent — 25 to 34 years	35 to 44 years	45 to 54 years	55 to 64 years	65 to 74 years	75 years and over	Percent female	Population–Change and components of change — Change 1980–1990 — Number	Percent	Total persons, 1986	Total persons, 1980	Components of change, 1980–1986 — Net change — Number	Percent	Natural increase — Births	Deaths
	14	15	16	17	18	19	20	21	22	23	24	25	26	27	28
TEXAS—Con.															
Walker	20.2	16.0	8.9	6.7	5.1	3.8	40.4	9 128	21.8	53 900	41 789	12 100	28.9	3 600	1 600
Waller	13.6	12.8	9.4	7.6	6.1	4.9	50.9	3 592	18.1	23 400	19 798	3 600	18.4	2 000	1 100
Ward	15.1	13.9	9.1	8.8	6.5	4.7	50.2	-861	-6.2	15 400	13 976	1 400	10.2	2 000	700
Washington	14.6	13.1	8.8	9.5	8.9	8.4	51.5	4 156	18.9	25 600	21 998	3 600	16.3	2 400	1 800
Webb	16.0	12.4	8.1	6.5	4.6	3.3	52.0	33 981	34.2	120 800	99 258	21 500	21.7	17 100	3 900
Wharton	14.8	13.6	9.6	8.7	7.6	6.8	51.2	-287	-0.7	41 300	40 242	1 100	2.7	4 700	2 400
Wheeler	12.4	12.4	10.7	10.1	9.8	12.0	52.5	-1 258	-17.6	6 800	7 137	-300	-4.4	800	500
Wichita	17.3	13.2	9.3	8.9	7.1	5.7	51.0	1 296	1.1	127 100	121 082	6 000	5.0	14 000	6 700
Wilbarger	14.5	12.7	9.7	9.2	9.2	9.6	50.6	-810	-5.1	17 000	15 931	1 100	6.9	1 700	1 300
Willacy	14.0	11.8	8.3	8.4	6.5	4.6	51.7	210	1.2	19 100	17 495	1 600	9.0	2 500	800
Williamson	19.6	17.4	9.4	5.6	4.1	3.5	50.8	63 025	82.4	114 600	76 526	38 100	49.8	10 500	3 700
Wilson	15.1	14.4	9.9	8.4	6.9	5.7	50.2	5 894	35.2	19 500	16 756	2 700	16.2	1 800	900
Winkler	15.4	12.4	9.2	9.2	7.4	5.4	50.6	-1 318	-13.3	10 200	9 944	300	2.5	1 500	500
Wise	15.8	14.8	11.4	8.7	7.1	5.5	49.6	8 104	30.5	34 100	26 575	7 500	28.3	3 000	1 500
Wood	12.3	12.4	10.7	11.7	11.7	9.3	51.9	4 683	19.0	28 700	24 697	4 000	16.1	2 300	2 300
Yoakum	17.3	13.9	9.7	7.4	5.0	3.7	49.6	487	5.9	10 000	8 299	1 700	19.9	1 200	400
Young	14.6	13.3	10.0	10.4	9.1	9.2	52.0	-957	-5.0	19 000	19 083	-100	-0.7	2 200	1 600
Zapata	13.2	11.7	7.9	7.7	9.0	5.9	50.9	2 651	40.0	8 600	6 628	2 000	30.2	1 000	400
Zavala	14.5	12.1	8.2	7.3	6.2	4.5	49.5	496	4.3	12 000	11 666	300	2.5	1 700	500
UTAH	16.0	13.0	8.0	6.2	5.1	3.6	50.3	261 850	17.9	1 665 000	1 461 000	204 000	14.0	248 000	54 000
Beaver	11.3	12.0	8.3	9.4	9.1	7.1	51.0	387	8.8	5 100	4 378	700	15.9	700	300
Box Elder	14.7	11.7	8.6	7.5	5.5	4.3	50.1	3 263	9.8	36 800	33 222	3 600	10.8	5 400	1 300
Cache	16.4	11.0	6.6	4.8	4.2	3.9	49.8	13 007	22.7	65 500	57 176	8 400	14.6	11 200	2 000
Carbon	13.5	14.3	8.2	7.6	7.8	5.6	51.4	-1 951	-8.8	22 700	22 179	500	2.2	3 300	1 100
Daggett	12.8	14.9	9.6	11.7	4.6	5.2	49.0	-79	-10.3	700	769	0	-3.1	100	0
Davis	15.9	13.1	8.5	6.1	4.0	2.1	49.7	41 401	28.3	180 100	146 540	33 600	22.9	24 300	3 700
Duchesne	13.9	12.4	9.1	6.2	5.0	3.5	49.5	80	0.6	15 200	12 565	2 600	20.7	2 700	500
Emery	14.1	13.8	8.7	6.1	4.4	3.5	49.0	-1 119	-9.8	12 200	11 451	800	6.7	2 400	400
Garfield	12.1	12.2	9.1	10.1	8.7	5.3	49.0	307	8.4	4 100	3 673	400	11.6	600	200
Grand	14.0	15.5	10.0	10.4	8.2	4.3	51.5	-1 621	-19.7	7 100	8 241	-1 200	-14.1	1 100	300
Iron	13.1	11.7	8.0	6.7	5.8	3.8	50.3	3 440	19.8	19 800	17 349	2 400	13.9	3 000	600
Juab	11.9	12.4	8.3	7.6	7.4	6.7	50.4	287	5.2	5 900	5 530	400	6.8	900	300
Kane	11.3	13.5	9.2	8.7	8.5	5.3	49.6	1 145	28.5	4 800	4 024	800	18.7	600	200
Millard	12.8	11.9	7.7	6.9	6.4	5.6	49.7	2 363	26.3	14 200	8 970	5 300	58.6	1 900	500
Morgan	12.8	12.6	10.5	7.5	4.8	3.5	49.7	611	12.4	5 200	4 917	300	6.2	700	200
Piute	7.6	9.7	12.5	11.7	11.8	7.6	48.9	-52	-3.9	1 500	1 329	200	13.2	200	100
Rich	13.6	13.7	7.1	6.6	6.3	4.9	49.0	-375	-17.9	2 300	2 100	200	7.8	400	100
Salt Lake	17.4	14.4	8.4	6.1	5.0	3.5	50.4	106 890	17.3	702 500	619 066	83 400	13.5	99 200	23 100
San Juan	14.3	11.6	7.9	6.3	4.0	3.0	50.5	368	3.0	11 300	12 253	-900	-7.5	2 000	400
Sanpete	10.5	11.7	7.3	6.5	7.0	6.2	50.9	1 639	11.2	16 600	14 620	2 000	13.8	2 400	800
Sevier	11.9	12.3	8.4	7.9	7.5	6.1	50.5	704	4.8	15 600	14 727	900	5.8	2 400	800
Summit	19.0	18.9	9.5	5.4	3.4	2.4	48.9	5 320	52.2	12 900	10 198	2 700	26.8	1 600	300
Tooele	14.8	13.5	10.1	7.7	5.5	3.1	49.5	568	2.2	29 200	26 033	3 200	12.2	3 700	900
Uintah	15.0	13.3	8.4	6.8	4.9	2.9	50.5	1 705	8.3	24 200	20 506	3 700	18.1	4 400	800
Utah	15.1	10.1	6.3	4.9	4.0	3.0	50.6	45 484	20.9	240 500	218 106	22 400	10.3	45 000	6 600
Wasatch	14.0	13.6	8.8	6.8	5.1	4.1	49.9	1 566	18.4	9 800	8 523	1 300	14.9	1 400	400
Washington	11.8	10.7	7.0	8.0	9.8	6.5	50.9	22 495	86.3	38 600	26 065	12 600	48.2	4 800	1 300
Wayne	12.4	13.2	7.7	7.6	8.8	6.6	48.4	266	13.9	2 100	1 911	200	10.3	300	100
Weber	15.6	13.1	8.6	7.5	6.6	4.5	50.8	13 714	9.5	158 800	144 616	14 100	9.8	21 600	6 300
VERMONT	16.9	16.4	10.2	8.0	6.6	5.2	51.0	51 758	10.1	541 000	511 000	29 000	5.8	50 000	28 000
Addison	15.9	16.8	9.7	7.3	6.1	4.3	50.2	3 547	12.1	31 400	29 406	2 000	6.9	3 000	1 400
Bennington	15.4	15.1	10.5	9.3	7.9	7.0	51.6	2 500	7.5	35 200	33 345	1 900	5.6	3 300	2 100
Caledonia	14.9	16.1	9.8	8.6	7.4	5.7	51.1	2 038	7.9	26 700	25 808	800	3.3	2 400	1 600
Chittenden	19.3	16.3	9.8	6.7	4.6	3.5	51.5	16 227	14.0	124 800	115 534	9 300	8.0	11 000	4 600
Essex	15.1	15.2	11.4	10.6	8.6	5.6	50.8	92	1.5	6 700	6 313	400	5.6	500	400
Franklin	18.0	15.7	9.5	7.7	6.2	4.6	50.7	5 192	14.9	37 200	34 788	2 400	6.9	3 800	2 000
Grand Isle	17.1	17.4	10.9	9.5	7.1	4.0	49.7	705	15.3	5 300	4 613	600	14.0	500	300
Lamoille	17.6	16.3	10.0	7.4	6.3	4.7	50.0	2 968	17.7	18 100	16 767	1 300	7.9	1 800	800
Orange	16.6	16.5	10.1	8.3	6.7	5.0	49.9	3 410	15.0	24 100	22 739	1 300	5.9	2 300	1 200
Orleans	14.6	15.9	10.5	8.8	8.0	5.5	50.7	613	2.6	24 100	23 440	700	2.8	2 300	1 300
Rutland	16.3	16.0	10.4	8.7	7.7	6.1	51.5	3 795	6.5	60 000	58 347	1 700	2.8	5 200	3 900
Washington	15.9	17.3	10.6	8.2	6.5	6.0	51.0	2 535	4.8	53 900	52 393	1 500	2.8	4 900	3 100
Windham	16.8	17.6	10.4	8.2	7.0	6.0	51.2	4 655	12.6	39 900	36 933	3 000	8.0	3 800	2 300

STATE County	Population—(cont'd) Components of change, 1980-1986 (cont'd) Net migration	Households, 1990 Number	Households, 1990 Percent change, 1980–1990	Households, 1990 Persons per household	Households, 1990 Percent Female family householder[1]	Households, 1990 Percent One-person	Births, 1988 Total	Births, 1988 Rate[2]	Births, 1988 Low birth weight[3] (Number)	Deaths, 1987 Number Total	Deaths, 1987 Number Infant[4]	Deaths, 1987 Rate Total[2]	Deaths, 1987 Rate Infant[5]	Marriages, 1984 Number	Marriages, 1984 Rate[2]
	29	30	31	32	33	34	35	36	37	38	39	40	41	42	43
TEXAS—Con.															
Walker	10 000	14 918	26.3	2.49	10.2	26.7	676	12.5	43	301	9	5.6	13.9	527	10.4
Waller	2 800	7 402	29.3	2.76	12.8	22.5	308	13.2	21	156	4	6.7	12.3	285	12.3
Ward	100	4 444	-6.7	2.88	9.1	20.9	253	18.3	20	111	1	7.8	4.7	178	11.3
Washington	3 000	9 619	23.1	2.55	10.6	26.3	369	14.2	13	269	5	10.3	13.1	253	10.1
Webb	8 300	34 438	33.0	3.81	17.6	12.7	3 263	25.3	215	699	25	5.6	8.0	1 630	13.9
Wharton	-1 300	14 210	2.3	2.77	11.7	23.8	610	15.4	42	371	6	9.3	9.6	432	10.4
Wheeler	-600	2 350	-14.2	2.45	6.6	28.3	82	13.0	5	84	0	12.9	0.0	241	31.7
Wichita	-1 300	45 271	5.0	2.55	10.8	25.3	2 004	16.1	138	1 201	26	9.5	12.4	2 737	21.6
Wilbarger	800	5 741	-4.0	2.50	8.5	28.3	233	14.9	20	179	2	11.1	8.7	501	29.6
Willacy	-100	5 049	6.1	3.48	14.2	16.6	381	20.2	26	115	3	6.1	7.2	179	9.5
Williamson	31 300	48 792	95.7	2.81	9.6	19.2	2 272	17.7	128	646	18	5.1	7.8	1 056	10.8
Wilson	1 800	7 481	37.8	3.00	8.1	16.6	288	14.0	28	183	4	9.2	12.2	163	8.9
Winkler	-700	2 941	-13.8	2.91	7.4	19.3	138	15.9	9	76	1	8.4	7.7	144	13.2
Wise	6 100	12 175	29.4	2.77	6.3	19.4	466	13.4	30	271	2	7.7	4.2	395	12.8
Wood	3 900	11 426	23.6	2.49	7.5	24.3	342	12.0	20	403	2	14.2	5.2	333	12.1
Yoakum	800	2 839	5.1	3.08	6.2	15.4	159	16.9	5	43	0	4.6	0.0	177	19.0
Young	-700	7 101	-3.5	2.51	7.5	25.0	277	15.2	14	208	2	11.1	7.1	257	13.1
Zapata	1 400	2 862	39.0	3.23	10.3	16.1	182	20.7	21	69	2	8.0	12.3	70	8.5
Zavala	-900	3 356	9.4	3.54	17.3	15.6	246	20.5	10	81	1	6.6	3.6	128	10.5
UTAH	10 000	537 273	19.8	3.15	9.1	18.9	36 055	21.3	2 048	9 120	312	5.4	8.8	17 981	11.1
Beaver	300	1 594	11.6	2.95	5.6	21.9	69	14.7	3	46	1	9.4	14.5	41	8.2
Box Elder	-400	10 954	11.7	3.31	6.6	16.6	777	20.2	36	226	4	5.9	5.3	335	9.2
Cache	-900	21 021	19.7	3.29	6.1	17.0	1 695	25.4	63	343	13	5.2	8.1	926	14.3
Carbon	-1 800	6 907	-4.6	2.89	9.5	21.8	308	14.3	22	137	1	6.2	2.7	192	8.1
Daggett	-100	253	3.7	2.73	4.7	25.7	13	18.6	0	1	0	1.2	0.0	23	28.8
Davis	13 000	53 598	34.0	3.45	8.9	13.3	3 945	21.3	213	674	26	3.7	6.8	1 012	5.9
Duchesne	400	3 707	5.9	3.40	7.7	15.7	289	21.4	18	87	6	6.1	19.5	121	8.0
Emery	-1 200	2 998	-8.5	3.43	6.6	15.4	187	16.5	10	68	3	5.9	14.9	68	5.3
Garfield	0	1 321	10.5	3.00	5.1	19.8	70	17.1	5	40	1	9.8	13.3	41	10.0
Grand	-2 000	2 489	-9.8	2.63	9.5	26.2	92	14.2	5	56	2	8.5	17.5	111	14.2
Iron	0	6 269	21.3	3.21	7.4	16.5	421	21.9	12	94	2	4.8	5.3	188	9.8
Juab	-200	1 801	5.5	3.18	6.6	20.7	90	15.8	4	62	0	10.7	0.0	38	6.4
Kane	300	1 724	34.1	2.98	5.2	20.4	92	18.8	10	41	0	8.4	0.0	50	11.1
Millard	3 900	3 349	22.8	3.36	5.7	18.7	244	19.8	7	82	2	6.4	8.0	79	6.0
Morgan	-200	1 555	14.8	3.55	4.8	11.6	84	15.6	2	30	2	5.6	22.7	30	5.8
Piute	100	449	3.2	2.84	3.6	20.7	17	12.1	0	15	0	10.7	0.0	11	7.9
Rich	-200	521	-20.3	3.26	3.8	18.4	29	14.5	1	8	0	3.8	0.0	43	17.2
Salt Lake	7 300	240 680	19.3	2.98	10.1	22.2	14 768	20.5	893	3 944	133	5.5	9.1	8 244	12.1
San Juan	-2 600	3 375	11.8	3.70	14.6	15.6	359	30.9	30	71	7	6.2	20.8	80	6.8
Sanpete	400	4 859	9.1	3.24	6.5	20.2	293	17.9	14	136	4	8.3	13.6	109	6.5
Sevier	-700	4 877	6.3	3.13	6.5	18.9	267	17.6	11	120	3	7.8	10.7	151	9.4
Summit	1 400	5 271	55.9	2.91	6.2	19.3	232	16.8	15	64	3	4.8	14.2	114	9.2
Tooele	500	8 581	7.7	3.06	10.0	18.4	464	16.2	23	153	6	5.3	11.9	233	8.2
Uintah	100	6 670	12.1	3.31	9.7	16.4	428	19.2	42	127	6	5.5	11.5	302	11.8
Utah	-16 000	70 168	19.9	3.63	7.8	12.2	6 599	27.2	304	1 077	44	4.5	7.3	2 704	11.4
Wasatch	300	3 074	18.5	3.26	6.8	16.9	173	17.5	14	66	1	6.8	4.7	101	10.6
Washington	9 100	15 256	95.6	3.14	7.9	17.0	938	21.6	47	285	5	6.8	5.7	540	16.6
Wayne	0	699	13.7	3.07	3.4	19.5	30	14.3	2	17	0	8.1	0.0	19	9.0
Weber	-1 100	53 253	11.8	2.93	10.4	21.1	3 082	19.2	242	1 050	37	6.5	12.2	2 075	13.3
VERMONT	8 000	210 650	18.1	2.57	9.2	23.4	8 111	14.6	406	4 768	69	8.7	8.5	5 421	10.2
Addison	500	11 410	21.6	2.68	8.2	20.7	463	14.2	21	215	5	6.6	9.7	276	8.8
Bennington	600	13 595	13.7	2.54	10.2	24.3	559	15.5	21	392	5	11.0	9.8	395	11.4
Caledonia	0	10 368	12.4	2.60	10.1	23.3	372	13.5	19	249	3	9.2	8.0	238	9.0
Chittenden	2 800	48 439	25.7	2.57	8.9	23.0	2 005	15.5	107	805	7	6.4	3.5	1 205	10.0
Essex	200	2 344	7.5	2.61	8.1	21.4	72	10.6	6	53	1	8.0	13.0	40	6.2
Franklin	700	14 326	23.6	2.76	9.8	19.8	634	16.5	22	359	8	9.5	13.4	355	9.8
Grand Isle	400	2 018	25.9	2.64	7.5	19.9	90	16.7	6	33	1	5.9	11.6	63	12.6
Lamoille	400	7 397	25.4	2.56	8.5	23.5	259	13.7	18	154	3	8.3	10.0	232	13.1
Orange	200	9 455	21.8	2.69	8.9	20.1	371	14.8	19	210	6	8.4	15.7	238	10.0
Orleans	-300	8 873	9.6	2.66	9.1	21.2	331	13.6	25	254	1	10.5	3.3	233	9.7
Rutland	300	23 690	15.0	2.52	9.6	24.6	833	13.5	41	636	7	10.5	8.5	567	9.6
Washington	-400	20 948	12.5	2.50	9.2	26.2	783	14.2	44	478	2	8.9	2.5	538	10.0
Windham	1 500	16 264	17.5	2.49	9.7	25.7	612	15.0	34	395	13	9.9	21.5	430	11.1

1. No spouse present. 2. Per 1,000 resident population estimated as of July 1 of the year shown. 3. Under 2,500 grams. 4. Deaths of infants under 1 year old. 5. Deaths of infants under 1 year old per 1,000 live births.

STATE County	Divorces, 1984 Number	Divorces, 1984 Rate[1]	Physicians, active non-Federal, 1989 Number[2]	Physicians Rate[3]	Hospitals, 1989 Number	Hospitals, 1989 Beds Number	Hospitals, 1989 Beds Rate[3]	Nursing homes,[4] 1986 Number	Nursing homes, 1986 Beds	Serious crimes known to police, 1988 Number Total[5]	Serious crimes Number Violent[6]	Serious crimes Rate[3]	Education Public school enrollment[7] 1986–1987	Public school enrollment 1980	Attainment,[8] 1980 Percent 12 yrs. or more	Attainment, 1980 Percent 16 yrs. or more
	44	45	46	47	48	49	50	51	52	53	54	55	56	57	58	59
TEXAS—Con.																
Walker	208	4.1	50	91	1	108	197	3	295	3 166	231	5 953	14 954	5 814	60.8	17.7
Waller	123	5.3	8	34	0	0	0	2	244	995	80	4 290	5 109	3 812	58.1	16.3
Ward	113	7.2	5	38	1	45	341	1	59	688	34	4 813	3 488	3 031	58.2	8.4
Washington	88	3.5	35	134	1	73	280	2	369	782	72	3 020	4 743	3 952	48.3	11.3
Webb	3	NA	101	76	3	451	340	2	328	10 847	796	8 757	30 552	26 940	41.5	9.8
Wharton	185	4.5	52	133	2	168	430	3	325	1 658	119	4 095	8 461	8 571	48.3	10.8
Wheeler	43	5.7	6	98	2	83	1 361	2	154	98	4	1 463	1 350	1 364	54.6	10.7
Wichita	1 089	8.6	246	199	6	1 384	1 117	16	1 491	11 234	803	8 940	21 276	21 905	65.4	14.4
Wilbarger	107	6.3	18	118	2	551	3 625	2	296	804	97	4 964	3 074	2 947	50.2	10.9
Willacy	54	2.9	5	26	0	0	0	1	48	573	77	3 001	5 264	4 896	33.6	8.9
Williamson	463	4.7	84	62	4	295	217	8	802	5 194	342	4 252	32 658	17 912	65.5	19.4
Wilson	58	3.2	6	28	1	33	156	2	152	428	54	2 141	4 399	3 757	45.2	6.6
Winkler	13	1.2	6	74	1	27	333	1	92	216	18	2 299	2 190	2 053	52.9	7.7
Wise	165	5.3	12	34	2	74	207	4	282	877	36	2 507	5 921	5 698	52.1	7.5
Wood	172	6.3	17	59	2	78	271	10	777	907	85	3 206	5 312	4 518	50.7	9.0
Yoakum	59	6.3	3	32	1	40	430	1	100	228	18	2 376	2 434	1 916	51.8	8.8
Young	135	6.9	19	106	2	84	469	7	523	698	17	3 714	3 802	3 424	51.9	10.3
Zapata	5	0.6	1	11	0	0	0	0	0	252	27	2 931	2 362	1 614	41.3	7.2
Zavala	35	2.9	4	33	0	0	0	0	0	142	14	1 174	2 863	3 319	25.9	7.5
UTAH	8 262	5.1	3 047	179	54	5 841	342	114	6 736	93 975	4 097	5 578	417 002	334 743	80.0	19.9
Beaver	17	3.4	5	109	2	70	1 522	1	34	112	5	2 226	1 375	976	76.0	8.6
Box Elder	178	4.9	25	64	2	69	176	3	160	856	46	2 233	10 026	9 040	77.8	15.3
Cache	262	4.1	82	121	1	125	185	2	215	2 105	43	3 189	16 161	11 945	84.4	27.1
Carbon	141	6.0	24	113	1	88	415	0	0	534	36	2 380	5 573	4 543	65.8	10.2
Daggett	4	5.0	0	0	0	0	0	0	0	36	2	3 974	173	175	81.3	14.6
Davis	735	4.3	147	78	3	275	146	5	297	5 862	298	3 229	49 559	38 958	85.8	20.4
Duchesne	69	4.5	8	62	1	42	323	0	0	527	28	3 637	4 855	3 390	74.8	12.5
Emery	64	5.0	3	27	0	0	0	1	48	372	30	3 106	3 494	2 761	75.0	9.8
Garfield	17	4.1	3	73	1	20	488	0	0	38	3	899	1 116	842	72.5	13.3
Grand	55	7.1	1	16	1	32	508	0	0	386	14	5 641	1 536	1 785	73.5	16.1
Iron	90	4.7	18	95	1	48	253	2	58	662	37	3 374	5 125	4 171	83.3	19.9
Juab	18	3.1	4	71	1	22	393	1	64	263	15	4 356	1 694	1 329	74.5	11.8
Kane	19	4.2	4	80	1	33	660	1	14	66	8	1 338	1 334	989	81.0	14.7
Millard	32	2.4	6	51	2	40	342	1	36	199	5	1 533	3 790	2 279	77.4	14.3
Morgan	17	3.3	5	91	0	0	0	0	0	80	4	1 445	1 640	1 472	83.3	16.0
Piute	5	3.6	0	0	0	0	0	0	0	21	4	1 490	371	332	73.9	12.1
Rich	6	2.4	1	53	0	0	0	0	0	55	6	2 484	567	478	76.0	13.1
Salt Lake	3 922	5.7	2 023	277	20	3 078	422	72	4 046	56 555	2 460	7 873	165 056	136 115	80.3	21.7
San Juan	35	3.0	6	52	2	45	388	1	78	92	4	1 091	3 480	3 386	58.8	14.3
Sanpete	66	4.0	13	79	2	41	250	1	37	353	6	2 287	4 500	3 433	74.2	13.7
Sevier	83	5.2	7	46	1	27	179	0	0	382	27	2 804	4 686	3 630	77.4	13.3
Summit	58	4.7	23	161	0	0	0	0	0	750	40	5 562	3 157	2 396	83.9	25.2
Tooele	135	4.7	14	49	1	97	340	1	48	929	48	3 183	7 254	6 909	72.2	12.5
Uintah	134	5.2	14	65	1	33	153	0	0	942	48	4 088	6 611	4 919	69.5	12.0
Utah	863	3.6	282	116	6	936	384	12	707	10 039	399	4 126	63 339	47 177	82.7	23.4
Wasatch	45	4.7	11	111	1	40	404	2	89	349	33	3 539	2 789	2 128	78.0	15.4
Washington	131	4.0	48	103	1	106	227	2	176	1 451	37	3 466	10 713	6 101	79.8	14.9
Wayne	7	3.3	0	0	0	0	0	0	0	35	2	1 581	607	426	71.7	12.9
Weber	1 054	6.8	270	168	2	574	356	6	629	9 924	409	6 152	36 421	32 658	77.8	15.6
VERMONT	2 334	4.4	1 397	247	19	2 319	409	153	4 508	X	783	4 172	91 308	101 936	71.0	19.0
Addison	129	4.1	47	142	1	95	288	10	163	494	12	3 477	5 273	6 217	70.4	20.5
Bennington	139	4.0	81	223	1	140	385	15	365	852	20	4 092	5 580	6 614	68.2	18.4
Caledonia	124	4.7	33	118	1	100	357	7	204	522	24	4 289	4 533	5 051	68.3	14.9
Chittenden	482	4.0	678	514	2	566	429	18	674	7 406	153	6 943	20 177	22 056	78.3	26.6
Essex	20	3.1	1	14	0	0	0	2	32	NA	NA	NA	833	1 285	56.3	8.2
Franklin	161	4.4	34	87	1	77	197	13	247	421	18	4 083	6 869	7 996	59.2	9.4
Grand Isle	20	4.0	5	91	0	0	0	0	0	NA	NA	NA	748	960	66.4	14.4
Lamoille	97	5.5	39	202	1	53	275	6	159	718	16	5 539	3 300	3 381	72.0	22.3
Orange	97	4.1	39	152	1	39	152	10	198	85	5	1 706	5 942	4 691	69.1	17.4
Orleans	114	4.8	28	114	1	80	327	11	367	294	17	4 014	4 543	4 904	60.1	11.2
Rutland	290	4.9	101	161	1	197	314	15	500	1 444	55	4 834	10 331	10 902	70.0	16.5
Washington	253	4.7	99	177	2	259	462	27	806	1 071	44	2 929	9 445	10 632	72.8	19.7
Windham	199	5.1	77	186	4	416	1 007	6	308	2 151	54	8 853	6 974	6 929	72.0	19.7

1. Per 1,000 resident population estimated as of July 1 of the year shown. 2. As of end of year. 3. Per 100,000 resident population as of July 1 of the year shown. 4. Preliminary. Covers nursing homes with 3 or more beds. 5. Data for serious crimes have not been adjusted for underreporting, this may affect comparability between geographic areas or over time. 6. Includes murder and nonnegligent manslaughter, forcible rape, robbery, and aggravated assault. 7. The 1986–1987 data are based on administrative reports obtained by the U.S. National Center for Education Statistics. The 1980 data are based on the 1980 Census of Population and Housing. 8. Persons 25 years old or older.

STATE County	Education (cont'd): Local government expenditures for education,[1] 1982: Total (Mil dol)	Education (cont'd): Local government expenditures for education,[1] 1982: Per capita (Dollars)	Social Security Program December 1988: Beneficiaries: Total	Social Security Program December 1988: Beneficiaries: Rate[2]	Social Security Program December 1988: Payments ($1,000)	Supplemental Security Income Program recipients June 1986	Money income: Per capita[3]: 1987 Income, (Dollars)	Money income: Per capita[3]: 1979: Current dollars	Money income: Per capita[3]: 1979: Constant 1987 dollars	Money income: Median household income 1979 (Dollars)	Money income: Percent below poverty level, 1979: Persons	Money income: Percent below poverty level, 1979: Families	Housing units, 1990: Total	Housing units, 1990: Percent change, 1980–1990
	60	61	62	63	64	65	66	67	68	69	70	71	72	73
TEXAS—Con.														
Walker	29.3	632	5 860	108.7	2 751	750	8 407	5 644	8 831	12 905	20.8	13.1	18 349	26.9
Waller	10.0	458	2 815	120.3	1 263	332	8 316	6 004	9 394	17 379	16.2	13.3	8 824	31.3
Ward	13.1	812	1 900	137.7	903	198	7 727	6 097	9 540	16 175	13.6	11.3	5 365	2.0
Washington	7.0	296	5 435	209.8	2 297	1 090	10 539	6 744	10 552	13 891	16.4	12.0	11 717	21.5
Webb	61.5	557	13 885	107.7	4 600	5 092	5 642	3 980	6 228	11 154	33.1	29.0	37 197	34.0
Wharton	21.0	512	7 105	179.0	3 120	1 086	8 863	6 285	9 834	15 358	17.2	13.6	16 277	6.4
Wheeler	6.3	800	1 645	261.1	720	146	9 816	7 484	11 710	13 691	14.0	11.3	3 071	-4.1
Wichita	47.2	375	19 490	156.4	9 100	1 762	10 215	7 059	11 045	15 361	12.3	9.4	51 413	6.3
Wilbarger	8.7	535	3 505	224.7	1 586	334	9 363	6 451	10 094	11 998	20.2	14.2	6 812	4.2
Willacy	12.5	681	2 500	132.3	864	896	5 943	4 133	6 467	10 083	34.8	29.6	6 072	13.6
Williamson	55.9	650	12 370	96.6	5 579	1 214	10 981	7 038	11 012	19 569	9.9	7.7	54 466	92.9
Wilson	6.4	371	2 920	142.4	1 098	552	8 273	5 234	8 190	13 458	17.7	15.6	8 516	37.2
Winkler	14.0	1 218	1 380	158.6	686	126	7 942	6 125	9 584	16 741	12.1	10.0	3 708	-3.8
Wise	12.2	429	4 890	140.1	2 201	308	9 791	6 671	10 438	16 381	12.3	9.3	14 219	29.1
Wood	14.8	576	7 435	260.9	3 335	688	9 230	6 180	9 670	12 798	14.6	10.6	14 541	27.1
Yoakum	8.9	1 044	960	102.1	456	78	8 822	6 343	9 925	17 697	17.6	12.7	3 372	11.5
Young	8.5	428	4 195	230.5	2 009	328	11 209	8 107	12 685	14 300	11.5	8.2	8 523	3.4
Zapata	5.9	772	1 620	184.1	598	344	5 962	4 395	6 877	10 289	28.3	23.8	4 225	38.3
Zavala	6.8	567	1 840	153.3	589	644	4 646	3 202	5 010	8 907	38.6	34.7	4 180	18.4
UTAH	791.8	508	180 007	106.5	87 753	9 232	9 288	6 305	9 865	17 671	10.3	7.7	598 388	22.1
Beaver	2.4	490	785	167.0	338	60	6 837	4 908	7 680	12 755	14.3	11.2	2 200	21.1
Box Elder	17.6	500	4 355	113.4	2 056	150	9 555	5 798	9 072	17 428	8.2	6.9	11 890	15.5
Cache	30.5	492	6 845	102.5	3 335	186	8 365	5 401	8 451	14 902	12.7	7.9	22 053	16.9
Carbon	11.1	458	3 385	156.7	1 700	122	9 014	6 883	10 770	20 149	7.1	5.1	8 713	6.4
Daggett	1.0	1 108	100	142.9	44	0	8 341	5 662	8 859	16 488	11.3	9.8	825	11.9
Davis	91.3	571	12 665	68.5	5 795	394	9 575	6 275	9 818	20 862	6.7	5.1	55 777	34.2
Duchesne	8.5	601	1 645	121.9	727	66	7 644	5 531	8 654	17 345	12.5	10.3	5 860	30.9
Emery	12.1	893	1 185	104.9	551	54	7 462	5 896	9 225	20 299	8.4	7.2	3 928	6.1
Garfield	2.9	732	755	184.1	333	32	7 280	4 969	7 775	12 364	12.0	9.4	2 488	40.6
Grand	3.8	451	1 145	176.2	558	56	8 452	6 495	10 163	17 163	11.0	10.3	2 992	-1.8
Iron	12.7	676	2 515	131.0	1 222	98	7 209	5 158	8 071	14 471	14.5	9.1	8 499	36.0
Juab	5.1	886	970	170.2	465	42	7 531	5 223	8 172	15 095	12.4	8.5	2 311	17.4
Kane	2.9	679	850	173.5	411	16	6 977	4 528	7 085	12 244	17.3	12.6	3 237	48.1
Millard	6.8	654	1 620	131.7	707	38	7 371	4 809	7 525	13 004	14.9	12.1	4 125	25.4
Morgan	3.0	589	515	95.4	232	12	9 081	6 237	9 759	20 882	7.0	6.0	1 681	20.1
Piute	1.2	864	340	242.9	144	12	7 021	4 893	7 656	11 420	11.3	10.1	704	13.7
Rich	1.8	723	245	122.5	122	6	8 094	5 821	9 108	16 142	14.2	11.4	1 859	24.2
Salt Lake	299.1	451	75 245	104.5	38 940	3 986	10 294	7 013	10 973	18 418	8.6	6.9	257 339	19.9
San Juan	15.1	1 209	1 120	96.6	420	378	5 095	3 701	5 791	13 216	31.9	25.9	4 650	24.1
Sanpete	10.1	627	2 725	166.2	1 204	120	6 431	4 531	7 090	12 224	16.0	11.7	6 570	16.5
Sevier	11.2	722	2 560	168.4	1 213	106	8 001	5 481	8 576	15 733	9.9	7.4	6 059	11.7
Summit	13.3	1 154	1 075	77.9	533	20	13 652	8 454	13 228	19 577	7.7	4.4	11 256	91.5
Tooele	14.1	504	2 660	92.7	1 048	110	9 792	6 458	10 105	19 682	7.6	6.7	9 510	11.0
Uintah	14.6	587	2 175	97.5	1 014	92	7 184	5 768	9 025	18 555	13.1	10.5	8 142	23.0
Utah	104.0	447	23 965	98.7	11 822	1 592	7 321	5 199	8 135	16 197	15.4	10.2	72 820	16.8
Wasatch	5.9	631	1 235	124.7	602	44	7 772	5 466	8 553	15 519	10.0	6.7	4 465	-0.2
Washington	17.5	595	7 880	181.1	3 734	200	6 961	4 869	7 619	13 507	15.8	11.9	19 523	100.8
Wayne	1.6	797	455	216.7	186	6	6 940	4 675	7 315	11 047	22.3	20.1	1 061	25.1
Weber	70.8	467	18 665	116.5	8 150	1 216	10 038	6 585	10 304	17 287	9.1	7.1	57 851	14.6
VERMONT	243.1	468	85 076	152.6	40 791	9 494	11 234	6 177	9 665	14 790	12.1	8.9	271 214	21.5
Addison	12.5	414	4 200	129.2	1 950	468	10 364	5 574	8 722	14 751	12.3	9.9	14 022	16.8
Bennington	13.2	385	6 525	181.2	3 224	552	11 524	6 468	10 120	14 719	9.3	6.5	18 501	18.6
Caledonia	11.0	423	4 810	174.3	2 210	562	9 387	5 453	8 532	13 131	15.3	11.2	13 449	15.8
Chittenden	60.4	511	13 920	107.7	6 905	1 530	13 195	6 925	10 836	17 569	10.3	6.5	52 095	26.0
Essex	2.1	328	1 160	170.6	513	144	8 267	4 929	7 712	12 369	17.2	11.9	4 403	18.9
Franklin	16.4	464	5 320	138.5	2 317	908	9 764	5 561	8 701	14 025	14.9	12.1	17 250	19.3
Grand Isle	1.5	310	855	158.3	385	62	11 334	5 896	9 225	14 768	12.2	10.0	4 135	16.3
Lamoille	6.9	408	2 780	147.1	1 269	378	10 148	5 586	8 740	13 238	14.8	10.5	9 872	31.0
Orange	10.2	442	3 700	147.4	1 674	388	9 767	5 245	8 207	12 867	13.7	10.8	12 336	17.7
Orleans	10.5	445	4 260	174.6	1 822	616	8 749	5 207	8 147	12 453	16.8	13.4	12 997	16.3
Rutland	26.8	459	11 310	183.0	5 523	1 442	11 047	6 089	9 527	14 765	11.1	8.4	31 181	21.0
Washington	25.0	469	9 390	169.8	4 601	1 150	10 953	6 078	9 510	14 382	11.5	8.8	25 328	14.5
Windham	19.8	528	6 705	163.9	3 368	528	11 370	6 323	9 894	13 696	12.8	9.9	25 796	31.9

1. Elementary and secondary. 2. Per 1,000 resident population estimated as of July 1 of the year shown. 3. Based on the resident population estimated as of July 1, 1988 for 1987 data and enumerated as of April 1, 1980 for 1979 data.

STATE County	Housing units, 1990 (cont'd): Occupied units: Total	Occupied units: Owner occupied: Percent	Owner occupied: Median value (Dollars)	Median rent (Dollars)	Civilian labor force, 1990: Total	Percent change, 1989–1990	Unemployment: Total	Unemployment: Rate[1]	Private nonfarm establishments, 1988: Number	Net change, 1987–1988	Employment[2]: Total	Per-cent change, 1987–1988	Manu-facturing	Retail trade
	74	75	76	77	78	79	80	81	82	83	84	85	86	87
TEXAS—Con.														
Walker	14 918	57.4	60 300	323	21 480	-0.4	743	3.5	709	-58	7 230	-11.5	643	2 939
Waller	7 402	68.7	54 300	237	9 985	1.4	500	5.0	333	3	3 327	17.4	821	1 255
Ward	4 444	76.9	33 300	223	5 776	-8.9	306	5.3	373	-5	2 794	4.2	45	633
Washington	9 619	72.4	58 600	262	12 909	-2.9	391	3.0	676	-20	7 197	-5.4	1 920	1 615
Webb	34 438	60.6	49 800	243	53 159	2.1	5 727	10.8	2 489	80	26 818	5.6	1 515	9 115
Wharton	14 210	66.4	49 300	227	21 969	2.7	938	4.3	955	-39	9 165	3.9	1 060	2 580
Wheeler	2 350	78.5	31 200	176	2 978	-1.8	115	3.9	183	-5	969	-5.0	16	355
Wichita	45 271	63.4	46 400	291	55 057	-2.0	3 334	6.1	3 499	-100	40 011	-0.8	8 135	10 118
Wilbarger	5 741	67.3	36 300	213	8 358	-0.4	362	4.3	360	-26	3 048	-11.8	646	846
Willacy	5 049	75.5	25 800	155	7 133	-0.1	1 083	15.2	226	-15	1 662	-3.0	0	582
Williamson	48 792	64.0	72 300	350	69 197	0.9	2 834	4.1	2 376	-89	21 589	-2.1	4 810	6 032
Wilson	7 481	80.6	49 900	196	9 330	3.7	394	4.2	266	-27	1 499	-6.6	119	567
Winkler	2 941	80.3	29 200	215	3 765	1.5	194	5.2	201	-21	1 452	-3.8	35	435
Wise	12 175	79.2	49 700	244	14 179	-0.8	661	4.7	594	-12	5 248	-4.5	732	1 333
Wood	11 426	79.6	47 400	221	12 751	0.4	733	5.7	591	-22	4 213	-6.9	503	1 204
Yoakum	2 839	74.1	45 100	259	4 546	0.6	160	3.5	240	1	2 310	9.8	65	367
Young	7 101	73.1	41 200	203	8 139	-2.1	339	4.2	637	-52	5 273	-1.1	979	1 064
Zapata	2 862	82.0	35 500	163	3 213	2.1	336	10.5	100	-3	706	11.0	0	288
Zavala	3 356	69.4	20 300	104	5 425	1.2	926	17.1	115	-6	1 325	-16.1	0	248
UTAH	537 273	68.1	68 900	300	792 000	0.4	34 000	4.3	X	X	507 545	3.0	94 934	112 193
Beaver	1 594	85.1	51 200	190	1 940	-1.3	94	4.8	112	-9	715	9.0	53	299
Box Elder	10 954	79.0	65 000	258	16 783	-6.3	734	4.4	563	18	14 699	14.1	0	2 041
Cache	21 021	62.6	67 100	268	32 114	0.2	1 247	3.9	1 231	5	16 514	4.8	5 932	3 767
Carbon	6 907	75.7	51 500	223	8 193	-3.6	527	6.4	465	-20	4 933	-1.7	300	1 241
Daggett	253	60.1	50 400	187	456	2.2	7	1.5	14	1	68	-11.7	0	41
Davis	53 598	74.1	75 700	329	79 339	-0.5	3 226	4.1	2 553	62	28 671	5.1	4 451	8 989
Duchesne	3 707	81.5	43 400	224	4 462	-0.2	357	8.0	283	-10	1 900	-4.0	171	535
Emery	2 998	82.3	48 500	209	3 543	-3.3	280	7.9	156	-5	2 643	-3.8	0	268
Garfield	1 321	81.9	49 800	202	1 509	-5.5	157	10.4	91	-1	674	10.0	0	115
Grand	2 489	73.6	49 700	226	3 088	4.5	221	7.2	205	-4	1 324	1.1	40	429
Iron	6 269	69.8	63 400	267	9 276	3.4	415	4.5	549	2	4 412	8.3	301	1 716
Juab	1 801	80.1	43 300	194	2 021	0.0	130	6.4	98	1	956	16.3	0	296
Kane	1 724	77.4	63 100	217	2 522	-1.7	152	6.0	126	12	746	15.8	59	293
Millard	3 349	79.3	50 400	199	5 197	0.7	217	4.2	210	-11	2 497	-3.4	320	527
Morgan	1 555	82.7	78 000	286	1 648	-0.8	97	5.9	62	2	569	2.0	0	140
Piute	449	85.7	45 500	150	374	6.2	43	11.5	13	-1	35	-14.6	0	16
Rich	521	78.7	45 900	192	803	-4.7	18	2.2	32	4	94	-4.1	0	52
Salt Lake	240 680	65.1	71 000	316	357 308	-0.7	13 748	3.8	18 387	-85	283 549	0.8	47 927	57 273
San Juan	3 375	77.3	37 800	184	3 960	-0.3	298	7.5	198	8	1 570	1.6	208	356
Sanpete	4 859	79.7	49 000	221	6 206	0.9	558	9.0	278	2	2 231	5.8	618	728
Sevier	4 877	82.4	51 600	224	6 041	-6.2	331	5.5	369	-7	3 413	1.2	317	1 026
Summit	5 271	71.2	107 800	451	8 493	1.2	481	5.7	560	44	7 201	8.4	106	2 040
Tooele	8 581	70.2	60 400	292	11 405	-1.0	605	5.3	288	-2	3 045	12.1	310	1 133
Uintah	6 670	75.7	44 400	183	7 920	-1.4	502	6.3	479	-49	3 279	-8.2	140	980
Utah	70 168	62.7	70 000	288	117 656	5.9	4 327	3.7	4 109	19	65 902	8.8	12 645	12 974
Wasatch	3 074	76.0	69 900	296	4 702	0.1	312	6.6	194	9	1 232	-3.4	82	407
Washington	15 256	70.8	78 400	346	19 571	7.4	833	4.3	976	11	9 105	5.9	1 115	2 790
Wayne	699	81.7	54 000	174	1 003	-6.0	76	7.6	41	1	295	-23.2	53	51
Weber	53 253	70.7	66 000	286	74 472	-0.5	4 005	5.4	3 124	-44	42 199	3.6	9 189	11 670
VERMONT	210 650	69.0	95 500	378	309 000	0.7	15 000	5.0	X	X	208 783	2.6	46 838	48 495
Addison	11 410	74.2	93 400	384	17 776	2.5	716	4.0	932	96	9 600	-7.5	2 785	1 960
Bennington	13 595	70.0	97 100	370	20 330	-2.2	1 099	5.4	1 465	54	14 889	5.8	3 895	4 494
Caledonia	10 368	71.3	72 700	278	13 628	0.5	846	6.2	885	55	7 601	11.2	1 471	2 012
Chittenden	48 439	64.4	117 500	457	78 664	0.1	2 590	3.3	4 500	207	64 291	0.6	15 880	14 229
Essex	2 344	78.3	56 500	249	3 195	2.1	241	7.5	129	9	1 241	1.3	963	120
Franklin	14 326	72.5	81 700	330	18 338	2.5	1 182	6.4	983	60	8 317	8.7	2 372	2 188
Grand Isle	2 018	77.7	105 100	367	2 736	1.9	183	6.7	135	19	365	25.0	27	142
Lamoille	7 397	69.8	89 900	363	12 159	1.4	698	5.7	837	19	7 019	5.9	602	1 877
Orange	9 455	77.6	86 400	338	13 146	0.4	643	4.9	806	15	6 950	14.1	1 895	1 562
Orleans	8 873	73.7	66 500	263	11 853	2.3	1 021	8.6	750	37	6 609	7.4	2 068	1 406
Rutland	23 690	68.5	94 000	376	35 028	3.3	1 558	4.4	2 276	103	23 409	-0.8	5 218	5 759
Washington	20 948	68.7	89 900	343	29 512	2.1	1 659	5.6	2 065	79	20 943	6.2	2 965	4 769
Windham	16 264	64.2	97 200	383	23 451	-0.2	1 197	5.1	1 837	24	20 550	2.2	3 745	4 265

1. Percent of total civilian labor force. 2. For week including March 12. Excludes government employees, self-employed persons, farm workers, domestic service workers, railroad employees subject to the Railroad Retirement Act, and employees on oceanborne vessels or in foreign countries.

STATE County	Private nonfarm establishments, 1988 (cont'd) — Employment[1] (cont'd): Finance, insurance, and real estate	Employment[1] (cont'd): Services	Annual payroll: Total (Mil dol)	Annual payroll: Average per employee (Dollars)	Personal income, 1989: Total (Mil dol)	Percent change, 1988–1989	Wages and salaries[2] (Mil dol)	Proprietor's income (Mil dol)	Dividends, interest, & rent (Mil dol)	Transfer payments (Mil dol)	Per capita[3]: Dollars	Per capita[3]: Rank	Earnings, 1989: Total (Mil dol)	Percent by selected industries: Farm	Goods-related[4]: Total
	88	89	90	91	92	93	94	95	96	97	98	99	100	101	102
TEXAS—Con.															
Walker	531	2 192	90	12 474	622	5.5	362	61	96	110	11 375	2 548	423	4.2	17.0
Waller	182	498	57	17 246	306	8.9	130	26	52	55	13 051	1 890	157	6.3	24.4
Ward	87	421	49	17 467	181	6.7	104	21	33	27	13 684	1 591	125	1.0	37.2
Washington	599	1 606	112	15 602	457	7.5	206	61	132	67	17 529	366	267	3.7	29.7
Webb	1 837	6 517	349	13 004	1 066	10.5	702	100	103	239	8 043	3 074	802	1.3	13.6
Wharton	515	2 395	139	15 147	574	5.9	240	81	125	93	14 670	1 144	321	11.6	22.1
Wheeler	53	195	12	12 554	101	2.8	31	28	25	20	16 605	503	59	33.2	13.0
Wichita	2 101	11 213	681	17 024	1 985	6.6	1 192	234	397	337	16 014	641	1 426	0.5	27.1
Wilbarger	177	646	47	15 528	219	4.1	106	26	53	47	14 357	1 266	132	6.0	20.8
Willacy	116	302	20	11 912	136	-0.9	53	21	21	38	7 199	3 095	74	20.6	8.8
Williamson	1 123	5 379	329	15 256	1 899	8.4	530	173	271	197	13 961	1 450	702	4.0	29.7
Wilson	128	323	17	11 538	259	7.5	47	34	41	46	12 317	2 192	81	21.1	17.4
Winkler	74	236	23	16 102	102	7.6	49	14	21	19	12 521	2 104	62	1.9	32.6
Wise	259	896	86	16 470	447	6.6	154	62	87	64	12 491	2 122	216	5.5	36.3
Wood	309	991	56	13 191	397	7.2	119	62	101	92	13 819	1 525	181	9.3	23.6
Yoakum	69	289	45	19 370	129	-4.3	87	20	20	15	13 982	1 444	108	10.1	44.0
Young	363	1 064	89	16 955	309	5.0	129	57	81	53	17 324	393	186	3.6	35.1
Zapata	0	159	7	9 642	65	3.2	22	5	17	22	7 334	3 093	27	8.1	NA
Zavala	39	183	12	8 719	81	4.3	41	11	8	26	6 739	3 102	52	16.5	NA
UTAH	31 550	156 507	9 365	X	22 353	8.1	15 124	1 794	3 137	3 234	13 104	X	16 918	1.2	24.6
Beaver	117	134	7	9 256	55	9.0	24	10	10	13	12 003	2 326	34	19.6	NA
Box Elder	221	1 129	399	27 161	534	4.8	488	45	63	68	13 651	1 601	533	3.9	73.1
Cache	660	3 078	245	14 813	808	9.7	467	79	118	117	11 971	2 335	546	3.5	35.8
Carbon	143	1 124	101	20 543	290	5.5	175	20	39	56	13 691	1 585	194	1.1	39.4
Daggett	0	7	1	10 824	10	6.5	5	1	1	2	13 903	1 473	6	6.2	NA
Davis	1 147	7 551	479	16 706	2 338	8.6	1 432	154	253	311	12 430	2 149	1 585	0.7	17.9
Duchesne	56	397	30	15 815	144	5.2	68	29	20	24	11 079	2 642	97	11.0	22.8
Emery	34	278	84	31 755	110	7.3	115	12	11	19	9 884	2 896	127	3.7	46.5
Garfield	0	259	11	15 820	49	9.1	25	7	8	9	11 975	2 334	32	12.6	NA
Grand	72	254	21	15 613	84	5.4	35	12	14	16	13 307	1 768	47	0.8	18.7
Iron	278	1 211	51	11 621	203	12.1	120	25	29	39	10 661	2 749	145	5.1	14.2
Juab	46	234	12	12 061	57	7.2	25	8	8	14	10 291	2 838	33	9.8	NA
Kane	36	238	8	10 550	56	6.7	22	6	11	10	11 189	2 607	28	4.3	NA
Millard	73	425	53	21 175	130	5.4	79	20	22	20	11 127	2 631	99	11.2	18.2
Morgan	0	28	11	19 373	73	4.0	20	8	11	11	13 220	1 805	27	18.1	27.7
Piute	0	0	0	8 543	13	3.1	3	2	3	4	9 257	2 984	5	39.1	NA
Rich	0	10	1	10 340	24	3.4	6	4	6	3	12 526	2 103	10	45.8	NA
Salt Lake	21 934	87 790	5 597	19 741	10 441	7.9	8 083	744	1 570	1 320	14 315	1 278	8 827	0.1	22.3
San Juan	24	414	22	14 252	95	6.3	60	11	11	22	8 179	3 064	71	6.2	32.0
Sanpete	199	326	28	12 715	159	4.4	60	23	24	35	9 745	2 919	83	16.3	22.5
Sevier	141	708	53	15 519	179	9.3	100	24	28	35	11 881	2 365	123	6.2	28.8
Summit	1 007	3 154	79	11 028	279	9.8	130	34	40	19	19 476	195	163	4.8	13.3
Tooele	134	827	46	15 013	373	6.2	284	18	30	63	13 121	1 853	302	1.5	NA
Uintah	146	754	56	17 229	229	3.4	133	39	31	36	10 670	2 746	172	5.9	25.6
Utah	2 261	29 908	1 062	16 117	2 721	9.9	1 640	250	335	415	11 171	2 614	1 890	1.1	24.6
Wasatch	61	469	14	11 419	113	3.8	40	10	17	18	11 358	2 551	50	6.2	NA
Washington	510	2 494	123	13 542	484	12.3	218	62	108	101	10 383	2 814	279	1.3	21.8
Wayne	0	27	3	9 010	21	-0.4	8	4	4	5	10 207	2 855	12	15.8	18.9
Weber	2 162	13 273	672	15 933	2 279	7.1	1 260	134	313	430	14 148	1 371	1 394	0.4	25.4
VERMONT	12 967	60 508	3 791	X	9 354	9.0	5 744	954	1 709	1 260	16 514	X	6 699	1.8	32.1
Addison	289	3 162	167	17 401	480	9.1	246	56	90	59	14 547	1 191	302	5.3	36.4
Bennington	582	3 734	241	16 204	659	9.5	344	65	155	90	18 124	281	409	1.1	35.8
Caledonia	475	1 981	126	16 595	381	9.3	203	47	73	66	13 597	1 632	250	2.4	31.7
Chittenden	3 812	18 382	1 381	21 481	2 498	9.7	2 034	220	371	238	18 937	224	2 254	0.4	35.9
Essex	17	49	23	18 208	75	8.9	34	11	11	16	10 844	2 702	46	10.8	NA
Franklin	323	1 810	137	16 517	543	9.1	241	56	73	85	13 916	1 462	297	5.7	30.5
Grand Isle	21	71	5	12 496	86	9.4	11	7	15	12	15 460	814	18	12.5	23.8
Lamoille	202	3 177	91	12 922	299	9.0	146	40	55	43	15 511	798	186	3.7	22.3
Orange	262	1 629	112	16 154	398	9.3	136	53	72	51	15 545	789	189	5.6	30.1
Orleans	194	1 829	93	14 067	309	9.3	153	41	61	62	12 612	2 069	194	5.0	32.2
Rutland	1 329	6 508	405	17 301	1 028	7.6	609	97	179	176	16 363	557	706	1.5	33.9
Washington	3 476	6 176	370	17 676	917	9.1	622	87	169	139	16 385	549	708	0.8	21.9
Windham	1 064	6 587	358	17 440	734	8.2	495	83	157	94	17 765	324	577	1.5	27.0

1. For week including March 12. Excludes government employees, self-employed persons, farm workers, domestic service workers, railroad employees subject to the Railroad Retirement Act, and employees on oceanborne vessels or in foreign countries. 2. Includes other labor income. 3. Based on the resident population estimated as of July 1 of the year shown. 4. Covers mining, construction, and manufacturing.

STATE County	Earnings, 1989 (cont'd)						Agriculture, 1987									
	Percent by selected industries (cont'd)						Farms			Farm operators, percent		Land in farms				
	Goods-related[1]	Service-related & other[2]						Percent with						Acres		
	Manu-facturing	Total	Retail trade	Finance, insur-ance, & real estate	Services	Govern-ment	Number	Less than 50 acres	500 acres and over	Whose principal occu-pation is farming	Residing on farm operated	Acreage (1,000)	Percent change, 1982–1987	Average size of farm	Total irrigated (1,000)	Total cropland (1,000)
	103	104	105	106	107	108	109	110	111	112	113	114	115	116	117	118
TEXAS—Con.																
Walker	8.1	30.2	9.1	2.6	14.3	48.6	747	36.7	12.7	30.3	52.1	270	3.9	361	0	56
Waller	17.4	35.8	12.2	4.3	13.5	33.5	893	39.8	12.2	43.3	59.5	277	16.1	310	5	121
Ward	1.1	43.2	8.0	2.3	13.3	18.5	82	29.3	41.5	30.5	50.0	469	5.2	5 715	1	6
Washington	19.0	48.1	10.0	6.4	20.7	18.5	1 983	30.3	5.7	36.7	54.7	339	11.1	171	0	149
Webb	3.8	62.0	17.3	5.2	18.7	23.1	494	12.3	57.5	38.5	22.9	2 022	23.0	4 093	3	50
Wharton	9.5	51.3	10.6	3.8	22.4	14.9	1 272	28.6	25.9	57.9	46.8	686	6.6	539	80	398
Wheeler	0.5	36.8	9.0	3.0	10.8	17.1	467	9.6	48.8	55.5	50.3	486	-1.3	1 041	5	173
Wichita	17.7	49.3	10.0	4.0	24.4	23.1	544	35.3	24.6	37.7	59.2	298	-5.8	549	4	131
Wilbarger	14.6	40.9	10.1	3.4	15.4	32.3	486	17.1	41.4	68.7	52.7	850	-3.6	1 748	8	264
Willacy	4.5	42.3	11.5	3.7	12.7	28.4	293	23.9	40.6	75.8	53.6	227	-3.0	776	14	201
Williamson	17.8	47.5	11.6	4.4	23.7	18.7	1 891	28.8	14.5	45.5	62.1	527	2.2	279	1	278
Wilson	3.9	37.3	12.5	4.1	14.2	24.2	1 746	24.7	10.8	40.7	52.8	448	1.1	257	10	204
Winkler	1.5	NA	9.1	2.9	18.2	20.9	30	20.0	73.3	56.7	66.7	467	-2.7	15 572	0	1
Wise	13.1	44.6	12.2	2.8	13.6	13.6	1 749	33.6	9.6	33.2	71.3	403	-0.8	230	1	165
Wood	9.3	51.8	10.8	5.1	20.5	15.2	1 303	34.6	5.3	40.0	63.1	207	-6.5	159	1	100
Yoakum	1.9	30.8	5.0	1.3	10.3	15.1	273	8.4	68.5	73.3	44.0	348	0.9	1 276	50	228
Young	18.8	50.0	8.3	5.6	22.8	11.4	713	12.5	34.2	42.2	45.9	586	6.4	822	0	130
Zapata	NA	NA	9.8	4.9	13.0	43.4	360	8.1	47.8	44.7	15.3	432	12.4	1 199	0	31
Zavala	22.2	31.5	5.3	1.6	10.5	25.1	272	8.1	53.3	51.1	27.6	826	8.1	3 036	26	67
UTAH	16.9	54.0	9.5	5.3	23.8	20.2	14 066	44.1	16.3	45.1	62.7	9 989	2.2	710	1 161	2 029
Beaver	3.8	47.5	11.0	2.0	10.0	20.0	226	30.5	22.6	58.8	45.6	187	-0.3	828	35	37
Box Elder	69.4	16.7	5.3	1.0	6.4	6.3	1 088	35.5	24.6	49.6	66.3	1 584	3.1	1 456	107	368
Cache	29.2	34.9	7.9	2.5	19.3	25.8	1 223	40.8	7.9	46.9	67.4	324	12.4	265	84	172
Carbon	2.5	42.3	8.7	2.2	16.3	17.3	210	41.4	20.5	36.7	64.8	224	-7.5	1 065	9	17
Daggett	0.0	NA	5.0	NA	17.7	52.0	36	11.1	47.2	61.1	63.9	25	-24.3	698	8	9
Davis	12.5	34.9	8.4	2.2	16.4	46.4	647	71.3	2.5	37.9	68.8	63	-43.4	98	25	30
Duchesne	3.8	45.1	8.2	2.1	15.8	21.1	753	27.2	19.4	47.7	70.9	366	16.3	487	97	107
Emery	0.2	38.8	2.9	0.6	6.5	11.0	446	27.1	19.3	39.0	58.1	216	10.2	484	39	52
Garfield	16.2	NA	6.5	2.1	23.8	25.5	263	30.0	18.6	46.4	43.0	139	1.7	527	23	32
Grand	1.6	56.6	14.5	2.4	26.3	23.8	81	55.6	17.3	40.7	70.4	169	8.2	2 090	4	D
Iron	6.8	53.1	13.9	3.4	19.9	27.6	380	28.9	36.6	49.5	39.2	483	13.5	1 271	62	74
Juab	NA	NA	11.0	2.3	17.2	19.4	215	20.9	35.8	55.3	52.1	274	2.7	1 274	23	69
Kane	3.7	NA	16.4	2.5	24.3	28.9	152	19.7	47.4	32.2	38.8	207	-0.8	1 365	8	18
Millard	4.8	55.6	7.0	1.6	9.9	15.0	630	19.2	30.5	60.8	63.8	480	-1.6	762	93	176
Morgan	16.6	37.1	6.4	3.0	10.5	17.1	261	51.3	13.8	42.1	71.6	283	10.9	1 085	10	23
Piute	3.7	NA	2.5	3.3	8.8	32.6	126	18.3	26.2	69.8	62.7	56	6.3	447	18	22
Rich	NA	NA	5.6	3.6	7.2	27.2	166	19.3	50.0	65.7	68.7	515	8.0	3 101	54	75
Salt Lake	15.4	62.8	10.0	7.6	24.5	14.8	734	81.3	3.3	34.9	68.8	155	-10.8	212	16	40
San Juan	3.2	32.2	6.9	0.9	17.1	29.6	218	15.6	58.7	56.4	46.3	340	-6.2	1 562	9	118
Sanpete	15.5	35.1	8.6	3.0	14.5	26.2	761	30.1	17.5	54.0	44.9	448	5.6	588	111	98
Sevier	7.7	45.6	10.5	3.1	14.6	19.4	476	39.9	7.4	44.3	46.2	161	-6.0	339	43	50
Summit	3.6	70.2	11.9	12.9	37.8	11.7	439	38.0	21.6	39.9	68.3	349	2.8	795	29	41
Tooele	10.0	18.3	4.3	1.0	9.5	63.6	299	40.8	29.1	44.8	63.2	487	-3.6	1 630	19	D
Uintah	2.7	50.5	9.4	1.5	20.1	18.1	693	38.7	15.9	41.4	75.0	1 319	-0.9	1 903	76	D
Utah	19.0	60.2	9.1	3.0	39.1	14.1	1 723	65.6	6.0	40.1	65.7	494	14.2	287	79	135
Wasatch	2.7	46.6	9.6	2.6	24.5	23.2	298	49.0	8.1	39.3	64.4	160	-22.8	536	17	20
Washington	8.9	59.7	15.7	3.5	25.8	17.3	414	43.7	19.3	37.7	45.7	178	7.7	430	14	28
Wayne	6.2	NA	5.3	NA	9.5	38.6	217	28.6	8.3	51.2	67.7	102	-3.7	468	18	23
Weber	20.0	47.3	10.6	4.1	24.6	26.8	891	69.9	3.9	39.6	74.0	199	12.7	224	32	46
VERMONT	22.3	52.0	11.0	4.9	24.8	14.1	5 877	19.0	10.9	64.0	87.1	1 408	-10.6	240	2	708
Addison	27.6	48.0	10.7	2.2	27.5	10.3	714	19.3	19.5	71.3	89.6	221	-4.6	309	0	146
Bennington	25.6	53.7	15.9	4.1	27.6	9.4	169	30.8	8.9	54.4	82.2	33	-20.5	194	0	13
Caledonia	20.7	53.3	12.2	3.9	23.1	12.7	461	17.1	9.1	64.2	88.1	102	-13.5	222	D	47
Chittenden	27.5	50.1	9.6	5.1	24.0	13.5	452	28.1	11.3	53.3	85.4	98	-14.3	217	0	53
Essex	52.3	19.6	5.6	0.6	7.2	12.3	81	9.9	13.6	64.2	84.0	22	-14.6	275	0	9
Franklin	22.8	46.4	12.3	2.5	17.9	17.5	786	13.7	12.2	76.3	85.5	214	-4.1	273	0	115
Grand Isle	3.1	40.1	11.0	2.1	18.0	23.5	127	20.5	10.2	70.1	90.6	28	-18.2	222	0	21
Lamoille	8.7	60.3	13.7	3.1	36.5	13.7	213	23.9	7.5	61.0	79.8	45	-16.7	211	0	22
Orange	14.4	49.0	12.4	3.3	24.9	15.3	560	16.4	6.4	62.9	90.5	113	-14.2	202	0	49
Orleans	22.5	47.6	10.8	2.3	22.6	15.2	616	10.2	12.2	75.0	86.9	168	-6.7	273	D	87
Rutland	23.9	53.1	11.1	4.6	24.6	11.6	516	19.4	15.1	59.9	85.7	140	-16.0	272	0	61
Washington	13.3	54.4	10.6	11.6	23.7	22.9	361	19.1	4.7	53.5	87.3	72	-9.6	198	0	29
Windham	15.5	63.1	11.6	4.2	28.5	8.3	287	27.5	7.7	57.5	86.1	53	-12.7	186	0	20

1. Covers mining, construction, and manufacturing. 2. Covers private sector earnings in agricultural services, forestry, and fisheries; transportation and public utilities; wholesale trade; retail trade; finance, insurance, and real estate; and services.

STATE County	Agriculture, 1987 (cont'd): Value of land and buildings: Average per farm ($1,000)	Value of land and buildings: Average per acre (Dollars)	Value of products sold: Total (Mil dol)	Value of products sold: Average per farm (Dollars)	Value of products sold: Percent from: Crops	Value of products sold: Percent from: Livestock and poultry[1]	Percent of farms with sales of: $10,000 or more	Percent of farms with sales of: $100,000 or more	Manufactures, 1987: Establishments: Total	Establishments: Percent with 20 or more employees	All employees: Number (1,000)	All employees: Percent change, 1982–1987	All employees: Annual payroll (Mil dol)	Production workers: Number (1,000)	Production workers: Work hours (Mil)
	119	120	121	122	123	124	125	126	127	128	129	130	131	132	133
TEXAS—Con.															
Walker	390	1 178	8	11 349	8.3	91.7	19.0	1.3	36	25.0	1.0	-52.4	22.9	0.7	1.5
Waller	570	1 680	24	26 816	45.4	54.6	28.6	5.2	21	23.8	D	D	D	D	D
Ward	616	108	3	35 055	D	D	31.7	3.7	8	12.5	0.1	-50.0	1.7	0.0	0.1
Washington	279	1 647	23	11 820	9.8	90.2	20.9	1.9	39	41.0	2.1	31.2	39.9	1.6	3.3
Webb	1 353	340	24	47 624	6.2	93.8	41.5	9.3	57	24.6	1.4	-6.7	20.4	8.0	1.8
Wharton	498	856	78	60 991	79.1	20.9	49.0	17.2	41	26.8	1.2	20.0	20.4	0.9	1.7
Wheeler	255	272	62	132 912	5.9	94.1	54.8	7.3	5	0.0	0.0	0.0	0.2	0.0	0.0
Wichita	219	406	17	31 699	47.4	52.6	35.1	7.5	155	25.2	7.9	0.0	182.6	5.8	11.5
Wilbarger	507	292	30	62 384	64.6	35.4	64.8	13.0	14	28.6	D	D	D	D	D
Willacy	670	933	48	164 523	89.2	10.8	67.6	39.2	8	12.5	0.3	0.0	2.5	0.2	0.3
Williamson	389	1 418	45	24 019	50.9	49.1	32.6	4.9	163	25.2	5.1	45.7	96.3	3.6	7.5
Wilson	231	928	56	32 209	20.3	79.7	30.2	4.2	10	10.0	0.1	-66.7	1.8	0.1	0.2
Winkler	1 972	127	2	57 657	D	D	60.0	3.3	5	20.0	0.0	-100.0	0.5	0.0	0.0
Wise	276	1 248	35	20 285	14.5	85.5	24.9	4.9	39	30.8	0.7	16.7	14.9	0.5	1.0
Wood	199	1 253	35	27 070	12.5	87.5	28.8	7.6	33	18.2	0.6	-25.0	7.9	0.5	1.0
Yoakum	469	361	32	116 102	92.4	7.6	74.0	34.1	7	14.3	0.1	0.0	1.5	0.0	0.1
Young	302	388	26	37 132	20.8	79.2	40.0	4.6	26	23.1	1.0	-28.6	24.3	0.7	1.7
Zapata	511	477	6	16 423	3.4	96.6	37.2	2.8	2	0.0	D	D	D	D	D
Zavala	1 262	411	46	168 937	35.8	64.2	62.1	26.8	6	33.3	D	D	D	D	D
UTAH	303	425	618	43 927	21.1	78.9	42.2	9.9	2 083	29.3	88.8	6.7	2 073.1	54.8	107.6
Beaver	282	386	19	86 235	24.2	75.8	61.1	22.1	7	0.0	D	D	D	D	D
Box Elder	409	282	60	55 229	33.9	66.1	54.9	14.6	25	28.0	8.7	0.0	309.5	4.4	9.5
Cache	213	814	67	54 480	12.2	87.8	49.8	15.4	79	31.6	5.3	29.3	92.3	4.1	7.8
Carbon	333	304	3	13 149	14.1	85.9	20.0	3.8	13	15.4	D	D	D	D	D
Daggett	277	396	D	D	NA	NA	63.9	5.6	1	0.0	D	D	D	D	D
Davis	193	2 242	29	44 191	49.1	50.9	29.8	7.9	152	36.2	4.5	12.5	90.6	3.3	6.4
Duchesne	215	418	20	26 083	8.9	91.1	45.3	6.2	9	11.1	D	D	D	D	D
Emery	208	442	8	17 392	12.4	87.6	37.9	2.7	2	0.0	D	D	D	D	D
Garfield	337	530	6	22 535	12.7	87.3	43.7	4.9	7	28.6	D	D	D	D	D
Grand	425	204	2	23 080	24.5	75.5	29.6	4.9	7	0.0	D	D	D	D	D
Iron	494	386	25	64 532	53.9	46.1	55.3	15.8	21	19.0	0.3	-25.0	4.6	0.2	0.4
Juab	325	281	8	38 237	33.4	66.5	52.1	9.3	8	25.0	0.2	-33.3	5.2	0.2	0.3
Kane	414	320	D	D	NA	NA	39.5	3.3	7	14.3	0.1	0.0	0.6	0.0	0.1
Millard	328	422	40	63 886	32.9	67.1	62.1	14.0	11	27.3	0.1	-75.0	1.2	0.1	0.2
Morgan	437	408	13	49 932	5.3	94.7	41.0	15.7	7	28.6	D	D	D	D	D
Piute	272	577	5	38 850	6.5	93.5	61.1	10.3	1	0.0	D	D	D	D	D
Rich	872	283	13	77 691	6.7	93.3	72.9	19.3	1	0.0	D	D	D	D	D
Salt Lake	358	1 580	24	32 417	33.7	66.3	21.4	5.3	1 145	29.8	47.5	3.3	1 130.3	26.6	52.5
San Juan	425	257	9	42 983	31.0	69.1	56.0	13.8	7	28.6	0.1	0.0	1.1	0.1	0.1
Sanpete	298	512	63	82 511	5.2	94.8	54.4	16.8	18	33.3	D	D	D	D	D
Sevier	225	667	36	75 712	9.6	90.4	50.8	7.8	16	31.2	0.4	33.3	7.9	0.2	0.5
Summit	329	464	15	35 264	3.2	96.8	40.3	10.0	10	10.0	0.1	0.0	1.3	0.1	0.1
Tooele	417	254	11	35 172	20.0	80.0	34.4	5.7	13	69.2	0.5	-50.0	10.2	0.4	0.7
Uintah	325	166	19	26 996	11.3	88.7	33.6	5.1	12	16.7	D	D	D	D	D
Utah	256	925	73	42 283	25.9	74.1	32.3	8.8	276	27.5	9.0	-21.7	167.2	6.4	12.2
Wasatch	311	517	8	27 810	6.5	93.5	32.6	7.4	15	0.0	0.1	0.0	1.4	0.1	0.1
Washington	346	730	7	16 428	18.7	81.3	30.9	2.9	45	17.8	0.8	33.3	14.5	0.6	1.1
Wayne	276	586	7	31 528	8.0	92.0	57.6	6.0	4	25.0	0.0	0.0	0.5	0.0	0.1
Weber	187	816	26	29 489	15.2	84.8	28.5	7.5	164	34.1	9.0	32.4	201.3	6.5	12.7
VERMONT	259	1 124	376	63 899	6.7	93.3	55.9	23.7	1 262	26.4	48.5	3.6	1 140.0	30.6	58.3
Addison	296	1 019	76	105 990	8.1	91.9	68.9	40.6	65	18.5	4.0	73.9	74.2	1.7	3.7
Bennington	246	1 297	7	39 446	22.6	77.4	38.5	13.6	103	35.0	3.8	-11.6	75.6	2.8	5.4
Caledonia	195	921	23	50 843	4.5	95.5	53.4	16.5	61	14.8	1.5	-21.1	33.5	1.0	2.1
Chittenden	331	1 768	22	48 753	11.4	88.6	46.2	17.9	193	26.4	16.2	5.9	500.4	7.4	12.9
Essex	214	778	5	61 281	8.2	91.8	55.6	22.2	24	16.7	1.0	0.0	18.2	0.8	1.6
Franklin	206	797	79	99 953	1.6	98.4	76.2	41.0	58	43.1	2.2	-8.3	47.3	1.6	3.2
Grand Isle	247	1 117	8	63 184	14.9	85.1	64.6	22.0	4	0.0	D	D	D	D	D
Lamoille	228	1 165	14	66 187	4.9	95.1	58.7	25.4	54	20.4	D	D	D	D	D
Orange	230	1 146	25	44 223	6.2	93.8	49.3	14.6	61	31.1	1.7	30.8	29.2	1.3	2.6
Orleans	222	841	49	79 799	2.6	97.4	72.9	27.9	51	31.4	2.0	5.3	32.0	1.7	3.3
Rutland	331	1 182	26	51 035	6.6	93.4	52.3	20.3	126	30.2	5.5	17.0	125.4	4.4	8.7
Washington	236	1 274	15	40 946	6.3	93.7	41.8	14.1	143	25.9	2.8	3.7	54.9	2.1	3.9
Windham	294	1 707	13	46 920	24.4	75.6	36.6	15.3	170	26.5	3.9	-2.5	68.9	3.0	5.7

1. Includes livestock and poultry products.

STATE County	Manufactures, 1987 (cont'd): Production workers (cont'd): Wages: Total (Mil dol)	Manufactures, 1987 (cont'd): Production workers (cont'd): Wages: Average per worker (Dollars)	Manufactures, 1987 (cont'd): Value added by manufacture (Mil dol)	Manufactures, 1987 (cont'd): Value of shipments (Mil dol)	Manufactures, 1987 (cont'd): New capital expenditures (Mil dol)	Value of construction authorized by building permits, 1990: Total[1] ($1,000)	Nonresidential: Total ($1,000)	Nonresidential: Percent: Office	Nonresidential: Percent: Industrial	Nonresidential: Percent: Stores	Residential: New construction ($1,000)	Residential: Number of housing units	Residential: Alterations and additions ($1,000)
	134	135	136	137	138	139	140	141	142	143	144	145	146
TEXAS—Con.													
Walker	15.6	22 286	20.4	80.2	0.6	3 686	1 413	3.1	0.0	80.5	483	10	330
Waller	D	D	D	D	D	521	2	0.0	0.0	0.0	283	4	29
Ward	0.9	NA	5.7	12.0	0.2	1 252	0	NA	NA	NA	125	2	230
Washington	27.8	17 375	112.8	257.6	6.0	4 840	278	18.0	61.1	0.0	1 771	23	164
Webb	10.9	1 362	73.2	122.4	2.5	100 260	51 187	9.1	0.0	85.6	30 729	824	5 161
Wharton	12.9	14 333	31.2	90.7	2.1	3 939	1 201	62.6	8.3	15.0	2 228	52	225
Wheeler	0.1	NA	0.4	1.1	0.0	298	184	100.0	0.0	0.0	0	0	24
Wichita	122.5	21 121	563.7	949.0	35.9	30 699	14 531	16.7	0.8	22.9	6 842	84	2 793
Wilbarger	D	D	D	D	D	689	390	0.0	0.0	0.0	105	2	106
Willacy	1.6	8 000	4.7	6.5	D	4 444	2 653	6.6	47.7	35.9	937	38	502
Williamson	52.9	14 694	255.8	448.2	11.9	31 735	7 167	21.1	14.9	35.0	13 713	174	998
Wilson	1.1	11 000	4.4	7.4	0.3	1 238	246	26.4	0.0	27.0	686	17	171
Winkler	0.2	NA	0.9	1.4	0.0	319	195	100.0	0.0	0.0	0	0	54
Wise	8.5	17 000	31.6	68.5	1.6	3 921	2 415	26.5	6.5	62.4	806	19	35
Wood	5.7	11 400	27.8	44.4	0.7	2 923	1 056	21.6	0.0	20.2	710	13	147
Yoakum	1.0	NA	4.7	6.7	0.1	451	66	0.0	0.0	0.0	160	2	123
Young	15.4	22 000	64.1	131.9	3.6	1 231	609	30.7	0.0	60.6	140	2	163
Zapata	D	D	D	D	D	NA	NA	NA	NA	NA	NA	NA	NA
Zavala	D	D	D	D	D	43	0	NA	NA	NA	0	0	15
UTAH	1 002.3	18 290	4 882.9	10 286.7	403.5	1 153 357	381 381	13.4	21.7	35.2	594 691	7 328	37 963
Beaver	D	D	D	D	D	2 807	191	0.0	0.0	26.9	1 204	12	459
Box Elder	122.9	27 932	582.6	1 069.8	D	7 686	1 689	0.0	25.1	17.8	3 658	44	731
Cache	63.5	15 488	345.0	1 095.1	10.8	34 397	10 855	1.9	37.9	21.9	19 182	286	1 048
Carbon	D	D	D	D	D	7 071	2 646	0.0	0.0	70.8	1 429	16	535
Daggett	D	D	D	D	D	172	38	0.0	0.0	0.0	90	1	12
Davis	57.5	17 424	316.2	903.9	25.1	123 304	21 735	1.6	36.0	29.9	88 627	948	3 117
Duchesne	D	D	D	D	D	2 169	436	11.4	0.0	49.0	908	21	305
Emery	D	D	D	D	D	1 514	849	0.0	1.5	76.6	281	6	164
Garfield	D	D	D	D	D	1 866	170	0.0	0.0	11.7	1 172	24	102
Grand	D	D	D	D	D	2 605	314	0.0	0.0	100.0	1 821	34	302
Iron	3.1	15 500	14.7	31.6	0.7	9 016	1 728	0.0	9.8	0.0	6 002	85	365
Juab	3.3	16 500	7.0	26.3	D	1 002	596	0.0	68.8	0.0	275	6	53
Kane	0.5	NA	1.1	2.4	0.0	3 879	106	0.0	0.0	0.0	3 236	70	141
Millard	1.0	10 000	2.8	9.2	D	1 515	147	0.0	0.0	0.0	559	7	219
Morgan	D	D	D	D	D	2 766	121	0.0	52.2	0.0	1 995	24	133
Piute	D	D	D	D	D	58	0	NA	NA	NA	40	1	18
Rich	D	D	D	D	D	561	14	0.0	0.0	100.0	399	15	59
Salt Lake	467.3	17 568	2 556.0	5 087.0	200.2	449 583	173 483	13.8	7.8	42.7	196 483	2 413	11 188
San Juan	0.7	7 000	2.7	4.9	0.1	2 146	1 240	15.3	0.0	84.7	286	8	54
Sanpete	D	D	D	D	D	6 794	215	0.0	0.0	48.9	4 236	74	454
Sevier	4.7	23 500	16.1	39.1	0.8	3 092	900	0.0	0.0	0.0	1 335	32	362
Summit	0.8	8 000	2.3	4.7	D	68 773	5 442	9.5	0.4	11.9	55 085	439	5 755
Tooele	7.3	18 250	26.9	47.3	1.2	23 816	16 435	2.9	68.9	5.3	5 757	90	550
Uintah	D	D	D	D	D	4 183	2 272	0.8	7.6	82.4	571	8	297
Utah	104.4	16 312	334.3	629.4	35.3	243 772	111 509	22.1	36.5	25.8	100 925	1 303	5 076
Wasatch	1.0	10 000	2.9	8.5	D	10 413	1 445	0.0	9.0	8.9	7 975	93	526
Washington	10.0	16 667	62.8	94.7	D	70 632	11 839	6.5	4.7	40.9	53 831	799	1 968
Wayne	0.4	NA	1.2	4.9	0.1	7	0	NA	NA	NA	3	1	0
Weber	129.3	19 892	523.1	994.2	42.1	67 760	14 967	0.6	20.4	63.3	37 329	468	3 970
VERMONT	551.6	18 026	2 543.1	4 752.7	334.4	369 340	83 093	18.9	26.0	16.5	188 860	2 371	41 628
Addison	32.2	18 941	179.2	292.0	9.7	25 557	4 611	8.0	41.1	13.9	16 140	261	1 564
Bennington	48.7	17 393	204.7	398.2	13.3	30 030	3 015	12.7	3.3	44.5	19 691	173	4 408
Caledonia	20.4	20 400	62.5	112.1	D	16 724	4 413	0.0	4.1	38.3	8 270	129	1 638
Chittenden	135.1	18 257	1 041.7	1 845.5	D	96 624	21 494	33.6	33.5	16.3	44 752	461	14 962
Essex	15.2	19 000	38.6	93.7	D	5 102	1 493	0.0	0.0	0.0	2 818	44	203
Franklin	32.0	20 000	115.2	289.2	8.0	28 486	9 360	57.2	1.7	16.9	14 319	201	1 902
Grand Isle	D	D	D	D	D	3 120	547	0.0	0.0	0.0	2 282	24	188
Lamoille	D	D	D	D	D	12 315	873	0.0	31.5	25.4	7 765	74	1 865
Orange	19.6	15 077	72.2	137.6	6.4	9 306	2 266	4.4	27.9	18.3	4 674	60	1 094
Orleans	24.5	14 412	68.6	133.3	D	16 030	4 112	0.0	30.8	10.4	7 653	130	479
Rutland	95.5	21 705	313.5	482.4	15.9	37 614	8 783	9.1	47.7	9.2	18 412	278	3 135
Washington	36.4	17 333	112.0	288.3	14.1	33 041	8 684	9.8	13.3	6.4	13 847	176	4 071
Windham	47.2	15 733	159.6	322.3	11.6	23 264	3 553	15.2	17.8	22.7	10 864	164	3 318

1. Includes nonresidential additions and alterations, residential nonhousekeeping buildings, and residential garages and carports not shown separately.

STATE County	Wholesale trade, 1987: Estab-lishments	Wholesale trade, 1987: Sales (Mil dol)	Wholesale trade, 1987: Paid employees[1]	Wholesale trade, 1987: Annual payroll (Mil dol)	Retail trade, all establishments, 1987: Number	Retail trade, all establishments, 1987: Sales: Total (Mil dol)	Retail trade, all establishments, 1987: Sales: Percent change, 1982–1987	Retail trade, all establishments, 1987: Sales: Per capita[2] (Dollars)	Retail trade, establishments with payroll, 1987: Number	Retail trade, establishments with payroll, 1987: Sales: Total (Mil dol)	Per capita[2] (Dollars): General merchan-dise stores	Per capita[2] (Dollars): Food stores	Per capita[2] (Dollars): Apparel & acces-sory stores	Per capita[2] (Dollars): Eating and drinking places
	147	148	149	150	151	152	153	154	155	156	157	158	159	160
TEXAS—Con.														
Walker	41	60.8	275	4.1	417	247.4	22.9	4 607	253	239.2	455	933	183	502
Waller	28	57.4	253	3.5	207	181.5	-0.5	7 756	107	178.5	D	1 084	26	389
Ward	31	109.1	269	5.1	166	46.2	-27.6	3 255	102	44.2	265	932	166	355
Washington	60	254.3	798	15.3	355	148.9	3.3	5 704	186	143.0	D	1 553	446	366
Webb	258	606.6	2 123	30.4	1 217	708.2	1.0	5 634	791	688.5	888	1 338	579	441
Wharton	90	232.6	841	14.3	528	199.1	-3.8	4 990	304	191.8	D	1 392	241	378
Wheeler	14	13.7	81	1.1	109	29.5	-16.7	4 532	68	26.9	D	1 435	108	357
Wichita	265	478.1	2 101	38.3	1 587	826.4	10.1	6 559	928	795.5	1 174	959	283	771
Wilbarger	38	48.4	217	2.9	203	78.8	7.9	4 892	111	73.8	484	1 021	270	384
Willacy	16	20.3	80	1.4	149	50.1	11.3	2 635	85	47.6	233	955	47	109
Williamson	127	196.5	852	14.7	1 238	531.3	77.9	4 223	609	506.8	D	1 307	180	341
Wilson	19	24.5	114	1.8	181	71.3	32.0	3 565	95	67.9	D	990	D	131
Winkler	18	27.6	100	1.7	112	32.1	-35.0	3 571	68	30.2	D	1 359	183	168
Wise	45	158.1	297	5.4	359	191.8	70.6	5 465	170	184.1	D	1 095	85	315
Wood	44	109.6	311	4.7	381	127.7	35.7	4 511	194	118.6	477	1 147	140	241
Yoakum	23	20.3	90	2.0	116	33.4	9.5	3 553	67	32.0	D	1 601	D	209
Young	51	117.6	307	4.6	315	97.8	6.8	5 231	163	91.2	708	1 297	229	291
Zapata	2	D	D	D	96	16.1	8.8	1 867	38	12.5	D	671	D	203
Zavala	7	9.7	113	1.6	95	21.4	-3.6	1 755	50	19.7	D	922	D	95
UTAH	2 956	11 094.3	34 180	718.4	13 827	8 619.8	36.2	5 132	8 519	8 378.8	609	1 131	242	450
Beaver	4	D	D	D	76	17.9	23.4	3 662	49	16.6	D	839	D	345
Box Elder	29	104.3	318	5.2	301	133.9	23.4	3 523	175	127.3	264	809	D	429
Cache	77	208.6	964	13.3	512	269.1	25.7	4 077	311	259.9	515	973	195	335
Carbon	53	58.4	267	5.1	234	94.6	-18.4	4 262	142	91.1	447	1 278	91	346
Daggett	0	0.0	0	0.0	11	D	D	D	7	2.3	D	D	0	D
Davis	158	796.9	1 838	36.9	1 111	766.3	51.3	4 229	603	740.8	411	939	73	256
Duchesne	27	37.4	161	2.3	145	48.5	-20.9	3 395	83	45.8	388	935	D	106
Emery	6	D	D	D	104	23.0	-16.1	1 981	50	20.3	D	428	D	196
Garfield	2	D	D	D	76	10.7	42.7	2 612	44	9.9	D	633	0	331
Grand	10	8.3	44	0.7	108	D	D	D	72	29.3	D	1 456	83	435
Iron	36	61.7	283	3.3	269	113.6	0.9	5 857	183	110.2	417	996	272	690
Juab	8	14.9	67	1.3	64	23.7	17.3	4 094	32	22.6	0	657	D	256
Kane	6	7.7	34	0.6	68	19.1	15.8	3 904	44	16.5	D	D	0	391
Millard	13	9.6	74	1.0	126	38.6	33.1	3 012	71	36.2	D	800	D	189
Morgan	2	D	D	D	43	8.7	19.2	1 617	18	7.2	D	721	0	154
Piute	0	0.0	0	0.0	14	2.0	81.8	1 409	6	1.6	0	D	0	D
Rich	1	D	D	D	23	4.5	12.5	2 147	13	4.0	D	D	0	D
Salt Lake	1 904	8 491.9	24 958	556.9	5 955	4 357.3	43.5	6 100	3 750	4 259.0	760	1 296	364	604
San Juan	8	16.1	64	0.8	94	20.9	-19.9	1 821	54	19.0	289	483	D	161
Sanpete	19	14.7	67	0.7	166	42.9	66.9	2 614	105	41.2	33	1 129	42	126
Sevier	27	84.8	255	3.3	186	78.9	16.7	5 155	119	76.6	D	767	463	300
Summit	16	23.4	72	2.5	269	103.6	91.1	7 788	171	97.1	0	2 399	D	1 343
Tooele	5	D	D	D	196	92.1	25.0	3 222	105	87.3	D	967	D	202
Uintah	57	66.3	263	6.2	220	87.5	-35.4	3 819	131	84.9	418	964	108	273
Utah	244	450.3	2 014	34.3	1 664	987.6	28.0	4 088	1 034	961.2	549	923	188	305
Wasatch	9	12.9	102	0.8	93	28.8	-3.7	2 972	56	27.3	D	828	D	387
Washington	48	92.1	474	7.4	429	230.5	86.5	5 514	237	220.1	356	1 180	185	396
Wayne	2	D	D	D	29	4.0	53.8	1 883	15	2.5	D	777	0	149
Weber	185	395.8	1 626	30.4	1 241	978.7	44.5	6 094	839	961.0	1 004	1 274	242	435
VERMONT	986	2 833.0	10 270	205.1	7 981	4 177.0	60.6	7 635	5 077	4 043.4	550	1 536	317	665
Addison	52	67.1	303	5.2	396	181.5	59.2	5 602	225	171.5	325	1 092	178	425
Bennington	49	43.1	313	4.8	621	401.6	56.8	11 313	413	392.1	647	2 038	610	858
Caledonia	51	D	D	D	367	175.3	41.6	6 470	238	168.7	516	1 492	361	443
Chittenden	267	D	D	D	1 587	1 089.4	61.9	8 694	1 131	1 073.5	895	1 713	507	892
Essex	3	D	D	D	67	9.9	57.1	1 499	32	8.2	0	D	D	327
Franklin	69	233.9	654	11.6	438	240.5	57.3	6 346	289	233.0	363	1 548	206	325
Grand Isle	2	D	D	D	80	16.3	69.8	2 909	37	14.1	226	D	0	245
Lamoille	32	19.1	121	1.9	361	133.0	48.3	7 152	239	129.6	447	1 773	186	872
Orange	37	51.0	284	5.3	324	117.0	60.7	4 663	179	109.1	87	1 247	D	371
Orleans	40	63.6	228	4.1	343	145.2	75.4	5 975	182	137.8	532	1 446	92	359
Rutland	125	251.9	1 357	24.9	1 020	514.0	63.2	8 454	623	493.1	647	1 532	351	771
Washington	110	197.8	971	19.0	818	419.5	60.4	7 768	528	406.7	636	1 513	234	574
Windham	59	636.2	1 533	31.0	749	375.9	75.1	9 373	479	362.2	404	1 846	414	870

1. For pay period including March 12. 2. Based on the estimated population as of July 1 of the year shown.

Table A. States and Counties — **Retail Trade, Services, and Banking**

STATE County	Retail trade, establishments with payroll, 1987 (cont'd): Paid employees[1]	Retail trade: Annual payroll (Mil dol)	Taxable service industries–establishments with payroll, 1987: Number	Receipts (Mil dol): Total	Receipts, selected kinds of business: Hotels, motels and other lodging places	Health services	Legal services	Paid employees	Annual payroll (Mil dol)	Bank deposits,[2] June 1989: Total (Mil dol)	Percent change, 1988–1989	Savings capital,[3] September 1989: Total (Mil dol)	Percent change, 1988–1989
	161	162	163	164	165	166	167	168	169	170	171	172	173
TEXAS—Con.													
Walker	3 109	27.0	196	49.0	2.2	22.5	3.0	1 435	18.2	291	-8.9	82.3	-2.4
Waller	1 294	12.9	76	13.0	D	4.7	0.3	427	4.3	110	2.7	28.6	-56.7
Ward	672	5.4	73	14.4	D	1.9	0.5	313	5.2	96	-4.9	30.8	6.3
Washington	1 757	17.0	152	41.4	2.5	17.2	2.9	1 134	14.8	345	-10.2	203.5	5.3
Webb	9 068	81.2	511	132.4	15.0	D	8.7	4 090	44.3	2 469	7.8	514.6	-16.1
Wharton	2 417	22.0	208	60.4	1.4	37.9	2.9	1 345	21.9	395	5.8	168.4	0.8
Wheeler	368	2.9	30	3.9	D	2.5	D	137	1.3	77	-3.0	22.5	-17.2
Wichita	10 471	99.2	861	279.6	D	108.1	22.3	6 803	105.2	1 163	-8.2	463.3	-35.9
Wilbarger	908	7.8	92	17.3	1.4	7.2	0.7	534	5.6	218	1.4	26.6	-95.6
Willacy	636	5.0	56	5.7	0.6	2.0	0.3	191	1.5	83	-0.6	7.8	-13.5
Williamson	5 936	54.7	606	145.0	2.4	53.4	6.5	3 576	49.2	928	-8.4	440.3	17.4
Wilson	668	6.3	55	7.6	D	3.3	0.5	252	2.9	114	12.0	28.2	-4.0
Winkler	383	3.3	41	6.7	D	2.5	0.8	195	2.0	83	-1.3	10.2	-14.5
Wise	1 441	14.4	104	25.2	1.0	12.1	1.6	692	8.4	202	4.9	94.7	-6.2
Wood	1 291	11.8	114	19.6	1.1	9.6	1.2	671	6.7	277	-2.9	85.6	-4.5
Yoakum	386	3.6	48	10.8	D	1.2	0.6	228	3.2	74	7.9	14.2	13.7
Young	1 111	10.0	135	26.3	1.8	7.6	2.1	865	9.0	230	1.9	322.6	-3.9
Zapata	189	1.5	24	3.2	1.6	D	0.0	119	0.8	80	17.3	9.7	-13.7
Zavala	301	2.2	13	2.8	D	0.6	D	59	0.9	25	-6.8	0.0	NA
UTAH	108 925	963.3	10 117	3 833.2	296.7	1 008.6	263.9	93 897	1 419.7	8 791	5.0	1 708.4	-7.4
Beaver	283	1.8	26	3.6	1.6	1.1	D	133	0.8	34	1.0	0.0	NA
Box Elder	1 879	14.7	128	25.3	0.9	16.2	0.8	748	8.2	187	4.7	32.8	13.8
Cache	3 900	30.0	323	70.6	2.6	27.5	2.5	1 743	22.9	342	5.5	87.8	-12.7
Carbon	1 201	10.4	128	38.7	3.0	24.4	1.9	1 011	13.0	167	4.9	16.1	-15.2
Daggett	28	0.4	3	D	D	0.0	0.0	D	D	NA	NA	0.0	NA
Davis	8 421	77.7	687	256.7	2.1	84.2	2.2	6 296	98.2	497	12.1	61.4	-9.7
Duchesne	658	4.8	51	13.4	0.4	4.2	0.3	291	4.0	76	5.9	5.8	-21.7
Emery	281	1.9	40	11.5	1.5	2.0	D	237	3.3	43	10.4	0.0	NA
Garfield	122	1.0	20	7.8	7.5	D	0.0	103	1.4	23	3.4	0.0	NA
Grand	408	3.5	45	7.6	4.3	1.0	D	253	1.7	40	5.8	7.8	-4.7
Iron	1 534	12.9	137	29.6	9.6	5.1	1.2	859	7.7	129	7.4	6.0	-4.5
Juab	269	1.7	19	3.5	D	1.4	D	98	1.0	39	11.2	0.0	NA
Kane	310	2.2	25	6.5	3.6	0.4	D	145	2.0	34	6.2	7.0	18.5
Millard	504	3.6	45	9.0	2.7	1.3	D	328	2.6	78	25.6	0.0	NA
Morgan	127	0.7	9	1.2	0.0	D	0.0	21	0.3	15	3.9	0.0	NA
Piute	15	0.1	0	0.0	0.0	0.0	0.0	0	0.0	4	14.9	0.0	NA
Rich	45	0.4	7	1.0	D	0.0	0.0	16	0.2	10	9.2	0.0	NA
Salt Lake	55 903	515.8	5 427	2 335.8	157.3	552.2	229.8	53 764	892.3	4 759	2.5	1 049.2	-1.6
San Juan	320	2.2	33	6.8	2.8	1.8	D	202	1.8	46	3.5	0.0	NA
Sanpete	733	4.3	45	5.2	0.3	2.4	D	159	1.2	90	4.7	0.0	NA
Sevier	991	7.0	89	21.0	7.0	4.2	D	591	5.6	131	6.0	0.0	NA
Summit	1 688	11.5	129	72.3	29.6	1.5	D	2 905	25.0	92	10.9	6.8	-10.9
Tooele	1 079	9.0	62	27.2	15.1	3.0	D	770	9.0	81	15.0	0.0	NA
Uintah	1 067	9.0	125	24.6	0.9	6.6	0.8	667	8.2	110	3.8	8.0	-15.6
Utah	12 671	107.0	1 232	510.9	12.2	145.5	11.7	12 113	186.2	894	7.2	120.7	-15.9
Wasatch	441	3.1	48	7.7	2.0	1.5	0.2	300	2.3	51	11.1	5.5	-14.5
Washington	2 704	23.4	282	65.6	15.7	21.7	2.9	1 844	19.1	210	13.8	57.6	-42.2
Wayne	36	0.2	7	D	0.5	0.0	0.0	D	D	8	-0.6	0.0	NA
Weber	11 307	103.1	945	269.0	12.2	98.7	7.9	8 283	101.4	601	8.4	236.1	-12.1
VERMONT	46 635	472.5	4 412	1 352.9	227.9	247.8	92.2	36 674	448.4	6 112	7.4	382.5	4.1
Addison	1 802	19.4	174	32.6	7.8	7.6	4.0	819	10.7	191	2.0	30.9	8.2
Bennington	4 217	47.4	333	79.9	17.7	19.8	4.6	2 121	27.7	384	0.8	53.9	6.7
Caledonia	1 812	17.8	153	30.4	3.4	11.3	4.2	854	11.7	356	9.3	0.0	NA
Chittenden	13 592	132.6	1 182	475.8	43.9	86.1	34.0	12 128	156.8	1 561	8.2	165.4	0.7
Essex	119	0.9	9	0.7	D	0.0	D	18	0.2	11	4.2	0.0	NA
Franklin	2 160	21.4	181	34.0	D	11.2	3.0	874	11.5	315	8.7	20.6	17.4
Grand Isle	141	1.2	25	3.2	2.0	D	D	51	0.7	25	-2.2	0.0	NA
Lamoille	1 894	17.2	191	68.3	47.2	D	2.3	2 584	21.7	175	4.8	0.0	NA
Orange	1 389	13.1	181	41.5	6.6	7.8	1.3	1 042	13.5	223	20.2	14.4	5.8
Orleans	1 274	13.7	139	28.7	7.5	7.9	D	1 077	9.4	253	10.5	0.0	NA
Rutland	5 822	56.6	523	179.3	26.9	32.1	13.4	5 015	64.9	768	-0.4	21.9	11.4
Washington	4 706	47.2	488	109.3	12.1	20.9	8.3	2 858	36.8	759	7.8	20.1	-6.0
Windham	4 079	44.2	396	150.3	24.7	18.2	6.7	4 050	44.1	555	16.8	30.3	16.2

1. For the period including March 12 of the year shown. 2. Includes deposits for all insured and reporting noninsured commercial and mutual savings banks. 3. Includes savings capital for all FSLIC insured savings institutions.

STATE County	Federal funds and grants, 1989: Expenditures: Total (Mil dol)	Federal funds and grants, 1989: Expenditures: Percent change, 1988–1989	Federal funds and grants, 1989: Per capita[1] (Dollars): Total	Per capita[1]: Direct payments for individuals	Per capita[1]: Procurement contract awards	Per capita[1]: Salaries and wages	Per capita[1]: Grant awards	Local government finances, 1981–1982: General revenue: Total (Mil dol)	General revenue: Intergovernmental: Total (Mil dol)	General revenue: Intergovernmental: Percent from state	General revenue: Taxes: Total (Mil dol)	Taxes: Per capita[2]: Total (Dollars)	Taxes: Per capita[2]: Property (Dollars)	Direct general expenditure: Total (Mil dol)	Direct general expenditure: Percent change, 1977–1982
	174	175	176	177	178	179	180	181	182	183	184	185	186	187	188
TEXAS—Con.															
Walker	86.5	9.3	1 581	1 328	17	85	140	71.8	20.8	84.7	18.3	395	353	66.6	-9.7
Waller	56.3	10.5	2 408	1 622	13	96	472	19.3	5.6	91.7	10.3	471	432	17.0	95.4
Ward	22.9	-8.0	1 738	1 476	10	74	169	23.0	3.1	86.9	14.3	890	840	25.2	161.2
Washington	62.2	9.8	2 385	1 912	30	98	317	22.9	10.2	89.3	5.1	217	150	22.9	93.2
Webb	256.1	6.9	1 931	1 112	67	224	520	113.8	59.1	87.4	30.9	279	186	116.7	97.8
Wharton	118.6	14.8	3 034	1 736	29	112	321	45.4	15.9	87.3	18.8	456	411	42.1	63.8
Wheeler	21.1	3.4	3 463	2 545	21	198	149	11.8	2.3	96.3	6.4	816	763	12.2	90.4
Wichita	507.1	8.3	4 093	2 061	556	1 301	148	115.7	39.3	75.0	40.5	322	247	109.6	98.0
Wilbarger	51.1	9.7	3 364	2 334	15	165	186	18.5	6.8	96.3	4.6	280	229	20.9	95.1
Willacy	47.1	7.8	2 494	1 214	29	80	438	21.1	12.0	76.8	4.6	252	222	18.4	83.1
Williamson	277.3	60.4	2 039	970	36	75	881	76.1	32.0	94.7	27.5	320	292	81.7	197.8
Wilson	42.3	12.4	2 003	1 510	25	85	200	10.5	6.2	89.2	2.8	163	135	9.5	91.0
Winkler	15.8	4.8	1 957	1 740	20	60	129	18.9	2.3	89.9	10.9	951	894	23.6	174.7
Wise	60.8	13.6	1 699	1 324	16	85	191	21.8	6.2	92.0	9.4	330	284	21.5	156.9
Wood	85.3	9.5	2 961	2 575	13	145	177	21.5	6.1	93.7	11.0	429	391	23.0	125.6
Yoakum	25.6	22.3	2 751	1 012	6	60	402	19.1	1.2	85.0	15.8	1 861	1 816	15.6	21.8
Young	47.6	4.3	2 657	2 253	19	109	202	18.6	4.9	94.1	8.1	409	340	16.9	55.7
Zapata	21.3	10.4	2 390	1 772	7	87	484	10.6	3.6	93.6	5.3	704	691	8.9	154.4
Zavala	29.5	9.8	2 458	1 397	5	40	612	11.4	6.2	85.9	3.2	263	236	9.8	1.6
UTAH	6 142.1	5.3	X	1 345	896	788	520	1 668.6	613.3	83.9	529.5	340	261	1 451.5	85.3
Beaver	13.6	9.1	2 965	2 074	12	322	518	6.7	2.7	78.4	1.4	284	236	5.9	110.6
Box Elder	796.9	23.7	20 381	1 245	18 073	265	538	29.1	13.7	86.3	9.6	271	224	29.4	59.3
Cache	167.0	21.9	2 475	1 131	637	167	457	41.3	19.4	92.5	12.4	199	156	45.7	102.3
Carbon	59.9	2.4	2 827	1 876	221	269	448	23.1	7.8	85.7	8.9	367	283	21.5	61.1
Daggett	4.3	5.0	6 161	1 771	1 059	2 834	409	1.3	0.5	77.5	0.6	712	677	1.4	108.3
Davis	939.4	-1.4	4 994	1 145	867	2 858	106	130.5	69.6	89.5	37.8	236	190	133.5	94.1
Duchesne	34.2	43.7	2 628	1 149	574	217	474	18.7	5.4	79.1	8.4	597	517	17.7	32.6
Emery	31.2	-64.6	2 810	1 058	46	127	1 368	24.4	2.6	71.6	12.2	906	847	26.1	227.8
Garfield	11.8	8.1	2 869	1 672	301	616	236	5.1	3.0	80.9	1.4	371	322	4.4	54.7
Grand	22.3	36.0	3 547	1 804	41	660	1 035	8.8	3.1	79.7	4.0	479	368	7.8	66.0
Iron	42.9	7.5	2 256	1 419	60	473	283	20.9	6.9	85.6	6.9	366	307	24.2	129.9
Juab	16.5	35.1	2 948	1 769	13	146	692	9.2	4.6	90.7	1.8	307	263	10.6	121.1
Kane	10.5	2.1	2 105	1 553	31	275	235	6.2	3.6	75.7	1.4	333	277	5.8	112.7
Millard	24.9	14.7	2 131	1 159	19	246	454	13.9	6.2	85.1	3.4	324	258	13.8	69.2
Morgan	9.8	-3.3	1 773	1 469	11	105	94	4.2	2.3	96.4	1.2	242	219	3.9	10.4
Piute	4.0	1.2	2 884	2 091	26	187	460	1.6	1.1	92.0	0.3	248	231	1.6	67.7
Rich	4.1	18.3	2 157	1 249	22	168	244	3.3	1.5	96.3	1.2	481	445	3.1	67.8
Salt Lake	1 980.7	0.8	2 716	1 190	504	458	556	836.0	234.9	81.8	262.9	397	290	618.4	90.3
San Juan	33.4	1.6	2 879	981	163	336	1 219	24.1	11.7	40.7	9.2	736	693	21.4	89.5
Sanpete	35.4	8.8	2 156	1 538	56	144	337	14.9	8.8	89.8	2.4	151	125	15.5	124.0
Sevier	39.0	-30.9	2 582	1 679	65	363	450	15.0	8.3	78.8	3.8	243	188	16.9	141.9
Summit	15.8	-3.8	1 107	781	31	124	120	22.0	3.0	71.5	11.7	1 016	811	25.4	178.7
Tooele	302.5	27.6	10 612	1 698	3 595	5 063	231	26.6	12.9	84.3	6.5	232	193	26.8	87.8
Uintah	40.1	-77.3	1 863	982	63	479	265	32.4	11.4	86.2	10.6	429	318	29.8	157.1
Utah	398.2	7.9	1 635	1 095	170	138	223	178.2	86.5	91.2	54.0	232	182	170.8	62.8
Wasatch	39.4	70.3	3 978	1 145	2 412	185	187	10.4	6.6	54.1	2.3	247	202	9.6	93.1
Washington	97.7	9.1	2 096	1 681	17	172	196	24.8	12.1	86.9	7.3	247	192	29.5	129.0
Wayne	6.7	-39.8	3 366	1 831	36	974	447	2.2	1.6	90.8	0.4	194	162	2.3	110.0
Weber	625.5	9.6	3 883	1 989	352	1 251	285	133.7	61.3	82.8	45.6	300	227	128.6	49.5
VERMONT	1 736.7	10.6	X	1 655	348	344	688	394.2	109.8	72.3	237.3	456	453	394.5	53.9
Addison	86.7	12.8	2 627	1 256	684	155	459	19.9	4.4	83.3	13.5	446	444	22.4	79.8
Bennington	91.5	13.7	2 514	1 813	174	132	385	24.1	6.0	67.9	15.1	442	439	21.8	29.1
Caledonia	64.7	-9.7	2 310	1 671	25	150	447	18.3	5.7	86.9	10.2	395	393	17.4	14.4
Chittenden	466.5	13.4	3 537	1 238	1 087	538	661	93.8	22.3	68.0	55.1	467	461	96.8	74.1
Essex	17.2	6.8	2 492	1 753	25	313	384	3.7	1.1	84.0	2.3	369	368	3.2	2.8
Franklin	90.0	-2.4	2 309	1 428	68	378	408	22.9	8.1	90.1	12.8	362	359	23.0	45.4
Grand Isle	11.4	19.9	2 078	1 571	18	156	258	3.1	0.5	79.0	2.4	482	480	2.5	79.0
Lamoille	39.2	0.2	2 029	1 487	16	139	354	12.4	3.3	79.4	8.0	469	466	12.0	49.3
Orange	51.2	10.0	2 000	1 419	24	160	378	15.5	4.7	87.4	9.7	416	414	15.3	51.7
Orleans	60.8	0.4	2 480	1 646	51	244	503	19.8	8.4	56.8	9.4	397	395	19.9	76.0
Rutland	154.9	2.4	2 467	1 854	53	202	347	40.9	12.6	67.3	24.4	419	417	41.0	48.5
Washington	209.8	7.3	3 746	1 690	43	264	1 736	41.1	13.7	75.2	22.2	418	414	40.5	46.9
Windham	101.4	12.3	2 455	1 587	183	170	500	35.7	9.1	65.6	23.2	617	614	34.6	51.6

1. Based on the estimated population as of July 1 of the year shown. 2. Based on the estimated population as of July 1, 1982.

STATE County	Local government finances, 1981–1982 (cont'd): Direct general expenditure (cont'd): Per capita[1] (Dollars)	Percent of total for– Education	Percent of total for– Health & hospitals	Percent of total for– Police protection	Percent of total for– Public welfare	Percent of total for– Highways	Debt outstanding: Total (Mil dol)	Debt outstanding: Per capita[1] (Dollars)	State and local government employment, 1989: Total	State and local government employment, 1989: Rate[2]	Federal government civilian employment 1989: Total	Federal government civilian employment 1989: Earnings ($1,000)	Elections, 1988[3]: Total vote cast for president	Elections, 1988[3]: Vote for lead party (Percent)
	189	190	191	192	193	194	195	196	197	198	199	200	201	202
TEXAS—Con.														
Walker	1 438	43.9	0.9	2.5	0.1	2.3	358.5	7 743	9 750	1 782.4	144	3 804	14 391	R—58.9
Waller	778	58.9	6.4	3.6	0.3	10.9	21.3	976	2 601	1 111.5	50	1 335	7 624	D—51.9
Ward	1 565	51.9	11.5	2.7	0.3	5.1	13.0	810	1 084	821.2	32	912	4 590	R—59.0
Washington	967	59.2	1.6	3.8	0.2	4.5	14.3	605	2 626	1 006.1	69	2 153	9 037	R—66.8
Webb	1 057	62.1	0.9	4.4	1.8	5.0	68.8	623	8 313	626.9	581	20 106	23 832	D—68.1
Wharton	1 025	66.2	8.2	3.4	0.2	7.4	19.8	481	2 290	585.7	116	3 207	12 991	R—53.7
Wheeler	1 547	51.7	27.0	2.4	0.2	5.3	3.3	419	494	809.8	38	987	2 777	R—61.3
Wichita	871	43.1	16.4	5.3	1.1	8.0	57.9	460	7 273	587.0	2 456	57 009	41 590	R—56.1
Wilbarger	1 283	59.3	17.8	2.2	0.0	3.4	9.4	579	2 135	1 404.6	93	2 781	4 929	R—54.1
Willacy	1 004	67.8	0.0	2.8	0.1	5.2	5.1	277	1 098	581.0	40	1 051	4 940	D—64.1
Williamson	949	68.4	5.2	2.3	0.1	4.5	123.5	1 436	6 112	449.4	258	7 528	47 230	R—57.8
Wilson	547	67.8	0.2	4.0	0.1	9.4	5.4	310	953	451.7	58	1 380	8 425	R—52.7
Winkler	2 051	59.4	15.1	2.3	0.1	4.2	13.8	1 203	625	771.6	15	499	2 611	R—63.4
Wise	755	56.8	14.0	3.4	0.1	11.0	12.5	439	1 350	377.1	86	2 327	11 395	R—53.2
Wood	896	64.3	5.5	4.6	0.0	7.7	16.7	651	1 315	456.6	79	2 224	11 366	R—54.7
Yoakum	1 838	56.8	8.5	2.7	0.0	14.0	0.9	107	670	720.4	28	759	2 507	R—70.3
Young	855	50.1	14.1	3.8	0.0	7.6	9.5	479	970	541.9	58	1 644	7 193	R—57.8
Zapata	1 170	66.0	0.5	3.7	0.4	10.7	8.5	1 124	699	785.4	27	793	3 135	D—69.3
Zavala	816	69.5	0.1	4.2	0.5	5.6	4.4	363	728	606.7	22	735	3 973	D—84.0
UTAH	932	54.6	3.8	5.6	0.3	5.8	2 916.6	1 872	105 270	617.1	40 097	1 177 408	647 008	R—66.2
Beaver	1 234	39.7	28.2	3.7	0.0	12.2	2.2	461	379	823.9	50	1 064	2 112	R—60.9
Box Elder	836	59.8	1.5	5.8	5.6	6.3	21.9	623	1 780	455.2	113	3 103	15 461	R—81.4
Cache	737	66.7	1.1	4.9	0.1	6.6	55.0	887	7 039	1 042.8	322	9 317	27 963	R—77.8
Carbon	890	51.5	0.6	5.8	4.0	9.0	27.4	1 134	1 711	807.1	178	5 644	8 603	D—64.2
Daggett	1 592	69.6	0.3	8.8	0.0	8.8	0.4	446	87	1 242.9	81	1 703	412	R—66.0
Davis	836	68.3	2.1	4.7	0.0	3.2	89.5	560	6 317	335.8	15 125	479 521	68 384	R—73.8
Duchesne	1 257	47.8	12.2	4.6	0.8	11.6	11.1	789	1 022	786.2	143	3 169	4 403	R—70.8
Emery	1 935	46.2	0.7	4.5	0.0	5.8	196.3	14 537	701	631.5	55	1 344	4 144	R—56.0
Garfield	1 132	64.7	0.6	3.7	0.0	10.6	3.1	800	296	722.0	164	3 546	1 855	R—79.2
Grand	933	48.4	0.5	9.0	0.0	10.3	5.9	698	357	566.7	163	4 762	3 248	R—58.3
Iron	1 292	52.4	12.6	3.7	0.3	6.4	18.4	986	1 798	946.3	285	9 337	7 868	R—76.7
Juab	1 822	48.6	15.6	4.2	0.0	6.2	19.1	3 293	359	641.1	25	658	2 523	R—59.7
Kane	1 348	50.4	0.0	4.2	0.0	4.7	4.0	940	386	772.0	63	1 707	2 255	R—79.3
Millard	1 331	49.1	12.9	4.3	0.0	9.3	6.6	634	727	621.4	100	2 429	4 710	R—74.6
Morgan	773	76.3	1.3	4.4	0.1	3.9	1.9	365	258	469.1	10	259	2 567	R—73.6
Piute	1 111	77.8	0.6	1.9	0.1	7.1	0.3	180	88	628.6	NA	152	687	R—69.3
Rich	1 244	58.1	1.1	5.2	0.0	10.0	1.3	522	151	794.7	16	304	860	R—72.2
Salt Lake	933	48.4	3.4	6.5	0.2	5.8	1 992.8	3 006	49 505	678.8	7 935	244 612	276 903	R—59.1
San Juan	1 713	70.6	5.7	2.6	0.0	8.4	6.0	483	955	823.3	190	4 416	3 837	R—61.9
Sanpete	960	65.3	7.3	4.2	0.1	6.7	11.9	738	1 301	793.3	80	2 027	6 517	R—70.3
Sevier	1 090	66.3	0.1	4.2	0.0	5.0	12.9	829	1 022	676.8	211	5 804	6 221	R—76.3
Summit	2 209	52.3	0.9	3.7	0.0	7.1	19.5	1 697	882	616.8	67	1 478	6 503	R—59.7
Tooele	957	52.6	14.6	5.0	0.0	6.9	13.8	492	1 125	394.7	5 154	161 892	9 804	R—56.5
Uintah	1 201	48.8	7.2	4.5	0.0	14.4	9.8	397	1 186	551.6	399	10 924	7 218	R—74.0
Utah	735	60.9	1.2	4.6	0.0	4.5	212.6	914	13 576	557.5	850	22 375	88 227	R—77.2
Wasatch	1 030	61.3	0.8	3.6	0.0	10.5	7.2	776	531	536.4	76	1 552	3 997	R—62.2
Washington	1 003	59.3	0.0	10.5	0.1	5.0	30.1	1 025	2 006	430.5	290	8 285	16 565	R—80.3
Wayne	1 141	69.9	1.1	3.4	0.0	15.3	0.1	63	188	940.0	107	2 317	1 143	R—68.6
Weber	847	55.1	6.8	5.7	0.9	3.8	135.3	891	9 537	592.0	7 838	183 707	62 018	R—64.0
VERMONT	759	61.6	0.4	3.3	0.0	10.8	276.7	532	35 270	622.7	5 405	161 570	243 326	R—51.1
Addison	743	55.7	0.1	1.5	0.1	13.2	8.3	274	1 353	410.0	140	3 225	13 791	D—49.2
Bennington	637	60.5	1.4	3.8	0.1	12.1	12.6	369	1 499	411.8	135	3 742	15 725	R—53.3
Caledonia	672	62.9	0.2	2.5	0.0	14.0	8.4	324	1 514	540.7	105	2 806	11 312	R—61.1
Chittenden	819	62.4	0.3	4.5	0.0	6.6	164.9	1 395	10 011	759.0	1 777	56 361	57 345	D—50.9
Essex	505	64.9	0.4	1.2	0.0	14.9	1.1	173	218	315.9	62	1 916	2 391	R—64.2
Franklin	651	71.3	0.1	2.1	0.0	9.4	8.4	239	1 792	459.5	516	14 785	14 834	D—49.7
Grand Isle	516	60.1	0.2	1.4	0.0	16.8	1.1	230	194	352.7	23	593	2 728	D—50.2
Lamoille	704	58.0	0.4	3.9	0.1	15.8	4.9	289	1 168	605.2	69	1 807	8 133	R—54.5
Orange	659	67.1	0.3	0.9	0.0	15.9	5.0	217	1 343	524.6	100	2 428	11 318	R—54.3
Orleans	842	52.9	0.1	2.4	0.0	12.3	4.8	204	1 302	531.4	164	5 101	9 611	R—54.7
Rutland	703	65.3	0.3	3.0	0.0	10.1	12.9	221	3 322	529.0	340	10 051	26 260	R—55.1
Washington	760	61.7	0.7	2.6	0.1	10.5	17.3	325	6 866	1 226.1	333	9 750	26 294	R—50.4
Windham	921	57.3	0.7	3.8	0.1	13.2	11.0	293	2 024	490.1	181	5 016	18 654	D—52.7

1. Based on the estimated population as of July 1, 1982. 2. Per 10,000 resident population estimated as of July 1 of the year shown. 3. Data subject to copyright.

STATE–County code	MSA/CMSA/NECMA code[1]	STATE County	Land Area,[2] 1990 (Sq. Km.)	Population, 1990 Total persons	Rank	Per square kilometer	Race White	Black	Am. Indian, Eskimo, Aleut	Asian & Pacific Islander	Other race	Hispanic[3]	Age of population Percent Under 5 years	5 to 14 years	15 to 24 years
			1	2	3	4	5	6	7	8	9	10	11	12	13
		VERMONT–Con.													
50 027	...	Windsor	2 516	54 055	796	21.5	53 439	135	124	280	77	255	6.9	14.0	11.0
51 000	...	VIRGINIA	102 558	6 187 358	X	60.3	4 791 739	1 162 994	15 282	159 053	58 290	160 288	7.2	13.3	15.5
51 001	...	Accomack	1 177	31 703	1 222	26.9	20 499	10 938	40	71	155	452	6.4	13.3	12.2
51 003	1540	Albemarle	1 872	68 040	650	36.3	59 264	6 824	75	1 643	234	786	6.8	12.4	18.5
51 005	...	Alleghany	1 155	13 176	2 125	11.4	12 792	329	13	40	2	54	5.8	13.7	13.3
51 007	...	Amelia	924	8 787	2 486	9.5	5 933	2 822	14	13	5	45	7.0	14.5	13.3
51 009	4640	Amherst	1 231	28 578	1 342	23.2	22 576	5 758	128	74	42	231	6.3	12.7	15.5
51 011	...	Appomattox	864	12 298	2 196	14.2	9 459	2 816	14	6	3	30	6.4	13.9	13.7
51 013	8840	Arlington	67	170 936	282	2 551.3	130 873	17 940	537	11 560	10 026	23 089	5.5	7.5	13.9
51 015	...	Augusta	2 517	54 677	787	21.7	52 434	2 006	48	132	57	239	6.4	13.9	13.1
51 017	...	Bath	1 378	4 799	2 859	3.5	4 533	251	2	8	5	23	5.4	11.9	13.5
51 019	...	Bedford	1 955	45 656	908	23.4	41 856	3 612	60	114	14	177	6.6	13.3	12.1
51 021	...	Bland	929	6 514	2 709	7.0	6 257	230	3	8	16	24	5.1	12.8	13.0
51 023	6800	Botetourt	1 406	24 992	1 463	17.8	23 745	1 121	15	75	36	143	5.8	13.0	12.9
51 025	...	Brunswick	1 466	15 987	1 923	10.9	6 605	9 349	9	12	12	47	6.1	13.5	16.7
51 027	...	Buchanan	1 305	31 333	1 233	24.0	31 107	63	26	47	90	257	5.5	16.3	16.0
51 029	...	Buckingham	1 505	12 873	2 150	8.6	7 564	5 259	17	27	6	38	6.9	12.6	13.3
51 031	4640	Campbell	1 307	47 572	881	36.4	40 418	6 876	44	168	66	216	6.7	13.3	15.0
51 033	...	Caroline	1 379	19 217	1 719	13.9	11 686	7 244	203	49	35	100	7.4	14.5	14.1
51 035	...	Carroll	1 234	26 594	1 405	21.6	26 380	109	24	26	55	151	5.5	12.1	13.7
51 036	6760	Charles City County	473	6 282	2 725	13.3	1 800	3 969	489	11	13	24	6.2	13.7	13.3
51 037	...	Charlotte	1 230	11 688	2 235	9.5	7 392	4 263	18	4	11	33	6.9	13.1	14.4
51 041	6760	Chesterfield	1 103	209 274	238	189.7	177 067	27 196	487	3 738	786	2 511	8.0	16.5	13.5
51 043	...	Clarke	457	12 101	2 208	26.5	10 984	1 054	14	30	19	82	6.4	12.7	12.2
51 045	...	Craig	855	4 372	2 888	5.1	4 354	8	5	4	1	5	6.5	12.8	12.5
51 047	...	Culpeper	987	27 791	1 360	28.2	22 569	4 783	87	292	60	192	7.8	14.7	13.5
51 049	...	Cumberland	773	7 825	2 595	10.1	4 765	3 027	8	13	12	45	7.0	14.3	13.8
51 051	...	Dickenson	862	17 620	1 810	20.4	17 519	68	13	14	6	58	5.9	16.0	14.6
51 053	6760	Dinwiddie	1 305	20 960	1 630	16.1	13 348	7 471	33	60	48	122	6.7	13.3	14.0
51 057	...	Essex	668	8 689	2 494	13.0	5 329	3 270	46	40	4	30	5.9	14.0	11.8
51 059	8840	Fairfax	1 025	818 584	45	798.6	665 399	63 325	2 038	69 338	18 484	51 874	7.1	13.3	13.9
51 061	...	Fauquier	1 684	48 741	860	28.9	42 657	5 462	113	291	218	602	8.0	14.9	12.7
51 063	...	Floyd	988	12 005	2 219	12.2	11 664	292	16	21	12	59	5.6	13.2	12.6
51 065	1540	Fluvanna	744	12 429	2 187	16.7	9 522	2 846	21	18	22	69	7.6	14.0	12.2
51 067	...	Franklin	1 793	39 549	1 011	22.1	35 142	4 231	41	71	64	137	6.2	12.6	15.6
51 069	...	Frederick	1 074	45 723	907	42.6	44 536	832	68	218	69	291	7.6	14.9	13.2
51 071	...	Giles	927	16 366	1 898	17.7	16 044	284	8	24	6	57	5.8	12.0	13.8
51 073	5720	Gloucester	561	30 131	1 291	53.7	26 448	3 354	70	195	64	287	7.5	15.5	12.1
51 075	6760	Goochland	737	14 163	2 040	19.2	9 895	4 210	16	33	9	33	6.5	11.3	11.7
51 077	...	Grayson	1 146	16 278	1 904	14.2	15 729	486	13	18	32	75	5.8	11.7	14.0
51 079	1540	Greene	406	10 297	2 358	25.4	9 579	664	13	27	14	53	8.6	14.8	12.3
51 081	...	Greensville	765	8 853	2 485	11.6	3 900	4 916	13	23	1	64	7.0	14.9	14.7
51 083	...	Halifax	2 108	29 033	1 327	13.8	17 504	11 393	79	23	34	164	5.8	14.1	13.3
51 085	6760	Hanover	1 224	63 306	690	51.7	56 440	6 405	143	269	49	321	6.9	13.9	13.8
51 087	6760	Henrico	617	217 881	227	353.1	168 453	43 827	626	4 364	611	2 171	6.9	12.4	13.5
51 089	...	Henry	990	56 942	765	57.5	43 529	13 155	63	110	85	253	6.4	12.7	14.3
51 091	...	Highland	1 077	2 635	3 016	2.4	2 630	3	0	2	0	5	5.6	12.5	9.1
51 093	...	Isle of Wight	818	25 053	1 460	30.6	16 975	7 925	51	69	33	172	7.6	14.3	12.6
51 095	5720	James City County	370	34 859	1 135	94.2	27 804	6 460	69	452	74	382	7.1	13.6	12.8
51 097	...	King and Queen	819	6 289	2 723	7.7	3 573	2 633	65	10	8	28	7.3	13.9	13.2
51 099	...	King George	466	13 527	2 099	29.0	10 597	2 734	37	119	40	156	8.4	15.5	13.9
51 101	...	King William	713	10 913	2 305	15.3	7 351	3 310	217	25	10	66	7.4	14.9	12.8
51 103	...	Lancaster	345	10 896	2 306	31.6	7 567	3 289	6	12	22	75	5.0	12.0	9.4
51 105	...	Lee	1 132	24 496	1 478	21.6	24 346	91	26	21	12	119	6.2	14.7	13.9
51 107	8840	Loudoun	1 347	86 129	530	63.9	77 095	6 168	177	2 101	588	2 156	8.8	14.3	13.0
51 109	...	Louisa	1 289	20 325	1 658	15.8	14 970	5 233	65	37	20	108	6.8	14.2	12.8
51 111	...	Lunenburg	1 118	11 419	2 260	10.2	7 081	4 292	11	24	11	83	6.6	14.9	12.0
51 113	...	Madison	833	11 949	2 224	14.3	10 182	1 697	29	22	19	35	6.7	14.6	12.1
51 115	...	Mathews	222	8 348	2 529	37.6	7 140	1 175	11	15	7	49	4.8	11.5	11.1
51 117	...	Mecklenburg	1 616	29 241	1 321	18.1	17 926	11 226	20	49	20	108	6.0	13.1	12.6
51 119	...	Middlesex	337	8 653	2 498	25.7	6 503	2 131	6	9	4	48	5.7	11.7	9.4
51 121	...	Montgomery	1 006	73 913	609	73.5	67 983	2 841	64	2 821	204	793	5.4	9.6	34.0
51 125	...	Nelson	1 223	12 778	2 158	10.4	10 246	2 406	15	26	85	118	6.4	13.7	11.8
51 127	6760	New Kent	543	10 445	2 343	19.2	8 078	2 151	136	34	46	78	7.1	13.7	12.5
51 131	...	Northampton	537	13 061	2 136	24.3	6 882	6 035	16	16	112	256	6.8	14.7	10.9

1. MSA = Metropolitan Statistical Area. CMSA = Consolidated MSA. NECMA = New England county metropolitan area. PMSA = Primary MSA. See Appendix A for explanation of these concepts. See Appendix B for list of metropolitan areas identified by type, with component counties. 2. Dry land or land partially or temporarily covered by water. 3. Hispanic persons may be of any race.

STATE County	Population, 1990 (cont'd): Age of population (cont'd), Percent: 25 to 34 years	35 to 44 years	45 to 54 years	55 to 64 years	65 to 74 years	75 years and over	Percent female	Population–Change and components of change: Change, 1980–1990: Number	Percent	Components of change, 1980–1986: Total persons, 1986	Total persons, 1980	Net change: Number	Net change: Percent	Natural increase: Births	Natural increase: Deaths
	14	15	16	17	18	19	20	21	22	23	24	25	26	27	28
VERMONT—Con.															
Windsor	16.2	17.0	11.0	9.1	8.4	6.3	51.0	3 025	5.9	53 700	51 030	2 600	5.1	4 800	3 100
VIRGINIA	18.4	16.0	10.7	8.1	6.5	4.3	51.0	840 358	15.7	5 787 000	5 347 000	440 000	8.2	511 000	273 000
Accomack	14.2	13.6	10.6	11.1	10.5	7.9	52.8	435	1.4	31 600	31 268	300	1.0	2 700	2 700
Albemarle	18.4	16.3	10.2	7.8	5.9	3.8	51.2	12 257	22.0	60 900	55 783	5 100	9.2	5 100	2 200
Alleghany	13.9	15.9	13.1	10.7	8.5	5.2	50.3	-1 157	-8.1	13 900	14 333	-500	-3.3	1 100	800
Amelia	16.0	14.5	12.0	9.6	7.5	5.6	50.6	382	4.5	8 500	8 405	100	1.1	700	600
Amherst	15.5	15.8	12.0	9.9	7.4	4.9	51.9	-544	-1.9	29 000	29 122	-100	-0.4	2 300	1 500
Appomattox	14.9	14.1	12.2	10.0	8.3	6.4	51.6	327	2.7	12 400	11 971	400	3.7	1 000	700
Arlington	25.8	18.1	10.7	7.0	6.5	4.8	50.9	18 337	12.0	158 700	152 599	6 100	4.0	13 900	7 000
Augusta	16.8	16.7	12.2	9.5	7.0	4.3	49.5	4 179	8.3	51 900	50 498	1 400	2.8	4 300	2 800
Bath	14.0	13.6	14.0	12.1	8.8	6.8	49.2	-1 061	-18.1	5 200	5 860	-600	-10.7	400	400
Bedford	16.8	16.8	12.3	10.0	7.5	4.7	50.2	10 729	30.7	39 300	34 927	4 400	12.6	3 000	1 900
Bland	16.4	17.0	12.0	10.1	7.8	5.8	46.7	165	2.6	6 400	6 349	0	0.5	500	400
Botetourt	15.2	17.5	13.2	10.3	7.7	4.5	49.8	1 722	7.4	24 700	23 270	1 400	6.2	1 600	1 200
Brunswick	14.9	14.3	9.9	10.2	8.7	5.6	50.4	355	2.3	16 000	15 632	300	2.1	1 300	1 100
Buchanan	17.2	16.1	11.9	8.3	5.4	3.3	50.5	-6 656	-17.5	35 800	37 989	-2 200	-5.7	3 200	1 600
Buckingham	17.1	15.5	10.7	9.3	8.4	6.2	47.8	1 122	9.5	12 300	11 751	500	4.5	1 000	800
Campbell	16.7	15.2	12.2	9.5	7.3	4.2	50.7	2 148	4.7	47 200	45 424	1 700	3.8	3 900	2 000
Caroline	17.1	14.6	11.3	9.1	7.2	4.6	50.4	1 313	7.3	19 000	17 904	1 100	6.0	1 700	1 000
Carroll	14.5	14.8	12.0	11.4	9.1	6.9	50.7	-676	-2.5	27 300	27 270	100	0.2	1 700	1 600
Charles City County	16.4	16.2	11.8	11.0	6.9	4.4	51.1	-410	-6.1	6 500	6 692	-200	-3.4	700	400
Charlotte	13.6	12.6	10.8	11.3	10.5	6.7	51.1	-578	-4.7	11 800	12 266	-500	-4.1	1 000	900
Chesterfield	18.0	19.8	11.3	6.6	4.1	2.0	51.1	67 902	48.0	172 400	141 372	31 000	21.9	15 200	4 500
Clarke	16.2	16.2	11.9	10.4	7.8	6.2	50.5	2 136	21.4	10 300	9 965	300	3.2	800	600
Craig	16.0	15.7	12.1	10.4	8.4	5.6	49.2	424	10.7	4 200	3 948	200	5.7	300	300
Culpeper	17.5	15.3	10.4	8.2	7.0	5.5	51.0	5 171	22.9	24 300	22 620	1 700	7.4	2 100	1 400
Cumberland	14.5	13.5	11.9	9.5	8.7	6.8	51.6	-56	-0.7	7 900	7 881	0	-0.1	600	500
Dickenson	15.2	15.4	11.2	9.4	7.2	5.0	51.0	-2 186	-11.0	19 800	19 806	0	0.2	1 600	1 100
Dinwiddie	16.4	14.9	12.6	9.7	8.1	4.3	50.8	-1 642	-7.3	21 100	22 602	-1 500	-6.7	1 500	1 200
Essex	14.6	14.1	11.3	10.5	9.4	8.4	53.0	-175	-2.0	8 900	8 864	0	0.0	800	600
Fairfax	19.4	19.3	13.2	7.4	4.4	2.1	50.3	222 830	37.4	710 500	595 754	114 800	19.3	59 500	16 600
Fauquier	17.9	17.0	12.2	8.1	5.6	3.7	49.6	12 852	35.8	42 000	35 889	6 200	17.1	3 600	1 900
Floyd	14.2	15.7	12.4	9.8	9.2	7.4	50.6	442	3.8	11 800	11 563	200	1.6	800	700
Fluvanna	17.3	15.1	10.7	10.0	8.3	4.7	50.7	2 185	21.3	10 700	10 244	500	4.4	900	600
Franklin	15.4	15.3	11.9	10.0	7.7	5.3	50.6	3 809	10.7	37 200	35 740	1 500	4.1	2 600	1 900
Frederick	18.2	16.4	11.8	8.5	6.1	3.4	50.1	11 573	33.9	36 900	34 150	2 800	8.1	3 100	1 500
Giles	14.1	14.8	12.1	10.7	10.3	6.5	51.3	-1 444	-8.1	17 600	17 810	-200	-1.3	1 300	1 100
Gloucester	17.7	16.6	11.1	8.2	6.5	4.6	50.6	10 024	49.9	28 300	20 107	8 100	40.5	2 200	1 200
Goochland	18.8	17.7	12.7	10.2	6.4	4.6	51.1	2 402	20.4	12 600	11 761	900	7.3	1 000	700
Grayson	14.1	14.6	12.0	11.3	9.7	6.9	51.2	-301	-1.8	16 600	16 579	0	0.0	1 100	1 100
Greene	19.1	17.0	10.8	8.0	6.0	3.4	50.4	2 672	35.0	8 700	7 625	1 100	14.6	900	400
Greensville	13.6	14.4	11.1	10.6	8.5	5.3	52.3	-2 050	-18.8	10 400	10 903	-500	-4.7	1 000	700
Halifax	14.0	14.6	11.6	10.0	9.6	6.9	51.9	-1 566	-5.1	29 900	30 599	-700	-2.3	2 300	1 900
Hanover	16.3	17.1	12.4	9.0	6.6	4.0	51.1	12 908	25.6	54 100	50 398	3 700	7.3	4 300	2 600
Henrico	19.4	16.5	10.4	8.5	7.3	5.1	53.5	37 146	20.6	195 500	180 735	14 800	8.2	15 900	10 200
Henry	16.3	14.7	12.9	10.3	7.6	4.8	51.5	-712	-1.2	56 200	57 654	-1 400	-2.5	4 300	2 600
Highland	14.4	15.3	12.0	11.8	11.3	8.1	50.5	-302	-10.3	2 800	2 937	-100	-3.6	200	200
Isle of Wight	17.9	15.6	11.7	9.1	7.0	4.2	50.9	3 450	16.0	24 100	21 603	2 500	11.5	2 100	1 200
James City County	17.8	16.4	11.1	9.7	7.4	4.1	51.1	12 520	56.0	26 600	22 339	4 300	19.3	2 000	900
King and Queen	15.2	13.9	11.1	10.3	9.5	5.6	51.1	321	5.4	6 400	5 968	500	7.8	500	400
King George	19.0	15.3	10.9	7.7	5.8	3.6	50.0	2 984	28.3	12 000	10 543	1 500	14.2	1 100	500
King William	16.3	16.0	11.3	8.5	7.2	5.4	51.7	1 579	16.9	10 300	9 334	1 000	10.6	900	600
Lancaster	11.2	11.9	10.6	14.0	14.8	11.1	53.2	767	7.6	11 100	10 129	1 000	9.8	900	1 000
Lee	14.6	14.3	11.2	9.4	8.8	6.8	52.3	-1 460	-5.6	26 600	25 956	600	2.3	2 000	1 800
Loudoun	21.3	18.4	11.8	6.3	3.5	2.5	50.3	28 702	50.0	66 800	57 427	9 300	16.3	6 400	2 100
Louisa	16.5	15.2	11.1	9.7	8.3	5.5	50.6	2 500	14.0	19 100	17 825	1 300	7.2	1 600	1 200
Lunenburg	13.1	14.8	10.8	10.7	10.9	6.2	51.5	-705	-5.8	12 200	12 124	100	1.0	1 100	900
Madison	15.6	14.9	11.3	9.9	8.1	6.8	50.9	1 717	16.8	10 700	10 232	500	4.6	900	600
Mathews	11.8	13.5	12.0	12.7	12.3	10.4	52.2	353	4.4	8 800	7 995	800	10.2	500	700
Mecklenburg	14.7	14.1	10.7	11.6	10.4	6.8	52.0	-203	-0.7	29 800	29 444	300	1.1	2 300	2 100
Middlesex	13.4	12.7	11.9	13.3	12.6	9.4	51.9	934	12.1	8 700	7 719	900	12.1	600	700
Montgomery	16.4	12.4	8.2	6.0	4.6	3.5	48.2	10 629	16.8	66 100	63 284	2 900	4.5	4 500	2 200
Nelson	14.7	15.8	11.3	10.5	9.3	6.5	51.1	574	4.7	12 300	12 204	100	0.7	1 000	1 000
New Kent	17.5	19.3	12.3	8.9	5.7	3.1	49.8	1 664	19.0	10 400	8 781	1 600	17.9	800	400
Northampton	14.0	12.4	9.3	11.9	11.4	8.5	53.6	-1 564	-10.7	14 500	14 625	-100	-0.6	1 200	1 300

STATE County	Population– (cont'd) Components of change, 1980-1986 (cont'd) Net migration	Households, 1990 Number	Households, 1990 Percent change, 1980–1990	Households, 1990 Persons per household	Households, 1990 Percent Female family householder[1]	Households, 1990 Percent One-person	Births, 1988 Total	Births, 1988 Rate[2]	Births, 1988 Low birth weight[3] (Number)	Deaths, 1987 Number Total	Deaths, 1987 Number Infant[4]	Deaths, 1987 Rate Total[2]	Deaths, 1987 Rate Infant[5]	Marriages, 1984 Number	Marriages, 1984 Rate[2]
	29	30	31	32	33	34	35	36	37	38	39	40	41	42	43
VERMONT—Con.															
Windsor	1 000	21 523	13.0	2.47	8.7	25.1	727	13.2	23	535	7	9.9	9.0	611	11.7
VIRGINIA	202 000	2 291 830	23.0	2.61	11.1	22.9	93 127	15.5	6 549	46 665	923	7.9	10.2	66 143	11.7
Accomack	400	12 653	9.1	2.46	13.1	27.4	434	13.8	45	474	3	15.1	6.9	237	7.6
Albemarle	2 200	24 433	29.4	2.53	8.6	23.0	[6]1 480	[6]14.4	[6]92	[6]749	[6]14	[6]7.4	[6]9.5	452	7.6
Alleghany	-800	4 942	1.9	2.62	7.9	20.3	[7]287	[7]11.3	[7]17	[7]335	[7]2	[7]13.0	[7]7.1	91	6.6
Amelia	-100	3 131	13.5	2.80	10.2	19.9	131	15.4	12	94	2	11.2	20.6	83	10.0
Amherst	-900	9 827	9.7	2.68	10.9	19.5	370	12.7	17	250	4	8.6	11.5	276	9.5
Appomattox	100	4 531	11.8	2.68	10.9	19.3	169	13.5	13	146	3	11.8	19.7	117	9.5
Arlington	-800	78 520	9.6	2.12	7.6	39.3	2 564	16.6	160	1 157	20	7.5	7.8	2 938	18.7
Augusta	-100	19 781	10.0	2.68	8.0	18.2	[8]1 125	[8]12.0	[8]69	[8]852	[8]4	[8]9.2	[8]3.4	380	7.0
Bath	-700	1 895	-3.4	2.51	7.9	24.2	57	11.2	3	65	0	12.7	0.0	127	23.5
Bedford	3 300	17 292	44.3	2.62	6.4	18.2	[9]588	[9]12.4	[9]39	[9]463	[9]6	[9]10.0	[9]9.6	355	9.5
Bland	-100	2 244	8.0	2.65	8.5	20.9	59	9.1	4	59	0	9.1	0.0	79	12.3
Botetourt	1 100	9 148	14.8	2.67	7.3	17.9	259	10.2	18	181	3	7.3	10.7	203	8.5
Brunswick	100	5 499	9.6	2.67	14.6	25.7	176	11.1	18	187	0	11.8	0.0	133	8.3
Buchanan	-3 700	11 061	-6.1	2.81	9.3	16.6	373	10.6	21	247	7	6.9	19.2	710	19.0
Buckingham	300	4 341	12.5	2.71	12.7	23.0	189	14.8	22	129	2	10.2	11.8	118	9.6
Campbell	-100	17 952	18.7	2.63	10.0	19.9	[10]1 609	[10]13.8	[10]106	[10]1 122	[10]15	[10]9.7	[10]9.6	363	7.8
Caroline	400	6 631	15.9	2.86	12.9	18.7	282	14.5	20	181	5	9.5	17.6	134	7.1
Carroll	-100	10 463	7.4	2.51	9.1	21.2	276	NA	21	281	2	NA	NA	264	9.4
Charles City County	-500	2 161	10.7	2.91	14.7	16.9	91	13.6	11	57	1	8.6	11.1	47	7.0
Charlotte	-700	4 312	6.5	2.68	12.3	23.0	181	15.1	10	142	2	11.9	12.4	107	9.0
Chesterfield	20 300	73 441	60.3	2.82	9.7	16.4	[11]3 198	([11])	[11]169	[11]1 021	[11]24	([11])	([11])	1 149	7.2
Clarke	200	4 236	20.5	2.78	9.7	18.8	138	12.4	6	130	0	11.9	0.0	104	10.3
Craig	200	1 676	15.4	2.59	7.3	19.0	50	11.9	3	41	0	9.8	0.0	38	9.3
Culpeper	900	9 757	28.3	2.79	10.0	19.0	407	15.7	24	246	2	9.8	5.2	221	9.5
Cumberland	-100	2 813	9.9	2.77	12.6	22.2	114	14.2	10	99	1	12.4	9.6	60	7.5
Dickenson	-500	6 457	0.9	2.71	10.8	19.7	207	11.1	14	155	3	8.2	15.2	1 387	69.0
Dinwiddie	-1 900	7 492	16.7	2.76	12.9	18.8	[12]1 006	([12])	[12]108	[12]668	[12]14	([12])	([12])	121	5.7
Essex	-200	3 258	7.2	2.62	11.3	24.8	105	11.8	11	121	1	13.6	9.1	56	6.3
Fairfax	71 900	292 345	42.5	2.75	8.4	18.7	[13]12 468	[13]15.6	[13]680	[13]3 173	[13]84	[13]4.1	[13]7.2	5 434	8.1
Fauquier	4 500	16 509	42.2	2.89	7.7	15.3	712	15.4	37	377	3	8.5	4.4	385	9.9
Floyd	100	4 763	15.0	2.51	8.1	23.0	131	11.1	13	142	1	12.1	9.8	91	7.8
Fluvanna	200	4 518	32.9	2.73	10.1	18.5	193	16.0	22	93	2	7.9	12.5	81	7.7
Franklin	800	14 655	23.6	2.59	8.9	20.0	492	12.1	51	314	5	7.8	10.9	332	9.0
Frederick	1 200	16 470	43.6	2.76	7.9	16.6	[14]955	[14]15.5	[14]56	[14]544	[14]13	[14]9.1	[14]14.2	279	7.9
Giles	-400	6 461	2.9	2.51	10.4	22.9	179	10.3	11	169	3	9.8	15.1	1 612	91.1
Gloucester	7 200	10 966	53.5	2.72	8.2	19.0	476	15.9	11	230	5	8.0	11.0	200	8.2
Goochland	600	4 880	32.7	2.70	9.4	17.1	188	13.5	11	97	1	7.1	5.2	99	7.9
Grayson	0	6 468	7.8	2.48	9.3	22.5	[15]274	([15])	[15]13	[15]242	[15]1	([15])	([15])	156	9.5
Greene	600	3 749	46.8	2.74	9.9	17.5	171	19.0	14	79	1	9.0	6.8	69	8.3
Greensville	-900	3 150	-8.6	2.80	15.5	20.9	[16]241	[16]15.9	[16]24	[16]193	[16]2	[16]12.7	[16]7.9	44	4.2
Halifax	-1 200	10 728	5.4	2.66	13.3	22.0	[17]423	[17]11.7	[17]35	[17]425	[17]5	[17]11.7	[17]10.9	236	7.9
Hanover	2 000	22 628	39.1	2.73	8.0	16.5	827	13.7	56	439	7	7.6	8.6	506	9.7
Henrico	9 100	89 138	33.0	2.41	11.8	26.6	6 699	15.9	611	4 392	90	10.5	14.0	1 380	7.2
Henry	-3 100	21 771	11.3	2.59	11.7	20.7	[18]969	[18]12.5	[18]77	[18]670	[18]7	[18]8.6	[18]6.8	449	8.0
Highland	-100	1 081	-2.5	2.43	6.4	25.3	30	12.5	2	43	0	17.9	0.0	37	12.3
Isle of Wight	1 600	9 032	28.2	2.75	12.3	18.6	369	14.1	22	181	4	7.2	10.5	178	7.7
James City County	3 200	12 968	69.8	2.60	9.4	19.6	[19]618	[19]13.6	[19]47	[19]266	[19]8	[19]6.1	[19]13.4	121	4.8
King and Queen	400	2 339	13.8	2.69	13.5	22.0	100	16.4	9	78	0	12.8	0.0	50	8.2
King George	1 000	4 736	34.8	2.79	9.3	19.7	221	17.8	9	108	0	8.9	0.0	109	9.7
King William	600	3 834	24.0	2.82	10.5	19.0	149	14.3	8	97	1	9.6	6.2	95	9.7
Lancaster	1 100	4 564	15.9	2.34	10.3	26.3	123	11.3	8	150	0	13.9	0.0	98	9.1
Lee	400	9 231	3.7	2.63	11.6	22.4	297	11.7	24	271	4	10.6	11.7	333	12.5
Loudoun	5 100	30 490	63.5	2.80	7.9	16.8	1 487	19.2	82	414	7	5.6	5.1	659	10.6
Louisa	800	7 427	24.6	2.71	10.4	20.7	269	13.5	12	190	3	9.6	10.5	136	7.2
Lunenburg	-100	4 423	3.9	2.58	10.9	25.4	133	11.1	11	152	2	12.6	13.4	92	7.5
Madison	200	4 144	21.5	2.83	8.7	19.2	151	13.9	13	115	3	10.6	20.1	98	9.2
Mathews	1 000	3 530	13.2	2.35	7.6	27.1	64	7.5	1	106	0	12.5	0.0	84	9.9
Mecklenburg	100	11 244	10.7	2.52	13.0	25.0	343	11.5	43	393	5	13.1	13.9	268	9.0
Middlesex	1 000	3 530	20.8	2.40	9.0	24.8	108	12.6	6	135	1	16.1	10.6	78	9.5
Montgomery	600	26 241	26.0	2.48	7.7	22.9	[20]983	[20]12.5	[20]45	[20]498	[20]5	[20]6.4	[20]5.5	559	8.6
Nelson	0	4 807	12.7	2.63	10.5	22.3	153	12.2	10	135	2	10.8	12.7	120	9.7
New Kent	1 100	3 718	26.7	2.77	8.6	14.7	136	11.8	5	67	2	6.1	13.6	83	8.5
Northampton	0	5 129	-4.9	2.50	16.1	27.8	203	14.8	16	218	2	15.7	10.7	132	9.2

1. No spouse present. 2. Per 1,000 resident population estimated as of July 1 of the year shown. 3. Under 2,500 grams. 4. Deaths of infants under 1 year old. 5. Deaths of infants under 1 year old per 1,000 live births. 6. Charlottesville included with Albemarle county. 7. Clifton Forge and Covington included with Allegheny County. 8. Staunton and Waynesboro included with Augusta County. 9. Bedford City included with Bedford County. 10. Lynchburg included with Campbell County. 11. Colonial Heights included with Chesterfield County. 12. Petersburg included with Dinwiddie County. 13. Fairfax City and Falls Church included with Fairfax County. 14. Winchester included with Frederick County. 15. Galax included with Grayson County. 16. Emporia included with Greensville County. 17. South Boston included with Halifax County. 18. Martinsville included with Henry County. 19. Williamsburg included with James City County. 20. Radford included with Montgomery County.

STATE County	Divorces, 1984		Physicians, active non-Federal, 1989		Hospitals, 1989			Nursing homes,[4] 1986		Serious crimes known to police, 1988			Education			
						Beds				Number			Public school enrollment[7]		Attainment,[8] 1980	
	Number	Rate[1]	Number[2]	Rate[3]	Number	Number	Rate[3]	Number	Beds	Total[5]	Violent[6]	Rate[3]	1986–1987	1980	Percent 12 yrs. or more	Percent 16 yrs. or more
	44	45	46	47	48	49	50	51	52	53	54	55	56	57	58	59
VERMONT—Con.																
Windsor	209	4.0	135	241	3	297	529	13	485	1 447	70	3 827	10 286	10 318	73.6	18.6
VIRGINIA	24 705	4.4	12 222	200	141	29 925	491	462	33 421	250 436	17 940	4 177	968 396	1 046 087	62.4	19.1
Accomack	112	3.6	18	57	0	0	0	4	272	538	37	1 640	5 151	5 568	41.2	8.0
Albemarle	276	4.7	[9]1 026	[9]997	[9]4	[9]1 050	[9]1 020	3	339	2 028	115	3 236	8 936	9 536	70.1	32.7
Alleghany	77	5.6	[10]43	[10]172	[10]1	[10]204	[10]816	2	220	176	13	1 284	3 381	3 331	50.0	8.4
Amelia	22	2.7	3	35	0	0	0	2	20	103	11	1 179	1 537	1 619	40.7	7.0
Amherst	103	3.6	9	31	1	1 465	5 034	1	51	665	96	2 258	4 671	5 682	42.4	9.1
Appomattox	41	3.3	5	40	0	0	0	3	74	103	12	818	2 355	2 675	43.3	7.3
Arlington	694	4.4	600	394	5	880	578	3	658	9 418	680	5 829	14 596	15 339	86.6	42.5
Augusta	235	4.3	[11]148	[11]158	[11]5	[11]1 070	[11]1 140	3	51	869	73	1 698	9 514	11 377	51.5	9.7
Bath	21	3.9	7	140	1	25	500	0	0	60	13	1 182	914	1 188	47.6	8.8
Bedford	175	4.7	[12]36	[12]75	[12]1	[12]166	[12]345	4	150	590	28	1 431	6 855	7 067	50.1	10.3
Bland	26	4.1	0	0	0	0	0	0	0	118	9	1 788	1 116	1 294	46.9	5.2
Botetourt	84	3.5	20	78	0	0	0	3	157	451	16	1 791	4 309	5 000	57.7	10.9
Brunswick	37	2.3	6	38	0	0	0	0	0	211	32	1 298	2 721	3 235	35.4	7.9
Buchanan	114	3.1	19	55	1	194	564	0	0	391	60	1 088	7 619	9 266	33.4	5.1
Buckingham	32	2.6	5	39	0	0	0	1	60	181	31	1 414	2 107	2 780	35.7	6.7
Campbell	213	4.6	[13]227	[13]195	[13]2	[13]728	[13]627			1 037	72	2 173	8 548	10 071	50.8	9.7
Caroline	51	2.7	3	15	0	0	0	2	52	280	44	1 428	3 433	4 313	42.8	6.3
Carroll	154	5.5	44	NA	2	187	NA	1	7	349	16	1 254	4 415	5 524	37.2	5.8
Charles City County	14	2.1	2	30	0	0	0	0	0	54	6	818	1 160	1 573	41.9	8.4
Charlotte	37	3.1	6	50	0	0	0	2	66	204	26	1 702	2 311	2 673	35.9	6.7
Chesterfield	912	5.7	[14]173	(14)	(14)	(14)	(14)	3	398	7 663	241	4 213	38 755	32 875	73.0	23.4
Clarke	30	3.0	7	62	0	0	0	2	137	143	8	1 316	1 596	1 825	57.3	15.7
Craig	20	4.9	1	24	0	0	0	0	0	19	1	445	726	825	49.8	8.3
Culpeper	105	4.5	34	128	1	84	317	3	233	572	60	2 253	4 409	4 783	50.1	11.4
Cumberland	31	3.9	2	25	0	0	0	1	12	45	3	540	1 317	1 755	39.4	7.2
Dickenson	81	4.0	6	33	1	50	275	0	0	111	14	560	4 097	4 722	33.5	4.5
Dinwiddie	63	3.0	[15]134	(15)	[15]3	[15]1 168	(15)	3	62	304	22	1 425	3 699	4 982	39.9	6.6
Essex	24	2.7	13	148	1	100	1 136	3	171	279	9	3 087	1 509	1 763	46.4	12.0
Fairfax	2 895	4.3	[16]1 632	[16]198	[16]4	[16]1 081	[16]131	12	1 260	27 599	1 044	3 676	128 241	125 621	88.5	41.8
Fauquier	162	4.2	51	106	1	98	204	2	177	730	40	1 619	7 745	7 591	60.3	15.5
Floyd	37	3.2	5	42	0	0	0	1	60	78	7	645	1 954	2 242	40.1	7.6
Fluvanna	47	4.5	9	72	0	0	0	1	7	119	2	1 001	2 053	2 224	51.8	11.3
Franklin	68	1.8	17	40	1	50	119	3	373	690	26	1 690	6 257	7 247	45.6	7.4
Frederick	163	4.6	[17]139	[17]220	[17]1	[17]359	[17]569	1	54	1 004	42	2 588	7 060	7 566	53.4	9.9
Giles	62	3.5	14	82	1	29	170	1	60	218	20	1 248	3 010	4 017	52.6	7.2
Gloucester	114	4.7	34	109	1	71	228	3	187	633	19	2 120	5 071	3 828	56.1	13.2
Goochland	43	3.4	12	84	0	0	0	1	21	242	13	1 833	1 770	2 001	47.1	13.4
Grayson	92	5.6	[18]5	(18)	(18)	(18)	(18)	1	18	42	2	254	2 463	3 410	38.3	4.9
Greene	33	4.0	4	43	0	0	0	0	0	134	22	1 482	1 667	1 644	49.2	10.4
Greensville	49	4.6	[19]14	[19]93	[19]1	[19]127	[19]847			182	23	1 757	2 934	2 607	32.8	5.1
Halifax	121	4.0	[20]47	[20]132	[20]1	[20]192	[20]538	4	42	270	31	901	5 765	6 788	36.3	5.0
Hanover	232	4.4	54	86	0	0	0	2	140	1 389	47	2 425	10 070	11 128	59.7	12.5
Henrico	893	4.7	2 050	484	18	4 573	1 079	9	1 550	9 174	477	4 519	30 887	33 441	69.3	20.8
Henry	315	5.6	[21]76	[21]97	[21]1	[21]176	[21]225	2	189	1 402	64	2 384	9 588	13 019	43.4	6.2
Highland	8	2.7	2	91	0	0	0	0	0	41	3	1 552	384	473	53.3	8.8
Isle of Wight	66	2.9	8	30	0	0	0	1	81	552	51	2 165	3 907	4 424	48.0	9.3
James City County	133	5.3	[22]134	[22]276	[22]2	[22]1 181	[22]2 430			1 085	87	3 928	5 407	4 457	64.3	23.4
King and Queen	19	3.1	0	0	0	0	0	0	0	49	11	766	921	1 130	42.6	7.6
King George	49	4.4	7	56	0	0	0	1	130	181	10	1 461	2 345	2 638	63.2	19.2
King William	24	2.4	7	67	0	0	0	0	0	157	13	1 501	2 065	2 057	52.8	12.4
Lancaster	26	2.4	30	278	1	76	704	2	132	222	43	1 969	1 633	1 691	50.6	14.3
Lee	81	3.0	16	65	1	84	340	2	160	231	43	868	5 205	5 801	34.3	6.2
Loudoun	294	4.7	87	106	3	328	400	4	249	2 166	114	2 983	13 236	14 086	75.3	23.5
Louisa	62	3.3	11	54	0	0	0	1	60	198	20	990	3 472	3 773	40.9	7.2
Lunenburg	43	3.5	3	25	0	0	0	0	0	139	18	1 122	2 157	2 467	39.4	6.8
Madison	23	2.2	7	64	0	0	0	5	108	176	5	1 590	1 762	2 241	45.4	9.9
Mathews	26	3.1	8	94	0	0	0	1	24	62	7	694	1 243	1 430	53.8	10.5
Mecklenburg	110	3.7	29	98	1	260	881	4	359	696	77	2 300	5 202	5 744	41.1	8.5
Middlesex	29	3.5	6	71	0	0	0	3	130	211	10	2 416	1 166	1 283	50.2	10.6
Montgomery	231	3.6	[23]133	[23]171	[23]3	[23]434	[23]556	5	497	3 140	76	4 670	8 544	9 201	62.0	26.8
Nelson	48	3.9	8	64	0	0	0	3	167	100	4	781	2 097	2 539	36.6	10.1
New Kent	34	3.5	7	59	1	84	706	1	19	215	49	1 978	1 753	1 885	54.9	9.1
Northampton	56	3.9	30	222	1	163	1 207	1	125	339	29	2 302	2 617	2 753	39.9	8.7

1. Per 1,000 resident population estimated as of July 1 of the year shown. 2. As of end of year. 3. Per 100,000 resident population as of July 1 of the year shown. 4. Preliminary. Covers nursing homes with 3 or more beds. 5. Data for serious crimes have not been adjusted for underreporting, this may affect comparability between geographic areas or over time. 6. Includes murder and nonnegligent manslaughter, forcible rape, robbery, and aggravated assault. 7. The 1986–1987 data are based on administrative reports obtained by the U.S. National Center for Education Statistics. The 1980 data are based on the 1980 Census of Population and Housing. 8. Persons 25 years old or older. 9. Charlottesville included with Albemarle county. 10. Clifton Forge and Covington included with Allegheny County. 11. Staunton and Waynesboro included with Augusta County. 12. Bedford City included with Bedford County. 13. Lynchburg included with Campbell County. 14. Colonial Heights included with Chesterfield County. 15. Petersburg included with Dinwiddie County. 16. Fairfax City and Falls Church included with Fairfax County. 17. Winchester included with Frederick County. 18. Galax included with Grayson County. 19. Emporia included with Greensville County. 20. South Boston included with Halifax County. 21. Martinsville included with Henry County. 22. Williamsburg included with James City County. 23. Radford included with Montgomery County.

STATE County	Education (cont'd): Local government expenditures for education,[1] 1982: Total (Mil dol)	Education (cont'd): Local government expenditures for education,[1] 1982: Per capita (Dollars)	Social Security Program December 1988: Beneficiaries: Total	Social Security Program December 1988: Beneficiaries: Rate[2]	Social Security Program December 1988: Payments ($1,000)	Supplemental Security Income Program recipients June 1986	Money income: Per capita[3]: 1987 Income, (Dollars)	Money income: Per capita[3]: 1979: Current dollars	Money income: Per capita[3]: 1979: Constant 1987 dollars	Money income: Median household income 1979 (Dollars)	Money income: Percent below poverty level, 1979: Persons	Money income: Percent below poverty level, 1979: Families	Housing units, 1990: Total	Housing units, 1990: Percent change, 1980–1990
	60	61	62	63	64	65	66	67	68	69	70	71	72	73
VERMONT—Con.														
Windsor	26.8	517	10 015	181.8	4 977	760	11 806	6 760	10 577	15 360	10.6	7.6	29 849	23.0
VIRGINIA	2 359.5	430	801 050	133.2	365 243	87 319	13 658	7 475	11 696	17 475	11.8	9.2	2 496 334	23.5
Accomack	11.1	355	7 220	229.2	3 017	1 164	9 852	5 254	8 221	10 873	21.1	15.8	15 840	14.7
Albemarle	23.8	413	13 320	129.7	2 744	626	15 368	7 852	12 286	17 808	9.8	7.1	25 958	27.5
Alleghany	6.0	436	5 130	201.2	159	268	10 190	6 085	9 521	15 925	10.0	8.0	5 481	0.9
Amelia	3.8	462	1 380	162.4	567	246	10 503	5 370	8 402	14 253	12.2	9.3	3 439	14.0
Amherst	9.8	336	4 485	153.6	2 008	1 018	10 158	5 752	9 000	16 587	10.0	7.5	10 598	9.6
Appomattox	4.9	406	2 170	173.6	903	328	11 118	6 207	9 712	16 324	10.2	7.5	4 913	9.0
Arlington	62.9	410	17 600	114.3	8 549	1 030	22 181	12 562	19 656	21 713	7.4	4.6	84 847	12.9
Augusta	20.7	384	17 295	185.0	3 192	702	11 832	6 226	9 742	16 026	10.0	7.3	21 202	8.1
Bath	3.2	623	1 085	212.7	484	112	10 409	6 211	9 718	13 293	12.7	9.6	2 596	2.3
Bedford	14.9	413	8 410	177.4	838	492	11 463	6 171	9 656	16 145	9.3	7.2	19 641	41.4
Bland	2.0	307	1 235	190.0	501	162	9 624	4 885	7 644	13 867	12.6	11.2	2 706	19.5
Botetourt	11.5	490	3 455	136.6	1 552	272	12 647	6 762	10 581	17 142	7.7	6.7	9 785	12.3
Brunswick	6.6	419	3 090	194.3	1 212	626	9 062	4 534	7 094	10 950	24.3	19.6	6 456	4.2
Buchanan	26.2	687	6 595	187.9	2 598	812	7 850	5 444	8 518	15 446	18.8	15.9	12 222	-4.3
Buckingham	5.1	439	2 105	164.5	828	428	8 928	4 605	7 205	11 461	19.8	16.4	5 013	10.4
Campbell	17.8	388	21 590	185.6	2 819	698	11 244	6 333	9 909	16 718	9.5	7.3	19 008	16.3
Caroline	7.0	381	2 780	143.3	1 197	322	9 973	5 431	8 498	14 482	16.7	13.6	7 292	11.7
Carroll	9.5	341	7 520	216.7	1 854	836	9 626	4 998	7 820	12 088	16.1	13.7	12 209	4.5
Charles City County	3.2	481	800	119.4	321	150	10 836	5 718	8 947	17 120	12.8	11.7	2 314	6.5
Charlotte	4.7	389	2 795	232.9	1 074	508	9 124	4 540	7 104	11 070	25.3	20.3	4 947	8.5
Chesterfield	68.0	446	11 355	61.8	5 736	594	14 774	8 419	13 173	23 924	4.6	3.8	77 329	58.2
Clarke	3.9	381	1 735	156.3	782	152	15 204	7 473	11 693	16 649	9.8	7.2	4 531	14.4
Craig	1.4	367	700	166.7	285	76	10 095	5 481	8 576	13 562	10.2	8.0	1 993	6.4
Culpeper	9.2	405	4 485	173.2	1 971	546	11 724	6 232	9 751	15 537	15.4	11.7	10 471	26.6
Cumberland	3.0	386	1 185	148.1	462	274	8 681	4 630	7 245	11 398	24.7	19.8	3 170	3.6
Dickenson	10.4	515	3 875	207.2	1 569	548	7 863	5 151	8 060	13 532	17.5	15.8	7 112	3.0
Dinwiddie	11.2	508	15 010	183.0	1 248	938	10 190	5 392	8 437	16 642	13.5	11.7	8 023	17.3
Essex	3.6	419	1 900	213.5	858	244	11 504	5 920	9 263	14 059	16.0	11.9	4 073	-0.2
Fairfax	390.4	611	43 090	53.8	2 820	2 124	20 805	11 498	17 991	30 011	3.9	3.0	307 966	42.7
Fauquier	17.5	466	5 130	111.3	2 315	410	14 597	7 331	11 471	19 331	10.6	8.1	17 716	41.0
Floyd	4.2	357	2 345	198.7	925	250	10 008	5 186	8 115	12 230	15.4	12.5	5 505	12.0
Fluvanna	4.1	402	2 025	167.4	862	250	10 230	5 446	8 521	13 276	19.0	13.6	5 035	31.5
Franklin	12.1	336	2 255	55.3	1 034	728	10 748	5 674	8 878	14 892	10.3	8.0	17 526	29.7
Frederick	14.5	414	9 370	151.9	1 952	336	12 461	6 503	10 175	17 110	9.8	7.9	17 864	40.0
Giles	9.9	557	3 725	215.3	1 716	404	10 041	5 640	8 825	13 589	12.5	10.1	7 098	5.4
Gloucester	7.7	348	3 965	132.2	1 716	296	11 072	6 566	10 274	16 126	11.6	9.5	12 451	49.8
Goochland	4.5	374	1 535	110.4	690	206	15 254	7 263	11 364	18 145	13.6	11.0	5 203	29.1
Grayson	4.8	289	3 235	197.3	1 226	578	10 060	5 266	8 240	11 732	14.0	11.4	7 529	10.9
Greene	3.4	427	1 295	143.9	551	180	10 776	5 820	9 107	16 293	12.2	9.4	4 154	35.8
Greensville	6.0	556	3 030	199.3	419	234	8 961	4 630	7 245	11 655	22.7	16.2	3 393	-10.5
Halifax	13.0	434	7 885	218.4	2 088	1 432	9 524	4 813	7 531	12 183	19.2	15.5	11 790	3.9
Hanover	19.2	375	8 065	133.7	4 018	414	14 207	7 636	11 948	21 349	7.9	6.0	23 727	37.3
Henrico	76.5	411	20 240	97.0	10 718	958	15 658	8 562	13 397	20 096	6.3	4.8	94 539	34.2
Henry	22.5	398	9 225	118.7	4 225	710	10 656	6 033	9 440	15 891	9.8	8.0	23 169	10.5
Highland	1.1	418	645	268.8	248	54	10 083	6 047	9 462	13 569	15.1	11.5	1 759	20.2
Isle of Wight	8.9	405	3 510	134.5	1 583	474	12 146	6 192	9 689	16 862	14.4	11.7	9 753	26.6
James City County	0.0	0	6 355	139.7	663	220	14 375	7 411	11 596	18 706	11.3	7.9	14 330	65.2
King and Queen	2.3	392	1 145	187.7	489	116	10 754	5 745	8 989	12 103	17.9	12.7	2 698	7.5
King George	4.4	410	1 225	98.8	463	122	11 699	6 720	10 515	18 050	13.6	12.2	5 280	32.1
King William	5.4	559	1 745	167.8	820	132	12 319	6 601	10 329	17 471	13.2	10.3	4 193	21.9
Lancaster	3.5	338	3 465	317.9	1 654	210	12 786	6 755	10 570	13 217	16.1	12.9	5 918	15.9
Lee	11.4	432	5 785	228.7	2 089	1 280	8 096	4 540	7 104	10 436	25.9	21.3	10 263	6.3
Loudoun	33.4	564	5 865	75.8	2 794	372	17 496	8 989	14 065	24 434	6.6	4.9	32 932	66.8
Louisa	8.6	471	3 565	179.1	1 510	526	10 277	5 488	8 587	13 871	16.1	12.5	9 080	28.6
Lunenburg	5.0	412	2 160	180.0	856	306	9 836	5 125	8 019	11 628	18.6	14.5	5 065	5.3
Madison	4.7	462	1 795	164.7	740	288	10 458	5 205	8 144	13 272	17.2	13.5	4 547	13.8
Mathews	2.8	331	2 130	250.6	966	116	12 558	7 171	11 220	15 051	9.0	5.5	4 725	11.8
Mecklenburg	10.7	367	6 550	220.5	2 650	1 250	10 437	5 266	8 240	12 561	20.7	16.8	14 589	11.9
Middlesex	2.7	344	2 225	258.7	1 022	140	10 488	5 887	9 211	12 171	17.0	11.6	5 486	11.1
Montgomery	17.7	274	9 860	125.6	3 432	682	10 429	5 658	8 853	13 082	19.7	8.7	27 770	24.1
Nelson	5.5	447	2 660	212.8	1 101	414	11 463	5 476	8 568	12 210	18.6	14.6	7 063	28.4
New Kent	4.0	439	1 430	124.3	651	124	12 085	6 736	10 540	18 629	9.3	7.6	3 968	21.9
Northampton	6.5	452	3 190	232.8	1 317	642	8 824	4 579	7 165	9 930	26.7	20.9	6 183	0.8

1. Elementary and secondary. 2. Per 1,000 resident population estimated as of July 1 of the year shown. 3. Based on the resident population estimated as of July 1, 1988 for 1987 data and enumerated as of April 1, 1980 for 1979 data.

STATE County	Housing units, 1990 (cont'd)				Civilian labor force, 1990				Private nonfarm establishments, 1988					
	Occupied units						Unemployment				Employment[2]			
		Owner occupied												
	Total	Percent	Median value (Dollars)	Median rent (Dollars)	Total	Percent change, 1989–1990	Total	Rate[1]	Number	Net change, 1987–1988	Total	Percent change, 1987–1988	Manufacturing	Retail trade
	74	75	76	77	78	79	80	81	82	83	84	85	86	87
VERMONT—Con.														
Windsor	21 523	69.4	97 300	386	29 185	-2.9	1 369	4.7	2 080	71	16 927	0.7	2 952	3 712
VIRGINIA	2 291 830	66.3	91 000	411	3 196 000	1.6	137 000	4.3	X	X	2 164 484	4.0	429 930	488 935
Accomack	12 653	74.8	52 700	219	14 475	2.0	869	6.0	707	10	8 523	0.9	3 328	1 892
Albemarle	24 433	64.1	111 200	454	35 249	2.5	927	2.6	877	41	10 280	-3.4	2 725	2 332
Alleghany	4 942	82.1	50 100	185	5 941	0.5	444	7.5	93	2	1 420	-0.9	0	279
Amelia	3 131	80.5	54 900	219	3 859	-1.6	178	4.6	187	4	1 238	-4.2	344	234
Amherst	9 827	78.6	56 900	250	13 251	0.7	670	5.1	462	-5	4 566	2.8	868	1 249
Appomattox	4 531	81.1	51 000	209	6 630	3.8	314	4.7	207	-1	2 574	0.0	0	537
Arlington	78 520	44.6	231 000	678	108 813	1.2	2 510	2.3	4 378	30	95 007	6.0	5 530	13 912
Augusta	19 781	80.5	70 500	265	21 780	3.4	1 189	5.5	821	3	10 742	3.5	4 925	1 720
Bath	1 895	76.6	46 700	214	1 948	0.1	244	12.5	138	-1	1 552	-9.5	0	166
Bedford	17 292	85.8	75 800	272	22 570	4.4	1 019	4.5	354	3	3 526	20.8	1 454	326
Bland	2 244	84.8	43 800	171	4 585	14.9	263	5.7	76	-4	1 113	-7.6	775	85
Botetourt	9 148	85.7	73 400	249	13 879	1.0	460	3.3	350	23	2 760	12.0	610	723
Brunswick	5 499	74.8	42 900	150	8 534	4.0	606	7.1	303	6	2 889	-2.3	1 298	490
Buchanan	11 061	80.8	41 700	188	11 448	3.3	969	8.5	700	-11	9 718	8.8	253	1 173
Buckingham	4 341	78.2	44 900	175	5 723	4.1	319	5.6	208	1	1 948	2.3	843	297
Campbell	17 952	77.5	61 800	260	25 165	0.7	1 324	5.3	676	5	10 616	1.4	5 398	1 977
Caroline	6 631	80.0	64 700	288	8 972	-4.4	637	7.1	302	17	2 487	-1.3	791	670
Carroll	10 463	82.7	44 000	200	13 770	1.7	890	6.5	342	2	3 007	4.6	1 519	552
Charles City County	2 161	86.2	52 100	229	3 756	1.6	187	5.0	47	1	247	-3.9	74	42
Charlotte	4 312	77.9	43 100	144	5 558	5.5	612	11.0	216	6	1 970	-4.0	1 140	213
Chesterfield	73 441	79.5	87 200	447	105 484	1.5	3 259	3.1	3 983	252	58 241	11.7	11 366	15 233
Clarke	4 236	74.2	104 300	335	4 834	6.0	172	3.6	245	7	2 257	5.0	699	330
Craig	1 676	83.1	49 500	185	1 899	-3.1	110	5.8	49	4	345	-12.9	0	40
Culpeper	9 757	67.3	95 200	402	11 981	4.2	608	5.1	674	49	7 703	6.8	1 594	2 000
Cumberland	2 813	79.3	50 600	222	3 540	6.8	210	5.9	134	12	1 289	5.7	100	285
Dickenson	6 457	81.4	39 300	189	5 057	3.6	695	13.7	303	5	2 965	2.0	271	575
Dinwiddie	7 492	80.1	56 900	239	9 031	0.7	552	6.1	194	-5	1 262	-3.9	432	259
Essex	3 258	78.9	68 200	277	4 681	3.4	275	5.9	302	15	3 138	9.6	845	1 050
Fairfax	292 345	70.7	213 800	748	493 398	1.3	10 319	2.1	18 104	1 230	302 765	5.6	14 961	65 829
Fauquier	16 509	73.3	146 500	498	26 295	3.8	859	3.3	1 215	87	10 198	6.8	980	2 472
Floyd	4 763	84.1	51 000	183	6 027	2.4	424	7.0	177	-13	1 578	-3.4	805	262
Fluvanna	4 518	79.8	75 100	329	6 511	2.6	256	3.9	195	4	1 371	0.4	116	203
Franklin	14 655	81.2	63 400	206	20 349	0.0	1 221	6.0	702	55	8 563	5.9	4 494	1 367
Frederick	16 470	79.1	90 100	351	22 998	3.6	1 110	4.8	567	39	7 645	7.1	2 256	1 134
Giles	6 461	80.5	46 300	198	8 634	0.7	814	9.4	309	14	4 711	3.2	2 628	805
Gloucester	10 966	80.5	84 000	356	15 612	1.2	465	3.0	642	7	4 823	0.7	346	1 610
Goochland	4 880	84.2	90 100	282	6 694	1.3	216	3.2	303	15	2 047	-0.6	140	381
Grayson	6 468	82.5	39 700	168	8 194	1.7	691	8.4	146	-4	1 933	-15.8	1 368	191
Greene	3 749	76.8	73 700	314	5 338	3.8	229	4.3	157	26	1 146	16.8	0	231
Greensville	3 150	78.6	45 200	160	4 696	3.2	286	6.1	62	5	771	13.5	281	110
Halifax	10 728	76.9	45 200	138	14 943	4.3	1 134	7.6	301	9	2 331	-3.6	646	530
Hanover	22 628	83.5	91 300	423	34 518	1.6	904	2.6	1 799	124	21 534	4.1	2 385	4 551
Henrico	89 138	63.8	83 900	436	125 924	1.5	3 492	2.8	4 999	177	80 915	5.2	9 031	21 730
Henry	21 771	77.9	51 800	239	34 969	1.3	2 717	7.8	765	11	18 322	-3.4	13 831	1 989
Highland	1 081	81.2	51 400	172	795	-2.5	49	6.2	72	-2	413	11.6	90	66
Isle of Wight	9 032	79.5	83 200	264	11 509	2.7	608	5.3	388	-4	7 025	3.1	0	864
James City County	12 968	73.3	119 500	455	17 395	0.8	494	2.8	352	6	5 874	7.1	1 048	2 055
King and Queen	2 339	81.9	55 600	228	2 813	0.1	158	5.6	69	-2	480	-6.6	134	59
King George	4 736	69.6	90 000	386	7 460	7.3	343	4.6	223	10	2 400	10.3	231	423
King William	3 834	81.2	70 200	247	5 192	0.3	188	3.6	224	-5	2 839	-3.9	0	621
Lancaster	4 564	81.7	90 000	309	4 946	-3.5	458	9.3	486	16	3 452	3.5	400	797
Lee	9 231	75.7	34 400	176	8 419	1.5	696	8.3	358	-9	3 366	-1.1	936	748
Loudoun	30 490	73.3	170 200	682	48 692	1.3	916	1.9	2 306	181	27 014	12.5	3 147	5 605
Louisa	7 427	79.9	64 400	283	11 047	-7.8	546	4.9	317	8	3 216	0.8	903	446
Lunenburg	4 423	77.6	37 600	154	5 082	-0.4	393	7.7	238	0	2 824	0.7	1 634	497
Madison	4 144	77.1	72 200	281	5 715	0.2	211	3.7	218	4	1 669	13.3	516	340
Mathews	3 530	83.3	79 900	280	3 760	5.1	83	2.2	181	9	875	5.2	197	219
Mecklenburg	11 244	71.7	50 700	149	14 759	-1.2	910	6.2	723	18	10 616	9.4	4 856	2 544
Middlesex	3 530	82.8	77 500	263	3 335	-0.2	137	4.1	264	-1	1 534	-5.5	338	428
Montgomery	26 241	55.4	71 700	341	33 144	1.4	2 131	6.4	1 288	40	21 230	8.1	8 183	6 260
Nelson	4 807	79.1	53 100	206	5 648	-0.7	282	5.0	283	10	3 213	0.3	832	378
New Kent	3 718	87.8	86 500	304	6 033	1.0	171	2.8	190	13	1 357	11.0	210	264
Northampton	5 129	65.7	47 700	151	5 874	0.7	334	5.7	310	11	2 852	-1.0	1 014	594

1. Percent of total civilian labor force. 2. For week including March 12. Excludes government employees, self-employed persons, farm workers, domestic service workers, railroad employees subject to the Railroad Retirement Act, and employees on oceanborne vessels or in foreign countries.

STATE / County	Private nonfarm establishments, 1988 (cont'd): Employment[1] (cont'd): Finance, insurance, and real estate	Employment[1] (cont'd): Services	Annual payroll: Total (Mil dol)	Annual payroll: Average per employee (Dollars)	Personal income, 1989: Total (Mil dol)	Per cent change, 1988–1989	Wages and salaries[2] (Mil dol)	Proprietor's income (Mil dol)	Dividends, interest, & rent (Mil dol)	Transfer payments (Mil dol)	Per capita[3]: Dollars	Per capita[3]: Rank	Earnings, 1989: Total (Mil dol)	Percent by selected industries: Farm	Percent by selected industries: Goods-related[4]: Total
	88	89	90	91	92	93	94	95	96	97	98	99	100	101	102
VERMONT—Con.															
Windsor	895	5 409	279	16 503	946	8.6	471	92	227	129	16 868	458	563	1.6	30.4
VIRGINIA	146 617	628 273	43 122	X	115 762	8.6	75 015	7 557	19 155	14 557	18 979	X	82 572	0.8	23.3
Accomack	357	1 570	119	13 962	441	7.6	222	61	106	86	14 022	1 427	284	6.2	27.4
Albemarle	148	3 040	190	18 490	[5]2 037	[5]8.9	[5]1 477	[5]162	[5]512	[5]241	[5]19 793	[5]179	(5)	[5]0.9	[5]20.1
Alleghany	0	683	24	16 982	[6]355	[6]5.8	[6]243	[6]25	[6]62	[6]79	[6]14 196	[6]1 345	(6)	[6]0.4	[6]45.2
Amelia	33	121	17	13 782	127	10.0	34	14	18	18	14 876	1 038	48	9.2	42.8
Amherst	157	1 149	71	15 451	349	6.7	188	28	58	61	12 012	2 323	216	2.0	27.4
Appomattox	103	235	38	14 605	171	8.2	71	14	27	28	13 653	1 599	85	3.3	47.3
Arlington	6 980	46 047	2 564	26 987	5 029	8.1	6 694	425	1 003	552	33 039	6	7 118	0.0	4.4
Augusta	230	1 217	205	19 110	[7]1 493	[7]7.3	[7]922	[7]136	[7]306	[7]226	[7]15 895	[7]679	(7)	[7]2.1	[7]42.2
Bath	31	0	31	19 977	84	6.4	49	7	18	14	16 836	466	56	3.1	12.2
Bedford	119	487	60	16 989	[8]799	[8]8.8	[8]223	[8]56	[8]147	[8]111	[8]16 605	[8]502	(8)	[8]4.0	[8]44.2
Bland	0	84	17	14 844	78	8.9	33	6	10	14	11 984	2 331	39	7.4	NA
Botetourt	95	652	36	12 900	413	8.5	109	29	61	50	16 146	604	139	3.6	NA
Brunswick	89	485	39	13 414	195	7.1	76	20	32	39	12 296	2 198	96	6.0	NA
Buchanan	278	1 157	235	24 145	407	6.9	329	51	61	88	11 825	2 387	380	0.1	64.6
Buckingham	0	261	26	13 246	159	7.4	47	15	24	35	12 403	2 159	62	10.8	NA
Campbell	166	720	163	15 373	[9]1 805	[9]7.8	[9]1 482	[9]133	[9]382	[9]284	[9]15 535	[9]792	(9)	[9]0.3	[9]45.2
Caroline	154	361	34	13 871	295	6.1	88	20	40	43	15 119	935	108	3.5	29.9
Carroll	69	325	36	11 881	[10]407	[10]7.0	[10]229	[10]43	[10]66	[10]84	[10]11 800	[10]2 401	(10)	[10]3.2	[10]46.8
Charles City County	0	56	3	11 336	110	12.3	17	5	12	14	16 374	555	21	9.2	NA
Charlotte	69	281	25	12 695	149	5.7	50	15	28	28	12 472	2 128	65	8.1	42.4
Chesterfield	3 138	10 948	1 207	20 730	3 921	10.3	1 840	194	479	267	20 696	137	2 034	0.1	38.6
Clarke	90	680	31	13 739	258	6.1	70	17	49	25	22 837	74	87	9.2	37.6
Craig	0	29	5	13 417	57	8.7	9	6	9	11	13 483	1 695	15	18.2	NA
Culpeper	460	2 055	125	16 168	453	9.0	212	39	83	60	17 081	424	251	5.2	24.5
Cumberland	28	625	19	14 424	100	8.7	15	14	17	24	12 530	2 099	29	25.7	15.8
Dickenson	96	408	58	19 634	211	0.6	82	26	31	55	11 591	2 475	108	0.6	56.6
Dinwiddie	106	139	18	13 868	[11]1 175	[11]7.3	[11]529	[11]72	[11]200	[11]279	[11]14 211	[11]1 338	(11)	[11]0.7	[11]19.1
Essex	171	681	40	12 743	140	6.4	55	15	33	25	15 794	713	70	4.9	30.8
Fairfax	25 974	123 629	7 879	26 024	[12]23 435	[12]10.4	[12]13 509	[12]1 311	[12]3 609	[12]1 999	[12]28 366	[12]19	(12)	(12)	[12]14.7
Fauquier	882	2 674	187	18 310	1 136	9.3	346	85	245	92	23 694	61	431	5.0	24.2
Floyd	83	167	20	12 845	168	5.9	34	20	28	30	14 290	1 292	55	17.0	33.5
Fluvanna	79	342	23	16 675	169	11.2	42	15	33	31	13 488	1 689	57	6.2	28.3
Franklin	224	1 455	124	14 482	542	8.2	193	58	94	78	12 905	1 952	251	3.0	50.7
Frederick	149	1 244	155	20 283	[13]1 046	[13]8.1	[13]763	[13]107	[13]194	[13]136	[13]16 567	[13]511	(13)	[13]0.9	[13]38.9
Giles	90	570	83	17 713	230	8.4	133	19	37	47	13 498	1 682	152	2.4	58.5
Gloucester	187	1 463	60	12 380	463	9.3	110	34	76	70	14 844	1 055	143	2.0	NA
Goochland	77	404	35	17 040	314	9.8	61	21	67	28	21 973	94	82	4.3	NA
Grayson	0	169	26	13 209	187	4.0	44	17	32	44	11 533	2 489	62	12.5	41.6
Greene	239	293	16	14 086	133	16.6	26	11	19	17	14 558	1 186	37	9.2	NA
Greensville	0	69	12	15 925	[14]209	[14]8.1	[14]125	[14]20	[14]32	[14]43	[14]13 881	[14]1 491	(14)	[14]3.0	(14)
Halifax	45	334	31	13 481	[15]503	[15]8.5	[15]246	[15]43	[15]86	[15]98	[15]14 103	[15]1 388	(15)	[15]3.8	[15]49.5
Hanover	658	4 760	406	18 838	1 285	9.1	621	92	196	101	20 532	147	714	1.5	35.6
Henrico	9 787	22 137	1 542	19 063	4 969	11.0	2 904	235	987	506	23 353	66	3 139	0.1	23.7
Henry	393	821	303	16 562	[16]1 146	[16]8.7	[16]857	[16]68	[16]231	[16]181	[16]14 647	[16]1 149	(16)	[16]0.3	[16]63.5
Highland	0	155	5	11 024	32	8.7	8	7	6	7	14 282	1 295	16	28.0	NA
Isle of Wight	155	743	103	14 718	424	5.9	263	29	59	51	15 839	700	292	4.2	64.7
James City County	0	1 820	86	14 613	[17]750	[17]8.8	[17]638	[17]49	[17]148	[17]119	[17]15 429	[17]824	(17)	[17]0.4	[17]25.8
King and Queen	0	158	5	10 248	93	3.7	14	8	16	17	15 513	797	22	17.6	34.2
King George	112	1 245	52	21 724	221	8.6	209	13	36	29	17 501	369	222	1.2	6.2
King William	143	422	67	23 630	181	7.8	97	13	31	21	17 374	382	110	2.9	65.2
Lancaster	269	1 348	49	14 134	226	9.4	77	25	91	42	20 874	131	102	1.7	24.8
Lee	165	585	47	14 009	264	5.8	78	24	37	73	10 667	2 748	103	7.4	27.8
Loudoun	1 187	7 813	583	21 583	2 099	14.9	991	124	319	124	25 642	33	1 115	1.7	24.6
Louisa	118	318	64	19 792	292	9.5	170	28	45	47	14 505	1 209	198	3.0	39.0
Lunenburg	56	143	35	12 233	139	7.1	55	14	27	29	11 593	2 474	69	6.6	50.0
Madison	41	439	21	12 385	164	8.1	32	25	35	28	14 902	1 025	57	17.6	29.3
Mathews	44	192	10	11 808	149	7.8	20	14	43	32	17 661	343	35	6.5	24.3
Mecklenburg	237	1 327	149	14 038	408	7.9	230	39	83	69	13 832	1 518	270	3.6	41.6
Middlesex	68	321	18	11 824	153	10.1	41	17	41	32	17 941	302	58	5.6	23.1
Montgomery	970	3 739	337	15 863	[18]1 132	[18]7.5	[18]842	[18]62	[18]176	[18]167	[18]14 513	[18]1 205	(18)	[18]0.8	[18]34.7
Nelson	195	1 200	50	15 561	178	7.4	54	18	29	31	14 219	1 328	72	7.8	21.0
New Kent	8	400	21	15 265	207	8.8	35	10	24	20	17 444	372	45	3.7	30.2
Northampton	60	569	36	12 606	177	7.0	72	26	46	43	13 086	1 871	98	12.3	16.7

1. For week including March 12. Excludes government employees, self-employed persons, farm workers, domestic service workers, railroad employees subject to the Railroad Retirement Act, and employees on oceanborne vessels or in foreign countries. 2. Includes other labor income. 3. Based on the resident population estimated as of July 1 of the year shown. 4. Covers mining, construction, and manufacturing. 5. Charlottesville included with Albemarle county. 6. Clifton Forge and Covington included with Allegheny County. 7. Staunton and Waynesboro included with Augusta County. 8. Bedford City included with Bedford County. 9. Lynchburg included with Campbell County. 10. Galax included with Carroll County. 11. Petersburg and Colonial Heights included with Dinwiddie County. 12. Fairfax City and Falls Church included with Fairfax County. 13. Winchester included with Frederick County. 14. Emporia included with Greensville County. 15. South Boston included with Halifax County. 16. Martinsville included with Henry County. 17. Williamsburg included with James City County. 18. Radford included with Montgomery County.

STATE County	Earnings, 1989 (cont'd) — Percent by selected industries (cont'd) — Goods-related[1] — Manu-facturing	Service-related & other[2] — Total	Service-related & other[2] — Retail trade	Service-related & other[2] — Finance, insur-ance, & real estate	Service-related & other[2] — Services	Govern-ment	Agriculture, 1987 — Farms — Number	Farms — Percent with — Less than 50 acres	Farms — Percent with — 500 acres and over	Farm operators, percent — Whose principal occu-pation is farming	Farm operators, percent — Residing on farm operated	Land in farms — Acreage (1,000)	Land in farms — Percent change, 1982–1987	Land in farms — Acres — Average size of farm	Land in farms — Acres — Total irrigated (1,000)	Land in farms — Acres — Total cropland (1,000)
	103	104	105	106	107	108	109	110	111	112	113	114	115	116	117	118
VERMONT—Con.																
Windsor	17.9	50.1	11.0	3.0	24.6	17.8	534	23.0	5.8	50.9	89.7	97	-12.6	182	0	37
VIRGINIA	14.6	51.9	9.3	5.4	24.5	24.0	44 799	31.6	8.6	46.0	72.3	8 676	-8.1	194	79	4 363
Accomack	20.5	44.4	10.1	2.3	16.9	22.0	323	35.0	16.7	64.4	65.3	90	-14.7	278	9	74
Albemarle	[3]12.9	[3]46.9	[3]10.2	[3]5.9	[3]22.5	[3]32.1	772	29.8	12.6	43.0	77.3	186	-7.4	242	0	73
Alleghany	[4]40.0	[4]43.2	[4]8.7	[4]1.7	[4]16.9	[4]11.2	150	18.0	4.7	38.0	68.0	28	-16.8	188	D	9
Amelia	20.1	30.0	7.9	0.6	10.3	18.0	322	21.1	12.4	50.9	77.3	73	-21.5	228	1	36
Amherst	17.9	39.0	10.7	1.1	16.5	31.7	408	20.8	9.6	40.4	67.2	94	-1.1	230	0	34
Appomattox	35.9	31.5	9.8	2.3	9.8	17.9	358	18.4	9.5	37.7	70.7	79	-9.6	221	0	37
Arlington	2.2	57.6	4.5	3.2	30.0	38.0	1	100.0	0.0	100.0	100.0	D	D	D	D	D
Augusta	[5]33.4	[5]39.5	[5]9.5	[5]2.2	[5]17.4	[5]16.3	1 536	32.0	7.7	45.9	77.0	292	-6.6	190	2	149
Bath	6.8	72.8	4.2	0.5	44.5	11.8	135	12.6	24.4	37.8	71.1	54	-10.5	396	D	18
Bedford	[6]29.6	[6]38.2	[6]9.0	[6]1.9	[6]19.3	[6]13.6	1 240	24.1	5.3	39.8	74.9	204	-6.6	165	0	97
Bland	33.2	NA	4.0	2.4	7.6	29.8	327	18.7	11.3	45.6	74.3	80	-7.3	246	0	25
Botetourt	16.4	NA	10.2	1.5	14.8	13.3	532	26.5	6.2	40.4	82.5	98	-0.3	183	0	40
Brunswick	25.0	NA	10.2	2.1	13.9	24.4	402	26.4	12.9	52.2	70.4	101	-17.5	252	2	40
Buchanan	2.0	NA	5.8	1.4	9.7	7.4	105	45.7	1.9	38.1	70.5	9	-7.3	83	0	3
Buckingham	10.4	NA	6.7	1.0	16.4	32.0	346	21.7	12.7	41.9	74.0	79	-7.7	229	0	35
Campbell	[7]39.5	[7]46.2	[7]10.3	[7]5.9	[7]20.2	[7]8.3	628	20.9	8.6	44.3	76.8	134	-6.3	214	1	65
Caroline	14.3	38.7	9.3	3.3	12.1	27.9	200	18.0	17.5	54.0	80.5	60	-19.3	298	1	36
Carroll	[8]42.3	[8]35.5	[8]10.6	[8]1.6	[8]17.4	[8]14.5	939	31.4	2.9	38.0	71.7	117	-4.2	125	1	67
Charles City County	21.9	NA	6.4	NA	12.9	26.2	47	23.4	40.4	61.7	72.3	25	0.7	538	1	16
Charlotte	39.0	31.8	6.8	2.6	12.3	17.8	518	23.9	9.1	51.7	67.4	119	-9.8	229	1	51
Chesterfield	25.2	42.6	10.4	3.6	16.5	18.7	169	47.9	3.6	37.9	75.7	20	-13.6	119	0	10
Clarke	26.0	41.2	8.1	1.3	21.1	12.0	315	30.8	11.4	47.0	75.9	73	-15.4	231	0	48
Craig	14.0	NA	7.5	NA	9.8	23.8	177	13.0	14.7	45.2	67.2	50	-10.6	284	0	20
Culpeper	15.9	53.7	12.0	4.1	21.3	16.5	492	29.5	12.8	48.0	76.2	121	-15.5	246	0	76
Cumberland	4.4	36.4	7.7	0.8	19.3	22.1	277	24.2	11.6	41.9	75.5	61	-8.8	221	0	27
Dickenson	2.8	28.0	6.9	1.7	10.2	14.7	120	40.8	0.8	29.2	71.7	10	-20.0	82	D	4
Dinwiddie	[9]11.5	[9]51.4	[9]15.7	[9]3.7	[9]21.7	[9]28.8	373	26.0	12.6	52.0	71.8	85	-9.6	228	2	41
Essex	23.6	51.6	16.4	4.5	23.9	12.6	142	16.9	32.4	59.9	68.3	69	-15.4	487	1	46
Fairfax	[10]4.7	[10]68.0	[10]9.4	[10]7.7	[10]37.0	[10]17.3	198	73.7	2.0	34.3	71.2	13	-28.4	64	0	6
Fauquier	4.8	45.3	10.0	4.8	22.6	25.5	978	32.7	11.8	44.3	82.0	241	-2.9	246	0	123
Floyd	23.9	34.1	10.5	3.0	10.5	15.4	772	23.1	4.8	40.4	75.3	118	-10.3	153	0	54
Fluvanna	10.6	49.2	5.6	1.8	21.3	16.3	261	17.2	11.9	48.3	78.5	61	-4.2	234	0	27
Franklin	39.9	34.8	9.4	2.3	16.7	11.5	1 016	20.8	6.1	49.1	74.8	180	-6.8	177	2	83
Frederick	[11]28.8	[11]51.5	[11]12.8	[11]3.0	[11]21.4	[11]8.7	555	30.5	9.2	44.1	75.3	111	-11.9	200	0	59
Giles	53.1	29.6	7.2	2.1	11.9	9.4	346	16.5	9.8	37.9	63.9	72	-8.6	207	D	25
Gloucester	3.2	NA	12.7	2.9	25.9	24.8	130	46.9	11.5	44.6	75.4	26	-21.5	199	0	18
Goochland	1.5	NA	10.6	1.4	18.6	24.3	253	27.7	11.9	38.3	75.1	58	-3.8	229	0	28
Grayson	33.3	27.6	7.4	2.3	14.3	18.4	865	32.7	5.8	42.0	72.9	140	-2.0	162	0	60
Greene	20.4	NA	9.8	1.3	15.2	21.2	225	21.3	6.7	43.1	72.4	39	-3.8	175	D	18
Greensville	[12]38.3	([12])	[12]11.3	[12]2.0	([12])	[12]10.4	201	23.9	21.9	57.7	67.2	74	-11.6	368	1	43
Halifax	[13]43.1	[13]34.4	[13]8.4	[13]1.2	[13]18.0	[13]12.3	1 252	26.8	8.5	58.9	63.8	242	-5.5	193	3	96
Hanover	12.9	54.5	11.1	2.5	17.8	8.5	554	38.6	7.8	41.9	81.4	105	-13.6	189	4	60
Henrico	15.4	67.7	14.0	13.9	24.0	8.5	158	51.3	6.3	41.1	66.5	30	-9.8	189	1	17
Henry	[14]58.9	[14]28.5	[14]7.6	[14]2.3	[14]12.0	[14]7.8	342	32.7	7.0	35.1	71.6	54	-14.9	157	0	22
Highland	11.3	NA	6.4	2.5	19.2	14.5	303	13.9	17.8	54.8	68.6	95	-8.3	313	D	34
Isle of Wight	58.0	23.6	4.9	4.6	6.3	7.4	245	21.6	24.5	73.9	67.8	84	-16.4	342	1	57
James City County	[15]17.2	[15]51.7	[15]13.5	[15]3.7	[15]31.4	[15]22.1	68	36.8	10.3	52.9	67.6	12	-25.4	182	0	7
King and Queen	21.2	NA	6.6	NA	16.6	19.8	157	25.5	15.9	48.4	72.0	53	1.3	339	D	38
King George	2.9	26.1	3.1	0.5	18.6	66.5	141	17.7	14.2	41.1	80.1	38	-9.2	270	0	21
King William	57.3	23.0	7.2	3.3	8.3	8.9	121	19.8	37.2	53.7	79.3	64	-2.4	525	2	42
Lancaster	10.8	65.7	10.9	6.3	36.6	7.8	84	23.8	14.3	53.6	70.2	19	-13.6	223	0	15
Lee	13.0	41.2	9.4	3.5	17.3	23.7	1 431	47.6	1.9	42.9	65.5	133	-11.0	93	0	59
Loudoun	6.7	55.1	9.2	3.1	24.0	18.6	934	47.4	10.1	38.7	82.4	207	1.5	221	0	141
Louisa	14.4	NA	4.5	4.2	NA	9.0	397	24.4	10.8	41.6	79.1	89	-5.5	223	0	43
Lunenburg	35.3	30.1	8.9	1.8	10.3	13.4	404	22.5	10.1	54.2	74.0	84	-18.9	207	2	37
Madison	13.7	38.6	8.5	0.9	21.4	14.4	441	25.6	12.2	47.6	72.8	106	-2.9	241	0	57
Mathews	9.8	51.3	13.3	1.1	21.6	17.9	77	57.1	6.5	40.3	77.9	8	-13.6	104	0	6
Mecklenburg	36.0	39.8	12.3	2.1	14.6	15.0	780	23.3	10.0	56.0	65.9	180	-4.1	230	4	86
Middlesex	10.9	50.0	13.4	1.9	19.0	21.3	83	34.9	14.5	50.6	71.1	20	-21.0	237	1	14
Montgomery	[16]29.9	[16]30.2	[16]9.9	[16]2.6	[16]14.2	[16]34.3	544	33.3	7.2	37.5	72.8	97	-4.4	179	0	41
Nelson	8.7	57.2	7.7	9.9	25.6	14.1	365	20.3	8.8	38.1	74.8	78	-8.8	214	0	32
New Kent	10.4	NA	10.4	-0.3	28.7	21.4	72	31.9	16.7	52.8	72.2	D	D	D	D	14
Northampton	11.8	51.2	11.3	1.4	26.2	19.8	180	21.1	18.3	69.4	57.8	51	-18.9	281	10	42

1. Covers mining, construction, and manufacturing. 2. Covers private sector earnings in agricultural services, forestry, and fisheries; transportation and public utilities; wholesale trade; retail trade; finance, insurance, and real estate; and services. 3. Charlottesville included with Albemarle county. 4. Clifton Forge and Covington included with Allegheny County. 5. Staunton and Waynesboro included with Augusta County. 6. Bedford City included with Bedford County. 7. Lynchburg included with Campbell County. 8. Galax included with Carroll County. 9. Petersburg and Colonial Heights included with Dinwiddie County. 10. Fairfax City and Falls Church included with Fairfax County. 11. Winchester included with Frederick County. 12. Emporia included with Greensville County. 13. South Boston included with Halifax County. 14. Martinsville included with Henry County. 15. Williamsburg included with James City County. 16. Radford included with Montgomery County.

STATE County	Agriculture, 1987 (cont'd)								Manufactures, 1987						
	Value of land and buildings		Value of products sold				Percent of farms with sales of		Establishments		All employees			Production workers	
					Percent from										
	Average per farm ($1,000)	Average per acre (Dollars)	Total (Mil dol)	Average per farm (Dollars)	Crops	Livestock and poultry[1]	$10,000 or more	$100,000 or more	Total	Percent with 20 or more employees	Number (1,000)	Percent change, 1982–1987	Annual payroll (Mil dol)	Number (1,000)	Work hours (Mil)
	119	120	121	122	123	124	125	126	127	128	129	130	131	132	133
VERMONT—Con.															
Windsor	306	1 622	14	25 407	12.4	87.6	32.0	9.0	149	20.1	3.4	-26.1	71.3	2.2	4.4
VIRGINIA	232	1 198	1 589	35 464	29.3	70.7	34.8	8.0	6 137	36.3	429.2	9.7	9 740.1	305.3	600.3
Accomack	419	1 378	50	153 939	57.8	42.2	67.5	33.4	34	38.2	3.4	3.0	41.8	2.9	5.1
Albemarle	465	1 939	19	24 704	25.4	74.6	30.2	4.0	44	20.5	3.1	10.7	70.2	2.3	4.6
Alleghany	137	765	2	10 202	6.8	93.3	21.3	1.3	7	28.6	0.3	0.0	5.3	0.3	0.5
Amelia	226	1 049	34	105 976	7.1	92.9	37.3	17.1	17	35.3	0.4	0.0	6.7	0.4	0.8
Amherst	175	760	4	10 616	16.1	83.9	24.3	1.5	45	26.7	1.1	57.1	18.7	0.7	1.3
Appomattox	184	839	5	14 877	13.3	86.7	26.0	4.5	21	28.6	1.4	7.7	21.7	1.1	2.3
Arlington	D	D	D	D	NA	NA	100.0	0.0	117	25.6	6.0	122.2	206.1	1.2	2.3
Augusta	241	1 205	83	54 229	7.4	92.6	45.6	13.1	56	51.8	4.9	-16.9	109.4	4.0	7.8
Bath	334	870	2	12 885	10.2	89.7	33.3	2.2	5	40.0	D	D	D	D	D
Bedford	171	1 007	19	15 291	10.0	90.0	22.9	3.8	36	19.4	1.0	11.1	24.0	0.8	1.6
Bland	153	601	5	16 625	3.3	96.7	34.9	3.4	8	62.5	0.9	0.0	12.7	0.7	1.3
Botetourt	203	1 070	12	22 432	17.5	82.5	24.4	5.6	15	40.0	D	D	D	D	D
Brunswick	182	697	14	34 000	58.7	41.3	45.3	9.0	48	33.3	1.2	-20.0	15.2	1.0	1.9
Buchanan	D	D	0	3 595	54.5	45.5	8.6	0.0	19	15.8	0.3	0.0	6.4	0.2	0.4
Buckingham	152	717	10	30 131	10.2	89.8	25.1	7.5	36	13.9	0.8	33.3	10.4	0.7	1.4
Campbell	153	731	14	21 606	33.2	66.8	32.3	4.1	61	32.8	5.5	-1.8	91.4	4.6	9.0
Caroline	272	1 001	5	26 576	73.6	26.4	36.5	6.0	35	34.3	0.8	14.3	11.9	0.7	1.4
Carroll	108	904	16	16 988	21.4	78.6	31.6	4.3	38	26.3	1.5	-6.3	18.7	1.4	2.4
Charles City County	556	1 035	2	52 616	86.5	13.5	51.1	21.3	9	33.3	0.1	0.0	1.6	0.1	0.2
Charlotte	181	714	12	23 431	44.4	55.6	37.1	6.0	41	12.2	1.2	33.3	17.8	1.0	2.0
Chesterfield	291	1 711	5	31 574	41.9	58.1	32.0	5.9	123	32.5	7.8	41.8	234.0	4.8	9.4
Clarke	437	2 090	14	45 576	35.1	64.9	45.4	10.5	15	13.3	D	D	D	D	D
Craig	196	699	2	13 642	4.0	95.9	38.4	1.7	4	50.0	D	D	D	D	D
Culpeper	427	1 738	18	37 109	26.4	73.6	33.5	7.1	38	34.2	1.7	6.2	32.5	1.3	2.3
Cumberland	220	954	22	80 773	3.0	97.0	35.4	16.2	11	18.2	0.1	0.0	1.2	0.1	0.2
Dickenson	77	876	D	D	NA	NA	1.7	0.0	11	9.1	0.3	50.0	2.6	0.2	0.4
Dinwiddie	189	968	14	37 338	60.6	39.4	45.6	9.7	14	42.9	0.4	0.0	6.1	0.3	0.7
Essex	483	932	7	52 194	82.7	17.3	54.9	13.4	32	34.4	0.9	12.5	12.3	0.8	1.5
Fairfax	480	8 428	6	31 826	D	19.5	17.7	4.5	464	25.0	17.7	56.6	552.6	7.5	14.8
Fauquier	600	2 390	31	32 202	13.7	86.3	34.3	7.5	29	37.9	0.9	28.6	19.3	0.6	1.2
Floyd	116	837	15	19 301	13.6	86.4	29.3	3.9	25	24.0	0.8	0.0	10.7	0.7	1.3
Fluvanna	253	1 144	5	17 980	9.5	90.5	24.9	1.9	11	18.2	D	D	D	D	D
Franklin	178	936	34	33 315	18.0	82.0	37.0	10.3	54	48.1	4.5	28.6	70.7	3.8	7.3
Frederick	298	1 431	18	31 818	63.6	36.4	28.5	6.5	39	46.2	2.3	64.3	50.2	1.7	3.1
Giles	116	574	4	11 037	7.6	92.4	28.6	1.2	16	56.2	D	D	D	D	D
Gloucester	460	2 198	4	27 464	81.7	18.3	41.5	7.7	31	22.6	D	D	D	D	D
Goochland	305	1 424	5	19 704	22.2	77.8	24.9	4.7	15	6.7	0.1	-50.0	1.8	0.1	0.2
Grayson	134	854	14	16 140	7.0	93.0	29.4	3.4	16	50.0	1.6	-11.1	20.8	1.4	2.7
Greene	234	1 679	4	19 926	4.9	95.1	30.7	3.6	9	22.2	D	D	D	D	D
Greensville	239	677	13	62 912	65.7	34.3	63.2	16.9	9	22.2	D	D	D	D	D
Halifax	122	594	22	17 658	76.9	23.1	39.1	3.0	16	31.2	1.5	0.0	29.4	1.1	2.3
Hanover	298	1 526	19	34 360	45.6	54.4	34.1	7.4	124	33.1	2.6	52.9	55.8	1.8	3.5
Henrico	350	1 947	6	35 713	83.5	16.5	23.4	8.2	174	36.2	8.0	6.7	208.7	5.4	11.0
Henry	116	729	3	10 022	49.6	50.4	21.1	1.2	75	40.0	14.6	17.7	263.9	12.6	26.1
Highland	193	707	7	23 238	1.2	98.8	49.8	4.6	8	25.0	0.1	-50.0	0.8	0.1	0.1
Isle of Wight	493	1 260	26	107 010	52.6	47.4	73.1	31.0	18	38.9	D	D	D	D	D
James City County	398	2 189	3	40 607	66.4	33.6	44.1	10.3	15	53.3	1.1	120.0	25.7	0.8	1.7
King and Queen	289	923	5	34 709	72.9	27.1	39.5	9.6	16	12.5	0.1	0.0	2.0	0.1	0.2
King George	375	1 396	2	16 640	66.2	33.8	34.0	4.3	12	33.3	D	D	D	D	D
King William	581	1 083	7	58 652	60.6	39.4	56.2	15.7	19	36.8	D	D	D	D	D
Lancaster	240	1 149	2	20 911	83.3	16.7	40.5	2.4	30	20.0	0.4	-33.3	3.9	0.3	0.4
Lee	78	839	11	7 509	50.2	49.8	18.4	0.3	30	33.3	1.0	11.1	14.0	0.8	1.4
Loudoun	659	3 012	28	29 560	34.7	65.3	29.8	5.2	94	34.0	2.7	125.0	73.8	1.3	2.8
Louisa	179	988	8	19 233	15.0	85.1	29.0	4.8	31	19.4	0.9	-18.2	10.6	0.8	1.6
Lunenburg	124	572	9	22 157	68.9	31.1	35.1	5.4	31	48.4	1.5	-31.8	19.8	1.3	2.5
Madison	344	1 490	16	35 915	8.4	91.6	42.2	9.5	17	29.4	0.5	25.0	6.4	0.4	0.8
Mathews	229	2 210	3	33 846	86.9	13.1	27.3	6.5	8	25.0	0.2	0.0	2.3	0.2	0.3
Mecklenburg	151	712	24	30 284	68.5	31.5	44.6	6.4	49	42.9	4.7	-2.1	74.4	3.9	8.5
Middlesex	377	1 552	3	36 725	64.0	36.0	39.8	9.6	22	27.3	0.3	-25.0	4.6	0.3	0.4
Montgomery	252	1 307	14	25 053	5.8	94.2	29.8	7.7	50	38.0	7.8	122.9	168.5	5.7	10.9
Nelson	196	838	5	14 805	38.7	61.3	24.4	2.7	36	19.4	0.8	33.3	19.8	0.7	1.3
New Kent	386	1 195	2	24 662	85.4	14.6	34.7	9.7	14	35.7	0.2	0.0	2.4	0.1	0.3
Northampton	435	1 547	20	110 114	99.3	0.7	66.1	26.1	10	70.0	1.1	-26.7	12.7	1.0	1.9

1. Includes livestock and poultry products.

STATE County	Manufactures, 1987 (cont'd): Production workers (cont'd): Wages: Total (Mil dol)	Manufactures, 1987 (cont'd): Production workers (cont'd): Wages: Average per worker (Dollars)	Manufactures, 1987 (cont'd): Value added by manufacture (Mil dol)	Manufactures, 1987 (cont'd): Value of shipments (Mil dol)	Manufactures, 1987 (cont'd): New capital expenditures (Mil dol)	Value of construction authorized by building permits, 1990: Total[1] ($1,000)	Nonresidential: Total ($1,000)	Nonresidential: Percent: Office	Nonresidential: Percent: Industrial	Nonresidential: Percent: Stores	Residential: New construction ($1,000)	Residential: Number of housing units	Residential: Alterations and additions ($1,000)
	134	135	136	137	138	139	140	141	142	143	144	145	146
VERMONT—Con.													
Windsor	38.7	17 591	152.0	316.7	8.0	32 126	9 888	1.4	39.5	17.7	17 373	196	2 801
VIRGINIA	5 728.2	18 763	26 857.3	51 902.1	1 542.7	5 783 955	1 603 375	32.1	18.2	24.0	2 799 346	42 151	453 614
Accomack	33.9	11 690	61.8	286.8	3.9	24 297	2 860	28.0	4.0	21.0	16 001	225	1 215
Albemarle	43.0	18 696	140.0	258.8	D	94 850	11 166	12.2	0.4	19.7	61 099	822	10 430
Alleghany	4.3	14 333	9.7	17.5	D	41 592	37 204	0.1	96.4	2.7	1 358	34	356
Amelia	4.8	12 000	14.3	25.0	0.8	6 762	1 156	0.0	0.0	10.4	4 609	81	526
Amherst	8.0	11 429	30.3	61.6	3.2	17 030	1 462	5.5	0.5	54.1	12 137	167	878
Appomattox	15.9	14 455	49.5	91.4	D	5 800	1 342	24.9	0.0	11.3	3 713	52	424
Arlington	23.9	19 917	269.5	432.3	26.0	210 878	59 838	93.6	0.0	4.3	39 769	1 024	17 254
Augusta	74.6	18 650	294.3	568.0	24.4	61 982	10 708	16.2	0.5	12.8	41 685	666	3 595
Bath	D	D	D	D	D	3 658	47	0.0	0.0	0.0	2 411	34	1 021
Bedford	16.4	20 500	80.2	151.6	D	30 370	4 062	4.5	0.0	0.0	21 303	401	2 265
Bland	9.3	13 286	35.2	97.2	2.4	3 003	1 080	0.0	0.0	98.9	1 584	23	97
Botetourt	D	D	D	D	D	22 796	7 563	32.4	7.6	5.2	10 391	145	1 255
Brunswick	12.1	12 100	28.5	54.6	2.6	4 457	0	NA	NA	NA	2 840	48	888
Buchanan	5.1	25 500	17.5	68.3	D	5 418	3 899	27.3	0.0	0.9	1 053	29	168
Buckingham	8.5	12 143	30.6	68.1	1.3	7 519	2 824	0.1	0.0	1.9	2 868	60	899
Campbell	65.2	14 174	442.2	737.1	18.8	45 461	29 928	0.6	7.3	1.5	10 244	131	1 741
Caroline	9.0	12 857	30.6	87.6	3.6	18 033	620	0.0	0.0	100.0	17 232	283	0
Carroll	15.6	11 143	32.2	63.9	1.3	14 387	3 228	0.0	0.9	9.0	8 841	162	852
Charles City County	1.0	10 000	4.8	10.7	0.4	3 305	251	0.0	0.0	79.7	2 430	40	479
Charlotte	14.5	14 500	28.4	69.3	D	3 424	141	19.8	54.5	8.5	2 766	50	224
Chesterfield	127.6	26 583	614.4	1 221.5	64.7	254 871	37 229	3.7	1.0	78.1	174 784	2 611	16 298
Clarke	D	D	D	D	D	11 736	1 553	0.0	40.6	1.4	5 764	55	3 476
Craig	D	D	D	D	D	2 364	397	0.0	0.0	14.6	1 584	35	325
Culpeper	20.8	16 000	122.1	275.8	4.0	41 983	2 748	26.7	23.0	7.8	35 991	315	1 314
Cumberland	1.0	10 000	3.4	6.1	D	6 325	1 694	0.0	4.9	0.0	3 768	69	734
Dickenson	2.2	11 000	4.7	6.9	D	1 714	46	0.0	0.0	0.0	1 029	38	590
Dinwiddie	4.9	16 333	15.5	37.2	1.1	25 657	16 489	0.0	3.6	82.2	8 029	146	750
Essex	9.9	12 375	18.2	94.3	2.8	11 663	2 737	0.0	87.7	0.0	5 261	68	2 830
Fairfax	173.4	23 120	821.5	1 372.1	46.3	1 015 728	446 294	64.2	0.1	22.6	327 910	4 199	96 259
Fauquier	11.9	19 833	34.3	82.5	2.8	59 289	7 624	10.9	9.4	35.4	41 630	394	6 601
Floyd	8.0	11 429	43.0	71.5	2.5	5 932	342	0.0	2.9	25.0	3 879	66	633
Fluvanna	D	D	D	D	D	25 147	2 817	9.8	0.0	0.0	20 713	272	1 242
Franklin	48.9	12 868	159.2	326.5	10.1	44 807	11 864	4.5	27.7	12.0	28 343	385	2 035
Frederick	34.1	20 059	104.9	371.4	8.4	61 078	11 963	0.0	69.2	7.9	44 093	750	2 292
Giles	D	D	D	D	D	6 376	941	16.9	7.4	5.8	2 971	52	731
Gloucester	D	D	D	D	D	29 643	3 171	16.6	0.0	72.4	22 586	229	2 701
Goochland	1.2	12 000	3.1	6.2	0.1	17 377	2 906	24.0	0.0	0.0	12 137	165	1 808
Grayson	16.5	11 786	47.5	73.1	1.1	6 679	323	0.0	0.0	0.0	4 595	77	426
Greene	D	D	D	D	D	13 085	1 758	10.1	5.1	19.3	10 519	157	511
Greensville	D	D	D	D	D	6 401	3 798	0.0	0.0	2.8	1 486	26	245
Halifax	18.6	16 909	65.5	114.9	D	3 615	0	NA	NA	NA	3 615	77	0
Hanover	31.9	17 722	149.6	304.0	D	100 090	33 127	5.8	51.0	35.9	53 856	836	6 876
Henrico	125.1	23 167	480.2	968.8	33.3	182 627	43 287	24.2	12.1	47.7	94 468	1 837	8 546
Henry	203.0	16 111	501.5	1 035.3	24.4	27 271	7 449	0.7	41.2	38.7	14 135	187	1 347
Highland	0.7	7 000	1.8	4.5	0.1	1 792	339	0.0	0.0	35.1	883	21	551
Isle of Wight	D	D	D	D	D	27 737	1 900	0.0	0.6	68.5	23 069	285	1 452
James City County	16.7	20 875	69.4	121.0	8.1	58 041	5 493	0.0	52.1	42.8	49 637	419	2 666
King and Queen	1.5	15 000	4.8	11.0	0.4	4 762	291	0.0	43.1	0.0	3 477	47	625
King George	D	D	D	D	D	11 645	1 037	24.0	0.0	0.0	9 345	197	457
King William	D	D	D	D	D	10 899	546	47.8	18.3	21.4	10 352	166	0
Lancaster	2.2	7 333	8.5	22.6	0.3	32 842	7 779	8.1	45.9	4.5	21 186	179	2 065
Lee	9.7	12 125	31.8	65.6	1.0	5 459	543	3.7	0.0	30.0	3 468	95	1 073
Loudoun	26.0	20 000	135.4	256.5	5.6	191 050	44 654	14.0	27.6	34.1	122 481	2 121	9 482
Louisa	8.7	10 875	19.2	35.4	0.9	22 831	1 121	21.0	32.1	36.3	18 446	411	1 048
Lunenburg	15.6	12 000	41.5	87.1	1.8	3 104	92	0.0	0.0	100.0	2 575	54	0
Madison	5.2	13 000	11.7	29.8	1.1	10 010	278	0.0	0.0	0.0	7 191	102	2 139
Mathews	2.0	10 000	4.2	6.1	D	21 263	1 175	0.0	0.0	0.0	17 069	194	2 111
Mecklenburg	53.6	13 744	201.8	632.4	5.4	133 896	120 570	0.5	97.9	0.1	9 570	148	3 420
Middlesex	3.5	11 667	9.9	25.0	0.4	23 412	2 083	14.3	6.0	0.0	18 478	180	2 851
Montgomery	107.2	18 807	408.2	528.5	5.4	36 142	8 364	33.7	0.0	29.8	20 560	412	2 271
Nelson	12.5	17 857	61.8	118.1	6.0	22 019	516	0.0	0.0	2.9	19 264	172	1 996
New Kent	1.6	16 000	5.2	11.2	0.2	15 230	3 106	5.6	0.0	66.9	10 097	122	1 107
Northampton	10.2	10 200	27.7	69.8	2.3	13 969	4 299	1.8	0.0	78.0	7 010	77	1 710

1. Includes nonresidential additions and alterations, residential nonhousekeeping buildings, and residential garages and carports not shown separately.

STATE County	Wholesale trade, 1987: Establishments	Wholesale trade, 1987: Sales (Mil dol)	Wholesale trade, 1987: Paid employees[1]	Wholesale trade, 1987: Annual payroll (Mil dol)	Retail trade, all establishments, 1987: Number	Retail trade, all establishments, 1987: Sales: Total (Mil dol)	Sales: Percent change, 1982–1987	Sales: Per capita[2] (Dollars)	Retail trade, establishments with payroll, 1987: Number	Sales: Total (Mil dol)	Per capita[2] (Dollars): General merchandise stores	Per capita: Food stores	Per capita: Apparel & accessory stores	Per capita: Eating and drinking places
	147	148	149	150	151	152	153	154	155	156	157	158	159	160
VERMONT—Con.														
Windsor	90	262.1	907	18.2	810	357.9	56.8	6 627	482	343.8	244	1 246	147	610
VIRGINIA	8 446	44 758.8	115 126	2 625.0	52 634	39 784.8	61.0	6 727	34 916	38 960.2	728	1 361	312	604
Accomack	55	73.0	549	7.1	413	148.5	45.2	4 743	232	138.6	425	1 561	250	469
Albemarle	41	D	D	D	1 107	902.5	485.3	8 883	813	886.1	985	1 815	D	785
Alleghany	2	D	D	D	241	161.6	22 985.7	6 264	180	159.9	D	D	D	448
Amelia	10	28.0	130	2.1	66	18.4	11.5	2 189	33	17.0	114	665	D	74
Amherst	12	32.5	128	1.9	208	106.7	18.4	3 666	127	102.5	D	1 223	33	339
Appomattox	7	4.3	34	0.5	120	42.3	13.4	3 413	63	40.7	56	D	52	250
Arlington	165	1 031.7	4 161	135.7	1 262	1 168.5	40.4	7 583	895	1 151.5	551	1 184	246	1 181
Augusta	46	87.4	430	8.0	965	568.3	296.9	6 138	609	551.8	704	1 203	125	521
Bath	4	3.3	11	0.2	63	14.1	53.3	2 772	41	13.0	212	577	165	259
Bedford	32	257.2	340	5.8	346	126.4	590.7	2 731	189	119.8	116	814	84	165
Bland	2	D	D	D	50	16.4	160.3	2 530	18	14.6	0	248	0	54
Botetourt	17	86.3	158	3.8	173	69.7	38.8	2 801	80	66.2	16	673	D	72
Brunswick	13	23.5	79	1.3	141	41.2	43.6	2 592	88	38.7	122	793	115	158
Buchanan	45	138.3	380	7.8	302	119.7	15.2	3 335	146	107.8	D	1 155	81	163
Buckingham	11	10.3	73	0.9	86	29.2	67.8	2 302	50	27.9	151	660	D	104
Campbell	43	91.7	483	9.5	1 191	796.1	731.9	6 857	840	781.1	D	1 346	314	603
Caroline	15	15.3	50	0.8	127	44.2	22.8	2 313	71	40.7	D	865	0	162
Carroll	15	D	D	D	433	169.2	276.0	4 904	219	155.9	635	1 120	216	321
Charles City County	1	D	D	D	24	4.2	90.9	631	7	3.0	D	D	0	D
Charlotte	13	31.6	104	1.6	136	22.9	32.4	1 923	48	17.4	D	587	D	62
Chesterfield	265	2 279.3	3 128	80.6	1 371	1 282.3	85.8	7 261	908	1 263.1	927	1 217	376	525
Clarke	11	D	D	D	110	22.6	-1.7	2 073	62	19.6	94	643	26	223
Craig	3	1.3	22	0.2	36	4.2	-6.7	993	10	3.4	0	575	0	D
Culpeper	29	70.7	328	5.0	252	145.0	84.7	5 753	167	139.1	779	1 406	188	495
Cumberland	6	4.9	22	0.2	50	24.7	71.5	3 091	34	24.0	D	1 025	D	79
Dickenson	11	6.5	30	0.5	151	56.0	0.4	2 948	80	51.1	398	881	17	147
Dinwiddie	9	D	D	D	737	577.8	2 338.0	7 055	527	565.3	D	1 487	D	509
Essex	16	24.4	98	1.4	120	81.5	47.4	9 155	80	78.9	D	2 355	431	766
Fairfax	913	9 177.2	15 950	499.1	6 237	6 847.8	105.7	8 756	4 078	6 748.2	D	D	573	D
Fauquier	45	130.7	531	10.1	361	240.4	92.8	5 427	212	232.1	262	1 770	137	486
Floyd	5	2.6	13	0.2	111	34.5	44.4	2 951	56	30.2	95	642	D	83
Fluvanna	9	D	D	D	72	16.9	-5.1	1 446	34	15.3	D	619	D	42
Franklin	31	32.5	183	2.8	332	123.2	71.3	3 064	162	111.2	213	814	112	197
Frederick	49	124.9	688	11.7	820	533.6	648.4	8 952	536	519.2	1 349	1 647	D	818
Giles	16	26.4	146	1.2	150	84.5	21.4	4 883	97	81.8	268	1 626	67	306
Gloucester	35	40.0	292	3.6	248	135.7	65.1	4 713	145	132.1	475	1 381	50	480
Goochland	21	66.9	276	3.5	89	41.3	79.6	3 039	56	40.3	D	1 124	0	78
Grayson	7	3.0	23	0.2	103	20.8	-3.7	1 267	41	17.0	D	457	D	43
Greene	6	D	D	D	80	20.4	29.1	2 315	32	17.2	D	644	D	93
Greensville	6	5.6	41	0.5	183	96.0	4 471.4	6 318	133	93.9	D	D	195	572
Halifax	19	26.9	114	1.8	371	149.2	624.3	4 110	207	141.8	510	953	D	318
Hanover	161	1 558.2	3 303	84.6	507	342.7	64.8	5 939	305	333.5	D	1 389	115	476
Henrico	472	2 583.8	6 488	169.1	1 611	1 610.2	51.5	7 916	1 123	1 585.8	1 723	1 598	515	640
Henry	39	103.9	282	5.8	837	418.5	233.5	5 387	455	397.0	586	1 153	180	367
Highland	3	D	D	D	41	6.0	36.4	2 507	20	5.0	D	319	0	D
Isle of Wight	30	D	D	D	189	77.8	53.5	3 074	98	75.1	145	1 182	45	217
James City County	21	29.5	107	2.0	543	465.0	441.3	10 740	416	461.6	D	D	1 010	1 927
King and Queen	4	D	D	D	36	5.4	10.2	880	14	4.7	D	247	0	D
King George	6	3.0	47	0.6	70	29.6	88.5	2 423	47	27.7	D	945	D	252
King William	12	25.6	85	1.6	105	61.2	57.7	6 063	67	59.1	D	1 391	D	144
Lancaster	34	55.9	281	3.5	201	74.9	56.0	6 934	124	71.9	233	2 218	305	359
Lee	21	26.3	136	1.9	222	77.3	64.5	3 033	123	72.6	167	1 332	20	167
Loudoun	97	574.1	884	20.9	745	556.0	113.1	7 494	444	543.9	281	1 820	181	673
Louisa	12	10.0	67	0.9	128	39.8	12.1	2 018	67	36.1	238	469	D	107
Lunenburg	12	13.9	72	0.9	109	35.8	35.1	2 958	80	34.5	140	915	61	135
Madison	8	18.8	85	1.0	87	34.2	47.4	3 169	48	32.4	66	670	12	136
Mathews	14	9.0	50	0.8	81	21.5	15.0	2 533	46	19.5	41	818	D	106
Mecklenburg	50	70.5	427	5.4	378	158.6	39.7	5 303	241	149.4	397	1 218	263	410
Middlesex	14	27.2	124	1.8	113	34.0	56.0	4 052	65	31.7	93	1 574	32	271
Montgomery	46	68.1	494	5.6	719	556.2	113.5	7 150	517	548.9	D	1 425	223	618
Nelson	16	20.7	70	0.9	152	55.7	84.4	4 459	68	50.7	D	686	127	42
New Kent	14	8.3	94	1.2	57	24.4	36.3	2 235	30	22.6	D	702	0	91
Northampton	24	23.0	197	2.2	175	52.2	17.3	3 755	100	46.9	179	1 366	61	278

1. For pay period including March 12. 2. Based on the estimated population as of July 1 of the year shown.

STATE County	Retail trade, establishments with payroll, 1987 (cont'd): Paid employees[1]	Retail trade, establishments with payroll, 1987 (cont'd): Annual payroll (Mil dol)	Taxable service industries–establishments with payroll, 1987: Number	Receipts (Mil dol): Total	Receipts (Mil dol), Selected kinds of business: Hotels, motels and other lodging places	Receipts (Mil dol), Selected kinds of business: Health services	Receipts (Mil dol), Selected kinds of business: Legal services	Paid employees	Annual payroll (Mil dol)	Bank deposits,[2] June 1989: Total (Mil dol)	Bank deposits,[2] June 1989: Percent change, 1988–1989	Savings capital,[3] September 1989: Total (Mil dol)	Savings capital,[3] September 1989: Percent change, 1988–1989
	161	162	163	164	165	166	167	168	169	170	171	172	173
VERMONT—Con.													
Windsor	3 628	39.8	437	118.9	26.4	19.9	8.7	3 183	38.8	536	7.5	25.0	-3.4
VIRGINIA	453 325	4 556.7	38 337	20 414.6	1 451.7	4 012.5	1 019.5	438 728	8 128.4	49 024	4.9	18 523.4	3.4
Accomack	1 968	17.1	148	39.5	6.8	3.3	2.1	1 096	19.9	304	5.2	28.1	27.1
Albemarle	10 450	104.0	205	64.8	D	11.9	0.4	1 747	24.0	158	4.9	110.6	4.9
Alleghany	1 734	16.9	20	6.2	D	5.3	0.0	98	3.0	7	6.6	0.0	NA
Amelia	194	1.7	26	4.2	0.0	0.5	0.2	78	0.8	50	9.2	0.0	NA
Amherst	1 217	10.5	95	19.0	D	3.9	1.0	554	6.4	126	3.0	45.0	4.1
Appomattox	478	4.3	42	4.8	D	1.4	0.4	154	1.5	104	13.5	13.7	-0.2
Arlington	13 119	161.2	1 815	2 027.8	231.7	143.1	76.8	35 488	816.4	1 856	1.6	789.1	-8.8
Augusta	6 355	63.3	133	32.5	6.4	7.8	D	940	9.6	161	23.8	0.0	NA
Bath	168	1.6	35	D	D	0.8	0.3	D	D	26	-7.2	0.0	NA
Bedford	1 423	13.2	59	9.7	0.5	1.8	D	272	3.3	40	-2.4	78.8	-0.8
Bland	94	0.8	16	3.6	D	0.8	D	66	0.9	21	2.8	0.0	NA
Botetourt	628	5.7	68	10.3	1.8	2.3	0.6	346	3.7	135	5.0	10.8	16.6
Brunswick	460	4.1	46	7.2	D	0.8	D	230	1.8	99	6.1	0.0	NA
Buchanan	1 195	10.6	120	26.9	D	12.9	3.1	491	10.4	289	7.9	9.6	-10.9
Buckingham	317	2.6	29	6.6	D	D	0.5	161	2.7	53	3.8	0.0	NA
Campbell	10 979	95.5	128	19.5	D	3.1	1.4	517	5.8	306	9.3	71.8	23.8
Caroline	513	4.4	45	10.4	3.2	2.7	0.5	220	3.5	120	11.8	20.2	8.4
Carroll	1 846	17.1	74	10.3	1.7	2.4	0.7	231	2.7	131	6.8	0.0	NA
Charles City County	41	0.3	6	1.0	0.0	D	0.0	29	0.2	NA	NA	0.0	NA
Charlotte	225	1.7	30	4.7	D	0.5	0.5	175	1.4	81	9.0	0.0	NA
Chesterfield	14 053	142.2	893	343.2	16.5	97.2	12.6	8 416	136.5	661	15.3	856.7	22.2
Clarke	321	2.8	42	7.9	D	3.7	0.4	278	2.9	92	9.9	0.0	NA
Craig	42	0.2	10	0.9	0.0	D	0.0	32	0.3	28	2.4	0.0	NA
Culpeper	1 771	15.6	131	53.9	2.2	14.8	2.0	1 300	18.4	265	8.1	34.7	-7.6
Cumberland	321	2.8	27	3.5	0.0	2.1	0.2	79	1.2	18	9.1	0.0	NA
Dickenson	603	5.1	51	12.9	D	D	0.6	316	4.6	124	6.9	0.0	NA
Dinwiddie	6 862	66.4	46	5.9	0.9	1.5	0.3	152	1.7	74	5.8	15.8	7.0
Essex	924	8.8	64	10.2	0.8	5.8	0.5	285	3.2	105	-2.7	13.5	7.9
Fairfax	72 210	818.7	6 078	5 712.4	134.1	543.7	135.6	96 059	2 372.4	5 003	7.0	3 059.4	5.2
Fauquier	2 397	26.7	301	84.4	3.6	22.1	4.6	2 030	35.6	306	3.6	197.3	4.9
Floyd	284	2.6	27	4.2	D	1.9	0.4	134	1.2	98	5.0	0.0	NA
Fluvanna	188	1.7	32	5.2	D	D	D	130	1.5	37	18.3	0.0	NA
Franklin	1 295	11.8	134	19.8	D	6.5	2.2	669	6.5	276	6.2	40.2	11.4
Frederick	5 945	60.9	95	40.8	2.7	3.1	D	918	16.0	107	14.7	12.6	-20.1
Giles	811	7.4	67	10.9	D	4.4	0.9	336	3.9	153	16.3	0.0	NA
Gloucester	1 571	14.3	146	32.4	D	11.5	2.1	981	11.1	156	-0.2	18.5	-4.0
Goochland	375	4.0	52	8.2	0.0	1.4	0.7	164	2.1	77	7.6	0.0	NA
Grayson	216	1.6	32	4.5	0.0	1.7	0.3	128	1.1	83	4.7	0.0	NA
Greene	239	2.1	18	3.1	D	D	D	116	1.1	42	7.4	0.0	NA
Greensville	1 169	10.4	5	1.5	D	0.0	0.0	43	0.4	9	11.2	47.4	-0.5
Halifax	1 958	16.8	69	9.6	D	2.2	1.3	254	2.7	82	6.2	76.3	1.6
Hanover	3 700	36.2	336	139.4	7.8	12.6	D	3 513	41.6	311	9.6	151.9	2.9
Henrico	18 582	181.6	1 368	701.4	29.3	304.3	15.3	18 263	273.1	1 045	8.8	967.0	0.0
Henry	4 827	45.2	125	34.0	4.5	6.1	D	582	8.6	249	5.1	33.5	-7.4
Highland	62	0.5	13	2.1	D	D	D	116	0.9	31	6.6	0.0	NA
Isle of Wight	810	7.2	76	17.2	D	2.0	1.0	398	5.2	148	13.1	5.0	-12.1
James City County	7 291	66.4	74	29.8	18.0	2.7	1.5	846	9.5	34	36.5	20.6	-16.7
King and Queen	56	0.5	10	D	D	0.0	0.0	D	D	7	-4.1	0.0	NA
King George	353	3.0	69	58.7	0.0	D	D	1 119	28.3	53	14.6	0.0	NA
King William	484	5.6	46	7.6	D	1.9	0.9	903	2.7	130	7.8	16.1	-4.2
Lancaster	722	8.2	100	29.7	12.1	9.2	2.6	666	10.7	172	1.9	13.6	23.3
Lee	838	6.9	75	10.2	D	5.4	1.3	307	3.9	185	6.8	12.7	20.9
Loudoun	5 840	64.3	591	295.3	20.5	42.0	8.7	5 707	102.6	777	14.7	129.3	36.1
Louisa	471	4.0	59	8.6	1.0	D	1.5	269	2.5	136	10.0	0.0	NA
Lunenburg	453	3.7	41	3.9	D	0.6	0.3	116	0.9	84	9.8	0.0	NA
Madison	334	2.9	37	5.4	D	1.1	0.7	151	1.6	61	8.8	0.0	NA
Mathews	237	2.1	35	4.6	D	1.2	0.3	136	1.1	72	15.1	0.0	NA
Mecklenburg	1 901	16.4	138	21.1	4.5	7.3	1.2	575	6.9	278	3.2	42.3	21.7
Middlesex	427	4.0	52	7.7	0.6	2.4	0.5	227	2.1	81	10.7	0.0	NA
Montgomery	6 836	59.9	323	88.4	10.4	36.7	3.1	2 780	34.4	540	6.2	37.4	-12.3
Nelson	366	4.5	52	13.7	D	2.1	0.6	1 065	7.6	63	21.3	0.0	NA
New Kent	248	2.4	35	14.2	D	D	0.7	337	5.8	35	10.1	0.0	NA
Northampton	631	4.8	71	14.1	1.8	8.7	0.6	423	5.6	114	9.0	19.4	11.6

1. For the period including March 12 of the year shown. 2. Includes deposits for all insured and reporting noninsured commercial and mutual savings banks. 3. Includes savings capital for all FSLIC insured savings institutions.

STATE County	Federal funds and grants, 1989							Local government finances, 1981–1982							
	Expenditures		Per capita[1] (Dollars)					General revenue						Direct general expenditure	
									Intergovernmental		Taxes				
												Per capita[2]			
	Total (Mil dol)	Percent change, 1988–1989	Total	Direct payments for individuals	Procurement contract awards	Salaries and wages	Grant awards	Total (Mil dol)	Total (Mil dol)	Percent from state	Total (Mil dol)	Total (Dollars)	Property (Dollars)	Total (Mil dol)	Percent change, 1977–1982
	174	175	176	177	178	179	180	181	182	183	184	185	186	187	188
VERMONT—Con.															
Windsor	167.5	0.2	2 986	1 784	102	803	267	43.0	9.8	66.7	29.1	560	558	44.2	54.7
VIRGINIA	32 095.6	-10.5	X	1 888	1 218	1 635	374	5 061.9	1 976.5	80.9	2 274.5	414	286	4 850.8	55.5
Accomack	177.8	21.2	5 664	2 676	1 416	1 169	379	19.8	10.4	92.1	6.0	192	131	19.6	52.0
Albemarle	320.1	-2.3	3 111	1 548	333	468	750	44.5	18.8	68.8	19.7	343	229	42.5	103.3
Alleghany	76.5	10.9	3 059	2 509	165	146	233	11.6	5.6	95.1	3.3	239	184	10.4	74.6
Amelia	16.7	6.7	1 966	1 500	12	93	278	4.3	2.7	91.6	1.4	166	128	5.1	39.6
Amherst	51.9	-7.1	1 783	1 449	92	63	170	14.5	8.3	94.3	4.7	161	118	13.2	32.9
Appomattox	24.6	0.8	1 969	1 574	16	132	226	7.2	4.5	95.3	2.0	166	131	6.8	65.5
Arlington	3 384.5	-4.4	22 237	2 934	4 543	14 456	303	191.2	56.4	64.0	115.3	752	541	167.8	51.0
Augusta	202.6	10.3	2 158	1 734	50	121	240	31.3	17.2	87.5	10.2	189	130	29.5	65.2
Bath	13.6	7.9	2 716	2 230	47	214	209	5.0	2.2	74.3	2.2	419	330	4.7	106.8
Bedford	104.3	11.6	2 169	1 887	19	113	129	19.4	11.2	97.0	5.8	160	138	19.6	67.0
Bland	15.7	15.9	2 423	1 968	84	114	223	3.1	2.2	85.9	0.8	118	99	2.8	100.1
Botetourt	42.6	-5.4	1 663	1 497	16	84	54	13.8	8.0	89.2	4.8	204	170	15.7	117.0
Brunswick	45.4	16.1	2 876	1 888	251	135	539	9.7	6.3	88.1	3.0	191	141	9.4	40.7
Buchanan	88.7	-4.8	2 579	2 044	140	84	302	38.3	15.4	93.9	19.7	515	173	37.9	109.6
Buckingham	28.0	5.3	2 191	1 600	9	67	480	6.8	4.8	91.6	1.7	145	102	7.1	62.7
Campbell	380.6	-50.0	3 275	1 765	1 096	185	217	27.1	15.4	94.2	8.8	193	158	25.6	52.9
Caroline	53.4	3.8	2 739	1 681	169	654	192	10.4	6.5	95.3	3.2	175	121	9.6	26.1
Carroll	78.1	8.5	2 262	1 833	20	103	293	13.6	9.2	94.4	3.4	122	97	12.9	70.8
Charles City County	11.0	-43.4	1 637	1 219	9	104	259	5.1	2.8	76.8	2.1	313	280	4.6	46.8
Charlotte	32.3	9.3	2 689	2 041	116	128	350	6.5	4.6	94.3	1.5	125	95	6.2	37.7
Chesterfield	201.9	4.0	1 066	802	112	77	72	131.8	45.4	92.6	59.7	392	310	152.5	99.0
Clarke	44.0	9.3	3 890	2 684	599	276	264	5.6	2.5	96.5	2.6	256	206	5.6	64.0
Craig	8.5	10.2	2 030	1 619	18	195	178	2.4	1.8	76.7	0.5	139	115	2.4	74.1
Culpeper	61.8	9.0	2 333	1 860	61	158	191	18.4	9.0	71.8	7.3	321	236	18.2	49.1
Cumberland	15.5	-0.4	1 933	1 318	7	69	388	4.1	3.1	97.5	0.7	87	70	3.8	46.0
Dickenson	49.7	6.7	2 731	2 200	14	94	409	17.3	8.1	94.0	7.8	388	164	16.2	48.7
Dinwiddie	228.0	7.3	2 757	2 258	29	121	337	14.0	8.1	95.2	4.9	223	185	14.3	47.6
Essex	24.2	2.3	2 745	2 198	13	152	247	5.6	2.8	88.7	2.6	296	212	5.3	35.8
Fairfax	4 994.1	2.7	6 045	1 779	2 922	1 073	260	797.4	193.7	79.3	470.6	736	591	711.2	70.9
Fauquier	117.7	0.5	2 453	1 314	248	691	168	26.5	10.1	91.9	13.9	370	292	24.7	78.0
Floyd	23.8	-2.7	2 017	1 673	16	129	183	5.5	3.2	85.0	1.9	160	111	5.4	69.0
Fluvanna	27.0	9.5	2 160	1 816	22	90	219	6.3	3.1	96.6	2.8	276	251	5.5	52.3
Franklin	65.6	7.8	1 561	1 306	21	81	142	18.6	10.9	94.6	5.8	161	102	18.8	41.6
Frederick	120.4	-1.9	1 909	1 416	60	297	125	22.7	10.1	95.7	9.7	275	210	21.3	46.2
Giles	41.2	6.1	2 410	2 029	45	103	224	12.4	7.0	94.0	4.2	240	200	13.8	84.5
Gloucester	88.1	4.8	2 824	1 757	114	769	127	11.6	5.7	94.7	5.2	237	160	12.0	92.3
Goochland	19.4	4.8	1 355	1 073	10	107	136	6.9	3.4	95.4	3.1	258	210	6.8	34.7
Grayson	31.9	-8.8	1 967	1 555	6	83	286	8.4	5.5	93.0	2.0	120	80	7.9	81.9
Greene	17.9	1.0	1 948	1 502	100	126	196	4.7	3.3	89.0	1.3	159	119	4.9	49.3
Greensville	36.8	4.9	2 456	1 919	14	99	374	8.2	5.8	87.4	1.8	169	121	8.7	72.5
Halifax	86.8	6.1	2 432	1 831	22	108	432	18.8	13.7	84.7	4.3	143	97	18.8	63.0
Hanover	96.5	8.5	1 542	1 353	18	85	64	32.6	14.3	93.6	15.2	298	227	28.8	38.9
Henrico	206.6	4.4	971	788	21	94	63	159.3	52.6	86.9	80.3	432	289	173.4	76.4
Henry	154.7	14.7	1 979	1 538	194	74	167	31.5	17.9	96.3	10.7	190	132	30.0	36.7
Highland	7.2	11.1	3 265	2 571	46	237	355	1.7	0.9	91.0	0.7	241	203	1.8	99.3
Isle of Wight	48.8	-4.6	1 822	1 425	69	116	175	14.3	7.3	92.8	6.0	273	222	13.6	60.9
James City County	140.1	11.0	2 883	2 190	184	338	162	17.4	3.6	73.0	11.3	474	371	9.0	36.8
King and Queen	40.1	-7.6	6 691	1 898	21	4 297	322	3.2	1.8	96.0	1.3	218	198	3.0	39.4
King George	248.2	-1.5	19 699	1 548	7 236	10 740	146	5.8	3.6	95.0	1.9	173	127	6.0	44.2
King William	23.0	5.4	2 210	1 771	11	90	247	7.9	3.5	94.8	3.7	386	302	7.2	72.5
Lancaster	48.5	14.4	4 487	4 048	21	170	206	5.5	2.8	95.8	2.2	217	153	5.7	55.2
Lee	79.4	6.0	3 214	2 271	273	85	574	15.6	11.4	96.4	3.5	134	102	14.9	62.8
Loudoun	202.9	-14.9	2 478	1 188	219	946	96	56.5	17.6	91.6	33.2	561	458	54.9	53.9
Louisa	43.3	3.5	2 145	1 776	10	91	247	13.1	5.1	91.5	6.5	355	316	12.1	86.5
Lunenburg	39.6	21.0	3 301	1 722	482	703	314	6.9	4.5	91.9	1.9	158	129	6.7	66.4
Madison	25.0	6.4	2 273	1 798	15	175	220	5.3	3.1	94.2	1.9	187	129	5.8	46.1
Mathews	53.3	5.2	6 275	5 825	63	245	123	4.0	1.9	96.3	1.8	217	183	3.9	60.7
Mecklenburg	127.7	26.8	4 330	1 921	1 882	152	351	17.3	11.2	83.8	5.0	171	110	15.8	48.3
Middlesex	26.7	5.0	3 146	2 659	30	223	153	4.8	2.4	94.6	2.1	260	211	4.3	36.6
Montgomery	393.5	23.1	5 045	1 414	2 795	199	627	35.8	17.5	89.8	13.8	214	150	33.0	62.2
Nelson	49.1	1.1	3 932	2 290	191	1 069	304	7.7	4.4	94.8	2.8	230	175	7.2	40.5
New Kent	20.3	9.9	1 702	1 417	12	102	146	6.0	2.9	89.2	2.7	296	241	5.4	69.6
Northampton	42.8	-21.8	3 173	2 217	315	196	413	33.1	6.6	81.4	3.4	234	175	24.6	27.8

1. Based on the estimated population as of July 1 of the year shown. 2. Based on the estimated population as of July 1, 1982.

STATE County	Local government finances, 1981–1982 (cont'd)								State and local government employment, 1989		Federal government civilian employment 1989		Elections, 1988[3]	
	Direct general expenditure (cont'd)						Debt outstanding							
	Per capita[1] (Dollars)	Percent of total for– Education	Health & hospitals	Police protection	Public welfare	Highways	Total (Mil dol)	Per capita[1] (Dollars)	Total	Rate[2]	Total	Earnings ($1,000)	Total vote cast for president	Vote for lead party (Percent)
	189	190	191	192	193	194	195	196	197	198	199	200	201	202
VERMONT—Con.														
Windsor	851	60.8	0.4	3.7	0.1	12.5	15.9	306	2 664	474.9	1 460	43 989	24 930	R–50.5
VIRGINIA	884	48.6	3.3	5.3	4.7	3.6	4 404.7	802	375 941	616.4	188 507	6 358 490	2 191 609	R–59.7
Accomack	630	56.4	2.0	2.3	17.6	0.4	3.1	101	1 528	486.6	762	27 620	11 542	R–60.0
Albemarle	739	55.9	0.0	2.2	3.3	0.8	40.0	695	20 536	1 995.7	1 293	40 390	25 753	R–58.7
Alleghany	752	57.9	1.2	3.9	7.5	0.1	36.4	2 637	1 480	592.0	108	2 761	4 926	R–51.9
Amelia	620	74.5	1.0	2.8	4.4	0.1	2.4	290	419	492.9	27	654	3 594	R–60.9
Amherst	454	74.1	0.0	4.3	3.5	0.1	9.5	325	3 441	1 182.5	51	1 325	10 151	R–64.1
Appomattox	560	72.5	0.6	4.4	5.1	0.5	1.8	150	665	532.0	58	1 183	5 040	R–63.6
Arlington	1 095	37.5	4.6	8.6	7.6	6.9	139.7	912	7 777	511.0	40 825	1 622 050	75 365	D–53.5
Augusta	548	70.2	0.0	2.9	3.9	0.7	21.2	393	7 858	836.8	296	7 826	17 634	R–75.1
Bath	906	68.8	0.6	2.7	3.7	0.0	0.7	136	296	592.0	50	1 061	2 167	R–58.7
Bedford	542	76.1	0.4	4.0	5.1	0.0	14.2	393	1 790	372.1	175	4 103	16 382	R–65.3
Bland	430	71.4	0.8	5.3	6.5	0.0	0.0	6	517	795.4	21	482	2 546	R–61.1
Botetourt	667	73.5	0.0	3.5	3.3	0.1	10.2	436	785	306.6	62	1 525	9 591	R–59.3
Brunswick	598	70.1	0.9	3.7	5.1	1.5	1.5	98	1 083	685.4	63	1 430	5 884	D–52.2
Buchanan	992	69.3	0.2	1.7	3.2	0.4	16.9	443	1 410	409.9	70	2 138	10 965	D–63.2
Buckingham	618	71.1	0.7	2.0	7.1	0.1	2.6	223	908	709.4	24	613	4 471	R–55.5
Campbell	557	69.7	2.3	4.1	4.5	1.6	9.1	198	5 536	476.4	494	15 985	17 533	R–72.5
Caroline	527	72.2	0.5	3.2	3.9	0.2	3.3	178	834	427.7	377	10 346	6 292	D–50.6
Carroll	461	74.0	0.6	3.6	5.0	1.2	5.7	204	1 893	548.7	92	2 303	9 637	R–66.2
Charles City County	690	69.6	0.6	2.6	6.8	0.0	0.4	53	283	422.4	20	569	2 700	D–68.1
Charlotte	515	75.5	0.0	3.3	6.2	0.6	0.5	38	570	475.0	50	1 201	4 699	R–57.4
Chesterfield	1 000	44.6	1.6	6.0	3.9	0.3	201.1	1 320	11 550	609.8	4 097	113 752	78 083	R–75.3
Clarke	554	68.8	0.5	5.8	3.7	1.4	0.8	84	384	339.8	81	2 722	4 020	R–62.2
Craig	608	60.3	0.0	3.6	5.8	0.5	0.6	148	143	340.5	36	806	2 005	R–55.5
Culpeper	799	50.7	1.8	5.1	2.4	2.2	12.9	564	1 796	677.7	105	2 874	8 599	R–68.6
Cumberland	493	78.4	1.5	3.0	5.9	0.0	0.3	35	313	391.2	21	502	3 159	R–62.6
Dickenson	803	64.1	0.0	2.1	4.2	13.8	4.6	226	754	414.3	41	942	7 604	D–58.7
Dinwiddie	649	78.2	0.2	2.5	4.9	0.2	6.1	276	8 122	982.1	305	8 255	7 659	R–54.4
Essex	608	68.9	0.0	3.2	4.9	0.6	1.4	162	417	473.9	38	911	3 365	R–60.6
Fairfax	1 113	54.9	3.1	4.4	2.9	0.6	572.0	895	40 560	490.9	35 042	1 240 194	328 365	R–61.1
Fauquier	659	70.7	0.0	4.6	2.9	1.7	25.7	685	1 938	403.7	1 241	45 937	16 796	R–69.9
Floyd	465	76.7	0.0	3.0	4.6	0.0	0.3	26	345	292.4	51	992	4 735	R–61.7
Fluvanna	531	75.7	0.0	3.8	5.9	0.0	2.2	210	457	365.6	37	843	4 059	R–60.3
Franklin	522	64.3	0.2	4.6	3.8	1.2	10.2	283	1 189	283.1	109	2 578	13 261	R–55.7
Frederick	607	68.3	0.3	3.4	3.0	0.1	13.7	389	2 947	467.0	446	14 169	13 717	R–72.3
Giles	780	71.5	1.0	4.9	4.0	2.7	5.6	316	646	377.8	47	1 155	6 648	R–52.5
Gloucester	543	64.0	0.2	4.1	4.3	0.0	6.2	282	1 717	550.3	83	1 984	11 181	R–68.4
Goochland	563	66.4	0.5	4.3	6.5	0.2	2.0	169	904	632.2	31	771	6 013	R–62.6
Grayson	474	60.9	0.3	5.3	7.4	0.7	2.3	139	495	305.6	38	860	6 451	R–61.5
Greene	618	69.1	0.1	3.0	4.6	0.1	1.8	226	331	359.8	41	674	3 224	R–69.3
Greensville	808	68.9	0.4	2.6	1.4	0.0	0.9	82	691	460.7	39	1 101	3 733	D–55.8
Halifax	626	69.4	0.3	3.7	6.0	0.1	4.5	152	1 591	445.7	127	3 111	10 124	R–56.0
Hanover	563	66.7	1.6	5.3	2.9	1.5	30.6	597	2 626	419.5	128	3 604	26 718	R–77.0
Henrico	932	44.1	1.5	7.0	3.2	4.2	160.1	861	9 650	453.5	562	19 481	89 887	R–69.3
Henry	530	75.0	0.0	4.1	4.3	0.1	25.1	444	3 118	398.7	150	4 335	18 729	R–58.0
Highland	655	63.8	0.2	4.9	4.9	0.0	0.0	0	117	531.8	13	222	1 286	R–62.8
Isle of Wight	619	65.4	0.3	4.8	8.3	1.6	6.7	304	830	309.7	99	2 899	9 621	R–60.1
James City County	380	0.0	4.0	12.5	11.7	1.2	11.7	493	5 602	1 152.7	368	11 088	13 773	R–64.9
King and Queen	515	76.1	0.3	1.3	9.9	0.0	0.7	118	222	370.0	25	481	2 727	R–50.5
King George	561	73.1	0.0	3.7	4.9	0.4	3.1	290	505	400.8	3 401	126 240	4 146	R–62.4
King William	749	74.7	0.0	4.2	3.5	0.0	3.4	358	551	529.8	22	526	4 349	R–62.9
Lancaster	554	61.1	0.4	3.7	7.6	1.0	2.1	201	369	341.7	44	1 037	5 043	R–67.0
Lee	565	76.5	0.1	3.4	7.6	0.3	2.4	92	1 132	458.3	62	1 459	9 045	D–54.2
Loudoun	928	60.8	2.7	4.0	4.7	1.5	36.1	609	4 719	576.2	1 816	83 005	30 862	R–66.3
Louisa	666	70.7	0.9	3.7	4.1	0.4	7.5	415	855	423.3	45	1 095	6 702	R–57.2
Lunenburg	545	75.6	0.0	4.2	3.6	0.8	1.5	124	466	388.3	34	790	4 496	R–56.3
Madison	571	81.0	0.3	4.0	4.1	0.0	2.3	224	368	334.5	77	1 155	4 026	R–62.1
Mathews	474	69.9	0.5	3.6	5.3	0.2	0.9	111	248	291.8	39	675	4 076	R–67.5
Mecklenburg	544	67.4	0.0	5.4	4.5	2.9	8.0	276	1 914	648.8	139	3 842	9 278	R–63.5
Middlesex	541	63.6	0.4	2.8	5.9	0.1	1.0	121	616	724.7	31	629	4 018	R–64.0
Montgomery	510	53.8	0.2	7.1	6.0	4.5	21.4	330	13 703	1 756.8	386	11 747	21 444	R–57.5
Nelson	585	76.3	0.0	3.5	4.2	0.0	2.0	162	506	404.8	51	1 152	4 849	R–51.6
New Kent	591	74.2	0.0	2.9	4.4	0.0	1.6	171	401	337.0	31	723	4 384	R–66.5
Northampton	1 706	26.5	0.2	1.8	3.1	15.6	181.7	12 615	933	691.1	52	1 384	4 927	R–52.0

1. Based on the estimated population as of July 1, 1982. 2. Per 10,000 resident population estimated as of July 1 of the year shown. 3. Data subject to copyright.

STATE–County code	MSA/ CMSA/ NECMA code[1]	STATE County	Land Area,[2] 1990 (Sq. Km.)	Population, 1990											
							Race						Age of population Percent		
				Total persons	Rank	Per square kilometer	White	Black	Am. Indian, Eskimo, Aleut	Asian & Pacific Islander	Other race	Hispanic[3]	Under 5 years	5 to 14 years	15 to 24 years
			1	2	3	4	5	6	7	8	9	10	11	12	13
		VIRGINIA—Con.													
51 133	...	Northumberland	498	10 524	2 334	21.1	7 388	3 098	9	19	10	51	5.3	11.8	9.0
51 135	...	Nottoway	815	14 993	1 987	18.4	8 740	6 155	35	45	18	83	5.8	12.8	12.5
51 137	...	Orange	885	21 421	1 608	24.2	18 233	3 079	31	48	30	142	6.5	14.0	12.0
51 139	...	Page	806	21 690	1 592	26.9	21 141	442	24	68	15	106	6.3	13.2	13.1
51 141	...	Patrick	1 251	17 473	1 823	14.0	16 128	1 263	14	19	49	123	5.4	12.4	13.5
51 143	1950	Pittsylvania	2 515	55 655	778	22.1	40 570	14 919	45	63	58	239	6.1	13.8	13.3
51 145	6760	Powhatan	677	15 328	1 969	22.6	11 954	3 290	32	26	26	59	6.2	12.3	13.9
51 147	...	Prince Edward	914	17 320	1 832	18.9	10 923	6 265	29	77	26	114	5.6	11.6	28.6
51 149	6760	Prince George	688	27 394	1 379	39.8	18 268	7 972	100	592	462	1 060	7.7	14.9	17.9
51 153	8840	Prince William	877	215 686	231	245.9	179 709	25 078	718	6 569	3 612	9 662	9.3	16.7	15.5
51 155	...	Pulaski	830	34 496	1 149	41.6	32 353	2 004	42	78	19	154	5.9	11.9	14.9
51 157	...	Rappahannock	690	6 622	2 695	9.6	6 095	491	10	14	12	67	6.8	12.4	11.5
51 159	...	Richmond	496	7 273	2 628	14.7	5 027	2 194	8	23	21	52	6.0	13.7	11.7
51 161	6800	Roanoke	649	79 332	574	122.2	76 520	2 021	74	645	72	440	5.4	12.8	13.3
51 163	...	Rockbridge	1 553	18 350	1 773	11.8	17 678	574	34	48	16	56	6.1	12.6	13.6
51 165	...	Rockingham	2 205	57 482	760	26.1	56 160	869	49	139	265	546	6.8	13.7	14.1
51 167	...	Russell	1 229	28 667	1 340	23.3	28 310	315	14	15	13	76	5.6	14.5	14.3
51 169	3660	Scott	1 390	23 204	1 530	16.7	23 030	143	17	4	10	74	5.2	12.3	14.0
51 171	...	Shenandoah	1 327	31 636	1 226	23.8	31 069	359	30	100	78	292	6.1	12.5	12.5
51 173	...	Smyth	1 171	32 370	1 202	27.6	31 596	660	34	68	12	104	5.8	12.5	14.6
51 175	...	Southampton	1 555	17 550	1 818	11.3	9 634	7 868	15	17	16	67	6.2	13.0	15.3
51 177	...	Spotsylvania	1 038	57 403	761	55.3	50 220	6 178	197	607	201	843	8.8	17.0	13.5
51 179	8840	Stafford	699	61 236	711	87.6	55 546	4 304	233	746	407	1 252	8.4	16.6	15.8
51 181	...	Surry	723	6 145	2 739	8.5	2 722	3 411	10	2	0	19	7.3	15.0	12.7
51 183	...	Sussex	1 271	10 248	2 364	8.1	4 253	5 955	11	16	13	23	7.0	13.4	14.3
51 185	...	Tazewell	1 346	45 960	903	34.1	44 454	1 196	49	245	16	134	5.8	14.3	14.4
51 187	...	Warren	554	26 142	1 416	47.2	24 646	1 292	45	72	87	248	7.8	13.1	13.2
51 191	3660	Washington	1 461	45 887	905	31.4	45 081	682	29	72	23	138	5.4	12.5	14.5
51 193	...	Westmoreland	594	15 480	1 956	26.1	10 257	5 104	31	67	21	100	6.8	13.0	11.6
51 195	...	Wise	1 045	39 573	1 009	37.9	38 674	713	36	128	22	113	6.1	15.3	15.6
51 197	...	Wythe	1 200	25 466	1 448	21.2	24 471	880	34	73	8	60	5.9	13.2	14.1
51 199	5720	York	274	42 422	949	154.8	34 487	6 613	112	988	222	723	7.0	17.3	13.6
		Independent Cities													
51 510	8840	Alexandria City	40	111 183	413	2 779.6	76 789	24 339	333	4 632	5 090	10 778	5.6	7.6	13.5
51 515	...	Bedford City	18	6 073	2 749	337.4	4 691	1 338	7	33	4	53	6.1	11.5	11.1
51 520	3660	Bristol City	30	18 426	1 767	614.2	17 240	1 063	13	91	19	64	6.0	11.7	14.2
51 530	...	Buena Vista City	18	6 406	2 717	355.9	6 093	282	5	21	5	12	5.0	12.2	17.5
51 540	1540	Charlottesville City	27	40 341	990	1 494.1	30 684	8 561	39	935	122	476	6.1	9.6	25.8
51 550	5720	Chesapeake City	882	151 976	307	172.3	107 399	41 662	444	1 899	572	1 913	8.3	16.1	13.9
51 560	...	Clifton Forge City	8	4 679	2 863	584.9	3 967	695	2	8	7	25	5.7	12.3	11.2
51 570	6760	Colonial Heights City	19	16 064	1 919	845.5	15 502	129	33	354	46	161	5.6	12.1	13.5
51 580	...	Covington City	11	6 991	2 661	635.5	5 953	969	6	51	12	27	5.8	11.1	13.2
51 590	1950	Danville City	112	53 056	803	473.7	33 247	19 431	72	262	44	276	6.5	12.3	13.3
51 595	...	Emporia City	18	5 306	2 819	294.8	2 849	2 420	11	24	2	59	7.6	13.1	12.2
51 600	8840	Fairfax City	16	19 622	1 691	1 226.4	16 830	966	43	1 409	374	1 159	5.6	10.4	16.4
51 610	8840	Falls Church City	5	9 578	2 426	1 915.6	8 533	298	42	456	249	604	5.8	10.7	10.3
51 620	...	Franklin City	20	7 864	2 587	393.2	3 637	4 199	6	20	2	15	7.4	15.4	12.3
51 630	...	Fredericksburg City	27	19 027	1 734	704.7	14 468	4 115	27	205	212	463	6.6	9.2	26.0
51 640	...	Galax City	21	6 670	2 687	317.6	6 219	387	8	15	41	65	6.8	11.1	12.4
51 650	5720	Hampton City	134	133 793	347	998.5	78 149	51 981	392	2 339	932	2 636	7.8	13.5	17.1
51 660	...	Harrisonburg City	45	30 707	1 257	682.4	27 968	2 018	37	469	215	481	4.8	8.4	39.5
51 670	6760	Hopewell City	27	23 101	1 533	855.6	16 687	5 910	64	307	133	417	8.2	14.0	14.6
51 678	...	Lexington City	6	6 959	2 666	1 159.8	6 027	811	22	89	10	62	2.9	6.6	44.1
51 680	4640	Lynchburg City	128	66 049	663	516.0	47 853	17 445	105	501	145	476	6.8	12.0	19.3
51 683	8840	Manassas City	26	27 957	1 353	1 075.3	23 332	2 889	90	867	779	1 601	9.8	15.3	15.3
51 685	8840	Manassas Park City	5	6 734	2 683	1 346.8	5 941	490	7	169	127	314	9.7	17.1	15.8
51 690	...	Martinsville City	28	16 162	1 913	577.2	10 134	5 954	21	32	21	59	6.4	12.3	11.9
51 700	5720	Newport News City	177	170 045	283	960.7	106 418	57 077	579	3 969	2 002	4 710	9.3	14.4	16.0
51 710	5720	Norfolk City	139	261 229	192	1 879.3	148 228	102 012	1 165	6 815	3 009	7 611	8.3	12.0	24.5
51 720	...	Norton City	19	4 247	2 897	223.5	3 923	269	13	35	7	31	6.2	15.0	15.1
51 730	6760	Petersburg City	59	38 386	1 043	650.6	10 194	27 688	83	289	132	472	7.5	12.6	14.8
51 735	5720	Poquoson City	40	11 005	2 292	275.1	10 728	84	24	161	8	96	6.1	15.8	14.0
51 740	5720	Portsmouth City	86	103 907	443	1 208.2	53 212	49 180	303	827	385	1 364	8.4	14.5	14.9
51 750	...	Radford City	25	15 940	1 928	637.6	14 643	957	16	272	52	175	3.5	6.9	50.2
51 760	6760	Richmond City	156	203 056	244	1 301.6	88 028	112 122	463	1 787	656	1 898	6.9	10.9	16.3
51 770	6800	Roanoke City	111	96 397	478	868.4	71 907	23 395	165	717	213	665	7.1	11.6	13.2
51 775	6800	Salem City	38	23 756	1 500	625.2	22 473	1 065	27	165	26	111	5.2	11.2	15.7

1. MSA = Metropolitan Statistical Area. CMSA = Consolidated MSA. NECMA = New England county metropolitan area. PMSA = Primary MSA. See Appendix A for explanation of these concepts. See Appendix B for list of metropolitan areas identified by type, with component counties. 2. Dry land or land partially or temporarily covered by water. 3. Hispanic persons may be of any race.

STATE County	Population, 1990 (cont'd): Age of population (cont'd) Percent: 25 to 34 years	35 to 44 years	45 to 54 years	55 to 64 years	65 to 74 years	75 years and over	Percent female	Population–Change and components of change: Change 1980–1990: Number	Percent	Components of change, 1980–1986: Total persons, 1986	Total persons, 1980	Net change: Number	Percent	Natural increase: Births	Deaths
	14	15	16	17	18	19	20	21	22	23	24	25	26	27	28
VIRGINIA—Con.															
Northumberland	12.0	11.4	10.9	14.6	15.6	9.3	52.9	696	7.1	10 200	9 828	300	3.3	700	900
Nottoway	16.3	14.1	10.5	9.9	10.3	7.8	49.1	327	2.2	14 900	14 666	200	1.3	1 100	1 200
Orange	15.4	14.7	11.1	10.4	9.7	6.1	51.5	3 358	18.6	19 800	18 063	1 700	9.6	1 700	1 300
Page	15.5	14.6	11.6	10.6	9.0	6.0	51.0	2 289	11.8	20 000	19 401	600	2.9	1 600	1 300
Patrick	14.5	14.3	13.0	10.7	9.1	7.1	50.8	-174	-1.0	17 600	17 647	-100	-0.5	1 100	1 000
Pittsylvania	16.0	15.6	11.9	10.0	8.2	5.2	51.0	-10 492	-15.9	65 600	66 147	-500	-0.8	5 400	3 500
Powhatan	20.4	18.4	12.3	7.8	5.7	3.1	43.8	2 266	17.3	13 100	13 062	100	0.5	900	500
Prince Edward	11.9	11.5	8.1	8.4	7.7	6.7	52.1	864	5.3	17 400	16 456	900	5.6	1 300	1 000
Prince George	19.4	16.5	10.6	6.8	4.2	2.0	46.9	1 661	6.5	26 200	25 733	500	2.0	2 300	600
Prince William	21.4	18.5	10.8	4.8	2.0	1.0	48.8	71 050	49.1	175 400	144 636	30 700	21.2	19 500	3 300
Pulaski	14.9	15.8	11.8	10.1	8.6	6.2	51.7	-733	-2.1	34 200	35 229	-1 000	-2.8	2 600	2 000
Rappahannock	15.0	17.2	13.8	10.2	8.0	5.0	50.0	529	8.7	6 200	6 093	100	2.3	500	400
Richmond	14.5	13.5	10.7	10.6	10.2	9.1	51.1	321	4.6	7 200	6 952	300	3.8	500	500
Roanoke	14.6	17.7	12.6	10.1	7.8	5.7	52.8	6 387	8.8	74 500	72 945	1 600	2.1	4 800	3 600
Rockbridge	15.2	14.9	12.2	11.7	9.0	4.8	50.1	626	3.5	17 600	17 724	-100	-0.6	1 400	1 100
Rockingham	16.2	15.4	11.1	9.3	7.5	5.7	50.8	5 414	10.4	54 400	52 068	2 300	4.5	4 800	2 600
Russell	16.3	15.8	11.7	9.5	7.2	5.0	51.0	-3 094	-9.7	32 200	31 761	400	1.3	2 500	1 600
Scott	14.0	14.4	12.5	10.8	9.6	7.2	51.7	-1 864	-7.4	25 500	25 068	400	1.8	1 700	1 600
Shenandoah	15.2	14.7	11.7	10.6	9.5	7.2	51.7	4 077	14.8	28 200	27 559	700	2.5	2 100	2 000
Smyth	14.9	14.4	11.8	10.9	8.8	6.3	52.2	-975	-2.9	33 000	33 345	-300	-0.9	2 400	2 100
Southampton	17.5	13.6	10.8	9.4	8.8	5.5	47.5	-766	-4.2	18 000	18 316	-300	-1.9	1 400	1 100
Spotsylvania	18.8	17.8	10.3	6.5	4.7	2.6	50.4	25 408	79.4	39 400	31 995	7 400	23.2	3 600	1 200
Stafford	18.3	17.9	11.1	6.0	3.7	2.2	48.4	20 766	51.3	50 100	40 470	9 600	23.8	4 000	1 400
Surry	16.0	14.6	10.6	9.1	8.9	5.8	51.9	99	1.6	6 300	6 046	200	4.1	600	400
Sussex	14.8	13.9	10.4	10.8	8.8	6.5	52.4	-626	-5.8	10 100	10 874	-800	-7.1	1 000	700
Tazewell	14.7	16.0	11.3	9.8	8.3	5.4	51.8	-4 551	-9.0	50 400	50 511	-100	-0.2	4 200	2 800
Warren	17.6	14.9	11.2	9.1	7.8	5.2	50.8	4 942	23.3	23 300	21 200	2 100	10.1	1 900	1 300
Washington	14.7	15.7	12.5	10.4	8.5	5.7	51.5	-600	-1.3	47 300	46 487	800	1.7	3 200	2 600
Westmoreland	13.9	13.0	11.2	11.6	11.7	7.3	51.9	1 439	10.2	14 400	14 041	400	2.6	1 200	1 100
Wise	14.7	15.4	10.7	9.1	7.7	5.4	51.7	-4 290	-9.8	44 800	43 863	900	2.1	4 300	2 500
Wythe	14.9	14.8	11.5	10.2	8.9	6.5	52.6	-56	-0.2	25 600	25 522	100	0.3	2 000	1 600
York	15.9	18.4	12.6	7.8	5.0	2.4	50.2	6 959	19.6	40 400	35 463	5 000	14.0	2 000	1 100
Independent Cities															
Alexandria City	27.0	18.3	10.6	7.1	5.8	4.5	52.6	7 966	7.7	107 800	103 217	4 600	4.5	9 700	5 000
Bedford City	14.9	11.9	9.3	10.4	11.6	13.3	53.0	82	1.4	6 300	5 991	300	4.4	500	700
Bristol City	14.4	13.1	10.8	10.9	10.4	8.3	55.4	-616	-3.2	18 000	19 042	-1 000	-5.3	1 300	1 500
Buena Vista City	13.2	14.2	11.1	10.6	8.9	7.2	54.6	-498	-7.2	6 500	6 904	-400	-6.4	400	400
Charlottesville City	19.8	12.3	7.5	6.9	6.5	5.7	53.1	425	1.1	41 100	39 916	1 200	2.9	3 500	2 300
Chesapeake City	19.0	16.8	10.3	7.2	5.4	3.0	51.0	37 490	32.7	134 400	114 486	19 900	17.4	13 000	5 400
Clifton Forge City	13.6	12.1	10.0	10.8	11.8	12.7	55.2	-367	-7.3	5 100	5 046	100	1.5	400	500
Colonial Heights City	14.0	15.1	12.2	12.1	10.2	5.3	53.2	-445	-2.7	16 700	16 509	200	0.9	1 200	900
Covington City	14.4	12.5	10.5	10.4	11.7	10.4	53.3	-2 072	-22.9	7 900	9 063	-1 100	-12.4	600	700
Danville City	14.4	13.8	10.2	10.9	10.9	7.8	54.4	7 414	16.2	44 700	45 642	-900	-2.0	3 600	3 600
Emporia City	14.1	11.9	9.4	10.5	11.8	9.3	53.2	466	9.6	4 700	4 840	-200	-3.2	400	500
Fairfax City	20.1	15.3	11.4	10.0	7.1	3.8	51.2	-915	-4.5	19 900	20 537	-600	-3.0	2 000	800
Falls Church City	17.6	20.0	12.2	8.5	8.3	6.7	52.3	63	0.7	9 700	9 515	200	2.4	700	500
Franklin City	15.0	14.1	9.9	9.9	9.0	6.9	54.9	141	1.8	7 600	7 723	-100	-1.3	800	500
Fredericksburg City	17.8	11.5	7.8	7.4	7.5	6.1	54.3	1 265	7.1	19 500	17 762	1 800	10.0	1 600	1 300
Galax City	13.9	12.9	10.8	11.6	10.6	9.9	54.9	146	2.2	6 900	6 524	400	5.9	500	600
Hampton City	19.6	14.4	10.0	8.0	6.3	3.3	51.2	11 176	9.1	126 000	122 617	3 400	2.8	13 500	5 400
Harrisonburg City	14.1	10.2	6.7	5.8	5.4	5.0	53.8	6 066	24.6	27 000	24 641	2 400	9.7	1 500	1 200
Hopewell City	17.4	13.7	10.1	9.0	7.5	5.5	52.6	-296	-1.3	24 100	23 397	700	3.1	2 600	1 400
Lexington City	7.9	8.3	7.2	8.1	7.8	7.1	41.6	-333	-4.6	7 000	7 292	-300	-4.6	300	400
Lynchburg City	14.6	13.0	9.0	8.8	8.5	7.9	55.0	-694	-1.0	68 000	66 743	1 200	1.8	5 500	4 700
Manassas City	23.7	17.1	9.2	4.6	2.8	2.1	49.0	12 452	80.3	20 100	15 505	4 600	29.9	2 500	600
Manassas Park City	25.7	13.4	8.4	6.3	2.6	1.1	50.3	210	3.2	7 100	6 524	600	9.5	800	100
Martinsville City	14.6	13.7	10.6	11.0	11.2	8.1	55.0	-1 987	-10.9	18 700	18 149	600	3.3	1 700	1 300
Newport News City	21.6	13.9	8.6	7.0	5.9	3.4	51.0	25 142	17.4	161 700	144 903	16 800	11.6	18 400	7 000
Norfolk City	19.9	11.8	6.6	6.5	6.4	4.1	46.7	-5 750	-2.2	274 800	266 979	7 900	2.9	33 300	14 100
Norton City	15.4	14.8	9.9	9.5	8.2	5.9	54.0	-510	-10.7	4 700	4 757	-100	-1.3	400	300
Petersburg City	17.2	13.7	9.7	9.6	9.1	5.9	53.8	-2 669	-6.5	39 800	41 055	-1 200	-3.0	4 300	2 900
Poquoson City	13.7	19.2	14.4	8.4	4.6	3.8	50.2	2 279	26.1	10 100	8 726	1 400	16.3	600	300
Portsmouth City	17.9	13.2	8.7	8.5	8.7	5.1	52.4	-670	-0.6	111 000	104 577	6 400	6.1	12 100	6 700
Radford City	9.9	8.6	6.4	5.8	5.2	3.3	55.7	2 483	18.5	13 700	13 457	300	1.9	700	600
Richmond City	19.2	14.3	8.6	8.5	8.3	7.0	54.3	-16 158	-7.4	217 700	219 214	-1 500	-0.7	21 400	16 400
Roanoke City	17.8	14.7	9.1	9.4	9.5	7.6	53.7	-3 823	-3.8	101 900	100 220	1 700	1.7	8 900	7 600
Salem City	14.6	14.9	11.0	10.8	9.7	6.9	52.1	-202	-0.8	23 700	23 958	-200	-0.9	1 600	1 500

STATE County	Population–(cont'd)	Households, 1990					Births, 1988			Deaths, 1987				Marriages, 1984	
	Components of change, 1980-1986 (cont'd)				Percent					Number		Rate			
	Net migration	Number	Percent change, 1980–1990	Persons per house-hold	Female family house-holder[1]	One-person	Total	Rate[2]	Low birth weight[3] (Number)	Total	Infant[4]	Total[2]	Infant[5]	Number	Rate[2]
	29	30	31	32	33	34	35	36	37	38	39	40	41	42	43
VIRGINIA—Con.															
Northumberland	500	4 492	17.8	2.34	9.1	26.1	104	10.3	9	145	2	14.5	16.9	73	7.4
Nottoway	200	5 244	4.5	2.58	13.9	24.8	204	13.7	17	189	1	12.7	6.2	115	8.0
Orange	1 300	7 930	26.8	2.67	9.7	20.0	278	13.2	16	217	2	10.5	7.2	163	8.6
Page	200	8 055	16.3	2.67	9.4	20.6	282	13.8	13	210	2	10.4	7.7	211	10.7
Patrick	-200	6 908	11.1	2.50	8.5	21.8	170	9.7	14	156	2	8.9	10.2	173	9.8
Pittsylvania	-2 400	20 613	-6.9	2.68	10.7	19.4	[6]1 384	[6]12.8	[6]145	[6]1 243	[6]16	[6]11.5	[6]11.6	522	7.9
Powhatan	-400	4 672	30.5	2.84	8.0	13.5	176	12.3	5	83	0	6.0	0.0	111	8.3
Prince Edward	700	5 373	8.8	2.59	14.5	26.7	212	12.4	23	181	3	10.6	13.2	129	7.6
Prince George	-1 100	8 250	26.8	2.93	10.1	13.5	[7]729	[7]14.6	[7]57	[7]358	[7]8	[7]7.2	[7]11.1	227	8.7
Prince William	14 500	69 709	59.2	3.04	8.4	13.2	[8]4 542	[8]19.9	[8]267	[8]746	[8]36	[8]3.5	[8]8.1	1 232	7.5
Pulaski	-1 600	13 349	7.8	2.51	11.1	22.9	412	11.7	30	339	4	9.7	10.9	360	10.3
Rappahannock	100	2 496	16.4	2.65	7.1	19.7	104	15.8	9	58	2	8.9	26.3	75	12.3
Richmond	300	2 645	9.1	2.62	11.3	23.4	90	12.7	10	83	1	11.9	11.5	46	6.6
Roanoke	400	30 355	20.3	2.54	8.4	21.2	[9]2 566	[9]26.1	[9]186	[9]2 165	[9]20	[9]22.1	[9]8.1	649	8.8
Rockbridge	-400	7 202	13.9	2.52	9.5	21.3	[10]355	[10]11.5	[10]21	[10]331	[10]2	[10]10.7	[10]6.3	131	7.3
Rockingham	200	20 750	8.8	2.69	7.3	19.0	[11]1 086	[11]13.4	[11]60	[11]704	[11]6	[11]8.8	[11]5.6	585	11.0
Russell	-500	10 641	0.1	2.66	9.6	19.2	315	9.9	16	256	4	7.9	11.7	451	13.9
Scott	300	8 966	2.5	2.57	9.8	21.0	239	9.5	16	246	2	9.8	7.9	675	26.5
Shenandoah	600	12 452	24.1	2.50	8.9	23.2	367	12.4	18	308	4	10.5	10.6	324	11.6
Smyth	-600	12 234	7.1	2.55	11.3	21.5	378	11.6	33	352	2	10.7	5.4	380	11.4
Southampton	-700	6 009	4.1	2.69	12.0	22.1	[12]373	[12]14.6	[12]34	[12]297	[12]5	[12]11.7	[12]14.2	146	7.8
Spotsylvania	5 000	18 945	74.4	3.01	7.9	13.2	[13]1 311	[13]20.5	[13]102	[13]512	[13]16	[13]8.4	[13]15.6	292	8.2
Stafford	7 000	19 415	59.5	3.05	7.3	12.2	832	14.1	45	259	9	4.7	11.6	331	7.0
Surry	100	2 283	13.6	2.69	13.4	22.6	84	12.9	5	72	1	11.2	9.7	47	7.5
Sussex	-1 000	3 795	6.2	2.65	17.3	24.0	167	15.8	24	126	3	11.9	17.4	71	6.8
Tazewell	-1 400	17 309	1.3	2.62	10.7	21.3	540	11.1	41	440	7	8.9	12.4	668	13.1
Warren	1 500	9 879	27.4	2.60	8.9	22.1	391	15.6	18	239	3	9.8	7.6	257	11.5
Washington	200	17 483	10.2	2.55	8.8	21.1	[14]703	[14]10.9	[14]46	[14]718	[14]2	[14]11.1	[14]2.8	545	11.6
Westmoreland	300	6 057	20.1	2.55	12.3	23.9	222	14.6	18	192	0	12.7	0.0	104	7.3
Wise	-800	14 513	-1.5	2.67	12.1	20.9	[15]600	[15]12.7	[15]38	[15]461	[15]5	[15]9.6	[15]8.9	848	18.8
Wythe	-300	9 852	9.4	2.55	10.4	22.9	283	10.9	19	282	3	10.9	10.5	317	12.4
York	4 000	14 474	32.8	2.90	8.8	15.1	[16]472	[16]8.7	[16]27	[16]256	[16]3	[16]4.8	[16]6.7	271	7.0
Independent Cities															
Alexandria City	-100	53 280	8.7	2.04	9.1	42.0	2 071	19.1	144	875	20	8.1	9.9	2 713	25.2
Bedford City	500	2 475	7.7	2.28	16.2	31.0	(17)	(17)	(17)	(17)	(17)	(17)	(17)	29	4.7
Bristol City	-900	7 591	4.9	2.33	14.2	30.7	(14)	(14)	(14)	(14)	(14)	(14)	(14)	446	24.5
Buena Vista City	-400	2 404	6.0	2.53	14.4	23.7	(10)	(10)	(10)	(10)	(10)	(10)	(10)	75	11.4
Charlottesville City	0	16 009	3.9	2.37	12.9	30.6	(18)	(18)	(18)	(18)	(18)	(18)	(18)	574	14.1
Chesapeake City	12 300	51 965	42.8	2.87	12.7	16.1	2 626	17.8	200	1 005	21	7.1	8.5	953	7.6
Clifton Forge City	200	1 930	1.8	2.28	13.8	34.5	(19)	(19)	(19)	(19)	(19)	(19)	(19)	216	44.1
Colonial Heights City	-100	6 363	8.4	2.49	10.9	23.0	(20)	(20)	(20)	(20)	(20)	(20)	(20)	278	16.3
Covington City	-1 100	2 998	-14.6	2.32	12.0	30.4	(19)	(19)	(19)	(19)	(19)	(19)	(19)	241	30.5
Danville City	-900	21 712	24.0	2.38	17.3	30.2	(6)	(6)	(6)	(6)	(6)	(6)	(6)	594	13.3
Emporia City	-100	2 031	15.8	2.51	19.4	27.5	(21)	(21)	(21)	(21)	(21)	(21)	(21)	271	56.5
Fairfax City	-1 900	7 362	7.0	2.60	10.2	20.1	(22)	(22)	(22)	(22)	(22)	(22)	(22)	94	4.6
Falls Church City	0	4 195	-1.3	2.27	8.4	33.1	(22)	(22)	(22)	(22)	(22)	(22)	(22)	365	38.4
Franklin City	-300	3 006	16.2	2.57	21.2	25.1	(12)	(12)	(12)	(12)	(12)	(12)	(12)	83	11.7
Fredericksburg City	1 400	7 450	25.7	2.24	12.3	34.7	(13)	(13)	(13)	(13)	(13)	(13)	(13)	390	20.7
Galax City	400	2 750	4.8	2.32	14.1	29.8	(13)	(13)	(13)	(13)	(13)	(13)	(13)	87	13.0
Hampton City	-4 700	49 673	19.7	2.58	13.5	23.7	2 349	18.0	199	926	20	7.2	8.7	1 239	9.8
Harrisonburg City	2 100	10 310	73.1	2.40	10.2	28.2	(11)	(11)	(11)	(11)	(11)	(11)	(11)	183	7.0
Hopewell City	-500	9 014	6.0	2.53	16.3	24.9	(7)	(7)	(7)	(7)	(7)	(7)	(7)	259	10.8
Lexington City	-200	2 172	-0.3	2.18	9.5	36.4	(10)	(10)	(10)	(10)	(10)	(10)	(10)	118	17.1
Lynchburg City	400	25 143	5.0	2.39	15.6	30.5	(23)	(23)	(23)	(23)	(23)	(23)	(23)	743	11.0
Manassas City	2 800	9 481	87.8	2.88	9.2	17.0	(8)	(8)	(8)	(8)	(8)	(8)	(8)	540	29.5
Manassas Park City	-100	2 182	17.4	3.09	13.1	13.1	(8)	(8)	(8)	(8)	(8)	(8)	(8)	9	1.3
Martinsville City	200	6 839	3.1	2.35	17.4	31.4	(24)	(24)	(24)	(24)	(24)	(24)	(24)	348	18.9
Newport News City	5 400	63 952	24.6	2.59	15.1	23.7	3 378	21.1	256	1 261	52	8.0	16.4	2 045	13.2
Norfolk City	-11 300	89 478	1.9	2.55	16.1	26.8	[25]7 533	[25]19.1	[25]669	[25]3 361	[25]122	[25]8.5	[25]16.1	3 803	13.5
Norton City	-200	1 697	2.7	2.49	16.4	28.4	(15)	(15)	(15)	(15)	(15)	(15)	(15)	76	16.9
Petersburg City	-2 600	14 730	-1.3	2.46	23.0	30.3	(26)	(26)	(26)	(26)	(26)	(26)	(26)	563	14.0
Poquoson City	1 100	3 769	35.5	2.90	7.6	13.2	(16)	(16)	(16)	(16)	(16)	(16)	(16)	55	5.7
Portsmouth City	1 000	38 741	5.4	2.62	19.3	24.5	(25)	(25)	(25)	(25)	(25)	(25)	(25)	1 179	10.8
Radford City	100	5 207	31.7	2.48	8.8	25.2	(27)	(27)	(27)	(27)	(27)	(27)	(27)	126	9.4
Richmond City	-6 500	85 337	-0.5	2.25	19.8	35.9	NA	NA	NA	NA	NA	NA	NA	3 116	14.3
Roanoke City	500	41 030	2.5	2.30	15.7	32.3	NA	NA	NA	NA	NA	NA	NA	1 321	13.1
Salem City	-300	9 161	6.0	2.37	10.6	26.5	(9)	(9)	(9)	(9)	(9)	(9)	(9)	263	10.9

1. No spouse present. 2. Per 1,000 resident population estimated as of July 1 of the year shown. 3. Under 2,500 grams. 4. Deaths of infants under 1 year old. 5. Deaths of infants under 1 year old per 1,000 live births. 6. Danville included with Pittsylvania County. 7. Hopewell included with Prince George County. 8. Manassas and Manassas Park included with Prince William County. 9. Salem included with Roanoke County. 10. Buena Vista and Lexington included with Rockbridge County. 11. Harrisonburg included with Rockingham County. 12. Franklin included with Southhampton County. 13. Galax included with Grayson County. 14. Bristol included with Washington County. 15. Norton included with Wise County. 16. Poquoson included with York County. 17. Bedford City included with Bedford County. 18. Charlottesville included with Albemarle county. 19. Clifton Forge and Covington included with Allegheny County. 20. Colonial Heights included with Chesterfield County. 21. Emporia included with Greensville County. 22. Fairfax City and Falls Church included with Fairfax County. 23. Lynchburg included with Campbell County. 24. Martinsville included with Henry County. 25. Portsmouth City included with Norfolk City. 26. Petersburg included with Dinwiddie County. 27. Radford included with Montgomery County.

STATE County	Divorces, 1984 Number	Divorces, 1984 Rate[1]	Physicians, active non-Federal, 1989 Number[2]	Physicians, active non-Federal, 1989 Rate[3]	Hospitals, 1989 Number	Hospitals, 1989 Beds Number	Hospitals, 1989 Beds Rate[3]	Nursing homes,[4] 1986 Number	Nursing homes,[4] 1986 Beds	Serious crimes known to police, 1988 Number Total[5]	Serious crimes known to police, 1988 Number Violent[6]	Serious crimes known to police, 1988 Rate[3]	Education Public school enrollment[7] 1986–1987	Education Public school enrollment[7] 1980	Education Attainment,[8] 1980 Percent 12 yrs. or more	Education Attainment,[8] 1980 Percent 16 yrs. or more
	44	45	46	47	48	49	50	51	52	53	54	55	56	57	58	59
VIRGINIA—Con.																
Northumberland	24	2.4	8	79	0	0	0	0	0	194	7	1 891	1 364	1 653	46.9	10.5
Nottoway	46	3.2	25	169	1	210	1 419	3	246	345	45	2 265	2 495	2 855	38.9	8.8
Orange	70	3.7	19	88	0	0	0	6	256	329	24	1 596	3 634	3 791	50.4	11.2
Page	87	4.4	9	44	1	34	165	6	213	247	39	1 198	3 367	3 699	40.9	6.1
Patrick	64	3.6	12	69	1	71	408	1	120	338	27	1 880	2 937	3 920	39.8	6.0
Pittsylvania	219	3.3	[9]133	[9]125	[9]1	[9]391	[9]366	1	56	906	69	1 370	11 454	14 235	37.8	5.7
Powhatan	56	4.2	7	48	0	0	0	0	0	143	7	1 043	2 091	2 895	52.2	8.8
Prince Edward	45	2.7	27	159	1	101	594	3	250	355	24	1 986	2 353	2 595	46.6	15.1
Prince George	122	4.7	[10]50	[10]100	[10]2	[10]186	[10]373			526	31	1 992	4 852	5 520	67.9	14.6
Prince William	926	5.6	[11]186	[11]78	[11]2	[11]328	[11]137	3	438	7 728	434	4 120	37 576	37 113	81.9	22.9
Pulaski	162	4.6	31	89	1	153	437	4	309	1 139	61	3 289	6 415	7 884	46.7	8.8
Rappahannock	21	3.4	6	90	0	0	0	0	0	98	14	1 508	917	1 202	46.7	11.2
Richmond	27	3.9	2	28	0	0	0	1	180	74	7	959	1 283	1 407	42.8	9.1
Roanoke	389	5.3	[12]604	[12]614	[12]8	[12]2 422	[12]2 461	5	1 128	2 201	128	2 874	13 613	15 611	70.0	17.7
Rockbridge	92	5.1	[13]30	[13]97	[13]1	[13]130	[13]422	2	110	508	11	2 779	2 744	3 780	48.4	12.3
Rockingham	270	5.1	[14]118	[14]145	[14]2	[14]279	[14]343	5	358	445	29	795	9 146	10 539	53.0	11.7
Russell	113	3.5	14	44	1	78	248	1	39	241	6	746	5 993	7 267	39.1	5.9
Scott	91	3.6	6	24	0	0	0	2	150	281	18	1 098	4 535	5 374	36.7	4.9
Shenandoah	107	3.8	23	76	1	132	439	11	365	414	25	1 401	4 705	5 337	49.9	8.9
Smyth	132	4.0	48	148	2	440	1 358	7	436	392	32	1 170	6 056	7 010	37.4	7.3
Southampton	81	4.4	[15]32	[15]125	[15]1	[15]214	[15]839	1	19	309	33	1 690	2 496	3 732	38.6	8.8
Spotsylvania	183	5.1	[16]134	[16]201	[16]1	[16]299	[16]449	1	177	1 874	44	4 545	9 613	8 842	58.2	12.9
Stafford	220	4.7	5	8	0	0	0	3	194	1 006	45	1 862	10 628	9 824	65.2	15.0
Surry	23	3.7	1	15	0	0	0	1	10	107	15	1 646	1 187	1 292	39.5	7.2
Sussex	42	4.0	3	28	0	0	0	0	0	233	40	2 206	1 744	2 398	37.1	8.1
Tazewell	204	4.0	93	195	3	332	695	2	360	687	81	1 369	9 790	11 191	43.9	7.6
Warren	110	4.9	27	105	1	112	438	4	82	887	41	3 579	3 880	4 146	54.0	9.4
Washington	181	3.9	[17]62	[17]97	[17]1	[17]154	[17]240	17	547	774	47	1 608	8 124	9 729	44.3	9.7
Westmoreland	36	2.5	7	45	0	0	0	1	20	341	30	2 254	2 410	2 860	44.5	8.8
Wise	258	5.7	[18]83	[18]178	[18]4	[18]389	[18]837	2	242	647	48	1 451	9 396	9 842	40.8	7.5
Wythe	100	3.9	26	100	1	106	409	4	207	483	32	1 858	4 645	5 535	45.3	8.6
York	196	5.0	[19]41	[19]73	(19)	(19)	(19)	1	8	1 359	96	3 256	8 792	9 037	76.0	21.6
Independent Cities																
Alexandria City	536	5.0	616	571	3	647	600	5	538	7 498	750	6 842	9 738	11 364	83.0	40.9
Bedford City	NA	NA	(20)	(20)	(20)	(20)	(20)	4	190	114	8	1 810	NA	980	52.6	13.2
Bristol City	99	5.4	(17)	(17)	(17)	(17)	(17)	2	160	876	44	4 792	2 990	3 524	51.0	9.7
Buena Vista City	34	5.2	(13)	(13)	(13)	(13)	(13)	1	3	109	5	1 677	1 291	1 397	43.4	7.1
Charlottesville City	165	4.1	(21)	(21)	(21)	(21)	(21)	7	481	3 491	234	8 363	4 379	5 370	65.1	31.0
Chesapeake City	617	4.9	179	117	1	210	137	16	904	7 016	538	4 882	26 348	26 301	60.7	11.5
Clifton Forge City	21	4.3	(22)	(22)	(22)	(22)	(22)			158	6	3 050	NA	875	52.7	10.3
Colonial Heights City	83	4.9	(23)	(23)	(23)	(23)	(23)	1	136	502	25	2 857	2 838	3 670	67.0	16.1
Covington City	NA	NA	(22)	(22)	(22)	(22)	(22)	2	69	181	20	2 315	1 158	1 767	48.5	5.1
Danville City	241	5.4	(9)	(9)	(9)	(9)	(9)	8	659	1 829	85	4 084	7 140	7 908	47.5	10.5
Emporia City	NA	NA	(24)	(24)	(24)	(24)	(24)	1	130	494	36	10 574	0	933	35.5	7.9
Fairfax City	NA	NA	(25)	(25)	(25)	(25)	(25)	2	204	1 702	52	8 215	NA	3 625	85.6	33.5
Falls Church City	NA	NA	(25)	(25)	(25)	(25)	(25)			592	42	5 948	1 130	1 056	86.1	44.9
Franklin City	NA	NA	(15)	(15)	(15)	(15)	(15)	2	127	418	24	5 276	1 879	1 621	41.6	10.8
Fredericksburg City	94	5.0	(16)	(16)	(16)	(16)	(16)	2	94	1 087	68	5 168	2 221	2 131	59.5	22.2
Galax City	NA	NA	(16)	(16)	(16)	(16)	(16)	2	255	139	3	2 043	1 207	1 066	38.2	7.5
Hampton City	578	4.6	168	127	4	980	742	5	336	7 239	455	5 569	20 490	25 592	67.5	15.4
Harrisonburg City	NA	NA	(14)	(14)	(14)	(14)	(14)	3	397	1 545	35	5 593	2 885	2 275	63.5	23.3
Hopewell City	121	5.0	(10)	(10)	(10)	(10)	(10)	2	254	1 435	124	5 839	4 006	4 712	54.8	9.9
Lexington City	NA	NA	(13)	(13)	(13)	(13)	(13)	1	38	221	9	3 200	729	789	67.4	28.7
Lynchburg City	291	4.3	(26)	(26)	(26)	(26)	(26)	12	1 070	3 587	356	5 295	9 515	10 685	58.9	18.7
Manassas City	NA	NA	(11)	(11)	(11)	(11)	(11)			1 136	35	5 276	3 987	3 324	79.2	23.6
Manassas Park City	NA	NA	(11)	(11)	(11)	(11)	(11)			245	18	3 351	1 403	1 670	59.1	5.3
Martinsville City	72	3.9	(27)	(27)	(27)	(27)	(27)	2	343	1 287	138	7 001	3 109	3 443	53.0	15.0
Newport News City	861	5.6	335	209	6	928	580	9	1 225	9 182	878	5 553	26 485	27 049	67.0	16.2
Norfolk City	1 192	4.2	[28]1 043	[28]264	[28]14	[28]3 134	[28]793	13	1 116	22 635	2 211	7 937	35 117	39 051	61.7	12.5
Norton City	NA	NA	(18)	(18)	(18)	(18)	(18)			184	14	4 026	994	1 024	46.2	10.4
Petersburg City	167	4.1	(29)	(29)	(29)	(29)	(29)	9	493	3 560	472	8 488	6 334	8 374	50.7	12.7
Poquoson City	NA	NA	(19)	(19)	(19)	(19)	(19)			257	20	2 322	2 375	2 280	69.0	20.6
Portsmouth City	480	4.4	(28)	(28)	(28)	(28)	(28)	7	571	8 992	915	8 042	18 797	19 827	54.6	9.9
Radford City	35	2.6	(30)	(30)	(30)	(30)	(30)			500	5	3 594	1 610	1 892	61.1	21.2
Richmond City	1 010	4.6	NA	NA	NA	NA	NA	65	3 263	20 895	2 604	9 499	27 157	31 899	57.1	19.8
Roanoke City	488	4.9	NA	NA	NA	NA	NA	14	1 113	8 376	500	8 239	13 879	16 668	57.5	12.5
Salem City	136	5.6	(12)	(12)	(12)	(12)	(12)	1	45	956	20	3 955	3 441	4 192	61.2	15.4

1. Per 1,000 resident population estimated as of July 1 of the year shown. 2. As of end of year. 3. Per 100,000 resident population as of July 1 of the year shown. 4. Preliminary. Covers nursing homes with 3 or more beds. 5. Data for serious crimes have not been adjusted for underreporting, this may affect comparability between geographic areas or over time. 6. Includes murder and nonnegligent manslaughter, forcible rape, robbery, and aggravated assault. 7. The 1986–1987 data are based on administrative reports obtained by the U.S. National Center for Education Statistics. The 1980 data are based on the 1980 Census of Population and Housing. 8. Persons 25 years old or older. 9. Danville included with Pittsylvania County. 10. Hopewell included with Prince George County. 11. Manassas and Manassas Park included with Prince William County. 12. Salem included with Roanoke County. 13. Buena Vista and Lexington included with Rockbridge County. 14. Harrisonburg included with Rockingham County. 15. Franklin included with Southhampton County. 16. Galax included with Grayson County. 17. Bristol included with Washington County. 18. Norton included with Wise County. 19. Poquoson included with York County. 20. Bedford City included with Bedford County. 21. Charlottesville included with Albemarle county. 22. Clifton Forge and Covington included with Allegheny County. 23. Colonial Heights included with Chesterfield County. 24. Emporia included with Greensville County. 25. Fairfax City and Falls Church included with Fairfax County. 26. Lynchburg included with Campbell County. 27. Martinsville included with Henry County. 28. Portsmouth City included with Norfolk City. 29. Petersburg included with Dinwiddie County. 30. Radford included with Montgomery County.

STATE County	Education (cont'd): Local government expenditures for education,[1] 1982: Total (Mil dol)	Education (cont'd): Local government expenditures for education,[1] 1982: Per capita (Dollars)	Social Security Program December 1988: Beneficiaries: Total	Social Security Program December 1988: Beneficiaries: Rate[2]	Social Security Program December 1988: Payments ($1,000)	Supplemental Security Income Program recipients June 1986	Money income: Per capita[3]: 1987 Income, (Dollars)	Money income: Per capita[3]: 1979: Current dollars	Money income: Per capita[3]: 1979: Constant 1987 dollars	Money income: Median household income 1979 (Dollars)	Money income: Percent below poverty level, 1979: Persons	Money income: Percent below poverty level, 1979: Families	Housing units, 1990: Total	Housing units, 1990: Percent change, 1980–1990
	60	61	62	63	64	65	66	67	68	69	70	71	72	73
VIRGINIA—Con.														
Northumberland	3.5	357	2 740	271.3	1 229	194	13 890	7 075	11 070	13 589	11.6	7.8	6 841	22.5
Nottoway	5.2	359	3 090	207.4	1 266	486	10 115	5 489	8 589	13 426	18.0	13.3	5 732	2.0
Orange	7.8	417	4 405	208.8	1 960	442	11 236	5 824	9 113	13 719	15.1	11.5	9 038	22.8
Page	8.6	443	3 890	189.8	1 653	458	10 517	5 391	8 435	12 646	14.9	11.3	8 948	7.4
Patrick	6.4	363	3 610	205.1	1 421	464	10 797	5 561	8 701	13 015	13.1	10.9	8 125	15.2
Pittsylvania	22.5	339	22 355	206.8	3 810	1 850	10 913	5 643	8 830	14 177	15.1	11.9	22 861	-5.7
Powhatan	4.3	330	1 595	111.5	743	122	12 110	5 836	9 132	19 507	10.8	7.7	4 910	27.9
Prince Edward	6.5	389	3 485	203.8	1 488	490	8 969	4 797	7 506	12 295	21.5	17.8	6 075	9.5
Prince George	11.4	442	5 725	114.5	706	170	10 306	5 715	8 942	17 453	9.5	8.1	8 640	24.4
Prince William	82.4	526	10 545	46.1	2 912	614	14 949	8 211	12 848	25 435	4.9	4.1	74 759	60.8
Pulaski	12.5	354	6 295	179.3	2 834	790	10 771	5 822	9 110	14 482	11.0	8.5	14 740	7.3
Rappahannock	2.0	345	1 140	172.7	465	140	12 247	6 226	9 742	14 583	14.3	11.0	2 964	9.6
Richmond	4.8	680	1 670	235.2	718	186	10 787	5 779	9 042	13 946	15.4	11.8	3 179	5.7
Roanoke	42.8	580	10 775	109.4	2 594	506	13 996	8 088	12 655	20 458	5.8	4.2	31 689	18.2
Rockbridge	7.1	400	5 950	191.9	1 124	346	10 650	5 524	8 643	13 522	14.7	11.6	7 975	11.9
Rockingham	20.5	388	12 915	158.9	3 794	790	12 143	6 090	9 529	15 505	10.7	7.7	22 614	8.4
Russell	12.9	399	5 780	181.8	2 248	954	8 829	5 338	8 352	13 787	14.8	13.5	11 558	0.3
Scott	9.2	364	5 320	212.0	2 062	1 160	8 260	4 649	7 274	10 851	22.2	19.6	10 003	2.3
Shenandoah	10.0	361	6 285	211.6	2 804	436	11 506	5 849	9 152	13 483	12.3	9.4	15 160	26.3
Smyth	11.1	332	6 790	207.6	2 855	1 088	10 133	5 271	8 248	12 577	13.7	10.7	13 132	6.7
Southampton	6.7	358	8 580	335.2	1 066	598	10 416	5 008	7 836	13 891	23.2	19.1	6 560	4.9
Spotsylvania	17.4	517	8 775	136.9	1 614	262	12 083	6 698	10 480	19 222	9.9	8.0	20 483	72.9
Stafford	21.7	492	3 680	62.4	1 626	240	13 594	7 321	11 455	21 667	6.6	4.9	20 529	54.7
Surry	3.9	635	1 095	168.5	460	124	10 847	5 515	8 629	13 373	22.5	17.0	2 982	9.5
Sussex	4.8	460	2 270	214.2	934	446	9 608	5 176	8 099	12 842	19.9	15.7	4 252	7.4
Tazewell	19.2	371	10 490	215.4	4 504	1 056	8 735	5 786	9 053	14 667	14.3	12.2	18 901	3.4
Warren	7.9	364	4 005	160.2	1 910	312	11 099	6 326	9 898	14 921	10.7	8.1	11 223	17.9
Washington	18.0	383	12 925	200.1	3 149	1 410	10 566	5 743	8 986	13 136	15.1	12.2	19 183	7.3
Westmoreland	6.1	438	3 465	228.0	1 472	258	10 849	5 851	9 155	13 361	18.8	13.4	8 378	12.1
Wise	19.0	428	10 475	221.0	3 804	1 256	8 817	5 725	8 958	14 810	15.4	12.5	15 927	1.7
Wythe	8.8	342	5 540	213.9	2 357	762	10 466	5 579	8 729	13 142	13.8	10.7	10 659	8.4
York	18.8	510	3 695	67.8	1 235	160	13 422	7 260	11 360	20 916	6.6	5.0	15 284	33.8
Independent Cities														
Alexandria City	45.1	431	21 595	199.2	10 360	1 128	22 200	12 177	19 053	21 016	9.0	6.8	58 252	11.9
Bedford City	0.0	0	0	0.0	3 024	80	10 187	6 120	9 576	12 495	15.2	12.2	2 625	0.7
Bristol City	7.3	388	0	0.0	2 375	688	10 693	6 212	9 720	13 284	16.1	12.6	8 174	5.6
Buena Vista City	2.6	384	0	0.0	665	162	8 793	5 337	8 351	14 321	9.0	6.4	2 494	3.7
Charlottesville City	16.5	408	0	0.0	3 760	742	12 591	6 935	10 851	13 942	21.0	7.5	16 785	4.9
Chesapeake City	55.9	467	15 115	102.3	6 508	1 498	11 761	6 646	10 399	18 831	11.2	9.2	55 742	46.5
Clifton Forge City	3.0	633	0	0.0	542	132	10 146	6 102	9 548	13 373	15.5	10.6	2 131	3.2
Colonial Heights City	8.2	481	0	0.0	1 523	120	13 590	7 981	12 488	21 078	4.3	3.7	6 592	8.5
Covington City	3.5	421	0	0.0	1 690	178	10 278	6 021	9 421	13 671	12.4	9.0	3 269	-12.5
Danville City	16.1	359	0	0.0	5 940	1 582	10 599	6 508	10 183	13 717	13.8	9.9	23 297	26.6
Emporia City	0.0	0	0	0.0	852	382	9 964	5 712	8 938	12 069	17.2	13.9	2 178	11.6
Fairfax City	0.1	6	0	0.0	14 309	296	19 251	10 385	16 249	25 810	4.9	3.4	7 677	8.9
Falls Church City	4.8	506	0	0.0	3 731	560	23 169	12 885	20 161	24 517	4.2	2.7	4 668	3.7
Franklin City	3.7	534	0	0.0	2 537	468	10 595	6 164	9 645	13 459	22.1	18.6	3 166	17.8
Fredericksburg City	8.0	443	0	0.0	2 456	340	12 485	7 056	11 041	14 262	11.8	8.1	8 063	27.0
Galax City	2.8	436	0	0.0	1 203	268	11 779	6 624	10 365	11 224	15.4	11.3	2 943	4.7
Hampton City	44.3	354	15 150	115.8	7 003	1 076	11 826	6 786	10 618	16 971	11.7	10.2	53 623	22.8
Harrisonburg City	6.5	256	0	0.0	2 094	260	10 649	6 108	9 557	13 884	16.4	6.8	10 900	76.7
Hopewell City	10.1	418	0	0.0	2 038	374	10 289	6 478	10 136	16 317	12.5	10.6	9 625	3.6
Lexington City	1.7	242	0	0.0	942	208	10 338	5 574	8 722	12 248	18.5	10.9	2 311	-3.3
Lynchburg City	25.5	378	0	0.0	7 360	1 448	11 695	6 896	10 790	15 312	13.1	9.6	27 233	7.1
Manassas City	7.8	455	0	0.0	X	230	16 051	8 562	13 397	24 703	7.7	6.1	10 232	85.7
Manassas Park City	3.3	513	0	0.0	X	NA	11 160	6 081	9 515	20 662	8.1	7.5	2 252	16.6
Martinsville City	7.1	389	0	0.0	0	436	12 205	6 789	10 623	14 527	13.3	10.4	7 310	3.3
Newport News City	63.4	420	19 530	122.0	9 322	2 108	11 396	6 856	10 728	15 974	13.5	11.1	69 728	26.8
Norfolk City	90.7	339	32 500	113.4	14 434	4 724	10 070	6 113	9 565	12 509	20.7	16.8	98 762	4.1
Norton City	2.0	426	0	0.0	547	162	9 633	6 250	9 779	13 120	18.8	14.3	1 845	0.3
Petersburg City	16.6	412	0	0.0	4 017	1 446	10 330	6 358	9 948	13 434	20.3	15.1	16 196	0.4
Poquoson City	3.9	407	0	0.0	452	24	13 884	7 870	12 314	23 963	5.1	3.8	3 890	31.7
Portsmouth City	38.3	361	16 840	156.7	6 781	2 482	9 809	6 104	9 551	14 195	19.2	15.8	42 283	9.5
Radford City	3.6	271	0	0.0	1 205	176	10 590	5 867	9 180	14 434	14.0	7.1	5 496	32.1
Richmond City	99.4	455	52 440	245.9	26 523	6 180	12 205	7 073	11 067	13 606	19.3	15.0	94 141	2.9
Roanoke City	35.5	353	24 055	246.2	11 433	2 406	11 600	6 816	10 665	13 271	16.3	12.4	44 384	4.0
Salem City	0.0	0	0	0.0	2 582	306	14 036	7 590	11 876	16 072	7.7	6.0	9 609	6.6

1. Elementary and secondary. 2. Per 1,000 resident population estimated as of July 1 of the year shown. 3. Based on the resident population estimated as of July 1, 1988 for 1987 data and enumerated as of April 1, 1980 for 1979 data.

STATE County	Housing units, 1990 (cont'd): Occupied units: Total	Owner occupied: Percent	Owner occupied: Median value (Dollars)	Median rent (Dollars)	Civilian labor force, 1990: Total	Percent change, 1989–1990	Unemployment: Total	Unemployment: Rate[1]	Private nonfarm establishments, 1988: Number	Net change, 1987–1988	Employment[2]: Total	Per-cent change, 1987–1988	Manu-facturing	Retail trade
	74	75	76	77	78	79	80	81	82	83	84	85	86	87
VIRGINIA—Con.														
Northumberland	4 492	87.1	80 300	224	4 356	-2.4	411	9.4	246	18	1 588	6.4	480	302
Nottoway	5 244	73.1	43 000	194	7 066	4.8	378	5.3	311	-1	3 121	11.5	877	864
Orange	7 930	76.3	83 200	321	9 950	6.7	559	5.6	486	41	5 762	14.6	2 667	981
Page	8 055	76.9	61 500	243	10 534	4.4	1 103	10.5	462	8	5 170	8.8	1 926	1 025
Patrick	6 908	81.5	51 700	174	9 264	1.6	491	5.3	306	9	4 107	-2.0	2 174	576
Pittsylvania	20 613	79.6	48 800	186	26 821	0.7	2 014	7.5	669	5	8 152	2.8	4 526	1 139
Powhatan	4 672	85.1	74 700	331	5 824	1.9	210	3.6	231	18	1 173	2.2	132	312
Prince Edward	5 373	70.9	54 200	221	7 677	7.7	666	8.7	455	3	5 339	2.2	957	1 644
Prince George	8 250	68.8	75 800	388	6 814	0.8	416	6.1	182	0	2 377	-3.5	0	1 007
Prince William	69 709	71.0	138 500	637	110 204	1.6	2 865	2.6	3 310	163	42 693	13.7	3 273	14 831
Pulaski	13 349	73.0	51 400	228	19 204	2.8	1 854	9.7	588	10	10 282	7.4	6 066	1 492
Rappahannock	2 496	72.2	89 300	345	3 099	14.9	187	6.0	136	6	852	4.9	302	165
Richmond	2 645	81.5	63 100	215	3 649	1.9	224	6.1	199	-6	1 968	-0.2	505	464
Roanoke	30 355	77.3	80 500	369	43 163	1.4	1 220	2.8	1 367	58	18 019	2.2	2 244	3 834
Rockbridge	7 202	74.9	54 700	234	9 297	3.9	418	4.5	312	1	4 606	2.2	2 248	667
Rockingham	20 750	78.2	71 800	281	35 706	5.1	1 650	4.6	954	39	13 582	9.9	7 018	1 395
Russell	10 641	80.2	45 000	182	11 782	-0.6	1 076	9.1	454	-6	5 312	1.0	1 505	951
Scott	8 966	77.8	41 400	171	10 441	1.8	577	5.5	335	15	3 169	5.5	912	921
Shenandoah	12 452	71.5	73 600	270	17 879	1.9	900	5.0	736	37	10 132	-1.7	4 517	1 985
Smyth	12 234	74.3	42 600	196	17 304	4.7	1 338	7.7	622	7	9 732	-1.9	5 429	1 638
Southampton	6 009	71.5	57 000	140	6 444	3.6	365	5.7	212	-11	3 895	4.2	2 875	320
Spotsylvania	18 945	81.9	104 000	565	23 224	8.5	1 348	5.8	388	28	3 877	16.3	362	1 531
Stafford	19 415	81.9	125 400	538	31 792	2.5	1 100	3.5	876	41	9 233	13.2	809	2 511
Surry	2 283	76.5	59 400	220	2 761	-5.2	191	6.9	77	0	1 684	5.4	241	201
Sussex	3 795	69.3	48 200	185	5 744	7.1	329	5.7	218	12	2 064	-10.3	786	528
Tazewell	17 309	77.0	48 600	209	19 616	2.5	1 345	6.9	1 102	9	10 934	0.9	1 522	3 037
Warren	9 879	72.3	85 100	328	11 381	-9.3	912	8.0	624	57	7 027	5.8	2 381	1 665
Washington	17 483	77.1	52 500	224	24 436	3.3	1 422	5.8	637	22	7 083	5.3	1 886	1 939
Westmoreland	6 057	79.3	68 800	309	6 012	7.7	478	8.0	314	14	2 346	1.0	957	535
Wise	14 513	76.4	43 500	211	15 665	0.3	1 231	7.9	900	18	9 237	-7.8	418	2 206
Wythe	9 852	77.1	48 900	213	14 471	-0.1	1 109	7.7	556	17	7 210	4.9	2 262	1 879
York	14 474	71.6	121 600	442	19 663	1.1	640	3.3	669	29	6 280	6.5	0	2 166
Independent Cities														
Alexandria City	53 280	40.5	228 600	667	80 759	1.6	2 407	3.0	3 886	74	69 848	2.0	3 203	15 909
Bedford City	2 475	62.3	55 700	191	2 922	3.2	93	3.2	579	31	6 221	7.9	2 344	1 126
Bristol City	7 591	63.1	48 400	232	9 301	2.4	522	5.6	807	9	14 917	6.0	7 689	2 882
Buena Vista City	2 404	72.2	43 300	194	3 324	3.6	247	7.4	116	4	1 820	-1.4	916	430
Charlottesville City	16 009	42.4	85 600	391	24 675	2.8	723	2.9	2 340	93	33 121	4.8	6 114	8 604
Chesapeake City	51 965	73.0	88 200	399	74 648	1.0	3 241	4.3	2 938	127	36 102	2.9	3 836	9 121
Clifton Forge City	1 930	62.0	35 200	173	1 965	1.6	129	6.6	130	0	1 074	14.7	0	302
Colonial Heights City	6 363	72.2	71 000	368	9 944	1.6	349	3.5	410	19	3 807	3.1	618	1 512
Covington City	2 998	69.2	38 700	197	3 443	-0.3	285	8.3	305	0	4 989	1.9	0	1 172
Danville City	21 712	59.4	47 000	195	25 986	0.8	2 007	7.7	1 524	-1	27 957	2.7	12 404	6 042
Emporia City	2 031	56.7	52 000	225	3 026	2.9	184	6.1	335	-1	4 242	-0.1	1 373	1 057
Fairfax City	7 362	65.9	184 300	729	14 770	1.0	268	1.8	1 809	93	29 380	7.1	3 590	7 876
Falls Church City	4 195	58.8	226 000	769	6 716	0.8	117	1.7	881	10	9 020	7.0	372	2 303
Franklin City	3 006	53.8	67 900	222	3 124	1.3	146	4.7	286	4	3 239	-2.6	378	1 062
Fredericksburg City	7 450	37.3	104 900	461	13 674	7.8	618	4.5	1 659	127	17 951	5.3	2 375	6 505
Galax City	2 750	68.3	45 200	187	3 349	2.5	256	7.6	321	2	9 045	12.0	5 807	1 471
Hampton City	49 673	59.2	78 200	385	60 841	1.1	3 428	5.6	2 426	10	37 658	3.3	3 480	14 193
Harrisonburg City	10 310	42.1	89 300	341	16 141	5.1	693	4.3	1 242	91	20 479	11.1	4 503	5 263
Hopewell City	9 014	56.9	54 300	288	11 833	1.0	720	6.1	494	-2	7 399	4.1	2 632	1 964
Lexington City	2 172	54.9	74 500	284	2 583	3.0	57	2.2	418	29	3 688	2.4	97	1 235
Lynchburg City	25 143	58.2	56 900	272	36 495	1.3	1 621	4.4	2 352	25	46 975	0.3	14 146	10 158
Manassas City	9 481	66.1	150 700	603	14 531	2.2	404	2.8	1 118	122	17 001	3.6	0	4 651
Manassas Park City	2 182	71.8	101 800	602	4 331	1.9	98	2.3	119	26	1 363	45.9	52	273
Martinsville City	6 839	60.7	52 700	255	8 900	3.2	861	9.7	723	-1	21 210	-1.2	12 919	3 101
Newport News City	63 952	50.0	85 200	368	76 894	1.1	4 185	5.4	3 569	33	74 141	3.8	30 836	12 933
Norfolk City	89 478	44.0	74 500	361	97 647	0.2	4 667	4.8	5 927	-5	112 793	0.4	15 997	23 234
Norton City	1 697	60.9	48 000	217	1 671	-0.1	115	6.9	252	14	3 331	9.2	0	754
Petersburg City	14 730	50.9	52 000	257	20 698	0.7	1 372	6.6	1 081	-36	13 226	-0.7	2 275	4 920
Poquoson City	3 769	82.7	113 700	475	5 748	1.4	202	3.5	160	0	956	10.9	72	329
Portsmouth City	38 741	55.9	67 400	327	50 801	0.6	3 256	6.4	1 883	-5	25 213	7.8	2 517	7 366
Radford City	5 207	47.8	64 500	339	6 821	2.9	565	8.3	353	-4	6 037	0.3	2 219	1 354
Richmond City	85 337	46.3	66 600	333	114 064	1.4	6 008	5.3	8 268	36	176 130	2.6	39 548	27 661
Roanoke City	41 030	56.6	54 000	278	53 427	1.0	2 261	4.2	4 007	77	69 740	1.3	10 728	15 809
Salem City	9 161	67.4	69 100	345	13 726	0.8	386	2.8	884	26	18 214	-3.7	6 213	3 166

1. Percent of total civilian labor force. 2. For week including March 12. Excludes government employees, self-employed persons, farm workers, domestic service workers, railroad employees subject to the Railroad Retirement Act, and employees on oceanborne vessels or in foreign countries.

STATE County	Private nonfarm establishments, 1988 (cont'd)				Personal income, 1989								Earnings, 1989		
	Employment[1] (cont'd)		Annual payroll								Per capita[3]			Percent by selected industries	
	Finance, insurance, and real estate	Services	Total (Mil dol)	Average per employee (Dollars)	Total (Mil dol)	Percent change, 1988–1989	Wages and salaries[2] (Mil dol)	Proprietor's income (Mil dol)	Dividends, interest, & rent (Mil dol)	Transfer payments (Mil dol)	Dollars	Rank	Total (Mil dol)	Farm	Goods-related[4] Total
	88	89	90	91	92	93	94	95	96	97	98	99	100	101	102
VIRGINIA—Con.															
Northumberland	123	224	27	16 823	180	8.9	41	18	62	42	17 890	310	59	8.0	38.7
Nottoway	122	719	39	12 342	217	8.2	121	15	41	42	14 707	1 123	136	3.8	15.3
Orange	114	966	92	15 983	348	8.7	131	36	68	54	16 099	620	166	4.5	43.5
Page	140	1 168	67	12 946	314	8.4	102	30	52	53	15 223	900	132	5.5	41.1
Patrick	118	633	59	14 349	253	6.5	85	20	35	37	14 543	1 193	105	4.8	50.0
Pittsylvania	109	1 015	130	16 000	[5]1 589	[5]7.4	[5]897	[5]115	[5]271	[5]263	[5]14 901	[5]1 026	(5)	[5]1.9	[5]48.2
Powhatan	63	146	18	15 010	246	9.5	63	19	30	20	16 739	479	81	6.7	27.5
Prince Edward	211	1 616	65	12 182	199	7.5	123	16	41	39	11 721	2 432	139	2.3	17.6
Prince George	61	625	31	13 227	[6]632	[6]6.3	[6]579	[6]35	[6]89	[6]113	[6]12 673	[6]2 046	(6)	[6]0.5	[6]27.5
Prince William	1 086	11 510	756	17 713	[7]4 855	[7]10.2	[7]2 032	[7]214	[7]377	[7]351	[7]20 278	[7]153	(7)	[7]0.1	[7]32.8
Pulaski	228	1 380	185	17 995	453	6.6	298	30	63	86	12 963	1 924	328	1.2	52.7
Rappahannock	21	153	12	14 257	119	8.5	18	13	31	15	17 648	344	31	14.1	29.6
Richmond	73	326	29	14 512	111	7.9	58	13	27	18	15 670	749	71	5.1	21.6
Roanoke	3 401	4 972	286	15 870	[8]1 906	[8]8.6	[8]1 099	[8]149	[8]395	[8]213	[8]19 378	[8]201	(8)	[8]0.2	[8]32.2
Rockbridge	62	422	71	15 410	[9]438	[9]9.4	[9]226	[9]37	[9]93	[9]82	[9]14 239	[9]1 307	(9)	[9]2.9	[9]34.9
Rockingham	330	2 267	225	16 532	[10]1 318	[10]9.0	[10]841	[10]149	[10]246	[10]174	[10]16 207	[10]593	(10)	[10]3.6	[10]37.9
Russell	176	840	97	18 259	352	5.1	145	29	44	79	11 161	2 618	174	5.6	36.1
Scott	122	555	50	15 722	260	6.9	71	21	40	59	10 446	2 801	93	8.0	31.8
Shenandoah	400	1 825	153	15 124	528	6.9	240	45	100	71	17 568	360	284	3.1	50.3
Smyth	205	1 434	150	15 426	431	9.6	254	44	60	76	13 285	1 778	299	2.7	51.1
Southampton	0	163	102	26 266	[11]332	[11]7.7	[11]139	[11]34	[11]72	[11]73	[11]13 030	[11]1 894	(11)	[11]10.4	[11]18.9
Spotsylvania	150	566	65	16 688	[12]1 176	[12]10.4	[12]626	[12]92	[12]172	[12]168	[12]17 647	[12]345	(12)	[12]0.3	[12]23.2
Stafford	233	1 912	161	17 403	1 205	12.4	234	55	103	95	19 267	206	289	0.8	28.9
Surry	19	156	50	29 879	107	9.9	105	8	17	15	16 347	560	113	3.2	NA
Sussex	79	202	34	16 542	144	5.9	48	16	27	25	13 596	1 634	64	10.0	31.8
Tazewell	533	2 629	188	17 202	628	7.6	285	58	102	126	13 141	1 844	343	2.1	27.1
Warren	289	1 644	108	15 427	398	6.7	156	28	65	57	15 528	793	184	1.1	39.8
Washington	266	1 900	113	15 895	[13]937	[13]8.6	[13]579	[13]85	[13]162	[13]178	[13]14 613	[13]1 159	(13)	[13]2.6	[13]38.4
Westmoreland	171	366	27	11 547	253	6.9	49	22	50	53	16 378	552	70	9.8	27.6
Wise	387	1 779	195	21 115	[14]638	[14]5.1	[14]409	[14]74	[14]81	[14]165	[14]13 734	[14]1 559	(14)	[14]0.2	[14]40.0
Wythe	238	1 506	104	14 491	342	7.6	175	28	59	59	13 208	1 808	203	4.1	32.3
York	210	1 338	99	15 770	[15]1 028	[15]7.1	[15]332	[15]48	[15]167	[15]122	[15]18 357	[15]261	(15)	[15]1.0	[15]21.8
Independent Cities															
Alexandria City	5 849	30 719	1 623	23 229	3 373	8.3	2 954	198	581	343	31 264	10	3 151	0.0	8.8
Bedford City	205	1 577	100	16 025	(16)	(16)	(16)	(16)	(16)	(16)	(16)	(16)	(16)	(16)	(16)
Bristol City	609	1 651	252	16 882	(13)	(13)	(13)	(13)	(13)	(13)	(13)	(13)	(13)	(13)	(13)
Buena Vista City	30	315	33	18 375	(9)	(9)	(9)	(9)	(9)	(9)	(9)	(9)	(9)	(9)	(9)
Charlottesville City	4 377	8 448	612	18 469	(17)	(17)	(17)	(17)	(17)	(17)	(17)	(17)	(17)	(17)	(17)
Chesapeake City	1 537	7 975	613	16 979	2 409	7.5	931	120	233	301	15 709	738	1 050	0.9	30.7
Clifton Forge City	73	366	16	15 230	(18)	(18)	(18)	(18)	(18)	(18)	(18)	(18)	(18)	(18)	(18)
Colonial Heights City	148	1 002	49	12 911	(19)	(19)	(19)	(19)	(19)	(19)	(19)	(19)	(19)	(19)	(19)
Covington City	154	438	110	22 141	(18)	(18)	(18)	(18)	(18)	(18)	(18)	(18)	(18)	(18)	(18)
Danville City	1 125	5 478	483	17 279	(5)	(5)	(5)	(5)	(5)	(5)	(5)	(5)	(5)	(5)	(5)
Emporia City	157	1 132	64	15 148	(20)	(20)	(20)	(20)	(20)	(20)	(20)	(20)	(20)	(20)	(20)
Fairfax City	2 753	10 258	745	25 357	(21)	(21)	(21)	(21)	(21)	(21)	(21)	(21)	(21)	(21)	(21)
Falls Church City	325	4 211	198	21 939	(21)	(21)	(21)	(21)	(21)	(21)	(21)	(21)	(21)	(21)	(21)
Franklin City	145	1 110	44	13 568	(11)	(11)	(11)	(11)	(11)	(11)	(11)	(11)	(11)	(11)	(11)
Fredericksburg City	1 201	3 992	301	16 779	(12)	(12)	(12)	(12)	(12)	(12)	(12)	(12)	(12)	(12)	(12)
Galax City	114	1 225	117	12 892	(22)	(22)	(22)	(22)	(22)	(22)	(22)	(22)	(22)	(22)	(22)
Hampton City	1 860	12 478	574	15 237	1 909	5.4	1 544	69	259	334	14 460	1 228	1 613	0.0	12.5
Harrisonburg City	935	5 815	323	15 755	(10)	(10)	(10)	(10)	(10)	(10)	(10)	(10)	(10)	(10)	(10)
Hopewell City	276	1 433	163	22 024	(6)	(6)	(6)	(6)	(6)	(6)	(6)	(6)	(6)	(6)	(6)
Lexington City	180	1 601	53	14 355	(9)	(9)	(9)	(9)	(9)	(9)	(9)	(9)	(9)	(9)	(9)
Lynchburg City	3 112	14 086	894	19 039	(23)	(23)	(23)	(23)	(23)	(23)	(23)	(23)	(23)	(23)	(23)
Manassas City	828	3 230	445	26 163	(7)	(7)	(7)	(7)	(7)	(7)	(7)	(7)	(7)	(7)	(7)
Manassas Park City	0	108	26	18 908	(7)	(7)	(7)	(7)	(7)	(7)	(7)	(7)	(7)	(7)	(7)
Martinsville City	700	2 627	342	16 115	(24)	(24)	(24)	(24)	(24)	(24)	(24)	(24)	(24)	(24)	(24)
Newport News City	3 871	17 447	1 515	20 429	2 517	5.6	2 240	118	356	378	15 721	733	2 358	0.0	44.0
Norfolk City	9 239	36 657	2 134	18 921	4 109	4.4	5 603	216	675	729	14 211	1 336	5 819	0.0	12.1
Norton City	135	922	57	17 200	(14)	(14)	(14)	(14)	(14)	(14)	(14)	(14)	(14)	(14)	(14)
Petersburg City	774	3 276	196	14 813	(19)	(19)	(19)	(19)	(19)	(19)	(19)	(19)	(19)	(19)	(19)
Poquoson City	36	204	13	13 771	(15)	(15)	(15)	(15)	(15)	(15)	(15)	(15)	(15)	(15)	(15)
Portsmouth City	1 177	8 950	379	15 013	1 533	5.9	1 346	59	220	349	14 448	1 234	1 404	0.0	8.7
Radford City	230	1 873	113	18 651	(25)	(25)	(25)	(25)	(25)	(25)	(25)	(25)	(25)	(25)	(25)
Richmond City	22 831	50 170	4 104	23 303	4 397	7.4	5 603	303	1 013	666	20 852	133	5 906	0.0	23.1
Roanoke City	5 137	19 163	1 251	17 945	1 693	7.8	1 626	135	351	286	17 607	354	1 761	0.0	20.8
Salem City	362	5 004	354	19 430	(8)	(8)	(8)	(8)	(8)	(8)	(8)	(8)	(8)	(8)	(8)

1. For week including March 12. Excludes government employees, self-employed persons, farm workers, domestic service workers, railroad employees subject to the Railroad Retirement Act, and employees on oceanborne vessels or in foreign countries. 2. Includes other labor income. 3. Based on the resident population estimated as of July 1 of the year shown. 4. Covers mining, construction, and manufacturing. 5. Danville included with Pittsylvania County. 6. Hopewell included with Prince George County. 7. Manassas and Manassas Park included with Prince William County. 8. Salem included with Roanoke County. 9. Buena Vista and Lexington included with Rockbridge County. 10. Harrisonburg included with Rockingham County. 11. Franklin included with Southhampton County. 12. Galax included with Grayson County. 13. Bristol included with Washington County. 14. Norton included with Wise County. 15. Poquoson included with York County. 16. Bedford City included with Bedford County. 17. Charlottesville included with Albemarle county. 18. Clifton Forge and Covington included with Allegheny County. 19. Petersburg and Colonial Heights included with Dinwiddie County. 20. Emporia included with Greensville County. 21. Fairfax City and Falls Church included with Fairfax County. 22. Galax included with Carroll County. 23. Lynchburg included with Campbell County. 24. Martinsville included with Henry County. 25. Radford included with Montgomery County.

STATE County	Earnings, 1989 (cont'd): Percent by selected industries (cont'd): Goods-related[1]: Manufacturing	Service-related & other[2]: Total	Service-related & other[2]: Retail trade	Service-related & other[2]: Finance, insurance, & real estate	Service-related & other[2]: Services	Government	Agriculture, 1987: Farms: Number	Farms: Percent with: Less than 50 acres	Farms: Percent with: 500 acres and over	Farm operators, percent: Whose principal occupation is farming	Farm operators, percent: Residing on farm operated	Land in farms: Acreage (1,000)	Land in farms: Percent change, 1982–1987	Acres: Average size of farm	Acres: Total irrigated (1,000)	Acres: Total cropland (1,000)
	103	104	105	106	107	108	109	110	111	112	113	114	115	116	117	118
VIRGINIA—Con.																
Northumberland	23.1	41.2	7.9	2.3	18.0	12.0	159	22.0	17.0	59.7	71.7	48	2.0	303	D	36
Nottoway	11.5	43.7	7.9	2.0	12.4	37.1	302	21.5	9.9	47.4	81.5	65	2.3	216	0	29
Orange	29.7	37.4	10.9	1.6	15.2	14.7	424	25.2	13.0	51.2	77.8	113	-4.6	267	0	60
Page	26.7	39.3	9.3	2.2	18.2	14.1	489	37.0	4.7	50.7	78.7	67	-4.3	138	0	39
Patrick	43.2	34.1	8.3	1.6	17.1	11.1	643	34.7	3.1	44.3	70.8	81	-17.3	126	0	32
Pittsylvania	[3]41.4	[3]38.3	[3]10.1	[3]2.7	[3]18.2	[3]11.6	1 583	21.7	7.6	54.5	70.4	301	-9.0	190	6	132
Powhatan	3.8	28.2	6.9	3.4	11.0	37.7	212	29.2	14.2	46.7	78.8	58	0.7	272	0	27
Prince Edward	10.0	56.2	16.9	3.3	27.5	23.9	353	22.7	8.8	48.7	72.8	71	-13.8	201	0	34
Prince George	[4]19.1	[4]21.1	[4]7.5	[4]1.0	[4]9.6	[4]50.9	167	25.1	15.0	47.9	77.2	41	-12.4	247	D	24
Prince William	[5]16.0	[5]42.0	[5]13.6	[5]2.8	[5]17.4	[5]25.0	272	42.3	4.8	37.1	80.5	37	-27.8	136	0	27
Pulaski	47.2	34.8	6.5	1.7	15.5	11.3	360	26.4	9.7	35.6	70.3	79	1.5	218	0	40
Rappahannock	10.0	40.2	13.3	1.4	20.4	16.1	288	29.2	14.2	43.1	74.0	77	-11.8	268	0	35
Richmond	13.5	57.4	10.6	3.0	14.0	15.8	148	18.9	11.5	53.4	74.3	39	-9.8	264	D	26
Roanoke	[6]24.7	[6]53.1	[6]9.9	[6]7.5	[6]22.9	[6]14.6	279	47.7	2.2	39.1	73.8	30	-11.1	107	0	14
Rockbridge	[7]29.1	[7]42.9	[7]10.4	[7]2.5	[7]23.5	[7]19.4	682	22.0	9.5	43.7	74.3	146	-7.4	215	0	64
Rockingham	[8]27.9	[8]45.1	[8]10.2	[8]2.4	[8]21.5	[8]13.4	1 895	38.0	3.4	56.2	76.8	242	-7.4	128	4	145
Russell	9.3	42.9	7.9	2.3	13.5	15.3	1 134	39.5	4.7	44.5	71.7	168	-8.9	148	0	52
Scott	25.6	38.4	12.2	5.2	13.1	21.8	1 667	46.0	1.1	37.1	63.0	143	-4.5	86	0	53
Shenandoah	42.3	36.6	10.1	2.8	14.5	10.0	830	30.6	5.7	46.3	73.6	139	-0.5	167	2	76
Smyth	44.8	30.6	8.5	1.8	14.4	15.6	873	44.0	5.0	41.6	70.2	123	-0.1	141	0	46
Southampton	[9]12.6	[9]44.2	[9]9.6	[9]3.4	[9]20.3	[9]26.5	407	18.4	32.4	69.5	61.4	189	-4.9	464	1	112
Spotsylvania	[10]9.8	[10]62.0	[10]19.1	[10]5.5	[10]25.5	[10]14.5	305	33.8	11.8	47.9	80.7	57	-4.3	188	1	31
Stafford	3.4	53.3	21.3	1.6	17.4	17.0	197	41.1	5.6	38.1	78.2	28	-2.2	141	0	15
Surry	1.5	NA	1.9	0.4	9.2	6.6	126	24.6	23.0	63.5	61.1	46	-17.2	365	1	33
Sussex	27.5	NA	13.8	1.7	10.6	19.0	196	13.3	27.6	73.0	66.3	81	-17.3	414	2	50
Tazewell	12.8	53.5	13.9	3.9	24.6	17.3	488	28.3	12.7	35.2	68.4	137	-3.5	281	0	45
Warren	23.5	45.8	12.4	3.6	22.2	13.2	223	26.5	7.6	37.2	64.6	41	-9.9	183	D	21
Washington	[11]33.7	[11]45.2	[11]11.1	[11]5.0	[11]16.7	[11]13.8	1 972	51.8	3.1	38.4	64.8	203	-5.9	103	0	90
Westmoreland	18.6	45.2	11.2	2.1	19.2	17.3	181	27.1	20.4	60.2	61.3	70	2.5	388	1	41
Wise	[12]2.6	[12]44.4	[12]9.2	[12]2.3	[12]19.7	[12]15.4	143	53.8	4.2	30.8	74.1	15	14.6	105	D	7
Wythe	23.8	45.6	12.9	2.7	21.0	17.9	746	28.0	8.3	46.2	74.3	143	-11.7	192	0	77
York	[13]7.9	[13]36.8	[13]8.8	[13]1.4	[13]16.5	[13]40.4	66	71.2	0.0	39.4	53.0	3	4.1	51	0	D
Independent Cities																
Alexandria City	3.0	65.0	9.5	6.9	38.3	26.1	NA	NA	NA	NA	NA	NA	NA	NA	NA	NA
Bedford City	(14)	(14)	(14)	(14)	(14)	(14)	NA	NA	NA	NA	NA	NA	NA	NA	NA	NA
Bristol City	(11)	(11)	(11)	(11)	(11)	(11)	NA	NA	NA	NA	NA	NA	NA	NA	NA	NA
Buena Vista City	(7)	(7)	(7)	(7)	(7)	(7)	NA	NA	NA	NA	NA	NA	NA	NA	NA	NA
Charlottesville City	(15)	(15)	(15)	(15)	(15)	(15)	NA	NA	NA	NA	NA	NA	NA	NA	NA	NA
Chesapeake City	11.4	46.3	10.8	3.5	17.8	22.1	223	55.2	16.6	51.6	67.7	53	-5.6	237	0	45
Clifton Forge City	(16)	(16)	(16)	(16)	(16)	(16)	NA	NA	NA	NA	NA	NA	NA	NA	NA	NA
Colonial Heights City	(17)	(17)	(17)	(17)	(17)	(17)	NA	NA	NA	NA	NA	NA	NA	NA	NA	NA
Covington City	(16)	(16)	(16)	(16)	(16)	(16)	NA	NA	NA	NA	NA	NA	NA	NA	NA	NA
Danville City	(3)	(3)	(3)	(3)	(3)	(3)	NA	NA	NA	NA	NA	NA	NA	NA	NA	NA
Emporia City	(18)	(18)	(18)	(18)	(18)	(18)	NA	NA	NA	NA	NA	NA	NA	NA	NA	NA
Fairfax City	(19)	(19)	(19)	(19)	(19)	(19)	NA	NA	NA	NA	NA	NA	NA	NA	NA	NA
Falls Church City	(19)	(19)	(19)	(19)	(19)	(19)	NA	NA	NA	NA	NA	NA	NA	NA	NA	NA
Franklin City	(9)	(9)	(9)	(9)	(9)	(9)	NA	NA	NA	NA	NA	NA	NA	NA	NA	NA
Fredericksburg City	(10)	(10)	(10)	(10)	(10)	(10)	NA	NA	NA	NA	NA	NA	NA	NA	NA	NA
Galax City	(20)	(20)	(20)	(20)	(20)	(20)	NA	NA	NA	NA	NA	NA	NA	NA	NA	NA
Hampton City	6.4	38.3	11.2	2.1	18.7	49.2	NA	NA	NA	NA	NA	NA	NA	NA	NA	NA
Harrisonburg City	(8)	(8)	(8)	(8)	(8)	(8)	NA	NA	NA	NA	NA	NA	NA	NA	NA	NA
Hopewell City	(4)	(4)	(4)	(4)	(4)	(4)	NA	NA	NA	NA	NA	NA	NA	NA	NA	NA
Lexington City	(7)	(7)	(7)	(7)	(7)	(7)	NA	NA	NA	NA	NA	NA	NA	NA	NA	NA
Lynchburg City	(21)	(21)	(21)	(21)	(21)	(21)	NA	NA	NA	NA	NA	NA	NA	NA	NA	NA
Manassas City	(5)	(5)	(5)	(5)	(5)	(5)	NA	NA	NA	NA	NA	NA	NA	NA	NA	NA
Manassas Park City	(5)	(5)	(5)	(5)	(5)	(5)	NA	NA	NA	NA	NA	NA	NA	NA	NA	NA
Martinsville City	(22)	(22)	(22)	(22)	(22)	(22)	NA	NA	NA	NA	NA	NA	NA	NA	NA	NA
Newport News City	39.2	33.2	6.6	3.0	18.3	22.9	NA	NA	NA	NA	NA	NA	NA	NA	NA	NA
Norfolk City	8.0	42.1	6.1	4.8	19.1	45.9	NA	NA	NA	NA	NA	NA	NA	NA	NA	NA
Norton City	(12)	(12)	(12)	(12)	(12)	(12)	NA	NA	NA	NA	NA	NA	NA	NA	NA	NA
Petersburg City	(17)	(17)	(17)	(17)	(17)	(17)	NA	NA	NA	NA	NA	NA	NA	NA	NA	NA
Poquoson City	(13)	(13)	(13)	(13)	(13)	(13)	NA	NA	NA	NA	NA	NA	NA	NA	NA	NA
Portsmouth City	5.7	33.0	6.6	1.6	15.9	58.3	NA	NA	NA	NA	NA	NA	NA	NA	NA	NA
Radford City	(23)	(23)	(23)	(23)	(23)	(23)	NA	NA	NA	NA	NA	NA	NA	NA	NA	NA
Richmond City	18.9	55.1	6.9	11.3	21.7	21.9	NA	NA	NA	NA	NA	NA	NA	NA	NA	NA
Roanoke City	13.7	68.8	12.0	7.6	27.3	10.4	NA	NA	NA	NA	NA	NA	NA	NA	NA	NA
Salem City	(6)	(6)	(6)	(6)	(6)	(6)	NA	NA	NA	NA	NA	NA	NA	NA	NA	NA

1. Covers mining, construction, and manufacturing. 2. Covers private sector earnings in agricultural services, forestry, and fisheries; transportation and public utilities; wholesale trade; retail trade; finance, insurance, and real estate; and services. 3. Danville included with Pittsylvania County. 4. Hopewell included with Prince George County. 5. Manassas and Manassas Park included with Prince William County. 6. Salem included with Roanoke County. 7. Buena Vista and Lexington included with Rockbridge County. 8. Harrisonburg included with Rockingham County. 9. Franklin included with Southhampton County. 10. Galax included with Grayson County. 11. Bristol included with Washington County. 12. Norton included with Wise County. 13. Poquoson included with York County. 14. Bedford City included with Bedford County. 15. Charlottesville included with Albemarle county. 16. Clifton Forge and Covington included with Allegheny County. 17. Petersburg and Colonial Heights included with Dinwiddie County. 18. Emporia included with Greensville County. 19. Fairfax City and Falls Church included with Fairfax County. 20. Galax included with Carroll County. 21. Lynchburg included with Campbell County. 22. Martinsville included with Henry County. 23. Radford included with Montgomery County.

STATE County	Agriculture, 1987 (cont'd)								Manufactures, 1987						
	Value of land and buildings		Value of products sold				Percent of farms with sales of		Establishments		All employees			Production workers	
					Percent from										
	Average per farm ($1,000)	Average per acre (Dollars)	Total (Mil dol)	Average per farm (Dollars)	Crops	Livestock and poultry[1]	$10,000 or more	$100,000 or more	Total	Percent with 20 or more employees	Number (1,000)	Percent change, 1982–1987	Annual payroll (Mil dol)	Number (1,000)	Work hours (Mil)
	119	120	121	122	123	124	125	126	127	128	129	130	131	132	133
VIRGINIA—Con.															
Northumberland	358	1 181	5	30 720	90.7	9.3	54.7	8.2	23	43.5	0.8	-20.0	12.3	0.6	1.0
Nottoway	180	864	16	54 311	12.1	87.9	37.1	10.6	21	33.3	0.7	-36.4	8.7	0.6	1.3
Orange	392	1 419	16	37 549	12.5	87.5	37.0	7.8	28	46.4	2.6	18.2	43.3	2.1	4.3
Page	234	1 465	45	91 757	1.5	98.5	46.0	23.5	19	57.9	2.0	0.0	24.6	1.7	3.3
Patrick	100	867	10	15 318	42.4	57.6	27.2	2.2	45	35.6	2.4	-4.0	37.0	2.0	4.0
Pittsylvania	139	757	40	24 977	69.6	30.4	40.6	5.4	57	35.1	4.9	-9.3	81.8	4.0	8.0
Powhatan	412	1 448	11	52 185	23.6	76.4	27.8	10.4	13	15.4	0.1	0.0	2.0	0.1	0.2
Prince Edward	178	818	10	27 979	24.9	75.1	30.9	6.8	27	22.2	0.8	-27.3	9.6	0.7	1.2
Prince George	292	1 116	5	28 412	80.5	19.5	44.9	7.8	13	23.1	0.2	0.0	3.9	0.2	0.3
Prince William	420	3 321	6	22 572	19.3	80.8	27.6	4.4	77	35.1	2.8	86.7	72.5	1.7	3.3
Pulaski	194	980	12	34 485	4.7	95.3	33.9	8.6	41	56.1	5.9	18.0	108.4	4.5	7.7
Rappahannock	408	1 696	5	18 072	36.7	63.3	35.4	3.5	9	11.1	0.3	0.0	3.1	0.3	0.6
Richmond	255	962	6	40 886	87.3	12.7	54.7	6.8	14	21.4	0.5	-16.7	5.0	0.4	0.7
Roanoke	183	2 043	16	56 595	10.5	89.5	25.4	3.9	52	30.8	D	D	D	D	D
Rockbridge	196	938	12	17 496	8.2	91.8	32.4	3.7	30	43.3	2.2	0.0	39.8	1.8	3.7
Rockingham	251	1 926	277	146 263	2.4	97.6	57.4	33.9	73	38.4	6.6	26.9	120.7	5.2	10.1
Russell	118	791	14	12 265	25.8	74.2	24.4	1.6	22	27.3	1.5	87.5	19.3	1.2	2.1
Scott	68	719	10	6 254	51.1	48.9	14.8	0.3	20	35.0	0.9	-30.8	14.7	0.8	1.4
Shenandoah	246	1 314	45	54 172	7.8	92.2	40.0	11.4	42	57.1	4.9	48.5	81.4	4.2	8.9
Smyth	120	802	16	18 078	13.8	86.2	27.1	4.6	48	54.2	5.4	17.4	87.6	4.5	8.9
Southampton	532	1 156	39	95 203	66.5	33.5	75.9	32.9	26	38.5	D	D	D	D	D
Spotsylvania	307	2 005	6	18 577	20.4	79.6	27.5	3.6	14	42.9	0.4	-55.6	6.7	0.3	0.6
Stafford	460	D	2	11 168	30.0	70.0	13.7	2.0	39	25.6	0.7	16.7	14.1	0.5	1.0
Surry	426	1 170	10	77 833	69.7	30.3	60.3	23.8	8	62.5	0.2	100.0	3.3	0.2	0.3
Sussex	343	840	14	72 500	86.6	13.4	77.0	28.6	15	46.7	1.0	11.1	18.0	0.9	1.8
Tazewell	202	709	11	21 873	3.9	96.1	35.0	5.5	53	37.7	1.3	-31.6	22.6	0.9	1.5
Warren	285	1 804	3	13 254	28.1	71.9	28.7	2.7	28	46.4	2.3	-17.9	46.6	1.9	4.3
Washington	120	1 201	39	19 897	18.7	81.3	24.4	3.0	33	39.4	1.7	-5.6	29.6	1.3	2.7
Westmoreland	376	967	11	61 017	91.0	9.0	54.7	13.8	29	48.3	0.8	0.0	10.4	0.7	1.2
Wise	105	1 005	1	5 602	16.9	83.1	7.0	1.4	21	9.5	0.5	25.0	5.4	0.4	0.8
Wythe	156	780	23	30 894	3.0	97.0	41.2	6.2	38	44.7	2.3	-14.8	35.7	1.9	3.6
York	312	6 100	3	43 818	77.4	22.6	27.3	9.1	18	16.7	D	D	D	D	D
Independent Cities															
Alexandria City	NA	NA	NA	NA	NA	NA	NA	NA	140	29.3	3.3	13.8	82.7	1.8	3.4
Bedford City	NA	NA	NA	NA	NA	NA	NA	NA	35	34.3	2.3	-8.0	44.3	1.7	3.4
Bristol City	NA	NA	NA	NA	NA	NA	NA	NA	58	53.4	6.9	21.1	131.3	4.8	8.8
Buena Vista City	NA	NA	NA	NA	NA	NA	NA	NA	10	70.0	1.0	0.0	22.0	0.8	1.6
Charlottesville City	NA	NA	NA	NA	NA	NA	NA	NA	82	32.9	6.2	44.2	130.6	3.7	7.7
Chesapeake City	475	2 035	15	65 412	83.8	16.2	46.2	17.5	101	37.6	3.8	40.7	79.7	2.5	5.1
Clifton Forge City	NA	NA	NA	NA	NA	NA	NA	NA	4	25.0	D	D	D	D	D
Colonial Heights City	NA	NA	NA	NA	NA	NA	NA	NA	9	55.6	0.6	-25.0	8.9	0.5	0.9
Covington City	NA	NA	NA	NA	NA	NA	NA	NA	13	61.5	D	D	D	D	D
Danville City	NA	NA	NA	NA	NA	NA	NA	NA	56	50.0	12.2	-9.0	253.8	9.9	20.5
Emporia City	NA	NA	NA	NA	NA	NA	NA	NA	28	39.3	1.3	-7.1	23.2	1.0	2.1
Fairfax City	NA	NA	NA	NA	NA	NA	NA	NA	35	28.6	D	D	D	D	D
Falls Church City	NA	NA	NA	NA	NA	NA	NA	NA	26	23.1	D	D	D	D	D
Franklin City	NA	NA	NA	NA	NA	NA	NA	NA	10	40.0	0.5	0.0	9.1	0.3	0.6
Fredericksburg City	NA	NA	NA	NA	NA	NA	NA	NA	45	46.7	2.1	133.3	50.6	1.6	3.4
Galax City	NA	NA	NA	NA	NA	NA	NA	NA	30	56.7	5.5	27.9	69.9	4.9	9.4
Hampton City	NA	NA	NA	NA	NA	NA	NA	NA	73	41.1	D	D	D	D	D
Harrisonburg City	NA	NA	NA	NA	NA	NA	NA	NA	45	51.1	4.5	7.1	80.4	3.5	6.9
Hopewell City	NA	NA	NA	NA	NA	NA	NA	NA	16	43.8	2.6	-39.5	91.7	1.9	3.7
Lexington City	NA	NA	NA	NA	NA	NA	NA	NA	11	9.1	0.1	-50.0	1.0	0.1	0.1
Lynchburg City	NA	NA	NA	NA	NA	NA	NA	NA	123	49.6	14.4	-13.8	364.0	9.3	18.8
Manassas City	NA	NA	NA	NA	NA	NA	NA	NA	37	35.1	D	D	D	D	D
Manassas Park City	NA	NA	NA	NA	NA	NA	NA	NA	6	0.0	0.0	0.0	0.7	0.0	0.1
Martinsville City	NA	NA	NA	NA	NA	NA	NA	NA	57	59.6	13.4	28.8	218.9	11.3	21.4
Newport News City	NA	NA	NA	NA	NA	NA	NA	NA	117	36.8	30.1	7.1	817.3	25.3	47.8
Norfolk City	NA	NA	NA	NA	NA	NA	NA	NA	235	39.6	16.5	21.3	385.1	12.1	25.2
Norton City	NA	NA	NA	NA	NA	NA	NA	NA	5	40.0	D	D	D	D	D
Petersburg City	NA	NA	NA	NA	NA	NA	NA	NA	50	40.0	2.1	-56.2	33.6	1.4	2.9
Poquoson City	NA	NA	NA	NA	NA	NA	NA	NA	6	16.7	0.1	0.0	0.8	0.0	0.1
Portsmouth City	NA	NA	NA	NA	NA	NA	NA	NA	65	33.8	2.2	0.0	37.6	1.7	3.2
Radford City	NA	NA	NA	NA	NA	NA	NA	NA	16	68.8	2.3	-59.6	50.3	1.6	3.1
Richmond City	NA	NA	NA	NA	NA	NA	NA	NA	428	43.7	41.5	5.9	1 302.0	22.4	43.8
Roanoke City	NA	NA	NA	NA	NA	NA	NA	NA	170	45.3	11.5	7.5	236.9	7.5	14.9
Salem City	NA	NA	NA	NA	NA	NA	NA	NA	50	50.0	5.9	3.5	148.2	4.2	8.3

1. Includes livestock and poultry products.

STATE County	Manufactures, 1987 (cont'd): Production workers (cont'd): Wages: Total (Mil dol)	Manufactures, 1987 (cont'd): Production workers (cont'd): Wages: Average per worker (Dollars)	Value added by manufacture (Mil dol)	Value of shipments (Mil dol)	New capital expenditures (Mil dol)	Value of construction authorized by building permits, 1990: Total[1] ($1,000)	Nonresidential: Total ($1,000)	Nonresidential: Percent: Office	Nonresidential: Percent: Industrial	Nonresidential: Percent: Stores	Residential: New construction ($1,000)	Residential: Number of housing units	Residential: Alterations and additions ($1,000)
	134	135	136	137	138	139	140	141	142	143	144	145	146
VIRGINIA—Con.													
Northumberland	8.4	14 000	30.1	56.1	D	29 948	1 277	0.0	99.0	0.0	27 874	302	676
Nottoway	7.3	12 167	22.2	62.4	2.7	3 916	451	0.0	0.0	0.0	3 278	57	0
Orange	30.6	14 571	84.5	209.6	17.9	32 015	3 234	25.4	0.0	29.6	24 493	298	2 614
Page	19.8	11 647	96.6	221.0	5.2	19 983	5 974	1.3	0.0	3.3	7 464	162	2 008
Patrick	28.2	14 100	83.2	157.3	3.2	5 305	493	0.0	44.6	10.7	3 518	61	580
Pittsylvania	63.6	15 900	262.4	760.5	11.4	30 813	8 968	2.5	6.7	6.4	17 131	284	2 377
Powhatan	1.2	12 000	4.0	9.3	D	17 653	5	0.0	0.0	0.0	15 390	234	1 190
Prince Edward	7.7	11 000	22.5	39.1	2.1	14 360	6 935	15.1	1.2	47.0	5 357	110	696
Prince George	2.7	13 500	8.8	20.4	1.6	20 601	1 881	15.6	0.0	6.6	16 305	219	990
Prince William	42.7	25 118	164.3	258.3	10.7	182 386	26 662	11.9	4.3	47.9	108 555	1 782	11 286
Pulaski	73.7	16 378	225.4	748.0	8.9	11 670	5 025	12.8	6.8	76.6	4 461	88	1 620
Rappahannock	2.7	9 000	7.3	9.1	0.1	7 734	1 049	0.0	0.0	0.0	5 283	62	1 203
Richmond	4.5	11 250	29.2	42.8	0.4	5 366	904	0.0	0.0	55.6	3 157	49	669
Roanoke	D	D	D	D	D	52 395	13 006	53.1	28.8	3.7	21 018	384	3 202
Rockbridge	27.1	15 056	151.5	319.2	7.3	15 980	4 106	0.0	61.6	20.8	9 978	139	1 158
Rockingham	82.2	15 808	553.8	1 519.0	43.3	61 068	9 903	2.4	2.0	22.6	29 927	446	3 750
Russell	13.8	11 500	43.2	66.8	2.4	7 237	830	60.7	0.0	27.1	5 476	131	37
Scott	12.0	15 000	31.4	106.0	D	4 328	671	0.0	0.0	95.1	3 122	72	228
Shenandoah	63.6	15 143	209.8	470.3	14.5	32 895	4 291	2.9	0.0	32.2	21 647	273	1 444
Smyth	64.4	14 311	208.9	398.2	8.2	9 285	1 363	4.0	5.9	77.0	5 598	143	752
Southampton	D	D	D	D	D	12 427	4 254	0.0	89.2	0.0	3 886	61	1 496
Spotsylvania	4.7	15 667	12.5	26.6	1.1	148 264	27 905	17.2	7.5	35.1	115 204	970	3 325
Stafford	8.8	17 600	40.9	93.1	5.6	104 609	10 270	19.0	0.6	58.9	78 642	1 184	8 075
Surry	2.3	11 500	10.6	29.1	1.8	11 635	7 599	92.1	0.0	0.0	2 513	46	1 013
Sussex	15.0	16 667	45.4	145.6	5.3	3 779	2 033	0.0	0.0	39.8	1 286	25	335
Tazewell	13.5	15 000	66.3	168.0	D	17 193	2 666	8.0	17.5	48.0	9 673	254	672
Warren	36.1	19 000	208.3	366.6	D	38 880	2 608	0.0	0.0	46.3	23 699	379	1 600
Washington	20.6	15 846	91.3	176.6	D	25 840	4 215	13.3	20.2	27.1	15 389	310	1 250
Westmoreland	7.3	10 429	19.6	71.3	D	12 750	0	NA	NA	NA	12 750	170	0
Wise	4.3	10 750	12.5	26.7	0.7	10 269	4 747	42.0	0.0	47.3	4 302	92	679
Wythe	26.6	14 000	88.4	160.6	5.0	10 915	3 564	0.0	85.3	5.3	4 598	112	670
York	D	D	D	D	D	43 850	4 458	9.7	0.0	34.1	32 986	403	3 335
Independent Cities													
Alexandria City	38.0	21 111	291.6	453.3	4.8	63 280	13 185	38.9	0.0	0.5	5 307	54	5 134
Bedford City	27.7	16 294	88.5	211.6	5.4	2 462	256	81.6	15.6	0.0	1 023	34	327
Bristol City	77.7	16 188	291.8	792.8	33.2	7 121	2 570	41.8	33.9	4.9	1 565	41	418
Buena Vista City	14.8	18 500	61.7	141.2	2.1	2 003	385	71.4	0.0	0.0	530	12	62
Charlottesville City	56.0	15 135	357.9	569.0	14.2	35 564	16 638	3.6	0.0	5.6	4 435	100	5 612
Chesapeake City	44.3	17 720	232.0	588.8	14.2	193 876	29 238	22.5	18.3	35.0	138 305	1 932	9 410
Clifton Forge City	D	D	D	D	D	223	2	0.0	0.0	0.0	0	0	144
Colonial Heights City	6.2	12 400	25.9	49.1	3.0	13 777	6 346	17.1	0.0	66.2	5 468	183	506
Covington City	D	D	D	D	D	991	719	2.9	94.6	0.0	115	2	67
Danville City	190.6	19 253	520.6	1 030.4	17.3	23 922	7 722	48.0	3.2	46.9	4 616	114	1 940
Emporia City	17.7	17 700	58.9	144.4	3.6	3 931	1 592	5.9	75.4	6.2	1 358	25	486
Fairfax City	D	D	D	D	D	19 600	6 268	10.7	0.0	71.2	629	5	3 731
Falls Church City	D	D	D	D	D	11 852	2 908	0.0	0.0	0.0	5 071	39	2 307
Franklin City	4.4	14 667	23.7	44.9	D	7 858	409	100.0	0.0	0.0	5 376	225	284
Fredericksburg City	35.4	22 125	145.1	330.2	6.8	16 769	3 118	29.2	19.1	37.4	2 812	92	2 636
Galax City	57.4	11 714	124.0	243.1	7.3	2 370	679	0.0	16.0	0.0	505	7	102
Hampton City	D	D	D	D	D	78 362	14 587	0.1	8.4	59.5	38 348	666	9 193
Harrisonburg City	54.9	15 686	239.2	537.8	23.4	37 208	10 453	32.7	0.1	56.7	18 086	393	1 226
Hopewell City	60.8	32 000	229.8	681.6	33.7	14 393	8 375	1.7	86.8	3.5	1 502	33	336
Lexington City	0.8	8 000	1.8	3.6	0.4	2 379	197	0.0	0.0	0.0	760	40	372
Lynchburg City	212.6	22 860	989.2	1 582.1	33.9	47 578	25 658	6.9	5.8	53.6	9 349	118	2 264
Manassas City	D	D	D	D	D	31 273	10 405	17.5	0.0	12.7	11 060	198	1 388
Manassas Park City	0.5	NA	1.2	2.5	0.0	2 527	671	0.0	90.9	0.0	1 279	34	262
Martinsville City	157.2	13 912	574.0	953.1	32.6	6 903	1 798	48.0	0.0	52.0	2 559	46	1 631
Newport News City	591.6	23 383	1 380.7	2 037.4	D	139 771	64 504	6.3	30.0	13.8	54 093	1 142	7 790
Norfolk City	261.4	21 603	1 345.3	3 425.0	42.4	131 058	27 658	34.4	0.0	43.0	24 174	462	18 408
Norton City	D	D	D	D	D	3 283	682	0.0	0.0	0.0	1 660	99	257
Petersburg City	18.0	12 857	85.2	175.6	6.0	12 399	7 287	7.9	70.4	0.9	2 100	60	1 373
Poquoson City	0.5	NA	1.6	2.7	0.1	7 203	469	0.0	0.0	0.0	5 448	52	901
Portsmouth City	26.1	15 353	133.1	338.7	3.7	26 974	6 225	47.7	8.0	8.3	9 813	238	5 941
Radford City	30.9	19 312	106.9	188.0	3.2	8 636	1 277	14.6	0.0	11.7	5 100	93	769
Richmond City	586.3	26 174	5 206.6	8 280.4	203.1	110 650	18 450	15.2	15.6	2.3	15 966	278	20 883
Roanoke City	135.2	18 027	653.2	1 196.0	43.0	102 474	59 157	74.2	5.1	6.2	7 829	220	9 029
Salem City	86.1	20 500	312.2	579.3	13.6	24 334	3 989	33.1	7.4	50.6	5 083	73	1 455

1. Includes nonresidential additions and alterations, residential nonhousekeeping buildings, and residential garages and carports not shown separately.

STATE County	Wholesale trade, 1987: Establishments	Wholesale trade, 1987: Sales (Mil dol)	Wholesale trade, 1987: Paid employees[1]	Wholesale trade, 1987: Annual payroll (Mil dol)	Retail trade, all establishments, 1987: Number	Retail trade, all establishments, 1987: Sales: Total (Mil dol)	Retail trade, all establishments, 1987: Sales: Percent change, 1982–1987	Retail trade, all establishments, 1987: Sales: Per capita[2] (Dollars)	Retail trade, establishments with payroll, 1987: Number	Retail trade, establishments with payroll, 1987: Sales: Total (Mil dol)	Retail trade, establishments with payroll, 1987: Sales: Per capita[2] (Dollars): General merchandise stores	Retail trade, establishments with payroll, 1987: Sales: Per capita[2] (Dollars): Food stores	Retail trade, establishments with payroll, 1987: Sales: Per capita[2] (Dollars): Apparel & accessory stores	Retail trade, establishments with payroll, 1987: Sales: Per capita[2] (Dollars): Eating and drinking places
	147	148	149	150	151	152	153	154	155	156	157	158	159	160
VIRGINIA—Con.														
Northumberland	19	20.0	151	1.4	88	32.4	14.5	3 240	54	31.6	D	1 101	D	135
Nottoway	16	60.3	133	2.4	164	75.2	57.0	5 048	112	73.7	408	1 386	189	278
Orange	23	D	D	D	200	91.2	51.0	4 427	113	87.0	188	992	100	256
Page	16	10.0	65	0.8	207	131.2	127.8	6 495	119	127.8	307	1 305	84	411
Patrick	12	42.7	247	3.7	178	51.3	80.6	2 918	83	46.6	353	800	D	131
Pittsylvania	49	79.9	312	4.1	1 090	588.1	552.0	5 436	661	567.4	695	1 237	176	449
Powhatan	10	36.5	64	1.4	69	30.5	67.6	2 211	38	29.5	D	861	0	D
Prince Edward	30	57.7	273	4.1	187	117.2	55.4	6 853	143	114.6	776	1 759	D	825
Prince George	12	9.5	130	1.7	272	180.0	391.8	3 643	178	176.3	427	D	D	D
Prince William	118	515.3	1 245	28.5	1 661	1 788.9	172.3	8 275	1 159	1 766.2	D	D	429	D
Pulaski	28	62.9	235	4.1	263	136.6	41.0	3 904	151	132.0	240	1 077	66	353
Rappahannock	8	17.5	43	0.7	79	13.0	97.0	1 998	26	11.7	D	496	0	D
Richmond	27	30.0	155	2.7	88	47.6	84.5	6 801	57	46.6	D	2 001	255	296
Roanoke	104	501.3	1 068	25.6	913	711.0	198.4	7 255	580	697.4	D	1 635	D	597
Rockbridge	22	264.8	597	9.9	417	188.9	189.3	6 132	240	180.0	360	1 183	D	613
Rockingham	44	74.9	469	7.6	946	500.2	403.2	6 253	563	477.6	876	1 219	170	513
Russell	26	31.4	175	2.9	224	93.3	47.9	2 890	125	86.6	200	854	55	193
Scott	13	26.5	125	1.2	212	93.3	13.5	3 702	109	88.8	86	1 308	18	185
Shenandoah	31	80.9	333	4.6	359	162.4	67.6	5 544	191	155.4	185	1 208	102	444
Smyth	31	36.3	221	3.6	363	151.5	45.0	4 590	212	144.2	420	1 167	134	229
Southampton	20	27.0	151	1.5	227	112.9	247.4	4 445	159	110.3	D	1 341	117	220
Spotsylvania	14	18.0	113	2.2	806	655.9	298.5	10 787	552	642.4	1 842	1 679	453	1 049
Stafford	41	D	D	D	322	241.4	144.3	4 421	178	236.0	D	D	37	D
Surry	8	7.8	63	0.9	43	10.3	51.5	1 602	22	8.8	0	802	0	D
Sussex	26	59.6	274	3.4	104	47.9	24.1	4 516	66	45.8	83	1 375	58	395
Tazewell	94	212.4	809	12.6	472	341.2	38.2	6 920	311	331.1	589	2 241	103	294
Warren	25	18.4	141	1.9	260	145.2	79.0	5 973	165	140.4	640	1 490	188	461
Washington	46	172.3	444	5.4	646	362.8	244.5	5 590	441	354.2	542	1 329	312	438
Westmoreland	21	16.6	119	1.4	140	51.0	46.6	3 375	78	48.6	120	957	D	306
Wise	54	198.9	582	9.4	514	288.3	81.2	5 993	311	278.8	692	1 930	192	327
Wythe	30	55.7	260	4.0	277	140.1	21.6	5 429	177	134.6	298	959	200	421
York	35	87.8	239	4.8	306	148.7	89.4	2 816	198	145.8	D	D	D	373
Independent Cities														
Alexandria City	213	1 080.5	4 322	99.9	1 036	1 241.9	57.1	11 488	747	1 226.4	1 503	1 522	458	1 406
Bedford City	28	50.9	225	3.3	0	0.0	0.0	0	0	0.0	0	0	0	0
Bristol City	68	336.5	1 137	22.1	0	0.0	0.0	0	0	0.0	0	0	0	0
Buena Vista City	6	7.5	56	0.8	0	0.0	0.0	0	0	0.0	0	0	0	0
Charlottesville City	109	D	D	D	0	0.0	0.0	0	0	0.0	0	0	0	0
Chesapeake City	225	1 186.2	2 855	61.6	973	801.0	88.7	5 637	607	791.7	594	1 125	139	404
Clifton Forge City	6	5.0	38	0.7	0	0.0	0.0	0	0	0.0	0	0	0	0
Colonial Heights City	13	70.6	292	6.1	0	0.0	0.0	0	0	0.0	0	0	0	0
Covington City	14	14.4	73	0.9	0	0.0	0.0	0	0	0.0	0	0	0	0
Danville City	102	314.0	1 137	20.8	0	0.0	0.0	0	0	0.0	0	0	0	0
Emporia City	19	56.0	136	2.3	0	0.0	0.0	0	0	0.0	0	0	0	0
Fairfax City	67	529.2	763	16.7	0	0.0	0.0	0	0	0.0	0	0	0	0
Falls Church City	34	79.4	351	7.9	0	0.0	0.0	0	0	0.0	0	0	0	0
Franklin City	15	55.6	230	3.5	0	0.0	0.0	0	0	0.0	0	0	0	0
Fredericksburg City	83	341.2	982	18.4	0	0.0	0.0	0	0	0.0	0	0	0	0
Galax City	14	22.2	131	2.0	0	0.0	0.0	0	0	0.0	0	0	0	0
Hampton City	118	266.3	1 225	27.4	974	1 165.7	61.1	9 036	735	1 156.1	1 026	1 304	455	639
Harrisonburg City	100	276.7	1 514	27.7	0	0.0	0.0	0	0	0.0	0	0	0	0
Hopewell City	19	206.2	275	6.6	0	0.0	0.0	0	0	0.0	0	0	0	0
Lexington City	15	19.7	126	1.9	0	0.0	0.0	0	0	0.0	0	0	0	0
Lynchburg City	157	440.8	1 867	37.7	0	0.0	0.0	0	0	0.0	0	0	0	0
Manassas City	57	291.7	790	18.8	0	0.0	0.0	0	0	0.0	0	0	0	0
Manassas Park City	3	D	D	D	0	0.0	0.0	0	0	0.0	0	0	0	0
Martinsville City	37	55.6	280	4.9	0	0.0	0.0	0	0	0.0	0	0	0	0
Newport News City	162	498.2	2 232	43.2	1 265	1 058.3	52.9	6 715	950	1 046.6	849	1 152	255	497
Norfolk City	472	2 738.7	9 602	196.8	1 956	1 739.5	43.7	6 076	1 581	1 725.7	958	1 127	357	657
Norton City	27	119.6	370	7.8	0	0.0	0.0	0	0	0.0	0	0	0	0
Petersburg City	60	154.1	711	13.9	0	0.0	0.0	0	0	0.0	0	0	0	0
Poquoson City	8	6.7	73	0.7	0	0.0	0.0	0	0	0.0	0	0	0	0
Portsmouth City	83	1 157.3	1 254	27.1	723	590.2	41.8	5 527	546	584.3	584	1 450	310	425
Radford City	11	22.4	98	1.5	0	0.0	0.0	0	0	0.0	0	0	0	0
Richmond City	696	4 791.8	10 816	279.3	2 256	1 945.0	49.0	9 076	1 787	1 926.2	351	1 724	409	924
Roanoke City	376	1 440.1	5 813	107.4	1 351	1 033.6	61.1	10 483	1 061	1 023.3	1 816	1 505	595	944
Salem City	78	499.7	2 143	39.4	0	0.0	0.0	0	0	0.0	0	0	0	0

1. For pay period including March 12. 2. Based on the estimated population as of July 1 of the year shown.

STATE County	Retail trade, establishments with payroll, 1987 (cont'd)		Taxable service industries–establishments with payroll, 1987							Bank deposits,[2] June 1989		Savings capital,[3] September 1989	
				Receipts (Mil dol)									
					Selected kinds of business								
	Paid employees[1]	Annual payroll (Mil dol)	Number	Total	Hotels, motels and other lodging places	Health services	Legal services	Paid employees	Annual payroll (Mil dol)	Total (Mil dol)	Percent change, 1988–1989	Total (Mil dol)	Percent change, 1988–1989
	161	162	163	164	165	166	167	168	169	170	171	172	173
VIRGINIA—Con.													
Northumberland	336	3.2	36	6.1	0.5	1.6	D	174	2.1	129	9.0	0.0	NA
Nottoway	790	7.4	66	18.0	1.8	6.3	D	469	5.4	164	5.2	11.0	-4.8
Orange	923	9.5	95	14.0	0.4	2.7	1.9	372	4.5	189	9.3	22.4	-5.2
Page	977	9.6	103	29.7	12.0	5.5	1.0	691	8.3	167	9.8	28.1	7.5
Patrick	493	4.6	54	12.5	D	6.6	0.7	360	4.6	134	4.6	0.0	NA
Pittsylvania	7 045	65.2	122	18.3	0.4	2.9	0.7	445	4.3	165	5.8	21.8	-1.9
Powhatan	298	2.9	35	4.6	D	1.5	D	117	1.7	79	7.8	12.3	11.9
Prince Edward	1 513	13.1	105	20.8	1.5	11.9	0.7	805	7.9	173	1.4	55.8	8.0
Prince George	2 362	23.4	33	24.5	0.0	D	0.8	565	10.1	61	11.9	52.2	16.8
Prince William	17 893	197.1	832	296.7	42.3	54.1	10.6	7 387	114.3	536	11.3	292.0	13.4
Pulaski	1 484	13.7	143	38.5	D	23.3	1.8	1 102	13.4	189	6.3	42.5	-2.5
Rappahannock	144	1.6	19	4.4	0.0	D	1.3	70	1.3	22	4.6	0.0	NA
Richmond	467	4.4	34	7.5	0.0	D	0.7	303	2.7	82	3.6	120.2	-43.9
Roanoke	7 455	70.2	319	95.3	17.3	25.0	3.0	2 654	38.3	490	2.9	246.8	2.4
Rockbridge	2 423	21.5	58	13.3	5.9	0.4	0.0	371	3.7	61	7.8	18.2	4.7
Rockingham	5 717	53.7	190	31.5	D	4.8	D	939	10.7	301	6.4	29.5	42.5
Russell	866	7.9	91	23.9	1.1	13.3	1.9	604	7.0	194	7.2	0.0	NA
Scott	842	7.9	55	12.3	D	4.4	0.8	336	3.8	151	7.0	0.0	NA
Shenandoah	1 838	17.3	156	36.1	11.7	9.0	1.4	1 142	11.0	355	7.9	20.3	11.0
Smyth	1 582	14.0	136	32.2	D	11.5	1.3	883	11.9	259	6.9	28.0	-1.9
Southampton	1 356	12.6	29	4.8	D	D	0.5	116	1.5	85	15.4	0.0	NA
Spotsylvania	7 751	76.7	74	20.6	6.3	4.1	0.9	464	6.4	134	23.9	116.9	149.4
Stafford	2 417	25.1	190	59.5	9.1	D	D	1 762	20.6	117	12.5	38.8	106.6
Surry	163	1.2	14	1.8	D	1.0	0.5	67	0.6	16	-3.1	0.0	NA
Sussex	485	5.2	34	3.9	0.5	1.0	0.3	109	0.9	104	5.9	0.0	NA
Tazewell	3 044	32.1	277	123.7	D	81.7	3.4	2 183	37.1	491	8.1	45.8	4.2
Warren	1 679	15.5	135	32.2	4.7	6.4	2.0	887	10.6	163	8.9	62.6	10.2
Washington	4 520	39.9	149	41.0	D	17.3	8.0	1 006	17.1	346	9.5	23.3	4.9
Westmoreland	523	4.8	62	7.5	0.8	1.2	1.2	257	2.5	122	3.9	0.0	NA
Wise	3 088	26.6	167	39.5	0.5	16.4	1.3	845	13.4	374	3.1	16.0	5.9
Wythe	1 600	14.1	128	30.5	8.2	7.8	1.3	745	8.7	230	4.6	44.9	-72.5
York	2 201	18.2	152	84.6	D	5.2	D	3 469	23.0	173	4.5	47.3	21.4
Independent Cities													
Alexandria City	13 183	154.8	1 501	1 063.7	80.2	125.7	65.8	20 760	426.4	1 394	-4.5	1 816.1	24.6
Bedford City	0	0.0	131	28.3	D	6.1	1.8	681	8.8	175	8.4	0.0	NA
Bristol City	0	0.0	187	39.2	6.8	4.9	3.1	1 133	13.0	276	-1.0	183.7	32.8
Buena Vista City	0	0.0	23	4.1	D	2.0	0.3	153	1.4	59	3.8	0.0	NA
Charlottesville City	0	0.0	671	214.3	D	54.9	19.8	5 796	83.1	685	5.5	232.2	-5.7
Chesapeake City	8 322	83.2	685	270.4	8.3	60.6	8.7	6 635	109.4	542	8.6	128.2	-5.2
Clifton Forge City	0	0.0	37	8.1	0.0	6.0	D	261	3.1	80	3.5	24.1	9.7
Colonial Heights City	0	0.0	114	24.2	D	9.8	0.9	851	8.8	118	12.4	91.9	0.4
Covington City	0	0.0	68	12.4	D	3.4	0.8	321	3.5	177	3.6	12.9	-5.7
Danville City	0	0.0	390	106.2	9.2	47.8	5.7	2 654	45.3	689	8.0	120.0	-1.8
Emporia City	0	0.0	71	25.8	8.6	10.1	1.1	723	8.4	88	6.1	0.0	NA
Fairfax City	0	0.0	665	482.6	12.2	85.2	52.1	8 319	216.0	699	3.4	289.5	-9.7
Falls Church City	0	0.0	361	189.7	D	26.9	12.8	3 229	72.0	353	14.0	165.8	35.5
Franklin City	0	0.0	71	13.8	D	6.6	1.0	403	5.8	130	-8.5	14.6	6.6
Fredericksburg City	0	0.0	408	133.6	14.7	49.7	7.0	3 582	55.2	382	9.7	297.4	-10.2
Galax City	0	0.0	81	23.9	D	13.2	D	616	8.8	210	4.6	9.6	9.9
Hampton City	12 906	125.3	677	293.3	22.9	59.3	9.8	7 695	131.3	511	7.6	163.1	-1.2
Harrisonburg City	0	0.0	324	144.2	14.2	42.6	8.6	3 332	48.4	517	7.2	115.8	5.8
Hopewell City	0	0.0	137	36.7	1.0	14.5	3.9	902	15.6	96	7.9	135.3	-34.1
Lexington City	0	0.0	97	15.9	5.8	3.3	1.7	453	5.1	163	8.4	0.0	NA
Lynchburg City	0	0.0	636	320.0	12.9	75.5	11.6	6 792	130.2	687	4.0	405.9	0.5
Manassas City	0	0.0	301	115.3	D	24.6	6.5	3 018	46.1	43	7.8	396.1	39.5
Manassas Park City	0	0.0	10	3.4	0.0	D	D	63	1.3	184	-2.9	0.0	NA
Martinsville City	0	0.0	217	59.0	D	27.5	4.7	1 629	23.2	493	5.9	20.7	-2.4
Newport News City	11 950	117.2	1 008	417.4	60.4	111.5	24.1	11 821	176.1	762	2.7	410.5	-11.0
Norfolk City	22 309	213.9	1 599	934.3	61.2	216.4	87.0	21 378	372.2	3 080	-0.6	992.3	-5.0
Norton City	0	0.0	63	19.4	D	9.4	3.5	372	7.3	52	4.2	29.7	9.9
Petersburg City	0	0.0	301	110.8	13.1	47.1	3.3	2 592	42.0	309	3.7	240.4	7.4
Poquoson City	0	0.0	44	5.0	0.0	1.9	D	144	1.5	52	5.2	0.0	NA
Portsmouth City	7 130	67.1	561	200.7	4.4	78.7	14.7	5 778	82.3	516	4.9	315.4	-2.3
Radford City	0	0.0	98	29.2	D	19.7	2.0	803	13.3	140	25.3	24.9	-2.4
Richmond City	23 684	245.5	2 414	1 561.4	60.9	404.9	199.5	34 366	599.3	7 527	1.4	1 334.6	-3.9
Roanoke City	13 530	129.5	1 049	436.1	33.5	110.9	35.3	11 698	179.1	1 715	4.0	329.4	15.8
Salem City	0	0.0	219	150.4	3.7	106.2	2.4	3 760	61.0	351	2.1	67.0	-1.9

1. For the period including March 12 of the year shown. 2. Includes deposits for all insured and reporting noninsured commercial and mutual savings banks. 3. Includes savings capital for all FSLIC insured savings institutions.

STATE County	Federal funds and grants, 1989: Expenditures: Total (Mil dol)	Federal funds and grants, 1989: Expenditures: Percent change, 1988–1989	Federal funds and grants, 1989: Per capita[1] (Dollars): Total	Per capita[1] (Dollars): Direct payments for individuals	Per capita[1] (Dollars): Procurement contract awards	Per capita[1] (Dollars): Salaries and wages	Per capita[1] (Dollars): Grant awards	Local government finances, 1981–1982: General revenue: Total (Mil dol)	General revenue: Intergovernmental: Total (Mil dol)	General revenue: Intergovernmental: Percent from state	General revenue: Taxes: Total (Mil dol)	Taxes: Per capita[2]: Total (Dollars)	Taxes: Per capita[2]: Property (Dollars)	Direct general expenditure: Total (Mil dol)	Direct general expenditure: Percent change, 1977–1982
	174	175	176	177	178	179	180	181	182	183	184	185	186	187	188
VIRGINIA—Con.															
Northumberland	32.4	-6.7	3 210	2 764	34	151	171	5.2	2.6	96.3	2.3	237	203	5.0	50.9
Nottoway	56.6	1.4	3 823	2 360	77	1 052	307	8.8	5.2	93.9	2.8	196	139	8.5	39.9
Orange	62.4	9.4	2 887	2 528	12	118	193	11.7	5.9	93.3	4.9	266	210	10.9	59.7
Page	52.2	9.4	2 536	1 987	166	167	190	12.2	7.5	77.5	3.5	182	144	13.6	106.8
Patrick	36.5	13.0	2 098	1 671	81	105	210	8.8	5.4	96.0	2.4	135	108	8.4	72.9
Pittsylvania	259.2	9.6	2 429	1 790	231	107	284	31.4	21.4	96.7	6.8	102	82	29.5	53.2
Powhatan	25.2	5.1	1 715	1 514	10	80	85	6.1	3.6	95.9	2.0	154	122	5.7	51.3
Prince Edward	69.3	33.8	4 075	1 919	1 620	195	295	8.5	5.0	92.1	3.0	178	90	10.2	60.1
Prince George	390.8	-18.1	7 847	1 580	702	5 369	185	15.0	9.7	80.8	3.7	144	106	14.6	5.9
Prince William	1 228.5	3.5	5 132	1 002	2 786	1 275	57	144.6	55.3	82.6	71.8	458	381	138.4	67.7
Pulaski	76.2	4.3	2 178	1 885	14	95	174	22.2	13.0	90.5	6.7	189	135	19.9	58.6
Rappahannock	18.5	17.0	2 767	2 089	125	251	231	2.9	1.6	93.7	1.1	190	131	2.7	49.1
Richmond	58.6	189.5	8 258	2 480	22	162	5 459	4.2	2.3	92.8	1.6	226	163	6.1	121.9
Roanoke	205.1	-21.7	2 084	1 316	-6	674	97	55.3	21.5	89.7	26.0	352	284	62.5	60.7
Rockbridge	75.6	6.6	2 456	1 859	70	267	245	10.4	5.7	83.2	3.9	217	147	10.2	48.5
Rockingham	162.5	9.5	1 996	1 607	100	149	119	31.4	15.3	94.3	11.6	219	148	29.3	78.0
Russell	70.1	6.8	2 224	1 827	19	73	284	24.2	13.0	88.0	5.9	181	118	20.9	47.1
Scott	61.4	7.4	2 474	1 888	21	158	397	14.1	9.4	92.4	3.4	132	88	12.7	31.9
Shenandoah	75.4	6.8	2 504	2 131	81	138	128	15.7	7.4	94.0	7.0	251	188	15.6	59.2
Smyth	123.3	-13.6	3 806	1 774	1 525	117	369	19.7	13.0	85.1	4.8	143	96	19.1	66.7
Southampton	69.5	1.6	2 725	1 905	124	121	488	10.8	6.7	92.3	3.1	168	144	10.4	37.8
Spotsylvania	156.1	6.7	2 344	1 915	199	165	52	25.3	13.0	96.6	9.7	288	213	25.4	108.7
Stafford	86.9	3.1	1 391	947	14	307	118	31.0	14.6	90.8	14.1	321	278	30.5	134.9
Surry	14.2	5.7	2 144	1 558	11	102	378	6.6	2.4	92.3	3.9	634	611	6.1	57.2
Sussex	28.5	6.2	2 693	2 029	21	119	444	7.7	4.8	90.6	2.6	245	204	7.5	36.1
Tazewell	141.1	5.3	2 951	2 496	12	129	303	32.9	17.9	92.2	12.0	232	140	30.3	47.0
Warren	56.5	8.0	2 208	1 836	50	181	129	14.8	7.8	84.1	5.3	244	185	14.7	47.5
Washington	158.2	0.9	2 468	1 851	89	214	291	26.0	16.4	93.5	7.7	164	120	26.3	62.5
Westmoreland	55.8	8.2	3 597	2 988	23	323	195	10.3	6.1	80.4	3.4	244	206	10.7	52.8
Wise	162.6	8.7	3 496	2 517	161	233	581	36.6	17.7	89.5	15.3	343	105	30.2	24.3
Wythe	64.9	3.3	2 508	2 034	15	147	274	14.8	8.9	92.7	4.8	186	118	14.3	42.0
York	285.4	9.2	5 097	2 122	980	1 759	234	31.8	16.2	67.5	11.1	303	246	31.7	48.2
Independent Cities															
Alexandria City	1 433.0	-5.0	13 280	3 857	3 809	5 326	268	150.2	36.9	62.9	95.5	914	671	149.0	46.4
Bedford City	0.0	0.0	0	0	0	0	0	3.6	1.1	55.7	1.7	278	182	2.9	128.3
Bristol City	0.0	0.0	0	0	0	0	0	18.1	6.5	86.5	7.6	404	218	15.9	54.1
Buena Vista City	0.0	0.0	0	0	0	0	0	4.4	2.1	75.4	1.7	251	156	4.5	39.9
Charlottesville City	0.0	0.0	0	0	0	0	0	38.9	13.3	78.2	20.8	514	305	34.8	26.5
Chesapeake City	345.1	12.1	2 250	1 568	283	217	173	131.4	51.2	88.0	45.2	377	241	132.2	93.5
Clifton Forge City	0.0	0.0	0	0	0	0	0	4.2	2.2	72.7	1.5	322	194	4.9	37.1
Colonial Heights City	0.0	0.0	0	0	0	0	0	13.3	5.4	91.1	6.6	389	287	13.2	52.4
Covington City	0.0	0.0	0	0	0	0	0	6.2	2.5	90.9	3.0	359	185	6.1	42.8
Danville City	0.0	0.0	0	0	0	0	0	35.7	17.5	79.5	10.6	236	131	40.5	64.7
Emporia City	0.0	0.0	0	0	0	0	0	3.1	0.7	83.1	2.0	409	187	2.3	43.1
Fairfax City	0.0	0.0	0	0	0	0	0	24.9	3.4	85.3	17.6	860	549	11.5	89.3
Falls Church City	0.0	0.0	0	0	0	0	0	13.6	2.0	86.4	8.7	928	559	12.5	47.9
Franklin City	0.0	0.0	0	0	0	0	0	4.4	1.0	71.7	2.2	317	191	6.2	10.3
Fredericksburg City	0.0	0.0	0	0	0	0	0	13.6	4.9	79.3	7.3	401	251	18.5	95.2
Galax City	0.0	0.0	0	0	0	0	0	5.2	2.3	82.2	2.5	383	222	5.4	70.9
Hampton City	1 066.8	-5.4	8 082	1 866	1 725	4 279	207	110.1	50.1	77.7	50.6	405	256	96.0	20.5
Harrisonburg City	0.0	0.0	0	0	0	0	0	13.5	3.8	77.8	6.5	256	115	20.9	121.2
Hopewell City	0.0	0.0	0	0	0	0	0	41.9	8.3	82.9	10.4	433	320	41.1	-2.1
Lexington City	0.0	0.0	0	0	0	0	0	3.7	1.4	86.3	2.1	292	174	4.1	18.9
Lynchburg City	0.0	0.0	0	0	0	0	0	64.7	23.6	79.4	32.1	476	249	67.5	50.1
Manassas City	0.0	0.0	0	0	0	0	0	18.2	4.6	87.9	10.1	585	438	16.6	54.6
Manassas Park City	0.0	0.0	0	0	0	0	0	9.4	2.7	95.0	2.5	387	316	6.4	71.4
Martinsville City	0.0	0.0	0	0	0	0	0	15.4	6.3	79.2	6.3	348	198	16.9	42.0
Newport News City	1 734.9	-69.9	10 836	1 681	6 560	2 324	268	139.1	58.2	77.2	62.1	412	288	145.7	67.9
Norfolk City	3 365.6	0.3	11 642	1 823	1 733	7 570	502	303.2	134.4	70.2	113.2	424	211	272.0	30.1
Norton City	0.0	0.0	0	0	0	0	0	3.8	1.6	88.1	1.8	385	190	3.7	108.2
Petersburg City	0.0	0.0	0	0	0	0	0	73.1	17.6	81.6	18.2	453	282	69.3	21.1
Poquoson City	0.0	0.0	0	0	0	0	0	7.1	3.9	79.5	2.5	262	204	6.0	77.9
Portsmouth City	941.8	0.2	8 876	2 420	919	5 236	297	118.7	50.2	71.1	41.3	390	220	118.9	40.3
Radford City	0.0	0.0	0	0	0	0	0	7.0	3.5	87.2	2.7	206	133	8.0	53.8
Richmond City	1 642.7	-0.4	7 789	3 499	612	1 618	2 032	297.2	102.4	73.5	146.3	669	392	282.2	15.6
Roanoke City	429.1	2.7	4 460	2 994	476	612	357	115.0	42.5	77.3	49.2	490	289	109.2	53.5
Salem City	0.0	0.0	0	0	0	0	0	17.5	3.0	80.8	11.3	470	319	11.2	7.3

1. Based on the estimated population as of July 1 of the year shown.
2. Based on the estimated population as of July 1, 1982.

STATE County	Local government finances, 1981–1982 (cont'd): Direct general expenditure (cont'd): Per capita[1] (Dollars)	Percent of total for– Education	Percent of total for– Health & hospitals	Percent of total for– Police protection	Percent of total for– Public welfare	Percent of total for– Highways	Debt outstanding: Total (Mil dol)	Debt outstanding: Per capita[1] (Dollars)	State and local government employment, 1989: Total	State and local government employment, 1989: Rate[2]	Federal government civilian employment 1989: Total	Federal government civilian employment 1989: Earnings ($1,000)	Elections, 1988[3]: Total vote cast for president	Elections, 1988[3]: Vote for lead party (Percent)
	189	190	191	192	193	194	195	196	197	198	199	200	201	202
VIRGINIA—Con.														
Northumberland	503	71.1	0.3	5.0	5.6	0.3	0.4	39	310	306.9	40	896	4 581	R—65.1
Nottoway	589	60.9	0.2	6.5	5.8	4.7	6.8	470	1 409	952.0	476	19 231	5 509	R—57.4
Orange	588	70.9	0.0	4.7	5.4	1.7	5.5	295	1 177	544.9	57	1 462	7 015	R—61.6
Page	703	63.0	0.0	5.8	3.5	2.6	3.3	170	811	393.7	139	2 566	7 575	R—66.2
Patrick	479	75.7	0.4	2.8	4.3	2.2	3.2	180	607	348.9	53	1 253	6 229	R—64.1
Pittsylvania	445	76.2	0.3	3.8	3.5	0.4	15.1	228	4 935	462.5	291	8 257	19 201	R—63.7
Powhatan	438	75.4	0.2	4.1	5.8	0.0	3.6	276	1 406	956.5	27	643	5 541	R—72.9
Prince Edward	609	63.9	0.7	6.1	6.8	3.6	6.0	362	1 536	903.5	97	2 780	5 720	R—55.0
Prince George	566	78.1	0.1	5.2	2.6	0.2	5.5	214	2 444	490.8	5 115	145 251	7 515	R—66.3
Prince William	883	59.6	1.7	6.5	2.5	0.2	117.5	750	10 651	444.9	3 643	99 980	59 453	R—66.7
Pulaski	563	62.9	0.0	6.4	5.4	1.7	4.9	139	1 729	494.0	69	1 899	11 719	R—58.4
Rappahannock	457	75.5	0.0	3.7	6.2	0.2	0.5	90	240	358.2	51	806	2 686	R—61.7
Richmond	875	77.7	0.1	2.9	4.6	0.0	2.7	388	493	694.4	32	779	2 811	R—66.2
Roanoke	847	68.5	0.1	4.4	3.1	0.8	20.1	272	5 621	571.2	1 760	57 662	35 157	R—62.6
Rockbridge	573	69.8	1.3	3.0	5.3	0.2	4.6	257	2 129	691.2	157	3 787	6 062	R—58.4
Rockingham	556	69.9	0.9	3.7	3.1	0.8	28.9	548	5 476	672.7	408	11 522	18 241	R—72.6
Russell	645	61.8	0.3	1.9	4.4	0.3	57.6	1 777	1 213	385.1	63	1 629	10 753	D—57.9
Scott	501	72.7	0.0	5.2	4.3	0.6	4.2	166	896	361.3	62	1 552	8 785	R—56.8
Shenandoah	565	63.9	0.4	4.8	4.0	1.3	10.5	379	1 205	400.3	146	3 649	12 004	R—71.7
Smyth	574	57.9	0.2	4.9	6.1	4.3	3.4	102	1 980	611.1	113	2 904	11 727	R—63.5
Southampton	559	64.1	0.2	4.3	8.3	0.8	2.2	117	2 035	798.0	95	2 434	6 493	R—53.0
Spotsylvania	755	68.5	0.2	2.5	3.0	0.0	33.2	986	4 221	633.8	264	7 272	16 593	R—66.2
Stafford	692	71.1	0.2	3.1	2.8	1.7	44.2	1 001	2 163	346.1	69	1 574	17 712	R—69.1
Surry	996	63.7	0.8	6.0	10.8	0.1	2.0	321	393	595.5	21	487	2 899	D—55.3
Sussex	711	64.7	0.0	5.6	6.5	0.4	1.0	99	529	499.1	42	1 022	3 896	D—50.3
Tazewell	586	63.3	0.0	4.1	5.9	5.7	16.5	319	2 828	591.6	160	4 851	15 453	D—52.4
Warren	679	53.5	0.3	6.2	4.5	3.6	9.3	428	1 019	398.0	147	4 398	7 598	R—61.9
Washington	559	68.4	0.2	3.8	5.2	1.4	16.8	358	3 625	565.5	387	12 003	16 899	R—63.4
Westmoreland	765	57.2	0.2	5.8	4.0	0.6	1.9	136	575	371.0	64	1 290	5 370	R—55.4
Wise	680	62.9	0.2	5.0	3.6	2.2	16.0	361	2 824	607.3	330	10 806	13 386	D—52.4
Wythe	557	61.5	0.3	4.3	5.4	4.3	4.9	190	1 588	613.1	132	3 374	9 225	R—63.2
York	860	59.3	0.8	2.5	4.6	0.8	53.0	1 441	2 135	381.2	2 152	64 839	15 871	R—70.0
Independent Cities														
Alexandria City	1 425	30.2	4.5	6.9	7.2	5.8	171.7	1 643	7 003	649.0	13 008	461 162	45 804	D—53.2
Bedford City	473	0.0	0.4	14.8	0.0	12.8	2.3	364	0	0.0	0	0	2 328	R—56.8
Bristol City	848	45.8	0.8	7.1	3.6	5.6	10.0	531	0	0.0	0	0	6 895	R—63.9
Buena Vista City	666	57.7	0.4	8.2	2.1	6.3	1.0	142	0	0.0	0	0	1 999	R—56.1
Charlottesville City	862	47.3	0.0	6.3	5.9	6.5	24.7	610	0	0.0	0	0	13 652	D—56.2
Chesapeake City	1 104	42.3	17.8	4.6	3.5	9.5	121.8	1 016	8 859	577.5	369	11 009	48 855	R—60.9
Clifton Forge City	1 028	61.6	0.3	4.6	3.4	4.1	1.2	255	0	0.0	0	0	1 739	D—55.3
Colonial Heights City	769	62.5	0.5	5.0	1.8	4.4	8.9	522	0	0.0	0	0	7 638	R—78.6
Covington City	726	58.0	0.0	6.5	0.0	9.2	0.1	13	0	0.0	0	0	2 915	D—53.8
Danville City	903	39.8	0.0	6.8	6.0	9.6	26.8	597	0	0.0	0	0	19 874	R—61.5
Emporia City	462	0.0	1.6	24.2	0.0	22.4	1.2	255	0	0.0	0	0	2 277	R—56.6
Fairfax City	566	1.0	0.0	21.0	0.2	20.6	19.3	946	0	0.0	0	0	9 101	R—61.3
Falls Church City	1 329	38.0	0.6	9.3	1.8	12.8	5.4	573	0	0.0	0	0	4 989	D—49.8
Franklin City	888	60.1	0.7	6.8	3.1	4.4	13.2	1 883	0	0.0	0	0	3 210	D—50.8
Fredericksburg City	1 019	43.4	0.9	5.5	3.3	7.7	28.4	1 568	0	0.0	0	0	6 154	R—55.3
Galax City	828	52.7	0.7	11.1	7.1	11.1	1.3	193	0	0.0	0	0	2 200	R—58.1
Hampton City	768	46.1	0.7	6.3	5.2	5.4	70.0	560	6 754	511.7	10 334	330 984	43 818	R—54.8
Harrisonburg City	819	31.3	0.6	3.6	1.6	5.2	18.3	717	0	0.0	0	0	8 288	R—64.9
Hopewell City	1 704	24.5	34.3	2.8	2.0	4.3	4.2	173	0	0.0	0	0	7 360	R—63.5
Lexington City	579	41.8	1.0	10.6	0.0	11.6	1.5	217	0	0.0	0	0	2 024	D—49.3
Lynchburg City	1 001	37.7	0.1	6.0	6.2	6.5	98.1	1 456	0	0.0	0	0	23 926	R—64.0
Manassas City	967	47.1	0.6	6.0	2.9	4.7	26.0	1 513	0	0.0	0	0	8 719	R—68.6
Manassas Park City	1 007	50.9	0.7	6.6	3.9	4.3	5.8	901	0	0.0	0	0	1 446	R—68.7
Martinsville City	926	42.0	0.7	7.3	4.8	4.4	13.9	762	0	0.0	0	0	6 264	R—53.6
Newport News City	965	43.5	1.2	4.0	3.6	2.9	113.3	751	8 435	526.9	6 201	167 407	54 395	R—59.9
Norfolk City	1 018	33.3	7.6	6.8	6.7	4.5	208.9	782	16 481	570.1	18 390	511 555	68 891	D—54.8
Norton City	799	53.3	0.7	7.8	5.2	8.7	0.8	170	0	0.0	0	0	1 423	D—55.9
Petersburg City	1 723	23.9	45.1	3.6	4.0	2.4	39.6	984	0	0.0	0	0	12 591	D—64.9
Poquoson City	635	64.0	0.9	4.9	0.0	5.2	4.1	431	0	0.0	0	0	4 751	R—80.8
Portsmouth City	1 123	32.2	2.7	7.9	4.6	3.7	100.8	952	6 085	573.5	16 549	550 043	36 059	D—54.6
Radford City	607	44.7	0.5	5.7	3.6	4.7	2.1	163	0	0.0	0	0	4 365	R—56.8
Richmond City	1 291	35.2	2.0	6.4	12.3	7.0	517.3	2 367	42 020	1 992.4	7 175	224 087	74 736	D—56.4
Roanoke City	1 087	32.5	0.5	4.1	6.8	4.5	73.0	727	5 642	586.5	1 593	52 537	32 813	D—52.4
Salem City	468	0.0	0.0	12.0	0.0	7.6	47.9	1 994	0	0.0	0	0	9 527	R—59.8

1. Based on the estimated population as of July 1, 1982. 2. Per 10,000 resident population estimated as of July 1 of the year shown. 3. Data subject to copyright.

STATE–County code	MSA/CMSA/NECMA code[1]	STATE County	Land Area,[2] 1990 (Sq. Km.)	Population, 1990: Total persons	Rank	Per square kilometer	Race: White	Black	Am. Indian, Eskimo, Aleut	Asian & Pacific Islander	Other race	Hispanic[3]	Age of population Percent: Under 5 years	5 to 14 years	15 to 24 years
			1	2	3	4	5	6	7	8	9	10	11	12	13
		VIRGINIA—Con.													
51 780	...	South Boston City	14	6 997	2 659	499.8	4 376	2 569	11	34	7	45	6.4	12.8	13.2
51 790	...	Staunton City	51	24 461	1 479	479.6	21 181	3 081	38	102	59	169	5.6	11.2	14.2
51 800	5720	Suffolk City	1 036	52 141	812	50.3	28 511	23 245	112	200	73	319	7.6	15.2	13.0
51 810	5720	Virginia Beach City	643	393 069	128	611.3	316 408	54 671	1 384	17 025	3 581	12 137	8.9	15.2	16.8
51 820	...	Waynesboro City	36	18 549	1 760	515.2	16 681	1 749	34	44	41	150	6.9	12.3	13.2
51 830	5720	Williamsburg City	22	11 530	2 253	524.1	9 368	1 754	25	335	48	151	2.7	5.0	49.9
51 840	...	Winchester City	24	21 947	1 578	914.5	19 453	2 199	26	209	60	219	7.0	11.4	15.6
53 000	...	WASHINGTON	172 447	4 866 692	X	28.2	4 308 937	149 801	81 483	210 958	115 513	214 570	7.5	14.6	13.9
53 001	...	Adams	4 986	13 603	2 092	2.7	9 100	31	64	93	4 315	4 467	9.2	19.7	13.1
53 003	...	Asotin	1 647	17 605	1 814	10.7	17 136	38	260	107	64	278	7.4	15.8	11.8
53 005	6740	Benton	4 411	112 560	408	25.5	102 832	1 085	861	2 246	5 536	8 624	8.3	17.2	13.1
53 007	...	Chelan	7 567	52 250	810	6.9	48 333	80	487	378	2 972	4 786	7.7	15.2	11.9
53 009	...	Clallam	4 520	56 464	770	12.5	52 509	321	2 695	614	325	1 150	6.4	14.2	10.6
53 011	6442	Clark	1 626	238 053	210	146.4	225 192	2 976	2 296	5 670	1 919	5 872	7.8	16.2	13.2
53 013	...	Columbia	2 250	4 024	2 915	1.8	3 874	1	27	16	106	463	5.5	14.6	11.1
53 015	...	Cowlitz	2 949	82 119	552	27.8	78 516	288	1 347	1 137	831	1 672	7.4	15.6	13.0
53 017	...	Douglas	4 715	26 205	1 412	5.6	24 341	45	226	163	1 430	2 721	7.8	16.7	12.7
53 019	...	Ferry	5 708	6 295	2 722	1.1	5 084	20	1 131	24	36	85	7.7	17.8	14.5
53 021	6740	Franklin	3 217	37 473	1 060	11.6	26 917	1 310	263	869	8 114	11 316	9.4	20.0	15.2
53 023	...	Garfield	1 840	2 248	3 050	1.2	2 222	0	12	7	7	22	5.2	16.1	8.3
53 025	...	Grant	6 932	54 758	785	7.9	46 976	599	568	641	5 974	9 427	8.8	17.8	13.5
53 027	...	Grays Harbor	4 966	64 175	685	12.9	60 230	119	2 682	712	432	1 173	7.3	15.5	12.1
53 029	...	Island	540	60 195	720	111.5	55 034	1 454	480	2 553	674	2 006	8.1	14.2	14.2
53 031	...	Jefferson	4 685	20 146	1 668	4.3	19 252	84	566	195	49	241	5.7	13.4	8.7
53 033	7602	King	5 507	1 507 319	13	273.7	1 278 532	76 289	17 305	118 784	16 409	44 337	7.0	12.4	13.4
53 035	1150	Kitsap	1 026	189 731	252	184.9	171 063	5 107	3 211	8 282	2 068	6 169	8.2	15.7	14.7
53 037	...	Kittitas	5 950	26 725	1 400	4.5	25 529	151	216	477	352	684	5.6	12.2	25.3
53 039	...	Klickitat	4 850	16 616	1 876	3.4	15 383	26	581	128	498	928	7.5	17.1	11.6
53 041	...	Lewis	6 236	59 358	730	9.5	57 663	189	641	372	493	1 366	7.3	16.4	12.7
53 043	...	Lincoln	5 986	8 864	2 481	1.5	8 657	15	134	33	25	83	6.2	16.1	8.8
53 045	...	Mason	2 489	38 341	1 046	15.4	35 769	332	1 430	478	332	883	6.4	14.8	11.3
53 047	...	Okanogan	13 645	33 350	1 179	2.4	27 615	52	3 597	166	1 920	2 779	7.6	16.8	11.6
53 049	...	Pacific	2 524	18 882	1 741	7.5	17 683	57	519	480	143	433	6.4	13.4	10.5
53 051	...	Pend Oreille	3 627	8 915	2 478	2.5	8 640	12	206	25	32	120	7.4	17.0	10.7
53 053	7602	Pierce	4 340	586 203	80	135.1	498 642	42 210	8 344	29 035	7 972	20 562	8.2	15.2	15.1
53 055	...	San Juan	453	10 035	2 382	22.2	9 811	23	79	86	36	121	5.8	11.9	6.6
53 057	...	Skagit	4 494	79 555	573	17.7	74 133	280	1 712	782	2 648	4 335	7.1	15.1	12.2
53 059	...	Skamania	4 290	8 289	2 537	1.9	7 987	5	198	52	47	172	7.6	17.6	11.3
53 061	7602	Snohomish	5 414	465 642	106	86.0	434 536	4 767	6 422	16 467	3 450	10 656	8.5	15.5	12.6
53 063	7840	Spokane	4 568	361 364	142	79.1	341 874	5 105	5 539	6 569	2 277	6 994	7.4	14.9	14.6
53 065	...	Stevens	6 419	30 948	1 247	4.8	28 747	65	1 807	179	150	483	7.3	19.0	11.3
53 067	5910	Thurston	1 883	161 238	295	85.6	148 221	2 864	2 498	6 101	1 554	4 873	7.1	15.6	13.5
53 069	...	Wahkiakum	684	3 327	2 970	4.9	3 218	3	53	15	38	71	6.0	14.6	10.4
53 071	...	Walla Walla	3 291	48 439	864	14.7	43 290	720	359	625	3 445	4 703	6.8	14.3	16.4
53 073	0860	Whatcom	5 491	127 780	364	23.3	119 229	650	4 014	2 363	1 524	3 718	6.9	14.4	16.8
53 075	...	Whitman	5 593	38 775	1 030	6.9	35 653	490	248	2 112	272	683	5.0	10.1	37.2
53 077	9260	Yakima	11 127	188 823	255	17.0	139 514	1 938	8 405	1 922	37 044	45 114	8.7	17.0	14.4
54 000	...	WEST VIRGINIA	62 384	1 793 477	X	28.7	1 725 523	56 295	2 458	7 459	1 742	8 489	5.9	14.2	14.6
54 001	...	Barbour	883	15 699	1 944	17.8	15 333	148	160	35	23	89	6.1	14.4	15.8
54 003	...	Berkeley	832	59 253	733	71.2	56 511	2 209	89	283	161	399	7.4	14.5	13.9
54 005	...	Boone	1 303	25 870	1 427	19.9	25 590	214	29	19	18	48	5.7	15.8	14.6
54 007	...	Braxton	1 330	12 998	2 143	9.8	12 905	46	17	23	7	37	6.7	14.3	13.0
54 009	8080	Brooke	230	26 992	1 391	117.4	26 673	202	29	60	28	85	4.9	13.2	15.3
54 011	3400	Cabell	729	96 827	475	132.8	92 103	3 966	112	534	112	442	5.5	12.4	16.7
54 013	...	Calhoun	727	7 885	2 583	10.8	7 836	2	14	30	3	18	6.4	16.1	12.4
54 015	...	Clay	887	9 983	2 388	11.3	9 968	1	7	6	1	14	7.0	17.5	14.4
54 017	...	Doddridge	830	6 994	2 660	8.4	6 952	2	31	8	1	12	5.9	16.1	12.6
54 019	...	Fayette	1 720	47 952	872	27.9	44 697	3 017	62	142	34	252	5.2	15.0	14.7
54 021	...	Gilmer	881	7 669	2 605	8.7	7 593	32	8	31	5	24	5.8	13.6	19.5
54 023	...	Grant	1 236	10 428	2 347	8.4	10 273	106	22	19	8	35	6.1	14.3	14.1
54 025	...	Greenbrier	2 645	34 693	1 143	13.1	33 296	1 277	42	63	15	137	5.6	13.9	12.6
54 027	...	Hampshire	1 662	16 498	1 893	9.9	16 314	112	30	18	24	93	7.0	15.0	14.2
54 029	8080	Hancock	215	35 233	1 124	163.9	34 135	901	41	113	43	199	5.2	13.1	13.0
54 031	...	Hardy	1 511	10 977	2 297	7.3	10 744	209	14	5	5	55	6.5	13.1	13.2

1. MSA = Metropolitan Statistical Area. CMSA = Consolidated MSA. NECMA = New England county metropolitan area. PMSA = Primary MSA. See Appendix A for explanation of these concepts. See Appendix B for list of metropolitan areas identified by type, with component counties. 2. Dry land or land partially or temporarily covered by water. 3. Hispanic persons may be of any race.

STATE County	Population, 1990 (cont'd): Age of population (cont'd), Percent: 25 to 34 years	35 to 44 years	45 to 54 years	55 to 64 years	65 to 74 years	75 years and over	Percent female	Population–Change and components of change: Change, 1980–1990: Number	Percent	Components of change, 1980–1986: Total persons, 1986	Total persons, 1980	Net change: Number	Percent	Natural increase: Births	Deaths
	14	15	16	17	18	19	20	21	22	23	24	25	26	27	28
VIRGINIA—Con.															
South Boston City	12.7	14.3	10.2	10.2	10.9	9.3	56.0	-96	-1.4	7 000	7 093	-100	-0.8	500	500
Staunton City	16.1	14.8	10.7	10.4	9.5	7.5	52.9	2 604	11.9	21 500	21 857	-300	-1.5	1 700	1 600
Suffolk City	16.5	14.4	11.0	9.3	7.9	5.0	52.6	4 520	9.5	51 300	47 621	3 700	7.8	4 600	3 200
Virginia Beach City	22.4	16.1	8.8	6.0	3.9	2.0	49.2	130 870	49.9	333 400	262 199	71 200	27.2	32 900	8 400
Waynesboro City	15.7	13.3	11.4	10.4	10.1	6.7	52.8	-14	-0.1	18 100	18 563	-500	-2.7	1 400	1 000
Williamsburg City	12.5	7.5	5.4	5.3	6.5	5.4	53.6	1 236	12.0	11 400	10 294	1 100	10.3	1 100	600
Winchester City	17.9	14.1	9.5	9.3	8.7	6.6	52.2	1 730	8.6	21 200	20 217	1 000	4.7	1 700	1 600
WASHINGTON	17.6	16.5	10.3	7.8	6.9	4.9	50.4	734 692	17.8	4 462 000	4 132 000	330 000	8.0	433 000	207 000
Adams	14.2	14.0	9.9	8.4	6.8	4.5	49.6	336	2.5	13 800	13 267	500	3.9	1 900	600
Asotin	15.1	14.1	9.9	9.3	8.9	7.7	52.4	782	4.6	17 100	16 823	300	1.8	1 600	1 000
Benton	16.6	16.0	10.7	8.1	6.2	3.9	50.6	3 116	2.8	112 700	109 444	3 300	3.0	13 000	3 700
Chelan	15.1	15.6	9.9	8.9	8.6	7.1	50.7	7 189	16.0	49 900	45 061	4 900	10.8	5 100	3 200
Clallam	13.4	14.9	9.9	10.3	12.2	8.2	50.3	4 816	9.3	53 700	51 648	2 100	4.0	5 100	3 200
Clark	16.5	17.2	10.9	7.5	6.3	4.3	50.6	45 826	23.8	211 300	192 227	19 100	9.9	20 100	8 800
Columbia	12.5	14.9	11.9	10.4	11.1	8.1	50.4	-33	-0.8	4 200	4 057	100	2.7	400	300
Cowlitz	15.2	15.7	10.8	8.8	7.7	5.8	50.6	2 571	3.2	78 700	79 548	-900	-1.1	7 600	4 000
Douglas	15.3	16.1	10.6	8.7	7.3	4.8	49.7	4 061	18.3	24 200	22 144	2 100	9.4	2 300	1 000
Ferry	13.5	16.9	11.0	8.1	6.7	3.9	47.9	484	8.3	5 900	5 811	0	0.8	600	300
Franklin	15.5	14.4	8.2	7.4	6.3	3.6	48.7	2 448	7.0	36 800	35 025	1 800	5.1	5 400	1 400
Garfield	10.9	15.2	10.0	12.1	12.3	10.0	51.0	-220	-8.9	2 500	2 468	0	-0.4	200	200
Grant	14.7	14.1	9.4	8.9	7.9	4.8	49.4	6 236	12.9	53 100	48 522	4 500	9.4	5 900	2 200
Grays Harbor	14.5	15.0	10.5	9.2	9.2	6.7	50.2	-2 139	-3.2	62 700	66 314	-3 600	-5.5	6 700	4 000
Island	18.2	14.5	8.7	8.2	9.1	4.7	47.9	16 147	36.7	49 600	44 048	5 500	12.6	5 300	2 100
Jefferson	11.7	17.3	10.9	11.7	13.6	7.1	50.6	4 181	26.2	18 500	15 965	2 500	15.8	1 400	1 000
King	20.0	17.9	10.8	7.6	6.5	4.6	50.7	237 421	18.7	1 362 300	1 269 898	92 400	7.3	117 300	61 800
Kitsap	17.0	16.6	10.1	7.1	6.3	4.4	48.9	42 579	28.9	169 200	147 152	22 100	15.0	17 100	6 800
Kittitas	13.1	13.6	9.7	7.3	7.4	5.8	50.4	1 848	7.4	24 700	24 877	-200	-0.8	2 100	1 300
Klickitat	14.5	16.5	10.6	8.4	7.8	5.8	49.7	794	5.0	16 200	15 822	400	2.4	1 700	800
Lewis	13.8	14.7	10.3	9.1	8.7	7.0	50.8	3 333	5.9	58 200	56 025	2 200	3.8	5 800	3 400
Lincoln	12.2	14.4	11.5	11.2	10.5	9.2	50.1	-740	-7.7	9 400	9 604	-200	-1.8	800	700
Mason	14.2	15.3	10.6	10.9	10.8	5.6	48.4	7 157	23.0	36 000	31 184	4 800	15.3	3 200	1 800
Okanogan	14.0	15.5	11.1	9.6	7.8	6.1	49.5	2 687	8.8	32 500	30 663	1 800	5.9	3 800	1 900
Pacific	12.0	13.7	10.2	12.3	12.9	8.7	50.6	1 645	9.5	17 400	17 237	200	1.1	1 600	1 400
Pend Oreille	13.0	16.0	11.6	10.3	8.4	5.5	50.4	335	3.9	9 000	8 580	500	5.4	800	500
Pierce	18.2	15.4	9.7	7.6	6.2	4.3	50.0	100 536	20.7	533 300	485 667	47 700	9.8	58 400	23 500
San Juan	11.0	19.3	12.4	11.6	13.8	7.7	50.5	2 197	28.0	9 200	7 838	1 400	17.3	600	400
Skagit	14.6	15.9	10.4	9.1	9.1	6.5	50.7	15 417	24.0	69 600	64 138	5 500	8.6	6 800	4 000
Skamania	15.9	16.9	11.5	8.5	6.3	4.5	49.0	370	4.7	7 700	7 919	-200	-2.4	800	300
Snohomish	19.2	17.4	10.3	7.1	5.7	3.8	50.1	127 922	37.9	388 800	337 720	51 100	15.1	38 400	14 800
Spokane	16.4	15.6	9.8	7.9	7.4	5.8	51.4	19 529	5.7	356 900	341 835	15 100	4.4	35 200	18 700
Stevens	13.2	16.8	11.5	8.4	7.1	5.4	50.1	1 969	6.8	31 600	28 979	2 600	9.1	3 300	1 500
Thurston	16.0	17.6	10.8	7.7	6.8	4.9	51.3	36 974	29.8	146 600	124 264	22 400	18.0	13 400	6 100
Wahkiakum	11.3	15.6	11.9	10.6	11.3	8.2	50.3	-505	-13.2	3 600	3 832	-300	-6.9	300	200
Walla Walla	14.8	14.3	9.4	8.3	8.4	7.3	49.7	1 004	2.1	48 000	47 435	600	1.2	4 300	2 900
Whatcom	15.7	16.4	9.6	7.6	7.0	5.5	50.8	21 079	19.8	113 700	106 701	7 000	6.6	10 400	5 200
Whitman	14.5	10.7	7.4	5.6	5.2	4.3	48.3	-1 328	-3.3	40 700	40 103	600	1.4	3 100	1 300
Yakima	15.3	14.1	9.6	7.9	7.1	5.9	50.3	16 315	9.5	183 200	172 508	10 700	6.2	21 000	9 700
WEST VIRGINIA	14.6	15.1	10.7	9.9	8.7	6.3	52.0	-156 523	-8.0	1 918 000	1 950 000	-31 000	-1.6	164 000	120 000
Barbour	13.8	14.3	10.4	9.2	8.6	7.4	52.2	-940	-5.6	16 500	16 639	-100	-0.7	1 400	1 100
Berkeley	17.3	15.6	10.4	9.1	7.2	4.5	50.4	12 478	26.7	51 500	46 775	4 700	10.0	4 500	3 000
Boone	14.7	16.6	10.7	9.3	7.8	4.7	51.4	-4 577	-15.0	29 900	30 447	-600	-1.8	2 600	1 700
Braxton	13.7	14.9	10.3	9.9	9.3	7.8	51.5	-896	-6.4	14 600	13 894	700	5.3	1 100	1 000
Brooke	12.9	15.4	10.8	11.1	9.8	6.6	52.1	-4 125	-13.3	29 500	31 117	-1 600	-5.2	2 100	1 700
Cabell	14.1	14.0	10.6	10.3	9.3	7.1	53.2	-10 008	-9.4	104 700	106 835	-2 100	-2.0	8 600	7 300
Calhoun	14.2	15.0	10.3	9.9	8.3	7.4	50.9	-365	-4.4	8 200	8 250	0	-0.3	900	600
Clay	14.2	14.9	9.7	9.4	7.2	5.7	50.7	-1 282	-11.4	11 400	11 265	100	1.2	1 100	700
Doddridge	14.8	14.2	10.3	9.9	9.4	6.8	50.5	-439	-5.9	7 700	7 433	300	3.7	700	500
Fayette	13.1	14.9	9.7	10.3	9.8	7.3	52.1	-9 911	-17.1	55 500	57 863	-2 400	-4.1	4 900	4 100
Gilmer	13.5	12.4	9.6	9.3	7.9	8.4	50.4	-665	-8.0	8 500	8 334	200	1.9	800	500
Grant	14.4	15.4	11.5	9.3	8.0	6.8	50.8	218	2.1	9 700	10 210	-500	-5.1	800	600
Greenbrier	14.4	15.0	11.1	10.4	9.1	7.8	52.1	-2 972	-7.9	38 400	37 665	700	2.0	3 000	2 600
Hampshire	14.6	14.6	10.8	10.1	8.4	5.3	50.5	1 631	11.0	16 200	14 867	1 300	8.7	1 300	900
Hancock	14.2	15.7	11.2	11.7	9.9	6.1	52.1	-5 820	-14.2	39 600	41 053	-1 400	-3.5	2 900	2 300
Hardy	15.6	14.6	10.8	10.8	9.0	6.3	50.7	947	9.4	10 000	10 030	0	-0.2	700	700

STATE County	Population–(cont'd) Components of change, 1980-1986 (cont'd) Net migration	Households, 1990 Number	Households, 1990 Percent change, 1980–1990	Households, 1990 Persons per household	Households, 1990 Percent Female family householder[1]	Households, 1990 Percent One-person	Births, 1988 Total	Births, 1988 Rate[2]	Births, 1988 Low birth weight[3] (Number)	Deaths, 1987 Number Total	Deaths, 1987 Number Infant[4]	Deaths, 1987 Rate Total[2]	Deaths, 1987 Rate Infant[5]	Marriages, 1984 Number	Marriages, 1984 Rate[2]
	29	30	31	32	33	34	35	36	37	38	39	40	41	42	43
VIRGINIA—Con.															
South Boston City	-100	2 795	6.8	2.43	17.5	29.6	(6)	(6)	(6)	(6)	(6)	(6)	(6)	51	7.1
Staunton City	-300	9 432	16.5	2.30	11.3	30.7	(7)	(7)	(7)	(7)	(7)	(7)	(7)	322	14.8
Suffolk City	2 300	18 516	17.6	2.78	17.1	20.4	NA	NA	NA	NA	NA	NA	NA	420	8.6
Virginia Beach City	46 700	135 566	59.2	2.82	9.5	17.1	7 112	19.5	466	1 651	83	4.7	12.1	3 741	12.2
Waynesboro City	-900	7 568	28.9	2.40	12.4	26.5	(7)	(7)	(7)	(7)	(7)	(7)	(7)	232	15.4
Williamsburg City	600	3 468	23.0	2.11	8.3	35.0	(8)	(8)	(8)	(8)	(8)	(8)	(8)	562	52.0
Winchester City	800	9 084	14.0	2.31	10.6	32.6	(9)	(9)	(9)	(9)	(9)	(9)	(9)	1 790	86.9
WASHINGTON	105 000	1 872 431	21.5	2.53	9.4	25.4	72 503	15.6	3 804	35 022	682	7.7	9.7	45 080	10.4
Adams	-800	4 586	2.2	2.94	7.3	20.4	259	19.6	15	99	2	7.5	7.2	125	9.2
Asotin	-300	7 003	8.2	2.47	12.6	25.9	251	14.8	13	164	8	9.6	33.3	157	9.1
Benton	-6 100	42 227	8.3	2.65	9.3	23.5	1 751	15.6	78	662	17	5.9	9.3	1 116	10.0
Chelan	3 000	20 645	16.0	2.49	8.4	26.8	833	17.2	39	433	11	9.0	13.7	677	13.9
Clallam	200	22 837	14.2	2.40	8.2	25.8	704	12.6	29	590	14	10.7	18.3	525	10.1
Clark	7 800	88 440	28.6	2.66	9.9	22.1	3 455	15.3	162	1 487	16	6.8	4.9	3 778	18.6
Columbia	100	1 582	0.3	2.44	7.0	28.4	52	12.7	2	42	0	10.2	0.0	37	9.0
Cowlitz	-4 400	31 640	7.2	2.56	9.7	23.9	1 254	15.6	72	716	10	9.1	8.5	809	10.2
Douglas	800	9 687	21.2	2.68	8.1	20.0	349	14.0	16	189	2	7.7	5.8	191	8.1
Ferry	-300	2 247	15.0	2.70	9.1	22.1	77	12.8	4	49	1	8.3	14.1	54	9.0
Franklin	-2 200	12 196	1.8	3.03	11.1	19.4	778	22.9	39	240	2	7.0	2.7	238	6.5
Garfield	-100	922	-2.1	2.39	5.0	27.3	14	5.8	1	23	0	9.6	0.0	28	11.2
Grant	900	19 745	15.1	2.74	8.4	22.6	892	17.3	45	364	10	7.1	10.7	441	8.5
Grays Harbor	-6 300	25 514	1.3	2.48	9.8	26.8	960	15.3	61	698	12	11.2	13.3	672	10.5
Island	2 300	21 787	37.4	2.61	6.2	18.7	931	17.1	29	397	4	7.5	4.4	520	10.9
Jefferson	2 100	8 627	35.7	2.31	7.9	26.8	230	11.8	15	173	2	9.1	9.2	183	10.5
King	36 900	615 792	23.8	2.40	9.0	29.2	21 209	14.7	1 188	10 240	188	7.3	9.2	13 705	10.3
Kitsap	11 900	69 267	31.2	2.65	8.5	22.1	2 850	15.8	136	1 129	27	6.5	9.6	1 715	10.4
Kittitas	-1 000	10 460	10.2	2.33	7.2	29.1	295	11.7	18	198	4	7.9	14.1	215	8.6
Klickitat	-500	6 210	7.9	2.64	8.8	22.7	221	13.9	11	136	2	8.6	9.3	193	11.8
Lewis	-300	22 478	8.8	2.60	9.1	23.7	852	14.4	40	569	8	9.7	9.5	548	9.5
Lincoln	-300	3 605	-2.2	2.43	5.2	26.0	102	11.9	0	123	0	14.0	0.0	71	7.3
Mason	3 400	14 565	23.7	2.52	7.9	22.1	443	11.7	19	304	3	8.3	6.3	308	8.8
Okanogan	0	12 654	11.4	2.59	9.3	24.0	542	16.7	28	294	7	9.1	13.2	309	9.5
Pacific	0	7 896	13.8	2.35	7.9	27.2	250	14.0	4	263	0	14.9	0.0	223	12.7
Pend Oreille	200	3 395	13.1	2.60	8.3	22.8	123	13.8	8	87	0	10.1	0.0	78	8.9
Pierce	12 800	214 652	23.2	2.62	10.9	23.4	9 925	17.8	674	4 065	109	7.5	11.3	5 774	11.2
San Juan	1 200	4 392	31.5	2.25	6.0	27.2	105	10.5	2	82	0	8.5	0.0	164	18.6
Skagit	2 700	30 573	24.9	2.55	8.6	23.5	1 102	15.2	46	690	13	9.8	12.3	779	11.4
Skamania	-700	3 066	8.8	2.69	7.8	20.2	109	14.2	5	64	0	8.4	0.0	133	17.5
Snohomish	27 600	171 713	42.3	2.68	9.1	20.9	7 371	17.4	341	2 696	73	6.7	10.7	3 293	9.0
Spokane	-1 500	141 619	10.3	2.47	10.8	27.5	5 316	14.9	273	3 131	64	8.8	11.9	3 058	8.6
Stevens	900	11 241	14.2	2.73	8.0	21.0	399	12.5	21	249	3	7.9	7.1	210	6.8
Thurston	15 100	62 150	34.0	2.55	9.7	24.0	2 189	14.0	97	1 064	13	7.0	6.0	1 305	9.4
Wahkiakum	-300	1 321	-2.4	2.48	5.5	23.1	39	10.8	2	38	0	10.9	0.0	29	7.8
Walla Walla	-800	17 623	3.8	2.50	9.2	26.9	630	13.6	22	510	11	10.9	17.3	505	10.5
Whatcom	1 900	48 543	22.5	2.53	8.0	24.9	1 673	14.1	56	911	18	7.9	11.3	1 049	9.4
Whitman	-1 200	13 546	2.0	2.39	5.2	26.6	411	11.0	17	244	4	6.5	10.3	199	5.0
Yakima	-600	65 985	7.6	2.80	11.3	22.7	3 557	19.2	176	1 609	24	8.8	7.0	1 666	9.2
WEST VIRGINIA	-74 000	688 557	0.3	2.55	10.7	24.5	21 846	11.6	1 389	19 767	219	10.4	9.8	15 513	8.0
Barbour	-500	5 835	2.9	2.60	10.7	24.0	189	12.3	12	185	3	11.8	18.0	131	7.8
Berkeley	3 200	22 350	36.0	2.60	9.5	23.2	857	15.5	49	470	3	8.8	3.7	305	6.1
Boone	-1 400	9 656	-5.2	2.68	11.2	21.2	315	11.2	18	293	4	10.2	12.9	268	8.9
Braxton	600	4 950	1.0	2.61	10.1	23.3	181	12.7	6	177	2	12.2	10.2	143	9.7
Brooke	-2 000	10 131	-4.6	2.56	9.1	23.6	245	8.7	11	298	3	10.4	11.3	189	6.3
Cabell	-3 400	39 146	-2.7	2.39	11.5	29.0	1 127	11.2	67	1 185	10	11.6	8.9	909	8.4
Calhoun	-300	2 978	2.2	2.64	11.9	22.7	103	12.4	10	101	3	12.0	31.6	77	9.3
Clay	-300	3 627	-1.0	2.75	11.8	21.7	138	12.3	12	105	0	9.4	0.0	97	8.4
Doddridge	100	2 623	2.0	2.67	8.6	22.8	51	7.2	5	82	0	11.2	0.0	76	10.1
Fayette	-3 200	18 292	-7.9	2.55	12.6	25.8	536	10.3	35	629	4	11.9	6.8	435	7.6
Gilmer	-100	2 717	-3.2	2.61	9.3	22.9	89	11.4	13	101	2	12.9	20.4	65	7.6
Grant	-700	3 925	11.5	2.62	8.6	21.4	121	11.2	7	91	0	8.3	0.0	65	6.7
Greenbrier	400	13 775	1.8	2.48	10.6	25.9	400	11.4	23	400	2	11.2	5.0	255	6.5
Hampshire	900	6 182	20.0	2.63	8.5	22.3	183	11.2	12	153	2	9.6	9.3	117	7.4
Hancock	-2 000	13 781	-3.3	2.54	10.5	23.6	332	8.9	20	381	3	10.2	8.0	387	9.7
Hardy	-100	4 286	19.9	2.55	8.6	22.6	148	13.8	9	106	1	10.0	9.0	99	9.9

1. No spouse present. 2. Per 1,000 resident population estimated as of July 1 of the year shown. 3. Under 2,500 grams. 4. Deaths of infants under 1 year old. 5. Deaths of infants under 1 year old per 1,000 live births. 6. South Boston included with Halifax County. 7. Staunton and Waynesboro included with Augusta County. 8. Williamsburg included with James City County. 9. Winchester included with Frederick County.

STATE County	Divorces, 1984		Physicians, active non-Federal, 1989		Hospitals, 1989			Nursing homes,[4] 1986		Serious crimes known to police, 1988			Education			
						Beds				Number			Public school enrollment[7]		Attainment,[8] 1980	
	Number	Rate[1]	Number[2]	Rate[3]	Number	Number	Rate[3]	Number	Beds	Total[5]	Violent[6]	Rate[3]	1986–1987	1980	Percent 12 yrs. or more	Percent 16 yrs. or more
	44	45	46	47	48	49	50	51	52	53	54	55	56	57	58	59
VIRGINIA—Con.																
South Boston City	NA	NA	(9)	(9)	(9)	(9)	(9)	6	435	109	12	1 533	1 377	1 434	49.1	13.4
Staunton City	86	4.0	(10)	(10)	(10)	(10)	(10)	10	363	752	55	3 035	3 033	3 754	58.1	16.5
Suffolk City	155	3.2	NA	NA	NA	NA	NA	8	463	2 573	362	4 853	8 709	9 709	46.8	9.9
Virginia Beach City	1 743	5.7	652	171	3	558	147	8	980	19 363	723	5 446	61 200	56 825	80.0	22.4
Waynesboro City	94	6.2	(10)	(10)	(10)	(10)	(10)	2	260	777	42	4 227	2 703	3 011	58.4	16.7
Williamsburg City	25	2.3	(11)	(11)	(11)	(11)	(11)	1	156	637	38	5 227	0	622	77.5	40.3
Winchester City	112	5.4	(12)	(12)	(12)	(12)	(12)	5	461	1 348	72	6 006	3 099	3 195	55.1	14.0
WASHINGTON	27 138	6.2	9 670	203	115	16 066	338	405	33 454	317 560	21 033	7 032	762 308	769 107	77.6	19.0
Adams	50	3.7	9	69	2	58	443	2	112	568	24	4 044	3 225	3 031	65.7	13.4
Asotin	127	7.3	18	106	1	58	341	4	307	1 195	69	6 866	3 255	3 549	73.5	11.8
Benton	738	6.6	147	130	4	303	268	4	311	6 417	298	5 565	22 283	23 266	81.3	22.6
Chelan	447	9.2	127	263	3	236	490	5	491	3 277	122	6 918	8 869	8 064	69.1	14.5
Clallam	325	6.2	86	150	2	118	205	5	470	2 653	90	4 757	9 218	9 413	73.3	13.8
Clark	1 430	7.0	243	104	1	307	131	19	1 398	11 219	584	5 113	42 929	40 877	75.8	14.2
Columbia	20	4.9	3	73	1	94	2 293	3	95	221	5	5 429	725	810	71.9	7.2
Cowlitz	573	7.2	121	149	1	188	232	10	730	4 456	196	5 521	15 552	16 453	71.1	11.0
Douglas	37	1.6	10	40	0	0	0	1	81	1 122	40	4 445	4 485	4 563	71.7	12.6
Ferry	36	6.0	5	82	1	25	410	1	12	167	18	2 781	1 181	1 451	72.0	15.2
Franklin	269	7.3	44	131	1	108	322	2	202	3 389	214	9 148	7 937	7 118	71.8	12.5
Garfield	9	3.6	2	83	1	54	2 250	1	40	97	3	3 971	452	475	76.3	12.7
Grant	289	5.6	48	93	4	165	319	5	247	1 805	132	4 368	10 716	10 803	68.1	11.5
Grays Harbor	415	6.5	55	87	2	161	255	7	644	3 787	170	6 043	12 166	13 327	67.3	9.8
Island	334	7.0	44	77	2	76	133	3	147	692	27	1 313	7 611	8 530	82.2	17.6
Jefferson	119	6.8	22	109	1	23	114	1	94	818	43	4 230	2 814	2 745	76.9	17.6
King	8 145	6.2	5 101	345	26	5 044	341	96	10 492	130 711	9 307	9 232	198 749	208 956	82.6	26.2
Kitsap	895	5.4	219	117	2	376	201	12	1 046	6 430	401	3 625	30 234	29 010	79.7	16.4
Kittitas	94	3.8	23	91	1	41	161	3	225	1 685	46	6 570	3 897	4 094	74.4	20.7
Klickitat	103	6.3	11	70	2	58	367	1	80	567	43	3 482	3 422	3 424	67.5	9.6
Lewis	386	6.7	59	98	2	189	314	12	623	1 782	114	3 867	11 583	11 598	67.4	10.5
Lincoln	309	31.9	5	60	2	137	1 631	2	216	199	7	2 080	1 986	1 994	76.8	14.9
Mason	146	4.2	27	69	1	54	138	2	174	2 053	92	5 467	6 258	5 975	71.2	11.6
Okanogan	219	6.7	34	105	3	185	569	4	246	632	59	2 842	7 589	6 082	69.9	12.7
Pacific	112	6.4	10	56	2	37	206	4	214	539	10	4 100	3 056	3 109	67.5	9.5
Pend Oreille	30	3.4	4	45	1	24	270	1	50	446	31	5 037	1 954	1 972	68.1	10.5
Pierce	3 572	6.9	874	152	11	3 257	568	61	3 868	45 291	4 471	8 253	94 626	91 314	76.3	15.1
San Juan	60	6.8	21	200	0	0	0	1	53	354	8	3 623	1 295	1 222	88.0	31.3
Skagit	450	6.6	157	211	3	277	372	9	579	3 740	139	5 190	12 677	12 250	74.5	13.2
Skamania	51	6.7	2	26	0	0	0	0	0	411	19	5 314	1 254	1 628	72.0	12.3
Snohomish	2 147	5.8	472	107	5	713	161	24	2 319	21 734	893	5 317	66 918	67 813	78.0	15.3
Spokane	2 078	5.9	824	230	10	1 987	555	42	3 140	23 928	1 327	6 870	62 006	63 477	78.2	17.9
Stevens	178	5.7	17	53	2	73	227	2	133	300	3	4 286	5 739	6 763	74.6	10.5
Thurston	878	6.3	268	165	3	500	307	10	751	7 922	352	5 228	28 133	25 832	80.0	20.3
Wahkiakum	29	7.8	1	29	0	0	0	1	53	78	3	2 190	473	946	63.8	8.6
Walla Walla	271	5.6	96	208	4	372	807	8	763	3 065	266	6 491	7 249	7 518	75.2	18.2
Whatcom	624	5.6	193	159	1	162	133	13	1 135	6 209	290	5 309	18 663	18 592	76.5	17.9
Whitman	109	2.7	36	98	2	74	202	4	260	1 199	61	3 264	4 646	5 288	85.8	36.8
Yakima	1 034	5.7	232	124	5	532	284	20	1 653	16 402	1 056	8 902	36 483	35 775	62.1	11.3
WEST VIRGINIA	9 629	4.9	3 116	168	71	10 783	580	163	9 819	42 185	2 476	2 239	351 837	390 653	56.0	10.4
Barbour	67	4.0	13	87	1	61	407	2	70	148	9	944	3 225	3 563	49.3	8.3
Berkeley	241	4.8	73	129	2	655	1 153	2	122	2 493	85	4 677	9 778	9 546	55.9	10.6
Boone	186	6.2	9	33	1	38	138	1	120	319	28	1 093	6 521	6 789	41.4	4.4
Braxton	62	4.2	7	50	1	30	213	2	71	92	8	635	2 887	3 004	45.1	8.1
Brooke	126	4.2	11	40	0	0	0	3	108	472	19	1 657	4 952	5 827	62.7	9.6
Cabell	604	5.6	368	372	6	1 235	1 249	10	628	5 178	366	5 124	16 343	18 860	61.6	13.9
Calhoun	42	5.1	6	72	1	45	542	0	0	69	14	818	1 756	1 690	42.9	5.3
Clay	57	4.9	2	18	0	0	0	0	0	134	27	1 195	2 589	2 779	36.7	5.2
Doddridge	28	3.7	2	29	0	0	0	2	6	64	13	883	1 470	1 667	51.8	9.6
Fayette	290	5.1	48	95	2	190	376	7	358	694	67	1 309	10 880	12 250	46.7	7.4
Gilmer	35	4.1	1	13	0	0	0	1	65	70	2	904	1 388	1 588	46.5	11.4
Grant	41	4.2	13	117	1	59	532	2	70	58	6	536	2 074	2 206	45.0	7.7
Greenbrier	190	4.8	52	153	1	122	360	4	273	311	29	878	6 716	7 396	53.3	10.5
Hampshire	60	3.8	8	48	1	47	285	1	18	314	24	1 989	2 920	3 577	53.1	10.2
Hancock	187	4.7	54	149	2	271	749	1	57	630	24	1 688	6 293	7 315	62.1	7.6
Hardy	39	3.9	2	18	0	0	0	1	28	63	7	604	1 861	2 072	43.8	5.6

1. Per 1,000 resident population estimated as of July 1 of the year shown. 2. As of end of year. 3. Per 100,000 resident population as of July 1 of the year shown. 4. Preliminary. Covers nursing homes with 3 or more beds. 5. Data for serious crimes have not been adjusted for underreporting, this may affect comparability between geographic areas or over time. 6. Includes murder and nonnegligent manslaughter, forcible rape, robbery, and aggravated assault. 7. The 1986–1987 data are based on administrative reports obtained by the U.S. National Center for Education Statistics. The 1980 data are based on the 1980 Census of Population and Housing. 8. Persons 25 years old or older. 9. South Boston included with Halifax County. 10. Staunton and Waynesboro included with Augusta County. 11. Williamsburg included with James City County. 12. Winchester included with Frederick County.

STATE County	Education (cont'd): Local government expenditures for education,[1] 1982: Total (Mil dol)	Education (cont'd): Local government expenditures for education,[1] 1982: Per capita (Dollars)	Social Security Program December 1988: Beneficiaries: Total	Social Security Program December 1988: Beneficiaries: Rate[2]	Social Security Program December 1988: Payments ($1,000)	Supplemental Security Income Program recipients June 1986	Money income: Per capita[3]: 1987 Income, (Dollars)	Money income: Per capita[3]: 1979: Current dollars	Money income: Per capita[3]: 1979: Constant 1987 dollars	Money income: Median household income 1979 (Dollars)	Money income: Percent below poverty level, 1979: Persons	Money income: Percent below poverty level, 1979: Families	Housing units, 1990: Total	Housing units, 1990: Percent change, 1980–1990
	60	61	62	63	64	65	66	67	68	69	70	71	72	73
VIRGINIA—Con.														
South Boston City	2.5	345	0	0.0	968	432	10 672	5 978	9 354	13 724	15.7	13.2	2 997	6.4
Staunton City	6.8	308	0	0.0	2 878	532	12 043	7 172	11 222	15 996	9.9	6.8	10 003	15.9
Suffolk City	17.8	375	8 600	164.8	3 647	1 598	11 420	6 023	9 424	15 202	17.3	13.6	20 011	19.7
Virginia Beach City	108.5	383	27 285	74.7	12 942	1 578	13 141	7 704	12 054	20 203	8.9	7.7	147 037	59.8
Waynesboro City	6.2	410	0	0.0	2 224	246	14 007	7 721	12 081	16 081	9.2	7.2	7 902	27.4
Williamsburg City	15.2	1 444	0	0.0	2 443	80	11 954	6 366	9 961	15 004	13.2	1.7	3 960	30.2
Winchester City	7.4	367	0	0.0	2 476	442	13 394	7 358	11 513	13 955	14.9	11.0	9 808	17.0
WASHINGTON	2 129.9	498	684 421	147.3	348 738	50 576	12 184	8 073	12 632	18 367	9.8	7.2	2 032 378	20.3
Adams	11.1	832	2 170	164.4	1 067	330	9 481	6 593	10 316	16 834	12.7	11.1	5 263	4.2
Asotin	8.0	471	3 555	209.1	1 748	294	10 080	6 859	10 732	15 292	14.4	11.0	7 519	6.8
Benton	60.4	517	13 595	121.0	7 361	698	12 355	8 729	13 658	22 898	7.2	5.6	44 877	5.2
Chelan	23.1	497	10 370	214.7	5 193	620	11 103	7 532	11 785	15 428	11.7	8.6	25 048	13.1
Clallam	23.0	447	13 400	239.3	6 646	564	10 819	7 665	11 993	16 890	10.2	7.8	25 225	15.4
Clark	107.8	539	30 780	136.1	15 428	2 178	11 244	7 515	11 759	18 959	9.1	7.1	92 849	27.5
Columbia	2.0	488	945	230.5	458	76	9 231	6 347	9 931	14 067	13.1	9.3	2 046	12.5
Cowlitz	42.0	531	14 335	178.3	7 385	1 024	11 002	7 608	11 904	18 593	10.7	8.2	33 304	4.9
Douglas	11.2	490	3 375	135.0	1 697	180	10 221	6 789	10 623	16 388	10.7	8.5	10 640	16.4
Ferry	3.5	593	870	145.0	381	60	8 138	5 583	8 736	14 665	18.9	18.6	3 239	35.3
Franklin	22.2	605	4 725	139.0	2 360	354	9 451	7 069	11 061	18 082	14.1	10.4	13 664	2.6
Garfield	1.4	570	585	243.8	312	18	11 567	7 048	11 028	16 270	8.2	5.7	1 209	5.9
Grant	30.0	608	8 460	163.6	4 050	566	9 060	6 136	9 601	15 191	14.6	11.4	22 809	12.5
Grays Harbor	34.2	522	13 205	209.9	6 752	978	10 407	7 446	11 651	17 080	10.6	8.0	29 932	4.7
Island	18.0	394	7 610	139.4	3 682	210	11 130	7 108	11 122	15 660	9.9	8.1	25 860	23.9
Jefferson	7.2	427	4 805	246.4	2 345	178	11 572	7 749	12 125	15 353	12.9	9.9	11 014	24.8
King	603.6	461	196 330	136.4	106 978	14 948	14 897	9 582	14 993	20 717	7.7	5.0	647 343	23.2
Kitsap	77.4	495	21 685	119.9	9 404	1 336	11 618	7 814	12 227	18 942	8.1	6.3	74 038	29.2
Kittitas	10.9	439	4 065	161.3	1 992	222	9 336	6 343	9 925	12 703	16.6	9.8	13 215	12.9
Klickitat	10.9	662	3 050	191.8	1 474	194	9 642	6 766	10 587	15 948	10.9	8.7	7 213	11.0
Lewis	30.5	531	11 835	199.6	5 725	856	9 337	6 675	10 444	15 116	11.9	9.5	25 487	10.2
Lincoln	8.1	838	2 065	240.1	1 097	58	11 392	7 712	12 067	16 556	8.8	6.7	4 607	6.2
Mason	15.3	464	7 515	198.3	3 724	324	10 238	7 113	11 130	16 137	10.3	8.1	22 292	27.2
Okanogan	20.1	632	6 350	196.0	2 909	454	9 030	6 284	9 833	13 843	15.4	12.2	16 629	22.4
Pacific	10.4	587	5 030	282.6	2 515	262	10 723	7 272	11 378	14 103	10.9	8.7	12 404	13.3
Pend Oreille	5.6	644	1 805	202.8	818	136	7 808	5 310	8 309	12 252	15.9	12.6	5 404	15.3
Pierce	288.8	569	73 770	131.9	36 657	7 048	11 103	7 409	11 593	17 221	10.6	8.4	228 842	22.1
San Juan	3.7	446	2 230	223.0	1 118	28	13 422	8 606	13 466	16 026	12.0	7.9	6 075	14.4
Skagit	33.2	499	15 175	209.0	7 573	746	10 825	7 466	11 682	16 472	10.8	8.4	33 580	20.9
Skamania	4.7	617	905	117.5	437	72	10 445	7 907	12 372	19 509	8.8	6.0	3 922	14.2
Snohomish	175.9	494	50 550	119.6	26 089	3 300	12 192	8 243	12 898	20 760	7.5	5.6	183 942	40.2
Spokane	160.6	461	58 140	163.1	28 786	5 046	10 718	7 180	11 235	15 930	11.5	8.4	150 105	9.0
Stevens	15.2	501	4 825	151.7	2 163	346	8 415	5 894	9 222	14 791	14.6	11.2	14 601	16.3
Thurston	70.0	525	22 875	146.1	11 435	1 370	11 401	7 775	12 166	17 946	9.8	7.2	66 464	31.1
Wahkiakum	1.5	389	770	213.9	385	30	11 180	8 176	12 793	19 452	12.5	10.8	1 496	-0.5
Walla Walla	19.8	409	8 550	184.7	4 204	570	10 426	6 908	10 809	15 660	12.0	8.7	19 029	4.9
Whatcom	52.5	477	18 840	158.7	9 369	1 254	10 879	7 270	11 375	16 051	13.2	8.6	55 742	17.4
Whitman	16.3	409	4 325	115.6	2 334	222	9 844	6 228	9 745	14 108	18.0	7.9	14 598	1.2
Yakima	89.7	509	30 490	164.4	14 449	3 352	9 632	6 555	10 257	14 780	15.4	11.8	70 852	6.0
WEST VIRGINIA	890.5	454	364 675	194.3	167 944	43 531	8 980	6 142	9 610	14 564	15.0	11.7	781 295	4.5
Barbour	7.7	462	3 235	210.1	1 366	646	6 597	4 860	7 604	11 996	20.0	16.1	6 956	12.4
Berkeley	22.3	459	8 650	156.7	3 895	792	9 907	6 373	9 972	15 390	13.9	10.7	25 385	36.7
Boone	15.9	519	5 220	185.1	2 384	640	8 496	5 887	9 211	16 362	14.8	12.4	10 705	-0.5
Braxton	7.8	542	2 815	196.9	1 119	632	6 895	4 527	7 083	10 286	24.6	21.4	5 708	2.2
Brooke	12.4	403	4 820	170.3	2 503	262	9 286	7 031	11 001	19 600	9.0	6.1	10 838	-3.2
Cabell	44.0	414	20 940	207.9	9 990	2 346	10 331	6 785	10 616	14 304	13.5	9.6	43 596	0.0
Calhoun	4.8	560	1 895	228.3	752	424	6 831	4 554	7 126	10 000	25.3	20.3	3 446	8.1
Clay	6.0	528	2 175	194.2	853	496	5 319	3 895	6 095	9 835	31.8	26.5	4 359	5.2
Doddridge	4.3	577	1 160	163.4	479	192	6 822	4 434	6 938	10 704	21.5	16.8	3 251	2.0
Fayette	24.9	434	11 800	227.4	5 289	1 346	7 297	5 295	8 285	12 564	17.0	13.3	20 841	-2.9
Gilmer	3.6	413	1 590	203.8	620	332	6 906	4 478	7 007	10 063	21.7	18.0	3 243	2.8
Grant	6.0	567	1 930	178.7	756	386	7 384	4 834	7 564	11 675	22.9	19.8	4 746	15.9
Greenbrier	16.3	443	7 545	215.0	3 239	1 032	8 422	5 588	8 744	12 197	15.0	12.4	16 757	10.2
Hampshire	7.1	456	2 830	172.6	1 157	508	8 318	5 125	8 019	11 926	16.9	13.5	8 817	26.0
Hancock	16.7	414	8 240	221.5	4 367	298	10 059	7 935	12 416	20 701	7.7	6.5	14 697	-1.8
Hardy	5.3	515	2 100	196.3	829	440	8 343	4 847	7 584	11 577	20.8	17.9	5 573	24.6

1. Elementary and secondary. 2. Per 1,000 resident population estimated as of July 1 of the year shown. 3. Based on the resident population estimated as of July 1, 1988 for 1987 data and enumerated as of April 1, 1980 for 1979 data.

STATE County	Housing units, 1990 (cont'd): Occupied units: Total	Housing units, 1990 (cont'd): Occupied units: Owner occupied: Percent	Housing units, 1990 (cont'd): Occupied units: Owner occupied: Median value (Dollars)	Housing units, 1990 (cont'd): Occupied units: Median rent (Dollars)	Civilian labor force, 1990: Total	Civilian labor force, 1990: Percent change, 1989–1990	Civilian labor force, 1990: Unemployment: Total	Civilian labor force, 1990: Unemployment: Rate[1]	Private nonfarm establishments, 1988: Number	Private nonfarm establishments, 1988: Net change, 1987–1988	Private nonfarm establishments, 1988: Employment[2]: Total	Private nonfarm establishments, 1988: Employment[2]: Percent change, 1987–1988	Private nonfarm establishments, 1988: Employment[2]: Manufacturing	Private nonfarm establishments, 1988: Employment[2]: Retail trade
	74	75	76	77	78	79	80	81	82	83	84	85	86	87
VIRGINIA—Con.														
South Boston City	2 795	64.2	44 000	188	3 626	3.2	264	7.3	403	7	7 739	1.2	4 384	1 430
Staunton City	9 432	61.2	62 700	284	14 280	3.3	510	3.6	900	27	10 776	2.9	878	3 278
Suffolk City	18 516	67.7	70 700	250	26 841	0.3	1 624	6.1	1 060	6	11 889	0.2	2 697	2 956
Virginia Beach City	135 566	62.5	96 500	484	170 736	1.0	6 819	4.0	8 406	337	101 959	4.7	4 587	32 973
Waynesboro City	7 568	62.3	68 100	297	12 375	2.7	418	3.4	587	29	11 177	4.3	5 341	1 990
Williamsburg City	3 468	36.4	121 000	428	7 090	1.8	432	6.1	1 085	119	15 771	2.8	0	5 399
Winchester City	9 084	45.4	89 100	349	12 902	3.6	656	5.1	1 437	45	20 842	-2.3	6 406	5 215
WASHINGTON	1 872 431	62.6	93 400	383	2 503 000	2.1	122 000	4.9	X	X	1 536 022	4.9	326 080	344 830
Adams	4 586	65.5	45 900	218	7 295	5.9	782	10.7	352	-2	2 940	14.3	918	621
Asotin	7 003	65.6	53 900	257	9 331	2.1	376	4.0	343	6	2 650	8.9	242	885
Benton	42 227	63.1	66 200	283	57 769	3.1	3 360	5.8	2 218	-71	34 579	18.9	11 800	7 169
Chelan	20 645	61.9	71 500	306	30 212	2.9	2 418	8.0	1 811	-17	18 537	3.1	2 590	4 131
Clallam	22 837	70.2	79 200	308	24 567	0.5	1 725	7.0	1 645	-13	12 000	1.4	3 148	3 374
Clark	88 440	64.3	74 200	378	128 148	4.9	6 254	4.9	4 682	149	57 478	11.4	17 525	12 574
Columbia	1 582	67.6	37 400	214	1 805	3.6	168	9.3	103	-7	717	-25.8	0	124
Cowlitz	31 640	65.4	61 300	296	38 943	1.8	2 705	6.9	1 892	-2	26 098	6.1	9 777	5 775
Douglas	9 687	68.7	68 700	338	15 194	3.8	1 063	7.0	401	12	3 053	1.7	36	1 557
Ferry	2 247	69.8	50 100	197	3 281	1.8	283	8.6	124	-11	1 121	-6.2	536	225
Franklin	12 196	59.7	56 000	234	16 877	3.4	1 771	10.5	901	-42	10 336	0.3	3 048	2 387
Garfield	922	68.8	36 900	191	998	1.9	40	4.0	61	-2	224	14.9	0	58
Grant	19 745	64.6	51 600	244	26 965	-0.1	2 243	8.3	1 252	11	10 468	5.5	2 224	2 879
Grays Harbor	25 514	67.0	49 100	253	26 382	-2.1	2 391	9.1	1 830	8	17 389	2.9	6 323	4 099
Island	21 787	65.6	103 400	397	21 660	4.5	783	3.6	1 007	62	6 129	3.0	468	2 261
Jefferson	8 627	73.9	88 700	312	9 099	7.9	434	4.8	603	11	3 314	2.6	745	1 029
King	615 792	58.8	140 100	457	888 357	1.8	29 849	3.4	48 027	1 191	725 944	4.2	149 546	139 291
Kitsap	69 267	64.3	89 100	380	83 007	3.9	3 525	4.2	3 461	141	29 814	4.7	1 376	10 714
Kittitas	10 460	57.2	60 500	260	12 280	1.9	878	7.1	733	17	4 669	-4.7	739	1 873
Klickitat	6 210	66.0	52 700	249	7 869	-0.4	899	11.4	367	14	2 710	35.9	1 453	432
Lewis	22 478	70.0	57 600	276	25 393	-1.0	2 013	7.9	1 616	12	15 111	3.3	3 770	3 751
Lincoln	3 605	72.6	41 100	198	4 327	2.4	174	4.0	257	-11	1 092	1.3	77	319
Mason	14 565	76.7	70 100	298	14 595	3.1	897	6.1	752	18	5 880	6.8	2 147	1 473
Okanogan	12 654	66.7	50 300	222	17 849	1.5	1 765	9.9	826	8	6 072	11.9	1 120	1 532
Pacific	7 896	71.9	49 300	240	7 720	4.1	622	8.1	557	6	3 822	-0.6	1 090	979
Pend Oreille	3 395	73.6	49 500	237	3 351	-30.8	422	12.6	162	11	886	2.9	266	250
Pierce	214 652	60.3	82 500	374	254 279	1.0	12 238	4.8	11 574	311	135 132	3.8	20 170	35 255
San Juan	4 392	71.9	166 400	384	6 174	7.5	162	2.6	472	16	2 155	12.3	157	638
Skagit	30 573	69.9	81 500	341	40 076	6.1	2 682	6.7	2 176	54	18 252	0.7	3 699	5 263
Skamania	3 066	73.5	67 100	264	2 186	-6.5	349	16.0	140	-3	1 314	17.0	809	167
Snohomish	171 713	66.3	127 200	467	237 411	2.0	9 324	3.9	9 907	401	118 704	10.0	37 778	29 297
Spokane	141 619	63.7	59 000	288	171 132	1.0	9 132	5.3	9 176	-84	117 893	1.9	19 506	27 211
Stevens	11 241	76.2	55 900	231	11 570	-2.5	1 068	9.2	613	16	5 099	4.2	1 912	1 068
Thurston	62 150	64.7	79 700	382	83 521	5.0	4 141	5.0	3 492	69	32 804	2.4	3 313	10 149
Wahkiakum	1 321	75.5	62 300	221	1 225	1.2	106	8.7	77	2	388	15.5	177	77
Walla Walla	17 623	62.3	56 500	259	23 582	-0.3	1 359	5.8	1 090	12	12 730	-2.7	1 970	2 965
Whatcom	48 543	64.3	90 800	361	68 263	5.6	3 321	4.9	3 505	134	36 387	6.6	7 520	9 999
Whitman	13 546	48.2	61 900	303	18 854	0.5	404	2.1	802	19	4 982	-4.6	157	1 815
Yakima	65 985	63.2	55 200	270	101 450	2.6	9 873	9.7	4 215	53	46 040	4.3	7 722	11 163
WEST VIRGINIA	688 557	74.1	47 900	221	772 000	0.7	64 000	8.3	X	X	455 915	2.2	86 217	111 892
Barbour	5 835	77.5	35 200	177	4 781	1.8	751	15.7	242	6	2 309	4.2	162	607
Berkeley	22 350	73.0	70 600	284	29 131	1.5	2 099	7.2	1 055	53	13 174	7.1	3 505	3 701
Boone	9 656	76.3	41 800	196	8 635	-0.9	776	9.0	370	-6	5 687	-14.8	100	963
Braxton	4 950	77.9	39 300	175	5 797	-0.2	688	11.9	290	6	2 468	4.6	254	841
Brooke	10 131	79.1	44 100	198	10 930	0.3	787	7.2	370	0	14 199	123.2	10 091	1 331
Cabell	39 146	64.7	52 800	241	45 161	1.3	2 798	6.2	2 752	4	36 188	1.0	5 839	10 616
Calhoun	2 978	76.7	33 200	145	3 071	-0.5	537	17.5	162	-1	1 525	-1.7	787	199
Clay	3 627	76.0	33 000	140	3 384	3.1	492	14.5	92	13	484	7.8	45	162
Doddridge	2 623	82.4	33 800	157	2 442	-3.2	209	8.6	64	5	309	-6.9	91	69
Fayette	18 292	76.4	34 500	180	17 221	-1.7	1 841	10.7	899	-20	7 771	4.8	1 040	2 517
Gilmer	2 717	71.4	42 100	193	3 039	5.9	264	8.7	149	3	1 000	-12.7	122	194
Grant	3 925	81.5	49 900	178	4 800	13.8	421	8.8	257	0	2 817	-1.4	287	325
Greenbrier	13 775	75.6	44 000	192	16 006	1.4	1 761	11.0	855	20	7 986	9.1	1 156	2 065
Hampshire	6 182	81.1	50 500	179	7 392	0.3	842	11.4	264	5	2 034	3.1	479	461
Hancock	13 781	76.7	45 600	221	14 521	0.2	936	6.4	625	-3	8 235	-48.6	2 084	1 936
Hardy	4 286	82.2	49 300	186	6 047	7.7	369	6.1	198	-1	2 654	8.5	1 697	346

1. Percent of total civilian labor force. 2. For week including March 12. Excludes government employees, self-employed persons, farm workers, domestic service workers, railroad employees subject to the Railroad Retirement Act, and employees on oceanborne vessels or in foreign countries.

STATE County	Private nonfarm establishments, 1988 (cont'd): Employment[1] (cont'd): Finance, insurance, and real estate	Private nonfarm establishments, 1988 (cont'd): Employment[1] (cont'd): Services	Private nonfarm establishments, 1988 (cont'd): Annual payroll: Total (Mil dol)	Private nonfarm establishments, 1988 (cont'd): Annual payroll: Average per employee (Dollars)	Personal income, 1989: Total (Mil dol)	Personal income, 1989: Percent change, 1988–1989	Personal income, 1989: Wages and salaries[2] (Mil dol)	Personal income, 1989: Proprietor's income (Mil dol)	Personal income, 1989: Dividends, interest, & rent (Mil dol)	Personal income, 1989: Transfer payments (Mil dol)	Personal income, 1989: Per capita[3]: Dollars	Personal income, 1989: Per capita[3]: Rank	Earnings, 1989: Total (Mil dol)	Earnings, 1989: Percent by selected industries: Farm	Earnings, 1989: Percent by selected industries: Goods-related[4]: Total
	88	89	90	91	92	93	94	95	96	97	98	99	100	101	102
VIRGINIA—Con.															
South Boston City	125	1 298	127	16 471	(5)	(5)	(5)	(5)	(5)	(5)	(5)	(5)	(5)	(5)	(5)
Staunton City	641	3 439	152	14 102	(6)	(6)	(6)	(6)	(6)	(6)	(6)	(6)	(6)	(6)	(6)
Suffolk City	587	2 821	193	16 239	830	6.4	334	51	114	141	15 751	721	385	3.4	25.8
Virginia Beach City	6 773	36 181	1 548	15 178	6 615	7.0	2 938	342	978	684	17 383	380	3 280	0.2	14.1
Waynesboro City	313	2 209	239	21 353	(6)	(6)	(6)	(6)	(6)	(6)	(6)	(6)	(6)	(6)	(6)
Williamsburg City	469	6 519	276	17 495	(7)	(7)	(7)	(7)	(7)	(7)	(7)	(7)	(7)	(7)	(7)
Winchester City	778	5 124	385	18 493	(8)	(8)	(8)	(8)	(8)	(8)	(8)	(8)	(8)	(8)	(8)
WASHINGTON	109 394	428 934	32 527	X	84 167	10.3	52 752	7 611	14 466	12 664	17 696	X	60 363	2.7	28.1
Adams	91	475	39	13 177	211	6.9	87	56	42	35	16 115	612	143	35.8	15.2
Asotin	106	982	37	13 789	253	8.9	60	33	49	56	14 880	1 036	93	10.3	22.2
Benton	1 090	11 287	845	24 442	1 770	6.4	1 253	164	268	248	15 644	763	1 417	4.1	41.3
Chelan	1 087	5 800	321	17 301	836	10.6	518	121	173	158	17 335	390	639	9.7	NA
Clallam	479	2 603	205	17 067	858	9.8	369	84	238	199	14 942	1 013	452	2.5	27.4
Clark	4 583	14 187	1 118	19 452	3 601	10.8	1 765	271	568	536	15 379	844	2 036	1.6	36.5
Columbia	66	223	12	17 358	67	3.1	26	19	14	13	16 544	517	45	35.0	NA
Cowlitz	848	5 889	551	21 118	1 241	9.3	840	117	193	227	15 276	881	957	2.1	48.0
Douglas	186	496	37	12 099	394	9.8	116	78	70	57	15 539	791	194	36.1	8.6
Ferry	0	106	23	20 897	73	17.0	38	17	10	15	11 951	2 340	54	23.0	34.3
Franklin	270	2 338	164	15 854	502	7.2	286	81	77	93	14 967	1 002	367	16.0	NA
Garfield	18	42	3	12 728	50	6.0	14	15	14	8	21 190	123	29	44.3	NA
Grant	403	2 235	157	14 984	769	8.3	343	181	129	145	14 828	1 064	523	28.2	NA
Grays Harbor	595	3 753	325	18 701	933	7.7	514	100	164	214	14 772	1 093	614	3.0	NA
Island	505	1 916	75	12 190	864	11.5	391	68	186	151	15 165	919	459	1.8	10.0
Jefferson	288	703	51	15 425	310	12.0	100	36	88	69	15 378	845	135	3.9	26.7
King	64 287	202 388	17 389	23 954	32 694	10.8	25 610	2 553	5 787	3 725	22 125	88	28 163	0.2	29.5
Kitsap	2 069	10 500	433	14 538	2 958	9.1	1 711	175	451	520	15 843	697	1 886	0.3	7.5
Kittitas	169	1 104	65	13 844	357	8.5	167	53	76	69	14 035	1 420	220	10.6	13.3
Klickitat	130	422	53	19 658	241	12.5	110	45	46	49	15 270	882	155	22.1	36.0
Lewis	513	3 329	284	18 796	837	10.0	448	115	149	179	13 920	1 460	563	7.7	32.6
Lincoln	94	191	17	15 367	182	-0.7	43	53	56	29	21 792	99	96	52.3	NA
Mason	324	1 036	103	17 517	511	10.0	195	43	107	121	13 072	1 879	238	2.9	36.0
Okanogan	246	1 169	86	14 172	492	13.9	226	102	83	103	15 163	920	328	22.7	15.4
Pacific	143	756	48	12 689	270	8.4	95	38	62	70	14 979	997	133	5.9	26.0
Pend Oreille	32	201	14	15 804	116	23.8	76	16	19	31	13 104	1 862	92	9.4	56.3
Pierce	8 464	43 378	2 492	18 442	8 916	8.9	4 693	617	1 343	1 638	15 546	788	5 309	0.7	19.5
San Juan	134	673	30	14 138	196	12.9	54	24	84	29	18 700	238	78	1.7	26.7
Skagit	642	4 737	322	17 649	1 202	13.0	587	163	260	236	16 163	602	750	6.4	27.3
Skamania	18	178	21	16 197	110	13.3	39	10	17	20	14 225	1 323	49	9.3	37.2
Snohomish	5 519	24 678	2 727	22 975	7 877	12.8	4 074	550	968	944	17 832	316	4 624	1.0	48.5
Spokane	8 715	38 953	2 109	17 890	5 553	9.0	3 307	455	1 037	1 068	15 507	801	3 762	1.4	21.7
Stevens	187	1 325	89	17 449	398	9.5	164	69	68	80	12 376	2 172	233	18.1	34.8
Thurston	2 299	10 776	549	16 722	2 548	11.0	1 374	209	436	460	15 663	754	1 582	3.1	12.7
Wahkiakum	0	43	7	17 080	56	14.4	16	13	12	10	15 715	736	29	25.6	NA
Walla Walla	634	5 320	207	16 269	747	7.7	413	80	153	142	16 200	594	493	9.6	25.5
Whatcom	1 769	10 201	638	17 539	1 876	11.5	1 024	282	358	300	15 457	815	1 307	4.6	28.4
Whitman	309	1 422	61	12 219	583	4.5	276	98	140	88	15 895	680	374	18.6	3.4
Yakima	1 941	13 096	788	17 109	2 719	10.5	1 333	407	470	530	14 494	1 218	1 740	16.1	17.6
WEST VIRGINIA	23 990	121 672	8 649	X	23 096	5.6	13 594	1 572	3 644	5 559	12 434	X	15 167	0.3	34.1
Barbour	102	650	42	18 035	151	7.6	64	11	25	49	10 098	2 868	75	1.3	35.7
Berkeley	605	3 028	227	17 202	746	6.7	403	46	99	136	13 120	1 854	449	0.9	23.6
Boone	165	763	169	29 779	342	4.4	251	23	31	85	12 424	2 155	274	NA	70.5
Braxton	0	493	42	16 957	151	7.4	72	12	20	41	10 651	2 751	84	1.4	40.3
Brooke	184	1 592	430	30 249	343	9.4	192	13	58	67	12 380	2 170	205	0.1	63.9
Cabell	2 079	10 301	654	18 076	1 434	6.0	1 052	98	252	335	14 501	1 212	1 151	0.1	24.7
Calhoun	46	172	23	14 944	67	5.7	30	4	11	24	8 079	3 073	34	1.7	37.2
Clay	0	102	8	15 709	82	6.7	22	5	10	31	7 427	3 090	27	0.8	29.5
Doddridge	0	42	3	10 964	65	4.5	13	4	10	16	9 382	2 972	17	2.7	19.6
Fayette	388	2 028	126	16 162	503	3.8	224	35	67	184	9 968	2 884	259	0.5	29.4
Gilmer	0	184	14	14 023	72	4.5	30	6	12	23	9 602	2 942	36	1.6	32.1
Grant	72	366	62	22 131	125	8.2	113	12	18	27	11 231	2 590	126	0.6	48.3
Greenbrier	350	2 802	130	16 277	424	6.1	217	43	70	114	12 487	2 123	260	1.4	24.6
Hampshire	131	571	27	13 033	193	5.7	56	13	27	41	11 740	2 425	70	3.6	18.5
Hancock	287	3 015	122	14 825	562	6.3	590	25	89	114	15 510	799	615	0.1	76.4
Hardy	115	221	35	13 149	134	6.4	60	12	19	25	12 217	2 223	72	2.9	57.0

1. For week including March 12. Excludes government employees, self-employed persons, farm workers, domestic service workers, railroad employees subject to the Railroad Retirement Act, and employees on oceanborne vessels or in foreign countries. 2. Includes other labor income. 3. Based on the resident population estimated as of July 1 of the year shown. 4. Covers mining, construction, and manufacturing. 5. South Boston included with Halifax County. 6. Staunton and Waynesboro included with Augusta County. 7. Williamsburg included with James City County. 8. Winchester included with Frederick County.

Table A. States and Counties — **Earnings and Agriculture**

STATE County	Earnings, 1989 (cont'd): Percent by selected industries (cont'd): Goods-related[1]: Manu-facturing	Service-related & other[2]: Total	Service-related & other[2]: Retail trade	Service-related & other[2]: Finance, insur-ance, & real estate	Service-related & other[2]: Services	Govern-ment	Agriculture, 1987: Farms: Number	Farms: Percent with: Less than 50 acres	Farms: Percent with: 500 acres and over	Farm operators, percent: Whose principal occu-pation is farming	Farm operators, percent: Residing on farm operated	Land in farms: Acreage (1,000)	Land in farms: Percent change, 1982–1987	Land in farms: Acres: Average size of farm	Land in farms: Acres: Total irrigated (1,000)	Land in farms: Acres: Total cropland (1,000)
	103	104	105	106	107	108	109	110	111	112	113	114	115	116	117	118
VIRGINIA—Con.																
South Boston City	(3)	(3)	(3)	(3)	(3)	(3)	NA	NA	NA	NA	NA	NA	NA	NA	NA	NA
Staunton City	(4)	(4)	(4)	(4)	(4)	(4)	NA	NA	NA	NA	NA	NA	NA	NA	NA	NA
Suffolk City	18.0	51.8	9.9	2.9	21.8	19.0	314	31.5	18.8	61.5	66.2	88	-6.9	279	1	67
Virginia Beach City	3.0	53.7	12.8	5.5	25.4	32.0	165	56.4	15.8	53.9	69.7	39	-23.2	239	0	32
Waynesboro City	(4)	(4)	(4)	(4)	(4)	(4)	NA	NA	NA	NA	NA	NA	NA	NA	NA	NA
Williamsburg City	(5)	(5)	(5)	(5)	(5)	(5)	NA	NA	NA	NA	NA	NA	NA	NA	NA	NA
Winchester City	(6)	(6)	(6)	(6)	(6)	(6)	NA	NA	NA	NA	NA	NA	NA	NA	NA	NA
WASHINGTON	21.1	51.2	9.8	5.4	21.9	18.0	33 559	51.9	15.3	52.6	79.7	16 116	-2.2	480	1 519	8 168
Adams	12.7	34.0	6.9	1.8	10.4	15.0	805	21.7	52.2	76.4	68.8	1 168	1.1	1 451	131	878
Asotin	6.3	49.5	14.2	2.5	26.9	18.0	149	31.5	54.4	59.1	75.2	274	-4.5	1 840	0	93
Benton	33.7	39.0	7.5	1.8	25.5	15.7	1 178	68.1	10.4	41.9	74.8	644	-4.9	547	112	433
Chelan	13.0	NA	10.1	3.7	22.3	17.8	1 411	74.9	1.8	58.5	73.2	116	-14.2	82	31	46
Clallam	20.7	46.3	12.5	2.3	18.9	23.7	375	62.7	1.6	41.3	86.1	27	-6.2	71	5	16
Clark	26.8	44.8	9.7	5.7	19.7	17.1	1 428	66.7	1.7	37.3	87.8	95	-6.9	66	4	57
Columbia	16.9	25.1	4.0	0.9	8.7	18.4	212	14.6	60.8	67.9	58.0	321	-5.1	1 516	2	206
Cowlitz	40.6	39.0	9.2	2.7	16.2	11.0	435	59.5	2.3	34.9	84.4	38	-7.8	86	4	16
Douglas	2.7	39.5	9.6	1.6	14.3	15.8	948	55.1	28.4	65.0	71.6	988	1.8	1 042	21	576
Ferry	14.0	22.3	7.5	0.7	10.1	20.4	218	22.0	24.8	40.8	83.9	761	-5.0	3 489	4	29
Franklin	8.2	NA	10.7	1.8	17.0	19.6	894	23.7	26.3	74.7	73.4	661	4.5	739	194	469
Garfield	NA	28.7	3.2	2.1	6.2	24.2	210	11.0	68.1	80.0	71.0	338	0.3	1 610	2	205
Grant	10.7	NA	8.0	1.7	11.7	20.7	1 881	26.3	23.2	69.2	71.9	1 108	-0.5	589	369	724
Grays Harbor	31.0	NA	10.1	NA	17.5	15.6	410	48.5	3.9	43.7	88.8	44	-9.8	108	3	26
Island	2.8	28.6	7.6	2.3	14.2	59.6	286	64.3	1.4	35.7	88.1	19	-10.5	65	1	12
Jefferson	17.9	46.3	13.0	1.4	23.1	23.0	120	54.2	2.5	38.3	81.7	12	-23.6	99	0	4
King	22.8	58.5	9.4	7.8	24.0	11.8	1 498	83.1	0.7	36.2	84.2	54	-9.4	36	3	32
Kitsap	2.4	34.4	8.6	2.2	19.0	57.9	404	88.4	0.0	32.4	91.1	10	-12.7	24	1	5
Kittitas	9.5	42.0	13.0	1.7	14.1	34.1	740	42.8	14.6	53.1	81.6	403	2.5	545	78	100
Klickitat	33.1	NA	4.8	1.2	9.0	18.5	545	31.4	31.2	54.9	83.7	698	-3.7	1 282	24	211
Lewis	20.0	44.1	11.7	2.1	17.1	15.6	1 162	47.9	2.5	42.5	85.6	122	-9.8	105	7	67
Lincoln	NA	26.3	5.7	2.2	7.0	19.4	799	6.9	78.8	86.2	70.8	1 479	5.3	1 851	54	931
Mason	29.3	36.3	9.6	2.7	15.2	24.9	165	67.3	2.4	38.2	87.3	12	-23.1	71	0	5
Okanogan	11.4	38.0	8.3	1.3	15.2	23.9	1 476	50.5	16.9	57.3	77.6	1 339	0.5	907	51	144
Pacific	21.8	46.0	11.6	1.8	14.9	22.1	270	52.6	3.3	52.6	81.5	35	-9.5	129	3	13
Pend Oreille	15.7	17.8	4.9	1.2	7.6	16.5	227	22.0	12.3	44.5	85.9	63	-2.2	276	3	23
Pierce	12.3	49.6	10.8	4.2	22.7	30.2	1 228	77.4	0.5	37.4	88.0	59	-14.8	48	6	29
San Juan	6.8	57.1	15.1	1.7	27.1	14.5	155	45.8	3.2	42.6	75.5	18	-6.7	114	0	9
Skagit	16.4	49.0	13.3	2.9	19.4	17.2	806	55.6	6.0	48.5	80.5	95	-13.2	118	6	74
Skamania	32.3	15.7	4.4	0.4	5.9	37.8	71	49.3	1.4	36.6	91.5	7	-24.8	95	0	D
Snohomish	40.7	38.8	10.5	2.8	16.1	11.7	1 473	73.7	1.4	40.1	85.7	82	-11.9	56	5	52
Spokane	14.9	57.9	11.2	5.5	26.4	19.1	1 901	42.1	18.0	43.2	85.0	613	-2.2	322	15	399
Stevens	29.4	29.8	7.2	1.3	13.6	17.3	1 073	27.2	17.9	45.8	84.3	526	-9.0	490	12	132
Thurston	6.6	41.2	10.1	3.1	20.6	43.0	806	68.9	1.4	36.6	89.1	57	-16.0	70	4	23
Wahkiakum	15.0	NA	5.3	NA	8.0	22.5	135	28.1	0.7	56.3	82.2	15	-8.2	108	0	10
Walla Walla	22.0	44.5	8.8	3.2	22.1	20.4	759	42.6	34.9	63.2	69.4	676	-10.6	890	75	569
Whatcom	19.3	52.7	12.6	3.2	20.9	14.3	1 463	50.9	1.4	54.8	84.8	125	-2.9	85	29	94
Whitman	1.1	29.0	6.2	2.0	11.7	48.9	1 204	11.0	67.7	81.9	71.3	1 405	0.3	1 167	10	1 110
Yakima	12.7	51.1	10.4	3.0	21.3	15.2	4 239	67.7	4.7	54.1	77.3	1 612	-6.0	380	247	D
WEST VIRGINIA	18.6	48.5	9.8	3.6	21.2	17.0	17 237	19.3	7.6	41.8	76.8	3 373	-5.2	196	3	1 286
Barbour	4.5	NA	9.8	3.0	24.4	18.9	459	13.7	5.4	44.9	73.6	83	6.8	181	0	37
Berkeley	18.4	49.9	11.6	4.0	18.4	25.6	453	26.5	6.4	45.9	72.8	80	-6.5	177	0	53
Boone	0.7	19.8	5.8	1.6	7.3	9.7	31	25.8	0.0	35.5	87.1	3	-16.7	85	0	1
Braxton	6.2	42.3	14.3	1.9	13.6	16.0	318	10.1	8.2	44.7	80.2	70	-11.3	220	0	25
Brooke	51.1	NA	7.9	1.5	11.5	9.8	79	20.3	2.5	32.9	81.0	13	10.8	163	0	7
Cabell	19.1	60.6	11.3	4.2	27.7	14.6	375	34.7	1.9	34.9	70.7	38	-10.0	101	0	12
Calhoun	15.8	NA	8.2	NA	12.8	25.3	158	4.4	8.9	36.7	82.9	35	-8.1	220	0	11
Clay	2.0	NA	14.7	NA	13.6	34.3	97	13.4	4.1	34.0	75.3	16	-5.8	165	0	5
Doddridge	11.5	43.4	9.2	4.8	14.7	34.3	272	10.3	6.6	39.0	79.8	58	-3.0	212	D	22
Fayette	10.8	48.4	12.4	3.2	22.4	21.7	185	27.6	2.2	38.9	76.8	21	-26.3	115	D	10
Gilmer	4.1	NA	11.3	2.2	13.2	32.1	237	9.7	11.0	46.0	77.2	58	-5.8	244	D	18
Grant	8.8	NA	5.3	2.4	NA	12.3	353	15.9	19.5	57.5	78.5	119	3.5	337	0	34
Greenbrier	13.7	59.0	12.5	3.4	33.2	15.0	729	19.8	12.5	47.2	77.0	192	-4.3	263	0	57
Hampshire	11.4	47.9	10.5	4.0	18.4	29.9	492	14.2	13.8	47.8	76.8	138	-8.5	280	0	47
Hancock	74.1	19.1	3.8	1.2	10.6	4.4	86	31.4	1.2	31.4	80.2	8	-22.0	97	D	4
Hardy	49.8	26.8	7.9	2.6	8.4	13.3	460	16.5	18.7	58.3	75.2	148	-2.2	321	0	49

1. Covers mining, construction, and manufacturing. 2. Covers private sector earnings in agricultural services, forestry, and fisheries; transportation and public utilities; wholesale trade; retail trade; finance, insurance, and real estate; and services. 3. South Boston included with Halifax County. 4. Staunton and Waynesboro included with Augusta County. 5. Williamsburg included with James City County. 6. Winchester included with Frederick County.

STATE County	Agriculture, 1987 (cont'd): Value of land and buildings: Average per farm ($1,000)	Average per acre (Dollars)	Value of products sold: Total (Mil dol)	Average per farm (Dollars)	Percent from: Crops	Livestock and poultry[1]	Percent of farms with sales of: $10,000 or more	$100,000 or more	Manufactures, 1987: Establishments: Total	Percent with 20 or more employees	All employees: Number (1,000)	Percent change, 1982–1987	Annual payroll (Mil dol)	Production workers: Number (1,000)	Work hours (Mil)
	119	120	121	122	123	124	125	126	127	128	129	130	131	132	133
VIRGINIA—Con.															
South Boston City	NA	NA	NA	NA	NA	NA	NA	NA	26	42.3	3.6	44.0	57.1	3.2	6.4
Staunton City	NA	NA	NA	NA	NA	NA	NA	NA	28	25.0	0.8	0.0	12.7	0.6	1.3
Suffolk City	441	1 552	32	100 585	67.7	32.3	68.2	27.1	66	43.9	2.4	-57.1	43.3	1.8	3.5
Virginia Beach City	442	1 932	15	88 489	44.3	55.7	47.9	17.0	164	22.6	4.2	0.0	72.1	3.0	5.7
Waynesboro City	NA	NA	NA	NA	NA	NA	NA	NA	34	50.0	5.2	30.0	139.5	3.8	7.4
Williamsburg City	NA	NA	NA	NA	NA	NA	NA	NA	21	23.8	D	D	D	D	D
Winchester City	NA	NA	NA	NA	NA	NA	NA	NA	52	53.8	7.3	17.7	155.7	5.4	10.9
WASHINGTON	356	739	2 920	87 000	57.8	42.2	45.6	17.7	7 630	25.6	309.7	6.1	8 841.6	184.2	353.5
Adams	613	430	182	226 706	41.6	58.4	73.5	26.6	9	22.2	D	D	D	D	D
Asotin	492	283	9	57 506	51.5	48.5	61.1	17.4	13	15.4	0.2	0.0	4.1	0.2	0.3
Benton	411	750	133	113 018	83.2	16.8	37.3	16.9	82	23.2	D	D	D	D	D
Chelan	237	2 853	103	72 893	99.2	0.8	59.7	21.6	105	19.0	2.5	13.6	63.1	1.9	3.7
Clallam	255	3 531	6	15 416	32.7	67.3	20.8	3.7	192	16.1	D	D	D	D	D
Clark	222	2 947	37	25 815	22.9	77.1	19.2	6.0	330	28.8	14.9	13.7	381.8	11.0	21.5
Columbia	984	657	19	88 588	91.0	9.0	67.5	25.9	5	20.0	D	D	D	D	D
Cowlitz	178	2 253	11	26 050	32.0	68.0	12.9	4.4	185	31.9	9.2	-5.2	280.9	7.3	14.5
Douglas	474	421	83	87 326	91.6	8.4	65.8	23.9	8	12.5	D	D	D	D	D
Ferry	1 140	331	5	22 155	7.2	92.8	28.9	2.8	21	38.1	0.6	20.0	13.9	0.5	1.0
Franklin	564	708	176	197 269	86.2	13.8	77.2	40.6	38	13.2	D	D	D	D	D
Garfield	660	431	19	91 868	84.2	15.8	79.0	34.3	2	0.0	D	D	D	D	D
Grant	417	723	351	186 586	61.1	38.9	72.3	32.4	39	25.6	2.2	15.8	44.5	1.7	3.6
Grays Harbor	208	2 045	17	41 146	20.8	79.2	29.5	9.5	252	20.2	6.0	-4.8	152.5	5.0	9.3
Island	240	3 980	8	28 944	9.4	90.6	17.1	4.9	36	13.9	D	D	D	D	D
Jefferson	204	2 110	3	21 774	7.7	92.3	18.3	6.7	52	11.5	0.7	-12.5	17.3	0.5	1.0
King	210	6 131	74	49 232	31.6	68.4	24.3	9.3	2 784	27.4	140.8	4.1	4 344.2	68.5	129.9
Kitsap	149	7 526	6	14 076	9.5	90.5	6.9	0.2	114	15.8	1.5	-6.3	29.2	1.0	1.8
Kittitas	403	760	60	81 438	32.6	67.4	50.9	14.6	52	23.1	0.9	50.0	18.2	0.7	1.3
Klickitat	417	331	30	54 437	63.5	36.5	47.3	11.0	49	16.3	1.0	-41.2	19.7	0.9	1.7
Lewis	191	1 705	50	42 653	10.2	89.8	24.2	8.8	213	18.8	3.6	-12.2	77.4	3.0	5.6
Lincoln	718	372	64	80 675	82.4	17.6	80.7	29.0	10	10.0	0.1	0.0	1.0	0.0	0.1
Mason	180	2 530	1	6 905	32.1	68.0	18.8	1.2	86	17.4	2.0	0.0	50.7	1.6	3.2
Okanogan	442	499	106	71 970	86.1	13.9	54.0	16.1	50	10.0	1.1	57.1	24.9	0.9	2.0
Pacific	215	1 491	11	40 175	47.8	52.2	45.6	13.0	60	21.7	1.0	25.0	17.9	0.9	1.5
Pend Oreille	173	818	2	10 367	22.2	77.8	22.0	1.8	18	22.2	0.3	-57.1	6.5	0.3	0.5
Pierce	199	4 553	79	64 316	25.0	75.0	21.8	9.4	644	30.0	19.7	-3.4	477.9	13.2	25.2
San Juan	358	2 556	1	6 590	26.3	73.8	20.0	0.0	28	0.0	0.1	0.0	2.9	0.1	0.1
Skagit	291	2 427	103	127 211	46.5	53.5	41.3	22.6	169	19.5	3.4	-8.1	82.2	2.6	5.0
Skamania	188	1 989	1	11 603	65.5	34.5	14.1	2.8	36	25.0	0.8	14.3	16.1	0.7	1.3
Snohomish	226	3 697	88	59 607	16.6	83.4	25.9	11.5	680	25.0	33.8	7.6	1 104.4	19.1	39.6
Spokane	300	905	64	33 442	67.8	32.2	32.2	9.5	497	26.2	19.6	22.5	462.0	12.6	24.2
Stevens	259	517	19	18 138	25.0	75.0	31.2	5.5	68	27.9	1.9	26.7	45.4	1.6	3.1
Thurston	203	2 813	58	72 424	19.8	80.2	19.6	7.3	148	21.6	3.4	17.2	81.7	2.7	5.6
Wahkiakum	159	1 626	5	38 398	3.1	96.9	33.3	14.8	15	26.7	0.2	-33.3	3.5	0.1	0.3
Walla Walla	563	717	132	173 958	67.5	32.5	59.3	32.1	57	28.1	2.4	-7.7	59.5	1.8	3.5
Whatcom	258	2 882	180	122 981	15.7	84.3	51.1	30.8	232	27.2	7.3	4.3	187.6	5.6	11.0
Whitman	847	706	126	104 732	88.5	11.5	83.9	40.9	20	0.0	0.1	-50.0	2.2	0.1	0.2
Yakima	317	837	498	117 496	62.6	37.4	55.2	18.6	231	37.2	8.0	11.1	167.7	6.1	11.9
WEST VIRGINIA	131	682	271	15 701	18.2	81.8	18.9	2.8	1 619	30.1	83.8	-12.5	2 107.6	58.8	115.4
Barbour	89	538	4	8 042	20.4	79.6	17.2	0.7	17	11.8	D	D	D	D	D
Berkeley	266	1 498	19	41 529	62.0	38.0	37.5	9.3	40	47.5	3.3	-10.8	71.9	2.5	5.1
Boone	107	1 265	0	1 695	37.7	60.4	0.0	0.0	9	0.0	0.1	0.0	1.1	0.1	0.1
Braxton	86	407	2	6 016	6.6	93.4	15.7	0.0	23	13.0	0.2	0.0	2.4	0.2	0.3
Brooke	115	704	1	14 093	11.9	88.1	20.3	3.8	24	70.8	D	D	D	D	D
Cabell	89	877	2	5 222	50.2	49.8	9.1	0.5	116	32.8	6.0	-33.3	161.2	4.0	7.9
Calhoun	91	446	1	4 226	12.1	87.7	10.8	0.0	15	20.0	0.5	66.7	5.4	0.4	0.7
Clay	72	470	0	4 541	13.0	87.3	5.2	0.0	5	20.0	0.0	0.0	0.4	0.0	0.1
Doddridge	114	548	1	3 319	14.3	85.7	6.6	0.0	5	40.0	D	D	D	D	D
Fayette	73	551	1	6 858	9.1	90.9	10.8	1.6	37	24.3	D	D	D	D	D
Gilmer	100	423	2	6 389	7.6	92.4	13.9	0.8	15	20.0	0.3	0.0	3.2	0.3	0.5
Grant	195	617	14	40 817	1.2	98.8	32.3	7.9	24	25.0	0.3	0.0	5.0	0.2	0.5
Greenbrier	183	711	14	19 049	4.2	95.8	32.6	4.5	39	17.9	0.9	-30.8	17.2	0.6	1.2
Hampshire	212	780	10	20 948	51.1	48.9	25.4	2.6	16	12.5	0.4	0.0	5.2	0.4	0.7
Hancock	104	1 065	1	10 022	82.4	17.6	11.6	2.3	29	62.1	10.3	-4.6	316.8	7.7	16.2
Hardy	240	764	40	87 543	2.3	97.7	42.0	17.4	18	22.2	1.4	27.3	20.7	1.3	2.5

1. Includes livestock and poultry products.

STATE / County	Manufactures, 1987 (cont'd): Production workers (cont'd): Wages: Total (Mil dol)	Manufactures, 1987 (cont'd): Production workers (cont'd): Wages: Average per worker (Dollars)	Manufactures, 1987 (cont'd): Value added by manufacture (Mil dol)	Manufactures, 1987 (cont'd): Value of shipments (Mil dol)	Manufactures, 1987 (cont'd): New capital expenditures (Mil dol)	Value of construction authorized by building permits, 1990: Total[1] ($1,000)	Nonresidential: Total ($1,000)	Nonresidential: Percent: Office	Nonresidential: Percent: Industrial	Nonresidential: Percent: Stores	Residential: New construction ($1,000)	Residential: Number of housing units	Residential: Alterations and additions ($1,000)
	134	135	136	137	138	139	140	141	142	143	144	145	146
VIRGINIA—Con.													
South Boston City	50.1	15 656	143.4	375.8	4.5	3 089	233	54.6	0.0	29.9	1 155	18	1 104
Staunton City	9.2	15 333	20.6	32.8	1.4	10 460	3 976	1.9	0.0	87.7	3 562	63	1 241
Suffolk City	29.8	16 556	274.7	494.4	6.7	34 282	2 242	1.3	8.9	37.0	18 589	272	3 709
Virginia Beach City	42.4	14 133	171.7	449.3	11.7	256 498	38 241	12.3	1.6	35.5	162 867	2 207	28 444
Waynesboro City	83.3	21 921	471.3	871.8	40.2	11 676	1 405	0.0	0.0	83.0	3 262	88	1 184
Williamsburg City	D	D	D	D	D	16 291	3 583	44.7	0.0	23.2	4 030	27	878
Winchester City	103.4	19 148	446.6	806.5	42.6	20 718	4 353	58.9	0.4	34.9	8 959	139	1 322
WASHINGTON	4 262.0	23 138	19 016.1	46 531.8	1 244.8	5 652 421	1 238 495	31.7	17.8	28.8	3 486 985	48 447	241 910
Adams	D	D	D	D	D	9 520	7 942	0.0	53.9	2.9	1 067	11	196
Asotin	3.3	16 500	11.4	30.2	1.0	7 182	3 120	2.2	2.3	3.3	2 255	36	1 003
Benton	D	D	D	D	D	74 596	18 067	31.6	26.6	19.3	39 261	389	6 192
Chelan	46.3	24 368	283.2	535.4	20.2	45 250	11 949	7.7	12.1	57.4	24 073	319	2 239
Clallam	D	D	D	D	D	63 390	6 537	16.1	5.4	21.2	44 354	526	4 292
Clark	250.3	22 755	1 096.9	2 407.2	67.8	361 287	58 179	25.3	33.1	25.4	269 054	3 851	9 239
Columbia	D	D	D	D	D	124	0	NA	NA	NA	26	1	56
Cowlitz	215.2	29 479	904.2	2 218.7	160.1	118 311	80 322	0.3	92.1	1.5	15 575	197	4 609
Douglas	D	D	D	D	D	12 997	3 497	0.3	3.6	30.4	7 921	107	768
Ferry	10.9	21 800	32.7	93.7	1.2	2 367	742	37.7	13.4	14.8	967	30	186
Franklin	D	D	D	D	D	15 998	4 320	0.2	29.0	0.6	8 282	89	690
Garfield	D	D	D	D	D	332	92	0.0	0.0	0.0	50	2	148
Grant	30.7	18 059	130.6	284.3	9.4	30 004	15 441	0.9	13.7	68.5	8 739	109	1 430
Grays Harbor	118.1	23 620	467.5	1 116.3	30.0	30 366	7 649	1.8	41.8	24.9	8 677	128	6 784
Island	D	D	D	D	D	80 139	3 300	0.0	19.2	46.7	71 650	1 068	2 584
Jefferson	12.9	25 800	55.5	115.3	D	39 249	2 916	3.7	8.8	2.6	24 605	387	7 164
King	1 628.2	23 769	7 659.7	16 979.8	439.5	2 415 642	551 813	47.4	11.1	24.0	1 379 614	15 789	111 105
Kitsap	16.8	16 800	61.2	133.1	3.0	182 128	29 638	17.0	0.6	54.3	129 482	2 582	6 036
Kittitas	13.1	18 714	48.0	168.0	1.7	24 123	3 881	10.8	19.5	23.4	14 508	180	1 798
Klickitat	16.2	18 000	42.3	114.3	4.9	7 838	2 287	0.0	31.9	13.7	4 204	46	592
Lewis	57.7	19 233	181.9	515.4	10.8	30 405	14 593	1.3	3.7	46.4	10 292	174	1 754
Lincoln	0.5	NA	2.0	3.2	0.1	1 483	378	0.0	29.1	0.0	843	14	97
Mason	35.5	22 188	111.4	248.2	5.3	34 857	4 315	3.4	13.9	42.4	26 520	465	2 241
Okanogan	20.7	23 000	49.0	120.1	3.0	11 718	1 706	17.7	1.2	23.2	7 441	149	1 190
Pacific	13.4	14 889	31.3	86.2	2.6	9 044	743	67.3	0.0	0.0	4 433	76	1 404
Pend Oreille	5.9	19 667	11.4	23.8	0.6	6 537	2 151	0.0	8.5	41.3	3 732	70	340
Pierce	274.1	20 765	1 075.8	2 567.9	84.3	511 214	100 584	33.0	3.4	41.9	351 134	5 530	17 332
San Juan	1.3	13 000	5.5	9.0	0.2	38 326	2 660	34.8	0.0	5.3	28 245	360	2 670
Skagit	53.9	20 731	296.1	1 646.4	28.4	116 626	14 896	0.7	26.4	50.2	85 215	1 146	6 458
Skamania	14.0	20 000	28.1	90.6	1.7	3 506	665	0.0	0.0	96.3	2 325	35	64
Snohomish	504.0	26 387	2 160.4	6 383.9	109.8	548 212	107 250	31.6	19.1	38.5	420 940	7 397	2 657
Spokane	248.0	19 683	1 053.0	2 359.4	61.7	286 017	71 616	9.5	8.9	44.2	140 888	1 792	12 216
Stevens	38.1	23 812	107.5	258.7	6.2	14 062	1 062	0.0	0.0	16.9	7 600	124	798
Thurston	60.8	22 519	239.4	609.8	24.0	215 836	25 894	65.3	0.1	8.9	170 350	2 622	8 474
Wahkiakum	2.6	26 000	15.0	33.0	0.9	551	0	NA	NA	NA	463	6	88
Walla Walla	43.0	23 889	173.0	385.6	15.7	16 579	5 789	31.7	18.5	8.1	6 195	62	2 021
Whatcom	131.4	23 464	738.5	2 865.4	73.5	193 889	46 323	12.5	11.1	38.2	124 314	1 974	8 046
Whitman	1.1	11 000	5.8	8.7	0.2	11 795	2 573	26.9	0.6	10.4	7 599	164	1 155
Yakima	114.1	18 705	464.8	1 276.4	28.3	80 918	23 603	3.7	15.6	38.1	34 091	440	5 791
WEST VIRGINIA	1 312.3	22 318	5 404.4	11 560.8	434.8	338 056	139 600	7.2	20.5	37.8	110 192	1 771	33 346
Barbour	D	D	D	D	D	475	183	0.0	0.0	53.6	203	9	26
Berkeley	50.1	20 040	160.6	294.5	13.7	34 029	30 428	2.6	0.0	95.9	2 269	88	512
Boone	0.7	7 000	2.6	5.9	0.1	1 005	358	0.0	0.0	97.7	530	11	109
Braxton	1.8	9 000	6.5	16.4	0.4	19	0	NA	NA	NA	0	0	13
Brooke	D	D	D	D	D	7 119	3 775	44.4	15.2	29.0	1 845	38	1 008
Cabell	98.6	24 650	355.2	622.9	33.5	11 865	2 910	34.6	5.9	25.8	2 630	33	1 246
Calhoun	4.3	10 750	12.9	20.6	D	NA	NA	NA	NA	NA	NA	NA	NA
Clay	0.4	NA	1.3	2.7	D	0	0	NA	NA	NA	0	0	0
Doddridge	D	D	D	D	D	NA	NA	NA	NA	NA	NA	NA	NA
Fayette	D	D	D	D	D	7 638	2 137	21.1	28.8	16.4	3 982	109	819
Gilmer	2.8	9 333	3.6	10.4	0.6	253	0	NA	NA	NA	0	0	241
Grant	4.1	20 500	14.7	37.2	0.3	644	332	47.0	0.0	15.0	299	9	0
Greenbrier	8.5	14 167	34.4	75.3	D	8 519	2 624	3.8	0.2	14.5	4 179	81	1 323
Hampshire	4.6	11 500	12.7	24.1	0.6	478	153	0.0	0.0	98.0	186	4	40
Hancock	235.4	30 571	709.3	1 574.6	D	18 528	9 780	5.9	88.8	4.0	3 520	47	2 090
Hardy	16.8	12 923	56.0	149.4	D	10 478	5 913	0.0	0.0	0.0	3 517	70	274

1. Includes nonresidential additions and alterations, residential nonhousekeeping buildings, and residential garages and carports not shown separately.

STATE County	Wholesale trade, 1987				Retail trade, all establishments, 1987				Retail trade, establishments with payroll, 1987					
						Sales				Sales				
											Per capita[2] (Dollars)			
	Establishments	Sales (Mil dol)	Paid employees[1]	Annual payroll (Mil dol)	Number	Total (Mil dol)	Percent change, 1982–1987	Per capita[2] (Dollars)	Number	Total (Mil dol)	General merchandise stores	Food stores	Apparel & accessory stores	Eating and drinking places
	147	148	149	150	151	152	153	154	155	156	157	158	159	160
VIRGINIA—Con.														
South Boston City	24	47.8	151	2.0	0	0.0	0.0	0	0	0.0	0	0	0	0
Staunton City	45	120.4	535	9.4	0	0.0	0.0	0	0	0.0	0	0	0	0
Suffolk City	74	328.7	1 056	20.9	398	248.9	22.6	4 833	260	243.4	248	1 028	263	272
Virginia Beach City	410	1 419.0	4 573	96.1	3 061	2 385.6	88.9	6 783	2 166	2 349.4	691	1 343	370	765
Waynesboro City	29	130.9	440	7.4	0	0.0	0.0	0	0	0.0	0	0	0	0
Williamsburg City	38	48.6	154	3.7	0	0.0	0.0	0	0	0.0	0	0	0	0
Winchester City	107	319.4	1 473	26.2	0	0.0	0.0	0	0	0.0	0	0	0	0
WASHINGTON	9 335	41 499.0	102 778	2 380.1	44 759	27 938.9	39.6	6 152	28 499	27 249.8	738	1 366	302	652
Adams	54	126.5	616	9.7	154	41.9	-9.9	3 174	102	40.4	D	1 016	90	613
Asotin	14	46.2	87	1.7	154	59.1	24.2	3 456	81	55.5	0	1 177	D	460
Benton	102	222.8	783	15.0	1 017	584.5	13.5	5 177	635	568.5	839	1 391	169	517
Chelan	131	595.4	2 012	37.8	793	343.4	33.2	7 154	543	331.5	657	1 501	224	725
Clallam	63	86.5	391	7.6	664	296.1	29.5	5 385	431	286.4	352	1 367	215	592
Clark	284	585.4	1 763	36.0	1 662	996.3	45.3	4 568	1 013	968.0	680	1 114	175	494
Columbia	20	14.7	61	1.0	57	9.3	-21.2	2 270	30	8.6	D	927	D	189
Cowlitz	105	529.8	1 041	22.1	784	452.4	18.2	5 727	492	439.4	814	1 499	169	651
Douglas	21	78.0	348	5.7	217	116.8	52.1	4 746	131	112.5	D	1 986	343	565
Ferry	5	1.5	9	0.1	71	17.4	91.2	2 954	47	16.7	0	1 031	74	454
Franklin	134	375.1	1 268	23.2	335	262.8	29.2	7 685	209	256.6	717	1 448	76	501
Garfield	11	37.6	84	1.6	30	4.5	45.2	1 856	16	2.4	0	D	0	163
Grant	124	358.9	1 404	25.2	557	246.9	28.2	4 804	364	238.0	218	1 455	162	447
Grays Harbor	92	148.7	709	15.2	742	312.9	8.2	5 023	490	302.9	427	1 454	171	596
Island	22	13.0	60	1.2	460	188.3	53.5	3 579	261	180.9	32	1 120	104	402
Jefferson	16	11.0	58	1.1	297	72.8	17.6	3 834	176	68.9	111	1 306	87	489
King	4 451	26 634.6	53 763	1 371.7	14 501	10 706.4	41.7	7 627	9 461	10 495.5	878	1 516	497	879
Kitsap	115	193.2	789	15.9	1 484	829.1	46.3	4 754	903	814.9	562	1 170	175	435
Kittitas	43	70.9	269	4.2	350	141.0	18.7	5 596	228	136.4	357	1 566	210	794
Klickitat	15	18.7	50	0.8	150	38.6	4.6	2 426	93	37.0	41	842	25	195
Lewis	81	202.9	781	15.6	737	320.8	23.8	5 474	450	308.5	604	1 465	127	600
Lincoln	61	109.7	290	5.7	125	24.7	5.6	2 806	77	23.0	D	1 156	D	266
Mason	20	24.6	114	3.0	367	126.5	23.9	3 438	197	122.0	122	1 391	72	372
Okanogan	51	123.9	713	11.1	437	150.7	27.9	4 679	274	141.5	187	1 665	144	343
Pacific	14	13.8	74	1.1	282	66.4	20.7	3 751	166	62.0	D	1 290	55	592
Pend Oreille	6	3.2	12	0.1	82	27.0	15.4	3 138	47	24.9	D	1 591	D	147
Pierce	686	3 127.2	8 936	205.2	4 516	3 110.9	46.7	5 716	2 805	3 034.5	832	1 124	235	569
San Juan	14	8.8	33	0.7	241	50.6	62.2	5 217	127	43.8	D	1 709	135	838
Skagit	123	188.3	930	19.7	942	456.8	28.0	6 461	615	439.5	273	1 535	272	733
Skamania	3	D	D	D	58	9.6	15.7	1 269	34	9.1	D	614	0	142
Snohomish	608	1 549.4	4 978	106.2	3 651	2 562.7	61.5	6 351	2 284	2 500.3	888	1 320	299	610
Spokane	851	3 314.7	10 263	224.1	3 275	2 317.1	40.1	6 518	2 150	2 266.9	1 002	1 390	312	624
Stevens	37	36.1	193	2.8	313	91.4	7.7	2 912	179	86.7	93	993	121	275
Thurston	155	276.6	1 446	29.8	1 387	853.8	45.0	5 651	879	836.2	693	1 365	169	551
Wahkiakum	1	D	D	D	35	5.2	-1.9	1 498	19	4.8	D	D	0	126
Walla Walla	96	221.6	708	12.1	440	220.7	15.2	4 726	286	212.3	538	1 316	214	452
Whatcom	239	511.0	1 988	36.6	1 359	771.9	43.1	6 689	897	751.0	830	1 614	230	698
Whitman	114	256.5	744	13.6	308	119.7	33.6	3 166	200	116.4	38	971	22	343
Yakima	353	1 381.6	5 003	96.0	1 725	931.8	22.8	5 083	1 107	905.3	595	1 273	228	461
WEST VIRGINIA	2 444	5 935.4	24 217	476.9	17 621	9 349.2	24.3	4 926	10 737	9 030.0	693	1 129	175	384
Barbour	14	D	D	D	167	48.4	36.0	3 081	81	43.9	181	1 028	27	250
Berkeley	46	D	D	D	545	301.2	66.1	5 652	330	287.7	633	1 315	452	441
Boone	12	D	D	D	244	109.7	10.7	3 810	139	104.7	440	1 282	64	125
Braxton	18	D	D	D	178	87.6	52.9	6 045	108	83.7	384	1 406	D	236
Brooke	14	D	D	D	213	96.9	28.3	3 388	131	93.9	251	972	61	393
Cabell	232	966.1	3 337	70.4	1 075	812.9	25.7	7 939	777	799.6	1 592	1 384	446	748
Calhoun	6	D	D	D	97	21.3	28.3	2 540	37	17.3	155	919	0	93
Clay	2	D	D	D	88	19.5	2.1	1 738	33	15.7	113	679	0	37
Doddridge	1	D	D	D	49	7.6	-3.8	1 041	21	6.0	0	280	D	24
Fayette	47	D	D	D	448	203.2	7.1	3 842	293	197.7	550	959	112	239
Gilmer	6	D	D	D	65	18.4	18.7	2 359	36	17.1	D	1 004	0	92
Grant	17	D	D	D	114	36.4	36.8	3 342	65	33.8	D	898	D	186
Greenbrier	54	D	D	D	444	188.5	17.8	5 296	275	180.8	543	1 397	154	335
Hampshire	19	14.6	102	1.6	163	45.9	26.8	2 869	67	40.7	102	532	D	184
Hancock	19	D	D	D	328	148.6	9.9	3 962	219	144.6	557	1 326	82	338
Hardy	11	17.2	85	0.9	110	34.3	14.7	3 240	57	32.0	D	1 196	50	145

1. For pay period including March 12. 2. Based on the estimated population as of July 1 of the year shown.

STATE County	Retail trade, establishments with payroll, 1987 (cont'd)		Taxable service industries–establishments with payroll, 1987							Bank deposits,[2] June 1989		Savings capital,[3] September 1989	
				Receipts (Mil dol)									
					Selected kinds of business								
	Paid employees[1]	Annual payroll (Mil dol)	Number	Total	Hotels, motels and other lodging places	Health services	Legal services	Paid employees	Annual payroll (Mil dol)	Total (Mil dol)	Percent change, 1988–1989	Total (Mil dol)	Percent change, 1988–1989
	161	162	163	164	165	166	167	168	169	170	171	172	173
VIRGINIA—Con.													
South Boston City	0	0.0	103	22.1	D	12.7	0.6	633	8.6	142	9.9	0.0	NA
Staunton City	0	0.0	241	50.9	1.9	19.3	3.5	1 536	20.5	348	-3.8	123.2	0.5
Suffolk City	2 834	27.3	245	50.7	2.3	23.2	3.3	1 446	20.5	225	4.8	110.9	7.3
Virginia Beach City	30 774	282.9	2 433	1 059.7	107.3	245.7	43.9	27 706	438.8	1 328	7.7	1 339.9	1.0
Waynesboro City	0	0.0	161	39.3	5.2	15.7	2.7	1 061	16.4	192	-3.1	48.9	-2.1
Williamsburg City	0	0.0	285	170.2	112.3	25.1	3.2	4 130	52.1	226	2.9	59.8	9.1
Winchester City	0	0.0	371	109.7	4.9	56.6	7.0	2 860	47.1	583	11.4	77.7	10.1
WASHINGTON	329 204	3 401.6	33 181	12 852.0	655.1	3 305.6	1 028.2	277 118	4 773.9	35 261	8.2	11 487.7	4.3
Adams	634	5.2	66	11.9	1.7	5.0	1.2	383	4.0	105	-4.9	9.3	12.0
Asotin	744	6.8	108	18.4	2.1	10.0	0.9	529	5.8	82	-1.2	62.3	-1.0
Benton	7 251	69.3	701	750.4	10.1	78.5	10.8	11 159	307.0	427	6.3	260.5	-2.7
Chelan	4 020	40.0	433	141.6	15.7	70.0	9.9	3 829	57.4	421	5.8	187.0	-6.7
Clallam	3 524	36.0	402	80.8	10.6	34.2	4.4	2 148	25.3	259	15.1	365.2	1.9
Clark	12 146	120.4	1 233	373.3	13.3	114.4	21.2	9 663	130.6	822	9.9	617.1	2.6
Columbia	131	1.1	27	3.9	D	1.0	0.3	218	1.1	44	3.4	10.8	-8.8
Cowlitz	5 467	55.2	487	177.1	5.4	111.4	6.7	3 827	56.8	361	12.4	183.9	16.5
Douglas	1 517	13.1	89	14.2	1.3	3.3	1.4	379	4.4	99	10.1	69.9	-9.4
Ferry	234	1.8	25	1.8	0.3	0.6	D	40	0.4	13	14.7	0.0	NA
Franklin	2 506	26.9	218	60.1	7.4	14.8	4.1	1 480	18.8	173	4.6	55.2	5.5
Garfield	41	0.3	15	0.7	D	D	D	26	0.1	25	-3.0	13.2	-3.4
Grant	3 102	27.8	273	50.1	4.9	15.5	5.8	1 385	16.9	297	5.5	41.1	-13.8
Grays Harbor	4 175	38.5	398	85.5	19.6	31.2	6.8	2 237	30.2	334	3.8	262.8	1.6
Island	2 246	21.8	231	36.8	3.1	14.3	3.0	1 066	12.1	154	6.4	146.2	-4.0
Jefferson	1 011	9.3	144	19.7	3.8	6.4	0.3	556	6.1	98	15.9	55.4	2.7
King	126 227	1 366.5	13 956	6 890.9	354.6	1 229.4	677.1	137 129	2 553.1	17 618	10.9	4 584.6	3.8
Kitsap	9 664	99.2	936	306.0	10.7	100.5	11.4	7 696	120.9	714	8.7	303.0	-1.0
Kittitas	2 049	17.9	159	27.9	5.4	10.2	1.9	882	8.4	151	-3.7	55.3	10.1
Klickitat	438	4.2	65	10.9	1.8	4.8	0.6	321	3.6	119	8.0	20.5	0.3
Lewis	3 779	37.8	349	92.5	7.2	45.3	4.3	2 150	32.2	337	5.1	213.0	-3.7
Lincoln	315	2.6	36	6.1	D	2.4	D	143	2.2	157	5.1	0.0	NA
Mason	1 468	13.0	146	24.3	2.9	10.4	0.9	788	7.9	142	-8.4	58.3	5.0
Okanogan	1 569	15.3	186	25.2	4.2	10.4	2.9	725	8.6	213	3.4	41.8	-9.3
Pacific	966	8.9	126	20.0	3.1	8.4	0.5	772	6.3	137	8.9	27.2	-16.8
Pend Oreille	243	2.3	32	4.4	D	1.7	0.2	133	1.4	51	6.7	0.0	NA
Pierce	34 891	370.2	3 235	1 039.4	34.0	397.6	80.3	25 253	392.0	3 502	3.2	1 044.7	41.0
San Juan	705	6.7	88	19.7	11.1	2.4	0.7	425	5.9	92	11.0	30.8	2.4
Skagit	5 405	53.3	519	142.2	4.1	61.0	8.6	3 274	51.8	519	6.0	250.3	2.1
Skamania	162	1.2	20	2.4	0.8	0.4	D	74	0.8	16	7.4	14.4	-2.2
Snohomish	28 893	307.4	2 430	640.5	19.5	218.8	25.8	14 951	229.0	2 120	6.1	831.2	10.6
Spokane	27 235	272.5	2 647	857.6	38.4	312.6	73.4	21 119	333.6	2 396	6.8	498.6	-7.5
Stevens	1 142	9.4	122	18.2	0.8	9.7	0.9	689	6.3	144	5.5	22.9	-1.8
Thurston	9 945	100.4	936	291.2	14.9	133.1	14.1	6 715	106.1	568	3.9	446.1	-0.6
Wahkiakum	71	0.5	10	0.7	D	D	D	25	0.3	15	24.4	8.0	-4.5
Walla Walla	3 091	27.7	261	54.7	2.1	27.0	5.7	1 371	22.9	315	0.2	190.3	-6.1
Whatcom	9 325	88.0	855	225.7	21.1	82.3	13.5	5 536	82.1	1 005	5.9	160.7	13.3
Whitman	2 030	14.9	162	29.4	2.1	13.9	2.6	953	9.9	312	1.0	18.0	7.0
Yakima	10 842	108.1	1 055	295.6	16.6	112.1	24.3	7 069	111.5	900	7.1	328.0	-14.0
WEST VIRGINIA	109 220	994.3	8 909	2 917.0	226.9	1 085.1	225.5	67 281	1 030.9	13 969	4.2	1 684.4	-9.5
Barbour	542	4.4	41	6.0	D	D	0.4	154	1.6	121	6.0	0.0	-100.0
Berkeley	3 093	30.5	249	59.4	2.4	21.9	5.4	1 344	21.4	334	1.8	45.7	-7.7
Boone	1 075	10.3	71	18.0	D	8.7	2.5	516	5.6	172	7.2	5.3	25.5
Braxton	756	8.3	60	13.0	D	3.1	1.0	308	4.0	116	9.5	0.0	NA
Brooke	1 336	10.4	88	25.9	D	15.0	1.5	677	10.0	94	5.6	52.6	-1.1
Cabell	10 814	94.2	740	244.1	9.8	113.0	20.5	5 744	98.1	854	4.4	192.2	-4.9
Calhoun	185	1.6	24	2.8	0.0	1.3	D	66	0.8	42	4.8	0.0	NA
Clay	163	1.4	8	2.8	0.0	D	D	52	0.8	37	8.4	0.0	NA
Doddridge	74	0.6	8	1.2	0.0	D	0.1	29	0.3	76	6.0	0.0	NA
Fayette	2 296	22.3	201	54.6	D	27.1	2.3	1 350	17.4	341	5.8	28.3	-2.9
Gilmer	221	1.5	30	4.1	D	1.9	0.3	183	1.5	58	-5.8	0.0	NA
Grant	371	3.0	50	12.2	1.2	1.9	0.7	270	4.0	116	5.8	6.7	0.7
Greenbrier	2 091	20.4	195	102.6	D	34.4	D	1 873	38.7	330	4.9	27.3	0.8
Hampshire	503	4.1	56	13.6	3.7	4.0	0.9	374	4.3	107	12.0	0.0	NA
Hancock	2 118	16.6	169	44.4	D	19.4	5.6	1 579	15.4	246	4.9	139.2	-3.5
Hardy	371	3.0	38	4.3	0.2	1.5	0.9	129	1.1	100	5.1	0.0	NA

1. For the period including March 12 of the year shown. 2. Includes deposits for all insured and reporting noninsured commercial and mutual savings banks. 3. Includes savings capital for all FSLIC insured savings institutions.

STATE County	Federal funds and grants, 1989: Expenditures: Total (Mil dol)	Federal funds and grants, 1989: Expenditures: Percent change, 1988–1989	Per capita[1] (Dollars): Total	Per capita[1] (Dollars): Direct payments for individuals	Per capita[1] (Dollars): Procurement contract awards	Per capita[1] (Dollars): Salaries and wages	Per capita[1] (Dollars): Grant awards	Local government finances, 1981–1982: General revenue: Total (Mil dol)	General revenue: Intergovernmental: Total (Mil dol)	General revenue: Intergovernmental: Percent from state	General revenue: Taxes: Total (Mil dol)	Taxes: Per capita[2]: Total (Dollars)	Taxes: Per capita[2]: Property (Dollars)	Direct general expenditure: Total (Mil dol)	Direct general expenditure: Percent change, 1977–1982
	174	175	176	177	178	179	180	181	182	183	184	185	186	187	188
VIRGINIA—Con.															
South Boston City	0.0	0.0	0	0	0	0	0	5.1	2.5	86.6	2.4	340	170	5.1	60.8
Staunton City	0.0	0.0	0	0	0	0	0	16.1	6.9	72.6	7.2	326	190	15.4	50.7
Suffolk City	134.0	13.1	2 542	1 965	74	101	382	37.0	21.6	76.3	13.3	280	174	31.8	42.6
Virginia Beach City	1 457.9	6.0	3 831	1 511	461	1 728	124	311.0	134.2	61.3	112.5	398	217	312.4	106.1
Waynesboro City	0.0	0.0	0	0	0	0	0	13.2	5.0	81.7	6.8	453	288	12.5	7.7
Williamsburg City	0.0	0.0	0	0	0	0	0	15.9	7.8	83.4	6.7	640	222	21.7	68.5
Winchester City	0.0	0.0	0	0	0	0	0	17.8	5.1	88.2	9.7	478	299	17.8	79.7
WASHINGTON	19 520.1	6.4	X	1 812	878	750	585	5 305.2	2 502.5	85.9	1 296.1	303	186	4 855.9	76.5
Adams	53.0	-5.8	4 045	1 467	23	161	1 227	28.3	14.6	75.4	4.8	357	295	28.7	74.8
Asotin	47.6	4.2	2 801	2 139	33	120	349	15.1	9.2	89.5	3.1	181	127	14.2	83.2
Benton	1 145.4	1.6	10 128	1 287	8 243	236	308	330.3	57.2	93.5	32.2	276	158	126.5	104.7
Chelan	149.9	11.8	3 111	2 276	97	365	330	77.7	25.0	94.4	14.2	306	181	50.8	60.5
Clallam	196.0	11.9	3 409	2 534	218	322	329	66.6	29.3	95.2	10.2	197	140	65.2	106.4
Clark	499.0	8.7	2 131	1 455	46	376	246	198.7	109.6	92.5	46.0	230	160	217.9	105.4
Columbia	20.6	-2.3	5 024	2 300	1 008	491	350	6.3	3.4	82.4	1.3	313	247	6.5	66.2
Cowlitz	250.3	-0.1	3 082	1 774	122	105	1 075	101.6	51.7	92.1	25.5	322	223	97.1	54.3
Douglas	58.3	-6.5	2 304	1 185	199	227	219	23.5	13.2	91.8	4.7	204	158	19.8	60.7
Ferry	16.2	-6.6	2 661	1 380	137	581	510	6.8	5.2	92.5	0.7	111	71	6.5	114.0
Franklin	91.9	-4.5	2 744	1 553	150	490	325	47.5	21.6	94.5	11.8	322	225	47.3	97.0
Garfield	12.8	-23.1	5 332	2 498	50	1 153	201	4.8	2.2	96.0	1.2	479	428	4.8	77.2
Grant	151.4	-5.0	2 923	1 719	76	505	362	82.0	34.9	86.8	13.5	274	186	71.9	82.1
Grays Harbor	191.0	10.8	3 022	2 200	140	178	495	113.2	59.2	66.7	21.6	329	180	114.5	137.4
Island	349.5	1.4	6 131	1 969	419	3 579	160	36.1	20.7	90.5	8.0	174	125	34.2	95.2
Jefferson	68.9	9.2	3 427	2 738	37	368	278	22.2	11.4	90.6	4.3	255	185	21.3	82.3
King	6 350.6	-1.1	4 298	1 570	1 455	518	689	1 793.1	743.6	83.5	551.0	421	238	1 615.5	62.3
Kitsap	1 374.7	5.7	7 363	2 050	563	4 533	213	134.2	85.0	84.9	30.6	196	130	138.4	100.3
Kittitas	60.5	-7.1	2 383	1 793	79	180	296	29.9	14.7	89.7	6.5	262	168	31.0	48.9
Klickitat	46.9	-4.8	2 969	1 935	85	278	370	25.4	13.5	90.4	4.0	245	181	24.1	108.6
Lewis	161.6	-6.6	2 689	1 970	131	167	407	66.4	43.8	85.9	12.5	218	137	62.5	89.4
Lincoln	41.7	-33.3	4 964	2 503	88	244	433	20.6	12.1	71.7	4.2	436	377	19.7	87.6
Mason	103.9	7.5	2 656	2 251	48	90	264	34.5	14.7	92.2	8.5	258	159	34.5	118.3
Okanogan	114.4	18.1	3 519	1 929	384	410	664	39.4	19.5	88.4	6.8	214	145	41.7	86.6
Pacific	69.0	14.3	3 834	2 838	45	207	726	28.6	14.5	91.6	5.4	305	220	25.3	89.6
Pend Oreille	27.4	4.8	3 074	2 255	147	276	381	12.6	6.5	95.6	1.6	188	147	12.8	105.5
Pierce	2 461.7	3.6	4 292	1 850	338	1 768	330	584.4	321.4	84.6	136.8	269	169	589.5	82.6
San Juan	26.6	6.6	2 537	2 193	66	164	105	10.4	5.1	95.8	3.8	449	337	10.2	147.5
Skagit	206.8	6.7	2 779	2 162	148	147	288	97.3	37.1	92.5	17.6	265	193	93.0	62.0
Skamania	24.0	-6.5	3 079	1 352	374	810	538	13.4	8.6	94.5	1.6	216	137	11.9	70.5
Snohomish	884.7	8.8	2 003	1 260	374	121	241	383.5	192.2	86.5	85.9	241	156	371.2	111.8
Spokane	1 154.3	9.7	3 224	1 993	236	635	338	323.0	178.3	89.6	85.8	247	147	322.7	61.3
Stevens	74.7	7.0	2 326	1 525	93	307	374	28.4	16.8	90.3	4.8	157	110	27.0	125.3
Thurston	718.1	1.5	4 413	1 774	51	214	2 367	138.3	88.1	78.7	33.2	249	175	136.7	100.4
Wahkiakum	9.3	5.1	2 645	2 099	17	155	333	4.2	2.6	96.4	0.5	136	116	4.0	89.0
Walla Walla	163.8	-0.1	3 554	2 124	141	638	383	50.4	29.6	80.9	13.0	269	186	49.9	88.5
Whatcom	611.2	97.3	5 035	1 613	2 882	203	312	114.9	55.5	88.9	34.6	315	185	110.0	56.0
Whitman	129.0	-7.8	3 515	1 407	360	247	1 151	36.3	19.7	91.0	9.5	238	176	36.3	65.1
Yakima	486.1	6.3	2 591	1 617	156	238	533	175.0	110.9	88.0	34.7	197	134	160.8	54.8
WEST VIRGINIA	6 222.8	8.1	X	2 238	199	300	586	1 620.2	814.1	83.5	393.1	200	158	1 591.1	87.1
Barbour	45.1	5.8	3 007	2 384	25	119	469	10.6	6.8	90.6	2.6	158	141	10.3	73.8
Berkeley	192.1	4.4	3 382	1 706	223	1 206	228	31.4	18.5	90.1	7.8	161	138	31.2	68.0
Boone	78.7	9.3	2 861	2 124	101	148	483	24.5	13.2	94.3	6.8	221	210	22.6	95.8
Braxton	41.0	0.6	2 908	2 063	37	189	598	10.1	7.6	86.4	1.8	125	113	9.8	87.0
Brooke	66.2	16.0	2 391	1 901	21	88	366	21.4	10.2	94.9	5.7	185	156	19.8	97.6
Cabell	381.7	14.6	3 860	2 380	568	555	349	131.8	49.9	67.3	27.1	255	164	138.3	155.2
Calhoun	24.5	2.4	2 957	2 025	160	160	592	8.1	4.3	96.3	0.8	91	89	8.0	57.6
Clay	30.3	6.5	2 726	2 036	17	123	539	7.2	5.5	87.1	1.1	99	97	7.2	47.9
Doddridge	15.6	0.3	2 266	1 734	14	106	391	5.2	3.2	94.1	1.4	188	184	5.4	107.0
Fayette	192.0	17.4	3 803	2 753	454	225	363	37.6	22.3	89.2	9.1	158	133	35.4	33.5
Gilmer	22.4	10.0	2 988	2 203	34	218	481	5.0	3.1	92.0	1.4	161	155	4.8	43.6
Grant	25.5	-0.8	2 298	1 650	47	205	362	16.8	8.4	94.2	3.4	321	306	15.3	119.6
Greenbrier	105.2	-8.0	3 104	2 541	26	143	348	21.8	13.8	93.2	4.3	117	107	21.5	76.4
Hampshire	37.7	5.8	2 287	1 765	13	150	284	15.0	10.6	56.9	1.9	122	117	14.6	210.8
Hancock	96.9	4.5	2 677	2 412	27	89	141	39.5	12.5	86.2	14.8	365	241	37.4	88.7
Hardy	27.4	-5.3	2 488	1 799	14	135	480	6.9	4.8	91.7	1.5	148	141	6.6	80.2

1. Based on the estimated population as of July 1 of the year shown. 2. Based on the estimated population as of July 1, 1982.

STATE County	Local government finances, 1981–1982 (cont'd): Direct general expenditure (cont'd): Per capita[1] (Dollars)	Percent of total for– Education	Percent of total for– Health & hospitals	Percent of total for– Police protection	Percent of total for– Public welfare	Percent of total for– Highways	Debt outstanding: Total (Mil dol)	Debt outstanding: Per capita[1] (Dollars)	State and local government employment, 1989: Total	State and local government employment, 1989: Rate[2]	Federal government civilian employment 1989: Total	Federal government civilian employment 1989: Earnings ($1,000)	Elections, 1988[3]: Total vote cast for president	Elections, 1988[3]: Vote for lead party (Percent)
	189	190	191	192	193	194	195	196	197	198	199	200	201	202
VIRGINIA–Con.														
South Boston City	713	48.4	1.0	9.0	0.1	19.0	3.2	454	0	0.0	0	0	2 645	R–64.0
Staunton City	698	44.2	0.5	9.9	4.8	5.7	7.0	315	0	0.0	0	0	8 334	R–69.3
Suffolk City	670	56.0	0.9	6.1	7.7	2.4	11.3	239	3 110	590.1	150	4 570	17 950	R–54.3
Virginia Beach City	1 104	34.7	1.5	5.1	1.9	7.9	362.3	1 280	14 999	394.1	3 527	94 011	111 018	R–68.9
Waynesboro City	825	49.8	0.3	6.4	3.7	10.4	16.2	1 072	0	0.0	0	0	6 799	R–68.7
Williamsburg City	2 065	69.9	0.4	3.0	1.7	2.6	0.5	49	0	0.0	0	0	3 237	R–50.9
Winchester City	882	41.6	0.2	7.5	3.4	4.4	12.0	596	0	0.0	0	0	6 862	R–65.5
WASHINGTON	1 135	43.9	6.1	4.9	0.2	6.7	14 145.5	3 307	305 197	641.7	72 014	2 253 053	1 865 253	D–50.0
Adams	2 161	38.5	10.6	3.6	0.0	11.0	76.5	5 755	1 064	812.2	80	2 171	4 288	R–60.9
Asotin	834	56.5	5.0	4.4	0.0	8.3	8.2	483	751	441.8	57	1 681	6 384	D–53.6
Benton	1 083	47.7	7.9	5.9	0.0	6.3	8 520.1	72 946	6 901	610.2	620	24 972	44 016	R–65.2
Chelan	1 095	45.4	4.8	7.7	0.0	6.7	1 004.9	21 658	3 876	804.1	705	20 656	20 065	R–57.8
Clallam	1 267	35.3	19.6	4.6	0.0	8.7	32.2	626	3 877	674.3	554	13 847	22 794	R–49.1
Clark	1 089	49.5	1.2	4.7	0.4	5.5	206.2	1 030	11 234	479.7	2 410	85 192	78 306	D–51.1
Columbia	1 637	29.8	26.3	4.7	0.0	13.5	1.5	371	392	956.1	66	1 791	1 944	R–60.3
Cowlitz	1 226	43.3	1.9	5.8	0.0	12.1	71.3	900	4 266	525.4	234	7 421	28 465	D–56.5
Douglas	863	56.8	3.1	4.6	0.0	11.6	217.2	9 485	1 149	454.2	156	4 861	9 247	R–58.2
Ferry	1 102	53.8	3.8	5.7	0.0	13.0	6.0	1 010	393	644.3	144	3 686	2 021	T–48.1
Franklin	1 288	47.0	1.0	4.8	0.0	7.3	79.3	2 160	2 685	801.5	448	14 660	11 452	R–56.7
Garfield	1 923	29.6	23.2	4.4	0.0	18.4	8.9	3 548	268	1 116.7	125	3 212	1 319	R–54.1
Grant	1 456	41.7	14.4	3.5	0.1	7.4	282.8	5 724	4 229	816.4	308	9 834	18 799	R–57.8
Grays Harbor	1 745	29.9	3.0	5.6	0.0	10.2	73.5	1 120	3 872	612.7	280	7 847	23 391	D–60.3
Island	748	52.7	14.1	4.4	0.0	7.9	14.8	323	2 126	373.0	1 343	34 039	21 353	R–58.8
Jefferson	1 259	33.9	17.3	5.2	0.0	16.3	8.4	497	1 357	675.1	127	3 563	9 636	D–54.7
King	1 233	37.4	6.4	5.4	0.3	5.5	1 839.7	1 404	101 347	685.8	19 807	674 578	648 957	D–53.9
Kitsap	886	55.9	2.0	3.4	0.0	5.9	66.0	422	8 054	431.4	20 026	643 626	69 649	R–49.9
Kittitas	1 245	35.3	12.3	4.3	0.0	9.6	19.3	774	3 190	1 255.9	205	5 396	10 496	D–50.7
Klickitat	1 469	45.1	13.3	3.8	0.0	11.8	16.5	1 004	1 180	746.8	198	5 053	6 086	D–49.1
Lewis	1 088	48.8	5.2	5.2	0.1	12.5	22.4	390	3 717	618.5	412	10 757	23 238	R–61.0
Lincoln	2 032	41.2	14.8	2.3	0.0	25.2	4.0	408	1 004	1 195.2	72	1 638	4 645	R–57.9
Mason	1 046	44.3	17.2	4.6	0.0	5.4	42.1	1 275	2 456	628.1	120	3 616	15 545	D–50.3
Okanogan	1 310	48.3	19.1	3.9	0.0	7.9	33.5	1 054	2 248	691.7	1 075	33 918	11 740	R–49.9
Pacific	1 428	41.1	19.6	4.6	0.1	9.5	7.6	428	1 198	665.6	51	1 309	8 200	D–61.2
Pend Oreille	1 474	43.7	20.9	3.8	0.0	13.3	19.6	2 247	614	689.9	121	3 070	3 794	D–50.7
Pierce	1 162	49.0	1.0	3.8	0.3	4.8	543.6	1 071	29 626	516.6	11 153	291 877	194 473	D–49.7
San Juan	1 214	36.7	3.6	5.1	0.0	16.3	7.6	907	572	544.8	52	1 282	5 814	D–51.7
Skagit	1 396	35.7	33.1	3.6	0.0	6.2	46.4	696	5 230	703.0	417	11 854	32 401	R–51.1
Skamania	1 569	39.3	3.9	5.4	0.0	21.1	2.8	368	469	601.3	367	9 134	3 162	D–55.3
Snohomish	1 043	47.4	9.3	4.4	0.2	5.4	408.6	1 148	19 992	452.6	1 407	43 523	167 165	R–50.3
Spokane	927	49.8	2.0	6.0	0.1	7.2	152.8	439	20 536	573.5	4 252	129 295	139 150	R–49.4
Stevens	891	56.3	1.6	3.4	0.0	11.1	10.2	336	1 634	509.0	348	9 250	11 962	R–55.0
Thurston	1 026	51.2	2.5	4.2	0.1	6.7	82.7	620	25 258	1 552.4	833	27 840	66 930	D–50.6
Wahkiakum	1 062	36.6	0.5	6.2	0.0	18.6	0.6	169	177	505.7	134	3 004	1 626	D–59.1
Walla Walla	1 030	39.7	2.3	5.2	0.0	10.7	26.4	546	3 324	721.0	906	27 656	17 403	R–55.6
Whatcom	1 000	47.7	3.1	4.9	0.0	9.9	92.0	837	7 085	583.6	721	24 109	50 094	D–51.0
Whitman	911	44.9	9.2	4.4	0.0	20.3	8.6	215	8 051	2 193.7	323	11 088	15 333	R–50.1
Yakima	912	55.8	1.7	5.1	0.0	4.1	80.9	459	9 795	522.1	1 357	40 747	53 910	R–55.7
WEST VIRGINIA	811	56.0	10.9	3.0	0.1	1.9	1 952.7	996	107 259	577.4	16 692	507 455	653 311	D–52.2
Barbour	615	75.1	1.8	2.3	0.5	0.9	3.0	179	676	450.7	54	1 400	6 261	D–51.4
Berkeley	643	71.4	0.6	3.8	0.0	1.0	48.6	1 000	2 088	367.6	2 355	73 260	17 135	R–62.8
Boone	736	70.6	7.9	2.3	0.0	0.7	7.9	258	1 253	455.6	112	3 151	9 345	D–70.0
Braxton	678	80.0	4.5	1.8	0.1	0.9	0.5	35	631	447.5	73	1 738	5 423	D–62.3
Brooke	643	62.6	1.8	3.9	0.1	2.4	48.3	1 569	1 058	381.9	57	1 579	10 306	D–60.7
Cabell	1 302	31.8	25.7	2.8	0.0	1.0	154.6	1 456	6 368	643.9	1 314	41 590	32 662	R–52.7
Calhoun	945	59.3	32.9	0.6	0.0	0.5	0.4	47	441	531.3	34	658	3 057	D–53.8
Clay	631	83.7	0.5	1.2	1.7	0.1	0.6	54	452	407.2	37	719	3 811	D–59.4
Doddridge	718	80.4	4.7	0.3	0.5	0.3	0.7	95	297	430.4	18	392	2 847	R–66.0
Fayette	616	70.4	1.0	3.5	0.0	2.6	43.9	764	2 473	489.7	312	9 288	16 205	D–67.9
Gilmer	553	74.8	1.5	3.0	0.5	1.1	0.0	0	615	820.0	41	802	3 064	D–54.2
Grant	1 459	38.9	40.9	0.9	0.7	0.3	24.7	2 350	802	722.5	83	1 944	4 130	R–77.8
Greenbrier	583	75.9	1.3	2.8	0.1	1.3	6.7	181	1 904	561.7	150	3 791	11 521	D–52.9
Hampshire	941	48.4	13.1	0.7	0.0	0.4	0.7	42	1 248	756.4	57	1 300	5 363	R–60.7
Hancock	925	44.8	0.3	5.9	0.5	5.1	127.1	3 146	1 262	348.6	89	2 640	14 280	D–58.4
Hardy	651	79.2	1.3	1.2	0.1	2.1	1.9	191	468	425.5	51	1 266	4 288	R–60.2

1. Based on the estimated population as of July 1, 1982. 2. Per 10,000 resident population estimated as of July 1 of the year shown. 3. Data subject to copyright.

STATE–County code	MSA/CMSA/NECMA code[1]	STATE County	Land Area,[2] 1990 (Sq. Km.)	Population, 1990: Total persons	Rank	Per square kilometer	Race: White	Black	Am. Indian, Eskimo, Aleut	Asian & Pacific Islander	Other race	Hispanic[3]	Age of population Percent: Under 5 years	5 to 14 years	15 to 24 years
			1	2	3	4	5	6	7	8	9	10	11	12	13
		WEST VIRGINIA—Con.													
54 033	...	Harrison	1 078	69 371	637	64.4	68 056	975	91	186	63	817	5.9	14.1	13.2
54 035	...	Jackson	1 206	25 938	1 424	21.5	25 817	16	40	57	8	65	6.5	15.1	13.0
54 037	...	Jefferson	543	35 926	1 101	66.2	32 959	2 661	58	140	108	428	7.1	14.1	16.7
54 039	1480	Kanawha	2 339	207 619	241	88.8	192 019	13 792	242	1 306	260	897	5.9	13.3	12.7
54 041	...	Lewis	1 007	17 223	1 841	17.1	17 086	48	26	52	11	67	5.8	13.8	13.3
54 043	...	Lincoln	1 133	21 382	1 611	18.9	21 337	6	16	19	4	48	6.0	16.5	15.0
54 045	...	Logan	1 176	43 032	938	36.6	41 377	1 366	52	187	50	281	5.7	16.4	15.2
54 047	...	McDowell	1 385	35 233	1 125	25.4	30 407	4 754	35	26	11	182	6.2	16.8	14.4
54 049	...	Marion	802	57 249	763	71.4	55 076	1 859	123	149	42	311	5.4	13.0	15.2
54 051	9000	Marshall	795	37 356	1 063	47.0	37 002	204	33	87	30	229	6.0	13.8	13.4
54 053	...	Mason	1 119	25 178	1 456	22.5	24 948	112	26	81	11	53	5.8	15.3	12.7
54 055	...	Mercer	1 089	64 980	674	59.7	60 420	4 133	88	306	33	269	5.4	13.9	14.9
54 057	1900	Mineral	849	26 697	1 401	31.4	25 866	735	12	70	14	101	6.3	14.1	15.5
54 059	...	Mingo	1 095	33 739	1 171	30.8	32 811	823	21	70	14	124	6.6	18.1	15.9
54 061	...	Monongalia	935	75 509	597	80.8	71 770	1 836	125	1 598	180	637	5.4	11.1	26.6
54 063	...	Monroe	1 226	12 406	2 189	10.1	12 210	159	25	9	3	41	6.0	14.0	13.6
54 065	...	Morgan	593	12 128	2 205	20.5	11 985	92	25	18	8	50	5.6	13.3	12.3
54 067	...	Nicholas	1 680	26 775	1 398	15.9	26 670	4	32	51	18	57	6.5	15.8	13.9
54 069	9000	Ohio	275	50 871	830	185.0	48 791	1 684	31	330	35	146	5.8	12.3	14.3
54 071	...	Pendleton	1 808	8 054	2 559	4.5	7 869	167	1	13	4	27	6.6	13.7	12.3
54 073	...	Pleasants	339	7 546	2 614	22.3	7 513	17	8	2	6	9	5.7	14.9	13.9
54 075	...	Pocahontas	2 435	9 008	2 470	3.7	8 920	69	13	3	3	31	6.0	13.5	11.3
54 077	...	Preston	1 679	29 037	1 326	17.3	28 896	73	27	31	10	77	6.4	15.9	13.6
54 079	1480	Putnam	897	42 835	941	47.8	42 499	127	50	144	15	145	6.8	15.3	13.0
54 081	...	Raleigh	1 572	76 819	586	48.9	70 354	5 883	101	412	69	320	5.7	15.2	13.6
54 083	...	Randolph	2 693	27 803	1 359	10.3	27 444	223	37	74	25	144	6.0	13.6	14.7
54 085	...	Ritchie	1 175	10 233	2 366	8.7	10 211	7	4	10	1	7	5.6	14.7	12.9
54 087	...	Roane	1 253	15 120	1 982	12.1	15 056	4	25	30	5	37	5.7	16.3	12.8
54 089	...	Summers	935	14 204	2 036	15.2	13 344	728	38	34	60	211	5.2	14.0	11.8
54 091	...	Taylor	448	15 144	1 977	33.8	14 993	96	18	32	5	64	6.5	14.6	13.1
54 093	...	Tucker	1 085	7 728	2 603	7.1	7 703	4	6	13	2	16	5.6	13.7	13.7
54 095	...	Tyler	667	9 796	2 406	14.7	9 757	4	16	14	5	22	6.2	14.5	13.4
54 097	...	Upshur	919	22 867	1 538	24.9	22 631	121	42	56	17	112	6.1	14.8	17.4
54 099	3400	Wayne	1 310	41 636	966	31.8	41 489	19	73	48	7	114	5.8	15.0	14.6
54 101	...	Webster	1 440	10 729	2 315	7.5	10 704	3	8	8	6	29	6.4	15.5	14.3
54 103	...	Wetzel	930	19 258	1 714	20.7	19 184	16	12	39	7	37	6.2	14.6	14.0
54 105	...	Wirt	604	5 192	2 826	8.6	5 184	4	0	4	0	3	6.5	15.2	13.1
54 107	6020	Wood	951	86 915	526	91.4	85 569	793	131	335	87	254	6.3	13.7	13.3
54 109	...	Wyoming	1 297	28 990	1 330	22.4	28 673	234	40	26	17	88	5.8	16.9	15.0
55 000	...	WISCONSIN	140 672	4 891 769	X	34.8	4 512 523	244 539	39 387	53 583	41 737	93 194	7.4	14.9	14.5
55 001	...	Adams	1 678	15 682	1 945	9.3	15 001	375	125	56	125	308	5.5	12.1	9.9
55 003	...	Ashland	2 704	16 307	1 902	6.0	14 749	17	1 478	46	17	106	7.3	15.9	14.1
55 005	...	Barron	2 235	40 750	982	18.2	40 346	40	209	95	60	164	7.1	16.4	12.3
55 007	...	Bayfield	3 824	14 008	2 055	3.7	12 707	29	1 240	24	8	50	6.7	15.8	10.4
55 009	3080	Brown	1 369	194 594	248	142.1	186 621	1 012	3 869	2 522	570	1 525	7.8	15.1	15.2
55 011	...	Buffalo	1 773	13 584	2 093	7.7	13 521	5	22	29	7	42	7.2	15.6	11.6
55 013	...	Burnett	2 128	13 084	2 133	6.1	12 497	22	532	24	9	43	6.2	14.5	10.4
55 015	0460	Calumet	828	34 291	1 157	41.4	33 910	29	146	173	33	149	8.3	17.7	13.0
55 017	2290	Chippewa	2 617	52 360	808	20.0	51 854	31	150	276	49	174	7.4	16.5	12.7
55 019	...	Clark	3 149	31 647	1 225	10.0	31 437	29	91	38	52	116	7.7	17.9	12.2
55 021	...	Columbia	2 004	45 088	911	22.5	44 469	243	136	136	104	358	6.9	15.1	12.2
55 023	...	Crawford	1 483	15 940	1 927	10.7	15 791	50	26	56	17	67	7.3	16.6	12.5
55 025	4720	Dane	3 114	367 085	141	117.9	344 617	10 511	1 201	8 666	2 090	5 744	7.0	12.5	18.9
55 027	...	Dodge	2 285	76 559	590	33.5	74 700	1 142	215	197	305	911	7.1	15.5	12.6
55 029	...	Door	1 250	25 690	1 433	20.6	25 387	29	178	47	49	153	6.7	15.2	10.4
55 031	2240	Douglas	3 391	41 758	961	12.3	40 454	170	805	266	63	201	6.8	14.7	13.8
55 033	...	Dunn	2 207	35 909	1 102	16.3	34 929	172	95	633	80	188	6.5	14.2	24.3
55 035	2290	Eau Claire	1 652	85 183	538	51.6	82 202	238	467	2 124	152	437	7.1	13.9	21.1
55 037	...	Florence	1 264	4 590	2 867	3.6	4 562	4	14	4	6	11	6.6	15.7	11.2
55 039	...	Fond du Lac	1 873	90 083	509	48.1	88 760	257	297	448	321	937	7.1	15.8	14.1
55 041	...	Forest	2 627	8 776	2 489	3.3	7 842	127	780	14	13	30	7.6	14.3	14.2
55 043	...	Grant	2 973	49 264	852	16.6	48 838	76	76	234	40	160	6.9	15.7	18.3
55 045	...	Green	1 513	30 339	1 276	20.1	30 173	23	51	66	26	119	7.1	15.7	12.2
55 047	...	Green Lake	918	18 651	1 757	20.3	18 386	21	42	103	99	192	6.4	15.5	11.4
55 049	...	Iowa	1 976	20 150	1 666	10.2	20 093	7	21	19	10	48	7.8	16.4	12.5

1. MSA = Metropolitan Statistical Area. CMSA = Consolidated MSA. NECMA = New England county metropolitan area. PMSA = Primary MSA. See Appendix A for explanation of these concepts. See Appendix B for list of metropolitan areas identified by type, with component counties. 2. Dry land or land partially or temporarily covered by water. 3. Hispanic persons may be of any race.

STATE County	Population, 1990 (cont'd)							Population–Change and components of change							
	Age of population (cont'd) Percent							Change		Components of change, 1980–1986					
								1980–1990				Net change		Natural increase	
	25 to 34 years	35 to 44 years	45 to 54 years	55 to 64 years	65 to 74 years	75 years and over	Percent female	Number	Percent	Total persons, 1986	Total persons, 1980	Number	Percent	Births	Deaths
	14	15	16	17	18	19	20	21	22	23	24	25	26	27	28
WEST VIRGINIA—Con.															
Harrison	14.1	14.4	10.5	10.2	10.0	7.8	52.6	-8 339	-10.7	75 200	77 710	-2 500	-3.2	6 700	5 500
Jackson	14.5	14.1	12.4	11.1	7.5	6.0	51.1	144	0.6	26 300	25 794	500	1.9	2 300	1 300
Jefferson	15.9	15.8	10.7	8.3	7.1	4.3	50.8	5 624	18.6	33 800	30 302	3 500	11.4	2 900	1 700
Kanawha	15.3	15.7	10.9	10.6	9.3	6.4	52.8	-23 795	-10.3	224 100	231 414	-7 300	-3.1	19 000	14 200
Lewis	14.8	14.6	11.0	10.1	9.0	7.5	51.3	-1 590	-8.5	18 700	18 813	-100	-0.4	1 600	1 400
Lincoln	14.9	14.9	10.9	9.3	7.2	5.3	50.9	-2 293	-9.7	21 100	23 675	-2 600	-10.9	2 200	1 300
Logan	14.5	16.2	9.7	9.7	7.7	4.9	51.8	-7 647	-15.1	49 500	50 679	-1 100	-2.3	4 500	3 000
McDowell	14.1	14.6	9.5	9.6	8.9	5.8	52.9	-14 666	-29.4	45 300	49 899	-4 600	-9.2	4 700	3 000
Marion	13.1	14.5	10.5	10.1	10.2	8.0	53.4	-8 540	-13.0	64 100	65 789	-1 700	-2.6	5 100	4 400
Marshall	14.2	16.1	11.0	10.4	9.2	6.0	51.5	-4 252	-10.2	39 200	41 608	-2 400	-5.7	3 300	2 300
Mason	14.9	15.1	11.5	10.5	8.2	5.9	51.4	-1 867	-6.9	25 900	27 045	-1 100	-4.1	2 400	1 600
Mercer	13.6	15.1	10.4	10.1	9.7	6.9	53.1	-8 891	-12.0	70 900	73 871	-3 000	-4.1	6 100	4 800
Mineral	13.6	14.7	11.6	9.5	8.7	6.0	51.6	-537	-2.0	27 700	27 234	500	1.7	2 300	1 600
Mingo	16.0	15.1	9.6	8.3	6.5	3.9	51.2	-3 597	-9.6	36 800	37 336	-500	-1.4	4 200	2 200
Monongalia	16.0	13.9	8.7	7.3	6.3	4.6	50.4	485	0.6	77 700	75 024	2 700	3.6	5 900	3 400
Monroe	12.9	14.6	11.2	10.8	9.9	7.0	51.5	-467	-3.6	12 200	12 873	-700	-5.1	1 100	900
Morgan	14.1	14.6	11.4	11.8	10.2	6.6	51.4	1 417	13.2	10 100	10 711	-600	-5.3	800	700
Nicholas	14.3	15.5	10.5	9.6	8.1	5.8	51.0	-1 351	-4.8	28 400	28 126	300	1.0	2 500	1 500
Ohio	13.4	14.5	10.1	10.7	10.8	8.1	53.5	-10 518	-17.1	58 000	61 389	-3 400	-5.5	4 500	4 600
Pendleton	14.9	14.4	10.4	10.5	9.2	8.1	50.1	144	1.8	7 900	7 910	0	-0.1	700	500
Pleasants	15.8	14.9	11.1	9.4	8.1	6.5	51.4	-690	-8.4	8 100	8 236	-200	-2.3	700	500
Pocahontas	14.2	14.5	11.2	10.6	9.9	9.0	50.2	-911	-9.2	9 500	9 919	-500	-4.6	800	700
Preston	14.9	15.0	10.7	9.5	8.0	6.0	50.7	-1 423	-4.7	30 400	30 460	-100	-0.2	3 000	1 800
Putnam	16.4	17.0	11.8	8.8	6.6	4.4	51.0	4 654	12.2	42 300	38 181	4 100	10.7	3 300	1 700
Raleigh	13.6	16.3	10.3	10.0	9.0	6.3	52.9	-10 002	-11.5	84 200	86 821	-2 600	-3.0	7 000	5 400
Randolph	15.1	15.1	11.0	8.8	8.7	7.1	50.6	-931	-3.2	28 300	28 734	-400	-1.3	2 600	1 800
Ritchie	14.7	14.4	10.9	9.5	8.9	8.4	51.4	-1 209	-10.6	11 200	11 442	-300	-2.5	900	800
Roane	13.5	15.1	11.3	9.7	8.6	7.0	50.8	-832	-5.2	15 500	15 952	-400	-2.8	1 500	1 100
Summers	15.1	15.3	10.2	10.9	9.9	7.6	55.0	-1 671	-10.5	14 400	15 875	-1 500	-9.2	1 200	1 100
Taylor	14.9	14.8	10.3	9.7	8.8	7.3	51.6	-1 440	-8.7	16 300	16 584	-300	-1.5	1 400	1 100
Tucker	13.6	15.3	11.5	9.8	8.7	8.1	51.4	-947	-10.9	8 600	8 675	-100	-1.3	700	700
Tyler	13.9	14.5	11.7	10.3	8.5	6.9	50.9	-1 524	-13.5	11 000	11 320	-300	-2.6	900	700
Upshur	13.9	14.5	10.3	8.2	7.8	6.9	51.1	-560	-2.4	24 700	23 427	1 300	5.5	2 200	1 400
Wayne	14.2	15.0	11.8	10.0	8.3	5.5	51.7	-4 385	-9.5	44 600	46 021	-1 400	-3.1	3 700	2 400
Webster	14.2	14.8	9.9	9.5	8.7	6.7	51.5	-1 516	-12.4	11 900	12 245	-400	-3.2	1 100	800
Wetzel	13.5	14.5	11.9	10.4	8.0	6.8	52.0	-2 616	-12.0	21 700	21 874	-100	-0.6	2 000	1 400
Wirt	16.1	13.9	11.8	9.1	8.0	6.4	51.0	270	5.5	4 600	4 922	-300	-6.5	500	300
Wood	15.0	15.2	11.9	9.6	8.3	6.5	52.4	-6 708	-7.2	92 000	93 623	-1 600	-1.7	7 900	5 400
Wyoming	14.8	16.5	10.5	9.7	7.0	3.9	51.4	-7 003	-19.5	34 700	35 993	-1 300	-3.5	3 100	1 700
WISCONSIN	16.8	14.8	9.8	8.5	7.3	6.0	51.1	185 769	3.9	4 785 000	4 706 000	79 000	1.7	460 000	256 000
Adams	15.1	13.5	11.3	13.2	12.4	7.0	46.9	2 225	16.5	14 200	13 457	700	5.3	1 100	1 000
Ashland	14.7	13.1	8.8	8.3	9.1	8.8	51.1	-476	-2.8	16 700	16 783	0	-0.3	1 700	1 300
Barron	15.0	13.8	9.6	8.9	8.9	8.0	50.6	2 020	5.2	40 500	38 730	1 800	4.7	4 200	2 700
Bayfield	13.6	15.0	10.7	10.1	9.8	7.8	49.4	186	1.3	14 200	13 822	400	2.8	1 300	900
Brown	18.5	15.6	9.6	7.4	5.9	4.9	51.2	19 314	11.0	187 200	175 280	11 900	6.8	17 800	7 800
Buffalo	15.7	13.5	9.9	9.8	8.7	8.0	49.8	-725	-5.1	14 500	14 309	200	1.4	1 400	900
Burnett	12.6	13.5	10.5	11.9	11.9	8.4	50.5	744	6.0	13 500	12 340	1 200	9.5	1 100	900
Calumet	17.9	14.9	9.4	7.9	6.3	4.7	50.2	3 424	11.1	35 400	30 867	4 500	14.5	3 300	1 300
Chippewa	16.0	14.8	9.6	8.7	7.6	6.7	50.7	233	0.4	53 600	52 127	1 500	2.9	5 500	2 900
Clark	14.0	12.8	9.3	8.9	8.8	8.4	49.9	-1 263	-3.8	33 000	32 910	0	0.1	3 400	2 200
Columbia	15.4	15.0	10.3	9.3	8.5	7.1	50.3	1 866	4.3	45 400	43 222	2 100	5.0	4 100	2 700
Crawford	13.8	13.7	9.8	9.5	9.3	7.6	50.5	-616	-3.7	16 700	16 556	200	1.0	1 700	1 100
Dane	19.9	16.6	9.2	6.6	5.2	4.1	50.9	43 540	13.5	344 900	323 545	21 300	6.6	29 700	12 600
Dodge	17.0	14.6	9.9	8.5	8.0	6.8	48.8	1 495	2.0	75 300	75 064	300	0.3	7 100	4 400
Door	15.2	15.1	10.1	9.4	9.3	8.4	50.9	661	2.6	26 500	25 029	1 500	5.9	2 500	1 600
Douglas	15.1	15.0	9.7	8.7	8.6	7.7	51.4	-2 663	-6.0	41 600	44 421	-2 800	-6.3	4 000	2 900
Dunn	14.2	13.3	8.2	7.2	6.1	5.9	50.2	1 595	4.6	35 000	34 314	700	2.1	3 200	1 700
Eau Claire	15.0	14.4	8.8	7.3	6.9	5.5	52.1	6 378	8.1	83 100	78 805	4 300	5.5	7 500	3 800
Florence	14.8	14.0	11.3	9.6	9.3	7.5	49.4	418	10.0	4 100	4 172	0	-1.1	400	300
Fond du Lac	15.6	14.8	9.8	8.7	7.5	6.5	51.5	1 119	1.3	90 400	88 964	1 400	1.6	8 700	4 900
Forest	13.0	12.0	9.5	10.5	10.4	8.5	49.6	-268	-3.0	9 200	9 044	100	1.6	1 000	700
Grant	14.2	12.7	9.0	8.5	7.8	6.9	49.5	-2 472	-4.8	51 300	51 736	-500	-0.9	5 000	2 900
Green	15.9	15.3	10.0	8.5	8.2	7.1	51.0	327	1.1	30 500	30 012	500	1.6	3 000	1 900
Green Lake	14.1	13.8	9.6	10.0	10.0	9.1	51.4	281	1.5	18 900	18 370	600	3.0	1 800	1 300
Iowa	16.4	15.1	8.9	8.7	8.0	6.2	50.3	348	1.8	20 600	19 802	800	4.0	2 100	1 200

STATE County	Population–(cont'd) Components of change, 1980-1986 (cont'd) Net migration	Households, 1990 Number	Households, 1990 Percent change, 1980–1990	Households, 1990 Persons per household	Households, 1990 Percent Female family householder[1]	Households, 1990 Percent One-person	Births, 1988 Total	Births, 1988 Rate[2]	Births, 1988 Low birth weight[3] (Number)	Deaths, 1987 Number Total	Deaths, 1987 Number Infant[4]	Deaths, 1987 Rate Total[2]	Deaths, 1987 Rate Infant[5]	Marriages, 1984 Number	Marriages, 1984 Rate[2]
	29	30	31	32	33	34	35	36	37	38	39	40	41	42	43
WEST VIRGINIA—Con.															
Harrison	-3 700	27 009	-5.0	2.53	11.0	25.8	827	11.1	52	884	12	11.7	13.2	573	7.5
Jackson	-500	9 645	10.7	2.66	9.2	19.4	318	12.5	21	260	3	10.2	9.6	215	8.1
Jefferson	2 200	12 914	29.4	2.68	9.5	21.5	532	15.0	37	290	7	8.4	13.1	219	6.8
Kanawha	-12 000	84 713	-2.0	2.42	11.8	27.4	2 558	11.7	174	2 364	22	10.6	8.0	2 220	9.6
Lewis	-200	6 615	-0.9	2.54	11.1	25.6	207	11.8	15	203	1	11.3	4.8	190	10.0
Lincoln	-3 500	7 647	0.0	2.79	10.6	18.9	276	11.9	19	231	3	9.9	10.1	193	9.0
Logan	-2 700	15 425	-5.9	2.77	13.2	20.0	531	11.2	37	449	5	9.2	9.7	420	8.3
McDowell	-6 300	12 880	-19.7	2.72	14.3	22.8	523	12.9	49	473	3	11.1	5.2	237	5.0
Marion	-2 500	22 667	-7.1	2.47	10.8	26.7	656	10.5	34	728	8	11.5	11.5	460	7.0
Marshall	-3 300	14 051	-2.0	2.59	10.1	23.3	470	12.1	34	409	3	10.4	7.1	339	8.4
Mason	-1 800	9 603	2.2	2.59	9.6	22.6	314	12.0	21	271	2	10.3	6.5	197	7.5
Mercer	-4 300	25 390	-4.2	2.50	11.7	25.3	756	10.7	41	740	7	10.3	9.0	413	5.7
Mineral	-300	9 981	5.8	2.62	9.2	22.4	327	12.0	22	317	3	11.7	8.9	132	4.8
Mingo	-2 500	11 830	-0.4	2.84	13.4	20.0	467	13.1	22	331	6	9.1	12.2	221	6.0
Monongalia	200	29 087	7.3	2.40	8.4	28.7	862	11.2	40	615	9	7.9	9.8	601	7.6
Monroe	-900	4 749	7.0	2.58	8.2	23.2	152	12.1	12	140	3	11.1	19.4	75	6.1
Morgan	-600	4 731	24.0	2.52	7.5	22.2	142	11.7	4	133	4	11.2	32.3	67	6.6
Nicholas	-600	9 970	5.3	2.67	10.3	21.1	326	11.9	23	272	3	9.9	8.3	276	9.7
Ohio	-3 300	20 646	-10.0	2.35	11.6	31.9	676	11.9	40	756	10	13.1	15.2	540	8.9
Pendleton	-200	3 061	8.7	2.58	8.1	21.7	114	14.2	7	90	1	11.2	8.8	66	8.5
Pleasants	-400	2 769	2.3	2.62	9.7	22.9	91	11.8	1	68	1	8.7	13.0	57	7.0
Pocahontas	-500	3 628	1.9	2.44	8.1	26.6	105	11.4	7	125	0	13.6	0.0	73	7.4
Preston	-1 200	10 619	3.6	2.70	8.9	21.2	384	12.8	32	304	6	10.0	16.8	135	4.4
Putnam	2 500	15 695	21.0	2.71	8.5	17.6	515	12.3	24	302	3	7.3	5.5	308	7.5
Raleigh	-4 200	29 483	-2.2	2.57	11.9	24.3	852	10.6	66	841	3	10.2	3.5	695	8.0
Randolph	-1 200	10 366	7.0	2.55	9.9	25.0	343	12.1	26	325	5	11.3	13.3	266	9.3
Ritchie	-400	3 928	-4.8	2.57	9.6	23.1	110	10.1	7	126	0	11.4	0.0	122	10.9
Roane	-800	5 740	4.2	2.62	9.1	22.9	190	12.4	13	168	0	11.0	0.0	105	6.7
Summers	-1 600	5 240	-1.8	2.52	11.0	25.7	130	8.5	7	197	2	12.7	14.0	92	6.3
Taylor	-600	5 741	-1.7	2.58	10.6	23.9	204	13.0	12	165	1	10.3	5.4	108	6.5
Tucker	-100	3 017	-2.7	2.51	8.3	25.5	72	8.9	1	92	1	11.2	13.5	71	8.2
Tyler	-500	3 709	-5.5	2.62	8.2	21.5	103	9.8	2	129	1	12.2	9.1	92	8.2
Upshur	500	8 245	3.1	2.61	9.2	24.0	279	12.1	15	255	6	10.8	20.7	229	9.1
Wayne	-2 800	15 626	-0.1	2.66	10.5	21.2	498	11.4	39	420	5	9.5	9.9	288	6.3
Webster	-700	3 996	-4.6	2.67	12.1	21.2	126	11.2	5	116	3	10.3	19.5	92	7.7
Wetzel	-700	7 303	-4.0	2.61	9.8	23.4	256	12.4	16	227	3	10.8	12.3	196	8.8
Wirt	-500	1 942	16.9	2.67	8.4	21.9	73	14.3	6	49	2	9.4	30.3	52	11.3
Wood	-4 000	34 168	1.0	2.52	10.2	24.2	1 126	12.4	80	886	15	9.7	13.2	993	10.6
Wyoming	-2 700	10 474	-8.7	2.76	11.0	19.2	340	10.4	17	259	5	7.7	14.6	267	7.5
WISCONSIN	-125 000	1 822 118	10.3	2.61	9.6	24.3	70 817	14.6	3 856	42 172	612	8.8	8.6	41 102	8.6
Adams	600	5 972	23.4	2.44	6.4	23.1	173	12.1	4	175	0	12.2	0.0	128	9.3
Ashland	-400	6 255	2.5	2.50	9.7	30.6	256	15.1	12	213	5	12.5	22.7	182	10.6
Barron	200	15 435	12.1	2.60	7.9	24.2	570	13.7	16	462	10	11.2	17.6	386	9.5
Bayfield	0	5 515	7.9	2.52	7.5	25.6	174	12.2	4	156	2	11.0	11.4	109	7.6
Brown	1 900	72 280	20.7	2.62	9.0	24.1	2 848	14.9	125	1 218	25	6.5	8.6	1 730	9.4
Buffalo	-300	5 123	2.8	2.61	6.6	23.9	169	11.7	9	137	1	9.5	4.6	72	4.9
Burnett	900	5 242	15.0	2.45	7.6	25.5	143	10.5	7	144	0	10.7	0.0	109	8.1
Calumet	2 500	11 772	21.4	2.89	6.7	17.8	537	15.9	24	231	5	6.9	9.2	202	6.0
Chippewa	-1 100	19 077	11.0	2.68	7.7	23.0	715	13.2	30	485	3	9.0	4.2	430	8.0
Clark	-1 200	11 209	1.7	2.77	6.2	23.8	518	15.6	22	313	2	9.4	4.1	257	7.6
Columbia	800	16 868	8.6	2.60	7.1	23.6	581	12.2	30	427	2	9.1	3.3	424	9.5
Crawford	-500	5 914	3.4	2.64	7.5	24.9	241	14.3	12	164	1	9.8	4.0	135	8.0
Dane	4 200	142 786	18.4	2.46	8.0	26.4	5 071	14.4	283	2 147	33	6.2	6.4	3 033	9.0
Dodge	-2 500	26 853	8.1	2.71	6.5	21.7	1 021	13.3	54	710	9	9.3	8.5	592	7.9
Door	600	10 066	9.3	2.52	6.6	25.1	317	11.8	15	258	5	9.6	13.3	299	11.5
Douglas	-4 000	16 374	-0.6	2.46	11.1	27.8	537	12.8	32	437	4	10.5	7.2	342	8.0
Dunn	-900	12 250	10.9	2.69	6.3	22.9	435	12.3	16	253	6	7.2	15.0	229	6.5
Eau Claire	600	31 282	14.5	2.58	8.6	24.9	1 238	14.7	58	619	10	7.4	8.5	762	9.2
Florence	-100	1 755	17.5	2.57	7.6	22.9	69	16.8	4	57	1	13.9	22.2	32	8.0
Fond du Lac	-2 400	32 644	9.3	2.67	7.8	23.3	1 248	13.8	55	786	6	8.8	4.8	765	8.5
Forest	-100	3 290	8.8	2.56	9.0	24.6	136	14.9	5	113	1	12.4	6.5	104	11.2
Grant	-2 500	17 169	2.9	2.69	6.8	23.5	624	12.2	31	486	6	9.5	8.5	449	8.6
Green	-600	11 541	7.3	2.59	7.2	24.2	403	13.0	19	281	6	9.1	14.9	283	9.2
Green Lake	0	7 189	6.8	2.56	6.7	24.9	237	12.5	20	218	2	11.5	8.7	178	9.4
Iowa	-100	7 406	9.4	2.69	7.5	23.2	306	14.9	13	202	1	9.9	3.2	188	9.1

1. No spouse present. 2. Per 1,000 resident population estimated as of July 1 of the year shown. 3. Under 2,500 grams. 4. Deaths of infants under 1 year old. 5. Deaths of infants under 1 year old per 1,000 live births.

STATE County	Divorces, 1984		Physicians, active non–Federal, 1989		Hospitals, 1989			Nursing homes,[4] 1986		Serious crimes known to police, 1988			Education			
						Beds				Number			Public school enrollment[7]		Attainment,[8] 1980	
	Number	Rate[1]	Number[2]	Rate[3]	Number	Number	Rate[3]	Number	Beds	Total[5]	Violent[6]	Rate[3]	1986–1987	1980	Percent 12 yrs. or more	Percent 16 yrs. or more
	44	45	46	47	48	49	50	51	52	53	54	55	56	57	58	59
WEST VIRGINIA–Con.																
Harrison	320	4.2	131	178	2	466	633	13	568	1 399	69	1 884	13 291	14 783	60.7	10.9
Jackson	130	4.9	17	67	1	79	313	3	209	253	11	992	5 152	5 531	57.9	8.7
Jefferson	171	5.3	28	77	1	56	154	4	225	955	57	2 797	6 225	6 303	56.7	16.3
Kanawha	1 280	5.5	571	264	6	1 569	726	9	935	9 107	542	4 172	37 399	41 382	65.0	15.3
Lewis	107	5.6	12	70	2	377	2 205	2	72	192	5	1 063	3 380	3 597	50.8	7.5
Lincoln	138	6.4	4	17	0	0	0	2	9	238	41	1 012	5 111	5 682	40.9	4.8
Logan	252	5.0	57	122	3	187	400	1	120	773	67	1 586	10 981	11 153	45.1	5.6
McDowell	235	5.0	25	65	1	124	320	0	0	349	51	812	9 912	12 252	35.9	5.2
Marion	264	4.0	60	98	1	230	375	9	413	1 462	78	2 327	10 303	12 112	61.8	11.1
Marshall	205	5.1	29	75	1	150	389	3	174	768	17	1 979	6 865	8 338	60.7	7.4
Mason	125	4.8	26	100	1	228	874	3	108	403	7	1 555	5 144	5 513	52.7	7.0
Mercer	400	5.5	136	194	4	595	849	5	380	1 364	127	1 916	13 131	14 711	53.2	10.1
Mineral	123	4.4	13	48	1	51	189	3	183	374	35	1 385	5 119	5 894	60.0	7.1
Mingo	251	6.8	34	96	1	76	215	1	120	372	60	1 032	8 771	8 805	39.4	6.4
Monongalia	336	4.3	507	658	3	632	821	5	462	2 289	48	3 022	10 353	11 241	66.2	23.9
Monroe	67	5.4	7	55	0	0	0	1	198	88	6	698	2 256	2 782	52.4	7.9
Morgan	56	5.5	9	70	1	42	326	3	140	192	3	1 667	2 114	2 245	54.0	9.6
Nicholas	140	4.9	23	86	2	142	528	2	164	450	29	1 625	5 640	6 492	47.9	6.0
Ohio	239	4.0	256	457	2	740	1 321	7	598	1 478	147	2 608	6 893	8 778	65.4	13.2
Pendleton	35	4.5	4	50	0	0	0	1	101	32	1	408	1 416	1 532	47.1	8.0
Pleasants	28	3.5	7	92	0	0	0	0	0	45	3	589	1 566	1 756	57.6	7.7
Pocahontas	43	4.3	2	22	1	40	444	2	235	52	3	569	1 627	1 997	46.8	9.5
Preston	113	3.7	23	77	1	58	193	3	120	315	10	1 040	6 240	6 712	50.4	6.9
Putnam	207	5.1	24	57	1	60	143	2	123	536	15	1 307	8 179	8 413	62.6	10.6
Raleigh	437	5.0	171	218	4	802	1 023	5	421	1 887	66	2 285	16 889	18 303	53.6	9.1
Randolph	148	5.2	45	160	1	115	408	3	286	369	11	1 309	5 208	5 741	52.8	10.2
Ritchie	48	4.3	1	9	0	0	0	2	84	108	10	971	2 065	2 361	50.5	5.7
Roane	83	5.3	14	92	2	220	1 447	3	110	121	9	792	3 259	3 132	47.8	6.7
Summers	64	4.4	10	65	1	80	516	1	120	88	4	568	2 467	2 793	48.1	6.4
Taylor	91	5.5	5	32	1	127	819	2	91	232	16	1 470	3 146	3 570	56.1	7.5
Tucker	36	4.1	6	76	0	0	0	1	94	55	2	676	1 527	1 922	53.5	7.8
Tyler	45	4.0	3	29	1	21	204	2	32	102	13	951	2 131	2 731	57.7	7.2
Upshur	132	5.3	26	116	1	95	422	4	35	271	10	1 152	4 772	4 635	57.1	11.6
Wayne	208	4.6	5	11	0	0	0	2	34	934	58	2 119	9 375	10 211	50.6	6.9
Webster	53	4.4	4	36	1	35	315	0	0	47	4	412	2 515	2 821	35.0	5.6
Wetzel	72	3.2	14	69	1	58	287	2	170	214	7	1 027	4 253	5 138	59.2	9.2
Wirt	29	6.3	0	0	0	0	0	0	0	62	2	1 201	1 115	1 210	51.7	6.9
Wood	502	5.4	127	141	3	575	638	13	691	2 692	83	2 951	16 379	19 483	65.1	11.4
Wyoming	161	4.5	11	35	0	0	0	0	0	408	21	1 223	8 015	8 469	42.1	5.1
WISCONSIN	16 625	3.5	8 995	184	156	25 044	512	522	53 965	X	10 365	3 929	767 819	857 301	69.6	14.8
Adams	47	3.4	7	49	1	58	403	3	149	588	14	4 185	1 733	2 621	57.3	7.4
Ashland	56	3.3	36	211	1	161	942	3	297	584	13	3 419	3 089	3 202	65.7	12.2
Barron	160	4.0	46	110	3	207	493	13	685	545	28	1 315	7 949	7 768	62.6	10.4
Bayfield	52	3.6	11	77	0	0	0	1	86	278	6	1 951	2 290	2 930	68.1	13.6
Brown	621	3.4	284	147	4	1 037	536	19	1 693	7 298	395	3 832	30 261	32 812	73.9	14.5
Buffalo	25	1.7	7	48	0	0	0	3	229	163	18	1 364	2 468	2 895	60.8	8.9
Burnett	55	4.1	3	22	1	84	613	3	173	398	9	2 939	2 084	2 431	61.0	7.8
Calumet	93	2.8	11	33	1	53	158	3	261	805	20	2 170	4 160	6 119	66.5	10.6
Chippewa	171	3.2	47	86	3	369	676	10	892	921	25	1 821	9 039	10 349	63.5	9.3
Clark	90	2.7	18	54	2	491	1 483	5	602	615	27	1 872	6 320	6 741	56.2	7.4
Columbia	160	3.6	39	81	2	224	463	5	561	1 157	35	2 664	9 478	8 462	69.2	11.1
Crawford	56	3.3	10	59	1	45	266	2	239	393	14	2 357	2 669	3 362	62.3	10.0
Dane	1 255	3.7	1 581	442	7	2 686	752	26	2 356	17 902	806	5 098	48 920	55 433	83.7	30.9
Dodge	213	2.8	52	67	2	316	408	9	1 056	1 417	21	1 862	7 657	12 959	61.8	9.2
Door	71	2.7	29	107	1	78	287	3	239	644	4	2 386	4 297	4 368	67.8	13.1
Douglas	170	4.0	25	60	1	55	131	7	696	1 725	17	4 103	7 298	8 385	69.2	11.8
Dunn	92	2.6	23	65	1	63	177	4	424	1 131	12	3 206	5 169	5 972	67.6	16.3
Eau Claire	314	3.8	202	238	2	529	625	14	910	4 000	93	4 734	12 694	13 377	75.0	17.9
Florence	15	3.8	1	24	0	0	0	2	82	101	19	2 498	932	916	62.4	8.3
Fond du Lac	305	3.4	109	120	4	474	523	9	1 063	3 091	71	3 402	14 953	15 933	68.1	11.3
Forest	31	3.3	5	55	0	0	0	2	165	336	10	3 653	1 898	2 209	57.1	8.0
Grant	126	2.4	34	67	3	286	561	9	773	825	23	1 585	8 988	10 013	67.5	13.8
Green	86	2.8	75	240	1	173	554	5	402	690	25	2 224	5 434	6 191	66.9	10.9
Green Lake	59	3.1	15	79	1	163	858	4	259	382	20	2 010	3 469	3 196	62.5	10.4
Iowa	54	2.6	12	58	1	83	403	3	233	288	7	1 397	3 444	4 511	70.5	11.4

1. Per 1,000 resident population estimated as of July 1 of the year shown. 2. As of end of year. 3. Per 100,000 resident population as of July 1 of the year shown. 4. Preliminary. Covers nursing homes with 3 or more beds. 5. Data for serious crimes have not been adjusted for underreporting, this may affect comparability between geographic areas or over time. 6. Includes murder and nonnegligent manslaughter, forcible rape, robbery, and aggravated assault. 7. The 1986–1987 data are based on administrative reports obtained by the U.S. National Center for Education Statistics. The 1980 data are based on the 1980 Census of Population and Housing. 8. Persons 25 years old or older.

STATE County	Education (cont'd): Local government expenditures for education,[1] 1982: Total (Mil dol)	Education (cont'd): Local government expenditures for education,[1] 1982: Per capita (Dollars)	Social Security Program December 1988: Beneficiaries: Total	Social Security Program December 1988: Beneficiaries: Rate[2]	Social Security Program December 1988: Payments ($1,000)	Supplemental Security Income Program recipients June 1986	Money income: Per capita[3]: 1987 Income, (Dollars)	Money income: Per capita[3]: 1979: Current dollars	Money income: Per capita[3]: 1979: Constant 1987 dollars	Money income: Median household income 1979 (Dollars)	Money income: Percent below poverty level, 1979: Persons	Money income: Percent below poverty level, 1979: Families	Housing units, 1990: Total	Housing units, 1990: Percent change, 1980–1990
	60	61	62	63	64	65	66	67	68	69	70	71	72	73
WEST VIRGINIA—Con.														
Harrison	33.3	426	16 255	219.1	7 751	1 474	9 185	6 193	9 690	13 794	14.3	11.5	29 988	-0.7
Jackson	13.8	522	4 585	179.8	2 055	638	8 267	6 347	9 931	17 223	13.3	11.6	10 571	13.1
Jefferson	12.1	390	5 075	143.0	2 270	486	10 350	6 139	9 606	15 803	13.4	9.6	14 606	26.5
Kanawha	101.4	439	44 035	201.1	22 049	4 228	11 044	7 541	11 799	17 291	10.6	8.2	92 747	2.1
Lewis	9.0	477	4 040	229.5	1 738	646	7 975	5 316	8 318	12 383	17.3	13.7	7 454	3.7
Lincoln	12.3	509	4 115	178.1	1 656	1 108	6 509	4 484	7 016	11 788	24.5	20.6	8 429	3.7
Logan	23.0	451	9 910	208.2	4 444	1 158	7 931	5 643	8 830	14 533	16.6	14.4	16 848	-1.9
McDowell	24.7	508	10 435	257.7	4 337	1 796	6 166	4 779	7 478	12 091	23.5	19.3	15 330	-11.1
Marion	25.7	391	13 870	223.0	6 852	950	8 902	6 239	9 762	14 418	13.8	9.8	25 491	-2.8
Marshall	19.4	471	6 575	169.0	3 266	478	8 957	6 526	10 211	17 331	10.1	7.8	15 630	0.8
Mason	12.8	473	4 520	173.2	2 064	672	8 102	5 977	9 352	15 082	13.3	10.1	10 932	6.8
Mercer	46.0	610	14 720	209.1	6 581	1 800	9 105	6 225	9 740	13 841	15.1	11.7	28 426	-0.1
Mineral	13.0	471	4 515	166.0	2 059	434	8 824	5 697	8 914	14 662	13.3	11.8	10 930	6.7
Mingo	23.3	614	7 005	196.2	2 915	1 212	7 215	5 058	7 914	12 541	23.6	20.5	13 087	4.3
Monongalia	25.9	333	9 870	127.7	4 794	738	9 943	6 459	10 106	13 371	16.3	8.1	31 563	8.5
Monroe	5.8	448	3 350	265.9	1 352	482	7 494	4 767	7 459	11 388	20.9	17.3	5 994	15.9
Morgan	5.0	446	2 195	181.4	974	192	9 558	6 242	9 767	13 632	16.7	13.0	6 757	38.3
Nicholas	13.5	474	5 525	202.4	2 422	654	7 672	5 405	8 457	13 565	16.7	13.1	11 235	7.8
Ohio	20.4	333	12 460	219.4	6 337	884	10 346	7 074	11 069	15 083	11.6	8.9	23 229	-4.8
Pendleton	3.7	474	1 615	201.9	615	326	7 540	4 618	7 226	10 956	20.3	17.0	4 516	22.2
Pleasants	6.3	773	1 520	197.4	726	204	8 731	5 871	9 186	16 182	13.8	11.4	3 134	3.4
Pocahontas	4.9	513	2 120	230.4	865	344	7 617	5 434	8 503	12 355	13.6	11.3	5 579	1.9
Preston	15.0	485	5 435	180.6	2 270	662	8 100	5 397	8 445	12 979	18.7	15.3	12 137	5.6
Putnam	19.5	501	5 625	134.6	2 683	636	9 638	6 578	10 293	18 186	10.0	8.4	16 884	22.8
Raleigh	36.7	421	17 785	221.8	8 198	1 688	8 904	6 224	9 739	15 164	13.0	10.4	33 278	3.7
Randolph	13.0	447	5 525	195.2	2 381	980	8 028	5 598	8 759	12 801	17.5	13.1	12 548	13.4
Ritchie	5.2	441	2 280	209.2	984	324	7 721	5 019	7 853	11 381	17.8	13.7	4 936	1.9
Roane	6.7	419	3 155	206.2	1 310	506	7 147	4 892	7 655	11 623	18.5	15.0	6 611	9.4
Summers	6.5	408	2 530	165.4	998	714	6 908	4 813	7 531	10 738	23.3	19.7	6 769	3.1
Taylor	7.9	476	2 650	168.8	1 110	368	7 369	5 224	8 174	12 678	15.4	11.9	6 528	0.2
Tucker	3.8	437	1 545	190.7	657	266	7 791	5 102	7 983	11 522	17.0	13.7	3 900	2.0
Tyler	5.4	474	1 675	159.5	765	194	8 709	5 867	9 180	15 107	14.7	11.8	4 441	-3.4
Upshur	10.6	436	4 200	181.8	1 802	560	7 421	5 316	8 318	13 074	17.0	12.9	9 506	5.4
Wayne	22.7	490	6 425	146.7	2 692	1 458	8 177	5 615	8 786	13 951	18.6	15.6	16 991	1.0
Webster	6.3	527	2 395	211.9	929	528	6 227	4 087	6 395	9 801	27.9	22.1	5 072	6.1
Wetzel	9.5	435	4 195	203.6	2 012	488	9 034	6 273	9 815	16 149	13.2	10.7	8 129	-1.3
Wirt	2.9	576	995	195.1	425	148	7 361	4 749	7 431	12 222	17.7	15.6	2 795	38.2
Wood	40.4	432	16 590	182.5	8 193	1 484	10 434	6 806	10 649	16 583	11.1	8.3	37 620	4.0
Wyoming	18.0	501	5 995	183.9	2 641	846	7 413	5 467	8 554	15 870	19.3	16.3	11 756	-3.2
WISCONSIN	2 259.7	476	820 997	169.1	412 607	75 603	11 417	7 241	11 330	17 680	8.7	6.3	2 055 774	10.3
Adams	4.4	315	2 645	185.0	1 257	412	9 362	5 647	8 836	12 990	12.9	10.0	12 418	23.1
Ashland	8.2	472	3 870	227.6	1 782	466	8 125	5 173	8 094	11 666	12.6	10.0	8 371	7.6
Barron	19.8	508	8 960	215.4	4 022	994	9 065	5 670	8 872	13 421	11.9	8.6	19 363	12.9
Bayfield	7.7	542	2 845	199.0	1 312	284	7 922	5 214	8 158	11 768	13.9	11.2	10 918	13.2
Brown	85.3	475	26 355	137.8	13 334	2 290	11 723	7 171	11 220	18 595	7.5	5.2	74 740	20.0
Buffalo	6.8	467	2 945	203.1	1 268	282	9 542	5 780	9 044	13 422	13.5	10.6	5 586	2.0
Burnett	5.5	416	3 160	232.4	1 438	328	7 922	5 021	7 856	11 129	15.6	12.5	11 743	13.4
Calumet	11.0	347	3 945	117.1	1 945	222	11 032	7 124	11 147	20 452	4.3	3.6	12 465	19.5
Chippewa	22.9	431	9 750	179.6	4 480	1 130	9 633	5 868	9 182	15 203	10.2	8.2	21 024	9.5
Clark	17.8	537	6 785	205.0	2 926	708	8 077	5 266	8 240	12 805	16.2	12.4	12 904	4.2
Columbia	30.2	698	9 710	204.4	4 737	622	10 325	6 617	10 354	16 385	7.8	6.2	19 258	8.2
Crawford	7.1	425	3 290	195.8	1 444	436	8 620	5 610	8 778	12 300	14.2	11.5	7 315	8.1
Dane	155.4	469	42 055	119.2	22 534	4 044	13 106	8 074	12 633	18 309	9.7	4.7	147 851	17.1
Dodge	20.0	264	11 325	147.1	5 645	674	10 539	6 903	10 801	18 126	6.1	4.7	28 720	6.4
Door	11.1	431	5 690	211.5	2 835	296	10 548	6 942	10 862	15 802	6.9	5.3	18 037	17.7
Douglas	20.3	455	8 025	191.1	3 829	992	9 256	6 340	9 920	15 066	10.0	7.9	20 610	2.3
Dunn	14.4	411	5 330	150.6	2 402	620	9 132	5 629	8 808	13 871	15.8	8.8	13 252	11.5
Eau Claire	34.5	424	13 700	162.9	6 832	1 486	10 089	6 410	10 030	15 300	12.9	7.3	32 741	13.0
Florence	2.2	530	855	208.5	381	84	8 452	5 281	8 263	11 903	13.8	11.3	3 775	13.0
Fond du Lac	38.3	429	15 630	172.9	7 800	1 080	10 626	6 802	10 643	18 159	6.7	4.8	34 548	8.9
Forest	5.2	577	2 180	239.6	1 000	302	6 756	4 427	6 927	11 214	17.0	13.1	7 203	6.7
Grant	25.8	497	9 845	192.7	4 341	888	8 995	5 918	9 260	15 122	12.3	8.9	18 450	1.4
Green	14.6	486	5 445	175.1	2 656	380	11 063	7 307	11 433	16 766	9.1	6.6	12 087	6.8
Green Lake	8.7	458	4 495	236.6	2 141	250	10 057	6 479	10 138	15 057	8.5	6.6	9 202	10.6
Iowa	9.8	484	3 135	152.2	1 381	286	9 320	5 974	9 348	14 350	11.8	9.1	8 220	8.6

1. Elementary and secondary. 2. Per 1,000 resident population estimated as of July 1 of the year shown. 3. Based on the resident population estimated as of July 1, 1988 for 1987 data and enumerated as of April 1, 1980 for 1979 data.

Table A. States and Counties — **Housing, Labor Force, and Employment**

STATE County	Housing units, 1990 (cont'd): Occupied units: Total	Owner occupied: Percent	Owner occupied: Median value (Dollars)	Median rent (Dollars)	Civilian labor force, 1990: Total	Percent change, 1989–1990	Unemployment: Total	Unemployment: Rate[1]	Private nonfarm establishments, 1988: Number	Net change, 1987–1988	Employment[2]: Total	Percent change, 1987–1988	Manufacturing	Retail trade
	74	75	76	77	78	79	80	81	82	83	84	85	86	87
WEST VIRGINIA—Con.														
Harrison	27 009	74.0	45 000	205	29 998	-3.0	2 636	8.8	1 858	2	20 763	-2.7	1 741	5 846
Jackson	9 645	78.4	51 400	226	9 558	-2.3	1 042	10.9	401	-1	5 596	7.1	0	1 138
Jefferson	12 914	71.9	84 100	294	20 435	2.5	1 113	5.4	644	36	6 956	9.6	2 263	1 700
Kanawha	84 713	68.5	56 400	259	102 182	1.4	6 112	6.0	5 445	11	78 861	-1.2	9 652	19 367
Lewis	6 615	69.8	42 200	174	7 537	1.7	807	10.7	354	15	3 010	2.7	756	834
Lincoln	7 647	77.1	38 200	172	8 044	2.1	1 022	12.7	212	-4	1 314	-2.4	121	424
Logan	15 425	73.2	42 100	196	14 334	0.0	1 584	11.1	855	-7	8 666	-8.9	550	2 289
McDowell	12 880	78.7	15 800	139	7 194	-2.8	1 132	15.7	448	-34	3 663	-15.9	41	1 265
Marion	22 667	75.5	42 300	201	23 212	1.2	1 994	8.6	1 222	-37	15 066	9.6	2 558	4 088
Marshall	14 051	77.9	42 700	182	15 264	-0.9	1 204	7.9	509	20	6 631	7.7	617	2 214
Mason	9 603	78.5	44 800	177	10 155	11.0	971	9.6	368	4	4 588	-0.5	1 035	864
Mercer	25 390	76.3	44 600	212	27 647	-0.6	2 209	8.0	1 418	13	16 277	6.4	1 794	5 061
Mineral	9 981	77.5	49 300	196	11 061	0.2	611	5.5	429	0	4 359	3.5	875	1 068
Mingo	11 830	72.8	39 400	193	11 598	4.4	1 074	9.3	675	12	6 288	-5.7	278	1 254
Monongalia	29 087	62.1	64 600	297	39 811	1.2	1 472	3.7	1 706	51	23 720	15.8	2 994	5 606
Monroe	4 749	84.3	42 500	151	5 401	0.9	382	7.1	166	16	892	12.2	0	226
Morgan	4 731	83.0	61 900	217	5 216	4.2	346	6.6	219	5	1 929	7.5	247	299
Nicholas	9 970	81.2	42 300	186	9 547	-4.6	1 314	13.8	623	37	5 788	8.7	988	1 407
Ohio	20 646	66.7	48 800	209	25 134	-1.5	1 312	5.2	1 590	18	22 344	5.2	3 094	4 533
Pendleton	3 061	79.3	51 600	190	4 175	-1.2	217	5.2	154	5	1 588	7.4	0	169
Pleasants	2 769	79.6	51 100	178	2 512	-1.5	328	13.1	131	12	1 850	22.8	0	305
Pocahontas	3 628	79.4	42 000	177	5 069	1.9	623	12.3	225	19	2 761	22.3	745	402
Preston	10 619	81.3	44 200	176	12 997	2.4	1 053	8.1	521	-9	4 717	2.5	640	1 027
Putnam	15 695	83.3	62 700	265	17 505	1.4	1 390	7.9	650	25	6 759	3.5	434	2 103
Raleigh	29 483	75.5	44 100	218	29 007	-2.1	2 636	9.1	1 693	-1	18 508	-3.5	816	5 391
Randolph	10 366	74.5	46 000	202	12 202	3.2	1 736	14.2	655	23	6 574	9.4	963	1 598
Ritchie	3 928	80.0	32 400	147	5 596	1.1	696	12.4	182	8	2 236	9.8	1 366	336
Roane	5 740	78.0	36 600	173	5 359	-10.2	862	16.1	337	-10	2 006	-7.4	474	638
Summers	5 240	76.7	34 800	166	4 425	-2.0	487	11.0	192	-6	1 161	-1.1	15	563
Taylor	5 741	76.2	34 200	159	5 987	-3.6	624	10.4	206	-9	1 420	-15.7	415	416
Tucker	3 017	80.4	38 200	168	3 917	-1.3	445	11.4	175	-2	2 367	2.1	587	308
Tyler	3 709	82.0	43 200	171	5 123	5.2	447	8.7	144	-2	1 498	6.2	0	249
Upshur	8 245	75.5	47 900	200	9 049	5.0	1 028	11.4	458	1	5 340	6.1	1 089	1 274
Wayne	15 626	76.6	46 700	213	16 588	1.6	1 390	8.4	518	28	4 828	4.0	1 502	1 085
Webster	3 996	78.4	29 700	144	3 342	-1.7	642	19.2	170	14	1 387	1.7	236	289
Wetzel	7 303	77.3	50 200	183	10 055	4.1	913	9.1	389	9	5 243	4.6	0	1 400
Wirt	1 942	81.3	36 300	149	2 732	1.8	422	15.4	54	5	290	-2.4	0	73
Wood	34 168	73.8	49 500	249	43 058	0.2	3 170	7.4	2 055	-4	34 071	8.3	11 703	7 575
Wyoming	10 474	80.5	34 300	164	7 613	-3.0	979	12.9	385	-22	4 053	-20.1	153	867
WISCONSIN	1 822 118	66.7	62 500	331	2 587 000	-0.9	113 000	4.4	X	X	1 796 474	4.0	530 128	386 310
Adams	5 972	81.4	46 500	235	5 390	5.5	313	5.8	180	3	1 540	7.2	374	358
Ashland	6 255	70.6	37 300	217	7 706	2.1	501	6.5	524	12	5 562	1.3	1 441	1 186
Barron	15 435	73.5	47 000	246	20 855	1.1	1 297	6.2	1 096	4	12 360	5.6	4 909	2 899
Bayfield	5 515	78.8	44 700	206	6 503	2.7	426	6.6	344	17	1 672	7.8	351	634
Brown	72 280	65.6	62 600	324	111 384	0.2	4 362	3.9	4 840	36	86 827	-0.4	23 042	18 956
Buffalo	5 123	75.2	43 000	202	7 294	7.8	382	5.2	296	12	2 907	8.6	291	499
Burnett	5 242	80.7	44 600	205	5 527	-1.2	320	5.8	313	4	2 510	0.9	934	577
Calumet	11 772	78.6	62 100	284	19 808	0.0	1 622	8.2	601	-16	10 552	11.6	5 690	1 620
Chippewa	19 077	74.2	46 500	248	26 130	-4.4	1 448	5.5	1 147	19	13 985	4.4	5 611	3 250
Clark	11 209	78.7	36 900	194	14 127	-2.3	940	6.7	763	22	6 933	1.5	1 843	1 229
Columbia	16 868	72.9	55 700	279	24 480	-1.4	1 302	5.3	1 247	30	13 245	11.6	4 136	3 344
Crawford	5 914	74.2	42 900	217	8 550	4.0	458	5.4	360	0	3 929	2.8	1 085	1 104
Dane	142 786	55.2	78 400	423	226 833	-0.3	5 766	2.5	9 651	135	147 040	4.6	22 339	36 945
Dodge	26 853	73.1	54 800	290	38 788	1.9	1 876	4.8	1 604	36	21 576	9.2	9 355	4 028
Door	10 066	77.5	66 500	269	13 977	0.5	881	6.3	1 064	28	8 001	-9.4	2 495	2 091
Douglas	16 374	69.6	38 700	237	18 994	-0.4	936	4.9	987	0	9 405	1.2	1 245	3 228
Dunn	12 250	67.2	49 000	270	17 943	3.1	773	4.3	718	13	6 293	8.9	1 103	2 034
Eau Claire	31 282	64.5	53 500	284	45 472	-4.0	2 070	4.6	2 199	54	30 912	4.1	5 020	9 504
Florence	1 755	82.8	45 400	223	1 813	5.2	67	3.7	70	1	470	5.9	172	131
Fond du Lac	32 644	71.8	56 000	298	47 428	1.5	2 320	4.9	2 053	25	32 468	1.4	11 430	6 770
Forest	3 290	76.9	38 400	183	3 664	3.9	229	6.3	252	1	1 285	2.8	368	303
Grant	17 169	69.5	43 600	227	25 350	0.5	1 561	6.2	1 164	-16	11 638	6.7	3 222	2 928
Green	11 541	69.3	53 600	273	16 376	-4.8	872	5.3	816	7	11 414	16.0	3 498	3 471
Green Lake	7 189	75.1	48 400	231	7 959	-7.6	568	7.1	533	3	5 628	2.0	2 219	1 157
Iowa	7 406	72.5	45 900	235	13 602	-6.2	593	4.4	456	4	4 831	1.2	749	2 137

1. Percent of total civilian labor force. 2. For week including March 12. Excludes government employees, self-employed persons, farm workers, domestic service workers, railroad employees subject to the Railroad Retirement Act, and employees on oceanborne vessels or in foreign countries.

STATE County	Private nonfarm establishments, 1988 (cont'd): Employment[1] (cont'd): Finance, insurance, and real estate	Employment[1] (cont'd): Services	Annual payroll: Total (Mil dol)	Annual payroll: Average per employee (Dollars)	Personal income, 1989: Total (Mil dol)	Percent change, 1988–1989	Wages and salaries[2] (Mil dol)	Proprietor's income (Mil dol)	Dividends, interest, & rent (Mil dol)	Transfer payments (Mil dol)	Per capita[3]: Dollars	Per capita[3]: Rank	Earnings, 1989: Total (Mil dol)	Percent by selected industries: Farm	Goods-related[4]: Total
	88	89	90	91	92	93	94	95	96	97	98	99	100	101	102
WEST VIRGINIA—Con.															
Harrison	1 199	5 547	382	18 412	970	5.6	548	83	187	233	13 182	1 821	631	0.2	21.3
Jackson	247	772	121	21 579	289	5.0	181	22	41	64	11 490	2 502	203	0.6	60.3
Jefferson	301	1 692	116	16 676	482	8.3	201	25	74	84	13 255	1 792	226	1.1	38.8
Kanawha	6 463	23 697	1 599	20 272	3 327	5.8	2 370	226	575	697	15 397	839	2 597	0.0	23.6
Lewis	129	558	46	15 300	192	4.3	96	15	40	53	11 221	2 596	112	0.5	24.3
Lincoln	83	213	17	13 312	192	5.0	44	11	20	60	8 100	3 071	54	1.2	22.9
Logan	338	2 449	185	21 381	524	4.2	312	30	53	160	11 210	2 598	342	0.1	43.4
McDowell	211	575	72	19 698	336	4.8	150	21	46	147	8 670	3 033	171	0.0	NA
Marion	687	3 772	274	18 168	752	4.5	401	47	142	199	12 265	2 208	448	0.1	35.9
Marshall	175	1 713	134	20 237	464	6.8	336	21	72	103	12 039	2 317	357	0.0	NA
Mason	110	985	93	20 378	282	7.2	155	14	41	67	10 797	2 717	169	0.7	33.3
Mercer	1 149	5 020	261	16 012	912	4.9	446	60	147	248	13 005	1 905	506	0.1	13.2
Mineral	164	1 557	73	16 707	321	3.1	141	21	42	76	11 887	2 363	162	1.2	45.9
Mingo	280	1 000	154	24 431	406	5.3	266	24	45	114	11 502	2 496	290	0.0	54.2
Monongalia	1 038	8 334	437	18 440	1 060	8.1	790	84	158	202	13 762	1 550	873	0.1	30.1
Monroe	44	194	11	12 456	134	6.6	35	11	18	39	10 480	2 795	46	4.5	22.4
Morgan	90	603	29	15 162	151	6.3	42	9	23	36	11 782	2 412	51	1.4	NA
Nicholas	204	922	112	19 339	297	0.7	180	27	41	78	11 038	2 657	207	0.4	51.6
Ohio	1 599	9 385	389	17 426	861	6.6	498	62	227	180	15 372	847	560	0.1	17.8
Pendleton	0	311	19	12 233	81	5.9	34	6	16	20	10 065	2 874	40	1.6	NA
Pleasants	59	241	46	24 775	92	3.5	74	5	14	23	12 103	2 287	79	0.3	NA
Pocahontas	0	1 222	32	11 535	109	5.1	54	12	16	30	12 177	2 247	65	5.8	29.0
Preston	250	888	81	17 199	284	3.5	134	28	45	78	9 455	2 963	162	0.9	36.7
Putnam	176	1 745	125	18 426	545	7.3	238	26	62	87	13 006	1 904	265	0.2	25.4
Raleigh	965	5 406	359	19 380	956	4.3	538	75	131	271	12 187	2 243	613	0.1	28.2
Randolph	305	2 102	89	13 610	323	7.2	161	28	51	89	11 464	2 517	189	0.4	27.3
Ritchie	78	191	25	11 193	111	5.5	42	7	18	30	10 271	2 842	49	1.4	41.6
Roane	118	382	28	13 912	147	3.0	58	13	24	43	9 668	2 932	71	1.3	33.9
Summers	88	271	12	10 444	121	4.5	39	8	20	49	7 791	3 083	46	2.8	3.3
Taylor	0	244	21	14 887	148	3.7	62	10	22	45	9 564	2 949	72	2.3	34.5
Tucker	112	774	26	11 090	89	4.6	44	7	13	24	11 164	2 617	51	0.6	41.7
Tyler	71	206	35	23 035	118	7.6	61	6	20	24	11 432	2 529	67	0.8	66.8
Upshur	0	1 669	78	14 525	228	6.2	130	22	40	59	10 105	2 866	152	0.5	44.8
Wayne	200	827	75	15 562	446	4.3	151	22	57	91	10 262	2 844	173	0.1	26.7
Webster	0	167	22	15 761	97	9.1	42	7	9	34	8 771	3 029	49	0.2	40.3
Wetzel	196	534	129	24 664	248	4.1	71	15	39	59	12 239	2 214	86	1.3	14.5
Wirt	0	60	3	9 672	45	2.9	14	2	5	13	8 534	3 037	16	1.4	44.4
Wood	1 419	8 496	676	19 842	1 281	4.2	902	85	201	247	14 211	1 337	987	0.1	40.3
Wyoming	113	586	107	26 481	281	1.8	160	14	31	92	8 853	3 020	174	0.6	53.3
WISCONSIN	113 604	472 477	34 834	X	80 457	7.6	50 404	7 071	13 653	12 095	16 454	X	57 475	3.4	34.9
Adams	63	396	25	16 097	172	15.2	55	41	25	38	11 945	2 345	96	29.4	15.7
Ashland	254	2 016	86	15 539	215	7.8	134	27	32	55	12 579	2 078	161	2.4	31.3
Barron	477	2 495	176	14 266	566	7.4	289	98	96	110	13 470	1 703	387	10.6	35.9
Bayfield	76	365	20	11 775	169	9.8	50	26	32	39	11 797	2 403	76	8.8	16.6
Brown	4 861	22 499	1 771	20 400	3 216	7.3	2 367	252	500	385	16 609	501	2 618	1.7	36.2
Buffalo	100	792	53	18 141	209	14.4	64	54	41	35	14 432	1 241	118	32.4	9.3
Burnett	115	567	37	14 646	157	3.2	55	21	31	40	11 435	2 527	76	6.4	31.7
Calumet	310	1 415	188	17 807	539	7.6	238	58	92	51	16 077	625	296	10.6	57.0
Chippewa	382	2 872	253	18 081	770	8.7	398	105	124	144	14 099	1 390	503	8.9	44.7
Clark	658	1 992	93	13 349	410	9.4	144	92	82	84	12 391	2 164	236	23.1	22.7
Columbia	597	2 884	208	15 724	715	8.3	302	86	131	120	14 766	1 100	388	8.9	33.9
Crawford	154	1 116	54	13 663	198	11.1	86	36	40	42	11 698	2 443	121	15.8	31.2
Dane	18 520	42 668	2 759	18 766	6 797	8.3	4 866	512	1 134	771	19 023	218	5 378	1.2	19.5
Dodge	726	4 338	408	18 929	1 097	6.4	539	115	206	147	14 147	1 372	654	7.1	48.0
Door	328	1 987	127	15 813	417	8.2	203	62	108	71	15 361	853	265	7.0	36.1
Douglas	420	2 503	145	15 379	576	8.1	320	37	81	142	13 732	1 561	357	0.6	18.5
Dunn	341	1 768	84	13 291	455	9.7	201	81	71	83	12 775	2 006	282	15.8	19.2
Eau Claire	1 379	9 561	513	16 602	1 223	6.6	803	105	202	216	14 438	1 240	908	1.7	19.6
Florence	0	103	5	11 421	50	8.9	14	4	9	12	12 251	2 210	19	7.9	NA
Fond du Lac	1 316	8 035	612	18 850	1 478	11.3	914	150	239	209	16 314	566	1 064	4.7	46.3
Forest	57	306	15	11 584	89	6.6	31	10	17	29	9 738	2 920	40	4.1	20.5
Grant	529	2 983	143	12 316	717	7.8	264	143	137	122	14 046	1 416	406	18.6	18.9
Green	373	2 329	185	16 173	531	11.5	243	101	115	66	16 996	438	344	15.3	23.4
Green Lake	172	1 128	84	14 917	279	10.0	128	42	68	52	14 695	1 133	170	11.2	42.0
Iowa	173	910	76	15 672	288	13.6	126	57	53	39	13 988	1 439	183	20.4	11.2

1. For week including March 12. Excludes government employees, self-employed persons, farm workers, domestic service workers, railroad employees subject to the Railroad Retirement Act, and employees on oceanborne vessels or in foreign countries. 2. Includes other labor income. 3. Based on the resident population estimated as of July 1 of the year shown. 4. Covers mining, construction, and manufacturing.

STATE County	Earnings, 1989 (cont'd): Percent by selected industries (cont'd): Goods-related[1]: Manufacturing	Service-related & other[2]: Total	Service-related & other[2]: Retail trade	Service-related & other[2]: Finance, insurance, & real estate	Service-related & other[2]: Services	Government	Agriculture, 1987: Farms: Number	Farms: Percent with: Less than 50 acres	Farms: Percent with: 500 acres and over	Farm operators, percent: Whose principal occupation is farming	Farm operators, percent: Residing on farm operated	Land in farms: Acreage (1,000)	Land in farms: Percent change, 1982–1987	Land in farms: Acres: Average size of farm	Land in farms: Acres: Total irrigated (1,000)	Land in farms: Acres: Total cropland (1,000)
	103	104	105	106	107	108	109	110	111	112	113	114	115	116	117	118
WEST VIRGINIA—Con.																
Harrison	8.1	62.6	11.2	4.5	23.9	16.0	554	24.9	4.5	37.7	77.6	89	-13.8	161	0	42
Jackson	48.9	27.9	8.6	1.9	12.3	11.2	679	19.9	3.8	38.4	73.6	104	-3.4	153	0	40
Jefferson	29.1	39.7	10.0	3.0	20.9	20.4	363	30.0	12.9	56.2	77.7	83	-5.2	229	0	63
Kanawha	15.7	60.4	9.5	6.2	27.2	15.9	177	28.2	2.3	39.0	71.8	21	-7.4	121	0	7
Lewis	13.6	49.7	11.6	1.8	18.0	25.5	335	14.6	13.4	44.5	72.8	75	-11.4	225	D	34
Lincoln	4.0	NA	11.5	2.8	16.5	32.6	304	30.3	1.0	36.5	57.2	32	-11.4	104	0	9
Logan	4.3	44.5	9.9	2.3	20.7	12.1	27	37.0	3.7	33.3	59.3	D	D	D	0	1
McDowell	0.6	NA	10.2	2.3	13.1	21.8	12	50.0	0.0	25.0	75.0	1	-12.8	76	0	D
Marion	16.8	46.9	10.7	3.9	17.9	17.0	362	23.8	1.1	29.8	81.2	42	-11.2	115	0	19
Marshall	34.9	NA	6.8	1.2	NA	10.9	425	12.5	1.6	41.4	84.5	71	-1.8	167	0	27
Mason	21.7	51.0	6.9	2.2	16.3	15.0	709	22.1	6.3	41.0	72.8	124	-8.5	174	0	55
Mercer	8.2	67.4	12.7	4.6	29.1	19.3	358	23.2	4.2	36.9	77.4	49	-3.1	138	D	18
Mineral	36.3	NA	7.9	1.7	14.3	16.5	315	15.2	11.4	39.4	79.0	76	0.9	242	0	25
Mingo	2.0	34.3	6.5	2.2	11.2	11.4	4	25.0	0.0	75.0	25.0	D	D	D	0	D
Monongalia	7.4	36.2	7.5	2.3	19.9	33.7	390	21.5	3.3	32.1	83.6	53	13.3	136	0	25
Monroe	14.7	32.1	6.3	2.3	14.0	41.0	610	18.0	11.3	46.2	71.8	144	-6.5	236	0	50
Morgan	8.1	NA	9.9	3.8	19.1	20.9	124	9.7	5.6	48.4	87.9	22	-16.4	176	D	9
Nicholas	9.1	33.8	10.4	2.3	12.0	14.1	291	28.2	1.4	35.4	78.7	34	-15.5	116	D	14
Ohio	12.5	69.2	12.5	5.3	36.8	12.9	142	9.2	3.5	42.3	88.7	22	0.5	157	D	12
Pendleton	29.6	NA	8.7	2.5	13.6	27.1	561	13.7	20.3	55.3	80.0	184	-5.4	329	0	53
Pleasants	32.3	NA	5.2	1.6	6.6	22.3	89	15.7	7.9	32.6	76.4	16	-2.4	177	D	6
Pocahontas	23.8	43.6	8.1	3.1	25.5	21.6	379	14.2	16.1	45.9	78.9	119	-8.6	313	D	29
Preston	9.0	44.3	9.0	3.4	12.4	18.1	714	16.4	6.4	44.8	79.1	135	1.1	189	0	56
Putnam	13.7	61.9	14.4	2.1	13.5	12.5	470	25.5	1.7	37.7	74.7	56	-10.9	118	0	19
Raleigh	3.0	55.6	11.7	4.0	26.6	16.1	260	36.5	2.3	37.7	73.5	29	2.3	112	D	12
Randolph	10.7	53.3	11.1	3.8	24.7	19.0	383	17.2	14.6	42.6	73.4	112	-2.9	292	0	36
Ritchie	33.1	NA	9.8	3.4	12.3	17.2	325	9.5	10.2	39.4	76.6	77	-5.7	235	D	30
Roane	20.1	45.0	11.9	3.3	20.1	19.8	460	9.1	5.2	37.8	78.3	90	-10.9	195	0	35
Summers	0.7	59.5	13.7	3.9	20.6	34.3	317	16.1	6.3	38.2	77.0	60	0.0	190	0	17
Taylor	30.0	41.9	8.8	3.1	12.8	21.3	245	31.8	6.9	40.0	77.6	42	-2.4	171	D	21
Tucker	24.2	NA	7.7	3.4	20.5	17.5	160	14.4	5.6	45.6	76.9	32	-12.5	201	0	11
Tyler	55.8	NA	4.3	1.6	7.6	13.9	260	13.8	5.8	47.3	83.8	49	-7.6	188	0	19
Upshur	21.1	41.5	9.7	2.5	22.4	13.2	354	20.1	5.9	39.8	77.7	60	1.7	170	0	26
Wayne	18.5	41.8	11.0	2.4	13.9	31.4	193	22.3	3.1	34.7	78.2	27	-4.4	138	0	10
Webster	9.2	NA	9.6	2.0	11.3	20.9	105	26.7	0.0	29.5	69.5	12	-5.8	112	D	3
Wetzel	6.2	61.3	19.3	3.5	19.7	22.9	203	11.3	4.4	30.0	77.8	36	-21.1	178	D	11
Wirt	38.2	25.9	6.5	2.5	12.8	28.3	221	13.6	5.9	39.8	84.2	37	0.5	166	0	15
Wood	33.1	45.1	10.3	3.5	21.4	14.4	520	24.4	2.5	28.7	78.8	71	7.5	136	0	31
Wyoming	1.0	NA	7.6	2.1	8.7	15.8	53	45.3	3.8	34.0	66.0	6	-27.7	107	D	2
WISCONSIN	29.3	47.9	9.2	5.4	21.1	13.7	75 131	17.0	8.0	71.0	84.8	16 607	-3.6	221	285	11 619
Adams	11.8	NA	NA	1.4	14.1	22.9	382	12.8	16.2	61.0	79.3	119	-0.3	311	28	82
Ashland	25.9	52.0	10.2	2.8	31.0	14.2	250	5.6	8.8	60.0	88.0	62	-10.2	249	D	29
Barron	31.2	40.4	9.8	2.7	17.4	13.2	1 659	12.5	5.8	78.4	88.2	375	-2.9	226	10	250
Bayfield	9.6	NA	11.7	2.0	25.0	23.8	396	8.3	14.6	60.6	90.2	105	-4.9	265	0	58
Brown	30.1	51.4	10.4	3.2	21.1	10.7	1 263	22.3	5.4	70.5	84.1	223	-2.6	176	0	193
Buffalo	6.1	45.5	5.4	1.8	12.7	12.7	1 036	9.2	20.6	79.4	84.8	352	-3.5	340	3	190
Burnett	24.4	46.0	14.3	3.2	19.9	15.9	427	10.8	8.0	63.9	88.1	97	-7.4	227	0	56
Calumet	51.3	25.0	6.3	2.0	10.1	7.4	941	20.0	5.1	74.9	85.5	169	-0.9	179	0	145
Chippewa	39.3	32.7	8.5	1.9	14.5	13.7	1 647	8.9	8.7	80.5	88.7	408	-3.2	248	2	269
Clark	18.2	38.8	8.1	2.2	14.3	15.4	2 195	12.4	4.8	81.8	89.5	445	-5.1	203	0	308
Columbia	26.5	43.1	11.5	3.0	17.7	14.0	1 513	20.0	10.4	67.1	83.5	335	-5.6	221	3	263
Crawford	26.0	40.5	10.9	2.1	18.7	12.5	1 033	10.8	11.0	75.3	85.0	264	-4.9	256	0	130
Dane	13.7	51.6	9.2	8.7	22.8	27.6	2 849	27.2	7.9	65.1	81.5	570	-5.3	200	3	475
Dodge	39.2	32.4	7.5	2.1	15.4	12.5	2 151	17.9	6.0	76.1	85.1	437	1.2	203	1	367
Door	27.3	45.0	14.7	1.9	22.4	12.0	911	20.5	3.7	64.2	83.8	148	-4.8	162	1	112
Douglas	11.7	57.2	12.1	2.1	16.4	23.8	312	13.5	11.5	38.1	89.7	75	-12.5	239	0	42
Dunn	14.7	36.4	7.7	2.2	16.4	28.6	1 515	12.5	10.8	76.8	88.1	401	-2.8	264	16	271
Eau Claire	14.5	60.1	15.8	3.3	25.9	18.6	1 001	12.9	5.7	68.1	87.0	216	0.8	216	1	148
Florence	19.6	NA	11.2	NA	15.3	30.4	83	7.2	12.0	57.8	90.4	21	-11.1	257	D	10
Fond du Lac	40.1	38.8	8.5	2.7	15.6	10.2	1 738	16.9	6.2	74.6	84.2	359	-2.4	207	1	308
Forest	15.6	NA	10.0	NA	17.2	28.9	135	14.1	8.9	55.6	74.8	30	0.5	220	0	15
Grant	13.8	39.8	9.3	2.7	18.1	22.7	2 470	12.7	11.1	78.1	82.3	648	-1.0	262	1	420
Green	19.3	51.9	15.1	2.6	21.0	9.4	1 418	10.4	6.9	82.4	86.7	329	-2.8	232	4	272
Green Lake	30.6	36.9	9.4	2.1	15.8	9.9	711	16.0	7.6	72.4	81.2	162	-1.4	228	1	129
Iowa	6.1	NA	NA	2.3	NA	10.8	1 351	11.2	12.7	78.8	81.8	392	-3.5	290	6	251

1. Covers mining, construction, and manufacturing. 2. Covers private sector earnings in agricultural services, forestry, and fisheries; transportation and public utilities; wholesale trade; retail trade; finance, insurance, and real estate; and services.

STATE County	Agriculture, 1987 (cont'd): Value of land and buildings: Average per farm ($1,000)	Agriculture, 1987 (cont'd): Value of land and buildings: Average per acre (Dollars)	Agriculture, 1987 (cont'd): Value of products sold: Total (Mil dol)	Agriculture, 1987 (cont'd): Value of products sold: Average per farm (Dollars)	Agriculture, 1987 (cont'd): Value of products sold: Percent from: Crops	Agriculture, 1987 (cont'd): Value of products sold: Percent from: Livestock and poultry[1]	Agriculture, 1987 (cont'd): Percent of farms with sales of: $10,000 or more	Agriculture, 1987 (cont'd): Percent of farms with sales of: $100,000 or more	Manufactures, 1987: Establishments: Total	Manufactures, 1987: Establishments: Percent with 20 or more employees	Manufactures, 1987: All employees: Number (1,000)	Manufactures, 1987: All employees: Percent change, 1982–1987	Manufactures, 1987: All employees: Annual payroll (Mil dol)	Manufactures, 1987: Production workers: Number (1,000)	Manufactures, 1987: Production workers: Work hours (Mil)
	119	120	121	122	123	124	125	126	127	128	129	130	131	132	133
WEST VIRGINIA—Con.															
Harrison	105	665	4	6 508	8.3	91.7	13.4	0.7	68	19.1	2.8	-12.5	58.8	2.2	4.1
Jackson	82	555	3	4 938	26.8	73.2	9.9	0.3	11	36.4	D	D	D	D	D
Jefferson	413	1 684	19	51 835	38.1	61.9	42.7	14.9	30	36.7	2.1	40.0	50.4	1.7	3.1
Kanawha	109	879	1	7 677	67.0	33.0	9.0	0.6	144	29.2	9.8	-25.2	310.4	4.6	9.5
Lewis	101	496	3	8 511	3.4	96.6	23.3	0.6	20	25.0	D	D	D	D	D
Lincoln	62	779	1	3 747	82.6	17.4	8.2	0.0	10	10.0	D	D	D	D	D
Logan	183	1 053	0	17 092	11.3	88.7	22.2	3.7	33	18.2	0.5	-37.5	9.8	0.3	0.6
McDowell	D	D	D	D	NA	NA	16.7	8.3	4	0.0	0.0	-100.0	0.5	0.0	0.1
Marion	78	651	2	5 101	29.3	70.7	5.2	0.8	58	27.6	2.5	-19.4	59.3	1.9	3.5
Marshall	82	577	3	7 958	19.1	80.9	14.4	0.5	17	41.2	0.6	-80.6	16.6	0.5	0.9
Mason	136	749	13	18 980	22.4	77.6	21.0	4.9	18	44.4	1.0	-23.1	25.5	0.8	1.6
Mercer	98	714	2	5 199	13.3	86.7	12.6	0.3	54	37.0	1.6	-20.0	33.5	1.1	2.1
Mineral	140	655	4	11 246	12.8	87.2	15.6	2.2	22	50.0	1.7	30.8	42.1	0.8	1.3
Mingo	D	D	D	D	NA	NA	0.0	0.0	20	15.0	0.2	0.0	3.9	0.2	0.4
Monongalia	130	914	2	5 558	17.8	82.2	11.0	0.3	63	25.4	2.6	4.0	49.8	2.0	3.8
Monroe	147	578	12	20 290	8.5	91.5	32.8	4.3	7	14.3	D	D	D	D	D
Morgan	220	1 271	1	10 182	56.5	43.5	16.1	2.4	13	23.1	0.3	50.0	4.7	0.2	0.4
Nicholas	85	768	2	6 542	7.7	92.3	10.0	0.7	35	28.6	1.0	-9.1	14.3	0.7	1.3
Ohio	135	966	2	13 046	16.0	84.0	21.1	2.8	68	39.7	2.7	-18.2	57.7	1.6	3.0
Pendleton	178	545	35	62 157	0.7	99.3	33.2	10.7	9	33.3	D	D	D	D	D
Pleasants	111	627	1	6 027	22.2	77.8	16.9	0.0	6	33.3	D	D	D	D	D
Pocahontas	184	606	5	12 957	7.9	92.1	28.2	1.6	21	23.8	0.7	40.0	9.7	0.6	1.2
Preston	116	614	10	14 399	8.3	91.6	23.5	3.8	29	20.7	0.6	-33.3	11.4	0.5	1.0
Putnam	86	741	2	5 235	64.0	36.0	9.6	0.2	21	28.6	0.9	-30.8	30.5	0.6	1.2
Raleigh	81	716	2	6 849	33.0	66.9	11.5	1.2	44	27.3	0.9	-43.8	19.3	0.5	1.1
Randolph	149	535	5	13 913	9.4	90.6	22.2	1.6	38	31.6	0.9	-10.0	11.7	0.8	1.5
Ritchie	112	456	2	7 291	7.4	92.5	13.8	0.6	25	40.0	0.9	12.5	11.1	0.7	1.4
Roane	88	448	2	4 450	8.9	91.1	12.4	0.0	18	33.3	0.8	-11.1	11.9	0.7	1.1
Summers	103	568	3	7 983	21.7	78.3	14.8	0.9	8	0.0	0.0	0.0	0.1	0.0	0.0
Taylor	96	586	3	12 777	32.0	68.0	17.6	3.3	15	46.7	0.5	0.0	8.0	0.4	0.7
Tucker	128	706	1	6 673	11.0	88.9	17.5	0.0	17	29.4	0.6	20.0	8.1	0.5	0.9
Tyler	73	421	2	6 042	11.5	88.4	12.3	0.0	13	30.8	D	D	D	D	D
Upshur	98	567	2	6 720	28.6	71.4	15.3	0.6	33	30.3	0.9	12.5	19.5	0.7	1.4
Wayne	128	870	1	4 593	22.2	77.8	7.8	0.5	39	25.6	1.2	-14.3	23.4	1.0	1.8
Webster	84	849	0	1 821	24.6	75.4	3.8	0.0	19	15.8	0.2	100.0	2.3	0.2	0.3
Wetzel	67	385	1	2 776	13.8	86.2	5.9	0.0	26	19.2	D	D	D	D	D
Wirt	85	486	3	13 393	D	D	18.1	1.4	4	25.0	D	D	D	D	D
Wood	101	797	3	6 170	15.9	84.1	8.8	0.8	89	44.9	9.3	0.0	289.0	5.9	12.3
Wyoming	99	928	0	2 340	19.4	80.6	1.9	0.0	18	16.7	D	D	D	D	D
WISCONSIN	183	826	4 910	65 351	19.1	80.9	68.9	20.4	9 157	37.8	514.0	3.5	12 763.4	349.9	693.6
Adams	252	835	27	70 545	72.7	27.3	52.4	15.4	14	28.6	0.4	33.3	9.3	0.3	0.6
Ashland	96	455	6	23 795	7.4	92.6	41.6	7.2	50	22.0	1.5	15.4	28.6	1.2	2.5
Barron	145	621	139	83 906	10.5	89.5	73.2	20.4	89	29.2	4.9	25.6	76.4	3.7	7.3
Bayfield	106	389	11	26 872	15.1	84.9	45.7	7.6	31	9.7	0.3	50.0	4.2	0.2	0.4
Brown	201	1 124	95	74 998	12.0	88.0	71.4	22.3	315	43.5	23.5	10.8	618.1	15.7	31.2
Buffalo	183	531	76	73 488	11.1	88.9	77.5	24.8	15	33.3	0.3	0.0	5.1	0.2	0.5
Burnett	133	671	13	30 113	14.1	85.9	49.4	9.4	33	30.3	0.9	12.5	15.5	0.7	1.5
Calumet	174	959	72	76 014	9.1	90.9	77.0	26.7	59	45.8	5.1	27.5	112.9	4.2	7.9
Chippewa	155	624	109	66 071	8.2	91.8	78.0	20.6	99	33.3	5.4	22.7	122.5	3.6	6.8
Clark	132	666	134	61 208	6.0	94.0	76.6	20.1	91	30.8	1.7	13.3	28.8	1.3	2.6
Columbia	213	914	97	64 162	28.0	72.0	67.2	21.6	87	47.1	3.9	25.8	74.8	3.0	5.9
Crawford	142	560	46	44 739	13.9	86.1	68.4	10.3	21	28.6	D	D	D	D	D
Dane	232	1 166	216	75 976	24.4	75.6	67.8	25.1	517	33.1	22.1	18.8	525.7	13.1	25.7
Dodge	202	1 036	181	84 216	15.3	84.7	77.7	28.2	137	46.7	8.6	6.2	210.3	6.5	13.3
Door	157	985	37	41 129	27.7	72.3	53.3	11.9	42	40.5	3.4	9.7	67.3	2.7	5.2
Douglas	106	413	8	25 638	20.7	79.3	31.4	6.1	54	22.2	1.2	-7.7	27.6	0.9	1.7
Dunn	171	642	104	68 639	15.2	84.8	72.2	22.6	40	22.5	1.0	0.0	23.6	0.7	1.4
Eau Claire	140	654	51	50 470	14.8	85.2	62.7	14.3	93	35.5	4.9	19.5	121.2	3.7	7.5
Florence	118	437	2	30 011	20.6	79.4	43.4	12.0	14	21.4	0.1	0.0	1.7	0.1	0.2
Fond du Lac	197	973	137	78 623	17.1	82.9	78.1	30.3	129	47.3	11.7	19.4	287.1	8.1	15.9
Forest	118	527	4	30 165	11.3	88.8	44.4	5.9	51	3.9	0.3	-40.0	4.5	0.3	0.5
Grant	200	760	193	78 089	8.5	91.5	80.9	28.9	65	30.8	2.9	11.5	43.9	2.5	4.6
Green	214	883	122	86 096	10.4	89.6	84.0	31.5	69	37.7	2.9	31.8	55.8	2.3	4.5
Green Lake	218	916	47	66 313	24.4	75.6	73.1	24.6	50	44.0	2.1	-8.7	33.4	1.6	3.2
Iowa	218	765	113	83 884	11.3	88.7	79.4	26.4	33	21.2	0.8	33.3	10.8	0.6	1.1

1. Includes livestock and poultry products.

STATE County	Manufactures, 1987 (cont'd): Production workers (cont'd): Wages: Total (Mil dol)	Manufactures, 1987 (cont'd): Production workers (cont'd): Wages: Average per worker (Dollars)	Manufactures, 1987 (cont'd): Value added by manu- facture (Mil dol)	Manufactures, 1987 (cont'd): Value of shipments (Mil dol)	Manufactures, 1987 (cont'd): New capital expend- itures (Mil dol)	Value of construction authorized by building permits, 1990: Total[1] ($1,000)	Value of construction authorized by building permits, 1990: Nonresidential: Total ($1,000)	Value of construction authorized by building permits, 1990: Nonresidential: Percent: Office	Value of construction authorized by building permits, 1990: Nonresidential: Percent: Industrial	Value of construction authorized by building permits, 1990: Nonresidential: Percent: Stores	Value of construction authorized by building permits, 1990: Residential: New construction ($1,000)	Value of construction authorized by building permits, 1990: Residential: Number of housing units	Value of construction authorized by building permits, 1990: Residential: Alterations and additions ($1,000)
	134	135	136	137	138	139	140	141	142	143	144	145	146
WEST VIRGINIA—Con.													
Harrison	43.9	19 955	160.5	255.8	10.1	12 920	6 337	7.5	0.0	51.8	2 529	43	571
Jackson	D	D	D	D	D	5 255	1 836	10.5	0.0	55.9	1 163	31	916
Jefferson	35.0	20 588	198.3	345.8	7.1	48 384	8 007	11.8	4.1	24.9	36 993	426	1 973
Kanawha	128.1	27 848	722.6	1 796.9	D	38 358	15 426	2.3	47.4	28.2	12 400	111	3 077
Lewis	D	D	D	D	D	1 164	250	12.0	0.0	85.4	468	9	312
Lincoln	D	D	D	D	D	120	0	NA	NA	NA	120	4	0
Logan	4.9	16 333	20.3	37.7	D	798	309	0.0	0.0	55.6	370	13	104
McDowell	0.3	NA	1.1	1.6	0.0	97	0	NA	NA	NA	0	0	38
Marion	42.1	22 158	124.3	288.7	D	2 477	103	0.0	0.0	40.7	529	14	1 074
Marshall	12.0	24 000	50.0	143.8	D	4 401	1 424	0.4	54.1	13.0	133	4	1 423
Mason	17.5	21 875	110.0	276.3	33.1	1 821	917	19.0	0.0	12.6	521	14	264
Mercer	19.2	17 455	77.4	140.1	4.5	3 176	1 058	0.0	0.0	20.2	278	8	455
Mineral	10.9	13 625	34.0	60.7	D	8 664	372	28.5	1.9	0.0	7 412	136	420
Mingo	2.9	14 500	8.1	19.1	0.3	1 288	610	0.0	0.0	1.6	347	3	55
Monongalia	34.0	17 000	140.4	253.6	9.0	44 901	29 568	0.4	33.0	1.7	3 765	79	2 962
Monroe	D	D	D	D	D	75	10	0.0	0.0	0.0	8	1	0
Morgan	3.0	15 000	9.5	17.2	0.2	477	214	0.0	0.0	100.0	173	4	0
Nicholas	8.1	11 571	38.3	64.6	1.7	4 025	1 695	0.0	0.0	95.4	1 299	13	71
Ohio	28.5	17 812	102.5	182.6	D	14 088	1 048	47.0	17.6	34.1	2 505	50	4 737
Pendleton	D	D	D	D	D	199	11	0.0	0.0	0.0	45	1	70
Pleasants	D	D	D	D	D	294	37	0.0	0.0	40.4	73	2	59
Pocahontas	8.3	13 833	14.8	56.8	1.8	335	40	0.0	0.0	100.0	0	0	0
Preston	7.5	15 000	26.4	48.1	1.1	1 141	541	0.0	0.0	52.7	341	6	177
Putnam	19.2	32 000	98.5	204.2	D	3 984	147	23.8	0.0	0.0	3 588	104	82
Raleigh	11.0	22 000	33.7	80.6	1.6	11 836	2 576	19.2	3.5	63.2	3 537	63	2 705
Randolph	9.2	11 500	32.0	64.1	1.8	4 247	518	57.9	7.3	30.3	682	11	863
Ritchie	8.4	12 000	25.6	47.4	D	412	96	0.0	15.5	72.5	124	3	105
Roane	8.4	12 000	27.3	62.5	2.5	75	0	NA	NA	NA	50	1	10
Summers	0.0	NA	0.2	0.4	0.0	51	31	0.0	0.0	0.0	0	0	19
Taylor	5.9	14 750	20.4	40.6	D	755	400	0.0	0.0	100.0	247	5	74
Tucker	6.7	13 400	32.4	54.1	D	280	10	0.0	0.0	0.0	106	2	81
Tyler	D	D	D	D	D	281	0	NA	NA	NA	75	1	37
Upshur	13.6	19 429	57.2	117.2	2.7	2 222	332	0.0	0.0	40.6	1 418	33	254
Wayne	16.6	16 600	84.5	167.0	8.9	2 813	2 452	33.3	0.0	0.4	52	2	241
Webster	1.9	9 500	4.5	12.2	0.2	0	0	NA	NA	NA	0	0	0
WetzelL/D	D	D	D	D	2 003	798	12.5	0.0	43.8	341	6	380	
Wirt	D	D	D	D	D	0	0	NA	NA	NA	0	0	0
Wood	164.9	27 949	1 030.1	1 816.6	99.4	13 350	3 821	17.0	0.0	67.9	5 318	68	1 881
Wyoming	D	D	D	D	D	238	12	0.0	0.0	0.0	22	1	153
WISCONSIN	7 615.5	21 765	31 653.0	69 595.8	2 027.4	3 584 759	953 978	23.7	23.8	22.1	1 796 149	27 346	218 168
Adams	6.2	20 667	18.5	51.9	D	17 966	3 135	0.0	80.7	5.8	12 609	203	840
Ashland	21.7	18 083	61.2	109.5	4.7	5 257	3 550	0.0	0.0	77.8	1 371	25	256
Barron	51.6	13 946	205.8	550.2	19.2	22 603	6 223	3.4	32.9	22.8	10 949	225	1 490
Bayfield	2.9	14 500	8.8	25.5	0.4	12 030	451	0.0	0.0	0.0	7 828	124	1 351
Brown	373.4	23 783	1 611.1	4 537.5	79.3	167 459	44 355	23.5	4.6	30.4	86 075	1 261	5 581
Buffalo	3.6	18 000	18.1	70.9	0.6	3 147	421	0.0	0.0	22.6	1 837	36	348
Burnett	10.9	15 571	43.8	88.6	2.0	9 860	920	32.6	0.0	4.7	6 679	107	1 423
Calumet	88.2	21 000	304.4	761.5	13.8	11 444	1 574	12.7	3.5	9.0	5 064	112	1 600
Chippewa	63.3	17 583	548.2	1 002.5	35.7	19 619	5 034	19.8	44.2	10.2	10 012	176	1 757
Clark	19.5	15 000	69.5	319.4	4.3	4 580	1 826	0.2	55.8	19.4	857	15	598
Columbia	49.9	16 633	215.0	617.8	14.3	26 783	8 481	14.1	4.0	3.9	13 784	220	1 882
Crawford	D	D	D	D	D	3 737	1 225	0.0	34.6	4.9	537	9	274
Dane	253.8	19 374	1 209.1	2 604.8	65.9	395 530	96 249	53.6	7.8	12.2	195 299	2 801	31 290
Dodge	141.7	21 800	900.9	1 846.8	73.9	31 792	6 422	14.2	24.6	3.1	16 097	368	3 345
Door	49.3	18 259	115.9	251.6	3.1	26 725	5 206	3.2	19.1	19.0	14 089	195	2 289
Douglas	18.6	20 667	89.8	345.8	D	39 939	10 537	0.1	0.7	55.9	14 507	185	3 161
Dunn	13.5	19 286	94.6	178.1	D	8 545	1 455	7.8	22.3	10.7	5 111	94	591
Eau Claire	85.8	23 189	252.7	614.0	16.8	64 895	21 395	12.0	2.0	79.8	29 090	334	3 348
Florence	1.1	11 000	5.0	13.8	0.2	2 546	418	0.0	0.0	21.5	1 511	31	511
Fond du Lac	175.9	21 716	804.4	1 615.2	53.1	47 052	9 087	6.6	22.0	32.5	20 281	397	4 527
Forest	3.9	13 000	10.9	21.6	0.6	1 669	357	1.4	0.0	58.3	1 060	36	78
Grant	35.0	14 000	203.7	437.4	6.4	9 871	2 755	21.8	22.9	30.5	5 672	78	690
Green	39.6	17 217	249.1	617.2	11.7	13 536	2 281	21.9	3.2	13.2	5 686	91	1 250
Green Lake	22.7	14 187	93.5	175.9	2.6	7 892	1 832	0.0	39.5	24.1	4 730	63	668
Iowa	7.1	11 833	21.5	110.6	1.2	9 024	2 583	25.2	0.0	13.3	4 266	82	1 293

1. Includes nonresidential additions and alterations, residential nonhousekeeping buildings, and residential garages and carports not shown separately.

STATE County	Wholesale trade, 1987: Establishments	Wholesale trade, 1987: Sales (Mil dol)	Wholesale trade, 1987: Paid employees[1]	Wholesale trade, 1987: Annual payroll (Mil dol)	Retail trade, all establishments, 1987: Number	Retail trade, all establishments, 1987: Sales: Total (Mil dol)	Retail trade, all establishments, 1987: Sales: Percent change, 1982–1987	Retail trade, all establishments, 1987: Sales: Per capita[2] (Dollars)	Retail trade, establishments with payroll, 1987: Number	Retail trade, establishments with payroll, 1987: Sales: Total (Mil dol)	Sales: Per capita[2] (Dollars): General merchandise stores	Sales: Per capita[2] (Dollars): Food stores	Sales: Per capita[2] (Dollars): Apparel & accessory stores	Sales: Per capita[2] (Dollars): Eating and drinking places
	147	148	149	150	151	152	153	154	155	156	157	158	159	160
WEST VIRGINIA—Con.														
Harrison	137	275.1	1 303	23.5	778	489.5	57.6	6 474	520	478.3	1 087	1 334	257	481
Jackson	23	27.3	147	2.0	274	109.0	38.3	4 258	139	100.0	216	1 229	97	338
Jefferson	18	18.1	169	2.0	329	126.3	71.6	3 660	184	118.4	164	1 037	133	557
Kanawha	506	1 333.1	5 623	129.6	1 938	1 524.9	27.3	6 860	1 368	1 504.7	1 039	1 411	298	604
Lewis	18	31.8	97	1.9	197	72.5	9.7	4 026	116	68.6	D	1 258	186	314
Lincoln	10	3.8	32	0.4	180	39.9	27.1	1 713	78	33.7	335	495	0	53
Logan	55	73.2	378	7.2	397	223.0	11.8	4 588	258	215.5	608	1 135	87	237
McDowell	27	35.2	183	2.8	309	127.0	9.9	2 974	172	121.0	276	1 178	63	130
Marion	75	143.9	708	13.4	612	325.7	5.0	5 145	379	317.5	926	1 054	203	310
Marshall	17	60.1	160	3.1	305	172.4	28.6	4 399	174	166.4	718	1 403	108	330
Mason	22	53.5	166	3.3	207	74.3	11.1	2 824	128	71.1	157	996	24	201
Mercer	101	374.7	1 373	26.1	613	412.9	13.5	5 774	423	404.3	1 220	1 050	225	412
Mineral	17	15.6	96	1.2	265	73.7	48.3	2 709	145	68.3	D	697	78	268
Mingo	49	62.8	286	5.2	391	137.8	-8.6	3 806	200	128.6	397	599	295	159
Monongalia	87	230.8	711	14.1	713	425.4	41.9	5 461	461	411.8	655	1 191	309	481
Monroe	8	8.5	34	0.3	101	17.4	40.3	1 384	50	15.5	91	417	D	25
Morgan	13	18.1	101	2.2	120	29.8	51.3	2 506	53	27.0	105	613	0	100
Nicholas	37	54.1	235	4.1	273	141.5	37.0	5 144	156	135.5	606	1 202	88	333
Ohio	122	340.1	1 401	28.0	595	320.0	10.1	5 566	387	310.0	430	1 022	197	650
Pendleton	11	7.5	50	0.6	84	20.7	36.2	2 587	39	18.0	119	715	D	64
Pleasants	4	D	D	D	69	29.7	70.7	3 814	36	28.9	D	1 282	D	170
Pocahontas	9	10.2	42	0.6	129	35.3	11.4	3 841	69	32.6	185	1 123	D	191
Preston	32	58.4	228	3.2	277	100.1	27.8	3 282	129	92.6	354	821	D	152
Putnam	52	179.4	769	14.8	276	180.7	40.5	4 364	163	175.6	223	1 034	43	404
Raleigh	145	284.8	1 386	28.3	664	474.6	13.4	5 760	440	464.6	1 069	1 123	149	415
Randolph	37	99.8	441	6.4	346	146.3	20.7	5 097	204	138.9	551	1 189	161	420
Ritchie	11	15.2	43	0.8	111	38.0	45.6	3 420	58	36.0	131	1 114	0	123
Roane	19	16.8	88	1.2	137	59.4	9.8	3 879	76	56.6	309	1 171	38	146
Summers	11	15.6	81	1.2	118	37.5	8.4	2 417	67	35.2	309	935	65	234
Taylor	9	17.7	165	2.7	151	45.5	22.0	2 847	77	43.0	D	1 066	33	165
Tucker	5	2.0	25	0.3	106	25.9	-5.8	3 158	56	23.3	D	D	D	286
Tyler	8	3.3	29	0.4	106	24.7	26.7	2 328	44	22.5	19	826	D	58
Upshur	29	72.5	202	3.2	240	108.6	22.7	4 603	123	103.7	386	1 170	109	566
Wayne	29	78.2	359	6.4	308	105.5	-1.6	2 382	157	96.7	376	696	66	169
Webster	5	9.8	68	1.1	134	29.7	-0.3	2 626	57	27.2	154	1 035	0	55
Wetzel	13	14.4	78	1.2	228	115.0	24.6	5 450	143	111.9	500	1 838	156	429
Wirt	1	D	D	D	49	8.0	50.9	1 542	16	6.3	D	D	0	48
Wood	143	492.6	1 475	27.5	908	656.4	36.5	7 166	585	642.0	1 546	1 212	235	587
Wyoming	11	29.8	90	1.6	255	84.2	-15.9	2 514	138	78.9	322	614	26	106
WISCONSIN	8 821	33 698.6	101 731	2 198.9	50 292	28 537.2	38.8	5 937	32 164	27 802.5	712	1 110	226	604
Adams	9	12.2	128	1.7	113	27.2	15.3	1 903	66	25.5	D	675	24	240
Ashland	28	38.6	182	2.9	300	100.4	34.0	5 869	168	94.1	507	1 200	315	558
Barron	80	86.7	566	8.7	545	215.7	23.8	5 249	361	208.8	454	775	173	507
Bayfield	12	4.5	57	0.5	225	39.7	35.0	2 794	120	35.9	D	644	26	600
Brown	441	2 086.2	6 013	131.8	1 843	1 353.5	54.6	7 188	1 245	1 327.2	1 350	1 095	294	674
Buffalo	23	33.3	165	3.0	139	34.8	9.8	2 420	84	32.6	D	491	D	360
Burnett	10	D	D	D	164	52.8	38.6	3 914	108	49.6	181	990	D	441
Calumet	51	75.8	527	9.6	288	127.3	46.0	3 811	170	123.9	D	1 480	31	427
Chippewa	83	236.6	854	18.3	565	324.6	60.5	6 001	344	314.6	481	1 002	92	436
Clark	83	196.8	605	8.6	376	92.1	23.3	2 774	192	84.9	73	717	14	244
Columbia	83	184.6	694	12.3	607	249.5	32.9	5 309	378	240.6	D	1 027	138	632
Crawford	37	27.0	186	2.4	210	84.7	45.8	5 043	111	80.6	D	1 010	267	523
Dane	660	2 394.1	8 554	198.3	3 398	2 566.8	43.9	7 399	2 448	2 531.2	849	1 180	373	793
Dodge	110	333.8	1 193	20.9	760	291.2	26.2	3 817	445	278.9	545	823	131	407
Door	40	33.2	178	3.1	544	166.5	39.2	6 189	360	158.9	404	1 295	288	927
Douglas	54	570.6	762	17.0	509	239.8	27.6	5 736	354	234.0	D	1 051	182	658
Dunn	55	74.6	352	5.4	316	133.6	24.9	3 807	203	129.0	692	894	97	475
Eau Claire	156	371.4	1 863	35.3	888	535.2	20.6	6 417	628	524.9	1 171	1 202	336	766
Florence	2	D	D	D	52	10.8	61.2	2 640	23	9.8	0	D	0	389
Fond du Lac	148	448.6	1 626	30.0	915	493.4	29.9	5 500	580	481.0	972	974	190	590
Forest	7	6.7	45	0.6	152	23.5	53.6	2 579	68	19.9	39	1 176	0	239
Grant	109	140.4	668	9.1	634	214.1	21.1	4 182	364	201.3	384	990	81	472
Green	89	385.1	842	15.9	369	308.6	53.5	9 989	231	301.4	619	1 190	153	460
Green Lake	39	30.1	199	2.8	250	80.1	-12.8	4 216	136	76.0	104	1 030	233	475
Iowa	51	61.7	324	5.7	237	387.2	182.4	18 889	133	381.1	D	D	D	D

1. For pay period including March 12. 2. Based on the estimated population as of July 1 of the year shown.

STATE County	Retail trade, establishments with payroll, 1987 (cont'd): Paid employees[1]	Retail trade, establishments with payroll, 1987 (cont'd): Annual payroll (Mil dol)	Taxable service industries–establishments with payroll, 1987: Number	Receipts (Mil dol): Total	Receipts, Selected kinds of business: Hotels, motels and other lodging places	Receipts, Selected kinds of business: Health services	Receipts, Selected kinds of business: Legal services	Paid employees	Annual payroll (Mil dol)	Bank deposits,[2] June 1989: Total (Mil dol)	Bank deposits,[2] June 1989: Percent change, 1988–1989	Savings capital,[3] September 1989: Total (Mil dol)	Savings capital,[3] September 1989: Percent change, 1988–1989
	161	162	163	164	165	166	167	168	169	170	171	172	173
WEST VIRGINIA—Con.													
Harrison	6 002	51.8	447	128.3	7.2	46.5	12.3	2 986	43.5	626	-1.6	62.7	-5.0
Jackson	1 128	10.4	75	13.1	D	5.6	1.1	389	4.0	202	56.7	3.8	-96.9
Jefferson	1 516	13.9	137	44.9	3.7	5.5	1.8	1 069	11.7	306	6.4	16.4	-2.3
Kanawha	17 648	167.8	1 487	588.1	31.0	195.8	83.7	12 982	210.3	2 003	0.9	312.6	11.8
Lewis	832	8.0	75	11.3	D	3.3	1.6	286	3.2	150	5.8	0.0	-100.0
Lincoln	417	3.0	35	7.1	0.0	2.4	0.6	134	1.7	91	4.6	0.0	NA
Logan	2 273	23.1	227	60.3	1.3	15.9	6.7	1 206	19.2	265	3.3	44.8	-9.7
McDowell	1 256	11.9	84	20.4	D	13.5	1.6	417	7.7	251	1.1	0.0	NA
Marion	3 777	33.3	302	77.9	2.2	31.4	3.9	1 793	27.2	448	1.1	76.7	-12.5
Marshall	2 004	16.8	114	25.2	D	12.3	2.7	649	9.1	190	5.4	35.2	-2.7
Mason	872	7.3	81	17.7	0.3	10.3	1.3	460	6.1	151	6.3	40.4	4.1
Mercer	4 818	46.3	397	146.9	10.8	78.1	9.8	2 915	57.2	603	1.9	32.4	-15.5
Mineral	1 030	6.9	105	97.2	D	D	1.1	1 418	34.6	144	7.4	0.0	NA
Mingo	1 422	14.5	137	33.8	1.4	15.6	2.9	639	10.7	356	6.0	0.0	NA
Monongalia	5 288	47.6	454	149.3	14.4	52.3	8.7	3 849	54.8	541	4.0	67.9	-7.8
Monroe	194	1.6	26	2.8	D	1.2	D	77	0.8	53	9.2	4.6	5.6
Morgan	284	2.5	38	12.1	7.4	2.1	0.7	495	3.9	73	5.6	11.0	-5.5
Nicholas	1 260	13.1	120	23.5	2.8	6.8	1.5	602	6.8	213	3.6	0.0	NA
Ohio	4 751	40.8	458	168.5	D	D	12.5	3 887	59.3	698	0.5	135.9	-2.9
Pendleton	176	1.5	33	4.8	D	1.5	0.6	126	1.5	74	4.4	0.0	NA
Pleasants	298	2.9	27	5.4	D	2.1	D	115	1.8	67	4.3	10.0	8.8
Pocahontas	370	2.9	46	16.0	D	2.6	D	774	4.4	73	11.5	0.0	NA
Preston	906	8.5	86	16.8	0.8	6.5	1.1	496	5.7	205	8.8	0.0	NA
Putnam	2 115	19.1	148	54.2	1.3	21.3	1.1	1 317	26.4	230	11.3	9.5	4.2
Raleigh	5 203	50.2	474	198.1	8.7	105.3	6.7	4 167	67.4	606	1.4	62.8	-0.4
Randolph	1 735	14.4	131	24.4	2.4	11.3	1.9	737	8.1	268	6.8	0.0	NA
Ritchie	341	3.2	27	3.5	0.0	2.0	D	162	1.1	65	8.0	0.0	NA
Roane	563	5.8	49	7.3	D	2.9	0.5	225	2.6	150	8.1	0.0	NA
Summers	462	4.4	46	7.2	D	4.3	0.3	234	2.4	106	4.0	6.4	9.0
Taylor	496	4.0	41	4.5	D	1.5	0.4	143	1.3	102	17.6	0.0	-100.0
Tucker	314	2.7	38	13.6	D	1.9	0.4	536	4.5	68	6.8	0.0	NA
Tyler	278	2.1	27	3.1	D	2.3	D	111	0.9	44	4.7	16.3	-1.3
Upshur	1 397	11.8	116	19.3	D	8.7	1.1	542	5.8	207	-0.9	0.0	NA
Wayne	1 205	9.9	92	21.1	1.0	4.1	0.2	532	7.1	230	6.2	14.5	-2.0
Webster	271	2.5	22	3.2	D	1.0	1.3	82	0.9	34	6.7	0.0	NA
Wetzel	1 388	11.6	75	13.6	D	6.7	1.4	389	3.8	123	6.1	53.3	-5.0
Wirt	70	0.5	8	0.6	0.0	D	D	17	0.2	17	7.8	0.0	NA
Wood	7 936	74.8	528	251.0	12.6	57.9	8.4	5 369	84.0	627	7.0	170.1	-7.3
Wyoming	915	8.2	68	11.9	0.1	6.6	1.3	306	4.6	163	-0.9	0.0	NA
WISCONSIN	372 205	3 206.4	28 126	10 025.7	569.3	3 233.6	713.5	265 298	4 108.5	35 305	3.6	14 052.4	0.4
Adams	381	2.7	29	5.4	D	1.9	0.4	108	1.7	73	4.4	12.7	14.3
Ashland	1 326	10.3	115	29.2	3.3	18.1	1.3	885	13.1	116	2.7	59.9	-4.3
Barron	2 643	21.6	218	44.0	1.8	21.2	2.8	1 192	15.6	313	4.7	104.3	3.5
Bayfield	601	4.6	54	5.9	1.8	D	D	168	1.8	67	3.2	13.4	-4.2
Brown	17 264	154.5	1 155	446.8	30.1	149.4	19.8	13 362	205.1	1 479	4.8	468.8	1.5
Buffalo	534	3.4	56	21.7	D	12.4	0.7	557	11.1	103	3.7	15.5	-4.9
Burnett	581	4.5	52	6.5	0.5	2.1	0.4	179	1.9	88	5.3	7.0	9.0
Calumet	1 807	13.3	117	22.5	D	9.5	1.3	628	7.5	196	1.2	41.8	5.5
Chippewa	3 221	28.4	221	56.7	1.1	36.7	2.0	1 728	22.9	311	2.0	103.5	2.3
Clark	1 153	8.8	123	18.7	D	7.4	1.2	524	7.1	247	1.5	71.8	8.7
Columbia	3 316	27.1	285	55.1	10.4	14.4	3.2	1 617	16.4	418	3.4	85.9	1.2
Crawford	1 048	8.8	70	15.5	0.7	8.0	1.2	570	6.2	107	3.1	59.9	-0.7
Dane	35 627	310.4	2 489	1 133.0	61.1	314.2	92.3	26 803	462.9	2 527	7.0	1 016.8	-4.5
Dodge	4 135	32.5	312	65.4	1.4	28.3	5.1	1 734	24.3	449	5.9	121.5	-3.7
Door	2 301	20.0	264	55.3	21.1	13.4	2.0	1 337	15.9	192	0.4	77.9	0.3
Douglas	3 330	26.0	205	44.6	D	12.7	2.8	1 564	16.8	250	3.3	35.2	-3.3
Dunn	1 920	12.9	136	29.6	D	7.5	1.3	885	9.8	190	6.5	40.5	0.3
Eau Claire	8 939	64.6	543	205.4	11.3	83.9	12.6	5 094	84.0	469	3.8	188.4	-2.6
Florence	138	0.8	8	D	D	D	D	D	D	17	3.8	0.0	NA
Fond du Lac	6 793	55.4	450	134.5	7.1	54.5	7.1	3 997	54.7	711	2.6	247.8	-6.5
Forest	324	2.0	39	7.5	0.6	3.9	D	292	2.9	57	0.9	5.9	21.2
Grant	2 906	23.2	232	32.3	2.5	11.9	3.7	1 162	9.1	438	-0.3	94.1	9.3
Green	2 840	39.6	161	62.3	1.4	26.1	2.7	1 187	19.1	356	7.5	85.2	-0.6
Green Lake	1 186	9.4	101	15.7	2.7	5.7	1.1	516	4.6	171	2.0	63.6	-1.0
Iowa	2 130	27.0	78	15.3	D	3.3	1.1	377	4.0	147	1.3	23.2	2.7

1. For the period including March 12 of the year shown. 2. Includes deposits for all insured and reporting noninsured commercial and mutual savings banks. 3. Includes savings capital for all FSLIC insured savings institutions.

STATE County	Federal funds and grants, 1989: Expenditures: Total (Mil dol)	Federal funds and grants, 1989: Expenditures: Percent change, 1988–1989	Per capita[1] (Dollars): Total	Per capita[1] (Dollars): Direct payments for individuals	Per capita[1] (Dollars): Procurement contract awards	Per capita[1] (Dollars): Salaries and wages	Per capita[1] (Dollars): Grant awards	Local government finances, 1981–1982: General revenue: Total (Mil dol)	General revenue: Intergovernmental: Total (Mil dol)	General revenue: Intergovernmental: Percent from state	General revenue: Taxes: Total (Mil dol)	Taxes: Per capita[2]: Total (Dollars)	Taxes: Per capita[2]: Property (Dollars)	Direct general expenditure: Total (Mil dol)	Direct general expenditure: Percent change, 1977–1982
	174	175	176	177	178	179	180	181	182	183	184	185	186	187	188
WEST VIRGINIA—Con.															
Harrison	234.8	9.3	3 190	2 318	61	457	338	50.8	26.4	86.2	17.1	219	162	50.6	63.9
Jackson	59.8	10.0	2 371	1 716	136	145	357	20.8	10.3	92.7	5.3	201	178	20.9	93.7
Jefferson	101.8	13.3	2 804	1 689	163	457	449	16.6	10.3	92.3	4.3	139	127	15.7	77.9
Kanawha	838.6	4.1	3 880	2 236	176	357	1 102	196.0	87.8	79.6	69.2	300	210	190.3	66.4
Lewis	50.0	-26.7	2 922	2 275	59	159	408	12.0	7.7	91.5	2.8	150	142	11.4	93.1
Lincoln	58.9	3.3	2 476	1 847	13	89	516	15.4	11.8	89.6	2.9	119	117	13.6	79.2
Logan	142.6	0.5	3 053	2 467	87	125	365	28.4	19.3	96.5	6.7	132	121	27.5	63.7
McDowell	142.0	3.7	3 669	2 910	18	127	580	33.3	23.4	91.9	7.7	159	138	32.0	37.3
Marion	186.4	6.8	3 041	2 481	103	129	321	70.0	26.9	82.6	13.7	208	162	68.3	75.6
Marshall	87.6	0.7	2 269	1 923	13	115	205	46.0	13.9	82.7	13.0	317	270	42.3	134.4
Mason	89.3	-24.4	3 422	1 964	871	252	290	35.1	13.8	89.0	4.8	179	157	30.6	209.0
Mercer	212.9	4.6	3 037	2 508	36	174	310	88.9	38.5	68.1	13.4	178	139	103.3	206.1
Mineral	110.5	-14.2	4 092	2 303	1 474	89	211	17.1	11.6	94.2	3.7	132	121	16.2	45.8
Mingo	116.5	5.4	3 299	2 176	499	120	496	30.8	20.9	78.7	6.6	174	139	32.3	121.6
Monongalia	241.9	3.4	3 141	1 455	547	553	580	48.9	26.2	79.4	14.8	190	140	51.0	40.2
Monroe	46.9	4.3	3 664	2 416	22	723	419	7.4	5.7	87.9	1.1	81	78	7.3	92.4
Morgan	39.3	6.8	3 044	2 670	9	77	273	9.7	4.7	81.8	1.5	134	130	9.4	146.9
Nicholas	81.1	13.8	3 015	2 099	240	181	480	24.7	13.0	85.8	5.3	186	163	22.2	97.8
Ohio	194.5	13.5	3 473	2 520	71	309	527	50.8	20.3	71.8	18.5	302	203	45.9	19.1
Pendleton	23.1	-1.5	2 889	1 775	108	596	341	5.7	4.5	71.9	0.6	71	68	4.7	41.0
Pleasants	55.7	243.8	7 325	1 838	5 127	74	273	8.7	3.0	92.3	4.8	593	551	8.4	102.6
Pocahontas	58.2	4.3	6 471	2 174	98	216	3 913	6.4	4.9	83.2	1.0	104	96	6.1	72.2
Preston	79.4	5.3	2 647	2 078	51	164	320	23.1	13.0	93.4	4.1	132	128	22.8	59.3
Putnam	70.3	-1.8	1 679	1 342	17	131	177	33.2	14.2	92.3	10.1	258	251	31.1	136.8
Raleigh	256.7	3.2	3 275	2 507	71	421	268	58.2	32.8	90.7	15.2	174	125	57.2	88.9
Randolph	83.5	4.1	2 961	2 196	71	283	395	18.3	12.3	86.4	3.8	131	105	17.3	44.4
Ritchie	28.7	5.1	2 662	2 012	129	152	344	6.1	4.0	94.5	1.5	127	123	6.6	52.0
Roane	37.2	1.7	2 445	1 922	12	115	380	17.1	13.8	40.3	2.0	124	102	19.4	307.7
Summers	48.9	14.7	3 156	2 239	25	134	740	13.9	5.5	93.3	2.0	125	111	14.7	197.9
Taylor	38.4	0.5	2 475	2 018	16	129	302	16.0	8.3	89.8	2.0	123	97	14.9	133.0
Tucker	21.2	1.8	2 686	2 045	25	228	377	5.0	3.6	93.4	0.7	87	81	4.7	19.9
Tyler	21.1	5.2	2 049	1 581	52	133	265	9.6	4.6	95.4	1.7	153	142	8.4	126.4
Upshur	99.7	88.8	4 429	1 822	22	196	2 379	17.6	11.3	78.3	3.9	161	152	15.3	47.0
Wayne	86.4	-3.1	1 985	1 502	16	106	352	25.7	18.1	92.9	5.4	118	104	25.9	89.3
Webster	38.9	23.2	3 508	2 270	20	74	1 135	7.7	5.8	91.8	1.4	119	107	7.7	22.2
Wetzel	55.6	12.4	2 750	2 065	40	126	510	20.0	8.5	94.4	4.3	196	166	18.9	63.8
Wirt	15.5	-21.3	2 926	1 801	532	133	443	3.9	2.9	96.2	0.7	132	128	3.3	71.7
Wood	270.6	13.0	3 003	1 938	107	519	432	104.9	39.3	78.2	18.5	199	147	102.7	104.9
Wyoming	84.4	4.5	2 653	2 122	27	143	356	23.8	16.9	96.4	5.4	151	139	22.0	58.5
WISCONSIN	14 617.2	11.3	X	1 759	295	229	524	6 316.4	2 921.7	87.3	2 002.0	422	416	6 179.7	50.3
Adams	46.6	4.0	3 233	1 794	100	639	445	12.4	5.6	87.5	5.2	372	364	11.8	54.4
Ashland	57.8	0.6	3 381	2 262	208	263	564	19.3	12.0	88.8	4.6	268	264	18.5	11.9
Barron	121.8	21.3	2 900	1 837	45	137	411	48.9	23.1	92.6	15.8	404	399	47.0	55.9
Bayfield	42.3	7.4	2 961	1 900	107	221	515	16.6	8.8	92.2	5.2	368	364	17.1	32.1
Brown	442.8	15.7	2 287	1 334	428	205	232	275.1	116.3	84.5	70.2	391	387	242.5	48.5
Buffalo	44.3	6.7	3 056	1 663	171	341	314	15.6	8.6	94.9	4.5	310	306	16.2	38.8
Burnett	42.0	-3.2	3 064	2 112	205	88	427	14.1	6.4	91.0	5.4	416	411	13.8	32.6
Calumet	54.3	-8.1	1 622	1 111	41	135	127	27.3	11.7	93.0	10.4	328	325	27.8	60.1
Chippewa	178.5	0.4	3 269	1 780	681	157	330	54.9	28.6	94.9	12.8	241	238	55.3	7.3
Clark	105.1	21.9	3 176	1 708	44	128	419	40.9	20.2	94.6	11.1	335	332	39.9	41.1
Columbia	126.7	7.1	2 617	1 800	97	139	235	51.0	22.9	96.5	19.3	446	442	53.1	43.5
Crawford	55.0	15.8	3 255	1 727	507	157	468	19.4	12.2	85.5	5.1	303	300	17.8	54.0
Dane	1 309.5	2.0	3 665	1 314	216	396	1 501	419.0	180.5	87.1	155.6	470	460	419.0	50.3
Dodge	136.5	8.3	1 761	1 275	20	88	194	66.5	28.3	92.5	22.3	295	291	65.6	47.0
Door	315.6	263.9	11 605	1 930	9 020	218	237	29.8	13.1	94.4	12.5	486	479	29.3	77.3
Douglas	148.0	15.5	3 532	2 380	245	132	738	71.3	38.7	83.3	20.0	447	421	68.2	89.0
Dunn	93.5	18.1	2 626	1 514	20	106	415	47.5	18.0	91.3	10.4	299	295	42.0	63.9
Eau Claire	218.0	22.7	2 574	1 550	90	173	353	108.5	53.5	88.7	30.7	377	371	107.6	58.4
Florence	11.5	14.3	2 808	1 860	31	173	624	4.9	2.8	95.8	1.5	358	354	4.8	36.9
Fond du Lac	212.8	11.5	2 348	1 640	236	105	216	107.6	50.8	91.1	35.8	400	396	115.9	61.2
Forest	32.1	8.8	3 524	2 253	196	320	708	10.7	6.1	91.0	3.4	374	372	12.7	74.2
Grant	136.1	12.2	2 668	1 683	55	123	313	74.3	31.6	88.8	22.2	429	426	70.8	78.5
Green	83.7	26.5	2 683	1 470	64	109	223	35.8	13.3	93.3	14.2	473	469	34.6	42.9
Green Lake	55.0	3.5	2 893	2 041	16	116	372	19.1	9.6	94.9	7.1	373	369	21.1	60.1
Iowa	54.3	-26.5	2 636	1 241	41	141	346	26.3	12.0	87.1	10.2	505	501	23.2	45.7

1. Based on the estimated population as of July 1 of the year shown. 2. Based on the estimated population as of July 1, 1982.

STATE County	Local government finances, 1981–1982 (cont'd): Direct general expenditure (cont'd): Per capita[1] (Dollars)	Percent of total for– Education	Percent of total for– Health & hospitals	Percent of total for– Police protection	Percent of total for– Public welfare	Percent of total for– Highways	Debt outstanding: Total (Mil dol)	Debt outstanding: Per capita[1] (Dollars)	State and local government employment, 1989: Total	State and local government employment, 1989: Rate[2]	Federal government civilian employment 1989: Total	Federal government civilian employment 1989: Earnings ($1,000)	Elections, 1988[3]: Total vote cast for president	Elections, 1988[3]: Vote for lead party (Percent)
	189	190	191	192	193	194	195	196	197	198	199	200	201	202
WEST VIRGINIA—Con.														
Harrison	649	65.7	0.9	5.1	0.0	4.0	17.2	221	3 152	428.3	1 131	37 981	30 418	D—55.9
Jackson	790	66.0	1.5	2.5	0.4	0.9	38.0	1 440	1 138	451.6	92	2 138	10 291	R—55.3
Jefferson	505	77.3	0.5	3.3	0.1	1.7	8.1	261	1 723	474.7	599	17 149	9 726	R—55.0
Kanawha	825	53.3	1.0	4.0	0.0	2.5	331.0	1 434	16 676	771.7	1 768	60 659	79 542	D—51.7
Lewis	603	79.0	0.7	2.8	0.7	1.9	2.9	154	1 508	881.9	70	1 718	6 908	R—52.1
Lincoln	563	90.4	0.3	1.4	0.0	0.2	6.7	279	845	355.0	59	1 318	8 529	D—59.2
Logan	539	83.5	2.2	2.8	0.0	1.1	4.0	79	1 905	407.9	163	4 453	15 608	D—72.5
McDowell	659	77.1	0.9	3.0	0.0	1.2	3.4	70	1 827	472.1	139	3 161	9 714	D—74.2
Marion	1 041	37.6	31.5	2.5	0.2	2.9	38.7	591	3 607	588.4	197	5 637	23 742	D—60.8
Marshall	1 030	45.7	0.5	2.9	0.1	1.5	187.2	4 554	1 869	484.2	80	2 237	14 779	D—53.5
Mason	1 130	41.8	0.3	1.7	0.0	0.8	205.6	7 586	1 211	464.0	150	4 053	10 825	D—50.5
Mercer	1 370	44.5	37.5	1.4	0.0	1.2	82.0	1 088	4 628	660.2	336	10 430	20 430	R—50.0
Mineral	585	80.5	3.4	2.2	0.2	1.5	6.0	216	1 495	553.7	71	1 905	10 111	R—59.5
Mingo	853	72.1	0.7	3.1	0.1	2.3	12.8	336	1 696	480.5	127	3 150	10 350	D—71.8
Monongalia	657	50.8	4.1	3.7	0.2	4.1	63.7	821	11 987	1 556.8	1 290	47 289	26 338	D—53.8
Monroe	562	79.7	8.0	1.8	0.0	0.2	0.3	20	540	421.9	300	9 144	5 168	R—52.6
Morgan	844	52.9	21.8	1.0	0.0	0.2	12.6	1 140	587	455.0	25	660	4 564	R—65.8
Nicholas	778	60.9	18.6	3.1	0.2	1.5	17.1	600	1 362	506.3	154	4 067	8 936	D—57.9
Ohio	749	44.4	0.4	5.1	0.0	4.8	100.0	1 635	3 276	585.0	469	15 431	20 578	R—50.3
Pendleton	599	79.1	1.3	0.7	0.1	0.2	1.6	207	331	413.8	78	2 034	3 503	R—54.3
Pleasants	1 039	74.5	0.4	2.4	0.2	2.7	1.7	204	1 053	1 385.5	16	408	3 187	R—55.3
Pocahontas	632	81.2	1.3	1.8	0.3	0.7	0.1	7	753	836.7	97	2 075	3 852	D—50.8
Preston	734	66.0	14.1	2.0	0.1	0.5	7.4	239	1 457	485.7	81	1 904	10 196	R—56.9
Putnam	798	62.8	1.5	1.9	0.9	0.2	101.5	2 603	1 380	329.4	151	4 363	14 841	R—55.0
Raleigh	656	64.3	0.4	5.0	0.1	2.6	62.4	716	3 263	416.2	901	29 901	24 782	D—57.7
Randolph	593	75.3	0.6	2.3	0.1	2.2	6.0	205	1 557	552.1	336	7 977	10 017	D—52.2
Ritchie	564	78.3	1.2	1.4	0.2	1.4	0.2	18	407	376.9	42	944	4 338	R—66.3
Roane	1 206	34.7	0.3	1.5	0.1	1.1	16.5	1 022	708	465.8	47	1 070	5 332	R—53.7
Summers	927	43.9	40.9	2.0	0.0	0.7	1.7	106	897	578.7	57	1 282	5 314	D—57.8
Taylor	897	53.0	28.1	2.0	0.0	1.4	8.7	523	837	540.0	52	1 287	5 694	D—50.1
Tucker	543	80.5	0.1	2.2	0.1	0.4	2.2	255	453	573.4	82	1 824	3 577	D—52.3
Tyler	735	64.6	13.7	1.9	0.0	0.8	12.3	1 076	496	481.6	37	814	3 874	R—61.0
Upshur	630	69.3	1.4	2.5	0.2	0.9	4.6	188	1 017	452.0	67	1 819	7 894	R—61.0
Wayne	560	87.5	0.6	2.4	0.1	0.6	7.3	158	1 484	341.1	760	24 390	15 775	D—54.6
Webster	648	81.3	0.9	1.9	0.1	0.9	1.3	105	545	491.0	23	516	3 217	D—67.9
Wetzel	863	50.5	29.8	3.2	0.1	2.2	13.8	629	1 009	499.5	66	1 649	7 350	D—53.4
Wirt	654	88.0	0.3	1.3	0.0	0.7	0.0	4	224	422.6	20	435	2 066	R—54.5
Wood	1 100	39.3	26.5	3.6	0.1	1.8	95.6	1 023	4 990	553.8	1 595	41 252	32 563	R—59.7
Wyoming	612	81.8	1.3	3.5	0.3	0.5	0.9	25	1 330	418.2	127	3 413	9 684	D—63.4
WISCONSIN	1 302	40.8	10.5	6.1	4.1	9.6	3 324.4	700	303 986	621.7	29 472	884 372	2 191 608	D—51.4
Adams	835	37.7	7.3	8.3	5.9	19.0	1.9	135	555	385.4	335	10 484	6 883	D—52.3
Ashland	1 068	44.2	3.6	5.6	4.5	13.5	8.1	467	1 025	599.4	102	2 764	7 489	D—60.4
Barron	1 206	42.1	4.9	3.3	7.1	14.3	36.1	926	2 304	548.6	150	3 814	17 579	D—50.9
Bayfield	1 207	44.9	3.5	6.7	4.5	16.6	11.0	771	840	587.4	120	2 717	7 471	D—57.9
Brown	1 352	42.3	5.4	5.5	2.8	11.2	166.7	929	10 217	527.7	946	31 640	85 953	R—50.8
Buffalo	1 116	41.9	4.8	3.2	4.6	29.5	7.4	510	669	461.4	132	3 097	6 322	D—55.1
Burnett	1 050	39.7	9.8	4.2	5.5	22.2	6.5	495	579	422.6	43	962	6 483	D—54.6
Calumet	873	39.7	10.3	5.1	3.0	22.0	12.5	392	1 052	314.0	68	1 683	14 712	R—55.1
Chippewa	1 040	41.5	15.5	4.4	4.3	15.8	25.8	485	2 975	544.9	171	4 559	21 367	D—53.6
Clark	1 204	44.6	15.3	3.0	6.1	13.7	13.8	416	1 833	553.8	116	2 771	13 058	D—50.9
Columbia	1 227	56.9	7.8	4.9	3.2	9.5	27.4	633	2 386	493.0	181	5 089	19 766	R—53.0
Crawford	1 065	39.9	8.8	4.2	2.2	18.2	6.2	371	712	421.3	74	1 755	6 912	D—52.2
Dane	1 265	43.5	7.5	6.7	5.1	7.4	190.1	574	59 107	1 654.3	4 242	135 747	176 158	D—59.8
Dodge	868	30.5	16.2	6.3	3.2	15.1	37.1	491	3 531	455.6	181	4 919	29 950	R—56.8
Door	1 141	37.7	4.8	4.8	3.2	16.6	19.0	740	1 239	455.5	161	4 047	12 430	R—55.6
Douglas	1 526	48.8	12.2	5.6	3.7	8.9	23.2	519	3 824	912.6	129	3 530	20 468	D—67.9
Dunn	1 204	34.2	19.7	3.6	3.8	17.9	24.4	700	4 096	1 150.6	108	2 574	16 625	D—55.4
Eau Claire	1 322	46.0	11.1	4.4	4.1	8.5	49.7	611	7 242	855.0	435	14 071	39 023	D—54.2
Florence	1 143	46.4	6.3	3.4	6.5	20.0	1.3	312	240	585.4	23	653	2 147	R—51.5
Fond du Lac	1 298	46.3	9.4	5.6	3.2	7.5	79.0	885	4 457	491.9	244	6 848	38 193	R—57.6
Forest	1 395	41.4	6.3	4.0	3.0	17.2	3.5	386	578	635.2	106	3 012	4 013	D—53.4
Grant	1 367	44.0	19.5	4.5	6.8	11.4	23.7	457	4 710	923.5	175	4 369	19 620	R—51.2
Green	1 154	42.1	14.1	8.7	3.1	15.5	18.4	615	1 518	486.5	101	2 716	11 908	R—55.7
Green Lake	1 109	41.3	4.2	5.2	2.9	11.1	8.3	434	817	430.0	62	1 560	8 299	R—62.7
Iowa	1 142	42.4	8.4	3.5	6.7	19.6	8.9	438	988	479.6	82	1 935	8 575	D—49.8

1. Based on the estimated population as of July 1, 1982. 2. Per 10,000 resident population estimated as of July 1 of the year shown. 3. Data subject to copyright.

STATE–County code	MSA/CMSA/NECMA code[1]	STATE County	Land Area,[2] 1990 (Sq. Km.)	Population, 1990: Total persons	Rank	Per square kilometer	Race: White	Black	Am. Indian, Eskimo, Aleut	Asian & Pacific Islander	Other race	Hispanic[3]	Age of population Percent: Under 5 years	5 to 14 years	15 to 24 years
			1	2	3	4	5	6	7	8	9	10	11	12	13
		WISCONSIN—Con.													
55 051	...	Iron	1 961	6 153	2 737	3.1	6 121	1	25	2	4	8	5.0	12.7	10.0
55 053	...	Jackson	2 557	16 588	1 880	6.5	15 814	47	674	30	23	145	7.0	15.8	12.3
55 055	...	Jefferson	1 443	67 783	654	47.0	66 702	189	176	287	429	1 160	6.9	14.7	16.1
55 057	...	Juneau	1 988	21 650	1 595	10.9	21 307	31	166	78	68	152	7.1	15.7	11.6
55 059	1602	Kenosha	707	128 181	363	181.3	119 187	5 295	472	669	2 558	5 580	7.9	14.8	14.4
55 061	...	Kewaunee	887	18 878	1 742	21.3	18 766	24	52	23	13	54	7.1	16.3	13.3
55 063	3870	La Crosse	1 173	97 904	469	83.5	94 319	438	340	2 667	140	640	7.1	14.0	19.1
55 065	...	Lafayette	1 641	16 076	1 917	9.8	16 009	14	21	19	13	37	7.4	17.5	11.8
55 067	...	Langlade	2 260	19 505	1 701	8.6	19 291	13	137	22	42	104	6.7	15.3	11.7
55 069	...	Lincoln	2 287	26 993	1 390	11.8	26 712	84	96	78	23	118	6.6	15.4	13.0
55 071	...	Manitowoc	1 532	80 421	567	52.5	78 730	115	318	1 071	187	582	7.0	15.5	12.7
55 073	8940	Marathon	4 002	115 400	399	28.8	112 189	89	490	2 499	133	470	7.4	16.3	13.7
55 075	...	Marinette	3 631	40 548	985	11.2	40 280	8	150	63	47	156	6.9	15.8	11.7
55 077	...	Marquette	1 180	12 321	2 193	10.4	12 174	31	49	18	49	149	5.9	14.7	10.5
55 078	...	Menominee	927	3 890	2 926	4.2	416	0	3 469	0	5	55	12.6	23.2	14.9
55 079	5082	Milwaukee	626	959 275	34	1 532.4	718 918	195 470	6 994	15 308	22 585	44 671	7.9	14.1	14.6
55 081	...	Monroe	2 333	36 633	1 085	15.7	35 983	141	301	143	65	234	7.9	16.8	12.4
55 083	...	Oconto	2 585	30 226	1 286	11.7	29 926	18	212	36	34	107	7.2	15.7	11.9
55 085	...	Oneida	2 913	31 679	1 223	10.9	31 320	58	223	56	22	90	6.3	13.6	10.2
55 087	0460	Outagamie	1 659	140 510	338	84.7	136 043	206	1 965	1 904	392	987	8.2	16.1	14.1
55 089	5082	Ozaukee	601	72 831	615	121.2	71 676	492	127	438	98	517	7.3	15.5	12.6
55 091	...	Pepin	602	7 107	2 644	11.8	7 070	2	18	9	8	20	7.1	17.3	11.2
55 093	...	Pierce	1 493	32 765	1 195	21.9	32 366	82	87	172	58	196	7.3	15.5	20.3
55 095	...	Polk	2 376	34 773	1 139	14.6	34 348	23	321	50	31	131	7.3	16.6	11.4
55 097	...	Portage	2 088	61 405	710	29.4	59 972	161	255	786	231	572	6.9	14.8	21.3
55 099	...	Price	3 244	15 600	1 947	4.8	15 479	7	77	27	10	59	6.6	15.4	11.3
55 101	5082	Racine	863	175 034	275	202.8	152 098	16 999	521	1 004	4 412	9 034	7.8	15.8	13.2
55 103	...	Richland	1 518	17 521	1 820	11.5	17 411	12	34	38	26	59	7.0	16.0	12.4
55 105	3620	Rock	1 866	139 510	341	74.8	130 803	6 638	369	985	715	1 754	7.7	15.1	14.1
55 107	...	Rusk	2 365	15 079	1 983	6.4	14 821	31	82	114	31	85	7.2	15.7	12.9
55 109	5120	St. Croix	1 870	50 251	839	26.9	49 895	44	121	148	43	192	8.2	17.3	13.1
55 111	...	Sauk	2 170	46 975	890	21.6	46 459	54	288	79	95	207	7.5	15.5	12.5
55 113	...	Sawyer	3 254	14 181	2 039	4.4	11 962	18	2 167	15	19	101	7.0	15.0	10.4
55 115	...	Shawano	2 312	37 157	1 068	16.1	35 251	42	1 762	70	32	129	7.0	15.2	12.6
55 117	7620	Sheboygan	1 330	103 877	444	78.1	100 389	430	357	2 061	640	1 668	7.1	15.4	13.1
55 119	...	Taylor	2 525	18 901	1 740	7.5	18 807	2	39	44	9	42	8.0	17.5	12.8
55 121	...	Trempealeau	1 901	25 263	1 453	13.3	25 160	12	32	46	13	53	7.0	14.7	12.5
55 123	...	Vernon	2 059	25 617	1 437	12.4	25 509	12	36	42	18	98	7.2	15.8	11.1
55 125	...	Vilas	2 261	17 707	1 804	7.8	16 116	9	1 534	38	10	61	5.9	12.6	9.2
55 127	...	Walworth	1 438	75 000	598	52.2	72 747	454	201	494	1 104	2 017	6.6	13.7	17.5
55 129	...	Washburn	2 097	13 772	2 074	6.6	13 585	25	122	33	7	34	6.5	15.6	10.4
55 131	5082	Washington	1 116	95 328	485	85.4	94 465	125	208	337	193	670	7.6	16.3	13.7
55 133	5082	Waukesha	1 439	304 715	163	211.8	298 313	1 096	672	2 699	1 935	5 448	7.2	15.5	13.1
55 135	...	Waupaca	1 945	46 104	901	23.7	45 695	22	125	92	170	406	7.0	15.6	12.2
55 137	...	Waushara	1 622	19 385	1 711	12.0	19 094	29	70	43	149	379	6.4	14.5	10.5
55 139	0460	Winnebago	1 136	140 320	339	123.5	136 822	697	685	1 728	388	1 144	7.0	13.5	16.3
55 141	...	Wood	2 053	73 605	611	35.9	72 157	90	481	722	155	386	7.5	16.0	12.9
56 000	...	WYOMING	251 501	453 588	X	1.8	427 061	3 606	9 479	2 806	10 636	25 751	7.7	17.5	13.8
56 001	...	Albany	11 069	30 797	1 250	2.8	28 829	253	235	643	837	1 988	6.3	12.0	28.9
56 003	...	Big Horn	8 125	10 525	2 333	1.3	10 209	2	58	24	232	551	7.6	17.5	11.8
56 005	...	Campbell	12 424	29 370	1 318	2.4	28 652	37	323	89	269	882	9.0	21.5	12.6
56 007	...	Carbon	20 452	16 659	1 872	0.8	15 114	100	133	87	1 225	2 315	7.0	17.8	12.3
56 009	...	Converse	11 020	11 128	2 282	1.0	10 716	15	101	33	263	565	8.0	19.6	12.3
56 011	...	Crook	7 404	5 294	2 820	0.7	5 258	1	27	3	5	26	8.1	19.4	10.6
56 013	...	Fremont	23 783	33 662	1 173	1.4	26 766	51	6 222	110	513	1 336	7.9	18.7	12.4
56 015	...	Goshen	5 764	12 373	2 191	2.1	11 750	25	99	16	483	1 078	6.8	16.5	13.2
56 017	...	Hot Springs	5 190	4 809	2 857	0.9	4 660	14	103	2	30	67	5.2	16.0	10.3
56 019	...	Johnson	10 791	6 145	2 738	0.6	6 057	1	61	7	19	78	6.7	15.3	11.3
56 021	1580	Laramie	6 957	73 142	614	10.5	66 280	2 218	528	821	3 295	7 310	8.0	15.6	14.2
56 023	...	Lincoln	10 540	12 625	2 175	1.2	12 431	10	65	38	81	252	9.1	23.0	12.2
56 025	1350	Natrona	13 831	61 226	712	4.4	59 323	458	404	280	761	2 252	7.6	17.1	12.8
56 027	...	Niobrara	6 801	2 499	3 023	0.4	2 449	8	20	3	19	36	6.2	13.5	10.4
56 029	...	Park	17 982	23 178	1 531	1.3	22 580	19	130	106	343	825	7.3	16.4	13.3
56 031	...	Platte	5 400	8 145	2 551	1.5	8 057	5	24	10	49	404	7.2	16.7	11.2
56 033	...	Sheridan	6 536	23 562	1 511	3.6	23 095	36	210	100	121	444	6.2	15.9	11.7

1. MSA = Metropolitan Statistical Area. CMSA = Consolidated MSA. NECMA = New England county metropolitan area. PMSA = Primary MSA. See Appendix A for explanation of these concepts. See Appendix B for list of metropolitan areas identified by type, with component counties. 2. Dry land or land partially or temporarily covered by water. 3. Hispanic persons may be of any race.

STATE County	Population, 1990 (cont'd): Age of population (cont'd), Percent: 25 to 34 years	35 to 44 years	45 to 54 years	55 to 64 years	65 to 74 years	75 years and over	Percent female	Population–Change and components of change: Change, 1980–1990: Number	Percent	Components of change, 1980–1986: Total persons, 1986	Total persons, 1980	Net change: Number	Percent	Natural increase: Births	Deaths
	14	15	16	17	18	19	20	21	22	23	24	25	26	27	28
WISCONSIN—Con.															
Iron	12.9	13.0	10.4	11.6	13.7	10.7	50.6	-577	-8.6	6 200	6 730	-500	-8.0	400	500
Jackson	14.2	14.1	9.9	9.6	9.4	7.7	49.2	-243	-1.4	16 400	16 831	-500	-2.8	1 600	1 100
Jefferson	15.8	14.7	10.5	8.2	7.2	5.9	50.6	1 631	2.5	68 000	66 152	1 800	2.8	6 200	3 500
Juneau	14.9	12.8	10.2	10.2	9.9	7.6	50.6	613	2.9	21 400	21 037	400	1.8	2 200	1 400
Kenosha	17.2	14.5	10.2	8.3	7.2	5.4	51.1	5 044	4.1	120 000	123 137	-3 100	-2.5	11 500	6 400
Kewaunee	15.3	13.9	9.5	8.7	8.5	7.3	49.8	-661	-3.4	20 000	19 539	400	2.2	2 000	1 100
La Crosse	16.2	14.4	8.9	7.6	6.8	6.0	52.0	6 848	7.5	94 100	91 056	3 100	3.4	8 700	4 900
Lafayette	15.6	13.2	9.3	9.6	8.7	6.7	50.6	-1 336	-7.7	17 100	17 412	-400	-2.0	1 900	1 000
Langlade	14.1	13.2	9.9	10.1	10.4	8.6	51.4	-473	-2.4	19 700	19 978	-300	-1.6	1 800	1 400
Lincoln	15.3	13.0	10.8	9.8	8.6	7.6	50.5	438	1.6	28 100	26 555	1 500	5.6	2 400	1 800
Manitowoc	15.4	14.3	10.0	9.2	8.5	7.5	51.1	-2 497	-3.0	82 200	82 918	-700	-0.8	7 900	4 800
Marathon	16.6	15.1	10.1	8.2	7.1	5.6	50.6	4 130	3.7	112 500	111 270	1 200	1.1	11 200	5 100
Marinette	14.7	13.7	10.2	9.4	9.3	8.3	51.1	1 234	3.1	41 000	39 314	1 700	4.3	3 700	2 700
Marquette	13.1	12.7	9.9	12.8	12.2	8.2	50.4	649	5.6	12 800	11 672	1 100	9.7	1 000	900
Menominee	15.1	10.0	7.8	7.9	5.7	2.7	51.1	517	15.3	4 000	3 373	600	17.2	700	200
Milwaukee	18.5	14.2	8.8	8.5	7.5	6.1	52.6	-5 713	-0.6	932 400	964 988	-32 600	-3.4	99 700	56 300
Monroe	14.9	14.6	9.8	8.8	8.4	6.3	49.8	1 559	4.4	36 700	35 074	1 600	4.7	3 700	2 300
Oconto	15.3	13.9	10.0	9.7	9.3	7.1	50.0	1 279	4.4	30 200	28 947	1 200	4.3	2 800	2 000
Oneida	14.3	14.3	11.4	11.8	10.4	7.6	50.8	463	1.5	31 500	31 216	300	0.8	2 800	2 100
Outagamie	18.2	15.1	9.7	7.6	6.1	5.0	50.6	11 778	9.1	135 800	128 732	7 000	5.5	14 000	5 700
Ozaukee	15.3	16.9	12.1	9.2	6.6	4.5	50.5	5 850	8.7	69 100	66 981	2 100	3.1	5 900	2 700
Pepin	14.2	13.7	9.1	8.8	9.0	9.6	50.6	-370	-4.9	7 200	7 477	-300	-3.7	800	500
Pierce	16.3	14.4	8.9	6.6	5.9	4.7	50.2	1 616	5.2	33 800	31 149	2 700	8.6	3 200	1 400
Polk	15.2	14.9	10.0	8.6	8.3	7.6	50.2	2 422	7.5	34 300	32 351	2 000	6.2	3 400	2 200
Portage	16.1	14.2	8.9	7.0	5.9	4.9	50.0	3 985	6.9	58 700	57 420	1 300	2.2	5 500	2 400
Price	14.1	13.3	9.5	10.3	10.1	9.4	49.8	-188	-1.2	16 500	15 788	700	4.7	1 500	1 200
Racine	17.1	15.1	10.4	8.6	6.9	5.1	51.5	1 902	1.1	172 300	173 132	-900	-0.5	17 200	8 400
Richland	14.1	13.8	9.6	9.5	9.4	8.0	50.5	45	0.3	17 100	17 476	-400	-2.2	1 800	1 100
Rock	16.4	14.6	10.6	8.9	7.0	5.6	51.3	90	0.1	137 800	139 420	-1 600	-1.1	13 400	7 300
Rusk	14.1	13.1	9.4	9.4	10.0	8.2	50.6	-510	-3.3	15 700	15 589	100	0.6	1 500	1 000
St. Croix	17.7	16.4	10.1	7.0	5.2	4.9	50.1	6 989	16.2	46 400	43 262	3 200	7.3	4 800	2 500
Sauk	15.9	14.5	9.8	8.6	8.5	7.3	50.8	3 506	8.1	45 500	43 469	2 100	4.8	4 300	1 700
Sawyer	13.1	13.3	10.1	11.7	10.9	8.4	49.5	1 338	10.4	14 200	12 843	1 300	10.2	1 300	1 900
Shawano	14.8	12.6	10.0	9.8	9.7	8.2	50.3	1 229	3.4	36 800	35 928	800	2.3	3 300	4 600
Sheboygan	16.6	14.9	9.9	8.6	7.9	6.7	50.5	2 942	2.9	102 700	100 935	1 700	1.7	9 700	3 600
Taylor	16.2	13.0	9.1	8.2	7.9	7.3	49.6	84	0.4	18 900	18 817	0	0.2	2 200	1 100
Trempealeau	14.7	13.8	10.1	8.8	9.2	9.1	50.2	-895	-3.4	25 900	26 158	-300	-1.0	2 400	1 800
Vernon	14.0	13.8	9.9	9.4	9.9	8.8	50.9	-25	-0.1	26 600	25 642	900	3.6	2 500	1 800
Vilas	11.8	13.0	11.2	13.3	13.6	9.3	50.4	1 172	7.1	17 500	16 535	900	5.7	1 400	1 300
Walworth	15.3	14.3	9.9	8.5	7.6	6.7	50.8	3 493	4.9	71 500	71 507	0	0.0	6 100	4 000
Washburn	13.0	14.2	10.5	10.8	11.0	8.1	50.2	598	4.5	13 800	13 174	600	4.8	1 300	900
Washington	17.0	16.1	11.1	7.8	5.8	4.6	50.2	10 480	12.4	89 400	84 848	4 600	5.4	8 700	3 500
Waukesha	15.9	17.4	12.1	9.0	5.8	4.0	50.4	24 512	8.7	288 800	280 203	8 600	3.1	23 400	10 900
Waupaca	15.2	14.0	9.5	8.9	9.0	8.7	50.7	3 273	7.6	44 500	42 831	1 600	3.8	4 100	3 700
Waushara	13.6	13.5	10.3	11.8	11.0	8.4	50.5	859	4.6	19 600	18 526	1 100	5.7	1 600	1 300
Winnebago	17.5	14.7	9.8	8.3	6.9	5.9	51.0	8 550	6.5	136 400	131 770	4 600	3.5	12 100	6 700
Wood	16.5	14.4	10.0	8.4	7.7	6.5	51.2	806	1.1	77 500	72 799	4 700	6.5	7 500	3 600
WYOMING	16.4	16.4	10.0	7.8	6.1	4.3	50.0	-16 412	-3.5	507 000	470 000	38 000	8.0	64 000	20 000
Albany	17.7	13.8	8.0	5.7	4.4	3.2	48.3	1 735	6.0	29 400	29 062	300	1.0	2 900	1 000
Big Horn	11.5	13.6	10.7	9.9	9.1	8.4	50.1	-1 371	-11.5	12 300	11 896	400	3.7	1 500	700
Campbell	20.5	18.8	8.8	5.1	2.2	1.5	49.1	5 003	20.5	36 700	24 367	12 400	50.7	5 400	700
Carbon	16.9	17.2	10.6	7.9	6.0	4.3	47.4	-5 237	-23.9	19 400	21 896	-2 500	-11.5	2 700	1 000
Converse	15.7	17.2	10.3	8.0	5.4	3.6	51.1	-2 941	-20.9	13 900	14 069	-100	-0.9	2 000	500
Crook	14.4	15.4	11.0	9.1	7.7	4.5	50.1	-14	-0.3	6 000	5 308	700	13.0	800	200
Fremont	14.4	15.5	10.7	8.9	6.9	4.6	50.3	-5 330	-13.7	35 300	38 992	-3 700	-9.5	5 000	1 700
Goshen	14.1	13.8	10.3	9.2	9.0	7.1	51.6	333	2.8	12 600	12 040	600	5.0	1 300	800
Hot Springs	13.0	14.9	11.4	10.5	9.7	9.0	50.8	-901	-15.8	6 100	5 710	300	6.0	600	400
Johnson	12.2	16.0	11.4	9.7	10.2	7.3	50.9	-555	-8.3	6 900	6 700	200	2.3	700	400
Laramie	17.8	15.8	10.2	8.1	6.1	4.2	50.2	4 493	6.5	75 200	68 649	6 600	9.6	8 500	3 200
Lincoln	14.2	14.9	9.7	6.9	6.4	3.6	49.1	448	3.7	15 600	12 177	3 400	28.0	2 200	500
Natrona	16.6	16.5	10.0	8.9	6.7	3.9	50.9	-10 630	-14.8	70 900	71 856	-900	-1.3	9 300	2 600
Niobrara	14.4	13.9	11.3	11.1	9.8	9.3	53.9	-425	-14.5	3 100	2 924	200	5.2	300	200
Park	14.8	15.9	10.6	8.5	7.5	5.8	50.9	1 539	7.1	24 900	21 639	3 200	14.9	2 800	1 000
Platte	12.6	15.8	11.6	9.2	8.5	7.2	50.5	-3 830	-32.0	9 900	11 975	-2 100	-17.4	1 200	500
Sheridan	13.7	17.5	10.8	9.3	8.3	6.7	50.9	-1 486	-5.9	26 000	25 048	900	3.7	2 800	1 400

STATE County	Population–(cont'd) Components of change, 1980-1986 (cont'd) Net migration	Households, 1990 Number	Households, 1990 Percent change, 1980–1990	Households, 1990 Persons per household	Households, 1990 Percent Female family householder[1]	Households, 1990 Percent One-person	Births, 1988 Total	Births, 1988 Rate[2]	Births, 1988 Low birth weight[3] (Number)	Deaths, 1987 Number Total	Deaths, 1987 Number Infant[4]	Deaths, 1987 Rate Total[2]	Deaths, 1987 Rate Infant[5]	Marriages, 1984 Number	Marriages, 1984 Rate[2]
	29	30	31	32	33	34	35	36	37	38	39	40	41	42	43
WISCONSIN—Con.															
Iron	-500	2 602	-2.3	2.32	6.5	29.2	70	11.1	6	86	0	13.7	0.0	62	10.0
Jackson	-1 000	6 253	3.0	2.59	8.3	25.5	249	15.2	8	187	2	11.5	8.7	169	10.3
Jefferson	-900	24 019	7.9	2.67	7.8	22.1	849	12.3	35	581	7	8.5	7.8	570	8.5
Juneau	-300	8 265	8.8	2.59	8.1	24.8	279	12.7	11	238	3	11.0	9.3	205	9.6
Kenosha	-8 200	47 029	9.2	2.67	11.6	23.2	1 934	15.8	105	1 074	21	8.9	10.9	1 221	10.1
Kewaunee	-400	6 756	4.4	2.77	6.1	22.4	227	11.3	6	178	3	8.8	10.0	144	7.1
La Crosse	-800	36 662	14.5	2.54	8.9	26.1	1 362	14.3	71	859	16	9.1	11.7	821	8.7
Lafayette	-1 200	5 876	0.1	2.72	6.8	24.3	215	12.9	8	159	1	9.5	4.3	117	6.8
Langlade	-700	7 563	7.0	2.55	7.5	26.2	280	14.1	12	207	2	10.5	8.0	184	9.2
Lincoln	900	10 159	8.4	2.60	7.2	23.4	316	11.0	15	313	1	11.0	2.9	256	9.1
Manitowoc	-3 800	30 112	5.6	2.62	7.0	24.9	1 040	12.9	59	830	6	10.3	5.3	645	7.8
Marathon	-4 900	41 547	10.2	2.75	7.2	21.0	1 620	14.3	75	881	14	7.8	8.5	900	8.0
Marinette	700	15 542	10.0	2.55	7.6	25.8	513	12.1	25	478	2	11.4	3.7	365	9.1
Marquette	1 000	4 831	10.8	2.52	5.6	23.4	141	10.6	6	146	4	11.1	23.7	100	7.9
Menominee	100	1 079	35.0	3.57	29.9	12.6	113	NA	6	37	2	NA	14.2	24	6.9
Milwaukee	-76 000	373 048	2.6	2.50	15.8	29.4	16 370	17.6	1 284	9 440	172	10.2	10.7	7 721	8.2
Monroe	200	13 144	10.5	2.70	8.2	23.3	568	15.1	22	346	3	9.4	5.4	296	8.2
Oconto	400	11 283	13.0	2.65	6.1	22.5	433	13.9	23	311	4	10.1	9.7	241	8.0
Oneida	-400	12 666	10.9	2.44	7.1	24.7	386	12.1	9	347	4	11.0	10.7	334	10.7
Outagamie	-1 300	50 527	18.2	2.73	7.4	21.4	2 269	16.1	126	930	13	6.7	5.8	1 277	9.6
Ozaukee	-1 100	25 707	18.1	2.79	6.4	17.0	948	13.1	32	462	8	6.5	8.4	588	8.7
Pepin	-500	2 612	2.4	2.66	6.2	25.0	98	13.2	3	72	0	9.9	0.0	73	9.9
Pierce	900	11 011	12.1	2.77	7.0	20.7	452	12.9	21	214	4	6.2	9.2	194	5.9
Polk	800	13 056	14.6	2.62	7.0	23.3	471	13.3	21	358	2	10.2	3.9	306	9.0
Portage	-1 800	21 306	16.3	2.71	7.7	22.0	850	14.2	26	430	5	7.3	6.1	476	8.2
Price	500	6 054	6.1	2.53	6.2	26.2	211	12.8	14	173	0	10.5	0.0	129	7.7
Racine	-9 600	63 736	7.3	2.70	12.3	22.0	2 641	15.2	178	1 428	23	8.3	8.6	1 496	8.7
Richland	-1 000	6 593	5.5	2.62	6.6	24.0	219	12.7	6	194	1	11.2	4.1	134	7.7
Rock	-7 700	52 252	6.6	2.62	10.6	23.4	2 084	15.3	116	1 200	24	8.9	11.4	1 290	9.3
Rusk	-400	5 693	6.7	2.59	7.6	24.6	202	12.9	14	159	5	10.1	24.6	150	9.4
St. Croix	900	17 638	24.6	2.81	6.4	19.7	736	14.9	29	394	4	8.2	4.8	414	9.2
Sauk	-600	17 703	14.1	2.61	7.4	23.8	663	14.3	27	434	5	9.4	7.5	456	10.2
Sawyer	1 900	5 569	19.3	2.50	9.6	25.0	196	13.5	8	169	0	11.9	0.0	112	8.1
Shawano	2 100	13 775	11.6	2.64	6.6	23.1	531	12.9	19	397	6	9.7	11.8	297	8.2
Sheboygan	-4 400	38 592	8.8	2.63	7.1	23.3	1 399	13.6	40	917	20	9.0	14.5	813	7.9
Taylor	-1 100	6 692	8.5	2.79	5.7	21.9	309	16.0	15	160	5	8.4	17.9	145	7.7
Trempealeau	-900	9 495	4.3	2.59	7.4	25.3	316	12.0	8	319	6	12.2	18.5	196	7.5
Vernon	200	9 725	4.8	2.59	6.8	25.8	344	12.9	13	288	3	10.8	9.1	203	7.6
Vilas	800	7 294	16.8	2.40	7.2	23.6	191	10.7	8	209	2	11.9	8.8	140	8.0
Walworth	-2 000	27 620	11.4	2.60	8.0	23.9	1 001	13.6	41	700	6	9.6	6.6	749	10.5
Washburn	300	5 456	11.7	2.49	6.9	26.9	157	11.4	9	154	1	11.1	5.8	117	8.5
Washington	-600	32 977	23.4	2.86	7.0	17.2	1 316	14.1	43	628	9	6.9	6.9	686	7.8
Waukesha	-3 800	105 990	19.7	2.83	6.7	16.6	3 941	13.0	179	1 839	20	6.2	5.3	2 408	8.5
Waupaca	1 200	17 037	13.9	2.62	7.0	23.8	603	13.2	31	626	1	13.8	1.7	438	10.0
Waushara	800	7 616	10.3	2.52	6.7	23.4	231	11.6	10	199	4	10.1	15.4	153	7.8
Winnebago	-800	53 216	13.5	2.52	8.1	25.1	1 901	13.7	91	1 091	11	8.0	5.8	1 155	8.6
Wood	900	27 473	9.6	2.65	8.0	23.5	1 005	12.6	42	638	11	8.1	10.4	712	9.1
WYOMING	-6 000	168 839	1.9	2.63	8.3	24.5	7 162	14.9	504	3 045	69	6.2	9.2	5 783	11.3
Albany	-1 500	11 957	12.4	2.35	8.0	29.3	418	14.6	39	161	1	5.6	2.5	293	9.7
Big Horn	-300	3 905	-5.4	2.65	5.7	25.0	170	14.8	9	117	2	9.9	12.9	88	7.0
Campbell	7 700	9 968	24.5	2.92	7.7	19.1	537	16.4	36	99	7	3.0	12.0	344	9.7
Carbon	-4 300	6 001	-19.7	2.63	7.6	24.7	252	13.7	28	111	2	5.9	7.7	180	8.6
Converse	-1 600	4 046	-13.5	2.73	8.9	21.7	162	13.3	16	79	2	6.2	11.0	181	12.4
Crook	200	1 892	2.2	2.77	5.3	20.6	89	15.3	5	25	0	4.2	0.0	50	8.5
Fremont	-7 000	12 002	-6.7	2.74	10.7	22.2	557	16.4	30	288	6	8.3	10.1	383	10.2
Goshen	200	4 790	7.2	2.54	7.9	25.5	155	12.4	11	133	0	10.5	0.0	227	18.2
Hot Springs	100	1 943	-10.1	2.38	7.8	29.2	44	8.0	2	50	0	8.8	0.0	77	12.6
Johnson	-100	2 397	-3.5	2.50	6.4	25.7	86	13.2	4	64	0	9.6	0.0	79	11.1
Laramie	1 300	28 092	11.1	2.55	9.7	25.3	1 236	16.4	112	466	15	6.2	11.4	1 008	13.8
Lincoln	1 800	4 137	7.2	3.05	5.7	19.3	238	16.4	14	77	4	5.1	15.0	88	5.9
Natrona	-7 700	23 837	-7.8	2.54	9.7	25.9	925	14.3	63	412	7	6.2	7.0	801	10.8
Niobrara	100	1 032	-10.6	2.31	7.7	31.8	31	10.7	2	38	0	12.7	0.0	31	9.1
Park	1 500	8 757	13.2	2.57	7.1	24.2	362	NA	13	164	3	NA	8.8	350	14.2
Platte	-2 700	3 179	-27.4	2.54	6.0	25.8	102	10.6	12	77	0	7.9	0.0	100	9.9
Sheridan	-400	9 426	1.1	2.43	8.4	28.3	287	11.4	11	227	4	8.9	13.2	343	12.6

1. No spouse present. 2. Per 1,000 resident population estimated as of July 1 of the year shown. 3. Under 2,500 grams. 4. Deaths of infants under 1 year old. 5. Deaths of infants under 1 year old per 1,000 live births.

STATE County	Divorces, 1984		Physicians, active non–Federal, 1989		Hospitals, 1989			Nursing homes,[4] 1986		Serious crimes known to police, 1988			Education			
						Beds				Number			Public school enrollment[7]		Attainment,[8] 1980	
	Number	Rate[1]	Number[2]	Rate[3]	Number	Number	Rate[3]	Number	Beds	Total[5]	Violent[6]	Rate[3]	1986–1987	1980	Percent 12 yrs. or more	Percent 16 yrs. or more
	44	45	46	47	48	49	50	51	52	53	54	55	56	57	58	59
WISCONSIN—Con.																
Iron	21	3.4	2	31	0	0	0	2	106	100	3	1 570	902	1 138	62.6	8.5
Jackson	57	3.5	9	55	1	51	311	4	340	483	18	2 932	3 394	3 568	61.2	8.0
Jefferson	207	3.1	56	81	1	92	132	4	583	1 668	57	2 399	10 907	11 374	67.7	12.6
Juneau	81	3.8	15	68	1	100	452	5	243	515	20	2 370	4 103	4 314	59.1	7.7
Kenosha	542	4.5	137	111	2	330	268	12	1 327	5 789	239	4 785	20 331	23 258	64.8	10.7
Kewaunee	37	1.8	9	45	1	23	114	2	157	168	5	839	3 429	3 709	63.0	7.7
La Crosse	364	3.9	326	339	2	625	650	10	1 240	4 157	123	4 343	13 384	14 377	73.5	17.3
Lafayette	38	2.2	5	30	1	28	170	4	163	135	2	819	3 639	3 976	66.8	9.3
Langlade	67	3.4	16	81	1	46	232	1	173	646	30	3 228	3 878	4 047	59.0	8.5
Lincoln	86	3.1	27	94	1	53	184	4	359	685	9	2 378	4 774	5 316	59.6	9.8
Manitowoc	228	2.8	86	107	3	367	456	6	943	2 466	48	3 016	10 961	14 045	66.9	9.9
Marathon	341	3.0	176	155	2	685	602	9	916	3 312	117	2 939	17 412	21 105	64.6	11.6
Marinette	120	3.0	39	91	1	99	230	8	715	1 192	22	2 821	7 319	7 815	64.9	8.6
Marquette	47	3.7	4	29	0	0	0	1	62	247	31	2 123	1 968	2 239	58.6	8.0
Menominee	1	0.3	2	NA	0	0	NA	0	0	193	62	4 657	889	699	40.5	1.6
Milwaukee	3 518	3.7	2 740	295	22	6 404	689	72	10 620	63 167	5 565	6 708	135 988	146 074	68.5	15.7
Monroe	157	4.3	20	53	3	793	2 087	4	494	754	26	2 027	6 099	6 868	64.0	8.9
Oconto	96	3.2	14	44	2	85	270	7	340	462	2	1 635	4 595	6 123	58.9	7.4
Oneida	151	4.8	74	230	2	262	814	4	326	1 247	33	3 868	5 321	6 303	70.5	13.2
Outagamie	460	3.4	213	149	4	526	367	14	1 235	4 358	171	3 316	22 729	23 943	72.3	13.3
Ozaukee	215	3.2	121	164	1	114	155	3	471	1 225	28	1 709	10 800	13 459	79.4	23.8
Pepin	25	3.4	7	95	1	90	1 216	2	190	81	1	1 098	1 707	1 520	58.8	8.6
Pierce	97	2.9	22	62	1	37	104	9	656	613	19	1 768	6 839	6 317	70.0	16.2
Polk	135	4.0	33	92	4	176	490	7	479	603	21	1 714	7 218	6 875	67.4	10.6
Portage	159	2.7	73	120	1	133	219	4	403	2 221	53	3 724	8 947	9 962	68.7	17.5
Price	41	2.4	6	36	1	41	248	3	277	263	23	1 577	3 018	3 291	60.9	8.3
Racine	752	4.4	222	127	3	543	311	12	1 416	9 340	654	5 341	28 573	31 461	67.7	14.0
Richland	38	2.2	13	75	1	37	213	2	201	368	29	2 105	2 193	3 356	63.3	10.4
Rock	632	4.6	168	124	6	541	398	12	1 689	6 746	300	5 055	24 906	29 380	71.1	12.4
Rusk	64	4.0	12	77	1	158	1 013	2	159	165	10	1 040	3 030	3 373	60.6	9.4
St. Croix	117	2.6	34	67	5	376	742	9	752	908	25	1 868	8 324	9 661	73.7	15.1
Sauk	148	3.3	40	85	3	209	445	6	663	1 111	23	2 384	8 221	8 317	65.8	11.2
Sawyer	48	3.5	11	75	1	117	796	4	146	455	7	3 148	2 261	2 441	64.8	11.7
Shawano	87	2.4	25	60	1	53	126	6	564	803	14	2 130	5 513	7 314	57.2	7.7
Sheboygan	329	3.2	110	106	3	376	364	11	1 429	3 468	141	3 559	17 241	18 761	67.8	11.2
Taylor	51	2.7	8	41	1	160	825	5	255	254	7	1 344	3 531	3 954	54.8	7.9
Trempealeau	92	3.5	15	57	3	317	1 205	11	691	350	6	1 332	5 449	5 539	59.9	9.5
Vernon	82	3.1	18	68	2	123	462	4	365	263	7	971	4 851	4 951	59.0	10.0
Vilas	59	3.4	13	72	2	136	751	2	178	611	32	3 494	2 088	3 015	69.9	11.7
Walworth	313	4.4	62	83	1	119	160	12	872	2 632	73	3 587	11 065	13 607	71.0	15.3
Washburn	43	3.1	13	94	2	185	1 331	2	116	293	11	2 085	2 803	2 655	64.5	10.4
Washington	263	3.0	72	76	2	181	190	5	820	2 479	55	2 701	16 107	16 940	72.1	13.8
Waukesha	892	3.2	645	209	7	838	272	17	1 860	7 017	230	2 348	49 943	59 345	81.1	21.5
Waupaca	135	3.1	37	80	3	138	298	13	2 307	1 141	28	2 470	9 316	7 788	62.3	9.3
Waushara	58	3.0	9	45	1	30	149	2	168	522	22	2 676	2 762	3 658	59.0	8.7
Winnebago	479	3.6	231	165	3	807	578	9	1 280	5 523	110	4 000	19 426	23 393	72.0	15.3
Wood	275	3.5	323	403	3	805	1 004	8	691	2 217	113	2 783	12 972	13 522	67.9	11.4
WYOMING	3 705	7.2	670	141	33	3 022	637	39	2 551	18 651	1 477	3 967	101 449	94 542	77.9	17.2
Albany	172	5.7	50	175	1	108	379	1	119	1 694	68	6 059	4 333	4 132	84.7	35.5
Big Horn	60	4.8	7	62	2	146	1 292	3	165	288	22	2 519	2 658	2 607	70.8	12.3
Campbell	299	8.5	31	97	1	104	325	1	120	1 178	143	3 627	7 750	5 235	80.1	13.5
Carbon	135	6.5	18	100	1	78	433	2	138	579	31	3 222	4 075	4 322	75.3	13.8
Converse	101	6.9	7	60	1	44	376	2	74	389	33	3 163	3 004	3 117	76.1	13.4
Crook	30	5.1	2	34	1	48	828	0	0	141	17	2 487	1 219	1 238	72.2	12.8
Fremont	254	6.8	62	186	3	218	653	3	200	1 183	141	3 528	7 561	8 441	73.0	16.3
Goshen	61	4.9	10	80	1	43	344	2	79	361	36	2 958	2 464	2 485	69.9	13.5
Hot Springs	44	7.2	6	111	1	49	907	2	194	240	31	4 382	1 148	1 104	70.3	8.5
Johnson	48	6.8	5	78	1	83	1 297	2	164	151	4	2 381	1 375	1 367	75.9	14.9
Laramie	669	9.1	143	187	4	422	552	3	278	3 192	143	4 394	13 853	13 799	80.1	17.7
Lincoln	54	3.6	10	69	2	33	229	0	0	304	48	2 109	3 799	3 008	74.8	12.5
Natrona	698	9.4	130	207	2	279	444	3	317	3 441	270	5 377	13 359	13 937	82.5	19.7
Niobrara	23	6.8	2	71	1	51	1 821	1	36	96	6	3 331	555	533	70.5	11.6
Park	128	5.2	35	NA	2	285	NA	2	178	705	40	3 020	4 631	4 540	77.9	16.4
Platte	53	5.2	5	52	1	86	896	1	43	240	39	2 549	1 940	2 388	73.5	11.7
Sheridan	196	7.2	48	194	2	427	1 722	5	156	666	50	2 718	4 800	4 755	76.3	17.0

1. Per 1,000 resident population estimated as of July 1 of the year shown. 2. As of end of year. 3. Per 100,000 resident population as of July 1 of the year shown. 4. Preliminary. Covers nursing homes with 3 or more beds. 5. Data for serious crimes have not been adjusted for underreporting, this may affect comparability between geographic areas or over time. 6. Includes murder and nonnegligent manslaughter, forcible rape, robbery, and aggravated assault. 7. The 1986–1987 data are based on administrative reports obtained by the U.S. National Center for Education Statistics. The 1980 data are based on the 1980 Census of Population and Housing. 8. Persons 25 years old or older.

STATE County	Education (cont'd): Local government expenditures for education,[1] 1982: Total (Mil dol)	Education (cont'd): Local government expenditures for education,[1] 1982: Per capita (Dollars)	Social Security Program December 1988: Beneficiaries: Total	Social Security Program December 1988: Beneficiaries: Rate[2]	Social Security Program December 1988: Payments ($1,000)	Supplemental Security Income Program recipients June 1986	Money income: Per capita[3]: 1987 Income, (Dollars)	Money income: Per capita[3]: 1979: Current dollars	Money income: Per capita[3]: 1979: Constant 1987 dollars	Money income: Median household income 1979 (Dollars)	Money income: Percent below poverty level, 1979: Persons	Money income: Percent below poverty level, 1979: Families	Housing units, 1990: Total	Housing units, 1990: Percent change, 1980–1990
	60	61	62	63	64	65	66	67	68	69	70	71	72	73
WISCONSIN—Con.														
Iron	3.3	504	1 845	292.9	864	188	7 397	4 796	7 504	9 944	13.9	10.1	5 243	2.8
Jackson	9.7	575	3 510	214.0	1 534	500	8 787	5 565	8 708	12 574	13.6	11.1	7 627	9.3
Jefferson	29.9	450	12 275	178.2	6 208	974	10 609	7 000	10 953	18 206	6.5	5.0	25 719	7.0
Juneau	10.5	496	4 795	218.9	2 201	502	9 097	5 590	8 747	12 528	11.6	9.1	11 422	14.9
Kenosha	58.9	485	20 450	166.8	10 794	1 682	11 789	7 756	12 136	20 084	7.0	5.6	51 262	7.9
Kewaunee	9.5	479	3 710	184.6	1 758	208	10 196	6 426	10 055	16 519	7.4	5.9	7 544	7.4
La Crosse	33.5	360	15 205	159.2	7 485	1 492	11 092	6 814	10 662	15 900	9.9	5.1	38 239	14.9
Lafayette	10.4	599	2 860	171.3	1 275	244	9 095	5 940	9 294	15 224	11.4	9.0	6 313	0.3
Langlade	11.2	562	4 605	232.6	2 111	526	8 548	5 386	8 427	12 738	13.2	10.4	10 825	10.2
Lincoln	12.9	481	6 135	214.5	2 953	536	9 680	6 160	9 639	14 267	9.3	6.9	13 256	3.7
Manitowoc	28.8	345	16 020	198.3	8 094	1 008	10 473	6 838	10 699	17 622	5.9	4.1	31 843	5.7
Marathon	45.1	402	17 575	155.0	8 563	1 594	10 608	6 697	10 479	17 344	8.1	6.2	43 774	10.1
Marinette	20.0	500	9 665	228.5	4 633	882	8 778	5 788	9 056	13 945	9.0	6.8	25 650	13.7
Marquette	4.3	352	3 450	259.4	1 646	200	9 090	5 708	8 931	12 586	11.9	10.3	8 035	12.7
Menominee	10.2	2 677	8 625	208.8	211	98	5 459	3 525	5 516	13 352	17.9	15.3	1 742	31.3
Milwaukee	471.3	491	169 970	182.7	89 354	21 456	12 278	7 952	12 442	18 122	10.2	8.0	390 715	3.4
Monroe	14.2	396	6 560	174.9	2 768	672	9 487	6 148	9 620	15 095	10.1	7.6	14 135	10.9
Oconto	12.4	425	5 985	192.4	2 736	558	8 707	5 439	8 510	13 463	11.1	8.5	18 832	11.2
Oneida	17.6	559	8 085	252.7	4 027	700	9 755	6 183	9 675	14 521	8.7	6.4	25 173	8.7
Outagamie	57.0	432	20 080	142.6	10 348	1 240	11 796	7 269	11 374	19 415	6.2	4.7	51 923	18.2
Ozaukee	34.3	511	9 465	131.1	5 307	254	15 547	9 640	15 084	25 554	3.3	2.3	26 482	17.6
Pepin	5.1	678	1 630	220.3	722	172	8 880	5 574	8 722	13 902	9.7	8.1	2 919	1.3
Pierce	17.3	546	4 820	137.7	2 248	360	10 415	6 315	9 881	16 801	11.2	6.7	11 536	11.4
Polk	20.1	602	6 950	196.3	3 149	590	9 432	5 795	9 067	14 106	10.7	8.5	18 562	14.4
Portage	23.2	410	7 905	131.8	3 810	682	10 135	6 249	9 778	16 659	11.2	6.8	22 910	15.1
Price	7.7	478	3 775	228.8	1 697	416	8 500	5 248	8 212	11 947	13.7	10.9	9 052	3.7
Racine	86.4	500	29 705	170.9	15 708	2 772	11 985	7 969	12 469	20 944	7.0	5.5	66 945	7.0
Richland	5.7	323	3 465	200.3	1 546	422	8 881	5 787	9 055	13 229	11.8	8.5	7 325	4.9
Rock	69.2	498	22 635	166.1	11 777	2 244	11 445	7 348	11 497	19 154	7.2	5.7	54 840	5.3
Rusk	8.7	551	3 435	220.2	1 498	428	7 811	5 039	7 885	11 565	14.2	11.3	7 904	9.9
St. Croix	21.9	492	5 670	114.8	2 707	468	12 461	7 063	11 051	19 568	6.5	5.3	18 519	24.1
Sauk	22.4	504	8 850	190.3	4 249	780	10 532	6 584	10 302	15 507	9.4	7.2	20 439	17.1
Sawyer	6.6	479	3 480	240.0	1 572	346	7 669	5 070	7 933	11 118	16.2	13.4	13 025	17.8
Shawano	15.5	429	0	0.0	3 681	792	9 170	5 800	9 075	13 932	10.7	8.5	16 737	9.8
Sheboygan	48.7	478	18 525	179.9	9 821	1 020	11 555	7 387	11 558	18 719	4.9	3.7	40 695	9.0
Taylor	9.6	501	3 310	171.5	1 466	296	8 958	5 703	8 923	14 217	11.6	9.3	7 710	7.6
Trempealeau	16.0	612	5 845	222.2	2 494	648	9 476	5 654	8 847	13 566	12.1	8.9	10 097	3.6
Vernon	12.6	480	5 675	213.3	2 397	662	8 766	5 707	8 930	12 546	13.7	10.7	10 830	6.8
Vilas	6.5	380	5 010	279.9	2 433	266	9 295	5 797	9 071	12 373	11.8	9.7	20 225	10.0
Walworth	33.3	467	12 325	167.5	6 441	778	11 168	7 123	11 145	17 457	8.2	5.1	36 937	10.6
Washburn	8.1	608	3 795	275.0	1 729	412	8 277	5 475	8 567	12 046	12.4	10.3	9 829	12.8
Washington	45.0	524	12 600	135.0	6 624	548	12 159	7 609	11 906	21 989	4.6	3.7	34 382	21.2
Waukesha	156.4	553	36 810	121.8	20 293	1 470	14 837	9 205	14 403	25 827	3.1	2.4	110 452	19.3
Waupaca	23.7	548	10 730	234.8	5 100	772	9 926	6 207	9 712	15 286	8.7	6.7	20 141	11.0
Waushara	6.8	364	4 485	225.4	2 106	420	9 552	5 924	9 269	12 734	11.4	8.7	12 246	8.9
Winnebago	55.6	418	22 235	160.7	11 552	1 554	11 811	7 321	11 455	18 063	6.7	4.6	56 123	12.9
Wood	35.8	479	14 020	176.4	6 988	1 178	11 218	6 854	10 724	17 482	7.6	5.8	28 839	10.1
WYOMING	434.0	851	58 571	122.2	28 801	2 519	9 826	7 927	12 403	19 994	7.9	5.8	203 411	8.1
Albany	14.5	479	2 705	94.6	1 352	134	8 841	6 672	10 440	14 644	15.6	8.4	13 844	15.8
Big Horn	12.4	968	2 140	186.1	1 010	88	7 404	6 050	9 466	14 682	12.7	10.9	5 048	4.4
Campbell	39.4	1 223	1 595	48.6	771	52	11 422	9 245	14 466	26 060	4.8	3.1	11 538	21.4
Carbon	25.4	1 120	2 040	110.9	992	78	9 232	8 227	12 873	21 972	6.7	5.1	8 190	-5.4
Converse	15.2	1 012	1 350	110.7	663	50	9 241	8 133	12 726	22 693	6.4	5.2	5 234	-2.2
Crook	5.5	980	790	136.2	356	18	8 287	6 854	10 724	16 557	9.9	7.5	2 605	7.0
Fremont	34.4	895	5 175	152.7	2 408	354	8 550	7 269	11 374	20 461	9.5	7.4	14 437	-0.9
Goshen	11.0	900	2 270	181.6	1 075	146	7 694	6 274	9 817	14 030	11.9	9.0	5 551	10.6
Hot Springs	5.7	950	1 155	210.0	563	70	8 829	7 001	10 954	16 147	7.5	5.0	2 429	-4.3
Johnson	5.5	771	1 105	170.0	532	26	9 644	8 023	12 554	16 506	8.3	5.8	3 112	2.7
Laramie	49.3	693	8 620	114.6	4 170	506	10 597	7 743	12 115	17 630	8.0	6.6	30 507	11.4
Lincoln	12.7	890	1 675	115.5	796	40	7 803	6 442	10 080	18 005	11.5	9.3	5 409	15.8
Natrona	57.0	733	8 375	129.4	4 442	334	10 773	9 353	14 635	22 867	5.8	4.0	29 082	2.1
Niobrara	2.3	730	595	205.2	266	12	8 139	6 481	10 141	12 830	16.0	13.8	1 456	1.5
Park	17.6	750	3 840	158.7	1 925	90	8 968	7 214	11 288	17 734	8.4	5.9	10 306	17.5
Platte	11.2	1 069	1 605	167.2	782	48	9 070	7 597	11 887	19 545	9.7	7.7	4 026	-20.3
Sheridan	16.5	624	4 335	172.7	2 061	184	9 860	7 785	12 181	18 111	6.1	3.8	11 154	2.1

1. Elementary and secondary. 2. Per 1,000 resident population estimated as of July 1 of the year shown. 3. Based on the resident population estimated as of July 1, 1988 for 1987 data and enumerated as of April 1, 1980 for 1979 data.

STATE County	Housing units, 1990 (cont'd)				Civilian labor force, 1990				Private nonfarm establishments, 1988					
	Occupied units						Unemployment				Employment[2]			
		Owner occupied												
	Total	Percent	Median value (Dollars)	Median rent (Dollars)	Total	Percent change, 1989–1990	Total	Rate[1]	Number	Net change, 1987–1988	Total	Percent change, 1987–1988	Manufacturing	Retail trade
	74	75	76	77	78	79	80	81	82	83	84	85	86	87
WISCONSIN—Con.														
Iron	2 602	79.2	30 800	171	2 761	0.7	159	5.8	199	19	1 362	7.4	196	483
Jackson	6 253	72.7	39 600	203	7 866	4.0	485	6.2	388	1	3 364	6.6	344	1 049
Jefferson	24 019	70.6	59 800	308	37 240	-0.8	1 581	4.2	1 526	-6	25 475	9.6	11 576	4 522
Juneau	8 265	75.9	40 700	224	11 526	1.1	688	6.0	471	-12	5 215	4.0	2 321	1 122
Kenosha	47 029	68.8	65 100	347	53 325	-2.1	3 382	6.3	2 439	52	36 902	8.4	13 914	8 199
Kewaunee	6 756	80.8	50 000	204	9 705	-0.3	454	4.7	427	17	4 335	2.4	1 706	859
La Crosse	36 662	62.9	58 400	290	52 593	-4.6	1 980	3.8	2 557	52	44 192	3.2	10 295	11 132
Lafayette	5 876	72.5	39 400	213	8 298	-3.2	428	5.2	345	-6	2 194	7.1	545	538
Langlade	7 563	77.5	37 600	227	9 295	0.2	452	4.9	521	22	4 735	6.5	1 322	1 296
Lincoln	10 159	76.3	43 200	222	15 099	10.5	788	5.2	677	33	7 861	5.1	3 320	1 650
Manitowoc	30 112	73.9	49 500	232	39 838	1.3	2 070	5.2	1 689	-2	27 765	-0.8	10 626	5 315
Marathon	41 547	74.7	54 800	301	63 698	-1.5	2 874	4.5	2 720	58	40 691	4.3	11 919	8 440
Marinette	15 542	77.4	41 400	221	16 762	0.5	1 121	6.7	963	2	14 251	3.9	7 229	2 574
Marquette	4 831	80.6	45 600	228	6 976	4.7	379	5.4	293	4	1 985	12.6	741	459
Menominee	1 079	64.4	48 600	103	923	-3.2	201	21.8	38	-1	438	20.3	257	89
Milwaukee	373 048	52.1	65 300	363	501 062	-2.1	20 603	4.1	21 829	142	432 695	1.5	104 375	84 874
Monroe	13 144	72.8	48 600	251	17 068	-1.1	1 009	5.9	756	13	9 435	3.8	3 102	2 284
Oconto	11 283	81.6	43 200	217	13 507	-7.3	934	6.9	644	-39	6 285	4.0	2 936	1 223
Oneida	12 666	77.4	52 900	258	16 425	1.1	716	4.4	1 035	9	9 115	-2.7	1 703	2 710
Outagamie	50 527	72.3	64 400	327	76 108	-0.7	2 876	3.8	3 114	0	56 287	7.0	18 062	11 515
Ozaukee	25 707	74.4	100 500	431	40 214	-2.3	1 152	2.9	1 949	106	25 145	8.0	10 445	5 264
Pepin	2 612	76.4	40 700	204	3 405	-1.8	160	4.7	181	-4	1 581	0.6	164	440
Pierce	11 011	70.7	65 500	331	16 981	1.7	662	3.9	738	18	6 329	3.9	1 176	1 851
Polk	13 056	77.9	53 600	254	14 998	-0.5	873	5.8	859	-3	7 875	7.7	2 116	1 776
Portage	21 306	70.3	58 800	309	33 019	1.6	1 419	4.3	1 343	59	21 017	6.0	4 155	5 272
Price	6 054	79.6	40 900	223	7 585	7.0	401	5.3	402	-10	4 702	4.6	2 598	680
Racine	63 736	68.3	64 200	327	89 824	-2.2	4 243	4.7	3 889	9	66 224	4.1	26 637	13 365
Richland	6 593	71.9	40 500	229	9 016	11.6	406	4.5	364	-10	3 443	5.4	1 258	886
Rock	52 252	68.2	52 300	303	74 176	-1.2	3 904	5.3	3 038	40	50 000	3.2	18 240	10 997
Rusk	5 693	75.0	36 700	205	7 308	9.7	513	7.0	329	3	3 475	11.1	1 406	680
St. Croix	17 638	74.9	74 400	352	25 481	-2.3	892	3.5	1 086	45	11 554	8.7	3 420	3 019
Sauk	17 703	72.3	55 600	281	28 984	0.7	1 402	4.8	1 325	3	17 182	7.5	5 672	3 659
Sawyer	5 569	74.9	49 500	183	6 715	12.9	449	6.7	452	2	2 302	0.9	304	773
Shawano	13 775	77.1	45 500	229	17 744	2.4	909	5.1	808	-4	8 071	6.5	2 129	1 978
Sheboygan	38 592	70.3	59 400	290	58 459	-2.3	2 687	4.6	2 261	8	42 520	2.5	18 825	7 467
Taylor	6 692	78.9	43 500	220	10 532	-1.3	639	6.1	423	6	5 284	0.5	2 453	667
Trempealeau	9 495	73.0	40 900	202	14 542	0.6	806	5.5	659	8	7 332	11.7	3 132	1 335
Vernon	9 725	76.2	43 600	196	13 410	11.1	622	4.6	590	14	4 662	9.7	943	1 326
Vilas	7 294	79.2	58 900	222	7 736	-2.1	433	5.6	797	33	4 632	4.8	661	1 479
Walworth	27 620	66.9	69 100	342	39 013	-1.0	1 294	3.3	2 010	15	23 006	5.4	8 085	5 626
Washburn	5 456	76.3	46 900	219	6 303	7.0	432	6.9	478	11	3 147	8.4	776	966
Washington	32 977	73.9	83 900	390	50 008	-2.1	1 848	3.7	2 073	92	28 286	7.2	10 865	5 946
Waukesha	105 990	77.3	96 300	480	167 852	-2.0	5 274	3.1	9 457	338	142 709	7.1	40 888	26 586
Waupaca	17 037	76.1	50 000	250	23 023	0.5	1 257	5.5	1 133	-4	13 168	-5.7	5 212	2 833
Waushara	7 616	80.3	45 300	221	8 094	-5.3	521	6.4	427	7	2 997	13.4	455	809
Winnebago	53 216	66.6	60 200	318	78 202	-0.7	3 020	3.9	3 718	115	69 820	7.8	28 963	12 783
Wood	27 473	73.3	50 500	272	38 349	-0.9	1 719	4.5	1 860	-9	31 836	4.1	9 737	7 125
WYOMING	168 839	67.8	61 600	270	246 000	2.9	13 000	5.4	X	X	121 556	-0.7	8 320	33 196
Albany	11 957	49.2	67 300	296	17 088	7.5	550	3.2	777	-16	6 465	3.4	508	2 397
Big Horn	3 905	73.9	44 300	204	5 265	2.8	351	6.7	246	-18	1 580	12.6	300	354
Campbell	9 968	70.5	68 500	299	16 504	4.5	1 058	6.4	909	-19	10 029	0.2	167	1 908
Carbon	6 001	69.1	52 700	231	8 213	4.0	490	6.0	488	1	3 556	-2.3	469	1 038
Converse	4 046	71.0	51 000	229	5 206	-2.5	335	6.4	343	0	2 419	-1.1	20	614
Crook	1 892	78.3	54 400	231	2 859	0.3	117	4.1	164	4	1 014	9.0	187	200
Fremont	12 002	69.6	50 600	236	16 303	-0.9	1 138	7.0	1 011	-10	7 196	2.6	582	2 139
Goshen	4 790	70.1	52 100	216	6 256	-0.4	284	4.5	324	-10	2 427	4.7	315	681
Hot Springs	1 943	67.1	53 400	219	2 778	-1.6	113	4.1	180	-10	1 097	-7.6	0	287
Johnson	2 397	69.7	56 600	242	3 546	-1.9	195	5.5	233	-5	1 227	4.4	39	300
Laramie	28 092	65.5	69 800	312	37 644	1.9	1 916	5.1	1 888	-12	19 306	0.9	1 209	6 435
Lincoln	4 137	80.0	60 200	248	6 015	3.2	408	6.8	351	-25	2 787	-6.4	460	673
Natrona	23 837	68.9	53 100	252	32 012	3.5	1 854	5.8	2 310	-60	19 111	-2.1	1 454	5 513
Niobrara	1 032	71.4	33 700	175	1 497	0.7	58	3.9	79	-6	350	-18.4	0	179
Park	8 757	67.7	65 600	266	13 842	0.9	657	4.7	848	-47	5 144	-0.1	501	1 514
Platte	3 179	75.6	52 100	223	4 458	0.9	231	5.2	253	6	1 723	0.8	14	369
Sheridan	9 426	68.4	58 200	245	13 203	3.2	681	5.2	809	20	5 717	1.1	362	1 803

1. Percent of total civilian labor force. 2. For week including March 12. Excludes government employees, self-employed persons, farm workers, domestic service workers, railroad employees subject to the Railroad Retirement Act, and employees on oceanborne vessels or in foreign countries.

STATE County	Private nonfarm establishments, 1988 (cont'd): Employment[1] (cont'd): Finance, insurance, and real estate	Employment[1] (cont'd): Services	Annual payroll: Total (Mil dol)	Annual payroll: Average per employee (Dollars)	Personal income, 1989: Total (Mil dol)	Percent change, 1988–1989	Wages and salaries[2] (Mil dol)	Proprietor's income (Mil dol)	Dividends, interest, & rent (Mil dol)	Transfer payments (Mil dol)	Per capita[3]: Dollars	Per capita[3]: Rank	Earnings, 1989: Total (Mil dol)	Percent by selected industries: Farm	Goods-related[4]: Total
	88	89	90	91	92	93	94	95	96	97	98	99	100	101	102
WISCONSIN—Con.															
Iron	60	443	13	9 583	71	7.3	22	6	16	22	11 141	2 624	28	2.2	23.6
Jackson	156	652	62	18 383	218	12.6	102	38	39	47	13 233	1 801	140	16.5	NA
Jefferson	634	5 620	423	16 617	1 065	7.7	603	100	176	165	15 317	868	703	4.5	47.1
Juneau	145	946	78	14 864	290	10.7	148	45	46	61	13 150	1 839	193	10.8	36.3
Kenosha	1 015	8 669	808	21 893	2 097	2.4	955	110	278	320	17 006	435	1 066	1.1	44.9
Kewaunee	215	887	63	14 541	289	10.7	105	51	57	43	14 337	1 272	156	22.0	31.6
La Crosse	1 648	13 201	797	18 025	1 550	7.3	1 140	117	265	238	16 127	610	1 257	1.2	29.3
Lafayette	134	255	32	14 470	244	17.5	67	67	56	34	14 760	1 105	133	39.1	15.6
Langlade	181	951	71	14 992	256	11.3	119	39	46	57	12 931	1 937	159	12.3	NA
Lincoln	457	1 386	130	16 528	360	5.3	187	33	56	77	12 506	2 113	220	3.3	39.9
Manitowoc	1 092	7 021	464	16 704	1 192	8.0	652	119	210	203	14 825	1 066	770	6.2	46.6
Marathon	3 632	8 841	797	19 583	1 734	9.7	1 140	191	261	233	15 243	888	1 331	5.9	36.5
Marinette	592	2 280	267	18 732	555	7.5	353	70	93	118	12 929	1 941	422	3.8	52.1
Marquette	71	333	30	15 124	171	13.8	53	30	31	38	12 557	2 092	83	18.8	36.2
Menominee	0	46	5	10 660	(5)	(5)	(5)	(5)	(5)	(5)	(5)	(5)	(5)	(5)	(5)
Milwaukee	35 416	144 371	9 177	21 209	16 783	6.5	13 591	909	2 923	3 022	18 062	287	14 501	0.1	29.8
Monroe	542	2 012	132	14 008	458	7.5	264	69	83	95	12 065	2 304	333	10.4	22.6
Oconto	223	1 233	94	14 940	397	10.5	144	67	66	71	12 629	2 062	212	15.8	36.5
Oneida	392	2 936	146	16 055	457	7.5	253	37	91	107	14 204	1 344	290	1.1	26.4
Outagamie	2 674	13 410	1 221	21 698	2 241	7.3	1 760	177	360	267	15 654	757	1 937	2.3	NA
Ozaukee	932	5 092	491	19 523	1 649	7.6	576	121	319	132	22 373	85	697	2.5	42.4
Pepin	212	256	23	14 361	100	9.5	38	21	20	20	13 630	1 612	59	22.5	NA
Pierce	343	1 652	90	14 147	523	7.0	164	61	80	66	14 726	1 114	225	10.2	17.7
Polk	305	2 550	116	14 681	489	7.4	170	72	91	89	13 619	1 621	242	11.8	28.1
Portage	4 391	3 903	372	17 694	876	6.7	538	94	125	125	14 419	1 244	632	6.4	25.0
Price	145	882	86	18 372	216	4.4	119	23	39	46	13 090	1 869	142	3.8	54.8
Racine	2 693	15 964	1 372	20 720	3 046	7.0	1 851	166	475	448	17 426	374	2 017	1.0	50.8
Richland	178	590	52	14 975	210	8.9	73	43	45	42	12 034	2 318	116	15.3	23.8
Rock	1 700	11 522	1 014	20 278	2 194	6.2	1 389	188	333	334	16 140	606	1 577	2.4	46.2
Rusk	117	865	53	15 156	180	6.4	87	27	28	44	11 486	2 505	114	9.7	38.4
St. Croix	461	2 812	193	16 688	916	9.6	308	104	145	88	18 055	289	412	10.4	31.9
Sauk	562	3 904	291	16 951	722	11.7	442	98	133	114	15 360	856	540	8.2	35.5
Sawyer	137	724	28	12 189	164	6.8	63	24	35	47	11 141	2 623	86	5.2	26.1
Shawano	428	1 660	119	14 792	[5]497	[5]7.3	[5]185	[5]68	[5]95	[5]106	[5]11 860	[5]2 374	(5)	[5]16.1	[5]24.9
Sheboygan	1 984	8 890	831	19 545	1 783	8.2	1 161	125	310	242	17 270	402	1 286	2.3	53.3
Taylor	222	896	102	19 316	263	7.0	149	44	41	42	13 552	1 660	193	10.3	43.8
Trempealeau	301	1 545	102	13 945	364	9.9	165	70	59	70	13 833	1 516	235	16.8	35.6
Vernon	225	1 236	60	12 826	328	10.0	103	61	67	66	12 345	2 184	164	19.5	13.0
Vilas	188	1 624	64	13 919	236	7.4	79	30	68	58	13 041	1 892	109	1.2	24.9
Walworth	803	5 017	364	15 842	1 204	7.9	593	125	209	169	16 171	600	718	4.3	35.8
Washburn	130	799	44	13 879	172	7.8	71	23	33	51	12 372	2 173	94	7.8	23.3
Washington	1 347	5 663	505	17 840	1 688	8.7	746	126	279	165	17 734	328	872	3.5	47.0
Waukesha	7 633	33 528	3 132	21 944	6 385	7.4	3 887	390	1 017	525	20 691	139	4 277	0.6	42.0
Waupaca	528	2 511	218	16 558	676	8.8	311	77	116	135	14 604	1 166	388	9.1	37.6
Waushara	153	839	37	12 195	281	13.6	72	53	50	54	14 013	1 431	125	28.1	9.0
Winnebago	4 696	15 052	1 471	21 068	2 291	6.6	1 694	141	400	314	16 410	543	1 835	1.1	53.5
Wood	958	8 898	661	20 761	1 243	6.2	880	110	222	185	15 507	802	989	3.0	40.3
WYOMING	7 211	30 051	2 259	X	6 903	4.7	4 273	602	1 391	999	14 554	X	4 875	0.9	28.1
Albany	358	2 371	85	13 190	404	5.6	238	30	79	64	14 170	1 361	267	0.6	11.0
Big Horn	82	188	27	16 997	130	2.0	65	12	28	29	11 495	2 501	77	2.1	26.6
Campbell	318	1 953	251	25 032	501	2.4	395	44	62	37	15 663	755	439	0.7	53.2
Carbon	176	835	64	18 081	262	8.3	173	25	47	38	14 564	1 182	199	4.5	30.2
Converse	174	441	46	19 069	154	0.3	97	10	33	22	13 180	1 823	107	0.6	40.2
Crook	48	98	18	17 490	77	-2.4	31	5	20	11	13 161	1 833	36	-0.7	34.0
Fremont	343	2 467	110	15 252	397	2.6	219	39	79	77	11 869	2 371	258	0.9	17.8
Goshen	110	770	32	13 176	155	2.5	65	17	38	33	12 428	2 152	82	7.6	15.7
Hot Springs	58	452	15	13 708	75	1.3	37	6	16	18	13 840	1 510	43	-0.7	25.5
Johnson	211	352	15	12 076	89	3.5	41	8	28	15	13 836	1 514	49	1.6	22.9
Laramie	1 757	5 346	304	15 756	1 158	5.7	776	71	194	189	15 139	931	848	0.5	11.3
Lincoln	104	321	62	22 146	161	0.2	102	18	32	24	11 209	2 599	121	3.0	40.9
Natrona	1 515	4 394	354	18 522	1 021	3.9	608	102	232	135	16 241	583	710	0.0	27.2
Niobrara	X	74	4	10 526	38	1.7	13	5	11	8	13 624	1 617	18	6.2	NA
Park	285	1 442	78	15 137	360	6.0	192	38	91	54	14 828	1 063	231	-0.2	29.9
Platte	68	517	29	16 581	115	6.4	65	9	28	21	12 042	2 316	74	3.5	8.7
Sheridan	501	1 808	84	14 659	376	6.1	166	38	111	66	15 173	916	205	0.7	18.8

1. For week including March 12. Excludes government employees, self-employed persons, farm workers, domestic service workers, railroad employees subject to the Railroad Retirement Act, and employees on oceanborne vessels or in foreign countries. 2. Includes other labor income. 3. Based on the resident population estimated as of July 1 of the year shown. 4. Covers mining, construction, and manufacturing. 5. Menominee County included with Shawano County.

STATE County	Earnings, 1989 (cont'd): Percent by selected industries (cont'd): Goods-related[1]: Manu-facturing	Service-related & other[2]: Total	Service-related & other[2]: Retail trade	Service-related & other[2]: Finance, insur-ance, & real estate	Service-related & other[2]: Services	Govern-ment	Agriculture, 1987: Farms: Number	Farms: Percent with: Less than 50 acres	Farms: Percent with: 500 acres and over	Farm operators, percent: Whose principal occu-pation is farming	Farm operators, percent: Residing on farm operated	Land in farms: Acreage (1,000)	Land in farms: Percent change, 1982–1987	Land in farms: Acres: Average size of farm	Land in farms: Acres: Total irrigated (1,000)	Land in farms: Acres: Total cropland (1,000)
	103	104	105	106	107	108	109	110	111	112	113	114	115	116	117	118
WISCONSIN—Con.																
Iron	11.1	51.7	20.3	3.3	20.5	22.5	57	14.0	10.5	49.1	77.2	14	-2.4	242	D	6
Jackson	6.7	NA	9.5	2.0	NA	14.2	793	10.5	11.3	73.6	85.0	229	-7.4	289	3	135
Jefferson	42.7	38.2	9.6	2.0	16.6	10.2	1 440	22.8	5.0	63.3	80.9	256	-5.0	178	3	207
Juneau	32.8	37.6	8.6	3.3	14.7	15.4	762	14.3	9.7	69.0	85.4	191	-3.1	250	8	120
Kenosha	38.6	38.6	10.3	2.4	18.9	15.3	505	33.9	10.1	57.4	79.0	101	-0.1	199	0	90
Kewaunee	24.8	34.3	7.2	1.9	12.9	12.1	991	14.7	4.7	73.4	86.0	184	0.9	185	0	151
La Crosse	22.9	56.8	10.3	3.4	26.0	12.6	821	15.7	8.5	67.6	83.8	193	-4.6	235	1	103
Lafayette	12.3	30.6	5.1	2.9	7.8	14.6	1 341	13.2	12.1	82.9	77.5	377	-2.5	281	0	294
Langlade	18.7	NA	13.7	2.6	17.9	13.8	510	14.3	9.8	76.5	85.7	132	-9.1	260	8	83
Lincoln	35.1	41.3	10.1	5.8	14.5	15.6	507	11.6	5.7	63.1	88.4	109	-11.8	215	0	56
Manitowoc	41.1	36.4	8.3	2.1	17.2	10.9	1 529	19.8	5.2	72.0	86.5	277	-2.3	181	1	236
Marathon	31.3	47.0	8.2	7.3	17.6	10.6	3 078	17.9	4.7	73.8	85.3	582	-4.0	189	5	367
Marinette	48.4	33.1	7.8	2.3	13.1	10.9	716	13.4	8.8	64.8	87.2	169	-6.9	236	2	102
Marquette	25.3	32.4	8.2	3.2	13.0	12.7	502	14.5	14.7	60.0	80.5	146	-3.4	290	5	96
Menominee	(3)	(3)	(3)	(3)	(3)	(3)	1	100.0	0.0	0.0	100.0	D	D	D	0	0
Milwaukee	25.9	58.0	8.6	9.0	26.9	12.1	132	62.1	1.5	50.8	62.1	D	D	D	0	9
Monroe	18.4	36.8	9.5	3.9	11.6	30.1	1 642	12.2	6.1	70.8	87.4	356	-3.5	217	2	197
Oconto	31.5	34.7	7.5	1.7	16.0	13.0	1 119	12.9	6.2	68.2	86.9	232	-4.9	208	1	164
Oneida	18.3	55.7	15.2	2.9	28.1	16.8	106	25.5	19.8	51.9	82.1	44	8.0	419	3	17
Outagamie	32.7	NA	9.0	7.0	18.4	8.4	1 584	23.5	5.0	68.8	85.9	282	-4.3	178	0	241
Ozaukee	36.4	44.6	9.5	3.7	21.3	10.5	483	28.4	6.4	64.4	77.0	85	-4.6	176	0	75
Pepin	4.5	51.3	9.2	5.4	15.2	15.9	446	11.2	9.2	78.5	85.4	113	-5.4	253	1	73
Pierce	12.5	43.3	8.6	2.7	18.9	28.8	1 240	17.4	7.9	65.2	85.6	270	-9.7	217	D	197
Polk	20.0	43.8	9.5	2.9	19.5	16.2	1 467	16.2	7.4	68.2	86.3	315	-6.9	215	1	201
Portage	20.9	52.6	9.8	13.9	16.1	15.9	1 081	11.8	9.9	68.1	87.8	282	-0.6	261	62	203
Price	51.7	29.0	6.7	1.8	12.6	12.4	485	8.0	8.7	62.5	87.2	125	-6.2	257	0	48
Racine	45.8	37.2	8.7	2.2	18.3	10.9	710	38.3	9.0	58.6	82.0	133	-2.7	188	1	118
Richland	18.8	45.4	10.5	2.3	21.2	15.4	1 165	9.9	8.5	74.0	85.2	291	-2.8	250	2	154
Rock	41.5	40.7	9.6	2.7	18.7	10.6	1 518	31.7	12.6	63.4	80.2	358	-1.2	236	10	320
Rusk	35.4	33.7	7.4	2.0	14.0	18.3	713	9.1	7.6	77.4	88.2	175	-7.3	245	0	90
St. Croix	25.3	45.5	11.1	2.5	21.0	12.1	1 576	19.7	8.2	61.8	85.7	334	-5.2	212	7	262
Sauk	25.6	46.7	9.7	2.5	20.4	9.6	1 502	14.2	10.3	72.4	85.4	370	-4.7	246	9	243
Sawyer	17.5	51.1	14.7	3.0	26.4	17.5	204	13.7	11.3	57.8	80.9	51	4.9	251	0	26
Shawano	[3]19.6	[3]43.3	[3]9.9	[3]2.3	[3]17.6	[3]15.7	1 631	11.8	5.3	76.0	87.5	326	-2.2	200	1	223
Sheboygan	47.9	34.9	8.6	4.5	14.7	9.5	1 213	28.6	6.6	65.3	84.3	210	-3.8	173	0	179
Taylor	39.0	36.6	7.7	2.4	12.9	9.2	1 079	9.8	8.9	79.5	90.6	265	2.6	246	0	142
Trempealeau	31.2	34.0	8.1	2.4	15.1	13.6	1 498	12.3	9.3	72.8	83.6	367	-4.5	245	4	233
Vernon	8.6	50.9	10.7	4.5	17.7	16.6	2 193	16.8	4.2	74.7	85.4	404	-3.0	184	0	234
Vilas	12.2	59.0	17.1	2.2	33.2	14.9	46	23.9	8.7	47.8	71.7	9	15.6	188	1	4
Walworth	28.3	41.4	10.4	1.7	19.1	18.5	980	29.3	13.8	65.2	79.6	239	-3.9	244	1	208
Washburn	17.9	47.6	13.9	3.2	20.6	21.3	372	10.8	13.7	64.5	86.8	101	-5.9	271	2	49
Washington	38.5	36.5	9.0	4.2	15.0	13.0	967	27.3	4.4	67.3	81.9	156	-4.6	162	0	132
Waukesha	33.1	49.2	7.8	4.5	20.0	8.3	818	40.7	6.1	54.4	77.9	127	-15.1	155	3	105
Waupaca	33.6	39.4	11.6	2.9	14.9	13.9	1 365	15.5	6.7	69.6	85.5	272	-0.7	200	7	193
Waushara	5.0	49.7	11.3	3.4	14.7	13.1	705	16.9	11.6	67.5	85.7	177	-4.5	252	44	131
Winnebago	48.2	33.4	6.7	2.8	16.5	12.0	994	21.6	7.4	69.2	86.1	190	-0.4	191	0	161
Wood	35.6	47.3	9.9	1.7	25.6	9.4	1 157	16.2	6.2	64.8	87.1	237	-2.2	205	3	147
WYOMING	5.0	46.0	9.4	3.6	17.3	25.1	9 205	19.4	49.2	64.7	75.4	33 595	0.3	3 650	1 518	2 839
Albany	5.3	42.8	10.2	3.6	20.6	45.5	287	21.6	61.3	59.6	75.3	1 820	0.2	6 342	118	96
Big Horn	12.0	41.7	6.7	3.0	11.2	29.6	570	22.8	28.1	66.1	75.6	468	-0.9	821	106	131
Campbell	0.6	32.7	6.7	1.9	12.6	13.4	489	14.1	69.9	68.5	77.3	2 894	1.8	5 918	3	159
Carbon	10.8	43.1	8.9	1.9	10.7	22.2	320	18.4	64.7	72.5	67.8	2 768	-0.9	8 652	146	161
Converse	1.6	39.9	8.4	2.2	9.5	19.2	337	14.8	63.5	68.0	78.9	2 473	3.3	7 337	52	78
Crook	14.0	36.0	9.1	2.9	8.1	30.6	461	9.8	73.3	70.1	77.0	1 509	-2.5	3 274	4	157
Fremont	4.6	52.2	11.1	3.4	25.7	29.0	908	26.2	27.4	55.1	80.7	2 465	0.7	2 714	136	D
Goshen	10.3	46.5	11.2	3.4	14.5	30.2	717	12.0	52.0	78.0	72.9	1 317	4.6	1 836	103	319
Hot Springs	0.7	47.8	8.5	2.7	19.8	27.4	158	20.9	36.7	59.5	74.7	981	-7.1	6 212	26	D
Johnson	2.2	47.4	12.9	4.1	13.6	28.1	272	14.0	64.0	72.1	71.0	1 936	0.1	7 119	36	48
Laramie	4.6	48.6	8.9	5.5	16.4	39.7	595	14.3	56.8	63.7	72.8	1 601	-2.9	2 691	48	342
Lincoln	11.9	36.3	7.8	2.8	8.1	19.8	528	23.1	26.5	57.8	74.6	592	7.7	1 121	91	129
Natrona	7.0	56.6	10.7	5.3	23.5	16.2	304	30.3	46.4	51.0	66.8	2 634	-7.9	8 663	35	49
Niobrara	NA	NA	12.4	4.2	14.3	36.7	282	9.9	81.9	76.2	73.4	1 358	1.7	4 816	8	79
Park	4.0	42.4	10.1	2.6	18.6	27.9	618	27.0	27.5	59.7	80.1	957	-11.0	1 549	112	135
Platte	0.6	62.7	8.3	1.8	12.6	25.2	484	15.7	57.6	66.3	74.6	1 337	2.7	2 762	64	207
Sheridan	3.3	50.6	11.2	5.0	20.8	29.9	586	25.3	45.2	63.7	75.9	1 337	2.3	2 281	53	119

1. Covers mining, construction, and manufacturing. 2. Covers private sector earnings in agricultural services, forestry, and fisheries; transportation and public utilities; wholesale trade; retail trade; finance, insurance, and real estate; and services. 3. Menominee County included with Shawano County.

STATE County	Agriculture, 1987 (cont'd)								Manufactures, 1987						
	Value of land and buildings		Value of products sold				Percent of farms with sales of		Establishments		All employees			Production workers	
	Average per farm ($1,000)	Average per acre (Dollars)	Total (Mil dol)	Average per farm (Dollars)	Percent from: Crops	Percent from: Livestock and poultry[1]	$10,000 or more	$100,000 or more	Total	Percent with 20 or more em-ployees	Number (1,000)	Percent change, 1982–1987	Annual payroll (Mil dol)	Number (1,000)	Work hours (Mil)
	119	120	121	122	123	124	125	126	127	128	129	130	131	132	133
WISCONSIN—Con.															
Iron	D	D	D	D	NA	NA	31.6	5.3	13	23.1	0.2	0.0	2.2	0.2	0.3
Jackson	210	736	61	76 592	35.9	64.1	69.6	19.9	22	22.7	0.4	-20.0	6.0	0.2	0.4
Jefferson	194	1 034	101	70 418	28.0	72.0	62.2	17.6	152	50.7	10.8	21.3	230.4	7.3	14.2
Juneau	217	860	42	54 962	29.1	70.9	64.7	13.3	36	44.4	2.0	11.1	38.0	1.6	3.2
Kenosha	282	1 349	33	65 212	41.2	58.8	60.8	24.4	160	33.8	12.6	-11.3	376.0	9.7	20.0
Kewaunee	182	970	70	70 313	16.3	83.7	72.1	23.0	35	34.3	1.6	-5.9	30.6	1.3	2.6
La Crosse	179	758	45	55 304	12.0	88.0	67.5	17.4	138	38.4	10.3	3.0	226.0	6.7	13.1
Lafayette	243	851	127	94 386	15.5	84.5	86.3	35.0	26	30.8	0.6	100.0	8.1	0.5	0.9
Langlade	177	666	41	81 235	44.6	55.4	71.0	22.9	44	36.4	1.3	0.0	22.7	1.0	2.1
Lincoln	128	576	22	43 908	12.4	87.6	59.6	9.5	73	35.6	3.4	21.4	68.8	2.7	5.4
Manitowoc	187	1 058	116	76 025	11.4	88.6	72.0	26.1	150	50.0	10.8	-12.2	233.8	7.7	15.3
Marathon	141	751	183	59 616	17.2	82.8	72.3	17.9	190	37.9	11.2	-7.4	276.7	8.2	16.2
Marinette	158	690	39	54 346	11.5	88.5	58.4	16.3	97	35.1	7.2	18.0	165.1	5.6	11.0
Marquette	197	674	28	55 585	34.1	65.9	53.6	17.3	23	21.7	0.6	0.0	9.3	0.4	0.8
Menominee	D	D	D	D	NA	NA	0.0	0.0	8	25.0	D	D	D	D	D
Milwaukee	199	2 802	9	67 232	94.1	5.9	45.5	15.2	1 683	38.6	107.0	-17.2	2 995.2	66.9	132.4
Monroe	162	732	88	53 379	21.0	79.0	68.6	15.1	48	31.2	2.8	55.6	44.4	1.9	3.7
Oconto	154	760	62	55 632	12.9	87.1	67.7	18.2	70	38.6	2.8	55.6	50.8	2.3	4.9
Oneida	247	566	9	89 153	65.5	34.5	35.8	17.9	54	20.4	1.7	-15.0	37.7	1.3	2.8
Outagamie	202	1 141	116	73 005	15.6	84.4	71.2	27.1	206	43.7	16.8	-7.7	439.7	11.7	24.1
Ozaukee	234	1 333	31	64 907	31.8	68.2	64.2	22.8	194	42.8	9.4	19.0	228.3	6.4	12.8
Pepin	145	560	25	56 818	16.4	83.6	75.6	17.9	10	30.0	0.2	100.0	2.9	0.1	0.2
Pierce	171	760	68	54 478	18.5	81.5	66.9	18.1	35	28.6	1.1	10.0	19.7	0.8	1.6
Polk	143	687	71	48 334	9.3	90.7	59.7	16.2	69	40.6	2.1	5.0	37.9	1.6	3.2
Portage	226	848	90	82 799	49.5	50.5	62.9	17.8	67	35.8	3.9	-2.5	95.8	3.1	6.3
Price	137	455	16	33 390	16.7	83.3	48.0	4.9	64	29.7	2.6	44.4	56.2	2.0	3.7
Racine	261	1 413	55	77 275	52.1	47.9	58.7	20.0	384	37.5	25.5	5.8	718.3	14.2	26.8
Richland	153	622	61	52 221	10.2	89.8	70.7	14.0	27	33.3	1.2	33.3	23.1	0.9	1.8
Rock	273	1 165	117	77 374	36.4	63.6	64.6	23.5	200	35.0	17.5	10.8	484.7	12.9	24.8
Rusk	124	491	31	43 101	5.4	94.6	66.5	9.7	36	30.6	1.4	75.0	24.7	1.2	2.4
St. Croix	170	780	89	56 625	15.7	84.3	64.5	19.0	91	31.9	3.1	-3.1	64.5	2.2	4.4
Sauk	201	827	112	74 546	11.3	88.7	72.5	23.0	102	41.2	5.1	37.8	90.3	4.0	7.8
Sawyer	123	493	10	47 024	27.5	72.5	51.5	16.2	39	7.7	0.4	33.3	8.3	0.3	0.7
Shawano	159	814	102	62 796	6.8	93.2	73.9	21.2	85	24.7	2.1	16.7	35.7	1.6	3.0
Sheboygan	177	1 005	81	66 950	14.1	85.9	63.7	24.2	236	53.0	18.7	14.0	443.8	12.4	24.9
Taylor	133	532	62	57 721	3.5	96.5	72.3	17.8	50	26.0	2.7	28.6	51.6	2.1	4.0
Trempealeau	149	618	95	63 677	12.7	87.3	72.2	18.2	53	28.3	2.5	66.7	40.6	2.1	4.7
Vernon	140	731	93	42 575	9.5	90.5	65.9	9.7	45	17.8	0.7	-12.5	11.0	0.6	1.0
Vilas	341	1 811	5	114 488	97.2	2.8	32.6	15.2	40	17.5	0.7	0.0	9.6	0.5	1.0
Walworth	287	1 252	81	82 263	34.6	65.4	69.1	25.9	192	39.6	7.0	12.9	147.1	5.3	10.7
Washburn	141	601	15	40 029	27.7	72.3	54.6	9.9	40	17.5	0.5	25.0	8.1	0.4	0.8
Washington	213	1 332	61	63 011	19.0	81.0	63.4	20.9	208	33.2	9.4	-4.1	213.3	6.7	13.6
Waukesha	250	1 650	41	49 512	42.9	57.1	49.0	13.8	938	40.2	38.2	14.4	1 005.8	24.9	50.7
Waupaca	170	834	77	56 673	13.4	86.6	64.7	18.2	102	36.3	4.7	30.6	93.4	3.7	7.3
Waushara	228	927	56	79 380	57.9	42.1	64.1	17.6	28	17.9	0.4	33.3	5.7	0.3	0.5
Winnebago	190	972	56	56 538	22.1	77.9	66.3	19.4	294	51.0	27.8	21.9	749.7	16.7	33.5
Wood	179	884	73	63 316	33.9	66.1	63.6	17.8	102	46.1	10.2	10.9	297.8	7.4	14.4
WYOMING	533	147	677	73 517	18.4	81.6	59.5	17.2	500	16.0	7.7	-22.2	179.7	5.4	10.7
Albany	1 013	159	32	111 359	2.4	97.6	58.9	16.7	27	22.2	0.4	-33.3	8.2	0.2	0.5
Big Horn	287	342	37	65 257	52.7	47.3	58.8	19.6	15	20.0	0.3	0.0	5.4	0.2	0.4
Campbell	504	83	28	57 940	10.1	89.9	60.3	16.2	22	4.5	0.1	-66.7	2.7	0.1	0.1
Carbon	1 021	119	45	139 579	3.9	96.1	65.9	30.6	21	23.8	D	D	D	D	D
Converse	748	106	26	75 988	4.5	95.5	62.3	22.8	6	0.0	0.0	0.0	0.2	0.0	0.0
Crook	315	98	23	50 386	8.2	91.8	67.0	15.2	13	23.1	0.2	0.0	3.1	0.1	0.3
Fremont	417	153	40	43 601	22.9	77.1	48.8	11.7	42	16.7	D	D	D	D	D
Goshen	358	212	86	119 272	26.8	73.2	78.7	25.0	14	7.1	D	D	D	D	D
Hot Springs	684	111	9	58 331	8.4	91.6	52.5	14.6	3	33.3	D	D	D	D	D
Johnson	676	95	20	73 679	2.8	97.2	70.6	24.6	12	8.3	0.1	0.0	1.3	0.1	0.1
Laramie	418	156	40	67 711	29.9	70.1	60.3	15.6	39	35.9	1.1	-21.4	25.6	0.7	1.6
Lincoln	333	311	21	40 285	13.0	87.0	54.7	11.2	29	10.3	0.4	33.3	14.3	0.3	0.6
Natrona	1 074	123	19	63 799	6.4	93.6	48.4	15.1	92	10.9	1.4	-36.4	33.8	0.9	1.8
Niobrara	421	89	18	63 647	7.6	92.4	74.8	16.3	3	0.0	D	D	D	D	D
Park	514	318	50	80 824	39.4	60.6	50.2	16.8	30	10.0	0.4	-60.0	7.4	0.3	0.6
Platte	456	174	51	106 202	14.8	85.2	64.0	16.5	6	0.0	0.0	0.0	0.2	0.0	0.0
Sheridan	570	248	26	44 499	6.7	93.3	50.2	10.4	26	11.5	D	D	D	D	D

1. Includes livestock and poultry products.

STATE County	Manufactures, 1987 (cont'd) — Production workers (cont'd) — Wages — Total (Mil dol)	Average per worker (Dollars)	Value added by manufacture (Mil dol)	Value of shipments (Mil dol)	New capital expenditures (Mil dol)	Value of construction authorized by building permits, 1990 — Total[1] ($1,000)	Nonresidential — Total ($1,000)	Nonresidential — Percent — Office	Industrial	Stores	Residential — New construction ($1,000)	Number of housing units	Alterations and additions ($1,000)
	134	135	136	137	138	139	140	141	142	143	144	145	146
WISCONSIN—Con.													
Iron	1.5	7 500	6.4	8.9	D	4 316	1 038	0.0	60.9	20.6	2 243	38	448
Jackson	3.8	19 000	12.5	47.1	0.5	1 382	25	0.0	0.0	0.0	816	31	159
Jefferson	136.2	18 658	609.2	1 426.3	45.4	44 345	9 153	11.1	28.1	28.1	22 439	316	3 226
Juneau	25.2	15 750	104.7	228.6	5.6	2 781	790	23.2	10.0	7.6	1 363	27	135
Kenosha	267.6	27 588	795.3	2 360.7	20.9	167 303	74 239	7.4	9.1	32.4	82 432	1 294	4 929
Kewaunee	21.8	16 769	61.8	134.8	3.4	7 703	2 932	2.2	7.6	42.5	3 615	61	591
La Crosse	125.2	18 687	494.2	1 026.8	29.7	66 504	23 676	11.3	10.0	29.5	29 989	451	2 593
Lafayette	5.3	10 600	72.1	203.3	1.3	2 592	878	0.0	83.5	10.8	1 346	25	168
Langlade	17.3	17 300	69.3	136.7	1.8	11 187	6 258	0.0	61.2	23.6	3 680	79	543
Lincoln	49.5	18 333	205.2	377.3	12.1	22 452	8 021	2.3	26.4	28.3	9 607	220	1 294
Manitowoc	151.4	19 662	473.9	984.6	35.8	36 239	7 920	4.2	12.3	39.0	15 680	247	4 524
Marathon	182.5	22 256	628.2	1 843.0	58.2	101 369	35 520	11.0	54.2	3.0	40 059	613	5 034
Marinette	118.2	21 107	476.8	976.8	25.8	13 795	4 200	61.8	10.0	4.3	6 519	132	1 299
Marquette	6.6	16 500	22.5	42.1	2.2	5 222	1 281	8.0	67.1	0.0	1 803	33	488
Menominee	D	D	D	D	D	1 580	5	0.0	0.0	0.0	1 332	29	147
Milwaukee	1 704.8	25 483	6 027.2	12 144.9	324.5	507 345	198 131	30.9	39.3	9.3	139 228	2 902	29 599
Monroe	26.5	13 947	173.0	421.6	5.3	12 970	5 150	1.9	85.4	3.5	6 443	110	293
Oconto	39.0	16 957	140.7	321.1	12.4	12 995	3 274	11.3	8.1	10.3	7 018	152	1 214
Oneida	27.4	21 077	78.5	191.0	7.7	25 154	1 705	12.3	2.1	33.5	13 979	277	4 524
Outagamie	281.1	24 026	1 109.8	2 714.6	121.3	125 903	41 663	18.1	25.5	46.9	58 916	854	4 421
Ozaukee	131.7	20 578	534.3	1 200.5	26.5	107 780	17 812	0.0	45.1	41.1	75 005	705	5 419
Pepin	2.1	21 000	10.2	37.0	0.4	1 655	392	46.8	0.0	0.0	531	8	129
Pierce	13.4	16 750	51.3	149.6	2.9	16 866	3 846	0.0	7.3	3.5	8 545	128	953
Polk	24.8	15 500	116.7	293.5	7.5	17 256	4 688	14.9	14.1	32.1	9 154	185	2 038
Portage	69.0	22 258	379.2	696.7	32.2	52 166	8 956	16.3	22.3	14.5	21 699	370	1 237
Price	35.6	17 800	109.5	251.3	D	10 204	3 495	10.5	20.9	48.9	5 301	111	1 154
Racine	297.7	20 965	1 943.3	3 071.7	126.9	134 104	36 628	50.9	7.3	13.6	75 810	866	7 954
Richland	14.4	16 000	61.7	200.6	2.8	4 806	2 208	8.3	28.6	14.7	1 978	35	250
Rock	323.7	25 093	1 602.6	4 289.2	43.2	67 559	18 636	12.2	30.2	16.2	37 429	618	2 716
Rusk	19.9	16 583	69.7	153.0	1.9	4 121	2 860	0.0	0.6	0.0	1 096	50	71
St. Croix	39.1	17 773	168.7	359.3	13.5	43 370	10 040	14.8	8.5	23.7	24 428	299	2 039
Sauk	61.4	15 350	226.0	558.6	20.6	32 108	10 709	6.7	49.1	14.3	14 595	274	1 834
Sawyer	6.3	21 000	36.5	62.8	D	11 587	834	4.7	0.0	4.2	7 611	175	1 235
Shawano	24.5	15 312	78.1	217.9	9.6	13 316	3 772	13.3	1.2	19.4	5 808	101	1 167
Sheboygan	262.8	21 194	945.0	2 077.3	84.5	56 882	11 997	5.5	23.0	37.2	26 314	326	7 580
Taylor	32.5	15 476	171.1	375.3	D	4 130	1 036	17.7	61.0	0.0	2 658	50	24
Trempealeau	29.4	14 000	97.6	342.3	11.3	6 805	861	18.0	61.0	2.0	4 868	116	328
Vernon	7.8	13 000	42.4	105.9	1.7	3 797	1 582	0.0	12.8	55.7	1 673	35	227
Vilas	6.4	12 800	23.9	44.4	1.8	21 441	2 568	7.4	13.6	42.7	11 870	224	3 580
Walworth	97.6	18 415	389.2	813.6	33.9	108 575	15 050	35.0	28.0	11.5	68 920	979	7 452
Washburn	6.1	15 250	18.8	32.7	1.1	12 435	4 411	22.4	5.1	2.2	5 897	142	735
Washington	130.0	19 403	471.6	979.6	25.9	152 413	38 173	40.7	25.1	14.8	92 574	1 376	5 208
Waukesha	570.6	22 916	2 633.1	4 779.3	164.9	405 109	59 646	19.6	30.3	35.1	274 675	3 183	16 179
Waupaca	65.1	17 595	206.4	516.9	13.3	19 113	4 952	3.2	24.8	39.5	9 750	262	1 511
Waushara	3.4	11 333	14.0	26.8	0.8	10 351	1 623	3.9	21.6	6.3	6 282	129	1 302
Winnebago	394.7	23 635	1 671.6	3 462.6	119.5	88 020	16 474	42.7	10.4	18.3	54 614	1 041	7 159
Wood	198.1	26 770	691.2	1 677.0	96.2	42 152	7 096	6.8	16.1	38.5	23 555	399	2 613
WYOMING	118.6	21 963	492.8	2 074.3	65.3	211 938	105 477	2.1	78.6	11.7	62 055	692	10 423
Albany	5.4	27 000	17.3	34.7	D	4 323	80	100.0	0.0	0.0	1 276	24	418
Big Horn	3.8	19 000	6.4	45.0	1.1	624	271	0.0	18.8	64.6	128	3	123
Campbell	1.3	13 000	5.4	11.5	0.1	9 399	4 749	0.0	3.6	54.7	1 720	15	661
Carbon	D	D	D	D	D	4 491	761	1.3	0.0	0.0	324	9	577
Converse	0.1	NA	0.5	0.8	0.0	371	74	0.0	0.0	40.4	3	0	56
Crook	2.5	25 000	6.6	17.0	0.4	292	34	0.0	0.0	0.0	45	1	46
Fremont	D	D	D	D	D	5 271	1 094	14.6	0.0	16.1	2 736	58	751
Goshen	D	D	D	D	D	1 658	1 032	33.9	0.0	14.5	369	6	98
Hot SpringsL/D	D	D	D	D	434	85	0.0	0.0	0.0	93	1	137	
Johnson	1.1	11 000	1.6	6.8	0.1	368	66	0.0	0.0	37.8	77	1	37
Laramie	16.8	24 000	34.2	306.1	5.4	101 947	86 871	0.0	93.4	5.3	7 618	79	1 032
Lincoln	9.9	33 000	42.2	114.5	D	620	240	0.0	0.0	5.0	167	3	106
Natrona	21.6	24 000	68.7	495.8	6.4	9 922	629	0.0	0.0	42.6	3 191	30	2 290
Niobrara	D	D	D	D	D	12	0	NA	NA	NA	0	0	2
Park	4.8	16 000	20.3	39.7	0.3	2 042	744	0.0	41.5	52.8	900	16	137
Platte	0.1	NA	0.5	1.0	0.0	1 161	33	0.0	0.0	0.0	122	2	61
Sheridan	D	D	D	D	D	4 961	3 154	15.4	0.0	75.9	738	10	331

1. Includes nonresidential additions and alterations, residential nonhousekeeping buildings, and residential garages and carports not shown separately.

STATE County	Wholesale trade, 1987				Retail trade, all establishments, 1987				Retail trade, establishments with payroll, 1987					
						Sales				Sales				
											Per capita[2] (Dollars)			
	Establishments	Sales (Mil dol)	Paid employees[1]	Annual payroll (Mil dol)	Number	Total (Mil dol)	Percent change, 1982–1987	Per capita[2] (Dollars)	Number	Total (Mil dol)	General merchandise stores	Food stores	Apparel & accessory stores	Eating and drinking places
	147	148	149	150	151	152	153	154	155	156	157	158	159	160
WISCONSIN—Con.														
Iron	11	8.3	46	0.8	128	35.0	11.8	5 553	66	33.1	D	1 996	0	578
Jackson	25	25.0	196	2.6	226	73.9	2.2	4 532	138	70.8	71	1 021	122	539
Jefferson	106	235.6	1 096	17.9	629	309.7	39.8	4 555	410	299.5	715	1 013	125	585
Juneau	39	41.7	249	3.4	306	92.1	11.1	4 262	167	86.5	121	712	42	393
Kenosha	117	489.6	1 221	25.7	1 126	587.4	29.2	4 882	753	572.1	480	916	261	559
Kewaunee	28	33.2	243	3.2	231	66.8	25.8	3 307	124	62.4	D	815	38	391
La Crosse	186	1 428.4	3 592	86.1	985	682.0	33.3	7 186	732	670.5	1 191	1 082	297	835
Lafayette	47	55.3	271	4.1	177	42.5	23.9	2 547	96	38.2	D	616	58	D
Langlade	50	95.8	444	7.0	288	111.2	4.9	5 643	144	105.1	689	1 248	168	468
Lincoln	33	55.1	320	5.2	372	123.1	41.0	4 334	187	116.8	253	1 173	91	371
Manitowoc	103	213.2	1 112	17.2	813	342.0	19.1	4 227	494	331.6	597	1 089	91	455
Marathon	235	659.6	2 920	57.2	1 143	653.3	44.1	5 818	691	638.2	1 009	1 071	222	488
Marinette	55	66.2	529	8.7	559	197.3	25.8	4 685	316	186.4	439	1 079	219	422
Marquette	12	35.0	118	2.5	171	32.6	43.6	2 489	83	29.6	70	611	D	506
Menominee	1	D	D	D	0	0.0	0.0	0	0	0.0	0	0	0	0
Milwaukee	1 700	8 928.6	24 774	571.2	8 181	5 941.9	30.9	6 396	5 680	5 839.6	809	1 192	334	726
Monroe	61	95.8	436	6.9	398	176.1	31.8	4 772	236	167.0	652	1 031	91	486
Oconto	41	35.0	179	2.8	382	98.9	44.6	3 222	178	89.2	51	884	D	384
Oneida	41	54.5	304	6.2	552	222.5	23.6	7 063	349	215.1	705	1 278	365	737
Outagamie	277	1 848.7	3 517	83.9	1 218	927.7	46.1	6 713	895	915.8	D	987	262	615
Ozaukee	177	449.1	1 302	30.2	712	383.2	42.0	5 420	423	371.1	237	1 023	117	512
Pepin	19	47.8	244	4.3	94	31.7	36.6	4 349	62	30.4	D	956	D	447
Pierce	43	74.7	394	8.1	382	129.8	39.3	3 741	244	123.2	22	766	54	499
Polk	49	59.7	336	5.9	445	145.3	29.8	4 151	260	136.9	74	1 081	61	464
Portage	92	422.8	1 400	26.5	629	337.0	38.6	5 693	377	327.6	858	924	193	677
Price	19	20.4	109	1.9	261	62.3	17.5	3 778	135	56.8	68	1 171	133	260
Racine	234	732.7	2 316	47.8	1 617	1 062.4	44.3	6 187	1 095	1 041.5	812	1 115	247	562
Richland	30	53.4	261	3.3	194	77.5	25.0	4 481	123	74.2	D	1 128	178	282
Rock	207	709.6	2 575	52.4	1 343	866.9	39.1	6 412	911	850.8	875	1 324	190	634
Rusk	30	17.3	120	1.8	188	50.8	14.9	3 235	95	45.2	D	909	143	D
St. Croix	51	64.8	433	7.8	452	240.0	59.9	4 989	279	231.0	450	970	60	486
Sauk	88	231.2	955	18.8	594	274.9	39.5	5 964	383	267.4	496	1 547	175	745
Sawyer	18	13.5	88	1.1	261	81.8	47.7	5 761	146	76.8	90	2 019	142	527
Shawano	56	136.5	565	9.2	462	147.0	30.9	3 594	251	138.6	240	908	88	417
Sheboygan	133	576.3	1 647	35.9	957	541.6	40.7	5 289	594	530.4	857	1 145	112	497
Taylor	27	66.1	368	5.8	242	65.2	42.0	3 412	99	57.0	D	867	44	268
Trempealeau	59	87.5	397	5.2	368	115.6	32.1	4 410	196	107.9	63	931	29	364
Vernon	47	63.7	391	5.1	291	79.4	25.4	2 986	179	76.3	D	698	186	274
Vilas	27	35.3	129	2.1	496	122.3	50.6	6 950	282	113.6	133	1 821	151	900
Walworth	122	357.3	1 163	23.3	883	402.4	28.3	5 520	566	389.3	422	1 178	292	770
Washburn	20	34.7	148	2.3	267	100.0	82.5	7 198	157	95.0	D	1 996	148	569
Washington	120	316.6	1 097	23.1	860	434.6	49.3	4 782	507	422.4	492	1 059	120	499
Waukesha	1 101	5 930.5	12 853	339.8	2 724	2 158.6	56.3	7 315	1 722	2 118.4	899	1 296	247	588
Waupaca	67	132.9	598	11.0	640	215.5	29.7	4 747	342	202.8	326	1 124	68	570
Waushara	32	39.2	245	3.5	227	69.0	17.1	3 503	131	64.5	63	875	D	297
Winnebago	220	461.3	2 334	44.4	1 457	879.2	55.5	6 431	940	859.9	812	1 053	274	624
Wood	105	321.3	1 054	21.1	962	593.9	45.1	7 537	606	580.5	1 222	1 246	184	513
WYOMING	1 024	2 224.7	6 369	125.6	6 023	2 614.2	-7.2	5 338	3 726	2 521.9	537	1 103	215	556
Albany	29	22.9	125	2.0	338	161.9	5.3	5 602	227	158.7	373	1 197	242	675
Big Horn	18	17.4	91	1.2	140	24.3	-18.5	2 056	74	22.2	75	730	63	283
Campbell	87	369.1	609	14.8	336	158.1	-15.9	4 718	187	153.8	441	1 212	184	470
Carbon	25	18.5	107	2.0	236	91.8	-23.9	4 909	157	87.5	D	1 221	108	490
Converse	14	11.7	85	1.3	154	48.5	-30.4	3 822	85	46.2	D	898	117	374
Crook	9	7.7	60	1.0	85	14.8	1.4	2 512	50	13.6	D	556	D	355
Fremont	54	83.3	274	3.8	456	167.2	-15.1	4 834	275	159.9	514	1 122	190	424
Goshen	33	88.5	278	3.5	153	46.1	-1.9	3 628	90	44.0	D	922	157	377
Hot Springs	8	D	D	D	87	23.0	-30.5	4 043	52	21.8	D	D	123	323
Johnson	11	D	D	D	116	26.0	-33.3	3 878	64	23.8	D	D	145	410
Laramie	116	198.2	793	14.8	722	484.6	23.4	6 401	464	474.0	864	960	247	681
Lincoln	23	17.2	122	1.5	207	53.5	-19.5	3 543	115	50.1	170	704	70	269
Natrona	276	776.6	1 947	44.0	785	449.1	-10.5	6 774	492	437.3	808	1 506	239	631
Niobrara	2	D	D	D	45	12.9	-25.0	4 312	28	12.2	D	D	D	422
Park	54	46.0	245	4.4	380	131.2	-3.7	5 422	235	124.8	1 020	882	203	626
Platte	13	15.8	86	0.9	138	36.4	-10.1	3 712	77	34.3	D	1 032	83	372
Sheridan	42	93.1	341	5.7	340	146.2	3.8	5 710	213	139.6	474	1 322	281	679

1. For pay period including March 12. 2. Based on the estimated population as of July 1 of the year shown.

STATE County	Retail trade, establishments with payroll, 1987 (cont'd): Paid employees[1]	Retail trade, establishments with payroll, 1987 (cont'd): Annual payroll (Mil dol)	Taxable service industries–establishments with payroll, 1987: Number	Taxable service industries: Receipts (Mil dol): Total	Receipts: Selected kinds of business: Hotels, motels and other lodging places	Receipts: Selected kinds of business: Health services	Receipts: Selected kinds of business: Legal services	Taxable service industries: Paid employees	Taxable service industries: Annual payroll (Mil dol)	Bank deposits,[2] June 1989: Total (Mil dol)	Bank deposits,[2] June 1989: Percent change, 1988–1989	Savings capital,[3] September 1989: Total (Mil dol)	Savings capital,[3] September 1989: Percent change, 1988–1989
	161	162	163	164	165	166	167	168	169	170	171	172	173
WISCONSIN—Con.													
Iron	448	3.0	32	7.0	D	2.6	0.2	337	2.1	37	2.7	9.0	-20.3
Jackson	1 048	7.7	60	12.0	2.3	5.7	1.1	392	4.5	99	4.1	19.8	3.0
Jefferson	4 498	33.6	329	76.2	6.0	22.8	3.8	2 206	26.6	518	4.5	112.8	-4.2
Juneau	1 150	8.9	102	21.8	3.0	5.9	1.1	652	6.8	139	4.1	39.7	0.1
Kenosha	7 830	69.4	659	151.6	3.8	76.3	8.6	4 436	60.0	619	6.4	332.1	1.3
Kewaunee	918	6.8	79	14.7	0.6	6.0	1.2	500	5.8	175	3.1	38.8	4.9
La Crosse	10 562	80.1	583	244.9	14.1	113.8	10.0	5 824	103.0	640	3.8	361.1	-1.4
Lafayette	467	4.2	46	4.6	D	2.1	0.8	149	1.0	166	-1.4	7.0	3.7
Langlade	1 224	11.1	95	20.3	1.0	8.9	0.6	572	6.9	104	4.9	37.5	11.1
Lincoln	1 558	12.6	142	24.4	1.5	11.8	2.6	855	9.4	130	6.7	65.1	9.8
Manitowoc	5 423	39.8	371	105.7	13.2	42.2	6.0	3 561	44.0	643	1.5	198.0	0.4
Marathon	8 200	70.2	609	231.0	7.8	77.8	18.1	5 329	89.0	816	7.1	232.8	9.3
Marinette	2 674	20.9	171	37.9	3.9	16.6	2.2	1 318	15.2	337	0.5	75.8	6.0
Marquette	439	3.1	54	7.9	2.1	2.7	D	239	2.4	82	3.1	9.3	3.0
Menominee	0	0.0	2	D	0.0	D	0.0	D	D	NA	NA	0.0	NA
Milwaukee	80 363	723.0	6 408	3 063.2	107.0	806.8	333.4	78 562	1 336.1	8 093	0.1	4 793.5	0.5
Monroe	2 306	17.9	143	33.8	3.5	9.7	2.1	1 088	12.8	217	4.3	74.2	-3.7
Oconto	1 181	9.0	122	19.1	1.5	10.0	1.6	694	6.4	164	2.1	21.1	4.4
Oneida	2 609	24.7	268	71.0	8.6	37.2	5.4	2 184	29.0	270	-0.6	85.9	3.5
Outagamie	12 041	105.0	774	288.7	17.4	86.5	15.8	8 396	113.1	985	9.0	381.8	3.5
Ozaukee	4 970	45.0	466	126.5	3.6	56.1	4.8	3 389	50.2	454	7.3	237.2	0.9
Pepin	381	3.2	21	4.6	0.0	2.7	D	174	1.8	75	1.5	22.6	1.1
Pierce	1 951	13.6	151	36.0	0.3	17.1	3.0	1 058	13.6	259	5.4	42.9	-12.3
Polk	1 812	15.8	193	40.4	1.2	15.5	2.9	1 476	16.4	252	1.0	63.5	7.2
Portage	5 031	38.4	276	81.9	9.9	26.3	3.0	2 205	31.9	386	9.0	203.5	0.2
Price	715	6.3	74	11.3	1.2	5.5	1.4	444	4.4	118	2.7	36.0	3.5
Racine	13 302	117.1	1 004	350.0	5.2	134.7	20.7	9 606	141.1	1 318	6.1	446.8	0.4
Richland	934	7.4	59	9.5	0.1	4.1	0.6	260	3.4	127	5.4	48.6	-5.4
Rock	10 984	96.6	702	209.3	17.7	87.3	13.5	6 739	92.4	901	5.4	255.5	0.0
Rusk	572	4.6	58	9.3	0.9	4.9	0.3	307	3.7	90	1.8	18.1	14.2
St. Croix	2 832	22.4	242	54.5	3.8	13.3	6.8	1 507	22.8	293	8.0	56.0	-8.6
Sauk	3 675	30.5	306	84.4	13.6	22.0	3.7	2 099	27.8	464	8.6	81.1	-1.7
Sawyer	767	8.7	109	11.9	3.7	3.4	0.4	358	3.8	103	1.3	21.5	5.3
Shawano	1 921	16.3	137	25.4	1.6	13.2	1.2	856	10.1	310	1.9	37.9	14.6
Sheboygan	7 349	59.9	488	191.7	15.1	56.1	7.0	5 037	73.8	837	3.5	236.9	-0.8
Taylor	671	5.6	78	15.0	D	7.1	1.1	423	6.2	135	2.9	61.8	4.6
Trempealeau	1 376	10.6	103	17.9	1.6	7.6	2.1	638	6.4	192	3.2	37.4	3.1
Vernon	1 170	8.7	86	11.2	0.3	4.6	1.1	363	4.6	175	0.3	63.1	-2.3
Vilas	1 460	13.4	164	30.0	7.5	12.8	0.9	811	10.8	144	3.7	10.5	16.5
Walworth	5 590	45.4	458	123.8	39.9	25.1	6.9	3 698	42.6	508	4.1	150.3	3.9
Washburn	1 091	9.3	94	15.4	2.5	3.9	0.8	454	5.6	93	3.7	20.0	-3.8
Washington	5 717	44.7	394	105.3	4.4	32.5	4.9	3 377	38.3	558	4.5	221.8	3.8
Waukesha	24 700	230.1	2 311	933.0	36.3	212.8	24.9	21 693	370.6	1 838	5.3	1 016.9	0.9
Waupaca	2 920	23.2	247	50.5	1.8	20.2	2.4	1 559	18.9	426	4.3	131.7	1.8
Waushara	808	6.8	76	12.3	1.2	5.2	0.9	480	4.0	112	-0.7	21.1	6.1
Winnebago	11 722	101.9	877	295.6	D	116.4	10.7	8 004	122.7	827	5.9	358.1	-0.2
Wood	6 401	58.1	390	202.3	D	129.2	5.6	4 437	87.1	581	2.6	211.7	4.9
WYOMING	33 263	307.8	3 802	883.5	184.0	217.0	80.9	21 791	289.7	3 621	-2.3	1 002.1	-16.0
Albany	2 453	18.4	231	61.8	8.8	17.3	3.4	1 468	22.5	176	-7.9	76.1	-14.4
Big Horn	405	2.7	51	5.0	D	1.6	0.3	123	1.5	88	-10.5	30.7	-12.0
Campbell	1 802	18.2	255	62.7	6.5	13.8	3.0	1 394	19.6	236	-1.7	23.3	-46.2
Carbon	1 151	10.6	113	31.0	9.8	7.5	1.1	770	9.3	151	-1.0	38.9	-12.8
Converse	603	5.4	83	11.0	3.3	2.9	0.8	366	3.1	90	-5.7	6.9	-34.8
Crook	223	1.5	24	3.0	1.0	D	D	83	0.6	50	-5.7	0.0	NA
Fremont	2 114	19.1	274	66.6	5.2	36.7	4.1	1 643	25.3	189	1.0	72.5	-11.4
Goshen	609	4.9	65	10.0	1.4	3.0	0.8	297	2.8	115	0.5	61.8	-2.3
Hot Springs	317	2.8	49	7.2	2.0	1.6	0.4	232	2.4	53	-7.6	8.7	-0.2
Johnson	331	3.1	62	7.1	3.2	0.6	1.2	181	1.8	70	-5.9	28.0	-11.0
Laramie	6 119	60.0	510	136.8	20.6	39.7	20.6	3 676	50.7	383	-1.6	252.6	-14.4
Lincoln	706	5.2	76	7.1	1.8	1.4	0.5	193	1.8	101	-10.1	5.6	-2.7
Natrona	5 315	53.9	595	147.5	9.3	36.9	16.2	3 562	54.2	495	-8.6	133.6	-20.3
Niobrara	156	1.4	19	1.5	0.5	D	0.1	68	0.5	32	-6.2	0.0	NA
Park	1 527	15.2	254	61.9	31.9	9.9	2.0	1 208	17.0	245	-1.8	36.2	-26.7
Platte	401	3.3	52	7.2	1.8	1.7	1.2	204	2.0	83	1.2	11.1	2.0
Sheridan	1 967	18.2	212	49.9	8.8	12.3	4.9	1 372	16.3	184	-4.3	103.2	-17.1

1. For the period including March 12 of the year shown. 2. Includes deposits for all insured and reporting noninsured commercial and mutual savings banks. 3. Includes savings capital for all FSLIC insured savings institutions.

STATE County	Federal funds and grants, 1989							Local government finances, 1981–1982							
	Expenditures		Per capita[1] (Dollars)					General revenue						Direct general expenditure	
									Intergovernmental		Taxes				
												Per capita[2]			
	Total (Mil dol)	Percent change, 1988–1989	Total	Direct payments for individuals	Procurement contract awards	Salaries and wages	Grant awards	Total (Mil dol)	Total (Mil dol)	Percent from state	Total (Mil dol)	Total (Dollars)	Property (Dollars)	Total (Mil dol)	Percent change, 1977–1982
	174	175	176	177	178	179	180	181	182	183	184	185	186	187	188
WISCONSIN—Con.															
Iron	22.8	12.0	3 558	2 577	297	173	460	8.0	4.2	94.1	2.8	437	432	8.3	53.8
Jackson	56.0	-12.5	3 412	1 901	43	147	912	21.5	11.2	95.1	6.1	365	361	20.7	35.6
Jefferson	172.9	12.8	2 488	1 656	129	94	378	76.2	33.1	95.1	26.1	392	387	70.6	37.3
Juneau	80.7	9.8	3 652	2 003	492	364	475	26.1	12.6	91.0	8.4	400	394	25.2	63.0
Kenosha	281.2	-0.8	2 281	1 767	37	88	326	175.8	84.7	89.7	54.8	451	448	169.1	71.6
Kewaunee	48.5	20.0	2 414	1 576	22	170	236	23.4	10.7	96.7	7.4	373	370	23.7	46.9
La Crosse	249.8	10.9	2 600	1 735	290	187	323	110.6	47.4	88.2	34.2	367	358	110.7	56.2
Lafayette	55.2	15.0	3 343	1 505	15	117	301	28.2	10.1	93.4	9.7	559	556	24.2	55.8
Langlade	57.1	3.0	2 883	2 130	19	107	466	22.6	12.7	92.3	7.2	360	356	22.3	39.0
Lincoln	77.1	13.8	2 678	1 946	182	102	378	31.3	15.4	90.0	9.6	359	355	30.7	45.2
Manitowoc	191.7	9.3	2 384	1 843	41	97	234	87.9	43.1	91.1	22.1	265	261	83.2	13.7
Marathon	266.0	22.9	2 339	1 400	213	154	379	134.7	63.9	78.9	42.3	377	374	148.5	86.3
Marinette	138.4	16.4	3 220	1 961	726	105	346	54.7	22.5	89.4	15.0	377	373	53.2	42.8
Marquette	40.1	4.1	2 949	2 173	37	118	256	10.8	4.6	93.3	4.8	395	391	10.0	32.6
Menominee	0.0	0.0	0	0	0	0	0	13.3	11.9	38.1	0.6	171	170	13.3	190.1
Milwaukee	3 109.4	3.9	3 346	2 098	190	395	638	1 633.5	777.9	83.7	493.0	514	505	1 565.3	44.2
Monroe	246.2	9.3	6 478	1 814	194	3 838	402	37.1	19.6	91.9	10.0	281	278	34.9	41.4
Oconto	74.5	13.4	2 364	1 596	57	102	343	31.8	17.5	93.2	8.7	300	296	30.5	52.0
Oneida	97.4	8.9	3 026	2 338	76	265	331	43.4	17.4	90.0	20.4	648	645	43.6	109.9
Outagamie	253.0	-1.3	1 767	1 288	65	96	225	168.9	83.2	92.1	48.5	368	363	170.4	55.3
Ozaukee	151.6	-0.8	2 057	1 347	427	84	128	72.5	25.2	95.7	32.5	485	481	69.6	41.0
Pepin	22.9	16.1	3 092	1 915	55	132	372	11.5	5.9	93.3	3.8	502	497	10.5	42.9
Pierce	73.4	15.7	2 069	1 260	18	120	386	38.1	18.5	95.9	12.9	408	403	38.1	50.8
Polk	95.9	10.8	2 672	1 754	33	122	311	40.1	18.3	94.8	13.5	404	399	41.8	53.7
Portage	118.6	9.9	1 950	1 380	30	140	278	53.3	25.3	93.6	18.4	324	316	59.3	84.8
Price	48.3	10.7	2 927	2 025	80	246	439	17.0	9.7	94.5	5.0	308	305	16.0	47.6
Racine	374.2	2.9	2 141	1 651	34	101	306	214.1	106.2	91.0	65.7	380	376	201.2	38.3
Richland	44.6	9.8	2 563	1 614	11	116	497	20.1	10.0	77.2	5.3	303	300	20.9	74.4
Rock	378.0	6.9	2 782	1 623	504	100	372	169.1	90.7	88.9	48.9	352	348	180.5	54.5
Rusk	49.6	14.0	3 180	1 983	19	151	601	22.7	10.7	94.1	4.9	309	305	22.6	55.5
St. Croix	95.0	6.8	1 873	1 078	38	95	286	52.5	22.6	96.1	16.2	366	361	50.1	59.1
Sauk	131.0	11.3	2 787	1 667	462	109	305	54.6	23.6	88.4	18.7	420	412	55.8	28.6
Sawyer	52.1	10.8	3 546	2 253	207	191	797	15.5	7.3	82.8	5.9	431	426	15.4	30.8
Shawano	122.9	14.6	2 934	1 700	135	95	639	33.7	16.4	93.1	11.1	308	304	34.2	42.8
Sheboygan	219.5	3.4	2 125	1 673	37	95	258	137.0	61.6	89.0	40.4	397	393	134.9	55.0
Taylor	44.2	19.3	2 277	1 465	15	145	268	18.8	10.5	91.4	5.5	288	286	20.4	63.8
Trempealeau	77.7	9.9	2 955	1 828	47	145	476	38.1	18.3	88.1	10.5	399	395	40.1	79.0
Vernon	70.7	-27.8	2 658	1 733	28	143	449	29.7	14.5	94.6	9.4	359	356	31.3	57.1
Vilas	63.5	3.1	3 509	2 535	47	142	770	16.9	5.7	81.4	8.9	518	514	15.3	37.9
Walworth	150.9	-0.5	2 025	1 536	29	88	235	113.9	41.1	59.3	37.3	522	513	113.9	90.7
Washburn	58.9	17.1	4 238	2 946	148	344	566	16.8	7.5	94.4	6.6	490	486	17.4	48.1
Washington	157.9	12.2	1 658	1 231	19	101	221	112.0	55.2	70.4	36.5	426	420	114.0	89.7
Waukesha	519.8	6.3	1 684	1 212	171	100	162	342.8	130.1	92.1	140.1	496	490	333.5	58.3
Waupaca	138.1	6.0	2 982	2 085	307	112	330	49.4	23.1	94.2	16.4	378	374	45.3	32.8
Waushara	52.9	-1.5	2 634	1 971	14	100	349	18.2	8.3	93.3	7.5	399	396	17.0	43.2
Winnebago	659.1	20.9	4 721	1 572	2 707	166	217	143.8	70.9	90.0	42.0	316	310	144.3	51.0
Wood	169.9	10.0	2 119	1 605	30	99	291	107.6	46.5	91.4	30.3	406	402	102.3	49.4
WYOMING	1 716.4	1.6	X	1 491	309	633	1 089	1 164.2	375.3	86.8	443.3	869	766	991.3	171.2
Albany	86.3	13.6	3 027	1 556	128	335	999	40.2	21.4	81.3	6.8	225	210	39.6	169.5
Big Horn	32.1	8.9	2 837	1 923	19	305	487	25.7	9.4	78.1	11.2	876	869	22.8	131.7
Campbell	29.7	-3.4	930	503	11	77	204	99.9	15.7	90.2	63.6	1 975	1 774	88.0	330.4
Carbon	48.7	-0.2	2 708	1 326	31	371	933	57.5	12.1	89.7	31.9	1 405	1 289	50.6	189.5
Converse	18.5	-7.5	1 579	1 092	20	143	187	41.1	6.4	80.6	23.9	1 595	1 510	33.0	144.8
Crook	15.5	5.0	2 679	1 285	57	242	399	12.4	5.0	90.8	5.4	969	873	9.9	133.6
Fremont	86.2	0.9	2 582	1 534	68	303	643	66.9	32.1	83.0	25.4	661	650	59.8	143.6
Goshen	37.2	-3.8	2 976	1 843	19	258	418	20.5	13.7	93.3	3.5	283	276	20.2	96.4
Hot Springs	18.3	-1.5	3 384	2 422	29	131	774	17.2	1.9	86.5	12.7	2 119	2 012	11.2	118.6
Johnson	26.6	40.6	4 150	1 777	15	272	1 845	13.0	3.4	73.3	7.9	1 119	1 034	10.2	120.7
Laramie	450.4	-6.3	5 888	1 763	577	2 080	1 392	119.5	62.6	87.0	27.5	387	300	100.0	104.2
Lincoln	26.9	-33.9	1 871	1 111	126	241	274	34.9	10.1	91.5	12.5	874	799	30.0	237.9
Natrona	169.3	0.4	2 696	1 445	390	400	440	171.1	69.0	94.1	47.3	609	404	157.0	155.5
Niobrara	9.4	11.2	3 340	1 873	35	348	226	6.2	1.0	82.7	3.3	1 058	1 001	3.9	85.8
Park	76.6	-16.1	3 166	1 577	578	765	212	53.1	14.1	77.9	26.8	1 145	1 136	44.6	162.1
Platte	27.7	-2.3	2 887	1 563	41	455	396	29.5	5.6	93.2	8.9	848	841	27.1	384.9
Sheridan	84.9	6.1	3 424	1 978	364	790	247	48.5	24.3	79.8	11.3	426	352	47.4	182.0

1. Based on the estimated population as of July 1 of the year shown. 2. Based on the estimated population as of July 1, 1982.

STATE County	Local government finances, 1981–1982 (cont'd)								State and local government employment, 1989		Federal government civilian employment 1989		Elections, 1988[3]	
	Direct general expenditure (cont'd)						Debt outstanding							
	Per capita[1] (Dollars)	Percent of total for– Education	Health & hospitals	Police protection	Public welfare	Highways	Total (Mil dol)	Per capita[1] (Dollars)	Total	Rate[2]	Total	Earnings ($1,000)	Total vote cast for president	Vote for lead party (Percent)
	189	190	191	192	193	194	195	196	197	198	199	200	201	202
WISCONSIN—Con.														
Iron	1 269	39.7	5.4	5.4	3.9	17.7	3.9	594	304	475.0	25	602	3 717	D—56.2
Jackson	1 230	46.8	11.4	4.1	6.3	17.9	5.2	309	992	604.9	58	1 391	7 523	D—52.2
Jefferson	1 062	42.4	15.1	5.9	2.3	12.8	40.2	605	3 151	453.4	164	4 633	26 361	R—54.3
Juneau	1 195	41.5	7.3	4.9	4.5	17.3	10.9	518	1 150	520.4	309	7 752	8 667	R—56.2
Kenosha	1 392	46.2	8.6	8.5	2.1	8.9	95.3	784	6 250	506.9	269	8 283	52 149	D—57.7
Kewaunee	1 189	40.3	14.7	3.8	2.0	20.6	9.6	483	814	405.0	81	2 020	9 191	D—52.1
La Crosse	1 190	43.8	11.2	4.5	4.9	8.0	73.7	792	7 216	750.9	442	13 774	44 111	D—50.3
Lafayette	1 401	42.7	9.7	2.8	5.2	21.0	10.3	596	1 016	615.8	66	1 580	7 235	R—50.7
Langlade	1 113	50.5	4.6	4.3	3.4	16.6	5.3	263	976	492.9	62	1 502	9 201	R—53.1
Lincoln	1 145	42.0	13.0	6.2	3.6	14.4	29.0	1 081	1 560	541.7	74	2 049	11 185	D—52.0
Manitowoc	997	34.6	12.8	6.1	4.2	15.6	36.0	432	3 536	439.8	189	5 221	36 025	D—54.6
Marathon	1 323	39.1	12.3	3.8	3.3	9.8	101.5	904	6 027	530.1	464	14 127	49 543	D—49.8
Marinette	1 334	37.5	22.5	3.8	3.1	11.2	27.6	692	1 994	463.7	134	3 554	17 791	R—54.2
Marquette	822	42.8	5.9	5.5	5.5	22.4	4.7	382	502	369.1	48	1 182	5 573	R—54.9
Menominee	3 500	76.5	5.5	2.0	5.0	3.5	2.7	699	0	0.0	0	0	1 422	D—72.3
Milwaukee	1 632	33.8	12.0	7.1	4.7	4.9	789.1	823	53 284	573.4	9 450	309 128	440 296	D—60.9
Monroe	977	40.6	14.4	4.8	5.9	17.4	7.2	202	1 610	423.7	2 722	64 237	13 591	R—52.0
Oconto	1 049	40.5	11.0	4.0	3.7	16.3	14.0	482	1 240	393.7	125	3 285	13 733	R—51.6
Oneida	1 384	53.7	5.8	9.2	2.3	9.5	12.9	409	1 798	558.4	222	6 541	15 670	R—51.9
Outagamie	1 292	43.5	7.4	4.7	3.4	12.0	128.0	971	6 212	433.8	390	11 561	61 304	R—54.0
Ozaukee	1 037	49.3	8.3	7.7	2.2	10.2	39.1	582	2 827	383.6	151	4 540	35 852	R—63.9
Pepin	1 404	48.3	5.9	3.3	5.2	17.0	5.2	699	464	627.0	36	868	3 255	D—58.6
Pierce	1 202	45.4	3.7	4.4	4.4	26.9	11.4	360	3 075	866.2	115	2 748	14 831	D—58.4
Polk	1 252	48.0	11.0	2.7	3.8	14.7	27.5	822	1 795	500.0	145	3 494	16 022	D—56.1
Portage	1 048	39.1	11.1	5.1	1.9	13.2	56.9	1 006	4 846	797.0	176	4 873	28 542	D—57.2
Price	990	48.3	6.3	3.7	4.7	16.5	7.5	461	820	497.0	133	3 790	7 516	D—53.0
Racine	1 163	42.9	10.1	9.1	4.5	8.6	60.7	351	7 593	434.4	445	13 663	76 631	D—51.7
Richland	1 190	27.2	14.6	13.5	3.7	14.1	10.0	569	924	531.0	58	1 347	7 718	R—52.2
Rock	1 300	41.6	9.1	6.0	4.6	6.2	92.5	666	6 589	484.8	379	11 166	58 227	D—50.8
Rusk	1 443	38.2	25.0	2.3	4.6	14.0	8.3	529	1 155	740.4	68	1 492	7 017	D—55.4
St. Croix	1 128	43.7	13.2	3.8	5.1	13.2	31.4	707	2 395	472.4	127	3 094	21 549	D—52.9
Sauk	1 257	40.1	12.7	5.3	3.7	12.5	25.0	563	2 616	556.6	142	3 682	18 699	R—54.7
Sawyer	1 123	42.7	8.0	4.5	4.9	16.0	10.6	775	649	441.5	77	1 969	6 545	R—49.8
Shawano	945	45.4	7.8	4.3	4.3	18.1	13.3	368	1 938	462.5	120	2 905	15 162	R—55.2
Sheboygan	1 323	43.5	10.8	6.7	3.4	6.9	116.3	1 141	4 898	474.2	240	7 138	47 234	R—49.7
Taylor	1 063	47.1	6.8	3.5	4.3	16.5	9.6	500	763	393.3	83	2 109	8 113	R—52.4
Trempealeau	1 530	40.0	13.9	5.0	4.4	12.6	21.2	808	1 569	596.6	115	2 750	11 183	D—55.5
Vernon	1 189	40.4	14.5	2.5	6.2	21.7	14.3	542	1 377	517.7	111	2 708	11 102	D—51.8
Vilas	890	42.7	5.7	7.4	3.6	20.3	7.6	442	671	370.7	75	1 985	9 730	R—60.0
Walworth	1 596	29.3	20.5	6.2	2.8	6.8	49.1	688	6 197	831.8	173	4 773	30 711	R—59.5
Washburn	1 297	46.9	5.3	3.2	3.5	17.4	8.0	593	848	610.1	123	3 265	6 521	D—52.0
Washington	1 329	39.4	8.0	4.8	2.9	7.8	48.7	567	3 778	396.8	807	25 580	40 575	R—60.0
Waukesha	1 180	52.6	6.2	6.6	2.7	7.7	219.9	778	12 859	416.7	738	23 327	148 935	R—60.7
Waupaca	1 045	52.4	7.0	4.8	3.2	13.8	27.2	629	2 654	573.2	141	3 653	18 784	R—61.5
Waushara	909	40.0	8.9	4.3	12.7	17.9	5.7	304	806	401.0	61	1 422	8 567	R—57.8
Winnebago	1 086	38.5	10.7	6.8	4.7	11.8	73.6	554	8 884	636.4	634	20 119	64 039	R—54.8
Wood	1 370	42.3	10.1	4.9	3.9	14.0	106.9	1 430	3 870	482.5	218	6 174	32 856	R—50.4
WYOMING	1 944	48.1	10.8	4.0	0.1	6.6	1 214.1	2 381	44 665	941.7	7 447	219 905	176 551	R—60.5
Albany	1 311	36.5	23.2	4.9	0.1	3.7	14.7	488	5 819	2 041.8	253	7 485	11 335	R—49.9
Big Horn	1 784	54.3	13.2	3.0	0.0	6.8	19.4	1 518	1 116	987.6	99	2 775	4 780	R—68.2
Campbell	2 733	44.7	11.5	3.6	0.0	16.6	87.9	2 730	2 653	829.1	79	2 212	9 112	R—73.6
Carbon	2 228	50.2	16.8	4.7	0.1	6.1	34.5	1 522	1 860	1 033.3	225	6 703	5 989	R—55.7
Converse	2 203	45.9	9.3	4.4	0.0	5.4	71.6	4 771	977	835.0	58	1 519	4 215	R—68.4
Crook	1 771	55.3	5.9	4.5	0.0	18.4	0.9	159	542	934.5	68	1 461	2 540	R—76.3
Fremont	1 558	62.7	0.2	4.6	0.0	5.9	47.8	1 246	3 305	989.5	379	10 493	12 889	R—59.6
Goshen	1 659	74.7	0.4	2.7	0.0	4.6	6.6	542	1 257	1 005.6	108	2 609	5 005	R—61.4
Hot Springs	1 874	50.7	12.4	5.1	0.0	8.6	2.4	403	565	1 046.3	17	516	2 324	R—64.1
Johnson	1 436	53.7	1.2	5.3	0.0	12.4	3.8	535	644	1 006.2	60	1 692	2 858	R—72.8
Laramie	1 407	56.6	11.4	3.7	0.0	4.3	71.1	999	7 485	978.4	2 718	80 300	27 770	R—56.0
Lincoln	2 095	42.5	6.4	4.1	0.0	5.8	95.5	6 682	1 068	741.7	115	2 912	4 897	R—66.1
Natrona	2 021	43.4	16.7	3.9	0.1	6.2	61.8	795	4 157	661.9	681	23 306	23 487	R—59.6
Niobrara	1 247	58.6	0.1	4.9	0.0	13.6	21.8	7 021	321	1 146.4	32	905	1 191	R—69.3
Park	1 908	53.4	10.3	3.2	0.2	5.4	46.4	1 983	2 126	878.5	778	21 989	9 702	R—71.0
Platte	2 578	41.5	1.3	2.4	0.0	6.9	162.1	15 437	835	869.8	120	3 465	3 808	R—59.2
Sheridan	1 795	43.2	15.6	6.5	0.2	4.0	12.8	483	1 972	795.2	693	20 763	10 778	R—55.5

1. Based on the estimated population as of July 1, 1982. 2. Per 10,000 resident population estimated as of July 1 of the year shown. 3. Data subject to copyright.

STATE–County code	MSA/CMSA/NECMA code[1]	STATE County	Land Area,[2] 1990 (Sq. Km.)	Population, 1990											
							Race						Age of population Percent		
				Total persons	Rank	Per square kilometer	White	Black	Am. Indian, Eskimo, Aleut	Asian & Pacific Islander	Other race	Hispanic[3]	Under 5 years	5 to 14 years	15 to 24 years
			1	2	3	4	5	6	7	8	9	10	11	12	13
		WYOMING—Con.													
56 035	...	Sublette	12 643	4 843	2 851	0.4	4 750	5	70	13	5	57	7.4	16.2	11.0
56 037	...	Sweetwater	27 003	38 823	1 028	1.4	36 564	289	305	254	1 411	3 470	8.1	20.7	13.2
56 039	...	Teton	10 381	11 172	2 279	1.1	10 989	17	95	49	22	158	7.9	13.2	10.8
56 041	...	Uinta	5 392	18 705	1 749	3.5	18 278	25	128	66	208	773	9.7	24.0	13.2
56 043	...	Washakie	5 802	8 388	2 523	1.4	7 864	14	59	41	410	801	7.0	17.6	12.1
56 045	...	Weston	6 211	6 518	2 708	1.0	6 390	3	79	11	35	83	6.5	18.7	10.9

1. MSA = Metropolitan Statistical Area. CMSA = Consolidated MSA. NECMA = New England county metropolitan area. PMSA = Primary MSA. See Appendix A for explanation of these concepts. See Appendix B for list of metropolitan areas identified by type, with component counties. 2. Dry land or land partially or temporarily covered by water. 3. Hispanic persons may be of any race.

Table A. States and Counties — **Population**

STATE County	Population, 1990 (cont'd): Age of population (cont'd), Percent: 25 to 34 years	35 to 44 years	45 to 54 years	55 to 64 years	65 to 74 years	75 years and over	Percent female	Population–Change and components of change: Change 1980–1990: Number	Percent	Components of change, 1980–1986: Total persons, 1986	Total persons, 1980	Net change: Number	Percent	Natural increase: Births	Deaths
	14	15	16	17	18	19	20	21	22	23	24	25	26	27	28
WYOMING—Con.															
Sublette	14.7	18.3	11.7	8.8	6.9	5.0	48.2	295	6.5	6 300	4 548	1 700	37.5	600	200
Sweetwater	17.3	17.8	9.7	6.1	4.3	2.9	49.5	-2 900	-7.0	47 000	41 723	5 300	12.7	6 200	1 300
Teton	22.1	21.8	10.8	7.0	4.2	2.3	47.8	1 817	19.4	10 800	9 355	1 400	15.4	1 200	300
Uinta	17.8	17.2	7.7	5.1	3.2	2.1	49.2	5 684	43.7	21 300	13 021	8 300	63.5	3 600	500
Washakie	14.0	15.3	10.8	9.3	8.0	5.8	49.8	-1 108	-11.7	10 000	9 496	500	5.1	1 100	400
Weston	15.1	16.3	10.9	9.0	7.8	4.9	50.2	-588	-8.3	7 900	7 106	700	10.5	1 000	400

STATE County	Population–(cont'd)	Households, 1990					Births, 1988			Deaths, 1987				Marriages, 1984	
	Components of change, 1980-1986 (cont'd)				Percent					Number		Rate			
	Net migration	Number	Percent change, 1980–1990	Persons per house-hold	Female family house-holder[1]	One-person	Total	Rate[2]	Low birth weight[3] (Number)	Total	Infant[4]	Total[2]	Infant[5]	Number	Rate[2]
	29	30	31	32	33	34	35	36	37	38	39	40	41	42	43
WYOMING—Con.															
Sublette	1 300	1 834	15.3	2.60	4.4	23.4	76	14.6	4	37	0	6.6	0.0	60	11.1
Sweetwater	400	13 616	-3.1	2.83	7.7	22.2	621	14.3	38	174	4	3.9	5.9	342	7.8
Teton	500	4 568	21.8	2.43	5.4	26.6	221	NA	16	43	1	NA	5.8	389	35.0
Uinta	5 200	5 885	44.2	3.12	7.8	18.7	373	19.8	28	84	5	4.2	12.4	168	7.1
Washakie	-200	3 156	-3.6	2.61	6.4	24.7	123	13.4	4	69	4	7.2	27.8	125	12.4
Weston	100	2 419	-4.2	2.65	7.2	22.1	97	13.3	7	50	2	6.6	18.0	65	8.1

1. No spouse present. 2. Per 1,000 resident population estimated as of July 1 of the year shown. 3. Under 2,500 grams. 4. Deaths of infants under 1 year old. 5. Deaths of infants under 1 year old per 1,000 live births.

STATE County	Divorces, 1984		Physicians, active non–Federal, 1989		Hospitals, 1989			Nursing homes,[4] 1986		Serious crimes known to police, 1988			Education			
						Beds				Number			Public school enrollment[7]		Attainment,[8] 1980	
	Number	Rate[1]	Number[2]	Rate[3]	Number	Number	Rate[3]	Number	Beds	Total[5]	Violent[6]	Rate[3]	1986–1987	1980	Percent 12 yrs. or more	Percent 16 yrs. or more
	44	45	46	47	48	49	50	51	52	53	54	55	56	57	58	59
WYOMING—Con.																
Sublette	32	5.9	4	80	0	0	0	1	34	94	2	1 779	1 399	1 065	78.2	18.3
Sweetwater	268	6.1	36	84	1	99	230	1	101	1 974	218	4 671	10 220	8 487	76.3	14.0
Teton	85	7.7	30	NA	1	51	NA	1	12	680	26	6 376	1 750	1 588	90.4	33.1
Uinta	186	7.9	18	102	2	277	1 574	1	26	629	65	3 306	5 759	2 744	77.8	11.8
Washakie	61	6.0	8	88	1	30	330	1	76	307	31	3 328	2 203	2 206	75.3	12.6
Weston	48	6.0	3	42	1	61	847	1	41	119	13	1 651	1 594	1 444	72.7	12.1

1. Per 1,000 resident population estimated as of July 1 of the year shown. 2. As of end of year. 3. Per 100,000 resident population as of July 1 of the year shown. 4. Preliminary. Covers nursing homes with 3 or more beds. 5. Data for serious crimes have not been adjusted for underreporting, this may affect comparability between geographic areas or over time. 6. Includes murder and nonnegligent manslaughter, forcible rape, robbery, and aggravated assault. 7. The 1986–1987 data are based on administrative reports obtained by the U.S. National Center for Education Statistics. The 1980 data are based on the 1980 Census of Population and Housing. 8. Persons 25 years old or older.

STATE County	Education (cont'd): Local government expenditures for education,[1] 1982: Total (Mil dol)	Education (cont'd): Local government expenditures for education,[1] 1982: Per capita (Dollars)	Social Security Program December 1988: Beneficiaries: Total	Social Security Program December 1988: Beneficiaries: Rate[2]	Social Security Program December 1988: Payments ($1,000)	Supplemental Security Income Program recipients June 1986	Money income: Per capita[3]: 1987 Income, (Dollars)	Money income: Per capita[3]: 1979: Current dollars	Money income: Per capita[3]: 1979: Constant 1987 dollars	Money income: Median household income 1979 (Dollars)	Money income: Percent below poverty level, 1979: Persons	Money income: Percent below poverty level, 1979: Families	Housing units, 1990: Total	Housing units, 1990: Percent change, 1980–1990
	60	61	62	63	64	65	66	67	68	69	70	71	72	73
WYOMING—Con.														
Sublette	5.7	1 099	620	119.2	312	10	8 385	7 059	11 045	17 430	9.7	8.3	2 911	21.6
Sweetwater	44.5	952	3 410	78.8	1 743	122	11 287	8 880	13 895	24 114	5.2	4.5	15 444	2.2
Teton	6.4	595	980	84.5	492	18	12 671	9 040	14 145	18 442	7.7	6.1	7 060	44.3
Uinta	28.4	1 418	1 270	67.6	617	40	8 887	7 518	11 763	22 584	3.9	2.5	7 246	61.1
Washakie	7.7	759	1 470	159.8	746	54	9 156	7 066	11 056	18 239	6.5	4.5	3 732	-1.4
Weston	6.2	791	1 085	148.6	544	38	9 045	7 357	11 511	20 021	7.4	5.8	3 090	6.6

1. Elementary and secondary. 2. Per 1,000 resident population estimated as of July 1 of the year shown. 3. Based on the resident population estimated as of July 1, 1988 for 1987 data and enumerated as of April 1, 1980 for 1979 data.

STATE County	Housing units, 1990 (cont'd)				Civilian labor force, 1990				Private nonfarm establishments, 1988					
	Occupied units						Unemployment				Employment[2]			
		Owner occupied												
	Total	Percent	Median value (Dollars)	Median rent (Dollars)	Total	Percent change, 1989–1990	Total	Rate[1]	Number	Net change, 1987–1988	Total	Percent change, 1987–1988	Manufacturing	Retail trade
	74	75	76	77	78	79	80	81	82	83	84	85	86	87
WYOMING–Con.														
Sublette	1 834	69.8	64 400	275	2 854	-1.7	110	3.9	200	-10	898	-4.6	20	238
Sweetwater	13 616	70.2	70 900	279	20 698	7.0	1 187	5.7	1 009	-28	11 919	-4.3	629	2 706
Teton	4 568	58.9	133 400	392	12 156	10.8	254	2.1	962	47	5 613	3.5	196	1 928
Uinta	5 885	72.2	59 300	258	9 758	-1.0	612	6.3	475	-14	3 862	3.8	167	1 129
Washakie	3 156	71.8	54 600	236	4 543	2.1	216	4.8	326	-10	2 264	-4.6	484	434
Weston	2 419	78.1	44 700	217	3 299	-0.8	184	5.6	232	-8	1 529	-0.4	230	357

1. Percent of total civilian labor force. 2. For week including March 12. Excludes government employees, self-employed persons, farm workers, domestic service workers, railroad employees subject to the Railroad Retirement Act, and employees on oceanborne vessels or in foreign countries.

STATE County	Private nonfarm establishments, 1988 (cont'd) — Employment[1] (cont'd): Finance, insurance, and real estate	Employment[1] (cont'd): Services	Annual payroll: Total (Mil dol)	Annual payroll: Average per employee (Dollars)	Personal income, 1989: Total (Mil dol)	Per cent change, 1988–1989	Wages and salaries[2] (Mil dol)	Proprietor's income (Mil dol)	Dividends, interest, & rent (Mil dol)	Transfer payments (Mil dol)	Per capita[3]: Dollars	Per capita[3]: Rank	Earnings, 1989: Total (Mil dol)	Percent by selected industries: Farm	Goods-related[4]: Total
	88	89	90	91	92	93	94	95	96	97	98	99	100	101	102
WYOMING—Con.															
Sublette	47	274	14	16 133	75	9.6	40	9	19	9	14 827	1 065	49	0.4	NA
Sweetwater	340	2 110	297	24 956	635	5.6	510	39	80	67	14 717	1 117	549	0.2	49.0
Teton	344	2 122	88	15 638	281	13.3	166	37	80	19	23 337	68	203	0.5	19.4
Uinta	135	959	68	17 504	216	3.9	154	16	25	26	12 282	2 204	170	0.7	34.3
Washakie	116	562	41	18 245	119	2.7	69	9	26	21	13 160	1 834	78	0.4	30.9
Weston	72	195	28	18 414	104	4.2	51	12	31	14	14 497	1 214	63	4.3	35.6

1. For week including March 12. Excludes government employees, self-employed persons, farm workers, domestic service workers, railroad employees subject to the Railroad Retirement Act, and employees on oceanborne vessels or in foreign countries. 2. Includes other labor income. 3. Based on the resident population estimated as of July 1 of the year shown. 4. Covers mining, construction, and manufacturing.

STATE County	Earnings, 1989 (cont'd) — Percent by selected industries (cont'd) — Goods-related[1] — Manufacturing	Service-related & other[2] — Total	Retail trade	Finance, insurance, & real estate	Services	Government	Agriculture, 1987 — Farms — Number	Percent with — Less than 50 acres	500 acres and over	Farm operators, percent — Whose principal occupation is farming	Residing on farm operated	Land in farms — Acreage (1,000)	Percent change, 1982–1987	Acres — Average size of farm	Total irrigated (1,000)	Total cropland (1,000)
	103	104	105	106	107	108	109	110	111	112	113	114	115	116	117	118
WYOMING—Con.																
Sublette	NA	NA	7.2	2.4	15.7	22.2	253	22.5	58.5	63.2	75.1	583	14.2	2 304	159	152
Sweetwater	2.9	36.2	6.8	1.8	9.7	14.5	183	23.5	39.3	56.8	74.9	1 683	-0.9	9 195	34	41
Teton	2.1	66.5	17.3	5.1	38.6	13.6	110	22.7	30.9	60.9	79.1	72	0.9	656	25	34
Uinta	3.3	41.1	9.5	2.3	14.6	24.0	283	19.8	51.9	63.3	74.6	873	16.5	3 086	107	83
Washakie	17.4	44.2	9.1	3.3	16.3	24.4	225	24.0	44.0	64.9	77.8	391	14.2	1 738	47	54
Weston	10.8	39.1	9.2	2.5	12.2	21.0	235	8.9	74.0	69.8	75.3	1 547	3.9	6 581	4	55

1. Covers mining, construction, and manufacturing. 2. Covers private sector earnings in agricultural services, forestry, and fisheries; transportation and public utilities; wholesale trade; retail trade; finance, insurance, and real estate; and services.

STATE County	Agriculture, 1987 (cont'd)								Manufactures, 1987						
	Value of land and buildings		Value of products sold				Percent of farms with sales of		Establishments		All employees			Production workers	
					Percent from										
	Average per farm ($1,000)	Average per acre (Dollars)	Total (Mil dol)	Average per farm (Dollars)	Crops	Livestock and poultry[1]	$10,000 or more	$100,000 or more	Total	Percent with 20 or more em-ployees	Number (1,000)	Percent change, 1982–1987	Annual payroll (Mil dol)	Number (1,000)	Work hours (Mil)
	119	120	121	122	123	124	125	126	127	128	129	130	131	132	133
WYOMING—Con.															
Sublette	612	286	21	82 195	4.4	95.6	57.3	17.8	8	0.0	0.0	0.0	0.4	0.0	0.0
Sweetwater	915	101	6	34 976	5.6	94.4	47.0	7.7	22	27.3	0.6	50.0	19.0	0.4	0.8
Teton	802	1 233	8	72 734	10.3	89.7	43.6	17.3	27	11.1	0.2	0.0	3.7	0.1	0.2
Uinta	496	147	15	53 179	2.9	97.1	62.2	12.0	13	23.1	0.1	-50.0	2.8	0.1	0.2
Washakie	475	299	27	120 447	50.3	49.7	63.1	36.4	12	33.3	0.4	-20.0	12.1	0.3	0.6
Weston	669	101	28	117 832	2.6	97.4	62.6	17.4	18	16.7	D	D	D	D	D

1. Includes livestock and poultry products.

STATE County	Manufactures, 1987 (cont'd)					Value of construction authorized by building permits, 1990							
	Production workers (cont'd)						Nonresidential				Residential		
	Wages							Percent					
	Total (Mil dol)	Average per worker (Dollars)	Value added by manu-facture (Mil dol)	Value of shipments (Mil dol)	New capital expend-itures (Mil dol)	Total[1] ($1,000)	Total ($1,000)	Office	Industrial	Stores	New construction ($1,000)	Number of housing units	Alterations and additions ($1,000)
	134	135	136	137	138	139	140	141	142	143	144	145	146
WYOMING—Con.													
Sublette	0.3	NA	0.8	2.0	0.0	4 903	1 325	4.2	95.5	0.0	3 035	37	86
Sweetwater	12.1	30 250	140.1	288.7	13.9	10 331	1 556	25.9	0.0	8.0	4 365	56	327
Teton	1.9	19 000	7.4	11.9	D	46 041	1 687	40.8	0.0	31.1	34 775	333	2 710
Uinta	1.9	19 000	22.2	37.9	0.2	1 202	46	0.0	0.0	0.0	224	4	287
Washakie	7.5	25 000	32.0	99.8	0.5	421	98	0.0	0.0	48.2	0	0	109
Weston	D	D	D	D	D	1 144	850	0.0	0.0	100.0	150	4	40

1. Includes nonresidential additions and alterations, residential nonhousekeeping buildings, and residential garages and carports not shown separately.

STATE County	Wholesale trade, 1987				Retail trade, all establishments, 1987				Retail trade, establishments with payroll, 1987					
						Sales				Sales				
											Per capita[2] (Dollars)			
	Estab-lishments	Sales (Mil dol)	Paid employees[1]	Annual payroll (Mil dol)	Number	Total (Mil dol)	Percent change, 1982–1987	Per capita[2] (Dollars)	Number	Total (Mil dol)	General merchan-dise stores	Food stores	Apparel & acces-sory stores	Eating and drinking places
	147	148	149	150	151	152	153	154	155	156	157	158	159	160
WYOMING—Con.														
Sublette	12	D	D	D	102	18.8	-22.0	3 361	62	17.0	199	1 223	121	480
Sweetwater	86	195.4	496	12.0	428	228.9	-8.1	5 087	287	223.5	513	1 012	242	448
Teton	24	15.7	153	2.3	345	120.4	5.2	10 752	235	116.2	D	1 216	877	2 013
Uinta	43	34.9	167	3.5	197	93.3	-37.5	4 714	114	88.6	355	1 079	182	383
Washakie	31	47.2	252	4.2	123	44.8	-16.9	4 665	83	42.8	D	D	265	383
Weston	14	D	D	D	110	32.4	-17.6	4 265	60	30.2	D	968	139	302

1. For pay period including March 12. 2. Based on the estimated population as of July 1 of the year shown.

Table A. States and Counties — **Retail Trade, Services, and Banking**

STATE County	Retail trade, establishments with payroll, 1987 (cont'd)		Taxable service industries–establishments with payroll, 1987							Bank deposits,[2] June 1989		Savings capital,[3] September 1989	
				Receipts (Mil dol)									
					Selected kinds of business								
	Paid employees[1]	Annual payroll (Mil dol)	Number	Total	Hotels, motels and other lodging places	Health services	Legal services	Paid employees	Annual payroll (Mil dol)	Total (Mil dol)	Percent change, 1988–1989	Total (Mil dol)	Percent change, 1988–1989
	161	162	163	164	165	166	167	168	169	170	171	172	173
WYOMING—Con.													
Sublette	319	2.2	49	7.0	1.0	1.3	D	144	2.2	38	5.8	0.0	NA
Sweetwater	2 916	26.3	256	69.3	22.4	14.1	2.8	1 612	20.6	362	5.0	55.5	-13.7
Teton	1 769	17.3	328	84.8	36.5	6.7	11.4	1 919	21.5	174	8.9	8.6	-25.8
Uinta	1 185	9.9	136	30.9	5.3	3.5	3.7	909	10.0	128	-0.2	15.9	-9.9
Washakie	502	4.3	69	9.2	1.3	2.5	0.7	225	2.7	98	7.3	28.7	-2.3
Weston	373	3.6	39	4.8	D	1.1	0.4	142	1.4	80	-0.5	4.3	-52.4

1. For the period including March 12 of the year shown. 2. Includes deposits for all insured and reporting noninsured commercial and mutual savings banks. 3. Includes savings capital for all FSLIC insured savings institutions.

Table A. States and Counties — Federal Funds and Local Government Finances

STATE County	Federal funds and grants, 1989							Local government finances, 1981–1982							
	Expenditures		Per capita[1] (Dollars)					General revenue						Direct general expenditure	
									Intergovernmental		Taxes				
												Per capita[2]			
	Total (Mil dol)	Percent change, 1988–1989	Total	Direct payments for individuals	Procurement contract awards	Salaries and wages	Grant awards	Total (Mil dol)	Total (Mil dol)	Percent from state	Total (Mil dol)	Total (Dollars)	Property (Dollars)	Total (Mil dol)	Percent change, 1977–1982
	174	175	176	177	178	179	180	181	182	183	184	185	186	187	188
WYOMING—Con.															
Sublette	10.1	15.2	2 018	1 382	31	439	139	11.4	2.3	81.8	8.0	1 542	1 521	9.8	90.7
Sweetwater	71.0	17.7	1 648	937	21	221	450	140.6	26.7	77.6	68.8	1 473	1 295	124.9	149.6
Teton	43.5	-4.1	3 622	940	1 578	663	426	21.8	8.2	81.2	5.6	524	368	19.7	272.0
Uinta	33.5	19.6	1 904	823	29	124	903	101.4	16.7	95.5	18.7	935	798	53.2	624.8
Washakie	26.0	14.7	2 857	1 634	16	511	652	17.0	9.2	93.5	5.8	571	558	14.9	156.3
Weston	41.4	27.0	5 746	1 387	3 308	246	643	15.0	4.4	87.3	6.6	847	736	13.3	115.2

1. Based on the estimated population as of July 1 of the year shown. 2. Based on the estimated population as of July 1, 1982.

STATE County	Local government finances, 1981–1982 (cont'd): Direct general expenditure (cont'd): Per capita[1] (Dollars)	Percent of total for– Education	Health & hospitals	Police protection	Public welfare	Highways	Debt outstanding: Total (Mil dol)	Per capita[1] (Dollars)	State and local government employment, 1989: Total	Rate[2]	Federal government civilian employment 1989: Total	Earnings ($1,000)	Elections, 1988[3]: Total vote cast for president	Vote for lead party (Percent)
	189	190	191	192	193	194	195	196	197	198	199	200	201	202
WYOMING—Con.														
Sublette	1 884	58.3	3.0	4.2	0.0	7.2	6.6	1 269	426	852.0	82	2 171	2 247	R—72.8
Sweetwater	2 675	41.1	8.8	3.4	0.4	3.6	276.6	5 923	3 417	792.8	262	8 642	13 705	R—49.5
Teton	1 840	32.3	30.0	5.6	0.0	5.8	6.9	642	905	754.2	324	9 343	5 926	R—61.0
Uinta	2 662	53.3	0.7	3.7	0.0	4.9	149.9	7 494	1 890	1 073.9	71	1 898	5 501	R—63.0
Washakie	1 478	51.3	1.3	5.2	0.1	10.1	6.3	619	749	823.1	157	4 946	3 768	R—67.4
Weston	1 699	46.6	13.0	5.3	0.1	12.2	6.8	871	576	800.0	68	1 800	2 724	R—73.0

1. Based on the estimated population as of July 1, 1982. 2. Per 10,000 resident population estimated as of July 1 of the year shown. 3. Data subject to copyright.

TABLE B:

Metropolitan Areas

(For explanation of symbols, see page ix)

MSA/ CMSA/ NECMA/ PMSA code[1]	Area name	Land Area,[2] 1990 (Sq. Km.)	Population, 1990: Total persons	Rank	Per square kilometer	Race: White	Race: Black	Race: Am. Indian, Eskimo, Aleut	Race: Asian & Pacific Islander	Race: Other race	Hispanic[3]	Age of population, Percent: Under 5 years	5 to 14 years	15 to 24 years	25 to 34 years	35 to 44 years
		1	2	3	4	5	6	7	8	9	10	11	12	13	14	15
0040	Abilene, TX	2 372	119 655	236	50.4	100 237	7 547	450	1 449	9 972	17 511	8.2	15.1	17.3	17.3	13.3
0120	Albany, GA	1 776	112 561	249	63.4	60 041	51 522	281	498	219	928	8.3	17.0	16.9	15.9	14.9
0160	Albany-Schenectady-Troy, NY	8 414	874 304	48	103.9	815 315	41 112	1 560	10 789	5 528	15 840	6.8	12.7	15.4	16.8	15.3
0200	Albuquerque, NM	3 020	480 577	79	159.1	369 445	13 199	16 296	7 386	74 251	178 310	7.7	14.5	14.3	18.7	16.2
0220	Alexandria, LA	3 426	131 556	212	38.4	92 989	36 805	564	908	290	1 526	7.7	16.9	14.8	16.5	13.8
0240	Allentown-Bethlehem, PA-NJ	3 784	686 688	60	181.5	649 890	13 466	688	7 293	15 351	28 885	6.7	12.8	13.5	16.4	15.3
0280	Altoona, PA	1 362	130 542	220	95.8	128 840	1 073	118	380	131	431	6.3	13.9	13.4	14.5	14.5
0320	Amarillo, TX	4 723	187 547	165	39.7	158 517	9 788	1 355	3 216	14 671	25 390	8.2	15.8	14.5	17.2	14.5
0380	Anchorage, AK	4 397	226 338	147	51.5	182 736	14 544	14 569	10 910	3 579	9 258	9.5	16.0	14.6	21.5	19.2
0400	Anderson, IN	1 171	130 669	218	111.6	119 734	9 870	299	415	351	885	6.4	13.9	14.8	15.2	14.8
0405	Anderson, SC	1 860	145 196	197	78.1	120 384	24 151	173	340	148	559	6.6	13.8	14.3	15.6	15.0
0450	Anniston, AL	1 576	116 034	242	73.6	92 873	21 578	296	869	418	1 282	6.4	14.1	17.4	15.9	14.5
0460	Appleton-Oshkosh-Neenah, WI	3 623	315 121	117	87.0	306 775	932	2 796	3 805	813	2 280	7.7	15.1	15.0	17.9	14.9
0480	Asheville, NC	1 700	174 821	171	102.8	158 979	14 336	486	765	255	1 173	6.3	12.1	13.3	15.4	15.7
0500	Athens, GA	2 418	156 267	182	64.6	124 076	29 003	257	2 352	579	2 011	6.6	12.8	24.2	16.9	13.9
0520	Atlanta, GA	13 265	2 833 511	12	213.6	2 020 017	736 153	5 532	51 486	20 323	57 169	7.7	14.1	15.0	20.3	17.5
0560	Atlantic City, NJ	2 114	319 416	115	151.1	260 185	44 398	778	5 389	8 666	17 972	7.0	12.1	13.4	17.6	14.2
0600	Augusta, GA-SC	5 042	396 809	92	78.7	264 801	123 482	941	5 438	2 147	5 620	7.9	15.5	15.5	17.7	15.4
0640	Austin, TX	7 231	781 572	53	108.1	600 023	72 254	2 827	18 770	87 698	159 942	7.8	13.8	19.0	21.2	16.4
0680	Bakersfield, CA	21 087	543 477	71	25.8	378 479	30 131	7 026	16 541	111 300	151 995	9.6	17.5	14.4	18.2	14.3
0720	Baltimore, MD	6 757	2 382 172	18	352.5	1 709 309	616 065	6 444	42 634	7 720	30 160	7.5	13.1	13.9	18.6	16.0
0733	Bangor, ME	8 796	146 601	195	16.7	143 678	536	1 273	932	182	701	6.5	13.6	17.5	16.6	15.2
0760	Baton Rouge, LA	4 108	528 264	72	128.6	363 692	156 509	902	5 657	1 504	7 532	7.8	16.4	17.3	17.5	15.3
0780	Battle Creek, MI	1 836	135 982	207	74.1	118 737	14 383	696	1 068	1 098	2 583	7.4	14.8	14.2	15.3	15.0
0840	Beaumont-Port Arthur, TX	5 579	361 226	103	64.7	264 365	84 665	890	5 687	5 619	15 241	7.3	16.0	13.7	15.9	14.2
0860	Bellingham, WA	5 491	127 780	222	23.3	119 229	650	4 014	2 363	1 524	3 718	6.9	14.4	16.8	15.7	16.4
0870	Benton Harbor, MI	1 479	161 378	177	109.1	133 259	24 872	685	1 487	1 075	2 683	7.4	15.1	14.2	15.5	14.4
0880	Billings, MT	6 825	113 419	247	16.6	107 921	511	3 235	612	1 140	3 158	7.4	15.6	13.0	16.7	16.0
0920	Biloxi-Gulfport, MS	2 740	197 125	157	71.9	156 255	35 055	595	4 495	725	3 488	7.9	15.3	15.9	17.4	13.8
0960	Binghamton, NY	3 174	264 497	129	83.3	254 447	4 647	450	3 990	963	2 845	7.0	13.2	14.9	16.8	14.2
1000	Birmingham, AL	10 313	907 810	46	88.0	655 609	245 726	1 506	4 014	955	3 989	7.0	14.2	14.1	16.8	15.5
1010	Bismarck, ND	9 219	83 831	272	9.1	81 306	79	2 016	286	144	435	7.4	16.5	13.8	17.2	15.7
1020	Bloomington, IN	1 021	108 978	252	106.7	102 752	2 835	216	2 713	462	1 367	5.5	10.2	31.8	16.8	12.8
1040	Bloomington-Normal, IL	3 066	129 180	221	42.1	121 057	5 563	203	1 624	733	1 671	6.6	13.0	24.1	16.3	14.0
1080	Boise City, ID	2 733	205 775	155	75.3	198 888	958	1 382	2 887	1 660	5 556	7.7	16.3	14.1	17.7	16.9
1123	Boston-Lawrence-Salem, MA-NH	6 321	3 783 817	9	598.6	3 331 834	233 819	6 921	116 597	94 646	186 652	6.7	11.5	15.5	19.2	15.4
1140	Bradenton, FL	1 920	211 707	153	110.3	190 328	16 400	501	1 227	3 251	9 424	5.8	10.4	10.2	13.7	12.0
1150	Bremerton, WA	1 026	189 731	161	184.9	171 063	5 107	3 211	8 282	2 068	6 169	8.2	15.7	14.7	17.0	16.6
1240	Brownsville-Harlingen, TX	2 345	260 120	131	110.9	214 424	825	413	750	43 708	212 995	8.9	19.9	17.7	14.6	12.8
1260	Bryan-College Station, TX	1 517	121 862	230	80.3	94 866	13 672	274	4 313	8 737	16 713	6.8	11.8	34.9	17.5	11.0
1282	Buffalo-Niagara Falls, NY	4 060	1 189 288	33	292.9	1 037 211	121 956	7 611	11 026	11 484	24 347	6.9	12.9	14.3	16.4	14.3
1280	Buffalo, NY	2 706	968 532	X	357.9	831 903	109 852	5 600	10 220	10 957	22 249	6.9	12.7	14.4	16.5	14.3
5700	Niagara Falls, NY	1 354	220 756	X	163.0	205 308	12 104	2 011	806	527	2 098	7.1	13.9	13.6	16.1	14.4
1300	Burlington, NC	1 115	108 213	254	97.1	86 373	20 822	303	487	228	736	6.3	11.8	15.2	15.8	14.8
1303	Burlington, VT	1 610	137 079	206	85.1	134 165	834	317	1 477	286	1 199	7.3	12.7	19.6	19.2	16.3
1320	Canton, OH	2 514	394 106	94	156.8	365 675	25 187	1 015	1 558	671	2 854	6.9	14.2	13.5	15.5	15.2
1350	Casper, WY	13 831	61 226	281	4.4	59 323	458	404	280	761	2 252	7.6	17.1	12.8	16.6	16.5
1360	Cedar Rapids, IA	1 858	168 767	174	90.8	163 164	3 334	363	1 401	505	1 591	7.1	14.1	14.9	17.2	15.5
1400	Champaign-Urbana-Rantoul, IL	2 583	173 025	172	67.0	146 506	16 559	331	8 033	1 596	3 485	6.8	11.8	25.8	18.9	13.6
1440	Charleston, SC	6 713	506 875	74	75.5	343 776	153 227	1 613	6 113	2 146	7 512	8.6	15.1	17.0	19.7	15.0
1480	Charleston, WV	3 236	250 454	137	77.4	234 518	13 919	292	1 450	275	1 042	6.0	13.6	12.7	15.5	15.9
1520	Charlotte-Gastonia-Rock Hill, NC-SC	8 751	1 162 093	34	132.8	911 904	231 654	4 107	11 304	3 124	10 671	7.3	13.4	15.1	18.3	15.8
1540	Charlottesville, VA	3 049	131 107	215	43.0	109 049	18 895	148	2 623	392	1 384	6.8	11.9	19.7	18.7	15.0
1560	Chattanooga, TN-GA	5 415	433 210	83	80.0	370 586	58 218	891	2 825	690	2 539	6.6	13.8	14.4	15.9	15.5
1580	Cheyenne, WY	6 957	73 142	279	10.5	66 280	2 218	528	821	3 295	7 310	8.0	15.6	14.2	17.8	15.8
1602	Chicago-Gary-Lake County, IL-IN-WI	14 553	8 065 633	3	554.2	5 772 110	1 547 725	15 758	256 050	473 990	893 422	7.7	14.3	14.5	18.3	15.2
0620	Aurora-Elgin, IL	2 179	356 884	X	163.8	307 694	19 216	693	4 698	24 583	45 340	8.6	16.6	14.3	17.7	16.2
1600	Chicago, IL	4 880	6 069 974	X	1 243.8	4 098 747	1 332 919	11 550	229 492	397 266	734 827	7.6	13.8	14.4	18.6	15.0
2960	Gary-Hammond, IN	2 370	604 526	X	255.1	460 532	117 142	1 108	3 716	22 028	48 384	7.1	16.1	14.5	15.9	15.0
3690	Joliet, IL	3 257	389 650	X	119.6	335 284	38 382	737	4 887	10 360	20 721	8.2	16.8	14.6	17.3	16.7
3800	Kenosha, WI	707	128 181	X	181.3	119 187	5 295	472	669	2 558	5 580	7.9	14.8	14.4	17.2	14.5
3965	Lake County, IL	1 160	516 418	X	445.2	450 666	34 771	1 198	12 588	17 195	38 570	8.5	15.1	14.9	18.0	16.9

1. MSA = Metropolitan Statistical Area. CMSA = Consolidated MSA. NECMA = New England county metropolitan area. PMSA = Primary MSA. See Appendix A for explanation of these concepts. See Appendix B for list of metropolitan areas identified by type, with component counties. 2. Dry land or land partially or temporarily covered by water. 3. Hispanic persons may be of any race.

Area name	Population, 1990 (cont'd): Age of population (cont'd), Percent: 45 to 54 years	55 to 64 years	65 to 74 years	75 years and over	Percent female	Population–change and components of change: Change, 1980–1990: Number	Percent	Components of change, 1980–1986: Total persons, 1986	Total persons, 1980	Net change: Number	Percent	Natural increase: Births	Deaths	Net migration	Households, 1990: Total
	16	17	18	19	20	21	22	23	24	25	26	27	28	29	30
Abilene, TX	8.8	7.9	6.6	5.4	51.4	8 723	7.9	125 900	110 932	14 900	13.4	15 300	6 000	5 600	43 301
Albany, GA	9.5	7.8	5.9	3.7	52.5	167	0.1	117 200	112 394	4 700	4.2	13 400	5 200	-3 500	39 362
Albany-Schenectady-Troy, NY	10.0	8.8	8.0	6.2	51.7	38 424	4.6	843 600	835 880	7 900	0.9	69 300	52 300	-9 100	335 823
Albuquerque, NM	10.1	7.9	6.4	4.1	51.2	60 315	14.4	474 400	420 262	54 100	12.9	48 100	17 500	23 500	185 582
Alexandria, LA	9.9	8.4	7.0	5.0	52.1	-3 726	-2.8	139 600	135 282	4 200	3.1	15 300	7 700	-3 400	45 941
Allentown-Bethlehem, PA-NJ	10.4	9.7	8.9	6.3	51.7	51 207	8.1	656 800	635 481	21 300	3.4	50 500	38 700	9 500	259 828
Altoona, PA	10.2	10.2	9.8	7.2	52.9	-6 079	-4.4	132 500	136 621	-4 100	-3.0	11 100	9 700	-5 500	50 332
Amarillo, TX	9.5	8.7	6.7	4.9	51.9	13 848	8.0	195 300	173 699	21 600	12.4	21 400	8 800	9 000	71 897
Anchorage, AK	10.3	5.3	2.7	1.0	48.6	51 907	29.8	235 000	174 431	60 600	34.7	29 900	4 100	34 800	82 702
Anderson, IN	11.2	9.5	8.2	5.8	51.1	-8 667	-6.2	132 700	139 336	-6 700	-4.8	11 000	7 700	-10 000	49 804
Anderson, SC	11.6	9.6	8.3	5.3	52.2	11 961	9.0	140 700	133 235	7 600	5.7	11 600	7 000	3 000	55 481
Anniston, AL	10.2	9.1	7.4	5.0	51.7	-3 727	-3.1	123 800	119 761	4 100	3.4	10 700	6 300	-300	42 983
Appleton-Oshkosh-Neenah, WI	9.7	8.0	6.5	5.4	50.8	23 752	8.2	307 600	291 369	16 100	5.5	29 400	13 700	400	115 515
Asheville, NC	11.2	9.9	9.2	6.9	52.5	13 887	8.6	170 000	160 934	9 000	5.6	12 500	10 300	6 800	70 802
Athens, GA	9.2	6.7	5.5	4.2	51.7	26 252	20.2	141 500	130 015	11 400	8.8	11 900	5 900	5 400	57 787
Atlanta, GA	10.7	6.9	4.8	3.2	51.3	695 368	32.5	2 560 300	2 138 143	422 200	19.7	227 700	97 600	292 100	1 056 427
Atlantic City, NJ	9.7	9.6	9.3	6.9	51.9	43 031	15.6	297 400	276 385	21 100	7.6	25 400	22 400	18 100	122 979
Augusta, GA-SC	9.9	8.1	6.2	3.7	51.3	50 886	14.7	390 000	345 923	44 000	12.7	39 300	17 900	22 600	142 669
Austin, TX	8.6	5.8	4.3	3.1	50.1	244 879	45.6	726 400	536 693	189 700	35.3	71 300	21 800	140 200	303 871
Bakersfield, CA	9.0	7.2	5.9	3.8	49.6	140 388	34.8	494 200	403 089	91 100	22.6	58 900	21 300	53 500	181 480
Baltimore, MD	10.7	8.6	7.1	4.6	51.7	182 675	8.3	2 279 900	2 199 497	80 200	3.6	205 200	126 200	1 200	880 145
Bangor, ME	10.1	8.8	6.5	5.0	51.1	9 586	7.0	138 200	137 015	1 300	0.9	12 100	7 100	-3 700	54 063
Baton Rouge, LA	9.6	7.1	5.5	3.4	51.7	34 113	6.9	545 700	494 151	51 600	10.4	62 300	20 900	10 200	188 377
Battle Creek, MI	10.4	9.4	7.7	5.6	51.6	-5 597	-4.0	136 900	141 579	-4 700	-3.3	12 900	7 800	-9 800	51 812
Beaumont-Port Arthur, TX	10.2	9.6	7.7	5.4	51.7	-11 984	-3.2	375 800	373 210	2 600	0.7	41 100	20 600	-17 900	134 238
Bellingham, WA	9.6	7.6	7.0	5.5	50.8	21 079	19.8	113 700	106 701	7 100	6.7	10 400	5 200	1 900	48 543
Benton Harbor, MI	10.4	9.3	8.0	5.7	52.1	-9 898	-5.8	163 600	171 276	-7 700	-4.5	15 700	9 400	-14 000	61 025
Billings, MT	10.3	8.6	7.2	5.2	51.5	5 384	5.0	120 100	108 035	12 200	11.3	12 200	4 800	4 800	44 689
Biloxi-Gulfport, MS	9.6	8.8	7.1	4.2	50.2	14 964	8.2	204 200	182 161	22 000	12.1	21 600	9 600	10 000	71 374
Binghamton, NY	10.4	9.3	8.1	6.1	51.6	1 037	0.4	261 800	263 460	-1 700	-0.6	22 700	15 100	-9 300	100 681
Birmingham, AL	10.2	9.0	7.6	5.6	52.7	23 817	2.7	911 000	883 993	27 100	3.1	84 100	53 000	-4 000	345 328
Bismarck, ND	9.6	8.3	6.3	5.1	51.2	3 843	4.8	85 900	79 988	5 900	7.4	9 500	3 300	-300	31 361
Bloomington, IN	8.0	6.5	4.9	3.7	51.7	10 193	10.3	101 700	98 785	3 000	3.0	7 400	3 400	-1 000	39 351
Bloomington-Normal, IL	8.6	6.9	5.7	4.8	52.3	10 031	8.4	122 700	119 149	3 600	3.0	11 000	5 500	-1 900	46 796
Boise City, ID	10.0	6.8	6.0	4.4	50.8	32 650	18.9	193 800	173 125	20 700	12.0	20 000	7 300	8 000	77 471
Boston-Lawrence-Salem, MA-NH	10.2	8.5	7.2	5.7	52.0	120 929	3.3	3 704 700	3 662 888	41 900	1.1	306 200	211 900	-52 400	1 412 190
Bradenton, FL	8.8	11.0	15.6	12.5	52.7	63 262	42.6	177 100	148 445	28 600	19.3	13 300	14 900	30 200	91 060
Bremerton, WA	10.1	7.1	6.3	4.4	48.9	42 579	28.9	169 200	147 152	22 200	15.1	17 100	6 800	11 900	69 267
Brownsville-Harlingen, TX	8.1	7.3	6.4	4.2	52.1	50 393	24.0	257 300	209 727	47 600	22.7	33 500	8 600	22 700	73 278
Bryan-College Station, TX	6.7	4.7	3.7	3.0	48.6	28 274	30.2	120 800	93 588	27 300	29.2	11 900	3 300	18 700	43 725
Buffalo-Niagara Falls, NY	10.0	9.9	9.0	6.2	52.3	-53 538	-4.3	1 181 600	1 242 826	-61 200	-4.9	102 700	78 700	-85 200	461 803
Buffalo, NY	10.0	9.9	9.0	6.2	52.4	-46 940	-4.6	964 700	1 015 472	-50 700	-5.0	83 100	64 800	-69 000	376 994
Niagara Falls, NY	10.0	9.7	9.0	6.1	52.1	-6 598	-2.9	216 900	227 354	-10 500	-4.6	19 600	13 900	-16 200	84 809
Burlington, NC	11.1	10.1	8.9	5.9	52.6	8 894	9.0	102 400	99 319	3 100	3.1	7 500	5 800	1 400	42 652
Burlington, VT	9.8	6.9	4.7	3.5	51.4	16 932	14.1	130 100	120 147	9 800	8.2	11 500	4 900	3 200	50 457
Canton, OH	10.7	9.6	8.5	5.8	52.1	-10 315	-2.6	400 300	404 421	-4 000	-1.0	35 700	23 100	-16 600	149 240
Casper, WY	10.0	8.9	6.7	3.9	50.9	-10 630	-14.8	70 900	71 856	-1 000	-1.4	9 300	2 600	-7 700	23 837
Cedar Rapids, IA	10.6	8.4	6.8	5.4	51.4	-1 008	-0.6	168 800	169 775	-1 000	-0.6	15 900	7 700	-9 200	65 501
Champaign-Urbana-Rantoul, IL	7.9	6.4	5.0	3.8	49.4	4 633	2.8	171 100	168 392	2 700	1.6	16 300	5 900	-7 700	63 900
Charleston, SC	9.2	6.9	5.5	3.1	50.1	76 529	17.8	485 600	430 346	55 200	12.8	54 000	18 500	19 700	177 668
Charleston, WV	11.0	10.3	8.9	6.0	52.5	-19 141	-7.1	266 400	269 595	-3 100	-1.1	22 300	15 900	-9 500	100 408
Charlotte-Gastonia-Rock Hill, NC-SC	10.7	8.4	6.6	4.3	51.8	190 646	19.6	1 065 400	971 447	93 900	9.7	90 600	49 500	52 800	440 670
Charlottesville, VA	9.4	7.7	6.3	4.5	51.7	17 539	15.4	121 400	113 568	7 900	7.0	10 400	5 500	3 000	48 709
Chattanooga, TN-GA	11.2	9.5	7.5	5.5	52.3	6 670	1.6	425 500	426 540	-1 100	-0.3	36 800	23 600	-14 300	166 404
Cheyenne, WY	10.2	8.1	6.1	4.2	50.2	4 493	6.5	75 200	68 649	6 600	9.6	8 500	3 200	1 300	28 092
Chicago-Gary-Lake County, IL-IN-WI	10.3	8.3	6.7	4.6	51.4	128 326	1.6	8 116 000	7 937 307	179 200	2.3	823 200	417 500	-226 500	2 908 063
Aurora-Elgin, IL	10.2	7.0	5.3	4.0	50.3	41 277	13.1	342 900	315 607	27 400	8.7	36 500	14 700	5 600	120 477
Chicago, IL	10.2	8.5	7.0	4.9	51.7	9 573	0.2	6 188 000	6 060 401	127 700	2.1	628 500	332 800	-168 000	2 221 772
Gary-Hammond, IN	10.5	9.1	7.4	4.4	51.8	-38 207	-5.9	614 800	642 733	-27 900	-4.3	63 300	31 700	-59 500	215 907
Joliet, IL	10.5	6.9	5.3	3.7	50.1	34 608	9.7	370 100	355 042	15 300	4.3	36 600	14 700	-6 600	128 912
Kenosha, WI	10.2	8.3	7.2	5.4	51.1	5 044	4.1	120 000	123 137	-3 100	-2.5	11 500	6 400	-8 200	47 029
Lake County, IL	10.8	7.5	5.1	3.3	49.4	76 031	17.3	480 200	440 387	39 800	9.0	46 800	17 200	10 200	173 966

Area name	Households, (cont'd): Percent change, 1980–1990	Households, (cont'd): Percent: Female family householder[1]	Households, (cont'd): Percent: One-person	Births, 1988: Total	Births, 1988: Rate[2]	Births, 1988: Low birth weight[3] (Number)	Deaths, 1987: Number: Total	Deaths, 1987: Number: Infant[4]	Deaths, 1987: Rate: Total[2]	Deaths, 1987: Rate: Infant[5]	Marriages, 1984: Number	Marriages, 1984: Rate[2]	Divorces, 1984: Number	Divorces, 1984: Rate[2]	Physicians, active non-Federal, 1989: Number[6]	Physicians, active non-Federal, 1989: Rate[7]
	31	33	34	35	36	37	38	39	40	41	42	43	44	45	46	47
Abilene, TX	12.4	9.3	24.7	2 290	18.8	173	993	15	8.0	6.5	1 840	15.0	954	7.8	215	177
Albany, GA	7.3	20.8	22.2	2 046	17.6	236	854	29	7.3	14.6	1 310	11.2	771	6.6	172	149
Albany-Schenectady-Troy, NY	11.1	10.7	26.9	11 782	13.8	709	8 422	94	10.0	8.1	6 880	8.2	2 700	3.2	2 144	251
Albuquerque, NM	22.9	11.9	26.1	8 157	16.5	636	3 102	71	6.4	8.4	4 996	11.0	3 972	8.7	1 503	300
Alexandria, LA	2.6	15.3	23.0	2 176	15.8	208	1 222	21	8.8	9.4	1 423	10.2	659	4.7	248	180
Allentown-Bethlehem, PA-NJ	12.8	9.3	23.5	9 233	13.6	522	6 486	75	9.7	8.5	5 158	8.0	2 121	3.3	1 214	177
Altoona, PA	2.5	11.4	25.9	1 601	12.1	95	1 612	14	12.1	8.5	953	7.1	373	2.8	215	163
Amarillo, TX	11.5	10.6	26.2	3 333	17.0	259	1 506	58	7.6	16.7	2 642	13.8	1 469	7.7	356	181
Anchorage, AK	36.8	10.1	22.9	NA	NA	NA	NA	NA	NA	NA	3 168	13.9	1 989	8.7	NA	NA
Anderson, IN	-0.4	11.4	24.9	1 678	12.7	132	1 253	25	9.5	15.0	1 393	10.4	890	6.6	137	104
Anderson, SC	18.2	11.7	22.7	1 859	13.0	166	1 253	21	8.9	11.4	1 477	10.7	673	4.9	190	132
Anniston, AL	8.4	12.4	23.2	1 645	13.3	117	1 010	21	8.2	12.6	1 413	11.3	1 088	8.7	136	111
Appleton-Oshkosh-Neenah, WI	16.3	7.7	22.7	4 707	15.0	241	2 252	29	7.3	6.2	2 634	8.7	1 032	3.4	455	144
Asheville, NC	17.5	10.9	26.6	2 358	13.6	145	1 755	23	10.2	10.0	1 634	9.8	937	5.6	452	259
Athens, GA	26.8	11.8	24.4	2 104	14.5	168	1 014	15	7.1	7.1	1 285	9.4	610	4.4	218	150
Atlanta, GA	39.6	13.0	22.9	47 093	17.2	3 700	17 567	524	6.6	11.7	27 536	11.6	12 246	5.1	5 698	202
Atlantic City, NJ	18.1	12.6	26.9	5 130	16.6	339	3 609	47	11.9	9.8	2 770	9.6	1 332	4.6	468	150
Augusta, GA-SC	24.0	15.0	22.8	6 955	17.5	600	3 179	91	8.1	13.7	5 201	14.0	2 362	6.4	1 295	323
Austin, TX	55.1	10.2	28.9	13 298	17.8	789	3 806	99	5.1	7.3	8 758	13.5	4 080	6.3	1 343	175
Bakersfield, CA	29.8	12.3	20.3	11 078	21.3	716	3 756	93	7.4	8.9	3 963	8.5	2 923	6.3	666	124
Baltimore, MD	14.9	14.6	23.5	37 786	16.1	3 219	21 527	458	9.3	12.6	21 129	9.4	8 787	3.9	8 279	350
Bangor, ME	17.6	9.9	22.6	1 920	13.6	103	1 227	16	8.8	8.7	1 386	10.0	709	5.1	285	199
Baton Rouge, LA	14.8	14.4	22.8	8 975	16.7	782	3 497	127	6.5	14.1	5 426	10.1	NA	0.0	876	164
Battle Creek, MI	1.3	13.1	25.3	2 017	14.5	146	1 360	25	9.8	12.6	1 367	10.0	765	5.6	161	115
Beaumont-Port Arthur, TX	1.8	12.9	23.9	5 485	15.1	408	3 517	61	9.6	11.0	5 247	13.7	2 555	6.7	497	139
Bellingham, WA	22.5	8.0	24.9	1 673	14.1	56	911	18	7.9	11.3	1 049	9.4	624	5.6	193	159
Benton Harbor, MI	1.2	13.3	24.4	2 530	15.2	203	1 562	35	9.4	13.7	1 685	10.3	814	5.0	193	115
Billings, MT	12.0	9.7	26.5	1 637	14.1	105	757	12	6.4	7.0	1 207	10.1	711	6.0	256	220
Biloxi-Gulfport, MS	18.2	13.4	24.0	3 252	15.9	216	1 695	30	8.2	8.9	2 759	14.0	1 498	7.6	317	154
Binghamton, NY	7.9	9.8	25.5	3 879	14.9	215	2 478	42	9.6	11.3	2 035	7.8	979	3.7	494	191
Birmingham, AL	9.1	13.9	24.7	13 727	14.9	1 162	8 877	161	9.6	11.9	9 966	11.1	5 568	6.2	2 602	281
Bismarck, ND	12.2	8.5	24.9	1 276	14.9	66	552	16	6.4	13.2	784	9.2	306	3.6	199	232
Bloomington, IN	15.9	8.3	28.5	1 278	12.4	75	571	10	5.6	8.7	977	9.6	536	5.3	167	161
Bloomington-Normal, IL	12.2	8.3	26.1	1 758	14.1	89	912	15	7.4	9.0	1 138	9.3	537	4.4	171	136
Boise City, ID	22.7	9.2	23.6	3 065	15.3	153	1 282	38	6.5	12.4	1 993	10.5	1 443	7.6	356	173
Boston-Lawrence-Salem, MA-NH	8.9	12.1	26.4	56 141	15.0	3 380	34 202	388	9.2	7.2	31 422	8.5	10 213	2.8	15 031	402
Bradenton, FL	46.9	8.4	27.0	2 695	14.4	190	2 655	38	14.5	14.8	1 890	11.1	1 041	6.1	305	160
Bremerton, WA	31.2	8.5	22.1	2 850	15.8	136	1 129	27	6.5	9.6	1 715	10.4	895	5.4	219	117
Brownsville-Harlingen, TX	25.4	16.1	16.0	5 853	22.2	304	1 558	39	6.0	7.1	2 885	11.7	916	3.7	267	100
Bryan-College Station, TX	34.6	9.1	25.2	1 827	15.7	115	568	12	4.8	7.0	1 175	9.9	457	3.8	163	142
Buffalo-Niagara Falls, NY	3.7	12.9	27.5	16 684	14.2	1 143	12 571	156	10.7	9.4	10 214	8.6	4 110	3.4	2 955	252
Buffalo, NY	3.2	13.3	27.9	13 572	14.2	957	10 380	137	10.9	10.1	8 006	8.2	3 390	3.5	2 714	284
Niagara Falls, NY	5.7	11.6	26.1	3 112	14.3	186	2 191	19	10.2	6.2	2 208	10.2	720	3.3	241	111
Burlington, NC	18.6	12.0	24.5	1 522	14.4	121	958	11	9.1	7.7	993	9.8	577	5.7	139	130
Burlington, VT	25.7	8.8	22.9	2 095	15.6	113	838	8	6.4	3.9	1 268	10.1	502	4.0	683	497
Canton, OH	4.6	10.7	23.7	5 519	13.7	396	3 722	53	9.3	9.9	3 661	9.1	1 986	4.9	601	150
Casper, WY	-7.8	9.7	25.9	925	14.3	63	412	7	6.2	7.0	801	10.8	698	9.4	130	207
Cedar Rapids, IA	6.0	8.5	25.0	2 465	14.4	139	1 269	19	7.5	8.0	1 614	9.6	576	3.4	249	143
Champaign-Urbana-Rantoul, IL	9.4	8.4	28.7	2 615	15.2	168	969	25	5.7	9.6	1 636	9.6	875	5.1	382	221
Charleston, SC	28.9	13.5	21.3	9 533	18.7	737	3 210	101	6.4	11.0	5 894	12.4	2 087	4.4	1 375	263
Charleston, WV	1.0	11.3	25.9	3 073	11.8	198	2 666	25	10.1	7.6	2 528	9.3	1 487	5.5	595	231
Charlotte-Gastonia-Rock Hill, NC-SC	28.7	12.0	23.1	17 814	16.0	1 570	8 910	214	8.2	12.8	11 292	10.9	5 633	5.5	1 614	142
Charlottesville, VA	21.0	10.2	24.6	1 844	14.9	128	921	17	7.5	9.5	1 176	9.9	521	4.4	1 039	834
Chattanooga, TN-GA	10.4	12.5	23.9	6 314	14.4	446	3 941	77	9.1	13.0	9 190	21.6	2 599	6.1	788	178
Cheyenne, WY	11.1	9.7	25.3	1 236	16.4	112	466	15	6.2	11.4	1 008	13.7	669	9.1	143	187
Chicago-Gary-Lake County, IL-IN-WI	5.1	13.4	25.3	139 057	17.0	10 934	67 772	1 649	8.3	12.3	70 159	8.7	32 325	4.0	20 299	247
Aurora-Elgin, IL	13.9	9.5	19.5	6 347	17.9	401	2 476	76	7.1	12.6	3 290	10.0	1 548	4.7	473	130
Chicago, IL	3.3	14.1	26.9	106 940	17.2	8 823	53 562	1 349	8.6	13.0	52 899	8.6	24 049	3.9	17 436	279
Gary-Hammond, IN	0.8	14.3	22.4	9 003	14.7	732	5 177	81	8.5	10.1	5 223	8.3	2 858	4.6	882	144
Joliet, IL	13.2	9.6	18.2	6 140	16.2	361	2 512	49	6.7	8.6	2 684	7.4	1 257	3.5	329	86
Kenosha, WI	9.2	11.6	23.2	1 934	15.8	105	1 074	21	8.9	10.9	1 221	10.1	542	4.5	137	111
Lake County, IL	24.5	8.7	18.5	8 693	17.6	512	2 971	73	6.1	8.8	4 842	10.5	2 071	4.5	1 042	206

1. No spouse present. 2. Per 1,000 resident population estimated as of July 1 of the year shown. 3. Under 2,500 grams. 4. Deaths of infants under 1 year old. 5. Deaths of infants under 1 year old per 1,000 live births. 6. As of end of year. 7. Per 100,000 resident population as of July 1 of the year shown.

Table B. Metropolitan Areas — **Health Resources, Crime, Education, and Social Security**

Area name	Hospitals, 1989: Number	Hospitals, 1989: Beds: Number	Hospitals, 1989: Beds: Rate[1]	Nursing homes,[2] 1986: Number	Nursing homes,[2] 1986: Beds	Serious crimes known to police, 1988: Number: Total[3]	Serious crimes known to police, 1988: Number: Violent[4]	Serious crimes known to police, 1988: Rate[5]	Education: Public school enrollment[6]: 1986–1987	Education: Public school enrollment[6]: 1980	Education: Attainment,[7] 1980: Percent 12 years or more	Education: Attainment,[7] 1980: Percent 16 years or more	Education: Local government expenditures for education,[8] 1982: Total (Mil dol)	Education: Local government expenditures for education,[8] 1982: Per capita (Dollars)	Social Security Program December 1988: Beneficiaries: Total	Social Security Program December 1988: Beneficiaries: Rate[9]
	48	49	50	51	52	53	54	55	56	57	58	59	60	61	62	63
Abilene, TX	4	663	546	8	932	6 937	701	5 695	22 061	20 021	64.5	17.4	40.0	336	17 990	147.7
Albany, GA	2	624	541	18	657	9 928	1 039	8 537	22 839	25 369	58.0	13.7	45.2	808	14 805	127.3
Albany-Schenectady-Troy, NY	19	4 647	544	68	5 857	29 609	2 459	3 480	122 185	148 427	69.7	17.9	444.2	3 275	151 360	177.9
Albuquerque, NM	21	2 863	571	34	1 562	40 185	4 364	8 149	79 919	79 654	76.5	22.8	225.9	521	62 110	126.0
Alexandria, LA	7	1 424	1 036	15	1 745	4 101	377	2 976	25 060	27 149	56.5	11.9	56.6	413	20 545	149.1
Allentown-Bethlehem, PA-NJ	12	3 303	482	37	5 165	18 952	1 227	2 799	94 214	109 029	63.3	12.7	277.6	1 732	127 680	188.6
Altoona, PA	7	909	687	29	2 070	3 137	176	2 368	20 992	23 974	65.4	8.1	55.1	406	22 365	168.8
Amarillo, TX	6	1 221	619	13	1 147	14 253	972	7 261	35 410	33 050	69.4	16.2	71.8	716	25 610	130.5
Anchorage, AK	NA	NA	NA	2	456	12 534	1 122	5 736	39 785	36 008	88.3	23.6	148.9	729	10 895	49.9
Anderson, IN	4	655	498	11	1 095	4 982	443	3 780	23 814	29 246	64.5	10.4	53.1	393	24 540	186.2
Anderson, SC	1	473	328	14	601	6 514	825	4 552	24 972	27 005	47.3	10.1	49.4	360	25 970	181.5
Anniston, AL	5	584	475	7	593	5 529	888	4 484	20 939	23 279	56.7	11.0	35.6	288	20 075	162.8
Appleton-Oshkosh-Neenah, WI	8	1 386	438	26	2 776	10 686	301	3 415	46 315	53 455	71.6	14.0	123.6	1 197	46 260	147.8
Asheville, NC	7	1 569	898	48	1 619	7 633	455	4 410	26 606	29 574	59.4	14.6	59.9	366	33 570	193.9
Athens, GA	5	742	509	11	782	6 557	521	4 531	22 393	22 199	57.1	23.6	45.7	1 353	20 090	138.8
Atlanta, GA	61	12 343	438	178	10 049	227 873	25 896	8 327	444 248	425 695	66.7	20.2	920.2	6 804	282 755	103.3
Atlantic City, NJ	7	2 107	673	37	2 928	31 713	2 260	10 256	43 321	46 890	61.7	12.7	148.2	1 026	60 900	197.0
Augusta, GA-SC	11	3 867	965	59	2 059	21 191	2 214	5 346	70 385	67 149	58.9	14.0	138.5	1 505	52 560	132.6
Austin, TX	20	3 272	427	41	4 123	65 951	3 459	8 811	123 609	95 812	73.1	28.1	246.9	1 424	69 125	92.4
Bakersfield, CA	12	1 268	237	63	2 162	36 756	4 547	7 068	100 462	81 814	62.1	11.8	236.6	544	68 775	132.3
Baltimore, MD	43	12 516	529	128	14 318	152 722	24 568	6 520	334 189	401 685	62.0	16.9	981.0	3 289	331 365	141.5
Bangor, ME	5	880	616	49	1 189	4 756	128	3 364	22 743	27 831	71.9	14.2	52.8	383	22 600	159.8
Baton Rouge, LA	12	2 170	406	28	3 279	41 137	5 033	7 668	94 813	96 228	68.2	19.6	228.4	1 915	62 875	117.2
Battle Creek, MI	6	1 670	1 194	74	1 385	8 535	918	6 131	25 564	29 333	67.8	11.9	66.4	476	24 015	172.5
Beaumont-Port Arthur, TX	10	2 070	577	23	2 602	26 270	2 579	7 219	72 369	77 268	62.5	12.1	207.0	1 645	62 240	171.0
Bellingham, WA	1	162	133	13	1 135	6 209	290	5 231	18 663	18 592	76.5	17.9	52.5	477	18 840	158.7
Benton Harbor, MI	5	818	488	60	1 310	11 328	1 461	6 800	30 962	34 385	64.8	13.3	86.9	525	30 625	183.8
Billings, MT	2	551	475	7	564	6 694	159	5 751	21 724	21 191	76.6	19.9	54.2	478	17 120	147.1
Biloxi-Gulfport, MS	9	2 044	991	7	757	8 819	765	4 302	33 421	33 792	66.4	13.5	56.0	575	29 565	144.2
Binghamton, NY	3	1 507	581	19	2 168	7 715	287	2 965	43 622	51 583	69.9	15.5	169.3	1 317	48 285	185.6
Birmingham, AL	24	5 589	603	73	5 560	51 083	6 478	5 532	154 595	165 337	61.7	14.4	284.7	1 543	158 285	171.4
Bismarck, ND	4	645	754	7	657	3 534	57	4 119	15 206	14 752	71.5	18.9	39.3	1 004	12 005	139.9
Bloomington, IN	1	285	275	4	601	3 744	199	3 631	12 855	14 246	74.7	31.3	29.2	289	11 240	109.0
Bloomington-Normal, IL	2	662	528	11	1 103	5 847	277	4 689	18 668	18 675	76.0	22.8	48.6	403	16 055	128.7
Boise City, ID	5	816	397	23	1 318	9 454	642	4 711	37 359	34 608	81.7	22.1	61.6	339	25 805	128.6
Boston-Lawrence-Salem, MA-NH	111	24 854	664	472	33 638	166 884	22 639	4 467	517 435	654 702	75.7	22.6	1 705.9	2 313	553 325	148.1
Bradenton, FL	2	895	469	31	1 789	NA	NA	0	22 873	20 920	66.5	12.4	54.2	336	54 425	291.2
Bremerton, WA	2	376	201	12	1 046	6 430	401	3 554	30 234	29 010	79.7	16.4	77.4	495	21 685	119.9
Brownsville-Harlingen, TX	6	993	371	8	907	19 275	1 979	7 301	67 350	55 312	43.8	10.5	106.8	462	33 220	125.8
Bryan-College Station, TX	4	390	339	4	589	10 744	635	9 214	15 847	13 688	69.1	31.9	32.2	287	9 470	81.2
Buffalo-Niagara Falls, NY	23	7 406	632	85	9 622	55 395	6 990	4 712	171 099	217 224	65.5	14.5	691.6	1 156	226 515	192.7
Buffalo, NY	18	6 539	685	62	7 662	45 677	6 164	4 764	136 448	173 760	65.4	15.1	559.4	560	183 360	191.3
Niagara Falls, NY	5	867	400	23	1 960	9 718	826	4 480	34 651	43 464	65.7	11.5	132.2	596	43 155	199.0
Burlington, NC	2	340	317	28	651	4 066	349	3 843	17 014	19 752	54.0	11.8	38.1	377	20 680	195.5
Burlington, VT	2	566	412	18	674	NA	NA	0	20 925	23 016	77.8	26.1	61.9	821	14 775	109.8
Canton, OH	7	2 123	529	51	3 951	16 594	1 722	4 134	70 873	79 261	67.1	11.0	167.4	695	73 105	182.1
Casper, WY	2	279	444	3	317	3 441	270	5 318	13 359	13 937	82.5	19.7	57.0	733	8 375	129.4
Cedar Rapids, IA	2	928	534	14	1 137	9 243	345	5 390	29 107	32 778	77.6	16.7	87.6	519	25 815	150.5
Champaign-Urbana-Rantoul, IL	4	1 032	597	13	1 399	9 393	1 001	5 458	23 263	25 200	80.9	30.0	61.1	355	17 375	101.0
Charleston, SC	11	2 328	445	39	1 662	29 742	3 574	5 823	81 945	85 479	63.2	15.0	174.5	1 159	55 380	108.4
Charleston, WV	7	1 629	631	11	1 058	9 643	557	3 697	45 578	49 795	64.7	14.7	120.9	940	49 660	190.4
Charlotte-Gastonia-Rock Hill, NC-SC	18	4 698	415	91	5 628	78 291	10 094	7 041	183 966	195 678	57.5	14.6	391.0	2 675	159 540	143.5
Charlottesville, VA	4	1 050	843	11	827	5 772	373	4 662	17 035	18 774	65.1	28.5	47.8	1 650	16 640	134.4
Chattanooga, TN-GA	19	2 489	563	35	2 358	NA	NA	0	75 152	78 385	58.3	12.6	133.9	1 938	71 945	164.2
Cheyenne, WY	4	422	552	3	278	3 192	143	4 245	13 853	13 799	80.1	17.7	49.3	693	8 620	114.6
Chicago-Gary-Lake County, IL-IN-WI	127	40 158	488	362	56 405	518 773	80 239	6 341	1 248 992	1 410 041	67.4	17.8	3 663.3	5 386	1 098 190	134.2
Aurora-Elgin, IL	6	2 091	577	21	2 328	17 773	1 210	5 001	76 034	63 498	71.3	16.4	172.0	972	42 050	118.3
Chicago, IL	99	30 860	494	264	43 515	427 885	72 289	6 883	887 228	1 031 474	66.6	18.4	2 722.1	1 352	847 285	136.3
Gary-Hammond, IN	7	2 995	490	25	3 438	28 883	3 759	4 718	114 313	130 851	65.3	10.9	294.7	910	96 770	158.1
Joliet, IL	4	895	233	18	2 520	17 689	1 521	4 665	67 029	73 816	69.9	13.9	175.8	1 136	40 310	106.3
Kenosha, WI	2	330	268	12	1 327	5 789	239	4 722	20 331	23 258	64.8	10.7	58.9	485	20 450	166.8
Lake County, IL	9	2 987	591	22	3 277	20 754	1 221	4 190	84 057	87 144	77.6	25.1	239.8	531	51 325	103.6

1. Per 100,000 resident population estimated as of July 1 of the year shown. 2. Covers nursing homes with 3 or more beds. 3. Data for serious crimes have not been adjusted for underreporting, this may affect comparability between geographic areas or over time. 4. Includes murder and nonnegligent manslaughter, forcible rape, robbery, and aggravated assault. 5. Per 100,000 resident population as of July 1 of the year shown. 6. The 1986–1987 data are based on administrative reports obtained by the U.S. National Center for Education Statistics. The 1980 data are based on the 1980 Census of Population and Housing. 7. Persons 25 years old or older. 8. Elementary and secondary. 9. Per 1,000 resident population estimated as of July 1 of the year shown.

Area name	Social Security Program, Dec. 1988 (cont'd)		Housing units, 1990				Civilian labor force, 1990				Private nonfarm establishments, 1988			
					Occupied units				Unemployment				Employment[2]	
	Payments ($1,000)	Supplemental Security Income Program recipients, June 1986	Total	Percent change, 1980–1990	Total	Percent owner-occupied	Total	Percent change, 1989–1990	Total	Rate[1]	Number	Net change, 1987–1988	Total	Percent change, 1987–1988
	64	65	72	73	74	75	78	79	80	81	82	83	84	85
Abilene, TX	8 353	2 172	49 988	20.1	43 301	62.2	50 932	-3.1	3 122	6.1	3 420	-23	38 469	-4.2
Albany, GA	6 180	3 590	42 910	11.1	39 362	55.7	54 083	0.8	3 544	6.6	2 727	-13	36 848	0.4
Albany-Schenectady-Troy, NY	77 826	11 506	371 571	10.7	335 823	64.1	440 590	0.8	15 996	3.6	20 430	478	298 092	-0.4
Albuquerque, NM	28 953	6 080	201 235	24.1	185 582	60.7	264 817	-0.3	13 225	5.0	13 300	15	181 695	0.1
Alexandria, LA	8 144	5 558	51 239	6.2	45 941	66.5	57 675	-4.1	3 670	6.4	2 846	-114	34 150	0.8
Allentown-Bethlehem, PA-NJ	66 926	6 626	277 649	13.3	259 828	71.6	335 581	2.1	18 496	5.5	16 239	425	252 978	2.2
Altoona, PA	10 301	2 260	54 349	4.4	50 332	72.6	61 796	2.4	4 472	7.2	2 958	-13	42 415	0.5
Amarillo, TX	12 604	1 696	80 734	16.0	71 897	64.2	96 218	-1.5	4 866	5.1	5 256	-65	63 289	0.7
Anchorage, AK	5 323	1 094	94 153	33.8	82 702	52.8	117 230	2.6	6 141	5.2	6 569	-113	73 502	-6.0
Anderson, IN	12 874	1 448	53 353	0.0	49 804	73.1	59 535	-1.8	3 805	6.4	2 548	-42	41 748	0.0
Anderson, SC	11 913	2 792	60 745	18.3	55 481	75.2	70 699	0.3	3 794	5.4	3 086	50	47 291	8.6
Anniston, AL	8 325	3 212	46 753	9.8	42 983	70.3	50 774	-1.7	3 569	7.0	2 200	20	30 650	2.0
Appleton-Oshkosh-Neenah, WI	23 845	3 016	120 511	15.8	115 515	70.3	174 118	-0.6	7 518	4.3	7 433	99	136 659	7.8
Asheville, NC	15 367	3 524	77 951	17.9	70 802	70.3	92 205	2.2	3 033	3.3	4 771	104	69 093	6.4
Athens, GA	8 756	3 554	62 735	31.6	57 787	58.6	77 064	-0.6	3 504	4.5	3 419	145	47 346	0.7
Atlanta, GA	135 804	36 904	1 174 007	45.1	1 056 427	62.3	1 521 859	0.7	77 235	5.1	76 270	2 708	1 271 674	3.1
Atlantic City, NJ	31 051	4 944	192 414	19.2	122 979	66.8	187 878	5.0	11 654	6.2	9 748	185	132 577	-1.4
Augusta, GA-SC	23 247	9 614	158 342	26.0	142 669	66.3	198 569	3.9	8 706	4.4	8 063	41	127 082	0.7
Austin, TX	32 993	8 472	343 886	57.9	303 871	49.6	435 282	0.9	19 806	4.6	19 368	-509	254 614	-3.1
Bakersfield, CA	32 024	16 448	198 636	27.6	181 480	59.3	232 418	-2.2	24 378	10.5	10 407	10	119 973	4.2
Baltimore, MD	168 317	33 366	938 979	16.0	880 145	63.7	1 214 498	0.5	61 616	5.1	54 429	564	903 266	1.2
Bangor, ME	10 316	2 538	61 359	14.9	54 063	69.7	69 543	3.5	3 737	5.4	3 780	143	51 551	7.5
Baton Rouge, LA	28 860	9 550	212 078	19.2	188 377	65.3	269 673	0.0	14 541	5.4	11 733	-236	164 967	1.1
Battle Creek, MI	12 247	2 392	55 619	2.6	51 812	71.0	64 725	-1.2	4 951	7.6	2 817	11	47 807	1.4
Beaumont-Port Arthur, TX	31 535	6 138	149 807	4.2	134 238	69.7	165 066	0.8	12 153	7.4	7 745	-123	117 329	1.4
Bellingham, WA	9 369	1 254	55 742	17.4	48 543	64.3	68 263	5.6	3 321	4.9	3 505	134	36 387	6.6
Benton Harbor, MI	15 500	3 304	69 532	1.1	61 025	69.6	78 014	-1.3	5 747	7.4	3 621	31	57 333	3.0
Billings, MT	8 434	912	48 781	14.1	44 689	65.7	64 473	0.1	3 078	4.8	3 981	-19	41 371	-1.8
Biloxi-Gulfport, MS	12 469	3 940	84 374	19.7	71 374	64.3	89 494	1.8	5 517	6.2	4 163	-54	46 708	-1.1
Binghamton, NY	24 571	3 452	108 223	8.3	100 681	67.9	122 834	-2.8	5 105	4.2	5 343	25	97 781	2.7
Birmingham, AL	74 779	20 892	376 897	10.5	345 328	69.0	439 185	-0.9	23 651	5.4	21 156	262	343 970	1.7
Bismarck, ND	5 467	782	33 270	10.1	31 361	67.1	47 179	0.2	1 833	3.9	2 506	-1	28 143	3.0
Bloomington, IN	5 816	662	41 948	15.8	39 351	54.8	60 553	-0.7	2 004	3.3	2 427	91	34 735	5.6
Bloomington-Normal, IL	8 360	772	49 164	8.3	46 796	63.5	75 503	1.7	3 005	4.0	2 868	42	50 505	-1.7
Boise City, ID	12 766	1 382	80 849	19.2	77 471	69.1	116 504	2.6	4 471	3.8	6 028	236	76 912	8.0
Boston-Lawrence-Salem, MA-NH	281 682	67 408	1 510 420	9.6	1 412 190	57.5	2 055 669	-0.7	112 148	5.5	103 312	1 108	1 950 594	1.3
Bradenton, FL	27 283	1 554	115 245	37.9	91 060	70.9	93 021	7.6	4 316	4.6	4 289	-29	50 686	-1.2
Bremerton, WA	9 404	1 336	74 038	29.2	69 267	64.3	83 007	3.9	3 525	4.2	3 461	141	29 814	4.7
Brownsville-Harlingen, TX	12 441	9 350	88 759	34.5	73 278	64.4	104 812	1.4	12 280	11.7	4 671	97	53 621	2.3
Bryan-College Station, TX	4 358	1 172	48 799	36.7	43 725	41.9	61 806	0.2	2 159	3.5	2 402	-43	27 974	3.4
Buffalo-Niagara Falls, NY	119 062	18 148	492 516	3.9	461 803	64.5	558 684	-0.7	27 770	5.0	26 761	586	432 552	3.3
Buffalo, NY	96 354	15 408	402 131	3.4	376 994	63.7	461 287	-0.8	22 100	4.8	22 254	447	366 032	3.5
Niagara Falls, NY	22 708	2 740	90 385	6.1	84 809	68.1	97 397	-0.2	5 670	5.8	4 507	139	66 520	2.2
Burlington, NC	9 944	2 092	45 312	18.7	42 652	71.8	65 594	-1.0	2 159	3.3	2 964	37	51 169	3.0
Burlington, VT	7 290	1 592	56 230	25.2	50 457	64.9	81 400	0.2	2 773	3.4	4 635	226	64 656	0.7
Canton, OH	37 308	4 282	158 446	3.2	149 240	70.7	193 782	-0.3	12 028	6.2	9 126	92	144 726	2.4
Casper, WY	4 442	334	29 082	2.1	23 837	68.9	32 012	3.5	1 854	5.8	2 310	-60	19 111	-2.1
Cedar Rapids, IA	13 599	1 376	68 357	5.5	65 501	70.4	96 835	-0.9	4 989	5.2	4 411	63	78 591	2.5
Champaign-Urbana-Rantoul, IL	8 219	1 208	68 416	9.4	63 900	54.5	91 966	0.7	3 577	3.9	3 726	22	53 659	2.5
Charleston, SC	23 546	9 490	199 879	31.6	177 668	62.6	237 256	3.7	8 055	3.4	10 905	125	137 781	3.1
Charleston, WV	24 732	4 864	109 631	4.8	100 408	70.8	119 687	1.4	7 502	6.3	6 095	36	85 620	-0.9
Charlotte-Gastonia-Rock Hill, NC-SC	77 848	14 240	472 913	29.9	440 670	66.8	646 683	0.9	22 560	3.5	31 154	1 182	553 984	4.3
Charlottesville, VA	7 917	1 798	51 932	20.1	48 709	59.4	71 773	2.7	2 135	3.0	3 569	164	45 918	3.0
Chattanooga, TN-GA	34 539	9 092	181 276	12.5	166 404	68.4	211 262	-0.6	9 850	4.7	10 040	130	165 221	4.6
Cheyenne, WY	4 170	506	30 507	11.4	28 092	65.5	37 644	1.9	1 916	5.1	1 888	-12	19 306	0.9
Chicago-Gary-Lake County, IL-IN-WI	592 232	103 226	3 105 919	5.6	2 908 063	61.8	4 321 385	0.4	250 903	5.8	186 219	3 442	3 380 339	4.0
Aurora-Elgin, IL	22 841	1 910	125 243	12.8	120 477	70.3	190 607	2.4	11 059	5.8	8 219	308	127 855	6.8
Chicago, IL	457 786	88 954	2 380 355	4.3	2 221 772	58.6	3 294 644	0.2	195 478	5.9	145 698	2 195	2 751 735	3.5
Gary-Hammond, IN	51 389	6 286	230 254	1.0	215 907	69.3	263 751	0.3	14 966	5.7	11 091	153	189 964	5.3
Joliet, IL	21 254	1 902	135 522	11.7	128 912	76.7	209 928	0.8	13 890	6.6	6 685	181	90 865	3.2
Kenosha, WI	10 794	1 682	51 262	7.9	47 029	68.8	53 325	-2.1	3 382	6.3	2 439	52	36 902	8.4
Lake County, IL	28 168	2 492	183 283	21.8	173 966	74.2	309 130	1.8	12 128	3.9	12 087	553	183 018	7.1

1. Percent of total civilian labor force. 2. For week including March 12. Excludes government employees, self-employed persons, farm workers, domestic service workers, railroad employees subject to the Railroad Retirement Act, and employees on oceanborne vessels or in foreign countries.

Area name	Private nonfarm establishments, 1987 (cont'd): Employment[1] (cont'd): Manufacturing	Employment[1] (cont'd): Retail trade	Employment[1] (cont'd): Finance, insurance, and real estate	Employment[1] (cont'd): Services	Annual payroll: Total (Mil dol)	Annual payroll: Average per employee	Personal income, 1989: Total (Mil dol)	Percent change, 1988–1989	Wages and salaries[2] (Mil dol)	Proprietor's income (Mil dol)	Dividends, interest, & rent (Mil dol)	Transfer payments (Mil dol)	Per capita[3]: Dollars	Per capita[3]: Rank (Dollars)
	86	87	88	89	90	91	92	93	94	95	96	97	98	99
Abilene, TX	4 877	10 312	2 503	11 445	633	16 455	1 820	5.0	1 081	248	357	282	15 001	182
Albany, GA	NA	9 258	NA	8 244	669	18 156	1 538	5.7	1 133	108	200	280	13 348	250
Albany-Schenectady-Troy, NY	42 318	70 434	24 803	105 592	5 947	19 950	16 062	8.2	10 732	942	2 861	2 775	18 802	40
Albuquerque, NM	19 601	41 845	13 411	65 042	3 402	18 724	7 929	7.0	5 724	497	1 396	1 178	15 806	134
Alexandria, LA	3 346	9 217	2 319	11 932	532	15 578	1 768	6.3	998	184	281	415	12 865	258
Allentown-Bethlehem, PA-NJ	77 638	51 111	11 248	68 746	5 291	20 915	12 537	7.6	7 130	921	2 331	1 781	18 294	52
Altoona, PA	10 588	10 546	1 899	11 031	681	16 056	1 810	7.2	1 094	160	290	425	13 685	236
Amarillo, TX	11 100	17 439	4 119	15 291	1 103	17 428	3 036	5.2	1 669	413	565	421	15 396	153
Anchorage, AK	1 709	17 906	6 438	24 014	2 062	28 054	5 313	12.1	3 793	612	665	659	24 773	2
Anderson, IN	16 386	9 536	1 508	10 149	949	22 732	2 048	8.1	1 377	122	314	335	15 558	147
Anderson, SC	20 509	9 992	1 407	9 125	773	16 346	1 932	7.1	1 084	149	260	298	13 388	247
Anniston, AL	10 474	7 537	1 160	6 386	465	15 171	1 518	5.3	1 049	102	185	311	12 353	269
Appleton-Oshkosh-Neenah, WI	52 715	25 918	7 680	29 877	2 880	21 074	5 071	7.0	3 691	377	852	633	16 032	122
Asheville, NC	19 542	16 298	2 766	18 620	1 187	17 180	2 730	9.1	1 796	201	508	440	15 627	144
Athens, GA	15 338	12 576	1 986	9 018	758	16 010	2 193	8.5	1 420	228	328	305	15 052	175
Atlanta, GA	199 323	274 097	107 660	341 594	28 660	22 537	53 715	6.6	41 311	3 845	7 709	4 788	19 055	35
Atlantic City, NJ	8 311	28 690	7 560	67 425	2 760	20 818	7 200	7.6	4 487	497	1 295	989	23 001	10
Augusta, GA-SC	37 987	31 043	6 182	32 718	2 413	18 988	5 999	9.8	4 426	362	753	948	14 970	184
Austin, TX	40 786	64 221	27 211	80 751	4 945	19 422	12 349	7.7	8 673	1 136	2 016	1 405	16 113	118
Bakersfield, CA	8 256	32 434	5 997	34 962	2 306	19 221	7 948	5.9	4 873	1 173	1 066	1 388	14 856	191
Baltimore, MD	147 163	195 516	76 431	293 160	19 201	21 257	47 996	7.7	30 726	2 781	7 466	6 453	20 267	19
Bangor, ME	13 668	12 462	2 114	13 021	950	18 428	2 177	9.2	1 462	186	309	373	15 239	168
Baton Rouge, LA	18 946	38 024	12 623	47 212	3 332	20 198	7 887	7.1	5 262	605	1 106	1 115	14 757	196
Battle Creek, MI	15 409	11 162	3 884	13 012	1 042	21 796	2 096	6.4	1 572	94	337	410	14 981	183
Beaumont-Port Arthur, TX	26 677	25 654	4 951	30 616	2 474	21 086	5 500	5.8	3 423	463	997	927	15 339	160
Bellingham, WA	7 520	9 999	1 769	10 201	638	17 534	1 876	11.6	1 024	282	358	300	15 457	152
Benton Harbor, MI	22 033	11 351	2 585	14 575	1 112	19 395	2 507	6.5	1 544	167	426	449	14 966	185
Billings, MT	2 991	11 109	2 785	13 181	710	17 162	1 811	8.0	1 090	185	373	273	15 595	145
Biloxi-Gulfport, MS	8 478	14 793	3 310	11 461	694	14 858	2 517	6.8	1 688	213	349	504	12 209	271
Binghamton, NY	37 079	20 909	3 469	22 317	2 127	21 753	4 491	7.3	3 046	323	778	751	17 318	83
Birmingham, AL	53 883	67 140	31 082	90 583	7 083	20 592	14 679	7.1	10 039	1 175	2 161	2 197	15 833	131
Bismarck, ND	2 016	7 259	1 734	11 226	470	16 700	1 236	6.3	784	129	191	192	14 447	205
Bloomington, IN	8 559	10 383	1 708	8 390	567	16 324	1 444	8.1	1 042	126	235	186	13 905	226
Bloomington-Normal, IL	6 241	12 096	12 124	11 896	1 035	20 493	2 302	12.6	1 557	232	379	254	18 357	50
Boise City, ID	12 386	17 812	6 323	20 755	1 579	20 530	3 538	10.0	2 323	448	542	429	17 194	87
Boston-Lawrence-Salem, MA-NH	378 224	373 576	170 657	693 141	47 840	24 526	88 889	6.4	64 868	7 079	16 048	11 360	23 746	7
Bradenton, FL	6 194	15 990	3 625	16 855	803	15 843	3 530	11.6	1 392	284	1 177	647	18 482	48
Bremerton, WA	1 376	10 714	2 069	10 500	433	14 523	2 958	9.2	1 711	175	451	520	15 843	129
Brownsville-Harlingen, TX	9 278	15 715	3 870	14 893	705	13 148	2 260	9.3	1 285	197	385	513	8 435	280
Bryan-College Station, TX	3 107	8 733	1 507	9 300	412	14 728	1 467	8.7	1 012	128	234	190	12 760	260
Buffalo-Niagara Falls, NY	102 503	99 852	31 140	128 585	8 533	19 727	20 431	7.4	12 789	1 273	3 748	3 797	17 439	79
Buffalo, NY	79 999	83 900	29 152	110 851	7 202	19 676	16 922	7.4	10 772	1 099	3 168	3 131	17 724	X
Niagara Falls, NY	22 504	15 952	1 988	17 734	1 331	20 009	3 508	7.3	2 016	174	580	666	16 183	X
Burlington, NC	24 138	9 993	1 253	9 216	806	15 752	1 775	7.0	1 055	138	266	237	16 576	103
Burlington, VT	15 907	14 371	3 833	18 453	1 386	21 437	2 584	9.7	2 045	227	386	250	18 797	41
Canton, OH	46 124	31 298	6 879	37 958	2 792	19 292	6 171	5.9	3 698	391	1 014	1 111	15 364	156
Casper, WY	1 454	5 513	1 515	4 394	354	18 523	1 021	3.9	608	102	232	135	16 241	112
Cedar Rapids, IA	24 527	16 498	5 264	19 027	1 669	21 237	2 980	7.8	2 237	217	508	355	17 143	89
Champaign-Urbana-Rantoul, IL	9 728	16 557	2 956	15 070	891	16 605	2 777	6.6	1 868	276	494	372	16 063	121
Charleston, SC	20 584	38 989	7 465	37 717	2 207	16 018	6 456	0.3	4 960	368	408	1 105	12 351	270
Charleston, WV	10 086	21 470	6 639	25 442	1 724	20 135	3 873	6.0	2 609	253	638	784	15 009	181
Charlotte-Gastonia-Rock Hill, NC-SC	156 986	100 679	39 533	111 644	11 337	20 464	19 686	7.9	15 440	1 425	2 562	2 105	17 377	81
Charlottesville, VA	NA	11 370	4 843	12 123	841	18 315	2 340	9.5	1 544	188	564	289	18 775	42
Chattanooga, TN-GA	48 310	34 405	NA	39 524	2 930	17 734	6 645	5.4	4 524	580	993	1 031	15 038	179
Cheyenne, WY	1 209	6 435	1 757	5 346	304	15 746	1 158	5.6	776	71	194	189	15 139	170
Chicago-Gary-Lake County, IL-IN-WI	786 903	648 811	303 115	974 801	82 830	24 503	165 475	7.2	114 246	12 543	28 713	19 623	20 109	23
Aurora-Elgin, IL	41 025	28 260	7 311	30 176	2 741	21 438	7 102	7.7	3 606	499	1 052	663	19 587	X
Chicago, IL	604 707	504 583	269 070	814 258	68 552	24 912	127 014	7.1	94 111	9 909	22 813	15 633	20 349	X
Gary-Hammond, IN	55 761	43 330	8 101	51 394	4 262	22 436	9 380	6.9	6 297	540	1 342	1 429	15 344	X
Joliet, IL	21 590	20 969	3 992	22 830	1 983	21 824	6 843	7.2	2 795	478	932	698	17 797	X
Kenosha, WI	13 914	8 199	1 015	8 669	808	21 896	2 097	2.4	955	110	278	320	17 006	X
Lake County, IL	49 906	43 470	13 626	47 474	4 484	24 500	13 039	9.5	6 483	1 007	2 296	880	25 804	X

1. For week including March 12. Excludes government employees, self-employed persons, farm workers, domestic service workers, railroad employees subject to the Railroad Retirement Act, and employees on oceanborne vessels or in foreign countries. 2. Includes other labor income. 3. Based on the resident population estimated as of July 1 of the year shown.

Area name	Earnings, 1989: Total (Mil. dol)	Earnings, 1989: Percent by selected industries: Farm	Goods-related[1]: Total	Goods-related[1]: Manu-facturing	Service-related & other[2]: Total	Service-related & other[2]: Retail trade	Service-related & other[2]: Finance, insurance, & real estate	Service-related & other[2]: Ser-vices	Govern-ment	Agriculture, 1987: Farms: Number	Farms: Percent with: Less than 50 acres	Farms: Percent with: 500 acres and over	Farm operators, Percent: Whose principal occupation is farming	Farm operators, Percent: Residing on farm operated	Land in farms: Acreage (1,000)	Land in farms: Percent change, 1982–1987	Acres: Average size of farm	Acres: Total irrigated (1,000)	Acres: Total cropland (1,000)
	100	101	102	103	104	105	106	107	108	109	110	111	112	113	114	115	116	117	118
Abilene, TX	1 330	2.4	18.2	9.9	55.7	11.1	4.0	27.4	23.7	903	23.8	24.5	38.2	58.6	431	-1.0	478	1	190
Albany, GA	1 242	1.1	NA	21.0	45.9	9.4	4.2	19.2	25.9	327	35.2	27.8	41.0	59.0	215	-22.0	658	34	117
Albany-Schenectady-Troy, NY	11 674	0.5	20.8	14.0	51.2	9.1	5.6	25.6	27.5	2 591	24.5	6.4	55.7	86.1	492	-9.5	190	1	317
Albuquerque, NM	6 221	0.3	16.0	9.4	62.5	10.2	5.8	32.7	21.2	434	74.9	9.9	33.6	69.1	D	D	D	7	17
Alexandria, LA	1 181	1.6	16.2	8.6	53.6	10.0	4.6	28.0	28.7	875	45.3	11.9	46.3	71.7	196	-6.8	224	5	136
Allentown-Bethlehem, PA-NJ	8 051	0.6	39.1	31.1	51.0	10.1	4.6	23.9	9.3	1 868	39.9	6.5	52.6	80.2	293	-4.2	157	3	234
Altoona, PA	1 254	0.9	26.9	20.6	59.0	12.7	3.4	23.4	13.2	489	22.9	6.3	66.5	84.3	87	-0.5	177	1	60
Amarillo, TX	2 081	3.0	20.6	10.5	61.1	11.7	5.1	25.6	15.3	796	33.4	35.8	48.0	55.2	992	2.0	1 247	38	321
Anchorage, AK	4 405	0.0	19.6	1.4	52.8	9.6	4.7	22.6	27.6	245	38.8	7.8	45.3	75.1	59	-76.9	242	1	17
Anderson, IN	1 499	0.9	56.6	53.5	32.9	8.5	2.3	16.7	9.5	956	39.1	15.0	50.1	74.8	226	1.6	236	1	206
Anderson, SC	1 233	0.7	46.4	40.2	39.8	11.9	2.6	17.9	13.0	1 038	33.5	5.7	37.1	75.7	157	-10.1	151	1	90
Anniston, AL	1 151	1.5	23.2	19.7	35.1	9.6	2.3	13.4	40.2	685	41.3	2.2	35.9	75.2	90	-3.0	132	0	41
Appleton-Oshkosh-Neenah, WI	4 068	2.4	47.8	41.1	39.2	7.8	4.7	16.9	10.0	3 519	22.0	5.7	70.6	85.8	641	-2.3	182	1	546
Asheville, NC	1 997	0.8	31.0	24.0	53.7	11.5	3.4	26.6	14.4	1 200	61.8	2.1	37.2	73.2	104	-7.0	87	0	40
Athens, GA	1 649	5.5	25.9	20.0	40.2	9.1	3.2	17.7	28.4	1 744	40.0	3.8	41.9	77.1	215	-5.3	123	1	109
Atlanta, GA	45 156	0.4	18.7	12.6	68.4	10.0	8.8	25.0	12.6	5 288	50.3	3.5	33.7	76.0	561	-14.8	106	D	251
Atlantic City, NJ	4 985	NA	NA	4.8	NA	11.4	3.4	NA	15.2	508	64.8	2.4	54.5	74.4	43	3.6	85	13	29
Augusta, GA-SC	4 788	0.7	39.6	29.3	37.6	8.7	3.2	18.8	21.7	1 107	35.6	8.2	35.0	71.3	221	-17.3	199	3	108
Austin, TX	9 809	0.5	21.2	15.7	51.9	9.4	6.7	26.8	26.5	3 626	31.8	15.5	42.0	62.2	1 131	3.9	312	3	446
Bakersfield, CA	6 046	9.2	24.0	6.3	44.7	8.9	3.2	19.2	22.1	2 255	39.5	26.5	56.4	49.4	3 037	-3.3	1 347	747	974
Baltimore, MD	33 507	0.3	21.6	13.8	57.6	9.8	7.7	26.7	20.5	4 369	48.0	6.4	47.8	80.7	627	-5.2	143	8	484
Bangor, ME	1 649	0.7	29.3	22.5	51.5	12.0	3.3	22.3	18.6	572	21.5	11.4	50.3	87.8	133	-9.1	232	1	54
Baton Rouge, LA	5 867	0.4	29.2	15.9	52.7	9.1	NA	25.3	17.7	1 369	52.4	7.1	36.4	71.4	221	-6.9	161	0	125
Battle Creek, MI	1 666	0.6	41.4	36.9	39.3	8.0	4.7	17.3	18.6	1 166	22.7	11.3	47.0	83.3	253	-5.0	217	8	194
Beaumont-Port Arthur, TX	3 886	0.3	38.4	29.3	49.1	9.3	3.3	23.5	12.1	1 178	52.6	15.2	34.9	63.4	430	-13.8	365	32	147
Bellingham, WA	1 307	4.6	28.4	19.3	52.7	12.6	3.2	20.9	14.3	1 463	50.9	1.4	54.8	84.8	125	-2.9	85	29	94
Benton Harbor, MI	1 711	1.5	43.0	38.7	43.8	9.3	3.8	19.9	11.7	1 479	50.4	4.7	54.5	81.9	180	-5.4	121	9	150
Billings, MT	1 275	2.0	14.4	7.7	70.2	13.1	6.1	28.7	13.4	1 043	33.3	32.2	59.9	73.3	1 398	8.5	1 340	70	376
Biloxi-Gulfport, MS	1 900	0.2	17.7	13.3	44.3	10.1	3.9	19.7	37.8	446	50.9	4.0	32.1	71.7	53	-26.9	118	0	22
Binghamton, NY	3 368	0.7	45.0	39.0	39.7	8.1	2.9	19.2	14.6	1 169	16.8	8.8	52.7	88.8	243	-11.0	208	0	134
Birmingham, AL	11 214	0.8	22.8	14.1	62.8	8.9	7.5	25.5	13.5	3 438	40.8	4.0	32.8	73.9	421	-7.7	122	D	201
Bismarck, ND	913	2.2	13.5	6.9	63.6	10.7	4.4	30.3	20.7	1 791	12.0	62.1	74.7	71.5	2 110	6.2	1 178	8	1 088
Bloomington, IN	1 167	0.2	29.2	22.7	41.7	10.6	3.3	19.2	28.9	583	31.0	3.1	31.7	76.5	73	-3.0	125	0	42
Bloomington-Normal, IL	1 789	3.1	18.3	13.7	65.7	8.9	24.0	21.5	12.9	1 906	16.8	30.0	72.2	68.0	741	-0.6	389	1	707
Boise City, ID	2 772	1.1	29.7	18.7	53.3	10.8	6.9	21.8	15.9	1 293	63.9	5.6	44.0	80.4	247	-0.1	191	86	D
Boston-Lawrence-Salem, MA-NH	71 947	0.1	24.3	18.6	64.1	8.9	8.8	33.6	11.5	2 000	63.7	1.7	53.2	72.7	D	D	D	D	67
Bradenton, FL	1 676	6.4	23.8	17.2	57.8	13.8	4.2	30.9	12.1	766	50.4	14.5	48.6	58.5	329	-6.9	430	41	93
Bremerton, WA	1 886	0.3	7.5	2.4	34.4	8.6	2.2	19.0	57.9	404	88.4	0.0	32.4	91.1	10	-12.7	24	1	5
Brownsville-Harlingen, TX	1 483	2.8	17.1	12.6	56.1	13.7	5.1	24.7	24.1	1 002	52.2	19.0	53.1	58.6	389	0.8	389	123	257
Bryan-College Station, TX	1 140	1.5	14.7	7.2	43.2	10.7	3.8	20.8	40.6	971	31.8	11.8	35.6	53.8	271	5.7	280	9	109
Buffalo-Niagara Falls, NY	14 061	0.4	30.3	24.7	51.7	9.5	5.9	24.0	17.6	2 124	37.2	5.8	50.0	84.3	313	-8.2	147	3	245
Buffalo, NY	11 871	0.3	27.3	21.8	54.3	9.5	6.7	25.2	18.1	1 201	36.3	5.0	52.2	83.4	166	-12.7	138	2	120
Niagara Falls, NY	2 190	0.9	46.5	40.5	37.6	9.4	2.1	17.6	15.0	923	38.4	6.8	47.0	85.5	147	-2.6	159	1	125
Burlington, NC	1 193	0.9	43.8	37.6	46.6	11.6	4.3	20.9	8.8	821	35.9	3.4	40.4	73.1	100	-13.2	122	2	54
Burlington, VT	2 272	0.5	35.8	27.3	50.0	9.6	5.1	24.0	13.6	579	26.4	11.1	57.0	86.5	126	-15.2	218	0	74
Canton, OH	4 089	0.4	43.0	35.8	46.5	9.9	3.8	21.7	10.1	2 009	35.5	4.0	46.3	81.6	270	-5.9	135	1	195
Casper, WY	710	0.0	27.2	7.0	56.6	10.7	5.3	23.5	16.2	304	30.3	46.4	51.0	66.8	2 634	-7.9	8 663	35	49
Cedar Rapids, IA	2 454	0.7	39.1	33.4	50.5	9.2	5.4	21.9	9.6	1 690	27.6	11.5	57.9	76.9	356	-3.4	211	0	308
Champaign-Urbana-Rantoul, IL	2 144	2.6	15.3	10.0	45.5	8.6	3.3	23.2	36.7	1 671	16.8	26.3	71.2	64.7	594	-1.0	356	2	574
Charleston, SC	5 327	0.6	17.6	11.5	42.9	9.4	4.0	19.0	39.0	914	47.9	9.6	38.1	65.8	181	-13.7	198	D	77
Charleston, WV	2 862	0.0	23.8	15.5	60.6	10.0	5.8	25.9	15.6	647	26.3	1.9	38.0	73.9	77	-10.0	119	0	26
Charlotte-Gastonia-Rock Hill, NC-SC	16 865	1.0	31.3	24.3	58.2	10.0	7.5	18.9	9.5	4 181	37.4	5.6	41.0	75.2	620	-13.6	148	3	386
Charlottesville, VA	1 732	1.3	20.8	13.0	46.6	10.0	5.7	22.3	31.3	1 258	25.7	11.4	44.1	76.7	287	-6.3	228	D	118
Chattanooga, TN-GA	5 104	0.6	29.5	23.3	52.4	10.4	6.6	22.2	17.6	2 039	36.5	4.9	32.2	74.8	295	-10.5	145	D	141
Cheyenne, WY	848	0.5	11.3	4.6	48.6	8.9	5.5	16.4	39.7	595	14.3	56.8	63.7	72.8	1 601	-2.9	2 691	48	342
Chicago-Gary-Lake County, IL-IN-WI	126 789	0.2	NA	20.5	NA	8.7	9.4	NA	10.8	6 983	33.6	16.2	59.1	73.0	1 810	-2.8	259	23	1 660
Aurora-Elgin, IL	4 105	1.2	39.7	30.4	49.3	10.4	5.1	23.0	9.9	1 359	24.7	19.2	65.3	72.1	414	-2.8	305	1	387
Chicago, IL	104 020	0.0	24.5	18.6	65.1	8.5	10.7	28.4	10.3	1 686	44.7	11.3	55.3	72.8	338	-4.0	201	8	303
Gary-Hammond, IN	6 837	0.3	45.1	36.7	44.2	8.6	2.6	20.5	10.4	1 148	33.7	17.8	57.1	75.8	308	-0.4	268	9	281
Joliet, IL	3 272	1.6	NA	21.9	NA	8.8	3.0	NA	13.1	1 837	23.8	20.7	63.0	70.5	566	-2.7	308	4	529
Kenosha, WI	1 066	1.1	44.9	38.6	38.6	10.3	2.4	18.9	15.3	505	33.9	10.1	57.4	79.0	101	-0.1	199	0	90
Lake County, IL	7 490	0.1	30.3	23.1	52.7	10.1	4.6	24.4	16.8	448	57.6	9.4	45.3	72.5	82	-10.6	184	0	69

1. Covers mining, construction, and manufacturing. 2. Covers private sector earnings in agricultural services, forestry, and fisheries; transportation and public utilities; wholesale trade; retail trade; finance, insurance, and real estate; and services.

Area name	Agriculture, 1987 (cont'd): Value of products sold: Total (Mil dol)	Average per farm (Dollars)	Percent from: Crops	Percent from: Livestock and poultry[1]	Percent of farms with sales of: $10,000 or more	$100,000 or more	Manufactures, 1987: Establishments: Total	Percent with 20 or more employees	All employees: Number (1,000)	Annual payroll (Mil dol)	Production workers: Number (1,000)	Work hours (Millions)	Wages: Total (Mil dol)	Average per worker (Dollars)	Value added by manufacture (Mil dol)
	121	122	123	124	125	126	127	128	129	131	132	133	134	135	136
Abilene, TX	72	79 740	8.5	91.5	32.7	4.0	122	27.0	4.9	93.6	2.9	5.5	44.6	15 379	330.7
Albany, GA	39	119 709	85.2	14.8	52.3	25.1	97	43.3	8.0	214.0	6.0	12.1	148.3	24 717	910.1
Albany-Schenectady-Troy, NY	119	46 080	21.1	78.9	45.8	13.9	828	35.7	48.0	1 233.9	25.7	53.5	575.2	22 381	3 109.0
Albuquerque, NM	27	61 505	11.1	88.9	15.0	4.4	592	23.3	19.2	421.4	12.8	25.2	251.7	19 664	648.1
Alexandria, LA	38	43 485	82.4	17.6	35.1	11.5	106	24.5	4.1	88.3	2.6	5.2	48.1	18 500	425.1
Allentown-Bethlehem, PA-NJ	109	58 521	43.6	56.4	46.1	13.7	1 091	46.7	78.1	1 948.4	50.3	94.0	1 032.7	20 531	4 693.8
Altoona, PA	33	67 910	13.8	86.2	61.6	24.5	145	42.1	10.3	204.0	7.8	14.2	139.6	17 897	607.1
Amarillo, TX	184	231 481	7.6	92.4	52.9	18.7	184	26.6	11.0	243.0	8.1	16.5	162.7	20 086	328.0
Anchorage, AK	13	53 600	59.0	41.0	32.7	11.0	146	15.1	2.3	59.8	1.3	2.4	30.0	23 077	234.8
Anderson, IN	58	60 274	75.3	24.7	57.5	17.3	132	31.8	16.8	599.0	12.5	25.5	433.3	34 664	973.4
Anderson, SC	32	30 881	46.5	53.5	20.6	4.2	204	43.6	19.9	386.7	16.5	33.0	289.1	17 521	812.7
Anniston, AL	27	39 185	9.5	90.5	20.4	7.9	143	46.9	10.7	176.6	8.3	16.3	122.5	14 759	352.9
Appleton-Oshkosh-Neenah, WI	243	69 158	15.2	84.8	71.4	24.8	559	47.8	49.7	1 302.2	32.7	65.6	764.1	23 367	3 085.7
Asheville, NC	19	16 089	35.1	64.9	16.8	3.5	285	44.6	18.7	353.5	13.7	26.6	220.7	16 109	927.0
Athens, GA	192	110 343	3.5	96.5	44.2	26.1	197	38.1	15.4	255.1	12.1	21.7	171.8	14 198	616.5
Atlanta, GA	219	41 359	10.1	89.9	26.0	D	3 878	35.8	200.4	5 073.3	122.1	243.3	2 569.2	21 042	13 345.7
Atlantic City, NJ	42	82 409	98.2	1.8	47.4	17.5	249	30.5	8.4	170.0	6.2	11.9	113.8	18 355	668.2
Augusta, GA-SC	38	34 221	37.9	62.1	25.2	6.6	347	45.8	38.9	999.6	24.5	50.5	521.2	21 273	2 830.5
Austin, TX	71	19 691	44.1	55.9	27.6	3.9	823	26.2	42.5	1 150.2	20.7	40.8	394.7	19 068	2 917.2
Bakersfield, CA	1 100	487 821	87.1	12.9	64.5	40.6	357	22.4	7.7	174.0	5.1	9.8	98.3	19 275	532.5
Baltimore, MD	178	40 785	41.8	58.2	37.8	10.7	2 311	37.4	145.2	3 975.3	86.6	169.2	1 994.4	23 030	9 675.6
Bangor, ME	26	46 045	31.0	69.0	37.6	13.8	234	27.8	13.4	307.8	10.2	20.9	209.9	20 578	721.2
Baton Rouge, LA	36	26 053	55.8	44.2	22.5	5.6	456	31.4	19.2	633.0	10.7	22.8	305.6	28 561	3 222.6
Battle Creek, MI	42	36 281	45.3	54.7	41.0	8.9	211	42.7	15.3	490.6	10.8	23.7	308.6	28 574	1 632.4
Beaumont-Port Arthur, TX	22	18 298	67.4	32.6	21.6	5.4	336	32.1	25.6	881.6	17.1	34.7	549.0	32 105	3 214.9
Bellingham, WA	180	122 981	15.7	84.3	51.1	30.8	232	27.2	7.3	187.6	5.6	11.0	131.4	23 464	738.5
Benton Harbor, MI	63	42 880	83.2	16.8	46.8	11.4	390	39.0	22.3	559.9	13.9	28.0	282.5	20 324	970.9
Billings, MT	100	95 458	19.7	80.3	52.1	15.5	147	18.4	3.0	70.0	1.8	3.6	40.7	22 611	159.9
Biloxi-Gulfport, MS	3	7 554	31.6	68.4	15.5	1.3	164	30.5	8.0	153.4	5.8	11.3	98.5	16 983	519.8
Binghamton, NY	53	45 601	9.2	90.8	41.5	16.5	312	41.0	36.5	1 065.4	14.7	29.2	290.1	19 735	2 483.8
Birmingham, AL	134	38 932	12.8	87.2	25.0	D	1 150	37.0	51.6	1 093.0	36.1	71.3	661.3	18 319	2 613.2
Bismarck, ND	93	51 748	33.0	67.0	72.6	13.8	83	27.7	1.9	42.7	1.1	2.2	22.3	20 273	149.1
Bloomington, IN	7	12 635	41.9	58.1	25.4	2.6	108	32.4	8.2	184.8	6.9	13.4	140.7	20 391	763.5
Bloomington-Normal, IL	164	86 208	83.1	16.9	82.2	31.2	99	34.3	6.4	132.9	3.5	6.9	74.3	21 229	323.1
Boise City, ID	113	87 282	17.0	83.0	36.8	12.2	284	25.7	11.1	293.3	6.1	12.0	117.5	19 262	633.7
Boston-Lawrence-Salem, MA-NH	158	78 754	D	D	46.5	D	6 796	37.3	377.7	10 313.3	207.5	411.5	4 425.3	21 327	24 076.4
Bradenton, FL	149	194 067	84.7	15.3	49.2	19.8	215	27.0	9.3	198.9	6.6	14.4	115.8	17 545	671.0
Bremerton, WA	6	14 077	9.5	90.5	6.9	0.2	114	15.8	1.5	29.2	1.0	1.8	16.8	16 800	61.2
Brownsville-Harlingen, TX	87	86 932	81.0	19.0	47.3	19.5	168	33.9	8.9	122.2	6.9	13.4	85.4	12 377	348.3
Bryan-College Station, TX	35	36 154	20.0	80.0	27.0	3.5	87	27.6	2.4	49.4	1.6	3.4	28.5	17 812	136.7
Buffalo-Niagara Falls, NY	115	54 121	48.5	51.5	44.0	15.1	1 604	37.5	103.2	2 896.7	69.4	138.9	1 798.2	25 911	7 025.5
Buffalo, NY	73	60 475	40.6	59.4	44.4	16.7	1 310	36.3	80.4	2 218.4	53.9	107.6	1 366.5	25 353	5 255.8
Niagara Falls, NY	42	45 854	62.1	37.9	43.4	13.0	294	42.5	22.7	678.3	15.5	31.3	431.6	27 845	1 769.7
Burlington, NC	28	34 311	22.5	77.5	31.7	9.1	303	53.8	24.3	425.6	19.1	37.1	283.5	14 843	942.5
Burlington, VT	30	51 917	12.4	87.6	50.3	18.8	197	25.9	16.2	500.4	7.4	12.9	135.1	18 257	1 041.7
Canton, OH	68	33 746	37.2	62.8	40.7	8.4	643	36.9	43.5	1 132.3	30.7	62.1	724.9	23 612	2 970.4
Casper, WY	19	63 799	6.4	93.6	48.4	15.1	92	10.9	1.4	33.8	0.9	1.8	21.6	24 000	68.7
Cedar Rapids, IA	93	54 922	46.2	53.8	65.7	14.9	234	38.9	23.4	669.8	11.4	23.0	289.3	25 377	2 110.7
Champaign-Urbana-Rantoul, IL	135	80 550	91.0	9.0	82.0	27.0	141	41.1	9.4	189.7	6.4	12.1	117.5	18 359	676.5
Charleston, SC	40	43 721	80.8	19.2	24.3	D	389	32.9	20.3	474.7	13.9	27.3	263.6	18 964	1 498.8
Charleston, WV	4	5 903	65.1	35.0	9.4	0.3	165	29.1	10.7	340.9	5.2	10.7	147.3	28 327	821.1
Charlotte-Gastonia-Rock Hill, NC-SC	289	69 056	17.3	82.7	29.5	12.6	2 276	41.3	155.4	3 223.5	111.3	225.7	1 888.6	16 969	8 153.6
Charlottesville, VA	28	22 455	19.5	80.5	29.2	D	146	27.4	9.6	204.4	6.1	12.7	101.6	16 656	508.1
Chattanooga, TN-GA	48	23 334	12.5	87.5	23.4	D	644	45.3	44.2	887.1	32.5	65.5	559.4	17 212	2 298.7
Cheyenne, WY	40	67 711	29.9	70.1	60.3	15.6	39	35.9	1.1	25.6	0.7	1.6	16.8	24 000	34.2
Chicago-Gary-Lake County, IL-IN-WI	521	74 567	71.3	28.7	65.4	20.3	14 350	39.6	755.4	20 580.3	454.4	923.8	10 211.5	22 472	49 773.3
Aurora-Elgin, IL	129	95 171	67.2	32.8	76.2	26.0	800	41.4	38.8	977.8	25.8	52.3	557.2	21 597	2 723.1
Chicago, IL	137	81 335	66.3	33.7	57.1	18.3	11 742	39.7	579.9	15 458.7	343.9	697.6	7 369.8	21 430	36 219.0
Gary-Hammond, IN	66	57 340	79.8	20.2	60.5	18.0	483	39.8	52.7	1 696.5	38.7	80.1	1 190.4	30 760	5 199.2
Joliet, IL	127	68 880	83.8	16.2	74.3	18.9	405	38.0	20.5	595.4	14.2	29.6	376.2	26 493	1 916.1
Kenosha, WI	33	65 212	41.2	58.8	60.8	24.4	160	33.8	12.6	376.0	9.7	20.0	267.6	27 588	795.3
Lake County, IL	29	64 603	72.8	27.2	45.3	17.0	760	38.0	50.9	1 476.1	22.1	44.2	450.4	20 380	2 920.7

1. Includes livestock and poultry products.

Area name	Manufactures, 1987 (cont'd)		Value of construction authorized by building permits, 1990								Wholesale trade, 1987				Retail trade, all establishments, 1987
				Nonresidential				Residential							
					Percent										
	Value of shipments (Mil dol)	New capital expenditures (Mil dol)	Total[1] ($1,000)	Total ($1,000)	Office	Industrial	Stores	New construction ($1,000)	Number of housing units	Alterations and additions ($1,000)	Establishments	Sales (Mil dol)	Paid employees[2]	Annual payroll (Mil dol)	Number
	137	138	139	140	141	142	143	144	145	146	147	148	149	150	151
Abilene, TX	900.6	11.8	41 628	8 979	30.0	3.4	50.2	10 162	118	2 657	296	1 319.5	2 960	59.8	1 427
Albany, GA	2 123.6	D	43 502	11 200	18.6	40.5	28.6	20 833	384	3 304	264	938.0	3 279	61.4	1 139
Albany-Schenectady-Troy, NY	5 512.4	201.7	626 660	216 598	32.8	37.1	15.7	266 377	3 150	64 139	1 408	5 702.1	18 152	425.1	8 888
Albuquerque, NM	1 646.1	98.1	269 703	49 993	15.0	14.8	15.1	151 742	1 890	10 106	1 149	3 032.1	12 616	271.6	4 490
Alexandria, LA	731.6	17.2	22 217	14 267	10.0	4.0	75.2	4 545	60	1 107	228	425.8	2 277	39.0	1 292
Allentown-Bethlehem, PA-NJ	9 083.5	312.7	431 987	142 455	10.8	30.6	25.5	183 497	2 151	38 171	1 026	4 012.8	12 669	314.3	6 873
Altoona, PA	1 127.5	31.0	41 241	10 758	17.7	7.7	38.5	20 938	337	2 203	194	1 026.9	2 596	56.3	1 432
Amarillo, TX	3 122.9	18.7	60 159	13 415	24.6	0.1	35.5	15 634	158	5 973	457	1 864.6	5 784	116.6	2 403
Anchorage, AK	714.1	9.3	122 642	20 612	2.1	1.7	80.0	62 476	399	8 930	479	1 708.5	4 965	146.8	2 314
Anderson, IN	2 119.1	45.4	30 953	10 675	19.1	11.9	33.3	16 584	221	1 725	127	274.5	1 370	26.0	1 256
Anderson, SC	2 026.9	57.4	165 980	98 299	6.0	71.5	11.4	53 769	915	4 164	196	551.5	1 400	24.7	1 691
Anniston, AL	773.5	16.7	27 399	9 717	15.2	33.2	30.3	10 312	231	2 646	139	528.4	1 549	28.0	1 258
Appleton-Oshkosh-Neenah, WI	6 938.7	254.7	225 367	59 711	24.8	20.7	38.0	118 594	2 007	13 180	548	2 385.8	6 378	138.0	2 963
Asheville, NC	1 773.0	D	172 291	57 295	6.7	0.2	16.3	72 764	816	11 570	325	872.1	3 486	69.0	1 977
Athens, GA	1 338.9	33.9	129 456	41 659	7.4	41.5	20.4	67 514	957	4 771	218	894.7	2 789	56.6	1 497
Atlanta, GA	28 085.7	900.2	3 597 858	962 050	36.3	10.7	29.8	1 887 923	26 828	172 451	7 963	69 999.9	118 263	3 045.9	25 453
Atlantic City, NJ	946.7	25.6	294 599	40 421	31.1	12.4	31.2	132 976	1 647	61 574	405	1 179.4	4 165	94.6	4 335
Augusta, GA-SC	5 047.9	192.3	348 060	108 277	26.2	11.3	46.6	179 144	2 367	16 987	476	1 361.6	5 305	100.7	3 574
Austin, TX	5 371.6	282.3	507 695	144 704	43.9	9.9	11.8	227 694	1 946	18 704	1 243	3 169.8	12 775	296.5	7 631
Bakersfield, CA	1 455.2	51.2	662 266	153 977	14.7	15.0	29.1	445 351	4 954	16 182	752	3 335.5	8 292	191.8	4 510
Baltimore, MD	19 215.2	509.6	2 127 708	440 100	33.3	20.7	30.0	904 026	13 561	259 273	3 657	23 407.1	54 805	1 357.9	19 681
Bangor, ME	1 447.3	174.9	63 840	14 971	10.1	39.0	18.1	30 759	559	6 860	243	884.4	3 040	64.9	1 651
Baton Rouge, LA	10 711.5	316.6	212 332	63 180	33.7	5.0	13.7	81 641	1 024	14 258	994	3 248.2	10 560	225.8	4 829
Battle Creek, MI	2 544.3	236.4	60 106	33 474	73.1	9.0	7.2	14 239	229	2 291	165	539.0	1 476	30.3	1 272
Beaumont-Port Arthur, TX	14 079.2	367.4	91 714	21 610	35.2	15.5	24.1	40 982	494	9 327	571	1 790.2	5 499	115.2	3 969
Bellingham, WA	2 865.4	73.5	193 889	46 323	12.5	11.1	38.2	124 314	1 974	8 046	239	511.0	1 988	36.6	1 359
Benton Harbor, MI	2 545.7	66.6	78 493	16 241	10.0	16.4	10.7	45 889	554	10 112	231	1 451.5	2 451	63.8	1 566
Billings, MT	1 109.6	25.3	41 964	7 557	9.3	8.8	79.2	16 028	160	4 096	391	1 393.7	4 581	94.7	1 406
Biloxi-Gulfport, MS	990.7	79.2	63 324	18 118	1.4	0.8	44.9	28 481	485	6 743	260	430.4	2 190	36.2	2 067
Binghamton, NY	3 820.5	110.3	130 116	35 264	20.7	40.1	20.3	49 699	596	10 742	358	1 084.3	4 567	91.8	2 621
Birmingham, AL	5 748.0	157.7	697 110	209 464	12.0	13.8	26.1	287 546	3 991	39 173	2 068	10 610.4	29 459	688.2	8 455
Bismarck, ND	600.6	7.8	48 302	7 833	26.7	4.5	52.3	27 275	392	2 606	208	533.9	1 753	32.8	910
Bloomington, IN	1 616.2	D	72 497	16 835	20.0	27.6	21.4	45 869	541	3 156	117	458.0	1 577	30.5	996
Bloomington-Normal, IL	786.3	D	102 456	33 163	36.1	4.9	30.8	46 220	747	4 727	241	1 111.3	3 526	73.3	1 202
Boise City, ID	1 473.7	48.4	310 645	65 155	41.2	27.1	17.5	183 212	2 570	10 108	536	1 746.1	5 479	115.4	1 961
Boston-Lawrence-Salem, MA-NH	41 855.0	1 479.5	1 873 275	398 318	34.0	6.4	16.2	608 230	6 305	385 399	7 937	62 075.6	119 494	3 438.8	34 390
Bradenton, FL	1 502.8	38.6	188 805	36 598	23.6	8.7	24.3	125 327	2 381	15 451	197	1 058.2	2 001	37.4	1 863
Bremerton, WA	133.1	3.0	182 128	29 638	17.0	0.6	54.3	129 482	2 582	6 036	115	193.2	789	15.9	1 484
Brownsville-Harlingen, TX	730.5	34.9	75 547	25 294	17.1	7.4	56.4	27 618	665	6 836	393	838.2	3 830	57.6	2 296
Bryan-College Station, TX	283.2	7.8	34 715	5 616	26.7	1.1	34.2	20 202	213	2 860	147	287.9	1 333	24.6	1 043
Buffalo-Niagara Falls, NY	14 189.7	368.6	647 716	154 257	22.2	18.6	33.6	330 401	3 640	46 224	2 092	10 795.8	25 685	566.3	11 256
Buffalo, NY	10 907.1	280.8	504 172	109 421	28.6	7.3	39.6	263 530	2 743	33 927	1 860	10 282.7	23 362	522.9	9 023
Niagara Falls, NY	3 282.5	87.9	143 542	44 836	6.5	46.2	18.9	66 871	897	12 296	232	513.1	2 323	43.3	2 233
Burlington, NC	2 262.3	72.7	83 685	33 127	30.5	39.3	20.4	24 756	370	6 212	185	545.1	1 782	32.7	1 332
Burlington, VT	1 845.5	D	99 744	22 041	32.8	32.6	15.9	47 034	485	15 150	269	0.0	D	D	1 667
Canton, OH	6 122.3	144.9	183 855	23 283	22.4	6.3	37.1	115 017	1 256	12 729	559	2 817.9	8 604	186.5	3 923
Casper, WY	495.8	6.4	9 922	629	0.0	0.0	42.6	3 191	30	2 290	276	776.6	1 947	44.0	785
Cedar Rapids, IA	3 862.5	117.1	103 405	24 086	15.0	31.5	37.3	43 797	682	8 638	432	1 731.6	4 639	101.5	1 700
Champaign-Urbana-Rantoul, IL	1 685.7	34.7	65 068	13 273	20.3	24.3	8.6	29 114	529	3 907	229	1 490.0	3 160	70.5	1 491
Charleston, SC	3 507.8	125.1	487 052	117 258	27.9	16.1	23.7	263 305	3 542	40 659	645	2 887.6	7 089	133.9	4 640
Charleston, WV	2 001.1	40.8	42 343	15 573	2.5	46.9	27.9	15 988	215	3 159	558	1 512.5	6 392	144.3	2 214
Charlotte-Gastonia-Rock Hill, NC-SC	17 637.7	530.4	1 482 296	444 646	20.6	15.0	26.3	694 767	10 752	53 693	3 394	25 749.2	43 031	1 084.2	10 994
Charlottesville, VA	848.5	27.2	168 645	32 379	7.4	0.4	10.7	96 766	1 351	17 795	165	2 132.5	1 856	40.9	1 259
Chattanooga, TN-GA	5 744.3	178.2	258 552	96 930	20.4	7.8	27.7	93 865	1 504	13 436	944	4 213.8	11 937	248.9	4 540
Cheyenne, WY	306.1	5.4	101 947	86 871	0.0	93.4	5.3	7 618	79	1 032	116	198.2	793	14.8	722
Chicago-Gary-Lake County, IL-IN-WI	100 463.9	2 921.2	7 149 762	2 037 987	36.9	15.2	22.0	3 081 788	30 996	534 972	17 043	139 810.3	257 310	6 798.1	63 461
Aurora-Elgin, IL	5 147.7	163.7	645 714	155 474	25.6	26.0	36.5	399 038	3 848	30 503	624	3 511.4	6 449	165.5	2 860
Chicago, IL	68 935.5	1 780.5	4 741 810	1 452 568	43.9	11.0	18.5	1 647 055	16 666	377 117	14 376	125 820.4	228 749	6 093.6	47 758
Gary-Hammond, IN	13 189.5	550.6	450 322	114 274	8.4	47.8	23.7	240 212	2 293	25 672	628	2 802.1	7 341	155.3	4 914
Joliet, IL	6 014.1	150.0	414 338	95 570	6.2	29.6	43.1	266 277	2 774	28 996	426	1 788.5	4 208	98.3	2 673
Kenosha, WI	2 360.7	20.9	167 303	74 239	7.4	9.1	32.4	82 432	1 294	4 929	117	489.6	1 221	25.7	1 126
Lake County, IL	4 816.3	255.4	730 276	145 861	36.6	14.2	21.0	446 775	4 121	67 756	872	5 398.3	9 342	259.7	4 130

1. Includes nonresidential additions and alterations, residential nonhousekeeping buildings, and residential garages and carports not shown separately. 2. For pay period including March 12.

Area name	Retail trade, all establishments, 1987 (cont'd) — Sales — Total (Mil dol)	Percent change, 1982–1987	Per capita[1] (Dollars)	Retail trade, establishments with payroll, 1987 — Number	Sales — Total (Mil dol)	Per capita[1] (Dollars) — General merchandise stores	Food stores	Apparel and accessory stores	Eating and drinking places	Paid employees[2]	Annual payroll (Mil dol)	Taxable service industries–establishments with payroll, 1987 — Number	Receipts (Mil dol) — Total	Selected kinds of business — Hotels, motels & other lodging places	Health services	Legal services
	152	153	154	155	156	157	158	159	160	161	162	163	164	165	166	167
Abilene, TX	799.5	-0.6	6 468	884	769.4	988	923	315	633	10 606	96.2	938	345.4	19.4	151.1	17.9
Albany, GA	753.7	43.8	6 431	787	734.1	984	1 388	260	549	9 463	85.3	734	287.1	D	105.6	15.7
Albany-Schenectady-Troy, NY	5 976.9	56.8	7 088	5 522	5 796.6	847	1 485	346	595	66 711	662.6	5 233	2 382.6	130.9	501.9	179.0
Albuquerque, NM	3 373.9	47.0	6 924	2 868	3 296.9	922	1 155	316	766	42 368	397.4	4 082	2 615.3	105.7	505.0	155.9
Alexandria, LA	775.8	25.1	5 557	832	746.2	1 010	1 112	345	404	9 178	86.2	788	289.4	12.8	133.0	29.4
Allentown-Bethlehem, PA-NJ	4 574.8	52.1	6 855	4 082	4 424.9	755	1 350	309	536	48 699	497.8	4 091	1 518.3	51.0	442.4	78.1
Altoona, PA	880.9	44.3	6 638	856	850.9	1 015	1 496	303	489	10 494	88.4	724	229.7	10.8	80.5	8.0
Amarillo, TX	1 553.2	27.3	7 868	1 477	1 509.4	1 157	1 449	499	744	17 805	171.6	1 401	513.4	26.3	167.2	55.2
Anchorage, AK	1 994.3	11.1	9 012	1 403	1 952.5	1 672	1 702	571	1 265	19 703	267.0	2 123	1 064.1	85.8	241.6	169.2
Anderson, IN	768.9	33.8	5 820	773	752.4	690	1 154	209	531	9 666	84.4	722	178.9	3.9	77.5	7.3
Anderson, SC	862.0	59.7	6 096	940	809.8	702	1 301	263	455	9 760	90.1	714	177.4	D	70.9	9.6
Anniston, AL	645.4	50.1	5 243	672	615.0	701	814	255	487	7 785	71.2	542	142.9	11.8	56.1	10.1
Appleton-Oshkosh-Neenah, WI	1 934.2	50.3	6 274	2 005	1 899.6	897	1 070	242	598	25 570	220.2	1 768	606.8	32.8	212.4	27.8
Asheville, NC	1 215.8	43.3	7 098	1 254	1 176.7	899	1 406	382	704	14 596	139.6	1 280	440.7	52.5	176.7	23.7
Athens, GA	887.2	58.0	6 243	994	860.7	800	1 108	246	638	11 962	103.1	790	236.8	11.0	97.0	13.8
Atlanta, GA	21 140.1	80.6	7 959	16 683	20 713.6	1 009	1 308	388	874	249 008	2 616.7	21 657	12 938.1	758.8	2 483.4	1 001.5
Atlantic City, NJ	2 763.5	58.0	9 105	3 077	2 692.9	786	1 741	523	1 226	28 353	341.9	2 650	3 820.3	3 146.3	174.7	75.0
Augusta, GA-SC	2 452.4	68.9	6 253	2 313	2 386.0	872	1 189	243	580	30 843	281.1	2 178	883.6	37.4	325.2	41.9
Austin, TX	4 972.6	46.3	6 667	4 833	4 851.5	726	1 562	383	793	64 188	616.4	6 052	3 009.6	160.1	603.4	418.0
Bakersfield, CA	2 851.0	36.9	5 637	2 745	2 762.8	569	1 287	196	519	32 031	335.2	2 795	1 185.4	54.8	329.7	61.0
Baltimore, MD	15 533.9	55.4	6 723	13 542	15 213.0	769	1 250	371	666	188 879	1 904.1	15 268	7 655.1	331.1	1 674.9	642.6
Bangor, ME	1 146.6	69.2	8 225	1 054	1 116.3	971	1 638	372	534	11 597	120.7	891	260.6	21.6	90.3	24.9
Baton Rouge, LA	3 149.7	19.9	5 848	2 939	3 071.5	890	1 428	263	477	37 289	357.7	3 580	1 417.2	48.1	406.2	149.5
Battle Creek, MI	883.9	58.9	6 373	878	866.3	1 099	1 126	216	606	11 039	97.3	757	221.1	14.4	81.3	9.2
Beaumont-Port Arthur, TX	2 253.1	7.6	6 126	2 251	2 187.6	946	1 160	335	523	25 491	242.6	2 219	878.7	25.5	386.8	113.0
Bellingham, WA	771.9	43.1	6 689	897	751.0	830	1 614	230	698	9 325	88.0	855	225.7	21.1	82.3	13.5
Benton Harbor, MI	982.4	46.6	5 922	1 012	957.7	808	1 067	208	620	11 223	103.9	867	258.8	14.2	83.9	16.6
Billings, MT	906.2	15.8	7 679	932	884.1	1 005	1 632	313	788	11 540	104.9	1 110	351.0	24.0	111.8	38.7
Biloxi-Gulfport, MS	1 051.2	29.6	5 088	1 292	1 015.6	736	1 143	132	581	14 633	125.6	1 165	389.7	34.8	128.8	36.2
Binghamton, NY	1 688.5	44.9	6 512	1 581	1 643.1	870	1 325	280	551	19 409	183.5	1 319	458.6	17.1	169.2	34.4
Birmingham, AL	5 759.5	57.5	6 258	5 364	5 585.6	745	1 154	413	531	64 600	631.6	5 429	2 947.7	81.0	845.6	243.0
Bismarck, ND	590.1	21.6	6 894	640	580.6	1 168	1 123	253	586	7 299	64.0	578	212.7	18.5	93.4	19.3
Bloomington, IN	632.0	45.1	6 154	680	617.0	916	1 211	383	731	9 986	76.9	629	168.3	7.7	63.5	9.9
Bloomington-Normal, IL	849.7	41.9	6 880	811	832.8	938	1 072	282	763	11 471	94.7	679	239.7	11.2	78.5	15.9
Boise City, ID	1 217.3	36.5	6 164	1 233	1 186.2	676	1 341	255	656	15 793	143.5	1 691	566.3	36.2	151.2	62.0
Boston-Lawrence-Salem, MA-NH	29 536.7	57.7	7 924	23 115	28 824.2	846	1 359	512	839	340 722	3 590.5	30 415	21 971.6	954.6	3 239.4	1 792.6
Bradenton, FL	1 367.9	54.4	7 483	1 172	1 320.8	818	1 570	251	769	15 890	152.1	1 201	462.5	29.1	217.8	24.8
Bremerton, WA	829.1	46.3	4 754	903	814.9	562	1 170	175	435	9 664	99.2	936	306.0	10.7	100.5	11.4
Brownsville-Harlingen, TX	1 132.8	10.5	4 350	1 462	1 095.3	642	1 046	334	400	15 334	132.2	1 069	353.4	34.8	144.0	29.2
Bryan-College Station, TX	665.4	12.5	5 644	693	649.3	799	1 289	307	579	9 103	78.9	724	255.5	14.4	73.4	14.4
Buffalo-Niagara Falls, NY	6 985.1	39.6	5 962	7 457	6 829.8	714	1 341	308	582	97 066	812.0	6 874	2 615.4	115.6	737.2	240.9
Buffalo, NY	5 772.0	39.2	6 035	6 006	5 648.3	713	1 362	309	596	81 128	678.6	5 819	2 325.0	83.0	640.5	223.7
Niagara Falls, NY	1 213.0	42.0	5 634	1 451	1 181.4	720	1 251	304	523	15 938	133.4	1 055	290.4	32.6	96.7	17.2
Burlington, NC	823.9	59.1	7 869	847	799.6	681	1 404	531	636	9 288	88.2	602	175.3	12.0	72.3	7.9
Burlington, VT	1 105.7	62.1	8 447	1 168	1 087.6	867	D	486	864	13 733	133.8	1 207	479.0	45.9	D	D
Canton, OH	2 363.0	31.7	5 930	2 445	2 302.4	793	1 303	250	569	30 574	267.7	2 399	767.4	21.8	281.5	41.9
Casper, WY	449.1	-10.5	6 774	492	437.3	808	1 506	239	631	5 315	53.9	595	147.5	9.3	36.9	16.2
Cedar Rapids, IA	1 162.2	39.9	6 868	1 100	1 138.1	1 098	1 299	277	680	15 459	135.2	1 167	545.3	25.4	111.4	34.9
Champaign-Urbana-Rantoul, IL	1 137.0	43.5	6 634	1 032	1 117.7	944	1 108	317	798	15 749	130.6	958	416.7	33.7	156.5	26.3
Charleston, SC	3 017.4	57.4	6 006	3 015	2 944.3	652	1 220	319	615	38 585	342.3	2 968	1 034.7	120.1	332.9	81.8
Charleston, WV	1 705.5	28.6	6 468	1 531	1 680.3	911	1 352	258	573	19 763	187.0	1 635	642.3	32.3	217.1	84.8
Charlotte-Gastonia-Rock Hill, NC-SC	7 709.3	63.3	7 073	6 992	7 515.9	694	1 323	365	658	86 631	851.0	7 260	3 249.1	195.4	759.9	181.7
Charlottesville, VA	939.8	57.3	7 697	879	918.5	826	1 616	452	664	10 877	107.8	926	287.4	34.4	67.5	20.6
Chattanooga, TN-GA	2 765.0	47.9	6 371	2 702	2 661.9	756	1 294	313	565	31 288	307.5	2 565	1 120.6	63.9	446.7	73.8
Cheyenne, WY	484.6	23.4	6 401	464	474.0	864	960	247	681	6 119	60.0	510	136.8	20.6	39.7	20.6
Chicago-Gary-Lake County, IL-IN-WI	51 322.6	40.7	6 301	41 936	50 221.2	686	1 083	421	649	593 067	6 064.9	53 806	31 498.2	1 408.3	5 530.0	3 348.7
Aurora-Elgin, IL	2 232.0	57.4	6 442	1 903	2 186.3	749	1 195	390	580	26 704	256.5	2 019	671.6	11.0	213.1	42.8
Chicago, IL	39 595.1	39.9	6 376	31 656	38 753.0	700	1 078	464	679	457 320	4 764.6	42 973	27 337.6	1 282.7	4 296.7	3 143.6
Gary-Hammond, IN	3 406.0	24.0	5 590	3 177	3 321.0	677	1 138	238	542	41 874	373.3	3 179	1 182.9	28.7	399.9	68.0
Joliet, IL	1 820.8	43.3	4 874	1 661	1 774.3	464	890	147	416	20 466	191.8	1 627	517.6	14.5	162.3	33.0
Kenosha, WI	587.4	29.2	4 882	753	572.1	480	916	261	559	7 830	69.4	659	151.6	3.8	76.3	8.6
Lake County, IL	3 681.3	60.3	7 581	2 786	3 614.6	703	1 189	370	655	38 873	409.3	3 349	1 636.9	67.3	381.7	52.7

1. Based on the estimated population as of July 1 of the year shown. 2. For the period including March 12 of the year shown.

Area name	Taxable service industries–establishments with payroll, 1987 (cont'd): Paid employees	Taxable service industries–establishments with payroll, 1987 (cont'd): Annual payroll (Mil dol)	Banking: Bank deposits,[1] June 1989 (Mil dol)	Banking: Savings capital,[2] September 1989 (Mil dol)	Federal funds and grants, 1989: Expenditures (Mil dol)	Federal funds and grants, 1989: Per capita[3] (Dollars): Total	Per capita[3] (Dollars): Direct payments for individuals	Per capita[3] (Dollars): Procurement contract awards	Per capita[3] (Dollars): Salaries and wages	Per capita[3] (Dollars): Grant awards	Local government finances, 1981–1982: General revenue: Total (Mil dol)	General revenue: Intergovernmental (Mil dol)	General revenue: Taxes: Total (Mil dol)	Taxes: Per capita[4]: Total (Dollars)	Taxes: Per capita[4]: Property (Dollars)
	168	169	170	172	174	176	177	178	179	180	181	182	184	185	186
Abilene, TX	7 241	112.8	978	411.4	519.0	4 275	1 754	1 086	1 255	141	86.5	33.7	37.2	312	219
Albany, GA	6 814	110.0	489	222.7	381.1	3 305	1 559	274	1 029	401	126.7	42.8	32.1	278	172
Albany-Schenectady-Troy, NY	48 418	858.1	8 975	2 909.6	4 791.1	5 609	1 945	1 045	519	2 083	1 169.4	539.6	470.7	564	453
Albuquerque, NM	48 102	1 031.2	3 298	2 462.5	3 368.2	6 715	1 795	3 455	1 140	317	506.0	297.9	103.8	239	203
Alexandria, LA	7 476	99.9	1 022	231.2	497.1	3 618	1 729	239	1 046	558	118.9	66.5	34.6	253	109
Allentown-Bethlehem, PA-NJ	37 066	568.6	6 780	1 863.3	1 642.0	2 396	1 864	124	154	240	632.7	226.0	276.6	431	335
Altoona, PA	6 376	79.4	987	235.9	399.1	3 017	2 283	48	253	413	112.7	48.8	38.1	280	199
Amarillo, TX	10 068	173.9	1 732	513.3	616.0	3 124	1 520	1 099	320	108	193.2	58.0	71.4	389	316
Anchorage, AK	18 302	420.4	2 024	171.5	1 151.1	5 366	917	720	2 881	835	430.8	225.8	63.5	320	279
Anderson, IN	5 231	71.3	698	387.7	323.6	2 459	1 934	40	112	299	115.1	62.7	37.9	280	279
Anderson, SC	4 634	72.9	636	525.6	294.2	2 039	1 586	98	108	227	76.3	38.7	26.8	196	183
Anniston, AL	3 985	51.5	749	94.3	752.6	6 124	2 080	980	2 830	226	100.1	36.3	18.0	147	58
Appleton-Oshkosh-Neenah, WI	17 028	243.3	2 008	781.7	966.4	3 055	1 394	1 229	131	212	340.0	165.8	100.9	341	336
Asheville, NC	10 426	184.4	1 270	474.5	491.4	2 813	1 955	192	435	219	134.4	71.5	41.1	251	192
Athens, GA	6 971	90.4	819	420.0	362.1	2 485	1 372	49	465	577	123.0	44.5	37.1	278	189
Atlanta, GA	267 493	4 805.3	25 547	7 348.1	7 397.9	2 624	1 176	413	583	438	2 664.1	821.3	983.9	438	333
Atlantic City, NJ	58 892	1 150.2	2 179	1 951.6	922.3	2 947	2 126	58	449	296	445.3	154.9	220.5	784	737
Augusta, GA-SC	21 804	365.0	1 805	1 059.7	3 240.1	8 086	1 684	4 750	1 350	291	335.9	112.5	81.8	230	158
Austin, TX	64 815	1 146.9	5 254	3 322.3	3 041.6	3 969	1 224	365	611	1 743	617.1	183.5	219.4	378	318
Bakersfield, CA	25 142	459.4	2 078	1 533.8	1 891.3	3 534	1 446	794	941	262	721.1	309.6	240.5	552	444
Baltimore, MD	176 385	3 137.1	21 533	8 695.6	10 162.0	4 291	1 840	861	949	627	2 800.9	1 330.6	1 070.3	483	284
Bangor, ME	6 504	101.0	1 508	0.0	404.3	2 829	1 728	142	392	551	114.8	44.2	50.7	367	364
Baton Rouge, LA	32 838	548.2	4 474	1 021.1	1 448.8	2 711	1 290	228	178	1 003	549.1	230.9	193.0	370	116
Battle Creek, MI	6 868	84.0	656	371.4	473.5	3 385	1 968	93	850	405	173.6	71.8	60.6	435	397
Beaumont-Port Arthur, TX	20 546	317.1	2 856	1 963.7	1 115.4	3 110	1 898	719	162	279	441.8	112.3	211.9	554	493
Bellingham, WA	5 536	82.1	1 005	160.7	611.2	5 035	1 613	2 882	203	312	114.9	55.5	34.6	315	186
Benton Harbor, MI	7 347	107.2	1 039	480.9	559.8	3 342	1 790	888	103	481	172.3	56.6	76.9	465	461
Billings, MT	7 857	127.1	938	180.5	303.7	2 616	1 581	140	554	267	126.5	40.9	48.6	428	412
Biloxi-Gulfport, MS	10 059	141.2	1 076	351.4	1 081.6	5 245	2 002	630	2 367	236	152.4	64.5	40.8	213	171
Binghamton, NY	11 923	184.1	2 142	173.2	1 131.3	4 363	1 825	1 951	185	388	380.3	181.4	143.1	544	399
Birmingham, AL	58 619	1 049.3	8 218	1 962.0	2 493.9	2 690	1 878	138	344	320	769.3	293.5	256.5	289	118
Bismarck, ND	5 058	94.0	642	244.5	339.1	3 961	1 464	84	499	1 540	92.0	40.5	27.9	340	329
Bloomington, IN	4 367	60.6	500	206.2	235.1	2 265	1 224	86	150	791	62.9	31.3	21.7	214	214
Bloomington-Normal, IL	5 835	89.1	821	779.8	284.4	2 268	1 364	89	232	108	108.4	26.5	57.3	475	403
Boise City, ID	14 169	213.1	1 463	261.4	674.6	3 278	1 524	151	753	823	141.2	55.1	50.5	278	266
Boston-Lawrence-Salem, MA-NH	399 233	8 523.7	84 907	5 254.1	17 873.1	4 775	1 762	1 745	521	737	4 728.5	2 020.0	2 103.5	574	567
Bradenton, FL	11 407	187.7	1 705	1 283.6	620.2	3 247	2 956	40	112	128	194.8	63.1	53.9	334	295
Bremerton, WA	7 696	120.9	714	303.0	1 374.7	7 363	2 049	563	4 533	213	134.2	85.0	30.6	196	130
Brownsville-Harlingen, TX	10 010	114.8	1 756	632.4	569.8	2 126	1 280	163	150	458	215.9	122.3	46.9	201	149
Bryan-College Station, TX	7 090	92.0	838	289.6	249.9	2 175	1 050	141	277	685	61.7	20.0	25.7	228	172
Buffalo-Niagara Falls, NY	70 659	1 032.3	14 136	3 209.5	3 704.0	3 162	2 090	164	313	580	2 090.6	1 043.0	776.5	636	449
Buffalo, NY	62 147	926.3	11 881	3 194.7	3 091.6	3 238	2 129	148	332	617	1 720.2	874.9	644.9	646	454
Niagara Falls, NY	8 512	106.0	2 255	14.8	612.4	2 825	1 917	234	231	418	370.4	168.1	131.6	593	428
Burlington, NC	5 539	68.8	789	441.5	257.7	2 406	1 703	312	100	279	91.8	51.1	25.1	249	203
Burlington, VT	12 179	157.5	1 586	165.4	477.9	3 476	1 250	1 044	522	644	96.9	22.8	57.5	467	461
Canton, OH	23 737	300.2	2 391	1 661.7	959.9	2 390	1 810	186	140	238	351.4	139.3	138.7	343	259
Casper, WY	3 562	54.2	495	133.6	169.3	2 696	1 444	390	400	439	171.1	69.0	47.3	607	403
Cedar Rapids, IA	11 320	174.6	1 426	530.0	624.9	3 596	1 470	1 452	241	211	235.1	94.0	94.0	558	548
Champaign-Urbana-Rantoul, IL	10 195	165.6	1 342	496.1	597.3	3 455	1 240	356	916	769	183.3	51.3	73.1	426	348
Charleston, SC	27 704	359.2	1 574	1 141.1	2 456.5	4 700	1 518	589	2 213	351	319.5	144.4	101.6	223	203
Charleston, WV	14 299	236.7	2 233	322.1	908.9	3 523	2 090	150	321	952	229.2	102.0	79.3	294	216
Charlotte-Gastonia-Rock Hill, NC-SC	81 064	1 262.9	11 237	3 206.3	2 153.6	1 901	1 338	116	209	225	995.4	455.3	295.9	295	247
Charlottesville, VA	7 789	109.7	922	342.8	365.0	2 929	1 571	285	405	657	94.4	38.5	44.6	384	249
Chattanooga, TN-GA	26 871	419.8	2 856	964.9	1 455.0	3 293	1 755	325	861	341	425.1	125.7	136.2	318	214
Cheyenne, WY	3 676	50.7	383	252.6	450.4	5 888	1 763	576	2 080	1 392	119.5	62.6	27.5	386	299
Chicago-Gary-Lake County, IL-IN-WI	598 861	11 834.2	91 850	43 697.4	20 866.1	2 536	1 588	208	379	319	10 510.1	3 910.2	4 938.3	618	459
Aurora-Elgin, IL	15 465	256.0	2 453	1 488.0	869.6	2 398	1 328	719	214	77	363.3	107.1	182.4	572	508
Chicago, IL	508 654	10 258.8	79 816	37 202.1	16 311.3	2 613	1 649	199	364	361	8 300.7	3 111.4	3 946.1	646	452
Gary-Hammond, IN	27 997	469.3	3 272	1 781.4	1 335.1	2 184	1 656	42	138	315	770.4	367.6	267.5	420	414
Joliet, IL	12 501	197.7	1 998	1 312.8	655.0	1 704	1 186	259	85	83	363.9	112.7	166.6	465	410
Kenosha, WI	4 436	60.0	619	332.1	281.2	2 281	1 767	37	88	326	175.8	84.7	54.8	450	447
Lake County, IL	29 808	592.4	3 692	1 581.0	1 413.9	2 798	1 205	159	1 270	153	536.0	126.7	320.9	710	632

1. Includes deposits for all insured and reporting noninsured commercial and mutual savings banks. 2. Includes savings capital for all FSLIC insured savings institutions. 3. Based on the estimated population as of July 1 of the year shown. 4. Based on the estimated population as of July 1, 1982.

Area name	Local government finances, 1981–1982, (cont'd): Direct general expenditure: Total (Mil dol)	Percent change, 1977–1982	Per capita[1] (Dollars)	Percent of total for–: Education	Health & hospitals	Police protection	Public welfare	Highways	Debt outstanding: Total (Mil dol)	Per capita[1] (Dollars)	State and local government employment, 1989: Total	Rate[2]	Federal government civilian employment, 1989: Total	Earnings ($1,000)	Elections,[3] 1988: Total vote cast for president	Vote for lead party (Percent)
	187	188	189	190	191	192	193	194	195	196	197	198	199	200	201	202
Abilene, TX	74.6	83.3	625	53.6	0.7	6.4	0.3	7.5	51	427	7 577	624.1	1 440	34 191	42 024	R—68.0
Albany, GA	144.3	109.4	1 249	31.3	17.1	4.5	0.1	3.3	50	434	9 187	796.8	3 531	112 914	34 400	R—53.5
Albany-Schenectady-Troy, NY	1 134.2	31.0	1 359	42.3	3.1	3.4	15.2	6.3	1 221	1 463	100 735	1 179.3	9 335	303 710	404 836	D—51.0
Albuquerque, NM	449.1	86.0	1 036	50.3	2.6	6.3	0.1	4.1	504	1 162	37 826	754.1	13 851	442 193	173 135	R—53.6
Alexandria, LA	107.1	78.8	782	52.8	1.1	5.4	0.2	5.7	133	974	9 619	700.1	2 956	86 481	48 891	R—61.3
Allentown-Bethlehem, PA-NJ	589.3	44.3	918	49.8	2.2	3.5	7.7	4.9	764	1 191	28 081	409.8	2 571	80 357	236 298	R—55.5
Altoona, PA	101.8	47.8	749	54.1	4.2	3.7	5.3	4.6	115	843	6 313	477.2	963	32 155	41 662	R—61.5
Amarillo, TX	180.7	68.6	985	47.5	15.5	6.0	0.7	6.8	83	451	12 202	618.8	1 753	62 948	62 797	R—70.7
Anchorage, AK	398.1	76.6	2 005	37.4	2.5	5.6	0.0	4.6	552	2 781	14 832	691.5	10 210	362 288	NA	
Anderson, IN	100.8	48.9	745	52.7	0.5	4.3	6.5	4.2	59	435	5 745	436.6	369	10 884	57 241	R—56.9
Anderson, SC	74.1	97.1	541	66.7	0.4	5.4	0.3	3.4	72	523	7 118	493.3	368	12 091	38 383	R—67.6
Anniston, AL	97.4	66.2	796	36.6	31.0	3.6	0.1	6.8	75	611	6 614	538.2	7 205	221 740	33 970	R—58.3
Appleton-Oshkosh-Neenah, WI	342.5	53.9	1 156	41.1	9.0	5.6	3.9	12.7	214	723	16 148	510.5	1 092	33 363	140 055	R—54.5
Asheville, NC	131.6	46.9	803	50.2	2.6	5.3	2.1	1.8	76	466	10 155	581.3	2 507	78 688	63 992	R—57.6
Athens, GA	118.2	91.3	885	38.7	28.8	4.7	1.3	3.5	57	427	15 896	1 091.0	2 164	72 663	41 168	R—57.2
Atlanta, GA	2 328.3	70.0	1 035	40.3	19.3	5.2	0.2	3.4	4 133	1 838	168 403	597.4	45 194	1 427 693	843 418	R—59.6
Atlantic City, NJ	440.5	67.9	1 566	37.0	1.2	6.7	6.5	5.4	577	2 052	23 807	760.6	2 912	110 591	123 559	R—59.5
Augusta, GA-SC	328.9	113.4	925	42.1	29.7	3.8	0.9	2.7	263	739	27 618	689.2	8 329	239 528	112 827	R—66.4
Austin, TX	615.7	100.8	1 061	43.4	10.9	5.7	0.7	4.3	1 852	3 192	92 404	1 205.7	11 754	334 451	306 578	D—51.7
Bakersfield, CA	703.7	52.4	1 615	39.3	9.7	5.0	9.4	4.1	304	699	30 137	563.2	12 125	410 775	147 293	R—61.5
Baltimore, MD	2 635.9	24.7	1 189	40.9	4.3	6.2	0.2	12.4	2 454	1 107	147 683	623.6	77 279	2 377 727	867 309	R—51.1
Bangor, ME	109.6	46.9	793	48.2	3.1	3.7	1.7	7.8	112	809	12 821	897.2	1 302	40 168	63 754	R—54.8
Baton Rouge, LA	515.6	81.7	989	44.3	5.7	6.3	0.4	4.5	788	1 511	49 328	922.9	2 363	77 698	205 368	R—57.1
Battle Creek, MI	176.2	75.3	1 264	43.1	7.2	6.9	1.7	7.2	120	857	6 444	460.6	4 328	152 628	49 787	R—53.8
Beaumont-Port Arthur, TX	422.3	90.1	1 103	49.0	3.8	5.6	0.3	6.4	659	1 723	19 084	532.2	1 404	45 258	136 774	D—59.8
Bellingham, WA	110.0	56.0	1 001	47.7	3.1	4.9	0.0	9.9	92	837	7 085	583.6	721	24 109	50 094	D—51.0
Benton Harbor, MI	163.4	34.8	987	56.7	7.7	5.4	1.5	4.7	128	773	8 117	484.6	482	13 623	60 183	R—62.8
Billings, MT	116.0	65.7	1 022	46.7	1.1	4.6	1.6	6.4	88	772	5 721	492.8	1 805	59 500	50 647	R—55.4
Biloxi-Gulfport, MS	146.4	46.5	764	38.3	17.9	4.6	0.6	10.5	216	1 128	9 847	477.5	8 631	252 020	59 441	R—68.4
Binghamton, NY	381.5	32.4	1 451	47.3	3.0	2.7	14.4	7.1	218	829	19 048	734.6	979	30 922	117 311	R—51.4
Birmingham, AL	745.7	55.9	841	38.2	9.5	6.2	0.9	7.1	1 011	1 139	54 549	588.4	9 488	297 560	343 621	R—60.0
Bismarck, ND	85.2	61.4	1 039	52.8	0.7	4.3	2.2	11.6	100	1 215	7 372	861.2	1 166	36 947	39 531	R—59.7
Bloomington, IN	54.9	44.9	542	53.2	0.5	4.2	4.4	4.0	29	288	16 233	1 563.9	367	11 224	37 038	R—56.0
Bloomington-Normal, IL	105.0	52.2	870	46.3	1.2	5.3	1.7	12.1	84	700	10 174	811.3	936	23 452	49 511	R—61.7
Boise City, ID	133.0	39.7	732	46.3	0.5	7.3	0.0	8.4	79	433	14 271	693.4	4 135	135 514	87 334	R—62.9
Boston-Lawrence-Salem, MA-NH	3 906.2	19.1	1 065	43.9	6.5	6.3	0.7	4.3	2 810	766	227 565	607.9	48 680	1 560 936	1 701 043	D—53.0
Bradenton, FL	161.0	38.0	998	40.1	19.6	5.6	0.4	5.7	241	1 492	9 012	471.8	567	17 398	78 113	R—65.5
Bremerton, WA	138.4	100.3	884	55.9	2.0	3.4	0.0	5.9	66	422	8 054	431.4	20 026	643 626	69 649	R—49.9
Brownsville-Harlingen, TX	198.7	88.0	852	58.2	3.8	3.3	0.5	3.2	197	845	15 862	591.9	1 233	42 197	55 552	D—55.8
Bryan-College Station, TX	64.3	61.6	570	50.1	0.5	5.9	0.2	5.6	139	1 236	21 464	1 868.1	888	31 913	44 690	R—65.7
Buffalo-Niagara Falls, NY	2 067.0	27.4	1 693	35.5	5.6	3.4	15.0	5.3	1 371	1 123	75 611	645.4	10 466	324 791	517 660	D—54.6
Buffalo, NY	1 684.8	28.1	1 687	35.0	5.8	3.5	15.3	4.8	1 102	1 103	64 483	675.4	9 105	284 065	430 792	D—55.4
Niagara Falls, NY	382.2	24.4	1 722	37.7	5.0	2.6	13.6	7.6	269	1 213	11 128	513.3	1 361	40 726	86 868	D—50.4
Burlington, NC	83.5	51.3	828	51.1	2.3	5.3	2.6	1.4	54	537	5 132	479.2	287	9 157	36 851	R—65.5
Burlington, VT	99.3	74.2	806	62.3	0.3	4.4	0.0	6.8	166	1 347	10 205	742.2	1 800	56 954	60 073	D—50.9
Canton, OH	342.0	48.8	846	48.9	5.5	4.3	4.7	6.5	260	643	17 314	431.0	1 370	43 193	169 090	R—55.2
Casper, WY	157.0	155.3	2 015	43.4	16.7	3.9	0.1	6.2	62	793	4 157	661.9	681	23 306	23 487	R—59.6
Cedar Rapids, IA	211.3	45.7	1 253	56.5	1.9	3.7	1.9	6.8	142	844	9 383	539.9	1 120	37 481	76 718	D—56.0
Champaign-Urbana-Rantoul, IL	174.8	60.1	1 019	43.0	13.7	4.6	2.7	7.4	101	588	29 229	1 690.5	2 923	78 957	63 499	R—52.4
Charleston, SC	336.1	117.1	738	51.9	6.2	4.9	0.3	1.8	338	743	33 375	638.5	20 183	701 586	131 445	R—61.4
Charleston, WV	221.4	73.6	820	54.6	1.1	3.7	0.2	2.2	432	1 602	18 056	699.8	1 919	65 022	94 383	D—50.6
Charlotte-Gastonia-Rock Hill, NC-SC	954.9	51.6	951	44.8	17.4	4.8	2.6	2.6	726	722	62 150	548.6	6 841	226 301	374 281	R—63.3
Charlottesville, VA	87.7	58.6	755	54.5	0.0	3.9	4.6	3.0	69	592	21 324	1 711.4	1 371	41 907	46 688	R—54.9
Chattanooga, TN-GA	473.6	74.2	1 107	28.3	27.0	3.8	3.9	4.0	359	838	24 382	551.8	9 068	357 845	153 087	R—63.1
Cheyenne, WY	100.0	104.1	1 403	56.6	11.4	3.7	0.0	4.3	71	997	7 485	978.4	2 718	80 300	27 770	R—56.0
Chicago-Gary-Lake County, IL-IN-WI	9 319.0	44.5	1 166	43.1	4.6	7.8	1.8	4.6	7 870	985	404 549	491.6	76 316	2 524 273	3 129 147	D—49.8
Aurora-Elgin, IL	338.9	40.8	1 062	56.8	0.4	4.6	0.2	7.3	206	646	14 123	389.5	1 912	76 557	118 496	R—64.9
Chicago, IL	7 337.4	43.1	1 202	40.9	4.9	8.3	1.1	4.2	6 198	1 015	314 861	504.4	62 163	2 081 045	2 405 697	D—51.7
Gary-Hammond, IN	672.6	54.9	1 055	43.8	6.6	4.9	10.2	3.7	594	933	29 617	484.5	2 152	68 560	235 080	D—52.9
Joliet, IL	341.0	49.6	953	55.7	1.1	6.0	1.5	7.0	476	1 329	17 498	455.1	762	23 282	138 092	R—59.3
Kenosha, WI	169.1	71.5	1 389	46.2	8.6	8.5	2.1	8.9	95	783	6 250	506.9	269	8 283	52 149	D—57.7
Lake County, IL	460.0	43.1	1 018	55.5	1.6	5.9	1.9	6.6	300	664	22 200	439.3	9 058	266 546	179 633	R—63.5

1. Based on the estimated population as of July 1, 1982. 2. Per 10,000 resident population estimated as of July 1 of the year shown. 3. Data subject to copyright.

MSA/ CMSA/ NECMA/ PMSA code[1]	Area name	Land Area,[2] 1990 (Sq. Km.)	Population, 1990													
			Total persons	Rank	Per square kilometer	Race: White	Race: Black	Race: Am. Indian, Eskimo, Aleut	Race: Asian & Pacific Islander	Race: Other race	Hispanic[3]	Age of population Percent: Under 5 years	5 to 14 years	15 to 24 years	25 to 34 years	35 to 44 years
		1	2	3	4	5	6	7	8	9	10	11	12	13	14	15
1620	Chico, CA	4 247	182 120	168	42.9	165 200	2 361	3 241	5 170	6 148	13 606	6.8	13.4	17.1	14.5	13.9
1642	Cincinnati-Hamilton, OH-KY-IN	6 715	1 744 124	23	259.7	1 521 061	203 607	2 457	14 260	2 739	9 376	7.8	14.9	14.8	17.5	14.9
1640	Cincinnati, OH-KY-IN	5 505	1 452 645	X	263.9	1 246 169	190 473	2 078	11 601	2 324	7 909	7.9	14.9	14.2	17.7	14.9
3200	Hamilton-Middletown, OH	1 210	291 479	X	240.9	274 892	13 134	379	2 659	415	1 467	7.4	14.7	17.3	16.7	15.2
1660	Clarksville-Hopkinsville, TN-KY	3 264	169 439	173	51.9	128 583	34 801	688	2 712	2 655	5 567	8.6	13.9	20.4	19.9	13.3
1692	Cleveland-Akron-Lorain, OH	7 537	2 759 823	13	366.2	2 261 217	441 940	5 133	28 187	23 346	52 997	7.1	13.8	13.9	16.6	15.0
0080	Akron, OH	2 344	657 575	X	280.5	583 900	65 091	1 357	6 180	1 047	3 815	6.9	13.6	15.7	16.5	15.2
1680	Cleveland, OH	3 917	1 831 122	X	467.5	1 435 768	355 619	3 038	20 528	16 169	33 921	7.1	13.6	13.1	16.7	14.9
4440	Lorain-Elyria, OH	1 276	271 126	X	212.5	241 549	21 230	738	1 479	6 130	15 261	7.4	15.3	14.9	16.2	15.5
1720	Colorado Springs, CO	5 508	397 014	91	72.1	341 400	28 593	3 242	9 841	13 938	34 473	8.5	15.0	16.2	19.6	16.1
1740	Columbia, MO	1 775	112 379	250	63.3	100 055	8 377	394	3 129	424	1 226	7.1	12.5	25.1	18.9	14.2
1760	Columbia, SC	3 774	453 331	81	120.1	307 454	137 906	1 013	4 820	2 138	5 949	7.1	13.6	17.5	19.0	16.2
1800	Columbus, GA-AL	2 865	243 072	140	84.8	144 326	91 484	765	3 107	3 390	7 388	8.1	14.7	17.8	18.0	13.7
1840	Columbus, OH	9 270	1 377 419	29	148.6	1 184 770	164 602	2 880	21 059	4 108	11 363	7.5	13.8	16.3	19.0	15.6
1880	Corpus Christi, TX	3 957	349 894	107	88.4	265 002	13 659	1 394	2 646	67 193	181 860	8.3	17.6	14.9	16.9	14.7
1900	Cumberland, MD-WV	1 951	101 643	260	52.1	98 821	2 270	71	391	90	420	6.0	12.7	15.6	13.2	13.5
1922	Dallas-Fort Worth, TX	18 046	3 885 415	8	215.3	2 924 673	554 616	18 972	97 578	289 576	518 917	8.4	14.8	15.0	21.0	16.1
1920	Dallas, TX	11 581	2 553 362	X	220.5	1 854 577	410 766	12 635	67 195	208 189	368 884	8.4	14.7	15.1	21.3	16.2
2800	Fort Worth-Arlington, TX	6 465	1 332 053	X	206.0	1 070 096	143 850	6 337	30 383	81 387	150 033	8.4	14.9	14.9	20.4	15.7
1950	Danville, VA	2 627	108 711	253	41.4	73 817	34 350	117	325	102	515	6.3	13.0	13.3	15.2	14.7
1960	Davenport-Rock Island-Moline, IA-IL	4 423	350 861	105	79.3	322 805	19 115	902	2 502	5 537	13 134	7.3	15.3	13.6	15.6	15.0
2000	Dayton-Springfield, OH	4 361	951 270	43	218.1	811 393	126 238	1 915	9 278	2 446	7 254	7.2	14.1	14.9	16.5	15.0
2020	Daytona Beach, FL	2 864	370 712	97	129.4	328 530	33 455	915	2 739	5 073	14 840	5.7	10.8	12.7	14.8	13.0
2030	Decatur, AL	3 304	131 556	213	39.8	113 685	14 879	2 434	389	169	686	7.0	14.8	14.3	16.7	15.0
2040	Decatur, IL	1 504	117 206	240	77.9	102 197	14 135	157	506	211	540	6.8	14.8	13.6	14.8	14.9
2082	Denver-Boulder, CO	11 663	1 848 319	22	158.5	1 599 734	97 755	13 884	42 642	94 304	226 200	7.8	14.1	13.5	19.6	18.0
1125	Boulder-Longmont, Co	1 923	225 339	X	117.2	210 190	1 959	1 313	5 508	6 369	15 195	7.0	12.7	17.9	19.6	18.7
2080	Denver, CO	9 740	1 622 980	X	166.6	1 389 544	95 796	12 571	37 134	87 935	211 005	7.9	14.3	12.9	19.6	17.9
2120	Des Moines, IA	4 475	392 928	95	87.8	368 386	14 952	1 015	6 218	2 357	6 614	7.5	14.3	14.4	18.2	15.6
2162	Detroit-Ann Arbor, MI	13 404	4 665 236	6	348.0	3 569 087	975 199	17 961	69 454	33 535	90 947	7.6	14.0	14.8	17.6	15.5
0440	Ann Arbor, MI	1 839	282 937	X	153.9	236 390	31 720	1 076	11 724	2 027	5 731	6.8	11.6	22.8	19.9	16.1
2160	Detroit, MI	11 565	4 382 299	X	378.9	3 332 697	943 479	16 885	57 730	31 508	85 216	7.6	14.2	14.3	17.4	15.5
2180	Dothan, AL	2 956	130 964	216	44.3	100 878	27 801	526	1 201	558	1 679	7.8	15.3	15.5	17.4	14.3
2200	Dubuque, IA	1 575	86 403	270	54.9	85 367	354	77	437	168	437	7.0	15.7	15.2	15.2	14.1
2240	Duluth, MN-WI	19 515	239 971	144	12.3	232 507	1 276	4 487	1 342	359	1 153	6.3	14.3	14.1	14.4	15.2
2290	Eau Claire, WI	4 269	137 543	205	32.2	134 056	269	617	2 400	201	611	7.2	14.9	17.9	15.4	14.5
2320	El Paso, TX	2 624	591 610	69	225.5	452 512	22 110	2 590	6 485	107 913	411 619	9.0	18.0	17.9	17.2	13.7
2330	Elkhart-Goshen, IN	1 201	156 198	183	130.1	146 505	7 106	453	997	1 137	2 932	8.5	15.6	14.6	16.6	15.2
2335	Elmira, NY	1 057	95 195	267	90.1	88 370	5 245	211	690	679	1 441	7.1	14.2	14.2	15.6	14.5
2340	Enid, OK	2 742	56 735	282	20.7	52 403	2 020	1 234	587	491	1 086	6.9	15.4	12.7	16.3	13.9
2360	Erie, PA	2 077	275 572	127	132.7	257 879	14 304	438	1 411	1 540	3 364	7.2	14.5	16.2	15.5	14.4
2400	Eugene-Springfield, OR	11 795	282 912	122	24.0	269 798	2 107	3 207	5 557	2 243	6 852	6.7	14.1	15.5	15.6	16.9
2440	Evansville, IN-KY	3 801	278 990	124	73.4	260 832	16 115	477	1 237	329	1 321	7.0	14.4	13.5	16.7	15.0
2520	Fargo-Moorhead, ND-MN	7 280	153 296	185	21.1	149 004	446	1 497	1 396	953	1 879	7.3	14.1	20.4	17.5	14.7
2560	Fayetteville, NC	1 692	274 566	128	162.3	170 069	87 496	4 425	5 769	6 807	13 298	9.1	14.9	21.1	20.3	13.6
2580	Fayetteville-Springdale, AR	2 461	113 409	248	46.1	108 743	1 676	1 486	1 043	461	1 526	6.9	13.9	19.1	16.8	14.4
2640	Flint, MI	1 657	430 459	85	259.8	336 651	84 257	3 132	2 902	3 517	8 877	7.8	15.6	15.0	16.9	15.0
2650	Florence, AL	3 274	131 327	214	40.1	114 380	16 263	302	289	93	500	6.5	13.5	14.8	15.1	14.2
2655	Florence, SC	2 070	114 344	246	55.2	69 501	44 276	145	307	115	508	7.3	16.1	15.6	15.6	15.5
2670	Fort Collins-Loveland, CO	6 738	186 136	166	27.6	175 971	1 114	1 063	2 777	5 211	12 227	7.3	14.3	18.0	17.9	16.9
2700	Fort Myers-Cape Coral, FL	2 081	335 113	113	161.0	306 200	22 184	672	1 894	4 163	15 094	5.9	10.7	10.3	14.1	12.5
2710	Fort Pierce, FL	2 922	251 071	136	85.9	214 278	30 709	526	1 565	3 993	10 680	6.2	11.4	10.5	14.6	12.8
2720	Fort Smith, AR-OK	4 676	175 911	170	37.6	155 580	6 831	9 054	3 755	691	2 120	7.3	15.4	13.9	16.0	14.5
2750	Fort Walton Beach, FL	2 424	143 776	198	59.3	125 191	13 007	776	3 658	1 144	4 427	7.8	14.2	14.9	19.8	14.6
2760	Fort Wayne, IN	3 511	363 811	101	103.6	326 568	30 380	1 056	2 769	3 038	6 268	7.9	15.6	14.2	17.3	15.5
2840	Fresno, CA	15 445	667 490	61	43.2	422 839	33 423	7 119	57 239	146 870	236 634	9.4	17.5	15.7	17.1	14.1
2880	Gadsden, AL	1 385	99 840	261	72.1	85 274	13 799	250	419	98	331	6.0	13.9	14.5	14.2	14.6
2900	Gainesville, FL	3 023	204 111	156	67.5	158 479	38 982	443	4 656	1 551	7 205	6.5	12.2	23.9	18.2	14.5
2975	Glens Falls, NY	4 417	118 539	239	26.8	115 157	2 352	214	392	424	1 789	7.0	14.0	14.5	16.7	14.9

1. MSA = Metropolitan Statistical Area. CMSA = Consolidated MSA. NECMA = New England county metropolitan area. PMSA = Primary MSA. See Appendix A for explanation of these concepts. See Appendix B for list of metropolitan areas identified by type, with component counties. 2. Dry land or land partially or temporarily covered by water. 3. Hispanic persons may be of any race.

Area name	Population, 1990 (cont'd): Age of population (cont'd), Percent: 45 to 54 years	55 to 64 years	65 to 74 years	75 years and over	Percent female	Population–change and components of change: Change, 1980–1990: Number	Percent	Components of change, 1980–1986: Total persons, 1986	Total persons, 1980	Net change: Number	Net change: Percent	Natural increase: Births	Natural increase: Deaths	Net migration	Households, 1990: Total
	16	17	18	19	20	21	22	23	24	25	26	27	28	29	30
Chico, CA	8.7	8.4	10.1	7.2	51.0	38 269	26.6	166 700	143 851	22 900	15.9	14 100	9 600	18 400	71 665
Cincinnati-Hamilton, OH-KY-IN	9.9	8.5	6.7	5.0	52.0	83 866	5.1	1 690 100	1 660 258	29 800	1.8	168 300	92 200	-46 300	652 920
Cincinnati, OH-KY-IN	9.8	8.6	6.9	5.2	52.0	51 174	3.7	1 418 600	1 401 471	17 100	1.2	143 100	79 800	-46 200	548 385
Hamilton-Middletown, OH	10.1	8.5	6.1	4.1	51.6	32 692	12.6	271 500	258 787	12 700	4.9	25 200	12 400	-100	104 535
Clarksville-Hopkinsville, TN-KY	8.3	6.9	5.0	3.7	47.7	19 219	12.8	154 400	150 220	4 200	2.8	19 400	6 600	-8 600	55 981
Cleveland-Akron-Lorain, OH	10.3	9.4	8.3	5.6	52.3	-74 239	-2.6	2 765 700	2 834 062	-68 600	-2.4	252 500	163 800	-157 300	1 057 653
Akron, OH	10.1	9.2	7.8	5.1	51.9	-2 753	-0.4	644 800	660 328	-15 600	-2.4	57 800	36 200	-37 200	249 227
Cleveland, OH	10.4	9.6	8.7	5.9	52.6	-67 703	-3.6	1 850 300	1 898 825	-48 700	-2.6	169 200	115 200	-102 700	712 362
Lorain-Elyria, OH	10.4	8.7	7.1	4.5	51.3	-3 783	-1.4	270 600	274 909	-4 300	-1.6	25 500	12 400	-17 400	96 064
Colorado Springs, CO	9.6	7.0	5.0	3.0	49.8	87 590	28.3	380 400	309 424	71 000	22.9	41 000	11 200	41 200	146 965
Columbia, MO	8.1	5.8	4.6	3.8	51.6	12 003	12.0	106 500	100 376	6 200	6.2	9 700	3 700	200	41 937
Columbia, SC	9.9	7.5	5.8	3.4	51.3	43 376	10.6	444 700	409 955	34 700	8.5	39 300	19 500	14 900	163 223
Columbus, GA-AL	9.0	8.3	6.4	4.2	50.4	3 876	1.6	250 600	239 196	11 300	4.7	26 400	12 900	-2 200	86 241
Columbus, OH	9.9	7.9	5.9	4.1	51.2	133 592	10.7	1 299 400	1 243 827	55 600	4.5	124 500	61 500	-7 400	524 535
Corpus Christi, TX	9.4	8.1	6.1	4.0	51.0	23 666	7.3	363 300	326 228	37 100	11.4	43 800	14 800	8 100	118 516
Cumberland, MD-WV	10.9	10.6	10.1	7.4	52.6	-6 139	-5.7	102 200	107 782	-5 700	-5.3	8 100	7 700	-6 100	39 615
Dallas-Fort Worth, TX	10.0	6.8	4.7	3.3	50.6	954 847	32.6	3 655 300	2 930 568	725 100	24.7	379 600	137 700	483 200	1 449 872
Dallas, TX	10.0	6.6	4.5	3.2	50.7	595 932	30.4	2 401 400	1 957 430	444 200	22.7	254 400	88 800	278 600	954 728
Fort Worth-Arlington, TX	10.0	7.1	5.1	3.5	50.5	358 915	36.9	1 253 900	973 138	280 900	28.9	125 200	48 900	204 600	495 144
Danville, VA	11.1	10.4	9.5	6.4	52.6	-3 078	-2.8	110 300	111 789	-1 400	-1.3	9 000	7 100	-3 300	42 325
Davenport-Rock Island-Moline, IA-IL	10.5	8.9	7.7	5.9	51.7	-33 888	-8.8	371 300	384 749	-13 300	-3.5	37 700	20 100	-30 900	136 269
Dayton-Springfield, OH	10.9	9.2	7.4	4.9	51.9	9 187	1.0	933 500	942 083	-8 400	-0.9	89 000	49 700	-47 700	364 300
Daytona Beach, FL	9.4	10.9	13.3	9.5	51.6	111 950	43.3	320 900	258 762	62 100	24.0	20 800	24 300	65 600	153 416
Decatur, AL	11.4	9.0	6.9	4.8	51.2	11 155	9.3	130 300	120 401	10 000	8.3	11 400	6 400	5 000	49 209
Decatur, IL	10.8	9.6	8.2	6.3	52.3	-14 169	-10.8	126 700	131 375	-4 700	-3.6	11 600	7 300	-9 000	45 996
Denver-Boulder, CO	10.5	7.4	5.5	3.7	50.8	229 858	14.2	1 847 400	1 618 461	228 800	14.1	185 800	65 700	108 700	737 806
Boulder-Longmont, Co	10.2	6.2	4.3	3.3	49.9	35 714	18.8	214 400	189 625	24 700	13.0	19 400	6 300	11 600	88 402
Denver, CO	10.6	7.6	5.6	3.7	50.9	194 144	13.6	1 633 000	1 428 836	204 100	14.3	166 400	59 400	97 100	649 404
Des Moines, IA	10.2	8.1	6.5	5.2	52.2	25 367	6.9	381 400	367 561	13 700	3.7	37 300	18 500	-5 100	153 100
Detroit-Ann Arbor, MI	10.4	8.6	7.0	4.6	51.8	-87 528	-1.8	4 600 800	4 752 764	-152 000	-3.2	421 100	248 000	-325 100	1 723 478
Ann Arbor, MI	9.3	6.1	4.4	3.1	50.5	18 197	6.9	266 000	264 740	1 200	0.5	24 200	9 000	-14 000	104 528
Detroit, MI	10.4	8.7	7.2	4.7	51.9	-105 725	-2.4	4 334 800	4 488 024	-153 200	-3.4	396 900	239 000	-311 100	1 618 950
Dothan, AL	10.1	8.3	6.6	4.7	51.4	8 511	7.0	129 900	122 453	7 400	6.0	13 300	5 900	0	48 418
Dubuque, IA	10.0	8.7	7.6	6.5	51.7	-7 342	-7.8	91 100	93 745	-2 700	-2.9	8 800	5 100	-6 400	30 799
Duluth, MN-WI	9.8	9.1	9.0	7.7	51.4	-26 679	-10.0	243 500	266 650	-23 200	-8.7	22 800	16 500	-29 500	95 275
Eau Claire, WI	9.1	7.8	7.2	5.9	51.5	6 611	5.0	136 700	130 932	5 800	4.4	13 000	6 700	-500	50 359
El Paso, TX	8.7	7.4	5.1	3.0	51.4	111 711	23.3	561 500	479 899	81 500	17.0	69 500	16 900	28 900	178 366
Elkhart-Goshen, IN	10.3	8.0	6.4	4.8	51.1	18 868	13.7	146 400	137 330	9 100	6.6	14 800	6 700	1 000	56 713
Elmira, NY	10.0	9.3	8.8	6.3	51.4	-2 461	-2.5	90 500	97 656	-7 100	-7.3	8 500	6 000	-9 600	35 275
Enid, OK	10.1	9.3	8.1	7.3	52.0	-6 085	-9.7	62 900	62 820	0	0.0	7 400	3 900	-3 500	22 460
Erie, PA	9.6	8.9	8.4	5.4	51.7	-4 208	-1.5	279 200	279 780	-600	-0.2	26 500	16 200	-10 900	101 564
Eugene-Springfield, OR	10.3	7.9	7.6	5.5	51.3	7 686	2.8	263 200	275 226	-12 000	-4.4	24 900	12 300	-24 600	110 799
Evansville, IN-KY	10.3	9.0	7.9	6.1	52.2	2 738	1.0	281 100	276 252	5 000	1.8	26 300	16 700	-4 600	108 663
Fargo-Moorhead, ND-MN	8.5	7.1	5.6	4.9	50.8	15 722	11.4	145 300	137 574	7 700	5.6	14 200	6 000	-500	57 771
Fayetteville, NC	8.4	6.5	4.1	2.1	48.3	27 406	11.1	258 500	247 160	11 400	4.6	33 300	8 300	-13 600	91 500
Fayetteville-Springdale, AR	9.8	7.7	6.3	4.9	50.6	12 915	12.9	107 400	100 494	6 900	6.9	9 900	5 000	2 000	43 372
Flint, MI	10.8	8.7	6.1	4.1	52.1	-19 990	-4.4	434 900	450 449	-15 600	-3.5	44 000	20 900	-38 700	161 296
Florence, AL	11.4	10.1	8.6	5.8	52.2	-3 738	-2.8	137 700	135 065	2 600	1.9	11 200	7 100	-1 500	51 001
Florence, SC	10.5	8.3	7.0	4.2	52.9	4 181	3.8	116 000	110 163	5 900	5.4	11 400	6 200	700	40 217
Fort Collins-Loveland, CO	9.4	6.5	5.5	4.1	50.5	36 952	24.8	174 600	149 184	25 400	17.0	16 400	5 600	14 600	70 472
Fort Myers-Cape Coral, FL	9.5	12.1	15.3	9.4	51.7	129 847	63.3	279 100	205 266	73 800	36.0	19 000	17 200	72 000	140 124
Fort Pierce, FL	9.3	11.6	14.9	8.7	51.0	99 875	66.1	205 700	151 196	54 400	36.0	16 000	12 800	51 200	101 196
Fort Smith, AR-OK	10.9	8.7	7.5	5.9	51.4	13 098	8.0	176 000	162 813	13 200	8.1	16 200	9 500	6 500	66 884
Fort Walton Beach, FL	10.4	9.1	6.3	3.0	49.4	33 856	30.8	141 300	109 920	31 300	28.5	13 500	4 400	22 200	53 313
Fort Wayne, IN	9.8	8.1	6.6	4.9	51.4	9 655	2.7	356 100	354 156	2 000	0.6	35 700	17 200	-16 500	136 068
Fresno, CA	8.8	7.1	6.1	4.3	50.4	152 869	29.7	587 600	514 621	73 000	14.2	70 100	25 300	28 200	220 933
Gadsden, AL	10.8	10.3	9.4	6.5	52.7	-3 217	-3.1	102 300	103 057	-700	-0.7	8 700	6 600	-2 800	38 675
Gainesville, FL	8.5	6.6	5.7	3.9	50.2	32 719	19.1	199 800	171 392	28 300	16.5	17 700	7 300	17 900	78 451
Glens Falls, NY	10.3	8.9	7.8	5.9	50.2	8 890	8.1	112 400	109 649	2 700	2.5	9 500	7 000	200	42 815

Area name	Households, (cont'd)			Births, 1988			Deaths, 1987				Marriages, 1984		Divorces, 1984		Physicians, active non-Federal, 1989	
		Percent					Number		Rate							
	Percent change, 1980–1990	Female family house-holder[1]	One-person	Total	Rate[2]	Low birth weight[3] (Number)	Total	Infant[4]	Total[2]	Infant[5]	Number	Rate[2]	Number	Rate[2]	Number[6]	Rate[7]
	31	33	34	35	36	37	38	39	40	41	42	43	44	45	46	47
Chico, CA	25.9	9.7	25.4	2 493	14.3	154	1 770	25	10.5	10.5	1 071	6.8	1 095	6.9	331	185
Cincinnati-Hamilton, OH-KY-IN	11.3	12.3	25.5	27 481	15.9	1 806	14 956	249	8.7	9.1	17 702	10.6	8 167	4.9	3 968	227
Cincinnati, OH-KY-IN	10.0	12.6	26.4	23 378	16.1	1 543	12 828	212	8.9	9.1	14 758	10.5	6 298	4.5	3 661	250
Hamilton-Middletown, OH	18.6	10.4	20.8	4 103	14.7	263	2 128	37	7.7	9.2	2 944	11.1	1 869	7.1	307	108
Clarksville-Hopkinsville, TN-KY	19.5	11.6	19.1	3 063	19.3	200	1 111	33	7.1	11.3	1 823	12.0	1 204	7.9	148	92
Cleveland-Akron-Lorain, OH	3.8	13.0	26.5	40 579	14.7	3 018	26 341	414	9.5	10.4	24 979	9.0	12 882	4.6	7 523	272
Akron, OH	6.5	11.8	24.7	9 028	13.8	594	5 785	88	8.9	10.0	6 189	9.5	3 335	5.1	1 282	195
Cleveland, OH	2.6	13.6	27.9	27 709	15.0	2 185	18 434	291	9.9	10.7	16 397	8.8	8 301	4.4	5 955	323
Lorain-Elyria, OH	5.8	11.7	20.8	3 842	14.2	239	2 122	35	7.9	9.1	2 393	8.8	1 246	4.6	286	106
Colorado Springs, CO	36.3	9.8	23.7	7 659	19.4	620	2 119	85	5.4	11.1	4 839	13.7	2 503	7.1	537	133
Columbia, MO	18.8	9.5	27.5	1 632	15.4	105	668	21	6.3	12.9	1 159	11.0	521	5.0	725	686
Columbia, SC	22.7	13.5	23.6	7 044	15.4	664	3 282	90	7.3	13.4	4 504	10.4	1 800	4.2	1 122	242
Columbus, GA-AL	10.0	17.5	23.9	4 462	18.1	402	2 219	73	9.0	16.3	3 425	13.9	1 793	7.3	374	152
Columbus, OH	16.8	11.6	25.6	21 450	16.0	1 508	10 442	178	7.9	8.8	13 886	10.9	7 499	5.9	2 921	214
Corpus Christi, TX	13.4	13.4	21.2	6 187	17.3	363	2 471	54	6.9	8.7	3 980	11.1	2 218	6.2	594	166
Cumberland, MD-WV	1.3	10.6	26.4	1 228	12.0	75	1 338	10	13.0	8.5	1 219	11.7	339	3.3	173	170
Dallas-Fort Worth, TX	36.8	11.1	25.3	71 958	19.1	5 089	23 846	675	6.4	9.4	46 029	13.6	24 059	7.1	6 929	180
Dallas, TX	34.3	11.4	26.1	47 760	19.3	3 487	15 298	443	6.2	9.3	31 168	14.0	15 699	7.0	5 189	205
Fort Worth-Arlington, TX	41.9	10.5	23.9	24 198	18.7	1 602	8 548	232	6.7	9.7	14 861	12.9	8 360	7.3	1 740	132
Danville, VA	6.7	14.1	24.9	1 384	12.8	145	1 243	16	11.5	11.6	1 116	10.0	460	4.1	133	125
Davenport-Rock Island-Moline, IA-IL	-1.4	10.8	26.4	5 134	14.1	278	3 261	44	8.9	8.6	3 567	9.4	1 940	5.1	443	122
Dayton-Springfield, OH	7.1	12.0	24.8	14 057	14.8	986	8 315	120	8.8	8.5	9 601	10.3	5 906	6.4	1 710	179
Daytona Beach, FL	45.0	9.5	26.4	4 401	12.6	323	4 465	45	13.3	10.7	3 180	10.6	1 870	6.2	472	131
Decatur, AL	19.5	10.3	21.5	1 872	14.1	145	1 142	15	8.7	8.1	1 518	12.1	866	6.9	131	98
Decatur, IL	-4.8	11.4	26.4	1 735	14.0	135	1 105	19	8.9	10.9	1 293	10.0	755	5.9	170	139
Denver-Boulder, CO	21.3	10.2	28.4	30 491	16.4	2 481	11 073	303	6.0	9.8	19 886	11.1	10 560	5.9	4 833	259
Boulder-Longmont, Co	28.2	7.9	26.3	3 232	14.8	200	1 062	17	4.9	5.2	2 686	12.8	1 286	6.1	430	196
Denver, CO	20.4	10.5	28.7	27 259	16.6	2 281	10 011	286	6.1	10.4	17 200	10.8	9 274	5.8	4 403	268
Des Moines, IA	11.7	9.9	25.9	5 867	15.0	348	3 031	72	7.9	12.2	3 889	10.3	1 816	4.8	661	166
Detroit-Ann Arbor, MI	4.8	14.7	24.4	70 432	15.2	5 796	40 778	843	8.8	11.8	37 736	8.2	18 797	4.1	10 872	235
Ann Arbor, MI	12.5	9.3	26.3	3 639	13.6	231	1 517	41	5.7	10.1	2 487	9.5	1 266	4.9	2 082	773
Detroit, MI	4.3	15.1	24.3	66 793	15.3	5 565	39 261	802	9.0	11.9	35 249	8.2	17 531	4.1	8 790	202
Dothan, AL	17.1	12.7	23.0	2 173	16.6	154	1 039	23	8.0	10.8	1 563	12.2	1 108	8.6	196	149
Dubuque, IA	2.6	8.5	24.4	1 192	13.1	66	782	7	8.6	5.6	924	10.0	261	2.8	146	160
Duluth, MN-WI	-2.7	9.5	28.7	2 835	11.7	149	2 571	38	10.6	13.0	1 962	7.8	995	3.9	416	174
Eau Claire, WI	13.1	8.3	24.2	1 953	14.1	88	1 104	13	8.0	6.9	1 192	8.7	485	3.6	249	179
El Paso, TX	26.7	15.8	17.0	12 981	22.2	889	2 973	122	5.2	10.0	7 996	14.9	3 166	5.9	774	129
Elkhart-Goshen, IN	17.8	9.1	21.6	2 722	18.0	160	1 162	24	7.8	9.4	1 592	11.1	960	6.7	159	104
Elmira, NY	2.2	11.5	25.5	1 349	14.7	91	1 000	3	11.0	2.3	871	9.4	367	4.0	190	207
Enid, OK	-5.8	9.1	26.9	824	14.1	54	632	7	10.6	8.3	772	11.7	479	7.3	96	170
Erie, PA	4.9	11.5	25.4	4 013	14.5	248	2 585	45	9.3	11.5	2 381	8.4	960	3.4	459	166
Eugene-Springfield, OR	7.0	9.4	25.1	3 817	14.1	172	2 256	36	8.5	9.6	2 354	8.8	1 825	6.9	467	170
Evansville, IN-KY	7.0	10.5	25.8	3 980	14.2	283	2 700	42	9.6	10.8	3 156	11.2	1 909	6.8	505	179
Fargo-Moorhead, ND-MN	18.4	7.9	26.7	2 164	14.6	103	951	19	6.5	8.8	1 387	9.7	532	3.7	366	245
Fayetteville, NC	22.1	14.1	19.4	5 663	22.1	442	1 598	73	6.2	13.7	2 004	7.9	1 611	6.3	281	110
Fayetteville-Springdale, AR	20.2	8.1	24.4	1 732	15.7	115	906	14	8.3	8.6	1 811	17.4	807	7.8	202	180
Flint, MI	4.3	16.7	23.9	6 705	15.6	553	3 601	83	8.3	12.4	4 372	10.1	2 285	5.3	695	162
Florence, AL	7.6	10.6	23.2	1 749	12.9	121	1 244	16	9.2	9.5	2 284	16.7	773	5.6	167	124
Florence, SC	12.6	17.3	21.8	1 818	15.4	195	1 105	26	9.4	15.2	1 185	10.4	405	3.5	214	180
Fort Collins-Loveland, CO	30.3	7.6	23.0	2 773	15.2	170	1 015	22	5.7	8.3	1 803	10.9	821	4.9	270	146
Fort Myers-Cape Coral, FL	69.8	8.2	23.0	4 148	13.4	295	3 431	41	11.6	10.7	2 856	11.2	1 745	6.8	501	154
Fort Pierce, FL	73.4	8.5	22.3	3 226	13.9	269	2 539	43	11.5	13.5	1 902	9.9	1 102	5.8	359	147
Fort Smith, AR-OK	13.7	10.1	23.6	2 719	15.0	201	1 686	30	9.5	11.0	2 799	16.4	1 320	7.7	276	151
Fort Walton Beach, FL	42.0	9.5	20.9	2 505	16.6	181	850	24	5.8	9.7	1 881	14.5	1 100	8.5	175	112
Fort Wayne, IN	8.9	10.3	24.2	5 998	16.3	387	2 897	56	7.9	9.6	3 365	9.6	1 682	4.8	568	152
Fresno, CA	23.8	13.9	21.0	13 095	21.3	851	4 604	107	7.7	8.6	6 146	10.9	3 187	5.6	1 143	182
Gadsden, AL	4.9	11.8	24.3	1 323	12.9	99	1 159	15	11.3	11.7	1 107	10.7	683	6.6	153	149
Gainesville, FL	28.8	12.0	27.4	2 926	14.1	202	1 370	26	6.7	8.9	1 949	10.1	1 198	6.2	1 163	552
Glens Falls, NY	14.8	10.0	22.9	1 633	14.1	93	1 123	11	9.8	6.5	1 135	10.3	374	3.4	178	151

1. No spouse present. 2. Per 1,000 resident population estimated as of July 1 of the year shown. 3. Under 2,500 grams. 4. Deaths of infants under 1 year old. 5. Deaths of infants under 1 year old per 1,000 live births. 6. As of end of year. 7. Per 100,000 resident population as of July 1 of the year shown.

Area name	Hospitals, 1989: Number	Hospitals, 1989: Beds: Number	Hospitals, 1989: Beds: Rate[1]	Nursing homes,[2] 1986: Number	Nursing homes,[2] 1986: Beds	Serious crimes known to police, 1988: Number: Total[3]	Serious crimes known to police, 1988: Number: Violent[4]	Serious crimes known to police, 1988: Rate[5]	Education: Public school enrollment[6]: 1986–1987	Education: Public school enrollment[6]: 1980	Education: Attainment,[7] 1980: Percent 12 years or more	Education: Attainment,[7] 1980: Percent 16 years or more	Education: Local government expenditures for education,[8] 1982: Total (Mil dol)	Education: Local government expenditures for education,[8] 1982: Per capita (Dollars)	Social Security Program December 1988: Beneficiaries: Total	Social Security Program December 1988: Beneficiaries: Rate[9]
	48	49	50	51	52	53	54	55	56	57	58	59	60	61	62	63
Chico, CA	5	592	331	54	1 323	10 554	745	6 048	26 097	22 479	71.6	16.9	70.4	462	37 505	214.9
Cincinnati-Hamilton, OH-KY-IN	30	8 781	503	147	13 745	NA	NA	0	271 593	292 212	63.5	15.6	684.6	3 030	259 535	150.2
Cincinnati, OH-KY-IN	26	7 890	540	122	11 630	NA	NA	0	223 828	242 483	63.3	15.9	573.5	2 607	220 285	152.0
Hamilton-Middletown, OH	4	891	314	25	2 115	12 859	1 093	4 597	47 765	49 729	64.7	14.1	111.1	423	39 250	140.3
Clarksville-Hopkinsville, TN-KY	4	981	611	16	1 028	NA	NA	0	29 661	28 769	63.5	12.0	38.9	500	18 905	119.0
Cleveland-Akron-Lorain, OH	55	15 242	550	182	17 891	114 127	12 738	4 122	419 049	498 270	68.5	15.2	1 330.0	3 295	470 245	169.8
Akron, OH	11	3 307	504	35	3 164	26 973	2 692	4 127	106 361	125 975	69.5	15.4	298.2	899	105 290	161.1
Cleveland, OH	38	10 939	594	120	12 549	79 534	9 308	4 311	262 604	313 865	68.3	15.7	907.5	1 942	324 775	176.0
Lorain-Elyria, OH	6	996	368	27	2 178	7 620	738	2 817	50 084	58 430	67.0	10.9	124.3	454	40 180	148.5
Colorado Springs, CO	6	1 373	341	26	1 636	25 816	1 542	6 554	69 625	60 963	82.7	20.9	159.4	481	40 035	101.6
Columbia, MO	7	1 564	1 480	12	776	5 636	343	5 327	15 079	15 466	79.7	34.7	31.0	299	12 130	114.7
Columbia, SC	13	4 058	875	49	2 908	32 377	4 651	7 092	74 963	79 040	66.3	21.0	179.0	882	55 330	121.2
Columbus, GA-AL	8	1 938	789	17	1 419	14 076	1 352	5 701	38 844	45 471	58.3	11.8	84.5	752	34 585	140.1
Columbus, OH	16	5 397	395	85	8 283	NA	NA	0	218 414	234 061	71.4	18.3	542.3	2 893	171 735	127.8
Corpus Christi, TX	13	1 757	492	14	1 710	32 183	2 265	8 990	77 163	73 052	57.7	13.9	169.3	1 008	46 045	128.6
Cumberland, MD-WV	5	663	651	9	816	2 508	197	2 449	16 502	20 025	59.5	8.8	51.2	957	21 010	205.2
Dallas-Fort Worth, TX	97	16 007	416	174	21 693	405 505	37 187	10 767	846 363	571 116	70.2	20.4	1 230.3	3 753	381 170	101.2
Dallas, TX	62	10 946	433	100	13 428	274 293	26 718	11 082	626 767	380 347	71.1	21.8	838.6	2 611	243 630	98.4
Fort Worth-Arlington, TX	35	5 061	383	74	8 265	131 212	10 469	10 164	219 596	190 769	68.5	17.5	391.7	1 142	137 540	106.5
Danville, VA	1	391	366	9	715	2 735	154	2 530	18 594	22 143	41.9	7.8	38.6	698	22 355	206.8
Davenport-Rock Island-Moline, IA-IL	8	1 577	436	31	3 356	16 870	1 436	4 632	64 076	74 572	71.2	14.5	169.2	1 307	59 485	163.3
Dayton-Springfield, OH	16	6 389	669	83	7 425	51 050	5 582	5 385	161 849	182 683	69.3	15.3	442.4	1 827	148 470	156.6
Daytona Beach, FL	8	1 399	387	64	2 768	NA	NA	0	40 192	37 538	66.5	13.0	96.4	342	92 620	265.8
Decatur, AL	5	601	449	8	790	4 601	394	3 467	24 936	26 354	55.8	9.9	43.8	718	20 575	155.0
Decatur, IL	3	906	741	10	1 185	7 323	625	5 920	21 608	25 078	68.5	12.9	49.4	380	20 865	168.7
Denver-Boulder, CO	32	6 820	366	134	10 728	124 076	9 916	6 678	299 563	297 826	81.3	25.9	885.4	3 337	199 495	107.4
Boulder-Longmont, Co	4	480	219	9	820	12 953	711	5 944	35 647	33 195	87.4	36.4	98.9	494	21 625	99.2
Denver, CO	28	6 340	385	125	9 908	111 123	9 205	6 776	263 916	264 631	80.5	24.6	786.5	2 843	177 870	108.5
Des Moines, IA	8	2 365	592	45	3 295	27 015	1 909	6 895	64 597	69 581	78.5	18.2	176.6	1 496	57 340	146.4
Detroit-Ann Arbor, MI	79	21 363	462	671	28 903	324 352	42 889	7 020	771 965	945 476	67.7	15.2	2 591.8	4 120	694 790	150.4
Ann Arbor, MI	7	2 726	1 013	57	1 448	18 802	2 030	7 021	39 065	44 030	80.9	36.1	125.1	480	27 040	101.0
Detroit, MI	72	18 637	428	614	27 455	305 550	40 859	7 020	732 900	901 446	67.0	14.1	2 466.7	3 640	667 750	153.4
Dothan, AL	5	799	607	9	545	6 960	804	5 309	23 321	25 142	60.7	12.3	39.8	622	19 155	146.1
Dubuque, IA	2	558	611	13	1 265	3 030	269	3 333	13 239	14 631	68.6	15.0	41.4	447	15 370	169.1
Duluth, MN-WI	10	1 452	606	28	3 179	8 856	342	3 669	42 129	50 678	71.5	14.3	144.8	1 026	48 005	198.9
Eau Claire, WI	5	898	645	24	1 802	4 921	118	3 556	21 733	23 726	70.3	14.4	57.4	855	23 450	169.4
El Paso, TX	10	2 288	382	12	1 179	53 558	4 743	9 141	128 355	117 799	59.5	14.0	203.6	397	61 740	105.4
Elkhart-Goshen, IN	3	605	394	9	1 100	7 573	384	5 012	26 856	27 890	65.6	12.3	60.9	445	20 965	138.7
Elmira, NY	3	717	781	17	828	4 005	253	4 368	14 855	18 931	69.5	13.3	53.2	558	18 695	203.9
Enid, OK	3	450	795	8	592	3 679	279	6 310	10 865	11 235	71.6	16.1	27.2	402	10 480	179.8
Erie, PA	10	1 830	663	23	2 258	9 592	853	3 463	41 151	46 792	69.9	13.2	114.5	407	48 430	174.8
Eugene-Springfield, OR	5	669	244	19	1 493	16 607	882	6 148	43 038	48 143	77.6	20.4	153.1	563	44 615	165.2
Evansville, IN-KY	7	2 238	795	26	3 047	NA	NA	0	44 298	47 776	64.2	12.1	104.5	1 554	49 685	176.7
Fargo-Moorhead, ND-MN	5	944	632	11	1 208	6 135	154	4 134	23 561	23 015	76.5	20.8	66.8	972	19 180	129.2
Fayetteville, NC	5	1 369	535	19	868	20 902	1 942	8 174	43 783	51 467	69.6	14.2	91.1	365	23 855	93.3
Fayetteville-Springdale, AR	5	837	746	9	701	5 200	231	4 702	18 220	17 551	63.8	18.0	33.7	332	17 360	157.0
Flint, MI	6	1 771	413	79	2 404	35 186	5 354	8 169	88 556	103 701	67.8	10.9	277.1	629	64 155	149.0
Florence, AL	4	899	669	10	832	4 211	315	3 108	22 813	27 141	56.9	11.5	48.2	715	24 900	183.8
Florence, SC	4	661	557	21	947	6 443	1 022	5 460	22 948	24 238	51.5	12.0	44.8	398	17 575	148.9
Fort Collins-Loveland, CO	3	384	207	17	1 183	8 941	583	4 913	29 505	26 160	82.7	28.8	72.7	459	21 150	116.2
Fort Myers-Cape Coral, FL	5	1 318	406	27	1 675	NA	NA	0	35 309	30 009	67.4	13.3	89.9	390	84 660	273.9
Fort Pierce, FL	6	806	331	9	864	NA	NA	0	27 384	22 845	66.1	13.2	68.2	791	58 470	252.2
Fort Smith, AR-OK	6	1 101	601	15	1 504	7 744	678	4 286	32 138	32 454	58.8	9.7	59.1	1 126	31 135	172.3
Fort Walton Beach, FL	5	627	402	8	551	NA	NA	0	23 889	24 205	77.4	16.6	52.8	444	16 755	111.3
Fort Wayne, IN	7	1 799	481	26	3 070	19 985	1 232	5 440	59 978	65 233	72.7	13.8	147.8	1 201	53 125	144.6
Fresno, CA	15	2 028	322	87	3 925	50 435	6 171	8 203	126 617	104 489	63.7	15.2	293.7	547	83 400	135.7
Gadsden, AL	3	570	554	7	814	3 679	525	3 575	18 288	20 502	54.9	8.9	29.0	282	21 310	207.1
Gainesville, FL	6	1 739	825	15	984	NA	NA	0	27 319	27 083	72.5	26.4	61.5	737	25 875	124.6
Glens Falls, NY	2	553	470	13	800	3 402	214	2 930	21 359	24 810	65.7	13.3	72.9	1 327	20 975	180.7

1. Per 100,000 resident population estimated as of July 1 of the year shown. 2. Covers nursing homes with 3 or more beds. 3. Data for serious crimes have not been adjusted for underreporting, this may affect comparability between geographic areas or over time. 4. Includes murder and nonnegligent manslaughter, forcible rape, robbery, and aggravated assault. 5. Per 100,000 resident population as of July 1 of the year shown. 6. The 1986–1987 data are based on administrative reports obtained by the U.S. National Center for Education Statistics. The 1980 data are based on the 1980 Census of Population and Housing. 7. Persons 25 years old or older. 8. Elementary and secondary. 9. Per 1,000 resident population estimated as of July 1 of the year shown.

Area name	Social Security Program, Dec. 1988 (cont'd)		Housing units, 1990				Civilian labor force, 1990				Private nonfarm establishments, 1988			
					Occupied units				Unemployment				Employment[2]	
	Payments ($1,000)	Supplemental Security Income Program recipients, June 1986	Total	Percent change, 1980–1990	Total	Percent owner-occupied	Total	Percent change, 1989–1990	Total	Rate[1]	Number	Net change, 1987–1988	Total	Percent change, 1987–1988
	64	65	72	73	74	75	78	79	80	81	82	83	84	85
Chico, CA	18 018	6 342	76 115	24.0	71 665	60.9	74 502	-3.0	5 625	7.6	4 337	51	40 959	4.9
Cincinnati-Hamilton, OH-KY-IN.	129 551	21 382	692 729	11.0	652 920	64.1	919 255	0.9	40 478	4.4	39 434	691	720 738	4.7
Cincinnati, OH-KY-IN	109 968	18 408	582 376	9.6	548 385	63.1	786 940	1.1	32 799	4.2	34 379	612	639 962	4.8
Hamilton-Middletown, OH	19 583	2 974	110 353	19.3	104 535	69.2	132 315	0.0	7 679	5.8	5 055	79	80 776	4.0
Clarksville-Hopkinsville, TN-KY	7 849	3 114	60 662	19.1	55 981	58.1	55 412	2.4	3 601	6.5	2 944	54	35 660	4.4
Cleveland-Akron-Lorain, OH	246 006	31 702	1 122 697	4.2	1 057 653	66.9	1 406 703	0.1	72 235	5.1	65 894	680	1 109 405	1.9
Akron, OH	54 601	6 676	263 776	6.4	249 227	69.0	332 254	0.2	17 320	5.2	14 904	174	241 815	6.2
Cleveland, OH	170 688	22 584	758 984	3.4	712 362	65.4	954 819	0.1	45 673	4.8	46 098	462	787 275	0.3
Lorain-Elyria, OH	20 717	2 442	99 937	4.2	96 064	71.9	119 630	0.1	9 242	7.7	4 892	44	80 315	6.0
Colorado Springs, CO	18 226	2 788	165 056	40.4	146 965	57.4	189 614	0.7	11 931	6.3	9 854	-277	122 359	0.4
Columbia, MO	6 031	938	44 695	19.4	41 937	55.0	68 555	2.2	1 934	2.8	2 814	33	36 772	-0.4
Columbia, SC	25 331	7 516	177 120	22.5	163 223	65.6	242 477	2.0	8 380	3.5	11 202	195	168 195	2.5
Columbus, GA-AL	14 901	6 154	93 643	10.3	86 241	55.0	100 606	1.0	6 055	6.0	5 055	59	74 093	0.6
Columbus, OH	83 057	15 982	559 446	16.1	524 535	60.1	739 532	0.8	32 630	4.4	31 606	1 001	558 867	3.6
Corpus Christi, TX	20 387	7 906	136 452	19.8	118 516	59.8	164 148	2.8	11 252	6.9	8 204	-250	96 242	-0.7
Cumberland, MD-WV	10 013	1 832	43 443	3.1	39 615	71.8	44 163	1.3	3 536	8.0	2 285	-23	26 632	-2.2
Dallas-Fort Worth, TX	188 830	32 768	1 627 055	41.2	1 449 872	56.9	2 166 752	0.0	111 983	5.2	99 380	-1 518	1 670 699	0.3
Dallas, TX	122 000	22 050	1 072 830	38.9	954 728	55.1	1 432 875	-0.7	73 575	5.1	69 427	-1 248	1 219 034	-0.4
Fort Worth-Arlington, TX	66 830	10 718	554 225	45.7	495 144	60.3	733 877	1.3	38 408	5.2	29 953	-270	451 665	2.1
Danville, VA	9 750	3 432	46 158	8.2	42 325	69.3	52 807	0.7	4 021	7.6	2 193	4	36 109	2.8
Davenport-Rock Island-Moline, IA-IL	30 312	3 178	145 587	0.5	136 269	67.8	182 179	-1.0	10 772	5.9	8 421	33	128 672	2.2
Dayton-Springfield, OH	72 408	11 472	385 420	6.3	364 300	65.7	476 808	-0.3	25 351	5.3	20 321	319	363 362	2.5
Daytona Beach, FL	45 178	3 994	180 972	45.4	153 416	71.9	160 040	2.6	8 899	5.6	9 177	160	101 107	5.0
Decatur, AL	8 761	4 176	52 631	17.5	49 209	73.9	61 364	1.1	4 465	7.3	2 631	-9	37 188	-0.7
Decatur, IL	10 771	1 638	50 049	-3.0	45 996	70.2	60 229	-1.1	4 247	7.1	2 745	5	47 978	3.5
Denver-Boulder, CO	99 983	14 464	810 771	24.3	737 806	61.5	1 033 253	2.9	46 160	4.5	54 983	-440	767 734	-0.3
Boulder-Longmont, Co	10 743	1 090	94 621	26.8	88 402	61.1	138 920	3.7	5 092	3.7	6 935	15	90 546	1.5
Denver, CO	89 240	13 374	716 150	24.0	649 404	61.6	894 333	2.8	41 068	4.6	48 048	-455	677 188	-0.5
Des Moines, IA	29 840	3 570	160 948	10.3	153 100	66.9	235 582	-0.5	7 624	3.2	10 812	64	194 611	7.2
Detroit-Ann Arbor, MI	370 708	63 848	1 825 607	5.0	1 723 478	69.0	2 314 100	-1.1	168 127	7.3	101 643	1 664	1 764 587	0.2
Ann Arbor, MI	14 965	2 434	111 256	13.3	104 528	55.3	163 414	1.8	7 396	4.5	6 590	150	116 427	3.5
Detroit, MI	355 743	61 414	1 714 351	4.5	1 618 950	69.8	2 150 686	-1.3	160 731	7.5	95 053	1 514	1 648 160	0.0
Dothan, AL	7 769	3 984	52 628	16.6	48 418	65.2	58 670	-0.7	3 359	5.7	3 122	0	42 436	-1.9
Dubuque, IA	7 699	858	32 053	1.7	30 799	71.2	44 513	-0.9	2 467	5.5	2 255	38	40 225	9.8
Duluth, MN-WI	23 381	3 178	116 013	0.5	95 275	73.4	112 806	2.5	6 522	5.8	5 876	85	68 627	5.9
Eau Claire, WI	11 312	2 616	53 765	11.6	50 359	68.2	71 602	-4.1	3 518	4.9	3 346	73	44 897	4.2
El Paso, TX	24 473	10 580	187 473	26.7	178 366	58.7	250 793	0.2	26 892	10.7	10 503	100	152 179	4.4
Elkhart-Goshen, IN	11 188	940	60 182	16.0	56 713	71.8	94 095	-3.9	5 364	5.7	4 522	165	94 211	4.8
Elmira, NY	9 476	1 734	37 290	1.6	35 275	68.3	44 163	0.3	1 963	4.4	2 030	32	32 637	7.3
Enid, OK	5 197	906	26 502	3.6	22 460	69.1	27 328	-1.4	1 191	4.4	1 630	-28	16 717	-3.7
Erie, PA	24 839	3 472	108 585	4.7	101 564	68.6	134 670	1.5	7 442	5.5	6 260	130	99 820	0.3
Eugene-Springfield, OR	22 543	2 606	116 676	5.0	110 799	60.8	149 171	1.1	8 748	5.9	7 954	25	87 564	6.2
Evansville, IN-KY	24 922	3 446	117 896	9.5	108 663	68.9	144 249	-1.1	7 713	5.3	7 266	-48	117 129	-0.2
Fargo-Moorhead, ND-MN	9 377	1 098	60 953	14.9	57 771	58.9	88 499	1.2	2 462	2.8	4 352	89	59 709	2.2
Fayetteville, NC	9 875	4 250	98 360	20.9	91 500	57.7	93 797	-1.9	4 414	4.7	4 670	106	59 912	-0.1
Fayetteville-Springdale, AR	7 568	1 440	47 349	23.0	43 372	61.6	64 170	1.3	2 224	3.5	2 844	81	38 391	3.9
Flint, MI	33 408	6 300	170 808	4.8	161 296	70.4	184 094	-1.1	17 951	9.8	8 226	95	144 932	-7.0
Florence, AL	11 474	3 902	55 334	7.8	51 001	74.1	61 498	0.1	4 392	7.1	2 956	48	36 189	5.6
Florence, SC	7 072	5 150	43 209	10.3	40 217	70.5	57 719	1.3	2 605	4.5	2 843	25	43 710	7.2
Fort Collins-Loveland, CO	9 987	1 124	77 811	25.1	70 472	62.9	102 596	5.8	4 484	4.4	5 168	-43	50 613	0.9
Fort Myers-Cape Coral, FL	43 127	2 310	189 051	70.3	140 124	72.1	152 616	4.9	6 739	4.4	9 525	413	98 786	8.7
Fort Pierce, FL	29 828	2 056	128 042	70.9	101 196	74.0	109 150	4.7	11 417	10.5	6 302	343	65 434	7.6
Fort Smith, AR-OK	13 568	3 756	74 646	15.2	66 884	69.4	93 069	-0.3	6 939	7.5	4 230	-22	70 048	5.3
Fort Walton Beach, FL	7 233	1 468	62 569	45.2	53 313	62.2	64 813	2.2	4 047	6.2	3 708	83	38 493	6.1
Fort Wayne, IN	27 832	2 654	147 376	10.6	136 068	72.1	204 324	-1.0	10 736	5.3	9 118	41	175 935	3.7
Fresno, CA	38 571	22 742	235 563	21.6	220 933	54.3	318 441	1.7	32 571	10.2	14 355	23	170 922	5.0
Gadsden, AL	9 652	3 518	41 787	4.8	38 675	74.0	42 291	-0.8	4 532	10.7	1 949	30	30 266	1.3
Gainesville, FL	11 708	3 886	87 121	31.6	78 451	56.2	109 069	3.2	3 803	3.5	4 855	76	60 592	2.9
Glens Falls, NY	10 447	1 778	55 953	14.8	42 815	71.4	53 598	0.7	3 120	5.8	3 290	96	37 087	3.7

1. Percent of total civilian labor force. 2. For week including March 12. Excludes government employees, self-employed persons, farm workers, domestic service workers, railroad employees subject to the Railroad Retirement Act, and employees on oceanborne vessels or in foreign countries.

Area name	Private nonfarm establishments, 1987 (cont'd): Employment[1] (cont'd): Manu-facturing	Retail trade	Finance, insurance, and real estate	Services	Annual payroll: Total (Mil dol)	Average per employee	Personal income, 1989: Total (Mil dol)	Percent change, 1988–1989	Wages and salaries[2] (Mil dol)	Propri-etor's income (Mil dol)	Dividends, Interest, & rent (Mil dol)	Transfer payments (Mil dol)	Per capita[3]: Dollars	Rank (Dollars)
	86	87	88	89	90	91	92	93	94	95	96	97	98	99
Chico, CA	5 645	12 551	2 348	12 950	643	15 699	2 590	9.4	1 175	296	559	614	14 471	204
Cincinnati-Hamilton, OH-KY-IN	178 207	151 945	46 599	198 419	15 810	21 936	30 310	6.9	20 607	1 827	5 296	4 408	17 365	82
Cincinnati, OH-KY-IN	155 883	134 278	40 051	180 577	14 087	22 012	25 760	7.0	18 314	1 591	4 644	3 751	17 624	X
Hamilton-Middletown, OH	22 324	17 667	6 548	17 842	1 723	21 331	4 550	6.2	2 292	236	652	657	16 029	X
Clarksville-Hopkinsville, TN-KY	9 400	11 328	2 190	7 224	513	14 386	2 006	6.8	1 316	174	238	332	12 495	268
Cleveland-Akron-Lorain, OH	299 676	220 680	69 715	318 631	25 176	22 693	50 896	6.7	34 136	3 394	8 727	8 218	18 380	49
Akron, OH	69 051	53 359	10 366	61 028	5 363	22 178	11 033	6.2	6 951	557	1 677	1 770	16 805	X
Cleveland, OH	200 529	150 355	56 256	237 190	18 045	22 921	35 726	7.0	24 854	2 644	6 490	5 777	19 395	X
Lorain-Elyria, OH	30 096	16 966	3 093	20 413	1 768	22 013	4 137	5.6	2 330	193	560	671	15 286	X
Colorado Springs, CO	21 994	30 057	8 752	42 876	2 249	18 380	6 479	6.7	4 183	475	1 067	984	16 105	119
Columbia, MO	4 276	10 620	5 079	10 784	587	15 963	1 781	7.4	1 173	163	299	224	16 851	95
Columbia, SC	26 685	36 527	18 243	44 886	3 029	18 009	7 314	8.2	5 502	494	903	1 008	15 775	135
Columbus, GA-AL	18 822	18 943	6 439	17 233	1 215	16 398	3 304	5.3	2 330	190	480	634	13 459	246
Columbus, OH	102 055	129 422	57 295	158 780	11 577	20 715	23 444	7.3	17 070	1 562	3 220	3 448	17 178	88
Corpus Christi, TX	10 609	24 921	6 202	29 922	1 721	17 882	4 741	5.6	2 963	473	791	804	13 272	253
Cumberland, MD-WV	4 908	7 981	1 231	7 837	450	16 897	1 384	6.7	788	91	236	348	13 576	241
Dallas-Fort Worth, TX	340 804	334 166	162 637	446 957	38 409	22 990	72 073	7.2	52 743	6 048	11 031	6 369	18 721	43
Dallas, TX	226 251	228 556	134 709	333 010	29 168	23 927	49 277	7.3	39 216	4 285	7 836	4 049	19 485	X
Fort Worth-Arlington, TX	114 553	105 610	27 928	113 947	9 241	20 460	22 795	7.0	13 527	1 762	3 195	2 320	17 259	X
Danville, VA	16 930	7 181	1 234	6 493	613	16 976	1 589	7.4	897	115	271	263	14 901	188
Davenport-Rock Island-Moline, IA-IL	30 147	31 600	8 413	34 008	2 627	20 416	5 928	7.4	3 890	567	1 091	929	16 387	109
Dayton-Springfield, OH	103 409	78 235	17 993	109 649	7 852	21 609	16 147	6.1	11 460	866	2 458	2 766	16 919	93
Daytona Beach, FL	12 956	32 158	6 634	31 462	1 463	14 470	5 553	10.5	2 317	420	1 587	1 194	15 364	157
Decatur, AL	NA	7 074	1 892	7 606	709	19 065	1 847	6.9	1 070	147	207	289	13 794	232
Decatur, IL	14 637	10 540	2 518	10 787	1 103	22 990	2 051	6.2	1 472	203	376	316	16 767	98
Denver-Boulder, CO	125 710	161 751	68 179	224 670	17 281	22 509	36 071	6.6	25 684	3 165	5 993	3 857	19 345	32
Boulder-Longmont, Co	29 704	20 585	4 785	24 213	1 974	21 801	4 428	6.9	2 867	393	769	382	20 203	X
Denver, CO	96 006	141 166	63 394	200 457	15 307	22 604	31 643	6.6	22 818	2 772	5 224	3 475	19 231	X
Des Moines, IA	27 753	39 320	32 576	53 596	3 812	19 588	7 204	8.5	5 278	642	1 082	894	18 039	58
Detroit-Ann Arbor, MI	493 164	367 670	112 329	501 988	45 359	25 705	91 617	6.7	64 828	4 825	14 488	12 804	19 826	28
Ann Arbor, MI	39 001	25 692	4 790	34 127	2 940	25 252	6 061	7.2	4 937	414	912	611	22 512	X
Detroit, MI	454 163	341 978	107 539	467 861	42 419	25 737	85 556	6.6	59 890	4 411	13 576	12 194	19 660	X
Dothan, AL	9 203	10 684	1 647	9 012	666	15 694	1 840	6.9	1 277	161	222	296	13 982	221
Dubuque, IA	12 694	7 990	1 430	13 086	725	18 024	1 299	7.4	939	134	273	198	14 207	214
Duluth, MN-WI	7 236	19 142	3 024	23 146	1 197	17 442	3 442	8.9	2 111	191	583	791	14 367	207
Eau Claire, WI	10 631	12 754	1 761	12 433	766	17 061	1 993	7.4	1 201	210	325	359	14 305	209
El Paso, TX	39 170	35 311	8 571	39 366	2 246	14 759	6 423	9.4	4 379	464	842	1 200	10 735	278
Elkhart-Goshen, IN	54 015	12 222	2 154	13 584	1 888	20 040	2 524	6.5	2 395	221	423	265	16 442	107
Elmira, NY	7 791	7 465	1 942	9 826	576	17 649	1 452	8.6	869	93	244	306	15 825	133
Enid, OK	1 344	4 277	1 014	4 538	284	16 989	896	4.0	467	121	178	171	15 840	130
Erie, PA	34 083	20 604	5 026	28 427	1 938	19 415	4 235	7.6	2 769	329	681	735	15 332	161
Eugene-Springfield, OR	21 213	22 560	4 380	24 343	1 547	17 667	4 132	9.2	2 463	453	724	682	15 049	176
Evansville, IN-KY	NA	25 396	5 728	30 801	2 393	20 430	4 612	6.4	3 116	432	866	674	16 377	110
Fargo-Moorhead, ND-MN	4 903	15 309	5 008	20 102	1 001	16 765	2 251	8.0	1 490	238	360	335	15 070	174
Fayetteville, NC	12 053	19 063	3 211	14 743	931	15 539	3 473	7.4	2 679	196	337	570	13 576	240
Fayetteville-Springdale, AR	10 201	9 234	1 639	7 159	602	15 681	1 546	9.5	1 062	161	256	240	13 775	234
Flint, MI	NA	33 651	5 900	37 535	3 746	25 847	6 993	6.2	5 279	312	1 042	1 261	16 315	111
Florence, AL	12 985	8 722	1 525	7 244	606	16 745	1 706	5.2	1 042	140	264	309	12 691	265
Florence, SC	13 385	8 970	2 695	10 387	732	16 747	1 500	5.2	1 118	117	136	276	12 635	266
Fort Collins-Loveland, CO	12 258	13 945	2 743	12 739	913	18 039	2 954	9.3	1 647	279	534	355	15 925	127
Fort Myers-Cape Coral, FL	6 014	30 623	8 797	28 656	1 647	16 672	5 858	12.4	2 570	429	1 966	1 032	18 063	57
Fort Pierce, FL	6 682	19 402	5 723	17 499	1 104	16 872	4 307	10.7	1 784	364	1 429	722	17 668	69
Fort Smith, AR-OK	26 615	12 698	2 600	15 813	1 190	16 988	2 335	5.7	1 595	248	357	417	12 749	262
Fort Walton Beach, FL	4 580	12 472	3 392	11 892	533	13 847	2 124	8.7	1 378	133	320	449	13 619	238
Fort Wayne, IN	49 735	34 169	12 949	43 630	3 668	20 849	6 440	7.6	4 938	416	1 068	723	17 236	86
Fresno, CA	21 827	42 743	12 466	49 184	3 204	18 745	10 023	8.2	5 706	1 491	1 567	1 828	15 927	126
Gadsden, AL	11 223	6 800	1 250	6 421	579	19 130	1 286	4.3	792	97	184	261	12 514	267
Gainesville, FL	6 547	18 750	4 414	21 019	931	15 365	2 986	9.8	1 990	225	468	493	14 163	215
Glens Falls, NY	10 550	9 170	2 103	9 206	727	19 603	1 748	7.9	1 071	148	349	325	14 865	189

1. For week including March 12. Excludes government employees, self-employed persons, farm workers, domestic service workers, railroad employees subject to the Railroad Retirement Act, and employees on oceanborne vessels or in foreign countries. 2. Includes other labor income. 3. Based on the resident population estimated as of July 1 of the year shown.

Area name	Earnings, 1989									Agriculture, 1987									
		Percent by selected industries								Farms			Farm operators, Percent		Land in farms				
			Goods-related[1]		Service-related & other[2]						Percent with						Acres		
	Total (Mil. dol)	Farm	Total	Manufacturing	Total	Retail trade	Finance, insurance, & real estate	Services	Government	Number	Less than 50 acres	500 acres and over	Whose principal occupation is farming	Residing on farm operated	Acreage (1,000)	Percent change, 1982–1987	Average size of farm	Total irrigated (1,000)	Total cropland (1,000)
	100	101	102	103	104	105	106	107	108	109	110	111	112	113	114	115	116	117	118
Chico, CA	1 471	4.2	18.1	9.8	59.1	13.8	4.9	29.1	18.5	2 030	60.1	9.9	55.2	66.4	495	5.8	244	179	256
Cincinnati-Hamilton, OH-KY-IN	22 434	0.2	33.9	27.6	54.5	9.8	5.8	23.8	11.4	5 892	40.2	3.6	38.3	75.7	701	-8.5	119	3	487
Cincinnati, OH-KY-IN	19 905	0.2	32.8	26.7	55.9	9.9	6.0	24.5	11.1	4 878	41.3	3.1	36.5	75.8	541	-9.6	111	2	362
Hamilton-Middletown, OH	2 529	0.3	42.1	34.1	43.6	8.9	4.3	18.6	14.0	1 014	34.7	5.9	47.0	75.5	160	-4.3	157	0	126
Clarksville-Hopkinsville, TN-KY	1 490	1.3	22.6	17.4	32.0	9.4	2.7	13.5	44.1	2 185	27.9	11.4	46.5	68.0	490	-2.8	224	2	344
Cleveland-Akron-Lorain, OH	37 529	0.2	34.5	29.3	53.8	8.3	5.6	26.4	11.5	4 234	45.8	3.6	47.9	82.5	478	-7.1	113	3	358
Akron, OH	7 508	0.1	37.5	32.3	49.1	9.5	3.7	22.7	13.3	1 117	48.8	3.2	40.5	82.2	122	-9.4	109	1	88
Cleveland, OH	27 498	0.1	32.4	27.3	56.6	8.0	6.4	28.1	10.9	2 132	46.1	2.6	50.5	83.3	213	-8.5	100	2	151
Lorain-Elyria, OH	2 523	0.9	49.1	43.3	37.6	8.1	2.5	19.1	12.4	985	42.0	6.4	50.5	81.2	144	-2.8	146	0	120
Colorado Springs, CO	4 658	0.2	23.1	16.9	46.9	9.1	5.0	24.7	29.7	711	26.6	39.5	46.8	77.6	918	2.4	1 291	13	90
Columbia, MO	1 336	0.7	14.3	8.5	51.1	9.4	8.0	25.2	33.9	1 344	26.1	9.2	38.7	73.8	280	-4.5	208	4	182
Columbia, SC	5 997	0.3	19.6	13.3	53.5	9.7	8.5	22.1	26.7	1 028	44.5	6.0	39.1	72.5	144	-20.9	140	5	82
Columbus, GA-AL	2 520	NA	NA	NA	NA	9.9	7.1	18.3	31.7	338	26.0	18.9	35.2	68.6	153	-3.1	453	D	D
Columbus, OH	18 632	0.7	24.6	18.9	57.7	11.4	9.3	24.3	17.0	6 424	32.2	12.8	52.1	74.6	1 516	-5.6	236	3	1 312
Corpus Christi, TX	3 436	0.9	25.6	13.6	51.1	10.2	4.3	25.5	22.4	1 205	24.9	36.0	55.0	46.7	806	-4.2	669	D	601
Cumberland, MD-WV	879	0.6	32.5	24.4	49.9	11.9	3.0	21.6	15.4	555	17.1	9.7	43.1	76.0	125	-2.3	226	0	47
Dallas-Fort Worth, TX	58 790	0.2	27.3	20.0	62.3	10.0	9.2	25.1	10.2	12 321	45.5	8.7	31.5	65.6	2 552	-6.1	207	7	1 236
Dallas, TX	43 501	0.2	25.3	17.9	65.1	9.6	10.6	26.2	9.4	7 394	42.6	9.4	31.6	62.8	1 638	-9.9	222	4	882
Fort Worth-Arlington, TX	15 289	0.3	33.1	26.0	54.4	11.2	5.3	22.1	12.2	4 927	49.7	7.6	31.2	69.9	914	1.7	185	3	355
Danville, VA	1 013	1.9	48.2	41.4	38.3	10.1	2.7	18.2	11.6	1 583	21.7	7.6	54.5	70.4	301	-9.0	190	6	132
Davenport-Rock Island-Moline, IA-IL	4 457	1.4	31.7	26.9	50.5	10.3	4.4	22.1	16.5	3 392	22.6	16.0	67.9	75.9	903	-0.6	266	7	807
Dayton-Springfield, OH	12 326	0.5	36.3	31.5	45.7	8.4	3.6	23.8	17.5	3 788	39.0	10.4	49.2	74.8	717	2.2	189	5	630
Daytona Beach, FL	2 737	2.4	20.4	11.3	60.9	16.1	4.9	31.0	16.3	920	71.0	5.1	47.3	66.6	193	-12.9	210	5	27
Decatur, AL	1 217	2.9	NA	37.9	37.2	9.4	3.2	15.7	13.4	2 366	40.1	5.4	32.1	72.8	348	-5.7	147	1	229
Decatur, IL	1 674	2.0	42.8	35.1	47.2	8.2	3.6	20.1	8.0	850	23.3	32.1	66.8	65.4	329	1.1	387	0	316
Denver-Boulder, CO	28 850	0.3	23.1	15.7	61.6	9.0	7.8	27.3	15.0	2 655	48.9	19.3	44.5	74.8	1 467	D	553	78	809
Boulder-Longmont, Co	3 260	0.8	39.5	33.9	43.5	8.8	3.2	25.5	16.3	752	55.7	6.8	37.5	79.1	155	-3.7	207	39	69
Denver, CO	25 590	0.2	21.0	13.4	63.9	9.1	8.4	27.5	14.9	1 903	46.2	24.2	47.2	73.1	1 311	D	689	39	741
Des Moines, IA	5 920	0.9	18.1	13.2	67.6	9.3	15.3	25.2	13.4	3 392	30.5	16.0	53.1	72.4	870	-4.8	257	D	737
Detroit-Ann Arbor, MI	69 653	NA	NA	33.8	NA	8.4	5.0	24.1	11.4	7 186	42.2	6.8	45.8	82.8	1 111	-9.9	155	16	934
Ann Arbor, MI	5 351	0.3	35.6	31.7	39.5	7.0	2.4	22.7	24.6	1 222	36.8	7.7	46.6	84.1	204	-8.7	167	4	171
Detroit, MI	64 302	NA	NA	34.0	NA	8.5	5.2	24.2	10.2	5 964	43.3	6.6	45.7	82.5	907	-10.1	152	12	763
Dothan, AL	1 439	2.9	29.2	22.6	48.0	9.9	3.0	20.4	19.9	1 352	26.5	14.6	48.5	68.1	337	-0.2	249	9	205
Dubuque, IA	1 073	3.1	40.7	36.0	48.5	9.1	3.5	25.2	7.7	1 689	18.5	5.7	75.5	81.2	334	-1.4	198	0	267
Duluth, MN-WI	2 302	0.3	24.8	9.5	52.7	10.9	3.0	23.3	22.3	1 233	16.1	7.9	37.4	87.4	255	-8.6	206	1	135
Eau Claire, WI	1 411	4.3	28.5	23.3	50.3	13.2	2.8	21.9	16.9	2 648	10.4	7.6	75.8	88.1	624	-1.8	236	4	417
El Paso, TX	4 842	0.5	20.9	16.1	50.4	10.8	4.1	21.0	28.2	422	68.7	10.9	39.8	63.5	237	-21.0	561	41	45
Elkhart-Goshen, IN	2 617	0.7	61.7	56.7	32.5	6.9	2.7	12.3	5.1	1 556	42.4	4.7	49.8	79.3	205	-4.1	131	20	179
Elmira, NY	962	0.8	30.9	24.5	50.3	10.6	3.3	24.9	18.0	327	21.1	7.3	48.6	86.5	64	-9.4	196	0	37
Enid, OK	589	5.4	16.7	6.8	58.3	10.9	4.3	24.3	19.7	1 182	12.9	35.3	64.1	57.3	633	-3.9	536	0	467
Erie, PA	3 097	0.6	40.7	35.7	48.1	9.1	4.8	22.9	10.7	1 355	29.9	3.0	56.4	84.1	185	-7.5	136	1	118
Eugene-Springfield, OR	2 916	1.7	27.4	21.7	53.7	12.0	3.6	25.2	17.2	2 039	62.0	4.9	37.0	86.9	277	1.6	136	24	122
Evansville, IN-KY	3 547	1.3	41.1	29.6	49.3	9.7	3.5	23.3	8.3	1 999	29.9	17.7	53.0	70.6	616	-1.9	308	D	527
Fargo-Moorhead, ND-MN	1 728	3.5	14.0	7.4	65.8	10.1	7.0	28.1	16.7	2 200	12.3	52.6	78.9	75.7	1 648	-1.4	749	16	1 536
Fayetteville, NC	2 874	0.6	15.5	11.7	33.6	9.5	2.8	11.4	50.3	524	38.2	10.3	42.2	70.8	100	-16.0	191	3	67
Fayetteville-Springdale, AR	1 224	2.3	30.2	25.0	48.0	10.3	3.2	17.3	19.5	2 853	40.2	4.1	44.2	77.3	363	5.0	127	1	182
Flint, MI	5 591	0.2	52.6	48.8	36.3	8.8	2.4	17.4	10.9	851	43.7	7.6	42.8	81.4	145	-9.7	171	2	127
Florence, AL	1 182	2.0	36.1	30.2	40.2	10.2	3.3	17.7	21.7	1 817	37.1	9.5	33.1	70.0	345	-8.0	190	2	220
Florence, SC	1 236	1.7	33.1	26.1	48.7	11.3	5.5	20.1	16.4	926	33.8	11.6	57.5	60.7	210	-15.3	226	1	136
Fort Collins-Loveland, CO	1 926	1.5	33.9	25.7	40.9	10.5	3.3	20.8	23.7	1 233	48.6	13.5	43.4	76.5	575	4.9	466	80	142
Fort Myers-Cape Coral, FL	3 000	1.7	18.1	4.8	66.5	16.4	6.9	31.7	13.7	415	61.0	9.9	45.5	61.2	133	11.9	320	17	33
Fort Pierce, FL	2 148	6.4	20.0	7.4	61.5	14.1	6.0	27.5	12.0	838	60.1	15.4	47.3	40.0	529	-7.0	631	168	196
Fort Smith, AR-OK	1 843	2.1	39.3	32.4	48.8	9.7	3.8	22.8	9.8	2 616	34.1	7.2	36.0	74.3	457	-6.1	175	6	214
Fort Walton Beach, FL	1 512	0.1	12.6	7.4	42.6	10.7	3.8	22.1	44.8	322	43.2	6.8	39.1	79.8	63	-11.3	195	1	29
Fort Wayne, IN	5 354	0.7	40.8	34.7	50.5	9.1	7.0	19.1	8.0	3 353	30.2	9.0	46.5	77.0	632	-5.5	188	D	551
Fresno, CA	7 197	10.1	16.6	8.8	55.8	10.8	5.1	23.1	17.5	7 590	62.7	8.4	56.5	67.8	1 975	-4.7	260	1 011	1 231
Gadsden, AL	888	1.3	42.0	37.2	44.9	9.5	3.4	21.6	11.8	928	52.5	2.6	33.2	72.8	101	-14.5	108	0	47
Gainesville, FL	2 214	1.3	11.4	6.4	49.3	10.5	4.3	28.6	37.7	1 510	54.8	6.8	37.0	74.9	233	-10.2	155	9	100
Glens Falls, NY	1 219	2.1	32.4	24.7	48.5	12.4	3.3	23.0	17.1	922	15.4	15.3	65.4	83.7	249	-6.7	271	0	150

1. Covers mining, construction, and manufacturing. 2. Covers private sector earnings in agricultural services, forestry, and fisheries; transportation and public utilities; wholesale trade; retail trade; finance, insurance, and real estate; and services.

Area name	Agriculture, 1987 (cont'd): Value of products sold: Total (Mil dol)	Value of products sold: Average per farm (Dollars)	Value of products sold: Percent from Crops	Value of products sold: Percent from Livestock and poultry[1]	Percent of farms with sales of $10,000 or more	Percent of farms with sales of $100,000 or more	Manufactures, 1987: Establishments: Total	Establishments: Percent with 20 or more employees	All employees: Number (1,000)	All employees: Annual payroll (Mil dol)	Production workers: Number (1,000)	Production workers: Work hours (Millions)	Production workers: Wages: Total (Mil dol)	Production workers: Wages: Average per worker (Dollars)	Value added by manufacture (Mil dol)
	121	122	123	124	125	126	127	128	129	131	132	133	134	135	136
Chico, CA	176	86 559	92.8	7.2	54.3	20.2	222	23.0	5.7	107.7	4.4	8.5	78.5	17 841	274.3
Cincinnati-Hamilton, OH-KY-IN	116	19 717	59.9	40.1	29.7	4.8	2 530	40.1	174.4	5 130.7	97.3	197.2	2 425.3	24 926	12 831.7
Cincinnati, OH-KY-IN	85	17 435	64.0	36.0	26.9	4.1	2 242	40.3	151.9	4 437.0	82.0	165.5	1 967.9	23 999	11 335.0
Hamilton-Middletown, OH	31	30 695	48.9	51.1	42.9	8.1	288	38.5	22.5	693.7	15.3	31.7	457.4	29 895	1 496.7
Clarksville-Hopkinsville, TN-KY	59	27 157	65.9	34.1	43.4	6.5	117	39.3	9.3	177.8	7.0	13.2	115.7	16 529	461.4
Cleveland-Akron-Lorain, OH	183	43 282	66.1	33.8	39.9	8.5	5 762	37.9	296.4	8 643.9	176.7	359.4	4 352.0	24 629	17 262.2
Akron, OH	32	28 512	46.5	53.5	32.3	6.8	1 225	39.3	64.6	1 979.4	35.3	70.4	772.5	21 884	2 900.9
Cleveland, OH	91	42 774	67.2	32.8	40.2	8.2	4 155	37.6	203.3	5 787.8	121.1	247.3	2 976.9	24 582	10 926.3
Lorain-Elyria, OH	60	61 130	75.0	25.0	47.8	11.3	382	37.2	28.5	876.7	20.3	41.7	602.6	29 685	3 435.0
Colorado Springs, CO	24	33 132	26.4	73.6	38.3	7.6	419	23.9	22.2	532.9	13.3	25.6	258.2	19 414	1 136.6
Columbia, MO	29	21 414	41.5	58.5	34.5	4.9	87	28.7	4.0	81.7	2.4	5.0	44.6	18 583	244.7
Columbia, SC	49	47 781	22.6	77.4	29.7	10.3	448	36.6	27.0	607.8	18.3	36.1	336.5	18 388	1 684.9
Columbus, GA-AL	8	23 006	45.0	55.0	29.3	D	204	47.5	19.8	411.3	14.3	30.1	262.8	18 378	1 139.7
Columbus, OH	364	56 629	53.0	47.0	51.7	12.8	1 573	38.6	98.7	2 689.6	62.7	126.2	1 463.5	23 341	7 079.1
Corpus Christi, TX	118	97 804	75.3	24.7	57.8	D	258	28.3	11.0	293.3	7.1	14.5	176.5	24 859	1 324.7
Cumberland, MD-WV	7	12 317	25.6	74.4	16.9	2.3	91	37.4	6.0	156.4	3.8	7.3	92.3	24 289	388.3
Dallas-Fort Worth, TX	242	19 637	27.6	72.4	21.8	3.4	6 491	32.9	329.3	8 886.8	183.6	371.1	3 831.7	20 870	19 641.4
Dallas, TX	131	17 762	35.5	64.5	23.0	3.0	4 352	32.4	219.3	5 921.3	117.2	234.3	2 344.8	20 007	12 667.0
Fort Worth-Arlington, TX	111	22 450	18.1	81.9	19.9	4.0	2 139	33.8	110.0	2 965.4	66.4	136.8	1 486.9	22 393	6 974.4
Danville, VA	40	24 977	69.6	30.4	40.6	5.4	113	42.5	17.1	335.6	13.9	28.5	254.2	18 288	782.9
Davenport-Rock Island-Moline, IA-IL	301	88 843	39.2	60.8	75.7	26.0	452	35.2	32.7	979.0	21.3	41.8	554.6	26 038	2 144.8
Dayton-Springfield, OH	209	55 267	60.0	40.0	52.1	11.9	1 588	39.5	105.9	3 028.7	63.5	127.3	1 651.5	26 008	6 284.6
Daytona Beach, FL	64	69 341	84.4	15.6	43.2	14.5	359	21.2	12.6	264.3	7.6	15.9	118.0	15 526	603.7
Decatur, AL	109	46 271	20.2	79.8	27.9	10.4	211	38.9	D	D	D	D	D	D	D
Decatur, IL	72	84 631	93.0	7.0	74.4	32.6	129	36.4	13.1	428.2	8.2	16.7	254.7	31 061	1 281.8
Denver-Boulder, CO	170	63 982	D	D	36.3	9.7	3 012	25.1	125.9	3 602.9	67.7	134.1	1 589.5	23 479	8 037.3
Boulder-Longmont, Co	40	52 693	29.7	70.3	31.1	6.9	507	27.4	29.5	776.0	11.6	23.4	211.3	18 216	1 451.0
Denver, CO	130	68 442	D	D	38.3	10.8	2 505	24.6	96.4	2 826.9	56.1	110.7	1 378.2	24 567	6 586.4
Des Moines, IA	189	55 706	59.1	40.9	59.2	D	474	33.3	24.4	587.1	14.5	28.0	322.2	22 221	1 480.9
Detroit-Ann Arbor, MI	299	41 540	63.3	36.7	40.5	9.6	8 500	35.3	518.3	17 586.5	301.4	623.8	8 759.0	29 061	31 043.7
Ann Arbor, MI	48	39 032	41.5	58.5	41.4	11.0	428	39.3	39.5	1 322.8	27.4	55.0	866.9	31 639	2 901.2
Detroit, MI	251	42 054	67.4	32.6	40.3	9.3	8 072	35.1	478.8	16 263.8	274.0	568.8	7 892.1	28 803	28 142.5
Dothan, AL	61	44 886	62.7	37.3	50.1	11.2	148	36.5	10.2	178.4	7.9	16.2	117.7	14 899	423.6
Dubuque, IA	153	90 636	8.8	91.2	81.9	31.1	143	40.6	12.2	318.4	8.3	16.2	199.9	24 084	775.1
Duluth, MN-WI	20	16 530	21.6	78.4	23.7	3.1	285	21.8	7.9	166.2	4.2	7.7	81.0	19 286	361.1
Eau Claire, WI	159	60 173	10.3	89.7	72.2	18.2	192	34.4	10.3	243.7	7.3	14.3	149.1	20 425	800.9
El Paso, TX	66	156 552	43.0	57.0	37.4	16.6	546	38.8	35.2	522.6	27.1	51.0	342.0	12 620	1 489.2
Elkhart-Goshen, IN	86	55 380	27.8	72.2	62.4	16.6	855	51.0	50.0	1 100.8	36.1	70.2	646.9	17 920	2 640.8
Elmira, NY	13	39 581	29.1	70.9	40.1	10.7	102	42.2	7.4	156.7	5.0	9.7	93.1	18 620	349.0
Enid, OK	57	48 541	35.7	64.3	65.1	13.1	56	16.1	1.3	28.4	0.8	1.7	16.6	20 750	92.4
Erie, PA	59	43 783	52.6	47.4	51.3	11.7	538	42.6	34.0	856.6	22.7	46.6	489.1	21 546	1 922.4
Eugene-Springfield, OR	60	29 314	50.5	49.5	20.7	5.8	769	23.3	20.3	444.2	15.5	29.6	310.1	20 006	1 060.3
Evansville, IN-KY	103	51 348	77.3	22.7	57.4	D	407	39.6	32.0	919.5	21.4	42.6	518.7	24 238	3 484.0
Fargo-Moorhead, ND-MN	234	106 368	80.1	19.9	82.6	33.0	155	31.0	4.9	97.4	3.3	6.2	55.8	16 909	256.0
Fayetteville, NC	24	45 200	62.6	37.4	42.6	9.9	146	43.8	11.6	274.8	8.8	17.0	196.8	22 364	1 002.8
Fayetteville-Springdale, AR	299	104 696	1.0	99.0	44.7	22.2	140	44.3	9.8	165.3	7.6	15.1	117.1	15 408	409.3
Flint, MI	29	34 643	52.6	47.4	34.7	7.1	323	30.0	D	D	D	D	D	D	D
Florence, AL	48	26 290	54.9	45.1	25.8	7.5	214	38.8	12.2	263.7	9.5	18.9	182.4	19 200	579.6
Florence, SC	44	47 392	84.9	15.1	53.2	13.9	143	46.2	11.5	217.3	8.7	17.8	146.0	16 782	581.6
Fort Collins-Loveland, CO	90	73 145	20.0	80.0	36.0	10.7	274	24.8	12.5	336.5	6.3	13.2	149.1	23 667	694.6
Fort Myers-Cape Coral, FL	73	176 894	96.6	3.4	41.7	14.9	305	23.6	5.6	100.8	3.6	7.1	55.1	15 306	239.3
Fort Pierce, FL	296	352 888	91.4	8.6	62.5	25.2	231	27.7	6.4	124.9	4.1	8.4	72.2	17 610	366.6
Fort Smith, AR-OK	67	25 651	16.8	83.2	25.8	6.6	298	41.6	25.9	527.6	21.0	41.6	370.6	17 648	1 529.1
Fort Walton Beach, FL	5	16 947	41.7	58.3	22.7	4.0	115	27.0	4.7	75.6	3.6	7.1	48.8	13 556	180.1
Fort Wayne, IN	148	43 993	48.1	51.9	56.7	D	674	42.3	45.7	1 187.3	29.6	58.4	642.6	21 709	2 361.8
Fresno, CA	1 682	221 545	72.8	27.2	68.1	25.2	678	30.2	21.1	442.4	14.8	28.7	262.5	17 736	1 309.9
Gadsden, AL	25	27 108	9.8	90.2	21.8	7.3	110	41.8	11.1	287.3	9.0	18.9	221.0	24 556	677.4
Gainesville, FL	47	31 326	35.1	64.9	27.7	6.9	198	25.8	5.9	116.9	4.3	8.3	72.7	16 907	341.0
Glens Falls, NY	75	80 919	7.3	92.7	59.8	28.0	213	33.3	10.9	254.5	7.8	15.7	161.3	20 679	618.3

1. Includes livestock and poultry products.

Area name	Manufactures, 1987 (cont'd) — Value of shipments (Mil dol)	Manufactures, 1987 (cont'd) — New capital expenditures (Mil dol)	Value of construction authorized by building permits, 1990 — Total[1] ($1,000)	Nonresidential — Total ($1,000)	Nonresidential — Percent — Office	Nonresidential — Percent — Industrial	Nonresidential — Percent — Stores	Residential — New construction ($1,000)	Residential — Number of housing units	Residential — Alterations and additions ($1,000)	Wholesale trade, 1987 — Establishments	Wholesale trade, 1987 — Sales (Mil dol)	Wholesale trade, 1987 — Paid employees[2]	Wholesale trade, 1987 — Annual payroll (Mil dol)	Retail trade, all establishments, 1987 — Number
	137	138	139	140	141	142	143	144	145	146	147	148	149	150	151
Chico, CA	671.0	20.5	199 001	36 337	19.9	8.2	43.5	141 182	1 912	9 411	238	569.2	1 849	36.8	1 848
Cincinnati-Hamilton, OH-KY-IN	25 735.1	770.7	1 361 180	397 753	17.1	19.8	33.9	657 276	9 136	54 255	3 283	26 928.3	50 835	1 189.8	14 221
Cincinnati, OH-KY-IN	22 532.6	701.0	1 160 422	347 505	19.2	14.3	35.0	562 694	7 601	48 759	2 955	25 745.6	46 880	1 097.3	12 160
Hamilton-Middletown, OH	3 202.3	69.7	200 757	50 248	2.5	58.3	26.2	94 582	1 535	5 495	328	1 182.7	3 955	92.5	2 061
Clarksville-Hopkinsville, TN-KY	945.1	28.1	69 743	15 265	33.7	9.5	41.2	45 019	913	2 638	195	468.9	1 824	29.4	1 513
Cleveland-Akron-Lorain, OH	37 097.1	1 155.4	2 055 298	443 165	31.2	13.5	21.2	926 706	9 958	140 125	5 675	34 195.7	79 337	1 986.3	23 985
Akron, OH	5 491.4	194.2	508 840	92 440	26.5	14.7	30.9	267 524	3 332	25 822	1 134	7 160.8	14 246	363.1	5 671
Cleveland, OH	22 055.9	841.6	1 383 894	330 614	33.4	12.6	18.1	554 829	5 593	104 916	4 311	26 254.6	63 023	1 582.3	16 229
Lorain-Elyria, OH	9 549.2	119.6	162 564	20 110	18.0	22.0	28.3	104 353	1 033	9 387	230	780.3	2 068	41.0	2 085
Colorado Springs, CO	2 111.9	97.9	152 459	17 632	38.0	1.8	12.8	87 655	1 049	7 802	537	986.4	4 483	88.8	3 825
Columbia, MO	439.7	14.4	125 396	49 544	68.6	0.2	20.0	57 232	787	4 267	143	392.8	1 615	28.7	1 055
Columbia, SC	3 622.0	236.1	330 212	87 458	17.5	1.4	40.6	170 624	2 480	20 031	927	3 201.6	12 113	260.4	4 291
Columbus, GA-AL	2 364.5	76.5	117 202	43 502	51.6	4.9	7.9	29 952	612	11 228	301	932.7	3 235	58.3	2 117
Columbus, OH	15 936.6	511.4	1 408 052	381 329	39.4	11.6	19.5	689 494	9 446	76 399	2 476	15 950.5	37 280	908.1	11 311
Corpus Christi, TX	6 756.2	91.6	96 922	18 497	22.0	7.4	18.9	37 628	552	15 854	725	1 832.7	6 748	132.4	3 539
Cumberland, MD-WV	678.2	D	27 885	4 122	16.6	5.6	33.4	18 161	323	1 778	119	527.8	1 203	22.5	1 186
Dallas-Fort Worth, TX	36 470.5	1 236.1	3 426 020	1 049 405	45.4	11.2	16.2	1 763 641	19 881	98 626	10 158	71 118.3	136 217	3 525.6	39 090
Dallas, TX	23 027.9	811.6	2 372 583	712 038	64.5	1.8	15.5	1 228 467	14 819	69 115	7 704	58 491.4	104 799	2 805.3	26 088
Fort Worth-Arlington, TX	13 442.6	424.5	1 053 437	337 367	5.2	31.0	17.6	535 174	5 062	29 511	2 454	12 626.9	31 418	720.3	13 002
Danville, VA	1 790.9	28.8	54 735	16 690	23.5	5.1	25.2	21 747	398	4 317	151	393.9	1 449	24.9	1 090
Davenport-Rock Island-Moline, IA-IL	5 905.9	176.8	212 134	62 557	18.3	34.4	23.3	67 526	649	22 482	810	4 420.2	9 318	209.5	3 462
Dayton-Springfield, OH	13 541.5	380.6	458 473	111 969	25.1	7.7	50.2	220 844	2 684	18 861	1 472	7 756.0	18 672	443.4	7 835
Daytona Beach, FL	1 029.7	42.3	410 941	42 153	14.4	6.5	27.8	304 875	3 860	20 255	449	662.3	3 627	63.9	3 972
Decatur, AL	D	D	53 920	10 423	18.0	11.3	31.1	34 412	581	2 577	197	0.0	NA	NA	1 412
Decatur, IL	3 345.0	135.6	55 132	18 544	16.2	20.4	32.2	23 513	242	2 375	189	3 662.4	2 038	42.9	1 149
Denver-Boulder, CO	14 864.2	585.8	1 077 399	105 967	26.5	14.3	27.0	628 400	5 956	82 512	4 715	25 204.0	56 956	1 436.0	18 430
Boulder-Longmont, Co	2 744.2	144.1	214 465	21 593	17.4	51.0	4.0	136 978	1 460	20 092	395	1 062.6	3 912	96.9	2 546
Denver, CO	12 120.0	441.7	862 932	84 374	28.8	5.0	32.9	491 422	4 496	62 419	4 320	24 141.4	53 044	1 339.2	15 884
Des Moines, IA	4 013.1	87.4	339 972	86 138	35.7	5.8	26.7	187 340	2 669	11 365	1 059	5 410.6	13 551	319.9	3 934
Detroit-Ann Arbor, MI	82 327.2	2 304.2	2 963 165	819 938	33.3	23.1	21.9	1 388 188	17 971	244 505	8 122	60 503.7	104 734	2 863.4	36 656
Ann Arbor, MI	7 348.1	227.1	246 672	54 311	36.5	32.3	19.9	136 665	1 809	19 569	376	986.0	3 813	84.0	2 231
Detroit, MI	74 979.1	2 077.1	2 716 494	765 627	33.1	22.4	22.0	1 251 523	16 162	224 936	7 746	59 517.7	100 921	2 779.4	34 425
Dothan, AL	895.0	38.1	52 094	17 962	5.7	19.9	40.8	20 528	376	3 252	260	759.2	3 314	54.4	1 467
Dubuque, IA	1 893.4	38.2	66 614	17 518	32.0	23.0	18.9	26 184	346	3 639	191	506.2	2 025	34.5	982
Duluth, MN-WI	839.5	D	109 765	20 238	3.5	1.4	55.0	42 335	652	12 569	375	1 533.3	3 923	84.5	2 754
Eau Claire, WI	1 616.4	52.4	84 514	26 429	13.5	10.1	66.5	39 102	510	5 106	239	608.0	2 717	53.6	1 453
El Paso, TX	4 455.4	65.6	235 648	72 008	29.1	8.6	52.2	102 566	2 111	15 550	909	2 699.6	10 024	187.6	4 346
Elkhart-Goshen, IN	5 760.2	113.5	108 529	26 840	2.4	31.8	32.0	55 067	744	7 138	397	1 640.4	5 285	120.0	1 562
Elmira, NY	623.1	19.7	47 724	9 571	47.2	6.4	29.4	10 267	113	13 599	147	549.1	2 432	48.9	935
Enid, OK	278.5	1.4	10 791	1 096	16.4	4.6	28.3	3 567	31	788	146	1 364.0	1 558	33.3	719
Erie, PA	3 382.3	100.8	108 861	31 518	8.9	16.2	37.7	44 215	678	7 820	402	861.1	4 069	82.5	2 763
Eugene-Springfield, OR	2 617.9	56.8	197 006	34 789	10.6	15.5	49.5	120 861	1 872	11 196	532	1 803.1	5 400	116.3	2 870
Evansville, IN-KY	6 949.8	319.1	136 870	38 795	19.2	31.5	7.2	72 631	1 167	7 675	614	2 671.0	7 406	161.0	2 771
Fargo-Moorhead, ND-MN	666.6	15.9	104 970	21 399	18.7	8.5	58.8	49 848	990	6 256	474	2 142.9	6 108	132.7	1 449
Fayetteville, NC	2 051.4	66.6	118 470	28 912	24.3	2.3	26.3	61 805	1 218	7 710	268	564.5	2 722	48.3	2 123
Fayetteville-Springdale, AR	1 027.1	37.9	81 463	26 555	41.4	0.9	34.7	40 000	753	1 883	225	904.4	2 813	52.6	1 208
Flint, MI	D	D	159 762	41 785	37.7	0.9	31.3	84 190	1 281	10 494	476	1 982.7	5 549	122.6	3 707
Florence, AL	2 037.2	41.5	40 522	11 754	18.7	11.9	59.9	14 483	366	4 062	213	433.1	1 949	34.8	1 502
Florence, SC	1 205.9	54.1	75 037	16 477	0.6	1.5	76.4	42 025	710	4 434	241	656.3	2 958	54.1	1 485
Fort Collins-Loveland, CO	1 124.3	40.4	149 840	16 406	10.1	31.0	28.0	85 567	1 236	6 427	293	522.9	2 006	39.1	2 154
Fort Myers-Cape Coral, FL	452.0	13.2	526 687	118 551	13.0	6.7	35.2	342 640	4 915	34 353	538	954.1	4 487	83.9	3 769
Fort Pierce, FL	700.2	12.0	413 745	61 518	12.8	14.9	23.3	295 428	3 778	13 827	309	659.8	2 784	51.7	2 580
Fort Smith, AR-OK	3 402.1	86.2	65 877	15 215	33.9	0.9	22.0	32 301	660	1 960	352	818.6	3 083	55.4	2 101
Fort Walton Beach, FL	290.8	8.5	84 606	19 005	27.6	3.3	31.9	54 353	1 065	4 222	163	328.3	1 173	18.4	1 650
Fort Wayne, IN	5 055.3	155.7	357 136	146 788	54.9	13.6	20.2	181 660	1 963	17 730	861	5 420.2	12 177	275.9	3 413
Fresno, CA	3 172.6	71.9	687 317	183 956	12.3	22.6	19.3	431 534	5 353	16 485	1 129	4 557.5	12 845	294.7	5 352
Gadsden, AL	1 341.1	19.4	18 877	8 948	4.4	11.2	80.4	6 974	132	596	137	333.0	1 340	24.8	1 110
Gainesville, FL	725.9	21.7	100 452	19 734	12.6	3.8	24.0	61 932	1 211	5 811	239	461.5	2 331	40.4	1 905
Glens Falls, NY	1 293.3	71.5	104 391	18 367	20.8	25.5	23.3	58 924	740	7 664	177	442.1	2 000	44.0	1 635

1. Includes nonresidential additions and alterations, residential nonhousekeeping buildings, and residential garages and carports not shown separately. 2. For pay period including March 12.

Area name	Retail trade, all establishments, 1987 (cont'd): Sales: Total (Mil dol)	Sales: Percent change, 1982–1987	Sales: Per capita[1] (Dollars)	Retail trade, establishments with payroll, 1987: Number	Sales: Total (Mil dol)	Sales: Per capita[1] (Dollars): General merchandise stores	Per capita: Food stores	Per capita: Apparel and accessory stores	Per capita: Eating and drinking places	Paid employees[2]	Annual payroll (Mil dol)	Taxable service industries–establishments with payroll, 1987: Number	Receipts (Mil dol): Total	Receipts: Selected kinds of business: Hotels, motels & other lodging places	Health services	Legal services
	152	153	154	155	156	157	158	159	160	161	162	163	164	165	166	167
Chico, CA	944.2	36.3	5 584	1 145	913.8	576	1 366	184	565	12 031	115.3	1 235	343.3	11.7	173.6	17.8
Cincinnati-Hamilton, OH-KY-IN	10 816.2	45.6	6 289	9 730	10 616.0	843	1 303	255	716	137 624	1 292.7	10 590	5 173.4	269.4	1 228.2	316.5
Cincinnati, OH-KY-IN	9 436.0	45.0	6 540	8 398	9 268.0	915	1 335	288	754	120 309	1 139.7	9 324	4 772.5	255.6	1 079.3	298.1
Hamilton-Middletown, OH	1 380.2	49.3	4 981	1 332	1 348.0	468	1 139	82	519	17 315	153.1	1 266	400.9	13.8	148.9	18.4
Clarksville-Hopkinsville, TN-KY	911.0	54.1	5 799	970	881.6	763	920	230	523	11 032	103.3	700	155.2	10.8	55.0	11.1
Cleveland-Akron-Lorain, OH	16 970.0	34.7	6 113	16 134	16 618.0	783	1 222	282	626	210 994	1 995.5	18 633	8 129.6	269.2	2 026.3	760.3
Akron, OH	3 904.7	35.8	6 019	3 795	3 821.3	765	1 289	226	662	49 602	454.6	4 173	1 451.7	59.1	419.6	87.3
Cleveland, OH	11 632.2	33.9	6 262	10 993	11 390.7	809	1 219	321	639	144 714	1 384.3	13 175	6 310.4	190.4	1 451.0	651.0
Lorain-Elyria, OH	1 433.1	38.0	5 318	1 346	1 406.1	650	1 079	142	453	16 678	156.6	1 285	367.5	19.7	155.7	22.0
Colorado Springs, CO	2 423.3	46.6	6 191	2 458	2 362.3	786	1 010	262	615	29 251	302.5	3 094	1 181.1	98.6	273.0	64.3
Columbia, MO	742.6	65.3	7 026	737	730.9	993	1 163	338	671	10 365	86.7	778	293.5	18.1	135.4	D
Columbia, SC	2 926.7	64.4	6 521	2 792	2 835.0	758	1 145	331	666	37 134	344.7	3 120	1 209.1	65.5	296.4	121.6
Columbus, GA-AL	1 506.7	59.4	6 102	1 485	1 478.7	775	1 103	311	576	18 163	176.3	1 306	515.5	21.5	173.6	32.8
Columbus, OH	9 089.8	52.5	6 856	7 410	8 922.5	875	1 171	300	728	115 219	1 091.0	8 559	4 336.6	177.7	990.2	359.6
Corpus Christi, TX	1 989.4	7.9	5 540	2 171	1 933.6	680	1 311	251	560	24 484	229.2	2 457	918.1	54.7	317.5	123.0
Cumberland, MD-WV	585.8	38.4	5 709	764	564.6	956	1 194	220	511	7 729	63.8	549	195.6	7.1	63.7	4.8
Dallas-Fort Worth, TX	27 663.9	44.2	7 412	23 007	26 866.4	902	1 382	391	760	307 990	3 232.5	29 313	16 748.7	862.8	3 613.2	1 473.7
Dallas, TX	18 891.3	44.6	7 686	15 523	18 375.0	923	1 382	438	808	210 525	2 254.8	20 802	13 256.2	734.1	2 558.6	1 219.7
Fort Worth-Arlington, TX	8 772.5	43.3	6 884	7 484	8 491.5	861	1 382	301	667	97 465	977.6	8 511	3 492.5	128.7	1 054.6	254.0
Danville, VA	588.1	49.0	5 436	661	567.4	695	1 237	176	449	7 045	65.2	512	124.5	9.6	50.7	6.4
Davenport-Rock Island-Moline, IA-IL	2 271.5	23.1	6 203	2 380	2 228.7	801	1 188	252	642	29 591	271.4	2 150	690.1	35.1	217.4	46.2
Dayton-Springfield, OH	5 976.9	43.0	6 344	5 229	5 876.9	894	1 225	238	653	74 520	683.8	5 592	2 690.4	83.5	706.0	123.2
Daytona Beach, FL	2 452.4	63.2	7 323	2 440	2 372.5	817	1 589	262	797	31 065	279.4	2 538	925.0	180.8	315.1	56.3
Decatur, AL	707.5	65.3	5 401	748	659.5	D	958	251	413	7 288	72.0	650	209.9	7.6	95.8	9.8
Decatur, IL	783.6	28.0	6 279	748	766.0	965	1 072	255	595	9 947	92.7	678	235.0	10.4	69.2	15.1
Denver-Boulder, CO	13 028.8	30.0	7 019	11 576	12 736.8	907	1 395	307	770	159 593	1 649.1	17 523	8 328.0	389.2	1 653.5	800.8
Boulder-Longmont, Co	1 638.1	44.7	7 570	1 585	1 599.6	720	1 571	298	819	20 555	205.0	2 244	847.2	26.2	149.9	48.3
Denver, CO	11 390.7	28.1	6 946	9 991	11 137.3	931	1 372	308	763	139 038	1 444.2	15 279	7 480.8	363.0	1 503.6	752.5
Des Moines, IA	2 781.5	38.0	7 225	2 596	2 724.8	981	1 471	346	680	35 096	320.7	2 972	1 310.2	67.9	303.8	124.0
Detroit-Ann Arbor, MI	30 595.8	47.7	6 613	24 811	29 973.6	866	1 075	386	657	349 048	3 583.2	30 359	15 839.5	399.9	3 532.2	1 210.1
Ann Arbor, MI	2 017.9	52.8	7 635	1 565	1 988.7	1 118	1 130	392	806	24 301	249.6	2 143	941.3	36.1	209.3	43.6
Detroit, MI	28 577.9	47.4	6 551	23 246	27 984.9	850	1 071	385	648	324 747	3 333.7	28 216	14 898.2	363.8	3 322.9	1 166.5
Dothan, AL	869.2	56.4	6 701	995	845.4	955	1 224	333	615	10 583	97.5	812	310.8	18.1	161.7	10.6
Dubuque, IA	572.9	31.8	6 323	650	556.2	1 204	1 187	231	601	7 436	67.0	481	217.0	11.0	97.4	8.2
Duluth, MN-WI	1 438.9	21.3	5 953	1 840	1 397.3	853	1 164	235	520	18 186	156.5	1 340	396.7	39.9	123.9	28.3
Eau Claire, WI	859.8	33.1	6 253	972	839.5	900	1 123	240	636	12 160	92.9	764	262.1	12.4	120.6	14.6
El Paso, TX	2 898.6	36.7	5 051	2 813	2 832.0	752	1 018	272	454	35 571	329.3	2 796	1 133.3	58.9	377.7	76.2
Elkhart-Goshen, IN	1 090.4	43.2	7 314	960	1 061.3	665	1 278	266	625	12 002	116.6	887	387.0	18.3	75.8	14.6
Elmira, NY	600.7	37.5	6 623	620	583.7	1 267	1 170	367	540	7 482	67.1	480	152.0	6.2	61.8	10.1
Enid, OK	351.8	-8.0	5 903	478	339.6	1 003	1 171	361	525	4 702	40.5	403	133.1	3.8	78.3	10.5
Erie, PA	1 621.8	36.9	5 847	1 753	1 571.9	774	1 234	235	549	20 569	174.0	1 553	655.2	40.3	226.5	29.5
Eugene-Springfield, OR	1 719.9	38.9	6 458	1 863	1 678.0	897	1 275	256	609	20 655	201.9	2 207	619.6	34.8	207.9	52.6
Evansville, IN-KY	1 840.6	32.1	6 555	1 812	1 803.4	947	1 245	317	672	24 217	220.1	1 824	702.0	23.6	216.1	35.6
Fargo-Moorhead, ND-MN	1 087.0	28.8	7 389	978	1 069.1	1 086	1 271	301	735	14 660	120.9	1 017	408.2	30.9	168.8	27.5
Fayetteville, NC	1 544.6	58.6	6 017	1 468	1 519.7	869	993	236	546	18 196	175.7	1 108	418.0	35.9	140.8	22.5
Fayetteville-Springdale, AR	776.3	55.8	7 129	732	750.2	1 431	1 317	269	498	8 585	80.9	751	191.2	9.0	81.3	14.1
Flint, MI	2 977.5	45.7	6 857	2 559	2 935.2	1 106	1 100	287	617	32 635	326.5	2 486	886.5	23.2	342.6	45.4
Florence, AL	751.9	41.4	5 549	879	715.6	889	1 170	233	439	8 560	75.4	747	206.0	6.5	115.0	9.7
Florence, SC	804.0	57.3	6 872	877	772.2	889	1 216	289	428	8 774	81.1	666	231.6	26.9	100.8	13.2
Fort Collins-Loveland, CO	1 136.8	47.0	6 347	1 269	1 101.9	611	1 275	214	656	14 593	138.7	1 558	358.0	23.0	105.5	19.5
Fort Myers-Cape Coral, FL	2 597.6	85.5	8 770	2 369	2 522.5	978	1 644	346	858	28 903	300.8	2 339	975.2	125.4	345.8	60.1
Fort Pierce, FL	1 713.5	82.6	7 743	1 563	1 656.1	705	1 513	261	639	18 296	188.8	1 590	572.8	35.3	219.1	43.1
Fort Smith, AR-OK	1 048.4	40.8	5 876	1 239	997.4	950	1 214	234	550	12 643	114.2	977	389.0	21.5	165.0	17.3
Fort Walton Beach, FL	961.9	70.7	6 584	1 142	933.3	895	1 080	219	812	12 694	110.7	995	424.4	63.2	138.6	15.8
Fort Wayne, IN	2 516.9	57.0	6 901	2 186	2 455.3	908	1 138	283	690	31 902	291.3	2 342	1 001.3	29.5	285.3	53.2
Fresno, CA	3 641.3	42.0	6 088	3 403	3 526.1	665	1 315	253	569	39 975	422.6	4 135	1 448.9	56.0	477.3	112.3
Gadsden, AL	566.3	43.1	5 520	616	537.0	724	1 215	277	443	6 539	56.0	495	141.3	4.2	78.6	9.9
Gainesville, FL	1 375.3	51.5	6 712	1 338	1 346.9	835	1 451	242	690	17 582	155.9	1 466	515.7	23.6	216.6	31.0
Glens Falls, NY	857.3	64.0	7 507	1 001	830.8	738	1 695	312	653	8 589	92.6	799	274.6	66.0	57.9	15.8

1. Based on the estimated population as of July 1 of the year shown. 2. For the period including March 12 of the year shown.

Area name	Taxable service Industries–establishments with payroll, 1987 (cont'd)		Banking		Federal funds and grants, 1989						Local government finances, 1981–1982				
						Per capita[3] (Dollars)					General revenue				
													Taxes		
														Per capita[4]	
	Paid employees	Annual payroll (Mil dol)	Bank deposits,[1] June 1989 (Mil dol)	Savings capital,[2] September 1989 (Mil dol)	Expenditures (Mil dol)	Total	Direct payments for individuals	Procurement contract awards	Salaries and wages	Grant awards	Total (Mil dol)	Intergovernmental (Mil dol)	Total (Mil dol)	Total (Dollars)	Property (Dollars)
	168	169	170	172	174	176	177	178	179	180	181	182	184	185	186
Chico, CA	8 463	126.1	972	834.2	494.8	2 764	2 214	31	103	267	176.0	103.5	49.8	326	247
Cincinnati-Hamilton, OH-KY-IN	131 620	2 062.3	14 087	7 658.3	6 400.5	3 667	1 589	1 377	326	359	1 736.7	682.4	719.9	431	296
Cincinnati, OH-KY-IN	116 510	1 904.1	12 695	6 812.2	5 883.9	4 026	1 628	1 632	373	379	1 494.4	584.3	627.1	445	304
Hamilton-Middletown, OH	15 110	158.2	1 392	846.1	516.6	1 820	1 389	64	87	260	242.3	98.1	92.8	353	251
Clarksville-Hopkinsville, TN-KY	4 361	54.2	832	302.6	1 052.8	6 555	1 521	370	4 344	241	113.3	55.5	26.5	171	93
Cleveland-Akron-Lorain, OH	181 271	3 274.3	22 557	15 022.7	8 138.5	2 939	1 882	338	321	386	3 736.9	1 458.4	1 573.6	561	384
Akron, OH	35 661	588.5	4 002	2 269.7	1 664.1	2 535	1 689	390	162	284	717.1	286.5	278.5	425	304
Cleveland, OH	136 252	2 541.1	17 146	11 987.5	5 880.0	3 192	1 999	354	393	435	2 769.5	1 065.2	1 195.9	638	425
Lorain-Elyria, OH	9 358	144.7	1 409	765.5	594.4	2 197	1 558	104	220	296	250.3	106.7	99.2	362	292
Colorado Springs, CO	27 353	475.2	1 727	1 663.0	2 445.2	6 078	1 775	1 543	2 564	186	348.8	135.6	126.2	381	287
Columbia, MO	8 093	113.1	756	287.9	282.0	2 668	1 361	75	588	535	108.5	42.0	32.9	319	204
Columbia, SC	33 881	493.5	2 999	1 206.4	1 835.3	3 958	1 532	368	1 238	806	389.3	142.4	115.8	274	256
Columbus, GA-AL	13 660	188.7	1 429	497.9	1 306.9	5 323	1 956	361	2 640	354	247.6	76.0	67.7	278	158
Columbus, OH	107 059	1 700.0	11 588	4 957.0	4 296.2	3 148	1 435	396	410	869	1 330.0	513.5	511.7	405	294
Corpus Christi, TX	21 129	346.5	2 388	1 251.6	1 115.0	3 122	1 562	768	426	260	418.5	149.8	148.9	430	362
Cumberland, MD-WV	3 788	72.3	612	294.6	365.3	3 585	2 543	569	154	304	86.7	44.1	27.9	262	175
Dallas-Fort Worth, TX	324 628	6 251.9	33 789	17 047.0	13 389.3	3 478	1 187	1 699	408	156	3 271.2	953.8	1 355.1	430	342
Dallas, TX	247 469	4 966.4	24 519	13 037.2	6 836.0	2 703	1 136	998	388	164	2 132.4	632.5	980.7	470	374
Fort Worth-Arlington, TX	77 159	1 285.5	9 270	4 009.8	6 553.3	4 962	1 283	3 042	445	142	1 138.8	321.3	374.4	350	279
Danville, VA	3 099	49.6	854	141.8	259.2	2 429	1 789	231	108	283	67.1	38.9	17.4	156	102
Davenport-Rock Island-Moline, IA-IL	17 700	256.3	3 229	869.8	1 233.8	3 411	1 854	297	884	205	452.4	151.8	165.8	429	386
Dayton-Springfield, OH	63 703	1 072.4	5 666	3 934.7	4 462.1	4 675	1 894	1 193	1 239	322	1 049.1	426.9	425.0	454	313
Daytona Beach, FL	22 549	320.0	2 493	2 197.3	1 206.9	3 340	2 711	380	120	116	326.6	112.2	94.4	335	276
Decatur, AL	6 267	83.9	737	201.0	408.1	3 048	1 559	176	989	252	115.2	40.8	22.7	185	84
Decatur, IL	5 505	92.6	969	406.4	284.4	2 325	1 809	73	150	159	117.0	43.8	51.0	392	315
Denver-Boulder, CO	170 256	3 165.3	12 798	8 927.6	8 166.3	4 380	1 402	1 668	810	484	2 327.5	712.3	1 077.9	626	399
Boulder-Longmont, Co	17 715	315.6	1 247	835.0	740.5	3 378	1 167	980	486	734	215.6	71.0	106.2	531	395
Denver, CO	152 541	2 849.7	11 551	8 092.6	7 425.8	4 513	1 433	1 759	853	450	2 111.9	641.3	971.7	638	400
Des Moines, IA	29 965	482.4	3 413	1 349.6	1 591.0	3 984	1 606	187	532	773	459.3	175.2	177.5	478	462
Detroit-Ann Arbor, MI	327 890	6 342.2	41 116	14 910.6	12 391.9	2 682	1 751	196	281	439	6 868.5	2 391.4	3 020.2	652	585
Ann Arbor, MI	22 266	386.1	1 832	855.5	758.4	2 817	1 219	354	349	868	297.8	74.4	167.6	643	635
Detroit, MI	305 624	5 956.1	39 284	14 055.1	11 633.5	2 673	1 784	186	277	412	6 570.7	2 317.0	2 852.6	653	582
Dothan, AL	6 921	117.5	954	217.1	673.1	5 115	1 812	366	2 659	239	117.4	41.1	23.5	186	80
Dubuque, IA	5 152	91.1	770	178.4	251.1	2 747	1 676	85	165	623	92.8	39.8	36.0	387	375
Duluth, MN-WI	11 218	160.8	1 591	509.6	779.0	3 251	2 141	119	304	669	455.8	254.7	84.2	321	293
Eau Claire, WI	6 822	106.9	780	291.9	396.5	2 846	1 640	322	167	344	163.4	82.1	43.5	323	318
El Paso, TX	28 896	413.7	3 378	1 224.4	2 031.9	3 396	1 516	387	1 227	260	488.5	249.6	137.8	267	217
Elkhart-Goshen, IN	8 377	111.7	1 609	99.5	249.2	1 623	1 269	45	82	195	120.2	53.2	50.6	369	311
Elmira, NY	3 750	58.5	710	199.6	272.0	2 963	2 136	63	227	523	121.8	54.6	53.7	562	408
Enid, OK	3 132	53.1	366	227.3	227.1	4 012	1 979	866	843	239	56.9	23.1	22.3	329	173
Erie, PA	13 234	216.0	1 710	652.8	681.6	2 468	1 835	111	214	296	263.3	118.8	99.2	352	274
Eugene-Springfield, OR	16 752	252.1	1 201	666.9	676.1	2 463	1 743	70	272	369	361.0	156.8	132.9	493	453
Evansville, IN-KY	16 748	265.0	2 423	924.5	694.7	2 467	1 751	141	161	351	239.0	112.7	85.5	307	297
Fargo-Moorhead, ND-MN	9 899	149.5	1 112	508.1	464.2	3 107	1 497	78	514	406	170.7	85.3	40.7	292	276
Fayetteville, NC	11 860	149.7	940	241.8	1 998.0	7 808	1 597	573	5 348	276	177.8	109.6	46.3	186	151
Fayetteville-Springdale, AR	4 378	68.4	834	252.8	289.2	2 578	1 661	190	297	409	87.2	27.2	18.6	183	151
Flint, MI	21 393	372.9	2 423	373.7	982.8	2 293	1 702	27	130	415	649.3	257.6	236.2	536	490
Florence, AL	4 969	72.9	943	282.9	412.8	3 071	1 978	87	716	201	121.2	42.1	22.4	164	73
Florence, SC	6 062	92.2	599	305.3	257.9	2 173	1 506	36	174	421	71.4	40.5	20.8	185	165
Fort Collins-Loveland, CO	9 854	135.4	879	516.3	391.7	2 112	1 247	155	315	383	201.4	52.6	76.9	487	354
Fort Myers-Cape Coral, FL	21 368	371.0	3 073	1 763.5	981.6	3 027	2 706	22	164	120	268.5	75.3	95.5	414	375
Fort Pierce, FL	14 049	223.5	1 780	1 324.0	703.0	2 884	2 469	209	106	94	150.4	58.7	62.0	356	321
Fort Smith, AR-OK	9 906	141.9	1 143	592.5	466.7	2 547	1 789	78	278	385	102.0	55.8	26.0	158	136
Fort Walton Beach, FL	9 063	139.4	892	159.4	1 170.4	7 503	2 298	1 791	3 294	108	101.7	63.7	18.3	154	123
Fort Wayne, IN	25 902	387.8	3 873	541.8	1 195.0	3 198	1 391	1 344	200	210	319.0	161.7	107.8	308	301
Fresno, CA	31 678	533.4	3 040	2 525.1	1 433.3	2 278	1 376	75	417	315	869.1	488.7	207.9	386	296
Gadsden, AL	3 920	58.7	595	103.7	266.8	2 595	2 007	209	157	211	69.7	33.8	24.3	237	71
Gainesville, FL	12 002	203.1	988	347.2	568.3	2 696	1 497	177	460	544	185.3	89.1	43.0	236	200
Glens Falls, NY	5 324	89.2	1 010	85.4	276.9	2 355	1 769	60	168	342	161.0	73.0	65.7	598	450

1. Includes deposits for all insured and reporting noninsured commercial and mutual savings banks. 2. Includes savings capital for all FSLIC insured savings institutions. 3. Based on the estimated population as of July 1 of the year shown. 4. Based on the estimated population as of July 1, 1982.

Area name	Local government finances, 1981–1982, (cont'd)										State and local government employment, 1989		Federal government civilian employment, 1989		Elections,[3] 1988	
	Direct general expenditure								Debt outstanding							
				Percent of total for–												
	Total (Mil dol)	Percent change, 1977–1982	Per capita[1] (Dollars)	Education	Health & hospitals	Police protection	Public welfare	Highways	Total (Mil dol)	Per capita[1] (Dollars)	Total	Rate[2]	Total	Earnings ($1,000)	Total vote cast for president	Vote for lead party (Percent)
	187	188	189	190	191	192	193	194	195	196	197	198	199	200	201	202
Chico, CA	171.6	66.8	1 123	48.6	3.5	5.2	13.0	6.3	114	745	10 903	609.1	572	16 584	71 631	R–56.0
Cincinnati-Hamilton, OH-KY-IN	1 635.9	18.0	979	41.8	5.3	5.9	3.9	4.9	1 471	880	89 387	512.1	16 608	495 592	682 858	R–64.8
Cincinnati, OH-KY-IN	1 395.4	15.8	991	41.1	5.7	6.1	3.9	4.6	1 162	825	74 246	508.0	16 049	478 557	572 650	R–64.1
Hamilton-Middletown, OH	240.5	32.7	916	46.2	3.2	4.9	3.8	6.9	309	1 177	15 141	533.3	559	17 035	110 208	R–68.7
Clarksville-Hopkinsville, TN-KY	106.0	90.6	685	36.7	14.7	4.2	0.8	6.0	135	875	7 743	482.1	4 251	92 935	36 864	R–59.3
Cleveland-Akron-Lorain, OH	3 579.7	43.9	1 276	39.1	9.5	6.1	6.2	4.6	2 376	847	147 399	532.3	24 433	860 287	1 154 118	D–53.6
Akron, OH	729.6	45.9	1 113	40.9	8.8	4.8	5.5	5.9	429	655	39 409	600.3	2 402	77 971	268 069	D–51.6
Cleveland, OH	2 606.9	44.5	1 390	37.1	10.3	6.7	6.5	4.2	1 733	924	95 956	520.9	20 745	724 953	779 123	D–54.5
Lorain-Elyria, OH	243.2	32.3	888	55.5	3.7	4.1	5.0	5.1	215	784	12 034	444.7	1 286	57 363	106 926	D–52.0
Colorado Springs, CO	327.2	70.7	988	48.7	6.7	5.1	6.3	5.7	426	1 288	20 104	499.7	9 783	252 748	138 466	R–70.0
Columbia, MO	117.7	113.2	1 141	26.3	28.0	3.2	1.4	4.2	120	1 167	19 303	1 826.2	2 299	72 879	47 458	D–51.4
Columbia, SC	384.1	80.4	908	46.6	22.0	4.5	0.2	1.5	306	724	54 608	1 177.7	8 046	240 230	136 361	R–62.6
Columbus, GA-AL	263.3	89.4	1 081	32.1	36.5	3.2	0.8	3.9	196	805	14 064	572.9	7 206	182 910	55 904	R–53.4
Columbus, OH	1 319.5	55.9	1 043	41.1	5.8	6.1	6.3	4.6	1 429	1 130	111 217	815.0	16 094	521 825	539 355	R–62.8
Corpus Christi, TX	399.7	87.7	1 154	47.7	12.4	4.4	0.4	4.5	463	1 338	21 426	599.8	7 379	229 014	115 390	D–51.2
Cumberland, MD-WV	83.6	18.4	786	67.7	3.0	3.3	0.0	4.5	54	506	5 953	584.2	310	9 429	39 614	R–59.3
Dallas-Fort Worth, TX	3 165.2	87.8	1 004	42.4	8.6	5.6	0.3	6.3	6 104	1 935	183 452	476.5	42 426	1 432 085	1 272 713	R–61.2
Dallas, TX	2 127.4	88.1	1 020	42.6	9.7	5.9	0.3	6.1	2 861	1 372	126 964	502.0	28 954	979 802	823 582	R–61.2
Fort Worth-Arlington, TX	1 037.8	87.2	971	41.9	6.5	4.9	0.3	6.6	3 242	3 033	56 488	427.7	13 472	452 283	449 131	R–61.1
Danville, VA	70.0	59.5	629	55.1	0.1	5.4	4.9	5.7	42	376	4 935	462.5	291	8 257	39 075	R–62.6
Davenport-Rock Island-Moline, IA-IL	435.2	53.3	1 126	45.0	11.1	4.3	1.4	7.1	352	910	16 654	460.4	10 176	367 500	156 984	D–54.9
Dayton-Springfield, OH	1 047.7	51.3	1 120	44.5	4.7	5.1	5.2	4.7	579	619	46 223	484.3	28 334	767 906	374 736	R–59.7
Daytona Beach, FL	303.7	90.1	1 077	39.4	20.9	6.4	0.2	5.1	188	666	18 924	523.6	1 025	34 207	131 182	R–56.6
Decatur, AL	112.7	65.5	917	38.9	21.5	3.2	0.3	5.9	215	1 747	7 384	551.5	453	12 924	37 824	R–58.9
Decatur, IL	117.4	60.2	903	46.9	1.3	4.9	1.9	6.0	128	983	5 567	455.2	401	12 649	49 489	D–51.3
Denver-Boulder, CO	2 077.9	59.3	1 206	42.6	4.9	5.6	6.8	5.3	2 165	1 257	118 230	634.1	36 488	1 219 240	790 853	R–49.7
Boulder-Longmont, Co	205.8	49.9	1 030	48.1	2.1	5.5	6.3	6.5	127	633	22 720	1 036.5	2 674	105 834	107 223	D–53.4
Denver, CO	1 872.1	60.5	1 230	42.0	5.2	5.6	6.8	5.2	2 039	1 339	95 510	580.5	33 814	1 113 406	683 630	R–50.4
Des Moines, IA	432.1	54.8	1 164	45.2	7.5	5.3	2.0	8.1	366	986	25 312	633.9	5 819	194 673	171 694	D–59.2
Detroit-Ann Arbor, MI	6 365.2	45.7	1 374	44.4	7.7	6.7	0.9	4.6	5 080	1 097	261 386	565.6	35 509	1 132 021	1 794 905	R–50.8
Ann Arbor, MI	274.5	54.2	1 053	52.8	1.4	5.8	1.5	5.9	237	908	56 896	2 113.5	2 781	93 133	117 920	D–52.4
Detroit, MI	6 090.7	45.3	1 393	44.0	7.9	6.7	0.8	4.5	4 844	1 108	204 490	469.9	32 728	1 038 888	1 676 985	R–51.1
Dothan, AL	119.9	93.7	949	33.2	28.8	3.9	0.3	4.3	161	1 274	8 017	609.2	4 670	124 139	39 970	R–73.2
Dubuque, IA	88.8	60.9	954	46.6	5.0	3.9	1.5	8.0	58	620	3 167	346.5	363	11 240	38 547	D–61.7
Duluth, MN-WI	465.0	50.1	1 770	33.9	6.1	3.6	14.6	9.1	256	976	20 950	874.4	1 907	57 953	123 776	D–68.1
Eau Claire, WI	162.9	36.3	1 209	44.4	12.6	4.4	4.2	11.0	76	561	10 217	733.5	606	18 630	60 390	D–54.0
El Paso, TX	425.7	82.6	824	52.6	5.4	5.2	0.2	2.9	424	820	32 621	545.2	9 421	311 677	118 781	D–52.7
Elkhart-Goshen, IN	111.6	46.5	814	54.6	0.8	5.8	6.4	4.0	62	451	5 292	344.8	361	11 056	48 200	R–70.1
Elmira, NY	124.6	13.0	1 305	42.7	2.3	3.0	16.2	6.5	75	786	6 293	685.5	436	14 914	37 139	R–56.4
Enid, OK	50.0	77.3	737	54.4	0.8	4.8	0.0	12.4	19	274	3 361	593.8	394	9 918	23 538	R–64.8
Erie, PA	236.1	18.1	838	48.5	4.1	3.6	5.3	5.5	236	838	12 120	438.8	1 588	51 026	103 300	D–52.2
Eugene-Springfield, OR	377.1	72.1	1 398	47.5	2.3	4.4	0.3	9.4	393	1 456	20 018	729.3	2 435	73 760	119 702	D–58.4
Evansville, IN-KY	232.5	64.2	834	44.9	0.9	4.0	5.9	5.5	312	1 120	11 289	400.9	1 195	37 905	114 127	R–54.6
Fargo-Moorhead, ND-MN	172.1	87.9	1 235	38.8	1.6	4.1	3.6	6.0	163	1 167	10 976	734.7	2 283	70 057	70 852	R–52.3
Fayetteville, NC	170.9	25.6	688	61.1	3.0	5.3	4.3	1.3	72	292	14 568	569.3	9 370	256 118	50 979	R–53.1
Fayetteville-Springdale, AR	82.9	80.2	814	40.7	31.8	3.3	0.1	4.8	84	822	9 940	885.9	1 052	34 092	36 658	R–64.4
Flint, MI	635.0	39.6	1 442	47.4	17.9	4.9	1.3	2.9	637	1 447	21 498	501.5	1 480	47 940	176 859	D–59.3
Florence, AL	130.1	62.6	952	37.0	31.7	3.5	0.1	5.0	112	817	7 853	584.3	2 697	92 410	44 599	D–52.2
Florence, SC	70.9	78.1	632	63.2	1.4	4.8	0.3	2.8	42	373	9 013	759.3	568	17 465	32 214	R–60.5
Fort Collins-Loveland, CO	189.6	91.3	1 202	38.3	14.7	4.0	5.9	6.4	594	3 766	16 382	883.1	1 931	65 205	83 066	R–55.3
Fort Myers-Cape Coral, FL	252.4	118.9	1 094	38.8	14.9	4.2	1.0	6.8	303	1 312	17 138	528.5	1 352	43 562	128 936	R–67.7
Fort Pierce, FL	154.0	98.2	883	56.0	1.1	7.5	0.8	6.2	227	1 304	10 951	449.2	700	22 232	93 087	R–68.3
Fort Smith, AR-OK	96.6	77.2	587	61.2	1.1	4.5	0.0	5.2	85	517	6 403	349.5	1 634	50 587	57 993	R–67.6
Fort Walton Beach, FL	93.2	45.2	785	64.3	0.4	3.9	0.1	6.2	44	366	6 272	402.1	6 721	174 670	50 462	R–80.0
Fort Wayne, IN	287.8	34.3	822	51.4	2.4	5.2	7.7	3.9	221	631	16 270	435.4	2 035	66 545	140 037	R–65.2
Fresno, CA	834.9	56.6	1 551	40.1	11.8	4.8	13.5	4.3	331	615	39 022	620.1	10 198	265 100	189 870	R–49.9
Gadsden, AL	64.0	60.4	624	45.3	0.9	6.2	0.3	5.6	46	446	4 553	442.9	356	11 060	35 891	R–49.7
Gainesville, FL	169.1	31.6	927	48.5	2.6	6.7	0.9	4.8	352	1 928	33 298	1 579.6	2 988	101 436	66 849	R–51.4
Glens Falls, NY	159.1	46.6	1 448	49.7	3.2	2.4	10.7	11.2	95	864	8 146	692.7	413	12 923	47 137	R–63.6

1. Based on the estimated population as of July 1, 1982. 2. Per 10,000 resident population estimated as of July 1 of the year shown. 3. Data subject to copyright.

MSA/ CMSA/ NECMA/ PMSA code[1]	Area name	Land Area,[2] 1990 (Sq. Km.)	Population, 1990													
						Race						Age of population Percent				
			Total persons	Rank	Per square kilometer	White	Black	Am. Indian, Eskimo, Aleut	Asian & Pacific Islander	Other race	Hispanic[3]	Under 5 years	5 to 14 years	15 to 24 years	25 to 34 years	35 to 44 years
		1	2	3	4	5	6	7	8	9	10	11	12	13	14	15
2985	Grand Forks, ND	3 724	70 683	280	19.0	66 766	1 446	1 244	881	346	1 053	8.4	14.3	22.4	20.0	13.3
3000	Grand Rapids, MI	3 683	688 399	59	186.9	623 787	41 311	3 394	7 831	12 076	22 631	8.7	15.8	15.2	18.3	14.9
3040	Great Falls, MT	6 988	77 691	277	11.1	72 345	1 061	3 072	792	421	1 398	8.2	15.7	13.0	17.0	14.6
3060	Greeley, CO	10 341	131 821	211	12.7	117 247	567	785	1 133	12 089	27 502	7.9	16.0	17.4	16.4	15.3
3080	Green Bay, WI	1 369	194 594	159	142.1	186 621	1 012	3 869	2 522	570	1 525	7.8	15.1	15.2	18.5	15.6
3120	Greensboro-Winston-Salem-High Pt.,NC	8 941	942 091	44	105.4	747 835	182 284	3 196	6 381	2 395	7 096	6.6	12.5	15.3	17.4	15.7
3160	Greenville-Spartanburg, SC	5 439	640 861	64	117.8	522 632	111 334	959	4 617	1 319	5 120	6.8	13.4	16.3	16.5	15.2
3180	Hagerstown, MD	1 187	121 393	231	102.3	112 828	7 245	241	793	286	905	6.7	12.4	14.2	17.8	15.0
3240	Harrisburg-Lebanon-Carlisle, PA	5 157	587 986	70	114.0	536 738	39 472	737	6 251	4 788	10 239	6.6	12.9	14.3	16.5	15.7
3283	Hartford-New Britain-Middletown, CT	3 923	1 123 678	35	286.4	968 589	95 882	1 876	17 331	40 000	76 672	6.8	12.1	14.6	17.9	15.6
3290	Hickory, NC	3 022	221 700	151	73.4	201 558	17 540	417	1 673	512	1 449	6.4	13.0	14.8	16.5	15.6
3320	Honolulu, HI	1 554	836 231	51	538.1	264 372	25 875	3 532	526 459	15 993	56 884	7.4	13.4	15.6	18.7	15.6
3350	Houma-Thibodaux, LA	6 061	182 842	167	30.2	147 453	26 735	6 814	1 370	470	2 625	8.5	18.1	16.0	17.3	14.0
3362	Houston-Galveston-Brazoria, TX	18 408	3 711 043	10	201.6	2 507 455	665 378	11 029	132 131	395 050	772 295	8.5	15.9	14.9	19.7	16.7
1145	Brazoria, TX	3 592	191 707	X	53.4	154 875	15 981	812	1 961	18 078	33 797	8.1	16.8	13.9	19.2	16.3
2920	Galveston-Texas City, TX	1 033	217 399	X	210.5	164 210	38 154	752	3 569	10 714	30 962	7.6	15.6	13.5	17.7	15.7
3360	Houston, TX	13 783	3 301 937	X	239.6	2 188 370	611 243	9 465	126 601	366 258	707 536	8.6	15.9	15.1	19.9	16.8
3400	Huntington-Ashland, WV-KY-OH	5 595	312 529	118	55.9	304 244	6 751	372	937	225	1 274	5.9	14.1	15.0	14.6	14.6
3440	Huntsville, AL	2 085	238 912	145	114.6	184 197	48 116	1 601	4 232	766	2 984	7.3	13.5	15.4	19.9	14.8
3480	Indianapolis, IN	7 955	1 249 822	31	157.1	1 061 142	172 326	2 510	10 081	3 763	11 084	7.7	14.5	14.1	18.8	15.4
3500	Iowa City, IA	1 592	96 119	266	60.4	89 649	1 979	176	3 837	478	1 435	6.4	11.1	27.5	20.3	14.5
3520	Jackson, MI	1 830	149 756	191	81.8	135 557	11 983	655	653	908	2 303	7.3	14.3	13.7	17.6	15.7
3560	Jackson, MS	6 120	395 396	93	64.6	224 999	167 899	346	1 754	398	1 944	7.6	15.9	15.9	17.6	15.1
3580	Jackson, TN	1 443	77 982	276	54.0	53 423	24 170	66	253	70	376	7.1	14.9	15.3	16.2	14.8
3600	Jacksonville, FL	6 826	906 727	47	132.8	701 911	181 265	2 587	15 362	5 602	22 479	7.8	14.2	14.8	18.6	15.5
3605	Jacksonville, NC	1 986	149 838	190	75.4	111 939	29 808	939	2 994	4 158	8 035	9.1	12.4	30.2	22.3	11.3
3610	Jamestown, NY	2 751	141 895	202	51.6	136 311	2 405	558	545	2 076	4 055	6.9	14.3	15.1	14.7	13.9
3620	Janesville-Beloit, WI	1 866	139 510	203	74.8	130 803	6 638	369	985	715	1 754	7.7	15.1	14.1	16.4	14.6
3660	Johnson City-Kingsport-Bristol,TN-VA	7 422	436 047	82	58.8	424 751	8 925	766	1 247	358	1 690	5.7	12.3	14.8	15.2	15.1
3680	Johnstown, PA	4 566	241 247	142	52.8	236 459	3 836	152	527	273	1 216	5.9	13.6	13.3	14.1	14.4
3710	Joplin, MO	3 280	134 910	209	41.1	130 093	1 327	2 452	751	287	1 150	6.9	14.7	14.1	15.4	14.1
3720	Kalamazoo, MI	1 455	223 411	149	153.5	197 427	19 879	1 017	3 168	1 920	3 950	7.3	13.4	19.2	16.9	15.1
3740	Kankakee, IL	1 755	96 255	265	54.8	80 194	14 399	150	644	868	1 946	7.6	15.9	14.5	15.3	14.3
3760	Kansas City, MO-KS	12 919	1 566 280	25	121.2	1 320 564	200 508	7 631	17 444	20 133	45 227	7.7	14.7	13.2	18.3	15.8
3810	Killeen-Temple, TX	5 467	255 301	133	46.7	181 144	49 687	1 405	7 201	15 864	31 238	9.3	15.1	20.8	20.3	13.0
3840	Knoxville, TN	7 186	604 816	67	84.2	561 535	36 400	1 505	4 540	836	3 232	6.3	12.7	15.4	16.5	15.5
3850	Kokomo, IN	1 433	96 946	264	67.7	91 410	4 408	246	508	374	1 178	7.0	14.9	13.7	15.5	15.1
3870	La Crosse, WI	1 173	97 904	263	83.5	94 319	438	340	2 667	140	640	7.1	14.0	19.1	16.2	14.4
3880	Lafayette, LA	2 615	208 740	154	79.8	154 146	51 378	440	1 915	861	3 115	8.6	16.9	16.1	18.6	14.8
3920	Lafayette-West Lafayette, IN	1 295	130 598	219	100.8	122 013	2 660	320	4 821	784	2 078	6.3	11.5	29.2	16.3	12.7
3960	Lake Charles, LA	2 774	168 134	175	60.6	128 181	38 445	387	590	531	1 847	7.8	17.0	14.6	16.5	14.5
3980	Lakeland-Winter Haven, FL	4 856	405 382	88	83.5	341 952	54 385	1 158	2 486	5 401	16 600	7.0	13.2	13.1	14.7	13.1
4000	Lancaster, PA	2 458	422 822	86	172.0	397 815	10 038	484	4 652	9 833	15 639	7.9	14.6	14.6	16.6	14.7
4040	Lansing-East Lansing, MI	4 421	432 674	84	97.9	381 371	31 365	2 655	8 320	8 963	16 963	7.3	14.3	20.1	17.3	15.4
4080	Laredo, TX	8 695	133 239	210	15.3	93 657	156	201	484	38 741	125 069	10.1	20.3	18.8	16.0	12.4
4100	Las Cruces, NM	9 861	135 510	208	13.7	123 434	2 172	1 009	1 164	7 731	76 448	8.6	17.0	19.2	16.9	13.3
4120	Las Vegas, NV	20 489	741 459	54	36.2	602 658	70 738	6 416	26 043	35 604	82 904	7.7	13.3	13.8	18.8	15.6
4150	Lawrence, KS	1 184	81 798	274	69.1	72 885	3 324	2 161	2 581	847	2 138	6.3	11.3	30.9	17.6	13.1
4200	Lawton, OK	2 770	111 486	251	40.2	79 666	19 908	5 153	3 065	3 694	6 923	8.5	15.7	19.6	19.0	13.1
4243	Lewiston-Auburn, ME	1 218	105 259	258	86.4	103 687	485	233	557	297	780	7.4	14.3	15.0	17.0	14.5
4280	Lexington-Fayette, KY	3 832	348 428	108	90.9	305 725	37 212	561	4 037	893	3 117	6.9	13.2	17.0	19.0	16.0
4320	Lima, OH	2 087	154 340	184	74.0	140 402	12 379	252	749	558	1 483	7.7	15.8	14.1	16.0	14.5
4360	Lincoln, NE	2 173	213 641	152	98.3	202 663	4 659	1 207	3 367	1 745	3 938	7.1	13.3	19.1	18.3	15.3
4400	Little Rock-North Little Rock, AR	7 534	513 117	73	68.1	404 808	101 862	1 870	3 347	1 230	4 164	7.3	14.8	15.0	17.8	15.5
4420	Longview-Marshall, TX	3 038	162 431	176	53.5	122 270	35 975	670	635	2 881	5 053	7.4	16.0	14.2	15.9	14.3
4472	Los Angeles-Anaheim-Riverside, CA	87 970	14 531 529	2	165.2	9 388 957	1 229 809	87 487	1 339 048	2 486 228	4 779 118	8.4	14.2	15.9	19.6	15.1
0360	Anaheim-Santa Ana, CA	2 045	2 410 556	X	1 178.8	1 894 593	42 681	12 165	249 192	211 925	564 828	7.7	12.9	16.4	20.1	15.6
4480	Los Angeles-Long Beach, CA	10 515	8 863 164	X	842.9	5 035 103	992 974	45 508	954 485	1 835 094	3 351 242	8.3	13.9	16.3	19.8	15.1
6000	Oxnard-Ventura, CA	4 781	669 016	X	139.9	529 166	15 629	4 909	34 579	84 733	176 952	8.0	15.1	15.0	18.1	16.4
6780	Riverside-San Bernardino, CA	70 629	2 588 793	X	36.7	1 930 095	178 525	24 905	100 792	354 476	686 096	9.4	16.4	14.5	18.7	14.6

1. MSA = Metropolitan Statistical Area. CMSA = Consolidated MSA. NECMA = New England county metropolitan area. PMSA = Primary MSA. See Appendix A for explanation of these concepts. See Appendix B for list of metropolitan areas identified by type, with component counties. 2. Dry land or land partially or temporarily covered by water. 3. Hispanic persons may be of any race.

Table B. Metropolitan Areas — **Population and Households**

Area name	Population, 1990 (cont'd)					Population–change and components of change										Households, 1990
	Age of population (cont'd) Percent					Change, 1980–1990		Components of change, 1980–1986							
										Net change		Natural increase			
	45 to 54 years	55 to 64 years	65 to 74 years	75 years and over	Percent female	Number	Percent	Total persons, 1986	Total persons, 1980	Number	Percent	Births	Deaths	Net migration	Total
	16	17	18	19	20	21	22	23	24	25	26	27	28	29	30
Grand Forks, ND	7.1	5.7	4.7	4.1	48.9	4 583	6.9	69 400	66 100	3 400	5.1	8 700	2 400	-2 900	25 340
Grand Rapids, MI	9.2	7.3	5.9	4.6	51.3	86 719	14.4	648 800	601 680	47 100	7.8	70 900	27 800	4 000	244 404
Great Falls, MT	10.3	8.6	7.2	5.4	50.7	-3 005	-3.7	79 400	80 696	-1 300	-1.6	9 200	3 900	-6 600	30 133
Greeley, CO	9.6	7.2	5.7	4.5	50.6	8 383	6.8	135 000	123 438	11 500	9.3	14 200	5 000	2 300	47 470
Green Bay, WI	9.6	7.4	5.9	4.9	51.2	19 314	11.0	187 200	175 280	11 900	6.8	17 800	7 800	1 900	72 280
Greensboro-Winston-Salem-High Pt.,NC	11.2	9.2	7.2	5.0	52.2	90 647	10.6	899 400	851 444	48 200	5.7	69 500	43 900	22 600	372 141
Greenville-Spartanburg, SC	11.0	8.7	7.3	4.8	51.7	70 650	12.4	606 400	570 211	36 300	6.4	52 000	29 300	13 600	240 803
Hagerstown, MD	10.6	9.5	8.1	5.7	49.5	8 307	7.3	114 100	113 086	1 000	0.9	8 900	6 600	-1 300	44 762
Harrisburg-Lebanon-Carlisle, PA	10.6	9.5	8.1	5.8	51.7	31 744	5.7	577 300	556 242	20 900	3.8	46 600	32 600	6 900	226 353
Hartford-New Britain-Middletown, CT	10.7	8.9	7.7	5.7	51.6	72 072	6.9	1 083 400	1 051 606	31 900	3.0	86 300	55 100	700	423 651
Hickory, NC	11.8	9.5	7.4	4.8	51.2	18 989	9.4	217 700	202 711	15 000	7.4	16 300	10 000	8 700	85 215
Honolulu, HI	9.8	8.5	7.0	4.0	49.1	73 666	9.7	816 700	762 565	54 200	7.1	88 900	24 700	-10 000	265 304
Houma-Thibodaux, LA	9.8	7.6	5.4	3.3	51.1	5 966	3.4	189 100	176 876	12 300	7.0	24 600	7 600	-4 700	60 672
Houston-Galveston-Brazoria, TX	9.9	6.9	4.5	2.8	50.2	611 101	19.7	3 634 100	3 099 942	534 400	17.2	429 600	126 800	231 600	1 331 845
Brazoria, TX	10.3	7.6	4.8	3.0	48.1	22 120	13.0	188 700	169 587	19 100	11.3	21 400	6 400	4 100	64 019
Galveston-Texas City, TX	10.5	8.8	6.5	4.0	50.8	21 661	11.1	214 800	195 738	19 100	9.8	23 900	10 500	5 700	81 451
Houston, TX	9.9	6.7	4.4	2.7	50.3	567 320	20.7	3 230 600	2 734 617	496 200	18.1	384 300	109 900	221 800	1 186 375
Huntington-Ashland, WV-KY-OH	11.4	10.1	8.4	6.0	52.2	-23 881	-7.1	328 200	336 410	-8 100	-2.4	28 200	20 400	-15 900	119 640
Huntsville, AL	11.3	8.8	5.6	3.3	50.7	41 946	21.3	233 700	196 966	36 700	18.6	19 400	8 600	25 900	91 208
Indianapolis, IN	10.2	8.2	6.5	4.6	51.9	83 247	7.1	1 212 700	1 166 575	46 100	4.0	119 200	61 100	-12 000	480 010
Iowa City, IA	7.5	5.4	4.1	3.4	50.5	14 402	17.6	85 300	81 717	3 600	4.4	8 200	2 700	-1 900	36 067
Jackson, MI	10.3	8.8	7.2	5.1	49.2	-1 739	-1.1	144 400	151 495	-7 000	-4.6	13 300	7 800	-12 500	53 660
Jackson, MS	9.5	7.8	6.0	4.5	52.7	33 358	9.2	392 000	362 038	30 000	8.3	41 500	18 300	6 800	140 157
Jackson, TN	9.6	8.4	7.5	6.3	52.9	3 436	4.6	78 000	74 546	3 500	4.7	7 300	4 600	800	29 609
Jacksonville, FL	10.0	8.1	6.7	4.2	51.1	184 475	25.5	852 700	722 252	130 400	18.1	83 900	41 200	87 700	343 526
Jacksonville, NC	5.8	4.5	2.9	1.5	40.2	37 054	32.9	126 600	112 784	13 800	12.2	19 400	3 000	-2 600	40 658
Jamestown, NY	9.8	9.5	8.5	7.2	51.8	NA	NA	143 100	146 925	-3 700	-2.5	12 900	9 600	-7 000	53 696
Janesville-Beloit, WI	10.6	8.9	7.0	5.6	51.3	90	0.1	137 800	139 420	-1 600	-1.1	13 400	7 300	-7 700	52 252
Johnson City-Kingsport-Bristol,TN-VA	12.1	10.2	8.6	6.0	51.9	2 409	0.6	443 400	433 638	9 500	2.2	31 900	24 500	2 100	170 569
Johnstown, PA	9.8	10.7	10.8	7.3	52.0	-23 259	-8.8	254 100	264 506	-10 400	-3.9	20 500	17 200	-13 700	91 578
Joplin, MO	10.3	9.2	8.3	6.9	52.0	7 397	5.8	132 900	127 513	5 400	4.2	11 700	8 700	2 400	53 020
Kalamazoo, MI	9.8	7.6	6.0	4.6	51.9	11 033	5.2	217 700	212 378	5 300	2.5	20 000	9 400	-5 300	83 702
Kankakee, IL	10.1	8.6	7.9	5.8	51.6	-6 671	-6.5	98 000	102 926	-5 000	-4.9	10 300	5 600	-9 700	34 623
Kansas City, MO-KS	10.4	8.3	6.7	5.0	51.7	132 816	9.3	1 517 800	1 433 464	84 200	5.9	147 300	76 700	13 600	602 347
Killeen-Temple, TX	7.7	6.0	4.6	3.4	47.7	40 714	19.0	233 700	214 587	19 000	8.9	35 200	8 500	-7 700	83 927
Knoxville, TN	11.2	9.3	7.8	5.4	52.0	38 846	6.9	591 200	565 970	25 100	4.4	46 000	31 000	10 100	237 822
Kokomo, IN	12.1	9.5	7.1	5.1	52.1	-6 769	-6.5	101 400	103 715	-2 300	-2.2	9 400	5 200	-6 500	37 549
La Crosse, WI	8.9	7.6	6.8	6.0	52.0	6 848	7.5	94 100	91 056	3 000	3.3	8 700	4 900	-800	36 662
Lafayette, LA	9.1	7.4	5.1	3.4	51.5	18 509	9.7	218 000	190 231	27 800	14.6	26 700	7 900	9 000	75 045
Lafayette-West Lafayette, IN	8.1	6.4	5.4	4.1	49.3	8 896	7.3	124 400	121 702	2 600	2.1	10 900	5 100	-3 200	45 618
Lake Charles, LA	10.0	8.9	6.6	4.3	51.4	911	0.5	173 100	167 223	5 900	3.5	21 100	8 400	-6 800	60 328
Lakeland-Winter Haven, FL	10.0	10.3	11.3	7.3	51.5	83 730	26.0	377 200	321 652	55 500	17.3	33 700	21 500	43 300	155 969
Lancaster, PA	9.9	8.6	7.4	5.7	51.4	60 476	16.7	393 500	362 346	31 200	8.6	36 800	20 000	14 400	150 956
Lansing-East Lansing, MI	9.6	6.9	5.2	3.8	51.6	12 924	3.1	424 700	419 750	5 100	1.2	40 600	15 900	-19 600	156 887
Laredo, TX	8.1	6.5	4.6	3.3	52.0	33 981	34.2	120 800	99 258	21 500	21.7	17 100	3 900	8 300	34 438
Las Cruces, NM	8.6	7.5	5.5	3.3	50.3	39 170	40.7	123 000	96 340	26 600	27.6	12 900	3 500	17 200	NA
Las Vegas, NV	11.3	9.1	7.2	3.3	49.3	278 372	60.1	569 500	463 087	106 400	23.0	53 300	22 800	75 900	287 025
Lawrence, KS	7.3	5.5	4.4	3.7	50.2	14 158	20.9	72 600	67 640	5 000	7.4	6 100	2 400	1 300	30 138
Lawton, OK	8.4	7.1	5.2	3.5	48.1	-970	-0.9	120 700	112 456	8 200	7.3	16 400	4 400	-3 800	37 569
Lewiston-Auburn, ME	9.8	8.6	7.4	6.0	51.6	5 750	5.8	101 100	99 509	1 600	1.6	9 300	6 100	-1 600	40 017
Lexington-Fayette, KY	10.0	7.7	6.0	4.3	52.0	30 880	9.7	332 000	317 548	14 400	4.5	29 800	15 200	-200	134 077
Lima, OH	9.7	8.8	7.7	5.7	50.7	-455	-0.3	154 200	154 795	-600	-0.4	15 800	8 600	-7 800	55 384
Lincoln, NE	8.8	7.2	5.9	4.9	51.1	20 757	10.8	206 100	192 884	13 200	6.8	19 600	8 600	2 200	82 759
Little Rock-North Little Rock, AR	10.3	7.9	6.6	4.8	52.0	38 653	8.1	505 600	474 464	31 200	6.6	50 900	24 500	4 800	195 437
Longview-Marshall, TX	10.0	8.7	7.3	6.0	52.0	10 671	7.0	170 300	151 760	18 500	12.2	17 300	9 600	10 800	60 732
Los Angeles-Anaheim-Riverside, CA	9.6	7.3	5.8	4.0	50.0	3 033 980	26.4	13 074 800	11 497 549	1 577 300	13.7	1 375 000	568 200	770 500	4 900 720
Anaheim-Santa Ana, CA	10.6	7.5	5.4	3.8	49.6	477 635	24.7	2 166 800	1 932 921	233 900	12.1	213 000	79 700	100 600	827 066
Los Angeles-Long Beach, CA	9.5	7.3	5.7	4.0	50.1	1 385 925	18.5	8 295 900	7 477 239	818 700	10.9	894 400	377 100	301 400	2 989 552
Oxnard-Ventura, CA	10.7	7.4	5.5	3.9	49.6	139 842	26.4	611 000	529 174	81 800	15.5	61 800	21 100	41 100	217 298
Riverside-San Bernardino, CA	8.6	7.0	6.5	4.3	49.9	1 030 578	66.1	2 001 100	1 558 215	442 900	28.4	205 800	90 300	327 400	866 804

Area name	Households, (cont'd): Percent change, 1980–1990	Households, (cont'd): Percent: Female family householder[1]	Households, (cont'd): Percent: One-person	Births, 1988: Total	Births, 1988: Rate[2]	Births, 1988: Low birth weight[3] (Number)	Deaths, 1987: Number: Total	Deaths, 1987: Number: Infant[4]	Deaths, 1987: Rate: Total[2]	Deaths, 1987: Rate: Infant[5]	Marriages, 1984: Number	Marriages, 1984: Rate[2]	Divorces, 1984: Number	Divorces, 1984: Rate[2]	Physicians, active non-Federal, 1989: Number[6]	Physicians, active non-Federal, 1989: Rate[7]
	31	33	34	35	36	37	38	39	40	41	42	43	44	45	46	47
Grand Forks, ND	14.6	8.0	25.6	1 304	18.5	60	469	9	6.7	6.8	654	9.5	284	4.1	171	242
Grand Rapids, MI	18.6	10.3	21.4	12 072	18.1	670	4 884	120	7.5	10.1	6 542	10.5	2 153	3.5	1 171	174
Great Falls, MT	2.5	9.3	26.2	1 333	17.0	91	616	13	7.9	9.7	821	10.1	425	5.2	154	197
Greeley, CO	11.0	9.1	22.3	2 122	15.6	157	873	30	6.4	14.0	1 018	7.6	559	4.2	169	124
Green Bay, WI	20.7	9.0	24.1	2 848	14.9	125	1 218	25	6.5	8.6	1 730	9.4	621	3.4	284	147
Greensboro-Winston-Salem-High Pt.,NC	21.2	11.8	25.0	13 006	14.1	1 096	7 889	142	8.6	11.4	8 279	9.4	4 871	5.5	2 019	216
Greenville-Spartanburg, SC	21.9	12.0	23.5	9 190	14.8	782	5 144	114	8.4	13.2	7 118	12.0	2 982	5.0	1 056	168
Hagerstown, MD	12.0	9.7	23.6	1 547	13.1	122	1 073	18	9.2	11.8	1 831	16.2	424	3.8	166	140
Harrisburg-Lebanon-Carlisle, PA	12.5	9.6	25.3	7 795	13.2	473	5 467	80	9.4	10.4	4 737	8.3	1 963	3.4	1 323	222
Hartford-New Britain-Middletown, CT	13.9	11.6	24.4	16 071	14.5	1 094	9 369	151	8.5	9.5	9 064	8.5	3 990	3.7	3 317	298
Hickory, NC	19.7	10.5	22.2	2 962	13.3	216	1 705	33	7.8	11.1	1 665	7.9	1 102	5.2	285	127
Honolulu, HI	15.2	10.5	19.2	14 538	17.3	1 000	4 591	137	5.5	9.6	10 009	12.5	3 779	4.7	1 947	230
Houma-Thibodaux, LA	11.0	12.3	17.4	3 206	17.5	252	1 175	32	6.4	9.8	1 843	9.8	1 083	5.7	186	103
Houston-Galveston-Brazoria, TX	21.5	12.2	24.6	66 886	18.4	4 880	21 205	606	5.9	9.2	43 540	12.1	23 367	6.5	8 899	244
Brazoria, TX	18.8	8.6	18.5	3 078	16.7	193	1 093	21	5.9	6.4	2 263	12.2	1 278	6.9	152	83
Galveston-Texas City, TX	17.6	12.6	24.3	3 493	16.6	271	1 787	30	8.5	8.5	2 689	12.6	722	3.4	965	463
Houston, TX	21.9	12.3	24.9	60 315	18.6	4 416	18 325	555	5.7	9.4	38 588	12.1	21 367	6.7	7 782	239
Huntington-Ashland, WV-KY-OH	0.5	11.1	23.8	3 670	11.4	224	3 280	32	10.1	8.3	2 979	8.9	1 744	5.2	526	165
Huntsville, AL	36.0	10.5	24.0	3 722	15.7	228	1 519	30	6.6	8.6	3 059	13.9	1 701	7.7	386	162
Indianapolis, IN	14.7	11.7	25.5	20 088	16.2	1 475	10 227	243	8.3	12.5	12 484	10.5	8 126	6.8	3 431	274
Iowa City, IA	19.3	6.7	27.8	1 330	15.3	55	450	9	5.3	7.0	961	11.3	289	3.4	1 211	1 378
Jackson, MI	5.3	11.5	23.2	2 124	14.2	145	1 287	15	8.7	7.0	1 362	9.4	645	4.5	127	84
Jackson, MS	16.5	17.1	23.8	6 614	16.7	625	3 036	77	7.7	12.0	3 775	9.9	2 026	5.3	1 217	305
Jackson, TN	10.8	15.2	25.0	1 198	15.3	101	854	10	10.9	8.8	768	10.0	462	6.0	202	258
Jacksonville, FL	32.3	12.6	24.4	15 813	17.6	1 194	7 148	170	8.1	10.9	8 219	10.3	6 802	8.5	1 813	196
Jacksonville, NC	34.2	9.5	15.4	3 322	26.3	241	557	36	4.4	10.8	1 553	12.9	683	5.7	109	85
Jamestown, NY	1.7	10.3	26.1	1 943	13.8	102	1 639	13	11.6	6.8	1 364	9.4	566	3.9	163	116
Janesville-Beloit, WI	6.6	10.6	23.4	2 084	15.3	116	1 200	24	8.9	11.4	1 290	9.3	632	4.6	168	124
Johnson City-Kingsport-Bristol,TN-VA	10.6	10.1	23.4	5 016	11.3	324	4 291	45	9.7	9.0	5 056	11.4	2 559	5.8	853	193
Johnstown, PA	-0.4	9.8	25.7	2 822	11.3	163	2 896	28	11.5	10.0	1 817	7.0	620	2.4	384	154
Joplin, MO	9.5	9.1	25.7	1 875	13.8	95	1 411	12	10.5	6.4	1 339	10.2	761	5.8	153	112
Kalamazoo, MI	11.0	10.9	24.7	3 359	15.4	215	1 594	35	7.4	10.5	2 087	9.8	818	3.8	607	278
Kankakee, IL	-0.9	12.5	24.3	1 600	16.3	136	965	16	9.9	10.7	900	9.0	354	3.5	132	135
Kansas City, MO-KS	13.9	11.3	26.0	25 182	16.0	1 714	12 677	280	8.2	11.4	15 347	10.4	7 919	5.4	3 525	221
Killeen-Temple, TX	25.7	10.1	20.4	5 672	23.7	429	1 430	46	6.0	7.8	4 044	17.7	2 394	10.5	523	216
Knoxville, TN	15.6	10.8	25.0	7 553	12.6	528	5 399	78	9.1	10.5	7 001	11.9	3 985	6.8	1 226	203
Kokomo, IN	1.4	10.7	24.5	1 300	13.1	85	837	8	8.4	5.9	1 096	10.8	944	9.3	103	105
La Crosse, WI	14.5	8.9	26.1	1 362	14.3	71	859	16	9.1	11.7	821	8.7	364	3.9	326	339
Lafayette, LA	20.1	13.1	23.4	3 831	18.3	315	1 275	32	6.0	8.7	2 058	9.6	648	3.0	377	182
Lafayette-West Lafayette, IN	12.1	7.9	25.4	1 761	14.0	91	841	12	6.8	6.9	1 147	9.2	572	4.6	226	179
Lake Charles, LA	7.0	13.2	22.2	2 864	16.6	238	1 406	25	8.2	9.0	1 740	9.9	890	5.1	254	148
Lakeland-Winter Haven, FL	36.3	10.8	22.4	6 122	15.5	493	3 826	68	9.9	12.0	4 439	12.4	2 553	7.1	555	137
Lancaster, PA	21.9	7.9	20.9	6 890	16.6	352	3 467	54	8.6	8.3	3 105	8.1	1 220	3.2	558	132
Lansing-East Lansing, MI	9.7	11.1	24.0	6 370	14.9	404	2 661	60	6.3	9.1	4 092	9.9	1 661	4.0	742	172
Laredo, TX	33.0	17.6	12.7	3 263	25.3	215	699	25	5.6	8.0	1 630	13.9	3	0.0	101	76
Las Cruces, NM	NA	NA	NA	2 552	19.3	167	656	17	5.1	7.1	1 209	10.6	859	7.5	164	120
Las Vegas, NV	65.1	11.2	25.5	10 997	17.4	851	4 633	101	7.7	10.0	58 078	107.4	7 844	14.5	903	135
Lawrence, KS	26.5	7.6	27.0	1 041	13.6	68	413	5	5.5	5.0	706	10.1	385	5.5	104	133
Lawton, OK	6.9	12.1	20.4	2 267	19.0	163	724	13	6.0	5.6	1 566	12.9	936	7.7	121	102
Lewiston-Auburn, ME	13.6	10.9	24.4	1 564	15.1	90	1 035	13	10.2	8.6	1 019	10.1	611	6.1	191	183
Lexington-Fayette, KY	17.8	11.7	25.8	5 000	14.4	324	2 548	43	7.4	8.5	3 781	11.6	1 881	5.8	1 314	371
Lima, OH	3.1	10.5	22.8	2 453	15.7	143	1 403	21	9.0	8.5	1 446	9.4	691	4.5	202	128
Lincoln, NE	15.3	8.7	27.5	2 966	14.0	149	1 399	38	6.7	12.6	1 852	9.1	957	4.7	375	174
Little Rock-North Little Rock, AR	15.7	12.1	24.9	8 109	15.8	685	4 144	94	8.1	11.5	6 835	13.9	3 867	7.8	1 547	299
Longview-Marshall, TX	12.6	12.2	24.9	2 510	15.1	184	1 559	22	9.3	8.7	3 254	19.2	938	5.5	204	123
Los Angeles-Anaheim-Riverside, CA	18.3	12.0	23.0	276 991	20.1	16 869	99 411	2 456	7.4	9.4	111 418	8.9	61 006	4.9	34 061	241
Anaheim-Santa Ana, CA	20.5	9.7	20.7	42 287	18.7	2 096	14 155	295	6.4	7.5	19 486	9.3	12 335	5.9	5 911	256
Los Angeles-Long Beach, CA	9.5	13.1	25.0	175 332	20.4	11 088	64 118	1 630	7.6	9.8	71 257	8.9	34 368	4.3	23 363	267
Oxnard-Ventura, CA	25.8	9.8	17.5	11 481	17.7	566	3 769	80	6.0	7.4	5 294	9.0	3 303	5.6	1 139	171
Riverside-San Bernardino, CA	57.1	11.0	19.7	47 891	21.0	3 119	17 369	451	8.1	10.5	15 381	8.5	11 000	6.1	3 648	151

1. No spouse present. 2. Per 1,000 resident population estimated as of July 1 of the year shown. 3. Under 2,500 grams. 4. Deaths of infants under 1 year old. 5. Deaths of infants under 1 year old per 1,000 live births. 6. As of end of year. 7. Per 100,000 resident population as of July 1 of the year shown.

Area name	Hospitals, 1989			Nursing homes,[2] 1986		Serious crimes known to police, 1988			Education						Social Security Program December 1988	
		Beds				Number			Public school enrollment[6]		Attainment,[7] 1980		Local government expenditures for education,[8] 1982		Beneficiaries	
	Number	Number	Rate[1]	Number	Beds	Total[3]	Violent[4]	Rate[5]	1986–1987	1980	Percent 12 years or more	Percent 16 years or more	Total (Mil dol)	Per capita (Dollars)	Total	Rate[9]
	48	49	50	51	52	53	54	55	56	57	58	59	60	61	62	63
Grand Forks, ND	5	582	823	6	678	2 974	43	4 218	11 120	11 248	76.2	22.6	29.2	434	7 425	105.3
Grand Rapids, MI	12	2 637	391	166	7 154	33 421	3 188	5 024	106 692	110 714	70.4	15.9	296.2	943	92 105	138.5
Great Falls, MT	2	610	782	3	578	4 890	164	6 253	13 865	15 966	75.2	17.4	40.6	507	12 690	162.3
Greeley, CO	1	281	206	14	872	7 971	636	5 852	22 127	24 920	68.8	16.8	58.7	464	16 430	120.6
Green Bay, WI	4	1 037	536	19	1 693	7 298	395	3 817	30 261	32 812	73.9	14.5	85.3	475	26 355	137.8
Greensboro-Winston-Salem-High Pt.,NC	19	3 629	388	116	6 117	45 587	4 925	4 930	147 204	167 211	57.4	15.1	337.2	2 643	143 160	154.8
Greenville-Spartanburg, SC	18	2 682	427	55	3 009	37 444	4 587	6 026	102 317	111 215	53.0	14.1	228.5	1 089	100 845	162.3
Hagerstown, MD	3	519	437	11	1 032	2 925	264	2 483	17 296	21 724	59.8	9.5	48.6	440	19 325	164.0
Harrisburg-Lebanon-Carlisle, PA	14	3 683	617	55	5 741	17 390	1 730	2 942	90 602	100 623	68.3	14.4	238.7	1 637	93 905	158.9
Hartford-New Britain-Middletown, CT	24	5 950	534	120	11 461	52 074	4 876	4 698	157 562	193 468	70.8	20.3	524.8	1 429	174 725	157.6
Hickory, NC	7	1 733	771	28	1 208	7 714	877	3 473	37 380	41 862	48.8	9.9	74.8	1 065	35 365	159.2
Honolulu, HI	15	3 176	375	147	2 880	49 469	2 186	5 900	164 336	126 860	75.6	21.7	0.0	0	100 455	119.8
Houma-Thibodaux, LA	6	761	420	9	1 142	4 821	750	2 633	37 739	38 038	49.5	9.8	90.6	959	25 440	138.9
Houston-Galveston-Brazoria, TX	87	18 697	512	101	12 329	290 957	27 976	7 990	778 711	623 411	69.3	21.5	1 671.4	3 689	337 300	92.6
Brazoria, TX	5	335	182	10	1 101	7 548	464	4 089	39 296	37 365	65.2	13.6	90.1	503	19 575	106.0
Galveston-Texas City, TX	6	1 575	755	10	1 067	15 601	1 251	7 429	103 819	39 143	65.3	15.4	131.9	633	28 715	136.7
Houston, TX	76	16 787	515	81	10 161	267 808	26 261	8 248	635 596	546 903	69.9	22.5	1 449.4	2 553	289 010	89.0
Huntington-Ashland, WV-KY-OH	9	1 822	570	50	1 787	NA	NA	0	61 620	68 231	56.9	9.8	133.0	2 334	58 170	180.5
Huntsville, AL	5	1 068	447	8	610	14 974	1 025	6 326	37 098	40 061	70.1	21.4	70.2	346	26 165	110.5
Indianapolis, IN	25	6 620	529	102	10 674	55 015	6 967	4 449	204 879	227 852	69.4	15.9	506.5	3 233	177 915	143.9
Iowa City, IA	4	1 443	1 642	6	434	5 144	443	5 933	10 420	11 618	85.6	38.6	28.0	334	8 125	93.7
Jackson, MI	2	491	325	59	1 299	7 415	1 226	4 960	24 355	30 208	69.2	12.2	65.9	444	24 225	162.0
Jackson, MS	16	4 873	1 222	24	2 039	18 435	1 791	4 653	66 256	65 072	67.3	20.8	114.5	904	54 425	137.4
Jackson, TN	3	861	1 098	11	600	5 416	772	6 926	13 979	14 291	57.6	12.8	11.1	146	13 825	176.8
Jacksonville, FL	19	3 537	383	71	4 945	NA	NA	0	139 811	138 139	67.0	14.1	323.9	1 797	119 090	132.6
Jacksonville, NC	3	379	297	12	423	5 786	649	4 574	16 511	18 659	66.4	11.4	27.3	236	8 795	69.5
Jamestown, NY	4	567	404	19	1 458	4 956	206	3 507	25 829	28 812	65.8	11.8	85.7	586	29 320	207.5
Janesville-Beloit, WI	6	541	398	12	1 689	6 746	300	4 949	24 906	29 380	71.1	12.4	69.2	498	22 635	166.1
Johnson City-Kingsport-Bristol,TN-VA	13	2 563	580	47	3 227	11 691	692	2 643	77 007	87 781	51.6	11.1	147.6	2 644	82 580	186.7
Johnstown, PA	9	1 553	625	23	2 041	3 664	394	1 462	40 072	47 492	60.1	8.2	103.4	778	54 650	218.1
Joplin, MO	5	739	540	25	1 402	5 200	308	3 824	23 919	24 407	62.3	10.5	46.8	688	26 280	193.2
Kalamazoo, MI	4	1 512	691	75	2 044	15 354	1 901	7 046	32 858	38 583	75.8	23.0	96.7	452	30 105	138.2
Kankakee, IL	2	556	569	11	1 197	5 351	694	5 466	17 609	20 484	61.0	10.6	42.7	418	17 645	180.2
Kansas City, MO-KS	49	9 317	583	163	11 294	108 516	12 920	6 888	250 488	262 839	73.6	17.9	588.7	4 156	218 565	138.7
Killeen-Temple, TX	7	1 577	652	19	1 766	12 327	855	5 145	45 412	38 349	68.3	15.0	74.5	598	24 375	101.7
Knoxville, TN	14	3 570	592	31	3 348	21 287	1 953	3 550	100 333	107 332	59.8	15.6	186.8	2 133	101 970	170.1
Kokomo, IN	3	485	493	8	871	3 013	223	3 047	19 025	22 833	68.3	10.5	46.3	915	16 025	162.0
La Crosse, WI	2	625	650	10	1 240	4 157	123	4 353	13 384	14 377	73.5	17.3	33.5	360	15 205	159.2
Lafayette, LA	10	1 150	554	13	1 575	10 624	1 088	5 069	37 378	36 215	59.1	17.7	109.2	1 086	24 095	115.0
Lafayette-West Lafayette, IN	5	770	611	11	1 591	4 501	157	3 589	16 871	18 627	76.8	25.5	41.1	332	15 185	121.1
Lake Charles, LA	7	868	506	11	1 539	11 388	1 226	6 606	32 819	33 968	58.5	13.6	86.4	494	26 405	153.2
Lakeland-Winter Haven, FL	8	1 519	375	39	2 564	NA	NA	0	59 233	60 487	59.8	11.4	142.1	417	80 120	202.4
Lancaster, PA	5	1 281	303	52	4 460	10 532	748	2 543	54 002	61 003	59.6	13.0	151.8	409	63 245	152.7
Lansing-East Lansing, MI	7	1 586	368	89	2 329	22 389	2 317	5 226	75 617	84 128	77.3	21.7	211.7	1 381	51 285	119.7
Laredo, TX	3	451	340	2	328	10 847	796	8 415	30 552	26 940	41.5	9.8	61.5	557	13 885	107.7
Las Cruces, NM	2	357	261	9	379	8 290	406	6 280	26 355	21 759	65.1	19.3	58.3	564	15 325	116.1
Las Vegas, NV	12	2 171	325	28	1 478	42 896	4 917	6 795	95 416	87 481	74.0	12.6	210.5	413	87 590	138.7
Lawrence, KS	1	200	255	7	497	4 862	230	6 356	9 535	9 215	82.3	35.1	20.5	296	7 695	100.6
Lawton, OK	4	546	458	8	632	6 426	555	5 386	22 307	22 417	73.3	15.1	46.6	388	11 905	99.8
Lewiston-Auburn, ME	3	547	524	34	1 416	5 008	195	4 848	17 151	19 857	58.5	10.5	32.6	327	18 975	183.7
Lexington-Fayette, KY	14	3 380	954	40	2 014	NA	NA	0	52 860	54 722	66.3	20.9	101.6	1 864	44 165	126.9
Lima, OH	5	853	541	18	1 721	7 825	1 212	4 994	29 778	31 127	67.4	9.6	68.3	853	26 355	168.2
Lincoln, NE	6	1 471	685	19	1 622	14 612	878	6 905	29 320	30 003	81.5	23.9	75.1	378	27 295	129.0
Little Rock-North Little Rock, AR	16	4 670	903	42	4 306	38 387	4 516	7 481	87 292	90 402	68.2	16.4	168.9	1 263	74 170	144.6
Longview-Marshall, TX	6	532	321	14	1 597	10 675	799	6 408	34 957	30 666	62.4	13.7	83.8	983	28 350	170.2
Los Angeles-Anaheim-Riverside, CA	261	54 302	384	1 389	80 888	913 633	157 376	6 635	2 260 277	2 042 777	71.9	18.4	5 445.7	2 306	1 518 680	110.3
Anaheim-Santa Ana, CA	41	6 931	301	147	9 651	131 837	10 643	5 841	378 000	359 838	80.4	22.6	876.4	434	241 775	107.1
Los Angeles-Long Beach, CA	169	36 881	421	919	58 377	594 139	120 668	6 918	1 368 386	1 276 117	69.8	18.5	3 513.2	456	885 925	103.2
Oxnard-Ventura, CA	11	2 845	428	67	2 756	22 469	2 345	3 471	108 831	110 075	75.9	18.2	272.9	488	73 130	113.0
Riverside-San Bernardino, CA	40	7 645	316	256	10 104	165 188	23 720	7 253	405 060	296 747	70.1	13.0	783.2	928	317 850	139.6

1. Per 100,000 resident population estimated as of July 1 of the year shown. 2. Covers nursing homes with 3 or more beds. 3. Data for serious crimes have not been adjusted for underreporting, this may affect comparability between geographic areas or over time. 4. Includes murder and nonnegligent manslaughter, forcible rape, robbery, and aggravated assault. 5. Per 100,000 resident population as of July 1 of the year shown. 6. The 1986–1987 data are based on administrative reports obtained by the U.S. National Center for Education Statistics. The 1980 data are based on the 1980 Census of Population and Housing. 7. Persons 25 years old or older. 8. Elementary and secondary. 9. Per 1,000 resident population estimated as of July 1 of the year shown.

Area name	Social Security Program, Dec. 1988 (cont'd)		Housing units, 1990				Civilian labor force, 1990				Private nonfarm establishments, 1988			
					Occupied units				Unemployment				Employment[2]	
	Payments ($1,000)	Supplemental Security Income Program recipients, June 1986	Total	Percent change, 1980–1990	Total	Percent owner-occupied	Total	Percent change, 1989–1990	Total	Rate[1]	Number	Net change, 1987–1988	Total	Percent change, 1987–1988
	64	65	72	73	74	75	78	79	80	81	82	83	84	85
Grand Forks, ND	3 615	490	27 085	10.3	25 340	48.7	35 804	-1.0	1 304	3.6	1 687	27	20 908	2.3
Grand Rapids, MI	48 071	6 656	259 322	18.3	244 404	72.5	377 513	0.9	22 868	6.1	16 629	493	309 410	2.5
Great Falls, MT	6 177	1 006	33 063	2.7	30 133	63.7	39 658	0.5	1 982	5.0	2 305	-17	22 313	-4.5
Greeley, CO	7 577	1 564	51 138	10.0	47 470	61.2	71 008	5.8	3 498	4.9	2 718	-59	34 501	3.0
Green Bay, WI	13 334	2 290	74 740	20.0	72 280	65.6	111 384	0.2	4 362	3.9	4 840	36	86 827	-0.4
Greensboro-Winston-Salem-High Pt.,NC	68 896	12 924	399 004	21.2	372 141	67.3	521 027	0.0	19 402	3.7	24 221	623	447 921	4.9
Greenville-Spartanburg, SC	47 749	11 140	257 437	21.4	240 803	68.4	343 080	1.3	13 535	3.9	15 553	342	306 823	3.9
Hagerstown, MD	9 605	1 404	47 448	11.9	44 762	63.8	60 964	1.8	4 078	6.7	2 737	60	40 582	1.6
Harrisburg-Lebanon-Carlisle, PA	47 129	5 330	241 489	11.6	226 353	68.8	332 446	0.4	14 511	4.4	13 394	239	237 328	3.9
Hartford-New Britain-Middletown, CT	95 217	10 264	450 082	15.4	423 651	64.7	621 291	1.6	29 451	4.7	30 712	762	559 442	0.1
Hickory, NC	16 469	3 158	91 964	18.4	85 215	74.7	131 115	-0.1	5 384	4.1	5 669	168	114 838	4.2
Honolulu, HI	47 849	9 002	281 683	11.8	265 304	52.0	391 387	2.0	9 999	2.6	20 395	383	297 324	4.5
Houma-Thibodaux, LA	11 118	3 758	66 748	15.4	60 672	74.4	69 110	-0.6	3 846	5.6	3 856	-102	42 744	7.4
Houston-Galveston-Brazoria, TX	170 228	36 288	1 529 776	22.6	1 331 845	56.1	1 920 153	2.1	101 797	5.3	83 959	-396	1 346 228	1.6
Brazoria, TX	9 922	1 524	74 504	23.2	64 019	69.2	87 156	1.1	4 819	5.5	3 171	-91	45 459	-0.7
Galveston-Texas City, TX	14 434	2 660	99 451	19.9	81 451	62.0	109 581	-0.6	7 797	7.1	4 025	-53	52 528	-4.0
Houston, TX	145 872	32 104	1 355 821	22.8	1 186 375	54.9	1 723 416	2.3	89 181	5.2	76 763	-252	1 248 241	1.9
Huntington-Ashland, WV-KY-OH	26 337	8 554	130 687	2.0	119 640	72.0	132 086	1.6	9 126	6.9	6 188	50	79 607	2.5
Huntsville, AL	10 869	4 010	97 855	37.6	91 208	65.1	133 346	-0.2	6 227	4.7	5 534	181	87 676	2.9
Indianapolis, IN	92 498	11 300	517 893	14.8	480 010	63.8	670 671	-3.3	28 018	4.2	30 739	799	537 072	4.9
Iowa City, IA	4 335	462	37 210	17.8	36 067	52.7	61 922	-0.1	1 020	1.6	1 997	13	25 941	6.3
Jackson, MI	12 725	1 922	57 979	4.0	53 660	73.7	65 723	-0.8	5 159	7.8	2 953	67	44 890	-0.3
Jackson, MS	23 947	11 288	152 493	17.7	140 157	65.7	201 631	1.2	10 597	5.3	9 711	-52	144 818	5.4
Jackson, TN	6 004	2 590	31 809	10.3	29 609	65.4	39 656	2.4	1 972	5.0	2 145	42	30 263	4.8
Jacksonville, FL	55 432	12 998	384 360	33.7	343 526	64.8	459 747	1.7	25 416	5.5	23 184	557	343 162	4.5
Jacksonville, NC	3 495	1 246	47 526	34.1	40 658	53.7	39 146	1.9	1 543	3.9	2 135	63	20 418	0.9
Jamestown, NY	14 803	2 330	62 682	2.9	53 696	68.6	65 040	-0.8	3 508	5.4	3 272	36	43 750	-0.5
Janesville-Beloit, WI	11 777	2 244	54 840	5.3	52 252	68.2	74 176	-1.2	3 904	5.3	3 038	40	50 000	3.2
Johnson City-Kingsport-Bristol,TN-VA	36 252	12 312	183 995	10.3	170 569	73.7	219 924	1.3	10 041	4.6	8 736	74	138 776	2.3
Johnstown, PA	26 246	4 122	103 087	2.5	91 578	74.6	97 762	1.0	7 472	7.6	5 204	65	64 244	1.4
Joplin, MO	12 015	2 186	57 938	10.8	53 020	71.7	71 747	1.3	3 921	5.5	3 546	22	52 011	7.1
Kalamazoo, MI	15 939	2 838	88 955	11.5	83 702	64.4	120 051	-0.4	6 161	5.1	5 131	93	92 096	0.2
Kankakee, IL	8 833	1 750	37 001	-1.6	34 623	66.8	47 600	2.8	3 388	7.1	1 935	-1	27 329	0.9
Kansas City, MO-KS	112 229	13 652	657 351	15.3	602 347	65.4	852 499	0.4	42 268	5.0	40 249	555	649 975	1.0
Killeen-Temple, TX	10 103	2 674	94 927	25.4	83 927	52.1	96 870	0.2	6 848	7.1	3 993	-69	49 820	-5.0
Knoxville, TN	47 482	13 194	260 970	16.5	237 822	68.7	287 597	-0.4	14 244	5.0	15 632	195	220 268	5.4
Kokomo, IN	8 384	806	40 247	2.2	37 549	72.8	47 589	-1.7	3 079	6.5	2 120	-12	38 029	-1.6
La Crosse, WI	7 485	1 492	38 239	14.9	36 662	62.9	52 593	-4.6	1 980	3.8	2 557	52	44 192	3.2
Lafayette, LA	9 940	5 228	85 023	27.2	75 045	64.9	104 456	2.7	4 915	4.7	5 576	-165	69 184	5.5
Lafayette-West Lafayette, IN	7 973	656	48 134	11.6	45 618	57.1	68 642	-1.1	1 967	2.9	2 610	29	44 580	1.8
Lake Charles, LA	12 245	3 640	66 426	9.2	60 328	70.4	77 844	1.8	5 048	6.5	3 610	-40	46 818	-0.1
Lakeland-Winter Haven, FL	38 396	5 464	186 225	38.1	155 969	70.5	182 628	1.6	17 738	9.7	8 906	191	130 560	8.2
Lancaster, PA	33 192	3 424	156 462	20.9	150 956	69.4	227 715	0.8	9 428	4.1	9 671	333	175 369	5.1
Lansing-East Lansing, MI	26 632	4 196	165 018	10.4	156 887	64.7	241 147	-0.3	14 594	6.1	8 853	112	144 746	0.8
Laredo, TX	4 600	5 092	37 197	34.0	34 438	60.6	53 159	2.1	5 727	10.8	2 489	80	26 818	5.6
Las Cruces, NM	6 353	2 092	NA	NA	NA	NA	59 168	1.5	3 961	6.7	2 460	127	24 754	5.1
Las Vegas, NV	44 298	5 672	317 188	66.4	287 025	51.9	385 330	7.1	19 043	4.9	14 470	812	270 247	6.6
Lawrence, KS	3 954	422	31 782	24.7	30 138	52.5	44 397	3.9	1 617	3.6	1 813	27	21 742	6.3
Lawton, OK	5 063	1 270	43 589	9.1	37 569	60.2	48 298	-0.6	2 625	5.4	2 026	-47	21 588	1.8
Lewiston-Auburn, ME	8 691	2 224	43 815	14.2	40 017	62.2	50 499	2.1	3 519	7.0	2 741	38	39 707	6.7
Lexington-Fayette, KY	20 321	5 380	145 229	18.4	134 077	57.8	199 227	0.3	7 260	3.6	9 551	281	147 284	6.3
Lima, OH	13 014	1 412	59 665	4.0	55 384	73.2	77 723	-0.8	5 259	6.8	3 668	18	60 664	1.4
Lincoln, NE	14 081	1 564	86 734	13.6	82 759	60.5	130 100	4.4	2 160	1.7	5 466	111	86 332	5.6
Little Rock-North Little Rock, AR	33 656	9 582	214 546	18.6	195 437	64.8	268 713	-0.1	15 879	5.9	13 178	98	190 132	3.2
Longview-Marshall, TX	13 265	3 558	68 170	14.0	60 732	67.3	79 634	-0.9	5 493	6.9	4 718	-112	56 526	2.3
Los Angeles-Anaheim-Riverside, CA	771 304	331 754	5 293 072	19.6	4 900 720	54.0	7 256 906	3.3	392 840	5.4	341 763	6 872	5 479 860	3.2
Anaheim-Santa Ana, CA	128 104	29 616	875 072	21.3	827 066	60.1	1 382 849	-1.9	46 443	3.4	68 128	1 607	1 098 300	3.3
Los Angeles-Long Beach, CA	452 837	240 902	3 163 343	10.8	2 989 552	48.2	4 428 000	4.9	255 000	5.8	216 117	3 146	3 628 164	2.3
Oxnard-Ventura, CA	36 058	10 114	228 478	24.6	217 298	65.5	374 422	0.6	20 768	5.5	14 332	537	186 813	5.7
Riverside-San Bernardino, CA	154 305	51 122	1 026 179	54.3	866 804	65.2	1 071 635	4.7	70 629	6.6	43 186	1 582	566 583	8.0

1. Percent of total civilian labor force. 2. For week including March 12. Excludes government employees, self-employed persons, farm workers, domestic service workers, railroad employees subject to the Railroad Retirement Act, and employees on oceanborne vessels or in foreign countries.

Table B. Metropolitan Areas — **Employment and Personal Income**

Area name	Private nonfarm establishments, 1987 (cont'd): Employment[1] (cont'd): Manufacturing	Employment[1] (cont'd): Retail trade	Employment[1] (cont'd): Finance, insurance, and real estate	Employment[1] (cont'd): Services	Annual payroll: Total (Mil dol)	Annual payroll: Average per employee	Personal income, 1989: Total (Mil dol)	Percent change, 1988–1989	Wages and salaries[2] (Mil dol)	Propri-etor's income (Mil dol)	Dividends, Interest, & rent (Mil dol)	Transfer payments (Mil dol)	Per capita[3]: Dollars	Per capita[3]: Rank (Dollars)
	86	87	88	89	90	91	92	93	94	95	96	97	98	99
Grand Forks, ND	1 766	6 630	1 137	7 333	330	15 783	956	8.0	683	93	135	138	13 521	244
Grand Rapids, MI	100 649	61 803	15 016	77 989	6 685	21 606	11 983	8.3	8 915	916	1 956	1 383	17 766	64
Great Falls, MT	906	6 614	1 834	7 884	355	15 910	1 245	7.7	674	151	238	227	15 962	125
Greeley, CO	8 440	7 269	3 057	7 596	698	20 231	1 943	6.9	1 027	223	303	269	14 230	212
Green Bay, WI	23 042	18 956	4 861	22 499	1 771	20 397	3 216	7.3	2 367	252	500	385	16 609	102
Greensboro-Winston-Salem-High Pt.,NC	156 446	84 003	30 915	91 409	8 574	19 142	16 513	7.2	11 996	1 340	2 643	1 841	17 652	70
Greenville-Spartanburg, SC	103 745	52 950	13 807	65 413	5 798	18 897	9 874	8.4	7 523	705	1 339	1 232	15 707	139
Hagerstown, MD	10 445	8 957	1 768	9 362	747	18 407	1 881	7.5	1 221	105	312	299	15 828	132
Harrisburg-Lebanon-Carlisle, PA	52 139	50 864	19 565	64 287	4 661	19 639	10 040	8.3	7 585	749	1 731	1 613	16 830	96
Hartford-New Britain-Middletown, CT	126 884	101 878	83 543	149 694	13 758	24 592	26 407	7.0	20 066	1 574	4 693	2 919	23 695	8
Hickory, NC	66 274	18 207	2 267	13 682	1 913	16 658	3 377	7.2	2 624	289	457	421	15 032	180
Honolulu, HI	16 613	79 379	28 088	101 289	5 905	19 860	16 251	10.5	11 488	1 098	2 408	2 043	19 171	33
Houma-Thibodaux, LA	3 895	11 384	2 775	8 276	732	17 125	2 147	5.0	1 199	197	344	353	11 850	275
Houston-Galveston-Brazoria, TX	184 943	267 288	109 206	386 061	32 617	24 228	64 063	8.9	46 842	5 349	9 606	5 898	17 538	75
Brazoria, TX	13 917	9 983	1 730	8 720	1 142	25 122	3 139	7.5	1 804	217	391	299	17 099	X
Galveston-Texas City, TX	8 406	15 449	4 507	14 031	995	18 942	3 545	8.3	1 872	199	512	474	16 995	X
Houston, TX	162 620	241 856	102 969	363 310	30 480	24 418	57 379	9.1	43 165	4 933	8 704	5 125	17 598	X
Huntington-Ashland, WV-KY-OH	16 884	21 049	4 019	19 858	1 553	19 508	4 073	5.9	2 523	272	596	904	12 755	261
Huntsville, AL	25 188	19 531	3 519	26 785	1 884	21 488	4 201	8.6	3 712	226	495	557	17 577	73
Indianapolis, IN	107 035	117 059	46 560	148 506	11 311	21 060	22 623	7.9	16 576	1 679	3 347	2 692	18 080	56
Iowa City, IA	3 764	9 010	1 464	8 457	385	14 841	1 572	9.9	1 131	150	230	149	17 890	61
Jackson, MI	13 183	10 753	1 868	11 046	928	20 673	2 261	6.8	1 344	117	384	376	14 950	187
Jackson, MS	19 872	30 368	14 397	43 124	2 576	17 788	5 775	7.9	3 980	518	810	839	14 479	203
Jackson, TN	8 807	7 168	1 363	7 283	542	17 910	1 102	7.1	857	109	166	196	14 062	218
Jacksonville, FL	35 620	81 777	39 269	96 470	6 457	18 816	14 964	7.9	10 575	820	2 144	2 148	16 215	114
Jacksonville, NC	2 842	8 628	1 044	4 188	242	11 852	1 554	7.9	1 264	116	102	214	12 157	272
Jamestown, NY	15 020	9 310	1 381	11 480	756	17 280	2 075	7.5	1 177	164	378	441	14 778	193
Janesville-Beloit, WI	18 240	10 997	1 700	11 522	1 014	20 280	2 194	6.2	1 389	188	333	334	16 140	115
Johnson City-Kingsport-Bristol,TN-VA	52 337	29 264	5 567	29 185	2 578	18 577	5 913	6.9	3 799	535	876	1 045	13 385	249
Johnstown, PA	13 120	14 416	4 634	17 594	1 103	17 169	3 300	7.5	1 690	320	595	859	13 276	252
Joplin, MO	17 419	11 277	1 577	11 175	836	16 074	1 817	5.9	1 119	227	329	336	13 285	251
Kalamazoo, MI	29 212	19 754	4 888	26 855	2 079	22 574	3 895	7.6	2 979	231	673	531	17 807	63
Kankakee, IL	6 732	6 055	1 453	8 441	503	18 405	1 474	6.5	770	134	251	281	15 078	173
Kansas City, MO-KS	114 394	133 845	57 634	189 722	13 663	21 021	28 612	6.3	19 828	2 350	4 852	3 423	17 899	60
Killeen-Temple, TX	7 691	14 477	3 136	15 649	745	14 954	3 186	5.8	2 182	231	382	527	13 179	255
Knoxville, TN	49 372	53 009	NA	65 486	4 121	18 709	9 111	6.4	5 940	871	1 424	1 413	15 110	171
Kokomo, IN	17 838	8 630	1 318	6 673	1 019	26 795	1 679	7.8	1 435	120	233	222	17 069	92
La Crosse, WI	10 295	11 132	1 648	13 201	797	18 035	1 550	7.3	1 140	117	265	238	16 127	117
Lafayette, LA	6 865	16 844	3 571	18 795	1 283	18 545	2 935	5.8	2 053	326	474	387	14 154	216
Lafayette-West Lafayette, IN	12 034	12 303	3 316	11 625	838	18 798	1 936	9.3	1 465	155	340	239	15 366	155
Lake Charles, LA	10 082	11 209	2 891	12 388	922	19 693	2 267	5.8	1 523	184	355	396	13 202	254
Lakeland-Winter Haven, FL	21 720	34 109	9 217	33 078	2 198	16 835	5 768	8.9	3 341	566	1 218	1 015	14 246	211
Lancaster, PA	61 042	35 892	7 599	37 349	3 424	19 525	7 467	8.7	4 540	744	1 324	862	17 645	71
Lansing-East Lansing, MI	32 183	38 353	11 495	38 769	3 206	22 149	7 186	7.5	5 329	389	1 042	1 015	16 659	101
Laredo, TX	1 515	9 115	1 837	6 517	349	13 014	1 066	10.5	702	100	103	239	8 043	281
Las Cruces, NM	2 585	7 181	1 759	7 623	346	13 978	1 419	9.1	826	118	237	291	10 389	279
Las Vegas, NV	8 604	52 958	13 012	143 088	5 065	18 742	12 378	15.0	8 651	633	1 881	1 678	18 508	47
Lawrence, KS	4 429	6 784	999	6 126	332	15 270	1 087	8.9	647	93	200	129	13 886	229
Lawton, OK	3 260	7 126	1 742	5 383	326	15 101	1 424	3.9	968	116	147	285	11 945	274
Lewiston-Auburn, ME	11 811	8 438	2 308	10 385	655	16 496	1 642	8.8	897	122	240	279	15 731	137
Lexington-Fayette, KY	29 552	34 366	9 306	39 741	2 831	19 221	5 938	7.9	4 193	767	955	702	16 760	99
Lima, OH	21 551	13 219	2 266	14 863	1 211	19 962	2 413	5.9	1 695	172	397	461	15 301	163
Lincoln, NE	14 675	21 278	9 416	25 541	1 468	17 004	3 452	8.6	2 442	323	541	427	16 067	120
Little Rock-North Little Rock, AR	31 967	41 887	15 110	58 196	3 428	18 030	8 101	7.4	5 652	662	1 071	1 257	15 657	142
Longview-Marshall, TX	15 107	13 018	2 678	12 643	1 051	18 593	2 386	6.2	1 538	268	470	400	14 405	206
Los Angeles-Anaheim-Riverside, CA	1 268 031	1 035 741	426 014	1 636 283	130 043	23 731	283 106	8.2	191 103	25 065	46 653	34 444	20 004	24
Anaheim-Santa Ana, CA	251 736	217 890	98 506	303 982	26 178	23 835	56 000	8.9	35 398	4 594	9 339	4 895	24 288	X
Los Angeles-Long Beach, CA	891 105	622 070	285 731	1 124 051	89 414	24 644	174 366	7.7	131 725	16 244	29 841	21 908	19 906	X
Oxnard-Ventura, CA	33 248	46 346	12 960	52 681	3 870	20 716	13 396	7.9	6 401	1 197	1 928	1 456	20 156	X
Riverside-San Bernardino, CA	91 942	149 435	28 817	155 569	10 581	18 675	39 344	9.6	17 580	3 030	5 546	6 185	16 238	X

1. For week including March 12. Excludes government employees, self-employed persons, farm workers, domestic service workers, railroad employees subject to the Railroad Retirement Act, and employees on oceanborne vessels or in foreign countries. 2. Includes other labor income. 3. Based on the resident population estimated as of July 1 of the year shown.

Area name	Earnings, 1989: Total (Mil. dol)	Earnings, 1989: Percent by selected industries: Farm	Goods-related[1]: Total	Goods-related[1]: Manufacturing	Service-related & other[2]: Total	Service-related & other[2]: Retail trade	Service-related & other[2]: Finance, insurance, & real estate	Service-related & other[2]: Services	Government	Agriculture, 1987: Farms: Number	Farms: Percent with Less than 50 acres	Farms: Percent with 500 acres and over	Farm operators, Percent: Whose principal occupation is farming	Farm operators, Percent: Residing on farm operated	Land in farms: Acreage (1,000)	Land in farms: Percent change, 1982–1987	Acres: Average size of farm	Acres: Total irrigated (1,000)	Acres: Total cropland (1,000)
	100	101	102	103	104	105	106	107	108	109	110	111	112	113	114	115	116	117	118
Grand Forks, ND	777	4.7	9.4	4.1	48.3	11.0	3.5	20.0	37.7	893	7.6	59.9	80.3	72.3	808	-5.5	904	5	740
Grand Rapids, MI	9 831	0.9	42.2	35.2	48.6	10.4	4.3	20.9	8.4	2 839	42.0	5.0	48.2	82.1	382	-6.1	134	18	309
Great Falls, MT	825	2.9	9.1	3.2	61.5	12.8	5.3	28.8	26.5	805	18.4	50.2	66.8	76.1	1 461	4.9	1 815	32	485
Greeley, CO	1 250	6.6	32.6	23.5	45.5	8.8	4.5	18.8	15.3	2 975	25.7	24.4	66.7	77.3	2 105	6.2	708	359	957
Green Bay, WI	2 618	1.7	36.2	30.1	51.4	10.4	3.2	21.1	10.7	1 263	22.3	5.4	70.5	84.1	223	-2.6	176	0	193
Greensboro-Winston-Salem-High Pt.,NC	13 337	0.8	39.7	32.8	50.5	9.8	5.1	20.4	9.0	7 089	43.2	2.4	45.0	72.5	720	-8.8	102	8	390
Greenville-Spartanburg, SC	8 228	0.7	40.9	32.9	47.2	10.5	4.2	20.2	11.3	2 178	43.6	3.0	36.3	75.7	240	-15.6	110	5	128
Hagerstown, MD	1 326	0.9	29.3	21.0	52.1	13.9	3.0	20.6	17.7	906	32.6	5.0	56.0	80.7	138	-5.8	152	1	103
Harrisburg-Lebanon-Carlisle, PA	8 334	0.9	25.0	18.7	52.3	9.0	6.3	21.2	21.8	3 351	29.2	4.1	62.1	81.3	485	-4.9	145	3	388
Hartford-New Britain-Middletown, CT	21 640	0.3	29.0	22.2	58.1	8.8	15.5	21.8	12.6	1 253	53.2	3.4	48.8	76.8	125	-8.0	100	6	72
Hickory, NC	2 913	1.6	52.9	48.4	34.7	9.3	1.8	13.2	10.8	1 527	44.6	3.0	40.9	74.5	160	-9.4	105	1	86
Honolulu, HI	12 585	0.4	12.3	4.2	58.2	11.1	7.6	26.2	29.1	938	92.0	2.5	70.4	56.8	131	3.8	139	36	50
Houma-Thibodaux, LA	1 396	1.5	28.7	8.5	55.6	11.0	3.3	23.1	14.2	511	34.1	17.6	44.8	47.2	163	-32.6	319	1	95
Houston-Galveston-Brazoria, TX	52 191	0.2	29.7	14.5	59.0	8.2	7.0	26.9	11.1	7 938	48.2	10.9	35.4	57.5	2 202	-4.1	277	92	907
Brazoria, TX	2 021	1.0	57.7	41.4	28.4	6.9	2.2	12.5	13.0	1 498	45.8	13.6	35.3	59.5	537	-14.9	359	33	196
Galveston-Texas City, TX	2 072	0.1	32.5	21.9	41.5	8.5	5.8	17.8	25.9	471	57.1	8.9	29.5	57.5	99	0.7	210	5	38
Houston, TX	48 098	0.2	28.4	13.1	61.0	8.3	7.2	27.9	10.4	5 969	48.1	10.4	35.9	57.0	1 566	-0.1	262	54	673
Huntington-Ashland, WV-KY-OH	2 794	0.5	34.4	26.6	51.1	9.7	3.3	21.4	14.0	3 197	32.5	2.3	32.8	70.3	373	-4.8	117	0	133
Huntsville, AL	3 938	0.3	32.1	28.4	40.7	6.8	2.3	25.2	26.9	977	40.8	12.2	39.5	68.4	235	-19.6	241	1	170
Indianapolis, IN	18 255	0.6	28.6	21.6	57.1	9.9	7.6	23.3	13.8	5 818	37.3	13.8	51.6	74.0	1 309	-0.6	225	D	1 168
Iowa City, IA	1 281	1.3	14.6	10.1	37.4	7.8	2.7	20.2	46.7	1 356	23.7	11.9	65.4	75.7	306	-6.9	225	0	265
Jackson, MI	1 461	1.0	NA	30.0	NA	10.0	2.6	NA	14.7	1 103	30.6	9.2	44.0	83.4	218	-7.1	198	5	161
Jackson, MS	4 498	0.8	17.1	11.7	61.8	10.0	9.3	24.5	20.3	1 852	24.7	15.1	38.2	64.1	613	-11.3	331	D	310
Jackson, TN	966	0.7	35.0	25.5	47.4	11.1	3.2	23.4	17.0	614	27.0	13.4	46.9	64.5	160	-14.5	261	2	110
Jacksonville, FL	11 395	0.5	16.6	9.6	62.1	10.7	10.7	23.9	20.8	1 167	63.9	7.1	37.6	76.1	224	-26.4	192	24	58
Jacksonville, NC	1 380	2.4	7.8	3.8	19.8	7.2	1.4	7.1	70.0	436	37.8	6.9	55.0	67.9	69	-9.1	158	0	43
Jamestown, NY	1 341	1.5	39.3	33.3	43.4	10.1	2.8	20.5	15.8	1 972	33.8	4.5	56.3	83.4	290	-5.6	147	1	169
Janesville-Beloit, WI	1 577	2.4	46.2	41.5	40.7	9.6	2.7	18.7	10.6	1 518	31.7	12.6	63.4	80.2	358	-1.2	236	10	320
Johnson City-Kingsport-Bristol,TN-VA	4 335	1.4	42.6	36.8	43.2	9.8	3.1	20.6	12.7	9 917	55.2	1.5	35.7	68.8	783	-4.2	79	2	396
Johnstown, PA	2 010	1.6	31.1	17.5	53.5	10.0	5.2	24.5	13.8	1 667	18.8	6.8	56.9	83.1	313	-1.4	188	0	193
Joplin, MO	1 346	1.8	34.3	28.7	53.7	11.0	3.0	22.2	10.2	3 186	31.6	7.3	41.1	78.4	542	5.7	170	6	345
Kalamazoo, MI	3 211	0.6	43.2	38.1	43.5	7.9	4.7	23.1	12.6	842	41.8	10.5	46.6	81.4	168	-5.0	200	15	133
Kankakee, IL	904	3.6	28.8	21.0	50.9	10.0	3.3	26.0	16.8	1 086	18.2	23.9	67.1	69.3	389	2.7	358	8	370
Kansas City, MO-KS	22 178	0.4	22.9	16.8	62.3	9.3	7.8	24.9	14.5	9 834	32.6	11.0	42.4	73.6	2 107	-6.3	214	11	1 520
Killeen-Temple, TX	2 413	0.8	14.1	9.0	34.2	8.0	2.6	17.4	50.8	2 664	25.2	16.9	42.2	60.5	1 032	-3.7	387	2	366
Knoxville, TN	6 811	0.7	29.2	21.0	54.1	11.1	3.7	26.0	16.0	7 011	50.1	1.4	35.6	72.5	586	-7.8	84	1	346
Kokomo, IN	1 555	2.0	62.8	59.8	27.0	7.3	2.0	12.2	8.2	1 228	30.3	16.6	60.8	71.9	315	-0.6	256	0	291
La Crosse, WI	1 257	1.2	29.3	22.9	56.8	10.3	3.4	26.0	12.6	821	15.7	8.5	67.6	83.8	193	-4.6	235	1	103
Lafayette, LA	2 379	0.5	29.2	7.4	59.3	10.2	4.0	30.2	11.0	973	60.5	11.1	48.1	60.4	163	-8.0	167	14	137
Lafayette-West Lafayette, IN	1 620	1.3	34.3	28.3	39.9	9.2	5.3	18.9	24.5	881	31.9	18.5	52.3	74.1	247	-5.1	280	1	222
Lake Charles, LA	1 707	0.6	39.2	28.9	48.6	9.3	3.7	22.9	11.6	772	45.3	19.3	38.9	65.5	326	-5.5	422	28	168
Lakeland-Winter Haven, FL	3 908	4.8	25.6	15.5	57.3	13.9	4.9	25.2	12.4	2 638	64.4	7.7	40.4	44.4	602	-11.4	228	115	201
Lancaster, PA	5 285	2.3	43.8	34.3	46.7	10.3	4.0	19.7	7.2	4 775	38.0	0.8	73.4	79.4	404	-3.2	85	4	345
Lansing-East Lansing, MI	5 718	0.6	30.1	25.4	41.3	8.6	5.6	18.7	28.0	3 512	30.2	9.0	45.2	83.2	698	-4.9	199	7	580
Laredo, TX	802	1.3	13.6	3.8	62.0	17.3	5.2	18.7	23.1	494	12.3	57.5	38.5	22.9	2 022	23.0	4 093	3	50
Las Cruces, NM	944	4.3	15.2	8.8	40.8	10.4	3.5	18.2	39.7	1 104	68.4	8.3	44.5	71.3	573	42.5	519	78	92
Las Vegas, NV	9 284	0.1	14.5	3.0	71.6	10.4	5.0	45.3	13.8	267	75.3	5.2	32.2	70.8	68	3.2	254	8	11
Lawrence, KS	740	0.2	24.7	17.6	46.9	11.6	3.9	23.9	28.1	852	24.1	14.0	42.3	75.9	223	0.3	262	1	155
Lawton, OK	1 084	1.8	13.9	9.9	33.0	8.8	3.1	13.4	51.4	959	18.1	22.6	49.8	68.2	374	-9.1	390	2	175
Lewiston-Auburn, ME	1 019	1.1	32.3	23.4	56.5	11.8	5.3	27.8	10.1	343	24.2	9.6	54.8	85.1	70	-6.3	203	0	31
Lexington-Fayette, KY	4 960	6.3	29.0	22.2	48.6	9.6	4.8	22.1	16.2	5 587	39.3	7.0	50.9	65.7	920	5.4	165	7	638
Lima, OH	1 867	1.8	48.6	42.4	38.7	9.0	2.3	17.4	10.9	2 267	28.7	8.6	48.3	74.0	418	0.5	184	D	376
Lincoln, NE	2 765	1.0	20.0	14.6	55.7	10.0	8.1	23.8	23.3	1 508	27.8	20.0	53.6	71.6	448	-0.2	297	11	379
Little Rock-North Little Rock, AR	6 315	1.0	18.8	13.2	60.2	9.9	7.4	24.6	20.0	2 945	28.7	15.9	43.9	67.8	803	-5.3	273	192	577
Longview-Marshall, TX	1 805	0.3	42.2	29.5	46.9	10.9	3.5	19.5	10.6	1 394	35.4	8.5	29.1	62.1	248	-5.3	178	1	104
Los Angeles-Anaheim-Riverside, CA	216 168	0.5	26.6	20.0	61.0	9.4	7.9	30.2	11.9	10 471	78.0	4.2	40.0	59.2	2 892	-15.1	276	378	576
Anaheim-Santa Ana, CA	39 992	0.2	30.9	22.7	59.8	10.6	9.6	28.3	9.0	504	79.6	2.4	42.1	44.8	109	-34.1	216	17	24
Los Angeles-Long Beach, CA	147 969	0.1	25.8	20.6	62.8	8.7	8.1	31.9	11.2	2 035	85.2	3.7	33.8	65.4	280	-11.8	138	23	64
Oxnard-Ventura, CA	7 598	4.9	24.5	14.3	52.8	10.5	5.3	24.4	17.8	2 120	70.8	5.5	44.6	53.1	329	9.4	155	104	134
Riverside-San Bernardino, CA	20 609	2.4	24.2	12.5	52.8	12.0	4.3	24.5	20.6	5 812	78.0	4.0	40.3	60.5	2 174	-17.1	374	234	354

1. Covers mining, construction, and manufacturing. 2. Covers private sector earnings in agricultural services, forestry, and fisheries; transportation and public utilities; wholesale trade; retail trade; finance, insurance, and real estate; and services.

Area name	Agriculture, 1987 (cont'd): Value of products sold: Total (Mil dol)	Agriculture, 1987 (cont'd): Value of products sold: Average per farm (Dollars)	Agriculture, 1987 (cont'd): Value of products sold: Percent from: Crops	Agriculture, 1987 (cont'd): Value of products sold: Percent from: Livestock and poultry[1]	Agriculture, 1987 (cont'd): Percent of farms with sales of: $10,000 or more	Agriculture, 1987 (cont'd): Percent of farms with sales of: $100,000 or more	Manufactures, 1987: Establishments: Total	Manufactures, 1987: Establishments: Percent with 20 or more employees	Manufactures, 1987: All employees: Number (1,000)	Manufactures, 1987: All employees: Annual payroll (Mil dol)	Manufactures, 1987: Production workers: Number (1,000)	Manufactures, 1987: Production workers: Work hours (Millions)	Manufactures, 1987: Production workers: Wages: Total (Mil dol)	Manufactures, 1987: Production workers: Wages: Average per worker (Dollars)	Manufactures, 1987: Value added by manufacture (Mil dol)
	121	122	123	124	125	126	127	128	129	131	132	133	134	135	136
Grand Forks, ND	91	102 111	90.9	9.1	83.4	31.5	48	22.9	1.5	27.6	1.1	2.2	17.5	15 909	97.6
Grand Rapids, MI	266	93 675	48.5	51.5	49.5	18.8	1 593	41.8	101.5	2 647.9	72.1	144.6	1 678.3	23 277	5 967.7
Great Falls, MT	51	63 062	32.8	67.2	59.0	14.9	60	20.0	1.0	19.6	0.6	1.1	10.6	17 667	45.6
Greeley, CO	865	290 624	14.0	86.0	66.6	24.9	142	22.5	7.9	202.0	5.0	9.7	104.2	20 840	1 457.4
Green Bay, WI	95	74 998	12.0	88.0	71.4	22.3	315	43.5	23.5	618.1	15.7	31.2	373.4	23 783	1 611.1
Greensboro-Winston-Salem-High Pt.,NC	207	29 165	29.4	70.6	32.5	8.0	1 977	44.8	149.9	3 188.0	106.0	203.5	1 870.7	17 648	10 910.7
Greenville-Spartanburg, SC	38	17 463	50.5	49.5	18.1	3.6	1 172	45.8	99.2	2 011.4	74.2	150.3	1 255.5	16 920	4 967.5
Hagerstown, MD	54	59 703	11.9	88.1	50.7	22.7	146	45.2	11.5	259.3	8.6	17.8	181.3	21 081	471.4
Harrisburg-Lebanon-Carlisle, PA	254	75 734	12.9	87.1	56.4	20.6	690	45.2	53.6	1 244.9	34.1	65.6	647.3	18 982	3 197.4
Hartford-New Britain-Middletown, CT	140	111 843	68.5	31.5	39.3	14.0	2 229	36.6	132.7	3 741.9	76.5	157.0	1 786.7	23 356	7 784.0
Hickory, NC	61	39 733	13.7	86.3	29.4	11.3	852	52.5	65.8	1 128.0	54.3	105.0	790.2	14 552	2 230.7
Honolulu, HI	169	179 983	59.4	40.6	53.5	12.7	800	22.8	16.5	330.7	10.9	19.9	178.2	16 349	1 077.1
Houma-Thibodaux, LA	27	53 020	87.9	12.1	38.0	13.9	178	28.1	3.7	74.1	2.6	5.3	45.3	17 423	215.7
Houston-Galveston-Brazoria, TX	181	22 812	62.4	37.6	23.6	4.2	4 777	28.8	183.2	5 612.1	97.2	201.1	2 453.9	25 246	18 596.9
Brazoria, TX	37	24 796	68.6	31.4	23.6	5.0	171	33.3	14.4	550.6	6.6	13.5	239.1	36 227	2 788.8
Galveston-Texas City, TX	6	11 904	56.8	43.2	21.2	2.5	138	26.8	8.5	298.2	5.7	11.7	188.4	33 053	1 652.9
Houston, TX	138	23 175	61.0	39.0	23.7	4.2	4 468	28.7	160.2	4 763.3	84.9	175.9	2 026.4	23 868	14 155.2
Huntington-Ashland, WV-KY-OH	27	8 307	36.3	63.7	13.3	1.0	275	32.7	16.6	467.0	12.2	23.9	323.5	26 516	1 263.7
Huntsville, AL	35	35 698	63.9	36.1	32.1	8.8	293	36.9	25.6	705.2	16.1	32.6	380.6	23 640	1 881.9
Indianapolis, IN	318	54 641	69.8	30.2	56.9	D	1 813	35.9	105.6	3 033.6	65.9	133.1	1 639.4	24 877	6 806.0
Iowa City, IA	95	69 959	29.5	70.5	71.3	19.9	76	23.7	3.7	84.5	2.5	4.6	54.3	21 720	614.1
Jackson, MI	46	41 690	29.0	71.0	36.5	9.1	324	41.4	13.3	327.7	9.0	18.2	184.2	20 467	627.9
Jackson, MS	89	48 079	35.3	64.7	34.6	D	394	34.0	19.5	390.7	13.7	27.5	238.9	17 438	1 138.7
Jackson, TN	23	37 596	84.4	15.6	39.3	11.2	100	44.0	8.5	191.4	6.2	13.2	121.0	19 516	621.1
Jacksonville, FL	112	96 340	39.3	60.7	27.4	13.7	942	30.1	35.4	807.8	24.4	49.3	491.6	20 148	2 834.8
Jacksonville, NC	30	69 752	43.7	56.3	49.5	16.1	48	29.2	3.0	40.1	2.6	4.9	31.2	12 000	116.2
Jamestown, NY	79	40 126	34.5	65.5	51.8	11.4	255	35.4	14.7	331.0	10.5	20.9	222.0	21 143	859.5
Janesville-Beloit, WI	117	77 374	36.4	63.6	64.6	23.5	200	35.0	17.5	484.7	12.9	24.8	323.7	25 093	1 602.6
Johnson City-Kingsport-Bristol,TN-VA	115	11 592	33.2	66.8	18.1	1.7	494	40.3	52.8	1 243.5	36.7	73.3	754.2	20 550	3 105.8
Johnstown, PA	66	39 663	20.8	79.2	45.5	12.7	280	32.9	12.7	232.8	10.0	18.7	162.9	16 290	424.2
Joplin, MO	111	34 957	17.0	83.0	34.3	5.5	265	36.6	16.0	300.2	12.6	24.6	211.2	16 762	779.6
Kalamazoo, MI	65	76 616	55.8	44.2	46.6	17.5	393	38.4	27.9	916.7	18.1	37.7	515.9	28 503	2 307.7
Kankakee, IL	94	86 250	85.9	14.1	80.4	25.5	111	40.5	7.0	170.7	4.7	9.1	108.0	22 979	606.5
Kansas City, MO-KS	301	30 603	50.4	49.6	40.0	6.8	2 254	35.7	115.4	3 121.2	68.1	135.6	1 580.1	23 203	9 124.0
Killeen-Temple, TX	69	25 924	19.7	80.3	29.2	3.4	148	37.2	7.4	143.9	5.5	10.9	90.8	16 509	454.4
Knoxville, TN	69	9 842	33.3	66.7	17.6	1.4	796	33.5	48.8	1 061.0	34.2	66.4	617.8	18 064	2 621.8
Kokomo, IN	99	80 511	64.9	35.1	70.7	22.6	85	37.6	18.5	677.1	13.7	29.4	477.6	34 861	1 169.0
La Crosse, WI	45	55 305	12.0	88.0	67.5	17.4	138	38.4	10.3	226.0	6.7	13.1	125.2	18 687	494.2
Lafayette, LA	32	33 020	88.1	11.9	27.4	8.2	208	20.7	5.9	111.9	4.3	8.4	72.7	16 907	316.6
Lafayette-West Lafayette, IN	60	68 452	65.1	34.9	62.0	21.0	106	44.3	11.7	328.9	8.1	16.1	200.8	24 790	941.4
Lake Charles, LA	16	21 063	72.2	27.8	29.3	5.8	121	34.7	9.5	311.5	6.6	13.6	202.9	30 742	1 425.3
Lakeland-Winter Haven, FL	261	98 813	84.0	16.0	48.1	11.4	469	40.7	20.7	416.4	14.9	30.4	253.4	17 007	1 517.4
Lancaster, PA	601	125 816	9.7	90.3	78.1	29.3	821	45.2	60.0	1 378.0	42.5	83.3	838.2	19 722	3 883.7
Lansing-East Lansing, MI	147	41 865	43.9	56.1	46.4	11.1	399	33.8	35.6	1 183.1	27.4	56.0	863.7	31 522	1 930.5
Laredo, TX	24	47 623	6.2	93.8	41.5	9.3	57	24.6	1.4	20.4	8.0	1.8	10.9	1 362	73.2
Las Cruces, NM	156	141 498	52.4	47.6	39.0	14.6	74	28.4	2.5	43.3	2.0	4.8	29.9	14 950	127.3
Las Vegas, NV	15	55 135	7.3	92.7	21.0	5.6	408	21.3	8.1	178.7	5.6	11.0	112.0	20 000	442.0
Lawrence, KS	28	32 892	44.1	55.9	39.1	8.0	82	35.4	4.5	98.8	3.1	6.5	60.5	19 516	549.4
Lawton, OK	24	25 195	22.1	77.9	41.6	4.8	52	26.9	3.3	83.8	2.5	5.2	61.5	24 600	337.3
Lewiston-Auburn, ME	71	207 239	8.2	91.8	44.3	20.7	200	43.0	11.3	193.4	8.7	17.0	130.4	14 989	434.2
Lexington-Fayette, KY	367	65 768	22.7	77.3	53.4	8.4	388	40.2	27.1	734.1	17.1	33.5	365.9	21 398	2 031.2
Lima, OH	111	49 172	54.2	45.8	65.6	D	247	39.7	21.3	601.0	15.4	31.8	403.7	26 214	1 713.0
Lincoln, NE	56	36 914	55.7	44.3	53.1	9.5	237	40.1	13.9	324.1	9.3	18.6	187.8	20 194	867.0
Little Rock-North Little Rock, AR	123	41 822	60.5	39.5	34.1	12.9	590	35.9	31.1	632.0	21.6	42.2	386.6	17 898	1 761.0
Longview-Marshall, TX	13	9 177	13.0	87.0	20.2	1.1	280	38.2	15.3	374.5	10.7	21.1	228.4	21 346	1 065.7
Los Angeles-Anaheim-Riverside, CA	2 135	203 915	56.3	43.7	41.9	17.8	28 938	34.0	1 255.9	32 746.0	781.8	1 538.3	15 817.6	20 232	72 520.5
Anaheim-Santa Ana, CA	188	372 825	98.4	1.6	44.8	25.0	5 855	31.4	254.6	6 786.3	147.0	294.4	3 081.8	20 965	14 860.0
Los Angeles-Long Beach, CA	194	95 394	82.1	17.9	28.8	10.1	19 753	35.2	881.0	23 114.7	557.2	1 089.9	11 239.9	20 172	50 905.6
Oxnard-Ventura, CA	538	253 547	89.5	10.5	55.8	23.3	836	30.7	34.6	920.2	19.9	39.6	414.7	20 839	2 201.3
Riverside-San Bernardino, CA	1 216	209 160	30.9	69.1	41.2	17.9	2 494	31.8	85.6	1 924.8	57.7	114.4	1 081.2	18 738	4 553.6

1. Includes livestock and poultry products.

Area name	Manufactures, 1987 (cont'd)		Value of construction authorized by building permits, 1990								Wholesale trade, 1987				Retail trade, all establishments, 1987
				Nonresidential				Residential							
					Percent										
	Value of shipments (Mil dol)	New capital expenditures (Mil dol)	Total[1] ($1,000)	Total ($1,000)	Office	Industrial	Stores	New construction ($1,000)	Number of housing units	Alterations and additions ($1,000)	Establishments	Sales (Mil dol)	Paid employees[2]	Annual payroll (Mil dol)	Number
	137	138	139	140	141	142	143	144	145	146	147	148	149	150	151
Grand Forks, ND	199.5	D	24 230	8 695	2.8	8.6	71.0	6 624	77	1 830	140	332.9	1 262	23.9	648
Grand Rapids, MI	11 135.5	609.8	681 345	150 847	21.6	29.2	18.1	348 744	4 876	37 608	1 541	8 740.2	22 939	599.3	5 724
Great Falls, MT	137.6	4.0	18 352	3 992	3.9	2.4	63.5	5 900	55	3 115	203	690.1	1 907	34.5	928
Greeley, CO	3 037.1	33.6	50 230	14 244	11.9	65.2	5.3	20 458	271	4 174	241	583.1	1 970	35.0	1 100
Green Bay, WI	4 537.5	79.3	167 459	44 355	23.5	4.6	30.4	86 075	1 261	5 581	441	2 086.2	6 013	131.8	1 843
Greensboro-Winston-Salem-High Pt.,NC	18 949.3	591.3	750 873	225 727	18.8	9.7	30.9	351 313	5 134	36 862	2 207	9 295.8	27 062	619.5	9 820
Greenville-Spartanburg, SC	10 545.5	392.4	510 617	141 814	20.5	29.9	21.7	259 001	4 116	20 739	1 384	5 676.4	15 189	341.4	6 704
Hagerstown, MD	1 112.9	63.3	100 253	20 847	21.2	7.2	48.6	56 624	678	8 716	212	724.4	2 850	58.2	1 179
Harrisburg-Lebanon-Carlisle, PA	6 332.3	176.9	512 931	202 470	34.4	8.9	33.1	207 242	2 988	28 953	872	5 090.2	14 006	316.1	6 060
Hartford-New Britain-Middletown, CT	13 012.6	488.6	585 466	121 112	29.8	10.8	14.2	203 667	2 226	95 805	2 003	9 976.3	29 357	783.6	10 673
Hickory, NC	4 821.1	132.8	135 075	40 120	6.1	41.0	27.9	68 626	1 083	7 190	384	1 756.0	6 145	125.3	2 450
Honolulu, HI	2 783.8	66.1	917 553	212 819	20.1	8.9	23.1	401 876	2 977	110 626	1 577	4 501.8	16 907	357.5	7 814
Houma-Thibodaux, LA	441.5	11.5	43 354	10 943	14.5	0.8	55.9	23 156	455	4 685	340	578.9	2 993	52.1	1 940
Houston-Galveston-Brazoria, TX	52 662.1	1 454.1	2 145 092	455 475	10.9	19.1	30.7	1 176 168	13 289	124 311	8 258	72 418.8	96 874	2 532.5	34 071
Brazoria, TX	7 732.6	271.5	130 469	45 538	1.3	80.9	5.4	74 935	940	3 511	230	388.0	1 710	40.0	1 811
Galveston-Texas City, TX	7 346.9	117.5	227 951	104 228	1.2	5.3	33.8	104 672	982	8 164	215	995.7	1 727	34.5	2 222
Houston, TX	37 582.6	1 065.1	1 786 673	305 708	15.7	14.6	33.4	996 560	11 367	112 637	7 813	71 035.1	93 437	2 458.0	30 038
Huntington-Ashland, WV-KY-OH	3 754.1	91.8	51 715	28 577	9.6	53.1	14.6	10 823	153	2 729	458	1 497.1	5 718	111.7	3 018
Huntsville, AL	3 427.2	158.5	187 250	58 592	53.7	0.5	22.5	57 311	1 865	8 809	404	1 506.2	4 155	90.7	2 248
Indianapolis, IN	13 274.7	513.7	1 670 848	535 687	25.9	25.0	30.5	795 181	8 478	43 130	2 795	16 532.4	35 934	877.6	11 326
Iowa City, IA	985.1	21.6	77 750	17 948	44.9	5.9	5.7	47 680	619	2 589	91	300.2	1 004	20.4	831
Jackson, MI	1 406.8	37.4	75 688	21 497	7.3	14.6	57.4	39 826	584	4 428	180	707.8	2 013	45.6	1 214
Jackson, MS	2 502.9	72.6	197 774	48 752	17.7	4.0	44.6	82 318	1 299	6 195	859	3 557.7	11 431	235.9	3 779
Jackson, TN	1 341.2	D	90 791	43 406	3.5	37.6	11.5	30 253	433	1 619	167	453.1	1 922	34.2	871
Jacksonville, FL	5 936.3	170.1	893 868	208 122	32.4	8.2	18.5	522 025	8 158	34 396	1 756	15 425.4	25 346	574.1	8 403
Jacksonville, NC	251.5	D	38 780	9 596	8.2	6.7	32.6	24 020	532	2 032	85	101.5	523	8.0	1 101
Jamestown, NY	1 887.7	55.8	46 325	17 121	1.3	6.8	52.7	16 141	237	6 625	207	0.0	NA	NA	1 629
Janesville-Beloit, WI	4 289.2	43.2	67 559	18 636	12.2	30.2	16.2	37 429	618	2 716	207	709.6	2 575	52.4	1 343
Johnson City-Kingsport-Bristol,TN-VA	6 594.6	318.4	198 228	69 711	8.1	26.2	42.2	79 934	1 330	10 865	605	3 622.2	9 230	191.0	4 262
Johnstown, PA	1 081.8	23.4	149 281	111 317	3.2	1.4	8.5	26 386	435	3 979	338	620.1	3 204	55.1	2 604
Joplin, MO	1 857.7	36.5	54 702	11 533	6.5	25.4	24.0	17 746	318	2 130	294	747.1	2 959	49.7	1 602
Kalamazoo, MI	3 970.6	206.7	161 670	36 513	46.0	10.2	18.5	79 217	728	8 469	394	1 270.2	4 788	108.7	1 943
Kankakee, IL	1 301.6	32.0	64 942	19 043	2.4	40.5	44.2	33 221	449	2 786	140	530.6	1 786	34.4	779
Kansas City, MO-KS	19 398.9	740.0	1 387 380	321 749	17.8	15.9	32.7	654 227	7 414	54 822	3 710	30 074.4	49 508	1 227.3	14 295
Killeen-Temple, TX	828.9	24.7	60 351	19 758	9.1	26.8	32.3	18 922	259	11 331	202	803.1	2 397	44.7	2 228
Knoxville, TN	5 336.3	191.7	406 314	95 078	25.3	29.1	20.6	215 616	3 277	15 910	1 178	4 637.6	15 264	352.2	6 939
Kokomo, IN	2 546.6	204.7	58 797	31 394	31.6	17.1	1.7	22 200	236	1 524	140	362.2	1 188	21.2	1 080
La Crosse, WI	1 026.8	29.7	66 504	23 676	11.3	10.0	29.5	29 989	451	2 593	186	1 428.4	3 592	86.1	985
Lafayette, LA	635.8	11.4	100 490	30 168	9.8	1.5	51.4	36 228	402	5 677	555	1 357.3	5 300	110.9	2 185
Lafayette-West Lafayette, IN	1 965.0	100.6	108 814	36 327	11.9	50.9	28.5	45 701	752	6 209	143	261.9	1 433	27.1	1 068
Lake Charles, LA	5 679.3	193.8	135 753	72 841	2.3	86.1	3.7	36 735	592	4 856	295	1 585.6	2 461	50.6	1 647
Lakeland-Winter Haven, FL	4 109.3	83.8	263 744	72 157	16.4	11.8	33.4	150 976	2 785	18 805	634	2 462.6	9 347	153.6	3 720
Lancaster, PA	7 429.1	264.7	421 148	141 063	8.5	32.6	27.9	192 580	2 692	33 967	700	3 466.7	10 527	210.3	4 713
Lansing-East Lansing, MI	7 378.5	148.9	235 821	61 794	44.4	15.9	17.6	115 714	1 634	15 320	574	2 572.8	8 746	207.3	3 562
Laredo, TX	122.4	2.5	100 260	51 187	9.1	0.0	85.6	30 729	824	5 161	258	606.6	2 123	30.4	1 217
Las Cruces, NM	262.5	5.5	53 443	13 822	14.5	9.1	35.7	33 369	553	3 098	129	229.8	1 141	17.9	1 004
Las Vegas, NV	839.8	34.2	1 833 693	367 907	7.4	9.7	58.0	1 055 766	20 703	21 083	805	3 079.7	10 005	209.6	5 413
Lawrence, KS	864.4	D	80 065	14 715	36.3	24.8	7.9	48 613	710	2 216	96	127.3	703	11.1	720
Lawton, OK	583.4	7.9	18 870	7 072	46.9	34.9	17.7	6 377	61	2 458	100	184.0	958	15.5	1 049
Lewiston-Auburn, ME	821.1	33.1	56 543	24 015	4.5	20.1	42.1	18 564	250	5 126	184	444.3	2 361	46.7	1 084
Lexington-Fayette, KY	4 112.4	796.6	283 025	77 474	14.9	33.5	33.9	159 477	2 165	11 599	650	3 637.1	8 809	179.1	3 530
Lima, OH	5 792.4	97.9	70 178	16 633	7.3	36.7	37.4	36 400	502	3 553	293	1 249.2	3 596	70.6	1 667
Lincoln, NE	1 805.2	62.4	169 127	26 873	20.4	13.1	33.9	107 567	2 070	5 141	353	1 808.4	5 041	104.0	1 998
Little Rock-North Little Rock, AR	3 785.0	112.3	268 539	96 139	22.7	19.3	29.5	121 968	1 559	11 929	1 140	6 156.1	14 402	295.8	5 258
Longview-Marshall, TX	2 340.5	87.6	35 628	7 592	16.9	2.9	30.1	8 661	117	6 417	424	1 176.1	3 773	80.4	2 325
Los Angeles-Anaheim-Riverside, CA	138 893.3	4 248.5	15 491 090	4 029 301	24.1	16.8	30.7	7 465 233	68 340	1 549 427	28 918	203 520.0	378 799	9 857.3	127 678
Anaheim-Santa Ana, CA	25 887.4	881.6	2 492 261	723 737	26.4	8.4	38.2	1 149 251	11 983	218 632	6 055	47 128.5	77 218	2 134.8	24 061
Los Angeles-Long Beach, CA	99 888.6	2 995.5	7 892 454	2 115 588	29.0	13.3	25.2	2 978 493	25 125	1 106 222	19 688	141 729.2	266 696	6 929.9	79 297
Oxnard-Ventura, CA	3 671.9	98.2	607 715	162 397	18.8	26.3	28.9	326 632	2 620	45 307	867	6 306.1	9 877	233.8	5 803
Riverside-San Bernardino, CA	9 445.3	273.2	4 498 660	1 027 579	13.2	28.3	37.2	3 010 857	28 612	179 266	2 308	8 356.1	25 008	558.9	18 517

1. Includes nonresidential additions and alterations, residential nonhousekeeping buildings, and residential garages and carports not shown separately. 2. For pay period including March 12.

Table B. Metropolitan Areas — **Retail Trade and Services**

Area name	Retail trade, all establishments, 1987 (cont'd)			Retail trade, establishments with payroll, 1987								Taxable service industries–establishments with payroll, 1987				
	Sales				Sales								Receipts (Mil dol)			
						Per capita[1] (Dollars)								Selected kinds of business		
	Total (Mil dol)	Percent change, 1982–1987	Per capita[1] (Dollars)	Number	Total (Mil dol)	General merchandise stores	Food stores	Apparel and accessory stores	Eating and drinking places	Paid employees[2]	Annual payroll (Mil dol)	Number	Total	Hotels, motels & other lodging places	Health services	Legal services
	152	153	154	155	156	157	158	159	160	161	162	163	164	165	166	167
Grand Forks, ND	526.4	36.4	7 531	494	518.9	1 473	1 108	399	624	6 611	59.3	355	133.4	13.5	52.4	9.0
Grand Rapids, MI	4 700.5	59.5	7 208	3 718	4 604.7	1 285	974	385	612	56 240	544.7	4 158	1 757.8	77.4	442.0	151.9
Great Falls, MT	515.9	13.9	6 589	599	503.4	999	1 252	262	688	6 528	60.3	635	167.8	16.4	46.7	24.7
Greeley, CO	591.0	29.3	4 355	672	570.2	591	1 051	117	418	7 381	69.2	697	165.6	5.3	57.7	7.5
Green Bay, WI	1 353.5	54.6	7 188	1 245	1 327.2	1 350	1 095	294	674	17 264	154.5	1 155	446.8	30.1	149.4	19.8
Greensboro-Winston-Salem-High Pt.,NC	6 455.8	64.1	7 055	6 032	6 236.6	722	1 176	370	660	74 400	735.6	5 710	2 236.4	143.6	575.1	151.5
Greenville-Spartanburg, SC	4 032.4	57.6	6 593	4 078	3 877.0	725	1 341	371	586	47 807	447.6	3 810	1 565.2	64.0	368.3	104.5
Hagerstown, MD	788.7	38.9	6 764	774	769.6	884	1 240	230	452	8 419	87.1	610	188.7	D	D	9.1
Harrisburg-Lebanon-Carlisle, PA	4 434.8	53.3	7 589	3 591	4 304.0	877	1 248	250	559	47 236	456.1	3 376	1 640.8	136.4	384.7	109.4
Hartford-New Britain-Middletown, CT	8 682.8	62.1	7 906	7 049	8 482.3	824	1 287	436	682	93 469	1 043.9	8 328	4 395.8	159.0	1 003.0	388.0
Hickory, NC	1 426.9	69.7	6 510	1 535	1 369.5	598	1 264	288	578	15 979	157.5	1 162	368.3	12.5	161.0	16.4
Honolulu, HI	6 207.7	56.7	7 488	4 918	6 079.6	1 357	1 219	517	1 247	74 485	752.8	5 704	3 234.3	868.9	601.3	283.7
Houma-Thibodaux, LA	937.2	-5.7	5 090	1 104	899.8	718	1 377	182	478	11 030	110.4	998	316.7	7.8	95.4	39.6
Houston-Galveston-Brazoria, TX	22 792.6	10.3	6 293	19 647	22 088.9	793	1 335	371	615	257 174	2 612.8	26 035	15 825.7	525.5	3 617.0	1 664.3
Brazoria, TX	914.4	14.9	4 972	953	873.6	685	1 354	193	391	10 147	98.0	884	256.7	5.7	70.3	16.5
Galveston-Texas City, TX	1 238.4	18.7	5 917	1 320	1 189.8	810	1 615	343	601	14 949	144.1	1 096	341.0	44.0	96.7	33.0
Houston, TX	20 639.8	9.6	6 393	17 374	20 025.6	798	1 315	383	628	232 078	2 370.7	24 055	15 228.0	475.8	3 450.0	1 614.8
Huntington-Ashland, WV-KY-OH	1 699.2	25.5	5 240	1 833	1 638.3	868	1 084	218	449	21 586	185.7	1 542	433.7	17.4	189.9	34.3
Huntsville, AL	1 586.7	77.6	6 866	1 460	1 547.7	1 003	1 236	433	681	18 683	181.5	1 582	1 247.6	49.2	254.1	D
Indianapolis, IN	9 210.2	57.8	7 518	7 317	9 034.0	950	1 120	303	771	107 308	1 035.4	8 188	3 989.2	210.0	1 078.1	270.2
Iowa City, IA	540.1	46.1	6 310	597	527.1	803	1 426	267	748	8 633	67.5	520	211.6	14.1	38.7	8.2
Jackson, MI	843.6	42.1	5 685	801	824.1	1 402	835	136	506	9 668	96.1	738	262.6	9.1	78.2	11.5
Jackson, MS	2 482.9	48.5	6 297	2 409	2 404.1	1 009	1 081	265	529	28 469	279.4	2 476	1 053.3	62.1	300.3	115.9
Jackson, TN	603.6	50.5	7 738	584	589.1	1 448	1 415	374	544	6 882	64.3	542	208.9	9.5	113.6	10.1
Jacksonville, FL	6 271.0	67.8	7 142	5 825	6 166.8	731	1 225	274	725	71 735	716.6	6 386	3 000.5	158.4	678.7	204.0
Jacksonville, NC	663.7	59.8	5 272	761	651.7	629	888	181	546	8 422	75.8	451	116.9	10.5	40.6	7.9
Jamestown, NY	744.1	33.4	5 259	1 004	719.8	627	1 262	182	440	9 312	79.6	732	198.9	23.9	67.7	12.4
Janesville-Beloit, WI	866.9	39.1	6 412	911	850.8	875	1 324	190	634	10 984	96.6	702	209.3	17.7	87.3	13.5
Johnson City-Kingsport-Bristol,TN-VA	2 346.1	31.3	5 306	2 459	2 256.2	761	1 072	207	461	27 664	247.7	2 184	681.9	45.8	320.2	41.0
Johnstown, PA	1 201.0	28.1	4 768	1 426	1 139.4	524	1 081	155	336	13 847	118.3	1 106	287.8	14.2	108.8	16.9
Joplin, MO	892.0	43.5	6 607	946	857.1	1 016	1 242	284	582	10 654	95.2	879	237.1	13.0	100.8	9.8
Kalamazoo, MI	1 539.0	38.7	7 125	1 343	1 514.4	1 374	993	399	718	19 791	178.5	1 426	730.3	19.0	317.1	51.0
Kankakee, IL	552.3	31.9	5 642	487	539.2	687	1 088	167	485	6 243	59.0	537	146.6	3.9	57.6	6.2
Kansas City, MO-KS	10 524.9	46.2	6 786	9 266	10 288.4	948	1 215	298	672	123 678	1 237.4	11 056	5 322.5	320.6	1 273.1	462.2
Killeen-Temple, TX	1 133.0	27.0	4 784	1 399	1 097.8	711	1 043	178	454	14 220	128.0	1 016	375.5	20.2	170.8	17.6
Knoxville, TN	4 337.7	50.6	7 300	4 296	4 216.8	885	1 338	367	743	50 694	482.4	4 209	2 136.4	175.3	531.1	90.3
Kokomo, IN	715.8	45.8	7 186	675	701.1	909	1 170	D	683	8 365	74.4	542	142.1	5.4	68.5	7.2
La Crosse, WI	682.0	33.3	7 186	732	670.5	1 191	1 082	297	835	10 562	80.1	583	244.9	14.1	113.8	10.0
Lafayette, LA	1 300.1	-4.5	6 118	1 345	1 257.8	986	1 436	369	634	17 365	156.6	1 849	710.5	15.8	208.1	108.8
Lafayette-West Lafayette, IN	864.4	46.0	6 943	743	851.3	1 133	1 128	277	727	11 746	95.9	654	277.9	17.0	94.7	13.2
Lake Charles, LA	930.9	3.1	5 402	966	896.6	830	1 441	246	428	11 491	104.2	1 038	366.5	17.1	134.7	44.9
Lakeland-Winter Haven, FL	2 431.8	49.3	6 292	2 329	2 357.2	758	1 285	213	518	27 872	264.4	2 198	842.0	100.0	254.7	57.0
Lancaster, PA	2 806.8	67.4	6 924	2 475	2 682.4	654	1 345	305	599	34 206	335.0	2 178	795.5	77.9	220.5	38.5
Lansing-East Lansing, MI	2 878.2	52.3	6 766	2 384	2 828.0	1 257	1 015	303	635	35 302	323.0	2 502	893.5	43.1	269.5	87.2
Laredo, TX	708.2	1.0	5 634	791	688.5	888	1 338	579	441	9 068	81.2	511	132.4	15.0	D	8.7
Las Cruces, NM	532.3	32.2	4 146	606	515.6	561	810	175	424	7 063	60.9	633	235.6	15.2	64.0	8.0
Las Vegas, NV	4 460.0	45.6	7 444	3 524	4 370.3	823	1 570	368	832	49 889	556.6	4 450	6 999.6	3 874.1	828.9	156.8
Lawrence, KS	392.3	39.0	5 244	488	383.3	621	1 102	218	661	6 070	48.2	463	121.8	6.7	35.7	5.4
Lawton, OK	565.8	13.6	4 715	669	547.7	931	866	205	447	7 107	63.5	568	164.7	9.0	61.6	8.8
Lewiston-Auburn, ME	723.1	58.0	7 146	700	702.7	891	1 630	224	522	7 716	75.9	659	199.9	9.6	73.4	20.7
Lexington-Fayette, KY	2 481.1	46.6	7 200	2 300	2 421.8	1 054	1 268	348	797	33 658	286.7	2 516	983.6	87.5	316.7	71.3
Lima, OH	1 041.9	45.1	6 679	1 074	1 016.1	1 000	1 241	252	608	12 637	110.9	840	253.5	D	108.9	10.5
Lincoln, NE	1 283.5	39.0	6 168	1 318	1 262.7	D	1 151	D	657	18 493	153.5	1 426	619.2	29.1	160.2	38.9
Little Rock-North Little Rock, AR	3 298.4	41.2	6 452	3 256	3 192.8	951	1 113	361	552	38 409	361.2	3 634	1 399.7	62.4	488.2	120.5
Longview-Marshall, TX	1 160.2	9.0	6 952	1 421	1 108.9	747	1 366	376	575	13 191	126.9	1 103	313.7	15.6	112.5	31.3
Los Angeles-Anaheim-Riverside, CA	91 937.3	52.7	6 831	71 008	88 645.4	802	1 290	372	730	971 960	10 913.4	111 383	73 134.3	2 643.5	15 488.1	5 868.5
Anaheim-Santa Ana, CA	18 099.1	54.9	8 167	13 385	17 426.8	1 000	1 414	457	941	197 763	2 177.0	21 771	13 959.7	716.8	3 326.5	798.5
Los Angeles-Long Beach, CA	56 140.7	46.2	6 619	43 606	54 071.8	738	1 250	393	719	591 714	6 740.6	73 951	52 548.6	1 504.9	10 095.0	4 784.9
Oxnard-Ventura, CA	4 376.6	69.0	6 957	3 328	4 251.3	929	1 301	249	607	44 843	487.9	4 269	1 910.4	75.7	555.7	84.2
Riverside-San Bernardino, CA	13 321.0	77.1	6 250	10 689	12 895.4	812	1 315	235	594	137 640	1 507.9	11 392	4 715.6	346.1	1 510.9	200.9

1. Based on the estimated population as of July 1 of the year shown. 2. For the period including March 12 of the year shown.

Area name	Taxable service Industries–establishments with payroll, 1987 (cont'd): Paid employees	Taxable service Industries–establishments with payroll, 1987 (cont'd): Annual payroll (Mil dol)	Banking: Bank deposits,[1] June 1989 (Mil dol)	Banking: Savings capital,[2] September 1989 (Mil dol)	Federal funds and grants, 1989: Expenditures (Mil dol)	Federal funds and grants, 1989: Per capita[3] (Dollars): Total	Per capita[3] (Dollars): Direct payments for individuals	Per capita[3] (Dollars): Procurement contract awards	Per capita[3] (Dollars): Salaries and wages	Per capita[3] (Dollars): Grant awards	Local government finances, 1981–1982: General revenue: Total (Mil dol)	General revenue: Intergovernmental (Mil dol)	General revenue: Taxes: Total (Mil dol)	Taxes: Per capita[4]: Total (Dollars)	Taxes: Per capita[4]: Property (Dollars)
	168	169	170	172	174	176	177	178	179	180	181	182	184	185	186
Grand Forks, ND	3 498	57.4	469	218.6	325.8	4 608	1 284	543	1 977	591	66.3	33.0	16.7	249	232
Grand Rapids, MI	43 976	683.4	6 292	700.3	1 459.5	2 164	1 356	348	184	242	688.3	212.4	281.2	460	426
Great Falls, MT	4 275	59.1	528	119.9	528.4	6 774	2 097	655	1 764	427	82.4	31.5	33.7	420	403
Greeley, CO	4 326	61.7	702	286.6	244.6	1 791	1 167	77	111	296	168.4	56.5	61.9	488	409
Green Bay, WI	13 362	205.1	1 479	468.8	442.8	2 287	1 334	428	205	232	275.1	116.3	70.2	390	385
Greensboro-Winston-Salem-High Pt.,NC	57 239	860.2	10 338	3 395.8	2 351.2	2 513	1 443	488	213	357	814.0	363.6	239.4	275	227
Greenville-Spartanburg, SC	41 197	627.9	3 153	2 141.0	1 186.4	1 887	1 483	48	146	202	454.3	180.0	143.5	246	228
Hagerstown, MD	5 050	71.6	858	364.0	370.9	3 122	1 747	458	672	226	99.5	48.2	37.4	338	206
Harrisburg-Lebanon-Carlisle, PA	37 133	601.9	5 031	1 783.2	2 918.8	4 893	1 893	155	1 127	1 698	549.5	205.0	198.8	352	224
Hartford-New Britain-Middletown, CT	89 861	1 755.4	22 642	2 596.0	4 569.9	4 101	1 622	1 456	287	701	1 045.9	327.1	592.0	559	554
Hickory, NC	9 495	135.6	1 377	790.6	386.0	1 718	1 370	59	105	172	166.2	90.3	39.6	191	158
Honolulu, HI	66 533	1 124.0	9 663	4 189.1	4 784.6	5 645	1 667	661	2 627	683	389.9	82.4	236.2	303	244
Houma-Thibodaux, LA	6 513	125.6	1 320	392.9	345.0	1 904	1 306	64	92	437	243.5	90.4	80.2	426	173
Houston-Galveston-Brazoria, TX	293 667	5 903.6	28 528	22 621.2	8 027.8	2 198	1 116	454	284	295	3 987.0	1 128.4	1 934.4	558	476
Brazoria, TX	6 242	100.3	893	646.3	278.7	1 518	1 136	82	90	125	196.3	51.9	99.0	552	502
Galveston-Texas City, TX	9 355	133.7	1 339	707.1	530.2	2 542	1 648	275	214	295	303.6	79.3	128.1	614	553
Houston, TX	278 070	5 669.6	26 296	21 267.8	7 218.9	2 214	1 081	487	300	305	3 487.1	997.2	1 707.3	554	469
Huntington-Ashland, WV-KY-OH	10 579	169.4	2 133	521.4	1 149.8	3 600	1 999	911	274	405	280.0	141.2	57.3	171	126
Huntsville, AL	25 086	476.9	1 406	360.4	2 711.1	11 344	1 839	6 290	2 869	310	221.9	68.8	49.7	237	106
Indianapolis, IN	95 363	1 577.8	11 519	2 238.4	4 097.9	3 275	1 567	545	635	482	1 216.2	545.6	411.7	349	332
Iowa City, IA	4 518	72.8	763	46.7	281.8	3 206	1 053	458	437	1 031	71.1	27.6	31.3	375	371
Jackson, MI	6 691	109.0	717	310.6	342.9	2 268	1 627	157	128	295	146.9	53.6	61.6	415	386
Jackson, MS	26 241	389.3	3 322	874.5	1 312.7	3 291	1 557	338	461	891	359.1	176.0	88.5	239	228
Jackson, TN	5 101	96.3	684	77.4	215.5	2 749	1 784	186	261	435	87.1	20.2	21.6	284	162
Jacksonville, FL	66 878	1 161.1	6 627	2 116.3	3 528.6	3 824	1 816	330	1 365	301	765.7	378.8	190.9	252	203
Jacksonville, NC	3 517	39.5	343	50.8	1 133.9	8 872	1 200	674	6 794	194	70.0	36.0	14.0	122	92
Jamestown, NY	5 551	69.5	1 058	206.0	418.0	2 977	1 980	226	140	608	219.2	103.3	82.8	566	424
Janesville-Beloit, WI	6 739	92.4	901	255.5	378.0	2 781	1 623	504	100	372	169.1	90.7	48.9	352	348
Johnson City-Kingsport-Bristol,TN-VA	16 841	261.5	2 545	1 454.2	1 605.5	3 634	1 791	1 275	245	306	286.3	110.9	113.6	258	184
Johnstown, PA	6 788	111.1	2 141	523.0	759.9	3 057	2 388	141	202	293	228.8	110.3	69.2	265	193
Joplin, MO	6 203	86.5	834	433.0	343.2	2 509	1 838	192	167	265	83.7	36.3	30.9	239	157
Kalamazoo, MI	17 888	310.9	1 327	500.0	487.7	2 230	1 514	164	211	305	230.8	71.6	112.2	524	511
Kankakee, IL	3 774	57.0	629	402.3	267.0	2 733	1 949	58	167	230	87.2	38.5	34.7	340	276
Kansas City, MO-KS	123 872	2 103.7	16 424	7 038.1	5 392.5	3 373	1 594	716	740	243	1 654.0	529.3	689.2	475	289
Killeen-Temple, TX	8 137	125.3	1 114	579.5	1 908.5	7 896	1 663	573	5 434	200	165.0	79.5	40.0	178	141
Knoxville, TN	41 410	746.2	4 080	1 402.9	3 258.4	5 405	1 768	2 789	500	336	441.2	173.8	179.0	307	198
Kokomo, IN	3 955	55.5	641	261.3	220.8	2 244	1 746	30	155	205	116.2	46.2	33.7	331	321
La Crosse, WI	5 824	103.0	640	361.1	249.8	2 599	1 736	290	187	324	110.6	47.4	34.2	368	358
Lafayette, LA	13 999	265.8	1 458	705.9	373.9	1 803	1 228	36	184	336	196.9	85.5	68.3	328	91
Lafayette-West Lafayette, IN	6 811	97.4	998	223.4	314.4	2 495	1 332	108	195	780	99.9	45.0	40.7	328	327
Lake Charles, LA	8 728	143.2	1 006	514.9	510.9	2 976	1 607	867	147	280	213.9	79.6	65.9	378	184
Lakeland-Winter Haven, FL	20 429	321.3	2 746	964.9	1 009.8	2 494	1 959	226	131	171	286.1	138.6	84.0	246	213
Lancaster, PA	18 836	292.9	3 848	713.6	809.5	1 913	1 446	157	141	158	275.8	102.1	116.6	314	222
Lansing-East Lansing, MI	21 925	359.6	2 411	760.8	1 550.6	3 594	1 291	68	275	1 888	496.0	155.6	209.4	505	466
Laredo, TX	4 090	44.3	2 469	514.6	256.1	1 931	1 112	67	224	520	113.8	59.1	30.9	278	185
Las Cruces, NM	5 903	90.2	560	220.3	649.4	4 754	1 567	1 472	1 332	365	123.9	66.3	10.5	100	65
Las Vegas, NV	135 439	2 344.4	3 928	2 003.2	2 544.6	3 805	1 717	1 231	616	235	676.3	299.0	157.9	310	178
Lawrence, KS	3 034	45.0	343	364.2	198.5	2 535	1 176	708	254	360	71.9	14.4	24.5	353	306
Lawton, OK	4 092	62.0	427	193.3	898.4	7 537	1 787	794	4 597	327	131.9	50.4	21.1	176	95
Lewiston-Auburn, ME	5 456	80.9	708	247.2	247.2	2 368	1 788	33	158	380	68.7	30.3	30.5	306	303
Lexington-Fayette, KY	25 421	378.1	3 148	472.1	866.7	2 446	1 366	152	484	418	233.8	101.3	100.6	311	136
Lima, OH	6 970	104.1	1 255	561.5	1 279.8	8 115	2 090	5 553	159	240	147.5	58.3	51.8	338	262
Lincoln, NE	14 176	216.7	1 740	693.7	693.6	3 228	1 772	126	467	797	231.7	59.1	94.8	477	399
Little Rock-North Little Rock, AR	33 129	550.0	3 511	1 869.0	1 742.0	3 367	1 749	124	819	610	366.1	151.1	109.9	228	188
Longview-Marshall, TX	8 624	112.1	1 567	702.9	443.4	2 678	1 779	452	146	290	165.5	55.1	77.4	466	393
Los Angeles-Anaheim-Riverside, CA	1 207 507	26 459.1	104 021	128 102.0	46 057.4	3 254	1 392	1 192	384	278	18 063.3	9 458.2	5 092.1	424	300
Anaheim-Santa Ana, CA	241 866	4 900.5	17 093	23 125.7	7 516.5	3 260	1 323	1 342	344	243	2 583.1	1 152.2	943.1	465	356
Los Angeles-Long Beach, CA	822 432	19 188.7	74 684	90 929.4	30 039.3	3 429	1 380	1 396	329	314	12 155.8	6 554.0	3 323.6	429	290
Oxnard-Ventura, CA	37 377	697.6	3 242	3 735.3	2 129.3	3 204	1 339	932	757	172	792.8	404.1	220.3	393	311
Riverside-San Bernardino, CA	105 832	1 672.3	9 002	10 311.6	6 372.3	2 630	1 512	385	518	209	2 531.6	1 347.9	605.1	358	272

1. Includes deposits for all insured and reporting noninsured commercial and mutual savings banks. 2. Includes savings capital for all FSLIC insured savings institutions. 3. Based on the estimated population as of July 1 of the year shown. 4. Based on the estimated population as of July 1, 1982.

Area name	Local government finances, 1981–1982, (cont'd) — Direct general expenditure — Total (Mil dol)	Percent change, 1977–1982	Per capita[1] (Dollars)	Percent of total for– Education	Health & hospitals	Police protection	Public welfare	Highways	Debt outstanding — Total (Mil dol)	Per capita[1] (Dollars)	State and local government employment, 1989 — Total	Rate[2]	Federal government civilian employment, 1989 — Total	Earnings ($1,000)	Elections,[3] 1988 — Total vote cast for president	Vote for lead party (Percent)
	187	188	189	190	191	192	193	194	195	196	197	198	199	200	201	202
Grand Forks, ND	60.0	52.7	894	48.7	0.7	4.0	1.0	7.3	45	671	7 132	1 008.8	1 505	34 578	27 531	R—53.8
Grand Rapids, MI	664.1	57.6	1 085	47.1	10.3	4.8	1.6	5.8	555	907	29 397	435.8	2 914	97 919	287 571	R—67.3
Great Falls, MT	75.8	15.5	945	53.6	1.7	4.2	7.4	5.0	31	392	3 669	470.4	1 756	47 568	32 124	R—49.6
Greeley, CO	164.1	75.5	1 294	40.0	17.6	4.3	7.9	6.8	213	1 677	8 387	614.0	442	12 430	47 807	R—55.4
Green Bay, WI	242.5	48.6	1 347	42.3	5.4	5.4	2.8	11.2	167	926	10 217	527.7	946	31 640	85 953	R—50.8
Greensboro-Winston-Salem-High Pt.,NC	796.1	46.5	916	45.7	13.1	5.6	3.1	2.8	554	637	49 021	524.0	5 009	165 943	325 541	R—61.6
Greenville-Spartanburg, SC	450.7	80.6	771	50.7	14.9	4.7	0.4	2.6	401	686	38 145	606.8	2 080	68 419	183 390	R—68.5
Hagerstown, MD	102.1	48.6	922	53.0	0.0	3.9	0.0	11.0	67	609	6 177	519.9	1 591	43 650	40 638	R—63.8
Harrisburg-Lebanon-Carlisle, PA	543.3	63.1	963	46.1	5.2	2.7	5.7	3.7	682	1 208	53 046	889.3	14 200	443 400	206 251	R—62.6
Hartford-New Britain-Middletown, CT	1 037.1	46.3	980	50.6	0.8	5.6	2.8	5.4	650	614	80 574	723.0	8 865	294 012	501 741	D—52.0
Hickory, NC	149.0	50.2	717	56.5	10.3	4.7	3.1	2.6	96	460	14 062	625.8	631	20 258	80 811	R—65.3
Honolulu, HI	330.7	9.5	425	0.0	1.6	15.6	0.0	10.8	249	319	51 284	605.0	32 479	1 039 629	261 577	D—53.1
Houma-Thibodaux, LA	233.8	147.7	1 242	38.8	29.3	3.9	0.2	3.8	262	1 391	10 065	555.5	460	13 772	64 391	R—54.2
Houston-Galveston-Brazoria, TX	3 878.1	108.1	1 118	45.8	6.2	5.2	0.4	5.6	5 827	1 680	205 964	563.9	26 942	973 730	1 094 810	R—57.1
Brazoria, TX	188.3	114.2	1 049	55.9	4.1	4.5	0.2	7.5	246	1 371	10 991	598.6	381	11 954	59 081	R—57.6
Galveston-Texas City, TX	298.5	88.9	1 431	50.1	7.8	3.6	0.3	4.1	389	1 866	21 591	1 035.0	1 012	32 996	74 042	D—52.2
Houston, TX	3 391.3	109.7	1 101	44.9	6.2	5.3	0.4	5.6	5 192	1 685	173 382	531.7	25 549	928 780	961 687	R—57.9
Huntington-Ashland, WV-KY-OH	291.0	117.8	869	45.7	16.2	3.0	1.0	2.4	405	1 209	15 165	474.8	2 896	90 660	114 695	R—50.2
Huntsville, AL	201.3	72.6	962	34.9	25.0	3.7	0.0	5.3	226	1 080	14 347	600.3	17 052	643 421	79 894	R—67.1
Indianapolis, IN	1 136.0	46.8	962	44.6	13.9	4.6	5.6	4.4	739	625	77 268	617.5	19 950	658 643	494 234	R—64.2
Iowa City, IA	66.1	68.2	793	42.4	3.2	4.7	3.5	10.4	60	724	22 217	2 527.5	1 612	47 554	44 647	D—64.4
Jackson, MI	148.7	23.6	1 001	52.5	6.0	4.6	1.6	5.2	104	700	7 643	505.5	466	14 248	56 127	R—60.4
Jackson, MS	360.2	96.4	972	40.3	10.5	3.9	1.3	9.6	261	703	37 735	946.0	4 997	159 713	144 085	R—60.4
Jackson, TN	77.1	27.0	1 014	14.4	47.5	4.4	0.5	4.4	64	847	7 020	895.4	531	18 751	28 039	R—60.5
Jacksonville, FL	769.2	56.9	1 015	48.6	8.0	6.0	0.2	4.7	1 088	1 436	43 872	475.4	18 091	554 639	277 739	R—65.4
Jacksonville, NC	62.1	45.4	541	56.0	19.2	4.3	3.7	1.0	28	246	5 321	416.4	5 111	109 081	19 488	R—62.9
Jamestown, NY	220.7	26.9	1 509	42.9	5.8	2.9	16.5	9.1	112	762	8 919	635.3	427	13 008	57 867	R—54.7
Janesville-Beloit, WI	180.5	54.5	1 300	41.7	9.1	6.0	4.6	6.1	92	666	6 589	484.8	379	11 166	58 227	D—50.8
Johnson City-Kingsport-Bristol,TN-VA	280.1	60.1	636	52.7	7.1	5.1	1.1	6.5	271	616	21 826	494.0	3 585	107 611	150 353	R—65.0
Johnstown, PA	209.7	36.8	804	49.3	1.9	2.3	6.4	5.5	298	1 144	11 432	459.9	1 269	37 677	95 320	D—54.9
Joplin, MO	81.7	49.1	631	60.3	6.4	5.1	0.1	5.9	20	158	6 488	474.3	500	14 057	47 684	R—64.1
Kalamazoo, MI	235.4	73.7	1 100	46.5	2.4	6.7	2.1	4.5	196	916	15 137	692.1	1 157	38 695	90 235	R—55.6
Kankakee, IL	84.6	54.4	829	60.6	0.4	5.9	0.5	9.0	37	358	6 327	647.6	429	13 943	35 755	R—56.8
Kansas City, MO-KS	1 551.4	51.9	1 070	41.0	7.0	6.5	0.4	7.5	2 091	1 442	86 232	539.5	33 033	1 033 494	622 953	D—50.8
Killeen-Temple, TX	164.6	114.3	734	64.8	5.5	4.2	0.2	3.5	127	566	14 696	608.0	8 463	219 233	59 178	R—62.3
Knoxville, TN	420.5	46.8	722	44.4	3.8	5.8	1.4	4.4	581	998	39 120	648.9	7 637	287 095	203 523	R—64.7
Kokomo, IN	104.1	58.9	1 024	44.5	20.5	3.8	5.0	4.6	38	369	5 456	554.5	380	11 530	39 286	R—63.9
La Crosse, WI	110.7	56.1	1 192	43.8	11.2	4.4	4.9	8.0	74	793	7 216	750.9	442	13 774	44 111	D—50.3
Lafayette, LA	206.2	128.1	991	53.0	1.4	5.2	0.3	9.8	541	2 602	11 310	545.3	903	30 401	79 787	R—55.4
Lafayette-West Lafayette, IN	95.2	91.9	768	43.2	0.4	4.1	3.7	5.6	43	345	16 748	1 329.2	588	18 835	44 364	R—62.9
Lake Charles, LA	205.1	71.8	1 176	42.1	6.6	4.7	0.0	7.8	377	2 162	9 034	526.2	616	19 875	64 100	D—52.9
Lakeland-Winter Haven, FL	277.7	54.6	813	54.3	8.2	6.9	1.0	5.6	266	780	19 850	490.2	1 360	41 969	116 041	R—66.4
Lancaster, PA	259.5	55.2	698	58.5	2.3	3.1	3.5	4.4	261	701	14 284	337.5	1 522	47 091	137 029	R—70.8
Lansing-East Lansing, MI	502.0	46.9	1 210	48.8	10.2	5.4	1.5	4.6	366	883	53 517	1 240.5	3 325	105 655	180 078	R—54.5
Laredo, TX	116.7	97.8	1 049	62.1	0.9	4.4	1.9	5.1	69	618	8 313	626.9	581	20 106	23 832	D—68.1
Las Cruces, NM	124.0	130.5	1 187	47.0	31.0	3.5	0.0	4.3	51	490	11 559	846.2	4 598	155 286	41 747	R—51.7
Las Vegas, NV	615.1	99.1	1 207	34.2	10.9	4.3	1.3	4.8	564	1 107	30 079	449.7	6 672	219 139	191 779	R—56.4
Lawrence, KS	66.4	32.0	955	30.9	23.2	4.4	2.0	9.5	70	1 001	9 546	1 219.2	544	15 268	32 361	R—49.9
Lawton, OK	130.1	108.2	1 086	35.8	30.8	3.8	0.0	6.8	109	912	6 306	529.0	5 495	132 432	29 099	R—60.0
Lewiston-Auburn, ME	68.1	46.5	682	47.9	0.1	5.1	0.9	9.7	59	592	4 323	414.1	342	9 829	44 585	R—51.7
Lexington-Fayette, KY	232.0	65.2	717	43.8	3.9	8.3	1.2	4.4	395	1 220	26 272	741.5	6 269	193 754	122 550	R—59.4
Lima, OH	139.5	31.1	911	49.0	8.5	4.5	3.8	6.3	81	529	8 685	550.7	688	21 071	63 454	R—70.3
Lincoln, NE	227.0	66.4	1 142	39.1	13.1	4.1	6.1	8.1	502	2 526	25 188	1 172.1	2 665	88 207	89 447	R—49.9
Little Rock-North Little Rock, AR	363.6	88.5	753	46.5	4.1	4.5	0.3	4.8	625	1 295	38 680	747.6	9 956	307 969	179 679	R—56.1
Longview-Marshall, TX	165.9	93.8	999	57.6	4.2	3.9	0.4	6.0	196	1 182	8 205	495.5	637	19 332	60 672	R—63.3
Los Angeles-Anaheim-Riverside, CA	16 678.1	56.3	1 388	37.8	8.1	6.8	11.9	3.5	9 810	816	688 489	486.5	123 067	3 969 227	4 477 807	R—53.8
Anaheim-Santa Ana, CA	2 344.1	54.3	1 157	46.0	2.1	6.9	7.3	5.4	1 401	691	98 671	427.9	16 091	499 325	865 307	R—67.7
Los Angeles-Long Beach, CA	11 169.8	50.8	1 443	36.1	8.4	7.2	12.9	2.9	6 857	886	444 584	507.5	74 627	2 504 949	2 644 671	D—51.9
Oxnard-Ventura, CA	774.8	68.0	1 381	40.1	7.8	5.8	7.5	4.1	342	610	29 755	447.7	11 944	391 332	239 473	R—61.6
Riverside-San Bernardino, CA	2 389.4	85.9	1 415	36.6	13.0	5.2	12.7	4.0	1 211	717	115 479	476.6	20 405	573 621	728 356	R—59.7

1. Based on the estimated population as of July 1, 1982. 2. Per 10,000 resident population estimated as of July 1 of the year shown. 3. Data subject to copyright.

MSA/ CMSA/ NECMA/ PMSA code[1]	Area name	Land Area,[2] 1990 (Sq. Km.)	Population, 1990: Total persons	Rank	Per square kilometer	Race: White	Race: Black	Race: Am. Indian, Eskimo, Aleut	Race: Asian & Pacific Islander	Race: Other race	Hispanic[3]	Age of population, Percent: Under 5 years	5 to 14 years	15 to 24 years	25 to 34 years	35 to 44 years
		1	2	3	4	5	6	7	8	9	10	11	12	13	14	15
4520	Louisville, KY-IN	5 869	952 662	42	162.3	818 898	124 761	1 576	5 640	1 787	5 765	6.8	14.2	13.8	17.2	15.8
4600	Lubbock, TX	2 330	222 636	150	95.6	176 037	17 154	686	2 722	26 037	51 011	7.7	14.8	20.4	17.7	13.3
4640	Lynchburg, VA	2 666	142 199	200	53.3	110 847	30 079	277	743	253	923	6.7	12.6	17.1	15.5	14.3
4680	Macon-Warner Robins, GA	3 035	281 103	123	92.6	180 383	97 294	571	1 941	914	2 832	7.7	15.0	15.3	17.4	14.9
4720	Madison, WI	3 114	367 085	100	117.9	344 617	10 511	1 201	8 666	2 090	5 744	7.0	12.5	18.9	19.9	16.6
4763	Manchester, NH	2 270	336 073	112	148.0	326 821	3 001	612	3 816	1 823	5 696	8.1	13.7	14.1	19.7	16.5
4800	Mansfield, OH	1 287	126 137	224	98.0	115 078	9 981	223	578	277	903	6.9	14.7	13.9	15.5	14.8
4880	McAllen-Edinburg-Mission, TX	4 064	383 545	96	94.4	286 858	806	668	1 088	94 125	326 972	9.3	20.8	18.2	14.6	12.7
4890	Medford, OR	7 214	146 389	196	20.3	140 188	340	1 863	1 429	2 569	5 949	6.7	14.4	12.5	13.7	16.3
4900	Melbourne-Titusville-Palm Bay, FL	2 638	398 978	90	151.2	358 391	31 417	1 369	5 379	2 422	12 261	6.6	12.0	12.1	17.5	13.6
4920	Memphis, TN-AR-MS	5 965	981 747	40	164.6	570 511	399 011	1 791	8 178	2 256	7 986	8.1	15.3	15.5	17.9	15.5
4940	Merced, CA	4 996	178 403	169	35.7	120 280	8 523	1 516	15 128	32 956	58 107	10.2	19.1	15.6	17.4	13.2
4992	Miami-Fort Lauderdale, FL	8 167	3 192 582	11	390.9	2 438 598	591 440	5 700	43 437	113 407	1 061 846	6.9	12.2	12.9	17.1	14.5
2680	Ft.Lauderdale-Hollywood-Pom.Beach,	3 131	1 255 488	X	401.0	1 025 583	193 447	2 634	17 130	16 694	108 439	6.3	11.0	11.3	17.1	14.8
5000	Miami-Hialeah, FL	5 036	1 937 094	X	384.6	1 413 015	397 993	3 066	26 307	96 713	953 407	7.2	13.0	14.0	17.1	14.4
5040	Midland, TX	2 332	106 611	256	45.7	86 977	8 281	414	888	10 051	22 780	9.4	17.8	12.7	18.4	15.3
5082	Milwaukee-Racine, WI	4 645	1 607 183	24	346.0	1 335 470	214 182	8 522	19 786	29 223	60 340	7.7	14.7	14.0	17.6	15.1
5080	Milwaukee, WI	3 782	1 432 149	X	378.7	1 183 372	197 183	8 001	18 782	24 811	51 306	7.7	14.6	14.1	17.7	15.1
6600	Racine, WI	863	175 034	X	202.8	152 098	16 999	521	1 004	4 412	9 034	7.8	15.8	13.2	17.1	15.1
5120	Minneaolis-St. Paul, MN-WI	13 085	2 464 124	16	188.3	2 270 360	89 710	23 956	65 204	14 894	37 448	8.1	14.5	13.8	20.2	16.4
5160	Mobile, AL	7 329	476 923	80	65.1	339 418	130 512	2 570	3 619	804	4 186	7.6	15.7	14.7	16.0	14.5
5170	Modesto, CA	3 871	370 522	98	95.7	297 315	6 450	4 039	19 223	43 495	80 897	9.1	17.2	14.1	17.6	14.7
5200	Monroe, LA	1 582	142 191	201	89.9	96 870	44 096	239	740	246	1 194	8.0	16.5	17.5	15.7	13.6
5240	Montgomery, AL	5 200	292 517	120	56.3	184 414	105 196	622	1 782	503	2 124	7.6	15.2	15.7	16.9	15.0
5280	Muncie, IN	1 019	119 659	235	117.4	111 232	7 167	274	641	345	853	6.1	12.1	22.8	13.9	13.0
5320	Muskegon, MI	1 319	158 983	181	120.5	133 931	21 617	1 338	555	1 542	3 623	8.1	15.7	13.6	16.4	14.7
5345	Naples, FL	5 246	152 099	186	29.0	139 073	6 986	428	584	5 028	20 734	6.0	10.9	10.8	14.6	12.8
5360	Nashville, TN	10 549	985 026	39	93.4	818 424	152 349	2 121	10 012	2 120	7 665	7.2	13.9	14.9	18.7	16.1
5403	New Bedford, MA	1 440	506 325	75	351.6	482 426	8 054	937	4 478	10 430	13 578	7.1	13.3	14.9	16.8	14.8
5483	New Haven-Waterbury-Meriden, CT	1 569	804 219	52	512.6	687 491	82 011	1 536	10 484	22 697	51 003	7.0	12.2	14.2	18.0	15.1
5523	New London-Norwich, CT-RI.	1 725	254 957	134	147.8	234 274	12 123	1 338	3 389	3 833	8 455	7.4	12.7	15.4	19.3	14.9
5560	New Orleans, LA	5 980	1 238 816	32	207.2	770 406	430 470	3 615	21 380	12 945	53 226	7.7	15.8	14.8	17.3	15.4
5602	N.Y.-North N.J.-Long Island,NY-NJ-CT	18 134	17 953 372	1	990.0	12 570 610	3 286 349	45 969	871 999	1 178 445	2 774 937	6.8	12.4	14.0	17.8	15.4
0875	Bergen-Passaic, NJ	1 086	1 278 440	X	1 177.2	1 043 437	106 108	2 221	66 743	59 931	147 868	6.4	11.6	13.4	16.9	15.3
1163	Bridgept-Stamfrd-Norwlk-Danbry,CT	1 621	827 645	X	510.6	700 350	81 519	1 226	17 332	27 218	70 818	6.9	12.0	13.2	17.1	15.7
3640	Jersey City, NJ	121	553 099	X	4 571.1	380 612	79 770	1 460	36 777	54 480	183 465	6.7	11.8	14.8	20.4	14.4
5015	Middlesex-Somerset-Hunterdon, NJ	2 708	1 019 835	X	376.6	865 158	70 670	1 420	56 804	25 783	71 695	6.8	11.6	14.3	19.4	16.2
5190	Monmouth-Ocean, NJ	2 870	986 327	X	343.7	895 986	59 264	1 327	19 098	10 652	36 357	6.9	12.9	12.4	15.6	15.4
5380	Nassau-Suffolk, NY	3 103	2 609 212	X	840.9	2 305 434	193 967	4 636	62 399	42 776	165 238	6.6	12.6	14.4	16.5	15.5
5600	New York, NY	2 972	8 546 846	X	2 875.8	4 826 081	2 250 026	29 711	556 399	884 629	1 889 662	6.9	12.4	14.2	18.4	15.3
5640	Newark, NJ	3 160	1 824 321	X	577.3	1 279 952	422 802	3 144	52 898	65 525	188 299	6.9	12.7	14.0	17.4	15.7
5950	Orange County, NY	2 114	307 647	X	145.5	273 600	22 223	824	3 549	7 451	21 535	8.3	15.2	14.8	17.3	16.1
5720	Norfolk-Virginia B.-Newport News, VA	4 364	1 396 107	28	319.9	947 160	398 093	4 679	35 205	10 970	32 329	8.4	14.3	17.5	20.1	14.7
5790	Ocala, FL	4 090	194 833	158	47.6	167 094	24 844	638	945	1 312	5 860	6.3	12.3	11.2	13.8	12.5
5800	Odessa, TX	2 334	118 934	237	51.0	91 309	5 557	647	662	20 759	37 315	9.1	18.0	14.2	17.5	14.3
5880	Oklahoma City, OK	11 002	958 839	41	87.2	777 589	101 082	45 720	17 742	16 706	34 152	7.4	15.0	15.2	17.8	15.2
5910	Olympia, WA	1 883	161 238	178	85.6	148 221	2 864	2 498	6 101	1 554	4 873	7.1	15.6	13.5	16.0	17.6
5920	Omaha, NE	4 963	618 262	65	124.6	550 758	51 426	3 159	6 374	6 545	16 371	8.1	15.5	14.4	18.3	15.4
5960	Orlando, FL	6 573	1 072 748	36	163.2	888 913	133 308	3 199	20 474	26 854	96 418	7.3	13.3	15.4	19.6	15.6
5990	Owensboro, KY	1 198	87 189	269	72.8	83 168	3 619	101	229	72	312	7.3	15.4	14.2	16.1	14.5
6015	Panama City, FL	1 978	126 994	223	64.2	109 570	13 713	949	2 229	533	2 256	7.3	14.0	14.0	17.8	14.5
6020	Parkersburg-Marietta, WV-OH	2 596	149 169	192	57.5	146 698	1 567	242	520	142	479	6.4	14.2	13.7	15.1	15.1
6025	Pascagoula, MS	1 882	115 243	244	61.2	90 114	23 581	254	1 115	179	1 060	7.6	16.8	15.0	16.1	15.1
6080	Pensacola, FL	4 350	344 406	109	79.2	277 620	55 893	3 347	6 021	1 525	6 236	7.5	14.2	15.4	17.4	14.4
6120	Peoria, IL	4 654	339 172	110	72.9	309 325	25 142	587	2 759	1 359	3 642	7.0	15.1	14.2	15.1	15.0
6162	Phila.-Willming.-Trenton,PA-NJ-DE-MD	13 844	5 899 345	5	426.1	4 540 541	1 100 347	11 307	123 458	123 692	225 868	7.2	13.3	14.4	17.5	15.0
6160	Philadelphia, PA-NJ	9 111	4 856 881	X	533.1	3 717 175	929 907	8 335	104 595	96 869	173 980	7.3	13.3	14.2	17.4	14.9
8480	Trenton, NJ	585	325 824	X	557.0	244 656	61 481	533	9 992	9 162	19 665	6.7	12.2	15.5	17.3	15.7
8760	Vineland-Millville-Bridgeton, NJ	1 267	138 053	X	109.0	101 467	23 318	1 311	1 134	10 823	18 348	7.3	14.4	14.5	16.6	14.5
9160	Wilmington, DE-NJ-MD	2 881	578 587	X	200.8	477 243	85 641	1 128	7 737	6 838	13 875	7.2	13.6	15.3	17.9	15.3

1. MSA = Metropolitan Statistical Area. CMSA = Consolidated MSA. NECMA = New England county metropolitan area. PMSA = Primary MSA. See Appendix A for explanation of these concepts. See Appendix B for list of metropolitan areas identified by type, with component counties. 2. Dry land or land partially or temporarily covered by water. 3. Hispanic persons may be of any race.

Table B. Metropolitan Areas — **Population and Households**

Area name	Population, 1990 (cont'd): Age of population (cont'd), Percent: 45 to 54 years	55 to 64 years	65 to 74 years	75 years and over	Percent female	Population–change and components of change: Change, 1980–1990: Number	Percent	Components of change, 1980–1986: Total persons, 1986	Total persons, 1980	Net change: Number	Percent	Natural increase: Births	Deaths	Net migration	Households, 1990: Total
	16	17	18	19	20	21	22	23	24	25	26	27	28	29	30
Louisville, KY-IN	10.5	9.1	7.4	5.3	52.3	-3 774	-0.4	962 700	956 436	6 500	0.7	87 500	53 500	-27 500	367 819
Lubbock, TX	8.7	7.5	5.7	4.1	50.7	10 985	5.2	224 800	211 651	13 200	6.2	26 200	8 800	-4 200	81 534
Lynchburg, VA	10.7	9.2	7.9	6.1	52.9	910	0.6	144 200	141 289	2 900	2.1	11 700	8 200	-600	52 922
Macon-Warner Robins, GA	10.3	8.5	6.6	4.2	52.4	17 512	6.6	282 200	263 591	18 600	7.1	26 900	14 000	5 700	103 182
Madison, WI	9.2	6.6	5.2	4.1	50.9	43 540	13.5	344 900	323 545	21 300	6.6	29 700	12 600	4 200	142 786
Manchester, NH	10.1	7.5	5.9	4.4	51.1	59 465	21.5	314 300	276 608	37 700	13.6	28 000	14 200	23 900	124 567
Mansfield, OH	11.3	9.8	7.7	5.2	51.0	-5 068	-3.9	128 800	131 205	-2 500	-1.9	11 700	6 900	-7 300	47 573
McAllen-Edinburg-Mission, TX	7.8	6.6	6.1	4.0	51.7	100 222	35.4	365 900	283 323	82 600	29.2	47 500	10 700	45 800	103 479
Medford, OR	10.9	9.4	9.5	6.7	51.2	13 933	10.5	140 000	132 456	7 600	5.7	12 200	7 100	2 500	57 238
Melbourne-Titusville-Palm Bay, FL	10.5	11.0	10.8	5.8	50.6	126 019	46.2	361 200	272 959	88 200	32.3	25 300	16 700	79 600	161 365
Memphis, TN-AR-MS	9.7	7.7	6.1	4.3	52.2	68 275	7.5	959 500	913 472	46 000	5.0	101 100	49 100	-6 000	356 997
Merced, CA	8.3	7.0	5.7	3.5	49.5	43 846	32.6	163 500	134 557	28 900	21.5	20 900	6 000	14 000	55 331
Miami-Fort Lauderdale, FL	10.5	9.2	8.8	7.9	52.1	548 816	20.8	2 911 900	2 643 766	268 300	10.1	243 800	184 000	208 500	1 220 797
Ft.Lauderdale-Hollywood-Pom.Beach,	9.9	8.8	10.6	10.1	52.1	237 231	23.3	1 142 400	1 018 257	124 200	12.2	82 100	78 300	120 400	528 442
Miami-Hialeah, FL	10.9	9.4	7.5	6.4	52.1	311 585	19.2	1 769 500	1 625 509	144 100	8.9	161 700	105 700	88 100	692 355
Midland, TX	9.1	8.4	5.5	3.5	51.5	23 975	29.0	111 300	82 636	28 600	34.6	14 200	3 700	18 100	38 920
Milwaukee-Racine, WI	9.9	8.6	7.0	5.4	51.8	37 031	2.4	1 552 000	1 570 152	-18 000	-1.1	154 900	81 800	-91 100	601 458
Milwaukee, WI	9.8	8.6	7.0	5.5	51.9	35 129	2.5	1 379 700	1 397 020	-17 200	-1.2	137 700	73 400	-81 500	537 722
Racine, WI	10.4	8.6	6.9	5.1	51.5	1 902	1.1	172 300	173 132	-800	-0.5	17 200	8 400	-9 600	63 736
Minneaolis-St. Paul, MN-WI	10.0	7.1	5.5	4.4	51.1	326 991	15.3	2 295 100	2 137 133	158 000	7.4	228 600	96 300	25 700	935 516
Mobile, AL	10.2	8.7	7.5	5.0	52.3	33 387	7.5	470 000	443 536	26 600	6.0	49 900	24 400	1 100	173 943
Modesto, CA	9.3	7.2	6.3	4.5	50.8	104 622	39.3	316 600	265 900	50 700	19.1	33 000	14 600	32 300	125 375
Monroe, LA	9.4	8.1	6.4	4.8	52.8	2 950	2.1	145 900	139 241	6 600	4.7	15 800	7 200	-2 000	50 518
Montgomery, AL	10.0	8.2	6.6	4.8	52.1	19 830	7.3	298 900	272 687	26 300	9.6	28 400	15 000	12 900	105 531
Muncie, IN	10.6	8.8	7.3	5.4	52.5	-8 928	-6.9	120 900	128 587	-7 700	-6.0	9 800	6 400	-11 100	45 177
Muskegon, MI	9.7	8.7	7.7	5.3	51.2	1 394	0.9	158 500	157 589	900	0.6	16 100	8 600	-6 600	57 798
Naples, FL	10.0	12.1	14.4	8.4	50.4	66 128	76.9	121 400	85 971	35 400	41.2	9 400	6 400	32 400	61 703
Nashville, TN	10.5	8.0	6.1	4.5	51.7	134 521	15.8	930 600	850 505	80 400	9.5	81 700	44 500	43 200	375 831
New Bedford, MA	10.0	8.7	8.3	6.1	52.2	31 684	6.7	484 900	474 641	10 200	2.1	40 400	28 900	-1 300	187 668
New Haven-Waterbury-Meriden, CT	10.1	8.7	8.4	6.3	52.0	42 894	5.6	778 900	761 325	17 500	2.3	64 200	45 500	-1 200	304 730
New London-Norwich, CT-RI	9.9	8.4	7.0	4.9	49.4	16 548	6.9	246 400	238 409	8 000	3.4	23 100	12 300	-2 800	93 245
New Orleans, LA	9.8	8.1	6.6	4.4	52.4	-17 852	-1.4	1 334 500	1 256 668	77 800	6.2	147 500	68 600	-1 100	455 178
N.Y.-North N.J.-Long Island,NY-NJ-CT	11.1	9.3	7.5	5.6	52.2	1 348 312	8.1	17 836 000	17 412 203	423 900	2.4	1 503 200	1 038 100	-41 200	6 570 875
Bergen-Passaic, NJ	11.5	10.3	8.5	6.0	51.9	-14 530	-1.1	1 297 800	1 292 970	4 800	0.4	97 400	74 800	-17 800	464 149
Bridgept-Stamfrd-Norwlk-Danbry,CT	12.0	9.8	7.7	5.6	51.8	20 502	2.5	821 000	807 143	13 900	1.7	64 400	43 500	-7 000	305 011
Jersey City, NJ	10.1	9.1	7.5	5.2	51.5	-3 873	-0.7	553 100	556 972	-3 900	-0.7	51 300	36 500	-18 700	208 739
Middlesex-Somerset-Hunterdon, NJ	11.2	9.2	7.1	4.1	50.7	133 452	15.1	950 100	886 383	63 800	7.2	71 400	42 700	35 100	365 085
Monmouth-Ocean, NJ	10.4	9.1	9.7	7.6	52.1	137 116	16.1	935 200	849 211	86 000	10.1	71 100	60 100	75 000	365 717
Nassau-Suffolk, NY	11.7	10.2	7.6	4.9	51.4	3 399	0.1	2 635 000	2 605 813	29 300	1.1	196 400	135 200	-31 900	856 234
New York, NY	10.8	9.0	7.3	5.8	52.9	271 885	3.3	8 473 400	8 274 961	198 600	2.4	770 100	525 600	-45 900	3 252 399
Newark, NJ	11.4	9.3	7.3	5.2	52.0	-54 826	-2.9	1 888 700	1 879 147	9 300	0.5	155 500	105 100	-41 100	652 035
Orange County, NY	10.3	7.4	5.9	4.5	49.7	48 044	18.5	281 700	259 603	22 100	8.5	25 600	14 600	11 100	101 506
Norfolk-Virginia B.-Newport News, VA	8.9	7.0	5.7	3.3	49.9	235 796	20.3	1 309 400	1 160 311	149 200	12.9	135 700	54 300	67 800	493 536
Ocala, FL	9.8	11.9	14.4	7.7	51.8	72 345	59.1	171 000	122 488	48 500	39.6	13 200	9 900	45 200	78 177
Odessa, TX	9.3	8.4	5.8	3.5	51.1	3 560	3.1	133 100	115 374	17 800	15.4	18 700	5 000	4 100	42 322
Oklahoma City, OK	10.1	8.2	6.3	4.7	51.3	97 870	11.4	983 000	860 969	121 800	14.1	106 100	45 200	60 900	367 775
Olympia, WA	10.8	7.7	6.8	4.9	51.3	36 974	29.8	146 600	124 264	22 400	18.0	13 400	6 100	15 100	62 150
Omaha, NE	9.7	7.9	6.1	4.5	51.5	33 140	5.7	614 300	585 122	29 300	5.0	65 600	29 000	-7 300	232 352
Orlando, FL	10.0	8.1	6.6	4.2	50.7	372 842	53.3	898 400	699 906	198 500	28.4	74 500	39 000	163 000	401 659
Owensboro, KY	10.4	9.3	7.5	5.4	52.2	1 240	1.4	87 500	85 949	1 600	1.9	9 100	4 700	-2 800	33 036
Panama City, FL	10.8	9.6	7.7	4.3	50.7	29 254	29.9	122 300	97 740	24 600	25.2	11 200	5 300	18 700	48 938
Parkersburg-Marietta, WV-OH.	11.6	9.6	8.1	6.2	52.2	-8 720	-5.5	156 200	157 889	-1 600	-1.0	13 700	9 000	-6 300	57 804
Pascagoula, MS	11.4	8.7	5.9	3.5	50.9	-2 772	-2.3	128 200	118 015	10 200	8.6	12 700	4 500	2 000	40 454
Pensacola, FL	10.7	9.0	7.1	4.2	51.1	54 624	18.9	337 100	289 782	47 400	16.4	32 200	14 100	29 300	128 508
Peoria, IL	10.6	9.2	7.7	6.2	51.8	-26 692	-7.3	340 400	365 864	-25 400	-6.9	34 700	18 700	-41 400	129 363
Phila.-Willming.-Trenton,PA-NJ-DE-MD	10.2	9.1	7.9	5.4	52.0	218 836	3.9	5 832 600	5 680 509	151 900	2.7	520 300	345 500	-22 900	2 154 104
Philadelphia, PA-NJ	10.2	9.1	8.0	5.5	52.1	140 322	3.0	4 825 800	4 716 559	108 800	2.3	433 600	292 000	-32 800	1 777 365
Trenton, NJ	10.7	9.0	7.8	5.2	51.6	17 961	5.8	320 800	307 863	13 000	4.2	26 300	17 900	4 600	116 941
Vineland-Millville-Bridgeton, NJ	10.3	8.9	7.9	5.6	51.2	5 187	3.9	135 300	132 866	2 600	2.0	13 000	8 100	-2 300	47 118
Wilmington, DE-NJ-MD	10.4	8.7	7.1	4.5	51.4	55 366	10.6	550 700	523 221	27 500	5.3	47 400	27 500	7 600	212 680

Area name	Households, (cont'd): Percent change, 1980–1990	Households, (cont'd): Percent: Female family house-holder[1]	Households, (cont'd): Percent: One-person	Births, 1988: Total	Births, 1988: Rate[2]	Births, 1988: Low birth weight[3] (Number)	Deaths, 1987: Number: Total	Deaths, 1987: Number: Infant[4]	Deaths, 1987: Rate: Total[2]	Deaths, 1987: Rate: Infant[5]	Marriages, 1984: Number	Marriages, 1984: Rate[2]	Divorces, 1984: Number	Divorces, 1984: Rate[2]	Physicians, active non-Federal, 1989: Number[6]	Physicians, active non-Federal, 1989: Rate[7]
	31	33	34	35	36	37	38	39	40	41	42	43	44	45	46	47
Louisville, KY-IN	7.9	13.5	25.3	13 108	13.6	934	8 905	110	9.2	8.5	10 512	10.9	5 978	6.2	2 391	247
Lubbock, TX	12.3	10.4	25.5	3 769	16.6	278	1 483	23	6.5	5.9	2 876	12.9	1 512	6.8	642	282
Lynchburg, VA	10.2	12.9	24.9	1 979	13.6	123	1 372	19	9.4	9.9	1 382	9.7	607	4.3	236	163
Macon-Warner Robins, GA	15.2	16.5	23.6	4 493	15.7	421	2 336	73	8.3	16.4	2 943	10.6	1 723	6.2	523	182
Madison, WI	18.4	8.0	26.4	5 071	14.4	283	2 147	33	6.2	6.4	3 033	9.0	1 255	3.7	1 581	442
Manchester, NH	30.0	8.9	22.1	5 805	17.5	284	2 455	40	7.6	7.2	3 364	11.4	1 343	4.5	556	164
Mansfield, OH	2.5	10.4	24.1	1 773	13.7	118	1 144	23	8.9	12.9	1 285	9.9	743	5.7	155	120
McAllen-Edinburg-Mission, TX	36.5	15.0	13.4	8 906	23.0	500	1 896	72	5.0	8.6	3 715	10.8	137	0.4	297	74
Medford, OR	16.8	9.1	24.0	1 913	13.1	99	1 344	12	9.4	6.4	1 297	9.5	981	7.2	256	171
Melbourne-Titusville-Palm Bay, FL	58.5	9.1	23.7	5 273	13.6	357	3 244	44	8.7	8.9	3 728	11.3	2 089	6.3	543	135
Memphis, TN-AR-MS	14.4	17.9	24.5	17 873	18.3	1 793	8 339	264	8.6	15.3	10 173	10.8	5 182	5.5	2 488	252
Merced, CA	24.2	12.5	17.7	3 771	22.2	190	1 171	30	7.1	8.1	955	6.2	739	4.8	187	107
Miami-Fort Lauderdale, FL	18.8	12.8	26.9	48 638	16.2	3 980	31 598	477	10.7	10.4	33 677	11.9	19 622	6.9	8 569	282
Ft.Lauderdale-Hollywood-Pom.Beach,	26.6	10.0	29.5	17 078	14.4	1 390	13 944	169	12.0	10.6	10 858	9.9	6 642	6.0	2 394	198
Miami-Hialeah, FL	13.5	14.9	24.9	31 560	17.4	2 590	17 654	308	9.9	10.3	22 819	13.2	12 980	7.5	6 175	336
Midland, TX	31.3	9.8	23.7	2 142	20.0	138	615	16	5.7	7.4	1 319	12.4	654	6.2	141	132
Milwaukee-Racine, WI	7.4	12.9	25.1	25 216	16.0	1 716	13 797	232	8.9	9.4	12 899	8.3	5 640	3.6	3 800	240
Milwaukee, WI	7.4	13.0	25.5	22 575	16.1	1 538	12 369	209	8.9	9.5	11 403	8.3	4 888	3.5	3 578	254
Racine, WI	7.3	12.3	22.0	2 641	15.2	178	1 428	23	8.3	8.6	1 496	8.7	752	4.4	222	127
Minneaolis-St. Paul, MN-WI	21.5	9.7	25.0	40 360	16.9	2 120	16 276	336	7.0	8.7	20 685	9.3	9 039	4.1	5 733	236
Mobile, AL	15.9	15.3	22.9	7 736	15.9	618	4 180	93	8.6	11.5	5 259	11.4	3 242	7.0	939	191
Modesto, CA	32.4	11.5	19.9	6 590	19.3	411	2 777	58	8.5	9.6	2 354	7.9	2 163	7.3	530	149
Monroe, LA	6.8	17.0	24.1	2 470	17.2	200	1 173	31	8.1	12.6	1 327	9.2	797	5.5	261	181
Montgomery, AL	13.9	15.7	24.5	5 009	16.7	420	2 438	67	8.2	14.0	3 312	11.4	1 976	6.8	460	152
Muncie, IN	1.1	10.6	25.9	1 458	12.1	86	1 080	15	9.0	10.0	1 170	9.5	409	3.3	214	179
Muskegon, MI	6.0	13.9	23.1	2 579	16.0	191	1 486	26	9.3	10.7	1 508	9.7	768	4.9	177	109
Naples, FL	81.7	7.1	22.6	2 012	14.5	141	1 338	27	10.2	14.4	1 219	10.9	646	5.8	256	175
Nashville, TN	24.5	12.2	24.6	15 266	15.7	1 184	7 675	146	8.0	9.9	12 333	13.8	5 844	6.5	2 757	278
New Bedford, MA	12.4	12.5	23.8	7 375	15.3	496	4 714	48	9.9	7.0	4 210	8.8	1 502	3.2	549	113
New Haven-Waterbury-Meriden, CT	12.2	12.5	25.9	12 090	15.2	890	7 663	110	9.7	9.3	6 267	8.1	3 083	4.0	3 100	388
New London-Norwich, CT-RI	14.0	9.6	23.1	4 151	16.8	239	1 997	41	8.1	10.3	2 495	10.1	1 110	4.5	472	191
New Orleans, LA	3.6	17.5	26.4	21 853	16.7	2 060	11 011	269	8.4	12.3	12 530	9.5	NA	0.0	4 059	312
N.Y.-North N.J.-Long Island,NY-NJ-CT	4.8	14.2	26.4	284 244	15.8	22 866	172 415	2 879	9.6	10.5	166 297	9.4	66 625	3.8	59 392	330
Bergen-Passaic, NJ	2.3	11.2	22.7	18 000	13.9	1 160	12 173	133	9.4	7.7	11 043	8.5	4 698	3.6	3 978	310
Bridgept-Stamfrd-Norwlk-Danbry,CT	8.7	11.3	22.9	11 943	14.6	797	6 938	87	8.5	7.4	7 151	8.8	2 663	3.3	2 347	289
Jersey City, NJ	0.4	16.5	28.7	9 207	17.0	811	5 920	88	10.8	10.0	5 184	9.3	2 001	3.6	1 041	195
Middlesex-Somerset-Hunterdon, NJ	24.8	9.2	20.8	14 826	15.2	837	7 400	112	7.7	7.9	7 441	8.1	3 792	4.1	2 514	254
Monmouth-Ocean, NJ	22.5	9.3	23.3	14 011	14.5	823	10 571	111	11.1	8.2	6 939	7.8	3 771	4.2	1 782	181
Nassau-Suffolk, NY	5.8	10.3	16.5	36 996	14.0	2 211	22 230	317	8.5	9.0	21 757	8.3	7 624	2.9	8 927	338
New York, NY	1.7	17.1	31.6	145 188	16.9	13 537	87 059	1 697	10.2	12.1	88 329	10.5	34 488	4.1	32 947	383
Newark, NJ	0.7	14.1	23.4	29 021	15.4	2 400	17 611	292	9.3	10.4	16 194	8.6	6 737	3.6	5 391	287
Orange County, NY	20.5	10.2	19.7	5 052	17.2	290	2 513	42	8.7	8.7	2 259	8.3	851	3.1	465	155
Norfolk-Virginia B.-Newport News, VA	27.9	13.1	21.1	17 031	12.3	1 206	8 956	314	6.6	19.3	14 589	11.5	6 094	4.8	2 586	183
Ocala, FL	72.0	10.3	22.9	2 640	13.9	200	2 045	24	11.2	9.1	1 858	12.0	1 147	7.4	213	107
Odessa, TX	4.6	11.3	22.5	2 383	19.1	183	785	19	6.2	8.4	1 932	14.4	1 202	9.0	153	126
Oklahoma City, OK	14.4	11.4	26.3	14 906	15.5	1 036	7 468	161	7.7	10.8	11 448	11.8	6 775	7.0	2 228	232
Olympia, WA	34.0	9.7	24.0	2 189	14.0	97	1 064	13	7.0	6.0	1 305	9.4	878	6.3	268	165
Omaha, NE	11.4	11.4	25.4	10 310	16.6	635	4 774	95	7.8	9.3	5 528	9.1	2 845	4.7	1 737	276
Orlando, FL	59.0	11.0	22.6	16 203	16.7	1 177	7 018	133	7.5	8.8	10 714	12.9	5 301	6.4	1 734	172
Owensboro, KY	9.4	11.5	24.8	1 248	14.2	70	747	8	8.5	6.0	990	11.3	527	6.0	134	153
Panama City, FL	40.8	11.1	23.0	2 070	16.5	125	998	16	8.1	8.1	1 658	15.0	1 072	9.7	163	126
Parkersburg-Marietta, WV-OH.	2.9	9.8	23.9	1 905	12.3	114	1 464	21	9.4	10.8	1 551	9.8	807	5.1	183	119
Pascagoula, MS	7.6	13.5	19.3	1 880	14.7	136	798	21	6.2	11.1	1 291	10.3	873	7.0	160	125
Pensacola, FL	28.9	13.1	22.4	5 657	16.2	431	2 734	69	7.9	12.7	4 196	13.0	2 486	7.7	571	160
Peoria, IL	-1.1	10.3	25.4	4 635	13.6	319	3 055	54	9.0	11.9	3 263	9.2	1 716	4.8	682	201
Phila.-Willming.-Trenton,PA-NJ-DE-MD	9.3	13.5	25.0	94 195	15.8	7 477	57 636	1 081	9.8	11.8	46 934	8.2	19 006	3.3	16 830	280
Philadelphia, PA-NJ	8.4	13.7	25.3	77 894	15.8	6 256	48 571	891	9.9	11.7	36 133	7.6	15 140	3.2	14 613	295
Trenton, NJ	10.5	13.2	24.2	5 080	15.3	400	3 101	73	9.5	15.3	2 590	8.3	1 074	3.4	905	271
Vineland-Millville-Bridgeton, NJ	6.4	15.8	21.6	2 291	16.6	176	1 294	29	9.4	13.3	1 034	7.7	571	4.3	179	129
Wilmington, DE-NJ-MD	17.7	11.9	23.1	8 930	15.6	645	4 670	88	8.3	10.6	7 177	13.3	2 221	4.1	1 133	194

1. No spouse present. 2. Per 1,000 resident population estimated as of July 1 of the year shown. 3. Under 2,500 grams. 4. Deaths of infants under 1 year old. 5. Deaths of infants under 1 year old per 1,000 live births. 6. As of end of year. 7. Per 100,000 resident population as of July 1 of the year shown.

Area name	Hospitals, 1989: Number	Hospitals, 1989: Beds: Number	Hospitals, 1989: Beds: Rate[1]	Nursing homes,[2] 1986: Number	Nursing homes,[2] 1986: Beds	Serious crimes known to police, 1988: Number: Total[3]	Serious crimes known to police, 1988: Number: Violent[4]	Serious crimes known to police, 1988: Rate[5]	Education: Public school enrollment[6]: 1986–1987	Education: Public school enrollment[6]: 1980	Education: Attainment,[7] 1980: Percent 12 years or more	Education: Attainment,[7] 1980: Percent 16 years or more	Education: Local government expenditures for education,[8] 1982: Total (Mil dol)	Education: Local government expenditures for education,[8] 1982: Per capita (Dollars)	Social Security Program December 1988: Beneficiaries: Total	Social Security Program December 1988: Beneficiaries: Rate[9]
	48	49	50	51	52	53	54	55	56	57	58	59	60	61	62	63
Louisville, KY-IN	24	5 282	545	147	8 100	NA	NA	0	147 618	161 238	63.0	13.8	324.9	2 543	155 645	161.0
Lubbock, TX	8	1 667	731	14	1 222	20 261	1 134	8 933	40 542	40 701	66.4	20.1	90.3	416	27 795	122.6
Lynchburg, VA	3	2 193	1 510	13	1 121	5 289	524	3 635	22 734	26 438	52.9	13.9	53.1	1 102	26 075	179.2
Macon-Warner Robins, GA	11	1 515	527	24	2 015	17 663	1 405	6 161	46 482	52 747	59.0	13.0	100.1	1 383	39 925	139.3
Madison, WI	7	2 686	752	26	2 356	17 902	806	5 074	48 920	55 433	83.7	30.9	155.4	469	42 055	119.2
Manchester, NH	9	1 548	457	41	2 575	13 144	385	3 957	52 072	52 549	71.1	18.5	109.6	384	42 535	128.0
Mansfield, OH	4	590	457	16	1 038	2 162	165	1 676	24 311	26 296	66.1	10.1	62.2	479	21 690	168.1
McAllen-Edinburg-Mission, TX	8	970	243	13	1 192	24 569	1 512	6 334	99 012	78 126	41.1	10.8	171.4	542	46 335	119.5
Medford, OR	3	517	345	13	727	7 151	548	4 901	23 905	24 990	73.9	15.3	73.2	543	28 210	193.4
Melbourne-Titusville-Palm Bay, FL	10	1 356	337	18	1 410	NA	NA	0	48 154	49 200	75.4	17.1	115.2	381	69 235	178.3
Memphis, TN-AR-MS	19	6 733	681	51	4 886	71 566	9 790	7 308	177 889	172 430	63.8	14.6	292.3	1 591	131 875	134.7
Merced, CA	6	361	207	21	677	8 298	949	4 881	36 955	29 356	60.4	10.5	89.9	631	20 040	117.9
Miami-Fort Lauderdale, FL	64	16 747	550	276	14 974	NA	NA	0	375 415	385 603	66.6	16.1	1 043.0	735	532 160	177.4
Ft.Lauderdale-Hollywood-Pom.Beach,	27	6 477	536	128	6 591	NA	NA	0	131 725	140 003	70.4	15.1	360.6	337	267 120	225.0
Miami-Hialeah, FL	37	10 270	560	148	8 383	NA	NA	0	243 690	245 600	64.0	16.8	682.4	398	265 040	146.1
Midland, TX	4	380	356	5	474	6 806	553	6 343	20 480	16 078	72.5	24.3	42.5	433	11 365	105.9
Milwaukee-Racine, WI	35	8 080	511	109	15 187	83 228	6 532	5 295	241 411	267 279	71.2	16.8	793.4	2 579	258 550	164.5
Milwaukee, WI	32	7 537	536	97	13 771	73 888	5 878	5 285	212 838	235 818	71.7	17.1	707.0	2 079	228 845	163.7
Racine, WI	3	543	311	12	1 416	9 340	654	5 374	28 573	31 461	67.7	14.0	86.4	500	29 705	170.9
Minneaolis-St. Paul, MN-WI	38	9 436	388	188	23 497	130 172	10 311	5 452	367 602	396 758	79.7	21.8	1 170.6	5 992	287 435	120.4
Mobile, AL	12	2 933	597	30	2 733	30 610	4 548	6 304	85 029	79 840	61.4	12.3	133.7	584	76 415	157.4
Modesto, CA	8	1 317	371	78	3 224	22 566	2 463	6 618	67 256	52 470	62.0	11.8	135.9	483	50 205	147.2
Monroe, LA	7	1 115	775	12	1 448	8 230	1 173	5 715	28 690	27 636	61.1	15.3	56.7	402	20 470	142.2
Montgomery, AL	11	1 712	567	20	1 641	14 165	970	4 709	52 840	52 646	64.5	17.5	82.5	947	44 050	146.4
Muncie, IN	1	552	461	11	1 066	4 348	291	3 620	21 440	25 300	66.4	14.9	49.3	392	19 870	165.4
Muskegon, MI	3	693	426	48	1 435	10 499	1 533	6 509	30 710	33 474	65.3	10.6	81.4	524	29 090	180.3
Naples, FL	2	543	371	7	473	NA	NA	0	16 087	13 110	71.2	18.5	47.8	475	32 215	232.6
Nashville, TN	26	7 289	734	76	5 626	48 577	6 637	4 999	154 682	151 304	63.5	16.8	259.8	2 387	128 930	132.7
New Bedford, MA	8	1 839	380	63	4 143	27 633	2 590	5 721	81 082	90 289	52.6	10.8	210.1	441	89 655	185.6
New Haven-Waterbury-Meriden, CT	15	3 928	492	103	8 503	49 746	4 519	6 262	106 990	131 483	67.8	17.9	329.7	432	135 165	170.1
New London-Norwich, CT-RI	5	1 109	449	31	2 068	7 435	488	3 003	34 677	45 090	71.0	16.9	111.7	465	36 410	147.1
New Orleans, LA	43	8 198	631	47	8 022	NA	NA	0	191 625	198 265	63.1	16.4	521.0	2 789	181 235	138.7
N.Y.-North N.J.-Long Island,NY-NJ-CT	260	102 632	570	930	112 966	NA	NA	0	2 476 392	NA	66.6	19.5	NA	NA	2 673 180	148.6
Bergen-Passaic, NJ	14	5 450	425	70	6 151	58 990	5 247	4 565	168 233	211 481	68.6	20.5	657.2	984	211 165	163.4
Bridgept-Stamfrd-Norwlk-Danbry,CT	13	3 299	406	56	5 461	41 516	3 319	5 080	113 090	146 984	73.0	25.9	410.1	506	121 535	148.7
Jersey City, NJ	10	3 050	570	11	1 849	41 310	5 432	7 619	68 286	81 864	51.5	11.2	228.5	408	80 945	149.3
Middlesex-Somerset-Hunterdon, NJ	15	4 899	495	60	5 094	35 743	2 339	3 654	131 736	160 630	72.3	20.7	507.7	1 781	129 595	132.5
Monmouth-Ocean, NJ	13	4 294	436	115	7 807	36 746	2 674	3 790	143 727	159 643	70.3	17.7	465.1	1 064	195 085	201.2
Nassau-Suffolk, NY	37	15 909	603	136	15 620	91 412	7 081	3 464	419 072	532 658	75.8	20.9	2 158.4	1 658	392 840	148.9
New York, NY	115	52 418	610	311	57 678	NA	NA	0	1 102 611	1 212 609	62.4	18.7	3 664.3	2 806	1 233 255	144.0
Newark, NJ	35	11 408	608	159	11 012	120 061	17 792	6 365	278 334	347 178	68.9	20.6	1 039.6	2 318	267 790	142.0
Orange County, NY	8	1 905	636	12	2 294	12 041	1 434	4 103	51 303	55 103	67.5	14.9	175.8	662	40 970	139.6
Norfolk-Virginia B.-Newport News, VA	31	7 062	501	71	5 946	80 971	6 342	5 867	218 791	224 578	66.2	15.8	464.5	5 408	149 035	108.0
Ocala, FL	4	612	308	21	831	NA	NA	0	25 456	22 078	59.5	9.6	56.7	407	49 265	259.6
Odessa, TX	2	455	374	4	445	12 552	482	10 066	25 579	23 143	61.1	12.0	65.5	485	14 715	118.0
Oklahoma City, OK	28	5 034	523	77	7 205	78 133	5 466	8 107	173 922	161 133	73.0	18.8	378.1	2 674	125 520	130.2
Olympia, WA	3	500	307	10	751	7 922	352	5 059	28 133	25 832	80.0	20.3	70.0	525	22 875	146.1
Omaha, NE	17	4 772	759	48	5 129	33 669	3 190	5 417	103 665	111 379	76.6	18.5	281.3	1 905	79 420	127.8
Orlando, FL	17	3 960	392	80	4 701	NA	NA	0	138 884	131 240	71.2	16.2	303.7	1 161	136 495	140.5
Owensboro, KY	3	545	621	14	925	NA	NA	0	13 278	14 581	61.3	11.0	27.2	313	15 310	174.4
Panama City, FL	3	505	391	10	644	NA	NA	0	21 341	20 384	65.8	13.2	47.3	454	18 855	150.2
Parkersburg-Marietta, WV-OH	5	855	557	20	1 324	4 120	136	2 668	28 775	32 970	66.4	11.4	67.6	852	27 935	180.9
Pascagoula, MS	2	536	417	4	284	4 736	646	3 697	24 871	26 579	67.5	11.3	45.1	367	14 435	112.7
Pensacola, FL	9	1 877	526	34	1 561	NA	NA	0	54 981	57 361	67.7	14.2	141.5	1 049	46 830	133.8
Peoria, IL	6	1 885	556	34	3 725	15 711	1 483	4 615	58 003	70 190	69.2	14.3	144.7	1 221	58 715	172.5
Phila.-Willming.-Trenton,PA-NJ-DE-MD	133	31 852	530	522	41 869	263 391	35 184	4 417	771 896	909 038	66.1	17.0	2 598.0	6 405	931 675	156.2
Philadelphia, PA-NJ	110	25 584	516	445	35 963	207 131	28 863	4 210	621 037	742 388	66.0	16.9	2 125.1	3 781	772 735	157.0
Trenton, NJ	8	2 186	654	26	1 608	22 003	2 765	6 647	44 052	48 487	67.8	21.8	165.0	534	52 310	158.0
Vineland-Millville-Bridgeton, NJ	3	645	464	7	844	8 056	1 002	5 821	25 007	27 165	53.3	8.7	75.1	562	25 310	182.9
Wilmington, DE-NJ-MD	12	3 437	590	44	3 454	26 201	2 554	4 569	81 800	90 998	69.6	18.0	232.8	1 528	81 320	141.8

1. Per 100,000 resident population estimated as of July 1 of the year shown. 2. Covers nursing homes with 3 or more beds. 3. Data for serious crimes have not been adjusted for underreporting, this may affect comparability between geographic areas or over time. 4. Includes murder and nonnegligent manslaughter, forcible rape, robbery, and aggravated assault. 5. Per 100,000 resident population as of July 1 of the year shown. 6. The 1986–1987 data are based on administrative reports obtained by the U.S. National Center for Education Statistics. The 1980 data are based on the 1980 Census of Population and Housing. 7. Persons 25 years old or older. 8. Elementary and secondary. 9. Per 1,000 resident population estimated as of July 1 of the year shown.

Table B. Metropolitan Areas — **Social Security, Housing, Labor Force, and Employment**

Area name	Social Security Program, Dec. 1988 (cont'd)		Housing units, 1990				Civilian labor force, 1990				Private nonfarm establishments, 1988			
					Occupied units				Unemployment				Employment[2]	
	Payments ($1,000)	Supplemental Security Income Program recipients, June 1986	Total	Percent change, 1980–1990	Total	Percent owner-occupied	Total	Percent change, 1989–1990	Total	Rate[1]	Number	Net change, 1987–1988	Total	Percent change, 1987–1988
	64	65	72	73	74	75	78	79	80	81	82	83	84	85
Louisville, KY-IN	76 412	14 276	392 033	8.1	367 819	67.5	520 695	0.6	26 563	5.1	22 472	349	374 907	2.0
Lubbock, TX	13 095	3 206	91 770	14.0	81 534	58.2	115 267	1.3	5 485	4.8	5 835	-80	72 150	1.8
Lynchburg, VA	12 187	3 164	56 839	10.5	52 922	68.5	74 911	1.0	3 615	4.8	3 490	25	62 157	0.7
Macon-Warner Robins, GA	16 423	7 692	111 506	16.8	103 182	62.6	134 830	1.4	6 390	4.7	6 544	97	89 063	3.6
Madison, WI	22 534	4 044	147 851	17.1	142 786	55.2	226 833	-0.3	5 766	2.5	9 651	135	147 040	4.6
Manchester, NH	21 739	1 726	135 622	34.0	124 567	63.7	189 253	2.2	11 542	6.1	10 304	271	164 160	1.8
Mansfield, OH	10 796	1 438	50 350	2.4	47 573	70.8	64 953	-1.7	4 733	7.3	2 866	9	49 839	1.8
McAllen-Edinburg-Mission, TX	16 465	13 154	128 241	44.0	103 479	70.3	164 362	2.7	31 324	19.1	5 757	228	67 775	3.6
Medford, OR	13 745	1 214	60 376	15.5	57 238	66.2	72 670	-0.7	4 954	6.8	3 977	72	42 578	6.4
Melbourne-Titusville-Palm Bay, FL	33 725	2 648	185 150	62.6	161 365	69.2	195 550	4.3	10 811	5.5	9 113	270	126 107	5.2
Memphis, TN-AR-MS	59 501	26 134	385 214	16.0	356 997	61.4	474 332	0.4	21 804	4.6	22 312	639	388 017	8.9
Merced, CA	8 886	5 852	58 410	16.7	55 331	54.4	73 095	-1.9	8 478	11.6	2 716	32	30 243	5.4
Miami-Fort Lauderdale, FL	269 538	78 440	1 399 948	21.6	1 220 797	60.2	1 612 477	1.5	100 080	6.2	96 708	2 172	1 153 702	2.3
Ft.Lauderdale-Hollywood-Pom.Beach,	143 139	8 994	628 660	29.3	528 442	68.0	660 159	2.0	36 231	5.5	37 956	1 456	426 412	2.7
Miami-Hialeah, FL	126 399	69 446	771 288	15.9	692 355	54.3	952 318	1.2	63 849	6.7	58 752	716	727 290	2.1
Midland, TX	5 891	860	45 181	44.1	38 920	65.9	47 885	-3.6	2 611	5.5	3 505	40	38 296	0.2
Milwaukee-Racine, WI	137 286	26 500	628 976	7.7	601 458	60.4	848 960	-2.1	33 120	3.9	39 197	687	695 059	3.3
Milwaukee, WI	121 578	23 728	562 031	7.8	537 722	59.4	759 136	-2.1	28 877	3.8	35 308	678	628 835	3.2
Racine, WI	15 708	2 772	66 945	7.0	63 736	68.3	89 824	-2.2	4 243	4.7	3 889	9	66 224	4.1
Minneaolis-St. Paul, MN-WI	148 922	15 764	988 735	22.8	935 516	68.7	1 410 227	1.5	59 991	4.3	61 696	1 339	1 161 171	2.6
Mobile, AL	34 488	10 630	202 153	22.4	173 943	69.3	211 224	-0.6	14 575	6.9	10 905	75	136 814	1.1
Modesto, CA	23 452	12 534	132 027	28.8	125 375	60.7	163 563	-0.8	18 552	11.3	7 280	171	91 621	4.8
Monroe, LA	8 935	4 144	56 300	9.4	50 518	64.8	68 722	-1.4	4 007	5.8	3 712	-107	47 655	-6.7
Montgomery, AL	19 090	8 642	116 754	14.6	105 531	67.1	137 333	-0.5	8 538	6.2	6 631	122	99 475	-1.0
Muncie, IN	10 245	1 502	48 793	2.5	45 177	66.8	60 611	-0.3	3 175	5.2	2 557	-52	41 732	4.1
Muskegon, MI	14 735	2 820	61 962	6.4	57 798	74.4	68 359	-0.3	6 350	9.3	3 190	50	48 938	-0.7
Naples, FL	17 261	846	94 165	85.6	61 703	70.2	78 307	8.7	4 225	5.4	5 323	416	51 027	11.3
Nashville, TN	60 599	15 736	410 968	28.5	375 831	63.2	532 706	0.7	21 140	4.0	26 058	654	440 110	4.1
New Bedford, MA	41 325	14 552	201 235	13.9	187 668	59.1	252 045	-0.3	21 880	8.7	11 914	255	189 101	1.5
New Haven-Waterbury-Meriden, CT	72 986	7 764	327 079	13.9	304 730	62.8	425 041	2.5	23 647	5.6	21 999	483	335 133	2.8
New London-Norwich, CT-RI	19 028	1 942	104 461	15.7	93 245	64.7	127 125	0.4	7 124	5.6	6 014	178	96 009	3.3
New Orleans, LA	84 479	27 076	524 056	9.5	455 178	58.0	577 471	-2.3	33 128	5.7	27 781	-427	418 412	-1.0
N.Y.-North N.J.-Long Island,NY-NJ-CT	1 449 349	344 276	7 042 994	5.8	6 570 875	50.8	9 031 741	0.3	481 752	5.3	506 668	5 425	7 500 371	1.1
Bergen-Passaic, NJ	119 625	12 828	487 329	4.5	464 149	63.9	706 663	-0.4	32 129	4.5	43 464	459	616 825	-0.2
Bridgept-Stamfrd-Norwlk-Danbry,CT	68 722	6 428	324 355	9.9	305 011	68.2	466 634	0.8	21 979	4.7	27 513	547	419 079	2.7
Jersey City, NJ	41 754	13 560	229 682	3.8	208 739	32.5	275 844	0.7	20 497	7.4	12 499	-20	208 827	2.1
Middlesex-Somerset-Hunterdon, NJ	72 195	7 176	382 814	26.2	365 085	70.7	590 322	3.3	21 980	3.7	26 958	908	465 450	3.0
Monmouth-Ocean, NJ	104 876	8 878	438 271	22.0	365 717	77.4	490 891	1.4	23 646	4.8	25 064	579	268 689	2.8
Nassau-Suffolk, NY	218 603	26 372	927 609	7.1	856 234	80.3	1 402 800	-2.1	53 556	3.8	85 062	1 212	1 014 260	2.6
New York, NY	656 556	238 878	3 449 058	2.3	3 252 399	33.3	4 010 467	0.8	250 584	6.2	225 619	672	3 581 907	0.1
Newark, NJ	146 450	26 280	693 062	1.6	652 035	59.1	952 533	0.3	51 118	5.4	53 301	812	844 174	1.7
Orange County, NY	20 568	3 876	110 814	18.8	101 506	67.5	135 587	-2.3	6 263	4.6	7 188	256	81 160	4.5
Norfolk-Virginia B.-Newport News, VA	67 146	15 844	537 101	29.9	493 536	58.9	623 916	0.9	29 453	4.7	29 117	664	433 459	3.1
Ocala, FL	23 599	2 630	94 567	70.9	78 177	75.6	80 781	2.9	5 583	6.9	4 510	136	49 432	9.0
Odessa, TX	7 394	1 234	48 789	14.5	42 322	65.8	51 268	-2.1	3 092	6.0	3 433	-73	35 936	4.1
Oklahoma City, OK	59 084	10 878	425 043	20.6	367 775	64.3	499 986	0.0	26 809	5.4	24 143	-356	309 956	0.4
Olympia, WA	11 435	1 370	66 464	31.1	62 150	64.7	83 521	5.0	4 141	5.0	3 492	69	32 804	2.4
Omaha, NE	40 039	5 468	247 538	11.8	232 352	64.2	340 743	3.0	8 791	2.6	15 682	227	261 232	4.0
Orlando, FL	65 251	9 254	448 490	62.1	401 659	61.9	640 528	4.1	33 994	5.3	28 219	1 030	441 127	6.8
Owensboro, KY	7 174	1 456	35 041	10.7	33 036	68.8	45 051	1.6	2 487	5.5	2 294	-34	32 094	9.4
Panama City, FL	8 358	1 914	65 999	53.8	48 938	65.5	60 531	-0.1	5 130	8.5	3 663	75	37 651	2.5
Parkersburg-Marietta, WV-OH	13 451	2 368	63 372	5.4	57 804	74.1	72 917	0.3	4 956	6.8	3 568	-27	52 482	6.8
Pascagoula, MS	6 739	1 342	45 542	6.8	40 454	73.5	54 895	2.5	4 224	7.7	2 039	-25	35 432	-2.1
Pensacola, FL	20 161	5 634	145 061	33.1	128 508	67.2	149 814	1.5	9 004	6.0	7 525	63	93 640	2.0
Peoria, IL	30 851	3 260	136 458	-2.6	129 363	68.0	166 435	0.7	9 839	5.9	7 498	60	128 613	10.8
Phila.-Willming.-Trenton,PA-NJ-DE-MD	489 904	88 106	2 307 675	9.2	2 154 104	69.4	2 997 565	0.9	142 480	4.8	140 480	3 169	2 375 108	2.5
Philadelphia, PA-NJ	406 582	74 796	1 907 150	8.4	1 777 365	69.6	2 446 469	0.7	113 682	4.6	114 851	2 395	1 925 759	2.2
Trenton, NJ	28 219	4 514	123 666	10.8	116 941	66.5	175 319	2.2	7 163	4.1	8 520	127	152 853	3.0
Vineland-Millville-Bridgeton, NJ	12 580	3 138	50 294	6.2	47 118	68.5	61 665	5.3	4 938	8.0	3 168	30	48 422	-1.2
Wilmington, DE-NJ-MD	42 523	5 658	226 565	15.8	212 680	69.5	314 112	0.4	16 697	5.3	13 941	617	248 074	5.1

1. Percent of total civilian labor force. 2. For week including March 12. Excludes government employees, self-employed persons, farm workers, domestic service workers, railroad employees subject to the Railroad Retirement Act, and employees on oceanborne vessels or in foreign countries.

Area name	Private nonfarm establishments, 1987 (cont'd)						Personal income, 1989							
	Employment[1] (cont'd)				Annual payroll								Per capita[3]	
	Manu-facturing	Retail trade	Finance, insurance, and real estate	Services	Total (Mil dol)	Average per employee	Total (Mil dol)	Percent change, 1988–1989	Wages and salaries[2] (Mil dol)	Propri-etor's income (Mil dol)	Dividends, Interest, & rent (Mil dol)	Transfer payments (Mil dol)	Dollars	Rank (Dollars)
	86	87	88	89	90	91	92	93	94	95	96	97	98	99
Louisville, KY-IN	86 774	82 085	27 226	104 834	7 375	19 672	16 246	7.1	10 838	1 300	2 871	2 318	16 768	97
Lubbock, TX	7 373	20 834	5 244	21 492	1 241	17 200	3 240	6.6	2 008	388	551	466	14 208	213
Lynchburg, VA	20 412	13 384	3 435	15 955	1 128	18 148	2 154	7.6	1 670	161	440	345	14 829	192
Macon-Warner Robins, GA	NA	23 677	7 550	22 949	1 631	18 313	4 386	6.9	3 073	321	624	764	15 261	164
Madison, WI	22 339	36 945	18 520	42 668	2 759	18 764	6 797	8.3	4 866	512	1 134	771	19 023	36
Manchester, NH	45 168	34 564	12 795	37 285	3 729	22 716	7 452	5.9	4 870	584	1 143	636	22 010	11
Mansfield, OH	18 422	10 693	2 756	11 067	1 015	20 366	1 982	5.6	1 426	139	304	329	15 366	154
McAllen-Edinburg-Mission, TX	10 031	20 734	3 645	14 856	847	12 497	3 118	10.0	1 730	310	507	722	7 814	282
Medford, OR	8 580	12 827	2 106	11 128	719	16 887	2 103	8.4	1 094	256	437	398	14 046	219
Melbourne-Titusville-Palm Bay, FL	25 352	31 217	5 260	45 054	2 624	20 808	6 618	10.4	4 100	327	1 297	1 127	16 445	106
Memphis, TN-AR-MS	60 847	80 916	30 828	112 737	7 782	20 056	16 302	7.4	11 700	1 281	2 126	2 452	16 484	105
Merced, CA	7 101	8 218	2 330	6 218	508	16 797	2 335	7.7	1 172	376	333	506	13 387	248
Miami-Fort Lauderdale, FL	139 119	268 883	112 236	354 450	23 023	19 956	59 433	8.6	34 500	3 844	15 156	8 386	19 526	30
Ft.Lauderdale-Hollywood-Pom.Beach,	44 740	116 148	42 365	131 110	8 323	19 519	26 470	9.2	12 086	1 396	7 970	3 652	21 898	X
Miami-Hialeah, FL	94 379	152 735	69 871	223 340	14 700	20 212	32 964	8.1	22 415	2 448	7 187	4 734	17 963	X
Midland, TX	2 905	7 915	2 690	9 090	852	22 248	1 898	4.7	1 218	200	467	170	17 765	65
Milwaukee-Racine, WI	193 210	136 035	48 021	204 618	14 677	21 116	29 551	6.9	20 651	1 712	5 013	4 292	18 686	44
Milwaukee, WI	166 573	122 670	45 328	188 654	13 305	21 158	26 506	6.9	18 800	1 547	4 538	3 844	18 842	X
Racine, WI	26 637	13 365	2 693	15 964	1 372	20 718	3 046	7.0	1 851	166	475	448	17 426	X
Minneaolis-St. Paul, MN-WI	263 312	232 038	98 439	339 139	26 939	23 200	49 234	7.5	37 124	2 984	7 434	5 404	20 227	20
Mobile, AL	24 647	33 677	7 632	39 012	2 357	17 228	6 380	7.3	3 758	565	987	1 153	12 985	256
Modesto, CA	21 819	22 863	3 944	23 306	1 750	19 100	5 212	8.8	2 864	587	873	962	14 689	199
Monroe, LA	7 241	11 269	5 637	13 130	846	17 753	1 839	5.1	1 202	165	292	332	12 783	259
Montgomery, AL	19 166	22 813	8 091	27 058	1 702	17 110	4 514	6.6	3 017	319	658	769	14 962	186
Muncie, IN	11 200	10 396	1 627	10 903	804	19 266	1 768	6.5	1 146	130	287	281	14 770	194
Muskegon, MI	17 376	10 995	1 743	11 702	1 013	20 700	2 258	6.6	1 403	143	353	473	13 895	228
Naples, FL	1 814	15 329	4 363	17 662	863	16 913	3 413	14.6	1 361	306	1 503	391	23 322	9
Nashville, TN	88 633	88 757	40 072	129 641	8 669	19 697	17 013	6.7	11 919	1 650	2 525	1 998	17 134	91
New Bedford, MA	65 257	45 850	8 300	40 299	3 512	18 572	9 117	6.7	4 666	590	1 263	1 576	18 845	39
New Haven-Waterbury-Meriden, CT	77 020	65 479	21 953	103 519	7 601	22 681	17 345	6.6	10 601	1 042	3 240	2 241	21 736	12
New London-Norwich, CT-RI	33 448	21 964	3 558	25 162	2 076	21 623	5 051	6.6	3 439	273	908	637	20 429	16
New Orleans, LA	43 793	103 414	31 665	140 257	8 139	19 452	19 165	4.9	12 601	1 644	3 170	3 053	14 745	197
N.Y.-North N.J.-Long Island,NY-NJ-CT	1 344 089	1 235 931	905 960	2 394 655	203 111	27 080	429 452	7.0	281 652	34 176	83 608	58 414	23 841	5
Bergen-Passaic, NJ	150 794	114 479	41 965	158 410	15 797	25 610	35 140	6.6	20 807	2 745	7 765	3 322	27 374	X
Bridgept-Stamfrd-Norwlk-Danbry,CT	115 854	78 447	34 663	110 470	12 211	29 138	25 545	6.6	15 549	1 881	5 456	2 068	31 438	X
Jersey City, NJ	45 157	36 183	13 412	41 890	4 754	22 765	9 861	7.2	7 183	458	1 630	1 630	18 440	X
Middlesex-Somerset-Hunterdon, NJ	112 520	87 240	37 357	108 234	12 470	26 791	26 442	6.8	17 002	1 655	4 184	2 093	26 716	X
Monmouth-Ocean, NJ	37 674	76 113	19 157	82 211	5 603	20 853	23 092	6.9	8 886	1 329	4 810	2 834	23 456	X
Nassau-Suffolk, NY	187 888	214 478	86 418	314 319	23 298	22 970	67 656	6.5	32 476	5 210	13 360	7 654	25 628	X
New York, NY	487 216	479 324	587 847	1 316 289	105 321	29 404	189 571	7.4	146 362	17 545	36 602	32 832	22 064	X
Newark, NJ	192 681	128 036	80 303	240 867	22 146	26 234	46 404	6.7	30 808	3 002	8 999	5 180	24 729	X
Orange County, NY	14 305	21 631	4 838	21 965	1 511	18 618	5 741	7.0	2 578	350	801	801	19 178	X
Norfolk-Virginia B.-Newport News, VA	65 416	114 335	25 946	133 853	7 490	17 280	22 161	6.3	16 015	1 106	3 224	3 227	15 721	138
Ocala, FL	8 347	14 652	2 765	12 309	731	14 788	2 525	10.8	1 194	187	603	572	12 699	264
Odessa, TX	4 012	9 473	1 991	8 150	646	17 976	1 685	5.6	1 032	175	284	220	13 850	231
Oklahoma City, OK	47 103	78 123	24 957	92 254	5 866	18 925	14 945	6.5	10 034	1 418	2 204	2 362	15 536	148
Olympia, WA	3 313	10 149	2 299	10 776	549	16 736	2 548	11.0	1 374	209	436	460	15 663	140
Omaha, NE	33 519	57 845	NA	85 745	4 851	18 570	10 534	7.5	7 650	788	1 626	1 393	16 753	100
Orlando, FL	53 506	103 544	29 424	158 803	8 304	18 825	17 705	10.2	12 960	1 355	2 613	2 165	17 540	74
Owensboro, KY	7 963	7 190	1 806	7 645	589	18 352	1 296	9.1	715	132	225	208	14 769	195
Panama City, FL	3 090	13 285	3 252	10 539	530	14 077	1 747	8.1	1 054	150	276	364	13 524	243
Parkersburg-Marietta, WV-OH	16 808	11 478	2 265	13 179	1 021	19 454	2 141	4.6	1 371	149	341	412	13 959	223
Pascagoula, MS	16 732	6 811	2 007	5 827	729	20 575	1 457	4.1	1 075	100	169	254	11 342	276
Pensacola, FL	10 743	26 600	4 824	30 549	1 496	15 976	4 824	7.8	2 994	341	690	985	13 509	245
Peoria, IL	36 599	26 707	7 839	34 968	2 871	22 323	5 850	8.2	3 898	463	1 122	853	17 266	85
Phila.-Willming.-Trenton,PA-NJ-DE-MD	480 478	459 532	201 447	790 697	54 089	22 773	119 714	7.6	78 451	8 251	21 148	17 302	19 909	25
Philadelphia, PA-NJ	374 653	377 305	162 415	649 360	43 373	22 523	97 903	7.4	62 798	6 830	17 265	14 598	19 750	X
Trenton, NJ	34 618	25 442	10 772	62 202	3 804	24 887	7 988	7.6	5 782	454	1 516	960	23 913	X
Vineland-Millville-Bridgeton, NJ	14 652	8 694	3 335	11 117	949	19 599	2 206	7.7	1 356	148	359	437	15 869	X
Wilmington, DE-NJ-MD	56 555	48 091	24 925	68 018	5 963	24 037	11 617	8.9	8 516	819	2 009	1 307	19 931	X

1. For week including March 12. Excludes government employees, self-employed persons, farm workers, domestic service workers, railroad employees subject to the Railroad Retirement Act, and employees on oceanborne vessels or in foreign countries. 2. Includes other labor income. 3. Based on the resident population estimated as of July 1 of the year shown.

Area name	Earnings, 1989: Total (Mil. dol)	Percent by selected industries: Farm	Goods-related[1]: Total	Goods-related[1]: Manu-fac-turing	Service-related & other[2]: Total	Service-related & other[2]: Retail trade	Service-related & other[2]: Finance, insurance, & real estate	Service-related & other[2]: Ser-vices	Govern-ment	Agriculture, 1987: Farms: Number	Farms: Percent with Less than 50 acres	Farms: Percent with 500 acres and over	Farm operators, Percent: Whose principal occupation is farming	Farm operators, Percent: Residing on farm operated	Land in farms: Acreage (1,000)	Land in farms: Percent change, 1982–1987	Acres: Average size of farm	Acres: Total irrigated (1,000)	Acres: Total cropland (1,000)
	100	101	102	103	104	105	106	107	108	109	110	111	112	113	114	115	116	117	118
Louisville, KY-IN	12 139	0.7	30.9	24.6	56.1	10.2	6.6	24.2	12.3	5 679	38.7	4.7	41.7	74.2	763	-2.6	134	2	509
Lubbock, TX	2 396	1.3	14.6	8.2	61.3	13.5	6.1	26.4	22.8	969	29.1	35.5	61.1	49.4	465	-15.6	480	124	411
Lynchburg, VA	1 831	0.5	43.1	36.9	45.3	10.3	5.3	19.8	11.0	1 036	20.8	9.0	42.8	73.0	228	-4.2	220	1	99
Macon-Warner Robins, GA	3 393	0.6	NA	18.4	NA	9.5	5.8	19.9	29.5	738	36.0	12.2	38.9	64.9	184	-16.6	249	11	112
Madison, WI	5 378	1.2	19.5	13.7	51.6	9.2	8.7	22.8	27.6	2 849	27.2	7.9	65.1	81.5	570	-5.3	200	3	475
Manchester, NH	5 454	0.2	38.6	31.0	53.0	10.5	6.5	24.2	8.2	338	42.3	4.1	43.5	85.5	43	-20.0	128	1	17
Mansfield, OH	1 564	0.7	47.0	41.9	41.7	9.1	4.0	17.4	10.6	1 022	26.6	6.4	47.5	80.7	169	-10.8	165	0	131
McAllen-Edinburg-Mission, TX	2 040	2.2	16.3	10.1	55.3	15.0	4.4	22.1	26.2	1 929	57.1	15.5	46.3	48.6	762	-8.5	395	231	448
Medford, OR	1 350	1.7	25.7	19.4	56.9	13.9	4.0	24.5	15.7	1 588	65.9	4.5	40.1	86.8	298	-1.1	188	53	73
Melbourne-Titusville-Palm Bay, FL	4 428	0.4	30.1	23.8	53.9	10.4	2.9	34.6	15.6	495	78.6	5.9	32.3	55.8	165	-14.9	333	17	28
Memphis, TN-AR-MS	12 981	0.4	20.1	14.4	63.2	10.1	NA	24.2	16.3	2 201	39.8	19.1	46.2	61.4	823	-14.2	374	53	701
Merced, CA	1 548	NA	13.9	13.8	33.6	8.9	3.7	13.5	25.1	3 048	55.1	10.7	59.0	68.5	1 049	-9.8	344	423	517
Miami-Fort Lauderdale, FL	38 344	0.5	15.2	9.0	70.8	12.2	8.9	32.4	13.4	2 071	84.2	2.6	43.1	55.6	119	-26.7	57	59	D
Ft.Lauderdale-Hollywood-Pom.Beach	13 482	0.2	18.4	9.8	69.7	14.0	8.9	33.2	11.7	448	82.1	3.6	38.8	55.8	36	-52.1	80	6	D
Miami-Hialeah, FL	24 862	0.7	13.5	8.5	71.4	11.2	8.9	31.9	14.4	1 623	84.8	2.3	44.3	55.5	83	-5.0	51	53	66
Midland, TX	1 418	0.2	36.5	5.2	51.2	8.6	5.2	23.1	12.1	343	49.0	29.4	39.1	53.6	733	-10.8	2 138	10	72
Milwaukee-Racine, WI	22 363	0.5	35.1	29.9	53.2	8.5	7.2	24.1	11.3	3 110	35.0	6.1	60.8	79.3	D	D	D	5	438
Milwaukee, WI	20 346	0.4	33.6	28.3	54.8	8.5	7.7	24.7	11.3	2 400	34.0	5.2	61.4	78.5	D	D	D	4	321
Racine, WI	2 017	1.0	50.8	45.8	37.2	8.7	2.2	18.3	10.9	710	38.3	9.0	58.6	82.0	133	-2.7	188	1	118
Minneaolis-St. Paul, MN-WI	40 108	0.4	30.3	24.4	57.1	9.1	8.0	23.8	12.2	10 295	31.5	6.1	51.7	83.1	1 717	-8.2	167	62	1 341
Mobile, AL	4 323	1.4	25.8	19.0	57.4	11.4	4.5	26.9	15.4	1 745	49.6	9.1	44.0	76.0	303	-11.4	174	17	201
Modesto, CA	3 451	7.1	30.2	21.1	48.7	11.3	4.1	21.2	14.0	4 630	68.6	5.0	50.9	75.3	720	-10.8	155	312	361
Monroe, LA	1 367	0.8	24.2	18.3	60.3	10.5	7.6	27.7	14.7	429	43.6	10.7	38.5	67.1	87	-6.8	204	5	59
Montgomery, AL	3 336	0.9	19.5	13.5	51.1	9.6	6.6	23.1	28.5	1 722	26.5	15.0	36.3	68.4	514	-15.8	298	3	234
Muncie, IN	1 276	0.9	36.9	32.1	45.6	11.1	2.9	22.3	16.5	834	37.1	12.0	46.6	71.8	179	-6.2	215	0	163
Muskegon, MI	1 546	1.0	43.7	37.9	41.4	10.0	2.2	19.9	14.0	460	35.9	7.8	45.9	79.3	82	-3.6	179	6	57
Naples, FL	1 667	4.8	18.7	3.6	67.0	14.4	7.5	34.2	9.5	224	43.3	34.4	61.2	38.4	332	18.7	1 483	43	60
Nashville, TN	13 569	0.6	26.0	18.9	61.3	10.9	7.3	28.0	12.1	10 341	35.8	4.3	36.3	72.4	1 395	-6.6	135	2	829
New Bedford, MA	5 256	0.5	36.9	29.3	50.0	12.4	3.6	20.5	12.7	675	59.0	0.7	53.0	80.7	43	1.6	63	2	21
New Haven-Waterbury-Meriden, CT	11 643	0.2	28.0	20.3	59.8	10.7	5.8	28.7	11.9	407	63.4	1.2	52.8	73.5	26	-12.7	64	1	15
New London-Norwich, CT-RI	3 712	1.0	36.2	29.6	40.0	9.5	2.4	19.7	22.8	556	34.4	3.2	55.8	79.5	74	-10.5	133	0	34
New Orleans, LA	14 244	0.2	20.7	10.5	64.6	10.2	6.6	30.2	14.5	733	61.1	5.6	36.7	60.2	136	-8.0	186	D	D
N.Y.-North N.J.-Long Island,NY-NJ-CT	315 828	0.1	19.7	14.2	67.3	7.6	14.5	29.8	12.9	6 578	63.2	3.0	47.2	77.4	D	D	D	D	D
Bergen-Passaic, NJ	23 552	0.1	29.4	22.6	61.9	9.7	7.1	25.6	8.7	183	89.6	0.0	45.9	69.9	4	-5.9	22	0	2
Bridgept-Stamfrd-Norwlk-Danbry,CT	17 430	0.0	33.0	26.7	59.7	9.1	9.8	27.0	7.3	261	69.7	0.0	49.4	79.7	14	-23.3	52	0	7
Jersey City, NJ	7 641	0.0	20.5	16.7	63.0	9.0	8.7	19.6	16.5	0	0.0	0.0	0.0	0.0	0	0.0	0	0	0
Middlesex-Somerset-Hunterdon, NJ	18 657	0.4	29.9	23.8	59.1	8.3	7.8	22.7	10.6	2 057	61.2	4.0	40.4	83.8	194	-4.0	94	3	142
Monmouth-Ocean, NJ	10 215	0.3	17.9	8.4	62.4	12.4	5.3	32.2	19.4	1 046	75.8	3.0	44.5	76.4	75	-4.6	71	8	55
Nassau-Suffolk, NY	37 685	0.2	22.0	14.8	62.5	10.3	7.7	30.1	15.3	763	70.1	1.2	66.8	60.3	43	-16.5	57	19	36
New York, NY	163 908	0.0	13.8	9.4	73.0	5.9	20.5	32.4	13.2	217	66.4	1.8	39.6	69.1	D	D	D	D	D
Newark, NJ	33 810	0.1	26.6	20.5	60.9	7.4	8.7	27.4	12.3	1 262	60.5	2.6	37.2	82.2	107	6.2	85	1	60
Orange County, NY	2 929	1.2	20.0	12.8	54.5	12.8	3.9	23.3	24.2	789	39.9	4.7	67.3	74.1	115	-11.5	146	3	79
Norfolk-Virginia B.-Newport News, VA	17 120	NA	18.8	11.8	42.8	8.8	3.9	20.4	38.1	966	46.4	14.9	53.5	67.6	222	-12.8	229	2	D
Ocala, FL	1 381	1.8	25.6	16.7	56.6	14.2	4.9	24.1	16.0	1 707	55.7	5.6	45.7	74.6	311	-6.5	182	6	112
Odessa, TX	1 207	0.2	37.3	16.6	48.5	11.2	3.7	20.4	14.0	223	69.1	17.0	26.5	69.1	589	0.7	2 641	2	6
Oklahoma City, OK	11 452	0.6	22.0	13.6	53.3	10.3	5.9	24.7	24.0	6 074	27.9	15.3	40.9	68.5	1 723	-0.9	284	11	834
Olympia, WA	1 582	3.1	12.7	6.6	41.2	10.1	3.1	20.6	43.0	806	68.9	1.4	36.6	89.1	57	-16.0	70	4	23
Omaha, NE	8 439	0.9	17.2	12.1	63.8	9.1	9.3	26.1	17.9	3 390	26.5	20.3	64.8	73.0	1 006	-0.8	297	33	900
Orlando, FL	14 315	1.6	20.6	12.6	65.4	11.8	6.9	32.6	12.4	2 018	72.5	7.9	47.0	56.7	1 009	-18.5	500	64	140
Owensboro, KY	847	2.8	29.0	19.3	54.8	11.5	4.0	23.1	13.4	1 288	43.7	9.5	45.2	66.1	249	3.6	193	1	208
Panama City, FL	1 204	0.0	15.2	8.3	53.2	14.8	4.5	24.9	31.6	85	57.6	3.5	32.9	68.2	11	-38.7	135	D	4
Parkersburg-Marietta, WV-OH	1 521	0.2	40.7	33.1	45.5	10.1	3.3	21.6	13.6	1 475	20.9	3.1	36.3	81.2	217	-3.8	147	1	100
Pascagoula, MS	1 175	0.3	53.4	47.9	30.3	6.9	2.3	15.1	16.1	206	56.8	4.4	27.2	77.7	21	-29.1	101	0	10
Pensacola, FL	3 335	0.1	18.0	10.9	49.7	10.2	3.6	25.3	32.2	937	48.0	8.1	44.0	76.2	147	-13.8	157	1	104
Peoria, IL	4 361	1.6	41.0	34.2	48.6	8.4	4.4	23.8	8.8	3 387	25.7	18.6	59.8	69.1	941	1.5	278	22	843
Phila.-Willming.-Trenton,PA-NJ-DE-MD	86 702	0.3	NA	20.8	NA	8.7	7.7	NA	13.8	7 291	50.8	5.4	55.2	79.3	905	D	124	69	707
Philadelphia, PA-NJ	69 628	0.3	25.9	19.2	60.7	9.0	7.9	30.2	13.1	4 792	53.0	4.0	56.6	79.4	515	D	108	30	393
Trenton, NJ	6 236	0.2	22.6	18.7	51.5	6.9	5.7	30.2	25.7	309	57.3	8.4	49.5	76.1	41	3.2	134	1	34
Vineland-Millville-Bridgeton, NJ	1 504	1.5	36.5	29.0	45.0	9.4	6.1	18.8	17.0	612	54.7	5.6	56.2	77.9	72	-3.7	118	19	57
Wilmington, DE-NJ-MD	9 334	0.6	NA	32.5	NA	7.8	7.9	NA	10.2	1 578	41.1	9.0	51.7	80.3	276	-5.9	175	19	223

1. Covers mining, construction, and manufacturing. 2. Covers private sector earnings in agricultural services, forestry, and fisheries; transportation and public utilities; wholesale trade; retail trade; finance, insurance, and real estate; and services.

Area name	Agriculture, 1987 (cont'd): Value of products sold: Total (Mil dol)	Agriculture, 1987 (cont'd): Value of products sold: Average per farm (Dollars)	Agriculture, 1987 (cont'd): Value of products sold: Percent from: Crops	Agriculture, 1987 (cont'd): Value of products sold: Percent from: Livestock and poultry[1]	Agriculture, 1987 (cont'd): Percent of farms with sales of: $10,000 or more	Agriculture, 1987 (cont'd): Percent of farms with sales of: $100,000 or more	Manufactures, 1987: Establishments: Total	Manufactures, 1987: Establishments: Percent with 20 or more employees	Manufactures, 1987: All employees: Number (1,000)	Manufactures, 1987: All employees: Annual payroll (Mil dol)	Manufactures, 1987: Production workers: Number (1,000)	Manufactures, 1987: Production workers: Work hours (Millions)	Manufactures, 1987: Production workers: Wages: Total (Mil dol)	Manufactures, 1987: Production workers: Wages: Average per worker (Dollars)	Manufactures, 1987: Value added by manufacture (Mil dol)
	121	122	123	124	125	126	127	128	129	131	132	133	134	135	136
Louisville, KY-IN	197	34 633	30.1	69.9	34.6	5.2	1 223	43.5	86.1	2 352.8	58.6	117.1	1 430.1	24 404	8 320.8
Lubbock, TX	140	144 460	44.4	55.6	64.1	25.2	270	23.3	6.9	141.2	4.2	8.0	69.7	16 595	410.6
Lynchburg, VA	18	17 279	29.1	70.9	29.2	3.1	229	40.6	21.0	474.1	14.6	29.0	285.8	19 575	1 461.7
Macon-Warner Robins, GA	36	48 947	48.2	51.8	34.0	12.9	262	35.9	18.7	471.6	13.7	27.9	323.2	23 591	2 310.3
Madison, WI	216	75 976	24.4	75.6	67.8	25.1	517	33.1	22.1	525.7	13.1	25.7	253.8	19 374	1 209.1
Manchester, NH	15	45 178	60.8	39.2	32.0	10.4	697	37.3	43.9	1 151.3	27.0	54.8	632.9	23 441	3 112.8
Mansfield, OH	37	35 899	47.4	52.6	48.7	10.1	219	43.4	18.1	511.0	13.6	28.5	362.2	26 632	775.7
McAllen-Edinburg-Mission, TX	233	120 837	94.3	5.7	41.1	15.1	190	33.7	10.4	138.9	8.2	15.9	91.6	11 171	338.4
Medford, OR	41	25 531	59.3	40.7	20.1	3.8	326	22.7	8.1	179.4	6.4	12.6	134.9	21 078	451.5
Melbourne-Titusville-Palm Bay, FL	22	43 471	77.1	22.9	31.9	6.9	387	25.1	24.3	665.0	10.5	19.7	206.6	19 676	1 412.6
Memphis, TN-AR-MS	128	58 114	89.9	10.1	40.4	15.1	1 178	44.1	60.3	1 330.8	40.1	79.8	741.9	18 501	4 114.2
Merced, CA	792	259 877	40.2	59.8	67.1	31.2	120	44.2	7.3	137.9	5.8	11.8	102.2	17 621	379.6
Miami-Fort Lauderdale, FL	294	141 894	94.9	5.1	46.4	17.7	5 185	25.8	132.6	2 504.3	88.4	170.8	1 326.1	15 001	5 700.2
Ft.Lauderdale-Hollywood-Pom.Beach,	43	96 748	81.7	18.3	43.5	14.7	1 790	22.2	43.3	936.0	26.2	51.9	446.1	17 027	2 138.3
Miami-Hialeah, FL	251	154 356	97.2	2.8	47.2	18.5	3 395	27.7	89.3	1 568.4	62.2	119.0	880.1	14 150	3 561.9
Midland, TX	15	42 373	44.2	55.8	38.2	11.1	111	20.7	2.5	72.9	1.2	2.5	26.8	22 333	135.0
Milwaukee-Racine, WI	197	63 191	38.6	61.4	57.9	18.9	3 407	38.8	189.5	5 160.9	119.0	236.4	2 834.9	23 823	11 609.4
Milwaukee, WI	142	59 024	33.4	66.6	57.7	18.5	3 023	39.0	164.0	4 442.6	104.8	209.6	2 537.2	24 210	9 666.1
Racine, WI	55	77 276	52.1	47.9	58.7	20.0	384	37.5	25.5	718.3	14.2	26.8	297.7	20 965	1 943.3
Minneaolis-St. Paul, MN-WI	458	44 518	35.3	64.7	51.2	13.0	4 494	36.7	250.1	7 486.3	128.0	253.4	2 989.8	23 358	15 732.2
Mobile, AL	94	53 715	78.4	21.6	34.3	8.8	517	30.8	25.0	598.5	18.3	36.4	393.8	21 519	2 114.0
Modesto, CA	786	169 745	38.5	61.5	59.1	22.1	379	35.4	23.2	531.9	17.4	34.1	354.9	20 397	2 209.2
Monroe, LA	17	39 096	73.0	27.0	30.8	10.0	161	31.1	7.1	190.7	4.8	9.6	121.5	25 312	527.5
Montgomery, AL	59	34 544	37.9	62.1	33.2	7.2	337	36.5	18.6	349.5	14.1	28.9	232.4	16 482	935.2
Muncie, IN	39	47 305	75.0	25.0	54.9	13.1	188	39.9	11.2	327.3	7.9	16.1	216.5	27 405	611.3
Muskegon, MI	27	57 622	57.0	43.0	42.6	14.3	275	36.7	17.7	481.7	12.0	24.1	291.4	24 283	1 151.6
Naples, FL	119	530 598	94.3	5.7	62.5	34.4	136	15.4	1.5	29.2	0.9	1.7	14.5	16 111	73.8
Nashville, TN	160	15 487	35.9	64.1	27.3	2.8	1 506	36.2	88.6	2 051.6	60.6	121.0	1 236.2	20 399	4 989.5
New Bedford, MA	30	44 401	64.0	36.0	42.1	9.5	1 072	43.3	66.8	1 347.0	46.6	89.4	741.6	15 914	2 882.9
New Haven-Waterbury-Meriden, CT	30	73 182	76.4	23.6	42.8	12.5	1 795	36.8	76.2	1 943.7	47.8	97.3	983.3	20 571	4 247.5
New London-Norwich, CT-RI	99	177 176	29.4	70.6	41.4	16.5	255	38.0	34.2	973.6	18.3	39.0	440.1	24 049	1 985.0
New Orleans, LA	17	23 322	D	D	24.7	D	937	29.1	43.1	1 145.4	27.3	55.6	676.1	24 766	4 314.7
N.Y.-North N.J.-Long Island,NY-NJ-CT	401	60 895	D	D	41.4	D	35 493	33.4	1 393.2	37 365.6	763.9	1 482.2	14 790.6	19 362	81 959.2
Bergen-Passaic, NJ	6	33 087	D	D	47.5	10.4	3 721	38.3	162.7	4 245.4	91.3	181.9	1 800.3	19 719	8 237.1
Bridgept-Stamfrd-Norwlk-Danbry,CT	15	58 529	42.7	57.3	35.6	10.7	1 796	36.9	117.0	3 813.6	52.5	105.6	1 201.1	22 878	6 441.4
Jersey City, NJ	0	0	0.0	0.0	0.0	0.0	1 385	37.0	46.0	977.8	32.1	61.4	536.7	16 720	2 635.9
Middlesex-Somerset-Hunterdon, NJ	74	36 171	64.7	35.3	31.2	6.2	1 753	42.7	110.2	3 250.4	57.2	115.9	1 315.4	22 997	8 799.1
Monmouth-Ocean, NJ	62	58 809	85.6	14.4	35.8	10.4	996	26.3	34.8	888.1	18.8	36.7	349.0	18 564	1 794.3
Nassau-Suffolk, NY	119	155 410	83.9	16.1	69.7	28.7	4 948	29.5	187.1	4 968.0	107.2	210.2	2 181.8	20 353	10 914.9
New York, NY	10	46 101	D	D	51.6	D	16 277	30.8	522.3	13 323.1	282.0	526.6	4 745.0	16 826	29 745.2
Newark, NJ	41	32 499	D	D	27.8	8.8	3 887	38.4	185.3	5 246.3	103.8	206.6	2 292.1	22 082	11 692.7
Orange County, NY	74	93 437	59.2	40.8	67.4	25.7	362	38.7	13.6	269.5	9.7	18.6	161.3	16 629	675.9
Norfolk-Virginia B.-Newport News, VA	70	72 459	67.3	32.7	51.6	18.1	912	34.6	66.0	1 625.6	51.4	100.1	1 112.7	21 648	4 285.3
Ocala, FL	94	54 894	14.2	85.8	28.4	6.9	208	28.8	6.5	113.4	4.6	8.9	69.3	15 065	247.7
Odessa, TX	3	15 583	9.6	90.4	19.3	3.6	223	24.2	4.0	107.3	2.2	4.6	48.8	22 182	386.5
Oklahoma City, OK	154	25 430	23.0	77.0	32.2	5.0	1 071	26.7	48.2	1 167.9	32.9	61.8	721.0	21 915	3 653.4
Olympia, WA	58	72 424	19.8	80.2	19.6	7.3	148	21.6	3.4	81.7	2.7	5.6	60.8	22 519	239.4
Omaha, NE	323	95 236	40.5	59.5	70.9	23.1	702	37.3	33.7	789.3	23.4	45.2	489.9	20 936	2 384.8
Orlando, FL	273	135 487	89.8	10.2	43.5	18.3	1 249	28.7	51.9	1 302.9	26.9	54.1	466.2	17 331	3 197.8
Owensboro, KY	45	35 068	84.3	15.7	44.2	9.2	97	44.3	7.5	194.0	5.2	10.1	127.7	24 558	635.6
Panama City, FL	0	0	NA	NA	18.8	D	114	19.3	2.8	64.8	2.2	4.6	47.9	21 773	170.3
Parkersburg-Marietta, WV-OH	19	13 192	21.9	78.1	18.7	2.6	195	36.9	14.4	420.4	9.3	19.2	243.0	26 129	1 430.2
Pascagoula, MS	3	12 451	18.8	81.2	16.5	1.5	89	38.2	16.8	463.1	10.8	21.0	277.8	25 722	1 332.4
Pensacola, FL	31	33 510	71.6	28.4	34.5	8.4	262	21.8	10.8	284.0	7.5	15.6	177.2	23 627	894.0
Peoria, IL	228	67 237	67.4	32.6	67.1	20.0	319	40.1	29.7	979.5	15.8	32.0	472.1	29 880	1 902.8
Phila.-Willming.-Trenton,PA-NJ-DE-MD	630	86 364	D	D	48.6	17.4	8 659	38.1	486.8	13 359.2	276.4	543.1	6 141.7	22 220	28 940.8
Philadelphia, PA-NJ	437	91 138	D	D	49.3	17.7	7 414	38.1	375.2	9 981.4	224.4	439.0	4 864.8	21 679	23 312.6
Trenton, NJ	14	45 165	80.6	19.4	41.1	12.0	468	37.2	39.8	1 058.1	15.9	32.7	377.8	23 761	1 359.2
Vineland-Millville-Bridgeton, NJ	58	95 155	89.6	10.4	52.0	22.9	235	40.9	15.2	308.4	11.6	22.5	211.2	18 207	820.4
Wilmington, DE-NJ-MD	121	76 522	50.3	49.7	46.5	15.2	542	38.7	56.6	2 011.3	24.5	48.9	687.9	28 078	3 448.6

1. Includes livestock and poultry products.

Area name	Manufactures, 1987 (cont'd): Value of shipments (Mil dol)	Manufactures, 1987 (cont'd): New capital expenditures (Mil dol)	Value of construction authorized by building permits, 1990: Total[1] ($1,000)	Nonresidential: Total ($1,000)	Nonresidential: Percent: Office	Nonresidential: Percent: Industrial	Nonresidential: Percent: Stores	Residential: New construction ($1,000)	Residential: Number of housing units	Residential: Alterations and additions ($1,000)	Wholesale trade, 1987: Establishments	Wholesale trade, 1987: Sales (Mil dol)	Wholesale trade, 1987: Paid employees[2]	Wholesale trade, 1987: Annual payroll (Mil dol)	Retail trade, all establishments, 1987: Number
	137	138	139	140	141	142	143	144	145	146	147	148	149	150	151
Louisville, KY-IN	18 210.7	332.3	670 084	208 448	28.7	10.5	34.8	365 329	4 796	18 758	1 896	11 140.1	23 736	516.1	8 774
Lubbock, TX	867.4	17.8	71 525	32 147	20.1	0.3	12.7	38 998	453	203	598	2 717.8	6 860	138.5	2 495
Lynchburg, VA	2 380.8	55.9	110 069	57 049	3.6	6.5	26.3	31 730	416	4 883	212	565.0	2 478	49.2	1 399
Macon-Warner Robins, GA	3 884.6	84.1	175 627	32 763	30.4	4.4	37.6	87 388	1 516	10 397	431	1 423.4	4 965	101.6	2 555
Madison, WI	2 604.8	65.9	395 530	96 249	53.6	7.8	12.2	195 299	2 801	31 290	660	2 394.1	8 554	198.3	3 398
Manchester, NH	4 690.2	146.3	227 525	39 529	10.4	4.9	47.4	104 956	1 202	33 305	742	3 301.0	10 323	278.6	3 356
Mansfield, OH	1 896.4	239.9	47 941	6 770	10.6	0.0	50.3	22 040	299	3 640	211	541.3	2 179	45.4	1 245
McAllen-Edinburg-Mission, TX	734.1	20.5	112 771	30 682	46.1	9.1	18.5	61 155	1 402	6 396	547	1 343.9	9 313	99.1	2 866
Medford, OR	1 163.2	25.7	157 843	24 352	42.5	8.9	14.9	111 423	1 511	8 279	263	579.4	1 991	40.7	1 604
Melbourne-Titusville-Palm Bay, FL	2 500.1	92.1	499 832	85 601	27.4	9.4	17.0	359 764	4 759	17 704	456	1 158.8	3 992	75.7	3 779
Memphis, TN-AR-MS	9 347.3	228.2	758 049	156 882	32.5	11.8	27.7	423 268	6 022	30 752	2 241	22 205.7	35 802	848.7	8 193
Merced, CA	1 322.6	21.9	141 154	21 077	15.1	10.0	26.1	101 691	1 178	7 208	154	578.4	1 588	33.6	1 192
Miami-Fort Lauderdale, FL	10 480.7	254.0	2 544 628	451 777	16.9	8.9	41.8	1 472 048	21 604	178 911	9 924	33 545.4	89 380	2 008.7	33 371
Ft.Lauderdale-Hollywood-Pom.Beach,	3 746.3	122.0	1 243 736	242 029	16.0	7.2	53.0	810 513	10 749	63 793	3 064	11 773.1	26 350	634.8	13 790
Miami-Hialeah, FL	6 734.4	132.0	1 300 893	209 748	17.9	11.0	29.0	661 535	10 855	115 119	6 860	21 772.3	63 030	1 373.9	19 581
Midland, TX	214.8	4.1	41 274	3 811	27.0	6.6	48.4	22 595	216	3 441	289	1 623.8	2 586	60.7	1 227
Milwaukee-Racine, WI	22 176.0	668.7	1 306 751	350 390	30.6	33.2	16.4	657 291	9 032	64 359	3 332	16 357.4	42 342	1 012.1	14 094
Milwaukee, WI	19 104.3	541.9	1 172 647	313 762	28.2	36.2	16.7	581 481	8 166	56 405	3 098	15 624.8	40 026	964.3	12 477
Racine, WI	3 071.7	126.9	134 104	36 628	50.9	7.3	13.6	75 810	866	7 954	234	732.7	2 316	47.8	1 617
Minneaolis-St. Paul, MN-WI	30 357.9	993.5	2 989 514	834 185	53.4	9.4	21.1	1 337 804	14 850	208 131	5 645	44 676.4	81 029	2 215.0	20 657
Mobile, AL	4 592.9	187.6	159 273	31 538	21.5	1.7	48.3	59 599	824	12 810	917	2 890.8	10 290	198.9	4 544
Modesto, CA	4 625.4	130.6	463 755	94 054	5.9	25.7	46.3	316 625	3 957	14 994	469	1 331.0	5 246	107.4	2 914
Monroe, LA	1 234.0	66.3	52 400	10 486	27.9	20.9	21.6	22 383	254	2 871	333	1 101.1	3 959	74.3	1 601
Montgomery, AL	1 895.2	56.8	145 841	47 815	24.0	13.9	33.9	50 359	936	11 254	521	2 486.3	7 047	142.8	2 578
Muncie, IN	1 177.3	44.9	43 861	12 462	17.5	3.0	45.3	20 414	258	1 633	163	445.4	1 905	37.1	1 184
Muskegon, MI	1 999.1	121.4	86 146	17 710	13.9	24.0	33.9	47 449	691	9 433	179	776.3	1 966	41.5	1 339
Naples, FL	129.7	5.5	534 561	78 111	25.3	7.4	16.9	415 803	5 846	19 351	214	346.6	1 378	25.3	1 886
Nashville, TN	11 727.8	342.3	973 734	302 125	21.4	10.2	35.4	430 328	6 261	50 909	2 101	10 742.9	29 652	679.1	9 713
New Bedford, MA	5 497.1	196.1	306 618	85 267	13.8	2.7	63.5	140 812	1 528	37 461	683	3 959.4	10 065	225.0	4 988
New Haven-Waterbury-Meriden, CT	7 374.4	295.5	386 153	58 811	11.9	10.6	35.5	129 173	1 875	52 737	1 577	7 734.3	21 518	548.8	7 817
New London-Norwich, CT-RI	2 930.9	87.3	131 249	22 630	6.6	17.1	33.3	62 450	751	25 126	261	636.5	2 701	63.7	2 687
New Orleans, LA	13 466.0	262.9	390 991	94 232	25.4	3.1	41.2	152 912	2 273	33 137	2 461	15 342.5	30 422	694.7	11 370
N.Y.-North N.J.-Long Island,NY-NJ-CT	149 611.3	3 916.0	6 712 390	1 543 669	29.7	7.9	32.2	2 224 185	26 887	1 283 995	47 647	398 584.4	606 092	17 445.2	167 778
Bergen-Passaic, NJ	14 998.9	380.8	508 490	88 568	63.6	4.1	14.3	127 285	1 545	152 678	4 828	57 696.7	76 838	2 233.7	13 646
Bridgept-Stamfrd-Norwlk-Danbry,CT	10 833.0	303.5	531 463	78 256	22.7	5.6	24.1	149 925	1 461	139 468	1 926	29 767.2	28 151	922.9	8 627
Jersey City, NJ	5 372.9	212.7	210 067	110 479	88.6	2.2	1.2	30 070	486	21 424	1 164	10 911.0	27 088	712.3	5 376
Middlesex-Somerset-Hunterdon, NJ	16 714.2	529.9	908 151	321 813	22.8	2.8	59.9	274 608	3 040	108 281	2 233	20 685.2	39 811	1 189.4	9 085
Monmouth-Ocean, NJ	3 282.9	97.5	561 529	89 247	17.1	10.5	26.8	275 767	3 353	124 067	1 412	4 056.4	12 390	292.2	9 525
Nassau-Suffolk, NY	17 949.2	559.5	1 069 688	234 176	13.5	18.9	35.2	331 141	5 024	240 605	8 194	33 527.9	86 288	2 312.4	28 813
New York, NY	54 138.0	1 101.6	1 706 825	269 163	29.5	4.8	24.8	763 645	9 090	273 461	22 937	207 016.9	256 900	7 633.3	72 839
Newark, NJ	23 336.3	605.3	1 048 678	305 832	26.4	11.8	23.5	191 454	1 813	207 586	4 505	31 039.3	68 304	1 917.4	16 974
Orange County, NY	1 344.3	48.8	167 500	46 134	14.6	1.1	56.1	80 290	1 075	16 426	448	2 789.6	6 838	148.1	2 893
Norfolk-Virginia B.-Newport News, VA	9 075.1	265.7	1 015 849	199 868	15.3	15.1	30.8	560 876	8 049	93 376	1 681	7 807.0	23 662	488.0	10 447
Ocala, FL	545.9	23.5	119 542	18 806	25.9	4.4	42.9	72 988	1 988	5 156	311	1 075.9	3 780	71.0	1 951
Odessa, TX	963.0	31.2	13 671	2 097	11.7	7.6	48.3	5 437	45	2 045	473	1 271.4	3 420	78.3	1 463
Oklahoma City, OK	9 348.3	140.9	344 548	64 351	23.9	5.7	39.1	178 538	2 067	20 694	1 981	8 274.8	21 566	471.1	10 009
Olympia, WA	609.8	24.0	215 836	25 894	65.3	0.1	8.9	170 350	2 622	8 474	155	276.6	1 446	29.8	1 387
Omaha, NE	5 553.9	118.9	383 716	106 700	49.0	2.8	19.8	171 509	3 370	18 177	1 381	8 550.6	19 904	441.3	5 401
Orlando, FL	5 655.3	203.4	2 007 111	362 803	12.4	4.7	35.0	1 236 617	18 831	65 683	2 306	11 433.1	27 838	626.4	9 808
Owensboro, KY	2 046.0	86.4	31 102	6 676	15.5	20.3	35.5	17 647	315	2 460	184	531.3	1 946	33.7	1 095
Panama City, FL	447.2	D	96 490	25 199	9.3	6.9	56.6	53 326	725	5 769	198	379.9	1 781	27.9	1 670
Parkersburg-Marietta, WV-OH	2 857.4	128.7	38 619	18 723	22.9	36.9	19.9	6 904	89	2 588	243	811.4	2 436	44.3	1 499
Pascagoula, MS	3 801.2	58.8	36 065	11 046	1.0	1.7	70.8	14 140	282	6 984	107	498.4	920	15.9	1 087
Pensacola, FL	1 836.7	D	171 031	32 437	34.3	19.9	20.7	112 354	1 997	8 677	495	1 193.3	5 017	94.0	3 336
Peoria, IL	4 165.4	192.3	252 245	104 023	41.6	8.9	26.8	77 422	849	9 846	645	4 710.3	8 556	214.0	3 240
Phila.-Willming.-Trenton,PA-NJ-DE-MD	63 287.5	1 647.8	3 427 530	1 054 879	43.8	16.0	21.0	1 225 402	17 115	371 369	11 192	73 631.8	150 974	3 999.6	52 334
Philadelphia, PA-NJ	49 790.0	1 271.1	2 615 767	824 101	47.9	14.9	17.8	946 858	11 907	310 282	9 641	63 054.2	127 406	3 334.2	43 261
Trenton, NJ	2 593.0	84.0	232 653	54 698	24.1	45.5	7.6	63 078	1 004	23 036	521	2 621.2	7 376	203.8	3 026
Vineland-Millville-Bridgeton, NJ	1 537.9	47.8	56 724	13 914	3.4	39.4	27.3	18 810	294	8 992	225	767.9	2 899	60.4	1 347
Wilmington, DE-NJ-MD	9 366.6	244.9	522 385	162 165	33.6	9.6	41.5	196 657	3 910	29 059	805	7 188.4	13 293	401.1	4 700

1. Includes nonresidential additions and alterations, residential nonhousekeeping buildings, and residential garages and carports not shown separately. 2. For pay period including March 12.

Area name	Retail trade, all establishments, 1987 (cont'd): Sales: Total (Mil dol)	Retail trade, all establishments, 1987 (cont'd): Sales: Percent change, 1982–1987	Retail trade, all establishments, 1987 (cont'd): Sales: Per capita[1] (Dollars)	Retail trade, establishments with payroll, 1987: Number	Retail trade, establishments with payroll, 1987: Sales: Total (Mil dol)	Sales: Per capita[1] (Dollars): General merchandise stores	Sales: Per capita[1] (Dollars): Food stores	Sales: Per capita[1] (Dollars): Apparel and accessory stores	Sales: Per capita[1] (Dollars): Eating and drinking places	Paid employees[2]	Annual payroll (Mil dol)	Taxable service industries–establishments with payroll, 1987: Number	Receipts (Mil dol): Total	Receipts (Mil dol): Selected kinds of business: Hotels, motels & other lodging places	Receipts (Mil dol): Selected kinds of business: Health services	Receipts (Mil dol): Selected kinds of business: Legal services
	152	153	154	155	156	157	158	159	160	161	162	163	164	165	166	167
Louisville, KY-IN	6 043.0	41.5	6 249	5 618	5 915.1	847	1 239	256	656	78 057	709.5	6 091	2 701.8	122.8	1 027.9	204.7
Lubbock, TX	1 661.1	23.5	7 305	1 487	1 587.1	986	1 324	380	739	19 022	186.7	1 586	597.1	19.3	238.5	45.9
Lynchburg, VA	902.8	35.4	6 217	967	883.6	937	1 321	258	550	12 196	106.0	859	358.5	14.6	82.5	14.0
Macon-Warner Robins, GA	1 913.1	55.1	6 762	1 855	1 879.4	867	1 174	276	609	22 747	212.9	1 717	701.9	37.1	337.7	41.0
Madison, WI	2 566.8	43.9	7 399	2 448	2 531.2	849	1 180	373	793	35 627	310.4	2 489	1 133.0	61.1	314.2	92.3
Manchester, NH	3 165.0	88.0	9 753	2 265	3 100.7	1 592	1 681	518	706	32 882	360.9	2 694	1 154.4	71.8	247.7	105.5
Mansfield, OH	851.6	41.6	6 622	800	830.9	1 126	1 200	223	592	10 291	96.8	707	212.9	4.6	83.1	9.3
McAllen-Edinburg-Mission, TX	1 552.4	14.8	4 086	1 657	1 495.0	692	932	304	308	18 700	168.0	1 268	452.3	32.2	208.6	43.7
Medford, OR	1 080.2	63.4	7 549	1 022	1 048.6	1 015	1 205	239	575	12 041	144.5	983	257.7	22.4	99.2	14.9
Melbourne-Titusville-Palm Bay, FL	2 514.0	68.9	6 724	2 387	2 446.7	885	1 258	169	680	29 636	284.3	2 533	1 751.4	79.5	266.1	45.3
Memphis, TN-AR-MS	6 429.7	49.2	6 645	5 404	6 280.1	891	1 162	349	549	72 495	712.3	5 810	2 672.7	171.0	730.0	149.3
Merced, CA	715.1	33.9	4 339	765	686.7	441	1 059	119	366	7 907	81.8	694	169.4	7.6	73.8	10.3
Miami-Fort Lauderdale, FL	23 736.7	47.2	8 046	21 761	23 188.1	862	1 385	481	818	251 671	2 735.5	29 812	13 391.7	1 118.7	3 952.5	1 576.4
Ft.Lauderdale-Hollywood-Pom.Beach,	10 410.9	55.0	8 950	8 625	10 140.8	829	1 546	419	940	109 968	1 162.1	11 840	5 457.1	442.7	1 751.6	448.6
Miami-Hialeah, FL	13 325.8	41.6	7 458	13 136	13 047.3	884	1 280	522	739	141 703	1 573.3	17 972	7 934.6	676.0	2 200.9	1 127.8
Midland, TX	730.3	2.4	6 826	724	704.4	1 062	1 626	361	572	7 521	79.8	874	319.9	13.3	73.5	36.6
Milwaukee-Racine, WI	9 980.7	38.2	6 409	9 427	9 792.9	782	1 188	285	659	129 052	1 159.9	10 583	4 578.0	156.5	1 242.9	388.7
Milwaukee, WI	8 918.3	37.6	6 436	8 332	8 751.4	779	1 197	290	671	115 750	1 042.8	9 579	4 228.0	151.3	1 108.2	368.0
Racine, WI	1 062.4	44.3	6 187	1 095	1 041.5	812	1 115	247	562	13 302	117.1	1 004	350.0	5.2	134.7	20.7
Minneaolis-St. Paul, MN-WI	17 071.3	49.3	7 312	13 311	16 762.0	1 017	1 226	343	736	214 355	1 992.8	17 075	9 269.5	405.7	2 030.0	818.9
Mobile, AL	2 793.8	43.3	5 775	2 982	2 714.7	720	1 223	241	525	33 903	318.2	2 802	1 061.1	62.9	383.4	95.3
Modesto, CA	2 036.8	56.2	6 217	1 812	1 977.7	775	1 344	224	535	21 461	238.6	1 943	747.8	20.0	361.8	32.2
Monroe, LA	935.2	36.3	6 454	1 012	901.3	920	1 304	393	592	11 912	104.4	973	380.9	13.3	143.6	29.8
Montgomery, AL	1 827.3	58.2	6 126	1 647	1 780.7	831	1 002	292	556	20 382	200.3	1 758	686.7	45.8	254.3	60.2
Muncie, IN	719.8	25.9	5 969	758	697.8	775	1 111	252	631	10 007	82.4	688	206.3	4.3	78.8	10.3
Muskegon, MI	860.4	46.0	5 384	912	837.6	1 079	977	159	553	10 831	96.4	807	236.1	12.0	94.1	17.6
Naples, FL	1 174.3	73.6	8 985	1 236	1 133.1	837	1 901	563	889	13 328	139.3	1 261	522.4	164.4	102.4	37.2
Nashville, TN	7 091.3	68.3	7 404	5 840	6 893.3	994	1 282	336	749	83 116	808.7	7 107	3 505.7	295.7	994.9	183.1
New Bedford, MA	3 680.0	60.4	7 710	3 234	3 582.9	841	1 531	463	681	42 101	422.1	2 775	825.6	41.6	263.2	66.2
New Haven-Waterbury-Meriden, CT	5 981.1	62.3	7 580	5 222	5 811.3	831	1 400	443	625	64 042	693.8	5 933	2 409.1	70.3	730.2	209.8
New London-Norwich, CT-RI	1 882.3	62.7	7 680	1 822	1 833.6	775	1 348	404	672	20 955	226.3	1 506	639.9	51.9	159.1	61.0
New Orleans, LA	7 537.1	19.1	5 720	7 220	7 342.2	671	1 332	319	647	101 987	952.3	9 038	4 573.6	475.1	1 375.1	673.0
N.Y.-North N.J.-Long Island,NY-NJ-CT	115 680.2	49.9	6 446	111 127	112 285.7	664	1 233	506	610	1 167 520	14 086.0	145 074	89 175.8	3 298.9	14 219.7	11 090.1
Bergen-Passaic, NJ	11 230.0	54.6	8 671	8 707	10 910.8	960	1 532	670	674	107 155	1 311.1	12 515	6 330.1	179.9	1 223.7	341.2
Bridgept-Stamfrd-Norwlk-Danbry,CT	7 465.6	61.3	9 119	5 838	7 272.6	931	1 579	638	676	71 464	918.8	8 304	4 791.6	158.9	775.8	338.3
Jersey City, NJ	2 805.7	46.6	5 133	3 365	2 683.7	288	1 119	632	394	28 538	318.5	2 858	1 224.5	44.3	212.6	90.4
Middlesex-Somerset-Hunterdon, NJ	7 506.0	59.7	7 770	5 785	7 311.7	918	1 556	521	614	75 698	857.1	7 409	4 143.4	133.0	708.1	260.7
Monmouth-Ocean, NJ	7 530.9	67.6	7 878	6 169	7 351.0	790	1 598	398	641	75 890	845.5	7 314	2 729.7	70.3	733.4	202.4
Nassau-Suffolk, NY	22 158.6	56.7	8 431	19 301	21 586.3	837	1 592	529	623	209 476	2 540.1	25 321	11 552.7	253.3	3 019.1	772.5
New York, NY	42 699.0	40.7	4 990	48 739	41 295.0	543	931	486	614	455 273	5 633.2	64 011	49 275.4	2 153.0	5 792.0	8 101.3
Newark, NJ	12 262.5	45.5	6 490	11 369	11 912.1	541	1 375	427	565	123 999	1 439.4	15 554	8 573.7	274.9	1 583.0	928.1
Orange County, NY	2 022.0	63.2	7 026	1 854	1 962.5	845	1 603	369	505	20 027	222.2	1 788	554.7	31.3	172.0	55.2
Norfolk-Virginia B.-Newport News, VA	8 738.6	62.7	6 474	7 604	8 636.6	730	1 253	330	631	107 288	1 015.8	7 909	3 548.5	405.0	841.8	199.6
Ocala, FL	1 204.1	64.1	6 602	1 216	1 165.3	766	1 346	186	564	13 986	134.8	1 110	376.2	38.2	135.5	25.1
Odessa, TX	805.3	-18.9	6 391	858	775.3	903	1 504	321	599	9 164	92.6	861	314.3	11.2	D	28.3
Oklahoma City, OK	6 097.2	5.2	6 303	6 058	5 897.7	764	1 172	363	673	75 191	701.3	7 124	2 626.6	110.7	812.6	336.6
Olympia, WA	853.8	45.0	5 651	879	836.2	693	1 365	169	551	9 945	100.4	936	291.2	14.9	133.1	14.1
Omaha, NE	3 905.9	33.8	6 364	3 733	3 831.6	853	1 165	269	679	52 704	456.6	4 285	2 153.7	80.3	524.9	149.8
Orlando, FL	8 296.0	91.2	8 852	6 388	8 095.3	947	1 500	371	1 034	92 505	946.1	8 268	6 453.6	1 148.2	1 034.1	303.4
Owensboro, KY	565.2	29.1	6 437	697	545.2	1 083	1 281	262	582	7 289	64.7	569	176.1	17.7	67.2	11.5
Panama City, FL	950.7	63.9	7 717	1 136	924.2	985	1 616	293	1 015	12 495	106.9	976	328.9	60.7	107.3	15.1
Parkersburg-Marietta, WV-OH	982.0	31.0	6 319	939	955.9	1 104	1 234	196	525	11 846	110.2	866	332.8	18.2	88.8	12.5
Pascagoula, MS	504.4	21.8	3 934	671	482.5	504	1 008	138	360	6 676	59.2	579	157.0	D	46.9	17.5
Pensacola, FL	2 084.8	54.2	6 027	2 154	2 031.3	787	1 135	223	570	25 517	231.8	1 989	778.3	54.0	307.4	58.7
Peoria, IL	2 141.1	30.5	6 320	2 096	2 096.1	829	1 139	236	556	24 780	232.3	1 861	701.5	30.3	219.6	62.8
Phila.-Willming.-Trenton,PA-NJ-DE-MD	39 445.8	54.2	6 673	33 440	38 361.6	780	1 276	374	565	432 561	4 558.2	39 922	21 996.1	782.5	4 689.2	2 162.1
Philadelphia, PA-NJ	31 960.7	52.9	6 544	27 382	31 052.9	757	1 259	380	560	353 974	3 731.0	32 820	18 353.0	636.1	3 875.9	1 883.7
Trenton, NJ	2 399.6	57.7	7 340	2 015	2 341.7	865	1 364	478	649	25 324	281.4	2 590	1 484.4	64.5	293.0	95.4
Vineland-Millville-Bridgeton, NJ	932.3	54.9	6 781	837	900.2	672	1 496	287	386	8 662	94.1	761	244.2	4.9	77.0	22.6
Wilmington, DE-NJ-MD	4 153.2	62.5	7 383	3 206	4 066.8	953	1 319	281	599	44 601	451.7	3 751	1 914.5	77.0	443.3	160.4

1. Based on the estimated population as of July 1 of the year shown. 2. For the period including March 12 of the year shown.

Area name	Taxable service industries–establishments with payroll, 1987 (cont'd): Paid employees	Taxable service industries–establishments with payroll, 1987 (cont'd): Annual payroll (Mil dol)	Banking: Bank deposits,[1] June 1989 (Mil dol)	Banking: Savings capital,[2] September 1989 (Mil dol)	Federal funds and grants, 1989: Expenditures (Mil dol)	Federal funds and grants, 1989: Per capita[3] (Dollars): Total	Per capita[3] (Dollars): Direct payments for individuals	Per capita[3] (Dollars): Procurement contract awards	Per capita[3] (Dollars): Salaries and wages	Per capita[3] (Dollars): Grant awards	Local government finances, 1981–1982: General revenue: Total (Mil dol)	General revenue: Intergovernmental (Mil dol)	General revenue: Taxes: Total (Mil dol)	Taxes: Per capita[4]: Total (Dollars)	Taxes: Per capita[4]: Property (Dollars)
	168	169	170	172	174	176	177	178	179	180	181	182	184	185	186
Louisville, KY-IN	65 984	976.4	9 938	2 262.1	2 507.6	2 588	1 685	244	387	255	797.4	337.1	293.7	306	178
Lubbock, TX	13 293	210.5	2 040	1 112.2	584.9	2 565	1 436	179	543	291	188.2	66.6	73.4	337	267
Lynchburg, VA	7 863	142.4	1 119	522.7	432.5	2 979	1 703	896	160	207	106.3	47.3	45.6	320	192
Macon-Warner Robins, GA	16 193	246.6	1 544	794.7	1 433.0	4 986	1 933	585	2 145	303	275.2	84.4	87.6	323	230
Madison, WI	26 803	462.9	2 527	1 016.8	1 309.5	3 665	1 313	216	395	1 500	419.0	180.5	155.6	471	461
Manchester, NH	24 753	458.3	4 868	447.2	1 093.0	3 228	1 372	1 192	435	215	241.7	51.1	156.6	549	541
Mansfield, OH	7 777	86.1	763	417.6	283.1	2 195	1 616	60	222	257	118.6	52.5	46.4	357	278
McAllen-Edinburg-Mission, TX	10 714	142.9	2 246	1 052.1	767.3	1 923	1 187	145	129	398	294.8	169.5	65.8	206	160
Medford, OR	6 095	97.9	645	425.8	390.7	2 610	1 983	65	330	224	148.9	67.8	53.6	398	364
Melbourne-Titusville-Palm Bay, FL	34 426	791.0	2 206	1 340.8	3 182.7	7 907	2 321	4 720	754	107	313.1	128.5	84.3	279	220
Memphis, TN-AR-MS	66 574	1 031.4	7 242	1 907.7	2 976.7	3 010	1 621	173	740	441	893.5	301.6	352.5	380	263
Merced, CA	4 037	58.8	706	366.1	516.5	2 962	1 399	259	780	349	264.2	142.8	45.4	317	254
Miami-Fort Lauderdale, FL	276 377	5 116.4	29 801	33 067.6	9 066.8	2 979	2 178	90	321	379	3 999.6	1 516.2	1 314.1	472	377
Ft.Lauderdale-Hollywood-Pom.Beach,	110 484	1 978.8	8 055	14 910.1	3 690.1	3 053	2 564	94	193	187	1 252.2	350.8	488.3	456	364
Miami-Hialeah, FL	165 893	3 137.6	21 746	18 157.5	5 376.7	2 930	1 923	87	406	506	2 747.4	1 165.4	825.8	482	385
Midland, TX	7 105	120.0	1 487	493.4	171.4	1 605	1 096	44	312	113	108.1	24.2	50.1	510	396
Milwaukee-Racine, WI	116 627	1 936.3	12 261	6 716.2	4 312.9	2 727	1 789	170	273	460	2 374.9	1 094.6	767.8	490	483
Milwaukee, WI	107 021	1 795.2	10 943	6 269.4	3 938.7	2 800	1 806	187	294	478	2 160.8	988.4	702.1	504	496
Racine, WI	9 606	141.1	1 318	446.8	374.2	2 141	1 650	34	101	307	214.1	106.2	65.7	380	377
Minneaolis-St. Paul, MN-WI	227 891	3 743.9	23 485	6 482.5	7 325.3	3 010	1 291	746	330	519	3 455.8	1 664.1	915.8	418	394
Mobile, AL	25 777	398.0	2 735	1 052.9	1 269.7	2 584	1 781	215	269	302	303.3	133.4	95.1	209	84
Modesto, CA	17 383	279.4	1 998	1 352.9	732.5	2 065	1 451	131	106	275	415.1	224.9	98.1	348	259
Monroe, LA	8 202	140.3	1 166	394.3	317.5	2 206	1 550	47	160	348	129.0	65.9	37.4	265	131
Montgomery, AL	16 412	268.9	2 200	315.9	1 377.7	4 566	1 915	242	1 159	1 214	188.1	93.5	58.7	207	51
Muncie, IN	5 561	81.6	725	338.4	265.5	2 218	1 687	50	150	282	103.8	55.9	34.7	276	275
Muskegon, MI	6 281	95.9	884	144.7	441.2	2 715	1 786	417	111	378	169.8	70.2	62.2	400	396
Naples, FL	12 608	189.2	1 708	978.5	443.8	3 033	2 242	161	135	485	107.5	29.8	56.2	559	510
Nashville, TN	81 033	1 275.1	9 075	1 916.4	2 134.2	2 149	1 414	72	366	258	763.0	228.6	322.7	372	216
New Bedford, MA	22 867	322.2	5 007	448.0	3 259.6	6 737	1 713	4 402	125	491	455.6	234.4	178.3	375	371
New Haven-Waterbury-Meriden, CT	59 858	975.3	13 701	728.6	2 313.7	2 899	1 764	228	280	617	724.1	220.8	414.7	543	536
New London-Norwich, CT-RI	14 532	266.7	2 767	317.7	3 613.2	14 617	1 655	10 877	1 774	301	200.8	66.7	109.9	456	451
New Orleans, LA	105 814	1 690.9	9 061	7 155.3	4 824.5	3 712	1 566	1 196	464	411	1 517.9	545.9	555.6	426	147
N.Y.-North N.J.-Long Island,NY-NJ-CT	1 477 419	33 010.8	382 576	64 185.6	60 891.9	3 380	1 764	591	351	659	33 879.3	12 805.4	16 193.6	926	635
Bergen-Passaic, NJ	112 875	2 329.6	17 994	8 642.8	3 584.9	2 793	1 815	581	187	200	1 471.4	458.0	842.3	650	643
Bridgept-Stamfrd-Norwlk-Danbry,CT	75 232	1 732.6	17 702	763.0	3 723.8	4 583	1 608	2 416	235	305	881.5	200.2	582.9	718	710
Jersey City, NJ	24 524	455.8	5 849	2 187.2	1 600.8	2 993	1 743	295	451	489	800.9	430.3	258.9	463	457
Middlesex-Somerset-Hunterdon, NJ	74 447	1 621.0	11 020	4 502.0	2 363.7	2 388	1 449	464	263	201	1 095.1	365.9	580.5	647	637
Monmouth-Ocean, NJ	54 155	1 054.9	9 676	5 468.7	3 345.9	3 399	2 136	421	654	179	1 092.0	413.4	506.2	582	571
Nassau-Suffolk, NY	214 108	4 127.0	43 908	10 159.1	10 087.0	3 821	1 656	1 552	276	325	4 891.4	1 634.2	2 748.2	1 054	884
New York, NY	749 646	18 256.0	249 643	18 631.0	29 610.7	3 446	1 824	205	344	1 055	20 696.9	8 004.3	9 340.3	1 125	574
Newark, NJ	160 094	3 232.6	24 177	13 016.3	5 653.6	3 013	1 703	518	403	378	2 595.0	1 127.6	1 189.2	634	615
Orange County, NY	12 338	201.3	2 607	815.5	921.5	3 078	1 461	237	1 003	357	355.1	171.5	145.1	546	529
Norfolk-Virginia B.-Newport News, VA	92 029	1 427.8	7 605	3 606.5	9 559.7	6 782	1 773	1 537	3 204	260	1 234.3	537.1	475.0	395	232
Ocala, FL	8 240	129.4	1 210	733.6	563.7	2 836	2 449	116	107	152	126.9	64.3	25.8	185	173
Odessa, TX	6 288	114.8	784	510.9	179.6	1 476	1 236	10	77	149	165.3	47.7	71.7	529	448
Oklahoma City, OK	57 904	1 039.0	6 315	2 365.3	3 574.5	3 716	1 731	277	1 185	505	1 012.9	336.4	326.1	351	186
Olympia, WA	6 715	106.1	568	446.1	718.1	4 414	1 774	51	215	2 367	138.3	88.1	33.2	249	176
Omaha, NE	51 791	852.7	4 859	2 137.5	2 166.1	3 445	1 630	433	992	305	748.0	220.7	295.5	496	414
Orlando, FL	116 175	2 008.0	6 756	3 875.8	3 859.6	3 824	1 660	1 392	591	171	803.7	351.5	231.1	303	250
Owensboro, KY	4 906	70.2	590	315.4	193.2	2 203	1 668	124	132	228	79.2	25.3	17.3	199	116
Panama City, FL	8 176	117.7	505	411.9	584.9	4 527	2 136	561	1 663	159	145.7	64.1	24.7	237	161
Parkersburg-Marietta, WV-OH.	7 546	113.4	1 141	291.0	508.4	3 314	1 849	670	359	417	155.6	60.7	41.0	259	211
Pascagoula, MS	4 056	65.1	456	220.0	981.2	7 642	1 446	5 667	365	139	138.0	42.4	31.8	255	232
Pensacola, FL	19 849	304.0	2 099	276.3	1 615.2	4 523	2 109	433	1 754	207	341.2	154.3	63.1	205	181
Peoria, IL	16 591	287.9	2 289	1 515.7	857.7	2 532	1 773	184	253	173	387.9	119.8	179.0	492	425
Phila.-Willming.-Trenton,PA-NJ-DE-MD	443 195	8 370.0	84 717	20 094.4	21 463.5	3 570	1 908	559	590	495	7 092.9	2 858.0	2 969.0	519	362
Philadelphia, PA-NJ	366 367	6 981.2	55 895	16 781.8	17 547.9	3 540	1 960	560	609	397	5 973.3	2 316.4	2 589.8	546	361
Trenton, NJ	29 629	600.2	3 422	1 718.2	1 852.2	5 546	1 788	1 087	415	2 242	443.9	201.4	183.3	593	584
Vineland-Millville-Bridgeton, NJ	6 746	95.5	701	895.6	354.3	2 549	1 863	106	125	429	163.5	95.2	49.9	373	367
Wilmington, DE-NJ-MD	40 453	693.1	24 699	698.8	1 709.1	2 932	1 548	360	637	345	512.2	245.0	146.0	276	243

1. Includes deposits for all insured and reporting noninsured commercial and mutual savings banks. 2. Includes savings capital for all FSLIC insured savings institutions. 3. Based on the estimated population as of July 1 of the year shown. 4. Based on the estimated population as of July 1, 1982.

Area name	Local government finances, 1981–1982, (cont'd)										State and local government employment, 1989		Federal government civilian employment, 1989		Elections,[3] 1988	
	Direct general expenditure								Debt outstanding							
				Percent of total for–												
	Total (Mil dol)	Percent change, 1977–1982	Per capita[1] (Dollars)	Education	Health & hospitals	Police protection	Public welfare	Highways	Total (Mil dol)	Per capita[1] (Dollars)	Total	Rate[2]	Total	Earnings ($1,000)	Total vote cast for president	Vote for lead party (Percent)
	187	188	189	190	191	192	193	194	195	196	197	198	199	200	201	202
Louisville, KY-IN	753.7	33.4	784	43.1	7.8	6.4	2.0	2.3	1 225	1 275	47 548	490.8	11 921	382 455	373 551	R–53.5
Lubbock, TX	175.6	66.0	806	51.4	12.3	5.6	0.1	3.7	133	610	20 075	880.5	2 232	64 199	73 292	R–69.3
Lynchburg, VA	106.3	48.5	746	50.0	0.7	5.3	5.6	4.5	117	819	8 977	618.3	545	17 310	51 610	R–66.9
Macon-Warner Robins, GA	262.3	71.2	966	38.2	28.9	5.7	0.2	3.2	138	508	17 058	593.5	18 187	525 644	81 091	R–54.7
Madison, WI	419.0	50.3	1 267	43.5	7.5	6.7	5.1	7.4	190	575	59 107	1 654.3	4 242	135 747	176 158	D–59.8
Manchester, NH	258.5	55.3	906	42.4	0.5	5.1	3.4	8.1	159	558	12 407	366.4	3 706	135 018	135 778	R–65.0
Mansfield, OH	118.0	43.2	908	52.7	5.7	4.0	4.6	5.8	50	386	6 781	525.7	748	23 298	50 047	R–60.0
McAllen-Edinburg-Mission, TX	281.3	98.5	882	60.9	4.7	3.2	0.3	3.3	216	678	24 210	606.6	2 137	73 042	83 870	D–64.8
Medford, OR	140.0	72.8	1 040	52.3	5.6	6.9	0.6	5.4	64	478	7 532	503.1	1 753	53 651	61 912	R–52.5
Melbourne-Titusville-Palm Bay, FL	299.0	62.3	988	47.0	8.6	5.3	0.6	4.5	454	1 501	16 588	412.1	6 372	220 558	149 159	R–70.3
Memphis, TN-AR-MS	882.7	55.5	952	33.1	5.0	7.7	0.1	5.2	1 695	1 827	59 750	604.1	20 441	588 608	353 540	R–52.5
Merced, CA	254.1	72.2	1 773	41.3	11.2	3.3	13.0	3.3	87	607	10 513	602.8	1 339	30 207	42 414	R–51.2
Miami-Fort Lauderdale, FL	3 704.1	87.5	1 331	31.8	11.2	7.4	0.6	3.4	3 302	1 186	155 063	509.4	25 340	870 337	930 870	R–52.8
Ft.Lauderdale-Hollywood-Pom.Beach,	1 150.3	84.0	1 074	34.4	16.7	9.9	0.2	5.6	932	870	57 163	472.9	5 928	197 008	440 605	R–50.0
Miami-Hialeah, FL	2 553.8	89.2	1 491	30.6	8.8	6.3	0.8	2.4	2 370	1 384	97 900	533.5	19 412	673 329	490 265	R–55.3
Midland, TX	100.7	165.7	1 024	49.8	18.9	5.4	0.1	3.8	93	946	5 908	553.2	1 015	35 294	39 326	R–77.9
Milwaukee-Racine, WI	2 283.6	47.2	1 457	38.1	10.7	7.1	4.2	6.0	1 158	739	80 341	508.0	11 591	376 238	742 289	D–53.1
Milwaukee, WI	2 082.4	48.1	1 493	37.7	10.8	6.9	4.2	5.7	1 097	787	72 748	517.2	11 146	362 575	665 658	D–53.2
Racine, WI	201.2	38.3	1 164	42.9	10.1	9.0	4.5	8.6	61	351	7 593	434.4	445	13 663	76 631	D–51.7
Minneaolis-St. Paul, MN-WI	3 356.9	60.4	1 531	34.9	7.0	4.2	10.5	6.6	4 337	1 978	156 451	642.8	22 161	754 700	1 195 170	D–54.5
Mobile, AL	312.1	57.2	685	42.8	7.3	7.1	0.1	6.5	640	1 404	25 150	511.8	3 232	106 978	154 286	R–63.6
Modesto, CA	396.0	60.9	1 405	40.9	10.9	5.2	14.8	3.2	143	507	19 609	552.7	876	27 259	97 315	R–53.1
Monroe, LA	110.9	63.8	785	51.1	3.2	6.2	0.0	4.4	195	1 380	10 375	721.0	613	19 587	50 292	R–67.3
Montgomery, AL	178.8	64.9	632	46.1	2.9	7.5	0.6	8.3	135	478	26 026	862.6	7 371	198 339	97 683	R–61.2
Muncie, IN	106.2	40.5	845	46.4	1.6	3.4	7.6	4.3	30	238	9 326	779.1	477	15 433	48 112	R–56.8
Muskegon, MI	166.4	26.4	1 071	54.7	4.9	4.4	2.9	2.8	149	959	8 156	501.9	428	13 661	62 907	R–53.4
Naples, FL	98.1	91.2	975	48.7	1.9	8.1	0.4	14.1	112	1 110	5 652	386.3	496	16 080	51 980	R–74.9
Nashville, TN	704.5	47.7	812	36.9	11.3	6.4	0.9	5.3	1 114	1 285	53 106	534.9	11 520	371 835	333 210	R–56.4
New Bedford, MA	417.5	17.2	879	50.3	0.8	6.1	0.7	3.6	318	669	25 002	516.8	1 376	42 532	193 530	D–55.7
New Haven-Waterbury-Meriden, CT	711.7	40.8	932	46.3	2.2	5.9	2.3	4.2	742	971	41 432	519.2	6 326	215 614	342 361	R–50.9
New London-Norwich, CT-RI	206.5	36.3	856	54.1	1.3	4.8	2.3	6.2	132	547	14 126	571.4	4 805	144 328	102 851	R–51.2
New Orleans, LA	1 393.2	86.1	1 068	37.4	9.5	6.6	0.7	4.8	1 657	1 270	71 809	552.5	15 892	527 087	470 943	R–53.3
N.Y.-North N.J.-Long Island,NY-NJ-CT	30 834.3	34.7	1 763	33.4	7.0	5.9	14.9	3.5	22 804	1 304	1 118 259	620.8	180 638	6 017 324	6 435 068	R–49.6
Bergen-Passaic, NJ	1 454.7	40.7	1 123	47.2	3.8	6.4	5.2	4.3	999	771	61 117	476.1	6 066	197 836	547 446	R–57.5
Bridgept-Stamfrd-Norwlk-Danbry,CT	880.1	46.3	1 084	46.6	2.5	6.2	2.8	4.7	543	669	36 738	452.1	4 910	161 585	374 878	R–59.0
Jersey City, NJ	781.6	54.9	1 397	29.8	10.2	6.8	11.9	1.5	443	792	30 993	579.5	11 676	382 692	184 463	D–53.4
Middlesex-Somerset-Hunterdon, NJ	1 091.4	46.4	1 216	49.2	3.0	5.5	4.6	5.7	974	1 085	63 232	638.8	6 793	220 838	416 494	R–58.3
Monmouth-Ocean, NJ	1 060.6	41.6	1 219	46.9	1.3	5.6	7.0	5.0	1 056	1 215	46 619	473.5	15 782	602 421	431 515	R–63.0
Nassau-Suffolk, NY	4 804.5	37.2	1 843	46.7	3.9	8.3	8.3	4.3	3 602	1 381	155 948	590.7	22 066	691 805	1 106 768	R–58.6
New York, NY	17 868.2	30.6	2 152	24.8	9.4	5.3	20.1	3.0	13 518	1 628	589 314	685.9	86 804	2 899 592	2 546 165	D–61.7
Newark, NJ	2 529.8	40.0	1 349	42.8	3.3	5.9	9.6	3.4	1 467	783	116 860	622.8	21 459	722 906	722 529	R–53.7
Orange County, NY	363.4	42.9	1 367	52.0	2.2	2.5	14.9	5.9	201	756	17 438	582.4	5 082	137 649	104 810	R–62.4
Norfolk-Virginia B.-Newport News, VA	1 189.4	58.0	989	39.1	4.7	5.6	4.3	5.5	1 064	884	74 177	526.2	58 123	1 747 490	429 799	R–58.7
Ocala, FL	123.7	90.0	888	52.7	18.2	6.2	0.2	3.4	41	297	10 320	519.1	604	16 175	62 520	R–66.4
Odessa, TX	154.8	131.0	1 142	51.2	17.5	4.0	1.0	2.9	73	538	7 623	626.4	258	8 021	34 152	R–67.8
Oklahoma City, OK	953.5	106.5	1 026	39.6	9.7	4.9	0.2	5.2	1 821	1 960	71 297	741.1	31 321	1 002 256	338 680	R–63.0
Olympia, WA	136.7	100.4	1 026	51.2	2.5	4.2	0.1	6.7	83	620	25 258	1 552.4	833	27 840	66 930	D–50.6
Omaha, NE	694.2	46.4	1 166	44.0	12.2	4.2	0.6	5.8	1 630	2 738	37 736	600.1	9 428	272 664	248 176	R–57.1
Orlando, FL	851.1	112.2	1 118	39.8	3.1	6.8	0.9	3.8	895	1 175	50 954	504.8	9 415	284 084	287 825	R–69.1
Owensboro, KY	87.8	81.0	1 009	31.0	39.9	5.0	0.6	2.4	230	2 649	4 935	562.7	304	9 339	32 445	R–53.5
Panama City, FL	136.1	86.2	1 305	40.9	22.3	4.6	0.4	4.0	61	589	7 239	560.3	3 754	104 335	43 851	R–72.5
Parkersburg-Marietta, WV-OH	152.6	93.4	965	44.3	20.3	3.4	1.8	3.9	113	717	7 759	505.8	1 851	48 279	57 479	R–59.5
Pascagoula, MS	120.5	65.7	967	37.4	28.7	4.6	0.3	6.2	191	1 533	7 108	553.6	816	27 591	40 364	R–73.9
Pensacola, FL	334.4	75.0	1 086	50.1	8.0	4.2	0.5	3.8	335	1 088	17 994	503.9	11 785	354 896	119 882	R–70.1
Peoria, IL	360.1	47.8	989	45.4	1.4	5.2	1.6	7.9	364	1 001	15 055	444.4	1 950	64 501	141 112	R–53.8
Phila.-Willming.-Trenton,PA-NJ-DE-MD	6 537.7	44.3	1 144	41.7	3.4	6.6	5.0	4.1	7 368	1 289	307 841	512.0	90 206	2 872 761	2 390 416	R–50.6
Philadelphia, PA-NJ	5 410.1	43.3	1 141	41.1	3.8	6.9	4.6	3.9	6 162	1 299	219 890	443.6	81 204	2 568 411	1 986 958	R–50.2
Trenton, NJ	460.1	65.1	1 489	39.9	1.7	4.9	9.8	4.3	414	1 339	46 580	1 394.6	3 594	120 546	135 345	D–50.8
Vineland-Millville-Bridgeton, NJ	163.8	50.3	1 224	48.7	1.2	4.2	16.9	4.0	123	917	9 642	693.7	491	15 732	48 349	R–53.8
Wilmington, DE-NJ-MD	503.7	37.3	951	47.3	0.5	6.0	0.6	6.0	669	1 263	31 729	544.3	4 917	168 072	219 764	R–55.1

1. Based on the estimated population as of July 1, 1982. 2. Per 10,000 resident population estimated as of July 1 of the year shown. 3. Data subject to copyright.

Table B. Metropolitan Areas — **Land Area and Population**

MSA/ CMSA/ NECMA/ PMSA code[1]	Area name	Land Area,[2] 1990 (Sq. Km.)	Population, 1990: Total persons	Population, 1990: Rank	Population, 1990: Per square kilometer	Race: White	Race: Black	Race: Am. Indian, Eskimo, Aleut	Race: Asian & Pacific Islander	Race: Other race	Hispanic[3]	Age of population, Percent: Under 5 years	5 to 14 years	15 to 24 years	25 to 34 years	35 to 44 years
		1	2	3	4	5	6	7	8	9	10	11	12	13	14	15
6200	Phoenix, AZ	23 838	2 122 101	20	89.0	1 799 420	74 257	38 017	36 294	174 113	345 498	8.0	14.3	14.6	18.5	14.8
6240	Pine Bluff, AR	2 292	85 487	271	37.3	47 878	36 877	227	352	153	427	7.3	16.0	16.5	15.0	13.7
6282	Pittsburgh-Beaver Valley, PA.	9 932	2 242 798	19	225.8	2 041 897	178 857	2 257	16 174	3 613	12 852	6.2	12.1	12.9	15.7	14.7
0845	Beaver County, PA	1 127	186 093	X	165.1	174 759	10 475	203	377	279	1 124	6.3	13.2	12.3	15.1	14.2
6280	Pittsburgh, PA	8 805	2 056 705	X	233.6	1 867 138	168 382	2 054	15 797	3 334	11 728	6.2	12.0	13.0	15.8	14.8
6323	Pittsfield, MA	2 412	139 352	204	57.8	135 122	2 534	242	1 001	453	1 407	6.3	12.6	14.8	15.1	14.7
6403	Portland, ME	2 164	243 135	139	112.4	238 403	1 565	628	2 147	392	1 560	7.0	12.8	14.5	18.2	16.3
6442	Portland-Vancouver, OR-WA	11 320	1 477 895	27	130.6	1 350 155	41 671	13 603	52 030	20 436	49 921	7.4	14.4	13.1	17.4	17.7
6440	Portland, OR	9 694	1 239 842	X	127.9	1 124 963	38 695	11 307	46 360	18 517	44 049	7.3	14.1	13.1	17.5	17.8
8725	Vancouver, WA	1 626	238 053	X	146.4	225 192	2 976	2 296	5 670	1 919	5 872	7.8	16.2	13.2	16.5	17.2
6453	Portsmouth-Dover-Rochester, NH-ME	2 756	350 078	106	127.0	342 511	2 901	607	3 203	856	3 232	7.9	13.7	14.8	19.6	16.8
6460	Poughkeepsie, NY	2 076	259 462	132	125.0	229 194	21 788	374	5 826	2 280	9 765	7.1	13.0	14.9	17.9	16.1
6483	Providence-Pawtucket-Fall Rvr, RI-MA	2 436	916 270	45	376.1	835 537	35 465	3 719	17 264	24 285	44 040	6.7	12.3	15.5	17.3	14.6
6520	Provo-Orem, UT	5 176	263 590	130	50.9	253 596	374	1 913	3 958	3 749	8 488	10.7	21.5	24.3	15.1	10.1
6560	Pueblo, CO	6 187	123 051	227	19.9	104 304	2 253	991	729	14 774	44 090	6.9	15.1	13.6	14.9	14.6
6640	Raleigh-Durham, NC	5 221	735 480	55	140.9	533 056	183 447	1 933	13 834	3 210	9 019	6.9	12.2	17.8	20.7	16.8
6660	Rapid City, SD	7 191	81 343	275	11.3	72 769	1 288	5 835	933	518	1 777	9.2	16.0	15.0	18.6	14.7
6680	Reading, PA	2 225	336 523	111	151.2	314 561	10 003	333	2 746	8 880	17 174	6.7	12.9	13.7	16.1	14.8
6690	Redding, CA	9 805	147 036	193	15.0	137 977	1 081	3 954	2 684	1 340	5 652	7.7	15.6	12.3	14.7	15.6
6720	Reno, NV	16 427	254 667	135	15.5	225 095	5 680	4 921	9 824	9 147	22 959	7.4	12.5	13.8	19.0	17.3
6740	Richland-Kennewick-Pasco, WA	7 628	150 033	189	19.7	129 749	2 395	1 124	3 115	13 650	19 940	8.5	17.9	13.6	16.3	15.6
6760	Richmond-Petersburg, VA	7 628	865 640	49	113.5	595 714	252 340	2 705	11 864	3 017	9 327	7.2	13.3	14.4	18.5	16.7
6800	Roanoke, VA	2 204	224 477	148	101.8	194 645	27 602	281	1 602	347	1 359	6.2	12.1	13.4	16.1	16.1
6820	Rochester, MN	1 691	106 470	257	63.0	101 880	788	295	3 237	270	970	8.6	15.3	13.0	20.1	15.4
6840	Rochester, NY	7 593	1 002 410	38	132.0	875 886	93 819	2 870	13 978	15 857	31 238	7.6	13.7	15.0	17.4	15.4
6880	Rockford, IL	2 060	283 719	121	137.7	251 783	23 383	697	3 136	4 720	9 836	7.6	14.5	13.8	16.9	15.3
6920	Sacramento, CA	13 193	1 481 102	26	112.3	1 170 505	101 940	17 021	114 520	77 116	172 374	7.8	14.6	14.2	18.5	16.3
6960	Saginaw-Bay City-Midland, MI	4 596	399 320	89	86.9	346 643	38 810	1 975	2 504	9 388	17 715	7.5	15.3	14.6	15.9	15.1
6980	St. Cloud, MN	5 670	190 921	160	33.7	188 080	738	637	1 171	295	910	8.0	16.8	19.5	17.1	13.7
7000	St. Joseph, MO	1 061	83 083	273	78.3	79 378	2 635	273	266	531	1 709	7.2	14.6	13.8	15.8	13.5
7040	St. Louis, MO-IL	13 805	2 444 099	17	177.0	1 985 500	423 182	4 947	23 686	6 784	26 014	7.6	14.7	13.5	17.5	14.9
7080	Salem, OR	4 988	278 024	125	55.7	255 212	2 332	4 041	4 746	11 693	21 027	7.3	15.0	14.0	15.6	15.6
7120	Salinas-Seaside-Monterey, CA	8 604	355 660	104	41.3	227 008	22 849	3 017	27 856	74 930	119 570	8.8	14.9	17.0	19.5	14.7
7160	Salt Lake City-Ogden, UT	4 190	1 072 227	37	255.9	1 000 082	10 464	8 337	25 598	27 746	61 964	9.7	20.8	15.4	16.9	14.0
7200	San Angelo, TX	3 942	98 458	262	25.0	79 533	4 136	373	998	13 418	25 501	7.8	15.3	16.8	16.4	13.9
7240	San Antonio, TX	6 526	1 302 099	30	199.5	978 505	88 778	4 648	16 058	214 110	620 290	8.3	16.1	16.0	17.7	14.6
7320	San Diego, CA	10 890	2 498 016	15	229.4	1 872 256	159 306	20 066	198 311	248 077	510 781	7.8	13.1	17.0	20.0	15.2
7362	San Francisco-Oakland-San Jose, CA	19 085	6 253 311	4	327.7	4 334 064	537 753	40 847	926 961	413 686	970 403	7.1	12.5	13.8	19.5	17.3
5775	Oakland, CA	3 776	2 082 914	X	551.6	1 372 818	303 826	14 230	269 566	122 474	273 087	7.5	13.2	13.9	18.8	17.3
7360	San Francisco, CA	2 630	1 603 678	X	609.8	1 058 796	122 494	7 232	329 599	85 557	233 274	5.9	10.1	12.6	20.0	17.9
7400	San Jose, CA	3 344	1 497 577	X	447.8	1 032 190	56 211	9 269	261 466	138 441	314 564	7.5	12.8	15.1	21.2	16.3
7485	Santa Cruz, CA	1 155	229 734	X	198.9	192 849	2 632	1 821	8 512	23 920	46 797	7.2	13.1	15.8	17.7	18.8
7500	Santa Rosa-Petaluma, CA.	4 082	388 222	X	95.1	351 650	5 547	4 397	10 774	15 854	41 223	7.3	13.9	12.5	16.8	18.4
8720	Vallejo-Fairfield-Napa, CA	4 098	451 186	X	110.1	325 761	47 043	3 898	47 044	27 440	61 458	8.2	15.3	13.9	18.4	16.9
7480	Santa Barbara-Santa Maria-Lompoc, CA	7 093	369 608	99	52.1	285 461	10 402	3 351	16 429	53 965	98 199	7.3	12.6	18.0	18.2	14.5
7490	Santa Fe, NM	5 228	117 043	241	22.4	96 454	711	2 948	941	15 989	50 947	7.1	14.8	12.2	16.1	19.0
7510	Sarasota, FL	1 481	277 776	126	187.6	262 836	12 073	483	1 430	954	5 882	4.6	8.6	8.8	12.0	12.0
7520	Savannah, GA	2 383	242 622	141	101.8	152 513	86 228	515	2 412	954	2 951	7.9	14.9	15.1	17.4	14.4
7560	Scranton-Wilkes Barre, PA	7 356	734 175	56	99.8	720 692	7 660	580	3 827	1 416	5 640	6.2	12.3	14.2	14.6	14.1
7602	Seattle-Tacoma, WA	15 261	2 559 164	14	167.7	2 211 710	123 266	32 071	164 286	27 831	75 555	7.5	13.6	13.6	19.4	17.3
7600	Seattle, WA	10 921	1 972 961	X	180.7	1 713 068	81 056	23 727	135 251	19 859	54 993	7.3	13.1	13.2	19.8	17.8
8200	Tacoma, WA	4 340	586 203	X	135.1	498 642	42 210	8 344	29 035	7 972	20 562	8.2	15.2	15.1	18.2	15.4
7610	Sharon, PA	1 740	121 003	232	69.5	114 479	5 882	115	393	134	506	6.2	13.1	14.5	14.2	13.8
7620	Sheboygan, WI	1 330	103 877	259	78.1	100 389	430	357	2 061	640	1 668	7.1	15.4	13.1	16.6	14.9
7640	Sherman-Dension, TX	2 418	95 021	268	39.3	85 553	6 565	1 046	412	1 445	2 795	6.8	14.5	13.6	15.1	13.9
7680	Shreveport, LA	4 457	334 341	114	75.0	213 610	116 892	865	2 023	951	4 394	8.0	16.2	14.3	16.3	14.4
7720	Sioux City, IA-NE	2 944	115 018	245	39.1	107 579	1 953	1 999	1 624	1 863	3 728	7.7	16.3	13.9	15.8	14.3
7760	Sioux Falls, SD	2 096	123 809	225	59.1	120 454	754	1 680	714	207	648	7.9	15.3	14.4	19.1	15.0
7800	South Bend-Mishawaka, IN	1 185	247 052	138	208.5	216 984	24 190	846	2 507	2 525	5 201	7.3	14.1	16.3	15.9	14.5
7840	Spokane, WA	4 568	361 364	102	79.1	341 874	5 105	5 539	6 569	2 277	6 994	7.4	14.9	14.6	16.4	15.6

1. MSA = Metropolitan Statistical Area. CMSA = Consolidated MSA. NECMA = New England county metropolitan area. PMSA = Primary MSA. See Appendix A for explanation of these concepts. See Appendix B for list of metropolitan areas identified by type, with component counties. 2. Dry land or land partially or temporarily covered by water. 3. Hispanic persons may be of any race.

Area name	Population, 1990 (cont'd): Age of population (cont'd), Percent: 45 to 54 years	55 to 64 years	65 to 74 years	75 years and over	Percent female	Population–change and components of change: Change, 1980–1990: Number	Percent	Components of change, 1980–1986: Total persons, 1986	Total persons, 1980	Net change: Number	Net change: Percent	Natural increase: Births	Natural increase: Deaths	Net migration	Households, 1990: Total
	16	17	18	19	20	21	22	23	24	25	26	27	28	29	30
Phoenix, AZ	9.6	7.7	7.4	5.1	50.7	612 874	40.6	1 900 200	1 509 227	390 900	25.9	186 600	79 300	283 600	807 560
Pine Bluff, AR	9.8	8.3	7.5	6.0	51.9	-5 231	-5.8	90 000	90 718	-800	-0.9	9 400	5 400	-4 800	30 001
Pittsburgh-Beaver Valley, PA	10.3	10.7	10.4	7.0	52.8	-180 513	-7.4	2 316 200	2 423 311	-107 300	-4.4	184 200	160 400	-131 100	891 923
Beaver County, PA	10.5	11.4	10.5	6.4	52.4	-18 348	-9.0	193 200	204 441	-11 300	-5.5	15 700	12 300	-14 700	71 939
Pittsburgh, PA	10.3	10.7	10.3	7.0	52.8	-162 165	-7.3	2 123 000	2 218 870	-96 000	-4.3	168 500	148 100	-116 400	819 984
Pittsfield, MA	10.1	9.6	9.3	7.6	52.1	-5 758	-4.0	141 300	145 110	-3 800	-2.6	11 000	9 400	-5 400	54 315
Portland, ME	9.9	8.3	7.2	5.8	51.9	27 346	12.7	228 100	215 789	12 300	5.7	20 300	13 200	5 200	94 512
Portland-Vancouver, OR-WA	10.5	7.5	6.7	5.2	51.0	179 918	13.9	1 364 100	1 297 977	66 100	5.1	128 900	67 400	4 600	575 531
Portland, OR	10.4	7.5	6.8	5.4	51.1	134 092	12.1	1 152 800	1 105 750	47 000	4.3	108 800	58 600	-3 200	487 091
Vancouver, WA	10.9	7.5	6.3	4.3	50.6	45 826	23.8	211 300	192 227	19 100	9.9	20 100	8 800	7 800	88 440
Portsmouth-Dover-Rochester, NH-ME	10.2	7.4	5.6	4.0	50.7	74 325	27.0	315 800	275 753	39 900	14.5	27 800	13 100	25 200	126 862
Poughkeepsie, NY	11.1	8.5	6.4	5.0	49.7	14 407	5.9	256 800	245 055	11 800	4.8	19 100	12 200	4 900	89 567
Providence-Pawtucket-Fall Rvr, RI-MA	9.6	8.9	8.6	6.6	52.2	50 499	5.8	890 200	865 771	24 300	2.8	71 700	53 900	6 500	345 290
Provo-Orem, UT	6.3	4.9	4.0	3.0	50.6	45 484	20.9	240 500	218 106	22 400	10.3	45 000	6 600	-16 000	70 168
Pueblo, CO	9.8	10.0	8.8	6.4	51.6	-2 921	-2.3	127 100	125 972	1 200	1.0	12 200	6 800	-4 200	47 057
Raleigh-Durham, NC	9.9	6.9	5.3	3.7	51.7	174 705	31.2	650 700	560 775	89 800	16.0	49 900	25 800	65 700	287 647
Rapid City, SD	8.9	7.5	5.7	4.3	50.5	10 982	15.6	76 900	70 361	6 600	9.4	10 100	3 200	-300	30 553
Reading, PA	10.3	9.9	8.8	6.8	51.7	24 014	7.7	321 000	312 509	8 400	2.7	25 800	19 600	2 200	127 649
Redding, CA	11.0	9.1	8.6	5.5	51.0	31 423	27.2	133 100	115 613	17 500	15.1	12 400	6 900	12 000	55 966
Reno, NV	11.2	8.5	6.7	3.6	49.3	61 044	31.5	224 600	193 623	31 100	16.1	20 500	9 400	20 000	102 294
Richland-Kennewick-Pasco, WA	10.1	7.9	6.2	3.9	50.1	5 564	3.9	149 500	144 469	5 000	3.5	18 400	5 100	-8 300	54 423
Richmond-Petersburg, VA	10.5	8.2	6.7	4.6	52.4	104 329	13.7	810 200	761 311	48 900	6.4	72 100	42 700	19 500	331 824
Roanoke, VA	11.0	9.9	8.7	6.5	52.8	4 084	1.9	224 800	220 393	4 700	2.1	16 900	13 900	1 700	89 694
Rochester, MN	10.5	7.1	5.3	4.7	51.5	14 464	15.7	98 000	92 006	5 900	6.4	10 900	3 700	-1 300	40 058
Rochester, NY	10.3	8.2	7.0	5.4	51.7	31 180	3.2	980 300	971 230	8 900	0.9	91 900	51 500	-31 500	374 475
Rockford, IL	10.7	8.7	7.3	5.2	51.4	4 205	1.5	280 300	279 514	800	0.3	27 200	14 200	-12 200	107 677
Sacramento, CA	9.9	7.9	6.6	4.1	50.8	381 288	34.7	1 291 400	1 099 814	191 500	17.4	123 000	55 400	123 900	556 448
Saginaw-Bay City-Midland, MI	10.9	8.6	7.0	5.0	51.8	-22 198	-5.3	403 600	421 518	-18 000	-4.3	39 800	19 500	-38 300	148 235
St. Cloud, MN	8.4	6.7	5.4	4.5	49.8	27 665	16.9	175 100	163 256	11 900	7.3	19 400	6 800	-700	64 354
St. Joseph, MO	9.5	9.2	8.7	7.7	52.6	-4 805	-5.5	85 800	87 888	-2 100	-2.4	8 200	6 300	-4 000	32 486
St. Louis, MO-IL	10.2	8.8	7.2	5.6	52.2	67 128	2.8	2 438 000	2 376 971	60 700	2.6	240 600	139 600	-40 300	924 733
Salem, OR	10.0	8.0	7.9	6.5	50.6	28 129	11.3	262 100	249 895	12 400	5.0	25 700	13 800	500	101 661
Salinas-Seaside-Monterey, CA	8.4	7.0	5.8	4.0	48.1	65 216	22.5	339 700	290 444	49 300	17.0	40 600	13 100	21 800	112 965
Salt Lake City-Ogden, UT	8.4	6.3	5.0	3.4	50.3	162 005	17.8	1 041 400	910 222	131 200	14.4	145 100	33 100	19 200	347 531
San Angelo, TX	9.0	8.1	7.0	5.7	51.5	13 674	16.1	98 100	84 784	13 400	15.8	11 000	5 000	7 400	35 408
San Antonio, TX	9.4	7.7	6.2	4.1	51.4	229 974	21.5	1 276 400	1 072 125	204 200	19.0	139 000	51 700	116 900	451 021
San Diego, CA	8.8	7.1	6.5	4.4	49.0	636 170	34.2	2 201 300	1 861 846	339 500	18.2	216 700	89 100	211 900	887 403
San Francisco-Oakland-San Jose, CA	10.8	7.9	6.5	4.6	50.2	885 411	16.5	5 877 800	5 367 900	510 000	9.5	543 000	271 400	238 400	2 329 808
Oakland, CA	10.8	7.7	6.3	4.4	50.8	321 204	18.2	1 933 800	1 761 710	172 100	9.8	180 100	89 300	81 300	779 806
San Francisco, CA	11.3	8.9	7.6	5.7	50.3	114 783	7.7	1 588 000	1 488 895	99 100	6.7	128 200	87 600	58 500	642 504
San Jose, CA	10.9	7.5	5.3	3.4	49.3	202 506	15.6	1 401 600	1 295 071	106 600	8.2	144 600	49 400	11 400	520 180
Santa Cruz, CA	9.7	6.6	6.1	5.2	50.3	41 593	22.1	218 500	188 141	30 400	16.2	21 600	10 500	19 300	83 566
Santa Rosa-Petaluma, CA	10.4	7.4	7.5	5.9	51.0	88 541	29.5	343 600	299 681	43 900	14.6	30 000	18 400	32 300	149 011
Vallejo-Fairfield-Napa, CA	9.9	7.2	6.1	4.1	49.2	116 784	34.9	392 300	334 402	57 900	17.3	38 500	16 200	35 600	154 741
Santa Barbara-Santa Maria-Lompoc, CA	9.3	7.8	6.9	5.4	49.8	70 914	23.7	339 400	298 694	40 700	13.6	30 500	15 000	25 200	129 802
Santa Fe, NM	12.3	8.5	6.2	3.8	50.7	23 925	25.7	106 200	93 118	13 100	14.1	9 700	3 500	6 900	45 053
Sarasota, FL	9.5	12.4	17.9	14.2	53.2	75 525	37.3	247 600	202 251	45 400	22.4	13 500	20 900	52 800	125 493
Savannah, GA	9.7	8.3	7.5	4.8	51.9	22 069	10.0	239 700	220 553	19 000	8.6	25 300	13 000	6 700	89 870
Scranton-Wilkes Barre, PA	10.1	10.3	10.5	7.8	52.5	5 379	0.7	725 900	728 796	-3 000	-0.4	53 400	53 600	-2 800	280 697
Seattle-Tacoma, WA	10.5	7.5	6.3	4.4	50.5	465 879	22.3	2 284 400	2 093 285	191 300	9.1	214 100	100 100	77 300	1 002 157
Seattle, WA	10.7	7.5	6.3	4.4	50.6	365 343	22.7	1 751 100	1 607 618	143 600	8.9	155 700	76 600	64 500	787 505
Tacoma, WA	9.7	7.6	6.2	4.3	50.0	100 536	20.7	533 300	485 667	47 700	9.8	58 400	23 500	12 800	214 652
Sharon, PA	10.3	10.7	10.0	7.2	51.5	-7 296	-5.7	123 600	128 299	-4 700	-3.7	9 800	7 800	-6 700	45 591
Sheboygan, WI	9.9	8.6	7.9	6.7	50.5	2 942	2.9	102 700	100 935	1 700	1.7	9 700	3 600	-4 400	38 592
Sherman-Denison, TX	10.3	9.5	8.8	7.5	52.3	5 225	5.8	98 300	89 796	8 400	9.4	9 000	6 600	6 000	36 847
Shreveport, LA	9.9	8.7	7.0	5.2	52.8	1 183	0.4	364 600	333 158	31 500	9.5	41 400	18 900	9 000	123 966
Sioux City, IA-NE	9.0	8.7	7.8	6.5	51.7	-2 439	-2.1	115 900	117 457	-1 600	-1.4	12 500	6 900	-7 200	42 934
Sioux Falls, SD	8.9	7.7	6.4	5.2	51.9	14 374	13.1	122 700	109 435	13 100	12.0	12 300	5 500	6 300	47 681
South Bend-Mishawaka, IN	9.1	8.8	8.0	6.1	51.8	5 435	2.2	241 400	241 617	-100	0.0	22 600	13 800	-8 900	92 365
Spokane, WA	9.8	7.9	7.4	5.8	51.4	19 529	5.7	356 900	341 835	15 000	4.4	35 200	18 700	-1 500	141 619

Area name	Households, (cont'd): Percent change, 1980–1990	Households, (cont'd): Percent: Female family householder[1]	Households, (cont'd): Percent: One-person	Births, 1988: Total	Births, 1988: Rate[2]	Births, 1988: Low birth weight[3] (Number)	Deaths, 1987: Number: Total	Deaths, 1987: Number: Infant[4]	Deaths, 1987: Rate: Total[2]	Deaths, 1987: Rate: Infant[5]	Marriages, 1984: Number	Marriages, 1984: Rate[2]	Divorces, 1984: Number	Divorces, 1984: Rate[2]	Physicians, active non-Federal, 1989: Number[6]	Physicians, active non-Federal, 1989: Rate[7]
	31	33	34	35	36	37	38	39	40	41	42	43	44	45	46	47
Phoenix, AZ	48.2	10.2	25.0	38 125	18.8	2 362	14 889	368	7.5	10.0	19 408	11.2	11 626	6.7	4 187	201
Pine Bluff, AR	-1.9	16.0	24.2	1 463	16.1	163	897	13	9.9	9.3	1 013	11.2	546	6.0	138	152
Pittsburgh-Beaver Valley, PA	0.8	11.7	27.6	28 156	12.3	1 944	25 736	279	11.2	9.9	17 397	7.3	6 919	2.9	6 200	274
Beaver County, PA	0.3	11.2	24.4	2 299	12.1	142	1 968	19	10.3	8.4	1 290	6.5	500	2.5	193	103
Pittsburgh, PA	0.8	11.8	27.9	25 857	12.3	1 802	23 768	260	11.3	10.0	16 107	7.4	6 419	3.0	6 007	289
Pittsfield, MA	3.7	10.8	27.5	1 723	12.4	100	1 553	11	11.1	6.4	1 325	9.3	485	3.4	371	269
Portland, ME	20.1	9.8	25.2	3 534	15.0	169	2 108	29	9.1	8.2	2 476	11.1	1 097	4.9	710	297
Portland-Vancouver, OR-WA	15.9	9.7	26.1	21 416	15.1	1 205	11 616	192	8.4	9.5	13 051	9.8	7 131	5.3	3 557	246
Portland, OR	13.8	9.7	26.8	17 961	15.1	1 043	10 129	176	8.7	10.4	9 273	8.2	5 701	5.0	3 314	273
Vancouver, WA	28.6	9.9	22.1	3 455	15.3	162	1 487	16	6.8	4.9	3 778	18.6	1 430	7.0	243	104
Portsmouth-Dover-Rochester, NH-ME	33.5	8.1	20.1	5 504	16.5	229	2 194	40	6.8	7.2	3 680	12.3	1 622	5.4	462	135
Poughkeepsie, NY	11.1	9.3	22.2	3 852	14.7	238	2 267	32	8.8	8.6	2 031	8.1	859	3.4	525	198
Providence-Pawtucket-Fall Rvr, RI-MA	11.3	11.9	26.3	13 059	14.4	800	8 988	110	10.0	8.5	6 967	7.9	3 320	3.8	2 351	257
Provo-Orem, UT	19.9	7.8	12.2	6 599	27.2	304	1 077	44	4.5	7.3	2 704	11.4	863	3.6	282	116
Pueblo, CO	4.4	13.7	25.8	1 752	13.7	135	1 205	10	9.5	5.6	1 111	8.8	587	4.7	259	203
Raleigh-Durham, NC	44.4	11.2	26.7	10 506	15.4	725	4 483	136	6.7	13.7	5 165	8.5	2 955	4.8	3 702	527
Rapid City, SD	21.4	10.2	23.4	1 708	20.8	90	546	16	6.8	8.8	1 202	15.9	473	6.3	165	197
Reading, PA	11.4	9.1	23.5	4 445	13.5	240	3 371	33	10.4	7.6	2 541	8.0	930	2.9	566	170
Redding, CA	30.1	11.0	22.3	2 184	15.6	87	1 374	29	10.1	14.6	958	7.5	1 136	9.0	260	182
Reno, NV	32.5	9.4	27.6	4 020	16.8	303	1 729	37	7.4	9.8	35 394	165.5	4 496	21.0	582	233
Richland-Kennewick-Pasco, WA	6.8	9.7	22.6	2 529	17.3	117	902	19	6.1	7.4	1 354	9.1	1 007	6.8	191	130
Richmond-Petersburg, VA	23.2	13.6	25.1	13 050	15.5	1 033	7 182	147	8.7	11.5	7 939	10.0	3 750	4.7	2 489	291
Roanoke, VA	9.5	11.9	26.5	2 825	12.7	204	2 346	23	10.6	8.4	2 436	11.0	1 097	4.9	624	284
Rochester, MN	22.6	7.5	24.6	1 886	18.7	79	635	20	6.4	11.2	1 094	11.4	382	4.0	1 790	1 750
Rochester, NY	9.4	11.7	24.9	15 435	15.7	895	8 173	133	8.4	8.8	8 399	8.6	3 523	3.6	2 662	271
Rockford, IL	8.6	10.6	23.9	4 293	15.2	304	2 396	41	8.5	9.6	2 723	9.8	1 367	4.9	511	180
Sacramento, CA	33.7	11.8	23.9	23 661	17.1	1 465	10 289	224	7.7	9.9	16 585	13.6	9 013	7.4	3 146	219
Saginaw-Bay City-Midland, MI	4.4	12.7	22.9	6 010	14.8	464	3 256	51	8.0	8.5	3 580	8.7	1 731	4.2	567	140
St. Cloud, MN	30.4	7.4	20.6	2 881	15.9	110	1 075	18	6.0	6.4	1 496	8.8	405	2.4	207	112
St. Joseph, MO	-1.3	11.4	27.7	1 253	14.7	70	985	9	11.5	7.5	961	11.2	598	6.9	136	160
St. Louis, MO-IL	9.5	12.6	25.8	39 316	15.9	2 857	23 011	384	9.4	9.9	23 240	9.7	10 184	4.2	6 178	249
Salem, OR	12.1	10.1	24.1	4 055	15.0	205	2 402	45	9.1	11.3	2 274	8.8	1 429	5.6	393	142
Salinas-Seaside-Monterey, CA	18.0	10.4	20.4	7 166	20.5	396	2 202	59	6.4	8.5	4 088	12.7	2 172	6.7	505	142
Salt Lake City-Ogden, UT	20.1	10.0	20.6	21 795	20.5	1 348	5 668	196	5.4	9.1	11 331	11.2	5 711	5.7	2 440	226
San Angelo, TX	16.6	10.5	24.8	1 751	17.6	120	860	18	8.7	10.9	1 319	13.6	712	7.3	162	162
San Antonio, TX	29.1	14.0	22.9	23 735	17.9	1 523	8 945	209	6.8	8.6	16 019	13.3	8 108	6.7	3 063	227
San Diego, CA	32.4	10.8	22.9	44 096	18.6	2 539	16 113	388	7.0	9.4	20 358	9.8	9 100	4.4	5 755	234
San Francisco-Oakland-San Jose, CA	14.1	10.7	25.9	99 474	16.5	5 983	46 242	737	7.8	7.8	43 741	7.7	37 072	6.5	18 268	298
Oakland, CA	16.8	12.1	25.1	33 934	16.9	2 357	15 269	267	7.8	8.2	11 674	6.2	11 781	6.3	4 818	236
San Francisco, CA	4.8	9.7	32.3	22 673	14.3	1 322	14 827	148	9.3	6.7	13 783	8.9	10 495	6.8	7 465	467
San Jose, CA	13.4	10.3	21.7	26 292	18.4	1 414	8 324	209	5.9	8.5	11 766	8.5	8 739	6.3	4 024	278
Santa Cruz, CA	16.4	9.6	24.1	3 976	17.5	191	1 749	16	7.9	4.2	1 923	9.3	1 404	6.8	415	179
Santa Rosa-Petaluma, CA	30.2	9.8	24.6	5 475	15.0	269	3 098	42	8.7	7.9	2 469	7.6	2 161	6.6	781	207
Vallejo-Fairfield-Napa, CA	32.2	10.9	20.2	7 124	16.9	430	2 975	55	7.3	8.1	2 126	5.8	2 492	6.8	765	175
Santa Barbara-Santa Maria-Lompoc, CA	18.7	9.3	23.0	5 887	17.2	273	2 507	40	7.3	7.4	3 364	10.4	2 084	6.4	864	248
Santa Fe, NM	38.3	10.5	26.3	1 670	14.8	133	695	8	6.2	4.9	1 204	12.0	951	9.5	265	229
Sarasota, FL	41.4	7.3	27.7	2 567	9.9	154	3 866	26	15.1	10.5	2 567	10.8	1 499	6.3	626	235
Savannah, GA	16.5	15.5	25.0	4 258	17.4	423	2 241	70	9.3	16.6	2 228	9.5	1 460	6.3	487	198
Scranton-Wilkes Barre, PA	6.6	11.0	26.8	8 938	12.1	519	8 863	72	12.1	8.6	5 571	7.7	1 887	2.6	1 246	168
Seattle-Tacoma, WA	26.5	9.4	26.5	38 505	15.9	2 203	17 001	370	7.2	10.0	22 772	10.3	13 864	6.3	6 447	259
Seattle, WA	27.4	9.0	27.4	28 580	15.4	1 529	12 936	261	7.2	9.6	16 998	10.0	10 292	6.1	5 573	290
Tacoma, WA	23.2	10.9	23.4	9 925	17.8	674	4 065	109	7.5	11.3	5 774	11.1	3 572	6.9	874	152
Sharon, PA	2.1	10.3	24.6	1 506	12.3	93	1 344	13	10.9	9.3	1 084	8.6	395	3.1	147	121
Sheboygan, WI	8.8	7.1	23.3	1 399	13.6	40	917	20	9.0	14.5	813	7.9	329	3.2	110	106
Sherman-Densison, TX	8.5	10.2	25.2	1 357	13.9	73	1 050	11	10.7	7.9	1 512	15.9	722	7.6	154	157
Shreveport, LA	5.6	16.9	25.6	6 127	17.1	554	3 095	81	8.5	12.8	2 966	8.3	1 748	4.9	994	278
Sioux City, IA-NE	1.4	10.5	25.5	1 877	16.2	127	1 121	23	9.8	12.7	995	8.5	495	4.2	185	159
Sioux Falls, SD	19.0	8.8	27.0	1 999	15.9	94	936	21	7.6	10.7	1 447	12.2	595	5.0	368	290
South Bend-Mishawaka, IN	7.1	11.4	26.4	3 717	15.2	228	2 367	40	9.7	11.1	2 358	9.8	1 424	5.9	415	169
Spokane, WA	10.3	10.8	27.5	5 316	14.9	273	3 131	64	8.8	11.9	3 058	8.6	2 078	5.9	824	230

1. No spouse present. 2. Per 1,000 resident population estimated as of July 1 of the year shown. 3. Under 2,500 grams. 4. Deaths of infants under 1 year old. 5. Deaths of infants under 1 year old per 1,000 live births. 6. As of end of year. 7. Per 100,000 resident population as of July 1 of the year shown.

Area name	Hospitals, 1989: Number	Hospitals, 1989: Beds: Number	Hospitals, 1989: Beds: Rate[1]	Nursing homes,[2] 1986: Number	Nursing homes,[2] 1986: Beds	Serious crimes known to police, 1988: Number: Total[3]	Serious crimes known to police, 1988: Number: Violent[4]	Serious crimes known to police, 1988: Rate[5]	Education: Public school enrollment[6]: 1986–1987	Education: Public school enrollment[6]: 1980	Education: Attainment,[7] 1980: Percent 12 years or more	Education: Attainment,[7] 1980: Percent 16 years or more	Education: Local government expenditures for education,[8] 1982: Total (Mil dol)	Education: Local government expenditures for education,[8] 1982: Per capita (Dollars)	Social Security Program December 1988: Beneficiaries: Total	Social Security Program December 1988: Beneficiaries: Rate[9]
	48	49	50	51	52	53	54	55	56	57	58	59	60	61	62	63
Phoenix, AZ	41	8 208	395	102	8 247	155 742	12 845	7 674	320 411	279 863	75.0	18.3	672.5	417	301 660	148.6
Pine Bluff, AR	1	425	468	6	505	4 757	668	5 239	18 487	19 441	57.6	11.9	33.7	373	14 950	164.6
Pittsburgh-Beaver Valley, PA	55	15 735	694	357	16 398	64 962	7 210	2 844	307 515	398 399	67.3	14.1	1 028.0	2 056	465 265	203.7
Beaver County, PA	2	660	351	19	1 550	3 172	349	1 671	29 380	38 029	64.8	9.4	82.1	406	38 295	201.8
Pittsburgh, PA	53	15 075	725	338	14 848	61 790	6 861	2 950	278 135	360 370	67.5	14.6	945.9	1 650	426 970	203.9
Pittsfield, MA	5	656	476	21	1 508	2 515	303	1 813	21 162	26 884	69.7	16.3	62.7	441	28 560	205.9
Portland, ME	10	1 612	674	49	2 138	14 517	821	6 164	34 545	41 498	75.0	19.0	81.2	372	39 170	166.3
Portland-Vancouver, OR-WA	27	5 042	348	151	10 167	117 878	11 128	8 335	225 879	230 027	78.3	19.8	752.8	2 948	209 295	148.0
Portland, OR	26	4 735	390	132	8 769	106 659	10 544	8 978	182 950	189 150	78.7	20.8	645.0	2 409	178 515	150.3
Vancouver, WA	1	307	131	19	1 398	11 219	584	4 960	42 929	40 877	75.8	14.2	107.8	539	30 780	136.1
Portsmouth-Dover-Rochester, NH-ME	11	1 095	320	37	1 930	10 254	589	3 066	42 509	52 666	75.2	18.7	110.0	725	40 650	121.6
Poughkeepsie, NY	7	2 888	1 091	20	1 800	8 831	999	3 368	39 756	48 061	70.6	18.9	150.5	605	37 940	144.7
Providence-Pawtucket-Fall Rvr, RI-MA	17	4 327	474	122	9 796	47 131	3 675	5 191	123 462	141 986	60.1	14.7	373.6	1 851	164 960	181.7
Provo-Orem, UT	6	936	384	12	707	10 039	399	4 136	63 339	47 177	82.7	23.4	104.0	447	23 965	98.7
Pueblo, CO	3	1 224	957	26	1 037	8 858	1 223	6 942	23 143	26 399	66.5	13.2	68.3	543	23 105	181.1
Raleigh-Durham, NC	18	4 776	680	112	3 509	37 273	2 729	5 453	100 641	99 542	68.9	26.6	215.8	1 481	82 825	121.2
Rapid City, SD	3	385	459	8	470	1 444	112	1 761	16 394	13 568	78.8	18.3	31.8	440	10 475	127.7
Reading, PA	6	1 800	541	24	2 817	8 863	842	2 693	47 966	53 493	58.5	11.4	145.6	463	61 870	188.0
Redding, CA	3	440	307	24	732	8 626	1 307	6 175	26 350	23 004	75.6	12.4	70.0	575	27 355	195.8
Reno, NV	9	1 457	583	13	1 017	16 451	1 985	6 863	33 712	31 465	80.1	19.7	91.2	439	30 830	128.6
Richland-Kennewick-Pasco, WA	5	411	280	6	513	9 806	512	6 698	30 220	30 384	79.1	20.2	82.6	1 122	18 320	125.1
Richmond-Petersburg, VA	24	6 011	702	96	6 336	46 102	4 118	5 460	135 372	144 955	62.3	18.4	336.6	5 572	118 195	140.0
Roanoke, VA	8	2 422	1 100	23	2 443	11 984	664	5 408	35 242	41 471	62.0	14.3	89.8	1 423	38 285	172.8
Rochester, MN	3	1 661	1 624	9	852	3 736	100	3 699	17 211	17 997	81.7	24.8	49.2	525	12 320	122.0
Rochester, NY	17	5 602	571	87	8 374	48 069	2 881	4 904	158 567	182 704	70.3	19.1	623.7	3 269	157 940	161.1
Rockford, IL	6	1 321	466	22	2 641	19 596	1 455	6 944	46 729	53 940	67.4	13.1	116.4	802	44 565	157.9
Sacramento, CA	21	3 676	256	224	8 009	98 559	9 383	7 115	230 240	195 556	77.8	19.6	541.3	1 922	185 565	134.0
Saginaw-Bay City-Midland, MI	7	2 014	496	115	2 885	21 871	2 796	5 384	73 655	89 496	67.3	12.6	210.9	1 492	64 275	158.2
St. Cloud, MN	6	1 322	717	15	1 453	5 368	164	2 962	33 156	33 005	68.0	14.1	95.0	1 582	23 000	126.9
St. Joseph, MO	3	916	1 078	29	1 211	4 382	314	5 131	14 226	15 263	63.4	10.6	33.1	382	17 505	205.0
St. Louis, MO-IL	51	14 529	587	228	20 880	133 963	17 553	5 431	361 187	412 538	64.1	15.6	1 004.1	3 898	390 190	158.2
Salem, OR	5	1 252	454	29	2 050	18 768	925	6 956	43 096	43 643	73.5	17.3	128.0	906	49 710	184.2
Salinas-Seaside-Monterey, CA	6	807	227	82	1 727	18 845	2 648	5 403	60 358	52 011	71.0	19.6	146.5	480	39 465	113.1
Salt Lake City-Ogden, UT	25	3 927	364	83	4 972	72 341	3 167	6 793	251 036	207 731	80.7	20.5	461.2	1 489	106 575	100.1
San Angelo, TX	5	880	882	5	830	6 514	467	6 560	17 462	15 960	59.8	14.7	31.1	342	15 110	152.2
San Antonio, TX	32	8 305	615	53	6 276	138 596	6 594	10 474	248 670	226 402	62.7	15.7	461.1	1 259	161 800	122.3
San Diego, CA	35	8 251	336	377	12 384	171 804	17 024	7 248	353 115	316 060	78.0	20.9	851.8	433	306 440	129.3
San Francisco-Oakland-San Jose, CA	108	25 211	411	1 345	38 501	388 333	43 956	6 427	883 706	880 207	78.6	25.0	2 443.9	4 272	761 710	126.1
Oakland, CA	36	6 101	299	412	13 694	154 244	16 668	7 688	309 511	308 141	78.1	23.5	815.5	897	254 065	126.6
San Francisco, CA	32	7 746	484	388	10 409	106 532	14 141	6 700	177 191	182 470	79.2	28.7	539.9	1 114	225 245	141.7
San Jose, CA	16	5 152	356	263	7 129	71 015	7 765	4 959	232 530	244 087	79.5	26.4	712.2	534	140 385	98.0
Santa Cruz, CA	4	597	257	57	1 798	13 443	1 067	5 930	37 449	28 955	77.8	23.5	82.1	418	30 920	136.4
Santa Rosa-Petaluma, CA	9	2 220	587	111	2 768	18 149	1 326	4 959	57 076	52 239	77.6	19.3	133.8	426	59 960	163.8
Vallejo-Fairfield-Napa, CA	11	3 395	777	114	2 703	24 950	2 989	5 931	69 949	64 315	76.3	15.0	160.4	883	51 135	121.5
Santa Barbara-Santa Maria-Lompoc, CA	11	1 185	341	72	2 464	18 554	1 723	5 408	50 904	48 089	79.1	24.6	134.5	435	49 895	145.4
Santa Fe, NM	4	348	301	9	496	NA	NA	0	17 083	18 585	79.4	31.3	46.1	1 174	13 335	118.5
Sarasota, FL	6	1 466	551	28	1 899	NA	NA	0	25 436	24 294	73.4	17.7	68.3	311	97 575	374.4
Savannah, GA	6	1 549	631	30	1 099	16 132	1 355	6 601	36 885	37 775	59.5	13.4	75.1	769	36 965	151.2
Scranton-Wilkes Barre, PA	23	4 769	644	98	6 730	13 833	1 053	1 878	99 705	116 043	63.1	10.2	272.0	2 021	163 580	222.1
Seattle-Tacoma, WA	42	9 014	362	181	16 679	197 736	14 671	8 168	360 293	368 083	80.5	22.1	1 068.3	1 524	320 650	132.5
Seattle, WA	31	5 757	300	120	12 811	152 445	10 200	8 188	265 667	276 769	81.7	24.0	779.5	955	246 880	132.6
Tacoma, WA	11	3 257	568	61	3 868	45 291	4 471	8 101	94 626	91 314	76.3	15.1	288.8	569	73 770	131.9
Sharon, PA	4	620	509	20	1 327	2 907	257	2 375	19 599	23 688	66.8	11.7	62.7	492	25 715	210.1
Sheboygan, WI	3	376	364	11	1 429	3 468	141	3 367	17 241	18 761	67.8	11.2	48.7	478	18 525	179.9
Sherman-Dension, TX	3	595	605	11	1 222	7 463	537	7 623	17 473	16 740	60.5	12.9	34.1	369	18 650	190.5
Shreveport, LA	15	2 877	804	25	2 979	30 293	2 778	8 436	71 291	64 895	63.3	15.3	155.1	896	50 900	141.7
Sioux City, IA-NE	2	795	684	14	1 340	8 106	580	7 006	20 224	21 646	71.2	14.1	53.5	860	21 270	183.8
Sioux Falls, SD	6	1 369	1 080	11	1 006	4 818	252	3 839	19 429	19 529	75.8	16.7	42.2	376	18 405	146.7
South Bend-Mishawaka, IN	4	1 114	453	18	2 201	17 059	998	6 986	37 838	41 804	67.6	14.6	94.6	395	44 045	180.4
Spokane, WA	10	1 987	555	42	3 140	23 928	1 327	6 714	62 006	63 477	78.2	17.9	160.6	461	58 140	163.1

1. Per 100,000 resident population estimated as of July 1 of the year shown. 2. Covers nursing homes with 3 or more beds. 3. Data for serious crimes have not been adjusted for underreporting, this may affect comparability between geographic areas or over time. 4. Includes murder and nonnegligent manslaughter, forcible rape, robbery, and aggravated assault. 5. Per 100,000 resident population as of July 1 of the year shown. 6. The 1986–1987 data are based on administrative reports obtained by the U.S. National Center for Education Statistics. The 1980 data are based on the 1980 Census of Population and Housing. 7. Persons 25 years old or older. 8. Elementary and secondary. 9. Per 1,000 resident population estimated as of July 1 of the year shown.

Area name	Social Security Program, Dec. 1988 (cont'd): Payments ($1,000)	Supplemental Security Income Program recipients, June 1986	Housing units, 1990: Total	Housing units, 1990: Percent change, 1980–1990	Housing units, 1990: Occupied units: Total	Housing units, 1990: Occupied units: Percent owner-occupied	Civilian labor force, 1990: Total	Civilian labor force, 1990: Percent change, 1989–1990	Civilian labor force, 1990: Unemployment: Total	Civilian labor force, 1990: Unemployment: Rate[1]	Private nonfarm establishments, 1988: Number	Private nonfarm establishments, 1988: Net change, 1987–1988	Private nonfarm establishments, 1988: Employment[2]: Total	Private nonfarm establishments, 1988: Employment[2]: Percent change, 1987–1988
	64	65	72	73	74	75	78	79	80	81	82	83	84	85
Phoenix, AZ	154 041	15 484	952 041	55.9	807 560	63.3	1 074 542	1.1	46 422	4.3	53 030	513	802 077	3.1
Pine Bluff, AR	6 074	3 378	33 311	0.8	30 001	67.1	37 676	-0.3	3 147	8.4	1 724	-63	24 287	3.8
Pittsburgh-Beaver Valley, PA	241 917	34 344	956 147	2.1	891 923	69.6	1 051 785	0.8	52 500	5.0	52 003	452	823 432	1.3
Beaver County, PA	20 267	2 298	76 336	1.7	71 939	73.3	59 982	0.0	4 655	7.8	3 283	71	40 700	2.2
Pittsburgh, PA	221 650	32 046	879 811	2.2	819 984	69.3	991 803	0.9	47 845	4.8	48 720	381	782 732	1.2
Pittsfield, MA	14 520	2 886	64 324	8.6	54 315	65.2	74 040	1.1	4 591	6.2	4 113	99	59 738	2.5
Portland, ME	18 964	3 468	109 890	19.7	94 512	64.3	143 802	2.6	5 207	3.6	8 680	313	118 933	6.7
Portland-Vancouver, OR-WA	108 533	13 362	605 513	15.0	575 531	61.3	812 040	1.8	34 988	4.3	40 163	651	555 551	5.5
Portland, OR	93 105	11 184	512 664	13.0	487 091	60.7	683 892	1.3	28 734	4.2	35 481	502	498 073	4.8
Vancouver, WA	15 428	2 178	92 849	27.5	88 440	64.3	128 148	4.9	6 254	4.9	4 682	149	57 478	11.4
Portsmouth-Dover-Rochester, NH-ME	19 860	1 476	144 160	32.8	126 862	70.0	195 164	2.5	11 698	6.0	10 075	199	124 668	7.3
Poughkeepsie, NY	20 015	4 264	97 632	12.4	89 567	69.1	129 091	-1.0	3 874	3.0	6 273	193	92 789	-1.3
Providence-Pawtucket-Fall Rvr, RI-MA	82 968	15 192	377 097	11.0	345 290	59.5	471 031	-1.4	32 248	6.8	25 425	386	377 658	1.9
Provo-Orem, UT	11 822	1 592	72 820	16.8	70 168	62.7	117 656	5.9	4 327	3.7	4 109	19	65 902	8.8
Pueblo, CO	10 426	2 750	50 872	3.6	47 057	67.9	53 671	8.8	3 575	6.7	2 720	-53	30 159	6.5
Raleigh-Durham, NC	39 649	10 256	308 496	45.8	287 647	58.9	418 532	0.8	10 288	2.5	19 525	706	324 280	7.9
Rapid City, SD	4 927	796	33 741	19.6	30 553	61.4	40 347	0.9	1 440	3.6	2 590	19	26 646	2.4
Reading, PA	32 368	3 236	134 482	12.1	127 649	73.9	175 804	-0.2	9 070	5.2	7 389	108	133 597	2.3
Redding, CA	12 968	4 854	60 552	27.6	55 966	64.5	61 526	-0.8	5 270	8.6	4 209	50	37 182	4.4
Reno, NV	15 549	1 552	112 193	30.4	102 294	54.1	135 849	-0.7	6 519	4.8	8 042	198	122 909	6.1
Richland-Kennewick-Pasco, WA	9 721	1 052	58 541	4.6	54 423	62.4	74 646	3.2	5 131	6.9	3 119	-113	44 915	14.0
Richmond-Petersburg, VA	58 932	11 796	355 207	23.9	331 824	65.0	460 617	1.4	17 856	3.9	22 181	612	369 715	4.4
Roanoke, VA	18 161	3 490	95 467	9.5	89 694	67.7	124 195	1.1	4 327	3.5	6 608	184	108 733	0.8
Rochester, MN	6 145	562	41 603	21.1	40 058	72.4	64 983	4.3	2 095	3.2	2 221	33	52 741	1.3
Rochester, NY	83 706	12 766	399 088	9.1	374 475	67.6	509 978	-0.9	18 900	3.7	21 584	447	415 692	4.6
Rockford, IL	23 812	2 790	113 143	9.6	107 677	68.5	156 659	0.3	10 052	6.4	6 884	114	124 525	6.3
Sacramento, CA	87 316	35 862	609 904	30.8	556 448	59.0	739 134	0.7	35 472	4.8	34 094	639	410 931	6.2
Saginaw-Bay City-Midland, MI	32 843	5 412	155 508	4.2	148 235	73.6	185 977	0.2	14 165	7.6	8 290	105	130 984	0.6
St. Cloud, MN	10 029	1 176	70 291	27.5	64 354	72.6	101 102	1.3	5 786	5.7	4 156	134	59 504	4.7
St. Joseph, MO	8 494	1 384	35 652	-1.5	32 486	68.0	42 757	0.6	2 661	6.2	2 066	7	32 384	7.4
St. Louis, MO-IL	200 083	31 230	1 006 011	10.9	924 733	68.5	1 272 232	-0.1	75 246	5.9	59 124	792	1 021 090	1.9
Salem, OR	24 465	3 738	105 847	8.9	101 661	63.5	140 687	2.1	7 621	5.4	6 603	179	72 277	6.2
Salinas-Seaside-Monterey, CA	18 890	6 076	121 224	17.1	112 965	50.6	160 646	-2.3	14 142	8.8	8 012	220	79 157	1.9
Salt Lake City-Ogden, UT	52 885	5 596	370 967	21.0	347 531	67.4	511 119	-0.6	20 979	4.1	24 064	-67	354 419	1.5
San Angelo, TX	6 917	1 670	40 135	22.1	35 408	62.3	43 827	-3.6	2 461	5.6	2 496	-39	31 425	5.7
San Antonio, TX	67 279	22 736	504 411	33.2	451 021	59.2	605 702	-1.6	41 753	6.9	27 766	-471	392 250	-1.5
San Diego, CA	148 668	46 216	946 240	31.4	887 403	53.8	1 174 417	0.2	52 771	4.5	57 667	1 768	767 646	4.5
San Francisco-Oakland-San Jose, CA	392 259	144 632	2 457 201	14.7	2 329 808	56.5	3 324 011	-1.5	136 062	4.1	173 901	2 952	2 621 281	3.4
Oakland, CA	130 002	51 900	820 279	17.8	779 806	58.8	1 092 277	-1.4	45 856	4.2	50 981	1 083	718 401	4.0
San Francisco, CA	120 564	47 182	680 010	5.8	642 504	48.3	873 199	-1.6	28 943	3.3	58 953	482	863 945	1.4
San Jose, CA	73 138	24 914	540 240	14.0	520 180	59.1	813 569	-4.0	32 854	4.0	38 070	699	769 907	4.3
Santa Cruz, CA	15 111	4 746	91 878	13.6	83 566	59.9	134 510	0.8	8 551	6.4	6 384	160	67 153	8.7
Santa Rosa-Petaluma, CA	29 815	8 006	161 062	29.7	149 011	62.9	209 955	3.3	9 155	4.4	11 024	284	109 801	4.5
Vallejo-Fairfield-Napa, CA	23 629	7 884	163 732	31.7	154 741	63.3	200 501	2.1	10 703	5.3	8 489	244	92 074	5.8
Santa Barbara-Santa Maria-Lompoc, CA	24 856	6 006	138 149	20.2	129 802	54.7	180 500	-1.3	8 109	4.5	10 210	102	121 331	0.7
Santa Fe, NM	6 191	1 352	49 029	40.5	45 053	68.8	70 676	4.2	2 457	3.5	3 475	23	33 833	3.5
Sarasota, FL	50 971	1 480	157 055	38.6	125 493	76.2	126 594	3.9	5 188	4.1	9 835	300	99 952	6.0
Savannah, GA	17 330	5 992	100 670	20.1	89 870	60.8	117 094	2.8	5 751	4.9	6 087	78	93 396	1.6
Scranton-Wilkes Barre, PA	78 847	10 120	322 709	8.5	280 697	70.0	365 581	0.7	25 334	6.9	17 274	542	256 691	4.8
Seattle-Tacoma, WA	169 724	25 296	1 060 127	25.6	1 002 157	60.4	1 380 047	1.7	51 411	3.7	69 508	1 903	979 780	4.8
Seattle, WA	133 067	18 248	831 285	26.6	787 505	60.4	1 125 768	1.8	39 173	3.5	57 934	1 592	844 648	5.0
Tacoma, WA	36 657	7 048	228 842	22.1	214 652	60.3	254 279	1.0	12 238	4.8	11 574	311	135 132	3.8
Sharon, PA	13 329	1 568	48 689	2.2	45 591	75.0	52 274	2.3	2 769	5.3	2 558	49	36 326	8.2
Sheboygan, WI	9 821	1 020	40 695	9.0	38 592	70.3	58 459	-2.3	2 687	4.6	2 261	8	42 520	2.5
Sherman-Dension, TX	8 390	1 758	44 223	12.0	36 847	69.3	47 282	-0.6	2 513	5.3	2 299	-128	30 488	0.5
Shreveport, LA	22 751	8 536	142 609	12.7	123 966	65.0	153 640	-3.0	10 260	6.7	8 155	-210	108 912	1.2
Sioux City, IA-NE	10 449	1 462	45 557	0.9	42 934	68.5	60 832	-0.1	2 339	3.8	3 026	-4	46 979	12.9
Sioux Falls, SD	9 027	1 196	49 780	16.6	47 681	62.3	75 833	0.8	2 070	2.7	3 882	89	60 739	2.3
South Bend-Mishawaka, IN	23 397	2 032	97 956	7.4	92 365	72.0	130 699	-1.0	7 104	5.4	6 153	39	102 432	4.6
Spokane, WA	28 786	5 046	150 105	9.0	141 619	63.7	171 132	1.0	9 132	5.3	9 176	-84	117 893	1.9

1. Percent of total civilian labor force. 2. For week including March 12. Excludes government employees, self-employed persons, farm workers, domestic service workers, railroad employees subject to the Railroad Retirement Act, and employees on oceanborne vessels or in foreign countries.

Area name	Private nonfarm establishments, 1987 (cont'd): Employment[1] (cont'd): Manu- facturing	Retail trade	Finance, insurance, and real estate	Services	Annual payroll: Total (Mil dol)	Average per employee	Personal income, 1989: Total (Mil dol)	Percent change, 1988–1989	Wages and salaries[2] (Mil dol)	Propri- etor's income (Mil dol)	Dividends, Interest, & rent (Mil dol)	Transfer payments (Mil dol)	Per capita[3]: Dollars	Rank (Dollars)
	86	87	88	89	90	91	92	93	94	95	96	97	98	99
Phoenix, AZ	133 471	176 787	70 083	243 566	16 228	20 232	36 804	7.8	24 296	2 376	7 099	4 768	17 705	67
Pine Bluff, AR	6 877	5 707	1 563	6 492	417	17 170	1 103	5.2	775	78	154	228	12 134	273
Pittsburgh-Beaver Valley, PA	135 443	178 552	56 038	281 459	17 476	21 223	39 553	6.9	23 990	3 175	7 432	7 398	17 455	78
Beaver County, PA	9 655	11 142	1 734	10 788	790	19 410	2 641	5.9	1 204	159	448	567	14 046	X
Pittsburgh, PA	125 788	167 410	54 304	270 671	16 686	21 318	36 912	7.0	22 786	3 015	6 983	6 831	17 763	X
Pittsfield, MA	16 076	14 285	3 158	18 810	1 210	20 255	2 724	7.8	1 584	212	549	475	19 783	29
Portland, ME	17 442	31 379	12 135	31 409	2 311	19 431	4 873	9.4	3 591	450	921	621	20 383	17
Portland-Vancouver, OR-WA	114 729	117 067	43 740	157 594	11 479	20 662	25 655	10.5	17 191	2 242	4 416	3 427	17 713	66
Portland, OR	97 204	104 493	39 157	143 407	10 361	20 802	22 053	10.4	15 426	1 971	3 847	2 891	18 163	X
Vancouver, WA	17 525	12 574	4 583	14 187	1 118	19 451	3 601	10.8	1 765	271	568	536	15 379	X
Portsmouth-Dover-Rochester, NH-ME	26 346	33 828	8 945	29 942	2 423	19 436	6 966	6.7	3 490	672	1 059	643	20 351	18
Poughkeepsie, NY	29 109	20 286	3 824	26 524	2 211	23 828	5 435	7.0	3 433	324	909	689	20 533	15
Providence-Pawtucket-Fall Rvr, RI-MA	108 119	76 423	26 267	104 981	7 238	19 165	16 366	7.2	10 194	1 110	3 015	2 737	17 923	59
Provo-Orem, UT	12 645	12 974	2 261	29 908	1 062	16 115	2 721	9.9	1 640	250	335	415	11 171	277
Pueblo, CO	3 981	9 529	1 426	10 104	462	15 319	1 659	7.6	856	127	314	443	12 974	257
Raleigh-Durham, NC	63 354	67 513	24 233	102 937	6 553	20 208	13 302	9.7	10 407	1 016	1 921	1 320	18 945	38
Rapid City, SD	3 366	7 799	1 478	8 385	413	15 500	1 170	8.0	813	142	200	176	13 944	224
Reading, PA	48 629	27 088	8 245	28 636	2 783	20 831	6 339	8.4	3 984	434	1 085	874	19 068	34
Redding, CA	5 006	10 167	1 784	10 538	709	19 068	2 229	9.8	1 175	292	402	475	15 567	146
Reno, NV	9 321	23 917	6 218	57 088	2 370	19 283	5 225	10.2	3 404	340	1 127	589	20 920	14
Richland-Kennewick-Pasco, WA	14 848	9 556	1 360	13 625	1 009	22 465	2 271	6.6	1 539	245	345	341	15 489	151
Richmond-Petersburg, VA	NA	79 836	37 927	95 496	7 793	21 078	17 255	9.3	12 252	985	3 096	2 013	20 164	22
Roanoke, VA	19 795	23 532	8 995	29 791	1 927	17 722	4 012	8.3	2 835	313	806	549	18 229	53
Rochester, MN	10 384	10 809	1 745	24 686	1 211	22 961	1 996	9.0	1 680	136	288	199	19 517	31
Rochester, NY	133 027	79 800	23 241	119 011	9 358	22 512	19 479	8.4	13 284	1 373	3 502	2 723	19 858	26
Rockford, IL	48 896	22 956	5 642	31 625	2 742	22 020	4 958	6.3	3 569	398	842	614	17 498	76
Sacramento, CA	42 950	111 967	33 390	125 775	8 047	19 582	26 230	10.5	16 626	2 288	3 918	4 589	18 299	51
Saginaw-Bay City-Midland, MI	NA	31 603	5 922	32 386	3 168	24 186	6 589	6.3	4 475	359	1 150	1 070	16 238	113
St. Cloud, MN	11 659	18 033	2 273	15 825	982	16 503	2 568	8.2	1 562	285	380	368	13 927	225
St. Joseph, MO	9 058	6 842	1 986	7 949	590	18 219	1 278	6.8	839	96	259	235	15 041	177
St. Louis, MO-IL	225 077	207 836	69 154	307 265	22 604	22 137	46 959	6.9	31 737	3 434	9 011	6 093	18 957	37
Salem, OR	12 077	18 896	6 120	23 089	1 128	15 607	4 057	9.6	2 195	377	748	725	14 708	198
Salinas-Seaside-Monterey, CA	8 562	23 269	4 526	25 440	1 492	18 849	6 274	5.2	3 448	976	1 251	858	17 622	72
Salt Lake City-Ogden, UT	61 567	77 932	25 243	108 614	6 748	19 040	15 058	7.9	10 774	1 031	2 136	2 061	13 962	222
San Angelo, TX	5 066	7 902	1 792	8 028	524	16 675	1 462	5.9	810	188	304	238	14 658	201
San Antonio, TX	44 516	101 393	38 940	121 846	6 869	17 512	19 106	7.2	12 362	1 320	3 185	3 423	14 144	217
San Diego, CA	124 379	184 606	64 541	243 821	16 145	21 032	45 868	9.6	28 784	3 633	8 709	6 614	18 651	45
San Francisco-Oakland-San Jose, CA	525 113	510 548	221 013	793 688	68 745	26 226	145 873	7.2	98 520	13 037	25 889	15 995	23 778	6
Oakland, CA	110 136	160 105	56 355	210 354	17 245	24 005	45 447	7.3	26 789	3 391	7 330	5 608	22 249	X
San Francisco, CA	84 294	154 488	116 217	298 589	23 153	26 799	45 051	7.1	32 739	5 392	9 979	4 542	28 170	X
San Jose, CA	286 410	120 608	31 173	208 860	23 116	30 024	35 544	7.4	29 885	2 348	5 190	3 043	24 581	X
Santa Cruz, CA	13 284	19 012	3 191	19 951	1 301	19 374	4 322	-0.1	1 986	485	615	572	18 637	X
Santa Rosa-Petaluma, CA	18 939	28 657	9 207	28 554	2 181	19 863	7 883	9.3	3 384	831	1 668	1 014	20 860	X
Vallejo-Fairfield-Napa, CA	12 050	27 678	4 870	27 380	1 749	18 996	7 626	8.3	3 737	590	1 106	1 217	17 454	X
Santa Barbara-Santa Maria-Lompoc, CA	20 831	30 395	9 246	39 094	2 518	20 753	7 478	9.0	4 163	910	1 911	905	21 504	13
Santa Fe, NM	1 435	10 016	2 079	14 926	550	16 256	1 979	8.6	1 370	156	437	247	17 137	90
Sarasota, FL	12 021	29 409	7 996	31 072	1 650	16 508	6 402	11.5	2 371	404	2 867	1 148	24 039	4
Savannah, GA	20 780	20 455	5 561	25 776	1 771	18 962	3 844	7.4	2 647	265	633	609	15 658	141
Scranton-Wilkes Barre, PA	NA	55 690	12 997	70 636	4 276	16 658	11 500	7.7	6 336	1 041	2 049	2 525	15 519	149
Seattle-Tacoma, WA	207 494	203 843	78 270	270 444	22 608	23 075	49 487	10.7	34 376	3 720	8 097	6 307	19 851	27
Seattle, WA	187 324	168 588	69 806	227 066	20 116	23 816	40 571	11.1	29 684	3 103	6 755	4 669	21 137	X
Tacoma, WA	20 170	35 255	8 464	43 378	2 492	18 441	8 916	8.9	4 693	617	1 343	1 638	15 546	X
Sharon, PA	11 449	8 183	1 276	9 604	663	18 251	1 744	8.1	950	166	325	362	14 322	208
Sheboygan, WI	18 825	7 467	1 984	8 890	831	19 544	1 783	8.2	1 161	125	310	242	17 270	84
Sherman-Densison, TX	10 168	6 892	1 855	7 167	604	19 811	1 478	5.5	866	121	281	271	15 040	178
Shreveport, LA	19 360	24 298	7 308	32 430	2 011	18 464	4 920	4.4	3 089	462	915	881	13 744	235
Sioux City, IA-NE	NA	10 056	2 736	14 540	811	17 263	1 771	7.9	1 125	233	294	299	15 242	167
Sioux Falls, SD	8 626	13 526	6 375	18 191	1 066	17 551	2 080	8.4	1 465	256	323	253	16 412	108
South Bend-Mishawaka, IN	23 957	22 889	5 350	33 620	1 954	19 076	4 067	6.2	2 641	282	682	555	16 545	104
Spokane, WA	19 506	27 211	8 715	38 953	2 109	17 889	5 553	9.0	3 307	455	1 037	1 068	15 507	150

1. For week including March 12. Excludes government employees, self-employed persons, farm workers, domestic service workers, railroad employees subject to the Railroad Retirement Act, and employees on oceanborne vessels or in foreign countries. 2. Includes other labor income. 3. Based on the resident population estimated as of July 1 of the year shown.

Area name	Earnings, 1989									Agriculture, 1987									
		Percent by selected industries								Farms			Farm operators, Percent		Land in farms				
			Goods-related[1]		Service-related & other[2]						Percent with						Acres		
	Total (Mil. dol)	Farm	Total	Manu-facturing	Total	Retail trade	Finance, insurance, & real estate	Services	Government	Number	Less than 50 acres	500 acres and over	Whose principal occupation is farming	Residing on farm operated	Acreage (1,000)	Percent change, 1982–1987	Average size of farm	Total irrigated (1,000)	Total cropland (1,000)
	100	101	102	103	104	105	106	107	108	109	110	111	112	113	114	115	116	117	118
Phoenix, AZ	26 672	0.8	24.4	17.1	60.8	11.0	8.7	27.2	14.0	2 334	65.9	11.7	44.6	61.3	1 391	-2.7	596	276	424
Pine Bluff, AR	854	2.6	27.0	21.4	49.8	8.7	3.3	19.4	20.6	417	27.3	40.3	63.8	51.3	280	-5.4	671	121	252
Pittsburgh-Beaver Valley, PA	27 165	0.2	26.2	18.3	62.5	9.8	6.1	32.5	11.1	4 852	29.3	2.4	44.9	82.9	602	-0.7	124	2	387
Beaver County, PA	1 364	0.6	33.4	24.5	53.9	9.8	2.6	23.2	12.2	570	33.5	1.8	46.8	87.2	59	-0.1	104	0	37
Pittsburgh, PA	25 801	0.2	25.8	17.9	63.0	9.8	6.3	33.0	11.0	4 282	28.7	2.5	44.6	82.3	543	-0.8	127	1	350
Pittsfield, MA	1 796	0.7	38.2	28.8	51.8	11.9	3.9	29.0	9.2	392	33.2	9.9	49.7	82.4	71	-3.6	181	0	32
Portland, ME	4 041	0.2	21.9	13.1	65.7	12.8	10.3	27.4	12.2	456	35.5	4.2	45.0	86.8	58	-7.0	127	1	27
Portland-Vancouver, OR-WA	19 433	1.3	26.4	20.0	59.5	10.1	6.8	25.1	12.8	8 527	70.0	2.5	38.7	85.8	626	-5.3	73	71	419
Portland, OR	17 397	1.2	25.3	19.2	61.2	10.2	7.0	25.7	12.3	7 099	70.7	2.6	39.0	85.4	531	-5.0	75	67	362
Vancouver, WA	2 036	1.6	36.5	26.8	44.8	9.7	5.7	19.7	17.1	1 428	66.7	1.7	37.3	87.8	95	-6.9	66	4	57
Portsmouth-Dover-Rochester, NH-ME	4 162	0.4	31.9	21.4	54.4	13.5	6.4	23.6	13.3	571	42.9	2.5	40.1	88.3	63	-15.5	111	1	23
Poughkeepsie, NY	3 756	0.5	43.6	36.0	38.1	8.2	3.2	20.8	17.8	613	33.8	10.6	54.8	83.0	124	-9.8	203	1	70
Providence-Pawtucket-Fall Rvr, RI-MA	11 304	0.2	30.4	23.6	55.9	10.4	7.0	27.3	13.5	564	55.0	2.0	48.2	78.0	48	-5.9	86	3	19
Provo-Orem, UT	1 890	1.1	24.6	19.0	60.2	9.1	3.0	39.1	14.1	1 723	65.6	6.0	40.1	65.7	494	14.2	287	79	135
Pueblo, CO	984	1.4	21.9	15.4	51.5	11.9	4.3	24.7	25.2	615	33.0	32.4	50.4	73.3	892	-8.5	1 451	32	103
Raleigh-Durham, NC	11 423	0.6	25.6	19.5	53.2	8.9	5.9	26.3	20.6	2 425	38.0	5.4	52.9	70.3	358	-16.5	148	12	187
Rapid City, SD	955	1.2	16.1	8.4	51.3	11.7	3.9	23.3	31.3	614	16.8	52.0	60.6	75.4	1 142	6.2	1 860	9	271
Reading, PA	4 418	1.5	41.1	34.3	48.2	9.5	5.5	21.0	9.3	1 809	36.7	3.8	62.0	81.0	243	-5.1	134	1	204
Redding, CA	1 467	1.1	24.6	12.0	56.8	12.0	3.0	27.1	17.4	899	57.4	14.2	43.3	82.2	377	-6.9	420	49	60
Reno, NV	3 744	0.2	16.0	6.6	71.1	11.1	5.2	38.8	12.7	346	57.5	14.7	38.2	75.1	881	0.8	2 546	32	42
Richland-Kennewick-Pasco, WA	1 784	6.5	35.2	28.4	40.4	8.1	1.8	23.7	16.5	2 072	48.9	17.3	56.1	74.2	1 305	-0.4	630	306	902
Richmond-Petersburg, VA	13 237	0.3	NA	18.2	54.0	9.8	NA	20.6	19.3	2 005	34.0	11.1	44.8	76.0	D	D	D	D	237
Roanoke, VA	3 148	0.2	25.4	18.2	61.4	11.1	7.3	25.0	12.2	811	33.8	4.8	40.0	79.5	127	-3.1	157	0	54
Rochester, MN	1 816	1.4	31.8	26.3	57.7	7.7	2.3	42.2	9.0	1 446	23.1	10.4	55.4	78.4	319	-3.5	220	D	258
Rochester, NY	14 657	NA	43.1	38.0	43.8	7.9	4.5	22.7	11.9	3 901	30.6	12.8	57.3	83.1	914	-5.9	234	4	728
Rockford, IL	3 967	NA	NA	43.6	42.5	8.0	3.4	20.6	7.7	1 368	28.8	15.1	63.5	78.6	357	-7.3	261	1	325
Sacramento, CA	18 914	0.9	16.6	7.7	51.0	10.1	6.2	23.4	31.4	4 568	62.9	10.6	44.0	76.7	1 214	-6.1	266	388	640
Saginaw-Bay City-Midland, MI	4 834	1.2	48.6	42.5	39.7	8.7	2.6	19.5	10.5	2 805	28.9	10.3	51.5	78.5	580	-2.7	207	9	513
St. Cloud, MN	1 847	4.8	NA	19.3	NA	14.8	3.1	19.8	16.4	4 743	17.7	5.8	67.3	82.6	981	-2.7	207	66	744
St. Joseph, MO	935	0.7	33.5	27.2	52.6	9.5	5.3	20.8	13.2	848	28.4	12.6	53.1	71.5	189	-4.6	223	D	149
St. Louis, MO-IL	35 171	0.4	31.5	24.5	56.6	9.1	6.5	25.0	11.5	8 708	27.8	12.1	49.9	72.5	1 959	-2.5	225	8	1 539
Salem, OR	2 572	4.5	21.4	15.4	45.9	10.5	4.4	21.2	28.2	3 658	60.0	6.7	48.3	82.8	483	-1.6	132	98	363
Salinas-Seaside-Monterey, CA	4 424	13.4	12.4	6.7	49.0	10.2	3.6	21.4	25.2	1 364	44.4	26.6	66.1	53.8	1 385	2.9	1 015	181	316
Salt Lake City-Ogden, UT	11 806	0.2	22.0	15.5	57.2	9.9	6.5	23.4	20.5	2 272	74.0	3.3	37.6	70.8	418	-9.7	184	72	116
San Angelo, TX	998	2.1	20.1	11.8	54.7	10.7	4.2	25.5	23.0	867	33.7	35.6	49.1	56.7	1 014	4.8	1 170	26	208
San Antonio, TX	13 683	0.3	15.1	8.8	54.5	11.4	8.2	24.9	30.2	4 372	40.0	9.6	38.3	63.7	1 032	-0.8	236	14	362
San Diego, CA	32 417	1.1	22.6	14.3	52.7	9.9	6.9	26.4	23.6	6 259	87.7	1.9	37.9	63.9	530	-15.1	85	73	123
San Francisco-Oakland-San Jose, CA	111 557	0.6	26.8	19.7	59.1	9.1	8.1	28.3	13.5	9 408	64.6	9.3	46.9	68.2	D	D	D	244	632
Oakland, CA	30 179	0.2	24.0	14.5	58.3	10.7	6.4	26.1	17.5	1 532	60.4	10.4	39.0	65.1	442	-21.6	288	33	110
San Francisco, CA	38 131	0.2	14.0	8.4	73.9	8.7	14.5	34.2	11.9	620	49.5	22.3	53.4	64.8	D	D	D	6	44
San Jose, CA	32 233	0.3	45.5	40.2	45.6	7.0	3.6	25.0	8.6	1 312	75.2	5.7	48.1	68.9	348	5.5	265	24	45
Santa Cruz, CA	2 471	6.3	26.1	16.2	52.5	12.0	3.0	28.6	15.0	813	75.4	2.1	59.8	61.1	55	-3.9	68	19	27
Santa Rosa-Petaluma, CA	4 215	3.4	27.5	14.5	54.2	12.5	6.3	24.1	14.9	3 039	65.1	7.9	45.1	73.0	550	-6.3	181	36	160
Vallejo-Fairfield-Napa, CA	4 327	2.9	20.2	9.5	44.1	11.7	3.2	20.8	32.8	2 092	60.6	11.6	47.5	66.7	579	-1.2	277	125	246
Santa Barbara-Santa Maria-Lompoc, CA	5 073	4.9	25.2	16.9	54.4	10.4	5.6	28.8	15.6	1 756	62.4	15.2	55.2	54.7	870	3.5	495	76	145
Santa Fe, NM	1 527	0.1	8.7	2.7	46.2	10.3	3.4	28.7	45.0	326	55.8	19.9	32.8	71.8	D	D	D	7	17
Sarasota, FL	2 775	0.4	20.0	7.9	67.8	16.5	6.6	35.9	11.7	352	69.3	8.8	36.4	69.6	167	-19.4	474	5	13
Savannah, GA	2 912	0.4	29.4	20.5	54.1	10.0	4.6	24.7	16.1	253	32.8	12.6	33.6	68.8	67	-23.5	264	D	30
Scranton-Wilkes Barre, PA	7 378	0.6	31.0	23.2	54.7	10.9	4.1	25.5	13.6	2 032	25.9	4.9	52.3	83.1	310	-10.1	153	1	202
Seattle-Tacoma, WA	38 096	0.3	30.5	23.5	54.9	9.7	6.7	22.9	14.4	4 199	78.1	0.9	37.9	85.8	195	-12.1	46	15	113
Seattle, WA	32 787	0.3	32.2	25.3	55.7	9.5	7.1	22.9	11.8	2 971	78.4	1.0	38.2	84.9	136	-10.9	46	9	84
Tacoma, WA	5 309	0.7	19.5	12.3	49.6	10.8	4.2	22.7	30.2	1 228	77.4	0.5	37.4	88.0	59	-14.8	48	6	29
Sharon, PA	1 116	1.5	39.1	33.3	49.3	10.6	2.8	25.5	10.0	1 267	18.7	3.2	56.3	83.7	183	2.6	144	0	122
Sheboygan, WI	1 286	2.3	53.3	47.9	34.9	8.6	4.5	14.7	9.5	1 213	28.6	6.6	65.3	84.3	210	-3.8	173	0	179
Sherman-Dension, TX	987	0.9	44.0	36.8	45.6	9.9	4.5	21.6	9.6	1 900	37.5	8.8	32.5	63.7	414	2.0	218	2	234
Shreveport, LA	3 551	0.5	24.3	16.0	54.7	9.5	4.4	26.2	20.4	958	33.9	17.5	43.3	59.2	295	-15.4	308	3	173
Sioux City, IA-NE	1 358	2.6	27.2	21.1	59.2	9.5	5.3	27.8	11.0	1 705	21.2	23.2	68.9	72.5	602	-4.3	353	16	528
Sioux Falls, SD	1 721	2.2	18.1	11.8	69.7	10.9	10.8	28.6	10.0	1 382	23.2	21.6	66.4	78.2	432	1.5	313	2	373
South Bend-Mishawaka, IN	2 922	0.6	32.1	25.1	58.0	10.2	5.3	28.4	9.2	897	37.9	10.6	50.2	80.8	174	0.2	194	11	156
Spokane, WA	3 762	1.4	21.7	14.9	57.9	11.2	5.5	26.4	19.1	1 901	42.1	18.0	43.2	85.0	613	-2.2	322	15	399

1. Covers mining, construction, and manufacturing. 2. Covers private sector earnings in agricultural services, forestry, and fisheries; transportation and public utilities; wholesale trade; retail trade; finance, insurance, and real estate; and services.

Area name	Agriculture, 1987 (cont'd)						Manufactures, 1987								
	Value of products sold				Percent of farms with sales of		Establishments		All employees		Production workers				Value added by manufacture (Mil dol)
			Percent from										Wages		
	Total (Mil dol)	Average per farm (Dollars)	Crops	Livestock and poultry[1]	$10,000 or more	$100,000 or more	Total	Percent with 20 or more employees	Number (1,000)	Annual payroll (Mil dol)	Number (1,000)	Work hours (Millions)	Total (Mil dol)	Average per worker (Dollars)	
	121	122	123	124	125	126	127	128	129	131	132	133	134	135	136
Phoenix, AZ	549	235 128	56.2	43.8	45.1	25.7	2 803	28.9	135.8	3 541.5	78.7	160.9	1 673.3	21 262	8 179.8
Pine Bluff, AR	57	136 353	93.6	6.4	60.7	36.2	87	43.7	5.8	142.8	4.5	9.6	102.9	22 867	388.7
Pittsburgh-Beaver Valley, PA	104	21 387	36.1	63.9	30.1	4.7	2 690	34.8	133.4	3 849.0	74.9	144.0	1 745.3	23 302	6 322.8
Beaver County, PA	12	21 295	35.5	64.5	30.4	5.4	172	36.6	9.8	258.2	7.0	12.6	167.6	23 943	562.4
Pittsburgh, PA	92	21 400	36.1	63.9	30.1	4.6	2 518	34.7	123.7	3 590.7	67.9	131.4	1 577.7	23 236	5 760.4
Pittsfield, MA	18	44 806	25.2	74.8	35.2	13.5	217	35.9	16.4	470.4	8.0	16.6	178.3	22 288	832.0
Portland, ME	13	28 678	42.7	57.3	30.7	9.0	381	26.0	16.2	372.6	10.9	21.0	201.7	18 505	1 015.2
Portland-Vancouver, OR-WA	364	42 634	67.6	32.4	26.3	7.7	2 961	28.3	109.0	2 758.7	69.4	134.9	1 469.6	21 176	6 445.4
Portland, OR	327	46 018	72.6	27.4	27.8	8.0	2 631	28.3	94.1	2 376.9	58.5	113.4	1 219.2	20 841	5 348.5
Vancouver, WA	37	25 815	22.9	77.1	19.2	6.0	330	28.8	14.9	381.8	11.0	21.5	250.3	22 755	1 096.9
Portsmouth-Dover-Rochester, NH-ME	21	37 215	58.8	41.2	27.5	7.5	576	29.0	24.7	557.3	16.0	31.0	295.7	18 481	3 271.2
Poughkeepsie, NY	38	61 248	36.7	63.3	51.5	17.9	207	38.6	30.9	1 102.8	10.0	19.5	198.1	19 810	2 063.3
Providence-Pawtucket-Fall Rvr, RI-MA	27	47 363	66.0	34.0	32.8	8.9	2 791	31.4	106.0	2 120.1	73.4	143.8	1 185.8	16 155	4 425.3
Provo-Orem, UT	73	42 283	25.9	74.1	32.3	8.8	276	27.5	9.0	167.2	6.4	12.2	104.4	16 312	334.3
Pueblo, CO	38	62 421	23.4	76.6	39.7	10.9	95	17.9	3.6	85.7	2.4	5.2	57.4	23 917	230.7
Raleigh-Durham, NC	111	45 969	60.3	39.7	45.6	12.1	834	33.5	59.4	1 491.7	30.5	58.6	561.4	18 407	4 728.5
Rapid City, SD	26	41 552	31.3	68.7	56.4	11.2	102	31.4	3.5	68.2	2.4	5.0	37.4	15 583	161.0
Reading, PA	168	92 735	45.7	54.3	60.4	23.2	624	47.3	47.3	1 180.5	34.5	69.8	752.5	21 812	2 628.6
Redding, CA	27	29 707	48.3	51.7	28.6	6.0	239	22.6	5.0	117.6	3.7	7.1	84.9	22 946	338.7
Reno, NV	12	34 147	28.0	72.0	25.7	8.7	357	27.2	9.1	203.8	6.0	11.9	114.7	19 117	564.5
Richland-Kennewick-Pasco, WA	309	149 370	84.9	15.1	54.5	27.1	120	20.0	15.4	493.2	8.0	12.2	195.5	24 438	1 220.6
Richmond-Petersburg, VA	69	34 406	51.1	48.9	34.7	D	1 002	38.2	66.4	1 952.3	39.1	77.0	968.6	24 772	6 833.0
Roanoke, VA	28	34 185	13.5	86.5	24.8	5.1	287	43.2	20.3	435.3	13.8	27.5	251.6	18 232	1 099.8
Rochester, MN	86	59 515	29.6	70.4	64.1	D	66	36.4	10.3	378.2	3.4	12.5	75.3	22 147	1 037.6
Rochester, NY	277	71 028	56.2	43.8	51.8	19.1	1 391	38.4	130.2	4 056.9	67.7	136.4	1 669.1	24 654	12 409.0
Rockford, IL	95	69 148	51.2	48.8	67.8	22.3	772	38.5	43.8	1 229.7	27.8	56.4	669.5	24 083	2 807.7
Sacramento, CA	418	91 435	65.3	34.7	33.7	13.0	1 415	23.6	41.6	1 002.9	25.3	49.8	513.1	20 281	2 802.3
Saginaw-Bay City-Midland, MI	122	43 657	81.6	18.4	56.9	11.6	412	37.1	38.9	1 375.2	27.1	56.4	904.7	33 384	3 337.6
St. Cloud, MN	323	68 067	14.3	85.7	65.8	19.4	250	32.0	11.1	233.1	8.3	16.4	151.9	18 301	608.1
St. Joseph, MO	26	30 846	65.9	34.1	48.6	D	102	42.2	8.1	181.5	6.0	11.5	123.5	20 583	645.1
St. Louis, MO-IL	376	43 216	53.7	46.3	50.6	12.2	3 351	37.1	221.7	6 461.1	124.9	249.4	3 097.6	24 801	14 115.0
Salem, OR	255	69 707	70.9	29.1	40.2	14.4	463	29.2	13.7	256.1	10.4	19.5	167.1	16 067	663.5
Salinas-Seaside-Monterey, CA	731	535 738	94.1	5.9	65.2	38.0	252	23.8	7.8	182.7	4.9	9.0	101.7	20 755	603.6
Salt Lake City-Ogden, UT	79	34 622	33.1	66.9	26.6	6.9	1 463	30.9	61.0	1 422.2	36.3	71.6	654.1	18 019	3 395.3
San Angelo, TX	76	87 196	24.3	75.7	48.6	14.4	102	27.5	4.1	68.0	2.9	5.1	44.0	15 172	204.1
San Antonio, TX	74	16 969	43.8	56.2	19.9	2.3	1 193	30.6	44.1	838.3	29.8	58.5	465.2	15 611	2 127.7
San Diego, CA	444	70 938	77.8	22.2	32.3	8.9	3 041	26.3	120.0	3 236.3	67.4	129.2	1 369.1	20 313	6 426.8
San Francisco-Oakland-San Jose, CA	910	96 680	74.3	25.7	42.0	15.1	11 124	29.1	507.1	16 113.2	239.0	468.6	5 497.8	23 003	38 913.2
Oakland, CA	106	69 250	74.6	25.4	36.3	9.3	3 211	29.0	107.0	3 068.8	62.0	122.7	1 490.7	24 044	9 479.3
San Francisco, CA	132	212 715	68.3	31.7	55.2	25.5	3 153	25.8	81.9	2 270.0	45.1	85.5	887.6	19 681	5 374.6
San Jose, CA	132	100 623	80.4	19.6	35.7	15.2	3 298	34.4	275.7	9 742.1	104.6	208.9	2 562.7	24 500	20 865.3
Santa Cruz, CA	162	198 677	96.9	3.1	50.9	24.5	375	21.6	12.2	288.2	8.4	15.2	147.6	17 571	995.7
Santa Rosa-Petaluma, CA	209	68 794	47.4	52.6	40.3	13.1	657	25.0	19.2	467.1	12.0	23.0	252.0	21 000	1 090.2
Vallejo-Fairfield-Napa, CA	169	80 778	85.5	14.5	45.0	15.4	430	25.8	11.0	277.1	7.0	13.3	157.3	22 471	1 108.2
Santa Barbara-Santa Maria-Lompoc, CA	288	163 876	84.9	15.1	48.4	17.8	523	24.3	20.2	563.0	8.6	17.1	163.9	19 058	1 023.6
Santa Fe, NM	7	22 399	27.9	72.1	19.3	3.4	130	12.3	1.5	25.2	1.0	1.8	13.6	13 600	59.3
Sarasota, FL	15	43 293	65.0	35.0	36.4	8.8	427	21.1	8.9	180.2	5.6	11.3	88.5	15 804	433.1
Savannah, GA	8	32 154	64.4	35.6	35.6	D	244	32.0	15.9	430.5	10.4	22.7	263.1	25 298	1 110.0
Scranton-Wilkes Barre, PA	84	41 237	39.1	60.9	42.4	8.5	1 166	48.5	69.3	1 324.3	53.2	101.7	900.2	16 921	3 522.9
Seattle-Tacoma, WA	241	57 282	23.9	76.1	24.1	10.1	4 108	27.4	194.2	5 926.6	100.8	194.7	2 406.4	23 873	10 895.9
Seattle, WA	162	54 375	23.4	76.6	25.1	10.4	3 464	27.0	174.5	5 448.7	87.6	169.4	2 132.3	24 341	9 820.1
Tacoma, WA	79	64 316	25.0	75.0	21.8	9.4	644	30.0	19.7	477.9	13.2	25.2	274.1	20 765	1 075.8
Sharon, PA	40	31 177	32.0	68.0	46.4	6.9	169	36.7	10.4	253.2	7.5	14.1	172.7	23 027	630.7
Sheboygan, WI	81	66 951	14.1	85.9	63.7	24.2	236	53.0	18.7	443.8	12.4	24.9	262.8	21 194	945.0
Sherman-Densison, TX	27	14 305	36.3	63.7	22.2	2.9	127	39.4	10.4	273.9	7.3	15.1	158.1	21 658	774.0
Shreveport, LA	33	34 228	63.4	36.6	33.9	8.9	344	31.1	19.3	490.3	13.9	26.7	338.0	24 317	1 961.2
Sioux City, IA-NE	151	88 309	42.2	57.8	75.0	24.2	119	49.6	9.9	204.9	6.1	13.4	104.7	17 164	329.5
Sioux Falls, SD	95	69 090	38.0	62.0	71.9	17.9	138	36.2	8.9	164.8	6.3	11.5	100.4	15 937	463.8
South Bend-Mishawaka, IN	47	52 787	60.1	39.9	51.8	13.4	489	38.7	23.2	599.5	14.8	28.9	313.2	21 162	1 189.9
Spokane, WA	64	33 442	67.8	32.2	32.2	9.5	497	26.2	19.6	462.0	12.6	24.2	248.0	19 683	1 053.0

1. Includes livestock and poultry products.

Area name	Manufactures, 1987 (cont'd)		Value of construction authorized by building permits, 1990								Wholesale trade, 1987				Retail trade, all establishments, 1987
				Nonresidential				Residential							
					Percent										
	Value of shipments (Mil dol)	New capital expenditures (Mil dol)	Total[1] ($1,000)	Total ($1,000)	Office	Industrial	Stores	New construction ($1,000)	Number of housing units	Alterations and additions ($1,000)	Establishments	Sales (Mil dol)	Paid employees[2]	Annual payroll (Mil dol)	Number
	137	138	139	140	141	142	143	144	145	146	147	148	149	150	151
Phoenix, AZ	14 061.8	655.2	2 167 246	469 475	17.8	19.4	35.6	1 285 519	12 950	62 131	3 984	16 991.1	49 119	1 141.4	17 682
Pine Bluff, AR	902.9	68.6	33 158	24 500	4.9	69.4	22.8	2 770	103	1 689	124	272.2	1 193	20.1	914
Pittsburgh-Beaver Valley, PA	14 198.2	345.2	1 060 295	357 446	16.0	30.8	26.2	458 106	4 887	81 687	4 051	26 537.2	49 582	1 215.3	21 361
Beaver County, PA	1 764.9	30.8	116 259	67 154	1.4	85.8	3.6	41 149	470	4 077	163	377.7	1 152	22.4	1 625
Pittsburgh, PA	12 433.2	314.4	944 036	290 292	19.3	18.0	31.4	416 958	4 417	77 610	3 888	26 159.5	48 430	1 193.0	19 736
Pittsfield, MA	1 442.6	53.9	104 126	30 172	29.8	6.1	5.5	35 935	377	15 229	152	277.9	1 416	28.3	1 764
Portland, ME	1 813.7	103.8	188 111	50 103	36.8	3.4	29.7	89 237	1 070	20 845	572	3 010.0	8 927	202.2	2 848
Portland-Vancouver, OR-WA	13 254.7	424.6	1 861 510	309 255	27.5	21.6	23.1	1 184 122	15 963	66 691	3 687	24 434.5	44 745	1 091.4	13 403
Portland, OR	10 847.5	356.9	1 500 223	251 076	28.0	18.9	22.6	915 067	12 112	57 452	3 403	23 849.1	42 982	1 055.4	11 741
Vancouver, WA	2 407.2	67.8	361 287	58 179	25.3	33.1	25.4	269 054	3 851	9 239	284	585.4	1 763	36.0	1 662
Portsmouth-Dover-Rochester, NH-ME	4 279.4	79.6	249 179	74 248	1.8	11.4	64.7	113 707	1 350	27 766	589	1 895.0	5 649	133.3	3 850
Poughkeepsie, NY	5 464.8	D	172 262	46 346	21.0	0.3	33.6	67 457	647	18 975	294	653.5	2 715	65.5	2 718
Providence-Pawtucket-Fall Rvr, RI-MA	8 611.0	263.2	399 990	50 518	16.7	11.0	29.9	209 428	2 747	62 812	1 644	5 903.2	21 890	481.8	9 175
Provo-Orem, UT	629.4	35.3	243 772	111 509	22.1	36.5	25.8	100 925	1 303	5 076	244	450.3	2 014	34.3	1 664
Pueblo, CO	467.2	12.3	23 526	4 243	3.6	23.2	27.6	10 355	224	1 491	137	247.8	1 347	23.3	1 252
Raleigh-Durham, NC	9 346.1	256.7	961 653	296 669	49.2	13.7	18.3	490 497	6 602	39 988	1 313	6 546.7	17 966	431.8	7 124
Rapid City, SD	398.2	6.2	47 732	16 207	5.7	19.1	50.3	17 280	297	1 745	167	388.2	1 558	29.9	1 034
Reading, PA	5 227.5	184.5	207 525	69 892	26.2	27.6	34.7	102 899	1 401	12 592	484	2 463.5	7 981	186.2	3 534
Redding, CA	732.1	17.3	286 451	58 005	22.0	10.6	22.0	204 371	2 368	8 866	262	651.1	2 118	44.5	1 621
Reno, NV	1 075.4	55.1	384 093	78 249	21.6	25.1	33.8	228 013	2 602	16 292	555	2 066.6	6 340	144.2	2 454
Richland-Kennewick-Pasco, WA	2 246.4	20.7	90 594	22 388	25.6	27.0	15.7	47 543	478	6 882	236	597.9	2 051	38.2	1 352
Richmond-Petersburg, VA	11 776.1	359.1	788 631	178 740	10.9	21.5	46.2	412 531	6 764	61 140	1 753	11 773.0	25 615	648.4	6 993
Roanoke, VA	2 012.2	61.2	201 999	83 714	65.2	9.1	7.8	44 320	822	14 941	575	2 527.4	9 182	176.2	2 437
Rochester, MN	1 762.1	47.0	185 989	7 733	18.3	9.1	36.8	99 098	1 107	5 025	140	357.9	1 304	26.7	985
Rochester, NY	18 962.8	696.7	747 260	240 527	30.8	13.3	30.3	336 568	3 516	44 260	1 652	7 598.8	18 391	434.0	9 071
Rockford, IL	5 274.1	441.9	181 113	47 137	41.2	17.6	29.2	93 853	1 472	11 099	606	1 435.4	6 267	141.0	2 607
Sacramento, CA	5 495.7	176.3	2 644 609	427 565	40.7	11.8	30.2	1 882 317	16 345	111 044	2 083	8 615.5	27 217	624.0	12 743
Saginaw-Bay City-Midland, MI	6 080.7	368.0	189 582	65 040	11.0	12.7	62.3	80 864	1 039	12 748	554	2 202.8	6 198	141.4	3 578
St. Cloud, MN	1 290.9	37.2	162 157	30 942	5.9	32.9	36.8	104 386	1 967	7 134	287	897.3	4 192	85.3	1 776
St. Joseph, MO	1 632.1	35.2	30 281	6 352	12.0	41.2	15.1	15 177	206	2 309	163	576.3	1 961	35.2	847
St. Louis, MO-IL	36 176.2	1 086.5	1 679 576	405 634	30.4	16.1	20.9	678 648	8 345	92 741	5 057	31 705.0	65 323	1 634.3	21 435
Salem, OR	1 500.6	43.4	165 524	33 299	21.6	37.2	16.5	106 065	2 156	6 477	403	1 431.8	3 885	85.5	2 459
Salinas-Seaside-Monterey, CA	1 195.1	30.7	274 255	61 556	33.2	12.7	24.0	132 562	1 183	44 502	460	1 680.2	5 025	120.1	3 393
Salt Lake City-Ogden, UT	6 985.1	267.4	640 647	210 185	11.6	11.6	42.9	322 439	3 829	18 275	2 247	9 684.6	28 422	624.2	8 307
San Angelo, TX	478.7	9.6	18 387	2 574	1.6	0.0	30.4	5 427	131	1 600	186	551.8	1 593	30.6	1 161
San Antonio, TX	4 500.9	96.3	410 651	138 096	2.9	14.6	24.2	105 857	1 749	23 938	2 111	9 235.5	27 346	572.3	11 892
San Diego, CA	10 996.6	429.0	3 008 354	566 216	26.2	19.0	28.5	1 820 448	15 732	226 345	3 415	9 950.2	37 917	894.1	21 117
San Francisco-Oakland-San Jose, CA	70 578.9	2 974.7	6 088 564	1 326 967	24.7	31.8	18.9	2 492 216	21 904	894 246	12 714	83 412.4	172 237	4 820.8	61 274
Oakland, CA	22 629.1	798.2	1 909 982	501 166	9.1	47.8	22.7	801 518	6 987	222 206	3 884	30 306.7	53 779	1 446.3	18 200
San Francisco, CA	9 053.1	224.6	1 525 420	269 144	57.0	1.7	6.5	411 416	2 715	379 692	4 621	27 282.5	56 796	1 568.3	19 690
San Jose, CA	32 056.6	1 742.9	1 433 337	349 747	21.8	39.5	18.1	498 957	4 983	172 117	2 886	21 700.5	47 875	1 488.0	13 339
Santa Cruz, CA	2 076.7	64.7	139 449	26 470	32.1	13.4	13.5	70 773	553	26 130	328	893.0	3 343	75.6	2 646
Santa Rosa-Petaluma, CA	2 088.0	58.6	483 189	74 549	33.0	8.6	26.0	325 178	3 645	41 894	596	1 690.5	6 024	137.2	3 973
Vallejo-Fairfield-Napa, CA	2 675.5	85.6	597 187	105 891	17.9	28.6	31.0	384 374	3 021	52 207	399	1 539.2	4 420	105.3	3 426
Santa Barbara-Santa Maria-Lompoc, CA	1 733.6	53.8	350 342	91 545	17.1	57.2	12.3	168 325	1 279	49 336	538	1 114.3	4 991	118.2	3 914
Santa Fe, NM	95.9	3.5	106 496	8 095	54.6	14.8	19.8	56 112	510	17 489	135	236.5	1 186	23.3	1 464
Sarasota, FL	692.2	24.9	439 327	82 541	12.3	6.2	26.2	290 064	3 487	27 305	470	788.6	3 208	62.3	3 528
Savannah, GA	3 194.5	252.6	181 019	65 476	49.2	4.1	27.0	78 153	1 229	10 511	464	1 752.5	5 568	116.7	2 236
Scranton-Wilkes Barre, PA	6 812.9	221.7	448 288	111 042	15.1	12.4	33.4	267 334	3 619	27 793	1 059	3 273.0	13 122	237.4	8 723
Seattle-Tacoma, WA	25 931.6	633.5	3 475 068	759 647	43.3	11.2	28.4	2 151 689	28 716	131 094	5 745	31 311.2	67 677	1 683.1	22 668
Seattle, WA	23 363.4	549.2	2 963 854	659 063	44.8	12.4	26.4	1 800 555	23 186	113 762	5 059	28 184.0	58 741	1 477.9	18 152
Tacoma, WA	2 567.9	84.3	511 214	100 584	33.0	3.4	41.9	351 134	5 530	17 332	686	3 127.2	8 936	205.2	4 516
Sharon, PA	1 521.5	30.8	48 116	18 904	23.2	20.0	35.8	16 898	272	3 213	168	873.2	1 938	31.7	1 232
Sheboygan, WI	2 077.3	84.5	56 882	11 997	5.5	23.0	37.2	26 314	326	7 580	133	576.3	1 647	35.9	957
Sherman-Dension, TX	1 591.8	54.8	24 852	4 842	11.7	13.5	25.3	3 720	61	2 645	167	283.4	1 195	20.0	1 248
Shreveport, LA	4 556.6	73.3	86 830	32 862	25.6	11.9	50.2	29 842	296	5 640	759	2 362.4	8 357	165.8	3 233
Sioux City, IA-NE	2 259.7	26.1	40 393	15 233	7.8	2.4	30.1	12 153	257	1 808	321	6 041.8	3 275	65.2	1 190
Sioux Falls, SD	1 518.2	20.7	114 573	33 837	12.9	3.1	30.3	43 290	692	5 572	375	1 439.8	4 255	86.6	1 293
South Bend-Mishawaka, IN	2 887.6	79.6	654 537	505 130	1.3	89.3	1.6	111 052	1 490	8 680	501	1 597.5	6 098	136.0	2 383
Spokane, WA	2 359.4	61.7	286 017	71 616	9.5	8.9	44.2	140 888	1 792	12 216	851	3 314.7	10 263	224.1	3 275

1. Includes nonresidential additions and alterations, residential nonhousekeeping buildings, and residential garages and carports not shown separately. 2. For pay period including March 12.

Area name	Retail trade, all establishments, 1987 (cont'd): Sales: Total (Mil dol)	Retail trade, all establishments, 1987 (cont'd): Sales: Percent change, 1982–1987	Retail trade, all establishments, 1987 (cont'd): Sales: Per capita[1] (Dollars)	Retail trade, establishments with payroll, 1987: Number	Retail trade, establishments with payroll, 1987: Sales: Total (Mil dol)	Retail trade, establishments with payroll, 1987: Sales: Per capita[1] (Dollars): General merchandise stores	Retail trade, establishments with payroll, 1987: Sales: Per capita[1] (Dollars): Food stores	Retail trade, establishments with payroll, 1987: Sales: Per capita[1] (Dollars): Apparel and accessory stores	Retail trade, establishments with payroll, 1987: Sales: Per capita[1] (Dollars): Eating and drinking places	Retail trade, establishments with payroll, 1987: Paid employees[2]	Retail trade, establishments with payroll, 1987: Annual payroll (Mil dol)	Taxable service industries–establishments with payroll, 1987: Number	Taxable service industries–establishments with payroll, 1987: Receipts (Mil dol): Total	Taxable service industries–establishments with payroll, 1987: Receipts (Mil dol): Selected kinds of business: Hotels, motels & other lodging places	Taxable service industries–establishments with payroll, 1987: Receipts (Mil dol): Selected kinds of business: Health services	Taxable service industries–establishments with payroll, 1987: Receipts (Mil dol): Selected kinds of business: Legal services
	152	153	154	155	156	157	158	159	160	161	162	163	164	165	166	167
Phoenix, AZ	14 229.8	66.7	7 194	11 133	13 889.3	777	1 551	277	729	163 886	1 703.1	16 684	7 765.1	681.0	1 723.7	703.4
Pine Bluff, AR	464.4	25.3	5 109	560	446.0	724	997	225	382	5 575	50.3	455	128.4	6.6	58.5	8.0
Pittsburgh-Beaver Valley, PA	13 689.2	28.5	5 973	13 672	13 308.2	850	1 188	302	557	172 562	1 527.9	14 306	7 894.8	260.0	1 616.1	534.0
Beaver County, PA	872.5	16.0	4 582	988	846.1	878	1 079	159	374	10 903	91.4	835	236.7	4.7	82.4	11.6
Pittsburgh, PA	12 816.8	29.4	6 099	12 684	12 462.1	847	1 197	315	574	161 659	1 436.5	13 471	7 658.1	255.3	1 533.7	522.4
Pittsfield, MA	1 087.1	52.9	7 799	1 165	1 054.2	808	1 495	373	749	13 326	129.3	1 021	347.5	48.9	108.4	20.5
Portland, ME	2 676.8	78.2	11 528	1 953	2 634.3	1 100	1 866	560	894	27 550	311.2	2 285	905.5	58.8	219.8	107.1
Portland-Vancouver, OR-WA	9 371.5	38.9	6 769	8 550	9 128.7	1 159	1 185	341	694	108 592	1 097.4	11 281	4 164.3	196.5	1 062.5	405.6
Portland, OR	8 375.2	38.2	7 180	7 537	8 160.7	1 249	1 198	372	731	96 446	977.1	10 048	3 791.0	183.2	948.1	384.4
Vancouver, WA	996.3	45.3	4 568	1 013	968.0	680	1 114	175	494	12 146	120.4	1 233	373.3	13.3	114.4	21.2
Portsmouth-Dover-Rochester, NH-ME	3 196.4	96.1	9 838	2 497	3 126.1	1 222	1 825	405	769	31 800	345.5	2 541	853.2	39.4	249.1	49.4
Poughkeepsie, NY	1 793.1	60.9	6 926	1 688	1 740.2	903	1 505	424	497	18 543	202.9	1 621	550.2	31.1	184.8	42.6
Providence-Pawtucket-Fall Rvr, RI-MA	5 897.2	55.5	6 538	5 947	5 711.2	D	1 204	365	611	68 697	692.9	6 530	2 289.9	D	642.3	237.9
Provo-Orem, UT	987.6	28.0	4 088	1 034	961.2	549	923	188	305	12 671	107.0	1 232	510.9	12.2	145.5	11.7
Pueblo, CO	690.9	27.7	5 423	842	671.7	786	1 246	170	548	8 621	81.4	804	193.4	12.4	90.6	11.3
Raleigh-Durham, NC	5 282.1	89.1	7 944	4 599	4 914.8	848	1 401	378	750	62 686	584.7	5 133	2 391.2	148.6	494.2	148.5
Rapid City, SD	668.9	41.5	8 279	678	654.9	1 134	1 413	351	733	7 570	76.2	741	192.2	29.6	54.9	17.6
Reading, PA	2 242.5	48.6	6 896	2 081	2 171.8	842	1 259	650	577	25 121	245.8	1 739	685.3	30.6	205.0	35.8
Redding, CA	904.2	50.0	6 663	972	871.8	659	1 578	191	527	9 345	103.4	1 162	348.8	28.4	135.7	26.4
Reno, NV	2 027.0	34.6	8 696	1 660	1 983.5	1 251	1 545	332	694	20 800	254.6	2 629	2 178.4	992.2	288.1	85.9
Richland-Kennewick-Pasco, WA	847.3	18.0	5 760	844	825.0	810	1 404	147	514	9 757	96.3	919	810.5	17.5	93.3	14.9
Richmond-Petersburg, VA	6 038.3	57.9	7 291	4 959	5 945.6	878	1 431	355	625	70 205	704.8	5 770	2 975.5	130.8	906.1	242.7
Roanoke, VA	1 814.3	64.3	8 191	1 721	1 786.9	1 001	1 469	398	692	21 613	205.4	1 655	692.1	56.3	244.4	41.3
Rochester, MN	838.7	46.3	8 498	648	823.3	1 500	1 381	397	706	10 416	90.2	524	184.0	44.2	40.1	13.0
Rochester, NY	6 468.0	49.5	6 639	5 565	6 301.2	701	1 415	307	586	75 759	715.3	5 654	2 200.8	91.3	516.4	187.0
Rockford, IL	1 779.7	39.7	6 334	1 663	1 739.5	882	1 236	255	596	22 360	206.8	1 706	675.0	26.8	204.6	40.8
Sacramento, CA	9 295.0	55.6	6 949	7 894	9 053.1	855	1 410	270	713	102 362	1 112.3	10 231	4 092.1	173.6	1 078.8	347.3
Saginaw-Bay City-Midland, MI	2 567.2	38.7	6 322	2 455	2 525.2	1 037	1 046	329	599	30 809	289.5	2 207	727.1	36.5	279.9	52.5
St. Cloud, MN	1 929.8	86.1	10 860	1 136	1 894.0	D	1 031	228	525	17 501	157.6	906	263.4	15.6	93.7	19.3
St. Joseph, MO	549.6	26.0	6 399	545	537.1	1 215	1 262	147	613	6 699	60.4	541	146.0	8.7	54.6	D
St. Louis, MO-IL	15 647.5	43.4	6 372	14 361	15 353.0	889	1 184	291	674	191 585	1 879.3	16 455	8 035.5	355.6	1 757.2	580.7
Salem, OR	1 431.5	38.3	5 410	1 535	1 389.6	837	1 110	214	530	17 402	170.8	1 786	485.7	10.4	199.6	33.6
Salinas-Seaside-Monterey, CA	1 970.4	38.2	5 736	2 220	1 905.1	623	975	327	710	22 953	256.7	2 293	933.5	236.5	183.9	51.0
Salt Lake City-Ogden, UT	6 102.3	44.6	5 778	5 192	5 960.9	737	1 231	296	519	75 631	696.6	7 059	2 861.5	171.6	735.1	239.9
San Angelo, TX	601.4	5.3	6 118	697	580.0	837	1 243	376	564	7 753	71.5	609	210.0	D	67.3	17.1
San Antonio, TX	7 514.7	35.8	5 711	7 292	7 336.1	656	1 246	353	684	96 190	926.5	8 483	3 498.4	200.2	1 034.1	308.5
San Diego, CA	15 641.6	65.0	6 842	12 733	15 213.1	895	1 239	363	729	174 403	1 867.1	17 874	8 938.0	679.8	2 148.0	665.8
San Francisco-Oakland-San Jose, CA	43 195.5	45.0	7 262	37 518	41 889.3	859	1 400	402	834	476 182	5 731.1	53 828	32 005.3	1 667.9	5 938.8	2 963.2
Oakland, CA	13 457.8	47.4	6 843	10 924	13 076.7	842	1 389	317	672	141 918	1 734.3	15 310	7 793.8	224.0	2 006.8	448.9
San Francisco, CA	12 864.2	41.2	8 111	12 455	12 413.4	931	1 448	581	1 206	149 154	1 849.7	18 959	13 378.9	1 027.1	1 706.4	1 890.0
San Jose, CA	10 501.9	40.3	7 432	7 991	10 226.2	944	1 321	444	763	114 281	1 346.7	12 323	8 516.4	260.7	1 411.2	506.8
Santa Cruz, CA	1 578.0	59.3	7 102	1 541	1 518.4	473	1 603	226	759	17 858	194.8	1 756	601.5	40.0	190.5	31.3
Santa Rosa-Petaluma, CA	2 562.4	58.8	7 234	2 427	2 480.9	827	1 609	271	660	27 526	317.9	3 161	931.9	46.7	326.2	55.0
Vallejo-Fairfield-Napa, CA	2 231.2	52.6	5 497	2 180	2 173.8	602	1 248	171	606	25 445	287.6	2 319	782.8	69.4	297.7	31.2
Santa Barbara-Santa Maria-Lompoc, CA	2 376.6	28.7	6 964	2 512	2 301.5	549	1 644	381	829	30 106	314.9	3 034	1 447.5	101.9	354.9	78.2
Santa Fe, NM	738.8	43.0	6 626	890	708.1	705	1 091	346	803	9 422	91.6	1 036	504.9	57.4	129.6	D
Sarasota, FL	2 431.5	69.8	9 528	2 217	2 360.1	1 044	1 623	388	966	27 670	288.6	2 896	1 046.3	75.3	375.7	84.4
Savannah, GA	1 670.4	55.8	6 914	1 657	1 642.6	913	1 291	355	715	20 452	193.0	1 543	625.8	65.2	209.4	45.2
Scranton-Wilkes Barre, PA	4 639.8	55.4	6 358	4 811	4 423.5	869	1 262	294	492	52 524	465.1	3 942	1 435.5	255.7	448.2	82.1
Seattle-Tacoma, WA	16 379.9	45.5	6 966	14 550	16 030.3	869	1 392	403	761	190 011	2 044.1	19 621	8 570.8	408.1	1 845.8	783.2
Seattle, WA	13 269.0	45.2	7 342	11 745	12 995.8	880	1 472	453	819	155 120	1 673.9	16 386	7 531.4	374.1	1 448.2	702.9
Tacoma, WA	3 110.9	46.7	5 716	2 805	3 034.5	832	1 124	235	569	34 891	370.2	3 235	1 039.4	34.0	397.6	80.3
Sharon, PA	639.1	26.2	5 204	751	615.8	719	1 038	262	437	7 997	66.0	642	169.3	10.2	72.6	6.8
Sheboygan, WI	541.6	40.7	5 289	594	530.4	857	1 145	112	497	7 349	59.9	488	191.7	15.1	56.1	7.0
Sherman-Dension, TX	633.0	29.6	6 426	700	604.1	933	1 297	253	446	7 278	68.8	622	192.8	10.3	98.1	13.9
Shreveport, LA	2 052.4	17.3	5 651	2 105	1 997.7	819	1 064	298	497	24 419	230.0	2 290	888.5	30.7	351.0	70.4
Sioux City, IA-NE	726.5	24.3	6 351	803	706.9	980	1 343	288	586	9 641	81.9	763	308.6	12.3	94.7	22.1
Sioux Falls, SD	977.0	40.1	7 943	875	963.2	1 085	1 276	362	705	12 672	109.8	932	351.7	26.3	136.5	21.6
South Bend-Mishawaka, IN	1 715.1	49.0	7 055	1 571	1 686.9	1 030	1 242	289	689	22 445	203.8	1 687	705.5	23.5	211.1	32.0
Spokane, WA	2 317.1	40.1	6 518	2 150	2 266.9	1 002	1 390	312	624	27 235	272.5	2 647	857.6	38.4	312.6	73.4

1. Based on the estimated population as of July 1 of the year shown. 2. For the period including March 12 of the year shown.

Area name	Taxable service Industries–establishments with payroll, 1987 (cont'd)		Banking		Federal funds and grants, 1989						Local government finances, 1981–1982				
						Per capita[3] (Dollars)					General revenue				
													Taxes		
														Per capita[4]	
	Paid employees	Annual payroll (Mil dol)	Bank deposits,[1] June 1989 (Mil dol)	Savings capital,[2] September 1989 (Mil dol)	Expenditures (Mil dol)	Total	Direct payments for individuals	Procurement contract awards	Salaries and wages	Grant awards	Total (Mil dol)	Intergovernmental (Mil dol)	Total (Mil dol)	Total (Dollars)	Property (Dollars)
	168	169	170	172	174	176	177	178	179	180	181	182	184	185	186
Phoenix, AZ	170 803	2 963.6	14 585	11 189.5	6 642.0	3 195	1 695	797	393	282	1 926.3	827.0	553.4	344	246
Pine Bluff, AR	2 839	49.2	609	424.3	370.9	4 080	1 920	790	689	455	69.6	29.2	22.1	244	213
Pittsburgh-Beaver Valley, PA	148 349	2 957.1	28 438	10 508.9	8 001.9	3 531	2 359	425	310	425	2 746.3	1 087.5	1 112.2	463	343
Beaver County, PA	5 247	94.3	1 073	628.5	491.6	2 615	2 179	39	105	285	215.0	73.9	73.0	360	261
Pittsburgh, PA	143 102	2 862.8	27 365	9 880.4	7 510.3	3 614	2 375	460	328	438	2 531.3	1 013.6	1 039.2	473	350
Pittsfield, MA	8 965	138.1	1 884	153.2	904.9	6 572	2 111	3 836	177	439	126.9	50.8	63.6	448	443
Portland, ME	19 654	340.3	4 173	378.6	768.6	3 215	1 812	242	748	396	185.7	62.1	98.9	453	448
Portland-Vancouver, OR-WA	96 475	1 556.9	8 841	4 788.4	3 830.8	2 645	1 673	160	444	351	1 717.9	585.6	744.0	559	480
Portland, OR	86 812	1 426.3	8 019	4 171.3	3 331.8	2 744	1 715	182	458	371	1 519.2	476.0	698.0	618	537
Vancouver, WA	9 663	130.6	822	617.1	499.0	2 131	1 455	46	376	246	198.7	109.6	46.0	230	160
Portsmouth-Dover-Rochester, NH-ME	19 266	309.7	3 423	521.5	1 084.9	3 169	1 406	251	1 275	228	220.2	41.1	153.9	536	529
Poughkeepsie, NY	12 256	202.1	1 963	992.0	578.7	2 186	1 492	57	282	343	313.8	130.6	142.6	576	506
Providence-Pawtucket-Fall Rvr, RI-MA	54 079	885.4	12 758	2 058.3	2 731.8	2 992	1 904	146	282	650	757.8	258.2	443.8	510	506
Provo-Orem, UT	12 113	186.2	894	120.7	398.2	1 635	1 095	170	138	223	178.2	86.5	54.0	234	184
Pueblo, CO	5 333	72.1	608	388.8	396.2	3 098	2 148	163	321	443	165.9	72.6	61.0	484	362
Raleigh-Durham, NC	58 445	936.8	5 253	1 697.0	2 323.1	3 309	1 320	318	425	1 233	577.1	239.5	192.3	332	273
Rapid City, SD	4 813	61.9	504	213.9	372.1	4 435	1 580	169	2 282	354	64.3	22.1	32.7	451	356
Reading, PA	15 336	266.5	3 768	931.4	777.8	2 339	1 835	156	145	190	320.0	117.8	118.9	378	270
Redding, CA	7 951	125.5	793	504.7	431.3	3 012	1 984	189	270	559	180.3	101.4	45.5	372	292
Reno, NV	46 735	722.9	1 553	804.5	567.2	2 271	1 528	50	408	275	319.3	134.5	71.7	343	202
Richland-Kennewick-Pasco, WA	12 639	325.8	600	315.7	1 237.3	8 440	1 348	6 394	294	312	377.8	78.8	44.0	286	174
Richmond-Petersburg, VA	70 267	1 138.5	10 393	3 858.1	2 842.4	3 321	1 718	226	775	588	802.3	276.5	355.2	456	304
Roanoke, VA	18 458	282.1	2 691	654.0	676.8	3 075	2 071	208	578	206	201.6	75.0	91.3	411	278
Rochester, MN	5 790	66.8	662	238.4	235.1	2 298	1 199	78	282	580	145.8	79.1	30.5	325	309
Rochester, NY	57 307	842.2	12 515	2 530.6	2 541.7	2 591	1 648	152	218	542	1 513.4	652.6	655.9	669	488
Rockford, IL	19 036	265.8	2 108	807.2	638.6	2 253	1 506	339	161	144	266.1	106.1	114.2	408	337
Sacramento, CA	83 849	1 493.0	8 143	6 279.0	7 746.4	5 404	1 716	879	799	1 983	1 741.5	953.0	426.8	365	272
Saginaw-Bay City-Midland, MI	17 435	301.1	2 253	1 003.5	924.9	2 279	1 642	57	170	367	475.8	150.4	221.5	533	513
St. Cloud, MN	7 389	104.2	1 314	269.8	381.1	2 067	1 219	39	277	261	202.4	122.1	41.4	247	236
St. Joseph, MO	4 144	56.0	822	367.0	226.4	2 664	2 105	66	231	213	63.6	25.5	26.7	308	201
St. Louis, MO-IL	177 092	3 057.3	21 273	10 481.5	12 915.5	5 214	1 817	2 424	596	352	2 343.4	852.4	1 049.3	441	281
Salem, OR	13 238	180.0	1 501	574.5	989.8	3 588	1 823	43	233	1 476	250.3	101.6	108.2	424	402
Salinas-Seaside-Monterey, CA	19 067	333.4	1 762	1 597.3	1 553.2	4 363	1 486	254	2 397	214	458.2	232.7	116.5	380	265
Salt Lake City-Ogden, UT	68 343	1 091.9	5 857	1 346.7	3 545.6	3 288	1 301	545	995	437	1 100.2	365.8	346.3	358	266
San Angelo, TX	4 436	73.1	818	294.5	340.1	3 408	1 843	185	1 077	195	66.3	27.1	25.5	279	217
San Antonio, TX	80 201	1 309.9	8 449	7 372.5	5 585.1	4 135	1 906	441	1 498	279	1 030.4	478.4	297.1	259	192
San Diego, CA	172 878	3 386.6	13 624	21 799.4	11 531.7	4 689	1 730	1 009	1 637	306	2 726.8	1 329.9	718.7	364	272
San Francisco-Oakland-San Jose, CA	559 803	12 371.7	62 083	46 851.8	23 358.4	3 808	1 582	1 174	682	347	9 333.4	4 271.6	2 811.7	508	345
Oakland, CA	143 553	3 034.5	16 704	11 583.3	7 222.9	3 536	1 578	836	705	375	3 188.0	1 541.6	889.2	489	347
San Francisco, CA	219 050	5 107.3	27 623	21 666.4	5 676.9	3 550	1 870	423	809	430	2 866.8	1 178.6	906.4	599	375
San Jose, CA	144 637	3 375.7	12 010	8 394.9	7 369.2	5 096	1 180	3 173	424	311	2 169.5	1 006.5	690.6	517	351
Santa Cruz, CA	13 884	221.2	1 243	1 265.0	431.5	1 861	1 433	93	94	236	228.9	115.2	72.3	366	265
Santa Rosa-Petaluma, CA	21 323	345.1	2 403	2 585.0	877.9	2 323	1 754	97	226	234	431.3	191.1	132.7	422	321
Vallejo-Fairfield-Napa, CA	17 356	287.9	2 100	1 357.2	1 780.0	4 074	1 800	394	1 676	191	448.9	238.6	120.5	338	256
Santa Barbara-Santa Maria-Lompoc, CA	27 572	539.9	2 484	3 165.4	1 526.0	4 388	1 744	1 794	579	260	432.2	192.6	137.1	442	333
Santa Fe, NM	10 965	200.7	777	265.5	1 389.4	12 029	1 358	8 717	510	1 438	85.8	59.8	12.9	134	84
Sarasota, FL	24 838	403.5	3 696	2 188.6	1 105.8	4 152	3 778	125	148	90	224.5	47.9	83.7	381	312
Savannah, GA	14 589	238.9	1 651	553.5	992.8	4 044	1 801	917	971	347	234.4	77.9	67.6	294	232
Scranton-Wilkes Barre, PA	37 011	514.9	7 946	1 471.3	2 915.6	3 935	2 525	246	383	767	576.0	242.7	229.1	315	224
Seattle-Tacoma, WA	177 333	3 174.1	23 240	6 460.5	9 697.0	3 890	1 580	1 007	735	527	2 761.0	1 257.2	773.7	356	208
Seattle, WA	152 080	2 782.1	19 738	5 415.8	7 235.3	3 770	1 499	1 206	427	586	2 176.6	935.8	636.9	382	220
Tacoma, WA	25 253	392.0	3 502	1 044.7	2 461.7	4 292	1 850	338	1 768	330	584.4	321.4	136.8	269	169
Sharon, PA	4 031	64.1	1 103	234.1	315.6	2 591	2 196	22	112	244	114.9	51.4	42.6	334	244
Sheboygan, WI	5 037	73.8	837	236.9	219.5	2 125	1 673	38	95	258	137.0	61.6	40.4	395	391
Sherman-Dension, TX	4 356	74.5	972	422.1	257.0	2 614	2 159	118	96	209	97.2	35.4	29.6	320	262
Shreveport, LA	22 597	332.9	2 991	423.4	1 308.9	3 656	1 722	724	764	413	381.8	181.3	117.8	339	156
Sioux City, IA-NE	7 667	113.2	881	289.1	340.8	2 933	1 892	194	292	326	136.8	54.8	53.5	455	434
Sioux Falls, SD	8 375	148.6	3 964	308.1	390.0	3 076	1 729	313	507	274	101.7	32.9	53.5	476	385
South Bend-Mishawaka, IN	17 168	273.1	1 900	483.0	867.5	3 529	1 712	1 277	203	305	202.2	94.8	76.8	320	319
Spokane, WA	21 119	333.6	2 396	498.6	1 154.3	3 223	1 992	236	635	338	323.0	178.3	85.8	247	147

1. Includes deposits for all insured and reporting noninsured commercial and mutual savings banks. 2. Includes savings capital for all FSLIC insured savings institutions. 3. Based on the estimated population as of July 1 of the year shown. 4. Based on the estimated population as of July 1, 1982.

Area name	Local government finances, 1981–1982, (cont'd): Direct general expenditure: Total (Mil dol)	Direct general expenditure: Percent change, 1977–1982	Direct general expenditure: Per capita[1] (Dollars)	Percent of total for– Education	Percent of total for– Health & hospitals	Percent of total for– Police protection	Percent of total for– Public welfare	Percent of total for– Highways	Debt outstanding: Total (Mil dol)	Debt outstanding: Per capita[1] (Dollars)	State and local government employment, 1989: Total	State and local government employment, 1989: Rate[2]	Federal government civilian employment, 1989: Total	Federal government civilian employment, 1989: Earnings ($1,000)	Elections,[3] 1988: Total vote cast for president	Elections,[3] 1988: Vote for lead party (Percent)
	187	188	189	190	191	192	193	194	195	196	197	198	199	200	201	202
Phoenix, AZ	1 885.2	78.4	1 172	40.4	5.4	7.2	1.3	5.8	5 245	3 260	115 221	554.3	18 691	588 648	681 518	R—64.9
Pine Bluff, AR	64.6	64.0	714	52.2	1.5	4.8	0.2	5.3	162	1 788	5 369	590.6	2 144	68 347	29 752	D—56.0
Pittsburgh-Beaver Valley, PA	2 446.7	57.4	1 019	44.1	4.8	4.5	2.6	5.2	3 953	1 646	93 522	412.7	18 816	618 096	928 812	D—59.9
Beaver County, PA	202.1	58.0	998	43.2	4.7	2.9	6.9	4.1	734	3 627	7 454	396.5	466	13 525	76 469	D—65.8
Pittsburgh, PA	2 244.6	57.4	1 021	44.2	4.9	4.6	2.2	5.3	3 218	1 464	86 068	414.2	18 350	604 571	852 343	D—59.4
Pittsfield, MA	122.1	7.6	859	51.4	0.7	4.8	0.5	8.1	56	395	6 009	436.4	636	18 798	62 859	D—60.8
Portland, ME	190.0	36.3	870	42.7	1.9	5.0	0.7	6.2	201	919	14 904	623.3	2 820	81 472	119 075	R—52.9
Portland-Vancouver, OR-WA	1 688.3	80.0	1 269	48.9	2.3	5.0	0.7	5.9	1 515	1 139	78 062	539.0	17 943	623 705	618 099	D—53.8
Portland, OR	1 470.4	76.8	1 301	48.9	2.5	5.0	0.8	6.0	1 309	1 158	66 828	550.4	15 533	538 513	539 793	D—54.2
Vancouver, WA	217.9	105.4	1 087	49.5	1.2	4.7	0.4	5.5	206	1 029	11 234	479.7	2 410	85 192	78 306	D—51.1
Portsmouth-Dover-Rochester, NH-ME	222.3	66.9	775	49.5	0.4	5.2	5.3	6.9	121	423	18 836	550.3	2 563	70 995	139 592	R—60.7
Poughkeepsie, NY	309.9	35.3	1 252	53.8	3.6	2.4	11.3	6.3	175	708	21 608	816.3	2 239	73 006	101 959	R—61.0
Providence-Pawtucket-Fall Rvr, RI-MA	738.1	52.5	848	50.6	0.2	6.9	2.8	4.5	551	634	50 080	548.5	6 837	215 809	369 905	D—56.1
Provo-Orem, UT	170.8	62.8	741	60.9	1.2	4.6	0.0	4.5	213	922	13 576	557.5	850	22 375	88 227	R—77.2
Pueblo, CO	153.6	57.7	1 218	44.5	1.6	4.9	15.6	4.2	436	3 458	8 946	699.5	1 286	38 864	53 318	D—61.5
Raleigh-Durham, NC	481.7	40.6	831	47.9	5.6	6.2	2.9	2.9	1 572	2 713	83 686	1 191.9	8 427	298 648	257 414	R—51.1
Rapid City, SD	58.9	31.5	812	54.0	0.7	6.3	1.0	8.1	15	211	4 497	536.0	1 991	52 406	31 757	R—61.4
Reading, PA	347.8	77.7	1 105	43.0	1.9	2.7	4.9	4.0	440	1 399	15 547	467.6	1 397	44 430	112 444	R—62.4
Redding, CA	184.6	75.6	1 509	44.8	9.1	4.4	14.8	5.6	51	419	8 754	611.3	1 306	39 940	54 585	R—59.4
Reno, NV	323.4	97.8	1 546	28.2	17.3	8.0	1.4	6.1	241	1 153	13 877	555.5	2 975	104 034	88 728	R—59.3
Richland-Kennewick-Pasco, WA	173.8	102.6	1 130	47.5	6.0	5.6	0.0	6.6	8 599	55 913	9 586	653.9	1 068	39 632	55 468	R—63.4
Richmond-Petersburg, VA	811.9	38.5	1 042	41.5	6.9	5.8	6.5	3.9	981	1 259	79 406	927.9	17 491	517 136	330 825	R—63.1
Roanoke, VA	198.6	55.5	895	45.2	0.3	4.6	4.9	3.2	151	681	12 048	547.4	3 415	111 724	87 088	R—56.0
Rochester, MN	139.1	109.8	1 483	35.4	3.7	3.3	8.1	7.2	127	1 357	5 623	549.7	858	27 928	47 609	R—58.1
Rochester, NY	1 531.9	44.8	1 563	42.9	3.2	3.4	13.3	6.6	1 013	1 033	58 268	594.0	5 135	168 291	423 555	R—52.1
Rockford, IL	249.4	43.3	892	50.6	1.3	6.7	2.4	7.7	126	450	11 053	390.0	1 170	38 362	112 772	R—55.5
Sacramento, CA	1 663.3	56.0	1 421	37.5	2.9	5.2	15.9	2.9	1 353	1 156	164 522	1 147.7	30 264	960 458	570 307	R—52.0
Saginaw-Bay City-Midland, MI	485.5	33.8	1 169	48.7	7.1	5.1	1.9	5.1	567	1 366	18 448	454.6	1 814	60 850	171 535	D—50.9
St. Cloud, MN	193.3	64.2	1 153	49.1	5.4	3.0	8.5	10.0	149	890	10 657	577.9	1 704	53 182	80 786	R—51.9
St. Joseph, MO	65.1	35.6	752	50.8	2.0	5.2	0.5	8.6	25	286	4 948	582.1	562	18 462	34 089	D—54.6
St. Louis, MO-IL	2 207.6	46.5	927	49.3	6.6	7.5	0.9	6.1	1 229	516	108 079	436.3	37 861	1 170 063	1 028 370	D—50.6
Salem, OR	255.6	57.1	1 002	57.0	3.1	5.0	0.0	5.5	120	471	28 601	1 036.6	1 779	54 464	109 113	R—51.2
Salinas-Seaside-Monterey, CA	455.7	71.3	1 485	37.5	13.8	5.2	8.6	4.3	95	310	16 426	461.4	8 784	221 194	100 381	R—49.8
Salt Lake City-Ogden, UT	880.5	83.5	911	52.4	3.7	6.1	0.2	5.1	2 218	2 294	65 359	606.0	30 898	907 840	407 305	R—62.3
San Angelo, TX	60.9	67.8	667	51.1	1.1	6.2	0.8	8.5	56	617	5 909	592.1	1 221	32 674	34 012	R—63.1
San Antonio, TX	1 024.5	69.2	893	50.1	7.8	4.7	0.4	3.5	1 900	1 656	72 795	538.9	45 925	1 600 366	410 338	R—53.7
San Diego, CA	2 500.2	72.9	1 265	40.5	10.0	4.6	11.1	3.0	928	469	125 687	511.1	46 047	1 353 428	869 195	R—60.2
San Francisco-Oakland-San Jose, CA	8 345.6	46.6	1 507	34.8	11.5	5.4	10.1	3.8	4 830	872	368 205	600.2	97 537	3 267 482	2 418 403	D—58.0
Oakland, CA	2 812.1	47.1	1 545	33.9	12.7	5.1	11.3	3.4	2 250	1 236	135 141	661.6	29 575	977 838	810 509	D—59.2
San Francisco, CA	2 399.4	41.0	1 584	27.8	13.9	6.1	8.8	2.8	1 297	856	100 393	627.8	35 723	1 196 281	649 794	D—63.6
San Jose, CA	2 031.7	45.9	1 521	41.5	9.8	4.8	9.6	4.4	686	513	75 110	519.4	13 894	469 719	541 528	D—51.3
Santa Cruz, CA	240.4	63.2	1 217	41.5	4.4	5.2	12.0	4.7	85	428	15 025	647.9	572	18 176	102 611	D—61.5
Santa Rosa-Petaluma, CA	405.1	53.7	1 288	39.1	12.6	5.2	10.5	6.2	166	528	20 541	543.6	1 906	60 312	161 583	D—56.5
Vallejo-Fairfield-Napa, CA	456.9	66.3	1 281	40.5	2.1	6.5	10.4	7.2	347	973	21 995	503.4	15 867	545 156	152 378	D—50.3
Santa Barbara-Santa Maria-Lompoc, CA	411.4	40.9	1 326	40.4	7.5	5.1	7.4	3.5	126	407	25 574	735.3	4 319	122 573	142 940	R—54.2
Santa Fe, NM	88.8	92.6	920	51.9	0.3	6.0	1.9	6.5	94	975	20 528	1 777.3	1 703	51 048	47 080	D—57.0
Sarasota, FL	207.3	82.6	943	32.9	27.5	6.6	0.4	4.9	116	526	12 158	456.6	1 074	34 961	127 483	R—66.4
Savannah, GA	244.6	78.4	1 063	30.7	29.1	5.2	1.1	5.7	255	1 108	13 361	544.2	2 989	89 367	67 148	R—58.9
Scranton-Wilkes Barre, PA	532.7	40.3	732	52.4	2.8	3.1	3.6	4.5	669	919	31 925	430.8	9 121	265 711	263 672	R—52.0
Seattle-Tacoma, WA	2 576.2	72.5	1 185	41.5	5.6	4.8	0.3	5.3	2 792	1 284	150 965	605.6	32 367	1 009 978	1 010 595	D—52.2
Seattle, WA	1 986.7	69.7	1 192	39.2	7.0	5.2	0.2	5.5	2 248	1 349	121 339	632.2	21 214	718 101	816 122	D—52.7
Tacoma, WA	589.5	82.6	1 160	49.0	1.0	3.7	0.3	4.8	544	1 070	29 626	516.6	11 153	291 877	194 473	D—49.7
Sharon, PA	106.9	48.7	839	58.7	2.7	3.6	4.3	5.9	115	903	4 771	391.7	334	9 561	45 880	D—52.9
Sheboygan, WI	134.9	55.1	1 320	43.4	10.7	6.7	3.4	7.0	116	1 138	4 898	474.2	240	7 138	47 234	R—49.7
Sherman-Dension, TX	92.0	100.0	994	45.8	18.3	3.3	0.0	7.6	140	1 506	3 986	405.5	280	7 974	33 287	R—56.6
Shreveport, LA	334.0	96.6	962	47.1	6.4	5.5	0.2	9.3	388	1 118	20 383	569.4	4 924	143 967	124 487	R—60.5
Sioux City, IA-NE	128.6	42.7	1 093	46.8	1.2	4.3	2.6	10.3	137	1 161	5 708	491.2	956	29 807	44 921	D—51.4
Sioux Falls, SD	92.4	67.4	823	45.7	1.0	4.8	1.1	6.6	26	236	5 044	397.8	1 932	63 947	56 095	D—51.9
South Bend-Mishawaka, IN	193.9	42.3	809	48.8	4.4	6.0	6.9	4.7	164	682	10 354	421.2	1 225	40 829	97 864	R—50.6
Spokane, WA	322.7	61.3	928	49.8	2.0	6.0	0.1	7.2	153	439	20 536	573.5	4 252	129 295	139 150	R—49.4

1. Based on the estimated population as of July 1, 1982. 2. Per 10,000 resident population estimated as of July 1 of the year shown. 3. Data subject to copyright.

MSA/ CMSA/ NECMA/ PMSA code[1]	Area name	Land Area,[2] 1990 (Sq. Km.)	Population, 1990: Total persons	Rank	Per square kilometer	Race: White	Black	Am. Indian, Eskimo, Aleut	Asian & Pacific Islander	Other race	Hispanic[3]	Age of population Percent: Under 5 years	5 to 14 years	15 to 24 years	25 to 34 years	35 to 44 years
		1	2	3	4	5	6	7	8	9	10	11	12	13	14	15
7880	Springfield, IL	3 063	189 550	162	61.9	173 114	14 373	319	1 391	353	1 311	7.2	14.6	12.5	17.0	16.0
7920	Springfield, MO	3 207	240 593	143	75.0	233 186	3 784	1 471	1 600	552	1 991	6.5	13.3	17.8	16.4	14.7
8003	Springfield, MA	2 972	602 878	68	202.9	525 290	36 841	1 051	8 363	31 333	49 672	6.9	13.0	17.5	16.4	14.5
8050	State College, PA	2 869	123 786	226	43.1	116 552	2 801	179	3 841	413	1 350	5.6	9.8	31.1	16.8	12.5
8080	Steubenville-Weirton, OH-WV	1 506	142 523	199	94.6	136 078	5 591	237	439	178	710	5.4	13.3	13.6	13.5	15.0
8120	Stockton, CA	3 625	480 628	78	132.6	353 169	27 094	5 085	59 690	35 590	112 673	8.8	16.5	14.7	17.3	14.9
8160	Syracuse, NY	6 189	659 864	63	106.6	605 924	39 095	3 948	7 740	3 157	8 926	7.5	13.9	16.5	17.0	14.6
8240	Tallahassee, FL	3 064	233 598	146	76.2	158 398	70 227	568	2 788	1 617	5 679	6.7	13.3	22.4	17.6	15.4
8280	Tampa-St. Petersburg-Clearwater, FL	6 617	2 067 959	21	312.5	1 827 492	185 503	5 467	23 055	26 442	139 248	6.0	11.1	11.9	15.8	13.8
8320	Terre Haute, IN	1 971	130 812	217	66.4	122 933	6 029	338	1 176	336	1 063	6.3	13.4	17.5	15.4	13.8
8360	Texarkana, TX-AR	3 916	120 132	234	30.7	92 342	26 423	560	405	402	1 644	7.2	15.8	13.8	15.4	14.5
8400	Toledo, OH	3 535	614 128	66	173.7	526 555	69 717	1 423	6 146	10 287	20 382	7.5	14.4	16.6	16.6	14.6
8440	Topeka, KS	1 424	160 976	179	113.0	141 189	13 365	1 836	1 179	3 407	7 785	7.2	14.6	13.2	17.0	15.5
8520	Tucson, AZ	23 794	666 880	62	28.0	524 976	20 795	20 330	11 964	88 815	163 262	7.5	13.7	15.6	17.1	14.7
8560	Tulsa, OK	12 988	708 954	58	54.6	590 612	58 186	48 196	6 563	5 397	14 534	7.6	15.1	13.7	17.2	15.7
8600	Tuscaloosa, AL	3 432	150 522	188	43.9	109 398	39 377	253	1 264	230	948	6.4	13.2	21.6	15.7	14.2
8640	Tyler, TX	2 405	151 309	187	62.9	113 676	31 572	520	638	4 903	8 986	7.4	15.0	14.5	16.0	14.4
8680	Utica-Rome, NY	6 798	316 633	116	46.6	297 746	13 849	613	2 314	2 111	6 174	6.9	13.6	14.9	16.0	13.9
8750	Victoria, TX	2 286	74 361	278	32.5	59 251	4 906	208	257	9 739	25 372	8.3	17.5	13.8	16.4	15.0
8780	Visalia-Tulare-Porterville, CA.	12 495	311 921	119	25.0	204 835	4 618	3 992	13 319	85 157	120 893	9.3	18.9	15.1	16.1	13.6
8800	Waco, TX	2 699	189 123	163	70.1	146 100	29 520	563	1 384	11 556	23 643	7.5	14.4	18.7	15.3	13.0
8840	Washington, DC-MD-VA	10 275	3 923 574	7	381.9	2 577 933	1 041 934	11 036	202 437	90 234	224 786	7.3	12.6	14.7	20.4	17.6
8920	Waterloo-Cedar Falls, IA	2 603	146 611	194	56.3	136 236	8 584	237	1 137	417	984	6.6	14.8	17.5	13.9	14.5
8940	Wausau, WI	4 002	115 400	243	28.8	112 189	89	490	2 499	133	470	7.4	16.3	13.7	16.6	15.1
8960	W. Palm Beach-Boca Raton-Delray, FL	5 269	863 518	50	163.9	732 231	107 705	1 211	9 020	13 351	66 613	6.2	10.5	10.4	15.8	13.6
9000	Wheeling, WV	2 462	159 301	180	64.7	155 313	3 196	145	546	101	569	5.9	13.2	13.2	13.8	14.9
9040	Wichita, KS	7 687	485 270	77	63.1	423 784	36 979	5 160	9 109	10 238	19 793	8.3	15.5	13.5	18.1	15.0
9080	Wichita Falls, TX	1 626	122 378	229	75.3	102 427	11 221	903	1 851	5 976	10 555	7.6	14.6	16.1	17.3	13.2
9140	Williamsport, PA	3 198	118 710	238	37.1	115 040	2 816	219	469	166	641	6.9	14.0	14.0	15.5	14.7
9200	Wilmington, NC	515	120 284	233	233.6	94 895	24 097	435	616	241	924	6.2	12.6	16.5	16.5	16.0
9243	Worcester-Fitchburg-Leominster, MA	3 919	709 705	57	181.1	665 768	15 096	1 446	11 439	15 956	32 940	7.5	13.2	15.0	17.9	15.1
9260	Yakima, WA	11 127	188 823	164	17.0	139 514	1 938	8 405	1 922	37 044	45 114	8.7	17.0	14.4	15.3	14.1
9280	York, PA	3 690	417 848	87	113.2	399 694	11 911	501	2 471	3 271	6 381	7.0	13.5	13.8	16.9	15.8
9320	Youngstown-Warren, OH	2 671	492 619	76	184.4	432 024	54 902	785	1 958	2 950	7 400	6.6	13.9	13.3	14.6	14.8
9340	Yuba City, CA	3 194	122 643	228	38.4	95 062	3 478	2 616	10 996	10 491	17 320	9.3	16.6	14.2	16.7	13.7
9360	Yuma, AZ	14 282	106 895	255	7.5	80 702	3 056	1 429	1 393	20 315	43 388	8.5	16.5	16.0	16.0	12.4

1. MSA = Metropolitan Statistical Area. CMSA = Consolidated MSA. NECMA = New England county metropolitan area. PMSA = Primary MSA. See Appendix A for explanation of these concepts. See Appendix B for list of metropolitan areas identified by type, with component counties. 2. Dry land or land partially or temporarily covered by water. 3. Hispanic persons may be of any race.

Area name	Population, 1990 (cont'd): Age of population (cont'd), Percent: 45 to 54 years	55 to 64 years	65 to 74 years	75 years and over	Percent female	Population–change and components of change: Change, 1980–1990: Number	Percent	Components of change, 1980–1986: Total persons, 1986	Total persons, 1980	Net change: Number	Percent	Natural increase: Births	Deaths	Net migration	Households, 1990: Total
	16	17	18	19	20	21	22	23	24	25	26	27	28	29	30
Springfield, IL	10.4	8.7	7.5	6.3	52.9	1 780	0.9	190 600	187 770	2 900	1.5	18 500	11 100	-4 500	76 345
Springfield, MO	10.0	8.3	7.2	5.9	52.0	32 889	15.8	225 300	207 704	17 600	8.5	19 100	11 500	10 000	93 400
Springfield, MA	9.3	8.3	8.1	5.9	52.5	21 047	3.6	586 400	581 831	4 500	0.8	48 300	34 000	-9 800	219 958
State College, PA	8.4	6.9	5.3	3.7	48.2	11 026	9.8	114 600	112 760	1 800	1.6	8 300	4 200	-2 300	42 683
Steubenville-Weirton, OH-WV	11.0	11.3	10.1	6.6	52.4	-21 211	-13.0	154 800	163 734	-8 800	-5.4	11 800	10 000	-10 600	55 223
Stockton, CA	9.3	7.4	6.5	4.6	49.4	133 286	38.4	432 700	347 342	85 400	24.6	45 400	20 200	60 200	158 156
Syracuse, NY	9.7	8.5	7.2	5.2	51.8	16 893	2.6	649 400	642 971	6 400	1.0	61 000	34 500	-20 100	243 899
Tallahassee, FL	9.1	6.6	5.4	3.6	52.0	43 269	22.7	218 000	190 329	27 600	14.5	19 600	7 900	15 900	88 233
Tampa-St. Petersburg-Clearwater, FL	9.8	10.0	12.2	9.4	52.3	454 359	28.2	1 914 200	1 613 600	300 700	18.6	135 800	138 600	303 500	869 481
Terre Haute, IN	9.5	8.7	8.6	6.8	51.2	-6 435	-4.7	134 200	137 247	-3 100	-2.3	12 000	9 200	-5 900	49 186
Texarkana, TX-AR	10.3	8.8	8.0	6.2	51.8	7 065	6.2	119 800	113 067	6 700	5.9	11 200	6 900	2 400	44 868
Toledo, OH	9.5	8.4	7.2	5.2	52.2	-2 736	-0.4	611 200	616 864	-5 700	-0.9	60 400	35 700	-30 400	230 681
Topeka, KS	10.2	9.1	7.2	5.9	51.8	6 060	3.9	160 800	154 916	5 800	3.7	15 200	8 500	-900	63 768
Tucson, AZ	9.3	8.4	8.2	5.5	51.1	135 437	25.5	602 400	531 443	71 000	13.4	59 700	28 300	39 600	261 792
Tulsa, OK	10.6	8.6	6.7	4.8	51.5	51 781	7.9	733 500	657 173	76 200	11.6	74 700	33 900	35 400	277 202
Tuscaloosa, AL	9.2	8.3	6.6	4.8	51.7	12 981	9.4	141 300	137 541	3 700	2.7	12 100	6 600	-1 800	55 354
Tyler, TX	10.0	9.0	7.8	5.9	51.9	22 943	17.9	152 100	128 366	23 800	18.5	15 000	7 700	16 500	56 800
Utica-Rome, NY	9.9	9.0	9.0	6.7	50.8	-3 547	-1.1	315 400	320 180	-4 700	-1.5	28 500	20 800	-12 400	117 498
Victoria, TX	9.8	8.3	6.4	4.5	51.3	5 554	8.1	76 000	68 807	7 200	10.5	9 600	3 300	900	26 228
Visalia-Tulare-Porterville, CA	9.0	7.2	6.2	4.6	50.1	66 183	26.9	287 300	245 738	41 600	16.9	35 300	13 000	19 300	97 861
Waco, TX	9.1	8.4	7.5	6.1	51.5	18 368	10.8	187 600	170 755	16 800	9.8	18 600	10 700	8 900	70 208
Washington, DC-MD-VA	11.5	7.4	5.2	3.3	51.3	672 653	20.7	3 563 000	3 250 921	312 100	9.6	322 400	137 000	126 700	1 459 358
Waterloo-Cedar Falls, IA	10.0	8.6	7.9	6.3	52.3	-16 170	-9.9	151 500	162 781	-11 400	-7.0	15 500	7 900	-19 000	55 326
Wausau, WI	10.1	8.2	7.1	5.6	50.6	4 130	3.7	112 500	111 270	1 200	1.1	11 200	5 100	-4 900	41 547
W. Palm Beach-Boca Raton-Delray, FL	9.3	9.8	13.5	10.9	52.0	286 764	49.7	755 600	576 754	178 700	31.0	53 700	49 800	174 800	365 558
Wheeling, WV	10.4	10.6	10.4	7.6	52.8	-26 265	-14.2	175 400	185 566	-10 100	-5.4	14 300	12 700	-11 700	62 858
Wichita, KS	9.3	8.3	6.9	5.0	51.1	42 869	9.7	469 900	442 401	27 600	6.2	52 600	22 000	-3 000	186 640
Wichita Falls, TX	9.3	8.9	7.1	5.7	51.0	1 296	1.1	127 100	121 082	6 000	5.0	14 000	6 700	-1 300	45 271
Williamsport, PA	10.1	9.7	8.7	6.4	51.8	294	0.2	116 300	118 416	-2 100	-1.8	10 600	7 200	-5 500	44 949
Wilmington, NC	10.7	9.0	7.8	4.7	52.6	16 813	16.2	114 100	103 471	10 600	10.2	8 800	5 800	7 600	48 139
Worcester-Fitchburg-Leominster, MA	9.5	8.1	7.7	6.0	51.3	63 353	9.8	661 100	646 352	14 800	2.3	56 300	38 400	-3 100	260 153
Yakima, WA	9.6	7.9	7.1	5.9	50.3	16 315	9.5	183 200	172 508	10 700	6.2	21 000	9 700	-600	65 985
York, PA	10.8	9.1	7.7	5.5	51.1	36 593	9.6	397 800	381 255	16 500	4.3	32 500	20 400	4 400	156 733
Youngstown-Warren, OH	10.5	10.4	9.8	6.0	52.4	-38 731	-7.3	510 100	531 350	-21 300	-4.0	44 600	31 900	-34 000	187 192
Yuba City, CA	9.8	8.5	6.8	4.5	50.3	20 664	20.3	114 200	101 979	12 200	12.0	13 100	5 300	4 400	42 887
Yuma, AZ	8.3	8.4	8.9	4.9	49.1	NA	NA	88 500	76 205	12 300	16.1	10 900	3 800	5 200	35 791

Area name	Households, (cont'd)			Births, 1988			Deaths, 1987				Marriages, 1984		Divorces, 1984		Physicians, active non-Federal, 1989	
		Percent					Number		Rate							
	Percent change, 1980–1990	Female family householder[1]	One-person	Total	Rate[2]	Low birth weight[3] (Number)	Total	Infant[4]	Total[2]	Infant[5]	Number	Rate[2]	Number	Rate[2]	Number[6]	Rate[7]
	31	33	34	35	36	37	38	39	40	41	42	43	44	45	46	47
Springfield, IL	5.7	11.1	29.0	2 910	15.2	231	1 765	28	9.3	10.1	1 810	9.5	1 020	5.4	601	312
Springfield, MO	21.0	9.1	25.4	3 181	13.6	189	1 999	24	8.7	7.6	2 533	11.7	1 440	6.6	468	197
Springfield, MA	8.7	14.1	25.4	8 468	14.3	570	5 726	62	9.7	7.5	4 737	8.1	1 766	3.0	1 226	206
State College, PA	18.2	6.2	23.6	1 413	12.2	70	758	14	6.6	9.9	855	7.5	327	2.9	173	149
Steubenville-Weirton, OH-WV	-4.1	10.9	24.7	1 550	10.5	106	1 705	21	11.5	13.4	1 326	8.4	666	4.2	157	108
Stockton, CA	26.9	12.7	20.9	8 974	19.7	607	3 704	76	8.3	8.7	2 188	5.5	2 475	6.2	670	142
Syracuse, NY	9.0	11.3	25.1	10 003	15.4	674	5 703	122	8.8	12.3	5 625	8.7	2 157	3.3	1 636	252
Tallahassee, FL	33.3	13.9	26.2	3 324	14.5	282	1 449	53	6.5	16.3	2 092	10.0	1 254	6.0	449	192
Tampa-St. Petersburg-Clearwater, FL	32.4	9.9	28.0	27 201	13.6	2 086	24 432	229	12.5	9.0	19 853	10.9	11 829	6.5	3 915	192
Terre Haute, IN	-0.7	10.3	27.5	1 806	13.6	111	1 495	22	11.2	12.7	1 322	9.8	784	5.8	190	144
Texarkana, TX-AR	9.6	13.8	24.2	1 817	15.2	148	1 135	10	9.5	5.7	1 889	16.0	850	7.2	195	163
Toledo, OH	4.7	12.5	26.1	9 948	16.1	723	5 663	81	9.2	8.3	NA	0.0	2 412	4.0	1 505	243
Topeka, KS	8.4	10.5	27.6	2 494	15.1	174	1 399	32	8.6	13.4	1 706	10.7	851	5.3	439	264
Tucson, AZ	33.9	10.9	27.8	11 222	17.6	675	5 313	85	8.5	7.8	6 292	10.9	3 747	6.5	1 778	275
Tulsa, OK	12.5	10.4	26.3	11 143	15.3	725	5 528	99	7.6	8.8	7 393	10.1	6 626	9.1	1 242	170
Tuscaloosa, AL	18.2	13.0	25.8	2 098	14.4	169	1 119	27	7.7	14.1	1 514	11.0	625	4.5	292	199
Tyler, TX	23.4	11.3	24.3	2 334	15.3	138	1 299	21	8.5	8.6	1 948	13.3	802	5.5	339	221
Utica-Rome, NY	5.2	10.9	26.6	4 342	13.9	276	3 394	51	10.8	11.3	2 745	8.6	1 004	3.2	493	159
Victoria, TX	14.1	11.1	21.2	1 355	18.2	99	518	16	6.9	12.7	949	12.7	520	7.0	150	203
Visalia-Tulare-Porterville, CA	21.3	12.8	18.1	6 072	20.4	349	2 299	53	7.9	9.0	1 812	6.6	1 617	5.9	364	120
Waco, TX	14.1	12.1	25.8	3 117	16.6	237	1 760	30	9.3	9.9	2 463	13.5	1 093	6.0	297	157
Washington, DC-MD-VA	24.4	12.0	25.2	64 052	17.2	5 191	24 640	656	6.7	10.8	35 569	10.3	13 953	4.1	12 778	336
Waterloo-Cedar Falls, IA	-2.4	9.6	25.4	1 861	12.6	108	1 318	15	8.9	8.0	1 450	9.1	640	4.0	213	145
Wausau, WI	10.2	7.2	21.0	1 620	14.3	75	881	14	7.8	8.5	900	8.0	341	3.0	176	155
W. Palm Beach-Boca Raton-Delray, FL	56.0	8.6	27.5	12 001	14.7	947	9 400	150	12.0	13.4	7 279	10.5	4 012	5.8	1 791	210
Wheeling, WV	-6.9	10.9	27.4	2 036	11.9	120	2 081	15	12.0	7.6	1 618	8.9	769	4.2	364	215
Wichita, KS	13.3	9.7	26.0	8 493	17.6	577	3 673	83	7.7	9.8	5 188	11.3	3 083	6.7	1 035	212
Wichita Falls, TX	5.0	10.8	25.3	2 004	16.1	138	1 201	26	9.5	12.4	2 737	21.6	1 089	8.6	246	199
Williamsport, PA	6.8	9.9	24.1	1 627	13.8	92	1 189	13	10.1	8.3	1 057	9.0	427	3.6	214	180
Wilmington, NC	27.7	13.3	25.8	1 642	14.0	135	1 060	17	9.1	11.3	996	9.0	676	6.1	292	245
Worcester-Fitchburg-Leominster, MA	15.5	11.2	23.9	10 841	16.1	563	6 335	82	9.5	8.1	5 729	8.8	2 280	3.5	1 874	275
Yakima, WA	7.6	11.3	22.7	3 557	19.2	176	1 609	24	8.8	7.0	1 666	9.2	1 034	5.7	232	124
York, PA	15.9	8.3	21.1	5 770	14.1	319	3 580	54	8.9	9.7	2 732	7.0	1 470	3.8	485	117
Youngstown-Warren, OH	0.3	12.8	24.6	6 317	12.6	463	5 259	67	10.5	10.7	4 559	8.8	NA	0.0	831	167
Yuba City, CA	18.1	11.8	21.1	2 404	20.3	122	941	20	8.1	8.7	741	6.7	472	4.3	163	135
Yuma, AZ	19.9	9.4	19.0	2 324	25.0	143	838	19	9.3	8.8	2 073	25.2	756	9.2	120	127

1. No spouse present. 2. Per 1,000 resident population estimated as of July 1 of the year shown. 3. Under 2,500 grams. 4. Deaths of infants under 1 year old. 5. Deaths of infants under 1 year old per 1,000 live births. 6. As of end of year. 7. Per 100,000 resident population as of July 1 of the year shown.

Area name	Hospitals, 1989			Nursing homes,[2] 1986		Serious crimes known to police, 1988			Education						Social Security Program December 1988	
		Beds				Number			Public school enrollment[6]		Attainment,[7] 1980		Local government expenditures for education,[8] 1982		Beneficiaries	
	Number	Number	Rate[1]	Number	Beds	Total[3]	Violent[4]	Rate[5]	1986–1987	1980	Percent 12 years or more	Percent 16 years or more	Total (Mil dol)	Per capita (Dollars)	Total	Rate[9]
	48	49	50	51	52	53	54	55	56	57	58	59	60	61	62	63
Springfield, IL	4	1 549	805	16	1 816	9 711	964	5 066	35 485	30 454	72.1	18.3	67.5	804	32 980	172.0
Springfield, MO	6	2 705	1 137	26	2 473	13 200	676	5 634	38 090	37 478	70.3	14.9	70.2	675	37 250	159.0
Springfield, MA	17	3 540	595	67	5 437	21 937	3 480	3 704	83 864	103 621	68.1	16.5	236.9	795	100 165	169.1
State College, PA	4	465	401	6	514	4 133	114	3 572	13 020	17 398	75.8	27.5	45.5	400	13 730	118.7
Steubenville-Weirton, OH-WV	4	694	479	13	704	3 482	198	2 357	25 672	29 928	62.3	8.0	69.5	1 265	31 050	210.2
Stockton, CA	8	1 086	231	136	3 619	36 506	3 173	8 011	88 704	66 466	62.6	11.5	184.3	495	63 880	140.2
Syracuse, NY	11	2 816	433	45	3 932	26 370	1 867	4 055	111 969	126 611	70.7	17.6	397.9	1 909	103 190	158.7
Tallahassee, FL	5	2 236	958	10	605	NA	NA	0	32 461	33 252	71.6	26.7	80.4	855	26 905	117.7
Tampa-St. Petersburg-Clearwater, FL	52	11 466	563	288	15 636	NA	NA	0	243 381	242 026	65.5	13.4	600.7	1 359	481 720	241.5
Terre Haute, IN	4	651	492	13	1 206	3 708	364	2 796	22 025	24 286	67.7	14.8	56.4	850	25 860	195.0
Texarkana, TX-AR	4	720	603	12	1 188	10 016	586	8 389	24 114	24 473	58.3	10.4	40.8	702	20 460	171.4
Toledo, OH	12	3 778	611	47	3 953	24 536	2 039	3 980	99 581	107 024	68.2	14.4	262.5	1 368	95 235	154.5
Topeka, KS	7	2 191	1 316	32	1 918	12 370	930	7 506	25 425	27 696	78.3	19.9	68.9	439	25 000	151.7
Tucson, AZ	16	2 708	420	23	2 678	62 325	4 475	9 800	96 300	95 851	74.6	20.7	226.5	400	104 435	164.2
Tulsa, OK	20	3 247	445	57	5 329	46 725	4 538	6 422	126 833	127 504	71.9	17.0	305.5	1 954	101 725	139.8
Tuscaloosa, AL	5	2 811	1 912	9	1 131	7 059	920	4 855	24 252	24 658	60.1	16.6	40.2	293	21 455	147.6
Tyler, TX	6	930	607	13	1 450	12 456	796	8 163	28 212	25 449	65.1	16.1	54.7	399	25 030	164.0
Utica-Rome, NY	9	2 840	913	39	3 656	8 967	418	2 869	52 328	62 862	64.5	12.6	173.6	1 124	63 665	203.7
Victoria, TX	5	749	1 014	4	504	4 762	476	6 409	14 675	14 404	58.4	12.0	28.1	382	10 475	141.0
Visalia-Tulare-Porterville, CA	8	1 874	615	41	1 397	16 699	2 087	5 606	64 722	54 719	55.8	10.1	159.1	615	43 335	145.5
Waco, TX	6	1 519	804	18	1 856	17 725	1 186	9 428	32 150	30 295	58.5	14.5	58.7	333	31 655	168.4
Washington, DC-MD-VA	55	16 213	426	122	13 677	210 620	25 382	5 640	554 367	601 381	79.2	31.9	1 773.1	531	336 529	90.1
Waterloo-Cedar Falls, IA	5	783	535	19	1 643	7 140	463	4 831	24 973	29 393	73.5	15.2	75.0	1 117	26 720	180.8
Wausau, WI	2	685	602	9	916	3 312	117	2 921	17 412	21 105	64.6	11.6	45.1	402	17 575	155.0
W. Palm Beach-Boca Raton-Delray, FL	22	3 711	436	64	4 670	NA	NA	0	84 685	73 748	70.7	17.1	227.3	352	203 305	248.4
Wheeling, WV	6	1 226	725	21	1 374	2 893	183	1 687	25 893	32 604	63.2	9.4	67.8	1 146	35 700	208.2
Wichita, KS	12	2 616	535	41	3 831	27 637	1 937	5 721	78 699	76 855	75.9	17.9	201.9	1 457	69 275	143.4
Wichita Falls, TX	6	1 384	1 117	16	1 491	11 234	803	9 016	21 276	21 905	65.4	14.4	47.2	375	19 490	156.4
Williamsport, PA	4	674	567	17	1 120	2 879	167	2 434	19 669	22 875	65.6	10.3	56.7	483	22 630	191.3
Wilmington, NC	3	549	461	17	994	9 885	668	8 427	19 457	20 953	64.9	16.3	40.8	380	19 180	163.5
Worcester-Fitchburg-Leominster, MA	20	3 959	580	119	7 509	22 058	2 533	3 266	104 395	121 739	66.7	15.4	286.4	443	114 735	169.9
Yakima, WA	5	532	284	20	1 653	16 402	1 056	8 842	36 483	35 775	62.1	11.3	89.7	509	30 490	164.4
York, PA	5	1 079	259	39	3 206	11 042	616	2 691	58 937	72 061	61.4	11.3	142.6	838	65 540	159.7
Youngstown-Warren, OH	10	2 493	501	46	4 353	17 684	2 964	3 525	85 632	96 970	66.7	10.4	228.1	875	98 790	196.9
Yuba City, CA	3	274	227	23	560	7 996	1 348	6 753	24 926	20 848	65.9	12.0	58.4	1 100	18 090	152.8
Yuma, AZ	3	314	332	4	222	5 546	593	5 963	18 696	18 723	61.6	10.9	45.5	477	15 085	162.2

1. Per 100,000 resident population estimated as of July 1 of the year shown. 2. Covers nursing homes with 3 or more beds. 3. Data for serious crimes have not been adjusted for underreporting, this may affect comparability between geographic areas or over time. 4. Includes murder and nonnegligent manslaughter, forcible rape, robbery, and aggravated assault. 5. Per 100,000 resident population as of July 1 of the year shown. 6. The 1986–1987 data are based on administrative reports obtained by the U.S. National Center for Education Statistics. The 1980 data are based on the 1980 Census of Population and Housing. 7. Persons 25 years old or older. 8. Elementary and secondary. 9. Per 1,000 resident population estimated as of July 1 of the year shown.

Area name	Social Security Program, Dec. 1988 (cont'd)	Supplemental Security Income Program recipients, June 1986	Housing units, 1990				Civilian labor force, 1990				Private nonfarm establishments, 1988			
	Payments ($1,000)		Total	Percent change, 1980–1990	Occupied units: Total	Occupied units: Percent owner-occupied	Total	Percent change, 1989–1990	Unemployment: Total	Unemployment: Rate[1]	Number	Net change, 1987–1988	Employment[2]: Total	Employment[2]: Percent change, 1987–1988
	64	65	72	73	74	75	78	79	80	81	82	83	84	85
Springfield, IL	16 364	2 172	81 523	5.2	76 345	67.1	114 856	0.2	5 103	4.4	4 740	10	66 377	0.7
Springfield, MO	17 095	3 378	100 722	20.6	93 400	65.4	130 058	2.6	5 760	4.4	6 764	142	98 975	5.8
Springfield, MA	49 428	11 896	233 093	9.0	219 958	60.7	297 204	0.5	16 983	5.7	14 293	294	237 282	4.0
State College, PA	6 892	882	46 195	16.8	42 683	59.8	67 569	2.9	3 590	5.3	2 669	51	35 182	3.4
Steubenville-Weirton, OH-WV	15 968	1 814	59 446	-3.8	55 223	75.4	56 358	0.3	3 614	6.4	2 642	18	43 644	0.5
Stockton, CA	29 974	16 334	166 274	22.3	158 156	57.6	196 738	-2.3	19 238	9.8	9 532	114	118 224	4.9
Syracuse, NY	53 692	8 442	266 067	9.1	243 899	66.2	325 524	0.5	13 322	4.1	15 277	371	259 554	6.1
Tallahassee, FL	11 931	4 292	96 184	31.9	88 233	59.7	137 198	3.1	5 690	4.1	5 837	119	67 380	6.0
Tampa-St. Petersburg-Clearwater, FL	237 333	22 070	1 025 064	34.2	869 481	69.3	1 017 874	2.4	52 108	5.1	53 599	959	717 829	4.9
Terre Haute, IN	12 716	1 702	54 809	2.7	49 186	71.2	61 023	-0.1	2 792	4.6	2 851	27	43 853	3.2
Texarkana, TX-AR	8 359	3 176	50 406	13.3	44 868	70.0	57 210	-1.6	3 632	6.3	2 557	-34	33 155	0.9
Toledo, OH	48 556	7 352	247 243	4.7	230 681	66.6	313 920	-0.7	21 804	6.9	14 371	174	245 465	3.0
Topeka, KS	12 464	1 994	68 991	7.1	63 768	66.6	92 966	0.7	4 490	4.8	4 382	111	67 491	6.6
Tucson, AZ	52 032	6 656	298 207	36.4	261 792	60.9	313 679	-0.2	12 924	4.1	15 466	181	209 786	2.6
Tulsa, OK	51 399	8 474	311 890	16.8	277 202	65.5	347 194	1.4	18 528	5.3	18 849	-171	264 621	1.1
Tuscaloosa, AL	9 539	4 170	58 740	16.7	55 354	61.5	73 097	1.3	3 693	5.1	3 101	64	39 442	5.2
Tyler, TX	11 862	2 668	64 369	25.8	56 800	66.5	74 118	-1.6	4 601	6.2	4 251	-120	50 934	-3.4
Utica-Rome, NY	31 133	6 254	132 050	6.2	117 498	66.5	137 933	-0.7	6 315	4.6	6 572	78	89 222	1.2
Victoria, TX	4 765	1 320	29 162	18.3	26 228	64.6	35 896	-0.9	1 787	5.0	2 059	-51	21 305	-1.8
Visalia-Tulare-Porterville, CA	19 031	13 742	105 013	18.3	97 861	60.1	136 767	-2.8	15 467	11.3	5 529	63	59 830	1.1
Waco, TX	14 116	3 760	78 857	19.6	70 208	58.9	92 420	-0.6	5 357	5.8	4 507	-69	66 628	-1.2
Washington, DC-MD-VA	157 271	33 749	1 556 749	0.0	1 459 358	0.0	2 209 784	-0.1	75 373	3.4	96 590	4 191	1 647 312	4.8
Waterloo-Cedar Falls, IA	13 663	1 720	58 535	-1.0	55 326	68.5	72 636	0.7	3 457	4.8	3 517	-3	49 533	7.7
Wausau, WI	8 563	1 594	43 774	10.1	41 547	74.7	63 698	-1.5	2 874	4.5	2 720	58	40 691	4.3
W. Palm Beach-Boca Raton-Delray, FL	111 467	5 674	461 665	56.1	365 558	71.9	430 148	2.1	28 086	6.5	26 188	1 229	311 676	5.7
Wheeling, WV	17 770	2 318	69 434	-3.3	62 858	72.4	71 708	-1.4	4 288	6.0	3 565	-17	44 789	2.7
Wichita, KS	36 415	3 932	202 521	16.1	186 640	65.2	257 368	0.9	11 224	4.4	12 542	120	215 491	1.8
Wichita Falls, TX	9 100	1 762	51 413	6.3	45 271	63.4	55 057	-2.0	3 334	6.1	3 499	-100	40 011	-0.8
Williamsport, PA	11 249	1 510	49 580	4.3	44 949	69.7	60 262	0.1	4 362	7.2	2 772	48	45 669	2.1
Wilmington, NC	9 144	2 220	57 076	31.8	48 139	62.7	64 990	0.1	2 756	4.2	3 912	92	51 418	5.3
Worcester-Fitchburg-Leominster, MA	57 758	12 364	279 428	16.5	260 153	61.4	340 284	-0.8	23 657	7.0	17 036	316	281 565	6.3
Yakima, WA	14 449	3 352	70 852	6.0	65 985	63.2	101 450	2.6	9 873	9.7	4 215	53	46 040	4.3
York, PA	33 492	4 004	164 902	16.1	156 733	74.2	223 941	0.0	10 958	4.9	9 094	105	160 145	3.0
Youngstown-Warren, OH	50 010	6 516	198 448	0.8	187 192	72.3	221 779	-0.6	15 922	7.2	10 816	138	170 784	3.3
Yuba City, CA	8 184	4 812	45 408	14.5	42 887	55.9	49 231	0.2	6 137	12.5	2 309	21	20 705	-0.8
Yuma, AZ	6 707	894	46 541	24.1	35 791	66.0	55 587	3.4	10 747	19.3	1 885	-5	22 502	1.1

Area name	Private nonfarm establishments, 1987 (cont'd)						Personal income, 1989							
	Employment[1] (cont'd)				Annual payroll								Per capita[3]	
	Manu-facturing	Retail trade	Finance, insurance, and real estate	Services	Total (Mil dol)	Average per employee	Total (Mil dol)	Percent change, 1988–1989	Wages and salaries[2] (Mil dol)	Propri-etor's income (Mil dol)	Dividends, Interest, & rent (Mil dol)	Transfer payments (Mil dol)	Dollars	Rank (Dollars)
	86	87	88	89	90	91	92	93	94	95	96	97	98	99
Springfield, IL	4 631	16 243	7 306	24 693	1 207	18 184	3 484	5.8	2 272	378	590	553	18 103	55
Springfield, MO	22 048	22 758	5 076	29 213	1 653	16 701	3 653	7.8	2 332	462	687	530	15 353	158
Springfield, MA	54 402	54 192	24 568	69 549	4 659	19 635	11 010	6.8	6 416	754	1 821	2 023	18 519	46
State College, PA	8 109	10 011	1 611	9 643	630	17 907	1 781	9.7	1 242	172	272	275	15 345	159
Steubenville-Weirton, OH-WV	17 086	8 856	1 568	10 474	925	21 194	2 013	7.0	1 360	106	354	461	13 899	227
Stockton, CA	24 073	28 984	8 769	29 922	2 277	19 260	6 998	7.7	3 891	793	1 190	1 411	14 861	190
Syracuse, NY	54 310	56 023	20 352	76 385	5 442	20 967	11 372	8.2	7 887	854	1 741	1 765	17 490	77
Tallahassee, FL	4 824	20 408	4 728	23 214	1 037	15 390	3 426	10.2	2 512	232	457	483	14 677	200
Tampa-St. Petersburg-Clearwater, FL	87 390	178 917	60 986	236 013	12 743	17 752	36 007	9.8	19 355	2 674	8 938	6 347	17 675	68
Terre Haute, IN	11 077	12 142	1 943	11 581	794	18 106	1 851	8.5	1 154	149	337	356	13 998	220
Texarkana, TX-AR	7 776	8 042	1 705	9 133	582	17 554	1 647	6.9	989	176	259	330	13 793	233
Toledo, OH	64 134	54 952	12 964	75 843	5 371	21 881	10 453	5.7	7 287	726	1 704	1 777	16 893	94
Topeka, KS	9 848	17 572	6 489	21 453	1 246	18 462	2 977	7.4	2 150	225	534	462	17 886	62
Tucson, AZ	31 618	52 459	12 837	71 527	3 565	16 994	9 814	7.3	5 657	648	2 143	1 707	15 203	169
Tulsa, OK	50 113	53 948	18 244	75 570	5 614	21 215	11 691	7.2	7 736	1 173	2 000	1 534	16 016	123
Tuscaloosa, AL	9 159	10 826	2 415	8 347	693	17 570	2 041	8.1	1 373	166	274	364	13 886	230
Tyler, TX	10 702	11 967	3 729	13 650	996	19 555	2 472	6.8	1 446	339	528	347	16 139	116
Utica-Rome, NY	24 050	21 742	6 602	23 905	1 608	18 022	4 867	7.5	2 828	330	872	1 020	15 648	143
Victoria, TX	2 728	5 834	1 472	5 838	378	17 742	1 164	6.6	597	138	244	155	15 749	136
Visalia-Tulare-Porterville, CA	11 869	15 766	2 688	13 048	986	16 480	4 164	6.6	1 976	730	632	868	13 668	237
Waco, TX	13 832	13 868	5 192	22 258	1 054	15 819	2 697	7.2	1 574	257	551	463	14 276	210
Washington, DC-MD-VA	96 306	348 116	132 736	719 601	39 544	24 005	94 454	8.8	73 526	6 123	14 851	10 459	24 845	1
Waterloo-Cedar Falls, IA	13 177	12 141	3 949	13 835	979	19 765	2 233	8.4	1 499	192	396	379	15 248	165
Wausau, WI	11 919	8 440	3 632	8 841	797	19 587	1 734	9.7	1 140	191	261	233	15 243	166
W. Palm Beach-Boca Raton-Delray, FL	38 396	80 806	32 392	94 341	6 378	20 464	20 707	11.3	9 322	1 308	8 282	2 555	24 319	3
Wheeling, WV	5 651	12 599	2 585	15 081	765	17 080	2 301	6.4	1 238	146	493	536	13 608	239
Wichita, KS	70 368	41 625	10 881	51 791	4 719	21 899	8 501	6.9	5 967	754	1 377	1 095	17 387	80
Wichita Falls, TX	8 135	10 118	2 101	11 213	681	17 020	1 985	6.6	1 192	234	397	337	16 014	124
Williamsport, PA	16 734	8 721	2 513	10 109	829	18 152	1 795	6.9	1 116	175	299	332	15 106	172
Wilmington, NC	11 260	12 545	2 088	14 130	936	18 204	1 894	9.6	1 263	188	345	295	15 896	128
Worcester-Fitchburg-Leominster, MA	76 735	60 380	19 102	75 553	5 811	20 638	13 788	6.3	7 735	882	2 037	1 989	20 200	21
Yakima, WA	7 722	11 163	1 941	13 096	788	17 116	2 719	10.5	1 333	407	470	530	14 494	202
York, PA	61 240	31 617	5 524	31 729	3 118	19 470	7 556	7.4	4 240	599	1 218	900	18 166	54
Youngstown-Warren, OH	50 104	41 797	9 650	44 295	3 571	20 909	7 625	7.1	4 947	460	1 263	1 581	15 308	162
Yuba City, CA	3 070	6 256	1 326	5 024	372	17 967	1 641	8.6	819	191	271	393	13 572	242
Yuma, AZ	1 725	7 337	969	6 541	315	13 999	1 204	2.3	778	124	194	222	12 725	263

1. For week including March 12. Excludes government employees, self-employed persons, farm workers, domestic service workers, railroad employees subject to the Railroad Retirement Act, and employees on oceanborne vessels or in foreign countries. 2. Includes other labor income. 3. Based on the resident population estimated as of July 1 of the year shown.

Area name	Earnings, 1989: Total (Mil. dol)	Earnings, 1989: Percent by selected industries: Farm	Goods-related[1]: Total	Goods-related[1]: Manu-facturing	Service-related & other[2]: Total	Service-related & other[2]: Retail trade	Service-related & other[2]: Finance, insurance, & real estate	Service-related & other[2]: Ser-vices	Govern-ment	Agriculture, 1987: Farms: Number	Farms: Percent with: Less than 50 acres	Farms: Percent with: 500 acres and over	Farm operators, Percent: Whose principal occupation is farming	Farm operators, Percent: Residing on farm operated	Land in farms: Acreage (1,000)	Land in farms: Percent change, 1982–1987	Acres: Average size of farm	Acres: Total irrigated (1,000)	Acres: Total cropland (1,000)
	100	101	102	103	104	105	106	107	108	109	110	111	112	113	114	115	116	117	118
Springfield, IL	2 650	2.7	10.0	4.2	58.8	10.4	7.9	28.4	28.5	1 714	26.6	30.0	67.9	69.5	683	2.0	398	1	627
Springfield, MO	2 794	0.7	24.0	17.9	63.4	11.8	4.7	29.0	11.9	3 620	36.3	4.8	35.3	80.1	519	-0.5	143	1	315
Springfield, MA	7 170	0.5	28.7	21.6	54.2	10.7	6.7	26.3	16.6	1 114	48.3	2.7	49.8	80.9	111	3.6	100	1	53
State College, PA	1 415	1.0	23.0	14.4	40.7	9.2	3.6	21.0	35.3	817	21.7	5.8	60.5	82.3	149	-6.4	182	0	104
Steubenville-Weirton, OH-WV	1 466	0.2	NA	50.9	34.2	7.3	2.2	14.7	8.0	605	18.3	4.5	36.9	85.5	97	-1.4	161	D	50
Stockton, CA	4 683	5.7	23.8	15.4	52.4	9.9	6.3	20.8	18.2	4 366	63.1	7.4	54.9	69.1	824	-7.6	189	449	551
Syracuse, NY	8 741	0.6	NA	21.7	NA	9.1	6.4	NA	15.5	2 306	23.6	10.2	60.1	85.4	494	-10.5	214	D	337
Tallahassee, FL	2 744	1.0	NA	3.9	44.5	9.9	5.0	25.8	41.3	650	42.0	7.5	32.2	67.1	164	-15.0	252	3	54
Tampa-St. Petersburg-Clearwater, FL	22 029	1.1	18.7	11.4	66.9	12.4	9.6	30.3	13.3	4 362	71.8	5.2	41.4	67.1	582	-18.2	133	48	198
Terre Haute, IN	1 303	1.6	32.4	24.6	49.4	13.3	3.3	21.1	16.6	1 269	32.9	16.1	50.0	72.5	310	-2.6	245	D	262
Texarkana, TX-AR	1 165	2.9	23.0	17.7	48.6	11.5	3.7	23.5	25.6	1 668	30.9	11.3	37.1	68.5	426	-4.0	255	8	229
Toledo, OH	8 013	0.6	36.4	30.4	50.2	9.3	3.9	24.0	12.8	2 814	31.7	12.9	53.9	69.6	621	-0.1	221	4	583
Topeka, KS	2 375	0.6	18.4	12.8	59.3	9.9	7.7	24.3	21.7	852	26.5	15.0	43.3	75.4	221	-3.8	260	11	150
Tucson, AZ	6 305	0.4	25.3	16.1	52.4	11.3	4.4	28.3	21.9	520	64.0	20.2	39.4	73.1	3 195	-8.1	6 144	27	39
Tulsa, OK	8 909	0.7	31.3	19.7	58.7	8.9	5.6	24.7	9.3	5 145	32.3	13.6	34.6	72.1	1 893	-11.1	368	D	522
Tuscaloosa, AL	1 538	0.8	34.6	20.3	37.9	9.3	3.0	17.3	26.7	521	28.0	12.3	36.5	67.8	121	-10.5	231	1	48
Tyler, TX	1 786	1.4	28.4	20.0	58.2	12.6	5.1	26.3	12.0	1 701	39.5	4.8	30.9	62.4	249	1.0	147	1	117
Utica-Rome, NY	3 158	0.9	27.2	22.0	45.4	9.9	5.7	20.9	26.5	1 959	16.4	9.3	69.2	88.0	462	-7.2	236	1	290
Victoria, TX	735	1.3	29.3	15.4	55.1	12.3	5.3	25.6	14.4	1 119	28.7	16.7	40.2	53.4	428	-13.2	382	7	155
Visalia-Tulare-Porterville, CA	2 706	18.0	17.7	11.6	45.9	9.7	3.0	16.1	18.4	5 911	61.5	8.2	54.0	61.1	1 410	5.5	239	597	762
Waco, TX	1 831	1.2	26.8	20.2	55.7	11.1	6.6	25.5	16.3	1 977	36.5	10.8	36.8	62.9	445	0.4	225	1	269
Washington, DC-MD-VA	79 649	0.1	11.2	4.2	59.1	8.2	5.7	34.1	29.6	5 458	46.7	5.6	46.6	78.9	D	D	D	D	D
Waterloo-Cedar Falls, IA	1 692	2.4	39.3	35.4	43.4	9.1	4.4	20.5	14.9	2 409	26.5	11.7	60.6	76.5	541	-3.3	224	0	491
Wausau, WI	1 331	5.9	36.5	31.3	47.0	8.2	7.3	17.6	10.6	3 078	17.9	4.7	73.8	85.3	582	-4.0	189	5	367
W. Palm Beach-Boca Raton-Delray, FL	10 630	3.0	21.4	12.5	64.8	12.2	8.1	33.0	10.8	975	71.7	11.3	54.6	42.6	659	-1.3	676	423	573
Wheeling, WV	1 384	0.1	22.9	17.9	NA	12.4	4.3	NA	12.8	1 235	14.8	4.0	45.4	82.9	220	-4.1	178	D	103
Wichita, KS	6 722	0.7	38.6	32.8	49.4	9.2	4.5	23.6	11.2	3 763	24.9	24.3	54.0	73.2	1 532	-0.2	407	52	1 061
Wichita Falls, TX	1 426	0.5	27.1	17.7	49.3	10.0	4.0	24.4	23.1	544	35.3	24.6	37.7	59.2	298	-5.8	549	4	131
Williamsport, PA	1 291	1.6	39.7	32.7	46.3	10.2	4.4	21.4	12.3	847	17.6	3.4	56.0	84.3	139	-9.9	165	1	90
Wilmington, NC	1 451	0.2	28.1	20.0	53.5	12.8	3.9	23.1	18.2	65	69.2	1.5	40.0	44.6	9	-29.0	136	0	4
Worcester-Fitchburg-Leominster, MA	8 618	0.4	35.9	28.6	52.6	10.0	5.6	24.6	11.1	1 191	41.6	2.3	47.5	83.1	135	0.8	113	1	62
Yakima, WA	1 740	16.1	17.6	12.7	51.1	10.4	3.0	21.3	15.2	4 239	67.7	4.7	54.1	77.3	1 612	-6.0	380	247	D
York, PA	4 839	0.9	44.8	36.1	45.3	11.5	2.6	19.2	9.0	3 145	38.9	5.3	54.0	79.6	465	-6.3	148	4	366
Youngstown-Warren, OH	5 407	0.3	44.4	38.7	45.2	9.4	3.4	21.6	10.1	1 619	33.5	2.5	47.5	86.3	203	-1.0	126	1	148
Yuba City, CA	1 010	10.1	16.6	8.2	44.0	9.8	3.6	18.3	29.3	2 092	48.9	12.3	59.9	62.8	579	2.5	277	286	394
Yuma, AZ	902	11.4	9.9	5.0	47.8	10.7	2.6	18.2	30.9	609	49.8	20.0	52.4	42.2	272	-46.6	447	194	223

1. Covers mining, construction, and manufacturing. 2. Covers private sector earnings in agricultural services, forestry, and fisheries; transportation and public utilities; wholesale trade; retail trade; finance, insurance, and real estate; and services.

Table B. Metropolitan Areas — **Agriculture and Manufactures**

Area name	Agriculture, 1987 (cont'd): Value of products sold: Total (Mil dol)	Agriculture: Value of products sold: Average per farm (Dollars)	Agriculture: Value of products sold: Percent from: Crops	Agriculture: Value of products sold: Percent from: Livestock and poultry[1]	Agriculture: Percent of farms with sales of: $10,000 or more	Agriculture: Percent of farms with sales of: $100,000 or more	Manufactures, 1987: Establishments: Total	Manufactures: Establishments: Percent with 20 or more employees	Manufactures: All employees: Number (1,000)	Manufactures: All employees: Annual payroll (Mil dol)	Manufactures: Production workers: Number (1,000)	Manufactures: Production workers: Work hours (Millions)	Manufactures: Production workers: Wages: Total (Mil dol)	Manufactures: Production workers: Wages: Average per worker (Dollars)	Manufactures: Value added by manufacture (Mil dol)
	121	122	123	124	125	126	127	128	129	131	132	133	134	135	136
Springfield, IL	164	95 728	74.3	25.7	70.8	29.7	133	29.3	4.4	92.6	2.8	5.4	48.9	17 464	203.7
Springfield, MO	66	18 363	8.1	91.9	31.8	4.0	378	33.3	21.2	412.7	14.8	27.7	258.3	17 453	953.4
Springfield, MA	47	41 820	62.9	37.1	34.6	10.1	1 066	39.7	51.4	1 196.5	34.8	70.8	689.0	19 799	3 586.5
State College, PA	37	45 436	20.1	79.9	58.4	14.2	141	38.3	7.8	153.9	5.6	10.6	94.2	16 821	333.0
Steubenville-Weirton, OH-WV	8	12 686	29.5	70.5	21.5	D	107	47.7	17.6	501.0	13.6	28.0	372.9	27 419	1 316.1
Stockton, CA	634	145 144	65.5	34.5	60.6	23.5	535	38.9	25.8	581.1	19.4	37.6	400.3	20 634	1 880.9
Syracuse, NY	153	66 564	22.3	77.7	53.5	D	759	37.7	51.9	1 480.7	31.0	61.6	748.0	24 129	3 431.6
Tallahassee, FL	44	67 212	84.1	15.9	23.5	4.6	205	23.4	4.5	76.3	3.4	6.6	47.8	14 059	179.4
Tampa-St. Petersburg-Clearwater, FL	316	72 427	D	D	32.3	10.8	2 546	26.7	84.5	1 834.5	51.2	103.9	854.2	16 684	4 139.8
Terre Haute, IN	53	41 876	76.5	23.5	52.2	D	161	40.4	10.9	296.4	7.0	15.2	176.1	25 157	1 012.8
Texarkana, TX-AR	65	39 008	17.7	82.3	30.5	9.5	106	32.1	7.3	171.9	5.3	9.4	111.7	21 075	465.8
Toledo, OH	178	63 112	64.6	35.4	66.8	16.2	988	40.1	63.2	2 002.2	42.9	92.2	1 204.7	28 082	4 925.1
Topeka, KS	22	25 656	58.5	41.5	39.8	6.8	130	38.5	9.0	234.6	6.6	12.8	160.5	24 318	980.9
Tucson, AZ	57	108 979	62.8	37.2	31.5	14.4	686	23.6	30.7	793.3	14.6	28.9	254.0	17 397	1 947.0
Tulsa, OK	112	21 856	19.4	80.6	25.9	D	1 322	27.9	48.7	1 324.3	30.3	62.8	692.7	22 861	2 735.9
Tuscaloosa, AL	13	24 906	34.3	65.7	23.8	6.1	152	36.8	8.7	214.5	6.5	13.0	149.2	22 954	579.6
Tyler, TX	33	19 108	54.5	45.5	22.8	2.5	172	28.5	11.5	296.8	7.8	13.8	182.0	23 333	634.6
Utica-Rome, NY	122	62 162	12.8	87.2	62.0	22.2	367	33.0	23.7	552.7	15.8	31.0	311.8	19 734	1 174.9
Victoria, TX	21	19 046	46.1	53.9	30.8	3.8	58	24.1	D	D	D	D	D	D	D
Visalia-Tulare-Porterville, CA	1 030	174 329	63.9	36.1	66.2	27.8	301	30.9	11.2	216.7	8.4	16.3	150.5	17 917	705.9
Waco, TX	79	39 984	28.3	71.7	26.0	4.5	249	39.8	13.8	263.5	10.0	19.7	165.2	16 520	837.9
Washington, DC-MD-VA	192	35 126	D	D	32.3	D	2 744	28.0	103.2	2 992.4	44.2	88.3	957.9	21 672	6 788.0
Waterloo-Cedar Falls, IA	175	72 628	46.4	53.6	75.1	21.7	188	33.5	11.9	369.8	8.2	15.7	230.6	28 122	857.5
Wausau, WI	183	59 616	17.2	82.8	72.3	17.9	190	37.9	11.2	276.7	8.2	16.2	182.5	22 256	628.2
W. Palm Beach-Boca Raton-Delray, FL	855	877 099	99.0	1.0	59.8	32.1	861	23.2	38.5	1 189.6	13.6	28.4	282.8	20 794	2 685.6
Wheeling, WV	15	12 353	17.5	82.4	23.0	D	139	34.5	5.3	117.2	3.5	6.7	69.9	19 971	357.3
Wichita, KS	211	56 068	30.5	69.5	51.7	11.5	697	34.4	69.0	1 952.3	35.6	76.7	940.6	26 421	4 122.8
Wichita Falls, TX	17	31 699	47.4	52.6	35.1	7.5	155	25.2	7.9	182.6	5.8	11.5	122.5	21 121	563.7
Williamsport, PA	34	40 425	29.4	70.6	46.5	9.0	231	48.5	17.2	344.7	12.5	23.5	205.9	16 472	950.4
Wilmington, NC	0	0	NA	NA	43.1	4.6	154	35.1	11.1	285.0	7.5	15.7	172.7	23 027	1 009.1
Worcester-Fitchburg-Leominster, MA	54	45 599	35.1	64.9	35.6	10.5	1 469	39.8	69.4	1 668.0	44.6	88.7	858.0	19 238	3 908.1
Yakima, WA	498	117 496	62.6	37.4	55.2	18.6	231	37.2	8.0	167.7	6.1	11.9	114.1	18 705	464.8
York, PA	219	69 621	30.6	69.4	48.4	15.1	759	51.8	59.2	1 360.7	41.2	83.5	808.6	19 626	2 975.3
Youngstown-Warren, OH	49	30 099	38.0	62.0	40.0	7.8	637	38.3	49.5	1 502.3	37.8	74.0	1 093.0	28 915	2 889.3
Yuba City, CA	267	127 820	91.4	8.6	63.0	26.5	117	23.1	3.1	67.2	2.4	4.5	47.0	19 583	197.6
Yuma, AZ	356	584 811	72.0	28.0	63.1	32.3	56	28.8	1.6	23.3	1.2	2.1	15.0	12 500	67.4

1. Includes livestock and poultry products.

Area name	Manufactures, 1987 (cont'd)		Value of construction authorized by building permits, 1990								Wholesale trade, 1987				Retail trade, all establishments, 1987
				Nonresidential				Residential							
					Percent										
	Value of shipments (Mil dol)	New capital expenditures (Mil dol)	Total[1] ($1,000)	Total ($1,000)	Office	Industrial	Stores	New construction ($1,000)	Number of housing units	Alterations and additions ($1,000)	Establishments	Sales (Mil dol)	Paid employees[2]	Annual payroll (Mil dol)	Number
	137	138	139	140	141	142	143	144	145	146	147	148	149	150	151
Springfield, IL	496.3	10.3	145 340	39 840	38.4	3.1	25.1	71 839	1 268	6 426	361	1 541.3	3 735	89.0	1 933
Springfield, MO	2 951.9	54.9	166 963	53 073	21.7	3.8	41.6	63 509	1 389	3 970	604	3 273.3	7 650	153.4	2 663
Springfield, MA	6 375.6	164.3	354 779	66 769	10.5	25.1	22.2	149 392	1 714	48 351	901	2 969.2	10 873	255.9	6 029
State College, PA	663.5	32.1	92 279	26 842	21.1	1.0	45.5	52 353	807	3 868	136	210.6	1 151	22.3	1 175
Steubenville-Weirton, OH-WV	3 176.7	111.0	48 064	26 796	21.4	35.5	33.1	6 498	103	4 850	122	296.1	1 168	23.8	1 381
Stockton, CA	3 974.3	139.0	588 474	185 031	17.4	10.4	54.2	338 037	3 187	23 240	631	2 672.7	7 176	164.0	3 629
Syracuse, NY	7 479.1	256.9	425 367	141 984	13.3	2.4	44.0	157 518	2 025	31 887	1 422	7 926.2	16 980	400.9	6 480
Tallahassee, FL	343.0	12.4	238 880	49 098	41.2	10.4	20.5	160 358	2 989	7 702	303	988.2	3 465	73.4	2 009
Tampa-St. Petersburg-Clearwater, FL	8 547.0	279.1	1 628 083	384 704	16.5	3.6	38.6	862 535	13 105	108 283	3 986	17 994.2	47 885	1 034.4	20 307
Terre Haute, IN	2 034.6	93.8	53 904	21 736	4.7	42.3	40.5	21 722	371	2 298	204	522.7	2 076	38.1	1 334
Texarkana, TX-AR	847.2	38.2	25 648	5 625	42.5	3.9	20.4	9 267	168	3 261	237	544.9	2 409	44.7	1 332
Toledo, OH	12 446.2	295.0	350 407	91 689	17.6	10.9	44.3	126 871	1 512	31 900	1 130	5 125.9	13 803	327.8	5 404
Topeka, KS	1 632.6	35.2	88 413	21 149	24.4	10.3	25.2	44 137	546	2 613	270	806.8	2 986	62.4	1 634
Tucson, AZ	3 608.8	126.1	345 807	72 735	41.2	10.3	23.8	195 457	2 678	16 264	911	1 607.4	8 470	161.4	5 464
Tulsa, OK	5 932.8	159.7	377 773	162 826	10.1	19.4	12.6	146 943	2 043	10 356	1 744	6 789.2	16 590	375.4	7 474
Tuscaloosa, AL	1 392.2	44.7	54 188	10 327	7.6	0.8	43.2	33 621	886	3 544	167	392.0	1 596	27.0	1 357
Tyler, TX	1 521.0	32.9	31 013	4 862	3.0	1.4	38.5	13 385	119	2 442	372	953.5	3 497	67.5	1 869
Utica-Rome, NY	2 449.0	63.7	119 893	33 432	13.9	6.9	23.1	59 364	942	8 923	462	1 019.7	4 697	96.7	3 567
Victoria, TX	D	D	27 121	8 369	5.2	72.9	2.6	11 641	107	2 732	186	594.3	1 850	33.1	959
Visalia-Tulare-Porterville, CA	1 688.6	32.4	305 796	79 283	16.5	28.7	34.5	171 520	2 138	13 455	390	1 558.6	6 075	104.6	2 575
Waco, TX	1 635.1	70.6	67 196	13 784	36.5	11.4	29.4	18 226	237	7 365	398	1 061.8	4 354	81.7	2 137
Washington, DC-MD-VA	10 859.3	352.0	3 586 222	980 995	48.0	2.7	26.5	1 651 559	24 621	424 277	4 353	31 241.9	72 958	2 021.8	28 843
Waterloo-Cedar Falls, IA	1 559.6	29.3	84 712	27 965	9.2	39.7	19.0	20 593	236	6 831	278	680.9	2 654	51.9	1 546
Wausau, WI	1 843.0	58.2	101 369	35 520	11.0	54.2	3.0	40 059	613	5 034	235	659.6	2 920	57.2	1 143
W. Palm Beach-Boca Raton-Delray, FL	6 405.7	160.0	1 353 935	185 910	13.4	3.5	30.0	731 379	9 861	219 797	1 440	4 101.6	12 664	279.1	9 115
Wheeling, WV	865.7	10.0	32 418	10 877	22.9	8.8	44.7	4 164	76	7 888	211	501.8	2 120	41.0	1 730
Wichita, KS	8 615.4	317.3	394 129	99 601	33.8	13.4	22.3	134 754	2 290	17 822	1 002	4 441.6	13 919	288.4	4 889
Wichita Falls, TX	949.0	35.9	30 699	14 531	16.7	0.8	22.9	6 842	84	2 793	265	478.1	2 101	38.3	1 587
Williamsport, PA	1 814.7	45.9	61 612	11 042	39.8	0.7	36.4	17 345	315	8 413	182	372.2	1 840	34.2	1 299
Wilmington, NC	2 004.5	81.0	133 920	27 400	35.6	2.7	35.4	92 626	1 406	4 512	282	820.8	3 110	60.7	1 607
Worcester-Fitchburg-Leominster, MA	6 736.0	237.0	385 250	70 424	17.9	17.3	24.5	182 698	2 453	47 508	1 075	4 815.2	16 552	387.4	6 713
Yakima, WA	1 276.4	28.3	80 918	23 603	3.7	15.6	38.1	34 091	440	5 791	353	1 381.6	5 003	96.0	1 725
York, PA	5 962.0	263.6	362 336	72 803	12.3	16.9	32.0	199 561	2 637	25 825	620	2 575.8	8 223	179.4	4 290
Youngstown-Warren, OH	8 107.2	151.6	196 456	70 131	30.3	17.8	24.7	94 871	1 131	8 778	695	2 859.9	8 986	177.7	4 787
Yuba City, CA	512.7	9.9	180 737	40 938	8.7	58.6	3.2	121 186	1 443	7 335	142	269.0	1 203	23.6	993
Yuma, AZ	144.6	3.8	76 760	24 768	11.7	15.8	45.1	43 321	819	2 752	159	0.0	NA	NA	812

1. Includes nonresidential additions and alterations, residential nonhousekeeping buildings, and residential garages and carports not shown separately. 2. For pay period including March 12.

Area name	Retail trade, all establishments, 1987 (cont'd) — Sales: Total (Mil dol)	Percent change, 1982–1987	Per capita[1] (Dollars)	Retail trade, establishments with payroll, 1987: Number	Sales: Total (Mil dol)	Per capita[1] (Dollars): General merchandise stores	Food stores	Apparel and accessory stores	Eating and drinking places	Paid employees[2]	Annual payroll (Mil dol)	Taxable service industries–establishments with payroll, 1987: Number	Receipts (Mil dol): Total	Selected kinds of business: Hotels, motels & other lodging places	Health services	Legal services
	152	153	154	155	156	157	158	159	160	161	162	163	164	165	166	167
Springfield, IL	1 290.0	35.2	6 775	1 222	1 264.5	1 065	1 188	259	711	15 686	145.0	1 243	547.3	44.6	173.7	37.7
Springfield, MO	1 759.4	62.0	7 620	1 648	1 716.1	1 279	1 233	270	696	21 515	202.8	1 782	638.1	42.0	225.0	40.3
Springfield, MA	4 074.3	54.9	6 932	3 946	3 960.7	858	1 260	359	657	50 391	478.4	3 518	1 304.1	53.4	413.4	95.9
State College, PA	719.4	46.2	6 272	732	697.0	712	1 143	301	666	9 531	77.5	619	324.7	20.9	68.7	8.4
Steubenville-Weirton, OH-WV	690.0	23.5	4 637	884	669.6	698	1 133	154	382	8 892	74.2	639	163.3	4.5	75.4	12.1
Stockton, CA	2 443.1	53.0	5 505	2 261	2 371.2	624	1 156	197	532	26 246	285.0	2 550	865.2	23.1	344.5	54.6
Syracuse, NY	4 116.7	48.9	6 380	4 007	4 011.3	607	1 389	368	613	49 715	475.4	3 781	1 564.1	78.9	357.4	130.8
Tallahassee, FL	1 485.4	61.3	6 655	1 398	1 451.3	896	1 252	285	664	19 449	169.1	1 781	670.5	40.1	172.0	108.8
Tampa-St. Petersburg-Clearwater, FL	14 461.5	66.0	7 392	12 759	14 110.7	862	1 449	262	715	168 176	1 641.0	16 013	7 526.7	497.7	2 393.1	491.7
Terre Haute, IN	1 283.4	65.4	9 628	817	1 264.3	872	1 143	D	630	11 949	111.8	701	246.1	6.6	124.1	11.7
Texarkana, TX-AR	743.6	26.9	6 202	771	695.9	1 100	1 075	278	480	8 281	75.1	630	223.6	14.2	112.1	16.3
Toledo, OH	4 081.0	33.6	6 650	3 847	4 018.0	1 070	1 279	269	709	50 851	483.2	3 967	1 655.6	50.2	514.1	112.0
Topeka, KS	1 088.7	34.7	6 704	1 088	1 063.3	941	1 270	244	674	13 504	126.7	1 158	425.1	23.7	141.0	39.5
Tucson, AZ	3 980.9	53.5	6 391	3 675	3 900.9	848	1 340	268	637	48 624	473.5	4 703	1 915.2	171.3	590.6	144.4
Tulsa, OK	4 269.8	12.3	5 863	4 479	4 127.2	680	1 264	347	593	53 077	495.4	5 280	2 118.1	103.7	553.6	213.0
Tuscaloosa, AL	881.9	52.4	6 094	920	857.2	816	1 120	316	524	10 433	97.7	744	244.8	13.1	112.5	17.2
Tyler, TX	1 036.4	29.3	6 774	1 012	990.6	1 047	1 269	378	608	12 029	120.6	1 248	414.9	10.5	159.6	37.9
Utica-Rome, NY	1 788.1	39.2	5 715	1 984	1 712.8	686	1 196	294	488	20 919	192.6	1 565	491.4	31.4	150.6	31.4
Victoria, TX	495.0	0.4	6 618	576	479.9	903	1 514	385	545	6 071	58.5	583	209.1	6.4	114.8	11.7
Visalia-Tulare-Porterville, CA	1 368.1	27.0	4 692	1 558	1 318.5	446	1 266	179	355	15 668	155.3	1 349	397.1	18.3	170.3	20.1
Waco, TX	1 141.7	21.0	6 054	1 236	1 096.9	943	1 255	289	606	14 391	131.9	1 184	395.2	18.5	127.1	29.5
Washington, DC-MD-VA	28 420.2	59.4	7 778	19 814	27 984.2	850	1 415	468	845	323 427	3 593.8	32 336	26 899.4	1 434.6	3 025.7	3 665.7
Waterloo-Cedar Falls, IA	865.3	16.7	5 834	1 012	847.8	899	1 068	201	526	11 506	97.3	875	263.4	14.5	98.4	18.7
Wausau, WI	653.3	44.1	5 818	691	638.2	1 009	1 071	222	488	8 200	70.2	609	231.0	7.8	77.8	18.1
W. Palm Beach-Boca Raton-Delray, FL	6 801.2	76.8	8 655	5 938	6 622.1	943	1 558	528	868	76 125	812.8	7 627	3 262.1	229.4	985.3	371.6
Wheeling, WV	950.9	18.8	5 493	1 106	923.2	896	1 266	225	501	12 571	105.6	878	256.0	12.0	20.1	20.1
Wichita, KS	3 021.7	27.2	6 371	3 093	2 936.2	907	1 225	279	683	39 347	360.3	3 244	1 471.7	53.3	588.4	100.0
Wichita Falls, TX	826.4	10.1	6 559	928	795.5	1 174	959	283	771	10 471	99.2	861	279.6	D	108.1	22.3
Williamsport, PA	783.0	51.7	6 669	793	754.7	778	1 371	351	446	8 617	77.4	607	174.6	11.9	70.6	12.5
Wilmington, NC	972.1	57.9	8 359	1 088	947.9	1 100	1 516	468	910	12 350	113.2	983	399.6	25.0	89.8	17.4
Worcester-Fitchburg-Leominster, MA	4 875.9	70.6	7 322	4 266	4 732.4	843	1 226	332	627	52 395	525.8	4 161	1 838.7	60.4	460.0	115.5
Yakima, WA	931.8	22.8	5 083	1 107	905.3	595	1 273	228	461	10 842	108.1	1 055	295.6	16.6	112.1	24.3
York, PA	2 659.1	68.3	6 593	2 424	2 564.9	691	1 224	216	528	29 194	263.0	2 086	662.6	40.2	200.5	36.5
Youngstown-Warren, OH	3 052.9	36.2	6 077	3 105	2 963.9	804	1 123	270	543	38 639	336.5	2 879	933.1	36.4	397.7	44.9
Yuba City, CA	566.1	33.9	4 888	609	544.6	573	1 338	144	404	6 242	64.3	599	153.2	5.1	66.7	9.6
Yuma, AZ	596.1	39.4	6 594	546	585.9	826	1 390	184	546	6 994	64.4	509	155.0	21.3	42.6	6.8

1. Based on the estimated population as of July 1 of the year shown. 2. For the period including March 12 of the year shown.

Area name	Taxable service Industries–establishments with payroll, 1987 (cont'd): Paid employees	Taxable service Industries–establishments with payroll, 1987 (cont'd): Annual payroll (Mil dol)	Banking: Bank deposits,[1] June 1989 (Mil dol)	Banking: Savings capital,[2] September 1989 (Mil dol)	Federal funds and grants, 1989: Expenditures (Mil dol)	Federal funds and grants, 1989: Per capita[3] (Dollars): Total	Per capita[3] (Dollars): Direct payments for individuals	Per capita[3] (Dollars): Procurement contract awards	Per capita[3] (Dollars): Salaries and wages	Per capita[3] (Dollars): Grant awards	Local government finances, 1981–1982: General revenue: Total (Mil dol)	General revenue: Intergovernmental (Mil dol)	General revenue: Taxes: Total (Mil dol)	Taxes: Per capita[4]: Total (Dollars)	Taxes: Per capita[4]: Property (Dollars)
	168	169	170	172	174	176	177	178	179	180	181	182	184	185	186
Springfield, IL	13 179	209.0	1 848	643.5	1 106.0	5 748	1 843	50	447	3 260	172.9	60.3	79.1	421	358
Springfield, MO	16 040	247.5	1 790	919.9	578.4	2 430	1 705	45	315	200	145.2	52.8	55.0	262	191
Springfield, MA	33 422	528.7	8 204	293.6	1 731.2	2 912	1 759	187	481	463	568.1	244.6	205.9	354	350
State College, PA	6 601	134.9	773	319.7	352.7	3 038	1 442	607	181	787	87.2	34.6	28.6	252	159
Steubenville-Weirton, OH-WV	4 772	58.5	1 018	347.8	447.7	3 092	2 444	27	132	472	145.2	53.7	58.2	361	286
Stockton, CA	20 858	331.8	2 758	5 026.3	1 109.7	2 357	1 528	143	357	305	596.8	343.0	132.6	355	257
Syracuse, NY	37 357	607.4	6 833	561.0	2 243.4	3 450	1 629	1 120	265	421	1 009.8	485.1	404.6	632	496
Tallahassee, FL	15 116	249.9	1 399	450.2	1 171.4	5 019	1 281	67	265	3 394	193.9	102.7	41.0	204	175
Tampa-St. Petersburg-Clearwater, FL	168 870	2 803.7	16 950	11 970.4	7 171.8	3 520	2 622	372	365	148	1 727.6	701.5	536.9	312	248
Terre Haute, IN	6 128	84.0	1 212	230.0	406.8	3 077	2 167	100	374	369	105.7	50.6	38.0	279	278
Texarkana, TX-AR	5 154	78.7	868	496.1	560.7	4 696	2 140	844	1 381	250	90.2	48.7	22.7	197	153
Toledo, OH	45 105	689.7	4 648	2 412.4	1 454.1	2 350	1 733	70	175	333	700.4	279.7	274.4	446	302
Topeka, KS	10 423	169.9	1 162	2 149.9	740.0	4 444	2 027	370	625	1 228	189.7	59.1	70.5	449	394
Tucson, AZ	48 712	740.9	3 429	4 243.9	3 071.9	4 759	1 969	1 875	554	351	655.3	283.7	231.3	415	304
Tulsa, OK	47 167	808.5	5 285	1 925.9	1 633.3	2 237	1 500	161	261	258	703.9	242.5	277.8	393	212
Tuscaloosa, AL	5 801	91.1	774	278.1	366.9	2 496	1 631	221	370	258	142.5	41.8	31.7	231	66
Tyler, TX	8 959	162.2	1 507	532.3	344.9	2 251	1 715	161	182	181	104.5	46.9	39.0	284	225
Utica-Rome, NY	13 134	188.4	3 200	194.3	1 196.6	3 848	2 092	558	734	443	430.0	223.3	133.4	419	396
Victoria, TX	4 382	75.1	979	912.7	141.6	1 916	1 478	39	131	192	76.9	21.6	29.6	402	319
Visalia-Tulare-Porterville, CA	10 302	148.3	1 324	823.2	678.4	2 227	1 355	57	115	375	438.7	255.4	74.6	287	208
Waco, TX	10 163	149.9	1 601	894.1	568.3	3 008	1 859	458	432	234	142.4	62.5	51.7	293	229
Washington, DC-MD-VA	469 851	10 764.8	35 048	20 103.3	38 226.1	10 055	1 999	2 896	4 129	597	6 140.8	2 263.4	2 979.0	891	467
Waterloo-Cedar Falls, IA	7 202	104.3	1 066	425.3	430.3	2 939	1 850	187	171	504	181.2	74.2	67.6	417	409
Wausau, WI	5 329	89.0	816	232.8	266.0	2 339	1 399	213	154	379	134.7	63.9	42.3	377	374
W. Palm Beach-Boca Raton-Delray, FL	70 529	1 290.1	7 595	8 761.1	3 040.2	3 570	2 551	710	194	104	713.0	196.7	328.1	508	444
Wheeling, WV	6 513	89.8	1 418	543.6	510.3	3 018	2 364	56	177	395	152.9	61.1	50.0	271	220
Wichita, KS	31 979	558.3	3 972	2 224.8	1 922.9	3 933	1 690	1 500	489	212	515.4	162.1	185.1	406	365
Wichita Falls, TX	6 803	105.2	1 163	463.3	507.1	4 093	2 061	556	1 301	148	115.7	39.3	40.5	321	247
Williamsport, PA	3 935	65.0	954	81.2	339.8	2 860	1 975	244	216	405	133.8	59.1	42.1	358	231
Wilmington, NC	9 838	174.5	937	340.7	309.4	2 598	1 796	249	318	229	99.5	52.5	34.3	319	252
Worcester-Fitchburg-Leominster, MA	40 030	664.5	7 807	680.1	1 754.0	2 570	1 766	211	161	423	636.2	298.2	244.5	378	375
Yakima, WA	7 069	111.5	900	328.0	486.1	2 591	1 617	156	238	533	175.0	110.9	34.7	196	133
York, PA	17 364	247.0	3 875	790.3	987.4	2 374	1 532	478	124	221	286.8	108.5	117.2	303	203
Youngstown-Warren, OH	23 285	364.7	3 282	2 003.8	1 303.0	2 616	2 063	45	163	332	453.7	204.1	170.1	324	247
Yuba City, CA	3 574	54.8	548	355.0	446.8	3 696	1 782	154	988	501	167.7	91.0	36.4	341	274
Yuma, AZ	4 132	56.4	621	153.3	417.4	4 412	1 797	220	2 038	292	105.9	54.9	27.7	299	231

1. Includes deposits for all insured and reporting noninsured commercial and mutual savings banks. 2. Includes savings capital for all FSLIC insured savings institutions. 3. Based on the estimated population as of July 1 of the year shown. 4. Based on the estimated population as of July 1, 1982.

Area name	Local government finances, 1981–1982, (cont'd) — Direct general expenditure — Total (Mil dol)	Percent change, 1977–1982	Per capita[1] (Dollars)	Percent of total for– Education	Health & hospitals	Police protection	Public welfare	Highways	Debt outstanding — Total (Mil dol)	Per capita[1] (Dollars)	State and local government employment, 1989 — Total	Rate[2]	Federal government civilian employment, 1989 — Total	Earnings ($1,000)	Elections,[3] 1988 — Total vote cast for president	Vote for lead party (Percent)
	187	188	189	190	191	192	193	194	195	196	197	198	199	200	201	202
Springfield, IL	171.0	52.8	910	46.0	1.9	5.6	1.8	7.3	308	1 637	24 704	1 284.0	2 287	73 064	94 108	R–57.1
Springfield, MO	137.9	36.1	657	50.9	1.5	5.3	1.6	5.5	193	919	11 905	500.2	2 008	66 412	100 400	R–59.6
Springfield, MA	521.0	23.0	896	45.5	2.8	5.9	1.4	4.2	1 140	1 960	41 252	693.9	6 996	218 884	238 335	D–57.6
State College, PA	83.4	86.2	735	54.6	2.2	2.9	5.0	4.4	144	1 272	21 827	1 880.0	430	13 243	42 527	R–56.1
Steubenville-Weirton, OH-WV	137.6	67.4	853	50.5	2.9	4.4	2.4	6.0	217	1 344	5 159	356.3	454	13 181	61 095	D–60.1
Stockton, CA	602.5	50.0	1 615	35.1	9.7	5.1	17.4	4.3	136	364	25 449	540.4	5 949	167 317	138 453	R–54.4
Syracuse, NY	1 039.5	50.9	1 624	40.0	3.3	2.9	15.3	7.4	764	1 194	46 392	713.5	4 220	142 996	270 450	R–53.4
Tallahassee, FL	220.8	60.6	1 098	39.4	1.9	5.2	0.6	5.0	290	1 444	48 722	2 087.5	1 629	54 128	82 725	R–50.8
Tampa-St. Petersburg-Clearwater, FL	1 668.3	67.3	971	39.5	6.9	6.7	1.2	4.5	1 510	878	90 807	445.7	17 745	561 621	767 751	R–58.1
Terre Haute, IN	109.0	68.2	800	51.7	4.4	3.1	4.7	6.6	70	516	9 047	684.3	1 345	45 149	50 922	R–54.6
Texarkana, TX-AR	89.1	74.0	772	54.0	0.8	4.9	0.2	5.9	111	959	5 366	449.4	7 219	189 077	40 570	R–55.6
Toledo, OH	704.2	50.3	1 145	37.3	3.7	5.6	6.6	5.4	542	881	40 493	654.4	2 652	86 352	245 456	D–50.3
Topeka, KS	184.8	34.7	1 176	46.6	1.8	5.8	0.1	6.9	280	1 780	18 867	1 133.2	2 983	96 700	70 197	R–50.6
Tucson, AZ	652.3	52.8	1 170	39.1	5.9	6.9	2.8	7.2	974	1 748	42 936	665.2	8 058	241 059	234 473	R–50.3
Tulsa, OK	678.0	92.0	960	45.1	2.4	4.8	0.1	5.8	1 063	1 505	32 134	440.2	4 938	160 543	273 369	R–61.9
Tuscaloosa, AL	128.0	27.7	934	31.4	34.6	5.6	0.0	5.0	72	528	15 882	1 080.4	1 882	53 061	45 758	R–59.9
Tyler, TX	104.7	73.1	761	64.4	0.5	3.8	0.2	5.8	125	911	9 144	596.9	793	26 331	53 592	R–64.7
Utica-Rome, NY	435.5	41.2	1 366	44.0	7.4	2.2	15.0	6.6	248	779	24 788	797.0	4 528	143 430	131 483	R–53.3
Victoria, TX	70.7	96.4	959	47.0	22.8	4.5	0.3	5.8	50	682	4 911	664.5	259	8 132	24 253	R–62.1
Visalia-Tulare-Porterville, CA	433.0	72.2	1 668	39.6	17.1	4.5	15.6	3.9	71	272	19 068	626.0	1 316	34 400	78 669	R–59.6
Waco, TX	131.7	71.3	747	51.5	5.4	5.2	0.5	5.6	71	401	9 909	524.6	2 807	88 595	66 423	R–58.1
Washington, DC-MD-VA	5 294.5	45.4	1 584	36.2	6.7	5.4	7.7	3.3	6 421	1 921	222 417	585.0	380 762	14 690 328	1 418 498	D–51.3
Waterloo-Cedar Falls, IA	175.6	59.9	1 083	48.1	7.5	4.6	2.8	7.9	102	629	11 304	772.1	626	19 571	66 270	D–55.3
Wausau, WI	148.5	86.3	1 322	39.1	12.3	3.8	3.3	9.8	102	904	6 027	530.1	464	14 127	49 543	D–49.8
W. Palm Beach-Boca Raton-Delray, FL	709.3	105.2	1 098	34.4	7.1	7.7	2.1	4.3	580	898	40 226	472.4	4 063	132 899	327 217	R–55.5
Wheeling, WV	143.7	52.4	780	47.2	1.9	3.8	2.3	5.2	321	1 740	8 314	491.7	734	22 924	67 330	D–55.8
Wichita, KS	505.9	72.9	1 109	41.1	2.9	4.1	0.0	9.6	1 071	2 346	23 929	489.4	4 573	146 537	187 512	R–55.5
Wichita Falls, TX	109.6	98.2	870	43.1	16.3	5.3	1.1	8.0	58	460	7 273	587.0	2 456	57 009	41 590	R–56.1
Williamsport, PA	118.8	41.9	1 010	59.8	2.0	1.8	3.8	4.4	116	987	6 160	518.5	531	16 826	38 735	R–64.0
Wilmington, NC	94.6	35.5	879	50.5	2.3	6.3	3.6	1.9	63	586	10 132	850.7	1 085	37 587	39 313	R–60.6
Worcester-Fitchburg-Leominster, MA	630.0	30.6	975	45.5	5.3	4.8	1.3	5.1	296	458	33 519	491.0	2 751	83 966	293 256	R–50.6
Yakima, WA	160.8	54.8	909	55.8	1.7	5.1	0.1	4.2	81	457	9 795	522.1	1 357	40 747	53 910	R–55.7
York, PA	270.4	49.1	698	52.7	3.8	3.3	4.0	6.0	261	674	13 067	314.1	5 199	143 955	135 221	R–65.1
Youngstown-Warren, OH	435.4	37.2	830	52.4	4.2	4.4	8.6	5.0	178	339	22 731	456.4	2 079	65 674	218 376	D–61.5
Yuba City, CA	166.3	51.5	1 559	45.5	8.1	4.6	13.4	3.4	177	1 655	6 720	555.8	1 574	36 259	35 461	R–65.0
Yuma, AZ	105.2	57.7	1 135	52.2	4.8	4.8	5.5	4.8	108	1 162	4 733	500.3	2 420	76 337	22 480	R–59.0

1. Based on the estimated population as of July 1, 1982. 2. Per 10,000 resident population estimated as of July 1 of the year shown. 3. Data subject to copyright.

TABLE C:

Cities of 25,000 or More

(For explanation of symbols, see page ix)

Table C. Cities — **Area and Population**

MSA/ CMSA Code[1]	State/ Place code	City	Land area,[2] 1990 (Sq. Km.)	Population: 1990: Total persons	Population: 1990: Rank	Population: 1990: Per sq. km.	Population: 1980	Population: Change 1980–1990: Number	Population: Change 1980–1990: Per-cent	Population characteristics, 1990: Percent: Race: White	Race: Black	Race: Am. Indian, Eskimo, Aleut	Race: Asian & Pacific Islander	Race: Other race	His-panic[3]	65 Years and over
			1	2	3	4	5	6	7	8	9	10	11	12	13	14
...	01 0000	ALABAMA	131 443.1	4 040 587	X	31	3 894 025	146 562	3.8	73.65	25.26	0.41	0.54	0.14	0.61	12.9
0450	01 0060	Anniston	52.3	26 623	897	509	29 135	-2 512	-8.6	54.50	44.33	0.18	0.68	0.31	0.80	17.4
...	01 0110	Auburn	84.2	33 830	743	402	28 471	5 359	18.8	79.86	16.35	0.18	3.36	0.25	0.93	5.6
1000	01 0175	Bessemer	100.2	33 497	756	334	31 729	1 768	5.6	41.41	58.37	0.11	0.07	0.04	0.23	17.5
1000	01 0185	Birmingham	384.6	265 968	60	692	284 413	-18 445	-6.5	35.96	63.27	0.12	0.56	0.09	0.39	14.8
...	01 0480	Decatur	122.3	48 761	508	399	42 002	6 759	16.1	82.40	16.48	0.27	0.61	0.23	0.79	12.0
2180	01 0500	Dothan	206.4	53 589	447	260	48 750	4 839	9.9	71.49	27.32	0.25	0.79	0.15	0.67	12.7
2650	01 0640	Florence	60.9	36 426	694	598	37 029	-603	-1.6	82.14	17.07	0.27	0.43	0.08	0.49	16.6
2880	01 0685	Gadsden	92.1	42 523	585	462	47 565	-5 042	-10.6	70.81	28.18	0.15	0.74	0.13	0.39	20.3
3440	01 0935	Huntsville	425.8	159 789	109	375	142 513	17 276	12.1	72.64	24.42	0.51	2.15	0.29	1.24	10.0
5160	01 1165	Mobile	305.7	196 278	79	642	200 452	-4 174	-2.1	59.62	38.93	0.23	1.01	0.21	1.02	13.7
5240	01 1180	Montgomery	349.6	187 106	86	535	177 857	9 249	5.2	56.53	42.34	0.19	0.73	0.21	0.80	11.7
1800	01 1365	Phenix City	52.8	25 312	916	479	26 928	-1 616	-6.0	59.43	39.97	0.17	0.30	0.12	0.61	14.0
5160	01 1420	Prichard	65.8	34 311	730	521	39 541	-5 230	-13.2	20.14	79.42	0.37	0.03	0.04	0.33	11.2
...	01 1555	Selma	36.0	23 755	939	660	26 684	-2 929	-11.0	41.00	58.44	0.09	0.43	0.04	0.29	15.9
8600	01 1720	Tuscaloosa	122.0	77 759	273	637	75 211	2 548	3.4	62.85	35.49	0.14	1.34	0.18	0.77	11.7
...	02 0000	ALASKA	1 477 267.5	550 043	X	0	401 851	148 192	36.9	75.54	4.08	15.58	3.59	1.21	3.24	4.1
0380	02 0140	Anchorage	4 396.9	226 338	69	51	174 431	51 907	29.8	80.74	6.43	6.44	4.82	1.58	4.09	3.6
...	04 0000	ARIZONA	294 333.5	3 665 228	X	12	2 716 546	948 682	34.9	80.85	3.02	5.55	1.51	9.08	18.78	13.1
6200	04 0050	Chandler	123.2	90 533	221	735	29 673	60 860	205.1	85.18	2.56	1.22	2.38	8.66	17.28	5.0
...	04 0115	Flagstaff	163.8	45 857	543	280	34 743	11 114	32.0	79.64	2.48	9.18	1.43	7.27	15.20	4.3
6200	04 0140	Glendale	135.2	148 134	117	1 096	97 172	50 962	52.4	84.98	3.01	0.95	2.13	8.94	15.47	7.9
6200	04 0215	Mesa	281.3	288 091	53	1 024	152 404	135 687	89.0	90.07	1.85	1.05	1.51	5.52	10.88	12.4
6200	04 0260	Phoenix	1 087.6	983 403	9	904	789 704	193 699	24.5	81.69	5.19	1.85	1.66	9.61	20.04	9.7
6200	04 0305	Scottsdale	477.5	130 069	139	272	88 622	41 447	46.8	96.02	0.76	0.61	1.23	1.37	4.77	16.3
6200	04 0360	Tempe	102.4	141 865	122	1 385	106 919	34 946	32.7	86.85	3.20	1.32	4.05	4.57	10.88	6.6
8520	04 0380	Tucson	404.8	405 390	33	1 001	330 537	74 853	22.6	75.25	4.28	1.59	2.20	16.68	29.25	12.6
9360	04 0415	Yuma	56.6	54 923	428	970	42 481	12 442	29.3	73.02	3.80	1.10	1.69	20.39	35.64	12.0
...	05 0000	ARKANSAS	134 875.1	2 350 725	X	17	2 286 357	64 368	2.8	82.73	15.91	0.54	0.53	0.29	0.85	14.9
...	05 0615	El Dorado	40.5	23 146	945	572	25 270	-2 124	-8.4	61.68	37.70	0.15	0.32	0.14	0.48	19.1
2580	05 0670	Fayetteville	104.2	42 099	591	404	36 608	5 491	15.0	93.13	3.75	1.14	1.56	0.42	1.43	9.7
2720	05 0700	Fort Smith	121.0	72 798	299	602	71 626	1 172	1.6	86.25	7.68	1.38	4.09	0.60	1.42	14.9
...	05 0985	Hot Springs	74.7	32 462	776	435	35 781	-3 319	-9.3	83.11	15.46	0.49	0.42	0.51	1.34	25.6
4400	05 1045	Jacksonville	50.9	29 101	841	572	27 589	1 512	5.5	79.42	16.99	0.47	2.30	0.81	2.30	6.1
...	05 1070	Jonesboro	189.8	46 535	531	245	31 530	15 005	47.6	90.77	7.95	0.34	0.82	0.13	0.53	11.2
4400	05 1195	Little Rock	266.4	175 795	96	660	159 159	16 636	10.5	64.68	33.98	0.26	0.87	0.21	0.76	12.6
4400	05 1475	North Little Rock	102.9	61 741	372	600	64 388	-2 647	-4.1	75.32	23.62	0.33	0.41	0.32	0.84	15.3
6240	05 1615	Pine Bluff	109.8	57 140	409	520	56 636	504	0.9	45.65	53.52	0.18	0.49	0.16	0.43	15.1
4920	05 3005	West Memphis	37.2	28 259	859	760	28 138	121	0.4	56.94	42.15	0.16	0.52	0.23	0.50	10.4
...	06 0000	CALIFORNIA	403 970.3	29 760 021	X	74	23 667 764	6 092 257	25.7	68.97	7.42	0.81	9.56	13.24	25.83	10.5
7362	06 0010	Alameda	27.8	76 459	278	2 750	63 852	12 607	19.7	69.91	6.72	0.70	19.25	3.42	9.09	11.8
4472	06 0025	Alhambra	19.7	82 106	257	4 168	64 767	17 339	26.8	40.85	2.00	0.43	38.14	18.58	36.08	13.0
4472	06 0070	Anaheim	114.7	266 406	59	2 323	219 494	46 912	21.4	71.44	2.54	0.53	9.39	16.09	31.44	8.4
7362	06 0085	Antioch	50.7	62 195	365	1 227	42 683	19 512	45.7	85.42	2.61	1.11	4.83	6.02	15.63	7.6
4472	06 0105	Arcadia	28.2	48 290	514	1 712	45 993	2 297	5.0	71.48	0.77	0.36	23.45	3.94	10.66	16.1
4472	06 0175	Azusa	23.3	41 333	603	1 774	29 380	11 953	40.7	66.00	3.84	0.69	6.63	22.83	53.45	6.9
0680	06 0180	Bakersfield	237.9	174 820	97	735	105 611	69 209	65.5	72.66	9.44	1.15	3.57	13.18	20.51	9.2
4472	06 0185	Baldwin Park	17.1	69 330	326	4 054	50 554	18 776	37.1	55.56	2.43	0.73	12.27	29.00	70.75	5.6
4472	06 0210	Bell	6.6	34 365	729	5 207	25 450	8 915	35.0	42.04	1.05	0.84	1.37	54.70	86.08	6.5
4472	06 0215	Bellflower	15.7	61 815	371	3 937	53 441	8 374	15.7	69.77	6.27	0.91	10.09	12.97	23.90	10.8
4472	06 0220	Bell Gardens	6.5	42 355	586	6 516	34 117	8 238	24.1	38.18	0.53	1.16	1.29	58.85	87.53	4.2
7362	06 0245	Berkeley	27.1	102 724	187	3 791	103 328	-604	-0.6	62.14	18.77	0.64	14.78	3.68	8.36	11.0
4472	06 0250	Beverly Hills	14.7	31 971	786	2 175	32 646	-675	-2.1	91.28	1.70	0.18	5.46	1.38	5.40	20.3
4472	06 0325	Brea	25.9	32 873	769	1 269	27 913	4 960	17.8	86.96	1.08	0.44	6.22	5.30	15.45	9.3
4472	06 0335	Buena Park	27.5	68 784	328	2 501	64 165	4 619	7.2	70.89	2.54	0.72	14.45	11.40	24.54	8.0
4472	06 0340	Burbank	44.9	93 643	213	2 086	84 625	9 018	10.7	82.59	1.75	0.54	6.77	8.36	22.61	14.5
7362	06 0345	Burlingame	11.3	26 801	892	2 372	26 173	628	2.4	87.45	0.97	0.37	8.87	2.35	10.19	18.8
4472	06 0379	Camarillo	47.8	52 303	464	1 094	37 797	14 506	38.4	86.34	1.60	0.55	6.35	5.16	12.09	16.7
7362	06 0390	Campbell	14.5	36 048	699	2 486	26 843	9 205	34.3	83.64	1.98	0.64	9.48	4.26	10.65	9.3
7320	06 0405	Carlsbad	97.6	63 126	364	647	35 490	27 636	77.9	89.76	1.18	0.47	3.17	5.41	13.78	13.1
4472	06 0440	Carson	48.8	83 995	252	1 721	81 221	2 774	3.4	34.72	26.14	0.59	24.97	13.59	27.87	8.0
4472	06 0487	Cerritos	22.3	53 240	452	2 387	53 020	220	0.4	42.35	7.44	0.33	45.19	4.70	12.52	5.7
1620	06 0500	Chico	58.1	40 079	629	690	26 716	13 363	50.0	89.47	1.82	1.10	4.00	3.62	8.69	9.0
4472	06 0510	Chino	44.2	59 682	390	1 350	40 165	19 517	48.6	67.31	9.75	0.46	3.44	19.03	36.17	5.0
7320	06 0525	Chula Vista	75.1	135 163	131	1 800	83 927	51 236	61.0	67.74	4.60	0.64	8.93	18.09	37.27	11.7
4472	06 0535	Claremont	28.5	32 503	775	1 140	31 028	1 475	4.8	82.24	5.00	0.41	8.51	3.85	10.26	12.4
2840	06 0550	Clovis	37.1	50 323	490	1 356	33 021	17 302	52.4	83.17	1.72	1.37	5.48	8.26	16.31	7.9

1. MSA = Metropolitan Statistical Area. CMSA = Consolidated MSA. 2. Dry land or land partially or temporarily covered by water. 3. Hispanic persons may be of any race.

City	Households, 1990				Births, 1984			Deaths, 1984				Hospitals, 1985		
			Percent–		Number			Number		Rate			Beds	
	Number	Persons per house-hold	Female family house-holder[1]	One-person[2]	Total	To mothers under 20 yrs. old (Percent)	Rate[3]	Total	Infant[4]	Total[3]	Infant[5]	Number	Number	Rate[6]
	15	16	17	18	19	20	21	22	23	24	25	26	27	28
ALABAMA	1 506 790	2.62	13.4	23.8	59 217	18.2	14.8	36 536	766	9.2	12.9	147	25 142	620
Anniston	10 807	2.42	18.6	30.5	615	24.1	20.5	437	7	14.5	11.4	2	393	1 338
Auburn	13 444	2.23	8.3	32.5	331	13.6	12.0	134	2	4.9	6.0	0	0	0
Bessemer	12 584	2.62	23.8	27.8	648	24.2	20.8	414	17	13.3	26.2	1	180	562
Birmingham	105 437	2.46	21.7	31.9	4 801	18.4	17.2	3 360	77	12.0	16.0	16	5 175	1 865
Decatur	19 134	2.50	12.2	26.1	644	16.6	15.0	380	8	8.8	12.4	3	442	982
Dothan	20 685	2.55	14.8	26.1	846	18.7	16.3	438	15	8.4	17.7	3	675	1 266
Florence	14 910	2.35	13.3	29.6	517	17.6	14.4	363	4	10.1	7.7	2	629	1 742
Gadsden	17 512	2.38	15.6	30.7	787	22.6	16.8	663	10	14.2	12.7	3	573	1 268
Huntsville	63 058	2.46	11.8	27.1	2 282	16.3	15.3	1 143	24	7.6	10.5	4	991	606
Mobile	75 442	2.53	18.3	28.4	3 332	17.3	16.3	1 949	37	9.5	11.1	8	2 005	986
Montgomery	69 968	2.59	17.7	27.4	3 139	15.7	17.0	1 604	43	8.7	13.7	6	1 509	777
Phenix City	9 745	2.55	20.5	27.1	474	20.5	17.1	383	8	13.8	16.9	1	234	859
Prichard	11 121	3.03	33.9	20.7	785	25.7	19.8	375	10	9.4	12.7	0	0	0
Selma	8 731	2.64	25.2	29.3	544	25.9	20.1	349	15	12.9	27.6	2	281	1 095
Tuscaloosa	29 467	2.35	14.5	31.9	1 166	18.1	15.9	618	21	8.4	18.0	4	2 717	3 680
ALASKA	188 915	2.80	9.6	22.1	12 455	9.6	24.5	1 929	140	3.8	11.2	27	1 881	352
Anchorage	82 702	2.68	10.1	22.9	5 194	8.5	22.9	704	55	3.1	10.6	6	981	417
ARIZONA	1 368 843	2.62	10.4	24.7	55 001	14.3	18.0	23 972	525	7.9	9.5	86	13 126	405
Chandler	31 490	2.86	10.4	17.9	1 499	9.9	30.1	256	16	5.1	10.7	1	90	132
Flagstaff	14 417	2.75	11.1	20.4	760	11.7	20.4	132	6	3.5	7.9	1	110	281
Glendale	53 669	2.73	11.8	22.0	2 694	11.1	23.7	810	18	7.1	6.7	3	271	215
Mesa	107 863	2.65	9.3	24.0	4 263	11.7	22.0	1 495	22	7.7	5.2	4	953	379
Phoenix	369 921	2.62	11.8	26.1	15 640	16.1	18.3	6 384	155	7.5	9.9	18	5 364	600
Scottsdale	57 583	2.24	8.4	29.7	1 283	5.6	12.9	963	7	9.7	5.5	4	510	459
Tempe	55 540	2.47	9.3	26.2	1 687	8.5	14.3	506	14	4.3	8.3	1	89	65
Tucson	162 685	2.42	12.4	31.3	6 878	12.9	18.8	3 371	74	9.2	10.8	12	2 498	696
Yuma	19 282	2.80	10.9	21.2	1 075	16.7	23.2	402	9	8.7	8.4	1	227	481
ARKANSAS	891 179	2.57	11.1	24.0	34 840	19.9	14.8	23 595	380	10.0	10.9	105	13 393	565
El Dorado	9 158	2.45	16.2	29.8	404	22.5	15.8	343	1	13.4	2.5	2	287	1 125
Fayetteville	16 894	2.26	8.8	32.2	521	9.6	14.6	313	2	8.8	3.8	4	628	1 566
Fort Smith	29 646	2.41	10.5	29.7	1 199	18.2	16.5	752	18	10.4	15.0	3	1 006	1 354
Hot Springs	14 488	2.14	12.2	36.7	481	18.7	13.1	698	8	18.9	16.6	3	484	1 311
Jacksonville	9 854	2.81	11.2	17.8	774	13.8	27.3	163	8	5.7	10.3	2	147	496
Jonesboro	17 976	2.46	11.2	25.3	507	17.4	16.7	295	4	9.7	7.9	2	357	1 188
Little Rock	72 573	2.37	14.5	32.1	3 044	15.0	17.9	1 718	38	10.1	12.5	9	3 942	2 178
North Little Rock	24 987	2.42	15.2	29.0	1 184	14.9	18.2	727	14	11.2	11.8	2	235	370
Pine Bluff	20 871	2.64	19.4	27.2	952	24.5	17.0	671	13	12.0	13.7	1	498	812
West Memphis	9 879	2.83	20.8	21.4	472	23.9	16.9	220	6	7.9	12.7	1	152	547
CALIFORNIA	10 381 206	2.79	11.5	23.4	447 730	11.2	17.5	195 531	4 224	7.6	9.4	578	110 309	409
Alameda	29 078	2.36	11.0	31.5	974	6.5	13.4	607	9	8.4	9.2	1	98	135
Alhambra	28 239	2.83	14.1	24.5	1 190	8.1	17.2	673	6	9.7	5.0	1	125	174
Anaheim	87 588	2.99	11.6	19.9	4 535	10.1	19.4	1 589	28	6.8	6.2	6	1 159	481
Antioch	21 401	2.89	12.2	16.9	879	11.6	18.9	312	6	6.7	6.8	1	53	106
Arcadia	18 352	2.60	9.7	23.9	492	5.7	10.5	569	4	12.2	8.1	1	315	660
Azusa	12 651	3.17	14.8	20.6	1 036	11.8	31.4	227	9	6.9	8.7	1	50	140
Bakersfield	62 467	2.75	14.0	23.0	5 706	15.9	43.8	2 053	77	15.8	13.5	6	980	652
Baldwin Park	16 614	4.13	16.3	10.5	1 540	14.9	26.8	334	17	5.8	11.0	1	95	151
Bell	9 013	3.78	15.1	17.3	730	13.2	26.3	186	4	6.7	5.5	0	0	0
Bellflower	22 905	2.67	13.8	25.3	1 212	8.9	21.3	542	14	9.5	11.6	4	651	1 112
Bell Gardens	9 244	4.52	18.2	9.3	1 044	18.6	28.2	200	12	5.4	11.5	0	0	0
Berkeley	43 453	2.10	10.7	39.8	1 157	6.4	11.2	739	10	7.1	8.6	3	440	423
Beverly Hills	14 564	2.19	8.1	38.1	251	0.8	7.7	407	3	12.4	12.0	0	0	0
Brea	12 224	2.68	8.0	21.7	384	9.4	12.1	193	8	6.1	20.8	2	304	930
Buena Park	22 210	3.08	12.8	15.1	1 134	11.6	17.4	386	3	5.9	2.6	2	124	187
Burbank	39 275	2.36	10.7	32.0	1 127	9.9	12.9	945	9	10.8	8.0	2	691	775
Burlingame	12 329	2.13	7.6	37.3	296	2.0	11.4	294	3	11.3	10.1	1	310	1 181
Camarillo	18 109	2.84	7.3	18.1	699	6.0	16.5	364	4	8.6	5.7	2	1 418	3 182
Campbell	15 306	2.35	10.6	29.0	602	8.8	17.8	253	5	7.5	8.3	0	0	0
Carlsbad	24 995	2.47	8.1	23.2	589	4.1	14.3	239	6	5.8	10.2	0	0	0
Carson	23 808	3.51	14.2	14.2	1 341	12.9	15.8	435	13	5.1	9.7	0	0	0
Cerritos	15 026	3.54	9.5	7.4	585	7.5	10.6	158	5	2.9	8.5	1	100	175
Chico	15 508	2.38	10.5	29.6	1 012	8.1	34.6	450	4	15.4	4.0	2	301	921
Chino	15 636	3.27	10.8	14.7	1 186	9.3	25.3	266	7	5.7	5.9	2	199	392
Chula Vista	47 824	2.79	12.4	21.8	2 165	9.3	24.0	900	17	10.0	7.9	4	436	367
Claremont	10 472	2.68	8.9	21.3	320	6.9	9.5	227	4	6.8	12.5	0	0	0
Clovis	18 259	2.75	12.7	21.5	832	9.1	21.8	275	5	7.2	6.0	1	63	153

1. No spouse present. 2. Householder living alone. 3. Per 1,000 resident population estimated as of July 1 of the year shown. 4. Deaths of infants under 1 year old. 5. Deaths of infants under 1 year old per 1,000 live births. 6. Per 100,000 resident population estimated as of July 1, 1986.

City	Serious crimes known to police, 1985: Number: Total	Serious crimes known to police, 1985: Number: Violent[1]	Serious crimes known to police, 1985: Rate[2]	Police officers, 1985: Number	Police officers, 1985: Rate[3]	Educational attainment,[4] 1980: Percent completing 12 years or more	Educational attainment,[4] 1980: Percent completing 16 years or more	Money income: Per capita[5]: 1985: Total (Dollars)	Money income: Per capita[5]: 1985: Percent of State average	Money income: Per capita[5]: 1979: Current dollars	Money income: Per capita[5]: 1979: Constant (1985) dollars	Money income: Percent below poverty level, 1979: Persons	Money income: Percent below poverty level, 1979: Families	Housing, 1990: Total units	Housing, 1990: Percent change, 1980–1990	Housing, 1990: Vacant units for sale or rent[6]
	29	30	31	32	33	34	35	36	37	38	39	40	41	42	43	44
ALABAMA	158 513	18 398	3 942	NA	NA	56.5	12.2	8 681	100.0	5 892	8 732	18.9	14.8	1 670 379	12.2	81 774
Anniston	3 662	611	11 869	82	26.6	56.1	15.2	8 731	100.6	5 842	8 658	23.5	18.0	12 100	2.3	815
Auburn	1 602	164	5 449	46	15.6	82.2	47.8	8 434	97.2	5 471	8 108	33.7	13.6	14 673	25.9	1 009
Bessemer	2 009	237	6 307	59	18.5	50.3	7.0	6 746	77.7	5 202	7 709	25.8	20.8	13 783	13.7	872
Birmingham	28 076	3 350	9 957	619	22.0	60.4	13.0	8 035	92.6	5 815	8 618	22.0	17.7	117 691	2.7	9 178
Decatur	1 938	81	4 542	72	16.9	67.8	17.5	10 884	125.4	7 077	10 488	13.3	9.6	20 640	21.3	1 258
Dothan	3 461	361	6 622	82	15.7	63.8	16.6	9 999	115.2	6 727	9 969	16.1	11.8	22 190	15.3	1 105
Florence	1 863	136	4 880	70	18.3	63.6	18.3	9 556	110.1	6 701	9 931	15.6	10.9	15 913	9.9	720
Gadsden	2 736	380	5 709	111	23.2	54.5	10.3	8 745	100.7	6 305	9 344	18.4	14.0	19 146	-3.0	1 088
Huntsville	10 875	684	7 217	239	15.9	74.9	25.5	12 467	143.6	7 661	11 354	12.8	9.8	67 827	21.4	3 863
Mobile	16 707	2 177	8 090	294	14.2	67.1	17.0	9 658	111.3	6 593	9 771	18.6	14.8	82 817	8.7	5 652
Montgomery	10 275	546	5 513	391	21.0	67.8	20.5	9 826	113.2	6 640	9 840	19.4	14.7	76 636	12.0	4 987
Phenix City	1 796	341	6 542	52	18.9	44.2	6.2	7 657	88.2	5 068	7 511	24.7	19.3	10 813	3.2	798
Prichard	2 728	532	6 710	50	12.3	42.2	4.0	4 674	53.8	3 432	5 086	38.8	35.1	13 037	-0.2	1 146
Selma	2 894	750	10 315	55	19.6	59.8	14.6	7 662	88.3	5 286	7 834	29.7	22.7	9 556	-2.4	602
Tuscaloosa	4 976	541	6 622	148	19.7	64.4	22.7	8 284	95.4	5 633	8 348	25.9	17.0	31 194	9.6	1 292
ALASKA	30 619	3 031	5 877	NA	NA	82.5	21.1	13 650	100.0	10 193	15 106	10.7	8.6	232 608	30.0	15 428
Anchorage	14 622	1 184	6 369	288	12.5	88.3	23.6	15 517	113.7	11 339	16 804	7.4	6.1	94 153	25.3	6 731
ARIZONA	226 793	19 202	7 116	NA	NA	72.4	17.4	10 561	100.0	7 042	10 436	13.2	9.5	1 659 430	33.1	143 067
Chandler	3 927	207	9 757	72	17.9	72.3	14.3	10 004	94.7	6 165	9 137	13.0	10.9	34 967	70.3	2 432
Flagstaff	3 193	182	8 301	58	15.1	82.0	31.2	8 670	82.1	6 155	9 122	14.7	9.4	16 313	30.6	792
Glendale	10 418	806	8 763	166	14.0	75.9	14.9	10 925	103.4	7 091	10 509	9.0	6.9	61 218	42.1	6 206
Mesa	14 158	1 121	6 993	281	13.9	78.5	18.5	10 889	103.1	7 142	10 584	8.5	6.2	140 468	53.5	13 269
Phoenix	82 523	7 521	9 264	1 704	19.1	73.3	16.5	11 363	107.6	7 552	11 192	11.1	8.1	422 036	26.9	41 553
Scottsdale	6 587	263	6 342	147	14.2	86.3	27.1	16 773	158.8	10 346	15 333	5.6	3.8	69 028	39.1	6 118
Tempe	2 673	137	2 164	168	13.6	87.6	32.8	12 419	117.6	7 908	11 720	10.9	5.5	61 452	34.6	4 593
Tucson	38 249	3 713	10 027	647	17.0	72.7	19.2	9 430	89.3	6 551	9 709	14.7	10.2	183 338	25.1	14 838
Yuma	4 683	349	9 495	NA	NA	70.6	13.7	9 088	86.1	6 391	9 471	11.8	8.8	22 689	29.1	1 450
ARKANSAS	84 571	8 199	3 585	NA	NA	55.5	10.8	8 389	100.0	5 613	8 318	19.0	14.9	1 000 667	10.2	58 062
El Dorado	997	29	3 850	44	17.0	61.2	14.5	9 801	116.8	6 521	9 664	21.2	15.4	10 269	-4.0	742
Fayetteville	1 962	37	5 283	49	13.2	78.0	34.5	9 358	111.6	5 896	8 738	18.9	10.0	18 835	24.4	1 492
Fort Smith	4 858	359	6 657	105	14.4	67.3	13.8	11 118	132.5	7 262	10 762	13.5	10.5	33 054	8.1	2 827
Hot Springs	3 114	347	8 434	64	17.3	57.2	11.8	8 971	106.9	6 142	9 102	20.1	13.9	17 543	-2.5	1 770
Jacksonville	1 327	96	4 475	44	14.8	77.2	12.0	8 515	101.5	5 639	8 357	8.7	6.9	10 890	15.8	885
Jonesboro	1 091	29	3 422	38	11.9	64.2	19.8	10 110	120.5	6 576	9 746	13.9	11.0	19 537	37.5	1 219
Little Rock	18 464	2 622	10 807	328	19.2	76.2	25.0	11 923	142.1	7 812	11 577	14.1	10.1	80 995	20.2	6 639
North Little Rock	4 937	608	7 497	121	18.4	67.5	15.5	10 468	124.8	6 966	10 324	12.7	9.5	27 255	4.9	1 849
Pine Bluff	3 513	461	6 115	115	20.0	59.8	14.4	7 826	93.3	5 606	8 308	24.3	19.4	23 189	8.1	1 564
West Memphis	1 779	104	6 248	41	14.4	54.0	8.1	8 141	97.0	5 619	8 327	26.2	20.4	10 505	8.3	489
CALIFORNIA	1 718 473	201 763	6 518	NA	NA	73.5	19.6	11 885	100.0	8 294	12 292	11.4	8.7	11 182 882	17.0	480 170
Alameda	4 891	405	6 752	99	13.7	79.8	21.0	13 494	113.5	9 288	13 765	8.1	6.6	30 520	8.9	1 177
Alhambra	4 148	469	5 769	87	12.1	71.6	18.6	10 363	87.2	7 788	11 542	11.8	8.9	29 604	8.1	1 113
Anaheim	17 571	1 162	7 313	316	13.2	75.6	15.3	12 155	102.3	8 535	12 649	7.7	6.0	93 177	11.2	5 016
Antioch	3 028	191	6 241	59	12.2	74.6	10.7	11 052	93.0	7 791	11 546	7.3	6.5	22 973	31.8	1 418
Arcadia	2 353	160	4 768	63	12.8	85.7	28.4	17 391	146.3	12 105	17 940	4.0	2.7	19 483	4.4	916
Azusa	2 358	236	7 044	54	16.1	58.9	8.3	8 665	72.9	6 421	9 516	11.4	9.3	13 232	20.7	502
Bakersfield	12 921	1 202	9 644	196	14.6	73.3	17.5	11 010	92.6	8 326	12 339	11.3	9.4	66 175	35.4	3 006
Baldwin Park	3 093	407	5 367	55	9.5	50.1	6.4	6 915	58.2	4 955	7 343	15.2	13.2	17 179	16.5	423
Bell	1 314	260	4 584	43	15.0	43.6	3.8	6 495	54.6	5 302	7 858	19.5	17.0	9 401	1.5	277
Bellflower	2 898	416	4 900	NA	NA	67.1	8.8	10 598	89.2	7 694	11 403	9.9	8.1	24 117	7.7	1 057
Bell Gardens	2 067	441	5 389	42	11.0	30.7	2.4	4 988	42.0	3 796	5 626	25.3	23.1	9 546	-2.3	241
Berkeley	13 199	1 164	12 362	173	16.2	86.4	52.3	12 695	106.8	8 461	12 539	21.0	11.7	45 735	-1.3	1 312
Beverly Hills	2 763	307	8 135	115	33.9	86.6	35.2	33 839	284.7	24 316	36 036	8.9	6.4	15 723	-0.2	870
Brea	1 923	173	5 817	71	21.5	83.4	23.0	15 006	126.3	10 032	14 867	3.4	2.0	12 648	11.4	339
Buena Park	3 660	339	5 315	85	12.3	73.2	11.8	11 905	100.2	8 261	12 243	7.5	5.9	23 200	5.2	886
Burbank	3 943	331	4 310	133	14.5	75.3	14.8	13 377	112.6	9 251	13 710	7.7	5.9	41 216	9.9	1 607
Burlingame	1 145	45	4 100	44	15.8	84.5	25.1	17 619	148.2	11 787	17 468	5.8	3.8	12 914	2.0	443
Camarillo	961	37	2 225	NA	NA	84.4	23.5	13 327	112.1	9 195	13 627	4.2	3.1	18 731	24.0	501
Campbell	2 093	194	6 014	40	11.5	82.2	21.5	15 147	127.4	9 598	14 224	7.6	5.5	15 860	24.5	486
Carlsbad	2 293	167	5 685	62	15.4	83.5	25.6	15 640	131.6	10 273	15 225	7.5	4.8	27 235	43.6	1 332
Carson	4 547	636	5 097	NA	NA	67.6	12.5	10 160	85.5	7 177	10 636	7.9	6.4	24 441	4.8	546
Cerritos	3 175	256	5 483	NA	NA	88.0	28.5	12 134	102.1	9 003	13 342	3.2	2.8	15 364	2.9	298
Chico	2 668	149	8 925	46	15.4	82.1	31.1	8 028	67.5	6 057	8 976	26.1	11.6	16 295	32.0	627
Chino	2 194	210	4 775	60	13.1	71.2	11.4	9 519	80.1	6 598	9 778	7.9	6.4	16 137	29.5	435
Chula Vista	5 443	489	5 845	97	10.4	73.9	15.9	10 485	88.2	7 172	10 629	8.4	6.9	49 849	36.0	1 679
Claremont	1 661	102	4 790	35	10.1	91.3	44.6	14 729	123.9	9 967	14 771	5.8	3.3	10 831	8.2	306
Clovis	2 481	144	6 518	49	12.9	77.5	17.6	9 450	79.5	6 913	10 245	9.2	6.9	18 888	29.3	535

1. Includes murder and nonnegligent manslaughter, forcible rape, robbery, and aggravated assault. 2. Per 100,000 resident population estimated for 1985 by the FBI. 3. Per 10,000 resident population estimated for 1985 by the FBI. 4. Persons 25 years old or older. 5. Based on the resident population estimated as of July 1, 1988 for 1987 data and enumerated as of April 1, 1980 for 1979 data. 6. Also includes units rented or sold, but not occupied.

City	Housing, 1990 (cont'd): Occupied units: Total	Percent with more than 1 person per room	Owner-occupied: Percent of total	Owner-occupied: Median value[1] (Dollars)	Median rent[2] (Dollars)	Construction authorized by building permits, 1990: New private housing units: Number	Value ($1,000)	Percent single family	Non-residential, value ($1,000)	Civilian labor force, 1990: Total	Percent change, 1989–1990	Unemployment: Total	Rate[3]
	45	46	47	48	49	50	51	52	53	54	55	56	57
ALABAMA	1 506 790	3.5	70.5	53 700	229	12 564	683 799	70.3	514 807	1 892 000	-0.8	128 000	6.8
Anniston	10 807	2.9	60.4	49 700	198	65	3 825	87.7	4 998	12 556	-2.0	1 500	11.9
Auburn	13 444	3.0	37.0	80 900	290	423	18 546	26.2	2 195	13 151	-2.8	636	4.8
Bessemer	12 584	5.1	59.1	40 500	164	19	1 039	100.0	6 859	15 121	-0.5	1 694	11.2
Birmingham	105 437	4.0	53.4	44 500	225	307	24 030	46.3	108 884	131 103	-1.0	9 787	7.5
Decatur	19 134	2.0	61.7	66 000	277	445	27 491	79.6	5 604	23 199	1.2	1 713	7.4
Dothan	20 685	3.4	60.9	58 600	229	264	15 015	95.5	14 718	27 784	-0.9	1 396	5.0
Florence	14 910	1.5	60.5	53 400	226	292	11 009	50.3	9 328	17 014	0.1	1 612	9.5
Gadsden	17 512	2.1	64.8	36 300	181	15	1 242	100.0	8 152	19 347	-0.8	2 917	15.1
Huntsville	63 058	2.7	59.8	78 200	329	1 563	48 282	69.5	53 494	94 881	-0.1	4 354	4.6
Mobile	75 442	3.9	58.1	55 400	248	366	31 088	100.0	13 607	95 409	-0.8	6 771	7.1
Montgomery	69 968	4.6	60.1	62 200	294	811	43 744	85.9	41 393	90 449	-0.6	5 717	6.3
Phenix City	9 745	4.7	55.1	46 900	196	151	6 461	49.7	3 564	13 189	1.6	1 027	7.8
Prichard	11 121	8.3	57.4	35 000	120	23	500	82.6	698	13 301	-1.9	1 159	8.7
Selma	8 731	5.8	53.4	45 500	161	11	314	45.5	5 233	10 371	-2.5	1 542	14.9
Tuscaloosa	29 467	3.5	46.9	62 900	258	520	21 419	53.7	8 578	36 859	1.2	2 196	6.0
ALASKA	188 915	8.6	56.1	94 400	503	876	102 115	82.6	59 144	257 000	1.6	18 000	6.9
Anchorage	82 702	4.9	52.8	109 700	528	399	62 476	100.0	20 612	117 230	2.6	6 141	5.2
ARIZONA	1 368 843	7.4	64.2	80 100	370	23 031	1 963 013	81.3	678 003	1 726 000	1.1	92 000	5.3
Chandler	31 490	6.2	67.7	90 300	437	973	98 551	100.0	22 058	20 123	1.1	784	3.9
Flagstaff	14 417	8.4	49.9	90 900	409	364	21 473	51.9	7 003	23 918	3.0	1 486	6.2
Glendale	53 669	6.1	62.1	84 900	370	688	62 083	100.0	26 918	70 319	1.1	3 059	4.4
Mesa	107 863	5.2	60.9	86 500	396	1 160	111 679	86.6	35 640	106 494	1.1	4 340	4.1
Phoenix	369 921	7.3	59.1	77 100	374	4 134	409 697	81.2	170 089	595 354	1.1	26 639	4.5
Scottsdale	57 583	1.5	64.1	115 200	525	1 934	266 029	60.3	84 673	72 793	1.1	2 305	3.2
Tempe	55 540	4.6	51.6	91 500	437	389	40 526	69.4	20 484	90 167	1.1	3 291	3.6
Tucson	162 685	7.3	51.4	66 800	327	477	32 215	92.2	40 401	203 475	-0.2	8 426	4.1
Yuma	19 282	10.4	58.5	65 400	376	526	26 234	39.0	19 074	30 488	2.7	4 623	15.2
ARKANSAS	891 179	3.7	69.6	46 300	230	6 000	343 289	81.2	328 103	1 133 000	-0.2	78 000	6.9
El Dorado	9 158	4.2	64.1	42 300	197	21	583	61.9	1 562	11 459	-1.6	815	7.1
Fayetteville	16 894	2.5	43.4	66 200	278	361	22 839	70.4	13 546	24 038	1.3	882	3.7
Fort Smith	29 646	3.4	59.2	50 600	246	366	17 627	45.1	7 607	41 500	-0.8	2 642	6.4
Hot Springs	14 488	2.3	59.9	45 000	223	70	4 352	71.4	48 159	NA	NA	NA	NA
Jacksonville	9 854	4.1	47.1	55 100	294	28	1 728	92.9	2 289	11 656	-0.1	936	8.0
Jonesboro	17 976	2.2	59.9	58 900	274	298	15 409	90.6	17 214	19 192	-0.8	898	4.7
Little Rock	72 573	3.1	56.2	64 200	318	472	51 009	94.5	61 280	94 197	0.0	5 154	5.5
North Little Rock	24 987	3.1	58.9	56 100	272	61	4 829	100.0	10 849	35 558	0.0	1 771	5.0
Pine Bluff	20 871	5.4	61.7	41 200	219	76	2 047	94.7	24 215	23 706	-0.3	2 101	8.9
West Memphis	9 879	6.3	57.7	50 900	248	75	4 125	89.3	2 722	14 148	-2.6	1 011	7.1
CALIFORNIA	10 381 206	12.3	55.6	195 500	561	163 175	17 233 076	64.3	7 600 432	14 670 000	1.0	823 000	5.6
Alameda	29 078	6.4	46.3	267 600	632	89	13 016	100.0	16 443	38 275	-1.4	1 094	2.9
Alhambra	28 239	21.5	40.6	231 000	587	173	15 311	29.5	13 867	38 592	4.5	1 469	3.8
Anaheim	87 588	15.8	49.2	218 700	661	527	51 679	23.5	65 314	162 631	-1.9	6 219	3.8
Antioch	21 401	4.9	64.3	156 900	565	826	93 349	100.0	12 963	25 605	-1.2	1 476	5.8
Arcadia	18 352	6.1	61.6	440 800	657	214	52 016	100.0	6 971	28 241	4.2	726	2.6
Azusa	12 651	21.6	48.2	150 800	585	31	2 039	61.3	590	16 996	4.9	1 009	5.9
Bakersfield	62 467	7.6	55.1	91 200	389	1 554	160 970	92.3	46 761	67 964	-2.3	4 793	7.1
Baldwin Park	16 614	37.5	60.1	151 100	588	152	10 002	50.7	12 072	24 797	5.3	1 851	7.5
Bell	9 013	46.0	30.4	171 200	514	15	820	0.0	454	12 638	5.1	868	6.9
Bellflower	22 905	14.1	39.6	195 200	581	183	15 063	31.7	5 568	33 073	4.8	1 827	5.5
Bell Gardens	9 244	59.5	22.5	165 200	542	108	6 903	17.6	8 092	13 770	5.7	1 292	9.4
Berkeley	43 453	4.5	43.6	261 000	392	75	7 315	34.7	1 520	67 135	-1.5	2 765	4.1
Beverly Hills	14 564	3.3	43.8	500 001	902	120	44 322	62.5	2 103	19 749	4.5	755	3.8
Brea	12 224	5.1	63.5	264 000	701	94	8 451	39.4	33 505	21 190	-2.0	580	2.7
Buena Park	22 210	14.1	56.2	206 000	675	93	6 377	7.5	5 475	46 522	-1.8	2 027	4.4
Burbank	39 275	9.7	45.7	262 500	612	43	7 809	76.7	109 403	53 970	4.5	2 186	4.1
Burlingame	12 329	4.5	47.6	461 500	682	16	2 967	43.8	0	15 650	-1.5	427	2.7
Camarillo	18 109	5.1	72.2	249 500	765	470	40 464	47.0	18 928	25 763	0.4	1 026	4.0
Campbell	15 306	5.9	47.0	276 700	688	53	7 021	100.0	4 571	19 417	-4.0	634	3.3
Carlsbad	24 995	4.1	62.2	255 900	711	539	64 636	50.6	34 534	25 103	0.1	902	3.6
Carson	23 808	20.7	79.0	188 100	648	135	15 573	98.5	15 515	47 501	4.8	2 614	5.5
Cerritos	15 026	11.0	83.4	300 000	1 001	4	1 062	100.0	18 162	32 508	4.3	911	2.8
Chico	15 508	4.7	32.9	106 100	402	1 026	62 554	28.8	22 641	15 605	-3.0	1 045	6.7
Chino	15 636	11.8	67.9	172 200	605	302	35 505	99.3	35 864	27 229	4.4	1 265	4.6
Chula Vista	47 824	10.9	53.3	164 000	540	665	95 247	67.4	21 751	52 771	0.2	2 478	4.7
Claremont	10 472	3.1	69.8	253 900	631	124	11 024	27.4	3 392	18 724	4.4	686	3.7
Clovis	18 259	5.7	53.2	92 300	405	795	94 633	93.7	19 646	22 619	1.6	1 564	6.9

1. Specified owner-occupied units. 2. Specified renter-occupied units. 3. Percent of total civilian labor force.

City	Employed,[1] 1980: Total	Employed,[1] 1980: Rate per 1,000 employees: Professional, specialty, and technical	Employed,[1] 1980: Rate per 1,000 employees: Precision production, craft, and operators	Manufactures, 1987: Establishments: Total	Manufactures, 1987: Establishments: Percent with 20 or more employees	Manufactures, 1987: All employees: Number (1,000)	Manufactures, 1987: All employees: Percent change, 1982–1987	Manufactures, 1987: All employees: Annual payroll (Mil. dol.)	Manufactures, 1987: Production workers: Number (1,000)	Manufactures, 1987: Production workers: Work-hours (Millions)	Manufactures, 1987: Production workers: Wages: Total (Mil. dol.)	Manufactures, 1987: Production workers: Wages: Average per production worker (Dollars)	Manufactures, 1987: Value added by manufacture (Mil. dol.)	Manufactures, 1987: Value of shipments (Mil. dol.)	Manufactures, 1987: New capital expenditures (Mil. dol.)
	58	59	60	61	62	63	64	65	66	67	68	69	70	71	72
ALABAMA	1 511 928	137.9	268.7	5 843	35.4	347.3	5.4	6 962.5	268.8	530.7	4 745.6	17 655	18 652.1	40 901.4	1 360.1
Anniston	10 262	171.1	202.8	71	53.5	6.9	25.5	121.7	5.2	10.2	79.7	15 327	246.8	534.0	12.2
Auburn	10 582	352.7	90.3	20	35.0	0.9	NA	14.9	0.7	1.3	9.8	14 000	32.6	54.0	3.0
Bessemer	10 365	114.2	251.6	44	43.2	2.0	25.0	46.1	1.7	3.5	34.4	20 235	127.5	261.1	20.6
Birmingham	114 568	152.2	175.9	442	42.5	25.4	-8.6	568.9	17.0	34.0	339.7	19 982	1 244.0	2 613.2	73.9
Decatur	17 978	175.8	232.1	99	46.5	8.4	2.4	206.3	6.4	12.7	134.4	21 000	792.8	1 903.4	40.6
Dothan	21 254	155.3	223.0	85	42.4	7.1	-4.1	128.0	5.4	11.2	81.1	15 019	334.6	690.5	35.1
Florence	15 470	168.3	233.2	72	33.3	4.2	40.0	79.3	3.4	6.9	53.0	15 588	180.6	351.3	7.2
Gadsden	17 763	135.7	257.3	66	50.0	9.9	2.1	269.2	8.2	17.4	210.2	25 634	645.8	1 282.5	18.3
Huntsville	63 006	257.1	172.9	226	38.5	23.9	12.7	674.7	14.8	30.3	360.6	24 365	1 718.2	3 168.9	155.0
Mobile	81 855	176.7	178.9	228	26.8	12.9	-13.4	354.3	9.2	18.4	235.1	25 554	1 430.8	2 526.6	100.3
Montgomery	72 437	177.4	155.4	219	42.5	13.3	16.7	245.8	10.1	21.3	163.3	16 168	624.4	1 313.9	31.2
Phenix City	10 106	112.5	317.6	33	45.5	2.8	21.7	61.6	2.4	5.1	48.4	20 167	216.6	500.1	16.3
Prichard	11 958	73.5	283.7	28	39.3	0.7	-12.5	11.4	0.5	1.1	7.0	14 000	27.8	67.2	0.9
Selma	9 708	163.6	224.7	48	58.3	4.6	4.5	75.0	3.5	6.7	45.8	13 086	238.3	571.5	22.2
Tuscaloosa	28 789	227.0	146.6	84	46.4	4.8	-18.6	101.4	3.4	6.8	60.7	17 853	256.0	823.6	25.5
ALASKA	164 874	193.7	153.7	427	24.8	11.1	-13.3	271.7	8.4	16.7	191.4	22 786	834.0	2 710.7	68.6
Anchorage	77 754	192.7	130.3	146	15.1	2.3	-17.9	59.8	1.3	2.4	30.0	23 077	234.8	714.1	9.3
ARIZONA	1 113 270	165.4	196.6	4 151	27.2	184.1	22.9	4 669.0	105.9	214.2	2 148.8	20 291	11 299.0	20 757.7	836.9
Chandler	12 487	132.4	237.2	79	39.2	7.2	157.1	208.7	3.5	7.0	68.0	19 429	473.2	805.1	69.1
Flagstaff	16 227	197.1	128.6	72	22.2	1.9	11.8	41.5	1.3	2.6	24.0	18 462	173.6	341.9	8.1
Glendale	43 417	142.3	209.7	122	25.4	5.3	47.2	133.9	3.0	5.8	52.4	17 467	317.2	518.1	16.6
Mesa	65 940	170.6	213.2	187	23.5	14.3	81.0	424.4	7.2	14.9	171.3	23 792	1 116.7	1 658.3	115.0
Phoenix	367 093	158.1	206.5	1 559	32.1	75.7	13.3	1 928.5	45.7	93.1	977.9	21 398	4 665.3	7 923.1	299.1
Scottsdale	45 498	189.1	113.6	226	15.0	7.1	-12.3	187.8	3.6	7.3	68.8	19 111	207.4	552.8	48.5
Tempe	56 077	239.7	146.1	416	29.3	18.4	41.5	481.7	10.9	23.1	246.3	22 596	992.6	1 724.7	73.8
Tucson	142 795	190.4	185.1	497	24.9	26.3	8.7	692.2	12.3	24.4	212.6	17 285	1 745.3	3 231.3	106.5
Yuma	15 405	159.8	164.9	38	39.5	D	D	D	D	D	D	D	D	D	D
ARKANSAS	875 733	120.2	262.5	3 390	35.7	205.5	8.3	3 814.6	161.7	326.3	2 651.6	16 398	10 826.9	25 307.6	891.5
El Dorado	9 944	152.9	206.8	41	34.1	2.9	-37.0	57.0	2.2	4.3	35.5	16 136	125.6	603.2	10.4
Fayetteville	16 328	253.9	140.4	54	48.1	4.5	12.5	77.3	3.7	7.2	56.8	15 351	243.0	519.2	23.8
Fort Smith	31 692	131.5	247.0	203	44.8	D	D	D	D	D	D	D	D	D	D
Hot Springs	13 540	151.1	172.1	58	34.5	2.1	16.7	37.2	1.5	2.9	20.6	13 733	81.3	367.2	5.2
Jacksonville	8 988	119.0	255.1	35	51.4	2.2	-8.3	43.6	1.7	3.3	30.2	17 765	101.2	215.5	3.4
Jonesboro	14 384	158.2	185.6	83	39.8	5.8	5.5	111.3	4.4	8.9	77.0	17 500	389.7	732.3	30.2
Little Rock	74 654	207.9	147.2	265	38.1	15.0	-10.2	323.9	9.4	18.4	183.3	19 500	784.2	1 986.5	59.2
North Little Rock	28 327	145.0	177.2	80	40.0	3.7	-9.8	69.2	2.6	5.3	43.4	16 692	339.1	572.7	13.1
Pine Bluff	20 978	143.0	222.8	74	47.3	5.5	12.2	135.2	4.2	9.0	97.3	23 167	368.7	851.7	D
West Memphis	10 763	90.1	237.0	36	50.0	1.5	0.0	27.0	1.1	2.1	16.7	15 182	70.3	239.4	7.6
CALIFORNIA	10 640 405	164.5	194.3	49 930	31.4	2 104.3	5.0	57 147.8	1 240.2	2 432.9	25 697.0	20 720	132 637.5	252 728.8	8 571.7
Alameda	29 554	150.7	164.5	52	11.5	0.7	-30.0	22.4	0.4	0.9	8.6	21 500	36.5	70.9	2.9
Alhambra	30 887	156.7	198.4	129	31.0	3.0	11.1	54.6	2.4	4.6	38.4	16 000	103.7	214.5	3.9
Anaheim	114 095	133.0	226.9	975	38.2	50.0	13.4	1 392.4	25.8	52.6	524.3	20 322	3 188.3	5 298.7	188.9
Antioch	18 470	107.5	274.2	36	33.3	1.6	14.3	44.0	1.2	2.1	31.2	26 000	114.1	313.6	10.8
Arcadia	22 893	206.4	112.9	74	21.6	1.6	6.7	40.5	1.1	2.2	22.6	20 545	75.1	127.0	4.1
Azusa	13 301	95.0	314.3	136	33.8	7.7	35.1	206.9	4.8	9.8	84.5	17 604	436.3	717.5	33.1
Bakersfield	49 249	166.8	164.8	157	17.2	2.8	-9.7	56.4	1.9	3.0	31.3	16 474	153.2	345.1	9.9
Baldwin Park	19 091	65.5	386.6	120	29.2	2.4	33.3	41.3	1.8	3.4	26.8	14 889	71.2	145.3	6.1
Bell	9 793	46.9	400.8	37	37.8	2.2	10.0	47.9	1.7	3.2	30.9	18 176	111.0	219.1	2.3
Bellflower	25 997	101.7	282.6	NA	NA	NA	NA	NA	NA	NA	NA	NA	NA	NA	NA
Bell Gardens	10 382	29.3	485.2	77	35.1	2.0	-16.7	42.7	1.6	3.0	26.5	16 562	79.8	142.2	4.8
Berkeley	51 165	377.7	82.6	236	20.8	5.6	-27.3	149.4	2.7	5.1	60.3	22 333	272.0	501.5	22.7
Beverly Hills	15 803	266.5	44.4	111	14.4	1.6	-27.3	49.2	0.9	1.5	12.0	13 333	82.4	140.9	D
Brea	15 034	166.4	173.7	198	34.8	9.4	28.8	208.8	5.3	11.2	89.5	16 887	405.6	718.1	17.1
Buena Park	32 457	117.7	234.1	179	31.3	7.3	12.3	180.1	4.5	9.1	101.3	22 511	423.1	1 054.8	23.2
Burbank	43 085	150.5	238.0	443	36.1	33.7	-5.3	1 129.7	18.4	35.8	462.7	25 147	2 187.6	3 242.2	120.6
Burlingame	13 909	179.2	126.8	76	25.0	1.6	-15.8	44.9	0.9	1.7	20.8	23 111	154.3	266.7	3.1
Camarillo	16 471	223.6	166.2	121	45.5	6.8	51.1	178.7	4.3	8.6	91.8	21 349	518.6	838.0	30.3
Campbell	15 904	165.1	216.7	169	19.5	3.3	-29.8	85.2	1.8	3.2	33.4	18 556	204.7	272.9	7.2
Carlsbad	16 320	178.6	140.6	109	45.0	5.1	41.7	124.6	3.2	6.4	63.7	19 906	316.6	537.2	23.6
Carson	37 346	130.8	280.1	343	45.2	16.5	3.1	401.7	11.3	22.6	226.7	20 062	1 168.8	4 261.8	172.6
Cerritos	26 289	195.4	177.0	140	42.1	4.5	-13.5	101.3	3.3	6.6	62.2	18 848	262.1	583.2	8.2
Chico	11 301	193.3	133.1	89	25.8	2.7	42.1	49.6	1.9	4.0	34.1	17 947	104.9	293.4	8.1
Chino	16 006	126.9	228.9	166	42.2	6.0	172.7	121.4	4.6	9.0	76.0	16 522	315.4	750.7	22.0
Chula Vista	33 916	142.6	204.8	68	25.0	6.6	D	210.2	3.8	7.7	97.5	25 658	351.8	515.1	22.6
Claremont	15 008	307.0	92.8	32	28.1	1.2	NA	38.7	0.5	1.0	9.4	18 800	169.8	193.6	D
Clovis	15 764	137.8	171.5	55	18.2	0.8	60.0	18.4	0.5	1.1	9.7	19 400	58.0	112.9	5.4

1. Persons 16 years old and over.

City	Wholesale trade, 1987				Retail trade–all establishments, 1987				Retail trade–establishments with payroll, 1987					
						Sales				Sales				
											Per capita[2] (Dollars)			
	Establishments	Sales (Mil. dol.)	Paid employees[1]	Annual payroll ($1,000)	Number	Total (Mil. dol.)	Percent change, 1982–1987	Per capita[2] (Dollars)	Number	Total (Mil. dol.)	General merchandise group stores	Food stores	Apparel and accessory stores	Eating and drinking places
	73	74	75	76	77	78	79	80	81	82	83	84	85	86
ALABAMA	6 671	24 343.6	77 559	1 548 477	40 218	22 268.2	53.8	5 494	24 092	21 260.9	654	1 104	284	449
Anniston	83	385.2	1 072	20 931	468	406.2	38.5	13 830	325	398.7	1 609	2 027	720	982
Auburn	27	28.8	167	2 711	266	279.3	69.2	9 385	218	274.6	1 730	1 667	358	813
Bessemer	61	D	D	D	393	298.5	52.3	9 319	266	292.6	1 138	2 193	185	480
Birmingham	1 030	6 026.0	18 428	413 993	2 438	2 226.2	41.4	8 022	1 887	2 199.6	884	1 186	581	790
Decatur	135	388.0	1 493	28 819	636	508.6	73.4	11 302	447	497.1	1 510	1 723	616	947
Dothan	201	506.5	2 323	42 292	803	648.4	60.7	12 163	636	640.4	D	2 036	660	1 067
Florence	77	136.3	759	12 599	559	388.8	41.1	10 770	397	380.1	2 357	1 867	655	827
Gadsden	106	260.4	1 011	18 995	763	440.2	50.5	9 743	454	422.9	1 243	2 046	424	730
Huntsville	344	D	D	D	1 765	1 450.6	73.5	8 877	1 235	1 426.7	1 413	1 465	563	832
Mobile	607	2 173.4	7 479	153 130	2 303	1 816.9	40.3	8 939	1 661	1 787.3	1 298	1 506	497	833
Montgomery	436	2 260.0	6 539	133 011	1 765	1 468.9	58.0	7 560	1 232	1 446.2	D	1 079	D	723
Phenix City	28	61.4	175	3 136	266	114.6	0.0	4 207	167	107.5	D	1 054	D	526
Prichard	35	144.6	628	11 115	210	81.5	14.0	2 099	126	77.1	49	742	13	78
Selma	56	223.8	586	10 162	371	210.5	30.7	8 200	260	205.7	1 246	2 123	D	488
Tuscaloosa	116	291.5	1 141	18 889	931	713.7	57.9	9 667	712	704.4	1 558	1 593	577	856
ALASKA	778	2 685.5	7 176	204 883	6 266	3 728.1	15.5	6 981	3 522	3 606.2	980	1 708	362	859
Anchorage	479	1 708.5	4 965	146 806	2 314	1 994.3	11.1	8 486	1 403	1 952.5	1 575	1 603	538	1 191
ARIZONA	5 874	20 776.8	64 687	1 420 256	31 519	22 359.9	60.9	6 893	19 798	21 778.4	764	1 536	257	681
Chandler	76	225.1	881	18 529	530	330.9	128.5	4 850	259	317.6	D	1 444	164	516
Flagstaff	90	D	D	D	639	417.9	47.8	10 666	471	408.9	1 519	2 036	D	1 331
Glendale	144	370.3	1 697	32 192	1 136	992.0	72.0	7 884	613	965.9	509	1 510	118	492
Mesa	249	553.1	2 146	41 717	2 300	2 291.0	104.4	9 112	1 466	2 250.8	1 678	1 673	401	755
Phoenix	2 412	12 583.2	34 695	828 140	8 427	6 905.9	54.0	7 724	5 503	6 758.7	822	1 652	348	826
Scottsdale	374	776.7	2 261	50 289	1 890	1 551.9	71.0	13 963	1 243	1 510.6	1 700	2 278	544	1 599
Tempe	507	1 729.8	5 262	121 205	1 266	1 136.6	55.0	8 328	906	1 115.2	365	2 136	174	1 023
Tucson	682	1 270.0	6 704	130 779	3 840	3 277.0	53.9	9 132	2 897	3 231.1	1 329	1 715	409	875
Yuma	112	219.3	1 145	19 145	602	492.9	60.3	10 434	416	485.1	1 520	1 972	321	965
ARKANSAS	4 024	12 780.7	38 940	705 452	27 040	12 318.7	35.2	5 193	15 096	11 631.7	724	1 051	213	384
El Dorado	70	108.0	478	7 989	407	244.5	35.1	9 584	272	237.1	1 015	2 033	617	531
Fayetteville	81	D	D	D	572	425.1	41.7	10 598	407	416.6	D	1 808	572	867
Fort Smith	278	D	D	D	1 153	748.2	36.7	10 067	818	728.7	D	1 773	D	999
Hot Springs	107	626.9	953	20 010	701	461.6	35.0	12 499	482	450.7	2 051	2 522	406	1 151
Jacksonville	22	D	D	D	268	194.8	68.8	6 570	168	189.6	D	1 014	185	539
Jonesboro	110	201.5	1 041	17 892	589	411.8	48.7	13 704	412	397.9	2 604	2 021	948	944
Little Rock	637	3 161.6	9 737	207 186	2 172	1 615.2	40.8	8 922	1 538	1 590.9	1 411	1 447	661	884
North Little Rock	261	2 466.7	2 808	56 178	939	686.1	32.8	10 798	606	663.5	2 257	1 732	503	846
Pine Bluff	111	259.2	1 115	18 984	713	439.8	29.3	7 172	503	429.2	1 073	1 388	D	539
West Memphis	54	D	D	D	323	276.9	34.9	9 957	212	270.9	D	1 607	D	713
CALIFORNIA	53 773	327 370.4	684 516	17 653 575	268 873	185 958.6	50.0	6 892	157 760	179 801.4	797	1 353	356	741
Alameda	52	346.0	407	11 244	964	716.1	52.7	9 860	664	700.0	2 826	1 410	1 201	878
Alhambra	223	465.9	1 376	27 611	764	658.7	75.3	9 188	378	639.5	1 317	1 104	231	728
Anaheim	916	7 792.9	10 599	279 961	2 517	1 855.7	37.3	7 709	1 411	1 783.3	532	1 484	162	1 114
Antioch	29	74.5	269	5 302	407	318.3	44.9	6 355	233	310.3	1 194	1 648	199	571
Arcadia	102	234.0	684	16 227	661	473.7	19.2	9 922	396	459.2	2 321	2 002	717	1 203
Azusa	55	139.8	795	18 642	261	287.3	165.8	8 036	153	282.0	D	1 051	198	538
Bakersfield	392	1 916.8	4 036	103 185	1 774	1 621.1	45.5	10 779	1 210	1 588.6	1 564	1 781	435	965
Baldwin Park	67	164.3	655	14 567	348	169.1	76.0	2 682	169	161.9	D	907	27	277
Bell	57	360.9	775	20 422	203	122.5	36.9	4 189	110	116.7	D	1 961	170	504
Bellflower	49	80.0	431	10 018	559	341.2	10.9	5 829	293	327.0	D	836	103	623
Bell Gardens	42	165.1	440	9 995	211	89.6	26.6	2 426	119	85.4	D	815	70	125
Berkeley	152	D	D	D	1 222	850.7	45.4	8 171	877	830.8	D	1 518	373	1 110
Beverly Hills	177	748.1	1 164	37 983	1 019	972.4	38.7	28 863	663	941.2	D	1 305	7 787	3 401
Brea	167	1 326.5	2 149	55 076	476	375.0	56.4	11 468	305	362.2	2 432	1 390	2 442	1 143
Buena Park	166	1 527.9	2 827	89 581	722	650.3	28.6	9 828	433	635.0	1 310	1 496	483	896
Burbank	323	1 159.0	3 562	97 879	1 033	788.7	70.9	8 850	511	760.3	D	1 662	144	1 118
Burlingame	259	1 093.9	3 006	65 988	423	450.1	55.4	17 140	291	441.0	D	2 494	615	2 295
Camarillo	78	302.7	1 455	27 941	463	324.6	85.2	7 285	259	312.1	D	1 597	108	754
Campbell	126	433.9	1 078	30 853	508	384.4	23.2	11 256	362	376.8	D	1 687	478	1 465
Carlsbad	112	296.8	1 270	30 298	744	675.4	70.3	13 295	398	658.7	2 043	1 763	529	841
Carson	363	12 141.7	8 769	257 646	636	588.0	35.9	6 694	367	578.9	782	1 070	291	450
Cerritos	253	2 379.8	4 423	119 422	831	1 183.2	96.2	20 693	330	1 146.9	4 217	1 043	1 556	933
Chico	131	430.5	1 155	25 185	695	419.8	42.5	12 846	477	407.8	714	2 630	582	1 461
Chino	98	350.7	1 058	25 810	522	306.6	98.7	6 032	223	291.6	D	1 360	344	591
Chula Vista	159	329.1	1 151	21 019	990	718.4	66.9	6 045	562	698.3	1 583	1 164	295	588
Claremont	30	188.2	253	8 610	320	256.6	123.7	7 405	173	247.6	D	1 681	76	1 280
Clovis	54	D	D	D	477	380.8	70.9	9 267	293	372.3	D	2 350	232	713

1. For the period including March 12 of the year shown. 2. Based on resident population estimated as of July 1, 1986.

City	Retail trade–establishment with payroll, 1987 (cont'd): Paid employees[1]: Number	Retail trade (cont'd): Paid employees[1]: Percent change, 1982–1987	Retail trade (cont'd): Annual payroll (Mil. dol.)	Taxable service industries–establishments with payroll, 1987: Number	Taxable service: Receipts (Mil. dol.): Total	Taxable service: Receipts: Selected kinds of business: Hotels, motels, and other lodging places	Taxable service: Receipts: Selected kinds of business: Health services	Taxable service: Receipts: Selected kinds of business: Legal services	Taxable service: Paid employees[1]	Taxable service: Annual payroll (Mil. dol.)	Federal grants, 1986: Procurement contract awards (Mil. dol.)	Federal grants, 1986: Grant awards (Mil. dol.)	Federal government civilian employment, 1984
	87	88	89	90	91	92	93	94	95	96	97	98	99
ALABAMA	249 847	29.9	2 357.5	20 474	8 397.2	350.7	2 874.5	562.0	189 566	3 066.9	2 266.3	1 825.1	59 771
Anniston	4 118	15.6	41.7	347	95.7	D	41.8	9.8	2 465	38.5	24.2	5.9	235
Auburn	3 486	28.6	30.3	139	35.9	D	D	D	954	12.6	6.8	19.5	201
Bessemer	2 867	26.1	31.6	189	47.9	3.8	21.2	4.2	1 313	17.8	0.4	2.4	170
Birmingham	26 495	21.2	266.3	2 428	2 085.6	52.1	583.1	211.7	35 830	722.0	176.1	115.6	7 581
Decatur	5 480	35.3	55.9	444	154.1	D	68.7	7.9	4 240	59.4	41.5	2.1	2 751
Dothan	7 486	38.1	73.6	571	D	D	D	8.3	D	D	11.4	3.2	352
Florence	4 579	10.3	41.3	379	115.4	D	66.5	D	2 680	42.3	3.4	2.2	217
Gadsden	4 986	28.5	43.7	402	117.9	D	66.9	D	3 195	50.8	61.7	4.9	288
Huntsville	16 901	41.8	166.6	1 451	D	D	250.9	D	D	D	1 048.5	20.7	2 208
Mobile	22 478	27.0	215.6	1 904	832.8	30.3	332.2	D	19 222	322.6	77.3	27.2	2 321
Montgomery	16 745	32.0	167.5	1 447	612.0	41.4	226.0	52.3	14 344	242.9	42.0	239.6	2 793
Phenix City	1 480	D	12.7	156	32.2	D	D	3.4	980	10.4	0.0	3.3	47
Prichard	841	10.2	8.6	75	22.3	D	4.6	0.0	577	7.4	NA	1.6	0
Selma	2 254	-10.2	21.7	243	77.9	3.0	D	3.9	1 914	26.9	59.7	2.7	130
Tuscaloosa	8 721	22.4	82.0	558	182.9	11.6	68.0	16.6	4 069	70.0	20.8	9.5	1 486
ALASKA	35 967	19.8	483.5	3 949	1 544.3	174.4	369.0	205.2	27 555	591.6	759.4	693.9	13 882
Anchorage	19 703	24.7	267.0	2 123	1 064.1	85.8	241.6	169.2	18 302	420.4	191.6	151.9	5 968
ARIZONA	260 512	31.5	2 624.3	25 250	10 639.5	1 072.7	2 570.9	888.7	243 999	4 011.3	3 252.7	1 340.7	34 565
Chandler	3 977	126.9	38.5	342	88.1	4.3	29.6	3.1	2 635	30.8	3.3	3.6	125
Flagstaff	5 763	26.7	51.5	467	135.8	24.2	27.6	7.1	3 490	41.5	3.1	9.2	649
Glendale	8 732	50.0	103.6	741	191.4	1.9	66.4	2.8	4 557	68.2	1.3	3.8	241
Mesa	24 258	58.7	253.2	1 811	625.0	38.0	237.0	29.3	15 075	233.5	411.2	4.1	549
Phoenix	82 287	27.9	856.1	9 130	5 049.9	339.4	958.0	621.6	103 944	1 959.3	262.4	247.4	10 553
Scottsdale	17 826	33.3	191.4	1 940	764.4	169.1	161.5	23.9	19 837	302.8	329.3	5.0	489
Tempe	14 668	32.7	144.0	1 309	598.1	42.3	108.0	14.8	14 608	210.8	200.4	16.9	307
Tucson	39 381	21.0	388.6	3 768	1 570.2	81.6	530.4	134.7	38 348	620.2	1 288.7	94.4	4 376
Yuma	5 957	35.3	55.4	431	123.0	14.3	41.6	6.8	3 374	47.1	53.0	3.8	1 070
ARKANSAS	138 671	21.6	1 245.8	12 437	3 703.2	237.8	1 515.5	241.1	93 960	1 365.9	1 021.4	1 097.4	18 260
El Dorado	3 088	28.9	26.0	256	68.8	3.6	28.5	D	1 641	23.7	4.1	2.2	156
Fayetteville	5 312	4.8	47.1	435	120.0	6.0	53.2	11.1	2 694	44.3	4.2	23.0	776
Fort Smith	9 386	20.9	86.0	699	317.4	D	D	14.5	7 725	119.4	9.2	2.5	683
Hot Springs	5 925	13.1	51.8	481	180.7	22.9	81.3	6.2	5 278	64.8	3.4	2.1	316
Jacksonville	2 030	39.1	18.9	135	26.0	D	11.6	0.8	909	10.1	0.3	2.1	234
Jonesboro	4 566	15.7	42.0	388	133.5	D	69.8	D	3 103	55.3	0.6	2.4	297
Little Rock	19 957	34.6	190.3	2 203	998.4	41.1	350.0	108.5	21 838	407.6	40.8	206.7	4 722
North Little Rock	8 208	32.1	77.3	536	159.6	11.8	56.0	5.7	4 473	58.8	5.7	3.6	1 816
Pine Bluff	5 310	15.8	48.4	423	118.3	D	58.0	8.0	2 582	44.5	5.4	11.6	1 551
West Memphis	2 863	27.6	24.7	181	79.0	7.1	18.4	2.6	1 417	21.9	0.1	1.7	64
CALIFORNIA	2 022 068	24.6	22 731.7	222 636	128 546.0	6 028.5	28 009.4	10 419.4	2 248 466	47 369.0	35 228.3	13 017.0	307 257
Alameda	8 745	25.1	94.6	480	226.3	2.1	42.0	6.9	4 573	95.2	24.4	2.8	6 483
Alhambra	5 609	35.5	67.2	453	572.8	D	47.1	D	4 013	93.6	1.6	1.9	1 102
Anaheim	22 070	19.1	238.4	2 172	1 941.3	244.7	408.0	13.9	39 993	680.7	1 047.1	5.6	985
Antioch	3 379	18.1	40.9	277	76.9	D	38.4	2.2	1 703	26.9	2.5	1.3	69
Arcadia	6 515	1.8	61.6	609	331.3	7.1	103.9	5.8	6 242	116.4	10.1	1.9	171
Azusa	2 085	25.6	25.4	141	51.7	1.1	12.6	D	1 101	17.5	131.4	0.6	94
Bakersfield	17 737	21.1	197.7	1 653	696.3	30.1	236.1	58.6	14 525	267.3	29.6	17.0	1 138
Baldwin Park	1 808	50.9	18.7	158	54.4	2.2	27.6	D	1 461	21.7	1.2	8.3	69
Bell	1 277	30.4	13.8	92	29.1	1.5	9.8	D	878	9.9	1.0	0.9	1 421
Bellflower	3 598	9.4	40.3	367	220.3	2.4	139.2	1.5	4 888	86.7	0.1	0.9	140
Bell Gardens	850	11.5	9.4	89	120.7	0.4	17.5	D	2 568	34.1	0.5	0.8	1
Berkeley	11 669	35.4	134.2	1 183	508.1	39.7	124.1	13.9	8 173	191.6	1 224.5	129.0	598
Beverly Hills	9 968	9.2	156.0	3 035	2 028.0	119.0	321.5	343.8	23 754	841.4	1.3	0.3	239
Brea	5 017	47.2	48.0	354	180.0	D	81.3	5.6	3 431	60.3	9.2	0.7	77
Buena Park	6 787	12.8	74.0	326	267.8	22.2	36.4	D	6 496	92.4	2.0	1.8	124
Burbank	7 732	32.0	83.3	1 230	2 859.5	23.0	140.1	6.5	35 422	1 049.2	314.8	4.9	483
Burlingame	4 009	5.0	57.2	579	434.3	66.9	71.5	22.5	7 694	142.7	12.0	3.8	257
Camarillo	3 290	44.0	34.6	393	276.9	5.5	38.7	2.8	5 880	111.1	132.4	0.5	103
Campbell	4 848	6.2	53.5	541	230.4	D	14.3	7.8	4 201	84.3	8.1	0.3	125
Carlsbad	6 783	31.2	76.8	483	253.4	64.7	24.1	9.0	5 276	92.5	35.6	0.7	79
Carson	5 336	22.8	63.7	326	337.8	D	17.3	1.4	5 089	91.0	415.1	3.4	258
Cerritos	8 753	23.9	117.2	300	200.8	D	55.6	6.8	6 100	80.7	8.6	1.2	1
Chico	5 867	18.0	52.7	571	214.2	7.8	122.3	8.3	4 925	79.2	1.7	3.2	212
Chino	3 275	93.9	32.3	278	97.5	1.5	32.3	0.8	1 938	31.5	0.9	1.5	119
Chula Vista	8 115	40.6	79.7	594	226.0	15.5	91.5	5.7	4 490	86.4	23.5	3.4	705
Claremont	2 889	51.3	30.1	274	89.2	D	30.2	20.7	1 702	32.1	1.4	2.6	13
Clovis	3 525	48.5	40.1	281	59.0	D	17.8	1.3	1 450	18.5	0.4	0.7	75

1. For the period including March 12 of the year shown.

City	City government employment, 1985 (October)			Form of government[2] (As of 1986)	City government finances, 1984–1985												
					General revenue							General expenditures					
						Intergovernmental		Taxes					Per capita[3] (Dol.)		Percent of total for–		
									Per capita[3] (Dollars)								
	Total	Rates[1]	Percent education		Total (Mil. dol.)	Total (Mil. dol.)	Percent from State government	Total (Mil. dol.)	Total	Property	Sales & gross receipts	Total (Mil. dol.)	Total	Capital outlays	Public welfare	Highways	Education
	100	101	102	103	104	105	106	107	108	109	110	111	112	113	114	115	116
ALABAMA	NA	NA	NA	NA	NA	NA	NA	NA	NA	NA	NA	NA	NA	NA	NA	NA	NA
Anniston	421	143.3	0.0	2	59.3	3.0	20.3	9.3	315	35	211	54.3	1 849	203	0.1	3.7	0.4
Auburn	338	113.6	0.0	2	12.1	1.5	17.6	6.8	228	48	76	10.4	349	55	0.6	9.9	12.1
Bessemer	358	111.8	0.0	3	11.6	2.9	27.9	7.1	222	61	120	17.4	544	165	0.0	2.4	4.2
Birmingham	3 658	131.8	0.0	1	202.0	32.1	20.7	105.1	379	67	120	200.4	722	127	0.0	8.8	2.9
Decatur	1 284	285.3	0.0	1	54.1	2.6	64.4	13.4	299	68	200	52.3	1 163	291	0.1	6.2	9.7
Dothan	778	145.9	0.0	1	22.5	3.0	27.0	12.3	230	23	181	24.4	458	50	0.0	5.2	9.4
Florence	657	182.0	0.0	1	13.1	2.0	43.1	7.5	208	56	121	13.2	366	25	0.0	13.4	13.5
Gadsden	793	175.5	0.0	3	23.0	3.9	23.7	14.0	310	28	9	21.1	467	36	0.1	4.7	1.2
Huntsville	3 881	237.5	0.0	1	81.9	10.1	31.1	49.1	300	49	212	74.2	454	93	0.1	18.1	5.4
Mobile	2 170	106.8	0.0	3	116.1	9.1	46.7	55.7	274	25	179	94.3	464	44	0.0	4.3	0.0
Montgomery	2 448	126.0	0.0	1	72.1	13.3	22.2	43.9	226	35	136	65.7	338	46	0.9	7.9	0.7
Phenix City	NA	NA	NA	2	38.0	1.8	42.8	4.9	178	27	113	34.7	1 273	38	NA	3.6	1.3
Prichard	321	82.7	0.0	1	7.8	1.9	38.3	4.1	107	6	74	7.3	188	14	0.6	8.8	0.0
Selma	411	160.1	0.0	1	17.7	3.0	39.4	10.0	390	95	230	16.2	629	159	0.0	3.2	8.1
Tuscaloosa	823	111.5	0.0	3	25.1	4.6	15.0	13.3	181	35	81	26.2	355	79	0.0	14.1	0.9
ALASKA	NA	NA	NA	NA	NA	NA	NA	NA	NA	NA	NA	NA	NA	NA	NA	NA	NA
Anchorage	9 202	391.6	57.7	1	722.4	387.7	94.7	124.0	528	492	14	684.0	2 911	742	1.0	5.0	42.5
ARIZONA	NA	NA	NA	NA	NA	NA	NA	NA	NA	NA	NA	NA	NA	NA	NA	NA	NA
Chandler	478	70.1	0.0	2	53.0	6.9	83.3	11.2	165	31	92	91.5	1 341	893	0.0	5.3	0.0
Flagstaff	508	129.7	0.0	2	26.8	11.1	71.0	7.6	193	66	116	26.8	683	255	0.0	18.4	0.0
Glendale	1 024	81.4	0.0	2	59.4	21.4	83.1	17.2	137	35	82	55.9	444	138	0.7	20.0	0.0
Mesa	1 805	71.8	0.0	2	120.1	33.3	82.8	33.0	131	8	111	131.7	524	185	0.1	12.0	0.0
Phoenix	9 788	109.5	0.0	2	673.8	240.3	68.1	197.2	221	75	131	668.8	748	252	0.1	15.8	0.7
Scottsdale	1 107	99.6	0.0	2	77.2	18.2	87.1	32.6	294	61	195	86.9	782	310	0.0	11.9	0.0
Tempe	1 217	89.2	0.0	2	75.7	23.5	81.2	26.2	192	56	123	61.3	450	144	0.0	13.6	0.0
Tucson	4 776	133.1	0.0	2	270.9	94.6	70.4	93.5	261	34	212	249.3	695	168	0.8	13.8	0.0
Yuma	561	118.8	0.0	2	25.8	9.6	88.0	9.4	199	57	133	23.6	500	128	0.0	17.8	0.0
ARKANSAS	NA	NA	NA	NA	NA	NA	NA	NA	NA	NA	NA	NA	NA	NA	NA	NA	NA
El Dorado	269	105.4	0.0	1	7.1	1.9	73.3	1.1	44	21	17	6.9	269	27	0.0	15.2	0.0
Fayetteville	345	86.0	0.0	2	22.0	7.0	28.1	8.5	211	25	181	21.8	543	162	3.5	10.4	0.0
Fort Smith	573	77.1	0.0	2	21.9	6.7	46.5	4.5	60	28	23	18.6	251	38	0.0	12.0	0.0
Hot Springs	457	123.7	0.0	1	15.4	2.9	58.2	6.0	164	18	102	12.6	341	43	0.1	12.8	0.0
Jacksonville	477	160.9	0.0	1	15.4	2.2	60.5	1.0	35	17	15	14.8	499	55	0.0	5.4	0.0
Jonesboro	363	120.8	0.0	1	14.9	4.1	32.8	1.7	57	23	20	11.1	370	23	0.0	9.0	0.0
Little Rock	2 042	112.8	0.0	2	88.6	21.9	58.3	28.1	155	46	78	79.2	438	39	0.0	12.7	0.0
North Little Rock	734	115.5	0.0	1	23.0	6.1	45.8	4.6	72	42	20	26.7	420	29	0.0	10.8	0.0
Pine Bluff	459	74.9	0.0	1	20.3	5.6	45.9	7.8	127	23	95	17.1	279	40	0.2	13.3	0.0
West Memphis	283	101.8	0.0	1	14.9	2.9	51.7	1.7	61	24	15	9.2	330	27	4.3	7.1	0.0
CALIFORNIA	NA	NA	NA	NA	NA	NA	NA	NA	NA	NA	NA	NA	NA	NA	NA	NA	NA
Alameda	604	83.2	0.0	2	32.7	7.7	50.5	15.5	214	82	97	28.4	391	6	0.0	5.9	0.0
Alhambra	499	69.6	0.0	2	30.9	7.5	62.1	14.7	205	74	120	27.9	390	53	0.0	13.8	0.0
Anaheim	3 437	142.8	0.0	2	154.4	21.0	59.9	66.6	277	90	171	156.9	652	50	0.0	5.5	0.0
Antioch	205	40.9	0.0	2	12.3	2.3	70.1	5.6	111	49	56	10.9	218	22	0.0	11.4	0.0
Arcadia	367	76.9	0.0	2	21.0	3.2	77.6	11.4	239	57	166	19.3	405	24	0.0	11.3	0.0
Azusa	275	76.9	0.0	2	14.9	3.3	41.1	4.6	129	44	73	16.6	465	6	0.0	13.7	0.0
Bakersfield	975	64.8	0.0	2	64.4	14.8	71.8	35.0	233	75	142	62.1	413	77	0.0	18.0	0.0
Baldwin Park	234	37.1	0.0	2	13.6	6.6	73.2	4.4	70	25	36	14.0	223	14	0.0	11.9	0.0
Bell	125	42.7	0.0	2	7.1	2.3	54.5	4.0	137	51	45	8.1	276	24	0.0	10.2	0.0
Bellflower	175	29.9	0.0	2	11.0	4.4	62.2	4.6	78	8	65	11.7	199	29	0.0	26.7	0.0
Bell Gardens	101	27.3	0.0	2	9.0	3.8	49.3	4.1	111	29	33	8.8	238	81	0.0	4.9	0.0
Berkeley	NA	NA	NA	2	76.2	15.5	61.6	30.6	294	107	112	78.5	754	27	0.0	5.5	0.0
Beverly Hills	902	267.7	0.0	2	63.4	2.9	77.0	36.7	1 090	270	412	81.1	2 407	949	0.0	8.1	0.0
Brea	330	100.9	0.0	2	23.5	3.0	76.9	17.4	532	336	169	19.2	587	116	0.0	12.3	0.0
Buena Park	469	70.9	0.0	2	26.8	4.8	60.8	17.2	260	64	181	27.5	415	75	0.0	12.8	0.0
Burbank	1 155	129.6	0.0	2	71.3	14.4	79.9	35.8	402	171	208	72.0	808	172	0.0	7.7	0.0
Burlingame	NA	NA	NA	2	19.0	1.9	77.0	11.8	451	100	329	17.7	673	154	0.0	17.5	0.0
Camarillo	114	25.6	0.0	2	12.1	2.6	92.9	4.8	107	22	62	9.9	223	51	0.0	25.7	0.0
Campbell	196	57.4	0.0	2	13.6	2.4	67.2	8.1	237	59	161	11.8	345	26	0.0	13.0	0.0
Carlsbad	440	86.6	0.0	2	36.1	4.0	75.4	21.5	423	106	143	24.0	472	94	0.0	20.1	0.0
Carson	531	60.5	0.0	2	39.1	7.4	72.1	20.9	238	63	149	31.2	355	27	0.0	10.5	0.0
Cerritos	290	50.7	0.0	2	36.9	4.4	79.1	23.5	411	185	209	43.7	764	416	0.0	2.6	0.0
Chico	270	82.6	0.0	2	17.8	4.0	52.8	7.8	238	57	169	17.8	544	122	0.0	16.7	0.0
Chino	264	51.9	0.0	2	18.1	3.8	76.6	7.7	152	58	60	16.4	323	36	0.0	10.8	0.0
Chula Vista	608	51.2	0.0	2	34.6	6.5	66.2	16.9	142	55	74	36.2	305	52	0.0	10.3	0.0
Claremont	187	54.0	0.0	2	11.8	2.1	79.8	5.1	148	71	52	9.7	279	46	0.0	9.3	0.0
Clovis	301	73.3	0.0	2	11.9	2.9	81.4	5.7	140	52	67	11.0	268	62	0.0	19.4	0.4

1. Per 10,000 population estimated as of July 1, 1986. 2. 1=Mayor-council; 2=Council-manager; 3=Commission. Data subject to copyright. 3. Based on resident population estimated as of July 1, 1986.

City	City government finances, 1984–1985 (cont'd)								Climate[2]							Typical monthly electric bills, 1986		
	General expenditure (cont'd)					Debt outstanding			Average daily temperature (Degrees Fahrenheit)							Residential[6]		
	Percent of total for (cont'd)								Mean		Limits							
	Health and hospitals	Police protection	Sewerage and sanitation	Parks and recreation	Housing and community development	Total (Mil. dol.)	Per capita[1] (Dollars)	Percent utility	Jan.	July	Jan.[3]	July[4]	Annual precipitation (Inches)	Heating degree days[5]	Cooling degree days[5]	Total (Dollars)	Percent change, 1980–1986	Commercial[7] (Dollars)
	117	118	119	120	121	122	123	124	125	126	127	128	129	130	131	132	133	134
ALABAMA	NA	NA	NA	NA	NA	NA	NA	NA	NA	NA	NA	NA	NA	NA	NA	51.26	50.8	NA
Anniston	69.0	3.9	1.9	2.2	2.0	55.3	1 883	27.0	43.0	79.8	32.3	91.0	53.25	2 872	1 809	54.94	46.9	NA
Auburn	2.5	15.4	16.5	6.4	4.5	11.5	385	49.3	44.6	79.6	33.7	90.6	56.10	2 611	1 921	54.94	46.9	NA
Bessemer	0.4	12.6	12.7	0.6	3.1	10.1	315	47.9	42.4	80.3	33.0	90.6	52.15	2 943	1 891	37.61	60.5	NA
Birmingham	0.8	10.7	9.4	10.4	4.9	435.8	1 571	0.0	42.4	80.3	33.0	90.6	52.15	2 943	1 891	54.94	46.9	498.0
Decatur	48.1	4.1	9.3	5.8	1.1	78.5	1 744	6.5	40.2	79.3	31.0	89.4	54.74	3 279	1 708	34.84	72.6	NA
Dothan	0.1	11.8	24.8	7.7	0.0	45.9	862	13.1	49.2	80.4	38.1	91.4	54.58	1 928	2 293	47.59	53.3	NA
Florence	0.8	16.9	12.9	10.5	0.0	36.8	1 018	66.0	39.8	79.9	30.6	90.5	51.58	3 315	1 788	39.66	69.2	NA
Gadsden	0.9	15.7	20.1	8.3	6.4	21.0	466	39.3	41.0	79.1	31.0	90.4	54.09	3 160	1 671	54.94	46.9	NA
Huntsville	2.1	10.1	11.0	8.0	6.4	119.3	730	8.7	40.2	79.3	31.0	89.4	54.74	3 279	1 708	36.51	76.0	327.4
Mobile	0.4	12.3	14.0	4.6	0.0	452.9	2 228	14.9	50.8	82.2	40.9	91.2	64.64	1 695	2 643	54.94	46.9	498.0
Montgomery	1.1	17.9	17.5	14.7	0.9	67.3	346	24.7	46.7	81.7	36.4	91.5	49.16	2 277	2 274	54.94	46.9	498.0
Phenix City	71.4	4.0	3.8	2.5	0.0	55.3	2 030	15.5	46.2	81.0	35.4	91.1	51.09	2 356	2 152	54.94	46.9	NA
Prichard	0.1	23.1	23.8	3.7	0.0	12.0	309	64.1	50.8	82.2	40.9	91.2	64.64	1 695	2 643	54.94	46.9	NA
Selma	NA	11.2	5.1	4.2	12.9	29.8	1 160	2.6	48.1	82.1	37.8	92.8	53.51	2 040	2 433	54.94	46.9	NA
Tuscaloosa	1.3	20.1	19.7	2.4	6.8	42.5	575	80.3	43.8	81.3	33.5	91.8	52.61	2 675	2 102	54.94	46.9	498.0
ALASKA	NA	NA	NA	NA	NA	NA	NA	NA	NA	NA	NA	NA	NA	NA	NA	52.62	57.0	NA
Anchorage	2.0	5.5	6.8	1.6	0.0	752.5	3 202	23.4	13.0	58.1	6.0	65.1	15.20	10 816	0	48.87	76.0	500.4
ARIZONA	NA	NA	NA	NA	NA	NA	NA	NA	NA	NA	NA	NA	NA	NA	NA	60.43	47.6	NA
Chandler	0.0	3.8	62.2	1.8	0.3	284.9	4 176	10.7	51.1	90.0	37.0	104.6	7.85	1 598	3 296	57.99	47.6	NA
Flagstaff	0.0	10.8	11.5	3.6	8.1	31.4	801	54.0	28.2	66.1	14.7	81.9	20.86	7 254	127	65.84	54.8	NA
Glendale	0.0	12.1	7.5	6.4	3.4	89.0	707	83.3	52.3	92.3	39.4	105.0	7.11	1 442	3 746	57.99	47.6	454.3
Mesa	0.0	17.0	23.2	7.5	3.1	343.3	1 365	57.0	51.1	90.0	37.0	104.6	7.85	1 598	3 296	57.99	47.6	454.3
Phoenix	0.1	14.3	14.2	8.3	4.5	1 311.8	1 467	16.4	52.3	92.3	39.4	105.0	7.11	1 442	3 746	58.91	47.8	648.8
Scottsdale	0.0	9.7	13.0	8.4	1.5	195.3	1 758	8.3	51.1	90.0	37.0	104.6	7.85	1 598	3 296	57.99	47.6	643.2
Tempe	0.1	21.4	16.6	10.2	8.2	103.5	759	49.5	50.9	89.7	36.2	105.0	8.00	1 654	3 160	57.99	47.6	454.3
Tucson	0.0	13.3	6.5	9.5	6.4	626.6	1 746	18.7	51.1	86.2	38.1	98.5	11.14	1 734	2 840	53.80	35.9	479.3
Yuma	0.1	15.5	20.3	17.2	2.1	12.4	263	62.5	55.9	93.6	43.2	106.8	2.65	983	4 244	65.84	53.4	NA
ARKANSAS	NA	NA	NA	NA	NA	NA	NA	NA	NA	NA	NA	NA	NA	NA	NA	55.25	93.3	NA
El Dorado	0.3	18.5	26.0	5.8	0.0	7.7	300	12.3	43.1	81.8	32.4	92.6	49.12	2 755	2 109	61.37	102.3	NA
Fayetteville	1.2	6.3	36.7	2.5	2.0	74.3	1 853	5.4	34.8	78.3	23.3	89.9	43.91	4 174	1 366	37.63	70.3	NA
Fort Smith	0.2	17.0	21.1	3.1	7.6	26.7	359	59.2	37.5	82.1	26.6	93.6	39.91	3 477	1 969	48.26	105.9	388.3
Hot Springs	0.7	13.2	25.3	0.7	0.0	16.1	436	26.7	41.4	82.2	31.3	93.4	55.38	2 932	2 147	61.37	102.3	NA
Jacksonville	48.8	8.6	9.6	2.1	3.2	11.9	403	19.8	39.5	81.7	30.3	91.6	46.26	3 163	1 999	61.37	102.3	NA
Jonesboro	0.5	9.4	13.2	1.3	25.8	111.0	3 693	61.8	37.6	81.5	28.6	92.1	47.62	3 521	1 946	40.38	41.9	NA
Little Rock	0.5	12.6	10.7	6.3	4.8	220.3	1 217	5.9	39.9	82.1	29.9	92.7	49.20	3 152	2 045	61.37	102.3	457.1
North Little Rock	0.6	17.4	20.1	5.6	0.0	71.6	1 126	13.2	39.5	81.7	30.3	91.6	46.26	3 163	1 999	57.52	128.5	450.1
Pine Bluff	0.3	18.0	13.6	11.1	10.1	23.5	383	0.0	42.9	82.7	33.0	93.6	50.28	2 729	2 272	61.37	102.3	457.1
West Memphis	1.5	12.7	14.8	1.1	4.7	75.6	2 717	34.2	39.6	82.1	30.9	91.5	51.57	3 207	2 067	51.41	46.6	NA
CALIFORNIA	NA	NA	NA	NA	NA	NA	NA	NA	NA	NA	NA	NA	NA	NA	NA	60.90	77.9	NA
Alameda	0.0	21.6	2.4	10.1	13.9	84.0	1 157	12.7	49.0	63.7	43.4	70.6	18.03	2 877	174	65.89	144.4	421.5
Alhambra	0.0	21.4	9.6	9.8	7.1	34.5	481	0.0	54.8	74.8	41.3	89.1	17.76	1 532	1 281	56.07	63.0	558.2
Anaheim	0.0	17.2	7.2	31.1	9.4	485.7	2 017	48.7	55.9	72.2	44.1	82.9	12.60	1 430	1 089	69.22	72.8	600.9
Antioch	0.0	34.7	5.5	15.2	0.0	2.7	54	54.4	45.2	78.0	37.5	95.0	13.77	2 674	1 448	66.97	148.4	NA
Arcadia	0.0	24.6	2.3	3.8	4.0	23.6	495	0.0	54.8	74.8	41.3	89.1	17.76	1 532	1 281	56.07	63.0	NA
Azusa	3.5	19.4	2.9	8.0	1.1	47.9	1 339	0.0	52.2	74.4	40.7	89.7	17.13	2 048	1 134	64.88	47.0	NA
Bakersfield	0.0	22.7	16.2	7.7	4.1	21.6	143	63.7	48.2	84.5	38.9	98.8	5.72	2 128	2 347	66.97	148.4	NA
Baldwin Park	NA	19.0	0.0	2.8	16.4	65.4	1 037	0.0	54.8	74.8	41.3	89.1	17.76	1 532	1 281	56.07	63.0	558.2
Bell	0.0	53.9	3.8	9.4	3.8	0.4	12	0.0	57.2	74.1	47.7	83.8	14.85	1 204	1 339	56.07	63.0	NA
Bellflower	0.0	23.0	0.0	15.0	18.8	0.0	0	0.0	57.2	74.1	47.7	83.8	14.85	1 204	1 339	56.07	63.0	558.2
Bell Gardens	0.0	27.9	1.6	4.6	37.9	0.0	0	0.0	57.2	74.1	47.7	83.8	14.85	1 204	1 339	56.07	63.0	NA
Berkeley	5.0	12.5	9.2	8.2	7.2	15.9	153	0.0	49.7	61.7	43.2	69.5	23.24	2 951	91	66.97	148.4	NA
Beverly Hills	0.0	14.4	4.1	6.4	0.1	104.6	3 104	6.3	57.5	68.7	49.7	76.7	17.39	1 509	796	56.07	63.0	NA
Brea	0.0	24.1	2.9	5.4	12.0	36.7	1 121	4.3	54.9	73.5	42.4	88.8	14.46	1 644	1 118	56.07	63.0	NA
Buena Park	0.0	23.3	4.0	5.6	12.3	21.3	322	8.7	54.9	73.5	42.4	88.8	14.46	1 644	1 118	56.07	63.0	558.2
Burbank	0.0	16.0	8.1	22.0	7.1	82.4	924	4.0	53.8	75.1	41.3	89.4	15.78	1 679	1 292	55.29	-10.3	439.0
Burlingame	0.0	15.1	17.1	11.1	0.0	3.9	147	0.0	48.5	62.2	41.5	71.0	19.71	3 161	115	66.97	148.4	NA
Camarillo	0.0	21.3	16.3	0.0	0.0	1.9	42	72.2	54.6	65.7	43.5	74.7	14.53	2 068	357	56.07	63.0	NA
Campbell	0.0	26.0	2.5	4.6	0.5	4.7	136	0.0	49.5	68.8	41.1	81.5	13.86	2 439	498	66.97	148.4	NA
Carlsbad	0.0	18.6	6.0	8.1	5.3	17.7	349	5.1	52.2	73.3	38.7	87.8	14.53	2 006	980	73.58	77.5	NA
Carson	0.3	12.6	0.3	17.7	7.9	97.2	1 106	0.0	55.1	69.1	44.1	78.3	13.13	1 719	677	56.07	63.0	558.2
Cerritos	0.0	7.1	3.4	7.8	57.8	57.7	1 010	2.8	56.0	69.0	47.3	75.3	12.08	1 595	728	56.07	63.0	558.2
Chico	0.0	19.8	6.5	4.1	3.3	44.0	1 345	0.0	44.8	78.1	36.0	95.4	25.93	2 878	1 414	66.97	148.4	NA
Chino	0.0	26.4	17.1	6.6	0.5	6.7	131	15.6	52.4	74.6	39.0	90.9	17.02	1 972	1 191	56.07	63.0	NA
Chula Vista	0.0	14.5	6.3	7.8	13.5	108.8	915	0.0	53.4	66.9	44.0	71.1	8.67	2 074	385	73.58	77.5	772.9
Claremont	0.0	25.3	9.3	15.8	7.2	4.4	127	0.0	52.2	74.4	40.7	89.7	17.13	2 048	1 134	56.07	63.0	NA
Clovis	0.0	22.8	22.7	6.4	0.0	4.9	120	0.0	45.5	81.0	36.8	97.9	10.52	2 647	1 769	66.97	148.4	NA

1. Based on resident population estimated as of July 1, 1986. 2. Represents normal values based on the 30-year period, 1951–1980 (see text). 3. Average daily minimum. 4. Average daily maximum. 5. For definition, see text. 6. As of January 1; based on consumption of 750 kWh. 7. Based on billing demand of 30 kW and consumption of 6,000 kWh.

MSA/ CMSA Code[1]	State/ Place code	City	Land area,[2] 1990 (Sq. Km.)	Population: 1990: Total persons	Population: 1990: Rank	Population: 1990: Per sq. km.	Population: 1980	Population: Change 1980–1990: Number	Population: Change 1980–1990: Per-cent	Population characteristics, 1990: Percent: Race: White	Race: Black	Race: Am. Indian, Eskimo, Aleut	Race: Asian & Pacific Islander	Race: Other race	His-panic[3]	65 Years and over
			1	2	3	4	5	6	7	8	9	10	11	12	13	14
		CALIFORNIA—Con.														
4472	06 0590	Compton	26.3	90 454	222	3 439	81 350	9 104	11.2	10.58	54.83	0.32	1.93	32.34	43.68	5.7
7362	06 0595	Concord	76.3	111 348	162	1 459	103 763	7 585	7.3	84.03	2.36	0.69	8.68	4.25	11.46	9.5
4472	06 0610	Corona	73.8	76 095	280	1 031	37 791	38 304	101.4	75.88	2.76	0.83	7.10	13.43	30.36	5.8
4472	06 0625	Costa Mesa	40.3	96 357	205	2 391	82 562	13 795	16.7	84.31	1.33	0.49	6.56	7.31	20.05	8.2
4472	06 0635	Covina	17.9	43 207	574	2 414	32 746	10 461	31.9	80.28	4.11	0.51	7.59	7.50	25.56	10.8
4472	06 0665	Culver City	13.2	38 793	651	2 939	38 139	654	1.7	69.22	10.38	0.58	12.04	7.79	19.76	13.3
7362	06 0670	Cupertino	26.7	40 263	623	1 508	34 297	5 966	17.4	74.44	0.91	0.33	23.01	1.30	4.93	8.8
4472	06 0685	Cypress	17.1	42 655	583	2 494	40 738	1 917	4.7	79.17	2.04	0.54	13.69	4.56	13.52	7.5
7362	06 0700	Daly City	19.5	92 311	219	4 734	78 519	13 792	17.6	39.45	7.70	0.42	43.84	8.59	22.35	10.5
6920	06 0715	Davis	21.9	46 209	536	2 110	36 640	9 569	26.1	79.75	3.01	0.73	13.16	3.35	7.41	6.2
4472	06 0795	Downey	32.2	91 444	220	2 840	82 602	8 842	10.7	72.53	3.36	0.64	8.83	14.65	32.34	13.4
7320	06 0850	El Cajon	37.3	88 693	227	2 378	73 892	14 801	20.0	87.36	2.92	0.98	2.82	5.93	13.97	10.9
4472	06 0880	El Monte	24.6	106 209	179	4 317	79 494	26 715	33.6	62.23	0.99	0.56	11.76	24.46	72.49	6.4
7320	06 0935	Escondido	92.3	108 635	174	1 177	64 355	44 280	68.8	85.15	1.46	0.83	3.72	8.84	23.36	13.0
7362	06 0960	Fairfield	92.9	77 211	275	831	58 099	19 112	32.9	68.17	13.80	1.02	10.70	6.31	13.22	6.4
4472	06 1030	Fontana	92.3	87 535	231	948	36 804	50 731	137.8	67.75	8.70	0.91	4.53	18.11	36.10	5.5
4472	06 1065	Fountain Valley	23.1	53 691	445	2 324	55 080	-1 389	-2.5	78.23	0.95	0.60	17.73	2.50	8.11	7.3
7362	06 1080	Fremont	199.5	173 339	98	869	131 945	41 394	31.4	70.60	3.79	0.70	19.42	5.49	13.32	6.7
2840	06 1090	Fresno	256.8	354 202	47	1 379	217 491	136 711	62.9	59.18	8.30	1.05	12.52	18.94	29.87	10.1
4472	06 1095	Fullerton	57.3	114 144	155	1 992	102 246	11 898	11.6	74.65	2.17	0.46	12.18	10.53	21.29	10.2
4472	06 1105	Gardena	13.7	49 847	493	3 638	45 165	4 682	10.4	32.16	23.50	0.55	33.23	10.56	23.08	10.9
4472	06 1110	Garden Grove	46.5	143 050	120	3 076	123 307	19 743	16.0	67.32	1.50	0.61	20.51	10.06	23.47	8.7
4472	06 1130	Glendale	79.3	180 038	92	2 270	139 060	40 978	29.5	74.02	1.30	0.35	14.14	10.19	20.96	13.3
4472	06 1135	Glendora	50.4	47 828	516	949	38 500	9 328	24.2	88.49	1.12	0.53	5.62	4.24	15.16	10.6
4472	06 1220	Hawthorne	15.4	71 349	310	4 633	56 437	14 912	26.4	42.28	28.33	0.46	10.96	17.98	31.14	7.3
7362	06 1225	Hayward	112.5	111 498	161	991	93 585	17 913	19.1	61.80	9.83	0.97	15.55	11.84	23.92	10.7
4472	06 1300	Huntington Beach	68.4	181 519	90	2 654	170 505	11 014	6.5	86.11	0.93	0.64	8.29	4.03	11.24	8.3
4472	06 1305	Huntington Park	7.9	56 065	418	7 097	45 932	10 133	22.1	31.19	1.06	0.54	1.85	65.37	91.85	5.6
4472	06 1340	Inglewood	23.7	109 602	167	4 625	94 162	15 440	16.4	17.40	51.88	0.39	2.51	27.82	38.55	6.8
4472	06 1347	Irvine	109.6	110 330	165	1 007	62 134	48 196	77.6	77.90	1.81	0.23	18.10	1.95	6.26	5.8
4472	06 1428	La Habra	19.0	51 266	478	2 698	45 232	6 034	13.3	76.55	0.95	0.70	4.06	17.75	33.93	10.7
4472	06 1455	Lakewood	24.3	73 557	295	3 027	74 511	-954	-1.3	81.15	3.69	0.66	9.36	5.14	14.63	12.1
7320	06 1460	La Mesa	23.9	52 931	458	2 215	50 308	2 623	5.2	90.24	3.00	0.53	3.09	3.14	9.78	18.3
4472	06 1462	La Mirada	20.3	40 452	618	1 993	40 986	-534	-1.3	81.23	1.39	0.60	8.24	8.54	25.86	11.4
4472	06 1476	Lancaster	230.0	97 291	202	423	48 027	49 264	102.6	79.38	7.41	0.94	3.72	8.56	15.23	7.9
4472	06 1480	La Puente	9.0	36 955	687	4 106	30 882	6 073	19.7	63.92	3.54	0.65	7.84	24.06	74.86	6.0
7362	06 1570	Livermore	50.8	56 741	413	1 117	48 349	8 392	17.4	89.39	1.52	0.73	4.60	3.76	9.85	7.1
8120	06 1585	Lodi	27.5	51 874	471	1 886	35 221	16 653	47.3	89.29	0.33	0.91	4.72	4.76	16.90	15.7
7480	06 1600	Lompoc	29.1	37 649	676	1 294	26 267	11 382	43.3	70.52	7.85	1.34	5.42	14.87	26.83	8.5
4472	06 1610	Long Beach	129.5	429 433	32	3 316	361 498	67 935	18.8	58.38	13.68	0.65	13.57	13.72	23.62	10.8
7362	06 1620	Los Altos	16.5	26 303	900	1 594	25 769	534	2.1	88.97	0.41	0.18	10.04	0.40	3.02	18.7
4472	06 1630	Los Angeles	1 215.6	3 485 398	2	2 867	2 968 528	516 870	17.4	52.83	13.99	0.47	9.81	22.91	39.92	10.0
7362	06 1640	Los Gatos town	26.9	27 357	877	1 017	26 906	451	1.7	92.75	0.70	0.38	5.04	1.12	5.00	12.7
4472	06 1660	Lynwood	12.6	61 945	367	4 916	48 289	13 656	28.3	23.96	23.65	0.42	2.22	49.75	70.33	5.1
4472	06 1690	Manhattan Beach	10.2	32 063	783	3 143	31 542	521	1.7	93.48	0.64	0.27	4.40	1.21	5.13	8.6
7362	06 1745	Menlo Park	26.1	28 040	869	1 074	26 438	1 602	6.1	79.09	12.36	0.38	5.95	2.22	9.66	17.9
4940	06 1750	Merced	41.8	56 216	416	1 345	36 423	19 793	54.3	61.68	6.87	0.93	15.23	15.29	29.86	9.0
7362	06 1770	Milpitas	35.6	50 686	485	1 424	37 820	12 866	34.0	52.11	5.86	0.95	34.67	6.42	18.61	4.9
5170	06 1790	Modesto	78.2	164 730	103	2 107	106 963	57 767	54.0	80.56	2.68	1.03	7.89	7.84	16.34	10.5
4472	06 1800	Monrovia	34.6	35 761	702	1 034	30 531	5 230	17.1	69.66	10.14	0.53	4.53	15.14	28.46	10.8
4472	06 1820	Montebello	21.4	59 564	392	2 783	52 929	6 635	12.5	47.05	0.97	0.47	15.11	36.40	67.60	11.9
7120	06 1825	Monterey	21.8	31 954	787	1 466	27 558	4 396	16.0	86.62	2.93	0.55	7.32	2.58	7.81	12.9
4472	06 1830	Monterey Park	19.8	60 738	379	3 068	54 338	6 400	11.8	26.75	0.64	0.33	57.46	14.83	31.33	13.8
7362	06 1860	Mountain View	31.2	67 460	336	2 162	58 655	8 805	15.0	72.73	5.03	0.58	14.72	6.94	16.04	9.8
7362	06 1884	Napa	45.1	61 842	369	1 371	50 879	10 963	21.5	90.30	0.38	0.77	2.09	6.46	15.24	14.9
7320	06 1885	National City	19.6	54 249	440	2 768	48 772	5 477	11.2	40.89	8.46	0.69	17.67	32.30	49.61	9.4
7362	06 1900	Newark	36.2	37 861	667	1 046	32 126	5 735	17.9	68.60	4.32	0.62	15.94	10.52	22.90	5.3
4472	06 1915	Newport Beach	36.3	66 643	341	1 836	62 556	4 087	6.5	95.81	0.35	0.26	2.89	0.70	3.97	15.5
4472	06 1950	Norwalk	25.3	94 279	212	3 726	84 901	9 378	11.0	55.83	3.25	0.86	12.41	27.65	47.86	8.6
7362	06 1955	Novato	71.4	47 585	519	666	43 916	3 669	8.4	89.57	2.79	0.50	5.02	2.12	7.27	9.8
7362	06 1970	Oakland	145.2	372 242	39	2 564	339 337	32 905	9.7	32.47	43.88	0.64	14.76	8.26	13.89	12.0
7320	06 1990	Oceanside	105.3	128 398	141	1 219	76 698	51 700	67.4	74.72	7.89	0.71	6.09	10.59	22.57	14.0
4472	06 2005	Ontario	95.2	133 179	134	1 399	88 820	44 359	49.9	64.62	7.30	0.69	3.89	23.50	41.70	6.4
4472	06 2015	Orange	60.4	110 658	164	1 832	91 450	19 208	21.0	82.99	1.40	0.54	7.90	7.17	22.84	8.7
4472	06 2050	Oxnard	63.3	142 216	121	2 247	108 195	34 021	31.4	58.66	5.25	0.77	8.58	26.74	54.37	7.7
7362	06 2060	Pacifica	32.7	37 670	675	1 152	36 866	804	2.2	76.28	5.21	0.73	13.63	4.15	13.54	7.4
4472	06 2085	Palm Springs	198.3	40 181	624	203	32 359	7 822	24.2	83.15	4.51	0.74	3.34	8.25	18.68	25.8
7362	06 2090	Palo Alto	61.3	55 900	419	912	55 225	675	1.2	84.90	2.88	0.27	10.44	1.51	4.99	15.5
4472	06 2115	Paramount	12.2	47 669	518	3 907	36 407	11 262	30.9	48.15	10.69	0.75	5.75	34.65	60.83	6.2
4472	06 2125	Pasadena	59.5	131 591	137	2 212	118 072	13 519	11.4	57.25	18.96	0.45	8.11	15.22	27.29	13.2
7362	06 2140	Petaluma	31.9	43 184	576	1 354	33 834	9 350	27.6	92.10	1.28	0.57	3.31	2.74	9.23	11.6

1. MSA = Metropolitan Statistical Area. CMSA = Consolidated MSA. 2. Dry land or land partially or temporarily covered by water. 3. Hispanic persons may be of any race.

City	Households, 1990				Births, 1984			Deaths, 1984				Hospitals, 1985		
	Number	Persons per house-hold	Percent–		Number		Rate[3]	Number		Rate		Number	Beds	
			Female family house-holder[1]	One-person[2]	Total	To mothers under 20 yrs. old (Percent)		Total	Infant[4]	Total[3]	Infant[5]		Number	Rate[6]
	15	16	17	18	19	20	21	22	23	24	25	26	27	28
CALIFORNIA—Con.														
Compton	22 323	4.02	27.5	13.6	2 888	21.5	32.9	729	45	8.3	15.6	0	0	0
Concord	41 940	2.63	11.1	22.4	1 594	4.5	15.4	678	10	6.5	6.3	1	303	286
Corona	23 920	3.16	9.3	14.4	1 189	11.4	27.9	338	13	7.9	10.9	3	330	710
Costa Mesa	37 467	2.51	9.9	27.2	1 361	6.3	15.9	542	9	6.3	6.6	2	1 284	1 455
Covina	15 531	2.74	13.0	22.5	944	8.5	24.0	480	10	12.2	10.6	2	357	874
Culver City	16 166	2.34	11.4	31.6	664	6.6	17.2	341	6	8.9	9.0	2	426	1 074
Cupertino	15 358	2.60	8.0	20.0	512	3.1	13.5	257	3	6.8	5.9	0	0	0
Cypress	14 279	2.98	11.5	15.0	583	8.2	14.0	206	1	4.9	1.7	0	0	0
Daly City	29 010	3.15	13.5	19.9	1 340	5.7	16.5	521	8	6.4	6.0	1	350	422
Davis	17 926	2.46	7.3	24.3	544	2.9	14.1	146	4	3.8	7.4	2	58	141
Downey	33 013	2.71	12.2	23.0	1 252	8.8	14.9	733	20	8.7	16.0	3	751	880
El Cajon	32 893	2.63	14.7	22.9	2 066	8.1	25.3	1 023	13	12.5	6.3	1	189	224
El Monte	26 131	4.00	16.3	13.7	2 816	14.6	31.4	620	27	6.9	9.6	0	0	0
Escondido	39 267	2.73	10.3	23.3	1 707	10.2	22.7	874	16	11.6	9.4	1	267	320
Fairfield	25 425	2.92	12.5	16.9	1 372	10.6	21.3	358	14	5.6	10.2	2	421	612
Fontana	26 385	3.30	13.7	14.6	1 545	15.5	33.0	484	8	10.3	5.2	1	448	809
Fountain Valley	17 407	3.07	9.6	13.5	528	9.1	9.5	239	6	4.3	11.4	1	287	518
Fremont	60 198	2.86	9.2	16.8	2 504	7.0	17.4	745	12	5.2	4.8	1	231	150
Fresno	121 807	2.84	16.2	24.1	7 318	14.8	27.4	2 786	59	10.4	8.1	6	1 790	629
Fullerton	40 872	2.74	9.7	22.4	1 709	8.9	16.0	700	15	6.5	8.8	2	357	328
Gardena	18 126	2.70	14.4	25.9	1 308	9.7	27.3	570	10	11.9	7.6	2	204	414
Garden Grove	44 538	3.17	11.9	16.7	2 484	9.2	19.2	954	21	7.4	8.5	1	175	130
Glendale	68 604	2.59	10.5	27.8	1 736	4.8	11.8	1 398	15	9.5	8.6	3	1 064	692
Glendora	16 327	2.88	9.7	17.5	620	4.5	15.6	364	4	9.1	6.5	2	269	653
Hawthorne	27 137	2.61	16.1	30.1	1 111	9.7	19.1	470	12	8.1	10.8	2	299	492
Hayward	40 117	2.75	13.1	22.3	2 418	11.3	24.3	1 069	22	10.7	9.1	3	495	488
Huntington Beach	68 879	2.62	9.5	21.5	2 447	5.0	13.6	901	14	5.0	5.7	2	250	136
Huntington Park	13 903	4.01	17.2	13.8	1 762	16.1	35.1	416	12	8.3	6.8	2	226	411
Inglewood	36 102	2.99	21.2	26.9	2 769	12.4	28.0	795	35	8.0	12.6	3	806	786
Irvine	40 257	2.69	9.2	19.7	1 206	1.7	15.5	254	7	3.3	5.8	0	0	0
La Habra	18 112	2.81	11.5	22.0	785	9.7	16.6	353	7	7.5	8.9	1	299	621
Lakewood	26 102	2.81	10.3	17.7	1 154	6.8	15.4	534	9	7.1	7.8	2	206	272
La Mesa	23 206	2.23	10.7	31.1	758	7.1	14.5	577	8	11.0	10.6	1	416	802
La Mirada	12 731	3.06	9.1	14.7	549	11.7	13.4	249	3	6.1	5.5	1	141	338
Lancaster	32 901	2.83	11.1	20.4	1 063	11.9	19.4	568	7	10.3	6.6	3	438	689
La Puente	9 019	4.06	16.4	11.5	1 735	18.4	53.9	389	16	12.1	9.2	0	0	0
Livermore	20 643	2.74	9.5	18.8	850	6.1	16.5	266	10	5.1	11.8	2	397	738
Lodi	19 001	2.63	11.3	24.0	746	10.5	18.7	485	6	12.2	8.0	2	192	436
Lompoc	12 504	2.81	13.0	22.1	650	9.5	22.2	225	7	7.7	10.8	3	240	771
Long Beach	158 975	2.61	13.0	30.8	7 654	13.0	20.2	3 833	78	10.1	10.2	12	4 004	1 010
Los Altos	9 837	2.63	5.4	16.3	238	5.0	8.5	277	3	9.9	12.6	0	0	0
Los Angeles	1 217 405	2.80	13.6	28.5	63 267	12.5	20.4	27 090	694	8.7	11.0	45	11 075	340
Los Gatos town	11 273	2.37	8.3	26.8	394	3.6	14.2	330	3	11.9	7.6	2	254	915
Lynwood	14 158	4.29	20.3	12.0	1 426	17.3	27.0	326	20	6.2	14.0	1	416	744
Manhattan Beach	13 992	2.29	6.4	27.2	392	2.6	11.8	193	4	5.8	10.2	0	0	0
Menlo Park	11 816	2.28	9.1	33.1	478	7.9	18.3	391	4	15.0	8.4	0	0	0
Merced	18 282	3.03	15.7	21.7	1 581	14.3	35.7	401	13	9.1	8.2	2	251	534
Milpitas	14 099	3.37	10.9	12.0	927	10.8	22.2	154	9	3.7	9.7	0	0	0
Modesto	57 958	2.79	12.1	22.1	2 927	13.9	23.9	1 330	29	10.9	9.9	4	805	606
Monrovia	13 242	2.68	14.1	25.8	748	10.7	23.3	330	5	10.3	6.7	1	49	148
Montebello	18 618	3.17	17.6	18.3	989	10.6	17.5	405	8	7.2	8.1	1	212	387
Monterey	12 693	2.26	7.6	31.8	466	3.4	16.2	238	2	8.3	4.3	1	170	566
Monterey Park	19 505	3.10	13.7	17.3	912	7.5	15.6	347	4	5.9	4.4	2	325	534
Mountain View	29 990	2.23	8.0	35.1	1 099	4.4	17.8	428	9	6.9	8.2	1	396	649
Napa	23 914	2.53	10.6	25.9	1 011	9.3	18.8	658	8	12.2	7.9	2	1 892	3 333
National City	14 773	3.22	19.7	17.9	1 343	12.5	24.0	343	17	6.1	12.7	1	210	366
Newark	12 015	3.15	10.4	13.8	738	9.5	20.7	134	4	3.8	5.4	0	0	0
Newport Beach	30 860	2.14	6.2	31.9	451	1.8	6.8	464	2	7.0	4.4	2	439	658
Norwalk	26 346	3.48	13.7	13.6	1 685	13.0	19.3	540	14	6.2	8.3	3	1 206	1 339
Novato	18 236	2.59	9.7	21.3	694	3.0	15.3	301	11	6.7	15.9	1	75	164
Oakland	144 521	2.52	18.5	33.2	6 715	14.0	19.1	3 710	95	10.5	14.1	10	1 947	545
Oceanside	46 741	2.72	9.7	20.8	2 471	15.6	27.4	707	25	7.8	10.1	2	338	341
Ontario	40 277	3.28	13.3	16.8	2 558	11.6	24.1	632	30	5.9	11.7	1	99	87
Orange	36 791	2.90	10.9	18.9	1 744	5.7	18.0	676	13	7.0	7.5	5	1 113	1 105
Oxnard	39 302	3.56	12.9	15.4	3 088	13.4	25.5	731	34	6.0	11.0	3	343	270
Pacifica	13 340	2.81	10.8	18.8	674	6.8	18.5	218	5	6.0	7.4	0	0	0
Palm Springs	18 622	2.13	8.0	36.6	482	13.7	13.3	461	5	12.7	10.4	1	330	1 064
Palo Alto	24 206	2.24	7.5	32.5	554	2.9	9.9	504	6	9.0	10.8	2	1 487	2 658
Paramount	12 993	3.64	17.2	17.6	1 005	18.1	25.0	246	7	6.1	7.0	1	184	430
Pasadena	50 199	2.53	12.2	32.0	2 342	10.8	18.7	1 415	26	11.3	11.1	4	922	710
Petaluma	16 062	2.66	9.7	22.5	662	6.3	18.1	371	7	10.2	10.6	1	99	257

1. No spouse present. 2. Householder living alone. 3. Per 1,000 resident population estimated as of July 1 of the year shown. 4. Deaths of infants under 1 year old. 5. Deaths of infants under 1 year old per 1,000 live births. 6. Per 100,000 resident population estimated as of July 1, 1986.

City	Serious crimes known to police, 1985: Number: Total	Serious crimes known to police, 1985: Number: Violent[1]	Serious crimes known to police, 1985: Rate[2]	Police officers, 1985: Number	Police officers, 1985: Rate[3]	Educational attainment,[4] 1980: Percent completing 12 years or more	Educational attainment,[4] 1980: Percent completing 16 years or more	Money income: Per capita[5]: 1985: Total (Dollars)	Money income: Per capita[5]: 1985: Percent of State average	Money income: Per capita[5]: 1979: Current dollars	Money income: Per capita[5]: 1979: Constant (1985) dollars	Money income: Percent below poverty level, 1979: Persons	Money income: Percent below poverty level, 1979: Families	Housing, 1990: Total units	Housing, 1990: Percent change, 1980–1990	Housing, 1990: Vacant units for sale or rent[6]
	29	30	31	32	33	34	35	36	37	38	39	40	41	42	43	44
CALIFORNIA—Con.																
Compton	7 855	2 530	8 665	121	13.3	56.8	5.5	6 161	51.8	4 266	6 322	26.4	23.8	23 239	3.5	778
Concord	6 508	406	6 092	133	12.5	84.8	21.4	13 030	109.6	8 879	13 159	6.0	4.6	43 715	9.7	1 524
Corona	3 556	190	8 286	57	13.3	70.3	12.6	10 758	90.5	7 251	10 746	9.9	8.4	26 538	52.8	2 408
Costa Mesa	6 369	456	7 001	131	14.4	82.4	21.2	13 516	113.7	8 985	13 316	8.5	5.7	39 611	14.1	1 890
Covina	2 172	265	5 236	48	11.6	78.0	15.9	12 253	103.1	8 573	12 705	6.3	4.6	16 110	21.7	513
Culver City	3 228	374	7 924	105	25.8	80.9	28.2	15 482	130.3	10 595	15 702	6.8	4.5	16 943	1.3	654
Cupertino	1 913	119	4 770	NA	NA	91.2	39.1	18 880	158.9	11 679	17 308	3.7	2.7	16 055	21.8	593
Cypress	1 785	116	4 055	49	11.1	83.8	20.6	13 640	114.8	9 155	13 568	4.9	3.7	14 715	12.2	355
Daly City	3 018	254	3 536	98	11.5	76.3	20.4	11 321	95.3	8 227	12 192	7.0	5.7	30 162	7.8	965
Davis	2 606	129	6 503	42	10.5	94.4	60.9	11 091	93.3	7 581	11 235	25.1	8.2	18 282	20.4	277
Downey	4 427	326	4 996	102	11.5	72.4	13.3	12 558	105.7	9 339	13 840	7.0	5.3	34 302	1.8	1 052
El Cajon	4 933	285	5 930	103	12.4	75.4	13.8	10 048	84.5	7 166	10 620	11.8	9.7	34 453	12.6	1 380
El Monte	5 809	1 085	6 399	106	11.7	45.9	4.7	6 823	57.4	4 902	7 265	19.9	16.6	27 167	6.5	867
Escondido	4 170	281	5 564	88	11.7	73.2	13.8	10 428	87.7	6 925	10 263	11.1	8.4	42 040	35.4	2 389
Fairfield	3 940	264	5 961	72	10.9	81.1	11.6	9 996	84.1	6 778	10 045	9.4	8.4	26 357	28.1	748
Fontana	3 642	328	7 866	58	12.5	65.7	6.2	8 761	73.7	6 589	9 765	11.6	9.6	29 383	52.5	2 644
Fountain Valley	2 811	159	4 785	59	10.0	87.0	26.0	14 132	118.9	9 423	13 965	3.8	2.8	18 019	7.0	526
Fremont	6 667	614	4 504	157	10.6	79.7	18.2	13 689	115.2	9 087	13 467	4.8	3.7	62 400	27.1	1 983
Fresno	28 821	2 311	10 476	350	12.7	67.9	16.5	8 973	75.5	6 708	9 941	15.7	12.6	129 404	31.4	6 274
Fullerton	6 629	416	6 026	145	13.2	81.7	26.9	14 699	123.7	10 151	15 044	7.5	4.7	42 956	8.0	1 858
Gardena	3 397	618	6 888	86	17.4	71.5	13.5	11 348	95.5	7 911	11 724	9.2	7.1	19 037	7.7	814
Garden Grove	9 321	823	7 008	153	11.5	74.4	13.4	11 410	96.0	7 931	11 754	8.3	6.1	45 984	6.8	1 221
Glendale	7 405	479	4 881	176	11.6	76.4	21.6	13 187	111.0	9 514	14 100	10.1	8.0	72 114	14.5	2 881
Glendora	1 584	192	3 785	47	11.2	79.3	17.4	12 960	109.0	8 804	13 048	5.2	4.0	16 876	21.7	462
Hawthorne	4 543	711	7 346	79	12.8	74.1	12.0	11 189	94.1	8 024	11 892	9.2	7.4	29 214	18.2	1 811
Hayward	7 445	671	7 274	144	14.1	69.9	13.5	11 261	94.7	8 067	11 955	9.2	8.0	42 216	15.0	1 900
Huntington Beach	8 499	466	4 606	202	10.9	86.3	25.2	14 928	125.6	9 782	14 497	6.5	4.9	72 736	12.4	3 043
Huntington Park	3 586	501	6 907	58	11.2	35.6	5.1	5 886	49.5	4 500	6 669	23.4	20.4	14 515	-7.5	542
Inglewood	8 165	1 891	8 015	183	18.0	73.7	13.0	9 407	79.2	6 965	10 322	15.4	13.0	38 713	1.2	2 176
Irvine	3 702	120	4 840	107	14.0	95.1	44.7	18 080	152.1	12 169	18 034	3.6	2.4	42 221	46.7	1 677
La Habra	2 261	129	4 525	51	10.2	73.7	16.1	12 462	104.9	8 824	13 077	6.1	4.9	18 670	7.9	493
Lakewood	3 257	391	4 089	NA	NA	75.6	11.0	12 045	101.3	8 510	12 612	5.2	4.2	26 795	2.0	573
La Mesa	2 501	132	4 559	53	9.7	81.6	21.1	12 455	104.8	8 761	12 984	9.9	6.0	24 154	6.4	791
La Mirada	1 323	141	3 043	NA	NA	78.5	14.3	11 712	98.5	8 199	12 151	4.9	4.5	13 354	6.5	591
Lancaster	2 777	311	5 097	NA	NA	76.4	15.5	11 680	98.3	8 097	12 000	8.7	7.4	36 217	49.9	2 868
La Puente	1 724	307	5 130	NA	NA	52.3	4.2	7 770	65.4	5 392	7 991	11.8	9.9	9 285	7.4	244
Livermore	2 549	185	4 804	51	9.6	84.2	22.6	13 414	112.9	8 839	13 099	4.4	4.0	21 489	22.6	733
Lodi	3 189	200	8 054	56	14.1	63.0	11.0	10 338	87.0	7 691	11 398	9.4	7.8	19 676	24.7	553
Lompoc	1 599	129	5 310	36	12.0	76.5	13.2	10 508	88.4	6 823	10 112	13.1	12.4	13 261	25.5	632
Long Beach	30 795	4 134	7 902	652	16.7	72.9	18.0	11 729	98.7	8 342	12 363	14.2	10.7	170 388	6.3	9 632
Los Altos	747	64	2 670	26	9.3	92.4	47.7	23 294	196.0	14 338	21 249	2.6	1.7	10 107	7.8	194
Los Angeles	294 404	52 832	9 239	7 051	22.1	68.6	19.8	12 084	101.7	8 415	12 471	16.4	13.0	1 299 963	8.5	69 406
Los Gatos town	1 544	87	5 318	39	13.4	89.2	40.3	19 606	165.0	12 771	18 927	5.4	3.3	11 822	7.2	399
Lynwood	3 502	953	6 438	NA	NA	53.5	5.6	6 222	52.4	4 938	7 318	20.6	18.3	14 525	-0.1	299
Manhattan Beach	1 779	129	5 147	57	16.5	93.1	41.7	22 529	189.6	13 789	20 435	4.4	2.4	14 695	6.7	528
Menlo Park	1 625	157	5 803	39	13.9	84.3	41.5	19 428	163.5	12 488	18 507	8.0	5.1	12 247	5.8	326
Merced	3 309	192	779	55	1.3	68.2	14.4	8 914	75.0	6 632	9 829	16.6	13.9	18 965	22.6	577
Milpitas	2 565	250	5 997	61	14.3	77.2	16.7	12 305	103.5	7 905	11 715	6.4	4.6	14 465	19.4	325
Modesto	9 791	557	7 784	154	12.2	71.7	15.1	10 526	88.6	7 730	11 456	10.3	8.3	60 878	30.4	2 542
Monrovia	2 208	269	6 657	50	15.1	72.2	15.4	11 062	93.1	7 525	11 152	11.1	7.7	13 944	10.1	595
Montebello	3 270	322	5 595	68	11.6	61.6	13.3	9 604	80.8	7 153	10 601	11.9	10.3	19 193	3.4	489
Monterey	2 126	127	7 026	51	16.9	83.4	32.3	12 470	104.9	8 771	12 999	7.1	4.6	13 497	10.4	564
Monterey Park	2 981	285	4 920	72	11.9	72.3	21.0	10 364	87.2	8 019	11 884	10.1	7.7	20 298	4.8	627
Mountain View	3 836	200	5 967	72	11.2	83.7	31.0	16 308	137.2	10 754	15 937	6.9	4.6	31 487	9.2	1 246
Napa	3 512	271	6 241	66	11.7	76.8	15.5	11 865	99.8	8 107	12 015	8.7	6.6	24 922	18.8	755
National City	4 658	497	8 105	66	11.5	58.0	7.5	6 977	58.7	5 046	7 478	19.0	17.3	15 243	3.2	371
Newark	2 270	199	6 354	46	12.9	75.6	12.8	11 731	98.7	7 806	11 568	5.3	4.8	12 284	23.0	240
Newport Beach	4 850	152	6 997	143	20.6	93.5	42.2	28 712	241.6	17 953	26 606	6.9	3.4	34 861	9.9	2 196
Norwalk	3 835	649	4 150	NA	NA	58.3	6.3	8 620	72.5	6 273	9 297	10.5	8.3	27 247	5.2	780
Novato	1 395	68	2 895	46	9.5	89.1	27.3	14 409	121.2	9 901	14 673	5.5	4.0	18 782	15.0	467
Oakland	42 823	6 703	11 826	617	17.0	71.5	21.8	10 911	91.8	7 701	11 413	18.5	16.0	154 737	2.9	7 668
Oceanside	4 841	572	5 378	120	13.3	74.5	14.2	10 407	87.6	7 040	10 433	12.3	8.8	51 109	36.0	2 899
Ontario	7 759	1 001	7 095	130	11.9	66.9	9.8	9 376	78.9	6 772	10 036	10.6	8.2	42 536	26.3	1 985
Orange	5 809	455	5 736	117	11.6	80.6	19.5	13 519	113.7	8 885	13 168	6.7	5.2	38 018	13.5	1 039
Oxnard	7 772	718	6 234	149	12.0	61.5	10.8	9 032	76.0	6 247	9 258	12.3	9.5	41 247	14.9	1 308
Pacifica	916	75	2 321	40	10.1	83.2	20.0	12 871	108.3	8 804	13 048	5.8	5.4	13 740	4.4	326
Palm Springs	3 168	224	8 756	83	22.9	77.2	18.0	16 109	135.5	11 666	17 289	10.4	7.4	30 517	19.8	2 318
Palo Alto	3 830	164	6 509	101	17.2	91.3	54.0	21 141	177.9	12 799	18 968	6.0	2.5	25 188	5.7	808
Paramount	2 588	436	6 217	NA	NA	46.5	3.8	7 267	61.1	5 294	7 846	18.9	16.0	13 726	14.5	631
Pasadena	11 279	1 488	8 768	202	15.7	77.3	29.5	13 557	114.1	9 184	13 611	14.1	10.7	53 032	6.2	2 202
Petaluma	1 949	113	5 145	45	11.9	77.4	16.2	11 887	100.0	7 992	11 844	6.3	4.9	16 546	24.2	363

1. Includes murder and nonnegligent manslaughter, forcible rape, robbery, and aggravated assault. 2. Per 100,000 resident population estimated for 1985 by the FBI. 3. Per 10,000 resident population estimated for 1985 by the FBI. 4. Persons 25 years old or older. 5. Based on the resident population estimated as of July 1, 1988 for 1987 data and enumerated as of April 1, 1980 for 1979 data. 6. Also includes units rented or sold, but not occupied.

City	Housing, 1990 (cont'd) — Occupied units — Total	Housing, 1990 (cont'd) — Occupied units — Percent with more than 1 person per room	Housing, 1990 (cont'd) — Occupied units — Owner-occupied — Percent of total	Housing, 1990 (cont'd) — Occupied units — Owner-occupied — Median value[1] (Dollars)	Housing, 1990 (cont'd) — Occupied units — Median rent[2] (Dollars)	Construction authorized by building permits, 1990 — New private housing units — Number	Construction authorized by building permits, 1990 — New private housing units — Value ($1,000)	Construction authorized by building permits, 1990 — New private housing units — Percent single family	Construction authorized by building permits, 1990 — Non-residential, value ($1,000)	Civilian labor force, 1990 — Total	Civilian labor force, 1990 — Percent change, 1989–1990	Civilian labor force, 1990 — Unemployment — Total	Civilian labor force, 1990 — Unemployment — Rate[3]
	45	46	47	48	49	50	51	52	53	54	55	56	57
CALIFORNIA—Con.													
Compton	22 323	35.3	56.8	108 000	477	68	3 858	27.9	11 616	36 777	6.2	4 357	11.8
Concord	41 940	5.2	60.9	195 300	618	295	24 368	24.7	11 774	70 046	-1.3	2 705	3.9
Corona	23 920	11.8	63.9	186 300	592	1 219	91 694	31.2	63 085	28 913	4.8	2 213	7.7
Costa Mesa	37 467	9.9	40.2	257 000	759	224	18 095	47.3	105 415	65 333	-2.0	1 979	3.0
Covina	15 531	8.3	58.1	200 700	601	24	1 894	12.5	10 014	21 561	4.5	833	3.9
Culver City	16 166	8.5	55.5	328 900	730	48	5 844	29.2	4 891	27 101	4.4	920	3.4
Cupertino	15 358	3.7	63.0	414 300	934	384	44 102	16.9	17 118	23 314	-4.1	492	2.1
Cypress	14 279	6.8	69.4	252 700	722	276	37 659	71.0	16 225	29 452	-2.0	883	3.0
Daly City	29 010	19.8	58.1	272 100	674	155	23 361	89.0	618	46 653	-1.5	1 819	3.9
Davis	17 926	5.5	40.8	191 300	547	747	69 282	43.8	4 496	25 858	0.7	940	3.6
Downey	33 013	11.9	52.5	231 600	602	304	27 350	24.7	35 760	52 146	4.7	2 457	4.7
El Cajon	32 893	8.8	40.7	158 000	507	54	6 219	96.3	9 624	49 667	0.3	2 670	5.4
El Monte	26 131	42.6	40.2	172 100	541	267	24 310	94.8	4 379	40 154	5.4	3 266	8.1
Escondido	39 267	10.2	51.9	169 500	570	390	57 807	71.8	21 624	41 899	0.2	1 968	4.7
Fairfield	25 425	6.2	56.2	139 900	501	578	55 524	38.9	16 976	32 081	2.1	2 280	7.1
Fontana	26 385	13.4	64.2	134 600	519	1 362	178 765	98.5	64 179	24 508	5.0	1 999	8.2
Fountain Valley	17 407	5.7	75.1	287 000	846	9	1 522	100.0	4 806	38 902	-2.0	1 149	3.0
Fremont	60 198	6.9	64.6	264 300	732	558	84 681	50.4	192 056	87 309	-1.4	3 098	3.5
Fresno	121 807	13.2	48.2	80 300	369	3 338	224 861	61.1	86 322	137 490	1.6	12 325	9.0
Fullerton	40 872	11.1	55.1	234 600	659	130	10 616	17.7	12 910	77 530	-1.9	2 685	3.5
Gardena	18 126	17.7	46.6	200 200	592	189	14 905	2.1	8 426	29 499	4.5	1 179	4.0
Garden Grove	44 538	18.4	59.6	199 700	694	347	18 237	3.5	6 565	87 921	-1.9	3 439	3.9
Glendale	68 604	18.3	38.7	343 600	626	511	50 777	12.7	88 161	86 962	4.5	3 391	3.9
Glendora	16 327	5.7	73.9	231 600	657	34	6 970	79.4	4 557	24 046	4.5	904	3.8
Hawthorne	27 137	19.1	25.5	226 100	593	156	17 222	32.7	3 928	37 088	4.7	1 782	4.8
Hayward	40 117	11.0	51.5	184 500	629	541	65 147	42.0	19 930	59 569	-1.5	2 597	4.4
Huntington Beach	68 879	5.2	58.5	287 100	808	204	26 148	44.1	11 471	128 051	-1.9	4 232	3.3
Huntington Park	13 903	54.8	28.5	163 700	482	37	2 408	56.8	11 882	23 491	5.5	2 038	8.7
Inglewood	36 102	24.5	36.3	170 400	556	111	9 781	12.6	12 937	56 513	5.0	3 642	6.4
Irvine	40 257	4.8	62.5	294 700	913	1 343	90 244	2.4	116 442	47 084	-2.1	1 022	2.2
La Habra	18 112	11.2	56.4	201 700	634	46	4 569	67.4	10 024	32 802	-1.9	1 159	3.5
Lakewood	26 102	7.0	72.1	215 600	735	67	3 860	4.5	5 463	46 911	4.7	2 187	4.7
La Mesa	23 206	4.4	48.2	163 700	552	193	19 836	10.9	37 325	37 228	0.1	1 360	3.7
La Mirada	12 731	7.0	82.4	209 700	699	370	29 758	42.2	8 459	25 864	4.7	1 273	4.9
Lancaster	32 901	6.6	62.9	133 700	542	971	99 150	86.6	41 733	26 629	5.0	1 695	6.4
La Puente	9 019	32.6	60.9	155 400	547	79	7 234	83.5	1 512	16 397	4.9	988	6.0
Livermore	20 643	3.6	67.1	217 300	680	272	45 620	93.4	25 706	30 089	-1.4	829	2.8
Lodi	19 001	8.6	54.3	126 300	426	123	16 310	98.4	6 961	21 523	-2.3	1 840	8.5
Lompoc	12 504	10.9	51.9	144 600	463	274	27 370	74.5	0	13 938	-1.1	1 012	7.3
Long Beach	158 975	16.5	41.0	222 900	551	1 269	138 292	16.8	20 711	207 215	4.8	11 523	5.6
Los Altos	9 837	1.1	87.8	500 001	1 001	49	9 901	57.1	745	15 637	-4.1	379	2.4
Los Angeles	1 217 405	22.3	39.4	244 500	544	11 826	1 357 248	16.0	813 458	1 792 321	5.0	115 830	6.5
Los Gatos town	11 273	2.0	64.2	439 900	800	37	9 083	100.0	5 222	17 188	-4.0	529	3.1
Lynwood	14 158	46.8	48.2	136 000	502	54	3 517	9.3	85	23 460	5.4	1 914	8.2
Manhattan Beach	13 992	1.4	62.5	500 001	1 001	255	49 784	69.4	4 440	23 961	4.3	692	2.9
Menlo Park	11 816	4.7	53.9	463 600	803	46	6 994	63.0	3 410	14 554	-1.5	375	2.6
Merced	18 282	16.9	44.6	91 100	374	345	28 414	97.7	6 440	20 977	-1.9	2 422	11.5
Milpitas	14 099	16.2	69.6	255 600	802	802	67 269	35.7	24 728	22 766	-4.0	761	3.3
Modesto	57 958	8.6	58.5	130 700	448	1 508	104 780	84.4	33 999	70 577	-0.9	6 905	9.8
Monrovia	13 242	11.9	47.0	234 900	590	84	11 711	69.0	2 391	18 473	4.9	1 048	5.7
Montebello	18 618	22.8	48.4	213 600	574	89	7 563	14.6	4 081	30 672	4.7	1 547	5.0
Monterey	12 693	4.3	35.8	266 600	654	52	5 425	44.2	12 527	15 797	-2.5	897	5.7
Monterey Park	19 505	23.4	54.9	238 800	606	142	9 629	17.6	10 920	32 176	4.6	1 388	4.3
Mountain View	29 990	8.6	37.8	347 000	715	241	29 825	24.5	18 184	43 508	-4.1	1 210	2.8
Napa	23 914	5.7	60.0	175 000	572	367	42 541	86.1	6 949	30 117	2.1	1 625	5.4
National City	14 773	29.1	35.5	114 700	441	78	5 964	35.9	3 517	22 307	0.4	1 413	6.3
Newark	12 015	9.6	72.2	225 500	728	46	4 914	82.6	25 586	19 781	-1.4	760	3.8
Newport Beach	30 860	1.6	55.8	500 001	961	300	42 425	79.7	18 845	49 190	-2.0	1 373	2.8
Norwalk	26 346	22.6	65.0	166 000	642	185	12 880	15.1	2 034	46 448	4.9	2 722	5.9
Novato	18 236	3.3	61.9	279 600	742	76	16 277	76.3	11 832	22 790	-1.6	637	2.8
Oakland	144 521	12.2	41.6	177 400	486	336	28 645	47.9	13 068	190 509	-1.5	10 982	5.8
Oceanside	46 741	9.6	58.4	170 200	599	1 015	129 604	68.7	18 216	45 288	0.3	2 285	5.0
Ontario	40 277	16.4	58.6	143 200	562	377	28 333	27.9	147 844	66 102	4.5	3 287	5.0
Orange	36 791	9.6	61.3	248 700	706	450	33 693	13.1	36 998	66 157	-2.0	2 025	3.1
Oxnard	39 302	25.0	53.7	204 600	634	376	41 304	67.8	27 518	74 804	0.8	6 071	8.1
Pacifica	13 340	6.2	66.7	266 800	749	44	6 232	54.5	636	22 501	-1.5	760	3.4
Palm Springs	18 622	7.4	58.9	141 200	498	154	20 791	95.5	4 004	26 764	4.6	1 771	6.6
Palo Alto	24 206	2.5	56.7	457 800	825	160	20 132	43.8	21 073	36 936	-4.1	901	2.4
Paramount	12 993	34.2	42.4	147 200	593	439	21 293	4.6	14 508	17 759	5.3	1 386	7.8
Pasadena	50 199	13.1	46.3	284 100	573	269	25 429	23.4	10 691	70 555	4.6	3 266	4.6
Petaluma	16 062	3.2	66.9	204 000	641	113	13 777	78.8	17 625	25 379	3.3	730	2.9

1. Specified owner-occupied units. 2. Specified renter-occupied units. 3. Percent of total civilian labor force.

City	Employed,[1] 1980: Total	Employed,[1] 1980: Rate per 1,000 employees: Professional, specialty, and technical	Employed,[1] 1980: Rate per 1,000 employees: Precision production, craft, and operators	Manufactures, 1987: Establishments: Total	Establishments: Percent with 20 or more employees	All employees: Number (1,000)	All employees: Percent change, 1982–1987	All employees: Annual payroll (Mil. dol.)	Production workers: Number (1,000)	Production workers: Work-hours (Millions)	Production workers: Wages: Total (Mil. dol.)	Production workers: Wages: Average per production worker (Dollars)	Value added by manufacture (Mil. dol.)	Value of shipments (Mil. dol.)	New capital expenditures (Mil. dol.)
	58	59	60	61	62	63	64	65	66	67	68	69	70	71	72
CALIFORNIA—Con.															
Compton	26 974	91.2	282.7	192	52.6	8.6	0.0	175.1	6.6	13.1	110.8	16 788	480.5	939.1	13.9
Concord	51 548	150.5	167.0	132	21.2	2.9	-34.1	77.9	1.5	2.9	31.8	21 200	131.7	214.9	7.9
Corona	16 002	143.7	234.7	163	36.2	4.9	53.1	100.9	3.7	7.5	65.5	17 703	236.2	477.4	24.6
Costa Mesa	46 214	175.9	195.4	376	27.4	13.1	-1.5	322.2	7.7	15.1	149.1	19 364	624.7	1 221.4	33.6
Covina	17 246	155.6	212.4	147	25.9	3.6	-2.7	78.5	2.6	5.0	45.2	17 385	145.4	244.4	7.6
Culver City	21 783	213.9	159.5	175	29.1	5.1	-7.3	112.0	2.7	5.2	44.8	16 593	177.3	307.6	5.9
Cupertino	19 324	273.7	131.8	58	46.6	14.2	44.9	659.0	2.7	4.2	62.4	23 111	710.4	1 059.8	D
Cypress	20 840	167.7	180.5	39	30.8	0.9	28.6	23.8	0.6	1.3	10.6	17 667	48.8	80.5	3.3
Daly City	40 964	124.3	133.1	NA	NA	NA	NA	NA	NA	NA	NA	NA	NA	NA	NA
Davis	18 266	423.7	61.8	26	23.1	0.6	D	14.8	0.5	0.8	9.1	18 200	61.2	124.6	2.3
Downey	41 342	124.7	232.6	139	29.5	11.5	-25.8	418.0	3.6	7.3	87.0	24 167	880.9	1 499.1	42.7
El Cajon	31 693	134.9	219.1	197	31.0	7.3	49.0	166.9	5.1	9.7	99.5	19 510	351.8	595.7	13.0
El Monte	30 691	56.8	395.8	216	36.6	9.2	-4.2	216.4	6.2	12.4	120.6	19 452	464.3	823.3	14.5
Escondido	26 928	138.0	236.0	204	19.1	3.7	27.6	77.8	2.5	4.8	42.1	16 840	186.5	368.1	12.1
Fairfield	19 606	113.0	224.7	41	36.6	2.1	31.2	63.5	1.4	2.7	39.1	27 929	386.3	660.4	15.2
Fontana	13 876	84.8	292.0	83	42.2	3.1	244.4	77.3	2.3	5.1	55.8	24 261	245.7	714.8	12.0
Fountain Valley	27 539	191.8	154.6	122	28.7	2.8	16.7	57.2	2.1	4.0	33.1	15 762	143.4	256.6	4.1
Fremont	66 936	153.8	241.5	282	36.9	13.8	245.0	398.4	8.2	16.4	191.4	23 341	2 523.1	4 855.4	92.4
Fresno	93 714	146.1	161.7	393	29.8	11.6	16.0	246.1	7.6	14.7	132.7	17 461	633.3	1 521.1	41.1
Fullerton	54 596	187.6	188.2	258	30.2	23.8	-5.2	770.8	16.3	33.7	510.0	31 288	1 648.2	2 596.5	69.2
Gardena	23 562	139.0	247.6	420	35.5	12.6	5.0	251.0	8.9	17.9	152.1	17 090	541.0	955.7	30.8
Garden Grove	61 626	126.2	244.0	241	30.3	7.7	-7.2	180.0	5.2	10.3	94.6	18 192	399.4	829.0	13.1
Glendale	69 532	175.1	178.1	316	32.9	11.6	-8.7	294.1	6.9	14.0	143.9	20 855	513.3	832.5	17.5
Glendora	19 254	156.4	201.5	61	32.8	1.9	5.6	53.9	1.0	2.0	18.5	18 500	107.3	209.0	5.5
Hawthorne	29 375	131.0	260.1	147	34.0	22.3	-9.3	825.6	10.2	19.0	295.5	28 971	1 567.3	2 376.1	D
Hayward	45 285	116.0	247.2	364	34.9	12.7	19.8	355.0	7.1	14.1	161.7	22 775	725.9	1 469.1	36.3
Huntington Beach	90 320	185.3	166.7	432	24.8	15.3	37.8	465.5	8.8	17.5	193.2	21 955	940.7	1 550.8	50.8
Huntington Park	17 849	31.0	496.9	168	38.1	5.2	-8.8	107.9	3.7	7.1	65.6	17 730	230.0	411.4	7.9
Inglewood	43 989	143.4	196.0	109	30.3	3.2	-5.9	71.4	2.1	4.2	35.6	16 952	161.8	275.8	5.6
Irvine	33 600	274.2	84.2	407	52.1	35.4	-1.9	1 053.2	19.1	37.9	420.8	22 031	2 423.2	4 079.9	190.6
La Habra	23 082	133.7	210.0	103	20.4	1.8	20.0	37.0	1.2	2.3	22.5	18 750	100.6	210.4	2.6
Lakewood	37 211	126.5	253.2	16	25.0	0.9	12.5	17.5	0.7	1.2	12.3	17 571	35.5	49.4	D
La Mesa	24 188	203.4	152.6	NA	NA	NA	NA	NA	NA	NA	NA	NA	NA	NA	NA
La Mirada	20 460	129.0	207.2	87	54.0	4.7	38.2	114.3	3.5	6.7	73.9	21 114	336.4	742.3	19.4
Lancaster	20 745	209.7	238.5	38	15.8	D	D	D	D	D	D	D	D	D	D
La Puente	12 820	56.0	383.7	NA	NA	NA	NA	NA	NA	NA	NA	NA	NA	NA	NA
Livermore	23 258	231.6	193.9	62	21.0	1.7	6.2	43.7	1.2	2.4	27.9	23 250	454.0	584.7	17.8
Lodi	15 096	116.7	233.8	89	29.2	4.4	46.7	100.8	3.5	6.7	72.8	20 800	401.8	648.6	39.4
Lompoc	10 308	160.5	184.0	NA	NA	NA	NA	NA	NA	NA	NA	NA	NA	NA	NA
Long Beach	162 817	174.2	195.5	404	31.9	40.1	46.9	1 324.0	23.0	43.9	721.1	31 352	2 091.0	5 040.7	220.0
Los Altos	12 919	286.1	79.7	NA	NA	NA	NA	NA	NA	NA	NA	NA	NA	NA	NA
Los Angeles	1 394 855	168.2	204.8	8 262	32.9	301.9	-7.8	7 343.0	198.9	382.0	3 593.9	18 069	16 084.6	32 108.1	695.1
Los Gatos town	14 106	283.9	115.4	53	18.9	1.3	-23.5	40.6	0.6	1.2	13.2	22 000	76.5	126.8	D
Lynwood	17 926	75.9	352.5	102	40.2	4.3	13.2	86.4	2.7	5.5	43.3	16 037	137.5	305.2	8.1
Manhattan Beach	19 360	278.5	122.7	21	14.3	D	D	D	D	D	D	D	D	D	D
Menlo Park	12 955	299.4	91.2	92	42.4	6.9	-4.2	228.7	3.1	6.7	59.0	19 032	719.1	968.0	29.2
Merced	14 137	145.4	165.7	57	45.6	3.0	57.9	61.4	2.4	5.1	43.9	18 292	172.8	450.4	11.4
Milpitas	18 633	161.9	300.9	184	51.6	15.0	97.4	474.2	6.6	13.1	157.1	23 803	1 077.4	1 877.0	124.1
Modesto	46 495	150.5	200.5	145	29.7	7.3	17.7	186.9	4.4	8.5	95.9	21 795	797.0	1 685.6	37.5
Monrovia	14 498	135.1	232.8	162	39.5	7.9	12.9	188.8	4.2	8.5	87.4	20 810	436.5	664.0	14.3
Montebello	24 232	130.0	233.2	104	52.9	6.0	7.1	139.2	4.0	7.4	72.7	18 175	282.7	572.4	21.9
Monterey	11 534	211.0	113.3	47	25.5	1.9	11.8	45.7	0.8	1.3	17.1	21 375	89.7	152.6	2.5
Monterey Park	25 616	181.4	178.7	75	38.7	2.5	-13.8	55.1	1.8	3.3	29.1	16 167	82.6	136.9	3.3
Mountain View	35 815	251.5	193.9	317	36.0	20.3	13.4	689.0	8.3	17.0	188.9	22 759	1 406.2	2 268.9	194.7
Napa	23 295	151.4	201.4	84	19.0	1.6	23.1	34.4	1.1	2.2	22.4	20 364	78.8	158.3	2.1
National City	14 090	81.8	272.4	111	29.7	2.7	35.0	55.4	2.1	3.9	36.0	17 143	98.0	219.6	3.0
Newark	15 119	122.6	316.7	75	44.0	3.0	-6.3	89.0	1.9	3.8	46.3	24 368	202.6	389.7	11.6
Newport Beach	34 880	235.0	81.4	141	17.7	8.0	-2.4	226.4	3.1	6.3	54.9	17 710	595.5	905.2	39.0
Norwalk	36 380	75.3	330.2	78	24.4	1.6	-30.4	33.4	1.1	2.2	17.5	15 909	70.0	145.0	2.7
Novato	20 949	170.5	128.7	83	15.7	1.5	0.0	35.9	0.8	1.5	14.4	18 000	78.5	142.2	3.8
Oakland	142 699	185.5	157.1	717	24.3	19.1	-21.1	521.8	11.8	22.7	265.6	22 508	1 095.7	2 135.2	52.1
Oceanside	29 000	119.3	208.9	115	31.3	2.9	16.0	52.6	1.8	3.6	26.6	14 778	122.2	195.0	4.5
Ontario	38 724	105.2	274.4	246	43.5	14.0	97.2	349.7	9.1	18.1	181.9	19 989	593.8	1 483.1	47.3
Orange	46 781	164.1	183.9	427	32.1	11.8	61.6	254.7	7.7	15.5	127.0	16 494	555.5	1 012.3	23.3
Oxnard	45 766	114.8	216.3	93	36.6	6.1	10.9	157.3	4.0	8.3	89.2	22 300	545.2	903.7	17.2
Pacifica	19 864	138.7	171.2	NA	NA	NA	NA	NA	NA	NA	NA	NA	NA	NA	NA
Palm Springs	14 979	141.9	128.2	36	13.9	0.6	0.0	12.3	0.3	0.5	3.9	13 000	33.3	51.6	1.0
Palo Alto	30 512	387.6	80.4	165	37.6	26.1	0.0	1 024.1	7.3	12.9	195.3	26 753	1 635.4	2 672.7	85.8
Paramount	13 622	54.0	403.5	286	32.2	6.1	1.7	128.2	4.6	9.1	79.7	17 326	276.7	548.5	11.9
Pasadena	55 985	229.4	148.6	212	33.0	8.5	-14.1	230.7	4.3	8.7	89.6	20 837	470.8	704.0	23.0
Petaluma	15 969	138.1	182.8	100	31.0	3.6	89.5	86.4	1.9	3.8	37.9	19 947	201.2	473.7	15.3

1. Persons 16 years old and over.

City	Wholesale trade, 1987				Retail trade–all establishments, 1987				Retail trade–establishments with payroll, 1987					
						Sales				Sales				
											Per capita[2] (Dollars)			
	Establishments	Sales (Mil. dol.)	Paid employees[1]	Annual payroll ($1,000)	Number	Total (Mil. dol.)	Percent change, 1982–1987	Per capita[2] (Dollars)	Number	Total (Mil. dol.)	General merchandise group stores	Food stores	Apparel and accessory stores	Eating and drinking places
	73	74	75	76	77	78	79	80	81	82	83	84	85	86
CALIFORNIA—Con.														
Compton	140	1 486.8	3 262	85 642	339	200.2	14.1	2 140	215	196.2	D	628	32	203
Concord	238	1 402.9	2 772	66 091	1 113	1 197.9	48.2	11 303	745	1 178.0	2 099	1 739	590	783
Corona	116	533.5	1 664	38 989	521	512.6	71.7	11 028	295	500.1	879	1 844	196	872
Costa Mesa	339	4 036.6	5 325	163 751	1 453	1 661.1	54.4	18 818	999	1 634.3	3 376	1 600	3 428	1 571
Covina	90	426.3	813	17 338	532	563.5	38.5	13 788	329	547.0	2 114	3 180	118	1 190
Culver City	221	1 310.6	4 254	131 030	759	694.6	41.0	17 505	532	681.0	2 832	2 298	1 911	1 455
Cupertino	70	279.5	540	19 635	545	446.6	7.0	11 713	388	438.5	3 562	1 398	1 066	1 642
Cypress	65	1 850.2	2 061	67 429	384	214.7	76.3	4 969	167	202.7	D	883	262	684
Daly City	38	149.8	592	16 159	684	616.9	38.8	7 433	361	592.8	1 715	861	621	695
Davis	13	25.6	78	2 181	318	230.6	33.8	5 593	216	226.9	0	1 516	D	719
Downey	114	295.8	1 017	21 684	1 015	963.1	34.2	11 281	522	929.4	978	1 207	281	822
El Cajon	169	356.2	1 816	34 990	1 047	1 112.6	54.0	13 173	770	1 094.2	1 503	2 331	526	960
El Monte	183	1 198.5	2 974	80 249	653	677.7	63.5	7 014	367	660.4	D	937	151	327
Escondido	169	352.4	1 490	31 470	1 246	1 318.6	124.8	15 782	807	1 290.8	2 320	1 781	1 234	883
Fairfield	41	185.8	403	8 543	605	533.7	87.7	7 763	434	526.8	2 096	816	425	550
Fontana	73	719.6	1 349	26 477	511	376.6	120.0	6 797	283	365.1	696	1 830	108	672
Fountain Valley	122	1 527.3	1 319	37 115	664	357.6	35.6	6 456	317	336.2	D	1 630	102	777
Fremont	230	4 101.1	4 229	105 592	1 366	1 132.0	72.0	7 371	714	1 097.7	445	1 441	124	640
Fresno	783	3 545.9	9 257	214 160	3 166	2 514.9	52.8	8 835	2 184	2 453.2	1 310	1 555	443	848
Fullerton	238	1 942.2	2 754	78 988	1 079	971.8	57.9	8 936	571	938.2	2 201	1 208	271	924
Gardena	268	745.2	2 818	69 392	626	462.0	27.1	9 377	361	448.3	D	2 103	160	791
Garden Grove	261	1 966.1	4 344	104 119	1 356	980.4	58.2	7 270	689	946.8	667	1 607	206	727
Glendale	328	1 235.2	3 292	88 893	1 944	1 482.4	60.4	9 647	930	1 413.9	1 167	1 428	951	883
Glendora	52	207.1	312	9 192	527	400.0	76.0	9 711	257	378.9	D	1 609	236	654
Hawthorne	72	620.2	1 681	42 885	556	420.5	42.1	6 915	355	411.0	945	1 788	582	602
Hayward	491	3 101.3	8 380	206 784	956	996.9	68.0	9 820	599	979.1	2 125	1 486	192	757
Huntington Beach	382	1 398.7	3 709	93 246	1 839	1 301.4	44.0	7 087	919	1 244.2	838	1 259	269	762
Huntington Park	73	286.5	1 038	25 353	403	261.8	36.6	4 759	237	253.3	143	713	588	330
Inglewood	127	510.6	1 553	40 561	594	587.2	38.8	5 726	387	577.1	D	986	101	469
Irvine	545	8 453.3	11 581	377 751	912	900.2	141.8	10 179	399	867.0	D	1 555	134	1 173
La Habra	72	157.4	623	11 877	551	348.4	49.3	7 234	338	338.4	1 012	1 766	129	753
Lakewood	30	76.5	456	8 506	729	688.4	43.4	9 077	453	669.0	1 842	1 603	626	997
La Mesa	52	92.6	462	8 740	709	734.5	55.8	14 169	494	723.8	1 979	2 089	540	1 099
La Mirada	133	1 844.1	2 907	94 175	404	218.8	13.3	5 252	197	205.3	D	1 525	129	575
Lancaster	92	157.4	788	15 887	755	678.9	83.7	10 686	458	662.7	1 568	1 992	420	703
La Puente	22	126.2	229	3 784	289	151.4	4.6	4 457	164	145.8	D	1 155	148	373
Livermore	73	258.9	1 380	21 342	418	305.5	59.4	5 679	235	297.5	D	1 471	157	499
Lodi	67	290.4	554	11 039	572	401.4	70.0	9 108	365	389.9	716	1 770	259	763
Lompoc	13	16.9	97	1 626	288	188.8	46.4	6 067	188	185.2	D	1 509	271	628
Long Beach	536	4 707.5	6 745	168 895	3 181	2 258.4	40.2	5 699	1 940	2 187.7	404	1 241	163	763
Los Altos	57	351.0	322	12 130	352	197.2	41.4	7 122	209	188.9	0	2 243	215	1 027
Los Angeles	8 683	53 109.5	106 932	2 707 549	32 203	20 564.5	38.1	6 309	17 625	19 729.0	604	1 224	428	767
Los Gatos town	46	118.1	297	8 349	528	496.1	67.7	17 865	339	487.3	D	2 842	391	1 596
Lynwood	34	104.9	514	11 146	235	139.5	-2.5	2 496	133	134.5	D	1 149	27	215
Manhattan Beach	50	366.3	216	8 399	446	318.3	27.4	9 205	273	304.5	1 466	1 885	474	1 381
Menlo Park	80	458.7	1 168	38 666	344	343.4	49.9	12 588	232	337.9	0	3 056	257	1 249
Merced	84	350.7	938	20 858	557	441.5	38.1	9 390	398	429.7	1 313	2 028	312	583
Milpitas	104	2 239.5	2 895	92 877	377	253.3	56.2	5 741	205	244.8	965	1 419	306	763
Modesto	213	635.8	2 634	56 208	1 529	1 257.8	52.1	9 461	1 003	1 230.0	1 598	1 853	429	819
Monrovia	77	202.1	901	24 293	304	313.5	72.0	9 466	197	306.8	D	2 131	130	854
Montebello	160	879.7	2 263	59 013	745	449.3	94.2	8 206	387	428.4	1 227	1 858	589	756
Monterey	55	142.2	564	13 924	547	390.7	48.7	13 006	425	384.0	D	2 433	564	2 513
Monterey Park	163	382.2	1 388	30 425	716	309.0	38.3	5 078	298	283.9	D	1 638	212	732
Mountain View	210	902.8	2 588	75 942	623	506.2	2.2	8 300	442	496.5	1 717	1 562	118	870
Napa	90	129.2	659	13 415	678	439.3	42.5	7 740	451	426.3	D	1 961	254	676
National City	116	490.5	1 617	31 111	558	796.3	50.5	13 875	451	790.2	2 415	1 453	506	866
Newark	45	262.2	486	12 685	322	286.1	140.0	7 646	180	278.0	1 378	2 091	335	511
Newport Beach	252	2 864.1	2 567	57 135	1 183	991.2	58.1	14 852	686	954.5	1 554	1 963	1 025	2 693
Norwalk	96	480.8	1 562	48 372	640	621.5	85.6	6 902	341	605.9	D	1 289	162	488
Novato	96	243.8	931	23 038	436	291.6	55.4	6 378	262	278.3	D	1 740	194	624
Oakland	756	5 684.0	13 327	384 741	2 973	1 825.5	17.7	5 114	1 921	1 768.7	323	1 094	170	697
Oceanside	80	145.4	630	12 110	830	530.5	58.5	5 351	485	516.1	D	1 385	200	665
Ontario	192	910.1	2 540	62 433	818	774.2	81.3	6 772	487	752.9	781	1 352	120	620
Orange	432	3 192.0	4 935	135 879	1 539	1 237.5	64.7	12 284	995	1 205.4	1 668	1 551	593	1 375
Oxnard	138	474.2	1 854	40 489	1 012	767.0	48.1	6 040	632	748.7	824	1 134	271	602
Pacifica	8	3.8	15	210	242	117.5	35.7	3 179	110	111.8	D	1 427	D	343
Palm Springs	72	79.1	410	8 529	707	499.3	33.1	16 101	485	486.6	1 460	2 979	1 282	2 276
Palo Alto	144	671.5	1 932	66 378	840	766.9	38.9	13 707	621	758.5	D	1 808	2 559	1 885
Paramount	202	635.7	2 350	51 825	297	174.9	48.0	4 091	156	167.6	D	1 540	131	338
Pasadena	199	704.8	3 448	72 813	1 304	1 345.9	49.3	10 361	872	1 322.8	1 912	1 381	446	1 150
Petaluma	82	401.9	1 027	25 826	536	323.5	48.5	8 390	327	314.1	840	2 010	218	958

1. For the period including March 12 of the year shown. 2. Based on resident population estimated as of July 1, 1986.

City	Retail trade–establishment with payroll, 1987 (cont'd): Paid employees[1]: Number	Retail trade: Paid employees[1]: Percent change, 1982–1987	Retail trade: Annual payroll (Mil. dol.)	Taxable service industries–establishments with payroll, 1987: Number	Taxable service: Receipts (Mil. dol.): Total	Receipts: Selected kinds of business: Hotels, motels, and other lodging places	Receipts: Selected kinds of business: Health services	Receipts: Selected kinds of business: Legal services	Taxable service: Paid employees[1]	Taxable service: Annual payroll (Mil. dol.)	Federal grants, 1986: Procurement contract awards (Mil. dol.)	Federal grants, 1986: Grant awards (Mil. dol.)	Federal government civilian employment, 1984
	87	88	89	90	91	92	93	94	95	96	97	98	99
CALIFORNIA—Con.													
Compton	2 165	10.5	23.0	220	154.9	D	23.8	0.2	2 824	50.6	62.7	6.1	228
Concord	11 113	18.0	147.2	929	366.4	15.9	104.3	12.3	8 653	147.6	18.9	3.6	1 479
Corona	4 327	27.9	51.0	432	200.5	D	83.6	3.6	3 284	66.7	8.5	1.3	896
Costa Mesa	18 428	38.4	215.9	1 277	859.0	44.6	78.9	81.8	13 854	322.6	70.9	2.1	487
Covina	5 863	22.7	65.2	551	277.4	D	109.8	11.8	6 225	109.2	4.4	0.6	123
Culver City	7 562	20.4	85.9	749	1 769.9	17.8	169.1	8.6	19 381	483.6	313.8	1.9	428
Cupertino	6 326	1.3	63.4	424	208.4	D	36.0	5.1	3 203	83.3	25.4	0.4	112
Cypress	2 493	35.2	25.9	220	138.2	D	27.5	D	2 707	50.7	7.3	0.3	82
Daly City	6 377	12.5	75.0	380	140.7	3.2	66.7	2.2	3 854	57.5	0.7	1.7	150
Davis	3 326	22.3	28.9	255	75.4	1.0	23.8	D	1 853	29.5	10.0	43.3	340
Downey	7 462	8.9	101.9	726	323.0	8.4	149.1	12.7	7 307	123.5	975.2	28.9	342
El Cajon	11 294	33.9	125.1	777	274.5	10.4	108.8	10.1	6 262	91.3	30.9	3.7	305
El Monte	4 297	2.4	55.2	358	221.6	1.9	47.2	2.6	3 851	71.4	116.8	8.9	627
Escondido	12 308	80.7	145.5	939	302.0	6.5	98.7	13.5	6 483	112.4	7.4	1.9	285
Fairfield	5 915	48.7	65.0	418	134.1	4.6	60.3	8.6	3 220	48.7	3.4	3.9	123
Fontana	3 852	88.4	41.6	203	122.1	2.1	59.9	1.1	2 714	60.0	9.8	0.8	143
Fountain Valley	4 364	35.4	41.9	555	356.3	D	219.3	4.1	6 361	137.2	9.6	1.4	6
Fremont	11 274	49.5	141.1	1 025	434.6	D	144.4	8.6	9 354	173.1	13.3	2.9	806
Fresno	28 911	28.4	303.5	3 095	1 215.4	44.3	397.5	105.6	25 953	455.9	46.5	26.1	7 478
Fullerton	9 964	19.2	104.8	1 033	529.0	19.3	180.3	17.4	10 570	206.3	995.7	4.0	491
Gardena	3 864	10.9	49.7	421	214.4	D	73.5	6.7	4 688	87.4	32.8	2.5	205
Garden Grove	9 763	27.2	111.0	872	426.4	20.8	132.0	3.4	9 448	139.0	19.8	20.9	288
Glendale	14 710	25.0	176.1	1 621	840.9	11.3	237.4	43.0	18 629	346.0	85.4	3.7	616
Glendora	3 148	23.1	35.2	358	159.1	0.7	64.5	2.0	3 046	59.1	5.4	0.4	174
Hawthorne	4 646	21.1	50.9	316	233.2	5.1	85.8	0.8	4 635	85.3	391.6	1.8	987
Hayward	8 107	25.6	109.7	825	503.0	6.5	147.8	20.1	9 665	184.8	11.9	5.0	502
Huntington Beach	13 850	19.4	149.7	1 337	541.8	9.5	227.4	10.0	9 389	193.5	342.4	3.5	495
Huntington Park	2 550	17.9	29.3	195	126.2	D	52.5	2.0	2 951	44.7	17.8	1.6	156
Inglewood	5 173	8.0	62.6	653	503.3	18.5	167.9	5.5	7 498	182.8	47.1	4.4	2 025
Irvine	7 667	67.6	98.6	1 357	2 113.2	72.1	77.5	57.0	22 958	590.2	123.6	35.2	52
La Habra	3 799	12.4	43.4	352	176.0	D	76.1	3.9	3 707	59.7	0.3	0.4	105
Lakewood	8 077	17.2	84.0	287	164.4	2.2	93.5	2.2	3 741	62.0	0.8	1.0	172
La Mesa	7 502	25.2	83.7	628	242.6	D	118.4	3.7	5 610	94.1	0.4	1.4	156
La Mirada	2 767	2.3	27.1	213	107.3	D	45.6	1.0	2 056	33.4	3.0	0.4	79
Lancaster	6 290	37.9	74.3	543	248.6	15.7	140.6	4.2	4 665	89.4	1.5	1.7	232
La Puente	1 407	-8.1	17.0	93	29.3	D	3.8	D	809	13.9	NA	0.5	250
Livermore	3 218	44.4	37.6	335	307.3	D	26.2	D	2 996	80.7	7.9	3.5	758
Lodi	4 077	39.1	46.8	392	117.9	D	66.8	3.5	2 956	44.0	3.5	1.1	117
Lompoc	2 429	43.2	23.9	178	75.4	5.8	15.5	0.9	1 156	19.1	29.7	4.0	457
Long Beach	26 693	18.0	287.6	2 816	1 622.2	92.7	597.5	96.1	32 110	612.9	1 278.6	28.4	14 447
Los Altos	2 370	1.3	29.5	423	166.8	D	35.2	6.8	2 186	57.5	1.2	0.8	91
Los Angeles	227 058	17.9	2 576.7	35 367	25 863.9	798.5	4 034.4	3 700.1	370 100	9 335.8	4 455.1	704.9	33 391
Los Gatos town	4 578	47.1	63.7	627	265.7	5.2	153.0	6.2	4 474	111.5	5.5	0.3	133
Lynwood	1 609	-2.9	16.2	165	59.7	0.7	42.2	0.2	1 425	24.8	1.9	2.2	86
Manhattan Beach	4 153	15.8	40.2	390	136.3	D	34.4	3.2	2 530	54.6	5.4	0.2	123
Menlo Park	3 068	23.8	42.9	402	231.5	1.1	44.1	13.4	3 137	98.7	102.6	17.1	2 763
Merced	4 579	11.1	49.9	437	119.0	4.3	59.5	8.5	2 893	44.3	1.2	6.0	192
Milpitas	3 246	50.9	31.9	258	262.2	9.4	32.0	0.5	4 185	91.6	22.5	1.0	66
Modesto	13 432	20.2	150.0	1 222	541.4	14.2	286.6	28.6	12 829	213.4	28.5	10.1	508
Monrovia	3 061	84.5	36.5	225	159.6	D	20.6	1.8	2 090	38.5	7.9	0.6	87
Montebello	5 101	76.3	52.3	375	162.7	D	61.3	1.6	3 717	60.9	2.5	3.8	83
Monterey	5 489	24.8	54.6	599	301.7	88.9	63.4	20.7	5 851	105.6	8.9	11.2	2 274
Monterey Park	3 551	22.9	34.6	413	231.2	7.3	133.7	5.4	4 729	79.4	1.2	2.4	150
Mountain View	5 707	-16.5	71.3	774	623.8	14.5	86.4	6.3	9 305	254.6	364.7	16.4	233
Napa	4 915	15.5	56.2	609	173.3	15.2	70.4	10.2	3 738	63.1	1.2	4.9	186
National City	7 093	31.2	91.2	332	149.6	4.6	36.2	D	3 276	53.4	12.8	4.6	83
Newark	2 651	52.9	29.6	125	40.3	5.6	5.1	D	743	10.8	0.7	0.4	51
Newport Beach	11 356	12.2	137.7	1 957	1 205.2	67.7	230.7	223.1	17 333	462.2	282.7	0.7	340
Norwalk	4 637	20.7	56.9	290	251.4	8.3	70.7	D	5 622	125.8	4.7	2.0	143
Novato	2 979	29.0	35.5	488	184.0	1.8	54.7	8.6	4 042	78.4	3.5	1.5	157
Oakland	20 216	4.7	253.8	3 038	1 794.9	75.6	470.9	213.8	32 422	742.7	316.3	115.2	12 083
Oceanside	5 965	29.3	60.6	517	175.3	6.7	71.0	6.4	3 989	58.8	17.9	10.2	254
Ontario	7 282	44.2	86.9	490	257.2	18.8	34.3	12.0	5 244	74.9	93.6	3.2	457
Orange	14 143	32.6	155.1	1 532	1 075.4	29.0	222.9	46.4	17 066	364.2	95.8	2.3	308
Oxnard	9 282	31.6	90.6	719	257.7	20.0	98.1	10.5	5 916	97.9	69.1	9.1	605
Pacifica	1 149	-7.6	15.0	104	22.0	4.2	4.9	D	560	7.6	0.0	0.4	70
Palm Springs	6 097	-7.0	67.6	619	268.3	59.0	72.8	19.1	7 060	96.1	1.1	3.0	405
Palo Alto	9 787	23.1	110.5	1 286	1 070.5	40.1	149.9	177.8	15 149	433.6	382.1	8.3	2 812
Paramount	1 755	38.1	21.6	201	154.5	0.0	45.8	1.4	2 299	49.3	15.6	1.0	54
Pasadena	14 950	21.2	173.4	1 814	1 339.7	31.1	310.5	80.5	23 627	484.5	1 058.9	54.1	1 492
Petaluma	3 779	19.0	42.3	410	113.4	4.5	37.1	3.9	2 692	42.5	3.7	1.3	172

1. For the period including March 12 of the year shown.

City	City government employment, 1985 (October): Total	City government employment, 1985 (October): Rates[1]	City government employment, 1985 (October): Percent education	Form of governments[2] (As of 1986)	City government finances, 1984–1985: General revenue: Total (Mil. dol.)	General revenue: Intergovernmental: Total (Mil. dol.)	General revenue: Intergovernmental: Percent from State government	General revenue: Taxes: Total (Mil. dol.)	General revenue: Taxes: Per capita[3] (Dollars): Total	General revenue: Taxes: Per capita[3] (Dollars): Property	General revenue: Taxes: Per capita[3] (Dollars): Sales & gross receipts	General expenditures: Total (Mil. dol.)	General expenditures: Per capita[3] (Dol.): Total	General expenditures: Per capita[3] (Dol.): Capital outlays	General expenditures: Percent of total for–: Public welfare	General expenditures: Percent of total for–: Highways	General expenditures: Percent of total for–: Education
	100	101	102	103	104	105	106	107	108	109	110	111	112	113	114	115	116
CALIFORNIA—Con.																	
Compton	694	74.2	0.0	2	51.1	14.4	59.5	18.1	193	106	74	45.6	487	89	0.0	8.1	0.0
Concord	876	82.7	0.0	2	61.8	6.7	74.8	29.3	277	95	149	50.9	480	108	0.0	10.4	0.0
Corona	461	99.2	0.0	2	35.0	4.1	69.9	10.3	221	100	94	46.7	1 004	457	0.0	3.2	0.0
Costa Mesa	734	83.2	0.0	2	49.6	5.7	72.4	28.8	326	82	220	42.0	476	135	0.0	29.6	0.0
Covina	337	82.5	0.0	2	20.0	3.0	76.1	10.2	250	92	138	16.3	398	52	0.0	7.6	0.0
Culver City	612	154.2	0.0	2	56.4	7.1	80.1	30.2	760	253	411	47.6	1 199	268	0.0	7.1	0.0
Cupertino	109	28.6	0.0	2	15.3	2.0	85.9	7.9	208	10	169	10.7	281	54	0.0	19.1	0.0
Cypress	192	44.4	0.0	2	14.0	2.3	81.9	6.9	161	70	58	12.8	296	21	0.0	27.4	0.0
Daly City	525	63.3	0.0	2	23.7	6.8	75.8	11.9	143	58	74	21.8	263	35	0.0	9.4	0.0
Davis	376	91.2	0.0	2	19.6	4.6	79.9	7.6	184	86	54	17.0	411	69	0.0	12.1	0.0
Downey	510	59.7	0.0	2	26.4	6.1	72.1	14.8	174	44	115	35.5	415	139	0.0	8.0	0.0
El Cajon	584	69.1	0.0	2	27.1	5.7	79.8	14.7	174	38	123	22.0	260	35	0.0	12.7	0.0
El Monte	492	50.9	0.0	2	30.8	12.9	73.8	14.6	151	52	88	25.1	260	16	0.0	12.3	0.0
Escondido	576	68.9	0.0	2	45.7	5.0	74.2	26.5	317	53	121	28.1	336	113	0.0	25.3	0.0
Fairfield	392	57.0	0.0	2	40.6	4.8	72.5	16.2	236	90	80	36.8	535	89	0.0	23.5	0.0
Fontana	286	51.6	0.0	2	17.2	3.6	74.5	7.0	126	43	60	15.0	271	62	0.0	18.5	0.0
Fountain Valley	281	50.7	0.0	2	14.2	3.1	79.9	7.8	140	56	73	13.6	245	24	0.0	17.5	0.0
Fremont	788	51.3	0.0	2	66.8	10.3	68.5	29.2	190	61	83	67.1	437	187	0.0	42.4	0.0
Fresno	2 584	90.8	0.0	2	139.7	32.4	59.3	65.2	229	90	115	145.0	509	123	0.0	11.2	0.0
Fullerton	861	79.2	0.0	2	47.8	9.7	50.8	24.5	226	104	109	45.3	416	66	0.0	17.5	0.0
Gardena	449	91.1	0.0	2	22.5	6.9	81.0	12.9	261	36	150	20.1	407	17	0.0	5.3	0.0
Garden Grove	771	57.2	0.0	2	44.1	12.5	46.9	23.4	174	80	83	37.9	281	45	0.0	15.4	0.0
Glendale	1 539	100.2	0.0	2	96.8	17.1	53.5	37.3	243	75	151	75.4	491	85	0.0	13.4	0.0
Glendora	246	59.7	0.0	2	13.9	2.8	78.9	7.3	178	74	87	13.5	327	74	0.0	22.7	0.0
Hawthorne	426	70.1	0.0	2	27.6	4.9	79.5	13.8	227	47	157	27.5	451	5	0.0	4.2	0.0
Hayward	738	72.7	0.0	2	48.2	8.6	65.9	25.0	246	80	142	39.9	393	34	0.0	12.2	0.0
Huntington Beach	1 194	65.0	0.0	2	75.0	11.8	75.6	45.0	245	92	134	68.5	373	39	0.0	12.6	0.0
Huntington Park	207	37.6	0.0	2	26.1	5.3	55.6	7.1	130	56	61	20.0	363	19	0.0	9.1	0.0
Inglewood	1 065	103.9	0.0	2	52.0	9.6	58.2	26.6	259	71	144	49.6	483	38	0.0	13.1	0.0
Irvine	734	83.0	0.0	2	50.6	4.7	85.7	33.2	376	56	186	47.7	539	247	0.0	38.9	0.0
La Habra	443	92.0	0.0	2	23.0	4.4	84.6	7.4	154	64	78	19.4	403	26	0.0	12.0	0.0
Lakewood	342	45.1	0.0	2	19.6	4.2	80.9	9.3	122	34	79	29.7	391	199	0.0	13.5	0.0
La Mesa	319	61.5	0.0	2	16.7	3.7	75.2	8.8	171	38	120	15.1	290	47	0.0	11.2	0.0
La Mirada	102	24.5	0.0	2	12.6	2.6	73.9	7.0	167	56	103	15.2	365	108	0.0	30.0	0.0
Lancaster	95	15.0	0.0	2	25.1	4.8	74.7	9.5	149	12	101	24.1	380	111	0.0	13.3	0.0
La Puente	46	13.5	0.0	2	5.5	2.0	69.3	2.0	59	6	49	4.5	133	5	0.0	17.7	0.0
Livermore	313	58.2	0.0	2	23.5	3.9	88.0	7.6	142	53	58	27.7	515	212	0.0	41.7	0.0
Lodi	420	95.3	0.0	2	18.1	3.4	86.4	8.1	183	60	84	24.9	564	231	0.0	7.1	0.0
Lompoc	326	104.8	0.0	2	15.1	3.0	76.8	4.4	141	39	69	10.9	350	25	0.0	12.2	0.0
Long Beach	5 197	131.1	0.0	2	423.1	80.3	55.3	118.3	299	114	152	364.6	920	148	0.0	6.1	0.1
Los Altos	168	60.7	0.0	2	9.7	1.4	92.3	4.5	161	73	75	9.3	336	35	0.0	10.5	0.0
Los Angeles	42 771	131.2	0.0	1	2 300.0	424.6	50.1	1 155.5	355	115	170	1 940.5	595	114	0.0	5.0	0.2
Los Gatos town	NA	NA	NA	2	11.7	1.9	85.1	7.1	255	64	160	9.3	333	47	0.0	22.3	0.0
Lynwood	170	30.4	0.0	2	12.2	3.9	68.5	4.9	87	39	43	10.9	195	16	0.0	15.9	0.0
Manhattan Beach	272	78.7	0.0	2	16.1	1.9	92.6	8.5	246	88	106	14.4	418	35	0.0	14.8	0.0
Menlo Park	251	92.0	0.0	2	13.4	2.1	93.4	7.3	266	88	138	15.1	555	193	0.0	28.0	0.0
Merced	364	77.4	0.0	2	20.9	5.1	82.5	8.9	190	75	102	16.1	343	32	0.0	12.1	0.0
Milpitas	307	69.6	0.0	2	33.9	2.7	69.8	17.9	405	229	116	20.4	463	69	0.0	11.4	0.0
Modesto	959	72.1	0.0	2	70.7	33.5	34.6	23.4	176	36	116	75.1	565	284	0.0	9.7	0.0
Monrovia	242	73.1	0.0	2	19.3	3.4	75.2	8.2	248	128	98	22.8	687	319	0.0	6.0	0.0
Montebello	451	82.4	0.0	2	29.1	6.7	63.6	16.9	308	149	128	25.9	473	94	0.0	5.3	0.0
Monterey	NA	NA	NA	2	23.0	2.0	64.2	14.7	488	108	339	22.3	742	124	0.0	9.4	0.0
Monterey Park	378	62.1	0.0	2	21.1	4.8	67.5	12.2	201	99	81	20.2	332	59	0.0	15.9	0.0
Mountain View	555	91.0	0.0	2	46.8	5.5	67.5	23.5	386	129	201	46.0	754	198	0.0	15.6	0.0
Napa	449	79.1	0.0	2	19.0	5.2	77.0	10.6	187	83	81	37.0	652	369	0.0	31.3	0.0
National City	303	52.8	0.0	2	19.4	4.4	65.8	10.5	183	29	146	20.7	361	101	0.0	14.3	0.0
Newark	219	58.5	0.0	2	16.2	3.1	67.4	7.4	197	63	106	16.0	428	75	0.0	25.3	0.0
Newport Beach	788	118.1	0.0	2	51.9	7.6	96.4	27.3	409	176	187	50.9	763	153	0.0	14.8	0.0
Norwalk	305	33.9	0.0	2	23.0	9.6	57.0	8.8	98	15	74	19.5	217	26	0.0	19.4	0.0
Novato	188	41.1	0.0	2	9.2	2.2	87.7	5.1	111	33	63	8.4	184	39	0.0	23.8	0.0
Oakland	4 186	117.3	0.0	2	372.5	57.3	43.3	135.6	380	164	141	336.8	943	246	0.0	5.4	0.4
Oceanside	686	69.2	0.0	2	64.7	6.7	64.3	22.3	225	86	56	58.6	591	99	0.0	11.3	0.0
Ontario	785	68.7	0.0	2	49.1	10.2	73.3	19.5	171	72	85	49.7	434	52	0.0	9.8	0.0
Orange	718	71.3	0.0	2	42.1	7.0	75.0	25.1	249	63	164	35.7	354	27	0.0	14.1	0.0
Oxnard	1 071	84.3	0.0	2	54.1	8.1	59.9	24.7	194	80	98	50.3	396	46	0.0	12.8	0.0
Pacifica	238	64.4	0.0	2	13.2	4.2	82.4	4.6	124	65	52	13.3	361	110	0.0	5.0	0.0
Palm Springs	501	161.6	0.0	2	35.6	3.4	45.3	20.1	648	250	310	38.4	1 238	189	0.0	9.9	0.0
Palo Alto	1 393	249.0	0.0	2	43.6	2.2	66.2	19.4	346	76	244	50.0	894	104	0.0	4.5	0.0
Paramount	217	50.8	0.0	2	16.9	6.0	58.1	7.0	165	69	88	16.5	385	97	0.0	23.2	0.0
Pasadena	1 766	136.0	0.0	2	104.4	20.2	48.0	47.9	369	116	206	95.4	735	138	0.0	10.1	0.0
Petaluma	237	61.5	0.0	2	14.3	4.0	50.0	6.7	173	53	84	14.3	371	80	0.0	14.9	0.0

1. Per 10,000 population estimated as of July 1, 1986. 2. 1=Mayor-council; 2=Council-manager; 3=Commission. Data subject to copyright. 3. Based on resident population estimated as of July 1, 1986.

City	City government finances, 1984–1985 (cont'd)								Climate[2]							Typical monthly electric bills, 1986		
	General expenditure (cont'd)					Debt outstanding			Average daily temperature (Degrees Fahrenheit)							Residential[6]		
	Percent of total for (cont'd)								Mean		Limits							
	Health and hos-pitals	Police protec-tion	Sew-erage and san-itation	Parks and recre-ation	Housing and com-munity dev-elopment	Total (Mil. dol.)	Per capita[1] (Dollars)	Per-cent utility	Jan.	July	Jan.[3]	July[4]	Annual precip-itation (Inches)	Heating degree days[5]	Cooling degree days[5]	Total (Dollars)	Percent change, 1980–1986	Commer-cial[7] (Dollars)
	117	118	119	120	121	122	123	124	125	126	127	128	129	130	131	132	133	134
CALIFORNIA—Con.																		
Compton	0.0	10.0	3.8	3.0	25.7	134.0	1 433	0.0	55.1	69.1	44.1	78.3	13.13	1 719	677	56.07	63.0	558.2
Concord	0.0	19.6	10.4	18.4	14.8	41.3	389	0.0	49.7	61.7	43.2	69.5	23.24	2 951	91	66.97	148.4	NA
Corona	0.0	8.9	4.1	3.5	1.8	209.4	4 505	3.6	53.2	75.2	40.2	91.9	11.60	1 795	1 225	56.07	63.0	NA
Costa Mesa	0.0	19.5	5.4	9.7	1.3	46.0	521	0.0	54.2	66.7	45.8	71.9	11.09	1 954	371	56.07	63.0	558.2
Covina	0.0	20.2	6.3	5.7	4.7	18.1	444	0.0	52.2	74.4	40.7	89.7	17.13	2 048	1 134	56.07	63.0	NA
Culver City	0.0	18.7	8.4	5.1	22.9	41.5	1 045	0.0	56.5	69.2	45.5	77.7	14.09	1 517	770	56.07	63.0	NA
Cupertino	0.0	24.5	1.4	25.4	1.0	4.8	127	0.0	49.5	68.8	41.1	81.5	13.86	2 439	498	66.97	148.4	NA
Cypress	0.0	30.5	1.9	11.1	NA	25.5	589	0.0	55.2	72.8	44.3	83.0	11.54	1 485	1 091	56.07	63.0	NA
Daly City	0.3	27.0	4.3	9.9	7.2	1.8	21	0.0	48.5	62.2	41.5	71.0	19.71	3 161	115	66.97	148.4	NA
Davis	0.0	14.6	22.3	8.4	0.1	19.0	462	0.8	45.1	74.3	37.2	93.2	17.14	2 843	1 059	66.97	148.4	NA
Downey	0.0	21.8	1.1	3.9	32.6	24.7	290	0.0	56.0	69.0	47.3	75.3	12.08	1 595	728	56.07	63.0	558.2
El Cajon	0.0	21.4	11.4	6.0	1.6	2.0	24	0.0	55.4	71.8	44.0	82.6	12.56	1 567	986	73.58	77.5	772.9
El Monte	0.0	27.5	0.5	9.7	9.3	7.1	73	0.0	54.8	74.8	41.3	89.1	17.76	1 532	1 281	56.07	63.0	558.2
Escondido	0.0	20.4	14.8	9.4	0.0	80.9	968	8.1	52.2	73.3	38.7	87.8	14.53	2 006	980	73.58	77.5	772.9
Fairfield	0.0	13.7	1.1	3.0	7.3	246.7	3 588	20.7	46.3	71.7	37.0	88.0	20.94	2 686	821	66.97	148.4	NA
Fontana	0.0	26.9	12.1	12.1	7.1	1.7	30	0.0	55.3	78.7	44.0	94.9	14.93	1 529	1 893	56.07	63.0	NA
Fountain Valley	0.0	30.3	8.6	7.5	4.6	0.6	11	100.0	55.9	72.2	44.1	82.9	12.60	1 430	1 089	56.07	63.0	558.2
Fremont	0.0	16.3	0.4	8.8	3.6	159.6	1 039	0.0	47.8	66.3	38.5	77.9	14.77	2 891	275	66.97	148.4	NA
Fresno	0.0	20.5	12.5	22.0	1.8	160.1	563	0.2	45.5	81.0	36.8	97.9	10.52	2 647	1 769	66.97	148.4	NA
Fullerton	0.0	23.6	9.2	8.6	6.6	12.1	111	2.3	54.9	73.5	42.4	88.8	14.46	1 644	1 118	56.07	63.0	558.2
Gardena	0.2	31.9	3.2	8.0	2.5	0.4	8	0.0	55.1	69.1	44.1	78.3	13.13	1 719	677	56.07	63.0	NA
Garden Grove	3.5	30.1	0.6	4.5	12.7	12.3	91	21.6	55.9	72.2	44.1	82.9	12.60	1 430	1 089	56.07	63.0	558.2
Glendale	NA	19.1	10.6	6.8	10.1	60.9	396	63.3	55.0	74.7	43.1	88.6	19.29	1 550	1 299	55.66	5.6	NA
Glendora	0.3	28.6	6.8	9.2	12.8	8.6	208	5.2	52.2	74.4	40.7	89.7	17.13	2 048	1 134	56.07	63.0	NA
Hawthorne	0.0	29.9	16.6	5.5	4.4	26.6	438	0.0	55.1	69.1	44.1	78.3	13.13	1 719	677	56.07	63.0	558.2
Hayward	0.0	28.1	10.7	0.5	2.2	36.3	357	2.5	45.9	71.3	34.7	90.0	14.11	3 011	734	66.97	148.4	NA
Huntington Beach	0.0	26.7	9.1	7.6	1.4	65.3	356	1.7	54.2	66.7	45.8	71.9	11.09	1 954	371	56.07	63.0	558.2
Huntington Park	0.0	21.5	2.4	4.5	6.1	153.8	2 797	0.0	56.5	69.2	45.5	77.7	14.09	1 517	770	56.07	63.0	NA
Inglewood	0.0	24.4	11.6	7.2	4.2	98.3	959	18.6	56.5	69.2	45.5	77.7	14.09	1 517	770	56.07	63.0	558.2
Irvine	0.0	15.4	4.2	15.0	0.4	121.8	1 378	0.0	55.9	72.2	44.1	82.9	12.60	1 430	1 089	56.07	63.0	558.2
La Habra	0.0	21.6	5.0	7.1	2.9	50.6	1 050	5.6	54.9	73.5	42.4	88.8	14.46	1 644	1 118	56.07	63.0	NA
Lakewood	0.0	18.8	6.2	25.7	19.3	8.8	117	25.1	55.2	72.8	44.3	83.0	11.54	1 485	1 091	56.07	63.0	558.2
La Mesa	0.0	21.7	13.1	17.6	0.4	14.2	275	0.0	55.4	71.8	44.0	82.6	12.56	1 567	986	73.58	77.5	772.9
La Mirada	0.0	17.9	0.7	21.4	14.1	10.3	248	0.0	54.9	73.5	42.4	88.8	14.46	1 644	1 118	56.07	63.0	NA
Lancaster	NA	11.1	1.0	11.3	4.7	169.1	2 661	0.0	45.4	81.4	32.2	97.7	7.38	2 908	1 760	56.07	63.0	NA
La Puente	0.7	33.1	2.4	11.5	11.9	0.0	0	0.0	54.8	74.8	41.3	89.1	17.76	1 532	1 281	56.07	63.0	NA
Livermore	0.0	13.9	13.1	3.2	0.5	49.1	912	0.0	45.9	71.3	34.7	90.0	14.11	3 011	734	66.97	148.4	NA
Lodi	0.0	12.2	16.7	8.0	0.0	13.5	307	0.0	45.4	73.9	37.0	91.8	16.27	2 861	1 001	52.85	70.2	NA
Lompoc	0.0	16.4	22.3	6.5	3.3	6.6	213	12.6	51.9	61.5	39.5	70.9	13.88	2 890	87	67.31	83.9	NA
Long Beach	1.6	16.8	4.1	8.4	8.3	423.2	1 068	1.5	55.2	72.8	44.3	83.0	11.54	1 485	1 091	56.07	63.0	558.2
Los Altos	0.0	15.3	10.1	12.4	0.0	2.6	94	0.0	48.7	68.4	39.2	82.9	19.27	2 600	432	66.97	148.4	NA
Los Angeles	0.3	21.8	11.5	5.6	7.9	3 670.6	1 126	51.1	57.2	74.1	47.7	83.8	14.85	1 204	1 339	58.55	28.4	487.2
Los Gatos town	0.0	29.5	2.5	7.2	1.8	1.8	63	0.0	48.1	69.8	38.1	86.3	25.59	2 740	591	66.97	148.4	NA
Lynwood	0.0	25.8	6.6	5.5	6.0	1.9	34	0.0	55.1	69.1	44.1	78.3	13.13	1 719	677	56.07	63.0	NA
Manhattan Beach	0.0	29.8	13.0	9.5	0.0	0.1	3	0.0	55.1	69.1	44.1	78.3	13.13	1 719	677	56.07	63.0	NA
Menlo Park	0.0	19.6	4.4	22.9	2.2	2.0	72	0.0	48.7	68.4	39.2	82.9	19.27	2 600	432	66.97	148.4	NA
Merced	1.6	14.3	18.0	11.7	6.5	18.8	400	14.9	45.6	78.7	36.0	97.3	12.05	2 653	1 465	66.97	148.4	NA
Milpitas	0.0	19.2	10.2	6.7	3.0	63.9	1 449	0.0	47.8	66.3	38.5	77.9	14.77	2 891	275	66.97	148.4	NA
Modesto	NA	13.1	40.5	7.2	8.5	67.1	505	0.0	45.7	76.8	37.5	94.4	11.70	2 671	1 287	32.77	84.0	531.5
Monrovia	0.0	14.8	4.6	3.6	48.5	38.3	1 157	0.2	55.0	74.7	43.1	88.6	19.29	1 550	1 299	56.07	63.0	NA
Montebello	0.0	20.5	0.0	12.1	24.3	24.9	454	0.0	54.8	74.8	41.3	89.1	17.76	1 532	1 281	56.07	63.0	558.2
Monterey	0.0	14.0	2.1	18.6	0.4	22.2	739	0.0	51.4	59.5	42.8	67.7	18.35	3 170	48	66.97	148.4	NA
Monterey Park	0.0	22.5	10.0	8.2	5.1	16.7	274	0.0	54.8	74.8	41.3	89.1	17.76	1 532	1 281	56.07	63.0	558.2
Mountain View	0.0	11.4	15.1	17.4	2.6	72.3	1 186	1.2	48.7	68.4	39.2	82.9	19.27	2 600	432	66.97	148.4	NA
Napa	0.0	11.1	0.0	2.7	18.3	56.8	1 001	34.5	47.6	67.7	37.9	82.4	24.34	2 749	416	66.97	148.4	NA
National City	0.0	22.0	5.1	7.5	20.4	9.3	163	0.0	56.8	70.3	48.4	75.6	9.32	1 284	842	73.58	77.5	NA
Newark	0.0	20.5	0.8	7.5	3.9	64.4	1 721	0.0	47.8	66.3	38.5	77.9	14.77	2 891	275	66.97	148.4	NA
Newport Beach	0.0	24.3	4.3	17.7	0.0	61.2	917	0.0	54.2	66.7	45.8	71.9	11.09	1 954	371	56.07	63.0	558.2
Norwalk	0.0	19.2	9.9	12.9	8.4	0.0	0	0.0	54.9	73.5	42.4	88.8	14.46	1 644	1 118	56.07	63.0	558.2
Novato	0.0	34.0	0.0	17.6	0.0	0.1	2	0.0	47.1	67.0	37.7	82.5	24.02	2 960	316	66.97	148.4	NA
Oakland	0.1	12.8	1.6	7.9	7.1	717.0	2 009	0.0	49.0	63.7	43.4	70.6	18.03	2 877	174	66.97	148.4	NA
Oceanside	0.0	14.3	24.5	2.7	6.0	80.0	807	7.8	52.2	73.3	38.7	87.8	14.53	2 006	980	73.58	77.5	772.9
Ontario	0.0	17.6	11.3	4.7	4.4	56.8	497	2.3	52.4	74.6	39.0	90.9	17.02	1 972	1 191	56.07	63.0	558.2
Orange	0.0	24.1	7.3	8.2	3.7	1.9	19	92.3	55.9	72.2	44.1	82.9	12.60	1 430	1 089	56.07	63.0	558.2
Oxnard	0.2	20.5	27.5	11.1	1.5	8.8	69	46.2	54.6	65.7	43.5	74.7	14.53	2 068	357	56.07	63.0	558.2
Pacifica	0.0	18.7	24.3	6.6	0.0	2.4	64	0.0	48.5	62.2	41.5	71.0	19.71	3 161	115	66.97	148.4	NA
Palm Springs	0.0	23.2	5.9	10.0	1.2	31.6	1 020	0.0	55.1	91.7	40.8	109.1	5.20	1 109	3 820	56.07	63.0	NA
Palo Alto	0.0	18.2	17.2	12.0	1.0	23.5	421	4.2	47.8	66.3	38.5	77.9	14.77	2 891	275	66.97	148.4	NA
Paramount	0.0	18.9	0.0	10.2	2.6	57.3	1 341	0.9	57.2	74.1	47.7	83.8	14.85	1 204	1 339	31.35	124.9	333.0
Pasadena	3.9	17.6	5.9	13.3	1.7	141.1	1 086	15.5	55.0	74.7	43.1	88.6	19.29	1 550	1 299	56.07	12.2	NA
Petaluma	0.0	20.4	15.0	6.6	1.2	15.8	410	7.2	47.1	67.0	37.7	82.5	24.02	2 960	316	66.97	148.4	NA

1. Based on resident population estimated as of July 1, 1986. 2. Represents normal values based on the 30-year period, 1951–1980 (see text). 3. Average daily minimum. 4. Average daily maximum. 5. For definition, see text. 6. As of January 1; based on consumption of 750 kWh. 7. Based on billing demand of 30 kW and consumption of 6,000 kWh.

MSA/ CMSA Code[1]	State/ Place code	City	Land area,[2] 1990 (Sq. Km.)	Population: 1990: Total persons	Population: 1990: Rank	Population: 1990: Per sq. km.	Population: 1980	Population: Change 1980–1990: Number	Population: Change 1980–1990: Percent	Population characteristics, 1990: Percent: Race: White	Race: Black	Race: Am. Indian, Eskimo, Aleut	Race: Asian & Pacific Islander	Race: Other race	Hispanic[3]	65 Years and over
			1	2	3	4	5	6	7	8	9	10	11	12	13	14
		CALIFORNIA—Con.														
4472	06 2145	Pico Rivera	20.7	59 177	396	2 859	53 387	5 790	10.8	58.78	0.69	0.56	3.16	36.81	83.20	9.6
7362	06 2175	Pittsburg	28.2	47 564	520	1 687	33 465	14 099	42.1	58.60	17.58	0.77	12.18	10.87	23.73	7.7
4472	06 2195	Placentia	17.1	41 259	604	2 413	35 041	6 218	17.7	76.18	1.85	0.49	8.19	13.29	24.66	7.2
7362	06 2210	Pleasant Hill	17.6	31 585	796	1 795	25 547	6 038	23.6	89.31	1.40	0.60	6.98	1.71	6.65	11.7
7362	06 2215	Pleasanton	42.0	50 553	488	1 204	35 160	15 393	43.8	90.67	1.37	0.43	5.78	1.75	6.69	5.4
4472	06 2230	Pomona	59.1	131 723	136	2 229	92 742	38 981	42.0	57.02	14.43	0.57	6.67	21.30	51.27	7.0
4472	06 2278	Rancho Cucamonga	97.9	101 409	189	1 036	55 250	46 159	83.5	78.59	5.87	0.57	5.44	9.53	20.02	5.1
4472	06 2284	Rancho Palos Verdes	35.4	41 659	601	1 177	36 577	5 082	13.9	76.19	1.89	0.24	20.51	1.17	5.32	12.0
6690	06 2290	Redding	132.7	66 462	343	501	42 103	24 359	57.9	92.60	1.05	2.16	3.27	0.92	3.96	14.5
4472	06 2295	Redlands	63.0	60 394	385	959	43 619	16 775	38.5	79.59	3.83	0.73	4.42	11.43	18.96	11.9
4472	06 2300	Redondo Beach	16.3	60 167	386	3 691	57 102	3 065	5.4	87.04	1.60	0.52	6.83	4.01	11.50	7.2
7362	06 2305	Redwood City	49.3	66 072	345	1 340	54 951	11 121	20.2	82.76	3.64	0.51	6.32	6.77	24.12	11.5
4472	06 2320	Rialto	55.0	72 388	302	1 316	37 862	34 526	91.2	57.93	20.35	0.87	3.53	17.33	31.48	6.6
7362	06 2330	Richmond	77.0	87 425	233	1 135	74 676	12 749	17.1	36.18	43.76	0.60	11.83	7.63	14.52	11.3
4472	06 2370	Riverside	201.2	226 505	68	1 126	170 591	55 914	32.8	70.79	7.39	0.84	5.22	15.76	25.97	8.9
4472	06 2400	Rosemead	13.3	51 638	472	3 883	42 604	9 034	21.2	35.44	0.62	0.48	34.33	29.13	49.66	9.0
6920	06 2420	Sacramento	249.4	369 365	41	1 481	275 741	93 624	34.0	60.09	15.30	1.23	15.01	8.36	16.25	12.1
7120	06 2435	Salinas	48.2	108 777	171	2 257	80 479	28 298	35.2	54.55	3.01	0.95	8.08	33.40	50.64	8.3
4472	06 2450	San Bernardino	142.7	164 164	105	1 150	118 794	45 370	38.2	60.64	16.01	0.97	4.00	18.38	34.57	10.0
7362	06 2455	San Bruno	16.7	38 961	647	2 333	35 417	3 544	10.0	71.62	4.08	0.75	17.93	5.62	18.61	10.5
4472	06 2460	San Buenaventura (Ventura)	53.1	92 575	218	1 743	73 774	18 801	25.5	86.10	1.68	1.06	2.71	8.46	17.55	12.5
4472	06 2470	San Clemente	45.2	41 100	606	909	27 325	13 775	50.4	91.56	0.67	0.43	2.71	4.64	12.86	13.0
7320	06 2475	San Diego	839.2	1 110 549	6	1 323	875 538	235 011	26.8	67.12	9.39	0.61	11.79	11.09	20.67	10.2
7362	06 2485	San Francisco	121.0	723 959	14	5 983	678 974	44 985	6.6	53.56	10.92	0.48	29.13	5.91	13.91	14.6
4472	06 2490	San Gabriel	10.7	37 120	683	3 469	30 072	7 048	23.4	47.96	1.06	0.54	32.45	17.99	36.29	13.4
7362	06 2510	San Jose	443.6	782 248	11	1 763	629 400	152 848	24.3	62.80	4.70	0.69	19.54	12.27	26.64	7.2
7362	06 2525	San Leandro	34.0	68 223	332	2 007	63 952	4 271	6.7	74.14	5.75	0.74	13.77	5.60	15.19	19.3
...	06 2535	San Luis Obispo	24.0	41 958	595	1 748	34 252	7 706	22.5	88.68	1.90	0.75	5.11	3.57	9.42	12.2
7362	06 2555	San Mateo	31.6	85 486	241	2 705	77 640	7 846	10.1	78.57	3.58	0.39	13.31	4.15	15.48	16.3
7362	06 2565	San Rafael	43.0	48 404	512	1 126	44 700	3 704	8.3	83.48	2.94	0.34	5.50	7.73	14.36	13.9
4472	06 2570	Santa Ana	70.2	293 742	52	4 184	204 023	89 719	44.0	67.99	2.62	0.52	9.73	19.14	65.15	5.6
7480	06 2575	Santa Barbara	48.9	85 571	239	1 750	74 414	11 157	15.0	77.75	2.24	0.89	2.33	16.79	31.46	16.2
7362	06 2580	Santa Clara	47.4	93 613	214	1 975	87 700	5 913	6.7	73.69	2.57	0.51	18.60	4.63	15.23	10.0
7362	06 2585	Santa Cruz	34.5	49 040	503	1 421	41 483	7 557	18.2	85.88	2.30	0.87	4.63	6.32	13.58	10.1
7480	06 2595	Santa Maria	44.5	61 284	377	1 377	39 685	21 599	54.4	61.55	2.20	0.95	6.06	29.23	45.71	12.0
4472	06 2600	Santa Monica	21.4	86 905	234	4 061	88 314	-1 409	-1.6	82.80	4.51	0.44	6.39	5.86	14.05	16.5
7362	06 2615	Santa Rosa	87.3	113 313	157	1 298	82 658	30 655	37.1	89.37	1.79	1.22	3.36	4.25	9.47	16.3
7362	06 2630	Saratoga	31.0	28 061	868	905	29 261	-1 200	-4.1	83.69	0.42	0.19	15.02	0.68	3.35	13.6
4472	06 2650	Seal Beach	30.4	25 098	920	826	25 975	-877	-3.4	93.70	0.98	0.20	4.21	0.91	4.99	37.0
7120	06 2655	Seaside	22.9	38 901	650	1 699	36 567	2 334	6.4	52.73	23.47	0.95	13.48	9.37	17.45	5.4
4472	06 2702	Simi Valley	85.6	100 217	193	1 171	77 500	22 717	29.3	88.15	1.52	0.61	5.46	4.25	12.68	5.3
4472	06 2730	South Gate	19.0	86 284	238	4 541	66 784	19 500	29.2	41.65	1.67	0.44	1.62	54.63	83.13	7.3
7362	06 2765	South San Francisco	23.2	54 312	438	2 341	49 393	4 919	10.0	61.49	4.00	0.66	24.61	9.24	27.12	11.4
8120	06 2805	Stockton	136.2	210 943	74	1 549	148 283	62 660	42.3	57.54	9.63	0.98	22.80	9.06	24.96	10.5
7362	06 2835	Sunnyvale	56.7	117 229	152	2 068	106 618	10 611	10.0	71.63	3.43	0.52	19.33	5.09	13.17	10.4
4472	06 2880	Temple City	10.4	31 100	803	2 990	28 972	2 128	7.3	71.93	0.62	0.37	19.51	7.58	18.85	14.9
4472	06 2897	Thousand Oaks	128.4	104 352	183	813	77 072	27 280	35.4	90.40	1.22	0.40	4.78	3.21	9.60	9.0
4472	06 2910	Torrance	53.2	133 107	135	2 502	129 881	3 226	2.5	72.98	1.45	0.40	21.86	3.30	10.07	11.9
5170	06 2960	Turlock	24.8	42 198	588	1 702	26 287	15 911	60.5	82.52	1.18	0.93	4.37	11.00	20.97	12.5
4472	06 2965	Tustin	29.2	50 689	484	1 736	32 248	18 441	57.2	73.24	5.71	0.54	10.38	10.13	20.73	7.5
7362	06 2985	Union City	48.6	53 762	444	1 106	39 406	14 356	36.4	43.92	8.58	0.59	33.44	13.47	25.08	7.1
4472	06 2990	Upland	39.1	63 374	361	1 621	47 647	15 727	33.0	78.85	5.33	0.45	7.03	8.33	17.54	9.2
7362	06 2995	Vacaville	58.6	71 479	308	1 220	43 367	28 112	64.8	78.84	8.91	0.99	3.81	7.45	15.90	6.8
7362	06 3000	Vallejo	78.3	109 199	169	1 395	80 303	28 896	36.0	50.46	21.15	0.74	22.95	4.70	10.78	10.9
8780	06 3015	Visalia	60.8	75 636	284	1 244	49 729	25 907	52.1	74.77	1.47	0.97	6.44	16.34	25.13	11.1
7320	06 3017	Vista	46.5	71 872	304	1 546	35 834	36 038	100.6	80.66	4.45	0.83	3.97	10.09	24.77	12.2
7362	06 3030	Walnut Creek	50.0	60 569	382	1 211	54 033	6 536	12.1	90.60	1.05	0.25	6.68	1.42	4.74	22.8
4472	06 3070	West Covina	42.0	96 086	207	2 288	80 292	15 794	19.7	59.78	8.54	0.50	17.20	13.99	34.61	8.7
4472	06 3085	Westminster	26.0	78 118	272	3 005	71 133	6 985	9.8	69.63	1.11	0.59	22.55	6.12	19.07	9.4
4472	06 3110	Whittier	32.5	77 671	274	2 390	68 558	9 113	13.3	73.45	1.28	0.59	3.32	21.36	38.98	13.9
6920	06 3150	Woodland	23.8	39 802	633	1 672	30 235	9 567	31.6	77.47	1.26	1.33	3.07	16.87	26.16	11.2
4472	06 3169	Yorba Linda	45.3	52 422	461	1 157	28 254	24 168	85.5	85.74	1.10	0.42	10.12	2.60	9.44	5.0
...	08 0000	COLORADO	268 659.5	3 294 394	X	12	2 889 735	404 659	14.0	88.19	4.04	0.84	1.82	5.10	12.88	10.0
2082	08 0040	Arvada	57.3	89 235	226	1 557	84 576	4 659	5.5	94.28	0.57	0.53	1.98	2.63	7.44	7.6
2082	08 0055	Aurora	343.2	222 103	72	647	158 588	63 515	40.1	82.41	11.43	0.64	3.77	1.74	6.65	6.8
2082	08 0110	Boulder	58.4	83 312	254	1 427	76 685	6 627	8.6	92.53	1.26	0.50	3.85	1.86	4.83	7.8
1720	08 0240	Colorado Springs	474.5	281 140	54	592	215 105	66 035	30.7	85.90	7.02	0.83	2.43	3.81	9.13	9.2
2082	08 0320	Denver	397.0	467 610	26	1 178	492 686	-25 076	-5.1	72.11	12.84	1.15	2.35	11.54	22.96	13.9
2082	08 0395	Englewood	16.9	29 387	837	1 739	30 021	-634	-2.1	93.83	1.21	0.91	1.53	2.51	7.99	15.9
2670	08 0455	Fort Collins	106.7	87 758	230	822	65 092	22 666	34.8	93.30	0.98	0.52	2.39	2.81	7.06	7.7

1. MSA = Metropolitan Statistical Area. CMSA = Consolidated MSA. 2. Dry land or land partially or temporarily covered by water. 3. Hispanic persons may be of any race.

City	Households, 1990: Number	Households, 1990: Persons per house-hold	Households, 1990: Percent– Female family house-holder[1]	Households, 1990: Percent– One-person[2]	Births, 1984: Number: Total	Births, 1984: Number: To mothers under 20 yrs. old (Percent)	Births, 1984: Rate[3]	Deaths, 1984: Number: Total	Deaths, 1984: Number: Infant[4]	Deaths, 1984: Rate: Total[3]	Deaths, 1984: Rate: Infant[5]	Hospitals, 1985: Number	Hospitals, 1985: Beds: Number	Hospitals, 1985: Beds: Rate[6]
	15	16	17	18	19	20	21	22	23	24	25	26	27	28
CALIFORNIA—Con.														
Pico Rivera	16 002	3.67	15.2	13.8	1 088	13.8	19.3	349	10	6.2	9.2	1	95	175
Pittsburg	15 643	3.02	14.3	17.8	1 182	12.2	30.6	364	3	9.4	2.5	1	81	196
Placentia	13 369	3.07	10.9	14.7	581	11.7	15.6	163	4	4.4	6.9	1	114	298
Pleasant Hill	13 004	2.39	8.3	26.7	406	3.9	15.2	197	2	7.4	4.9	0	0	0
Pleasanton	18 484	2.73	8.0	16.8	420	5.7	10.9	177	2	4.6	4.8	0	0	0
Pomona	36 443	3.52	14.2	18.2	2 704	14.5	25.3	779	22	7.3	8.1	4	1 714	1 483
Rancho Cucamonga	33 635	3.01	9.8	16.1	398	4.0	6.3	164	10	2.6	25.1	0	0	0
Rancho Palos Verdes	14 943	2.76	6.2	14.0	292	3.4	6.3	188	5	4.0	17.1	0	0	0
Redding	26 105	2.48	12.2	25.6	1 125	11.8	23.3	594	14	12.3	12.4	3	405	787
Redlands	21 985	2.65	11.0	24.4	763	12.1	15.4	420	9	8.5	11.8	1	195	369
Redondo Beach	26 717	2.25	9.0	29.4	977	4.3	16.0	400	4	6.5	4.1	1	203	318
Redwood City	25 493	2.52	10.0	27.5	1 358	7.7	24.4	578	9	10.4	6.6	3	545	950
Rialto	21 893	3.30	13.9	15.7	988	14.4	22.1	320	14	7.2	14.2	0	0	0
Richmond	32 749	2.63	20.3	27.2	1 464	15.8	19.2	766	17	10.1	11.6	1	43	55
Riverside	75 463	2.92	12.5	20.6	4 626	12.6	25.4	1 611	54	8.8	11.7	5	1 017	517
Rosemead	13 701	3.72	15.4	14.3	1 096	11.1	23.9	330	10	7.2	9.1	2	227	478
Sacramento	144 444	2.50	14.3	30.9	9 566	13.6	31.5	4 569	83	15.0	8.7	6	1 937	599
Salinas	33 360	3.21	14.2	19.3	2 511	15.2	28.7	766	21	8.7	8.4	3	426	439
San Bernardino	54 482	2.90	17.5	23.4	3 434	16.7	26.3	1 413	48	10.8	14.0	3	915	660
San Bruno	14 640	2.58	10.0	27.0	582	4.8	16.8	232	5	6.7	8.6	0	0	0
San Buenaventura (Ventura)	35 408	2.55	10.7	24.6	1 401	8.8	16.8	796	8	9.5	5.7	0	0	0
San Clemente	16 701	2.46	7.0	23.5	526	8.7	17.7	222	6	7.4	11.4	1	116	349
San Diego	406 096	2.61	11.2	26.3	15 928	9.6	16.6	6 622	155	6.9	9.7	18	4 465	440
San Francisco	305 584	2.29	9.9	39.3	9 679	8.1	13.6	7 984	85	11.2	8.8	19	6 131	819
San Gabriel	12 216	3.00	13.8	20.5	826	5.6	26.2	454	6	14.4	7.3	1	184	557
San Jose	250 218	3.08	11.9	18.4	14 598	10.7	21.3	3 865	115	5.6	7.9	6	1 802	253
San Leandro	29 128	2.33	10.4	30.8	1 022	5.1	15.5	929	6	14.1	5.9	3	505	767
San Luis Obispo	16 952	2.39	7.4	27.9	361	7.8	10.2	290	4	8.2	11.1	4	422	1 134
San Mateo	35 480	2.36	9.0	31.1	1 098	4.7	13.8	798	15	10.1	13.7	2	477	589
San Rafael	20 295	2.31	8.9	30.8	597	3.0	13.5	563	8	12.7	13.4	1	235	525
Santa Ana	71 611	4.00	11.8	16.6	6 931	13.8	30.7	1 473	65	6.5	9.4	5	741	313
Santa Barbara	34 348	2.41	9.5	32.4	1 497	8.8	19.5	1 236	12	16.1	8.0	7	784	989
Santa Clara	36 545	2.49	10.2	27.0	1 290	5.1	14.3	604	12	6.7	9.3	1	318	359
Santa Cruz	18 121	2.50	10.1	27.2	1 132	8.8	25.7	723	9	16.4	8.0	2	405	883
Santa Maria	19 907	3.04	12.6	19.7	1 354	13.3	29.1	539	9	11.6	6.6	2	154	300
Santa Monica	44 860	1.88	7.9	49.6	975	5.8	10.7	1 002	7	11.0	7.2	2	824	884
Santa Rosa	45 708	2.44	10.6	27.5	1 965	8.3	21.5	1 258	12	13.8	6.1	4	525	538
Saratoga	10 050	2.76	5.4	13.7	220	1.8	7.4	213	0	7.2	0.0	0	0	0
Seal Beach	13 370	1.86	5.0	46.9	144	1.4	5.5	558	1	21.4	6.9	0	0	0
Seaside	10 641	3.10	12.3	16.5	1 392	10.8	37.0	205	22	5.4	15.8	0	0	0
Simi Valley	31 998	3.12	9.5	12.6	1 400	9.0	16.5	339	11	4.0	7.9	2	209	232
South Gate	22 428	3.84	15.4	15.1	1 938	11.0	25.6	524	15	6.9	7.7	0	0	0
South San Francisco	18 519	2.91	12.4	20.9	796	6.8	15.7	359	6	7.1	7.5	1	120	233
Stockton	68 794	3.00	15.5	23.4	4 868	15.1	28.4	2 014	47	11.7	9.7	4	714	389
Sunnyvale	48 296	2.42	9.0	28.1	1 722	5.3	15.6	694	14	6.3	8.1	0	0	0
Temple City	11 055	2.77	12.3	21.9	424	8.0	14.0	304	2	10.0	4.7	0	0	0
Thousand Oaks	36 457	2.82	8.2	17.2	813	5.4	8.7	310	2	3.3	2.5	1	212	220
Torrance	52 615	2.51	9.3	25.3	2 059	6.0	15.5	1 058	25	8.0	12.1	5	1 269	936
Turlock	14 689	2.81	12.0	21.6	845	14.2	26.9	338	6	10.8	7.1	1	319	939
Tustin	18 332	2.66	11.6	23.6	868	5.8	22.1	274	10	7.0	11.5	1	150	357
Union City	15 701	3.39	12.1	12.8	896	8.9	19.0	190	8	4.0	8.9	0	0	0
Upland	23 077	2.73	11.2	20.9	762	8.4	14.5	390	4	7.4	5.2	1	310	542
Vacaville	22 627	2.82	10.4	17.3	859	8.8	17.7	250	7	5.1	8.1	1	84	153
Vallejo	37 383	2.85	13.1	21.7	1 766	13.0	19.9	840	14	9.5	7.9	2	328	352
Visalia	26 111	2.84	12.3	21.2	1 434	15.5	25.7	532	10	9.5	7.0	2	282	458
Vista	25 371	2.78	10.4	20.0	1 215	10.4	28.3	536	13	12.5	10.7	0	0	0
Walnut Creek	28 347	2.11	6.3	35.8	622	1.3	11.1	802	6	14.3	9.6	3	526	897
West Covina	30 096	3.18	13.5	14.7	1 603	7.9	17.9	496	15	5.5	9.4	3	402	415
Westminster	25 077	3.10	10.8	17.5	1 126	8.9	15.4	474	8	6.5	7.1	1	182	249
Whittier	27 637	2.72	12.0	22.8	2 722	9.1	38.8	1 168	16	16.6	5.9	2	521	717
Woodland	14 198	2.75	12.1	20.9	601	14.1	18.2	287	3	8.7	5.0	2	240	698
Yorba Linda	16 774	3.12	7.2	10.8	563	3.2	16.4	119	4	3.5	7.1	0	0	0
COLORADO	1 282 489	2.51	9.7	26.6	54 364	10.7	17.1	20 394	552	6.4	10.2	100	14 732	451
Arvada	32 744	2.71	9.9	19.5	1 525	7.9	17.0	396	11	4.4	7.2	0	0	0
Aurora	89 132	2.47	11.8	28.1	4 313	7.7	22.1	848	42	4.4	9.7	3	756	347
Boulder	34 681	2.18	7.1	33.4	1 008	5.1	13.0	432	3	5.6	3.0	4	279	365
Colorado Springs	110 862	2.49	10.1	26.7	5 233	11.9	21.1	1 565	62	6.3	11.8	6	1 387	509
Denver	210 952	2.17	11.5	40.4	8 927	13.9	17.7	4 629	106	9.2	11.9	22	5 424	1 074
Englewood	13 252	2.19	10.9	35.9	724	11.3	23.7	338	10	11.1	13.8	2	385	1 263
Fort Collins	33 689	2.44	7.6	26.2	1 260	7.2	17.8	424	14	6.0	11.1	1	202	272

1. No spouse present. 2. Householder living alone. 3. Per 1,000 resident population estimated as of July 1 of the year shown. 4. Deaths of infants under 1 year old. 5. Deaths of infants under 1 year old per 1,000 live births. 6. Per 100,000 resident population estimated as of July 1, 1986.

City	Serious crimes known to police, 1985 — Number — Total	Violent[1]	Rate[2]	Police officers, 1985 — Number	Rate[3]	Educational attainment,[4] 1980 — Percent completing 12 years or more	Percent completing 16 years or more	Money income — Per capita[5] — 1985 — Total (Dollars)	Percent of State average	1979 — Current dollars	Constant (1985) dollars	Percent below poverty level, 1979 — Persons	Families	Housing, 1990 — Total units	Percent change, 1980–1990	Vacant units for sale or rent[6]
	29	30	31	32	33	34	35	36	37	38	39	40	41	42	43	44
CALIFORNIA—Con.																
Pico Rivera	2 295	412	3 912	NA	NA	54.3	5.0	8 111	68.2	5 878	8 711	10.7	8.9	16 316	2.6	255
Pittsburg	2 966	643	7 629	52	13.4	71.1	11.3	9 821	82.6	6 867	10 177	12.9	10.6	16 709	28.6	915
Placentia	1 429	96	3 655	44	11.3	81.5	25.7	13 499	113.6	8 993	13 328	5.1	3.7	13 733	17.1	330
Pleasant Hill	1 809	90	6 336	37	13.0	84.9	25.5	14 945	125.7	9 784	14 500	4.5	2.8	13 653	25.7	444
Pleasanton	1 611	72	4 216	51	13.3	87.8	24.8	15 560	130.9	9 619	14 255	3.5	3.1	19 356	39.7	804
Pomona	9 705	1 912	8 816	149	13.5	61.9	10.7	8 574	72.1	5 819	8 624	17.2	13.5	38 466	16.4	1 592
Rancho Cucamonga	2 697	166	4 247	NA	NA	82.0	16.8	11 832	99.6	8 240	12 212	5.5	4.6	36 367	50.9	2 282
Rancho Palos Verdes	751	77	1 912	NA	NA	95.3	51.2	22 822	192.0	15 222	22 559	2.8	2.2	15 468	20.6	416
Redding	3 528	275	7 544	71	15.2	79.7	16.4	9 972	83.9	7 535	11 167	10.1	7.8	27 238	34.2	781
Redlands	2 411	181	4 808	63	12.6	79.0	27.0	12 118	102.0	8 545	12 664	9.7	7.7	23 189	26.1	1 008
Redondo Beach	3 494	249	5 544	95	15.1	83.2	24.0	17 313	145.7	10 287	15 245	7.8	5.6	28 220	8.3	1 228
Redwood City	2 841	210	4 830	70	11.9	76.8	18.6	14 542	122.4	9 720	14 405	7.2	5.2	26 847	12.5	1 133
Rialto	3 227	316	7 227	50	11.2	74.2	9.2	9 517	80.1	7 046	10 442	8.5	7.0	23 836	41.8	1 707
Richmond	9 453	1 960	11 630	158	19.4	67.3	13.7	9 854	82.9	6 977	10 340	16.5	14.9	34 532	15.8	1 390
Riverside	15 688	1 870	8 366	254	13.5	76.6	18.7	10 802	90.9	7 597	11 259	11.3	8.7	80 240	19.9	4 013
Rosemead	2 317	369	4 895	NA	NA	54.7	8.6	7 904	66.5	5 641	8 360	14.9	11.6	14 134	3.5	318
Sacramento	33 908	3 681	10 835	502	16.0	71.6	18.7	10 627	89.4	7 558	11 201	15.0	11.7	153 362	19.6	6 874
Salinas	7 736	634	8 558	138	15.3	60.6	12.5	8 852	74.5	6 795	10 070	12.5	9.5	34 577	17.9	1 018
San Bernardino	15 001	2 248	11 181	238	17.7	66.7	12.4	8 876	74.7	6 339	9 394	16.3	13.8	58 804	21.0	3 398
San Bruno	1 435	129	3 834	46	12.3	81.2	18.4	14 121	118.8	9 655	14 309	5.0	3.8	15 178	3.4	438
San Buenaventura (Ventura)	4 711	419	5 449	106	12.3	81.2	20.5	12 516	105.3	8 543	12 661	7.7	5.8	37 343	18.0	1 430
San Clemente	1 046	70	3 402	38	12.4	86.5	25.1	16 721	140.7	10 545	15 628	7.8	6.2	18 726	29.3	1 055
San Diego	67 893	6 250	6 870	1 407	14.2	78.9	24.0	11 766	99.0	8 016	11 880	12.4	9.2	431 722	20.8	20 212
San Francisco	58 590	9 502	7 988	1 929	26.3	74.0	28.2	13 575	114.2	9 265	13 731	13.7	10.3	328 471	3.6	15 836
San Gabriel	1 822	253	5 529	47	14.3	67.9	15.8	11 100	93.4	7 742	11 474	11.1	8.8	12 736	9.3	431
San Jose	40 224	3 470	5 697	976	13.8	76.4	21.1	12 583	105.9	8 382	12 422	8.2	6.3	259 365	16.5	7 715
San Leandro	4 784	411	6 917	87	12.6	69.9	10.6	13 199	111.1	9 453	14 009	4.8	3.5	30 189	7.0	876
San Luis Obispo	2 055	87	5 604	49	13.4	84.1	30.1	10 831	91.1	7 324	10 854	23.3	7.1	17 877	18.9	631
San Mateo	4 916	499	5 894	105	12.6	82.5	24.5	16 261	136.8	11 080	16 421	5.8	4.4	36 928	7.2	1 201
San Rafael	2 383	153	5 015	70	14.7	88.2	33.2	17 218	144.9	11 542	17 105	7.7	5.4	21 139	9.2	720
Santa Ana	22 459	1 558	9 683	352	15.2	59.7	12.0	9 395	79.0	6 567	9 732	14.0	10.1	74 973	10.4	2 878
Santa Barbara	4 732	360	5 920	132	16.5	77.9	28.0	13 733	115.5	9 103	13 491	11.0	6.3	36 226	6.4	1 296
Santa Clara	5 407	278	5 728	141	14.9	76.9	20.7	14 367	120.9	9 360	13 872	5.8	4.0	37 873	8.0	1 112
Santa Cruz	5 835	306	12 870	59	13.0	79.4	24.7	11 149	93.8	7 535	11 167	16.5	10.1	19 364	7.7	713
Santa Maria	3 628	223	8 034	59	13.1	65.1	10.5	9 501	79.9	6 507	9 643	11.7	9.5	21 144	29.0	874
Santa Monica	9 795	915	10 259	146	15.3	82.0	33.6	17 755	149.4	11 126	16 489	9.9	6.6	47 753	2.8	1 531
Santa Rosa	6 405	356	6 878	120	12.9	81.1	22.0	12 291	103.4	8 471	12 554	9.3	6.5	47 726	26.3	1 541
Saratoga	701	41	2 236	NA	NA	92.5	48.1	25 572	215.2	15 059	22 317	2.2	1.4	10 315	7.5	177
Seal Beach	902	89	3 296	38	13.9	78.8	26.0	16 594	139.6	11 128	16 492	6.0	2.3	14 407	3.3	510
Seaside	2 009	559	4 966	36	8.9	76.3	11.3	7 950	66.9	5 546	8 219	14.7	12.8	11 238	8.2	358
Simi Valley	2 636	114	3 026	77	8.8	82.9	14.1	12 104	101.8	7 801	11 561	4.9	4.0	33 111	31.6	1 008
South Gate	3 828	548	4 965	90	11.7	48.0	4.9	7 070	59.5	5 734	8 498	14.2	12.2	22 946	-2.8	420
South San Francisco	2 055	101	3 828	73	13.6	73.3	14.3	11 981	100.8	8 478	12 564	6.2	5.0	19 081	5.6	422
Stockton	19 389	1 561	10 977	253	14.3	65.7	14.0	9 333	78.5	6 757	10 014	16.6	13.5	72 525	15.5	2 664
Sunnyvale	4 004	224	3 518	117	10.3	83.1	26.6	16 073	135.2	10 359	15 352	4.8	3.7	50 789	13.3	2 231
Temple City	923	66	2 912	NA	NA	76.9	13.2	11 980	100.8	8 574	12 707	4.8	3.4	11 548	4.4	390
Thousand Oaks	3 154	127	3 251	NA	NA	89.3	29.6	15 178	127.7	9 879	14 641	4.4	3.4	37 765	27.2	1 066
Torrance	7 178	635	5 250	234	17.1	83.6	22.1	15 333	129.0	10 285	15 242	4.7	3.6	54 927	7.2	1 846
Turlock	2 354	118	7 667	42	13.7	65.3	15.9	8 998	75.7	6 953	10 304	12.9	11.6	15 400	29.1	614
Tustin	3 114	346	7 581	59	14.4	85.0	23.9	13 429	113.0	9 342	13 845	6.6	4.2	19 300	31.8	858
Union City	2 813	231	6 195	48	10.6	72.9	14.8	10 784	90.7	7 565	11 211	7.1	6.3	16 259	24.1	502
Upland	2 566	138	4 809	57	10.7	79.5	22.3	13 504	113.6	9 641	14 288	6.8	5.6	24 496	24.1	1 203
Vacaville	1 825	124	3 631	47	9.4	79.3	16.0	10 891	91.6	7 499	11 114	8.5	6.7	23 660	35.1	890
Vallejo	6 424	623	6 992	104	11.3	72.9	12.5	10 185	85.7	7 226	10 709	10.7	9.3	39 902	24.0	2 031
Visalia	4 780	260	8 387	73	12.8	72.3	17.4	10 038	84.5	7 474	11 076	10.8	9.0	27 154	28.2	842
Vista	NA	NA	NA	NA	NA	73.1	15.1	10 212	85.9	7 207	10 681	11.0	8.8	27 418	45.4	1 815
Walnut Creek	2 654	117	4 408	73	12.1	91.3	37.5	19 265	162.1	12 764	18 916	4.0	2.9	29 968	18.6	1 316
West Covina	5 551	442	5 993	104	11.2	81.8	18.4	11 844	99.7	8 697	12 889	5.3	4.2	31 112	12.0	918
Westminster	4 378	317	5 633	81	10.4	76.9	15.5	12 181	102.5	8 454	12 529	7.2	5.6	25 852	5.0	693
Whittier	3 085	258	4 173	85	11.5	76.4	19.7	13 763	115.8	9 648	14 298	7.4	5.3	28 758	3.3	929
Woodland	2 022	161	5 996	46	13.6	69.2	14.7	10 499	88.3	7 774	11 521	8.3	6.9	14 818	24.1	510
Yorba Linda	760	82	2 270	NA	NA	89.6	29.0	16 160	136.0	10 308	15 276	3.0	2.3	17 341	47.8	503
COLORADO	223 555	15 219	6 919	NA	NA	78.6	23.0	11 713	100.0	7 998	11 853	10.1	7.4	1 477 349	19.2	98 422
Arvada	3 654	268	3 918	113	12.1	85.6	21.8	12 927	110.4	8 754	12 973	3.9	2.8	34 541	15.0	1 462
Aurora	16 906	2 250	8 537	340	17.2	87.8	25.0	13 133	112.1	8 925	13 227	5.4	4.1	99 890	37.1	9 494
Boulder	5 862	239	7 113	121	14.7	91.9	50.5	13 054	111.4	8 385	12 427	16.3	6.9	36 270	16.5	1 306
Colorado Springs	21 835	1 169	8 669	386	15.3	82.3	22.4	11 334	96.8	7 405	10 974	10.3	7.8	124 442	29.1	11 451
Denver	53 234	4 252	10 376	1 349	26.3	74.7	24.8	12 490	106.6	8 553	12 676	13.7	10.3	239 636	4.9	22 955
Englewood	3 921	197	11 833	75	22.6	74.9	16.3	11 657	99.5	7 837	11 614	7.8	5.3	14 908	10.4	1 412
Fort Collins	4 446	331	6 154	83	11.5	85.6	38.5	10 444	89.2	7 130	10 567	15.3	6.5	35 357	28.2	1 284

1. Includes murder and nonnegligent manslaughter, forcible rape, robbery, and aggravated assault. 2. Per 100,000 resident population estimated for 1985 by the FBI. 3. Per 10,000 resident population estimated for 1985 by the FBI. 4. Persons 25 years old or older. 5. Based on the resident population estimated as of July 1, 1988 for 1987 data and enumerated as of April 1, 1980 for 1979 data. 6. Also includes units rented or sold, but not occupied.

City	Housing, 1990 (cont'd): Occupied units: Total	Percent with more than 1 person per room	Owner-occupied: Percent of total	Owner-occupied: Median value[1] (Dollars)	Median rent[2] (Dollars)	Construction authorized by building permits, 1990: New private housing units: Number	Value ($1,000)	Percent single family	Non-residential, value ($1,000)	Civilian labor force, 1990: Total	Percent change, 1989–1990	Unemployment: Total	Rate[3]
	45	46	47	48	49	50	51	52	53	54	55	56	57
CALIFORNIA—Con.													
Pico Rivera	16 002	25.9	70.1	165 000	561	9	767	33.3	409	28 344	5.1	1 883	6.6
Pittsburg	15 643	11.1	61.4	138 900	566	205	21 265	98.5	33 265	18 726	-1.2	1 121	6.0
Placentia	13 369	9.8	65.2	255 800	735	58	3 758	31.0	6 054	25 007	-2.0	767	3.1
Pleasant Hill	13 004	2.3	62.2	229 400	696	11	1 599	100.0	2 955	18 290	-1.3	596	3.3
Pleasanton	18 484	1.7	70.2	297 200	760	96	17 084	100.0	23 589	22 318	-1.4	491	2.2
Pomona	36 443	25.5	57.4	134 200	527	238	25 664	64.3	20 712	47 486	5.2	3 423	7.2
Rancho Cucamonga	33 635	5.5	70.3	182 800	644	897	106 497	60.4	43 179	42 013	4.3	1 573	3.7
Rancho Palos Verdes	14 943	2.7	81.7	500 001	1 001	49	16 247	100.0	3 177	22 630	4.2	535	2.4
Redding	26 105	4.5	53.5	95 300	373	1 721	140 035	70.5	39 482	25 498	-0.7	1 913	7.5
Redlands	21 985	5.4	59.2	144 300	527	309	35 627	37.9	10 950	31 160	4.3	1 235	4.0
Redondo Beach	26 717	4.1	46.4	348 300	828	271	61 049	100.0	11 562	42 693	4.5	1 636	3.8
Redwood City	25 493	10.5	50.8	349 500	670	41	5 915	63.4	53 557	33 561	-1.6	798	2.4
Rialto	21 893	11.5	70.0	125 500	510	538	57 254	91.8	19 673	27 433	4.7	1 729	6.3
Richmond	32 749	9.9	54.5	144 300	506	609	32 227	17.4	16 780	41 866	-1.2	2 893	6.9
Riverside	75 463	10.8	56.3	134 800	512	1 253	108 821	51.6	84 259	137 927	4.8	10 338	7.5
Rosemead	13 701	35.9	49.3	193 900	581	71	9 112	85.9	8 977	21 969	4.9	1 313	6.0
Sacramento	144 444	8.5	51.3	115 800	429	2 181	174 145	86.4	166 874	175 542	0.6	9 515	5.4
Salinas	33 360	22.2	46.3	161 500	528	205	19 690	94.6	16 731	49 282	-2.1	5 051	10.2
San Bernardino	54 482	14.5	52.3	96 200	422	1 050	99 829	80.8	22 304	75 159	4.8	5 229	7.0
San Bruno	14 640	8.8	62.5	294 600	709	5	733	60.0	6 564	22 273	-1.5	596	2.7
San Buenaventura (Ventura)	35 408	6.1	56.3	242 300	671	266	33 127	58.3	20 122	NA	NA	NA	NA
San Clemente	16 701	5.2	58.6	308 500	721	136	28 173	69.1	21 282	18 888	-1.9	662	3.5
San Diego	406 096	10.5	48.3	189 400	560	8 312	756 845	26.1	299 091	556 688	0.2	25 124	4.5
San Francisco	305 584	10.7	34.5	298 900	613	1 077	143 432	14.9	164 032	393 245	-1.8	15 695	4.0
San Gabriel	12 216	21.1	48.5	251 600	620	19	3 514	100.0	20 042	17 120	4.7	823	4.8
San Jose	250 218	14.9	61.3	259 100	692	1 725	117 052	21.3	118 559	381 968	-3.9	18 088	4.7
San Leandro	29 128	5.2	58.5	193 700	608	34	2 958	23.5	6 891	40 635	-1.4	1 346	3.3
San Luis Obispo	16 952	6.5	44.1	241 100	546	80	7 720	63.7	5 394	24 622	-1.6	792	3.2
San Mateo	35 480	7.1	53.2	349 800	738	12	2 108	66.7	3 032	47 227	-1.6	1 101	2.3
San Rafael	20 295	5.9	54.5	342 700	691	443	36 626	7.9	1 902	26 459	-1.6	711	2.7
Santa Ana	71 611	38.1	48.3	185 400	679	94	9 577	63.8	76 435	137 686	-1.8	6 064	4.4
Santa Barbara	34 348	10.6	42.2	346 900	670	57	8 975	87.7	2 604	48 507	-1.4	1 713	3.5
Santa Clara	36 545	9.3	47.1	270 400	737	503	35 967	8.5	92 466	60 140	-4.0	2 070	3.4
Santa Cruz	18 121	7.1	47.4	263 200	651	51	6 631	88.2	4 677	30 276	0.8	2 022	6.7
Santa Maria	19 907	16.8	53.8	141 900	505	358	28 256	48.6	24 245	22 900	-1.1	1 679	7.3
Santa Monica	44 860	5.4	27.5	500 001	498	308	45 099	23.1	65 748	60 558	4.5	2 501	4.1
Santa Rosa	45 708	4.3	57.9	193 800	579	1 197	108 274	63.7	17 712	58 551	3.3	2 285	3.9
Saratoga	10 050	1.5	89.4	500 001	994	40	15 523	100.0	902	17 096	-4.1	421	2.5
Seal Beach	13 370	1.3	75.9	353 600	790	9	1 933	100.0	839	14 661	-2.0	427	2.9
Seaside	10 641	14.6	38.0	150 100	565	17	1 826	88.2	1 103	13 886	-2.2	1 276	9.2
Simi Valley	31 998	5.5	76.4	233 000	844	134	12 265	9.7	29 951	57 294	0.5	2 747	4.8
South Gate	22 428	42.2	48.5	162 500	508	68	3 163	17.6	14 572	33 782	5.0	2 192	6.5
South San Francisco	18 519	12.8	61.4	271 900	670	54	6 045	72.2	7 596	29 442	-1.5	935	3.2
Stockton	68 794	16.8	48.5	107 200	404	1 418	128 632	88.2	58 700	85 252	-2.3	8 269	9.7
Sunnyvale	48 296	8.4	48.9	332 700	728	354	38 519	35.9	15 166	74 178	-4.0	2 314	3.1
Temple City	11 055	9.4	63.7	255 900	641	53	5 246	79.2	1 365	16 992	4.4	557	3.3
Thousand Oaks	36 457	3.7	73.7	297 000	840	769	87 736	17.7	28 910	59 917	0.4	2 473	4.1
Torrance	52 615	6.4	56.3	340 000	740	187	33 478	86.1	45 722	88 027	4.4	2 915	3.3
Turlock	14 689	10.3	52.5	123 300	406	752	61 112	83.4	13 118	16 913	-0.9	1 595	9.4
Tustin	18 332	11.3	40.9	254 500	701	1 504	117 334	71.8	5 627	23 955	-1.9	792	3.3
Union City	15 701	15.0	67.4	229 300	703	209	20 876	100.0	10 450	24 001	-1.5	895	3.7
Upland	23 077	6.4	60.3	226 500	562	185	16 518	57.3	7 313	40 290	4.2	1 247	3.1
Vacaville	22 627	4.9	64.5	147 900	561	582	84 733	100.0	13 735	26 519	2.1	1 766	6.7
Vallejo	37 383	9.3	61.9	140 600	511	456	34 446	60.1	30 669	50 470	2.1	2 164	4.3
Visalia	26 111	8.8	60.5	90 300	384	910	89 905	86.8	31 034	30 277	-3.1	2 401	7.9
Vista	25 371	11.0	53.9	183 400	582	411	55 566	68.9	29 315	22 567	0.2	1 102	4.9
Walnut Creek	28 347	1.6	67.7	291 500	675	213	25 630	24.4	2 047	33 979	-1.3	956	2.8
West Covina	30 096	13.2	66.7	205 000	672	125	13 649	31.2	2 886	52 719	4.6	2 374	4.5
Westminster	25 077	14.6	62.8	226 100	690	72	6 518	0.0	31 181	48 586	-1.9	1 733	3.6
Whittier	27 637	10.1	57.7	213 600	583	61	10 861	68.9	10 610	42 229	4.6	1 801	4.3
Woodland	14 198	9.7	57.2	131 300	431	283	18 858	54.1	4 421	19 077	0.6	1 313	6.9
Yorba Linda	16 774	3.0	84.3	326 200	893	200	52 658	100.0	15 448	19 746	-2.1	379	1.9
COLORADO	1 282 489	3.0	62.2	82 700	362	12 012	1 172 594	84.3	225 314	1 756 000	3.6	87 000	4.9
Arvada	32 744	1.7	72.8	89 800	400	268	22 298	84.7	876	54 112	2.8	2 274	4.2
Aurora	89 132	2.9	58.7	80 200	393	115	12 946	100.0	11 075	114 573	2.9	4 946	4.3
Boulder	34 681	2.3	46.2	122 700	480	514	33 656	48.2	12 457	58 686	3.7	2 251	3.8
Colorado Springs	110 862	2.8	54.6	81 900	360	NA	NA	NA	NA	142 865	0.8	8 780	6.1
Denver	210 952	4.2	49.2	79 000	339	198	15 852	81.8	15 310	266 954	2.8	14 482	5.4
Englewood	13 252	2.4	51.8	72 800	367	4	153	100.0	714	22 918	2.9	1 005	4.4
Fort Collins	33 689	2.0	52.7	85 000	376	728	46 978	74.2	8 822	45 394	5.9	1 748	3.9

1. Specified owner-occupied units. 2. Specified renter-occupied units. 3. Percent of total civilian labor force.

City	Employed,[1] 1980: Total	Employed,[1] 1980: Rate per 1,000 employees: Professional, specialty, and technical	Employed,[1] 1980: Rate per 1,000 employees: Precision production, craft, and operators	Manufactures, 1987: Establishments: Total	Manufactures, 1987: Establishments: Percent with 20 or more employees	Manufactures, 1987: All employees: Number (1,000)	Manufactures, 1987: All employees: Percent change, 1982–1987	Manufactures, 1987: All employees: Annual payroll (Mil. dol.)	Manufactures, 1987: Production workers: Number (1,000)	Manufactures, 1987: Production workers: Work-hours (Millions)	Manufactures, 1987: Production workers: Wages: Total (Mil. dol.)	Manufactures, 1987: Production workers: Wages: Average per production worker (Dollars)	Manufactures, 1987: Value added by manufacture (Mil. dol.)	Manufactures, 1987: Value of shipments (Mil. dol.)	Manufactures, 1987: New capital expenditures (Mil. dol.)
	58	59	60	61	62	63	64	65	66	67	68	69	70	71	72
CALIFORNIA—Con.															
Pico Rivera	22 016	65.5	321.9	82	46.3	3.3	10.0	65.0	2.5	4.9	39.3	15 720	149.0	339.7	8.5
Pittsburg	13 476	108.0	246.1	40	32.5	1.8	-25.0	51.6	0.8	1.6	24.9	31 125	136.0	320.0	D
Placentia	17 682	184.9	171.4	106	36.8	2.7	50.0	59.2	1.9	4.1	33.0	17 368	143.8	234.9	5.1
Pleasant Hill	13 544	180.1	160.1	31	32.3	0.6	20.0	10.8	0.4	0.8	5.8	14 500	23.1	37.1	1.1
Pleasanton	17 349	182.2	143.5	76	25.0	2.0	66.7	66.3	0.6	1.2	12.2	20 333	99.0	167.4	2.7
Pomona	36 661	125.4	287.0	232	41.8	18.5	24.2	477.0	12.5	24.8	268.9	21 512	1 132.1	2 070.2	72.9
Rancho Cucamonga	24 930	153.5	223.9	172	40.1	8.5	107.3	221.6	4.6	9.0	87.8	19 087	593.3	936.5	22.1
Rancho Palos Verdes	18 383	299.9	64.8	NA	NA	NA	NA	NA	NA	NA	NA	NA	NA	NA	NA
Redding	17 614	170.9	137.6	115	26.1	2.3	35.3	41.4	1.5	2.5	23.1	15 400	99.7	229.5	6.2
Redlands	18 448	238.5	142.6	42	28.6	1.5	25.0	23.9	1.1	2.2	16.9	15 364	55.9	119.0	2.5
Redondo Beach	34 160	190.0	188.7	55	20.0	D	D	D	D	D	D	D	D	D	D
Redwood City	29 935	155.6	204.9	124	28.2	3.7	-17.8	136.6	1.5	3.0	37.9	25 267	180.0	293.6	18.7
Rialto	15 846	114.9	224.0	51	37.3	1.2	33.3	23.6	0.8	1.7	15.7	19 625	53.8	137.3	1.6
Richmond	29 833	144.3	185.9	139	34.5	6.6	D	223.2	3.5	6.6	101.4	28 971	813.5	2 867.8	57.0
Riverside	76 468	181.9	203.2	254	32.7	15.4	20.3	373.1	10.1	19.1	198.0	19 604	744.8	1 423.2	45.7
Rosemead	17 186	81.5	303.7	57	19.3	1.5	0.0	25.1	1.3	2.4	18.3	14 077	51.9	91.2	1.8
Sacramento	113 333	175.2	138.0	448	30.6	21.0	15.4	542.3	11.4	22.7	238.7	20 939	1 408.6	2 703.4	93.7
Salinas	34 240	103.0	164.9	87	29.9	3.3	-2.9	74.7	2.2	4.1	44.3	20 136	317.3	598.8	16.8
San Bernardino	43 110	148.8	180.9	144	37.5	4.9	25.6	87.0	3.4	6.5	51.3	15 088	209.2	425.6	15.4
San Bruno	19 806	122.4	183.1	NA	NA	NA	NA	NA	NA	NA	NA	NA	NA	NA	NA
San Buenaventura (Ventura)	34 777	190.7	168.2	162	16.0	2.5	25.0	53.1	1.5	2.9	25.8	17 200	124.5	202.7	4.7
San Clemente	13 295	187.1	177.4	NA	NA	NA	NA	NA	NA	NA	NA	NA	NA	NA	NA
San Diego	358 469	206.4	161.8	1 397	29.2	77.5	0.9	2 266.6	39.2	74.3	844.1	21 533	4 302.9	7 398.8	314.6
San Francisco	342 484	191.5	116.2	1 695	27.8	43.8	-16.4	1 174.9	25.5	46.0	458.4	17 976	2 745.0	4 727.9	84.3
San Gabriel	13 559	132.5	205.8	86	26.7	1.3	-18.8	22.3	0.9	1.8	12.6	14 000	58.1	91.1	D
San Jose	308 112	183.2	225.7	1 056	31.7	68.3	16.8	2 335.7	31.7	62.3	759.4	23 956	4 645.1	7 864.4	384.2
San Leandro	31 229	99.0	223.0	263	41.4	11.8	-11.3	329.4	7.6	14.9	182.9	24 066	914.3	1 969.8	37.6
San Luis Obispo	15 801	212.6	117.6	74	27.0	1.9	D	37.4	1.1	2.0	18.9	17 182	77.4	142.3	4.8
San Mateo	42 144	145.9	150.2	94	13.8	1.4	-33.3	43.5	0.6	1.2	10.7	17 833	47.1	77.6	1.5
San Rafael	24 348	197.7	118.5	145	15.9	2.0	11.1	49.7	1.0	2.0	19.8	19 800	86.0	147.1	4.3
Santa Ana	96 012	112.9	315.4	1 013	32.3	39.1	20.3	890.1	24.6	49.6	477.9	19 427	1 974.9	3 632.8	114.6
Santa Barbara	37 315	198.5	153.6	197	16.2	3.0	-25.0	68.9	1.7	3.3	33.9	19 941	185.8	280.9	11.0
Santa Clara	49 170	204.5	244.5	662	35.6	48.8	-16.2	1 631.7	20.9	46.4	510.0	24 402	3 741.3	5 482.3	284.1
Santa Cruz	19 010	205.9	177.2	108	28.7	3.1	-18.4	75.6	2.0	4.0	46.5	23 250	300.5	499.0	11.8
Santa Maria	16 922	109.4	199.6	72	36.1	2.9	26.1	54.9	1.8	3.6	31.6	17 556	147.1	318.6	4.4
Santa Monica	48 304	279.1	111.8	203	26.1	8.6	2.4	253.9	5.4	11.1	113.1	20 944	472.7	762.9	20.5
Santa Rosa	36 452	176.6	165.1	192	24.0	7.4	17.5	186.8	4.6	8.8	103.8	22 565	413.1	697.2	21.8
Saratoga	14 119	282.4	98.9	NA	NA	NA	NA	NA	NA	NA	NA	NA	NA	NA	NA
Seal Beach	10 383	262.4	98.9	12	8.3	D	D	D	D	D	D	D	D	D	D
Seaside	9 762	92.0	160.3	NA	NA	NA	NA	NA	NA	NA	NA	NA	NA	NA	NA
Simi Valley	36 320	156.0	252.6	157	26.8	5.7	171.4	144.1	3.2	6.2	56.9	17 781	273.9	472.7	14.4
South Gate	26 283	53.5	391.6	214	38.8	8.3	0.0	178.2	6.3	12.2	118.3	18 778	417.3	856.7	16.4
South San Francisco	26 046	96.8	190.1	187	38.0	7.4	15.6	199.7	3.9	7.8	92.1	23 615	584.6	1 146.2	48.0
Stockton	59 044	137.9	164.9	230	37.0	9.5	17.3	207.8	7.1	13.6	142.5	20 070	650.3	1 420.2	32.0
Sunnyvale	60 850	235.3	206.8	406	42.1	71.6	-15.7	2 620.0	20.6	40.2	554.3	26 908	6 864.0	9 535.2	553.3
Temple City	13 674	128.6	194.2	41	17.1	D	D	D	D	D	D	D	D	D	D
Thousand Oaks	38 249	209.0	148.1	114	36.0	5.9	90.3	189.7	2.6	4.9	64.0	24 615	398.8	603.7	13.3
Torrance	70 814	182.2	175.1	345	35.1	30.6	34.8	1 035.4	19.0	36.0	545.9	28 732	2 070.0	4 276.2	287.8
Turlock	11 186	154.6	216.0	67	38.8	3.4	17.2	59.5	2.7	5.6	42.1	15 593	186.0	413.4	8.7
Tustin	16 896	172.3	172.8	136	34.6	8.5	3.7	242.3	4.0	7.5	91.4	22 850	448.9	847.9	38.8
Union City	18 366	116.8	262.9	77	48.1	2.7	35.0	72.9	2.0	4.2	47.2	23 600	234.3	541.8	14.8
Upland	24 069	188.5	192.6	92	23.9	1.5	-11.8	33.2	1.1	2.3	21.2	19 273	73.9	194.2	3.4
Vacaville	16 285	148.4	249.4	37	40.5	1.5	D	29.4	1.0	1.6	18.0	18 000	79.7	149.3	3.6
Vallejo	31 781	137.2	214.3	47	14.9	0.7	D	15.0	0.5	0.9	9.1	18 200	44.8	97.4	D
Visalia	21 808	172.4	159.4	117	32.5	4.3	19.4	80.3	3.2	6.2	54.7	17 094	258.8	581.0	13.7
Vista	14 475	122.1	224.1	53	15.1	0.9	80.0	15.2	0.5	1.0	7.7	15 400	40.8	64.9	1.3
Walnut Creek	25 278	222.3	89.8	75	24.0	4.2	35.5	113.7	1.2	2.9	29.1	24 250	233.0	316.8	12.5
West Covina	41 887	152.2	207.3	30	20.0	1.6	0.0	42.8	0.4	0.7	7.1	17 750	42.7	126.5	2.9
Westminster	34 177	161.1	233.5	110	18.2	1.9	-20.8	33.7	1.3	2.4	18.4	14 154	79.2	134.5	3.8
Whittier	33 636	168.4	202.4	117	32.5	3.3	13.8	65.1	2.4	4.5	40.6	16 917	174.6	301.3	5.3
Woodland	13 022	130.1	190.8	70	38.6	2.8	7.7	55.6	2.0	4.0	37.0	18 500	213.1	431.6	11.6
Yorba Linda	14 127	202.0	141.7	NA	NA	NA	NA	NA	NA	NA	NA	NA	NA	NA	NA
COLORADO	1 362 017	173.6	183.9	4 718	23.4	183.8	-4.0	4 958.4	103.3	204.0	2 285.6	22 126	12 045.8	23 235.9	791.5
Arvada	43 404	169.0	196.8	105	21.0	2.0	D	52.5	1.2	2.5	27.6	23 000	116.1	199.2	5.7
Aurora	81 613	165.2	145.9	131	16.8	3.8	26.7	102.4	1.9	4.1	38.7	20 368	310.7	454.4	9.2
Boulder	41 817	304.3	121.4	225	28.0	14.5	3.6	463.9	4.4	8.6	85.5	19 432	723.0	1 300.2	83.0
Colorado Springs	90 846	173.8	188.9	352	25.6	20.8	20.9	509.6	12.2	23.4	240.7	19 730	1 046.7	1 954.1	92.7
Denver	244 838	193.4	156.0	1 146	26.9	37.9	-14.3	935.9	20.4	39.0	397.6	19 490	2 034.8	3 798.2	109.1
Englewood	15 915	145.5	231.0	226	24.3	5.3	10.4	140.1	3.2	6.6	63.3	19 781	316.1	571.8	12.8
Fort Collins	32 096	238.8	141.8	103	17.5	6.0	-4.8	180.5	2.9	5.8	67.2	23 172	385.2	601.3	23.5

1. Persons 16 years old and over.

City	Wholesale trade, 1987: Establishments	Wholesale trade, 1987: Sales (Mil. dol.)	Wholesale trade, 1987: Paid employees[1]	Wholesale trade, 1987: Annual payroll ($1,000)	Retail trade–all establishments, 1987: Number	Retail trade–all establishments, 1987: Sales: Total (Mil. dol.)	Retail trade–all establishments, 1987: Sales: Percent change, 1982–1987	Retail trade–all establishments, 1987: Sales: Per capita[2] (Dollars)	Retail trade–establishments with payroll, 1987: Number	Retail trade–establishments with payroll, 1987: Sales: Total (Mil. dol.)	Retail trade–establishments with payroll, 1987: Sales: Per capita[2] (Dollars): General merchandise group stores	Retail trade–establishments with payroll, 1987: Sales: Per capita[2] (Dollars): Food stores	Retail trade–establishments with payroll, 1987: Sales: Per capita[2] (Dollars): Apparel and accessory stores	Retail trade–establishments with payroll, 1987: Sales: Per capita[2] (Dollars): Eating and drinking places
	73	74	75	76	77	78	79	80	81	82	83	84	85	86
CALIFORNIA—Con.														
Pico Rivera	96	467.9	1 832	47 761	347	169.1	7.8	3 112	181	160.9	513	1 076	133	475
Pittsburg	24	148.5	383	10 237	239	167.6	59.6	4 064	131	163.2	D	1 216	56	338
Placentia	103	327.2	897	22 171	352	176.7	26.8	4 620	155	165.9	0	778	258	444
Pleasant Hill	50	256.2	435	10 414	346	321.3	27.8	11 282	217	316.5	3 216	1 826	620	1 158
Pleasanton	145	2 725.1	2 210	69 563	519	363.6	191.3	8 198	317	352.9	D	2 058	222	933
Pomona	161	624.4	1 753	41 975	776	605.6	35.4	5 241	466	590.1	D	1 102	113	575
Rancho Cucamonga	100	414.7	1 246	29 214	534	256.0	71.1	3 379	259	240.5	D	993	119	578
Rancho Palos Verdes	30	38.3	100	2 640	327	66.0	72.3	1 418	82	50.5	0	577	34	205
Redding	184	382.0	1 616	33 994	1 001	699.0	61.6	13 575	671	682.1	1 654	2 599	445	1 102
Redlands	33	59.0	279	4 286	518	443.7	72.4	8 388	311	435.4	972	1 497	150	827
Redondo Beach	62	228.9	730	21 202	736	507.0	83.0	7 943	466	492.8	D	1 740	1 449	1 126
Redwood City	141	675.9	1 729	57 883	628	779.6	65.2	13 596	416	767.7	D	2 146	286	1 287
Rialto	41	297.5	506	13 700	354	205.7	73.3	3 824	184	199.4	D	1 536	206	403
Richmond	128	766.2	1 781	46 124	546	487.9	37.8	6 266	359	479.0	1 940	866	369	320
Riverside	273	1 307.0	4 243	102 490	1 766	1 793.4	68.7	9 115	1 154	1 756.9	1 323	1 346	312	737
Rosemead	51	264.1	606	9 035	411	224.7	32.8	4 729	183	211.8	D	881	79	562
Sacramento	792	4 054.9	13 239	311 964	2 940	2 395.7	44.3	7 404	2 074	2 351.4	1 262	1 558	285	888
Salinas	240	1 184.6	3 061	75 906	1 131	800.6	36.9	8 257	713	778.2	1 160	1 469	440	672
San Bernardino	211	965.5	3 206	73 417	1 457	1 442.3	49.3	10 405	1 078	1 419.2	2 329	1 479	447	976
San Bruno	53	693.7	745	24 324	415	361.4	37.5	10 270	273	353.9	2 768	1 354	595	674
San Buenaventura (Ventura)	262	657.9	2 529	58 591	1 192	1 045.2	69.6	12 197	755	1 023.6	1 387	1 789	460	978
San Clemente	61	117.7	214	5 881	438	207.1	54.0	6 238	228	195.1	D	1 809	134	942
San Diego	1 832	6 644.3	23 875	606 323	9 396	6 790.1	56.4	6 689	5 890	6 614.2	766	1 161	436	868
San Francisco	2 257	13 943.4	28 131	759 142	10 194	5 726.7	34.7	7 646	6 884	5 513.0	766	1 307	674	1 494
San Gabriel	87	175.9	605	11 411	406	231.3	7.7	6 998	219	221.5	D	893	122	849
San Jose	1 132	7 687.3	18 631	551 823	5 977	4 031.3	27.7	5 661	3 308	3 893.5	657	1 240	290	560
San Leandro	355	2 046.8	5 641	158 070	807	755.9	53.7	11 488	536	742.1	2 284	2 474	355	974
San Luis Obispo	82	93.7	681	12 471	677	530.1	72.1	14 242	516	519.2	1 300	2 665	679	1 389
San Mateo	201	1 583.8	2 080	69 472	1 089	857.5	47.3	10 584	696	836.4	2 220	1 564	1 425	975
San Rafael	229	614.2	2 160	52 260	869	764.7	36.9	17 096	626	746.8	2 814	1 938	716	1 188
Santa Ana	711	3 769.1	10 043	265 802	2 068	1 817.7	53.8	7 677	1 310	1 774.2	1 399	1 277	292	778
Santa Barbara	195	331.3	1 718	37 370	1 433	894.8	36.1	11 285	975	866.3	915	2 172	893	1 599
Santa Clara	520	3 965.2	9 876	317 316	1 011	1 376.3	92.0	15 541	703	1 360.9	2 533	1 480	1 239	1 072
Santa Cruz	75	134.1	806	16 095	747	523.3	32.5	11 403	510	510.8	791	2 087	447	1 537
Santa Maria	136	294.7	1 234	28 706	648	525.3	12.6	10 246	447	513.5	1 288	1 857	493	822
Santa Monica	268	2 030.2	2 368	61 694	1 532	1 297.6	38.2	13 927	1 046	1 266.4	1 154	1 492	900	1 890
Santa Rosa	245	786.9	2 630	59 187	1 654	1 439.9	100.4	14 753	1 097	1 406.7	2 462	2 507	698	1 017
Saratoga	40	325.0	226	6 822	274	87.0	15.8	2 947	120	80.0	D	965	64	D
Seal Beach	19	15.5	44	1 150	255	109.7	19.0	4 083	152	104.1	D	1 214	394	747
Seaside	17	23.2	160	2 782	222	248.2	60.0	6 699	142	244.4	D	204	50	397
Simi Valley	69	150.7	557	11 877	849	557.3	76.5	6 190	437	537.8	675	1 623	215	610
South Gate	100	1 328.8	1 743	45 179	509	534.0	139.0	6 627	240	517.3	D	1 142	73	292
South San Francisco	464	4 042.9	7 810	218 035	516	520.5	91.2	10 097	310	506.8	1 697	1 889	74	1 993
Stockton	346	1 544.7	4 357	98 175	1 701	1 335.3	46.9	7 280	1 141	1 303.4	1 175	1 254	334	758
Sunnyvale	272	3 796.1	7 006	232 662	1 047	987.0	49.9	8 802	648	971.1	1 474	1 405	309	944
Temple City	31	24.3	115	2 063	364	168.6	37.1	5 425	167	157.6	D	939	524	449
Thousand Oaks	133	D	D	D	1 081	1 019.2	61.5	10 586	621	997.0	1 638	1 331	440	822
Torrance	488	13 655.3	8 686	287 985	1 913	2 127.7	65.2	15 694	1 235	2 083.7	2 573	2 107	1 115	1 175
Turlock	59	96.0	542	8 077	416	269.4	56.5	7 933	260	262.5	742	2 068	354	756
Tustin	188	1 083.8	2 758	82 947	516	389.4	45.3	9 278	332	380.7	D	2 287	280	1 325
Union City	83	704.1	1 846	51 586	259	104.9	31.8	2 068	111	96.9	0	941	0	219
Upland	89	184.7	828	13 586	617	442.2	82.7	7 736	325	421.5	699	1 489	187	717
Vacaville	20	76.1	169	3 477	399	262.8	50.8	4 786	244	257.2	D	1 354	182	773
Vallejo	47	203.9	542	14 906	757	565.1	35.6	6 059	467	552.5	D	1 280	98	517
Visalia	145	607.3	1 549	33 193	931	630.8	27.0	10 249	605	615.7	1 532	2 005	435	793
Vista	57	85.4	401	7 382	532	258.3	54.8	5 381	263	246.2	D	1 849	56	494
Walnut Creek	162	1 246.2	1 243	34 924	785	859.7	43.8	14 658	517	847.4	D	1 934	2 187	1 197
West Covina	53	86.7	234	4 979	870	836.0	49.0	8 628	481	816.3	1 165	1 540	364	644
Westminster	89	156.4	601	12 416	933	758.4	43.4	10 356	574	736.1	1 823	1 949	638	714
Whittier	101	1 474.6	1 820	57 926	756	608.7	22.5	8 377	440	587.3	899	1 277	323	614
Woodland	82	280.7	975	19 704	390	286.5	66.3	8 331	277	281.1	952	1 784	454	656
Yorba Linda	51	246.0	1 433	11 756	367	151.9	99.9	3 816	137	133.6	0	1 420	58	428
COLORADO	7 100	29 972.0	76 393	1 770 867	36 131	21 287.1	28.4	6 516	22 389	20 688.6	774	1 309	275	729
Arvada	134	D	D	D	763	444.7	47.9	4 870	371	428.2	1 112	1 722	137	352
Aurora	250	2 051.6	3 585	98 367	1 932	1 632.6	45.7	7 489	1 226	1 607.0	D	1 415	383	609
Boulder	176	404.8	1 222	34 109	1 156	876.3	33.3	11 458	838	863.4	1 246	2 050	603	1 384
Colorado Springs	468	864.8	3 942	78 905	3 212	2 221.4	47.8	8 147	2 141	2 172.8	D	1 324	349	803
Denver	2 028	11 108.0	28 205	685 486	5 115	3 300.8	16.8	6 536	3 527	3 224.0	681	1 437	361	1 069
Englewood	313	4 074.4	4 850	147 689	696	753.3	51.8	24 706	531	744.3	4 901	2 701	962	1 113
Fort Collins	163	201.8	1 124	21 442	1 149	726.9	46.0	9 804	718	711.1	1 126	2 064	420	1 016

1. For the period including March 12 of the year shown. 2. Based on resident population estimated as of July 1, 1986.

City	Retail trade–establishment with payroll, 1987 (cont'd)			Taxable service industries–establishments with payroll, 1987							Federal grants, 1986		Federal government civilian employment, 1984
	Paid employees[1]				Receipts (Mil. dol.)								
						Selected kinds of business							
	Number	Percent change, 1982–1987	Annual payroll (Mil. dol.)	Number	Total	Hotels, motels, and other lodging places	Health services	Legal services	Paid employees[1]	Annual payroll (Mil. dol.)	Procurement contract awards (Mil. dol.)	Grant awards (Mil. dol.)	
	87	88	89	90	91	92	93	94	95	96	97	98	99
CALIFORNIA–Con.													
Pico Rivera	2 206	0.4	22.4	191	141.3	2.3	57.5	D	2 828	48.4	4.9	1.7	101
Pittsburg	1 592	25.6	24.4	141	35.8	0.0	11.4	2.7	791	12.8	1.4	0.4	106
Placentia	1 943	19.8	21.3	218	105.9	D	41.5	2.0	3 508	40.8	3.8	0.3	68
Pleasant Hill	3 859	20.9	39.2	304	119.5	D	25.6	4.2	2 514	45.6	4.4	0.2	34
Pleasanton	4 141	111.1	42.3	440	309.1	19.8	82.7	5.8	5 547	115.6	4.2	0.8	357
Pomona	6 055	10.6	69.3	565	302.2	5.5	131.7	21.1	5 551	103.5	926.9	6.0	759
Rancho Cucamonga	3 467	70.5	32.5	323	110.6	D	20.8	7.2	2 440	40.7	2.3	1.0	0
Rancho Palos Verdes	762	58.8	7.1	234	62.9	D	19.4	6.8	1 038	27.3	0.8	0.5	10
Redding	7 225	32.3	81.4	923	300.1	22.5	122.5	D	6 770	110.5	5.6	4.7	619
Redlands	4 799	30.5	52.9	394	159.3	1.4	84.0	3.4	2 751	59.9	0.7	0.9	125
Redondo Beach	7 275	58.2	67.0	464	270.8	6.4	104.2	9.8	3 800	91.9	611.7	1.5	333
Redwood City	6 754	27.7	90.1	644	458.7	13.0	99.8	32.6	6 215	168.7	9.9	3.1	305
Rialto	2 420	38.2	23.8	195	62.9	D	16.7	D	1 420	23.5	0.1	4.0	71
Richmond	4 532	12.1	58.8	359	156.3	D	48.0	6.1	3 560	62.2	207.0	4.1	2 978
Riverside	17 163	33.1	202.4	1 502	634.9	15.2	213.8	55.7	14 566	247.3	14.4	29.1	1 096
Rosemead	2 734	14.4	27.0	142	57.1	4.0	20.7	D	1 177	16.7	1.3	7.2	66
Sacramento	28 156	16.6	302.6	3 386	1 674.4	D	393.7	D	32 165	642.9	285.4	1 576.1	9 517
Salinas	8 199	14.4	99.9	823	268.6	8.3	81.9	21.2	5 328	97.2	5.4	5.0	654
San Bernardino	15 147	12.3	165.1	1 168	503.6	7.0	170.5	55.5	10 576	192.6	20.5	19.4	1 456
San Bruno	3 667	7.7	45.5	240	100.6	D	24.1	1.8	1 940	35.2	3.7	0.4	1 978
San Buenaventura (Ventura)	10 031	38.3	120.5	1 070	432.2	18.4	127.2	41.6	8 742	163.2	0.0	1.1	307
San Clemente	2 479	27.9	23.8	346	111.7	D	46.8	4.0	2 128	45.3	9.3	0.3	161
San Diego	81 946	27.6	873.0	9 762	6 103.1	448.0	1 243.4	583.0	113 239	2 388.3	2 342.4	295.1	27 632
San Francisco	74 733	24.2	910.3	10 538	8 794.5	794.6	829.4	1 706.6	139 602	3 444.7	556.8	521.7	23 185
San Gabriel	2 341	10.8	27.0	294	86.5	1.6	39.6	D	2 292	33.2	0.7	0.4	99
San Jose	45 148	14.6	515.2	4 970	2 722.8	78.1	579.9	271.1	52 535	1 109.5	1 027.8	120.3	3 829
San Leandro	7 440	33.3	98.1	642	449.5	D	130.8	5.4	6 667	163.2	46.3	1.5	258
San Luis Obispo	6 459	29.8	66.9	587	249.6	25.5	130.4	26.8	5 106	90.3	43.7	4.1	198
San Mateo	9 804	20.7	118.7	1 141	626.0	28.8	116.6	30.3	12 562	247.5	8.9	2.0	376
San Rafael	7 315	15.7	98.1	908	399.4	1.4	81.6	28.1	7 145	162.4	3.2	2.7	518
Santa Ana	18 004	21.8	213.3	2 521	1 484.2	31.4	386.3	234.8	26 796	555.4	114.0	16.8	3 287
Santa Barbara	12 368	13.7	125.4	1 419	674.2	47.9	179.1	65.7	12 115	256.9	77.5	28.9	1 032
Santa Clara	12 524	48.3	170.5	951	1 126.4	63.0	127.9	9.6	21 194	433.7	94.7	4.7	336
Santa Cruz	7 064	14.9	77.7	555	265.1	27.3	78.1	19.5	6 084	98.4	4.5	30.0	278
Santa Maria	5 589	9.1	64.7	531	234.6	15.6	119.4	6.9	6 164	100.1	8.7	2.9	228
Santa Monica	14 277	17.6	179.5	2 430	1 339.3	59.2	287.4	133.9	19 470	542.0	87.6	13.5	329
Santa Rosa	14 320	45.5	175.6	1 590	513.7	20.2	199.9	42.0	12 190	203.2	9.7	8.7	773
Saratoga	1 183	5.6	12.4	222	45.8	D	12.6	1.6	872	17.1	0.1	0.2	78
Seal Beach	1 683	8.3	14.6	143	53.1	D	12.6	1.9	1 286	21.7	330.2	0.2	1 162
Seaside	2 007	15.3	26.0	140	50.9	4.8	3.2	D	1 222	22.6	0.0	1.0	39
Simi Valley	5 969	46.8	61.1	445	135.6	3.7	36.1	D	2 873	48.8	21.6	3.3	132
South Gate	3 467	55.8	42.6	242	77.9	0.7	25.4	0.6	1 720	29.2	2.7	2.6	116
South San Francisco	5 714	70.1	70.6	439	466.7	54.3	69.6	3.7	8 309	165.2	9.2	2.4	170
Stockton	14 777	15.3	160.5	1 458	527.2	15.8	208.6	48.0	13 269	213.9	16.2	19.2	2 039
Sunnyvale	9 722	13.1	117.9	924	1 403.1	33.1	102.6	7.7	20 277	551.4	2 687.3	2.4	993
Temple City	2 071	36.2	19.2	158	47.0	D	21.9	0.6	1 508	18.3	0.1	0.1	61
Thousand Oaks	10 210	30.1	115.6	864	461.2	16.7	169.5	17.4	7 996	173.5	23.3	1.9	271
Torrance	19 425	19.0	232.1	1 892	970.6	28.2	343.5	48.2	22 899	406.1	368.9	15.1	468
Turlock	3 251	46.3	34.2	281	78.7	4.0	34.1	2.3	1 782	25.8	0.1	1.3	86
Tustin	4 702	10.8	47.1	863	461.0	2.5	124.3	31.9	9 947	184.2	22.8	0.4	122
Union City	1 180	0.7	13.4	136	62.5	D	14.0	D	1 504	23.9	0.7	0.8	54
Upland	4 213	22.5	46.7	536	202.4	D	93.1	6.1	4 678	82.1	3.1	0.5	181
Vacaville	3 548	44.3	37.3	226	45.0	1.6	13.5	2.0	1 116	14.4	0.2	0.9	81
Vallejo	5 394	9.6	69.3	481	253.2	6.0	115.8	6.9	5 293	99.2	23.9	9.3	11 039
Visalia	7 278	14.5	73.2	682	256.9	10.9	108.6	13.3	7 013	104.2	5.9	8.6	268
Vista	2 711	40.5	30.3	453	131.4	D	49.3	7.5	2 560	46.3	0.6	0.5	90
Walnut Creek	8 668	34.6	112.6	1 168	636.0	6.5	191.6	75.5	12 256	268.3	8.9	7.4	570
West Covina	7 879	12.9	95.2	485	252.7	2.4	144.1	8.3	5 127	103.9	25.0	1.6	167
Westminster	7 478	11.0	80.8	520	226.4	3.9	112.7	6.6	4 253	70.0	0.3	1.2	152
Whittier	6 238	0.3	73.1	718	303.5	1.5	151.6	21.5	5 478	118.0	4.8	61.4	332
Woodland	2 954	47.8	35.7	254	89.0	2.2	39.6	4.5	1 842	28.2	2.0	1.3	135
Yorba Linda	1 635	113.4	17.8	210	55.1	D	24.8	0.4	1 032	18.4	0.0	0.2	73
COLORADO	267 899	12.7	2 668.0	28 596	11 532.8	824.8	2 430.7	972.9	256 147	4 341.8	3 555.4	1 312.9	50 511
ArvadaL/4 922	16.2	46.8	499	D	D	D	4.9	D	D	7.6	1.2	306	
Aurora	18 316	16.2	188.6	1 417	549.1	D	238.0	D	11 588	185.8	7.9	4.6	3 087
Boulder	12 134	15.1	116.4	1 258	563.1	D	87.5	37.3	11 796	207.6	168.0	47.0	1 724
Colorado Springs	26 151	28.9	276.7	2 818	1 014.0	95.7	263.4	D	24 624	414.4	328.8	13.9	1 760
Denver	48 853	6.3	505.5	6 471	3 927.6	261.6	695.7	619.4	78 075	1 517.6	1 375.9	418.6	11 537
Englewood	6 779	22.3	81.9	890	781.4	12.5	73.9	35.7	12 346	304.3	47.3	8.2	501
Fort Collins	9 280	24.8	88.5	917	224.1	5.9	74.3	15.8	6 083	87.3	22.1	34.1	1 048

1. For the period including March 12 of the year shown.

City	City government employment, 1985 (October): Total	City government employment, 1985 (October): Rates[1]	City government employment, 1985 (October): Percent education	Form of governments[2] (As of 1986)	City government finances, 1984–1985: General revenue: Total (Mil. dol.)	General revenue: Intergovernmental: Total (Mil. dol.)	General revenue: Intergovernmental: Percent from State government	General revenue: Taxes: Total (Mil. dol.)	General revenue: Taxes: Per capita[3] (Dollars): Total	General revenue: Taxes: Per capita[3] (Dollars): Property	General revenue: Taxes: Per capita[3] (Dollars): Sales & gross receipts	General expenditures: Total (Mil. dol.)	General expenditures: Per capitl[3](Dol.): Total	General expenditures: Per capitl[3](Dol.): Capital outlays	General expenditures: Percent of total for–: Public welfare	General expenditures: Percent of total for–: Highways	General expenditures: Percent of total for–: Education
	100	101	102	103	104	105	106	107	108	109	110	111	112	113	114	115	116
CALIFORNIA—Con.																	
Pico Rivera	319	58.7	0.0	2	16.1	4.0	61.6	8.9	164	58	82	14.8	272	21	0.0	12.9	0.0
Pittsburg	229	55.5	0.0	2	31.4	4.8	88.6	7.0	171	117	43	30.4	737	88	0.0	3.5	0.0
Placentia	176	46.0	0.0	2	10.5	2.0	82.4	7.2	189	49	96	8.9	233	20	0.0	12.4	0.0
Pleasant Hill	130	45.6	0.0	2	10.9	1.5	89.0	5.9	206	30	142	9.0	316	27	0.0	15.5	0.0
Pleasanton	326	73.5	0.0	2	37.2	3.9	91.3	10.3	232	84	70	47.9	1 080	456	0.0	7.6	0.0
Pomona	832	72.0	0.0	2	84.8	10.4	50.3	24.7	213	76	118	79.8	690	13	0.0	6.7	0.0
Rancho Cucamonga	141	18.6	0.0	2	20.3	4.8	82.3	11.7	155	43	44	12.8	169	39	0.0	17.2	0.0
Rancho Palos Verdes	51	11.0	0.0	2	5.6	2.1	92.3	2.3	49	8	15	7.3	156	61	0.0	19.2	0.0
Redding	594	115.4	0.0	2	28.7	7.4	59.2	12.4	241	56	156	23.5	457	73	0.0	16.4	0.0
Redlands	387	73.2	0.0	2	22.2	3.7	84.3	10.6	200	102	70	20.5	387	95	0.0	12.1	0.0
Redondo Beach	595	93.2	0.0	2	40.2	5.0	74.3	18.3	287	94	159	36.7	575	39	0.0	10.6	0.0
Redwood City	561	97.8	0.0	2	38.8	4.8	74.2	21.8	380	156	173	30.2	526	64	0.0	8.6	0.0
Rialto	276	51.3	0.0	2	17.7	2.7	71.2	9.3	173	58	46	14.7	273	48	0.0	15.0	0.0
Richmond	723	92.9	0.0	2	69.6	7.9	47.3	30.3	390	234	139	55.6	714	69	0.0	5.6	0.0
Riverside	2 008	102.1	0.0	2	96.9	15.3	67.4	42.7	217	48	133	100.4	511	92	0.0	15.9	0.0
Rosemead	90	18.9	0.0	2	12.8	3.6	55.2	6.0	127	57	61	10.3	216	34	0.0	27.6	0.0
Sacramento	3 413	105.5	0.0	2	177.3	24.9	68.8	89.6	277	81	159	165.0	510	83	0.0	13.2	0.0
Salinas	658	67.9	0.0	2	42.9	12.5	73.0	21.2	218	56	134	34.5	355	66	0.0	19.0	0.0
San Bernardino	1 608	116.0	0.0	1	108.4	17.9	58.5	42.9	309	106	179	103.4	746	209	0.0	5.3	0.0
San Bruno	232	65.9	0.0	2	12.8	1.9	84.9	6.1	173	47	107	13.1	373	49	0.0	10.6	0.0
San Buenaventura (Ventura)	686	80.1	0.0	2	46.9	6.8	77.7	23.9	279	71	185	36.9	431	69	0.0	12.5	0.0
San Clemente	300	90.4	0.0	2	14.3	1.2	86.4	5.4	163	84	54	13.3	399	24	0.0	9.2	0.0
San Diego	8 473	83.5	0.0	2	600.6	121.4	56.9	211.7	209	72	118	503.6	496	100	NA	6.0	0.0
San Francisco	24 914	332.6	0.0	1	1 745.9	643.5	69.9	563.5	752	383	190	1 352.6	1 806	207	12.1	0.8	2.5
San Gabriel	209	63.2	0.0	2	8.4	2.0	84.9	5.1	153	54	86	8.2	247	31	0.0	16.9	0.0
San Jose	4 966	69.7	0.0	2	446.3	71.3	59.7	213.5	300	99	139	416.0	584	167	0.0	20.8	0.0
San Leandro	590	89.7	0.0	2	40.2	6.8	70.8	21.2	322	61	248	39.3	597	34	0.0	13.6	0.0
San Luis Obispo	409	109.9	0.0	2	18.7	3.9	61.4	10.2	274	55	193	16.6	445	104	0.0	11.3	0.0
San Mateo	730	90.1	0.0	2	47.2	8.8	88.1	26.3	325	108	162	42.1	520	147	0.0	24.7	0.0
San Rafael	461	103.1	0.0	2	25.0	3.0	82.5	13.6	305	74	204	39.4	882	424	0.0	28.4	0.0
Santa Ana	1 885	79.6	0.0	2	113.0	25.5	40.4	58.5	247	91	128	125.8	531	181	0.0	6.7	0.0
Santa Barbara	1 158	146.0	0.0	2	57.7	5.7	62.3	28.1	354	94	228	66.5	839	338	0.0	5.5	0.0
Santa Clara	1 120	126.5	0.0	2	80.3	7.5	72.3	34.8	393	104	272	83.6	944	243	0.0	13.1	0.0
Santa Cruz	745	162.3	0.0	2	28.6	4.7	88.9	11.9	260	71	171	52.8	1 150	596	0.0	42.2	0.0
Santa Maria	455	88.7	0.0	2	24.5	4.1	80.4	10.0	195	39	142	26.4	515	88	0.0	8.4	0.0
Santa Monica	1 634	175.4	0.0	2	82.3	15.5	70.5	36.7	394	95	225	74.0	794	103	0.0	6.1	0.0
Santa Rosa	825	84.5	0.0	2	59.8	9.5	53.7	25.3	259	73	166	49.1	503	91	0.0	11.4	0.0
Saratoga	70	23.7	0.0	2	4.3	1.5	86.4	2.4	82	16	38	5.5	185	28	0.0	27.9	0.0
Seal Beach	141	52.5	0.0	2	9.5	2.2	88.7	5.4	199	83	97	9.8	363	63	0.0	8.0	0.0
Seaside	163	44.0	0.0	2	8.5	2.1	70.3	5.2	140	33	99	8.0	215	18	0.0	11.3	0.0
Simi Valley	342	38.0	0.0	2	27.8	6.6	79.8	10.4	115	32	50	49.2	546	192	0.0	34.4	0.0
South Gate	440	54.6	0.0	2	27.3	12.4	72.5	8.5	106	38	55	19.3	240	12	0.0	16.3	0.0
South San Francisco	579	112.3	0.0	2	32.6	3.6	78.8	14.9	290	90	179	30.9	600	100	0.0	14.7	0.0
Stockton	1 605	87.5	0.0	2	88.7	15.6	54.7	41.4	226	57	147	87.2	476	61	0.0	11.2	0.0
Sunnyvale	875	78.0	0.0	2	79.5	10.2	58.2	42.2	376	115	220	68.1	607	108	0.0	14.3	0.0
Temple City	53	17.1	0.0	2	5.2	1.5	90.1	2.6	83	26	49	4.8	154	37	0.0	21.5	0.0
Thousand Oaks	477	49.5	0.0	2	37.2	7.0	82.0	16.3	169	44	104	28.4	295	50	0.0	20.5	0.0
Torrance	1 519	112.0	0.0	2	77.6	14.7	52.9	50.5	373	69	261	77.2	569	87	0.0	18.5	0.0
Turlock	229	67.4	0.0	2	10.9	2.4	84.5	4.3	128	33	81	9.8	289	27	0.0	17.1	0.0
Tustin	210	50.0	0.0	2	16.3	4.3	83.7	10.1	240	92	131	13.7	326	61	0.0	24.2	0.0
Union City	214	42.2	0.0	2	13.5	3.7	79.6	7.3	144	58	64	11.4	226	17	0.0	11.2	0.0
Upland	349	61.1	0.0	2	19.8	3.7	77.0	9.9	174	61	77	18.5	323	37	0.0	10.0	0.0
Vacaville	294	53.5	0.0	2	21.1	4.3	80.7	8.5	155	62	46	14.3	260	34	0.0	16.0	0.0
Vallejo	453	48.6	0.0	2	31.4	6.7	53.9	18.1	194	59	99	34.8	373	106	0.0	30.1	0.0
Visalia	503	81.7	0.0	2	31.1	7.2	67.2	10.7	174	35	120	32.7	531	180	0.0	9.5	0.0
Vista	224	46.7	0.0	2	15.4	2.7	78.4	7.6	159	47	49	13.9	290	62	0.0	21.7	0.0
Walnut Creek	335	57.1	0.0	2	26.5	3.1	86.3	15.7	267	67	147	23.7	405	138	0.0	22.4	0.0
West Covina	530	54.7	0.0	2	33.4	5.9	76.2	16.9	175	62	87	44.3	458	175	0.0	9.2	0.0
Westminster	311	42.5	0.0	2	18.8	4.8	81.5	11.3	154	30	113	18.8	256	31	0.0	19.6	0.0
Whittier	496	68.3	0.0	2	22.5	5.0	62.4	11.1	153	37	105	33.1	456	207	0.0	10.7	0.0
Woodland	252	73.3	0.0	2	14.5	2.9	76.7	6.1	179	77	78	14.5	421	26	0.0	16.7	0.0
Yorba Linda	102	25.6	0.0	2	9.8	1.8	94.7	3.8	96	32	30	10.2	257	84	0.0	19.4	0.0
COLORADO	NA	NA	NA	NA	NA	NA	NA	NA	NA	NA	NA	NA	NA	NA	NA	NA	NA
Arvada	507	55.5	0.0	2	34.3	3.8	50.6	20.8	228	26	157	30.8	338	86	2.5	10.8	0.0
Aurora	1 889	86.7	0.0	2	135.4	9.8	58.4	75.7	347	52	234	137.4	630	185	0.0	18.7	0.0
Boulder	1 155	151.0	0.0	2	52.7	5.1	48.1	31.3	409	71	308	56.1	733	259	2.2	13.8	0.0
Colorado Springs	4 564	167.4	0.0	2	210.6	25.9	22.4	62.7	230	42	184	161.7	593	177	0.3	7.9	0.0
Denver	12 100	239.6	0.0	1	738.6	140.5	74.1	280.1	555	170	337	675.1	1 337	248	11.7	4.2	0.0
Englewood	508	166.6	0.0	2	30.2	2.6	76.7	15.7	514	55	447	28.9	947	321	0.0	8.6	0.0
Fort Collins	1 118	150.8	0.0	2	43.1	4.8	39.5	22.1	299	70	214	44.5	600	202	0.0	20.6	0.0

1. Per 10,000 population estimated as of July 1, 1986. 2. 1 = Mayor-council; 2 = Council-manager; 3 = Commission. Data subject to copyright. 3. Based on resident population estimated as of July 1, 1986.

City	City government finances, 1984–1985 (cont'd): General expenditure (cont'd): Percent of total for (cont'd): Health and hospitals	Police protection	Sewerage and sanitation	Parks and recreation	Housing and community development	Debt outstanding: Total (Mil. dol.)	Per capita[1] (Dollars)	Percent utility	Climate[2]: Average daily temperature (Degrees Fahrenheit): Mean: Jan.	Mean: July	Limits: Jan.[3]	Limits: July[4]	Annual precipitation (Inches)	Heating degree days[5]	Cooling degree days[5]	Typical monthly electric bills, 1986: Residential[6]: Total (Dollars)	Residential: Percent change, 1980–1986	Commercial[7] (Dollars)
	117	118	119	120	121	122	123	124	125	126	127	128	129	130	131	132	133	134
CALIFORNIA—Con.																		
Pico Rivera	0.0	17.6	0.9	16.6	16.1	25.9	477	0.0	57.2	74.1	47.7	83.8	14.85	1 204	1 339	56.07	63.0	558.2
Pittsburg	0.0	10.8	1.0	3.0	22.4	213.5	5 177	NA	45.2	78.0	37.5	95.0	13.77	2 674	1 448	66.97	148.4	NA
Placentia	0.0	33.0	1.0	14.4	0.2	2.8	73	0.0	54.9	73.5	42.4	88.8	14.46	1 644	1 118	56.07	63.0	NA
Pleasant Hill	0.0	28.1	0.2	0.9	5.6	34.0	1 194	0.0	49.7	61.7	43.2	69.5	23.24	2 951	91	66.97	148.4	NA
Pleasanton	0.0	7.1	11.0	3.9	0.1	143.3	3 231	0.4	45.9	71.3	34.7	90.0	14.11	3 011	734	66.97	148.4	NA
Pomona	0.3	14.5	3.3	2.7	3.1	559.5	4 842	0.0	52.4	74.6	39.0	90.9	17.02	1 972	1 191	56.07	63.0	558.2
Rancho Cucamonga	0.0	26.6	0.0	2.6	2.3	114.7	1 513	0.0	52.0	75.0	40.6	91.8	19.89	2 175	1 223	56.07	NA	558.2
Rancho Palos Verdes	0.0	20.3	0.0	43.5	0.0	0.0	0	0.0	55.1	69.1	44.1	78.3	13.13	1 719	677	56.07	63.0	NA
Redding	0.0	18.8	14.5	9.4	2.5	55.7	1 082	67.2	46.5	83.5	37.3	99.5	40.95	2 544	2 139	32.48	111.0	NA
Redlands	0.0	20.5	16.9	5.9	11.8	31.1	588	6.0	51.9	78.2	39.1	95.9	12.89	1 992	1 571	56.07	63.0	NA
Redondo Beach	0.0	20.5	3.4	3.3	5.4	50.2	786	0.0	55.1	69.1	44.1	78.3	13.13	1 719	677	56.07	63.0	558.2
Redwood City	0.0	17.3	10.1	9.7	0.7	80.2	1 398	8.5	48.7	68.4	39.2	82.9	19.27	2 600	432	66.97	148.4	NA
Rialto	0.0	22.3	5.2	7.8	3.0	16.1	299	0.0	55.3	78.7	44.0	94.9	14.93	1 529	1 893	56.07	63.0	NA
Richmond	0.0	11.9	4.4	4.9	5.8	139.8	1 796	0.0	49.7	62.4	42.0	69.7	21.83	2 687	162	66.97	148.4	NA
Riverside	0.0	16.6	13.4	12.5	4.1	328.0	1 667	45.2	52.8	77.2	39.5	94.2	9.64	1 818	1 471	72.66	85.6	654.9
Rosemead	1.3	24.1	2.7	13.1	10.0	6.4	134	0.0	54.8	74.8	41.3	89.1	17.76	1 532	1 281	56.07	63.0	NA
Sacramento	0.0	22.4	16.2	12.1	2.1	125.8	389	13.4	47.1	76.6	40.2	93.1	17.87	2 398	1 379	42.55	148.8	278.4
Salinas	0.0	22.1	2.9	8.8	6.7	36.1	373	0.0	51.4	59.5	42.8	67.7	18.35	3 170	48	66.97	148.4	NA
San Bernardino	0.5	14.2	12.1	7.1	11.3	201.6	1 454	0.0	52.9	79.3	39.4	97.6	15.68	1 777	1 718	56.07	63.0	558.2
San Bruno	0.0	21.9	8.3	12.1	0.0	0.0	0	0.0	48.5	62.2	41.5	71.0	19.71	3 161	115	66.97	148.4	NA
San Buenaventura (Ventura)	0.0	23.2	13.7	12.0	1.5	45.3	529	9.7	54.6	65.7	43.5	74.7	14.53	2 068	357	56.07	63.0	558.2
San Clemente	0.0	19.8	23.4	11.0	3.6	2.0	59	0.0	53.2	66.7	41.6	75.0	12.34	2 221	375	73.58	77.5	NA
San Diego	NA	16.0	14.3	12.1	10.6	1 087.7	1 071	0.2	56.8	70.3	48.4	75.6	9.32	1 284	842	74.98	77.5	787.5
San Francisco	19.5	8.6	9.5	6.1	3.6	1 388.9	1 854	2.8	48.5	62.2	41.5	71.0	19.71	3 161	115	66.97	148.4	NA
San Gabriel	0.0	34.0	1.5	10.7	0.0	0.0	0	0.0	54.8	74.8	41.3	89.1	17.76	1 532	1 281	56.07	63.0	NA
San Jose	1.3	13.9	12.8	6.9	8.5	510.8	717	NA	49.5	68.8	41.1	81.5	13.86	2 439	498	66.97	148.4	NA
San Leandro	NA	13.6	9.6	11.3	2.2	37.8	575	0.0	49.0	63.7	43.4	70.6	18.03	2 877	174	66.97	148.4	NA
San Luis Obispo	0.0	21.5	11.5	13.3	0.3	2.6	69	93.4	52.1	64.8	41.7	77.4	23.00	2 498	285	66.97	148.4	NA
San Mateo	0.0	18.3	10.4	9.7	1.4	15.2	187	0.0	48.7	68.4	39.2	82.9	19.27	2 600	432	66.97	148.4	NA
San Rafael	0.0	9.1	0.2	5.8	2.0	45.5	1 018	0.0	49.5	67.8	41.4	82.3	37.48	2 439	483	66.97	148.4	NA
Santa Ana	0.0	21.2	3.1	5.4	34.9	226.2	955	1.6	55.9	72.2	44.1	82.9	12.60	1 430	1 089	56.07	63.0	558.2
Santa Barbara	0.0	13.3	4.4	6.6	17.1	48.1	606	24.3	54.0	66.6	42.7	76.0	17.70	1 993	393	56.07	63.0	558.2
Santa Clara	0.0	10.5	15.1	4.3	4.8	229.5	2 592	50.4	49.5	68.8	41.1	81.5	13.86	2 439	498	40.29	58.9	NA
Santa Cruz	0.0	7.4	8.0	7.8	0.9	41.8	911	16.0	49.0	62.8	38.4	75.0	28.98	3 136	95	66.97	148.4	NA
Santa Maria	0.0	15.5	10.7	10.1	5.1	49.2	959	0.2	50.8	62.3	38.8	72.1	12.35	3 054	76	66.97	148.4	NA
Santa Monica	0.0	14.2	10.6	8.0	4.7	30.4	326	0.0	56.4	65.8	48.8	70.5	13.69	1 873	438	56.07	63.0	558.2
Santa Rosa	0.0	14.3	12.7	7.8	4.1	157.7	1 615	0.6	46.7	67.4	36.0	84.3	29.88	2 980	382	66.97	148.4	NA
Saratoga	0.0	22.6	0.0	13.8	1.9	1.8	61	0.0	49.5	68.8	41.1	81.5	13.86	2 439	498	66.97	148.4	NA
Seal Beach	0.0	26.3	9.7	20.0	1.0	4.3	159	16.8	55.2	72.8	44.3	83.0	11.54	1 485	1 091	56.07	63.0	NA
Seaside	0.0	25.2	0.0	15.0	4.4	1.7	46	0.0	51.4	59.5	42.8	67.7	18.35	3 170	48	66.97	148.4	NA
Simi Valley	0.0	11.9	7.6	0.1	0.5	165.8	1 842	0.8	54.6	65.7	43.5	74.7	14.53	2 068	357	56.07	63.0	558.2
South Gate	0.0	35.2	5.6	11.3	6.2	0.0	0	0.0	57.2	74.1	47.7	83.8	14.85	1 204	1 339	56.07	63.0	558.2
South San Francisco	1.1	16.6	12.2	10.4	5.6	30.0	581	0.0	48.5	62.2	41.5	71.0	19.71	3 161	115	NA	NA	NA
Stockton	0.0	20.5	17.3	8.5	2.5	95.1	519	0.0	45.2	78.0	37.5	95.0	13.77	2 674	1 448	66.97	148.4	NA
Sunnyvale	0.0	15.5	19.3	11.2	1.5	48.8	435	0.3	49.5	68.8	41.1	81.5	13.86	2 439	498	66.97	148.4	NA
Temple City	0.0	22.8	1.3	7.6	0.1	2.6	85	0.0	54.8	74.8	41.3	89.1	17.76	1 532	1 281	56.07	63.0	NA
Thousand Oaks	0.0	16.8	17.0	3.5	3.7	20.1	209	11.3	54.6	65.7	43.5	74.7	14.53	2 068	357	56.07	63.0	558.2
Torrance	0.1	23.9	3.9	10.5	0.6	42.4	313	26.0	55.1	69.1	44.1	78.3	13.13	1 719	677	56.07	63.0	558.2
Turlock	0.0	26.3	20.4	8.5	0.1	13.4	395	0.0	45.7	76.8	37.5	94.4	11.70	2 671	1 287	37.13	95.8	NA
Tustin	0.0	28.2	1.2	7.1	0.2	10.7	256	0.0	53.6	70.9	40.3	83.4	11.97	1 854	813	56.07	63.0	NA
Union City	0.0	32.4	0.0	5.3	3.1	13.7	270	0.0	45.9	71.3	34.7	90.0	14.11	3 011	734	66.97	148.4	NA
Upland	0.0	21.6	27.2	6.9	1.1	59.6	1 042	5.3	52.0	75.0	40.6	91.8	19.89	2 175	1 223	56.07	63.0	NA
Vacaville	0.0	27.0	12.2	10.2	4.9	63.8	1 162	2.5	45.2	75.6	36.1	95.1	24.29	2 788	1 174	66.97	148.4	NA
Vallejo	0.0	23.3	6.1	2.8	2.7	60.1	644	7.1	47.1	67.0	37.7	82.5	24.02	2 960	316	66.97	148.4	NA
Visalia	0.0	13.4	21.2	8.4	14.5	52.8	857	0.0	46.0	80.9	36.9	97.7	9.86	2 460	1 804	56.07	63.0	NA
Vista	0.0	12.9	7.7	10.4	3.0	27.9	582	0.0	52.2	73.3	38.7	87.8	14.53	2 006	980	73.58	77.5	NA
Walnut Creek	0.0	20.3	0.6	19.5	0.5	27.0	460	0.0	49.7	61.7	43.2	69.5	23.24	2 951	91	66.97	148.4	NA
West Covina	0.0	22.6	0.9	28.4	10.4	43.6	451	0.0	52.2	74.4	40.7	89.7	17.13	2 048	1 134	56.07	63.0	558.2
Westminster	0.0	34.4	1.5	7.3	0.0	1.4	19	100.0	55.2	72.8	44.3	83.0	11.54	1 485	1 091	56.07	63.0	558.2
Whittier	0.0	19.3	5.0	6.6	41.0	15.2	209	0.0	57.2	74.1	47.7	83.8	14.85	1 204	1 339	56.07	63.0	558.2
Woodland	0.0	17.6	18.1	8.6	0.0	27.4	796	0.0	45.1	76.6	36.6	96.2	17.89	2 709	1 321	66.97	148.4	NA
Yorba Linda	0.0	17.9	10.6	15.5	1.4	6.9	172	0.0	54.9	73.5	42.4	88.8	14.46	1 644	1 118	56.07	63.0	NA
COLORADO	NA	NA	NA	NA	NA	NA	NA	NA	NA	NA	NA	NA	NA	NA	NA	52.06	58.4	NA
Arvada	0.0	17.7	11.5	11.9	9.9	55.8	611	61.8	30.9	72.6	17.5	87.5	15.15	5 883	639	55.82	51.0	500.3
Aurora	0.3	12.9	15.6	6.8	1.3	437.0	2 005	28.2	29.5	73.3	15.9	88.0	15.31	6 014	680	55.82	51.0	500.3
Boulder	0.6	10.8	4.4	20.5	0.5	47.9	627	22.8	32.6	74.0	20.1	88.1	18.12	5 460	790	55.82	51.0	500.3
Colorado Springs	24.5	10.9	25.6	6.3	0.4	328.0	1 203	82.6	28.8	71.2	16.2	84.9	15.42	6 346	501	33.03	20.9	NA
Denver	15.6	11.5	7.9	6.8	1.5	670.2	1 327	42.0	29.5	73.3	15.9	88.0	15.31	6 014	680	55.82	63.8	500.3
Englewood	0.0	12.7	11.9	9.8	30.5	45.3	1 485	13.3	29.5	73.3	15.9	88.0	15.31	6 014	680	55.82	63.8	NA
Fort Collins	0.0	9.8	15.9	13.8	3.1	86.4	1 165	25.9	26.9	71.4	13.2	85.8	14.47	6 483	471	45.21	60.0	385.1

1. Based on resident population estimated as of July 1, 1986. 2. Represents normal values based on the 30-year period, 1951–1980 (see text). 3. Average daily minimum. 4. Average daily maximum. 5. For definition, see text. 6. As of January 1; based on consumption of 750 kWh. 7. Based on billing demand of 30 kW and consumption of 6,000 kWh.

MSA/ CMSA Code[1]	State/ Place code	City	Land area,[2] 1990 (Sq. Km.)	Population: 1990: Total persons	Population: 1990: Rank	Population: 1990: Per sq. km.	Population: 1980	Population: Change 1980–1990: Number	Population: Change 1980–1990: Per-cent	Population characteristics, 1990: Percent: Race: White	Race: Black	Race: Am. Indian, Eskimo, Aleut	Race: Asian & Pacific Islander	Race: Other race	His-panic[3]	65 Years and over
			1	2	3	4	5	6	7	8	9	10	11	12	13	14
		COLORADO—Con.														
...	08 0555	Grand Junction	38.5	29 034	844	754	27 956	1 078	3.9	91.82	0.82	0.83	0.99	5.55	11.11	19.5
3060	08 0570	Greeley	73.6	60 536	384	823	53 006	7 530	14.2	89.10	0.67	0.60	1.00	8.62	20.36	11.2
2082	08 0760	Lakewood	105.7	126 481	143	1 197	113 808	12 673	11.1	93.15	1.04	0.69	1.93	3.19	9.10	10.5
2082	08 0810	Littleton	31.9	33 685	750	1 056	28 631	5 054	17.7	96.09	0.88	0.56	1.39	1.07	5.21	12.1
2082	08 0820	Longmont	34.0	51 555	473	1 516	42 942	8 613	20.1	92.74	0.38	0.74	1.23	4.92	11.09	9.9
2670	08 0830	Loveland	55.4	37 352	681	674	30 215	7 137	23.6	94.87	0.30	0.48	0.71	3.64	6.77	13.0
2082	08 0943	Northglenn	18.1	27 195	884	1 502	29 847	-2 652	-8.9	90.68	1.64	0.82	2.03	4.83	14.58	7.0
6560	08 1085	Pueblo	93.0	98 640	200	1 061	101 686	-3 046	-3.0	82.95	2.18	0.83	0.63	13.41	39.51	16.0
2082	08 1285	Thornton	53.5	55 031	425	1 029	40 343	14 688	36.4	89.69	1.27	0.91	1.66	6.47	16.92	5.3
2082	08 1355	Westminster	69.4	74 625	293	1 075	50 211	24 414	48.6	90.64	0.99	0.63	3.69	4.04	11.48	4.8
2082	08 1360	Wheat Ridge	23.0	29 419	836	1 279	30 293	-874	-2.9	94.68	0.57	0.61	1.49	2.66	7.26	19.4
...	09 0000	CONNECTICUT	12 549.6	3 287 116	X	262	3 107 564	179 552	5.8	86.99	8.34	0.20	1.54	2.92	6.48	13.6
5602	09 0200	Bridgeport	41.5	141 686	123	3 414	142 546	-860	-0.6	58.54	26.60	0.29	2.32	12.26	26.50	13.6
3282	09 0230	Bristol	68.7	60 640	380	883	57 370	3 270	5.7	96.05	2.08	0.17	0.77	0.94	2.72	13.6
5602	09 0530	Danbury	109.1	65 585	350	601	60 470	5 115	8.5	86.75	6.57	0.20	3.94	2.54	7.69	11.6
3282	09 0970	Hartford	44.8	139 739	127	3 119	136 392	3 347	2.5	39.98	38.89	0.32	1.45	19.36	31.59	9.9
5480	09 1210	Meriden	61.5	59 479	393	967	57 118	2 361	4.1	89.66	4.29	0.18	0.70	5.17	13.69	14.7
3282	09 1250	Middletown	105.9	42 762	582	404	39 040	3 722	9.5	85.43	11.10	0.17	1.93	1.36	3.30	12.0
5602	09 1270	Milford	57.7	48 168	515	835	49 101	-933	-1.9	96.77	1.54	0.15	1.05	0.50	2.29	13.9
8880	09 1370	Naugatuck borough	42.5	30 625	819	721	26 456	4 169	15.8	96.23	1.85	0.24	0.86	0.82	3.10	12.1
3282	09 1390	New Britain	34.5	75 491	286	2 188	73 840	1 651	2.2	81.61	7.58	0.17	1.79	8.86	16.27	16.9
5480	09 1450	New Haven	48.8	130 474	138	2 674	126 089	4 385	3.5	53.85	36.14	0.31	2.41	7.29	13.22	12.3
5520	09 1480	New London	14.3	28 540	854	1 996	28 842	-302	-1.0	72.98	16.84	0.68	2.15	7.35	12.12	12.8
5602	09 1630	Norwalk	59.1	78 331	270	1 325	77 767	564	0.7	79.29	15.48	0.13	1.65	3.46	9.37	12.6
5520	09 1650	Norwich	73.4	37 391	680	509	38 074	-683	-1.8	91.32	5.28	0.64	1.07	1.69	3.11	15.7
5602	09 2030	Shelton	79.2	35 418	711	447	31 314	4 104	13.1	97.11	0.97	0.19	1.29	0.44	2.48	12.6
5602	09 2180	Stamford	97.7	108 056	175	1 106	102 466	5 590	5.5	76.28	17.78	0.12	2.60	3.21	9.77	13.3
...	09 2330	Torrington	103.1	33 687	749	327	30 987	2 700	8.7	96.72	1.68	0.18	1.23	0.19	1.06	18.6
8880	09 2460	Waterbury	74.0	108 961	170	1 472	103 266	5 695	5.5	79.55	12.97	0.32	0.72	6.44	13.38	16.5
5480	09 2535	West Haven	28.1	54 021	442	1 922	53 184	837	1.6	84.12	12.43	0.23	2.03	1.19	3.57	14.8
...	10 0000	DELAWARE	5 062.5	666 168	X	132	594 338	71 830	12.1	80.32	16.88	0.30	1.36	1.13	2.37	12.1
6162	10 0195	Newark	22.3	25 098	921	1 125	25 247	-149	-0.6	90.39	5.71	0.14	3.52	0.24	1.47	8.5
6162	10 0255	Wilmington	27.9	71 529	307	2 564	70 195	1 334	1.9	42.13	52.35	0.22	0.44	4.86	7.09	14.8
8840	11 0000	DISTRICT OF COLUMBIA	159.1	606 900	X	3 815	638 432	-31 532	-4.9	29.60	65.84	0.24	1.85	2.46	5.39	12.8
8840	11 0005	District of Columbia	159.1	606 900	19	3 815	638 333	-31 433	-4.9	29.60	65.84	0.24	1.85	2.46	5.39	12.8
...	12 0000	FLORIDA	139 852.4	12 937 926	X	93	9 746 961	3 190 965	32.7	83.08	13.60	0.28	1.19	1.84	12.17	18.3
8960	12 0180	Boca Raton	70.4	61 492	374	873	49 447	12 045	24.4	94.38	2.90	0.07	1.90	0.75	5.59	21.5
8960	12 0200	Boynton Beach	39.2	46 194	537	1 178	35 624	10 570	29.7	77.74	20.12	0.11	0.63	1.39	6.76	30.3
1140	12 0215	Bradenton	29.7	43 779	566	1 474	30 228	13 551	44.8	82.89	14.42	0.18	0.64	1.87	5.39	28.5
2700	12 0293	Cape Coral	272.2	74 991	290	275	32 103	42 888	133.6	97.47	1.01	0.17	0.62	0.73	3.67	22.0
8280	12 0375	Clearwater	64.4	98 784	199	1 534	85 170	13 614	16.0	89.13	8.97	0.24	1.03	0.62	2.92	25.6
4992	12 0425	Coral Gables	30.6	40 091	627	1 310	43 241	-3 150	-7.3	93.05	3.42	0.10	1.74	1.69	41.85	17.4
4992	12 0427	Coral Springs	60.8	79 443	268	1 307	37 349	42 094	112.7	93.08	3.48	0.18	2.12	1.14	7.12	7.0
2020	12 0485	Daytona Beach	83.5	61 921	368	742	54 176	7 745	14.3	67.37	30.72	0.24	1.14	0.53	2.48	21.4
4992	12 0495	Deerfield Beach	27.0	46 325	534	1 716	39 193	7 132	18.2	81.57	16.68	0.11	0.84	0.80	3.86	36.3
8960	12 0510	Delray Beach	38.4	47 181	524	1 229	34 329	12 852	37.4	71.99	26.28	0.14	0.68	0.91	6.08	31.7
8280	12 0530	Dunedin	26.8	34 012	737	1 269	30 203	3 809	12.6	98.12	1.07	0.21	0.43	0.16	1.83	33.3
4992	12 0645	Fort Lauderdale	81.2	149 377	116	1 840	153 279	-3 902	-2.5	69.61	28.11	0.21	0.87	1.19	7.15	17.8
2700	12 0655	Fort Myers	56.9	45 206	549	794	36 638	8 568	23.4	64.24	32.16	0.21	0.81	2.58	7.72	16.1
2710	12 0665	Fort Pierce	31.8	36 830	689	1 158	33 802	3 028	9.0	53.68	42.37	0.32	0.54	3.09	6.43	19.2
2900	12 0695	Gainesville	90.3	84 770	245	939	81 371	3 399	4.2	73.36	21.44	0.18	3.94	1.07	4.40	9.4
4992	12 0815	Hallandale	10.9	30 996	806	2 844	36 517	-5 521	-15.1	84.01	14.17	0.14	0.47	1.21	8.76	48.5
4992	12 0860	Hialeah	49.8	188 004	85	3 775	145 254	42 750	29.4	89.93	1.93	0.10	0.54	7.50	87.58	14.0
4992	12 0915	Hollywood	70.6	121 697	148	1 724	121 323	374	0.3	88.25	8.52	0.21	1.32	1.70	11.86	23.1
3600	12 1000	Jacksonville	1 965.0	635 230	15	323	540 920	94 310	17.4	71.87	25.23	0.28	1.92	0.70	2.59	10.6
3980	12 1136	Lakeland	99.4	70 576	317	710	47 406	23 170	48.9	78.12	20.20	0.17	0.90	0.61	3.26	22.9
8960	12 1165	Lake Worth	14.5	28 564	853	1 970	27 048	1 516	5.6	80.51	14.91	0.26	0.88	3.44	15.71	23.7
8280	12 1175	Largo	36.6	65 674	348	1 794	57 958	7 716	13.3	97.62	0.99	0.19	0.84	0.35	1.95	32.4
4992	12 1183	Lauderdale Lakes	9.3	27 341	878	2 940	25 426	1 915	7.5	51.64	45.60	0.21	1.40	1.14	5.98	30.5
4992	12 1185	Lauderhill	19.0	49 708	495	2 616	37 271	12 437	33.4	58.59	38.54	0.14	1.49	1.23	6.79	21.3
4992	12 1300	Margate	22.9	42 985	577	1 877	35 900	7 085	19.7	93.09	3.74	0.19	1.47	1.51	7.68	30.4
4900	12 1350	Melbourne	74.3	59 646	391	803	46 536	13 110	28.2	87.42	9.50	0.32	2.05	0.70	3.48	17.0
4992	12 1370	Miami	92.1	358 548	46	3 893	346 681	11 867	3.4	65.64	27.39	0.15	0.63	6.18	62.46	16.6
4992	12 1375	Miami Beach	18.2	92 639	217	5 090	96 298	-3 659	-3.8	88.30	5.18	0.15	1.21	5.15	46.79	30.1
4992	12 1420	Miramar	76.8	40 663	615	529	32 813	7 850	23.9	79.29	15.66	0.17	2.30	2.58	17.33	9.7

1. MSA = Metropolitan Statistical Area. CMSA = Consolidated MSA. 2. Dry land or land partially or temporarily covered by water. 3. Hispanic persons may be of any race.

City	Households, 1990				Births, 1984			Deaths, 1984				Hospitals, 1985		
			Percent–		Number			Number		Rate			Beds	
	Number	Persons per house-hold	Female family house-holder[1]	One-person[2]	Total	To mothers under 20 yrs. old (Percent)	Rate[3]	Total	Infant[4]	Total[3]	Infant[5]	Number	Number	Rate[6]
	15	16	17	18	19	20	21	22	23	24	25	26	27	28
COLORADO—Con.														
Grand Junction	12 810	2.15	11.6	37.2	515	10.1	15.5	409	10	12.3	19.4	3	499	1 538
Greeley	22 647	2.50	10.1	27.0	1 058	15.2	19.3	458	6	8.4	5.7	2	340	597
Lakewood	51 657	2.38	10.7	27.5	1 618	9.8	13.4	815	12	6.7	7.4	1	32	26
Littleton	13 905	2.39	9.8	29.5	647	9.0	20.4	259	5	8.2	7.7	0	0	0
Longmont	19 570	2.61	10.0	23.7	854	10.2	17.5	322	10	6.6	11.7	1	128	253
Loveland	14 049	2.62	9.4	21.9	572	8.6	16.9	285	5	8.4	8.7	1	100	282
Northglenn	9 829	2.75	10.9	20.3	485	15.1	16.0	137	0	4.5	0.0	0	0	0
Pueblo	38 324	2.50	14.9	27.9	1 619	18.9	16.2	995	17	10.0	10.5	3	1 247	1 232
Thornton	19 055	2.87	12.2	18.4	891	10.9	19.2	184	10	4.0	11.2	1	250	500
Westminster	27 828	2.67	10.2	21.9	1 018	7.5	17.0	198	10	3.3	9.8	0	0	0
Wheat Ridge	13 138	2.20	10.4	33.2	422	9.5	13.9	290	6	9.5	14.2	1	401	1 334
CONNECTICUT	1 230 479	2.59	11.4	24.2	42 220	9.4	13.4	27 851	438	8.8	10.4	65	16 210	508
Bridgeport	52 328	2.63	20.6	29.4	2 744	20.4	19.3	1 585	45	11.2	16.4	4	1 125	793
Bristol	23 956	2.51	10.3	24.9	779	8.7	13.4	479	5	8.2	6.4	1	200	339
Danbury	24 094	2.60	10.5	25.8	882	8.5	13.9	489	10	7.7	11.3	1	420	651
Hartford	51 464	2.55	27.6	32.8	2 776	23.6	20.5	1 352	55	10.0	19.8	6	2 723	1 973
Meriden	23 240	2.51	12.8	26.8	905	11.2	15.6	524	12	9.0	13.3	3	317	544
Middletown	16 821	2.31	11.9	31.0	524	9.7	13.5	338	5	8.7	9.5	3	991	2 551
Milford	18 116	2.63	9.8	22.7	660	5.0	13.3	441	2	8.9	3.0	1	149	303
Naugatuck borough	11 330	2.69	10.4	23.1	408	7.4	14.1	205	7	7.1	17.2	0	0	0
New Britain	30 170	2.40	14.6	29.9	1 042	13.6	14.4	777	14	10.7	13.4	2	580	805
New Haven	48 986	2.41	21.6	34.0	2 204	17.9	17.7	1 393	38	11.2	17.2	5	1 413	1 145
New London	10 712	2.29	15.5	34.7	513	14.2	18.0	309	7	10.8	13.6	1	325	1 136
Norwalk	30 560	2.53	11.7	25.8	1 137	8.5	14.5	643	16	8.2	14.1	1	427	553
Norwich	15 018	2.44	13.0	27.8	666	11.9	17.3	386	6	10.1	9.0	3	923	2 428
Shelton	12 454	2.79	8.0	18.1	408	3.9	12.3	242	3	7.3	7.4	0	0	0
Stamford	41 945	2.54	12.4	26.5	1 462	8.5	14.3	873	13	8.6	8.9	2	485	480
Torrington	13 883	2.38	9.8	29.0	414	6.5	13.2	356	5	11.4	12.1	1	188	605
Waterbury	43 164	2.48	15.4	29.7	1 631	15.1	15.9	1 210	16	11.8	9.8	2	848	829
West Haven	21 284	2.48	13.0	27.5	794	7.6	14.9	545	10	10.2	12.6	1	731	1 372
DELAWARE	247 497	2.61	11.8	23.2	9 266	13.8	15.1	5 098	100	8.3	10.8	13	3 760	594
Newark	7 469	2.57	7.5	23.4	227	9.3	9.4	188	12	7.8	52.9	0	0	0
Wilmington	28 556	2.44	21.8	36.4	1 732	20.6	24.9	1 130	26	16.2	15.0	6	2 001	2 871
DISTRICT OF COLUMBIA	249 634	2.26	19.5	41.5	9 666	18.0	15.5	6 762	203	10.9	21.0	17	8 309	1 327
District of Columbia	249 634	2.26	19.5	41.5	9 666	18.0	15.5	6 762	203	10.9	21.0	17	8 309	1 327
FLORIDA	5 134 869	2.46	10.7	25.5	155 397	14.7	14.2	115 227	1 684	10.5	10.8	279	62 668	537
Boca Raton	26 297	2.27	6.7	28.3	583	2.2	10.4	706	9	12.6	15.4	1	390	667
Boynton Beach	20 292	2.25	9.5	30.0	481	17.7	12.3	614	3	15.7	6.2	1	350	815
Bradenton	18 871	2.23	10.1	30.9	586	20.0	16.4	754	7	21.2	11.9	2	895	2 390
Cape Coral	29 748	2.50	7.8	17.1	429	8.2	9.8	496	4	11.3	9.3	1	174	347
Clearwater	44 138	2.17	10.2	33.0	1 215	13.9	12.6	1 587	14	16.5	11.5	3	1 151	1 180
Coral Gables	15 460	2.33	9.5	31.2	281	3.6	6.8	423	5	10.2	17.8	3	539	1 288
Coral Springs	27 014	2.94	9.9	16.5	621	3.1	11.7	212	4	4.0	6.4	0	0	0
Daytona Beach	27 546	2.10	12.9	37.6	844	23.2	15.0	877	8	15.5	9.5	2	734	1 264
Deerfield Beach	23 118	2.00	7.4	38.1	408	14.5	9.8	692	8	16.6	19.6	0	0	0
Delray Beach	21 390	2.19	9.2	31.8	595	16.8	14.0	657	11	15.5	18.5	1	211	476
Dunedin	15 888	2.08	8.0	34.1	239	8.4	7.6	552	0	17.5	0.0	1	278	868
Fort Lauderdale	66 440	2.17	11.3	38.2	4 357	15.4	29.1	2 260	33	15.1	7.6	10	2 522	1 697
Fort Myers	18 144	2.40	16.5	32.3	895	22.0	23.4	545	13	14.3	14.5	3	961	2 431
Fort Pierce	14 171	2.54	18.6	27.8	784	25.6	21.5	542	17	14.9	21.7	3	300	813
Gainesville	31 924	2.35	12.8	30.0	1 351	12.8	16.3	535	26	6.4	19.2	5	1 771	2 079
Hallandale	17 135	1.79	7.2	45.7	262	19.1	7.1	742	0	20.0	0.0	0	0	0
Hialeah	59 381	3.13	14.9	13.9	1 960	9.0	12.9	1 249	10	8.2	5.1	3	984	608
Hollywood	52 904	2.28	9.9	33.4	1 739	12.1	14.5	1 810	12	15.1	6.9	5	1 457	1 205
Jacksonville	241 384	2.55	13.9	25.8	10 544	16.1	18.2	4 912	125	8.5	11.9	13	3 235	530
Lakeland	29 656	2.29	12.3	30.6	1 072	21.3	19.7	677	12	12.5	11.2	2	682	1 102
Lake Worth	12 565	2.21	9.5	36.7	727	14.0	25.9	598	2	21.3	2.8	2	272	993
Largo	31 921	2.02	8.0	34.7	689	13.1	11.0	918	8	14.6	11.6	3	515	825
Lauderdale Lakes	11 962	2.26	13.5	33.8	175	12.0	6.6	393	4	14.7	22.9	0	0	0
Lauderhill	21 131	2.33	13.0	30.4	518	6.4	12.6	377	6	9.2	11.6	0	0	0
Margate	18 930	2.26	7.4	28.1	305	6.2	7.9	529	4	13.7	13.1	1	155	391
Melbourne	25 065	2.32	10.8	29.1	745	14.9	14.2	563	9	10.7	12.1	2	495	872
Miami	130 252	2.70	18.6	28.9	13 463	15.5	36.1	4 882	97	13.1	7.2	20	6 205	1 659
Miami Beach	49 305	1.85	9.1	50.7	929	9.5	9.7	2 346	7	24.5	7.5	4	1 370	1 442
Miramar	14 395	2.82	13.3	17.7	569	5.3	15.9	270	5	7.6	8.8	0	0	0

1. No spouse present. 2. Householder living alone. 3. Per 1,000 resident population estimated as of July 1 of the year shown. 4. Deaths of infants under 1 year old. 5. Deaths of infants under 1 year old per 1,000 live births. 6. Per 100,000 resident population estimated as of July 1, 1986.

City	Serious crimes known to police, 1985			Police officers, 1985		Educational attainment,[4] 1980		Money income						Housing, 1990		
	Number							Per capita[5]				Percent below poverty level, 1979				
								1985		1979						
	Total	Violent[1]	Rate[2]	Number	Rate[3]	Percent completing 12 years or more	Percent completing 16 years or more	Total (Dollars)	Percent of State average	Current dollars	Constant (1985) dollars	Persons	Families	Total units	Percent change, 1980–1990	Vacant units for sale or rent[6]
	29	30	31	32	33	34	35	36	37	38	39	40	41	42	43	44
COLORADO—Con.																
Grand Junction	2 263	89	6 922	63	19.3	73.7	16.4	9 088	77.6	6 995	10 367	13.2	9.3	13 698	7.2	567
Greeley	5 207	302	9 232	93	16.5	74.0	24.9	9 726	83.0	6 561	9 723	17.6	10.6	23 991	13.6	1 026
Lakewood	10 261	718	8 333	193	15.7	85.2	26.2	14 478	123.6	9 716	14 399	5.0	3.6	55 678	22.0	3 204
Littleton	2 055	59	6 136	55	16.4	85.4	27.9	13 834	118.1	9 357	13 867	6.3	3.8	14 778	23.7	777
Longmont	3 386	144	7 027	71	14.7	79.7	18.6	11 235	95.9	7 686	11 391	6.1	4.1	20 480	20.2	771
Loveland	1 944	147	5 702	39	11.4	76.2	18.9	11 220	95.8	7 746	11 480	7.3	5.1	14 711	17.0	515
Northglenn	2 405	111	7 554	48	15.1	81.9	14.2	11 462	97.9	7 867	11 659	5.6	4.2	10 442	5.9	545
Pueblo	7 343	850	7 224	171	16.8	66.0	13.6	8 685	74.1	6 696	9 923	14.3	11.3	40 862	2.1	1 688
Thornton	3 558	92	7 599	66	14.1	78.2	12.5	10 794	92.2	7 424	11 002	6.4	5.8	20 974	30.9	1 402
Westminster	4 808	261	8 278	94	16.2	84.4	19.0	12 161	103.8	8 075	11 967	5.6	4.4	29 868	37.9	1 738
Wheat Ridge	2 631	173	8 159	50	15.5	80.8	19.1	13 424	114.6	9 329	13 826	7.0	5.3	14 130	7.5	826
CONNECTICUT	149 330	12 758	4 705	NA	NA	70.3	20.7	14 090	100.0	8 511	12 613	8.0	6.2	1 320 850	12.3	55 167
Bridgeport	15 808	2 194	11 052	401	28.0	50.7	8.7	9 427	66.9	6 081	9 012	20.4	17.4	57 224	3.4	3 971
Bristol	1 572	136	2 699	93	16.0	63.0	10.8	12 361	87.7	7 721	11 443	5.9	4.7	24 989	15.9	780
Danbury	2 742	96	4 347	117	18.6	67.4	18.7	13 337	94.7	7 957	11 792	6.7	5.1	25 950	13.0	1 229
Hartford	17 886	2 727	13 096	501	36.7	50.8	11.9	8 677	61.6	5 559	8 238	25.2	22.5	56 098	1.5	4 053
Meriden	2 384	101	4 076	103	17.6	61.3	12.0	11 952	84.8	7 496	11 109	7.4	6.5	24 826	10.6	1 147
Middletown	1 758	132	4 473	85	21.6	63.9	17.2	11 530	81.8	7 160	10 611	9.7	5.9	18 102	18.4	1 057
Milford	1 909	75	3 802	104	20.7	74.2	17.9	13 534	96.1	8 231	12 198	4.0	2.9	19 339	8.5	665
Naugatuck borough	571	28	2 063	42	15.2	63.9	11.0	11 418	81.0	7 031	10 420	7.1	5.7	11 930	18.5	519
New Britain	4 571	464	6 165	148	20.0	55.8	12.3	10 945	77.7	7 156	10 605	11.8	8.9	32 335	8.0	1 679
New Haven	14 495	2 169	11 599	351	28.1	60.9	19.8	9 378	66.6	5 822	8 628	23.2	19.4	54 057	6.3	3 507
New London	2 255	154	7 605	75	25.3	62.2	14.8	10 629	75.4	6 451	9 560	16.9	13.0	11 970	4.6	941
Norwalk	4 896	284	6 143	146	18.3	69.6	22.1	15 907	112.9	9 482	14 052	7.0	5.5	32 224	8.6	1 341
Norwich	1 665	103	4 276	73	18.7	60.5	10.9	10 870	77.1	6 641	9 842	12.6	10.3	16 472	7.3	961
Shelton	637	11	1 950	40	12.2	73.6	18.7	13 833	98.2	8 251	12 228	3.5	2.9	12 981	19.4	388
Stamford	6 118	499	5 965	275	26.8	72.7	25.6	18 246	129.5	10 711	15 874	7.7	6.1	44 279	9.5	1 874
Torrington	715	52	2 251	61	19.2	58.3	11.0	11 646	82.7	7 307	10 829	6.9	5.5	15 161	15.6	739
Waterbury	6 887	409	6 654	251	24.2	55.4	9.4	10 187	72.3	6 429	9 528	14.1	11.6	47 205	13.5	3 387
West Haven	2 379	205	4 407	103	19.1	64.7	11.9	11 556	82.0	7 200	10 670	9.4	7.9	22 679	7.8	1 017
DELAWARE	30 859	2 695	4 961	NA	NA	68.6	17.5	11 375	100.0	7 449	11 039	11.9	8.9	289 919	17.7	12 178
Newark	1 792	62	6 846	51	19.5	86.2	43.5	10 560	92.8	6 789	10 061	18.5	4.5	7 860	3.8	320
Wilmington	6 821	815	9 405	255	35.2	55.2	13.1	9 410	82.7	6 301	9 338	24.6	20.2	31 244	2.4	1 827
DISTRICT OF COLUMBIA	50 123	10 179	8 007	3 837	61.3	67.1	27.5	13 530	100.0	8 959	13 277	18.6	15.1	278 489	0.5	19 907
District of Columbia	50 123	10 179	8 007	3 837	61.3	67.1	27.5	13 530	100.0	8 959	13 277	18.6	15.1	278 489	0.5	19 907
FLORIDA	860 889	106 971	7 574	NA	NA	66.7	14.9	11 271	100.0	7 260	10 759	13.5	9.9	6 100 262	28.2	425 736
Boca Raton	3 601	177	6 196	103	17.7	84.3	27.8	21 112	187.3	12 549	18 598	5.1	3.4	33 043	21.8	1 981
Boynton Beach	3 399	601	8 265	86	20.9	65.0	12.8	11 560	102.6	7 266	10 768	9.9	7.1	25 544	29.1	1 557
Bradenton	3 896	500	10 539	51	13.8	65.2	11.9	10 321	91.6	6 699	9 928	14.4	10.5	22 123	31.5	1 530
Cape Coral	1 400	69	3 326	69	16.4	74.4	15.0	11 845	105.1	8 340	12 360	5.9	4.8	34 486	53.8	1 851
Clearwater	7 381	644	7 545	206	21.1	73.3	18.0	13 213	117.2	8 223	12 186	8.6	5.7	53 833	17.9	4 707
Coral Gables	5 078	376	10 827	126	26.9	86.0	40.3	21 089	187.1	12 900	19 118	9.0	6.1	16 561	-6.7	740
Coral Springs	1 849	74	3 813	112	23.1	86.3	27.9	14 567	129.2	8 928	13 231	4.1	3.9	29 785	57.1	2 117
Daytona Beach	8 952	1 103	14 878	177	29.4	65.0	15.0	9 170	81.4	5 853	8 674	22.7	15.9	32 167	19.4	2 896
Deerfield Beach	2 707	348	6 050	88	19.7	65.8	12.9	12 695	112.6	7 872	11 666	8.5	5.5	28 796	22.5	1 732
Delray Beach	5 263	549	12 251	92	21.4	72.6	17.6	14 258	126.5	9 261	13 725	12.4	7.8	27 527	29.0	2 217
Dunedin	1 395	95	4 140	49	14.5	72.7	16.4	12 913	114.6	8 106	12 013	6.0	3.2	18 411	15.0	993
Fort Lauderdale	21 844	2 233	14 074	434	28.0	72.1	18.6	15 135	134.3	9 752	14 452	14.2	9.7	81 268	1.4	6 119
Fort Myers	4 344	510	10 470	96	23.1	61.7	12.0	9 892	87.8	6 483	9 608	21.7	15.7	21 388	23.6	1 987
Fort Pierce	5 483	715	14 049	78	20.0	52.5	9.1	7 705	68.4	5 547	8 221	27.6	20.8	17 250	12.1	1 584
Gainesville	7 370	948	8 122	188	20.7	78.8	35.4	9 460	83.9	6 150	9 114	24.2	14.0	34 608	13.9	2 072
Hallandale	3 075	537	7 638	98	24.3	62.8	12.4	15 529	137.8	10 047	14 890	11.1	7.4	24 798	6.3	1 722
Hialeah	13 332	1 358	8 456	304	19.3	50.1	8.2	8 256	73.2	5 915	8 766	13.2	12.0	62 187	19.2	2 394
Hollywood	11 366	1 032	9 133	291	23.4	66.8	14.0	13 350	118.4	8 727	12 933	8.5	5.9	63 303	8.3	4 487
Jacksonville	48 924	7 301	8 140	945	15.7	66.2	13.6	10 466	92.9	6 767	10 029	16.0	12.9	267 148	20.1	20 020
Lakeland	6 041	641	10 760	137	24.4	66.9	17.4	10 345	91.8	7 142	10 584	15.3	11.2	34 933	37.5	2 484
Lake Worth	3 395	425	11 199	69	22.8	62.9	13.7	11 542	102.4	7 186	10 650	11.8	7.6	15 632	-1.5	1 221
Largo	2 785	307	4 258	99	15.1	69.1	12.9	11 874	105.4	7 577	11 229	7.0	4.7	38 711	19.0	2 567
Lauderdale Lakes	1 515	144	5 225	NA	NA	66.4	10.5	11 667	103.5	7 456	11 050	8.4	6.3	13 921	11.7	918
Lauderhill	2 564	259	6 070	NA	NA	78.3	18.0	13 301	118.0	8 627	12 785	7.9	5.5	26 274	23.7	2 358
Margate	1 505	79	3 582	78	18.6	66.6	9.9	11 983	106.3	7 430	11 011	4.4	2.9	21 647	21.9	1 077
Melbourne	4 748	516	8 771	97	17.9	70.2	12.8	10 287	91.3	6 430	9 529	11.9	8.0	28 070	33.2	2 023
Miami	58 355	11 186	15 122	1 040	27.0	50.0	13.0	8 904	79.0	6 084	9 016	24.5	19.9	144 550	-0.8	10 802
Miami Beach	12 447	1 021	12 254	285	28.1	57.0	13.4	13 307	118.1	8 904	13 196	17.7	12.4	62 413	-3.4	8 028
Miramar	1 251	175	3 324	63	16.7	71.9	10.0	12 081	107.2	7 830	11 604	5.9	4.6	15 243	20.3	602

1. Includes murder and nonnegligent manslaughter, forcible rape, robbery, and aggravated assault. 2. Per 100,000 resident population estimated for 1985 by the FBI. 3. Per 10,000 resident population estimated for 1985 by the FBI. 4. Persons 25 years old or older. 5. Based on the resident population estimated as of July 1, 1988 for 1987 data and enumerated as of April 1, 1980 for 1979 data. 6. Also includes units rented or sold, but not occupied.

City	Housing, 1990 (cont'd)					Construction authorized by building permits, 1990				Civilian labor force, 1990			
	Occupied units					New private housing units						Unemployment	
			Owner-occupied										
	Total	Percent with more than 1 person per room	Percent of total	Median value[1] (Dollars)	Median rent[2] (Dollars)	Number	Value ($1,000)	Percent single family	Non-residential, value ($1,000)	Total	Percent change, 1989–1990	Total	Rate[3]
	45	46	47	48	49	50	51	52	53	54	55	56	57
COLORADO—Con.													
Grand Junction	12 810	2.3	50.4	54 100	266	28	2 138	92.9	5 366	15 893	7.3	983	6.2
Greeley	22 647	3.8	53.9	70 400	314	132	9 956	85.6	7 157	30 988	5.6	1 806	5.8
Lakewood	51 657	2.0	60.5	91 400	407	172	18 407	80.2	12 082	73 773	2.8	2 940	4.0
Littleton	13 905	1.8	60.6	97 700	379	61	8 487	100.0	0	21 226	3.0	817	3.8
Longmont	19 570	2.9	62.2	85 900	392	75	7 581	100.0	189	29 053	3.7	1 151	4.0
Loveland	14 049	2.0	63.8	73 400	348	151	9 981	97.4	1 886	19 895	5.6	1 073	5.4
Northglenn	9 829	2.5	63.5	71 500	379	0	0	NA	356	19 697	2.8	832	4.2
Pueblo	38 324	3.7	64.8	48 700	250	NA	NA	NA	NA	42 991	8.8	2 879	6.7
Thornton	19 055	3.4	69.9	75 600	398	64	4 605	100.0	1 490	24 764	2.7	1 204	4.9
Westminster	27 828	2.6	65.2	85 700	418	321	27 439	100.0	4 897	32 644	2.7	1 496	4.6
Wheat Ridge	13 138	1.7	53.5	88 600	375	11	1 598	100.0	3 666	19 476	2.8	829	4.3
CONNECTICUT	1 230 479	2.3	65.6	177 800	510	7 584	648 770	72.9	309 974	1 789 000	1.6	91 000	5.1
Bridgeport	52 328	6.7	44.2	145 900	496	85	3 536	43.5	377	66 903	1.7	6 198	9.3
Bristol	23 956	1.4	62.4	153 500	465	90	6 588	88.9	1 884	30 425	1.6	2 030	6.7
Danbury	24 094	4.1	60.1	190 300	589	67	6 299	65.7	17 439	43 879	3.2	2 169	4.9
Hartford	51 464	9.2	23.6	133 800	443	333	11 135	2.7	13 253	64 988	3.0	5 677	8.7
Meriden	23 240	2.4	60.5	146 300	453	91	4 986	97.8	1 338	34 374	3.0	1 801	5.2
Middletown	16 821	1.5	50.7	157 000	500	83	7 731	100.0	241	24 591	-1.4	1 086	4.4
Milford	18 116	1.0	76.6	172 400	654	40	2 762	80.0	11 811	29 830	0.6	1 424	4.8
Naugatuck borough	11 330	1.8	67.1	143 100	478	99	6 253	88.9	635	14 204	1.1	1 047	7.4
New Britain	30 170	4.2	43.1	139 200	427	22	732	50.0	0	37 109	0.7	2 736	7.4
New Haven	48 986	4.9	31.8	145 000	487	134	5 123	29.9	3 957	59 744	3.6	3 927	6.6
New London	10 712	4.5	36.9	131 600	455	16	896	43.8	1 392	13 314	0.5	972	7.3
Norwalk	30 560	3.8	62.0	241 300	647	141	5 859	9.9	6 356	48 660	-0.9	2 049	4.2
Norwich	15 018	2.0	52.7	126 200	444	192	8 095	19.8	1 751	19 405	0.2	1 279	6.6
Shelton	12 454	0.9	79.5	208 600	549	114	6 972	93.0	7 414	19 213	1.3	1 076	5.6
Stamford	41 945	4.9	57.9	295 700	716	408	22 367	17.4	7 681	62 907	0.1	2 762	4.4
Torrington	13 883	1.0	62.7	141 700	428	186	11 630	100.0	5 009	19 527	3.1	1 167	6.0
Waterbury	43 164	3.3	49.0	131 800	404	354	13 041	81.4	2 312	50 958	1.6	4 465	8.8
West Haven	21 284	2.5	56.1	147 000	534	36	1 825	77.8	2 309	30 975	3.4	1 704	5.5
DELAWARE	247 497	2.3	70.2	100 100	425	5 142	274 461	80.7	187 368	362 000	0.0	19 000	5.1
Newark	7 469	2.0	56.3	134 600	486	315	12 435	26.3	4 813	13 807	-0.3	754	5.5
Wilmington	28 556	4.3	53.2	77 800	374	144	6 562	98.6	29 101	34 247	1.9	2 610	7.6
DISTRICT OF COLUMBIA	249 634	8.2	38.9	123 900	441	368	20 801	48.9	19 378	298 000	-5.4	20 000	6.6
District of Columbia	249 634	8.2	38.9	123 900	441	368	20 801	48.9	19 378	298 000	-5.4	20 000	6.6
FLORIDA	5 134 869	5.8	67.2	77 100	402	126 384	8 426 844	65.4	2 654 097	6 365 000	2.8	378 000	5.9
Boca Raton	26 297	1.9	74.5	165 300	581	861	66 813	33.1	10 916	36 861	1.9	1 516	4.1
Boynton Beach	20 292	4.8	76.5	79 400	537	299	20 648	34.4	19 004	21 340	2.2	1 591	7.5
Bradenton	18 871	4.0	61.1	71 700	406	424	20 309	51.7	6 144	18 862	7.6	1 165	6.2
Cape Coral	29 748	1.7	75.1	91 100	438	1 263	61 093	90.5	20 232	22 863	4.9	951	4.2
Clearwater	44 138	2.1	61.8	82 100	396	1 020	64 954	9.7	18 701	51 456	2.5	2 260	4.4
Coral Gables	15 460	6.3	63.6	223 500	476	104	32 077	100.0	1 117	25 372	1.1	1 090	4.3
Coral Springs	27 014	3.7	62.4	160 200	576	843	83 801	51.5	7 306	23 846	1.9	1 066	4.5
Daytona Beach	27 546	4.2	46.8	63 000	355	210	16 477	68.6	6 302	34 998	2.6	2 126	6.1
Deerfield Beach	23 118	3.7	72.1	97 400	536	366	12 948	19.7	6 868	18 382	2.2	1 467	8.0
Delray Beach	21 390	5.3	70.3	92 900	513	561	37 892	32.8	28 735	23 215	2.3	1 898	8.2
Dunedin	15 888	1.1	70.5	76 500	395	240	12 784	34.6	2 531	15 292	2.6	691	4.5
Fort Lauderdale	66 440	8.2	54.4	99 200	420	232	18 226	15.9	29 550	109 005	2.0	6 013	5.5
Fort Myers	18 144	8.0	42.4	60 500	373	455	13 365	9.2	18 932	30 775	4.9	1 350	4.4
Fort Pierce	14 171	9.8	51.8	56 100	324	98	4 091	22.4	1 659	26 485	6.4	4 323	16.3
Gainesville	31 924	4.9	47.1	63 800	305	128	4 512	93.8	4 807	51 993	3.1	1 890	3.6
Hallandale	17 135	4.7	66.8	76 600	431	83	4 106	18.1	1 178	16 184	2.2	1 378	8.5
Hialeah	59 381	30.3	49.9	80 100	407	848	32 901	52.8	6 473	95 477	1.3	7 749	8.1
Hollywood	52 904	5.9	64.7	82 100	446	437	16 321	16.0	19 515	77 018	2.0	4 462	5.8
Jacksonville	241 384	4.4	62.1	62 900	353	5 168	281 123	68.7	175 646	331 417	1.7	18 600	5.6
Lakeland	29 656	3.4	59.0	61 600	316	275	16 034	80.7	14 024	27 596	1.5	2 577	9.3
Lake Worth	12 565	7.8	55.6	66 900	387	6	382	100.0	2 050	20 311	2.3	1 728	8.5
Largo	31 921	1.3	65.8	71 500	401	54	2 429	77.8	8 057	34 194	2.5	1 416	4.1
Lauderdale Lakes	11 962	7.0	66.0	79 600	473	0	0	NA	915	13 967	2.2	1 052	7.5
Lauderhill	21 131	7.1	57.9	93 500	496	53	4 994	100.0	906	26 474	2.0	1 380	5.2
Margate	18 930	2.7	78.3	83 000	538	370	26 370	90.3	8 725	20 138	2.2	1 476	7.3
Melbourne	25 065	2.7	58.1	65 100	391	809	60 567	53.2	13 902	33 705	4.2	1 503	4.5
Miami	130 252	26.9	33.1	79 200	346	975	50 703	8.1	53 025	207 691	1.3	17 203	8.3
Miami Beach	49 305	15.5	28.5	191 300	379	346	57 605	3.2	794	36 345	1.3	2 876	7.9
Miramar	14 395	7.2	77.8	81 200	519	191	17 383	100.0	10 481	23 750	2.0	1 176	5.0

1. Specified owner-occupied units. 2. Specified renter-occupied units. 3. Percent of total civilian labor force.

Table C. Cities — **Labor Force and Manufactures**

City	Employed,[1] 1980: Total	Employed, 1980: Rate per 1,000 employees: Professional, specialty, and technical	Employed, 1980: Rate per 1,000 employees: Precision production, craft, and operators	Manufactures, 1987: Establishments: Total	Manufactures, 1987: Establishments: Percent with 20 or more employees	Manufactures, 1987: All employees: Number (1,000)	Manufactures, 1987: All employees: Percent change, 1982–1987	Manufactures, 1987: All employees: Annual payroll (Mil. dol.)	Manufactures, 1987: Production workers: Number (1,000)	Manufactures, 1987: Production workers: Work-hours (Millions)	Manufactures, 1987: Production workers: Wages: Total (Mil. dol.)	Manufactures, 1987: Production workers: Wages: Average per production worker (Dollars)	Manufactures, 1987: Value added by manufacture (Mil. dol.)	Manufactures, 1987: Value of shipments (Mil. dol.)	Manufactures, 1987: New capital expenditures (Mil. dol.)
	58	59	60	61	62	63	64	65	66	67	68	69	70	71	72
COLORADO—Con.															
Grand Junction	13 156	172.6	201.4	68	23.5	1.6	-23.8	29.9	0.9	1.8	14.8	16 444	60.7	100.5	6.3
Greeley	23 227	177.6	152.2	60	25.0	D	D	D	D	D	D	D	D	D	D
Lakewood	59 296	193.3	162.6	139	12.2	3.0	-9.1	71.9	1.3	2.2	18.4	14 154	200.9	285.6	D
Littleton	14 804	199.4	155.6	59	20.3	1.9	D	47.1	1.3	2.6	30.1	23 154	74.9	139.7	3.9
Longmont	20 674	175.1	260.3	94	34.0	4.5	21.6	95.7	3.2	6.7	58.8	18 375	187.1	592.6	21.0
Loveland	13 841	168.1	282.9	66	31.8	4.5	4.7	116.0	2.2	4.8	58.8	26 727	237.0	383.3	13.2
Northglenn	15 995	120.3	238.8	24	25.0	D	D	D	D	D	D	D	D	D	D
Pueblo	38 813	162.7	204.8	68	17.6	2.8	-47.2	70.6	2.0	4.4	50.9	25 450	157.9	343.1	7.5
Thornton	19 976	104.3	246.5	14	14.3	D	D	D	D	D	D	D	D	D	D
Westminster	26 286	148.7	218.3	38	23.7	D	D	D	D	D	D	D	D	D	D
Wheat Ridge	15 610	165.9	206.0	56	23.2	1.2	-25.0	29.9	0.8	1.5	15.8	19 750	96.4	160.2	7.5
CONNECTICUT	1 482 309	175.6	239.1	6 747	36.5	388.9	-8.4	11 110.6	216.5	440.6	4 825.6	22 289	22 348.9	37 400.3	1 293.3
Bridgeport	59 711	110.5	325.8	343	36.7	18.6	-18.8	538.2	11.6	23.8	257.8	22 224	834.1	1 451.9	27.8
Bristol	28 457	131.0	367.9	160	35.0	6.4	-11.1	173.5	4.6	9.1	105.9	23 022	302.9	503.6	17.1
Danbury	29 572	171.4	288.8	160	40.6	13.7	-14.4	443.9	5.7	12.2	118.6	20 807	585.9	1 021.5	45.6
Hartford	56 896	131.8	245.4	162	40.7	8.6	-18.1	236.1	4.6	9.0	84.5	18 370	468.0	749.1	31.8
Meriden	27 727	140.6	333.7	122	37.7	5.0	6.4	121.5	2.8	5.7	49.1	17 536	221.0	373.0	20.2
Middletown	19 472	177.4	272.9	59	50.8	6.9	-11.5	208.9	4.6	9.5	132.9	28 891	527.8	850.7	22.5
Milford	25 120	164.3	265.8	185	37.3	7.6	7.0	214.0	4.5	9.1	98.4	21 867	471.4	686.0	26.6
Naugatuck borough	12 206	149.6	337.8	49	46.9	2.6	-7.1	66.6	1.8	3.7	38.4	21 333	197.3	440.5	13.7
New Britain	36 769	126.3	323.2	165	35.2	7.9	-35.2	186.4	4.9	10.2	96.0	19 592	400.9	700.0	26.9
New Haven	50 266	203.3	226.2	186	37.1	8.6	-26.5	193.7	5.7	11.5	99.6	17 474	390.0	667.7	20.7
New London	11 326	164.6	249.2	26	26.9	D	D	D	D	D	D	D	D	D	D
Norwalk	41 619	159.9	214.2	207	41.5	16.0	2.6	483.7	6.7	13.2	134.3	20 045	815.9	1 313.6	49.9
Norwich	16 315	152.4	299.5	49	40.8	D	D	D	D	D	D	D	D	D	D
Shelton	15 198	179.8	275.3	78	42.3	3.6	-5.3	103.6	1.6	3.4	32.1	20 062	133.2	250.4	7.7
Stamford	52 811	165.3	171.2	313	37.7	22.9	-3.4	848.4	7.7	14.5	169.1	21 961	1 529.2	2 268.9	55.2
Torrington	15 111	118.2	336.8	75	40.0	3.4	-2.9	75.5	2.3	4.8	42.0	18 261	262.6	533.2	11.0
Waterbury	45 386	120.3	345.2	242	38.8	11.4	-17.4	261.8	7.8	16.1	151.7	19 449	631.1	1 087.3	35.4
West Haven	26 026	143.1	242.0	72	44.4	3.6	5.9	112.8	1.4	2.8	26.5	18 929	240.1	316.5	31.1
DELAWARE	262 809	181.5	203.3	673	38.9	66.6	-1.9	2 090.8	32.8	65.2	760.0	23 171	3 866.0	10 729.7	276.9
Newark	11 599	298.0	99.1	35	40.0	D	D	D	D	D	D	D	D	D	D
Wilmington	26 948	173.1	179.6	128	34.4	19.2	-11.9	785.2	2.4	4.8	47.2	19 667	245.0	473.0	29.6
DISTRICT OF COLUMBIA	298 107	239.7	75.9	486	25.5	17.0	1.8	494.1	5.2	10.7	118.8	22 846	1 525.4	2 128.3	43.6
District of Columbia	298 107	239.7	75.9	486	25.5	17.0	1.8	494.1	5.2	10.7	118.8	22 846	1 525.4	2 128.3	43.6
FLORIDA	4 002 330	142.0	186.3	15 603	25.9	499.3	9.9	10 954.0	308.7	614.7	5 222.7	16 918	27 574.2	56 612.7	1 910.7
Boca Raton	21 077	197.2	131.3	170	20.6	D	D	D	D	D	D	D	D	D	D
Boynton Beach	11 776	135.8	189.1	44	25.0	2.7	350.0	67.7	1.3	2.6	23.1	17 769	268.7	416.0	D
Bradenton	10 775	120.9	199.2	60	40.0	5.9	51.3	124.7	4.2	9.2	74.0	17 619	544.4	1 232.6	24.7
Cape Coral	11 840	114.8	183.7	81	17.3	1.1	83.3	16.4	0.8	1.5	10.5	13 125	28.9	54.1	D
Clearwater	34 855	154.8	150.2	241	24.9	6.7	86.1	139.3	4.5	9.2	74.0	16 444	301.4	527.4	26.7
Coral Gables	20 294	275.0	61.6	74	14.9	1.3	0.0	37.6	0.6	1.2	12.6	21 000	53.0	99.0	1.5
Coral Springs	15 928	181.6	140.6	34	26.5	1.2	-20.0	27.6	0.7	1.6	12.5	17 857	77.9	108.6	1.8
Daytona Beach	20 904	144.2	153.3	77	23.4	4.7	34.3	120.5	2.0	4.0	33.4	16 700	292.0	435.1	18.6
Deerfield Beach	11 829	107.8	183.8	69	24.6	1.5	-25.0	33.2	1.0	2.1	16.2	16 200	73.8	158.4	4.6
Delray Beach	12 713	142.9	125.9	62	19.4	0.8	NA	17.0	0.6	1.2	11.0	18 333	39.7	88.7	1.2
Dunedin	10 345	141.4	172.8	24	16.7	D	D	D	D	D	D	D	D	D	D
Fort Lauderdale	72 011	139.7	170.5	407	31.0	12.8	-6.6	297.4	7.5	14.9	136.8	18 240	598.1	1 064.4	60.4
Fort Myers	15 899	141.5	179.1	100	34.0	3.1	34.8	60.8	1.8	3.7	30.8	17 111	158.5	284.3	9.7
Fort Pierce	13 043	105.3	194.1	68	32.4	1.9	18.7	35.0	1.2	2.6	18.7	15 583	144.5	316.2	3.5
Gainesville	35 045	295.0	95.2	100	26.0	D	D	D	D	D	D	D	D	D	D
Hallandale	10 351	92.3	145.9	51	21.6	1.1	37.5	13.6	0.8	1.3	8.3	10 375	27.6	54.8	0.6
Hialeah	73 327	68.8	346.1	805	32.5	21.8	-8.4	341.7	17.4	32.3	227.2	13 057	797.9	1 450.7	22.8
Hollywood	50 730	134.0	191.4	175	25.7	4.4	22.2	92.1	3.0	6.2	50.1	16 700	182.7	503.5	10.2
Jacksonville	227 571	134.2	177.1	720	33.6	29.7	9.2	689.3	20.2	41.0	411.8	20 386	2 384.2	4 855.3	130.0
Lakeland	20 349	183.5	185.6	125	29.6	4.8	45.5	107.0	3.3	6.5	58.2	17 636	211.3	508.0	12.8
Lake Worth	11 081	137.0	213.2	56	23.2	0.7	16.7	11.5	0.5	0.9	6.8	13 600	29.2	54.5	1.0
Largo	23 222	143.7	196.9	122	25.4	7.1	446.2	191.6	2.7	5.3	43.2	16 000	308.7	460.7	27.5
Lauderdale Lakes	9 031	139.4	183.7	NA	NA	NA	NA	NA	NA	NA	NA	NA	NA	NA	NA
Lauderhill	17 544	169.0	146.4	NA	NA	NA	NA	NA	NA	NA	NA	NA	NA	NA	NA
Margate	13 048	112.0	236.7	NA	NA	NA	NA	NA	NA	NA	NA	NA	NA	NA	NA
Melbourne	19 861	168.2	240.8	95	32.6	6.3	65.8	165.8	2.8	5.9	46.8	16 714	365.4	738.0	33.1
Miami	159 214	110.0	233.0	884	22.5	21.8	-15.2	373.6	13.5	25.6	196.5	14 556	942.4	1 712.2	32.8
Miami Beach	27 977	146.3	114.6	40	20.0	1.1	120.0	30.3	0.3	0.5	4.2	14 000	87.6	131.4	0.5
Miramar	15 783	129.8	219.2	NA	NA	NA	NA	NA	NA	NA	NA	NA	NA	NA	NA

1. Persons 16 years old and over.

City	Wholesale trade, 1987				Retail trade–all establishments, 1987				Retail trade–establishments with payroll, 1987					
						Sales				Sales				
											Per capita[2] (Dollars)			
	Establishments	Sales (Mil. dol.)	Paid employees[1]	Annual payroll ($1,000)	Number	Total (Mil. dol.)	Percent change, 1982–1987	Per capita[2] (Dollars)	Number	Total (Mil. dol.)	General merchandise group stores	Food stores	Apparel and accessory stores	Eating and drinking places
	73	74	75	76	77	78	79	80	81	82	83	84	85	86
COLORADO—Con.														
Grand Junction	146	290.2	1 243	22 483	637	453.4	-6.8	13 977	462	444.1	D	2 102	551	2 243
Greeley	124	312.4	1 145	21 272	627	443.6	34.3	7 793	419	433.6	D	1 989	275	668
Lakewood	216	973.9	1 581	42 606	1 468	1 221.1	11.8	9 998	974	1 195.6	1 491	1 365	447	1 010
Littleton	89	259.0	408	9 649	550	416.2	72.7	12 897	320	407.8	D	2 416	265	D
Longmont	65	121.8	498	8 642	639	409.0	52.9	8 073	374	398.2	948	1 731	253	665
Loveland	56	155.6	389	8 148	545	288.1	57.0	8 113	274	276.4	647	D	D	644
Northglenn	33	33.4	126	2 896	264	273.3	18.9	9 271	186	271.2	2 086	1 051	628	647
Pueblo	118	228.7	1 211	20 961	1 066	645.3	27.8	6 374	749	629.7	989	1 460	179	621
Thornton	25	281.1	585	15 159	355	312.9	5.6	6 258	212	308.8	866	1 583	179	481
Westminster	59	81.2	260	5 670	521	366.9	95.6	5 493	333	360.7	D	D	439	522
Wheat Ridge	74	132.7	546	12 570	394	307.3	6.2	10 226	284	300.8	D	2 432	D	D
CONNECTICUT	6 138	49 235.6	84 714	2 384 527	32 816	25 785.1	62.9	8 086	21 688	25 101.8	821	1 412	473	656
Bridgeport	234	929.8	3 244	76 967	1 060	698.3	28.1	4 922	707	670.2	392	972	219	464
Bristol	55	D	D	D	555	620.6	83.4	10 529	374	613.9	D	1 671	295	456
Danbury	145	625.7	2 064	57 469	860	978.7	91.4	15 167	676	968.3	2 584	1 623	1 160	900
Hartford	288	1 804.2	5 770	157 669	1 091	725.0	34.6	5 254	856	704.2	604	484	334	874
Meriden	88	378.3	1 084	30 273	512	448.6	83.2	7 692	354	435.5	1 385	777	437	427
Middletown	55	175.3	602	14 519	340	349.6	73.8	8 999	254	345.8	D	1 152	748	652
Milford	149	562.6	2 259	57 237	598	599.6	76.5	12 175	433	589.1	994	1 218	556	1 082
Naugatuck borough	21	102.7	437	11 257	243	112.0	64.9	3 671	156	105.9	D	1 094	101	275
New Britain	59	412.0	1 143	29 859	491	341.2	50.5	4 736	332	333.2	217	932	111	364
New Haven	216	1 732.2	3 034	72 744	1 106	654.9	51.4	5 305	852	637.8	663	667	439	810
New London	37	153.3	605	12 588	334	326.9	43.6	11 430	270	321.2	789	953	547	921
Norwalk	225	2 260.8	3 643	133 712	862	974.9	75.1	12 625	594	957.1	D	2 155	744	741
Norwich	66	194.6	856	22 048	421	369.2	41.6	9 713	304	362.4	1 027	2 168	320	520
Shelton	51	536.7	2 071	82 489	238	225.2	171.3	6 464	141	218.3	D	1 710	71	317
Stamford	370	11 030.3	5 448	208 450	1 106	1 138.8	72.8	11 266	780	1 111.7	2 073	1 405	1 097	749
Torrington	60	D	D	D	408	306.2	62.0	9 849	271	297.8	1 231	1 767	428	578
Waterbury	166	428.2	1 962	47 374	1 061	855.6	45.0	8 364	713	833.4	1 296	1 803	637	506
West Haven	96	455.1	2 388	48 031	390	237.7	24.3	4 461	236	226.6	D	418	57	581
DELAWARE	999	7 899.6	15 526	452 623	6 380	5 076.8	62.2	8 020	4 416	4 975.7	1 100	1 424	346	693
Newark	48	934.7	2 263	48 230	349	418.1	74.0	17 291	260	414.3	1 433	3 350	508	1 720
Wilmington	199	3 061.8	3 259	99 302	792	678.4	76.2	9 735	605	666.6	D	1 232	310	901
DISTRICT OF COLUMBIA	554	2 846.2	8 856	231 591	4 478	3 464.9	30.5	5 534	3 681	3 423.0	502	943	521	1 336
District of Columbia	554	2 846.2	8 856	231 591	4 478	3 464.9	30.5	5 534	3 681	3 423.0	502	943	521	1 336
FLORIDA	25 636	97 360.0	261 765	5 554 657	130 508	90 295.0	62.8	7 734	83 808	87 925.6	849	1 456	343	778
Boca Raton	281	601.4	1 526	41 377	1 705	788.9	95.1	13 483	1 048	748.6	524	3 458	1 108	2 118
Boynton Beach	80	D	D	D	579	350.0	137.3	8 153	370	340.6	1 868	1 798	555	894
Bradenton	65	656.2	916	18 298	544	561.5	124.6	14 993	379	551.2	1 041	3 689	324	1 271
Cape Coral	99	94.0	613	10 188	669	264.1	106.3	5 260	336	248.9	640	1 625	217	422
Clearwater	320	676.5	2 545	51 304	1 632	2 278.7	110.4	23 366	1 234	2 254.3	2 469	2 195	989	1 578
Coral Gables	209	1 609.3	1 663	54 602	610	558.5	59.5	13 345	442	551.2	264	1 536	878	1 345
Coral Springs	112	131.5	358	8 294	725	400.5	287.7	6 624	385	384.8	1 220	1 405	667	670
Daytona Beach	120	242.8	1 452	25 376	975	959.4	56.3	16 527	754	945.4	2 425	1 596	973	1 791
Deerfield Beach	135	D	D	D	486	356.6	81.9	8 103	298	346.5	682	1 876	165	949
Delray Beach	118	178.4	847	18 099	854	827.1	87.0	18 649	523	807.7	549	2 033	709	1 092
Dunedin	28	17.9	128	2 163	328	134.3	8.8	4 193	196	128.4	D	1 747	121	485
Fort Lauderdale	701	3 858.2	8 364	202 523	2 593	2 576.3	47.9	17 335	1 844	2 525.3	1 002	1 755	946	2 190
Fort Myers	241	576.2	2 445	48 710	1 125	1 325.4	81.8	33 529	855	1 308.6	5 593	3 790	1 455	2 311
Fort Pierce	134	415.1	1 691	31 244	866	663.0	61.0	17 972	564	647.0	D	2 820	537	1 530
Gainesville	146	349.3	1 733	29 990	985	897.4	49.6	10 537	764	885.3	1 238	1 921	343	929
Hallandale	78	119.1	539	10 156	391	246.4	0.0	6 703	277	240.8	D	1 655	621	1 147
Hialeah	542	1 093.1	4 972	92 108	1 931	1 062.5	20.9	6 568	1 248	1 035.3	1 250	1 381	539	490
Hollywood	289	686.5	1 970	44 942	1 461	1 281.5	24.6	10 599	937	1 257.4	1 397	1 532	362	765
Jacksonville	1 498	14 796.0	23 088	533 980	5 720	4 686.9	63.6	7 685	4 097	4 620.6	D	1 204	294	746
Lakeland	211	1 027.8	3 179	54 356	1 258	931.4	62.8	15 049	807	910.1	2 446	2 417	669	1 316
Lake Worth	93	134.2	653	12 858	602	384.5	55.4	14 043	370	373.3	D	2 116	285	1 137
Largo	153	328.1	1 455	31 861	624	445.7	63.6	7 140	444	437.4	571	2 877	130	720
Lauderdale Lakes	22	27.2	158	3 674	304	323.1	76.8	11 775	191	317.9	D	1 898	560	413
Lauderhill	64	63.9	252	4 692	496	536.3	151.5	12 619	286	528.9	1 363	1 662	215	802
Margate	51	46.7	237	4 312	433	225.0	41.4	5 680	261	218.5	635	1 969	107	546
Melbourne	129	420.8	1 382	27 622	807	752.4	57.4	13 260	563	738.7	2 487	1 419	509	987
Miami	2 131	6 610.0	18 439	394 895	5 143	3 204.9	20.7	8 571	3 805	3 149.2	920	1 407	671	851
Miami Beach	102	179.3	636	14 130	885	345.7	-7.3	3 639	617	337.1	D	1 103	285	725
Miramar	52	76.5	275	6 064	286	99.5	14.0	2 693	139	94.2	D	1 086	48	309

1. For the period including March 12 of the year shown. 2. Based on resident population estimated as of July 1, 1986.

City	Retail trade–establishment with payroll, 1987 (cont'd)			Taxable service industries–establishments with payroll, 1987							Federal grants, 1986		
	Paid employees[1]				Receipts (Mil. dol.)								
						Selected kinds of business							
	Number	Percent change, 1982–1987	Annual payroll (Mil. dol.)	Number	Total	Hotels, motels, and other lodging places	Health services	Legal services	Paid employees[1]	Annual payroll (Mil. dol.)	Procurement contract awards (Mil. dol.)	Grant awards (Mil. dol.)	Federal government civilian employment, 1984
	87	88	89	90	91	92	93	94	95	96	97	98	99
COLORADO—Con.													
Grand Junction	6 234	-2.1	61.4	588	163.1	14.8	48.6	D	4 122	64.8	35.7	2.9	1 045
Greeley	5 219	16.1	52.5	501	130.8	2.9	49.6	7.0	3 346	49.0	31.6	4.2	245
Lakewood	14 460	10.3	151.0	1 336	452.9	15.1	104.3	21.1	11 223	186.9	76.0	2.1	8 818
Littleton	4 275	44.5	48.4	474	131.2	D	D	6.9	3 354	50.1	22.5	3.0	356
Longmont	4 536	40.5	44.8	408	100.2	3.5	41.3	6.1	2 417	40.1	1.7	0.7	692
Loveland	3 638	55.5	33.9	368	83.8	1.0	27.1	3.0	2 510	32.8	7.1	0.5	309
Northglenn	3 097	3.3	33.2	139	37.1	D	10.0	D	991	12.6	0.4	1.2	0
Pueblo	7 943	5.0	75.0	741	179.7	9.0	89.9	11.3	5 041	68.2	31.0	6.8	1 360
Thornton	3 420	5.8	34.3	221	139.0	3.6	58.2	D	2 303	42.8	0.1	0.7	0
Westminster	4 599	69.6	42.9	276	85.3	D	24.6	4.1	2 432	32.1	1.1	2.3	70
Wheat Ridge	3 780	1.1	36.6	486	171.8	D	58.5	5.3	3 954	65.9	1.4	0.3	139
CONNECTICUT	267 611	27.1	3 081.1	25 756	12 692.3	458.0	2 819.4	1 033.1	250 198	4 888.4	959.6	1 688.2	21 323
Bridgeport	7 390	9.7	90.4	896	456.3	D	153.2	85.5	8 380	182.9	27.2	17.5	1 154
Bristol	4 444	22.9	48.2	339	104.5	D	46.3	D	2 447	42.8	1.5	1.0	125
Danbury	9 846	64.7	122.1	631	337.4	22.1	104.2	25.3	7 513	150.5	59.6	3.0	478
Hartford	9 706	4.5	111.6	1 410	1 166.3	44.3	251.4	254.0	22 972	509.8	102.9	146.3	3 788
Meriden	4 325	32.7	49.0	352	111.9	D	48.7	9.6	2 817	46.6	0.8	2.4	154
Middletown	3 534	8.7	40.6	321	119.9	D	52.4	8.9	2 600	50.1	20.0	5.5	111
Milford	6 344	32.9	73.2	400	239.4	11.9	51.7	9.8	8 097	97.6	7.5	2.3	198
Naugatuck borough	1 165	28.4	10.6	137	32.8	D	11.4	3.0	718	11.1	1.7	0.6	53
New Britain	3 572	12.8	41.4	399	200.4	D	88.9	12.5	4 176	87.8	13.5	3.7	191
New Haven	8 760	12.4	93.0	1 209	634.4	20.6	197.0	99.3	13 932	271.4	23.4	166.6	2 024
New London	3 216	6.8	42.6	303	160.6	D	44.7	36.8	2 991	69.7	34.8	1.8	1 704
Norwalk	7 531	30.9	106.6	898	513.4	D	88.1	17.2	8 099	191.8	159.3	2.0	359
Norwich	3 812	22.6	41.3	314	112.5	9.3	52.0	12.2	2 853	49.6	1.9	2.4	129
Shelton	1 653	118.1	21.6	177	58.7	0.0	9.4	2.6	1 228	24.3	22.2	0.0	67
Stamford	10 499	33.3	142.6	1 448	1 467.2	65.0	99.0	91.8	18 516	463.0	18.4	3.8	1 021
Torrington	2 994	28.7	33.8	275	82.5	D	39.0	6.8	2 082	30.9	1.8	0.8	105
Waterbury	9 040	19.7	93.8	765	350.7	D	149.9	35.5	9 840	149.8	30.6	9.1	604
West Haven	2 653	1.3	30.7	288	95.9	4.0	25.5	6.3	2 532	36.1	7.6	3.2	1 737
DELAWARE	56 077	33.6	565.7	4 447	2 108.1	95.4	497.3	171.5	46 209	767.0	259.7	321.4	4 997
Newark	4 685	47.6	47.1	315	121.6	D	33.1	D	2 847	49.8	20.0	16.0	200
Wilmington	6 809	20.3	73.9	967	580.1	28.6	160.9	142.3	13 823	265.5	37.4	26.5	2 070
DISTRICT OF COLUMBIA	54 549	21.6	575.4	7 486	7 882.5	679.4	564.6	2 992.4	120 844	2 993.0	2 759.2	1 912.2	215 926
District of Columbia	54 549	21.6	575.4	7 486	7 882.5	679.4	564.6	2 992.4	120 844	2 993.0	2 759.2	1 912.2	215 926
FLORIDA	1 022 862	35.7	10 297.0	98 713	45 530.9	4 474.6	12 901.0	3 697.5	974 746	16 909.6	7 223.2	3 599.9	90 972
Boca Raton	11 587	64.1	107.1	1 656	673.3	45.3	180.1	61.2	14 623	273.5	6.9	1.6	306
Boynton Beach	4 909	105.0	46.7	376	118.8	3.5	44.4	4.3	2 189	44.8	6.4	0.3	98
Bradenton	5 603	104.0	57.4	455	250.5	8.6	132.3	D	6 368	107.9	7.9	7.8	346
Cape Coral	3 432	87.8	30.2	430	110.0	6.4	38.4	4.2	2 514	43.1	3.8	0.6	1
Clearwater	22 712	48.4	230.7	1 550	738.0	81.9	230.1	48.0	15 216	265.7	247.4	12.9	594
Coral Gables	5 019	7.5	70.0	1 460	593.2	28.4	173.9	114.9	11 614	246.1	5.4	34.3	113
Coral Springs	4 950	204.6	44.7	610	170.3	D	60.2	9.2	3 546	64.7	3.2	0.4	1
Daytona Beach	11 835	22.9	110.2	801	395.5	90.3	120.0	38.5	9 361	135.6	151.2	7.6	435
Deerfield Beach	4 133	36.5	41.3	441	180.9	15.5	30.9	6.2	3 639	61.2	1.0	0.5	70
Delray Beach	6 396	35.6	81.9	642	226.2	7.4	109.6	7.4	4 839	78.6	0.4	0.9	191
Dunedin	2 043	29.1	18.2	268	192.8	D	36.0	4.9	2 983	54.8	0.3	0.3	69
Fort Lauderdale	25 636	6.5	291.3	2 874	1 603.0	210.7	313.2	290.2	31 500	617.8	93.4	18.7	2 637
Fort Myers	12 491	38.2	142.4	905	516.8	15.2	244.1	48.3	10 313	220.0	1.1	7.9	869
Fort Pierce	6 791	30.9	70.2	464	212.1	9.9	92.4	16.2	5 231	77.0	0.4	3.3	305
Gainesville	10 902	24.6	100.0	920	363.4	6.5	146.8	28.8	8 527	141.2	32.9	63.3	2 651
Hallandale	3 736	D	35.5	308	D	2.9	42.7	5.5	D	D	0.3	0.3	79
Hialeah	11 753	11.4	119.9	1 306	417.4	4.0	208.3	7.9	9 309	139.5	16.2	6.8	377
Hollywood	11 973	-5.0	136.2	1 402	699.2	51.3	294.0	60.5	14 009	270.6	3.0	5.4	657
Jacksonville	51 369	32.5	539.0	4 815	2 451.0	82.9	498.9	189.8	54 279	990.0	151.5	38.9	11 838
Lakeland	10 999	42.6	101.9	841	314.6	D	126.3	28.9	7 392	120.5	22.9	0.6	551
Lake Worth	3 480	11.0	43.8	442	126.4	1.1	56.9	3.2	3 255	45.3	0.9	0.3	233
Largo	5 585	55.6	50.2	525	227.7	D	134.3	5.1	4 742	85.8	12.5	0.9	290
Lauderdale Lakes	2 605	23.1	28.5	174	134.0	0.0	113.0	D	2 480	53.0	0.1	0.2	1
Lauderhill	3 353	15.6	37.6	287	218.7	D	31.8	D	2 064	33.4	NA	0.3	1
Margate	2 909	29.3	26.1	313	107.8	D	57.4	1.3	2 785	36.8	0.1	0.4	1
Melbourne	8 293	42.5	86.3	625	261.1	D	97.8	20.8	5 180	110.5	379.3	3.3	492
Miami	34 726	9.4	401.7	5 329	2 592.2	205.7	466.1	823.8	50 515	1 103.4	130.8	108.0	13 395
Miami Beach	5 577	-9.7	52.7	926	416.0	136.3	141.0	32.8	8 343	160.0	3.6	5.5	87
Miramar	1 178	-7.1	10.6	219	38.3	D	10.3	D	1 047	14.4	0.0	0.3	0

1. For the period including March 12 of the year shown.

City	City government employment, 1985 (October): Total	City government employment, 1985 (October): Rates[1]	City government employment, 1985 (October): Percent education	Form of governments[2] (As of 1986)	City government finances, 1984–1985: General revenue: Total (Mil. dol.)	General revenue: Intergovernmental: Total (Mil. dol.)	General revenue: Intergovernmental: Percent from State government	General revenue: Taxes: Total (Mil. dol.)	General revenue: Taxes: Per capita[3] (Dollars): Total	General revenue: Taxes: Per capita[3] (Dollars): Property	General revenue: Taxes: Per capita[3] (Dollars): Sales & gross receipts	General expenditures: Total (Mil. dol.)	General expenditures: Per capita[3] (Dol.): Total	General expenditures: Per capita[3] (Dol.): Capital outlays	General expenditures: Percent of total for–: Public welfare	General expenditures: Percent of total for–: Highways	General expenditures: Percent of total for–: Education
	100	101	102	103	104	105	106	107	108	109	110	111	112	113	114	115	116
COLORADO—Con.																	
Grand Junction	469	144.6	0.0	2	20.2	2.3	59.9	10.2	314	57	249	22.1	683	169	0.0	26.1	0.0
Greeley	571	100.3	0.0	2	27.9	3.9	41.0	14.9	261	46	208	30.5	536	181	0.4	10.6	0.0
Lakewood	941	77.0	0.0	2	36.5	4.9	66.0	26.5	217	20	181	39.8	326	70	0.0	22.5	0.0
Littleton	344	106.6	0.0	2	25.3	1.3	76.9	13.1	405	48	239	27.3	847	297	0.3	7.5	0.0
Longmont	NA	NA	NA	2	26.2	2.5	52.7	12.3	242	49	165	23.5	464	57	1.2	10.9	0.0
Loveland	475	133.8	0.0	2	14.2	1.3	79.3	5.6	158	36	113	15.2	429	44	0.0	5.8	0.0
Northglenn	232	78.7	0.0	2	15.7	1.0	64.4	7.7	261	18	236	15.1	512	70	0.0	11.5	0.0
Pueblo	1 083	107.0	0.0	2	46.5	11.4	34.0	23.1	228	53	171	45.6	451	139	3.0	11.0	0.0
Thornton	471	94.2	0.0	2	28.6	1.5	57.0	14.1	282	44	222	23.3	466	113	0.0	16.0	0.0
Westminster	616	92.2	0.0	2	40.5	2.0	58.6	28.9	433	17	218	34.1	510	167	0.0	26.2	0.0
Wheat Ridge	201	66.9	0.0	1	9.8	1.1	76.4	7.7	256	18	225	10.0	333	116	0.0	37.1	0.1
CONNECTICUT	NA	NA	NA	NA	NA	NA	NA	NA	NA	NA	NA	NA	NA	NA	NA	NA	NA
Bridgeport	4 559	321.4	50.0	1	200.9	80.5	78.7	94.5	666	657	0	211.5	1 491	138	6.0	1.6	34.7
Bristol	1 601	271.6	67.0	1	62.9	20.2	93.0	37.5	637	633	0	58.3	989	141	2.7	4.7	48.5
Danbury	1 866	289.2	63.1	1	63.6	13.7	89.8	42.8	663	657	0	74.9	1 161	117	0.9	8.4	45.2
Hartford	7 075	512.8	57.9	2	280.3	132.1	81.7	114.9	833	813	0	284.5	2 062	171	8.8	2.3	38.1
Meriden	2 156	369.7	47.0	2	77.8	22.2	87.1	33.8	579	567	0	75.8	1 300	86	1.6	2.4	37.5
Middletown	1 142	294.0	60.3	1	43.6	12.8	92.8	25.5	657	653	0	40.7	1 048	110	4.0	7.5	45.4
Milford	1 372	278.6	57.5	1	65.7	22.0	55.3	40.6	824	809	0	64.0	1 299	299	1.0	3.1	39.3
Naugatuck borough	863	282.9	70.0	1	23.9	7.3	94.2	14.6	479	473	0	26.4	866	50	0.2	7.1	54.6
New Britain	1 850	256.8	56.9	1	79.0	29.0	96.5	40.2	558	552	0	77.9	1 081	42	2.2	6.2	38.1
New Haven	4 328	350.6	49.8	1	220.1	101.7	90.0	86.7	702	693	0	204.8	1 659	380	6.8	4.7	29.3
New London	983	343.7	56.0	2	33.7	12.4	79.8	14.9	522	517	0	33.5	1 172	88	7.3	3.0	36.7
Norwalk	2 234	289.3	57.0	1	101.9	17.8	94.2	76.8	995	977	0	94.0	1 218	107	3.4	4.2	46.3
Norwich	960	252.6	48.4	2	33.0	14.2	88.3	14.3	377	370	0	37.0	974	27	6.4	7.4	46.3
Shelton	764	219.3	72.9	1	26.6	7.0	96.3	18.0	518	505	0	25.9	742	80	0.6	4.3	52.4
Stamford	3 347	331.1	54.6	1	165.9	33.4	86.5	117.3	1 161	1 141	0	168.0	1 662	167	5.7	5.7	38.6
Torrington	790	254.1	66.2	1	29.8	9.8	89.1	18.4	592	585	0	29.7	955	112	1.5	7.4	56.2
Waterbury	3 372	329.6	52.4	1	124.5	56.7	87.4	61.0	596	582	0	114.3	1 117	28	6.2	2.3	45.5
West Haven	1 395	261.8	63.4	1	49.7	13.8	92.9	32.9	618	614	0	44.3	832	22	1.5	4.9	50.4
DELAWARE	NA	NA	NA	NA	NA	NA	NA	NA	NA	NA	NA	NA	NA	NA	NA	NA	NA
Newark	278	115.0	0.0	2	7.4	0.8	60.0	2.1	85	77	0	8.6	354	3	0.0	5.9	0.0
Wilmington	1 385	198.7	0.0	1	81.7	15.0	6.7	31.8	457	154	12	86.6	1 243	248	0.0	2.3	0.0
DISTRICT OF COLUMBIA	43 839	700.3	32.4	1	2 850.9	996.1	0.0	1 574.4	2 515	727	789	2 834.7	4 528	349	17.2	3.2	16.7
District of Columbia	43 839	700.3	32.4	1	2 850.9	996.1	0.0	1 574.4	2 515	727	789	2 834.7	4 528	349	17.2	3.2	16.7
FLORIDA	NA	NA	NA	NA	NA	NA	NA	NA	NA	NA	NA	NA	NA	NA	NA	NA	NA
Boca Raton	963	164.6	0.0	2	39.0	4.5	75.5	22.0	377	201	141	36.4	623	64	0.0	8.8	0.0
Boynton Beach	547	127.4	0.0	2	20.1	3.0	85.4	8.3	194	108	64	17.4	405	68	0.0	3.2	0.0
Bradenton	435	116.2	0.0	1	17.2	3.5	67.6	6.6	177	67	97	12.8	341	62	0.0	9.8	0.0
Cape Coral	490	97.6	0.0	1	25.5	3.4	80.6	7.5	150	108	21	11.9	236	38	0.0	22.4	0.0
Clearwater	1 435	147.1	0.0	2	62.4	7.6	75.1	23.3	239	111	110	58.0	595	77	0.1	11.9	0.0
Coral Gables	802	191.6	0.0	2	37.4	2.8	87.9	22.0	525	281	189	33.1	790	37	0.0	6.2	0.0
Coral Springs	533	88.2	0.0	2	17.6	3.5	82.3	9.0	149	58	70	14.8	245	57	0.0	15.6	0.0
Daytona Beach	841	144.9	0.0	2	37.5	9.1	37.9	12.4	214	87	106	30.0	516	56	0.0	13.2	0.0
Deerfield Beach	468	106.3	0.0	2	17.7	3.5	69.2	7.8	178	116	45	15.3	347	22	1.2	4.8	0.0
Delray Beach	540	121.8	0.0	2	22.6	4.0	87.6	11.8	266	158	94	18.6	420	51	0.0	6.0	0.0
Dunedin	403	125.8	0.0	2	18.7	2.1	88.7	4.7	146	77	58	17.9	558	37	0.0	7.0	0.0
Fort Lauderdale	NA	NA	NA	2	112.6	28.1	32.7	53.0	356	160	172	86.8	584	46	0.0	5.2	0.0
Fort Myers	742	187.7	0.0	1	38.3	18.8	16.4	8.2	208	71	108	22.6	571	65	0.0	8.6	0.0
Fort Pierce	600	162.6	0.0	2	15.1	2.9	74.8	3.5	94	43	43	21.5	583	230	0.0	8.0	0.0
Gainesville	1 439	169.0	0.0	2	47.3	8.7	60.7	11.9	139	60	70	45.4	533	103	0.0	9.9	0.0
Hallandale	447	121.6	0.0	2	18.0	3.2	66.8	9.0	246	117	118	17.0	462	43	0.0	4.8	0.0
Hialeah	NA	NA	NA	1	71.5	16.0	61.2	36.9	228	125	86	61.8	382	45	0.0	3.6	0.0
Hollywood	1 444	119.4	0.0	2	64.8	12.3	69.0	27.7	229	100	115	56.5	467	7	0.2	8.9	0.0
Jacksonville	9 262	151.9	0.0	1	528.9	117.5	57.2	136.9	224	159	52	379.7	623	87	1.6	6.8	NA
Lakeland	1 265	204.4	0.0	2	120.0	5.1	77.7	7.0	113	43	62	117.9	1 904	280	0.0	3.3	0.0
Lake Worth	571	208.5	0.0	2	15.0	2.2	87.7	3.7	134	60	60	18.2	665	125	0.0	4.1	0.0
Largo	627	100.4	0.0	2	37.6	4.6	85.0	7.3	117	16	91	40.3	646	311	0.0	2.6	0.0
Lauderdale Lakes	88	32.1	0.0	1	5.6	1.8	89.4	2.6	95	31	50	4.9	179	16	0.0	6.9	0.0
Lauderhill	324	76.2	0.0	1	10.4	2.5	89.5	5.7	133	34	83	13.6	320	51	0.0	4.0	0.0
Margate	368	92.9	0.0	2	19.0	3.6	89.0	6.7	170	59	89	11.4	289	42	0.0	13.6	0.0
Melbourne	705	124.3	0.0	2	23.4	5.8	56.5	9.1	161	62	85	21.3	375	119	0.0	23.0	0.0
Miami	4 423	118.3	0.0	2	236.1	53.4	52.2	138.4	370	249	97	225.8	604	82	0.6	6.2	0.1
Miami Beach	1 489	156.7	0.0	2	92.7	12.4	54.9	50.0	526	328	172	89.2	939	108	0.1	1.4	0.0
Miramar	304	82.3	0.0	1	10.9	2.8	79.3	5.2	142	36	94	9.0	245	19	0.0	6.4	0.0

1. Per 10,000 population estimated as of July 1, 1986. 2. 1=Mayor-council; 2=Council-manager; 3=Commission. Data subject to copyright. 3. Based on resident population estimated as of July 1, 1986.

City	City government finances, 1984–1985 (cont'd): General expenditure (cont'd): Percent of total for (cont'd): Health and hos-pitals	Police protec-tion	Sew-erage and san-itation	Parks and recre-ation	Housing and com-munity dev-elopment	Debt outstanding: Total (Mil. dol.)	Per capita[1] (Dollars)	Per-cent utility	Climate[2]: Average daily temperature (Degrees Fahrenheit): Mean: Jan.	July	Limits: Jan.[3]	July[4]	Annual precip-itation (Inches)	Heating degree days[5]	Cooling degree days[5]	Typical monthly electric bills, 1986: Residential[6]: Total (Dollars)	Percent change, 1980–1986	Commer-cial[7] (Dollars)
	117	118	119	120	121	122	123	124	125	126	127	128	129	130	131	132	133	134
COLORADO—Con.																		
Grand Junction	0.0	18.3	17.7	12.5	0.7	10.5	324	49.4	25.5	78.9	15.2	94.0	8.00	5 683	1 205	55.82	51.0	NA
Greeley	0.4	15.2	10.8	29.3	6.9	55.1	969	37.7	25.0	73.6	10.6	89.6	12.68	6 442	647	53.52	68.0	565.4
Lakewood	0.0	25.4	4.7	9.3	1.9	39.2	321	0.0	30.9	72.6	17.5	87.5	15.15	5 883	639	55.82	63.8	500.3
Littleton	0.0	8.9	14.5	3.9	19.8	12.4	384	0.0	30.9	72.6	17.5	87.5	15.15	5 883	639	55.82	63.8	NA
Longmont	0.2	15.3	17.2	11.7	NA	16.3	323	85.6	26.5	72.2	11.6	88.6	13.00	6 432	555	43.23	48.9	NA
Loveland	0.0	11.5	17.1	9.7	0.0	32.5	915	80.8	26.9	71.4	13.2	85.8	14.47	6 483	471	50.56	60.5	NA
Northglenn	0.3	15.8	23.4	10.2	0.0	60.6	2 055	88.8	29.5	73.3	15.9	88.0	15.31	6 014	680	55.82	63.8	NA
Pueblo	1.1	14.8	17.2	6.8	4.2	83.3	823	32.3	29.8	76.9	14.3	92.2	10.87	5 465	1 042	53.99	71.0	457.3
Thornton	0.0	14.3	15.8	11.9	0.0	81.0	1 619	39.1	29.5	73.3	15.9	88.0	15.31	6 014	680	55.82	63.8	NA
Westminster	0.0	11.4	15.2	12.5	2.3	52.3	782	21.2	30.9	72.6	17.5	87.5	15.15	5 883	639	55.82	63.8	500.3
Wheat Ridge	0.0	20.8	0.2	9.6	3.1	0.0	0	0.0	30.9	72.6	17.5	87.5	15.15	5 883	639	55.82	63.8	NA
CONNECTICUT	NA	NA	NA	NA	NA	NA	NA	NA	NA	NA	NA	NA	NA	NA	NA	71.96	60.7	NA
Bridgeport	7.6	6.9	4.2	1.8	3.6	76.5	539	0.0	29.5	74.0	22.5	82.1	41.56	5 501	746	77.27	55.8	724.7
Bristol	0.8	5.9	5.9	1.9	8.7	31.4	533	12.3	26.2	72.7	17.2	83.5	43.18	6 156	600	69.77	58.9	660.3
Danbury	0.8	6.2	2.1	1.5	1.1	23.5	365	30.6	26.6	71.7	18.3	83.2	48.17	6 100	521	69.77	58.9	660.3
Hartford	1.8	6.2	1.0	5.1	8.6	82.7	600	0.0	26.2	72.7	17.2	83.5	43.18	6 156	600	69.77	68.9	660.3
Meriden	17.7	4.0	2.6	1.0	1.9	56.1	961	10.6	27.4	72.5	19.8	82.7	50.10	5 976	611	69.77	58.9	660.3
Middletown	0.9	7.8	6.9	2.3	2.2	30.9	795	11.8	27.4	72.5	19.8	82.7	50.10	5 976	611	69.77	68.9	NA
Milford	0.9	5.6	25.6	0.6	0.0	38.1	773	0.0	29.5	74.0	22.5	82.1	41.56	5 501	746	77.27	55.8	NA
Naugatuck borough	2.0	4.4	6.7	1.5	0.0	20.7	679	0.0	27.4	72.5	19.8	82.7	50.10	5 976	611	69.77	58.9	NA
New Britain	0.8	6.7	8.4	2.7	2.8	47.9	665	1.4	26.2	72.7	17.2	83.5	43.18	6 156	600	69.77	58.9	660.3
New Haven	0.9	6.6	10.0	2.0	8.8	124.6	1 009	0.0	29.5	74.0	22.5	82.1	41.56	5 501	746	77.27	55.8	724.7
New London	2.1	9.9	8.2	5.0	3.8	12.3	430	4.1	NA	NA	NA	NA	NA	NA	NA	69.77	68.9	NA
Norwalk	1.7	6.2	9.1	3.0	0.1	95.9	1 242	0.0	28.0	72.7	18.7	83.6	46.90	5 847	598	69.77	58.9	660.3
Norwich	0.8	6.7	5.8	3.0	1.6	12.1	317	47.8	NA	NA	NA	NA	NA	NA	NA	71.89	74.3	NA
Shelton	0.4	4.2	11.0	1.0	2.3	20.0	573	0.0	29.5	74.0	22.5	82.1	41.56	5 501	746	77.27	55.8	NA
Stamford	2.0	7.9	5.6	3.1	1.6	121.6	1 203	0.0	28.0	72.7	18.7	83.6	46.90	5 847	598	69.77	68.9	660.3
Torrington	0.0	6.2	7.3	1.2	0.0	12.6	406	0.0	24.2	69.5	15.0	80.0	48.10	6 671	359	69.77	68.9	NA
Waterbury	1.1	8.1	5.2	2.1	1.0	68.9	674	4.5	27.4	72.5	19.8	82.7	50.10	5 976	611	69.77	58.9	660.3
West Haven	0.5	9.1	8.3	2.8	0.0	18.7	350	0.0	29.5	74.0	22.5	82.1	41.56	5 501	746	77.27	55.8	724.7
DELAWARE	NA	NA	NA	NA	NA	NA	NA	NA	NA	NA	NA	NA	NA	NA	NA	68.18	38.7	NA
Newark	0.0	20.7	33.6	7.3	0.0	7.7	320	0.0	31.7	75.7	23.1	86.9	42.59	4 906	1 003	61.14	44.3	547.3
Wilmington	0.0	13.0	24.9	3.6	1.9	137.4	1 972	26.5	31.2	76.0	23.2	85.6	41.38	4 986	1 015	72.29	43.9	555.6
DISTRICT OF COLUMBIA	9.4	6.4	4.2	1.4	5.8	2 390.6	3 819	3.8	35.2	78.9	27.5	87.9	39.00	4 122	1 430	42.85	56.9	548.6
District of Columbia	9.4	6.4	4.2	1.4	5.8	2 390.6	3 819	3.8	35.2	78.9	27.5	87.9	39.00	4 122	1 430	42.85	56.9	548.6
FLORIDA	NA	NA	NA	NA	NA	NA	NA	NA	NA	NA	NA	NA	NA	NA	NA	64.45	75.7	NA
Boca Raton	0.0	14.7	10.5	15.2	3.9	75.5	1 290	0.0	66.8	82.1	57.1	90.9	61.38	243	3 957	70.47	119.6	NA
Boynton Beach	0.5	20.0	8.3	24.7	0.0	15.5	360	0.0	66.8	82.1	57.1	90.9	61.38	243	3 957	70.47	119.6	NA
Bradenton	0.0	15.2	12.3	6.8	5.5	29.5	787	29.2	60.9	81.2	50.0	90.6	55.67	616	3 162	70.47	119.6	NA
Cape Coral	0.0	14.0	0.0	10.0	2.5	95.9	1 910	5.2	63.4	82.6	52.5	91.0	53.64	441	3 699	NA	NA	NA
Clearwater	0.0	16.0	25.9	13.5	1.6	48.6	498	14.6	59.8	82.2	49.5	90.0	46.73	739	3 324	59.82	66.1	435.8
Coral Gables	0.0	22.4	16.0	18.2	0.0	22.7	542	0.0	67.1	82.4	59.2	88.7	57.55	199	4 095	70.47	119.6	NA
Coral Springs	0.0	25.3	0.0	18.8	0.0	40.5	670	0.0	66.8	82.1	57.1	90.9	61.38	243	3 957	70.47	NA	NA
Daytona Beach	0.3	26.5	16.7	13.6	2.9	62.0	1 068	82.0	57.9	81.1	47.4	89.6	48.46	900	2 878	70.47	119.6	555.0
Deerfield Beach	NA	21.6	9.9	7.3	2.7	41.0	932	0.0	66.8	82.1	57.1	90.9	61.38	243	3 957	70.47	119.6	NA
Delray Beach	0.2	25.9	6.2	23.7	0.0	15.1	341	24.1	66.8	82.1	57.1	90.9	61.38	243	3 957	70.47	119.6	NA
Dunedin	0.0	11.5	10.7	12.9	0.0	73.2	2 284	0.0	59.8	82.2	49.5	90.0	46.73	739	3 324	59.82	66.1	NA
Fort Lauderdale	0.0	28.7	4.2	15.0	2.2	116.4	783	0.0	66.2	82.3	56.6	90.1	60.83	254	3 933	70.47	119.6	555.0
Fort Myers	0.0	17.0	8.3	13.4	0.0	67.6	1 710	1.9	63.4	82.6	52.5	91.0	53.64	441	3 699	70.47	119.6	NA
Fort Pierce	0.0	12.8	47.1	3.6	1.8	62.8	1 702	68.5	62.7	81.0	52.4	89.4	52.55	500	3 352	50.23	52.7	NA
Gainesville	0.4	19.0	23.3	4.0	0.0	550.6	6 465	0.0	56.4	81.4	44.2	91.6	52.84	1 069	2 856	53.02	33.9	495.4
Hallandale	0.0	25.4	22.3	4.1	0.0	2.0	53	0.0	66.2	82.3	56.6	90.1	60.83	254	3 933	70.47	119.6	NA
Hialeah	0.0	25.0	21.5	8.7	0.6	43.7	270	0.0	65.7	81.7	56.2	89.2	63.47	284	3 815	70.47	119.6	555.0
Hollywood	0.0	28.1	17.9	10.0	0.8	39.0	322	14.3	66.2	82.3	56.6	90.1	60.83	254	3 933	70.47	119.6	555.0
Jacksonville	6.0	12.0	11.4	7.1	11.3	2 713.6	4 450	59.4	53.2	81.3	41.7	90.7	52.77	1 402	2 520	57.23	10.8	463.7
Lakeland	71.4	3.9	3.8	6.0	0.4	574.0	9 275	15.5	61.0	82.4	50.3	92.2	48.34	618	3 461	56.17	38.8	NA
Lake Worth	0.0	17.0	31.9	9.9	0.1	35.4	1 294	0.0	66.8	82.1	57.1	90.9	61.38	243	3 957	63.80	42.5	NA
Largo	0.0	9.3	52.6	8.6	1.1	34.1	546	0.0	59.8	82.2	49.5	90.0	46.73	739	3 324	59.82	66.1	435.8
Lauderdale Lakes	0.0	27.4	0.0	21.3	0.0	0.0	0	0.0	66.2	82.3	56.6	90.1	60.83	254	3 933	70.47	119.6	NA
Lauderhill	2.1	20.8	0.0	18.9	0.0	33.5	788	0.0	66.2	82.3	56.6	90.1	60.83	254	3 933	70.47	119.6	NA
Margate	0.0	26.7	0.0	5.3	0.0	43.3	1 094	0.0	66.8	82.1	57.1	90.9	61.38	243	3 957	70.47	119.6	NA
Melbourne	0.0	17.0	0.0	14.6	3.9	36.0	634	0.0	61.5	81.3	51.3	90.2	48.17	607	3 225	70.47	119.6	NA
Miami	0.1	22.7	11.5	10.8	6.3	236.6	633	0.0	67.1	82.4	59.2	88.7	57.55	199	4 095	70.47	119.6	555.0
Miami Beach	0.2	15.5	9.8	18.8	3.4	111.1	1 170	0.9	68.0	82.6	62.2	87.0	46.05	133	4 150	70.47	119.6	555.0
Miramar	2.9	23.9	10.5	6.8	0.0	3.8	103	0.0	65.7	81.7	56.2	89.2	63.47	284	3 815	70.47	119.6	NA

1. Based on resident population estimated as of July 1, 1986. 2. Represents normal values based on the 30-year period, 1951–1980 (see text). 3. Average daily minimum. 4. Average daily maximum. 5. For definition, see text. 6. As of January 1; based on consumption of 750 kWh. 7. Based on billing demand of 30 kW and consumption of 6,000 kWh.

MSA/ CMSA Code[1]	State/ Place code	City	Land area,[2] 1990 (Sq. Km.)	Population						Population characteristics, 1990						
				1990				Change 1980–1990		Percent						
										Race						
				Total persons	Rank	Per sq. km.	1980	Number	Per-cent	White	Black	Am. Indian, Eskimo, Aleut	Asian & Pacific Islander	Other race	His-panic[3]	65 Years and over
			1	2	3	4	5	6	7	8	9	10	11	12	13	14
		FLORIDA—Con.														
4992	12 1498	North Miami	21.8	49 998	492	2 293	42 566	7 432	17.5	62.42	31.88	0.22	2.41	3.07	24.56	15.1
4992	12 1500	North Miami Beach	12.9	35 359	712	2 741	36 553	-1 194	-3.3	71.57	21.80	0.16	3.41	3.06	22.11	19.9
5790	12 1545	Ocala	74.7	42 045	592	563	37 170	4 875	13.1	74.89	23.79	0.26	0.63	0.43	2.17	20.8
5960	12 1600	Orlando	174.2	164 693	104	945	128 291	36 402	28.4	68.76	26.90	0.31	1.56	2.48	8.74	11.4
6015	12 1675	Panama City	40.1	34 378	728	857	33 346	1 032	3.1	75.50	21.82	0.63	1.70	0.37	1.34	17.0
4992	12 1700	Pembroke Pines	82.7	65 452	352	791	35 776	29 676	82.9	91.28	5.26	0.16	1.99	1.31	11.51	19.4
6080	12 1715	Pensacola	58.6	58 165	400	993	57 619	546	0.9	65.67	31.90	0.52	1.56	0.34	1.59	16.4
8280	12 1750	Pinellas Park	35.9	43 426	572	1 210	32 811	10 615	32.4	96.08	0.96	0.31	1.87	0.78	3.26	23.1
4992	12 1755	Plantation	56.3	66 692	340	1 185	48 653	18 039	37.1	90.70	6.17	0.12	1.83	1.18	8.14	14.4
4992	12 1780	Pompano Beach	52.7	72 411	301	1 374	52 618	19 793	37.6	69.97	28.48	0.14	0.57	0.83	5.36	25.2
8960	12 1855	Riviera Beach	19.4	27 639	871	1 425	26 489	1 150	4.3	28.70	69.68	0.17	0.78	0.68	2.61	15.4
8280	12 1900	St. Petersburg	153.3	238 629	65	1 557	238 647	-18	0.0	78.00	19.58	0.25	1.66	0.51	2.62	22.2
7510	12 1930	Sarasota	37.9	50 961	481	1 345	48 868	2 093	4.3	81.99	16.22	0.23	0.69	0.87	4.73	25.2
4992	12 2047	Sunrise	47.2	64 407	354	1 365	39 681	24 726	62.3	89.30	7.39	0.09	1.94	1.28	8.64	23.0
8240	12 2070	Tallahassee	163.9	124 773	146	761	81 548	43 225	53.0	68.24	29.09	0.23	1.75	0.69	3.00	8.8
4992	12 2072	Tamarac	29.8	44 822	555	1 504	29 376	15 446	52.6	95.96	2.31	0.10	0.89	0.75	5.44	47.6
8280	12 2075	Tampa	281.5	280 015	55	995	271 577	8 438	3.1	70.90	25.05	0.30	1.35	2.40	15.00	14.6
4900	12 2105	Titusville	50.5	39 394	640	780	31 910	7 484	23.5	87.26	10.97	0.42	0.84	0.50	2.75	15.9
8960	12 2215	West Palm Beach	127.8	67 643	334	529	63 305	4 338	6.9	63.40	32.62	0.14	0.93	2.91	14.16	18.2
...	13 0000	GEORGIA	150 009.5	6 478 216	X	43	5 462 982	1 015 234	18.6	71.01	26.96	0.21	1.17	0.65	1.68	10.1
0120	13 0045	Albany	143.6	78 122	271	544	74 425	3 697	5.0	44.22	54.99	0.20	0.43	0.16	0.83	10.8
0500	13 0145	Athens	43.0	45 734	544	1 064	42 549	3 185	7.5	66.37	29.62	0.13	3.34	0.54	1.61	10.2
0520	13 0150	Atlanta	341.3	394 017	36	1 154	425 022	-31 005	-7.3	31.05	67.07	0.14	0.89	0.85	1.91	11.3
0600	13 0165	Augusta	50.9	44 639	559	877	47 532	-2 893	-6.1	43.04	55.99	0.15	0.61	0.20	0.75	18.8
1800	13 0660	Columbus	559.8	178 681	93	319	169 441	9 240	5.5	58.86	38.14	0.32	1.40	1.27	2.96	10.8
0520	13 0960	East Point	35.6	34 402	727	966	37 486	-3 084	-8.2	31.63	66.34	0.22	0.72	1.09	1.90	11.6
4680	13 1725	Macon	124.0	106 612	178	860	116 896	-10 284	-8.8	47.15	52.19	0.12	0.42	0.12	0.62	14.6
0520	13 1750	Marietta	52.8	44 129	562	836	30 821	13 308	43.2	76.27	20.53	0.29	1.84	1.08	3.21	10.4
...	13 2455	Rome	62.7	30 326	826	484	28 915	1 411	4.9	68.79	29.71	0.18	0.75	0.58	1.65	17.9
7520	13 2540	Savannah	162.1	137 560	129	849	141 654	-4 094	-2.9	46.85	51.31	0.20	1.15	0.50	1.42	13.8
...	13 2910	Valdosta	68.6	39 806	632	580	37 596	2 210	5.9	55.19	43.48	0.24	0.87	0.23	1.13	10.8
4680	13 2970	Warner Robins	43.2	43 726	568	1 012	39 893	3 833	9.6	72.68	24.95	0.31	1.44	0.62	1.80	8.2
...	15 0000	HAWAII	16 636.5	1 108 229	X	67	964 691	143 538	14.9	33.35	2.45	0.46	61.83	1.90	7.34	11.3
3320	15 0005	Aiea (CDP)	4.3	8 906	NA	2 071	32 879	-23 973	-72.9	24.35	0.94	0.08	73.41	1.21	6.39	NA
...	15 0090	Hilo (CDP)	140.6	37 808	670	269	35 269	2 539	7.2	26.65	0.57	0.56	70.18	2.05	8.53	14.6
3320	15 0110	Honolulu (CDP)	214.5	365 272	44	1 703	365 048	224	0.1	26.70	1.32	0.31	70.51	1.16	4.57	16.0
3320	15 0144	Kailua (CDP)	17.2	36 818	690	2 141	35 812	1 006	2.8	57.69	1.36	0.52	39.10	1.33	5.48	10.8
3320	15 0164	Kaneohe (CDP)	17.0	35 448	709	2 085	29 919	5 529	18.5	31.18	1.17	0.44	65.62	1.59	6.91	10.9
3320	15 0384	Pearl City (CDP)	12.9	30 993	807	2 403	42 575	-11 582	-27.2	21.40	2.54	0.27	74.11	1.69	6.59	8.8
3320	15 0474	Waipahu (CDP)	6.7	31 435	799	4 692	29 139	2 296	7.9	11.56	1.97	0.47	83.79	2.20	11.53	10.5
...	16 0000	IDAHO	214 325.0	1 006 749	X	5	944 127	62 622	6.6	94.41	0.33	1.37	0.93	2.96	5.26	12.0
1080	16 0090	Boise City	119.5	125 738	145	1 052	102 249	23 489	23.0	96.44	0.58	0.64	1.57	0.77	2.72	11.9
...	16 0440	Idaho Falls	37.6	43 929	563	1 168	39 739	4 190	10.5	95.34	0.58	0.60	1.22	2.27	4.18	10.3
...	16 0530	Lewiston	42.6	28 082	867	659	27 986	96	0.3	97.38	0.14	1.41	0.68	0.40	1.22	16.1
...	16 0660	Nampa	28.0	28 365	855	1 013	25 112	3 253	13.0	89.50	0.26	0.97	1.05	8.21	12.76	16.4
...	16 0780	Pocatello	71.5	46 080	539	644	46 340	-260	-0.6	94.07	0.86	1.41	1.27	2.39	4.53	10.9
...	16 0970	Twin Falls	27.3	27 591	875	1 011	26 209	1 382	5.3	94.76	0.17	0.68	1.60	2.79	6.75	15.5
...	17 0000	ILLINOIS	143 986.6	11 430 602	X	79	11 427 409	3 193	0.0	78.32	14.82	0.19	2.50	4.17	7.91	12.6
1602	17 0015	Addison village	22.3	32 058	784	1 438	29 826	2 232	7.5	87.86	1.69	0.14	5.94	4.37	13.37	6.7
7040	17 0115	Alton	38.9	32 905	767	846	34 171	-1 266	-3.7	75.61	23.06	0.53	0.34	0.46	1.13	17.3
1602	17 0190	Arlington Heights village	41.9	75 460	287	1 801	66 116	9 344	14.1	94.77	0.63	0.07	3.71	0.82	2.71	12.2
1602	17 0280	Aurora	86.7	99 581	196	1 149	81 293	18 288	22.5	74.07	11.86	0.24	1.32	12.51	22.96	8.6
7040	17 0430	Belleville	36.2	42 785	581	1 182	41 580	1 205	2.9	92.08	6.75	0.25	0.61	0.31	1.31	19.0
1602	17 0495	Berwyn	10.1	45 426	546	4 498	46 849	-1 423	-3.0	95.56	0.12	0.14	1.74	2.44	7.87	21.4
1040	17 0540	Bloomington	43.3	51 972	469	1 200	44 189	7 783	17.6	90.91	6.70	0.17	1.47	0.75	1.62	12.0
1602	17 0563	Bolingbrook village	29.1	40 843	611	1 404	37 261	3 582	9.6	76.76	15.63	0.30	5.01	2.29	5.85	3.5
1602	17 0743	Burbank	10.7	27 600	874	2 579	28 462	-862	-3.0	97.49	0.04	0.18	1.13	1.16	4.73	13.6
1602	17 0800	Calumet City	18.8	37 840	668	2 013	39 697	-1 857	-4.7	73.28	23.68	0.15	0.56	2.33	6.41	15.5
...	17 0865	Carbondale	26.4	27 033	889	1 024	26 414	619	2.3	74.34	17.41	0.13	7.11	1.01	2.50	7.1
1400	17 0990	Champaign	33.5	63 502	360	1 896	58 267	5 235	9.0	80.71	14.18	0.18	4.11	0.82	1.95	8.2
1602	17 1051	Chicago	588.5	2 783 726	3	4 730	3 005 072	-221 346	-7.4	45.39	39.07	0.25	3.74	11.54	19.61	11.9
1602	17 1055	Chicago Heights	23.4	33 072	766	1 413	37 026	-3 954	-10.7	54.99	35.10	0.18	0.30	9.44	15.05	12.6
1602	17 1085	Cicero town	15.1	67 436	337	4 466	61 232	6 204	10.1	75.17	0.21	0.39	1.62	22.62	36.97	13.7
...	17 1395	Danville	39.3	33 828	744	861	38 985	-5 157	-13.2	78.34	19.07	0.23	1.07	1.29	2.10	17.5
2040	17 1410	Decatur	96.0	83 885	253	874	93 939	-10 054	-10.7	82.45	16.68	0.14	0.49	0.23	0.53	16.1
...	17 1435	De Kalb	20.8	34 925	719	1 679	33 157	1 768	5.3	88.88	4.66	0.15	4.48	1.83	4.08	6.9
1602	17 1460	Des Plaines	36.8	53 223	453	1 446	53 568	-345	-0.6	92.02	0.61	0.12	4.70	2.55	6.61	15.4

1. MSA = Metropolitan Statistical Area. CMSA = Consolidated MSA. 2. Dry land or land partially or temporarily covered by water. 3. Hispanic persons may be of any race.

City	Households, 1990				Births, 1984			Deaths, 1984				Hospitals, 1985		
			Percent–		Number			Number		Rate			Beds	
	Number	Persons per house-hold	Female family house-holder[1]	One-person[2]	Total	To mothers under 20 yrs. old (Percent)	Rate[3]	Total	Infant[4]	Total[3]	Infant[5]	Number	Number	Rate[6]
	15	16	17	18	19	20	21	22	23	24	25	26	27	28
FLORIDA—Con.														
North Miami	20 127	2.44	13.9	33.2	485	5.4	11.4	695	3	16.3	6.2	2	631	1 479
North Miami Beach	13 968	2.47	13.9	29.2	575	3.8	16.0	1 109	4	30.9	7.0	2	636	1 774
Ocala	17 393	2.34	15.3	31.3	820	21.2	19.1	562	17	13.1	20.7	3	482	1 068
Orlando	65 703	2.29	14.2	33.0	3 685	19.1	26.9	1 579	53	11.5	14.4	6	2 592	1 777
Panama City	14 053	2.38	15.0	30.5	967	18.2	28.4	471	7	13.8	7.2	3	510	1 431
Pembroke Pines	26 722	2.40	8.5	24.6	520	4.2	12.0	296	0	6.9	0.0	1	301	612
Pensacola	23 983	2.40	16.6	29.8	1 528	17.1	24.6	653	14	10.5	9.2	5	1 696	2 657
Pinellas Park	18 185	2.34	10.3	26.4	469	13.0	12.1	489	2	12.6	4.3	1	154	379
Plantation	26 489	2.50	8.7	22.9	474	6.3	9.2	405	5	7.8	10.5	3	627	1 122
Pompano Beach	32 157	2.17	10.5	34.7	1 509	15.4	23.1	1 030	13	15.8	8.6	2	592	887
Riviera Beach	10 333	2.65	21.8	25.7	481	22.9	17.3	270	8	9.7	16.6	0	0	0
St. Petersburg	105 703	2.19	12.4	35.1	3 299	16.7	13.7	4 357	45	18.1	13.6	9	2 045	854
Sarasota	22 822	2.14	12.6	34.2	871	14.7	16.6	898	12	17.2	13.8	3	894	1 736
Sunrise	26 314	2.43	8.9	25.1	579	3.3	12.1	572	4	12.0	6.9	1	108	205
Tallahassee	50 442	2.26	13.2	31.6	1 501	10.7	13.4	693	20	6.2	13.3	2	900	753
Tamarac	22 906	1.94	5.2	31.4	137	7.3	4.3	607	1	19.0	7.3	1	210	607
Tampa	114 800	2.35	15.5	32.3	5 163	18.5	18.7	3 355	68	12.2	13.2	15	3 855	1 389
Titusville	16 207	2.42	10.9	25.6	478	15.7	12.5	342	1	9.0	2.1	1	210	501
West Palm Beach	28 787	2.27	13.3	35.2	1 858	16.0	27.5	1 133	27	16.8	14.5	4	852	1 243
GEORGIA	2 366 615	2.66	13.9	22.7	92 013	17.8	15.8	46 595	1 189	8.0	12.9	206	34 818	570
Albany	27 926	2.69	24.1	25.0	1 593	22.4	18.7	697	28	8.2	17.6	2	601	707
Athens	17 012	2.25	14.7	34.7	544	17.6	12.8	346	2	8.1	3.7	4	572	1 327
Atlanta	155 752	2.40	23.4	35.0	7 967	20.7	18.7	4 721	148	11.1	18.6	25	5 539	1 313
Augusta	18 819	2.26	23.1	39.2	1 108	24.0	24.1	773	20	16.8	18.1	6	3 242	7 135
Columbus	65 634	2.61	17.9	24.5	2 792	19.9	16.0	1 573	44	9.0	15.8	6	1 342	745
East Point	13 373	2.55	22.5	28.2	579	11.1	15.0	320	13	8.3	22.5	1	427	1 136
Macon	41 175	2.50	22.7	29.6	1 972	22.1	16.4	1 246	28	10.4	14.2	6	1 122	947
Marietta	19 866	2.17	11.3	35.8	1 041	12.9	27.0	392	11	10.2	10.6	1	517	1 208
Rome	12 008	2.39	17.1	32.0	459	22.7	15.2	412	3	13.7	6.5	3	876	2 834
Savannah	51 938	2.55	19.8	29.5	2 629	21.8	18.1	1 599	53	11.0	20.2	5	1 457	993
Valdosta	14 143	2.65	19.6	24.8	735	23.7	19.0	412	8	10.6	10.9	3	354	958
Warner Robins	16 721	2.60	14.0	24.2	711	19.4	16.0	296	8	6.7	11.3	1	181	397
HAWAII	356 267	3.01	10.5	19.4	18 707	10.4	18.0	5 640	185	5.4	9.9	26	4 090	385
Aiea (CDP)	NA	NA	NA	NA	549	8.4	NA	149	12	NA	21.9	0	0	NA
Hilo (CDP)	13 324	2.79	13.9	22.1	638	13.0	NA	285	8	NA	12.5	1	274	NA
Honolulu (CDP)	134 563	2.63	11.0	27.4	5 911	7.6	15.8	2 468	60	6.6	10.2	10	2 549	NA
Kailua (CDP)	11 843	3.11	10.3	11.4	596	10.1	NA	208	9	NA	15.1	1	156	NA
Kaneohe (CDP)	10 610	3.26	10.8	11.7	917	9.1	NA	252	2	NA	2.2	1	220	NA
Pearl City (CDP)	8 876	3.49	9.1	8.2	559	9.7	NA	143	3	NA	5.4	0	0	NA
Waipahu (CDP)	7 567	4.13	17.7	9.2	935	13.0	NA	137	3	NA	3.2	0	0	NA
IDAHO	360 723	2.73	8.0	22.4	18 028	10.7	18.0	7 251	176	7.2	9.8	52	4 157	414
Boise City	50 852	2.42	9.7	27.8	2 137	7.9	19.9	909	19	8.5	8.9	5	887	818
Idaho Falls	16 017	2.71	8.4	24.6	983	12.4	23.5	345	12	8.3	12.2	1	364	850
Lewiston	11 515	2.40	8.2	27.8	415	11.3	14.8	280	5	10.0	12.0	1	139	501
Nampa	10 213	2.61	11.7	26.7	489	17.0	17.9	319	10	11.7	20.4	2	196	694
Pocatello	17 183	2.62	9.5	26.5	1 002	8.9	22.1	347	11	7.7	11.0	2	257	579
Twin Falls	10 472	2.55	9.7	26.3	478	15.5	17.0	261	2	9.3	4.2	2	192	692
ILLINOIS	4 202 240	2.65	12.0	25.7	179 274	13.0	15.6	100 911	2 161	8.8	12.1	276	66 888	579
Addison village	10 722	2.98	10.3	17.5	515	7.8	16.7	116	3	3.8	5.8	0	0	0
Alton	12 969	2.47	15.4	30.5	608	17.4	18.3	395	8	11.9	13.2	4	854	2 591
Arlington Heights village	28 810	2.58	6.2	23.7	884	1.7	12.8	510	9	7.4	10.2	1	420	598
Aurora	33 710	2.90	12.2	22.7	1 971	14.9	23.0	765	29	8.9	14.7	2	584	684
Belleville	17 739	2.32	11.6	33.5	673	9.4	15.9	582	12	13.8	17.8	2	997	2 327
Berwyn	19 298	2.34	10.7	34.0	541	4.8	11.8	626	3	13.7	5.5	1	427	949
Bloomington	21 480	2.31	9.6	33.7	860	11.6	18.5	474	8	10.2	9.3	2	356	770
Bolingbrook village	12 387	3.30	9.9	13.2	674	8.2	17.1	117	8	3.0	11.9	0	0	0
Burbank	9 171	2.98	10.9	17.0	322	8.1	11.5	229	3	8.2	9.3	0	0	0
Calumet City	15 434	2.45	14.6	29.5	514	7.8	12.9	361	5	9.0	9.7	0	0	0
Carbondale	9 606	2.12	9.0	38.0	283	11.3	11.2	152	3	6.0	10.6	1	151	625
Champaign	24 173	2.30	8.8	34.2	800	9.8	13.3	340	11	5.6	13.8	2	267	451
Chicago	1 025 174	2.67	19.6	32.1	53 912	19.1	18.0	28 834	887	9.6	16.5	63	20 033	666
Chicago Heights	10 932	2.97	22.0	21.1	699	19.6	19.6	325	12	9.1	17.2	1	420	1 182
Cicero town	23 179	2.85	14.3	26.5	965	13.3	15.8	749	9	12.2	9.3	0	0	0
Danville	13 791	2.40	14.0	32.4	623	21.3	16.5	467	11	12.4	17.7	3	1 411	3 849
Decatur	34 013	2.39	13.4	29.9	1 481	16.7	16.1	979	19	10.7	12.8	3	845	935
De Kalb	10 557	2.43	8.1	29.5	303	8.6	9.6	153	5	4.9	16.5	1	132	418
Des Plaines	19 990	2.61	8.2	23.6	960	5.1	16.8	658	5	11.5	5.2	2	466	830

1. No spouse present. 2. Householder living alone. 3. Per 1,000 resident population estimated as of July 1 of the year shown. 4. Deaths of infants under 1 year old. 5. Deaths of infants under 1 year old per 1,000 live births. 6. Per 100,000 resident population estimated as of July 1, 1986.

Table C. Cities — **Crime, Police Officers, Education, Money Income, and Housing**

City	Serious crimes known to police, 1985: Number: Total	Serious crimes known to police, 1985: Number: Violent[1]	Serious crimes known to police, 1985: Rate[2]	Police officers, 1985: Number	Police officers, 1985: Rate[3]	Educational attainment,[4] 1980: Percent completing 12 years or more	Educational attainment,[4] 1980: Percent completing 16 years or more	Money income: Per capita[5]: 1985: Total (Dollars)	Money income: Per capita[5]: 1985: Percent of State average	Money income: Per capita[5]: 1979: Current dollars	Money income: Per capita[5]: 1979: Constant (1985) dollars	Money income: Percent below poverty level, 1979: Persons	Money income: Percent below poverty level, 1979: Families	Housing, 1990: Total units	Housing, 1990: Percent change, 1980–1990	Housing, 1990: Vacant units for sale or rent[6]
	29	30	31	32	33	34	35	36	37	38	39	40	41	42	43	44
FLORIDA—Con.																
North Miami	4 578	554	9 796	100	21.4	70.6	15.3	13 102	116.2	8 738	12 950	10.5	7.0	22 107	7.1	1 466
North Miami Beach	3 592	433	9 083	91	23.0	67.7	13.9	12 618	112.0	8 070	11 960	9.0	6.9	15 821	-7.5	846
Ocala	5 363	497	12 148	93	21.1	64.6	14.8	9 171	81.4	6 175	9 151	21.0	15.9	19 478	24.7	1 403
Orlando	16 122	2 931	11 352	423	29.8	69.1	16.1	10 894	96.7	6 735	9 981	17.8	14.2	73 425	29.8	6 200
Panama City	3 560	268	9 501	70	18.7	62.4	14.0	8 875	78.7	5 937	8 799	20.7	15.7	15 928	11.2	1 314
Pembroke Pines	1 978	208	4 366	85	18.8	77.8	17.9	13 562	120.3	8 956	13 273	3.5	2.4	29 546	51.3	1 196
Pensacola	4 282	603	6 699	128	20.0	69.0	20.5	10 591	94.0	6 881	10 198	19.5	14.6	26 366	11.6	1 626
Pinellas Park	2 703	176	7 011	50	13.0	63.4	7.8	10 590	94.0	6 408	9 497	8.9	6.6	20 593	29.1	1 171
Plantation	4 836	268	8 664	109	19.5	84.5	26.7	17 110	151.8	10 494	15 552	3.8	3.0	29 399	38.0	1 824
Pompano Beach	8 524	1 379	13 548	155	24.6	72.8	18.2	14 474	128.4	9 245	13 701	11.2	7.3	42 719	22.7	2 434
Riviera Beach	4 925	788	15 976	76	24.7	57.5	11.7	10 481	93.0	6 804	10 084	16.2	12.5	14 078	14.9	1 105
St. Petersburg	21 130	3 202	8 456	419	16.8	65.7	14.6	11 109	98.6	6 966	10 324	14.0	9.9	125 452	4.8	10 299
Sarasota	5 394	478	9 827	127	23.1	70.3	17.8	12 650	112.2	8 071	11 961	14.9	9.5	26 974	6.0	1 776
Sunrise	1 653	122	3 417	113	23.4	69.9	11.9	12 624	112.0	7 727	11 451	5.0	3.7	29 295	40.5	1 504
Tallahassee	11 013	1 194	9 473	201	17.3	79.0	35.2	10 352	91.8	6 777	10 044	24.0	15.0	55 221	38.9	3 941
Tamarac	1 031	52	3 100	67	20.1	67.0	11.7	15 187	134.7	8 979	13 307	4.5	3.3	26 141	40.6	1 393
Tampa	41 770	6 855	14 642	692	24.3	61.0	12.8	9 902	87.9	6 385	9 463	18.7	14.8	129 681	11.9	11 234
Titusville	2 828	276	7 495	56	14.8	72.5	15.1	11 171	99.1	7 001	10 375	12.7	10.7	18 183	31.3	1 308
West Palm Beach	12 984	1 807	18 081	178	24.8	65.7	16.2	12 188	108.1	7 528	11 156	15.8	11.2	34 971	14.1	3 090
GEORGIA	305 381	30 311	5 110	NA	NA	56.4	14.6	10 191	100.0	6 380	9 455	16.6	13.2	2 638 418	23.1	173 937
Albany	5 274	581	5 874	177	19.7	54.8	13.3	8 757	85.9	5 797	8 591	24.3	19.0	30 603	14.4	2 324
Athens	3 029	333	6 672	90	19.8	62.8	34.1	8 586	84.3	5 613	8 318	26.6	17.7	18 499	16.1	1 121
Atlanta	57 505	11 610	13 183	1 278	29.3	60.2	20.5	10 341	101.5	6 539	9 691	27.5	23.7	182 754	2.1	21 547
Augusta	2 860	219	5 813	159	32.3	45.6	13.8	8 100	79.5	5 165	7 655	30.4	23.7	21 588	3.5	1 476
Columbus	9 636	878	5 384	344	19.2	61.0	12.9	9 182	90.1	6 048	8 963	18.0	14.5	70 657	10.0	4 096
East Point	3 733	370	9 203	78	19.2	64.6	15.5	9 878	96.9	7 002	10 377	13.2	10.5	15 671	-1.0	2 019
Macon	7 737	609	6 286	258	21.0	53.0	12.6	9 174	90.0	5 936	8 797	22.4	17.1	45 499	2.4	3 308
Marietta	4 019	288	11 264	96	26.9	63.8	22.0	13 257	130.1	8 007	11 866	13.1	9.7	23 158	40.5	2 999
Rome	1 741	91	5 409	63	19.6	47.9	15.4	9 177	90.1	6 032	8 939	19.3	15.4	13 099	8.7	773
Savannah	12 009	1 064	8 089	291	19.6	58.5	13.6	9 028	88.6	5 896	8 738	22.4	18.2	58 762	7.6	4 386
Valdosta	3 800	83	9 304	72	17.6	58.8	16.6	8 368	82.1	5 523	8 185	23.0	18.0	15 608	12.4	1 046
Warner Robins	2 304	154	5 154	66	14.8	72.6	13.5	10 821	106.2	6 953	10 304	10.3	8.3	18 086	18.3	1 222
HAWAII	54 814	2 313	5 201	NA	NA	73.8	20.3	11 003	100.0	7 740	11 471	9.9	7.8	389 810	14.3	14 817
Aiea (CDP)	NA	NA	NA	NA	NA	77.7	22.1	NA	NA	8 734	12 944	7.7	5.9	NA	NA	NA
Hilo (CDP)	2 296	63	6 162	141	37.8	72.2	18.0	NA	NA	6 925	10 263	13.9	11.3	14 134	16.7	471
Honolulu (CDP)	42 048	1 801	5 146	1 639	20.1	74.5	24.0	NA	NA	8 948	13 261	10.0	7.4	145 796	2.4	6 669
Kailua (CDP)	NA	NA	NA	NA	NA	82.8	28.6	NA	NA	9 021	13 369	7.1	5.8	12 225	9.0	196
Kaneohe (CDP)	NA	NA	NA	NA	NA	78.1	20.7	NA	NA	8 216	12 176	5.2	4.4	10 849	21.4	147
Pearl City (CDP)	NA	NA	NA	NA	NA	81.9	20.3	NA	NA	8 078	11 972	3.6	2.8	8 999	-26.3	81
Waipahu (CDP)	NA	NA	NA	NA	NA	59.3	8.7	NA	NA	5 771	8 553	13.7	14.4	7 739	8.0	155
IDAHO	39 276	2 360	3 908	NA	NA	73.7	15.8	8 567	100.0	6 248	9 260	12.6	9.6	413 327	9.2	16 815
Boise City	6 393	384	5 939	NA	NA	83.4	25.4	11 740	137.0	8 268	12 253	8.8	6.1	53 271	18.7	1 916
Idaho Falls	2 305	100	5 493	69	16.4	80.7	22.9	10 309	120.3	7 169	10 624	7.9	6.3	16 845	10.6	605
Lewiston	1 518	47	5 303	42	14.7	72.3	13.3	9 635	112.5	7 063	10 467	11.5	8.7	12 054	4.8	367
Nampa	1 845	54	6 819	30	11.1	62.8	11.9	7 584	88.5	5 460	8 092	17.3	13.1	10 760	9.1	367
Pocatello	2 448	136	5 107	64	13.4	80.2	20.3	9 344	109.1	6 986	10 353	9.6	6.9	18 768	1.6	1 118
Twin Falls	1 569	75	5 647	45	16.2	70.4	15.1	9 600	112.1	6 781	10 049	11.6	7.7	11 009	4.0	394
ILLINOIS	611 324	81 119	5 300	NA	NA	66.5	16.2	11 302	100.0	8 064	11 951	11.0	8.4	4 506 275	4.1	208 467
Addison village	NA	NA	NA	50	16.3	71.6	12.6	12 183	107.8	8 518	12 624	3.8	3.3	11 025	9.0	265
Alton	NA	NA	NA	62	18.3	58.2	9.3	9 129	80.8	6 430	9 529	15.7	12.2	14 212	2.5	834
Arlington Heights village	NA	NA	NA	90	13.4	86.6	32.7	16 278	144.0	11 136	16 504	2.6	1.9	30 428	23.7	1 268
Aurora	NA	NA	NA	175	21.2	63.4	13.7	10 836	95.9	7 842	11 622	8.7	6.6	35 621	17.4	1 539
Belleville	NA	NA	NA	56	13.4	61.6	13.0	11 043	97.7	7 733	11 460	7.8	5.2	19 080	10.2	1 014
Berwyn	NA	NA	NA	68	14.7	56.8	9.4	12 659	112.0	8 903	13 194	5.4	4.0	20 044	-2.1	488
Bloomington	NA	NA	NA	68	14.9	73.9	21.9	11 989	106.1	8 327	12 341	9.9	6.5	22 640	11.4	850
Bolingbrook village	NA	NA	NA	48	12.3	85.9	24.0	10 235	90.6	7 994	11 847	3.3	2.8	12 889	8.7	433
Burbank	NA	NA	NA	36	12.7	60.5	5.0	10 483	92.8	7 806	11 568	4.0	2.8	9 298	6.6	88
Calumet City	NA	NA	NA	55	13.8	64.8	9.4	11 414	101.0	9 312	13 800	6.0	5.0	16 587	2.0	992
Carbondale	NA	NA	NA	52	19.5	82.7	43.8	7 287	64.5	5 270	7 810	34.7	14.3	10 416	10.0	676
Champaign	NA	NA	NA	85	14.3	82.0	34.9	10 211	90.3	7 301	10 820	18.5	7.8	25 996	13.3	1 516
Chicago	277 260	58 446	9 246	11 871	39.6	56.2	13.8	9 642	85.3	6 933	10 275	20.3	16.8	1 133 039	-3.7	83 759
Chicago Heights	NA	NA	NA	79	21.7	59.7	10.2	8 943	79.1	6 795	10 070	14.7	12.9	11 620	-9.6	412
Cicero town	NA	NA	NA	92	14.9	49.1	6.2	9 412	83.3	7 528	11 156	8.9	6.8	24 841	-4.1	1 091
Danville	NA	NA	NA	66	17.2	63.1	13.8	9 941	88.0	7 339	10 876	13.4	10.4	15 326	-8.0	972
Decatur	NA	NA	NA	121	13.0	67.0	14.2	11 143	98.6	7 955	11 789	11.8	9.2	37 470	-2.6	2 586
De Kalb	NA	NA	NA	45	13.6	80.0	36.4	8 906	78.8	6 411	9 501	19.3	5.2	10 915	9.3	277
Des Plaines	NA	NA	NA	95	16.9	75.4	16.7	13 628	120.6	9 668	14 328	3.2	2.1	20 509	6.0	419

1. Includes murder and nonnegligent manslaughter, forcible rape, robbery, and aggravated assault. 2. Per 100,000 resident population estimated for 1985 by the FBI. 3. Per 10,000 resident population estimated for 1985 by the FBI. 4. Persons 25 years old or older. 5. Based on the resident population estimated as of July 1, 1988 for 1987 data and enumerated as of April 1, 1980 for 1979 data. 6. Also includes units rented or sold, but not occupied.

City	Housing, 1990 (cont'd): Occupied units: Total	Percent with more than 1 person per room	Owner-occupied: Percent of total	Owner-occupied: Median value[1] (Dollars)	Median rent[2] (Dollars)	Construction authorized by building permits, 1990: New private housing units: Number	Value ($1,000)	Percent single family	Non-residential, value ($1,000)	Civilian labor force, 1990: Total	Percent change, 1989–1990	Unemployment: Total	Rate[3]
	45	46	47	48	49	50	51	52	53	54	55	56	57
FLORIDA–Con.													
North Miami	20 127	15.5	48.7	71 800	423	8	1 310	100.0	994	27 157	1.1	1 498	5.5
North Miami Beach	13 968	12.2	61.0	72 700	439	3	598	100.0	1 000	20 329	1.2	1 422	7.0
Ocala	17 393	5.2	57.2	62 900	294	132	8 275	90.9	15 023	26 450	2.8	1 692	6.4
Orlando	65 703	5.8	41.1	74 300	428	1 247	46 185	29.7	51 654	105 110	4.3	5 968	5.7
Panama City	14 053	3.5	58.3	49 800	279	NA	NA	NA	NA	21 612	-0.2	1 901	8.8
Pembroke Pines	26 722	3.0	76.8	93 800	608	1 247	91 442	34.4	9 347	NA	NA	NA	NA
Pensacola	23 983	3.4	60.5	63 600	312	169	11 700	75.1	11 109	30 839	1.5	1 655	5.4
Pinellas Park	18 185	2.6	73.6	61 900	411	139	5 295	92.1	3 590	18 478	2.6	906	4.9
Plantation	26 489	2.5	72.6	130 100	617	703	64 106	74.7	7 287	33 543	1.9	1 342	4.0
Pompano Beach	32 157	7.6	63.3	99 300	470	742	37 958	4.9	31 282	31 876	1.9	1 385	4.3
Riviera Beach	10 333	11.4	58.6	61 600	411	45	2 821	100.0	3 370	21 222	2.1	1 276	6.0
St. Petersburg	105 703	3.3	63.0	63 000	353	463	24 617	30.9	29 248	139 129	2.6	7 916	5.7
Sarasota	22 822	3.9	56.9	71 600	411	309	24 287	18.1	6 378	34 939	4.0	1 614	4.6
Sunrise	26 314	3.3	75.6	89 100	562	1 411	82 458	51.2	30 376	NA	NA	NA	NA
Tallahassee	50 442	4.3	45.2	72 400	353	1 722	71 022	46.5	46 055	62 837	3.0	3 020	4.8
Tamarac	22 906	1.5	78.2	77 600	557	553	19 820	16.8	3 227	12 699	2.1	894	7.0
Tampa	114 800	6.0	55.5	59 000	334	1 106	87 522	38.3	30 344	188 769	2.2	10 069	5.3
Titusville	16 207	2.9	64.2	66 100	380	293	23 765	81.2	7 042	22 232	4.4	1 417	6.4
West Palm Beach	28 787	7.5	50.3	72 000	434	111	11 388	87.4	56 763	52 820	2.1	3 037	5.7
GEORGIA	2 366 615	4.0	64.9	71 300	344	43 265	2 847 696	80.9	1 534 764	3 216 000	0.7	175 000	5.4
Albany	27 926	7.5	47.2	56 200	218	209	11 341	76.1	6 151	33 678	0.6	2 429	7.2
Athens	17 012	4.6	33.4	64 900	289	287	16 519	69.7	26 362	21 909	-1.0	1 065	4.9
Atlanta	155 752	6.5	43.1	71 200	342	2 525	145 649	16.8	201 365	227 915	0.5	16 429	7.2
Augusta	18 819	5.4	42.9	49 000	217	35	2 478	94.3	24 949	23 033	2.8	1 628	7.1
Columbus	65 634	4.5	53.8	59 000	275	461	23 491	96.5	39 938	76 197	0.9	4 191	5.5
East Point	13 373	6.3	49.7	64 500	369	4	317	100.0	4 428	22 120	0.4	1 372	6.2
Macon	41 175	4.7	49.7	49 300	238	NA	NA	NA	NA	57 993	1.3	3 189	5.5
Marietta	19 866	2.9	33.4	87 500	455	211	11 967	43.1	12 208	26 794	0.3	1 449	5.4
Rome	12 008	2.8	51.4	51 300	198	NA	NA	NA	NA	13 985	0.1	1 150	8.2
Savannah	51 938	4.9	50.7	54 800	281	525	21 802	55.8	48 889	72 334	2.7	3 915	5.4
Valdosta	14 143	5.6	50.1	59 600	264	163	8 808	100.0	7 021	20 897	-0.5	1 015	4.9
Warner Robins	16 721	3.8	57.1	56 000	323	100	3 614	100.0	4 789	21 143	1.4	926	4.4
HAWAII	356 267	15.9	53.9	245 300	599	8 718	1 007 598	63.5	460 524	539 000	2.7	15 000	2.8
Aiea (CDP)L/NA	NA	NA	NA	NA	NA	NA	NA	NA	NA	NA	NA	NA	
Hilo (CDP)	13 324	10.6	60.1	111 800	371	NA	NA	NA	NA	NA	NA	NA	NA
Honolulu (CDP)	134 563	16.2	47.0	353 900	582	NA	NA	NA	NA	391 387	2.0	9 999	2.6
Kailua (CDP)	11 843	8.3	70.0	318 900	850	NA	NA	NA	NA	NA	NA	NA	NA
Kaneohe (CDP)	10 610	12.9	70.2	242 700	776	NA	NA	NA	NA	NA	NA	NA	NA
Pearl City (CDP)	8 876	15.3	67.8	252 300	716	NA	NA	NA	NA	NA	NA	NA	NA
Waipahu (CDP)	7 567	32.4	51.5	234 800	558	NA	NA	NA	NA	NA	NA	NA	NA
IDAHO	360 723	4.2	70.1	58 200	261	5 712	445 609	82.0	175 775	496 000	1.4	29 000	5.8
Boise City	50 852	2.2	63.1	67 700	346	1 763	112 886	59.2	55 000	NA	NA	NA	NA
Idaho Falls	16 017	3.3	64.8	63 400	293	347	25 707	98.0	8 811	23 003	2.7	1 062	4.6
Lewiston	11 515	1.6	65.0	56 900	251	59	4 866	91.5	1 676	14 255	0.0	656	4.6
Nampa	10 213	6.2	60.6	45 600	242	162	9 840	96.3	2 772	12 885	1.0	1 106	8.6
Pocatello	17 183	3.0	64.0	51 300	234	93	6 633	95.7	2 192	22 315	-2.3	1 358	6.1
Twin Falls	10 472	3.6	62.8	51 600	246	96	7 806	91.7	4 696	13 880	0.6	763	5.5
ILLINOIS	4 202 240	4.0	64.2	80 900	369	38 289	3 517 201	71.6	2 434 138	6 029 000	0.2	371 000	6.2
Addison village	10 722	6.6	63.6	126 000	494	90	14 275	100.0	8 556	18 553	0.3	1 150	6.2
Alton	12 969	3.0	64.8	37 500	231	22	833	36.4	2 127	15 399	-1.3	1 159	7.5
Arlington Heights village	28 810	1.0	72.6	169 100	655	121	16 648	76.0	18 547	42 561	0.2	1 415	3.3
Aurora	33 710	7.6	61.4	81 900	425	1 241	98 392	60.8	24 630	45 954	2.0	3 603	7.8
Belleville	17 739	1.7	61.3	58 500	301	104	5 364	48.1	4 529	23 699	-0.9	2 435	10.3
Berwyn	19 298	1.7	61.9	90 200	412	29	1 503	58.6	1 500	23 695	0.6	1 308	5.5
Bloomington	21 480	1.4	58.3	66 100	322	421	24 613	84.8	22 620	31 218	1.6	1 221	3.9
Bolingbrook village	12 387	2.8	79.4	94 300	492	197	15 495	100.0	14 599	22 408	-1.1	781	3.5
Burbank	9 171	3.1	82.9	89 600	462	51	2 693	68.6	244	15 639	0.0	980	6.3
Calumet City	15 434	2.8	62.4	64 300	401	13	647	100.0	4 006	NA	NA	NA	NA
Carbondale	9 606	2.9	29.0	54 800	279	76	2 957	10.5	1 225	10 169	-0.8	406	4.0
Champaign	24 173	2.2	47.2	66 500	345	334	14 008	24.6	4 616	33 134	1.1	737	2.2
Chicago	1 025 174	8.8	41.5	78 700	377	3 240	251 070	17.6	666 592	1 442 230	0.2	110 664	7.7
Chicago Heights	10 932	7.2	62.5	62 500	326	9	814	100.0	4 381	16 416	-0.3	662	4.0
Cicero town	23 179	9.5	53.3	73 200	349	8	295	25.0	4 471	32 488	0.6	2 531	7.8
Danville	13 791	2.4	63.1	38 800	228	26	2 810	84.6	23 344	16 406	1.0	1 848	11.3
Decatur	34 013	1.8	65.9	42 800	251	109	10 405	81.7	14 870	43 111	-1.1	3 517	8.2
De Kalb	10 557	3.9	42.5	78 500	371	180	11 613	44.4	643	15 019	-3.5	537	3.6
Des Plaines	19 990	2.5	79.8	130 000	529	98	9 426	69.4	2 964	33 671	0.5	1 738	5.2

1. Specified owner-occupied units. 2. Specified renter-occupied units. 3. Percent of total civilian labor force.

City	Employed,[1] 1980: Total	Employed, 1980: Rate per 1,000 employees: Professional, specialty, and technical	Employed, 1980: Rate per 1,000 employees: Precision production, craft, and operators	Manufactures, 1987: Establishments: Total	Manufactures, 1987: Establishments: Percent with 20 or more employees	Manufactures, 1987: All employees: Number (1,000)	Manufactures, 1987: All employees: Percent change, 1982–1987	Manufactures, 1987: All employees: Annual payroll (Mil. dol.)	Manufactures, 1987: Production workers: Number (1,000)	Manufactures, 1987: Production workers: Work-hours (Millions)	Manufactures, 1987: Production workers: Wages: Total (Mil. dol.)	Manufactures, 1987: Production workers: Wages: Average per production worker (Dollars)	Manufactures, 1987: Value added by manufacture (Mil. dol.)	Manufactures, 1987: Value of shipments (Mil. dol.)	Manufactures, 1987: New capital expenditures (Mil. dol.)
	58	59	60	61	62	63	64	65	66	67	68	69	70	71	72
FLORIDA—Con.															
North Miami	21 445	150.9	143.8	68	20.6	1.0	0.0	20.6	0.7	1.3	12.2	17 429	52.5	84.8	1.4
North Miami Beach	15 806	138.2	116.6	69	23.2	2.0	100.0	32.1	1.6	3.1	19.7	12 312	60.9	149.0	1.8
Ocala	14 325	148.3	167.1	133	30.8	4.8	6.7	82.6	3.4	6.7	53.0	15 588	175.2	414.7	19.0
Orlando	55 487	152.4	143.7	277	33.9	26.4	193.3	767.7	11.0	21.8	201.0	18 273	1 959.3	3 136.0	134.7
Panama City	12 935	162.9	158.4	84	21.4	2.4	-27.3	57.6	1.9	4.0	42.6	22 421	153.5	413.4	5.8
Pembroke Pines	16 405	149.8	146.4	NA	NA	NA	NA	NA	NA	NA	NA	NA	NA	NA	NA
Pensacola	22 352	205.9	121.2	99	23.2	3.1	-16.2	71.9	2.0	4.1	41.8	20 900	198.1	421.9	D
Pinellas Park	12 449	111.7	270.8	85	34.1	2.8	12.0	55.6	1.8	3.6	28.6	15 889	121.0	227.5	7.3
Plantation	22 513	201.0	123.0	56	21.4	D	D	D	D	D	D	D	D	D	D
Pompano Beach	21 320	131.9	175.4	288	27.1	6.7	76.3	135.8	4.5	8.3	71.9	15 978	272.9	507.5	12.9
Riviera Beach	11 894	117.5	188.9	80	35.0	2.6	0.0	50.4	1.6	3.2	25.4	15 875	96.7	178.4	6.0
St. Petersburg	92 963	157.6	170.5	250	23.6	9.6	11.6	202.8	5.2	9.7	84.7	16 288	402.5	770.1	40.5
Sarasota	20 504	155.6	172.4	238	18.1	4.1	7.9	82.4	2.6	5.3	42.4	16 308	194.4	307.5	9.7
Sunrise	15 590	121.0	174.6	24	4.2	D	D	D	D	D	D	D	D	D	D
Tallahassee	39 342	224.3	79.4	122	19.7	2.4	50.0	42.8	1.6	3.1	23.8	14 875	100.2	183.4	5.8
Tamarac	8 255	123.1	154.5	NA	NA	NA	NA	NA	NA	NA	NA	NA	NA	NA	NA
Tampa	113 245	135.0	186.7	610	31.3	22.9	-2.6	492.5	13.6	27.2	230.1	16 919	1 087.9	2 459.7	77.9
Titusville	12 838	222.3	196.1	36	16.7	D	D	D	D	D	D	D	D	D	D
West Palm Beach	29 686	141.2	183.7	165	23.0	12.5	184.1	411.4	4.1	8.7	95.6	23 317	588.5	834.4	83.7
GEORGIA	2 335 835	136.1	245.1	9 187	38.4	569.9	13.3	11 933.1	409.4	820.1	7 239.9	17 684	33 708.1	75 709.2	2 471.5
Albany	29 361	136.3	220.5	85	41.2	5.9	-39.8	151.8	4.3	8.6	100.1	23 279	596.2	1 334.0	26.3
Athens	17 413	257.5	147.9	79	45.6	9.1	49.2	161.0	6.9	12.4	104.5	15 145	423.7	876.4	22.2
Atlanta	174 839	171.1	148.1	703	39.7	40.3	-2.2	1 128.0	20.7	41.4	472.2	22 812	2 413.3	4 803.4	191.8
Augusta	17 315	189.1	165.8	105	53.3	9.8	6.5	235.8	6.6	13.7	131.3	19 894	667.1	1 508.5	60.7
Columbus	62 065	144.5	212.2	157	51.0	D	D	D	D	D	D	D	D	D	D
East Point	17 211	144.3	171.1	42	42.9	D	D	D	D	D	D	D	D	D	D
Macon	46 824	149.0	194.5	136	39.0	11.5	16.2	317.5	8.2	17.2	215.6	26 293	1 994.8	3 042.2	59.2
Marietta	15 987	167.9	174.9	156	35.3	5.2	20.9	112.1	3.2	6.4	55.1	17 219	335.1	657.3	16.2
Rome	12 029	150.1	229.8	91	57.1	7.9	-3.7	174.0	6.0	12.0	118.9	19 817	444.1	948.2	19.8
Savannah	54 173	163.5	178.6	143	32.9	10.5	1.0	278.2	6.6	14.5	162.4	24 606	652.2	1 936.2	60.7
Valdosta	15 368	154.1	196.2	82	39.0	D	D	D	D	D	D	D	D	D	D
Warner Robins	15 875	165.7	218.8	27	37.0	D	D	D	D	D	D	D	D	D	D
HAWAII	415 181	146.7	149.8	1 022	22.0	22.2	-5.9	440.2	15.2	28.8	254.2	16 724	1 405.3	3 447.9	102.0
Aiea (CDP)	14 874	157.3	159.7	29	27.6	0.8	33.3	16.1	0.5	0.8	8.1	16 200	52.8	119.7	3.5
Hilo (CDP)	14 983	174.1	141.2	53	20.8	D	D	D	D	D	D	D	D	D	D
Honolulu (CDP)	179 765	162.5	127.8	628	22.8	12.9	-13.4	256.8	8.5	15.5	136.3	16 035	768.3	1 812.9	41.2
Kailua (CDP)	16 524	183.9	127.0	NA	NA	NA	NA	NA	NA	NA	NA	NA	NA	NA	NA
Kaneohe (CDP)	13 858	156.5	164.2	24	20.8	0.5	NA	7.9	0.4	0.7	4.3	10 750	23.6	37.2	0.2
Pearl City (CDP)	19 793	152.0	174.1	NA	NA	NA	NA	NA	NA	NA	NA	NA	NA	NA	NA
Waipahu (CDP)	11 373	74.7	240.9	26	26.9	0.7	D	11.1	0.4	0.8	5.8	14 500	32.4	66.0	D
IDAHO	383 652	141.3	188.4	1 491	24.9	52.9	11.1	1 148.5	38.3	72.4	698.3	18 232	3 057.0	7 004.7	234.8
Boise City	51 071	177.9	139.1	189	21.7	8.8	22.2	247.9	4.4	8.6	89.9	20 432	523.5	978.2	41.8
Idaho Falls	17 233	225.8	152.0	54	31.5	2.5	25.0	78.5	1.5	2.7	37.0	24 667	178.2	239.5	D
Lewiston	11 992	134.3	211.6	40	17.5	D	D	D	D	D	D	D	D	D	D
Nampa	9 672	122.4	208.9	47	38.3	2.4	71.4	41.0	1.6	3.1	24.7	15 437	173.0	287.2	8.7
Pocatello	20 784	173.3	182.4	45	22.2	D	D	D	D	D	D	D	D	D	D
Twin Falls	11 725	132.1	176.5	49	24.5	1.7	21.4	29.0	1.4	2.4	19.9	14 214	85.8	199.7	D
ILLINOIS	5 068 428	148.3	219.7	18 404	39.1	989.6	-8.1	26 234.7	609.3	1 227.5	13 401.4	21 995	63 350.1	132 204.3	4 425.8
Addison village	15 806	106.0	282.7	378	34.1	9.8	16.7	214.9	7.0	14.2	130.3	18 614	510.9	899.8	27.0
Alton	12 655	155.9	234.1	41	34.1	D	D	D	D	D	D	D	D	D	D
Arlington Heights village	34 122	197.0	104.7	117	29.9	6.5	51.2	186.3	2.9	5.7	59.6	20 552	442.7	682.9	22.5
Aurora	37 586	129.6	309.7	143	42.7	7.5	-17.6	173.5	4.8	9.2	99.2	20 667	440.0	785.8	17.6
Belleville	18 132	152.6	165.4	60	28.3	D	D	D	D	D	D	D	D	D	D
Berwyn	21 719	122.7	208.6	31	12.9	0.5	NA	9.2	0.3	0.6	5.1	17 000	19.0	27.6	0.8
Bloomington	22 485	152.7	165.4	53	47.2	D	D	D	D	D	D	D	D	D	D
Bolingbrook village	17 151	174.8	196.5	NA	NA	NA	NA	NA	NA	NA	NA	NA	NA	NA	NA
Burbank	13 408	75.3	278.0	NA	NA	NA	NA	NA	NA	NA	NA	NA	NA	NA	NA
Calumet City	19 439	123.3	270.0	NA	NA	NA	NA	NA	NA	NA	NA	NA	NA	NA	NA
Carbondale	10 615	295.9	61.4	14	50.0	0.8	-11.1	11.8	0.6	1.0	8.2	13 667	21.9	63.5	D
Champaign	29 016	265.6	101.3	76	40.8	6.0	93.5	123.0	4.0	7.3	81.9	20 475	482.9	1 251.0	D
Chicago	1 235 865	141.3	224.0	4 377	40.7	220.6	-20.4	5 632.9	135.2	270.6	2 769.1	20 482	14 333.2	27 747.7	504.8
Chicago Heights	15 095	120.1	255.0	74	58.1	4.9	-16.9	126.0	3.6	7.6	83.3	23 139	307.6	724.6	14.5
Cicero town	27 352	82.1	313.0	135	53.3	8.3	-42.8	209.5	5.9	11.8	128.7	21 814	332.5	945.8	22.8
Danville	16 074	153.4	219.5	62	50.0	5.3	-15.9	143.9	3.7	7.6	97.4	26 324	493.0	1 088.0	17.3
Decatur	40 059	155.4	227.3	105	38.1	D	D	D	D	D	D	D	D	D	D
De Kalb	15 380	245.6	108.5	39	46.2	2.0	-4.8	42.2	1.5	2.9	27.7	18 467	102.2	194.9	D
Des Plaines	29 306	147.8	201.7	219	46.1	13.7	-0.7	395.6	6.9	14.5	143.0	20 725	570.5	1 116.7	37.8

1. Persons 16 years old and over.

Table C. Cities — **Wholesale Trade and Retail Trade**

City	Wholesale trade, 1987				Retail trade–all establishments, 1987				Retail trade–establishments with payroll, 1987					
						Sales				Sales				
											Per capita[2] (Dollars)			
	Establishments	Sales (Mil. dol.)	Paid employees[1]	Annual payroll ($1,000)	Number	Total (Mil. dol.)	Percent change, 1982–1987	Per capita[2] (Dollars)	Number	Total (Mil. dol.)	General merchandise group stores	Food stores	Apparel and accessory stores	Eating and drinking places
	73	74	75	76	77	78	79	80	81	82	83	84	85	86
FLORIDA–Con.														
North Miami	138	348.8	930	23 223	610	424.5	48.9	9 953	402	417.5	D	2 211	351	1 182
North Miami Beach	162	639.7	2 099	57 603	662	413.7	4.8	11 540	414	401.8	1 498	1 692	830	1 087
Ocala	218	460.6	2 116	40 913	1 082	882.3	56.7	19 555	777	865.9	2 593	3 326	595	1 854
Orlando	642	3 222.8	8 767	197 825	1 803	1 745.6	40.9	11 964	1 428	1 720.1	1 897	2 309	664	1 578
Panama City	152	326.9	1 456	23 708	1 006	674.6	61.3	18 933	703	658.1	D	2 937	740	1 968
Pembroke Pines	56	69.3	287	5 421	474	212.3	89.4	4 319	239	202.1	D	1 683	89	653
Pensacola	229	588.5	2 581	50 673	991	644.7	54.0	10 102	655	626.2	1 190	1 447	229	1 060
Pinellas Park	70	161.2	848	16 425	442	328.9	63.3	8 087	306	323.1	2 247	1 703	262	490
Plantation	131	203.2	618	15 621	779	745.9	55.9	13 348	515	735.6	2 999	1 993	981	857
Pompano Beach	401	1 212.2	4 009	89 060	1 032	929.7	49.0	13 930	704	912.5	1 351	1 794	830	915
Riviera Beach	112	776.3	1 475	35 986	229	114.1	29.2	4 107	162	110.8	D	952	188	579
St. Petersburg	329	680.4	2 955	56 686	2 229	1 758.3	41.0	7 344	1 411	1 721.2	1 029	1 392	279	615
Sarasota	297	545.2	2 233	45 311	1 735	1 198.6	116.0	23 274	1 172	1 166.3	3 004	3 767	1 354	2 795
Sunrise	59	140.7	374	11 679	518	247.7	73.6	4 697	284	237.8	D	1 366	144	618
Tallahassee	231	541.4	2 394	51 594	1 334	1 140.0	67.6	9 544	1 047	1 123.1	D	1 631	434	1 080
Tamarac	77	106.4	348	7 540	520	232.4	62.9	6 719	295	219.7	694	2 127	638	842
Tampa	1 352	10 959.0	21 781	499 754	3 614	3 118.3	47.3	11 234	2 679	3 073.5	1 548	1 590	437	1 230
Titusville	25	23.9	208	3 256	448	315.9	66.1	7 530	309	309.9	1 180	1 585	92	863
West Palm Beach	261	969.8	3 453	68 291	1 146	1 271.0	50.9	18 536	779	1 250.9	3 538	1 176	691	1 420
GEORGIA	13 678	86 854.0	178 235	4 116 577	61 686	41 186.2	68.7	6 747	39 782	39 994.9	806	1 263	305	652
Albany	244	822.1	2 937	57 332	1 012	723.7	42.3	8 519	726	707.1	1 347	1 787	D	729
Athens	119	452.0	1 316	29 527	673	452.0	38.9	10 487	543	445.9	1 526	1 880	451	1 384
Atlanta	1 543	13 590.9	25 328	676 231	3 843	3 239.1	32.3	7 677	2 914	3 196.1	D	1 035	575	1 290
Augusta	203	653.0	2 538	51 834	635	549.2	73.1	12 086	515	541.5	1 481	2 317	345	1 172
Columbus	268	867.8	3 026	54 775	1 692	1 361.1	63.8	7 554	1 256	1 343.1	D	D	402	D
East Point	59	1 279.4	798	18 489	213	128.2	2.5	3 410	143	125.0	D	993	38	751
Macon	308	1 201.6	4 076	83 605	1 462	1 186.3	49.9	10 018	1 114	1 168.0	D	1 642	485	930
Marietta	327	1 654.9	4 601	123 902	791	1 002.0	80.2	23 406	603	993.7	1 920	3 391	758	1 944
Rome	127	314.2	1 125	21 739	673	451.3	55.7	14 600	466	440.8	D	2 655	D	1 347
Savannah	335	1 312.8	4 345	90 490	1 490	1 296.7	48.0	8 833	1 215	1 283.1	1 410	1 524	537	903
Valdosta	132	311.5	1 415	24 641	656	458.5	48.0	12 402	523	451.6	D	2 349	593	1 243
Warner Robins	32	77.4	228	5 449	488	416.7	60.0	9 134	361	412.5	D	1 796	223	715
HAWAII	1 998	5 362.5	20 157	415 114	11 143	8 267.4	59.2	7 785	7 195	8 084.4	1 181	1 480	545	1 272
Aiea (CDP)	67	172.7	749	16 654	380	426.1	67.5	NA	246	420.6	NA	NA	NA	NA
Hilo (CDP)	116	275.9	1 144	20 491	511	408.8	43.0	NA	378	403.4	NA	NA	NA	NA
Honolulu (CDP)	1 293	3 816.7	14 266	297 270	5 538	4 544.1	58.9	12 205	3 644	4 451.5	2 470	1 681	953	2 169
Kailua (CDP)	31	21.4	105	2 269	300	180.9	18.5	NA	173	175.8	NA	NA	NA	NA
Kaneohe (CDP)	24	14.3	97	1 613	309	297.6	63.3	NA	188	292.8	NA	NA	NA	NA
Pearl City (CDP)	40	117.9	376	8 160	232	141.4	15.1	NA	101	137.3	NA	NA	NA	NA
Waipahu (CDP)	49	135.1	428	9 554	242	211.8	59.0	NA	154	208.7	NA	NA	NA	NA
IDAHO	2 128	5 078.2	20 814	353 438	10 953	5 082.2	25.2	5 067	6 587	4 891.0	483	1 129	193	447
Boise City	420	1 476.8	4 469	95 152	1 503	969.2	36.9	8 942	1 007	948.9	823	1 835	D	1 061
Idaho Falls	176	404.8	1 918	33 197	732	471.6	30.6	11 011	478	459.9	D	D	505	D
Lewiston	70	235.1	699	12 879	406	251.5	24.2	9 070	284	247.5	1 118	D	322	803
Nampa	68	165.9	714	12 563	424	280.1	34.6	9 915	271	272.2	2 160	1 547	494	776
Pocatello	102	322.8	1 012	19 421	561	313.9	16.6	7 067	357	307.4	595	1 521	255	653
Twin Falls	139	265.4	1 453	23 063	460	317.1	32.2	11 427	342	313.3	D	D	728	883
ILLINOIS	23 620	167 460.9	319 497	8 080 982	99 468	69 937.2	37.8	6 056	63 945	68 263.9	696	1 078	352	604
Addison village	245	862.8	3 298	86 348	331	189.4	23.4	6 169	223	182.5	1 150	1 476	355	715
Alton	44	D	D	D	416	322.5	30.5	9 785	323	318.4	1 831	1 049	415	902
Arlington Heights village	344	3 352.2	4 543	146 188	675	813.4	94.1	11 590	455	803.0	881	2 170	762	946
Aurora	137	D	D	D	844	813.9	48.0	9 536	634	803.3	1 956	1 124	978	754
Belleville	87	D	D	D	556	428.1	39.6	9 993	392	423.2	D	1 894	213	772
Berwyn	39	D	D	D	391	272.5	54.7	6 054	247	265.9	620	613	360	681
Bloomington	116	632.2	2 554	52 978	607	563.3	35.1	12 179	474	558.9	1 829	2 053	525	1 262
Bolingbrook village	20	D	D	D	172	0.0	0.0	D	96	D	D	1 155	51	D
Burbank	7	D	D	D	185	214.3	127.5	7 511	114	210.7	D	2 165	D	749
Calumet City	34	D	D	D	412	498.1	49.0	12 509	311	492.6	4 589	1 103	1 692	983
Carbondale	29	28.4	194	3 155	330	304.6	17.3	12 602	275	301.8	D	1 609	1 083	1 386
Champaign	91	D	D	D	730	598.1	45.4	10 106	572	590.9	2 034	1 558	783	1 350
Chicago	4 509	32 702.1	70 313	1 902 220	19 585	12 371.3	19.9	4 111	12 785	12 021.2	431	792	303	598
Chicago Heights	54	D	D	D	260	290.8	19.4	8 182	188	286.1	D	413	D	734
Cicero town	66	D	D	D	397	158.3	15.5	2 570	231	150.9	14	607	63	456
Danville	73	D	D	D	443	348.8	27.5	9 514	336	344.3	1 795	1 732	509	924
Decatur	147	D	D	D	906	680.2	35.1	7 528	620	666.1	1 023	1 364	275	759
De Kalb	29	26.0	182	3 631	296	214.3	40.1	6 788	216	211.3	D	1 680	315	813
Des Plaines	375	5 165.1	6 972	211 910	586	492.0	54.7	8 759	388	482.6	D	1 318	313	1 485

1. For the period including March 12 of the year shown. 2. Based on resident population estimated as of July 1, 1986.

City	Retail trade–establishment with payroll, 1987 (cont'd)			Taxable service industries–establishments with payroll, 1987							Federal grants, 1986		
	Paid employees[1]				Receipts (Mil. dol.)								
						Selected kinds of business							
	Number	Percent change, 1982–1987	Annual payroll (Mil. dol.)	Number	Total	Hotels, motels, and other lodging places	Health services	Legal services	Paid employees[1]	Annual payroll (Mil. dol.)	Procurement contract awards (Mil. dol.)	Grant awards (Mil. dol.)	Federal government civilian employment, 1984
	87	88	89	90	91	92	93	94	95	96	97	98	99
FLORIDA—Con.													
North Miami	4 698	18.8	52.3	518	184.7	4.4	70.8	13.1	4 746	71.6	1.6	0.4	11
North Miami Beach	4 591	13.0	49.4	768	350.4	3.4	203.9	26.9	6 495	140.2	2.1	0.6	6
Ocala	10 613	50.5	102.5	786	273.0	18.1	117.8	24.9	6 190	102.3	8.5	0.7	253
Orlando	22 872	40.5	221.8	2 482	2 045.3	212.5	387.2	247.3	36 243	763.1	1 593.8	42.6	4 352
Panama City	8 041	40.0	73.7	639	224.7	23.7	100.1	14.5	5 350	87.2	71.4	3.1	1 416
Pembroke Pines	2 991	102.2	24.5	339	93.5	D	29.1	2.5	2 312	33.7	0.1	0.3	1
Pensacola	7 693	38.3	74.1	918	395.3	18.7	166.3	54.9	9 150	168.7	61.3	10.5	8 663
Pinellas Park	3 452	17.7	35.4	313	90.1	3.3	23.9	1.4	2 955	35.0	23.0	0.4	110
Plantation	7 657	7.2	79.2	858	431.2	D	275.4	12.5	7 168	168.1	3.5	0.3	0
Pompano Beach	8 505	5.4	104.4	885	452.8	46.9	100.1	15.0	9 320	159.0	20.6	3.4	470
Riviera Beach	1 461	22.2	14.0	181	76.6	18.6	5.2	1.4	2 068	27.2	6.4	3.6	80
St. Petersburg	19 460	10.3	200.3	2 336	956.5	54.1	376.7	92.5	22 172	393.3	235.4	27.3	2 038
Sarasota	14 927	67.8	153.7	1 746	704.4	38.4	244.3	71.0	17 132	281.9	36.8	2.9	634
Sunrise	3 255	41.0	30.3	400	111.4	D	46.2	8.3	2 897	42.7	NA	0.6	2
Tallahassee	15 943	30.1	137.5	1 468	604.7	D	154.0	D	13 384	227.4	22.9	496.7	1 129
Tamarac	3 298	44.7	29.6	391	170.6	0.0	110.9	2.8	3 362	63.7	0.1	0.2	0
Tampa	35 927	25.2	374.9	4 015	2 752.4	132.9	526.7	281.2	58 394	1 057.3	203.1	53.2	6 323
Titusville	4 152	51.8	37.1	275	511.2	D	36.3	D	8 177	251.7	50.9	3.2	168
West Palm Beach	12 061	15.1	149.7	1 448	851.2	35.0	221.5	206.0	16 838	365.7	1 004.0	14.5	1 916
GEORGIA	486 992	46.9	4 791.6	39 189	18 645.8	1 234.8	4 756.6	1 346.7	414 969	6 908.9	3 956.6	2 583.4	80 210
Albany	9 078	25.6	82.8	693	280.5	D	105.2	D	6 647	107.8	17.7	6.1	3 150
Athens	7 115	28.1	58.9	506	171.8	8.7	83.8	12.5	5 339	70.7	17.9	41.2	1 229
Atlanta	46 713	17.5	499.6	4 913	4 344.2	D	539.9	682.1	90 984	1 662.9	305.5	306.0	21 036
Augusta	7 492	53.7	68.7	781	336.8	11.7	126.5	29.5	7 998	148.8	21.0	19.6	2 948
Columbus	16 345	41.8	160.7	1 123	D	19.8	160.6	29.4	D	D	10.6	11.4	475
East Point	1 708	-23.9	19.8	285	182.9	20.0	42.1	2.4	3 348	59.2	2.1	0.4	875
Macon	14 781	32.5	139.6	1 109	533.8	D	279.8	34.6	11 141	187.2	24.3	12.0	1 095
Marietta	9 335	29.7	114.1	939	494.2	D	126.9	23.1	8 695	189.8	2 155.9	0.1	1 877
Rome	5 440	25.0	52.8	363	159.7	D	98.7	8.9	4 518	63.4	2.7	1.5	158
Savannah	16 210	25.8	155.2	1 170	510.5	51.4	182.1	43.4	11 537	197.3	266.9	12.2	1 976
Valdosta	6 311	44.7	53.7	467	142.7	15.1	D	7.1	3 804	53.6	7.0	2.3	230
Warner Robins	4 726	27.5	46.5	309	103.3	8.6	38.4	4.2	2 681	37.8	10.4	4.2	127
HAWAII	101 969	24.4	1 016.1	7 458	4 456.0	1 562.0	742.5	315.5	91 673	1 499.5	619.0	500.7	26 768
Aiea (CDP)	4 593	23.1	47.6	188	70.3	2.6	18.9	D	1 589	23.0	NA	NA	329
Hilo (CDP)	5 077	28.5	49.4	388	131.1	12.5	50.0	9.0	2 901	46.5	NA	NA	291
Honolulu (CDP)	54 846	12.9	559.4	4 529	2 848.9	828.4	473.4	276.5	57 050	986.0	NA	NA	6 004
Kailua (CDP)	2 383	15.6	23.0	242	57.5	0.0	24.7	D	1 154	22.5	NA	NA	78
Kaneohe (CDP)	3 036	57.1	31.6	143	36.2	D	14.7	D	931	12.4	NA	NA	754
Pearl City (CDP)	1 806	4.0	17.0	144	45.7	0.0	18.7	D	1 228	16.5	NA	NA	151
Waipahu (CDP)	2 014	22.7	22.9	116	26.7	0.0	9.2	D	743	9.9	NA	NA	70
IDAHO	62 535	11.8	556.1	6 239	2 063.9	131.6	574.6	145.5	47 621	789.5	642.4	463.4	9 800
Boise City	13 160	20.2	117.8	1 434	516.2	34.7	143.6	61.1	12 435	196.5	25.6	94.5	3 489
Idaho Falls	5 844	19.8	51.3	510	537.2	D	D	15.2	8 104	231.7	491.0	3.0	596
Lewiston	3 013	10.0	28.6	293	76.9	2.8	36.6	6.6	1 978	27.8	5.0	1.7	153
Nampa	3 324	18.6	31.1	237	51.5	D	25.0	2.5	1 475	20.5	2.6	2.6	78
Pocatello	4 062	6.5	35.5	360	92.4	D	39.1	12.0	2 409	36.6	19.9	3.6	371
Twin Falls	3 778	13.3	36.5	365	105.6	7.1	48.8	D	2 748	40.1	5.3	2.8	249
ILLINOIS	820 197	15.9	8 078.4	70 738	36 499.6	1 695.4	7 270.4	3 771.9	729 655	13 682.5	3 013.5	5 083.4	101 407
Addison village	3 104	27.6	24.4	278	99.5	D	8.8	1.3	2 210	33.6	3.0	0.0	80
Alton	3 955	4.4	37.5	280	98.5	6.8	45.6	9.9	2 113	34.7	75.9	1.7	162
Arlington Heights village	8 210	68.9	90.0	845	413.4	19.7	122.6	9.1	8 015	159.0	28.8	1.2	472
Aurora	10 222	30.5	93.8	552	213.7	D	D	16.5	5 164	88.4	4.7	2.6	813
Belleville	4 674	19.2	50.0	560	207.0	3.2	97.1	44.8	4 675	92.5	61.5	0.7	222
Berwyn	3 300	20.3	33.1	251	84.9	D	49.4	1.6	1 553	30.0	NA	0.4	114
Bloomington	7 358	13.4	62.5	450	182.2	6.5	57.8	15.3	4 249	69.1	1.0	2.6	391
Bolingbrook village	D	D	D	130	D	0.0	7.0	2.7	D	D	0.1	0.5	1
Burbank	2 354	88.6	20.3	76	21.8	D	10.3	D	589	7.2	NA	0.2	1
Calumet City	6 077	26.3	56.5	172	41.8	D	9.5	1.9	1 025	12.9	0.0	0.4	96
Carbondale	4 456	11.1	37.3	188	71.1	3.9	33.9	6.1	2 003	28.8	2.2	10.9	313
Champaign	9 476	24.0	72.4	546	226.4	21.1	D	17.7	5 675	89.8	7.9	6.7	793
Chicago	154 253	4.8	1 647.2	17 126	13 583.1	695.0	1 434.1	2 844.5	241 623	5 367.0	431.2	902.4	44 369
Chicago Heights	3 110	-1.8	33.3	240	109.8	D	53.2	6.2	2 507	42.5	1.1	6.7	125
Cicero town	2 220	-1.9	20.8	196	120.8	1.8	11.4	D	2 338	35.5	1.9	2.3	1
Danville	4 398	12.6	40.1	308	138.0	D	41.0	8.0	2 906	47.5	26.2	1.9	1 625
Decatur	8 732	23.5	81.8	598	213.2	10.4	64.0	D	4 963	85.4	10.1	41.7	413
De Kalb	3 120	22.1	24.4	172	35.7	D	15.5	2.1	965	12.6	0.4	4.5	86
Des Plaines	6 039	25.4	63.7	733	725.9	9.0	88.6	5.4	12 253	181.8	11.8	1.2	923

1. For the period including March 12 of the year shown.

City	City government employment, 1985 (October): Total	City government employment, 1985 (October): Rates[1]	City government employment, 1985 (October): Percent education	Form of governments[2] (As of 1986)	City government finances, 1984–1985: General revenue: Total (Mil. dol.)	General revenue: Intergovernmental: Total (Mil. dol.)	General revenue: Intergovernmental: Percent from State government	General revenue: Taxes: Total (Mil. dol.)	Taxes: Per capita[3] (Dollars): Total	Taxes: Per capita[3] (Dollars): Property	Taxes: Per capita[3] (Dollars): Sales & gross receipts	General expenditures: Total (Mil. dol.)	General expenditures: Per capita[3] (Dol.): Total	General expenditures: Per capita[3] (Dol.): Capital outlays	Percent of total for–: Public welfare	Percent of total for–: Highways	Percent of total for–: Education
	100	101	102	103	104	105	106	107	108	109	110	111	112	113	114	115	116
FLORIDA—Con.																	
North Miami	470	110.2	0.0	2	17.8	3.5	89.6	10.4	245	114	117	16.8	394	61	0.0	6.4	0.0
North Miami Beach	440	122.7	0.0	2	19.6	2.9	87.2	8.0	222	96	115	17.5	489	41	0.0	2.1	0.0
Ocala	834	184.8	0.0	2	15.6	4.1	74.4	3.8	83	49	22	17.2	381	36	0.0	5.4	0.0
Orlando	3 419	234.3	0.0	1	223.2	31.9	43.1	38.5	264	95	142	191.6	1 313	309	0.0	3.6	0.0
Panama City	460	129.1	0.0	2	18.8	4.0	59.3	7.5	210	49	75	14.8	415	75	NA	13.8	0.0
Pembroke Pines	522	106.2	0.0	2	15.7	3.1	79.3	7.1	145	39	81	15.7	319	74	2.4	20.1	0.0
Pensacola	845	132.4	0.0	2	34.8	9.1	57.0	9.2	144	20	113	48.8	765	132	0.0	5.9	0.0
Pinellas Park	394	96.9	0.0	2	13.0	2.7	85.3	5.3	131	37	71	12.5	307	18	0.0	16.1	0.0
Plantation	454	81.2	0.0	1	20.3	3.3	89.9	11.2	200	55	122	17.5	313	59	0.0	6.4	0.0
Pompano Beach	887	132.9	0.0	2	42.0	4.6	69.9	19.5	293	148	127	38.9	583	107	0.1	5.3	0.0
Riviera Beach	391	140.7	0.0	2	17.7	2.3	79.7	8.4	301	198	90	16.6	597	20	0.0	7.0	0.0
St. Petersburg	3 160	132.0	0.0	2	138.6	37.2	41.0	44.7	187	101	78	119.5	499	81	0.0	9.9	0.0
Sarasota	961	186.6	0.0	2	38.6	6.4	59.9	15.3	298	127	153	32.8	636	45	0.0	7.3	0.0
Sunrise	585	110.9	0.0	1	23.8	3.2	81.5	11.3	215	55	115	31.4	595	122	0.0	3.7	0.0
Tallahassee	2 097	175.6	0.0	2	62.6	13.9	49.5	12.0	100	38	53	64.2	537	98	1.5	12.8	0.0
Tamarac	325	94.0	0.0	2	11.5	2.0	86.7	4.9	140	52	49	9.7	281	20	0.0	5.6	0.0
Tampa	3 964	142.8	0.0	1	222.2	44.1	51.8	76.3	275	96	155	250.2	901	349	0.0	5.7	0.0
Titusville	415	98.9	0.0	2	12.0	2.8	77.9	5.2	123	38	73	12.2	291	41	0.0	15.7	0.0
West Palm Beach	1 174	171.2	0.0	2	42.9	6.8	64.3	20.4	297	161	112	43.8	639	135	0.0	5.5	0.0
GEORGIA	NA	NA	NA	NA	NA	NA	NA	NA	NA	NA	NA	NA	NA	NA	NA	NA	NA
Albany	1 782	209.8	0.0	2	25.2	4.5	20.7	9.6	113	61	41	32.7	385	60	0.0	5.5	0.0
Athens	585	135.7	0.0	1	15.1	4.1	41.8	4.6	106	4	82	15.5	360	31	7.7	8.1	0.0
Atlanta	7 626	180.7	0.0	1	491.8	93.2	17.7	167.0	396	154	190	417.9	990	242	0.8	4.7	3.6
Augusta	1 047	230.4	0.0	1	32.4	9.6	7.0	9.7	213	105	88	29.3	645	149	0.8	8.9	0.0
Columbus	2 292	127.2	0.0	2	72.4	11.2	20.1	48.6	270	91	144	68.2	379	44	0.2	7.2	0.0
East Point	440	117.1	0.0	2	11.1	1.1	17.3	4.5	121	56	52	15.5	411	23	0.0	3.5	0.0
Macon	1 424	120.2	0.0	1	47.6	10.3	14.9	30.5	258	65	174	42.1	355	47	0.0	4.5	0.0
Marietta	580	135.5	0.0	2	16.0	1.3	20.9	7.3	170	81	61	15.6	365	32	4.5	7.1	0.0
Rome	588	190.2	0.0	2	17.3	6.2	19.3	7.7	250	117	107	16.7	540	99	0.0	10.4	0.0
Savannah	1 830	124.7	0.0	2	59.7	11.9	31.0	22.3	152	66	68	68.4	466	86	0.9	7.6	0.0
Valdosta	435	117.7	0.0	2	10.5	1.6	50.7	4.3	116	37	65	12.5	339	45	0.0	16.5	0.0
Warner Robins	496	108.7	0.0	1	11.0	1.0	56.3	5.7	125	75	40	10.5	231	10	0.0	8.6	0.0
HAWAII	NA	NA	NA	NA	NA	NA	NA	NA	NA	NA	NA	NA	NA	NA	NA	NA	NA
Aiea (CDP)	NA	NA	NA	NA	NA	NA	NA	NA	NA	NA	NA	NA	NA	NA	NA	NA	NA
Hilo (CDP)	NA	NA	NA	1	NA	NA	NA	NA	NA	NA	NA	NA	NA	NA	NA	NA	NA
Honolulu (CDP)	NA	NA	NA	1	NA	NA	NA	NA	NA	NA	NA	NA	NA	NA	NA	NA	NA
Kailua (CDP)	NA	NA	NA	NA	NA	NA	NA	NA	NA	NA	NA	NA	NA	NA	NA	NA	NA
Kaneohe (CDP)	NA	NA	NA	NA	NA	NA	NA	NA	NA	NA	NA	NA	NA	NA	NA	NA	NA
Pearl City (CDP)	NA	NA	NA	NA	NA	NA	NA	NA	NA	NA	NA	NA	NA	NA	NA	NA	NA
Waipahu (CDP)	NA	NA	NA	NA	NA	NA	NA	NA	NA	NA	NA	NA	NA	NA	NA	NA	NA
IDAHO	NA	NA	NA	NA	NA	NA	NA	NA	NA	NA	NA	NA	NA	NA	NA	NA	NA
Boise City	777	71.7	0.0	1	48.0	12.5	21.6	14.8	137	118	11	44.5	411	81	0.0	0.9	0.0
Idaho Falls	513	119.8	0.0	1	15.9	3.8	47.0	5.5	128	116	5	18.0	419	73	0.0	12.4	0.0
Lewiston	260	93.8	0.0	2	12.9	5.2	39.8	4.2	151	144	0	14.6	526	186	0.0	7.4	0.0
Nampa	179	63.4	0.0	1	9.1	2.2	77.0	2.7	95	82	4	9.2	327	87	0.0	11.5	0.0
Pocatello	445	100.2	0.0	2	14.8	3.3	68.4	6.6	148	134	8	15.4	347	30	0.0	10.3	0.0
Twin Falls	188	67.7	0.0	2	9.7	2.3	71.2	3.7	132	112	0	8.9	320	40	0.0	11.2	0.0
ILLINOIS	NA	NA	NA	NA	NA	NA	NA	NA	NA	NA	NA	NA	NA	NA	NA	NA	NA
Addison village	223	72.6	0.0	1	15.6	2.0	80.0	5.4	177	58	92	12.1	394	51	0.0	8.6	0.0
Alton	315	95.6	0.0	1	18.9	2.6	76.4	7.4	224	74	130	17.6	534	39	0.8	8.6	0.0
Arlington Heights village	516	73.5	0.0	2	29.4	4.0	73.2	18.6	265	128	95	21.4	305	38	0.0	7.2	0.0
Aurora	736	86.2	0.0	1	26.9	6.6	62.6	16.1	189	121	63	25.7	301	73	0.0	24.7	0.0
Belleville	355	82.9	0.0	1	12.5	2.2	86.8	6.4	150	37	102	10.8	252	24	0.0	13.9	0.0
Berwyn	NA	NA	NA	1	11.6	2.0	82.1	7.5	167	73	77	9.6	214	6	0.2	17.6	0.0
Bloomington	475	102.7	0.0	2	22.7	3.3	77.3	12.5	270	105	147	19.2	415	71	2.9	12.9	0.0
Bolingbrook village	246	62.9	0.0	2	21.8	2.0	74.6	7.5	193	108	62	16.5	422	19	0.5	10.6	0.0
Burbank	162	56.8	0.0	1	4.8	1.2	81.2	3.2	113	57	36	4.8	168	11	0.0	21.6	0.0
Calumet City	396	99.4	0.0	1	13.9	2.0	84.3	9.0	225	69	130	16.1	405	191	8.1	7.7	0.0
Carbondale	342	141.5	0.0	2	16.9	4.6	29.1	5.7	235	56	173	17.1	706	291	0.0	6.1	0.0
Champaign	1 396	235.9	0.0	2	53.8	4.4	58.0	13.4	227	85	127	53.9	910	106	2.5	9.1	0.0
Chicago	45 260	150.4	0.0	1	2 146.3	627.4	49.4	1 160.4	386	132	214	1 992.2	662	96	2.8	9.2	1.4
Chicago Heights	NA	NA	NA	1	18.2	5.0	44.1	9.6	270	118	139	23.9	673	354	0.0	4.5	0.0
Cicero town	529	85.9	0.0	1	14.8	3.3	83.4	9.6	155	97	39	12.6	205	1	1.6	20.0	0.0
Danville	307	83.7	0.0	3	15.8	4.4	66.1	7.2	196	79	111	14.7	402	14	0.1	17.9	0.0
Decatur	570	63.1	0.0	2	32.7	6.9	64.2	16.0	177	69	81	31.3	346	88	0.0	18.9	0.0
De Kalb	224	71.0	0.0	2	11.7	2.4	62.7	5.8	185	45	134	8.8	279	37	0.0	7.8	0.0
Des Plaines	489	87.1	0.0	1	19.7	2.9	78.5	12.3	218	102	86	16.1	287	2	0.0	16.5	0.0

1. Per 10,000 population estimated as of July 1, 1986. 2. 1 = Mayor-council; 2 = Council-manager; 3 = Commission. Data subject to copyright. 3. Based on resident population estimated as of July 1, 1986.

City	City government finances, 1984–1985 (cont'd): General expenditure (cont'd), Percent of total for (cont'd): Health and hospitals	Police protection	Sewerage and sanitation	Parks and recreation	Housing and community development	Debt outstanding: Total (Mil. dol.)	Per capita[1] (Dollars)	Percent utility	Climate[2]: Average daily temperature (Degrees Fahrenheit), Mean: Jan.	Mean: July	Limits: Jan.[3]	Limits: July[4]	Annual precipitation (Inches)	Heating degree days[5]	Cooling degree days[5]	Typical monthly electric bills, 1986: Residential[6]: Total (Dollars)	Residential: Percent change, 1980–1986	Commercial[7] (Dollars)
	117	118	119	120	121	122	123	124	125	126	127	128	129	130	131	132	133	134
FLORIDA—Con.																		
North Miami	0.0	23.5	11.9	22.2	0.0	30.1	705	0.0	65.7	81.7	56.2	89.2	63.47	284	3 815	70.47	119.6	NA
North Miami Beach	0.0	26.4	20.2	9.9	0.0	11.8	329	75.0	68.0	82.6	62.2	87.0	46.05	133	4 150	70.47	119.6	NA
Ocala	0.0	21.0	10.7	11.5	3.8	53.1	1 178	27.0	58.3	81.8	46.1	92.2	53.86	881	3 134	56.33	51.6	NA
Orlando	0.0	10.9	19.9	4.5	1.1	1 101.1	7 547	51.9	60.5	82.4	49.3	91.7	47.83	656	3 401	53.41	65.4	414.6
Panama City	0.8	14.4	11.3	6.9	3.7	20.3	569	0.0	51.7	82.3	42.7	90.1	61.16	1 571	2 680	51.18	51.1	NA
Pembroke Pines	0.1	24.7	0.0	17.5	0.0	21.7	441	0.0	65.7	81.7	56.2	89.2	63.47	284	3 815	70.47	119.6	NA
Pensacola	0.4	11.1	5.5	9.6	2.7	146.1	2 290	10.1	51.7	82.3	42.7	90.1	61.16	1 571	2 680	51.18	51.1	423.5
Pinellas Park	0.2	16.0	14.4	7.0	NA	8.7	213	0.0	61.9	83.1	53.7	90.1	53.10	545	3 686	59.82	66.1	NA
Plantation	0.0	34.8	0.0	16.6	0.0	76.0	1 360	0.0	66.2	82.3	56.6	90.1	60.83	254	3 933	70.47	119.6	NA
Pompano Beach	0.0	23.2	16.2	10.5	1.0	40.0	600	44.1	66.8	82.1	57.1	90.9	61.38	243	3 957	70.47	119.6	555.0
Riviera Beach	0.0	20.2	11.0	8.0	0.0	31.7	1 141	0.0	65.2	82.0	55.9	89.7	59.72	262	3 769	70.47	119.6	NA
St. Petersburg	0.0	19.1	13.8	14.3	5.6	185.7	775	0.0	61.9	83.1	53.7	90.1	53.10	545	3 686	59.82	66.1	435.8
Sarasota	0.0	20.2	16.7	17.3	2.8	41.9	813	33.6	60.9	81.2	50.0	90.6	55.67	616	3 162	70.47	119.6	NA
Sunrise	0.0	13.5	7.0	5.1	0.0	105.9	2 008	0.0	66.2	82.3	56.6	90.1	60.83	254	3 933	70.47	119.6	NA
Tallahassee	0.0	13.2	24.2	8.9	1.5	380.8	3 188	30.0	51.6	81.2	39.9	90.9	64.59	1 652	2 492	63.37	78.1	578.5
Tamarac	0.0	30.4	7.8	5.2	0.0	13.0	377	0.0	66.2	82.3	56.6	90.1	60.83	254	3 933	70.47	119.6	NA
Tampa	NA	13.7	35.9	8.2	2.5	571.6	2 059	23.0	59.8	82.2	49.5	90.0	46.73	739	3 324	58.19	38.9	416.5
Titusville	0.5	16.3	10.1	1.8	2.6	15.0	358	0.0	60.2	81.5	48.6	92.0	56.69	712	3 184	70.47	119.6	NA
West Palm Beach	0.0	15.9	8.8	28.1	0.3	48.5	707	0.0	65.2	82.0	55.9	89.7	59.72	262	3 769	70.47	119.6	555.0
GEORGIA	NA	NA	NA	NA	NA	NA	NA	NA	NA	NA	NA	NA	NA	NA	NA	46.07	53.2	NA
Albany	0.0	17.1	19.9	8.4	5.2	8.7	102	60.0	48.7	81.4	36.8	92.2	49.76	2 062	2 396	37.45	29.9	303.7
Athens	0.9	19.2	21.8	11.8	6.0	19.6	455	97.6	42.4	79.2	32.6	89.3	50.15	2 965	1 680	46.00	56.9	NA
Atlanta	0.1	9.2	18.3	5.8	3.7	1 019.2	2 416	13.4	41.9	78.6	32.6	87.9	48.61	3 021	1 670	46.00	56.9	612.7
Augusta	0.0	13.4	14.7	1.9	1.2	15.8	348	54.6	45.0	80.6	33.2	91.4	43.07	2 568	1 935	46.00	56.9	NA
Columbus	10.1	14.1	10.6	2.8	4.8	82.6	459	59.2	46.2	81.0	35.4	91.1	51.09	2 356	2 152	46.00	56.9	612.7
East Point	0.0	19.9	14.1	2.4	4.2	12.9	344	75.9	41.9	78.6	32.6	87.9	48.61	3 021	1 670	44.57	38.9	NA
Macon	0.0	21.6	10.4	11.3	7.6	27.0	228	12.8	46.6	81.4	35.5	92.2	44.86	2 279	2 217	46.00	47.9	612.7
Marietta	0.0	17.8	21.2	7.0	0.5	14.5	338	55.8	41.9	78.6	32.6	87.9	48.61	3 021	1 670	43.17	62.1	NA
Rome	0.4	14.8	16.5	1.5	8.0	14.5	471	80.7	41.7	78.3	30.8	89.7	54.21	3 122	1 601	46.00	56.9	NA
Savannah	0.0	16.1	16.2	7.5	7.7	42.7	291	61.6	49.2	81.2	37.9	90.8	49.70	1 921	2 290	64.75	39.4	599.6
Valdosta	0.0	15.7	22.0	6.3	1.2	7.8	211	81.1	51.3	80.9	39.0	91.8	51.76	1 672	2 430	46.00	56.9	NA
Warner Robins	1.9	19.0	19.9	6.9	6.8	9.0	198	82.9	46.6	81.4	35.5	92.2	44.86	2 279	2 217	NA	NA	NA
HAWAII	NA	NA	NA	NA	NA	NA	NA	NA	NA	NA	NA	NA	NA	NA	NA	77.93	45.6	NA
Aiea (CDP)	NA	NA	NA	NA	NA	NA	NA	NA	72.6	80.1	65.3	87.1	23.47	0	4 389	75.19	45.4	NA
Hilo (CDP)	NA	NA	NA	NA	NA	NA	NA	NA	71.4	75.4	63.2	82.8	128.15	0	3 134	98.37	40.5	NA
Honolulu (CDP)	NA	NA	NA	NA	NA	NA	NA	NA	72.6	80.1	65.3	87.1	23.47	0	4 389	75.19	45.4	627.2
Kailua (CDP)	NA	NA	NA	NA	NA	NA	NA	NA	71.1	76.6	65.1	81.9	74.01	0	3 329	75.19	45.4	627.2
Kaneohe (CDP)	NA	NA	NA	NA	NA	NA	NA	NA	71.1	76.6	65.1	81.9	74.01	0	3 329	75.19	45.4	NA
Pearl City (CDP)	NA	NA	NA	NA	NA	NA	NA	NA	72.6	80.1	65.3	87.1	23.47	0	4 389	75.19	45.4	627.2
Waipahu (CDP)	NA	NA	NA	NA	NA	NA	NA	NA	72.6	80.1	65.3	87.1	23.47	0	4 389	75.19	45.4	NA
IDAHO	NA	NA	NA	NA	NA	NA	NA	NA	NA	NA	NA	NA	NA	NA	NA	31.14	68.7	NA
Boise City	NA	13.4	26.7	9.9	3.1	23.2	214	0.0	29.9	74.6	22.6	90.6	11.71	5 802	742	31.36	58.9	281.7
Idaho Falls	3.4	17.6	17.2	8.5	0.0	44.8	1 045	88.2	18.7	68.9	10.3	86.4	9.77	7 995	288	27.60	120.1	255.0
Lewiston	0.0	10.7	36.3	4.8	4.2	3.7	134	69.9	32.1	74.1	25.6	89.5	12.78	5 436	734	28.14	106.0	NA
Nampa	0.0	13.8	28.7	4.7	2.7	4.6	161	3.0	29.9	74.6	22.6	90.6	11.71	5 802	742	31.36	58.9	NA
Pocatello	0.0	14.3	18.7	6.4	3.3	1.7	39	23.3	23.8	71.2	15.1	88.6	10.86	7 123	445	31.36	58.9	281.7
Twin Falls	0.0	16.7	23.2	4.6	0.0	0.5	18	0.4	27.6	73.6	19.0	91.3	10.12	6 234	658	31.36	58.9	NA
ILLINOIS	NA	NA	NA	NA	NA	NA	NA	NA	NA	NA	NA	NA	NA	NA	NA	57.90	72.8	NA
Addison village	0.0	18.2	21.0	0.5	0.0	62.8	2 047	2.9	21.4	73.0	13.6	83.3	33.34	6 455	740	59.60	90.4	NA
Alton	0.5	13.2	15.4	6.8	0.0	61.5	1 865	0.0	27.7	78.7	19.0	88.7	36.32	5 129	1 410	49.63	56.0	NA
Arlington Heights village	1.2	20.6	0.0	0.0	3.8	46.2	658	4.5	21.4	73.0	13.6	83.3	33.34	6 455	740	59.60	90.4	618.3
Aurora	0.0	21.3	4.4	3.3	2.9	19.4	227	21.8	20.1	73.0	11.3	84.2	35.62	6 618	733	59.60	90.4	618.3
Belleville	0.0	16.3	18.8	5.6	0.0	8.9	208	0.0	29.8	77.7	20.8	89.1	36.75	4 818	1 320	51.89	37.5	NA
Berwyn	0.0	26.9	18.2	5.7	0.0	4.7	103	11.0	22.6	75.0	15.3	84.3	35.51	6 177	955	62.36	99.2	NA
Bloomington	3.5	13.8	10.5	9.8	0.0	34.0	734	6.3	24.6	76.1	15.9	87.4	36.79	5 640	1 084	52.69	39.7	NA
Bolingbrook village	0.3	15.2	4.5	0.5	0.0	88.0	2 252	5.5	20.1	73.0	11.3	84.2	35.62	6 618	733	62.25	98.8	NA
Burbank	0.0	34.6	0.0	0.0	0.0	4.0	141	0.0	22.6	75.0	15.3	84.3	35.51	6 177	955	59.60	90.4	NA
Calumet City	0.0	14.1	4.1	0.0	0.0	19.5	489	35.3	21.4	73.4	13.1	83.9	35.24	6 483	791	59.60	90.4	NA
Carbondale	1.5	9.5	10.6	0.8	0.0	41.8	1 728	7.3	31.7	78.1	22.1	89.7	42.59	4 563	1 395	59.51	39.6	NA
Champaign	56.7	8.4	1.7	3.3	0.8	9.7	164	0.0	24.7	75.2	17.0	85.5	37.04	5 758	1 019	52.81	35.9	391.2
Chicago	2.5	23.9	7.1	0.6	4.5	1 901.4	632	8.3	21.4	73.0	13.6	83.3	33.34	6 455	740	56.84	83.3	645.0
Chicago Heights	0.6	11.8	13.2	0.0	0.0	28.6	806	0.0	21.4	73.4	13.1	83.9	35.24	6 483	791	62.06	87.9	NA
Cicero town	1.1	24.0	3.3	0.0	0.0	6.4	104	20.3	22.6	75.0	15.3	84.3	35.51	6 177	955	59.60	90.4	618.3
Danville	0.9	16.3	8.4	4.4	7.2	23.8	648	0.0	25.7	75.2	16.8	86.9	38.54	5 599	1 009	51.36	36.1	NA
Decatur	0.0	13.9	4.6	0.5	4.1	97.5	1 079	25.4	25.8	76.6	17.1	88.0	39.12	5 453	1 175	51.36	36.1	380.4
De Kalb	0.0	19.2	10.9	0.0	0.0	7.4	235	12.3	19.2	73.4	10.6	84.9	36.29	6 703	767	62.67	89.8	NA
Des Plaines	0.7	24.0	9.9	0.0	0.0	27.6	492	0.0	21.4	73.0	13.6	83.3	33.34	6 455	740	59.60	90.4	618.3

1. Based on resident population estimated as of July 1, 1986. 2. Represents normal values based on the 30-year period, 1951–1980 (see text). 3. Average daily minimum. 4. Average daily maximum. 5. For definition, see text. 6. As of January 1; based on consumption of 750 kWh. 7. Based on billing demand of 30 kW and consumption of 6,000 kWh.

MSA/ CMSA Code[1]	State/ Place code	City	Land area,[2] 1990 (Sq. Km.)	Population: 1990: Total persons	Population: 1990: Rank	Population: 1990: Per sq. km.	Population: 1980	Population: Change 1980–1990: Number	Population: Change 1980–1990: Per-cent	Population characteristics, 1990: Percent: Race: White	Race: Black	Race: Am. Indian, Eskimo, Aleut	Race: Asian & Pacific Islander	Race: Other race	His-panic[3]	65 Years and over
			1	2	3	4	5	6	7	8	9	10	11	12	13	14
		ILLINOIS—Con.														
1602	17 1540	Downers Grove village	35.3	46 858	527	1 327	42 691	4 167	9.8	93.19	1.73	0.09	4.21	0.78	2.43	12.2
7040	17 1660	East St. Louis	36.4	40 944	610	1 125	55 200	-14 256	-25.8	1.62	98.10	0.12	0.06	0.10	0.39	10.8
1602	17 1720	Elgin	56.8	77 010	276	1 356	63 668	13 342	21.0	77.80	7.31	0.22	3.47	11.20	18.93	10.5
1602	17 1735	Elk Grove Village village	27.8	33 429	758	1 202	28 679	4 750	16.6	91.50	0.79	0.10	6.84	0.77	3.57	7.2
1602	17 1770	Elmhurst	26.3	42 029	593	1 598	44 276	-2 247	-5.1	95.90	0.42	0.08	3.04	0.56	2.73	14.3
1602	17 1845	Evanston	20.1	73 233	297	3 643	73 706	-473	-0.6	70.57	22.87	0.18	4.83	1.55	3.67	12.4
...	17 2070	Freeport	26.7	25 840	911	968	26 266	-426	-1.6	87.06	11.63	0.15	0.89	0.27	0.79	18.4
...	17 2100	Galesburg	43.7	33 530	754	767	35 305	-1 775	-5.0	88.59	8.37	0.17	0.87	2.00	3.85	18.0
1602	17 2225	Glenview village	31.0	37 093	684	1 197	32 060	5 033	15.7	91.00	0.77	0.15	7.42	0.66	2.42	12.8
7040	17 2305	Granite City	32.4	32 862	770	1 014	36 815	-3 953	-10.7	98.41	0.21	0.35	0.54	0.49	1.80	15.3
1602	17 2445	Hanover Park village	15.7	32 895	768	2 095	28 719	4 176	14.5	85.46	3.61	0.23	7.40	3.30	10.99	3.0
1602	17 2490	Harvey	16.0	29 771	831	1 861	35 810	-6 039	-16.9	15.08	79.99	0.25	0.27	4.41	6.49	8.3
1602	17 2595	Highland Park	31.2	30 575	821	980	30 599	-24	-0.1	93.70	2.57	0.06	2.36	1.30	4.70	12.4
1602	17 2647	Hoffman Estates village	48.4	46 561	530	962	37 272	9 289	24.9	87.21	2.87	0.19	8.00	1.73	5.46	4.3
1602	17 2865	Joliet	72.0	76 836	277	1 067	77 956	-1 120	-1.4	69.23	21.60	0.19	0.97	8.01	12.68	14.5
3740	17 2915	Kankakee	26.5	27 575	876	1 041	29 633	-2 058	-6.9	62.04	36.11	0.16	0.48	1.21	2.44	15.9
1602	17 3130	Lansing village	17.0	28 086	866	1 652	29 039	-953	-3.3	95.75	2.96	0.07	0.44	0.78	2.77	14.8
1602	17 3315	Lombard village	24.1	39 408	639	1 635	36 879	2 529	6.9	93.43	1.32	0.12	4.44	0.68	2.77	12.7
1602	17 3635	Maywood village	7.0	27 139	885	3 877	27 998	-859	-3.1	12.00	83.77	0.09	0.50	3.64	6.61	8.6
1960	17 3805	Moline	38.9	43 202	575	1 111	46 407	-3 205	-6.9	94.11	2.00	0.22	0.85	2.82	6.80	16.0
1602	17 3930	Mount Prospect village	26.7	53 170	454	1 991	52 634	536	1.0	90.19	1.14	0.14	6.43	2.11	6.42	11.9
1602	17 3990	Naperville	72.4	85 351	243	1 179	42 601	42 750	100.3	92.56	2.10	0.09	4.84	0.41	1.79	5.6
1602	17 4135	Niles village	15.1	28 284	858	1 873	30 363	-2 079	-6.8	91.61	0.43	0.08	7.03	0.86	3.59	24.6
1040	17 4160	Normal town	31.5	40 023	630	1 271	35 672	4 351	12.2	92.37	4.95	0.14	1.95	0.58	1.48	6.3
1602	17 4190	Northbrook village	32.7	32 308	778	988	30 778	1 530	5.0	93.03	0.21	0.05	6.43	0.27	1.58	14.6
1602	17 4195	North Chicago	19.2	34 978	718	1 822	38 774	-3 796	-9.8	56.67	34.43	0.53	3.63	4.74	9.19	5.2
1602	17 4270	Oak Forest	14.0	26 203	902	1 872	25 040	1 163	4.6	97.15	0.60	0.16	1.48	0.62	2.47	7.3
1602	17 4290	Oak Lawn village	21.7	56 182	417	2 589	60 590	-4 408	-7.3	98.25	0.12	0.08	1.09	0.46	2.35	20.2
1602	17 4295	Oak Park village	12.2	53 648	446	4 397	54 887	-1 239	-2.3	77.01	18.27	0.14	3.33	1.25	3.57	11.5
1602	17 4465	Palatine village	25.5	39 253	643	1 539	32 176	7 077	22.0	94.25	0.94	0.11	3.25	1.46	3.59	8.9
1602	17 4535	Park Forest village	12.8	24 656	930	1 926	26 222	-1 566	-6.0	73.00	24.63	0.17	1.13	1.07	3.12	10.6
1602	17 4540	Park Ridge	17.8	36 175	698	2 032	38 704	-2 529	-6.5	97.43	0.13	0.06	2.19	0.19	1.31	19.0
6120	17 4585	Pekin	28.3	32 254	780	1 140	33 967	-1 713	-5.0	99.16	0.08	0.24	0.39	0.12	0.60	15.6
6120	17 4590	Peoria	105.9	113 504	156	1 072	124 160	-10 656	-8.6	76.52	20.87	0.18	1.68	0.75	1.60	14.4
...	17 4780	Quincy	32.9	39 681	636	1 206	42 554	-2 873	-6.8	94.91	4.15	0.18	0.51	0.25	0.44	20.2
6880	17 4965	Rockford	116.5	139 426	128	1 197	139 712	-286	-0.2	81.13	14.97	0.26	1.54	2.10	4.19	14.7
1960	17 4970	Rock Island	39.2	40 552	617	1 034	46 821	-6 269	-13.4	80.71	17.22	0.24	0.58	1.24	3.78	17.3
1602	17 5215	Schaumburg village	48.7	68 586	330	1 408	53 355	15 231	28.5	90.60	2.14	0.12	6.49	0.64	2.67	7.3
1602	17 5365	Skokie village	26.0	59 432	395	2 286	60 278	-846	-1.4	81.21	2.21	0.10	15.57	0.91	4.13	20.7
7880	17 5480	Springfield	110.2	105 227	181	955	100 054	5 173	5.2	85.59	13.01	0.16	0.98	0.25	0.83	14.9
1602	17 5745	Tinley Park village	27.1	37 121	682	1 370	26 178	10 943	41.8	96.16	1.62	0.08	1.39	0.74	2.54	8.9
1400	17 5845	Urbana	20.2	36 344	696	1 799	35 978	366	1.0	75.74	11.44	0.15	11.72	0.95	2.75	9.0
1602	17 6075	Waukegan	57.4	69 392	325	1 209	67 653	1 739	2.6	64.32	19.85	0.39	3.06	12.38	23.70	11.0
1602	17 6190	Wheaton	28.7	51 464	474	1 793	43 043	8 421	19.6	92.97	2.53	0.10	3.78	0.62	2.04	9.3
1602	17 6255	Wilmette village	13.9	26 690	896	1 920	28 221	-1 531	-5.4	92.36	0.49	0.04	6.91	0.21	1.68	16.2
...	18 0000	INDIANA	92 903.7	5 544 159	X	60	5 490 212	53 947	1.0	90.56	7.79	0.23	0.68	0.74	1.78	12.6
0400	18 0065	Anderson	98.1	59 459	394	606	64 695	-5 236	-8.1	84.87	14.20	0.27	0.40	0.26	0.63	16.1
1020	18 0195	Bloomington	39.1	60 633	381	1 551	52 044	8 589	16.5	91.16	4.03	0.20	4.04	0.58	1.64	6.9
...	18 0515	Columbus	52.4	31 802	792	607	30 614	1 188	3.9	95.38	2.51	0.17	1.60	0.34	0.86	14.0
1602	18 0680	East Chicago	31.0	33 892	740	1 093	39 786	-5 894	-14.8	38.01	33.57	0.24	0.23	27.95	47.79	13.2
2330	18 0740	Elkhart	44.4	43 627	570	983	41 305	2 322	5.6	83.95	13.95	0.41	0.79	0.90	2.04	13.2
2440	18 0775	Evansville	105.4	126 272	144	1 198	130 496	-4 224	-3.2	89.56	9.53	0.19	0.57	0.16	0.58	17.2
2760	18 0825	Fort Wayne	162.3	173 072	99	1 066	172 391	681	0.4	80.45	16.75	0.32	1.01	1.46	2.70	13.3
1602	18 0905	Gary	130.1	116 646	153	897	151 968	-35 322	-23.2	16.31	80.57	0.15	0.18	2.79	5.74	11.4
1602	18 1040	Hammond	59.4	84 236	249	1 418	93 714	-9 478	-10.1	84.84	9.19	0.24	0.41	5.31	11.80	14.3
1602	18 1080	Highland town	17.6	23 696	941	1 346	25 935	-2 239	-8.6	97.76	0.24	0.07	0.87	1.06	3.88	13.1
3480	18 1145	Indianapolis	936.7	731 327	13	781	700 807	30 520	4.4	75.81	22.64	0.22	0.94	0.40	1.05	11.4
3850	18 1255	Kokomo	37.3	44 962	552	1 205	47 808	-2 846	-6.0	89.54	8.90	0.30	0.68	0.58	1.73	13.6
3920	18 1285	Lafayette	34.7	43 764	567	1 261	43 011	753	1.8	95.84	2.14	0.33	1.06	0.63	1.67	13.2
3480	18 1340	Lawrence	52.0	26 763	894	515	25 591	1 172	4.6	86.68	10.72	0.26	1.69	0.65	1.70	9.0
...	18 1470	Marion	32.3	32 618	773	1 010	35 874	-3 256	-9.1	82.62	14.83	0.44	0.66	1.44	3.18	16.6
1602	18 1536	Merrillville town	80.3	27 257	881	339	27 677	-420	-1.5	91.71	5.02	0.12	0.85	2.30	6.90	15.8
...	18 1550	Michigan City	50.8	33 822	746	666	36 850	-3 028	-8.2	75.77	22.54	0.33	0.67	0.68	1.76	13.9
7800	18 1610	Mishawaka	36.0	42 608	584	1 184	40 201	2 407	6.0	97.06	1.59	0.37	0.67	0.32	1.07	14.8
5280	18 1735	Muncie	59.0	71 035	313	1 204	77 216	-6 181	-8.0	89.12	9.54	0.26	0.71	0.38	0.88	13.3
4520	18 1760	New Albany	34.6	36 322	697	1 050	37 103	-781	-2.1	93.17	6.20	0.19	0.26	0.18	0.49	16.5
1602	18 2080	Portage	53.9	29 060	842	539	27 409	1 651	6.0	97.14	0.40	0.20	0.52	1.74	6.38	10.1
...	18 2140	Richmond	47.6	38 705	653	813	41 349	-2 644	-6.4	89.59	9.18	0.28	0.60	0.35	0.68	16.6
7800	18 2375	South Bend	94.3	105 511	180	1 119	109 727	-4 216	-3.8	76.03	20.90	0.37	0.87	1.84	3.36	16.8
8320	18 2505	Terre Haute	71.6	57 483	406	803	61 125	-3 642	-6.0	88.63	9.42	0.42	1.14	0.39	1.31	16.9

1. MSA = Metropolitan Statistical Area. CMSA = Consolidated MSA. 2. Dry land or land partially or temporarily covered by water. 3. Hispanic persons may be of any race.

City	Households, 1990: Number	Households, 1990: Persons per household	Households, 1990: Percent– Female family householder[1]	Households, 1990: Percent– One-person[2]	Births, 1984: Number: Total	Births, 1984: Number: To mothers under 20 yrs. old (Percent)	Births, 1984: Rate[3]	Deaths, 1984: Number: Total	Deaths, 1984: Number: Infant[4]	Deaths, 1984: Rate: Total[3]	Deaths, 1984: Rate: Infant[5]	Hospitals, 1985: Number	Hospitals, 1985: Beds: Number	Hospitals, 1985: Beds: Rate[6]
	15	16	17	18	19	20	21	22	23	24	25	26	27	28
ILLINOIS—Con.														
Downers Grove village	17 660	2.63	6.4	23.8	726	3.0	17.1	357	11	8.4	15.2	1	287	677
East St. Louis	13 057	3.12	39.7	25.4	1 474	33.2	28.7	602	34	11.7	23.1	2	495	1 001
Elgin	26 865	2.79	10.9	24.2	1 342	11.9	19.9	553	20	8.2	14.9	3	1 413	1 960
Elk Grove Village village	12 002	2.77	7.2	20.0	461	2.6	15.1	118	5	3.9	10.8	1	373	1 158
Elmhurst	15 135	2.72	7.6	20.3	548	2.9	12.6	379	3	8.7	5.5	1	408	962
Evanston	27 954	2.31	10.7	34.2	996	5.3	13.8	698	17	9.7	17.1	3	1 035	1 446
Freeport	10 843	2.33	10.9	32.1	408	15.4	15.8	297	3	11.5	7.4	1	183	708
Galesburg	13 272	2.30	11.2	33.3	467	17.6	14.0	400	2	12.0	4.3	2	374	1 175
Glenview village	13 348	2.75	7.0	18.7	453	2.6	13.3	343	4	10.0	8.8	0	0	0
Granite City	13 008	2.50	12.9	26.6	560	18.2	15.7	352	5	9.9	8.9	1	389	1 107
Hanover Park village	10 053	3.27	9.5	12.0	696	6.3	21.5	93	5	2.9	7.2	0	0	0
Harvey	9 052	3.25	28.9	21.6	742	24.1	21.0	307	12	8.7	16.2	1	594	1 679
Highland Park	11 023	2.73	6.1	17.0	362	2.2	11.7	188	3	6.1	8.3	1	263	860
Hoffman Estates village	15 924	2.91	8.0	17.4	716	2.8	17.7	135	1	3.3	1.4	1	223	537
Joliet	26 779	2.71	14.7	27.0	1 453	17.1	19.0	836	30	10.9	20.6	3	923	1 214
Kankakee	10 397	2.52	19.3	32.5	543	24.1	19.1	337	13	11.9	23.9	2	582	2 138
Lansing village	10 881	2.58	8.8	23.8	363	5.8	12.7	207	5	7.2	13.8	0	0	0
Lombard village	15 046	2.60	7.7	24.4	606	2.0	16.1	251	3	6.7	5.0	0	0	0
Maywood village	8 036	3.35	26.6	18.4	516	23.6	18.8	188	9	6.9	17.4	1	497	1 823
Moline	18 265	2.35	10.7	31.0	667	9.3	14.5	423	0	9.2	0.0	2	357	802
Mount Prospect village	20 281	2.62	6.8	22.3	706	4.1	13.2	334	0	6.3	0.0	0	0	0
Naperville	29 101	2.89	5.5	17.6	843	1.5	15.7	315	2	5.9	2.4	1	163	244
Niles village	10 776	2.48	8.1	25.5	226	2.7	7.6	418	4	14.0	17.7	0	0	0
Normal town	11 856	2.64	8.2	21.0	368	5.7	9.8	164	5	4.4	13.6	1	213	579
Northbrook village	11 391	2.78	5.6	15.8	435	2.1	13.7	296	4	9.3	9.2	0	0	0
North Chicago	7 142	3.10	18.3	19.0	303	20.1	7.6	130	6	3.3	19.8	1	1 254	2 903
Oak Forest	8 865	2.95	8.8	17.8	354	5.4	13.1	134	1	5.0	2.8	1	1 054	4 213
Oak Lawn village	21 459	2.59	9.6	26.2	665	4.8	11.3	637	1	10.9	1.5	1	873	1 499
Oak Park village	22 607	2.35	12.0	34.3	867	3.7	15.8	464	7	8.4	8.1	2	749	1 379
Palatine village	15 158	2.58	7.6	24.8	756	4.9	23.5	224	4	6.9	5.3	0	0	0
Park Forest village	9 119	2.65	15.0	23.4	423	5.9	16.0	160	10	6.1	23.6	0	0	0
Park Ridge	13 466	2.63	8.2	21.0	355	0.8	9.4	360	1	9.6	2.8	2	735	1 964
Pekin	13 078	2.43	10.4	28.4	513	15.2	15.6	347	9	10.6	17.5	1	231	738
Peoria	44 976	2.42	14.7	31.6	1 931	18.6	16.5	1 146	21	9.8	10.9	4	1 788	1 621
Quincy	16 086	2.33	11.1	33.4	626	13.9	15.1	616	10	14.9	16.0	2	472	1 192
Rockford	54 839	2.47	13.4	28.6	2 294	15.7	16.8	1 360	23	10.0	10.0	4	1 269	935
Rock Island	16 239	2.37	13.8	32.6	695	18.3	15.3	493	5	10.8	7.2	1	265	606
Schaumburg village	27 589	2.48	7.8	28.4	932	2.9	16.3	267	10	4.7	10.7	0	0	0
Skokie village	22 708	2.58	8.5	22.2	554	1.6	9.3	597	6	10.0	10.8	2	321	540
Springfield	45 006	2.29	12.7	35.0	1 817	13.0	17.9	1 213	27	11.9	14.9	4	1 594	1 589
Tinley Park village	12 678	2.84	7.9	20.2	547	4.9	18.9	184	2	6.4	3.7	1	290	1 021
Urbana	13 210	2.20	8.3	35.4	560	8.8	16.4	232	5	6.8	8.9	2	505	1 412
Waukegan	24 545	2.75	13.3	25.7	1 418	16.1	20.2	550	21	7.8	14.8	2	640	859
Wheaton	17 770	2.74	7.2	20.6	755	2.9	16.4	306	7	6.7	9.3	1	91	191
Wilmette village	9 720	2.71	7.4	18.6	291	0.3	10.7	233	1	8.6	3.4	0	0	0
INDIANA	2 065 355	2.61	10.5	24.1	80 084	14.1	14.6	47 449	890	8.6	11.1	137	29 839	542
Anderson	24 311	2.36	14.2	30.8	828	20.2	13.4	688	19	11.1	22.9	2	578	947
Bloomington	20 983	2.19	8.5	35.5	688	12.9	13.2	322	4	6.2	5.8	1	257	490
Columbus	12 850	2.42	11.1	27.7	482	14.5	15.7	295	4	9.6	8.3	2	224	725
East Chicago	12 122	2.78	25.8	27.4	617	14.6	16.6	358	9	9.6	14.6	1	409	1 107
Elkhart	17 519	2.45	14.0	29.7	866	20.7	20.1	454	7	10.5	8.1	1	354	801
Evansville	52 948	2.30	12.8	32.9	1 954	14.8	15.0	1 678	21	12.9	10.7	5	2 024	1 563
Fort Wayne	69 627	2.43	13.8	31.0	3 166	14.6	19.1	1 669	41	10.1	13.0	5	2 407	1 392
Gary	40 968	2.83	29.1	25.6	2 574	22.3	18.0	1 341	37	9.4	14.4	2	968	708
Hammond	32 146	2.61	14.4	27.7	1 224	14.0	13.7	849	20	9.5	16.3	1	487	564
Highland town	8 728	2.71	8.6	20.1	296	7.1	12.1	170	3	6.9	10.1	0	0	0
Indianapolis	291 946	2.46	14.1	29.4	12 812	16.6	18.0	6 390	170	9.0	13.3	14	5 269	732
Kokomo	18 664	2.37	13.9	31.0	843	15.7	18.6	553	9	12.2	10.7	2	413	906
Lafayette	18 074	2.37	9.6	31.1	848	10.8	19.2	505	11	11.5	13.0	2	641	1 449
Lawrence	10 612	2.47	12.0	25.6	72	12.5	2.8	40	1	1.5	13.9	0	0	0
Marion	12 693	2.42	15.0	30.1	527	23.5	14.5	470	8	13.0	15.2	2	1 052	2 938
Merrillville town	10 006	2.69	9.1	21.2	328	7.9	12.1	250	6	9.2	18.3	0	0	0
Michigan City	12 562	2.51	15.9	29.3	585	16.1	16.2	386	4	10.7	6.8	3	381	1 070
Mishawaka	18 001	2.33	11.7	33.3	602	13.8	14.6	419	8	10.2	13.3	1	117	283
Muncie	27 188	2.34	12.7	31.0	969	19.7	13.1	715	18	9.6	18.6	1	622	857
New Albany	14 691	2.41	16.0	28.3	566	15.9	14.9	412	3	10.9	5.3	1	222	596
Portage	10 520	2.74	10.8	19.9	404	12.1	14.0	189	5	6.6	12.4	0	0	0
Richmond	15 579	2.38	14.3	30.2	598	19.9	15.0	471	9	11.8	15.1	2	925	2 370
South Bend	42 260	2.45	14.9	30.7	1 862	16.5	17.4	1 261	24	11.8	12.9	4	1 148	1 071
Terre Haute	21 488	2.32	13.4	33.5	891	18.1	15.2	814	9	13.9	10.1	3	674	1 164

1. No spouse present. 2. Householder living alone. 3. Per 1,000 resident population estimated as of July 1 of the year shown. 4. Deaths of infants under 1 year old. 5. Deaths of infants under 1 year old per 1,000 live births. 6. Per 100,000 resident population estimated as of July 1, 1986.

City	Serious crimes known to police, 1985: Number: Total	Serious crimes known to police, 1985: Number: Violent[1]	Serious crimes known to police, 1985: Rate[2]	Police officers, 1985: Number	Police officers, 1985: Rate[3]	Educational attainment,[4] 1980: Percent completing 12 years or more	Educational attainment,[4] 1980: Percent completing 16 years or more	Money income: Per capita[5]: 1985: Total (Dollars)	Money income: Per capita[5]: 1985: Percent of State average	Money income: Per capita[5]: 1979: Current dollars	Money income: Per capita[5]: 1979: Constant (1985) dollars	Money income: Percent below poverty level, 1979: Persons	Money income: Percent below poverty level, 1979: Families	Housing, 1990: Total units	Housing, 1990: Percent change, 1980–1990	Housing, 1990: Vacant units for sale or rent[6]
	29	30	31	32	33	34	35	36	37	38	39	40	41	42	43	44
ILLINOIS—Con.																
Downers Grove village	1 559	53	3 616	57	13.2	85.4	32.6	16 160	143.0	10 954	16 234	2.5	1.9	18 166	12.6	386
East St. Louis	NA	NA	NA	78	14.5	46.3	6.7	5 381	47.6	3 681	5 455	43.3	38.9	15 622	-21.0	1 506
Elgin	NA	NA	NA	95	14.6	69.1	16.2	11 169	98.8	8 120	12 034	7.6	5.3	27 936	10.9	807
Elk Grove Village village	NA	NA	NA	76	25.5	84.3	22.6	14 207	125.7	9 721	14 407	1.7	1.2	12 416	21.3	378
Elmhurst	NA	NA	NA	60	13.5	80.9	28.3	15 395	136.2	10 340	15 324	3.0	1.3	15 486	3.1	252
Evanston	NA	NA	NA	150	20.4	82.6	46.2	15 458	136.8	11 028	16 343	7.1	3.8	29 164	-0.4	1 001
Freeport	NA	NA	NA	42	15.9	66.8	12.7	10 772	95.3	7 517	11 140	7.9	5.3	11 722	5.1	687
Galesburg	NA	NA	NA	47	13.7	68.4	11.8	10 313	91.2	7 462	11 059	9.4	7.5	14 322	-1.3	754
Glenview village	750	10	2 235	56	16.7	90.3	39.7	21 429	189.6	13 704	20 309	1.8	1.6	13 763	20.1	306
Granite City	NA	NA	NA	50	13.8	57.6	8.5	10 019	88.6	7 189	10 654	10.7	8.4	13 886	-1.9	657
Hanover Park village	NA	NA	NA	36	11.7	81.9	18.6	11 014	97.5	8 178	12 120	3.6	2.9	10 405	10.1	314
Harvey	NA	NA	NA	64	17.8	56.1	5.4	7 615	67.4	5 946	8 812	18.2	16.7	10 286	-11.3	982
Highland Park	NA	NA	NA	54	17.5	90.2	49.4	26 207	231.9	17 475	25 898	2.1	1.5	11 436	7.7	260
Hoffman Estates village	NA	NA	NA	57	14.6	88.5	29.4	13 882	122.8	9 600	14 227	2.8	2.6	16 608	20.4	626
Joliet	NA	NA	NA	160	20.7	62.6	12.8	10 412	92.1	7 629	11 306	12.0	9.1	29 043	-2.7	1 650
Kankakee	3 259	438	11 036	58	19.6	56.3	12.3	9 235	81.7	6 688	9 912	18.0	14.7	11 380	-3.4	582
Lansing village	NA	NA	NA	45	15.7	72.5	12.7	11 998	106.2	9 305	13 790	2.9	2.0	11 184	4.6	261
Lombard village	NA	NA	NA	52	13.6	81.9	23.8	14 221	125.8	9 775	14 487	2.5	1.5	15 848	15.2	716
Maywood village	NA	NA	NA	52	18.6	58.4	8.2	8 776	77.6	6 496	9 627	13.5	11.0	8 547	-2.7	405
Moline	NA	NA	NA	64	13.7	73.3	14.8	11 769	104.1	9 097	13 482	6.8	4.6	19 235	3.2	709
Mount Prospect village	NA	NA	NA	62	11.7	82.6	24.3	15 229	134.7	10 767	15 957	2.6	2.2	20 949	6.9	581
Naperville	NA	NA	NA	74	16.1	92.3	46.4	16 598	146.9	11 151	16 526	1.9	1.5	30 906	54.5	1 617
Niles village	849	37	2 809	50	16.5	69.2	15.1	13 545	119.8	9 598	14 224	3.2	2.2	11 052	2.9	231
Normal town	NA	NA	NA	42	11.7	88.4	39.4	9 673	85.6	6 709	9 943	17.2	3.6	12 300	15.7	325
Northbrook village	1 029	13	3 253	54	17.1	91.0	45.7	23 643	209.2	15 565	23 067	2.0	1.5	11 673	14.9	200
North Chicago	NA	NA	NA	43	10.4	69.4	9.7	8 488	75.1	5 606	8 308	9.4	7.5	7 925	5.8	545
Oak Forest	NA	NA	NA	28	10.4	75.6	13.9	11 562	102.3	8 637	12 800	2.4	2.2	9 058	11.2	172
Oak Lawn village	NA	NA	NA	95	15.9	70.1	13.7	13 185	116.7	9 405	13 938	3.3	2.6	21 835	2.9	282
Oak Park village	NA	NA	NA	125	22.7	84.0	39.4	14 194	125.6	10 110	14 983	5.1	2.8	23 571	0.5	711
Palatine village	NA	NA	NA	52	15.5	87.4	32.6	15 504	137.2	10 742	15 920	2.0	1.6	15 851	30.0	605
Park Forest village	NA	NA	NA	34	12.8	86.4	27.5	11 247	99.5	8 598	12 742	4.8	3.4	9 442	2.1	282
Park Ridge	NA	NA	NA	49	12.8	84.1	30.4	17 555	155.3	12 141	17 993	1.9	1.3	13 821	2.0	230
Pekin	NA	NA	NA	50	14.8	65.8	10.6	10 008	88.6	7 858	11 646	8.5	7.1	13 776	-0.1	436
Peoria	8 684	1 109	7 399	194	16.5	69.6	19.4	11 140	98.6	8 422	12 481	12.3	9.4	48 260	-5.4	2 445
Quincy	NA	NA	NA	70	16.4	62.5	11.3	9 359	82.8	6 829	10 121	11.9	9.0	17 530	-2.6	1 080
Rockford	12 669	1 130	9 259	243	17.8	66.8	14.9	10 704	94.7	7 850	11 634	10.3	7.9	58 146	6.0	2 189
Rock Island	NA	NA	NA	81	17.2	69.1	13.8	10 419	92.2	7 879	11 677	12.3	8.9	17 901	-2.5	1 076
Schaumburg village	2 596	72	4 605	100	17.7	86.4	27.3	14 410	127.5	10 064	14 915	2.6	1.9	29 499	29.0	1 606
Skokie village	NA	NA	NA	107	17.8	81.6	28.6	16 593	146.8	12 081	17 904	2.5	1.9	23 170	1.6	341
Springfield	NA	NA	NA	198	19.5	71.9	20.8	11 642	103.0	8 227	12 192	10.5	7.6	48 534	9.3	2 692
Tinley Park village	NA	NA	NA	32	11.7	73.8	12.7	10 983	97.2	8 061	11 946	3.9	2.7	13 222	34.8	495
Urbana	NA	NA	NA	42	11.7	84.5	49.6	9 409	83.3	6 717	9 955	17.7	8.1	14 006	8.9	649
Waukegan	NA	NA	NA	105	15.0	65.8	13.9	10 509	93.0	7 649	11 336	9.5	7.2	25 800	0.5	972
Wheaton	1 113	14	2 492	50	11.2	88.3	40.4	15 742	139.3	10 672	15 816	3.3	1.9	18 630	18.2	767
Wilmette village	881	6	3 163	43	15.4	92.8	54.0	26 117	231.1	16 520	24 483	2.8	2.0	10 046	0.6	235
INDIANA	215 234	17 014	3 914	NA	NA	66.4	12.5	9 978	100.0	7 141	10 583	9.7	7.3	2 246 046	6.9	97 102
Anderson	2 656	116	4 265	NA	NA	61.5	10.7	10 173	102.0	6 843	10 141	12.7	10.0	26 362	-0.9	1 175
Bloomington	2 227	220	4 190	55	10.3	82.3	47.8	8 513	85.3	5 804	8 602	23.3	11.1	22 025	19.6	820
Columbus	2 162	44	6 985	62	20.0	69.7	18.9	12 005	120.3	8 443	12 513	10.6	8.1	13 458	8.6	455
East Chicago	2 854	190	7 406	98	25.4	44.9	5.5	7 905	79.2	6 499	9 632	16.8	15.9	13 484	-10.8	957
Elkhart	3 252	85	7 915	96	23.4	65.2	13.7	10 194	102.2	7 196	10 664	12.0	9.2	19 147	7.7	1 316
Evansville	6 846	684	5 252	231	17.7	61.1	11.2	10 048	100.7	7 040	10 433	12.2	8.5	58 188	6.8	3 865
Fort Wayne	12 226	808	7 391	308	18.6	68.7	13.3	10 276	103.0	7 049	10 447	11.0	8.5	77 166	8.5	5 408
Gary	8 984	1 456	6 278	273	19.1	55.0	7.6	7 488	75.0	6 170	9 144	20.4	18.0	47 082	-15.6	4 009
Hammond	5 229	714	5 700	187	20.4	58.9	7.0	9 845	98.7	7 799	11 558	9.3	6.9	33 924	-6.4	1 316
Highland town	1 037	30	4 113	33	13.1	79.0	14.4	11 945	119.7	9 425	13 968	2.9	2.3	8 892	2.9	101
Indianapolis	29 651	4 622	6 287	951	20.2	66.7	16.4	10 836	108.6	7 585	11 241	11.5	8.8	319 980	11.5	20 085
Kokomo	2 410	56	5 224	99	21.5	62.2	9.8	10 714	107.4	7 244	10 736	11.3	9.1	20 340	4.0	1 179
Lafayette	2 310	70	5 250	79	18.0	70.5	16.0	10 272	102.9	7 307	10 829	9.0	5.9	19 259	4.9	908
Lawrence	481	55	1 887	34	13.3	74.7	13.1	10 850	108.7	7 718	11 438	7.4	6.1	11 621	13.3	873
Marion	1 774	77	5 102	63	18.1	57.7	8.8	9 265	92.9	6 474	9 594	13.6	10.4	14 000	-1.9	764
Merrillville town	983	63	3 564	34	12.3	72.3	13.4	11 514	115.4	9 130	13 531	3.2	2.5	10 322	10.0	270
Michigan City	2 435	121	6 638	83	22.6	56.9	8.9	8 852	88.7	6 605	9 789	12.0	8.9	13 995	2.4	752
Mishawaka	2 585	99	6 308	71	17.3	63.4	10.2	10 037	100.6	7 035	10 426	9.3	7.3	19 028	9.1	755
Muncie	4 181	219	5 526	124	16.4	62.0	15.6	8 979	90.0	6 225	9 225	17.7	12.5	29 828	1.3	1 462
New Albany	2 553	173	6 728	58	15.3	58.5	10.0	9 499	95.2	6 615	9 803	11.7	9.5	15 593	4.9	682
Portage	1 075	36	3 779	36	12.7	68.5	6.6	10 139	101.6	8 295	12 293	5.1	4.6	10 864	11.6	245
Richmond	1 744	56	4 271	75	18.4	60.5	11.2	9 126	91.5	6 373	9 445	14.2	10.7	16 942	0.3	906
South Bend	9 593	666	8 955	230	21.5	65.6	14.7	10 154	101.8	7 140	10 581	12.1	8.5	45 757	2.1	2 641
Terre Haute	3 413	132	5 649	121	20.0	63.2	14.3	8 643	86.6	6 067	8 991	13.7	9.5	24 077	-2.1	1 496

1. Includes murder and nonnegligent manslaughter, forcible rape, robbery, and aggravated assault. 2. Per 100,000 resident population estimated for 1985 by the FBI. 3. Per 10,000 resident population estimated for 1985 by the FBI. 4. Persons 25 years old or older. 5. Based on the resident population estimated as of July 1, 1988 for 1987 data and enumerated as of April 1, 1980 for 1979 data. 6. Also includes units rented or sold, but not occupied.

City	Housing, 1990 (cont'd)					Construction authorized by building permits, 1990				Civilian labor force, 1990			
	Occupied units					New private housing units						Unemployment	
			Owner-occupied										
	Total	Percent with more than 1 person per room	Percent of total	Median value[1] (Dollars)	Median rent[2] (Dollars)	Number	Value ($1,000)	Percent single family	Non-residential, value ($1,000)	Total	Percent change, 1989–1990	Total	Rate[3]
	45	46	47	48	49	50	51	52	53	54	55	56	57
ILLINOIS—Con.													
Downers Grove village	17 660	1.1	78.5	143 900	520	119	20 364	100.0	55 495	26 217	0.3	1 093	4.2
East St. Louis	13 057	11.1	50.5	26 400	183	1	75	100.0	0	14 321	-1.1	1 845	12.9
Elgin	26 865	7.1	62.3	96 800	434	817	53 844	91.4	46 464	35 986	2.5	2 073	5.8
Elk Grove Village village	12 002	1.6	76.6	137 900	591	97	7 133	36.1	4 594	20 270	0.0	678	3.3
Elmhurst	15 135	1.4	83.6	135 600	561	121	9 842	25.6	6 451	24 333	0.2	904	3.7
Evanston	27 954	2.6	51.1	184 800	584	176	8 625	3.4	50 857	41 986	-0.2	1 750	4.2
Freeport	10 843	1.0	64.9	46 800	230	88	1 677	42.0	1 452	13 466	-1.0	1 241	9.2
Galesburg	13 272	1.0	63.0	37 100	220	11	1 163	100.0	4 119	15 687	0.7	1 079	6.9
Glenview village	13 348	1.1	85.4	235 600	694	65	10 625	64.6	804	19 312	0.0	703	3.6
Granite City	13 008	2.5	68.4	42 700	253	17	1 373	100.0	4 063	16 626	-0.3	1 541	9.3
Hanover Park village	10 053	5.5	79.9	101 900	533	277	20 446	100.0	750	17 895	0.3	881	4.9
Harvey	9 052	11.3	58.8	49 900	357	0	0	NA	3 047	15 763	0.8	1 708	10.8
Highland Park	11 023	1.4	80.4	257 000	629	82	21 597	56.1	1 577	19 803	1.8	509	2.6
Hoffman Estates village	15 924	2.8	73.8	133 800	638	112	9 642	92.9	2 760	27 120	-0.1	799	2.9
Joliet	26 779	5.3	63.1	64 500	331	453	38 819	87.6	26 741	40 127	0.9	4 109	10.2
Kankakee	10 397	4.3	50.7	40 000	257	146	8 412	2.7	1 584	12 679	2.9	1 129	8.9
Lansing village	10 881	1.2	73.0	77 900	458	46	3 599	100.0	340	16 357	0.6	763	4.7
Lombard village	15 046	1.5	73.0	118 000	604	27	2 518	100.0	24 621	24 331	0.2	1 089	4.5
Maywood village	8 036	9.0	62.6	67 900	396	0	0	NA	177	14 227	-0.1	1 463	10.3
Moline	18 265	1.5	64.3	49 600	277	51	7 476	100.0	8 118	22 419	0.8	1 429	6.4
Mount Prospect village	20 281	3.1	69.1	155 100	564	55	6 771	72.7	4 995	33 245	0.0	1 088	3.3
Naperville	29 101	0.7	76.1	176 500	628	931	106 907	64.6	36 030	43 465	-0.4	962	2.2
Niles village	10 776	2.3	75.6	140 700	536	35	2 920	40.0	2 562	16 847	0.0	604	3.6
Normal town	11 856	1.2	55.0	74 000	370	202	10 575	40.6	8 089	23 195	1.9	510	2.2
Northbrook village	11 391	0.5	90.6	271 000	824	58	12 416	93.1	2 292	17 343	-0.2	566	3.3
North Chicago	7 142	8.5	33.0	64 000	422	128	6 919	4.7	5 374	12 087	1.0	989	8.2
Oak Forest	8 865	1.6	78.0	104 300	492	130	13 964	100.0	2 892	13 623	0.3	771	5.7
Oak Lawn village	21 459	1.4	81.9	108 100	487	173	10 359	47.4	4 445	30 883	-0.3	1 550	5.0
Oak Park village	22 607	1.3	53.5	138 700	495	193	16 744	0.5	1 672	31 572	0.3	1 270	4.0
Palatine village	15 158	1.4	69.4	149 600	607	221	18 003	45.7	5 237	21 210	0.5	1 180	5.6
Park Forest village	9 119	1.6	69.7	58 800	397	6	566	100.0	14	14 853	-0.1	698	4.7
Park Ridge	13 466	0.6	87.3	185 700	581	25	5 520	92.0	1 090	20 426	-0.4	598	2.9
Pekin	13 078	1.6	63.7	41 200	219	26	2 094	84.6	1 444	15 309	0.5	1 179	7.7
Peoria	44 976	2.2	56.5	49 200	277	227	23 512	78.4	50 662	54 697	1.2	3 825	7.0
Quincy	16 086	1.6	64.1	41 800	203	105	10 632	77.1	5 969	19 403	0.4	1 209	6.2
Rockford	54 839	2.6	59.6	56 300	291	551	30 396	42.6	22 525	75 041	0.1	6 256	8.3
Rock Island	16 239	1.8	62.0	44 100	233	19	3 475	89.5	1 235	20 258	-0.3	1 202	5.9
Schaumburg village	27 589	1.4	65.2	133 500	675	513	32 640	67.3	38 942	39 182	0.1	1 242	3.2
Skokie village	22 708	2.8	75.3	149 400	575	35	4 110	37.1	7 767	36 207	0.0	1 223	3.4
Springfield	45 006	2.0	58.3	59 200	316	944	48 515	35.8	26 481	61 534	0.2	3 356	5.5
Tinley Park village	12 678	1.1	79.0	115 900	503	299	30 173	71.6	19 702	16 477	-0.1	778	4.7
Urbana	13 210	4.2	39.5	69 000	340	35	2 422	34.3	4 277	21 373	0.7	845	4.0
Waukegan	24 545	8.4	53.6	72 600	428	83	8 139	90.4	6 291	46 323	2.0	2 511	5.4
Wheaton	17 770	1.3	74.5	148 700	590	414	24 358	16.9	14 515	28 643	0.2	891	3.1
Wilmette village	9 720	0.4	85.9	280 800	723	5	1 130	100.0	750	14 437	-0.2	359	2.5
INDIANA	2 065 355	2.2	70.2	53 900	291	25 065	2 038 260	77.4	1 855 379	2 832 000	-1.7	150 000	5.3
Anderson	24 311	1.9	63.8	37 000	253	68	3 757	22.1	5 339	27 151	-1.6	2 095	7.7
Bloomington	20 983	2.8	34.2	76 300	348	353	28 619	72.2	9 351	29 980	-0.7	933	3.1
Columbus	12 850	1.6	61.8	59 900	317	NA	NA	NA	NA	14 921	-4.2	771	5.2
East Chicago	12 122	7.8	45.4	42 600	208	0	0	NA	22 002	14 167	0.5	1 043	7.4
Elkhart	17 519	2.6	55.9	49 200	333	48	2 964	83.3	6 890	27 875	-3.6	2 053	7.4
Evansville	52 948	2.0	59.0	45 500	264	104	6 708	100.0	15 386	66 851	-1.0	3 995	6.0
Fort Wayne	69 627	2.2	59.6	47 800	312	392	23 686	49.5	37 040	98 933	-0.8	5 844	5.9
Gary	40 968	6.8	58.6	31 700	223	11	859	45.5	5 343	53 388	0.8	5 206	9.8
Hammond	32 146	3.7	64.1	45 500	297	16	986	100.0	1 789	38 519	0.4	2 244	5.8
Highland town	8 728	1.6	79.5	72 300	408	14	1 395	85.7	143	NA	NA	NA	NA
Indianapolis	291 946	2.5	56.7	60 800	342	4 039	313 773	61.2	409 120	397 234	-3.3	18 073	4.5
Kokomo	18 664	1.9	62.7	42 400	276	66	5 069	39.4	21 651	21 170	-1.8	1 736	8.2
Lafayette	18 074	1.8	59.4	51 700	317	153	7 774	60.1	10 310	26 409	-1.1	877	3.3
Lawrence	10 612	2.1	62.7	64 400	366	284	27 326	98.6	3 199	14 627	-3.3	621	4.2
Marion	12 693	2.5	59.8	34 500	235	16	1 496	87.5	1 096	14 894	-0.3	1 181	7.9
Merrillville town	10 006	1.8	73.6	62 300	459	103	5 692	35.9	5 995	12 351	0.2	473	3.8
Michigan City	12 562	3.1	59.8	43 700	272	42	2 001	42.9	2 015	16 651	-2.5	1 100	6.6
Mishawaka	18 001	1.6	59.6	46 800	317	441	12 599	15.2	4 608	22 424	-1.0	1 282	5.7
Muncie	27 188	2.1	57.5	34 500	249	97	5 125	25.8	9 748	35 781	-0.2	2 156	6.0
New Albany	14 691	1.9	59.3	48 100	268	266	13 495	49.6	4 073	20 669	-0.6	1 023	4.9
Portage	10 520	2.4	70.7	62 000	338	107	5 273	96.3	2 091	12 733	0.1	631	5.0
Richmond	15 579	1.5	58.8	38 800	235	75	6 157	66.7	1 374	18 125	-3.1	1 501	8.3
South Bend	42 260	2.4	65.9	40 300	325	175	12 880	60.6	16 282	58 622	-0.9	3 643	6.2
Terre Haute	21 488	2.2	62.1	32 300	224	12	863	100.0	9 344	26 984	-0.1	1 412	5.2

1. Specified owner-occupied units. 2. Specified renter-occupied units. 3. Percent of total civilian labor force.

City	Employed,[1] 1980: Total	Employed, 1980: Rate per 1,000 employees: Professional, specialty, and technical	Employed, 1980: Rate per 1,000 employees: Precision production, craft, and operators	Manufactures, 1987: Establishments: Total	Establishments: Percent with 20 or more employees	All employees: Number (1,000)	All employees: Percent change, 1982–1987	All employees: Annual payroll (Mil. dol.)	Production workers: Number (1,000)	Production workers: Work-hours (Millions)	Production workers: Wages: Total (Mil. dol.)	Production workers: Wages: Average per production worker (Dollars)	Value added by manufacture (Mil. dol.)	Value of shipments (Mil. dol.)	New capital expenditures (Mil. dol.)
	58	59	60	61	62	63	64	65	66	67	68	69	70	71	72
ILLINOIS—Con.															
Downers Grove village	22 306	209.5	142.0	105	50.5	6.5	25.0	183.9	3.3	6.4	68.0	20 606	369.0	533.5	18.2
East St. Louis	13 178	138.6	199.7	26	34.6	D	D	D	D	D	D	D	D	D	D
Elgin	30 837	164.6	257.2	176	45.5	7.2	-2.7	181.6	4.4	9.0	90.5	20 568	371.3	684.4	23.7
Elk Grove Village village	15 545	154.7	164.9	545	46.4	23.6	18.6	616.7	15.5	32.5	335.7	21 658	1 389.0	2 652.3	89.3
Elmhurst	22 607	196.9	162.1	94	45.7	3.1	19.2	83.4	1.9	3.8	40.5	21 316	142.7	266.6	7.2
Evanston	39 010	323.5	80.4	90	36.7	3.6	-41.0	89.7	1.6	3.3	30.0	18 750	189.7	307.5	9.1
Freeport	12 785	132.4	301.3	39	48.7	7.3	-6.4	184.1	5.1	10.2	116.7	22 882	458.4	802.0	D
Galesburg	15 287	153.4	218.8	49	44.9	D	D	D	D	D	D	D	D	D	D
Glenview village	15 985	212.5	94.2	63	23.8	6.1	117.9	206.6	1.0	2.0	28.2	28 200	311.0	389.5	D
Granite City	14 420	118.0	251.5	35	42.9	4.8	-9.4	160.3	3.5	7.2	102.3	29 229	406.0	1 116.5	46.9
Hanover Park village	14 185	136.7	239.8	NA	NA	NA	NA	NA	NA	NA	NA	NA	NA	NA	NA
Harvey	13 464	112.4	275.4	39	41.0	2.2	-52.2	59.2	1.4	3.0	33.6	24 000	139.9	395.2	3.9
Highland Park	15 108	270.4	70.3	46	19.6	1.2	0.0	23.6	1.0	2.0	15.8	15 800	54.3	136.4	3.2
Hoffman Estates village	20 173	162.4	167.2	NA	NA	NA	NA	NA	NA	NA	NA	NA	NA	NA	NA
Joliet	31 508	147.5	262.6	105	38.1	8.3	-24.5	266.1	5.6	11.4	169.5	30 268	916.8	2 980.7	88.9
Kankakee	11 886	179.2	225.4	40	57.5	3.1	-22.5	81.5	2.3	4.5	56.0	24 348	224.1	529.2	12.0
Lansing village	14 186	144.6	252.2	30	40.0	1.2	-7.7	29.3	0.8	1.6	14.2	17 750	78.0	134.2	5.6
Lombard village	20 178	170.7	164.3	100	23.0	1.7	54.5	42.0	0.9	1.7	15.9	17 667	71.7	134.5	7.8
Maywood village	12 022	99.0	248.6	31	32.3	0.6	20.0	11.1	0.4	0.8	6.4	16 000	21.9	39.9	0.8
Moline	21 795	150.6	228.5	60	40.0	3.6	-47.8	128.6	1.1	2.2	22.3	20 273	71.1	123.7	D
Mount Prospect village	29 302	160.8	160.5	58	22.4	2.7	8.0	68.7	1.1	2.1	28.2	25 636	275.8	401.6	8.6
Naperville	20 619	233.8	91.4	75	36.0	5.6	-15.2	222.0	1.2	2.5	26.8	22 333	244.5	343.2	D
Niles village	15 896	140.0	197.0	106	48.1	8.9	-19.1	228.7	5.3	10.8	112.6	21 245	474.9	885.2	25.6
Normal town	16 942	213.6	85.5	NA	NA	NA	NA	NA	NA	NA	NA	NA	NA	NA	NA
Northbrook village	14 962	213.5	77.3	155	43.2	6.0	-14.3	170.5	3.4	6.9	66.7	19 618	333.6	626.5	20.2
North Chicago	7 962	106.4	256.6	36	50.0	12.8	16.4	447.6	3.5	7.0	91.2	26 057	1 087.5	1 443.5	D
Oak Forest	11 875	144.8	224.6	13	38.5	0.5	NA	10.3	0.3	0.6	4.8	16 000	13.0	29.4	1.0
Oak Lawn village	28 436	136.1	212.4	30	23.3	0.5	NA	11.6	0.3	0.6	6.4	21 333	36.3	54.7	2.7
Oak Park village	28 508	290.3	98.7	42	28.6	0.6	NA	12.4	0.4	0.7	6.2	15 500	21.7	34.3	0.8
Palatine village	16 671	180.8	121.9	88	29.5	2.8	12.0	70.4	1.7	3.3	29.0	17 059	138.4	252.6	6.4
Park Forest village	13 109	215.1	153.9	NA	NA	NA	NA	NA	NA	NA	NA	NA	NA	NA	NA
Park Ridge	19 222	194.3	123.8	48	4.2	0.8	NA	20.1	0.1	0.2	2.6	26 000	11.1	22.7	0.3
Pekin	14 583	118.4	248.2	19	26.3	0.6	0.0	15.3	0.4	0.8	9.9	24 750	68.3	170.4	D
Peoria	55 103	182.0	183.5	121	44.6	14.0	-31.4	454.0	4.3	8.8	109.9	25 558	427.1	961.0	67.0
Quincy	18 386	141.2	190.1	61	44.3	4.8	D	110.1	3.1	6.1	61.5	19 839	270.2	940.4	D
Rockford	63 988	149.8	279.5	477	39.2	26.6	-1.8	731.7	16.0	31.5	364.0	22 750	1 581.4	2 859.4	D
Rock Island	20 614	142.9	239.6	62	27.4	2.2	-47.6	43.5	1.8	3.3	30.3	16 833	107.4	225.7	3.8
Schaumburg village	28 768	156.8	152.3	206	28.2	9.7	D	305.8	3.5	7.2	68.8	19 657	548.7	891.4	29.4
Skokie village	33 102	205.0	105.6	251	39.4	14.7	9.7	444.7	6.1	12.6	127.9	20 967	669.0	1 197.4	24.2
Springfield	49 112	180.9	110.5	93	32.3	3.4	-24.4	73.6	2.2	4.3	40.6	18 455	173.8	424.1	D
Tinley Park village	12 054	123.8	238.8	22	50.0	1.9	90.0	54.3	1.1	1.7	34.9	31 727	140.9	171.8	3.1
Urbana	17 949	372.0	85.0	26	42.3	1.4	100.0	30.0	0.9	1.7	11.9	13 222	49.3	119.2	D
Waukegan	31 028	154.9	240.3	86	45.3	5.8	-26.6	178.5	3.2	6.5	77.5	24 219	447.8	715.4	14.6
Wheaton	22 426	233.6	90.6	44	25.0	2.4	26.3	54.0	1.4	2.8	27.0	19 286	129.6	178.9	7.4
Wilmette village	13 680	293.3	47.0	25	16.0	0.9	80.0	21.9	0.2	0.3	4.5	22 500	51.3	69.4	1.6
INDIANA	2 366 263	130.4	274.1	8 641	41.8	602.0	2.9	15 756.5	426.7	858.9	9 874.1	23 141	39 278.8	83 787.9	3 363.9
Anderson	24 643	128.2	317.4	58	34.5	D	D	D	D	D	D	D	D	D	D
Bloomington	22 022	325.9	89.0	71	32.4	6.0	-1.6	129.3	5.0	9.6	100.4	20 080	590.1	1 341.0	18.2
Columbus	13 741	181.1	228.7	92	45.7	14.7	2.1	441.6	8.4	16.2	225.8	26 881	1 088.3	2 053.0	57.9
East Chicago	14 259	94.9	288.5	42	61.9	D	D	D	D	D	D	D	D	D	D
Elkhart	18 259	116.5	302.1	412	46.6	22.9	13.9	544.2	14.9	28.6	270.9	18 181	1 443.7	2 615.5	66.5
Evansville	58 261	129.3	256.3	220	39.1	19.2	23.9	554.2	11.6	23.1	260.5	22 457	1 915.6	3 056.8	D
Fort Wayne	77 431	139.3	231.0	357	40.3	26.8	-2.5	740.5	15.8	30.8	359.5	22 753	1 348.9	2 887.7	89.6
Gary	52 348	106.1	282.2	54	57.4	8.7	-58.4	278.8	6.7	13.9	208.3	31 090	829.1	1 970.5	32.1
Hammond	39 411	99.0	303.1	93	49.5	5.4	D	151.4	3.6	7.6	101.7	28 250	488.8	1 244.6	27.8
Highland town	12 311	150.5	269.8	NA	NA	NA	NA	NA	NA	NA	NA	NA	NA	NA	NA
Indianapolis	323 462	151.8	208.1	1 186	36.4	74.3	-2.9	2 257.1	45.1	91.7	1 207.5	26 774	5 268.9	10 270.9	352.6
Kokomo	18 827	114.0	352.4	61	42.6	D	D	D	D	D	D	D	D	D	D
Lafayette	21 545	163.9	230.2	74	48.6	7.5	27.1	206.2	5.5	11.0	139.8	25 418	473.0	1 195.0	69.4
Lawrence	11 950	126.7	255.1	22	40.9	0.9	D	19.9	0.6	1.2	9.9	16 500	19.5	70.0	1.4
Marion	13 956	127.9	317.8	63	42.9	10.1	-2.9	309.3	8.1	17.0	243.2	30 025	424.7	1 122.3	D
Merrillville town	12 905	150.7	252.7	NA	NA	NA	NA	NA	NA	NA	NA	NA	NA	NA	NA
Michigan City	15 244	117.0	282.4	84	52.4	6.5	1.6	149.2	4.2	8.5	80.8	19 238	369.7	789.4	20.5
Mishawaka	18 242	127.8	275.7	111	40.5	5.3	-3.6	133.9	3.5	7.3	74.9	21 400	246.5	473.7	14.4
Muncie	31 548	170.7	226.7	132	43.2	D	D	D	D	D	D	D	D	D	D
New Albany	16 034	120.7	264.3	87	52.9	D	D	D	D	D	D	D	D	D	D
Portage	11 824	94.0	333.7	21	23.8	D	D	D	D	D	D	D	D	D	D
Richmond	16 588	122.6	250.4	97	49.5	7.7	-7.2	175.5	5.9	12.0	127.2	21 559	334.0	726.4	19.9
South Bend	47 437	154.9	220.0	235	40.0	13.2	-15.4	367.5	7.7	15.2	176.7	22 948	719.5	1 606.9	55.9
Terre Haute	25 999	145.2	214.2	97	51.5	7.2	-11.1	179.8	4.6	9.6	109.5	23 804	582.7	1 157.1	68.8

1. Persons 16 years old and over.

City	Wholesale trade, 1987: Establishments	Wholesale trade, 1987: Sales (Mil. dol.)	Wholesale trade, 1987: Paid employees[1]	Wholesale trade, 1987: Annual payroll ($1,000)	Retail trade–all establishments, 1987: Number	Retail trade–all establishments, 1987: Sales: Total (Mil. dol.)	Retail trade–all establishments, 1987: Sales: Percent change, 1982–1987	Retail trade–all establishments, 1987: Sales: Per capita[2] (Dollars)	Retail trade–establishments with payroll, 1987: Number	Retail trade–establishments with payroll, 1987: Sales: Total (Mil. dol.)	Per capita[2] (Dollars): General merchandise group stores	Per capita[2] (Dollars): Food stores	Per capita[2] (Dollars): Apparel and accessory stores	Per capita[2] (Dollars): Eating and drinking places
	73	74	75	76	77	78	79	80	81	82	83	84	85	86
ILLINOIS—Con.														
Downers Grove village	164	1 405.9	2 073	58 369	464	620.5	81.4	14 634	364	616.9	1 424	2 189	927	1 217
East St. Louis	41	127.9	547	11 431	208	87.6	-14.2	1 771	142	85.0	46	427	63	263
Elgin	148	978.3	1 676	40 213	513	516.3	44.7	7 160	339	506.5	659	D	131	416
Elk Grove Village village	657	6 568.8	13 778	356 563	265	249.2	44.1	7 734	177	244.1	D	657	123	788
Elmhurst	217	1 126.6	3 511	112 428	372	481.1	65.6	11 344	254	476.0	0	1 321	239	724
Evanston	94	256.4	992	24 209	646	474.9	18.4	6 635	465	462.5	89	1 314	710	762
Freeport	40	D	D	D	314	227.0	34.1	8 788	225	221.1	D	2 080	D	686
Galesburg	59	D	D	D	390	297.2	21.7	9 337	298	293.1	D	1 850	438	717
Glenview village	138	354.6	837	21 683	404	326.4	72.2	9 461	236	317.9	0	1 605	247	1 240
Granite City	39	319.5	621	15 023	313	221.7	28.6	6 307	214	216.1	478	1 843	162	657
Hanover Park village	16	8.1	25	613	169	0.0	0.0	D	104	D	D	D	91	D
Harvey	35	119.8	426	9 113	164	187.3	30.3	5 295	119	184.8	D	351	D	508
Highland Park	117	D	D	D	417	450.0	38.5	14 716	265	439.2	D	1 630	982	748
Hoffman Estates village	57	1 520.2	13 921	30 130	246	208.0	76.7	5 013	151	200.2	D	1 045	311	574
Joliet	130	411.1	1 658	38 682	791	757.3	41.2	9 963	608	749.1	1 408	1 811	433	793
Kankakee	53	135.4	589	11 159	274	235.0	15.9	8 633	205	232.4	1 298	1 454	517	748
Lansing village	67	391.5	830	21 130	265	315.2	114.6	10 903	191	309.4	1 254	2 711	395	690
Lombard village	190	1 264.5	3 239	90 219	469	534.1	32.3	14 096	370	528.2	3 351	902	2 085	1 317
Maywood village	22	33.9	149	3 760	109	86.0	22.5	3 154	78	84.5	D	648	D	403
Moline	103	1 116.7	1 456	40 908	593	466.9	29.8	10 492	444	462.0	2 086	1 430	640	1 255
Mount Prospect village	139	1 377.6	1 643	50 741	457	448.4	13.7	8 208	308	438.9	1 449	1 687	575	601
Naperville	193	D	D	D	598	0.0	0.0	D	421	602.5	786	2 044	456	936
Niles village	119	1 352.4	2 828	79 400	467	755.2	91.7	25 617	355	747.6	5 462	2 483	2 100	1 353
Normal town	31	126.9	386	8 091	288	176.4	52.5	4 795	207	173.0	850	D	287	809
Northbrook village	372	2 449.6	4 442	132 369	539	447.9	23.9	14 032	370	433.3	1 338	1 766	2 683	954
North Chicago	15	D	D	D	100	52.8	37.9	1 223	73	51.7	D	259	D	436
Oak Forest	28	90.7	183	6 695	160	107.7	41.9	4 305	88	104.4	0	1 152	D	815
Oak Lawn village	65	108.9	389	8 109	496	819.9	67.8	14 078	332	809.1	1 279	2 472	491	776
Oak Park village	84	300.7	475	11 664	440	252.7	7.4	4 652	309	247.1	39	1 083	289	565
Palatine village	140	692.6	854	25 695	363	249.6	68.1	7 324	204	242.0	563	1 588	74	975
Park Forest village	16	D	D	D	123	0.0	0.0	D	62	116.6	D	1 689	56	166
Park Ridge	124	651.4	722	22 939	357	317.0	74.2	8 471	220	310.8	0	2 596	345	322
Pekin	38	149.6	311	6 597	333	293.9	0.0	9 396	246	290.6	1 476	2 248	206	681
Peoria	316	2 765.6	4 407	106 675	1 173	938.3	24.7	8 508	861	921.7	1 399	1 255	486	834
Quincy	123	D	D	D	559	365.9	15.5	9 240	382	359.6	D	1 965	562	818
Rockford	382	954.0	4 302	101 624	1 392	1 098.9	32.9	8 094	958	1 078.5	1 076	1 727	280	772
Rock Island	94	420.2	1 640	33 825	327	182.6	20.6	4 177	226	178.4	D	854	94	490
Schaumburg village	346	4 202.9	5 965	194 314	739	1 430.5	59.4	23 794	589	1 424.9	4 265	1 863	D	D
Skokie village	310	3 342.4	4 150	118 364	879	751.1	39.7	12 638	508	731.8	2 382	1 023	1 863	832
Springfield	229	1 271.4	3 000	73 375	1 255	1 113.1	41.7	11 099	923	1 100.8	1 921	1 791	482	1 191
Tinley Park village	23	D	D	D	232	241.7	57.4	8 511	146	232.3	D	1 905	483	448
Urbana	38	D	D	D	250	178.0	38.3	4 976	186	175.9	D	1 241	136	732
Waukegan	78	327.9	908	24 728	611	604.0	33.5	8 110	484	599.0	1 425	1 039	444	650
Wheaton	84	209.2	463	14 489	319	246.0	40.9	5 167	186	240.1	D	1 065	D	346
Wilmette village	63	128.7	258	7 449	285	231.8	40.1	8 617	182	226.0	D	1 278	488	631
INDIANA	9 678	40 500.7	108 208	2 344 024	53 633	33 992.3	43.3	6 176	33 083	33 097.1	739	1 101	235	591
Anderson	75	194.5	932	19 455	701	540.5	32.1	8 858	497	533.1	1 005	1 856	402	894
Bloomington	88	D	D	D	770	578.4	49.4	11 017	594	570.3	1 792	2 170	D	1 343
Columbus	94	190.9	755	15 987	571	375.2	45.5	12 146	353	367.2	D	D	529	1 387
East Chicago	44	389.6	963	20 893	224	94.1	-0.4	2 547	136	90.1	D	657	37	409
Elkhart	202	758.1	2 651	59 948	703	637.1	35.6	14 421	487	625.5	1 644	2 297	553	1 084
Evansville	415	1 702.0	5 486	122 887	1 620	1 303.2	34.6	10 065	1 173	1 285.3	D	1 724	D	1 102
Fort Wayne	607	4 782.7	9 948	230 211	2 070	1 885.4	65.1	10 905	1 494	1 856.0	1 708	1 483	523	1 101
Gary	74	361.1	1 325	32 478	591	299.6	-19.3	2 190	401	292.4	238	483	55	223
Hammond	107	623.1	1 250	23 906	677	408.0	1.5	4 723	467	398.5	547	886	191	561
Highland town	33	52.6	269	5 227	299	367.6	71.9	15 215	211	362.3	D	D	904	927
Indianapolis	1 952	14 059.5	29 287	724 195	6 894	6 692.3	61.7	9 297	4 760	6 592.1	D	1 245	397	963
Kokomo	85	203.5	782	14 740	791	582.9	44.3	12 780	530	572.8	D	2 175	D	1 298
Lafayette	104	182.5	1 133	21 418	714	623.9	49.3	14 103	510	615.5	D	1 690	733	1 201
Lawrence	37	134.4	549	12 523	152	113.5	11.4	4 286	114	111.7	D	D	D	591
Marion	69	95.2	522	9 317	500	366.9	38.1	10 246	347	361.8	D	1 683	498	915
Merrillville town	54	106.9	568	12 155	456	555.7	46.3	20 946	359	552.6	3 984	2 689	1 211	1 933
Michigan City	58	96.4	507	9 890	444	317.6	24.3	8 921	329	312.2	1 499	1 638	554	618
Mishawaka	84	172.7	818	16 379	604	682.3	79.4	16 481	442	677.3	D	2 255	991	1 259
Muncie	129	289.8	1 612	32 355	905	639.5	30.5	8 809	629	626.6	D	1 766	345	969
New Albany	72	217.9	689	12 690	406	250.7	34.3	6 728	258	247.1	D	1 740	D	631
Portage	25	45.2	149	4 070	212	112.6	36.5	3 962	133	109.6	D	1 270	D	500
Richmond	72	388.4	1 046	22 005	535	430.4	29.9	11 027	359	424.7	1 939	1 842	301	1 041
South Bend	309	1 085.7	4 507	103 322	1 111	790.9	30.1	7 378	790	780.2	832	1 548	225	792
Terre Haute	159	407.7	1 724	31 977	745	1 066.3	96.3	18 410	561	1 058.8	D	2 202	D	D

1. For the period including March 12 of the year shown. 2. Based on resident population estimated as of July 1, 1986.

City	Retail trade–establishment with payroll, 1987 (cont'd)			Taxable service industries–establishments with payroll, 1987							Federal grants, 1986		
	Paid employees[1]				Receipts (Mil. dol.)								
						Selected kinds of business							
	Number	Percent change, 1982–1987	Annual payroll (Mil. dol.)	Number	Total	Hotels, motels, and other lodging places	Health services	Legal services	Paid employees[1]	Annual payroll (Mil. dol.)	Procurement contract awards (Mil. dol.)	Grant awards (Mil. dol.)	Federal government civilian employment, 1984
	87	88	89	90	91	92	93	94	95	96	97	98	99
ILLINOIS—Con.													
Downers Grove village	6 746	72.4	74.5	533	807.5	D	63.0	4.4	8 940	171.2	6.8	8.0	201
East St. Louis	1 152	-11.7	11.1	108	76.0	D	14.4	D	1 000	20.0	13.7	4.5	346
Elgin	5 067	10.3	56.3	516	197.7	D	73.8	11.9	4 225	73.8	1.0	1.5	207
Elk Grove Village village	2 607	19.8	32.8	373	228.6	7.5	22.6	3.1	3 435	77.2	59.5	0.4	25
Elmhurst	4 007	25.9	48.3	490	237.7	D	58.3	4.2	5 211	89.7	5.2	0.3	142
Evanston	5 930	8.5	59.3	716	279.8	D	118.8	13.6	5 118	121.8	7.4	54.6	321
Freeport	2 529	6.7	24.1	182	47.7	D	23.8	D	1 302	20.3	5.8	0.7	97
Galesburg	3 567	-1.7	33.2	213	63.9	3.4	32.3	3.9	1 579	29.2	8.4	1.3	182
Glenview village	3 338	42.2	36.3	378	121.4	D	44.9	3.5	2 395	50.2	24.3	0.4	437
Granite City	2 611	9.9	26.1	229	64.7	0.4	23.0	9.1	1 677	25.0	5.9	0.6	312
Hanover Park village	D	D	D	95	D	0.0	D	0.7	D	D	0.0	0.2	0
Harvey	1 710	12.5	19.3	142	90.2	8.8	35.3	D	1 836	35.0	3.1	0.9	84
Highland Park	3 710	19.3	50.2	453	134.9	D	56.7	4.8	2 391	54.6	0.5	0.4	106
Hoffman Estates village	2 832	87.2	23.5	279	192.7	D	89.0	1.5	3 367	72.1	0.4	0.2	1
Joliet	8 697	15.5	84.5	591	259.1	9.4	105.0	24.0	6 201	107.9	10.2	8.2	330
Kankakee	2 934	-13.6	27.0	286	87.5	0.3	36.1	5.6	1 772	35.6	1.8	6.2	201
Lansing village	3 511	79.2	36.2	189	64.9	6.5	10.8	3.2	1 487	21.0	11.4	0.1	60
Lombard village	6 519	2.7	63.5	390	257.9	D	44.1	D	4 885	97.5	0.7	0.5	264
Maywood village	947	20.9	10.1	69	40.9	D	4.7	D	755	14.1	0.3	0.7	126
Moline	6 576	7.6	60.4	413	145.7	D	56.4	6.3	3 246	55.5	3.2	3.1	107
Mount Prospect village	4 945	-6.1	49.6	352	125.1	D	29.4	2.4	2 701	43.8	1.3	0.7	162
Naperville	7 561	D	72.2	667	415.6	21.9	54.0	8.6	9 983	147.6	1.1	0.6	147
Niles village	6 996	27.4	77.1	277	244.5	D	56.2	D	5 323	84.7	5.5	0.5	35
Normal town	2 890	24.2	21.4	148	45.7	4.8	17.4	D	1 299	16.9	0.0	2.6	6
Northbrook village	5 492	6.5	60.4	800	540.6	20.0	65.9	11.1	7 724	179.3	11.2	0.2	140
North Chicago	1 015	58.6	8.1	35	12.3	1.9	1.5	0.0	428	5.0	14.8	7.1	2 329
Oak Forest	1 537	42.6	13.9	114	33.9	D	8.0	2.0	749	12.4	0.9	0.1	44
Oak Lawn village	7 038	26.4	77.0	481	168.3	10.4	91.2	4.3	4 601	70.9	0.3	0.5	333
Oak Park village	3 525	10.3	33.9	542	173.8	D	85.7	5.2	5 786	78.7	0.2	1.8	234
Palatine village	3 189	37.6	30.7	375	155.6	4.2	19.3	3.5	3 697	62.5	0.3	0.1	180
Park Forest village	1 349	D	14.2	64	D	0.0	1.1	D	D	D	0.6	0.4	87
Park Ridge	2 762	32.2	32.3	469	273.1	D	62.8	8.3	5 309	119.8	1.3	0.5	142
Pekin	3 091	D	31.5	201	48.0	D	20.0	3.4	1 296	17.3	0.2	1.1	93
Peoria	12 008	2.5	108.9	945	468.0	D	151.1	54.4	9 932	201.8	73.9	13.2	1 535
Quincy	4 923	9.3	41.6	349	93.2	5.6	33.0	D	2 614	37.3	28.3	4.2	245
Rockford	13 768	13.2	131.8	1 179	537.6	23.1	168.0	37.7	15 220	223.6	143.9	9.0	927
Rock Island	2 422	-3.0	20.9	236	85.9	D	18.0	13.3	1 950	32.7	6.3	5.4	9 572
Schaumburg village	13 394	32.6	157.7	733	532.9	D	75.5	D	9 540	185.2	89.5	0.6	105
Skokie village	8 003	10.6	88.4	818	472.4	21.8	103.7	6.7	9 910	162.3	13.4	1.0	207
Springfield	13 581	17.7	126.8	1 013	502.7	44.3	163.2	36.3	11 529	194.7	86.1	413.9	1 873
Tinley Park village	2 682	34.6	25.1	174	D	0.0	13.6	1.0	D	D	0.4	0.2	88
Urbana	2 762	10.4	20.7	180	140.1	9.9	D	D	3 009	57.1	26.1	99.5	216
Waukegan	6 570	4.6	66.7	465	177.4	5.1	62.6	23.4	4 479	74.3	4.1	5.5	214
Wheaton	2 746	35.5	27.9	501	184.0	0.0	36.1	40.5	3 632	82.3	0.2	0.4	168
Wilmette village	2 384	1.0	29.5	287	65.2	D	18.3	2.3	1 334	27.8	1.0	0.1	104
INDIANA	412 466	22.1	3 726.7	30 336	11 204.5	516.3	3 649.7	631.5	282 483	4 239.8	2 996.8	2 162.1	39 226
Anderson	6 995	28.6	61.6	505	128.1	3.9	59.5	5.9	3 601	52.7	3.1	2.6	242
Bloomington	9 353	39.1	71.7	509	145.2	D	58.8	D	3 629	52.7	6.1	49.5	305
Columbus	5 015	25.6	41.5	366	119.1	D	47.4	5.8	2 669	43.0	18.7	2.6	197
East Chicago	1 186	-3.9	10.4	133	59.7	D	14.1	2.4	1 289	24.5	0.4	11.9	88
Elkhart	6 494	24.3	65.6	478	240.7	11.5	53.5	10.3	5 319	70.3	10.1	1.6	187
Evansville	17 306	14.3	162.0	1 213	516.0	D	171.1	27.5	12 622	203.7	15.3	10.0	769
Fort Wayne	23 939	33.0	224.7	1 695	785.1	25.1	243.6	47.1	20 304	313.9	250.3	9.7	1 688
Gary	4 022	-18.3	34.6	303	71.5	1.6	31.1	3.2	2 199	27.9	5.5	9.6	889
Hammond	5 277	-15.5	46.4	396	157.9	3.7	25.6	14.1	3 721	57.6	1.1	6.8	311
Highland town	3 497	19.8	36.3	220	71.0	0.0	15.7	6.6	2 376	28.6	NA	4.9	0
Indianapolis	75 915	32.1	754.3	5 723	3 270.8	196.9	814.1	241.5	76 677	1 312.9	1 052.4	339.6	11 951
Kokomo	7 149	22.9	63.3	433	124.4	D	61.0	6.7	3 486	49.8	0.7	1.6	279
Lafayette	7 736	26.1	67.2	449	222.1	5.4	85.1	D	4 722	76.6	4.5	6.2	392
Lawrence	1 392	19.3	14.3	89	26.5	D	1.6	D	628	8.6	0.1	0.5	0
Marion	4 408	13.1	39.3	296	77.3	D	40.5	D	2 364	30.7	5.8	0.6	1 531
Merrillville town	6 238	17.2	61.0	473	218.5	17.4	87.6	21.4	4 864	89.7	0.1	0.2	33
Michigan City	3 713	5.5	34.3	273	106.8	5.2	51.6	1.9	2 803	41.9	2.3	1.3	114
Mishawaka	7 809	48.9	74.2	341	95.3	D	26.6	D	2 767	31.7	420.9	1.2	96
Muncie	9 081	16.0	75.0	590	182.9	3.8	67.2	10.3	4 710	73.2	14.7	6.5	360
New Albany	3 185	6.0	30.0	284	90.3	D	40.5	D	2 317	34.2	1.9	1.5	124
Portage	1 562	10.7	11.8	126	52.4	D	9.0	1.8	1 458	19.7	0.3	0.4	39
Richmond	5 216	14.6	49.1	305	101.7	6.8	30.9	4.2	2 961	39.0	11.9	2.3	126
South Bend	11 032	15.5	99.7	1 037	517.9	19.2	164.2	28.6	12 219	211.4	275.1	11.1	953
Terre Haute	9 540	15.8	90.9	476	166.0	D	75.2	10.6	4 398	57.0	18.4	6.5	1 000

1. For the period including March 12 of the year shown.

City	City government employment, 1985 (October): Total	City government employment, 1985 (October): Rates[1]	City government employment, 1985 (October): Percent education	Form of governments[2] (As of 1986)	City government finances, 1984–1985: General revenue: Total (Mil. dol.)	General revenue: Intergovernmental: Total (Mil. dol.)	General revenue: Intergovernmental: Percent from State government	General revenue: Taxes: Total (Mil. dol.)	General revenue: Taxes: Per capita[3] (Dollars): Total	General revenue: Taxes: Per capita[3] (Dollars): Property	General revenue: Taxes: Per capita[3] (Dollars): Sales & gross receipts	General expenditures: Total (Mil. dol.)	General expenditures: Per capita[3] (Dol.): Total	General expenditures: Per capita[3] (Dol.): Capital outlays	General expenditures: Percent of total for–: Public welfare	General expenditures: Percent of total for–: Highways	General expenditures: Percent of total for–: Education
	100	101	102	103	104	105	106	107	108	109	110	111	112	113	114	115	116
ILLINOIS—Con.																	
Downers Grove village	383	90.3	0.0	2	22.2	2.2	85.4	10.5	248	98	140	15.6	368	4	0.0	17.8	0.0
East St. Louis	429	86.7	0.0	1	19.4	9.0	27.8	6.2	126	57	58	17.3	350	106	2.6	9.2	0.0
Elgin	564	78.2	0.0	2	23.6	4.8	64.2	12.6	175	101	61	23.3	324	79	0.0	12.3	0.0
Elk Grove Village village	367	113.9	0.0	2	18.0	3.2	54.4	12.1	375	157	173	15.1	468	53	0.0	27.8	0.0
Elmhurst	397	93.6	0.0	2	16.2	2.5	80.1	8.8	207	88	101	15.8	374	22	0.3	24.1	0.0
Evanston	865	120.9	0.0	2	46.5	6.2	52.6	29.2	408	258	120	53.2	743	154	3.9	7.7	0.0
Freeport	218	84.4	0.0	1	7.5	1.3	97.9	3.6	140	55	79	6.6	254	10	1.0	17.5	0.0
Galesburg	296	93.0	0.0	2	14.6	2.5	79.5	6.5	203	105	85	13.5	424	29	0.0	15.3	0.0
Glenview village	278	80.6	0.0	2	10.8	1.3	88.5	7.7	223	91	114	11.5	332	78	0.0	35.2	0.0
Granite City	292	83.1	0.0	1	13.6	3.5	71.6	6.5	184	81	93	12.3	349	15	0.0	16.3	0.0
Hanover Park village	132	42.2	0.0	2	7.0	1.4	78.4	3.3	107	61	37	5.1	162	6	0.0	12.4	0.0
Harvey	NA	NA	NA	3	12.5	3.1	59.7	8.1	228	124	95	12.0	339	68	0.5	11.8	0.0
Highland Park	346	113.1	0.0	2	18.4	1.5	87.5	12.8	419	216	180	23.6	772	382	0.5	8.3	0.0
Hoffman Estates village	NA	NA	NA	1	10.6	1.8	90.5	6.6	159	98	37	11.7	283	48	1.0	15.5	0.0
Joliet	652	85.8	0.0	2	52.6	6.9	59.9	19.4	255	137	103	37.8	498	40	0.0	14.6	0.0
Kankakee	249	91.5	0.0	1	13.2	3.2	44.2	7.1	260	82	171	12.3	453	30	10.7	12.7	0.0
Lansing village	264	91.3	0.0	1	8.6	1.4	84.4	5.1	176	118	52	7.2	248	24	0.4	16.0	0.0
Lombard village	283	74.7	0.0	2	17.0	1.9	81.2	8.8	233	106	108	17.0	450	77	0.0	11.1	0.0
Maywood village	261	95.7	0.0	2	11.2	3.2	41.7	6.3	231	142	74	9.7	354	57	0.0	18.6	0.0
Moline	1 066	239.6	0.0	1	49.3	5.5	53.6	11.5	259	139	105	44.8	1 007	121	1.0	8.1	0.0
Mount Prospect village	367	67.2	0.0	2	19.3	2.8	79.3	12.4	227	130	75	15.9	291	25	4.2	18.0	0.0
Naperville	444	66.3	0.0	2	33.2	2.6	84.6	17.3	259	109	124	29.4	439	125	0.0	17.6	0.0
Niles village	276	93.6	0.0	2	12.8	1.7	74.5	9.8	334	73	242	12.6	427	28	9.0	3.5	0.0
Normal town	261	70.9	0.0	2	12.5	2.4	64.8	5.8	159	62	87	9.9	269	45	NA	13.2	0.0
Northbrook village	321	100.6	0.0	2	12.7	1.5	92.3	8.8	275	130	118	17.4	546	201	0.0	6.5	0.0
North Chicago	172	39.8	0.0	1	7.1	2.6	68.0	3.4	79	26	46	7.2	166	26	0.0	18.3	0.0
Oak Forest	160	63.9	0.0	1	5.8	1.1	90.6	2.8	110	48	40	4.8	192	10	0.5	15.7	0.0
Oak Lawn village	471	80.9	0.0	2	23.7	4.1	87.4	14.2	244	118	94	21.9	376	62	0.4	15.6	0.0
Oak Park village	753	138.6	0.0	2	27.3	5.4	56.1	15.7	290	162	99	30.3	557	152	0.0	7.5	0.0
Palatine village	219	64.3	0.0	2	22.7	9.5	13.6	8.8	259	151	59	35.4	1 039	721	0.0	4.1	0.0
Park Forest village	258	99.7	0.0	2	6.7	1.2	81.1	4.1	158	84	53	6.9	266	27	0.0	9.2	0.0
Park Ridge	315	84.2	0.0	2	15.6	2.0	87.6	10.5	280	129	122	11.3	303	6	0.0	17.6	0.0
Pekin	267	85.4	0.0	3	22.0	2.7	71.7	7.2	230	148	75	18.7	597	11	0.0	8.3	0.0
Peoria	1 164	105.5	0.0	2	61.5	16.6	60.6	28.6	259	134	92	69.1	626	114	0.4	15.2	0.0
Quincy	443	111.9	0.0	1	20.8	6.1	42.1	6.1	155	68	84	18.0	456	64	0.0	11.5	0.0
Rockford	1 090	80.3	0.0	1	59.2	15.1	51.8	35.6	262	151	79	51.4	378	63	6.8	16.8	0.0
Rock Island	527	120.5	0.0	2	33.2	5.2	58.9	10.7	245	178	58	28.9	661	116	NA	9.4	0.0
Schaumburg village	437	72.7	0.0	2	22.7	2.6	84.5	15.4	255	0	216	18.0	300	38	0.0	22.1	0.0
Skokie village	597	100.5	0.0	2	23.4	3.9	78.6	17.8	299	168	108	24.0	404	98	0.3	7.5	0.0
Springfield	1 776	177.1	0.0	3	51.3	10.2	55.3	25.0	249	102	125	44.0	439	10	0.0	11.1	0.0
Tinley Park village	164	57.7	0.0	1	7.1	1.6	69.4	3.9	138	62	59	7.8	274	79	1.7	12.3	0.0
Urbana	286	80.0	0.0	1	16.2	2.9	55.9	7.0	197	67	110	13.7	384	56	0.4	13.3	0.0
Waukegan	564	75.7	0.0	1	37.3	7.4	60.4	17.2	231	80	131	40.0	537	143	0.0	12.0	0.0
Wheaton	316	66.4	0.0	2	13.6	2.1	85.7	7.4	154	76	61	11.3	237	28	2.3	11.7	0.0
Wilmette village	254	94.4	0.0	2	10.8	1.3	92.1	7.9	293	152	122	11.1	413	77	0.2	15.0	0.0
INDIANA	NA	NA	NA	NA	NA	NA	NA	NA	NA	NA	NA	NA	NA	NA	NA	NA	NA
Anderson	852	139.6	0.0	1	25.1	8.3	61.5	9.4	154	149	0	23.0	378	19	0.0	8.0	0.0
Bloomington	690	131.4	0.0	1	21.1	7.0	48.7	4.8	92	89	0	19.4	369	60	0.7	6.5	0.0
Columbus	456	147.6	0.0	1	13.2	3.1	79.6	5.7	185	182	0	14.3	464	39	0.0	9.9	0.0
East Chicago	929	251.4	0.0	1	52.3	11.8	52.6	17.9	484	480	0	41.9	1 135	17	0.0	2.6	0.0
Elkhart	572	129.5	0.0	1	23.1	11.0	34.4	5.5	124	121	0	26.1	591	210	0.0	7.8	0.0
Evansville	1 300	100.4	0.0	1	63.3	22.0	58.4	16.8	130	127	0	53.0	410	37	NA	9.6	0.0
Fort Wayne	1 801	104.2	0.0	1	71.7	26.5	41.8	22.7	131	129	0	70.2	406	63	0.0	7.3	0.0
Gary	1 707	124.8	0.0	1	82.4	31.2	62.4	24.3	177	176	0	83.4	609	48	0.0	6.5	0.0
Hammond	1 067	123.5	0.0	1	43.8	14.2	66.1	18.7	217	210	0	48.2	558	95	0.0	6.5	0.0
Highland town	192	79.5	0.0	1	5.3	1.4	94.1	2.0	83	78	0	5.9	243	7	0.0	10.2	0.0
Indianapolis	12 183	169.3	0.0	1	536.8	183.2	71.7	197.9	275	250	16	511.4	710	99	10.4	6.0	0.3
Kokomo	574	125.8	0.0	1	26.4	9.5	44.7	9.1	200	199	0	24.3	533	24	0.0	6.8	0.0
Lafayette	615	139.0	0.0	1	17.9	6.3	39.6	5.5	124	121	0	17.0	384	30	0.0	9.0	0.0
Lawrence	114	43.1	0.0	1	4.3	1.2	89.4	1.8	69	67	0	4.6	173	31	0.0	18.2	0.0
Marion	325	90.8	0.0	1	10.6	3.9	71.4	3.9	110	109	0	10.4	291	13	0.0	10.6	0.0
Merrillville town	NA	NA	NA	1	3.0	1.3	93.4	1.5	56	53	0	2.8	107	6	0.0	29.7	0.0
Michigan City	463	130.1	0.0	1	16.8	4.1	81.5	6.9	193	189	0	15.4	434	46	0.0	5.8	0.0
Mishawaka	460	111.1	0.0	1	13.0	4.2	64.4	6.1	148	146	0	11.8	286	45	0.0	11.1	0.0
Muncie	758	104.4	0.0	1	24.0	7.9	60.4	11.4	157	156	0	24.8	341	12	0.0	7.0	0.0
New Albany	356	95.5	0.0	1	11.0	3.4	75.7	4.0	108	106	0	9.9	265	54	0.0	7.1	0.0
Portage	178	62.6	0.0	1	8.7	2.1	83.9	3.4	119	117	0	9.1	319	76	0.0	15.3	0.0
Richmond	627	160.6	0.0	1	15.7	4.9	59.4	4.7	119	117	0	14.1	362	18	0.0	8.5	0.0
South Bend	1 259	117.5	0.0	1	42.9	9.4	84.5	20.7	193	188	2	54.9	512	35	0.0	6.1	0.1
Terre Haute	639	110.3	0.0	1	25.7	9.9	48.0	10.6	182	180	0	27.0	466	105	0.0	7.2	0.0

1. Per 10,000 population estimated as of July 1, 1986. 2. 1 = Mayor-council; 2 = Council-manager; 3 = Commission. Data subject to copyright. 3. Based on resident population estimated as of July 1, 1986.

City	City government finances, 1984–1985 (cont'd)								Climate[2]							Typical monthly electric bills, 1986		
	General expenditure (cont'd)					Debt outstanding			Average daily temperature (Degrees Fahrenheit)							Residential[6]		
	Percent of total for (cont'd)								Mean		Limits							
	Health and hospitals	Police protection	Sewerage and sanitation	Parks and recreation	Housing and community development	Total (Mil. dol.)	Per capita[1] (Dollars)	Percent utility	Jan.	July	Jan.[3]	July[4]	Annual precipitation (Inches)	Heating degree days[5]	Cooling degree days[5]	Total (Dollars)	Percent change, 1980–1986	Commercial[7] (Dollars)
	117	118	119	120	121	122	123	124	125	126	127	128	129	130	131	132	133	134
ILLINOIS—Con.																		
Downers Grove village	0.9	13.8	0.6	0.0	0.0	58.6	1 382	0.7	22.6	75.0	15.3	84.3	35.51	6 177	955	59.60	90.4	NA
East St. Louis	0.2	11.8	12.6	2.6	24.6	15.9	321	0.0	29.8	77.7	20.8	89.1	36.75	4 818	1 320	51.69	62.5	416.0
Elgin	1.5	21.0	3.2	10.4	2.2	50.3	698	35.1	21.4	73.0	13.6	83.3	33.34	6 455	740	59.60	90.4	618.3
Elk Grove Village village	0.7	21.3	4.9	0.0	0.0	0.2	5	0.0	21.4	73.0	13.6	83.3	33.34	6 455	740	59.60	90.4	618.3
Elmhurst	0.7	19.5	13.2	0.6	0.0	4.1	96	0.0	21.4	73.0	13.6	83.3	33.34	6 455	740	59.60	90.4	NA
Evanston	2.8	11.8	4.9	8.4	2.6	77.5	1 083	21.1	24.6	76.1	15.9	87.4	36.79	5 640	1 084	62.67	84.5	650.2
Freeport	1.4	16.4	21.3	1.1	0.0	2.5	96	0.0	17.4	72.5	9.2	83.2	34.55	7 055	648	59.60	90.4	NA
Galesburg	0.0	13.1	4.0	6.7	0.0	34.9	1 097	4.6	20.9	74.8	12.1	85.3	35.99	6 302	917	51.36	36.1	NA
Glenview village	0.5	18.7	5.6	0.0	0.0	11.6	337	52.6	21.4	73.0	13.6	83.3	33.34	6 455	740	62.67	89.8	NA
Granite City	4.0	17.3	26.5	0.0	0.0	5.4	154	0.0	28.8	78.9	19.9	89.0	33.91	4 938	1 468	51.36	36.1	NA
Hanover Park village	0.1	29.7	13.4	0.0	1.3	11.0	350	31.3	21.4	73.0	13.6	83.3	33.34	6 455	740	59.60	90.4	NA
Harvey	0.4	22.7	6.0	0.0	0.4	2.2	63	11.2	21.4	73.4	13.1	83.9	35.24	6 483	791	62.67	89.8	NA
Highland Park	0.0	11.4	4.1	0.0	0.0	14.5	474	0.0	20.2	71.5	12.1	81.4	33.65	6 881	591	62.67	89.8	NA
Hoffman Estates village	0.0	17.7	10.7	NA	0.0	5.0	120	56.6	21.4	73.0	13.6	83.3	33.34	6 455	740	59.60	80.5	NA
Joliet	0.0	16.2	7.8	0.3	3.6	124.3	1 635	9.4	21.4	73.4	13.1	83.9	35.24	6 483	791	59.60	90.4	618.3
Kankakee	1.1	15.5	20.9	0.3	0.0	11.7	430	0.0	21.4	73.4	13.1	83.9	35.24	6 483	791	62.67	100.2	NA
Lansing village	0.1	28.3	9.9	0.0	0.0	10.4	361	44.0	22.9	74.0	15.1	83.7	35.48	6 251	875	59.60	90.4	NA
Lombard village	0.0	13.7	15.5	0.0	0.0	45.2	1 192	0.0	21.4	73.0	13.6	83.3	33.34	6 455	740	59.60	90.4	NA
Maywood village	0.0	21.8	6.8	1.5	0.0	6.5	238	25.8	22.6	75.0	15.3	84.3	35.51	6 177	955	62.67	89.8	NA
Moline	51.1	6.6	11.2	2.6	0.0	36.1	811	2.5	19.5	74.9	11.0	85.4	37.17	6 498	899	57.11	74.6	NA
Mount Prospect village	0.4	16.8	8.6	0.2	0.0	21.9	402	0.0	21.4	73.0	13.6	83.3	33.34	6 455	740	59.60	90.4	618.3
Naperville	0.0	9.9	7.5	3.0	0.0	91.5	1 368	31.8	20.1	73.0	11.3	84.2	35.62	6 618	733	61.33	42.8	NA
Niles village	21.9	17.8	4.6	0.0	0.0	3.1	105	29.2	21.4	73.0	13.6	83.3	33.34	6 455	740	61.44	90.0	NA
Normal town	0.0	15.5	6.7	7.6	12.2	31.8	865	3.2	24.6	76.1	15.9	87.4	36.79	5 640	1 084	54.01	35.8	NA
Northbrook village	0.2	15.8	3.6	0.0	0.0	19.1	598	15.9	21.4	73.0	13.6	83.3	33.34	6 455	740	59.60	90.4	NA
North Chicago	0.4	29.9	4.1	0.0	7.2	3.9	91	64.6	20.2	71.5	12.1	81.4	33.65	6 881	591	62.67	89.8	NA
Oak Forest	0.0	26.3	13.3	0.0	0.0	2.7	107	77.5	21.4	73.4	13.1	83.9	35.24	6 483	791	59.60	90.4	NA
Oak Lawn village	0.0	17.4	8.1	0.0	0.0	30.2	519	35.0	22.6	75.0	15.3	84.3	35.51	6 177	955	59.60	90.4	618.3
Oak Park village	1.5	21.2	5.9	6.3	12.4	24.4	448	7.3	22.6	75.0	15.3	84.3	35.51	6 177	955	62.67	86.2	650.2
Palatine village	0.2	7.0	1.0	0.0	0.8	79.0	2 317	5.9	21.4	73.0	13.6	83.3	33.34	6 455	740	59.60	90.4	NA
Park Forest village	2.7	18.3	3.5	17.7	1.4	4.6	177	0.0	21.4	73.4	13.1	83.9	35.24	6 483	791	61.44	90.0	NA
Park Ridge	0.6	17.5	9.2	0.0	0.3	11.4	305	0.0	21.4	73.0	13.6	83.3	33.34	6 455	740	62.06	90.9	NA
Pekin	0.1	11.6	11.2	0.1	0.0	84.4	2 697	0.1	21.5	75.0	13.3	85.5	34.89	6 226	948	61.60	56.9	NA
Peoria	0.1	13.1	6.7	1.8	9.5	141.8	1 286	0.0	21.5	75.0	13.3	85.5	34.89	6 226	948	61.60	56.9	519.9
Quincy	0.0	12.5	13.7	0.1	3.2	64.2	1 621	2.5	23.6	76.7	15.1	87.0	37.65	5 789	1 120	56.60	40.0	NA
Rockford	0.0	18.2	7.0	0.0	6.7	50.5	372	10.7	18.3	73.0	9.8	83.7	36.78	6 952	714	59.60	90.4	618.3
Rock Island	NA	11.8	8.4	6.8	4.9	77.3	1 769	2.6	19.5	74.9	11.0	85.4	37.17	6 498	899	57.70	76.5	NA
Schaumburg village	2.2	26.4	0.0	1.0	1.2	2.9	48	84.0	21.4	73.0	13.6	83.3	33.34	6 455	740	59.60	90.4	618.3
Skokie village	2.7	25.5	5.7	0.0	1.8	5.4	91	0.0	21.4	73.0	13.6	83.3	33.34	6 455	740	59.60	90.4	618.3
Springfield	5.8	19.6	1.8	4.1	8.0	218.8	2 182	58.5	24.6	76.5	16.3	87.1	33.78	5 654	1 165	44.05	62.4	477.3
Tinley Park village	0.0	19.0	0.0	0.0	0.0	9.0	318	32.6	21.4	73.4	13.1	83.9	35.24	6 483	791	59.60	90.4	NA
Urbana	0.0	12.5	4.7	0.0	1.8	41.7	1 167	0.0	24.7	75.2	17.0	85.5	37.04	5 758	1 019	54.01	35.8	NA
Waukegan	0.0	13.8	2.9	0.0	5.4	92.8	1 245	5.8	20.2	71.5	12.1	81.4	33.65	6 881	591	62.67	100.2	650.2
Wheaton	0.0	22.2	11.2	1.3	0.0	7.8	165	15.7	20.9	73.5	12.6	85.4	35.46	6 427	787	61.44	90.0	NA
Wilmette village	0.6	17.6	17.3	0.2	1.7	4.1	154	69.7	24.6	76.1	15.9	87.4	36.79	5 640	1 084	62.67	89.8	NA
INDIANA	NA	NA	NA	NA	NA	NA	NA	NA	NA	NA	NA	NA	NA	NA	NA	56.12	59.3	NA
Anderson	0.2	17.8	17.6	5.2	12.3	35.5	582	28.6	25.6	73.8	17.7	84.5	37.54	5 884	890	45.85	42.7	NA
Bloomington	2.0	9.3	28.0	9.0	6.1	28.2	536	18.3	27.6	74.9	18.1	86.4	40.25	5 509	964	57.62	63.1	NA
Columbus	1.8	13.9	21.3	12.1	0.6	12.1	393	37.9	27.6	74.9	18.1	86.4	40.25	5 509	964	57.62	63.1	NA
East Chicago	1.6	6.4	15.4	5.4	12.1	204.2	5 528	2.0	22.9	74.0	15.1	83.7	35.48	6 251	875	80.03	79.5	NA
Elkhart	0.1	11.4	43.0	3.9	5.5	11.4	258	24.3	23.2	72.5	15.9	82.7	38.16	6 377	710	54.84	73.4	NA
Evansville	2.7	12.4	14.0	6.1	10.9	46.3	357	10.8	30.6	78.1	21.9	88.8	41.55	4 729	1 378	40.80	28.9	343.3
Fort Wayne	0.9	15.0	16.7	8.6	8.8	78.6	454	28.4	23.3	73.3	15.8	84.1	34.40	6 320	786	54.84	73.4	471.8
Gary	1.8	9.2	14.9	5.0	4.1	154.9	1 132	0.0	22.9	74.0	15.1	83.7	35.48	6 251	875	80.03	79.5	NA
Hammond	1.0	12.2	28.8	4.3	8.8	53.3	617	6.7	22.9	74.0	15.1	83.7	35.48	6 251	875	80.03	79.5	NA
Highland town	0.0	20.6	30.0	10.3	0.0	1.2	50	44.7	21.4	73.4	13.1	83.9	35.24	6 483	791	80.03	79.5	NA
Indianapolis	20.9	9.3	9.9	3.0	3.5	431.9	600	2.8	26.0	75.1	17.8	85.2	39.12	5 650	988	42.18	28.6	358.2
Kokomo	0.0	11.3	17.9	4.3	16.9	25.3	555	0.0	24.6	74.2	16.3	85.7	38.11	6 035	962	57.62	63.1	NA
Lafayette	0.8	13.1	21.0	6.6	10.8	11.7	265	39.1	23.0	73.6	14.6	84.5	36.60	6 223	818	57.62	63.1	NA
Lawrence	0.0	28.7	17.6	6.7	0.0	4.8	182	63.1	26.0	75.1	17.8	85.2	39.12	5 650	988	42.18	28.6	NA
Marion	0.0	17.2	17.6	2.9	7.4	9.4	263	40.3	23.6	72.9	15.1	84.7	36.73	6 318	734	54.84	73.4	NA
Merrillville town	11.4	43.3	0.0	2.0	0.0	0.0	0	0.0	21.4	73.4	13.1	83.9	35.24	6 483	791	80.03	79.5	NA
Michigan City	0.0	13.7	24.1	9.5	5.9	30.5	858	13.2	22.9	74.0	15.1	83.7	35.48	6 251	875	80.03	79.5	NA
Mishawaka	2.2	14.6	12.5	7.7	16.4	4.2	101	74.0	23.2	72.5	15.9	82.7	38.16	6 377	710	54.44	78.1	NA
Muncie	0.3	11.4	31.1	4.2	3.1	6.5	89	0.0	23.9	72.8	15.3	83.6	37.77	6 262	746	54.84	73.4	471.8
New Albany	3.6	17.9	29.7	4.1	3.0	6.0	160	0.0	32.5	77.6	24.1	87.6	43.56	4 525	1 342	57.62	63.1	NA
Portage	0.4	14.8	18.6	13.6	1.3	10.1	356	0.0	22.9	74.0	15.1	83.7	35.48	6 251	875	80.03	79.5	NA
Richmond	0.0	14.5	26.3	8.7	1.1	15.4	394	0.0	25.6	72.8	16.9	84.3	38.70	5 973	728	37.72	28.9	NA
South Bend	0.8	14.0	19.6	10.8	17.7	28.1	262	0.2	23.2	72.5	15.9	82.7	38.16	6 377	710	54.84	73.4	471.8
Terre Haute	0.0	8.7	16.4	8.2	19.8	28.2	486	0.0	26.2	75.6	17.3	86.8	38.14	5 521	1 049	57.62	63.1	NA

1. Based on resident population estimated as of July 1, 1986. 2. Represents normal values based on the 30-year period, 1951–1980 (see text). 3. Average daily minimum. 4. Average daily maximum. 5. For definition, see text. 6. As of January 1; based on consumption of 750 kWh. 7. Based on billing demand of 30 kW and consumption of 6,000 kWh.

MSA/ CMSA Code[1]	State/ Place code	City	Land area,[2] 1990 (Sq. Km.)	Population						Population characteristics, 1990						
				1990				Change 1980–1990		Percent						
										Race						
				Total persons	Rank	Per sq. km.	1980	Number	Per-cent	White	Black	Am. Indian, Eskimo, Aleut	Asian & Pacific Islander	Other race	His-panic[3]	65 Years and over
			1	2	3	4	5	6	7	8	9	10	11	12	13	14
...	19 0000	IOWA	144 716.0	2 776 755	X	19	2 913 808	-137 053	-4.7	96.63	1.73	0.26	0.92	0.46	1.18	15.3
...	19 0115	Ames	50.9	47 198	523	927	45 775	1 423	3.1	89.88	2.45	0.14	6.89	0.64	1.56	6.8
1960	19 0395	Bettendorf	55.0	28 132	865	511	27 381	751	2.7	96.80	1.37	0.17	0.96	0.69	2.15	10.0
...	19 0560	Burlington	34.3	27 208	883	793	29 529	-2 321	-7.9	94.12	4.48	0.20	0.66	0.54	1.28	17.3
8920	19 0665	Cedar Falls	73.7	34 298	731	465	36 322	-2 024	-5.6	96.92	1.12	0.19	1.41	0.36	0.75	11.1
1360	19 0670	Cedar Rapids	138.5	108 751	172	785	110 243	-1 492	-1.4	95.52	2.88	0.24	0.98	0.38	1.14	13.2
...	19 0810	Clinton	91.9	29 201	839	318	32 828	-3 627	-11.0	96.49	2.43	0.33	0.50	0.26	0.70	17.7
5920	19 0945	Council Bluffs	95.3	54 315	437	570	56 449	-2 134	-3.8	97.80	0.80	0.28	0.42	0.71	2.42	13.7
1960	19 1040	Davenport	158.9	95 333	210	600	103 264	-7 931	-7.7	89.13	7.89	0.41	1.05	1.53	3.46	12.7
2120	19 1130	Des Moines	194.9	193 187	80	991	191 003	2 184	1.1	89.25	7.11	0.36	2.38	0.89	2.40	13.4
2200	19 1215	Dubuque	59.7	57 546	405	964	62 374	-4 828	-7.7	98.40	0.58	0.12	0.64	0.26	0.64	16.0
...	19 1515	Fort Dodge	37.3	25 894	909	694	29 423	-3 529	-12.0	95.37	3.29	0.31	0.53	0.50	1.52	18.8
3500	19 2040	Iowa City	57.0	59 738	388	1 048	50 508	9 230	18.3	91.08	2.54	0.19	5.59	0.59	1.70	6.6
...	19 2685	Marshalltown	39.1	25 178	919	644	26 938	-1 760	-6.5	97.13	1.00	0.34	1.07	0.45	0.98	18.4
...	19 2710	Mason City	66.3	29 040	843	438	30 144	-1 104	-3.7	97.28	0.93	0.11	0.52	1.17	2.91	17.3
...	19 3275	Ottumwa	40.6	24 488	931	603	27 381	-2 893	-10.6	97.82	1.02	0.29	0.58	0.30	0.74	20.7
7720	19 3980	Sioux City	140.6	80 505	262	573	82 003	-1 498	-1.8	92.57	2.30	2.02	1.48	1.63	3.26	14.7
8920	19 4455	Waterloo	156.9	66 467	342	424	75 985	-9 518	-12.5	86.63	12.14	0.18	0.68	0.38	0.80	15.7
...	20 0000	KANSAS	211 921.6	2 477 574	X	12	2 364 236	113 338	4.8	90.09	5.77	0.89	1.28	1.97	3.78	13.8
...	20 0840	Emporia	23.8	25 512	913	1 072	25 287	225	0.9	89.29	2.75	0.58	2.59	4.78	7.80	12.0
...	20 1350	Hutchinson	53.6	39 308	642	733	40 284	-976	-2.4	91.46	4.09	0.64	0.41	3.41	5.41	16.6
3760	20 1430	Kansas City	279.2	149 767	115	536	161 148	-11 381	-7.1	65.00	29.27	0.68	1.24	3.80	7.15	13.0
4150	20 1535	Lawrence	59.4	65 608	349	1 105	52 738	12 870	24.4	87.11	4.87	2.96	3.86	1.20	2.96	7.0
3760	20 1540	Leavenworth	58.8	38 495	655	655	33 656	4 839	14.4	79.75	15.83	0.71	2.00	1.71	4.69	9.7
...	20 1775	Manhattan	28.6	37 712	673	1 319	32 644	5 068	15.5	90.05	4.98	0.54	3.26	1.17	2.81	8.1
3760	20 2120	Olathe	109.5	63 352	362	579	37 258	26 094	70.0	94.28	3.02	0.44	1.68	0.57	1.81	5.2
3760	20 2194	Overland Park	144.2	111 790	160	775	81 784	30 006	36.7	95.40	1.83	0.31	1.92	0.54	1.97	9.9
...	20 2540	Salina	54.4	42 303	587	778	41 843	460	1.1	93.07	3.55	0.51	1.24	1.64	2.67	14.4
3760	20 2635	Shawnee	108.2	37 993	665	351	29 653	8 340	28.1	94.85	2.15	0.35	1.73	0.92	2.65	7.1
8440	20 2795	Topeka	142.9	119 883	149	839	118 690	1 193	1.0	84.71	10.64	1.28	0.79	2.57	5.78	14.7
9040	20 3040	Wichita	298.2	304 011	51	1 019	279 838	24 173	8.6	82.29	11.28	1.16	2.56	2.71	5.02	12.4
...	21 0000	KENTUCKY	102 906.8	3 685 296	X	36	3 660 324	24 972	0.7	92.04	7.13	0.16	0.48	0.19	0.60	12.7
3400	21 0050	Ashland	27.8	23 622	944	850	27 064	-3 442	-12.7	97.00	2.50	0.09	0.32	0.09	0.25	20.1
...	21 0200	Bowling Green	75.0	40 641	616	542	40 450	191	0.5	86.39	12.18	0.17	1.12	0.14	0.68	13.1
1642	21 0465	Covington	34.3	43 264	573	1 261	49 585	-6 321	-12.7	91.48	7.67	0.18	0.43	0.23	0.65	14.3
...	21 0735	Frankfort	37.7	25 968	906	689	25 973	-5	0.0	87.43	11.65	0.18	0.57	0.17	0.56	14.2
1660	21 0955	Hopkinsville	52.6	29 809	830	567	27 318	2 491	9.1	69.88	29.00	0.23	0.60	0.29	0.88	15.2
4280	21 1160	Lexington-Fayette	736.9	225 366	70	306	204 165	21 201	10.4	84.51	13.38	0.16	1.65	0.32	1.13	9.9
4520	21 1230	Louisville	160.9	269 063	58	1 672	298 694	-29 631	-9.9	69.21	29.65	0.19	0.73	0.22	0.65	16.6
5990	21 1495	Owensboro	38.8	53 549	448	1 380	54 450	-901	-1.7	93.00	6.43	0.13	0.32	0.11	0.39	15.0
...	21 1520	Paducah	45.5	27 256	882	599	29 315	-2 059	-7.0	78.40	20.89	0.20	0.33	0.18	0.57	22.2
...	22 0000	LOUISIANA	112 836.0	4 219 973	X	37	4 206 116	13 857	0.3	67.28	30.79	0.44	0.97	0.52	2.20	11.1
0220	22 0025	Alexandria	64.1	49 188	502	767	51 565	-2 377	-4.6	49.64	49.29	0.19	0.70	0.20	1.03	14.3
0760	22 0095	Baton Rouge	191.5	219 531	73	1 146	220 394	-863	-0.4	53.95	43.89	0.14	1.67	0.35	1.57	11.5
7680	22 0140	Bossier City	98.5	52 721	459	535	50 817	1 904	3.7	79.32	18.06	0.38	1.51	0.73	2.63	8.9
3350	22 0605	Houma	35.1	30 495	823	869	32 602	-2 107	-6.5	71.00	24.96	3.03	0.77	0.23	1.41	11.9
5560	22 0675	Kenner	39.2	72 033	303	1 838	66 382	5 651	8.5	77.42	18.08	0.28	1.69	2.54	10.05	6.6
3880	22 0700	Lafayette	106.0	94 440	211	891	80 584	13 856	17.2	70.80	27.19	0.20	1.35	0.45	1.71	9.5
3960	22 0715	Lake Charles	83.1	70 580	316	849	75 226	-4 646	-6.2	57.30	41.64	0.21	0.53	0.32	1.15	13.2
5200	22 0890	Monroe	67.8	54 909	429	810	57 597	-2 688	-4.7	43.31	55.55	0.12	0.85	0.16	0.77	13.4
...	22 0950	New Iberia	26.3	31 828	790	1 210	32 766	-938	-2.9	64.22	33.32	0.21	1.97	0.27	2.28	12.4
5560	22 0956	New Orleans	467.9	496 938	24	1 062	557 927	-60 989	-10.9	34.92	61.92	0.15	1.95	1.05	3.47	13.0
7680	22 1240	Shreveport	255.4	198 525	77	777	205 820	-7 295	-3.5	54.32	44.76	0.20	0.51	0.21	1.09	13.7
5560	22 1280	Slidell	24.2	24 124	934	997	26 718	-2 594	-9.7	87.86	10.84	0.38	0.61	0.31	2.53	10.5
...	23 0000	MAINE	79 939.2	1 227 928	X	15	1 125 043	102 885	9.1	98.41	0.42	0.49	0.54	0.14	0.56	13.3
0730	23 0270	Bangor	89.2	33 181	763	372	31 643	1 538	4.9	97.11	0.92	0.74	1.00	0.23	0.64	13.6
4240	23 2470	Lewiston	88.3	39 757	634	450	40 481	-724	-1.8	98.16	0.67	0.23	0.69	0.24	0.71	16.4
6400	23 3750	Portland	58.6	64 358	355	1 098	61 572	2 786	4.5	96.59	1.12	0.41	1.66	0.22	0.80	15.0
...	24 0000	MARYLAND	25 316.3	4 781 468	X	189	4 216 933	564 535	13.4	70.98	24.89	0.27	2.92	0.94	2.62	10.8
0720	24 0011	Annapolis	16.4	33 187	762	2 024	31 740	1 447	4.6	64.94	33.04	0.23	1.34	0.45	1.46	12.2
0720	24 0025	Baltimore	209.3	736 014	12	3 517	786 741	-50 727	-6.4	39.10	59.21	0.35	1.08	0.27	1.03	13.7
8840	24 0085	Bowie	33.3	37 589	677	1 129	33 695	3 894	11.6	91.36	5.70	0.30	2.27	0.36	2.20	6.3
1900	24 0245	Cumberland	21.4	23 706	940	1 108	25 933	-2 227	-8.6	94.79	4.42	0.09	0.54	0.16	0.45	22.3
8840	24 0355	Frederick	47.1	40 148	626	852	28 086	12 062	42.9	84.25	12.83	0.29	1.93	0.70	2.11	12.1
8840	24 0385	Gaithersburg	23.6	39 542	637	1 676	26 424	13 118	49.6	72.15	12.88	0.40	10.17	4.40	9.34	6.4

1. MSA = Metropolitan Statistical Area. CMSA = Consolidated MSA. 2. Dry land or land partially or temporarily covered by water. 3. Hispanic persons may be of any race.

Table C. Cities — Households, Vital Statistics, and Hospitals

City	Households, 1990				Births, 1984			Deaths, 1984				Hospitals, 1985		
	Number	Persons per household	Percent–		Number		Rate[3]	Number		Rate		Number	Beds	
			Female family householder[1]	One-person[2]	Total	To mothers under 20 yrs. old (Percent)		Total	Infant[4]	Total[3]	Infant[5]		Number	Rate[6]
	15	16	17	18	19	20	21	22	23	24	25	26	27	28
IOWA	1 064 325	2.52	8.0	25.9	42 367	9.4	14.6	27 020	374	9.3	8.8	139	18 596	652
Ames	15 613	2.36	5.3	26.9	599	2.3	13.3	145	4	3.2	6.7	1	217	488
Bettendorf	10 663	2.62	8.2	22.1	323	5.0	11.5	159	1	5.7	3.1	0	0	0
Burlington	10 986	2.43	11.7	29.4	423	11.6	14.8	333	7	11.7	16.5	1	388	1 386
Cedar Falls	11 689	2.50	8.1	23.8	433	9.0	12.2	223	4	6.3	9.2	1	91	274
Cedar Rapids	43 674	2.43	9.2	27.5	1 668	10.1	15.3	827	11	7.6	6.6	2	959	885
Clinton	11 667	2.44	11.2	28.0	469	14.1	14.8	361	2	11.4	4.3	2	294	977
Council Bluffs	21 131	2.52	13.4	26.1	969	15.4	17.0	565	11	9.9	11.4	2	460	808
Davenport	37 205	2.50	12.9	28.0	1 876	13.2	18.4	902	22	8.8	11.7	3	653	661
Des Moines	78 453	2.38	11.9	30.7	3 638	11.9	19.1	1 884	39	9.9	10.7	7	2 416	1 258
Dubuque	21 437	2.52	9.6	27.7	889	11.0	14.8	656	8	10.9	9.0	2	611	1 023
Fort Dodge	10 502	2.35	11.2	31.2	413	14.3	14.9	334	5	12.0	12.1	1	194	717
Iowa City	21 951	2.34	6.8	29.7	735	3.4	14.4	283	5	5.6	6.8	3	1 413	2 799
Marshalltown	9 974	2.40	9.8	29.1	398	7.3	14.8	293	1	10.9	2.5	1	176	675
Mason City	12 027	2.32	9.5	31.5	430	8.1	14.3	334	9	11.1	20.9	2	393	1 301
Ottumwa	10 280	2.32	10.7	30.1	364	14.0	13.6	393	4	14.7	11.0	2	240	949
Sioux City	30 488	2.55	11.4	27.1	1 361	12.9	16.6	776	15	9.5	11.0	2	855	1 074
Waterloo	27 037	2.42	12.4	28.9	1 302	13.4	17.2	644	13	8.5	10.0	3	681	973
KANSAS	944 726	2.53	8.6	25.9	40 010	11.8	16.4	22 307	404	9.1	10.1	163	17 278	702
Emporia	9 753	2.42	8.8	31.5	522	9.8	19.3	172	2	6.3	3.8	2	225	914
Hutchinson	15 656	2.36	9.8	30.3	637	14.6	15.8	425	3	10.5	4.7	1	230	554
Kansas City	57 146	2.59	16.9	28.0	2 995	19.7	18.7	1 586	51	9.9	17.0	4	1 213	748
Lawrence	24 513	2.35	8.0	28.8	783	8.2	14.4	267	9	4.9	11.5	2	215	381
Leavenworth	11 475	2.70	10.7	24.5	405	13.8	11.5	305	1	8.7	2.5	4	698	1 927
Manhattan	14 689	2.39	6.7	28.2	688	10.6	21.2	176	6	5.4	8.7	3	184	545
Olathe	21 445	2.89	8.7	17.4	972	5.5	20.8	208	13	4.4	13.4	2	137	263
Overland Park	44 936	2.47	7.9	25.6	1 208	4.6	13.5	446	9	5.0	7.5	1	400	414
Salina	17 287	2.40	10.1	28.9	714	11.3	16.6	371	10	8.6	14.0	2	362	845
Shawnee	14 567	2.60	8.1	22.8	508	7.9	17.0	134	4	4.5	7.9	1	383	1 267
Topeka	49 936	2.33	11.9	32.0	1 914	12.8	16.1	1 217	21	10.2	11.0	7	2 265	1 910
Wichita	123 249	2.43	11.1	30.0	6 239	13.2	22.0	2 583	74	9.1	11.9	6	2 074	718
KENTUCKY	1 379 782	2.60	11.6	23.3	53 290	18.3	14.3	33 631	615	9.0	11.5	122	19 532	524
Ashland	10 128	2.30	12.9	30.3	303	17.2	11.6	371	4	14.2	13.2	3	440	1 688
Bowling Green	15 973	2.29	13.3	31.8	554	19.7	12.6	357	9	8.1	16.2	2	541	1 310
Covington	17 319	2.43	16.7	34.0	893	23.0	19.2	613	14	13.2	15.7	2	627	1 373
Frankfort	11 037	2.26	13.9	32.9	358	20.1	13.4	277	0	10.3	0.0	1	157	583
Hopkinsville	11 402	2.50	17.4	26.7	519	22.5	18.6	359	9	12.9	17.3	2	647	2 223
Lexington-Fayette	89 529	2.38	12.2	29.1	3 171	13.3	15.1	1 517	38	7.2	12.0	10	3 200	1 503
Louisville	113 065	2.31	18.3	35.0	4 244	19.6	14.6	3 690	51	12.7	12.0	16	4 948	1 727
Owensboro	21 672	2.39	13.8	30.1	1 036	17.7	18.6	583	5	10.5	4.8	3	639	1 135
Paducah	11 955	2.21	15.4	35.7	376	21.8	12.9	426	6	14.6	16.0	2	669	2 358
LOUISIANA	1 499 269	2.74	15.6	23.7	81 472	17.6	18.3	35 741	982	8.0	12.1	174	27 482	611
Alexandria	18 134	2.63	21.1	28.0	1 126	21.2	21.4	596	16	11.3	14.2	3	995	1 934
Baton Rouge	83 340	2.51	17.7	29.7	5 210	14.7	21.8	1 916	71	8.0	13.6	5	1 596	432
Bossier City	19 032	2.67	13.8	22.4	1 074	14.9	19.7	305	12	5.6	11.2	2	277	485
Houma	10 658	2.82	16.7	22.2	806	23.6	22.9	303	4	8.6	5.0	2	425	418
Kenner	25 056	2.85	14.0	21.8	1 171	12.6	15.8	329	7	4.5	6.0	0	0	0
Lafayette	36 326	2.50	13.8	28.9	1 667	13.0	20.2	616	17	7.5	10.2	8	1 125	1 252
Lake Charles	26 815	2.57	17.2	27.7	1 372	15.3	18.3	711	21	9.5	15.3	4	753	1 026
Monroe	19 131	2.67	24.2	29.7	1 257	23.0	22.5	615	18	11.0	14.3	3	779	1 386
New Iberia	11 143	2.82	18.0	23.1	729	17.6	20.3	316	11	8.8	15.1	2	241	666
New Orleans	188 235	2.55	24.1	32.2	10 432	18.7	18.7	5 798	167	10.4	16.0	21	5 755	1 038
Shreveport	75 645	2.57	19.9	28.7	4 053	21.3	18.4	2 112	57	9.6	14.1	10	2 684	1 218
Slidell	8 322	2.85	11.8	17.1	541	11.3	16.4	215	9	6.5	16.6	3	310	866
MAINE	465 312	2.56	9.5	23.3	16 770	12.2	14.5	10 873	141	9.4	8.4	48	6 444	549
Bangor	13 392	2.31	12.7	31.1	489	11.9	15.9	295	5	9.6	10.2	4	931	3 087
Lewiston	15 823	2.37	12.6	29.7	579	15.4	14.7	461	5	11.7	8.6	2	483	1 239
Portland	28 235	2.21	12.2	35.3	943	14.1	15.3	763	11	12.3	11.7	3	916	1 462
MARYLAND	1 748 991	2.67	13.3	22.6	65 409	12.8	15.0	35 466	773	8.2	11.8	86	22 700	509
Annapolis	14 061	2.33	16.7	31.8	550	15.3	17.2	360	8	11.3	14.5	1	303	908
Baltimore	276 484	2.59	24.6	30.5	12 954	23.7	17.0	9 624	217	12.6	16.8	31	9 342	1 241
Bowie	12 891	2.92	8.0	12.7	444	5.9	12.9	155	3	4.5	6.8	0	0	0
Cumberland	10 266	2.25	15.0	35.1	324	19.8	13.4	453	4	18.8	12.3	3	654	2 815
Frederick	15 671	2.45	12.4	27.3	629	11.3	19.7	368	11	11.5	17.5	1	239	707
Gaithersburg	15 202	2.57	11.6	25.7	1 440	5.7	48.7	274	5	9.3	3.5	0	0	0

1. No spouse present. 2. Householder living alone. 3. Per 1,000 resident population estimated as of July 1 of the year shown. 4. Deaths of infants under 1 year old. 5. Deaths of infants under 1 year old per 1,000 live births. 6. Per 100,000 resident population estimated as of July 1, 1986.

City	Serious crimes known to police, 1985: Number: Total	Serious crimes known to police, 1985: Number: Violent[1]	Serious crimes known to police, 1985: Rate[2]	Police officers, 1985: Number	Police officers, 1985: Rate[3]	Educational attainment,[4] 1980: Percent completing 12 years or more	Educational attainment,[4] 1980: Percent completing 16 years or more	Money income: Per capita[5]: 1985: Total (Dollars)	Money income: Per capita[5]: 1985: Percent of State average	Money income: Per capita[5]: 1979: Current dollars	Money income: Per capita[5]: 1979: Constant (1985) dollars	Money income: Percent below poverty level, 1979: Persons	Money income: Percent below poverty level, 1979: Families	Housing, 1990: Total units	Housing, 1990: Percent change, 1980–1990	Housing, 1990: Vacant units for sale or rent[6]
	29	30	31	32	33	34	35	36	37	38	39	40	41	42	43	44
IOWA	113 713	6 106	3 943	NA	NA	71.5	13.9	10 096	100.0	7 136	10 576	10.1	7.5	1 143 669	1.1	41 387
Ames	1 876	175	4 142	48	10.6	91.6	48.3	10 009	99.1	6 698	9 926	15.8	6.6	16 058	7.8	337
Bettendorf	996	39	3 650	28	10.3	85.5	26.3	14 430	142.9	9 831	14 570	2.7	2.0	11 063	12.6	314
Burlington	1 730	186	6 008	33	11.5	69.1	11.8	10 411	103.1	7 362	10 910	9.4	7.2	11 777	-2.7	477
Cedar Falls	1 077	27	3 005	44	12.3	83.2	27.0	10 462	103.6	7 727	11 451	8.3	4.7	12 066	-1.0	241
Cedar Rapids	8 058	172	7 482	158	14.7	77.4	17.7	12 301	121.8	8 269	12 255	7.6	5.3	45 473	4.2	1 386
Clinton	1 789	28	5 571	44	13.7	69.9	12.1	10 516	104.2	7 350	10 893	7.6	5.1	12 584	-2.5	649
Council Bluffs	4 031	287	7 182	89	15.9	65.2	8.7	9 996	99.0	6 709	9 943	10.3	8.3	22 244	1.3	865
Davenport	7 029	1 058	6 944	145	14.3	71.8	18.2	11 338	112.3	7 896	11 702	9.9	7.2	40 343	0.1	2 137
Des Moines	19 989	1 117	10 569	332	17.6	74.8	16.6	12 134	120.2	7 838	11 616	10.6	7.8	83 289	4.1	3 450
Dubuque	3 283	82	5 418	73	12.0	69.8	17.4	10 317	102.2	7 341	10 879	8.2	5.4	22 377	1.0	690
Fort Dodge	2 476	182	8 668	44	15.4	72.5	15.4	10 244	101.5	7 291	10 805	10.3	7.4	11 212	-3.8	524
Iowa City	2 491	184	4 880	54	10.6	89.5	48.1	11 280	111.7	7 247	10 740	19.7	6.3	22 464	14.4	352
Marshalltown	1 078	91	4 000	40	14.8	74.3	16.8	11 320	112.1	7 801	11 561	8.2	5.3	10 630	-1.3	506
Mason City	2 489	198	8 337	43	14.4	72.1	14.7	10 430	103.3	7 312	10 836	9.4	5.8	12 669	0.4	515
Ottumwa	1 109	24	4 157	32	12.0	64.3	10.9	9 969	98.7	7 187	10 651	9.6	6.0	10 912	-5.0	360
Sioux City	6 370	352	7 838	105	12.9	71.9	15.9	10 146	100.5	7 087	10 503	11.4	9.0	32 177	0.5	1 192
Waterloo	4 178	245	5 524	130	17.2	71.2	13.2	10 478	103.8	7 872	11 666	10.4	7.9	29 023	-1.8	1 391
KANSAS	107 190	8 716	4 375	NA	NA	73.3	17.0	10 684	100.0	7 349	10 891	10.1	7.4	1 044 112	8.5	60 956
Emporia	1 416	50	5 260	39	14.5	77.9	23.5	9 706	90.8	7 124	10 558	11.4	5.9	10 732	5.2	617
Hutchinson	2 831	120	6 903	46	11.2	71.7	13.4	10 326	96.6	7 190	10 656	9.7	6.7	17 163	0.4	1 082
Kansas City	14 451	2 119	8 961	NA	NA	61.4	8.9	8 757	82.0	6 398	9 482	14.4	11.4	64 457	0.0	5 980
Lawrence	3 355	199	6 087	76	13.8	85.0	41.4	9 372	87.7	6 384	9 461	19.1	8.3	25 893	22.1	1 107
Leavenworth	1 337	137	3 918	40	11.7	72.1	20.5	9 537	89.3	6 480	9 603	11.8	7.7	12 568	9.1	887
Manhattan	1 282	68	3 794	67	19.8	88.0	40.9	9 950	93.1	6 786	10 057	17.2	6.9	15 558	12.3	685
Olathe	2 197	120	5 124	65	15.2	84.2	24.3	11 615	108.7	7 922	11 740	5.3	3.9	22 497	42.1	948
Overland Park	4 084	190	4 776	NA	NA	91.1	35.1	16 404	153.5	10 623	15 743	2.8	2.1	48 043	35.0	2 495
Salina	2 031	75	4 719	58	13.5	76.2	16.3	10 446	97.8	7 418	10 993	8.4	5.8	18 411	4.0	850
Shawnee	1 295	57	4 163	47	15.1	86.3	26.2	13 861	129.7	9 224	13 670	3.9	3.1	15 217	26.8	555
Topeka	9 277	694	7 761	221	18.5	76.6	20.9	11 248	105.3	7 733	11 460	9.3	6.5	54 664	7.9	3 527
Wichita	21 751	1 672	7 634	474	16.6	75.9	19.0	11 764	110.1	8 127	12 044	10.2	7.2	135 069	13.6	9 508
KENTUCKY	109 812	11 384	2 947	NA	NA	53.1	11.1	8 614	100.0	5 973	8 852	17.6	14.6	1 506 845	9.1	65 649
Ashland	1 407	162	5 265	54	20.2	60.4	12.2	10 122	117.5	7 628	11 305	15.0	12.0	11 021	-3.6	639
Bowling Green	2 368	215	5 351	73	16.5	63.5	19.8	9 089	105.5	6 021	8 923	18.4	13.3	17 501	13.3	1 265
Covington	3 425	312	7 015	82	16.8	44.9	6.9	8 016	93.1	5 618	8 326	17.4	14.9	19 117	-6.7	1 164
Frankfort	1 193	146	4 537	45	17.1	67.7	20.6	11 042	128.2	7 762	11 503	11.0	8.2	11 880	5.6	659
Hopkinsville	1 868	206	6 531	41	14.3	61.1	11.4	8 825	102.4	6 142	9 102	18.9	13.6	12 236	14.0	567
Lexington-Fayette	12 711	1 121	6 042	322	15.3	71.6	25.6	11 454	133.0	7 395	10 959	13.5	9.5	97 742	16.4	6 427
Louisville	16 814	1 945	5 797	650	22.4	55.5	13.3	9 129	106.0	6 283	9 311	19.3	15.5	124 018	-1.7	6 928
Owensboro	2 756	100	4 969	102	18.4	60.9	12.4	9 233	107.2	6 550	9 707	13.8	10.8	23 074	8.3	1 042
Paducah	2 191	209	7 425	68	23.0	58.9	11.9	10 056	116.7	6 770	10 033	18.7	13.2	13 150	3.0	907
LOUISIANA	249 303	31 108	5 564	NA	NA	57.7	13.9	8 836	100.0	6 425	9 522	18.6	15.1	1 716 241	9.8	120 665
Alexandria	4 987	418	9 316	122	22.8	55.6	14.7	8 592	97.2	6 116	9 064	24.2	20.2	20 348	3.5	1 543
Baton Rouge	31 279	4 331	12 724	575	23.4	69.6	25.0	10 505	118.9	7 519	11 143	18.7	14.5	97 115	13.4	9 376
Bossier City	3 740	478	6 681	125	22.3	73.1	12.1	9 361	105.9	6 439	9 543	11.6	9.7	21 815	17.7	1 971
Houma	2 052	224	5 215	59	15.0	55.2	13.0	8 772	99.3	6 710	9 944	17.3	13.3	11 476	-0.5	647
Kenner	3 743	303	5 140	134	18.4	71.5	17.3	10 157	115.0	7 246	10 739	9.8	8.5	27 259	18.2	1 721
Lafayette	8 761	1 119	9 991	157	17.9	64.5	23.9	11 876	134.4	8 166	12 102	15.4	11.3	40 379	26.1	2 824
Lake Charles	4 578	198	5 849	114	14.6	58.6	16.9	9 816	111.1	7 146	10 590	15.3	12.4	29 844	5.6	2 178
Monroe	3 784	707	6 474	117	20.0	59.0	18.6	8 020	90.8	5 817	8 621	29.6	23.8	21 610	2.3	1 707
New Iberia	1 163	66	3 210	60	16.6	49.1	10.7	8 652	97.9	6 376	9 449	16.6	12.9	12 426	9.1	866
New Orleans	48 732	8 222	8 681	1 378	24.5	59.2	17.7	8 975	101.6	6 463	9 578	26.4	21.8	225 573	-0.4	26 583
Shreveport	20 366	1 750	9 220	418	18.9	62.5	17.3	10 240	115.9	7 169	10 624	17.7	13.8	87 473	8.5	8 730
Slidell	NA	NA	NA	NA	NA	78.0	22.8	11 414	129.2	7 877	11 674	8.7	6.9	9 087	3.1	541
MAINE	42 739	1 950	3 672	NA	NA	68.7	14.4	9 042	100.0	5 766	8 545	13.0	9.8	587 045	14.6	22 097
Bangor	2 054	47	6 393	62	19.3	78.6	17.9	9 494	105.0	6 185	9 166	14.6	9.8	14 366	11.0	719
Lewiston	3 204	227	7 817	67	16.3	49.9	8.4	8 796	97.3	5 600	8 299	13.3	10.0	17 118	7.3	1 126
Portland	7 368	670	11 730	148	23.6	72.9	19.4	10 386	114.9	6 416	9 509	15.4	10.2	31 293	10.6	1 764
MARYLAND	235 973	36 655	5 373	NA	NA	67.4	20.4	12 967	100.0	8 293	12 290	9.8	7.5	1 891 917	17.0	77 134
Annapolis	2 963	427	9 026	94	28.6	69.7	26.4	13 874	107.0	8 581	12 717	15.4	12.1	15 252	12.3	647
Baltimore	66 121	15 498	8 575	2 965	38.5	48.4	11.3	8 647	66.7	5 877	8 710	22.9	18.9	303 706	0.3	19 025
Bowie	NA	NA	NA	NA	NA	90.5	35.3	15 473	119.3	9 612	14 245	1.7	1.3	13 066	26.8	139
Cumberland	934	21	3 598	50	19.3	56.2	8.5	9 002	69.4	6 201	9 190	15.0	10.8	11 431	-1.1	745
Frederick	2 275	420	7 220	67	21.3	60.5	18.3	11 414	88.0	7 502	11 118	10.3	7.9	16 611	32.0	754
Gaithersburg	NA	NA	NA	NA	NA	82.7	31.8	14 625	112.8	9 279	13 751	6.4	5.0	16 059	32.6	781

1. Includes murder and nonnegligent manslaughter, forcible rape, robbery, and aggravated assault. 2. Per 100,000 resident population estimated for 1985 by the FBI. 3. Per 10,000 resident population estimated for 1985 by the FBI. 4. Persons 25 years old or older. 5. Based on the resident population estimated as of July 1, 1988 for 1987 data and enumerated as of April 1, 1980 for 1979 data. 6. Also includes units rented or sold, but not occupied.

City	Housing, 1990 (cont'd)					Construction authorized by building permits, 1990				Civilian labor force, 1990			
	Occupied units					New private housing units			Non-residential, value ($1,000)	Total	Percent change, 1989–1990	Unemployment	
	Total	Percent with more than 1 person per room	Owner-occupied		Median rent[2] (Dollars)	Number	Value ($1,000)	Percent single family				Total	Rate[3]
			Percent of total	Median value[1] (Dollars)									
	45	46	47	48	49	50	51	52	53	54	55	56	57
IOWA	1 064 325	1.5	70.0	45 900	261	7 637	530 765	68.7	354 194	1 496 000	-1.1	63 000	4.2
Ames	15 613	3.2	44.1	72 500	357	200	12 132	37.5	2 802	26 681	-1.0	507	1.9
Bettendorf	10 663	0.8	73.7	67 500	335	225	25 904	100.0	447	14 649	-2.1	486	3.3
Burlington	10 986	1.3	69.6	38 700	239	27	2 446	100.0	2 308	13 935	-2.8	772	5.5
Cedar Falls	11 689	1.4	63.7	56 600	276	117	9 919	59.8	2 975	17 070	0.8	628	3.7
Cedar Rapids	43 674	1.4	67.2	56 900	318	331	17 132	67.4	13 420	63 384	-0.9	3 221	5.1
Clinton	11 667	1.1	68.4	36 700	239	23	2 523	100.0	3 910	13 688	-2.0	1 076	7.9
Council Bluffs	21 131	2.4	66.2	44 500	309	103	6 199	48.5	3 812	31 554	-1.0	1 546	4.9
Davenport	37 205	2.0	61.2	48 800	283	136	12 721	100.0	31 105	51 845	-2.5	2 895	5.6
Des Moines	78 453	2.7	62.0	49 500	346	491	34 200	55.4	39 763	122 241	-0.4	4 676	3.8
Dubuque	21 437	1.3	66.1	51 600	255	209	14 750	53.6	12 149	30 434	-1.0	1 871	6.1
Fort Dodge	10 502	1.0	64.7	38 500	228	23	1 834	100.0	650	13 406	-1.5	635	4.7
Iowa City	21 951	3.2	44.7	79 000	368	341	22 618	39.9	11 315	38 303	-0.1	688	1.8
Marshalltown	9 974	1.3	68.3	43 500	250	22	1 968	100.0	1 369	13 076	-1.5	490	3.7
Mason City	12 027	0.9	65.8	44 100	258	56	4 080	89.3	699	16 255	-1.3	870	5.4
Ottumwa	10 280	1.3	72.8	26 400	226	16	904	87.5	2 237	10 756	-1.1	659	6.1
Sioux City	30 488	2.7	67.0	41 000	259	159	5 253	62.9	6 890	42 866	-0.8	1 738	4.1
Waterloo	27 037	2.1	65.4	39 800	250	40	4 085	95.0	19 455	33 845	0.7	1 915	5.7
KANSAS	944 726	2.5	67.9	52 200	285	8 496	661 281	75.1	307 969	1 300 000	1.2	57 000	4.4
Emporia	9 753	2.9	54.2	47 400	237	17	1 444	100.0	4 342	14 662	1.1	704	4.8
Hutchinson	15 656	1.6	64.5	39 000	241	81	3 655	23.5	1 646	19 499	1.0	1 015	5.2
Kansas City	57 146	4.6	61.9	41 200	285	125	8 402	97.6	3 715	83 150	-0.8	6 608	7.9
Lawrence	24 513	2.9	46.2	69 400	348	535	37 657	48.8	11 572	34 945	3.9	1 297	3.7
Leavenworth	11 475	2.7	51.7	57 500	348	144	9 760	68.1	1 770	15 396	1.4	789	5.1
Manhattan	14 689	2.6	44.3	65 900	333	261	14 552	30.7	1 038	19 880	3.3	632	3.2
Olathe	21 445	1.7	66.3	83 300	385	704	63 139	89.2	6 869	27 590	2.5	992	3.6
Overland Park	44 936	0.9	64.4	95 300	469	1 256	120 199	66.2	19 938	64 308	2.4	1 780	2.8
Salina	17 287	1.9	64.1	45 100	250	168	8 575	51.2	3 656	24 487	1.7	1 077	4.4
Shawnee	14 567	1.3	67.2	84 800	410	219	17 417	100.0	9 258	23 492	2.4	697	3.0
Topeka	49 936	2.2	60.8	48 800	304	287	20 449	69.0	18 189	69 133	0.7	3 464	5.0
Wichita	123 249	3.9	58.9	56 700	299	1 609	89 809	62.8	65 677	167 594	1.0	7 936	4.7
KENTUCKY	1 379 782	2.6	69.6	50 500	250	11 944	778 348	74.0	482 341	1 767 000	1.4	103 000	5.8
Ashland	10 128	1.0	65.3	43 800	218	25	1 725	64.0	1 834	11 073	2.2	624	5.6
Bowling Green	15 973	2.5	50.6	58 200	267	170	10 886	51.8	30 678	21 343	-0.4	572	2.7
Covington	17 319	4.4	50.8	41 600	248	50	2 209	100.0	544	21 298	0.8	948	4.5
Frankfort	11 037	1.8	53.9	61 500	282	133	5 975	100.0	4 278	15 915	3.7	660	4.1
Hopkinsville	11 402	3.4	57.3	43 500	227	80	4 879	92.5	1 720	13 010	2.3	796	6.1
Lexington-Fayette	89 529	2.3	53.0	73 900	338	1 347	113 135	94.3	52 430	134 047	0.3	4 228	3.2
Louisville	113 065	3.3	54.9	44 300	244	180	10 288	55.6	48 843	143 169	1.1	8 434	5.9
Owensboro	21 672	2.4	60.1	46 100	230	154	8 648	61.0	5 277	29 857	1.8	1 688	5.7
Paducah	11 955	1.8	54.4	37 800	190	31	3 115	61.3	4 408	13 213	1.2	581	4.4
LOUISIANA	1 499 269	6.0	65.9	58 500	260	6 451	440 227	88.5	375 495	1 874 000	-1.4	117 000	6.2
Alexandria	18 134	5.5	56.6	54 300	233	42	3 727	95.2	10 295	23 115	-4.2	1 548	6.7
Baton Rouge	83 340	5.3	52.8	67 900	273	30	2 141	63.3	46 490	121 003	0.1	6 387	5.3
Bossier City	19 032	4.3	57.4	58 400	293	114	8 669	98.2	4 883	22 613	-2.8	1 427	6.3
Houma	10 658	7.2	64.5	53 700	218	36	1 993	100.0	627	13 380	-0.5	827	6.2
Kenner	25 056	5.8	58.8	74 200	347	67	6 950	100.0	3 387	33 446	-2.1	1 695	5.1
Lafayette	36 326	4.6	53.3	66 000	254	NA	NA	NA	NA	47 378	2.5	2 346	5.0
Lake Charles	26 815	4.6	58.4	52 200	254	120	9 865	59.2	5 830	36 768	1.8	2 410	6.6
Monroe	19 131	8.5	51.9	50 100	203	45	6 440	100.0	3 496	26 547	-1.7	1 841	6.9
New Iberia	11 143	8.1	61.1	46 700	193	17	1 010	100.0	8 726	13 837	0.7	860	6.2
New Orleans	188 235	7.9	43.7	69 600	277	204	16 537	90.7	27 036	222 249	-2.5	13 365	6.0
Shreveport	75 645	5.1	60.5	54 800	269	68	9 832	100.0	25 604	96 345	-3.0	6 344	6.6
Slidell	8 322	2.1	75.2	67 800	353	3	225	100.0	9 900	15 994	-2.0	768	4.8
MAINE	465 312	1.7	70.5	87 400	358	4 816	329 551	85.1	169 400	635 000	3.1	33 000	5.1
Bangor	13 392	1.3	48.5	76 800	365	162	7 147	14.8	3 352	17 160	4.4	857	5.0
Lewiston	15 823	1.4	47.0	87 200	329	64	4 732	84.4	4 968	19 210	1.9	1 404	7.3
Portland	28 235	1.3	42.1	112 200	450	70	4 570	85.7	5 138	39 298	2.8	1 646	4.2
MARYLAND	1 748 991	3.0	65.0	116 500	473	32 111	2 185 336	73.9	892 215	2 535 000	0.5	118 000	4.6
Annapolis	14 061	3.2	47.8	138 500	533	92	5 849	60.9	5 225	19 678	0.3	816	4.1
Baltimore	276 484	4.6	48.6	54 700	321	240	10 764	66.2	91 310	346 599	0.9	26 767	7.7
Bowie	12 891	0.9	84.2	143 200	822	NA	NA	NA	NA	20 268	0.1	615	3.0
Cumberland	10 266	0.8	55.4	40 700	211	56	2 299	14.3	225	NA	NA	NA	NA
Frederick	15 671	2.1	45.5	113 400	517	795	39 888	50.4	14 104	19 968	1.5	1 081	5.4
Gaithersburg	15 202	5.0	49.6	147 300	639	350	25 096	56.6	15 328	21 626	-0.2	408	1.9

1. Specified owner-occupied units. 2. Specified renter-occupied units. 3. Percent of total civilian labor force.

City	Employed,[1] 1980			Manufactures, 1987											
		Rate per 1,000 employees		Establishments		All employees			Production workers						
											Wages				
	Total	Professional, specialty, and technical	Precision production, craft, and operators	Total	Percent with 20 or more employees	Number (1,000)	Percent change, 1982–1987	Annual payroll (Mil. dol.)	Number (1,000)	Work-hours (Millions)	Total (Mil. dol.)	Average per production worker (Dollars)	Value added by manufacture (Mil. dol.)	Value of shipments (Mil. dol.)	New capital expenditures (Mil. dol.)
	58	59	60	61	62	63	64	65	66	67	68	69	70	71	72
IOWA	1 304 638	135.4	204.0	3 569	35.3	206.1	-3.4	4 971.1	140.1	277.5	3 043.4	21 723	14 469.0	35 408.6	834.2
Ames	21 672	303.8	100.6	35	28.6	D	D	D	D	D	D	D	D	D	D
Bettendorf	13 703	181.9	169.8	31	25.8	D	D	D	D	D	D	D	D	D	D
Burlington	12 856	129.3	273.7	46	50.0	4.9	-3.9	132.9	3.8	7.3	97.6	25 684	538.3	1 009.6	D
Cedar Falls	17 454	205.1	180.1	47	27.7	1.3	-23.5	32.4	0.9	1.7	19.8	22 000	62.6	98.5	3.7
Cedar Rapids	54 474	161.5	228.9	164	46.3	22.2	-9.4	640.5	10.7	21.4	272.2	25 439	1 846.4	3 331.7	106.8
Clinton	14 715	126.7	290.7	34	58.8	3.7	-19.6	95.4	2.9	6.2	69.3	23 897	506.2	1 016.1	D
Council Bluffs	24 989	114.5	213.8	60	38.3	D	D	D	D	D	D	D	D	D	D
Davenport	47 361	145.1	229.1	117	37.6	8.7	-17.9	257.1	6.0	11.9	159.9	26 650	696.0	1 704.0	D
Des Moines	93 366	145.4	174.6	272	36.0	17.6	0.0	419.0	9.8	18.9	220.1	22 459	1 153.5	3 097.7	67.0
Dubuque	28 363	162.9	227.8	107	40.2	D	D	D	D	D	D	D	D	D	D
Fort Dodge	13 557	137.4	181.9	43	44.2	2.0	-20.0	41.9	1.0	2.1	18.4	18 400	170.4	283.2	D
Iowa City	27 210	324.9	88.6	46	28.3	3.0	7.1	72.5	2.2	3.8	49.0	22 273	596.9	886.8	19.5
Marshalltown	12 592	175.0	214.0	42	42.9	4.4	-25.4	129.4	2.6	5.2	66.7	25 654	231.7	645.4	11.3
Mason City	13 754	162.9	185.8	44	54.5	D	D	D	D	D	D	D	D	D	D
Ottumwa	10 901	139.7	226.3	22	50.0	D	D	D	D	D	D	D	D	D	D
Sioux City	36 233	151.0	181.0	88	52.3	4.8	0.0	103.3	3.1	6.6	60.6	19 548	310.8	1 146.9	14.0
Waterloo	33 895	141.0	271.5	94	38.3	9.1	D	301.3	6.2	11.6	184.1	29 694	673.5	1 200.9	23.6
KANSAS	1 078 741	145.8	214.0	3 275	34.8	189.1	10.8	4 597.2	120.7	245.3	2 608.5	21 611	12 908.8	31 055.8	1 011.2
Emporia	12 712	153.9	217.0	24	58.3	D	D	D	D	D	D	D	D	D	D
Hutchinson	18 795	112.1	260.2	48	41.7	2.4	-33.3	50.3	1.6	3.3	31.0	19 375	137.7	232.1	7.2
Kansas City	68 218	109.9	241.2	282	42.2	16.5	0.6	467.6	12.1	23.1	323.6	26 744	1 446.9	3 416.5	D
Lawrence	25 534	267.6	133.0	67	37.3	D	D	D	D	D	D	D	D	D	D
Leavenworth	10 764	179.8	177.6	22	40.9	D	D	D	D	D	D	D	D	D	D
Manhattan	15 257	283.3	97.3	20	45.0	0.9	D	16.6	0.7	1.2	9.5	13 571	74.2	107.1	2.7
Olathe	18 589	175.7	185.5	92	39.1	5.4	8.0	117.9	3.7	7.4	68.7	18 568	297.3	513.4	D
Overland Park	43 698	198.5	104.3	119	24.4	3.3	43.5	66.2	1.5	3.2	20.7	13 800	295.2	450.8	D
Salina	20 610	140.2	235.1	64	37.5	3.1	-3.1	61.4	2.5	4.9	45.1	18 040	178.1	430.8	D
Shawnee	15 931	175.0	153.6	43	20.9	1.1	22.2	27.1	0.6	1.1	10.4	17 333	65.0	136.2	D
Topeka	56 388	178.9	163.0	118	40.7	D	D	D	D	D	D	D	D	D	D
Wichita	139 460	165.9	259.6	509	36.5	56.5	78.8	1 620.6	27.7	61.1	768.0	27 726	3 554.5	6 684.4	240.0
KENTUCKY	1 388 046	128.3	257.9	3 693	41.0	251.6	2.0	5 865.2	184.8	356.2	3 752.3	20 305	18 091.7	41 827.1	1 746.0
Ashland	10 153	154.8	207.2	28	42.9	1.3	-53.6	26.0	0.8	1.4	12.0	15 000	40.5	86.7	D
Bowling Green	18 327	171.1	200.3	66	42.4	7.3	-5.2	172.1	5.4	10.0	116.8	21 630	597.8	1 346.6	D
Covington	18 856	100.4	231.7	52	38.5	1.8	-14.3	31.5	1.2	2.2	18.4	15 333	58.2	164.6	D
Frankfort	13 090	157.0	155.6	26	46.2	3.0	D	53.5	2.6	4.8	41.8	16 077	158.2	298.2	D
Hopkinsville	10 980	128.5	214.1	41	53.7	3.9	34.5	71.3	3.1	6.1	51.7	16 677	160.3	385.7	12.5
Lexington-Fayette	98 868	212.7	144.5	250	35.6	15.8	-5.4	481.2	9.0	17.8	213.1	23 678	1 284.1	2 644.6	D
Louisville	120 393	156.0	211.4	541	45.7	51.4	-18.2	1 519.2	34.0	68.2	917.6	26 988	5 319.0	11 891.4	187.4
Owensboro	23 002	137.2	233.8	73	42.5	5.1	10.9	113.4	3.4	6.2	68.1	20 029	418.8	1 103.7	D
Paducah	11 244	146.7	206.2	41	46.3	D	D	D	D	D	D	D	D	D	D
LOUISIANA	1 639 394	144.4	225.0	3 816	29.1	161.4	-20.1	4 175.9	110.8	224.9	2 587.8	23 356	16 425.8	50 699.7	1 419.8
Alexandria	19 175	148.8	132.9	58	24.1	D	D	D	D	D	D	D	D	D	D
Baton Rouge	96 825	200.9	168.2	236	26.7	8.7	D	265.3	4.2	8.5	99.4	23 667	1 059.3	2 345.7	73.4
Bossier City	20 018	123.2	202.3	62	30.6	1.5	-6.3	25.4	1.1	2.1	16.2	14 727	49.3	131.1	D
Houma	13 399	130.4	247.0	66	22.7	1.1	-60.7	27.0	0.7	1.3	12.7	18 143	56.6	87.7	D
Kenner	30 550	127.6	196.5	54	24.1	1.3	0.0	30.8	0.9	2.0	20.0	22 222	73.6	126.2	D
Lafayette	38 040	205.8	159.0	134	18.7	2.7	-30.8	52.8	1.3	2.7	23.0	17 692	129.9	244.8	4.6
Lake Charles	33 039	162.0	215.9	66	28.8	D	D	D	D	D	D	D	D	D	D
Monroe	20 582	173.1	145.1	62	40.3	3.7	19.4	90.9	2.4	4.8	58.9	24 542	247.6	585.8	D
New Iberia	13 208	121.4	273.5	43	34.9	D	D	D	D	D	D	D	D	D	D
New Orleans	218 693	175.8	148.3	371	31.0	16.8	-23.6	431.0	10.2	19.1	228.0	22 353	1 133.9	2 307.7	72.9
Shreveport	89 444	152.6	207.8	202	29.7	12.9	-30.6	325.5	8.8	16.5	209.4	23 795	1 067.2	2 091.1	63.8
Slidell	11 196	202.5	173.2	25	28.0	0.7	0.0	11.1	0.6	1.0	7.9	13 167	26.1	47.7	0.4
MAINE	459 522	145.3	271.6	2 172	27.8	101.6	-7.8	2 192.1	77.4	151.3	1 457.0	18 824	5 270.6	10 661.5	539.4
Bangor	14 156	172.8	158.8	47	36.2	2.1	-19.2	43.0	1.5	3.1	24.9	16 600	116.7	194.1	D
Lewiston	17 922	117.1	347.1	84	52.4	D	D	D	D	D	D	D	D	D	D
Portland	28 143	181.4	161.5	133	21.8	4.0	-14.9	88.7	2.4	4.7	47.3	19 708	237.1	442.1	10.3
MARYLAND	1 946 612	190.1	169.6	4 244	34.7	230.4	-1.7	5 955.7	139.6	273.5	2 994.3	21 449	14 020.0	28 009.4	875.2
Annapolis	15 314	226.1	118.9	66	15.2	1.1	57.1	24.5	0.5	1.0	9.8	19 600	59.5	107.1	3.8
Baltimore	306 248	148.2	192.5	963	44.5	50.4	-15.0	1 252.7	33.6	67.6	733.7	21 836	4 064.2	8 893.1	193.4
Bowie	16 358	248.7	104.7	NA	NA	NA	NA	NA	NA	NA	NA	NA	NA	NA	NA
Cumberland	9 542	148.0	188.8	26	42.3	D	D	D	D	D	D	D	D	D	D
Frederick	13 612	186.1	171.2	68	35.3	2.7	17.4	56.5	1.7	3.5	29.5	17 353	177.5	352.6	12.2
Gaithersburg	15 290	233.9	135.6	94	31.9	4.2	13.5	104.6	1.7	3.3	36.4	21 412	161.4	239.6	6.4

1. Persons 16 years old and over.

City	Wholesale trade, 1987				Retail trade–all establishments, 1987				Retail trade–establishments with payroll, 1987					
						Sales				Sales				
											Per capita[2] (Dollars)			
	Establishments	Sales (Mil. dol.)	Paid employees[1]	Annual payroll ($1,000)	Number	Total (Mil. dol.)	Percent change, 1982–1987	Per capita[2] (Dollars)	Number	Total (Mil. dol.)	General merchandise group stores	Food stores	Apparel and accessory stores	Eating and drinking places
	73	74	75	76	77	78	79	80	81	82	83	84	85	86
IOWA	7 015	24 483.5	65 941	1 281 004	32 338	15 581.5	23.2	5 465	20 311	15 081.6	678	1 153	219	480
Ames	56	121.5	577	10 229	461	335.2	31.3	7 539	354	332.5	D	1 496	388	962
Bettendorf	95	803.2	834	19 159	254	186.2	21.9	6 667	177	182.6	D	1 666	D	705
Burlington	68	258.1	733	13 793	319	197.1	21.1	7 039	225	192.9	D	1 848	255	910
Cedar Falls	44	150.7	454	10 278	402	269.3	27.5	8 111	273	264.0	D	888	D	778
Cedar Rapids	331	1 535.8	4 043	90 685	1 208	948.6	36.6	8 753	846	934.0	D	1 634	376	911
Clinton	45	117.1	343	5 575	358	240.9	9.8	8 009	257	235.5	D	1 794	374	682
Council Bluffs	89	659.0	979	21 083	575	421.4	19.5	7 406	413	415.3	D	1 155	209	662
Davenport	284	1 064.7	3 296	72 643	1 024	774.7	25.2	7 845	765	764.1	1 092	1 420	391	755
Des Moines	577	2 754.3	7 519	173 817	2 069	1 619.2	30.8	8 431	1 496	1 595.9	1 195	1 722	429	889
Dubuque	128	371.5	1 545	26 904	761	504.9	31.9	8 457	533	492.8	D	1 578	348	842
Fort Dodge	73	118.7	662	12 866	394	245.9	9.3	9 084	289	241.6	2 137	1 558	D	777
Iowa City	48	189.7	674	14 092	585	402.5	47.9	7 972	453	395.1	D	1 866	437	985
Marshalltown	55	77.7	525	9 655	357	202.9	15.9	7 783	244	198.9	D	1 715	D	701
Mason City	79	362.6	955	18 660	412	297.5	31.4	9 851	300	293.7	D	1 883	525	755
Ottumwa	44	63.4	385	6 586	318	181.3	7.3	7 169	209	176.6	1 041	1 755	D	514
Sioux City	253	D	D	D	846	634.9	26.1	7 977	622	623.1	D	1 678	D	639
Waterloo	154	329.2	1 731	33 450	732	459.7	8.8	6 566	491	451.7	1 257	1 332	214	592
KANSAS	5 754	30 239.8	60 810	1 282 783	27 556	13 863.4	27.9	5 633	16 797	13 396.6	728	1 139	226	523
Emporia	35	99.5	385	7 177	304	187.8	17.2	7 631	218	184.0	D	1 593	274	755
Hutchinson	82	273.2	864	16 604	561	338.3	24.3	8 152	345	330.0	1 293	1 643	D	661
Kansas City	325	3 193.8	6 171	149 281	1 143	707.0	24.9	4 362	740	687.3	D	909	D	443
Lawrence	77	88.5	593	8 880	632	378.2	39.5	6 695	450	371.4	D	1 380	285	861
Leavenworth	21	20.2	116	1 692	274	189.9	44.0	5 242	189	186.7	879	1 139	D	452
Manhattan	38	D	D	D	447	278.4	0.0	8 249	335	273.6	1 323	1 539	D	877
Olathe	134	461.3	1 760	41 911	446	434.7	100.7	8 331	263	429.0	810	1 746	84	521
Overland Park	497	9 571.3	4 690	134 794	1 405	1 275.8	68.7	13 219	961	1 254.8	2 740	1 350	1 128	1 166
Salina	113	625.1	1 452	26 659	585	364.7	23.8	8 515	400	357.2	1 217	1 512	553	D
Shawnee	53	300.7	465	13 170	333	237.2	98.8	7 844	186	229.7	D	2 537	157	581
Topeka	244	D	D	D	1 428	1 056.5	40.3	8 910	1 035	1 038.0	1 288	1 683	D	898
Wichita	805	3 453.2	10 351	217 040	3 379	2 449.4	28.0	8 479	2 304	2 399.2	1 305	1 563	421	925
KENTUCKY	5 650	24 461.5	63 606	1 240 003	38 507	19 871.7	36.4	5 332	21 731	18 939.9	690	1 150	200	484
Ashland	78	189.5	1 066	16 260	482	329.1	43.0	12 629	309	322.2	D	1 869	D	1 026
Bowling Green	144	1 069.2	1 492	28 071	841	561.1	44.5	13 586	546	547.3	D	2 411	D	D
Covington	58	326.8	775	14 299	412	293.8	20.4	6 433	299	289.3	298	1 312	33	1 150
Frankfort	35	D	D	D	430	231.4	38.3	8 596	280	225.6	1 018	2 118	D	930
Hopkinsville	86	267.3	1 003	16 032	464	246.9	34.9	8 485	292	236.8	D	1 728	D	772
Lexington-Fayette	520	3 083.4	7 257	151 253	2 373	1 939.6	45.7	9 110	1 656	1 902.8	1 414	1 451	511	1 082
Louisville	826	7 178.9	12 189	267 936	2 894	1 793.3	31.0	6 260	2 020	1 754.9	422	1 534	232	896
Owensboro	157	365.2	1 602	27 962	921	488.9	28.7	8 687	612	474.7	D	1 793	D	838
Paducah	131	708.2	2 071	43 195	737	467.8	49.1	16 489	478	451.5	D	2 990	1 347	1 638
LOUISIANA	7 643	31 477.3	80 533	1 652 536	40 465	22 445.8	12.3	4 987	24 262	21 627.1	673	1 206	239	450
Alexandria	177	368.7	1 889	33 110	777	594.5	23.5	11 557	581	582.3	2 320	1 875	903	838
Baton Rouge	678	2 047.0	7 993	173 520	2 515	2 215.8	19.9	9 189	1 832	2 186.1	D	2 012	515	818
Bossier City	85	404.3	823	14 701	601	381.6	22.6	6 688	407	373.4	D	1 184	D	749
Houma	149	228.9	1 159	20 850	603	317.3	-28.9	9 040	397	307.9	1 673	2 587	577	871
Kenner	197	761.4	1 656	32 020	705	494.6	91.3	6 533	448	483.8	1 266	867	406	800
Lafayette	369	970.2	3 862	76 801	1 463	1 067.4	-3.3	11 882	1 023	1 047.7	D	2 632	826	1 282
Lake Charles	200	421.7	1 778	37 167	933	645.6	3.9	8 796	633	629.8	1 482	1 960	468	770
Monroe	204	555.2	2 737	50 305	848	636.6	34.7	11 325	614	623.3	1 474	1 885	677	1 059
New Iberia	87	141.0	753	14 889	490	261.7	-12.6	7 229	290	253.9	D	1 990	D	656
New Orleans	793	4 180.7	10 501	239 758	4 264	2 674.1	10.1	4 823	2 920	2 611.6	442	992	339	727
Shreveport	601	1 869.8	7 107	144 063	2 141	0.0	0.0	D	1 466	1 453.9	921	1 215	374	571
Slidell	66	193.8	495	8 552	597	428.4	59.1	11 973	371	418.5	1 984	2 979	539	902
MAINE	1 865	6 525.0	22 665	461 796	15 242	8 939.7	67.7	7 615	9 204	8 651.0	696	1 541	287	587
Bangor	140	582.8	1 835	40 529	593	631.1	75.3	20 925	449	623.8	3 413	3 544	1 177	1 557
Lewiston	87	267.3	1 361	26 428	429	254.9	30.0	6 539	313	247.2	D	1 461	D	626
Portland	255	1 654.9	5 202	117 183	861	606.4	35.4	9 676	660	592.8	424	2 200	562	1 389
MARYLAND	6 667	41 128.0	99 512	2 495 769	39 495	32 680.2	55.7	7 322	26 538	32 009.4	839	1 370	396	673
Annapolis	101	230.3	794	18 948	647	619.3	66.4	18 564	501	610.9	1 916	2 915	857	1 700
Baltimore	NA	NA	NA	NA	5 570	3 167.2	19.8	4 207	4 096	3 091.6	280	833	289	617
Bowie	18	12.3	58	1 169	218	137.4	32.0	3 844	110	132.9	D	1 416	230	384
Cumberland	53	92.2	512	8 787	324	208.2	24.2	8 963	248	204.8	948	1 421	335	643
Frederick	109	332.2	1 433	30 528	774	660.1	73.8	19 530	557	651.3	D	3 832	819	1 722
Gaithersburg	156	631.7	1 864	53 551	750	829.1	100.9	25 629	473	817.4	4 260	3 629	1 869	1 585

1. For the period including March 12 of the year shown. 2. Based on resident population estimated as of July 1, 1986.

City	Retail trade–establishment with payroll, 1987 (cont'd)			Taxable service industries–establishments with payroll, 1987							Federal grants, 1986		
	Paid employees[1]				Receipts (Mil. dol.)								
						Selected kinds of business							
	Number	Percent change, 1982–1987	Annual payroll (Mil. dol.)	Number	Total	Hotels, motels, and other lodging places	Health services	Legal services	Paid employees[1]	Annual payroll (Mil. dol.)	Procure-ment contract awards (Mil. dol.)	Grant awards (Mil. dol.)	Federal govern-ment civilian employ-ment, 1984
	87	88	89	90	91	92	93	94	95	96	97	98	99
IOWA	203 517	6.9	1 705.2	16 387	5 121.0	262.0	1 568.0	382.1	131 041	1 828.7	821.9	1 214.7	18 240
Ames	5 510	13.0	40.7	269	82.9	10.0	37.7	D	2 252	33.3	23.5	36.1	842
Bettendorf	2 753	10.2	23.6	183	58.2	D	12.0	D	2 553	22.4	7.0	0.4	52
Burlington	2 912	14.2	24.6	220	72.3	4.7	24.0	4.8	1 546	25.4	0.8	1.8	156
Cedar Falls	3 418	8.3	30.3	197	54.7	D	17.5	D	1 395	21.4	0.4	2.0	68
Cedar Rapids	13 261	14.9	115.0	960	488.4	24.7	100.2	33.5	9 643	156.6	385.8	5.9	859
Clinton	3 113	-1.6	26.4	194	98.3	D	23.5	3.1	1 915	27.3	0.1	0.6	92
Council Bluffs	5 350	18.4	47.5	361	121.4	8.2	35.9	11.3	3 002	43.0	21.2	2.3	193
Davenport	9 941	5.6	95.0	790	284.6	12.9	97.5	19.7	6 635	107.2	36.2	5.7	352
Des Moines	21 465	13.5	195.8	1 726	965.5	43.8	219.4	112.1	19 908	356.1	42.8	189.0	4 690
Dubuque	6 798	12.6	61.4	398	204.2	10.7	94.5	7.7	4 802	87.1	11.9	3.9	272
Fort Dodge	3 417	-6.5	29.2	235	57.2	4.4	21.3	D	1 773	22.1	0.3	1.1	242
Iowa City	6 762	31.5	51.6	388	185.6	6.6	32.0	D	3 488	63.6	49.5	58.8	1 373
Marshalltown	2 694	-1.1	23.6	194	55.9	D	25.5	5.2	1 258	19.5	0.6	4.0	80
Mason City	4 176	22.9	34.1	239	95.0	3.4	36.1	5.8	2 011	33.1	2.7	1.1	186
Ottumwa	2 266	-1.7	20.1	165	46.3	1.8	D	4.0	1 157	17.5	0.3	1.5	173
Sioux City	8 269	8.0	72.0	616	225.2	D	87.1	D	5 394	86.4	5.0	5.2	755
Waterloo	6 357	-1.9	53.8	521	182.6	8.3	73.5	14.2	5 000	75.4	23.2	4.5	428
KANSAS	174 947	12.7	1 569.5	15 523	5 250.9	264.0	1 799.4	337.7	128 013	1 967.7	2 166.4	901.0	23 398
Emporia	2 485	7.0	21.2	212	48.0	D	D	3.1	1 414	19.0	NA	1.3	116
Hutchinson	4 366	9.2	39.1	267	89.5	8.7	34.9	4.1	2 292	39.0	30.0	2.4	204
Kansas City	8 392	12.2	86.3	759	331.4	D	99.3	25.1	7 473	128.4	24.3	23.7	1 492
Lawrence	5 880	16.6	47.0	429	116.3	D	33.3	D	2 847	43.2	16.1	18.3	342
Leavenworth	2 098	23.0	18.9	166	49.6	D	12.1	D	1 827	22.0	13.5	1.1	1 709
Manhattan	4 163	D	31.6	270	D	4.9	25.3	2.1	D	D	6.0	18.9	299
Olathe	3 990	57.4	41.5	369	106.7	D	42.5	5.8	2 463	40.6	12.1	2.5	738
Overland Park	15 145	44.2	158.1	1 252	747.5	51.4	178.2	50.2	18 309	303.1	18.9	0.9	176
Salina	4 731	11.4	41.5	361	120.6	D	39.8	9.8	2 984	49.9	3.2	1.9	324
Shawnee	2 710	56.9	24.1	216	45.6	D	4.9	0.4	1 154	15.8	1.3	8.8	0
Topeka	13 069	15.0	124.0	1 092	412.6	D	137.6	38.5	10 114	166.1	12.8	139.9	2 941
Wichita	32 139	15.2	298.8	2 596	1 319.8	D	519.4	95.0	27 990	498.7	1 588.8	24.6	3 136
KENTUCKY	243 641	24.2	2 132.2	18 415	6 325.3	377.1	2 443.0	459.1	166 228	2 315.5	3 300.0	1 698.6	35 128
Ashland	4 337	23.1	37.1	328	88.5	D	41.4	7.0	1 919	36.2	0.5	2.0	427
Bowling Green	6 815	21.2	60.2	440	215.0	D	132.9	12.3	5 374	81.5	10.0	4.1	320
Covington	3 945	18.3	38.7	250	72.4	5.5	19.6	14.6	1 902	29.8	9.4	22.9	2 168
Frankfort	3 167	22.9	25.7	239	90.4	D	32.4	D	2 321	30.5	2.1	286.8	457
Hopkinsville	3 140	33.7	27.5	250	54.6	D	23.2	4.4	1 600	20.8	3.9	1.7	156
Lexington-Fayette	27 198	23.1	231.6	1 968	885.3	83.5	280.7	64.2	22 760	346.2	63.0	93.7	5 038
Louisville	26 362	19.1	234.3	2 834	1 619.0	82.6	604.2	179.7	36 146	587.6	95.9	62.7	8 502
Owensboro	6 524	16.6	58.1	528	168.5	D	66.8	11.5	4 756	68.0	18.3	3.7	264
Paducah	6 153	43.5	49.8	373	139.4	D	59.9	9.4	3 407	59.7	767.4	1.6	852
LOUISIANA	277 708	2.8	2 569.8	25 513	10 243.3	663.1	3 365.4	1 268.2	240 551	3 788.2	2 561.5	2 206.5	32 062
Alexandria	7 120	10.4	68.3	615	245.2	D	110.0	27.9	6 002	84.1	34.7	5.4	1 457
Baton Rouge	27 343	7.1	265.2	2 483	1 077.2	32.7	297.6	122.2	24 755	427.5	229.4	316.1	1 743
Bossier City	4 975	29.8	45.5	341	137.4	11.6	35.7	D	3 011	42.7	1.1	1.9	99
Houma	4 216	-34.2	38.4	481	192.8	D	54.6	D	3 487	79.2	4.6	31.3	235
Kenner	6 483	87.2	58.3	451	254.2	19.6	92.6	D	4 958	69.3	1.2	1.3	124
Lafayette	14 733	-12.1	134.3	1 542	609.2	15.1	198.8	D	11 847	235.8	5.4	8.1	776
Lake Charles	8 283	-8.5	75.4	760	271.4	12.9	113.5	43.3	6 028	108.7	134.0	5.2	502
Monroe	8 104	29.4	71.4	642	275.7	D	98.1	27.0	5 411	101.7	2.3	3.9	428
New Iberia	3 127	-37.5	29.9	341	91.6	D	41.7	8.9	2 027	30.9	8.5	0.8	117
New Orleans	40 794	1.9	394.4	3 920	2 318.1	400.1	511.2	546.3	53 756	887.3	1 298.5	130.7	12 720
Shreveport	17 441	1.9	167.3	1 790	721.5	D	302.2	D	18 414	278.9	111.0	15.2	2 286
Slidell	5 347	67.7	44.9	399	138.7	2.9	78.3	5.0	3 067	44.9	12.9	0.0	182
MAINE	91 991	36.1	958.5	8 164	2 321.0	269.4	668.2	233.6	57 526	842.2	645.0	688.8	17 365
Bangor	6 603	33.4	70.7	486	179.0	13.6	68.1	20.5	4 005	72.2	11.2	7.7	775
Lewiston	3 417	11.6	31.5	365	109.8	D	49.0	15.1	3 057	46.3	0.9	2.8	102
Portland	8 143	20.0	85.6	1 020	506.4	23.1	121.1	97.9	10 920	204.3	10.0	13.8	1 421
MARYLAND	377 862	32.8	3 945.2	31 178	17 466.8	683.3	3 397.7	997.2	368 662	7 108.4	6 776.4	2 342.3	128 753
Annapolis	7 368	31.4	74.5	654	250.2	19.3	68.5	24.7	5 400	102.0	132.8	75.6	3 087
Baltimore	44 285	4.3	437.0	4 414	2 499.7	137.1	511.9	458.3	62 345	1 043.3	1 193.3	885.8	15 555
Bowie	1 888	18.5	16.2	200	48.7	D	23.4	3.1	1 151	18.2	2.4	1.0	76
Cumberland	2 441	16.5	24.1	275	64.8	D	D	D	1 364	26.3	41.2	2.7	215
Frederick	7 877	44.2	78.0	541	210.2	10.3	57.4	10.8	4 752	77.1	19.5	8.5	503
Gaithersburg	8 677	67.3	98.6	665	587.1	D	44.0	10.3	10 188	301.5	646.1	2.3	3 146

1. For the period including March 12 of the year shown.

Table C. Cities — **City Government Employment and Finances**

City	City government employment, 1985 (October): Total	City government employment, 1985 (October): Rates[1]	City government employment, 1985 (October): Percent education	Form of governments[2] (As of 1986)	City government finances, 1984–1985: General revenue: Total (Mil. dol.)	General revenue: Intergovernmental: Total (Mil. dol.)	General revenue: Intergovernmental: Percent from State government	General revenue: Taxes: Total (Mil. dol.)	Taxes: Per capita[3] (Dollars): Total	Taxes: Per capita[3] (Dollars): Property	Taxes: Per capita[3] (Dollars): Sales & gross receipts	General expenditures: Total (Mil. dol.)	General expenditures: Per capita[3] (Dol.): Total	General expenditures: Per capita[3] (Dol.): Capital outlays	General expenditures: Percent of total for–: Public welfare	General expenditures: Percent of total for–: Highways	General expenditures: Percent of total for–: Education
	100	101	102	103	104	105	106	107	108	109	110	111	112	113	114	115	116
IOWA	NA	NA	NA	NA	NA	NA	NA	NA	NA	NA	NA	NA	NA	NA	NA	NA	NA
Ames	1 292	290.6	0.0	2	42.5	5.8	45.4	6.2	139	133	0	35.8	805	66	1.0	4.2	0.0
Bettendorf	215	77.0	0.0	1	10.6	2.0	81.4	5.0	178	165	5	11.9	427	84	0.0	12.7	0.0
Burlington	302	107.9	0.0	2	13.9	3.5	65.3	5.2	185	175	7	12.6	451	54	0.4	14.3	0.0
Cedar Falls	715	215.4	0.0	1	20.8	3.6	62.1	4.8	144	140	0	27.2	821	152	0.0	6.3	0.0
Cedar Rapids	1 477	136.3	0.0	1	86.3	17.5	44.2	28.1	259	250	5	65.7	606	113	0.0	14.7	0.0
Clinton	264	87.8	0.0	1	33.0	3.8	63.2	5.6	187	183	0	14.9	495	67	0.0	11.2	0.0
Council Bluffs	534	93.8	0.0	2	29.0	7.6	53.0	10.5	185	175	5	26.9	473	108	0.0	10.0	0.0
Davenport	1 038	105.1	0.0	1	60.9	15.5	54.4	25.1	254	239	6	58.9	596	76	0.0	11.8	0.0
Des Moines	2 250	117.2	0.0	2	134.7	30.5	52.3	54.2	282	250	25	156.2	813	229	0.0	14.5	0.0
Dubuque	613	102.7	0.0	2	38.1	11.8	41.3	11.2	187	175	5	46.1	772	316	0.0	9.8	0.0
Fort Dodge	279	103.1	0.0	3	14.1	4.0	50.1	5.4	198	191	0	12.1	447	65	NA	8.9	0.0
Iowa City	677	134.1	0.0	2	27.1	6.8	46.5	9.3	185	175	3	25.7	508	89	0.0	14.3	0.0
Marshalltown	264	101.3	0.0	1	12.7	3.3	60.3	6.1	235	231	1	12.0	459	86	0.0	23.4	0.0
Mason City	NA	NA	NA	1	13.0	4.0	56.7	4.5	149	143	0	16.9	560	197	0.3	14.5	0.0
Ottumwa	310	122.6	0.0	3	9.7	3.2	84.7	3.4	134	124	7	10.2	402	78	0.0	18.9	0.0
Sioux City	901	113.2	0.0	2	52.0	13.9	50.3	19.8	249	223	22	52.8	663	152	0.0	18.6	0.0
Waterloo	762	108.8	0.0	1	41.5	11.8	51.5	18.1	259	250	4	68.7	982	132	0.0	13.0	0.0
KANSAS	NA	NA	NA	NA	NA	NA	NA	NA	NA	NA	NA	NA	NA	NA	NA	NA	NA
Emporia	258	104.8	0.0	2	11.5	1.6	47.9	4.9	199	159	32	9.4	384	83	0.0	8.3	0.0
Hutchinson	361	87.0	0.0	2	25.4	5.0	28.0	7.1	171	137	31	23.6	568	116	0.1	5.8	0.0
Kansas City	1 964	121.2	0.0	2	114.7	15.5	45.6	46.3	286	176	106	101.5	626	64	0.0	10.2	0.0
Lawrence	1 031	182.5	0.0	2	50.2	3.4	47.8	10.4	185	116	66	40.8	723	74	0.0	5.5	0.0
Leavenworth	266	73.4	0.0	2	10.0	1.8	48.5	5.0	139	73	63	8.2	226	23	0.8	18.5	0.0
Manhattan	291	86.2	0.0	2	14.8	1.9	59.5	6.0	178	84	88	16.0	473	86	0.0	8.3	0.0
Olathe	398	76.3	0.0	2	22.5	1.8	49.8	8.6	165	100	58	23.4	448	124	1.2	15.1	0.0
Overland Park	393	40.7	0.0	2	30.6	3.2	71.3	19.4	201	41	152	28.6	297	80	1.8	40.0	0.0
Salina	404	94.3	0.0	2	16.8	2.0	61.9	6.2	144	109	30	15.5	363	55	0.0	14.7	0.0
Shawnee	124	41.0	0.0	2	5.4	0.9	82.0	3.5	114	54	53	6.0	198	34	1.0	28.2	0.0
Topeka	1 580	133.2	0.0	3	82.4	17.2	25.8	33.5	283	138	140	84.5	713	146	0.0	10.9	0.0
Wichita	2 929	101.4	0.0	2	261.0	34.3	42.6	62.6	217	145	64	246.3	853	165	0.0	9.5	0.0
KENTUCKY	NA	NA	NA	NA	NA	NA	NA	NA	NA	NA	NA	NA	NA	NA	NA	NA	NA
Ashland	389	149.3	0.0	2	35.5	3.5	17.0	5.2	198	90	75	31.1	1 194	12	0.0	3.4	0.0
Bowling Green	517	125.2	0.0	2	32.6	4.1	23.4	11.0	266	55	32	24.9	602	59	1.3	5.8	0.0
Covington	369	80.8	0.0	2	20.8	7.0	12.3	10.1	221	46	43	17.6	385	26	0.0	6.8	0.0
Frankfort	358	133.0	0.0	2	12.9	3.0	15.4	5.2	194	48	26	10.2	378	84	0.0	6.8	0.0
Hopkinsville	330	113.4	0.0	1	11.3	2.7	20.4	3.6	122	43	14	8.7	298	13	0.2	9.2	0.0
Lexington-Fayette	3 613	169.7	0.0	1	135.2	26.1	29.5	67.8	318	57	48	128.9	606	52	2.4	0.0	0.0
Louisville	4 818	168.2	0.0	1	179.2	37.8	15.6	93.0	325	102	39	165.0	576	51	3.8	4.1	0.0
Owensboro	2 020	358.9	0.0	2	41.6	4.4	23.3	9.8	174	73	20	72.5	1 287	244	0.1	2.7	0.0
Paducah	547	192.8	0.0	2	17.1	2.2	34.4	9.9	348	117	0	16.8	592	101	0.6	8.0	0.0
LOUISIANA	NA	NA	NA	NA	NA	NA	NA	NA	NA	NA	NA	NA	NA	NA	NA	NA	NA
Alexandria	879	170.9	0.0	1	25.7	8.1	11.0	11.1	216	32	161	27.7	539	105	0.0	3.7	0.0
Baton Rouge	5 344	144.7	0.0	1	271.4	54.3	44.1	120.5	326	78	225	262.2	710	96	0.4	15.2	0.0
Bossier City	1 098	192.4	0.0	1	52.8	11.8	10.0	11.5	202	51	131	51.0	894	248	0.0	5.8	0.0
Houma	1 042	102.6	0.0	1	101.9	20.0	56.2	37.3	367	192	165	98.9	974	166	NA	10.6	9.8
Kenner	619	81.8	0.0	1	17.0	3.1	48.2	6.4	84	55	14	26.3	348	70	0.0	15.1	0.0
Lafayette	1 330	148.1	0.0	1	68.9	9.1	32.7	21.8	243	47	165	86.8	966	301	0.2	23.1	0.0
Lake Charles	655	89.2	0.0	1	28.0	5.0	34.0	16.5	225	68	135	25.7	351	53	0.3	13.1	0.0
Monroe	1 065	189.5	0.0	1	49.8	9.6	17.4	21.5	383	86	270	46.1	820	187	0.0	16.4	0.0
New Iberia	306	84.5	0.0	1	12.7	3.4	33.9	7.7	214	49	144	15.5	428	150	1.1	21.3	0.0
New Orleans	11 217	202.3	0.0	1	582.0	148.7	43.0	256.9	463	133	309	567.6	1 024	197	1.9	9.0	0.0
Shreveport	3 027	137.4	0.0	1	124.1	14.6	36.7	71.2	323	118	186	114.4	519	107	0.0	16.2	0.0
Slidell	265	74.1	0.0	1	11.2	3.0	24.6	6.5	181	68	96	8.5	239	28	0.0	18.4	0.0
MAINE	NA	NA	NA	NA	NA	NA	NA	NA	NA	NA	NA	NA	NA	NA	NA	NA	NA
Bangor	1 296	429.7	48.7	2	37.8	10.9	58.3	17.4	576	568	0	33.7	1 118	31	5.3	6.6	38.3
Lewiston	1 252	321.2	52.2	2	31.2	11.2	72.2	16.2	415	412	0	31.6	811	90	2.2	8.4	41.3
Portland	2 563	409.0	51.3	2	87.9	25.4	72.8	45.4	724	711	0	81.5	1 300	159	2.8	8.1	32.8
MARYLAND	NA	NA	NA	NA	NA	NA	NA	NA	NA	NA	NA	NA	NA	NA	NA	NA	NA
Annapolis	461	138.2	0.0	1	21.1	3.2	55.6	11.1	334	275	30	22.4	670	64	0.0	6.9	0.0
Baltimore	31 420	417.4	42.8	1	1 316.1	674.7	87.7	457.8	608	400	47	1 178.2	1 565	319	NA	12.8	30.8
Bowie	141	39.5	0.0	2	6.9	1.4	65.4	2.8	78	73	1	5.5	153	17	0.0	15.0	0.0
Cumberland	313	134.7	0.0	1	10.6	3.5	39.1	4.8	206	197	4	11.3	487	55	0.0	18.2	0.0
Frederick	394	116.6	0.0	1	17.5	5.4	37.5	6.2	184	168	6	16.5	489	153	0.0	11.0	0.0
Gaithersburg	179	55.3	0.0	2	6.1	0.6	81.2	3.6	112	87	6	6.0	186	40	0.0	16.5	0.0

1. Per 10,000 population estimated as of July 1, 1986. 2. 1=Mayor-council; 2=Council-manager; 3=Commission. Data subject to copyright. 3. Based on resident population estimated as of July 1, 1986.

City	City government finances, 1984–1985 (cont'd)								Climate[2]							Typical monthly electric bills, 1986		
	General expenditure (cont'd)					Debt outstanding			Average daily temperature (Degrees Fahrenheit)							Residential[6]		
	Percent of total for (cont'd)								Mean		Limits							
	Health and hospitals	Police protection	Sewerage and sanitation	Parks and recreation	Housing and community development	Total (Mil. dol.)	Per capita[1] (Dollars)	Percent utility	Jan.	July	Jan.[3]	July[4]	Annual precipitation (Inches)	Heating degree days[5]	Cooling degree days[5]	Total (Dollars)	Percent change, 1980–1986	Commercial[7] (Dollars)
	117	118	119	120	121	122	123	124	125	126	127	128	129	130	131	132	133	134
IOWA	NA	NA	NA	NA	NA	NA	NA	NA	NA	NA	NA	NA	NA	NA	NA	55.49	50.8	NA
Ames	59.5	6.7	6.1	2.7	2.1	63.1	1 419	68.2	17.1	74.0	7.9	85.0	31.69	6 874	792	54.10	13.9	NA
Bettendorf	1.6	11.7	16.0	11.9	0.0	16.5	592	0.0	20.6	75.8	12.6	85.0	33.67	6 274	1 017	52.94	85.4	NA
Burlington	5.0	11.3	14.1	7.8	12.4	12.3	440	26.8	21.0	75.5	11.8	86.9	35.12	6 181	992	44.61	38.2	NA
Cedar Falls	32.4	6.0	20.2	4.1	3.0	44.8	1 350	37.5	14.0	72.6	4.7	83.4	33.10	7 537	667	33.65	-18.4	NA
Cedar Rapids	0.0	11.2	17.8	7.7	5.1	116.8	1 077	0.0	18.5	74.3	9.7	85.3	36.01	6 671	828	55.45	23.6	368.9
Clinton	2.3	10.7	10.8	5.2	5.0	66.8	2 222	0.0	19.5	74.4	10.9	85.1	35.78	6 482	872	47.79	21.6	NA
Council Bluffs	2.9	17.3	17.7	6.5	7.0	50.8	892	4.7	20.2	77.7	10.2	88.5	30.34	6 194	1 166	64.68	81.5	561.4
Davenport	2.6	13.9	12.5	2.6	7.7	201.1	2 036	0.0	20.6	75.8	12.6	85.0	33.67	6 274	1 017	52.94	85.4	504.5
Des Moines	0.0	10.8	7.7	14.3	7.2	173.0	901	4.7	18.6	76.3	10.1	86.2	30.83	6 554	1 019	65.32	81.4	567.0
Dubuque	31.5	7.3	10.4	5.9	3.8	68.4	1 146	6.1	15.6	71.9	7.4	82.0	38.58	7 375	580	47.79	21.6	350.2
Fort Dodge	0.0	14.1	13.2	7.6	11.4	20.1	741	13.3	15.8	73.9	6.3	85.2	32.28	7 175	785	52.94	85.4	NA
Iowa City	0.0	11.6	11.2	5.8	3.3	54.3	1 075	1.6	19.8	75.4	10.5	86.8	34.55	6 376	968	52.94	85.4	504.5
Marshalltown	1.6	13.6	15.2	5.8	4.8	23.5	902	8.9	16.8	73.8	7.0	85.2	33.03	7 013	761	55.45	23.6	NA
Mason City	2.3	11.4	11.9	6.9	31.1	9.2	306	0.0	12.5	72.2	3.5	83.2	30.81	7 881	619	49.47	21.4	NA
Ottumwa	7.1	12.6	14.9	6.2	3.9	10.2	404	30.5	19.9	76.2	11.2	86.2	33.25	6 339	1 028	44.61	36.5	NA
Sioux City	0.0	13.1	10.0	5.4	14.2	137.5	1 727	1.8	16.2	75.6	6.3	86.5	25.37	6 947	940	66.19	65.8	496.8
Waterloo	0.7	8.9	7.3	4.2	3.0	106.7	1 524	0.0	14.0	72.6	4.7	83.4	33.10	7 537	667	64.89	65.7	487.0
KANSAS	NA	NA	NA	NA	NA	NA	NA	NA	NA	NA	NA	NA	NA	NA	NA	59.14	71.8	NA
Emporia	0.5	12.8	17.0	5.0	11.4	11.4	463	6.2	27.7	79.0	17.4	90.4	34.76	5 121	1 405	57.04	66.3	NA
Hutchinson	0.2	7.2	24.9	4.5	0.0	90.9	2 191	0.0	29.5	81.2	18.8	93.9	30.96	4 792	1 690	57.04	66.3	NA
Kansas City	1.1	14.3	14.1	3.2	4.7	469.2	2 895	0.0	28.4	80.9	19.4	90.5	29.27	4 812	1 681	49.23	60.8	563.4
Lawrence	40.9	6.9	6.7	3.7	2.9	85.5	1 514	14.6	28.4	80.1	18.6	91.3	36.81	4 819	1 583	57.04	66.3	387.0
Leavenworth	0.4	18.9	17.9	6.8	0.9	16.2	447	31.4	26.6	78.7	16.5	90.1	37.47	5 184	1 355	57.04	66.3	NA
Manhattan	0.3	14.0	4.7	13.6	3.6	68.2	2 021	3.7	27.1	79.9	16.5	91.7	32.88	5 119	1 525	57.04	66.3	NA
Olathe	0.0	20.1	8.5	4.3	1.8	98.2	1 882	28.9	27.6	78.3	17.8	89.3	37.22	5 057	1 363	57.04	66.3	NA
Overland Park	0.6	19.8	0.0	10.1	NA	39.8	412	0.0	28.4	80.9	19.4	90.5	29.27	4 812	1 681	55.24	62.6	671.1
Salina	0.0	10.8	9.6	4.3	0.5	44.6	1 042	6.2	27.3	80.8	16.8	92.7	28.95	5 187	1 566	57.04	66.3	NA
Shawnee	0.0	35.5	0.0	3.9	0.1	11.1	368	0.0	28.4	80.9	19.4	90.5	29.27	4 812	1 681	55.24	62.6	NA
Topeka	4.0	12.1	18.5	7.9	6.2	219.5	1 851	9.7	26.1	78.6	15.7	89.6	33.38	5 319	1 380	57.04	66.3	387.0
Wichita	1.7	6.5	7.0	8.9	1.9	1 181.7	4 091	2.7	29.6	81.4	19.4	92.9	28.61	4 787	1 684	69.48	93.0	574.3
KENTUCKY	NA	NA	NA	NA	NA	NA	NA	NA	NA	NA	NA	NA	NA	NA	NA	42.44	53.2	NA
Ashland	0.0	4.7	4.8	1.1	8.5	324.9	12 466	0.0	32.0	74.9	21.6	87.0	41.16	4 900	1 071	44.28	45.1	NA
Bowling Green	0.7	10.6	9.9	6.7	7.2	215.6	5 220	18.8	33.9	78.2	24.6	89.2	49.02	4 309	1 429	38.24	84.4	NA
Covington	0.0	16.8	5.9	3.2	29.4	28.6	627	0.0	28.9	75.4	20.4	85.8	40.14	5 247	1 037	48.73	66.8	NA
Frankfort	0.0	12.8	22.0	8.1	18.6	23.4	868	16.2	30.9	75.6	20.9	87.5	42.93	5 001	1 067	38.53	58.7	NA
Hopkinsville	1.6	13.8	13.1	2.1	20.6	38.1	1 309	53.3	33.2	78.1	23.1	90.0	49.16	4 361	1 451	35.60	76.3	NA
Lexington-Fayette	8.1	11.2	7.9	5.0	9.1	289.4	1 359	0.0	31.5	76.0	23.1	85.9	45.68	4 814	1 170	37.72	41.1	NA
Louisville	3.7	17.1	7.3	5.3	5.0	564.4	1 970	45.0	32.5	77.6	24.1	87.6	43.56	4 525	1 342	46.86	60.7	NA
Owensboro	50.6	5.0	21.4	1.6	1.3	282.4	5 017	84.9	33.2	78.3	24.4	89.8	44.79	4 279	1 460	35.77	27.1	NA
Paducah	0.2	10.5	9.4	4.3	25.0	50.6	1 784	66.4	34.3	79.3	24.9	90.6	45.79	4 130	1 573	40.48	53.9	NA
LOUISIANA	NA	NA	NA	NA	NA	NA	NA	NA	NA	NA	NA	NA	NA	NA	NA	50.22	89.7	NA
Alexandria	NA	14.6	12.5	10.5	8.0	71.1	1 382	33.0	48.4	82.5	37.7	92.9	55.90	1 961	2 521	51.06	34.9	459.6
Baton Rouge	6.3	9.2	7.6	4.9	2.9	629.1	1 704	NA	50.8	82.1	40.5	91.4	55.77	1 673	2 605	52.54	83.3	435.0
Bossier City	36.3	12.3	16.3	2.0	2.6	82.0	1 438	0.4	46.0	82.9	36.2	93.3	43.84	2 269	2 444	47.04	146.8	NA
Houma	22.8	6.1	19.8	3.6	1.8	165.0	1 624	19.4	54.2	81.7	44.0	90.8	63.89	1 315	2 755	57.31	84.2	NA
Kenner	0.2	14.5	20.1	11.2	6.6	16.0	211	0.0	52.4	82.1	43.0	90.7	59.74	1 490	2 686	51.93	99.4	508.4
Lafayette	0.0	5.5	15.9	3.8	2.3	536.0	5 966	52.1	51.7	82.1	42.0	91.2	57.69	1 560	2 675	49.23	56.6	406.2
Lake Charles	0.0	13.3	18.2	10.8	8.6	7.8	106	0.0	51.5	82.3	42.2	91.0	53.03	1 579	2 682	52.54	83.3	435.0
Monroe	5.9	8.7	14.7	9.3	4.3	145.1	2 581	13.6	45.3	82.4	35.6	92.7	49.56	2 404	2 340	51.93	99.4	508.4
New Iberia	0.0	10.3	32.5	4.1	2.2	12.2	336	0.0	51.9	81.8	41.8	91.2	57.25	1 555	2 649	49.85	50.1	NA
New Orleans	2.3	10.2	14.4	4.8	9.0	796.4	1 436	4.1	52.4	82.1	43.0	90.7	59.74	1 490	2 686	46.01	68.1	526.9
Shreveport	NA	11.1	12.0	5.8	3.2	244.7	1 110	12.7	46.0	82.9	36.2	93.3	43.84	2 269	2 444	47.04	146.8	NA
Slidell	0.0	25.6	7.5	10.1	0.0	10.0	279	9.0	52.4	82.1	43.0	90.7	59.74	1 490	2 686	49.85	50.1	NA
MAINE	NA	NA	NA	NA	NA	NA	NA	NA	NA	NA	NA	NA	NA	NA	NA	61.29	70.3	NA
Bangor	0.7	6.3	3.1	1.9	0.4	13.8	459	0.0	18.2	68.0	9.3	77.9	41.62	7 947	250	68.06	75.7	NA
Lewiston	0.2	6.1	7.6	1.6	2.1	15.5	397	16.4	20.6	70.2	12.0	79.9	45.76	7 351	390	60.06	69.8	535.1
Portland	5.5	5.4	7.3	5.3	0.5	70.9	1 132	0.0	21.5	68.1	11.9	78.9	43.52	7 501	254	60.06	69.8	535.1
MARYLAND	NA	NA	NA	NA	NA	NA	NA	NA	NA	NA	NA	NA	NA	NA	NA	52.88	44.4	NA
Annapolis	0.1	16.1	15.4	3.8	1.0	14.9	448	31.6	35.5	79.9	28.6	88.0	43.39	4 083	1 545	55.85	52.7	NA
Baltimore	3.4	9.5	8.7	3.7	2.6	1 037.3	1 378	5.4	35.5	79.9	28.6	88.0	43.39	4 083	1 545	55.85	52.7	430.5
Bowie	0.6	0.0	36.5	14.3	5.8	10.6	298	33.9	33.2	75.6	22.4	88.1	43.75	4 649	1 008	55.85	52.7	NA
Cumberland	0.0	14.1	18.0	3.5	8.9	5.8	248	0.0	30.9	74.4	21.8	87.5	36.50	5 106	902	47.89	24.2	NA
Frederick	0.0	14.7	8.3	8.5	3.4	17.8	526	4.1	29.5	73.6	19.8	85.6	39.99	5 415	759	47.89	24.2	NA
Gaithersburg	0.0	4.9	6.8	24.2	2.6	1.7	54	0.0	33.3	75.7	24.1	87.4	40.91	4 663	1 063	47.21	30.3	NA

1. Based on resident population estimated as of July 1, 1986. 2. Represents normal values based on the 30-year period, 1951–1980 (see text). 3. Average daily minimum. 4. Average daily maximum. 5. For definition, see text. 6. As of January 1; based on consumption of 750 kWh. 7. Based on billing demand of 30 kW and consumption of 6,000 kWh.

MSA/ CMSA Code[1]	State/ Place code	City	Land area,[2] 1990 (Sq. Km.)	Population: 1990: Total persons	Population: 1990: Rank	Population: 1990: Per sq. km.	Population: 1980	Population: Change 1980–1990: Number	Population: Change 1980–1990: Per- cent	Population characteristics, 1990: Percent: Race: White	Race: Black	Race: Am. Indian, Eskimo, Aleut	Race: Asian & Pacific Islander	Race: Other race	His- panic[3]	65 Years and over
			1	2	3	4	5	6	7	8	9	10	11	12	13	14
		MARYLAND—Con.														
3180	24 0450	Hagerstown	25.7	35 445	710	1 379	34 132	1 313	3.8	92.55	6.30	0.14	0.74	0.27	0.78	16.0
8840	24 0850	Rockville	31.4	44 835	554	1 428	43 811	1 024	2.3	79.16	8.25	0.27	9.80	2.52	8.62	10.5
...	25 0000	MASSACHUSETTS	20 300.3	6 016 425	X	296	5 737 093	279 332	4.9	89.84	4.99	0.20	2.38	2.58	4.78	13.6
6482	25 0210	Attleboro	71.3	38 383	657	538	34 196	4 187	12.2	95.52	1.01	0.19	2.40	0.89	2.94	12.1
1122	25 0390	Beverly	40.0	38 195	659	955	37 655	540	1.4	97.63	0.86	0.13	1.02	0.37	1.15	15.0
1122	25 0440	Boston	125.4	574 283	20	4 580	562 994	11 289	2.0	62.84	25.59	0.33	5.29	5.95	10.79	11.5
1122	25 0540	Brockton	55.6	92 788	215	1 669	95 172	-2 384	-2.5	80.24	12.96	0.29	1.71	4.80	6.32	12.4
1122	25 0610	Cambridge	16.7	95 802	208	5 737	95 322	480	0.5	75.28	13.50	0.30	8.44	2.49	6.79	10.5
1122	25 0700	Chelsea	5.7	28 710	850	5 037	25 431	3 279	12.9	69.68	5.20	0.30	5.00	19.83	31.41	13.8
8000	25 0760	Chicopee	59.3	56 632	414	955	55 112	1 520	2.8	95.41	1.83	0.12	0.58	2.06	3.62	17.2
1122	25 1200	Everett	8.8	35 701	706	4 057	37 195	-1 494	-4.0	93.50	3.17	0.25	1.80	1.28	3.84	16.4
6482	25 1220	Fall River	80.3	92 703	216	1 154	92 574	129	0.1	97.17	1.03	0.10	1.33	0.38	1.70	18.1
2600	25 1280	Fitchburg	71.9	41 194	605	573	39 580	1 614	4.1	89.45	3.43	0.24	2.57	4.33	9.61	15.4
1122	25 1430	Gloucester	67.3	28 716	849	427	27 768	948	3.4	99.28	0.23	0.09	0.27	0.13	0.95	15.4
1122	25 1710	Haverhill	86.3	51 418	475	596	46 865	4 553	9.7	94.86	2.01	0.19	0.84	2.10	5.28	14.2
8000	25 1830	Holyoke	55.1	43 704	569	793	44 678	-974	-2.2	73.08	3.59	0.24	0.81	22.27	31.06	16.8
1122	25 2030	Lawrence	18.0	70 207	321	3 900	63 175	7 032	11.1	64.98	6.40	0.52	1.93	26.15	41.64	12.6
2600	25 2100	Leominster	74.8	38 145	660	510	34 508	3 637	10.5	93.08	2.25	0.19	1.63	2.85	8.29	13.0
1122	25 2180	Lowell	35.7	103 439	186	2 897	92 418	11 021	11.9	81.07	2.39	0.17	11.11	5.26	10.15	12.1
1122	25 2210	Lynn	28.0	81 245	259	2 902	78 471	2 774	3.5	83.06	8.06	0.28	3.70	4.91	9.15	15.1
1122	25 2230	Malden	13.2	53 884	443	4 082	53 386	498	0.9	89.39	4.18	0.16	5.22	1.04	2.63	15.3
1122	25 2305	Marlborough	54.6	31 813	791	583	30 617	1 196	3.9	94.81	1.80	0.16	1.94	1.29	4.21	11.2
1122	25 2400	Medford	21.1	57 407	407	2 721	58 076	-669	-1.2	93.41	4.07	0.12	2.01	0.40	1.72	16.8
1122	25 2430	Melrose	12.2	28 150	863	2 307	30 055	-1 905	-6.3	98.11	0.56	0.05	1.14	0.13	0.80	16.9
5400	25 2770	New Bedford	52.2	99 922	194	1 914	98 478	1 444	1.5	87.55	4.07	0.40	0.40	7.56	6.66	17.4
1122	25 2830	Newton	46.8	82 585	255	1 765	83 622	-1 037	-1.2	92.78	2.08	0.12	4.55	0.47	1.98	14.9
8000	25 2865	Northampton	89.3	29 289	838	328	29 286	3	0.0	92.97	1.78	0.19	2.90	2.16	4.10	14.6
1122	25 3260	Peabody	42.5	47 039	525	1 107	45 976	1 063	2.3	96.78	1.21	0.04	1.08	0.88	2.86	14.1
6320	25 3370	Pittsfield	105.5	48 622	511	461	51 974	-3 352	-6.4	95.46	3.14	0.20	0.77	0.42	1.10	17.3
1122	25 3460	Quincy	43.5	84 985	244	1 954	84 743	242	0.3	91.68	1.09	0.21	6.56	0.46	1.41	16.7
1122	25 3510	Revere	15.3	42 786	580	2 796	42 423	363	0.9	93.20	1.40	0.25	3.67	1.48	3.81	17.0
1122	25 3670	Salem	21.0	38 091	663	1 814	38 276	-185	-0.5	92.96	2.67	0.28	1.37	2.72	6.69	15.2
1122	25 3920	Somerville	10.6	76 210	279	7 190	77 372	-1 162	-1.5	88.73	5.60	0.15	3.71	1.81	6.28	12.3
8000	25 4090	Springfield	83.2	156 983	111	1 887	152 319	4 664	3.1	68.56	19.15	0.21	1.04	11.04	16.90	13.7
...	25 4220	Taunton	120.7	49 832	494	413	45 001	4 831	10.7	95.29	2.01	0.16	0.46	2.09	4.74	14.1
1122	25 4440	Waltham	32.9	57 878	404	1 759	58 200	-322	-0.6	91.37	3.07	0.13	3.55	1.88	5.60	13.1
8000	25 4690	Westfield	120.7	38 372	658	318	36 465	1 907	5.2	96.53	0.88	0.11	0.77	1.70	4.08	13.8
1122	25 5010	Woburn	32.8	35 943	701	1 096	36 626	-683	-1.9	96.59	0.97	0.16	1.52	0.77	2.32	12.7
9240	25 5030	Worcester	97.3	169 759	101	1 745	161 799	7 960	4.9	87.08	4.52	0.32	2.81	5.27	9.58	16.1
...	26 0000	MICHIGAN	147 135.8	9 295 297	X	63	9 262 044	33 253	0.4	83.44	13.90	0.60	1.13	0.93	2.17	11.9
2162	26 0050	Allen Park	18.2	31 092	804	1 708	34 196	-3 104	-9.1	97.98	0.46	0.21	0.75	0.59	3.17	20.3
2162	26 0080	Ann Arbor	67.1	109 592	168	1 633	107 969	1 623	1.5	81.98	9.04	0.35	7.69	0.95	2.58	7.2
0780	26 0160	Battle Creek	110.9	53 540	449	483	35 724	17 816	49.9	80.74	16.54	0.64	1.25	0.84	1.83	14.4
6960	26 0165	Bay City	26.9	38 936	648	1 447	41 593	-2 657	-6.4	93.60	2.45	0.80	0.45	2.70	5.62	15.4
2640	26 0378	Burton	60.8	27 617	873	454	29 976	-2 359	-7.9	95.21	2.57	1.00	0.46	0.76	2.09	11.0
2162	26 0655	Dearborn	63.1	89 286	225	1 415	90 660	-1 374	-1.5	97.55	0.55	0.33	0.94	0.63	2.78	18.0
2162	26 0658	Dearborn Heights	30.3	60 838	378	2 008	67 706	-6 868	-10.1	97.33	0.46	0.41	1.29	0.51	2.30	16.8
2162	26 0680	Detroit	359.3	1 027 974	7	2 861	1 203 368	-175 394	-14.6	21.63	75.67	0.36	0.82	1.52	2.77	12.2
2162	26 0740	East Detroit	13.2	35 283	714	2 673	38 280	-2 997	-7.8	98.68	0.25	0.37	0.56	0.13	0.82	18.8
4040	26 0765	East Lansing	24.6	50 677	486	2 060	51 392	-715	-1.4	84.59	6.93	0.34	6.99	1.15	2.50	4.5
2162	26 0877	Farmington Hills	86.2	74 652	292	866	58 056	16 596	28.6	93.87	1.91	0.17	3.84	0.20	1.19	11.8
2162	26 0895	Ferndale	10.0	25 084	922	2 508	26 227	-1 143	-4.4	95.76	1.39	0.86	1.43	0.57	1.70	12.1
2640	26 0920	Flint	87.6	140 761	125	1 607	159 611	-18 850	-11.8	49.58	47.94	0.74	0.49	1.25	2.85	10.7
2162	26 1030	Garden City	15.2	31 846	789	2 095	35 640	-3 794	-10.6	98.58	0.24	0.42	0.51	0.26	1.52	9.9
3000	26 1085	Grand Rapids	114.6	189 126	83	1 650	181 843	7 283	4.0	76.39	18.54	0.83	1.14	3.09	4.97	13.1
2162	26 1225	Highland Park	7.7	20 121	950	2 613	27 909	-7 788	-27.9	6.39	92.80	0.20	0.27	0.33	0.68	14.1
3000	26 1240	Holland	36.7	30 745	816	838	26 281	4 464	17.0	87.72	1.05	0.34	3.18	7.70	14.14	13.8
2162	26 1320	Inkster	16.2	30 772	813	1 900	35 190	-4 418	-12.6	36.13	62.39	0.43	0.67	0.38	1.08	11.3
3520	26 1360	Jackson	28.6	37 446	679	1 309	39 739	-2 293	-5.8	80.17	17.67	0.58	0.41	1.17	2.55	14.1
3720	26 1370	Kalamazoo	63.6	80 277	265	1 262	79 722	555	0.7	77.28	18.75	0.56	1.87	1.53	2.68	10.9
3000	26 1392	Kentwood	54.5	37 826	669	694	30 438	7 388	24.3	91.27	5.59	0.42	1.96	0.77	2.01	9.6
4040	26 1485	Lansing	87.8	127 321	142	1 450	130 414	-3 093	-2.4	73.94	18.56	1.02	1.78	4.71	7.94	9.6
2162	26 1550	Lincoln Park	15.1	41 832	598	2 770	45 105	-3 273	-7.3	97.32	0.92	0.52	0.43	0.80	3.80	14.4
2162	26 1565	Livonia	92.5	100 850	191	1 090	104 814	-3 964	-3.8	98.04	0.26	0.18	1.34	0.18	1.34	13.1
2162	26 1610	Madison Heights	18.6	32 196	781	1 731	35 375	-3 179	-9.0	95.91	0.91	0.49	2.45	0.25	1.24	11.6
6960	26 1770	Midland	71.5	38 053	664	532	37 269	784	2.1	95.56	1.72	0.35	1.91	0.46	1.68	11.9
5320	26 1875	Muskegon	37.2	40 283	622	1 083	40 823	-540	-1.3	69.88	27.10	0.97	0.35	1.71	3.52	14.7
2162	26 1985	Oak Park	13.0	30 462	824	2 343	31 537	-1 075	-3.4	62.84	34.30	0.12	2.36	0.37	1.46	12.8

1. MSA = Metropolitan Statistical Area. CMSA = Consolidated MSA. 2. Dry land or land partially or temporarily covered by water. 3. Hispanic persons may be of any race.

City	Households, 1990				Births, 1984			Deaths, 1984				Hospitals, 1985		
			Percent–		Number			Number		Rate			Beds	
	Number	Persons per house-hold	Female family house-holder[1]	One-person[2]	Total	To mothers under 20 yrs. old (Percent)	Rate[3]	Total	Infant[4]	Total[3]	Infant[5]	Number	Number	Rate[6]
	15	16	17	18	19	20	21	22	23	24	25	26	27	28
MARYLAND—Con.														
Hagerstown	15 063	2.30	14.4	32.3	613	20.7	18.6	526	3	15.9	4.9	3	492	1 461
Rockville	15 660	2.77	9.9	20.0	1 104	5.8	24.5	598	6	13.3	5.4	3	421	898
MASSACHUSETTS	2 247 110	2.58	12.1	25.8	78 279	9.0	13.5	55 332	701	9.5	9.0	179	40 683	698
Attleboro	14 180	2.66	10.6	23.1	570	11.1	16.8	303	4	8.9	7.0	1	208	596
Beverly	14 796	2.48	11.2	26.7	487	6.8	13.0	398	4	10.6	8.2	1	233	630
Boston	228 464	2.37	16.8	35.5	8 530	13.3	14.9	5 734	100	10.0	11.7	31	9 175	1 600
Brockton	32 850	2.76	17.4	24.6	1 622	13.9	16.9	962	24	10.0	14.8	3	1 605	1 710
Cambridge	39 405	2.08	10.7	42.3	1 080	5.8	11.7	803	10	8.7	9.3	7	1 103	1 209
Chelsea	10 553	2.65	20.7	30.4	479	14.2	18.4	362	4	13.9	8.4	1	159	620
Chicopee	22 625	2.44	13.4	28.3	756	9.5	13.4	565	7	10.0	9.3	0	0	0
Everett	14 528	2.43	14.8	29.7	528	5.9	14.5	391	1	10.7	1.9	1	173	476
Fall River	37 303	2.44	14.8	30.1	1 381	16.9	15.0	1 064	7	11.6	5.1	3	617	682
Fitchburg	15 363	2.54	14.0	27.6	589	13.6	14.8	429	4	10.8	6.8	1	226	579
Gloucester	11 579	2.46	11.2	28.2	442	6.6	15.7	279	3	9.9	6.8	1	124	439
Haverhill	19 575	2.55	12.8	25.8	746	12.5	15.6	570	8	11.9	10.7	2	289	594
Holyoke	15 850	2.65	23.0	28.2	749	18.8	17.4	654	10	15.2	13.4	3	840	2 000
Lawrence	24 270	2.83	24.2	26.2	1 303	18.9	20.2	759	21	11.8	16.1	1	365	576
Leominster	14 834	2.54	10.4	24.5	509	11.4	14.7	309	3	8.9	5.9	1	150	428
Lowell	37 019	2.68	17.0	27.5	1 721	14.4	18.4	1 045	20	11.2	11.6	4	991	1 067
Lynn	31 554	2.53	16.9	31.1	1 317	11.8	16.6	996	11	12.6	8.4	2	599	762
Malden	21 921	2.43	12.4	31.1	718	6.1	13.4	560	5	10.4	7.0	1	241	451
Marlborough	12 152	2.55	10.0	25.1	451	8.2	14.3	272	1	8.6	2.2	1	164	526
Medford	21 829	2.54	12.2	26.0	706	4.5	12.3	622	7	10.8	9.9	1	200	352
Melrose	10 941	2.54	10.0	27.7	368	2.7	12.6	312	2	10.7	5.4	1	253	879
New Bedford	38 788	2.51	17.1	28.1	1 476	15.7	15.1	1 153	12	11.8	8.1	3	594	616
Newton	29 455	2.60	9.0	22.4	818	1.2	9.9	744	3	9.0	3.7	1	325	396
Northampton	11 164	2.28	10.5	33.5	296	5.1	10.1	292	1	10.0	3.4	3	1 051	3 706
Peabody	17 556	2.65	10.8	22.4	547	5.7	11.9	404	6	8.8	11.0	1	86	186
Pittsfield	19 916	2.41	12.7	29.1	677	11.5	13.4	540	5	10.7	7.4	2	495	998
Quincy	35 678	2.34	12.1	33.6	988	5.5	11.8	1 027	14	12.3	14.2	1	334	404
Revere	17 438	2.43	13.6	29.9	451	6.2	10.5	458	2	10.6	4.4	1	161	370
Salem	15 806	2.34	12.7	31.6	530	9.2	13.7	416	4	10.8	7.5	3	560	1 472
Somerville	30 319	2.44	12.3	30.1	998	7.8	13.2	842	4	11.1	4.0	2	237	328
Springfield	57 769	2.60	21.2	27.8	2 604	19.4	17.3	1 592	35	10.6	13.4	4	1 592	1 066
Taunton	18 849	2.59	13.5	24.9	720	13.2	15.9	411	7	9.1	9.7	2	500	1 093
Waltham	20 728	2.42	10.6	30.4	626	6.7	10.8	514	5	8.9	8.0	4	1 791	3 137
Westfield	13 823	2.60	11.4	23.7	509	9.8	13.8	302	6	8.2	11.8	2	264	700
Woburn	13 485	2.65	11.5	24.4	508	3.5	13.6	287	8	7.7	15.7	2	503	1 346
Worcester	63 884	2.46	15.7	30.1	2 407	13.0	15.1	1 926	27	12.0	11.2	8	2 458	1 558
MICHIGAN	3 419 331	2.66	12.9	23.7	136 076	12.4	15.0	76 588	1 597	8.4	11.7	228	46 555	509
Allen Park	12 030	2.55	9.2	23.5	387	4.9	12.2	344	4	10.9	10.3	1	611	1 963
Ann Arbor	41 657	2.32	8.1	31.4	1 414	4.2	13.1	489	11	4.5	7.8	3	1 845	1 711
Battle Creek	21 457	2.45	16.4	29.3	948	19.1	17.4	558	10	10.3	10.5	5	1 577	2 916
Bay City	15 570	2.48	14.4	29.9	701	13.7	17.6	433	5	10.8	7.1	2	464	1 169
Burton	10 447	2.64	14.2	22.4	383	13.3	13.1	233	5	8.0	13.1	0	0	0
Dearborn	35 442	2.51	10.4	29.0	1 158	6.2	13.3	1 024	14	11.8	12.1	2	660	764
Dearborn Heights	23 432	2.58	10.6	23.4	616	7.1	9.8	573	7	9.1	11.4	0	0	0
Detroit	374 057	2.71	30.3	29.8	18 523	20.4	17.0	12 907	387	11.9	20.9	25	7 880	725
East Detroit	13 443	2.62	11.5	23.0	474	5.7	13.2	388	7	10.8	14.8	0	0	0
East Lansing	13 500	2.43	6.5	28.7	404	3.7	8.6	135	1	2.9	2.5	0	0	0
Farmington Hills	29 234	2.52	6.0	25.5	694	3.9	11.0	411	5	6.5	7.2	1	300	459
Ferndale	9 858	2.54	13.9	28.5	474	10.1	18.8	315	5	12.5	10.5	1	91	363
Flint	53 894	2.56	26.3	29.3	3 129	20.5	21.0	1 539	58	10.3	18.5	5	1 741	1 196
Garden City	11 213	2.84	11.1	17.6	451	7.8	13.6	223	5	6.7	11.1	1	349	1 073
Grand Rapids	69 029	2.60	16.1	27.2	3 937	15.1	21.5	1 944	50	10.6	12.7	9	2 524	1 353
Highland Park	8 033	2.44	31.8	41.7	424	24.5	16.4	337	13	13.0	30.7	1	209	816
Holland	10 572	2.71	9.6	23.4	474	15.4	16.8	214	6	7.6	12.7	1	209	722
Inkster	11 201	2.73	24.2	26.8	503	19.1	15.2	302	11	9.1	21.9	0	0	0
Jackson	14 723	2.47	18.7	31.4	705	22.7	18.7	484	10	12.8	14.2	2	459	1 242
Kalamazoo	29 409	2.41	15.2	31.1	1 416	13.5	18.3	638	29	8.3	20.5	3	1 598	2 069
Kentwood	15 247	2.47	9.7	28.3	426	8.7	12.5	126	3	3.7	7.0	0	0	0
Lansing	50 635	2.50	16.6	29.1	2 566	15.3	20.1	978	36	7.6	14.0	4	1 527	1 184
Lincoln Park	16 257	2.57	12.6	25.2	614	9.4	14.2	373	5	8.6	8.1	2	325	758
Livonia	35 916	2.77	7.7	17.7	1 164	5.2	11.6	781	4	7.8	3.4	2	354	352
Madison Heights	12 850	2.49	11.1	28.7	532	9.4	15.5	267	9	7.8	16.9	2	190	566
Midland	14 812	2.49	7.7	25.4	537	6.0	14.2	235	2	6.2	3.7	1	307	855
Muskegon	14 770	2.46	20.2	31.6	867	22.7	21.9	460	7	11.6	8.1	3	755	1 897
Oak Park	10 885	2.80	15.9	22.0	482	5.4	15.8	258	6	8.5	12.4	0	0	0

1. No spouse present. 2. Householder living alone. 3. Per 1,000 resident population estimated as of July 1 of the year shown. 4. Deaths of infants under 1 year old. 5. Deaths of infants under 1 year old per 1,000 live births. 6. Per 100,000 resident population estimated as of July 1, 1986.

City	Serious crimes known to police, 1985: Number: Total	Serious crimes known to police, 1985: Number: Violent[1]	Serious crimes known to police, 1985: Rate[2]	Police officers, 1985: Number	Police officers, 1985: Rate[3]	Educational attainment,[4] 1980: Percent completing 12 years or more	Educational attainment,[4] 1980: Percent completing 16 years or more	Money income: Per capita[5]: 1985: Total (Dollars)	Money income: Per capita[5]: 1985: Percent of State average	Money income: Per capita[5]: 1979: Current dollars	Money income: Per capita[5]: 1979: Constant (1985) dollars	Money income: Percent below poverty level, 1979: Persons	Money income: Percent below poverty level, 1979: Families	Housing, 1990: Total units	Housing, 1990: Percent change, 1980–1990	Housing, 1990: Vacant units for sale or rent[6]
	29	30	31	32	33	34	35	36	37	38	39	40	41	42	43	44
MARYLAND—Con.																
Hagerstown	1 782	162	5 200	84	24.5	52.7	7.8	8 561	66.0	6 264	9 283	16.1	11.7	16 361	9.4	949
Rockville	547	11	1 212	27	6.0	82.8	38.2	16 456	126.9	10 368	15 365	4.9	3.6	16 238	8.3	480
MASSACHUSETTS	276 999	31 334	4 758	NA	NA	72.2	20.0	12 510	100.0	7 457	11 051	9.6	7.6	2 472 711	10.7	103 550
Attleboro	743	105	2 173	63	18.4	63.5	12.9	11 264	90.0	7 081	10 494	7.0	5.7	15 045	16.9	631
Beverly	825	30	2 157	76	19.9	81.2	20.1	13 907	111.2	8 078	11 972	7.3	5.8	15 652	10.0	667
Boston	68 073	11 887	11 877	1 829	31.9	68.4	20.3	10 774	86.1	6 555	9 715	20.2	16.7	250 863	3.8	17 557
Brockton	8 198	829	8 391	177	18.1	68.0	9.8	9 944	79.5	6 132	9 088	12.6	11.3	35 376	1.9	2 049
Cambridge	6 630	713	7 015	260	27.5	76.2	43.1	13 494	107.9	7 957	11 792	15.1	11.0	41 979	1.6	1 518
Chelsea	1 858	383	7 141	NA	NA	50.5	7.1	8 259	66.0	5 389	7 986	21.4	19.7	11 574	9.5	865
Chicopee	2 042	189	3 628	109	19.4	56.1	8.1	9 946	79.5	6 378	9 452	8.8	7.7	23 690	11.0	765
Everett	1 426	106	3 839	87	23.4	61.9	8.0	10 676	85.3	6 520	9 663	10.4	9.5	15 416	4.9	679
Fall River	5 772	642	6 186	211	22.6	35.3	6.7	8 050	64.3	5 197	7 702	14.8	13.1	40 375	8.3	2 434
Fitchburg	1 402	114	3 477	70	17.4	58.8	9.7	9 766	78.1	6 074	9 002	12.9	9.2	16 665	7.9	934
Gloucester	718	62	2 539	NA	NA	65.5	14.2	12 225	97.7	7 602	11 266	9.8	8.8	13 125	8.3	555
Haverhill	2 930	366	6 118	79	16.5	63.3	10.5	11 075	88.5	6 433	9 534	10.5	9.0	21 321	13.1	1 405
Holyoke	NA	NA	NA	NA	NA	59.7	10.4	9 611	76.8	6 137	9 095	19.3	16.6	16 917	-6.5	883
Lawrence	NA	NA	NA	NA	NA	51.8	7.6	8 624	68.9	5 485	8 129	19.3	17.0	26 915	3.4	2 230
Leominster	1 408	126	4 018	55	15.7	62.8	11.3	11 277	90.1	6 758	10 015	9.3	7.9	15 533	16.4	541
Lowell	4 377	750	4 684	140	15.0	57.7	10.4	10 106	80.8	6 016	8 916	13.5	11.3	40 302	13.4	2 733
Lynn	6 353	364	7 894	144	17.9	66.3	9.5	10 607	84.8	6 487	9 614	13.8	12.3	34 670	5.9	2 614
Malden	1 997	259	3 722	105	19.6	68.9	11.3	12 163	97.2	7 165	10 619	9.4	7.8	23 217	7.6	1 054
Marlborough	466	26	1 502	51	16.4	75.6	18.6	13 645	109.1	7 679	11 380	7.3	5.4	13 027	11.7	749
Medford	1 892	175	3 247	114	19.6	69.3	13.2	12 038	96.2	7 130	10 567	7.6	6.1	22 650	8.8	596
Melrose	544	16	1 838	56	18.9	83.2	21.6	14 151	113.1	8 294	12 292	4.5	3.3	11 297	2.9	280
New Bedford	5 200	738	5 247	244	24.6	38.1	6.2	8 156	65.2	5 431	8 049	16.2	14.1	41 760	5.4	2 178
Newton	2 843	152	3 410	204	24.5	87.4	45.9	20 601	164.7	11 609	17 205	5.8	2.8	30 497	4.5	673
Northampton	1 162	94	3 956	50	17.0	75.2	24.8	10 829	86.6	6 637	9 836	12.7	7.8	11 747	9.3	355
Peabody	1 973	100	4 203	83	17.7	74.4	15.8	12 681	101.4	7 728	11 453	5.9	5.1	18 240	10.9	532
Pittsfield	1 955	207	3 817	85	16.6	72.4	15.7	11 751	93.9	7 105	10 530	10.3	8.7	21 272	3.7	857
Quincy	3 781	256	4 483	194	23.0	76.2	15.8	12 840	102.6	7 652	11 340	8.2	6.9	37 732	9.0	1 572
Revere	1 190	87	2 758	NA	NA	64.3	7.7	10 760	86.0	6 660	9 870	10.6	9.5	18 726	8.3	1 055
Salem	NA	NA	NA	NA	NA	66.6	14.2	11 863	94.8	7 038	10 430	10.5	7.9	17 161	7.5	1 129
Somerville	3 701	266	4 783	143	18.5	62.0	16.4	10 759	86.0	6 349	9 409	12.4	9.6	31 786	2.7	1 137
Springfield	7 923	1 846	5 244	446	29.5	63.5	11.8	9 088	72.6	5 819	8 624	17.8	15.6	61 320	4.3	2 833
Taunton	1 300	136	2 846	90	19.7	51.4	8.0	9 742	77.9	6 132	9 088	10.5	9.4	20 281	17.3	1 105
Waltham	2 327	103	3 968	127	21.7	73.2	19.1	12 897	103.1	7 666	11 361	8.1	5.2	21 723	2.3	823
Westfield	1 094	30	2 938	67	18.0	70.5	15.8	10 825	86.5	6 843	10 141	7.8	6.4	14 470	10.1	465
Woburn	1 175	93	3 180	69	18.7	77.3	15.3	12 904	103.1	7 562	11 207	5.8	4.5	14 105	9.8	494
Worcester	11 701	1 521	7 290	368	22.9	62.6	14.8	10 454	83.6	6 443	9 549	14.4	11.2	69 336	11.1	4 116
MICHIGAN	578 566	66 714	6 366	NA	NA	68.0	14.3	10 902	100.0	7 688	11 394	10.4	8.2	3 847 926	6.7	134 958
Allen Park	1 256	50	3 886	52	16.1	71.9	11.9	13 550	124.3	10 163	15 062	2.1	1.8	12 233	0.8	164
Ann Arbor	9 193	635	8 525	151	14.0	90.7	56.2	12 911	118.4	8 729	12 936	14.7	5.3	44 010	8.8	2 051
Battle Creek	4 982	489	9 000	101	18.2	60.0	8.8	10 548	96.8	7 504	11 121	17.9	14.6	23 252	35.1	1 151
Bay City	2 144	190	5 266	76	18.7	59.2	8.0	9 539	87.5	6 818	10 104	13.2	10.6	16 372	0.3	527
Burton	2 030	170	6 964	34	11.7	61.8	6.0	11 021	101.1	7 742	11 474	8.9	7.8	10 840	1.9	278
Dearborn	7 132	394	8 266	179	20.7	68.7	17.8	13 524	124.1	9 852	14 601	6.0	4.1	36 929	3.3	1 069
Dearborn Heights	3 018	196	4 678	82	12.7	67.0	11.7	12 882	118.2	9 488	14 061	3.8	3.2	23 939	1.8	352
Detroit	149 954	25 904	13 750	4 640	42.5	54.2	8.3	8 852	81.2	6 215	9 211	21.9	18.9	410 027	-15.0	23 665
East Detroit	2 700	162	7 313	47	12.7	60.4	7.0	11 726	107.6	8 342	12 363	4.5	3.6	13 684	1.7	204
East Lansing	1 744	49	3 583	54	11.1	96.4	65.4	8 985	82.4	6 305	9 344	27.2	10.0	14 403	8.9	775
Farmington Hills	3 193	169	5 255	76	12.5	84.2	31.6	18 260	167.5	12 632	18 721	3.6	2.3	31 171	30.9	1 678
Ferndale	1 766	186	6 933	49	19.2	64.7	10.5	10 649	97.7	7 455	11 048	8.6	6.4	10 207	0.3	260
Flint	22 354	4 348	14 980	336	22.5	60.5	9.2	10 450	95.9	7 093	10 512	16.9	15.0	58 724	-3.8	3 277
Garden City	1 319	86	3 913	40	11.9	65.0	6.4	11 375	104.3	8 310	12 315	3.6	2.6	11 374	0.4	104
Grand Rapids	15 870	2 214	8 659	259	14.1	67.1	16.4	9 625	88.3	6 691	9 916	13.5	10.3	73 716	5.2	3 316
Highland Park	4 224	1 047	16 464	52	20.3	56.6	7.0	7 947	72.9	5 494	8 142	30.7	29.0	9 162	-28.0	715
Holland	1 257	48	4 698	50	18.7	63.8	19.0	10 717	98.3	7 313	10 838	8.6	5.4	11 243	14.1	477
Inkster	2 819	787	8 368	43	12.8	59.1	6.9	9 511	87.2	6 736	9 983	15.4	12.4	12 045	-1.7	602
Jackson	3 489	529	9 086	72	18.8	63.0	11.2	9 002	82.6	6 469	9 587	15.9	13.3	15 689	-1.6	688
Kalamazoo	8 800	1 253	11 152	253	32.1	73.4	26.8	10 068	92.4	6 945	10 292	19.6	13.7	31 488	4.1	1 557
Kentwood	1 841	61	5 769	34	10.7	78.7	19.5	11 691	107.2	8 145	12 071	6.8	6.0	16 337	25.9	997
Lansing	9 877	1 064	7 707	240	18.7	72.6	17.3	10 398	95.4	7 280	10 789	13.1	10.3	53 919	3.7	2 487
Lincoln Park	3 264	291	7 520	60	13.8	59.0	6.0	10 815	99.2	8 277	12 267	5.0	3.5	16 763	-0.5	409
Livonia	4 828	259	4 803	NA	NA	78.8	18.9	13 934	127.8	9 969	14 774	2.2	1.6	36 641	9.9	615
Madison Heights	2 577	181	7 468	54	15.6	66.6	9.0	11 986	109.9	8 326	12 339	6.2	4.9	13 220	1.5	285
Midland	1 382	45	3 709	41	11.0	84.6	35.0	13 621	124.9	9 548	14 150	5.7	4.0	15 447	10.7	469
Muskegon	4 173	862	10 465	64	16.0	59.2	7.8	7 827	71.8	5 507	8 161	19.3	15.5	16 019	-2.1	873
Oak Park	2 375	269	7 755	69	22.5	75.5	21.2	11 649	106.9	8 773	13 002	7.0	5.1	11 344	0.4	263

1. Includes murder and nonnegligent manslaughter, forcible rape, robbery, and aggravated assault. 2. Per 100,000 resident population estimated for 1985 by the FBI. 3. Per 10,000 resident population estimated for 1985 by the FBI. 4. Persons 25 years old or older. 5. Based on the resident population estimated as of July 1, 1988 for 1987 data and enumerated as of April 1, 1980 for 1979 data. 6. Also includes units rented or sold, but not occupied.

City	Housing, 1990 (cont'd)					Construction authorized by building permits, 1990				Civilian labor force, 1990			
	Occupied units					New private housing units						Unemployment	
			Owner-occupied										
	Total	Percent with more than 1 person per room	Percent of total	Median value[1] (Dollars)	Median rent[2] (Dollars)	Number	Value ($1,000)	Percent single family	Non-residential, value ($1,000)	Total	Percent change, 1989–1990	Total	Rate[3]
	45	46	47	48	49	50	51	52	53	54	55	56	57
MARYLAND—Con.													
Hagerstown	15 063	1.4	41.2	68 200	281	123	5 417	65.9	4 322	18 675	2.3	1 657	8.9
Rockville	15 660	4.5	66.2	180 900	730	205	9 549	28.3	7 377	31 746	-0.1	766	2.4
MASSACHUSETTS	2 247 110	2.5	59.3	162 800	506	14 290	1 321 152	75.2	708 453	3 166 000	-0.4	189 000	6.0
Attleboro	14 180	2.5	61.3	143 200	465	93	6 020	76.3	1 540	19 189	1.1	1 401	7.3
Beverly	14 796	0.9	58.9	177 200	583	34	5 022	100.0	585	23 093	0.0	1 003	4.3
Boston	228 464	6.9	30.9	161 400	546	279	16 120	30.5	81 415	302 527	-0.5	16 740	5.5
Brockton	32 850	4.0	53.3	131 700	491	55	1 502	89.1	5 651	48 744	-0.1	4 149	8.5
Cambridge	39 405	4.2	30.3	263 800	483	2	150	100.0	30	53 184	-1.1	2 007	3.8
Chelsea	10 553	10.8	28.1	142 000	501	0	0	NA	69	12 040	1.0	1 061	8.8
Chicopee	22 625	2.0	58.1	113 800	389	128	6 013	30.5	11 998	29 546	0.4	1 802	6.1
Everett	14 528	2.5	41.3	156 100	521	99	4 358	0.0	417	18 731	0.2	1 262	6.7
Fall River	37 303	2.5	33.0	127 800	277	177	8 829	48.0	2 048	43 595	0.5	5 158	11.8
Fitchburg	15 363	3.6	48.3	124 000	431	52	3 546	88.5	1 361	18 203	-1.2	1 672	9.2
Gloucester	11 579	1.5	57.8	177 100	501	44	3 911	81.8	6 160	16 996	1.6	1 682	9.9
Haverhill	19 575	1.9	58.6	140 100	504	143	7 661	59.4	3 193	23 990	-1.3	1 858	7.7
Holyoke	15 850	7.1	38.9	116 800	377	99	8 208	28.3	4 317	17 697	1.2	1 385	7.8
Lawrence	24 270	10.4	32.0	129 600	470	18	955	33.3	850	28 163	-1.2	3 228	11.5
Leominster	14 834	2.3	57.6	137 200	462	158	6 784	37.3	4 249	17 720	-1.2	1 452	8.2
Lowell	37 019	6.7	41.9	131 100	494	44	2 364	81.8	13 431	52 163	-2.4	4 235	8.1
Lynn	31 554	4.3	46.2	139 200	507	47	3 095	44.7	1 830	40 069	0.3	2 879	7.2
Malden	21 921	2.6	43.2	162 900	575	36	1 766	36.1	493	29 070	0.1	1 778	6.1
Marlborough	12 152	1.8	58.2	166 300	635	115	11 426	96.5	1 848	19 147	-0.2	1 026	5.4
Medford	21 829	1.2	57.1	182 400	579	7	545	71.4	12 658	30 810	-0.6	1 591	5.2
Melrose	10 941	0.6	65.4	196 100	588	3	171	100.0	119	15 662	-1.0	667	4.3
New Bedford	38 788	2.8	43.8	115 900	313	96	4 609	40.6	5 161	47 818	0.1	5 284	11.1
Newton	29 455	0.8	68.9	293 400	809	39	4 035	15.4	6 101	47 619	-1.3	1 450	3.0
Northampton	11 164	1.4	50.9	132 900	468	95	5 833	91.6	2 198	14 186	0.1	692	4.9
Peabody	17 556	1.3	70.4	177 100	523	56	7 818	92.9	2 906	29 420	0.4	1 540	5.2
Pittsfield	19 916	0.9	59.6	111 100	388	29	1 979	82.8	15 426	25 261	1.7	1 702	6.7
Quincy	35 678	2.2	48.8	161 100	599	141	8 510	12.1	3 671	46 933	-0.3	2 719	5.8
Revere	17 438	2.8	48.9	160 500	554	45	2 330	11.1	270	23 399	0.0	1 559	6.7
Salem	15 806	2.2	46.0	163 600	539	68	3 472	23.5	4 116	23 594	0.0	1 213	5.1
Somerville	30 319	3.9	31.0	165 800	591	35	1 187	100.0	0	39 293	-0.3	2 073	5.3
Springfield	57 769	4.1	49.4	105 500	418	256	12 812	39.1	5 255	68 674	0.4	4 939	7.2
Taunton	18 849	2.2	57.7	138 900	449	296	16 896	77.7	37 030	23 854	-2.0	2 237	9.4
Waltham	20 728	2.8	45.9	191 100	633	74	6 307	64.9	38 711	33 563	-0.4	1 692	5.0
Westfield	13 823	1.4	65.4	136 000	450	109	7 771	38.5	3 937	18 833	0.2	892	4.7
Woburn	13 485	1.6	61.1	172 600	651	108	7 688	38.0	4 343	22 512	-0.2	1 220	5.4
Worcester	63 884	3.3	43.3	128 900	451	405	22 428	68.1	19 481	79 387	-0.9	5 661	7.1
MICHIGAN	3 419 331	2.6	71.0	60 600	343	38 945	2 751 708	72.9	1 475 330	4 578 000	-0.3	344 000	7.5
Allen Park	12 030	1.2	87.2	67 400	447	84	3 817	26.2	2 076	16 777	-1.6	807	4.8
Ann Arbor	41 657	3.2	43.2	116 400	529	502	27 886	15.5	24 839	68 823	1.6	1 876	2.7
Battle Creek	21 457	2.2	62.9	39 300	307	82	4 709	86.6	28 006	25 450	-1.2	1 913	7.5
Bay City	15 570	1.7	67.5	32 600	268	9	555	100.0	2 317	17 991	-0.2	1 718	9.5
Burton	10 447	2.3	76.1	44 400	328	20	942	100.0	1 924	12 540	-1.2	1 298	10.4
Dearborn	35 442	3.0	74.4	69 600	388	115	8 282	58.3	20 251	41 815	-1.6	2 155	5.2
Dearborn Heights	23 432	1.9	84.3	64 500	471	18	1 650	100.0	2 920	32 834	-1.6	1 846	5.6
Detroit	374 057	5.4	52.9	25 600	265	633	48 115	0.0	199 472	450 341	-1.6	49 285	10.9
East Detroit	13 443	1.9	87.5	55 300	404	8	455	100.0	2 522	20 457	-0.4	1 624	7.9
East Lansing	13 500	5.8	33.2	97 000	414	32	3 756	68.8	5 709	29 426	-0.4	1 383	4.7
Farmington Hills	29 234	1.2	65.6	145 900	598	520	44 263	91.2	23 054	35 115	-1.5	1 659	4.7
Ferndale	9 858	2.7	68.1	38 400	407	0	0	NA	1 392	14 102	-1.3	1 106	7.8
Flint	53 894	4.4	58.1	33 900	300	156	6 139	3.8	19 177	60 281	-1.4	7 886	13.1
Garden City	11 213	2.6	86.3	59 700	414	12	703	100.0	1 388	17 608	-1.6	1 115	6.3
Grand Rapids	69 029	2.8	59.9	58 300	346	449	22 206	48.3	25 671	108 337	1.1	8 230	7.6
Highland Park	8 033	4.8	33.6	19 500	235	0	0	NA	0	9 631	-1.6	1 469	15.3
Holland	10 572	3.8	68.0	68 200	400	487	32 888	24.2	9 644	17 995	1.4	969	5.4
Inkster	11 201	7.0	58.6	36 500	337	8	749	100.0	18	14 287	-1.6	1 486	10.4
Jackson	14 723	2.4	55.8	32 100	283	7	438	100.0	9 006	17 151	-0.7	1 505	8.8
Kalamazoo	29 409	3.3	47.4	48 600	357	61	4 864	50.8	3 920	43 121	-0.3	2 599	6.0
Kentwood	15 247	2.1	57.7	78 100	432	588	25 008	41.5	7 288	21 127	0.6	969	4.6
Lansing	50 635	3.4	54.8	48 400	356	97	5 490	80.4	12 094	73 655	-0.3	5 309	7.2
Lincoln Park	16 257	2.2	78.5	44 500	370	7	239	42.9	0	20 797	-1.6	1 552	7.5
Livonia	35 916	1.1	88.9	94 800	531	240	30 118	100.0	27 475	52 508	-1.7	2 106	4.0
Madison Heights	12 850	3.0	69.5	59 800	435	27	1 028	59.3	3 647	20 892	-1.4	1 453	7.0
Midland	14 812	1.0	69.1	74 200	370	260	26 255	59.2	17 524	19 698	-0.1	877	4.5
Muskegon	14 770	3.9	54.6	32 400	289	44	2 534	63.6	3 718	16 268	-0.3	1 547	9.5
Oak Park	10 885	5.2	73.8	48 000	456	0	0	NA	5 480	18 298	-1.4	1 114	6.1

1. Specified owner-occupied units. 2. Specified renter-occupied units. 3. Percent of total civilian labor force.

City	Employed,[1] 1980: Total	Employed,[1] 1980: Rate per 1,000 employees: Professional, specialty, and technical	Employed,[1] 1980: Rate per 1,000 employees: Precision production, craft, and operators	Manufactures, 1987: Establishments: Total	Manufactures, 1987: Establishments: Percent with 20 or more employees	Manufactures, 1987: All employees: Number (1,000)	Manufactures, 1987: All employees: Percent change, 1982–1987	Manufactures, 1987: All employees: Annual payroll (Mil. dol.)	Manufactures, 1987: Production workers: Number (1,000)	Manufactures, 1987: Production workers: Work-hours (Millions)	Manufactures, 1987: Production workers: Wages: Total (Mil. dol.)	Manufactures, 1987: Production workers: Wages: Average per production worker (Dollars)	Manufactures, 1987: Value added by manufacture (Mil. dol.)	Manufactures, 1987: Value of shipments (Mil. dol.)	Manufactures, 1987: New capital expenditures (Mil. dol.)
	58	59	60	61	62	63	64	65	66	67	68	69	70	71	72
MARYLAND—Con.															
Hagerstown	14 398	115.4	280.7	79	48.1	4.5	2.3	86.0	3.0	5.9	49.1	16 367	207.8	380.7	10.3
Rockville	22 325	265.6	108.4	114	25.4	D	D	D	D	D	D	D	D	D	D
MASSACHUSETTS	2 674 275	188.9	213.7	11 006	38.0	591.3	-8.1	15 211.3	348.3	690.5	7 018.9	20 152	35 769.7	62 793.7	2 169.0
Attleboro	16 712	134.1	367.8	147	42.2	13.0	-12.2	286.7	8.0	16.0	136.5	17 062	588.4	1 236.4	34.3
Beverly	18 964	198.2	197.1	72	40.3	3.5	9.4	93.0	1.7	3.2	38.6	22 706	181.1	283.3	5.6
Boston	256 047	203.0	144.9	858	35.7	42.5	-10.3	1 156.0	21.0	38.8	407.3	19 395	2 517.4	4 204.1	123.6
Brockton	40 787	122.5	254.1	142	35.2	3.7	-30.2	76.1	2.4	4.5	41.3	17 208	161.1	290.5	5.7
Cambridge	49 682	353.3	115.8	196	40.3	11.7	-26.4	369.8	4.1	7.8	80.4	19 610	391.9	678.6	33.4
Chelsea	9 864	95.8	266.5	70	45.7	1.9	-20.8	42.9	1.2	2.4	23.2	19 333	98.0	246.1	5.3
Chicopee	25 896	99.2	340.8	97	45.4	4.7	-4.1	110.5	2.9	5.6	57.9	19 966	324.7	543.3	17.4
Everett	16 655	117.1	220.6	90	44.4	4.8	-2.0	131.8	3.3	6.5	84.7	25 667	289.1	617.6	9.9
Fall River	38 608	99.7	433.2	227	47.6	16.1	-10.1	257.4	13.2	24.5	182.2	13 803	572.5	1 046.5	29.0
Fitchburg	17 544	137.2	292.0	90	41.1	D	D	D	D	D	D	D	D	D	D
Gloucester	12 470	148.2	221.3	66	40.9	3.4	-10.5	85.5	2.2	4.5	46.1	20 955	225.6	470.5	11.4
Haverhill	20 617	150.5	335.0	127	42.5	3.9	-7.1	77.6	2.9	6.0	47.4	16 345	153.6	320.1	9.7
Holyoke	17 446	150.8	269.6	115	54.8	6.9	-11.5	138.1	5.0	10.6	85.1	17 020	325.3	687.7	9.2
Lawrence	25 782	110.9	375.5	135	45.9	9.2	-12.4	175.7	6.6	12.8	104.9	15 894	702.7	1 224.1	13.4
Leominster	15 973	136.9	317.8	158	44.3	6.8	-10.5	143.6	5.2	10.6	89.6	17 231	318.7	666.8	27.5
Lowell	41 621	139.7	321.3	161	43.5	19.1	-14.0	543.3	11.3	22.3	209.7	18 558	1 735.8	3 159.0	80.2
Lynn	34 459	131.4	271.7	109	33.0	15.0	-6.8	521.6	7.2	14.7	175.1	24 319	1 941.6	2 865.3	52.9
Malden	25 053	140.9	197.1	72	45.8	2.2	-18.5	59.2	1.6	3.2	37.1	23 188	118.4	286.5	5.1
Marlborough	16 163	178.6	237.0	81	46.9	3.4	3.0	97.4	1.6	3.0	33.8	21 125	187.7	336.2	10.7
Medford	27 577	149.4	188.5	54	22.2	0.8	-42.9	18.3	0.5	1.0	8.5	17 000	37.8	68.7	0.8
Melrose	14 501	211.8	157.2	25	28.0	D	D	D	D	D	D	D	D	D	D
New Bedford	40 440	90.5	392.8	206	54.4	17.3	-18.8	325.0	12.9	24.5	209.0	16 202	699.3	1 367.1	38.2
Newton	43 173	342.1	88.1	113	36.3	4.7	-13.0	124.0	2.3	4.6	39.8	17 304	244.2	435.1	9.4
Northampton	13 820	256.3	168.7	54	40.7	2.3	-8.0	55.8	1.4	3.0	28.6	20 429	94.8	253.8	4.3
Peabody	22 858	153.9	223.8	110	40.0	4.6	21.1	121.4	2.9	5.8	62.2	21 448	248.0	464.1	27.1
Pittsfield	22 670	188.4	217.9	71	42.3	10.1	-1.0	316.3	3.9	8.2	90.7	23 256	537.3	808.8	32.4
Quincy	41 686	173.3	164.0	104	25.0	4.6	-39.5	112.7	2.6	5.2	60.0	23 077	231.3	409.1	29.3
Revere	19 318	113.6	190.2	NA	NA	NA	NA	NA	NA	NA	NA	NA	NA	NA	NA
Salem	18 630	150.7	247.1	86	23.3	3.7	-22.9	95.0	2.5	5.0	51.5	20 600	282.5	423.1	9.1
Somerville	37 797	175.7	202.5	111	30.6	3.0	-16.7	68.0	2.1	4.2	37.6	17 905	151.7	287.3	4.8
Springfield	63 055	139.9	255.8	200	36.0	11.9	-27.9	299.5	7.7	15.2	163.1	21 182	631.1	1 251.4	52.1
Taunton	20 450	129.2	341.8	84	52.4	4.7	-7.8	86.2	3.2	5.8	46.5	14 531	183.1	325.5	8.0
Waltham	30 222	193.0	200.3	214	38.8	19.2	2.1	612.4	10.7	21.8	281.2	26 280	1 403.5	2 122.9	58.0
Westfield	16 526	153.6	286.7	97	41.2	6.1	3.4	144.2	4.2	8.3	81.5	19 405	1 038.5	1 494.7	15.3
Woburn	19 130	160.5	206.3	203	46.3	7.7	0.0	193.6	4.8	9.5	97.6	20 333	389.5	709.3	23.0
Worcester	70 998	173.0	231.4	342	38.6	18.7	-19.7	472.2	11.1	21.8	225.3	20 297	964.4	1 578.0	80.6
MICHIGAN	3 750 732	152.1	255.8	16 010	35.9	980.1	10.9	30 627.8	635.5	1 300.7	17 393.0	27 369	60 258.6	146 338.8	4 793.5
Allen Park	15 717	137.5	221.2	18	16.7	D	D	D	D	D	D	D	D	D	D
Ann Arbor	55 162	392.5	81.2	167	32.9	5.3	39.5	154.9	1.9	3.8	33.3	17 526	208.8	350.4	15.1
Battle Creek	13 201	129.4	230.4	87	46.0	9.5	-10.4	350.7	6.4	14.8	215.3	33 641	1 309.4	1 915.0	201.6
Bay City	15 243	118.1	281.8	68	38.2	3.9	D	112.9	2.9	5.7	76.1	26 241	250.6	536.3	D
Burton	11 625	93.5	370.8	NA	NA	NA	NA	NA	NA	NA	NA	NA	NA	NA	NA
Dearborn	39 032	213.0	200.2	149	46.3	D	D	D	D	D	D	D	D	D	D
Dearborn Heights	30 497	145.5	247.4	30	20.0	0.5	0.0	11.9	0.4	0.8	8.6	21 500	23.8	42.4	1.2
Detroit	394 707	129.1	252.4	1 255	36.2	102.2	-3.3	3 519.1	50.4	101.7	1 430.6	28 385	4 829.0	14 334.9	257.8
East Detroit	16 538	105.0	274.3	51	21.6	D	D	D	D	D	D	D	D	D	D
East Lansing	24 048	318.3	46.9	NA	NA	NA	NA	NA	NA	NA	NA	NA	NA	NA	NA
Farmington Hills	28 742	216.0	147.1	173	36.4	5.7	26.7	158.5	2.8	5.6	59.5	21 250	341.1	595.3	7.5
Ferndale	11 165	116.1	268.2	106	36.8	2.9	-25.6	68.5	1.9	3.8	38.9	20 474	152.9	317.1	7.2
Flint	54 180	119.3	366.8	132	31.1	D	D	D	D	D	D	D	D	D	D
Garden City	16 232	98.7	305.0	37	21.6	0.5	NA	15.1	0.3	0.7	8.2	27 333	26.6	45.6	1.0
Grand Rapids	78 555	150.5	242.8	489	42.1	35.8	20.5	979.8	25.2	49.0	608.7	24 155	2 145.8	3 759.7	201.6
Highland Park	8 033	133.8	235.9	24	54.2	9.3	10.7	367.1	0.4	0.9	9.4	23 500	33.2	61.2	0.7
Holland	12 175	150.4	265.8	142	45.8	11.1	22.0	263.5	8.1	16.4	168.3	20 778	743.8	1 307.1	46.9
Inkster	12 598	114.5	291.0	22	40.9	0.9	28.6	26.0	0.7	1.3	20.1	28 714	50.9	76.4	4.1
Jackson	15 539	135.5	246.2	150	42.0	7.1	1.4	180.3	4.6	9.3	104.6	22 739	363.9	785.5	17.1
Kalamazoo	35 203	204.5	167.2	190	39.5	D	D	D	D	D	D	D	D	D	D
Kentwood	15 818	129.8	225.4	96	56.2	6.5	71.1	160.4	4.4	9.3	84.2	19 136	379.9	677.1	26.8
Lansing	58 458	153.4	210.4	150	36.0	D	D	D	D	D	D	D	D	D	D
Lincoln Park	18 940	95.5	294.1	NA	NA	NA	NA	NA	NA	NA	NA	NA	NA	NA	NA
Livonia	49 604	176.5	217.3	354	36.7	21.3	11.5	753.9	16.0	34.3	537.9	33 619	1 585.7	3 487.3	162.8
Madison Heights	16 700	123.0	305.4	242	39.7	8.2	3.8	249.6	4.7	9.8	115.5	24 574	440.6	940.4	21.1
Midland	16 635	298.5	148.7	38	50.0	D	D	D	D	D	D	D	D	D	D
Muskegon	14 604	126.8	276.8	117	41.9	7.8	-4.9	224.7	5.0	10.2	127.3	25 460	592.2	1 006.8	87.7
Oak Park	14 763	203.3	168.2	93	35.5	2.4	-7.7	61.8	1.5	3.1	36.0	24 000	114.8	178.7	5.0

1. Persons 16 years old and over.

Table C. Cities — **Wholesale Trade and Retail Trade**

City	Wholesale trade, 1987				Retail trade–all establishments, 1987				Retail trade–establishments with payroll, 1987					
						Sales				Sales				
											Per capita[2] (Dollars)			
	Estab-lishments	Sales (Mil. dol.)	Paid employees[1]	Annual payroll ($1,000)	Number	Total (Mil. dol.)	Percent change, 1982–1987	Per capita[2] (Dollars)	Number	Total (Mil. dol.)	General merchan-dise group stores	Food stores	Apparel and accessory stores	Eating and drinking places
	73	74	75	76	77	78	79	80	81	82	83	84	85	86
MARYLAND—Con.														
Hagerstown	116	326.2	1 612	31 898	585	388.9	32.3	11 550	416	381.2	1 245	2 304	500	931
Rockville	206	3 722.5	3 022	92 667	587	684.8	44.3	14 601	459	677.5	688	2 383	540	1 470
MASSACHUSETTS	11 087	74 697.6	160 791	4 389 944	58 623	45 997.2	59.6	7 887	38 905	44 818.5	845	1 385	476	807
Attleboro	44	138.0	486	11 255	322	352.6	37.6	10 100	209	347.0	D	1 221	D	630
Beverly	43	109.7	589	16 936	328	278.2	49.7	7 523	222	272.1	D	1 753	225	669
Boston	1 072	8 160.6	17 565	482 768	4 837	3 910.4	41.1	6 817	3 772	3 837.1	687	1 080	603	1 410
Brockton	116	D	D	D	839	838.2	40.8	8 929	590	825.8	D	1 503	613	778
Cambridge	176	920.1	2 780	84 609	1 022	858.7	37.6	9 409	826	844.2	1 383	1 745	733	1 523
Chelsea	142	1 319.1	2 187	53 850	203	160.9	17.2	6 275	154	158.1	D	2 133	252	522
Chicopee	58	311.2	934	21 432	516	342.8	44.7	6 004	347	334.9	614	911	328	686
Everett	76	691.1	1 406	39 617	257	110.0	36.5	3 028	176	105.6	0	552	D	352
Fall River	97	345.2	1 467	28 342	858	548.6	49.6	6 067	598	532.7	532	1 514	453	480
Fitchburg	69	219.2	763	19 773	409	375.3	99.0	9 613	294	363.9	D	2 487	347	D
Gloucester	71	278.4	442	10 921	350	194.9	46.2	6 904	225	187.0	D	1 536	D	870
Haverhill	57	136.0	592	13 744	413	375.0	61.1	7 713	275	366.6	450	1 275	147	660
Holyoke	63	198.3	938	19 813	531	455.8	62.4	10 852	412	450.6	3 514	1 352	1 332	701
Lawrence	109	409.3	1 933	47 834	507	327.5	34.9	5 164	340	313.4	D	454	289	393
Leominster	43	129.3	583	12 902	383	315.3	80.4	8 993	266	308.4	D	D	920	840
Lowell	97	322.5	1 469	33 614	657	556.2	43.0	5 988	454	540.2	410	871	94	506
Lynn	95	543.6	1 708	41 691	570	552.2	34.3	7 029	397	539.6	165	911	173	559
Malden	63	403.1	1 107	30 174	382	299.9	49.5	5 607	246	289.9	D	1 134	147	474
Marlborough	84	493.9	1 841	66 901	318	245.2	70.5	7 864	225	241.1	676	1 298	305	910
Medford	83	425.4	1 476	41 796	458	466.1	62.2	8 202	291	452.7	D	1 951	637	361
Melrose	33	78.0	319	6 569	158	98.5	38.5	3 421	90	93.0	0	944	17	112
New Bedford	174	569.3	2 239	42 764	884	488.8	27.4	5 068	612	471.6	D	1 234	281	549
Newton	273	1 833.2	3 252	99 968	949	831.1	38.7	10 118	609	808.7	D	1 537	1 292	880
Northampton	35	88.8	437	9 322	429	304.6	75.5	10 740	307	298.3	960	1 699	404	1 352
Peabody	109	1 130.6	2 607	79 213	535	570.3	78.3	12 317	352	559.0	3 939	1 539	1 017	823
Pittsfield	66	154.0	724	14 720	524	458.9	41.6	9 256	398	452.6	D	1 907	501	868
Quincy	127	780.4	1 448	31 633	634	615.1	41.7	7 444	441	605.1	412	1 925	205	807
Revere	41	1 064.2	414	10 548	364	238.9	22.5	5 491	228	228.9	D	1 459	153	779
Salem	72	161.1	748	18 300	436	324.7	18.5	8 534	314	314.1	D	1 978	300	882
Somerville	111	508.1	1 707	41 241	509	432.2	57.3	5 980	362	424.4	781	1 256	300	444
Springfield	285	1 168.8	4 051	103 106	1 379	1 196.4	39.2	8 007	1 034	1 175.6	1 080	1 331	434	731
Taunton	60	291.3	1 060	27 766	360	243.3	52.8	5 317	245	236.9	D	1 289	162	342
Waltham	230	4 970.7	5 181	176 642	501	474.1	38.6	8 304	391	465.7	426	1 436	221	1 143
Westfield	60	243.3	797	20 847	370	288.4	58.6	7 648	232	282.9	985	1 420	144	649
Woburn	383	2 720.3	6 662	198 203	351	475.2	69.6	12 713	240	468.7	1 529	2 209	348	743
Worcester	347	1 839.1	6 587	146 787	1 647	1 498.7	72.9	9 499	1 165	1 469.1	875	1 230	474	848
MICHIGAN	14 811	86 064.5	179 452	4 571 465	80 743	58 025.6	48.0	6 338	53 399	56 697.3	878	1 084	321	606
Allen Park	29	73.8	243	4 986	309	172.9	39.4	5 554	239	168.5	D	1 126	222	760
Ann Arbor	191	552.5	2 138	48 946	1 111	1 081.7	59.8	10 033	857	1 070.0	D	1 360	895	1 191
Battle Creek	60	308.9	730	15 784	483	392.1	100.7	7 250	369	386.6	D	944	462	549
Bay City	84	458.8	1 199	25 050	502	290.1	28.9	7 307	352	285.8	D	1 326	461	668
Burton	50	94.9	443	10 501	290	277.9	52.2	9 446	221	274.9	3 988	870	660	799
Dearborn	196	2 364.3	3 115	90 281	1 177	1 262.2	46.7	14 605	872	1 241.0	2 712	1 568	1 422	1 221
Dearborn Heights	46	99.1	462	10 835	464	277.1	29.4	4 480	315	269.3	49	1 440	108	824
Detroit	1 176	10 210.0	17 664	447 435	5 202	3 159.5	9.6	2 909	3 847	3 094.5	117	681	119	426
East Detroit	43	D	D	D	298	302.4	15.9	8 610	213	297.5	D	1 594	169	699
East Lansing	31	151.6	264	9 569	221	224.1	77.4	4 657	161	221.1	D	439	148	609
Farmington Hills	378	3 904.1	5 203	165 267	680	579.7	92.1	8 872	432	560.9	D	677	349	1 047
Ferndale	100	293.1	1 374	31 470	225	212.0	56.7	8 456	163	208.6	D	1 337	311	631
Flint	224	1 183.5	3 386	77 232	1 499	1 247.7	45.4	8 570	1 205	1 238.1	1 472	1 564	371	940
Garden City	20	D	D	D	238	246.0	76.6	7 562	158	243.4	D	363	81	516
Grand Rapids	577	3 148.5	8 460	218 216	1 677	1 297.5	48.6	6 956	1 186	1 274.7	841	993	344	712
Highland Park	33	357.2	892	23 815	114	122.9	27.5	4 797	97	122.4	D	1 019	97	316
Holland	88	222.0	839	20 874	590	386.6	72.1	13 359	363	378.2	D	D	667	1 222
Inkster	13	9.3	64	1 315	125	78.1	25.6	2 448	84	76.6	77	799	D	229
Jackson	95	446.6	1 353	32 931	467	331.6	37.0	8 969	358	326.8	1 175	1 152	218	1 075
Kalamazoo	214	834.7	2 937	65 737	733	586.6	28.2	7 595	540	579.5	327	1 076	462	953
Kentwood	124	769.5	2 120	54 606	424	541.2	75.6	15 138	313	534.3	4 025	1 637	1 708	1 131
Lansing	252	1 138.6	4 017	97 665	1 088	0.0	0.0	D	799	1 022.5	D	904	230	762
Lincoln Park	25	154.9	252	6 301	353	310.4	36.7	7 244	274	306.1	D	1 781	332	590
Livonia	407	3 319.6	7 236	191 707	1 061	1 157.6	50.8	11 514	802	1 142.4	1 937	1 858	693	990
Madison Heights	176	730.9	2 680	70 516	304	317.7	67.5	9 472	223	313.6	D	1 620	267	1 294
Midland	59	120.6	461	10 488	476	0.0	0.0	D	329	D	D	1 686	D	D
Muskegon	86	496.8	1 213	26 809	433	289.0	42.3	7 259	345	283.5	1 042	949	391	778
Oak Park	125	925.9	1 937	49 462	429	295.5	67.7	9 496	269	285.6	77	3 018	427	575

1. For the period including March 12 of the year shown. 2. Based on resident population estimated as of July 1, 1986.

Table C. Cities — **Retail Trade, Taxable Service Industries, and Federal Grants**

City	Retail trade–establishment with payroll, 1987 (cont'd): Paid employees[1]: Number	Retail trade: Paid employees[1]: Percent change, 1982–1987	Retail trade: Annual payroll (Mil. dol.)	Taxable service industries–establishments with payroll, 1987: Number	Taxable service: Receipts (Mil. dol.): Total	Taxable service: Receipts: Selected kinds of business: Hotels, motels, and other lodging places	Taxable service: Receipts: Selected kinds of business: Health services	Taxable service: Receipts: Selected kinds of business: Legal services	Taxable service: Paid employees[1]	Taxable service: Annual payroll (Mil. dol.)	Federal grants, 1986: Procurement contract awards (Mil. dol.)	Federal grants, 1986: Grant awards (Mil. dol.)	Federal government civilian employment, 1984
	87	88	89	90	91	92	93	94	95	96	97	98	99
MARYLAND—Con.													
Hagerstown	4 434	19.7	44.2	401	131.5	D	48.8	D	3 468	51.7	2.9	2.8	195
Rockville	7 008	22.2	89.5	1 021	1 147.5	D	94.4	61.6	17 086	420.4	483.6	62.6	8 541
MASSACHUSETTS	529 891	25.0	5 492.7	44 387	27 016.0	1 326.1	4 680.6	2 137.4	523 188	10 434.4	9 460.7	3 649.0	56 341
Attleboro	3 135	16.6	43.8	218	68.9	D	30.1	7.4	1 692	27.0	2.7	8.9	88
Beverly	3 193	20.9	34.9	268	132.9	D	68.6	4.1	3 254	68.8	27.1	0.6	96
Boston	56 240	15.8	585.0	5 738	6 358.2	D	509.8	1 338.6	115 138	2 537.8	298.5	751.5	21 857
Brockton	10 028	18.0	97.8	599	263.2	D	118.8	25.3	6 592	102.8	5.4	7.9	2 193
Cambridge	12 690	15.7	120.6	1 167	1 872.7	77.3	115.0	18.1	29 933	741.5	601.8	263.9	888
Chelsea	1 919	17.7	18.2	128	44.7	D	3.9	D	761	15.3	22.0	4.7	39
Chicopee	4 161	15.6	41.8	235	64.7	6.2	16.9	1.9	1 825	22.7	5.8	2.8	147
Everett	1 405	15.0	14.2	168	121.0	0.0	D	0.7	2 393	54.3	51.4	1.7	20
Fall River	6 035	23.4	60.9	557	145.8	D	67.6	12.8	3 797	62.3	9.4	6.4	274
Fitchburg	3 895	30.0	38.5	277	89.6	D	39.9	6.3	2 394	35.8	64.8	8.9	140
Gloucester	2 209	22.9	24.3	197	48.8	2.8	D	6.1	1 084	16.7	15.4	1.3	243
Haverhill	3 537	5.8	37.9	310	118.7	D	48.6	10.8	2 824	45.9	2.4	4.5	150
Holyoke	5 757	23.0	52.4	303	131.4	D	49.6	4.8	3 429	58.9	4.4	7.5	135
Lawrence	3 356	4.6	40.8	367	133.8	D	44.7	9.0	3 460	47.1	1.7	8.1	386
Leominster	3 674	45.9	35.7	240	D	D	D	3.5	D	D	0.9	2.3	64
Lowell	5 570	-2.3	61.8	498	247.5	D	57.4	23.9	5 335	99.9	561.4	10.5	429
Lynn	5 178	19.6	58.1	437	164.5	D	74.9	13.9	4 113	68.9	1 226.7	5.4	528
Malden	3 125	11.2	34.8	332	142.2	2.7	28.6	10.9	4 578	58.1	3.9	2.7	42
Marlborough	2 784	23.0	28.0	255	105.4	D	23.9	3.4	2 178	39.6	122.3	0.7	100
Medford	4 616	23.1	46.1	322	118.7	0.0	33.0	3.9	2 569	44.9	7.4	30.3	6
Melrose	1 066	17.3	10.0	210	71.0	0.0	33.1	4.1	1 609	30.8	0.9	0.6	12
New Bedford	6 417	11.9	59.7	585	184.2	D	66.1	22.4	5 227	76.9	83.4	7.6	401
Newton	8 853	7.0	104.2	1 106	558.6	45.6	110.7	13.9	10 154	215.1	13.8	7.3	209
Northampton	4 342	58.2	38.3	266	84.9	4.0	36.4	8.2	2 267	36.1	28.5	3.1	1 082
Peabody	6 035	33.0	60.3	345	121.4	3.4	29.6	10.3	3 289	50.4	9.5	1.4	127
Pittsfield	6 048	29.6	56.6	450	160.9	D	56.7	D	3 930	74.4	494.9	7.5	337
Quincy	7 545	23.4	78.0	636	305.2	2.1	69.2	18.4	6 071	107.9	68.7	41.9	121
Revere	3 051	8.7	28.6	180	85.0	D	25.1	2.2	1 939	25.1	12.9	1.3	2
Salem	3 755	0.5	39.2	400	138.4	D	52.9	16.9	3 184	56.7	3.4	2.5	149
Somerville	5 250	36.4	51.8	369	183.8	D	23.9	6.6	4 640	74.0	2.7	5.6	5
Springfield	14 413	13.7	146.8	1 129	533.6	D	166.3	66.5	12 746	225.0	13.0	17.2	3 031
Taunton	2 591	23.2	26.1	255	72.6	0.0	21.1	9.5	1 692	28.2	2.7	4.3	105
Waltham	6 109	13.2	68.9	651	697.9	7.3	37.1	12.1	13 492	296.8	120.8	23.1	799
Westfield	3 408	26.8	33.8	233	85.0	D	37.6	2.7	2 121	32.3	7.7	2.2	318
Woburn	4 678	36.8	52.3	444	433.1	10.8	56.7	6.3	8 537	181.7	60.3	3.7	83
Worcester	15 632	19.1	157.1	1 356	718.7	17.4	214.8	78.3	15 254	280.2	21.9	51.4	1 062
MICHIGAN	673 265	29.9	6 583.5	55 367	23 859.8	893.7	6 219.9	1 769.9	533 061	9 469.9	3 101.2	4 452.5	54 392
Allen Park	2 425	22.8	20.0	268	87.4	D	30.8	1.5	2 161	34.8	2.2	0.3	1 764
Ann Arbor	14 573	32.2	143.8	1 226	556.8	34.0	97.2	35.1	12 421	213.7	75.7	117.8	2 684
Battle Creek	5 011	68.0	43.3	325	118.0	12.0	45.3	5.3	4 104	47.8	28.0	5.2	3 927
Bay City	3 449	0.3	33.1	335	97.6	D	36.2	D	1 967	41.5	3.7	3.3	208
Burton	3 506	25.4	32.7	165	55.4	D	13.7	1.7	1 139	16.9	0.4	0.3	0
Dearborn	14 250	17.6	152.3	813	455.1	43.0	132.4	7.6	10 687	189.9	7.7	4.8	374
Dearborn Heights	4 014	20.9	39.1	292	77.0	D	26.5	2.8	1 754	29.3	0.6	1.3	73
Detroit	38 529	1.9	387.4	3 734	2 580.7	82.3	513.0	479.6	53 411	1 067.3	368.4	319.5	12 861
East Detroit	2 802	12.4	31.0	296	93.2	D	30.8	3.0	2 164	29.3	0.1	0.6	83
East Lansing	3 791	17.6	28.4	197	70.9	D	31.1	6.3	1 681	31.6	8.8	53.6	361
Farmington Hills	6 692	73.1	68.3	987	549.7	10.7	90.5	33.4	8 744	215.6	4.7	0.6	2
Ferndale	2 204	66.3	25.3	174	64.3	D	7.2	0.8	1 692	20.9	1.8	0.6	3
Flint	15 586	39.2	148.4	1 220	507.0	14.3	193.5	36.1	11 770	215.1	17.1	14.6	1 121
Garden City	2 216	30.6	24.5	199	53.4	0.0	29.7	D	1 095	21.7	0.7	0.3	60
Grand Rapids	16 666	30.2	161.0	1 618	894.7	46.4	213.8	134.4	19 877	351.8	137.1	16.0	1 968
Highland Park	1 144	8.0	14.3	86	77.5	1.1	14.3	0.0	1 591	25.2	11.9	1.2	57
Holland	4 878	D	44.2	350	127.7	D	40.4	6.0	4 198	52.2	10.9	1.6	105
Inkster	844	0.4	8.8	77	16.2	1.9	2.8	1.2	442	5.4	2.0	0.5	107
Jackson	4 164	15.7	42.6	398	171.6	6.0	50.9	9.5	4 565	78.4	33.3	4.5	357
Kalamazoo	8 134	10.6	75.0	773	495.3	12.6	220.7	43.2	11 665	211.7	39.7	5.6	887
Kentwood	6 562	35.4	62.9	256	113.9	14.1	18.5	D	3 386	44.6	1.4	0.2	8
Lansing	11 910	15.6	119.4	1 009	492.1	D	D	67.9	12 114	208.1	6.1	309.6	1 486
Lincoln Park	3 828	12.9	35.5	256	95.4	0.9	25.0	1.5	2 204	33.6	0.2	1.2	81
Livonia	14 211	56.2	143.0	1 069	809.4	14.6	126.1	11.8	12 961	246.1	30.1	1.6	370
Madison Heights	4 060	43.5	37.2	319	310.8	6.1	36.6	D	6 064	144.9	5.2	0.5	2
Midland	D	D	D	338	123.2	D	47.1	4.4	3 268	53.0	9.1	1.3	118
Muskegon	3 711	23.1	33.4	404	137.4	D	61.7	16.7	3 618	62.7	59.4	2.4	342
Oak Park	2 978	61.4	34.5	224	128.7	D	23.2	0.6	3 696	49.3	0.4	1.2	39

1. For the period including March 12 of the year shown.

City	City government employment, 1985 (October)			Form of governments[2] (As of 1986)	City government finances, 1984–1985												
					General revenue							General expenditures					
						Intergovernmental		Taxes					Per capitl[3](Dol.)		Percent of total for–		
									Per capita[3] (Dollars)								
	Total	Rates[1]	Percent education		Total (Mil. dol.)	Total (Mil. dol.)	Percent from State government	Total (Mil. dol.)	Total	Property	Sales & gross receipts	Total (Mil. dol.)	Total	Capital outlays	Public welfare	Highways	Education
	100	101	102	103	104	105	106	107	108	109	110	111	112	113	114	115	116
MARYLAND—Con.																	
Hagerstown	455	135.1	0.0	1	13.1	3.3	45.4	4.9	146	132	6	13.5	402	56	0.0	11.7	0.0
Rockville	408	87.0	0.0	2	24.0	2.0	62.3	10.3	220	198	8	25.1	536	131	0.0	26.5	0.1
MASSACHUSETTS	NA	NA	NA	NA	NA	NA	NA	NA	NA	NA	NA	NA	NA	NA	NA	NA	NA
Attleboro	NA	NA	NA	1	32.8	12.4	92.4	16.7	477	471	0	30.1	861	9	0.4	3.8	57.9
Beverly	1 033	279.3	65.1	1	40.1	11.0	82.3	24.6	664	659	0	34.5	932	55	0.3	6.3	47.9
Boston	20 704	360.9	38.9	1	1 088.5	558.5	87.1	372.6	650	611	14	937.7	1 635	218	0.2	3.4	30.6
Brockton	2 685	286.0	62.6	1	102.3	52.6	91.6	43.3	461	456	0	94.3	1 004	42	1.7	3.8	48.2
Cambridge	3 710	406.5	37.7	2	182.8	60.0	75.2	76.6	840	792	0	159.5	1 748	129	4.7	3.3	30.7
Chelsea	933	363.9	53.2	1	30.0	18.5	88.0	9.5	370	361	0	30.2	1 180	93	0.4	7.6	39.3
Chicopee	1 679	294.0	60.9	1	47.1	23.5	93.0	19.9	348	344	0	41.4	725	25	3.8	3.3	50.8
Everett	990	272.5	51.8	1	40.9	11.8	84.2	27.7	762	759	0	39.2	1 079	9	0.4	6.1	42.5
Fall River	2 693	297.8	61.2	1	95.6	63.8	81.7	22.7	251	246	0	84.1	930	35	0.8	3.8	43.6
Fitchburg	847	217.0	52.7	1	38.7	20.4	86.7	13.6	349	345	0	34.8	891	70	0.5	7.8	42.6
Gloucester	872	308.9	60.1	1	37.3	15.1	69.7	19.7	698	692	0	35.0	1 238	294	0.6	6.2	37.2
Haverhill	2 226	457.8	40.8	1	77.6	23.6	81.5	20.6	424	413	0	69.8	1 435	70	1.9	2.8	28.9
Holyoke	1 705	406.0	53.4	1	50.5	29.7	76.7	13.1	312	309	0	49.5	1 179	42	9.8	5.2	48.8
Lawrence	2 080	328.0	61.9	3	74.5	50.8	73.5	19.1	301	297	0	89.2	1 407	375	0.2	2.5	57.7
Leominster	822	234.5	60.7	1	32.0	14.3	86.5	14.2	405	399	0	32.4	925	137	0.4	7.4	42.3
Lowell	2 657	286.1	59.2	2	102.3	56.1	91.2	38.3	412	407	0	93.4	1 006	112	0.6	2.6	44.2
Lynn	2 283	290.6	50.9	1	93.4	49.2	86.3	36.4	464	456	0	83.6	1 064	10	4.1	3.6	42.4
Malden	1 350	252.4	56.2	1	54.9	26.1	84.3	24.1	450	443	0	48.0	897	9	2.4	6.4	43.7
Marlborough	793	254.3	58.8	1	35.5	9.8	93.3	21.3	683	678	1	29.2	938	32	0.2	5.8	49.3
Medford	1 337	235.3	60.2	2	55.0	23.2	86.9	28.5	501	496	0	55.6	978	11	0.3	3.4	43.2
Melrose	1 016	352.9	71.9	1	28.3	10.1	92.3	16.7	582	581	0	26.2	911	14	0.2	3.4	57.1
New Bedford	3 201	331.9	56.9	1	97.0	66.3	88.0	26.9	279	273	0	94.2	977	3	0.7	3.9	46.0
Newton	2 844	346.2	56.6	1	106.6	17.7	82.9	82.5	1 005	988	0	99.4	1 210	37	0.2	9.5	47.1
Northampton	769	271.2	63.7	1	25.2	10.2	95.2	12.1	426	414	0	22.2	782	15	0.5	7.6	50.1
Peabody	1 158	250.1	51.7	1	69.7	22.6	75.3	26.2	566	562	0	62.1	1 342	17	0.2	3.5	33.1
Pittsfield	1 476	297.7	65.4	1	48.2	22.6	89.2	20.7	417	412	0	45.0	908	36	0.4	5.2	53.7
Quincy	3 495	423.0	43.7	1	148.5	44.8	76.6	48.1	582	574	0	139.1	1 683	86	0.2	2.1	29.2
Revere	989	227.3	57.2	1	50.7	21.7	80.6	26.5	609	602	0	42.5	977	44	0.7	1.1	48.1
Salem	1 398	367.4	44.8	1	51.3	15.2	78.9	22.4	590	581	0	44.5	1 168	11	0.3	3.0	35.1
Somerville	1 875	259.4	57.2	1	81.9	50.4	84.3	29.0	401	393	0	77.1	1 067	182	0.3	5.1	42.8
Springfield	6 706	448.8	52.1	1	157.9	80.4	95.6	55.4	371	367	0	163.2	1 092	18	0.4	3.3	47.6
Taunton	1 358	296.8	52.1	1	41.2	21.9	94.4	14.3	312	308	0	38.7	847	30	2.3	5.4	48.6
Waltham	1 483	259.8	57.9	1	59.8	16.7	90.1	38.5	674	663	0	55.6	974	25	0.2	3.5	48.4
Westfield	1 076	285.3	59.8	1	34.3	14.6	89.6	17.0	450	446	0	30.7	814	59	0.3	4.3	57.2
Woburn	1 156	309.3	68.9	1	35.4	10.1	91.9	23.9	639	632	0	31.9	855	33	0.3	9.9	56.6
Worcester	6 562	415.9	43.0	2	238.1	115.3	80.6	68.3	433	423	0	230.8	1 463	114	2.1	4.2	32.8
MICHIGAN	NA	NA	NA	NA	NA	NA	NA	NA	NA	NA	NA	NA	NA	NA	NA	NA	NA
Allen Park	233	74.8	0.0	1	13.3	3.5	87.1	8.0	259	252	0	10.8	348	27	NA	14.5	0.0
Ann Arbor	1 237	114.7	0.0	2	65.6	16.6	63.7	25.9	241	232	0	67.5	626	106	0.1	9.6	0.0
Battle Creek	769	142.2	0.0	2	47.2	17.3	38.0	14.1	261	134	0	42.7	790	237	0.0	5.2	0.0
Bay City	434	109.3	0.0	2	27.3	10.1	69.9	7.8	196	193	0	20.4	515	65	0.0	15.2	0.0
Burton	158	53.7	0.0	1	9.9	2.8	81.9	3.2	109	102	0	7.5	256	57	0.0	8.1	0.0
Dearborn	1 066	123.4	0.0	1	93.6	14.5	69.5	31.4	363	345	0	67.9	785	27	0.8	2.4	0.0
Dearborn Heights	394	63.7	0.0	1	19.6	7.5	74.7	10.0	161	155	0	20.0	324	19	1.8	6.8	0.0
Detroit	20 332	187.2	0.0	1	1 244.1	533.4	68.3	484.6	446	163	47	1 144.6	1 054	103	0.0	10.5	0.6
East Detroit	259	73.7	0.0	2	12.1	3.5	86.9	6.1	174	170	0	10.1	288	26	0.0	6.7	0.0
East Lansing	437	90.8	0.0	2	17.7	6.3	78.5	4.9	103	97	0	16.9	351	15	0.9	9.0	0.0
Farmington Hills	392	60.0	0.0	2	22.7	6.3	77.1	9.2	140	124	0	21.8	333	53	0.0	11.8	0.0
Ferndale	233	92.9	0.0	2	12.4	3.6	82.5	5.7	225	221	0	12.3	489	23	0.0	10.6	0.0
Flint	4 224	290.1	0.0	1	215.7	39.6	48.8	42.8	294	134	0	234.3	1 609	263	0.0	3.2	0.0
Garden City	NA	NA	NA	1	9.5	3.3	92.2	4.9	151	144	0	11.5	354	24	0.0	10.3	0.0
Grand Rapids	2 083	111.7	0.0	2	112.4	33.3	55.1	37.3	200	92	0	100.2	537	50	0.0	8.5	0.0
Highland Park	387	151.1	0.0	1	20.2	7.9	80.3	10.5	408	177	0	17.9	699	8	1.0	4.9	0.0
Holland	473	163.4	0.0	2	17.9	3.7	78.0	5.2	179	174	0	13.3	459	66	0.2	8.1	0.0
Inkster	211	66.1	0.0	2	10.1	4.1	85.3	4.4	137	134	0	9.3	291	11	0.0	11.5	0.0
Jackson	512	138.5	0.0	2	20.4	7.7	63.5	8.1	220	117	0	19.6	531	31	0.0	9.4	0.0
Kalamazoo	928	120.2	0.0	2	58.2	26.1	46.5	14.3	186	183	0	67.7	877	326	0.0	6.2	0.0
Kentwood	143	40.0	0.0	1	8.9	2.5	92.4	2.9	81	75	0	6.8	191	24	0.0	13.5	0.4
Lansing	2 459	190.6	0.0	1	103.2	19.4	72.2	30.8	238	103	0	89.3	693	56	0.8	7.5	0.0
Lincoln Park	NA	NA	NA	1	15.7	4.7	92.7	7.0	163	149	0	15.7	367	39	NA	16.9	0.0
Livonia	826	82.2	0.0	1	48.0	11.1	85.5	19.5	194	185	0	40.9	407	19	0.0	4.1	0.0
Madison Heights	282	84.1	0.0	2	13.4	4.0	81.8	6.1	182	173	0	12.9	384	23	0.0	5.3	0.0
Midland	424	118.1	0.0	2	21.0	4.8	78.6	9.7	271	266	0	21.2	591	138	0.0	10.5	0.0
Muskegon	362	90.9	0.0	2	16.5	5.0	85.1	5.6	140	136	0	17.1	430	0	0.0	9.2	0.0
Oak Park	296	95.1	0.0	2	15.2	4.1	83.3	7.2	231	231	0	15.2	487	24	0.5	6.9	0.0

1. Per 10,000 population estimated as of July 1, 1986. 2. 1=Mayor-council; 2=Council-manager; 3=Commission. Data subject to copyright. 3. Based on resident population estimated as of July 1, 1986.

City	City government finances, 1984–1985 (cont'd): General expenditure (cont'd): Percent of total for (cont'd): Health and hos-pitals	Police protec-tion	Sew-erage and san-itation	Parks and recre-ation	Housing and com-munity dev-elopment	Debt outstanding: Total (Mil. dol.)	Per capita[1] (Dollars)	Per-cent utility	Climate[2]: Average daily temperature (Degrees Fahrenheit): Mean: Jan.	July	Limits: Jan.[3]	July[4]	Annual precip-itation (Inches)	Heating degree days[5]	Cooling degree days[5]	Typical monthly electric bills, 1986: Residential[6]: Total (Dollars)	Percent change, 1980–1986	Commer-cial[7] (Dollars)
	117	118	119	120	121	122	123	124	125	126	127	128	129	130	131	132	133	134
MARYLAND—Con.																		
Hagerstown	0.0	23.3	22.2	5.4	0.7	6.6	197	7.8	30.6	74.9	22.4	86.8	38.84	5 086	935	41.76	52.0	NA
Rockville	0.0	4.6	18.9	12.3	2.4	33.3	709	4.7	33.3	75.7	24.1	87.4	40.91	4 663	1 063	47.21	30.3	NA
MASSACHUSETTS	NA	NA	NA	NA	NA	NA	NA	NA	NA	NA	NA	NA	NA	NA	NA	63.45	43.2	NA
Attleboro	0.3	5.7	3.8	1.3	0.0	16.5	473	6.5	27.0	71.3	17.2	82.5	45.77	6 276	455	56.56	27.7	NA
Beverly	0.8	6.8	7.0	4.3	0.0	8.7	236	44.7	27.8	69.6	20.8	77.4	45.44	6 294	328	56.56	27.7	NA
Boston	11.8	8.6	4.6	1.8	7.3	615.5	1 073	1.8	29.6	73.5	22.8	81.8	43.81	5 593	699	69.65	52.9	677.1
Brockton	0.7	8.0	7.2	1.6	1.5	40.4	431	11.3	27.0	71.3	17.2	82.5	45.77	6 276	455	71.69	49.8	667.4
Cambridge	17.9	6.7	3.4	2.2	5.8	56.9	623	0.0	29.6	73.5	22.8	81.8	43.81	5 593	699	68.88	59.1	619.8
Chelsea	0.8	8.1	3.4	2.0	4.8	7.9	308	6.2	29.6	73.5	22.8	81.8	43.81	5 593	699	69.65	52.9	NA
Chicopee	0.7	8.3	6.0	3.3	0.0	27.4	480	59.1	26.6	73.6	18.1	84.6	44.87	5 953	699	55.20	73.1	492.1
Everett	0.6	6.7	2.1	3.5	4.3	13.1	360	9.7	29.6	73.5	22.8	81.8	43.81	5 593	699	56.56	27.7	NA
Fall River	2.4	8.1	6.4	1.1	6.0	27.2	301	6.1	31.6	73.4	24.8	80.8	43.94	5 305	721	71.69	50.0	667.4
Fitchburg	1.0	6.1	9.2	1.0	5.7	8.3	213	4.1	24.1	71.9	13.8	84.0	45.78	6 619	523	83.98	32.5	NA
Gloucester	0.4	6.0	23.8	1.1	1.5	20.9	742	13.4	27.8	69.6	20.8	77.4	45.44	6 294	328	56.56	27.7	NA
Haverhill	32.5	4.5	4.7	0.8	3.4	44.4	913	15.7	26.4	73.5	17.8	84.6	42.69	6 024	667	56.56	27.7	NA
Holyoke	0.4	6.7	3.4	2.5	0.0	31.8	758	26.8	26.6	73.6	18.1	84.6	44.87	5 953	699	65.03	50.5	NA
Lawrence	0.2	4.6	3.5	1.0	15.2	50.9	803	2.8	25.8	72.6	16.8	82.8	42.56	6 232	563	56.56	27.7	507.6
Leominster	0.5	6.1	22.0	0.9	0.0	10.2	291	9.0	24.1	71.9	13.8	84.0	45.78	6 619	523	56.56	27.7	NA
Lowell	0.8	8.1	10.1	4.7	0.0	51.7	557	16.8	25.8	72.6	16.8	82.8	42.56	6 232	563	56.56	27.7	507.6
Lynn	0.6	7.3	2.7	1.9	5.2	47.9	610	73.9	29.6	73.5	22.8	81.8	43.81	5 593	699	56.56	27.7	507.6
Malden	0.3	7.4	3.4	2.5	0.0	21.5	403	9.5	29.6	73.5	22.8	81.8	43.81	5 593	699	56.56	27.7	507.6
Marlborough	0.6	6.6	5.9	1.2	1.6	36.2	1 160	13.1	25.6	73.1	15.8	84.3	45.34	6 205	613	56.56	27.7	NA
Medford	0.3	8.5	4.6	1.8	3.0	2.5	44	0.0	29.6	73.5	22.8	81.8	43.81	5 593	699	56.56	27.7	507.6
Melrose	0.4	7.4	3.6	2.5	1.7	4.4	152	42.1	29.6	73.5	22.8	81.8	43.81	5 593	699	56.56	27.7	NA
New Bedford	1.2	7.6	4.0	1.2	12.1	36.9	382	33.1	31.6	73.4	24.8	80.8	43.94	5 305	721	61.42	22.4	NA
Newton	0.8	8.3	4.2	4.3	1.9	10.1	124	8.5	29.6	73.5	22.8	81.8	43.81	5 593	699	69.65	52.9	677.1
Northampton	1.2	6.7	3.5	1.6	0.1	8.6	304	3.3	26.6	73.6	18.1	84.6	44.87	5 953	699	56.56	27.7	NA
Peabody	19.6	5.0	9.7	1.7	8.3	24.7	533	8.1	29.6	73.5	22.8	81.8	43.81	5 593	699	54.28	51.8	NA
Pittsfield	0.8	6.9	5.6	1.1	0.0	16.8	338	1.8	21.1	71.4	11.9	83.2	35.74	6 927	494	67.71	67.5	706.9
Quincy	31.6	6.0	3.4	1.3	1.4	38.3	464	2.7	29.6	73.5	22.8	81.8	43.81	5 593	699	56.56	27.7	507.6
Revere	0.4	7.5	1.1	1.7	2.2	11.3	259	8.4	29.6	73.5	22.8	81.8	43.81	5 593	699	56.56	27.7	NA
Salem	18.2	6.0	8.0	2.2	3.2	18.2	478	23.3	29.6	73.5	22.8	81.8	43.81	5 593	699	56.56	27.7	NA
Somerville	0.5	6.7	3.7	1.5	9.1	42.4	586	1.1	29.6	73.5	22.8	81.8	43.81	5 593	699	69.65	52.9	677.1
Springfield	7.4	8.3	5.3	3.3	0.0	42.9	287	6.5	26.6	73.6	18.1	84.6	44.87	5 953	699	67.71	67.5	706.9
Taunton	0.8	6.0	6.4	1.9	0.0	45.2	989	54.9	27.0	71.3	17.2	82.5	45.77	6 276	455	49.19	-3.7	NA
Waltham	0.3	8.1	5.2	2.3	0.0	7.8	136	29.5	29.6	73.5	22.8	81.8	43.81	5 593	699	69.65	52.9	677.1
Westfield	0.4	7.3	3.5	1.1	0.7	13.2	351	21.3	26.6	73.6	18.1	84.6	44.87	5 953	699	64.38	96.6	NA
Woburn	0.4	7.4	2.8	1.0	0.0	3.2	86	1.4	29.6	73.5	22.8	81.8	43.81	5 593	699	69.65	52.9	NA
Worcester	13.8	5.4	5.9	2.3	2.4	83.2	527	12.1	23.3	69.9	15.6	79.0	47.60	6 950	359	56.56	27.7	507.6
MICHIGAN	NA	NA	NA	NA	NA	NA	NA	NA	NA	NA	NA	NA	NA	NA	NA	53.58	58.8	NA
Allen Park	0.7	18.9	4.3	8.9	1.5	2.4	78	18.6	23.4	71.9	16.1	83.1	30.97	6 563	615	56.32	79.6	NA
Ann Arbor	0.0	11.1	18.1	4.2	0.1	66.7	619	24.7	23.8	72.9	16.8	83.6	30.22	6 346	723	56.32	79.6	570.0
Battle Creek	0.2	11.2	13.7	5.8	0.0	32.5	600	9.2	22.4	71.7	15.1	82.9	33.90	6 723	599	49.52	21.3	NA
Bay City	0.0	16.3	17.1	2.2	0.0	26.1	657	18.1	20.7	71.0	14.2	81.7	29.77	7 103	501	38.80	22.8	NA
Burton	0.0	20.6	24.1	0.1	0.0	6.6	225	24.0	21.3	70.1	14.0	81.2	29.21	7 068	456	49.52	NA	NA
Dearborn	0.7	15.4	13.5	7.6	2.3	21.7	251	0.0	23.4	71.9	16.1	83.1	30.97	6 563	615	56.32	79.6	570.0
Dearborn Heights	0.6	27.3	9.1	2.6	6.3	0.0	0	0.0	23.4	71.9	16.1	83.1	30.97	6 563	615	56.32	79.6	570.0
Detroit	6.0	16.3	15.3	7.0	9.2	935.8	861	15.5	23.4	71.9	16.1	83.1	30.97	6 563	615	56.32	79.6	570.0
East Detroit	0.0	28.6	13.3	7.1	0.0	0.0	0	0.0	23.4	71.9	16.1	83.1	30.97	6 563	615	56.32	79.6	NA
East Lansing	0.0	13.5	20.4	2.9	3.1	7.9	164	2.1	21.6	70.8	14.1	82.6	29.58	6 987	530	37.49	17.7	340.0
Farmington Hills	0.0	22.5	4.4	4.4	0.0	14.8	226	5.1	14.0	64.5	4.8	75.8	30.97	6 563	615	56.32	79.6	570.0
Ferndale	0.0	22.2	19.2	4.6	2.5	2.9	114	1.2	14.0	64.5	4.8	75.8	30.97	6 563	615	56.32	79.6	NA
Flint	46.7	8.4	5.4	1.5	0.0	116.8	802	1.5	21.3	70.1	14.0	81.2	29.21	7 068	456	49.52	21.3	589.4
Garden City	0.9	19.9	18.3	10.6	0.0	0.6	18	0.0	14.0	64.5	4.8	75.8	30.97	6 563	615	56.32	79.6	NA
Grand Rapids	0.0	14.3	7.5	5.8	3.1	45.1	242	17.6	22.0	71.4	14.9	83.0	34.36	6 927	570	49.52	21.3	589.4
Highland Park	0.0	19.1	0.0	1.5	0.0	0.9	37	0.0	20.2	67.4	12.6	80.2	30.97	6 563	615	56.32	79.6	NA
Holland	1.4	17.5	11.2	8.5	0.0	32.2	1 114	51.0	24.1	71.0	17.6	82.3	35.69	6 569	587	36.90	31.3	NA
Inkster	0.0	23.1	1.6	3.8	3.6	3.9	123	0.0	20.2	67.4	12.6	80.2	30.97	6 563	615	56.32	79.6	NA
Jackson	0.0	21.9	13.5	5.2	0.0	4.5	122	23.8	21.6	71.9	14.6	82.9	29.11	6 833	609	49.52	21.3	NA
Kalamazoo	0.2	14.2	44.3	2.4	0.0	79.5	1 029	2.6	23.7	73.2	16.5	84.9	34.83	6 281	751	49.52	21.3	589.4
Kentwood	0.0	18.7	17.4	4.1	0.0	3.8	106	33.0	22.0	71.4	14.9	83.0	34.36	6 927	570	49.52	21.3	NA
Lansing	0.0	10.2	20.8	5.1	2.7	90.1	698	15.5	21.6	70.8	14.1	82.6	29.58	6 987	530	37.49	17.7	340.0
Lincoln Park	0.0	24.4	18.5	5.5	0.0	6.6	154	0.0	20.2	67.4	12.6	80.2	30.97	6 563	615	56.32	79.6	NA
Livonia	0.0	19.4	23.2	4.6	0.3	45.5	452	2.2	20.2	67.4	12.6	80.2	30.97	6 563	615	56.32	79.6	570.0
Madison Heights	0.0	22.7	21.8	3.7	0.0	1.2	34	0.0	20.2	67.4	12.6	80.2	30.97	6 563	615	56.32	79.6	NA
Midland	0.0	12.1	12.1	7.7	1.6	34.1	950	71.3	22.0	71.5	14.9	82.9	28.75	6 847	555	49.52	21.3	NA
Muskegon	0.0	19.8	15.3	2.6	0.0	20.6	517	23.3	23.1	70.1	17.2	80.3	31.50	6 925	451	49.52	21.3	NA
Oak Park	0.0	22.0	18.4	4.3	0.0	2.5	80	0.0	20.2	67.4	12.6	80.2	30.97	6 563	615	56.32	79.6	NA

1. Based on resident population estimated as of July 1, 1986. 2. Represents normal values based on the 30-year period, 1951–1980 (see text). 3. Average daily minimum. 4. Average daily maximum. 5. For definition, see text. 6. As of January 1; based on consumption of 750 kWh. 7. Based on billing demand of 30 kW and consumption of 6,000 kWh.

MSA/ CMSA Code[1]	State/ Place code	City	Land area,[2] 1990 (Sq. Km.)	Population							Population characteristics, 1990						
				1990				Change 1980–1990		Percent						
										Race						
				Total persons	Rank	Per sq. km.	1980	Number	Per-cent	White	Black	Am. Indian, Eskimo, Aleut	Asian & Pacific Islander	Other race	His-panic[3]	65 Years and over
			1	2	3	4	5	6	7	8	9	10	11	12	13	14
		MICHIGAN—Con.														
2162	26 2200	Pontiac	51.8	71 166	312	1 374	76 715	-5 549	-7.2	51.25	42.20	0.83	1.36	4.35	8.01	8.7
3720	26 2206	Portage	83.4	41 042	607	492	38 157	2 885	7.6	94.30	2.78	0.36	2.06	0.50	1.44	8.5
2162	26 2220	Port Huron	20.7	33 694	748	1 628	33 981	-287	-0.8	90.05	6.81	0.85	0.59	1.70	3.49	13.9
2162	26 2360	Roseville	25.4	51 412	476	2 024	54 311	-2 899	-5.3	97.27	1.00	0.46	1.11	0.17	1.22	13.7
2162	26 2365	Royal Oak	30.6	65 410	353	2 138	70 893	-5 483	-7.7	97.90	0.51	0.25	1.11	0.23	1.06	15.7
6960	26 2370	Saginaw	45.2	69 512	323	1 538	77 508	-7 996	-10.3	52.26	40.35	0.54	0.43	6.42	10.51	11.9
2162	26 2385	St. Clair Shores	29.9	68 107	333	2 278	76 210	-8 103	-10.6	98.67	0.21	0.34	0.64	0.14	0.95	18.6
2162	26 2490	Southfield	67.9	75 728	282	1 115	75 568	160	0.2	67.89	29.12	0.25	2.38	0.36	1.72	17.0
2162	26 2495	Southgate	17.8	30 771	814	1 729	32 058	-1 287	-4.0	96.50	1.18	0.50	1.09	0.74	2.78	13.5
2162	26 2583	Sterling Heights	94.9	117 810	151	1 241	108 999	8 811	8.1	96.30	0.40	0.24	2.86	0.20	1.12	9.2
2162	26 2633	Taylor	61.2	70 811	314	1 157	77 568	-6 757	-8.7	93.23	4.21	0.57	1.26	0.73	2.81	8.0
2162	26 2675	Troy	86.9	72 884	298	839	67 102	5 782	8.6	91.52	1.35	0.16	6.78	0.19	1.27	8.4
2162	26 2790	Warren	88.8	144 864	118	1 631	161 134	-16 270	-10.1	97.33	0.72	0.46	1.34	0.15	1.09	14.9
2162	26 2827	Westland	53.0	84 724	246	1 599	84 603	121	0.1	94.66	3.34	0.55	0.98	0.47	1.88	10.8
2162	26 2920	Wyandotte	13.7	30 938	810	2 258	34 006	-3 068	-9.0	98.19	0.24	0.60	0.40	0.58	2.11	16.2
3000	26 2925	Wyoming	62.9	63 891	357	1 016	59 616	4 275	7.2	93.52	2.72	0.55	1.49	1.72	3.50	9.7
...	27 0000	MINNESOTA	206 207.1	4 375 099	X	21	4 075 970	299 129	7.3	94.41	2.17	1.14	1.78	0.50	1.23	12.5
5120	27 0370	Blaine	87.9	38 975	646	443	28 558	10 417	36.5	97.15	0.33	0.79	1.37	0.37	1.02	3.1
5120	27 0385	Bloomington	92.0	86 335	237	938	81 831	4 504	5.5	94.71	1.61	0.29	3.09	0.30	0.93	10.3
5120	27 0460	Brooklyn Center	20.6	28 887	845	1 402	31 230	-2 343	-7.5	90.94	5.20	0.94	2.31	0.61	1.27	12.3
5120	27 0465	Brooklyn Park	67.5	56 381	415	835	43 332	13 049	30.1	90.60	4.94	0.62	3.40	0.45	1.15	3.3
5120	27 0537	Burnsville	64.4	51 288	477	796	35 674	15 614	43.8	94.80	2.27	0.33	2.28	0.33	1.03	3.9
5120	27 0820	Coon Rapids	59.1	52 978	457	896	35 826	17 152	47.9	97.33	0.48	0.80	1.09	0.30	0.94	4.6
5120	27 0870	Crystal	14.9	23 788	938	1 597	25 543	-1 755	-6.9	95.30	1.82	0.61	1.85	0.44	0.95	12.4
2240	27 1040	Duluth	175.1	85 493	240	488	92 811	-7 318	-7.9	95.89	0.87	2.15	0.90	0.19	0.60	17.1
5120	27 1105	Edina	40.8	46 070	540	1 129	46 073	-3	0.0	97.19	0.72	0.14	1.73	0.22	0.71	20.4
5120	27 1385	Fridley	26.2	28 335	856	1 081	30 228	-1 893	-6.3	95.69	0.98	0.70	2.24	0.38	1.04	7.8
...	27 2420	Mankato	30.0	31 477	798	1 049	28 646	2 831	9.9	96.26	0.69	0.30	2.27	0.48	1.05	10.9
5120	27 2455	Maplewood	44.9	30 954	808	689	26 990	3 964	14.7	94.39	2.52	0.57	2.03	0.49	1.55	11.9
5120	27 2585	Minneapolis	142.3	368 383	42	2 589	370 951	-2 568	-0.7	78.44	13.02	3.35	4.27	0.93	2.14	13.0
5120	27 2610	Minnetonka	70.2	48 370	513	689	38 683	9 687	25.0	97.06	0.92	0.18	1.59	0.26	0.81	9.8
2520	27 2645	Moorhead	26.1	32 295	779	1 237	29 998	2 297	7.7	95.33	0.47	1.37	1.10	1.74	2.76	11.1
5120	27 3105	Plymouth	85.3	50 889	482	597	31 615	19 274	61.0	95.66	1.61	0.36	2.04	0.32	1.02	5.0
5120	27 3210	Richfield	17.8	35 710	704	2 006	37 851	-2 141	-5.7	93.49	2.61	0.61	2.81	0.48	1.07	16.9
6820	27 3235	Rochester	76.3	70 745	315	927	57 906	12 839	22.2	94.21	1.03	0.30	4.14	0.32	1.16	11.0
5120	27 3290	Roseville	34.3	33 485	757	976	35 820	-2 335	-6.5	95.09	1.64	0.30	2.55	0.41	1.13	16.8
6980	27 3380	St. Cloud	37.6	48 812	507	1 298	42 566	6 246	14.7	96.84	0.97	0.58	1.35	0.27	0.59	10.2
5120	27 3405	St. Louis Park	27.7	43 787	565	1 581	42 931	856	2.0	95.26	1.89	0.41	2.10	0.34	1.03	16.1
5120	27 3425	St. Paul	136.7	272 235	57	1 991	270 230	2 005	0.7	82.26	7.38	1.36	7.05	1.95	4.22	13.7
...	27 4145	Winona	30.7	25 399	914	827	25 075	324	1.3	97.59	0.66	0.24	1.24	0.27	0.86	16.2
...	28 0000	MISSISSIPPI	121 506.4	2 573 216	X	21	2 520 770	52 446	2.1	63.48	35.56	0.33	0.51	0.12	0.62	12.5
0920	28 0110	Biloxi	50.9	46 319	535	910	49 311	-2 992	-6.1	74.58	18.62	0.33	5.74	0.73	2.77	11.4
...	28 0265	Columbus	29.7	23 799	937	801	27 503	-3 704	-13.5	48.29	51.17	0.07	0.32	0.15	0.78	14.2
...	28 0495	Greenville	67.6	45 226	548	669	40 613	4 613	11.4	39.76	59.63	0.10	0.43	0.08	0.56	12.3
0920	28 0515	Gulfport	58.6	40 775	613	696	39 676	1 099	2.8	69.89	28.59	0.28	0.92	0.33	1.55	14.4
...	28 0535	Hattiesburg	65.8	41 882	596	637	40 829	1 053	2.6	58.22	40.43	0.11	1.06	0.17	0.98	12.7
3560	28 0615	Jackson	282.3	196 637	78	697	202 895	-6 258	-3.1	43.57	55.75	0.10	0.50	0.08	0.45	11.6
...	28 0805	Meridian	92.3	41 036	608	445	46 577	-5 541	-11.9	53.97	45.35	0.13	0.44	0.10	0.57	16.5
6025	28 0975	Pascagoula	39.3	25 899	908	659	29 318	-3 419	-11.7	77.22	21.46	0.19	0.92	0.22	0.97	11.4
...	28 1390	Vicksburg	34.8	20 908	949	601	25 434	-4 526	-17.8	40.54	58.98	0.07	0.34	0.08	0.49	18.6
...	29 0000	MISSOURI	178 446.0	5 117 073	X	29	4 916 762	200 311	4.1	87.67	10.71	0.39	0.81	0.42	1.21	14.0
3760	29 0425	Blue Springs	41.7	40 153	625	963	25 936	14 217	54.8	95.60	2.44	0.38	1.07	0.51	1.59	5.9
...	29 0695	Cape Girardeau	59.6	34 438	726	578	34 361	77	0.2	90.21	8.05	0.22	1.29	0.24	0.56	14.6
1740	29 0930	Columbia	114.8	69 101	327	602	62 061	7 040	11.3	85.14	9.93	0.33	4.12	0.48	1.31	8.7
7040	29 1465	Florissant	26.4	51 206	479	1 940	55 721	-4 515	-8.1	95.02	4.06	0.18	0.52	0.23	0.96	13.9
3760	29 2125	Independence	202.5	112 301	159	555	111 797	504	0.5	96.20	1.45	0.61	0.98	0.77	1.97	14.4
...	29 2180	Jefferson City	68.9	35 481	708	515	33 619	1 862	5.5	88.84	10.09	0.34	0.46	0.26	0.78	15.8
3710	29 2205	Joplin	76.9	40 961	609	533	39 023	1 938	5.0	95.03	2.13	1.89	0.64	0.31	1.16	17.2
3760	29 2220	Kansas City	806.9	435 146	31	539	448 028	-12 882	-2.9	66.78	29.59	0.49	1.20	1.94	3.91	12.9
7040	29 2280	Kirkwood	23.4	27 291	880	1 166	27 739	-448	-1.6	93.13	5.93	0.11	0.74	0.10	0.69	18.2
3760	29 2435	Lee's Summit	153.1	46 418	532	303	28 741	17 677	61.5	96.94	1.74	0.30	0.62	0.40	0.99	10.9
3760	29 3615	Raytown	25.7	30 601	820	1 191	31 831	-1 230	-3.9	95.34	3.25	0.41	0.51	0.49	1.44	17.8
7040	29 3830	St. Charles	42.9	54 555	435	1 272	37 379	17 176	46.0	95.95	2.79	0.27	0.74	0.25	1.00	9.9
7000	29 3865	St. Joseph	112.3	71 852	305	640	76 691	-4 839	-6.3	94.98	3.64	0.33	0.35	0.70	2.21	17.1
7040	29 3875	St. Louis	160.4	396 685	34	2 473	452 801	-56 116	-12.4	50.94	47.50	0.24	0.94	0.38	1.29	16.6
7920	29 4075	Springfield	176.0	140 494	126	798	133 116	7 378	5.5	95.65	2.51	0.67	0.90	0.27	0.95	15.2
7040	29 4320	University City	15.2	40 087	628	2 637	42 690	-2 603	-6.1	49.09	48.23	0.11	2.20	0.37	1.11	13.9
...	30 0000	MONTANA	376 990.9	799 065	X	2	786 690	12 375	1.6	92.75	0.30	5.97	0.53	0.45	1.52	13.3

1. MSA = Metropolitan Statistical Area. CMSA = Consolidated MSA. 2. Dry land or land partially or temporarily covered by water. 3. Hispanic persons may be of any race.

City	Households, 1990: Number	Households, 1990: Persons per household	Households, 1990: Percent– Female family householder[1]	Households, 1990: Percent– One-person[2]	Births, 1984: Number: Total	Births, 1984: Number: To mothers under 20 yrs. old (Percent)	Births, 1984: Rate[3]	Deaths, 1984: Number: Total	Deaths, 1984: Number: Infant[4]	Deaths, 1984: Rate: Total[3]	Deaths, 1984: Rate: Infant[5]	Hospitals, 1985: Number	Hospitals, 1985: Beds: Number	Hospitals, 1985: Beds: Rate[6]
	15	16	17	18	19	20	21	22	23	24	25	26	27	28
MICHIGAN—Con.														
Pontiac	24 777	2.76	25.5	26.3	1 469	24.6	20.7	653	27	9.2	18.4	5	1 781	2 507
Portage	15 467	2.64	8.6	21.6	515	4.7	12.9	227	6	5.7	11.7	0	0	0
Port Huron	13 158	2.51	18.2	28.5	689	19.7	20.6	374	9	11.2	13.1	2	372	1 102
Roseville	19 537	2.62	12.6	24.7	824	7.9	15.8	468	10	9.0	12.1	0	0	0
Royal Oak	28 344	2.29	9.2	32.3	1 005	4.7	14.9	639	11	9.5	10.9	1	929	1 404
Saginaw	26 179	2.61	26.0	28.1	1 557	22.1	21.1	745	32	10.1	20.6	6	1 538	2 122
St. Clair Shores	27 218	2.49	9.8	26.3	785	5.7	10.9	728	6	10.2	7.6	1	68	94
Southfield	32 112	2.34	9.7	32.3	821	3.5	11.2	829	4	11.3	4.9	3	599	822
Southgate	12 128	2.52	9.5	26.9	369	6.0	12.0	232	5	7.5	13.6	0	0	0
Sterling Heights	40 835	2.87	8.4	19.1	1 388	5.0	12.7	563	17	5.1	12.2	0	0	0
Taylor	24 861	2.82	16.4	18.2	1 154	13.3	15.8	429	17	5.9	14.7	1	242	334
Troy	26 167	2.78	6.3	20.5	864	2.5	12.8	320	6	4.7	6.9	1	189	281
Warren	54 602	2.63	11.4	22.7	1 722	8.5	11.3	1 288	21	8.5	12.2	3	419	280
Westland	33 110	2.53	11.7	27.1	1 256	9.5	15.5	620	13	7.6	10.4	2	612	754
Wyandotte	12 319	2.50	12.4	28.3	506	12.8	15.9	307	4	9.6	7.9	1	359	1 145
Wyoming	24 168	2.63	10.4	23.6	1 118	9.6	18.2	374	7	6.1	6.3	0	0	0
MINNESOTA	1 647 853	2.58	8.6	25.1	66 716	7.9	16.0	33 766	596	8.1	8.9	179	27 323	648
Blaine	12 825	3.04	10.0	12.8	657	5.5	19.7	71	5	2.1	7.6	0	0	0
Bloomington	34 488	2.47	8.2	23.4	1 098	4.7	13.1	452	7	5.4	6.4	0	0	0
Brooklyn Center	11 226	2.56	12.8	21.8	412	7.5	12.9	176	1	5.5	2.4	0	0	0
Brooklyn Park	20 386	2.76	11.7	19.2	1 070	6.2	21.3	145	11	2.9	10.3	0	0	0
Burnsville	19 127	2.67	9.2	19.5	620	3.9	15.9	99	2	2.5	3.2	1	97	239
Coon Rapids	17 449	3.01	10.6	13.3	767	7.7	18.7	142	10	3.5	13.0	0	0	0
Crystal	9 272	2.55	9.4	20.8	325	5.8	13.2	172	2	7.0	6.2	0	0	0
Duluth	34 563	2.36	11.1	31.7	1 298	11.2	15.2	1 025	14	12.0	10.8	3	744	903
Edina	19 860	2.30	6.2	29.7	415	1.2	9.0	419	4	9.1	9.6	0	0	0
Fridley	10 909	2.58	11.7	20.6	448	5.1	15.3	140	8	4.8	17.9	0	0	0
Mankato	11 220	2.46	8.7	27.2	426	8.2	15.5	198	3	7.2	7.0	1	186	623
Maplewood	11 496	2.62	11.0	21.5	408	8.1	13.9	225	8	7.7	19.6	0	0	0
Minneapolis	160 682	2.19	12.7	38.5	6 301	10.7	17.6	3 935	60	11.0	9.5	13	5 829	1 634
Minnetonka	18 687	2.56	6.7	21.3	526	0.6	12.6	186	8	4.5	15.2	0	0	0
Moorhead	11 063	2.56	10.3	24.8	426	7.3	14.6	222	4	7.6	9.4	1	68	240
Plymouth	18 361	2.72	7.5	17.7	573	1.7	14.2	114	4	2.8	7.0	0	0	0
Richfield	15 551	2.29	9.8	29.8	515	5.8	14.1	270	3	7.4	5.8	0	0	0
Rochester	27 913	2.45	8.3	29.1	1 297	4.7	22.3	480	17	8.3	13.1	3	1 847	3 177
Roseville	13 562	2.37	7.8	27.0	385	6.2	11.1	269	2	7.8	5.2	0	0	0
St. Cloud	17 926	2.46	10.4	27.9	718	10.2	17.1	315	5	7.5	7.0	2	975	2 275
St. Louis Park	19 925	2.16	8.4	33.4	638	4.4	14.9	429	7	10.0	11.0	1	387	887
St. Paul	110 249	2.37	13.0	34.7	5 040	10.6	19.0	2 663	53	10.0	10.5	8	1 791	679
Winona	9 334	2.36	8.3	32.3	354	8.8	14.4	282	0	11.5	0.0	1	230	955
MISSISSIPPI	911 374	2.75	15.9	23.4	43 841	21.2	16.9	23 939	632	9.2	14.4	128	17 497	667
Biloxi	16 644	2.50	13.0	28.9	1 065	18.2	21.9	366	17	7.5	16.0	4	1 314	2 752
Columbus	9 138	2.51	21.7	30.7	486	24.1	17.0	290	2	10.1	4.1	3	360	1 273
Greenville	15 322	2.91	24.8	24.3	873	28.3	21.5	489	16	12.0	18.3	2	405	1 013
Gulfport	15 797	2.45	16.5	29.6	812	20.4	19.7	450	6	10.9	7.4	3	461	1 062
Hattiesburg	15 911	2.36	19.0	33.4	687	21.7	16.4	449	6	10.7	8.7	2	643	1 578
Jackson	71 865	2.64	20.4	27.5	3 698	18.5	17.7	1 622	43	7.8	11.6	11	2 924	1 403
Meridian	16 170	2.46	20.7	31.0	759	24.6	16.0	570	9	12.0	11.9	6	1 456	3 388
Pascagoula	9 774	2.59	16.3	25.7	552	19.0	18.3	232	4	7.7	7.2	1	324	1 050
Vicksburg	8 268	2.49	21.7	33.3	489	22.7	18.7	320	17	12.2	34.8	3	448	1 722
MISSOURI	1 961 206	2.54	10.6	26.0	74 736	14.0	14.9	49 131	777	9.8	10.4	177	33 255	656
Blue Springs	13 529	2.95	9.5	14.9	520	6.9	17.3	131	3	4.4	5.8	1	72	217
Cape Girardeau	13 442	2.34	10.1	30.5	417	12.5	12.1	319	6	9.3	14.4	2	526	1 531
Columbia	25 841	2.27	9.7	32.2	828	8.3	13.1	421	10	6.7	12.1	7	1 607	2 545
Florissant	19 177	2.61	9.8	21.6	758	5.8	13.5	406	8	7.3	10.6	0	0	0
Independence	45 322	2.46	10.3	26.1	1 696	12.1	15.1	952	15	8.5	8.8	2	526	466
Jefferson City	14 162	2.28	9.5	34.4	446	8.3	12.7	329	8	9.4	17.9	5	595	1 643
Joplin	17 474	2.26	10.9	32.7	565	17.3	14.2	503	8	12.7	14.2	3	596	1 482
Kansas City	177 607	2.40	15.1	32.5	7 749	16.8	17.5	4 454	101	10.1	13.0	19	4 834	1 096
Kirkwood	11 212	2.41	8.8	28.6	420	3.3	15.0	275	1	9.8	2.4	1	332	1 210
Lee's Summit	17 632	2.60	8.6	23.4	478	6.1	14.6	341	4	10.4	8.4	1	92	255
Raytown	12 697	2.39	9.3	26.0	337	9.2	10.8	271	3	8.7	8.9	0	0	0
St. Charles	21 670	2.45	9.2	27.6	617	11.0	13.1	278	8	5.9	13.0	2	506	1 205
St. Joseph	28 411	2.44	12.2	29.1	1 061	19.5	14.2	867	14	11.6	13.2	4	1 060	1 431
St. Louis	164 931	2.34	20.5	39.2	7 931	21.7	18.5	6 225	119	14.5	15.0	26	9 637	2 261
Springfield	57 353	2.28	10.1	31.5	1 923	13.8	14.0	1 387	21	10.1	10.9	6	2 677	1 921
University City	16 556	2.40	16.2	30.1	608	12.2	14.2	404	9	9.4	14.8	0	0	0
MONTANA	306 163	2.53	8.6	26.3	14 141	10.3	17.2	6 711	125	8.1	8.8	67	4 949	604

1. No spouse present. 2. Householder living alone. 3. Per 1,000 resident population estimated as of July 1 of the year shown. 4. Deaths of infants under 1 year old. 5. Deaths of infants under 1 year old per 1,000 live births. 6. Per 100,000 resident population estimated as of July 1, 1986.

City	Serious crimes known to police, 1985: Number: Total	Serious crimes known to police, 1985: Number: Violent[1]	Serious crimes known to police, 1985: Rate[2]	Police officers, 1985: Number	Police officers, 1985: Rate[3]	Educational attainment,[4] 1980: Percent completing 12 years or more	Educational attainment,[4] 1980: Percent completing 16 years or more	Money income: Per capita[5]: 1985: Total (Dollars)	Money income: Per capita[5]: 1985: Percent of State average	Money income: Per capita[5]: 1979: Current dollars	Money income: Per capita[5]: 1979: Constant (1985) dollars	Money income: Percent below poverty level, 1979: Persons	Money income: Percent below poverty level, 1979: Families	Housing, 1990: Total units	Housing, 1990: Percent change, 1980–1990	Housing, 1990: Vacant units for sale or rent[6]
	29	30	31	32	33	34	35	36	37	38	39	40	41	42	43	44
MICHIGAN—Con.																
Pontiac	9 067	2 227	12 431	184	25.2	52.2	6.5	9 432	86.5	6 252	9 265	17.6	15.3	26 593	-4.3	1 263
Portage	1 639	62	4 237	47	12.1	82.7	25.5	12 811	117.5	8 733	12 942	3.6	3.3	16 133	15.3	532
Port Huron	1 961	143	5 864	55	16.4	63.0	10.6	9 485	87.0	6 735	9 981	16.0	13.3	14 026	4.5	630
Roseville	4 544	264	8 634	79	15.0	61.3	5.2	10 617	97.4	7 539	11 173	6.0	4.7	20 025	7.7	396
Royal Oak	3 794	189	5 564	90	13.2	78.1	20.7	13 900	127.5	9 766	14 473	4.2	2.8	29 163	1.3	609
Saginaw	8 191	1 592	10 899	127	16.9	57.6	8.4	8 652	79.4	6 101	9 042	20.8	18.4	27 986	-2.7	1 166
St. Clair Shores	3 307	127	4 516	89	12.2	69.0	10.3	13 158	120.7	9 191	13 621	3.5	2.8	27 929	2.8	543
Southfield	8 112	663	11 098	150	20.5	82.6	30.4	17 068	156.6	12 668	18 774	3.7	2.5	35 054	10.7	2 320
Southgate	1 883	103	6 156	41	13.4	65.7	9.1	11 776	108.0	8 978	13 305	3.1	2.4	12 504	9.4	319
Sterling Heights	5 199	305	4 744	160	14.6	76.9	14.6	12 760	117.0	8 996	13 332	3.2	3.1	42 317	18.4	1 333
Taylor	5 192	479	7 057	100	13.6	60.6	6.8	10 117	92.8	7 413	10 986	8.5	8.2	25 727	1.4	688
Troy	4 859	178	7 270	107	16.0	85.0	34.0	16 945	155.4	11 642	17 253	2.8	2.1	27 197	12.7	896
Warren	11 050	1 002	7 257	236	15.5	64.1	8.8	12 546	115.1	8 690	12 879	4.9	4.2	56 189	2.9	1 296
Westland	4 132	295	5 083	90	11.1	67.5	9.6	11 669	107.0	8 308	12 312	5.2	4.4	34 514	13.2	1 210
Wyandotte	1 726	44	5 322	46	14.2	56.4	6.9	10 468	96.0	7 957	11 792	7.7	6.3	12 822	-3.6	324
Wyoming	3 248	161	5 392	70	11.6	66.1	9.4	10 327	94.7	7 452	11 044	5.9	4.6	25 056	9.4	700
MINNESOTA	173 348	10 751	4 134	NA	NA	73.1	17.4	11 186	100.0	7 450	11 041	9.5	7.0	1 848 445	12.7	67 710
Blaine	1 790	17	5 733	29	9.3	80.5	10.1	11 117	99.4	7 318	10 845	4.6	3.7	13 176	34.0	320
Bloomington	3 545	89	4 198	91	10.8	88.8	25.0	15 854	141.7	10 220	15 146	3.0	2.2	35 815	17.4	1 083
Brooklyn Center	1 878	50	5 868	30	9.4	81.3	13.6	12 148	108.6	8 290	12 286	5.4	4.6	11 713	6.3	435
Brooklyn Park	2 284	109	4 843	43	9.1	87.2	18.4	12 166	108.8	8 182	12 126	6.0	5.4	21 265	25.7	805
Burnsville	2 107	56	5 467	44	11.4	93.1	33.5	14 840	132.7	9 881	14 644	3.1	2.4	20 244	36.5	998
Coon Rapids	1 904	32	4 863	43	11.0	82.6	13.5	11 614	103.8	7 554	11 195	4.1	3.5	18 098	40.7	591
Crystal	974	28	3 839	30	11.8	80.7	14.3	12 940	115.7	8 672	12 852	3.0	2.5	9 541	4.7	240
Duluth	4 324	202	4 730	129	14.1	72.3	18.4	10 051	89.9	7 176	10 635	12.0	7.3	36 022	-3.0	947
Edina	1 668	39	3 597	43	9.3	93.0	44.6	24 935	222.9	15 703	23 272	2.5	1.7	20 983	11.1	774
Fridley	1 589	44	5 260	32	10.6	82.9	19.6	12 850	114.9	8 654	12 825	4.2	3.6	11 418	6.6	456
Mankato	2 050	22	7 099	29	10.0	80.1	23.7	9 603	85.8	6 550	9 707	15.8	6.9	11 688	9.1	385
Maplewood	1 711	47	6 021	39	13.7	79.7	16.2	12 363	110.5	8 346	12 369	4.0	3.3	12 120	25.4	530
Minneapolis	37 977	5 135	10 519	677	18.8	74.8	23.7	12 302	110.0	7 940	11 767	13.5	9.0	172 666	2.2	9 494
Minnetonka	1 910	26	4 651	43	10.5	90.7	35.9	18 289	163.5	11 422	16 927	2.2	1.5	20 119	34.2	1 299
Moorhead	1 339	29	4 461	36	12.0	77.9	23.9	9 487	84.8	6 670	9 885	11.5	4.1	11 511	8.1	384
Plymouth	1 278	25	3 449	31	8.4	90.6	36.4	16 329	146.0	10 562	15 653	2.8	2.4	19 616	43.7	1 125
Richfield	1 434	39	3 809	43	11.4	83.5	17.6	13 770	123.1	9 233	13 683	3.7	2.4	16 094	4.1	478
Rochester	2 590	61	4 337	97	16.2	83.9	29.1	13 380	119.6	8 471	12 554	6.8	3.5	28 961	20.2	822
Roseville	1 705	35	4 740	37	10.3	86.2	30.8	15 197	135.9	10 136	15 022	3.1	2.4	14 216	7.4	593
St. Cloud	2 629	82	6 105	55	12.8	74.1	20.7	9 663	86.4	6 246	9 257	14.1	6.3	18 828	23.1	783
St. Louis Park	2 007	42	4 617	48	11.0	84.5	25.1	15 933	142.4	10 490	15 546	4.4	2.9	20 678	12.7	632
St. Paul	20 854	2 095	7 784	517	19.3	72.4	19.8	11 557	103.3	7 694	11 403	10.9	8.0	117 583	5.7	5 905
Winona	1 411	15	5 619	33	13.1	65.0	19.6	9 252	82.7	6 087	9 021	13.6	6.2	9 682	5.0	239
MISSISSIPPI	85 333	7 079	3 266	NA	NA	54.8	12.3	7 483	100.0	5 182	7 680	23.9	18.7	1 010 423	9.8	49 635
Biloxi	311	17	605	76	14.8	70.4	14.3	8 557	114.4	5 687	8 428	16.1	12.7	18 864	5.0	1 655
Columbus	927	48	3 149	54	18.3	54.6	16.9	7 633	102.0	5 097	7 554	26.5	21.0	9 901	0.3	580
Greenville	2 981	166	7 140	75	18.0	50.6	11.8	6 327	84.6	4 663	6 911	31.1	25.6	16 492	16.4	934
Gulfport	4 244	320	10 235	52	12.5	66.7	16.3	9 734	130.1	6 229	9 231	17.1	13.3	18 236	11.8	1 883
Hattiesburg	2 037	123	4 769	74	17.3	67.2	24.1	8 047	107.5	5 558	8 237	24.8	17.5	17 675	9.3	1 329
Jackson	13 307	1 399	6 336	401	19.1	71.3	24.2	9 927	132.7	6 920	10 255	18.4	14.0	79 374	4.7	5 977
Meridian	2 021	98	4 289	94	19.9	60.5	12.6	8 932	119.4	5 912	8 762	22.8	17.7	17 740	-4.3	1 063
Pascagoula	1 969	232	6 394	53	17.2	69.7	13.3	9 565	127.8	6 754	10 009	12.3	10.3	11 053	-3.0	956
Vicksburg	1 127	109	4 274	49	18.6	56.9	16.5	8 270	110.5	5 893	8 733	25.1	18.0	9 250	-8.3	713
MISSOURI	219 568	25 321	4 366	NA	NA	63.5	13.9	10 283	100.0	6 915	10 248	12.2	9.1	2 199 129	9.6	124 286
Blue Springs	1 213	41	4 310	33	11.7	85.0	19.3	11 916	115.9	8 336	12 354	3.7	3.2	14 246	38.2	634
Cape Girardeau	1 954	95	5 577	55	15.7	68.1	21.0	10 130	98.5	6 821	10 109	13.9	7.7	14 627	8.2	953
Columbia	4 525	230	7 035	96	14.9	83.5	42.9	10 292	100.1	6 706	9 938	17.5	7.2	27 551	17.6	1 417
Florissant	1 103	70	1 963	72	12.8	73.2	13.8	12 640	122.9	7 961	11 798	2.5	2.0	19 797	8.8	542
Independence	5 328	362	4 732	149	13.2	71.0	11.6	11 010	107.1	7 839	11 617	6.6	4.9	48 262	8.0	2 347
Jefferson City	1 439	93	4 096	56	15.9	72.9	22.4	11 516	112.0	7 640	11 322	7.1	4.6	15 437	12.7	977
Joplin	3 037	131	7 577	64	16.0	65.2	13.3	9 312	90.6	6 273	9 297	15.0	10.5	19 367	10.3	1 311
Kansas City	46 616	8 012	10 477	1 114	25.0	69.6	16.6	11 153	108.5	7 480	11 085	13.2	9.4	201 789	4.9	18 091
Kirkwood	862	18	3 047	NA	NA	81.5	32.9	16 426	159.7	10 316	15 288	3.1	1.9	11 699	5.0	381
Lee's Summit	1 030	61	3 314	49	15.8	83.0	22.4	12 985	126.3	8 715	12 916	5.2	3.7	18 755	36.4	1 024
Raytown	1 142	62	3 583	47	14.7	79.1	15.9	13 164	128.0	9 213	13 654	2.5	1.7	13 216	6.0	434
St. Charles	1 573	81	3 372	72	15.4	67.2	15.5	12 469	121.3	7 888	11 690	6.0	4.1	23 246	38.3	1 322
St. Joseph	4 238	237	5 519	113	14.7	63.0	10.8	9 382	91.2	6 367	9 436	11.8	8.1	31 276	-2.1	1 681
St. Louis	49 113	8 642	11 392	1 627	37.7	48.2	10.0	8 799	85.6	5 877	8 710	21.8	16.6	194 919	-3.7	19 858
Springfield	9 591	306	6 974	181	13.2	70.2	16.2	9 634	93.7	6 468	9 586	14.3	9.6	62 472	10.2	3 874
University City	2 424	247	5 583	77	17.7	75.5	32.8	13 742	133.6	8 572	12 704	10.3	6.6	17 706	1.8	997
MONTANA	37 577	1 722	4 549	NA	NA	74.4	17.5	8 781	100.0	6 589	9 765	12.3	9.2	361 155	9.1	20 004

1. Includes murder and nonnegligent manslaughter, forcible rape, robbery, and aggravated assault. 2. Per 100,000 resident population estimated for 1985 by the FBI. 3. Per 10,000 resident population estimated for 1985 by the FBI. 4. Persons 25 years old or older. 5. Based on the resident population estimated as of July 1, 1988 for 1987 data and enumerated as of April 1, 1980 for 1979 data. 6. Also includes units rented or sold, but not occupied.

City	Housing, 1990 (cont'd): Occupied units: Total	Housing, 1990 (cont'd): Occupied units: Percent with more than 1 person per room	Housing, 1990 (cont'd): Occupied units: Owner-occupied: Percent of total	Housing, 1990 (cont'd): Occupied units: Owner-occupied: Median value[1] (Dollars)	Housing, 1990 (cont'd): Occupied units: Median rent[2] (Dollars)	Construction authorized by building permits, 1990: New private housing units: Number	Construction authorized by building permits, 1990: New private housing units: Value ($1,000)	Construction authorized by building permits, 1990: New private housing units: Percent single family	Construction authorized by building permits, 1990: Non-residential, value ($1,000)	Civilian labor force, 1990: Total	Civilian labor force, 1990: Percent change, 1989–1990	Civilian labor force, 1990: Unemployment: Total	Civilian labor force, 1990: Unemployment: Rate[3]
	45	46	47	48	49	50	51	52	53	54	55	56	57
MICHIGAN—Con.													
Pontiac	24 777	6.9	49.7	36 300	362	171	3 726	11.1	5 219	34 962	-1.1	4 194	12.0
Portage	15 467	1.4	71.6	71 800	395	180	17 810	83.3	8 835	23 055	-0.4	944	4.1
Port Huron	13 158	2.2	54.5	41 400	316	54	3 415	66.7	4 792	16 546	-1.2	1 684	10.2
Roseville	19 537	2.5	74.6	55 400	415	152	3 810	26.3	318	28 961	-0.1	2 786	9.6
Royal Oak	28 344	1.2	70.0	75 600	465	29	1 684	37.9	21 041	44 220	-1.5	2 029	4.6
Saginaw	26 179	4.2	57.5	32 800	267	11	269	27.3	1 477	28 791	0.9	3 289	11.4
St. Clair Shores	27 218	1.3	84.7	69 700	460	33	3 459	100.0	985	43 076	-0.7	2 722	6.3
Southfield	32 112	2.3	53.9	85 100	614	257	9 588	9.3	6 515	46 328	-1.5	2 039	4.4
Southgate	12 128	2.0	70.2	58 700	447	30	3 323	100.0	2 121	15 806	-1.6	904	5.7
Sterling Heights	40 835	1.8	77.6	97 000	478	422	28 110	93.8	16 570	59 334	-0.7	3 763	6.3
Taylor	24 861	3.2	67.7	48 400	387	18	1 128	100.0	10 969	33 374	-1.6	2 691	8.1
Troy	26 167	1.3	74.7	128 900	584	351	41 231	100.0	10 353	39 519	-1.5	1 410	3.6
Warren	54 602	2.4	79.5	69 500	436	121	5 037	85.1	9 253	89 781	-0.4	7 006	7.8
Westland	33 110	2.6	60.2	63 400	457	365	19 587	98.9	5 390	40 612	-1.6	2 651	6.5
Wyandotte	12 319	1.6	70.0	49 400	347	88	3 541	42.0	2 620	14 936	-1.6	992	6.6
Wyoming	24 168	2.6	67.4	57 700	397	496	20 450	24.6	4 997	39 702	0.8	2 190	5.5
MINNESOTA	1 647 853	2.1	71.8	74 000	384	23 713	1 881 458	77.1	1 120 736	2 404 000	2.6	116 000	4.8
Blaine	12 825	2.5	90.2	80 600	491	378	26 988	69.8	7 527	20 864	1.9	1 024	4.9
Bloomington	34 488	1.4	70.3	97 500	545	231	18 080	45.0	62 569	58 516	1.4	2 299	3.9
Brooklyn Center	11 226	2.3	69.5	79 400	475	1	65	100.0	870	20 106	1.2	738	3.7
Brooklyn Park	20 386	2.6	67.4	88 400	447	466	33 555	53.2	16 485	35 955	1.3	1 374	3.8
Burnsville	19 127	1.6	64.9	108 100	537	241	26 563	99.2	19 378	29 042	1.4	1 201	4.1
Coon Rapids	17 449	2.1	80.0	82 500	520	701	48 148	75.5	26 024	28 081	1.7	1 324	4.7
Crystal	9 272	1.8	77.3	78 000	478	13	926	100.0	629	NA	NA	NA	NA
Duluth	34 563	1.3	64.4	46 300	287	127	9 707	85.8	5 081	40 400	3.1	2 098	5.2
Edina	19 860	0.4	76.4	156 700	634	254	20 481	12.2	17 151	27 557	1.3	795	2.9
Fridley	10 909	2.2	67.5	86 000	463	11	1 101	100.0	4 298	18 240	1.5	814	4.5
Mankato	11 220	2.9	51.5	62 100	348	84	3 896	40.5	15 247	16 941	2.4	588	3.5
Maplewood	11 496	1.4	75.9	87 800	473	192	21 024	100.0	53 048	19 914	1.4	529	2.7
Minneapolis	160 682	3.6	49.7	71 700	390	823	46 791	14.1	360 842	207 165	1.5	9 415	4.5
Minnetonka	18 687	0.7	76.6	121 000	631	169	6 399	100.0	4 517	28 930	1.4	975	3.4
Moorhead	11 063	2.9	60.2	62 000	310	129	6 576	50.4	3 424	16 546	2.6	500	3.0
Plymouth	18 361	1.2	73.6	127 400	578	606	57 878	63.7	16 233	31 949	1.6	1 085	3.4
Richfield	15 551	1.6	66.9	84 800	438	7	632	100.0	487	24 124	1.4	924	3.8
Rochester	27 913	1.9	66.2	71 900	387	845	68 377	62.6	6 476	40 617	4.4	1 491	3.7
Roseville	13 562	1.1	68.4	97 000	483	42	5 093	81.0	22 991	21 215	1.0	629	3.0
St. Cloud	17 926	2.0	51.3	59 400	369	417	14 144	22.1	14 146	27 938	1.4	1 585	5.7
St. Louis Park	19 925	1.4	62.6	87 100	511	8	863	100.0	2 805	28 851	1.3	992	3.4
St. Paul	110 249	4.0	53.9	70 900	389	102	6 569	72.5	12 193	145 191	1.6	6 932	4.8
Winona	9 334	1.8	63.6	50 400	285	145	6 795	24.8	2 204	NA	NA	NA	NA
MISSISSIPPI	911 374	5.8	71.5	45 600	215	5 950	298 514	74.9	194 456	1 184 000	1.5	88 000	7.5
Biloxi	16 644	4.8	43.8	55 400	279	70	3 961	100.0	2 127	16 279	0.4	1 209	7.4
Columbus	9 138	5.7	52.7	44 900	238	12	520	100.0	2 103	14 541	4.8	1 154	7.9
Greenville	15 322	9.7	58.3	42 500	207	51	3 159	92.2	1 878	18 697	-1.8	1 871	10.0
Gulfport	15 797	4.1	56.7	52 100	274	50	3 783	100.0	1 818	21 261	1.2	1 765	8.3
Hattiesburg	15 911	4.9	46.1	47 100	254	13	1 116	100.0	4 491	19 867	1.7	1 358	6.8
Jackson	71 865	6.2	57.3	54 600	290	271	18 653	58.3	23 198	106 948	1.4	5 732	5.4
Meridian	16 170	4.2	57.7	45 900	213	39	3 789	100.0	6 051	20 697	2.0	1 247	6.0
Pascagoula	9 774	5.1	59.3	49 100	265	5	385	100.0	1 575	14 444	1.5	1 434	9.9
Vicksburg	8 268	5.8	55.5	42 200	192	12	678	83.3	5 569	11 520	-1.0	997	8.7
MISSOURI	1 961 206	2.5	68.8	59 800	282	15 294	1 090 290	80.7	813 779	2 634 000	0.8	151 000	5.7
Blue Springs	13 529	1.3	72.0	76 700	396	430	28 448	86.5	6 282	14 242	-0.2	564	4.0
Cape Girardeau	13 442	1.5	57.4	58 300	254	166	7 839	49.4	14 709	21 942	3.8	1 017	4.6
Columbia	25 841	2.4	43.8	73 400	306	441	36 081	77.3	45 392	41 862	2.2	1 193	2.8
Florissant	19 177	1.4	79.0	67 200	411	55	4 613	100.0	2 044	33 571	0.0	1 420	4.2
Independence	45 322	1.8	67.1	56 000	311	258	20 118	62.8	33 446	62 080	-0.2	2 793	4.5
Jefferson City	14 162	1.0	59.5	61 500	252	141	11 953	85.8	9 855	21 199	0.8	804	3.8
Joplin	17 474	1.7	60.4	41 100	251	162	10 649	91.4	5 853	22 558	1.2	1 216	5.4
Kansas City	177 607	3.2	56.9	56 100	324	802	83 682	85.8	137 356	250 725	-0.3	14 521	5.8
Kirkwood	11 212	0.8	78.0	100 500	469	183	12 213	20.2	0	16 364	-0.2	415	2.5
Lee's Summit	17 632	1.4	65.9	84 700	417	696	47 452	88.2	6 693	NA	NA	NA	NA
Raytown	12 697	0.8	75.0	63 900	352	17	1 370	64.7	3	18 854	-0.2	581	3.1
St. Charles	21 670	1.5	59.7	80 700	390	220	20 749	87.7	8 738	30 332	0.1	1 454	4.8
St. Joseph	28 411	1.7	65.8	39 800	230	156	11 902	67.9	6 017	37 304	0.6	2 400	6.4
St. Louis	164 931	5.3	45.1	50 700	252	39	2 608	94.9	48 152	187 334	-0.4	15 337	8.2
Springfield	57 353	2.1	55.5	53 900	280	668	30 052	51.0	46 756	82 024	2.5	3 648	4.4
University City	16 556	2.1	58.8	75 200	400	12	1 146	100.0	1 783	24 719	0.1	1 167	4.7
MONTANA	306 163	2.9	67.3	56 600	251	1 223	87 980	60.9	65 791	402 000	-0.7	23 000	5.8

1. Specified owner-occupied units. 2. Specified renter-occupied units. 3. Percent of total civilian labor force.

City	Employed,[1] 1980: Total	Employed,[1] 1980: Rate per 1,000 employees: Professional, specialty, and technical	Employed,[1] 1980: Rate per 1,000 employees: Precision production, craft, and operators	Manufactures, 1987: Establishments: Total	Manufactures, 1987: Establishments: Percent with 20 or more employees	Manufactures, 1987: All employees: Number (1,000)	Manufactures, 1987: All employees: Percent change, 1982–1987	Manufactures, 1987: All employees: Annual payroll (Mil. dol.)	Manufactures, 1987: Production workers: Number (1,000)	Manufactures, 1987: Production workers: Work-hours (Millions)	Manufactures, 1987: Production workers: Wages: Total (Mil. dol.)	Manufactures, 1987: Production workers: Wages: Average per production worker (Dollars)	Manufactures, 1987: Value added by manufacture (Mil. dol.)	Manufactures, 1987: Value of shipments (Mil. dol.)	Manufactures, 1987: New capital expenditures (Mil. dol.)
	58	59	60	61	62	63	64	65	66	67	68	69	70	71	72
MICHIGAN—Con.															
Pontiac	26 433	90.7	348.1	75	37.3	D	D	D	D	D	D	D	D	D	D
Portage	19 209	195.4	221.3	72	38.9	D	D	D	D	D	D	D	D	D	D
Port Huron	12 645	126.8	234.6	76	46.1	5.2	20.9	127.0	3.6	7.4	73.7	20 472	269.6	647.3	24.5
Roseville	22 985	96.4	308.8	214	42.1	6.0	22.4	160.8	4.5	9.9	104.4	23 200	319.6	567.4	18.7
Royal Oak	36 247	216.8	185.3	121	19.0	2.2	0.0	53.3	1.5	2.9	27.4	18 267	137.0	266.4	16.2
Saginaw	24 364	115.2	283.7	79	38.0	D	D	D	D	D	D	D	D	D	D
St. Clair Shores	35 436	131.3	250.5	92	27.2	2.4	41.2	56.6	1.9	3.9	37.3	19 632	124.8	246.9	D
Southfield	38 049	254.0	112.3	209	36.8	6.9	-13.7	224.9	3.2	6.7	72.5	22 656	220.7	561.2	20.9
Southgate	14 666	117.1	290.5	NA	NA	NA	NA	NA	NA	NA	NA	NA	NA	NA	NA
Sterling Heights	48 799	170.5	251.4	220	37.3	22.0	58.3	786.8	17.9	39.4	614.6	34 335	1 495.6	4 765.3	108.4
Taylor	30 197	87.8	312.8	93	33.3	2.7	12.5	72.3	1.6	3.3	25.9	16 187	103.4	199.4	4.6
Troy	32 740	246.8	149.6	424	45.3	19.1	34.5	589.6	8.2	17.0	189.4	23 098	687.7	1 241.4	31.9
Warren	72 688	140.2	281.0	640	33.3	47.2	9.8	1 711.8	22.6	47.6	657.8	29 106	2 051.8	5 954.3	86.1
Westland	37 360	118.6	289.8	54	29.6	1.1	83.3	26.1	0.8	1.7	15.8	19 750	54.5	113.2	3.9
Wyandotte	13 723	97.0	302.9	56	39.3	2.8	7.7	80.1	1.4	2.8	29.9	21 357	158.9	323.3	43.0
Wyoming	29 436	103.5	315.4	191	42.4	14.2	-3.4	427.9	11.0	22.5	323.2	29 382	715.0	1 500.0	D
MINNESOTA	1 885 521	159.2	190.0	7 112	34.1	374.2	6.4	10 141.7	214.9	428.0	4 512.7	20 999	23 322.1	47 774.1	1 765.5
Blaine	14 263	119.4	317.1	76	15.8	0.8	NA	17.8	0.6	1.2	12.4	20 667	35.4	57.6	2.0
Bloomington	47 334	156.2	155.9	198	36.9	15.7	-9.2	529.0	6.3	11.5	134.2	21 302	812.1	1 368.3	52.7
Brooklyn Center	17 290	115.8	204.2	49	42.9	1.8	50.0	50.1	1.2	2.5	26.7	22 250	128.8	199.1	5.1
Brooklyn Park	23 622	144.5	224.2	67	31.3	2.2	83.3	69.1	0.9	1.8	19.5	21 667	160.4	261.8	12.1
Burnsville	19 644	183.0	124.5	81	24.7	2.6	36.8	66.6	1.1	2.3	19.2	17 455	170.2	265.7	11.8
Coon Rapids	18 017	151.5	260.8	44	43.2	1.3	44.4	30.3	0.9	1.8	18.9	21 000	65.5	105.0	4.6
Crystal	14 530	134.7	215.0	42	16.7	0.7	-12.5	16.1	0.5	1.1	9.8	19 600	44.5	71.7	1.5
Duluth	39 072	195.3	148.6	87	32.2	4.5	21.6	98.9	1.8	3.3	37.8	21 000	198.1	331.1	D
Edina	23 125	222.1	57.3	104	30.8	2.9	-34.1	74.8	1.5	2.8	27.4	18 267	186.0	316.3	6.8
Fridley	16 497	149.7	231.3	140	43.6	11.7	1.7	373.8	6.1	12.2	168.5	27 623	646.5	1 176.1	64.9
Mankato	14 154	176.7	159.5	55	52.7	2.7	-3.6	59.0	1.6	3.1	30.6	19 125	183.5	570.4	D
Maplewood	13 791	158.4	211.4	NA	NA	NA	NA	NA	NA	NA	NA	NA	NA	NA	NA
Minneapolis	190 727	202.2	157.9	860	39.5	44.3	-3.7	1 281.2	21.7	43.5	495.5	22 834	2 343.0	4 032.3	210.4
Minnetonka	20 686	190.3	119.9	115	39.1	11.0	86.4	355.2	3.7	7.2	83.2	22 486	826.8	1 456.6	47.6
Moorhead	14 695	186.1	121.5	NA	NA	NA	NA	NA	NA	NA	NA	NA	NA	NA	NA
Plymouth	16 582	186.2	135.1	137	46.7	7.5	29.3	214.6	4.5	9.3	101.0	22 444	404.4	643.2	32.5
Richfield	22 317	140.8	168.4	NA	NA	NA	NA	NA	NA	NA	NA	NA	NA	NA	NA
Rochester	31 062	315.8	111.5	49	42.9	10.1	3.1	374.2	3.2	12.2	72.4	22 625	1 029.2	1 747.7	D
Roseville	19 773	232.2	124.3	69	44.9	7.9	-23.3	283.0	3.8	7.9	101.8	26 789	835.7	1 455.5	D
St. Cloud	20 373	181.1	135.1	68	47.1	3.9	21.9	74.7	2.8	5.2	47.0	16 786	145.6	360.1	10.8
St. Louis Park	24 782	178.6	137.9	127	37.8	4.5	15.4	122.3	2.8	5.6	59.0	21 071	300.8	504.0	13.1
St. Paul	129 705	178.5	172.1	485	37.9	34.6	1.5	975.6	20.8	40.3	526.0	25 288	2 938.9	6 367.7	157.7
Winona	11 124	178.1	214.5	75	53.3	5.9	31.1	111.7	4.2	8.4	67.6	16 095	234.2	484.5	14.4
MISSISSIPPI	937 206	133.9	267.5	3 318	37.6	218.9	8.5	3 827.3	171.4	337.4	2 620.6	15 289	10 502.6	24 380.6	647.7
Biloxi	13 875	166.2	172.8	40	30.0	D	D	D	D	D	D	D	D	D	D
Columbus	10 664	137.6	228.3	43	48.8	5.3	12.8	96.7	4.2	7.8	63.2	15 048	263.6	446.1	9.0
Greenville	14 711	143.8	249.2	57	40.4	2.9	-27.5	58.3	2.3	4.8	41.1	17 870	249.1	397.3	D
Gulfport	15 498	156.1	178.2	61	27.9	2.3	-23.3	39.8	1.4	2.5	21.3	15 214	128.7	221.7	5.4
Hattiesburg	16 648	208.2	159.2	51	35.3	3.6	D	63.0	2.6	5.7	38.6	14 846	132.5	342.4	7.7
Jackson	91 358	180.2	157.1	220	36.4	10.9	D	207.9	7.3	14.9	118.5	16 233	627.1	1 252.6	38.6
Meridian	18 508	164.5	180.6	77	46.8	D	D	D	D	D	D	D	D	D	D
Pascagoula	12 041	159.2	289.3	35	45.7	D	D	D	D	D	D	D	D	D	D
Vicksburg	9 774	211.4	190.0	25	56.0	1.6	-11.1	27.5	1.4	2.6	22.4	16 000	79.6	176.4	6.1
MISSOURI	2 103 907	142.2	216.6	7 290	35.4	418.8	3.2	10 390.0	264.5	519.0	5 401.6	20 422	25 916.7	59 889.3	1 620.1
Blue Springs	12 427	143.0	222.4	41	19.5	0.9	12.5	17.8	0.6	1.2	9.3	15 500	41.7	71.6	2.0
Cape Girardeau	15 989	174.2	154.9	64	31.2	1.8	-14.3	33.4	1.4	2.6	22.8	16 286	84.3	173.5	5.9
Columbia	31 133	282.9	81.6	67	34.3	D	D	D	D	D	D	D	D	D	D
Florissant	27 849	147.9	189.6	NA	NA	NA	NA	NA	NA	NA	NA	NA	NA	NA	NA
Independence	53 863	114.5	251.1	102	25.5	4.8	-9.4	123.3	3.5	7.1	87.9	25 114	436.8	563.4	16.8
Jefferson City	15 784	182.1	125.8	48	35.4	3.2	D	68.9	2.2	4.0	42.9	19 500	283.5	490.5	D
Joplin	16 681	143.2	211.3	108	33.3	6.0	5.3	119.3	4.5	9.2	81.4	18 089	281.4	619.8	13.6
Kansas City	210 754	151.5	182.0	720	36.0	45.0	-10.7	1 329.1	21.7	43.0	502.8	23 171	3 185.1	5 902.0	140.6
Kirkwood	13 815	239.3	107.1	45	60.0	1.8	0.0	52.6	1.1	2.4	24.6	22 364	98.3	167.7	3.7
Lee's Summit	13 419	166.6	214.0	48	33.3	4.0	D	124.7	2.5	5.5	76.0	30 400	294.4	507.8	16.2
Raytown	16 601	142.3	195.8	39	20.5	D	D	D	D	D	D	D	D	D	D
St. Charles	18 263	181.5	230.6	53	20.8	D	D	D	D	D	D	D	D	D	D
St. Joseph	31 891	119.7	215.4	99	43.4	D	D	D	D	D	D	D	D	D	D
St. Louis	173 066	141.5	200.4	980	43.0	82.6	19.9	2 422.0	43.7	88.9	1 132.8	25 922	5 232.2	11 964.0	318.3
Springfield	58 146	150.3	184.0	278	37.1	18.4	11.5	371.4	12.6	23.4	229.3	18 198	859.8	2 781.8	49.6
University City	20 401	315.2	120.0	NA	NA	NA	NA	NA	NA	NA	NA	NA	NA	NA	NA
MONTANA	328 316	147.3	156.5	1 239	14.9	20.1	-0.5	425.8	14.8	28.8	296.2	20 014	1 112.0	3 497.9	97.0

1. Persons 16 years old and over.

City	Wholesale trade, 1987				Retail trade–all establishments, 1987				Retail trade–establishments with payroll, 1987					
						Sales				Sales				
											Per capita[2] (Dollars)			
	Estab-lishments	Sales (Mil. dol.)	Paid employees[1]	Annual payroll ($1,000)	Number	Total (Mil. dol.)	Percent change, 1982–1987	Per capita[2] (Dollars)	Number	Total (Mil. dol.)	General merchan-dise group stores	Food stores	Apparel and accessory stores	Eating and drinking places
	73	74	75	76	77	78	79	80	81	82	83	84	85	86
MICHIGAN—Con.														
Pontiac	87	1 024.2	2 719	71 493	463	419.1	10.1	5 900	355	411.9	823	880	185	628
Portage	73	194.8	748	18 738	498	477.1	48.4	11 801	379	470.7	4 063	1 280	880	974
Port Huron	68	114.0	521	12 517	528	379.7	55.8	11 244	365	372.2	D	2 200	646	944
Roseville	95	278.6	1 227	33 098	513	615.6	45.7	11 886	376	608.0	3 363	1 532	1 130	895
Royal Oak	153	665.2	1 166	35 234	526	530.4	42.4	8 013	327	521.1	D	1 190	157	631
Saginaw	110	476.4	1 556	38 253	572	338.7	31.5	4 674	428	332.2	D	1 009	254	440
St. Clair Shores	109	485.6	1 077	30 095	651	413.2	56.2	5 731	407	399.0	D	1 337	111	643
Southfield	633	9 722.7	9 844	329 536	1 403	1 399.0	43.9	19 188	1 003	1 370.5	2 485	2 091	2 088	1 846
Southgate	23	93.3	252	5 624	305	501.2	75.7	16 492	224	497.3	1 687	1 423	501	790
Sterling Heights	103	309.2	1 113	31 244	876	1 103.5	65.6	9 856	585	1 087.4	2 599	1 023	853	660
Taylor	69	1 161.6	1 598	38 262	572	685.2	52.2	9 459	413	676.0	3 257	1 056	505	736
Troy	483	5 609.1	6 500	198 164	845	1 225.8	57.1	18 222	597	1 208.4	3 479	1 351	2 229	1 402
Warren	296	1 204.3	3 923	98 784	1 289	1 243.4	40.4	8 300	897	1 220.1	698	1 598	357	895
Westland	44	124.4	376	8 743	601	663.3	58.5	8 170	423	655.0	1 530	1 723	687	651
Wyandotte	43	218.2	744	19 136	277	105.0	-3.7	3 349	188	101.2	D	885	148	413
Wyoming	249	1 830.6	5 122	136 839	549	589.9	58.2	9 450	390	581.6	1 825	885	864	1 043
MINNESOTA	9 478	55 276.7	114 343	2 822 664	42 874	28 007.7	42.9	6 643	27 005	27 279.8	811	1 160	288	613
Blaine	52	D	D	D	299	311.1	109.6	9 036	200	307.4	1 612	2 882	603	608
Bloomington	430	4 778.6	7 581	232 947	758	829.4	30.7	9 673	486	814.9	1 219	830	316	1 370
Brooklyn Center	49	207.8	618	15 925	284	584.3	63.7	18 351	194	579.9	4 726	1 208	748	943
Brooklyn Park	60	250.9	811	22 885	309	341.2	233.9	6 372	164	333.5	D	1 685	95	388
Burnsville	153	890.0	2 060	55 010	571	658.6	75.0	16 234	393	653.0	4 701	2 061	1 192	1 016
Coon Rapids	27	71.1	224	6 018	291	310.9	100.1	7 195	149	306.2	D	1 304	81	544
Crystal	29	55.0	220	4 863	204	149.7	9.5	6 073	149	148.1	D	1 029	510	834
Duluth	173	734.0	2 063	45 726	989	660.5	29.3	8 018	710	646.2	1 629	1 444	400	752
Edina	341	3 678.4	4 859	150 280	664	736.1	29.6	15 888	439	724.6	4 287	1 391	2 298	739
Fridley	68	652.5	1 400	42 189	238	312.0	44.2	10 623	150	308.1	D	280	79	808
Mankato	96	D	D	D	415	0.0	0.0	D	323	D	D	3 103	D	1 192
Maplewood	34	123.6	406	10 342	364	417.8	83.2	13 056	280	415.3	D	4 359	892	968
Minneapolis	1 123	12 083.1	18 413	485 038	3 368	2 349.7	31.8	6 585	2 441	2 316.0	747	1 220	373	1 031
Minnetonka	229	4 307.7	2 461	77 381	586	763.8	67.5	17 230	422	757.8	4 719	2 571	1 203	1 049
Moorhead	35	144.1	291	5 983	260	192.1	30.5	6 774	188	189.6	D	1 588	181	626
Plymouth	244	2 113.9	4 576	125 404	284	335.7	184.3	7 205	126	330.7	0	1 683	21	312
Richfield	65	93.3	479	10 714	323	388.2	17.0	10 777	206	382.9	658	1 005	531	961
Rochester	115	D	D	D	816	792.5	61.2	13 633	567	782.0	2 547	2 235	654	1 138
Roseville	119	506.5	1 602	38 376	524	718.1	58.7	21 177	413	712.6	5 557	1 140	2 373	1 711
St. Cloud	120	D	D	D	626	0.0	0.0	D	468	1 383.3	D	885	D	1 156
St. Louis Park	220	963.1	2 087	52 797	473	412.3	39.9	9 450	315	405.4	1 507	1 371	624	949
St. Paul	599	3 336.0	8 710	231 915	2 352	1 741.3	25.6	6 604	1 692	1 715.9	1 112	1 147	263	841
Winona	59	157.7	529	8 383	327	174.8	22.8	7 256	227	169.2	D	1 527	D	938
MISSISSIPPI	3 850	12 249.8	39 936	733 066	26 522	11 990.5	32.6	4 568	15 729	11 357.7	624	1 052	182	337
Biloxi	60	D	D	D	530	349.3	36.1	7 315	408	341.0	1 753	1 361	306	1 246
Columbus	86	197.3	978	18 217	512	316.8	29.9	11 198	377	309.6	D	2 013	736	918
Greenville	87	242.4	929	18 599	550	315.3	28.8	7 882	354	302.2	D	1 593	503	527
Gulfport	115	172.6	899	14 994	742	398.3	19.0	9 175	489	387.5	1 223	1 517	204	866
Hattiesburg	132	306.8	1 591	23 519	659	464.4	30.6	11 399	490	454.5	D	D	D	1 158
Jackson	603	2 557.5	8 502	175 749	2 184	0.0	0.0	D	1 520	1 714.3	1 307	1 195	347	713
Meridian	132	727.4	1 795	35 373	720	462.7	32.3	10 768	512	453.6	D	2 129	D	863
Pascagoula	64	440.2	571	10 656	412	233.7	10.0	7 573	268	224.1	431	1 859	220	683
Vicksburg	55	147.0	533	10 124	457	281.0	38.3	10 799	318	275.5	1 934	2 475	D	850
MISSOURI	10 696	53 546.4	125 247	2 820 903	52 540	31 142.2	43.8	6 147	32 524	30 175.6	823	1 149	250	600
Blue Springs	43	79.0	246	5 273	335	290.1	81.5	8 730	186	280.9	1 098	1 850	29	707
Cape Girardeau	129	350.6	1 582	28 017	524	444.9	62.9	12 948	405	440.5	D	1 828	698	1 093
Columbia	112	289.0	1 327	24 153	814	674.5	63.6	10 683	641	667.3	D	1 749	D	1 076
Florissant	50	91.5	334	7 715	488	364.2	48.4	6 169	323	358.4	401	2 041	183	618
Independence	114	223.2	704	16 488	1 054	823.8	36.0	7 293	725	809.9	1 225	D	302	690
Jefferson City	102	D	D	D	543	584.6	76.7	16 145	399	577.7	D	1 978	515	1 045
Joplin	179	530.5	2 120	37 671	729	550.1	42.6	13 677	510	537.9	2 600	2 000	D	1 399
Kansas City	1 166	8 248.3	18 975	468 209	4 153	3 417.6	36.6	7 747	3 077	3 353.9	D	D	508	1 001
Kirkwood	82	197.3	541	14 333	289	288.8	37.1	10 529	194	284.6	D	835	60	575
Lee's Summit	71	359.0	596	10 628	337	219.3	83.4	6 080	202	213.2	D	1 568	D	544
Raytown	66	231.3	469	13 952	318	317.8	64.9	10 301	188	312.2	D	1 265	D	478
St. Charles	99	97.1	480	7 595	740	536.5	70.9	12 777	483	526.1	872	1 416	404	1 422
St. Joseph	149	550.7	1 912	34 402	767	525.3	23.7	7 092	524	515.3	1 409	D	171	689
St. Louis	NA	NA	NA	NA	3 422	2 159.1	27.1	5 065	2 532	2 124.0	504	1 038	209	942
Springfield	504	3 132.9	7 040	144 269	1 958	1 506.5	59.4	10 810	1 349	1 480.6	2 028	1 654	D	1 069
University City	56	142.7	551	13 378	276	123.2	54.0	2 915	166	119.3	D	890	D	376
MONTANA	1 804	4 392.1	14 824	264 178	10 720	4 510.6	14.0	5 507	6 790	4 344.4	518	1 251	208	577

1. For the period including March 12 of the year shown. 2. Based on resident population estimated as of July 1, 1986.

City	Retail trade–establishment with payroll, 1987 (cont'd): Paid employees[1]: Number	Retail trade: Paid employees[1]: Percent change, 1982–1987	Retail trade: Annual payroll (Mil. dol.)	Taxable service industries–establishments with payroll, 1987: Number	Taxable service: Receipts (Mil. dol.): Total	Receipts: Selected kinds of business: Hotels, motels, and other lodging places	Receipts: Selected kinds of business: Health services	Receipts: Selected kinds of business: Legal services	Taxable service: Paid employees[1]	Taxable service: Annual payroll (Mil. dol.)	Federal grants, 1986: Procurement contract awards (Mil. dol.)	Federal grants, 1986: Grant awards (Mil. dol.)	Federal government civilian employment, 1984
	87	88	89	90	91	92	93	94	95	96	97	98	99
MICHIGAN—Con.													
Pontiac	4 275	-1.3	46.8	410	218.6	D	66.5	4.8	4 277	100.0	81.6	7.2	524
Portage	6 053	37.8	52.7	241	93.3	2.3	26.7	4.1	3 203	38.1	0.0	0.6	4
Port Huron	4 541	23.8	46.5	373	104.7	3.5	49.2	9.5	2 227	43.8	6.2	2.6	235
Roseville	7 063	34.9	67.6	294	97.4	5.9	22.8	0.7	2 636	35.9	26.4	1.3	175
Royal Oak	5 165	25.6	65.2	509	211.5	3.2	87.2	3.7	3 903	80.6	1.8	2.3	1 401
Saginaw	4 345	22.8	39.2	457	179.8	6.9	71.9	13.6	3 861	77.0	10.1	9.7	1 153
St. Clair Shores	5 136	44.1	49.2	559	148.9	D	57.4	6.5	3 706	62.7	0.3	1.9	167
Southfield	16 450	27.0	176.1	2 393	1 903.6	34.6	363.9	210.4	35 762	767.3	16.9	1.9	379
Southgate	4 213	45.8	48.6	180	64.3	D	24.5	2.5	1 725	24.9	0.0	0.4	4
Sterling Heights	11 730	51.8	112.7	516	453.9	D	62.7	10.5	8 232	182.2	16.1	2.1	560
Taylor	7 735	34.8	75.2	280	126.9	D	49.7	2.0	2 865	45.4	1.6	1.8	135
Troy	12 225	29.6	144.1	1 210	1 139.0	31.9	114.4	55.0	18 971	501.0	941.8	0.6	226
Warren	15 288	36.3	151.0	960	591.6	11.1	174.2	7.4	12 708	272.1	212.4	4.1	5 658
Westland	7 331	35.0	72.6	328	96.2	0.0	44.8	1.4	2 704	36.6	1.8	2.1	1
Wyandotte	1 394	2.0	12.4	185	48.0	0.0	17.0	2.0	1 388	20.0	0.9	0.5	177
Wyoming	7 559	36.1	74.5	348	155.8	3.2	18.7	2.7	3 363	50.4	1.1	1.1	66
MINNESOTA	347 038	17.9	3 085.8	26 458	11 621.0	653.9	2 853.5	986.9	294 807	4 591.6	2 673.8	2 197.6	29 478
Blaine	3 395	37.9	31.6	137	41.9	0.0	8.0	D	950	12.9	0.1	0.2	1
Bloomington	10 879	22.0	98.2	927	816.7	112.2	79.6	29.0	18 961	306.5	19.0	0.9	42
Brooklyn Center	5 660	40.9	59.2	178	72.4	4.9	17.5	3.4	2 034	24.7	0.3	0.2	128
Brooklyn Park	3 410	129.3	34.5	200	70.2	D	8.8	1.5	3 363	26.7	3.8	0.3	0
Burnsville	7 841	34.0	72.7	346	141.9	3.4	35.2	1.7	4 105	52.8	11.8	0.3	4
Coon Rapids	3 243	54.9	29.3	202	71.0	D	43.8	1.2	1 933	29.3	0.1	0.4	1
Crystal	2 336	15.7	18.0	142	36.7	D	7.9	1.1	1 080	14.1	0.2	0.1	14
Duluth	8 715	6.9	77.7	656	212.4	19.0	57.8	18.9	5 824	85.6	27.7	9.3	1 215
Edina	8 978	11.3	92.5	840	479.0	D	112.2	21.4	10 891	206.7	9.7	0.5	2
Fridley	3 360	23.8	32.9	213	93.5	1.1	35.3	1.0	2 037	37.2	18.3	0.2	81
Mankato	D	D	D	302	D	D	44.6	9.5	D	D	11.4	2.4	260
Maplewood	4 966	39.7	43.9	203	74.0	D	31.4	1.9	1 932	25.9	0.0	0.3	1
Minneapolis	33 898	10.3	325.0	3 771	2 837.1	124.5	520.8	515.6	61 402	1 219.1	667.7	83.4	10 155
Minnetonka	9 197	35.1	91.0	453	250.9	D	30.2	5.4	4 873	98.7	282.9	0.4	2
Moorhead	2 711	11.2	22.1	171	40.7	2.1	10.8	D	1 126	14.4	2.6	2.1	64
Plymouth	2 775	114.6	33.8	282	130.3	D	19.8	D	4 498	52.3	15.9	0.3	4
Richfield	4 532	13.1	44.3	238	82.5	D	21.8	2.3	2 077	27.2	0.1	0.2	3
Rochester	9 788	20.0	85.4	473	175.6	D	36.6	13.0	5 561	64.7	53.1	37.1	484
Roseville	8 959	30.6	83.3	338	155.4	9.7	28.5	4.0	3 943	56.3	30.8	0.2	3
St. Cloud	11 601	59.9	108.2	464	D	D	D	D	D	D	3.2	3.6	1 385
St. Louis Park	5 493	14.0	50.2	615	367.3	16.6	134.3	14.8	9 741	147.5	44.9	0.3	11
St. Paul	24 935	9.9	223.9	2 092	1 193.7	45.5	326.9	144.5	36 414	508.6	557.1	336.7	6 068
Winona	2 494	5.2	19.4	187	46.0	1.5	D	D	1 076	14.7	1.0	0.8	96
MISSISSIPPI	140 361	17.7	1 264.6	11 663	3 331.6	205.3	1 239.0	305.1	84 293	1 208.4	1 835.2	1 343.6	24 244
Biloxi	5 943	37.1	47.5	333	118.2	26.3	44.9	9.2	3 464	39.9	4.6	6.8	1 198
Columbus	4 058	19.9	35.6	298	79.4	D	D	5.3	1 893	28.1	17.3	1.0	192
Greenville	3 724	5.4	34.7	310	78.2	D	28.2	D	2 100	27.8	1.1	6.9	302
Gulfport	5 030	8.9	46.5	504	154.8	5.2	63.4	24.9	3 399	54.1	19.1	15.3	1 867
Hattiesburg	6 099	21.5	54.0	427	D	D	D	D	D	D	6.7	6.2	250
Jackson	19 221	11.6	200.6	1 827	821.5	D	222.4	106.4	20 451	312.2	97.4	222.7	4 162
Meridian	5 590	21.2	54.0	445	139.3	D	D	6.9	3 057	54.2	5.2	2.5	947
Pascagoula	2 890	-0.4	28.2	300	90.4	3.2	32.5	15.6	2 048	38.4	1 168.0	9.1	651
Vicksburg	3 483	19.4	30.8	221	79.5	D	40.2	4.3	1 863	27.6	46.0	0.5	3 113
MISSOURI	375 917	24.7	3 538.2	32 930	13 707.2	863.0	3 452.6	992.1	323 658	5 238.0	6 633.0	2 012.5	66 441
Blue Springs	3 062	62.0	29.6	223	49.2	3.8	18.4	2.5	1 314	18.6	2.5	0.3	53
Cape Girardeau	6 015	27.3	49.2	385	134.2	D	59.3	6.0	3 121	58.9	1.2	0.7	226
Columbia	9 664	33.6	80.1	679	271.4	D	133.4	D	7 436	105.9	6.3	37.3	2 087
Florissant	4 568	40.5	41.7	378	98.5	D	48.6	D	2 739	37.8	0.6	0.7	229
Independence	10 050	17.7	97.1	732	D	8.9	65.5	12.3	D	D	0.0	8.0	509
Jefferson City	5 650	D	51.7	416	129.7	D	46.7	10.5	3 290	52.0	4.4	246.9	536
Joplin	7 158	32.7	62.8	555	171.6	D	67.6	6.9	4 232	62.8	9.3	1.6	227
Kansas City	44 120	12.6	439.0	3 787	2 627.6	D	D	330.9	57 105	1 083.5	885.4	58.1	19 051
Kirkwood	2 857	26.4	29.9	296	72.0	D	32.3	1.1	1 606	31.1	NA	0.2	16
Lee's Summit	2 530	82.5	22.4	215	46.7	D	15.0	1.3	1 242	18.1	0.0	0.3	62
Raytown	2 441	27.5	33.4	289	63.7	D	18.8	0.9	2 118	25.8	1.2	0.2	17
St. Charles	6 354	53.6	61.6	560	157.3	D	64.9	9.7	4 670	62.4	1.7	7.6	196
St. Joseph	6 489	8.9	58.4	531	143.5	8.7	D	D	4 106	55.2	6.2	4.3	502
St. Louis	32 536	16.8	305.9	2 673	2 060.3	139.8	249.3	281.7	44 148	801.8	5 248.5	359.5	24 096
Springfield	19 303	35.4	181.2	1 512	576.5	D	196.5	39.9	14 547	229.7	10.1	6.5	1 545
University City	1 813	32.1	16.0	239	60.9	D	12.9	2.0	1 552	23.0	0.0	1.5	0
MONTANA	56 985	2.4	503.4	6 248	1 402.1	174.5	422.5	148.9	36 499	479.2	157.9	570.4	11 289

1. For the period including March 12 of the year shown.

City	City government employment, 1985 (October): Total	City government employment, 1985 (October): Rates[1]	City government employment, 1985 (October): Percent education	Form of governments[2] (As of 1986)	City government finances, 1984–1985: General revenue: Total (Mil. dol.)	General revenue: Intergovernmental: Total (Mil. dol.)	General revenue: Intergovernmental: Percent from State government	General revenue: Taxes: Total (Mil. dol.)	Taxes: Per capita[3] (Dollars): Total	Taxes: Per capita[3] (Dollars): Property	Taxes: Per capita[3] (Dollars): Sales & gross receipts	General expenditures: Total (Mil. dol.)	General expenditures: Per capita[3] (Dol.): Total	General expenditures: Per capita[3] (Dol.): Capital outlays	General expenditures: Percent of total for–: Public welfare	Percent of total for–: Highways	Percent of total for–: Education
	100	101	102	103	104	105	106	107	108	109	110	111	112	113	114	115	116
MICHIGAN—Con.																	
Pontiac	2 892	407.2	0.0	1	136.8	19.7	67.2	35.9	506	347	0	132.0	1 858	114	0.0	2.3	0.0
Portage	310	76.7	0.0	2	14.8	4.2	80.3	6.3	155	150	0	13.9	343	43	0.3	11.1	0.0
Port Huron	430	127.3	0.0	2	27.1	7.1	57.9	8.5	251	160	0	24.3	718	132	0.2	6.1	0.1
Roseville	312	60.2	0.0	2	18.0	7.4	67.5	8.6	166	160	0	19.2	372	11	0.0	8.7	0.0
Royal Oak	516	78.0	0.0	2	28.6	8.8	76.1	11.6	175	170	0	29.7	449	41	0.1	10.8	0.0
Saginaw	823	113.6	0.0	2	46.1	16.3	55.7	15.0	207	97	0	41.3	570	46	0.0	6.0	0.0
St. Clair Shores	482	66.9	0.0	2	23.9	7.7	86.0	11.0	152	148	0	26.7	370	23	0.0	11.7	0.0
Southfield	786	107.8	0.0	2	46.7	9.9	76.7	26.3	360	344	0	40.4	554	39	0.7	7.8	0.0
Southgate	242	79.6	0.0	1	12.0	4.1	81.0	6.0	196	187	0	10.8	355	31	0.0	10.8	0.0
Sterling Heights	674	60.2	0.0	2	41.8	18.1	50.1	18.1	162	154	0	42.5	379	110	0.0	12.5	0.0
Taylor	NA	NA	NA	1	33.8	9.1	76.9	14.0	193	188	0	26.9	372	59	0.3	12.7	0.0
Troy	501	74.5	0.0	2	34.1	6.9	92.2	15.8	234	217	0	34.4	512	110	0.0	13.3	0.0
Warren	1 089	72.7	0.0	1	57.9	17.4	83.7	29.4	196	186	0	51.2	342	23	0.0	11.3	0.0
Westland	414	51.0	0.0	1	25.7	9.9	72.9	11.2	139	134	0	22.1	272	2	0.8	9.8	0.0
Wyandotte	NA	NA	NA	1	74.2	3.3	82.5	6.9	220	218	0	60.6	1 933	105	0.0	0.9	0.0
Wyoming	505	80.9	0.0	2	22.3	6.5	78.9	6.7	107	103	0	20.8	333	63	0.1	11.9	0.0
MINNESOTA	NA	NA	NA	NA	NA	NA	NA	NA	NA	NA	NA	NA	NA	NA	NA	NA	NA
Blaine	121	35.1	0.0	2	13.2	2.8	85.4	2.2	63	53	0	8.8	256	25	0.0	12.7	0.0
Bloomington	607	70.8	0.0	2	47.1	8.0	76.6	15.7	183	132	26	39.2	457	72	0.0	16.8	0.0
Brooklyn Center	247	77.6	0.0	2	15.8	3.6	86.3	3.1	99	90	0	11.9	375	51	0.0	12.0	0.0
Brooklyn Park	365	68.2	0.0	2	25.8	4.5	82.1	5.6	104	90	0	19.4	362	118	0.0	29.0	0.0
Burnsville	197	48.6	0.0	2	44.2	4.0	94.5	13.3	327	311	0	35.2	867	237	0.0	9.1	0.0
Coon Rapids	239	55.3	0.0	2	31.8	4.3	88.3	4.1	94	69	17	28.8	667	147	0.0	13.9	0.0
Crystal	125	50.7	0.0	2	7.3	2.3	86.6	1.8	73	63	0	5.1	208	13	0.0	7.1	0.0
Duluth	1 321	160.4	0.0	1	80.8	29.8	72.1	19.1	232	146	82	74.6	905	136	0.0	13.4	0.0
Edina	306	66.0	0.0	2	15.6	1.8	88.2	7.1	152	143	0	13.3	287	20	0.0	12.3	0.0
Fridley	220	74.9	0.0	2	15.0	3.5	85.8	3.3	112	98	0	10.7	365	84	0.0	32.8	0.0
Mankato	293	98.1	0.0	2	23.8	10.9	64.4	5.7	191	182	0	18.5	618	183	0.0	9.1	0.0
Maplewood	NA	NA	NA	2	20.9	2.5	91.5	4.2	130	114	0	14.5	453	26	0.0	10.3	0.0
Minneapolis	5 394	151.2	0.0	1	517.5	145.5	66.7	117.7	330	274	35	415.2	1 164	135	0.0	9.5	0.0
Minnetonka	249	56.2	0.0	2	26.6	4.0	91.4	7.4	168	147	0	25.2	569	220	0.0	11.5	0.0
Moorhead	275	97.0	0.0	1	21.0	6.3	73.3	3.0	104	98	0	19.4	683	172	0.0	11.3	0.0
Plymouth	195	41.9	0.0	2	27.8	2.5	77.5	5.3	114	98	0	18.3	393	57	0.0	8.1	0.0
Richfield	394	109.4	0.0	2	15.8	5.4	81.5	4.8	132	118	0	12.0	334	30	0.0	11.9	0.0
Rochester	826	142.1	0.0	1	50.1	10.7	79.1	14.2	243	136	103	47.0	809	261	0.0	11.7	0.0
Roseville	249	73.4	0.0	2	11.5	2.0	92.3	4.1	121	103	0	9.1	267	37	0.0	16.1	0.0
St. Cloud	381	88.9	0.0	1	29.4	9.2	83.6	7.5	174	135	27	25.5	595	145	0.0	25.9	0.0
St. Louis Park	269	61.7	0.0	2	20.3	5.5	85.7	6.7	153	134	2	13.7	314	12	0.0	10.5	0.9
St. Paul	3 403	129.1	0.0	1	268.2	85.9	63.8	68.1	258	177	68	264.4	1 003	201	0.0	7.6	0.0
Winona	230	95.5	0.0	2	12.9	5.2	81.6	3.3	135	118	11	12.0	498	81	0.0	17.2	0.0
MISSISSIPPI	NA	NA	NA	NA	NA	NA	NA	NA	NA	NA	NA	NA	NA	NA	NA	NA	NA
Biloxi	477	99.9	0.0	1	20.1	8.5	56.2	7.7	161	122	31	19.0	399	108	3.7	30.6	0.0
Columbus	NA	NA	NA	1	9.2	4.5	89.3	2.1	76	68	3	8.0	282	11	0.5	7.7	0.0
Greenville	461	115.3	0.0	1	12.6	5.3	67.4	3.7	93	76	13	13.5	338	57	0.9	15.0	0.0
Gulfport	1 344	309.6	0.0	3	44.8	5.0	87.5	4.8	111	83	23	56.2	1 295	318	0.0	4.5	0.0
Hattiesburg	669	164.2	0.0	3	18.0	8.2	79.2	6.4	157	121	31	17.1	421	104	0.0	21.6	0.0
Jackson	3 094	148.5	0.0	3	109.5	45.0	57.6	32.3	155	133	13	111.2	533	129	2.9	11.5	0.0
Meridian	622	144.8	0.0	1	20.5	7.8	82.7	6.0	140	97	38	15.4	357	23	0.0	12.4	0.0
Pascagoula	343	111.1	0.0	2	10.4	3.7	83.9	3.9	126	96	26	9.7	316	7	0.0	7.4	0.0
Vicksburg	427	164.1	0.0	3	10.2	5.1	65.2	2.6	101	85	11	9.1	349	80	2.4	10.4	0.0
MISSOURI	NA	NA	NA	NA	NA	NA	NA	NA	NA	NA	NA	NA	NA	NA	NA	NA	NA
Blue Springs	150	45.1	0.0	2	9.5	1.1	67.2	6.6	198	48	140	8.1	245	84	1.1	28.1	0.0
Cape Girardeau	364	105.9	0.0	2	12.7	2.3	28.8	7.0	205	30	163	12.0	348	60	0.0	12.6	0.0
Columbia	1 063	168.4	0.0	2	37.3	6.9	26.9	16.5	261	22	233	38.4	608	177	1.5	11.9	0.0
Florissant	272	46.1	0.0	1	5.0	1.2	46.0	2.6	44	10	28	9.0	152	21	0.0	18.9	0.0
Independence	990	87.6	0.0	2	37.7	5.6	35.8	21.0	186	31	146	37.7	333	81	0.0	18.0	0.0
Jefferson City	367	101.4	0.0	1	17.9	4.6	44.9	9.3	257	62	189	15.9	440	147	0.0	22.6	0.0
Joplin	401	99.7	0.0	2	23.0	9.8	18.2	9.9	247	20	216	19.9	496	237	1.1	13.0	0.0
Kansas City	7 622	172.8	0.0	2	442.4	69.4	31.7	242.2	549	71	262	380.5	863	155	NA	9.7	5.2
Kirkwood	299	109.0	0.0	2	6.2	0.6	69.0	3.7	135	40	75	8.7	317	26	0.0	17.9	0.0
Lee's Summit	243	67.4	0.0	1	12.8	0.9	56.5	7.0	193	77	112	11.3	313	31	0.0	14.0	0.0
Raytown	172	55.8	0.0	1	8.1	0.7	73.9	5.1	165	35	124	6.9	223	38	0.0	20.3	0.0
St. Charles	344	81.9	0.0	1	14.1	1.3	50.0	9.2	220	49	155	13.1	313	51	0.6	22.3	0.0
St. Joseph	650	87.8	0.0	2	30.6	8.9	20.6	13.7	185	60	112	28.9	391	67	1.3	18.4	0.0
St. Louis	8 719	204.5	0.0	1	464.1	106.3	37.9	235.2	552	73	247	461.3	1 082	214	0.4	6.5	0.4
Springfield	2 269	162.8	0.0	2	66.3	12.3	61.7	27.0	194	27	155	55.6	399	74	7.6	13.7	0.0
University City	359	84.9	0.0	2	11.8	1.8	39.0	6.3	150	60	75	12.4	294	9	0.0	12.2	0.0
MONTANA	NA	NA	NA	NA	NA	NA	NA	NA	NA	NA	NA	NA	NA	NA	NA	NA	NA

1. Per 10,000 population estimated as of July 1, 1986. 2. 1 = Mayor-council; 2 = Council-manager; 3 = Commission. Data subject to copyright. 3. Based on resident population estimated as of July 1, 1986.

City	City government finances, 1984–1985 (cont'd)								Climate[2]							Typical monthly electric bills, 1986		
	General expenditure (cont'd)					Debt outstanding			Average daily temperature (Degrees Fahrenheit)							Residential[6]		
	Percent of total for (cont'd)								Mean		Limits							
	Health and hospitals	Police protection	Sewerage and sanitation	Parks and recreation	Housing and community development	Total (Mil. dol.)	Per capita[1] (Dollars)	Percent utility	Jan.	July	Jan.[3]	July[4]	Annual precipitation (Inches)	Heating degree days[5]	Cooling degree days[5]	Total (Dollars)	Percent change, 1980–1986	Commercial[7] (Dollars)
	117	118	119	120	121	122	123	124	125	126	127	128	129	130	131	132	133	134
MICHIGAN—Con.																		
Pontiac	40.9	8.8	6.5	7.2	1.5	155.1	2 184	1.2	22.4	72.1	15.3	83.6	29.30	6 658	636	56.32	79.6	570.0
Portage	0.0	19.2	12.8	3.6	0.0	12.5	310	3.3	23.7	73.2	16.5	84.9	34.83	6 281	751	49.52	21.3	NA
Port Huron	0.6	12.7	14.7	14.3	4.8	29.9	886	3.5	23.6	72.0	16.9	82.2	30.62	6 611	621	56.32	79.6	NA
Roseville	0.0	22.9	18.3	4.1	0.4	3.7	71	0.0	20.0	67.9	11.2	79.8	30.97	6 563	615	56.32	79.6	570.0
Royal Oak	0.0	12.0	21.8	4.9	2.3	14.0	211	16.1	20.0	67.9	11.2	79.8	30.97	6 563	615	56.32	79.6	570.0
Saginaw	0.0	18.0	10.6	4.2	13.1	68.6	947	21.2	20.7	71.0	14.2	81.7	29.77	7 103	501	49.52	21.3	589.4
St. Clair Shores	0.0	19.0	18.1	7.0	2.9	6.4	88	0.0	20.0	67.9	11.2	79.8	30.97	6 563	615	56.32	79.6	570.0
Southfield	0.0	20.4	2.5	11.4	0.0	24.4	335	0.0	20.0	67.9	11.2	79.8	30.97	6 563	615	56.32	79.6	570.0
Southgate	0.5	25.3	7.2	7.0	0.0	4.9	160	38.5	20.0	67.9	11.2	79.8	30.97	6 563	615	56.32	79.6	NA
Sterling Heights	0.0	24.3	4.9	3.4	0.0	2.4	21	30.0	22.4	72.1	15.3	83.6	29.30	6 658	636	56.32	79.6	570.0
Taylor	0.0	19.4	9.1	3.5	0.0	11.3	156	11.9	23.4	72.6	16.5	83.2	30.97	6 563	615	56.32	79.6	570.0
Troy	0.0	21.0	19.5	8.4	0.0	4.0	60	6.4	22.4	72.1	15.3	83.6	29.30	6 658	636	56.32	79.6	570.0
Warren	0.0	26.8	7.3	3.2	0.0	14.1	94	0.0	23.4	72.6	16.5	83.2	30.97	6 563	615	56.32	79.6	570.0
Westland	0.6	22.0	7.9	5.6	0.0	5.7	71	0.0	23.4	72.6	16.5	83.2	30.97	6 563	615	56.32	79.6	570.0
Wyandotte	79.1	3.2	4.4	1.1	0.0	30.2	963	39.2	23.4	72.6	16.5	83.2	30.97	6 563	615	54.85	15.2	NA
Wyoming	NA	19.9	16.0	6.7	3.3	17.3	277	55.4	22.0	71.4	14.9	83.0	34.36	6 927	570	49.52	21.3	589.4
MINNESOTA	NA	NA	NA	NA	NA	NA	NA	NA	NA	NA	NA	NA	NA	NA	NA	48.17	42.6	NA
Blaine	0.0	15.7	18.5	7.7	0.0	35.5	1 031	4.3	11.2	73.1	2.4	83.4	26.36	8 007	662	49.58	48.7	NA
Bloomington	3.2	11.9	11.2	12.4	3.7	185.6	2 165	1.3	11.2	73.1	2.4	83.4	26.36	8 007	662	49.58	48.7	361.2
Brooklyn Center	0.3	12.9	10.3	11.5	2.3	42.6	1 339	0.8	11.2	73.1	2.4	83.4	26.36	8 007	662	49.58	48.7	NA
Brooklyn Park	0.2	12.5	6.7	17.1	2.7	84.7	1 583	0.0	11.2	73.1	2.4	83.4	26.36	8 007	662	49.58	48.7	NA
Burnsville	0.2	7.3	19.0	8.3	0.0	270.8	6 676	1.9	11.2	73.1	2.4	83.4	26.36	8 007	662	49.58	48.7	NA
Coon Rapids	0.9	7.5	13.7	5.6	2.4	149.0	3 449	1.0	11.2	73.1	2.4	83.4	26.36	8 007	662	51.07	48.7	NA
Crystal	1.8	22.1	16.5	12.0	3.8	0.9	37	0.0	11.2	73.1	2.4	83.4	26.36	8 007	662	49.58	48.7	NA
Duluth	0.0	8.7	8.3	8.4	4.2	134.4	1 631	13.3	6.3	65.3	NA	76.4	29.68	9 901	150	42.21	21.3	387.7
Edina	1.5	17.0	18.0	18.7	0.0	12.0	258	0.0	11.2	73.1	2.4	83.4	26.36	8 007	662	49.58	48.7	NA
Fridley	0.0	17.5	11.5	5.5	0.0	22.2	756	0.8	11.2	73.1	2.4	83.4	26.36	8 007	662	49.58	48.7	NA
Mankato	0.0	11.9	34.5	6.6	4.2	32.0	1 071	3.1	11.0	72.8	0.4	84.5	28.11	7 967	654	49.58	48.7	NA
Maplewood	2.0	12.4	12.1	5.2	0.0	88.4	2 763	0.0	11.2	73.1	2.4	83.4	26.36	8 007	662	49.58	48.7	NA
Minneapolis	1.8	8.8	9.3	6.5	15.1	1 573.8	4 410	0.7	11.2	73.1	2.4	83.4	26.36	8 007	662	51.07	48.7	372.0
Minnetonka	0.0	8.8	8.4	7.1	4.6	83.0	1 872	2.0	11.2	73.1	2.4	83.4	26.36	8 007	662	49.58	48.7	NA
Moorhead	0.2	6.5	17.4	4.4	14.6	76.9	2 713	5.2	4.3	70.6	NA	82.7	19.59	9 343	476	22.95	20.8	NA
Plymouth	0.0	9.5	29.4	4.6	0.0	103.2	2 215	0.0	11.2	73.1	2.4	83.4	26.36	8 007	662	49.58	48.7	NA
Richfield	1.2	13.8	9.0	17.6	1.4	45.5	1 264	0.2	11.2	73.1	2.4	83.4	26.36	8 007	662	49.58	48.7	NA
Rochester	0.0	8.3	11.3	20.8	5.5	109.2	1 879	0.0	10.8	70.7	1.9	81.4	28.26	8 277	479	48.75	44.7	396.0
Roseville	0.3	17.3	18.6	15.2	0.0	21.6	638	0.0	11.2	73.1	2.4	83.4	26.36	8 007	662	49.58	48.7	NA
St. Cloud	1.0	7.4	9.7	6.5	0.0	69.5	1 622	0.5	7.0	69.8	NA	81.8	27.72	8 965	397	51.07	48.7	NA
St. Louis Park	0.5	15.9	22.1	12.1	1.6	67.5	1 547	0.0	11.2	73.1	2.4	83.4	26.36	8 007	662	49.58	48.7	NA
St. Paul	2.1	8.8	10.1	10.2	5.3	838.2	3 179	0.9	11.2	73.1	2.4	83.4	26.36	8 007	662	49.58	38.7	392.6
Winona	0.2	13.6	4.6	8.3	5.3	32.9	1 364	0.0	12.7	72.8	2.0	84.5	32.71	7 819	653	49.58	48.7	NA
MISSISSIPPI	NA	NA	NA	NA	NA	NA	NA	NA	NA	NA	NA	NA	NA	NA	NA	48.99	49.7	NA
Biloxi	0.0	11.0	9.9	7.4	2.9	29.1	609	36.5	52.0	82.3	43.2	90.2	61.00	1 498	2 652	46.94	47.7	489.0
Columbus	1.6	14.4	31.0	1.9	0.0	4.9	174	97.8	42.4	80.9	31.6	92.7	56.75	2 860	2 003	37.04	71.2	NA
Greenville	0.4	17.9	25.8	2.7	3.8	7.0	176	25.5	43.0	82.2	33.0	92.7	53.26	2 635	2 246	53.19	46.7	NA
Gulfport	73.9	4.3	3.7	1.7	2.3	61.2	1 409	32.3	51.6	82.2	42.2	91.2	62.85	1 539	2 631	46.94	47.7	NA
Hattiesburg	0.8	16.4	13.7	4.0	2.3	8.6	211	14.8	48.4	81.4	36.9	92.4	59.85	2 027	2 338	46.94	47.7	NA
Jackson	1.1	11.6	21.5	5.0	0.3	236.9	1 137	7.5	45.7	81.9	34.9	92.5	52.82	2 389	2 290	53.19	46.7	537.1
Meridian	0.6	18.3	18.7	7.1	2.2	34.9	812	32.8	45.5	81.3	34.2	92.5	53.30	2 479	2 158	46.94	47.7	489.0
Pascagoula	0.2	18.7	11.2	3.4	0.0	20.0	648	8.5	52.0	82.3	43.2	90.2	61.00	1 498	2 652	46.94	47.7	NA
Vicksburg	0.1	16.5	13.7	4.7	17.3	4.7	181	43.9	46.7	81.7	37.0	91.4	52.42	2 201	2 306	53.19	46.7	NA
MISSOURI	NA	NA	NA	NA	NA	NA	NA	NA	NA	NA	NA	NA	NA	NA	NA	49.42	46.7	NA
Blue Springs	1.4	15.9	12.7	11.0	0.1	12.2	367	53.5	28.4	80.9	19.4	90.5	29.27	4 812	1 681	62.38	52.3	NA
Cape Girardeau	1.3	17.4	16.6	8.6	2.9	7.9	229	0.0	32.2	78.0	21.0	90.9	44.37	4 466	1 330	49.47	38.1	NA
Columbia	3.2	10.4	24.6	10.0	1.8	56.9	901	61.0	27.5	77.8	18.6	88.6	36.06	5 206	1 269	56.29	38.2	407.8
Florissant	1.6	27.0	5.1	14.6	2.5	2.3	38	0.0	28.8	78.9	19.9	89.0	33.91	4 938	1 468	48.96	64.3	396.8
Independence	3.0	16.3	17.7	3.6	2.7	56.9	504	77.1	28.4	80.9	19.4	90.5	29.27	4 812	1 681	42.74	30.1	412.3
Jefferson City	1.5	13.4	21.0	7.7	0.0	5.7	157	0.0	29.5	78.0	18.0	90.9	36.08	4 897	1 330	49.81	43.8	NA
Joplin	2.3	9.2	46.7	4.6	0.9	3.8	95	0.0	32.6	80.1	23.3	90.3	39.54	4 321	1 628	39.41	39.7	NA
Kansas City	6.8	15.6	8.4	6.9	8.6	429.8	974	5.5	28.4	80.9	19.4	90.5	29.27	4 812	1 681	50.33	35.2	577.0
Kirkwood	0.0	23.1	9.5	8.5	0.0	4.1	149	50.4	28.8	78.9	19.9	89.0	33.91	4 938	1 468	50.81	35.0	NA
Lee's Summit	0.0	18.4	12.1	4.2	0.5	33.3	922	51.6	28.4	80.9	19.4	90.5	29.27	4 812	1 681	63.72	52.3	NA
Raytown	3.5	25.6	26.0	4.6	0.0	2.7	88	0.0	28.4	80.9	19.4	90.5	29.27	4 812	1 681	64.00	51.3	NA
St. Charles	1.1	19.1	10.2	9.1	0.1	7.2	171	9.0	28.8	78.4	19.1	89.8	34.99	4 949	1 412	50.54	59.2	NA
St. Joseph	2.2	10.3	15.5	6.7	4.4	11.8	159	0.0	24.9	78.5	15.0	89.5	34.51	5 453	1 347	45.44	15.5	NA
St. Louis	13.2	15.7	2.6	4.0	8.3	406.3	953	3.1	28.8	78.9	19.9	89.0	33.91	4 938	1 468	48.96	59.3	421.8
Springfield	4.2	13.6	16.3	7.2	1.3	169.0	1 213	78.7	31.5	78.0	20.8	89.8	39.47	4 660	1 374	37.72	5.1	NA
University City	0.0	22.5	8.6	9.7	0.1	11.1	262	0.0	28.8	78.9	19.9	89.0	33.91	4 938	1 468	51.65	59.2	NA
MONTANA	NA	NA	NA	NA	NA	NA	NA	NA	NA	NA	NA	NA	NA	NA	NA	40.59	91.5	NA

1. Based on resident population estimated as of July 1, 1986. 2. Represents normal values based on the 30-year period, 1951–1980 (see text). 3. Average daily minimum. 4. Average daily maximum. 5. For definition, see text. 6. As of January 1; based on consumption of 750 kWh. 7. Based on billing demand of 30 kW and consumption of 6,000 kWh.

MSA/ CMSA Code[1]	State/ Place code	City	Land area,[2] 1990 (Sq. Km.)	Population: 1990: Total persons	Population: 1990: Rank	Population: 1990: Per sq. km.	Population: 1980	Population: Change 1980–1990: Number	Population: Change 1980–1990: Per-cent	Population characteristics, 1990: Percent: Race: White	Race: Black	Race: Am. Indian, Eskimo, Aleut	Race: Asian & Pacific Islander	Race: Other race	His-panic[3]	65 Years and over
			1	2	3	4	5	6	7	8	9	10	11	12	13	14
		MONTANA—Con.														
0880	30 0050	Billings	84.4	81 151	260	962	66 813	14 338	21.5	94.56	0.54	3.17	0.59	1.14	3.06	13.6
...	30 0110	Butte-Silver Bow	1 854.9	33 336	761	18	37 205	-3 869	-10.4	97.28	0.10	1.55	0.41	0.66	2.41	17.0
3040	30 0295	Great Falls	40.0	55 097	423	1 377	56 884	-1 787	-3.1	93.11	0.96	4.63	0.83	0.47	1.68	14.5
...	30 0455	Missoula	43.1	42 918	578	996	33 351	9 567	28.7	95.49	0.34	2.43	1.45	0.28	1.28	12.3
...	31 0000	NEBRASKA	199 113.2	1 578 385	X	8	1 569 825	8 560	0.5	93.80	3.64	0.79	0.79	0.99	2.34	14.1
...	31 1045	Grand Island	53.2	39 386	641	740	33 180	6 206	18.7	96.05	0.34	0.32	1.30	1.99	4.79	14.6
4360	31 1425	Lincoln	163.9	191 972	81	1 171	171 932	20 040	11.7	94.45	2.35	0.60	1.71	0.89	1.96	10.9
5920	31 1825	Omaha	260.7	335 795	48	1 288	313 939	21 856	7.0	83.86	13.10	0.68	1.02	1.35	3.06	12.9
...	32 0000	NEVADA	284 397.2	1 201 833	X	4	800 508	401 325	50.1	84.26	6.55	1.63	3.17	4.38	10.35	10.6
...	32 0025	Carson City	371.8	40 443	619	109	32 022	8 421	26.3	90.73	1.73	2.73	1.41	3.40	7.69	14.9
4120	32 0065	Las Vegas	215.7	258 295	63	1 197	164 674	93 621	56.9	78.42	11.43	0.88	3.61	5.66	12.53	10.3
4120	32 0080	North Las Vegas	157.9	47 707	517	302	42 739	4 968	11.6	45.23	37.37	1.05	2.36	13.99	22.20	6.8
6720	32 0090	Reno	148.9	133 850	132	899	100 756	33 094	32.8	86.07	2.88	1.43	4.86	4.77	11.11	11.8
6720	32 0100	Sparks	36.9	53 367	450	1 446	40 780	12 587	30.9	88.43	2.38	1.44	4.49	3.26	8.56	9.3
...	33 0000	NEW HAMPSHIRE	23 230.7	1 109 252	X	48	920 610	188 642	20.5	98.03	0.65	0.19	0.84	0.28	1.02	11.3
...	33 0520	Concord	166.5	36 006	700	216	30 400	5 606	18.4	98.18	0.63	0.28	0.67	0.24	0.99	14.0
4760	33 1610	Manchester	85.5	99 567	197	1 165	90 936	8 631	9.5	96.97	0.97	0.21	1.10	0.75	2.13	13.7
1122	33 1770	Nashua	80.1	79 662	267	995	67 865	11 797	17.4	95.15	1.62	0.22	1.93	1.07	3.02	10.1
6450	33 2170	Portsmouth	40.4	25 925	907	642	26 254	-329	-1.3	92.63	4.60	0.27	1.72	0.77	2.00	12.2
...	34 0000	NEW JERSEY	19 214.8	7 730 188	X	402	7 365 011	365 177	5.0	79.31	13.41	0.19	3.53	3.56	9.57	13.4
0560	34 0075	Atlantic City	29.4	37 986	666	1 292	40 199	-2 213	-5.5	35.45	51.31	0.51	3.97	8.76	15.30	19.2
5602	34 1135	Bayonne	14.6	61 444	375	4 208	65 047	-3 603	-5.5	90.44	4.71	0.13	1.84	2.88	9.50	18.7
5602	34 1155	Belleville township	8.7	34 213	733	3 933	35 367	-1 154	-3.3	86.07	3.67	0.25	6.01	4.01	10.06	14.6
5602	34 1175	Bergenfield borough	7.5	24 458	932	3 261	25 568	-1 110	-4.3	83.92	4.19	0.15	9.09	2.64	9.21	15.4
5602	34 1235	Bloomfield township	13.8	45 061	550	3 265	47 792	-2 731	-5.7	89.06	4.30	0.12	5.00	1.53	5.13	18.0
6162	34 1390	Camden	22.8	87 492	232	3 837	84 910	2 582	3.0	19.00	56.42	0.41	1.32	22.85	31.17	8.4
5602	34 1490	Clifton	29.3	71 742	306	2 449	74 388	-2 646	-3.6	92.76	1.40	0.10	3.50	2.24	6.80	20.9
5602	34 1665	East Orange	10.2	73 552	296	7 211	77 878	-4 326	-5.6	7.21	89.95	0.42	0.63	1.79	4.05	11.5
5602	34 1715	Elizabeth	31.9	110 002	166	3 448	106 201	3 801	3.6	65.54	19.85	0.27	2.73	11.61	39.14	12.1
5602	34 1790	Fair Lawn borough	13.4	30 548	822	2 280	32 229	-1 681	-5.2	95.96	0.59	0.07	2.93	0.45	3.48	20.0
5602	34 1850	Fort Lee borough	6.6	31 997	785	4 848	32 449	-452	-1.4	77.21	1.31	0.06	20.33	1.10	5.56	20.1
5602	34 1920	Garfield	5.5	26 727	895	4 859	26 803	-76	-0.3	93.83	2.24	0.09	1.66	2.19	9.05	17.6
5602	34 2010	Hackensack	10.7	37 049	686	3 463	36 039	1 010	2.8	66.36	24.77	0.23	3.67	4.98	15.10	14.3
5602	34 2185	Hoboken	3.3	33 397	760	10 120	42 460	-9 063	-21.3	78.97	5.52	0.17	4.43	10.91	30.05	11.1
5602	34 2265	Irvington township	7.5	59 774	387	7 970	61 493	-1 719	-2.8	22.61	69.86	0.24	2.20	5.09	10.56	9.4
5602	34 2290	Jersey City	38.5	228 537	67	5 936	223 532	5 005	2.2	48.25	29.69	0.34	11.36	10.35	24.24	11.1
5602	34 2300	Kearny town	23.7	34 874	721	1 471	35 735	-861	-2.4	90.49	1.24	0.17	4.70	3.41	17.06	13.3
5602	34 2440	Linden	28.0	36 701	691	1 311	37 836	-1 135	-3.0	76.76	20.01	0.13	1.50	1.59	7.36	19.3
5602	34 2500	Long Branch	13.5	28 658	851	2 123	29 819	-1 161	-3.9	73.50	19.50	0.21	1.47	5.32	13.57	15.4
5602	34 2780	Montclair township	16.3	37 729	672	2 315	38 321	-592	-1.5	65.50	31.00	0.25	2.27	0.98	3.31	15.2
5602	34 2895	Newark	61.7	275 221	56	4 461	329 248	-54 027	-16.4	28.62	58.46	0.24	1.19	11.49	26.07	9.3
5602	34 2900	New Brunswick	13.5	41 711	599	3 090	41 442	269	0.6	57.37	29.58	0.31	3.96	8.78	19.33	9.3
5602	34 3000	Nutley township	8.7	27 099	887	3 115	28 998	-1 899	-6.5	92.73	1.76	0.04	4.70	0.76	3.27	17.1
5602	34 3065	Orange township	5.7	29 925	828	5 250	31 136	-1 211	-3.9	23.96	70.33	0.40	1.29	4.03	10.82	12.5
5602	34 3090	Paramus borough	27.1	25 067	923	925	26 474	-1 407	-5.3	88.23	0.79	0.03	10.48	0.48	3.65	17.4
5602	34 3110	Passaic	8.0	58 041	402	7 255	52 463	5 578	10.6	45.32	20.60	0.50	7.05	26.53	50.01	10.4
5602	34 3115	Paterson	21.9	140 891	124	6 433	137 970	2 921	2.1	41.15	36.01	0.31	1.44	21.10	40.96	9.6
5602	34 3160	Perth Amboy	12.4	41 967	594	3 384	38 951	3 016	7.7	59.82	11.76	0.41	1.57	26.44	55.54	13.8
5602	34 3205	Plainfield	15.6	46 567	529	2 985	45 555	1 012	2.2	26.50	65.65	0.54	1.06	6.25	15.02	9.9
5602	34 3275	Rahway	10.3	25 325	915	2 459	26 723	-1 398	-5.2	75.39	20.21	0.15	2.39	1.86	7.55	15.3
5602	34 3335	Ridgewood village	15.0	24 152	933	1 610	25 208	-1 056	-4.2	90.35	1.99	0.07	7.23	0.36	2.83	12.8
5602	34 3475	Sayreville borough	41.8	34 986	717	837	29 969	5 017	16.7	93.11	3.23	0.11	3.02	0.53	4.01	12.3
6162	34 3770	Trenton	19.8	88 675	228	4 479	92 124	-3 449	-3.7	42.17	49.27	0.25	0.66	7.65	14.13	12.7
5602	34 3802	Union City	3.3	58 012	403	17 579	55 593	2 419	4.4	74.68	5.11	0.24	2.09	17.88	75.62	10.0
6162	34 3870	Vineland	177.9	54 780	433	308	53 753	1 027	1.9	73.01	11.48	0.33	0.88	14.31	23.60	14.1
5602	34 4015	Westfield town	17.4	28 870	846	1 659	30 447	-1 577	-5.2	91.47	4.58	0.07	3.53	0.35	2.04	13.4
5602	34 4030	West New York town	2.6	38 125	662	14 663	39 194	-1 069	-2.7	76.72	4.00	0.38	1.95	16.96	73.26	13.7
5602	34 4035	West Orange township	31.4	39 103	645	1 245	39 510	-407	-1.0	87.64	5.73	0.15	5.58	0.91	4.42	18.9
...	35 0000	NEW MEXICO	314 334.1	1 515 069	X	5	1 303 302	211 767	16.2	75.64	1.99	8.87	0.93	12.56	38.23	10.8
0200	35 0015	Albuquerque	342.4	384 736	38	1 124	332 920	51 816	15.6	78.24	2.98	3.04	1.73	14.00	34.49	11.1
...	35 0055	Carlsbad	70.6	24 952	924	353	25 496	-544	-2.1	81.24	2.58	0.49	0.65	15.04	33.39	18.4
...	35 0085	Clovis	35.8	30 954	809	865	31 194	-240	-0.8	72.84	7.03	0.65	1.74	17.74	26.77	12.3
...	35 0135	Farmington	60.9	33 997	738	558	31 222	2 775	8.9	77.09	0.81	13.81	0.36	7.93	15.97	8.7
...	35 0180	Hobbs	48.9	29 115	840	595	29 153	-38	-0.1	78.71	7.45	0.56	0.47	12.81	30.13	10.8
4100	35 0220	Las Cruces	97.1	62 126	366	640	45 086	17 040	37.8	88.19	1.95	0.87	1.11	7.88	46.88	11.3

1. MSA = Metropolitan Statistical Area. CMSA = Consolidated MSA. 2. Dry land or land partially or temporarily covered by water. 3. Hispanic persons may be of any race.

City	Households, 1990				Births, 1984			Deaths, 1984				Hospitals, 1985		
	Number	Persons per house-hold	Percent– Female family house-holder[1]	Percent– One-person[2]	Number Total	Number To mothers under 20 yrs. old (Percent)	Rate[3]	Number Total	Number Infant[4]	Rate Total[3]	Rate Infant[5]	Number	Beds Number	Beds Rate[6]
	15	16	17	18	19	20	21	22	23	24	25	26	27	28
MONTANA—Con.														
Billings	33 181	2.39	10.5	29.4	1 302	9.9	18.6	541	10	7.7	7.7	2	531	661
Butte-Silver Bow	13 651	2.39	9.4	31.9	454	12.1	13.2	434	5	12.6	11.0	1	274	821
Great Falls	22 639	2.39	10.4	29.5	980	12.4	16.7	529	12	9.0	12.2	2	593	1 035
Missoula	17 677	2.28	10.2	33.3	638	12.1	19.1	351	7	10.5	11.0	3	366	1 078
NEBRASKA	602 363	2.54	8.3	26.5	26 127	9.7	16.3	14 673	252	9.1	9.6	110	11 585	725
Grand Island	15 244	2.51	9.3	27.8	667	12.0	16.7	382	9	9.6	13.5	3	459	1 174
Lincoln	75 402	2.40	9.1	28.8	2 884	8.9	16.0	1 244	31	6.9	10.7	7	1 459	797
Omaha	133 842	2.45	13.3	30.6	5 759	13.4	17.2	3 247	84	9.7	14.6	14	4 460	1 277
NEVADA	466 297	2.53	10.2	25.7	14 803	12.2	16.3	6 755	156	7.4	10.5	31	4 085	424
Carson City	15 895	2.39	9.6	27.2	507	10.5	14.1	309	3	8.6	5.9	1	97	263
Las Vegas	99 735	2.55	12.0	26.2	5 433	13.9	29.7	1 812	31	9.9	5.7	8	1 828	955
North Las Vegas	14 525	3.24	23.2	17.1	1 057	23.4	22.7	274	15	5.9	14.2	1	163	324
Reno	57 286	2.26	9.6	33.7	1 727	9.6	16.4	1 057	22	10.0	12.7	4	1 198	1 085
Sparks	20 561	2.56	11.2	23.7	740	7.8	15.5	338	10	7.1	13.5	3	271	521
NEW HAMPSHIRE	411 186	2.62	8.5	22.0	14 250	8.6	14.6	8 039	145	8.2	10.2	38	4 764	464
Concord	14 222	2.35	9.9	30.4	451	8.0	14.6	372	4	12.0	8.9	2	768	2 344
Manchester	40 338	2.40	11.1	29.2	1 477	11.0	15.6	996	17	10.5	11.5	3	887	912
Nashua	31 051	2.53	9.3	24.8	1 118	9.0	15.4	538	13	7.4	11.6	2	382	499
Portsmouth	10 329	2.39	9.9	28.6	442	10.0	15.9	197	4	7.1	9.0	2	161	620
NEW JERSEY	2 794 711	2.70	12.1	23.1	101 334	10.2	13.5	69 437	1 109	9.2	10.9	129	41 720	548
Atlantic City	15 731	2.30	22.8	40.6	677	29.5	18.4	772	16	21.0	23.6	2	709	1 971
Bayonne	25 309	2.42	13.7	31.4	715	7.1	11.2	869	3	13.6	4.2	1	299	475
Belleville township	13 374	2.55	12.2	26.7	412	3.4	11.7	346	4	9.8	9.7	1	567	1 582
Bergenfield borough	8 799	2.77	10.6	19.8	283	2.5	11.0	243	1	9.5	3.5	0	0	0
Bloomfield township	18 455	2.42	10.7	30.8	535	2.6	11.4	546	3	11.6	5.6	0	0	0
Camden	26 626	3.15	36.9	23.6	2 164	29.2	26.2	863	47	10.5	21.7	3	1 072	1 295
Clifton	29 041	2.44	10.3	28.1	747	3.5	9.9	857	4	11.4	5.4	0	0	0
East Orange	27 210	2.63	26.4	35.1	1 355	21.4	17.8	774	27	10.1	19.9	2	1 213	1 567
Elizabeth	39 101	2.76	17.2	26.7	1 695	13.0	15.8	1 133	26	10.5	15.3	3	907	851
Fair Lawn borough	11 493	2.64	8.7	20.4	286	1.0	9.1	342	3	10.9	10.5	0	0	0
Fort Lee borough	15 236	2.10	6.6	38.6	398	0.0	12.0	321	4	9.7	10.1	0	0	0
Garfield	10 946	2.44	11.8	28.9	380	6.1	14.1	355	2	13.2	5.3	0	0	0
Hackensack	16 464	2.16	11.9	39.7	488	5.3	13.7	399	6	11.2	12.3	1	505	1 410
Hoboken	15 036	2.17	12.8	37.8	499	17.2	11.9	360	3	8.6	6.0	1	330	792
Irvington township	21 693	2.75	23.1	28.5	1 006	17.2	16.3	662	18	10.7	17.9	1	157	252
Jersey City	82 381	2.73	20.4	28.7	3 958	17.0	17.7	2 436	67	10.9	16.9	5	1 630	743
Kearny town	12 470	2.77	12.2	22.1	480	4.4	13.6	362	4	10.2	8.3	1	218	624
Linden	14 369	2.53	13.1	26.9	419	7.2	11.2	404	2	10.8	4.8	0	0	0
Long Branch	11 544	2.44	15.5	32.1	554	16.4	18.8	326	5	11.1	9.0	1	506	1 715
Montclair township	14 518	2.52	12.9	28.9	436	8.3	11.5	443	7	11.6	16.1	2	519	1 348
Newark	91 552	2.91	28.6	27.5	5 500	25.5	17.5	2 936	103	9.3	18.7	6	2 298	727
New Brunswick	12 711	2.70	17.5	28.3	585	15.7	14.4	302	8	7.4	13.7	3	803	1 996
Nutley township	10 594	2.55	10.1	26.7	275	3.3	9.6	281	2	9.8	7.3	0	0	0
Orange township	11 580	2.56	21.3	35.2	521	17.9	16.7	342	6	11.0	11.5	2	560	1 773
Paramus borough	7 776	3.07	8.3	11.3	200	2.0	7.6	215	1	8.2	5.0	1	1 089	4 214
Passaic	18 735	3.06	20.2	23.3	1 064	18.5	19.8	560	20	10.4	18.8	3	777	1 442
Paterson	43 946	3.14	23.7	21.3	2 833	23.4	20.4	1 234	40	8.9	14.1	2	958	689
Perth Amboy	14 207	2.91	17.6	24.2	677	17.1	17.6	408	7	10.6	10.3	1	539	1 436
Plainfield	15 146	3.02	21.5	21.8	819	17.1	17.7	370	11	8.0	13.4	1	425	924
Rahway	9 623	2.62	12.8	24.9	349	9.7	13.1	290	4	10.9	11.5	1	307	1 151
Ridgewood village	8 354	2.87	7.7	17.8	263	0.4	10.5	181	1	7.2	3.8	1	387	1 557
Sayreville borough	12 749	2.72	9.9	19.7	327	3.7	10.6	272	2	8.8	6.1	0	0	0
Trenton	30 744	2.76	24.6	28.8	1 861	26.0	20.2	1 109	33	12.0	17.7	5	1 572	1 724
Union City	20 612	2.80	18.5	23.7	915	11.6	16.1	443	14	7.8	15.3	1	201	360
Vineland	18 732	2.81	15.2	21.1	776	18.7	14.6	462	9	8.7	11.6	2	353	658
Westfield town	10 289	2.78	7.3	17.2	334	1.5	11.0	245	1	8.0	3.0	0	0	0
West New York town	14 419	2.64	16.2	26.6	495	10.7	12.0	341	9	8.3	18.2	0	0	0
West Orange township	14 821	2.59	9.6	24.7	416	2.6	10.5	439	3	11.0	7.2	1	178	437
NEW MEXICO	542 709	2.74	11.9	23.0	27 373	15.7	19.2	9 562	263	6.7	9.6	63	6 840	462
Albuquerque	153 818	2.46	12.1	28.2	7 207	13.8	20.6	2 674	64	7.6	8.9	17	2 498	681
Carlsbad	9 273	2.63	11.0	23.9	459	23.1	16.1	284	4	10.0	8.7	1	144	517
Clovis	11 676	2.62	12.5	23.9	764	21.6	22.9	278	5	8.3	6.5	1	106	314
Farmington	11 979	2.83	10.1	20.6	895	14.0	24.0	167	4	4.5	4.5	1	124	318
Hobbs	10 242	2.81	12.6	22.2	870	16.2	24.8	251	8	7.2	9.2	1	244	700
Las Cruces	23 797	2.59	12.7	25.1	1 288	13.7	25.6	383	11	7.6	8.5	1	286	529

1. No spouse present. 2. Householder living alone. 3. Per 1,000 resident population estimated as of July 1 of the year shown. 4. Deaths of infants under 1 year old. 5. Deaths of infants under 1 year old per 1,000 live births. 6. Per 100,000 resident population estimated as of July 1, 1986.

Table C. Cities — **Crime, Police Officers, Education, Money Income, and Housing**

City	Serious crimes known to police, 1985: Number: Total	Serious crimes known to police, 1985: Number: Violent[1]	Serious crimes known to police, 1985: Rate[2]	Police officers, 1985: Number	Police officers, 1985: Rate[3]	Educational attainment,[4] 1980: Percent completing 12 years or more	Educational attainment,[4] 1980: Percent completing 16 years or more	Money income: Per capita[5]: 1985: Total (Dollars)	Money income: Per capita[5]: 1985: Percent of State average	Money income: Per capita[5]: 1979: Current dollars	Money income: Per capita[5]: 1979: Constant (1985) dollars	Money income: Percent below poverty level, 1979: Persons	Money income: Percent below poverty level, 1979: Families	Housing, 1990: Total units	Housing, 1990: Percent change, 1980–1990	Housing, 1990: Vacant units for sale or rent[6]
	29	30	31	32	33	34	35	36	37	38	39	40	41	42	43	44
MONTANA—Con.																
Billings	5 788	147	8 193	100	14.2	78.1	21.9	11 002	125.3	7 914	11 729	10.1	7.3	35 964	22.1	2 132
Butte-Silver Bow	NA	NA	NA	NA	NA	69.5	14.3	8 785	100.0	6 552	9 710	10.3	7.8	15 180	-3.4	1 000
Great Falls	4 407	73	7 509	64	10.9	75.0	18.6	10 381	118.2	7 369	10 921	9.6	7.1	24 157	0.6	1 081
Missoula	2 838	133	8 354	56	16.5	82.5	28.9	9 532	108.6	7 135	10 574	15.0	7.7	18 488	21.3	542
NEBRASKA	59 335	3 821	3 695	NA	NA	73.4	15.5	10 546	100.0	6 934	10 276	10.7	8.0	660 621	5.4	28 503
Grand Island	2 267	21	6 485	45	12.9	73.7	12.8	10 453	99.1	7 223	10 704	6.9	4.3	15 855	13.5	448
Lincoln	10 785	607	5 914	229	12.6	81.8	24.8	11 772	111.6	7 631	11 309	8.9	5.4	79 079	12.6	2 826
Omaha	22 720	2 498	6 261	574	15.8	73.9	18.4	12 886	122.2	7 714	11 432	11.4	8.2	143 612	12.7	6 845
NEVADA	61 538	6 244	6 575	NA	NA	75.5	14.4	11 200	100.0	8 453	12 527	8.7	6.3	518 858	34.5	32 551
Carson City	NA	NA	NA	NA	NA	78.5	15.8	10 937	97.7	8 148	12 075	7.0	5.3	16 628	19.6	550
Las Vegas	35 191	3 624	7 705	1 021	22.4	72.1	11.5	10 990	98.1	8 132	12 052	10.5	7.8	109 670	38.8	8 370
North Las Vegas	3 597	695	7 417	105	21.7	60.7	4.8	7 480	66.8	5 458	8 089	14.4	11.7	15 837	10.8	981
Reno	10 333	865	9 520	271	25.0	80.7	22.7	11 916	106.4	9 620	14 257	8.1	5.0	61 384	22.8	3 341
Sparks	3 076	260	6 359	74	15.3	78.0	12.9	11 074	98.9	8 578	12 713	5.7	4.0	21 660	25.3	764
NEW HAMPSHIRE	32 454	1 405	3 252	NA	NA	72.3	18.2	11 659	100.0	6 966	10 324	8.5	6.1	503 904	23.3	28 301
Concord	1 601	51	4 960	64	19.8	76.7	21.5	11 662	100.0	7 119	10 550	9.0	5.1	15 697	22.7	1 261
Manchester	5 591	200	5 774	159	16.4	61.4	13.3	11 481	98.5	6 841	10 138	10.4	7.5	44 361	19.1	3 485
Nashua	2 655	59	3 588	137	18.5	72.4	18.4	13 521	116.0	7 844	11 625	6.5	5.4	33 383	23.8	2 057
Portsmouth	1 472	171	5 167	57	20.0	76.9	17.5	10 972	94.1	6 416	9 509	9.3	6.8	11 369	13.1	780
NEW JERSEY	385 239	41 172	5 094	NA	NA	67.4	18.3	13 129	100.0	8 127	12 044	9.5	7.6	3 075 310	9.9	146 561
Atlantic City	14 823	996	38 379	405	104.9	48.1	7.7	9 205	70.1	5 708	8 459	24.9	18.8	21 626	0.5	2 456
Bayonne	1 871	200	2 891	188	29.0	61.4	11.0	11 826	90.1	7 751	11 487	9.6	7.6	26 468	0.4	872
Belleville township	1 812	156	5 152	90	25.6	60.8	13.0	11 927	90.8	7 741	11 472	6.8	6.0	14 058	4.7	590
Bergenfield borough	815	45	3 154	47	18.2	73.8	17.8	13 713	104.4	8 670	12 849	3.2	2.5	9 035	0.7	186
Bloomfield township	2 015	142	4 241	110	23.2	66.5	16.6	13 175	100.4	8 409	12 462	5.3	3.7	19 293	1.5	733
Camden	11 025	2 346	12 874	267	31.2	41.4	4.8	5 731	43.7	3 966	5 878	36.9	32.3	30 138	-8.1	2 026
Clifton	2 714	206	3 581	138	18.2	61.5	14.4	13 512	102.9	8 803	13 046	4.4	3.4	29 999	1.9	766
East Orange	7 917	1 607	10 277	222	28.8	66.1	11.5	8 841	67.3	6 240	9 248	20.1	18.4	28 987	-7.2	1 539
Elizabeth	8 291	1 123	7 668	307	28.4	53.6	10.2	9 572	72.9	6 712	9 947	15.8	13.2	41 315	1.7	1 757
Fair Lawn borough	845	56	2 641	50	15.6	74.6	22.7	16 104	122.7	10 019	14 848	3.5	2.9	11 759	0.7	198
Fort Lee borough	1 624	97	4 932	86	26.1	76.9	29.7	22 239	169.4	13 284	19 687	4.6	2.6	16 847	8.1	1 388
Garfield	317	15	1 169	46	17.0	44.9	7.4	11 062	84.3	7 029	10 417	6.8	5.9	11 458	3.0	366
Hackensack	2 492	93	6 870	106	29.2	68.1	20.5	14 971	114.0	9 462	14 023	8.7	6.5	17 705	7.9	1 087
Hoboken	2 117	232	5 042	140	33.3	43.6	11.8	9 795	74.6	5 421	8 034	23.5	21.3	17 421	3.4	1 874
Irvington township	5 749	933	9 180	161	25.7	58.0	9.8	10 281	78.3	6 611	9 798	14.7	12.6	23 792	-7.3	1 861
Jersey City	17 474	3 374	7 787	920	41.0	51.2	11.7	8 605	65.5	5 812	8 613	21.2	18.9	90 723	3.0	6 831
Kearny town	1 875	150	5 223	121	33.7	57.4	8.0	11 333	86.3	7 415	10 989	8.1	7.1	13 435	1.0	749
Linden	1 835	144	4 849	128	33.8	58.0	8.6	12 491	95.1	8 280	12 271	7.0	5.3	14 917	2.1	430
Long Branch	2 083	310	6 880	83	27.4	65.4	16.0	11 360	86.5	6 970	10 330	19.8	16.5	13 632	3.4	1 351
Montclair township	1 753	104	4 578	100	26.1	80.6	40.2	17 814	135.7	11 508	17 055	7.2	4.4	15 069	0.9	426
Newark	38 798	9 736	12 264	1 122	35.5	44.6	6.3	6 494	49.5	4 525	6 706	32.8	29.9	102 473	-18.5	8 054
New Brunswick	2 891	265	6 836	142	33.6	56.8	18.7	8 701	66.3	5 782	8 569	23.5	16.2	13 556	-4.3	703
Nutley township	617	17	2 140	61	21.2	71.3	18.9	14 152	107.8	8 870	13 145	3.9	2.5	11 001	3.1	319
Orange township	3 619	768	11 726	96	31.1	63.5	14.9	10 499	80.0	6 753	10 008	16.9	14.0	12 318	-5.1	624
Paramus borough	3 731	103	14 014	96	36.1	78.1	22.9	15 547	118.4	9 692	14 364	3.0	2.3	7 892	2.5	103
Passaic	3 631	464	6 691	152	28.0	48.5	11.2	8 027	61.1	5 813	8 615	23.5	21.0	19 619	-1.2	742
Paterson	10 790	1 825	7 724	366	26.2	42.4	6.2	7 216	55.0	5 060	7 499	25.2	21.9	46 138	-4.4	1 776
Perth Amboy	1 587	285	3 943	95	23.6	45.3	7.6	9 232	70.3	6 067	8 991	17.7	15.4	15 017	6.0	607
Plainfield	3 879	589	8 387	118	25.5	67.7	17.0	10 835	82.5	7 143	10 586	13.0	10.9	16 063	-0.6	770
Rahway	1 072	96	3 980	74	27.5	69.1	11.5	12 657	96.4	8 295	12 293	6.0	4.3	9 989	-0.7	307
Ridgewood village	203	7	803	49	19.4	90.8	48.2	24 001	182.8	13 947	20 669	1.9	1.1	8 666	2.3	253
Sayreville borough	972	90	3 133	72	23.2	68.2	11.5	13 414	102.2	8 267	12 252	3.1	2.9	13 347	27.6	541
Trenton	7 662	1 309	8 190	367	39.2	49.6	7.7	8 699	66.3	5 400	8 003	21.2	18.8	33 578	-6.7	1 887
Union City	4 026	410	7 012	142	24.7	42.2	8.3	7 992	60.9	5 625	8 336	20.3	18.5	22 592	4.8	1 560
Vineland	4 200	363	7 663	113	20.6	52.5	10.3	9 551	72.7	6 153	9 119	13.9	11.9	19 548	7.3	635
Westfield town	602	19	1 973	56	18.4	86.4	43.6	21 299	162.2	12 622	18 706	3.1	2.1	10 588	1.2	244
West New York town	2 272	219	5 487	98	23.7	43.6	10.5	8 804	67.1	6 084	9 016	18.3	15.5	15 794	-0.2	1 069
West Orange township	1 615	90	4 063	92	23.1	75.2	27.9	16 768	127.7	10 837	16 060	3.7	2.4	15 256	5.5	338
NEW MEXICO	94 050	10 207	6 486	NA	NA	68.9	17.6	8 814	100.0	6 120	9 070	17.6	14.0	632 058	19.7	38 093
Albuquerque	33 158	4 105	9 287	644	18.0	79.1	24.9	11 133	126.3	7 440	11 026	12.4	9.3	166 870	20.4	9 707
Carlsbad	1 798	120	6 379	34	12.1	66.5	12.3	8 606	97.6	6 107	9 051	13.0	9.5	10 575	7.2	925
Clovis	1 881	113	5 451	53	15.4	68.4	11.3	8 728	99.0	6 156	9 123	16.3	12.7	12 978	2.7	961
Farmington	3 020	244	7 980	74	19.6	77.3	16.6	9 807	111.3	7 618	11 290	9.1	6.6	13 119	8.5	755
Hobbs	2 285	201	6 828	NA	NA	63.1	11.7	10 198	115.7	7 246	10 739	12.4	9.5	12 327	9.4	1 327
Las Cruces	4 565	249	9 255	83	16.8	72.9	24.4	9 290	105.4	6 097	9 036	20.3	15.3	25 676	31.0	1 532

1. Includes murder and nonnegligent manslaughter, forcible rape, robbery, and aggravated assault. 2. Per 100,000 resident population estimated for 1985 by the FBI. 3. Per 10,000 resident population estimated for 1985 by the FBI. 4. Persons 25 years old or older. 5. Based on the resident population estimated as of July 1, 1988 for 1987 data and enumerated as of April 1, 1980 for 1979 data. 6. Also includes units rented or sold, but not occupied.

City	Housing, 1990 (cont'd) — Occupied units — Total	Housing, 1990 (cont'd) — Occupied units — Percent with more than 1 person per room	Housing, 1990 (cont'd) — Occupied units — Owner-occupied — Percent of total	Housing, 1990 (cont'd) — Occupied units — Owner-occupied — Median value[1] (Dollars)	Housing, 1990 (cont'd) — Occupied units — Median rent[2] (Dollars)	Construction authorized by building permits, 1990 — New private housing units — Number	Construction authorized by building permits, 1990 — New private housing units — Value ($1,000)	Construction authorized by building permits, 1990 — New private housing units — Percent single family	Construction authorized by building permits, 1990 — Non-residential, value ($1,000)	Civilian labor force, 1990 — Total	Civilian labor force, 1990 — Percent change, 1989–1990	Civilian labor force, 1990 — Unemployment — Total	Civilian labor force, 1990 — Unemployment — Rate[3]
	45	46	47	48	49	50	51	52	53	54	55	56	57
MONTANA—Con.													
Billings	33 181	1.7	61.2	63 600	294	144	15 196	94.4	7 349	41 492	0.1	1 952	4.7
Butte-Silver Bow	13 651	1.8	70.6	44 800	189	50	4 911	84.0	2 785	13 272	1.4	978	7.4
Great Falls	22 639	2.0	62.8	60 600	266	55	5 900	96.4	3 322	30 108	0.5	1 452	4.8
Missoula	17 677	2.4	49.5	64 500	272	316	19 621	61.4	4 633	18 573	1.1	911	4.9
NEBRASKA	602 363	1.7	66.5	50 400	282	6 756	355 401	59.8	225 424	839 000	3.3	18 000	2.2
Grand Island	15 244	2.1	60.8	47 600	256	77	6 883	87.0	3 097	18 911	1.2	489	2.6
Lincoln	75 402	1.6	58.1	61 700	323	2 048	105 999	46.3	26 721	117 094	4.4	1 980	1.7
Omaha	133 842	2.2	59.2	54 600	326	2 309	118 375	58.5	82 498	186 525	3.5	4 814	2.6
NEVADA	466 297	6.4	54.8	95 700	445	25 096	1 427 079	58.0	483 494	626 000	4.0	31 000	4.9
Carson City	15 895	3.9	60.3	99 300	406	491	36 733	86.2	8 335	21 794	-0.7	1 166	5.4
Las Vegas	99 735	7.9	50.4	89 200	434	9 219	438 044	51.7	137 999	137 984	7.1	7 110	5.2
North Las Vegas	14 525	17.8	49.9	58 100	351	741	78 421	99.7	16 660	30 626	7.1	2 096	6.8
Reno	57 286	6.7	42.6	109 600	419	1 829	134 132	61.7	39 733	73 145	-0.7	3 377	4.6
Sparks	20 561	5.1	54.2	97 300	443	200	18 613	98.0	25 830	28 674	-0.7	1 362	4.7
NEW HAMPSHIRE	411 186	1.6	68.2	129 400	479	4 201	367 943	83.6	179 959	630 000	3.1	36 000	5.6
Concord	14 222	1.2	52.3	112 400	485	99	5 732	85.9	2 195	19 603	5.7	1 040	5.3
Manchester	40 338	1.6	46.0	118 600	467	362	23 596	32.9	7 686	59 406	3.1	3 855	6.5
Nashua	31 051	1.6	57.7	138 800	574	79	5 744	97.5	17 957	47 183	1.3	3 074	6.5
Portsmouth	10 329	1.7	41.9	137 600	497	5	564	100.0	0	14 913	2.4	646	4.3
NEW JERSEY	2 794 711	3.9	64.9	162 300	521	17 524	1 397 723	73.0	1 190 179	4 048 000	1.5	202 000	5.0
Atlantic City	15 731	8.8	30.4	73 400	394	52	11 258	57.7	314	25 748	5.4	2 012	7.8
Bayonne	25 309	3.0	40.5	168 500	413	13	715	7.7	1 000	33 051	0.5	1 945	5.9
Belleville township	13 374	4.1	53.2	163 800	551	4	158	50.0	63	19 100	0.1	904	4.7
Bergenfield borough	8 799	3.4	71.1	184 000	647	0	0	NA	62	14 303	-0.3	597	4.2
Bloomfield township	18 455	2.0	54.8	172 500	541	6	390	33.3	1 542	25 731	0.0	1 167	4.5
Camden	26 626	15.2	48.4	31 300	323	1	55	100.0	0	30 735	3.5	3 584	11.7
Clifton	29 041	2.1	60.8	185 000	537	7	536	71.4	4 127	44 239	-0.6	1 874	4.2
East Orange	27 210	10.7	27.5	116 200	478	11	550	45.5	11 957	37 466	0.6	2 694	7.2
Elizabeth	39 101	11.5	31.7	145 400	456	42	1 911	23.8	21 221	55 010	0.9	4 471	8.1
Fair Lawn borough	11 493	0.9	81.0	199 000	539	1	100	100.0	0	18 257	-0.5	634	3.5
Fort Lee borough	15 236	4.1	58.4	283 000	702	34	3 491	17.6	9 660	18 646	-0.4	704	3.8
Garfield	10 946	3.6	42.6	172 900	544	13	800	23.1	0	14 597	0.2	959	6.6
Hackensack	16 464	6.3	34.6	186 300	639	3	224	33.3	1 062	21 678	-0.2	968	4.5
Hoboken	15 036	6.2	21.6	250 000	511	229	18 478	0.0	425	19 554	1.2	2 042	10.4
Irvington township	21 693	10.2	32.5	117 000	501	5	149	100.0	3 007	30 154	0.4	1 890	6.3
Jersey City	82 381	11.4	29.6	127 700	464	171	7 236	4.1	101 109	102 469	0.8	8 494	8.3
Kearny town	12 470	3.9	49.6	165 700	535	15	867	6.7	1 826	18 922	0.4	961	5.1
Linden	14 369	3.2	61.2	151 800	528	7	485	71.4	3 705	19 799	0.3	1 078	5.4
Long Branch	11 544	5.5	44.1	149 100	540	12	1 320	33.3	0	17 810	1.5	1 079	6.1
Montclair township	14 518	2.0	55.8	271 700	670	6	886	66.7	809	20 835	-0.1	763	3.7
Newark	91 552	13.6	23.1	110 000	385	258	8 834	8.5	65 322	127 046	1.1	13 085	10.3
New Brunswick	12 711	10.5	32.3	126 700	569	2	71	0.0	78	24 599	3.9	1 519	6.2
Nutley township	10 594	1.4	67.3	186 600	583	1	111	100.0	375	15 420	0.0	634	4.1
Orange township	11 580	8.8	28.1	123 600	500	6	240	0.0	100	15 810	0.4	983	6.2
Paramus borough	7 776	1.3	91.1	246 200	958	11	1 262	100.0	0	14 799	-0.5	469	3.2
Passaic	18 735	16.9	28.1	165 100	443	9	370	11.1	346	26 613	0.2	2 492	9.4
Paterson	43 946	14.3	33.6	138 700	444	106	5 763	23.6	1 854	65 601	0.2	6 043	9.2
Perth Amboy	14 207	11.3	42.0	125 500	486	38	2 027	31.6	1 125	22 927	4.2	1 770	7.7
Plainfield	15 146	10.4	51.0	141 400	558	5	276	100.0	26	23 387	0.8	1 759	7.5
Rahway	9 623	3.1	65.7	151 100	558	8	276	50.0	753	14 851	0.3	790	5.3
Ridgewood village	8 354	1.1	78.6	299 800	867	3	800	100.0	486	13 053	-0.7	299	2.3
Sayreville borough	12 749	1.2	71.3	156 800	580	74	5 016	100.0	15 073	19 780	3.3	781	3.9
Trenton	30 744	8.0	51.1	71 300	387	10	547	100.0	137	43 816	3.0	3 198	7.3
Union City	20 612	17.0	21.8	150 400	451	8	385	0.0	2 562	28 817	0.8	2 312	8.0
Vineland	18 732	5.8	67.0	83 600	435	87	4 906	73.6	2 020	24 584	5.1	1 612	6.6
Westfield town	10 289	0.6	81.3	257 300	753	3	463	100.0	347	15 439	0.1	626	4.1
West New York town	14 419	15.0	22.7	162 000	394	0	0	NA	0	20 976	0.7	1 506	7.2
West Orange township	14 821	1.9	68.9	202 800	619	179	7 638	13.4	6 050	21 187	-0.2	721	3.4
NEW MEXICO	542 709	7.9	67.4	70 100	312	5 988	463 625	83.8	121 568	700 000	0.3	44 000	6.3
Albuquerque	153 818	4.9	57.3	85 900	353	1 555	116 785	73.0	44 424	217 036	-0.3	10 237	4.7
Carlsbad	9 273	5.5	70.3	44 200	257	33	2 536	100.0	1 471	10 446	-2.3	782	7.5
Clovis	11 676	6.1	64.2	51 300	265	236	22 249	100.0	3 103	13 566	-2.4	928	6.8
Farmington	11 979	7.3	65.1	66 100	305	49	3 392	100.0	2 117	15 765	0.6	913	5.8
Hobbs	10 242	8.9	66.0	41 600	258	0	0	NA	1 636	11 426	-2.9	650	5.7
Las Cruces	23 797	6.0	56.2	68 300	301	361	21 281	69.0	8 087	30 574	1.5	1 904	6.2

1. Specified owner-occupied units. 2. Specified renter-occupied units. 3. Percent of total civilian labor force.

City	Employed,[1] 1980			Manufactures, 1987											
		Rate per 1,000 employees		Establishments		All employees			Production workers						
											Wages				
	Total	Professional, specialty, and technical	Precision production, craft, and operators	Total	Percent with 20 or more employees	Number (1,000)	Percent change, 1982–1987	Annual payroll (Mil. dol.)	Number (1,000)	Work-hours (Millions)	Total (Mil. dol.)	Average per production worker (Dollars)	Value added by manufacture (Mil. dol.)	Value of shipments (Mil. dol.)	New capital expenditures (Mil. dol.)
	58	59	60	61	62	63	64	65	66	67	68	69	70	71	72
MONTANA—Con.															
Billings	31 819	154.4	142.5	119	18.5	2.3	-23.3	52.2	1.3	2.6	29.0	22 308	121.0	779.5	20.3
Butte-Silver Bow	14 556	171.0	170.9	26	15.4	0.5	-16.7	11.6	0.3	0.5	5.8	19 333	26.8	67.4	3.7
Great Falls	24 886	161.9	135.6	53	22.6	1.0	D	19.3	0.6	1.1	10.3	17 167	44.9	136.2	4.0
Missoula	14 791	186.7	126.5	72	20.8	1.4	-26.3	25.9	1.0	1.9	16.7	16 700	69.2	136.4	1.8
NEBRASKA	716 633	137.9	177.8	1 876	33.6	90.7	-0.4	1 937.6	64.2	128.8	1 211.9	18 877	5 819.2	16 076.2	317.9
Grand Island	16 138	116.6	206.2	61	42.6	4.3	D	83.9	3.2	6.2	58.0	18 125	384.9	1 401.4	19.9
Lincoln	91 335	189.0	168.0	222	39.6	12.8	14.3	303.2	8.5	16.8	173.6	20 424	809.1	1 518.7	60.7
Omaha	145 459	165.0	170.7	507	40.0	26.7	-2.6	651.2	18.4	35.3	406.0	22 065	2 004.1	4 547.5	100.3
NEVADA	398 566	124.1	147.0	975	24.7	23.7	16.2	521.4	15.8	30.9	299.6	18 962	1 279.3	2 470.4	114.0
Carson City	15 541	164.9	182.6	98	33.7	3.1	63.2	65.2	2.1	3.9	36.4	17 333	128.5	273.6	18.0
Las Vegas	80 345	105.7	134.6	159	19.5	2.8	7.7	57.2	1.7	3.3	33.0	19 412	138.5	257.2	7.4
North Las Vegas	17 514	71.2	154.6	25	24.0	0.5	NA	9.2	0.4	0.6	5.9	14 750	28.4	42.2	D
Reno	58 338	153.6	118.2	162	26.5	4.6	-2.1	103.6	2.8	5.6	49.9	17 821	215.3	431.5	35.4
Sparks	22 837	96.1	169.2	164	28.7	3.6	44.0	79.2	2.6	4.9	50.9	19 577	300.5	539.4	17.3
NEW HAMPSHIRE	432 622	164.3	273.3	2 328	31.6	107.9	0.5	2 508.7	71.5	141.6	1 426.8	19 955	8 188.6	12 214.2	339.8
Concord	14 789	183.3	199.9	74	37.8	4.9	22.5	106.4	2.8	5.0	46.2	16 500	196.0	360.8	13.0
Manchester	44 584	127.8	272.5	189	39.2	9.6	-22.6	197.1	6.7	13.6	109.9	16 403	484.4	983.5	24.1
Nashua	34 831	175.4	268.5	164	37.8	17.8	-1.7	553.5	9.8	20.2	305.1	31 133	1 617.3	1 984.6	58.7
Portsmouth	10 666	169.7	236.3	51	35.3	2.2	-12.0	51.4	1.1	2.1	21.9	19 909	112.6	243.4	5.3
NEW JERSEY	3 288 302	166.8	206.0	14 442	37.9	690.8	-8.4	18 549.9	394.4	780.9	8 389.3	21 271	42 526.6	82 451.0	2 312.5
Atlantic City	15 257	111.9	128.3	NA	NA	NA	NA	NA	NA	NA	NA	NA	NA	NA	NA
Bayonne	29 208	124.8	223.4	61	47.5	3.6	-14.3	89.2	2.3	4.4	45.1	19 609	376.1	687.0	D
Belleville township	17 571	137.9	220.8	83	32.5	3.0	-31.8	77.6	1.9	3.8	39.1	20 579	197.3	328.1	6.5
Bergenfield borough	12 848	149.8	180.8	28	21.4	0.6	20.0	13.1	0.3	0.6	5.5	18 333	18.8	30.6	0.6
Bloomfield township	23 721	162.0	189.6	80	32.5	3.6	-35.7	81.5	2.3	4.5	33.4	14 522	196.1	324.5	3.9
Camden	23 609	106.8	253.4	122	37.7	10.5	2.9	293.0	7.0	13.0	163.0	23 286	695.7	1 171.3	32.1
Clifton	37 525	145.4	224.3	307	43.0	13.0	-8.5	337.8	8.3	16.8	166.2	20 024	701.4	1 413.8	37.9
East Orange	33 579	145.8	194.9	40	37.5	1.0	-47.4	18.6	0.7	1.5	11.7	16 714	41.0	81.5	3.6
Elizabeth	48 490	104.9	342.0	166	45.2	9.3	-35.4	210.5	6.4	13.3	122.9	19 203	548.3	1 224.3	27.2
Fair Lawn borough	16 519	177.3	151.9	72	51.4	4.4	-13.7	116.0	2.8	5.6	60.4	21 571	305.1	502.5	12.5
Fort Lee borough	16 820	202.3	108.3	39	15.4	0.6	-14.3	15.6	0.2	0.4	3.8	19 000	26.2	50.6	0.8
Garfield	12 786	97.1	332.2	118	33.9	3.4	-17.1	77.1	2.6	5.0	50.8	19 538	199.9	365.1	7.8
Hackensack	19 410	165.6	183.3	178	30.3	5.5	-5.2	138.2	3.0	6.0	55.8	18 600	340.0	539.4	16.3
Hoboken	16 443	133.2	284.4	123	52.0	5.9	-24.4	106.3	4.5	8.6	66.0	14 667	377.4	741.5	16.8
Irvington township	27 293	112.9	250.2	80	42.5	2.1	-8.7	45.3	1.4	2.9	25.0	17 857	96.9	175.5	3.8
Jersey City	88 239	124.3	220.7	296	46.3	11.8	-18.6	273.3	7.7	14.7	143.6	18 649	771.3	1 407.5	D
Kearny town	16 864	101.5	254.0	95	45.3	3.6	-61.7	90.6	2.3	4.7	45.8	19 913	246.5	683.4	9.1
Linden	17 962	105.5	301.0	198	43.4	12.0	D	392.3	8.5	17.7	250.4	29 459	680.1	4 532.9	45.9
Long Branch	12 315	189.5	174.6	35	31.4	0.7	-30.0	12.3	0.5	1.1	7.2	14 400	23.0	41.6	0.6
Montclair township	19 385	283.0	91.9	NA	NA	NA	NA	NA	NA	NA	NA	NA	NA	NA	NA
Newark	110 052	94.5	296.7	644	43.3	26.7	-21.9	656.8	17.9	35.4	359.6	20 089	1 568.7	3 150.7	120.8
New Brunswick	17 784	187.1	184.2	95	42.1	5.7	-10.9	174.1	2.6	5.1	52.9	20 346	245.1	447.8	9.7
Nutley township	14 280	179.1	170.3	36	41.7	11.0	5.8	497.6	3.9	7.1	186.9	47 923	759.7	1 166.6	D
Orange township	14 319	164.8	206.0	NA	NA	NA	NA	NA	NA	NA	NA	NA	NA	NA	NA
Paramus borough	13 434	176.3	153.0	51	33.3	2.6	-18.8	80.5	0.6	1.2	15.5	25 833	104.0	183.6	5.8
Passaic	21 365	119.8	352.8	176	44.9	6.6	-24.1	121.7	4.8	9.5	75.6	15 750	255.7	496.4	11.2
Paterson	52 753	84.8	368.5	450	41.1	16.0	-7.5	311.4	12.4	24.0	205.8	16 597	692.2	1 438.1	26.8
Perth Amboy	16 301	104.2	326.5	88	40.9	3.8	-5.0	80.0	3.0	5.8	57.6	19 200	198.9	739.2	8.9
Plainfield	20 751	154.5	255.0	57	33.3	3.1	6.9	95.4	1.6	2.8	39.0	24 375	177.1	315.2	8.4
Rahway	13 491	122.6	258.9	83	36.1	6.5	51.2	248.1	2.2	4.3	50.3	22 864	517.6	713.4	19.7
Ridgewood village	11 954	253.7	75.8	NA	NA	NA	NA	NA	NA	NA	NA	NA	NA	NA	NA
Sayreville borough	14 639	131.8	265.7	32	34.4	3.6	-20.0	116.7	2.6	5.4	77.2	29 692	377.8	750.6	14.8
Trenton	34 495	119.2	221.1	135	38.5	9.3	-6.1	208.9	5.3	11.7	104.0	19 623	360.8	608.9	19.5
Union City	24 888	81.6	348.8	197	23.9	2.8	-20.0	38.8	2.4	4.0	27.4	11 417	76.3	163.6	3.1
Vineland	21 408	135.5	274.2	118	42.4	6.5	-15.6	137.0	5.1	10.1	96.6	18 941	371.9	725.3	17.9
Westfield town	14 211	279.9	96.9	NA	NA	NA	NA	NA	NA	NA	NA	NA	NA	NA	NA
West New York town	18 282	86.3	359.8	216	18.1	3.2	-15.8	51.0	2.6	5.0	35.2	13 538	83.3	179.3	2.7
West Orange township	19 764	196.5	131.0	50	28.0	1.3	8.3	35.2	0.7	1.4	14.1	20 143	94.0	141.3	6.9
NEW MEXICO	508 238	179.6	190.5	1 322	21.5	34.7	5.2	713.3	23.7	47.3	432.5	18 249	1 652.9	4 226.4	196.4
Albuquerque	151 542	217.7	155.4	499	22.8	13.8	-10.4	291.3	9.2	18.0	165.5	17 989	673.6	1 303.3	56.6
Carlsbad	9 329	140.4	291.7	NA	NA	NA	NA	NA	NA	NA	NA	NA	NA	NA	NA
Clovis	11 873	108.5	185.4	27	37.0	D	D	D	D	D	D	D	D	D	D
Farmington	14 443	161.6	261.6	31	19.4	D	D	D	D	D	D	D	D	D	D
Hobbs	12 564	114.0	280.4	35	11.4	0.5	D	12.4	0.2	0.4	3.8	19 000	12.8	26.1	D
Las Cruces	18 056	232.4	136.2	59	23.7	1.6	D	24.9	1.3	3.3	20.0	15 385	98.0	156.9	4.0

1. Persons 16 years old and over.

City	Wholesale trade, 1987				Retail trade–all establishments, 1987				Retail trade–establishments with payroll, 1987					
						Sales				Sales				
											Per capita[2] (Dollars)			
	Estab- lishments	Sales (Mil. dol.)	Paid employees[1]	Annual payroll ($1,000)	Number	Total (Mil. dol.)	Percent change, 1982–1987	Per capita[2] (Dollars)	Number	Total (Mil. dol.)	General merchan- dise group stores	Food stores	Apparel and accessory stores	Eating and drinking places
	73	74	75	76	77	78	79	80	81	82	83	84	85	86
MONTANA—Con.														
Billings	348	1 231.2	4 049	85 091	1 193	828.5	18.2	10 316	806	809.5	D	2 082	D	1 057
Butte-Silver Bow	63	164.0	485	7 743	453	206.9	13.4	6 198	303	201.7	432	1 295	169	769
Great Falls	177	602.2	1 740	31 898	797	472.0	22.7	8 236	530	462.1	D	1 659	D	826
Missoula	131	325.0	1 384	25 552	695	468.3	27.8	13 790	533	459.5	D	2 534	D	1 517
NEBRASKA	3 973	21 358.9	43 148	836 124	17 896	8 776.4	25.5	5 492	11 485	8 486.3	679	1 047	228	543
Grand Island	123	401.7	1 567	30 824	578	333.2	25.6	8 522	393	324.9	D	992	430	925
Lincoln	325	D	D	D	1 848	1 248.4	39.3	6 820	1 254	1 229.5	952	1 284	D	724
Omaha	1 075	7 333.4	17 095	384 837	3 420	2 827.5	42.2	8 095	2 526	2 783.9	1 125	1 528	397	891
NEVADA	1 589	5 506.9	17 627	379 113	10 054	7 494.7	40.3	7 775	6 442	7 321.0	871	1 594	334	788
Carson City	NA	NA	NA	NA	497	352.5	62.5	9 553	301	341.4	1 082	2 046	121	744
Las Vegas	349	1 172.3	3 936	82 498	2 236	1 920.9	53.7	10 030	1 521	1 883.2	1 063	1 932	473	1 025
North Las Vegas	39	242.9	468	10 427	173	143.5	53.5	2 853	118	141.6	D	742	33	354
Reno	275	1 157.5	3 214	72 391	1 570	1 496.9	39.3	13 555	1 143	1 472.2	1 776	2 267	591	1 016
Sparks	226	832.8	2 745	63 069	478	374.1	44.5	7 197	303	368.0	D	1 560	158	585
NEW HAMPSHIRE	1 966	6 771.3	22 548	560 562	12 928	10 211.7	90.7	9 943	8 403	9 961.3	1 150	1 853	424	735
Concord	86	D	D	D	527	542.5	91.0	16 555	384	534.7	1 633	3 427	674	1 198
Manchester	263	1 374.7	4 419	110 344	1 049	1 097.3	61.7	11 280	770	1 078.8	1 974	1 505	707	969
Nashua	178	1 129.0	2 585	75 871	860	1 159.4	127.7	15 154	645	1 142.6	3 037	2 208	1 052	855
Portsmouth	78	321.3	932	23 165	462	555.6	67.3	21 394	374	551.2	2 727	1 990	1 067	1 929
NEW JERSEY	17 643	144 620.7	270 976	7 528 610	74 524	56 326.2	55.1	7 392	48 395	54 778.6	750	1 459	484	612
Atlantic City	40	D	D	D	545	421.5	33.9	11 715	456	415.6	139	903	1 149	1 750
Bayonne	71	1 483.0	1 487	48 951	621	229.6	9.3	3 650	403	215.9	61	1 043	372	367
Belleville township	67	139.4	683	15 818	287	216.1	11.6	6 028	155	207.1	D	D	141	335
Bergenfield borough	53	D	D	D	236	165.5	57.9	6 578	166	161.4	231	1 093	493	309
Bloomfield township	75	175.0	833	24 358	444	288.8	27.8	6 061	290	279.9	39	1 264	487	483
Camden	121	D	D	D	382	164.3	7.4	1 984	256	156.2	71	450	33	256
Clifton	267	D	D	D	778	585.8	48.2	7 665	474	568.1	D	1 432	323	732
East Orange	44	109.5	480	11 973	265	136.9	-0.7	1 768	180	132.5	23	531	50	212
Elizabeth	197	D	D	D	965	516.3	33.5	4 846	654	497.3	96	1 219	399	412
Fair Lawn borough	91	676.3	960	26 940	372	244.5	56.1	7 816	200	227.8	D	2 267	174	470
Fort Lee borough	236	13 056.7	1 542	58 357	463	249.6	34.0	7 668	273	236.2	D	3 035	357	908
Garfield	70	166.4	808	16 155	243	199.5	77.3	7 571	138	190.9	D	1 560	D	501
Hackensack	303	1 878.1	3 788	105 561	573	583.3	51.2	16 284	429	575.6	3 589	1 610	2 240	1 399
Hoboken	85	434.0	690	18 388	355	134.3	29.4	3 224	234	128.1	43	1 355	542	484
Irvington township	71	387.6	1 406	38 616	398	194.2	21.1	3 122	271	186.4	196	448	385	228
Jersey City	325	2 551.8	5 430	142 150	1 783	1 072.8	50.2	4 888	1 108	1 032.1	375	951	418	307
Kearny town	116	646.6	1 661	42 221	322	239.5	46.6	6 857	205	233.4	839	1 951	439	294
Linden	154	2 030.3	2 866	69 583	400	228.0	30.4	6 048	287	222.0	D	1 587	610	536
Long Branch	45	76.3	390	7 080	262	140.6	32.3	4 766	165	136.8	D	2 206	99	772
Montclair township	53	81.3	264	7 367	421	276.2	68.3	7 176	294	269.7	D	1 672	402	489
Newark	509	2 421.3	7 358	185 426	1 778	824.2	16.3	2 606	1 332	796.7	245	499	233	488
New Brunswick	75	236.9	867	20 715	328	202.4	13.5	5 031	244	197.3	D	399	107	732
Nutley township	56	844.5	1 749	62 060	269	139.5	32.1	4 794	158	133.6	D	1 797	287	540
Orange township	NA	NA	NA	NA	0	0.0	0.0	NA	NA	NA	NA	NA	NA	NA
Paramus borough	145	2 610.3	3 691	128 931	810	1 717.8	64.1	66 478	665	1 708.3	19 594	2 854	10 942	2 400
Passaic	97	250.7	886	21 106	436	179.8	20.2	3 338	260	168.3	80	911	343	142
Paterson	274	1 024.7	3 825	96 348	944	370.6	9.0	2 664	575	347.1	59	613	170	186
Perth Amboy	81	986.9	1 118	31 505	344	196.5	28.4	5 236	218	187.7	76	1 182	153	597
Plainfield	58	135.3	544	12 477	288	194.7	29.5	4 234	211	190.4	926	601	138	503
Rahway	73	270.9	972	25 960	254	199.4	56.4	7 477	169	195.6	D	407	D	532
Ridgewood village	45	107.2	191	5 648	274	228.9	36.6	9 211	181	222.3	D	D	1 279	352
Sayreville borough	29	45.7	216	5 997	262	155.2	52.9	4 523	157	151.5	97	1 800	231	386
Trenton	145	560.0	2 137	52 604	674	252.4	3.5	2 769	451	237.8	136	559	125	457
Union City	115	195.7	741	16 568	732	224.0	9.9	4 015	460	205.2	73	599	562	279
Vineland	125	408.0	1 637	34 963	668	531.3	58.9	9 905	438	515.8	1 468	2 231	580	534
Westfield town	59	238.7	542	19 515	312	213.7	50.4	7 053	202	207.1	D	1 165	690	336
West New York town	73	96.9	364	6 580	500	184.5	46.9	4 525	298	172.5	D	628	911	243
West Orange township	95	875.4	1 214	40 789	420	268.2	23.0	6 582	251	258.6	D	1 634	612	1 124
NEW MEXICO	2 398	5 102.4	22 137	421 783	15 168	8 202.1	29.8	5 546	9 032	7 919.6	633	1 127	230	578
Albuquerque	1 031	2 717.0	11 426	250 022	3 999	3 205.6	49.1	8 741	2 653	3 141.2	D	1 412	D	949
Carlsbad	44	47.4	271	4 407	337	149.4	-5.7	5 364	207	145.9	D	1 292	234	551
Clovis	63	104.7	505	6 412	458	252.0	34.5	7 460	311	245.8	991	D	D	700
Farmington	128	234.5	1 003	19 447	515	379.4	9.8	9 716	341	371.0	1 590	2 079	D	826
Hobbs	121	255.9	716	14 745	435	219.8	-15.8	6 303	251	212.7	D	1 699	357	460
Las Cruces	101	182.4	961	15 202	784	474.2	33.1	8 767	516	461.8	D	1 654	402	875

1. For the period including March 12 of the year shown. 2. Based on resident population estimated as of July 1, 1986.

City	Retail trade–establishment with payroll, 1987 (cont'd): Paid employees[1]: Number	Retail trade: Paid employees[1]: Percent change, 1982–1987	Retail trade: Annual payroll (Mil. dol.)	Taxable service industries–establishments with payroll, 1987: Number	Taxable service: Receipts (Mil. dol.): Total	Receipts: Selected kinds of business: Hotels, motels, and other lodging places	Receipts: Selected kinds of business: Health services	Receipts: Selected kinds of business: Legal services	Taxable service: Paid employees[1]	Taxable service: Annual payroll (Mil. dol.)	Federal grants, 1986: Procurement contract awards (Mil. dol.)	Federal grants, 1986: Grant awards (Mil. dol.)	Federal government civilian employment, 1984
	87	88	89	90	91	92	93	94	95	96	97	98	99
MONTANA—Con.													
Billings	10 610	13.0	97.1	996	331.9	D	106.8	38.4	7 241	120.9	5.9	9.8	1 654
Butte-Silver Bow	2 489	0.9	25.2	308	84.4	10.1	27.3	8.9	2 034	32.4	0.2	1.1	325
Great Falls	5 945	13.9	55.9	600	163.0	D	D	D	4 123	57.9	3.4	4.3	772
Missoula	6 185	9.7	56.0	625	155.2	13.3	50.3	D	4 107	55.3	3.0	5.8	1 156
NEBRASKA	117 936	11.8	970.4	10 148	3 547.0	173.6	984.5	245.0	89 254	1 336.9	507.3	663.5	14 991
Grand Island	4 887	16.2	37.7	364	102.6	7.8	D	4.8	2 771	37.9	10.8	4.9	753
Lincoln	18 023	19.2	150.1	1 378	600.7	D	159.7	D	13 919	213.1	33.7	128.6	2 460
Omaha	38 875	26.0	339.7	3 130	1 772.6	66.8	453.5	132.8	42 228	695.7	124.1	52.0	5 644
NEVADA	81 491	21.0	923.8	8 308	10 192.2	5 417.5	1 186.5	261.9	205 709	3 405.7	1 426.4	397.6	9 312
Carson City	3 438	38.6	38.4	438	162.9	52.6	32.7	9.8	3 935	55.8	3.6	70.6	399
Las Vegas	20 443	24.4	237.9	2 157	2 121.6	937.2	327.9	145.0	43 107	754.1	1 224.3	21.5	2 717
North Las Vegas	1 735	28.4	18.4	122	252.3	D	28.3	0.0	5 345	89.9	0.4	1.1	76
Reno	15 174	12.6	195.2	1 879	1 652.1	731.3	221.9	79.9	35 154	566.0	28.6	36.1	2 518
Sparks	3 955	34.0	41.6	432	337.1	160.7	49.8	0.5	7 747	100.6	3.2	0.9	154
NEW HAMPSHIRE	102 082	47.7	1 121.6	8 439	3 031.2	249.3	756.1	234.4	68 191	1 136.3	518.0	412.4	6 707
Concord	5 094	38.2	57.8	446	205.1	7.6	57.5	37.4	4 105	84.2	2.3	71.3	484
Manchester	11 701	26.3	129.0	1 017	507.4	D	100.7	74.0	9 740	194.8	11.4	10.4	2 039
Nashua	10 655	60.2	124.1	679	324.1	32.6	83.8	20.3	7 415	136.2	254.9	2.8	743
Portsmouth	5 386	32.7	63.4	376	155.0	9.5	65.5	15.0	3 193	59.4	20.4	3.0	416
NEW JERSEY	566 214	26.9	6 467.2	59 624	32 175.1	4 059.5	5 833.2	2 252.1	595 807	11 940.6	4 124.0	3 533.3	71 985
Atlantic City	4 656	16.8	54.4	422	3 126.3	2 963.1	25.5	39.4	44 548	901.9	8.1	12.6	1 850
Bayonne	2 747	-2.7	28.5	356	110.7	D	34.6	5.1	2 878	44.7	21.4	3.9	4 204
Belleville township	1 824	2.5	21.6	185	74.8	1.8	29.1	D	1 577	27.6	0.2	0.7	2
Bergenfield borough	1 578	27.7	16.3	168	46.7	0.0	6.5	1.7	1 211	16.0	5.8	0.3	68
Bloomfield township	2 863	11.3	32.7	358	185.8	0.0	23.4	11.3	4 110	64.5	1.2	2.1	209
Camden	1 940	-0.4	20.4	229	126.9	D	45.2	16.3	2 269	54.1	303.2	14.2	2 081
Clifton	5 449	15.7	67.5	754	464.9	D	60.0	23.7	11 248	185.2	12.2	1.7	335
East Orange	1 567	-5.0	17.7	345	262.4	4.4	52.4	14.1	4 244	91.8	14.2	5.3	2 457
Elizabeth	4 788	7.1	59.3	570	217.9	25.0	53.2	17.4	4 586	80.2	15.7	5.3	584
Fair Lawn borough	1 939	11.4	26.6	430	203.9	D	71.5	8.6	3 588	74.0	5.4	0.2	159
Fort Lee borough	2 646	15.7	32.5	612	390.4	13.1	43.9	12.7	5 329	136.1	1.8	0.2	105
Garfield	1 779	67.7	35.9	151	32.0	0.0	4.1	0.6	790	10.3	0.5	0.3	50
Hackensack	6 105	15.3	71.3	926	529.9	D	102.1	104.9	10 015	201.4	9.7	2.1	986
Hoboken	1 927	46.8	18.2	215	93.8	D	6.9	6.9	1 369	40.4	11.9	2.5	121
Irvington township	2 162	12.3	21.9	260	94.9	0.0	26.2	D	2 425	38.9	5.3	2.8	33
Jersey City	10 005	28.2	113.3	935	390.3	D	82.5	46.4	7 909	145.0	5.8	16.8	6 713
Kearny town	2 052	25.4	25.1	235	99.8	D	16.0	4.1	1 663	27.6	1.1	0.2	116
Linden	2 465	7.3	25.9	255	116.1	D	18.3	3.6	2 420	37.6	15.4	0.2	97
Long Branch	1 745	16.8	18.7	237	75.6	1.0	40.9	2.3	1 409	31.3	1.1	1.2	91
Montclair township	2 946	45.8	31.9	542	202.8	D	60.0	17.4	3 374	74.1	0.5	3.8	186
Newark	10 972	15.9	119.1	1 113	970.6	56.8	82.1	227.4	17 366	351.2	78.4	229.3	6 347
New Brunswick	2 857	23.3	26.4	310	142.6	D	44.9	28.5	3 500	59.2	16.9	36.3	892
Nutley township	1 793	39.3	17.1	249	85.8	D	20.4	D	3 648	32.7	9.2	0.6	48
Orange township	NA	NA	NA	NA	NA	NA	NA	NA	NA	NA	0.0	1.3	177
Paramus borough	15 346	19.6	184.9	483	373.9	6.5	39.6	13.8	8 700	139.3	3.8	13.0	109
Passaic	1 694	-30.3	19.8	260	78.5	D	25.6	9.8	1 679	30.4	2.5	3.1	188
Paterson	3 810	-2.6	50.2	542	193.7	D	41.5	18.5	3 573	69.6	30.6	16.0	1 100
Perth Amboy	1 761	10.8	20.6	209	69.7	D	32.6	6.6	1 498	29.5	2.3	1.8	246
Plainfield	2 312	25.2	22.6	269	83.2	0.0	27.7	5.0	1 270	28.9	79.1	1.9	264
Rahway	1 465	11.6	20.4	159	61.9	1.2	16.1	13.7	1 174	26.5	11.2	0.3	138
Ridgewood village	1 823	-5.6	26.0	411	165.4	D	59.9	7.8	2 707	57.4	0.0	0.2	122
Sayreville borough	1 692	26.7	15.4	180	57.3	1.0	11.8	2.0	851	17.3	0.5	0.3	41
Trenton	3 405	-9.5	31.4	463	203.0	0.9	70.4	19.3	4 123	80.6	37.4	370.6	2 491
Union City	2 229	-5.3	24.4	311	58.3	D	16.3	8.2	1 136	16.4	1.1	3.3	117
Vineland	5 301	36.5	54.9	409	144.4	D	36.9	14.5	4 324	56.7	21.8	5.0	176
Westfield town	2 118	13.3	25.0	362	124.3	D	50.1	23.0	2 307	50.1	1.4	0.1	150
West New York town	1 837	6.3	21.6	216	51.8	0.0	22.1	5.8	1 193	19.7	0.3	0.7	71
West Orange township	3 480	4.5	36.7	535	237.3	D	62.7	48.5	4 683	98.8	1.2	0.6	112
NEW MEXICO	104 620	21.1	941.2	9 471	4 223.2	306.1	970.3	261.6	88 313	1 602.5	2 984.1	828.0	25 169
Albuquerque	39 858	33.0	378.1	3 815	D	D	498.0	154.6	D	D	1 491.3	80.7	8 072
Carlsbad	2 157	0.8	17.2	198	62.8	D	37.3	2.8	1 439	21.7	72.4	2.0	292
Clovis	4 812	73.4	29.0	239	44.7	4.4	19.1	2.8	1 161	15.1	0.4	1.3	120
Farmington	4 130	-0.4	42.0	345	96.5	D	25.3	4.7	2 551	30.6	7.6	1.9	325
Hobbs	2 533	-25.8	24.8	258	108.6	D	51.5	3.5	2 053	32.9	0.1	0.7	91
Las Cruces	6 293	17.8	54.4	548	169.7	D	55.1	D	4 547	64.7	47.7	20.6	516

1. For the period including March 12 of the year shown.

City	City government employment, 1985 (October): Total	City government employment, 1985 (October): Rates[1]	City government employment, 1985 (October): Percent education	Form of governments[2] (As of 1986)	City government finances, 1984–1985: General revenue: Total (Mil. dol.)	General revenue: Intergovernmental: Total (Mil. dol.)	General revenue: Intergovernmental: Percent from State government	General revenue: Taxes: Total (Mil. dol.)	Taxes: Per capita[3] (Dollars): Total	Taxes: Per capita[3] (Dollars): Property	Taxes: Per capita[3] (Dollars): Sales & gross receipts	General expenditures: Total (Mil. dol.)	General expenditures: Per capita[3] (Dol.): Total	General expenditures: Per capita[3] (Dol.): Capital outlays	Percent of total for–: Public welfare	Percent of total for–: Highways	Percent of total for–: Education
	100	101	102	103	104	105	106	107	108	109	110	111	112	113	114	115	116
MONTANA—Con.																	
Billings	776	96.6	0.0	2	42.7	5.4	49.5	10.4	129	111	0	57.4	715	336	0.0	9.3	0.0
Butte-Silver Bow	NA	NA	NA	1	24.4	5.3	33.0	13.2	397	365	0	21.2	634	26	3.2	12.4	21.2
Great Falls	457	79.7	0.0	2	20.8	4.7	49.8	7.1	123	103	0	18.1	316	33	0.0	13.8	0.0
Missoula	291	85.7	0.0	1	22.6	3.3	32.4	7.5	221	203	0	19.3	567	97	0.0	8.2	0.0
NEBRASKA	NA	NA	NA	NA	NA	NA	NA	NA	NA	NA	NA	NA	NA	NA	NA	NA	NA
Grand Island	373	95.4	0.0	1	13.2	3.0	70.9	4.1	105	83	13	12.4	316	56	0.0	21.9	0.0
Lincoln	3 113	170.1	0.0	1	113.2	19.1	70.7	39.1	214	123	75	108.4	592	149	0.0	14.4	NA
Omaha	3 126	89.5	0.0	1	179.9	39.8	46.7	101.7	291	140	131	176.0	504	94	0.0	14.2	NA
NEVADA	NA	NA	NA	NA	NA	NA	NA	NA	NA	NA	NA	NA	NA	NA	NA	NA	NA
Carson City	874	236.9	0.0	1	38.0	13.0	49.5	4.6	125	53	39	41.4	1 123	298	0.3	6.8	0.0
Las Vegas	1 471	76.8	0.0	2	87.3	41.8	87.8	26.5	139	48	41	94.0	491	67	0.0	9.7	0.0
North Las Vegas	456	90.7	0.0	2	19.9	10.4	75.3	3.3	66	24	23	23.8	474	69	0.0	11.5	0.0
Reno	1 072	97.1	0.0	2	66.9	23.1	79.3	19.4	176	48	27	60.3	546	91	0.0	7.4	0.0
Sparks	435	83.7	0.0	2	23.7	8.5	92.7	8.0	153	66	23	21.2	409	28	0.0	11.1	0.0
NEW HAMPSHIRE	NA	NA	NA	NA	NA	NA	NA	NA	NA	NA	NA	NA	NA	NA	NA	NA	NA
Concord	486	148.3	0.0	2	18.2	4.7	68.9	8.3	253	242	0	21.7	661	66	2.5	10.7	0.0
Manchester	2 766	284.3	51.0	1	79.9	19.9	51.9	57.4	590	584	0	79.8	821	0	1.4	9.8	37.0
Nashua	1 938	253.3	61.6	1	56.3	7.6	51.2	42.7	559	550	0	63.6	831	61	0.9	7.8	46.7
Portsmouth	931	358.5	61.8	2	30.8	6.9	43.5	19.3	742	728	0	36.8	1 417	340	1.6	3.9	42.4
NEW JERSEY	NA	NA	NA	NA	NA	NA	NA	NA	NA	NA	NA	NA	NA	NA	NA	NA	NA
Atlantic City	2 868	797.1	28.0	3	95.9	18.4	93.5	68.2	1 894	1 823	0	99.7	2 771	16	0.9	3.6	26.9
Bayonne	1 949	309.9	55.0	1	56.7	21.8	96.6	29.8	474	467	0	56.8	903	15	0.5	1.5	49.9
Belleville township	390	108.8	0.0	3	13.1	4.9	86.5	7.1	198	194	0	13.1	366	1	1.0	6.7	0.0
Bergenfield borough	224	89.0	0.0	1	7.7	2.1	87.6	5.2	208	204	0	7.9	312	14	0.3	14.6	0.0
Bloomfield township	515	108.1	0.0	1	17.2	5.7	86.2	10.6	223	218	0	16.9	355	7	2.9	3.7	0.0
Camden	1 150	138.9	0.0	1	47.7	22.6	90.3	17.7	214	208	0	46.9	567	19	3.3	6.2	0.0
Clifton	1 476	193.1	57.0	2	53.6	16.2	95.9	32.5	425	419	0	58.6	767	83	0.2	7.9	46.3
East Orange	2 510	324.2	54.1	1	88.5	49.0	98.2	35.0	451	446	0	89.8	1 160	18	4.6	1.1	50.0
Elizabeth	4 800	450.5	73.3	1	108.4	61.9	98.0	37.8	354	350	0	109.0	1 023	36	0.6	1.6	56.2
Fair Lawn borough	271	86.6	0.0	2	9.8	4.4	96.1	4.7	151	146	0	10.0	320	12	1.5	7.4	0.0
Fort Lee borough	302	92.8	0.0	1	11.7	1.9	92.8	8.8	269	260	0	12.4	381	41	0.3	8.5	0.0
Garfield	148	56.2	0.0	2	9.5	2.5	91.8	3.7	139	135	0	9.3	352	31	1.2	4.5	0.0
Hackensack	1 107	309.0	57.9	2	39.1	8.2	93.8	28.3	791	776	0	40.6	1 134	35	0.6	1.5	55.0
Hoboken	572	137.3	NA	1	41.9	24.3	96.7	13.6	326	316	0	41.6	998	28	0.5	1.4	55.4
Irvington township	624	100.3	0.0	1	21.0	7.2	80.2	11.4	183	176	0	19.9	319	0	1.3	8.4	0.0
Jersey City	9 391	427.9	48.8	1	319.9	162.8	97.5	84.0	383	371	0	379.0	1 727	149	1.3	1.1	40.7
Kearny town	428	122.5	0.0	1	22.1	18.9	98.7	1.7	50	20	0	20.7	593	71	0.8	1.5	0.0
Linden	722	191.5	0.0	1	24.2	20.8	98.7	1.3	33	27	0	30.1	799	69	0.7	12.0	0.0
Long Branch	301	102.0	0.0	1	11.2	3.6	92.2	6.4	215	206	0	10.2	345	24	0.5	14.2	0.0
Montclair township	1 469	381.7	59.9	2	44.2	11.1	96.3	29.7	771	754	0	44.0	1 143	64	0.5	4.4	58.5
Newark	5 056	159.9	0.0	1	271.0	159.0	83.2	73.2	232	163	16	257.8	815	23	13.8	0.5	0.3
New Brunswick	1 371	340.8	55.1	3	40.4	19.7	97.2	17.6	437	429	0	47.0	1 169	98	0.7	1.6	49.5
Nutley township	286	98.3	0.0	3	9.4	2.9	92.5	5.7	195	191	0	10.4	357	40	0.2	5.9	0.0
Orange township	1 014	321.0	63.0	1	30.9	17.0	97.1	11.8	372	366	0	29.5	933	3	0.8	2.7	49.7
Paramus borough	344	133.1	0.0	1	13.2	4.5	95.6	5.8	223	207	0	13.5	521	16	0.4	7.0	0.0
Passaic	505	93.7	0.0	2	22.5	8.9	89.7	12.0	223	216	0	17.6	326	2	0.6	5.4	0.0
Paterson	4 558	327.6	62.8	1	141.1	82.9	97.1	47.4	340	337	0	156.6	1 126	69	0.4	1.6	54.1
Perth Amboy	489	130.3	0.0	1	15.5	5.3	90.5	7.8	207	200	0	14.5	386	11	3.0	8.4	0.0
Plainfield	1 573	342.1	62.0	1	50.1	27.7	97.5	19.3	420	416	0	52.2	1 134	55	0.8	2.2	60.2
Rahway	386	144.7	0.0	1	11.6	3.6	91.0	6.8	257	252	0	11.2	418	25	0.1	15.1	0.0
Ridgewood village	364	146.5	0.0	2	10.6	2.4	94.1	6.3	255	245	0	12.0	483	94	0.1	8.7	0.0
Sayreville borough	336	97.9	0.0	1	14.3	11.4	99.0	0.9	28	17	0	12.9	376	10	0.4	11.7	0.0
Trenton	1 718	188.5	0.0	1	56.1	24.7	93.8	22.5	247	239	0	57.2	627	47	3.8	3.6	0.0
Union City	714	128.0	0.0	3	24.5	9.0	83.4	14.7	264	261	0	21.8	391	NA	2.3	3.8	0.0
Vineland	2 111	393.5	70.1	1	16.1	6.4	87.1	5.7	105	98	0	51.1	952	33	0.4	3.9	69.9
Westfield town	272	89.8	0.0	1	10.6	2.9	96.0	4.5	148	139	0	9.5	313	27	0.6	14.7	0.0
West New York town	1 235	302.9	51.8	3	37.3	20.4	95.4	15.9	390	386	0	39.4	967	57	0.3	3.3	54.7
West Orange township	399	97.9	0.0	1	18.6	5.0	91.9	10.4	255	248	0	16.2	397	20	0.2	7.0	0.0
NEW MEXICO	NA	NA	NA	NA	NA	NA	NA	NA	NA	NA	NA	NA	NA	NA	NA	NA	NA
Albuquerque	6 494	177.1	0.0	1	341.8	117.4	65.7	85.4	233	97	124	313.7	855	237	0.0	5.6	0.0
Carlsbad	312	112.0	0.0	2	12.0	6.7	76.0	3.3	118	10	106	10.9	391	83	0.0	26.9	0.0
Clovis	316	93.5	0.0	2	15.1	7.3	87.7	2.4	71	7	61	12.7	376	95	0.0	19.0	0.0
Farmington	728	186.4	0.0	2	156.7	10.0	78.9	7.9	202	9	187	95.7	2 452	146	0.0	4.6	0.0
Hobbs	410	117.6	0.0	2	21.9	11.3	93.6	4.5	128	17	106	20.0	572	257	0.0	47.2	0.0
Las Cruces	758	140.1	0.0	2	38.4	21.0	62.1	7.8	144	27	110	34.4	637	213	0.0	11.8	0.0

1. Per 10,000 population estimated as of July 1, 1986. 2. 1 = Mayor-council; 2 = Council-manager; 3 = Commission. Data subject to copyright. 3. Based on resident population estimated as of July 1, 1986.

City	City government finances, 1984–1985 (cont'd): General expenditure (cont'd): Percent of total for (cont'd): Health and hospitals	Police protection	Sewerage and sanitation	Parks and recreation	Housing and community development	Debt outstanding: Total (Mil. dol.)	Per capita[1] (Dollars)	Percent utility	Climate[2]: Average daily temperature (Degrees Fahrenheit): Mean: Jan.	July	Limits: Jan.[3]	July[4]	Annual precipitation (Inches)	Heating degree days[5]	Cooling degree days[5]	Typical monthly electric bills, 1986: Residential[6]: Total (Dollars)	Percent change, 1980–1986	Commercial[7] (Dollars)
	117	118	119	120	121	122	123	124	125	126	127	128	129	130	131	132	133	134
MONTANA—Con.																		
Billings	0.3	6.2	18.6	2.5	1.9	73.7	917	28.9	20.9	72.3	11.8	86.6	15.09	7 212	553	39.39	88.9	330.8
Butte-Silver Bow	6.4	9.3	8.5	3.6	3.5	3.2	95	0.0	15.5	63.0	3.7	80.1	11.73	9 613	107	39.39	88.9	330.8
Great Falls	0.0	12.7	13.0	5.6	8.1	31.7	553	49.5	18.7	69.3	9.2	84.2	15.24	7 766	391	39.39	88.9	330.8
Missoula	1.5	9.9	7.1	3.8	6.5	39.1	1 152	0.0	21.3	67.2	13.7	84.8	13.29	7 839	216	39.39	88.9	NA
NEBRASKA	NA	NA	NA	NA	NA	NA	NA	NA	NA	NA	NA	NA	NA	NA	NA	44.11	49.5	NA
Grand Island	0.7	10.0	10.2	7.2	4.1	100.2	2 562	89.4	20.6	76.6	9.9	88.8	23.31	6 482	1 028	47.43	12.9	NA
Lincoln	27.5	9.2	9.6	6.8	3.4	417.7	2 282	80.7	21.9	78.5	12.7	88.6	28.36	5 967	1 263	42.98	44.5	329.0
Omaha	0.9	13.8	19.2	7.7	7.2	172.9	495	0.0	20.2	77.7	10.2	88.5	30.34	6 194	1 166	44.76	64.1	321.0
NEVADA	NA	NA	NA	NA	NA	NA	NA	NA	NA	NA	NA	NA	NA	NA	NA	53.53	48.8	NA
Carson City	36.8	6.5	24.2	3.6	NA	29.7	806	32.9	33.5	69.7	20.5	89.1	10.79	5 766	373	66.91	43.0	NA
Las Vegas	0.0	22.2	13.5	5.1	2.3	23.3	122	0.0	44.6	90.3	33.0	104.5	4.19	2 532	3 029	47.63	48.4	400.3
North Las Vegas	0.1	19.3	13.3	7.0	8.9	10.7	214	41.3	44.6	90.3	33.0	104.5	4.19	2 532	3 029	47.78	48.9	NA
Reno	0.6	25.5	15.2	6.5	5.5	69.3	628	0.0	32.2	69.5	19.5	91.3	7.49	6 030	357	66.91	43.0	520.0
Sparks	0.0	16.9	21.9	7.0	0.0	24.7	476	0.0	32.2	69.5	19.5	91.3	7.49	6 030	357	66.91	43.0	NA
NEW HAMPSHIRE	NA	NA	NA	NA	NA	NA	NA	NA	NA	NA	NA	NA	NA	NA	NA	65.12	45.7	NA
Concord	0.8	9.9	17.8	4.8	0.0	40.8	1 244	15.6	19.9	69.5	9.0	82.6	36.53	7 482	353	51.99	17.7	557.5
Manchester	0.6	6.4	7.0	2.1	0.0	46.7	480	10.4	22.6	69.8	11.4	82.7	43.27	7 081	351	67.43	49.1	534.9
Nashua	0.8	8.7	4.9	1.4	0.0	27.1	354	0.0	22.6	69.8	11.4	82.7	43.27	7 081	351	67.43	49.1	534.9
Portsmouth	0.1	5.7	3.9	1.4	9.8	11.9	458	0.3	19.9	69.5	9.0	82.6	36.53	7 482	353	67.43	49.1	NA
NEW JERSEY	NA	NA	NA	NA	NA	NA	NA	NA	NA	NA	NA	NA	NA	NA	NA	74.83	60.5	NA
Atlantic City	1.6	20.9	2.6	2.5	0.0	30.5	848	1.0	31.8	74.4	22.9	84.0	41.93	5 086	792	70.85	46.4	NA
Bayonne	1.3	9.4	4.3	3.2	2.5	15.8	251	0.2	30.6	74.6	24.5	82.1	43.77	5 285	854	75.19	61.1	694.2
Belleville township	4.2	23.1	9.9	4.2	0.4	0.5	13	0.0	31.3	76.8	24.2	85.6	42.34	4 972	1 091	75.19	61.1	NA
Bergenfield borough	1.4	24.0	18.3	4.7	0.0	3.3	132	0.0	30.6	74.6	24.5	82.1	43.77	5 285	854	75.19	61.1	NA
Bloomfield township	3.6	22.1	11.7	2.2	0.0	6.8	143	8.5	31.3	76.8	24.2	85.6	42.34	4 972	1 091	75.19	61.1	NA
Camden	0.4	25.1	14.7	0.4	0.7	23.2	280	9.1	31.2	76.5	23.8	86.1	41.42	4 947	1 075	75.19	61.1	694.2
Clifton	0.9	8.4	8.3	1.5	0.1	31.0	405	NA	31.3	76.8	24.2	85.6	42.34	4 972	1 091	75.19	61.1	694.2
East Orange	1.0	6.4	3.9	1.6	0.0	33.5	432	0.0	31.3	76.8	24.2	85.6	42.34	4 972	1 091	75.19	61.1	694.2
Elizabeth	1.6	9.4	6.6	3.0	NA	53.6	503	0.0	30.6	74.6	24.5	82.1	43.77	5 285	854	75.19	61.1	694.2
Fair Lawn borough	1.7	18.9	20.6	6.8	0.0	4.9	156	0.0	30.6	74.6	24.5	82.1	43.77	5 285	854	75.19	61.1	NA
Fort Lee borough	1.6	22.5	20.6	4.3	0.0	11.0	338	0.0	30.6	74.6	24.5	82.1	43.77	5 285	854	75.19	61.1	NA
Garfield	0.9	18.7	44.9	6.8	0.0	3.3	126	11.8	31.3	76.8	24.2	85.6	42.34	4 972	1 091	75.19	61.1	NA
Hackensack	0.6	8.9	5.6	0.7	1.0	16.9	471	0.0	31.3	76.8	24.2	85.6	42.34	4 972	1 091	75.19	61.1	NA
Hoboken	1.1	9.5	6.1	0.6	0.0	10.9	262	8.8	30.6	74.6	24.5	82.1	43.77	5 285	854	75.19	61.1	NA
Irvington township	1.4	22.0	8.0	1.3	0.0	11.3	182	0.0	31.3	76.8	24.2	85.6	42.34	4 972	1 091	75.19	61.1	694.2
Jersey City	20.5	7.3	4.9	0.7	0.3	137.5	627	25.9	30.6	74.6	24.5	82.1	43.77	5 285	854	75.19	61.1	694.2
Kearny town	2.5	21.9	19.3	2.1	0.0	28.6	820	3.0	31.3	76.8	24.2	85.6	42.34	4 972	1 091	75.19	61.1	NA
Linden	1.2	14.9	7.6	5.6	0.0	14.8	394	0.0	31.3	76.8	24.2	85.6	42.34	4 972	1 091	75.19	61.1	NA
Long Branch	2.5	24.4	4.6	3.5	0.0	9.3	316	0.0	31.6	74.0	23.9	82.8	46.92	5 158	770	75.96	76.9	NA
Montclair township	1.2	5.5	5.1	1.9	0.0	20.6	534	5.8	31.3	76.8	24.2	85.6	42.34	4 972	1 091	75.19	61.1	NA
Newark	2.3	15.9	11.0	1.4	7.1	156.6	495	3.0	31.3	76.8	24.2	85.6	42.34	4 972	1 091	75.19	61.1	694.2
New Brunswick	0.5	9.2	8.1	2.1	0.0	29.4	730	15.4	30.2	74.7	22.0	85.2	45.50	5 239	832	75.19	61.1	NA
Nutley township	3.1	18.3	19.3	6.0	0.0	3.0	103	0.0	31.3	76.8	24.2	85.6	42.34	4 972	1 091	75.19	61.1	NA
Orange township	2.1	10.2	3.9	1.0	0.0	8.4	267	8.1	31.3	76.8	24.2	85.6	42.34	4 972	1 091	75.19	61.1	NA
Paramus borough	1.5	30.3	12.7	4.9	0.0	17.0	660	0.0	30.6	74.6	24.5	82.1	43.77	5 285	854	75.19	61.1	NA
Passaic	3.2	21.3	0.0	1.7	2.0	4.2	78	33.0	31.3	76.8	24.2	85.6	42.34	4 972	1 091	75.19	61.1	694.2
Paterson	0.6	7.3	5.7	1.0	2.8	88.7	638	3.5	31.3	76.8	24.2	85.6	42.34	4 972	1 091	75.19	61.1	694.2
Perth Amboy	1.5	21.3	12.3	2.5	0.0	10.2	271	23.8	30.2	74.7	22.0	85.2	45.50	5 239	832	75.19	61.1	NA
Plainfield	0.6	7.2	3.5	0.8	0.1	15.4	335	0.0	30.1	74.8	22.2	86.1	48.76	5 253	863	75.19	61.1	NA
Rahway	2.9	22.9	12.4	1.0	0.0	7.9	296	27.2	31.3	76.8	24.2	85.6	42.34	4 972	1 091	75.19	61.1	NA
Ridgewood village	1.0	15.1	8.4	3.6	0.0	11.2	449	27.8	31.3	76.8	24.2	85.6	42.34	4 972	1 091	75.19	61.1	NA
Sayreville borough	0.7	23.0	14.8	4.6	0.2	19.7	573	17.3	30.2	74.7	22.0	85.2	45.50	5 239	832	75.96	76.9	NA
Trenton	4.6	20.4	16.0	3.1	2.0	65.8	722	20.8	31.6	75.9	24.9	84.9	42.40	4 950	983	75.19	61.1	694.2
Union City	2.2	19.4	10.9	2.0	0.0	1.9	34	0.0	30.6	74.6	24.5	82.1	43.77	5 285	854	75.19	61.1	694.2
Vineland	1.9	6.2	0.9	0.8	2.3	29.2	544	32.8	31.8	75.8	23.1	85.6	42.95	4 945	981	54.12	23.2	516.8
Westfield town	1.6	19.7	6.5	11.3	1.4	1.5	50	0.0	31.3	76.8	24.2	85.6	42.34	4 972	1 091	75.19	61.1	NA
West New York town	0.6	9.1	2.4	3.3	2.4	11.9	293	0.0	30.6	74.6	24.5	82.1	43.77	5 285	854	75.19	61.1	NA
West Orange township	3.0	18.6	9.3	2.8	0.0	8.2	201	0.0	31.3	76.8	24.2	85.6	42.34	4 972	1 091	75.19	61.1	NA
NEW MEXICO	NA	NA	NA	NA	NA	NA	NA	NA	NA	NA	NA	NA	NA	NA	NA	62.73	45.0	NA
Albuquerque	1.1	10.7	21.5	8.4	3.5	818.1	2 231	17.6	34.8	78.8	22.3	92.8	8.12	4 414	1 254	68.14	40.5	547.8
Carlsbad	0.7	14.5	12.7	14.1	3.6	6.8	243	63.7	43.2	82.5	29.2	95.6	10.66	2 833	2 155	44.64	20.5	NA
Clovis	0.1	16.0	16.0	9.1	0.0	24.7	730	0.0	37.0	77.2	22.6	91.1	16.48	4 076	1 194	44.64	20.5	NA
Farmington	0.0	3.8	4.8	2.9	0.0	1 194.7	30 595	12.4	28.5	74.7	14.7	92.6	9.31	5 732	738	59.47	51.2	NA
Hobbs	1.6	16.1	3.2	5.5	0.0	30.8	884	2.1	42.9	80.1	28.0	93.3	14.77	2 881	1 838	44.64	38.3	NA
Las Cruces	0.0	11.2	36.3	7.0	3.5	34.7	641	24.5	42.5	80.3	27.9	95.2	11.18	3 059	1 756	64.17	87.2	526.2

1. Based on resident population estimated as of July 1, 1986. 2. Represents normal values based on the 30-year period, 1951–1980 (see text). 3. Average daily minimum. 4. Average daily maximum. 5. For definition, see text. 6. As of January 1; based on consumption of 750 kWh. 7. Based on billing demand of 30 kW and consumption of 6,000 kWh.

MSA/ CMSA Code[1]	State/ Place code	City	Land area,[2] 1990 (Sq. Km.)	Population: 1990: Total persons	Population: 1990: Rank	Population: 1990: Per sq. km.	Population: 1980	Population: Change 1980–1990: Number	Population: Change 1980–1990: Per-cent	Population characteristics, 1990: Percent: Race: White	Race: Black	Race: Am. Indian, Eskimo, Aleut	Race: Asian & Pacific Islander	Race: Other race	His-panic[3]	65 Years and over
			1	2	3	4	5	6	7	8	9	10	11	12	13	14
		NEW MEXICO—Con.														
...	35 0334	Roswell	75.5	44 654	558	591	39 676	4 978	12.5	81.68	2.56	0.71	0.60	14.45	36.49	16.0
7490	35 0360	Santa Fe	94.8	55 859	420	589	49 160	6 699	13.6	81.20	0.59	2.24	0.63	15.34	47.43	12.8
...	36 0000	NEW YORK	122 309.7	17 990 455	X	147	17 558 165	432 290	2.5	74.40	15.89	0.35	3.86	5.50	12.31	13.1
0160	36 0030	Albany	55.4	101 082	190	1 825	101 727	-645	-0.6	75.51	20.65	0.27	2.30	1.27	3.15	15.3
...	36 0180	Auburn	21.7	31 258	802	1 440	32 548	-1 290	-4.0	91.94	6.81	0.30	0.52	0.43	2.15	18.3
0960	36 0325	Binghamton	26.9	53 008	456	1 971	55 860	-2 852	-5.1	91.94	4.89	0.31	2.05	0.81	1.83	19.1
1282	36 0450	Buffalo	105.2	328 123	50	3 119	357 870	-29 747	-8.3	64.75	30.65	0.78	0.99	2.83	4.92	14.8
2335	36 1105	Elmira	19.0	33 724	747	1 775	35 327	-1 603	-4.5	85.44	12.34	0.30	0.57	1.35	2.67	15.0
5602	36 1285	Freeport village	11.9	39 894	631	3 352	38 272	1 622	4.2	56.45	32.30	0.41	1.27	9.57	21.20	10.4
5602	36 1545	Hempstead village	9.5	49 453	497	5 206	40 404	9 049	22.4	32.37	58.82	0.45	1.67	6.69	19.12	8.5
...	36 1745	Ithaca	14.1	29 541	833	2 095	28 732	809	2.8	81.80	6.49	0.35	10.01	1.35	3.62	7.7
3610	36 1755	Jamestown	22.9	34 681	722	1 514	35 775	-1 094	-3.1	94.92	2.60	0.50	0.45	1.53	2.98	17.2
5602	36 1980	Lindenhurst village	9.7	26 879	890	2 771	26 919	-40	-0.1	97.90	0.47	0.07	0.95	0.61	4.14	10.7
5602	36 2035	Long Beach	5.5	33 510	755	6 093	34 073	-563	-1.7	87.03	7.76	0.28	1.67	3.27	10.77	18.6
5602	36 2390	Mount Vernon	11.4	67 153	339	5 891	66 713	440	0.7	39.76	55.30	0.39	1.84	2.70	7.80	14.9
5602	36 2495	New Rochelle	26.8	67 265	338	2 510	70 794	-3 529	-5.0	76.03	18.09	0.12	2.92	2.84	10.77	17.3
5602	36 2505	New York	800.2	7 322 564	1	9 151	7 071 639	250 925	3.5	52.26	28.71	0.38	7.00	11.65	24.36	13.0
1282	36 2515	Niagara Falls	36.4	61 840	370	1 699	71 384	-9 544	-13.4	82.19	15.58	1.63	0.26	0.34	1.20	19.2
1282	36 2595	North Tonawanda	26.2	34 989	716	1 335	35 760	-771	-2.2	98.92	0.16	0.32	0.37	0.23	0.79	14.5
6460	36 2985	Poughkeepsie	13.3	28 844	847	2 169	29 757	-913	-3.1	65.38	31.47	0.35	1.52	1.27	3.77	15.8
6840	36 3100	Rochester	92.7	231 636	66	2 499	241 741	-10 105	-4.2	61.09	31.53	0.48	1.76	5.15	8.66	12.1
5602	36 3105	Rockville Centre village	8.5	24 727	928	2 909	25 412	-685	-2.7	93.76	3.91	0.07	1.11	1.15	5.69	17.5
8680	36 3120	Rome	194.1	44 350	561	228	43 826	524	1.2	89.42	7.95	0.24	1.27	1.12	3.86	13.7
0160	36 3285	Schenectady	28.1	65 566	351	2 333	67 972	-2 406	-3.5	88.60	8.69	0.29	1.06	1.36	2.69	17.1
8160	36 3565	Syracuse	65.0	163 860	106	2 521	170 105	-6 245	-3.7	74.98	20.33	1.26	2.17	1.25	2.89	14.9
0160	36 3625	Troy	27.0	54 269	439	2 010	56 638	-2 369	-4.2	88.35	7.61	0.23	3.02	0.80	2.07	14.0
8680	36 3690	Utica	42.3	68 637	329	1 623	75 632	-6 995	-9.2	86.66	10.49	0.26	1.12	1.47	3.40	19.4
5602	36 3710	Valley Stream village	8.9	33 946	739	3 814	35 769	-1 823	-5.1	94.95	0.44	0.04	3.61	0.97	4.46	17.1
...	36 3835	Watertown	22.5	29 429	835	1 308	27 861	1 568	5.6	93.79	3.81	0.51	0.82	1.07	2.02	14.9
5602	36 3970	White Plains	25.4	48 718	510	1 918	46 999	1 719	3.7	73.65	19.03	0.17	3.07	4.08	14.16	15.5
5602	36 4075	Yonkers	46.8	188 082	84	4 019	195 351	-7 269	-3.7	76.21	14.11	0.18	3.00	6.50	16.74	16.4
...	37 0000	NORTH CAROLINA	126 179.9	6 628 637	X	53	5 880 415	748 222	12.7	75.56	21.97	1.21	0.79	0.48	1.16	12.1
0480	37 0095	Asheville	90.5	61 607	373	681	54 022	7 585	14.0	79.09	19.81	0.27	0.61	0.22	0.87	20.1
1300	37 0390	Burlington	52.7	39 498	638	749	37 266	2 232	6.0	76.34	22.56	0.20	0.78	0.13	0.59	17.2
6640	37 0475	Chapel Hill town	42.8	38 719	652	905	32 421	6 298	19.4	82.32	12.53	0.32	4.35	0.48	1.57	8.6
1520	37 0480	Charlotte	451.3	395 934	35	877	315 474	80 460	25.5	65.61	31.78	0.36	1.82	0.43	1.41	9.8
6640	37 0750	Durham	179.4	136 611	130	761	101 149	35 462	35.1	51.71	45.71	0.24	1.96	0.38	1.18	11.3
2560	37 0910	Fayetteville	105.1	75 695	283	720	59 507	16 188	27.2	57.57	38.28	1.29	1.52	1.34	3.15	10.7
1520	37 0990	Gastonia	78.7	54 732	434	695	47 218	7 514	15.9	74.00	24.88	0.19	0.70	0.23	0.54	14.4
...	37 1035	Goldsboro	54.5	40 709	614	747	31 871	8 838	27.7	50.33	47.44	0.32	1.32	0.58	1.47	11.0
3120	37 1065	Greensboro	206.7	183 521	88	888	155 642	27 879	17.9	63.88	33.95	0.46	1.43	0.27	0.96	11.8
...	37 1070	Greenville	46.7	44 972	551	963	35 740	9 232	25.8	64.19	34.10	0.23	1.17	0.31	0.84	8.7
3120	37 1195	High Point	111.4	69 496	324	624	63 479	6 017	9.5	68.13	30.19	0.54	0.94	0.20	0.79	14.1
...	37 1355	Kinston	34.0	25 295	917	744	25 234	61	0.2	41.56	57.78	0.13	0.41	0.12	0.47	16.5
6640	37 2020	Raleigh	228.3	207 951	75	911	150 255	57 696	38.4	69.18	27.58	0.28	2.47	0.49	1.41	8.8
...	37 2115	Rocky Mount	64.7	48 997	504	757	41 526	7 471	18.0	49.62	49.59	0.25	0.39	0.14	0.54	13.1
9200	37 2755	Wilmington	76.9	55 530	422	722	44 000	11 530	26.2	64.94	33.88	0.30	0.57	0.31	0.86	15.9
...	37 2760	Wilson	47.9	36 930	688	771	34 424	2 506	7.3	52.36	46.92	0.11	0.31	0.31	0.70	13.8
3120	37 2785	Winston-Salem	184.2	143 485	119	779	131 885	11 600	8.8	59.47	39.26	0.23	0.76	0.28	0.86	14.2
...	38 0000	NORTH DAKOTA	178 695.2	638 800	X	4	652 717	-13 917	-2.1	94.57	0.55	4.06	0.54	0.27	0.73	14.3
1010	38 0195	Bismarck	63.0	49 256	501	782	44 485	4 771	10.7	96.67	0.11	2.56	0.44	0.22	0.66	11.4
2520	38 0545	Fargo	77.2	74 111	294	960	61 383	12 728	20.7	97.11	0.35	1.07	1.25	0.21	0.73	10.1
2985	38 0693	Grand Forks	37.4	49 425	498	1 322	43 765	5 660	12.9	95.49	0.80	2.26	1.07	0.39	1.19	9.2
...	38 1140	Minot	34.3	34 544	724	1 007	32 843	1 701	5.2	95.81	1.10	2.10	0.76	0.23	0.78	13.9
...	39 0000	OHIO	106 067.2	10 847 115	X	102	10 797 603	49 512	0.5	87.78	10.65	0.19	0.84	0.54	1.29	13.0
1692	39 0035	Akron	161.1	223 019	71	1 384	237 177	-14 158	-6.0	73.76	24.51	0.27	1.21	0.25	0.72	14.9
1692	39 0230	Barberton	19.7	27 623	872	1 402	29 751	-2 128	-7.2	94.08	5.26	0.27	0.29	0.10	0.33	16.9
2000	39 0288	Beavercreek village	66.7	33 626	751	504	31 589	2 037	6.4	96.35	0.92	0.18	2.34	0.21	1.02	9.1
8400	39 0480	Bowling Green	20.5	28 176	862	1 374	25 728	2 448	9.5	93.88	2.63	0.18	2.13	1.18	2.22	6.7
1692	39 0550	Brook Park	20.2	22 865	946	1 132	26 195	-3 330	-12.7	97.14	1.40	0.11	0.79	0.56	1.60	9.8
1692	39 0570	Brunswick	29.8	28 230	860	947	28 104	126	0.4	98.57	0.44	0.07	0.77	0.15	0.80	6.2
1320	39 0705	Canton	52.4	84 161	250	1 606	93 077	-8 916	-9.6	80.67	18.21	0.51	0.32	0.30	1.06	16.4
1642	39 0865	Cincinnati	200.0	364 040	45	1 820	385 409	-21 369	-5.5	60.51	37.94	0.18	1.11	0.26	0.66	13.9
1692	39 0900	Cleveland	199.5	505 616	23	2 534	573 822	-68 206	-11.9	49.49	46.56	0.31	1.01	2.63	4.59	14.0
1692	39 0905	Cleveland Heights	21.0	54 052	441	2 574	56 438	-2 386	-4.2	60.19	37.10	0.18	2.11	0.43	1.08	12.8
1840	39 0960	Columbus	494.5	632 910	16	1 280	565 032	67 878	12.0	74.42	22.55	0.23	2.37	0.42	1.07	9.2

1. MSA = Metropolitan Statistical Area. CMSA = Consolidated MSA. 2. Dry land or land partially or temporarily covered by water. 3. Hispanic persons may be of any race.

City	Households, 1990				Births, 1984			Deaths, 1984				Hospitals, 1985		
			Percent–		Number			Number		Rate			Beds	
	Number	Persons per house-hold	Female family house-holder[1]	One-person[2]	Total	To mothers under 20 yrs. old (Percent)	Rate[3]	Total	Infant[4]	Total[3]	Infant[5]	Number	Number	Rate[6]
	15	16	17	18	19	20	21	22	23	24	25	26	27	28
NEW MEXICO—Con.														
Roswell	16 195	2.67	12.8	24.9	838	18.5	18.3	427	11	9.3	13.1	4	374	848
Santa Fe	22 789	2.39	12.3	31.0	938	13.4	17.9	392	6	7.5	6.4	2	247	441
NEW YORK	6 639 322	2.63	13.8	27.2	251 053	10.4	14.2	170 762	2 765	9.6	11.0	328	114 928	647
Albany	42 121	2.17	14.7	38.6	1 461	14.7	14.7	1 279	20	12.9	13.7	6	2 424	2 498
Auburn	11 936	2.41	14.5	32.2	475	11.6	14.8	389	6	12.1	12.6	1	294	938
Binghamton	22 617	2.25	13.2	36.2	868	12.7	15.9	747	9	13.7	10.4	2	982	1 856
Buffalo	136 436	2.33	20.2	35.6	5 757	15.8	17.0	4 574	80	13.5	13.9	14	6 321	1 946
Elmira	12 428	2.46	17.2	32.1	544	20.6	16.3	423	7	12.6	12.9	3	749	2 308
Freeport village	13 240	3.00	15.4	22.4	607	13.8	15.2	336	6	8.4	9.9	1	52	129
Hempstead village	14 586	3.11	22.6	23.5	829	14.1	19.6	441	13	10.4	15.7	1	222	520
Ithaca	9 617	2.26	8.3	36.5	240	9.6	8.9	186	1	6.9	4.2	1	191	721
Jamestown	14 269	2.37	13.3	31.9	620	13.7	17.4	513	7	14.4	11.3	2	394	1 135
Lindenhurst village	8 600	3.11	10.9	14.6	437	4.1	16.3	262	3	9.7	6.9	0	0	0
Long Beach	13 592	2.35	10.2	34.3	443	8.8	12.9	616	6	18.0	13.5	1	370	1 125
Mount Vernon	25 175	2.64	20.5	29.0	1 039	14.4	15.6	685	12	10.3	11.5	1	245	358
New Rochelle	25 317	2.57	11.8	28.8	792	6.1	11.1	810	5	11.3	6.3	1	311	450
New York	2 819 401	2.54	18.0	32.9	109 610	12.1	15.3	74 762	1 420	10.4	13.0	88	46 187	636
Niagara Falls	25 970	2.35	16.5	33.1	1 126	15.4	16.9	804	10	12.1	8.9	1	423	655
North Tonawanda	13 635	2.56	10.6	26.0	496	10.7	14.1	353	3	10.0	6.0	1	237	686
Poughkeepsie	11 874	2.36	17.1	33.8	559	14.1	18.5	431	7	14.3	12.5	3	1 609	5 365
Rochester	93 607	2.37	20.6	35.3	5 164	16.5	21.3	2 741	68	11.3	13.2	8	4 056	1 719
Rockville Centre village	9 167	2.67	8.7	26.5	345	4.3	13.3	266	3	10.3	8.7	1	398	1 564
Rome	15 754	2.55	11.8	27.2	852	15.0	19.5	383	8	8.8	9.4	3	940	2 236
Schenectady	27 748	2.26	14.6	36.0	1 089	12.5	16.0	877	17	12.9	15.6	4	834	1 241
Syracuse	64 945	2.33	16.9	35.8	2 895	17.0	17.6	1 943	39	11.8	13.5	7	2 306	1 435
Troy	20 761	2.37	14.8	33.7	932	13.1	16.8	676	13	12.2	13.9	3	636	1 179
Utica	28 358	2.31	15.4	35.6	1 169	13.3	16.0	1 106	11	15.2	9.4	4	1 847	2 660
Valley Stream village	11 851	2.86	9.9	18.4	494	1.8	14.0	399	0	11.3	0.0	1	305	878
Watertown	11 430	2.50	13.6	29.3	475	16.6	17.4	375	7	13.7	14.7	2	682	2 522
White Plains	19 432	2.39	11.7	33.9	618	7.0	13.5	506	5	11.1	8.1	3	631	1 392
Yonkers	72 101	2.57	15.3	28.3	2 393	10.4	12.5	1 999	36	10.5	15.0	3	666	358
NORTH CAROLINA	2 517 026	2.54	12.3	23.7	86 042	16.5	14.0	51 046	1 066	8.3	12.4	166	32 008	506
Asheville	27 027	2.19	13.9	35.2	725	19.2	12.4	845	6	14.4	8.3	6	1 532	2 541
Burlington	16 627	2.35	13.7	28.9	529	19.8	14.2	390	7	10.5	13.2	2	369	1 002
Chapel Hill town	13 780	2.18	8.1	32.8	268	6.3	8.1	165	7	5.0	26.1	1	576	1 694
Charlotte	158 991	2.45	14.0	28.0	5 021	16.2	15.2	2 549	53	7.7	10.6	8	2 120	602
Durham	56 001	2.30	16.1	32.6	1 511	16.3	14.8	1 110	29	10.9	19.2	5	1 935	1 699
Fayetteville	29 639	2.47	16.8	26.3	1 658	17.9	25.1	638	32	9.6	19.3	4	1 142	1 507
Gastonia	20 983	2.56	17.0	24.5	785	27.4	16.2	586	23	12.1	29.3	1	340	643
Goldsboro	13 423	2.56	20.0	26.8	691	16.8	19.2	350	8	9.7	11.6	3	1 130	3 229
Greensboro	74 905	2.33	13.8	30.5	2 060	14.2	12.9	1 358	28	8.5	13.6	6	1 128	639
Greenville	17 017	2.35	14.4	30.6	476	10.9	12.8	261	11	7.0	23.1	2	636	1 642
High Point	27 529	2.46	16.6	27.0	867	21.1	13.0	737	17	11.0	19.6	1	318	478
Kinston	9 987	2.42	23.0	31.6	348	19.5	13.9	308	8	12.3	23.0	2	1 354	5 405
Raleigh	85 822	2.26	11.3	32.2	2 201	10.6	13.0	1 158	34	6.8	15.4	7	2 112	1 171
Rocky Mount	18 871	2.58	19.9	26.4	708	18.2	15.3	464	8	10.1	11.3	2	330	686
Wilmington	23 557	2.26	18.0	32.8	671	23.8	15.0	532	7	11.9	10.4	2	557	1 023
Wilson	14 461	2.44	20.5	29.4	496	20.0	14.1	358	5	10.2	10.1	1	277	790
Winston-Salem	59 919	2.27	16.7	33.8	1 980	16.3	13.8	1 406	23	9.8	11.6	6	1 629	1 100
NORTH DAKOTA	240 878	2.55	7.3	26.5	11 825	8.5	17.2	5 546	96	8.0	8.1	60	6 190	910
Bismarck	19 315	2.48	9.5	27.5	865	5.2	18.2	297	10	6.2	11.6	2	547	1 139
Fargo	30 149	2.32	7.7	31.4	1 053	4.7	16.0	472	5	7.2	4.7	4	1 037	1 525
Grand Forks	18 531	2.43	9.5	29.1	860	8.5	19.4	260	6	5.9	7.0	3	409	907
Minot	13 965	2.39	9.9	30.8	666	9.6	17.9	305	3	8.2	4.5	2	744	2 075
OHIO	4 087 546	2.59	11.7	25.0	158 519	13.4	14.7	96 996	1 653	9.0	10.4	235	60 245	560
Akron	89 923	2.42	16.6	30.8	3 451	15.3	15.2	2 633	45	11.6	13.0	5	1 848	832
Barberton	11 082	2.47	14.3	28.2	426	15.7	15.0	332	8	11.7	18.8	1	327	1 177
Beavercreek village	11 693	2.84	5.5	13.6	280	7.9	8.4	157	3	4.7	10.7	0	0	0
Bowling Green	8 502	2.39	6.8	29.0	211	7.1	8.6	98	1	4.0	4.7	1	125	498
Brook Park	7 892	2.88	11.6	16.1	289	11.4	11.4	171	2	6.7	6.9	0	0	0
Brunswick	9 032	3.09	8.1	12.7	459	5.7	16.0	138	2	4.8	4.4	0	0	0
Canton	33 452	2.44	17.0	31.2	1 508	19.8	16.9	1 061	17	11.9	11.3	2	1 242	1 426
Cincinnati	154 342	2.26	18.2	39.5	7 312	19.2	19.7	4 562	94	12.3	12.9	20	6 753	1 826
Cleveland	199 787	2.48	22.7	33.5	10 162	19.6	18.6	6 826	171	12.5	16.8	21	8 185	1 528
Cleveland Heights	21 012	2.52	13.0	29.5	714	4.8	12.5	533	8	9.4	11.2	0	0	0
Columbus	256 996	2.38	14.2	31.3	10 406	14.4	18.4	4 588	100	8.1	9.6	9	4 959	876

1. No spouse present. 2. Householder living alone. 3. Per 1,000 resident population estimated as of July 1 of the year shown. 4. Deaths of infants under 1 year old. 5. Deaths of infants under 1 year old per 1,000 live births. 6. Per 100,000 resident population estimated as of July 1, 1986.

City	Serious crimes known to police, 1985			Police officers, 1985		Educational attainment,[4] 1980		Money income						Housing, 1990		
	Number							Per capita[5]				Percent below poverty level, 1979				
								1985		1979						
	Total	Violent[1]	Rate[2]	Number	Rate[3]	Percent completing 12 years or more	Percent completing 16 years or more	Total (Dollars)	Percent of State average	Current dollars	Constant (1985) dollars	Persons	Families	Total units	Percent change, 1980–1990	Vacant units for sale or rent[6]
	29	30	31	32	33	34	35	36	37	38	39	40	41	42	43	44
NEW MEXICO—Con.																
Roswell	3 563	292	7 937	73	16.3	66.1	14.8	8 796	99.8	6 064	8 987	17.8	13.0	18 242	10.7	1 487
Santa Fe	4 790	440	8 857	101	18.7	77.3	30.0	11 002	124.8	7 170	10 626	14.1	11.1	24 681	22.9	1 006
NEW YORK	993 811	165 365	5 589	NA	NA	66.3	17.9	11 765	100.0	7 496	11 109	13.4	10.8	7 226 891	5.0	276 872
Albany	5 778	626	5 763	324	32.3	66.8	22.4	10 675	90.7	6 708	9 941	17.5	11.2	46 199	0.0	2 850
Auburn	775	36	2 358	NA	NA	57.2	9.3	8 763	74.5	5 782	8 569	12.8	9.4	12 682	3.2	510
Binghamton	2 547	43	4 585	135	24.3	63.4	13.9	10 231	87.0	6 495	9 626	15.5	10.1	24 626	1.5	1 436
Buffalo	24 055	3 411	7 077	993	29.2	53.8	11.1	8 840	75.1	5 929	8 787	20.7	17.0	151 971	-3.0	8 513
Elmira	2 286	58	6 594	86	24.8	64.0	10.3	7 856	66.8	5 161	7 649	17.5	14.9	13 301	-3.1	586
Freeport village	2 069	221	5 233	NA	NA	71.0	16.8	11 582	98.4	7 535	11 167	12.5	9.5	13 660	3.9	344
Hempstead village	1 490	228	3 635	NA	NA	70.0	15.8	10 765	91.5	7 236	10 724	14.4	11.5	15 117	1.6	447
Ithaca	1 954	82	6 830	NA	NA	81.0	43.1	7 675	65.2	4 923	7 296	32.3	11.1	10 075	5.5	322
Jamestown	1 728	47	4 770	74	20.4	62.2	10.3	8 785	74.7	5 807	8 606	13.6	9.6	15 461	-0.1	937
Lindenhurst village	NA	NA	NA	NA	NA	66.3	7.7	11 631	98.9	6 941	10 287	4.3	4.0	8 847	2.1	173
Long Beach	1 342	102	3 922	NA	NA	69.0	18.7	13 518	114.9	8 285	12 278	13.3	10.0	15 358	1.0	869
Mount Vernon	3 965	575	5 909	166	24.7	63.9	14.0	11 701	99.5	7 492	11 103	14.6	12.6	26 232	0.2	865
New Rochelle	2 405	228	3 356	182	25.4	74.6	27.3	17 018	144.6	10 343	15 328	8.0	6.2	26 398	0.7	908
New York	601 467	135 152	8 372	26 073	36.3	60.2	17.3	11 188	95.1	7 271	10 776	20.0	17.2	2 992 169	1.5	130 092
Niagara Falls	4 708	437	6 782	143	20.6	59.8	9.1	9 333	79.3	6 443	9 549	13.7	11.4	28 635	-3.0	1 277
North Tonawanda	980	22	2 730	54	15.0	66.5	10.6	10 191	86.6	6 966	10 324	7.0	5.0	14 001	5.5	224
Poughkeepsie	2 305	203	7 669	76	25.3	58.7	14.8	11 234	95.5	6 904	10 232	17.2	13.9	13 112	-0.4	730
Rochester	22 491	2 967	9 247	570	23.4	58.0	13.9	9 967	84.7	6 492	9 621	17.5	14.5	101 154	-1.5	5 833
Rockville Centre village	1 031	35	4 014	54	21.0	82.5	34.8	18 477	157.1	11 285	16 724	5.7	3.9	9 497	3.2	245
Rome	1 123	25	2 545	NA	NA	64.2	12.6	8 922	75.8	5 976	8 856	10.8	9.2	16 661	5.1	646
Schenectady	3 091	176	4 508	NA	NA	63.8	13.1	10 224	86.9	6 494	9 624	14.4	10.2	30 232	-0.1	1 618
Syracuse	12 050	1 013	7 318	423	25.7	63.6	17.9	9 644	82.0	6 232	9 236	18.4	12.9	71 502	-2.3	5 148
Troy	3 000	209	5 314	122	21.6	59.9	12.3	8 681	73.8	5 536	8 204	18.2	12.9	22 871	1.2	1 364
Utica	2 246	173	3 004	NA	NA	56.4	10.4	8 689	73.9	5 592	8 287	16.8	13.3	31 127	-2.1	1 791
Valley Stream village	NA	NA	NA	NA	NA	71.8	12.6	13 861	117.8	8 563	12 690	3.7	3.0	12 165	-0.6	228
Watertown	1 185	20	4 275	NA	NA	65.9	13.0	9 046	76.9	5 982	8 865	14.1	10.9	12 405	8.8	672
White Plains	2 660	175	5 702	201	43.1	75.0	29.4	17 637	149.9	10 876	16 118	7.8	6.2	20 714	7.3	1 092
Yonkers	9 235	984	4 816	NA	NA	67.5	17.6	13 112	111.4	8 339	12 358	9.8	8.2	75 562	-0.5	2 690
NORTH CAROLINA	257 792	26 327	4 121	NA	NA	54.8	13.2	9 517	100.0	6 132	9 088	14.8	11.6	2 818 193	19.3	136 083
Asheville	4 327	355	7 811	134	24.2	59.8	17.4	10 350	108.8	6 529	9 676	16.7	12.3	29 713	21.8	1 764
Burlington	1 978	177	5 088	85	21.9	56.1	15.9	10 886	114.4	7 055	10 456	11.6	7.5	17 696	14.9	887
Chapel Hill town	1 739	99	5 149	61	18.1	92.4	68.7	11 954	125.6	7 282	10 792	16.3	7.6	14 850	29.4	906
Charlotte	33 087	4 575	9 856	608	18.1	70.1	22.4	12 259	128.8	7 952	11 785	12.4	9.5	170 430	27.2	9 616
Durham	9 781	678	9 451	275	26.6	62.2	24.5	10 257	107.8	6 511	9 649	19.1	13.0	60 607	34.4	3 639
Fayetteville	7 739	824	12 086	173	27.0	65.5	19.6	9 695	101.9	6 180	9 159	21.8	18.7	31 712	27.3	1 468
Gastonia	5 654	419	11 271	123	24.5	49.1	11.7	10 024	105.3	6 651	9 857	13.6	11.1	22 196	19.7	982
Goldsboro	2 293	194	6 328	70	19.3	62.0	13.3	8 040	84.5	5 165	7 655	21.5	17.4	14 345	19.9	600
Greensboro	9 989	1 004	6 179	366	22.6	68.6	24.6	11 686	122.8	7 630	11 308	12.8	9.1	80 411	25.6	4 297
Greenville	2 818	208	7 398	87	22.8	65.9	28.7	8 781	92.3	5 858	8 682	24.5	15.6	18 054	31.5	840
High Point	4 855	485	7 366	156	23.7	51.8	13.5	10 419	109.5	6 804	10 084	14.0	11.5	29 408	17.3	1 489
Kinston	2 096	263	7 998	63	24.0	54.9	14.8	8 467	89.0	5 707	8 458	23.4	18.1	10 826	10.3	550
Raleigh	10 280	1 035	5 983	345	20.1	76.4	33.0	12 904	135.6	7 873	11 668	12.2	7.9	92 643	37.5	5 891
Rocky Mount	3 736	397	8 395	104	23.4	56.7	15.5	10 044	105.5	6 320	9 366	19.7	15.6	20 173	19.9	1 064
Wilmington	4 985	328	10 733	110	23.7	57.2	16.2	9 358	98.3	6 391	9 471	24.4	19.5	26 469	27.4	2 117
Wilson	NA	NA	NA	NA	NA	51.0	14.8	9 312	97.8	6 226	9 227	19.7	13.9	15 383	15.3	704
Winston-Salem	10 588	1 889	7 279	325	22.3	62.2	21.9	11 790	123.9	7 387	10 948	16.4	11.9	65 631	18.3	4 697
NORTH DAKOTA	18 354	322	2 679	NA	NA	66.4	14.8	9 635	100.0	6 417	9 510	12.6	9.8	276 340	6.4	15 360
Bismarck	2 576	36	5 515	65	13.9	78.2	23.8	11 836	122.8	8 159	12 092	6.6	4.3	20 038	13.2	548
Fargo	3 856	50	6 057	86	13.5	80.0	25.6	11 493	119.3	7 950	11 782	9.7	4.8	31 711	20.5	1 338
Grand Forks	2 108	35	4 692	59	13.1	76.5	26.3	10 526	109.2	7 037	10 429	12.0	7.8	19 589	12.3	924
Minot	1 626	13	4 782	57	16.8	74.9	18.8	10 099	104.8	7 197	10 666	9.3	7.5	15 040	12.8	843
OHIO	449 882	41 000	4 187	NA	NA	67.0	13.7	10 371	100.0	7 284	10 795	10.3	8.0	4 371 945	6.0	178 706
Akron	15 134	1 873	6 676	439	19.4	62.4	12.5	9 798	94.5	6 784	10 054	15.0	11.8	96 372	-0.3	4 480
Barberton	1 562	214	5 375	40	13.8	61.1	6.7	8 891	85.7	6 391	9 471	10.9	8.4	11 731	0.2	369
Beavercreek village	863	21	2 650	29	8.9	85.3	30.1	13 417	129.4	9 234	13 685	2.2	1.7	12 148	16.1	398
Bowling Green	826	36	3 272	31	12.3	88.2	42.2	7 599	73.3	5 537	8 206	26.0	5.9	8 964	17.2	413
Brook Park	896	29	3 516	42	16.5	69.1	6.1	10 260	98.9	7 541	11 176	3.4	2.9	8 036	1.7	125
Brunswick	386	30	1 357	24	8.4	76.5	13.1	10 668	102.9	7 634	11 314	2.9	2.8	9 444	10.4	280
Canton	6 117	563	6 760	172	19.0	57.8	8.5	8 731	84.2	6 347	9 406	15.5	12.2	36 527	-7.5	2 202
Cincinnati	28 533	3 275	7 707	883	23.9	57.9	17.6	10 247	98.8	6 874	10 187	19.7	16.0	169 088	-2.1	11 558
Cleveland	43 071	6 580	7 887	1 742	31.9	50.9	6.4	8 018	77.3	5 770	8 551	22.1	18.8	224 311	-6.8	17 358
Cleveland Heights	2 064	53	3 717	NA	NA	83.4	39.6	13 233	127.6	9 233	13 683	7.5	4.8	21 862	2.1	693
Columbus	43 374	4 392	7 668	1 223	21.6	68.9	18.6	9 909	95.5	6 783	10 052	16.5	12.1	278 084	14.9	16 781

1. Includes murder and nonnegligent manslaughter, forcible rape, robbery, and aggravated assault. 2. Per 100,000 resident population estimated for 1985 by the FBI. 3. Per 10,000 resident population estimated for 1985 by the FBI. 4. Persons 25 years old or older. 5. Based on the resident population estimated as of July 1, 1988 for 1987 data and enumerated as of April 1, 1980 for 1979 data. 6. Also includes units rented or sold, but not occupied.

City	Housing, 1990 (cont'd) — Occupied units — Total	Percent with more than 1 person per room	Owner-occupied — Percent of total	Owner-occupied — Median value[1] (Dollars)	Median rent[2] (Dollars)	Construction authorized by building permits, 1990 — New private housing units — Number	Value ($1,000)	Percent single family	Non-residential, value ($1,000)	Civilian labor force, 1990 — Total	Percent change, 1989–1990	Unemployment — Total	Rate[3]
	45	46	47	48	49	50	51	52	53	54	55	56	57
NEW MEXICO—Con.													
Roswell	16 195	7.0	69.1	44 600	274	67	5 134	100.0	1 977	18 056	-1.3	963	5.3
Santa Fe	22 789	4.7	59.6	99 000	437	483	52 281	67.7	7 448	38 266	4.1	1 533	4.0
NEW YORK	6 639 322	6.5	52.2	131 600	428	36 637	2 892 990	71.0	1 687 133	8 673 000	-0.1	451 000	5.2
Albany	42 121	2.2	38.3	101 800	388	162	10 233	35.2	16 630	53 476	0.7	1 790	3.3
Auburn	11 936	1.4	52.0	53 600	312	18	555	44.4	4 720	14 994	0.5	1 074	7.2
Binghamton	22 617	1.4	44.4	71 500	316	12	844	100.0	236	25 356	-3.0	1 289	5.1
Buffalo	136 436	2.1	43.1	46 700	255	128	7 485	59.4	17 513	146 707	-1.2	9 962	6.8
Elmira	12 428	2.0	48.1	43 600	282	9	807	100.0	3 588	14 322	0.2	838	5.9
Freeport village	13 240	9.9	65.2	170 800	595	9	914	100.0	12 705	20 885	-2.2	941	4.5
Hempstead village	14 586	16.6	45.4	156 600	602	10	650	100.0	1 715	22 353	-2.3	1 187	5.3
Ithaca	9 617	2.7	28.9	95 600	444	39	1 641	23.1	18 744	17 853	2.1	447	2.5
Jamestown	14 269	1.3	51.9	43 300	243	5	281	100.0	306	15 689	-0.8	863	5.5
Lindenhurst village	8 600	2.4	80.5	156 800	654	5	543	100.0	78	14 911	-2.2	796	5.3
Long Beach	13 592	6.2	50.9	187 600	678	31	1 897	29.0	1 400	17 138	-2.2	774	4.5
Mount Vernon	25 175	8.6	36.8	227 200	480	10	579	20.0	842	35 429	-1.9	1 358	3.8
New Rochelle	25 317	5.2	51.6	321 400	527	13	2 670	100.0	1 162	39 432	-1.9	1 445	3.7
New York	2 819 401	12.3	28.6	189 600	448	6 858	519 928	18.3	169 369	3 339 000	1.4	228 000	6.8
Niagara Falls	25 970	1.7	56.0	45 100	257	12	715	100.0	18 502	29 574	-0.2	1 827	6.2
North Tonawanda	13 635	1.3	67.9	68 100	331	68	5 895	69.1	2 568	16 096	0.0	822	5.1
Poughkeepsie	11 874	4.6	40.2	128 700	459	44	3 644	6.8	40	15 145	-1.2	781	5.2
Rochester	93 607	2.9	44.0	65 200	377	193	7 635	52.3	43 605	118 045	-0.9	6 244	5.3
Rockville Centre village	9 167	2.0	68.3	278 900	565	1	200	100.0	2 795	13 618	-2.1	363	2.7
Rome	15 754	2.2	53.4	69 200	325	52	1 823	23.1	1 646	16 201	-0.7	848	5.2
Schenectady	27 748	1.4	46.6	82 100	346	95	2 814	28.4	1 270	33 968	1.0	1 582	4.7
Syracuse	64 945	2.7	41.1	67 600	347	63	2 967	68.3	74 486	82 952	0.6	3 529	4.3
Troy	20 761	2.2	39.6	84 400	325	101	5 134	54.5	2 774	26 504	0.8	1 374	5.2
Utica	28 358	1.7	48.9	65 900	271	53	2 307	28.3	4 614	31 205	-0.7	1 589	5.1
Valley Stream village	11 851	1.6	81.1	187 300	686	10	939	100.0	90	19 535	-2.1	606	3.1
Watertown	11 430	1.9	45.5	60 100	340	53	2 291	22.6	543	15 076	-3.1	1 069	7.1
White Plains	19 432	6.1	51.6	296 000	545	152	14 319	15.1	500	27 381	-1.9	753	2.8
Yonkers	72 101	6.9	43.5	228 100	482	273	24 333	47.3	1 529	103 214	-2.0	4 574	4.4
NORTH CAROLINA	2 517 026	2.9	68.0	65 800	284	41 504	2 805 340	80.2	1 674 605	3 401 000	0.3	139 000	4.1
Asheville	27 027	1.6	56.6	57 000	283	88	5 971	95.5	5 451	29 865	2.2	1 169	3.9
Burlington	16 627	1.8	61.8	66 000	292	75	4 856	72.0	26 493	24 729	-1.0	742	3.0
Chapel Hill town	13 780	1.8	40.5	141 100	413	211	21 291	92.4	1 124	19 913	0.6	360	1.8
Charlotte	158 991	3.3	55.0	81 300	377	NA	NA	NA	NA	221 108	0.6	6 855	3.1
Durham	56 001	3.1	44.2	80 600	353	1 252	86 408	50.0	65 812	65 195	0.5	1 911	2.9
Fayetteville	29 639	3.1	54.2	67 900	309	309	22 200	70.2	16 966	27 304	-1.9	1 118	4.1
Gastonia	20 983	3.5	58.2	60 200	272	534	34 334	53.9	10 457	28 824	1.6	1 272	4.4
Goldsboro	13 423	3.9	40.2	55 300	235	107	5 418	38.3	8 722	12 603	1.9	776	6.2
Greensboro	74 905	2.4	53.7	78 500	358	748	44 221	73.5	49 533	93 241	0.0	3 755	4.0
Greenville	17 017	3.6	42.1	73 300	290	807	35 167	32.7	40 138	24 058	1.1	894	3.7
High Point	27 529	2.5	54.4	65 200	279	496	37 599	87.9	53 235	37 215	-0.1	1 373	3.7
Kinston	9 987	3.7	52.0	54 000	176	77	3 654	66.2	9 624	11 610	1.4	710	6.1
Raleigh	85 822	2.6	46.9	96 600	394	1 931	104 923	55.2	121 061	121 200	1.0	3 498	2.9
Rocky Mount	18 871	4.2	52.6	60 300	234	264	17 641	67.8	18 203	22 301	-0.9	1 152	5.2
Wilmington	23 557	2.5	47.1	63 300	304	NA	NA	NA	NA	25 819	0.2	1 357	5.3
Wilson	14 461	3.8	49.3	64 500	222	214	13 264	73.8	5 385	19 196	4.7	1 625	8.5
Winston-Salem	59 919	2.3	51.8	69 600	301	427	27 528	70.5	49 004	75 519	-0.1	3 509	4.6
NORTH DAKOTA	240 878	2.0	65.6	50 800	266	1 512	88 505	56.7	55 028	325 000	-1.8	13 000	3.9
Bismarck	19 315	1.4	60.7	67 900	316	299	19 693	60.2	6 463	29 096	0.3	1 017	3.5
Fargo	30 149	1.7	48.1	70 300	321	717	34 421	32.4	12 542	45 279	0.6	1 032	2.3
Grand Forks	18 531	2.0	48.7	64 700	320	66	5 937	93.9	8 436	27 966	-1.0	1 008	3.6
Minot	13 965	1.6	60.2	56 200	279	32	2 210	81.2	3 045	17 284	-1.0	698	4.0
OHIO	4 087 546	1.8	67.5	63 500	296	38 491	3 039 006	68.6	1 676 680	5 433 000	0.3	307 000	5.7
Akron	89 923	1.6	58.7	43 800	281	253	16 836	56.9	18 600	111 533	0.1	7 301	6.5
Barberton	11 082	1.5	64.3	44 000	255	36	2 943	100.0	1 279	14 166	0.1	924	6.5
Beavercreek village	11 693	0.5	86.1	97 100	467	NA	NA	NA	NA	16 686	-0.5	562	3.4
Bowling Green	8 502	2.8	42.2	81 700	347	NA	NA	NA	NA	NA	NA	NA	NA
Brook Park	7 892	1.9	85.5	71 500	390	18	1 290	100.0	6 266	13 796	0.1	643	4.7
Brunswick	9 032	1.2	81.0	83 700	406	170	15 037	71.8	4 220	15 321	0.3	794	5.2
Canton	33 452	1.6	57.3	37 700	233	19	1 585	100.0	3 879	43 069	-0.2	3 687	8.6
Cincinnati	154 342	3.8	38.3	61 900	283	528	31 050	25.8	104 301	204 491	1.0	10 646	5.2
Cleveland	199 787	2.9	47.9	40 900	237	225	10 881	31.6	100 034	244 682	0.1	18 338	7.5
Cleveland Heights	21 012	1.2	62.6	71 500	423	2	700	100.0	82	29 755	0.2	962	3.2
Columbus	256 996	2.3	46.6	66 000	348	4 676	204 696	45.1	254 707	340 774	0.7	15 398	4.5

1. Specified owner-occupied units. 2. Specified renter-occupied units. 3. Percent of total civilian labor force.

City	Employed,[1] 1980			Manufactures, 1987										
		Rate per 1,000 employees		Establishments		All employees			Production workers					
											Wages			
	Total	Professional, specialty, and technical	Precision production, craft, and operators	Total	Percent with 20 or more employees	Number (1,000)	Percent change, 1982–1987	Annual payroll (Mil. dol.)	Number (1,000)	Work-hours (Millions)	Total (Mil. dol.)	Average per production worker (Dollars)	Value added by manufacture (Mil. dol.)	Value of shipments (Mil. dol.)	New capital expenditures (Mil. dol.)
	58	59	60	61	62	63	64	65	66	67	68	69	70	71	72
NEW MEXICO—Con.															
Roswell	14 641	154.4	192.2	39	25.6	D	D	D	D	D	D	D	D	D	D
Santa Fe	22 183	237.7	122.7	95	13.7	1.2	9.1	21.7	0.8	1.5	11.8	14 750	51.4	82.4	D
NEW YORK	7 440 768	174.7	185.1	29 608	32.1	1 278.7	-9.9	33 915.8	723.3	1 403.5	14 408.2	19 920	80 033.3	145 656.5	4 296.5
Albany	45 602	213.7	101.4	106	34.0	4.7	6.8	123.8	2.3	4.5	46.7	20 304	390.0	616.4	18.6
Auburn	12 513	140.7	251.8	59	40.7	3.5	-2.8	87.4	2.1	4.4	46.4	22 095	209.6	427.4	14.4
Binghamton	23 957	180.7	193.6	95	40.0	D	D	D	D	D	D	D	D	D	D
Buffalo	131 329	146.0	239.9	591	39.3	34.9	-5.4	922.4	24.1	48.4	586.9	24 353	2 339.8	4 794.2	95.7
Elmira	12 394	169.7	198.6	45	42.2	3.7	-19.6	75.9	2.4	4.5	43.8	18 250	173.6	287.3	8.8
Freeport village	17 453	143.5	202.0	133	36.1	3.5	0.0	77.4	2.5	5.8	43.0	17 200	189.5	412.0	8.4
Hempstead village	18 519	158.0	155.5	55	27.3	0.8	0.0	15.7	0.6	1.1	9.1	15 167	40.2	76.7	1.7
Ithaca	12 524	325.9	79.4	74	24.3	2.0	-23.1	45.5	1.2	2.4	20.4	17 000	97.3	180.0	5.3
Jamestown	14 599	130.4	284.6	95	40.0	4.8	-11.1	105.7	3.2	6.7	69.7	21 781	213.7	373.7	10.5
Lindenhurst village	11 975	102.8	258.9	85	28.2	1.8	-5.3	31.5	1.3	2.5	20.3	15 615	62.5	117.4	2.9
Long Beach	14 321	161.9	134.3	NA	NA	NA	NA	NA	NA	NA	NA	NA	NA	NA	NA
Mount Vernon	31 245	146.8	187.8	207	38.2	7.5	-13.8	171.6	5.2	10.7	90.3	17 365	439.5	867.1	14.2
New Rochelle	34 839	200.1	138.5	96	34.4	3.1	-13.9	81.2	1.8	3.7	34.1	18 944	158.1	349.5	5.0
New York	2 918 183	168.7	161.3	14 595	30.9	436.1	-17.6	10 530.1	245.6	455.2	3 993.9	16 262	24 542.8	44 693.6	697.6
Niagara Falls	28 602	122.6	260.4	76	51.3	7.4	-31.5	228.7	4.3	8.6	117.5	27 326	711.0	1 273.4	37.7
North Tonawanda	15 745	141.4	297.6	75	41.3	D	D	D	D	D	D	D	D	D	D
Poughkeepsie	12 141	186.6	198.8	56	42.9	D	D	D	D	D	D	D	D	D	D
Rochester	101 003	165.1	265.7	594	35.7	72.3	-17.0	2 331.7	36.2	74.0	972.2	26 856	5 249.2	8 269.5	521.8
Rockville Centre village	11 599	256.6	89.9	40	27.5	0.7	16.7	12.1	0.4	0.7	5.6	14 000	28.3	44.4	0.9
Rome	14 664	166.1	212.1	44	27.3	2.4	-35.1	56.5	1.5	2.9	32.6	21 733	96.5	310.5	D
Schenectady	28 222	174.6	184.2	83	31.3	12.3	D	345.5	4.6	10.5	119.4	25 957	570.9	895.0	13.1
Syracuse	70 437	189.8	185.8	233	39.1	21.9	-13.8	678.6	9.9	19.2	237.7	24 010	1 069.5	2 056.1	64.6
Troy	21 990	160.5	172.7	58	31.0	2.3	9.5	45.7	1.0	1.7	19.3	19 300	119.3	215.9	5.8
Utica	28 286	157.6	207.8	97	30.9	9.3	16.3	249.3	5.1	10.3	104.7	20 529	525.3	880.6	22.8
Valley Stream village	16 564	116.6	184.0	80	21.2	2.2	10.0	46.7	1.7	3.9	34.1	20 059	90.3	151.7	2.4
Watertown	10 702	174.5	208.5	35	37.1	D	D	D	D	D	D	D	D	D	D
White Plains	24 422	219.1	97.0	90	38.9	10.7	24.4	490.9	1.1	2.1	18.4	16 727	133.1	219.8	D
Yonkers	90 467	164.6	172.2	200	32.0	5.9	-18.1	142.7	4.1	8.5	85.3	20 805	322.2	812.9	21.2
NORTH CAROLINA	2 607 925	128.7	306.1	10 995	43.4	842.4	5.4	16 293.4	637.3	1 258.8	10 293.0	16 151	47 007.4	95 317.3	2 958.7
Asheville	23 060	166.3	217.5	134	43.3	6.7	-4.3	129.5	4.7	9.3	77.3	16 447	376.0	677.2	D
Burlington	18 797	139.5	314.6	131	52.7	10.4	11.8	173.8	8.2	15.4	113.4	13 829	380.2	945.4	28.3
Chapel Hill town	14 195	451.6	40.6	31	19.4	0.5	NA	6.7	0.3	0.4	2.8	9 333	16.2	24.2	D
Charlotte	161 107	157.0	172.9	856	34.6	44.0	11.4	1 114.4	22.9	46.3	437.7	19 114	2 079.0	4 969.5	172.2
Durham	47 014	244.1	157.5	131	33.6	D	D	D	D	D	D	D	D	D	D
Fayetteville	21 138	192.8	158.1	83	50.6	6.9	23.2	142.2	5.0	10.1	90.6	18 120	591.6	1 346.2	55.8
Gastonia	22 765	103.5	361.4	222	41.4	14.6	6.6	285.0	11.3	23.9	198.6	17 575	668.2	1 377.2	36.8
Goldsboro	10 124	164.3	229.6	50	52.0	5.0	16.3	80.1	3.7	7.2	46.7	12 622	174.2	326.5	12.3
Greensboro	75 694	164.3	192.8	396	43.4	26.8	11.2	656.1	16.2	33.6	332.8	20 543	2 258.8	3 679.9	71.4
Greenville	16 197	233.5	136.3	49	34.7	D	D	D	D	D	D	D	D	D	D
High Point	30 312	104.5	332.3	371	52.8	25.0	14.2	454.2	19.7	38.1	294.4	14 944	932.0	1 845.0	47.8
Kinston	10 067	165.6	239.7	42	64.3	D	D	D	D	D	D	D	D	D	D
Raleigh	76 191	238.1	117.8	273	28.6	12.9	7.5	298.9	8.0	16.3	147.9	18 488	819.9	1 507.5	41.6
Rocky Mount	17 917	142.8	251.8	73	57.5	8.9	36.9	144.9	7.4	15.1	104.6	14 135	406.1	908.2	D
Wilmington	17 705	153.8	208.8	107	34.6	D	D	D	D	D	D	D	D	D	D
Wilson	14 678	144.4	240.8	69	46.4	5.0	4.2	89.8	3.8	7.8	54.8	14 421	217.9	1 015.7	11.2
Winston-Salem	59 205	193.1	215.3	234	45.3	39.7	0.3	1 100.6	22.3	38.6	544.5	24 417	5 187.3	8 145.8	327.1
NORTH DAKOTA	272 620	141.5	151.6	627	22.2	15.4	4.1	310.4	10.4	20.4	180.1	17 317	979.0	2 574.0	47.0
Bismarck	23 094	184.6	139.5	53	24.5	D	D	D	D	D	D	D	D	D	D
Fargo	31 250	199.6	135.4	79	34.2	3.1	14.8	59.3	2.1	4.0	34.5	16 429	176.7	386.7	6.8
Grand Forks	20 553	200.5	128.0	36	27.8	1.3	30.0	25.7	1.0	2.0	16.3	16 300	93.8	191.6	2.6
Minot	14 610	160.8	146.8	33	33.3	D	D	D	D	D	D	D	D	D	D
OHIO	4 558 442	146.6	253.5	17 544	39.2	1 100.2	-0.7	30 765.2	713.4	1 447.9	17 490.4	24 517	71 707.4	158 559.9	4 742.2
Akron	95 086	147.9	232.2	420	37.1	28.8	-8.0	1 037.4	11.5	21.2	241.9	21 035	1 131.3	1 799.5	56.5
Barberton	12 080	115.6	296.9	62	43.5	5.5	-28.6	132.9	3.6	6.3	73.3	20 361	259.6	489.3	13.2
Beavercreek village	13 772	243.5	192.9	NA	NA	NA	NA	NA	NA	NA	NA	NA	NA	NA	NA
Bowling Green	11 119	257.1	95.9	34	44.1	2.1	50.0	44.8	1.3	2.5	22.9	17 615	142.0	241.1	6.4
Brook Park	12 427	93.1	286.1	61	54.1	9.4	-3.1	388.0	7.7	17.0	313.5	40 714	802.3	2 048.9	D
Brunswick	12 338	135.5	284.2	NA	NA	NA	NA	NA	NA	NA	NA	NA	NA	NA	NA
Canton	36 931	129.9	268.9	218	34.9	19.3	-17.5	541.5	13.4	27.7	339.5	25 336	1 483.4	2 877.4	44.7
Cincinnati	159 396	185.5	184.6	843	41.2	57.8	-6.8	1 722.4	24.7	49.0	554.7	22 457	3 349.8	6 041.0	167.8
Cleveland	213 852	101.2	283.1	1 598	36.5	75.6	-18.3	2 110.4	43.6	88.4	1 014.5	23 268	3 974.6	8 083.7	235.6
Cleveland Heights	27 204	337.2	132.6	NA	NA	NA	NA	NA	NA	NA	NA	NA	NA	NA	NA
Columbus	261 852	172.2	168.7	747	40.2	47.1	-6.7	1 309.8	28.9	58.1	679.0	23 495	3 353.0	6 228.2	180.6

1. Persons 16 years old and over.

City	Wholesale trade, 1987: Establishments	Wholesale trade, 1987: Sales (Mil. dol.)	Wholesale trade, 1987: Paid employees[1]	Wholesale trade, 1987: Annual payroll ($1,000)	Retail trade–all establishments, 1987: Number	Retail trade–all establishments, 1987: Sales: Total (Mil. dol.)	Retail trade–all establishments, 1987: Sales: Percent change, 1982–1987	Retail trade–all establishments, 1987: Sales: Per capita[2] (Dollars)	Retail trade–establishments with payroll, 1987: Number	Retail trade–establishments with payroll, 1987: Sales: Total (Mil. dol.)	Sales: Per capita[2] (Dollars): General merchandise group stores	Sales: Per capita[2] (Dollars): Food stores	Sales: Per capita[2] (Dollars): Apparel and accessory stores	Sales: Per capita[2] (Dollars): Eating and drinking places
	73	74	75	76	77	78	79	80	81	82	83	84	85	86
NEW MEXICO—Con.														
Roswell	86	353.5	1 479	19 136	526	267.8	-3.1	6 071	326	257.6	771	1 446	250	627
Santa Fe	112	D	D	D	1 101	624.7	43.4	11 159	711	602.7	1 343	1 578	D	D
NEW YORK	41 765	283 745.4	466 027	12 644 098	171 579	106 452.7	47.3	5 990	110 562	103 212.2	646	1 198	422	590
Albany	270	1 477.3	4 368	110 313	1 116	964.3	100.1	9 939	867	951.4	1 678	1 381	651	1 037
Auburn	72	128.0	627	11 438	423	285.4	37.0	9 104	285	278.7	D	2 432	705	623
Binghamton	135	304.5	1 777	34 011	679	465.7	33.8	8 802	446	453.1	1 080	1 889	212	801
Buffalo	667	2 729.3	9 479	209 477	2 674	1 323.1	24.7	4 073	1 875	1 289.2	273	1 249	170	552
Elmira	77	201.7	1 138	21 602	348	245.2	35.6	7 556	265	241.5	715	1 638	230	657
Freeport village	128	406.4	1 440	33 027	364	275.5	71.4	6 833	262	270.7	D	955	95	567
Hempstead village	90	285.5	1 411	40 800	318	480.7	39.2	11 250	249	477.5	D	1 307	280	324
Ithaca	53	100.2	488	10 095	596	388.7	55.5	14 679	467	378.7	D	2 780	839	1 410
Jamestown	73	133.9	697	11 977	419	278.9	48.4	8 035	296	272.4	730	1 635	254	499
Lindenhurst village	83	280.3	846	18 773	281	118.0	43.4	4 438	176	111.5	D	568	47	659
Long Beach	41	32.8	161	3 326	294	110.5	57.4	3 360	149	105.1	D	1 282	62	251
Mount Vernon	196	755.6	3 073	69 274	501	404.6	65.1	5 915	340	396.2	101	752	454	165
New Rochelle	204	879.0	1 950	55 354	695	545.3	47.2	7 883	472	532.7	881	740	398	497
New York	20 062	186 441.0	223 693	6 707 411	60 453	33 735.0	39.6	4 645	40 453	32 576.2	501	867	496	627
Niagara Falls	74	214.6	672	12 879	725	343.1	29.8	5 315	502	333.4	380	1 435	432	714
North Tonawanda	52	105.7	559	12 690	293	144.0	12.7	4 169	173	139.7	D	D	62	290
Poughkeepsie	84	308.2	1 057	26 512	610	494.1	83.7	16 475	456	485.3	D	1 185	2 003	1 158
Rochester	622	2 292.1	8 112	190 274	2 022	1 247.3	34.2	5 286	1 453	1 213.6	210	1 048	203	688
Rockville Centre village	127	742.0	1 067	29 505	361	304.7	66.0	11 972	250	299.6	111	1 912	354	777
Rome	46	77.9	367	6 088	445	268.2	34.8	6 381	275	258.8	D	1 405	183	483
Schenectady	108	620.4	1 636	41 760	683	434.6	17.9	6 466	476	421.0	D	1 723	258	528
Syracuse	476	4 344.4	7 167	174 453	1 507	989.3	0.0	6 154	1 126	969.1	D	1 068	258	750
Troy	74	D	D	D	496	294.8	58.3	5 463	355	289.4	387	1 582	132	669
Utica	165	458.9	2 262	51 356	883	359.3	8.5	5 174	550	342.9	449	1 264	401	649
Valley Stream village	160	398.9	979	25 865	478	446.2	56.1	12 844	340	438.0	D	1 012	700	905
Watertown	76	143.7	712	13 289	514	448.8	106.6	16 598	392	442.4	2 608	2 886	1 184	1 405
White Plains	210	2 477.4	3 564	97 705	914	997.5	31.7	22 000	704	982.9	7 108	985	2 396	1 551
Yonkers	279	821.0	2 894	70 940	1 521	1 106.4	37.4	5 946	1 016	1 077.9	712	1 516	434	408
NORTH CAROLINA	12 109	57 027.6	140 158	3 064 076	69 125	40 651.5	62.6	6 421	42 991	39 051.8	637	1 240	298	566
Asheville	230	640.7	2 561	50 747	1 175	871.4	45.4	14 453	849	856.5	2 277	2 216	1 028	1 512
Burlington	116	357.5	1 165	22 731	730	590.7	58.7	16 039	567	583.7	1 871	2 448	1 368	1 298
Chapel Hill town	24	58.0	258	7 311	445	0.0	0.0	D	335	D	531	2 254	D	D
Charlotte	2 120	21 127.2	30 394	790 722	4 035	3 652.9	63.7	10 375	2 820	3 590.8	1 047	1 534	607	1 015
Durham	185	910.7	2 676	60 195	1 307	1 052.2	63.6	9 239	1 039	1 040.4	D	1 819	553	941
Fayetteville	185	D	D	D	1 130	1 052.0	64.9	13 884	897	1 043.8	2 376	1 990	703	1 323
Gastonia	158	723.9	1 301	30 006	846	687.6	69.8	13 010	568	671.9	2 095	2 329	582	1 069
Goldsboro	120	D	D	D	574	359.5	41.0	10 274	398	349.3	1 722	1 725	543	750
Greensboro	742	4 353.8	11 256	278 640	2 281	2 042.0	68.4	11 560	1 651	2 008.0	1 534	1 760	731	1 168
Greenville	118	439.5	1 170	23 103	636	615.4	84.5	15 885	507	609.6	1 638	2 502	763	1 460
High Point	337	1 169.1	3 108	74 691	896	757.9	70.8	11 387	642	739.7	D	1 544	314	985
Kinston	58	371.4	1 118	14 965	420	299.2	80.8	11 944	308	295.7	1 698	2 051	731	953
Raleigh	661	3 754.1	9 252	235 705	2 736	2 495.7	116.5	13 832	1 715	2 196.8	1 538	1 778	724	1 270
Rocky Mount	121	569.6	1 788	35 681	726	483.7	47.4	10 052	521	471.3	D	1 623	D	989
Wilmington	215	679.4	2 447	49 079	1 063	665.8	41.3	12 232	771	654.1	1 697	1 766	810	1 455
Wilson	117	376.4	1 361	26 386	532	379.1	53.9	10 813	401	373.5	D	1 826	475	897
Winston-Salem	393	1 328.6	5 123	104 284	2 009	1 725.1	58.7	11 650	1 453	1 702.3	1 491	1 597	849	1 136
NORTH DAKOTA	2 049	6 011.0	17 525	324 728	7 803	3 848.8	14.3	5 660	5 235	3 729.6	733	1 002	244	499
Bismarck	139	405.2	1 335	26 780	608	457.5	22.5	9 523	455	450.7	2 057	1 448	D	796
Fargo	282	1 483.3	4 499	104 122	798	791.5	32.6	11 636	596	783.3	D	1 804	538	1 137
Grand Forks	95	199.4	993	19 069	515	488.6	34.9	10 836	414	483.1	2 284	1 619	D	881
Minot	115	512.6	1 397	24 874	535	390.0	15.2	10 879	384	385.9	1 908	1 753	491	916
OHIO	18 748	104 110.7	248 661	5 774 132	96 973	64 705.2	39.7	6 018	63 025	63 190.8	776	1 207	241	607
Akron	426	3 344.2	6 322	163 826	2 033	1 517.0	32.5	6 831	1 511	1 494.6	1 092	1 467	285	744
Barberton	33	D	D	D	226	119.2	8.5	4 289	165	117.5	780	1 085	81	629
Beavercreek village	25	D	D	D	242	144.6	105.4	4 203	136	141.9	D	1 044	34	356
Bowling Green	27	D	D	D	277	186.8	31.7	7 442	197	182.6	732	1 541	499	801
Brook Park	60	241.1	874	21 682	156	93.2	84.9	3 760	81	89.8	D	424	D	492
Brunswick	24	55.0	208	4 955	224	137.6	41.9	4 813	130	133.9	D	1 245	131	370
Canton	185	731.9	3 022	62 855	881	603.0	17.7	6 922	625	593.5	764	1 280	295	738
Cincinnati	1 074	8 680.2	19 346	485 988	3 071	2 384.6	33.0	6 449	2 341	2 351.2	801	1 509	339	836
Cleveland	1 230	5 708.2	20 775	528 057	3 956	2 075.2	8.9	3 873	2 952	2 026.7	288	924	151	617
Cleveland Heights	44	40.4	201	4 154	426	268.8	12.8	4 912	285	263.7	D	947	321	471
Columbus	1 322	D	D	D	4 710	4 764.7	52.3	8 418	3 452	4 711.6	1 289	1 128	D	D

1. For the period including March 12 of the year shown. 2. Based on resident population estimated as of July 1, 1986.

City	Retail trade–establishment with payroll, 1987 (cont'd): Paid employees[1]: Number	Retail trade–establishment with payroll, 1987 (cont'd): Paid employees[1]: Percent change, 1982–1987	Retail trade–establishment with payroll, 1987 (cont'd): Annual payroll (Mil. dol.)	Taxable service industries–establishments with payroll, 1987: Number	Taxable service industries: Receipts (Mil. dol.): Total	Receipts: Selected kinds of business: Hotels, motels, and other lodging places	Receipts: Selected kinds of business: Health services	Receipts: Selected kinds of business: Legal services	Taxable service industries: Paid employees[1]	Taxable service industries: Annual payroll (Mil. dol.)	Federal grants, 1986: Procurement contract awards (Mil. dol.)	Federal grants, 1986: Grant awards (Mil. dol.)	Federal government civilian employment, 1984
	87	88	89	90	91	92	93	94	95	96	97	98	99
NEW MEXICO—Con.													
Roswell	3 339	-10.2	30.8	336	82.3	8.0	D	11.5	2 123	30.4	5.6	1.6	350
Santa Fe	7 880	35.4	78.5	839	310.2	D	113.5	50.9	7 049	118.7	4.7	95.9	1 234
NEW YORK	1 150 448	21.0	12 774.2	126 684	74 289.4	3 384.9	12 344.6	9 948.4	1 292 626	27 386.7	11 679.0	13 252.3	153 806
Albany	11 554	57.9	117.6	1 082	645.4	20.3	153.5	107.7	11 947	247.0	22.4	1 143.5	4 596
Auburn	3 316	9.3	32.1	277	76.7	3.5	27.2	5.0	1 975	27.4	2.1	2.1	122
Binghamton	5 440	18.9	53.9	538	207.9	4.3	76.2	23.5	5 160	84.9	189.2	9.9	685
Buffalo	21 697	11.9	175.6	2 020	1 029.3	18.9	254.1	200.5	27 737	432.9	209.5	106.0	7 662
Elmira	3 137	28.2	29.2	266	89.5	D	43.0	9.3	2 196	39.6	7.4	1.1	377
Freeport village	2 266	15.9	29.2	332	104.8	2.9	34.2	5.2	1 967	36.2	20.0	0.7	161
Hempstead village	3 452	-6.4	52.1	374	189.0	D	75.1	27.4	4 188	72.9	1.0	5.5	294
Ithaca	5 007	18.5	46.4	366	111.7	D	32.3	8.3	2 564	38.0	63.8	96.4	267
Jamestown	2 985	6.1	28.8	296	93.1	D	39.6	7.5	2 541	35.7	15.0	1.9	216
Lindenhurst village	1 488	41.3	14.5	182	44.6	D	12.7	3.4	815	13.7	1.2	0.5	88
Long Beach	1 061	20.2	12.6	213	68.9	D	35.0	2.2	1 381	24.8	0.1	1.0	86
Mount Vernon	3 249	34.3	52.1	426	150.1	D	23.4	7.2	2 739	49.7	9.9	5.6	1 738
New Rochelle	4 431	3.5	58.8	666	221.0	D	74.1	13.7	4 487	77.5	9.2	2.3	258
New York	370 283	13.9	4 586.5	52 626	44 343.4	1 960.8	4 584.2	7 786.6	663 153	16 542.2	2 317.1	6 510.1	76 084
Niagara Falls	5 055	6.6	39.1	420	136.2	28.6	42.5	10.4	4 036	51.3	11.6	5.0	1 011
North Tonawanda	1 880	-4.8	15.7	163	31.5	D	8.1	1.3	978	10.1	6.3	1.0	85
Poughkeepsie	4 807	54.7	56.1	471	192.3	11.9	64.5	27.8	4 263	75.5	13.2	5.2	720
Rochester	16 798	14.7	169.0	2 029	1 017.8	30.4	178.4	158.0	25 888	421.3	138.1	147.5	2 627
Rockville Centre village	2 298	0.9	31.4	555	212.8	3.6	92.8	15.2	4 523	84.9	1.2	0.3	165
Rome	3 057	14.5	27.4	250	71.5	2.8	30.9	3.3	1 893	24.7	20.8	4.1	162
Schenectady	5 165	3.3	51.3	565	211.8	4.3	77.6	19.6	4 539	87.0	598.0	6.3	761
Syracuse	12 838	17.7	124.2	1 577	843.8	38.3	206.9	105.4	19 557	354.7	344.2	45.5	3 596
Troy	4 265	39.2	37.2	386	116.1	D	45.4	12.4	2 771	47.2	11.5	15.0	249
Utica	5 370	8.0	45.1	603	231.7	19.7	81.8	20.5	5 945	96.5	159.5	8.9	575
Valley Stream village	3 973	12.5	46.7	439	161.3	0.0	37.6	5.1	3 163	56.7	51.1	0.3	250
Watertown	5 087	74.9	49.9	258	85.4	8.9	33.2	7.8	1 659	34.1	4.9	3.4	224
White Plains	10 124	-2.3	125.7	1 231	873.9	42.4	141.3	122.3	16 444	312.8	35.6	14.7	603
Yonkers	10 767	10.1	121.0	1 135	422.4	10.3	148.5	16.9	7 033	139.3	184.3	5.7	681
NORTH CAROLINA	464 862	37.5	4 422.8	36 016	12 829.8	929.7	3 580.9	754.1	331 402	4 928.3	1 529.6	2 577.6	43 337
Asheville	10 907	25.7	103.8	918	354.7	43.9	155.4	22.4	8 177	156.2	23.9	18.6	2 320
Burlington	6 853	38.2	66.1	390	129.9	6.5	65.3	4.9	3 889	53.2	14.5	2.2	178
Chapel Hill town	D	D	D	354	D	16.2	51.2	8.1	D	D	17.5	88.9	111
Charlotte	40 767	33.3	418.9	3 905	2 300.9	166.7	455.7	143.0	52 065	904.2	42.9	17.9	2 729
Durham	13 830	44.9	130.8	993	D	D	89.3	24.5	D	D	39.9	106.7	3 976
Fayetteville	13 054	42.7	121.7	708	325.3	24.7	127.1	21.0	9 108	120.4	11.7	9.8	1 442
Gastonia	7 716	32.0	74.8	510	157.5	D	58.8	10.0	9 226	68.4	1.4	1.3	183
Goldsboro	4 547	21.4	42.1	302	90.5	3.2	29.4	D	2 526	36.2	0.6	3.7	163
Greensboro	25 055	41.7	250.2	1 867	849.2	59.1	207.5	52.6	21 367	327.8	408.7	14.1	2 730
Greenville	7 843	55.1	67.2	439	148.0	D	64.2	8.8	3 985	64.1	6.8	3.7	266
High Point	7 960	36.6	86.8	565	D	1.7	D	9.3	D	D	7.4	1.8	175
Kinston	3 642	25.8	32.3	269	86.0	D	D	D	2 252	35.4	2.5	2.2	194
Raleigh	27 592	65.7	263.1	2 264	1 197.5	86.2	284.3	102.3	30 490	499.6	78.7	344.8	2 348
Rocky Mount	5 973	23.4	54.8	401	D	D	D	D	D	D	4.3	1.2	293
Wilmington	9 052	34.1	81.9	749	346.7	16.6	79.8	D	8 419	157.3	43.5	3.5	712
Wilson	4 789	33.1	42.9	274	92.6	D	41.2	5.5	2 210	35.8	7.0	0.9	119
Winston-Salem	21 127	33.6	206.0	1 415	738.2	57.1	200.6	73.4	17 694	293.7	44.5	26.8	976
NORTH DAKOTA	48 163	5.3	407.7	3 881	1 090.4	96.5	453.1	76.2	27 753	419.4	314.1	416.2	7 513
Bismarck	5 897	13.0	50.9	452	182.8	D	D	D	4 203	83.6	7.5	62.2	827
Fargo	10 541	25.8	88.1	671	336.7	27.0	149.2	D	7 827	124.0	14.8	11.2	1 760
Grand Forks	6 196	21.1	56.1	313	127.8	13.5	D	8.5	3 352	56.1	8.1	18.8	311
Minot	4 693	4.1	43.2	325	87.3	D	36.0	D	2 305	35.3	23.9	4.3	288
OHIO	804 182	20.7	7 434.2	63 858	26 449.4	1 024.3	7 324.4	1 897.6	648 361	10 473.2	7 451.6	4 789.5	88 222
Akron	19 895	16.1	182.8	1 541	638.4	14.5	205.0	69.4	15 340	287.9	416.3	22.0	1 493
Barberton	1 865	-0.9	14.5	141	34.4	D	19.2	0.7	839	14.3	5.4	18.6	83
Beavercreek village	1 802	99.8	15.2	154	100.1	0.0	11.5	D	1 722	33.9	0.2	0.1	0
Bowling Green	2 724	14.6	21.7	160	49.9	2.9	17.7	3.4	1 802	19.9	0.3	3.4	66
Brook Park	1 187	27.4	10.4	85	86.4	2.7	6.2	D	1 395	21.7	5.2	0.7	178
Brunswick	1 610	12.9	15.2	119	34.9	D	14.1	D	1 113	13.3	NA	0.2	41
Canton	8 273	12.3	75.7	694	271.7	7.3	103.7	27.1	11 005	120.9	95.3	7.4	916
Cincinnati	32 914	13.0	320.8	3 406	2 229.9	89.3	483.2	243.8	52 009	953.9	2 948.3	111.2	10 184
Cleveland	30 413	0.6	293.0	3 488	2 600.9	77.1	315.4	584.9	49 398	1 106.9	465.0	220.9	15 626
Cleveland Heights	3 267	-7.9	33.9	318	87.3	D	36.1	0.5	2 303	33.9	0.1	1.9	32
Columbus	62 594	35.0	611.0	4 517	2 876.0	126.3	609.6	319.0	65 784	1 158.2	330.6	542.5	5 853

1. For the period including March 12 of the year shown.

City	City government employment, 1985 (October): Total	City government employment, 1985 (October): Rates[1]	City government employment, 1985 (October): Percent education	Form of governments[2] (As of 1986)	City government finances, 1984–1985: General revenue: Total (Mil. dol.)	General revenue: Intergovernmental: Total (Mil. dol.)	General revenue: Intergovernmental: Percent from State government	General revenue: Taxes: Total (Mil. dol.)	Taxes: Per capita[3] (Dollars): Total	Taxes: Per capita[3] (Dollars): Property	Taxes: Per capita[3] (Dollars): Sales & gross receipts	General expenditures: Total (Mil. dol.)	General expenditures: Per capita[3] (Dol.): Total	General expenditures: Per capita[3] (Dol.): Capital outlays	General expenditures: Percent of total for–: Public welfare	General expenditures: Percent of total for–: Highways	General expenditures: Percent of total for–: Education
	100	101	102	103	104	105	106	107	108	109	110	111	112	113	114	115	116
NEW MEXICO—Con.																	
Roswell	541	122.6	0.0	2	29.5	13.8	58.3	4.8	108	14	90	29.9	677	274	0.0	13.6	0.0
Santa Fe	800	142.9	0.0	2	45.1	17.6	84.6	10.9	195	22	164	42.3	755	119	0.0	8.2	0.0
NEW YORK	NA	NA	NA	NA	NA	NA	NA	NA	NA	NA	NA	NA	NA	NA	NA	NA	NA
Albany	1 872	192.9	0.0	1	68.3	19.6	67.8	30.2	311	282	17	79.7	822	34	0.2	5.1	0.0
Auburn	429	136.8	0.0	2	15.7	5.1	62.2	7.5	238	221	15	17.5	558	86	0.0	10.2	0.0
Binghamton	973	183.9	0.0	1	37.3	15.4	38.8	14.7	277	259	13	43.2	817	242	0.0	4.6	0.0
Buffalo	12 021	370.1	58.0	1	447.2	271.9	74.7	107.7	332	294	29	530.3	1 633	319	0.0	5.8	41.0
Elmira	432	133.1	0.0	2	18.1	6.9	56.9	8.0	247	149	95	19.4	599	67	0.0	8.0	0.0
Freeport village	494	122.5	0.0	1	17.1	2.0	78.9	12.1	300	290	3	19.1	472	55	0.0	12.5	0.0
Hempstead village	448	104.8	0.0	1	19.3	3.0	55.1	14.2	332	322	8	20.5	480	93	0.0	13.6	0.0
Ithaca	436	164.7	0.0	1	13.5	2.8	79.8	7.6	288	147	134	18.9	712	224	0.0	8.5	0.0
Jamestown	1 444	416.0	31.9	1	40.7	15.6	55.1	6.4	184	171	8	52.0	1 497	414	0.0	3.7	22.7
Lindenhurst village	130	48.9	0.0	1	3.9	0.8	72.2	2.2	84	73	7	4.7	175	39	0.0	26.9	0.0
Long Beach	502	152.6	0.0	2	20.7	4.5	70.6	12.0	366	350	11	23.0	699	128	0.0	2.4	0.0
Mount Vernon	982	143.6	0.0	1	39.2	10.9	70.1	21.8	319	243	67	38.1	558	52	0.0	2.0	0.0
New Rochelle	922	133.3	0.0	2	47.8	10.6	70.6	29.6	427	324	91	45.3	655	63	0.0	7.8	0.0
New York	39 329	541.5	30.7	1	22 981.4	9 254.0	83.4	10 634.4	1 464	588	369	20 590.1	2 835	242	20.6	2.8	21.0
Niagara Falls	990	153.4	0.0	2	51.9	17.4	67.2	16.3	253	223	24	60.5	938	116	0.0	4.5	0.0
North Tonawanda	452	130.9	0.0	1	14.1	5.1	93.1	4.8	140	116	18	18.0	521	69	0.0	13.1	0.0
Poughkeepsie	481	160.4	0.0	2	21.7	7.2	61.1	10.0	332	187	133	17.8	593	33	0.0	7.7	0.0
Rochester	8 670	367.4	59.0	2	329.6	159.4	78.8	125.9	534	473	6	362.9	1 538	194	0.2	5.1	47.9
Rockville Centre village	339	133.2	0.0	1	11.5	1.1	85.3	7.7	303	292	3	13.9	547	66	0.0	11.6	0.0
Rome	1 058	251.7	0.0	1	37.5	6.8	75.2	9.6	229	134	90	37.1	882	82	0.0	9.5	0.0
Schenectady	1 027	152.8	0.0	1	44.1	13.1	72.8	24.2	361	175	179	39.4	586	90	0.0	3.9	0.0
Syracuse	5 911	367.7	56.8	1	208.4	117.0	63.1	56.8	353	333	14	249.4	1 552	284	0.0	5.0	41.2
Troy	731	135.5	0.0	2	22.5	10.1	64.6	9.3	173	157	9	29.1	538	122	0.0	11.5	0.0
Utica	1 079	155.4	0.0	1	50.1	28.1	29.2	17.5	252	161	87	41.9	604	132	0.0	5.7	0.0
Valley Stream village	240	69.1	0.0	1	9.7	1.3	81.3	7.3	209	196	7	10.9	315	42	0.0	15.3	0.0
Watertown	458	169.4	0.0	2	15.0	6.0	47.9	5.7	211	191	11	18.3	678	132	0.0	7.8	0.0
White Plains	1 129	249.0	0.0	1	62.7	7.4	62.6	38.0	837	468	346	59.7	1 316	132	0.0	7.2	0.0
Yonkers	4 583	246.3	52.1	2	244.4	68.2	82.4	157.4	846	534	167	246.1	1 322	56	0.0	1.3	43.6
NORTH CAROLINA	NA	NA	NA	NA	NA	NA	NA	NA	NA	NA	NA	NA	NA	NA	NA	NA	NA
Asheville	1 032	171.2	0.0	2	27.9	9.3	43.0	11.2	186	167	0	28.3	469	97	0.0	7.9	0.0
Burlington	527	143.1	0.0	2	18.5	5.6	53.5	5.9	161	153	0	17.8	483	128	0.0	6.9	0.0
Chapel Hill town	433	127.4	0.0	2	12.8	4.5	63.2	6.2	181	171	0	12.5	368	57	0.0	6.7	0.0
Charlotte	4 113	116.8	0.0	2	219.6	44.9	49.3	102.7	292	228	52	190.0	540	133	0.1	12.4	0.0
Durham	1 511	132.7	0.0	2	48.8	10.3	58.7	18.4	162	150	0	53.3	468	77	0.0	12.8	0.0
Fayetteville	1 230	162.3	0.0	2	25.7	9.6	41.5	6.9	92	84	0	38.4	506	226	0.0	5.9	0.0
Gastonia	726	137.4	0.0	2	13.7	5.5	64.7	6.0	114	109	0	16.8	318	63	0.0	15.1	0.0
Goldsboro	391	111.7	0.0	2	12.2	4.2	66.3	4.3	124	118	0	13.0	373	93	0.0	11.4	0.0
Greensboro	2 935	166.1	0.0	2	71.2	19.6	63.7	31.6	179	166	0	82.2	465	34	0.0	9.6	0.0
Greenville	785	202.6	0.0	2	16.2	4.4	74.0	5.5	141	132	0	14.5	374	68	0.0	15.6	0.0
High Point	1 164	174.9	0.0	2	48.9	15.2	40.6	12.5	188	176	0	46.8	703	165	0.0	5.0	0.0
Kinston	471	188.0	0.0	2	8.6	2.9	51.6	3.0	120	109	0	10.5	420	45	0.0	3.9	0.0
Raleigh	2 198	121.8	0.0	2	88.7	17.7	68.4	43.5	241	219	0	76.0	421	92	0.5	13.3	0.0
Rocky Mount	760	157.9	0.0	2	14.4	4.3	66.9	4.6	96	90	0	20.0	415	91	0.1	16.7	0.0
Wilmington	714	131.2	0.0	2	25.9	8.8	38.4	10.0	184	174	0	21.0	386	54	0.0	13.9	0.0
Wilson	612	174.6	0.0	2	18.7	3.5	68.3	4.3	121	115	0	17.6	501	54	0.0	7.2	0.0
Winston-Salem	2 366	159.8	0.0	2	102.7	35.5	36.5	34.2	231	209	0	100.3	678	208	0.0	9.0	0.0
NORTH DAKOTA	NA	NA	NA	NA	NA	NA	NA	NA	NA	NA	NA	NA	NA	NA	NA	NA	NA
Bismarck	481	100.1	0.0	3	24.9	6.4	51.1	6.3	131	122	0	22.3	465	128	0.0	17.6	0.0
Fargo	534	78.5	0.0	3	40.9	13.3	31.1	7.1	104	76	19	37.0	543	198	0.1	9.5	0.0
Grand Forks	408	90.5	0.0	1	27.8	9.6	28.4	4.5	99	75	16	27.5	609	278	0.1	16.6	0.0
Minot	350	97.6	0.0	2	17.1	5.5	39.9	4.3	120	105	6	15.9	444	143	0.7	5.6	0.0
OHIO	NA	NA	NA	NA	NA	NA	NA	NA	NA	NA	NA	NA	NA	NA	NA	NA	NA
Akron	2 930	131.9	0.0	1	149.7	34.3	34.1	67.8	305	49	1	153.8	693	72	0.0	8.8	0.0
Barberton	329	118.4	0.0	1	12.5	2.3	66.2	5.2	187	28	0	12.1	436	58	0.3	16.4	0.0
Beavercreek village	81	23.5	0.0	1	3.6	1.2	89.2	1.9	56	54	0	4.1	119	19	0.0	30.2	0.0
Bowling Green	277	110.4	0.0	1	18.0	1.5	65.4	3.9	155	19	2	10.7	426	103	0.0	5.3	0.0
Brook Park	363	146.4	0.0	1	13.4	1.6	66.1	10.8	435	77	4	12.1	487	71	0.0	16.8	0.0
Brunswick	107	37.4	0.0	2	5.4	1.3	81.1	2.6	90	31	0	4.7	165	32	0.0	27.4	0.0
Canton	1 183	135.8	0.0	1	48.1	8.6	51.8	25.0	287	22	0	41.5	476	50	0.0	5.3	0.0
Cincinnati	6 186	167.3	0.0	2	328.2	78.6	29.7	150.2	406	78	4	333.7	902	196	0.0	6.6	0.0
Cleveland	9 348	174.5	0.0	1	421.5	128.2	34.2	208.7	390	79	3	392.3	732	74	0.3	7.2	0.0
Cleveland Heights	544	99.4	0.0	2	27.5	4.9	52.0	16.2	297	88	3	30.0	548	83	0.0	11.5	0.0
Columbus	6 784	119.9	0.0	1	351.8	74.8	41.4	168.7	298	24	5	333.5	589	98	0.0	8.5	0.0

1. Per 10,000 population estimated as of July 1, 1986. 2. 1 = Mayor-council; 2 = Council-manager; 3 = Commission. Data subject to copyright. 3. Based on resident population estimated as of July 1, 1986.

Table C. Cities — **City Government Finances, Climate, and Electric Bills**

City	City government finances, 1984–1985 (cont'd): General expenditure (cont'd): Percent of total for (cont'd): Health and hospitals	Police protection	Sewerage and sanitation	Parks and recreation	Housing and community development	Debt outstanding: Total (Mil. dol.)	Per capita[1] (Dollars)	Percent utility	Climate[2]: Average daily temperature (Degrees Fahrenheit): Mean: Jan.	Mean: July	Limits: Jan.[3]	Limits: July[4]	Annual precipitation (Inches)	Heating degree days[5]	Cooling degree days[5]	Typical monthly electric bills, 1986: Residential[6]: Total (Dollars)	Residential: Percent change, 1980–1986	Commercial[7] (Dollars)
	117	118	119	120	121	122	123	124	125	126	127	128	129	130	131	132	133	134
NEW MEXICO—Con.																		
Roswell	0.0	9.7	34.5	6.6	0.7	67.6	1 532	17.1	41.4	81.4	27.4	93.7	9.70	3 126	1 863	44.64	20.5	NA
Santa Fe	0.0	17.2	11.2	6.3	0.2	83.2	1 486	0.0	29.2	68.3	18.5	80.6	17.81	6 387	297	68.14	40.5	547.8
NEW YORK	NA	NA	NA	NA	NA	NA	NA	NA	NA	NA	NA	NA	NA	NA	NA	78.55	51.3	NA
Albany	0.2	20.5	10.9	5.8	9.9	152.0	1 567	11.0	21.1	71.4	11.9	83.2	35.74	6 927	494	52.64	72.7	545.9
Auburn	NA	12.0	14.3	6.9	10.2	7.9	251	3.6	22.8	70.9	15.0	81.6	39.11	6 787	506	62.43	79.2	NA
Binghamton	NA	11.8	15.7	3.9	17.3	44.6	844	0.5	21.2	68.9	14.3	78.4	36.79	7 344	330	62.43	79.2	587.6
Buffalo	0.2	6.0	9.2	4.9	12.0	253.9	782	7.0	23.5	70.7	17.0	80.2	37.52	6 798	476	52.64	72.7	545.9
Elmira	NA	13.8	2.8	3.8	21.3	15.8	487	0.0	23.5	69.8	14.3	83.5	33.10	6 927	411	62.43	79.2	NA
Freeport village	0.2	19.9	14.4	11.9	4.8	23.8	591	17.6	31.3	75.0	25.1	82.7	41.76	5 169	886	41.74	37.7	NA
Hempstead village	NA	20.8	9.3	4.9	3.2	8.8	207	1.9	31.3	75.0	25.1	82.7	41.76	5 169	886	84.99	66.4	NA
Ithaca	NA	11.6	35.8	7.3	0.1	22.2	839	0.2	22.2	68.8	13.8	80.3	35.27	7 177	328	62.43	79.2	NA
Jamestown	23.1	4.2	24.8	3.8	0.2	15.5	448	16.3	22.3	66.5	13.3	79.6	44.00	7 379	239	22.25	18.3	NA
Lindenhurst village	0.0	0.0	11.1	13.4	0.0	0.2	8	0.0	29.7	72.6	21.0	82.1	45.71	5 664	608	84.99	66.4	NA
Long Beach	0.0	16.7	13.9	7.3	1.8	24.1	734	20.1	31.3	75.0	25.1	82.7	41.76	5 169	886	84.99	66.4	NA
Mount Vernon	1.1	15.1	7.1	4.3	3.4	32.3	472	1.1	31.8	76.7	25.6	85.3	44.12	4 868	1 089	86.97	39.2	927.6
New Rochelle	1.0	18.0	7.8	5.4	6.0	37.2	537	0.0	29.6	74.1	20.9	86.0	47.42	5 419	778	86.97	39.2	927.6
New York	10.5	5.7	4.8	1.5	6.4	12 937.1	1 781	18.5	31.8	76.7	25.6	85.3	44.12	4 868	1 089	86.37	NA	939.4
Niagara Falls	0.0	7.8	13.9	11.2	14.8	83.0	1 286	0.6	23.5	70.7	17.0	80.2	37.52	6 798	476	52.64	72.7	545.9
North Tonawanda	0.2	10.2	20.1	5.8	3.0	25.7	745	5.0	23.5	70.7	17.0	80.2	37.52	6 798	476	52.64	72.7	NA
Poughkeepsie	0.4	11.7	12.8	2.9	4.0	9.3	309	7.7	24.4	72.4	14.8	84.1	40.16	6 366	591	84.93	65.3	NA
Rochester	0.0	6.8	2.8	1.9	4.4	237.9	1 008	9.6	23.6	71.3	16.3	82.3	31.27	6 713	531	63.68	92.1	694.0
Rockville Centre village	0.1	19.6	12.3	8.3	1.4	12.1	477	19.1	31.3	75.0	25.1	82.7	41.76	5 169	886	36.42	20.5	NA
Rome	49.0	5.4	3.8	2.4	2.3	29.2	696	2.8	20.1	69.8	12.7	79.9	43.44	7 368	425	52.64	72.7	NA
Schenectady	2.2	16.9	14.2	4.2	4.5	26.1	388	2.7	21.1	71.4	11.9	83.2	35.74	6 927	494	52.64	72.7	545.9
Syracuse	0.0	6.4	2.8	1.8	15.6	154.7	963	0.0	22.8	70.9	15.0	81.6	39.11	6 787	506	52.64	72.7	545.9
Troy	0.1	16.6	5.6	4.3	11.7	28.5	528	19.1	21.1	71.4	11.9	83.2	35.74	6 927	494	52.64	72.7	545.9
Utica	0.2	11.6	6.6	4.9	20.2	33.5	483	0.0	20.1	69.8	12.7	79.9	43.44	7 368	425	52.64	72.7	545.9
Valley Stream village	0.1	1.0	15.7	10.7	0.0	6.7	192	0.0	31.3	75.0	25.1	82.7	41.76	5 169	886	84.99	66.4	NA
Watertown	0.5	9.5	9.6	3.1	13.1	12.6	466	18.2	18.4	70.2	8.9	79.9	40.53	7 480	424	52.64	72.7	NA
White Plains	0.0	19.8	6.8	5.7	8.1	45.3	1 000	4.8	31.8	76.7	25.6	85.3	44.12	4 868	1 089	86.97	39.2	NA
Yonkers	0.1	8.5	2.7	1.7	4.2	139.0	747	1.4	31.8	76.7	25.6	85.3	44.12	4 868	1 089	88.62	19.3	945.2
NORTH CAROLINA	NA	NA	NA	NA	NA	NA	NA	NA	NA	NA	NA	NA	NA	NA	NA	56.15	72.1	NA
Asheville	0.0	16.5	4.6	11.7	6.0	11.0	182	64.2	36.8	73.2	26.0	84.0	47.72	4 294	842	56.21	74.9	427.7
Burlington	0.0	22.6	26.8	7.2	4.6	7.8	211	52.8	39.2	78.3	29.0	89.3	45.04	3 537	1 479	55.82	73.3	NA
Chapel Hill town	0.0	16.4	9.1	7.0	4.1	9.4	276	0.0	38.7	77.2	27.3	88.7	45.49	3 724	1 310	55.82	73.3	NA
Charlotte	0.6	12.5	11.2	10.3	1.5	296.7	843	12.8	40.5	78.5	30.7	88.3	43.16	3 342	1 546	55.82	73.3	434.4
Durham	1.6	23.7	15.5	7.2	6.1	45.8	402	63.6	39.5	77.7	28.0	89.6	47.06	3 612	1 387	55.82	73.3	434.4
Fayetteville	0.0	12.3	48.6	4.1	3.1	19.5	258	88.9	41.4	79.3	29.6	89.8	47.67	3 155	1 657	56.50	69.6	479.0
Gastonia	0.0	18.7	11.5	10.7	7.0	3.9	74	42.5	41.7	78.7	31.1	89.6	47.17	3 158	1 589	54.92	69.1	NA
Goldsboro	0.0	16.6	30.5	7.9	3.5	2.1	61	52.9	41.5	79.7	30.5	90.2	50.19	3 102	1 704	56.21	74.9	NA
Greensboro	0.0	18.6	17.7	15.6	4.2	21.2	120	15.3	37.5	77.2	27.3	87.4	42.47	3 874	1 303	55.82	73.3	434.4
Greenville	0.0	18.1	23.3	7.7	4.4	19.2	495	78.7	41.3	78.9	30.5	89.6	47.09	3 233	1 615	59.33	16.2	NA
High Point	0.0	10.1	24.9	5.8	2.2	33.1	498	52.5	39.8	77.6	29.9	88.3	44.15	3 422	1 387	55.82	99.1	434.4
Kinston	0.4	22.2	11.2	11.3	7.1	4.2	167	37.8	41.8	78.7	30.7	89.5	51.59	3 124	1 611	56.21	66.2	NA
Raleigh	0.2	14.6	20.0	14.9	3.0	107.3	595	53.2	39.6	77.7	29.1	88.2	41.76	3 531	1 394	56.21	74.9	427.7
Rocky Mount	0.0	16.0	26.8	6.5	2.8	11.6	242	56.9	41.3	78.9	30.5	89.6	47.09	3 233	1 615	53.74	75.4	NA
Wilmington	0.0	17.0	8.3	11.1	1.8	11.8	216	32.8	45.6	80.3	35.3	89.3	53.35	2 469	1 904	56.21	74.9	NA
Wilson	0.0	11.8	32.4	4.7	2.0	5.9	167	42.7	41.3	78.9	30.5	89.6	47.09	3 233	1 615	53.97	62.6	NA
Winston-Salem	0.0	16.3	34.4	9.9	4.3	65.2	440	28.8	39.8	77.6	29.9	88.3	44.15	3 422	1 387	55.82	73.3	434.4
NORTH DAKOTA	NA	NA	NA	NA	NA	NA	NA	NA	NA	NA	NA	NA	NA	NA	NA	45.56	44.7	NA
Bismarck	2.0	11.9	8.5	0.9	0.0	37.8	786	4.8	6.7	70.4	NA	84.4	15.36	9 075	473	51.03	49.7	452.0
Fargo	3.7	9.9	13.6	0.4	5.7	96.3	1 416	6.3	4.3	70.6	NA	82.7	19.59	9 343	476	41.99	34.5	362.3
Grand Forks	0.9	7.7	29.6	1.1	3.1	43.6	967	3.0	2.2	68.8	NA	81.6	18.29	9 881	418	41.99	34.5	362.3
Minot	0.3	11.3	19.5	4.1	1.5	23.8	665	7.7	6.3	69.4	NA	81.7	17.86	9 415	423	41.17	34.5	NA
OHIO	NA	NA	NA	NA	NA	NA	NA	NA	NA	NA	NA	NA	NA	NA	NA	59.92	50.0	NA
Akron	2.2	12.2	11.7	2.4	20.9	131.5	592	12.5	25.1	71.6	17.2	82.3	35.90	6 241	625	65.19	70.7	697.7
Barberton	2.9	16.9	16.9	5.7	2.3	16.2	581	3.5	25.1	71.6	17.2	82.3	35.90	6 241	625	65.19	70.7	NA
Beavercreek village	1.1	29.2	0.0	3.9	0.0	0.5	15	0.0	26.6	74.7	18.8	84.9	34.71	5 689	947	63.53	NA	NA
Bowling Green	0.6	11.5	30.1	1.9	0.0	6.8	269	24.3	25.0	73.7	17.2	85.4	32.20	6 023	817	42.33	7.6	NA
Brook Park	2.7	14.9	15.4	9.7	0.0	2.7	108	0.0	25.5	71.6	18.5	81.7	35.40	6 178	612	60.26	37.5	NA
Brunswick	0.1	17.9	8.2	6.6	1.5	5.7	199	0.0	25.1	71.6	17.2	82.3	35.90	6 241	625	65.19	70.7	NA
Canton	2.6	16.9	17.3	2.6	13.3	43.6	501	1.4	25.1	71.6	17.2	82.3	35.90	6 241	625	52.70	67.4	379.6
Cincinnati	7.1	13.6	14.6	7.5	14.6	200.4	542	17.3	30.3	76.1	22.5	86.3	40.10	4 950	1 159	54.25	76.5	596.5
Cleveland	3.1	23.8	7.9	7.1	11.5	390.3	728	35.0	25.5	71.6	18.5	81.7	35.40	6 178	612	60.26	37.5	535.1
Cleveland Heights	1.0	14.3	18.9	2.7	5.3	24.5	447	0.0	25.5	71.6	18.5	81.7	35.40	6 178	612	60.26	37.5	NA
Columbus	4.2	17.9	21.2	5.2	3.6	753.0	1 330	48.9	27.1	73.8	19.4	84.4	36.97	5 686	862	60.10	32.5	501.7

1. Based on resident population estimated as of July 1, 1986. 2. Represents normal values based on the 30-year period, 1951–1980 (see text). 3. Average daily minimum. 4. Average daily maximum. 5. For definition, see text. 6. As of January 1; based on consumption of 750 kWh. 7. Based on billing demand of 30 kW and consumption of 6,000 kWh.

MSA/ CMSA Code[1]	State/ Place code	City	Land area,[2] 1990 (Sq. Km.)	Population: 1990: Total persons	Population: 1990: Rank	Population: 1990: Per sq. km.	Population: 1980	Population: Change 1980–1990: Number	Population: Change 1980–1990: Per-cent	Population characteristics, 1990: Percent: Race: White	Race: Black	Race: Am. Indian, Eskimo, Aleut	Race: Asian & Pacific Islander	Race: Other race	His-panic[3]	65 Years and over
			1	2	3	4	5	6	7	8	9	10	11	12	13	14
		OHIO—Con.														
1692	39 1075	Cuyahoga Falls	66.1	48 950	505	741	43 890	5 060	11.5	98.09	1.06	0.13	0.63	0.09	0.43	15.3
2000	39 1110	Dayton	142.5	182 044	89	1 278	193 536	-11 492	-5.9	58.37	40.43	0.23	0.64	0.34	0.74	13.1
1692	39 1225	East Cleveland	8.0	33 096	765	4 137	36 957	-3 861	-10.4	5.34	93.69	0.11	0.66	0.20	0.56	10.5
1692	39 1300	Elyria	50.3	56 746	412	1 128	57 538	-792	-1.4	84.97	13.68	0.24	0.53	0.57	1.51	11.8
1692	39 1320	Euclid	27.7	54 875	430	1 981	59 999	-5 124	-8.5	82.91	15.97	0.09	0.85	0.17	0.83	22.2
2000	39 1330	Fairborn	29.0	31 300	800	1 079	29 702	1 598	5.4	92.37	4.12	0.39	2.60	0.51	1.34	9.4
1642	39 1340	Fairfield	54.0	39 729	635	736	30 777	8 952	29.1	94.96	3.29	0.13	1.41	0.21	0.73	8.5
...	39 1380	Findlay	35.1	35 703	705	1 017	35 594	109	0.3	95.93	1.26	0.17	0.83	1.81	3.44	13.6
1692	39 1495	Garfield Heights	18.7	31 739	793	1 697	34 938	-3 199	-9.2	84.40	14.77	0.12	0.54	0.17	0.84	19.4
1642	39 1705	Hamilton	51.7	61 368	376	1 187	63 189	-1 821	-2.9	91.93	7.32	0.15	0.39	0.21	0.50	14.2
2000	39 1881	Huber Heights	53.9	38 696	654	718	35 480	3 216	9.1	90.73	6.89	0.25	1.74	0.40	1.54	5.9
1692	39 2015	Kent	22.6	28 835	848	1 276	26 164	2 671	10.2	89.91	7.11	0.17	2.51	0.30	0.91	7.0
2000	39 2025	Kettering	48.3	60 569	383	1 254	61 186	-617	-1.0	97.78	0.72	0.13	1.23	0.14	0.79	16.9
1692	39 2120	Lakewood	14.4	59 718	389	4 147	61 963	-2 245	-3.6	97.50	0.85	0.19	1.02	0.44	1.50	13.5
1840	39 2125	Lancaster	40.5	34 507	725	852	34 953	-446	-1.3	98.75	0.51	0.23	0.38	0.13	0.54	15.7
4320	39 2205	Lima	32.8	45 549	545	1 389	47 827	-2 278	-4.8	74.53	24.04	0.22	0.50	0.70	1.50	13.4
1692	39 2285	Lorain	62.3	71 245	311	1 144	75 416	-4 171	-5.5	78.22	13.77	0.42	0.32	7.27	16.93	13.4
4800	39 2440	Mansfield	72.3	50 627	487	700	53 927	-3 300	-6.1	80.73	18.08	0.23	0.61	0.35	0.94	15.0
1692	39 2455	Maple Heights	13.4	27 089	888	2 022	29 735	-2 646	-8.9	83.76	14.72	0.09	1.06	0.36	0.70	19.0
...	39 2485	Marion	20.8	34 075	736	1 638	37 040	-2 965	-8.0	94.72	4.22	0.27	0.45	0.33	0.85	13.0
1320	39 2525	Massillon	34.2	31 007	805	907	30 557	450	1.5	89.41	9.84	0.24	0.24	0.27	0.87	15.8
1692	39 2580	Mentor	69.3	47 358	522	683	42 065	5 293	12.6	98.58	0.34	0.06	0.91	0.10	0.61	9.4
1642	39 2635	Middletown	52.3	46 022	541	880	43 719	2 303	5.3	88.32	10.98	0.13	0.43	0.14	0.45	14.5
1840	39 2925	Newark	46.7	44 389	560	951	41 200	3 189	7.7	95.98	3.21	0.23	0.39	0.19	0.66	15.1
1692	39 3145	North Olmsted	29.8	34 204	734	1 148	36 486	-2 282	-6.3	97.13	0.69	0.11	1.73	0.34	1.18	12.9
1642	39 3195	Norwood	8.0	23 674	942	2 959	26 342	-2 668	-10.1	97.99	1.01	0.16	0.69	0.16	0.55	13.4
1692	39 3360	Parma	51.8	87 876	229	1 696	92 548	-4 672	-5.0	97.90	0.73	0.10	1.09	0.19	0.87	19.1
...	39 3530	Portsmouth	27.9	22 676	947	813	25 943	-3 267	-12.6	93.97	5.17	0.45	0.34	0.07	0.41	21.4
...	39 3830	Sandusky	26.0	29 764	832	1 145	31 360	-1 596	-5.1	79.72	18.93	0.21	0.26	0.88	2.27	14.7
1692	39 3905	Shaker Heights	16.3	30 831	812	1 891	32 487	-1 656	-5.1	66.92	30.66	0.20	1.92	0.30	1.14	14.7
1692	39 4035	South Euclid	12.1	23 866	936	1 972	25 713	-1 847	-7.2	89.14	9.13	0.12	1.42	0.18	0.83	18.8
2000	39 4100	Springfield	50.6	70 487	318	1 393	72 563	-2 076	-2.9	81.61	17.38	0.22	0.51	0.28	0.65	15.4
8080	39 4115	Steubenville	21.0	22 125	948	1 054	26 400	-4 275	-16.2	83.41	15.45	0.22	0.68	0.24	0.99	21.8
1692	39 4135	Stow	44.4	27 702	870	624	25 303	2 399	9.5	97.10	1.08	0.08	1.62	0.12	0.51	9.5
1692	39 4150	Strongsville	63.8	35 308	713	553	28 577	6 731	23.6	96.60	0.78	0.10	2.36	0.16	0.95	7.9
8400	39 4265	Toledo	208.7	332 943	49	1 595	354 635	-21 692	-6.1	76.96	19.70	0.28	1.05	2.01	3.97	13.6
1840	39 4355	Upper Arlington	24.9	34 128	735	1 371	35 648	-1 520	-4.3	97.28	0.25	0.07	2.27	0.12	0.74	18.7
9320	39 4480	Warren	41.4	50 793	483	1 227	56 629	-5 836	-10.3	77.90	21.33	0.18	0.32	0.27	0.71	16.9
9320	39 4845	Youngstown	87.5	95 732	209	1 094	115 511	-19 779	-17.1	59.31	38.11	0.24	0.30	2.04	3.99	18.2
...	39 4860	Zanesville	27.0	26 778	893	992	28 655	-1 877	-6.6	88.29	10.76	0.53	0.20	0.23	0.40	16.8
...	40 0000	OKLAHOMA	177 877.5	3 145 585	X	18	3 025 487	120 098	4.0	82.13	7.43	8.02	1.07	1.34	2.74	13.5
...	40 0145	Bartlesville	54.7	34 256	732	626	34 568	-312	-0.9	88.58	3.33	6.36	1.12	0.61	1.76	16.7
8560	40 0290	Broken Arrow	104.5	58 043	401	555	35 761	22 282	62.3	91.69	3.12	3.58	0.96	0.65	2.12	5.5
5880	40 0660	Del City	19.5	23 928	935	1 227	28 523	-4 595	-16.1	81.31	10.97	4.54	1.78	1.41	2.95	11.5
5880	40 0755	Edmond	220.9	52 315	463	237	34 637	17 678	51.0	91.76	3.10	2.52	2.02	0.60	1.76	7.0
2340	40 0790	Enid	187.0	45 309	547	242	50 363	-5 054	-10.0	91.02	4.41	2.33	1.26	0.99	2.12	15.8
4200	40 1405	Lawton	132.5	80 561	261	608	80 054	507	0.6	70.78	19.33	3.33	3.25	3.30	6.34	9.2
5880	40 1630	Midwest City	63.5	52 267	465	823	49 559	2 708	5.5	77.07	16.27	3.89	1.74	1.03	2.67	11.3
5880	40 1655	Moore	55.7	40 318	621	724	35 063	5 255	15.0	90.19	1.78	5.30	1.28	1.45	3.36	5.0
...	40 1700	Muskogee	89.3	37 708	674	422	40 011	-2 303	-5.8	69.02	18.85	10.99	0.53	0.61	1.50	18.6
5880	40 1755	Norman	458.5	80 071	266	175	68 020	12 051	17.7	87.49	3.57	4.83	3.21	0.90	2.38	8.2
5880	40 1815	Oklahoma City	1 575.1	444 719	29	282	404 014	40 705	10.1	74.78	15.98	4.23	2.36	2.66	4.95	11.9
...	40 1935	Ponca City	45.0	26 359	899	586	26 238	121	0.5	90.16	2.93	5.52	0.69	0.70	1.93	17.1
5880	40 2195	Shawnee	108.2	26 017	904	240	26 506	-489	-1.8	82.62	3.41	12.46	0.77	0.73	1.96	18.1
...	40 2300	Stillwater	70.6	36 676	692	519	38 268	-1 592	-4.2	87.56	3.73	3.44	4.63	0.64	1.80	8.2
8560	40 2465	Tulsa	475.3	367 302	43	773	360 919	6 383	1.8	79.35	13.57	4.65	1.40	1.04	2.60	12.7
...	41 0000	OREGON	248 646.7	2 842 321	X	11	2 633 156	209 165	7.9	92.77	1.62	1.35	2.44	1.82	3.97	13.8
...	41 0010	Albany	29.7	29 462	834	992	26 511	2 951	11.1	96.13	0.34	1.14	1.28	1.11	3.01	14.1
6442	41 0095	Beaverton	35.8	53 310	451	1 489	31 962	21 348	66.8	89.44	1.00	0.54	7.66	1.36	3.30	9.1
...	41 0225	Corvallis	33.5	44 757	556	1 336	40 960	3 797	9.3	89.13	1.18	0.69	8.05	0.96	2.76	9.4
2400	41 0360	Eugene	98.5	112 669	158	1 144	105 664	7 005	6.6	93.43	1.25	0.89	3.46	0.97	2.71	12.7
6442	41 0465	Gresham	57.1	68 235	331	1 195	33 005	35 230	106.7	93.83	1.08	0.96	2.75	1.38	3.35	10.0
6442	41 0520	Hillsboro	49.9	37 520	678	752	27 664	9 856	35.6	88.58	0.49	0.56	2.20	8.17	11.20	8.7
4890	41 0720	Medford	47.3	46 951	526	993	39 746	7 205	18.1	94.78	0.26	1.20	1.15	2.60	5.08	17.4
6442	41 0905	Portland	322.9	437 319	30	1 354	368 148	69 171	18.8	84.64	7.67	1.23	5.30	1.16	3.17	14.6
7080	41 1005	Salem	107.6	107 786	176	1 002	89 091	18 695	21.0	91.18	1.51	1.64	2.39	3.27	6.11	14.5
2400	41 1085	Springfield	34.8	44 683	557	1 284	41 621	3 062	7.4	95.35	0.66	1.52	1.55	0.91	2.91	10.8
...	42 0000	PENNSYLVANIA	116 082.8	11 881 643	X	102	11 864 720	16 923	0.1	88.54	9.17	0.12	1.16	1.01	1.95	15.4

1. MSA = Metropolitan Statistical Area. CMSA = Consolidated MSA. 2. Dry land or land partially or temporarily covered by water. 3. Hispanic persons may be of any race.

City	Households, 1990: Number	Households, 1990: Persons per household	Households, 1990: Percent– Female family householder[1]	Households, 1990: Percent– One-person[2]	Births, 1984: Number: Total	Births, 1984: Number: To mothers under 20 yrs. old (Percent)	Births, 1984: Rate[3]	Deaths, 1984: Number: Total	Deaths, 1984: Number: Infant[4]	Deaths, 1984: Rate: Total[3]	Deaths, 1984: Rate: Infant[5]	Hospitals, 1985: Number	Hospitals, 1985: Beds: Number	Hospitals, 1985: Beds: Rate[6]
	15	16	17	18	19	20	21	22	23	24	25	26	27	28
OHIO—Con.														
Cuyahoga Falls	20 383	2.38	9.7	29.1	590	5.9	13.9	349	4	8.2	6.8	2	389	930
Dayton	72 670	2.41	20.6	33.4	3 535	21.7	19.5	2 083	55	11.5	15.6	9	4 766	2 664
East Cleveland	13 362	2.45	31.4	34.3	668	19.2	18.2	322	12	8.8	18.0	0	0	0
Elyria	21 423	2.61	13.9	24.8	980	13.7	17.1	463	12	8.1	12.2	1	359	627
Euclid	24 894	2.17	11.9	37.1	696	5.6	12.0	700	6	12.1	8.6	1	345	601
Fairborn	12 673	2.43	11.4	26.1	446	14.3	15.6	178	3	6.2	6.7	0	0	0
Fairfield	15 289	2.56	8.3	22.9	496	7.3	15.3	150	3	4.6	6.0	0	0	0
Findlay	14 117	2.46	9.2	28.0	622	11.6	17.3	328	7	9.1	11.3	1	239	652
Garfield Heights	12 483	2.52	13.7	26.0	454	8.4	13.5	372	6	11.0	13.2	1	279	836
Hamilton	23 992	2.52	14.9	26.7	1 208	17.8	18.9	643	11	10.1	9.1	2	604	929
Huber Heights	13 509	2.85	9.9	15.5	610	7.7	14.3	165	10	3.9	16.4	0	0	0
Kent	8 808	2.46	12.9	28.0	338	7.7	12.1	122	1	4.4	3.0	0	0	0
Kettering	26 098	2.30	8.5	30.0	720	4.9	12.0	512	6	8.5	8.3	1	618	1 033
Lakewood	26 999	2.20	10.7	41.0	860	4.8	14.2	626	8	10.3	9.3	1	410	689
Lancaster	13 981	2.44	12.4	27.4	541	15.9	15.6	358	8	10.3	14.8	1	177	511
Lima	16 311	2.57	17.9	28.3	881	22.5	19.1	594	13	12.9	14.8	3	827	1 798
Lorain	26 198	2.69	16.7	24.5	1 114	19.7	15.3	645	13	8.9	11.7	2	642	889
Mansfield	20 197	2.36	13.8	32.1	955	18.5	18.4	606	10	11.7	10.5	3	611	1 190
Maple Heights	10 551	2.55	12.0	25.2	364	6.9	12.7	326	4	11.4	11.0	0	0	0
Marion	13 179	2.56	13.3	26.5	623	18.5	17.4	365	9	10.2	14.4	2	419	1 194
Massillon	12 110	2.49	13.2	27.5	477	14.0	15.5	375	4	12.2	8.4	3	850	2 666
Mentor	16 730	2.82	8.4	17.2	602	5.5	14.0	278	8	6.5	13.3	0	0	0
Middletown	18 362	2.48	14.4	26.4	818	18.1	18.7	388	12	8.9	14.7	1	361	783
Newark	17 802	2.44	12.3	29.1	772	14.0	18.7	514	4	12.5	5.2	1	254	617
North Olmsted	12 657	2.68	8.9	22.4	393	5.9	10.9	260	7	7.2	17.8	0	0	0
Norwood	9 689	2.43	15.6	31.7	420	19.3	16.5	323	3	12.7	7.1	0	0	0
Parma	34 685	2.50	10.0	24.7	1 055	4.7	11.7	888	7	9.8	6.6	2	391	437
Portsmouth	9 667	2.29	15.4	35.2	335	24.5	13.7	383	2	15.7	6.0	3	528	2 289
Sandusky	12 059	2.44	14.7	31.8	535	15.7	17.5	348	2	11.4	3.7	3	488	1 599
Shaker Heights	12 648	2.43	11.2	27.7	327	4.3	10.4	306	2	9.7	6.1	0	0	0
South Euclid	9 388	2.52	10.3	24.6	356	2.5	14.2	288	3	11.5	8.4	0	0	0
Springfield	27 247	2.47	15.7	29.5	1 158	19.9	16.5	826	14	11.8	12.1	2	650	935
Steubenville	8 979	2.30	15.2	33.3	319	18.8	13.1	368	3	15.1	9.4	2	569	2 413
Stow	10 086	2.72	8.2	19.6	333	4.5	12.9	131	5	5.1	15.0	0	0	0
Strongsville	12 284	2.87	6.0	16.7	353	4.8	11.3	154	4	4.9	11.3	0	0	0
Toledo	130 883	2.50	15.7	29.7	5 594	17.0	16.3	3 548	51	10.3	9.1	7	2 915	856
Upper Arlington	13 956	2.43	6.8	25.6	366	1.4	10.1	318	3	8.8	8.2	0	0	0
Warren	20 314	2.45	17.2	29.6	934	18.3	17.3	663	6	12.3	6.4	4	995	1 881
Youngstown	37 037	2.52	21.5	29.5	1 641	17.9	15.2	1 463	31	13.5	18.9	6	1 814	1 733
Zanesville	10 819	2.42	17.4	32.3	520	22.9	18.4	443	5	15.6	9.6	2	579	2 074
OKLAHOMA	1 206 135	2.53	10.4	25.6	54 477	16.2	16.5	29 343	598	8.9	11.0	145	17 310	524
Bartlesville	14 013	2.41	8.3	26.8	587	9.5	16.4	345	12	9.7	20.4	1	312	1 040
Broken Arrow	19 256	2.99	8.4	13.3	1 055	6.5	22.5	247	8	5.3	7.6	1	73	142
Del City	9 193	2.59	13.9	22.9	471	15.1	17.4	162	2	6.0	4.2	0	0	0
Edmond	18 756	2.71	9.3	19.1	902	5.5	19.5	228	10	4.9	11.1	1	88	173
Enid	18 215	2.40	9.7	28.6	944	13.3	18.0	483	14	9.2	14.8	3	412	818
Lawton	29 566	2.66	13.2	21.9	2 168	16.7	25.3	596	28	7.0	12.9	3	365	441
Midwest City	20 390	2.54	13.7	25.7	1 015	15.0	19.0	310	16	5.8	15.8	1	146	273
Moore	13 567	2.96	11.5	14.3	693	13.4	17.2	157	5	3.9	7.2	1	76	182
Muskogee	15 088	2.42	14.5	30.7	725	23.4	16.9	559	6	13.1	8.3	2	512	1 205
Norman	31 907	2.34	9.2	30.3	1 155	8.3	15.3	418	11	5.5	9.5	3	869	1 109
Oklahoma City	178 662	2.44	12.6	30.0	8 357	15.8	18.9	3 897	96	8.8	11.5	12	3 798	851
Ponca City	10 733	2.41	8.4	28.9	456	8.8	15.9	281	6	9.8	13.2	1	167	592
Shawnee	10 337	2.39	12.1	30.9	495	18.6	17.7	384	5	13.7	10.1	2	182	660
Stillwater	14 172	2.19	7.2	32.9	538	7.6	14.1	205	5	5.4	9.3	2	164	448
Tulsa	155 447	2.31	11.8	32.7	6 376	14.2	17.0	3 246	69	8.7	10.8	9	2 985	799
OREGON	1 103 313	2.52	9.2	25.3	39 563	10.9	14.8	23 162	390	8.7	9.9	83	11 138	413
Albany	11 786	2.46	11.5	26.8	537	13.6	19.1	261	7	9.3	13.0	1	106	365
Beaverton	22 100	2.39	9.4	28.7	779	5.9	23.3	248	7	7.4	9.0	0	0	0
Corvallis	16 743	2.30	7.3	30.4	536	3.4	13.5	214	3	5.4	5.6	1	143	359
Eugene	46 274	2.30	9.2	31.0	1 483	6.5	14.6	807	10	7.9	6.7	2	454	431
Gresham	25 705	2.62	10.3	22.5	549	7.8	15.1	248	8	6.8	14.6	1	108	278
Hillsboro	12 849	2.87	10.8	19.4	583	9.8	19.4	206	8	6.9	13.7	1	137	443
Medford	18 867	2.44	10.7	26.8	738	11.9	17.6	427	5	10.2	6.8	2	473	1 085
Portland	187 268	2.27	11.0	34.9	6 116	10.7	16.7	4 318	73	11.8	11.9	17	3 950	1 018
Salem	40 936	2.41	11.2	29.9	1 732	12.2	19.2	1 027	26	11.4	15.0	2	1 153	1 228
Springfield	17 447	2.54	13.5	24.9	869	13.5	21.7	327	5	8.2	5.8	1	114	297
PENNSYLVANIA	4 495 966	2.57	11.3	25.6	157 110	11.7	13.2	122 009	1 638	10.3	10.4	306	75 198	633

1. No spouse present. 2. Householder living alone. 3. Per 1,000 resident population estimated as of July 1 of the year shown. 4. Deaths of infants under 1 year old. 5. Deaths of infants under 1 year old per 1,000 live births. 6. Per 100,000 resident population estimated as of July 1, 1986.

City	Serious crimes known to police, 1985: Number: Total	Serious crimes known to police, 1985: Number: Violent[1]	Serious crimes known to police, 1985: Rate[2]	Police officers, 1985: Number	Police officers, 1985: Rate[3]	Educational attainment,[4] 1980: Percent completing 12 years or more	Educational attainment,[4] 1980: Percent completing 16 years or more	Money income: Per capita[5]: 1985: Total (Dollars)	Money income: Per capita[5]: 1985: Percent of State average	Money income: Per capita[5]: 1979: Current dollars	Money income: Per capita[5]: 1979: Constant (1985) dollars	Money income: Percent below poverty level, 1979: Persons	Money income: Percent below poverty level, 1979: Families	Housing, 1990: Total units	Housing, 1990: Percent change, 1980–1990	Housing, 1990: Vacant units for sale or rent[6]
	29	30	31	32	33	34	35	36	37	38	39	40	41	42	43	44
OHIO—Con.																
Cuyahoga Falls	1 235	91	2 860	51	11.8	77.9	16.6	11 443	110.3	7 978	11 823	4.3	2.7	21 269	18.3	595
Dayton	17 077	2 295	9 434	440	24.3	59.3	10.4	8 621	83.1	5 816	8 619	20.8	17.4	80 370	-8.0	5 699
East Cleveland	2 561	304	6 976	63	17.2	64.5	10.4	8 806	84.9	6 173	9 148	22.6	22.3	15 168	-4.7	1 353
Elyria	1 716	124	3 006	71	12.4	67.3	11.3	9 744	94.0	7 208	10 682	10.1	8.6	22 544	2.4	854
Euclid	2 387	99	4 121	101	17.4	68.5	14.4	11 736	113.2	8 693	12 883	6.0	4.4	26 586	0.6	1 513
Fairborn	1 032	53	3 538	35	12.0	69.8	17.7	10 517	101.4	7 117	10 547	11.5	8.9	13 288	12.3	532
Fairfield	1 384	74	4 391	38	12.1	78.0	20.6	12 972	125.1	9 057	13 422	2.9	2.6	16 281	30.5	904
Findlay	NA	NA	NA	NA	NA	75.1	17.5	11 398	109.9	7 557	11 199	7.3	5.4	15 003	4.9	624
Garfield Heights	1 174	119	3 436	48	14.1	61.7	7.4	10 092	97.3	7 476	11 079	5.9	4.5	13 000	0.8	398
Hamilton	4 806	528	7 555	103	16.2	56.2	9.1	9 596	92.5	6 634	9 832	13.4	10.9	25 362	1.6	1 046
Huber Heights	NA	NA	NA	NA	NA	80.2	15.8	10 909	105.2	7 633	11 312	5.1	4.5	14 306	15.3	733
Kent	1 149	63	4 191	30	10.9	81.9	32.7	8 196	79.0	5 873	8 704	21.4	11.3	9 275	0.8	374
Kettering	2 540	119	4 225	80	13.3	81.1	23.9	14 751	142.2	9 794	14 515	4.2	2.9	27 096	6.5	822
Lakewood	1 967	95	3 214	79	12.9	77.0	22.0	12 631	121.8	9 008	13 350	6.3	4.6	28 521	0.2	1 104
Lancaster	1 764	358	5 028	57	16.2	64.8	9.9	10 364	99.9	7 186	10 650	9.9	7.5	14 754	5.1	483
Lima	3 525	346	7 547	82	17.6	60.2	8.3	8 748	84.4	6 077	9 006	16.9	13.7	18 666	-2.1	1 468
Lorain	2 395	175	3 219	81	10.9	58.8	7.5	9 007	86.8	6 727	9 969	13.4	11.3	27 544	-0.2	879
Mansfield	4 133	653	7 844	79	15.0	63.2	11.3	9 814	94.6	6 536	9 686	13.6	10.4	21 909	-2.6	1 210
Maple Heights	697	85	2 405	48	16.6	63.3	6.8	10 553	101.8	7 720	11 441	4.8	3.7	10 791	-1.3	180
Marion	2 510	128	6 858	40	10.9	60.8	9.4	8 502	82.0	6 226	9 227	14.8	11.5	14 243	-3.7	628
Massillon	1 668	162	5 427	47	15.3	63.1	7.6	9 165	88.4	6 356	9 420	10.0	7.7	12 814	4.1	481
Mentor	1 235	39	2 909	56	13.2	80.8	18.9	12 504	120.6	8 852	13 119	2.8	2.3	17 172	17.6	352
Middletown	2 761	107	6 330	79	18.1	60.8	12.1	10 028	96.7	7 447	11 036	12.8	9.8	19 385	8.0	774
Newark	1 731	62	4 149	61	14.6	63.8	11.2	9 919	95.6	6 915	10 248	11.6	8.7	18 967	9.7	897
North Olmsted	1 226	37	3 409	43	12.0	81.3	21.1	12 761	123.0	8 974	13 299	2.8	2.3	13 081	3.5	341
Norwood	1 290	56	5 004	53	20.6	49.7	5.4	9 606	92.6	6 909	10 239	9.7	7.3	10 260	-6.2	409
Parma	2 345	138	2 600	87	9.6	68.9	10.9	11 521	111.1	8 503	12 601	3.0	2.1	35 589	3.7	702
Portsmouth	1 489	104	5 959	37	14.8	56.7	9.3	8 838	85.2	5 969	8 846	19.5	15.2	10 758	-4.9	669
Sandusky	1 888	126	6 117	40	13.0	61.7	9.0	9 913	95.6	7 051	10 450	11.0	8.5	13 416	1.8	784
Shaker Heights	NA	NA	NA	NA	NA	90.7	50.6	22 648	218.4	15 668	23 220	3.4	2.2	13 374	0.9	618
South Euclid	726	19	2 876	37	14.7	78.5	24.3	12 964	125.0	9 204	13 640	3.2	2.4	9 565	0.1	126
Springfield	5 508	989	7 753	97	13.7	59.7	10.3	9 108	87.8	6 283	9 311	17.6	14.1	29 562	0.7	1 613
Steubenville	1 141	160	4 492	38	15.0	61.3	11.3	9 687	93.4	7 619	11 291	14.3	11.5	9 996	-11.6	641
Stow	848	11	3 337	24	9.4	82.0	26.5	12 260	118.2	8 530	12 641	2.8	2.1	10 462	15.2	312
Strongsville	788	16	2 651	38	12.8	83.3	22.7	13 986	134.9	9 911	14 688	2.1	1.8	13 099	25.5	734
Toledo	24 934	2 159	7 255	758	22.1	63.9	12.2	10 050	96.9	7 050	10 448	13.6	10.7	142 125	-0.8	7 550
Upper Arlington	1 173	10	3 323	43	12.2	95.3	52.0	21 696	209.2	14 448	21 412	2.4	1.7	14 376	3.3	293
Warren	2 774	362	4 994	81	14.6	64.6	9.3	10 030	96.7	7 166	10 620	13.9	11.8	21 785	-2.7	1 150
Youngstown	7 351	1 211	6 809	206	19.1	56.0	7.3	7 968	76.8	5 912	8 762	18.2	14.6	40 802	-10.5	2 407
Zanesville	1 817	106	6 354	54	18.9	54.0	7.4	8 025	77.4	5 512	8 169	18.7	14.4	11 770	-3.6	670
OKLAHOMA	179 080	13 930	5 425	NA	NA	66.0	15.1	9 754	100.0	6 854	10 158	13.4	10.3	1 406 499	12.0	112 149
Bartlesville	2 075	98	5 412	51	13.3	79.3	29.9	14 551	149.2	9 683	14 350	6.4	4.0	15 908	6.9	1 212
Broken Arrow	1 698	105	3 905	55	12.6	83.8	21.9	11 237	115.2	8 051	11 932	4.4	3.2	20 420	38.0	894
Del City	1 633	111	5 525	35	11.8	75.0	9.4	10 355	106.2	6 983	10 349	7.2	5.3	10 773	-0.1	1 052
Edmond	1 870	35	4 553	64	15.6	87.5	36.3	13 168	135.0	9 148	13 557	7.3	5.3	20 598	38.2	1 429
Enid	4 094	156	7 316	79	14.1	71.7	17.2	10 852	111.3	7 822	11 592	8.5	6.0	21 680	4.1	2 188
Lawton	5 444	511	6 182	143	16.2	74.1	15.8	8 976	92.0	5 904	8 750	15.2	12.4	34 622	7.8	3 898
Midwest City	3 915	239	7 210	89	16.4	75.7	13.5	11 003	112.8	7 359	10 906	7.4	5.7	22 846	14.7	2 007
Moore	2 396	173	6 010	52	13.0	78.8	13.8	9 758	100.0	6 746	9 998	5.8	5.1	14 824	20.7	1 014
Muskogee	2 776	244	6 659	58	13.9	61.7	13.8	8 706	89.3	6 203	9 193	19.4	15.2	17 674	1.6	1 851
Norman	4 466	127	5 946	103	13.7	81.6	36.6	11 236	115.2	7 410	10 982	12.5	6.7	35 650	24.6	3 044
Oklahoma City	49 633	4 328	11 189	732	16.5	72.4	18.9	11 527	118.2	7 998	11 853	12.0	9.3	212 367	16.6	23 602
Ponca City	1 056	38	3 687	48	16.8	72.2	20.0	11 822	121.2	7 923	11 742	7.3	5.0	12 294	7.2	974
Shawnee	2 531	128	8 943	46	16.3	62.8	13.0	9 037	92.6	6 255	9 270	18.0	13.3	11 784	3.4	930
Stillwater	1 369	56	3 375	47	11.6	83.6	41.7	8 023	82.3	5 517	8 176	20.7	9.9	15 771	11.0	1 219
Tulsa	32 652	2 902	8 710	694	18.5	77.3	21.7	12 670	129.9	8 842	13 104	10.4	7.4	176 211	11.3	15 096
OREGON	180 830	14 807	6 730	NA	NA	75.6	17.9	9 925	100.0	7 556	11 198	10.7	7.7	1 193 567	9.2	40 232
Albany	1 967	60	6 898	31	10.9	75.0	12.7	8 828	88.9	6 909	10 239	14.5	11.7	12 322	8.7	410
Beaverton	2 162	64	6 459	47	14.0	88.2	29.1	12 273	123.7	9 395	13 923	7.3	5.1	24 083	43.8	1 853
Corvallis	2 272	52	5 476	40	9.6	89.4	45.2	9 512	95.8	6 675	9 892	17.7	7.8	17 307	11.2	403
Eugene	8 592	377	8 417	132	12.9	85.3	33.7	10 305	103.8	7 818	11 586	14.7	8.0	47 991	6.4	1 315
Gresham	2 277	132	6 504	46	13.1	81.4	17.9	10 349	104.3	7 802	11 563	6.4	4.3	26 978	54.1	850
Hillsboro	1 667	56	5 661	39	13.2	78.4	16.8	9 781	98.5	7 525	11 152	7.8	6.5	13 347	24.3	398
Medford	3 522	141	8 673	62	15.3	76.1	17.3	10 255	103.3	7 657	11 348	12.1	9.1	19 684	15.9	613
Portland	62 255	8 634	16 937	758	20.6	75.8	22.1	10 770	108.5	8 123	12 038	13.0	8.5	198 368	15.4	7 344
Salem	8 406	228	9 250	129	14.2	76.8	21.8	9 824	99.0	7 310	10 833	11.8	8.1	42 601	12.9	1 311
Springfield	3 526	155	8 513	47	11.3	69.6	9.7	8 206	82.7	6 365	9 433	15.2	12.0	18 121	3.6	505
PENNSYLVANIA	360 028	39 240	3 037	NA	NA	64.7	13.6	10 288	100.0	7 075	10 485	10.5	7.8	4 938 140	6.9	195 284

1. Includes murder and nonnegligent manslaughter, forcible rape, robbery, and aggravated assault. 2. Per 100,000 resident population estimated for 1985 by the FBI. 3. Per 10,000 resident population estimated for 1985 by the FBI. 4. Persons 25 years old or older. 5. Based on the resident population estimated as of July 1, 1988 for 1987 data and enumerated as of April 1, 1980 for 1979 data. 6. Also includes units rented or sold, but not occupied.

City	Housing, 1990 (cont'd)					Construction authorized by building permits, 1990				Civilian labor force, 1990			
	Occupied units					New private housing units						Unemployment	
			Owner-occupied										
	Total	Percent with more than 1 person per room	Percent of total	Median value[1] (Dollars)	Median rent[2] (Dollars)	Number	Value ($1,000)	Percent single family	Non-residential, value ($1,000)	Total	Percent change, 1989–1990	Total	Rate[3]
	45	46	47	48	49	50	51	52	53	54	55	56	57
OHIO—Con.													
Cuyahoga Falls	20 383	0.8	66.6	61 500	370	238	10 558	99.2	4 816	23 515	0.2	904	3.8
Dayton	72 670	3.0	51.0	43 200	253	66	5 208	59.1	19 278	89 823	-0.4	7 060	7.9
East Cleveland	13 362	2.3	32.3	42 200	289	0	0	NA	0	17 770	0.1	1 546	8.7
Elyria	21 423	2.1	62.9	56 300	298	67	6 522	100.0	7 632	26 153	0.1	2 220	8.5
Euclid	24 894	1.0	58.7	65 000	384	12	645	66.7	1 295	32 502	0.2	1 101	3.4
Fairborn	12 673	4.2	51.3	61 800	359	33	1 535	45.5	7 602	14 863	-0.5	881	5.9
Fairfield	15 289	0.8	64.0	86 300	438	134	12 981	73.1	8 951	18 524	0.0	773	4.2
Findlay	14 117	1.2	67.7	62 700	288	103	5 214	47.6	0	22 394	0.3	1 048	4.7
Garfield Heights	12 483	1.2	80.8	58 500	352	7	370	42.9	846	17 945	0.2	606	3.4
Hamilton	23 992	2.6	60.5	53 700	286	91	7 043	45.1	7 000	30 994	0.0	2 123	6.8
Huber Heights	13 509	1.4	70.8	65 900	439	NA	NA	NA	NA	18 678	-0.5	671	3.6
Kent	8 808	2.5	38.6	68 400	339	211	7 038	9.0	309	15 099	0.5	698	4.6
Kettering	26 098	0.8	65.9	77 900	381	53	5 659	49.1	8 308	34 963	-0.5	991	2.8
Lakewood	26 999	1.0	44.5	73 200	352	0	0	NA	3 198	34 064	0.2	1 092	3.2
Lancaster	13 981	1.5	59.9	51 700	279	22	1 256	90.9	0	20 147	0.8	1 238	6.1
Lima	16 311	2.1	59.1	38 900	252	68	2 572	33.8	6 540	22 074	-0.6	2 085	9.4
Lorain	26 198	3.5	61.1	52 300	278	115	7 818	55.7	2 480	30 541	0.2	2 717	8.9
Mansfield	20 197	1.7	58.0	42 300	257	78	4 804	38.5	3 232	25 380	-1.5	2 118	8.3
Maple Heights	10 551	1.5	85.0	57 900	359	23	1 857	100.0	11	15 604	0.2	533	3.4
Marion	13 179	1.7	61.5	34 500	232	5	181	100.0	0	15 542	0.8	1 552	10.0
Massillon	12 110	1.3	67.3	43 600	241	71	3 790	49.3	606	14 483	-0.2	1 095	7.6
Mentor	16 730	0.7	85.9	89 800	470	288	33 147	88.2	12 900	24 138	0.0	1 136	4.7
Middletown	18 362	2.2	60.0	57 600	280	109	7 478	92.7	12 362	21 282	0.0	1 659	7.8
Newark	17 802	1.5	56.8	49 500	269	120	7 324	61.7	2 829	22 232	0.9	1 629	7.3
North Olmsted	12 657	0.8	79.0	94 700	446	37	5 051	100.0	2 664	19 125	0.2	591	3.1
Norwood	9 689	2.7	51.7	51 800	273	84	1 156	0.0	4 149	14 675	1.0	720	4.9
Parma	34 685	1.0	77.8	74 200	408	68	7 002	94.1	4 444	48 709	0.2	1 779	3.7
Portsmouth	9 667	1.4	56.7	32 800	203	7	400	42.9	735	NA	NA	NA	NA
Sandusky	12 059	2.1	57.5	48 800	273	194	5 782	7.2	20 476	16 234	0.4	1 051	6.5
Shaker Heights	12 648	0.5	64.9	138 100	504	2	240	100.0	6 950	17 009	0.2	386	2.3
South Euclid	9 388	0.5	87.4	71 200	433	5	592	100.0	0	13 415	0.2	342	2.5
Springfield	27 247	2.1	55.8	42 000	247	116	7 159	93.1	5 088	33 503	0.0	2 390	7.1
Steubenville	8 979	0.9	59.1	44 100	186	10	758	100.0	8 350	NA	NA	NA	NA
Stow	10 086	0.8	72.2	83 700	414	311	21 907	45.0	3 896	13 565	0.2	489	3.6
Strongsville	12 284	0.7	82.4	117 300	414	513	65 670	72.5	5 409	14 803	0.1	468	3.2
Toledo	130 883	1.9	60.7	48 900	286	208	6 077	37.5	22 887	174 118	-0.6	13 898	8.0
Upper Arlington	13 956	0.3	81.7	141 800	495	31	6 524	87.1	348	21 520	1.0	349	1.6
Warren	20 314	1.8	58.6	42 900	255	41	1 722	12.2	1 680	23 543	-0.6	2 134	9.1
Youngstown	37 037	1.9	64.6	31 000	204	5	402	100.0	15 269	42 291	-0.3	3 991	9.4
Zanesville	10 819	2.2	56.3	34 600	224	170	5 554	4.7	5 727	13 646	2.6	1 479	10.8
OKLAHOMA	1 206 135	3.3	68.1	48 100	259	5 284	400 621	89.7	287 939	1 540 000	1.1	86 000	5.6
Bartlesville	14 013	1.4	71.4	55 300	273	82	13 216	100.0	759	17 426	5.8	668	3.8
Broken Arrow	19 256	2.3	74.3	67 700	385	433	27 173	100.0	19 979	19 186	1.4	924	4.8
Del City	9 193	3.9	68.0	43 300	285	3	201	100.0	65	15 847	0.1	768	4.8
Edmond	18 756	1.9	67.8	80 000	332	479	55 301	100.0	3 282	20 400	0.0	956	4.7
Enid	18 215	2.3	65.6	38 400	243	31	3 567	100.0	1 062	22 171	-1.5	985	4.4
Lawton	29 566	4.4	57.9	55 000	298	57	6 256	100.0	7 055	38 615	-0.5	2 170	5.6
Midwest City	20 390	3.7	63.0	48 300	300	80	4 579	100.0	4 315	27 550	0.3	1 759	6.4
Moore	13 567	3.2	74.1	51 200	353	111	6 535	100.0	2 499	22 440	-0.4	907	4.0
Muskogee	15 088	2.7	63.7	40 300	229	82	3 485	100.0	0	18 625	1.0	1 227	6.6
Norman	31 907	2.4	51.0	65 600	294	235	18 928	99.1	4 416	45 281	-0.3	2 395	5.3
Oklahoma City	178 662	4.1	59.5	54 900	282	886	72 547	100.0	35 015	233 789	0.2	13 418	5.7
Ponca City	10 733	2.0	70.0	48 600	261	49	7 021	100.0	0	14 121	1.1	602	4.3
Shawnee	10 337	2.7	64.3	40 200	236	69	3 198	53.6	870	12 719	-0.2	900	7.1
Stillwater	14 172	2.2	39.7	64 900	312	46	4 092	100.0	4 859	20 269	0.4	994	4.9
Tulsa	155 447	2.8	55.8	60 500	293	984	78 468	69.5	78 248	200 929	1.4	9 893	4.9
OREGON	1 103 313	3.6	63.1	67 100	344	22 858	1 657 464	58.2	536 000	1 492 000	1.2	82 000	5.5
Albany	11 786	3.5	51.9	52 000	316	92	8 255	81.5	5 851	14 314	0.5	904	6.3
Beaverton	22 100	2.8	47.0	89 800	455	1 293	97 409	47.9	18 587	23 652	2.0	841	3.6
Corvallis	16 743	3.4	43.2	71 000	334	308	19 695	41.2	63 120	22 876	2.4	837	3.7
Eugene	46 274	2.6	50.7	73 200	375	1 434	86 779	31.7	15 210	61 013	1.1	2 942	4.8
Gresham	25 705	2.8	58.4	71 100	386	981	52 552	28.4	8 207	19 314	1.0	655	3.4
Hillsboro	12 849	5.6	58.6	71 900	397	563	38 446	63.1	12 966	18 557	2.0	659	3.6
Medford	18 867	3.4	56.7	71 500	358	842	63 491	46.0	15 697	22 662	-0.7	1 540	6.8
Portland	187 268	3.5	53.0	59 200	340	1 323	84 451	55.1	89 110	212 783	0.7	10 722	5.0
Salem	40 936	4.0	54.7	60 300	325	1 023	47 205	47.1	22 997	51 844	2.1	2 768	5.3
Springfield	17 447	5.0	49.3	51 000	362	178	12 264	98.9	9 590	22 544	1.2	1 746	7.7
PENNSYLVANIA	4 495 966	1.8	70.6	69 700	322	37 244	2 898 341	83.4	2 206 297	5 901 000	0.8	318 000	5.4

1. Specified owner-occupied units. 2. Specified renter-occupied units. 3. Percent of total civilian labor force.

City	Employed,[1] 1980			Manufactures, 1987											
		Rate per 1,000 employees		Establishments		All employees			Production workers						
											Wages				
	Total	Profes-sional, specialty, and technical	Precision pro-duction, craft, and opera-tors	Total	Percent with 20 or more employ-ees	Number (1,000)	Percent change, 1982–1987	Annual payroll (Mil. dol.)	Number (1,000)	Work-hours (Millions)	Total (Mil. dol.)	Average per pro-duction worker (Dollars)	Value added by manu-facture (Mil. dol.)	Value of shipments (Mil. dol.)	New capital expend-itures (Mil. dol.)
	58	59	60	61	62	63	64	65	66	67	68	69	70	71	72
OHIO—Con.															
Cuyahoga Falls	20 627	183.0	209.0	58	43.1	2.1	-69.6	61.5	1.3	2.4	24.0	18 462	82.4	183.7	9.9
Dayton	72 704	148.4	217.9	466	42.3	36.4	-5.9	1 155.6	20.9	43.5	622.4	29 780	1 935.1	3 589.1	119.9
East Cleveland	15 328	144.9	222.9	19	36.8	1.7	-51.4	67.6	0.2	0.4	4.7	23 500	12.9	21.1	D
Elyria	24 161	146.2	316.9	129	45.7	10.7	11.5	300.5	6.5	13.1	163.4	25 138	731.5	1 436.0	32.3
Euclid	29 668	168.5	239.6	126	45.2	11.5	-21.2	392.2	6.9	14.5	214.8	31 130	722.2	1 346.7	37.0
Fairborn	11 942	186.5	199.2	17	35.3	0.8	NA	17.5	0.5	1.0	10.2	20 400	54.1	99.6	3.0
Fairfield	15 389	176.0	210.3	47	36.2	2.8	-3.4	96.6	2.2	4.4	73.6	33 455	167.9	378.4	3.1
Findlay	16 717	150.3	245.6	61	34.4	5.3	-24.3	140.3	3.6	6.9	80.4	22 333	365.4	744.2	52.7
Garfield Heights	16 382	118.3	259.4	50	40.0	1.5	25.0	33.4	1.0	2.1	20.3	20 300	86.6	164.1	4.3
Hamilton	25 029	116.9	264.3	87	40.2	7.1	-14.5	194.4	4.3	9.1	112.7	26 209	368.7	742.8	24.4
Huber Heights	15 744	172.1	219.1	22	27.3	1.1	37.5	26.3	0.6	1.1	11.4	19 000	72.4	120.7	2.3
Kent	12 543	251.7	148.8	67	44.8	2.4	4.3	55.1	1.7	3.3	33.2	19 529	91.0	233.1	3.8
Kettering	29 703	230.9	168.7	68	30.9	6.0	7.1	209.0	4.0	8.1	126.5	31 625	359.9	710.0	D
Lakewood	31 152	192.7	169.3	46	23.9	1.1	-26.7	31.5	0.5	1.1	14.9	29 800	65.7	101.5	D
Lancaster	15 141	117.0	300.7	66	30.3	D	D	D	D	D	D	D	D	D	D
Lima	17 978	109.5	271.7	62	33.9	D	D	D	D	D	D	D	D	D	D
Lorain	28 089	119.2	323.3	56	30.4	D	D	D	D	D	D	D	D	D	D
Mansfield	21 334	132.5	278.3	140	43.6	9.8	-10.1	244.9	6.9	14.4	155.2	22 493	473.6	1 019.3	D
Maple Heights	14 239	97.7	274.1	39	33.3	2.0	17.6	51.6	1.4	3.1	34.7	24 786	89.3	222.1	3.9
Marion	14 818	124.0	286.8	46	41.3	3.4	-54.1	92.0	2.0	4.1	48.4	24 200	214.2	478.5	11.7
Massillon	12 555	126.2	281.2	58	34.5	3.3	-23.3	77.5	2.5	5.2	51.9	20 760	233.0	489.2	D
Mentor	20 568	173.0	246.7	189	36.5	4.8	-18.6	109.6	3.2	6.2	57.8	18 062	209.7	362.0	10.1
Middletown	17 012	135.3	249.6	62	46.8	8.8	-21.4	315.0	6.3	13.5	217.3	34 492	785.6	1 699.6	25.2
Newark	17 113	143.6	237.1	66	39.4	3.9	-23.5	106.3	2.9	6.4	79.8	27 517	351.2	622.2	12.8
North Olmsted	17 511	159.2	166.6	NA	NA	NA	NA	NA	NA	NA	NA	NA	NA	NA	NA
Norwood	11 475	80.8	367.0	49	46.9	5.9	-33.7	157.0	4.2	7.7	109.0	25 952	554.8	1 499.0	6.7
Parma	44 340	143.0	242.8	41	22.0	D	D	D	D	D	D	D	D	D	D
Portsmouth	8 477	162.6	176.8	30	30.0	D	D	D	D	D	D	D	D	D	D
Sandusky	13 246	120.8	305.5	86	46.5	4.1	13.9	98.0	2.8	5.7	60.9	21 750	212.0	537.5	D
Shaker Heights	15 705	343.5	63.9	NA	NA	NA	NA	NA	NA	NA	NA	NA	NA	NA	NA
South Euclid	12 351	208.6	154.6	18	22.2	D	D	D	D	D	D	D	D	D	D
Springfield	27 699	151.6	252.8	134	41.8	10.3	8.4	294.4	7.9	14.9	216.9	27 456	1 022.7	2 755.4	78.3
Steubenville	10 306	153.5	196.1	21	28.6	D	D	D	D	D	D	D	D	D	D
Stow	11 929	211.3	212.5	54	51.9	2.3	15.0	61.7	1.5	3.3	34.8	23 200	123.0	244.8	11.7
Strongsville	13 544	161.8	199.1	57	50.9	3.4	21.4	92.2	2.0	3.9	46.7	23 350	136.3	293.5	4.8
Toledo	141 698	158.3	225.8	560	38.4	39.5	-6.0	1 366.0	25.6	56.7	790.1	30 863	3 355.6	9 198.1	184.4
Upper Arlington	17 038	326.5	46.7	NA	NA	NA	NA	NA	NA	NA	NA	NA	NA	NA	NA
Warren	21 682	132.9	312.5	87	33.3	15.8	-7.1	571.6	11.8	23.7	423.0	35 847	1 069.7	2 096.1	56.9
Youngstown	39 246	120.0	278.2	163	34.4	6.0	-26.8	145.3	4.2	8.1	86.7	20 643	261.3	619.4	13.0
Zanesville	10 622	125.9	258.4	58	36.2	5.9	11.3	119.6	4.9	9.6	91.4	18 653	337.3	594.2	7.0
OKLAHOMA	1 287 857	140.9	229.8	3 728	27.3	151.2	-23.4	3 629.3	104.8	207.0	2 195.6	20 950	9 856.9	24 073.9	538.4
Bartlesville	16 600	259.3	154.1	29	27.6	2.4	D	78.3	0.9	1.6	19.3	21 444	86.2	156.0	4.9
Broken Arrow	17 193	148.8	191.1	93	24.7	2.4	33.3	55.9	1.7	3.2	34.2	20 118	125.4	211.7	7.6
Del City	13 273	111.1	249.2	NA	NA	NA	NA	NA	NA	NA	NA	NA	NA	NA	NA
Edmond	17 114	210.4	134.2	NA	NA	NA	NA	NA	NA	NA	NA	NA	NA	NA	NA
Enid	22 689	131.8	231.5	46	15.2	D	D	D	D	D	D	D	D	D	D
Lawton	27 917	145.5	189.7	47	25.5	D	D	D	D	D	D	D	D	D	D
Midwest City	22 701	137.4	229.6	21	28.6	0.7	-22.2	13.6	0.5	0.9	7.5	15 000	26.5	45.5	0.6
Moore	16 658	122.8	236.4	NA	NA	NA	NA	NA	NA	NA	NA	NA	NA	NA	NA
Muskogee	15 535	140.3	201.6	55	30.9	3.6	-14.3	87.1	2.7	5.3	66.6	24 667	297.5	612.2	17.4
Norman	33 177	246.0	131.3	65	23.1	2.0	-39.4	41.6	1.3	2.6	23.3	17 923	239.2	412.7	8.7
Oklahoma City	191 843	151.5	203.1	727	27.4	39.7	-4.8	1 000.4	27.0	50.7	619.8	22 956	3 089.5	8 216.6	116.9
Ponca City	12 163	181.5	207.4	36	41.7	2.1	D	58.3	1.5	2.9	36.3	24 200	155.8	1 194.7	20.0
Shawnee	10 470	151.6	248.8	36	44.4	2.3	35.3	52.1	1.8	3.2	37.2	20 667	140.6	311.3	10.1
Stillwater	17 216	286.0	136.6	28	25.0	D	D	D	D	D	D	D	D	D	D
Tulsa	180 789	167.4	193.6	868	27.2	33.4	-33.2	966.9	19.4	41.4	470.2	24 237	1 864.9	3 836.7	112.8
OREGON	1 138 425	149.5	197.9	6 353	25.9	202.9	9.6	4 767.2	144.3	280.0	2 948.6	20 434	11 610.3	25 351.7	735.4
Albany	11 683	137.0	232.5	81	32.1	4.0	0.0	110.6	2.8	5.4	68.8	24 571	284.9	515.6	14.5
Beaverton	16 517	176.7	174.2	153	29.4	13.1	403.8	369.8	5.4	11.0	110.6	20 481	587.0	1 130.3	64.0
Corvallis	17 559	318.5	101.4	73	19.2	3.3	-19.5	92.3	1.9	3.4	40.2	21 158	140.4	262.4	D
Eugene	48 559	228.1	131.7	336	23.2	8.6	38.7	180.3	5.8	10.8	103.1	17 776	346.8	848.6	17.7
Gresham	16 062	135.6	200.2	52	15.4	D	D	D	D	D	D	D	D	D	D
Hillsboro	12 959	156.0	237.7	89	32.6	2.8	55.6	58.3	1.8	3.6	30.6	17 000	229.4	475.8	24.1
Medford	16 152	148.0	163.1	92	20.7	2.1	16.7	51.2	1.6	3.2	36.2	22 625	124.9	322.4	6.9
Portland	173 812	173.7	173.0	1 084	28.1	32.7	-7.1	806.1	21.9	42.2	456.6	20 849	1 831.0	4 135.0	78.1
Salem	37 688	173.8	159.1	208	29.8	5.9	7.3	114.7	4.2	7.7	65.7	15 643	307.4	594.1	22.0
Springfield	17 391	86.2	238.7	97	36.1	4.5	-2.2	117.1	3.7	7.5	91.9	24 838	340.0	844.7	22.8
PENNSYLVANIA	4 961 501	149.7	252.1	17 844	40.5	1 037.5	-12.1	25 301.6	681.9	1 330.1	13 731.1	20 137	57 605.2	118 651.3	3 440.5

1. Persons 16 years old and over.

City	Wholesale trade, 1987				Retail trade–all establishments, 1987				Retail trade–establishments with payroll, 1987					
						Sales				Sales				
											Per capita[2] (Dollars)			
	Establishments	Sales (Mil. dol.)	Paid employees[1]	Annual payroll ($1,000)	Number	Total (Mil. dol.)	Percent change, 1982–1987	Per capita[2] (Dollars)	Number	Total (Mil. dol.)	General merchandise group stores	Food stores	Apparel and accessory stores	Eating and drinking places
	73	74	75	76	77	78	79	80	81	82	83	84	85	86
OHIO—Con.														
Cuyahoga Falls	56	D	D	D	386	351.5	77.6	8 405	296	347.4	D	2 033	541	839
Dayton	401	3 099.5	6 868	168 623	1 277	1 056.4	19.5	5 904	982	1 046.1	807	1 057	137	634
East Cleveland	13	61.0	114	2 974	143	77.0	17.7	2 119	103	75.1	D	715	92	379
Elyria	65	117.4	593	10 603	505	489.5	52.0	8 547	366	484.8	2 037	1 100	388	625
Euclid	84	383.4	1 028	30 053	420	278.5	6.3	4 853	294	273.7	844	585	363	503
Fairborn	16	93.3	249	4 924	249	243.5	41.2	8 678	177	240.8	846	1 621	115	822
Fairfield	64	D	D	D	345	443.5	104.2	12 987	227	436.7	D	1 744	100	1 035
Findlay	64	D	D	D	548	339.0	35.7	9 247	355	331.3	D	1 113	D	1 161
Garfield Heights	54	180.5	767	17 794	198	109.2	2.2	3 273	125	106.3	798	1 047	103	336
Hamilton	99	D	D	D	662	381.8	32.0	5 869	436	371.4	763	1 674	160	617
Huber Heights	24	70.4	278	4 673	256	163.6	65.8	3 593	160	159.8	D	1 169	116	370
Kent	28	D	D	D	255	262.7	73.9	9 399	182	257.4	D	1 256	82	857
Kettering	120	326.5	798	17 978	581	0.0	0.0	D	409	431.2	D	1 584	254	928
Lakewood	93	186.2	663	14 445	459	270.3	33.6	4 540	267	262.7	D	834	94	535
Lancaster	49	58.9	316	5 575	530	323.1	33.0	9 319	333	316.5	D	2 224	D	887
Lima	111	715.3	1 753	36 896	467	251.0	21.5	5 458	315	244.4	624	1 126	135	629
Lorain	42	310.1	484	10 908	438	244.9	0.3	3 391	297	240.0	238	731	131	375
Mansfield	146	411.5	1 638	33 770	679	451.3	27.3	8 790	470	441.8	1 053	1 359	341	817
Maple Heights	31	287.4	1 287	27 459	275	190.5	21.3	6 720	217	187.7	D	2 099	434	550
Marion	51	106.2	514	10 172	457	266.2	56.1	7 588	302	259.5	932	1 521	307	711
Massillon	34	315.9	999	22 408	341	274.9	42.9	8 623	233	270.4	1 284	2 627	217	548
Mentor	118	573.9	1 617	46 734	563	621.5	48.4	14 390	401	612.8	3 713	1 618	821	1 074
Middletown	49	158.1	608	13 565	436	271.8	27.8	5 897	265	264.0	1 272	1 130	76	697
Newark	70	149.7	629	13 219	511	336.4	26.0	8 165	318	329.0	1 478	1 757	200	704
North Olmsted	50	332.5	342	7 275	496	594.4	78.4	16 566	383	591.0	3 921	2 316	1 537	1 215
Norwood	36	91.3	533	11 675	191	127.5	7.7	5 104	138	125.3	D	1 744	78	715
Parma	87	613.6	1 478	38 102	825	687.5	41.3	7 685	594	676.3	1 420	1 395	552	663
Portsmouth	60	163.8	627	9 427	402	226.4	9.4	9 814	280	220.1	1 129	1 968	480	1 396
Sandusky	61	151.3	668	12 979	499	378.4	50.8	12 398	367	372.7	3 189	1 899	660	1 149
Shaker Heights	62	609.0	480	12 689	241	193.1	19.8	6 259	165	190.2	D	1 453	422	520
South Euclid	48	47.9	162	3 248	262	103.7	29.5	4 156	167	99.6	D	1 476	190	658
Springfield	100	451.0	1 222	25 731	631	456.0	42.0	6 561	461	449.5	666	1 610	95	747
Steubenville	50	117.2	488	10 058	333	260.4	33.4	11 043	264	256.1	D	1 524	731	878
Stow	46	293.1	533	19 067	216	159.8	31.0	6 201	126	157.1	D	1 517	135	406
Strongsville	87	701.3	1 163	31 286	257	156.4	40.6	4 784	151	150.8	D	1 200	29	469
Toledo	656	3 096.3	8 928	219 782	2 881	2 042.6	23.4	5 996	2 194	2 018.6	1 249	1 217	356	816
Upper Arlington	47	234.1	389	10 568	297	180.7	7.5	4 934	189	177.5	D	1 477	876	538
Warren	95	210.8	977	17 579	716	462.4	42.1	8 741	475	452.6	396	1 907	230	909
Youngstown	238	766.0	3 051	60 544	932	504.9	11.7	4 822	658	488.4	223	1 313	188	495
Zanesville	80	359.5	1 232	26 253	644	377.1	56.8	13 506	413	364.6	D	2 238	696	1 562
OKLAHOMA	5 974	20 212.6	54 918	1 117 781	35 949	16 912.5	5.2	5 117	20 235	16 073.5	630	1 103	268	484
Bartlesville	40	D	D	D	464	278.2	12.1	9 270	313	272.7	1 497	2 388	D	813
Broken Arrow	96	D	D	D	543	0.0	0.0	D	271	D	D	D	241	482
Del City	24	D	D	D	224	113.3	-1.2	4 338	136	111.1	D	1 318	D	728
Edmond	56	77.5	221	4 479	569	245.4	4.4	4 814	294	232.8	D	1 144	229	603
Enid	124	D	D	D	635	338.7	-7.3	6 727	439	327.8	D	1 332	D	617
Lawton	90	176.1	920	15 059	871	528.6	12.0	6 382	583	514.5	1 348	1 120	253	619
Midwest City	30	22.6	141	1 676	540	527.6	49.1	9 867	353	517.8	2 288	2 129	458	674
Moore	37	46.0	269	5 166	356	209.9	45.5	5 014	203	203.4	D	1 132	D	477
Muskogee	104	172.7	1 090	18 027	541	306.0	7.3	7 203	354	296.4	1 076	1 582	D	675
Norman	80	214.2	673	14 218	768	551.7	-10.0	7 038	535	541.2	D	911	423	759
Oklahoma City	1 471	D	D	D	4 687	3 164.9	-1.4	7 094	3 043	3 079.8	884	D	D	810
Ponca City	52	133.2	418	7 389	392	192.3	4.3	6 822	246	183.9	D	1 704	345	612
Shawnee	47	D	D	D	394	235.1	0.5	8 527	263	229.1	D	2 878	D	946
Stillwater	50	59.3	395	6 073	376	208.6	5.6	5 695	278	201.7	D	1 396	392	776
Tulsa	1 345	D	D	D	4 384	3 073.1	11.2	8 222	2 940	3 007.2	944	D	574	D
OREGON	5 952	29 884.8	64 115	1 465 515	29 488	17 339.8	37.2	6 427	18 712	16 821.0	936	1 233	283	636
Albany	65	131.2	517	9 538	422	0.0	0.0	D	275	D	D	1 467	D	D
Beaverton	214	1 639.2	2 231	56 756	619	720.3	60.7	20 988	434	710.2	2 819	2 478	1 406	1 772
Corvallis	57	66.7	398	7 418	480	281.4	21.8	7 056	350	276.9	D	1 697	D	891
Eugene	379	1 324.4	3 973	89 670	1 507	1 077.1	43.8	10 218	1 103	1 060.9	1 764	1 551	541	950
Gresham	46	51.4	227	3 360	405	371.0	74.6	9 550	249	362.2	1 926	1 260	326	902
Hillsboro	53	149.1	491	8 993	319	239.0	35.6	7 727	221	233.7	468	1 546	132	618
Medford	170	435.0	1 259	26 657	732	606.7	31.2	13 922	539	593.2	D	1 999	D	1 165
Portland	1 774	14 411.2	24 284	611 055	4 286	2 842.7	22.5	7 329	2 993	2 773.3	1 179	1 111	411	954
Salem	237	1 140.7	2 664	64 435	1 264	899.0	41.2	9 572	875	877.8	D	1 223	517	916
Springfield	58	164.7	530	11 831	417	267.5	21.9	6 966	266	261.0	1 126	1 755	171	772
PENNSYLVANIA	19 793	104 454.3	247 599	5 832 479	118 675	73 786.7	45.3	6 206	70 823	71 216.6	737	1 213	308	524

1. For the period including March 12 of the year shown. 2. Based on resident population estimated as of July 1, 1986.

Table C. Cities — **Retail Trade, Taxable Service Industries, and Federal Grants**

City	Retail trade–establishment with payroll, 1987 (cont'd): Paid employees[1]: Number	Retail trade (cont'd): Paid employees[1]: Percent change, 1982–1987	Retail trade (cont'd): Annual payroll (Mil. dol.)	Taxable service industries–establishments with payroll, 1987: Number	Taxable service: Receipts (Mil. dol.): Total	Taxable service: Receipts: Selected kinds of business: Hotels, motels, and other lodging places	Taxable service: Receipts: Selected kinds of business: Health services	Taxable service: Receipts: Selected kinds of business: Legal services	Taxable service: Paid employees[1]	Taxable service: Annual payroll (Mil. dol.)	Federal grants, 1986: Procurement contract awards (Mil. dol.)	Federal grants, 1986: Grant awards (Mil. dol.)	Federal government civilian employment, 1984
	87	88	89	90	91	92	93	94	95	96	97	98	99
OHIO—Con.													
Cuyahoga Falls	4 413	43.8	40.4	380	101.3	0.0	44.8	3.4	2 614	42.7	4.0	0.8	138
Dayton	12 680	-5.2	129.5	1 443	908.8	25.4	256.8	89.8	23 745	385.8	248.2	33.2	4 126
East Cleveland	1 106	11.8	8.9	65	17.1	0.7	10.4	D	452	6.5	0.0	0.6	0
Elyria	5 830	24.2	53.7	361	101.8	8.2	39.2	7.0	2 577	38.4	28.0	8.3	172
Euclid	3 683	-3.0	34.1	390	138.8	D	76.1	1.1	3 827	62.8	0.2	1.6	38
Fairborn	2 725	29.9	25.5	169	79.9	9.8	8.2	1.2	2 193	33.3	24.6	1.2	65
Fairfield	4 254	74.4	44.6	251	D	2.1	D	1.2	D	D	1.9	0.3	0
Findlay	4 412	15.2	38.8	321	108.5	D	32.0	6.2	2 526	41.2	31.7	1.5	153
Garfield Heights	1 528	-5.9	12.8	155	59.6	D	32.8	0.6	1 141	24.3	0.6	0.3	0
Hamilton	4 758	3.1	44.4	370	107.5	D	40.2	9.7	2 456	45.5	5.3	0.9	230
Huber Heights	2 298	65.1	19.0	153	35.5	D	14.4	0.4	992	12.3	5.1	0.2	0
Kent	2 690	12.3	26.6	169	46.6	4.5	15.5	1.4	1 434	17.5	1.5	4.8	74
Kettering	5 927	D	52.8	472	249.7	D	D	1.2	5 338	122.0	2.7	0.8	2 803
Lakewood	3 284	18.6	33.3	395	148.9	0.4	55.5	2.4	3 458	63.7	NA	1.8	4
Lancaster	4 074	19.7	37.1	325	83.0	D	36.2	4.6	3 070	33.5	1.6	1.1	95
Lima	3 276	2.2	29.3	391	144.3	D	74.2	7.1	3 901	68.3	142.9	2.4	482
Lorain	3 509	-6.5	30.2	348	115.9	D	64.2	11.0	2 722	50.7	4.0	6.4	212
Mansfield	5 714	12.4	53.5	469	146.6	D	55.5	8.5	6 110	62.2	16.9	3.9	618
Maple Heights	2 566	1.2	23.4	194	63.4	0.0	33.8	D	1 321	21.1	3.2	0.4	7
Marion	3 280	24.4	30.5	286	80.8	D	42.1	D	2 145	34.0	2.8	0.9	128
Massillon	3 092	31.2	28.8	185	47.2	D	22.3	1.9	1 257	19.2	1.0	1.3	103
Mentor	7 350	21.1	68.7	322	135.1	D	27.3	2.3	3 306	48.8	1.6	0.6	107
Middletown	3 649	6.3	30.5	311	93.5	3.0	47.0	6.3	3 408	38.6	1.7	1.5	136
Newark	4 046	-1.3	37.5	340	116.5	2.4	48.7	5.8	3 685	48.8	15.0	18.1	278
North Olmsted	6 625	34.5	64.8	262	77.3	1.2	19.9	0.9	2 053	29.8	0.1	0.3	70
Norwood	1 880	11.0	16.9	109	34.4	D	6.1	1.0	911	11.7	0.0	1.1	0
Parma	8 076	10.5	76.3	534	168.6	D	79.2	1.0	4 569	71.8	0.1	0.9	10
Portsmouth	3 321	18.6	29.1	250	65.5	1.4	41.6	D	1 559	29.0	0.2	2.3	145
Sandusky	4 798	32.6	43.3	322	211.8	21.2	36.8	D	2 936	70.2	10.6	0.5	122
Shaker Heights	2 161	12.9	22.6	235	77.1	D	15.6	1.7	1 455	32.2	3.0	0.3	1
South Euclid	1 732	24.2	14.8	230	69.5	0.0	41.6	D	1 400	29.5	0.0	0.2	1
Springfield	6 440	33.2	51.4	490	142.1	D	65.8	10.5	4 541	58.4	34.1	3.8	552
Steubenville	3 424	10.3	30.3	234	64.7	D	32.6	D	1 751	24.6	1.2	1.9	193
Stow	1 836	22.7	18.7	134	41.6	D	11.4	0.8	1 098	15.9	2.3	0.2	13
Strongsville	1 846	14.7	18.1	206	59.3	4.8	10.7	0.9	1 354	19.6	0.5	0.2	3
Toledo	29 032	14.2	262.5	2 395	1 117.8	18.1	344.0	91.1	30 854	488.4	61.1	40.4	1 823
Upper Arlington	3 196	20.2	24.8	251	60.3	D	23.2	1.5	1 262	22.7	0.0	0.1	3
Warren	5 440	16.2	50.2	562	203.7	14.9	89.5	12.1	4 683	81.7	13.6	1.7	196
Youngstown	6 414	-6.6	55.9	746	268.3	D	123.1	25.6	6 295	114.9	5.0	13.8	953
Zanesville	5 171	36.7	43.0	350	98.9	D	41.9	7.4	2 078	39.3	0.4	0.9	232
OKLAHOMA	206 897	0.5	1 859.3	19 456	6 347.9	308.5	2 049.5	670.9	149 370	2 416.2	973.4	1 463.7	46 326
Bartlesville	3 819	11.9	34.0	268	D	5.0	32.4	D	D	D	4.1	9.9	130
Broken Arrow	D	D	D	304	D	0.5	22.7	1.0	D	D	3.1	0.8	102
Del City	1 465	-9.1	13.8	99	24.9	D	5.0	1.4	993	10.7	5.8	0.3	0
Edmond	3 189	13.9	28.3	407	106.1	3.5	45.3	3.7	2 321	38.7	2.8	0.9	116
Enid	4 598	-10.2	39.7	387	131.1	D	77.6	D	3 060	52.2	0.1	2.0	180
Lawton	6 651	-0.6	60.4	531	157.7	D	60.8	D	3 903	59.7	3.7	7.7	457
Midwest City	5 546	12.6	52.9	280	79.3	D	40.4	2.3	2 187	32.6	20.5	3.0	31
Moore	2 446	38.3	20.9	156	32.4	1.3	11.8	D	810	11.6	0.7	0.7	9
Muskogee	3 836	-0.9	35.2	320	75.6	D	38.6	D	2 316	28.1	4.0	2.0	1 168
Norman	7 121	-5.0	60.3	597	166.2	3.7	55.5	18.2	3 743	59.7	6.7	13.1	590
Oklahoma City	40 644	-5.5	391.9	4 291	D	91.7	D	D	D	D	104.1	216.7	9 680
Ponca City	2 394	1.5	21.3	238	62.0	D	22.0	7.6	1 435	22.2	4.9	1.0	121
Shawnee	3 103	-11.0	27.3	228	63.3	D	30.3	4.2	1 847	24.3	4.8	5.0	191
Stillwater	3 664	8.7	25.0	261	62.9	D	D	3.8	1 929	24.4	10.4	34.1	297
Tulsa	38 727	8.7	371.7	3 985	1 841.6	98.4	450.0	199.4	39 701	710.7	191.8	28.1	3 603
OREGON	203 847	16.5	2 027.1	20 741	6 471.3	421.8	1 930.6	552.9	157 257	2 402.4	592.7	1 392.6	27 433
Albany	D	D	D	302	71.9	2.2	27.4	4.4	2 175	27.7	25.9	1.1	274
Beaverton	7 116	39.0	82.0	480	220.2	9.8	34.5	2.8	5 435	91.7	84.9	4.8	220
Corvallis	4 129	8.6	34.2	416	150.2	4.4	48.9	4.5	3 077	58.7	7.2	38.4	547
Eugene	13 241	8.2	130.6	1 475	461.8	18.3	152.3	47.8	12 434	197.3	7.3	54.2	1 170
Gresham	3 780	40.4	41.1	291	58.8	1.7	25.5	1.4	1 842	20.6	0.3	1.6	61
Hillsboro	2 680	31.6	26.0	319	73.3	2.6	25.5	5.9	1 922	25.2	0.4	1.0	158
Medford	6 737	-2.4	69.5	582	189.0	14.3	80.1	12.9	4 228	74.8	0.9	4.0	797
Portland	36 681	11.3	368.1	4 696	2 240.0	108.8	D	343.0	47 381	843.1	176.4	84.7	12 360
Salem	10 955	15.3	110.7	1 131	354.6	9.2	140.2	D	8 922	131.7	1.5	251.7	1 105
Springfield	3 339	-4.1	31.2	276	77.8	6.3	32.1	3.3	1 931	30.0	0.1	9.8	77
PENNSYLVANIA	847 907	21.5	8 096.8	70 071	33 232.2	1 649.2	7 998.4	2 747.9	693 760	12 407.8	5 580.9	5 737.3	126 720

1. For the period including March 12 of the year shown.

City	City government employment, 1985 (October): Total	City government employment, 1985 (October): Rates[1]	City government employment, 1985 (October): Percent education	Form of governments[2] (As of 1986)	City government finances, 1984–1985: General revenue: Total (Mil. dol.)	General revenue: Intergovernmental: Total (Mil. dol.)	General revenue: Intergovernmental: Percent from State government	General revenue: Taxes: Total (Mil. dol.)	Taxes: Per capita[3] (Dollars): Total	Taxes: Per capita[3] (Dollars): Property	Taxes: Per capita[3] (Dollars): Sales & gross receipts	General expenditures: Total (Mil. dol.)	General expenditures: Per capita[3] (Dol.): Total	General expenditures: Per capita[3] (Dol.): Capital outlays	General expenditures: Percent of total for–: Public welfare	Percent of total for–: Highways	Percent of total for–: Education
	100	101	102	103	104	105	106	107	108	109	110	111	112	113	114	115	116
OHIO–Con.																	
Cuyahoga Falls	541	129.4	0.0	1	20.3	2.8	72.6	7.1	169	69	0	21.3	508	37	0.0	9.5	0.0
Dayton	2 785	155.7	0.0	2	157.2	28.1	39.8	79.6	445	64	2	126.7	708	51	0.0	7.2	0.0
East Cleveland	299	82.3	0.0	2	13.8	2.3	71.8	7.1	194	42	0	13.6	373	9	0.0	6.7	0.0
Elyria	526	91.8	0.0	1	22.1	3.6	60.1	9.1	159	37	3	19.7	344	22	0.0	12.2	0.0
Euclid	796	138.7	0.0	1	35.0	5.8	61.5	20.3	354	116	1	33.3	581	79	0.0	6.3	0.0
Fairborn	247	88.0	0.0	2	10.6	2.3	51.7	3.9	137	50	2	10.2	364	61	0.0	9.1	0.0
Fairfield	234	68.5	0.0	2	16.9	1.7	67.3	7.7	225	43	0	13.5	394	61	0.0	14.5	0.0
Findlay	353	96.3	0.0	1	16.5	2.0	67.7	6.4	173	31	3	15.1	413	139	0.0	14.4	0.0
Garfield Heights	312	93.5	0.0	1	10.9	2.1	78.5	6.5	194	82	0	10.7	321	29	0.6	11.0	0.0
Hamilton	709	109.0	0.0	2	30.0	8.6	33.8	11.6	178	30	0	27.6	424	79	NA	6.4	0.0
Huber Heights	119	26.1	0.0	1	5.4	1.2	90.6	3.6	78	47	0	6.0	133	49	0.0	15.7	0.0
Kent	168	60.1	0.0	2	13.5	4.0	38.1	4.5	161	31	0	12.3	442	155	0.0	13.5	0.0
Kettering	508	84.9	0.0	2	21.6	3.7	75.1	15.0	252	52	0	18.1	303	29	0.0	15.4	0.0
Lakewood	1 695	284.7	0.0	1	79.6	10.8	56.5	15.3	257	106	0	80.7	1 355	180	NA	3.9	0.0
Lancaster	386	111.3	0.0	1	13.5	3.7	57.4	5.0	145	28	0	12.5	360	18	0.0	11.2	0.0
Lima	486	105.7	0.0	1	23.5	4.6	42.3	8.4	183	22	1	20.9	454	37	0.0	7.4	0.0
Lorain	549	76.0	0.0	1	24.9	5.9	51.5	10.2	141	43	0	25.1	348	32	0.0	9.4	0.0
Mansfield	550	107.1	0.0	1	25.2	8.8	36.7	8.1	157	27	0	24.6	478	67	0.0	6.9	0.0
Maple Heights	298	105.1	0.0	1	10.6	2.1	73.3	7.1	251	96	1	14.8	522	184	0.0	32.2	0.0
Marion	275	78.4	0.0	1	12.3	3.3	46.8	4.4	124	25	0	11.6	332	43	0.0	9.3	0.0
Massillon	263	82.5	0.0	1	11.4	2.4	51.1	5.1	159	21	0	10.9	342	56	0.0	14.2	0.0
Mentor	376	87.1	0.0	2	17.8	2.9	84.7	9.5	220	62	6	15.2	351	25	0.0	13.7	0.0
Middletown	533	115.6	0.0	2	36.7	5.2	34.4	12.8	278	74	0	30.9	671	90	0.1	9.6	0.0
Newark	363	88.1	0.0	1	13.7	3.7	49.5	6.3	153	28	0	13.0	316	64	0.0	16.7	0.0
North Olmsted	445	124.0	0.0	1	18.4	7.1	23.2	7.2	200	109	0	14.9	415	104	0.0	10.5	0.0
Norwood	249	99.7	0.0	1	11.9	2.2	54.7	7.9	315	35	0	11.1	445	23	0.0	9.2	0.0
Parma	627	70.1	0.0	1	26.5	5.1	70.8	17.1	191	34	1	25.2	282	24	0.1	14.3	0.0
Portsmouth	257	111.4	0.0	2	9.9	2.3	72.3	3.8	165	56	1	9.6	414	59	0.0	8.5	0.0
Sandusky	295	96.7	0.0	2	10.8	1.8	74.3	5.6	184	34	30	10.8	355	40	0.0	13.5	0.0
Shaker Heights	424	137.4	0.0	1	21.6	2.0	89.9	15.4	499	141	1	18.1	585	48	0.0	8.5	0.0
South Euclid	169	67.7	0.0	1	7.2	1.6	82.3	4.7	190	98	1	5.6	225	17	0.0	9.5	0.0
Springfield	672	96.7	0.0	2	34.0	7.3	35.0	17.1	246	10	1	28.5	411	61	0.2	8.3	0.0
Steubenville	265	112.4	0.0	2	10.4	2.8	55.8	4.6	193	56	3	10.0	423	36	0.0	11.0	0.0
Stow	175	67.9	0.0	1	7.3	1.6	87.3	4.4	173	56	0	6.4	250	32	0.0	18.9	0.0
Strongsville	222	67.9	0.0	1	12.3	1.5	89.4	7.2	220	96	1	12.5	383	53	0.1	16.5	0.0
Toledo	3 384	99.3	0.0	2	215.6	46.2	37.3	103.7	304	32	1	195.8	575	111	0.0	9.4	0.0
Upper Arlington	269	73.5	0.0	2	12.8	2.3	93.1	7.8	214	65	0	11.3	308	32	0.0	9.6	0.0
Warren	525	99.2	0.0	1	22.8	6.2	31.9	10.9	206	24	0	22.5	425	41	0.0	13.2	0.0
Youngstown	997	95.2	0.0	1	48.3	17.6	36.2	22.4	214	28	0	43.8	418	53	0.0	9.1	0.0
Zanesville	301	107.8	0.0	1	12.2	2.9	42.0	5.6	200	19	0	11.4	409	65	0.0	8.2	0.0
OKLAHOMA	NA	NA	NA	NA	NA	NA	NA	NA	NA	NA	NA	NA	NA	NA	NA	NA	NA
Bartlesville	402	134.0	0.0	2	20.8	1.1	45.9	11.7	391	45	341	18.0	598	201	0.0	27.3	0.0
Broken Arrow	326	63.3	0.0	2	14.3	0.9	27.4	10.4	202	15	170	15.0	292	158	0.0	6.2	0.0
Del City	210	80.4	0.0	2	6.2	0.4	27.1	3.3	126	10	108	7.1	272	18	0.0	5.4	0.0
Edmond	527	103.4	0.0	2	15.7	0.7	45.8	7.5	147	16	126	15.0	294	51	2.1	16.4	0.0
Enid	568	112.8	0.0	2	24.2	2.5	17.8	14.0	277	0	274	19.5	388	51	0.0	14.1	0.0
Lawton	813	98.2	0.0	2	30.0	5.0	16.7	17.2	207	9	194	26.2	316	42	1.6	13.1	0.0
Midwest City	1 148	214.7	0.0	2	53.5	3.8	9.1	14.0	261	39	214	51.9	971	292	0.3	5.0	0.0
Moore	419	100.1	0.0	2	18.6	1.4	5.9	6.4	154	19	132	21.4	512	130	0.0	10.2	0.0
Muskogee	484	113.9	0.0	2	61.7	10.1	5.0	11.1	262	14	244	55.4	1 304	208	0.1	3.2	0.0
Norman	1 626	207.4	0.0	2	61.6	3.2	50.2	18.0	230	13	210	59.2	755	94	NA	7.1	0.0
Oklahoma City	4 928	110.5	0.0	2	317.3	44.7	12.0	129.5	290	53	226	291.0	652	195	0.0	6.6	0.0
Ponca City	450	159.6	0.0	2	12.4	0.8	42.1	4.5	160	9	148	12.6	448	73	0.0	11.9	0.0
Shawnee	411	149.1	0.0	2	28.7	2.2	37.6	7.1	256	1	250	25.9	940	64	0.0	4.9	0.0
Stillwater	913	249.2	0.0	2	24.8	1.1	30.6	8.5	231	19	210	23.0	629	29	0.5	4.3	0.0
Tulsa	NA	NA	NA	3	335.3	34.4	24.9	138.7	371	45	319	299.3	801	250	0.0	12.1	NA
OREGON	NA	NA	NA	NA	NA	NA	NA	NA	NA	NA	NA	NA	NA	NA	NA	NA	NA
Albany	277	95.4	0.0	2	12.0	2.3	72.6	5.3	181	141	34	12.9	444	112	0.0	7.1	0.0
Beaverton	275	80.1	0.0	1	28.8	2.6	59.0	15.5	452	378	32	25.1	731	205	0.0	23.1	0.0
Corvallis	407	102.1	0.0	2	25.0	4.0	48.9	8.0	200	156	33	22.0	553	139	0.5	20.4	0.0
Eugene	1 500	142.3	0.0	2	73.9	16.8	30.6	27.3	259	236	14	77.3	733	161	0.0	19.7	0.0
Gresham	203	52.3	0.0	2	19.0	2.0	72.2	10.7	275	126	25	13.6	349	67	0.0	6.5	0.0
Hillsboro	243	78.6	0.0	2	11.4	1.7	70.4	6.2	199	98	25	9.1	293	56	0.0	14.5	0.0
Medford	352	80.8	0.0	2	17.7	3.1	60.1	8.1	185	119	39	18.6	426	100	0.0	12.7	0.0
Portland	4 805	123.9	0.0	3	256.6	47.7	41.7	118.7	306	220	50	256.4	661	89	0.0	6.9	0.0
Salem	1 031	109.8	0.0	2	61.6	13.8	32.4	26.8	286	242	33	55.5	590	81	0.0	12.0	0.0
Springfield	429	111.7	0.0	2	29.1	8.6	18.6	7.0	183	168	10	22.2	578	113	0.0	6.4	0.0
PENNSYLVANIA	NA	NA	NA	NA	NA	NA	NA	NA	NA	NA	NA	NA	NA	NA	NA	NA	NA

1. Per 10,000 population estimated as of July 1, 1986. 2. 1=Mayor-council; 2=Council-manager; 3=Commission. Data subject to copyright. 3. Based on resident population estimated as of July 1, 1986.

City	City government finances, 1984–1985 (cont'd)								Climate[2]							Typical monthly electric bills, 1986		
	General expenditure (cont'd)					Debt outstanding			Average daily temperature (Degrees Fahrenheit)							Residential[6]		
	Percent of total for (cont'd)								Mean		Limits							
	Health and hospitals	Police protection	Sewerage and sanitation	Parks and recreation	Housing and community development	Total (Mil. dol.)	Per capita[1] (Dollars)	Percent utility	Jan.	July	Jan.[3]	July[4]	Annual precipitation (Inches)	Heating degree days[5]	Cooling degree days[5]	Total (Dollars)	Percent change, 1980–1986	Commercial[7] (Dollars)
	117	118	119	120	121	122	123	124	125	126	127	128	129	130	131	132	133	134
OHIO—Con.																		
Cuyahoga Falls	0.6	13.8	15.9	8.2	2.3	3.4	81	0.0	25.1	71.6	17.2	82.3	35.90	6 241	625	52.58	47.7	NA
Dayton	0.0	14.3	10.0	5.6	7.0	167.8	938	25.5	26.6	74.7	18.8	84.9	34.71	5 689	947	63.53	55.8	526.2
East Cleveland	0.9	21.1	24.8	2.6	4.3	1.7	46	29.6	25.5	71.6	18.5	81.7	35.40	6 178	612	60.26	37.5	NA
Elyria	1.8	13.5	17.8	3.5	0.2	18.2	317	8.8	25.9	72.6	18.0	84.3	35.08	6 020	707	65.19	70.7	697.7
Euclid	0.8	14.5	28.1	4.8	3.8	21.2	370	0.0	25.5	71.6	18.5	81.7	35.40	6 178	612	60.26	37.5	NA
Fairborn	0.4	19.0	12.6	0.9	8.9	5.3	190	23.6	26.6	74.7	18.8	84.9	34.71	5 689	947	63.53	55.8	NA
Fairfield	0.2	13.4	14.0	4.5	0.0	49.3	1 444	0.0	29.9	75.4	20.7	87.3	38.20	5 052	1 059	54.25	76.5	NA
Findlay	1.2	14.1	6.2	2.7	0.0	43.3	1 180	49.5	23.8	72.5	15.9	83.8	35.60	6 376	699	52.70	67.4	NA
Garfield Heights	0.5	18.2	10.1	4.7	1.3	23.6	706	0.0	25.5	71.6	18.5	81.7	35.40	6 178	612	60.26	37.5	NA
Hamilton	1.9	14.8	17.9	4.1	6.1	63.1	971	11.9	29.9	75.4	20.7	87.3	38.20	5 052	1 059	51.38	71.2	493.0
Huber Heights	0.0	22.6	0.0	0.0	0.0	2.1	45	0.0	26.6	74.7	18.8	84.9	34.71	5 689	947	63.53	55.8	NA
Kent	1.0	14.1	28.2	2.5	9.6	16.1	574	24.4	25.1	71.6	17.2	82.3	35.90	6 241	625	65.19	70.7	NA
Kettering	0.2	23.7	0.0	11.8	3.2	3.4	57	0.0	26.6	74.7	18.8	84.9	34.71	5 689	947	63.53	55.8	526.2
Lakewood	64.6	4.9	4.9	1.3	2.6	52.0	873	0.1	25.5	71.6	18.5	81.7	35.40	6 178	612	60.26	37.5	NA
Lancaster	1.6	15.4	15.8	5.2	9.0	2.8	81	0.0	27.2	73.1	17.9	85.4	35.35	5 803	832	52.70	67.4	NA
Lima	1.8	12.2	18.1	2.2	8.0	72.3	1 571	4.6	25.5	73.7	17.5	85.1	35.38	5 910	849	52.70	67.4	NA
Lorain	2.8	12.1	21.5	4.1	5.3	43.8	606	6.2	25.9	72.6	18.0	84.3	35.08	6 020	707	65.19	70.7	697.7
Mansfield	1.7	12.3	22.2	1.2	14.0	24.2	471	10.6	24.8	72.0	17.4	82.1	34.88	6 249	652	65.19	70.7	697.7
Maple Heights	0.3	14.0	12.6	4.2	0.0	11.8	416	0.0	25.5	71.6	18.5	81.7	35.40	6 178	612	60.26	37.5	NA
Marion	1.9	15.4	29.8	2.4	1.4	5.4	154	0.0	25.4	72.6	16.4	84.6	36.52	6 113	732	65.19	70.7	NA
Massillon	1.8	17.6	22.0	2.8	5.4	3.7	117	0.0	24.8	70.5	16.8	81.8	35.71	6 404	515	65.19	70.7	NA
Mentor	1.1	19.3	1.5	9.1	0.0	38.5	892	0.0	26.9	71.5	19.6	81.0	35.70	5 987	612	60.26	37.5	NA
Middletown	2.2	13.1	11.7	4.1	5.7	113.5	2 462	2.1	29.9	75.4	20.7	87.3	38.20	5 052	1 059	54.25	76.5	NA
Newark	3.4	15.9	11.3	1.8	0.0	6.7	162	20.2	27.4	73.2	18.7	85.4	40.31	5 686	780	52.70	67.4	NA
North Olmsted	0.2	12.4	34.1	5.7	1.2	19.2	535	0.0	25.5	71.6	18.5	81.7	35.40	6 178	612	60.26	37.5	NA
Norwood	2.0	19.2	16.0	2.4	3.9	1.8	70	54.3	30.3	76.1	22.5	86.3	40.10	4 950	1 159	54.25	76.5	NA
Parma	0.6	14.7	9.0	10.1	3.8	33.8	378	0.0	25.5	71.6	18.5	81.7	35.40	6 178	612	60.26	37.5	NA
Portsmouth	5.7	11.0	13.0	1.7	9.6	7.8	338	25.9	32.0	75.9	23.4	86.4	41.33	4 702	1 137	52.70	67.4	NA
Sandusky	2.9	15.8	15.0	5.6	3.8	6.2	203	17.8	25.7	73.9	18.7	82.7	33.90	6 016	821	65.19	70.7	NA
Shaker Heights	0.6	20.9	10.6	5.2	4.0	13.7	446	0.0	25.5	71.6	18.5	81.7	35.40	6 178	612	60.26	37.5	NA
South Euclid	0.8	25.5	15.2	3.8	0.0	1.5	59	0.0	25.5	71.6	18.5	81.7	35.40	6 178	612	60.26	37.5	NA
Springfield	1.5	14.6	11.4	4.8	8.4	15.4	221	44.2	26.6	74.7	18.8	84.9	34.71	5 689	947	65.19	70.7	697.7
Steubenville	3.9	13.7	12.0	3.1	7.2	12.5	529	6.5	28.1	72.9	19.4	84.0	39.33	5 587	762	52.70	67.4	NA
Stow	3.7	22.8	NA	7.5	0.0	5.0	195	0.0	25.1	71.6	17.2	82.3	35.90	6 241	625	65.19	70.7	NA
Strongsville	0.3	13.8	17.0	8.2	0.0	21.7	664	0.1	25.5	71.6	18.5	81.7	35.40	6 178	612	60.26	37.5	NA
Toledo	1.9	19.7	20.1	4.1	8.2	188.9	554	6.1	23.1	71.8	15.5	83.4	31.77	6 570	622	71.68	44.5	675.9
Upper Arlington	0.3	16.5	10.9	10.2	0.8	5.0	137	0.0	27.1	73.8	19.4	84.4	36.97	5 686	862	60.10	23.4	NA
Warren	1.6	16.6	17.2	3.3	15.8	10.2	193	28.4	25.6	70.9	16.9	83.7	35.03	6 241	579	65.19	70.7	697.7
Youngstown	2.0	19.1	9.3	3.1	12.5	34.7	332	6.2	24.2	70.1	16.9	81.2	37.33	6 560	485	65.19	70.7	697.7
Zanesville	0.8	17.6	24.5	3.1	8.4	5.4	193	11.1	27.3	72.5	18.6	83.7	38.36	5 777	716	52.70	67.4	NA
OKLAHOMA	NA	NA	NA	NA	NA	NA	NA	NA	NA	NA	NA	NA	NA	NA	NA	52.39	76.5	NA
Bartlesville	0.0	16.7	22.2	9.3	0.0	8.1	270	70.6	34.6	82.0	22.5	94.7	34.49	3 842	1 886	46.88	56.9	NA
Broken Arrow	0.0	9.5	60.5	2.0	0.0	17.4	339	15.5	35.2	83.2	24.8	93.9	38.77	3 731	2 043	46.88	56.9	NA
Del City	0.0	18.2	23.8	4.8	0.0	6.7	258	5.9	35.9	82.1	25.2	93.5	30.89	3 735	1 914	56.59	97.6	NA
Edmond	0.0	16.1	13.8	12.2	0.0	8.7	170	34.6	35.9	82.1	25.2	93.5	30.89	3 735	1 914	48.63	90.1	NA
Enid	0.2	13.8	18.4	4.8	3.3	66.7	1 325	83.6	35.4	83.5	24.8	95.6	31.23	3 764	2 075	56.59	97.6	377.6
Lawton	0.6	21.1	17.0	5.0	2.8	23.1	279	69.5	38.8	83.7	26.3	96.4	29.20	3 237	2 216	46.88	56.9	326.4
Midwest City	49.2	8.3	19.5	2.8	0.5	51.6	964	16.1	35.9	82.1	25.2	93.5	30.89	3 735	1 914	56.04	97.6	NA
Moore	25.9	8.5	27.2	2.6	0.0	28.5	681	8.4	35.9	82.1	25.2	93.5	30.89	3 735	1 914	56.04	97.6	NA
Muskogee	60.3	4.5	18.0	2.2	0.5	4.9	116	100.0	37.7	82.6	27.3	94.1	40.00	3 409	2 038	56.59	97.6	NA
Norman	47.0	7.6	9.2	5.1	0.8	43.9	560	10.4	37.4	81.7	25.3	94.1	30.89	3 735	1 914	56.04	97.6	373.9
Oklahoma City	15.7	10.3	23.2	7.6	4.3	389.6	873	18.7	35.9	82.1	25.2	93.5	30.89	3 735	1 914	56.59	97.6	377.6
Ponca City	0.0	14.4	14.7	14.9	5.5	32.2	1 142	96.0	32.4	82.5	22.1	93.8	33.01	4 279	1 886	52.09	56.7	NA
Shawnee	63.4	5.2	4.4	2.3	1.9	16.3	593	63.6	37.4	81.7	25.3	94.1	30.89	3 735	1 914	56.59	99.5	NA
Stillwater	45.7	7.6	6.3	5.1	2.7	45.8	1 249	63.2	35.3	82.1	23.5	93.9	32.32	3 793	1 920	57.80	85.0	NA
Tulsa	1.2	10.0	13.8	6.8	3.0	848.4	2 270	4.7	35.2	83.2	24.8	93.9	38.77	3 731	2 043	46.88	56.9	326.4
OREGON	NA	NA	NA	NA	NA	NA	NA	NA	NA	NA	NA	NA	NA	NA	NA	35.58	58.3	NA
Albany	NA	12.0	26.0	7.0	2.6	29.5	1 017	65.0	39.0	65.6	32.9	80.7	42.55	4 987	202	39.30	70.6	NA
Beaverton	0.0	9.9	10.0	0.0	5.5	39.7	1 155	42.2	38.9	67.7	33.5	79.5	37.39	4 691	332	36.11	43.5	NA
Corvallis	0.0	12.2	12.6	7.4	4.4	34.2	858	20.3	39.0	65.6	32.9	80.7	42.55	4 987	202	39.30	70.6	NA
Eugene	0.0	9.8	8.6	8.1	3.4	243.8	2 313	80.6	40.1	66.8	33.8	82.6	46.04	4 799	261	24.58	77.5	211.4
Gresham	0.0	21.5	29.1	0.1	0.0	13.0	336	13.4	38.9	67.7	33.5	79.5	37.39	4 691	332	36.11	43.5	NA
Hillsboro	0.0	18.8	25.0	7.9	0.0	12.8	415	58.2	38.9	67.7	33.5	79.5	37.39	4 691	332	36.11	43.5	NA
Medford	0.0	18.1	19.0	7.1	1.9	12.9	297	17.2	37.6	72.5	30.2	90.7	19.84	4 798	645	39.30	70.6	NA
Portland	4.4	18.8	10.4	12.5	3.8	506.1	1 305	29.8	38.9	67.7	33.5	79.5	37.39	4 691	332	36.72	45.9	401.7
Salem	0.0	12.7	13.0	7.0	11.6	84.7	902	10.0	39.3	66.3	32.8	82.2	40.35	4 974	238	36.11	43.5	395.0
Springfield	0.0	12.6	41.3	0.0	2.3	39.5	1 029	38.2	40.1	66.8	33.8	82.6	46.04	4 799	261	30.45	104.4	NA
PENNSYLVANIA	NA	NA	NA	NA	NA	NA	NA	NA	NA	NA	NA	NA	NA	NA	NA	66.77	67.3	NA

1. Based on resident population estimated as of July 1, 1986. 2. Represents normal values based on the 30-year period, 1951–1980 (see text). 3. Average daily minimum. 4. Average daily maximum. 5. For definition, see text. 6. As of January 1; based on consumption of 750 kWh. 7. Based on billing demand of 30 kW and consumption of 6,000 kWh.

MSA/ CMSA Code[1]	State/ Place code	City	Land area,[2] 1990 (Sq. Km.)	Population: 1990: Total persons	Population: 1990: Rank	Population: 1990: Per sq. km.	Population: 1980	Population: Change 1980–1990: Number	Population: Change 1980–1990: Per- cent	Population characteristics, 1990: Percent: Race: White	Race: Black	Race: Am. Indian, Eskimo, Aleut	Race: Asian & Pacific Islander	Race: Other race	His- panic[3]	65 Years and over
			1	2	3	4	5	6	7	8	9	10	11	12	13	14
		PENNSYLVANIA—Con.														
0240	42 0165	Allentown	45.9	105 090	182	2 290	103 758	1 332	1.3	86.17	4.98	0.18	1.35	7.33	11.68	16.9
0280	42 0190	Altoona	25.3	51 881	470	2 051	57 078	-5 197	-9.1	97.96	1.53	0.11	0.27	0.13	0.37	18.6
6282	42 0826	Bethel Park borough	30.3	33 823	745	1 116	34 755	-932	-2.7	98.08	1.04	0.05	0.77	0.07	0.49	13.6
0240	42 0855	Bethlehem	49.9	71 428	309	1 431	70 419	1 009	1.4	87.56	2.91	0.08	1.72	7.73	13.02	17.2
6162	42 1855	Chester	12.5	41 856	597	3 348	45 794	-3 938	-8.6	32.00	65.17	0.21	0.39	2.23	3.77	13.9
0240	42 3295	Easton	11.0	26 276	901	2 389	26 027	249	1.0	86.78	9.44	0.17	1.70	1.91	4.41	14.2
2360	42 3685	Erie	56.9	108 718	173	1 911	119 123	-10 405	-8.7	86.05	12.04	0.21	0.47	1.23	2.40	16.1
3240	42 4920	Harrisburg	21.0	52 376	462	2 494	53 264	-888	-1.7	42.59	50.60	0.28	1.76	4.78	7.68	13.0
7560	42 5006	Hazleton	15.5	24 730	927	1 595	27 318	-2 588	-9.5	98.63	0.21	0.04	0.67	0.44	1.01	23.9
3680	42 5453	Johnstown	15.2	28 134	864	1 851	35 496	-7 362	-20.7	90.29	8.95	0.14	0.18	0.45	1.40	23.1
4000	42 5624	Lancaster	19.1	55 551	421	2 908	54 725	826	1.5	70.87	12.24	0.25	1.96	14.68	20.56	12.2
3240	42 5714	Lebanon	10.9	24 800	926	2 275	25 711	-911	-3.5	94.17	1.44	0.09	0.96	3.35	6.90	17.6
6282	42 6158	McKeesport	13.0	26 016	905	2 001	31 012	-4 996	-16.1	81.91	17.23	0.16	0.18	0.52	1.21	23.2
...	42 6744	New Castle	22.1	28 334	857	1 282	33 621	-5 287	-15.7	91.54	8.00	0.07	0.22	0.17	0.50	22.7
6162	42 6842	Norristown borough	9.1	30 749	815	3 379	34 684	-3 935	-11.3	70.83	26.43	0.16	1.65	0.93	2.69	14.6
6162	42 7180	Philadelphia	350.0	1 585 577	5	4 530	1 688 210	-102 633	-6.1	53.52	39.86	0.22	2.74	3.66	5.63	15.2
6282	42 7234	Pittsburgh	144.1	369 879	40	2 567	423 959	-54 080	-12.8	72.13	25.78	0.18	1.61	0.30	0.94	17.9
6282	42 7264	Plum borough	74.2	25 609	912	345	25 390	219	0.9	97.05	1.98	0.04	0.77	0.16	0.57	8.0
6680	42 7418	Reading	25.3	78 380	269	3 098	78 686	-306	-0.4	78.64	9.71	0.14	1.42	10.09	18.48	16.6
7560	42 7698	Scranton	65.3	81 805	258	1 253	88 117	-6 312	-7.2	97.18	1.58	0.09	0.91	0.24	0.67	21.9
8050	42 8050	State College borough	11.6	38 923	649	3 355	36 130	2 793	7.7	88.51	3.42	0.15	7.29	0.64	1.96	4.7
6282	42 8800	West Mifflin borough	36.7	23 644	943	644	26 322	-2 678	-10.2	92.17	7.45	0.05	0.22	0.11	0.36	19.9
7560	42 8904	Wilkes-Barre	17.7	47 523	521	2 685	51 551	-4 028	-7.8	96.11	2.91	0.09	0.58	0.31	0.74	21.0
9140	42 8918	Williamsport	23.0	31 933	788	1 388	33 401	-1 468	-4.4	92.34	6.71	0.21	0.52	0.23	0.77	15.0
9280	42 9034	York	13.5	42 192	589	3 125	44 619	-2 427	-5.4	72.49	21.26	0.23	1.11	4.91	7.69	13.5
...	44 0000	RHODE ISLAND	2 706.5	1 003 464	X	371	947 154	56 310	5.9	91.42	3.87	0.41	1.83	2.47	4.56	15.0
6482	44 0090	Cranston	74.0	76 060	281	1 028	71 992	4 068	5.7	95.08	2.42	0.18	1.77	0.55	2.01	18.6
6482	44 0120	East Providence	34.7	50 380	489	1 452	50 980	-600	-1.2	92.11	4.35	0.48	0.58	2.47	1.68	18.9
...	44 0310	Newport	20.6	28 227	861	1 370	29 259	-1 032	-3.5	88.65	8.08	0.74	1.41	1.11	2.80	13.2
6482	44 0380	Pawtucket	22.6	72 644	300	3 214	71 204	1 440	2.0	89.25	3.59	0.28	0.65	6.23	7.17	16.3
6482	44 0400	Providence	47.8	160 728	107	3 363	156 804	3 924	2.5	69.93	14.83	0.93	5.94	8.37	15.54	13.6
6482	44 0500	Warwick	92.0	85 427	242	929	87 123	-1 696	-1.9	97.97	0.79	0.21	0.83	0.19	0.99	16.8
6482	44 0560	Woonsocket	20.0	43 877	564	2 194	45 914	-2 037	-4.4	93.30	2.64	0.18	2.98	0.90	2.63	16.2
...	45 0000	SOUTH CAROLINA	77 987.8	3 486 703	X	45	3 120 730	365 973	11.7	69.03	29.82	0.24	0.64	0.26	0.88	11.4
0405	45 0035	Anderson	32.1	26 184	903	816	27 546	-1 362	-4.9	65.09	34.26	0.16	0.31	0.18	0.53	19.9
1440	45 0245	Charleston	111.9	80 414	263	719	69 779	10 635	15.2	57.23	41.58	0.11	0.85	0.22	0.81	12.8
1760	45 0305	Columbia	303.4	98 052	201	323	101 229	-3 177	-3.1	53.67	43.69	0.35	1.43	0.87	1.98	11.8
2655	45 0465	Florence	38.2	29 813	829	780	29 842	-29	-0.1	52.28	47.04	0.14	0.45	0.08	0.57	14.3
3160	45 0565	Greenville	65.0	58 282	399	897	58 242	40	0.1	63.62	35.16	0.14	0.85	0.23	1.04	15.9
1440	45 0987	North Charleston	129.6	70 218	320	542	62 504	7 714	12.3	62.67	34.35	0.49	1.63	0.87	2.48	5.9
1520	45 1195	Rock Hill	60.0	41 643	602	694	35 327	6 316	17.9	60.42	38.14	0.45	0.82	0.17	0.64	12.4
3160	45 1340	Spartanburg	46.9	43 467	571	927	43 826	-359	-0.8	53.11	45.63	0.11	0.91	0.25	0.78	15.3
...	46 0000	SOUTH DAKOTA	196 575.2	696 004	X	4	690 768	5 236	0.8	91.60	0.47	7.27	0.45	0.22	0.75	14.7
...	46 0005	Aberdeen	21.7	24 927	925	1 149	25 851	-924	-3.6	95.98	0.16	3.26	0.50	0.10	0.35	15.8
6660	46 1125	Rapid City	91.5	54 523	436	596	46 492	8 031	17.3	88.19	1.27	8.90	0.99	0.65	2.23	11.5
7760	46 1225	Sioux Falls	116.7	100 814	192	864	81 343	19 471	23.9	96.84	0.73	1.56	0.68	0.19	0.57	11.7
...	47 0000	TENNESSEE	106 758.5	4 877 185	X	46	4 591 023	286 162	6.2	83.00	15.95	0.21	0.65	0.19	0.67	12.7
1560	47 0245	Chattanooga	306.7	152 466	113	497	169 514	-17 048	-10.1	64.97	33.67	0.22	0.97	0.17	0.64	15.3
1660	47 0250	Clarksville	189.3	75 494	285	399	54 777	20 717	37.8	74.96	20.90	0.42	2.18	1.54	3.86	7.1
...	47 0255	Cleveland	51.4	30 354	825	591	26 415	3 939	14.9	91.55	7.17	0.27	0.47	0.54	1.44	14.7
...	47 0290	Columbia	76.2	28 583	852	375	26 571	2 012	7.6	78.55	20.60	0.18	0.38	0.29	0.74	15.1
5360	47 0637	Hendersonville	57.2	32 188	782	563	26 561	5 627	21.2	96.70	2.33	0.25	0.56	0.16	0.83	8.3
3580	47 0705	Jackson	104.5	48 949	506	468	49 258	-309	-0.6	59.13	40.25	0.08	0.44	0.10	0.53	15.5
3660	47 0730	Johnson City	79.2	49 381	499	623	39 753	9 628	24.2	93.09	5.90	0.20	0.65	0.15	0.64	15.9
3660	47 0750	Kingsport	83.8	36 365	695	434	32 027	4 338	13.5	94.82	4.43	0.11	0.58	0.06	0.34	20.0
3840	47 0760	Knoxville	200.1	165 121	102	825	175 045	-9 924	-5.7	82.73	15.78	0.24	1.04	0.21	0.67	15.4
4920	47 0940	Memphis	663.2	610 337	18	920	646 174	-35 837	-5.5	44.01	54.84	0.16	0.79	0.20	0.73	12.2
5360	47 1010	Murfreesboro	78.6	44 922	553	572	32 845	12 077	36.8	82.31	14.49	0.18	2.79	0.23	0.80	9.9
5360	47 1016	Nashville-Davidson	1 225.9	488 374	25	398	455 651	32 723	7.2	73.77	24.29	0.23	1.40	0.30	0.95	11.4
3840	47 1080	Oak Ridge	221.6	27 310	879	123	27 662	-352	-1.3	89.38	7.98	0.36	2.06	0.23	0.97	18.4
...	48 0000	TEXAS	678 357.8	16 986 510	X	25	14 225 513	2 760 997	19.4	75.21	11.90	0.39	1.88	10.62	25.55	10.1
0040	48 0015	Abilene	267.0	106 654	177	399	98 315	8 339	8.5	82.40	7.01	0.38	1.31	8.89	15.52	11.8
0320	48 0100	Amarillo	227.8	157 615	110	692	149 230	8 385	5.6	82.71	5.99	0.75	1.88	8.67	14.74	12.0
1922	48 0175	Arlington	240.9	261 721	61	1 086	160 113	101 608	63.5	82.64	8.41	0.51	3.92	4.52	8.91	5.0

1. MSA = Metropolitan Statistical Area. CMSA = Consolidated MSA. 2. Dry land or land partially or temporarily covered by water. 3. Hispanic persons may be of any race.

City	Households, 1990				Births, 1984			Deaths, 1984				Hospitals, 1985		
	Number	Persons per household	Percent–		Number		Rate[3]	Number		Rate		Number	Beds	
			Female family householder[1]	One-person[2]	Total	To mothers under 20 yrs. old (Percent)		Total	Infant[4]	Total[3]	Infant[5]		Number	Rate[6]
	15	16	17	18	19	20	21	22	23	24	25	26	27	28
PENNSYLVANIA—Con.														
Allentown	42 775	2.36	12.7	31.7	1 598	12.7	15.4	1 213	16	11.7	10.0	6	1 809	1 733
Altoona	20 684	2.47	14.0	28.9	715	16.1	13.1	702	8	12.9	11.2	4	826	1 554
Bethel Park borough	12 692	2.65	7.5	20.5	396	2.3	11.5	233	3	6.8	7.6	0	0	0
Bethlehem	27 268	2.44	12.0	27.9	845	13.1	12.1	766	7	10.9	8.3	2	567	806
Chester	14 537	2.74	29.4	27.8	899	26.1	20.4	569	18	12.9	20.0	2	641	1 467
Easton	9 397	2.51	14.3	29.8	410	15.4	15.7	325	2	12.5	4.9	1	389	1 466
Erie	42 131	2.47	15.6	30.8	2 110	14.5	18.0	1 299	22	11.1	10.4	7	1 663	1 443
Harrisburg	21 520	2.39	23.1	37.9	1 015	23.5	19.5	634	16	12.2	15.8	4	1 662	3 225
Hazleton	10 574	2.32	13.0	33.4	322	11.5	12.3	432	7	16.5	21.7	2	352	1 393
Johnstown	12 536	2.22	15.8	37.6	403	17.6	12.2	526	2	15.9	5.0	3	982	3 084
Lancaster	21 189	2.49	16.4	32.5	1 070	20.6	19.0	607	12	10.8	11.2	3	1 115	1 949
Lebanon	10 468	2.34	13.5	32.9	398	13.8	15.1	315	7	12.0	17.6	3	1 230	4 661
McKeesport	10 543	2.36	18.7	32.8	421	13.3	14.6	481	6	16.7	14.3	1	449	1 652
New Castle	11 374	2.42	15.6	30.9	459	14.4	14.3	474	9	14.8	19.6	2	374	1 220
Norristown borough	12 187	2.44	15.0	35.2	653	13.3	19.0	422	11	12.3	16.8	6	1 870	5 536
Philadelphia	603 075	2.56	20.3	31.6	25 013	17.9	15.2	20 090	388	12.2	15.5	48	13 260	807
Pittsburgh	153 483	2.27	17.2	36.2	5 489	14.0	13.6	5 457	83	13.6	15.1	28	9 364	2 417
Plum borough	9 067	2.82	8.4	16.2	369	1.9	14.6	138	2	5.5	5.4	0	0	0
Reading	31 403	2.44	16.4	32.6	1 423	20.8	18.2	1 012	20	12.9	14.1	4	1 177	1 516
Scranton	32 637	2.37	13.8	34.0	1 128	11.7	13.5	1 368	15	16.3	13.3	5	1 239	1 506
State College borough	10 938	2.43	3.4	27.4	164	4.9	4.8	118	2	3.4	12.2	1	200	583
West Mifflin borough	9 638	2.45	13.0	24.6	257	7.4	10.1	293	4	11.5	15.6	0	0	0
Wilkes-Barre	19 435	2.31	14.5	36.1	577	13.2	11.7	833	2	16.9	3.5	5	1 581	3 301
Williamsport	12 588	2.42	15.1	31.3	499	18.4	15.5	356	4	11.0	8.0	2	543	1 712
York	16 887	2.47	17.9	31.9	756	22.9	17.0	538	12	12.1	15.9	3	820	1 846
RHODE ISLAND	377 977	2.55	11.7	26.2	12 659	10.3	13.2	9 435	125	9.8	9.9	21	5 394	553
Cranston	29 349	2.46	11.2	27.1	744	4.4	10.2	734	5	10.1	6.7	1	79	107
East Providence	19 950	2.48	11.0	28.5	635	9.1	12.3	585	3	11.3	4.7	0	0	0
Newport	11 196	2.31	14.0	33.8	430	12.6	14.5	291	7	9.8	16.3	2	347	1 183
Pawtucket	29 711	2.42	13.7	30.6	1 066	11.7	14.6	806	7	11.1	6.6	1	306	421
Providence	58 905	2.52	18.4	31.8	2 590	15.3	16.8	1 850	30	12.0	11.6	7	2 240	1 425
Warwick	33 437	2.52	9.6	26.5	964	8.7	11.1	840	7	9.6	7.3	1	359	413
Woonsocket	17 572	2.45	14.1	29.3	657	19.9	14.5	511	16	11.3	24.4	1	245	545
SOUTH CAROLINA	1 258 044	2.68	14.0	22.4	50 670	17.2	15.4	26 374	743	8.0	14.7	94	16 046	475
Anderson	10 509	2.36	18.0	33.3	406	23.4	14.9	384	10	14.1	24.6	1	454	1 583
Charleston	30 753	2.43	17.0	30.8	1 806	21.5	26.9	910	35	13.6	19.4	8	2 239	3 250
Columbia	33 919	2.31	16.5	34.0	2 053	17.0	20.8	1 300	38	13.2	18.5	10	4 244	4 562
Florence	11 074	2.57	20.7	27.7	446	18.8	14.3	353	12	11.3	26.9	3	630	1 989
Greenville	24 101	2.25	16.7	36.6	1 230	18.7	21.4	669	15	11.7	12.2	6	1 260	2 159
North Charleston	23 499	2.59	16.6	24.9	1 074	19.0	16.1	206	16	3.1	14.9	1	104	169
Rock Hill	14 669	2.64	18.4	24.6	595	20.2	15.8	364	8	9.6	13.4	1	273	651
Spartanburg	16 712	2.45	21.0	31.2	760	24.9	17.3	525	15	12.0	19.7	3	820	1 855
SOUTH DAKOTA	259 034	2.59	8.0	26.4	12 445	10.8	17.6	6 533	124	9.3	10.0	69	5 800	820
Aberdeen	9 998	2.35	9.1	32.0	419	11.2	16.3	241	4	9.4	9.5	2	292	1 138
Rapid City	21 152	2.51	11.3	26.4	948	13.7	19.3	404	12	8.2	12.7	3	463	882
Sioux Falls	39 790	2.43	9.4	28.7	1 599	8.5	18.2	722	8	8.2	5.0	4	1 304	1 337
TENNESSEE	1 853 725	2.56	12.6	23.9	65 006	17.4	13.8	42 334	769	9.0	11.8	173	31 390	654
Chattanooga	62 177	2.37	17.1	31.1	2 471	20.6	15.0	1 709	40	10.4	16.2	11	2 057	1 268
Clarksville	25 442	2.70	11.4	19.4	1 125	16.1	19.2	356	15	6.1	13.3	1	194	319
Cleveland	11 996	2.41	12.1	27.4	376	25.3	14.0	290	4	10.8	10.6	2	321	1 228
Columbia	11 267	2.48	15.2	26.3	343	21.0	12.7	312	2	11.5	5.8	1	235	834
Hendersonville	11 441	2.77	9.3	16.7	358	10.9	12.7	128	2	4.5	5.6	1	75	249
Jackson	19 206	2.43	18.8	29.2	764	15.3	15.0	547	9	10.7	11.8	3	849	1 608
Johnson City	19 675	2.30	12.0	30.7	511	15.3	11.5	475	6	10.7	11.7	4	591	1 322
Kingsport	15 629	2.28	12.6	30.1	349	19.8	11.0	392	3	12.4	8.6	4	777	2 469
Knoxville	69 973	2.20	14.3	35.5	2 259	17.8	13.0	1 922	27	11.0	12.0	8	2 931	1 692
Memphis	229 829	2.59	21.9	28.3	11 407	18.5	17.6	6 317	169	9.7	14.8	17	6 823	1 045
Murfreesboro	17 110	2.38	12.0	29.9	490	16.5	13.4	305	14	8.3	28.6	2	871	2 126
Nashville-Davidson	198 585	2.35	14.5	30.7	7 232	14.9	15.6	4 213	90	9.1	12.4	15	5 122	1 081
Oak Ridge	11 763	2.30	10.4	29.8	270	11.5	9.7	221	2	8.0	7.4	2	308	1 144
TEXAS	6 070 937	2.73	11.6	23.9	299 025	15.7	18.7	117 021	3 127	7.3	10.5	569	86 824	520
Abilene	38 395	2.60	9.6	25.0	2 225	16.8	20.6	834	24	7.7	10.8	4	760	676
Amarillo	61 137	2.54	11.0	27.2	3 092	16.5	19.0	1 294	36	7.9	11.6	5	1 230	742
Arlington	100 651	2.58	9.4	24.8	3 873	8.7	18.1	873	29	4.1	7.5	3	649	260

1. No spouse present. 2. Householder living alone. 3. Per 1,000 resident population estimated as of July 1 of the year shown. 4. Deaths of infants under 1 year old. 5. Deaths of infants under 1 year old per 1,000 live births. 6. Per 100,000 resident population estimated as of July 1, 1986.

City	Serious crimes known to police, 1985 — Number — Total	Violent[1]	Rate[2]	Police officers, 1985 — Number	Rate[3]	Educational attainment,[4] 1980 — Percent completing 12 years or more	Percent completing 16 years or more	Money income — Per capita[5] — 1985 — Total (Dollars)	Percent of State average	1979 — Current dollars	Constant (1985) dollars	Percent below poverty level, 1979 — Persons	Families	Housing, 1990 — Total units	Percent change, 1980–1990	Vacant units for sale or rent[6]
	29	30	31	32	33	34	35	36	37	38	39	40	41	42	43	44
PENNSYLVANIA—Con.																
Allentown	5 585	396	5 397	161	15.6	59.7	10.9	10 575	102.8	7 134	10 573	11.7	8.4	45 636	4.1	2 324
Altoona	1 863	107	3 344	81	14.5	62.8	7.7	8 334	81.0	5 874	8 705	12.3	9.2	22 698	0.9	1 383
Bethel Park borough	532	24	1 558	29	8.5	83.1	27.1	13 452	130.8	9 269	13 737	2.4	2.0	12 997	7.7	220
Bethlehem	2 627	170	3 749	125	17.8	61.9	15.1	10 575	102.8	7 556	11 198	11.1	7.8	28 486	3.8	877
Chester	4 468	1 394	9 959	90	20.1	49.1	4.9	6 815	66.2	4 984	7 386	25.9	22.0	16 512	-8.0	1 377
Easton	1 364	111	5 248	49	18.9	57.1	10.6	8 490	82.5	5 727	8 487	15.6	11.9	10 309	2.2	684
Erie	5 422	564	4 635	203	17.4	64.8	11.3	8 995	87.4	6 218	9 215	13.4	10.2	45 424	-3.1	2 064
Harrisburg	5 129	873	9 796	140	26.7	60.7	11.4	9 099	88.4	6 190	9 174	23.1	20.4	24 590	-5.9	1 630
Hazleton	812	28	3 066	21	7.9	61.4	7.0	9 198	89.4	6 360	9 426	9.7	7.2	11 343	-1.1	440
Johnstown	1 137	137	3 345	NA	NA	55.8	5.5	7 426	72.2	5 625	8 336	16.5	12.9	14 667	-3.4	1 623
Lancaster	3 450	231	6 231	114	20.6	51.9	9.8	8 442	82.1	5 594	8 290	16.9	12.6	22 468	2.3	1 012
Lebanon	913	26	3 487	39	14.9	53.4	7.7	9 301	90.4	6 543	9 697	12.1	8.8	10 996	2.4	359
McKeesport	1 085	123	3 674	46	15.6	56.4	6.8	8 628	83.9	6 433	9 534	14.4	11.1	12 535	-5.3	1 051
New Castle	1 610	152	4 925	39	11.9	57.8	8.5	8 351	81.2	5 967	8 843	15.5	12.6	12 463	-6.9	774
Norristown borough	2 240	444	6 471	68	19.6	53.0	8.5	9 556	92.9	6 129	9 083	11.8	9.3	13 080	-1.2	661
Philadelphia	83 667	16 209	5 101	6 966	42.5	54.3	11.1	8 807	85.6	6 053	8 971	20.6	16.6	674 899	-1.6	44 060
Pittsburgh	28 931	4 353	7 215	1 210	30.2	61.1	14.6	9 998	97.2	6 845	10 144	16.5	11.9	170 159	-5.3	12 288
Plum borough	251	24	991	18	7.1	78.9	17.9	10 592	103.0	7 397	10 962	3.8	3.1	9 289	10.4	155
Reading	5 843	651	7 438	199	25.3	46.8	6.9	9 060	88.1	6 083	9 015	17.2	12.6	34 276	0.4	1 976
Scranton	2 721	175	3 174	143	16.7	61.4	9.6	8 511	82.7	5 780	8 566	12.9	9.2	35 357	-2.3	1 708
State College borough	1 599	13	3 560	52	11.6	93.0	59.5	7 065	68.7	4 686	6 945	39.2	13.5	11 623	12.8	544
West Mifflin borough	848	30	3 320	28	11.0	68.8	8.8	9 822	95.5	7 637	11 318	6.6	5.4	9 948	3.3	227
Wilkes-Barre	2 388	145	4 725	90	17.8	58.5	9.3	8 261	80.3	5 610	8 314	13.5	9.4	20 734	-3.2	839
Williamsport	1 777	89	5 446	49	15.0	63.0	11.4	8 479	82.4	5 863	8 689	16.6	11.9	13 326	-2.7	463
York	2 928	190	6 582	89	20.0	50.8	7.7	8 781	85.4	5 969	8 846	17.5	13.6	18 407	-4.9	1 222
RHODE ISLAND	45 723	3 355	4 723	NA	NA	61.1	15.4	10 892	100.0	6 897	10 221	10.3	7.7	414 572	10.1	19 071
Cranston	3 166	150	4 334	137	18.8	66.3	15.5	11 673	107.2	7 512	11 133	7.3	6.0	30 516	10.6	843
East Providence	1 600	86	3 058	89	17.0	57.3	12.1	10 804	99.2	6 879	10 195	7.1	5.9	20 808	6.8	621
Newport	2 400	127	7 931	82	27.1	73.7	26.1	11 867	109.0	7 035	10 426	16.1	13.0	13 094	9.2	1 018
Pawtucket	3 263	252	4 454	136	18.6	49.8	8.6	9 511	87.3	6 328	9 378	11.7	9.2	31 615	5.8	1 413
Providence	15 321	1 756	9 877	412	26.6	53.4	15.7	9 501	87.2	6 169	9 142	20.4	15.3	66 794	-1.1	5 760
Warwick	4 415	201	4 984	163	18.4	68.7	15.1	12 090	111.0	7 540	11 174	6.6	5.2	35 141	7.7	1 119
Woonsocket	1 597	145	3 457	99	21.4	44.8	7.0	8 837	81.1	5 690	8 433	14.3	11.0	18 739	2.1	1 058
SOUTH CAROLINA	162 013	21 121	4 841	NA	NA	53.7	13.4	8 890	100.0	5 884	8 720	16.6	13.1	1 424 155	19.0	78 102
Anderson	2 254	253	7 806	59	20.4	46.2	15.0	9 561	107.5	6 003	8 896	19.8	14.8	11 503	5.5	710
Charleston	5 005	802	6 789	225	30.5	63.6	24.6	10 600	119.2	6 908	10 238	21.8	17.1	34 322	20.6	2 025
Columbia	10 160	1 399	10 158	210	21.0	63.8	26.0	8 986	101.1	5 865	8 692	20.9	15.5	36 928	11.8	2 082
Florence	3 112	469	9 807	69	21.7	58.4	19.4	9 306	104.7	6 271	9 294	20.1	16.1	11 790	6.8	475
Greenville	5 901	715	9 854	156	26.1	58.4	22.8	10 976	123.5	6 924	10 261	19.6	14.9	26 453	11.2	1 820
North Charleston	5 602	764	7 952	95	13.5	64.0	9.4	8 850	99.6	5 739	8 505	20.2	17.3	26 608	24.0	1 997
Rock Hill	3 705	444	9 763	66	17.4	49.6	13.2	8 258	92.9	5 477	8 117	14.7	11.5	15 682	21.5	747
Spartanburg	4 564	483	10 067	107	23.6	53.8	20.9	9 688	109.0	6 367	9 436	20.9	16.5	17 950	4.4	1 009
SOUTH DAKOTA	18 697	967	2 641	NA	NA	67.9	14.0	8 553	100.0	5 696	8 441	16.9	13.1	292 436	5.3	13 361
Aberdeen	990	33	3 704	37	13.8	71.5	15.6	9 748	114.0	6 419	9 513	9.5	6.3	10 689	3.2	555
Rapid City	3 608	202	7 380	73	14.9	80.9	20.8	10 804	126.3	6 906	10 235	11.1	7.8	22 530	16.9	1 112
Sioux Falls	4 080	192	4 810	125	2.6	77.1	18.8	11 508	134.5	7 460	11 056	8.6	6.1	41 568	20.7	1 306
TENNESSEE	198 419	22 592	4 167	NA	NA	56.2	12.6	9 290	100.0	6 212	9 206	16.5	13.1	2 026 067	13.8	104 351
Chattanooga	13 461	1 509	8 110	364	21.9	60.5	14.1	9 340	100.5	6 331	9 383	17.9	13.4	69 601	4.3	5 765
Clarksville	2 630	253	4 303	91	14.9	70.5	16.6	8 612	92.7	5 716	8 471	12.8	10.5	27 642	29.8	1 832
Cleveland	1 359	118	4 998	47	17.3	55.6	13.9	10 555	113.6	6 551	9 709	16.6	12.9	13 050	18.7	841
Columbia	1 031	79	3 777	49	18.0	54.3	11.2	9 579	103.1	6 543	9 697	15.3	12.5	12 142	15.8	645
Hendersonville	NA	NA	NA	NA	NA	77.5	17.9	12 492	134.5	8 037	11 911	4.0	3.2	12 472	29.9	901
Jackson	4 310	647	8 526	130	25.7	59.3	14.8	9 097	97.9	6 104	9 046	18.1	13.5	20 739	6.5	1 315
Johnson City	2 308	107	5 125	96	21.3	57.2	18.9	10 121	108.9	6 703	9 934	16.8	12.2	21 241	29.2	1 028
Kingsport	2 160	123	6 603	71	21.7	59.5	18.7	11 528	124.1	7 416	10 991	14.3	11.1	16 742	20.6	738
Knoxville	10 838	1 078	6 170	288	16.4	61.4	17.4	9 438	101.6	6 378	9 452	19.6	13.9	76 453	4.2	4 788
Memphis	59 965	9 738	9 160	1 154	17.6	63.3	14.6	9 362	100.8	6 466	9 583	21.8	17.1	248 573	1.7	15 120
Murfreesboro	2 021	98	5 700	74	20.9	69.1	21.4	10 354	111.5	6 569	9 735	15.9	10.8	18 708	33.5	1 335
Nashville-Davidson	31 863	3 376	6 620	984	20.4	65.4	18.6	11 253	121.1	7 276	10 783	12.6	9.5	219 528	18.4	17 844
Oak Ridge	1 163	49	4 078	44	15.4	80.7	34.3	13 565	146.0	9 243	13 698	8.4	6.1	12 694	9.5	769
TEXAS	1 075 295	90 030	6 569	NA	NA	62.6	16.9	10 373	100.0	7 203	10 675	14.7	11.1	7 008 999	20.8	541 918
Abilene	6 511	355	5 849	162	14.6	65.7	18.6	9 685	93.4	6 704	9 935	12.1	8.6	44 436	17.9	3 957
Amarillo	10 843	759	6 503	229	13.7	68.7	15.7	10 975	105.8	7 776	11 524	9.9	7.1	68 592	12.1	5 645
Arlington	19 634	1 110	8 968	304	13.9	83.3	27.3	12 796	123.4	8 728	12 935	5.9	3.8	112 767	42.0	10 112

1. Includes murder and nonnegligent manslaughter, forcible rape, robbery, and aggravated assault. 2. Per 100,000 resident population estimated for 1985 by the FBI. 3. Per 10,000 resident population estimated for 1985 by the FBI. 4. Persons 25 years old or older. 5. Based on the resident population estimated as of July 1, 1988 for 1987 data and enumerated as of April 1, 1980 for 1979 data. 6. Also includes units rented or sold, but not occupied.

City	Housing, 1990 (cont'd)					Construction authorized by building permits, 1990				Civilian labor force, 1990			
	Occupied units					New private housing units						Unemployment	
			Owner-occupied										
	Total	Percent with more than 1 person per room	Percent of total	Median value[1] (Dollars)	Median rent[2] (Dollars)	Number	Value ($1,000)	Percent single family	Non-residential, value ($1,000)	Total	Percent change, 1989–1990	Total	Rate[3]
	45	46	47	48	49	50	51	52	53	54	55	56	57
PENNSYLVANIA—Con.													
Allentown	42 775	3.0	56.6	76 600	377	119	3 491	39.5	5 188	53 673	1.9	3 399	6.3
Altoona	20 684	1.1	66.1	31 600	218	79	3 057	63.3	1 968	23 840	2.5	1 830	7.7
Bethel Park borough	12 692	0.4	80.8	82 200	458	44	5 504	100.0	0	17 856	0.8	511	2.9
Bethlehem	27 268	2.5	61.0	90 600	391	88	4 855	72.7	9 468	34 431	2.1	1 957	5.7
Chester	14 537	5.9	53.1	38 400	291	1	28	100.0	491	17 857	-0.1	1 152	6.5
Easton	9 397	2.6	52.1	80 500	388	29	967	6.9	5 520	11 460	2.6	704	6.1
Erie	42 131	2.1	56.6	43 300	231	24	1 399	58.3	6 618	54 270	1.9	3 517	6.5
Harrisburg	21 520	4.9	42.4	38 400	296	125	5 330	28.0	4 999	25 296	0.5	1 456	5.8
Hazleton	10 574	1.0	60.3	43 900	242	30	1 796	100.0	255	12 490	0.5	810	6.5
Johnstown	12 536	1.2	47.7	26 600	169	0	0	NA	281	11 223	0.5	935	8.3
Lancaster	21 189	5.3	47.2	59 200	329	92	4 972	93.5	4 124	29 885	1.7	1 957	6.5
Lebanon	10 468	1.7	52.1	45 000	267	7	254	14.3	315	14 686	0.4	845	5.8
McKeesport	10 543	1.8	60.1	27 800	210	0	0	NA	42	10 990	0.8	649	5.9
New Castle	11 374	1.4	63.3	29 100	201	0	0	NA	542	13 500	1.0	760	5.6
Norristown borough	12 187	2.7	55.0	80 600	438	7	240	100.0	0	17 504	0.5	919	5.3
Philadelphia	603 075	4.7	61.9	49 400	358	747	46 205	24.0	53 831	732 351	0.3	44 110	6.0
Pittsburgh	153 483	2.0	52.3	41 200	298	81	5 039	60.5	31 677	174 025	0.8	7 895	4.5
Plum borough	9 067	0.7	79.4	63 700	401	81	6 518	100.0	3 955	12 690	0.6	531	4.2
Reading	31 403	4.1	55.9	37 700	292	127	3 568	15.0	2 542	37 968	0.5	2 772	7.3
Scranton	32 637	1.2	53.7	57 100	252	60	3 660	100.0	6 656	39 664	0.8	2 691	6.8
State College borough	10 938	11.1	23.8	115 800	449	223	9 583	9.0	100	16 684	2.4	704	4.2
West Mifflin borough	9 638	0.8	80.9	49 100	198	15	824	100.0	9 124	11 771	1.1	549	4.7
Wilkes-Barre	19 435	1.2	52.7	44 200	259	26	1 552	100.0	6 571	22 696	0.2	1 636	7.2
Williamsport	12 588	2.2	46.5	44 900	248	0	0	NA	0	15 830	0.7	1 224	7.7
York	16 887	3.0	49.8	41 600	281	0	0	NA	0	22 159	0.3	1 260	5.7
RHODE ISLAND	377 977	2.3	59.5	133 500	416	3 042	233 137	77.3	52 754	516 000	-1.7	35 000	6.7
Cranston	29 349	1.0	66.4	129 700	461	152	15 994	93.4	5 701	39 964	-1.2	2 565	6.4
East Providence	19 950	1.7	60.3	122 500	414	122	6 283	32.8	6 622	28 488	-1.3	1 823	6.4
Newport	11 196	1.4	41.6	155 000	525	58	2 182	15.5	140	15 271	-4.9	869	5.7
Pawtucket	29 711	2.9	45.8	112 500	374	74	2 121	29.7	0	37 372	-1.8	3 076	8.2
Providence	58 905	6.0	36.2	113 000	389	313	8 848	34.5	2 496	76 229	-1.1	5 533	7.3
Warwick	33 437	1.1	74.4	116 600	511	236	20 407	77.1	10 182	46 591	-1.4	2 816	6.0
Woonsocket	17 572	2.3	35.5	118 800	371	48	1 968	50.0	7 243	21 248	-1.6	2 082	9.8
SOUTH CAROLINA	1 258 044	4.1	69.8	61 100	276	21 251	1 445 118	80.5	787 959	1 724 000	1.7	81 000	4.7
Anderson	10 509	4.0	52.3	53 100	229	189	9 735	31.7	2 867	13 643	0.6	951	7.0
Charleston	30 753	4.1	48.1	86 600	341	391	26 520	88.0	22 658	38 918	3.3	1 313	3.4
Columbia	33 919	4.4	45.0	72 600	302	164	14 532	100.0	29 134	47 349	1.7	1 956	4.1
Florence	11 074	4.8	57.4	59 200	243	168	9 085	51.2	12 901	15 917	1.3	678	4.3
Greenville	24 101	2.9	46.8	68 700	274	273	10 120	19.8	23 026	34 418	1.2	1 472	4.3
North Charleston	23 499	5.9	37.5	60 100	319	285	11 450	57.2	24 739	23 148	2.6	1 222	5.3
Rock Hill	14 669	5.4	53.9	56 300	314	194	14 197	93.3	24 007	22 950	0.6	1 035	4.5
Spartanburg	16 712	3.9	48.2	58 300	257	25	2 128	100.0	11 138	23 655	1.5	1 263	5.3
SOUTH DAKOTA	259 034	3.0	66.1	45 200	242	2 830	139 723	50.0	122 240	360 000	-0.3	13 000	3.7
Aberdeen	9 998	1.3	56.6	47 900	247	55	2 487	52.7	2 768	14 430	-2.3	770	5.3
Rapid City	21 152	2.9	57.3	56 800	335	207	12 449	74.9	12 244	28 113	1.0	878	3.1
Sioux Falls	39 790	1.6	58.8	59 100	336	587	38 395	69.0	31 059	57 863	0.8	1 601	2.8
TENNESSEE	1 853 725	2.7	68.0	58 400	273	21 977	1 430 895	81.9	880 640	2 397 000	1.2	125 000	5.2
Chattanooga	62 177	2.8	54.2	54 100	271	305	21 486	89.8	81 865	82 345	-0.5	3 780	4.6
Clarksville	25 442	3.7	54.7	59 000	302	623	29 267	82.7	11 685	21 386	2.6	1 491	7.0
Cleveland	11 996	2.3	55.1	60 900	247	91	9 116	61.5	1 429	15 514	5.4	748	4.8
Columbia	11 267	2.3	61.3	61 500	303	225	15 070	97.3	3 255	15 797	11.6	991	6.3
Hendersonville	11 441	1.0	72.8	86 300	399	494	24 002	26.3	12 586	17 733	0.9	678	3.8
Jackson	19 206	2.5	55.9	50 600	240	114	7 633	94.7	34 522	26 595	2.4	1 422	5.3
Johnson City	19 675	1.4	56.8	60 000	245	214	14 146	74.8	19 469	20 421	1.0	903	4.4
Kingsport	15 629	1.2	62.9	55 400	231	154	14 111	93.5	7 817	16 265	1.2	488	3.0
Knoxville	69 973	2.3	49.9	49 800	261	452	19 001	76.3	18 050	86 974	-0.4	4 156	4.8
Memphis	229 829	5.5	55.1	55 700	282	NA	NA	NA	NA	333 822	0.4	15 908	4.8
Murfreesboro	17 110	2.5	47.6	78 200	326	404	24 991	79.2	12 414	24 443	1.1	1 247	5.1
Nashville-Davidson	198 585	2.6	52.8	74 400	358	1 597	111 602	75.0	169 793	NA	NA	NA	NA
Oak Ridge	11 763	1.4	66.5	64 100	307	135	18 901	100.0	16 339	15 640	-0.2	582	3.7
TEXAS	6 070 937	8.1	60.9	59 600	328	47 195	3 879 086	81.0	2 316 470	8 443 000	0.2	521 000	6.2
Abilene	38 395	4.7	59.5	45 800	292	82	8 470	89.0	8 979	45 216	-3.1	2 970	6.6
Amarillo	61 137	5.0	62.6	50 700	291	121	13 383	95.0	11 399	81 961	-1.5	4 039	4.9
Arlington	100 651	5.0	51.8	82 800	382	1 156	113 065	100.0	55 573	132 039	1.3	5 739	4.3

1. Specified owner-occupied units. 2. Specified renter-occupied units. 3. Percent of total civilian labor force.

City	Employed,[1] 1980			Manufactures, 1987											
	Total	Rate per 1,000 employees		Establishments		All employees			Production workers				Value added by manufacture (Mil. dol.)	Value of shipments (Mil. dol.)	New capital expenditures (Mil. dol.)
		Professional, specialty, and technical	Precision production, craft, and operators	Total	Percent with 20 or more employees	Number (1,000)	Percent change, 1982–1987	Annual payroll (Mil. dol.)	Number (1,000)	Work-hours (Millions)	Wages: Total (Mil. dol.)	Wages: Average per production worker (Dollars)			
	58	59	60	61	62	63	64	65	66	67	68	69	70	71	72
PENNSYLVANIA–Con.															
Allentown	47 564	132.0	294.0	241	43.6	19.9	-22.0	531.0	12.4	23.2	288.3	23 250	1 490.0	2 832.4	132.6
Altoona	21 193	129.7	256.4	56	42.9	4.5	-16.7	78.4	3.2	5.6	50.1	15 656	264.9	457.7	9.1
Bethel Park borough	15 896	211.4	143.3	41	14.6	0.5	0.0	8.7	0.3	0.6	5.1	17 000	21.6	35.5	0.9
Bethlehem	30 323	161.7	271.9	80	47.5	10.8	-37.2	315.3	6.8	13.0	172.8	25 412	569.5	1 093.9	28.4
Chester	15 913	104.9	254.3	53	49.1	D	D	D	D	D	D	D	D	D	D
Easton	9 844	130.5	292.3	74	36.5	5.7	5.6	133.4	3.7	7.2	76.8	20 757	334.0	552.3	15.3
Erie	48 922	136.0	273.1	238	42.0	13.2	-14.8	353.9	8.1	16.5	194.4	24 000	658.6	1 307.6	53.5
Harrisburg	21 131	131.7	144.8	74	43.2	4.2	-17.6	96.1	2.5	4.6	47.2	18 880	264.8	462.2	16.7
Hazleton	11 035	108.8	301.9	72	54.2	4.1	-21.2	67.3	3.2	5.9	46.2	14 438	144.6	313.3	8.7
Johnstown	11 653	127.2	232.8	50	42.0	4.6	-35.2	105.1	3.7	7.1	76.0	20 541	155.0	473.1	8.4
Lancaster	23 308	113.3	290.9	137	43.8	15.9	0.0	415.5	10.5	21.3	250.2	23 829	1 176.1	2 082.6	87.3
Lebanon	11 404	112.3	322.5	79	57.0	5.2	-13.3	95.5	3.9	7.6	62.3	15 974	231.6	586.4	14.2
McKeesport	10 892	122.5	260.9	30	20.0	0.6	D	17.0	0.4	0.8	10.2	25 500	33.7	67.4	2.0
New Castle	11 889	120.4	256.0	87	41.4	3.9	-13.3	91.7	2.8	5.7	60.4	21 571	239.3	429.0	17.0
Norristown borough	15 266	111.2	249.1	58	39.7	2.8	-34.9	58.8	1.6	3.1	27.5	17 188	171.8	268.1	3.9
Philadelphia	624 706	155.4	203.4	1 887	38.4	95.9	-23.3	2 425.1	60.7	116.3	1 210.5	19 942	5 084.5	11 567.6	213.3
Pittsburgh	170 591	185.2	155.5	607	36.4	30.8	-41.1	1 001.1	12.4	23.6	272.1	21 944	1 185.7	2 383.3	54.0
Plum borough	11 333	196.8	228.3	25	16.0	0.7	NA	15.1	0.3	0.6	3.5	11 667	20.4	31.9	0.4
Reading	33 354	101.2	323.7	191	51.3	19.1	10.4	561.1	13.2	26.8	358.3	27 144	1 260.9	2 318.3	78.5
Scranton	35 073	121.5	269.4	168	44.6	7.9	-17.7	137.5	6.2	11.3	96.5	15 565	321.3	551.9	12.0
State College borough	13 274	361.9	59.0	43	41.9	2.6	-13.3	58.7	1.6	3.1	32.1	20 062	145.0	248.4	22.2
West Mifflin borough	11 060	129.4	273.6	18	50.0	D	D	D	D	D	D	D	D	D	D
Wilkes-Barre	20 197	121.4	265.4	111	48.6	6.8	-20.9	123.7	4.6	8.5	66.3	14 413	274.3	520.1	7.6
Williamsport	13 254	149.3	251.6	89	62.9	9.2	16.5	186.4	6.7	12.2	117.1	17 478	564.7	1 116.5	16.7
York	18 638	101.6	335.4	169	60.9	21.9	-8.4	558.1	13.4	26.1	294.2	21 955	1 141.8	2 156.9	73.4
RHODE ISLAND	426 812	146.6	283.0	2 878	31.2	112.0	-2.3	2 292.0	76.3	149.4	1 252.3	16 413	4 787.5	9 166.4	276.4
Cranston	32 916	144.8	226.5	253	30.8	7.7	0.0	153.6	5.0	9.5	74.3	14 860	333.7	793.5	14.8
East Providence	24 319	127.6	312.8	149	36.2	6.0	-21.1	127.3	3.7	7.3	58.4	15 784	309.2	537.3	16.8
Newport	11 277	204.5	158.8	NA	NA	NA	NA	NA	NA	NA	NA	NA	NA	NA	NA
Pawtucket	33 233	94.1	379.2	247	40.9	14.7	10.5	295.0	10.0	20.7	157.6	15 760	525.6	1 160.1	28.0
Providence	65 786	158.7	284.0	844	26.4	24.6	-8.2	461.1	16.2	30.7	237.2	14 642	870.4	1 608.3	87.9
Warwick	40 748	141.3	247.8	237	27.8	7.8	-6.0	152.8	5.7	11.1	95.2	16 702	429.6	734.7	21.0
Woonsocket	19 742	87.9	387.2	40	57.5	3.3	-25.0	55.4	2.7	4.8	37.9	14 037	117.5	280.6	5.0
SOUTH CAROLINA	1 319 970	135.1	309.5	4 534	41.7	365.8	-0.4	7 323.9	279.6	566.2	4 742.2	16 961	19 111.9	41 211.7	1 586.0
Anderson	11 652	143.2	288.8	77	39.0	6.9	-11.5	132.6	5.6	10.9	99.3	17 732	285.7	606.5	18.8
Charleston	29 233	231.0	136.0	82	39.0	6.3	90.9	161.4	3.8	7.2	71.6	18 842	557.8	1 463.5	38.5
Columbia	37 818	232.0	125.5	146	40.4	11.7	15.8	277.1	8.3	16.5	166.5	20 060	951.0	1 802.7	170.4
Florence	12 622	192.1	183.6	53	39.6	5.0	28.2	104.2	3.6	7.6	69.2	19 222	222.2	438.7	42.2
Greenville	26 186	189.6	208.6	235	48.1	20.9	-3.2	422.7	15.0	30.5	252.3	16 820	1 152.5	2 276.5	100.5
North Charleston	17 040	107.4	249.5	58	31.0	3.1	-32.6	87.9	2.0	4.0	48.0	24 000	250.8	444.7	D
Rock Hill	15 561	149.7	333.7	72	33.3	4.3	59.3	95.2	3.3	6.6	63.0	19 091	191.1	403.8	17.7
Spartanburg	18 309	183.7	232.2	136	44.1	8.8	-20.7	188.4	6.1	12.5	113.3	18 574	363.6	894.4	37.3
SOUTH DAKOTA	296 679	130.2	159.3	764	30.2	27.5	12.2	497.9	19.9	38.8	312.6	15 709	1 476.1	3 858.7	79.3
Aberdeen	12 701	132.4	190.6	25	40.0	2.0	11.1	40.1	1.4	2.9	25.5	18 214	122.2	225.8	D
Rapid City	20 334	158.1	168.1	82	31.7	2.9	0.0	58.1	2.0	4.1	31.2	15 600	134.7	339.8	4.6
Sioux Falls	40 543	153.3	162.7	112	38.4	8.5	7.6	156.7	6.1	11.0	96.4	15 803	444.7	1 462.7	19.8
TENNESSEE	1 914 920	138.1	270.0	6 864	40.8	484.9	5.0	9 869.2	359.2	707.4	6 282.6	17 491	27 049.7	57 752.9	1 904.7
Chattanooga	71 921	150.7	224.4	368	46.2	25.3	-21.2	562.9	18.5	37.0	352.5	19 054	1 416.6	3 130.3	62.0
Clarksville	16 966	137.5	232.2	55	34.5	4.6	D	90.7	3.3	6.0	53.8	16 303	260.9	422.7	12.8
Cleveland	11 467	161.8	275.1	96	50.0	9.6	-5.0	178.3	7.0	14.2	107.7	15 386	566.0	1 276.1	43.2
Columbia	11 750	138.6	288.6	45	44.4	3.7	19.4	77.9	3.2	6.2	62.8	19 625	142.1	466.2	13.0
Hendersonville	12 598	168.1	182.7	60	18.3	1.5	-6.3	29.2	1.1	2.2	19.3	17 545	52.7	117.7	2.4
Jackson	21 091	154.4	215.5	88	47.7	8.4	9.1	188.5	6.1	13.0	119.3	19 557	616.4	1 331.1	71.0
Johnson City	16 189	195.3	202.6	82	54.9	9.2	10.8	175.5	6.4	12.5	100.8	15 750	532.6	981.9	22.1
Kingsport	13 199	211.7	226.6	55	38.2	15.0	-12.3	471.2	10.0	21.0	278.2	27 820	980.7	2 572.6	D
Knoxville	74 746	187.1	189.0	332	33.7	18.6	3.9	334.7	14.0	26.8	210.0	15 000	944.8	1 957.1	41.4
Memphis	269 138	148.1	181.8	853	43.3	43.4	-7.9	988.5	28.1	56.4	536.9	19 107	3 138.7	6 941.7	180.2
Murfreesboro	15 397	169.3	207.3	86	43.0	5.3	-3.6	110.3	3.8	7.4	72.0	18 947	321.4	658.9	13.0
Nashville-Davidson	219 225	174.2	172.7	827	35.3	D	D	D	D	D	D	D	D	D	D
Oak Ridge	13 261	363.0	161.7	64	26.6	8.5	D	265.7	3.9	8.1	107.9	27 667	752.6	826.8	4.5
TEXAS	6 311 845	145.8	223.4	20 370	30.4	914.0	-13.6	23 240.9	560.8	1 125.2	11 443.9	20 406	63 899.1	162 750.9	4 548.0
Abilene	42 574	147.6	191.7	111	28.8	4.7	-19.0	91.5	2.7	5.2	42.7	15 815	324.1	885.6	11.7
Amarillo	71 986	127.6	216.2	160	25.0	7.1	-24.5	128.7	5.6	11.7	95.7	17 089	103.5	1 810.7	17.5
Arlington	86 976	179.1	187.7	328	32.9	11.6	-6.5	329.6	7.6	15.9	191.7	25 224	983.5	1 911.2	88.8

1. Persons 16 years old and over.

City	Wholesale trade, 1987				Retail trade–all establishments, 1987				Retail trade–establishments with payroll, 1987					
						Sales				Sales				
											Per capita[2] (Dollars)			
	Establishments	Sales (Mil. dol.)	Paid employees[1]	Annual payroll ($1,000)	Number	Total (Mil. dol.)	Percent change, 1982–1987	Per capita[2] (Dollars)	Number	Total (Mil. dol.)	General merchandise group stores	Food stores	Apparel and accessory stores	Eating and drinking places
	73	74	75	76	77	78	79	80	81	82	83	84	85	86
PENNSYLVANIA–Con.														
Allentown	325	D	D	D	1 206	950.0	48.3	9 103	821	932.8	932	1 862	569	868
Altoona	104	D	D	D	681	470.0	50.6	8 841	419	457.8	1 448	2 002	286	675
Bethel Park borough	70	D	D	D	308	221.0	32.4	6 502	218	217.7	1 025	2 488	262	657
Bethlehem	82	D	D	D	612	401.4	29.4	5 707	395	389.4	D	1 486	153	588
Chester	39	110.1	559	11 905	230	120.7	5.9	2 763	163	117.1	40	618	49	252
Easton	67	174.5	896	23 362	384	228.6	72.3	8 613	245	221.1	D	2 562	576	726
Erie	224	490.8	2 562	51 241	1 069	650.4	29.1	5 642	739	632.7	494	1 479	183	596
Harrisburg	161	D	D	D	556	515.5	65.2	10 004	424	509.6	1 115	1 786	322	623
Hazleton	63	90.1	627	9 511	408	221.7	21.1	8 773	242	210.4	2 184	2 066	100	566
Johnstown	92	199.1	1 063	18 283	380	224.1	5.9	7 038	272	219.3	560	2 000	223	569
Lancaster	150	685.4	2 127	45 602	748	575.8	48.5	10 066	540	563.9	2 353	834	1 073	713
Lebanon	63	131.2	677	12 983	546	303.6	71.1	11 504	305	292.0	D	2 702	368	801
McKeesport	40	108.1	448	6 918	235	136.0	-5.3	5 004	170	132.5	D	1 534	112	426
New Castle	94	124.1	698	11 771	545	261.6	27.2	8 535	326	249.6	523	2 121	171	741
Norristown borough	78	359.3	1 042	27 962	288	216.1	3.9	6 397	207	212.2	D	1 864	43	389
Philadelphia	2 197	12 518.2	35 693	901 156	12 793	7 207.9	33.7	4 387	8 388	6 958.1	443	936	374	539
Pittsburgh	1 138	14 132.8	17 713	467 974	3 662	2 584.2	21.3	6 669	2 759	2 538.9	745	1 358	492	900
Plum borough	22	37.9	153	3 205	117	32.9	15.4	1 308	52	29.1	0	246	D	133
Reading	176	845.0	3 164	76 667	893	489.4	34.9	6 305	611	475.8	57	1 285	789	636
Scranton	208	729.6	3 041	52 493	1 027	658.8	56.9	8 009	623	637.4	1 710	1 402	508	496
State College borough	36	46.7	290	5 139	440	396.3	35.3	11 544	343	390.7	2 171	2 167	744	1 355
West Mifflin borough	21	122.1	376	6 638	320	481.8	49.7	19 577	269	479.6	7 340	2 631	1 628	963
Wilkes-Barre	120	462.9	1 780	35 185	701	509.8	52.2	10 645	495	499.3	2 504	1 674	1 037	815
Williamsport	84	160.3	814	15 252	423	315.7	65.7	9 956	304	309.8	D	2 424	470	547
York	141	397.8	1 773	38 694	510	272.2	46.7	6 126	369	265.5	D	761	434	666
RHODE ISLAND	1 724	6 056.7	22 284	490 802	10 276	6 521.0	56.6	6 688	6 682	6 314.7	793	1 209	368	659
Cranston	169	459.4	1 983	43 159	778	457.3	55.3	6 200	476	439.0	276	1 267	404	561
East Providence	157	717.9	2 393	64 450	470	361.5	44.1	7 167	299	353.9	418	1 106	448	561
Newport	31	71.5	167	4 451	517	211.6	58.0	7 217	393	203.6	D	958	688	1 939
Pawtucket	125	345.8	1 775	37 025	617	458.4	53.3	6 311	422	446.1	D	1 149	121	431
Providence	438	1 965.4	6 923	155 061	1 546	830.0	38.4	5 280	1 116	801.4	353	857	300	603
Warwick	198	606.0	2 244	52 176	1 121	1 097.6	65.6	12 622	771	1 078.1	3 487	1 410	1 197	924
Woonsocket	34	109.5	323	6 848	205	260.1	23.2	5 784	188	259.0	776	1 240	195	343
SOUTH CAROLINA	5 271	17 084.4	54 551	1 064 842	36 493	19 750.4	58.0	5 847	21 859	18 949.6	597	1 212	302	544
Anderson	86	D	D	D	693	481.2	42.3	16 778	469	462.7	2 633	2 406	965	1 346
Charleston	200	804.4	2 231	42 491	1 279	997.8	36.9	14 482	1 017	983.8	1 972	3 149	1 220	2 010
Columbia	403	1 656.3	6 255	133 930	1 339	971.9	57.5	10 448	1 030	950.9	1 304	1 331	735	1 217
Florence	128	309.2	1 409	26 644	764	528.5	55.1	16 688	554	517.4	2 624	2 971	832	1 341
Greenville	424	D	D	D	1 245	1 140.5	56.1	19 539	1 013	1 128.0	3 622	2 545	1 362	1 582
North Charleston	126	795.9	1 981	39 089	589	549.5	22.7	8 945	448	545.0	1 511	1 169	407	766
Rock Hill	84	183.2	1 257	18 728	618	427.0	64.6	10 184	412	416.9	1 275	2 254	560	963
Spartanburg	164	735.0	1 474	30 630	809	628.8	46.0	14 223	596	614.7	1 125	2 621	D	1 297
SOUTH DAKOTA	1 793	5 194.0	15 311	255 040	8 736	3 822.3	27.9	5 406	5 514	3 683.4	551	1 039	217	477
Aberdeen	70	D	D	D	351	244.3	34.7	9 517	243	238.4	D	1 761	386	993
Rapid City	139	364.4	1 408	27 520	811	623.5	44.4	11 881	564	612.0	D	2 098	D	997
Sioux Falls	321	1 354.1	3 820	79 171	1 069	879.5	39.9	9 016	768	869.9	D	1 518	423	882
TENNESSEE	8 782	48 278.9	115 927	2 518 097	50 423	29 694.4	51.5	6 182	29 373	28 532.9	792	1 177	278	540
Chattanooga	717	D	D	D	2 217	1 769.6	49.3	10 912	1 537	1 735.9	1 490	1 768	627	952
Clarksville	81	151.7	660	9 940	779	564.6	68.9	9 297	541	551.7	D	1 231	375	767
Cleveland	82	570.2	1 184	20 251	631	380.0	42.8	14 537	357	362.9	D	2 887	706	1 384
Columbia	66	100.4	514	8 819	460	281.4	64.3	9 989	319	271.3	D	2 066	565	716
Hendersonville	62	74.8	299	5 757	354	176.2	83.5	5 840	184	166.8	D	1 861	D	625
Jackson	149	420.4	1 680	30 821	787	579.1	53.3	10 966	555	569.0	D	2 033	D	D
Johnson City	142	501.3	2 122	35 699	657	484.0	29.0	10 828	469	473.4	D	1 858	D	1 132
Kingsport	114	2 028.8	1 709	47 210	834	0.0	0.0	D	526	611.9	4 283	2 695	1 022	1 745
Knoxville	753	3 129.0	9 568	203 653	2 877	2 227.3	51.4	12 859	2 008	2 185.3	1 783	2 156	753	1 306
Memphis	1 840	18 447.6	30 227	721 381	5 470	4 900.5	45.7	7 509	3 875	4 811.3	985	1 143	394	638
Murfreesboro	95	173.4	866	15 716	660	504.2	85.4	12 310	415	488.9	D	2 133	560	1 108
Nashville-Davidson	1 454	8 124.5	23 360	552 492	5 156	4 481.1	61.8	9 460	3 414	4 397.4	1 383	1 402	474	1 067
Oak Ridge	31	29.3	155	2 632	308	256.8	0.0	9 539	222	254.6	1 476	2 016	467	754
TEXAS	35 029	192 193.7	396 138	9 098 340	173 677	100 682.1	22.4	6 035	101 150	97 175.8	748	1 276	325	586
Abilene	280	D	D	D	1 266	764.1	1.2	6 796	821	737.7	1 082	957	336	685
Amarillo	426	D	D	D	2 151	1 466.9	27.0	8 845	1 372	1 430.6	D	D	D	D
Arlington	492	3 970.5	6 370	157 467	2 447	1 956.0	60.6	7 831	1 311	1 898.9	905	1 454	318	777

1. For the period including March 12 of the year shown. 2. Based on resident population estimated as of July 1, 1986.

City	Retail trade–establishment with payroll, 1987 (cont'd)			Taxable service industries–establishments with payroll, 1987							Federal grants, 1986		
	Paid employees[1]				Receipts (Mil. dol.)								
						Selected kinds of business							
	Number	Percent change, 1982–1987	Annual payroll (Mil. dol.)	Number	Total	Hotels, motels, and other lodging places	Health services	Legal services	Paid employees[1]	Annual payroll (Mil. dol.)	Procure-ment contract awards (Mil. dol.)	Grant awards (Mil. dol.)	Federal govern-ment civilian employ-ment, 1984
	87	88	89	90	91	92	93	94	95	96	97	98	99
PENNSYLVANIA—Con.													
Allentown	11 031	17.4	118.3	1 020	487.0	18.3	102.7	34.4	14 151	184.5	35.4	7.9	465
Altoona	5 574	36.9	46.9	439	131.5	2.5	58.8	4.9	3 876	49.2	5.8	3.8	315
Bethel Park borough	3 064	41.8	24.4	219	59.1	D	18.3	1.6	1 504	22.8	0.3	0.4	67
Bethlehem	4 729	15.7	46.7	521	201.2	D	50.6	9.5	4 319	69.0	2.2	5.3	255
Chester	1 201	-7.9	13.0	144	53.2	D	30.4	1.3	1 119	22.1	116.3	5.5	323
Easton	2 530	16.5	25.4	246	74.0	3.4	23.4	10.6	1 780	27.9	12.0	1.5	135
Erie	8 634	12.9	72.9	868	478.7	12.0	166.8	26.9	8 288	158.9	35.2	12.4	1 071
Harrisburg	5 505	21.1	57.9	596	328.3	13.6	61.9	78.6	7 823	129.5	19.6	709.2	2 034
Hazleton	2 802	9.2	23.6	232	70.7	D	36.0	4.0	1 792	30.6	26.9	1.1	116
Johnstown	3 032	6.8	26.4	322	102.4	4.8	51.2	8.2	2 248	47.2	3.3	4.1	573
Lancaster	7 492	13.7	72.9	564	241.2	D	86.7	32.1	5 154	109.8	132.7	9.1	846
Lebanon	3 218	32.9	29.9	273	85.3	4.3	41.1	D	1 930	32.2	5.5	1.2	123
McKeesport	1 581	-27.5	15.3	192	60.4	0.0	36.6	1.4	1 464	25.2	4.9	0.6	181
New Castle	3 147	3.7	27.8	292	75.9	D	33.4	D	2 712	29.7	2.2	1.9	347
Norristown borough	2 147	-3.9	24.0	308	113.0	0.5	50.2	29.5	2 098	45.7	2.9	0.6	329
Philadelphia	93 684	18.5	954.1	8 633	6 132.5	256.0	1 043.6	1 343.7	113 123	2 327.3	1 230.8	1 371.6	48 799
Pittsburgh	38 705	5.7	360.5	3 780	3 063.7	97.6	603.4	450.1	54 117	1 221.9	285.8	186.6	11 704
Plum borough	500	12.6	3.8	88	43.9	0.0	2.8	D	1 234	15.0	0.0	0.1	1
Reading	5 844	16.6	57.5	571	284.4	11.0	54.9	29.4	5 812	104.4	23.3	24.0	698
Scranton	7 894	25.9	68.5	641	280.0	16.3	108.6	27.9	6 795	113.3	22.0	16.1	738
State College borough	5 892	14.9	43.9	335	231.1	15.4	36.1	4.9	4 305	97.7	51.7	35.2	277
West Mifflin borough	5 395	26.7	48.5	88	D	D	7.7	D	D	D	440.0	0.5	80
Wilkes-Barre	6 629	24.7	57.5	491	230.3	26.2	79.2	23.3	5 840	94.6	9.9	9.1	1 862
Williamsport	3 377	23.2	32.4	329	113.6	6.2	57.7	11.5	2 227	46.2	26.0	3.6	311
York	3 426	17.2	31.8	425	195.3	10.1	35.4	22.2	4 440	79.7	422.3	24.8	434
RHODE ISLAND	76 449	25.8	772.4	7 133	2 603.8	96.2	679.7	248.0	60 638	1 006.6	448.4	668.7	9 201
Cranston	5 260	18.6	48.8	678	165.5	D	51.1	8.8	4 219	60.1	3.9	12.4	18
East Providence	3 576	10.3	38.3	378	154.4	D	37.0	6.5	3 630	59.7	1.8	1.7	4
Newport	3 645	38.5	34.4	280	119.3	24.9	18.6	6.9	2 645	41.1	52.5	2.7	3 498
Pawtucket	5 173	37.9	53.4	443	151.9	D	32.0	8.0	4 339	55.9	7.8	6.1	217
Providence	11 021	9.0	108.2	1 635	815.5	30.3	178.1	181.6	16 217	345.8	50.3	143.2	3 643
Warwick	12 314	27.3	123.1	840	320.6	4.6	101.3	10.9	7 492	117.2	3.4	6.1	277
Woonsocket	2 520	-9.0	27.5	30	10.8	0.0	6.8	D	424	4.8	0.8	3.5	183
SOUTH CAROLINA	237 122	37.7	2 177.5	18 810	6 355.0	668.7	1 775.0	473.6	169 535	2 397.0	1 783.8	1 403.8	32 696
Anderson	5 899	20.8	54.6	428	130.6	2.4	60.1	9.3	3 348	56.7	8.6	3.2	198
Charleston	15 417	36.7	127.9	1 061	487.7	65.3	198.6	61.6	11 436	167.7	69.3	34.4	15 536
Columbia	13 845	47.2	130.4	1 526	673.5	30.8	176.3	111.7	18 256	282.0	62.5	218.2	3 873
Florence	6 454	28.3	58.2	494	181.3	13.3	91.9	11.9	4 516	76.2	1.8	3.6	440
Greenville	13 832	25.8	139.9	1 250	672.1	35.7	108.9	75.4	16 387	268.0	11.6	11.4	975
North Charleston	6 262	-6.6	58.9	401	D	D	18.8	4.7	D	D	82.2	2.4	59
Rock Hill	5 131	48.4	47.3	370	149.2	D	78.4	7.6	3 403	57.3	2.0	4.5	130
Spartanburg	8 125	25.8	74.0	626	238.4	10.0	81.7	23.1	8 777	108.1	9.6	4.7	287
SOUTH DAKOTA	49 324	9.1	407.7	4 296	1 001.5	112.0	361.2	78.5	26 538	355.6	212.7	480.5	9 132
Aberdeen	3 445	13.8	28.2	292	72.9	D	D	D	1 828	23.9	1.6	12.8	533
Rapid City	7 020	17.2	69.7	647	177.0	25.3	54.3	D	4 468	57.7	24.4	5.4	678
Sioux Falls	12 071	24.5	102.0	843	328.1	D	131.1	21.1	7 586	136.5	11.4	6.1	1 780
TENNESSEE	338 168	29.8	3 198.1	27 829	12 010.2	814.4	3 797.9	605.8	282 908	4 486.9	4 550.3	2 199.3	57 089
Chattanooga	19 829	22.7	208.1	1 710	878.8	37.6	333.8	65.6	20 854	335.9	158.4	16.3	5 900
Clarksville	6 288	35.8	62.4	386	87.0	6.4	D	6.7	2 300	28.6	1.2	3.4	143
Cleveland	4 252	22.7	40.2	342	141.6	6.9	53.1	4.6	3 720	50.3	1.0	2.1	272
Columbia	3 387	34.6	28.8	262	89.5	D	35.8	6.3	2 083	30.2	7.6	1.5	171
Hendersonville	2 282	81.7	19.5	282	108.0	D	48.7	D	2 691	40.9	1.2	0.1	91
Jackson	6 615	17.0	62.4	517	205.9	D	113.6	10.1	5 026	95.5	1.9	3.6	419
Johnson City	6 158	16.9	56.0	480	157.8	D	78.0	9.0	4 551	61.7	6.9	4.3	1 732
Kingsport	7 458	16.8	69.8	521	204.2	9.5	112.2	12.6	4 432	81.4	1.6	2.1	320
Knoxville	26 998	26.7	255.2	2 142	838.4	45.6	266.8	76.4	19 451	325.3	111.3	38.4	6 904
Memphis	54 387	18.3	559.0	4 475	2 255.6	147.2	559.9	132.4	56 983	877.8	63.5	78.0	14 383
Murfreesboro	5 751	48.1	52.3	403	136.1	D	D	8.2	3 319	48.7	2.9	2.2	1 435
Nashville-Davidson	54 041	36.4	538.6	4 633	2 678.4	D	670.3	157.0	61 156	956.3	79.0	352.2	6 295
Oak Ridge	2 790	D	28.1	327	D	6.2	D	D	D	D	2 873.1	6.7	1 019
TEXAS	1 174 108	10.9	11 496.0	108 431	50 953.3	2 369.0	13 497.1	4 852.0	1 060 911	18 808.1	12 692.3	5 750.4	163 109
Abilene	10 221	3.4	93.1	903	337.2	D	149.4	17.9	6 972	110.3	324.5	5.7	510
Amarillo	16 798	11.4	162.7	1 304	487.3	D	D	D	9 584	168.4	245.1	7.8	1 703
Arlington	20 170	25.2	211.3	1 748	847.1	43.8	230.7	29.5	20 519	303.1	48.3	5.7	639

1. For the period including March 12 of the year shown.

City	City government employment, 1985 (October): Total	City government employment, 1985 (October): Rates[1]	City government employment, 1985 (October): Percent education	Form of governments[2] (As of 1986)	City government finances, 1984–1985: General revenue: Total (Mil. dol.)	General revenue: Intergovernmental: Total (Mil. dol.)	General revenue: Intergovernmental: Percent from State government	General revenue: Taxes: Total (Mil. dol.)	Taxes: Per capita[3] (Dollars): Total	Taxes: Per capita[3] (Dollars): Property	Taxes: Per capita[3] (Dollars): Sales & gross receipts	General expenditures: Total (Mil. dol.)	General expenditures: Per capita[3] (Dol.): Total	General expenditures: Per capita[3] (Dol.): Capital outlays	General expenditures: Percent of total for–: Public welfare	Percent of total for–: Highways	Percent of total for–: Education
	100	101	102	103	104	105	106	107	108	109	110	111	112	113	114	115	116
PENNSYLVANIA—Con.																	
Allentown	961	92.1	0.0	1	45.0	9.9	34.3	21.0	201	120	0	61.2	586	21	0.0	10.6	0.0
Altoona	NA	NA	NA	1	14.5	3.5	28.5	7.9	148	104	0	14.7	277	25	0.0	17.5	0.0
Bethel Park borough	153	45.0	0.0	2	6.8	0.8	70.6	4.2	125	45	0	6.8	199	NA	0.0	14.9	0.0
Bethlehem	685	97.4	0.0	1	26.2	4.8	26.4	12.8	181	126	0	23.2	329	41	0.0	8.7	0.0
Chester	379	86.8	0.0	1	24.1	11.0	6.3	9.9	227	103	0	25.7	589	33	0.0	7.8	0.0
Easton	294	110.8	0.0	1	9.6	2.1	18.7	3.6	136	82	0	9.9	374	20	0.0	9.5	0.0
Erie	1 171	101.6	0.0	1	47.1	12.4	38.8	21.8	189	141	0	47.6	413	58	0.0	13.1	0.0
Harrisburg	800	155.2	0.0	1	29.5	4.7	33.4	8.9	173	116	0	29.0	562	60	0.0	10.5	0.0
Hazleton	133	52.6	0.0	1	6.2	2.3	27.8	2.6	102	61	0	8.3	330	76	0.0	9.6	0.0
Johnstown	292	91.7	0.0	1	16.2	7.8	45.5	4.8	152	107	0	14.6	458	171	0.0	9.5	0.0
Lancaster	592	103.5	0.0	1	18.2	4.2	15.3	8.3	146	105	0	20.3	356	38	0.0	8.0	0.0
Lebanon	167	63.3	0.0	3	8.1	0.9	49.0	2.6	98	62	0	7.0	264	13	0.0	20.0	0.0
McKeesport	169	62.2	0.0	1	8.3	1.9	55.7	4.7	172	99	0	9.3	343	NA	0.0	15.2	0.0
New Castle	197	64.3	0.0	1	10.6	3.0	44.9	5.7	184	138	0	10.5	344	8	0.0	9.7	0.0
Norristown borough	NA	NA	NA	1	7.9	0.9	46.1	4.8	142	61	0	9.0	266	17	0.0	14.8	0.0
Philadelphia	32 854	200.0	0.0	1	1 954.2	438.7	65.3	1 141.4	695	139	10	1 839.2	1 119	103	5.6	4.1	1.1
Pittsburgh	6 152	158.8	0.0	1	300.6	69.4	43.6	188.1	485	215	38	306.0	790	129	NA	11.6	0.0
Plum borough	70	27.8	0.0	2	3.6	0.5	66.6	1.7	69	23	0	3.7	146	12	0.0	22.4	0.0
Reading	869	112.0	0.0	3	33.1	11.3	9.3	13.8	178	120	0	31.2	402	120	0.0	14.0	0.0
Scranton	854	103.8	0.0	1	34.6	10.4	16.4	17.1	208	69	0	39.7	483	70	0.0	10.9	0.0
State College borough	208	60.6	0.0	1	8.8	1.6	25.5	2.6	77	26	0	8.3	242	54	0.0	13.2	0.0
West Mifflin borough	152	61.8	0.0	1	5.8	0.7	55.0	4.5	182	115	0	5.6	229	8	0.0	23.9	0.0
Wilkes-Barre	445	92.9	0.0	1	18.5	5.5	22.8	10.9	228	85	0	18.2	380	56	0.0	8.2	0.0
Williamsport	224	70.6	0.0	1	10.6	4.7	19.4	4.4	138	88	0	10.2	322	6	0.0	27.7	0.0
York	434	97.7	0.0	1	20.8	4.0	29.4	7.9	178	120	0	28.8	648	226	0.0	6.8	0.0
RHODE ISLAND	NA	NA	NA	NA	NA	NA	NA	NA	NA	NA	NA	NA	NA	NA	NA	NA	NA
Cranston	2 025	274.5	58.0	1	71.8	20.0	78.3	45.3	615	601	0	78.5	1 064	170	1.3	4.2	44.1
East Providence	1 233	244.4	61.8	2	44.6	12.0	75.9	30.9	613	608	0	46.3	917	81	1.7	5.0	47.0
Newport	963	328.4	56.2	2	31.8	8.6	78.9	20.3	693	677	0	32.5	1 109	4	0.3	3.3	52.2
Pawtucket	1 727	237.7	56.2	1	65.5	25.3	86.0	37.8	520	517	0	64.2	884	23	0.5	4.0	53.1
Providence	3 970	252.5	48.8	1	202.1	79.2	71.9	100.9	642	635	0	182.1	1 158	94	6.3	3.2	41.0
Warwick	2 488	286.1	63.1	1	91.2	25.3	86.7	61.2	704	697	0	94.8	1 090	53	1.9	3.3	55.6
Woonsocket	1 288	286.4	63.4	1	45.4	21.0	85.5	20.6	458	454	0	45.6	1 014	11	4.2	3.2	51.3
SOUTH CAROLINA	NA	NA	NA	NA	NA	NA	NA	NA	NA	NA	NA	NA	NA	NA	NA	NA	NA
Anderson	286	99.7	0.0	2	10.3	3.3	24.7	5.0	173	122	15	10.3	359	40	0.0	5.9	0.0
Charleston	1 378	200.0	0.0	1	52.8	15.2	7.9	19.2	279	189	37	52.3	758	207	0.0	5.8	0.0
Columbia	1 530	164.5	0.0	2	55.3	20.2	13.0	17.3	186	122	27	55.5	597	207	0.0	5.6	0.0
Florence	303	95.7	0.0	2	10.9	2.1	35.4	5.8	183	120	27	8.8	277	17	0.0	10.6	0.0
Greenville	892	152.8	0.0	2	28.8	6.1	22.8	15.9	273	183	25	26.5	453	55	0.0	12.4	0.0
North Charleston	428	69.7	0.0	1	12.4	4.0	29.9	7.4	121	71	20	11.5	187	34	0.0	8.8	0.0
Rock Hill	528	125.9	0.0	2	10.6	2.9	19.8	4.2	99	81	0	15.2	362	47	0.0	3.8	0.0
Spartanburg	669	151.3	0.0	2	18.8	4.3	26.2	10.9	247	170	26	15.9	359	26	0.0	10.8	0.0
SOUTH DAKOTA	NA	NA	NA	NA	NA	NA	NA	NA	NA	NA	NA	NA	NA	NA	NA	NA	NA
Aberdeen	276	107.5	0.0	3	11.8	1.8	36.8	7.5	292	138	146	10.9	424	136	0.2	15.0	0.0
Rapid City	NA	NA	NA	1	45.9	3.1	43.3	14.6	278	74	192	25.2	480	108	0.0	9.0	0.0
Sioux Falls	928	95.1	0.0	3	54.9	13.1	11.7	28.5	292	129	153	46.0	472	183	0.1	16.1	0.0
TENNESSEE	NA	NA	NA	NA	NA	NA	NA	NA	NA	NA	NA	NA	NA	NA	NA	NA	NA
Chattanooga	5 964	367.8	47.5	3	134.5	57.2	57.7	46.5	287	250	32	155.6	959	104	5.8	4.6	41.4
Clarksville	545	89.7	0.0	1	17.2	5.3	56.2	4.2	69	43	24	14.5	238	24	0.8	22.3	0.0
Cleveland	847	324.0	51.7	3	18.8	7.2	87.3	5.7	219	81	124	19.3	737	85	0.4	10.3	47.3
Columbia	381	135.3	0.0	2	6.9	1.8	80.1	2.1	74	47	26	8.2	293	25	0.0	19.7	0.0
Hendersonville	135	44.7	0.0	2	4.9	1.7	83.3	1.5	49	31	15	6.6	217	42	0.5	12.8	0.4
Jackson	NA	NA	NA	3	32.5	11.9	77.7	10.2	193	149	35	36.0	682	63	0.2	6.0	39.4
Johnson City	1 535	343.4	50.4	2	24.7	8.6	81.4	9.4	211	133	70	32.0	715	63	0.1	5.4	46.8
Kingsport	1 186	376.9	62.2	2	26.5	9.3	84.6	9.4	297	250	43	35.5	1 128	136	0.0	4.6	46.5
Knoxville	5 936	342.7	52.3	1	110.7	40.3	63.6	43.7	252	213	26	143.5	829	69	0.4	1.4	42.1
Memphis	23 167	355.0	54.7	1	483.0	224.3	78.9	140.2	215	156	41	560.1	858	75	NA	2.9	47.9
Murfreesboro	839	204.8	45.3	2	15.6	6.4	74.1	6.5	158	123	32	19.6	478	55	0.0	15.2	35.8
Nashville-Davidson	18 040	380.9	46.5	1	576.6	142.6	76.5	271.4	573	273	247	561.4	1 185	220	1.0	3.2	33.0
Oak Ridge	NA	NA	NA	2	26.9	11.9	63.0	9.5	353	267	83	31.6	1 172	273	0.5	3.5	66.5
TEXAS	NA	NA	NA	NA	NA	NA	NA	NA	NA	NA	NA	NA	NA	NA	NA	NA	NA
Abilene	1 172	104.2	0.0	2	49.0	8.4	5.6	23.1	205	96	105	42.4	377	50	0.0	8.1	0.0
Amarillo	3 020	182.1	0.0	2	144.0	13.0	6.4	43.3	261	150	105	133.9	807	132	1.2	13.4	0.0
Arlington	2 006	80.3	0.0	2	129.0	9.3	12.5	52.8	211	111	92	107.6	431	107	0.0	20.2	0.0

1. Per 10,000 population estimated as of July 1, 1986. 2. 1 = Mayor-council; 2 = Council-manager; 3 = Commission. Data subject to copyright. 3. Based on resident population estimated as of July 1, 1986.

City	City government finances, 1984–1985 (cont'd): General expenditure (cont'd): Percent of total for (cont'd): Health and hospitals	Police protection	Sewerage and sanitation	Parks and recreation	Housing and community development	Debt outstanding: Total (Mil. dol.)	Per capita[1] (Dollars)	Percent utility	Climate[2]: Average daily temperature (Degrees Fahrenheit): Mean: Jan.	Mean: July	Limits: Jan.[3]	Limits: July[4]	Annual precipitation (Inches)	Heating degree days[5]	Cooling degree days[5]	Typical monthly electric bills, 1986: Residential[6]: Total (Dollars)	Residential[6]: Percent change, 1980–1986	Commercial[7] (Dollars)
	117	118	119	120	121	122	123	124	125	126	127	128	129	130	131	132	133	134
PENNSYLVANIA—Con.																		
Allentown	1.1	10.4	10.2	4.5	7.4	26.7	256	10.3	27.2	73.8	19.5	84.6	44.31	5 815	751	60.37	88.8	576.5
Altoona	0.3	22.0	11.1	2.6	6.4	1.0	19	0.0	27.9	72.9	19.2	85.6	45.66	5 768	728	63.38	61.0	603.4
Bethel Park borough	4.5	17.4	19.8	1.9	0.7	0.6	16	0.0	26.7	72.0	19.2	82.7	36.29	5 950	645	38.75	34.9	NA
Bethlehem	1.6	17.3	12.8	4.3	3.9	14.2	202	0.0	27.2	73.8	19.5	84.6	44.31	5 815	751	60.37	88.8	576.5
Chester	2.6	18.2	3.4	3.4	33.4	8.0	184	0.0	31.2	76.5	23.8	86.1	41.42	4 947	1 075	72.99	55.7	NA
Easton	0.1	13.9	13.8	4.9	11.2	12.3	465	79.6	27.2	73.8	19.5	84.6	44.31	5 815	751	63.14	73.8	NA
Erie	0.0	15.8	18.8	3.3	10.8	22.5	195	46.3	24.5	69.1	18.0	78.2	39.39	6 768	402	63.38	61.0	603.4
Harrisburg	0.0	15.4	14.7	1.5	9.6	40.3	781	0.0	29.4	75.8	22.1	86.2	39.09	5 335	1 006	60.37	88.8	576.5
Hazleton	0.4	6.9	2.6	1.2	20.7	0.6	23	0.0	23.3	69.4	15.3	79.1	46.49	6 911	371	60.37	88.8	NA
Johnstown	0.0	10.0	12.0	3.2	32.3	0.3	10	0.0	27.9	72.9	19.2	85.6	45.66	5 768	728	63.38	61.0	NA
Lancaster	0.6	17.2	13.3	3.2	8.2	1.4	25	0.0	30.0	74.7	20.7	87.2	40.63	5 203	901	60.37	88.8	576.5
Lebanon	0.4	17.0	9.9	1.3	0.2	2.4	92	0.0	29.4	75.8	22.1	86.2	39.09	5 335	1 006	63.14	73.8	NA
McKeesport	0.0	18.2	11.6	1.2	3.5	6.7	247	0.0	26.7	72.0	19.2	82.7	36.29	5 950	645	73.98	89.4	NA
New Castle	0.1	15.5	13.6	3.0	11.9	2.6	86	0.0	27.1	71.6	18.2	84.5	38.22	5 885	642	59.98	46.6	NA
Norristown borough	1.1	25.3	16.7	5.6	0.0	1.9	58	0.0	31.2	76.5	23.8	86.1	41.42	4 947	1 075	72.99	55.7	NA
Philadelphia	8.4	12.8	9.4	4.0	6.1	2 381.4	1 449	34.5	31.2	76.5	23.8	86.1	41.42	4 947	1 075	72.99	55.7	677.5
Pittsburgh	1.9	15.5	5.1	6.7	5.7	378.3	976	0.0	26.7	72.0	19.2	82.7	36.29	5 950	645	73.98	89.4	643.7
Plum borough	0.0	21.7	31.7	1.4	0.0	0.3	14	0.0	26.7	72.0	19.2	82.7	36.29	5 950	645	73.98	89.4	NA
Reading	0.6	16.6	11.5	5.0	17.2	13.6	175	0.0	25.8	70.8	15.3	84.7	48.76	6 406	486	63.14	73.8	591.5
Scranton	1.3	10.1	11.3	2.3	3.8	2.2	26	0.0	25.2	71.8	18.2	82.1	35.08	6 330	569	60.37	88.8	576.5
State College borough	0.5	21.0	20.5	4.7	0.3	10.2	298	0.0	25.9	71.5	18.4	82.2	37.65	6 247	559	38.75	34.9	NA
West Mifflin borough	0.3	20.2	23.4	2.9	0.0	0.3	13	0.0	26.7	72.0	19.2	82.7	36.29	5 950	645	73.98	89.4	NA
Wilkes-Barre	2.8	17.1	6.2	8.8	11.2	0.3	6	0.0	25.2	71.8	18.2	82.1	35.08	6 330	569	60.37	88.8	576.5
Williamsport	0.0	20.9	0.0	2.8	3.2	7.6	239	0.0	26.2	72.5	18.3	83.7	41.28	6 047	659	60.37	88.8	NA
York	0.2	10.0	19.5	4.9	22.9	28.5	641	0.0	30.0	74.7	20.7	87.2	40.63	5 203	901	63.14	73.8	NA
RHODE ISLAND	NA	NA	NA	NA	NA	NA	NA	NA	NA	NA	NA	NA	NA	NA	NA	62.46	40.8	NA
Cranston	0.0	9.8	14.3	1.3	3.3	62.6	849	1.5	28.2	72.5	20.0	81.7	45.32	5 908	574	60.25	34.3	538.5
East Providence	0.2	10.8	12.6	2.0	2.9	12.7	253	22.8	28.2	72.5	20.0	81.7	45.32	5 908	574	60.25	34.3	538.5
Newport	0.1	12.3	7.3	1.8	3.0	13.4	457	27.9	28.2	70.1	18.6	80.6	48.49	6 121	382	67.07	82.6	NA
Pawtucket	0.1	8.6	5.3	2.5	1.1	24.4	335	16.7	28.2	72.5	20.0	81.7	45.32	5 908	574	68.27	49.9	NA
Providence	0.1	6.8	2.5	4.0	4.0	96.5	614	9.4	28.2	72.5	20.0	81.7	45.32	5 908	574	60.25	34.3	538.5
Warwick	0.2	8.0	6.6	1.3	1.0	72.4	833	1.6	28.2	72.5	20.0	81.7	45.32	5 908	574	60.25	34.3	538.5
Woonsocket	0.0	6.5	4.5	0.7	2.6	47.6	1 059	8.1	28.2	72.5	20.0	81.7	45.32	5 908	574	68.27	49.9	NA
SOUTH CAROLINA	NA	NA	NA	NA	NA	NA	NA	NA	NA	NA	NA	NA	NA	NA	NA	55.24	58.9	NA
Anderson	0.0	19.4	22.4	7.1	13.6	3.9	136	0.0	42.2	79.8	32.2	89.9	46.79	3 021	1 774	51.72	58.3	NA
Charleston	0.0	14.7	25.9	7.3	12.4	118.4	1 719	63.9	49.2	81.6	41.4	87.9	47.34	1 868	2 304	59.71	51.4	429.3
Columbia	0.5	13.0	34.3	6.0	4.2	72.7	781	88.7	44.7	81.0	33.2	91.9	49.12	2 629	2 033	59.71	51.4	429.3
Florence	0.0	24.3	14.0	7.9	0.0	13.4	422	89.3	45.0	80.6	34.4	90.5	43.98	2 561	1 998	57.03	72.4	NA
Greenville	0.0	20.6	9.6	7.9	10.3	49.9	855	89.4	41.1	78.2	31.2	88.2	50.52	3 239	1 501	51.72	58.3	455.7
North Charleston	0.0	30.6	13.9	6.9	3.2	0.9	15	0.0	49.2	81.6	41.4	87.9	47.34	1 868	2 304	59.71	51.4	429.3
Rock Hill	0.0	11.5	17.8	12.4	4.6	5.9	141	52.1	41.9	78.4	31.2	89.3	46.93	3 110	1 533	46.54	52.9	NA
Spartanburg	0.0	25.6	12.9	9.8	1.2	18.0	408	93.7	41.1	78.2	31.2	88.2	50.52	3 239	1 501	51.72	58.3	NA
SOUTH DAKOTA	NA	NA	NA	NA	NA	NA	NA	NA	NA	NA	NA	NA	NA	NA	NA	50.64	52.0	NA
Aberdeen	0.2	9.0	15.4	11.5	0.1	11.1	431	53.1	8.3	72.1	NA	85.3	17.79	8 570	589	70.15	55.9	NA
Rapid City	0.3	10.7	13.8	31.5	3.3	5.1	98	50.2	20.8	72.6	9.2	86.5	16.27	7 301	667	55.93	57.9	482.2
Sioux Falls	2.1	8.7	27.4	10.6	2.8	21.0	215	0.0	12.4	74.0	1.9	86.2	24.12	7 885	749	46.59	52.8	380.4
TENNESSEE	NA	NA	NA	NA	NA	NA	NA	NA	NA	NA	NA	NA	NA	NA	NA	38.28	70.6	NA
Chattanooga	0.4	7.3	7.9	2.4	1.9	101.0	623	3.0	38.7	78.7	29.2	89.3	52.60	3 583	1 578	38.24	56.8	338.1
Clarksville	1.7	16.8	9.9	6.2	5.8	41.6	685	32.7	35.7	78.7	25.4	90.7	49.64	4 014	1 514	38.24	69.7	338.1
Cleveland	0.2	7.6	11.8	3.3	3.3	11.1	424	66.0	38.7	78.7	29.2	89.3	52.60	3 583	1 578	37.61	73.9	NA
Columbia	0.2	15.4	21.7	7.0	0.2	6.3	225	38.7	37.6	78.2	27.4	89.8	53.93	3 761	1 497	36.04	66.5	NA
Hendersonville	0.2	21.7	13.8	7.3	0.0	5.7	188	0.0	37.1	79.4	27.8	89.8	48.49	3 756	1 661	37.61	NA	NA
Jackson	NA	9.7	14.5	7.1	1.9	78.2	1 480	88.5	37.8	80.4	28.5	91.3	50.99	3 540	1 802	36.04	73.8	NA
Johnson City	0.0	10.8	8.7	7.7	0.0	27.1	606	39.4	37.0	75.7	27.3	87.4	44.12	3 920	1 164	37.04	83.5	NA
Kingsport	2.4	6.5	8.2	3.3	1.3	38.6	1 226	22.5	37.0	75.7	27.3	87.4	44.12	3 920	1 164	39.82	37.1	NA
Knoxville	0.0	9.3	12.7	4.7	3.9	209.8	1 211	21.1	38.2	77.6	29.5	87.2	47.29	3 658	1 449	38.24	69.7	338.1
Memphis	2.1	9.5	9.7	5.7	1.8	674.2	1 033	25.6	39.6	82.1	30.9	91.5	51.57	3 207	2 067	39.66	76.0	368.2
Murfreesboro	0.3	9.0	4.6	3.9	1.9	56.7	1 384	60.6	37.7	78.6	27.7	90.2	51.95	3 734	1 573	36.51	80.8	NA
Nashville-Davidson	8.0	7.1	15.9	3.9	2.0	1 177.2	2 485	35.2	37.1	79.4	27.8	89.8	48.49	3 756	1 661	37.61	73.8	333.9
Oak Ridge	0.1	5.6	5.0	2.5	0.9	13.7	508	1.9	36.7	76.6	27.7	87.2	54.76	4 006	1 294	36.04	66.6	NA
TEXAS	NA	NA	NA	NA	NA	NA	NA	NA	NA	NA	NA	NA	NA	NA	NA	55.56	63.7	NA
Abilene	1.4	13.3	22.0	8.8	1.0	113.0	1 005	14.3	43.3	84.1	31.2	95.4	23.26	2 621	2 467	52.21	73.1	410.8
Amarillo	45.9	7.0	11.3	2.6	0.7	109.1	658	1.7	35.4	78.8	21.7	91.4	19.10	4 231	1 428	49.39	34.3	449.8
Arlington	0.5	10.4	6.8	7.9	9.1	348.4	1 395	22.3	44.0	86.3	33.9	97.8	29.45	2 407	2 809	53.81	61.6	456.3

1. Based on resident population estimated as of July 1, 1986. 2. Represents normal values based on the 30-year period, 1951–1980 (see text). 3. Average daily minimum. 4. Average daily maximum. 5. For definition, see text. 6. As of January 1; based on consumption of 750 kWh. 7. Based on billing demand of 30 kW and consumption of 6,000 kWh.

MSA/ CMSA Code[1]	State/ Place code	City	Land area,[2] 1990 (Sq. Km.)	Population: 1990: Total persons	Population: 1990: Rank	Population: 1990: Per sq. km.	Population: 1980	Population: Change 1980–1990: Number	Population: Change 1980–1990: Per-cent	Population characteristics, 1990: Percent: Race: White	Race: Black	Race: Am. Indian, Eskimo, Aleut	Race: Asian & Pacific Islander	Race: Other race	His-panic[3]	65 Years and over
			1	2	3	4	5	6	7	8	9	10	11	12	13	14
		TEXAS—Con.														
0640	48 0210	Austin	564.0	465 622	27	826	345 890	119 732	34.6	70.56	12.43	0.38	3.04	13.60	22.95	7.4
3362	48 0315	Baytown	81.1	63 850	358	787	56 923	6 927	12.2	72.97	12.02	0.33	0.75	13.94	23.15	9.7
0840	48 0320	Beaumont	207.3	114 323	154	551	118 102	-3 779	-3.2	54.97	41.26	0.21	1.67	1.90	4.30	13.8
1240	48 0595	Brownsville	72.3	98 962	198	1 369	84 997	13 965	16.4	84.77	0.20	0.14	0.30	14.58	90.14	8.7
1260	48 0610	Bryan	84.6	55 002	427	650	44 337	10 665	24.1	69.88	17.18	0.25	1.55	11.14	19.80	9.8
1922	48 0740	Carrollton	90.0	82 169	256	913	40 595	41 574	102.4	83.12	4.89	0.42	6.81	4.76	10.25	3.4
1260	48 0905	College Station	76.3	52 456	460	687	37 272	15 184	40.7	82.96	6.28	0.21	6.54	4.02	8.92	2.8
1880	48 0980	Corpus Christi	349.6	257 453	64	736	232 134	25 319	10.9	76.14	4.80	0.43	0.93	17.71	50.38	10.1
1922	48 1085	Dallas	886.8	1 006 877	8	1 135	904 599	102 278	11.3	55.30	29.50	0.48	2.18	12.55	20.88	9.7
...	48 1130	Del Rio	38.2	30 705	818	804	30 034	671	2.2	65.51	1.38	0.35	0.42	32.33	77.18	10.2
1922	48 1140	Denton	136.3	66 270	344	486	48 063	18 207	37.9	81.96	9.53	0.45	2.81	5.25	8.96	8.1
1922	48 1230	Duncanville	29.2	35 748	703	1 224	27 781	7 967	28.7	82.54	12.06	0.35	2.14	2.90	6.65	6.8
2320	48 1340	El Paso	635.5	515 342	22	811	425 259	90 083	21.2	76.87	3.44	0.43	1.16	18.11	69.02	8.7
1922	48 1500	Fort Worth	728.0	447 619	28	615	385 164	62 455	16.2	63.79	22.01	0.43	1.99	11.78	19.51	11.2
3362	48 1570	Galveston	119.6	59 070	397	494	61 902	-2 832	-4.6	61.48	29.05	0.24	2.35	6.88	21.41	13.5
1922	48 1580	Garland	148.5	180 650	91	1 216	138 857	41 793	30.1	79.67	8.87	0.53	4.47	6.45	11.63	5.5
1922	48 1695	Grand Prairie	177.4	99 616	195	562	71 462	28 154	39.4	75.82	9.73	0.78	3.01	10.66	20.55	6.4
1922	48 1800	Haltom City	32.0	32 856	771	1 027	29 014	3 842	13.2	89.83	1.28	0.74	4.84	3.32	8.53	12.0
1240	48 1820	Harlingen	69.7	48 735	509	699	43 543	5 192	11.9	80.06	0.76	0.21	0.42	18.55	71.02	13.2
3362	48 1975	Houston	1 398.3	1 630 553	4	1 166	1 595 138	35 415	2.2	52.69	28.09	0.25	4.12	14.86	27.63	8.3
1922	48 2015	Hurst	25.6	33 574	753	1 311	31 420	2 154	6.9	93.35	2.61	0.46	1.24	2.34	5.18	8.9
1922	48 2060	Irving	175.1	155 037	112	885	109 943	45 094	41.0	78.73	7.52	0.65	4.61	8.49	16.28	5.4
3810	48 2230	Killeen	71.7	63 535	359	886	46 296	17 239	37.2	58.09	30.08	0.54	5.75	5.55	14.00	4.0
...	48 2235	Kingsville	32.9	25 276	918	768	28 808	-3 532	-12.3	66.81	3.76	0.25	1.56	27.62	62.37	10.0
4080	48 2400	Laredo	85.1	122 899	147	1 444	91 449	31 450	34.4	70.83	0.12	0.16	0.38	28.51	93.87	8.2
4420	48 2530	Longview	135.5	70 311	319	519	62 762	7 549	12.0	76.64	19.90	0.44	0.59	2.44	4.12	13.0
4600	48 2565	Lubbock	269.7	186 206	87	690	173 873	12 333	7.1	77.63	8.56	0.31	1.41	12.10	22.51	9.8
...	48 2575	Lufkin	61.1	30 206	827	494	28 562	1 644	5.8	65.22	27.22	0.19	0.79	6.57	9.64	15.3
4880	48 2595	McAllen	84.0	84 021	251	1 000	66 281	17 740	26.8	70.94	0.34	0.20	0.69	27.84	76.97	10.4
1922	48 2795	Mesquite	110.9	101 484	188	915	67 053	34 431	51.3	87.21	5.83	0.55	2.63	3.79	8.77	5.3
5040	48 2810	Midland	170.5	89 443	224	525	70 525	18 918	26.8	79.81	9.14	0.37	0.96	9.72	21.31	9.4
...	48 2945	Nacogdoches	64.6	30 872	811	478	27 149	3 723	13.7	73.53	22.47	0.21	0.87	2.92	5.06	10.8
1922	48 3050	North Richland Hills	47.2	45 895	542	972	30 592	15 303	50.0	93.64	1.81	0.51	1.64	2.39	5.84	6.8
5800	48 3080	Odessa	91.6	89 699	223	979	90 027	-328	-0.4	75.39	5.97	0.50	0.68	17.46	31.13	10.1
...	48 3195	Paris	70.4	24 699	929	351	25 498	-799	-3.1	75.92	22.12	0.97	0.56	0.43	1.16	20.1
3362	48 3200	Pasadena	113.4	119 363	150	1 053	112 560	6 803	6.0	83.73	0.97	0.49	1.57	13.24	28.83	7.7
1922	48 3310	Plano	171.6	128 713	140	750	72 331	56 382	77.9	88.48	4.14	0.34	4.01	3.04	6.23	3.6
0840	48 3335	Port Arthur	200.0	58 724	398	294	61 251	-2 527	-4.1	49.31	42.19	0.25	4.81	3.44	8.22	17.1
1922	48 3520	Richardson	73.2	74 840	291	1 022	72 496	2 344	3.2	86.78	4.68	0.32	6.61	1.61	4.35	7.5
7200	48 3740	San Angelo	124.0	84 474	247	681	73 240	11 234	15.3	78.81	4.80	0.38	1.14	14.88	27.99	13.1
7240	48 3745	San Antonio	862.6	935 933	10	1 085	785 940	149 993	19.1	72.24	7.04	0.35	1.14	19.23	55.59	10.5
7640	48 3920	Sherman	96.8	31 601	795	326	30 413	1 188	3.9	83.22	12.63	0.94	0.77	2.45	4.39	16.4
3810	48 4205	Temple	111.3	46 109	538	414	42 354	3 755	8.9	72.81	17.13	0.36	0.92	8.79	13.71	16.4
8360	48 4225	Texarkana	54.5	31 656	794	581	31 271	385	1.2	62.97	35.89	0.36	0.45	0.32	1.12	17.1
3362	48 4230	Texas City	160.9	40 822	612	254	41 201	-379	-0.9	67.10	25.14	0.40	1.15	6.21	15.94	11.3
8640	48 4350	Tyler	102.7	75 450	288	735	70 508	4 942	7.0	66.12	28.17	0.28	0.51	4.91	8.91	14.8
8750	48 4405	Victoria	78.0	55 076	424	706	50 695	4 381	8.6	76.92	7.94	0.26	0.41	14.47	37.85	11.4
8800	48 4415	Waco	196.3	103 590	185	528	101 261	2 329	2.3	67.60	23.14	0.28	0.92	8.05	16.35	14.9
9080	48 4605	Wichita Falls	140.2	96 259	206	687	94 201	2 058	2.2	80.42	11.21	0.72	1.83	5.82	10.04	12.6
...	49 0000	UTAH	212 815.5	1 722 850	X	8	1 461 037	261 813	17.9	93.79	0.67	1.41	1.94	2.19	4.91	8.7
7160	49 0075	Bountiful	27.6	36 659	693	1 328	32 877	3 782	11.5	98.24	0.10	0.27	0.95	0.45	1.60	10.8
...	49 0520	Logan	36.6	32 762	772	895	26 844	5 918	22.0	91.36	0.59	1.26	5.11	1.68	3.13	8.8
7160	49 0640	Murray	24.7	31 282	801	1 266	25 750	5 532	21.5	95.80	0.66	0.54	1.48	1.52	4.24	10.3
7160	49 0695	Ogden	67.6	63 909	356	945	64 407	-498	-0.8	87.44	2.72	1.07	1.76	7.00	12.00	14.6
6520	49 0720	Orem	46.5	67 561	335	1 453	52 399	15 162	28.9	96.39	0.13	0.79	1.54	1.15	3.02	6.2
6520	49 0800	Provo	100.0	86 835	236	868	74 111	12 724	17.2	94.07	0.26	1.07	2.73	1.87	4.17	6.5
7160	49 0870	Salt Lake City	282.4	159 936	108	566	163 034	-3 098	-1.9	87.02	1.72	1.59	4.73	4.94	9.70	14.5
7160	49 0875	Sandy City	51.8	75 058	289	1 449	52 210	22 848	43.8	97.05	0.19	0.31	1.69	0.76	2.54	3.5
7160	49 1075	West Jordan	69.5	42 892	579	617	27 325	15 567	57.0	94.01	0.28	0.63	1.92	3.15	6.49	2.7
...	50 0000	VERMONT	23 955.7	562 758	X	23	511 456	51 302	10.0	98.64	0.35	0.30	0.57	0.14	0.65	11.8
1305	50 0460	Burlington	27.3	39 127	644	1 433	37 712	1 415	3.8	96.80	1.00	0.31	1.49	0.40	1.23	10.6
...	51 0000	VIRGINIA	102 558.3	6 187 358	X	60	5 346 797	840 561	15.7	77.44	18.80	0.25	2.57	0.94	2.59	10.7
8840	51 0025	Alexandria	39.6	111 183	163	2 808	103 217	7 966	7.7	69.07	21.89	0.30	4.17	4.58	9.69	10.3
...	51 0100	Blacksburg town	48.6	34 590	723	712	30 638	3 952	12.9	87.43	4.27	0.11	7.70	0.49	1.76	4.2
1540	51 0225	Charlottesville	26.6	40 341	620	1 517	39 916	425	1.1	76.06	21.22	0.10	2.32	0.30	1.18	12.2
5720	51 0242	Chesapeake	882.4	151 976	114	172	114 486	37 490	32.7	70.67	27.41	0.29	1.25	0.38	1.26	8.5

1. MSA = Metropolitan Statistical Area. CMSA = Consolidated MSA. 2. Dry land or land partially or temporarily covered by water. 3. Hispanic persons may be of any race.

City	Households, 1990				Births, 1984			Deaths, 1984				Hospitals, 1985		
			Percent–		Number			Number		Rate			Beds	
	Number	Persons per house-hold	Female family house-holder[1]	One-person[2]	Total	To mothers under 20 yrs. old (Percent)	Rate[3]	Total	Infant[4]	Total[3]	Infant[5]	Number	Number	Rate[6]
	15	16	17	18	19	20	21	22	23	24	25	26	27	28
TEXAS—Con.														
Austin	192 148	2.33	11.0	34.1	8 375	13.6	21.1	2 377	73	6.0	8.7	13	3 778	810
Baytown	22 422	2.82	12.5	22.0	1 283	16.4	21.1	399	9	6.6	7.0	3	516	822
Beaumont	43 357	2.55	15.9	28.1	2 171	16.3	17.6	1 142	37	9.3	17.0	4	1 153	962
Brownsville	26 322	3.70	20.3	15.2	2 493	14.3	26.3	515	19	5.4	7.6	2	265	260
Bryan	20 705	2.61	12.2	25.5	1 168	15.8	19.8	416	9	7.1	7.7	3	293	471
Carrollton	30 452	2.69	9.0	19.2	1 265	5.1	23.9	198	12	3.7	9.5	1	79	128
College Station	17 878	2.31	6.3	26.7	600	7.8	13.1	83	2	1.8	3.3	0	0	0
Corpus Christi	89 468	2.83	13.8	22.5	4 907	14.8	19.0	1 788	59	6.9	12.0	9	1 635	620
Dallas	402 060	2.46	13.9	34.2	19 274	19.1	19.8	7 823	226	8.0	11.7	30	7 375	735
Del Rio	9 465	3.23	14.2	17.8	703	16.4	20.4	231	9	6.7	12.8	2	106	305
Denton	25 719	2.31	8.6	32.5	911	14.8	19.8	359	4	7.8	4.4	2	361	654
Duncanville	12 509	2.85	11.7	16.9	496	8.5	15.6	155	5	4.9	10.1	0	0	0
El Paso	160 545	3.17	16.4	17.9	10 414	14.8	22.5	2 650	100	5.7	9.6	13	2 360	480
Fort Worth	168 274	2.58	13.3	29.0	9 069	19.3	21.9	4 154	129	10.0	14.2	17	3 029	705
Galveston	24 157	2.37	16.6	34.3	1 107	18.4	17.7	663	11	10.6	9.9	3	1 288	2 139
Garland	63 193	2.85	11.3	18.4	3 246	12.2	20.3	653	19	4.1	5.9	3	358	203
Grand Prairie	34 958	2.83	11.4	20.6	1 721	17.7	20.0	448	18	5.2	10.5	2	386	403
Haltom City	12 756	2.55	11.2	25.7	411	16.3	13.0	209	3	6.6	7.3	0	0	0
Harlingen	15 398	3.09	14.6	20.1	934	15.4	18.0	399	8	7.7	8.6	3	615	1 119
Houston	616 877	2.60	14.6	31.0	37 685	16.2	22.1	11 714	449	6.9	11.9	45	13 601	787
Hurst	12 779	2.61	10.5	20.1	517	11.2	15.0	177	5	5.1	9.7	0	0	0
Irving	63 236	2.44	9.9	30.1	2 403	13.7	20.0	690	25	5.7	10.4	2	281	219
Killeen	23 248	2.72	11.3	20.3	2 234	18.0	40.1	235	27	4.2	12.1	1	78	131
Kingsville	8 529	2.85	13.5	22.8	713	19.6	23.8	172	4	5.7	5.6	1	136	476
Laredo	32 029	3.78	18.2	12.9	2 566	13.6	23.6	586	23	5.4	9.0	3	446	381
Longview	27 206	2.52	12.3	26.7	1 253	15.6	17.1	600	14	8.2	11.2	2	363	491
Lubbock	69 143	2.56	10.7	26.8	3 581	17.0	20.1	1 179	44	6.6	12.3	9	1 550	832
Lufkin	11 222	2.61	13.6	27.1	660	21.4	21.6	309	10	10.1	15.2	2	371	1 156
McAllen	24 905	3.34	15.0	17.4	1 585	10.4	20.6	463	25	6.0	15.8	4	543	652
Mesquite	35 856	2.81	11.7	19.1	1 666	12.8	21.6	386	15	5.0	9.0	3	409	461
Midland	33 169	2.67	10.3	25.0	1 922	12.3	19.8	558	16	5.7	8.3	3	305	311
Nacogdoches	11 306	2.34	12.6	30.8	396	18.4	13.8	230	2	8.0	5.1	2	348	1 228
North Richland Hills	16 901	2.71	9.5	18.6	430	11.4	11.6	141	4	3.8	9.3	1	160	364
Odessa	32 826	2.71	12.2	24.2	2 398	17.9	22.1	623	26	5.7	10.8	2	470	464
Paris	9 806	2.43	15.1	30.3	410	24.1	15.7	352	3	13.4	7.3	2	387	1 477
Pasadena	42 044	2.82	11.5	21.6	2 338	16.1	19.6	631	22	5.3	9.4	4	805	682
Plano	44 352	2.89	7.6	15.7	1 709	5.7	18.3	314	9	3.4	5.3	1	233	210
Port Arthur	22 326	2.60	17.2	28.6	1 103	17.8	17.2	725	11	11.3	10.0	2	501	803
Richardson	27 220	2.73	9.9	17.1	1 008	5.1	13.1	303	5	3.9	5.0	1	242	310
San Angelo	30 661	2.59	11.3	26.1	1 641	17.5	19.5	720	13	8.5	7.9	4	787	912
San Antonio	326 761	2.80	15.7	25.0	16 838	18.6	20.0	6 408	216	7.6	12.8	23	7 352	804
Sherman	12 454	2.42	12.6	29.4	581	20.1	18.6	356	3	11.4	5.2	2	388	1 231
Temple	18 153	2.45	12.8	29.2	782	16.1	17.4	476	8	10.6	10.2	3	1 792	3 847
Texarkana	12 475	2.47	17.6	29.1	573	21.8	17.4	450	13	13.7	22.7	3	573	1 730
Texas City	15 110	2.68	14.7	23.7	679	18.3	15.6	335	6	7.7	8.8	2	424	1 004
Tyler	29 381	2.49	13.5	30.1	1 354	16.5	18.5	753	21	10.3	15.5	6	966	1 280
Victoria	19 777	2.75	12.7	23.3	1 201	17.7	21.8	393	4	7.1	3.3	3	546	964
Waco	39 482	2.45	14.9	30.8	2 259	21.3	21.7	1 214	23	11.7	10.2	5	1 580	1 502
Wichita Falls	35 470	2.53	11.6	26.6	1 816	14.4	18.4	920	30	9.3	16.5	4	1 136	1 137
UTAH	537 273	3.15	9.1	18.9	38 299	8.7	23.2	8 997	350	5.4	9.1	47	5 423	326
Bountiful	11 152	3.25	8.3	14.8	625	6.9	18.2	192	5	5.6	8.0	1	128	371
Logan	11 034	2.87	6.5	21.7	861	5.9	29.9	164	7	5.7	8.1	1	154	533
Murray	11 712	2.66	10.8	25.6	618	10.5	22.9	160	1	5.9	1.6	1	243	1 024
Ogden	24 239	2.57	12.5	28.8	1 566	15.4	23.0	706	23	10.4	14.7	2	550	815
Orem	17 584	3.82	8.7	10.8	1 803	6.0	29.6	207	18	3.4	10.0	1	20	32
Provo	23 805	3.32	7.6	12.8	2 395	5.0	32.3	352	23	4.7	9.6	2	654	844
Salt Lake City	66 657	2.33	10.2	35.8	3 795	10.0	23.0	1 685	43	10.2	11.3	10	2 300	1 452
Sandy City	19 423	3.85	7.1	8.1	1 382	5.1	21.8	116	8	1.8	5.8	1	50	74
West Jordan	11 143	3.83	10.3	10.0	957	6.9	24.6	78	13	2.0	13.6	1	50	113
VERMONT	210 650	2.57	9.2	23.4	8 020	10.0	15.1	4 532	70	8.6	8.7	19	2 857	528
Burlington	14 680	2.29	10.2	32.1	466	12.4	12.3	330	7	8.7	15.0	1	491	1 282
VIRGINIA	2 291 830	2.61	11.1	22.9	82 719	12.6	14.7	44 310	1 005	7.9	12.1	138	30 096	520
Alexandria	53 280	2.04	9.1	42.0	1 945	8.5	18.2	813	35	7.6	18.0	4	766	711
Blacksburg town	11 175	2.37	5.4	24.5	246	9.3	8.1	83	3	2.7	12.2	1	146	481
Charlottesville	16 009	2.37	12.9	30.6	580	11.7	14.3	391	7	9.6	12.1	3	1 039	2 528
Chesapeake	51 965	2.87	12.7	16.1	2 135	13.5	16.9	886	21	7.0	9.8	1	210	156

1. No spouse present. 2. Householder living alone. 3. Per 1,000 resident population estimated as of July 1 of the year shown. 4. Deaths of infants under 1 year old. 5. Deaths of infants under 1 year old per 1,000 live births. 6. Per 100,000 resident population estimated as of July 1, 1986.

Table C. Cities — Crime, Police Officers, Education, Money Income, and Housing

City	Serious crimes known to police, 1985: Number: Total	Serious crimes known to police, 1985: Number: Violent[1]	Serious crimes known to police, 1985: Rate[2]	Police officers, 1985: Number	Police officers, 1985: Rate[3]	Educational attainment,[4] 1980: Percent completing 12 years or more	Educational attainment,[4] 1980: Percent completing 16 years or more	Money income: Per capita[5]: 1985: Total (Dollars)	Money income: Per capita[5]: 1985: Percent of State average	Money income: Per capita[5]: 1979: Current dollars	Money income: Per capita[5]: 1979: Constant (1985) dollars	Money income: Percent below poverty level, 1979: Persons	Money income: Percent below poverty level, 1979: Families	Housing, 1990: Total units	Housing, 1990: Percent change, 1980–1990	Housing, 1990: Vacant units for sale or rent[6]
	29	30	31	32	33	34	35	36	37	38	39	40	41	42	43	44
TEXAS—Con.																
Austin	39 044	2 363	9 606	681	16.8	74.8	30.6	11 633	112.1	7 368	10 919	15.8	9.8	217 054	32.5	20 339
Baytown	3 902	239	5 934	91	13.8	65.5	14.7	11 333	109.3	8 324	12 336	10.3	8.0	25 020	12.7	2 010
Beaumont	9 185	975	7 272	218	17.3	65.0	17.3	10 139	97.7	7 581	11 235	15.7	11.9	49 021	4.0	3 466
Brownsville	8 237	995	8 408	116	11.8	43.3	11.2	5 490	52.9	4 129	6 119	33.3	27.7	28 992	15.7	1 488
Bryan	4 119	396	7 239	78	13.7	62.2	24.7	9 395	90.6	6 447	9 554	18.7	11.5	23 007	24.4	1 664
Carrollton	3 196	102	6 126	93	17.8	85.3	28.4	15 454	149.0	10 132	15 016	2.9	2.3	32 992	53.2	2 178
College Station	2 403	93	5 254	62	13.6	88.0	54.0	7 558	72.9	5 057	7 494	32.3	10.2	19 845	34.6	1 555
Corpus Christi	21 311	932	8 066	339	12.8	61.4	15.4	9 546	92.0	6 753	10 008	15.7	12.5	100 205	18.6	7 550
Dallas	129 496	14 364	12 982	2 170	21.8	68.5	22.0	12 816	123.6	8 610	12 760	14.2	10.8	465 600	16.1	50 329
Del Rio	1 692	155	4 958	47	13.8	47.7	11.6	6 002	57.9	4 324	6 408	32.2	26.4	10 691	9.2	866
Denton	4 840	356	9 065	78	14.6	78.2	35.9	10 854	104.6	7 247	10 740	14.1	6.9	28 791	33.0	2 077
Duncanville	1 979	70	6 282	41	13.0	79.4	22.3	14 146	136.4	8 965	13 286	3.2	2.4	13 358	31.6	783
El Paso	33 697	3 662	7 096	686	14.4	60.1	14.5	7 670	73.9	5 439	8 061	21.2	17.7	168 625	20.3	6 103
Fort Worth	58 858	6 352	13 867	771	18.2	62.2	17.3	10 515	101.4	7 336	10 872	13.9	10.3	194 429	19.7	19 335
Galveston	6 654	867	9 910	152	22.6	60.2	17.9	10 286	99.2	7 292	10 807	15.9	11.9	30 898	9.9	3 522
Garland	9 209	444	5 614	173	10.5	77.5	20.3	12 419	119.7	8 108	12 016	5.1	3.9	69 595	30.6	5 687
Grand Prairie	7 266	520	8 791	107	12.9	65.2	12.6	11 072	106.7	7 232	10 718	8.7	6.7	38 721	35.2	3 051
Haltom City	2 962	112	9 065	43	13.2	56.0	6.6	10 396	100.2	7 028	10 415	9.4	6.6	14 030	21.0	970
Harlingen	3 862	207	7 656	67	13.3	49.3	12.7	7 163	69.1	4 968	7 363	26.4	20.8	17 798	18.4	1 229
Houston	155 910	16 461	8 928	4 363	25.0	68.4	23.1	12 115	116.8	8 817	13 067	12.7	10.0	726 435	6.6	84 106
Hurst	2 789	169	7 945	56	16.0	79.9	20.6	13 778	132.8	9 331	13 829	3.7	2.9	13 801	10.9	921
Irving	12 025	845	9 783	182	14.8	74.0	17.6	13 175	127.0	8 498	12 594	6.0	4.5	71 059	39.3	6 474
Killeen	4 137	277	7 637	98	18.1	76.4	15.5	7 981	76.9	5 301	7 856	17.9	16.2	26 439	25.4	2 742
Kingsville	1 679	84	5 246	38	11.9	59.5	18.5	7 619	73.5	5 527	8 191	21.7	16.5	10 100	1.5	1 035
Laredo	7 978	600	7 170	152	13.7	39.3	8.7	5 275	50.9	3 910	5 795	34.5	30.4	33 998	25.7	1 091
Longview	5 139	265	6 948	138	18.7	68.5	16.2	10 452	100.8	7 380	10 937	11.8	9.3	30 293	17.1	2 199
Lubbock	17 579	1 522	9 617	246	13.5	69.3	22.4	10 067	97.1	6 970	10 330	14.4	9.7	77 852	14.0	7 303
Lufkin	2 005	128	6 212	49	15.2	58.5	15.8	9 575	92.3	6 756	10 012	16.3	11.6	12 488	12.3	916
McAllen	5 480	257	7 098	126	16.3	54.6	16.0	7 941	76.6	5 608	8 311	26.4	20.8	28 597	23.6	1 498
Mesquite	6 790	449	8 905	130	17.0	68.7	11.3	11 616	112.0	7 330	10 863	5.2	4.2	39 251	43.3	2 699
Midland	4 487	459	4 975	165	18.3	73.5	26.1	14 404	138.9	10 159	15 056	8.7	6.1	38 453	29.9	4 435
Nacogdoches	1 311	129	4 359	47	15.6	64.4	23.8	8 457	81.5	5 901	8 745	22.5	12.8	12 253	17.9	721
North Richland Hills	2 489	112	7 041	53	15.0	79.7	18.5	12 939	124.7	8 782	13 015	4.1	2.9	18 121	37.7	1 087
Odessa	9 483	367	8 522	194	17.4	62.6	13.8	10 606	102.2	7 969	11 810	11.5	8.6	37 751	11.4	3 854
Paris	3 180	391	11 647	33	12.1	54.1	11.0	8 438	81.3	5 733	8 496	21.2	16.1	11 191	2.1	1 010
Pasadena	6 803	706	5 569	208	17.0	66.4	10.8	10 818	104.3	8 192	12 141	7.7	5.8	47 539	6.7	4 020
Plano	5 539	151	6 141	136	15.1	89.6	37.1	14 980	144.4	9 150	13 560	3.8	3.0	47 370	48.8	2 500
Port Arthur	3 157	305	4 524	102	14.6	53.3	8.4	8 519	82.1	6 704	9 935	17.7	14.4	25 746	6.3	2 022
Richardson	4 343	119	5 328	112	13.7	91.3	41.7	16 625	160.3	10 690	15 843	3.1	2.3	28 734	11.6	1 342
San Angelo	5 416	404	6 381	132	15.6	60.3	15.5	9 658	93.1	6 710	9 944	13.0	9.0	34 619	18.2	2 688
San Antonio	83 591	5 393	9 687	1 273	14.8	58.6	13.6	8 499	81.9	5 758	8 533	20.9	16.9	365 414	24.0	29 506
Sherman	2 626	131	7 940	48	14.5	65.1	17.4	10 638	102.6	7 247	10 740	9.5	6.8	14 261	9.6	1 381
Temple	2 710	141	6 014	99	22.0	60.0	18.2	10 047	96.9	6 703	9 934	15.1	11.3	20 718	16.3	2 062
Texarkana	2 953	250	8 674	75	22.0	61.3	13.4	8 992	86.7	6 279	9 305	20.7	15.5	14 313	8.8	1 433
Texas City	3 283	195	7 157	53	11.6	63.1	10.2	9 724	93.7	7 560	11 204	10.2	8.0	16 676	9.9	1 159
Tyler	7 282	449	9 295	125	16.0	68.1	19.5	11 048	106.5	7 451	11 042	13.5	9.2	32 860	13.6	2 840
Victoria	3 947	328	6 704	80	13.6	59.0	13.7	10 179	98.1	7 031	10 420	14.2	10.7	21 802	16.4	1 546
Waco	9 795	791	9 187	169	15.9	58.5	16.0	8 894	85.7	6 106	9 049	21.6	13.7	45 088	11.3	4 451
Wichita Falls	8 512	614	8 406	151	14.9	66.1	15.5	10 042	96.8	7 108	10 534	12.9	9.9	40 364	6.0	3 379
UTAH	87 470	4 398	5 317	NA	NA	80.0	19.9	8 535	100.0	6 305	9 344	10.3	7.7	598 388	18.1	28 928
Bountiful	1 242	107	3 488	29	8.1	90.0	28.6	10 335	121.1	7 312	10 836	4.1	3.5	11 488	17.9	248
Logan	897	35	3 009	32	10.7	86.6	35.3	7 489	87.7	5 552	8 228	18.1	9.3	11 440	13.5	286
Murray	3 136	142	11 096	46	16.3	78.2	18.1	10 260	120.2	7 373	10 927	7.7	5.7	12 347	21.3	534
Ogden	6 322	322	9 071	106	15.2	72.6	15.4	9 233	108.2	6 539	9 691	13.1	9.9	27 194	5.6	2 183
Orem	2 324	26	3 913	59	9.9	86.8	28.1	7 094	83.1	5 311	7 871	11.5	9.8	17 965	17.5	260
Provo	2 986	109	3 662	64	7.8	87.0	30.8	6 347	74.4	4 814	7 134	27.6	15.1	24 578	13.4	531
Salt Lake City	19 037	1 083	11 593	341	20.8	76.7	25.5	10 248	120.1	7 409	10 980	14.2	10.5	73 762	1.3	5 494
Sandy City	2 495	90	4 162	60	10.0	89.5	26.0	9 391	110.0	6 462	9 577	5.4	4.4	20 110	32.0	518
West Jordan	1 836	119	5 366	43	12.6	82.4	12.8	7 256	85.0	5 280	7 825	6.8	6.0	11 640	39.3	405
VERMONT	20 801	790	3 888	NA	NA	71.0	19.0	9 619	100.0	6 177	9 154	12.1	8.9	271 214	17.7	10 000
Burlington	3 976	100	10 217	85	21.8	74.6	27.9	9 542	99.2	6 143	9 104	16.2	7.8	15 480	11.1	507
VIRGINIA	215 634	16 813	3 779	NA	NA	62.4	19.1	11 894	100.0	7 475	11 078	11.8	9.2	2 496 334	19.0	118 944
Alexandria	7 670	802	7 079	214	19.8	83.0	40.9	19 783	166.3	12 177	18 046	9.0	6.8	58 252	10.7	4 099
Blacksburg town	1 286	25	4 036	39	12.2	85.5	56.2	8 219	69.1	5 158	7 644	31.8	8.8	11 857	17.5	595
Charlottesville	3 109	221	7 562	88	21.4	65.1	31.0	10 733	90.2	6 935	10 278	21.0	7.5	16 785	4.7	487
Chesapeake	5 112	407	4 007	212	16.6	60.7	11.5	10 501	88.3	6 646	9 849	11.2	9.2	55 742	31.7	2 988

1. Includes murder and nonnegligent manslaughter, forcible rape, robbery, and aggravated assault. 2. Per 100,000 resident population estimated for 1985 by the FBI. 3. Per 10,000 resident population estimated for 1985 by the FBI. 4. Persons 25 years old or older. 5. Based on the resident population estimated as of July 1, 1988 for 1987 data and enumerated as of April 1, 1980 for 1979 data. 6. Also includes units rented or sold, but not occupied.

City	Housing, 1990 (cont'd)					Construction authorized by building permits, 1990				Civilian labor force, 1990			
	Occupied units					New private housing units						Unemployment	
			Owner-occupied										
	Total	Percent with more than 1 person per room	Percent of total	Median value[1] (Dollars)	Median rent[2] (Dollars)	Number	Value ($1,000)	Percent single family	Non-residential, value ($1,000)	Total	Percent change, 1989–1990	Total	Rate[3]
	45	46	47	48	49	50	51	52	53	54	55	56	57
TEXAS—Con.													
Austin	192 148	6.8	40.6	72 600	346	923	103 114	96.1	91 266	279 528	0.9	13 344	4.8
Baytown	22 422	9.3	56.7	50 400	307	69	5 591	100.0	6 015	32 292	2.0	2 621	8.1
Beaumont	43 357	4.5	60.0	44 500	275	154	17 199	100.0	11 191	53 270	1.3	3 423	6.4
Brownsville	26 322	28.7	55.8	39 900	236	413	14 684	95.2	14 814	42 520	1.4	4 847	11.4
Bryan	20 705	7.1	48.3	58 400	312	80	5 286	100.0	2 800	30 995	0.2	1 106	3.6
Carrollton	30 452	4.9	60.7	99 700	466	589	65 362	100.0	10 265	33 542	-0.5	979	2.9
College Station	17 878	6.0	24.0	79 500	356	133	14 916	100.0	2 816	21 628	0.1	811	3.7
Corpus Christi	89 468	9.4	56.6	56 500	305	472	32 615	89.2	13 583	122 746	3.0	8 236	6.7
Dallas	402 060	9.8	44.1	78 800	375	2 756	162 804	52.4	71 310	638 035	-0.8	38 333	6.0
Del Rio	9 465	17.4	61.5	43 600	240	58	2 770	100.0	1 148	11 875	-1.9	1 606	13.5
Denton	25 719	4.5	39.1	77 300	362	121	15 937	86.0	8 909	44 659	-0.6	2 881	6.5
Duncanville	12 509	3.3	67.7	86 200	456	33	3 791	100.0	2 510	19 112	-0.6	652	3.4
El Paso	160 545	14.0	57.6	58 500	303	2 092	101 720	87.6	69 728	230 772	0.2	24 442	10.6
Fort Worth	168 274	7.9	54.5	59 900	337	1 104	80 578	70.7	224 494	278 970	1.2	18 164	6.5
Galveston	24 157	6.1	42.0	57 200	309	39	3 984	100.0	50 808	34 762	-0.6	2 334	6.7
Garland	63 193	6.4	64.2	73 100	411	407	33 673	100.0	2 861	98 418	-0.6	3 912	4.0
Grand Prairie	34 958	8.4	60.9	68 600	377	449	41 109	100.0	20 644	47 942	-0.5	2 511	5.2
Haltom City	12 756	5.6	59.2	52 300	334	64	3 188	100.0	2 250	21 222	1.3	972	4.6
Harlingen	15 398	16.1	59.0	42 700	262	124	8 151	100.0	9 228	23 050	1.4	2 399	10.4
Houston	616 877	11.7	44.6	58 000	328	2 156	195 651	56.8	124 108	1 022 979	2.3	57 272	5.6
Hurst	12 779	3.0	62.7	82 800	379	77	8 440	100.0	2 564	26 147	1.4	950	3.6
Irving	63 236	8.0	37.1	79 400	424	2 089	111 133	15.7	114 299	81 988	-0.6	3 371	4.1
Killeen	23 248	8.1	41.5	58 600	313	90	6 059	97.8	4 396	20 843	-0.3	2 433	11.7
Kingsville	8 529	9.9	56.9	40 800	277	6	318	100.0	442	13 300	3.6	904	6.8
Laredo	32 029	26.4	59.0	52 500	245	824	30 729	73.2	51 187	48 970	2.0	5 573	11.4
Longview	27 206	4.2	58.1	56 700	274	73	6 298	100.0	4 067	36 195	-0.5	2 785	7.7
Lubbock	69 143	6.6	55.3	55 500	316	401	36 068	92.0	32 004	97 556	1.3	4 649	4.8
Lufkin	11 222	6.7	60.5	47 800	274	58	3 576	100.0	5 002	15 661	-1.1	875	5.6
McAllen	24 905	19.6	60.3	56 300	283	435	26 734	88.5	10 868	40 904	2.2	6 299	15.4
Mesquite	35 856	4.7	63.5	68 700	397	613	38 630	84.8	4 793	46 977	-0.7	2 348	5.0
Midland	33 169	6.2	62.5	62 300	285	216	22 595	100.0	3 811	40 902	-3.6	2 269	5.5
Nacogdoches	11 306	4.6	41.8	59 100	284	34	2 872	100.0	1 567	16 656	0.9	952	5.7
North Richland Hills	16 901	2.8	62.8	82 500	400	428	42 467	100.0	11 520	24 570	1.3	1 124	4.6
Odessa	32 826	8.1	61.3	43 700	241	45	5 437	100.0	2 097	40 747	-1.9	2 292	5.6
Paris	9 806	3.7	59.3	37 100	261	59	3 005	71.2	11 869	13 151	-1.6	984	7.5
Pasadena	42 044	10.8	51.5	49 000	323	492	45 497	100.0	8 391	69 448	2.3	4 081	5.9
Plano	44 352	2.7	70.1	114 100	503	3 323	261 829	50.8	309 252	62 537	-0.4	2 514	4.0
Port Arthur	22 326	6.5	65.0	30 400	226	14	1 248	100.0	3 232	25 576	0.4	2 872	11.2
Richardson	27 220	2.7	70.3	110 000	516	208	26 789	100.0	79 579	52 879	-0.6	1 905	3.6
San Angelo	30 661	6.6	59.2	48 300	302	131	5 427	100.0	2 574	38 180	-3.7	2 305	6.0
San Antonio	326 761	10.4	54.0	49 700	308	1 141	58 180	93.0	103 114	443 713	-1.6	33 432	7.5
Sherman	12 454	3.4	57.8	49 800	305	29	2 182	100.0	4 360	17 057	-0.5	807	4.7
Temple	18 153	4.9	52.9	55 800	283	33	3 131	100.0	11 150	27 769	0.4	993	3.6
Texarkana	12 475	4.1	57.7	46 000	275	55	3 635	81.8	2 705	16 315	-1.6	1 146	7.0
Texas City	15 110	5.8	61.9	50 300	296	42	3 938	100.0	39 963	23 276	-0.7	2 242	9.6
Tyler	29 381	5.5	52.8	60 000	300	94	12 222	74.5	4 309	41 803	-1.6	2 565	6.1
Victoria	19 777	7.6	58.2	54 400	278	107	11 641	100.0	8 369	27 013	-0.9	1 418	5.2
Waco	39 482	6.1	46.5	43 100	281	81	6 328	96.3	5 042	53 467	-0.6	3 417	6.4
Wichita Falls	35 470	3.7	59.4	47 700	297	79	6 562	97.5	14 266	41 879	-2.0	2 660	6.4
UTAH	537 273	5.5	68.1	68 900	300	7 328	594 691	88.0	381 381	792 000	0.4	34 000	4.3
Bountiful	11 152	2.8	76.4	87 100	336	110	17 688	90.9	3 031	19 082	-0.5	602	3.2
Logan	11 034	8.9	43.2	67 900	267	135	7 359	37.8	6 821	16 324	0.2	729	4.5
Murray	11 712	3.2	61.0	74 900	339	88	6 805	100.0	21 653	16 582	-0.6	552	3.3
Ogden	24 239	4.5	58.8	54 700	266	44	5 822	100.0	3 469	33 015	-0.5	2 213	6.7
Orem	17 584	6.5	67.9	73 100	292	433	42 399	94.2	20 033	28 068	6.0	995	3.5
Provo	23 805	11.8	39.9	74 000	289	364	22 882	31.9	31 192	43 639	6.0	1 549	3.5
Salt Lake City	66 657	4.4	49.4	67 200	282	69	7 401	89.9	96 889	100 325	-0.7	4 338	4.3
Sandy City	19 423	3.2	87.3	87 500	397	565	40 954	99.3	7 563	NA	NA	NA	NA
West Jordan	11 143	6.9	78.8	67 600	330	151	9 351	100.0	3 489	13 034	-0.7	528	4.1
VERMONT	210 650	1.7	69.0	95 500	378	2 371	188 860	87.7	83 093	309 000	0.7	15 000	5.0
Burlington	14 680	1.9	40.2	113 500	435	6	668	100.0	5	22 303	-0.2	793	3.6
VIRGINIA	2 291 830	2.8	66.3	91 000	411	42 151	2 799 346	74.8	1 603 375	3 196 000	1.6	137 000	4.3
Alexandria	53 280	5.0	40.5	228 600	667	54	5 307	63.0	13 185	80 759	1.6	2 407	3.0
Blacksburg town	11 175	1.8	31.6	94 300	365	158	7 395	31.6	2 383	14 521	1.3	842	5.8
Charlottesville	16 009	3.0	42.4	85 600	391	100	4 435	46.0	16 638	24 675	2.8	723	2.9
Chesapeake	51 965	2.8	73.0	88 200	399	1 932	138 305	68.9	29 238	74 648	1.0	3 241	4.3

1. Specified owner-occupied units. 2. Specified renter-occupied units. 3. Percent of total civilian labor force.

Table C. Cities — **Labor Force and Manufactures**

City	Employed,[1] 1980: Total	Employed,[1] 1980: Rate per 1,000 employees: Professional, specialty, and technical	Employed,[1] 1980: Rate per 1,000 employees: Precision production, craft, and operators	Manufactures, 1987: Establishments: Total	Manufactures, 1987: Establishments: Percent with 20 or more employees	Manufactures, 1987: All employees: Number (1,000)	Manufactures, 1987: All employees: Percent change, 1982–1987	Manufactures, 1987: All employees: Annual payroll (Mil. dol.)	Manufactures, 1987: Production workers: Number (1,000)	Manufactures, 1987: Production workers: Work-hours (Millions)	Manufactures, 1987: Production workers: Wages: Total (Mil. dol.)	Manufactures, 1987: Production workers: Wages: Average per production worker (Dollars)	Manufactures, 1987: Value added by manufacture (Mil. dol.)	Manufactures, 1987: Value of shipments (Mil. dol.)	Manufactures, 1987: New capital expenditures (Mil. dol.)
	58	59	60	61	62	63	64	65	66	67	68	69	70	71	72
TEXAS—Con.															
Austin	174 459	213.0	146.9	549	26.0	33.2	21.2	951.3	14.6	28.3	299.8	20 534	2 212.4	4 197.8	238.5
Baytown	25 503	150.3	304.7	34	35.3	D	D	D	D	D	D	D	D	D	D
Beaumont	52 169	169.6	208.0	126	28.6	4.4	-57.7	102.2	2.5	4.9	56.6	22 640	171.2	536.2	15.6
Brownsville	29 070	128.5	234.5	64	37.5	4.5	-29.7	63.9	3.5	6.9	45.0	12 857	174.9	383.3	24.4
Bryan	20 171	199.6	198.6	56	35.7	2.0	-20.0	43.5	1.3	2.9	25.4	19 538	122.8	257.6	6.7
Carrollton	22 728	170.1	172.3	156	42.9	10.0	D	264.8	5.2	9.8	97.8	18 808	568.8	1 120.4	30.8
College Station	14 048	332.6	100.2	NA	NA	NA	NA	NA	NA	NA	NA	NA	NA	NA	NA
Corpus Christi	101 464	153.1	217.7	218	28.4	7.8	-13.3	189.8	4.9	9.9	107.6	21 959	482.2	4 379.9	43.5
Dallas	464 936	146.8	184.7	2 105	32.8	105.8	-12.6	2 871.4	57.3	116.5	1 199.2	20 928	6 023.1	10 626.5	403.0
Del Rio	9 146	127.9	207.0	NA	NA	NA	NA	NA	NA	NA	NA	NA	NA	NA	NA
Denton	24 149	227.5	162.7	68	32.4	4.3	-2.3	95.2	3.0	6.0	57.6	19 200	289.9	725.6	8.1
Duncanville	14 319	157.0	188.1	49	26.5	1.2	20.0	20.9	0.9	1.7	11.8	13 111	44.7	97.0	1.8
El Paso	154 211	152.1	218.7	507	39.1	33.0	-9.3	484.0	25.3	47.2	311.9	12 328	1 377.8	4 206.1	61.1
Fort Worth	179 603	148.4	240.7	907	37.7	71.9	9.8	2 069.1	40.3	84.3	967.3	24 002	4 616.4	8 646.9	247.1
Galveston	29 218	198.0	156.1	42	28.6	1.6	-38.5	35.6	1.1	1.9	23.3	21 182	114.4	189.0	1.1
Garland	73 307	158.1	227.4	359	34.8	18.9	15.2	488.4	10.2	19.8	193.9	19 010	1 151.3	2 083.9	57.6
Grand Prairie	34 866	105.3	275.7	223	36.3	11.2	49.3	314.1	6.3	12.8	119.9	19 032	704.6	1 300.0	29.7
Haltom City	13 945	84.0	321.3	107	24.3	1.8	0.0	38.8	1.3	2.8	23.2	17 846	81.4	151.3	2.4
Harlingen	15 935	134.4	202.6	52	36.5	2.3	-8.0	31.3	1.5	3.0	19.4	12 933	92.8	175.8	3.0
Houston	827 110	167.6	198.8	3 142	29.5	112.8	-35.4	3 264.5	56.5	116.4	1 239.3	21 935	7 192.9	16 814.4	374.9
Hurst	17 352	167.5	194.8	57	29.8	1.5	15.4	30.4	1.0	2.1	18.0	18 000	90.9	154.0	2.7
Irving	60 982	121.0	218.7	266	32.0	12.8	23.1	384.2	6.2	11.1	104.5	16 855	865.8	1 594.3	69.9
Killeen	12 762	150.0	176.7	NA	NA	NA	NA	NA	NA	NA	NA	NA	NA	NA	NA
Kingsville	10 826	182.7	202.9	NA	NA	NA	NA	NA	NA	NA	NA	NA	NA	NA	NA
Laredo	30 232	113.3	171.9	54	20.4	D	D	D	D	D	D	D	D	D	D
Longview	30 170	131.7	265.9	133	39.8	6.5	-12.2	154.9	4.5	9.1	97.1	21 578	407.7	945.7	20.2
Lubbock	83 239	170.0	182.9	226	23.0	6.4	-41.3	133.2	3.8	7.3	64.6	17 000	392.5	822.4	16.7
Lufkin	12 471	127.9	258.0	68	32.4	4.1	-26.8	82.7	3.3	6.7	59.1	17 909	139.3	381.0	10.2
McAllen	24 985	141.8	190.9	78	35.9	5.2	85.7	75.0	3.7	7.7	42.1	11 378	199.9	381.6	11.9
Mesquite	34 618	97.6	267.6	52	38.5	3.2	-28.9	80.0	2.2	4.4	48.3	21 955	232.6	498.5	17.6
Midland	35 628	194.8	182.1	101	19.8	D	D	D	D	D	D	D	D	D	D
Nacogdoches	12 067	165.0	201.2	44	52.3	3.0	-14.3	51.3	2.3	4.7	35.6	15 478	125.4	369.9	6.6
North Richland Hills	16 146	168.3	209.2	26	26.9	1.2	140.0	28.1	0.7	1.5	13.0	18 571	67.5	142.5	1.1
Odessa	44 720	120.1	280.5	122	18.0	2.0	-64.9	49.6	1.1	2.3	24.3	22 091	218.1	405.9	23.9
Paris	10 318	130.6	266.9	44	52.3	D	D	D	D	D	D	D	D	D	D
Pasadena	56 184	113.4	311.8	101	39.6	6.7	-8.2	224.2	4.2	9.3	129.9	30 929	1 433.9	4 043.6	230.2
Plano	35 545	220.6	124.3	108	25.9	5.6	166.7	156.9	1.8	3.6	30.4	16 889	154.3	380.5	10.5
Port Arthur	23 086	114.2	266.7	36	33.3	5.9	-41.0	205.2	4.5	8.5	144.6	32 133	834.6	5 826.8	144.0
Richardson	38 481	235.1	97.3	169	29.0	13.9	D	486.4	4.5	8.5	107.8	23 956	639.4	1 151.9	43.3
San Angelo	33 508	131.6	229.3	94	29.8	4.1	D	67.7	2.9	5.1	43.8	15 103	203.5	477.6	9.6
San Antonio	305 911	140.7	202.8	927	30.9	34.9	-17.9	659.2	23.0	44.3	354.1	15 396	1 636.2	3 474.1	61.4
Sherman	14 767	144.9	273.0	44	50.0	7.5	2.7	215.5	5.3	11.0	122.0	23 019	559.1	1 148.1	46.4
Temple	18 561	186.2	197.6	66	45.5	5.6	3.7	118.8	4.1	8.5	75.1	18 317	390.4	702.7	22.6
Texarkana	12 435	152.1	193.2	53	39.6	1.6	D	23.2	1.1	2.2	13.0	11 818	64.9	154.2	5.8
Texas City	18 952	120.8	284.3	24	41.7	6.0	-22.1	245.4	4.0	8.6	155.6	38 900	1 500.9	7 079.9	D
Tyler	32 772	158.1	214.9	108	35.2	10.6	-3.6	280.8	7.2	12.5	171.7	23 847	598.9	1 433.2	31.6
Victoria	23 494	142.6	256.1	47	25.5	D	D	D	D	D	D	D	D	D	D
Waco	42 176	152.5	224.4	178	44.4	10.7	5.9	206.2	7.6	14.9	128.9	16 961	712.2	1 351.8	49.8
Wichita Falls	38 819	132.2	241.1	121	23.1	4.9	-32.9	99.7	3.5	6.9	63.0	18 000	339.1	528.2	8.4
UTAH	585 921	159.9	221.6	2 083	29.3	88.8	6.7	2 073.1	54.8	107.6	1 002.3	18 290	4 882.9	10 286.7	403.5
Bountiful	13 450	176.3	153.8	NA	NA	NA	NA	NA	NA	NA	NA	NA	NA	NA	NA
Logan	11 425	231.3	171.8	55	30.9	D	D	D	D	D	D	D	D	D	D
Murray	12 648	143.1	220.3	84	20.2	1.7	-5.6	27.9	1.3	2.6	19.3	14 846	66.2	122.2	4.4
Ogden	25 526	157.9	200.3	127	33.9	6.7	15.5	139.8	4.9	9.4	90.0	18 367	412.0	782.6	30.3
Orem	18 526	196.7	233.3	70	17.1	2.4	0.0	50.0	1.8	3.4	29.8	16 556	27.5	92.1	D
Provo	28 803	229.0	170.9	81	30.9	2.5	8.7	41.7	1.9	3.3	26.4	13 895	106.8	199.4	7.4
Salt Lake City	75 738	210.7	169.0	576	34.7	27.6	11.7	663.5	15.1	29.8	268.9	17 808	1 495.0	3 170.5	80.1
Sandy City	19 467	158.2	200.4	NA	NA	NA	NA	NA	NA	NA	NA	NA	NA	NA	NA
West Jordan	9 867	104.0	328.4	50	34.0	2.5	-19.4	59.6	1.7	3.2	27.0	15 882	137.6	218.6	9.6
VERMONT	227 195	174.9	231.7	1 262	26.4	48.5	3.6	1 140.0	30.6	58.3	551.6	18 026	2 543.1	4 752.7	334.4
Burlington	17 456	220.3	147.1	58	25.9	3.4	-19.0	101.9	1.7	3.6	39.7	23 353	255.9	361.3	D
VIRGINIA	2 348 401	168.8	213.7	6 137	36.3	429.2	9.7	9 740.1	305.3	600.3	5 728.2	18 763	26 857.3	51 902.1	1 542.7
Alexandria	60 138	256.4	77.8	140	29.3	3.3	13.8	82.7	1.8	3.4	38.0	21 111	291.6	453.3	4.8
Blacksburg town	11 658	415.5	76.9	10	60.0	2.0	5.3	38.3	1.5	3.3	26.7	17 800	98.6	129.4	3.7
Charlottesville	19 473	279.1	127.1	82	32.9	6.2	44.2	130.6	3.7	7.7	56.0	15 135	357.9	569.0	14.2
Chesapeake	47 390	139.1	255.2	101	37.6	3.8	40.7	79.7	2.5	5.1	44.3	17 720	232.0	588.8	14.2

1. Persons 16 years old and over.

City	Wholesale trade, 1987: Establishments	Wholesale trade, 1987: Sales (Mil. dol.)	Wholesale trade, 1987: Paid employees[1]	Wholesale trade, 1987: Annual payroll ($1,000)	Retail trade–all establishments, 1987: Number	Retail trade–all establishments, 1987: Sales: Total (Mil. dol.)	Retail trade–all establishments, 1987: Sales: Percent change, 1982–1987	Retail trade–all establishments, 1987: Sales: Per capita[2] (Dollars)	Retail trade–establishments with payroll, 1987: Number	Retail trade–establishments with payroll, 1987: Sales: Total (Mil. dol.)	Sales per capita[2] (Dollars): General merchandise group stores	Sales per capita[2] (Dollars): Food stores	Sales per capita[2] (Dollars): Apparel and accessory stores	Sales per capita[2] (Dollars): Eating and drinking places
	73	74	75	76	77	78	79	80	81	82	83	84	85	86
TEXAS—Con.														
Austin	984	D	D	D	5 171	3 968.0	44.8	8 505	3 536	3 896.4	D	1 999	503	1 039
Baytown	53	270.8	519	15 134	639	450.4	12.0	7 175	362	438.6	936	1 570	202	649
Beaumont	342	1 229.2	3 642	78 607	1 432	1 041.1	9.3	8 683	988	1 023.5	1 547	1 277	597	864
Brownsville	186	310.0	1 472	19 055	1 033	525.0	0.1	5 142	671	510.8	903	1 314	427	385
Bryan	117	188.6	990	18 179	579	355.2	0.3	5 709	365	344.8	D	1 357	D	469
Carrollton	337	6 014.7	7 700	157 956	761	567.2	0.0	9 154	392	548.6	D	1 940	304	791
College Station	18	54.1	167	3 057	406	305.0	33.1	6 643	313	302.2	D	1 451	572	848
Corpus Christi	620	1 660.9	5 947	119 779	2 663	1 658.8	10.8	6 286	1 692	1 616.4	D	1 367	304	666
Dallas	4 422	D	D	D	11 137	8 820.9	30.5	8 790	7 327	8 631.7	1 088	D	640	1 060
Del Rio	35	D	D	D	387	166.9	-0.9	4 810	218	159.9	660	1 215	247	D
Denton	114	D	D	D	739	581.8	53.8	10 547	520	570.9	D	2 160	483	917
Duncanville	55	55.3	278	5 849	358	288.8	31.0	8 233	196	282.8	D	1 832	184	471
El Paso	876	2 629.4	9 726	182 667	4 078	2 823.8	37.2	5 742	2 706	2 764.8	D	1 144	D	508
Fort Worth	1 022	4 608.4	15 188	325 563	4 694	3 271.4	17.6	7 616	3 089	3 190.0	847	1 209	376	825
Galveston	66	195.7	626	13 671	720	376.7	1.5	6 256	485	364.6	616	1 775	375	908
Garland	293	789.2	2 206	51 039	1 476	875.1	30.3	4 958	761	842.8	420	1 394	173	464
Grand Prairie	299	2 715.1	5 527	143 631	707	454.0	57.1	4 735	374	439.0	D	1 273	D	375
Haltom City	119	280.6	1 206	24 580	328	223.1	31.2	6 672	204	211.4	481	1 273	153	331
Harlingen	130	265.2	1 494	24 456	641	401.0	17.5	7 294	432	391.1	1 204	1 485	609	707
Houston	5 981	D	D	D	18 531	14 049.1	7.7	8 126	11 502	13 693.1	992	1 534	543	863
Hurst	55	73.1	243	5 719	563	572.4	39.6	16 284	379	562.8	4 429	2 502	1 268	815
Irving	475	8 573.3	11 285	378 461	1 529	1 361.6	66.8	10 594	913	1 331.2	1 158	1 652	360	884
Killeen	32	34.4	238	2 738	700	457.6	32.1	7 683	502	451.7	1 222	1 303	326	744
Kingsville	17	37.1	379	4 715	282	144.5	-2.2	5 052	196	142.0	D	1 698	326	535
Laredo	252	603.1	2 085	29 704	1 185	702.3	1.7	5 999	776	683.2	954	1 429	614	D
Longview	253	D	D	D	1 215	0.0	0.0	D	811	659.3	D	1 738	642	913
Lubbock	541	2 612.9	6 359	129 700	2 166	1 551.2	25.3	8 322	1 353	1 492.7	D	1 500	454	872
Lufkin	89	D	D	D	539	348.6	13.2	10 867	381	339.1	1 726	2 186	580	896
McAllen	258	544.8	5 051	47 558	1 109	773.9	7.6	9 291	794	759.4	1 557	1 428	1 042	744
Mesquite	92	394.7	1 783	36 017	997	857.6	67.5	9 669	630	841.6	2 303	1 356	805	753
Midland	249	1 506.5	2 226	52 138	1 174	705.7	4.5	7 197	697	682.4	1 158	1 741	D	D
Nacogdoches	63	116.4	644	9 694	465	270.1	32.1	9 527	312	262.8	D	2 124	D	982
North Richland Hills	39	39.8	221	5 582	410	394.8	84.6	8 981	283	387.2	1 440	1 051	486	973
Odessa	343	1 069.3	2 480	57 745	1 209	728.0	-21.1	7 193	718	701.9	D	1 763	306	625
Paris	70	142.6	589	9 181	412	233.3	23.1	8 901	278	224.9	1 185	1 733	756	795
Pasadena	144	313.6	1 001	21 731	1 043	603.8	-15.9	5 115	632	588.9	1 096	1 341	269	511
Plano	248	1 196.7	2 175	68 821	1 258	1 118.6	146.1	10 075	786	1 099.3	D	1 960	557	824
Port Arthur	56	191.5	710	12 190	558	369.2	10.8	5 920	347	361.9	D	1 189	458	455
Richardson	414	D	D	D	1 083	860.4	26.2	11 025	639	840.3	1 226	D	560	D
San Angelo	169	543.4	1 502	29 427	1 094	575.8	2.9	6 675	672	556.1	D	1 389	D	D
San Antonio	1 785	8 702.4	24 913	525 934	9 041	6 020.9	32.8	6 585	5 743	5 895.4	830	1 440	421	809
Sherman	81	204.2	692	12 489	527	376.1	40.7	11 928	362	365.8	D	1 907	577	924
Temple	105	676.2	1 747	36 100	651	406.3	24.1	8 723	457	396.2	1 531	1 673	404	768
Texarkana	140	332.4	1 467	26 982	505	418.3	26.1	12 626	356	406.0	2 998	1 197	652	995
Texas City	48	D	D	D	354	244.1	2.7	5 778	217	232.4	D	1 393	311	452
Tyler	284	802.4	2 885	57 851	1 215	934.2	30.1	12 383	824	914.1	2 116	2 187	751	1 171
Victoria	167	576.2	1 750	31 293	833	479.9	-0.2	8 473	542	469.3	D	1 948	D	697
Waco	288	903.4	3 668	70 099	1 313	874.9	16.2	8 315	892	853.5	D	1 526	479	906
Wichita Falls	227	428.1	1 902	35 440	1 255	718.5	9.1	7 189	798	695.3	D	1 008	352	839
UTAH	2 956	11 094.3	34 180	718 412	13 827	8 619.8	36.2	5 177	8 519	8 378.8	614	1 141	244	454
Bountiful	48	55.3	335	6 413	339	273.0	52.9	7 911	188	259.8	D	1 760	D	462
Logan	57	165.5	716	10 992	339	226.0	25.6	7 825	237	221.1	D	1 956	445	647
Murray	129	375.8	1 416	33 397	465	555.3	42.6	23 401	341	548.6	2 374	1 280	2 689	745
Ogden	137	342.6	1 315	24 873	803	675.7	30.0	10 012	589	666.4	2 105	1 476	534	687
Orem	82	80.8	538	8 713	541	375.3	37.9	6 094	374	367.3	1 222	990	603	358
Provo	79	156.5	663	13 621	451	315.4	16.3	4 071	296	310.0	381	843	22	334
Salt Lake City	1 047	6 279.1	16 535	376 105	2 270	1 732.1	37.7	10 932	1 632	1 702.5	1 179	1 926	762	1 584
Sandy City	67	58.3	336	7 074	480	260.4	109.8	3 862	208	248.8	570	1 190	91	303
West Jordan	27	142.7	402	8 451	182	108.5	47.8	2 441	80	104.3	D	1 061	D	D
VERMONT	986	2 833.0	10 270	205 053	7 981	4 177.0	60.6	7 721	5 077	4 043.4	557	1 553	321	673
Burlington	72	295.7	1 174	23 820	508	338.9	53.7	8 846	414	336.0	1 628	1 216	1 007	1 207
VIRGINIA	8 446	44 758.8	115 126	2 625 045	52 634	39 784.8	61.0	6 875	34 916	38 960.2	744	1 391	319	617
Alexandria	213	1 080.5	4 322	99 874	1 036	1 241.9	57.1	11 520	747	1 226.4	1 507	1 526	460	1 410
Blacksburg town	11	6.6	72	953	260	191.0	54.2	6 287	201	189.3	647	1 445	252	730
Charlottesville	109	D	D	D	774	710.2	73.3	17 280	610	701.1	1 400	3 699	837	1 595
Chesapeake	225	1 186.2	2 855	61 644	973	801.0	88.7	5 960	607	791.7	628	1 190	147	427

1. For the period including March 12 of the year shown. 2. Based on resident population estimated as of July 1, 1986.

City	Retail trade–establishment with payroll, 1987 (cont'd)			Taxable service industries–establishments with payroll, 1987							Federal grants, 1986		
	Paid employees[1]				Receipts (Mil. dol.)								
						Selected kinds of business							
	Number	Percent change, 1982–1987	Annual payroll (Mil. dol.)	Number	Total	Hotels, motels, and other lodging places	Health services	Legal services	Paid employees[1]	Annual payroll (Mil. dol.)	Procure-ment contract awards (Mil. dol.)	Grant awards (Mil. dol.)	Federal govern-ment civilian employ-ment, 1984
	87	88	89	90	91	92	93	94	95	96	97	98	99
TEXAS—Con.													
Austin	51 330	25.5	506.3	4 767	2 640.5	147.1	502.1	D	56 438	1 022.9	157.2	995.5	7 700
Baytown	5 019	4.7	49.1	428	144.9	D	82.1	7.8	2 967	51.3	19.0	5.7	116
Beaumont	12 192	-4.3	119.8	1 118	491.4	18.5	192.7	76.2	11 370	184.4	229.5	6.0	901
Brownsville	6 971	-14.8	60.6	472	170.5	10.7	74.2	18.5	4 074	50.6	12.1	14.1	543
Bryan	3 997	-10.1	38.9	481	140.6	2.2	49.4	13.1	3 893	52.5	2.4	1.9	264
Carrollton	6 368	D	64.9	550	D	D	66.2	D	D	D	5.8	0.5	106
College Station	5 054	7.4	39.6	223	110.6	12.2	24.0	1.2	3 115	38.1	14.1	49.7	363
Corpus Christi	20 422	-0.5	194.7	2 130	D	48.1	289.2	D	D	D	380.4	17.0	6 603
Dallas	100 859	15.0	1 109.1	11 554	D	D	1 476.6	1 122.3	D	D	1 181.9	107.4	18 411
Del Rio	2 153	-9.7	18.6	159	31.0	D	7.6	1.5	903	9.8	0.5	2.1	335
Denton	7 203	43.5	66.3	506	173.9	8.2	82.6	8.5	4 632	66.9	2.2	6.8	410
Duncanville	2 884	46.3	32.3	252	54.4	1.6	21.4	1.4	1 439	19.7	0.0	0.3	60
El Paso	34 813	12.6	321.3	2 747	1 107.5	D	376.9	76.2	28 151	400.7	222.5	35.7	3 714
Fort Worth	37 977	7.2	389.4	3 789	1 703.4	53.2	511.0	193.0	34 568	651.0	4 622.3	25.4	8 689
Galveston	5 395	-2.1	51.2	403	146.9	41.6	28.5	22.7	4 788	60.5	43.7	22.2	668
Garland	10 244	25.7	103.9	968	D	6.0	108.1	4.6	D	D	169.7	2.4	341
Grand Prairie	4 496	28.8	49.6	453	D	D	43.5	5.8	D	D	81.0	1.7	428
Haltom City	2 207	6.2	24.6	169	54.8	D	9.8	1.6	1 370	18.4	0.0	0.3	0
Harlingen	5 240	8.4	47.9	405	130.8	6.3	D	9.8	3 283	45.5	9.9	7.4	290
Houston	158 181	-1.0	1 666.3	17 003	D	418.6	D	1 530.0	D	D	1 034.6	314.9	17 218
Hurst	5 887	11.6	61.0	347	112.6	3.0	28.2	9.1	3 063	48.9	3.4	0.3	77
Irving	13 804	71.9	153.0	1 181	946.3	88.0	102.8	14.6	17 914	365.7	27.8	1.5	294
Killeen	5 835	18.0	51.5	303	87.8	8.1	12.3	4.8	2 276	26.2	1.7	13.2	123
Kingsville	2 139	-4.2	17.3	148	30.1	D	D	1.0	897	11.6	3.0	2.3	459
Laredo	8 957	-16.9	80.5	503	129.2	D	D	8.7	4 028	43.2	24.9	18.6	631
Longview	8 620	0.6	80.2	695	219.6	9.6	86.4	18.5	6 441	79.0	3.2	1.7	394
Lubbock	18 131	4.8	177.3	1 483	580.4	D	236.9	D	12 900	205.9	5.6	19.8	1 247
Lufkin	4 328	8.3	41.5	350	115.4	D	55.9	11.5	2 613	43.8	0.4	2.5	307
McAllen	9 389	-13.7	90.6	654	304.9	23.2	D	27.7	6 614	98.6	52.3	4.0	350
Mesquite	9 513	48.9	99.0	474	179.8	4.7	87.1	D	4 381	65.5	3.0	1.3	184
Midland	7 324	-7.1	77.1	836	301.1	D	73.5	36.6	6 768	113.3	1.8	3.8	784
Nacogdoches	3 406	25.3	29.7	273	80.2	3.9	D	4.0	1 984	23.7	0.7	3.8	126
North Richland Hills	4 772	91.2	46.8	198	91.4	1.9	43.9	0.3	1 658	29.8	0.2	0.3	0
Odessa	7 902	-29.5	83.0	718	D	D	D	28.3	D	D	0.4	2.1	320
Paris	2 907	20.5	27.2	265	60.8	3.4	37.4	2.8	1 814	24.1	19.4	0.7	112
Pasadena	8 103	-11.4	75.6	727	361.2	2.4	185.6	11.9	9 523	142.0	23.4	2.4	472
Plano	12 483	93.7	124.2	899	670.2	12.9	142.4	D	10 419	237.1	12.2	1.4	177
Port Arthur	4 200	2.6	40.2	290	112.9	3.2	70.5	D	2 467	40.7	94.9	8.6	199
Richardson	8 535	3.6	98.8	957	494.8	17.4	82.6	D	9 512	180.4	248.9	4.5	264
San Angelo	7 457	1.3	69.0	585	206.4	8.4	66.6	17.1	4 317	72.0	3.2	2.9	293
San Antonio	77 541	20.7	755.0	6 974	3 109.8	188.5	913.8	296.8	70 322	1 173.6	229.7	148.1	8 110
Sherman	4 400	18.2	43.2	340	122.9	5.1	67.3	12.0	2 658	48.4	11.1	0.9	134
Temple	4 784	4.0	45.5	408	206.3	7.6	139.5	9.6	3 704	72.5	21.3	3.9	2 110
Texarkana	4 635	3.8	44.5	389	149.1	6.5	75.2	D	3 374	57.1	24.9	1.8	538
Texas City	2 648	-8.8	25.6	211	84.3	1.0	37.1	8.0	1 999	32.5	132.0	1.4	66
Tyler	11 083	14.2	112.2	1 099	392.3	D	150.9	37.5	8 283	153.9	35.1	4.2	525
Victoria	5 914	-8.5	57.4	557	205.5	6.4	114.8	11.7	4 315	74.4	0.7	1.9	231
Waco	11 739	4.3	108.4	937	334.1	17.2	111.7	28.5	8 324	132.5	19.0	6.5	2 664
Wichita Falls	9 332	9.5	87.7	755	253.4	D	D	21.8	5 921	95.8	3.4	4.8	429
UTAH	108 925	22.7	963.3	10 117	3 833.2	296.7	1 008.6	263.9	93 897	1 419.7	1 623.9	865.7	35 717
Bountiful	2 787	23.7	26.0	286	99.8	D	42.4	1.5	2 196	37.4	2.1	0.6	72
Logan	3 197	18.2	25.4	261	62.2	2.6	24.4	2.5	1 566	20.5	18.3	16.1	204
Murray	5 335	16.1	58.3	419	131.8	D	44.7	2.1	2 907	49.8	0.8	0.7	26
Ogden	8 004	10.3	71.9	663	186.8	9.9	72.7	D	4 694	69.8	42.7	6.8	5 386
Orem	4 734	13.7	40.1	335	218.7	1.4	24.4	1.8	4 047	68.3	0.9	1.9	83
Provo	3 968	2.9	36.7	506	185.6	9.0	64.5	6.8	4 925	76.7	15.7	7.9	525
Salt Lake City	24 983	26.8	227.5	2 787	1 513.8	125.0	281.7	216.9	30 973	581.4	398.4	261.0	6 819
Sandy City	3 196	90.1	27.8	268	51.9	D	17.4	D	1 739	19.6	4.9	1.0	100
West Jordan	1 441	38.8	11.9	113	18.4	0.0	10.4	0.0	664	6.8	1.9	0.6	77
VERMONT	46 635	33.2	472.5	4 412	1 352.9	227.9	247.8	92.2	36 674	448.4	151.3	360.7	4 474
Burlington	5 142	15.4	46.7	459	174.3	10.9	50.1	26.2	4 496	65.7	104.8	32.5	913
VIRGINIA	453 325	36.1	4 556.7	38 337	20 414.6	1 451.7	4 012.5	1 019.5	438 728	8 128.4	7 260.4	2 297.4	155 038
Alexandria	13 183	27.0	154.8	1 501	1 063.7	80.2	125.7	65.8	20 760	426.4	428.5	21.2	10 931
Blacksburg town	3 073	40.6	22.6	191	65.4	8.0	31.1	D	1 984	26.0	13.5	26.0	79
Charlottesville	8 145	36.1	83.7	671	214.3	D	54.9	19.8	5 796	83.1	54.0	54.5	974
Chesapeake	8 322	57.5	83.2	685	270.4	8.3	60.6	8.7	6 635	109.4	41.2	20.2	223

1. For the period including March 12 of the year shown.

City	City government employment, 1985 (October): Total	City government employment, 1985 (October): Rates[1]	City government employment, 1985 (October): Percent education	Form of governments[2] (As of 1986)	City government finances, 1984–1985: General revenue: Total (Mil. dol.)	General revenue: Intergovernmental: Total (Mil. dol.)	General revenue: Intergovernmental: Percent from State government	General revenue: Taxes: Total (Mil. dol.)	Taxes: Per capita[3] (Dollars): Total	Taxes: Per capita[3] (Dollars): Property	Taxes: Per capita[3] (Dollars): Sales & gross receipts	General expenditures: Total (Mil. dol.)	General expenditures: Per capita[3] (Dol.): Total	General expenditures: Per capita[3] (Dol.): Capital outlays	General expenditures: Percent of total for–: Public welfare	Percent of total for–: Highways	Percent of total for–: Education
	100	101	102	103	104	105	106	107	108	109	110	111	112	113	114	115	116
TEXAS—Con.																	
Austin	10 445	223.9	0.0	2	356.8	33.7	18.0	119.6	256	140	99	362.0	776	145	0.2	3.0	0.2
Baytown	534	85.1	0.0	2	33.7	1.1	16.8	18.7	299	200	93	30.2	481	79	0.5	15.6	0.0
Beaumont	1 365	113.8	0.0	2	72.2	13.9	5.0	34.4	286	154	119	65.5	546	104	0.0	15.6	0.0
Brownsville	1 227	120.2	0.0	2	36.0	11.9	4.5	11.5	113	66	44	28.6	280	36	0.1	4.8	0.0
Bryan	813	130.7	0.0	2	24.3	2.5	24.3	9.8	157	90	63	25.8	414	149	0.4	18.4	0.0
Carrollton	478	77.1	0.0	2	32.2	0.6	21.8	20.4	329	198	112	33.9	547	196	0.0	23.4	0.0
College Station	550	119.8	0.0	2	18.9	1.2	25.0	7.2	156	73	80	28.1	612	263	0.0	12.2	0.0
Corpus Christi	3 172	120.2	0.0	2	128.1	22.7	9.9	56.8	215	114	96	130.7	495	99	0.1	9.9	0.0
Dallas	14 912	148.6	0.0	2	629.7	67.8	21.0	376.4	375	197	166	585.1	583	133	0.0	7.9	0.0
Del Rio	282	81.3	0.0	2	5.9	0.9	4.1	3.2	91	38	53	8.2	235	41	0.7	14.7	0.0
Denton	1 117	202.5	0.0	2	35.0	0.8	42.6	11.4	206	116	85	36.2	656	47	0.2	10.6	0.0
Duncanville	230	65.6	0.0	2	2.1	0.0	0.0	0.0	0	0	0	7.6	216	15	0.0	9.5	0.0
El Paso	4 547	92.5	0.0	1	206.9	40.5	15.7	70.6	144	80	58	181.3	369	81	0.1	10.9	NA
Fort Worth	5 273	122.8	0.0	2	268.5	50.9	20.4	120.2	280	156	113	246.1	573	136	0.0	11.5	0.0
Galveston	1 061	176.2	0.0	2	96.7	6.8	7.0	16.9	281	138	131	76.9	1 277	107	0.0	4.2	0.0
Garland	1 561	88.4	0.0	2	59.8	5.3	25.6	29.8	169	100	64	66.0	374	95	2.7	13.2	0.0
Grand Prairie	720	75.1	0.0	2	45.0	5.0	1.8	17.0	177	100	73	41.4	432	45	0.0	9.4	0.0
Haltom City	201	60.1	0.0	2	9.4	0.3	7.0	6.2	185	75	106	7.1	213	25	NA	16.0	0.0
Harlingen	540	98.2	0.0	2	23.7	4.3	1.7	8.1	148	65	79	19.8	361	71	0.7	7.1	0.0
Houston	21 405	123.8	0.0	1	1 168.2	106.5	32.0	597.7	346	195	142	1 024.2	592	109	0.0	6.5	0.0
Hurst	299	85.1	0.0	2	14.7	0.5	43.9	9.8	280	112	157	14.3	406	78	0.0	7.2	0.0
Irving	1 196	93.1	0.0	2	62.0	1.7	24.0	37.4	291	146	133	60.5	471	107	0.0	11.5	0.1
Killeen	426	71.5	0.0	2	14.8	1.9	6.4	7.5	126	61	61	12.8	214	30	0.3	13.1	0.0
Kingsville	308	107.7	0.0	2	9.0	0.9	2.7	4.4	155	86	66	8.6	301	39	0.0	8.4	0.0
Laredo	1 287	109.9	0.0	2	36.7	9.4	19.2	12.1	103	43	59	31.4	269	46	5.1	13.9	0.0
Longview	773	104.6	0.0	2	28.7	3.0	3.7	16.7	226	109	113	27.2	368	87	0.3	13.0	0.0
Lubbock	1 958	105.0	0.0	2	88.3	6.4	46.7	37.1	199	102	92	71.8	385	61	0.0	12.9	0.0
Lufkin	330	102.9	0.0	2	13.5	0.6	6.3	6.9	214	86	123	10.4	323	6	0.0	13.1	0.0
McAllen	836	100.4	0.0	2	40.3	4.6	6.8	14.4	173	71	99	29.9	359	83	0.0	8.7	0.0
Mesquite	758	85.5	0.0	2	39.2	3.6	5.2	17.0	191	92	93	35.9	404	79	0.0	13.3	0.0
Midland	956	97.5	0.0	2	53.4	2.3	12.8	23.2	236	121	110	68.2	695	292	0.0	8.9	0.0
Nacogdoches	274	96.6	0.0	2	10.5	0.9	5.3	6.2	218	106	105	9.9	349	16	0.0	15.4	0.0
North Richland Hills	286	65.1	0.0	1	16.4	0.8	69.6	7.6	173	80	80	13.3	302	99	0.0	23.3	0.0
Odessa	942	93.1	0.0	2	45.2	2.6	8.4	19.5	192	92	99	39.7	393	47	0.4	5.0	0.0
Paris	262	100.0	0.0	2	8.5	0.9	3.2	4.4	168	56	110	9.6	364	83	0.3	15.1	0.0
Pasadena	936	79.3	0.0	1	44.7	3.6	4.4	22.8	193	106	83	54.5	462	100	0.4	13.1	0.0
Plano	994	89.5	0.0	2	39.0	1.0	39.1	23.7	213	131	70	50.2	452	198	0.0	28.7	0.0
Port Arthur	849	136.1	0.0	2	70.7	15.6	4.3	30.4	488	408	79	49.3	790	231	0.0	6.6	0.0
Richardson	847	108.5	0.0	2	36.4	0.7	29.3	22.0	282	130	146	39.5	506	130	0.0	25.9	0.0
San Angelo	890	103.2	0.0	2	27.0	3.4	21.7	17.4	202	116	79	24.5	284	32	1.8	17.0	0.0
San Antonio	12 761	139.6	0.0	2	387.8	59.2	30.7	132.6	145	71	68	407.4	446	108	0.8	7.3	0.8
Sherman	402	127.5	0.0	2	15.7	1.2	19.1	8.2	259	120	136	15.3	487	53	0.0	10.3	0.0
Temple	472	101.3	0.0	2	18.6	1.9	8.9	9.8	211	101	107	16.7	358	46	0.6	8.4	0.0
Texarkana	432	130.4	0.0	2	20.4	1.9	22.2	7.4	225	111	109	11.4	345	32	0.1	15.1	0.0
Texas City	439	103.9	0.0	3	25.7	1.5	3.1	13.6	322	178	129	20.4	484	21	0.0	10.7	0.0
Tyler	921	122.1	0.0	2	40.0	3.9	21.7	19.5	259	124	130	37.9	502	46	2.9	9.4	0.0
Victoria	587	103.6	0.0	2	27.3	2.4	15.6	14.1	249	128	115	26.6	469	79	0.7	20.5	0.0
Waco	1 276	121.3	0.0	2	54.3	5.2	18.6	22.7	216	96	110	50.0	475	65	1.6	12.6	0.0
Wichita Falls	1 031	103.2	0.0	2	42.4	4.5	7.2	24.3	243	144	95	38.9	390	44	0.0	16.9	0.0
UTAH	NA	NA	NA	NA	NA	NA	NA	NA	NA	NA	NA	NA	NA	NA	NA	NA	NA
Bountiful	291	84.3	0.0	2	10.1	1.2	48.3	5.0	145	47	91	10.5	303	126	0.0	13.6	0.0
Logan	292	101.1	0.0	1	13.1	0.8	43.8	3.4	117	26	85	12.0	417	31	0.0	12.5	0.0
Murray	371	156.3	0.0	3	13.4	2.1	43.7	6.9	292	76	194	13.9	587	221	0.0	14.7	0.0
Ogden	608	90.1	0.0	2	32.6	5.2	71.8	17.8	264	95	156	29.4	435	45	0.0	11.1	0.0
Orem	397	64.5	0.0	2	19.1	4.4	21.1	7.9	128	43	78	19.1	310	98	0.0	10.3	0.0
Provo	463	59.8	0.0	1	27.1	9.6	8.7	9.6	124	48	71	28.6	370	151	0.0	5.7	0.0
Salt Lake City	2 298	145.0	0.0	3	145.5	16.1	17.5	63.8	402	171	212	161.5	1 019	316	0.0	16.7	0.0
Sandy City	397	58.9	0.0	1	16.6	1.9	38.3	7.8	116	37	65	15.3	227	55	0.0	25.8	0.0
West Jordan	166	37.4	0.0	2	10.7	1.6	51.9	4.2	94	30	44	7.1	161	27	0.0	26.3	0.0
VERMONT	NA	NA	NA	NA	NA	NA	NA	NA	NA	NA	NA	NA	NA	NA	NA	NA	NA
Burlington	629	164.2	0.0	1	18.4	2.1	26.1	8.0	208	199	0	18.9	494	44	0.0	6.8	0.0
VIRGINIA	NA	NA	NA	NA	NA	NA	NA	NA	NA	NA	NA	NA	NA	NA	NA	NA	NA
Alexandria	3 678	341.2	41.9	2	197.5	41.0	86.5	125.1	1 160	840	218	189.9	1 762	198	5.8	7.6	28.9
Blacksburg town	259	85.3	0.0	2	6.9	1.6	72.3	2.8	91	31	38	6.7	221	35	0.0	17.0	0.0
Charlottesville	1 600	389.3	43.6	2	45.6	15.6	78.2	24.3	591	351	173	41.2	1 004	36	5.8	6.4	46.8
Chesapeake	5 057	376.3	61.1	2	147.1	63.2	93.8	64.4	479	311	100	135.5	1 008	52	4.0	9.1	51.0

1. Per 10,000 population estimated as of July 1, 1986. 2. 1 = Mayor-council; 2 = Council-manager; 3 = Commission. Data subject to copyright. 3. Based on resident population estimated as of July 1, 1986.

City	City government finances, 1984–1985 (cont'd): General expenditure (cont'd): Percent of total for (cont'd): Health and hospitals	Police protection	Sewerage and sanitation	Parks and recreation	Housing and community development	Debt outstanding: Total (Mil. dol.)	Per capita[1] (Dollars)	Percent utility	Climate[2]: Average daily temperature (Degrees Fahrenheit): Mean: Jan.	Mean: July	Limits: Jan.[3]	Limits: July[4]	Annual precipitation (Inches)	Heating degree days[5]	Cooling degree days[5]	Typical monthly electric bills, 1986: Residential[6]: Total (Dollars)	Residential: Percent change, 1980–1986	Commercial[7] (Dollars)
	117	118	119	120	121	122	123	124	125	126	127	128	129	130	131	132	133	134
TEXAS—Con.																		
Austin	24.5	10.4	20.2	5.6	2.1	1 514.8	3 247	52.8	49.1	84.7	38.8	95.4	31.50	1 760	2 914	37.19	24.7	511.9
Baytown	0.8	15.2	12.2	5.5	3.5	67.6	1 077	3.1	51.4	83.1	40.8	93.6	44.77	1 549	2 761	64.11	75.4	493.6
Beaumont	2.3	14.1	21.3	5.3	3.9	137.6	1 148	13.5	51.9	83.1	42.1	92.5	52.79	1 477	2 861	65.89	77.7	504.7
Brownsville	12.7	13.8	16.2	4.5	12.5	56.8	556	61.3	60.3	84.1	50.8	92.6	25.44	609	3 772	51.50	27.2	453.9
Bryan	1.3	10.4	19.8	9.2	4.7	114.3	1 838	59.3	49.2	84.2	39.3	94.8	39.08	1 786	2 806	60.66	43.1	NA
Carrollton	0.9	10.3	20.3	11.8	0.0	47.2	761	21.7	45.0	86.3	34.9	96.3	34.16	2 301	2 846	53.81	103.8	NA
College Station	0.1	8.5	21.3	14.5	0.9	63.1	1 374	54.2	49.2	84.2	39.3	94.8	39.08	1 786	2 806	67.96	88.6	NA
Corpus Christi	2.9	11.2	20.2	7.8	2.1	290.2	1 099	10.8	56.3	84.9	46.1	94.2	30.18	970	3 574	50.00	39.5	536.6
Dallas	1.3	19.2	13.1	12.0	2.3	900.4	897	20.6	45.0	86.3	34.9	96.3	34.16	2 301	2 846	53.81	57.2	456.3
Del Rio	5.9	14.6	4.8	5.2	7.0	1.4	39	100.0	50.8	86.0	38.3	97.7	17.19	1 510	3 272	50.00	39.5	NA
Denton	37.7	7.3	13.7	3.9	0.2	46.3	839	47.3	43.9	84.5	31.8	95.9	33.53	2 460	2 540	62.00	69.1	NA
Duncanville	0.0	21.0	9.3	9.5	0.0	8.1	231	36.9	45.0	86.3	34.9	96.3	34.16	2 301	2 846	53.81	103.8	NA
El Paso	3.7	14.8	16.4	6.3	1.6	344.5	701	8.8	44.2	82.5	30.4	95.3	7.82	2 664	2 096	63.24	61.8	632.0
Fort Worth	1.8	12.4	13.7	8.8	6.0	515.1	1 199	15.6	44.0	86.3	33.9	97.8	29.45	2 407	2 809	53.81	61.6	456.3
Galveston	0.9	6.6	6.6	0.9	NA	290.7	4 828	1.7	53.6	83.2	47.9	87.3	40.24	1 253	2 967	64.11	75.4	493.6
Garland	2.9	12.2	21.4	9.5	3.2	173.8	985	41.5	45.0	86.3	34.9	96.3	34.16	2 301	2 846	66.58	97.7	508.1
Grand Prairie	1.8	12.9	12.6	7.5	6.8	124.1	1 295	14.5	44.0	86.3	33.9	97.8	29.45	2 407	2 809	53.81	61.6	456.3
Haltom City	0.5	16.6	9.8	8.1	0.0	24.0	717	35.1	44.0	86.3	33.9	97.8	29.45	2 407	2 809	53.81	61.6	NA
Harlingen	1.8	9.3	19.3	5.4	1.5	28.8	523	7.9	58.7	84.2	48.0	95.1	26.48	786	3 770	50.00	39.5	NA
Houston	2.8	17.9	17.8	6.0	1.0	2 338.2	1 352	25.1	51.4	83.1	40.8	93.6	44.77	1 549	2 761	64.11	75.4	493.6
Hurst	0.0	15.3	15.9	15.9	0.0	16.4	467	34.7	44.0	86.3	33.9	97.8	29.45	2 407	2 809	53.81	61.6	NA
Irving	0.8	8.9	21.0	13.1	0.0	82.7	644	25.6	45.0	86.3	34.9	96.3	34.16	2 301	2 846	53.81	103.8	456.3
Killeen	0.5	29.2	11.0	7.8	0.1	6.8	115	58.6	46.6	84.6	35.7	95.7	33.75	2 125	2 740	53.81	103.8	NA
Kingsville	1.5	21.8	23.2	3.7	4.5	12.5	437	49.5	57.5	84.8	45.6	95.4	27.50	867	3 608	50.00	39.5	NA
Laredo	3.0	13.5	13.0	5.6	6.8	37.9	324	0.0	56.2	87.4	44.5	99.3	20.14	926	4 043	50.00	39.5	536.6
Longview	2.7	15.7	14.0	12.8	0.0	66.6	902	23.7	44.1	82.8	33.3	94.1	46.41	2 542	2 335	46.67	99.7	NA
Lubbock	2.7	13.6	10.8	9.4	4.7	362.1	1 943	17.2	38.8	79.8	24.3	91.9	17.76	3 516	1 676	49.40	40.5	449.8
Lufkin	3.3	12.7	14.5	10.4	0.0	22.5	702	24.4	48.6	83.3	38.0	93.8	41.48	1 930	2 651	53.81	103.8	NA
McAllen	2.3	15.2	13.5	8.3	1.1	50.8	610	6.3	58.8	84.4	47.6	95.1	23.04	755	3 833	50.00	39.5	536.6
Mesquite	1.1	12.8	13.1	7.9	5.2	91.3	1 029	10.7	45.0	86.3	34.9	96.3	34.16	2 301	2 846	53.81	103.8	456.3
Midland	1.7	11.4	27.9	4.2	0.6	137.5	1 402	26.5	43.7	81.7	29.7	94.2	13.70	2 658	2 126	53.81	61.6	456.3
Nacogdoches	0.3	15.3	16.8	4.5	2.6	18.5	654	56.0	48.6	83.3	38.0	93.8	41.48	1 930	2 651	53.81	103.8	NA
North Richland Hills	NA	13.3	15.6	11.5	0.0	31.7	722	46.5	44.0	86.3	33.9	97.8	29.45	2 407	2 809	53.81	61.6	NA
Odessa	0.0	20.9	19.4	NA	3.6	93.3	921	24.4	43.7	81.7	29.7	94.2	13.70	2 658	2 126	53.81	61.6	456.3
Paris	5.3	12.0	29.2	2.2	5.7	3.0	116	0.0	40.6	83.5	30.2	94.3	44.97	2 935	2 296	53.81	103.8	NA
Pasadena	1.9	20.2	16.9	6.3	4.4	56.8	481	20.2	51.4	83.1	40.8	93.6	44.77	1 549	2 761	64.11	75.4	493.6
Plano	0.7	10.7	9.3	16.4	0.0	111.1	1 001	22.9	45.0	86.3	34.9	96.3	34.16	2 301	2 846	53.81	103.8	456.3
Port Arthur	3.8	8.0	27.5	4.1	2.8	152.7	2 449	1.6	51.9	83.1	42.1	92.5	52.79	1 477	2 861	65.89	77.7	504.7
Richardson	1.2	17.0	13.1	9.0	0.0	82.3	1 054	17.0	45.0	86.3	34.9	96.3	34.16	2 301	2 846	53.81	103.8	456.3
San Angelo	4.4	17.6	7.4	8.1	1.7	18.9	219	27.5	45.5	84.3	32.2	96.5	18.19	2 313	2 596	52.21	73.1	410.8
San Antonio	5.3	13.8	17.8	10.3	3.5	2 258.4	2 470	75.0	50.4	84.6	39.0	94.9	29.13	1 606	2 983	52.08	46.1	440.4
Sherman	0.1	12.9	15.8	6.5	3.4	8.9	283	56.0	40.7	83.9	29.7	95.3	38.18	2 934	2 331	53.81	103.8	NA
Temple	0.9	14.6	17.4	4.2	1.6	12.4	266	36.3	46.6	84.6	35.7	95.7	33.75	2 125	2 740	53.81	103.8	NA
Texarkana	2.2	20.3	9.8	3.3	0.0	60.9	1 839	48.1	44.1	82.9	34.7	93.0	45.25	2 501	2 314	46.67	99.7	NA
Texas City	0.6	12.5	16.4	8.0	0.3	63.8	1 511	0.0	53.6	83.2	47.9	87.3	40.24	1 253	2 967	58.93	66.1	NA
Tyler	2.6	11.4	11.6	5.1	1.0	122.2	1 619	15.9	45.8	82.4	35.0	93.1	44.74	2 326	2 308	53.81	103.8	456.3
Victoria	4.7	16.1	15.9	3.3	0.0	64.4	1 138	19.6	53.4	84.5	43.1	93.7	36.90	1 273	3 184	50.00	39.5	536.6
Waco	4.1	12.5	13.9	9.4	4.7	103.0	978	23.0	46.2	85.9	35.7	96.5	30.95	2 126	2 891	53.81	103.8	456.3
Wichita Falls	3.4	16.3	13.1	8.4	1.1	22.8	228	32.2	40.3	85.6	28.2	98.5	26.73	3 011	2 506	53.81	61.6	456.3
UTAH	NA	NA	NA	NA	NA	NA	NA	NA	NA	NA	NA	NA	NA	NA	NA	60.30	91.4	NA
Bountiful	0.0	16.0	7.5	13.0	3.3	0.7	20	0.0	28.6	77.5	19.7	93.2	15.31	5 802	981	34.50	97.8	NA
Logan	0.3	11.7	13.0	10.6	0.0	44.1	1 527	32.8	24.7	73.0	16.3	87.2	17.36	6 751	593	47.85	26.2	NA
Murray	0.0	17.4	15.4	14.1	6.3	20.3	856	48.3	28.6	77.5	19.7	93.2	15.31	5 802	981	48.65	101.9	NA
Ogden	1.1	15.4	7.6	11.5	5.4	64.7	959	1.9	28.6	77.0	19.5	91.6	20.58	5 866	955	67.81	97.9	488.4
Orem	0.0	12.1	25.2	6.5	6.9	13.8	224	0.0	28.6	77.5	19.7	93.2	15.31	5 802	981	65.89	100.0	474.6
Provo	0.0	12.0	10.4	6.3	21.9	32.3	417	75.7	28.6	77.5	19.7	93.2	15.31	5 802	981	24.46	82.3	193.4
Salt Lake City	0.0	12.1	6.7	4.6	10.5	140.6	887	18.0	28.6	77.5	19.7	93.2	15.31	5 802	981	67.81	90.5	488.4
Sandy City	0.0	18.4	4.1	5.7	1.0	78.9	1 170	3.1	28.6	77.5	19.7	93.2	15.31	5 802	981	67.17	96.0	483.8
West Jordan	0.0	24.2	13.4	3.9	0.8	9.0	202	59.1	28.6	77.5	19.7	93.2	15.31	5 802	981	63.97	94.1	NA
VERMONT	NA	NA	NA	NA	NA	NA	NA	NA	NA	NA	NA	NA	NA	NA	NA	61.08	81.6	NA
Burlington	1.4	12.3	6.3	6.5	3.9	109.7	2 862	85.2	16.6	69.6	7.7	80.5	33.69	7 953	379	62.52	134.2	730.0
VIRGINIA	NA	NA	NA	NA	NA	NA	NA	NA	NA	NA	NA	NA	NA	NA	NA	55.02	18.8	NA
Alexandria	3.4	6.5	7.3	4.4	4.0	208.0	1 929	0.0	35.2	78.9	27.5	87.9	39.00	4 122	1 430	57.03	16.0	467.1
Blacksburg town	0.0	21.3	22.0	6.6	0.0	4.7	154	33.3	30.9	71.0	20.6	82.6	39.98	5 507	585	47.92	46.8	NA
Charlottesville	0.9	6.2	7.1	3.8	2.9	24.7	600	6.7	35.3	76.8	26.4	87.0	45.72	4 189	1 220	57.03	16.0	NA
Chesapeake	3.1	6.2	4.4	1.9	0.7	88.3	657	43.7	38.9	77.9	29.0	87.9	46.93	3 608	1 377	57.03	16.0	467.1

1. Based on resident population estimated as of July 1, 1986. 2. Represents normal values based on the 30-year period, 1951–1980 (see text). 3. Average daily minimum. 4. Average daily maximum. 5. For definition, see text. 6. As of January 1; based on consumption of 750 kWh. 7. Based on billing demand of 30 kW and consumption of 6,000 kWh.

Table C. Cities — **Area and Population**

MSA/ CMSA Code[1]	State/ Place code	City	Land area,[2] 1990 (Sq. Km.)	Population: 1990: Total persons	Population: 1990: Rank	Population: 1990: Per sq. km.	Population: 1980	Population: Change 1980–1990: Number	Population: Change 1980–1990: Per- cent	Population characteristics, 1990: Percent: Race: White	Race: Black	Race: Am. Indian, Eskimo, Aleut	Race: Asian & Pacific Islander	Race: Other race	His- panic[3]	65 Years and over
			1	2	3	4	5	6	7	8	9	10	11	12	13	14
		VIRGINIA—Con.														
1950	51 0370	Danville	111.5	53 056	455	476	45 642	7 414	16.2	62.66	36.62	0.14	0.49	0.08	0.52	18.7
5720	51 0590	Hampton	134.2	133 793	133	997	122 617	11 176	9.1	58.41	38.85	0.29	1.75	0.70	1.97	9.6
4640	51 0760	Lynchburg	127.9	66 049	346	516	66 743	-694	-1.0	72.45	26.41	0.16	0.76	0.22	0.72	16.4
5720	51 0860	Newport News	177.0	170 045	100	961	144 903	25 142	17.4	62.58	33.57	0.34	2.33	1.18	2.77	9.3
5720	51 0875	Norfolk	139.2	261 229	62	1 877	266 979	-5 750	-2.2	56.74	39.05	0.45	2.61	1.15	2.91	10.5
6760	51 0960	Petersburg	59.3	38 386	656	647	41 055	-2 669	-6.5	26.56	72.13	0.22	0.75	0.34	1.23	15.0
5720	51 0990	Portsmouth	85.8	103 907	184	1 211	104 577	-670	-0.6	51.21	47.33	0.29	0.80	0.37	1.31	13.9
6760	51 1035	Richmond	155.7	203 056	76	1 304	219 214	-16 158	-7.4	43.35	55.22	0.23	0.88	0.32	0.93	15.4
6800	51 1045	Roanoke	111.1	96 397	204	868	100 220	-3 823	-3.8	74.59	24.27	0.17	0.74	0.22	0.69	17.1
5720	51 1200	Suffolk	1 036.2	52 141	467	50	47 621	4 520	9.5	54.68	44.58	0.21	0.38	0.14	0.61	12.9
5720	51 1280	Virginia Beach	643.2	393 069	37	611	262 199	130 870	49.9	80.50	13.91	0.35	4.33	0.91	3.09	5.9
...	53 0000	WASHINGTON	172 447.2	4 866 692	X	28	4 132 353	734 339	17.8	88.54	3.08	1.67	4.33	2.37	4.41	11.8
7602	53 0055	Auburn	51.0	33 102	764	649	26 417	6 685	25.3	92.35	1.37	2.08	3.01	1.19	3.05	11.6
7602	53 0075	Bellevue	68.4	86 874	235	1 270	73 903	12 971	17.6	86.50	2.23	0.44	9.95	0.87	2.52	10.4
0860	53 0080	Bellingham	57.0	52 179	466	915	45 794	6 385	13.9	93.76	0.79	1.81	2.78	0.86	2.41	14.1
1150	53 0115	Bremerton	51.5	38 142	661	741	36 208	1 934	5.3	83.93	7.13	1.68	5.28	1.99	4.85	13.6
7602	53 0365	Edmonds	18.9	30 744	817	1 627	27 679	3 065	11.1	93.53	0.92	0.95	4.03	0.57	1.96	14.8
7602	53 0420	Everett	77.4	69 961	322	904	54 413	15 548	28.6	91.73	1.66	1.74	3.91	0.95	2.82	13.0
6740	53 0610	Kennewick	52.1	42 155	590	809	34 397	7 758	22.6	89.89	1.13	0.77	1.99	6.23	8.74	9.1
...	53 0695	Longview	31.1	31 499	797	1 013	31 052	447	1.4	94.69	0.54	1.51	2.13	1.13	2.04	15.5
5910	53 0920	Olympia	41.8	33 840	742	810	27 447	6 393	23.3	92.04	1.24	1.19	4.79	0.73	2.64	14.5
7602	53 1070	Renton	42.1	41 688	600	990	30 612	11 076	36.2	83.45	6.55	1.18	7.74	1.08	2.96	10.5
6740	53 1080	Richland	83.0	32 315	777	389	33 578	-1 263	-3.8	93.00	1.43	0.68	3.31	1.58	3.04	12.6
7602	53 1140	Seattle	217.3	516 259	21	2 376	493 846	22 413	4.5	75.32	10.06	1.42	11.78	1.42	3.55	15.2
7840	53 1220	Spokane	144.8	177 196	94	1 224	171 300	5 896	3.4	93.28	1.93	2.04	2.08	0.67	2.08	16.2
7602	53 1280	Tacoma	124.4	176 664	95	1 420	158 501	18 163	11.5	78.14	11.38	2.02	6.91	1.54	3.78	13.7
6442	53 1350	Vancouver	36.6	46 380	533	1 267	42 834	3 546	8.3	92.27	2.26	1.28	3.18	1.01	3.02	16.3
...	53 1365	Walla Walla	26.7	26 478	898	992	25 618	860	3.4	88.10	2.25	0.99	1.31	7.35	10.20	17.0
9260	53 1485	Yakima	38.7	54 827	432	1 417	49 826	5 001	10.0	82.55	2.40	2.02	1.28	11.76	16.26	16.4
...	54 0000	WEST VIRGINIA	62 384.2	1 793 477	X	29	1 950 186	-156 709	-8.0	96.21	3.14	0.14	0.42	0.10	0.47	15.0
1480	54 0280	Charleston	76.3	57 287	408	751	63 968	-6 681	-10.4	84.10	14.25	0.19	1.28	0.18	0.62	18.4
3400	54 0760	Huntington	38.6	54 844	431	1 421	63 684	-8 840	-13.9	92.52	6.75	0.12	0.46	0.15	0.54	19.9
...	54 1095	Morgantown	20.0	25 879	910	1 294	27 605	-1 726	-6.3	91.95	3.48	0.14	4.07	0.36	1.09	11.5
6020	54 1215	Parkersburg	28.9	33 862	741	1 172	39 946	-6 084	-15.2	97.70	1.70	0.19	0.30	0.11	0.29	19.9
9000	54 1690	Wheeling	35.7	34 882	720	977	43 070	-8 188	-19.0	94.67	4.46	0.07	0.72	0.08	0.30	21.9
...	55 0000	WISCONSIN	140 672.5	4 891 769	X	35	4 705 642	186 127	4.0	92.25	5.00	0.81	1.10	0.85	1.91	13.3
0460	55 0080	Appleton	44.4	65 695	347	1 480	58 913	6 782	11.5	96.59	0.25	0.42	2.41	0.32	0.88	11.9
3620	55 0215	Beloit	41.9	35 573	707	849	35 207	366	1.0	81.81	15.67	0.30	1.16	1.06	1.94	13.4
5082	55 0355	Brookfield	69.5	35 184	715	506	34 035	1 149	3.4	96.87	0.39	0.15	2.44	0.15	0.74	12.6
2290	55 0770	Eau Claire	71.7	56 856	411	793	51 509	5 347	10.4	95.05	0.37	0.58	3.78	0.21	0.60	12.7
...	55 0905	Fond du Lac	33.1	37 757	671	1 141	35 863	1 894	5.3	97.80	0.30	0.51	0.77	0.62	1.52	16.3
3080	55 1055	Green Bay	113.5	96 466	203	850	87 899	8 567	9.7	94.22	0.47	2.54	2.32	0.46	1.10	12.6
5082	55 1065	Greenfield	29.9	33 403	759	1 117	31 353	2 050	6.5	97.61	0.41	0.36	0.95	0.66	2.00	17.1
3620	55 1235	Janesville	60.9	52 133	468	856	51 071	1 062	2.1	98.08	0.55	0.22	0.82	0.33	1.15	11.9
1602	55 1280	Kenosha	55.8	80 352	264	1 440	77 685	2 667	3.4	89.78	6.39	0.37	0.56	2.90	5.89	13.5
3870	55 1325	La Crosse	47.5	51 003	480	1 074	48 347	2 656	5.5	93.78	0.72	0.45	4.85	0.20	0.88	15.7
4720	55 1475	Madison	149.6	191 262	82	1 278	170 616	20 646	12.1	90.72	4.24	0.39	3.91	0.75	2.03	9.3
...	55 1490	Manitowoc	37.3	32 520	774	872	32 547	-27	-0.1	96.37	0.22	0.54	2.52	0.36	1.15	19.8
5082	55 1585	Menomonee Falls village	86.2	26 840	891	311	27 845	-1 005	-3.6	98.83	0.28	0.20	0.54	0.15	0.60	11.7
5082	55 1645	Milwaukee	248.8	628 088	17	2 524	636 297	-8 209	-1.3	63.37	30.45	0.93	1.88	3.36	6.27	12.4
5082	55 1785	New Berlin	95.4	33 592	752	352	30 529	3 063	10.0	98.40	0.24	0.22	0.99	0.16	0.83	8.5
0460	55 1930	Oshkosh	46.5	55 006	426	1 183	49 620	5 386	10.9	96.25	0.79	0.50	2.18	0.28	0.83	14.1
5082	55 2105	Racine	40.0	84 298	248	2 107	85 725	-1 427	-1.7	76.37	18.45	0.32	0.54	4.32	8.13	13.1
7620	55 2300	Sheboygan	34.3	49 676	496	1 448	48 085	1 591	3.3	94.41	0.21	0.43	3.88	1.06	2.52	17.0
2240	55 2500	Superior	95.7	27 134	886	284	29 571	-2 437	-8.2	96.09	0.53	2.38	0.84	0.15	0.52	17.5
5082	55 2665	Waukesha	44.8	56 958	410	1 271	50 365	6 593	13.1	95.37	0.56	0.28	1.26	2.53	5.91	9.8
8940	55 2690	Wausau	36.5	37 060	685	1 015	32 426	4 634	14.3	93.05	0.13	0.70	5.98	0.14	0.65	17.3
5082	55 2705	Wauwatosa	34.3	49 366	500	1 439	51 308	-1 942	-3.8	97.32	1.24	0.18	1.02	0.24	0.99	19.8
5082	55 2720	West Allis	29.3	63 221	363	2 158	63 982	-761	-1.2	98.23	0.30	0.48	0.63	0.36	1.45	17.9
...	56 0000	WYOMING	251 500.8	453 588	X	2	469 557	-15 969	-3.4	94.15	0.79	2.09	0.62	2.34	5.68	10.4
1350	56 0045	Casper	53.4	46 742	528	875	51 016	-4 274	-8.4	96.52	0.93	0.55	0.54	1.46	3.94	11.4
1580	56 0050	Cheyenne	48.7	50 008	491	1 027	47 283	2 725	5.8	89.61	3.12	0.70	1.17	5.40	11.82	12.0

1. MSA = Metropolitan Statistical Area. CMSA = Consolidated MSA. 2. Dry land or land partially or temporarily covered by water. 3. Hispanic persons may be of any race.

City	Households, 1990: Number	Households, 1990: Persons per household	Households, 1990: Percent– Female family householder[1]	Households, 1990: Percent– One-person[2]	Births, 1984: Number: Total	Births, 1984: Number: To mothers under 20 yrs. old (Percent)	Births, 1984: Rate[3]	Deaths, 1984: Number: Total	Deaths, 1984: Number: Infant[4]	Deaths, 1984: Rate: Total[3]	Deaths, 1984: Rate: Infant[5]	Hospitals, 1985: Number	Hospitals, 1985: Beds: Number	Hospitals, 1985: Beds: Rate[6]
	15	16	17	18	19	20	21	22	23	24	25	26	27	28
VIRGINIA—Con.														
Danville	21 712	2.38	17.3	30.2	588	17.5	13.2	577	9	12.9	15.3	1	383	857
Hampton	49 673	2.58	13.5	23.7	2 119	13.5	16.8	869	30	6.9	14.2	4	1 067	847
Lynchburg	25 143	2.39	15.6	30.5	868	15.7	12.9	734	13	10.9	15.0	2	695	1 022
Newport News	63 952	2.59	15.1	23.7	2 950	15.2	19.1	1 153	37	7.5	12.5	5	942	583
Norfolk	89 478	2.55	16.1	26.8	5 456	17.7	19.5	2 279	87	8.1	15.9	11	2 092	761
Petersburg	14 730	2.46	23.0	30.3	699	24.0	17.1	490	19	12.0	27.2	3	1 176	2 955
Portsmouth	38 741	2.62	19.3	24.5	1 929	18.2	17.9	1 118	39	10.4	20.2	4	1 214	1 094
Richmond	85 337	2.25	19.8	35.9	3 414	16.7	15.6	2 685	64	12.3	18.7	18	4 730	2 173
Roanoke	41 030	2.30	15.7	32.3	1 417	18.8	14.1	1 148	20	11.4	14.1	3	1 021	1 002
Suffolk	18 516	2.78	17.1	20.4	760	20.9	15.6	493	6	10.1	7.9	1	202	394
Virginia Beach	135 566	2.82	9.5	17.1	5 622	9.3	18.2	1 400	73	4.5	13.0	3	537	161
WASHINGTON	1 872 431	2.53	9.4	25.4	68 927	10.4	15.8	33 814	703	7.8	10.2	120	17 029	382
Auburn	13 357	2.43	12.8	27.6	535	13.6	18.4	207	11	7.1	20.6	1	111	372
Bellevue	35 756	2.41	7.9	26.0	839	5.2	10.7	491	6	6.2	7.2	1	218	269
Bellingham	21 189	2.27	9.1	31.6	629	8.7	13.9	431	5	9.6	7.9	2	225	500
Bremerton	14 718	2.34	10.9	32.6	858	13.1	24.4	397	11	11.3	12.8	2	318	933
Edmonds	12 628	2.41	8.7	25.1	421	4.5	15.0	280	3	10.0	7.1	1	183	643
Everett	28 679	2.38	12.2	30.1	1 287	12.5	22.7	650	15	11.5	11.7	2	397	658
Kennewick	16 074	2.61	11.5	25.7	847	11.3	21.7	214	12	5.5	14.2	1	65	165
Longview	12 875	2.40	10.7	29.2	490	14.7	16.6	298	6	10.1	12.2	2	261	896
Olympia	14 951	2.22	10.0	34.5	773	10.9	26.5	358	8	12.3	10.3	2	441	1 484
Renton	18 219	2.27	9.9	32.5	595	8.9	17.8	253	6	7.6	10.1	1	313	910
Richland	13 162	2.44	8.4	28.0	516	10.3	15.6	214	4	6.5	7.8	2	176	540
Seattle	236 702	2.09	9.0	39.8	6 685	8.9	13.7	5 225	81	10.7	12.1	19	4 205	865
Spokane	75 147	2.29	12.4	33.8	2 989	11.1	17.2	2 080	34	12.0	11.4	8	1 770	1 024
Tacoma	69 939	2.44	13.3	31.3	3 053	14.3	19.1	1 799	38	11.3	12.4	8	2 150	1 353
Vancouver	20 138	2.22	13.2	35.7	1 211	16.4	27.9	661	8	15.2	6.6	1	411	936
Walla Walla	9 912	2.38	10.5	32.1	392	13.3	15.3	347	8	13.6	20.4	4	412	1 631
Yakima	21 596	2.47	12.1	30.7	969	15.8	19.8	593	6	12.1	6.2	3	441	893
WEST VIRGINIA	688 557	2.55	10.7	24.5	24 585	17.7	12.6	19 207	270	9.8	11.0	74	12 001	625
Charleston	25 306	2.21	13.9	35.7	723	14.8	12.2	802	7	13.5	9.7	5	1 425	2 460
Huntington	23 419	2.21	13.2	35.6	825	19.4	13.5	879	8	14.4	9.7	6	1 364	2 300
Morgantown	9 588	2.21	6.9	34.8	362	9.9	13.0	242	2	8.7	5.5	2	674	2 511
Parkersburg	14 463	2.30	13.0	31.5	512	16.2	13.0	533	8	13.5	15.6	2	555	1 440
Wheeling	15 038	2.24	12.5	36.3	527	14.8	12.5	593	7	14.1	13.3	2	910	2 276
WISCONSIN	1 822 118	2.61	9.6	24.3	73 187	10.1	15.4	41 047	725	8.6	9.9	170	28 543	597
Appleton	24 818	2.57	8.6	24.8	1 052	6.7	16.9	429	9	6.9	8.6	2	471	734
Beloit	13 307	2.58	16.1	26.3	583	17.5	17.1	304	7	8.9	12.0	2	189	560
Brookfield	11 939	2.92	5.1	11.3	289	4.8	8.7	230	0	6.9	0.0	1	136	407
Eau Claire	21 118	2.49	9.4	27.8	793	10.7	14.7	439	5	8.1	6.3	2	562	1 030
Fond du Lac	14 637	2.49	9.9	28.4	590	10.0	16.4	397	2	11.0	3.4	2	379	1 038
Green Bay	38 383	2.45	10.8	29.1	1 542	9.2	17.1	761	19	8.5	12.3	4	1 120	1 198
Greenfield	13 785	2.36	8.0	28.6	343	5.2	10.5	305	2	9.3	5.8	0	0	0
Janesville	20 388	2.54	10.0	25.2	901	8.8	17.5	374	9	7.3	10.0	3	672	1 298
Kenosha	29 919	2.61	14.0	25.7	1 232	13.2	16.3	744	10	9.8	8.1	2	425	567
La Crosse	19 970	2.34	10.1	33.2	710	8.9	14.9	533	3	11.2	4.2	2	750	1 574
Madison	77 361	2.30	8.3	31.2	2 580	6.1	15.1	1 227	27	7.2	10.5	7	2 242	1 275
Manitowoc	13 144	2.39	8.4	31.1	496	9.3	15.3	435	7	13.4	14.1	2	229	714
Menomonee Falls village	9 817	2.71	7.0	17.9	301	5.6	11.1	159	0	5.9	0.0	1	208	778
Milwaukee	240 540	2.53	19.8	30.5	11 800	17.6	19.0	6 000	168	9.7	14.2	22	7 170	1 185
New Berlin	11 695	2.86	5.4	13.7	341	4.4	11.2	134	2	4.4	5.9	1	126	408
Oshkosh	20 957	2.39	9.2	29.7	741	11.1	14.8	465	10	9.3	13.5	1	241	471
Racine	31 767	2.62	17.0	26.1	1 642	15.7	19.7	748	19	9.0	11.6	3	440	534
Sheboygan	19 703	2.47	8.7	28.3	812	9.1	17.0	550	10	11.5	12.3	2	295	622
Superior	11 001	2.36	13.5	31.6	397	16.9	13.9	350	7	12.3	17.6	1	52	193
Waukesha	21 235	2.59	10.0	25.4	956	6.8	18.5	356	9	6.9	9.4	2	423	802
Wausau	14 718	2.45	9.4	29.0	519	10.0	16.3	370	7	11.6	13.5	2	739	2 292
Wauwatosa	19 848	2.39	7.7	29.0	614	2.6	12.1	571	4	11.2	6.5	1	119	240
West Allis	26 797	2.32	10.0	31.7	971	7.6	14.9	685	7	10.5	7.2	1	232	363
WYOMING	168 839	2.63	8.3	24.5	9 754	11.6	19.1	3 189	108	6.2	11.1	32	3 119	615
Casper	18 504	2.49	10.2	27.6	1 112	10.2	22.4	346	11	7.0	9.9	2	336	710
Cheyenne	20 243	2.44	10.3	28.4	1 037	15.8	20.4	447	12	8.8	11.6	4	487	903

1. No spouse present. 2. Householder living alone. 3. Per 1,000 resident population estimated as of July 1 of the year shown. 4. Deaths of infants under 1 year old. 5. Deaths of infants under 1 year old per 1,000 live births. 6. Per 100,000 resident population estimated as of July 1, 1986.

City	Serious crimes known to police, 1985: Number: Total	Serious crimes known to police, 1985: Number: Violent[1]	Serious crimes known to police, 1985: Rate[2]	Police officers, 1985: Number	Police officers, 1985: Rate[3]	Educational attainment,[4] 1980: Percent completing 12 years or more	Educational attainment,[4] 1980: Percent completing 16 years or more	Money income: Per capita[5]: 1985: Total (Dollars)	Money income: Per capita[5]: 1985: Percent of State average	Money income: Per capita[5]: 1979: Current dollars	Money income: Per capita[5]: 1979: Constant (1985) dollars	Money income: Percent below poverty level, 1979: Persons	Money income: Percent below poverty level, 1979: Families	Housing, 1990: Total units	Housing, 1990: Percent change, 1980–1990	Housing, 1990: Vacant units for sale or rent[6]
	29	30	31	32	33	34	35	36	37	38	39	40	41	42	43	44
VIRGINIA—Con.																
Danville	1 408	63	3 111	84	18.6	47.5	10.5	9 848	82.8	6 508	9 645	13.8	9.9	23 297	21.0	1 012
Hampton	7 094	370	5 560	186	14.6	67.5	15.4	10 883	91.5	6 786	10 057	11.7	10.2	53 623	18.6	3 288
Lynchburg	3 220	368	4 725	136	20.0	58.9	18.7	10 655	89.6	6 896	10 220	13.1	9.6	27 233	6.7	1 483
Newport News	7 301	757	4 664	231	14.8	67.0	16.2	10 640	89.5	6 856	10 161	13.5	11.1	69 728	21.1	4 688
Norfolk	18 427	2 064	6 506	617	21.8	61.7	12.5	9 340	78.5	6 113	9 059	20.7	16.8	98 762	3.9	7 825
Petersburg	2 851	341	6 901	88	21.3	50.7	12.7	9 346	78.6	6 358	9 423	20.3	15.1	16 196	0.4	985
Portsmouth	6 255	583	5 720	199	18.2	54.6	9.9	9 274	78.0	6 104	9 046	19.2	15.8	42 283	8.7	2 961
Richmond	17 596	2 647	7 931	612	27.6	57.1	19.8	10 947	92.0	7 073	10 482	19.3	15.0	94 141	2.8	6 457
Roanoke	8 130	467	7 973	220	21.6	57.5	12.5	10 644	89.5	6 816	10 101	16.3	12.4	44 384	3.8	2 558
Suffolk	2 210	266	4 472	73	14.8	46.8	9.9	9 465	79.6	6 023	8 926	17.3	13.6	20 011	16.5	897
Virginia Beach	15 889	550	5 083	440	14.1	80.0	22.4	12 039	101.2	7 704	11 417	8.9	7.7	147 037	37.4	8 805
WASHINGTON	287 856	18 757	6 529	NA	NA	77.6	19.0	10 866	100.0	8 073	11 964	9.8	7.2	2 032 378	16.9	72 094
Auburn	2 514	118	8 373	51	17.0	75.6	11.7	10 771	99.1	8 048	11 927	9.9	7.0	13 977	18.8	494
Bellevue	5 581	197	7 318	111	14.6	93.0	40.9	16 277	149.8	11 666	17 289	4.9	3.5	37 428	21.7	1 373
Bellingham	3 850	149	8 255	70	15.0	79.4	22.8	10 037	92.4	7 207	10 681	17.0	9.0	22 114	10.7	660
Bremerton	2 284	203	6 437	59	16.6	76.0	10.9	9 778	90.0	7 165	10 619	12.9	10.1	15 693	4.7	610
Edmonds	1 158	43	4 141	38	13.6	84.2	25.0	14 149	130.2	10 477	15 527	4.4	3.0	12 945	17.3	251
Everett	6 250	230	10 731	105	18.0	71.3	11.9	10 223	94.1	7 819	11 588	12.1	8.9	30 795	22.4	1 675
Kennewick	2 833	134	7 194	46	11.7	81.0	18.7	10 523	96.8	8 416	12 473	9.2	7.2	17 209	16.0	575
Longview	2 467	79	7 751	47	14.8	73.6	13.2	10 638	97.9	8 073	11 964	11.7	8.7	13 441	2.4	332
Olympia	2 290	71	7 951	50	17.4	81.0	25.0	11 140	102.5	8 467	12 548	11.5	7.6	15 928	21.1	730
Renton	3 585	198	10 465	62	18.1	77.6	16.4	12 279	113.0	8 837	13 096	8.3	6.7	19 243	29.4	748
Richland	1 257	29	3 474	43	11.9	86.7	32.4	13 878	127.7	9 837	14 578	5.0	3.7	13 872	3.5	396
Seattle	63 102	6 523	12 743	1 039	21.0	79.7	28.1	12 919	118.9	9 282	13 756	11.2	6.6	249 032	7.6	9 058
Spokane	14 861	933	8 457	236	13.4	76.2	17.8	9 751	89.7	7 161	10 613	13.9	9.7	79 875	4.8	3 470
Tacoma	21 002	2 010	12 994	276	17.1	71.1	13.6	9 365	86.2	7 050	10 448	14.1	10.6	75 147	9.8	3 753
Vancouver	3 533	272	7 956	73	16.4	70.9	15.1	10 288	94.7	7 585	11 241	13.0	9.4	21 025	5.4	646
Walla Walla	2 128	113	8 047	30	11.3	74.2	17.7	9 453	87.0	6 817	10 103	12.5	8.9	10 649	4.5	490
Yakima	6 251	305	12 115	88	17.1	67.0	14.5	9 681	89.1	7 105	10 530	15.1	11.2	22 968	6.9	961
WEST VIRGINIA	43 615	3 214	2 253	NA	NA	56.0	10.4	8 141	100.0	6 142	9 102	15.0	11.7	781 295	4.3	39 062
Charleston	6 229	491	10 190	149	24.4	70.5	23.7	12 930	158.8	8 946	13 258	12.6	9.0	28 111	0.3	1 987
Huntington	4 511	537	7 345	107	17.4	61.5	14.9	9 577	117.6	6 867	10 177	15.3	10.0	26 674	-3.6	2 081
Morgantown	928	48	3 294	50	17.7	77.7	37.3	8 736	107.3	6 015	8 914	24.3	7.4	10 422	0.9	617
Parkersburg	2 110	95	5 404	61	15.6	61.8	10.3	9 410	115.6	6 651	9 857	14.2	10.5	16 341	-4.5	1 224
Wheeling	1 203	75	2 867	83	19.8	64.8	13.3	9 823	120.7	7 179	10 639	12.7	9.6	17 128	-7.1	1 335
WISCONSIN	191 798	9 880	4 017	NA	NA	69.6	14.8	10 298	100.0	7 241	10 731	8.7	6.3	2 055 774	9.3	55 030
Appleton	2 304	68	3 792	85	14.0	76.7	18.5	11 659	113.2	7 867	11 659	5.9	4.1	25 528	15.3	528
Beloit	3 136	276	9 060	64	18.5	66.2	12.1	9 539	92.6	6 704	9 935	11.6	9.3	14 033	4.4	506
Brookfield	1 355	24	4 003	53	15.7	87.9	32.3	17 135	166.4	11 551	17 119	2.1	1.9	12 254	14.0	220
Eau Claire	2 628	55	4 939	85	16.0	77.3	20.4	9 162	89.0	6 345	9 403	14.8	7.1	21 880	12.1	504
Fond du Lac	1 759	29	4 872	62	17.2	70.2	12.6	10 200	99.0	7 055	10 456	6.9	4.5	15 176	10.8	400
Green Bay	4 869	205	5 407	164	18.2	71.5	13.0	10 662	103.5	6 991	10 361	9.6	6.6	39 726	13.3	1 065
Greenfield	1 620	39	5 084	48	15.1	75.0	15.7	12 869	125.0	9 263	13 728	2.7	2.0	14 301	13.3	445
Janesville	2 891	80	5 615	69	13.4	75.5	14.5	11 556	112.2	7 716	11 435	5.6	4.3	21 153	8.8	484
Kenosha	5 296	295	6 904	152	19.8	64.0	10.3	10 326	100.3	7 543	11 179	8.0	6.4	31 197	5.7	898
La Crosse	3 126	44	6 471	83	17.2	71.3	17.4	9 701	94.2	6 467	9 584	14.0	6.2	20 897	10.2	705
Madison	12 358	445	7 225	294	17.2	86.3	38.1	11 824	114.8	8 012	11 874	13.4	5.3	80 047	13.8	2 143
Manitowoc	1 508	23	4 582	64	19.4	66.8	12.1	10 192	99.0	7 119	10 550	6.4	4.1	13 728	6.2	421
Menomonee Falls village	940	18	3 411	56	20.3	78.8	16.8	13 341	129.5	9 097	13 482	1.4	0.9	10 043	9.7	176
Milwaukee	43 943	4 056	7 066	2 041	32.8	63.6	12.3	9 765	94.8	7 029	10 417	13.8	11.2	254 204	0.3	9 278
New Berlin	681	27	2 226	52	17.0	83.4	19.9	13 602	132.1	9 359	13 870	1.8	1.3	12 102	21.1	374
Oshkosh	3 182	44	6 315	87	17.3	70.0	16.1	10 058	97.7	6 822	10 110	9.0	4.6	21 827	12.7	612
Racine	7 265	701	8 572	204	24.1	63.8	12.9	10 407	101.1	7 588	11 245	9.4	7.8	33 156	0.5	976
Sheboygan	2 915	35	6 013	93	19.2	65.8	11.3	10 585	102.8	7 323	10 853	5.7	4.1	20 588	8.6	534
Superior	NA	NA	NA	NA	NA	69.4	12.7	8 935	86.8	6 616	9 805	10.6	8.2	11 684	-2.6	349
Waukesha	1 140	16	2 212	88	17.1	77.4	20.4	11 418	110.9	7 895	11 700	5.1	4.0	22 065	16.9	683
Wausau	1 781	90	5 529	53	16.5	66.4	14.8	10 732	104.2	7 334	10 869	8.7	5.5	15 318	13.2	402
Wauwatosa	2 297	88	4 508	89	17.5	81.9	28.7	15 065	146.3	10 264	15 211	2.6	1.8	20 289	3.3	308
West Allis	2 756	118	4 256	131	20.2	68.2	9.3	11 268	109.4	8 311	12 317	4.5	3.0	27 502	4.4	471
WYOMING	20 437	1 307	4 015	NA	NA	77.9	17.2	9 782	100.0	7 927	11 748	7.9	5.8	203 411	7.5	15 866
Casper	2 757	176	5 158	80	15.0	84.2	21.8	11 825	120.9	9 471	14 036	6.0	4.2	21 700	6.6	2 326
Cheyenne	2 843	111	5 770	83	16.8	79.6	18.9	10 827	110.7	8 050	11 930	7.8	6.5	21 859	10.3	1 289

1. Includes murder and nonnegligent manslaughter, forcible rape, robbery, and aggravated assault. 2. Per 100,000 resident population estimated for 1985 by the FBI. 3. Per 10,000 resident population estimated for 1985 by the FBI. 4. Persons 25 years old or older. 5. Based on the resident population estimated as of July 1, 1988 for 1987 data and enumerated as of April 1, 1980 for 1979 data. 6. Also includes units rented or sold, but not occupied.

Table C. Cities — **Housing and Labor Force**

City	Housing, 1990 (cont'd)					Construction authorized by building permits, 1990				Civilian labor force, 1990			
	Occupied units					New private housing units						Unemployment	
			Owner-occupied										
	Total	Percent with more than 1 person per room	Percent of total	Median value[1] (Dollars)	Median rent[2] (Dollars)	Number	Value ($1,000)	Percent single family	Non-residential, value ($1,000)	Total	Percent change, 1989–1990	Total	Rate[3]
	45	46	47	48	49	50	51	52	53	54	55	56	57
VIRGINIA—Con.													
Danville	21 712	2.6	59.4	47 000	195	114	4 616	31.6	7 722	25 986	0.8	2 007	7.7
Hampton	49 673	2.7	59.2	78 200	385	666	38 348	72.4	14 587	60 841	1.1	3 428	5.6
Lynchburg	25 143	1.8	58.2	56 900	272	118	9 349	83.9	25 658	36 495	1.3	1 621	4.4
Newport News	63 952	3.6	50.0	85 200	368	1 142	54 093	86.3	64 504	76 894	1.1	4 185	5.4
Norfolk	89 478	5.3	44.0	74 500	361	462	24 174	43.3	27 658	97 647	0.2	4 667	4.8
Petersburg	14 730	4.3	50.9	52 000	257	60	2 100	46.7	7 287	20 698	0.7	1 372	6.6
Portsmouth	38 741	4.3	55.9	67 400	327	238	9 813	42.9	6 225	50 801	0.6	3 256	6.4
Richmond	85 337	3.1	46.3	66 600	333	278	15 966	92.8	18 450	114 064	1.4	6 008	5.3
Roanoke	41 030	2.0	56.6	54 000	278	220	7 829	56.4	59 157	53 427	1.0	2 261	4.2
Suffolk	18 516	3.4	67.7	70 700	250	272	18 589	84.6	2 242	26 841	0.3	1 624	6.1
Virginia Beach	135 566	2.5	62.5	96 500	484	2 207	162 867	68.1	38 241	170 736	1.0	6 819	4.0
WASHINGTON	1 872 431	3.9	62.6	93 400	383	48 447	3 486 985	59.2	1 238 495	2 503 000	2.1	122 000	4.9
Auburn	13 357	4.2	48.8	91 500	398	270	15 318	39.6	8 242	17 570	1.6	675	3.8
Bellevue	35 756	2.5	58.2	192 800	542	620	60 560	31.8	34 510	55 150	2.0	1 528	2.8
Bellingham	21 189	2.8	50.9	89 100	371	579	34 456	28.3	16 524	30 267	5.5	1 576	5.2
Bremerton	14 718	5.1	39.1	64 200	329	86	5 219	57.0	1 153	18 153	3.7	924	5.1
Edmonds	12 628	2.0	67.0	160 100	476	170	22 160	51.2	394	21 305	2.3	629	3.0
Everett	28 679	4.7	45.5	98 000	418	1 752	80 046	10.8	19 527	36 650	1.8	1 709	4.7
Kennewick	16 074	4.5	53.1	64 800	279	156	15 579	84.6	4 630	18 940	2.7	1 326	7.0
Longview	12 875	3.2	57.2	61 100	308	47	4 226	91.5	19 522	15 608	1.9	1 048	6.7
Olympia	14 951	2.5	52.0	77 800	382	563	34 657	44.2	16 580	19 666	4.9	1 003	5.1
Renton	18 219	3.8	48.5	106 300	440	961	39 156	8.4	36 385	21 621	1.8	716	3.3
Richland	13 162	1.9	62.0	69 200	293	134	15 578	100.0	8 303	17 994	3.6	807	4.5
Seattle	236 702	4.0	48.9	137 900	425	3 162	228 135	18.5	144 807	349 689	1.7	12 965	3.7
Spokane	75 147	2.5	57.2	51 100	278	812	62 237	53.4	45 519	87 415	1.0	4 789	5.5
Tacoma	69 939	4.9	52.7	66 200	350	817	52 324	43.1	47 797	85 888	0.9	4 509	5.2
Vancouver	20 138	3.5	43.1	61 300	332	112	5 288	36.6	21 111	29 128	4.6	1 680	5.8
Walla Walla	9 912	4.3	56.6	50 800	259	11	869	100.0	2 638	12 028	-0.4	760	6.3
Yakima	21 596	6.8	53.3	56 700	283	93	5 133	51.6	2 187	30 085	2.7	2 884	9.6
WEST VIRGINIA	688 557	1.9	74.1	47 900	221	1 771	110 192	83.6	139 600	772 000	0.7	64 000	8.3
Charleston	25 306	1.1	55.5	66 100	261	85	10 695	90.6	4 761	29 322	1.5	1 402	4.8
Huntington	23 419	1.1	57.1	46 700	235	15	1 763	100.0	2 387	26 717	1.3	1 530	5.7
Morgantown	9 588	1.4	44.4	69 500	306	62	3 261	83.9	17 560	14 616	1.2	518	3.5
Parkersburg	14 463	0.9	62.9	42 600	247	19	1 075	100.0	2 385	18 088	0.2	1 440	8.0
Wheeling	15 038	1.1	61.3	47 000	207	39	1 714	28.2	1 048	17 819	-1.5	903	5.1
WISCONSIN	1 822 118	2.1	66.7	62 500	331	27 346	1 796 149	58.5	953 978	2 587 000	-0.9	113 000	4.4
Appleton	24 818	1.6	66.3	64 400	341	225	17 564	62.2	11 524	37 915	-0.8	1 554	4.1
Beloit	13 307	2.4	60.2	37 900	293	38	1 756	52.6	2 286	18 561	-0.8	885	4.8
Brookfield	11 939	0.5	91.5	121 900	668	213	43 335	80.3	3 309	19 259	-2.1	465	2.4
Eau Claire	21 118	2.3	57.5	52 600	284	222	19 563	66.2	19 347	30 464	-3.9	1 566	5.1
Fond du Lac	14 637	1.3	62.5	51 700	320	254	11 298	36.2	4 493	19 918	1.8	1 253	6.3
Green Bay	38 383	2.2	56.6	55 500	314	289	25 451	63.3	28 729	57 197	0.3	3 155	5.5
Greenfield	13 785	1.0	62.5	80 300	484	496	18 698	16.1	2 306	20 041	-2.2	486	2.4
Janesville	20 388	1.4	65.6	56 000	327	385	21 930	46.2	7 234	27 092	-1.3	1 695	6.3
Kenosha	29 919	3.2	62.0	58 700	338	807	41 591	32.3	39 614	33 640	-2.8	2 941	8.7
La Crosse	19 970	3.1	49.6	53 500	286	118	5 042	16.1	13 161	26 661	-4.6	1 198	4.5
Madison	77 361	3.0	47.0	75 200	430	1 131	66 775	40.6	64 887	116 816	-0.3	3 048	2.6
Manitowoc	13 144	1.5	66.0	48 100	237	105	5 970	74.3	4 532	15 665	1.1	840	5.4
Menomonee Falls village	9 817	1.0	79.6	87 600	443	266	20 412	50.4	9 677	16 048	-2.2	132	0.8
Milwaukee	240 540	4.4	44.8	53 500	342	517	25 261	22.6	140 045	312 606	-2.1	15 485	5.0
New Berlin	11 695	0.7	84.6	96 700	575	211	23 398	84.8	2 867	19 284	-2.1	557	2.9
Oshkosh	20 957	1.5	57.0	53 800	315	588	15 172	18.5	2 958	29 679	-0.6	1 482	5.0
Racine	31 767	3.2	59.6	52 300	307	96	8 921	38.5	21 026	42 536	-2.4	2 756	6.5
Sheboygan	19 703	2.0	61.6	53 500	290	60	4 869	86.7	3 099	27 381	-2.1	1 476	5.4
Superior	11 001	1.1	61.2	37 300	238	100	6 150	57.0	7 472	NA	NA	NA	NA
Waukesha	21 235	2.3	55.5	81 600	469	476	25 118	25.6	8 269	NA	NA	NA	NA
Wausau	14 718	2.5	63.0	51 000	301	160	8 061	28.7	3 716	19 737	-1.3	870	4.4
Wauwatosa	19 848	0.5	68.7	89 300	460	158	11 969	1.9	28 100	27 441	-2.2	511	1.9
West Allis	26 797	1.3	59.4	63 100	391	103	4 954	15.5	2 327	36 661	-2.4	1 237	3.4
WYOMING	168 839	2.8	67.8	61 600	270	692	62 055	78.6	105 477	246 000	2.9	13 000	5.4
Casper	18 504	1.4	66.3	53 100	255	30	3 191	100.0	629	22 993	3.5	1 401	6.1
Cheyenne	20 243	1.8	63.9	68 700	316	49	4 366	100.0	5 573	26 760	1.9	1 318	4.9

1. Specified owner-occupied units. 2. Specified renter-occupied units. 3. Percent of total civilian labor force.

City	Employed,[1] 1980: Total	Employed,[1] 1980: Rate per 1,000 employees: Professional, specialty, and technical	Employed,[1] 1980: Rate per 1,000 employees: Precision production, craft, and operators	Manufactures, 1987: Establishments: Total	Manufactures, 1987: Establishments: Percent with 20 or more employees	Manufactures, 1987: All employees: Number (1,000)	Manufactures, 1987: All employees: Percent change, 1982–1987	Manufactures, 1987: All employees: Annual payroll (Mil. dol.)	Manufactures, 1987: Production workers: Number (1,000)	Manufactures, 1987: Production workers: Work-hours (Millions)	Manufactures, 1987: Production workers: Wages: Total (Mil. dol.)	Manufactures, 1987: Production workers: Wages: Average per production worker (Dollars)	Manufactures, 1987: Value added by manufacture (Mil. dol.)	Manufactures, 1987: Value of shipments (Mil. dol.)	Manufactures, 1987: New capital expenditures (Mil. dol.)
	58	59	60	61	62	63	64	65	66	67	68	69	70	71	72
VIRGINIA—Con.															
Danville	20 300	124.8	312.7	56	50.0	12.2	-9.0	253.8	9.9	20.5	190.6	19 253	520.6	1 030.4	17.3
Hampton	48 363	161.7	237.0	73	41.1	D	D	D	D	D	D	D	D	D	D
Lynchburg	30 318	189.1	190.1	123	49.6	14.4	-13.8	364.0	9.3	18.8	212.6	22 860	989.2	1 582.1	33.9
Newport News	58 981	171.9	243.7	117	36.8	30.1	7.1	817.3	25.3	47.8	591.6	23 383	1 380.7	2 037.4	D
Norfolk	86 015	146.9	185.3	235	39.6	16.5	21.3	385.1	12.1	25.2	261.4	21 603	1 345.3	3 425.0	42.4
Petersburg	16 789	132.6	222.3	50	40.0	2.1	-56.2	33.6	1.4	2.9	18.0	12 857	85.2	175.6	6.0
Portsmouth	40 003	138.9	251.5	65	33.8	2.2	D	37.6	1.7	3.2	26.1	15 353	133.1	338.7	3.7
Richmond	99 667	177.7	169.7	428	43.7	41.5	5.9	1 302.0	22.4	43.8	586.3	26 174	5 206.6	8 280.4	203.1
Roanoke	43 674	138.6	212.8	170	45.3	11.5	7.5	236.9	7.5	14.9	135.2	18 027	653.2	1 196.0	43.0
Suffolk	19 439	113.9	273.5	66	43.9	2.4	-57.1	43.3	1.8	3.5	29.8	16 556	274.7	494.4	6.7
Virginia Beach	105 894	186.8	158.9	164	22.6	4.2	D	72.1	3.0	5.7	42.4	14 133	171.7	449.3	11.7
WASHINGTON	1 794 354	164.6	199.2	7 630	25.6	309.7	6.1	8 841.6	184.2	353.5	4 262.0	23 138	19 016.1	46 531.8	1 244.8
Auburn	12 549	144.5	266.5	119	22.7	D	D	D	D	D	D	D	D	D	D
Bellevue	39 831	234.8	113.3	183	23.5	10.0	7.5	341.6	1.8	3.4	35.1	19 500	316.5	554.5	6.7
Bellingham	19 587	174.9	173.9	123	21.1	D	D	D	D	D	D	D	D	D	D
Bremerton	12 059	154.8	245.1	NA	NA	NA	NA	NA	NA	NA	NA	NA	NA	NA	NA
Edmonds	13 902	167.7	154.3	NA	NA	NA	NA	NA	NA	NA	NA	NA	NA	NA	NA
Everett	23 493	145.0	249.9	140	30.7	19.3	157.3	748.9	10.1	21.3	331.0	32 772	1 422.4	5 036.8	58.5
Kennewick	16 844	181.1	233.3	25	20.0	0.7	-22.2	13.0	0.3	0.6	6.5	21 667	57.4	92.1	D
Longview	12 673	133.2	238.5	62	41.9	3.9	-13.3	121.7	3.0	6.0	90.1	30 033	420.3	1 092.3	90.7
Olympia	12 354	193.2	116.0	64	21.9	1.9	-9.5	53.2	1.6	3.3	42.0	26 250	168.5	411.7	20.2
Renton	15 527	174.1	248.1	63	41.3	D	D	D	D	D	D	D	D	D	D
Richland	16 435	318.8	178.9	23	21.7	D	D	D	D	D	D	D	D	D	D
Seattle	250 117	215.5	154.3	1 261	27.8	35.2	-43.0	902.5	22.8	44.0	508.8	22 316	1 852.2	3 726.0	85.6
Spokane	71 099	160.9	162.1	323	20.1	D	D	D	D	D	D	D	D	D	D
Tacoma	61 161	153.2	221.7	339	35.7	13.4	-19.3	338.8	8.9	17.1	193.4	21 730	761.4	1 866.8	66.7
Vancouver	18 098	143.9	198.8	106	35.8	5.0	-2.0	113.8	3.7	7.2	73.5	19 865	278.3	714.8	26.0
Walla Walla	10 185	158.5	167.0	39	25.6	D	D	D	D	D	D	D	D	D	D
Yakima	20 745	164.4	176.7	97	33.0	3.7	12.1	77.1	2.7	5.3	50.9	18 852	205.9	453.3	13.4
WEST VIRGINIA	689 461	136.0	263.5	1 619	30.1	83.8	-12.5	2 107.6	58.8	115.4	1 312.3	22 318	5 404.4	11 560.8	434.8
Charleston	28 362	202.6	125.8	54	29.6	3.0	-34.8	83.1	2.0	4.0	50.2	25 100	81.3	579.6	14.8
Huntington	24 488	178.7	182.5	87	35.6	5.7	-35.2	150.2	4.0	7.7	94.8	23 700	342.7	580.5	31.0
Morgantown	11 208	292.0	103.2	25	40.0	2.1	16.7	38.2	1.6	3.0	26.8	16 750	105.0	182.0	5.9
Parkersburg	15 568	137.2	222.4	44	54.5	3.9	2.6	116.7	2.1	4.3	53.7	25 571	371.5	632.6	D
Wheeling	18 011	162.5	194.3	61	41.0	2.5	-21.9	55.4	1.5	2.8	27.4	18 267	95.8	171.4	2.4
WISCONSIN	2 114 473	141.0	240.6	9 157	37.8	514.0	3.5	12 763.4	349.9	693.6	7 615.5	21 765	31 653.0	69 595.8	2 027.4
Appleton	27 693	164.2	228.1	118	40.7	8.2	D	219.7	5.3	10.8	125.0	23 585	546.1	1 155.6	54.5
Beloit	14 802	143.4	316.8	52	38.5	5.4	-22.9	148.1	3.2	6.0	68.5	21 406	472.4	844.5	19.2
Brookfield	16 458	180.6	142.5	89	40.4	4.0	11.1	120.2	2.2	4.6	54.0	24 545	150.4	286.5	9.3
Eau Claire	23 154	181.3	151.5	73	38.4	4.6	7.0	114.8	3.4	7.0	81.3	23 912	205.5	483.0	16.0
Fond du Lac	16 130	142.3	226.9	69	53.6	7.7	10.0	203.5	5.1	10.3	123.4	24 196	620.5	1 180.0	38.6
Green Bay	39 842	138.5	212.1	183	45.9	16.7	7.7	457.9	10.8	22.1	275.9	25 546	1 233.7	3 711.9	54.7
Greenfield	17 096	138.0	244.6	NA	NA	NA	NA	NA	NA	NA	NA	NA	NA	NA	NA
Janesville	20 061	149.5	264.8	85	42.4	10.1	44.3	295.8	8.2	15.9	228.5	27 866	960.0	3 143.3	20.7
Kenosha	34 492	135.4	307.9	117	35.0	11.0	-12.7	339.3	8.6	18.0	245.7	28 570	706.2	2 222.4	17.9
La Crosse	22 816	167.8	185.4	88	39.8	7.9	-8.1	187.8	4.8	9.3	97.4	20 292	425.8	862.9	26.1
Madison	91 175	269.8	97.4	257	32.7	12.3	11.8	331.9	6.6	13.2	142.0	21 515	662.5	1 497.4	39.6
Manitowoc	14 827	135.5	299.2	83	55.4	7.1	-14.5	156.9	5.2	10.5	106.7	20 519	317.5	673.1	30.0
Menomonee Falls village	14 630	134.2	256.4	172	40.1	6.7	21.8	175.6	4.9	10.1	119.1	24 306	388.9	679.3	27.7
Milwaukee	285 291	132.6	256.6	1 054	39.5	63.9	-18.0	1 746.0	37.1	73.7	901.2	24 291	3 353.6	6 502.3	155.2
New Berlin	15 882	166.4	232.3	144	48.6	6.0	7.1	163.4	4.0	8.5	96.6	24 150	541.0	954.2	18.4
Oshkosh	23 054	145.3	230.0	117	52.1	9.4	19.0	217.2	5.8	11.0	118.2	20 379	451.2	1 189.2	30.2
Racine	38 376	135.1	321.4	247	37.7	17.6	23.1	528.5	8.6	16.3	184.2	21 419	848.6	1 371.8	87.8
Sheboygan	22 777	121.0	301.0	117	53.0	7.7	5.5	182.7	5.3	10.7	107.1	20 208	420.2	810.9	37.6
Superior	12 064	142.2	184.8	40	27.5	1.1	-15.4	26.2	0.8	1.6	17.6	22 000	82.9	335.4	D
Waukesha	25 345	176.4	236.0	177	42.9	10.3	17.0	284.9	6.3	12.7	150.7	23 921	849.7	1 553.9	47.7
Wausau	14 592	152.6	189.2	75	44.0	4.8	-25.0	109.2	3.3	6.6	65.6	19 879	237.2	564.6	16.6
Wauwatosa	25 166	241.0	132.5	93	36.6	10.8	33.3	330.7	8.0	16.3	239.2	29 900	501.3	905.9	49.0
West Allis	32 021	127.5	273.4	143	34.3	5.7	-43.0	149.5	3.7	7.6	88.0	23 784	313.7	595.8	13.4
WYOMING	217 374	142.9	234.6	500	16.0	7.7	-22.2	179.7	5.4	10.7	118.6	21 963	492.8	2 074.3	65.3
Casper	26 295	173.2	208.9	48	12.5	0.8	-42.9	20.3	0.5	1.0	12.1	24 200	48.3	303.6	5.3
Cheyenne	21 583	176.9	150.2	30	36.7	D	D	D	D	D	D	D	D	D	D

1. Persons 16 years old and over.

City	Wholesale trade, 1987				Retail trade–all establishments, 1987				Retail trade–establishments with payroll, 1987					
						Sales				Sales				
											Per capita[2] (Dollars)			
	Establishments	Sales (Mil. dol.)	Paid employees[1]	Annual payroll ($1,000)	Number	Total (Mil. dol.)	Percent change, 1982–1987	Per capita[2] (Dollars)	Number	Total (Mil. dol.)	General merchandise group stores	Food stores	Apparel and accessory stores	Eating and drinking places
	73	74	75	76	77	78	79	80	81	82	83	84	85	86
VIRGINIA—Con.														
Danville	102	314.0	1 137	20 769	692	487.1	59.9	10 897	494	478.0	1 582	2 272	392	924
Hampton	118	266.3	1 225	27 372	974	1 165.7	61.1	9 252	735	1 156.1	1 050	1 335	466	654
Lynchburg	157	440.8	1 867	37 742	852	627.1	30.3	9 222	638	618.3	1 678	1 638	488	863
Newport News	162	498.2	2 232	43 171	1 265	1 058.3	52.9	6 545	950	1 046.6	828	1 122	249	484
Norfolk	472	2 738.7	9 602	196 822	1 956	1 739.5	43.7	6 330	1 581	1 725.7	998	1 174	372	684
Petersburg	60	154.1	711	13 858	472	445.1	67.5	11 183	375	438.7	1 980	2 083	365	706
Portsmouth	83	1 157.3	1 254	27 083	723	590.2	41.8	5 317	546	584.3	562	1 395	299	409
Richmond	696	4 791.8	10 816	279 334	2 256	1 945.0	49.0	8 934	1 787	1 926.2	345	1 697	403	910
Roanoke	376	1 440.1	5 813	107 435	1 351	1 033.6	61.1	10 143	1 061	1 023.3	1 757	1 456	576	913
Suffolk	74	328.7	1 056	20 893	398	248.9	22.6	4 852	260	243.4	249	1 032	264	273
Virginia Beach	410	1 419.0	4 573	96 112	3 061	2 385.6	88.9	7 155	2 166	2 349.4	729	1 417	390	807
WASHINGTON	9 335	41 499.0	102 778	2 380 144	44 759	27 938.9	39.6	6 260	28 499	27 249.8	751	1 391	307	664
Auburn	87	566.8	1 589	32 195	339	364.4	46.5	12 204	225	361.2	D	2 189	D	823
Bellevue	599	4 064.6	6 269	185 698	1 227	1 294.1	61.0	15 988	887	1 280.8	2 134	1 810	2 033	1 264
Bellingham	142	315.9	1 181	21 334	810	517.6	36.1	11 512	555	506.6	1 845	2 570	420	1 160
Bremerton	46	87.6	426	8 993	430	331.0	7.9	9 707	307	328.3	1 685	1 660	178	1 026
Edmonds	65	203.5	371	8 376	344	156.4	44.3	5 499	193	149.5	D	1 567	D	1 047
Everett	159	627.3	1 637	39 004	906	676.8	39.7	11 209	636	664.4	1 765	2 312	279	1 180
Kennewick	65	127.5	489	8 716	541	371.8	22.0	9 425	371	362.9	D	2 337	401	818
Longview	62	217.2	616	11 252	397	315.6	16.8	10 830	278	308.9	D	2 411	D	1 037
Olympia	79	139.9	628	12 903	740	504.4	54.6	16 977	471	495.7	D	3 047	631	1 505
Renton	111	720.1	1 714	39 533	535	614.4	45.5	17 855	387	605.9	D	2 274	359	1 524
Richland	14	21.4	71	1 965	281	165.3	6.5	5 074	182	161.1	D	1 421	D	711
Seattle	2 004	13 085.1	25 687	645 317	5 834	3 976.3	29.2	8 178	4 076	3 898.6	1 008	1 510	686	1 158
Spokane	573	1 816.1	7 049	148 814	2 015	1 556.5	45.2	9 003	1 396	1 527.8	1 576	1 670	535	907
Tacoma	362	2 240.2	5 648	140 356	1 616	1 430.8	36.8	9 002	1 180	1 409.9	1 620	1 262	637	919
Vancouver	126	372.0	1 028	22 701	459	291.1	24.3	6 626	301	284.4	D	1 090	D	949
Walla Walla	72	139.8	481	8 467	330	203.0	14.9	8 036	238	198.5	994	2 267	396	708
Yakima	181	846.1	2 557	54 640	715	551.4	25.1	11 169	524	542.4	1 583	2 335	528	1 063
WEST VIRGINIA	2 444	5 935.4	24 217	476 934	17 621	9 349.2	24.3	4 872	10 737	9 030.0	685	1 117	173	380
Charleston	264	884.0	3 211	79 763	900	763.1	21.9	13 175	711	755.2	3 011	1 724	907	1 288
Huntington	194	597.4	2 636	55 357	747	485.5	11.0	8 186	528	476.0	D	D	D	961
Morgantown	50	58.8	372	6 501	444	296.5	39.9	11 047	338	291.6	D	2 624	D	1 038
Parkersburg	105	D	D	D	520	426.3	28.7	11 061	357	416.7	1 451	2 204	160	1 017
Wheeling	111	D	D	D	501	265.5	0.0	6 641	347	258.5	618	1 338	283	851
WISCONSIN	8 821	33 698.6	101 731	2 198 938	50 292	28 537.2	38.8	5 964	32 164	27 802.5	715	1 115	227	607
Appleton	182	D	D	D	646	418.3	35.4	6 516	478	412.5	846	1 479	273	664
Beloit	29	D	D	D	344	293.8	33.0	8 703	257	289.7	D	2 309	220	832
Brookfield	254	2 268.3	2 943	83 886	470	569.1	55.4	17 044	352	562.0	4 120	2 884	1 344	1 113
Eau Claire	134	D	D	D	727	521.5	27.7	9 555	548	514.9	1 781	1 755	493	1 089
Fond du Lac	67	283.6	987	22 265	517	362.6	35.6	9 926	361	357.0	D	1 593	387	1 080
Green Bay	273	1 190.9	3 545	79 982	1 100	817.0	54.6	8 741	780	802.0	1 486	1 623	386	832
Greenfield	31	27.2	187	3 310	290	407.7	47.6	12 785	199	404.3	D	1 641	663	1 090
Janesville	110	467.1	1 405	29 198	612	458.2	39.4	8 847	433	451.4	1 393	1 542	318	824
Kenosha	76	351.5	824	16 452	846	421.4	23.0	5 622	580	411.1	D	1 140	397	682
La Crosse	136	1 318.1	3 158	78 984	719	552.1	31.8	11 587	586	546.2	D	1 498	568	1 379
Madison	366	1 373.2	5 048	117 192	2 003	1 613.2	51.5	9 175	1 547	1 595.9	1 463	1 537	633	1 106
Manitowoc	54	95.7	610	8 712	421	224.7	18.1	7 007	282	220.3	D	1 705	166	660
Menomonee Falls village	126	584.2	1 311	36 737	279	277.2	48.5	10 374	185	274.3	1 558	1 357	162	673
Milwaukee	1 006	5 399.6	14 898	345 102	4 939	3 048.3	22.4	5 038	3 419	2 987.4	551	1 065	260	726
New Berlin	153	733.1	2 513	67 024	201	104.5	58.6	3 382	111	99.4	D	691	69	387
Oshkosh	91	225.0	1 241	22 079	618	450.0	40.7	8 791	435	441.7	1 394	1 535	279	998
Racine	131	351.5	1 286	28 125	903	579.8	31.0	7 033	670	570.4	1 445	1 627	445	728
Sheboygan	60	379.2	1 186	27 231	504	337.5	28.6	7 119	338	332.7	1 554	1 625	214	691
Superior	48	562.4	691	16 488	337	213.7	29.5	7 929	264	211.6	D	1 469	282	864
Waukesha	197	1 079.3	2 170	54 754	608	643.6	91.9	12 196	403	635.5	1 503	1 699	115	852
Wausau	102	252.5	1 131	23 782	532	386.9	39.7	12 001	374	382.2	D	D	692	879
Wauwatosa	174	1 678.2	3 805	80 645	571	656.2	35.8	13 219	425	650.1	1 708	1 292	634	989
West Allis	177	538.1	2 290	50 905	662	620.4	60.2	9 703	504	612.9	1 235	1 655	133	758
WYOMING	1 024	2 224.7	6 369	125 624	6 023	2 614.2	-7.2	5 156	3 726	2 521.9	519	1 066	208	537
Casper	208	647.5	1 370	29 314	679	417.0	-10.4	8 814	441	407.7	D	2 074	D	D
Cheyenne	89	173.7	645	12 560	612	429.3	24.3	7 956	401	420.4	D	1 117	D	858

1. For the period including March 12 of the year shown. 2. Based on resident population estimated as of July 1, 1986.

City	Retail trade–establishment with payroll, 1987 (cont'd): Paid employees[1]: Number	Retail trade–establishment with payroll, 1987 (cont'd): Paid employees[1]: Percent change, 1982–1987	Retail trade (cont'd): Annual payroll (Mil. dol.)	Taxable service industries–establishments with payroll, 1987: Number	Receipts (Mil. dol.): Total	Receipts: Selected kinds of business: Hotels, motels, and other lodging places	Receipts: Selected kinds of business: Health services	Receipts: Selected kinds of business: Legal services	Paid employees[1]	Annual payroll (Mil. dol.)	Federal grants, 1986: Procurement contract awards (Mil. dol.)	Federal grants, 1986: Grant awards (Mil. dol.)	Federal government civilian employment, 1984
	87	88	89	90	91	92	93	94	95	96	97	98	99
VIRGINIA—Con.													
Danville	5 916	35.7	55.0	390	106.2	9.2	47.8	5.7	2 654	45.3	17.5	12.1	175
Hampton	12 906	38.6	125.3	677	293.3	22.9	59.3	9.8	7 695	131.3	231.8	34.8	6 612
Lynchburg	9 190	23.2	79.5	636	320.0	12.9	75.5	11.6	6 792	130.2	294.0	15.1	394
Newport News	11 950	30.4	117.2	1 008	417.4	60.4	111.5	24.1	11 821	176.1	534.2	33.4	947
Norfolk	22 309	12.1	213.9	1 599	934.3	61.2	216.4	87.0	21 378	372.2	618.4	92.2	19 306
Petersburg	5 130	35.2	50.7	301	110.8	13.1	47.1	3.3	2 592	42.0	12.5	20.2	213
Portsmouth	7 130	17.3	67.1	561	200.7	4.4	78.7	14.7	5 778	82.3	90.0	40.6	15 878
Richmond	23 684	23.5	245.5	2 414	1 561.4	60.9	404.9	199.5	34 366	599.3	96.7	677.1	9 713
Roanoke	13 530	29.9	129.5	1 049	436.1	33.5	110.9	35.3	11 698	179.1	14.5	33.1	1 333
Suffolk	2 834	31.7	27.3	245	50.7	2.3	23.2	3.3	1 446	20.5	3.5	14.6	152
Virginia Beach	30 774	62.6	282.9	2 433	1 059.7	107.3	245.7	43.9	27 706	438.8	150.8	33.1	2 574
WASHINGTON	329 204	22.6	3 401.6	33 181	12 852.0	655.1	3 305.6	1 028.2	277 118	4 773.9	4 761.2	2 340.9	64 088
Auburn	3 327	38.7	40.0	276	104.6	D	57.2	2.9	2 505	41.3	9.2	2.9	1 189
Bellevue	14 631	44.3	160.8	1 779	989.1	41.8	159.5	46.9	17 604	388.5	16.8	4.0	274
Bellingham	6 550	14.1	61.8	621	170.3	16.0	74.0	11.2	4 415	64.1	1.2	7.6	260
Bremerton	4 059	-0.9	43.4	342	169.1	6.0	58.5	4.1	4 284	73.5	10.1	2.2	13 803
Edmonds	2 719	58.5	23.0	321	87.3	1.2	40.4	2.4	1 874	35.2	0.4	0.4	84
Everett	8 194	23.3	84.5	707	236.3	11.1	86.4	14.0	4 775	86.6	48.5	8.7	536
Kennewick	4 397	8.9	44.2	337	92.7	D	30.0	6.6	2 363	37.6	15.1	1.8	25
Longview	3 674	3.5	37.6	339	147.8	1.7	104.8	6.2	3 022	47.6	1.8	1.5	130
Olympia	5 648	35.0	58.9	604	218.8	12.1	111.2	11.9	4 515	82.3	5.1	305.2	694
Renton	5 884	26.0	74.6	462	216.0	D	59.1	6.6	4 332	97.0	11.5	1.6	224
Richland	2 334	1.9	20.4	293	D	8.5	D	3.9	D	D	1 740.1	6.2	512
Seattle	52 060	13.1	558.7	6 533	3 415.7	181.5	553.3	588.7	70 492	1 324.8	1 863.8	300.2	15 521
Spokane	19 048	23.6	190.5	1 880	663.2	33.0	247.2	66.8	16 310	269.6	64.7	16.3	2 587
Tacoma	16 386	19.8	179.8	1 539	632.5	22.9	251.0	67.3	13 986	249.0	53.3	70.0	3 083
Vancouver	3 798	15.4	38.2	527	210.9	7.2	62.8	17.3	5 437	74.7	14.4	3.4	2 219
Walla Walla	2 795	13.8	25.7	226	50.4	D	26.0	D	1 262	21.7	4.4	1.0	958
Yakima	6 489	12.1	66.7	679	221.9	14.3	85.5	21.9	5 063	87.6	8.4	9.0	656
WEST VIRGINIA	109 220	12.2	994.3	8 909	2 917.0	226.9	1 085.1	225.5	67 281	1 030.9	321.4	1 004.9	14 713
Charleston	9 653	10.1	91.7	921	429.8	24.6	145.9	80.6	9 153	157.6	12.7	187.5	1 484
Huntington	6 884	0.5	60.6	607	227.3	D	D	20.2	5 211	93.8	71.8	9.6	1 742
Morgantown	3 938	33.6	35.0	298	95.8	4.3	31.7	D	2 642	34.8	42.0	18.2	1 027
Parkersburg	4 973	6.7	49.6	382	199.3	D	51.7	D	3 705	60.8	5.4	4.0	1 500
Wheeling	4 149	D	35.4	436	D	D	D	12.5	D	D	1.5	4.5	332
WISCONSIN	372 205	16.9	3 206.4	28 126	10 025.7	569.3	3 233.6	713.5	265 298	4 108.5	1 603.7	2 357.4	25 731
Appleton	6 046	15.5	50.3	566	221.3	9.9	D	10.5	5 974	98.5	0.0	3.7	244
Beloit	3 543	13.1	30.6	158	46.5	3.0	23.9	2.9	1 305	21.0	5.6	1.5	91
Brookfield	6 707	27.2	65.1	565	320.9	21.2	52.4	5.8	6 796	132.5	2.3	0.3	132
Eau Claire	8 524	16.3	63.1	484	D	11.3	81.4	D	D	D	0.0	3.7	380
Fond du Lac	4 873	14.7	41.3	297	106.8	6.3	44.4	5.4	3 021	44.7	5.5	1.2	128
Green Bay	11 003	17.9	97.4	744	299.1	14.2	108.2	15.7	8 200	143.0	115.3	6.5	695
Greenfield	4 456	39.3	43.0	181	74.7	D	31.6	3.6	1 811	27.4	0.1	0.2	0
Janesville	5 975	11.5	53.7	353	115.7	11.1	46.2	9.0	3 876	54.2	21.1	1.3	175
Kenosha	6 131	7.0	51.9	569	134.8	3.6	74.0	8.1	3 827	54.4	9.8	7.6	200
La Crosse	8 545	12.4	67.5	449	219.7	13.7	104.9	D	5 002	93.8	17.3	5.3	311
Madison	24 400	23.5	200.9	1 594	852.7	55.2	247.7	86.4	19 980	362.3	69.7	364.5	3 476
Manitowoc	3 497	3.1	26.3	227	75.9	D	32.6	5.1	2 488	33.2	21.4	1.2	100
Menomonee Falls village	2 533	33.4	25.8	239	97.5	D	39.1	2.5	2 207	40.7	1.5	0.3	46
Milwaukee	45 603	11.4	392.3	3 589	1 920.1	79.5	447.5	302.3	44 130	827.4	199.5	110.8	9 411
New Berlin	1 335	26.2	13.1	182	108.1	0.0	8.4	1.3	2 271	42.5	16.1	0.2	5
Oshkosh	6 474	16.7	56.6	374	99.1	11.7	37.1	5.9	3 163	41.8	177.0	2.6	354
Racine	8 707	15.8	71.6	560	183.7	D	56.2	15.0	6 289	80.3	19.1	6.2	296
Sheboygan	4 856	6.6	39.9	309	138.4	3.6	36.8	5.5	3 414	54.7	5.5	3.3	125
Superior	2 942	2.4	23.2	172	40.8	D	D	2.8	1 461	15.8	0.0	0.7	95
Waukesha	6 218	48.7	62.9	568	196.0	3.8	59.7	11.1	5 244	78.1	37.5	4.6	214
Wausau	4 923	21.0	43.7	368	136.0	3.9	65.2	17.2	3 271	60.5	0.2	2.3	328
Wauwatosa	7 321	-2.7	79.8	776	350.3	15.8	119.4	9.8	13 196	181.9	0.3	0.8	4
West Allis	6 542	22.3	64.6	552	288.7	D	51.3	8.3	6 851	110.9	0.4	2.0	1
WYOMING	33 263	-9.7	307.8	3 802	883.5	184.0	217.0	80.9	21 791	289.7	182.4	451.0	6 470
Casper	4 994	-14.1	50.7	539	134.4	D	D	D	3 312	50.3	20.5	13.9	702
Cheyenne	5 416	5.7	53.8	461	128.6	20.2	39.2	D	3 339	47.5	13.4	53.8	1 491

1. For the period including March 12 of the year shown.

City	City government employment, 1985 (October)			Form of governments[2] (As of 1986)	City government finances, 1984–1985												
					General revenue							General expenditures					
						Intergovernmental		Taxes					Per capita[3] (Dol.)		Percent of total for–		
									Per capita[3] (Dollars)								
	Total	Rates[1]	Percent education		Total (Mil. dol.)	Total (Mil. dol.)	Percent from State government	Total (Mil. dol.)	Total	Property	Sales & gross receipts	Total (Mil. dol.)	Total	Capital outlays	Public welfare	Highways	Education
	100	101	102	103	104	105	106	107	108	109	110	111	112	113	114	115	116
VIRGINIA–Con.																	
Danville	1 901	425.3	48.9	2	43.2	22.0	83.7	13.8	309	174	87	50.9	1 139	76	6.4	3.0	39.9
Hampton	4 709	373.7	61.2	2	137.8	59.8	74.6	62.5	496	303	139	137.0	1 088	108	4.6	4.8	45.6
Lynchburg	2 453	360.7	49.0	2	78.7	28.7	82.9	37.3	549	291	200	83.8	1 232	119	4.5	5.1	36.1
Newport News	6 122	378.6	57.2	2	185.7	80.7	72.6	80.9	500	338	105	181.2	1 120	165	3.6	3.4	47.4
Norfolk	11 081	403.2	45.4	2	362.0	141.7	73.9	145.3	529	269	198	363.3	1 322	162	5.5	4.7	32.9
Petersburg	1 768	444.2	52.0	2	48.4	21.9	85.9	21.4	538	318	159	45.9	1 154	24	7.5	4.4	44.8
Portsmouth	4 542	409.2	51.9	2	138.4	61.8	77.1	52.5	473	276	148	145.6	1 312	143	6.9	6.4	36.0
Richmond	10 061	462.1	42.8	2	371.0	138.8	76.7	178.2	819	489	223	365.6	1 679	132	10.7	4.2	35.7
Roanoke	4 161	408.3	48.3	2	128.7	54.5	77.6	58.5	574	321	171	141.8	1 392	252	5.6	5.7	33.3
Suffolk	1 718	334.9	66.2	2	49.9	25.6	83.2	19.2	375	221	107	50.8	990	143	6.0	1.6	45.6
Virginia Beach	10 769	323.0	62.5	2	357.6	131.3	85.7	175.8	527	312	150	326.1	978	108	2.5	8.2	45.2
WASHINGTON	NA	NA	NA	NA	NA	NA	NA	NA	NA	NA	NA	NA	NA	NA	NA	NA	NA
Auburn	250	83.7	0.0	1	17.2	2.2	80.9	7.5	252	103	142	20.3	681	209	0.0	5.5	0.0
Bellevue	956	118.1	0.0	2	55.4	5.4	73.7	33.7	416	114	245	50.2	620	94	0.1	21.7	0.0
Bellingham	611	135.9	0.0	1	29.5	5.8	58.5	14.2	316	74	181	34.2	760	274	0.0	19.9	0.0
Bremerton	360	105.6	0.0	3	29.9	14.0	90.0	8.3	244	64	152	38.8	1 139	621	0.0	9.0	0.0
Edmonds	204	71.7	0.0	1	10.6	2.5	89.3	4.9	173	73	91	12.3	431	150	0.0	7.8	0.0
Everett	776	128.5	0.0	1	45.4	10.6	54.7	23.7	393	118	218	39.5	654	226	0.2	14.0	0.0
Kennewick	249	63.1	0.0	2	16.1	3.7	68.2	6.9	175	67	90	14.7	373	71	0.0	16.5	0.0
Longview	356	122.2	0.0	2	16.6	2.6	72.3	7.9	271	76	166	16.4	564	114	0.0	14.6	0.0
Olympia	362	121.8	0.0	2	20.4	3.4	46.8	10.3	346	100	198	24.4	820	198	0.0	14.8	0.0
Renton	464	134.8	0.0	1	29.5	4.2	78.3	15.1	440	136	276	29.3	852	240	0.0	24.2	0.0
Richland	379	116.3	0.0	2	30.8	15.7	84.9	5.8	177	81	78	36.0	1 105	619	0.0	5.1	0.0
Seattle	10 001	205.7	0.0	1	440.0	88.8	64.3	213.6	439	131	205	379.5	781	67	0.0	3.9	0.0
Spokane	2 010	116.3	0.0	2	95.4	25.6	69.2	41.7	241	68	152	87.1	504	89	0.0	13.4	0.0
Tacoma	2 995	188.4	0.0	2	131.1	33.9	35.0	52.6	331	99	160	124.5	783	74	0.3	11.4	0.0
Vancouver	NA	NA	NA	2	28.9	4.0	71.7	10.6	241	96	109	29.2	666	165	0.0	16.1	0.0
Walla Walla	246	97.4	0.0	2	11.6	2.6	56.2	4.5	177	57	101	10.1	399	58	0.0	9.6	0.0
Yakima	549	111.2	0.0	2	28.3	4.2	46.9	14.1	285	83	173	22.0	445	41	0.0	11.2	0.0
WEST VIRGINIA	NA	NA	NA	NA	NA	NA	NA	NA	NA	NA	NA	NA	NA	NA	NA	NA	NA
Charleston	1 141	197.0	0.0	1	44.9	8.9	15.4	21.1	364	76	32	42.8	739	145	0.0	7.2	0.0
Huntington	605	102.0	0.0	2	31.6	6.1	1.8	10.9	184	29	26	31.9	538	80	0.0	5.6	0.0
Morgantown	285	106.2	0.0	2	11.9	1.6	28.0	4.0	151	18	19	13.4	499	56	0.0	11.3	0.0
Parkersburg	1 364	353.9	0.0	1	53.8	2.2	3.1	5.6	146	24	17	46.4	1 204	82	NA	3.2	0.0
Wheeling	555	138.8	0.0	2	15.8	1.5	5.4	7.5	189	40	30	17.7	442	60	0.4	11.4	0.0
WISCONSIN	NA	NA	NA	NA	NA	NA	NA	NA	NA	NA	NA	NA	NA	NA	NA	NA	NA
Appleton	799	124.5	0.0	1	35.7	17.3	92.0	9.3	145	135	0	35.5	553	150	1.3	21.6	0.0
Beloit	411	121.7	0.0	2	20.3	11.5	80.1	4.0	119	113	0	22.0	653	97	0.0	11.6	0.0
Brookfield	NA	NA	NA	1	20.4	9.0	97.4	6.4	191	171	13	25.6	768	384	0.0	9.5	0.0
Eau Claire	699	128.1	0.0	2	37.6	16.2	82.2	6.8	125	112	5	30.4	557	96	0.0	22.1	0.0
Fond du Lac	460	125.9	0.0	2	20.6	10.4	83.7	5.2	141	128	3	20.9	573	60	1.8	13.8	0.0
Green Bay	1 198	128.2	0.0	1	70.3	30.6	85.3	16.6	177	170	2	70.2	751	157	1.3	19.4	0.0
Greenfield	NA	NA	NA	1	14.8	5.0	91.4	4.4	138	130	0	19.4	608	135	0.0	18.0	0.0
Janesville	526	101.6	0.0	2	25.4	11.7	82.6	6.7	130	125	0	26.8	517	137	0.0	16.5	0.0
Kenosha	810	108.1	0.0	1	46.4	24.9	82.5	12.4	165	161	1	47.2	630	144	0.0	16.5	0.0
La Crosse	665	139.6	0.0	1	32.3	12.0	81.7	9.9	208	192	9	28.5	598	47	0.0	15.1	0.0
Madison	2 577	146.6	0.0	1	121.1	53.3	78.1	38.2	217	200	9	107.6	612	95	7.4	12.0	0.0
Manitowoc	479	149.4	0.0	1	21.1	10.5	94.5	4.0	126	116	0	18.2	568	177	NA	17.9	0.0
Menomonee Falls village	294	110.0	0.0	1	13.5	4.1	91.9	5.0	186	178	1	13.4	502	72	0.0	19.8	0.0
Milwaukee	9 362	154.7	0.0	1	466.3	224.1	84.4	117.8	195	183	3	428.7	708	113	0.0	10.8	0.0
New Berlin	211	68.3	0.0	1	13.8	4.1	95.6	3.7	121	114	0	11.7	380	37	0.0	14.4	0.0
Oshkosh	629	122.9	0.0	2	26.9	14.4	81.4	6.0	117	107	4	26.9	526	68	0.9	15.3	0.0
Racine	1 142	138.5	0.0	1	55.9	28.4	83.7	15.1	183	177	1	48.1	583	58	NA	15.6	0.0
Sheboygan	677	142.8	0.0	1	33.9	15.6	82.5	7.1	150	143	2	32.2	678	151	0.8	12.5	0.0
Superior	361	134.0	0.0	1	18.1	10.7	83.5	4.3	158	125	6	23.9	886	87	NA	16.6	0.0
Waukesha	503	95.3	0.0	1	26.6	9.0	93.4	9.2	175	160	4	24.2	458	67	0.0	19.7	0.0
Wausau	373	115.7	0.0	1	26.0	8.2	79.9	5.0	155	148	3	21.4	663	109	2.1	18.6	0.0
Wauwatosa	NA	NA	NA	1	29.0	6.4	89.3	13.2	265	248	12	27.9	561	67	0.0	14.0	0.0
West Allis	778	121.7	0.0	1	35.9	14.9	85.6	11.2	175	165	0	37.1	580	45	0.0	15.0	0.0
WYOMING	NA	NA	NA	NA	NA	NA	NA	NA	NA	NA	NA	NA	NA	NA	NA	NA	NA
Casper	672	142.0	0.0	2	28.6	17.4	89.7	2.5	52	32	15	33.7	712	204	0.0	9.9	0.0
Cheyenne	754	139.7	0.0	1	35.5	17.8	85.5	2.9	54	26	22	37.8	700	234	0.0	9.3	0.0

1. Per 10,000 population estimated as of July 1, 1986. 2. 1=Mayor-council; 2=Council-manager; 3=Commission. Data subject to copyright. 3. Based on resident population estimated as of July 1, 1986.

City	City government finances, 1984–1985 (cont'd)								Climate[2]							Typical monthly electric bills, 1986		
	General expenditure (cont'd)					Debt outstanding			Average daily temperature (Degrees Fahrenheit)							Residential[6]		
	Percent of total for (cont'd)								Mean		Limits							
	Health and hospitals	Police protection	Sewerage and sanitation	Parks and recreation	Housing and community development	Total (Mil. dol.)	Per capita[1] (Dollars)	Percent utility	Jan.	July	Jan.[3]	July[4]	Annual precipitation (Inches)	Heating degree days[5]	Cooling degree days[5]	Total (Dollars)	Percent change, 1980–1986	Commercial[7] (Dollars)
	117	118	119	120	121	122	123	124	125	126	127	128	129	130	131	132	133	134
VIRGINIA—Con.																		
Danville	0.0	6.2	9.6	2.5	4.3	21.8	487	36.1	37.6	77.8	27.0	89.7	42.94	3 856	1 384	37.64	43.2	NA
Hampton	1.3	6.8	3.1	2.9	7.4	100.4	797	0.0	39.9	78.4	31.7	86.9	45.22	3 446	1 458	57.03	16.0	467.1
Lynchburg	0.6	4.8	3.9	3.1	2.5	125.0	1 839	0.0	35.1	75.7	25.9	86.1	39.91	4 323	1 074	46.42	42.2	373.5
Newport News	1.0	5.6	7.0	2.9	6.5	181.8	1 124	17.6	40.4	79.7	31.7	88.8	45.21	3 297	1 676	57.03	16.0	467.1
Norfolk	5.3	5.9	3.4	5.5	11.0	362.7	1 320	14.4	39.9	78.4	31.7	86.9	45.22	3 446	1 458	57.03	16.0	467.1
Petersburg	1.4	8.0	6.3	3.0	0.7	14.7	368	22.5	39.7	79.0	29.2	89.9	44.81	3 371	1 571	57.03	16.0	NA
Portsmouth	3.6	5.1	8.6	3.2	5.2	103.4	932	0.0	38.9	77.9	29.0	87.9	46.93	3 608	1 377	57.03	16.0	467.1
Richmond	1.5	7.4	5.9	3.9	6.7	393.5	1 808	21.5	36.6	77.8	26.5	88.4	44.07	3 960	1 336	57.03	16.0	467.1
Roanoke	0.6	5.1	6.8	2.9	10.7	81.7	802	1.5	35.5	75.7	26.2	86.7	39.15	4 315	1 085	46.42	42.2	373.5
Suffolk	0.7	5.4	3.8	1.2	15.4	61.7	1 204	0.0	38.9	77.9	29.0	87.9	46.93	3 608	1 377	57.03	16.0	NA
Virginia Beach	2.3	6.5	6.4	3.7	0.1	323.7	971	30.9	39.9	78.4	31.7	86.9	45.22	3 446	1 458	57.03	16.0	467.1
WASHINGTON	NA	NA	NA	NA	NA	NA	NA	NA	NA	NA	NA	NA	NA	NA	NA	30.41	135.6	NA
Auburn	0.2	13.3	37.2	4.1	0.9	18.1	607	15.4	38.9	65.0	32.6	78.4	39.92	5 073	146	38.83	124.3	NA
Bellevue	0.5	12.5	10.1	12.1	1.2	67.3	832	34.3	40.6	65.3	35.9	74.6	38.85	4 681	200	39.90	126.4	311.1
Bellingham	1.4	10.3	12.2	9.3	2.2	34.1	758	60.8	36.6	62.1	30.9	71.5	35.26	5 724	62	40.54	125.3	NA
Bremerton	0.8	7.5	58.4	3.6	1.4	29.5	865	87.0	38.4	64.1	33.0	75.3	50.41	5 193	133	40.43	124.7	NA
Edmonds	2.0	15.1	20.9	6.3	0.0	10.5	369	56.1	40.6	65.3	35.9	74.6	38.85	4 681	200	34.28	155.6	NA
Everett	1.7	13.9	25.8	8.3	NA	62.8	1 040	87.0	38.4	62.9	32.6	72.7	36.23	5 352	76	34.28	158.1	254.1
Kennewick	2.2	12.8	5.9	9.5	3.5	26.6	673	58.8	33.1	75.0	26.4	91.1	7.55	4 845	824	30.75	78.3	NA
Longview	1.3	15.0	15.4	10.5	1.8	12.5	428	65.0	38.8	64.1	32.8	77.2	46.14	5 059	139	NA	NA	NA
Olympia	0.8	11.7	22.1	12.5	1.7	22.1	743	43.4	37.2	63.0	30.8	77.2	50.96	5 709	94	39.78	126.4	NA
Renton	0.4	11.3	11.0	6.7	3.8	30.1	874	16.4	39.1	64.8	34.3	75.2	38.60	5 121	184	39.97	124.3	NA
Richland	0.6	6.0	56.8	2.9	1.2	54.5	1 672	75.3	33.5	75.7	25.9	91.6	6.78	4 700	940	33.44	129.2	NA
Seattle	1.0	14.6	13.3	13.1	4.3	636.9	1 310	61.0	40.6	65.3	35.9	74.6	38.85	4 681	200	21.77	154.3	225.0
Spokane	1.6	12.7	14.6	11.7	3.5	41.7	241	37.6	25.7	69.7	20.0	84.0	16.71	6 882	411	29.26	112.6	368.1
Tacoma	5.6	10.7	14.7	7.8	2.3	287.6	1 810	78.3	40.3	65.0	35.0	76.0	37.17	4 796	158	26.35	112.5	NA
Vancouver	0.9	11.7	31.3	8.4	0.2	31.0	706	76.8	38.2	65.7	32.3	78.4	41.07	5 026	269	34.15	191.4	NA
Walla Walla	1.0	12.6	21.5	7.0	6.9	6.3	251	87.9	33.3	75.1	27.1	89.5	18.36	5 049	843	34.20	87.5	NA
Yakima	1.1	20.3	15.4	7.8	3.1	18.0	364	43.6	28.2	70.4	19.7	87.8	7.98	6 031	484	34.03	91.9	NA
WEST VIRGINIA	NA	NA	NA	NA	NA	NA	NA	NA	NA	NA	NA	NA	NA	NA	NA	46.94	52.7	NA
Charleston	1.1	11.2	10.2	8.9	14.5	53.1	917	0.0	32.9	74.5	23.9	85.2	42.43	4 697	1 007	48.08	55.2	422.0
Huntington	0.2	12.9	18.4	3.5	12.5	70.3	1 185	0.0	32.8	75.4	24.5	85.6	40.72	4 676	1 121	48.08	55.2	422.0
Morgantown	NA	12.8	21.2	6.2	4.1	17.7	661	45.0	29.7	73.1	21.4	83.6	40.59	5 348	826	44.36	47.3	NA
Parkersburg	65.5	5.7	8.1	0.4	0.6	57.2	1 485	34.0	30.4	74.4	22.1	84.3	40.67	5 107	964	44.65	46.9	NA
Wheeling	0.0	13.1	23.3	3.4	1.1	22.9	573	14.0	29.1	73.6	20.6	84.8	38.06	5 450	840	51.96	65.6	378.9
WISCONSIN	NA	NA	NA	NA	NA	NA	NA	NA	NA	NA	NA	NA	NA	NA	NA	47.07	57.5	NA
Appleton	1.9	12.3	14.6	6.1	9.0	36.5	568	5.0	15.3	71.4	7.0	81.4	30.41	7 728	515	49.48	70.0	431.1
Beloit	6.7	16.9	14.0	10.1	4.4	18.4	544	0.0	19.5	73.7	11.1	84.9	32.00	6 611	791	52.22	83.6	NA
Brookfield	0.1	9.8	50.4	2.5	0.0	44.4	1 330	0.0	18.1	71.8	10.1	82.5	32.02	7 194	570	49.48	58.6	NA
Eau Claire	5.0	14.4	8.6	6.6	4.1	59.5	1 091	11.2	9.8	70.8	NA	82.3	30.31	8 463	472	43.70	49.8	330.8
Fond du Lac	3.2	13.5	17.7	4.1	6.4	32.5	888	3.6	15.8	71.3	7.2	81.9	28.82	7 568	521	52.22	83.6	NA
Green Bay	1.3	12.4	19.7	7.6	1.9	84.5	904	9.7	14.0	69.5	5.4	80.9	28.00	8 143	381	43.90	48.2	371.3
Greenfield	2.3	16.7	10.0	3.8	0.0	30.1	945	0.0	19.7	73.4	12.1	83.1	31.27	6 848	707	49.48	58.6	NA
Janesville	2.7	13.0	20.0	5.0	6.4	45.0	870	8.7	18.9	73.9	10.3	85.5	32.29	6 762	784	52.22	83.6	NA
Kenosha	4.1	16.7	18.1	5.4	5.3	53.2	710	9.0	20.4	70.1	12.1	79.4	32.24	7 090	485	49.48	58.6	431.1
La Crosse	0.0	12.4	11.8	11.7	5.6	52.6	1 105	0.0	14.0	73.0	5.0	83.5	30.25	7 540	683	43.70	49.8	NA
Madison	3.6	16.4	12.7	8.2	6.6	94.7	539	13.9	15.6	70.6	6.7	82.8	30.84	7 642	467	41.46	52.4	424.8
Manitowoc	1.4	13.6	14.8	9.0	6.9	23.7	740	71.2	18.3	69.7	10.5	79.6	28.83	7 517	388	36.65	56.2	NA
Menomonee Falls village	0.0	21.8	19.2	2.8	0.0	26.9	1 006	0.0	17.5	72.2	8.9	84.0	32.21	7 166	616	49.48	58.6	NA
Milwaukee	3.8	19.3	17.3	2.1	7.2	511.9	846	3.6	18.7	70.5	11.3	79.8	30.94	7 326	470	49.48	58.6	431.1
New Berlin	0.0	22.2	14.7	6.6	0.0	29.2	946	0.1	19.7	73.4	12.1	83.1	31.27	6 848	707	49.48	58.6	NA
Oshkosh	2.8	14.4	12.6	6.5	4.0	38.2	746	0.0	15.4	71.4	6.6	82.2	29.48	7 692	523	43.90	48.2	NA
Racine	1.9	23.1	14.5	11.5	1.9	31.0	376	28.3	20.4	71.7	12.6	81.6	34.19	6 919	591	49.48	58.6	431.1
Sheboygan	1.7	13.1	10.1	8.1	8.9	45.5	960	0.0	19.5	70.5	12.0	80.1	30.54	7 232	428	52.22	83.6	NA
Superior	0.0	12.0	13.1	5.0	4.8	93.8	3 479	0.0	9.2	65.8	NA	78.0	28.73	9 378	192	42.66	61.6	NA
Waukesha	NA	16.7	17.1	7.8	1.6	29.2	554	20.4	18.1	71.8	10.1	82.5	32.02	7 194	570	49.48	58.6	431.1
Wausau	0.1	9.0	15.6	4.4	3.4	60.1	1 864	3.8	11.2	69.4	1.8	80.3	31.62	8 565	371	43.90	48.2	NA
Wauwatosa	3.5	17.8	16.2	1.5	0.3	69.8	1 406	6.6	18.7	70.5	11.3	79.8	30.94	7 326	470	49.48	58.6	431.1
West Allis	3.5	19.3	17.6	0.8	4.9	37.6	588	0.0	19.7	73.4	12.1	83.1	31.27	6 848	707	49.48	58.6	431.1
WYOMING	NA	NA	NA	NA	NA	NA	NA	NA	NA	NA	NA	NA	NA	NA	NA	40.93	88.8	NA
Casper	2.2	11.5	18.0	18.4	2.8	12.8	270	31.3	22.2	70.9	11.9	87.1	11.43	7 642	457	39.38	89.1	336.5
Cheyenne	2.2	10.0	24.6	5.6	5.9	72.0	1 335	35.4	26.1	68.9	14.8	83.1	13.31	7 310	309	41.54	112.9	321.6

TABLE D:

Places of 2,500 or More

(For explanation of symbols, see page ix)

* Includes minor civil divisions (MCDs) of 2,500 or more.

Table D. Places — **Population, Housing, Money Income, and Land Area**

State/ Place/ MCD[1] code	Place	Population: 1990	Population: Places of 10,000 or more: 1980	Population: Places of 10,000 or more: Percent change, 1980–1990	Population characteristics, 1990: Race: White	Population characteristics, 1990: Race: Black	Population characteristics, 1990: Race: Am. Indian, Eskimo Aleut	Population characteristics, 1990: Race: Asian & Pacific Islander	Population characteristics, 1990: Race: Other race	Population characteristics, 1990: Hispanic[2]	Total housing units, 1990	Per capita income, 1985 (Dollars)	Land area,[3] 1990 (Sq. Km.)
		1	2	3	4	5	6	7	8	9	10	11	12
01	ALABAMA	4 040 587	3 894 025	3.8	2 975 797	1 020 705	16 506	21 797	5 782	24 629	1 670 379	8 681	131 443.1
0005	Abbeville	3 173	NA	NA	2 039	1 115	6	1	12	15	1 320	8 052	40.3
0010	Adamsville	4 161	NA	NA	3 493	659	5	3	1	12	1 554	8 854	7.9
0025	Alabaster	14 732	NA	NA	13 032	1 617	30	48	5	80	5 144	9 729	48.8
0030	Albertville	14 507	12 039	20.5	14 267	182	33	22	3	77	6 238	8 133	66.1
0035	Alexander City	14 917	13 807	8.0	10 684	4 184	16	27	6	18	6 170	8 876	100.6
0040	Aliceville	3 009	NA	NA	1 374	1 620	0	15	0	3	1 293	6 199	11.6
0055	Andalusia	9 269	10 415	-11.0	7 090	2 119	28	13	19	47	4 181	8 260	47.0
0060	Anniston	26 623	29 523	-9.8	14 509	11 801	49	181	83	212	12 100	8 731	52.3
0065	Arab	6 321	NA	NA	6 301	0	9	9	2	22	2 745	10 169	33.0
0095	Athens	16 901	14 558	16.1	13 687	3 041	52	113	8	77	7 271	9 901	77.6
0100	Atmore	8 046	NA	NA	4 489	3 266	278	11	2	19	3 394	7 412	21.4
0105	Attalla	6 859	NA	NA	5 801	1 032	19	0	7	31	2 874	7 621	15.5
0110	Auburn	33 830	28 471	18.8	27 016	5 531	60	1 138	85	314	14 673	8 434	84.2
0135	Bay Minette	7 168	NA	NA	4 960	2 122	59	24	3	43	2 682	7 192	19.7
0175	Bessemer	33 497	31 729	5.6	13 872	19 552	37	22	14	76	13 783	6 746	100.2
0185	Birmingham	265 968	284 413	-6.5	95 655	168 277	321	1 478	237	1 038	117 691	8 035	384.6
0210	Boaz	6 928	NA	NA	6 819	56	30	17	6	25	3 053	7 705	29.4
0240	Brent	2 776	NA	NA	1 639	1 129	2	0	6	11	1 103	5 721	21.2
0245	Brewton	5 885	NA	NA	3 572	2 261	12	25	15	19	2 482	10 348	25.7
0250	Bridgeport	2 936	NA	NA	2 593	256	74	12	1	0	1 241	7 191	7.8
0255	Brighton	4 518	NA	NA	595	3 902	2	12	7	6	1 735	5 368	3.6
0283	Cahaba Heights CDP	4 778	NA	NA	4 694	45	9	27	3	16	2 229	NA	5.4
0335	Center Point CDP	22 658	23 317	-2.8	21 648	878	41	69	22	107	9 081	NA	22.0
0340	Centre	2 893	NA	NA	2 581	284	11	3	14	19	1 254	NA	28.0
0345	Centreville	2 508	NA	NA	1 877	625	1	5	0	10	907	6 993	24.7
0365	Chickasaw	6 649	NA	NA	6 547	27	47	25	3	48	2 992	8 864	9.3
0370	Childersburg	4 579	NA	NA	3 419	1 152	1	7	0	12	1 899	7 877	20.1
0375	Citronelle	3 671	NA	NA	2 932	690	46	2	1	8	1 397	7 667	63.2
0380	Clanton	7 669	NA	NA	6 172	1 462	7	15	13	25	3 262	7 590	49.1
0415	Columbiana	2 968	NA	NA	2 338	613	6	7	4	8	1 132	8 096	24.8
0420	Cordova	2 623	NA	NA	2 305	316	2	0	0	4	1 175	8 036	15.3
0450	Cullman	13 367	13 084	2.2	13 271	27	18	40	11	71	5 933	10 574	40.5
0455	Dadeville	3 276	NA	NA	2 007	1 263	2	3	1	8	1 254	7 578	41.4
0460	Daleville	5 117	NA	NA	3 899	876	18	246	78	176	2 330	9 642	22.8
0465	Daphne	11 290	NA	NA	9 406	1 794	29	47	14	107	4 874	9 077	28.6
0480	Decatur	48 761	42 002	16.1	40 180	8 038	132	299	112	386	20 640	10 884	122.3
0485	Demopolis	7 512	NA	NA	3 882	3 616	6	5	3	36	3 015	8 693	31.6
0500	Dothan	53 589	48 750	9.9	38 312	14 639	136	424	78	359	22 190	9 999	206.4
0515	East Brewton	2 579	NA	NA	2 452	107	14	1	5	7	1 164	6 512	9.1
0530	Elba	4 011	NA	NA	2 935	1 052	21	0	3	10	1 755	7 583	39.8
0545	Enterprise	20 123	18 060	11.4	15 398	4 265	61	279	120	403	8 466	9 889	80.4
0560	Eufaula	13 220	12 097	9.3	8 585	4 556	23	42	14	74	5 457	7 974	153.9
0575	Evergreen	3 911	NA	NA	2 029	1 858	14	6	4	29	1 735	7 797	39.4
0590	Fairfield	12 200	13 040	-6.4	3 019	9 152	7	15	7	22	4 988	8 174	8.7
0595	Fairhope	8 485	NA	NA	7 850	580	17	26	12	91	3 808	11 536	19.9
0610	Fayette	4 909	NA	NA	3 806	1 072	2	5	24	54	2 170	8 429	22.1
0640	Florence	36 426	37 029	-1.6	29 922	6 219	98	157	30	179	15 913	9 556	60.9
0645	Foley	4 937	NA	NA	3 957	920	15	16	29	91	2 127	8 375	21.7
0647	Forestdale CDP	10 395	10 814	-3.9	8 482	1 872	8	28	5	31	4 160	NA	20.8
0652	Fort McClellan CDP	4 128	NA	NA	2 486	1 355	26	134	127	314	576	NA	18.3
0655	Fort Payne	11 838	11 485	3.1	11 077	569	114	46	32	54	5 236	9 652	139.9
0657	Fort Rucker CDP	7 593	NA	NA	5 660	1 429	47	212	245	595	1 553	NA	28.2
0675	Fultondale	6 400	NA	NA	6 261	107	14	17	1	34	2 462	10 420	19.6
0685	Gadsden	42 523	47 565	-10.6	30 111	11 981	62	314	55	167	19 146	8 745	92.1
0705	Gardendale	9 251	NA	NA	9 098	123	16	9	5	36	3 682	10 666	39.2
0720	Geneva	4 681	NA	NA	3 961	691	22	2	5	34	2 093	7 594	36.1
0745	Glencoe	4 670	NA	NA	4 562	94	7	6	1	6	1 797	9 993	41.4
0773	Grand Bay CDP	3 383	NA	NA	2 998	355	13	12	5	33	1 245	NA	22.4
0785	Greensboro	3 047	NA	NA	1 136	1 903	4	4	0	14	1 185	6 296	6.2
0790	Greenville	7 492	NA	NA	4 146	3 325	7	13	1	13	3 058	6 841	37.6
0810	Gulf Shores	3 261	NA	NA	3 242	1	7	6	5	20	4 976	NA	33.9
0815	Guntersville	7 038	NA	NA	6 184	789	32	26	7	29	3 154	8 637	55.6
0830	Haleyville	4 452	NA	NA	4 382	44	11	14	1	17	1 981	9 688	18.0
0835	Hamilton	5 787	NA	NA	5 442	315	14	12	4	17	2 414	9 204	67.9
0860	Hartselle	10 795	NA	NA	10 024	683	53	28	7	36	4 349	9 724	32.6
0870	Headland	3 266	NA	NA	2 172	1 088	2	0	4	27	1 311	7 738	41.2
0880	Heflin	2 906	NA	NA	2 499	400	3	4	0	1	1 218	8 505	26.8
0885	Helena	3 918	NA	NA	3 625	264	13	16	0	12	1 366	NA	35.6
0905	Hokes Bluff	3 739	NA	NA	3 728	0	5	6	0	11	1 460	10 191	29.2
0920	Holt CDP	4 125	NA	NA	2 704	1 408	6	4	3	24	1 602	NA	8.4
0925	Homewood	22 922	21 412	7.1	20 630	1 887	48	305	52	191	10 731	14 058	19.1
0927	Hoover	39 788	19 792	101.0	37 886	1 318	47	474	63	366	17 038	14 850	61.8
0930	Hueytown	15 280	13 309	14.8	13 204	2 029	15	30	2	32	5 970	9 610	22.4

1. Codes shown are 2-digit FIPS codes for states; 4-digit census place codes for places; and 3-digit FIPS county codes followed by 3-digit census MCD codes for minor civil divisions (MCDs). MCD names are followed by county names in parentheses. 2. Hispanic persons may be of any race. 3. Dry land or land partially or temporarily covered by water.

State/ Place/ MCD[1] code	Place	Population: 1990	Population: Places of 10,000 or more: 1980	Population: Places of 10,000 or more: Percent change, 1980–1990	Race: White	Race: Black	Race: Am. Indian, Eskimo Aleut	Race: Asian & Pacific Islander	Race: Other race	Hispanic[2]	Total housing units, 1990	Per capita income, 1985 (Dollars)	Land area,[3] 1990 (Sq. Km.)
		1	2	3	4	5	6	7	8	9	10	11	12
	ALABAMA—Con.												
0932	Huguley CDP	3 161	NA	NA	2 569	582	2	4	4	14	1 197	NA	22.7
0935	Huntsville	159 789	142 513	12.1	116 065	39 016	816	3 432	460	1 979	67 827	12 467	425.8
0944	Inverness CDP	2 528	NA	NA	2 449	46	4	27	2	11	1 050	NA	7.8
0945	Irondale	9 454	NA	NA	7 687	1 626	22	104	15	75	3 742	12 742	22.9
0950	Jackson	5 819	NA	NA	3 750	2 046	12	8	3	36	2 217	9 070	39.1
0955	Jacksonville	10 283	NA	NA	8 280	1 815	21	122	45	183	3 920	7 548	17.4
0960	Jasper	13 553	11 894	13.9	11 490	1 978	24	55	6	57	5 815	9 777	59.3
0997	Ladonia CDP	2 905	NA	NA	2 847	29	10	4	15	24	1 152	NA	8.3
1000	Lafayette	3 151	NA	NA	1 147	1 999	3	1	1	7	1 236	7 367	22.9
1005	Lanett	8 985	NA	NA	4 710	4 258	0	3	14	44	3 694	8 432	13.0
1015	Leeds	9 946	NA	NA	8 440	1 469	18	5	14	50	4 120	8 579	55.6
1030	Lincoln	2 941	NA	NA	1 948	987	5	1	0	2	1 335	7 207	47.7
1035	Linden	2 548	NA	NA	1 482	1 066	0	0	0	3	1 047	8 786	8.5
1045	Lipscomb	2 892	NA	NA	1 540	1 342	2	8	0	2	1 245	6 808	3.0
1060	Livingston	3 530	NA	NA	1 638	1 861	2	23	6	28	1 271	7 441	18.5
1080	Luverne	2 555	NA	NA	1 922	626	3	4	0	3	1 088	8 671	23.1
1095	Madison	14 904	NA	NA	13 209	1 164	77	400	54	248	6 616	12 498	51.8
1120	Marion	4 211	NA	NA	1 847	2 338	7	13	6	15	1 459	5 849	27.4
1127	Meadowbrook CDP	4 621	NA	NA	4 455	92	2	68	4	27	1 760	NA	7.1
1132	Meridianville CDP	2 852	NA	NA	2 573	239	19	21	0	8	1 005	NA	40.5
1135	Midfield	5 559	NA	NA	4 956	554	17	32	0	10	2 415	9 783	6.3
1152	Millbrook	6 050	NA	NA	5 015	992	12	20	11	54	2 153	8 145	18.3
1162	Minor CDP	3 313	NA	NA	2 244	1 058	8	3	0	4	1 349	NA	8.2
1165	Mobile	196 278	200 396	-2.1	117 022	76 407	443	1 992	414	2 002	82 817	9 658	305.7
1170	Monroeville	6 993	NA	NA	4 161	2 777	32	22	1	24	2 709	10 111	33.2
1175	Montevallo	4 239	NA	NA	3 191	1 004	9	29	6	29	1 308	7 161	16.8
1180	Montgomery	187 106	177 857	5.2	105 778	79 217	355	1 371	385	1 504	76 636	9 826	349.6
1183	Moody town	4 921	NA	NA	4 765	127	9	16	4	12	1 845	NA	28.6
1184	Moores Mill CDP	3 362	NA	NA	2 960	334	54	13	1	20	1 237	NA	34.7
1195	Moulton	3 248	NA	NA	2 572	521	155	0	0	13	1 364	8 964	15.3
1205	Mountain Brook	19 810	19 718	0.5	19 620	38	12	128	12	120	8 127	29 261	30.1
1225	Muscle Shoals	9 611	NA	NA	8 328	1 225	13	38	7	60	3 838	9 914	30.4
1275	Northport	17 366	14 291	21.5	13 191	3 964	25	160	26	64	6 793	9 413	27.3
1305	Oneonta	4 844	NA	NA	4 394	394	9	11	36	71	2 114	8 126	28.6
1310	Opelika	22 122	21 896	1.0	13 140	8 656	19	289	18	74	8 956	9 183	116.5
1315	Opp	6 985	NA	NA	5 918	1 051	8	7	1	11	2 902	8 017	46.3
1325	Oxford	9 362	NA	NA	8 524	777	19	30	12	32	3 810	9 029	29.8
1330	Ozark	12 922	13 188	-2.0	9 521	3 165	62	112	62	193	5 621	8 696	42.9
1347	Pelham	9 765	NA	NA	9 399	234	27	96	9	71	3 758	12 711	35.7
1350	Pell City	8 118	NA	NA	6 713	1 365	12	21	7	31	3 557	8 891	51.3
1365	Phenix City	25 312	26 941	-6.0	15 044	10 118	42	77	31	154	10 813	7 657	52.8
1375	Piedmont	5 288	NA	NA	4 763	507	5	8	5	19	2 392	7 773	22.0
1394	Pinson-Clay-Chalkville CDP	10 987	NA	NA	10 738	185	16	44	4	49	3 807	NA	29.4
1405	Pleasant Grove	8 458	NA	NA	8 282	152	14	6	4	6	2 992	10 736	16.0
1415	Prattville	19 587	18 631	5.1	16 654	2 730	48	118	37	153	7 184	9 503	47.6
1420	Prichard	34 311	39 518	-13.2	6 909	27 249	126	12	15	113	13 037	4 674	65.8
1430	Rainbow City	7 673	NA	NA	7 459	125	22	62	5	8	3 172	9 807	62.4
1435	Rainsville	3 875	NA	NA	3 844	1	22	7	1	11	1 629	7 482	47.3
1450	Red Bay	3 451	NA	NA	3 387	56	7	0	1	4	1 452	7 546	24.2
1457	Redstone Arsenal CDP	4 909	NA	NA	3 060	1 487	33	147	182	379	1 154	NA	20.5
1490	Roanoke	6 362	NA	NA	4 039	2 292	18	10	3	10	2 723	6 618	48.0
1510	Russellville	7 812	NA	NA	6 840	958	4	7	3	39	3 406	8 786	33.2
1519	Saks CDP	11 138	11 127	0.1	9 890	1 026	31	141	50	201	4 390	NA	31.8
1530	Saraland	11 751	NA	NA	10 838	789	101	21	2	58	4 494	9 695	29.5
1535	Satsuma	5 194	NA	NA	4 932	226	29	4	3	16	1 815	9 704	15.5
1540	Scottsboro	13 786	14 758	-6.6	12 876	792	57	51	10	86	5 909	9 414	120.3
1555	Selma	23 755	26 684	-11.0	9 739	13 882	22	102	10	68	9 556	7 662	36.0
1557	Selmont-West Selmont CDP	3 823	NA	NA	644	3 165	2	10	2	12	1 579	NA	8.5
1565	Sheffield	10 380	11 903	-12.8	7 864	2 455	29	24	8	39	4 709	9 283	17.0
1586	Smiths CDP	3 456	NA	NA	3 095	336	5	16	4	27	1 331	NA	41.6
1595	Southside	5 580	NA	NA	5 535	8	17	9	11	36	1 998	9 653	48.7
1602	Spanish Fort CDP	3 732	NA	NA	3 495	205	26	5	1	20	1 673	NA	24.4
1630	Sumiton	2 604	NA	NA	2 465	130	1	6	2	4	1 077	8 218	12.9
1645	Sylacauga	12 520	12 708	-1.5	9 380	3 071	42	20	7	41	5 422	8 796	46.2
1655	Talladega	18 175	19 113	-4.9	10 607	7 429	31	59	49	355	6 463	6 766	56.5
1665	Tallassee	5 112	NA	NA	4 352	738	10	10	2	19	2 302	8 031	25.0
1670	Tarrant	8 046	NA	NA	6 994	1 026	16	5	5	36	3 461	8 831	16.5
1674	Theodore CDP	6 509	NA	NA	4 828	1 640	22	18	1	21	2 451	NA	31.7
1680	Thomasville	4 301	NA	NA	2 491	1 800	3	7	0	5	1 752	8 230	22.1
1687	Tillmans Corner CDP	17 988	15 941	12.8	17 496	245	104	116	27	156	6 898	NA	54.9
1710	Troy	13 051	12 945	0.8	8 555	4 404	30	51	11	59	5 150	7 325	61.2
1715	Trussville	8 266	NA	NA	8 147	89	8	19	3	37	2 977	10 353	38.4
1720	Tuscaloosa	77 759	75 211	3.4	48 871	27 598	106	1 043	141	602	31 194	8 284	122.0

1. Codes shown are 2-digit FIPS codes for states; 4-digit census place codes for places; and 3-digit FIPS county codes followed by 3-digit census MCD codes for minor civil divisions (MCDs). MCD names are followed by county names in parentheses. 2. Hispanic persons may be of any race. 3. Dry land or land partially or temporarily covered by water.

State/ Place/ MCD[1] code	Place	Population 1990	Places of 10,000 or more: 1980	Places of 10,000 or more: Percent change, 1980–1990	Race: White	Race: Black	Race: Am. Indian, Eskimo Aleut	Race: Asian & Pacific Islander	Race: Other race	Hispanic[2]	Total housing units, 1990	Per capita income, 1985 (Dollars)	Land area,[3] 1990 (Sq. Km.)
		1	2	3	4	5	6	7	8	9	10	11	12
	ALABAMA—Con.												
1725	Tuscumbia	8 413	NA	NA	6 577	1 810	14	10	2	16	3 593	8 464	18.6
1730	Tuskegee	12 257	13 327	-8.0	329	11 849	12	57	10	37	4 713	6 578	39.4
1731	Underwood-Petersville CDP	3 092	NA	NA	2 970	102	7	6	7	10	1 168	NA	15.6
1735	Union Springs	3 975	NA	NA	1 020	2 949	2	3	1	36	1 695	6 457	17.8
1743	Valley	8 173	NA	NA	6 741	1 409	16	0	7	24	3 482	8 612	16.5
1755	Vestavia Hills	19 749	15 722	25.6	19 176	223	14	294	42	149	8 034	21 156	22.9
1785	Warrior	3 280	NA	NA	2 684	587	3	5	1	6	1 330	7 614	15.1
1800	Weaver	2 715	NA	NA	2 479	147	13	66	10	44	1 053	9 077	6.3
1816	West End-Cobb Town CDP	4 034	NA	NA	3 028	978	19	8	1	12	1 629	NA	13.1
1825	Wetumpka	4 670	NA	NA	3 178	1 455	13	21	3	8	1 642	7 403	18.1
1840	Winfield	3 689	NA	NA	3 467	210	1	11	0	15	1 629	8 488	29.9
1850	York	3 160	NA	NA	955	2 201	2	2	0	15	1 245	8 239	15.7
02	ALASKA	550 043	401 851	36.9	415 492	22 451	85 698	19 728	6 674	17 803	232 608	13 650	1 477 267.5
0010	Adak Station CDP	4 633	NA	NA	3 655	501	55	331	91	255	1 051	NA	316.8
0140	Anchorage	226 338	174 431	29.8	182 736	14 544	14 569	10 910	3 579	9 258	94 153	15 517	4 396.9
0250	Barrow	3 469	NA	NA	906	28	2 217	277	41	100	1 184	NA	48.7
0310	Bethel	4 674	NA	NA	1 551	39	2 986	81	17	59	1 624	11 460	114.7
0790	College CDP	11 249	NA	NA	9 479	290	950	421	109	285	4 255	NA	41.2
0975	Eielson AFB CDP	5 251	NA	NA	4 276	642	48	154	131	278	1 415	NA	31.8
1080	Fairbanks	30 843	22 645	36.2	22 316	3 997	2 830	1 013	687	1 656	12 537	13 211	81.1
1370	Homer	3 660	NA	NA	3 463	8	130	54	5	71	1 673	NA	28.3
1510	Juneau	26 751	19 528	37.0	21 570	292	3 462	1 154	273	749	10 638	17 070	6 717.3
1630	Kenai	6 327	NA	NA	5 604	37	535	96	55	176	2 681	13 847	67.9
1650	Ketchikan	8 263	NA	NA	6 471	48	1 296	401	47	205	3 360	13 691	7.9
1750	Kodiak	6 365	NA	NA	4 028	47	811	1 282	197	407	2 177	13 830	8.4
1800	Kotzebue	2 751	NA	NA	635	8	2 067	39	2	29	911	NA	69.8
2327	Nikiski CDP	2 743	NA	NA	2 551	4	168	19	1	36	1 045	NA	72.8
2370	Nome	3 500	NA	NA	1 574	6	1 824	49	47	95	1 334	NA	35.7
2510	Palmer	2 866	NA	NA	2 539	66	220	26	15	67	1 169	NA	9.5
2585	Petersburg	3 207	NA	NA	2 777	3	334	73	20	66	1 222	13 869	112.4
2960	Seward	2 699	NA	NA	2 173	69	410	37	10	56	1 010	NA	39.9
3040	Sitka	8 588	NA	NA	6 359	39	1 797	333	60	209	3 222	13 899	7 463.0
3070	Soldotna	3 482	NA	NA	3 267	11	158	37	9	94	1 460	NA	18.0
3140	Sterling CDP	3 802	NA	NA	3 673	1	79	33	16	38	2 179	NA	220.9
3430	Unalaska	3 089	NA	NA	1 917	63	259	593	257	394	682	NA	270.1
3470	Valdez	4 068	NA	NA	3 609	38	239	128	54	129	1 499	14 778	566.7
3520	Wasilla	4 028	NA	NA	3 728	24	212	36	28	79	1 723	NA	29.0
04	ARIZONA	3 665 228	2 716 598	34.9	2 963 186	110 524	203 527	55 206	332 785	688 338	1 659 430	10 561	294 333.5
0005	Ajo CDP	2 919	NA	NA	2 492	4	293	18	112	1 256	1 809	NA	14.0
0007	Apache Junction	18 100	NA	NA	17 447	69	150	64	370	1 018	12 760	9 188	42.6
0013	Avondale	16 169	NA	NA	9 528	747	217	203	5 474	8 271	5 579	6 931	57.3
0014	Avra Valley CDP	3 403	NA	NA	2 958	40	74	14	317	526	1 343	NA	120.3
0020	Benson	3 824	NA	NA	3 704	12	35	14	59	831	1 872	8 499	22.0
0022	Big Park CDP	3 024	NA	NA	2 983	4	20	16	1	98	1 924	NA	11.9
0025	Bisbee	6 288	NA	NA	5 967	30	59	24	208	2 292	3 181	8 595	12.5
0030	Buckeye town	5 038	NA	NA	3 791	204	111	44	888	1 389	2 605	9 404	48.3
0031	Bullhead City	21 951	10 364	111.8	20 915	115	176	158	587	1 426	13 453	9 846	111.6
0036	Camp Verde town	6 243	NA	NA	5 702	13	433	9	86	293	2 839	8 995	110.3
0041	Casa Grande	19 082	14 971	27.5	14 524	984	628	154	2 792	6 582	7 404	8 226	56.4
0043	Catalina CDP	4 864	NA	NA	4 198	28	44	24	570	775	1 923	NA	35.9
0044	Cave Creek town	2 925	NA	NA	2 871	5	15	10	24	152	1 363	NA	64.2
0046	Central Heights-Midland City CDP	2 969	NA	NA	2 509	3	24	1	432	669	1 267	NA	5.7
0050	Chandler	90 533	29 720	204.6	77 114	2 321	1 105	2 153	7 840	15 642	34 967	10 004	123.2
0052	Chinle CDP	5 059	NA	NA	298	16	4 711	3	31	58	1 521	NA	43.2
0053	Chino Valley town	4 837	NA	NA	4 695	11	60	12	59	199	2 156	6 817	48.1
0065	Clifton town	2 840	NA	NA	2 278	5	56	8	493	1 744	1 246	7 452	38.5
0070	Coolidge	6 927	NA	NA	4 398	567	389	64	1 509	2 307	2 806	7 034	12.4
0073	Cottonwood	5 918	NA	NA	5 513	14	77	33	281	740	2 768	7 423	13.7
0074	Cottonwood-Verde Village CDP	7 037	NA	NA	6 814	5	55	31	132	361	3 200	NA	22.0
0078	Dewey-Humboldt CDP	3 640	NA	NA	3 563	4	10	9	54	129	1 937	NA	64.6
0080	Douglas	12 822	13 058	-1.8	9 163	137	42	60	3 420	10 703	4 327	6 643	12.3
0090	Eagar town	4 025	NA	NA	3 683	2	177	8	155	524	1 504	6 415	26.4
0100	El Mirage town	5 001	NA	NA	1 764	131	20	10	3 076	3 948	2 117	4 510	25.0
0105	Eloy	7 211	NA	NA	2 224	566	404	36	3 981	4 862	2 333	5 183	179.5
0115	Flagstaff	45 857	34 743	32.0	36 519	1 135	4 210	657	3 336	6 972	16 313	8 670	163.8
0120	Florence town	7 510	NA	NA	5 637	746	312	39	776	2 359	2 143	5 397	15.0
0121	Flowing Wells CDP	14 013	NA	NA	12 993	64	151	75	730	1 721	6 657	NA	9.1
0122	Fort Defiance CDP	4 489	NA	NA	256	8	4 201	12	12	50	1 265	NA	13.9
0123	Fortuna Foothills CDP	7 737	NA	NA	7 437	40	33	37	190	495	6 957	NA	122.6
0124	Fountain Hills town	10 030	NA	NA	9 842	41	59	56	32	257	5 061	NA	43.3

1. Codes shown are 2-digit FIPS codes for states; 4-digit census place codes for places; and 3-digit FIPS county codes followed by 3-digit census MCD codes for minor civil divisions (MCDs). MCD names are followed by county names in parentheses. 2. Hispanic persons may be of any race. 3. Dry land or land partially or temporarily covered by water.

State/ Place/ MCD[1] code	Place	Population: 1990	Population: Places of 10,000 or more: 1980	Population: Places of 10,000 or more: Percent change, 1980–1990	Population characteristics, 1990: Race: White	Race: Black	Race: Am. Indian, Eskimo Aleut	Race: Asian & Pacific Islander	Race: Other race	Hispanic[2]	Total housing units, 1990	Per capita income, 1985 (Dollars)	Land area,[3] 1990 (Sq. Km.)
		1	2	3	4	5	6	7	8	9	10	11	12
	ARIZONA—Con.												
0135	Gilbert town	29 188	NA	NA	26 362	464	141	500	1 721	3 382	10 655	8 917	70.3
0140	Glendale	148 134	97 172	52.4	125 884	4 455	1 402	3 150	13 243	22 911	61 218	10 925	135.2
0145	Globe	6 062	NA	NA	5 069	34	170	53	736	2 005	2 615	8 324	21.6
0147	Golden Valley CDP	2 619	NA	NA	2 511	5	32	19	52	107	1 264	NA	72.6
0150	Goodyear	6 258	NA	NA	4 470	452	163	92	1 081	1 780	1 607	11 491	297.9
0157	Green Valley CDP	13 231	NA	NA	12 957	30	41	41	162	382	10 047	NA	57.5
0158	Guadalupe town	5 458	NA	NA	1 382	21	2 139	10	1 906	3 971	1 171	4 148	1.9
0165	Holbrook	4 686	NA	NA	2 900	138	955	51	642	1 065	1 814	7 452	15.7
0178	Kayenta CDP	4 372	NA	NA	491	7	3 839	19	16	75	1 294	NA	28.6
0185	Kingman	12 722	NA	NA	11 923	36	224	145	394	949	5 473	9 294	53.8
0188	Lake Havasu City	24 363	15 909	53.1	23 850	59	147	113	194	892	12 845	11 060	111.5
0191	Litchfield Park	3 303	NA	NA	3 171	21	9	82	20	106	1 433	NA	7.6
0195	Luke AFB CDP	4 371	NA	NA	3 370	588	31	207	175	410	1 192	NA	9.5
0215	Mesa	288 091	152 453	89.0	259 472	5 342	3 018	4 355	15 904	31 357	140 468	10 889	281.3
0227	Mohave Valley CDP	6 962	NA	NA	6 419	24	399	35	85	497	4 397	NA	117.9
0232	New Kingman-Butler CDP	11 627	NA	NA	11 182	31	128	48	238	618	5 148	NA	37.4
0235	Nogales	19 489	15 683	24.3	13 642	76	39	70	5 662	17 924	5 537	6 765	54.0
0237	Oracle CDP	3 043	NA	NA	2 829	0	28	4	182	1 084	1 185	NA	24.8
0238	Oro Valley town	6 670	NA	NA	6 449	37	26	65	93	431	3 576	NA	61.4
0240	Page	6 598	NA	NA	4 810	35	1 534	51	168	329	2 307	11 847	43.0
0242	Paradise Valley town	11 671	11 085	5.3	11 377	31	36	178	49	237	4 750	28 387	39.4
0245	Parker town	2 897	NA	NA	1 956	57	664	46	174	723	1 120	9 718	56.9
0252	Payson town	8 377	NA	NA	8 208	7	47	29	86	259	4 792	8 348	33.8
0255	Peoria	50 618	12 251	313.2	44 012	1 107	300	733	4 466	7 856	21 944	10 241	159.2
0260	Phoenix	983 403	789 704	24.5	803 332	51 053	18 225	16 303	94 490	197 103	422 036	11 363	1 087.6
0262	Picture Rocks CDP	4 026	NA	NA	3 794	15	53	10	154	430	1 597	NA	142.3
0280	Prescott	26 455	20 055	31.9	25 198	128	330	149	650	1 889	13 393	9 991	83.9
0282	Prescott Valley town	8 858	NA	NA	8 553	40	68	38	159	503	3 913	NA	42.8
0284	Queen Creek town	2 667	NA	NA	1 935	31	23	20	658	784	769	NA	28.3
0290	Safford	7 359	NA	NA	6 337	131	70	51	770	2 781	2 857	7 163	18.3
0295	St. Johns	3 294	NA	NA	2 587	10	128	10	559	744	1 237	7 042	17.1
0297	San Carlos CDP	2 918	NA	NA	84	11	2 804	1	18	48	875	NA	23.1
0299	San Luis	4 212	NA	NA	3 891	0	2	11	308	4 196	998	NA	5.3
0300	San Manuel CDP	4 009	NA	NA	3 623	16	42	2	326	1 903	1 676	NA	54.1
0305	Scottsdale	130 069	88 412	47.1	124 895	992	799	1 600	1 783	6 203	69 028	16 773	477.5
0307	Sedona	7 720	NA	NA	7 607	26	31	36	20	405	4 658	NA	50.9
0309	Sells CDP	2 750	NA	NA	96	4	2 634	4	12	105	778	NA	24.3
0313	Show Low	5 019	NA	NA	4 738	12	174	23	72	299	3 116	7 357	71.2
0315	Sierra Vista	32 983	24 937	32.3	25 518	3 949	204	1 722	1 590	3 884	12 927	9 434	368.7
0316	Sierra Vista Southeast CDP	9 237	NA	NA	8 481	163	62	185	346	1 144	3 814	NA	295.8
0320	Snowflake town	3 679	NA	NA	3 228	11	402	5	33	210	1 158	6 533	76.9
0325	Somerton	5 282	NA	NA	4 250	12	24	42	954	5 044	1 352	3 898	2.1
0340	South Tucson	5 093	NA	NA	1 471	126	502	19	2 975	4 244	1 861	4 886	2.6
0351	Sun City CDP	38 126	40 576	-6.0	37 960	63	26	49	28	191	27 353	NA	38.1
0352	Sun City West CDP	15 997	NA	NA	15 897	59	12	27	2	33	10 367	NA	23.8
0353	Sun Lakes CDP	6 578	NA	NA	6 517	31	13	11	6	66	4 356	NA	13.5
0355	Superior town	3 468	NA	NA	2 430	2	25	10	1 001	2 432	1 730	8 488	4.6
0356	Surprise town	7 122	NA	NA	3 896	113	37	9	3 067	3 916	5 256	5 069	161.3
0360	Tempe	141 865	106 743	32.9	123 209	4 542	1 877	5 748	6 489	15 430	61 452	12 419	102.4
0365	Thatcher town	3 763	NA	NA	3 589	37	73	23	41	742	1 263	6 055	8.2
0370	Tolleson	4 434	NA	NA	1 728	20	57	43	2 586	3 308	1 359	6 343	12.9
0378	Tuba City CDP	7 323	NA	NA	593	19	6 647	36	28	112	2 226	NA	28.1
0380	Tucson	405 390	330 537	22.6	305 055	17 366	6 464	8 901	67 604	118 595	183 338	9 430	404.8
0381	Tucson Estates CDP	2 662	NA	NA	2 637	3	5	9	8	55	1 866	NA	3.9
0382	Valencia West CDP	3 277	NA	NA	2 442	50	39	7	739	1 501	1 066	NA	29.1
0387	Whiteriver CDP	3 775	NA	NA	131	4	3 636	2	2	44	1 064	NA	28.4
0390	Wickenburg town	4 515	NA	NA	4 332	2	52	17	112	281	2 595	10 651	28.5
0395	Willcox	3 122	NA	NA	2 551	18	12	17	524	962	1 371	7 126	15.0
0400	Williams	2 532	NA	NA	2 254	102	49	34	93	669	1 118	NA	74.2
0403	Window Rock CDP	3 306	NA	NA	141	1	3 147	14	3	26	990	NA	13.4
0410	Winslow	8 190	NA	NA	5 240	304	1 929	81	636	2 176	3 108	8 092	30.4
0412	Youngtown town	2 542	NA	NA	2 424	25	2	4	87	169	1 669	NA	3.3
0415	Yuma	54 923	42 433	29.4	40 103	2 088	603	929	11 200	19 577	22 689	9 088	56.6
05	ARKANSAS	2 350 725	2 286 358	2.8	1 944 744	373 912	12 773	12 530	6 766	19 876	1 000 667	8 389	134 875.1
0025	Alma	2 959	NA	NA	2 846	81	16	6	10	26	1 221	7 731	10.2
0065	Arkadelphia	10 014	10 005	0.1	7 319	2 570	30	55	40	81	3 742	8 560	17.9
0075	Ashdown	5 150	NA	NA	3 559	1 519	47	6	19	49	2 049	9 064	18.4
0090	Atkins	2 834	NA	NA	2 776	26	23	6	3	4	1 176	7 445	15.9
0095	Augusta	2 759	NA	NA	1 439	1 318	2	0	0	3	1 162	5 946	5.7
0105	Bald Knob	2 653	NA	NA	2 461	159	20	13	0	6	1 143	6 906	9.6
0115	Barling	4 078	NA	NA	3 663	48	87	248	32	76	1 499	8 740	27.6

1. Codes shown are 2-digit FIPS codes for states; 4-digit census place codes for places; and 3-digit FIPS county codes followed by 3-digit census MCD codes for minor civil divisions (MCDs). MCD names are followed by county names in parentheses. 2. Hispanic persons may be of any race. 3. Dry land or land partially or temporarily covered by water.

State/ Place/ MCD[1] code	Place	Population: 1990	Places of 10,000 or more: 1980	Places of 10,000 or more: Percent change, 1980–1990	Race: White	Race: Black	Race: Am. Indian, Eskimo Aleut	Race: Asian & Pacific Islander	Race: Other race	Hispanic[2]	Total housing units, 1990	Per capita income, 1985 (Dollars)	Land area,[3] 1990 (Sq. Km.)
		1	2	3	4	5	6	7	8	9	10	11	12
	ARKANSAS—Con.												
0125	Batesville	9 187	NA	NA	8 602	482	23	56	24	69	3 947	8 982	27.0
0150	Beebe	4 455	NA	NA	4 153	264	17	17	4	29	1 799	7 052	10.9
0154	Bella Vista CDP	9 083	NA	NA	9 031	7	34	9	2	25	5 391	NA	165.9
0170	Benton	18 177	17 685	2.8	17 244	791	69	38	35	113	7 453	9 245	40.6
0175	Bentonville	11 257	NA	NA	10 975	27	102	98	55	161	4 482	8 641	37.9
0180	Berryville	3 212	NA	NA	3 155	0	26	21	10	41	1 468	8 930	10.6
0230	Blytheville	22 906	23 844	-3.9	13 757	8 765	79	211	94	333	8 902	7 393	30.0
0245	Booneville	3 804	NA	NA	3 767	0	23	6	8	22	1 689	7 367	10.0
0270	Brinkley	4 234	NA	NA	2 253	1 970	6	4	1	7	1 768	5 373	11.9
0280	Bryant	5 269	NA	NA	5 163	63	11	25	7	16	1 935	11 549	12.0
0300	Cabot	8 319	NA	NA	8 174	17	58	55	15	88	3 114	8 870	28.1
0315	Camden	14 380	15 356	-6.4	8 422	5 904	17	33	4	37	6 390	8 506	40.0
0383	Cherokee Village-Hidden Valley CDP	4 416	NA	NA	4 377	7	30	2	0	10	2 891	NA	80.3
0405	Clarksville	5 833	NA	NA	5 405	286	19	61	62	103	2 597	8 023	38.5
0440	Conway	26 481	20 375	30.0	23 521	2 658	84	173	45	143	10 139	9 180	62.4
0445	Corning	3 323	NA	NA	3 301	2	13	6	1	9	1 504	7 536	4.9
0475	Crossett	6 282	NA	NA	4 269	1 978	8	24	3	29	2 530	9 969	14.0
0500	Dardanelle	3 722	NA	NA	3 428	246	25	14	9	44	1 662	7 396	7.6
0540	De Queen	4 633	NA	NA	3 762	334	87	9	441	506	1 949	7 952	14.4
0545	Dermott	4 715	NA	NA	1 237	3 462	3	11	2	34	1 801	5 100	7.3
0560	De Witt	3 553	NA	NA	2 784	753	9	5	2	5	1 564	7 130	6.6
0585	Dumas	5 520	NA	NA	2 612	2 858	15	19	16	23	2 049	6 033	7.6
0600	Earle	3 393	NA	NA	1 140	2 237	6	9	1	22	1 300	5 034	8.4
0615	El Dorado	23 146	25 270	-8.4	14 277	8 727	35	74	33	110	10 269	9 801	40.5
0635	England	3 351	NA	NA	2 335	1 006	6	0	4	12	1 286	7 504	4.8
0645	Eudora	3 155	NA	NA	719	2 420	4	4	8	14	1 262	4 311	7.9
0670	Fayetteville	42 099	36 608	15.0	39 206	1 580	481	657	175	603	18 835	9 358	104.2
0685	Fordyce	4 729	NA	NA	2 571	2 133	7	5	13	21	1 966	8 542	14.5
0695	Forrest City	13 364	13 803	-3.2	5 682	7 572	14	68	28	93	5 195	6 972	35.8
0700	Fort Smith	72 798	71 626	1.6	62 790	5 590	1 001	2 981	436	1 032	33 054	11 118	121.0
0773	Gibson CDP	4 288	NA	NA	4 039	162	40	21	26	71	1 479	NA	20.5
0797	Gosnell	3 783	NA	NA	3 262	401	20	76	24	51	1 381	6 507	3.8
0813	Gravel Ridge CDP	3 846	NA	NA	3 440	352	12	26	16	69	1 573	NA	6.6
0845	Greenwood	3 984	NA	NA	3 873	3	93	12	3	25	1 526	8 770	22.1
0880	Hamburg	3 098	NA	NA	2 107	979	1	2	9	20	1 254	6 426	8.4
0905	Harrison	9 922	NA	NA	9 834	0	58	14	16	69	4 584	9 010	22.6
0940	Heber Springs	5 628	NA	NA	5 599	2	17	9	1	25	2 654	8 748	16.4
0945	Helena	7 491	NA	NA	2 700	4 744	8	32	7	36	2 987	6 333	22.5
0975	Hope	9 643	10 290	-6.3	5 667	3 860	24	29	63	128	4 207	7 380	23.4
0985	Hot Springs	32 462	35 781	-9.3	26 978	5 020	160	137	167	434	17 543	8 971	74.7
0987	Hot Springs Village CDP	6 361	NA	NA	6 324	14	17	6	0	16	3 761	NA	99.1
1000	Hoxie	2 676	NA	NA	2 643	21	12	0	0	14	1 116	5 277	8.9
1045	Jacksonville	29 101	27 589	5.5	23 113	4 944	138	670	236	670	10 890	8 515	50.9
1070	Jonesboro	46 535	31 530	47.6	42 238	3 701	156	381	59	247	19 537	10 110	189.8
1140	Lake Village	2 791	NA	NA	1 098	1 645	8	26	14	25	1 105	7 012	5.0
1195	Little Rock	175 795	158 461	10.9	113 707	59 742	449	1 529	368	1 337	80 995	11 923	266.4
1210	Lonoke	4 022	NA	NA	2 945	1 048	22	3	4	17	1 616	8 721	6.5
1250	McGehee	4 997	NA	NA	3 197	1 764	15	16	5	21	2 048	8 922	15.4
1285	Magnolia	11 151	11 909	-6.4	7 265	3 800	26	48	12	44	4 689	9 197	21.9
1290	Malvern	9 256	10 163	-8.9	6 865	2 338	29	17	7	37	4 244	7 764	18.8
1300	Manila	2 635	NA	NA	2 607	6	10	3	9	17	1 133	7 347	8.3
1310	Marianna	5 910	NA	NA	1 845	4 010	4	40	11	35	2 237	5 509	9.3
1315	Marion	4 391	NA	NA	4 032	318	2	18	21	45	1 568	10 135	9.4
1320	Marked Tree	3 100	NA	NA	2 076	1 014	6	4	0	8	1 246	7 853	6.0
1337	Maumelle	6 714	NA	NA	6 497	140	28	36	13	66	2 668	NA	22.8
1355	Mena	5 475	NA	NA	5 396	0	45	20	14	44	2 619	7 466	17.4
1380	Monticello	8 116	NA	NA	5 779	2 303	8	19	7	33	3 267	7 446	25.5
1395	Morrilton	6 551	NA	NA	5 386	1 121	24	11	9	45	2 891	8 096	21.1
1405	Mountain Home	9 027	NA	NA	8 974	0	28	14	11	47	4 561	10 685	17.9
1435	Nashville	4 639	NA	NA	3 167	1 394	14	56	8	37	1 908	7 774	11.1
1445	Newport	7 459	NA	NA	5 660	1 763	15	13	8	26	3 179	8 533	33.2
1473	North Crossett CDP	3 358	NA	NA	3 172	160	9	7	10	35	1 386	NA	25.7
1475	North Little Rock	61 741	64 288	-4.0	46 502	14 584	202	253	200	516	27 255	10 468	102.9
1530	Osceola	8 930	NA	NA	4 928	3 933	22	20	27	54	3 299	7 078	14.9
1545	Ozark	3 330	NA	NA	3 281	18	18	4	9	39	1 518	7 810	16.3
1560	Paragould	18 540	15 248	21.6	18 427	17	37	34	25	95	7 904	8 491	75.1
1570	Paris	3 674	NA	NA	3 589	55	12	4	14	27	1 654	7 705	11.0
1577	Parkers-Iron Springs CDP	3 611	NA	NA	3 231	335	22	14	9	14	1 377	NA	20.8
1610	Piggott	3 777	NA	NA	3 768	3	2	0	4	21	1 777	9 253	9.3
1615	Pine Bluff	57 140	56 636	0.9	26 084	30 583	103	280	90	244	23 189	7 826	109.8
1621	Piney CDP	2 500	NA	NA	2 420	44	20	3	13	35	1 300	NA	17.0
1640	Pocahontas	6 151	NA	NA	6 012	93	27	11	8	27	2 736	8 107	17.5
1680	Prescott	3 673	NA	NA	2 184	1 471	11	0	7	38	1 567	8 273	12.3

1. Codes shown are 2-digit FIPS codes for states; 4-digit census place codes for places; and 3-digit FIPS county codes followed by 3-digit census MCD codes for minor civil divisions (MCDs). MCD names are followed by county names in parentheses. 2. Hispanic persons may be of any race. 3. Dry land or land partially or temporarily covered by water.

State/ Place/ MCD[1] code	Place	Population: 1990	Population: Places of 10,000 or more: 1980	Population: Places of 10,000 or more: Percent change, 1980–1990	Population characteristics, 1990: Race: White	Race: Black	Race: Am. Indian, Eskimo Aleut	Race: Asian & Pacific Islander	Race: Other race	Hispanic[2]	Total housing units, 1990	Per capita income, 1985 (Dollars)	Land area,[3] 1990 (Sq. Km.)
		1	2	3	4	5	6	7	8	9	10	11	12
	ARKANSAS—Con.												
1741	Rockwell CDP	2 514	NA	NA	2 472	18	9	9	6	20	1 266	NA	8.2
1745	Rogers	24 692	17 429	41.7	24 128	16	224	191	133	460	10 291	10 205	57.5
1770	Russellville	21 260	14 031	51.5	19 897	1 000	139	155	69	237	8 653	9 601	66.4
1791	Salem CDP	2 950	NA	NA	2 893	17	13	22	5	18	1 008	NA	9.5
1805	Searcy	15 180	13 612	11.5	14 265	717	55	70	73	167	5 572	8 483	35.3
1815	Sheridan	3 098	NA	NA	3 061	2	15	10	10	30	1 279	9 890	8.4
1825	Sherwood	18 893	10 586	78.5	17 691	992	65	88	57	206	7 375	11 529	30.3
1845	Siloam Springs	8 151	NA	NA	7 498	29	399	37	188	282	3 241	8 938	18.3
1875	Springdale	29 941	23 440	27.7	29 095	33	338	292	183	446	12 008	9 699	76.8
1905	Stuttgart	10 420	10 941	-4.8	7 222	3 139	29	22	8	36	4 408	9 578	14.5
1945	Texarkana	22 631	21 459	5.5	15 211	7 184	65	120	51	172	9 854	8 423	43.0
1970	Trumann	6 304	NA	NA	6 126	143	11	10	14	36	2 636	6 908	10.5
2005	Van Buren	14 979	12 020	24.6	14 120	241	237	327	54	250	5 763	7 936	38.0
2040	Waldron	3 024	NA	NA	2 977	0	28	11	8	20	1 405	7 807	10.1
2050	Walnut Ridge	4 388	NA	NA	4 311	52	19	4	2	16	1 982	9 138	6.4
2060	Warren	6 455	NA	NA	3 821	2 588	3	2	41	75	2 819	6 620	16.9
3000	West Helena	9 695	11 367	-14.7	4 645	5 013	14	14	9	98	3 671	6 460	11.5
3005	West Memphis	28 259	28 138	0.4	16 090	11 911	45	148	65	142	10 505	8 141	37.2
3023	White Hall	3 849	NA	NA	3 606	215	9	10	9	18	1 391	9 148	15.2
3085	Wynne	8 187	NA	NA	5 434	2 700	17	32	4	57	3 079	8 645	17.2
06	CALIFORNIA	29 760 021	23 667 764	25.7	20 524 327	2 208 801	242 164	2 845 659	3 939 070	7 687 938	11 182 882	11 885	403 970.3
0003	Adelanto	8 517	NA	NA	6 034	1 191	132	355	805	1 475	3 227	NA	95.5
0007	Agoura Hills	20 390	NA	NA	18 377	238	64	1 396	315	1 243	6 927	14 670	21.2
0010	Alameda	76 459	63 852	19.7	53 454	5 140	534	14 717	2 614	6 950	30 520	13 494	27.8
0015	Alamo CDP	12 277	NA	NA	11 467	72	36	637	65	474	4 337	NA	48.4
0020	Albany	16 327	15 130	7.9	11 543	982	119	3 193	490	1 324	7 468	12 711	4.4
0025	Alhambra	82 106	64 615	27.1	33 543	1 643	351	31 313	15 256	29 626	29 604	10 363	19.7
0027	Aliso Viejo CDP	7 612	NA	NA	6 560	127	30	620	275	940	3 884	NA	25.4
0032	Alondra Park CDP	12 215	12 096	1.0	6 896	1 081	77	2 334	1 827	3 362	4 290	NA	4.1
0035	Alpine CDP	9 695	NA	NA	9 180	48	91	119	257	762	3 820	NA	67.6
0040	Altadena CDP	42 658	40 510	5.3	20 892	16 551	218	1 786	3 211	6 019	15 164	NA	22.5
0047	Alta Sierra CDP	5 709	NA	NA	5 575	17	30	46	41	218	2 327	NA	21.6
0050	Alturas	3 231	NA	NA	2 975	13	123	21	99	212	1 413	9 157	5.7
0067	American Canyon CDP	7 706	NA	NA	5 595	455	71	1 227	358	781	2 857	NA	9.7
0070	Anaheim	266 406	219 311	21.5	190 309	6 780	1 425	25 018	42 874	83 755	93 177	12 155	114.7
0075	Anderson	8 299	NA	NA	7 775	62	290	58	114	393	3 234	7 176	15.8
0083	Angwin CDP	3 503	NA	NA	2 867	90	17	385	144	353	867	NA	12.7
0085	Antioch	62 195	42 683	45.7	53 130	1 626	691	3 005	3 743	9 719	22 973	11 052	50.7
0090	Apple Valley town	46 079	14 305	222.1	39 980	1 778	481	1 138	2 702	5 813	16 672	NA	174.1
0092	Aptos CDP	9 061	NA	NA	8 522	68	50	232	189	572	4 309	NA	21.0
0105	Arcadia	48 290	45 994	5.0	34 519	374	174	11 322	1 901	5 146	19 483	17 391	28.2
0110	Arcata	15 197	12 340	23.2	13 923	185	408	409	272	721	6 302	7 937	20.9
0115	Arden-Arcade CDP	92 040	87 570	5.1	82 031	3 577	941	3 686	1 805	6 369	44 235	NA	48.8
0125	Armona CDP	3 122	NA	NA	2 297	108	22	96	599	1 001	978	NA	5.0
0128	Arnold CDP	3 788	NA	NA	3 667	8	50	40	23	123	3 937	NA	50.0
0130	Arroyo Grande	14 378	11 290	27.4	13 330	88	118	524	318	1 298	6 059	11 344	14.7
0135	Artesia	15 464	14 301	8.1	8 653	412	84	2 514	3 801	6 194	4 534	8 922	4.2
0139	Arvin	9 286	NA	NA	3 311	102	72	162	5 639	6 960	2 450	5 284	7.9
0143	Ashland CDP	16 590	13 893	19.4	11 183	2 131	225	1 867	1 184	3 528	7 061	NA	4.8
0145	Atascadero	23 138	16 232	42.5	21 757	260	270	262	589	1 972	8 875	10 525	65.4
0150	Atherton town	7 163	NA	NA	6 514	57	11	523	58	295	2 518	34 915	12.7
0155	Atwater	22 282	17 530	27.1	16 311	2 064	208	1 514	2 185	4 124	7 422	8 294	13.4
0160	Auburn	10 592	NA	NA	10 175	65	116	161	75	454	4 771	12 753	15.8
0162	August CDP	6 376	NA	NA	5 046	60	153	219	898	2 003	2 536	NA	3.4
0165	Avalon	2 918	NA	NA	2 877	5	12	24	0	1 170	1 888	NA	3.1
0170	Avenal	9 770	NA	NA	4 877	1 656	44	38	3 155	5 224	1 776	6 415	49.5
0172	Avocado Heights CDP	14 232	11 721	21.4	8 342	120	89	1 707	3 974	9 596	3 798	NA	6.9
0175	Azusa	41 333	29 380	40.7	27 281	1 586	286	2 742	9 438	22 092	13 232	8 665	23.3
0180	Bakersfield	174 820	105 611	65.5	127 018	16 509	2 005	6 247	23 041	35 854	66 175	11 010	237.9
0185	Baldwin Park	69 330	50 554	37.1	38 523	1 687	509	8 508	20 103	49 051	17 179	6 915	17.1
0190	Banning	20 570	14 020	46.7	14 204	1 955	428	1 520	2 463	4 776	8 278	8 292	47.8
0195	Barstow	21 472	17 690	21.4	14 402	2 245	479	738	3 608	6 726	8 509	9 696	59.3
0200	Bayview-Montalvin CDP	3 988	NA	NA	2 543	626	64	479	276	693	1 203	NA	1.6
0202	Baywood-Los Osos CDP	14 377	10 933	31.5	13 214	118	128	649	268	995	6 097	NA	19.7
0203	Beale AFB CDP	6 912	NA	NA	5 052	1 017	54	512	277	568	1 856	NA	28.1
0205	Beaumont	9 685	NA	NA	8 137	242	216	195	895	2 323	3 718	7 872	19.4
0210	Bell	34 365	25 450	35.0	14 448	360	287	472	18 798	29 583	9 401	6 495	6.6
0215	Bellflower	61 815	53 441	15.7	43 129	3 874	560	6 235	8 017	14 776	24 117	10 598	15.7
0220	Bell Gardens	42 355	34 117	24.1	16 171	223	491	545	24 925	37 075	9 546	4 988	6.5
0225	Belmont	24 127	24 505	-1.5	20 950	384	100	2 414	279	1 755	10 320	17 609	11.7
0235	Benicia	24 437	15 376	58.9	20 533	1 300	184	1 942	478	1 808	9 587	13 718	33.1
0240	Ben Lomond CDP	7 884	NA	NA	7 572	58	53	95	106	344	3 038	NA	36.4

1. Codes shown are 2-digit FIPS codes for states; 4-digit census place codes for places; and 3-digit FIPS county codes followed by 3-digit census MCD codes for minor civil divisions (MCDs). MCD names are followed by county names in parentheses. 2. Hispanic persons may be of any race. 3. Dry land or land partially or temporarily covered by water.

State/ Place/ MCD[1] code	Place	Population: 1990	Population: Places of 10,000 or more: 1980	Population: Places of 10,000 or more: Percent change, 1980–1990	Population characteristics, 1990: Race: White	Race: Black	Race: Am. Indian, Eskimo Aleut	Race: Asian & Pacific Islander	Race: Other race	Hispanic[2]	Total housing units, 1990	Per capita income, 1985 (Dollars)	Land area,[3] 1990 (Sq. Km.)
		1	2	3	4	5	6	7	8	9	10	11	12
	CALIFORNIA—Con.												
0245	Berkeley	102 724	103 328	-0.6	63 833	19 281	653	15 178	3 779	8 589	45 735	12 695	27.1
0248	Bermuda Dunes CDP	4 571	NA	NA	4 144	53	32	118	224	552	2 555	NA	9.3
0250	Beverly Hills	31 971	32 367	-1.2	29 182	543	59	1 745	442	1 725	15 723	33 839	14.7
0252	Big Bear City CDP	4 920	11 151	-55.9	4 744	5	57	41	73	419	4 670	NA	9.1
0255	Big Bear Lake	5 351	NA	NA	5 111	20	70	35	115	420	8 564	9 830	16.2
0275	Bishop	3 475	NA	NA	3 226	8	53	59	129	395	1 779	10 718	4.5
0276	Blackhawk CDP	6 199	NA	NA	5 304	93	19	698	85	243	2 144	NA	23.7
0277	Bloomington CDP	15 116	12 781	18.3	11 125	448	200	202	3 141	5 974	4 745	NA	14.7
0290	Blythe	8 428	NA	NA	4 842	733	87	59	2 707	3 909	2 904	7 567	9.9
0296	Bonadelle Ranchos-Madera Ranchos CD	5 705	NA	NA	4 970	79	52	76	528	870	1 741	NA	28.1
0297	Bonita CDP	12 542	NA	NA	9 924	342	56	1 036	1 184	2 737	4 261	NA	12.8
0304	Bostonia CDP	13 670	NA	NA	12 450	372	139	209	500	1 370	5 445	NA	5.1
0305	Boulder Creek CDP	6 725	NA	NA	6 423	45	61	114	82	337	2 961	NA	31.6
0308	Boyes Hot Springs CDP	5 973	NA	NA	5 371	26	58	118	400	1 131	2 612	NA	3.3
0320	Brawley	18 923	14 946	26.6	13 720	470	119	217	4 397	13 076	6 124	7 515	12.9
0325	Brea	32 873	27 913	17.8	28 586	355	145	2 044	1 743	5 078	12 648	15 006	25.9
0327	Brentwood	7 563	NA	NA	6 182	53	53	131	1 144	2 405	2 628	9 656	12.9
0328	Brisbane	2 952	NA	NA	2 534	52	15	239	112	415	1 382	16 586	8.6
0331	Broadmoor CDP	3 739	NA	NA	2 300	86	12	1 154	187	586	1 274	NA	1.1
0334	Buellton CDP	3 506	NA	NA	2 948	11	26	59	462	660	1 424	NA	12.0
0335	Buena Park	68 784	64 165	7.2	48 760	1 750	497	9 939	7 838	16 879	23 200	11 905	27.5
0340	Burbank	93 643	84 625	10.7	77 342	1 638	501	6 335	7 827	21 172	41 216	13 377	44.9
0341	Burbank CDP	4 902	NA	NA	3 776	130	44	280	672	1 511	2 132	NA	1.7
0345	Burlingame	26 801	26 173	2.4	23 437	261	98	2 376	629	2 731	12 914	17 619	11.3
0350	Burney CDP	3 423	NA	NA	3 250	5	113	16	39	158	1 382	NA	13.4
0365	Calexico	18 633	14 412	29.3	12 628	39	35	483	5 448	17 806	4 832	4 420	10.7
0367	California City	5 955	NA	NA	4 707	682	49	249	268	611	2 384	10 373	478.1
0368	Calimesa CDP	4 647	NA	NA	4 319	2	42	54	230	488	1 959	NA	6.5
0370	Calipatria	2 690	NA	NA	1 841	89	15	43	702	1 995	767	5 095	4.8
0375	Calistoga	4 468	NA	NA	3 913	12	29	40	474	1 098	2 157	9 889	6.7
0379	Camarillo	52 303	37 797	38.4	45 158	839	286	3 319	2 701	6 326	18 731	13 327	47.8
0386	Cambria CDP	5 382	NA	NA	5 160	12	31	59	120	498	3 081	NA	19.1
0387	Cambrian Park CDP	2 998	NA	NA	2 762	15	23	113	85	343	1 072	NA	1.6
0388	Cameron Park CDP	11 897	NA	NA	11 477	43	66	183	128	621	4 759	NA	16.8
0390	Campbell	36 048	27 067	33.2	30 150	712	230	3 419	1 537	3 839	15 860	15 147	14.5
0392	Camp Pendleton North CDP	10 373	NA	NA	7 050	1 896	158	462	807	1 259	1 496	NA	23.4
0393	Camp Pendleton South CDP	11 299	NA	NA	6 828	2 569	186	793	923	1 789	2 176	NA	10.0
0397	Canyon Lake CDP	7 938	NA	NA	7 577	84	48	117	112	506	3 471	NA	6.5
0400	Capitola	10 171	NA	NA	9 314	148	100	303	306	848	5 282	11 690	4.2
0405	Carlsbad	63 126	35 490	77.9	56 664	745	296	2 003	3 418	8 700	27 235	15 640	97.6
0410	Carmel-by-the-Sea	4 239	NA	NA	4 105	13	22	72	27	132	3 324	18 178	2.8
0420	Carmel Valley Village CDP	4 407	NA	NA	4 202	14	27	72	92	248	1 907	NA	50.9
0430	Carmichael CDP	48 702	43 108	13.0	44 968	1 048	405	1 569	712	2 446	20 661	NA	27.9
0433	Carpinteria	13 747	10 835	26.9	11 184	105	105	296	2 057	5 026	5 457	10 855	7.0
0440	Carson	83 995	81 221	3.4	29 160	21 953	496	20 972	11 414	23 413	24 441	10 160	48.8
0444	Casa Conejo CDP	3 286	NA	NA	2 995	26	21	130	114	328	1 013	NA	1.2
0446	Casa de Oro-Mount Helix CDP	30 727	19 651	56.4	28 170	784	125	810	838	2 502	11 108	NA	33.3
0455	Castro Valley CDP	48 619	44 011	10.5	41 778	1 386	253	4 169	1 033	4 463	19 682	NA	34.3
0460	Castroville CDP	5 272	NA	NA	2 234	86	56	310	2 586	4 185	1 320	NA	2.6
0465	Cathedral City	30 085	NA	NA	22 349	666	299	1 092	5 679	11 197	15 229	9 751	49.0
0467	Cayucos CDP	2 960	NA	NA	2 833	10	23	44	50	131	2 133	NA	7.9
0475	Central Valley CDP	4 340	NA	NA	4 028	6	228	21	57	202	1 668	NA	8.0
0480	Ceres	26 314	13 281	98.1	20 513	451	378	1 323	3 649	5 960	9 075	8 483	14.4
0487	Cerritos	53 240	53 020	0.4	22 545	3 960	178	24 057	2 500	6 666	15 364	12 134	22.3
0489	Channel Islands Beach CDP	3 317	NA	NA	3 143	34	31	53	56	218	1 738	NA	1.1
0491	Charter Oak CDP	8 858	NA	NA	6 960	381	55	666	796	2 010	3 382	NA	2.3
0492	Cherryland CDP	11 088	NA	NA	8 028	653	137	715	1 555	3 047	4 585	NA	3.0
0493	Cherry Valley CDP	5 945	NA	NA	5 710	32	49	40	114	623	2 530	NA	28.4
0500	Chico	40 079	26 603	50.7	35 858	731	439	1 602	1 449	3 484	16 295	8 028	58.1
0510	Chino	59 682	40 165	48.6	40 171	5 820	277	2 056	11 358	21 588	16 137	9 519	44.2
0511	Chino Hills CDP	27 608	NA	NA	20 482	1 381	156	3 755	1 834	4 591	9 757	NA	40.2
0515	Chowchilla	5 930	NA	NA	5 186	41	102	62	539	840	2 271	7 205	7.6
0525	Chula Vista	135 163	83 927	61.0	91 563	6 216	863	12 075	24 446	50 376	49 849	10 485	75.1
0528	Citrus CDP	9 481	12 450	-23.8	6 186	343	98	668	2 186	4 557	2 537	NA	2.3
0530	Citrus Heights CDP	107 439	85 911	25.1	97 979	2 473	1 181	3 545	2 261	7 368	43 004	NA	50.5
0535	Claremont	32 503	30 950	5.0	26 730	1 624	133	2 765	1 251	3 334	10 831	14 729	28.5
0537	Clayton	7 317	NA	NA	6 779	73	17	363	85	388	2 361	16 318	10.1
0538	Clearlake	11 804	NA	NA	10 748	514	214	125	203	672	7 315	7 130	26.8
0545	Cloverdale	4 924	NA	NA	4 488	8	78	30	320	791	2 033	10 335	6.0
0550	Clovis	50 323	33 021	52.4	41 855	865	690	2 757	4 156	8 206	18 888	9 450	37.1
0555	Coachella	16 896	NA	NA	5 329	172	89	156	11 150	16 107	3 830	5 181	52.0
0560	Coalinga	8 212	NA	NA	7 093	66	117	118	818	2 593	3 223	9 203	8.1
0580	Colton	40 213	21 310	88.7	23 411	3 506	368	1 717	11 211	20 000	14 767	7 859	36.6

1. Codes shown are 2-digit FIPS codes for states; 4-digit census place codes for places; and 3-digit FIPS county codes followed by 3-digit census MCD codes for minor civil divisions (MCDs). MCD names are followed by county names in parentheses. 2. Hispanic persons may be of any race. 3. Dry land or land partially or temporarily covered by water.

State/ Place/ MCD[1] code	Place	Population			Population characteristics, 1990									
		1990	Places of 10,000 or more		Race						Hispanic[2]	Total housing units, 1990	Per capita income, 1985 (Dollars)	Land area,[3] 1990 (Sq. Km.)
			1980	Percent change, 1980–1990	White	Black	Am. Indian, Eskimo Aleut	Asian & Pacific Islander	Other race					
		1	2	3	4	5	6	7	8		9	10	11	12
	CALIFORNIA—Con.													
0585	Colusa	4 934	NA	NA	4 004	22	112	145	651		1 580	1 896	8 539	3.8
0587	Commerce	12 135	10 510	15.5	4 724	95	107	156	7 053		11 006	3 330	6 481	16.9
0590	Compton	90 454	81 286	11.3	9 571	49 598	287	1 748	29 250		39 510	23 239	6 161	26.3
0595	Concord	111 348	103 255	7.8	93 565	2 624	763	9 668	4 728		12 765	43 715	13 030	76.3
0600	Corcoran	13 364	NA	NA	4 838	2 289	96	77	6 064		6 919	2 714	7 262	14.7
0605	Corning	5 870	NA	NA	5 491	17	100	44	218		882	2 428	6 748	7.5
0610	Corona	76 095	37 791	101.4	57 744	2 102	634	5 399	10 216		23 101	26 538	10 758	73.8
0615	Coronado	26 540	16 859	57.4	22 868	1 819	162	912	779		2 191	9 145	16 357	20.0
0617	Corralitos CDP	2 513	NA	NA	2 327	2	12	39	133		353	967	NA	22.4
0620	Corte Madera town	8 272	NA	NA	7 666	76	16	430	84		348	3 717	17 817	8.2
0625	Costa Mesa	96 357	82 562	16.7	81 238	1 282	475	6 318	7 044		19 319	39 611	13 516	40.3
0628	Cotati	5 714	NA	NA	5 127	148	76	211	152		487	2 433	9 584	4.7
0630	Coto De Caza CDP	2 853	NA	NA	2 682	17	10	103	41		144	1 088	NA	26.3
0633	Country Club CDP	9 325	NA	NA	7 726	238	119	671	571		1 818	3 747	NA	5.0
0635	Covina	43 207	33 751	28.0	34 687	1 776	221	3 281	3 242		11 042	16 110	12 253	17.9
0640	Crescent City	4 380	NA	NA	3 914	27	229	137	73		334	1 779	7 178	3.5
0647	Crescent City North CDP	3 853	NA	NA	3 342	5	223	164	119		253	1 656	NA	5.1
0649	Crestline CDP	8 594	NA	NA	8 245	57	66	67	159		685	6 586	NA	28.1
0652	Crockett CDP	3 228	NA	NA	2 947	36	24	70	151		355	1 552	NA	4.2
0658	Cudahy	22 817	17 984	26.9	6 932	262	216	402	15 005		20 288	5 416	4 831	2.9
0665	Culver City	38 793	38 139	1.7	26 853	4 026	224	4 669	3 021		7 667	16 943	15 482	13.2
0670	Cupertino	40 263	34 015	18.4	29 971	368	134	9 266	524		1 986	16 055	18 880	26.7
0675	Cutler CDP	4 450	NA	NA	2 565	9	8	49	1 819		4 234	936	NA	2.0
0685	Cypress	42 655	40 391	5.6	33 768	871	231	5 841	1 944		5 765	14 715	13 640	17.1
0700	Daly City	92 311	78 594	17.5	36 421	7 106	384	40 466	7 934		20 634	30 162	11 321	19.5
0705	Dana Point	31 896	10 602	200.8	28 579	191	176	718	2 232		4 425	14 666	NA	17.2
0706	Danville	31 306	26 446	18.4	28 673	259	97	2 029	248		1 288	11 466	18 972	45.8
0715	Davis	46 209	36 640	26.1	36 851	1 391	337	6 083	1 547		3 425	18 282	11 091	21.9
0718	Day Valley CDP	2 842	NA	NA	2 588	26	16	66	146		257	998	NA	43.9
0722	Del Aire CDP	8 040	NA	NA	6 411	185	48	702	694		1 884	2 849	NA	2.6
0725	Delano	22 762	16 491	38.0	5 521	534	134	4 903	11 670		14 214	6 482	5 739	22.1
0730	Delhi CDP	3 280	NA	NA	2 020	35	36	110	1 079		1 407	952	NA	4.9
0735	Del Mar	4 860	NA	NA	4 656	36	13	126	29		177	2 514	18 954	4.6
0738	Del Monte Forest CDP	5 069	NA	NA	4 799	11	15	231	13		127	2 739	NA	21.0
0760	Denair CDP	3 693	NA	NA	3 297	3	30	34	329		620	1 202	NA	5.1
0765	Desert Hot Springs	11 668	NA	NA	9 653	466	183	226	1 140		2 378	5 494	9 890	26.5
0771	Diamond Bar	53 672	28 045	91.4	34 165	3 036	190	13 360	2 921		9 136	17 664	NA	39.1
0773	Diamond Springs CDP	2 872	NA	NA	2 772	3	38	13	46		207	1 126	NA	8.6
0775	Dinuba	12 743	NA	NA	7 116	30	85	396	5 116		7 693	3 836	6 215	6.9
0777	Discovery Bay CDP	5 351	NA	NA	5 090	66	34	95	66		275	2 646	NA	17.4
0780	Dixon	10 401	NA	NA	8 461	136	94	275	1 435		2 958	3 555	9 437	9.8
0781	Dixon Lane-Meadow Creek CDP	2 561	NA	NA	2 462	2	31	25	41		164	1 141	NA	8.8
0790	Dos Palos	4 196	NA	NA	2 630	213	31	32	1 290		1 706	1 418	8 949	3.7
0795	Downey	91 444	82 602	10.7	66 323	3 068	586	8 070	13 397		29 569	34 302	12 558	32.2
0800	Duarte	20 688	16 724	23.7	12 717	1 850	130	2 417	3 574		7 160	6 758	9 709	18.7
0802	Dublin	23 229	13 496	72.1	18 060	2 668	197	1 404	900		2 429	6 992	11 597	22.2
0806	Durham CDP	4 784	NA	NA	4 537	6	56	45	140		381	1 766	NA	357.8
0810	Earlimart CDP	5 881	NA	NA	795	82	23	707	4 274		4 804	1 420	NA	5.2
0812	East Compton CDP	7 967	NA	NA	941	3 169	20	155	3 682		4 632	1 848	NA	1.3
0813	East Foothills CDP	14 898	NA	NA	10 090	479	159	1 051	3 119		6 224	4 709	NA	8.1
0814	East Hemet CDP	17 611	14 712	19.7	15 746	99	206	257	1 303		2 595	6 404	NA	10.6
0818	East La Mirada CDP	9 367	NA	NA	8 027	96	43	323	878		2 433	3 405	NA	2.9
0820	East Los Angeles CDP	126 379	110 017	14.9	53 330	1 772	527	1 591	69 159		119 684	30 196	NA	19.5
0827	East Palo Alto	23 451	18 191	28.9	7 431	10 071	154	2 252	3 543		8 527	7 351	8 927	6.6
0828	East Pasadena CDP	5 910	NA	NA	3 871	112	34	915	978		1 738	2 180	NA	3.4
0830	East Porterville CDP	5 790	NA	NA	3 048	37	170	352	2 183		2 646	1 706	NA	8.2
0834	East Richmond Heights CDP	3 266	NA	NA	2 243	558	17	382	66		220	1 364	NA	1.5
0838	East San Gabriel CDP	12 736	NA	NA	8 391	255	42	2 980	1 068		2 426	5 298	NA	4.0
0847	Edwards AFB CDP	7 423	NA	NA	5 775	851	53	518	226		576	2 107	NA	38.7
0850	El Cajon	88 693	73 892	20.0	77 483	2 589	865	2 499	5 257		12 387	34 453	10 048	37.3
0855	El Centro	31 384	23 996	30.8	18 817	1 409	208	784	10 166		20 482	10 180	7 802	16.2
0860	El Cerrito	22 869	22 731	0.6	14 999	2 117	83	5 154	516		1 518	10 311	15 171	9.4
0861	El Cerrito CDP	4 490	NA	NA	3 928	33	19	96	414		1 236	1 298	NA	8.5
0862	El Dorado Hills CDP	6 395	NA	NA	6 132	37	30	134	62		258	2 204	NA	22.2
0864	El Granada CDP	4 426	NA	NA	4 177	27	28	135	59		327	1 697	NA	12.6
0870	Elk Grove CDP	17 483	10 959	59.5	15 798	369	159	735	422		1 680	5 867	NA	10.2
0880	El Monte	106 209	79 494	33.6	66 096	1 047	600	12 489	25 977		76 991	27 167	6 823	24.6
0885	El Paso de Robles (Paso Robles) cit	18 583	NA	NA	15 759	655	260	342	1 567		3 367	7 599	9 670	34.1
0890	El Rio CDP	6 419	NA	NA	3 520	66	122	148	2 563		4 116	1 762	NA	4.2
0895	El Segundo	15 223	13 752	10.7	13 780	154	65	764	460		1 382	7 190	17 417	14.4
0902	El Sobrante CDP	9 852	10 535	-6.5	8 064	543	106	789	350		928	4 011	NA	8.6
0903	El Toro CDP	62 685	38 153	64.3	53 655	1 116	256	5 770	1 888		6 464	22 809	NA	30.5
0904	El Toro Station CDP	6 869	NA	NA	4 796	1 125	89	324	535		974	1 208	NA	15.6

1. Codes shown are 2-digit FIPS codes for states; 4-digit census place codes for places; and 3-digit FIPS county codes followed by 3-digit census MCD codes for minor civil divisions (MCDs). MCD names are followed by county names in parentheses. 2. Hispanic persons may be of any race. 3. Dry land or land partially or temporarily covered by water.

State/ Place/ MCD[1] code	Place	Population			Population characteristics, 1990						Total housing units, 1990	Per capita income, 1985 (Dollars)	Land area,[3] 1990 (Sq. Km.)
			Places of 10,000 or more		Race								
		1990	1980	Percent change, 1980–1990	White	Black	Am. Indian, Eskimo Aleut	Asian & Pacific Islander	Other race	Hispanic[2]			
		1	2	3	4	5	6	7	8	9	10	11	12
	CALIFORNIA—Con.												
0905	El Verano CDP	3 498	NA	NA	3 180	11	52	103	152	426	1 432	NA	3.0
0908	Emerald Lake Hills CDP	3 328	NA	NA	3 150	24	5	123	26	192	1 248	NA	3.1
0910	Emeryville	5 740	NA	NA	3 001	1 325	33	1 068	313	567	3 640	15 498	3.2
0920	Encinitas	55 386	10 796	413.0	49 506	316	246	1 621	3 697	8 446	22 123	NA	46.5
0930	Escalon	4 437	NA	NA	4 093	14	46	41	243	697	1 640	9 446	4.5
0935	Escondido	108 635	64 355	68.8	92 504	1 585	902	4 040	9 604	25 380	42 040	10 428	92.3
0945	Eureka	27 025	24 074	12.3	23 833	387	1 254	1 186	365	1 298	11 781	9 669	24.5
0950	Exeter	7 276	NA	NA	5 621	16	95	135	1 409	1 893	2 651	8 250	5.1
0955	Fairfax town	6 931	NA	NA	6 593	90	42	143	63	337	3 225	15 450	5.4
0960	Fairfield	77 211	58 099	32.9	52 636	10 656	786	8 262	4 871	10 208	26 357	9 996	92.9
0965	Fair Oaks CDP	26 867	22 602	18.9	25 105	379	197	879	307	1 306	10 718	NA	25.6
0970	Fairview CDP	9 045	NA	NA	6 092	1 708	65	856	324	927	3 206	NA	12.6
0980	Fallbrook CDP	22 095	14 006	57.8	17 542	413	142	416	3 582	6 201	7 767	NA	28.2
0986	Farmersville	6 235	NA	NA	3 517	10	98	33	2 577	3 636	1 732	5 011	4.3
0995	Felton CDP	5 350	NA	NA	5 164	37	26	75	48	202	2 348	NA	15.5
1010	Fillmore	11 992	NA	NA	9 046	25	94	104	2 723	7 111	3 528	7 967	6.8
1015	Firebaugh	4 429	NA	NA	1 414	83	32	27	2 873	3 573	1 243	6 423	7.3
1020	Florence-Graham CDP	57 147	48 662	17.4	11 676	13 722	172	213	31 364	44 097	13 488	NA	9.2
1023	Florin CDP	24 330	16 523	47.2	15 336	3 091	298	3 840	1 765	3 326	9 007	NA	14.5
1025	Folsom	29 802	11 003	170.9	25 026	2 949	195	1 031	601	3 245	9 418	10 826	55.5
1030	Fontana	87 535	37 111	135.9	59 304	7 616	800	3 963	15 852	31 597	29 383	8 761	92.3
1032	Foothill Farms CDP	17 135	13 700	25.1	14 075	1 557	223	686	594	1 504	6 792	NA	5.9
1035	Ford City CDP	3 781	NA	NA	3 477	10	52	50	192	323	1 508	NA	3.9
1050	Fort Bragg	6 078	NA	NA	5 411	29	98	47	493	833	2 629	8 814	6.9
1060	Fortuna	8 788	NA	NA	8 342	45	226	84	91	457	3 711	9 140	12.3
1062	Foster City	28 176	23 287	21.0	20 704	909	56	6 192	315	1 627	11 747	19 475	9.7
1065	Fountain Valley	53 691	55 080	-2.5	42 000	510	322	9 519	1 340	4 357	18 019	14 132	23.1
1070	Fowler	3 208	NA	NA	1 472	103	22	173	1 438	1 874	1 102	NA	5.1
1075	Freedom CDP	8 361	NA	NA	5 351	56	79	390	2 485	5 199	2 374	NA	4.2
1080	Fremont	173 339	131 945	31.4	122 376	6 562	1 218	33 671	9 512	23 091	62 400	13 689	199.5
1085	French Camp CDP	3 018	NA	NA	2 010	478	61	185	284	1 644	543	NA	8.0
1090	Fresno	354 202	218 202	62.3	209 604	29 409	3 729	44 358	67 102	105 787	129 404	8 973	256.8
1095	Fullerton	114 144	102 034	11.9	85 212	2 479	528	13 900	12 025	24 304	42 956	14 699	57.3
1100	Galt	8 889	NA	NA	7 778	53	100	223	735	2 187	3 073	7 833	14.5
1105	Gardena	49 847	45 165	10.4	16 033	11 713	272	16 566	5 263	11 506	19 037	11 348	13.7
1107	Garden Acres CDP	8 547	NA	NA	7 194	66	171	375	741	2 641	2 816	NA	6.7
1110	Garden Grove	143 050	123 307	16.0	96 304	2 144	872	29 337	14 393	33 579	45 984	11 410	46.5
1111	George AFB CDP	5 085	NA	NA	3 585	819	41	440	200	449	1 180	NA	7.2
1115	Gilroy	31 487	21 641	45.5	21 465	378	212	1 263	8 169	14 885	9 767	9 984	26.6
1120	Glen Avon CDP	12 663	NA	NA	10 005	419	105	245	1 889	3 128	4 768	NA	19.1
1130	Glendale	180 038	139 060	29.5	133 270	2 334	629	25 453	18 352	37 731	72 114	13 187	79.3
1135	Glendora	47 828	38 654	23.7	42 323	537	255	2 687	2 026	7 250	16 876	12 960	50.4
1139	Golden Hills CDP	5 423	NA	NA	4 885	114	73	55	296	634	1 923	NA	10.9
1140	Gonzales	4 660	NA	NA	1 243	60	11	157	3 189	3 828	1 222	7 064	2.9
1147	Grand Terrace	10 946	NA	NA	8 779	413	79	642	1 033	1 991	4 059	13 325	9.0
1148	Granite Hills CDP	3 157	NA	NA	3 032	27	17	25	56	213	1 035	NA	7.7
1150	Grass Valley	9 048	NA	NA	8 763	13	144	84	44	358	4 385	8 349	9.1
1157	Greenacres CDP	7 379	NA	NA	6 936	24	131	54	234	518	2 499	NA	10.2
1160	Greenfield	7 464	NA	NA	3 225	58	82	128	3 971	5 763	1 926	5 689	2.8
1170	Gridley	4 631	NA	NA	3 369	27	82	244	909	1 219	1 810	7 000	3.6
1173	Groveland-Big Oak Flat CDP	2 753	NA	NA	2 669	4	38	26	16	90	2 420	NA	56.6
1175	Grover City	11 656	NA	NA	10 041	203	167	527	718	2 280	4 941	9 238	6.0
1180	Guadalupe	5 479	NA	NA	1 624	37	22	528	3 268	4 546	1 378	6 763	2.3
1185	Gustine	3 931	NA	NA	3 484	27	15	63	342	779	1 583	10 567	3.6
1188	Hacienda Heights CDP	52 354	49 422	5.9	30 956	1 100	305	14 283	5 710	16 763	16 091	NA	28.6
1195	Half Moon Bay	8 886	NA	NA	8 110	46	19	333	378	1 978	3 402	14 286	16.8
1200	Hanford	30 897	20 995	47.2	22 887	1 628	239	947	5 196	9 131	11 610	8 439	29.9
1217	Hawaiian Gardens	13 639	10 548	29.3	8 379	620	121	1 285	3 234	9 078	3 518	6 968	2.5
1220	Hawthorne	71 349	56 447	26.4	30 166	20 212	326	7 819	12 826	22 219	29 214	11 189	15.4
1223	Hayfork CDP	2 605	NA	NA	2 395	3	168	22	17	80	1 166	NA	404.5
1225	Hayward	111 498	94 167	18.4	68 911	10 965	1 084	17 335	13 203	26 671	42 216	11 261	112.5
1230	Healdsburg	9 469	NA	NA	8 250	15	100	65	1 039	2 026	3 766	10 336	8.8
1232	Heber CDP	2 566	NA	NA	1 634	18	2	5	907	2 483	600	NA	3.8
1235	Hemet	36 094	22 454	60.7	32 802	244	319	425	2 304	5 383	19 692	10 011	45.5
1245	Hercules	16 829	NA	NA	6 700	2 150	53	7 288	638	1 758	5 652	13 482	14.3
1250	Hermosa Beach	18 219	18 070	0.8	16 858	211	87	693	370	1 267	9 689	21 588	3.7
1251	Hesperia	50 418	13 540	272.4	43 191	1 249	464	712	4 802	9 573	17 359	NA	125.1
1258	Highgrove CDP	3 175	NA	NA	2 081	174	22	142	756	1 367	1 086	NA	2.9
1260	Highland	34 439	10 908	215.7	25 190	3 778	374	1 657	3 440	7 839	12 562	NA	35.1
1263	Highlands CDP	2 644	NA	NA	2 065	96	13	402	68	174	880	NA	3.2
1265	Hillsborough town	10 667	10 451	2.1	8 476	74	5	2 028	84	436	3 789	37 147	16.1
1267	Hilmar-Irwin CDP	3 392	NA	NA	3 097	13	42	79	161	359	1 154	NA	9.3
1270	Hollister	19 212	11 488	67.2	12 205	119	147	481	6 260	10 786	6 222	7 955	14.6

1. Codes shown are 2-digit FIPS codes for states; 4-digit census place codes for places; and 3-digit FIPS county codes followed by 3-digit census MCD codes for minor civil divisions (MCDs). MCD names are followed by county names in parentheses. 2. Hispanic persons may be of any race. 3. Dry land or land partially or temporarily covered by water.

State/ Place/ MCD[1] code	Place	Population: 1990	Population: Places of 10,000 or more: 1980	Population: Places of 10,000 or more: Percent change, 1980–1990	Population characteristics, 1990: Race: White	Race: Black	Race: Am. Indian, Eskimo Aleut	Race: Asian & Pacific Islander	Race: Other race	Hispanic[2]	Total housing units, 1990	Per capita income, 1985 (Dollars)	Land area,[3] 1990 (Sq. Km.)
		1	2	3	4	5	6	7	8	9	10	11	12
	CALIFORNIA—Con.												
1280	Holtville	4 820	NA	NA	2 449	10	23	53	2 285	3 011	1 477	7 045	2.8
1285	Home Gardens CDP	7 780	NA	NA	5 675	118	44	276	1 667	4 497	2 042	NA	2.8
1286	Homeland CDP	3 312	NA	NA	3 047	4	23	24	214	392	1 613	NA	7.4
1295	Hughson	3 259	NA	NA	2 261	4	44	64	886	1 161	1 088	6 454	2.3
1297	Humboldt Hill CDP	2 865	NA	NA	2 656	13	103	57	36	113	1 027	NA	10.6
1300	Huntington Beach	181 519	170 505	6.5	156 314	1 687	1 157	15 048	7 313	20 397	72 736	14 928	68.4
1305	Huntington Park	56 065	46 223	21.3	17 486	594	301	1 035	36 649	51 496	14 515	5 886	7.9
1310	Huron	4 766	NA	NA	596	22	10	57	4 081	4 597	962	3 847	4.0
1314	Idyllwild-Pine Cove CDP	2 853	NA	NA	2 769	8	12	23	41	130	3 668	NA	35.3
1317	Imperial	4 113	NA	NA	2 938	145	41	33	956	2 176	1 372	7 920	6.2
1320	Imperial Beach	26 512	22 689	16.8	19 338	1 310	330	2 203	3 331	7 502	9 525	7 655	11.0
1327	Indian Wells	2 647	NA	NA	2 591	9	0	36	11	54	3 019	NA	34.6
1330	Indio	36 793	21 611	70.3	20 045	1 482	281	588	14 397	25 068	13 028	7 347	44.1
1340	Inglewood	109 602	94 245	16.3	19 073	56 861	427	2 754	30 487	42 249	38 713	9 407	23.7
1342	Interlaken CDP	6 404	NA	NA	4 155	54	72	536	1 587	3 321	1 657	NA	24.3
1345	Ione	6 516	NA	NA	4 243	1 567	98	51	557	1 445	910	NA	12.3
1347	Irvine	110 330	62 134	77.6	85 945	2 002	259	19 970	2 154	6 902	42 221	18 080	109.6
1353	Isla Vista CDP	20 395	NA	NA	15 899	595	142	2 453	1 306	2 993	5 513	NA	5.5
1360	Ivanhoe CDP	3 293	NA	NA	1 661	1	39	48	1 544	1 721	971	NA	5.2
1365	Jackson	3 545	NA	NA	3 463	10	37	19	16	144	1 618	NA	7.9
1377	Joshua Tree CDP	3 898	NA	NA	3 644	57	43	28	126	347	1 975	NA	15.9
1380	Kelseyville CDP	2 861	NA	NA	2 437	14	57	29	324	438	1 179	NA	12.4
1386	Kensington CDP	4 974	NA	NA	4 315	150	18	444	47	152	2 251	NA	3.0
1388	Kentfield CDP	6 030	NA	NA	5 791	28	7	173	31	165	2 492	NA	6.2
1390	Kerman	5 448	NA	NA	3 907	21	33	338	1 149	2 871	1 748	6 882	4.7
1395	Keyes CDP	2 878	NA	NA	2 359	0	49	80	390	613	1 007	NA	3.3
1400	King City	7 634	NA	NA	3 655	64	85	106	3 724	5 091	2 444	8 405	7.2
1403	Kings Beach CDP	2 796	NA	NA	2 256	7	30	21	482	922	2 155	NA	8.9
1405	Kingsburg	7 205	NA	NA	6 134	24	54	129	864	2 265	2 584	9 395	5.3
1410	La Canada Flintridge	19 378	20 153	-3.8	16 645	81	27	2 397	228	892	6 918	24 509	22.4
1412	La Crescenta-Montrose CDP	16 968	16 531	2.6	14 857	59	78	1 490	484	1 507	6 808	NA	8.7
1413	Ladera Heights CDP	6 316	NA	NA	2 326	3 634	15	236	105	240	2 677	NA	5.8
1415	Lafayette	23 501	20 879	12.6	21 804	135	73	1 368	121	761	9 270	21 518	39.4
1418	Laguna CDP	9 828	NA	NA	7 617	580	45	1 268	318	1 046	3 939	NA	14.3
1420	Laguna Beach	23 170	17 901	29.4	22 191	163	71	404	341	1 590	12 846	23 208	22.5
1423	Laguna Hills CDP	46 731	33 600	39.1	42 559	449	131	2 930	662	2 701	24 057	NA	27.9
1424	Laguna Niguel	44 400	12 237	262.8	39 277	604	129	3 442	948	3 451	18 892	NA	37.9
1428	La Habra	51 266	45 232	13.3	39 245	485	358	2 080	9 098	17 395	18 670	12 462	19.0
1429	La Habra Heights	6 226	NA	NA	5 603	21	23	425	154	678	2 161	21 476	16.5
1433	Lake Arrowhead CDP	6 539	NA	NA	6 299	21	45	64	110	626	8 015	NA	29.7
1434	Lake Elsinore	18 285	NA	NA	14 053	706	200	419	2 907	4 757	6 981	7 519	60.7
1437	Lake Isabella CDP	3 323	NA	NA	3 211	2	71	16	23	112	1 992	NA	20.3
1440	Lakeland Village CDP	5 159	NA	NA	4 646	56	47	51	359	733	2 216	NA	5.3
1441	Lake Los Angeles CDP	7 977	NA	NA	6 273	539	58	196	911	1 560	2 313	NA	12.6
1443	Lake Of The Pines CDP	3 890	NA	NA	3 790	1	19	58	22	150	1 616	NA	3.9
1445	Lakeport	4 390	NA	NA	4 113	31	62	73	111	306	2 145	10 923	6.3
1447	Lake San Marcos CDP	3 802	NA	NA	3 684	7	8	47	56	130	2 326	NA	4.7
1450	Lakeside CDP	39 412	23 921	64.8	37 036	289	332	537	1 218	3 671	14 620	NA	34.8
1455	Lakewood	73 557	74 654	-1.5	59 690	2 712	487	6 884	3 784	10 763	26 795	12 045	24.3
1460	La Mesa	52 931	50 308	5.2	47 763	1 589	281	1 635	1 663	5 176	24 154	12 455	23.9
1462	La Mirada	40 452	40 986	-1.3	32 858	562	244	3 332	3 456	10 459	13 354	11 712	20.3
1470	Lamont CDP	11 517	NA	NA	3 536	18	110	226	7 627	8 826	3 053	NA	12.0
1476	Lancaster	97 291	48 027	102.6	77 225	7 207	913	3 618	8 328	14 816	36 217	11 680	230.0
1477	La Palma	15 392	15 399	0.0	9 222	642	55	4 789	684	1 872	4 935	14 265	4.7
1480	La Puente	36 955	30 882	19.7	23 620	1 308	240	2 896	8 891	27 663	9 285	7 770	9.0
1482	La Quinta	11 215	NA	NA	8 941	206	134	170	1 764	2 944	6 426	12 867	63.1
1483	La Riviera CDP	10 986	10 906	0.7	8 891	714	104	1 013	264	941	4 427	NA	4.6
1484	Larkfield-Wikiup CDP	6 779	NA	NA	6 374	37	49	216	103	403	2 680	NA	11.7
1485	Larkspur	11 070	11 064	0.1	10 566	88	19	320	77	432	5 966	21 769	8.1
1490	Lathrop	6 841	NA	NA	4 566	203	154	1 066	852	2 568	2 040	NA	16.8
1500	La Verne	30 897	23 508	31.4	25 658	926	178	2 217	1 918	5 675	11 113	12 419	20.2
1505	Lawndale	27 331	23 460	16.5	16 568	2 273	233	3 309	4 948	9 359	9 778	10 130	5.1
1510	Lemon Grove	23 984	20 780	15.4	18 376	1 920	218	1 343	2 127	4 764	8 638	9 639	9.8
1515	Lemoore	13 622	NA	NA	9 570	789	130	1 141	1 992	2 886	4 887	8 978	14.7
1520	Lennox CDP	22 757	18 445	23.4	9 179	1 433	90	679	11 376	19 478	5 228	NA	3.0
1525	Lenwood CDP	3 190	NA	NA	2 484	89	68	40	509	900	1 221	NA	6.8
1535	Lincoln	7 248	NA	NA	6 410	12	76	76	674	1 796	2 602	7 486	16.7
1537	Lincoln Village CDP	4 236	NA	NA	3 842	99	24	174	97	396	1 651	NA	1.9
1540	Linda CDP	13 033	10 225	27.5	8 599	394	334	2 730	976	1 855	4 297	NA	15.0
1550	Lindsay	8 338	NA	NA	3 741	5	54	84	4 454	5 410	2 678	7 297	6.1
1561	Live Oak	4 320	NA	NA	2 486	43	74	440	1 277	1 606	1 428	6 041	3.4
1566	Live Oak CDP	15 212	11 482	32.5	13 502	236	143	532	799	2 096	5 997	NA	8.5
1570	Livermore	56 741	48 349	17.4	50 721	863	414	2 610	2 133	5 587	21 489	13 414	50.8

1. Codes shown are 2-digit FIPS codes for states; 4-digit census place codes for places; and 3-digit FIPS county codes followed by 3-digit census MCD codes for minor civil divisions (MCDs). MCD names are followed by county names in parentheses. 2. Hispanic persons may be of any race. 3. Dry land or land partially or temporarily covered by water.

State/ Place/ MCD[1] code	Place	Population			Population characteristics, 1990							Total housing units, 1990	Per capita income, 1985 (Dollars)	Land area,[3] 1990 (Sq. Km.)
		1990	Places of 10,000 or more		Race					Hispanic[2]				
			1980	Percent change, 1980–1990	White	Black	Am. Indian, Eskimo Aleut	Asian & Pacific Islander	Other race					
		1	2	3	4	5	6	7	8	9		10	11	12
	CALIFORNIA—Con.													
1575	Livingston	7 317	NA	NA	2 476	55	41	1 055	3 690	5 354		1 719	5 139	5.0
1581	Lockeford CDP	2 722	NA	NA	2 492	4	58	53	115	489		990	NA	19.9
1585	Lodi	51 874	35 221	47.3	46 317	171	472	2 446	2 468	8 766		19 676	10 338	27.5
1588	Loma Linda	17 400	10 694	62.7	11 150	1 108	91	3 726	1 325	2 365		6 524	10 300	18.1
1590	Lomita	19 382	18 807	3.1	15 358	566	141	1 762	1 555	3 756		8 255	12 786	4.9
1600	Lompoc	37 649	26 267	43.3	26 551	2 954	506	2 039	5 599	10 100		13 261	10 508	29.1
1610	Long Beach	429 433	361 334	18.8	250 716	58 761	2 781	58 266	58 909	101 419		170 388	11 729	129.5
1612	Loomis town	5 705	NA	NA	5 266	23	79	197	140	414		2 030	10 693	18.9
1615	Los Alamitos	11 676	11 529	1.3	9 910	350	50	838	528	1 460		4 279	13 509	10.4
1620	Los Altos	26 303	25 769	2.1	23 403	107	47	2 642	104	795		10 107	23 294	16.5
1625	Los Altos Hills town	7 514	NA	NA	6 266	58	5	1 163	22	202		2 682	34 254	21.8
1630	Los Angeles	3 485 398	2 966 850	17.5	1 841 182	487 674	16 379	341 807	798 356	1 391 411		1 299 963	12 084	1 215.6
1635	Los Banos	14 519	10 341	40.4	10 278	390	94	271	3 486	5 218		5 070	8 270	18.1
1640	Los Gatos town	27 357	26 906	1.7	25 374	192	104	1 380	307	1 367		11 822	19 606	26.9
1645	Los Serranos CDP	7 099	NA	NA	5 538	144	56	189	1 172	2 200		2 539	NA	4.3
1654	Loyola CDP	3 076	NA	NA	2 690	9	1	362	14	90		1 166	NA	3.6
1656	Lucas Valley-Marinwood CDP	5 982	NA	NA	5 463	72	6	399	42	279		2 225	NA	9.7
1660	Lynwood	61 945	48 548	27.6	14 844	14 652	258	1 373	30 818	43 565		14 525	6 222	12.6
1670	McFarland	7 005	NA	NA	1 983	12	22	97	4 891	5 809		1 747	4 305	5.3
1674	McKinleyville CDP	10 749	NA	NA	9 992	41	543	93	80	355		4 218	NA	43.5
1680	Madera	29 281	21 732	34.7	16 873	1 357	277	473	10 301	15 759		9 530	7 417	26.7
1681	Madera Acres CDP	5 245	NA	NA	3 875	164	56	123	1 027	1 676		1 535	NA	30.7
1684	Magalia CDP	8 987	NA	NA	8 823	11	58	48	47	318		4 191	NA	41.6
1687	Mammoth Lakes town	4 785	NA	NA	4 629	9	30	69	48	692		7 102	13 405	63.8
1690	Manhattan Beach	32 063	31 542	1.7	29 972	206	86	1 410	389	1 645		14 695	22 529	10.2
1695	Manteca	40 773	24 925	63.6	36 502	605	477	1 412	1 777	7 241		13 981	9 439	22.8
1697	March AFB CDP	5 523	NA	NA	3 737	1 142	27	386	231	530		1 175	NA	15.7
1705	Marina	26 436	20 647	28.0	14 169	5 016	190	5 508	1 553	2 837		8 261	7 747	22.7
1706	Marina del Rey CDP	7 431	NA	NA	6 666	311	23	337	94	321		5 419	NA	2.3
1710	Martinez	31 808	22 582	40.9	27 910	1 055	266	1 821	756	2 676		12 970	14 688	29.0
1720	Marysville	12 324	NA	NA	9 906	637	220	828	733	1 347		5 083	10 144	9.1
1722	Mather AFB CDP	4 885	NA	NA	3 605	840	33	279	128	369		1 279	NA	24.8
1727	Mayflower Village CDP	4 978	NA	NA	3 970	71	21	510	406	973		1 949	NA	1.7
1730	Maywood	27 850	21 810	27.7	8 733	114	161	213	18 629	25 931		6 680	5 902	3.0
1734	Meadow Vista CDP	3 067	NA	NA	3 019	3	20	20	5	117		1 187	NA	14.2
1736	Meiners Oaks CDP	3 329	NA	NA	3 045	6	41	49	188	448		1 299	NA	3.5
1740	Mendota	6 821	NA	NA	1 190	98	64	96	5 373	6 405		1 758	4 139	4.5
1745	Menlo Park	28 040	26 369	6.3	22 176	3 467	106	1 668	623	2 710		12 247	19 428	26.1
1747	Mentone CDP	5 675	NA	NA	4 898	155	53	133	436	1 048		2 251	NA	8.9
1750	Merced	56 216	36 499	54.0	34 675	3 860	522	8 564	8 595	16 786		18 965	8 914	41.8
1760	Millbrae	20 412	20 058	1.8	15 972	235	51	3 447	707	2 279		8 158	16 818	8.3
1765	Mill Valley	13 038	12 967	0.5	12 234	183	28	499	94	365		6 139	20 690	12.1
1770	Milpitas	50 686	37 820	34.0	26 413	2 970	479	17 572	3 252	9 434		14 465	12 305	35.6
1780	Mira Loma CDP	15 786	NA	NA	12 964	201	124	217	2 280	4 125		4 574	NA	16.7
1782	Mira Monte CDP	7 744	NA	NA	7 236	55	64	99	290	892		2 906	NA	11.1
1784	Mission Hills CDP	3 112	NA	NA	2 532	193	32	110	245	468		1 023	NA	3.2
1786	Mission Viejo	72 820	50 666	43.7	65 756	680	228	4 552	1 604	5 615		26 393	NA	45.2
1790	Modesto	164 730	106 602	54.5	132 701	4 413	1 694	13 001	12 921	26 920		60 878	10 526	78.2
1795	Mojave CDP	3 763	NA	NA	2 974	83	65	56	585	772		1 530	NA	35.1
1799	Mono Vista CDP	2 599	NA	NA	2 506	10	33	23	27	152		1 172	NA	7.7
1800	Monrovia	35 761	30 531	17.1	24 912	3 626	188	1 621	5 414	10 177		13 944	11 062	34.6
1813	Montara CDP	2 552	NA	NA	2 424	13	16	64	35	203		947	NA	10.1
1815	Montclair	28 434	22 628	25.7	17 523	2 682	237	1 932	6 060	10 849		8 915	9 256	13.1
1820	Montebello	59 564	52 929	12.5	28 023	579	279	9 001	21 682	40 263		19 193	9 604	21.4
1825	Monterey	31 954	27 558	16.0	27 680	937	176	2 338	823	2 495		13 497	12 470	21.8
1830	Monterey Park	60 738	54 338	11.8	16 245	389	198	34 898	9 008	19 031		20 298	10 364	19.8
1835	Monte Sereno	3 287	NA	NA	2 901	9	6	320	51	139		1 190	27 850	4.2
1840	Moorpark	25 494	NA	NA	20 109	396	137	1 689	3 163	5 613		7 915	10 383	31.8
1845	Morada CDP	3 570	NA	NA	3 267	14	16	146	127	270		1 339	NA	7.8
1847	Moraga Town	15 852	15 014	5.6	14 165	110	31	1 454	92	553		5 687	20 156	24.0
1849	Moreno Valley	118 779	NA	NA	80 116	16 402	856	7 895	13 510	27 165		37 945	9 486	127.3
1850	Morgan Hill	23 928	17 060	40.3	19 868	383	178	1 271	2 228	5 594		8 157	12 717	27.1
1855	Morro Bay	9 664	NA	NA	9 054	54	104	168	284	744		5 694	11 723	13.2
1857	Moss Beach CDP	3 002	NA	NA	2 797	33	22	70	80	338		1 113	NA	5.9
1860	Mountain View	67 460	58 655	15.0	49 062	3 390	391	9 932	4 685	10 821		31 487	16 308	31.2
1870	Mount Shasta	3 460	NA	NA	3 280	64	26	31	59	148		1 663	10 818	9.7
1881	Muscoy CDP	7 541	NA	NA	4 751	702	151	177	1 760	2 989		2 233	NA	7.5
1883	Myrtletown CDP	4 413	NA	NA	4 098	49	139	77	50	207		1 697	NA	5.0
1884	Napa	61 842	50 879	21.5	55 846	237	474	1 292	3 993	9 425		24 922	11 865	45.1
1885	National City	54 249	48 772	11.2	22 182	4 588	372	9 585	17 522	26 914		15 243	6 977	19.6
1890	Needles	5 191	NA	NA	4 262	63	341	85	440	887		2 337	10 451	77.1
1895	Nevada City	2 855	NA	NA	2 795	6	32	12	10	94		1 399	NA	5.0
1900	Newark	37 861	32 126	17.9	25 974	1 635	235	6 035	3 982	8 672		12 284	11 731	36.2

1. Codes shown are 2-digit FIPS codes for states; 4-digit census place codes for places; and 3-digit FIPS county codes followed by 3-digit census MCD codes for minor civil divisions (MCDs). MCD names are followed by county names in parentheses. 2. Hispanic persons may be of any race. 3. Dry land or land partially or temporarily covered by water.

State/ Place/ MCD[1] code	Place	Population			Population characteristics, 1990						Total housing units, 1990	Per capita income, 1985 (Dollars)	Land area,[3] 1990 (Sq. Km.)
			Places of 10,000 or more		Race					Hispanic[2]			
		1990	1980	Percent change, 1980–1990	White	Black	Am. Indian, Eskimo Aleut	Asian & Pacific Islander	Other race				
		1	2	3	4	5	6	7	8	9	10	11	12
	CALIFORNIA—Con.												
1910	Newman	4 151	NA	NA	2 959	18	29	86	1 059	1 784	1 520	7 470	3.1
1915	Newport Beach	66 643	62 556	6.5	63 850	230	170	1 927	466	2 648	34 861	28 712	36.3
1918	Nipomo CDP	7 109	NA	NA	6 054	50	79	138	788	2 498	2 386	NA	17.0
1919	Norco	23 302	21 126	10.3	19 206	1 852	163	317	1 764	4 556	5 785	10 769	35.5
1924	North Auburn CDP	10 301	NA	NA	9 822	59	146	149	125	512	4 368	NA	20.0
1926	North El Monte CDP	3 384	NA	NA	2 749	20	10	420	185	713	1 228	NA	1.1
1927	North Fair Oaks CDP	13 912	10 308	35.0	10 605	447	103	627	2 130	8 466	3 954	NA	3.0
1935	North Highlands CDP	42 105	37 825	11.3	32 768	4 194	647	2 828	1 668	3 901	16 138	NA	33.2
1950	Norwalk	94 279	85 286	10.5	52 636	3 061	813	11 702	26 067	45 118	27 247	8 620	25.3
1955	Novato	47 585	43 916	8.4	42 622	1 328	237	2 390	1 008	3 460	18 782	14 409	71.4
1957	Nuevo CDP	3 010	NA	NA	2 758	40	37	43	132	552	1 069	NA	13.7
1965	Oakdale	11 961	NA	NA	10 594	29	117	133	1 088	2 038	4 606	9 116	10.5
1967	Oakhurst CDP	2 602	NA	NA	2 447	11	82	22	40	109	1 181	NA	15.3
1970	Oakland	372 242	339 337	9.7	120 849	163 335	2 371	54 931	30 756	51 711	154 737	10 911	145.2
1975	Oakley CDP	18 374	NA	NA	15 425	288	209	643	1 809	3 950	6 143	NA	35.8
1980	Oak View CDP	3 606	NA	NA	3 336	19	55	46	150	467	1 251	NA	4.3
1985	Oceano CDP	6 169	NA	NA	5 190	54	82	175	668	2 232	2 433	NA	4.0
1990	Oceanside	128 398	76 698	67.4	95 935	10 129	910	7 825	13 599	28 982	51 109	10 407	105.3
1992	Oildale CDP	26 553	23 382	13.6	24 851	40	686	136	840	1 765	11 322	NA	15.5
1995	Ojai	7 613	NA	NA	7 020	20	51	126	396	928	3 130	12 388	11.5
2000	Olivehurst CDP	9 738	NA	NA	7 711	242	485	516	784	1 367	3 373	NA	9.1
2005	Ontario	133 179	88 820	49.9	86 056	9 724	914	5 183	31 302	55 542	42 536	9 376	95.2
2010	Opal Cliffs CDP	5 940	NA	NA	5 583	70	56	109	122	453	3 030	NA	2.0
2015	Orange	110 658	91 788	20.6	91 838	1 551	596	8 740	7 933	25 278	38 018	13 519	60.4
2020	Orange Cove	5 604	NA	NA	1 755	1	69	161	3 618	4 820	1 316	4 270	4.0
2022	Orangevale CDP	26 266	20 585	27.6	24 772	234	270	567	423	1 469	9 724	NA	25.9
2030	Orinda	16 642	16 825	-1.1	15 272	138	39	1 134	59	403	6 475	27 632	32.6
2035	Orland	5 052	NA	NA	4 586	12	72	70	312	1 073	2 008	8 761	5.7
2040	Orosi CDP	5 486	NA	NA	1 392	12	34	819	3 229	3 964	1 399	NA	6.4
2045	Oroville	11 960	NA	NA	9 667	385	433	1 229	246	679	4 831	8 587	28.1
2047	Oroville East CDP	8 462	NA	NA	8 116	41	174	69	62	295	3 797	NA	54.7
2050	Oxnard	142 216	108 195	31.4	83 428	7 464	1 092	12 198	38 034	77 320	41 247	9 032	63.3
2055	Pacheco CDP	3 325	NA	NA	2 959	74	48	168	76	262	1 536	NA	3.8
2060	Pacifica	37 670	36 866	2.2	28 733	1 964	275	5 133	1 565	5 099	13 740	12 871	32.7
2065	Pacific Grove	16 117	15 755	2.3	14 760	223	109	778	247	967	7 916	12 704	7.2
2070	Pajaro CDP	3 332	NA	NA	1 113	11	8	75	2 125	3 113	746	NA	2.7
2071	Palermo CDP	5 260	NA	NA	4 707	26	286	49	192	522	2 015	NA	102.4
2072	Palmdale	68 842	12 277	460.7	52 101	4 398	648	3 030	8 665	15 154	24 400	11 427	201.0
2077	Palmdale East CDP	3 052	NA	NA	2 316	129	38	88	481	691	917	NA	1.2
2080	Palm Desert	23 252	11 801	97.0	21 240	223	104	421	1 264	3 196	18 248	17 884	49.4
2082	Palm Desert Country CDP	5 626	NA	NA	5 211	40	32	84	259	664	4 947	NA	6.6
2085	Palm Springs	40 181	32 271	24.5	33 411	1 814	297	1 343	3 316	7 504	30 517	16 109	198.3
2090	Palo Alto	55 900	55 225	1.2	47 458	1 612	150	5 835	845	2 792	25 188	21 141	61.3
2095	Palos Verdes Estates	13 512	14 376	-6.0	11 436	156	15	1 841	64	398	5 131	29 616	12.4
2100	Paradise town	25 408	22 571	12.6	24 673	36	234	264	201	874	11 633	9 564	48.3
2115	Paramount	47 669	36 407	30.9	22 955	5 098	356	2 743	16 517	28 998	13 726	7 267	12.2
2117	Parkway-South Sacramento CDP	31 903	26 815	19.0	16 544	5 982	567	4 090	4 720	8 044	11 575	NA	12.3
2120	Parlier	7 938	NA	NA	4 086	17	30	82	3 723	7 707	1 818	3 845	3.7
2125	Pasadena	131 591	118 550	11.0	75 342	24 952	591	10 678	20 028	35 912	53 032	13 557	59.5
2130	Patterson	8 626	NA	NA	5 941	159	46	291	2 189	4 156	2 703	7 272	4.4
2133	Pedley CDP	8 869	NA	NA	7 309	378	77	306	799	1 671	2 754	NA	13.1
2138	Perris	21 460	NA	NA	15 119	2 788	218	713	2 622	7 704	7 761	7 259	76.9
2140	Petaluma	43 184	33 834	27.6	39 774	551	245	1 429	1 185	3 985	16 546	11 887	31.9
2142	Phoenix Lake-Cedar Ridge CDP	3 569	NA	NA	3 424	16	50	30	49	165	1 597	NA	26.0
2145	Pico Rivera	59 177	53 459	10.7	34 782	408	334	1 872	21 781	49 237	16 316	8 111	20.7
2150	Piedmont	10 602	10 498	1.0	9 051	147	22	1 323	59	341	3 848	27 502	4.4
2156	Pine Hills CDP	2 947	NA	NA	2 805	8	85	14	35	102	1 105	NA	26.4
2160	Pinole	17 460	14 253	22.5	12 403	1 234	157	3 082	584	1 715	6 496	13 411	13.3
2170	Pismo Beach	7 669	NA	NA	7 319	38	43	152	117	495	4 548	13 188	8.9
2175	Pittsburg	47 564	33 034	44.0	27 874	8 363	366	5 792	5 169	11 288	16 709	9 821	28.2
2195	Placentia	41 259	35 041	17.7	31 431	765	201	3 378	5 484	10 174	13 733	13 499	17.1
2200	Placerville	8 355	NA	NA	7 949	22	158	63	163	548	3 565	9 721	14.0
2205	Planada CDP	3 531	NA	NA	2 317	9	16	17	1 172	3 104	1 013	NA	5.5
2210	Pleasant Hill	31 585	25 124	25.7	28 209	442	190	2 205	539	2 099	13 653	14 945	17.6
2215	Pleasanton	50 553	35 160	43.8	45 835	694	216	2 924	884	3 383	19 356	15 560	42.0
2224	Point Dume CDP	2 809	NA	NA	2 656	24	10	70	49	138	1 351	NA	4.4
2229	Pollock Pines CDP	4 291	NA	NA	4 186	9	51	34	11	134	2 119	NA	13.4
2230	Pomona	131 723	92 742	42.0	75 113	19 013	745	8 791	28 061	67 533	38 466	8 574	59.1
2245	Porterville	29 563	19 692	50.1	19 223	288	382	1 936	7 734	10 299	10 073	7 291	29.1
2250	Port Hueneme	20 319	17 803	14.1	14 941	1 127	206	1 381	2 664	6 063	7 481	10 078	11.5
2256	Portola Hills CDP	2 677	NA	NA	2 417	17	10	156	77	213	970	NA	4.7
2257	Portola Valley town	4 194	NA	NA	4 011	13	13	134	23	124	1 675	36 269	23.7
2260	Poway	43 516	32 263	34.9	39 102	625	220	2 679	890	3 023	14 386	13 396	101.7

1. Codes shown are 2-digit FIPS codes for states; 4-digit census place codes for places; and 3-digit FIPS county codes followed by 3-digit census MCD codes for minor civil divisions (MCDs). MCD names are followed by county names in parentheses. 2. Hispanic persons may be of any race. 3. Dry land or land partially or temporarily covered by water.

State/ Place/ MCD[1] code	Place	Population: 1990	Population: Places of 10,000 or more: 1980	Population: Places of 10,000 or more: Percent change, 1980–1990	Population characteristics, 1990: Race: White	Population characteristics, 1990: Race: Black	Population characteristics, 1990: Race: Am. Indian, Eskimo Aleut	Population characteristics, 1990: Race: Asian & Pacific Islander	Population characteristics, 1990: Race: Other race	Population characteristics, 1990: Hispanic[2]	Total housing units, 1990	Per capita income, 1985 (Dollars)	Land area,[3] 1990 (Sq. Km.)
		1	2	3	4	5	6	7	8	9	10	11	12
	CALIFORNIA—Con.												
2263	Prunedale CDP	7 393	NA	NA	6 604	99	117	307	266	980	2 472	NA	26.7
2265	Quartz Hill CDP	9 626	NA	NA	8 430	364	96	195	541	1 028	3 465	NA	10.1
2270	Quincy-East Quincy CDP	4 271	NA	NA	3 950	116	95	34	76	212	1 872	NA	40.4
2275	Ramona CDP	13 040	NA	NA	11 236	98	208	186	1 312	2 354	4 405	NA	27.0
2277	Rancho Cordova CDP	48 731	42 881	13.6	38 446	4 907	553	3 577	1 248	3 806	19 072	NA	26.4
2278	Rancho Cucamonga	101 409	55 250	83.5	79 698	5 952	580	5 518	9 661	20 298	36 367	11 832	97.9
2281	Rancho Mirage	9 778	NA	NA	9 245	143	36	89	265	674	9 360	29 191	60.8
2284	Rancho Palos Verdes	41 659	36 577	13.9	31 738	788	100	8 546	487	2 215	15 468	22 822	35.4
2285	Rancho Rinconada CDP	4 206	NA	NA	3 242	61	25	715	163	457	1 479	NA	1.3
2286	Rancho San Diego CDP	6 977	NA	NA	6 035	213	32	465	232	725	2 474	NA	10.9
2288	Rancho Santa Margarita CDP	11 390	NA	NA	9 683	162	68	962	515	1 319	4 951	NA	10.8
2289	Red Bluff	12 363	NA	NA	11 277	69	287	131	599	1 106	5 062	8 506	18.8
2290	Redding	66 462	41 995	58.3	61 545	699	1 433	2 173	612	2 632	27 238	9 972	132.7
2295	Redlands	60 394	43 619	38.5	48 067	2 313	441	2 668	6 905	11 450	23 189	12 118	63.0
2300	Redondo Beach	60 167	57 102	5.4	52 371	960	311	4 111	2 414	6 917	28 220	17 313	16.3
2305	Redwood City	66 072	54 951	20.2	54 684	2 406	336	4 175	4 471	15 935	26 847	14 542	49.3
2315	Reedley	15 791	11 071	42.6	9 388	61	118	958	5 266	9 196	4 763	6 766	10.1
2320	Rialto	72 388	37 474	93.2	41 931	14 734	628	2 553	12 542	22 787	23 836	9 517	55.0
2330	Richmond	87 425	74 676	17.1	31 633	38 260	522	10 341	6 669	12 690	34 532	9 854	77.0
2335	Ridgecrest	27 725	15 929	74.1	24 347	883	277	1 152	1 066	2 198	11 249	11 825	53.8
2337	Rio Dell	3 012	NA	NA	2 793	7	104	14	94	225	1 244	7 674	4.8
2340	Rio del Mar CDP	8 919	NA	NA	8 487	34	35	255	108	422	4 580	NA	7.7
2345	Rio Linda CDP	9 481	NA	NA	8 568	139	224	229	321	696	3 288	NA	14.2
2350	Rio Vista	3 316	NA	NA	3 110	3	30	69	104	264	1 406	11 614	4.7
2355	Ripon	7 455	NA	NA	6 850	25	44	144	392	1 009	2 567	9 037	7.4
2360	Riverbank	8 547	NA	NA	6 080	24	141	99	2 203	3 619	2 647	7 090	4.5
2370	Riverside	226 505	170 876	32.6	160 344	16 740	1 910	11 821	35 690	58 826	80 240	10 802	201.2
2375	Rocklin	19 033	NA	NA	17 815	143	184	503	388	1 333	7 559	13 407	32.7
2376	Rodeo CDP	7 589	NA	NA	5 376	833	52	1 036	292	984	2 804	NA	19.4
2377	Rohnert Park	36 326	22 965	58.2	32 411	961	347	1 732	875	3 247	13 915	10 984	16.6
2390	Rolling Hills Estates	7 789	NA	NA	6 389	61	6	1 264	69	339	2 873	26 243	9.2
2392	Rosamond CDP	7 430	NA	NA	6 239	240	99	174	678	1 288	3 117	NA	52.2
2393	Rosedale CDP	4 673	NA	NA	4 326	37	56	67	187	388	1 523	NA	98.7
2395	Roseland CDP	8 779	NA	NA	6 897	340	252	458	832	2 267	2 934	NA	3.6
2400	Rosemead	51 638	42 604	21.2	18 300	320	250	17 725	15 043	25 641	14 134	7 904	13.3
2402	Rosemont CDP	22 851	18 888	21.0	17 343	1 902	266	2 633	707	2 253	8 454	NA	10.0
2405	Roseville	44 685	24 347	83.5	40 899	407	430	1 483	1 466	4 825	17 789	11 386	77.4
2411	Rossmoor CDP	9 893	10 457	-5.4	9 298	43	44	436	72	477	3 793	NA	4.1
2412	Rowland Heights CDP	42 647	28 203	51.2	22 959	2 220	177	12 504	4 787	12 687	13 595	NA	21.1
2414	Rubidoux CDP	24 367	16 763	45.4	15 750	2 357	292	733	5 235	8 436	7 872	NA	23.6
2417	Running Springs CDP	4 195	NA	NA	4 051	18	42	44	40	256	3 522	NA	10.3
2420	Sacramento	369 365	275 741	34.0	221 963	56 521	4 561	55 426	30 894	60 007	153 362	10 627	249.4
2425	St. Helena	4 990	NA	NA	4 417	22	22	72	457	1 034	2 364	12 401	12.4
2430	Salida CDP	4 499	NA	NA	3 544	56	51	137	711	1 195	1 468	NA	13.2
2435	Salinas	108 777	80 479	35.2	59 343	3 276	1 031	8 794	36 333	55 084	34 577	8 852	48.2
2445	San Anselmo town	11 743	12 053	-2.6	11 162	96	59	316	110	530	5 330	15 497	7.2
2447	San Antonio Heights CDP	2 935	NA	NA	2 612	39	19	163	102	207	1 078	NA	3.6
2450	San Bernardino	164 164	117 490	39.7	99 550	26 281	1 596	6 562	30 175	56 755	58 804	8 876	142.7
2455	San Bruno	38 961	35 417	10.0	27 904	1 589	293	6 987	2 188	7 252	15 178	14 121	16.7
2460	San Buenaventura (Ventura)	92 575	74 393	24.4	79 709	1 551	977	2 508	7 830	16 251	37 343	12 516	53.1
2465	San Carlos	26 167	24 710	5.9	23 891	245	73	1 589	369	1 691	11 338	18 301	14.6
2470	San Clemente	41 100	27 325	50.4	37 630	274	175	1 113	1 908	5 285	18 726	16 721	45.2
2475	San Diego	1 110 549	875 538	26.8	745 406	104 261	6 800	130 945	123 137	229 519	431 722	11 766	839.2
2476	San Diego Country Estates CDP	6 874	NA	NA	6 589	48	12	113	112	467	2 504	NA	39.9
2477	San Dimas	32 397	24 014	34.9	26 469	1 221	163	2 774	1 770	5 612	11 479	13 096	40.2
2480	San Fernando	22 580	17 731	27.3	8 799	266	165	322	13 028	18 683	5 794	8 186	6.2
2485	San Francisco	723 959	678 974	6.6	387 783	79 039	3 456	210 876	42 805	100 717	328 471	13 575	121.0
2490	San Gabriel	37 120	30 072	23.4	17 804	394	199	12 044	6 679	13 471	12 736	11 100	10.7
2495	Sanger	16 839	12 542	34.3	8 033	18	115	418	8 255	12 269	4 930	6 679	11.9
2500	San Jacinto	16 210	NA	NA	12 099	193	342	156	3 420	5 455	6 845	6 909	27.4
2510	San Jose	782 248	629 442	24.3	491 280	36 790	5 416	152 815	95 947	208 388	259 365	12 583	443.6
2519	San Juan Capistrano	26 183	18 959	38.1	23 406	95	211	564	1 907	5 703	9 612	15 531	36.9
2525	San Leandro	68 223	63 952	6.7	50 582	3 923	508	9 392	3 818	10 363	30 189	13 199	34.0
2530	San Lorenzo CDP	19 987	20 545	-2.7	16 233	249	170	2 173	1 162	3 177	7 471	NA	6.3
2535	San Luis Obispo	41 958	34 252	22.5	37 207	796	315	2 143	1 497	3 951	17 877	10 831	24.0
2537	San Marcos	38 974	17 479	123.0	33 014	567	297	1 142	3 954	10 702	14 476	10 537	60.1
2545	San Marino	12 959	13 307	-2.6	8 559	32	12	4 189	167	655	4 465	33 050	9.8
2555	San Mateo	85 486	77 561	10.2	67 170	3 060	330	11 377	3 549	13 235	36 928	16 261	31.6
2560	San Pablo	25 158	19 750	27.4	12 432	5 368	315	4 329	2 714	6 737	9 417	8 352	6.7
2565	San Rafael	48 404	44 800	8.0	40 409	1 425	166	2 661	3 743	6 951	21 139	17 218	43.0
2567	San Ramon	35 303	22 356	57.9	30 750	711	123	3 175	544	2 064	13 531	14 781	29.5
2570	Santa Ana	293 742	203 713	44.2	199 727	7 685	1 536	28 585	56 209	191 383	74 973	9 395	70.2
2575	Santa Barbara	85 571	74 414	15.0	66 529	1 920	758	1 997	14 367	26 920	36 226	13 733	48.9

1. Codes shown are 2-digit FIPS codes for states; 4-digit census place codes for places; and 3-digit FIPS county codes followed by 3-digit census MCD codes for minor civil divisions (MCDs). MCD names are followed by county names in parentheses. 2. Hispanic persons may be of any race. 3. Dry land or land partially or temporarily covered by water.

State/ Place/ MCD[1] code	Place	Population: 1990	Population: Places of 10,000 or more: 1980	Population: Places of 10,000 or more: Percent change, 1980–1990	Population characteristics, 1990: Race: White	Population characteristics, 1990: Race: Black	Population characteristics, 1990: Race: Am. Indian, Eskimo Aleut	Population characteristics, 1990: Race: Asian & Pacific Islander	Population characteristics, 1990: Race: Other race	Population characteristics, 1990: Hispanic[2]	Total housing units, 1990	Per capita income, 1985 (Dollars)	Land area,[3] 1990 (Sq. Km.)
		1	2	3	4	5	6	7	8	9	10	11	12
	CALIFORNIA—Con.												
2580	Santa Clara	93 613	87 746	6.7	68 984	2 404	473	17 416	4 336	14 260	37 873	14 367	47.4
2583	Santa Clarita	110 642	NA	NA	96 555	1 695	624	4 607	7 161	14 771	41 133	NA	104.8
2585	Santa Cruz	49 040	41 483	18.2	42 115	1 129	425	2 272	3 099	6 662	19 364	11 149	34.5
2590	Santa Fe Springs	15 520	14 520	6.9	8 811	322	117	756	5 514	10 456	4 817	8 269	22.4
2595	Santa Maria	61 284	39 685	54.4	37 722	1 350	582	3 716	17 914	28 014	21 144	9 501	44.5
2600	Santa Monica	86 905	88 314	-1.6	71 961	3 920	384	5 550	5 090	12 210	47 753	17 755	21.4
2605	Santa Paula	25 062	20 552	21.9	14 858	78	208	257	9 661	14 753	8 062	8 529	11.9
2615	Santa Rosa	113 313	83 320	36.0	101 270	2 031	1 382	3 811	4 819	10 727	47 726	12 291	87.3
2617	Santa Venetia CDP	3 362	NA	NA	2 896	95	15	205	151	334	1 349	NA	5.1
2619	Santa Ynez CDP	4 200	NA	NA	4 037	3	30	42	88	329	1 564	NA	20.2
2623	Santee	52 902	47 080	12.4	48 193	893	414	1 587	1 815	5 685	18 275	10 266	41.1
2630	Saratoga	28 061	29 261	-4.1	23 484	118	52	4 215	192	940	10 315	25 572	31.0
2640	Sausalito	7 152	NA	NA	6 752	77	11	245	67	225	4 378	31 766	4.8
2647	Scotts Valley	8 615	NA	NA	8 184	41	36	242	112	421	3 556	14 311	11.7
2650	Seal Beach	25 098	25 975	-3.4	23 516	245	51	1 057	229	1 253	14 407	16 594	30.4
2653	Searles Valley CDP	2 740	NA	NA	2 543	20	69	29	79	337	1 095	NA	30.4
2655	Seaside	38 901	36 567	6.4	20 513	9 129	371	5 244	3 644	6 787	11 238	7 950	22.9
2665	Sebastopol	7 004	NA	NA	6 666	26	77	104	131	560	2 942	10 744	4.7
2667	Sedco Hills CDP	3 008	NA	NA	2 610	144	28	46	180	517	1 203	NA	4.3
2670	Selma	14 757	10 942	34.9	9 514	205	180	493	4 365	9 043	4 696	7 019	9.8
2675	Shafter	8 409	NA	NA	4 626	26	51	33	3 673	4 179	2 641	6 941	4.9
2690	Sierra Madre	10 762	10 837	-0.7	9 873	92	43	549	205	1 050	4 868	17 834	7.8
2693	Signal Hill	8 371	NA	NA	5 375	884	73	950	1 089	1 822	3 670	11 920	5.8
2702	Simi Valley	100 217	77 500	29.3	88 345	1 527	615	5 474	4 256	12 707	33 111	12 104	85.6
2704	Solana Beach	12 962	13 047	-0.7	11 480	61	42	379	1 000	1 907	6 346	12 651	9.1
2705	Soledad	7 146	NA	NA	2 036	29	33	330	4 718	6 394	1 650	5 773	4.6
2710	Solvang	4 741	NA	NA	4 476	14	23	56	172	757	2 076	18 969	6.4
2715	Sonoma	8 121	NA	NA	7 839	28	26	145	83	418	4 164	12 999	6.2
2720	Sonora	4 153	NA	NA	3 943	9	61	64	76	352	2 084	10 628	6.3
2722	Soquel CDP	9 188	NA	NA	8 552	48	74	266	248	724	3 925	NA	11.8
2725	South El Monte	20 850	16 623	25.4	13 727	102	104	1 088	5 829	17 633	4 867	6 454	7.5
2730	South Gate	86 284	66 784	29.2	35 936	1 437	382	1 394	47 135	71 727	22 946	7 070	19.0
2737	South Lake Tahoe	21 586	20 681	4.4	18 496	223	226	1 367	1 274	4 003	14 066	10 278	26.1
2745	South Oroville CDP	7 463	NA	NA	6 003	569	323	315	253	594	2 771	NA	11.8
2755	South Pasadena	23 936	22 681	5.5	16 711	745	97	5 086	1 297	3 213	10 719	17 015	8.9
2765	South San Francisco	54 312	49 393	10.0	33 398	2 172	357	13 368	5 017	14 731	19 081	11 981	23.2
2770	South San Gabriel CDP	7 700	NA	NA	2 646	50	37	2 567	2 400	4 002	2 159	NA	2.2
2772	South San Jose Hills CDP	17 814	16 049	11.0	8 946	433	113	1 295	7 027	13 514	3 825	NA	3.7
2773	South Santa Rosa CDP	4 128	NA	NA	3 341	192	129	121	345	760	1 431	NA	21.0
2782	South Whittier CDP	49 514	43 815	13.0	33 253	579	351	2 101	13 230	25 627	14 656	NA	13.9
2785	South Yuba City CDP	8 816	NA	NA	7 036	102	92	1 161	425	771	3 035	NA	7.0
2795	Spring Valley CDP	55 331	40 191	37.7	40 745	4 704	449	4 380	5 053	10 474	18 521	NA	31.5
2798	Stanford CDP	18 097	11 045	63.8	12 640	961	112	3 861	523	1 436	4 770	NA	7.1
2800	Stanton	30 491	23 723	28.5	22 302	692	159	3 682	3 656	10 209	10 755	10 549	8.1
2805	Stockton	210 943	149 779	40.8	121 372	20 321	2 061	48 087	19 102	52 653	72 525	9 333	136.2
2817	Strawberry CDP	4 377	NA	NA	3 967	103	9	263	35	162	2 241	NA	3.5
2820	Suisun City	22 686	11 087	104.6	13 510	3 236	250	3 869	1 821	3 645	7 029	9 373	9.2
2823	Sun City CDP	14 930	NA	NA	14 161	168	56	152	393	983	8 506	NA	20.9
2834	Sunnyslope CDP	3 766	NA	NA	2 791	101	30	128	716	1 362	1 112	NA	3.6
2835	Sunnyvale	117 229	106 618	10.0	83 972	4 022	608	22 655	5 972	15 444	50 789	16 073	56.7
2845	Susanville	7 279	NA	NA	6 653	73	277	102	174	547	3 124	9 444	7.2
2850	Sutter CDP	2 606	NA	NA	2 411	17	60	36	82	229	888	NA	5.6
2860	Taft	5 902	NA	NA	5 422	62	91	120	207	433	2 370	11 779	9.2
2869	Tamalpais-Homestead Valley CDP	9 601	NA	NA	8 963	132	31	391	84	331	4 251	NA	7.5
2871	Tara Hills CDP	4 998	NA	NA	3 624	589	49	471	265	640	1 825	NA	2.0
2873	Tehachapi	5 791	NA	NA	4 927	64	74	51	675	1 226	2 430	9 663	15.2
2878	Temecula	27 099	NA	NA	24 583	414	170	758	1 174	3 939	10 659	NA	68.4
2880	Temple City	31 100	28 972	7.3	22 369	192	114	6 067	2 358	5 862	11 548	11 980	10.4
2882	Templeton CDP	2 887	NA	NA	2 753	11	27	28	68	239	1 100	NA	7.2
2885	Terra Bella CDP	2 740	NA	NA	1 634	4	12	171	919	1 940	706	NA	4.5
2892	Thermalito CDP	5 646	NA	NA	5 044	33	232	257	80	252	2 184	NA	33.5
2897	Thousand Oaks	104 352	77 072	35.4	94 332	1 270	414	4 990	3 346	10 019	37 765	15 178	128.4
2899	Thousand Palms CDP	4 122	NA	NA	3 181	28	31	43	839	1 263	2 257	NA	10.4
2903	Tiburon town	7 532	NA	NA	7 139	69	12	278	34	256	3 433	27 657	11.3
2906	Tierra Buena CDP	2 878	NA	NA	2 358	25	20	318	157	254	1 033	NA	6.4
2910	Torrance	133 107	129 881	2.5	97 144	1 933	539	29 097	4 394	13 398	54 927	15 333	53.2
2912	Trabuco Highlands CDP	3 191	NA	NA	2 783	37	14	233	124	280	1 302	NA	14.7
2915	Tracy	33 558	18 428	82.1	28 944	855	347	1 550	1 862	8 145	12 174	9 638	24.8
2940	Truckee CDP	3 484	NA	NA	3 372	3	37	31	41	571	1 664	NA	15.6
2945	Tulare	33 249	22 498	47.8	21 798	2 045	351	831	8 224	11 250	11 316	7 633	36.9
2960	Turlock	42 198	26 278	60.6	34 820	500	393	1 845	4 640	8 849	15 400	8 998	24.8
2965	Tustin	50 689	32 317	56.8	37 127	2 895	274	5 260	5 133	10 508	19 300	13 429	29.2
2967	Tustin Foothills CDP	24 358	26 174	-6.9	22 314	128	57	1 491	368	1 506	8 442	NA	17.5

1. Codes shown are 2-digit FIPS codes for states; 4-digit census place codes for places; and 3-digit FIPS county codes followed by 3-digit census MCD codes for minor civil divisions (MCDs). MCD names are followed by county names in parentheses. 2. Hispanic persons may be of any race. 3. Dry land or land partially or temporarily covered by water.

State/ Place/ MCD[1] code	Place	Population: 1990	Population: Places of 10,000 or more: 1980	Population: Places of 10,000 or more: Percent change, 1980–1990	Race: White	Race: Black	Race: Am. Indian, Eskimo Aleut	Race: Asian & Pacific Islander	Race: Other race	Hispanic[2]	Total housing units, 1990	Per capita income, 1985 (Dollars)	Land area,[3] 1990 (Sq. Km.)
		1	2	3	4	5	6	7	8	9	10	11	12
	CALIFORNIA—Con.												
2971	Twentynine Palms	11 821	NA	NA	9 633	1 030	162	508	488	1 219	5 958	NA	140.1
2972	Twentynine Palms Base CDP	10 606	NA	NA	7 494	1 960	140	427	585	1 414	1 533	NA	3.7
2975	Twin Lakes CDP	5 379	NA	NA	4 726	94	34	133	392	947	2 723	NA	1.8
2980	Ukiah	14 599	12 035	21.3	12 846	146	551	256	800	1 709	5 825	9 327	12.3
2985	Union City	53 762	39 406	36.4	23 613	4 612	318	17 978	7 241	13 484	16 259	10 784	48.6
2990	Upland	63 374	47 647	33.0	49 972	3 380	286	4 457	5 279	11 115	24 496	13 504	39.1
2995	Vacaville	71 479	43 367	64.8	56 351	6 370	707	2 724	5 327	11 366	23 660	10 891	58.6
2998	Valinda CDP	18 735	18 700	0.2	11 353	967	85	2 048	4 282	10 876	4 666	NA	5.2
3000	Vallejo	109 199	80 303	36.0	55 100	23 098	810	25 063	5 128	11 777	39 902	10 185	78.3
3001	Valle Vista CDP	8 751	NA	NA	8 383	27	60	113	168	637	4 444	NA	9.0
3004	Vandenberg AFB CDP	9 846	NA	NA	7 467	1 360	61	523	435	888	3 036	NA	57.3
3005	Vandenberg Village CDP	5 971	NA	NA	5 220	348	52	218	133	360	2 368	NA	13.5
3007	Victorville	40 674	14 229	185.9	29 724	3 899	442	1 491	5 118	9 353	15 627	9 495	108.3
3008	View Park-Windsor Hills CDP	11 769	12 101	-2.7	1 014	10 325	37	183	210	402	4 749	NA	4.7
3009	Villa Park	6 299	NA	NA	5 525	27	14	666	67	331	1 966	21 768	5.4
3011	Vincent CDP	13 713	NA	NA	9 662	391	88	974	2 598	6 253	3 862	NA	3.8
3013	Vine Hill CDP	3 214	NA	NA	2 782	62	62	107	201	541	1 163	NA	9.6
3015	Visalia	75 636	49 729	52.1	56 554	1 114	737	4 869	12 362	19 005	27 154	10 038	60.8
3017	Vista	71 872	35 834	100.6	57 972	3 201	593	2 853	7 253	17 804	27 418	10 212	46.5
3025	Walnut	29 105	12 478	133.3	13 979	1 925	102	10 909	2 190	6 836	8 091	12 100	23.0
3030	Walnut Creek	60 569	53 643	12.9	54 878	635	152	4 046	858	2 869	29 968	19 265	50.0
3040	Walnut Park CDP	14 722	11 811	24.6	4 747	54	59	152	9 710	13 566	3 544	NA	1.9
3045	Wasco	12 412	NA	NA	4 788	684	108	97	6 735	7 858	3 597	6 646	8.3
3050	Waterford	4 771	NA	NA	3 878	15	83	64	731	1 152	1 458	7 280	3.6
3055	Watsonville	31 099	23 543	32.1	17 147	228	299	1 727	11 698	18 927	9 909	9 234	15.3
3060	Weaverville CDP	3 370	NA	NA	3 237	10	84	25	14	69	1 502	NA	91.7
3063	Weed	3 062	NA	NA	2 393	371	71	144	83	318	1 255	8 271	10.3
3065	West Athens CDP	8 859	NA	NA	722	5 575	44	262	2 256	2 906	2 643	NA	3.5
3066	West Bishop CDP	2 908	NA	NA	2 826	2	42	19	19	120	1 133	NA	22.6
3067	West Carson CDP	20 143	17 997	11.9	11 353	1 993	130	4 271	2 396	4 621	7 137	NA	5.9
3068	West Compton CDP	5 451	NA	NA	499	4 104	13	92	743	1 270	1 591	NA	4.2
3070	West Covina	96 086	80 291	19.7	57 436	8 203	485	16 522	13 440	33 253	31 112	11 844	42.0
3080	West Hollywood	36 118	35 703	1.2	32 571	1 235	130	1 119	1 063	3 153	23 821	18 019	4.9
3082	Westlake Village	7 455	NA	NA	6 895	56	11	426	67	313	3 006	20 908	13.5
3084	West Menlo Park CDP	3 959	NA	NA	3 641	30	5	252	31	168	1 701	NA	1.4
3085	Westminster	78 118	71 133	9.8	54 396	868	464	17 612	4 778	14 896	25 852	12 181	26.0
3091	Westmont CDP	31 044	27 916	11.2	1 729	22 417	95	210	6 593	8 530	10 174	NA	4.8
3094	West Pittsburg CDP	17 453	NA	NA	11 676	2 047	229	1 925	1 576	3 768	6 291	NA	26.0
3097	West Puente Valley CDP	20 254	20 445	-0.9	13 021	884	146	1 732	4 471	15 208	4 538	NA	4.6
3098	West Sacramento	28 898	10 875	165.7	20 595	692	576	2 626	4 409	7 060	11 652	9 561	54.3
3099	West Whittier-Los Nietos CDP	24 164	21 001	15.1	13 386	126	142	593	9 917	18 015	6 927	NA	6.8
3110	Whittier	77 671	69 717	11.4	57 048	992	462	2 581	16 588	30 278	28 758	13 763	32.5
3112	Wildomar CDP	10 411	NA	NA	9 601	94	96	176	444	1 312	4 065	NA	31.8
3120	Willits	5 027	NA	NA	4 516	18	138	41	314	629	1 968	7 919	7.2
3121	Willowbrook CDP	32 772	30 845	6.2	3 615	18 096	66	195	10 800	14 618	8 538	NA	9.7
3125	Willows	5 988	NA	NA	4 759	33	161	660	375	647	2 240	9 385	6.7
3127	Wilton CDP	3 858	NA	NA	3 582	36	65	98	77	260	1 283	NA	76.7
3131	Windsor CDP	13 371	NA	NA	11 329	124	227	289	1 402	2 597	5 252	NA	25.4
3135	Winters	4 639	NA	NA	3 351	14	38	78	1 158	1 868	1 564	8 814	6.0
3137	Winton CDP	7 559	NA	NA	5 186	278	47	609	1 439	3 035	2 242	NA	7.4
3140	Woodbridge CDP	3 456	NA	NA	3 045	12	42	164	193	788	1 238	NA	11.5
3142	Woodcrest CDP	7 796	NA	NA	6 838	276	70	227	385	1 049	2 467	NA	26.9
3145	Woodlake	5 678	NA	NA	2 387	1	38	114	3 138	4 238	1 585	4 983	4.8
3150	Woodland	39 802	30 235	31.6	30 836	500	531	1 222	6 713	10 413	14 818	10 499	23.8
3155	Woodside town	5 035	NA	NA	4 766	17	13	201	38	192	1 892	33 864	30.4
3163	Wrightwood CDP	3 308	NA	NA	3 224	4	34	21	25	153	2 184	NA	5.7
3169	Yorba Linda	52 422	28 254	85.5	44 949	579	222	5 307	1 365	4 948	17 341	16 160	45.3
3177	Yountville town	3 259	NA	NA	3 021	56	22	45	115	326	980	8 770	4.2
3180	Yreka	6 948	NA	NA	6 510	35	330	41	32	238	3 102	9 443	23.4
3185	Yuba City	27 437	18 731	46.5	20 876	713	457	2 117	3 274	4 905	11 068	8 898	17.9
3186	Yucaipa	32 824	23 345	40.6	30 403	172	299	323	1 627	3 609	14 276	NA	68.7
3187	Yucca Valley CDP	13 701	NA	NA	12 781	204	139	182	395	976	6 422	NA	36.0
08	COLORADO	3 294 394	2 889 735	14.0	2 905 474	133 146	27 776	59 862	168 136	424 302	1 477 349	11 713	268 659.5
0007	Air Force Academy CDP	9 062	NA	NA	7 797	758	40	306	161	539	1 280	NA	26.0
0015	Alamosa	7 579	NA	NA	5 953	50	69	97	1 410	3 306	2 874	7 734	9.0
0029	Applewood CDP	11 069	12 040	-8.1	10 664	86	59	122	138	415	4 582	NA	18.9
0040	Arvada	89 235	84 619	5.5	84 129	513	475	1 768	2 350	6 643	34 541	12 927	57.3
0045	Aspen	5 049	NA	NA	4 883	15	24	73	54	239	4 004	20 963	5.2
0055	Aurora	222 103	158 588	40.1	183 046	25 394	1 426	8 376	3 861	14 768	99 890	13 133	343.2
0080	Berthoud town	2 990	NA	NA	2 783	3	20	21	163	271	1 168	NA	3.1
0088	Black Forest CDP	8 143	NA	NA	7 934	51	41	52	65	204	2 854	NA	330.4

1. Codes shown are 2-digit FIPS codes for states; 4-digit census place codes for places; and 3-digit FIPS county codes followed by 3-digit census MCD codes for minor civil divisions (MCDs). MCD names are followed by county names in parentheses. 2. Hispanic persons may be of any race. 3. Dry land or land partially or temporarily covered by water.

State/ Place/ MCD[1] code	Place	Population	Places of 10,000 or more		Population characteristics, 1990						Total housing units, 1990	Per capita income, 1985 (Dollars)	Land area,[3] 1990 (Sq. Km.)
					Race								
		1990	1980	Percent change, 1980–1990	White	Black	Am. Indian, Eskimo Aleut	Asian & Pacific Islander	Other race	Hispanic[2]			
		1	2	3	4	5	6	7	8	9	10	11	12
	COLORADO—Con.												
0110	Boulder	83 312	76 685	8.6	77 090	1 048	414	3 208	1 552	4 022	36 270	13 054	58.4
0130	Brighton	14 203	12 773	11.2	11 689	154	95	200	2 065	4 916	5 321	9 196	38.7
0143	Broomfield	24 638	20 722	18.9	23 236	166	159	528	549	1 381	9 098	12 116	57.8
0150	Brush	4 165	NA	NA	3 749	9	16	22	369	845	1 720	7 970	6.3
0160	Burlington	2 941	NA	NA	2 672	8	8	3	250	365	1 288	8 331	4.4
0175	Canon City	12 687	13 037	-2.7	12 143	171	91	43	239	999	5 609	8 160	20.4
0180	Carbondale town	3 004	NA	NA	2 898	10	6	18	72	249	1 119	NA	4.3
0185	Castle Rock	8 708	NA	NA	8 471	36	47	55	99	363	3 529	13 033	79.9
0187	Castlewood CDP	24 392	16 413	48.6	23 461	288	58	483	102	598	8 642	NA	16.2
0210	Cherry Hills Village	5 245	NA	NA	5 171	30	5	29	10	76	1 789	45 061	16.1
0218	Cimarron Hills CDP	11 160	NA	NA	9 571	875	69	303	342	922	4 439	NA	15.5
0221	Clifton CDP	12 671	NA	NA	12 036	33	94	97	411	1 034	4 922	NA	17.9
0240	Colorado Springs	281 140	215 150	30.7	241 513	19 746	2 335	6 845	10 701	25 662	124 442	11 334	474.5
0242	Columbine CDP	23 969	23 463	2.2	23 172	121	65	305	306	1 106	8 112	NA	16.6
0245	Commerce City	16 466	16 234	1.4	13 976	471	219	187	1 613	5 916	6 414	7 971	51.7
0250	Cortez	7 284	NA	NA	6 273	3	699	23	286	822	3 142	9 262	13.9
0255	Craig	8 091	NA	NA	7 770	10	54	33	224	527	3 559	10 480	12.5
0315	Delta	3 789	NA	NA	3 363	8	28	12	378	804	1 842	7 838	7.1
0320	Denver	467 610	492 365	-5.0	337 198	60 046	5 381	11 005	53 980	107 382	239 636	12 490	397.0
0325	Derby CDP	6 043	NA	NA	5 240	88	48	47	620	1 894	2 283	NA	4.6
0350	Durango	12 430	11 426	8.8	11 149	39	370	135	737	1 444	4 917	9 624	12.1
0380	Edgewater	4 613	NA	NA	4 124	38	60	83	308	794	2 385	10 586	1.9
0387	El Jebel CDP	2 605	NA	NA	2 490	1	17	9	88	262	921	NA	14.9
0395	Englewood	29 387	30 021	-2.1	27 573	357	267	451	739	2 348	14 908	11 657	16.9
0405	Estes Park town	3 184	NA	NA	3 144	5	9	19	7	33	2 006	13 436	13.2
0415	Evans	5 877	NA	NA	4 832	26	51	57	911	1 491	2 283	8 740	7.0
0420	Evergreen CDP	7 582	NA	NA	7 459	19	20	51	33	157	3 176	NA	26.8
0430	Federal Heights	9 342	NA	NA	8 421	87	77	382	375	1 167	4 955	10 782	4.7
0450	Florence	2 990	NA	NA	2 849	13	49	24	55	467	1 293	7 832	5.3
0452	Fort Carson CDP	11 309	13 219	-14.4	7 491	2 725	129	413	551	1 224	1 841	NA	24.3
0455	Fort Collins	87 758	65 092	34.8	81 877	856	459	2 098	2 468	6 197	35 357	10 444	106.7
0465	Fort Lupton	5 159	NA	NA	3 789	21	41	72	1 236	2 246	1 795	7 913	7.5
0470	Fort Morgan	9 068	NA	NA	7 534	26	76	41	1 391	1 917	3 761	9 420	11.2
0475	Fountain	9 984	NA	NA	8 007	1 057	80	320	520	1 311	3 789	7 497	36.6
0505	Fruita	4 045	NA	NA	3 775	5	27	14	224	622	1 583	7 243	10.5
0507	Fruitvale CDP	5 222	NA	NA	5 061	8	31	21	101	327	1 954	NA	8.2
0512	Gateway CDP	7 510	NA	NA	7 189	82	27	125	87	264	2 588	NA	13.8
0514	Genesee CDP	2 737	NA	NA	2 684	4	10	35	4	51	1 105	NA	17.2
0535	Glenwood Springs	6 561	NA	NA	6 389	17	32	32	91	270	2 882	11 689	11.9
0540	Golden	13 116	12 237	7.2	12 323	130	108	344	211	647	5 825	11 979	19.5
0555	Grand Junction	29 034	28 144	3.2	26 658	237	242	286	1 611	3 227	13 698	9 088	38.5
0570	Greeley	60 536	53 006	14.2	53 936	408	366	607	5 219	12 327	23 991	9 726	73.6
0580	Greenwood Village	7 589	NA	NA	7 293	89	9	174	24	139	2 687	26 331	20.0
0587	Gunbarrel CDP	9 388	NA	NA	8 818	158	44	265	103	283	3 981	NA	15.9
0590	Gunnison	4 636	NA	NA	4 459	46	39	28	64	247	1 853	7 145	8.2
0618	Highlands Ranch CDP	10 181	NA	NA	9 841	113	15	116	96	340	3 751	NA	12.5
0702	Ken Caryl CDP	24 391	10 661	128.8	23 186	192	82	445	486	1 403	8 612	NA	24.8
0735	Lafayette	14 548	NA	NA	12 942	143	107	316	1 040	2 163	5 775	10 920	17.9
0745	La Junta	7 637	NA	NA	6 597	67	79	59	835	2 958	3 255	8 469	6.7
0760	Lakewood	126 481	112 860	12.1	117 819	1 316	872	2 435	4 039	11 506	55 678	14 478	105.7
0765	Lamar	8 343	NA	NA	7 040	43	60	24	1 176	2 167	3 599	8 250	10.7
0790	Leadville	2 629	NA	NA	2 451	6	20	7	145	590	1 519	9 585	2.7
0805	Lincoln Park CDP	3 728	NA	NA	3 677	5	18	4	24	142	1 649	NA	9.8
0810	Littleton	33 685	28 655	17.6	32 369	296	189	469	362	1 755	14 778	13 834	31.9
0820	Longmont	51 555	42 942	20.1	47 810	197	379	632	2 537	5 715	20 480	11 235	34.0
0825	Louisville	12 361	NA	NA	11 689	103	48	306	215	666	4 785	12 409	19.9
0830	Loveland	37 352	30 244	23.5	35 436	111	179	266	1 360	2 527	14 711	11 220	55.4
0850	Manitou Springs	4 535	NA	NA	4 363	24	47	46	55	170	2 524	13 413	7.9
0900	Monte Vista	4 324	NA	NA	3 570	0	20	8	726	2 387	1 760	6 706	4.1
0910	Montrose	8 854	NA	NA	8 209	40	60	34	511	1 365	3 915	10 215	15.1
0942	Niwot CDP	2 666	NA	NA	2 582	15	5	43	21	64	1 104	NA	10.5
0943	Northglenn	27 195	29 847	-8.9	24 661	447	222	552	1 313	3 966	10 442	11 462	18.1
0990	Orchard Mesa CDP	5 977	NA	NA	5 675	19	23	26	234	382	2 219	NA	14.5
1039	Parker town	5 450	NA	NA	5 272	37	24	44	73	210	2 095	NA	34.3
1085	Pueblo	98 640	101 686	-3.0	81 824	2 147	822	622	13 225	38 969	40 862	8 685	93.0
1087	Pueblo West CDP	4 386	NA	NA	4 224	33	28	38	63	346	1 701	NA	196.1
1112	Redlands CDP	9 355	NA	NA	9 086	12	33	42	182	416	3 666	NA	49.9
1125	Rifle	4 636	NA	NA	4 498	4	45	29	60	302	1 984	8 658	10.0
1135	Rocky Ford	4 162	NA	NA	2 696	17	51	16	1 382	2 357	1 829	7 159	4.1
1160	Salida	4 737	NA	NA	4 552	1	36	19	129	595	2 350	8 456	5.7
1182	Security-Widefield CDP	23 822	18 768	26.9	19 601	2 271	202	987	761	2 298	8 435	NA	38.2
1200	Sheridan	4 976	NA	NA	4 365	100	89	37	385	1 097	2 253	9 496	5.7
1207	Sherrelwood CDP	16 636	17 629	-5.6	14 486	121	163	542	1 324	4 436	6 224	NA	6.4

1. Codes shown are 2-digit FIPS codes for states; 4-digit census place codes for places; and 3-digit FIPS county codes followed by 3-digit census MCD codes for minor civil divisions (MCDs). MCD names are followed by county names in parentheses. 2. Hispanic persons may be of any race. 3. Dry land or land partially or temporarily covered by water.

State/ Place/ MCD[1] code	Place	Population 1990	Places of 10,000 or more 1980	Places of 10,000 or more Percent change, 1980–1990	Race: White	Race: Black	Race: Am. Indian, Eskimo Aleut	Race: Asian & Pacific Islander	Race: Other race	Hispanic[2]	Total housing units, 1990	Per capita income, 1985 (Dollars)	Land area,[3] 1990 (Sq. Km.)
		1	2	3	4	5	6	7	8	9	10	11	12
	COLORADO—Con.												
1238	Southglenn CDP	43 087	37 787	14.0	41 562	324	137	821	243	1 315	15 763	NA	25.5
1250	Steamboat Springs	6 695	NA	NA	6 616	6	20	28	25	133	5 345	13 151	23.2
1255	Sterling	10 362	11 385	-9.0	9 689	19	33	24	597	1 100	4 791	9 356	14.0
1257	Stratmoor CDP	5 854	NA	NA	4 349	738	88	287	392	811	2 233	NA	7.6
1283	The Pinery CDP	4 885	NA	NA	4 808	19	17	27	14	91	1 561	NA	14.2
1285	Thornton	55 031	40 343	36.4	49 357	699	501	911	3 563	9 309	20 974	10 794	53.5
1295	Trinidad	8 580	NA	NA	7 088	31	77	50	1 334	4 264	3 903	6 878	11.0
1307	Vail town	3 659	NA	NA	3 539	10	13	25	72	140	6 102	18 320	12.1
1330	Walsenburg	3 300	NA	NA	2 976	18	45	11	250	1 814	1 654	7 188	6.0
1344	Welby CDP	10 218	NA	NA	8 416	228	114	158	1 302	2 484	4 138	NA	9.9
1355	Westminster	74 625	50 176	48.7	67 643	742	468	2 755	3 017	8 570	29 868	12 161	69.4
1356	Westminster East CDP	5 197	NA	NA	4 469	31	60	217	420	1 417	2 164	NA	4.3
1360	Wheat Ridge	29 419	30 280	-2.8	27 854	168	178	437	782	2 135	14 130	13 424	23.0
1375	Windsor town	5 062	NA	NA	4 682	18	28	29	305	662	1 917	8 869	12.3
1380	Woodland Park	4 610	NA	NA	4 496	5	35	21	53	128	2 018	10 393	10.2
1382	Woodmoor CDP	3 858	NA	NA	3 752	20	5	55	26	82	1 328	NA	15.9
1395	Yuma	2 719	NA	NA	2 648	2	13	3	53	113	1 256	6 918	5.9
09	CONNECTICUT	3 287 116	3 107 564	5.8	2 859 353	274 269	6 654	50 698	96 142	213 116	1 320 850	14 090	12 549.6
0020	Ansonia	18 403	19 039	-3.3	16 562	1 524	41	123	153	474	7 503	10 981	15.6
0125	Bethel CDP	8 835	NA	NA	8 407	154	16	221	37	193	3 615	NA	10.5
0155	Blue Hills CDP	3 206	NA	NA	561	2 524	8	34	79	140	1 046	NA	3.0
0182	Branford Center CDP	5 688	NA	NA	5 523	89	5	48	23	115	3 000	NA	4.8
0200	Bridgeport	141 686	142 546	-0.6	82 945	37 684	405	3 288	17 364	37 547	57 224	9 427	41.5
0230	Bristol	60 640	57 370	5.7	58 242	1 263	102	465	568	1 652	24 989	12 361	68.7
0250	Broad Brook CDP	3 585	NA	NA	3 389	98	11	65	22	80	1 497	NA	15.3
0353	Central Manchester CDP	30 934	NA	NA	29 132	1 038	67	469	228	730	13 443	NA	16.7
0357	Central Waterford CDP	2 939	NA	NA	2 824	62	8	31	14	50	1 338	NA	5.2
0379	Cheshire Village CDP	5 759	NA	NA	5 596	47	0	98	18	59	2 294	NA	8.7
0410	Clinton CDP	3 439	NA	NA	3 329	27	8	29	46	149	1 578	NA	6.3
0430	Colchester borough	3 212	NA	NA	3 088	96	9	13	6	29	1 219	11 377	5.9
0460	Collinsville CDP	2 591	NA	NA	2 551	16	1	17	6	26	1 075	NA	7.9
0480	Conning Towers-Nautilus Park CDP	10 013	NA	NA	8 780	661	53	376	143	457	2 769	NA	4.7
0505	Coventry Lake CDP	2 895	NA	NA	2 844	27	6	4	14	37	1 272	NA	7.6
0530	Danbury	65 585	60 470	8.5	56 897	4 311	132	2 582	1 663	5 045	25 950	13 337	109.1
0550	Danielson borough	4 441	NA	NA	4 240	51	26	110	14	56	1 912	9 971	2.9
0560	Darien CDP	18 130	18 892	-4.0	17 615	75	9	371	60	337	6 627	NA	33.3
0570	Deep River Center CDP	2 520	NA	NA	2 427	68	0	17	8	30	1 064	NA	6.8
0590	Derby	12 199	12 346	-1.2	11 571	301	22	94	211	539	5 269	12 311	12.9
0605	Durham CDP	2 650	NA	NA	2 607	11	2	23	7	23	954	NA	16.2
0680	East Hartford CDP	50 452	52 563	-4.0	43 791	4 235	110	1 120	1 196	3 006	21 274	NA	46.7
0690	East Haven CDP	26 144	25 028	4.5	25 635	231	26	101	151	507	10 580	NA	31.8
0760	Essex Village CDP	2 500	NA	NA	2 477	16	3	4	0	19	1 247	NA	9.1
0848	Glastonbury Center CDP	7 082	NA	NA	6 892	37	11	113	29	135	3 228	NA	12.4
0900	Groton	9 837	10 086	-2.5	8 602	812	87	158	178	427	4 479	12 479	8.3
0920	Guilford Center CDP	2 588	NA	NA	2 549	11	1	2	25	71	1 253	NA	5.8
0970	Hartford	139 739	136 392	2.5	55 869	54 338	450	2 024	27 058	44 137	56 098	8 677	44.8
1003	Hazardville CDP	5 179	NA	NA	5 032	75	6	58	8	67	1 891	NA	7.5
1015	Heritage Village CDP	3 623	NA	NA	3 605	9	1	2	6	27	2 700	NA	5.9
1040	Jewett City borough	3 349	NA	NA	3 256	48	5	17	23	50	1 469	9 041	1.9
1056	Kensington CDP	8 306	NA	NA	8 198	18	4	72	14	124	3 159	NA	13.6
1090	Lake Pocotopaug CDP	3 029	NA	NA	2 985	13	1	15	15	42	1 527	NA	7.0
1210	Meriden	59 479	57 118	4.1	53 327	2 553	107	417	3 075	8 144	24 826	11 952	61.5
1250	Middletown	42 762	39 040	9.5	36 533	4 747	74	826	582	1 413	18 102	11 530	105.9
1270	Milford	48 168	49 101	-1.9	46 610	741	71	505	241	1 105	19 339	13 534	57.7
1330	Moosup CDP	3 289	NA	NA	3 252	6	3	23	5	45	1 323	NA	6.0
1360	Mystic CDP	2 618	NA	NA	2 561	17	5	32	3	23	1 211	NA	7.7
1370	Naugatuck borough	30 625	26 456	15.8	29 471	567	73	264	250	950	11 930	11 418	42.5
1390	New Britain	75 491	73 840	2.2	61 605	5 723	130	1 348	6 685	12 284	32 335	10 945	34.5
1450	New Haven	130 474	126 109	3.5	70 263	47 157	402	3 141	9 511	17 243	54 057	9 378	48.8
1470	Newington CDP	29 208	28 841	1.3	28 197	413	39	408	151	612	11 609	NA	34.1
1480	New London	28 540	28 842	-1.0	20 828	4 807	194	614	2 097	3 459	11 970	10 629	14.3
1500	New Milford CDP	5 775	NA	NA	5 489	127	35	84	40	139	2 563	NA	7.5
1540	Niantic CDP	3 048	NA	NA	2 994	13	14	20	7	41	1 690	NA	3.8
1610	North Haven CDP	22 249	22 080	0.8	21 308	474	12	394	61	257	8 244	NA	53.8
1625	Northwest Harwinton CDP	3 299	NA	NA	3 281	9	0	7	2	24	1 233	NA	22.5
1630	Norwalk	78 331	77 767	0.7	62 106	12 123	100	1 290	2 712	7 339	32 224	15 907	59.1
1650	Norwich	37 391	38 074	-1.8	34 145	1 974	240	400	632	1 161	16 472	10 870	73.4
1666	Oakville CDP	8 741	NA	NA	8 569	85	7	52	28	153	3 218	NA	8.2
1700	Orange CDP	12 830	13 237	-3.1	12 391	107	4	304	24	148	4 544	NA	44.5
1720	Pawcatuck CDP	5 289	NA	NA	5 218	33	14	14	10	78	2 324	NA	9.6
1730	Plainfield Village CDP	2 856	NA	NA	2 811	8	9	14	14	30	1 025	NA	4.3

1. Codes shown are 2-digit FIPS codes for states; 4-digit census place codes for places; and 3-digit FIPS county codes followed by 3-digit census MCD codes for minor civil divisions (MCDs). MCD names are followed by county names in parentheses. 2. Hispanic persons may be of any race. 3. Dry land or land partially or temporarily covered by water.

State/ Place/ MCD[1] code	Place	Population: 1990	Places of 10,000 or more: 1980	Places of 10,000 or more: Percent change, 1980–1990	Race: White	Race: Black	Race: Am. Indian, Eskimo Aleut	Race: Asian & Pacific Islander	Race: Other race	Hispanic[2]	Total housing units, 1990	Per capita income, 1985 (Dollars)	Land area,[3] 1990 (Sq. Km.)
		1	2	3	4	5	6	7	8	9	10	11	12
	CONNECTICUT—Con.												
1805	Poquonock Bridge CDP	2 770	NA	NA	2 247	383	33	68	39	84	1 028	NA	3.9
1818	Portland CDP	5 645	NA	NA	5 401	166	15	32	31	83	2 222	NA	12.8
1855	Putnam District CDP	6 835	NA	NA	6 619	90	31	29	66	99	3 020	NA	8.3
1890	Ridgefield CDP	6 363	NA	NA	6 219	45	5	81	13	125	2 717	NA	14.5
2030	Shelton	35 418	31 314	13.1	34 396	342	67	457	156	880	12 981	13 833	79.2
2053	Sherwood Manor CDP	6 357	NA	NA	6 185	98	11	61	2	84	2 226	NA	8.1
2060	Simsbury Center CDP	5 577	NA	NA	5 426	53	3	81	14	84	2 196	NA	11.6
2143	Southwood Acres CDP	8 963	NA	NA	8 827	52	5	75	4	84	3 015	NA	10.6
2160	Stafford Springs borough	4 100	NA	NA	3 928	20	6	110	36	95	1 747	10 279	6.3
2180	Stamford	108 056	102 453	5.5	82 421	19 217	135	2 811	3 472	10 562	44 279	18 246	97.7
2240	Storrs CDP	12 198	11 338	7.6	10 512	487	21	1 059	119	362	1 717	NA	15.5
2250	Stratford CDP	49 389	50 541	-2.3	44 483	3 899	74	400	533	1 771	20 152	NA	45.5
2278	Terryville CDP	5 426	NA	NA	5 370	19	2	28	7	27	2 267	NA	7.2
2315	Thompsonville CDP	8 458	NA	NA	8 169	134	8	90	57	237	3 635	NA	5.7
2330	Torrington	33 687	30 987	8.7	32 581	567	61	415	63	357	15 161	11 646	103.1
2350	Trumbull CDP	32 000	32 989	-3.0	30 967	408	25	537	63	564	11 090	NA	60.2
2360	Uncasville-Oxoboxo Valley CDP	2 975	NA	NA	2 860	36	21	35	23	59	1 283	NA	11.2
2420	Wallingford Center CDP	17 827	17 821	0.0	17 198	169	27	182	251	915	7 716	NA	18.6
2460	Waterbury	108 961	103 266	5.5	86 681	14 133	344	787	7 016	14 578	47 205	10 187	74.0
2505	Weatogue CDP	2 521	NA	NA	2 436	18	1	57	9	49	917	NA	7.8
2530	West Hartford CDP	60 110	61 301	-1.9	56 493	1 310	46	1 710	551	1 891	25 021	NA	56.9
2535	West Haven	54 021	53 184	1.6	45 443	6 713	125	1 098	642	1 928	22 679	11 556	28.1
2550	West Mystic CDP	3 595	NA	NA	3 481	39	16	49	10	53	1 584	NA	6.2
2570	Westport CDP	24 407	25 290	-3.5	23 668	262	28	399	50	547	9 840	NA	51.8
2580	Wethersfield CDP	25 651	26 013	-1.4	25 021	293	31	200	106	422	10 790	NA	32.1
2590	Willimantic CDP	14 746	14 652	0.6	12 629	460	59	186	1 412	2 343	5 887	NA	11.4
2640	Windsor Locks CDP	12 358	12 190	1.4	11 884	185	16	214	59	163	4 929	NA	23.4
2660	Winsted CDP	8 254	NA	NA	8 145	39	24	33	13	110	3 643	NA	12.1
0010	Bethel town (Fairfield)	17 541	16 004	9.6	16 847	223	19	383	69	375	6 399	14 459	43.5
0010	Bridgeport town (Fairfield)	141 686	142 546	-0.6	82 945	37 684	405	3 288	17 364	37 547	57 224	NA	41.5
0010	Brookfield town (Fairfield)	14 113	12 872	9.6	13 720	101	5	238	49	220	5 354	17 038	51.3
0010	Danbury town (Fairfield)	65 585	60 470	8.5	56 897	4 311	132	2 582	1 663	5 045	25 950	NA	109.1
0010	Darien town (Fairfield)	18 196	18 892	-3.7	17 678	75	9	371	63	340	6 653	33 448	33.3
0010	Easton town (Fairfield)	6 303	NA	NA	6 165	19	2	104	13	81	2 215	21 633	71.0
0010	Fairfield town (Fairfield)	53 418	54 849	-2.6	52 134	437	40	674	133	993	20 204	18 107	77.8
0010	Greenwich town (Fairfield)	58 441	59 578	-1.9	54 503	1 245	46	2 039	608	2 583	23 515	29 764	124.0
0010	Monroe town (Fairfield)	16 896	14 010	20.6	16 324	279	23	220	50	357	5 596	15 023	67.6
0010	New Canaan town (Fairfield)	17 864	17 931	-0.4	17 232	230	13	349	40	247	6 856	36 250	57.3
0010	New Fairfield town (Fairfield)	12 911	11 260	14.7	12 684	31	16	159	21	213	5 081	15 718	53.0
0010	Newtown town (Fairfield)	20 779	19 107	8.8	20 221	206	34	265	53	351	7 194	15 963	149.6
0010	Norwalk town (Fairfield)	78 331	77 767	0.7	62 106	12 123	100	1 290	2 712	7 339	32 224	NA	59.1
0010	Redding town (Fairfield)	7 927	NA	NA	7 758	32	5	121	11	100	2 990	22 607	81.6
0010	Ridgefield town (Fairfield)	20 919	20 120	4.0	20 439	123	34	276	47	324	7 999	21 539	89.2
0010	Shelton town (Fairfield)	35 418	31 314	13.1	34 396	342	67	457	156	880	12 981	NA	79.2
0010	Sherman town (Fairfield)	2 809	NA	NA	2 768	13	4	14	10	42	1 451	NA	56.5
0010	Stamford town (Fairfield)	108 056	102 453	5.5	82 421	19 217	135	2 811	3 472	10 562	44 279	NA	97.7
0010	Stratford town (Fairfield)	49 389	50 541	-2.3	44 483	3 899	74	400	533	1 771	20 152	13 784	45.5
0011	Trumbull town (Fairfield)	32 016	32 989	-2.9	30 983	408	25	537	63	564	11 095	16 647	60.4
0011	Weston town (Fairfield)	8 648	NA	NA	8 421	98	2	104	23	125	3 278	32 007	51.3
0011	Westport town (Fairfield)	24 410	25 290	-3.5	23 671	262	28	399	50	547	9 841	30 072	51.8
0011	Wilton town (Fairfield)	15 989	15 328	4.3	15 554	161	8	251	15	212	5 824	27 925	69.8
0030	Avon town (Hartford)	13 937	11 201	24.4	13 552	129	12	210	34	118	5 709	22 841	59.9
0030	Berlin town (Hartford)	16 787	15 121	11.0	16 492	84	12	167	32	224	6 204	13 928	68.5
0030	Bloomfield town (Hartford)	19 483	18 608	4.7	10 835	8 084	36	271	257	590	7 738	15 615	67.4
0030	Bristol town (Hartford)	60 640	57 370	5.7	58 242	1 263	102	465	568	1 652	24 989	NA	68.7
0030	Burlington town (Hartford)	7 026	NA	NA	6 937	40	5	32	12	56	2 372	14 070	77.2
0030	Canton town (Hartford)	8 268	NA	NA	8 145	49	3	60	11	89	3 323	15 631	63.6
0030	East Granby town (Hartford)	4 302	NA	NA	4 214	63	4	16	5	51	1 685	15 205	45.3
0030	East Hartford town (Hartford)	50 452	52 563	-4.0	43 791	4 235	110	1 120	1 196	3 006	21 274	12 544	46.7
0030	East Windsor town (Hartford)	10 081	NA	NA	9 510	342	39	131	59	164	4 115	12 464	68.1
0030	Enfield town (Hartford)	45 532	42 695	6.6	43 582	1 208	55	472	215	1 039	16 614	12 094	86.6
0030	Farmington town (Hartford)	20 608	16 407	25.6	19 830	270	23	428	57	240	8 654	18 717	72.7
0030	Glastonbury town (Hartford)	27 901	24 327	14.7	26 779	259	25	677	161	562	10 948	18 999	133.0
0030	Granby town (Hartford)	9 369	NA	NA	9 224	48	16	66	15	88	3 492	17 010	105.4
0030	Hartford town (Hartford)	139 739	136 392	2.5	55 869	54 338	450	2 024	27 058	44 137	56 098	NA	44.8
0030	Manchester town (Hartford)	51 618	49 761	3.7	48 262	2 005	101	869	381	1 229	21 704	13 664	70.6
0030	Marlborough town (Hartford)	5 535	NA	NA	5 441	52	4	29	9	68	1 869	14 487	60.3
0030	New Britain town (Hartford)	75 491	73 840	2.2	61 605	5 723	130	1 348	6 685	12 284	32 335	NA	34.5
0030	Newington town (Hartford)	29 208	28 841	1.3	28 197	413	39	408	151	612	11 609	14 490	34.1
0031	Plainville town (Hartford)	17 392	16 401	6.0	16 686	417	16	162	111	371	7 452	12 176	25.2
0031	Rocky Hill town (Hartford)	16 554	14 559	13.7	15 762	431	19	267	75	326	7 107	15 254	34.9
0031	Simsbury town (Hartford)	22 023	21 161	4.1	21 432	184	9	370	28	254	8 175	19 044	87.8
0031	Southington town (Hartford)	38 518	36 879	4.4	37 736	350	32	260	140	508	14 250	13 083	93.2

1. Codes shown are 2-digit FIPS codes for states; 4-digit census place codes for places; and 3-digit FIPS county codes followed by 3-digit census MCD codes for minor civil divisions (MCDs). MCD names are followed by county names in parentheses. 2. Hispanic persons may be of any race. 3. Dry land or land partially or temporarily covered by water.

State/ Place/ MCD[1] code	Place	Population: 1990	Places of 10,000 or more: 1980	Places of 10,000 or more: Percent change, 1980–1990	Population characteristics, 1990 — Race: White	Black	Am. Indian, Eskimo Aleut	Asian & Pacific Islander	Other race	Hispanic[2]	Total housing units, 1990	Per capita income, 1985 (Dollars)	Land area,[3] 1990 (Sq. Km.)
		1	2	3	4	5	6	7	8	9	10	11	12
	CONNECTICUT—Con.												
0031	South Windsor town (Hartford)	22 090	17 198	28.4	20 890	509	42	560	89	370	8 044	15 299	72.4
0031	Suffield town (Hartford)	11 427	NA	NA	11 073	177	9	138	30	98	4 384	16 059	109.3
0031	West Hartford town (Hartford)	60 110	61 301	-1.9	56 493	1 310	46	1 710	551	1 891	25 021	19 864	56.9
0031	Wethersfield town (Hartford)	25 651	26 013	-1.4	25 021	293	31	200	106	422	10 790	15 612	32.1
0031	Windsor town (Hartford)	27 817	25 204	10.4	21 981	4 792	36	662	346	953	10 233	14 159	76.8
0031	Windsor Locks town (Hartford)	12 358	12 190	1.4	11 884	185	16	214	59	163	4 929	12 720	23.4
0050	Barkhamsted town (Litchfield)	3 369	NA	NA	3 344	11	3	8	3	14	1 334	13 163	93.8
0050	Bethlehem town (Litchfield)	3 071	NA	NA	3 043	14	1	9	4	23	1 262	13 923	50.1
0050	Harwinton town (Litchfield)	5 228	NA	NA	5 200	9	1	16	2	28	1 883	13 111	79.6
0050	Kent town (Litchfield)	2 918	NA	NA	2 812	20	14	64	8	52	1 414	16 559	125.5
0050	Litchfield town (Litchfield)	8 365	NA	NA	8 187	78	24	46	30	71	3 430	15 167	145.2
0050	New Hartford town (Litchfield)	5 769	NA	NA	5 688	27	4	42	8	48	2 319	14 057	95.9
0050	New Milford town (Litchfield)	23 629	19 420	21.7	22 822	350	47	303	107	449	9 295	13 515	159.5
0050	North Canaan town (Litchfield)	3 284	NA	NA	3 232	37	3	11	1	16	1 405	10 113	50.4
0050	Plymouth town (Litchfield)	11 822	10 732	10.2	11 696	44	21	47	14	111	4 556	11 538	56.3
0050	Salisbury town (Litchfield)	4 090	NA	NA	3 938	98	8	36	10	27	2 469	16 937	148.5
0050	Sharon town (Litchfield)	2 928	NA	NA	2 901	12	5	9	1	20	1 595	14 251	152.0
0051	Thomaston town (Litchfield)	6 947	NA	NA	6 894	18	7	17	11	66	2 736	12 085	31.1
0051	Torrington town (Litchfield)	33 687	30 987	8.7	32 581	567	61	415	63	357	15 161	NA	103.1
0051	Washington town (Litchfield)	3 905	NA	NA	3 843	22	11	26	3	39	1 856	17 339	98.9
0051	Watertown town (Litchfield)	20 456	19 489	5.0	20 071	151	38	161	35	245	7 522	12 279	75.5
0051	Winchester town (Litchfield)	11 524	10 841	6.3	11 379	52	26	36	31	143	5 093	10 982	83.6
0051	Woodbury town (Litchfield)	8 131	NA	NA	7 972	45	29	74	11	87	3 445	17 982	94.5
0070	Chester town (Middlesex)	3 417	NA	NA	3 360	20	15	19	3	39	1 379	13 785	41.5
0070	Clinton town (Middlesex)	12 767	11 282	13.2	12 354	130	31	132	120	374	5 411	12 826	42.2
0070	Cromwell town (Middlesex)	12 286	10 265	19.7	11 767	308	12	147	52	223	5 090	14 208	32.1
0070	Deep River town (Middlesex)	4 332	NA	NA	4 211	87	3	20	11	43	1 786	14 223	35.1
0070	Durham town (Middlesex)	5 732	NA	NA	5 611	67	8	38	8	51	1 927	14 410	61.1
0070	East Haddam town (Middlesex)	6 676	NA	NA	6 578	45	12	25	16	73	3 289	12 157	140.8
0070	East Hampton town (Middlesex)	10 428	NA	NA	10 274	71	13	42	28	139	4 205	12 664	92.2
0070	Essex town (Middlesex)	5 904	NA	NA	5 814	59	5	21	5	60	2 728	17 593	26.8
0070	Haddam town (Middlesex)	6 769	NA	NA	6 670	33	14	42	10	70	2 598	14 065	114.1
0070	Killingworth town (Middlesex)	4 814	NA	NA	4 749	23	13	26	3	41	1 879	14 717	91.5
0070	Middlefield town (Middlesex)	3 925	NA	NA	3 854	37	4	22	8	53	1 587	13 116	32.9
0070	Middletown town (Middlesex)	42 762	39 040	9.5	36 533	4 747	74	826	582	1 413	18 102	NA	105.9
0070	Old Saybrook town (Middlesex)	9 552	NA	NA	9 275	145	7	93	32	108	5 092	15 099	38.9
0070	Portland town (Middlesex)	8 418	NA	NA	8 120	191	18	46	43	110	3 289	13 437	60.6
0070	Westbrook town (Middlesex)	5 414	NA	NA	5 319	39	1	39	16	84	3 231	13 482	40.7
0090	Ansonia town (New Haven)	18 403	19 039	-3.3	16 562	1 524	41	123	153	474	7 503	NA	15.6
0090	Beacon Falls town (New Haven)	5 083	NA	NA	5 016	47	2	4	14	62	1 990	11 489	25.3
0090	Bethany town (New Haven)	4 608	NA	NA	4 420	114	8	60	6	46	1 581	15 176	54.3
0090	Branford town (New Haven)	27 603	23 363	18.1	26 765	329	29	352	128	436	13 056	15 723	57.0
0090	Cheshire town (New Haven)	25 684	21 788	17.9	23 902	1 002	28	486	266	709	8 590	15 183	85.2
0090	Derby town (New Haven)	12 199	12 346	-1.2	11 571	301	22	94	211	539	5 269	NA	12.9
0090	East Haven town (New Haven)	26 144	25 028	4.5	25 635	231	26	101	151	507	10 580	11 217	31.8
0090	Guilford town (New Haven)	19 848	17 375	14.2	19 454	110	19	168	97	308	7 765	16 426	122.2
0090	Hamden town (New Haven)	52 434	51 071	2.7	46 624	4 556	53	934	267	1 058	21 738	13 720	84.9
0090	Madison town (New Haven)	15 485	14 031	10.4	15 264	55	14	120	32	185	6 511	17 229	93.7
0090	Meriden town (New Haven)	59 479	57 118	4.1	53 327	2 553	107	417	3 075	8 144	24 826	NA	61.5
0090	Middlebury town (New Haven)	6 145	NA	NA	6 058	19	3	63	2	47	2 365	16 419	46.0
0090	Milford town (New Haven)	49 938	50 898	-1.9	48 337	757	74	514	256	1 154	20 149	NA	58.5
0090	Naugatuck town (New Haven)	30 625	26 456	15.8	29 471	567	73	264	250	950	11 930	NA	42.5
0090	New Haven town (New Haven)	130 474	126 109	3.5	70 263	47 157	402	3 141	9 511	17 243	54 057	NA	48.8
0090	North Branford town (New Haven)	12 996	11 554	12.5	12 735	164	19	66	12	116	4 610	13 035	64.6
0090	North Haven town (New Haven)	22 247	22 080	0.8	21 306	474	12	394	61	257	8 243	14 970	53.8
0090	Orange town (New Haven)	12 830	13 237	-3.1	12 391	107	4	304	24	148	4 544	17 862	44.5
0090	Oxford town (New Haven)	8 685	NA	NA	8 569	15	21	50	30	132	2 930	13 621	85.2
0091	Prospect town (New Haven)	7 775	NA	NA	7 555	157	11	35	17	93	2 624	12 030	37.1
0091	Seymour town (New Haven)	14 288	13 434	6.4	14 008	114	10	112	44	187	5 877	12 379	37.7
0091	Southbury town (New Haven)	15 818	14 156	11.7	15 567	95	14	108	34	152	6 826	16 214	101.2
0091	Wallingford town (New Haven)	40 822	37 274	9.5	39 652	412	45	374	339	1 316	15 936	13 013	101.1
0091	Waterbury town (New Haven)	108 961	103 266	5.5	86 681	14 133	344	787	7 016	14 578	47 205	NA	74.0
0091	West Haven town (New Haven)	54 021	53 184	1.6	45 443	6 713	125	1 098	642	1 928	22 679	NA	28.1
0091	Wolcott town (New Haven)	13 700	13 008	5.3	13 368	215	18	58	41	143	4 870	11 211	52.9
0091	Woodbridge town (New Haven)	7 924	NA	NA	7 547	90	12	257	18	91	2 825	25 606	48.8
0110	Colchester town (New London)	10 980	NA	NA	10 700	157	35	59	29	118	4 150	12 298	127.1
0110	East Lyme town (New London)	15 340	13 870	10.6	14 437	543	49	213	98	365	6 772	14 651	88.2
0110	Griswold town (New London)	10 384	NA	NA	10 184	80	41	46	33	102	4 211	9 890	90.6
0110	Groton town (New London)	45 144	41 062	9.9	40 291	2 985	302	974	592	1 649	16 598	11 343	81.1
0110	Lebanon town (New London)	6 041	NA	NA	5 941	47	21	19	13	57	2 422	11 522	140.2
0110	Ledyard town (New London)	14 913	13 735	8.6	14 216	313	87	248	49	230	5 250	13 397	98.8
0110	Lisbon town (New London)	3 790	NA	NA	3 723	28	16	13	10	43	1 400	10 809	42.1
0110	Montville town (New London)	16 673	16 436	1.4	15 666	468	149	239	151	435	6 283	11 316	108.8

1. Codes shown are 2-digit FIPS codes for states; 4-digit census place codes for places; and 3-digit FIPS county codes followed by 3-digit census MCD codes for minor civil divisions (MCDs). MCD names are followed by county names in parentheses. 2. Hispanic persons may be of any race. 3. Dry land or land partially or temporarily covered by water.

State/ Place/ MCD[1] code	Place	Population 1990	Population: Places of 10,000 or more 1980	Population: Places of 10,000 or more Percent change, 1980–1990	Population characteristics, 1990: Race White	Black	Am. Indian, Eskimo Aleut	Asian & Pacific Islander	Other race	Hispanic[2]	Total housing units, 1990	Per capita income, 1985 (Dollars)	Land area,[3] 1990 (Sq. Km.)
		1	2	3	4	5	6	7	8	9	10	11	12
	CONNECTICUT—Con.												
0110	New London town (New London)	28 540	28 842	-1.0	20 828	4 807	194	614	2 097	3 459	11 970	NA	14.3
0110	North Stonington town (New London)	4 884	NA	NA	4 788	27	24	43	2	39	1 858	12 810	140.7
0110	Norwich town (New London)	37 391	38 074	-1.8	34 145	1 974	240	400	632	1 161	16 472	NA	73.4
0110	Old Lyme town (New London)	6 535	NA	NA	6 421	34	16	57	7	42	4 336	18 951	59.8
0110	Preston town (New London)	5 006	NA	NA	4 831	104	13	46	12	93	1 689	10 773	80.0
0110	Salem town (New London)	3 310	NA	NA	3 229	28	9	32	12	40	1 245	NA	75.0
0110	Sprague town (New London)	3 008	NA	NA	2 930	34	23	13	8	38	1 109	11 514	34.2
0110	Stonington town (New London)	16 919	16 220	4.3	16 665	98	43	89	24	220	7 923	13 910	100.2
0111	Waterford town (New London)	17 930	17 862	0.4	17 194	372	55	250	59	310	7 357	14 005	84.8
0130	Andover town (Tolland)	2 540	NA	NA	2 512	14	9	5	0	16	980	NA	40.0
0130	Bolton town (Tolland)	4 575	NA	NA	4 488	31	3	42	11	74	1 704	16 221	37.3
0130	Columbia town (Tolland)	4 510	NA	NA	4 459	18	0	25	8	61	1 754	13 600	55.3
0130	Coventry town (Tolland)	10 063	NA	NA	9 899	78	24	25	37	118	3 894	12 245	97.7
0130	Ellington town (Tolland)	11 197	NA	NA	10 964	147	11	58	17	91	4 562	13 275	88.2
0130	Hebron town (Tolland)	7 079	NA	NA	6 965	62	14	26	12	67	2 489	13 916	95.6
0130	Mansfield town (Tolland)	21 103	20 634	2.3	18 912	690	31	1 281	189	573	5 158	9 297	115.2
0130	Somers town (Tolland)	9 108	NA	NA	8 291	710	10	66	31	275	2 739	13 212	73.4
0130	Stafford town (Tolland)	11 091	NA	NA	10 844	39	25	131	52	155	4 310	11 174	150.1
0130	Tolland town (Tolland)	11 001	NA	NA	10 752	104	14	107	24	97	3 747	13 454	102.9
0130	Vernon town (Tolland)	29 841	27 974	6.7	28 298	674	59	586	224	600	12 748	12 714	45.9
0130	Willington town (Tolland)	5 979	NA	NA	5 796	57	17	94	15	85	2 301	11 461	86.1
0150	Ashford town (Windham)	3 765	NA	NA	3 663	39	13	30	20	52	1 562	11 892	100.5
0150	Brooklyn town (Windham)	6 681	NA	NA	6 481	90	17	82	11	170	2 405	11 877	75.0
0150	Canterbury town (Windham)	4 467	NA	NA	4 395	19	22	22	9	31	1 556	11 002	103.3
0150	Killingly town (Windham)	15 889	14 548	9.2	15 473	115	73	202	26	123	6 480	9 944	125.7
0150	Plainfield town (Windham)	14 363	12 774	12.4	14 120	66	32	79	66	213	5 342	9 422	109.5
0150	Pomfret town (Windham)	3 102	NA	NA	3 065	17	4	10	6	17	1 258	11 173	104.4
0150	Putnam town (Windham)	9 031	NA	NA	8 788	103	37	37	66	108	3 790	9 185	52.6
0150	Thompson town (Windham)	8 668	NA	NA	8 572	19	30	26	21	73	3 563	10 726	121.6
0150	Windham town (Windham)	22 039	21 062	4.6	19 390	593	83	223	1 750	3 321	8 727	9 714	70.1
0150	Woodstock town (Windham)	6 008	NA	NA	5 948	14	23	13	10	40	2 615	13 623	156.8
10	DELAWARE	666 168	594 338	12.1	535 094	112 460	2 019	9 057	7 538	15 820	289 919	11 375	5 062.5
0034	Brookside CDP	15 307	15 255	0.3	13 576	1 421	30	207	73	247	5 601	NA	10.1
0053	Claymont CDP	9 800	10 022	-2.2	8 691	944	22	88	55	157	4 075	NA	5.5
0075	Dover	27 630	23 504	17.6	18 107	8 544	131	549	299	778	10 488	10 484	55.2
0076	Dover Base Housing CDP	4 376	NA	NA	3 157	926	23	139	131	230	1 260	NA	1.8
0079	Edgemoor CDP	5 853	NA	NA	4 522	1 188	16	80	47	100	2 727	NA	4.7
0085	Elsmere town	5 935	NA	NA	5 468	324	2	35	106	205	2 471	10 318	2.6
0115	Georgetown town	3 732	NA	NA	2 651	1 011	15	23	32	75	1 376	NA	6.3
0132	Highland Acres CDP	3 151	NA	NA	2 821	218	4	90	18	73	1 139	NA	4.0
0145	Laurel town	3 226	NA	NA	1 997	1 191	9	16	13	43	1 322	7 002	3.7
0170	Middletown town	3 834	NA	NA	2 928	869	6	5	26	54	1 475	9 746	8.8
0175	Milford	6 040	NA	NA	4 763	1 130	22	42	83	225	2 601	8 754	12.7
0195	Newark	25 098	25 247	-0.6	22 687	1 433	36	883	59	370	7 860	10 560	22.3
0200	New Castle	4 837	NA	NA	3 969	817	8	9	34	61	2 006	10 828	5.8
0216	Pike Creek CDP	10 163	NA	NA	9 380	371	18	363	31	162	4 732	NA	7.7
0225	Seaford	5 689	NA	NA	4 291	1 319	9	29	41	74	2 360	9 689	8.6
0237	Smyrna town	5 231	NA	NA	4 089	1 064	7	29	42	131	1 878	8 535	7.3
0241	Stanton CDP	5 028	NA	NA	4 673	209	10	101	35	77	1 997	NA	3.1
0244	Talleyville CDP	6 346	NA	NA	6 044	111	6	176	9	90	2 318	NA	7.8
0255	Wilmington	71 529	70 195	1.9	30 134	37 446	156	315	3 478	5 072	31 244	9 410	27.9
0256	Wilmington Manor CDP	8 568	NA	NA	7 801	572	11	44	140	231	3 173	NA	4.5
11	DISTRICT OF COLUMBIA	606 900	638 432	-4.9	179 667	399 604	1 466	11 214	14 949	32 710	278 489	13 530	159.1
0005	Washington	606 900	638 333	-4.9	179 667	399 604	1 466	11 214	14 949	32 710	278 489	13 530	159.1
12	FLORIDA	12 937 926	9 746 959	32.7	10 749 285	1 759 534	36 335	154 302	238 470	1 574 143	6 100 262	11 271	139 852.4
0002	Aberdeen CDP	2 572	NA	NA	2 489	43	0	28	12	60	1 336	NA	6.1
0005	Alachua	4 529	NA	NA	2 764	1 744	8	12	1	66	1 770	7 886	64.6
0015	Altamonte Springs	34 879	22 028	58.3	31 350	2 073	90	631	735	2 980	17 140	13 892	22.1
0024	Andover CDP	6 251	NA	NA	3 241	2 769	12	136	93	598	3 058	NA	4.3
0030	Apalachicola	2 602	NA	NA	1 604	973	10	12	3	25	1 190	6 505	4.9
0033	Apollo Beach CDP	6 025	NA	NA	5 909	29	5	59	23	263	2 799	NA	14.7
0035	Apopka	13 512	NA	NA	10 995	1 890	42	176	409	1 133	5 712	10 426	23.6
0040	Arcadia	6 488	NA	NA	4 258	1 958	43	26	203	591	2 835	7 150	10.4
0055	Atlantic Beach	11 636	NA	NA	9 333	1 792	34	383	94	355	4 948	11 380	7.9
0065	Auburndale	8 858	NA	NA	7 937	801	16	62	42	240	3 865	8 647	10.6
0066	Aventura CDP	14 914	NA	NA	14 732	58	8	70	46	1 067	12 829	NA	6.6
0067	Avon Park	8 042	NA	NA	5 301	2 431	33	24	253	559	3 964	6 855	11.9
0069	Azalea Park CDP	8 926	NA	NA	7 829	217	31	226	623	1 632	3 610	NA	8.2

1. Codes shown are 2-digit FIPS codes for states; 4-digit census place codes for places; and 3-digit FIPS county codes followed by 3-digit census MCD codes for minor civil divisions (MCDs). MCD names are followed by county names in parentheses. 2. Hispanic persons may be of any race. 3. Dry land or land partially or temporarily covered by water.

State/ Place/ MCD[1] code	Place	Population			Population characteristics, 1990							Total housing units, 1990	Per capita income, 1985 (Dollars)	Land area,[3] 1990 (Sq. Km.)
			Places of 10,000 or more		Race						Hispanic[2]			
		1990	1980	Percent change, 1980–1990	White	Black	Am. Indian, Eskimo Aleut	Asian & Pacific Islander	Other race					
		1	2	3	4	5	6	7	8	9	10	11	12	
	FLORIDA—Con.													
0080	Bal Harbour village	3 045	NA	NA	2 996	29	1	8	11	291	2 797	42 259	0.9	
0085	Bartow	14 716	14 780	-0.4	10 018	4 339	36	88	235	502	5 874	9 049	22.3	
0087	Baskin CDP	3 834	NA	NA	1 102	2 699	1	14	18	53	1 596	NA	2.8	
0088	Bassville Park CDP	2 752	NA	NA	2 724	15	4	4	5	21	1 608	NA	8.1	
0090	Bay Harbor Islands town	4 703	NA	NA	4 593	42	1	27	40	719	3 179	24 792	1.0	
0091	Bay Hill CDP	5 346	NA	NA	4 794	96	9	411	36	254	2 095	NA	10.4	
0094	Bayonet Point CDP	21 860	16 455	32.8	21 651	45	32	85	47	349	12 489	NA	14.5	
0096	Bay Pines CDP	4 171	NA	NA	4 072	72	6	16	5	62	1 893	NA	4.1	
0098	Bayshore Gardens CDP	17 062	14 894	14.6	16 525	237	56	157	87	391	10 058	NA	9.1	
0102	Beacon Square CDP	6 265	NA	NA	6 201	12	15	29	8	93	3 968	NA	5.2	
0107	Bee Ridge CDP	6 406	NA	NA	6 329	24	8	27	18	103	3 102	NA	10.1	
0113	Bellair-Meadowbrook Terrace CDP	15 606	12 144	28.5	13 941	920	58	516	171	680	6 170	NA	14.5	
0115	Belleair town	3 968	NA	NA	3 949	3	2	8	6	64	2 286	25 087	4.7	
0130	Belle Glade	16 177	16 535	-2.2	5 085	9 404	26	39	1 623	3 489	6 045	7 704	11.6	
0140	Belle Isle	5 272	NA	NA	5 052	119	7	84	10	163	2 114	14 824	4.8	
0145	Belleview	2 666	NA	NA	2 511	84	8	21	42	115	1 396	NA	3.4	
0147	Bellview CDP	19 386	15 439	25.6	17 173	1 253	261	608	91	429	7 474	NA	30.6	
0162	Beverly Hills CDP	6 163	NA	NA	6 088	27	18	24	6	126	3 704	NA	7.2	
0164	Big Pine Key CDP	4 206	NA	NA	4 126	38	11	22	9	187	2 453	NA	25.3	
0165	Biscayne Park village	3 068	NA	NA	2 686	235	5	92	50	573	1 338	12 847	1.6	
0170	Bithlo CDP	4 834	NA	NA	4 661	19	26	24	104	316	1 968	NA	27.6	
0173	Bloomingdale CDP	13 912	NA	NA	12 969	576	38	224	105	789	4 651	NA	20.2	
0177	Boca Del Mar CDP	17 754	NA	NA	17 166	126	12	310	140	930	10 353	NA	10.4	
0180	Boca Raton	61 492	49 505	24.2	58 035	1 784	44	1 167	462	3 438	33 043	21 112	70.4	
0182	Boca West CDP	2 847	NA	NA	2 833	8	0	6	0	69	3 338	NA	5.9	
0185	Bonifay	2 612	NA	NA	2 279	280	41	6	6	37	1 184	7 053	8.7	
0187	Bonita Springs CDP	13 600	NA	NA	13 157	35	27	56	325	1 038	8 813	NA	29.7	
0200	Boynton Beach	46 194	35 624	29.7	35 912	9 296	52	290	644	3 124	25 544	11 560	39.2	
0215	Bradenton	43 779	30 170	45.1	36 290	6 312	79	280	818	2 360	22 123	10 321	29.7	
0225	Brandon CDP	57 985	41 826	38.6	53 924	2 230	150	980	701	3 996	22 493	NA	75.3	
0234	Brent CDP	21 624	21 872	-1.1	15 092	5 872	229	342	89	404	7 838	NA	27.2	
0243	Broadview Park CDP	6 109	NA	NA	4 952	803	14	69	271	1 363	2 236	NA	2.5	
0244	Broadview-Pompano Park CDP	5 230	NA	NA	4 710	323	8	50	139	715	2 260	NA	2.0	
0253	Brookridge CDP	2 805	NA	NA	2 802	0	0	3	0	9	1 789	NA	5.3	
0255	Brooksville	7 440	NA	NA	5 857	1 496	29	23	35	112	3 953	9 175	11.9	
0258	Browardale CDP	6 257	NA	NA	121	6 107	13	6	10	46	1 807	NA	2.5	
0261	Brownsville CDP	15 607	18 058	-13.6	535	14 940	28	4	100	666	5 596	NA	5.9	
0263	Buena Ventura Lakes CDP	14 148	NA	NA	11 572	1 034	35	319	1 188	4 462	5 804	NA	14.2	
0264	Bunche Park CDP	4 388	NA	NA	11	4 361	4	4	8	24	1 440	NA	2.0	
0272	Butler Beach CDP	3 377	NA	NA	3 348	9	5	10	5	71	2 924	NA	6.6	
0277	Callaway	12 253	NA	NA	10 368	1 223	88	466	108	429	5 219	8 404	13.9	
0279	Campbell CDP	3 884	NA	NA	3 831	11	8	10	24	78	2 146	NA	6.4	
0292	Cape Canaveral	8 014	NA	NA	7 630	164	81	92	47	285	6 077	13 452	6.1	
0293	Cape Coral	74 991	32 103	133.6	73 090	758	126	467	550	2 749	34 486	11 845	272.2	
0295	Carol City CDP	53 331	47 349	12.6	20 729	29 090	114	327	3 071	19 186	15 405	NA	19.7	
0302	Carrollwood CDP	7 195	NA	NA	6 951	70	12	129	33	550	3 318	NA	5.9	
0303	Carrollwood Village CDP	15 051	NA	NA	14 013	421	27	378	212	1 490	6 670	NA	13.4	
0310	Casselberry	18 911	15 247	24.0	17 733	520	67	296	295	1 595	8 089	12 231	15.7	
0336	Century Village CDP	8 363	10 619	-21.2	8 348	10	2	3	0	68	7 621	NA	2.6	
0343	Charlotte Harbor CDP	3 327	NA	NA	3 253	28	8	25	13	57	2 167	NA	6.1	
0345	Chattahoochee	4 382	NA	NA	2 422	1 897	2	40	21	53	1 240	5 680	14.1	
0355	Chipley	3 866	NA	NA	2 757	1 007	33	42	27	53	1 641	7 082	10.3	
0375	Clearwater	98 784	85 528	15.5	88 046	8 863	240	1 019	616	2 886	53 833	13 213	64.4	
0380	Clermont	6 910	NA	NA	5 683	1 138	8	36	45	119	3 049	10 648	9.8	
0383	Cleveland CDP	2 896	NA	NA	2 876	5	5	7	3	26	1 765	NA	14.2	
0385	Clewiston	6 085	NA	NA	4 763	555	27	46	694	1 769	2 413	10 941	12.1	
0395	Cocoa	17 722	16 096	10.1	12 326	5 057	56	178	105	380	8 248	9 503	19.4	
0400	Cocoa Beach	12 123	10 926	11.0	11 882	61	31	110	39	334	8 266	17 277	12.7	
0405	Cocoa West CDP	6 160	NA	NA	3 610	2 503	18	23	6	109	2 391	NA	11.2	
0407	Coconut Creek	27 485	NA	NA	26 686	407	37	210	145	1 125	15 773	16 640	28.9	
0414	Collier Manor-Cresthaven CDP	7 322	NA	NA	6 870	185	5	58	204	788	3 365	NA	3.1	
0415	Combee Settlement CDP	5 463	NA	NA	5 265	100	36	35	27	87	2 551	NA	5.5	
0417	Conway CDP	13 159	24 010	-45.2	12 425	222	28	229	255	1 018	4 891	NA	9.0	
0420	Cooper City	20 791	10 140	105.0	19 598	418	29	555	191	2 215	7 348	14 365	16.4	
0425	Coral Gables	40 091	43 241	-7.3	37 304	1 372	40	697	678	16 778	16 561	21 089	30.6	
0427	Coral Springs	79 443	37 349	112.7	73 949	2 764	142	1 684	904	5 658	29 785	14 567	60.8	
0429	Coral Terrace CDP	23 255	22 702	2.4	21 662	185	27	143	1 238	18 215	7 789	NA	8.9	
0430	Cortez CDP	4 509	NA	NA	4 474	5	5	14	11	41	3 230	NA	5.7	
0432	Country Club CDP	3 408	NA	NA	2 770	467	3	68	100	1 225	1 393	NA	2.9	
0433	Country Club Trail CDP	4 599	NA	NA	4 539	32	2	20	6	158	3 319	NA	3.5	
0440	Crestview	9 886	NA	NA	7 750	1 930	64	99	43	131	4 171	6 989	26.8	
0448	Crystal Lake CDP	5 300	NA	NA	4 820	348	22	76	34	169	2 466	NA	7.0	
0450	Crystal River	4 044	NA	NA	3 473	507	13	37	14	56	2 178	9 058	11.2	

1. Codes shown are 2-digit FIPS codes for states; 4-digit census place codes for places; and 3-digit FIPS county codes followed by 3-digit census MCD codes for minor civil divisions (MCDs). MCD names are followed by county names in parentheses. 2. Hispanic persons may be of any race. 3. Dry land or land partially or temporarily covered by water.

State/ Place/ MCD[1] code	Place	Population: 1990	Places of 10,000 or more: 1980	Places of 10,000 or more: Percent change, 1980–1990	Race: White	Race: Black	Race: Am. Indian, Eskimo Aleut	Race: Asian & Pacific Islander	Race: Other race	Hispanic[2]	Total housing units, 1990	Per capita income, 1985 (Dollars)	Land area,[3] 1990 (Sq. Km.)
		1	2	3	4	5	6	7	8	9	10	11	12
	FLORIDA—Con.												
0454	Cutler CDP	16 201	15 593	3.9	15 072	556	10	400	163	2 575	5 530	NA	18.8
0455	Cutler Ridge CDP	21 268	20 886	1.8	18 084	2 043	53	450	638	4 032	7 615	NA	12.3
0458	Cypress Gardens CDP	9 188	NA	NA	8 963	42	7	126	50	240	4 268	NA	13.2
0460	Cypress Lake CDP	10 491	NA	NA	10 266	88	12	62	63	238	6 526	NA	10.3
0465	Dade City	5 633	NA	NA	3 725	1 725	11	12	160	435	2 330	10 551	7.9
0468	Dade City North CDP	3 058	NA	NA	2 102	223	19	13	701	1 093	1 063	NA	4.7
0470	Dania	13 024	11 811	10.3	8 748	4 076	30	65	105	793	7 699	10 243	13.3
0477	Davie town	47 217	20 877	126.2	43 829	1 820	100	826	642	4 713	19 889	12 247	83.7
0485	Daytona Beach	61 921	54 176	14.3	41 718	19 020	146	706	331	1 535	32 167	9 170	83.5
0490	De Bary CDP	7 176	NA	NA	7 060	45	29	24	18	133	3 404	NA	19.2
0495	Deerfield Beach	46 325	39 193	18.2	37 787	7 728	49	391	370	1 789	28 796	12 695	27.0
0500	De Funiak Springs	5 120	NA	NA	3 847	1 178	49	38	8	40	2 465	7 020	27.3
0505	De Land	16 491	15 354	7.4	12 556	3 611	49	68	207	623	7 724	8 517	25.0
0510	Delray Beach	47 181	34 325	37.5	33 965	12 398	66	323	429	2 868	27 527	14 258	38.4
0511	Del Rio CDP	8 248	NA	NA	4 689	3 356	27	65	111	663	4 037	NA	4.8
0512	Deltona CDP	50 828	15 710	223.5	47 683	1 683	139	355	968	5 139	20 744	NA	136.1
0514	Desoto Lakes CDP	2 807	NA	NA	2 720	36	12	24	15	92	1 098	NA	5.3
0517	Destin	8 080	NA	NA	7 915	48	33	56	28	97	7 269	13 062	19.3
0519	Doctor Phillips CDP	7 963	NA	NA	7 123	251	8	478	103	556	3 239	NA	9.5
0522	Doral CDP	3 126	NA	NA	2 837	53	4	109	123	1 306	1 699	NA	6.0
0524	Dover CDP	2 606	NA	NA	1 860	6	1	8	731	954	859	NA	6.8
0530	Dunedin	34 012	30 203	12.6	33 372	365	72	147	56	621	18 411	12 913	26.8
0543	East Lake-Orient Park CDP	6 171	NA	NA	4 679	1 252	91	40	109	442	2 316	NA	11.3
0544	East Naples CDP	22 951	12 127	89.3	21 759	670	60	110	352	2 136	14 639	NA	37.3
0565	Edgewater	15 337	NA	NA	15 087	112	50	61	27	163	6 888	8 854	18.9
0573	Eglin AFB CDP	8 347	NA	NA	6 109	1 589	57	441	151	497	2 363	NA	7.9
0574	Egypt Lake CDP	14 580	11 932	22.2	12 999	838	32	239	472	3 408	7 264	NA	7.0
0576	Elfers CDP	12 356	11 396	8.4	12 196	55	30	56	19	211	6 649	NA	9.2
0578	Ellenton CDP	2 573	NA	NA	2 519	4	8	2	40	139	1 360	NA	9.7
0590	Englewood CDP	15 025	10 227	46.9	14 919	38	15	45	8	86	9 854	NA	25.5
0595	Ensley CDP	16 362	14 422	13.5	11 430	4 612	173	116	31	154	6 771	NA	29.8
0598	Estero CDP	3 177	NA	NA	3 134	8	6	0	29	112	3 314	NA	15.9
0605	Eustis	12 967	NA	NA	10 207	2 597	31	68	64	215	6 318	10 795	19.2
0611	Fairview Shores CDP	13 192	10 174	29.7	11 645	1 134	30	205	178	716	6 094	NA	10.3
0614	Feather Sound CDP	2 690	NA	NA	2 616	16	6	47	5	97	1 535	NA	10.9
0620	Fernandina Beach	8 765	NA	NA	6 706	1 975	20	47	17	110	4 477	11 426	27.6
0622	Fern Park CDP	8 294	NA	NA	7 716	330	20	84	144	720	3 706	NA	5.5
0623	Ferry Pass CDP	26 301	16 910	55.5	23 719	1 805	198	483	96	553	11 428	NA	38.6
0630	Flagler Beach	3 820	NA	NA	3 794	8	4	10	4	46	2 661	NA	9.4
0638	Floral City CDP	2 609	NA	NA	2 538	49	13	5	4	22	1 612	NA	14.3
0640	Florida City	5 806	NA	NA	2 006	3 540	15	15	230	1 028	2 045	5 901	6.4
0642	Florida Ridge CDP	12 218	NA	NA	11 096	1 013	24	33	52	286	6 006	NA	28.0
0643	Forest City CDP	10 638	NA	NA	9 865	310	17	209	237	1 140	4 231	NA	11.1
0644	Forest Island Park CDP	5 988	NA	NA	5 937	10	9	29	3	51	4 086	NA	19.2
0645	Fort Lauderdale	149 377	153 279	-2.5	103 980	41 995	321	1 297	1 784	10 681	81 268	15 135	81.2
0650	Fort Meade	4 976	NA	NA	3 493	1 191	2	2	288	507	2 114	6 687	8.2
0655	Fort Myers	45 206	36 638	23.4	29 042	14 539	93	366	1 166	3 489	21 388	9 892	56.9
0656	Fort Myers Beach CDP	9 284	NA	NA	9 248	7	12	11	6	110	9 977	NA	15.4
0658	Fort Myers Shores CDP	5 460	NA	NA	5 192	98	9	41	120	346	2 194	NA	5.6
0665	Fort Pierce	36 830	33 802	9.0	19 772	15 604	118	198	1 138	2 370	17 250	7 705	31.8
0667	Fort Pierce North CDP	5 833	NA	NA	2 219	3 529	12	17	56	100	2 441	NA	9.2
0668	Fort Pierce South CDP	5 320	NA	NA	4 940	262	13	46	59	194	2 251	NA	11.2
0670	Fort Walton Beach	21 471	20 871	2.9	17 555	2 999	115	627	175	672	9 112	11 150	19.2
0680	Frostproof	2 808	NA	NA	2 574	57	44	2	131	234	1 472	8 932	6.2
0683	Fruit Cove CDP	5 904	NA	NA	5 803	38	12	45	6	82	2 182	NA	45.2
0685	Fruitland Park	2 754	NA	NA	2 702	23	7	12	10	42	1 155	NA	5.0
0690	Fruitville CDP	9 808	NA	NA	9 632	104	7	41	24	290	3 664	NA	18.6
0692	Fussels Corner CDP	3 840	NA	NA	3 452	291	15	17	65	140	1 646	NA	18.0
0695	Gainesville	84 770	81 371	4.2	62 186	18 177	153	3 343	911	3 732	34 608	9 460	90.3
0698	Gandy CDP	3 164	NA	NA	3 042	67	7	41	7	72	2 444	NA	7.7
0725	Gibsonia CDP	5 168	NA	NA	5 002	56	25	35	50	137	2 244	NA	6.9
0728	Gibsonton CDP	7 706	NA	NA	7 315	63	46	43	239	743	3 258	NA	20.4
0735	Gifford CDP	6 278	NA	NA	1 802	4 365	8	13	90	173	2 358	NA	18.2
0737	Gladeview CDP	15 637	18 919	-17.3	1 870	13 539	21	20	187	1 662	5 516	NA	6.6
0743	Glenvar Heights CDP	14 823	13 216	12.2	13 702	369	19	370	363	5 906	7 512	NA	10.9
0745	Golden Gate CDP	14 148	NA	NA	13 150	677	29	61	231	1 450	6 124	NA	10.6
0746	Golden Glades CDP	25 474	23 154	10.0	14 019	9 729	77	804	845	5 133	9 728	NA	12.8
0747	Golden Lakes CDP	3 867	13 682	-71.7	3 663	170	3	14	17	81	2 759	NA	6.1
0748	Goldenrod CDP	12 362	NA	NA	11 570	326	42	244	180	950	5 260	NA	6.7
0752	Gonzalez CDP	7 669	NA	NA	7 123	404	70	65	7	56	2 873	NA	29.2
0757	Goulding CDP	4 159	NA	NA	877	3 256	13	12	1	21	1 616	NA	3.2
0758	Goulds CDP	7 284	NA	NA	1 106	6 004	5	32	137	892	2 287	NA	7.7
0759	Graceville	2 675	NA	NA	2 110	556	7	1	1	8	1 090	7 602	11.0

1. Codes shown are 2-digit FIPS codes for states; 4-digit census place codes for places; and 3-digit FIPS county codes followed by 3-digit census MCD codes for minor civil divisions (MCDs). MCD names are followed by county names in parentheses. 2. Hispanic persons may be of any race. 3. Dry land or land partially or temporarily covered by water.

State/ Place/ MCD[1] code	Place	Population: 1990	Population: Places of 10,000 or more: 1980	Population: Places of 10,000 or more: Percent change, 1980–1990	Population characteristics, 1990: Race: White	Race: Black	Race: Am. Indian, Eskimo Aleut	Race: Asian & Pacific Islander	Race: Other race	Hispanic[2]	Total housing units, 1990	Per capita income, 1985 (Dollars)	Land area,[3] 1990 (Sq. Km.)
		1	2	3	4	5	6	7	8	9	10	11	12
	FLORIDA—Con.												
0763	Greater Northdale CDP	16 318	NA	NA	14 912	693	29	445	239	1 741	5 833	NA	15.7
0765	Greenacres City	18 683	NA	NA	17 768	344	30	198	343	1 545	11 186	11 152	10.5
0770	Green Cove Springs	4 497	NA	NA	3 233	1 200	26	19	19	78	1 819	7 128	16.5
0792	Gulf Breeze	5 530	NA	NA	5 463	4	22	29	12	55	2 365	14 408	12.3
0793	Gulf Gate Estates CDP	11 622	NA	NA	11 439	25	30	85	43	203	6 417	NA	7.3
0795	Gulfport	11 727	11 180	4.9	11 161	391	42	61	72	263	7 077	10 692	7.4
0810	Haines City	11 683	10 799	8.2	6 767	4 623	24	25	244	969	5 101	6 963	20.8
0815	Hallandale	30 996	36 511	-15.1	26 040	4 392	43	146	375	2 714	24 798	15 529	10.9
0818	Hammocks CDP	10 897	NA	NA	9 173	901	20	318	485	4 860	5 089	NA	4.0
0821	Hamptons at Boca Raton CDP	11 686	NA	NA	11 376	87	7	200	16	319	7 546	NA	6.4
0822	Harbor Bluffs CDP	2 659	NA	NA	2 652	1	1	5	0	46	1 260	NA	1.8
0823	Harbour Heights CDP	2 523	NA	NA	2 437	44	14	17	11	56	1 164	NA	5.7
0825	Harlem CDP	2 826	NA	NA	9	2 815	1	0	1	32	904	NA	1.2
0860	Hialeah	188 004	145 254	29.4	169 072	3 636	185	1 013	14 098	164 652	62 187	8 256	49.8
0865	Hialeah Gardens	7 713	NA	NA	7 048	106	14	77	468	6 328	2 883	11 819	6.4
0870	Highland Beach town	3 209	NA	NA	3 192	5	0	9	3	46	3 451	NA	1.3
0883	High Point CDP	2 814	NA	NA	2 811	1	1	0	1	33	1 717	NA	5.1
0885	Highpoint CDP	13 818	NA	NA	13 034	396	63	224	101	430	7 563	NA	11.4
0886	High Springs	3 144	NA	NA	2 264	861	9	7	3	64	1 317	NA	23.8
0887	Hiland Park CDP	3 865	NA	NA	3 479	283	47	52	4	45	1 632	NA	13.1
0905	Hobe Sound CDP	11 507	NA	NA	10 541	838	31	63	34	176	5 866	NA	14.2
0906	Holden Heights CDP	4 387	13 864	-68.4	3 848	409	18	52	60	277	1 748	NA	4.5
0909	Holiday CDP	19 360	18 392	5.3	19 146	56	28	76	54	349	12 160	NA	13.4
0910	Holly Hill	11 141	NA	NA	10 355	605	21	119	41	206	5 652	9 171	9.0
0915	Hollywood	121 697	121 323	0.3	107 396	10 365	256	1 611	2 069	14 430	63 303	13 350	70.6
0925	Holmes Beach	4 810	NA	NA	4 786	1	6	11	6	96	3 850	16 153	4.2
0930	Homestead	26 866	20 668	30.0	17 832	6 178	80	241	2 535	9 478	10 775	8 118	30.1
0931	Homestead AFB CDP	5 153	NA	NA	3 760	941	26	207	219	611	1 322	NA	11.3
0933	Homosassa Springs CDP	6 271	NA	NA	6 225	4	15	17	10	93	3 217	NA	33.5
0937	Hudson CDP	7 344	NA	NA	7 245	5	30	49	15	113	4 660	NA	9.4
0938	Hutchinson Island South CDP	3 893	NA	NA	3 863	10	3	9	8	33	5 700	NA	11.7
0945	Immokalee CDP	14 120	11 038	27.9	7 518	3 386	148	56	3 012	9 315	4 507	NA	20.5
0950	Indialantic town	2 844	NA	NA	2 787	11	8	26	12	73	1 414	17 490	2.7
0957	Indian Harbour Beach	6 933	NA	NA	6 719	62	30	102	20	163	3 893	14 621	5.5
0959	Indian River Estates CDP	4 858	NA	NA	4 749	51	15	28	15	80	1 975	NA	8.3
0965	Indian Rocks Beach	3 963	NA	NA	3 923	8	8	12	12	96	3 145	15 260	2.4
0975	Indiantown CDP	4 794	NA	NA	2 252	1 354	35	15	1 138	1 669	1 673	NA	15.5
0990	Inverness	5 797	NA	NA	5 308	389	21	26	53	214	3 099	8 612	18.9
0992	Inwood CDP	6 824	NA	NA	5 757	898	19	60	90	281	3 134	NA	5.1
0993	Iona CDP	9 565	NA	NA	9 466	44	17	25	13	89	7 823	NA	18.5
0998	Ives Estates CDP	13 531	12 623	7.2	11 911	1 053	25	351	191	2 027	6 650	NA	6.8
1002	Jacksonville Beach	17 839	15 462	15.4	16 268	1 166	47	289	69	390	8 709	11 986	19.9
1000	Jacksonville	635 230	540 920	17.4	456 529	160 283	1 801	12 182	4 435	16 455	267 148	10 466	1 965.0
1007	Jan Phyl Village CDP	5 308	NA	NA	4 912	260	8	95	33	165	1 955	NA	12.2
1008	Jasmine Estates CDP	17 136	11 995	42.9	16 743	182	16	108	87	547	9 309	NA	9.3
1022	Jensen Beach CDP	9 884	NA	NA	9 580	200	5	76	23	173	5 191	NA	11.0
1025	June Park CDP	4 080	NA	NA	4 015	16	8	30	11	71	1 770	NA	10.2
1035	Jupiter town	24 986	NA	NA	24 430	238	27	216	75	732	14 602	13 571	34.0
1044	Kathleen CDP	2 743	NA	NA	2 728	0	2	4	9	53	1 037	NA	8.6
1047	Kendale Lakes CDP	48 524	32 769	48.1	43 094	1 560	63	1 141	2 666	30 854	17 129	NA	21.4
1048	Kendall CDP	87 271	73 758	18.3	78 423	4 075	88	2 596	2 089	27 379	35 271	NA	61.0
1049	Kendall Green CDP	3 815	NA	NA	3 166	547	11	16	75	331	1 915	NA	1.9
1050	Kendall Lakes West CDP	6 038	NA	NA	5 098	471	4	110	355	3 671	2 753	11 585	2.4
1052	Kenneth City town	4 462	NA	NA	4 351	25	8	64	14	108	2 298	NA	1.9
1055	Kensington Park CDP	3 026	NA	NA	2 911	74	4	18	19	94	1 464	NA	2.6
1058	Key Biscayne CDP	8 854	NA	NA	8 687	36	13	42	76	3 790	5 724	NA	3.3
1063	Key Largo CDP	11 336	NA	NA	10 929	266	37	36	68	1 085	7 594	NA	24.1
1070	Key West	24 832	24 382	1.8	21 368	2 579	84	349	452	4 097	12 221	10 346	14.2
1074	Kings Point CDP	12 422	NA	NA	12 394	14	1	11	2	60	9 521	NA	4.6
1075	Kissimmee	30 050	15 487	94.0	25 121	2 806	105	707	1 311	4 355	13 602	10 035	32.2
1080	La Belle	2 703	NA	NA	2 126	425	15	2	135	338	1 157	NA	7.4
1095	Lady Lake town	8 071	NA	NA	7 852	184	17	15	3	88	4 519	NA	15.4
1100	Lake Alfred	3 622	NA	NA	3 008	535	21	30	28	82	1 558	8 205	6.5
1110	Lake City	10 005	NA	NA	6 010	3 848	30	84	33	141	4 494	8 667	27.3
1115	Lake Clarke Shores town	3 364	NA	NA	3 289	17	2	35	21	365	1 433	17 556	2.5
1136	Lakeland	70 576	47 406	48.9	55 133	14 255	123	636	429	2 302	34 933	10 345	99.4
1137	Lakeland Highlands CDP	9 972	10 426	-4.4	9 699	105	8	125	35	341	3 818	NA	14.5
1139	Lake Lorraine CDP	6 779	NA	NA	5 867	529	41	276	66	216	2 768	NA	5.3
1142	Lake Lucerne CDP	9 478	NA	NA	1 311	7 895	14	14	244	1 442	2 739	NA	6.6
1143	Lake Magdalene CDP	15 973	13 331	19.8	15 148	422	43	178	182	1 289	7 399	NA	12.4
1144	Lake Mary	5 929	NA	NA	5 711	108	12	67	31	174	2 296	13 074	22.0
1147	Lake Panasoffkee CDP	2 705	NA	NA	2 676	4	15	3	7	32	1 897	NA	10.4
1148	Lake Park town	6 704	NA	NA	4 988	1 398	21	220	77	320	3 363	15 247	4.7

1. Codes shown are 2-digit FIPS codes for states; 4-digit census place codes for places; and 3-digit FIPS county codes followed by 3-digit census MCD codes for minor civil divisions (MCDs). MCD names are followed by county names in parentheses. 2. Hispanic persons may be of any race. 3. Dry land or land partially or temporarily covered by water.

State/ Place/ MCD[1] code	Place	Population: 1990	Population: Places of 10,000 or more: 1980	Population: Places of 10,000 or more: Percent change, 1980–1990	Population characteristics, 1990: Race: White	Race: Black	Race: Am. Indian, Eskimo Aleut	Race: Asian & Pacific Islander	Race: Other race	Hispanic[2]	Total housing units, 1990	Per capita income, 1985 (Dollars)	Land area,[3] 1990 (Sq. Km.)
		1	2	3	4	5	6	7	8	9	10	11	12
	FLORIDA—Con.												
1151	Lake Sarasota CDP	4 117	NA	NA	4 034	21	4	36	22	111	1 396	NA	3.7
1152	Lakes by the Bay CDP	5 615	NA	NA	4 758	525	10	136	186	1 546	2 411	NA	12.5
1156	Lakeside CDP	29 137	10 534	176.6	26 902	1 177	94	761	203	907	9 811	NA	39.2
1158	Lakeside Green CDP	2 994	NA	NA	2 672	196	6	87	33	224	1 398	NA	1.4
1160	Lake Wales	9 670	NA	NA	6 147	3 310	12	36	165	372	4 235	8 703	16.6
1163	Lakewood Park CDP	7 211	NA	NA	6 780	344	30	41	16	104	3 096	NA	16.1
1165	Lake Worth	28 564	27 048	5.6	22 998	4 258	74	252	982	4 488	15 632	11 542	14.5
1168	Land O' Lakes CDP	7 892	NA	NA	7 649	71	29	48	95	494	3 238	NA	27.1
1170	Lantana town	8 392	NA	NA	7 879	394	11	38	70	504	4 374	12 432	5.9
1175	Largo	65 674	58 977	11.4	64 113	651	127	553	230	1 280	38 711	11 874	36.6
1180	Lauderdale-by-the-Sea town	2 990	NA	NA	2 963	8	2	8	9	86	3 345	21 367	1.2
1183	Lauderdale Lakes	27 341	25 426	7.5	14 120	12 468	58	384	311	1 635	13 921	11 667	9.3
1185	Lauderhill	49 708	37 271	33.4	29 124	19 158	71	743	612	3 376	26 274	13 301	19.0
1193	Laurel CDP	8 245	NA	NA	7 933	246	18	42	6	55	4 827	NA	12.6
1208	Lealman CDP	21 748	19 873	9.4	20 946	262	75	352	113	550	12 297	NA	13.7
1215	Leesburg	14 903	13 191	13.0	10 642	4 108	32	56	65	292	7 326	9 680	23.2
1217	Lehigh Acres CDP	13 611	NA	NA	12 663	671	34	100	143	585	7 519	NA	21.8
1219	Leisure City CDP	19 379	17 905	8.2	14 859	2 074	46	279	2 121	9 369	7 133	NA	9.0
1220	Lely CDP	3 014	NA	NA	2 994	13	0	2	5	39	2 145	NA	3.9
1225	Lighthouse Point	10 378	11 488	-9.7	10 262	18	9	61	28	257	5 757	19 295	5.9
1227	Lindgren Acres CDP	22 290	11 986	86.0	19 699	1 007	17	794	773	8 764	8 226	NA	9.7
1230	Live Oak	6 332	NA	NA	3 735	2 490	23	36	48	115	2 639	7 653	18.0
1232	Lochmoor Waterway Estates CDP	4 091	NA	NA	3 995	21	10	41	24	84	1 907	NA	5.8
1233	Lockhart CDP	11 636	10 569	10.1	10 043	1 089	44	149	311	995	4 448	NA	11.3
1245	Longboat Key town	5 937	NA	NA	5 906	4	7	20	0	48	7 067	27 630	12.7
1250	Longwood	13 316	10 029	32.8	12 611	294	25	234	152	824	4 924	11 552	13.6
1253	Lower Grand Lagoon CDP	3 329	NA	NA	3 267	20	11	20	11	75	5 152	NA	5.7
1254	Lutz CDP	10 552	NA	NA	10 185	172	18	110	67	573	4 046	NA	34.3
1255	Lynn Haven	9 298	NA	NA	8 179	935	61	103	20	98	3 632	8 724	13.1
1260	Macclenny	3 966	NA	NA	3 081	850	17	18	0	44	1 480	8 001	8.3
1263	McGregor CDP	6 504	NA	NA	6 395	16	11	56	26	123	3 603	NA	6.6
1270	Madeira Beach	4 225	NA	NA	4 160	10	7	32	16	105	3 788	14 688	2.6
1275	Madison	3 345	NA	NA	1 309	2 028	3	5	0	26	1 338	6 996	6.4
1280	Maitland	9 110	NA	NA	8 304	662	16	83	45	243	3 890	19 041	9.8
1294	Mango CDP	8 700	NA	NA	8 026	468	47	40	119	418	3 415	NA	11.9
1298	Marathon CDP	8 857	NA	NA	8 053	580	31	55	138	1 040	5 208	NA	13.5
1299	Marco CDP	9 493	NA	NA	9 360	12	8	44	69	254	11 096	NA	19.0
1300	Margate	42 985	36 044	19.3	40 015	1 609	82	630	649	3 301	21 647	11 983	22.9
1305	Marianna	6 292	NA	NA	3 789	2 421	32	23	27	65	2 678	7 579	17.0
1320	Mary Esther	4 139	NA	NA	3 628	285	40	148	38	134	1 652	9 834	4.0
1333	Meadow Wood CDP	4 876	NA	NA	3 483	520	18	119	736	1 758	1 654	NA	2.4
1338	Medulla CDP	3 977	NA	NA	3 459	487	8	13	10	72	1 617	NA	14.7
1350	Melbourne	59 646	46 497	28.3	52 145	5 666	192	1 224	419	2 075	28 070	10 287	74.3
1353	Melbourne Beach town	3 021	NA	NA	2 971	9	2	33	6	54	1 476	19 611	2.6
1358	Melrose Park CDP	6 477	NA	NA	2 014	4 311	14	64	74	419	2 079	NA	2.3
1360	Memphis CDP	6 760	NA	NA	3 253	3 192	23	8	284	842	2 763	NA	8.5
1365	Merritt Island CDP	32 886	30 708	7.1	30 397	1 786	121	428	154	909	14 424	NA	45.7
1370	Miami	358 548	346 865	3.4	235 358	98 207	545	2 272	22 166	223 964	144 550	8 904	92.1
1375	Miami Beach	92 639	96 298	-3.8	81 800	4 798	142	1 124	4 775	43 342	62 413	13 307	18.2
1377	Miami Gardens-Utopia-Carver CDP	7 448	NA	NA	2 439	4 759	9	90	151	911	2 545	NA	3.8
1378	Miami Lakes CDP	12 750	NA	NA	11 780	318	11	314	327	4 743	6 040	NA	10.2
1380	Miami Shores village	10 084	NA	NA	7 683	2 056	16	188	141	1 363	3 918	19 107	6.5
1385	Miami Springs	13 268	12 350	7.4	12 282	250	21	261	454	5 549	5 342	14 717	7.6
1391	Micco CDP	8 757	NA	NA	8 693	30	11	12	11	52	5 693	NA	24.1
1392	Middleburg CDP	6 223	NA	NA	5 815	289	27	65	27	108	2 187	NA	47.4
1393	Mid Florida Lakes CDP	2 776	NA	NA	2 763	4	1	2	6	30	1 855	NA	5.4
1400	Milton	7 216	NA	NA	5 943	1 056	54	109	54	125	2 879	8 929	9.9
1405	Mims CDP	9 412	NA	NA	8 092	1 194	54	38	34	140	3 780	NA	51.5
1420	Miramar	40 663	32 813	23.9	32 243	6 368	69	934	1 049	7 048	15 243	12 081	76.8
1425	Monticello	2 573	NA	NA	1 245	1 322	1	2	3	17	1 057	6 042	8.2
1436	Morse Shores CDP	3 771	NA	NA	3 557	80	4	6	124	311	2 395	NA	5.9
1440	Mount Dora	7 196	NA	NA	5 571	1 504	14	36	71	221	3 644	12 305	11.4
1445	Mulberry	2 988	NA	NA	2 232	715	5	15	21	58	1 444	7 373	7.4
1447	Myrtle Grove CDP	17 402	14 238	22.2	14 722	1 521	134	827	198	619	6 471	NA	17.1
1455	Naples	19 505	17 581	10.9	18 309	1 089	23	42	42	411	15 312	27 299	28.4
1456	Naples Manor CDP	4 574	NA	NA	3 711	561	4	45	253	1 316	2 001	NA	14.0
1457	Naples Park CDP	8 002	NA	NA	7 841	30	12	23	96	600	5 162	NA	5.7
1458	Naranja CDP	5 790	10 381	-44.2	3 890	1 556	10	109	225	1 010	2 883	NA	3.9
1459	Nassau Village-Ratliff CDP	4 047	NA	NA	4 000	19	20	6	2	26	1 438	NA	40.8
1465	Neptune Beach	6 816	NA	NA	6 617	96	10	70	23	126	3 265	15 715	6.3
1475	New Port Richey	14 044	11 196	25.4	13 808	67	41	82	46	285	7 824	9 703	10.9
1476	New Port Richey East CDP	9 683	NA	NA	9 473	62	18	63	67	316	4 990	NA	9.8
1480	New Smyrna Beach	16 543	13 449	23.0	15 095	1 343	20	66	19	170	11 476	10 739	38.0

1. Codes shown are 2-digit FIPS codes for states; 4-digit census place codes for places; and 3-digit FIPS county codes followed by 3-digit census MCD codes for minor civil divisions (MCDs). MCD names are followed by county names in parentheses. 2. Hispanic persons may be of any race. 3. Dry land or land partially or temporarily covered by water.

State/ Place/ MCD[1] code	Place	Population			Population characteristics, 1990						Total housing units, 1990	Per capita income, 1985 (Dollars)	Land area,[3] 1990 (Sq. Km.)
		1990	Places of 10,000 or more		Race					Hispanic[2]			
			1980	Percent change, 1980–1990	White	Black	Am. Indian, Eskimo Aleut	Asian & Pacific Islander	Other race				
		1	2	3	4	5	6	7	8	9	10	11	12
	FLORIDA—Con.												
1481	Niceville	10 507	NA	NA	9 600	490	43	318	56	321	4 257	10 790	27.4
1486	Nokomis CDP	3 448	NA	NA	3 432	1	5	8	2	21	1 814	NA	4.4
1488	Norland CDP	22 109	19 471	13.5	7 225	13 955	38	315	576	3 181	7 977	NA	9.4
1489	North Andrews Gardens CDP	9 002	NA	NA	8 558	101	19	163	161	1 231	3 618	NA	2.9
1490	North Bay Village	5 383	NA	NA	4 862	227	11	121	162	1 944	3 401	15 723	0.9
1493	North Fort Myers CDP	30 027	22 808	31.7	29 674	74	89	117	73	410	19 020	NA	59.3
1496	North Lauderdale	26 506	NA	NA	21 219	3 853	65	763	606	3 217	9 800	NA	10.0
1498	North Miami	49 998	42 566	17.5	31 210	15 941	108	1 206	1 533	12 279	22 107	13 102	21.8
1500	North Miami Beach	35 359	36 553	-3.3	25 308	7 707	55	1 207	1 082	7 817	15 821	12 618	12.9
1504	North Naples CDP	13 422	NA	NA	13 159	59	20	61	123	733	8 183	NA	19.2
1510	North Palm Beach village	11 343	11 344	0.0	11 219	30	13	58	23	259	6 781	19 548	8.6
1520	North Port	11 973	NA	NA	11 340	501	38	46	48	271	6 524	10 233	193.7
1524	North River Shores CDP	3 250	NA	NA	3 212	17	5	15	1	25	1 718	NA	3.4
1526	North Sarasota CDP	6 702	NA	NA	4 588	1 987	25	40	62	230	3 181	NA	9.8
1540	Oakland Park	26 326	23 035	14.3	21 895	3 386	57	447	541	3 143	13 875	13 351	16.5
1543	Oak Ridge CDP	15 388	15 477	-0.6	11 221	2 239	49	733	1 146	3 806	6 298	NA	11.7
1545	Ocala	42 045	37 161	13.1	31 488	10 003	110	263	181	914	19 478	9 171	74.7
1549	Ocean City CDP	5 422	NA	NA	4 870	308	31	161	52	163	2 511	NA	4.1
1560	Ocoee	12 778	NA	NA	12 088	168	21	126	375	1 075	4 439	8 830	23.4
1563	Ojus CDP	15 519	17 344	-10.5	15 018	243	4	118	136	1 718	8 142	NA	7.6
1565	Okeechobee	4 943	NA	NA	4 099	568	26	40	210	464	1 935	8 231	10.6
1570	Oldsmar	8 361	NA	NA	8 044	153	24	93	47	336	3 507	11 239	21.8
1573	Olympia Heights CDP	37 792	33 112	14.1	35 243	323	21	509	1 696	29 922	12 237	NA	17.5
1585	Opa-locka	15 283	14 460	5.7	3 803	10 603	26	55	796	4 186	5 709	6 615	11.2
1587	Opa-locka North CDP	6 568	NA	NA	1 286	5 125	12	21	124	855	1 553	NA	5.6
1590	Orange City	5 347	NA	NA	5 115	173	14	29	16	124	3 041	8 315	14.5
1595	Orange Park town	9 488	NA	NA	8 363	897	27	144	57	237	3 712	12 881	10.1
1600	Orlando	164 693	128 291	28.4	113 243	44 303	506	2 564	4 077	14 401	73 425	10 894	174.2
1603	Orlovista CDP	5 990	NA	NA	4 677	986	49	133	145	484	2 294	NA	5.0
1605	Ormond Beach	29 721	21 378	39.0	28 275	1 046	32	305	63	506	14 190	15 031	65.3
1607	Ormond-By-The-Sea CDP	8 157	NA	NA	8 096	13	8	23	17	137	5 241	NA	5.1
1610	Osprey CDP	2 597	NA	NA	2 576	0	5	9	7	20	1 517	NA	5.3
1615	Oviedo	11 114	NA	NA	9 356	1 360	17	177	204	768	4 212	11 893	34.7
1622	Pace CDP	6 277	NA	NA	6 132	29	62	37	17	92	2 526	NA	24.3
1624	Page Park-Pine Manor CDP	5 116	NA	NA	4 529	291	28	42	226	722	2 181	NA	2.7
1625	Pahokee	6 822	NA	NA	2 391	3 776	16	35	604	1 369	2 422	9 041	13.8
1630	Palatka	10 201	10 175	0.3	5 366	4 755	15	28	37	172	4 325	7 000	16.3
1640	Palm Bay	62 632	18 560	237.5	55 902	4 689	158	1 104	779	3 315	26 273	11 114	164.8
1645	Palm Beach town	9 814	NA	NA	9 705	58	1	36	14	266	9 191	38 945	10.2
1650	Palm Beach Gardens	22 965	14 407	59.4	22 331	187	26	339	82	800	12 171	16 737	68.1
1657	Palm City CDP	3 925	NA	NA	3 888	12	8	16	1	98	1 921	NA	8.7
1658	Palm Coast CDP	14 287	NA	NA	13 133	854	23	193	84	879	7 522	NA	51.5
1660	Palmetto	9 268	NA	NA	7 308	1 346	16	17	581	1 402	4 873	8 497	9.9
1661	Palmetto Estates CDP	12 293	11 116	10.6	6 496	4 967	31	499	300	2 380	4 016	NA	5.5
1663	Palm Harbor CDP	50 256	NA	NA	49 495	205	102	308	146	1 073	23 953	NA	46.4
1665	Palm River CDP	3 507	NA	NA	3 460	11	1	13	22	96	1 736	NA	5.2
1666	Palm River-Clair Mel CDP	13 691	14 447	-5.2	9 335	3 656	72	126	502	2 221	4 939	NA	21.0
1670	Palm Springs village	9 763	NA	NA	9 317	222	5	84	135	902	5 431	12 941	3.5
1672	Palm Springs North CDP	5 300	NA	NA	5 086	39	9	31	135	2 599	1 618	NA	1.8
1673	Palm Valley CDP	9 960	NA	NA	9 714	120	16	86	24	225	4 814	NA	34.7
1675	Panama City	34 378	33 346	3.1	25 954	7 500	215	583	126	460	15 928	8 875	40.1
1678	Panama City Beach	4 051	NA	NA	3 993	10	6	35	7	63	6 013	NA	14.8
1685	Parker	4 598	NA	NA	4 126	280	40	109	43	131	2 251	9 350	5.0
1686	Parkland	3 558	NA	NA	3 456	34	10	44	14	152	1 115	NA	22.4
1695	Pembroke Park town	4 933	NA	NA	4 109	709	13	28	74	557	3 467	11 693	3.5
1700	Pembroke Pines	65 452	35 776	82.9	59 746	3 441	103	1 304	858	7 532	29 546	13 562	82.7
1715	Pensacola	58 165	57 619	0.9	38 198	18 557	302	908	200	922	26 366	10 591	58.6
1720	Perrine CDP	15 576	16 129	-3.4	7 334	7 661	19	331	231	2 151	5 226	NA	10.4
1725	Perry	7 151	NA	NA	4 140	2 931	41	27	12	73	2 898	8 485	24.1
1735	Pierson town	2 988	NA	NA	896	136	6	5	1 945	1 995	410	NA	19.8
1740	Pine Castle CDP	8 276	NA	NA	6 690	746	51	213	576	1 601	3 323	NA	6.9
1746	Pine Hills CDP	35 322	35 771	-1.3	25 518	8 059	116	747	882	2 958	13 336	NA	20.0
1748	Pine Island Ridge CDP	5 244	NA	NA	5 121	40	6	45	32	417	3 193	NA	2.0
1750	Pinellas Park	43 426	32 811	32.4	41 725	419	135	810	337	1 414	20 593	10 590	35.9
1753	Pinewood CDP	15 518	16 252	-4.5	3 709	11 181	42	101	485	3 325	5 346	NA	4.4
1755	Plantation	66 692	48 501	37.5	60 491	4 112	80	1 219	790	5 430	29 399	17 110	56.3
1757	Plantation Key CDP	4 405	NA	NA	4 340	23	4	25	13	266	2 961	NA	8.4
1760	Plant City	22 754	19 270	18.1	17 193	4 837	53	129	542	1 888	9 350	8 200	54.8
1765	Poinciana Place CDP	3 618	NA	NA	2 828	513	4	54	219	796	1 490	NA	21.1
1780	Pompano Beach	72 411	52 618	37.6	50 666	20 625	104	415	601	3 878	42 719	14 474	52.7
1781	Pompano Beach Highlands CDP	17 915	16 154	10.9	13 572	3 634	33	230	446	2 075	7 946	NA	8.4
1790	Port Charlotte CDP	41 535	25 770	61.2	39 073	1 813	67	403	179	1 439	21 479	NA	57.7
1795	Port Orange	35 317	18 756	88.3	34 512	354	97	275	79	689	17 019	10 401	52.1

1. Codes shown are 2-digit FIPS codes for states; 4-digit census place codes for places; and 3-digit FIPS county codes followed by 3-digit census MCD codes for minor civil divisions (MCDs). MCD names are followed by county names in parentheses. 2. Hispanic persons may be of any race. 3. Dry land or land partially or temporarily covered by water.

State/ Place/ MCD[1] code	Place	Population: 1990	Population: Places of 10,000 or more: 1980	Population: Places of 10,000 or more: Percent change, 1980–1990	Race: White	Race: Black	Race: Am. Indian, Eskimo Aleut	Race: Asian & Pacific Islander	Race: Other race	Hispanic[2]	Total housing units, 1990	Per capita income, 1985 (Dollars)	Land area,[3] 1990 (Sq. Km.)
		1	2	3	4	5	6	7	8	9	10	11	12
	FLORIDA—Con.												
1800	Port Richey	2 523	NA	NA	2 469	26	6	7	15	65	1 607	NA	5.3
1805	Port St. Joe	4 044	NA	NA	2 542	1 480	10	8	4	27	1 638	8 106	8.6
1806	Port St. John CDP	8 933	NA	NA	8 446	291	29	123	44	220	3 445	NA	9.9
1807	Port St. Lucie	55 866	14 690	280.3	52 633	2 130	109	516	478	2 250	24 241	11 409	196.6
1808	Port St. Lucie-River Park CDP	4 874	NA	NA	4 690	102	2	67	13	89	2 668	NA	6.0
1809	Port Salerno CDP	7 786	NA	NA	6 997	540	13	31	205	345	4 136	NA	9.4
1814	Pretty Bayou CDP	3 839	NA	NA	3 666	96	26	49	2	60	1 548	NA	5.4
1817	Princeton CDP	7 073	NA	NA	4 852	1 622	22	195	382	2 300	2 220	NA	19.0
1820	Punta Gorda	10 747	NA	NA	10 037	631	24	39	16	171	6 936	15 622	36.5
1825	Quincy	7 444	NA	NA	2 871	4 504	10	12	47	73	2 883	7 444	16.1
1845	Richmond Heights CDP	8 583	NA	NA	933	7 485	7	78	80	644	2 696	NA	4.3
1847	Ridge Wood Heights CDP	4 851	NA	NA	4 769	13	21	33	15	87	2 232	NA	3.7
1851	Riverland CDP	5 376	NA	NA	5 176	54	17	45	84	617	2 180	NA	3.0
1853	Riverview CDP	6 478	NA	NA	6 280	64	41	36	57	342	2 921	NA	22.9
1855	Riviera Beach	27 639	26 473	4.4	7 932	19 258	47	215	187	720	14 078	10 481	19.4
1860	Rockledge	16 023	11 877	34.9	13 449	2 210	49	227	88	385	6 533	11 640	25.3
1862	Rotonda CDP	3 576	NA	NA	3 549	4	6	13	4	31	2 235	NA	31.3
1870	Royal Palm Beach village	14 589	NA	NA	13 139	1 050	24	205	171	1 201	5 985	15 317	22.8
1875	Ruskin CDP	6 046	NA	NA	5 688	45	16	19	278	1 453	2 800	NA	19.3
1880	Safety Harbor	15 124	NA	NA	14 095	790	21	147	71	437	6 373	12 289	11.7
1885	St. Augustine	11 692	11 985	-2.4	9 135	2 365	26	84	82	433	5 181	9 282	18.2
1886	St. Augustine Beach	3 657	NA	NA	3 609	11	7	21	9	101	2 562	NA	4.9
1887	St. Augustine Shores CDP	4 411	NA	NA	4 255	90	3	45	18	114	2 261	NA	8.9
1888	St. Augustine South CDP	4 218	NA	NA	4 138	14	10	48	8	106	1 623	NA	4.5
1890	St. Cloud	12 453	NA	NA	12 059	128	52	70	144	482	5 996	9 944	19.5
1900	St. Petersburg	238 629	238 647	0.0	186 125	46 726	596	3 967	1 215	6 255	125 452	11 109	153.3
1902	St. Petersburg Beach	9 200	NA	NA	9 120	17	9	40	14	147	7 205	16 041	5.8
1910	Samoset CDP	3 119	NA	NA	2 273	776	12	5	53	169	1 067	NA	5.0
1913	Samsula-Spruce Creek CDP	3 404	NA	NA	3 367	0	9	23	5	56	1 475	NA	60.3
1917	San Carlos Park CDP	11 785	NA	NA	11 515	77	19	76	98	390	4 722	NA	15.4
1918	Sandalfoot Cove CDP	14 214	NA	NA	13 716	173	20	244	61	845	7 179	NA	7.6
1920	Sanford	32 387	23 176	39.7	22 287	9 228	132	299	441	1 586	13 834	7 893	44.8
1923	Sanibel	5 468	NA	NA	5 375	68	7	14	4	70	6 422	24 164	44.6
1930	Sarasota	50 961	48 876	4.3	41 784	8 266	118	350	443	2 408	26 974	12 650	37.9
1934	Sarasota Springs CDP	16 088	13 860	16.1	15 853	78	22	95	40	384	6 795	NA	9.4
1935	Satellite Beach	9 889	NA	NA	9 555	105	25	171	33	271	4 205	14 076	6.2
1936	Sawgrass CDP	2 999	NA	NA	2 973	4	5	15	2	45	2 039	NA	8.0
1937	Scott Lake CDP	14 588	14 154	3.1	1 384	12 907	6	108	183	895	4 124	NA	8.5
1945	Sebastian	10 205	NA	NA	9 938	108	19	106	34	183	4 611	10 738	32.5
1950	Sebring	8 900	NA	NA	7 349	1 331	16	44	160	434	4 999	9 772	11.9
1952	Seffner CDP	5 371	NA	NA	5 075	232	11	16	37	248	2 095	NA	9.4
1953	Seminole	9 251	NA	NA	9 178	14	5	43	11	120	5 399	11 268	5.8
1963	Sharpes CDP	3 348	NA	NA	3 189	118	17	17	7	29	1 582	NA	7.7
1964	Siesta Key CDP	7 772	NA	NA	7 751	4	1	7	9	78	8 077	NA	5.9
1968	Silver Springs Shores CDP	6 421	NA	NA	5 058	1 136	27	32	168	516	3 326	NA	12.5
1969	Sky Lake CDP	6 202	NA	NA	5 074	649	12	126	341	1 270	2 262	NA	3.3
1985	South Apopka CDP	6 360	NA	NA	1 813	4 275	11	8	253	528	2 073	NA	9.4
1990	South Bay	3 558	NA	NA	784	2 204	9	15	546	1 061	1 213	5 565	5.0
1991	South Beach CDP	2 754	NA	NA	2 721	6	2	24	1	24	1 671	NA	7.0
1992	South Bradenton CDP	20 398	14 285	42.8	19 714	348	72	167	97	418	13 354	NA	11.8
1995	South Daytona	12 482	11 252	10.9	11 841	438	31	115	57	252	6 122	10 797	9.2
1997	Southeast Arcadia CDP	4 145	NA	NA	3 872	44	12	10	207	670	1 940	NA	19.0
2002	Southgate CDP	7 324	NA	NA	7 225	15	14	56	14	139	4 024	NA	5.3
2003	South Gate Ridge CDP	5 924	NA	NA	5 821	47	5	40	11	108	2 592	NA	4.7
2005	South Miami	10 404	10 944	-4.9	6 950	3 078	22	185	169	2 472	4 346	13 136	6.0
2007	South Miami Heights CDP	30 030	23 559	27.5	18 988	8 396	75	644	1 927	14 668	10 188	NA	12.8
2015	South Pasadena	5 644	NA	NA	5 604	15	5	15	5	43	4 398	17 313	1.8
2017	South Patrick Shores CDP	10 249	NA	NA	9 182	660	28	286	93	455	4 092	NA	5.3
2023	South Sarasota CDP	5 298	NA	NA	5 215	29	2	35	17	134	2 684	NA	5.4
2024	South Venice CDP	11 951	NA	NA	11 836	12	17	72	14	114	5 637	NA	15.9
2028	Springfield	8 715	NA	NA	6 375	1 950	80	284	26	98	3 673	6 469	9.9
2029	Spring Hill CDP	31 117	NA	NA	30 395	393	43	129	157	1 260	14 863	NA	58.8
2030	Starke	5 226	NA	NA	3 721	1 432	8	51	14	75	2 113	7 138	17.2
2032	Stock Island CDP	3 613	NA	NA	2 907	386	25	41	254	1 264	1 567	NA	2.3
2035	Stuart	11 936	NA	NA	9 960	1 807	16	80	73	463	7 021	12 775	11.4
2036	Sugarmill Woods CDP	4 073	NA	NA	4 026	15	1	22	9	60	2 258	NA	68.3
2037	Sun City Center CDP	8 326	NA	NA	8 312	2	1	10	1	52	5 665	NA	14.5
2038	Suncoast Estates CDP	4 483	NA	NA	4 379	7	40	12	45	217	2 000	NA	7.4
2043	Sunny Isles CDP	11 772	12 579	-6.4	11 459	83	13	83	134	1 997	10 309	NA	3.2
2047	Sunrise	64 407	39 681	62.3	57 517	4 759	58	1 247	826	5 565	29 295	12 624	47.2
2048	Sunset CDP	15 810	13 531	16.8	14 449	328	19	465	549	9 523	5 206	NA	9.2
2049	Sun Valley CDP	2 735	NA	NA	2 563	34	1	111	26	151	1 327	NA	1.5
2050	Surfside town	4 108	NA	NA	3 898	55	1	50	104	1 231	2 814	15 033	1.3

1. Codes shown are 2-digit FIPS codes for states; 4-digit census place codes for places; and 3-digit FIPS county codes followed by 3-digit census MCD codes for minor civil divisions (MCDs). MCD names are followed by county names in parentheses. 2. Hispanic persons may be of any race. 3. Dry land or land partially or temporarily covered by water.

State/ Place/ MCD[1] code	Place	Population: 1990	Population: Places of 10,000 or more: 1980	Population: Places of 10,000 or more: Percent change, 1980–1990	Population characteristics, 1990: Race: White	Race: Black	Race: Am. Indian, Eskimo Aleut	Race: Asian & Pacific Islander	Race: Other race	Hispanic[2]	Total housing units, 1990	Per capita income, 1985 (Dollars)	Land area,[3] 1990 (Sq. Km.)
		1	2	3	4	5	6	7	8	9	10	11	12
	FLORIDA—Con.												
2055	Sweetwater	13 909	NA	NA	10 857	142	15	71	2 824	12 938	4 145	7 073	2.1
2070	Tallahassee	124 773	81 548	53.0	85 140	36 298	283	2 189	863	3 738	55 221	10 352	163.9
2072	Tamarac	44 822	29 376	52.6	43 013	1 034	43	397	335	2 438	26 141	15 187	29.8
2073	Tamiami CDP	33 845	17 607	92.2	31 316	267	17	231	2 014	27 964	10 916	NA	15.5
2075	Tampa	280 015	271 523	3.1	198 542	70 131	834	3 794	6 714	42 009	129 681	9 902	281.5
2077	Tangelo Park CDP	2 663	NA	NA	250	2 383	1	3	26	90	791	NA	0.9
2080	Tarpon Springs	17 906	13 251	35.1	16 227	1 439	39	124	77	323	9 116	10 518	22.5
2085	Tavares	7 383	NA	NA	6 842	461	6	22	52	134	4 420	10 253	10.8
2088	Taylor Creek CDP	4 081	NA	NA	3 972	6	9	10	84	121	2 807	NA	10.1
2090	Temple Terrace	16 444	11 097	48.2	14 997	885	44	323	195	1 423	6 850	14 068	12.8
2095	Tequesta village	4 499	NA	NA	4 473	5	0	15	6	87	2 454	23 522	4.4
2098	The Meadows CDP	3 437	NA	NA	3 378	39	2	8	10	48	2 655	NA	4.0
2100	Tice CDP	3 971	NA	NA	3 474	236	5	39	217	577	1 867	NA	3.0
2103	Timber Pines CDP	3 182	NA	NA	3 171	0	5	6	0	24	1 895	NA	6.9
2105	Titusville	39 394	31 910	23.5	34 377	4 323	166	331	197	1 084	18 183	11 171	50.5
2108	Town 'n' Country CDP	60 946	37 834	61.1	55 129	2 648	142	1 290	1 737	10 926	26 939	NA	61.2
2115	Treasure Island	7 266	NA	NA	7 208	7	20	20	11	103	5 525	19 687	4.1
2123	Tyndall AFB CDP	4 318	NA	NA	3 371	703	26	146	72	263	943	NA	35.5
2126	Union Park CDP	6 890	19 175	-64.1	6 395	83	29	161	222	855	2 385	NA	7.9
2127	University West CDP	23 760	24 514	-3.1	17 148	5 362	94	566	590	2 748	14 910	NA	10.0
2132	Upper Grand Lagoon CDP	7 855	NA	NA	7 510	130	82	94	39	177	4 331	NA	21.4
2135	Valparaiso	4 672	NA	NA	4 220	239	25	154	34	146	1 937	10 675	31.0
2137	Vamo CDP	3 325	NA	NA	3 277	5	5	31	7	36	1 925	NA	4.6
2140	Venice	16 922	12 153	39.2	16 630	215	13	51	13	115	12 449	14 525	19.2
2143	Venice Gardens CDP	7 701	NA	NA	7 616	13	19	49	4	45	4 085	NA	6.5
2150	Vero Beach	17 350	16 176	7.3	16 596	571	25	98	60	435	10 064	16 195	28.7
2152	Vero Beach South CDP	16 973	12 636	34.3	16 620	141	38	130	44	317	7 767	NA	26.8
2153	Villages of Oriole CDP	5 698	NA	NA	5 698	0	0	0	0	21	4 249	NA	2.5
2155	Villas CDP	9 898	NA	NA	9 686	70	9	94	39	212	5 773	NA	12.2
2160	Wahneta CDP	4 024	NA	NA	3 699	5	23	1	296	834	1 511	NA	5.5
2172	Warm Mineral Springs CDP	4 041	NA	NA	4 035	0	3	2	1	20	3 200	NA	7.0
2175	Warrington CDP	16 040	15 792	1.6	12 313	2 998	136	440	153	443	7 553	NA	18.9
2177	Washington Park CDP	6 930	NA	NA	266	6 630	5	10	19	84	2 400	NA	2.9
2180	Watertown CDP	3 340	NA	NA	2 361	950	4	14	11	27	1 473	NA	8.0
2185	Wauchula	3 253	NA	NA	3 012	52	5	11	173	622	1 385	9 330	6.1
2193	Wekiva Springs CDP	23 026	13 386	72.0	22 275	254	39	381	77	787	8 716	NA	22.4
2197	Wellington CDP	20 670	NA	NA	19 617	515	24	377	137	1 332	9 377	NA	29.2
2201	West Bradenton CDP	4 528	NA	NA	4 452	1	11	52	12	115	1 836	NA	3.5
2202	Westchester CDP	29 883	29 272	2.1	28 051	153	18	150	1 511	24 554	9 564	NA	10.4
2203	West De Land CDP	3 389	NA	NA	3 212	113	13	27	24	82	1 319	NA	6.1
2206	Westgate-Belvedere Homes CDP	6 880	NA	NA	6 193	430	32	62	163	821	2 906	NA	5.3
2208	West Little River CDP	33 575	32 492	3.3	9 292	22 846	50	105	1 282	9 866	10 254	NA	11.8
2209	West Melbourne	8 399	NA	NA	8 207	69	14	81	28	175	4 059	11 676	14.8
2210	West Miami	5 727	NA	NA	5 326	64	5	27	305	4 549	2 082	10 992	1.8
2215	West Palm Beach	67 643	63 305	6.9	42 889	22 063	94	626	1 971	9 577	34 971	12 188	127.8
2217	West Park CDP	10 347	NA	NA	9 195	257	20	146	729	5 194	3 785	NA	6.0
2219	West Pensacola CDP	22 107	24 371	-9.3	16 257	4 748	324	678	100	459	10 032	NA	19.1
2221	West Samoset CDP	3 819	NA	NA	3 037	604	16	48	114	271	1 666	NA	3.6
2222	Westview CDP	9 668	NA	NA	1 961	7 369	26	57	255	1 761	3 068	NA	8.1
2230	Westwood Lakes CDP	11 522	11 478	0.4	10 775	91	2	141	513	7 811	3 420	NA	4.5
2237	Whiskey Creek CDP	5 061	NA	NA	5 000	13	2	44	2	68	2 391	NA	4.1
2239	Whisper Walk CDP	3 037	NA	NA	2 907	27	3	81	19	127	1 783	NA	2.6
2242	White City CDP	4 645	NA	NA	4 447	124	15	29	30	137	1 916	NA	19.2
2246	Whitfield CDP	3 152	NA	NA	3 094	24	5	22	7	32	1 446	NA	3.6
2250	Wildwood	3 421	NA	NA	2 155	1 252	7	1	6	36	1 794	6 953	8.7
2253	Williamsburg CDP	3 093	NA	NA	3 041	22	1	17	12	97	1 828	NA	3.4
2257	Willow Oak CDP	4 017	NA	NA	3 742	215	17	9	34	143	1 483	NA	10.6
2260	Wilton Manors	11 804	12 741	-7.4	10 373	1 103	18	134	176	733	5 983	13 547	5.0
2264	Wimauma CDP	2 932	NA	NA	2 306	445	11	0	170	1 887	861	NA	7.5
2275	Winston CDP	9 118	NA	NA	7 333	1 530	50	21	184	466	4 638	NA	14.2
2280	Winter Garden	9 745	NA	NA	8 226	1 159	27	63	270	735	3 875	8 909	12.4
2285	Winter Haven	24 725	21 169	16.8	18 795	5 598	58	138	136	620	12 752	11 232	31.6
2290	Winter Park	22 242	22 339	-0.4	18 912	2 988	31	204	107	557	10 057	16 265	18.0
2291	Winter Springs	22 151	10 475	111.5	20 876	664	48	340	223	1 274	8 706	13 047	35.1
2292	Woodville CDP	2 760	NA	NA	2 422	322	11	5	0	21	1 097	NA	16.6
2294	Wright CDP	18 945	13 011	45.6	15 897	2 142	109	611	186	639	8 289	NA	14.2
2297	Yulee CDP	6 915	NA	NA	6 376	473	28	19	19	71	2 591	NA	59.9
2300	Zephyrhills	8 220	NA	NA	7 933	164	27	35	61	199	5 209	8 732	15.1
2302	Zephyrhills South CDP	2 514	NA	NA	2 474	6	15	14	5	40	1 818	NA	3.7
2303	Zephyrhills West CDP	4 249	NA	NA	4 210	6	9	13	11	26	3 165	NA	6.2
13	GEORGIA	6 478 216	5 462 989	18.6	4 600 148	1 746 565	13 348	75 781	42 374	108 922	2 638 418	10 191	150 009.5

1. Codes shown are 2-digit FIPS codes for states; 4-digit census place codes for places; and 3-digit FIPS county codes followed by 3-digit census MCD codes for minor civil divisions (MCDs). MCD names are followed by county names in parentheses. 2. Hispanic persons may be of any race. 3. Dry land or land partially or temporarily covered by water.

State/ Place/ MCD[1] code	Place	Population: 1990	Population: Places of 10,000 or more: 1980	Population: Places of 10,000 or more: Percent change, 1980–1990	Population characteristics, 1990: Race: White	Race: Black	Race: Am. Indian, Eskimo Aleut	Race: Asian & Pacific Islander	Race: Other race	Hispanic[2]	Total housing units, 1990	Per capita income, 1985 (Dollars)	Land area,[3] 1990 (Sq. Km.)
		1	2	3	4	5	6	7	8	9	10	11	12
	GEORGIA—Con.												
0010	Acworth	4 519	NA	NA	4 158	311	13	11	26	55	2 093	11 335	12.0
0020	Adel	5 093	NA	NA	2 505	2 529	12	18	29	89	1 972	7 697	16.3
0045	Albany	78 122	74 059	5.5	34 544	42 962	155	335	126	647	30 603	8 757	143.6
0065	Alma	3 663	NA	NA	2 444	1 186	7	12	14	45	1 573	6 052	14.5
0070	Alpharetta	13 002	NA	NA	12 380	332	27	177	86	240	5 887	13 155	49.3
0100	Americus	16 512	16 120	2.4	7 646	8 737	43	64	22	79	6 317	7 247	25.0
0140	Ashburn	4 827	NA	NA	1 918	2 893	5	11	0	17	1 835	6 561	11.7
0145	Athens	45 734	42 549	7.5	30 354	13 547	60	1 528	245	736	18 499	8 586	43.0
0150	Atlanta	394 017	425 022	-7.3	122 327	264 262	563	3 498	3 367	7 525	182 754	10 341	341.3
0160	Auburn	3 139	NA	NA	2 988	46	1	39	65	108	1 358	NA	13.0
0165	Augusta	44 639	47 532	-6.1	19 213	24 993	69	273	91	336	21 588	8 100	50.9
0170	Austell	4 173	NA	NA	3 747	381	21	16	8	37	1 708	8 740	12.9
0195	Bainbridge	10 712	10 532	1.7	5 612	5 032	23	18	27	200	4 457	8 551	40.0
0210	Barnesville	4 747	NA	NA	2 295	2 437	9	2	4	13	1 842	7 048	10.7
0230	Baxley	3 841	NA	NA	2 403	1 397	2	17	22	45	1 654	7 442	15.8
0239	Belvedere Park CDP	18 089	17 766	1.8	4 547	13 041	29	327	145	280	6 840	NA	12.9
0275	Blackshear	3 263	NA	NA	2 638	620	3	2	0	13	1 405	6 927	9.3
0285	Blakely	5 595	NA	NA	2 813	2 758	16	7	1	35	2 095	7 023	29.3
0355	Bremen	4 356	NA	NA	3 851	488	8	7	2	11	1 813	8 181	22.3
0390	Brunswick	16 433	17 605	-6.7	6 726	9 570	37	70	30	146	6 901	7 172	44.6
0415	Buford	8 771	NA	NA	7 332	1 261	32	38	108	213	3 670	8 866	34.6
0435	Cairo	9 035	NA	NA	4 572	4 349	32	8	74	188	3 551	6 281	23.2
0440	Calhoun	7 135	NA	NA	6 370	670	13	73	9	39	3 109	10 317	26.8
0450	Camilla	5 008	NA	NA	1 768	3 223	3	2	12	51	1 830	6 894	12.5
0458	Candler-McAfee CDP	29 491	27 306	8.0	1 682	27 623	31	123	32	155	9 543	NA	18.1
0470	Canton	4 817	NA	NA	4 297	443	14	4	59	98	2 026	8 947	33.4
0495	Carrollton	16 029	14 078	13.9	11 108	4 724	14	102	81	247	6 580	8 752	38.3
0505	Cartersville	12 035	NA	NA	9 788	2 122	16	50	59	131	5 171	10 138	61.6
0520	Cedartown	7 978	NA	NA	5 930	1 808	5	37	198	279	3 462	7 597	16.1
0535	Centerville	3 251	NA	NA	3 029	168	13	33	8	52	1 166	10 445	6.0
0550	Chamblee	7 668	NA	NA	4 142	1 482	14	922	1 108	1 833	3 046	11 181	8.1
0560	Chatsworth	2 865	NA	NA	2 830	20	1	11	3	8	1 210	NA	9.4
0562	Chattanooga Valley CDP	4 088	NA	NA	4 066	8	7	7	0	10	1 597	NA	19.5
0585	Clarkston	5 385	NA	NA	2 012	3 015	13	313	32	119	2 461	11 960	2.7
0625	Cochran	4 390	NA	NA	2 690	1 651	1	46	2	16	1 781	7 729	10.2
0645	College Park	20 457	24 632	-16.9	4 310	15 231	47	663	206	405	10 077	10 588	25.1
0660	Columbus	178 681	169 434	5.5	105 172	68 157	568	2 508	2 276	5 290	70 657	9 182	559.8
0670	Commerce	4 108	NA	NA	3 442	625	12	18	11	24	1 724	8 926	12.0
0677	Conley CDP	5 528	NA	NA	3 503	1 859	21	113	32	81	1 900	NA	4.9
0680	Conyers	7 380	NA	NA	5 619	1 608	12	107	34	104	3 262	10 552	18.9
0690	Cordele	10 321	10 914	-5.4	3 993	6 294	23	5	6	35	4 181	6 832	14.3
0700	Cornelia	3 219	NA	NA	2 504	423	9	273	10	41	1 456	11 336	7.1
0706	Country Club Estates CDP	7 500	NA	NA	5 198	2 158	15	83	46	99	2 946	NA	12.3
0710	Covington	10 026	10 586	-5.3	5 426	4 554	13	15	18	99	3 913	8 323	31.1
0740	Cumming	2 828	NA	NA	2 691	5	15	1	116	143	1 031	NA	12.3
0750	Cuthbert	3 730	NA	NA	1 122	2 550	1	41	16	28	1 426	5 103	7.9
0760	Dahlonega	3 086	NA	NA	2 873	156	21	22	14	109	890	8 013	12.1
0770	Dallas	2 810	NA	NA	2 412	391	4	3	0	10	1 160	8 958	8.7
0775	Dalton	21 761	20 939	3.9	18 155	2 317	62	223	1 004	1 422	9 555	11 964	46.6
0810	Dawson	5 295	NA	NA	1 535	3 743	6	10	1	24	2 011	6 177	9.4
0825	Decatur	17 336	18 404	-5.8	10 386	6 716	31	155	48	186	8 230	10 887	10.8
0870	Dock Junction CDP	7 094	NA	NA	5 649	1 387	15	35	8	27	2 923	NA	24.7
0880	Donalsonville	2 761	NA	NA	1 213	1 546	2	0	0	7	1 058	7 271	10.3
0885	Doraville	7 626	NA	NA	5 324	1 421	33	545	303	704	3 197	10 822	9.3
0890	Douglas	10 464	10 980	-4.7	5 711	4 649	18	69	17	80	4 232	7 926	30.0
0895	Douglasville	11 635	NA	NA	9 187	2 261	26	117	44	153	4 682	9 402	31.1
0898	Druid Hills CDP	12 174	12 700	-4.1	11 073	553	24	460	64	236	4 794	NA	10.9
0900	Dublin	16 312	16 083	1.4	8 639	7 531	13	117	12	86	6 495	8 766	32.6
0915	Duluth	9 029	NA	NA	8 271	473	22	188	75	217	3 930	12 267	19.1
0918	Dunwoody CDP	26 302	17 768	48.0	24 609	722	21	868	82	429	10 427	NA	31.3
0927	East Boundary CDP	3 271	NA	NA	44	3 208	8	3	8	17	1 298	NA	2.5
0930	East Dublin town	2 524	NA	NA	1 651	864	8	1	0	5	1 095	7 313	7.6
0950	Eastman	5 153	NA	NA	3 646	1 455	4	22	26	39	2 257	7 873	12.5
0960	East Point	34 402	37 486	-8.2	10 881	22 823	74	249	375	653	15 671	9 878	35.6
0975	Eatonton	4 737	NA	NA	1 916	2 776	6	34	5	30	1 843	7 519	13.1
1000	Elberton	5 682	NA	NA	3 547	2 109	1	24	1	50	2 602	8 328	11.1
1044	Evans CDP	13 713	NA	NA	12 381	904	27	330	71	252	4 795	NA	25.7
1045	Experiment CDP	3 762	NA	NA	1 679	2 080	3	0	0	2	1 429	NA	7.9
1050	Fairburn	4 013	NA	NA	2 606	1 312	17	20	58	129	1 593	9 886	11.6
1057	Fair Oaks CDP	6 996	NA	NA	5 846	931	30	93	96	218	3 646	NA	5.1
1060	Fairview CDP	6 444	NA	NA	6 060	349	29	4	2	28	2 548	NA	19.4
1075	Fayetteville	5 827	NA	NA	5 414	338	6	45	24	82	2 609	11 598	21.8
1085	Fitzgerald	8 612	10 187	-15.5	4 507	4 076	5	20	4	26	3 721	7 503	14.9

1. Codes shown are 2-digit FIPS codes for states; 4-digit census place codes for places; and 3-digit FIPS county codes followed by 3-digit census MCD codes for minor civil divisions (MCDs). MCD names are followed by county names in parentheses. 2. Hispanic persons may be of any race. 3. Dry land or land partially or temporarily covered by water.

State/ Place/ MCD[1] code	Place	Population			Population characteristics, 1990						Total housing units, 1990	Per capita income, 1985 (Dollars)	Land area,[3] 1990 (Sq. Km.)
		1990	Places of 10,000 or more		Race					Hispanic[2]			
			1980	Percent change, 1980–1990	White	Black	Am. Indian, Eskimo Aleut	Asian & Pacific Islander	Other race				
		1	2	3	4	5	6	7	8	9	10	11	12
	GEORGIA—Con.												
1110	Forest Park	16 925	18 782	-9.9	13 006	3 240	47	411	221	455	6 993	10 173	22.3
1115	Forsyth	4 268	NA	NA	1 915	2 330	3	16	4	20	1 654	7 909	10.4
1117	Fort Benning South CDP	14 617	15 074	-3.0	8 657	4 375	99	464	1 022	1 768	2 143	NA	22.2
1121	Fort Gordon CDP	9 140	14 069	-35.0	4 892	3 399	64	271	514	768	879	NA	31.6
1125	Fort Oglethorpe	5 880	NA	NA	5 797	39	9	21	14	29	2 402	9 024	30.7
1127	Fort Stewart CDP	13 774	15 017	-8.3	6 871	5 755	91	368	689	1 188	2 137	NA	17.1
1130	Fort Valley	8 198	NA	NA	2 387	5 716	30	19	46	97	3 074	7 977	13.7
1153	Gaines School CDP	11 354	NA	NA	9 801	1 183	14	291	65	259	5 219	NA	16.2
1155	Gainesville	17 885	15 280	17.0	12 300	4 203	19	215	1 148	1 415	7 651	12 920	58.8
1165	Garden City	7 410	NA	NA	4 803	2 525	18	26	38	55	3 129	9 088	13.2
1187	Georgetown CDP	5 554	NA	NA	4 698	737	17	63	39	107	2 370	NA	29.7
1205	Glennville	3 676	NA	NA	2 477	1 100	10	23	66	80	1 586	6 990	15.8
1260	Greensboro	2 860	NA	NA	1 303	1 551	2	0	4	15	1 097	7 481	14.8
1267	Gresham Park CDP	9 000	NA	NA	480	8 498	4	7	11	34	3 039	NA	7.3
1270	Griffin	21 347	20 728	3.0	10 930	10 205	34	139	39	124	8 749	8 719	33.9
1275	Grovetown	3 596	NA	NA	2 905	564	27	52	48	108	1 499	7 944	5.6
1300	Hampton	2 694	NA	NA	2 192	479	4	13	6	14	984	NA	11.1
1305	Hapeville	5 483	NA	NA	4 194	570	10	566	143	217	2 670	10 718	6.1
1325	Hartwell	4 555	NA	NA	2 985	1 552	2	11	5	15	1 918	8 312	10.1
1330	Hawkinsville	3 527	NA	NA	1 754	1 750	1	10	12	25	1 564	8 062	6.5
1335	Hazlehurst	4 202	NA	NA	3 096	1 092	2	10	2	21	1 698	8 127	10.6
1380	Hinesville	21 603	11 309	91.0	12 380	7 695	108	708	712	1 481	8 037	8 073	32.0
1395	Hogansville	2 976	NA	NA	1 763	1 210	2	1	0	14	1 283	7 744	15.6
1415	Homerville	2 560	NA	NA	1 619	939	0	1	1	15	1 027	7 066	5.7
1447	Irondale CDP	3 352	NA	NA	3 021	249	5	63	14	64	1 137	NA	8.2
1455	Isle Of Hope-Dutch Island CDP	2 637	NA	NA	2 581	41	2	10	3	30	997	NA	4.9
1465	Jackson	4 076	NA	NA	2 259	1 775	3	23	16	21	1 491	8 036	10.3
1485	Jefferson	2 763	NA	NA	2 168	580	12	2	1	6	1 136	NA	41.2
1505	Jesup	8 958	NA	NA	5 524	3 375	22	27	10	87	3 607	7 938	42.4
1510	Jonesboro	3 635	NA	NA	2 832	768	9	17	9	39	1 495	9 472	6.2
1520	Kennesaw	8 936	NA	NA	8 458	305	21	107	45	129	3 558	10 874	14.5
1524	Kings Bay Base CDP	3 463	NA	NA	2 724	552	38	64	85	147	419	NA	5.3
1525	Kingsland	4 699	NA	NA	3 418	1 172	28	55	26	98	1 989	NA	29.5
1540	La Fayette	6 313	NA	NA	5 829	452	9	19	4	24	2 627	9 004	20.1
1545	La Grange	25 597	24 163	5.9	14 516	10 840	19	197	25	150	10 949	9 098	67.2
1550	Lake City	2 733	NA	NA	2 285	408	1	27	12	31	1 107	12 977	4.6
1562	Lakeview CDP	5 237	NA	NA	5 205	1	13	14	4	26	2 185	NA	5.9
1570	Lawrenceville	16 848	NA	NA	15 428	957	35	319	109	307	6 674	11 449	32.0
1600	Lilburn	9 301	NA	NA	8 626	247	16	366	46	216	3 633	12 997	16.0
1617	Lindale CDP	4 187	NA	NA	4 107	52	15	10	3	25	1 782	NA	14.0
1627	Lithia Springs CDP	11 403	NA	NA	10 494	761	46	53	49	124	5 027	NA	40.1
1640	Loganville	3 180	NA	NA	2 962	168	14	20	16	36	1 245	NA	13.8
1695	Lyons	4 502	NA	NA	2 709	1 408	9	9	367	414	1 765	6 491	19.4
1698	Mableton CDP	25 725	25 111	2.4	22 926	2 368	41	282	108	361	10 293	NA	54.6
1705	McDonough	2 929	NA	NA	2 069	850	3	3	4	19	1 067	10 065	8.1
1725	Macon	106 612	116 903	-8.8	50 265	55 645	127	444	131	657	45 499	9 174	124.0
1727	McRae	3 007	NA	NA	1 872	1 131	0	4	0	15	1 302	8 495	8.2
1730	Madison	3 483	NA	NA	1 668	1 798	1	9	7	28	1 348	8 447	21.4
1740	Manchester	4 104	NA	NA	2 416	1 671	2	2	13	39	1 768	8 396	14.4
1750	Marietta	44 129	30 829	43.1	33 655	9 059	126	814	475	1 418	23 158	13 257	52.8
1768	Martinez CDP	33 731	16 472	104.8	30 212	2 105	65	1 235	114	470	12 764	NA	41.4
1815	Metter	3 707	NA	NA	2 239	1 427	2	9	30	50	1 480	6 341	18.9
1835	Midway-Hardwick CDP	4 910	NA	NA	1 671	3 220	3	13	3	4	1 978	NA	12.7
1845	Milledgeville	17 727	12 176	45.6	8 730	8 741	25	202	29	228	4 873	8 617	51.4
1850	Millen	3 808	NA	NA	1 580	2 217	3	8	0	6	1 496	6 227	9.1
1890	Monroe	9 759	NA	NA	5 686	3 991	12	54	16	116	3 933	8 294	24.6
1895	Montezuma	4 506	NA	NA	1 502	2 975	8	14	7	26	1 705	6 703	11.6
1897	Montgomery CDP	4 327	NA	NA	3 898	363	14	44	8	52	1 655	NA	13.5
1925	Morrow	5 168	NA	NA	4 378	584	2	161	43	121	2 425	12 905	7.3
1935	Moultrie	14 865	15 703	-5.3	8 040	6 703	22	26	74	237	6 030	8 397	33.8
1947	Mountain Park CDP	11 025	NA	NA	10 709	58	21	212	25	158	4 002	NA	15.0
1985	Nashville	4 782	NA	NA	3 881	868	10	9	14	38	2 030	7 450	11.7
2015	Newnan	12 497	11 499	8.7	6 464	5 951	19	38	25	78	4 983	9 493	32.2
2035	Norcross	5 947	NA	NA	4 377	1 134	11	303	122	292	2 757	11 747	10.1
2053	North Atlanta CDP	27 812	30 521	-8.9	19 319	5 851	85	1 562	995	2 295	14 358	NA	19.8
2056	North Decatur CDP	13 936	11 830	17.8	13 083	470	16	288	79	345	7 462	NA	13.0
2057	North Druid Hills CDP	14 170	12 438	13.9	12 467	1 067	19	460	157	619	8 741	NA	12.9
2100	Ocilla	3 182	NA	NA	1 248	1 928	0	4	2	31	1 238	6 006	6.0
2155	Palmetto	2 612	NA	NA	1 695	885	11	5	16	74	1 014	NA	13.0
2156	Panthersville CDP	9 874	11 366	-13.1	469	9 348	13	17	27	62	4 069	NA	9.7
2177	Peachtree City	19 027	NA	NA	17 576	756	23	611	61	455	6 541	14 698	60.4
2185	Pelham	3 869	NA	NA	1 923	1 885	19	0	42	65	1 514	6 256	10.2
2210	Perry	9 452	NA	NA	5 793	3 582	26	38	13	51	3 732	8 561	38.9

1. Codes shown are 2-digit FIPS codes for states; 4-digit census place codes for places; and 3-digit FIPS county codes followed by 3-digit census MCD codes for minor civil divisions (MCDs). MCD names are followed by county names in parentheses. 2. Hispanic persons may be of any race. 3. Dry land or land partially or temporarily covered by water.

State/ Place/ MCD[1] code	Place	Population: 1990	Population: Places of 10,000 or more: 1980	Population: Places of 10,000 or more: Percent change, 1980–1990	Population characteristics, 1990: Race: White	Race: Black	Race: Am. Indian, Eskimo Aleut	Race: Asian & Pacific Islander	Race: Other race	Hispanic[2]	Total housing units, 1990	Per capita income, 1985 (Dollars)	Land area,[3] 1990 (Sq. Km.)
		1	2	3	4	5	6	7	8	9	10	11	12
	GEORGIA—Con.												
2280	Pooler	4 453	NA	NA	4 292	117	15	22	7	21	1 593	10 572	28.7
2295	Port Wentworth	4 012	NA	NA	3 313	667	9	13	10	37	1 647	9 990	43.5
2305	Powder Springs	6 893	NA	NA	5 732	1 010	25	90	36	118	2 485	10 843	13.8
2322	Putney CDP	3 108	NA	NA	2 536	547	11	11	3	13	1 153	NA	60.4
2325	Quitman	5 292	NA	NA	2 078	3 178	4	19	13	41	1 942	5 771	9.8
2347	Redan CDP	24 376	NA	NA	9 546	13 917	40	671	202	637	9 626	NA	24.8
2402	Richmond Hill	2 934	NA	NA	2 771	119	5	26	13	42	1 047	NA	24.0
2410	Rincon town	2 697	NA	NA	2 250	423	4	7	13	30	1 061	NA	14.8
2420	Riverdale	9 359	NA	NA	6 632	2 221	41	389	76	203	4 053	11 791	10.6
2432	Robins AFB CDP	3 092	NA	NA	2 376	576	16	84	40	131	738	NA	7.0
2440	Rockmart	3 356	NA	NA	2 698	642	3	7	6	12	1 442	8 798	10.6
2455	Rome	30 326	29 609	2.4	20 860	9 010	55	226	175	501	13 099	9 177	62.7
2465	Rossville	3 601	NA	NA	3 550	30	8	13	0	15	1 679	9 020	4.6
2470	Roswell	47 923	23 337	105.4	44 162	2 327	64	851	519	1 285	20 318	16 656	84.4
2475	Royston	2 758	NA	NA	2 138	605	5	10	0	25	1 064	NA	8.7
2500	St. Marys	8 187	NA	NA	6 478	1 407	42	173	87	228	3 166	8 708	47.9
2505	St. Simons CDP	12 026	NA	NA	11 290	631	14	60	31	170	6 764	NA	43.0
2515	Sandersville	6 290	NA	NA	2 528	3 739	3	20	0	16	2 401	8 599	20.2
2518	Sandy Springs CDP	67 842	46 877	44.7	60 797	5 152	74	1 106	713	1 973	35 011	NA	97.3
2540	Savannah	137 560	141 378	-2.7	64 446	70 580	270	1 581	683	1 956	58 762	9 028	162.1
2557	Scottdale CDP	8 636	NA	NA	4 740	3 496	10	315	75	169	3 865	NA	9.0
2601	Skidaway Island CDP	4 495	NA	NA	4 466	10	3	15	1	35	2 176	NA	42.6
2615	Smyrna	30 981	20 312	52.5	24 854	4 918	83	699	427	1 099	16 822	13 628	29.5
2620	Snellville	12 084	NA	NA	11 879	71	27	85	22	94	4 185	13 663	23.6
2625	Social Circle	2 755	NA	NA	1 491	1 257	3	1	3	24	1 047	8 249	28.7
2630	Soperton	2 797	NA	NA	1 418	1 377	2	0	0	5	1 095	7 080	8.5
2631	South Augusta CDP	55 998	51 072	9.6	27 001	27 314	154	1 047	482	1 141	21 485	NA	70.4
2665	Statesboro	15 854	14 866	6.6	10 608	5 009	21	170	46	135	5 758	8 182	20.3
2680	Stockbridge	3 359	NA	NA	2 977	308	1	61	12	33	1 438	NA	8.2
2685	Stone Mountain	6 494	NA	NA	4 726	1 501	18	186	63	150	2 584	12 122	4.2
2690	Sugar Hill	4 557	NA	NA	4 477	41	5	12	22	80	1 750	NA	15.3
2700	Summerville	5 025	NA	NA	3 720	1 291	2	9	3	21	2 099	6 183	9.7
2725	Swainsboro	7 361	NA	NA	4 169	3 143	2	26	21	35	2 930	7 626	28.5
2735	Sylvania	2 871	NA	NA	1 603	1 256	9	3	0	3	1 237	8 429	9.7
2740	Sylvester	5 702	NA	NA	2 364	3 278	8	11	41	94	2 139	7 118	14.8
2755	Tallapoosa	2 805	NA	NA	2 539	236	4	22	4	11	1 256	8 393	18.1
2800	Thomaston	9 127	NA	NA	6 588	2 485	13	27	14	23	4 025	9 143	22.2
2805	Thomasville	17 457	18 463	-5.4	8 193	9 175	29	29	31	85	7 427	8 333	37.5
2810	Thomson	6 862	NA	NA	3 300	3 536	15	10	1	23	2 710	7 118	8.9
2815	Thunderbolt town	2 786	NA	NA	1 270	1 478	10	26	2	11	862	NA	3.3
2820	Tifton	14 215	13 749	3.4	10 404	3 523	18	129	141	364	5 677	8 488	19.8
2835	Toccoa	8 266	NA	NA	6 392	1 787	18	56	13	59	3 836	8 317	18.8
2861	Tucker CDP	25 781	25 399	1.5	23 127	1 310	25	1 192	127	601	10 416	NA	31.1
2873	Tybee Island	2 842	NA	NA	2 751	44	20	23	4	41	2 150	NA	6.6
2875	Tyrone town	2 724	NA	NA	2 660	40	8	15	1	16	968	NA	24.0
2890	Union City	8 375	NA	NA	3 942	4 304	10	61	58	188	4 358	10 590	20.8
2900	Unionville CDP	2 710	NA	NA	63	2 640	2	2	3	27	898	NA	2.0
2910	Valdosta	39 806	37 533	6.1	21 968	17 307	94	347	90	450	15 608	8 368	68.6
2925	Vidalia	11 078	10 388	6.6	7 287	3 622	16	129	24	71	4 544	9 020	45.4
2935	Vienna	2 708	NA	NA	845	1 854	1	7	1	1	1 065	6 356	11.3
2940	Villa Rica	6 542	NA	NA	5 442	1 053	17	20	10	28	2 503	7 628	50.0
2942	Vinings CDP	7 417	NA	NA	6 478	811	6	86	36	142	4 658	NA	8.2
2970	Warner Robins	43 726	39 879	9.6	31 779	10 910	134	631	272	787	18 086	10 821	43.2
2985	Washington	4 279	NA	NA	1 697	2 566	6	8	2	21	1 776	8 392	20.2
3000	Waycross	16 410	19 330	-15.1	8 299	7 995	20	75	21	109	7 519	8 102	29.3
3005	Waynesboro	5 701	NA	NA	2 360	3 320	5	15	1	21	2 223	7 143	13.8
3012	West Augusta CDP	27 637	24 242	14.0	20 786	6 019	60	603	169	515	13 062	NA	36.0
3020	West Point	3 571	NA	NA	1 558	1 983	2	26	2	20	1 524	12 342	11.4
3035	Whitemarsh Island CDP	2 824	NA	NA	2 583	171	3	60	7	36	1 252	NA	15.3
3063	Wilmington Island CDP	11 230	NA	NA	10 827	188	22	182	11	131	4 552	NA	21.9
3065	Winder	7 373	NA	NA	6 003	1 282	27	55	6	41	3 202	8 879	24.1
3090	Woodstock	4 361	NA	NA	4 092	216	20	32	1	48	1 652	10 886	13.9
15	HAWAII	1 108 229	964 691	14.9	369 616	27 195	5 099	685 236	21 083	81 390	389 810	11 003	16 636.5
0003	Ahuimanu CDP	8 387	NA	NA	3 019	131	43	5 013	181	646	2 537	NA	4.6
0005	Aiea CDP	8 906	32 879	-72.9	2 169	84	7	6 538	108	569	2 678	NA	4.3
0007	Aliamanu CDP	8 835	NA	NA	4 624	1 931	43	1 799	438	1 030	2 353	NA	1.9
0014	Captain Cook CDP	2 595	NA	NA	921	5	11	1 618	40	228	949	NA	31.5
0029	Ewa Beach CDP	14 315	14 455	-1.0	3 296	207	39	10 389	384	1 640	3 426	NA	3.7
0032	Ewa Villages CDP	3 780	NA	NA	318	7	14	3 381	60	445	939	NA	2.5
0034	Fort Shafter CDP	2 952	NA	NA	1 887	619	28	278	140	283	917	NA	5.7
0039	Haiku-Pauwela CDP	4 509	NA	NA	2 634	28	71	1 664	112	536	1 649	NA	40.8

1. Codes shown are 2-digit FIPS codes for states; 4-digit census place codes for places; and 3-digit FIPS county codes followed by 3-digit census MCD codes for minor civil divisions (MCDs). MCD names are followed by county names in parentheses. 2. Hispanic persons may be of any race. 3. Dry land or land partially or temporarily covered by water.

State/ Place/ MCD[1] code	Place	Population: 1990	Population: Places of 10,000 or more: 1980	Population: Places of 10,000 or more: Percent change, 1980–1990	Population characteristics, 1990: Race: White	Race: Black	Race: Am. Indian, Eskimo Aleut	Race: Asian & Pacific Islander	Race: Other race	Hispanic[2]	Total housing units, 1990	Per capita income, 1985 (Dollars)	Land area,[3] 1990 (Sq. Km.)
		1	2	3	4	5	6	7	8	9	10	11	12
	HAWAII—Con.												
0045	Halawa CDP	13 408	NA	NA	3 256	279	27	9 602	244	1 053	4 094	NA	6.0
0069	Hanamaulu CDP	3 611	NA	NA	527	3	4	3 039	38	381	907	NA	2.9
0078	Hauula CDP	3 479	NA	NA	864	38	22	2 520	35	330	1 021	NA	15.6
0081	Hawaiian Beaches CDP	2 846	NA	NA	1 223	16	41	1 488	78	521	1 005	NA	65.8
0083	Hawaiian Paradise Park CDP	3 389	NA	NA	1 793	32	39	1 457	68	340	1 342	NA	58.2
0085	Heeia CDP	5 010	NA	NA	1 710	27	12	3 218	43	232	1 557	NA	5.3
0087	Hickam Housing CDP	6 553	NA	NA	4 554	863	27	879	230	454	1 841	NA	3.2
0090	Hilo CDP	37 808	35 269	7.2	10 075	214	210	26 533	776	3 226	14 134	NA	140.6
0095	Holualoa CDP	3 834	NA	NA	2 472	10	34	1 261	57	236	1 926	NA	36.4
0110	Honolulu CDP	365 272	365 048	0.1	97 527	4 821	1 126	257 552	4 246	16 704	145 796	NA	214.5
0123	Iroquois Point CDP	4 188	NA	NA	3 332	304	39	401	112	268	1 180	NA	1.4
0135	Kahaluu CDP	3 068	NA	NA	1 146	34	36	1 788	64	245	960	NA	3.2
0140	Kahului CDP	16 889	12 988	30.0	2 658	79	42	13 809	301	1 491	5 136	NA	39.3
0143	Kailua CDP	9 126	NA	NA	4 977	30	76	3 848	195	907	3 739	NA	90.4
0144	Kailua CDP	36 818	35 812	2.8	21 242	501	192	14 395	488	2 016	12 225	NA	17.2
0159	Kalaheo CDP	3 592	NA	NA	1 618	16	6	1 845	107	476	1 199	NA	7.6
0161	Kalaoa CDP	4 490	NA	NA	2 916	26	26	1 464	58	273	1 685	NA	95.0
0164	Kaneohe CDP	35 448	29 919	18.5	11 052	416	155	23 261	564	2 449	10 849	NA	17.0
0165	Kaneohe Station CDP	11 662	NA	NA	7 940	2 026	112	771	813	1 474	2 030	NA	11.4
0169	Kapaa CDP	8 149	NA	NA	2 836	39	45	5 064	165	1 174	2 736	NA	25.3
0184	Kaunakakai CDP	2 658	NA	NA	337	6	9	2 292	14	134	997	NA	5.3
0219	Kekaha CDP	3 506	NA	NA	718	3	4	2 669	112	573	1 106	NA	2.6
0225	Kihei CDP	11 107	NA	NA	6 853	87	99	3 869	199	862	6 497	NA	26.3
0264	Lahaina CDP	9 073	NA	NA	2 863	39	22	6 002	147	595	2 982	NA	14.9
0269	Laie CDP	5 577	NA	NA	1 851	48	50	3 572	56	173	1 122	NA	3.3
0289	Lihue CDP	5 536	NA	NA	1 674	27	17	3 755	63	344	2 227	NA	16.4
0307	Maili CDP	6 059	NA	NA	1 235	63	30	4 362	369	1 119	1 490	NA	2.5
0308	Makaha CDP	7 990	NA	NA	2 555	147	55	4 945	288	1 192	3 178	NA	6.0
0311	Makakilo City CDP	9 828	NA	NA	4 631	327	51	4 606	213	815	3 050	NA	7.6
0314	Makawao CDP	5 405	NA	NA	2 927	27	28	2 250	173	628	1 801	NA	12.1
0321	Maunawili CDP	4 847	NA	NA	2 298	34	15	2 444	56	214	1 443	NA	9.0
0322	Mililani Town CDP	29 359	21 365	37.4	10 032	842	102	17 973	410	1 573	8 900	NA	10.1
0324	Mountain View CDP	3 075	NA	NA	1 485	29	56	1 434	71	455	1 326	NA	217.1
0334	Nanakuli CDP	9 575	NA	NA	1 392	162	64	7 675	282	1 175	2 128	NA	6.5
0338	Napili-Honokowai CDP	4 332	NA	NA	2 733	37	26	1 445	91	309	3 080	NA	15.2
0384	Pearl City CDP	30 993	42 575	-27.2	6 632	786	83	22 968	524	2 043	8 999	NA	12.9
0397	Pukalani CDP	5 879	NA	NA	2 455	22	26	3 272	104	501	1 898	NA	11.4
0402	Pupukea CDP	4 111	NA	NA	2 647	21	39	1 321	83	400	1 488	NA	8.8
0405	Schofield Barracks CDP	19 597	18 851	4.0	11 921	4 955	179	1 145	1 397	2 099	3 556	NA	7.1
0407	Village Park CDP	7 407	NA	NA	1 622	114	16	5 506	149	727	2 176	NA	2.5
0409	Wahiawa CDP	17 386	16 911	2.8	3 998	712	105	12 013	558	1 861	5 765	NA	5.5
0424	Waialua CDP	3 943	NA	NA	922	20	19	2 937	45	264	1 205	NA	3.2
0429	Waianae CDP	8 758	NA	NA	1 751	101	56	6 502	348	1 250	2 264	NA	8.9
0434	Waihee-Waiehue CDP	4 004	NA	NA	851	14	17	3 048	74	318	1 076	NA	11.0
0447	Wailea-Makena CDP	3 799	NA	NA	3 052	20	18	669	40	146	3 070	NA	58.6
0450	Wailua Homesteads CDP	3 870	NA	NA	1 935	25	9	1 787	114	443	1 299	NA	18.2
0454	Wailuku CDP	10 688	10 232	4.5	2 486	47	44	7 942	169	687	3 848	NA	13.1
0456	Waimalu CDP	29 967	NA	NA	8 418	684	125	20 317	423	1 683	10 613	NA	15.3
0459	Waimanalo CDP	3 508	NA	NA	678	11	11	2 722	86	497	832	NA	1.0
0461	Waimanalo Beach CDP	4 185	NA	NA	728	25	15	3 346	71	290	965	NA	4.2
0463	Waimea CDP	5 972	NA	NA	2 525	19	28	3 326	74	701	2 140	NA	100.4
0474	Waipahu CDP	31 435	29 139	7.9	3 634	619	149	26 340	693	3 626	7 739	NA	6.7
0482	Waipio CDP	11 812	NA	NA	3 405	357	24	7 847	179	648	4 087	NA	3.1
0484	Waipio Acres CDP	5 304	NA	NA	2 000	510	49	2 532	213	523	1 836	NA	2.7
0488	Wheeler AFB CDP	2 600	NA	NA	1 933	322	11	237	97	168	704	NA	5.9
0491	Whitmore Village CDP	3 373	NA	NA	345	46	12	2 895	75	215	839	NA	2.4
16	IDAHO	1 006 749	944 127	6.6	950 451	3 370	13 780	9 365	29 783	52 927	413 327	8 567	214 325.0
0025	American Falls	3 757	NA	NA	3 300	4	32	30	391	552	1 453	8 452	3.8
0030	Ammon	5 002	NA	NA	4 898	8	18	27	51	122	1 336	7 566	5.8
0075	Blackfoot	9 646	10 065	-4.2	8 704	9	269	131	533	935	3 617	7 768	13.7
0090	Boise City	125 738	102 451	22.7	121 262	730	808	1 974	964	3 423	53 271	11 740	119.5
0105	Buhl	3 516	NA	NA	3 318	2	20	16	160	236	1 549	7 767	3.5
0110	Burley	8 702	NA	NA	7 436	1	100	44	1 121	1 785	3 346	7 793	9.2
0120	Caldwell	18 400	17 699	4.0	15 727	59	122	225	2 267	3 785	7 131	8 041	23.0
0150	Chubbuck	7 791	NA	NA	7 344	27	186	74	160	316	2 593	7 708	8.6
0170	Coeur d'Alene	24 563	20 054	22.5	24 088	37	187	142	109	432	10 956	8 767	27.6
0252	Eagle	3 327	NA	NA	3 266	4	11	34	12	77	1 238	10 677	13.0
0275	Emmett	4 601	NA	NA	4 309	1	34	26	231	374	1 957	8 066	3.7
0305	Fort Hall CDP	2 681	NA	NA	925	2	1 709	7	38	315	883	NA	106.4
0320	Garden City	6 369	NA	NA	6 050	29	85	94	111	240	2 724	7 550	8.6
0340	Gooding	2 820	NA	NA	2 755	1	12	10	42	147	1 291	8 371	3.4

1. Codes shown are 2-digit FIPS codes for states; 4-digit census place codes for places; and 3-digit FIPS county codes followed by 3-digit census MCD codes for minor civil divisions (MCDs). MCD names are followed by county names in parentheses. 2. Hispanic persons may be of any race. 3. Dry land or land partially or temporarily covered by water.

State/ Place/ MCD[1] code	Place	Population: 1990	Population: Places of 10,000 or more: 1980	Population: Places of 10,000 or more: Percent change, 1980–1990	Population characteristics, 1990: Race: White	Race: Black	Race: Am. Indian, Eskimo Aleut	Race: Asian & Pacific Islander	Race: Other race	Hispanic[2]	Total housing units, 1990	Per capita income, 1985 (Dollars)	Land area,[3] 1990 (Sq. Km.)
		1	2	3	4	5	6	7	8	9	10	11	12
	IDAHO—Con.												
0350	Grangeville	3 226	NA	NA	3 177	0	33	10	6	30	1 389	9 139	3.5
0360	Hailey	3 687	NA	NA	3 581	3	9	59	35	93	1 480	NA	6.6
0385	Hayden	3 744	NA	NA	3 687	6	22	15	14	48	1 556	7 907	10.2
0405	Heyburn	2 714	NA	NA	2 300	7	30	10	367	672	904	5 969	3.5
0440	Idaho Falls	43 929	39 590	11.0	41 882	256	262	534	995	1 837	16 845	10 309	37.6
0465	Jerome	6 529	NA	NA	6 139	4	68	20	298	476	2 706	6 784	5.4
0480	Kellogg	2 591	NA	NA	2 496	8	50	18	19	49	1 353	7 937	5.0
0490	Ketchum	2 523	NA	NA	2 491	2	8	13	9	50	2 439	NA	6.8
0530	Lewiston	28 082	27 986	0.3	27 347	38	395	190	112	342	12 054	9 635	42.6
0590	Meridian	9 596	NA	NA	9 377	31	42	71	75	235	3 746	8 455	18.1
0615	Montpelier	2 656	NA	NA	2 602	0	8	3	43	72	1 121	7 621	4.6
0625	Moscow	18 519	16 513	12.1	17 509	163	111	643	93	335	6 748	8 535	12.4
0630	Mountain Home	7 913	NA	NA	7 300	228	51	159	175	398	3 392	8 973	9.2
0631	Mountain Home AFB CDP	5 936	NA	NA	5 045	506	51	210	124	295	1 528	NA	25.7
0660	Nampa	28 365	25 112	13.0	25 388	75	275	299	2 328	3 618	10 760	7 584	28.0
0705	Orofino	2 868	NA	NA	2 788	1	59	9	11	44	1 231	8 209	6.2
0745	Payette	5 592	NA	NA	5 100	3	77	55	357	527	2 270	7 481	5.7
0780	Pocatello	46 080	46 340	-0.6	43 346	395	651	585	1 103	2 086	18 768	9 344	71.5
0790	Post Falls	7 349	NA	NA	7 227	17	57	27	21	96	2 790	7 991	15.1
0800	Preston	3 710	NA	NA	3 640	2	16	10	42	92	1 392	7 363	14.2
0820	Rexburg	14 302	11 559	23.7	13 730	41	86	219	226	441	3 554	5 733	11.0
0830	Rigby	2 681	NA	NA	2 524	2	25	10	120	218	969	7 761	2.3
0855	Rupert	5 455	NA	NA	4 301	12	71	21	1 050	1 415	2 129	7 032	4.7
0860	St. Anthony	3 010	NA	NA	2 853	5	25	19	108	179	1 135	7 016	3.1
0875	Salmon	2 941	NA	NA	2 901	2	15	9	14	47	1 469	7 844	4.4
0880	Sandpoint	5 203	NA	NA	5 110	10	55	13	15	80	2 451	7 151	10.0
0885	Shelley	3 536	NA	NA	3 225	7	18	14	272	322	1 070	6 633	3.1
0900	Soda Springs	3 111	NA	NA	3 088	2	8	9	4	54	1 244	8 801	11.7
0970	Twin Falls	27 591	26 209	5.3	26 144	47	188	442	770	1 863	11 009	9 600	27.3
1000	Weiser	4 571	NA	NA	3 866	6	30	67	602	765	1 945	7 392	5.9
17	ILLINOIS	11 430 602	11 427 429	0.0	8 952 978	1 694 273	21 836	285 311	476 204	904 446	4 506 275	11 302	143 986.6
0005	Abingdon	3 597	NA	NA	3 560	20	5	5	7	31	1 508	8 217	3.5
0015	Addison village	32 058	29 759	7.7	28 167	541	45	1 905	1 400	4 287	11 025	12 183	22.3
0040	Aledo	3 681	NA	NA	3 637	11	11	20	2	9	1 538	9 823	5.2
0050	Algonquin village	11 663	NA	NA	11 434	20	21	150	38	202	3 975	13 857	13.6
0080	Alorton village	2 960	NA	NA	91	2 858	7	0	4	12	985	NA	4.6
0095	Alsip village	18 227	17 134	6.4	16 862	885	30	296	154	730	7 144	11 570	16.3
0115	Alton	32 905	34 171	-3.7	24 880	7 589	173	113	150	371	14 212	9 129	38.9
0150	Anna	4 805	NA	NA	4 744	21	11	22	7	33	2 291	11 479	7.9
0160	Antioch village	6 105	NA	NA	5 984	9	10	54	48	120	2 348	11 333	17.4
0170	Arcola	2 678	NA	NA	2 554	6	4	13	101	243	1 055	9 613	3.5
0190	Arlington Heights village	75 460	66 116	14.1	71 514	479	52	2 797	618	2 046	30 428	16 278	41.9
0270	Auburn	3 724	NA	NA	3 702	3	6	6	7	30	1 409	8 265	7.1
0280	Aurora	99 581	81 293	22.5	73 761	11 814	237	1 314	12 455	22 864	35 621	10 836	86.7
0320	Barrington village	9 504	NA	NA	9 340	16	10	119	19	157	3 660	20 716	11.6
0323	Barrington Hills village	4 202	NA	NA	4 063	7	1	116	15	55	1 450	32 870	72.8
0340	Bartlett village	19 373	13 254	46.2	18 151	303	32	669	218	654	6 659	12 368	36.3
0345	Bartonville village	5 643	NA	NA	5 534	82	5	10	12	42	2 290	10 011	20.1
0355	Batavia	17 076	12 574	35.8	16 190	423	19	214	230	506	6 449	12 571	17.9
0368	Beach Park village	9 513	NA	NA	8 824	312	22	117	238	559	3 405	NA	16.9
0375	Beardstown	5 270	NA	NA	5 246	1	5	12	6	31	2 276	8 660	7.5
0430	Belleville	42 785	41 580	2.9	39 398	2 890	106	259	132	562	19 080	11 043	36.2
0445	Bellwood village	20 241	19 811	2.2	4 817	14 352	21	330	721	1 197	6 566	9 773	6.2
0450	Belvidere	15 958	15 176	5.2	14 883	101	25	71	878	1 644	6 414	10 353	14.3
0465	Bensenville village	17 767	16 115	10.3	15 395	171	56	1 115	1 030	3 333	6 825	13 023	15.0
0480	Benton	7 216	NA	NA	7 171	2	12	25	6	24	3 386	9 291	12.8
0485	Berkeley village	5 137	NA	NA	4 606	231	7	221	72	304	1 918	13 358	3.7
0495	Berwyn	45 426	46 849	-3.0	43 409	54	64	790	1 109	3 573	20 044	12 659	10.1
0500	Bethalto village	9 507	NA	NA	9 372	58	25	42	10	38	3 773	9 526	15.4
0535	Bloomingdale village	16 614	12 659	31.2	15 366	275	16	845	112	452	6 221	13 955	16.6
0540	Bloomington	51 972	44 189	17.6	47 250	3 480	89	762	391	843	22 640	11 989	43.3
0545	Blue Island	21 203	21 855	-3.0	16 001	2 978	39	73	2 112	5 280	8 600	9 820	10.5
0563	Bolingbrook village	40 843	37 245	9.7	31 353	6 384	124	2 046	936	2 391	12 889	10 235	29.1
0578	Boulder Hill CDP	8 894	NA	NA	8 602	81	8	94	109	286	2 969	NA	3.8
0580	Bourbonnais village	13 934	13 280	4.9	13 149	363	16	330	76	217	4 649	10 357	9.6
0600	Bradley village	10 792	11 008	-2.0	10 570	32	26	71	93	183	4 224	9 337	8.0
0605	Braidwood	3 584	NA	NA	3 522	21	9	8	24	56	1 261	10 067	8.5
0610	Breese	3 567	NA	NA	3 546	7	7	5	2	27	1 322	9 693	4.7
0620	Bridgeview village	14 402	14 157	1.7	14 014	24	24	170	170	674	5 355	10 253	10.7
0640	Broadview village	8 713	NA	NA	3 799	4 667	21	167	59	187	3 581	11 486	4.6
0655	Brookfield village	18 876	19 395	-2.7	18 505	33	22	178	138	583	7 680	12 495	8.0
0725	Buffalo Grove village	36 427	22 238	63.8	34 298	373	31	1 595	130	711	13 866	15 404	20.7

1. Codes shown are 2-digit FIPS codes for states; 4-digit census place codes for places; and 3-digit FIPS county codes followed by 3-digit census MCD codes for minor civil divisions (MCDs). MCD names are followed by county names in parentheses. 2. Hispanic persons may be of any race. 3. Dry land or land partially or temporarily covered by water.

State/ Place/ MCD[1] code	Place	Population: 1990	Population: Places of 10,000 or more: 1980	Population: Places of 10,000 or more: Percent change, 1980–1990	Population characteristics, 1990: Race: White	Race: Black	Race: Am. Indian, Eskimo Aleut	Race: Asian & Pacific Islander	Race: Other race	Hispanic[2]	Total housing units, 1990	Per capita income, 1985 (Dollars)	Land area,[3] 1990 (Sq. Km.)
		1	2	3	4	5	6	7	8	9	10	11	12
	ILLINOIS—Con.												
0743	Burbank	27 600	28 462	-3.0	26 906	11	50	312	321	1 305	9 298	10 483	10.7
0755	Burnham village	3 916	NA	NA	3 106	636	3	31	140	557	1 458	10 178	4.8
0759	Burr Ridge village	7 669	NA	NA	6 947	55	4	649	14	148	2 657	23 546	15.3
0765	Bushnell	3 288	NA	NA	3 275	3	3	3	4	33	1 499	8 538	5.1
0785	Cahokia village	17 550	18 904	-7.2	16 429	849	51	140	81	315	6 411	8 506	25.0
0790	Cairo	4 846	NA	NA	2 176	2 614	11	43	2	21	2 251	7 087	15.4
0800	Calumet City	37 840	39 697	-4.7	27 729	8 962	56	212	881	2 426	16 587	11 414	18.8
0805	Calumet Park village	8 418	NA	NA	1 968	6 061	17	9	363	715	3 140	9 720	2.8
0845	Canton	13 922	14 600	-4.6	13 079	654	28	64	97	159	5 907	9 630	18.9
0865	Carbondale	27 033	26 287	2.8	20 097	4 706	34	1 922	274	676	10 416	7 287	26.4
0875	Carlinville	5 416	NA	NA	5 294	72	14	29	7	24	2 224	9 136	5.8
0880	Carlyle	3 474	NA	NA	3 366	79	7	21	1	9	1 385	9 616	5.4
0885	Carmi	5 564	NA	NA	5 509	17	20	15	3	27	2 740	10 309	5.8
0890	Carol Stream village	31 716	15 514	104.4	28 050	1 081	53	1 853	679	1 801	12 098	12 419	20.2
0895	Carpentersville village	23 049	23 275	-1.0	19 612	1 009	63	294	2 071	3 840	7 171	9 469	14.0
0905	Carrollton	2 507	NA	NA	2 494	5	5	3	0	12	1 117	8 424	4.0
0910	Carterville	3 630	NA	NA	3 574	4	9	23	20	48	1 652	9 069	7.4
0915	Carthage	2 657	NA	NA	2 642	2	6	1	6	11	1 316	10 867	4.1
0920	Cary village	10 043	NA	NA	9 868	26	8	48	93	219	3 539	13 616	12.0
0925	Casey	2 914	NA	NA	2 891	1	8	10	4	17	1 387	10 143	5.5
0930	Caseyville village	4 419	NA	NA	4 178	192	12	11	26	85	1 779	9 040	11.9
0965	Centralia	14 274	15 119	-5.6	12 614	1 498	38	97	27	124	6 317	10 396	16.8
0975	Centreville	7 489	NA	NA	493	6 967	6	5	18	35	2 781	5 713	11.0
0990	Champaign	63 502	58 133	9.2	51 254	9 006	113	2 608	521	1 238	25 996	10 211	33.5
0997	Channahon village	4 266	NA	NA	4 214	18	3	8	23	95	1 344	11 441	11.2
1010	Charleston	20 398	19 355	5.4	19 507	613	30	209	39	190	6 726	8 019	19.0
1015	Chatham village	6 074	NA	NA	6 008	11	4	36	15	58	2 107	10 698	7.3
1045	Chester	8 194	NA	NA	6 114	2 014	19	18	29	226	2 247	7 915	15.2
1051	Chicago	2 783 726	3 005 078	-7.4	1 263 524	1 087 711	7 064	104 118	321 309	545 852	1 133 039	9 642	588.5
1055	Chicago Heights	33 072	37 026	-10.7	18 187	11 607	58	99	3 121	4 976	11 620	8 943	23.4
1060	Chicago Ridge village	13 643	13 473	1.3	13 371	41	17	106	108	502	5 499	10 655	5.8
1065	Chillicothe	5 959	NA	NA	5 847	17	5	11	79	231	2 382	10 381	9.0
1080	Christopher	2 774	NA	NA	2 762	2	7	3	0	5	1 387	8 758	3.1
1085	Cicero town	67 436	61 232	10.1	50 692	141	260	1 092	15 251	24 931	24 841	9 412	15.1
1115	Clarendon Hills village	6 994	NA	NA	6 783	41	2	161	7	132	2 810	18 769	4.4
1145	Clinton	7 437	NA	NA	7 359	13	17	29	19	54	3 311	10 572	6.8
1150	Coal City village	3 907	NA	NA	3 859	1	4	2	41	70	1 588	11 774	5.5
1160	Coal Valley village	2 683	NA	NA	2 629	7	3	32	12	47	972	10 516	6.1
1205	Collinsville	22 446	19 613	14.4	21 370	778	42	150	106	383	9 700	11 538	29.0
1220	Columbia	5 524	NA	NA	5 487	7	6	15	9	44	2 306	13 298	18.2
1270	Country Club Hills	15 431	14 676	5.1	6 061	8 871	17	338	144	388	5 002	10 726	11.9
1272	Countryside	5 716	NA	NA	5 533	57	5	60	61	195	2 596	14 161	6.5
1295	Crest Hill	10 643	NA	NA	8 358	1 979	33	66	207	635	3 827	10 963	18.5
1305	Crestwood village	10 823	10 852	-0.3	10 208	436	12	92	75	291	4 180	10 920	7.7
1310	Crete village	6 773	NA	NA	6 376	303	6	45	43	151	2 505	14 672	12.0
1315	Creve Coeur village	5 938	NA	NA	5 849	15	16	25	33	87	2 467	9 506	12.4
1325	Crystal Lake	24 512	18 590	31.9	23 934	49	27	287	215	610	8 973	13 225	36.6
1327	Crystal Lawns CDP	3 037	NA	NA	2 985	0	0	6	46	145	1 041	NA	2.5
1395	Danville	33 828	39 019	-13.3	26 500	6 451	79	363	435	709	15 326	9 941	39.3
1397	Darien	18 341	14 536	26.2	16 378	204	16	1 657	86	380	6 787	15 119	12.0
1410	Decatur	83 885	94 081	-10.8	69 164	13 994	120	411	196	447	37 470	11 143	96.0
1420	Deerfield village	17 327	17 413	-0.5	16 813	91	9	379	35	246	6 052	23 045	14.2
1430	Deer Park village	2 887	NA	NA	2 775	38	0	74	0	25	917	NA	9.4
1435	De Kalb	34 925	33 099	5.5	31 043	1 628	51	1 563	640	1 425	10 915	8 906	20.8
1460	Des Plaines	53 223	53 568	-0.6	48 976	325	63	2 504	1 355	3 520	20 509	13 628	36.8
1495	Dixmoor village	3 647	NA	NA	1 355	2 106	4	2	180	258	1 393	9 252	3.2
1500	Dixon	15 144	15 701	-3.5	13 509	1 186	44	120	285	455	5 862	9 877	14.9
1505	Dolton village	23 930	24 766	-3.4	13 998	9 127	25	279	501	1 085	8 594	11 404	11.7
1540	Downers Grove village	46 858	42 572	10.1	43 667	809	43	1 975	364	1 140	18 166	16 160	35.3
1565	Dupo village	3 164	NA	NA	3 142	6	5	6	5	25	1 358	9 881	7.8
1570	Du Quoin	6 697	NA	NA	6 269	378	7	31	12	37	3 015	8 760	14.8
1580	Dwight village	4 230	NA	NA	4 137	41	7	19	26	74	1 618	11 006	6.0
1595	East Alton village	7 063	NA	NA	7 030	11	6	12	4	30	3 180	9 770	13.5
1620	East Dundee village	2 721	NA	NA	2 654	11	0	15	41	85	1 029	12 637	6.5
1640	East Moline	20 147	20 907	-3.6	16 759	2 045	57	215	1 071	1 921	8 548	10 087	22.1
1650	East Peoria	21 378	22 385	-4.5	21 156	60	37	69	56	205	8 924	10 500	44.2
1660	East St. Louis	40 944	55 200	-25.8	664	40 167	50	23	40	159	15 622	5 381	36.4
1685	Edwardsville	14 579	12 480	16.8	13 289	1 065	25	171	29	112	6 109	12 103	22.6
1690	Effingham	11 851	11 270	5.2	11 742	7	22	66	14	52	5 059	11 342	17.6
1710	Eldorado	4 536	NA	NA	4 516	7	11	1	1	15	2 278	8 161	5.8
1720	Elgin	77 010	63 798	20.7	59 916	5 630	172	2 670	8 622	14 576	27 936	11 169	56.8
1735	Elk Grove Village village	33 429	28 907	15.6	30 586	263	35	2 287	258	1 192	12 416	14 207	27.8
1770	Elmhurst	42 029	44 276	-5.1	40 307	175	34	1 278	235	1 148	15 486	15 395	26.3

1. Codes shown are 2-digit FIPS codes for states; 4-digit census place codes for places; and 3-digit FIPS county codes followed by 3-digit census MCD codes for minor civil divisions (MCDs). MCD names are followed by county names in parentheses. 2. Hispanic persons may be of any race. 3. Dry land or land partially or temporarily covered by water.

State/ Place/ MCD[1] code	Place	Population: 1990	Population: Places of 10,000 or more: 1980	Population: Places of 10,000 or more: Percent change, 1980–1990	Population characteristics, 1990: Race: White	Race: Black	Race: Am. Indian, Eskimo Aleut	Race: Asian & Pacific Islander	Race: Other race	Hispanic[2]	Total housing units, 1990	Per capita income, 1985 (Dollars)	Land area,[3] 1990 (Sq. Km.)
		1	2	3	4	5	6	7	8	9	10	11	12
	ILLINOIS—Con.												
1780	Elmwood Park village	23 206	24 016	-3.4	22 651	21	20	239	275	1 001	9 781	12 678	4.9
1840	Eureka	4 435	NA	NA	4 378	21	10	14	12	50	1 609	9 980	5.7
1845	Evanston	73 233	73 706	-0.6	51 684	16 749	131	3 535	1 134	2 689	29 164	15 458	20.1
1855	Evergreen Park village	20 874	22 260	-6.2	20 459	85	15	205	110	432	7 667	12 806	8.2
1870	Fairbury	3 643	NA	NA	3 581	11	7	11	33	102	1 426	10 497	3.0
1875	Fairfield	5 439	NA	NA	5 393	5	9	30	2	16	2 670	9 607	7.8
1883	Fairmont CDP	2 894	NA	NA	1 075	1 656	14	13	136	219	957	NA	4.7
1893	Fairview Heights	14 351	12 414	15.6	12 902	1 158	32	203	56	224	5 725	11 165	26.3
1920	Farmington	2 535	NA	NA	2 522	0	7	5	1	17	1 108	8 788	3.2
1975	Flora	5 054	NA	NA	5 032	2	5	14	1	23	2 291	8 330	10.3
1985	Flossmoor village	8 651	NA	NA	7 264	910	6	446	25	97	3 061	25 777	8.9
1993	Ford Heights village	4 259	NA	NA	26	4 208	9	2	14	43	1 146	4 577	2.7
2005	Forest Park village	14 918	15 177	-1.7	11 421	1 942	22	1 260	273	734	7 817	13 154	6.3
2030	Fox Lake village	7 478	NA	NA	7 304	26	16	30	102	230	3 801	11 417	15.4
2031	Fox Lake Hills CDP	2 681	NA	NA	2 636	4	2	15	24	62	908	NA	4.3
2035	Fox River Grove village	3 551	NA	NA	3 491	10	4	30	16	99	1 331	12 816	3.8
2040	Frankfort village	7 180	NA	NA	7 022	10	13	122	13	89	2 317	12 172	21.6
2042	Frankfort Square CDP	6 227	NA	NA	6 016	76	18	93	24	167	1 892	NA	5.1
2055	Franklin Park village	18 485	17 507	5.6	15 970	30	28	242	2 215	3 849	6 685	11 458	11.8
2060	Freeburg village	3 115	NA	NA	3 081	2	7	12	13	28	1 157	9 344	4.5
2070	Freeport	25 840	26 266	-1.6	22 496	3 005	39	231	69	204	11 722	10 772	26.7
2075	Fulton	3 698	NA	NA	3 670	1	1	12	14	24	1 533	10 068	5.7
2086	Gages Lake CDP	8 349	NA	NA	8 100	55	18	121	55	194	2 948	NA	7.9
2095	Galena	3 647	NA	NA	3 623	5	6	6	7	26	1 732	10 008	7.8
2100	Galesburg	33 530	35 305	-5.0	29 705	2 805	58	291	671	1 290	14 322	10 313	43.7
2105	Galva	2 742	NA	NA	2 706	0	0	0	36	65	1 296	9 945	4.3
2130	Geneseo	5 990	NA	NA	5 961	5	2	13	9	33	2 590	12 197	9.2
2135	Geneva	12 617	NA	NA	12 409	13	13	146	36	177	4 802	15 408	17.0
2140	Genoa	3 083	NA	NA	3 018	2	11	4	48	104	1 226	9 381	3.1
2145	Georgetown	3 678	NA	NA	3 482	169	12	5	10	20	1 544	8 101	4.1
2160	Gibson	3 396	NA	NA	3 336	30	6	16	8	25	1 520	10 445	5.4
2175	Gillespie	3 645	NA	NA	3 635	1	2	0	7	12	1 561	9 515	3.7
2203	Glenbard South CDP	3 957	NA	NA	3 787	55	0	108	7	60	1 395	NA	3.5
2205	Glen Carbon village	7 731	NA	NA	7 063	455	21	155	37	88	2 975	12 326	15.9
2210	Glencoe village	8 499	NA	NA	8 000	275	4	198	22	129	3 159	38 101	9.8
2217	Glendale Heights village	27 973	23 163	20.8	22 845	776	44	3 718	590	1 725	10 210	11 773	13.3
2220	Glen Ellyn village	24 944	23 649	5.5	23 450	497	27	780	190	659	9 747	17 682	15.9
2225	Glenview village	37 093	32 060	15.7	33 756	285	54	2 752	246	898	13 763	21 429	31.0
2230	Glenwood village	9 289	10 538	-11.9	6 759	2 330	15	70	115	293	3 325	12 893	5.7
2235	Godfrey CDP	5 436	NA	NA	5 089	294	8	30	15	48	2 027	NA	23.1
2272	Goodings Grove CDP	14 054	NA	NA	13 744	17	9	222	62	309	3 952	NA	24.4
2305	Granite City	32 862	36 815	-10.7	32 341	69	116	176	160	591	13 886	10 019	32.4
2330	Grayslake village	7 388	NA	NA	7 189	59	16	70	54	204	3 019	12 534	10.7
2345	Green Rock	2 615	NA	NA	2 529	3	1	5	77	117	934	7 603	1.7
2365	Greenville	4 806	NA	NA	4 553	206	11	12	24	55	2 015	9 422	6.8
2385	Gurnee village	13 701	NA	NA	12 562	432	33	529	145	426	5 571	15 973	28.7
2405	Hamilton	3 281	NA	NA	3 247	13	1	19	1	17	1 350	9 381	9.4
2445	Hanover Park village	32 895	28 850	14.0	28 113	1 188	75	2 435	1 084	3 616	10 405	11 014	15.7
2460	Harrisburg	9 289	10 410	-10.8	8 676	533	19	26	35	63	4 517	8 765	13.1
2475	Harvard	5 975	NA	NA	5 331	20	18	16	590	847	2 243	10 762	6.6
2490	Harvey	29 771	35 779	-16.8	4 490	23 813	73	81	1 314	1 932	10 286	7 615	16.0
2495	Harwood Heights village	7 680	NA	NA	7 400	5	10	209	56	264	3 404	12 318	2.1
2500	Havana	3 610	NA	NA	3 581	4	5	14	6	17	1 640	10 120	5.5
2505	Hawthorn Woods village	4 423	NA	NA	4 269	51	1	96	6	29	1 330	NA	14.2
2510	Hazel Crest village	13 334	13 973	-4.6	6 120	6 869	23	158	164	401	4 811	11 624	8.7
2545	Henry	2 591	NA	NA	2 571	2	8	1	9	16	1 064	9 996	3.2
2555	Herrin	10 857	10 549	2.9	10 735	49	7	60	6	40	4 939	9 063	18.5
2580	Hickory Hills	13 021	13 778	-5.5	12 621	41	15	204	140	532	4 758	12 046	7.3
2590	Highland	7 525	NA	NA	7 478	4	5	28	10	54	3 047	10 247	8.1
2595	Highland Park	30 575	30 611	-0.1	28 650	787	17	723	398	1 438	11 436	26 207	31.2
2600	Highwood	5 331	NA	NA	4 554	223	12	89	453	1 272	2 101	10 975	2.9
2610	Hillsboro	4 400	NA	NA	4 323	39	5	18	15	46	1 943	9 393	6.8
2620	Hillside village	7 672	NA	NA	6 610	482	17	374	189	440	3 145	13 327	5.6
2640	Hinsdale village	16 029	16 726	-4.2	15 238	128	22	605	36	245	6 251	22 980	12.0
2647	Hoffman Estates village	46 561	37 272	24.9	40 608	1 334	87	3 727	805	2 543	16 608	13 882	48.4
2665	Hometown	4 769	NA	NA	4 725	2	10	20	12	85	1 951	10 176	1.2
2670	Homewood village	19 278	19 724	-2.3	17 618	1 233	13	344	70	280	7 545	15 062	13.6
2675	Hoopeston	5 871	NA	NA	5 677	19	11	24	140	295	2 550	8 576	6.0
2760	Indian Head Park village	3 503	NA	NA	3 409	22	4	58	10	52	1 518	23 658	2.1
2771	Ingalls Park CDP	3 173	NA	NA	3 046	36	7	4	80	185	1 295	NA	2.8
2774	Inverness village	6 503	NA	NA	6 195	20	3	270	15	83	2 151	26 213	15.7
2805	Island Lake village	4 449	NA	NA	4 351	19	6	46	27	195	1 655	NA	6.5
2810	Itasca village	6 947	NA	NA	6 552	92	11	224	68	350	2 587	14 996	11.8

1. Codes shown are 2-digit FIPS codes for states; 4-digit census place codes for places; and 3-digit FIPS county codes followed by 3-digit census MCD codes for minor civil divisions (MCDs). MCD names are followed by county names in parentheses. 2. Hispanic persons may be of any race. 3. Dry land or land partially or temporarily covered by water.

State/ Place/ MCD[1] code	Place	Population: 1990	Population: Places of 10,000 or more: 1980	Population: Places of 10,000 or more: Percent change, 1980–1990	Population characteristics, 1990: Race: White	Race: Black	Race: Am. Indian, Eskimo Aleut	Race: Asian & Pacific Islander	Race: Other race	Hispanic[2]	Total housing units, 1990	Per capita income, 1985 (Dollars)	Land area,[3] 1990 (Sq. Km.)
		1	2	3	4	5	6	7	8	9	10	11	12
	ILLINOIS—Con.												
2825	Jacksonville	19 324	20 284	-4.7	18 045	1 071	17	98	93	175	7 898	10 318	21.6
2845	Jerseyville	7 382	NA	NA	7 344	7	16	11	4	20	3 056	9 801	10.1
2860	Johnston City	3 706	NA	NA	3 689	4	6	5	2	16	1 733	7 939	4.4
2865	Joliet	76 836	77 956	-1.4	53 190	16 600	148	742	6 156	9 741	29 043	10 412	72.0
2895	Justice village	11 137	10 552	5.5	9 185	1 608	11	176	157	540	4 390	10 631	7.4
2915	Kankakee	27 575	30 141	-8.5	17 108	9 957	45	132	333	673	11 380	9 235	26.5
2980	Kewanee	12 969	14 508	-10.6	12 212	573	13	46	125	317	5 875	9 312	15.0
3045	Knoxville	3 243	NA	NA	3 216	10	5	6	6	15	1 232	10 074	5.7
3062	La Grange village	15 362	15 445	-0.5	14 174	968	18	141	61	251	5 635	15 910	6.5
3064	La Grange Park village	12 861	13 359	-3.7	12 544	52	14	203	48	245	5 223	16 421	5.8
3080	Lake Barrington village	3 855	NA	NA	3 804	9	5	35	2	27	1 702	NA	13.4
3085	Lake Bluff village	5 513	NA	NA	5 411	35	3	55	9	48	2 079	23 132	10.3
3090	Lake Forest	17 836	15 245	17.0	17 018	226	15	465	112	316	6 131	32 215	42.4
3095	Lake in the Hills village	5 866	NA	NA	5 801	5	10	38	12	127	1 938	10 243	13.1
3102	Lake of the Woods CDP	2 748	NA	NA	2 719	9	3	15	2	19	1 078	NA	5.3
3105	Lake Villa village	2 857	NA	NA	2 797	20	11	18	11	53	1 089	NA	11.3
3115	Lake Zurich village	14 947	NA	NA	14 320	125	14	359	129	565	4 920	13 321	14.7
3130	Lansing village	28 086	29 039	-3.3	26 891	832	20	124	219	779	11 184	11 998	17.0
3145	La Salle	9 717	10 347	-6.1	9 456	36	13	60	152	457	4 472	9 562	7.7
3155	Lawrenceville	4 897	NA	NA	4 814	60	16	5	2	26	2 330	9 394	4.4
3165	Lebanon	3 688	NA	NA	2 915	704	10	47	12	60	1 450	9 499	5.1
3185	Lemont village	7 348	NA	NA	7 241	6	16	52	33	181	2 714	11 549	10.1
3190	Lena village	2 605	NA	NA	2 601	0	0	3	1	10	1 065	NA	3.6
3210	Le Roy	2 777	NA	NA	2 760	8	3	3	3	10	1 117	10 850	5.0
3215	Lewistown	2 572	NA	NA	2 560	4	3	2	3	11	1 188	7 688	4.7
3230	Libertyville village	19 174	16 520	16.1	18 199	101	19	711	144	436	6 899	16 603	21.2
3240	Lincoln	15 418	16 327	-5.6	14 888	363	19	110	38	107	6 293	9 871	14.2
3245	Lincolnshire village	4 931	NA	NA	4 748	18	1	133	31	109	1 717	32 722	9.2
3250	Lincolnwood village	11 365	11 921	-4.7	9 499	13	5	1 770	78	368	4 188	23 923	6.9
3255	Lindenhurst village	8 038	NA	NA	7 845	57	19	86	31	147	2 594	12 398	6.8
3265	Lisle village	19 512	13 625	43.2	17 668	562	31	1 104	147	593	8 338	16 286	15.3
3270	Litchfield	6 883	NA	NA	6 829	27	10	17	0	32	2 915	8 381	7.9
3300	Lockport	9 401	NA	NA	9 241	30	4	48	78	276	3 689	12 258	10.6
3315	Lombard village	39 408	37 295	5.7	36 820	519	49	1 751	269	1 090	15 848	14 221	24.1
3325	Long Grove village	4 740	NA	NA	4 546	29	1	131	33	120	1 421	NA	31.6
3331	Long Lake CDP	2 888	NA	NA	2 803	12	12	3	58	150	1 086	NA	3.3
3360	Loves Park	15 462	13 192	17.2	15 068	150	26	121	97	329	6 430	10 438	30.6
3385	Lynwood village	6 535	NA	NA	5 380	1 017	5	57	76	284	2 327	10 817	11.1
3390	Lyons village	9 828	NA	NA	9 540	8	25	109	146	569	4 035	11 629	5.7
3405	McHenry	16 177	10 908	48.3	15 963	10	28	95	81	347	6 171	11 703	23.4
3406	Machesney Park village	19 033	NA	NA	18 572	134	58	155	114	367	6 723	9 746	22.9
3415	McLeansboro	2 677	NA	NA	2 663	1	4	9	0	7	1 461	8 451	5.3
3435	Macomb	19 952	19 863	0.4	17 820	1 226	48	740	118	282	6 592	7 763	23.8
3445	Madison	4 629	NA	NA	3 599	978	10	10	32	98	2 269	8 357	8.6
3460	Mahomet village	3 103	NA	NA	3 070	0	11	13	9	17	1 159	NA	6.0
3505	Manteno village	3 488	NA	NA	3 458	6	5	12	7	23	1 422	10 706	2.9
3525	Marengo	4 768	NA	NA	4 581	7	8	16	156	358	1 920	10 079	8.8
3540	Marion	14 545	14 031	3.7	13 920	483	24	91	27	123	6 666	9 539	27.7
3560	Markham	13 136	15 172	-13.4	2 926	10 040	19	64	87	193	3 980	8 221	13.5
3570	Marquette Heights	3 077	NA	NA	3 049	7	2	8	11	29	978	9 178	2.3
3575	Marseilles	4 811	NA	NA	4 779	7	14	5	6	53	1 991	10 103	10.5
3580	Marshall	3 555	NA	NA	3 539	2	5	9	0	8	1 610	9 342	6.9
3595	Maryville village	2 576	NA	NA	2 509	52	2	11	2	42	1 048	NA	6.4
3600	Mascoutah	5 511	NA	NA	5 116	308	13	48	26	64	2 150	9 711	11.0
3620	Matteson village	11 378	10 223	11.3	5 871	5 035	14	311	147	365	3 762	11 552	16.7
3625	Mattoon	18 441	19 055	-3.2	17 979	287	48	73	54	155	8 301	10 004	17.5
3635	Maywood village	27 139	27 998	-3.1	3 258	22 733	24	136	988	1 795	8 547	8 776	7.0
3652	Medinah CDP	2 512	NA	NA	2 449	0	0	59	4	46	853	NA	4.0
3660	Melrose Park village	20 859	20 735	0.6	17 498	184	28	491	2 658	6 303	7 843	10 915	10.9
3675	Mendota	7 018	NA	NA	6 592	9	14	28	375	642	2 839	10 493	8.0
3695	Metamora village	2 520	NA	NA	2 513	1	2	2	2	2	942	NA	3.1
3705	Metropolis	6 734	NA	NA	6 188	498	27	14	7	24	3 137	9 097	12.7
3725	Midlothian village	14 372	14 274	0.7	13 736	352	19	109	156	542	5 004	10 217	7.3
3730	Milan village	5 831	NA	NA	5 623	124	21	26	37	124	2 427	9 146	14.3
3760	Millstadt village	2 566	NA	NA	2 525	26	7	5	3	31	1 002	10 463	2.5
3790	Minooka village	2 561	NA	NA	2 524	1	7	14	15	27	821	NA	4.5
3800	Mokena village	6 128	NA	NA	6 069	10	11	18	20	90	2 113	11 216	11.8
3805	Moline	43 202	45 709	-5.5	40 658	865	93	368	1 218	2 939	19 235	11 769	38.9
3810	Momence	2 968	NA	NA	2 827	84	2	10	45	102	1 186	8 649	3.4
3820	Monmouth	9 489	10 706	-11.4	8 987	340	10	60	92	165	4 097	9 204	9.7
3830	Montgomery village	4 267	NA	NA	3 995	91	3	45	133	247	1 705	11 521	9.1
3835	Monticello	4 549	NA	NA	4 538	1	5	3	2	16	1 880	12 792	5.0
3845	Morris	10 270	NA	NA	10 037	10	15	67	141	383	4 307	11 954	14.3

1. Codes shown are 2-digit FIPS codes for states; 4-digit census place codes for places; and 3-digit FIPS county codes followed by 3-digit census MCD codes for minor civil divisions (MCDs). MCD names are followed by county names in parentheses. 2. Hispanic persons may be of any race. 3. Dry land or land partially or temporarily covered by water.

State/ Place/ MCD[1] code	Place	Population 1990	Population, Places of 10,000 or more 1980	Population, Places of 10,000 or more Percent change, 1980–1990	Population characteristics, 1990, Race: White	Black	Am. Indian, Eskimo Aleut	Asian & Pacific Islander	Other race	Hispanic[2]	Total housing units, 1990	Per capita income, 1985 (Dollars)	Land area,[3] 1990 (Sq. Km.)
		1	2	3	4	5	6	7	8	9	10	11	12
	ILLINOIS—Con.												
3850	Morrison	4 363	NA	NA	4 324	6	3	11	19	71	1 859	10 283	5.0
3872	Morton village	13 799	14 178	-2.7	13 702	13	10	60	14	72	5 482	13 335	31.0
3873	Morton Grove village	22 408	23 724	-5.5	18 787	58	13	3 370	180	618	8 242	15 874	13.2
3900	Mount Carmel	8 287	NA	NA	8 151	37	6	74	19	46	3 579	10 086	10.8
3920	Mount Morris village	2 919	NA	NA	2 885	5	9	5	15	27	1 248	12 207	2.9
3930	Mount Prospect village	53 170	52 634	1.0	47 953	606	73	3 417	1 121	3 411	20 949	15 229	26.7
3945	Mount Vernon	16 988	17 193	-1.2	14 970	1 854	25	102	37	100	7 922	10 106	27.9
3947	Mount Zion village	4 522	NA	NA	4 474	26	2	17	3	8	1 666	11 166	6.7
3975	Mundelein village	21 215	17 053	24.4	18 980	198	40	608	1 389	2 867	7 397	13 051	19.5
3980	Murphysboro	9 176	NA	NA	8 042	1 016	28	51	39	134	4 114	8 986	12.0
3990	Naperville	85 351	42 346	101.6	78 998	1 795	78	4 133	347	1 527	30 906	16 598	72.4
4005	Nashville	3 202	NA	NA	3 173	7	5	14	3	11	1 362	10 696	5.9
4055	New Baden village	2 602	NA	NA	2 475	78	8	29	12	33	974	NA	2.3
4105	New Lenox village	9 627	NA	NA	9 550	13	5	18	41	181	3 397	12 407	15.4
4125	Newton	3 154	NA	NA	3 148	0	1	4	1	14	1 456	10 132	4.6
4135	Niles village	28 284	30 363	-6.8	25 910	122	22	1 988	242	1 016	11 052	13 545	15.1
4150	Nokomis	2 534	NA	NA	2 527	2	3	1	1	14	1 140	8 859	3.3
4160	Normal town	40 023	35 672	12.2	36 971	1 982	57	779	234	592	12 300	9 673	31.5
4165	Norridge village	14 459	16 483	-12.3	14 153	12	14	234	46	321	5 552	12 906	4.7
4180	North Aurora village	5 940	NA	NA	5 496	184	9	158	93	307	2 391	12 531	9.6
4190	Northbrook village	32 308	30 778	5.0	30 057	68	16	2 079	88	510	11 673	23 643	32.7
4195	North Chicago	34 978	38 774	-9.8	19 822	12 043	186	1 268	1 659	3 213	7 925	8 488	19.2
4210	Northfield village	4 635	NA	NA	4 407	11	3	200	14	53	1 852	27 431	7.3
4220	Northlake	12 505	12 169	2.8	10 801	177	19	486	1 022	2 028	4 344	10 506	7.9
4240	North Riverside village	6 005	NA	NA	5 902	10	0	63	30	173	2 842	13 182	4.0
4262	Oak Brook village	9 178	NA	NA	7 487	74	3	1 576	38	244	3 112	33 356	21.1
4270	Oak Forest	26 203	26 096	0.4	25 455	158	41	387	162	647	9 058	11 562	14.0
4290	Oak Lawn village	56 182	60 590	-7.3	55 200	66	46	614	256	1 322	21 835	13 185	21.7
4295	Oak Park village	53 648	54 887	-2.3	41 313	9 804	73	1 785	673	1 915	23 571	14 194	12.2
4330	O'Fallon	16 073	12 241	31.3	14 317	1 351	43	289	73	291	6 326	12 121	15.9
4340	Oglesby	3 619	NA	NA	3 577	13	8	11	10	65	1 591	10 276	9.1
4385	Olney	8 664	NA	NA	8 604	16	12	14	18	42	4 028	10 871	12.4
4390	Olympia Fields village	4 248	NA	NA	3 282	685	5	252	24	55	1 434	30 646	7.4
4425	Oregon	3 891	NA	NA	3 843	3	9	23	13	39	1 632	11 056	4.5
4437	Orland Hills village	5 510	NA	NA	5 161	216	5	60	68	239	1 752	9 208	2.8
4440	Orland Park village	35 720	23 045	55.0	34 088	140	21	1 273	198	826	12 484	13 714	34.6
4445	Oswego village	3 876	NA	NA	3 819	7	17	22	11	86	1 377	13 268	9.8
4450	Ottawa	17 451	18 166	-3.9	17 009	141	25	123	153	677	7 511	11 318	15.5
4465	Palatine village	39 253	32 166	22.0	36 995	370	42	1 274	572	1 410	15 851	15 504	25.5
4485	Palos Heights	11 478	11 096	3.4	11 119	37	4	299	19	129	3 980	17 871	9.0
4490	Palos Hills	17 803	16 654	6.9	16 939	373	27	352	112	575	6 892	13 248	10.8
4495	Palos Park village	4 199	NA	NA	4 072	7	4	97	19	74	1 458	20 577	9.2
4500	Pana	5 796	NA	NA	5 773	1	6	16	0	15	2 542	8 648	6.3
4520	Paris	8 987	NA	NA	8 896	63	7	13	8	26	4 150	8 761	10.8
4525	Park City	4 677	NA	NA	3 871	220	22	215	349	736	2 215	11 591	3.0
4535	Park Forest village	24 656	26 222	-6.0	18 000	6 072	42	278	264	769	9 442	11 247	12.8
4540	Park Ridge	36 175	38 704	-6.5	35 245	48	21	791	70	474	13 821	17 555	17.8
4560	Paxton	4 289	NA	NA	4 265	1	4	13	6	21	1 826	10 521	5.8
4585	Pekin	32 254	33 967	-5.0	31 982	26	79	127	40	194	13 776	10 008	28.3
4590	Peoria	113 504	124 160	-8.6	86 852	23 692	206	1 906	848	1 813	48 260	11 140	105.9
4595	Peoria Heights village	6 930	NA	NA	6 556	273	11	65	25	83	3 350	13 151	6.8
4600	Peotone village	2 947	NA	NA	2 931	1	1	12	2	17	1 105	10 567	3.4
4615	Peru	9 302	10 869	-14.4	9 172	33	6	52	39	173	3 954	10 584	12.6
4650	Pinckneyville	3 372	NA	NA	3 341	10	7	8	6	20	1 586	11 718	4.5
4663	Pistakee Highlands CDP	3 848	NA	NA	3 815	2	14	9	8	54	1 336	NA	4.0
4670	Pittsfield	4 231	NA	NA	4 205	0	3	17	6	36	1 946	10 154	6.0
4675	Plainfield village	4 557	NA	NA	4 516	4	2	24	11	65	1 691	11 653	10.1
4690	Plano	5 104	NA	NA	4 462	6	12	21	603	832	1 832	9 826	5.5
4715	Polo	2 514	NA	NA	2 484	2	15	7	6	18	1 060	9 945	3.4
4720	Pontiac	11 428	11 227	1.8	9 479	1 585	22	49	293	427	3 932	9 438	11.9
4724	Pontoon Beach village	4 013	NA	NA	3 891	72	14	20	16	80	1 628	8 972	17.2
4740	Posen village	4 226	NA	NA	3 963	87	5	21	150	311	1 612	9 303	2.9
4758	Preston Heights CDP	2 750	NA	NA	1 445	1 257	11	4	33	80	983	NA	4.3
4760	Princeton	7 197	NA	NA	7 132	12	12	23	18	70	3 208	12 724	9.8
4772	Prospect Heights	15 239	11 808	29.1	13 351	262	12	677	937	2 190	6 270	15 714	11.0
4780	Quincy	39 681	42 554	-6.8	37 662	1 645	73	202	99	173	17 530	9 359	32.9
4810	Rantoul village	17 212	20 174	-14.7	14 065	2 018	73	418	638	863	6 059	8 287	17.0
4830	Red Bud	2 918	NA	NA	2 892	1	5	19	1	13	1 174	11 441	4.3
4855	Richton Park village	10 523	NA	NA	7 839	2 335	26	185	138	351	4 026	11 384	7.3
4890	Riverdale village	13 671	13 233	3.3	7 896	5 557	27	29	162	460	5 623	11 849	9.3
4895	River Forest village	11 669	12 392	-5.8	11 053	224	8	309	75	279	4 197	19 773	6.5
4900	River Grove village	9 961	10 368	-3.9	9 706	6	14	141	94	411	4 433	11 902	6.2
4905	Riverside village	8 774	NA	NA	8 638	2	5	85	44	243	3 647	17 767	5.1

1. Codes shown are 2-digit FIPS codes for states; 4-digit census place codes for places; and 3-digit FIPS county codes followed by 3-digit census MCD codes for minor civil divisions (MCDs). MCD names are followed by county names in parentheses. 2. Hispanic persons may be of any race. 3. Dry land or land partially or temporarily covered by water.

State/ Place/ MCD[1] code	Place	Population			Population characteristics, 1990						Total housing units, 1990	Per capita income, 1985 (Dollars)	Land area,[3] 1990 (Sq. Km.)
		1990	Places of 10,000 or more		Race					Hispanic[2]			
			1980	Percent change, 1980–1990	White	Black	Am. Indian, Eskimo Aleut	Asian & Pacific Islander	Other race				
		1	2	3	4	5	6	7	8	9	10	11	12
	ILLINOIS—Con.												
4910	Riverton village	2 638	NA	NA	2 629	3	5	1	0	8	1 060	9 628	4.1
4911	Riverwoods village	2 868	NA	NA	2 757	10	2	98	1	45	913	31 896	9.3
4920	Robbins village	7 498	NA	NA	109	7 367	10	4	8	20	2 322	6 452	3.8
4930	Robinson	6 740	NA	NA	6 647	46	15	22	10	27	3 174	11 418	9.0
4935	Rochelle	8 769	NA	NA	8 087	29	15	58	580	909	3 605	10 613	10.8
4940	Rochester village	2 676	NA	NA	2 645	7	3	17	4	14	938	NA	4.5
4960	Rock Falls	9 654	10 633	-9.2	9 013	82	21	37	501	964	3 891	8 729	7.8
4965	Rockford	139 426	139 712	-0.2	113 118	20 868	356	2 151	2 933	5 841	58 146	10 704	116.5
4970	Rock Island	40 552	47 036	-13.8	32 731	6 983	99	235	504	1 531	17 901	10 419	39.2
4975	Rockton village	2 928	NA	NA	2 878	18	9	20	3	27	1 221	NA	7.3
4985	Rolling Meadows	22 591	20 167	12.0	20 910	362	39	785	495	2 522	8 584	14 321	13.6
4995	Romeoville village	14 074	15 519	-9.3	12 831	376	38	125	704	1 434	3 959	9 286	20.6
5010	Roselle village	20 819	16 950	22.8	19 346	232	24	1 110	107	550	7 398	14 498	11.9
5015	Rosemont village	3 995	NA	NA	3 245	31	8	180	531	785	1 797	12 191	4.5
5025	Rosewood Heights CDP	4 821	NA	NA	4 789	1	8	12	11	56	1 858	NA	6.4
5043	Round Lake village	3 550	NA	NA	3 402	10	17	26	95	418	1 348	10 183	8.8
5045	Round Lake Beach village	16 434	12 921	27.2	15 054	169	47	218	946	2 347	5 041	8 991	10.2
5050	Round Lake Park village	4 045	NA	NA	3 825	9	13	4	194	522	1 356	9 648	8.5
5075	Rushville	3 229	NA	NA	3 218	2	4	5	0	2	1 493	9 013	3.9
5110	St. Charles	22 501	17 487	28.7	21 989	87	33	261	131	576	8 505	13 689	26.7
5160	Salem	7 470	NA	NA	7 321	19	21	101	8	38	3 202	9 676	13.6
5170	Sandwich	5 567	NA	NA	5 414	11	14	25	103	201	2 158	10 387	6.2
5180	Sauk Village village	9 926	10 906	-9.0	7 484	1 790	32	77	543	964	2 998	8 204	6.8
5190	Savanna	3 819	NA	NA	3 660	65	13	29	52	186	1 807	9 557	6.3
5195	Savoy village	2 674	NA	NA	2 355	105	1	208	5	36	1 150	NA	3.1
5215	Schaumburg village	68 586	53 303	28.7	62 140	1 471	80	4 454	441	1 829	29 499	14 410	48.7
5220	Schiller Park village	11 189	11 458	-2.3	9 996	124	38	439	592	1 382	4 315	11 376	7.2
5233	Scott AFB CDP	7 245	NA	NA	5 570	1 190	30	334	121	326	1 877	NA	9.7
5290	Shelbyville	4 943	NA	NA	4 921	7	4	11	0	13	2 159	10 422	6.5
5310	Shiloh village	2 655	NA	NA	2 485	79	9	67	15	51	1 101	NA	5.4
5320	Shorewood village	6 264	NA	NA	5 996	124	8	96	40	117	2 032	12 907	6.9
5350	Silvis	6 926	NA	NA	6 260	194	17	46	409	922	2 850	8 359	7.4
5365	Skokie village	59 432	60 278	-1.4	48 265	1 311	61	9 253	542	2 457	23 170	16 593	26.0
5370	Sleepy Hollow village	3 241	NA	NA	3 156	23	7	48	7	41	1 064	NA	4.9
5397	South Barrington village	2 937	NA	NA	2 650	26	1	260	0	14	871	NA	16.3
5400	South Beloit	4 072	NA	NA	3 679	223	22	20	128	201	1 789	9 264	8.1
5405	South Chicago Heights village	3 597	NA	NA	3 326	45	2	6	218	483	1 491	9 247	4.0
5410	South Elgin village	7 474	NA	NA	6 881	178	19	204	192	428	2 503	10 305	7.2
5420	South Holland village	22 105	24 977	-11.5	18 986	2 564	21	398	136	454	7 546	13 390	18.9
5425	South Jacksonville village	3 187	NA	NA	3 118	36	11	16	6	22	1 452	11 465	3.4
5455	Sparta	4 853	NA	NA	4 084	721	9	20	19	22	2 006	10 321	24.7
5480	Springfield	105 227	99 637	5.6	90 069	13 687	172	1 033	266	870	48 534	11 642	110.2
5490	Spring Valley	5 246	NA	NA	5 151	18	6	29	42	174	2 283	9 952	10.0
5510	Staunton	4 806	NA	NA	4 781	3	9	12	1	8	2 045	8 975	5.9
5520	Steger village	8 584	NA	NA	8 067	207	18	41	251	595	3 470	8 538	4.6
5525	Sterling	15 132	16 281	-7.1	13 484	260	19	50	1 319	2 397	6 364	10 364	10.5
5540	Stickney village	5 678	NA	NA	5 379	12	10	40	237	392	2 262	11 241	5.0
5560	Stone Park village	4 383	NA	NA	2 673	25	2	153	1 530	2 544	1 340	8 093	0.9
5585	Streamwood village	30 987	23 456	32.1	28 245	616	52	1 315	759	2 298	10 324	10 575	17.6
5590	Streator	14 121	14 789	-4.5	13 541	268	21	39	252	621	6 053	9 447	12.4
5610	Sullivan	4 354	NA	NA	4 343	0	7	3	1	8	1 884	9 773	4.7
5620	Summit village	9 971	10 110	-1.4	6 688	1 360	26	201	1 696	3 115	3 514	9 096	5.5
5635	Swansea village	8 201	NA	NA	7 697	380	13	96	15	104	3 294	11 692	8.0
5640	Sycamore	9 708	NA	NA	9 230	313	18	85	62	195	3 935	11 324	9.7
5680	Taylorville	11 133	11 386	-2.2	11 003	57	16	52	5	28	5 019	9 910	18.3
5725	Thornton village	2 778	NA	NA	2 758	2	5	5	8	86	1 037	11 803	6.1
5735	Tilton village	2 729	NA	NA	2 712	1	4	6	6	23	1 196	NA	6.7
5745	Tinley Park village	37 121	26 169	41.9	35 697	601	31	516	276	944	13 222	10 983	27.1
5760	Tolono village	2 605	NA	NA	2 586	5	3	8	3	12	1 047	NA	4.0
5810	Troy	6 046	NA	NA	5 957	26	27	27	9	45	2 283	10 024	6.6
5820	Tuscola	4 155	NA	NA	4 143	1	1	4	6	21	1 825	11 953	3.5
5838	University Park village	6 204	NA	NA	1 183	4 910	12	37	62	114	2 227	10 920	20.7
5845	Urbana	36 344	35 978	1.0	27 527	4 159	55	4 259	344	999	14 006	9 409	20.2
5870	Vandalia	6 114	NA	NA	5 432	590	17	10	65	120	2 341	9 299	13.5
5885	Venetian Village CDP	3 133	NA	NA	3 101	6	5	12	9	63	1 116	NA	9.3
5890	Venice	3 571	NA	NA	335	3 221	2	11	2	31	1 445	5 983	4.9
5920	Vernon Hills village	15 319	NA	NA	13 875	259	25	954	206	589	6 057	14 793	17.8
5945	Villa Grove	2 734	NA	NA	2 711	2	9	12	0	11	1 076	9 690	2.4
5950	Villa Park village	22 253	23 185	-4.0	20 967	252	30	711	293	1 125	8 214	12 890	12.0
5960	Virden	3 635	NA	NA	3 618	2	10	3	2	10	1 523	8 280	4.2
6020	Warrenville	11 333	NA	NA	10 663	215	22	362	71	345	4 126	14 076	13.8
6035	Washington	10 099	10 364	-2.6	10 004	24	10	44	17	46	3 903	11 014	16.5
6040	Washington Park village	7 431	NA	NA	1 065	6 293	4	10	59	115	2 597	6 366	6.3

1. Codes shown are 2-digit FIPS codes for states; 4-digit census place codes for places; and 3-digit FIPS county codes followed by 3-digit census MCD codes for minor civil divisions (MCDs). MCD names are followed by county names in parentheses. 2. Hispanic persons may be of any race. 3. Dry land or land partially or temporarily covered by water.

State/ Place/ MCD[1] code	Place	Population: 1990	Population: Places of 10,000 or more: 1980	Population: Places of 10,000 or more: Percent change, 1980–1990	Population characteristics, 1990: Race: White	Race: Black	Race: Am. Indian, Eskimo Aleut	Race: Asian & Pacific Islander	Race: Other race	Hispanic[2]	Total housing units, 1990	Per capita income, 1985 (Dollars)	Land area,[3] 1990 (Sq. Km.)
		1	2	3	4	5	6	7	8	9	10	11	12
	ILLINOIS—Con.												
6050	Waterloo	5 072	NA	NA	5 033	4	13	16	6	27	2 040	11 879	6.9
6060	Watseka	5 424	NA	NA	5 367	9	4	20	24	80	2 303	9 878	6.5
6070	Wauconda village	6 294	NA	NA	6 195	0	6	29	64	250	2 584	11 285	8.3
6075	Waukegan	69 392	67 653	2.6	44 633	13 772	274	2 123	8 590	16 443	25 800	10 509	57.4
6125	Westchester village	17 301	17 730	-2.4	16 605	144	10	467	75	315	6 948	15 307	8.1
6130	West Chicago	14 796	12 550	17.9	12 245	270	32	190	2 059	4 510	4 877	10 713	24.5
6140	West Dundee village	3 728	NA	NA	3 687	10	1	15	15	76	1 526	11 812	3.5
6145	Western Springs village	11 984	12 876	-6.9	11 868	19	7	76	14	127	4 370	20 092	6.8
6155	West Frankfort	8 526	NA	NA	8 483	2	18	14	9	22	4 070	7 989	11.0
6165	Westmont village	21 228	16 718	27.0	18 563	710	27	1 721	207	731	9 393	14 109	11.4
6168	West Peoria CDP	5 314	NA	NA	4 944	266	11	60	33	66	2 141	NA	3.3
6185	Westville village	3 387	NA	NA	3 357	24	5	1	0	8	1 542	9 820	4.1
6190	Wheaton	51 464	43 043	19.6	47 847	1 304	50	1 945	318	1 051	18 630	15 742	28.7
6200	Wheeling village	29 911	23 270	28.5	26 955	504	55	1 376	1 021	2 508	12 998	13 743	21.0
6215	White Hall	2 814	NA	NA	2 804	1	5	2	2	9	1 230	8 636	6.3
6240	Willowbrook village	8 598	NA	NA	7 630	97	10	814	47	186	4 102	21 225	6.5
6250	Willow Springs village	4 509	NA	NA	4 403	10	4	48	44	128	1 657	12 989	9.3
6255	Wilmette village	26 690	28 229	-5.5	24 651	130	10	1 843	56	449	10 046	26 117	13.9
6260	Wilmington	4 743	NA	NA	4 689	12	10	10	22	54	1 875	10 428	12.1
6295	Winfield village	7 096	NA	NA	6 875	67	8	121	25	147	2 486	15 739	5.8
6305	Winnetka village	12 174	12 772	-4.7	11 766	45	3	347	13	105	4 477	38 204	9.9
6315	Winthrop Harbor village	6 240	NA	NA	6 050	7	23	124	36	137	2 140	12 052	10.8
6325	Wonder Lake CDP	6 664	NA	NA	6 566	7	14	34	43	154	2 745	NA	18.2
6330	Wood Dale	12 425	11 251	10.4	11 790	27	15	381	212	870	4 697	14 725	11.0
6350	Woodridge village	26 256	22 322	17.6	22 682	1 599	36	1 617	322	1 078	10 198	13 476	19.5
6355	Wood River	11 490	12 449	-7.7	11 371	23	44	35	17	69	4 961	10 236	13.8
6365	Woodstock	14 353	11 725	22.4	13 532	56	38	201	526	1 114	5 541	11 587	26.0
6375	Worth village	11 208	11 592	-3.3	11 016	18	18	72	84	315	4 500	11 722	6.2
6402	York Center CDP	4 818	NA	NA	4 320	177	18	254	49	169	1 853	NA	3.2
6405	Yorkville	3 925	NA	NA	3 883	8	4	8	22	51	1 479	11 392	8.1
6415	Zion	19 775	17 861	10.7	14 512	4 304	101	332	526	1 253	6 845	10 353	19.7
18	INDIANA	5 544 159	5 490 212	1.0	5 020 700	432 092	12 720	37 617	41 030	98 788	2 246 046	9 978	92 903.7
0030	Alexandria	5 709	NA	NA	5 688	4	6	4	7	23	2 433	8 851	6.6
0065	Anderson	59 459	64 714	-8.1	50 460	8 442	161	239	157	374	26 362	10 173	98.1
0075	Angola	5 824	NA	NA	5 662	27	22	87	26	61	2 448	9 313	7.5
0100	Attica	3 457	NA	NA	3 426	0	4	17	10	34	1 503	9 160	3.9
0105	Auburn	9 379	NA	NA	9 295	2	28	29	25	73	3 853	10 629	11.7
0110	Aurora	3 825	NA	NA	3 801	2	14	4	4	30	1 599	8 658	7.2
0115	Austin town	4 310	NA	NA	4 273	1	6	1	29	61	1 645	6 166	5.4
0135	Batesville	4 720	NA	NA	4 680	1	5	28	6	22	1 848	10 731	10.7
0145	Bedford	13 817	14 410	-4.1	13 665	60	30	51	11	52	6 158	9 860	30.8
0150	Beech Grove	13 383	13 196	1.4	13 232	33	25	65	28	99	5 757	10 596	10.7
0155	Berne	3 559	NA	NA	3 527	2	1	13	16	33	1 353	10 612	4.3
0170	Bicknell	3 357	NA	NA	3 344	1	7	4	1	7	1 584	7 885	3.9
0185	Bloomfield town	2 592	NA	NA	2 566	1	3	13	9	18	1 246	9 769	3.6
0195	Bloomington	60 633	52 044	16.5	55 271	2 441	122	2 449	350	993	22 025	8 513	39.1
0210	Bluffton	9 020	NA	NA	8 934	6	12	26	42	121	3 777	10 209	14.4
0215	Boonville	6 724	NA	NA	6 656	39	7	17	5	17	2 843	10 128	7.7
0240	Brazil	7 640	NA	NA	7 523	97	10	4	6	27	3 467	7 953	7.1
0245	Bremen town	4 725	NA	NA	4 651	0	13	6	55	111	1 839	9 179	5.1
0248	Bright CDP	3 945	NA	NA	3 924	7	4	8	2	7	1 244	NA	37.9
0285	Brookville town	2 529	NA	NA	2 496	1	22	6	4	12	1 144	9 746	2.5
0290	Brownsburg town	7 628	NA	NA	7 563	4	17	38	6	17	2 923	11 986	9.3
0295	Brownstown town	2 872	NA	NA	2 862	2	5	0	3	3	1 140	8 069	3.3
0325	Butler	2 601	NA	NA	2 571	3	3	5	19	41	1 019	7 791	3.8
0370	Carmel	25 380	18 272	38.9	24 609	132	23	576	40	226	9 645	18 988	32.6
0392	Cedar Lake town	8 885	NA	NA	8 793	2	29	20	41	195	3 344	8 687	17.4
0415	Chandler town	3 099	NA	NA	3 083	6	9	0	1	8	1 197	8 227	2.7
0420	Charlestown	5 889	NA	NA	5 733	108	16	13	19	45	2 239	7 543	5.6
0425	Chesterfield town	2 730	NA	NA	2 709	3	1	8	9	22	1 175	10 351	3.0
0430	Chesterton town	9 124	NA	NA	9 038	9	23	33	21	206	3 507	10 488	18.4
0445	Cicero town	3 268	NA	NA	3 254	4	4	5	1	10	1 345	11 608	3.3
0455	Clarksville town	19 833	15 164	30.8	18 889	737	46	97	64	156	8 635	9 412	22.0
0490	Clinton	5 040	NA	NA	5 006	8	19	6	1	23	2 359	8 395	5.8
0510	Columbia City	5 706	NA	NA	5 650	14	18	13	11	46	2 450	9 414	7.3
0515	Columbus	31 802	30 614	3.9	30 334	798	53	508	109	273	13 458	12 005	52.4
0520	Connersville	15 550	17 023	-8.7	15 086	401	22	39	2	56	6 683	8 918	19.3
0535	Corydon town	2 661	NA	NA	2 613	36	8	4	0	10	1 202	9 050	4.1
0540	Covington	2 747	NA	NA	2 740	1	2	4	0	3	1 146	9 628	3.0
0550	Crawfordsville	13 584	13 325	1.9	13 250	173	39	97	25	92	5 842	9 727	19.6
0565	Crown Point	17 728	16 455	7.7	17 257	259	8	129	75	405	6 568	11 313	20.4

1. Codes shown are 2-digit FIPS codes for states; 4-digit census place codes for places; and 3-digit FIPS county codes followed by 3-digit census MCD codes for minor civil divisions (MCDs). MCD names are followed by county names in parentheses. 2. Hispanic persons may be of any race. 3. Dry land or land partially or temporarily covered by water.

State/ Place/ MCD[1] code	Place	Population			Population characteristics, 1990						Total housing units, 1990	Per capita income, 1985 (Dollars)	Land area,[3] 1990 (Sq. Km.)
		1990	Places of 10,000 or more		Race					Hispanic[2]			
			1980	Percent change, 1980–1990	White	Black	Am. Indian, Eskimo Aleut	Asian & Pacific Islander	Other race				
		1	2	3	4	5	6	7	8	9	10	11	12
	INDIANA—Con.												
0580	Cumberland town	2 933	NA	NA	2 635	225	2	48	23	42	1 166	NA	1.9
0605	Danville town	4 345	NA	NA	4 325	5	7	5	3	25	1 719	10 856	7.3
0615	Decatur	8 644	NA	NA	8 266	15	19	23	321	585	3 532	8 868	10.4
0625	Delphi	2 531	NA	NA	2 521	1	2	0	7	29	1 079	8 991	3.8
0655	Dunkirk	2 739	NA	NA	2 702	12	8	9	8	16	1 227	8 209	2.4
0660	Dunlap CDP	5 705	NA	NA	5 560	71	19	31	24	93	2 000	NA	12.0
0670	Dyer town	10 923	NA	NA	10 658	63	16	87	99	427	3 461	11 480	14.5
0680	East Chicago	33 892	39 786	-14.8	12 881	11 379	80	79	9 473	16 196	13 484	7 905	31.0
0715	Edinburgh town	4 536	NA	NA	4 508	6	10	8	4	18	1 801	7 733	4.8
0740	Elkhart	43 627	41 305	5.6	36 626	6 088	178	343	392	888	19 147	10 194	44.4
0745	Ellettsville town	3 275	NA	NA	3 225	24	8	4	14	28	1 226	8 626	3.2
0755	Elwood	9 494	10 865	-12.6	9 423	0	8	27	36	122	3 946	8 960	8.3
0775	Evansville	126 272	130 496	-3.2	113 090	12 031	239	716	196	732	58 188	10 048	105.4
0780	Fairmount town	3 130	NA	NA	3 109	3	13	5	0	10	1 262	8 881	3.4
0803	Fishers town	7 508	NA	NA	7 315	77	11	94	11	78	2 898	NA	21.4
0820	Fortville town	2 690	NA	NA	2 680	2	2	1	5	10	1 103	8 789	2.6
0825	Fort Wayne	173 072	172 196	0.5	139 244	28 989	560	1 744	2 535	4 679	77 166	10 276	162.3
0855	Frankfort	14 754	15 168	-2.7	14 516	32	26	31	149	362	6 146	9 642	11.8
0860	Franklin	12 907	11 563	11.6	12 633	195	28	32	19	83	4 661	9 438	18.6
0900	Garrett	5 349	NA	NA	5 286	11	18	21	13	47	2 080	8 907	5.9
0905	Gary	116 646	151 953	-23.2	19 020	93 982	175	213	3 256	6 690	47 082	7 488	130.1
0910	Gas City	6 296	NA	NA	6 240	7	23	9	17	82	2 535	8 783	6.5
0932	Georgetown CDP	3 993	NA	NA	3 634	188	23	129	19	49	1 994	NA	5.0
0950	Goshen	23 797	19 665	21.0	22 769	253	69	184	522	1 156	9 523	9 534	29.3
0967	Granger CDP	20 241	NA	NA	19 548	223	35	411	24	146	6 375	NA	68.8
0970	Greencastle	8 984	NA	NA	8 581	235	13	116	39	83	3 159	8 045	13.3
0975	Greendale town	3 881	NA	NA	3 852	16	3	10	0	14	1 610	11 322	5.4
0980	Greenfield	11 657	11 439	1.9	11 546	12	23	59	17	135	4 425	10 231	15.9
0990	Greensburg	9 286	NA	NA	9 163	8	6	105	4	50	3 637	8 844	9.3
1010	Greenwood	26 265	19 327	35.9	25 872	20	45	279	49	223	11 399	11 591	28.0
1020	Griffith town	17 916	17 026	5.2	16 959	434	27	171	325	946	6 914	11 437	22.6
1022	Grissom AFB CDP	4 271	NA	NA	3 506	564	33	81	87	204	1 129	NA	10.9
1024	Gulivoire Park CDP	2 788	NA	NA	2 770	1	3	13	1	16	1 095	NA	3.8
1040	Hammond	84 236	93 714	-10.1	71 465	7 743	203	348	4 477	9 941	33 924	9 845	59.4
1045	Hanover town	3 610	NA	NA	3 463	97	11	23	16	19	1 039	6 233	4.4
1055	Hartford City	6 960	NA	NA	6 914	5	24	8	9	54	3 033	9 102	8.9
1075	Hebron town	3 183	NA	NA	3 155	3	6	4	15	55	1 190	9 938	3.6
1080	Highland town	23 696	25 935	-8.6	23 165	56	16	207	252	919	8 892	11 945	17.6
1082	Highland CDP	3 508	NA	NA	3 427	23	0	53	5	10	1 211	NA	6.0
1095	Hobart	21 822	22 987	-5.1	21 467	48	15	47	245	1 058	8 302	10 454	40.0
1125	Huntingburg	5 242	NA	NA	5 204	10	9	11	8	48	2 119	9 018	8.2
1130	Huntington	16 389	16 202	1.2	16 116	33	93	103	44	144	6 529	9 223	19.0
1145	Indianapolis	731 327	700 719	4.4	554 423	165 570	1 574	6 852	2 908	7 681	319 980	10 836	936.7
1148	Indian Heights CDP	3 669	NA	NA	3 568	61	11	16	13	45	1 283	NA	2.8
1170	Jasper	10 030	NA	NA	9 993	15	5	11	6	47	4 162	11 879	21.6
1175	Jeffersonville	21 841	21 220	2.9	18 864	2 764	36	106	71	140	9 375	8 636	24.7
1200	Kendallville	7 773	NA	NA	7 704	9	9	32	19	70	3 163	8 730	11.4
1250	Knox	3 705	NA	NA	3 691	1	1	5	7	36	1 520	7 236	8.7
1255	Kokomo	44 962	47 808	-6.0	40 260	4 001	133	305	263	780	20 340	10 714	37.3
1285	Lafayette	43 764	43 011	1.8	41 945	936	145	464	274	733	19 259	10 272	34.7
1304	Lakes of the Four Seasons CDP	6 556	NA	NA	6 469	1	9	42	35	204	2 201	NA	6.9
1307	Lake Station	13 899	14 294	-2.8	12 867	31	65	31	905	1 834	5 066	8 250	21.5
1325	La Porte	21 507	21 755	-1.1	20 927	329	57	39	155	450	9 135	10 245	29.2
1340	Lawrence	26 763	25 591	4.6	23 199	2 868	69	453	174	455	11 621	10 850	52.0
1345	Lawrenceburg	4 375	NA	NA	4 161	200	3	11	0	16	1 867	8 228	10.9
1355	Lebanon	12 059	11 454	5.3	11 912	30	45	33	39	119	4 910	9 294	15.6
1375	Ligonier	3 443	NA	NA	3 301	2	11	20	109	321	1 365	9 596	5.2
1385	Linton	5 814	NA	NA	5 788	1	4	12	9	30	2 739	8 524	7.7
1405	Logansport	16 812	17 899	-6.1	16 482	197	62	38	33	101	7 356	8 973	16.6
1415	Loogootee	2 884	NA	NA	2 874	0	1	6	3	4	1 245	8 930	4.0
1420	Lowell town	6 430	NA	NA	6 386	0	6	14	24	135	2 184	10 402	10.0
1460	Madison	12 006	12 472	-3.7	11 645	230	19	68	44	56	5 151	9 360	20.8
1470	Marion	32 618	35 874	-9.1	26 950	4 838	143	216	471	1 036	14 000	9 265	32.3
1490	Martinsville	11 677	11 311	3.2	11 610	0	34	18	15	59	4 604	8 799	10.5
1522	Melody Hill CDP	2 932	NA	NA	2 896	29	2	2	3	16	1 043	NA	3.5
1536	Merrillville town	27 257	27 677	-1.5	24 998	1 367	32	233	627	1 880	10 322	11 514	80.3
1550	Michigan City	33 822	36 833	-8.2	25 628	7 625	112	228	229	596	13 995	8 852	50.8
1610	Mishawaka	42 608	40 201	6.0	41 354	678	157	284	135	457	19 028	10 037	36.0
1615	Mitchell	4 669	NA	NA	4 641	19	4	3	2	12	1 931	8 553	8.3
1660	Monticello	5 237	NA	NA	5 193	0	13	16	15	50	2 303	8 536	7.2
1680	Mooresville town	5 541	NA	NA	5 509	5	6	19	2	20	2 220	9 494	6.2
1725	Mount Vernon	7 217	NA	NA	6 917	262	13	15	10	29	3 236	10 376	6.1
1735	Muncie	71 035	77 216	-8.0	63 304	6 774	186	501	270	625	29 828	8 979	59.0

1. Codes shown are 2-digit FIPS codes for states; 4-digit census place codes for places; and 3-digit FIPS county codes followed by 3-digit census MCD codes for minor civil divisions (MCDs). MCD names are followed by county names in parentheses. 2. Hispanic persons may be of any race. 3. Dry land or land partially or temporarily covered by water.

State/ Place/ MCD[1] code	Place	Population			Population characteristics, 1990						Total housing units, 1990	Per capita income, 1985 (Dollars)	Land area,[3] 1990 (Sq. Km.)
			Places of 10,000 or more		Race								
		1990	1980	Percent change, 1980–1990	White	Black	Am. Indian, Eskimo Aleut	Asian & Pacific Islander	Other race	Hispanic[2]			
		1	2	3	4	5	6	7	8	9	10	11	12
	INDIANA—Con.												
1740	Munster town	19 949	20 671	-3.5	18 993	87	15	720	134	528	7 393	16 214	19.5
1750	Nappanee	5 510	NA	NA	5 478	3	2	11	16	62	2 196	9 506	9.4
1760	New Albany	36 322	37 103	-2.1	33 842	2 251	68	96	65	178	15 593	9 499	34.6
1775	Newburgh town	2 880	NA	NA	2 832	26	6	15	1	9	1 288	11 402	2.9
1785	New Castle	17 753	20 056	-11.5	17 275	382	33	29	34	101	7 829	8 407	14.8
1800	New Haven	9 320	NA	NA	9 203	24	25	26	42	111	3 531	10 598	15.1
1855	New Whiteland town	4 097	NA	NA	4 083	0	5	6	3	27	1 343	8 855	2.8
1860	Noblesville	17 655	12 056	46.4	17 312	174	41	110	18	85	7 128	12 699	22.4
1885	North Manchester town	6 383	NA	NA	6 239	48	18	49	29	71	2 169	9 685	8.1
1892	North Terre Haute CDP	4 331	NA	NA	4 236	71	2	15	7	23	1 852	NA	8.5
1895	North Vernon	5 311	NA	NA	5 181	95	6	18	11	40	2 262	8 293	8.3
1905	Oakland City	2 810	NA	NA	2 766	17	0	23	4	6	1 235	8 746	2.8
1911	Oak Park CDP	5 630	NA	NA	5 118	468	6	31	7	27	2 078	NA	6.6
1995	Paoli town	3 542	NA	NA	3 531	3	7	0	1	3	1 596	8 352	9.8
2035	Peru	12 843	13 764	-6.7	11 988	414	332	61	48	140	5 732	9 084	10.0
2060	Plainfield town	10 433	NA	NA	10 301	46	33	43	10	42	4 303	11 358	9.6
2070	Plymouth	8 303	NA	NA	7 969	17	22	70	225	420	3 466	8 787	13.9
2080	Portage	29 060	27 409	6.0	28 229	117	58	150	506	1 854	10 864	10 139	53.9
2085	Porter town	3 118	NA	NA	3 085	1	4	12	16	74	1 245	11 262	16.4
2090	Portland	6 483	NA	NA	6 405	9	11	27	31	58	2 850	8 396	8.3
2110	Princeton	8 127	NA	NA	7 680	362	18	50	17	50	3 734	9 520	9.2
2130	Rensselaer	5 045	NA	NA	4 998	5	17	9	16	72	2 096	10 626	6.3
2140	Richmond	38 705	41 327	-6.3	34 677	3 553	107	233	135	264	16 942	9 126	47.6
2180	Rochester	5 969	NA	NA	5 917	16	10	16	10	16	2 928	9 390	10.5
2190	Rockville town	2 706	NA	NA	2 689	3	14	0	0	15	1 344	9 738	3.7
2220	Rushville	5 533	NA	NA	5 397	99	5	29	3	7	2 313	8 200	4.9
2240	St. John town	4 921	NA	NA	4 859	2	5	29	26	136	1 567	11 688	15.8
2260	Salem	5 619	NA	NA	5 587	15	4	9	4	25	2 496	9 142	9.7
2280	Schererville town	19 926	13 209	50.9	19 330	143	28	254	171	711	7 703	12 297	33.6
2290	Scottsburg	5 334	NA	NA	5 284	12	10	27	1	16	2 240	9 039	10.4
2300	Sellersburg town	5 745	NA	NA	5 704	3	22	12	4	28	2 153	10 009	5.8
2310	Seymour	15 576	15 050	3.5	15 250	124	27	149	26	67	6 384	9 081	14.5
2325	Shelbyville	15 336	14 989	2.3	14 934	301	22	68	11	51	6 567	8 906	16.6
2366	Simonton Lake CDP	3 554	NA	NA	3 440	47	22	39	6	40	1 340	NA	9.1
2375	South Bend	105 511	109 727	-3.8	80 221	22 049	386	916	1 939	3 546	45 757	10 154	94.3
2378	South Haven CDP	6 112	NA	NA	6 012	16	18	11	55	289	1 934	NA	2.6
2390	Speedway town	13 092	12 641	3.6	12 214	715	21	109	33	93	6 728	13 545	12.3
2395	Spencer town	2 609	NA	NA	2 599	1	5	3	1	8	1 173	8 682	3.1
2455	Sullivan	4 663	NA	NA	4 636	7	11	5	4	14	2 255	8 965	5.0
2490	Syracuse town	2 729	NA	NA	2 688	9	0	18	14	43	1 235	10 885	4.2
2495	Tell City	8 088	NA	NA	8 044	7	8	24	5	22	3 446	9 096	9.7
2505	Terre Haute	57 483	61 125	-6.0	50 947	5 415	239	658	224	755	24 077	8 643	71.6
2515	Tipton	4 751	NA	NA	4 701	8	3	13	26	53	2 120	10 226	3.9
2540	Tri-Lakes CDP	3 299	NA	NA	3 288	0	6	1	4	7	1 450	NA	91.1
2555	Union City	3 612	NA	NA	3 546	13	12	7	34	82	1 659	9 574	3.9
2570	Upland town	3 295	NA	NA	3 227	32	7	21	8	20	798	5 984	9.6
2575	Valparaiso	24 414	22 247	9.7	23 873	142	50	275	74	346	9 293	11 174	26.3
2610	Vincennes	19 859	20 857	-4.8	19 167	465	36	151	40	116	8 350	8 067	16.6
2615	Wabash	12 127	12 985	-6.6	11 839	66	131	50	41	140	4 944	9 544	13.8
2650	Warsaw	10 968	10 647	3.0	10 606	117	32	90	123	312	4 498	10 502	24.4
2655	Washington	10 838	11 325	-4.3	10 727	70	16	17	8	50	4 787	8 208	11.0
2685	Westfield town	3 304	NA	NA	3 244	19	14	18	9	27	1 312	9 798	6.1
2695	West Lafayette	25 907	21 247	21.9	22 974	559	40	2 151	183	511	9 465	11 050	12.7
2715	Westville town	5 255	NA	NA	3 990	1 232	14	4	15	107	879	7 242	7.8
2745	Whiting	5 155	NA	NA	4 699	3	7	28	418	735	2 318	10 701	4.6
2770	Winchester	5 095	NA	NA	5 057	10	18	4	6	33	2 286	9 377	6.1
2785	Winona Lake town	4 053	NA	NA	3 934	22	9	43	45	145	1 392	7 864	6.0
2840	Yorktown town	4 106	NA	NA	4 072	10	7	17	0	15	1 573	10 486	7.4
2845	Zionsville town	5 281	NA	NA	5 241	14	3	20	3	23	1 923	17 106	6.5
19	IOWA	2 776 755	2 913 808	-4.7	2 683 090	48 090	7 349	25 476	12 750	32 647	1 143 669	10 096	144 716.0
0020	Adel	3 304	NA	NA	3 289	4	1	3	7	24	1 285	10 464	8.2
0050	Albia	3 870	NA	NA	3 832	9	11	16	2	6	1 772	10 334	8.0
0075	Algona	6 015	NA	NA	5 940	6	2	46	21	45	2 572	9 582	11.1
0105	Altoona	7 191	NA	NA	7 092	24	16	30	29	80	2 582	10 803	11.4
0115	Ames	47 198	45 775	3.1	42 421	1 155	66	3 254	302	738	16 058	10 009	50.9
0120	Anamosa	5 100	NA	NA	4 751	296	23	8	22	52	1 610	9 105	4.6
0140	Ankeny	18 482	15 429	19.8	18 259	72	24	94	33	109	6 983	12 256	34.1
0230	Atlantic	7 432	NA	NA	7 393	3	14	14	8	42	3 356	10 780	21.1
0240	Audubon	2 524	NA	NA	2 521	1	1	1	0	9	1 185	9 361	4.4
0355	Belle Plaine	2 834	NA	NA	2 823	3	4	1	3	6	1 289	9 591	7.9
0365	Belmond	2 500	NA	NA	2 474	4	4	12	6	13	1 171	10 570	5.0
0395	Bettendorf	28 132	27 376	2.8	27 233	386	49	271	193	606	11 063	14 430	55.0

1. Codes shown are 2-digit FIPS codes for states; 4-digit census place codes for places; and 3-digit FIPS county codes followed by 3-digit census MCD codes for minor civil divisions (MCDs). MCD names are followed by county names in parentheses. 2. Hispanic persons may be of any race. 3. Dry land or land partially or temporarily covered by water.

State/ Place/ MCD[1] code	Place	Population			Population characteristics, 1990						Total housing units, 1990	Per capita income, 1985 (Dollars)	Land area,[3] 1990 (Sq. Km.)
		1990	Places of 10,000 or more		Race					Hispanic[2]			
			1980	Percent change, 1980–1990	White	Black	Am. Indian, Eskimo Aleut	Asian & Pacific Islander	Other race				
		1	2	3	4	5	6	7	8	9	10	11	12
	IOWA—Con.												
0440	Bloomfield	2 580	NA	NA	2 546	1	5	19	9	21	1 174	9 361	5.3
0465	Boone	12 392	12 602	-1.7	12 305	19	8	49	11	48	5 332	10 475	22.9
0560	Burlington	27 208	29 529	-7.9	25 609	1 219	55	179	146	348	11 777	10 411	34.3
0595	Camanche	4 436	NA	NA	4 400	7	9	16	4	30	1 769	10 710	22.3
0615	Carlisle	3 241	NA	NA	3 214	1	7	6	13	39	1 230	10 387	7.9
0625	Carroll	9 579	NA	NA	9 519	5	6	38	11	35	3 779	10 312	13.6
0635	Carter Lake	3 200	NA	NA	3 112	2	53	8	25	76	1 149	9 283	4.7
0665	Cedar Falls	34 298	36 310	-5.5	33 241	385	64	485	123	258	12 066	10 462	73.7
0670	Cedar Rapids	108 751	110 217	-1.3	103 884	3 127	260	1 067	413	1 243	45 473	12 301	138.5
0685	Centerville	5 936	NA	NA	5 828	72	7	17	12	47	2 821	8 414	10.7
0700	Chariton	4 616	NA	NA	4 576	3	8	12	17	15	2 199	9 948	9.0
0705	Charles City	7 878	NA	NA	7 825	4	6	14	29	54	3 505	9 008	14.1
0730	Cherokee	6 026	NA	NA	5 951	20	30	20	5	30	2 663	10 301	15.9
0765	Clarinda	5 104	NA	NA	4 944	71	17	62	10	27	2 164	9 894	14.1
0770	Clarion	2 703	NA	NA	2 680	1	1	9	12	39	1 264	10 488	7.1
0790	Clear Lake	8 183	NA	NA	8 039	19	6	87	32	106	3 964	11 380	26.4
0810	Clinton	29 201	32 828	-11.0	28 175	709	96	145	76	205	12 584	10 516	91.9
0820	Clive	7 462	NA	NA	7 210	66	6	149	31	63	2 927	16 132	12.4
0910	Coralville	10 347	NA	NA	9 523	384	37	340	63	190	4 757	12 372	20.3
0945	Council Bluffs	54 315	56 449	-3.8	53 118	434	154	226	383	1 313	22 244	9 996	95.3
0965	Cresco	3 669	NA	NA	3 659	3	1	5	1	15	1 651	11 101	8.2
0970	Creston	7 911	NA	NA	7 823	8	18	45	17	35	3 618	10 241	13.2
1040	Davenport	95 333	103 264	-7.7	84 968	7 521	388	1 000	1 456	3 300	40 343	11 338	158.9
1065	Decorah	8 063	NA	NA	7 832	39	3	170	19	32	2 836	9 934	15.3
1115	Denison	6 604	NA	NA	6 435	57	25	75	12	54	2 725	10 006	14.1
1130	Des Moines	193 187	191 003	1.1	172 417	13 741	699	4 602	1 728	4 629	83 289	12 134	194.9
1140	De Witt	4 514	NA	NA	4 473	9	10	17	5	21	1 902	10 083	12.3
1215	Dubuque	57 546	62 321	-7.7	56 626	331	69	368	152	370	22 377	10 317	59.7
1255	Dyersville	3 703	NA	NA	3 698	1	2	2	0	1	1 457	10 996	12.1
1265	Eagle Grove	3 671	NA	NA	3 652	4	3	5	7	15	1 641	9 126	10.3
1315	Eldora	3 038	NA	NA	2 964	41	12	8	13	33	1 293	10 661	11.3
1320	Eldridge	3 378	NA	NA	3 352	2	8	9	7	26	1 170	10 942	24.4
1385	Emmetsburg	3 940	NA	NA	3 912	4	14	6	4	16	1 740	8 549	9.2
1400	Estherville	6 720	NA	NA	6 648	17	9	27	19	51	2 907	8 590	13.4
1405	Evansdale	4 638	NA	NA	4 589	10	18	13	8	50	1 755	7 974	10.9
1435	Fairfield	9 768	NA	NA	9 513	82	16	133	24	114	4 087	9 562	13.4
1505	Forest City	4 430	NA	NA	4 349	30	5	35	11	30	1 727	10 020	10.1
1515	Fort Dodge	25 894	29 423	-12.0	24 694	852	81	137	130	394	11 212	10 244	37.3
1520	Fort Madison	11 618	13 520	-14.1	10 678	565	21	48	306	552	5 209	10 274	24.0
1585	Garner	2 916	NA	NA	2 894	0	0	8	14	21	1 202	9 155	4.9
1640	Glenwood	4 571	NA	NA	4 533	13	7	5	13	34	1 792	9 128	5.1
1755	Grimes	2 653	NA	NA	2 620	3	3	17	10	33	1 005	NA	18.3
1760	Grinnell	8 902	NA	NA	8 612	80	17	169	24	58	3 407	10 410	9.8
1810	Hampton	4 133	NA	NA	4 056	3	1	7	66	114	1 916	10 378	9.9
1840	Harlan	5 148	NA	NA	5 118	1	11	14	4	11	2 253	10 902	11.3
1925	Hiawatha	4 986	NA	NA	4 875	48	19	34	10	33	2 189	10 649	7.8
1990	Humboldt	4 438	NA	NA	4 403	2	8	22	3	17	1 993	10 593	11.7
2020	Independence	5 972	NA	NA	5 943	10	1	6	12	31	2 480	10 023	8.7
2025	Indianola	11 340	10 843	4.6	11 227	32	17	48	16	56	4 304	10 433	21.7
2040	Iowa City	59 738	50 508	18.3	54 410	1 516	116	3 341	355	1 018	22 464	11 280	57.0
2045	Iowa Falls	5 424	NA	NA	5 312	68	6	25	13	27	2 400	10 496	12.8
2075	Jefferson	4 292	NA	NA	4 261	3	4	22	2	14	2 029	10 605	13.3
2089	Johnston	4 702	NA	NA	4 623	19	9	41	10	39	1 881	14 312	36.1
2145	Keokuk	12 451	13 536	-8.0	11 832	497	26	73	23	80	5 582	10 286	23.9
2210	Knoxville	8 232	NA	NA	8 130	45	14	38	5	36	3 420	10 162	10.9
2325	Le Claire	2 734	NA	NA	2 703	3	7	7	14	65	1 076	10 385	10.9
2355	Le Mars	8 454	NA	NA	8 386	33	2	23	10	27	3 280	10 667	13.6
2615	Manchester	5 137	NA	NA	5 101	4	12	17	3	21	2 102	9 081	10.6
2645	Maquoketa	6 111	NA	NA	6 065	10	10	13	13	38	2 724	9 680	8.7
2670	Marion	20 403	19 474	4.8	20 127	72	30	138	36	150	7 998	11 865	24.7
2685	Marshalltown	25 178	26 938	-6.5	24 455	253	86	270	114	248	10 630	11 320	39.1
2710	Mason City	29 040	30 144	-3.7	28 249	269	31	151	340	844	12 669	10 430	66.3
2850	Missouri Valley	2 888	NA	NA	2 880	1	2	3	2	6	1 232	9 814	5.9
2900	Monticello	3 522	NA	NA	3 510	2	1	8	1	14	1 529	9 921	9.2
2960	Mount Pleasant	8 027	NA	NA	7 627	198	27	143	32	62	3 031	9 603	18.6
2975	Mount Vernon	3 657	NA	NA	3 564	21	6	54	12	28	1 033	9 950	9.0
2990	Muscatine	22 881	23 467	-2.5	21 450	166	52	139	1 074	1 863	9 297	11 016	44.5
3015	Nevada	6 009	NA	NA	5 886	17	16	74	16	24	2 558	9 915	8.6
3035	New Hampton	3 660	NA	NA	3 649	0	3	3	5	9	1 550	9 591	6.5
3070	Newton	14 789	15 292	-3.3	14 607	32	20	99	31	113	6 477	11 311	23.2
3115	North Liberty	2 926	NA	NA	2 896	6	0	11	13	48	1 162	NA	12.4
3130	Norwalk	5 726	NA	NA	5 640	29	3	39	15	70	1 921	10 123	13.2
3165	Oelwein	6 493	NA	NA	6 421	7	7	14	44	140	2 918	8 590	9.4

1. Codes shown are 2-digit FIPS codes for states; 4-digit census place codes for places; and 3-digit FIPS county codes followed by 3-digit census MCD codes for minor civil divisions (MCDs). MCD names are followed by county names in parentheses. 2. Hispanic persons may be of any race. 3. Dry land or land partially or temporarily covered by water.

State/ Place/ MCD[1] code	Place	Population 1990	Places of 10,000 or more 1980	Places of 10,000 or more Percent change, 1980–1990	Race: White	Race: Black	Race: Am. Indian, Eskimo Aleut	Race: Asian & Pacific Islander	Race: Other race	Hispanic[2]	Total housing units, 1990	Per capita income, 1985 (Dollars)	Land area,[3] 1990 (Sq. Km.)
		1	2	3	4	5	6	7	8	9	10	11	12
	IOWA—Con.												
3200	Onawa	2 936	NA	NA	2 912	1	16	4	3	15	1 354	8 225	12.6
3215	Orange City	4 940	NA	NA	4 858	18	7	53	4	7	1 590	8 546	6.3
3235	Osage	3 439	NA	NA	3 428	0	0	7	4	20	1 594	11 754	5.4
3240	Osceola	4 164	NA	NA	4 144	3	1	14	2	6	1 945	9 266	12.9
3245	Oskaloosa	10 632	10 989	-3.2	10 415	39	11	146	21	70	4 638	9 509	14.3
3275	Ottumwa	24 488	27 381	-10.6	23 954	249	71	141	73	180	10 912	9 969	40.6
3360	Pella	9 270	NA	NA	9 013	26	9	211	11	73	3 179	9 938	11.1
3370	Perry	6 652	NA	NA	6 586	25	4	17	20	47	2 860	10 144	8.8
3420	Pleasant Hill	3 671	NA	NA	3 550	42	8	53	18	81	1 322	12 644	12.6
3595	Red Oak	6 264	NA	NA	6 242	2	10	5	5	31	2 911	10 486	9.5
3695	Rock Rapids	2 601	NA	NA	2 577	2	6	15	1	2	1 157	10 506	10.2
3700	Rock Valley	2 540	NA	NA	2 494	1	4	39	2	6	1 022	7 767	4.0
3862	Saylorville CDP	2 709	NA	NA	2 667	27	1	10	4	9	1 021	NA	24.6
3890	Sergeant Bluff	2 772	NA	NA	2 671	16	30	44	11	37	922	NA	5.7
3930	Sheldon	4 937	NA	NA	4 895	5	10	27	0	14	2 008	8 637	10.9
3945	Shenandoah	5 572	NA	NA	5 487	9	22	9	45	139	2 591	11 010	8.1
3955	Sibley	2 815	NA	NA	2 802	0	2	8	3	7	1 184	8 974	3.6
3975	Sioux Center	5 074	NA	NA	4 995	4	8	61	6	11	1 620	7 574	13.6
3980	Sioux City	80 505	82 003	-1.8	74 525	1 848	1 624	1 195	1 313	2 624	32 177	10 146	140.6
4025	Spencer	11 066	11 726	-5.6	10 968	6	16	67	9	31	4 824	9 887	25.9
4035	Spirit Lake	3 871	NA	NA	3 847	14	7	1	2	10	1 730	9 619	6.6
4105	Storm Lake	8 769	NA	NA	8 391	42	9	304	23	102	3 557	9 723	9.4
4110	Story City	2 959	NA	NA	2 914	1	4	40	0	1	1 240	10 814	5.4
4185	Tama	2 697	NA	NA	2 565	7	83	31	11	42	1 159	8 535	7.9
4245	Tipton	2 998	NA	NA	2 988	0	4	2	4	25	1 313	10 851	4.5
4330	Urbandale	23 500	17 869	31.5	22 837	229	25	355	54	183	9 296	15 786	27.8
4390	Vinton	5 103	NA	NA	5 059	7	15	17	5	35	2 089	11 697	10.9
4445	Washington	7 074	NA	NA	6 943	58	4	29	40	123	3 014	11 659	12.0
4455	Waterloo	66 467	75 985	-12.5	57 581	8 068	118	449	251	531	29 023	10 478	156.9
4470	Waukee	2 512	NA	NA	2 503	0	1	7	1	8	1 008	NA	9.0
4475	Waukon	4 019	NA	NA	4 003	0	6	10	0	8	1 758	10 008	6.5
4480	Waverly	8 539	NA	NA	8 354	64	8	100	13	37	3 160	11 030	28.5
4500	Webster City	7 894	NA	NA	7 807	2	13	65	7	48	3 435	10 541	22.1
4540	West Burlington	3 083	NA	NA	3 025	29	1	12	16	37	1 443	10 593	12.7
4550	West Des Moines	31 702	21 894	44.8	30 539	425	41	496	201	612	13 668	17 302	46.4
4565	West Liberty	2 935	NA	NA	2 479	7	10	117	322	679	1 103	11 105	3.9
4640	Wilton	2 577	NA	NA	2 539	0	3	7	28	34	1 074	10 580	4.7
4645	Windsor Heights	5 190	NA	NA	5 077	41	8	52	12	43	2 302	20 644	3.6
4655	Winterset	4 196	NA	NA	4 166	1	15	7	7	20	1 806	9 373	8.0
20	KANSAS	2 477 574	2 364 236	4.8	2 231 986	143 076	21 965	31 750	48 797	93 670	1 044 112	10 684	211 921.6
0010	Abilene	6 242	NA	NA	6 077	58	22	23	62	117	2 856	10 144	9.2
0090	Andover	4 047	NA	NA	3 989	8	22	11	17	70	1 499	11 149	9.4
0095	Anthony	2 516	NA	NA	2 467	8	23	4	14	47	1 257	9 119	3.9
0110	Arkansas City	12 762	13 201	-3.3	11 481	641	370	45	225	457	5 774	9 433	19.2
0135	Atchison	10 656	11 407	-6.6	9 557	848	66	85	100	270	4 267	8 416	16.8
0160	Augusta	7 876	NA	NA	7 682	24	88	33	49	132	3 251	10 570	7.4
0175	Baldwin City	2 961	NA	NA	2 856	38	19	25	23	41	961	7 406	3.9
0200	Baxter Springs	4 351	NA	NA	4 042	39	252	11	7	27	1 999	8 199	7.1
0212	Bel Aire	3 695	NA	NA	3 297	301	21	43	33	66	1 280	NA	5.6
0220	Belleville	2 517	NA	NA	2 497	2	6	11	1	5	1 260	10 938	4.9
0225	Beloit	4 066	NA	NA	3 997	44	16	5	4	15	1 820	8 772	9.0
0300	Bonner Springs	6 413	NA	NA	5 875	386	61	12	79	171	2 509	9 508	40.8
0355	Burlington	2 735	NA	NA	2 709	5	13	4	4	18	1 221	9 495	4.8
0445	Chanute	9 488	10 506	-9.7	9 098	171	81	28	110	313	4 426	9 796	15.2
0500	Clay Center	4 613	NA	NA	4 579	10	9	10	5	19	2 213	9 096	6.0
0535	Coffeyville	12 917	15 185	-14.9	10 726	1 625	400	51	115	253	6 203	9 044	18.2
0540	Colby	5 396	NA	NA	5 284	28	15	29	40	66	2 272	9 727	8.0
0560	Columbus	3 268	NA	NA	3 168	10	70	10	10	61	1 537	8 671	5.0
0570	Concordia	6 167	NA	NA	6 075	34	13	2	43	59	2 848	9 011	8.0
0680	Derby	14 699	NA	NA	14 214	155	93	119	118	333	5 002	12 506	12.0
0695	Dodge City	21 129	18 001	17.4	16 759	458	124	635	3 153	3 845	8 258	10 162	31.3
0765	Edwardsville	3 979	NA	NA	3 702	234	12	4	27	88	1 520	9 198	23.2
0780	El Dorado	11 504	10 510	9.5	11 072	172	74	61	125	252	5 241	9 928	15.6
0840	Emporia	25 512	25 287	0.9	22 780	702	149	662	1 219	1 989	10 732	9 706	23.8
0875	Eudora	3 006	NA	NA	2 911	9	64	5	17	61	1 136	8 795	3.8
0880	Eureka	2 974	NA	NA	2 907	6	33	0	28	60	1 630	8 486	5.0
0895	Fairway	4 173	NA	NA	4 074	25	6	34	34	77	1 863	23 338	3.0
0924	Fort Riley North CDP	12 848	16 063	-20.0	7 180	4 240	143	409	876	1 262	1 855	NA	13.2
0925	Fort Scott	8 362	NA	NA	7 901	398	28	16	19	51	4 034	9 872	13.0
0945	Fredonia	2 599	NA	NA	2 551	12	17	1	18	29	1 354	9 461	5.9
0955	Frontenac	2 588	NA	NA	2 546	1	31	6	4	25	1 134	9 214	8.8
0970	Galena	3 308	NA	NA	3 151	29	123	1	4	29	1 442	6 902	11.8

1. Codes shown are 2-digit FIPS codes for states; 4-digit census place codes for places; and 3-digit FIPS county codes followed by 3-digit census MCD codes for minor civil divisions (MCDs). MCD names are followed by county names in parentheses. 2. Hispanic persons may be of any race. 3. Dry land or land partially or temporarily covered by water.

State/ Place/ MCD[1] code	Place	Population 1990	Places of 10,000 or more 1980	Places of 10,000 or more Percent change, 1980–1990	Race White	Race Black	Race Am. Indian, Eskimo Aleut	Race Asian & Pacific Islander	Race Other race	Hispanic[2]	Total housing units, 1990	Per capita income, 1985 (Dollars)	Land area,[3] 1990 (Sq. Km.)
		1	2	3	4	5	6	7	8	9	10	11	12
	KANSAS—Con.												
0985	Garden City	24 097	18 256	32.0	18 859	405	158	962	3 713	6 092	8 583	9 564	19.1
0995	Gardner	3 191	NA	NA	3 112	33	20	8	18	70	1 251	NA	7.5
1005	Garnett	3 210	NA	NA	3 144	16	36	0	14	34	1 550	8 884	7.8
1035	Girard	2 794	NA	NA	2 748	23	18	5	0	6	1 258	8 254	4.8
1070	Goodland	4 983	NA	NA	4 706	17	4	15	241	371	2 360	8 820	11.2
1090	Great Bend	15 427	16 608	-7.1	14 731	232	85	61	318	575	7 050	11 253	25.1
1210	Hays	17 767	16 301	9.0	17 503	85	37	104	38	122	7 770	10 388	15.6
1215	Haysville	8 364	NA	NA	8 072	24	132	64	72	189	2 907	9 884	8.4
1230	Herington	2 685	NA	NA	2 617	30	10	3	25	68	1 360	9 617	5.6
1240	Hesston	3 012	NA	NA	2 866	47	8	36	55	82	1 014	8 485	6.1
1245	Hiawatha	3 603	NA	NA	3 419	88	59	10	27	48	1 623	9 949	5.1
1260	Hillsboro	2 704	NA	NA	2 650	20	9	15	10	16	1 093	9 307	4.4
1265	Hoisington	3 182	NA	NA	3 125	17	9	9	22	79	1 532	10 752	2.9
1280	Holton	3 196	NA	NA	3 112	8	73	2	1	19	1 453	10 773	6.0
1325	Hugoton	3 179	NA	NA	2 805	17	26	14	317	392	1 360	11 109	3.6
1350	Hutchinson	39 308	40 284	-2.4	35 951	1 607	250	160	1 340	2 127	17 163	10 326	53.6
1355	Independence	9 942	10 598	-6.2	8 933	677	155	47	130	315	4 735	10 208	11.7
1370	Iola	6 351	NA	NA	6 071	196	38	27	19	73	2 886	9 223	9.2
1415	Junction City	20 604	19 305	6.7	13 336	5 592	128	978	570	1 274	8 870	8 914	17.5
1430	Kansas City	149 767	161 093	-7.0	97 356	43 834	1 025	1 854	5 698	10 705	64 457	8 757	279.2
1450	Kingman	3 196	NA	NA	3 151	2	10	7	26	44	1 500	9 159	8.0
1515	Lansing	7 120	NA	NA	5 965	887	59	100	109	167	2 012	8 354	22.1
1520	Larned	4 490	NA	NA	4 179	144	11	43	113	198	2 231	10 748	6.0
1535	Lawrence	65 608	52 738	24.4	57 149	3 192	1 945	2 533	789	1 941	25 893	9 372	59.4
1540	Leavenworth	38 495	33 656	14.4	30 700	6 094	275	769	657	1 806	12 568	9 537	58.8
1545	Leawood	19 693	13 360	47.4	19 022	191	31	433	16	177	7 210	26 246	38.8
1570	Lenexa	34 034	18 639	82.6	32 193	821	144	693	183	580	13 496	15 740	75.2
1610	Liberal	16 573	14 911	11.1	12 578	1 097	132	442	2 324	3 369	6 663	10 513	24.6
1630	Lindsborg	3 076	NA	NA	3 017	22	4	17	16	25	1 182	8 567	3.6
1715	Lyons	3 688	NA	NA	3 496	56	17	5	114	167	1 808	10 524	5.3
1745	McPherson	12 422	11 753	5.7	11 992	182	70	77	101	224	5 118	10 681	13.3
1775	Manhattan	37 712	32 645	15.5	33 960	1 877	204	1 231	440	1 059	15 558	9 950	28.6
1810	Marysville	3 359	NA	NA	3 329	0	19	4	7	30	1 615	10 642	4.9
1860	Merriam	11 821	10 794	9.5	10 950	434	52	199	186	345	5 366	14 811	11.1
1900	Mission	9 504	NA	NA	9 081	170	24	85	144	292	5 239	16 783	6.6
1905	Mission Hills	3 446	NA	NA	3 408	1	5	31	1	28	1 333	48 966	5.2
1985	Mulvane	4 674	NA	NA	4 573	19	39	10	33	105	1 695	11 157	4.6
2020	Neodesha	2 837	NA	NA	2 800	3	22	5	7	19	1 407	8 548	2.9
2050	Newton	16 700	16 332	2.3	15 379	410	92	114	705	1 325	6 955	10 233	20.5
2075	Norton	3 017	NA	NA	2 968	1	6	13	29	52	1 485	9 996	4.9
2093	Oaklawn-Sunview CDP	3 240	NA	NA	2 527	314	85	264	50	119	1 166	NA	1.4
2120	Olathe	63 352	37 258	70.0	59 731	1 912	279	1 066	364	1 145	22 497	11 615	109.5
2155	Osage City	2 689	NA	NA	2 662	3	13	1	10	40	1 210	9 310	7.9
2160	Osawatomie	4 590	NA	NA	4 188	291	42	20	49	117	1 844	9 109	7.1
2185	Ottawa	10 667	11 016	-3.2	10 025	242	119	83	198	376	4 553	8 798	16.8
2194	Overland Park	111 790	81 784	36.7	106 648	2 051	341	2 145	605	2 198	48 043	16 404	144.2
2215	Paola	4 698	NA	NA	4 408	252	14	3	21	61	1 892	10 627	8.9
2230	Park City	5 050	NA	NA	4 764	76	94	13	103	162	1 741	9 966	7.5
2245	Parsons	11 924	12 898	-7.6	10 668	913	109	68	166	421	5 451	9 087	16.6
2285	Phillipsburg	2 828	NA	NA	2 778	11	8	25	6	23	1 398	9 503	3.9
2290	Pittsburg	17 775	18 770	-5.3	16 745	408	146	391	85	208	8 445	8 495	25.9
2335	Prairie Village	23 186	24 657	-6.0	22 615	153	44	264	110	360	10 031	19 906	16.1
2340	Pratt	6 687	NA	NA	6 448	110	33	14	82	108	3 209	10 934	8.2
2465	Roeland Park	7 706	NA	NA	7 215	192	30	90	179	385	3 317	13 963	4.2
2500	Russell	4 781	NA	NA	4 708	34	20	5	14	35	2 495	11 934	11.1
2540	Salina	42 303	41 843	1.1	39 371	1 500	217	523	692	1 128	18 411	10 446	54.4
2575	Scott City	3 785	NA	NA	3 672	4	9	19	81	99	1 692	9 793	4.1
2635	Shawnee	37 993	29 625	28.2	36 038	815	133	656	351	1 005	15 217	13 861	108.2
2795	Topeka	119 883	115 266	4.0	101 550	12 761	1 538	948	3 086	6 930	54 664	11 248	142.9
2840	Ulysses	5 474	NA	NA	4 527	2	57	39	849	1 372	1 979	10 613	6.7
2855	Valley Center	3 624	NA	NA	3 554	7	17	14	32	70	1 340	11 026	4.2
2925	Wamego	3 706	NA	NA	3 653	20	17	13	3	59	1 468	8 975	3.3
2960	Wellington	8 411	NA	NA	7 777	130	88	26	390	664	3 754	10 547	12.7
3040	Wichita	304 011	279 272	8.9	250 176	34 301	3 527	7 773	8 234	15 250	135 069	11 764	298.2
3090	Winfield	11 931	10 736	11.1	10 933	379	109	274	236	475	4 835	10 201	27.0
21	KENTUCKY	3 685 296	3 660 334	0.7	3 391 832	262 907	5 769	17 812	6 976	21 984	1 506 845	8 614	102 906.8
0020	Alexandria	5 592	NA	NA	5 577	1	2	11	1	8	1 949	10 116	14.6
0050	Ashland	23 622	27 064	-12.7	22 914	590	21	76	21	60	11 021	10 122	27.8
0070	Barbourville	3 658	NA	NA	3 486	134	18	14	6	17	1 523	7 627	8.1
0075	Bardstown	6 801	NA	NA	5 502	1 236	6	49	8	44	2 803	9 650	11.7
0095	Beaver Dam	2 904	NA	NA	2 796	95	6	7	0	11	1 297	9 004	5.4

1. Codes shown are 2-digit FIPS codes for states; 4-digit census place codes for places; and 3-digit FIPS county codes followed by 3-digit census MCD codes for minor civil divisions (MCDs). MCD names are followed by county names in parentheses. 2. Hispanic persons may be of any race. 3. Dry land or land partially or temporarily covered by water.

State/ Place/ MCD[1] code	Place	Population			Population characteristics, 1990						Total housing units, 1990	Per capita income, 1985 (Dollars)	Land area,[3] 1990 (Sq. Km.)
			Places of 10,000 or more		Race								
		1990	1980	Percent change, 1980–1990	White	Black	Am. Indian, Eskimo Aleut	Asian & Pacific Islander	Other race	Hispanic[2]			
		1	2	3	4	5	6	7	8	9	10	11	12
	KENTUCKY—Con.												
0130	Bellevue	6 997	NA	NA	6 950	6	8	22	11	52	2 939	8 842	2.4
0145	Benton	3 899	NA	NA	3 874	7	6	6	6	18	1 813	10 139	9.2
0150	Berea	9 126	NA	NA	8 682	323	18	86	17	36	3 481	8 213	20.1
0200	Bowling Green	40 641	40 450	0.5	35 110	4 950	69	454	58	275	17 501	9 089	75.0
0252	Buechel CDP	7 081	NA	NA	6 156	829	14	58	24	63	3 416	NA	6.6
0272	Burlington CDP	6 070	NA	NA	5 935	62	11	49	13	48	2 170	NA	22.0
0305	Calvert City	2 531	NA	NA	2 521	0	9	0	1	11	1 048	NA	24.2
0320	Campbellsville	9 577	NA	NA	8 733	822	11	11	0	19	4 205	8 262	11.9
0340	Carrollton	3 715	NA	NA	3 588	107	6	14	0	15	1 663	8 858	5.8
0380	Central City	4 979	NA	NA	4 660	307	5	5	2	9	2 196	8 864	10.1
0430	Cold Spring	2 880	NA	NA	2 864	6	0	8	2	9	1 047	NA	5.6
0435	Columbia	3 845	NA	NA	3 531	294	6	11	3	16	1 648	9 006	8.7
0450	Corbin	7 419	NA	NA	7 385	4	9	18	3	34	3 446	9 293	13.3
0465	Covington	43 264	49 569	-12.7	39 579	3 319	80	187	99	282	19 117	8 016	34.3
0490	Crestview Hills	2 546	NA	NA	2 492	34	0	15	5	9	945	NA	4.9
0505	Cumberland	3 112	NA	NA	2 876	227	2	3	4	16	1 384	6 122	11.9
0510	Cynthiana	6 497	NA	NA	6 092	386	6	6	7	18	2 778	8 200	7.0
0515	Danville	12 420	12 942	-4.0	10 402	1 939	11	54	14	67	5 210	9 298	14.4
0520	Dawson Springs	3 129	NA	NA	3 084	29	10	6	0	11	1 429	8 277	9.6
0525	Dayton	6 576	NA	NA	6 547	7	11	6	5	24	2 449	7 341	3.4
0547	Douglass Hills	5 549	NA	NA	5 230	207	1	83	28	68	2 334	18 192	3.5
0595	Edgewood	8 143	NA	NA	8 039	22	4	77	1	43	2 510	13 704	10.8
0610	Elizabethtown	18 167	15 380	18.1	16 322	1 407	43	355	40	161	7 914	9 841	53.9
0625	Elsmere	6 847	NA	NA	6 509	313	5	11	9	23	2 394	8 424	6.5
0635	Erlanger	15 979	14 433	10.7	15 701	161	21	61	35	88	6 081	10 067	21.5
0649	Fairdale CDP	6 563	NA	NA	6 468	42	14	28	11	42	2 467	NA	14.8
0672	Fern Creek CDP	16 406	16 866	-2.7	15 459	814	21	70	42	109	5 996	NA	15.1
0675	Flatwoods	7 799	NA	NA	7 751	13	8	16	11	19	3 115	8 935	8.9
0685	Flemingsburg	3 071	NA	NA	2 880	186	1	2	2	13	1 365	8 244	5.8
0690	Florence	18 624	15 553	19.7	18 225	170	18	178	33	144	7 336	10 356	21.5
0706	Fort Campbell North CDP	18 861	17 211	9.6	11 751	5 230	167	580	1 133	1 777	2 957	NA	10.2
0708	Fort Knox CDP	21 495	31 055	-30.8	14 239	5 634	170	555	897	1 646	4 346	NA	54.2
0710	Fort Mitchell	7 438	NA	NA	7 310	58	4	56	10	35	3 354	14 708	7.8
0715	Fort Thomas	16 032	16 010	0.1	15 907	60	10	48	7	58	6 544	13 283	14.6
0720	Fort Wright	6 570	NA	NA	6 510	17	3	34	6	35	2 637	13 511	9.0
0735	Frankfort	25 968	25 973	0.0	22 705	3 026	47	147	43	146	11 880	11 042	37.7
0740	Franklin	7 607	NA	NA	6 188	1 387	14	11	7	27	3 257	8 651	18.2
0765	Fulton	3 078	NA	NA	2 417	639	5	15	2	4	1 474	8 534	6.8
0775	Georgetown	11 414	10 972	4.0	10 240	1 068	12	69	25	41	4 506	8 743	11.7
0795	Glasgow	12 351	12 958	-4.7	11 214	1 073	16	39	9	34	5 395	9 235	27.3
0823	Graymoor-Devondale	2 911	NA	NA	2 808	54	1	45	3	17	1 117	NA	1.9
0825	Grayson	3 510	NA	NA	3 471	16	9	8	6	19	1 343	7 361	5.5
0840	Greenville	4 689	NA	NA	4 227	448	1	8	5	8	2 025	10 490	8.6
0865	Harlan	2 686	NA	NA	2 481	185	4	16	0	3	1 277	8 638	4.4
0870	Harrodsburg	7 335	NA	NA	6 607	680	11	35	2	49	3 317	8 022	12.0
0875	Hartford	2 532	NA	NA	2 475	48	2	6	1	28	1 104	7 948	6.7
0890	Hazard	5 416	NA	NA	5 007	363	3	40	3	15	2 277	9 188	16.8
0915	Henderson	25 945	24 834	4.5	23 075	2 720	47	81	22	99	11 355	10 306	33.7
0917	Hendron CDP	3 712	NA	NA	3 662	31	3	12	4	14	1 576	NA	13.5
0920	Hickman	2 689	NA	NA	1 869	812	5	0	3	18	1 155	7 085	7.7
0930	Highland Heights	4 223	NA	NA	4 191	5	7	17	3	25	1 797	9 997	5.4
0931	Highview CDP	14 814	13 276	11.6	13 929	771	15	77	22	82	5 513	NA	16.9
0933	Hillview	6 119	NA	NA	6 049	32	11	23	4	39	1 887	7 215	5.0
0945	Hodgenville	2 721	NA	NA	2 340	370	9	0	2	18	1 174	7 590	3.6
0955	Hopkinsville	29 809	27 318	9.1	20 830	8 645	69	178	87	261	12 236	8 825	52.6
0968	Hurstbourne	4 420	NA	NA	4 182	98	4	128	8	74	1 898	24 300	4.8
0980	Independence	10 444	NA	NA	10 328	43	17	41	15	47	3 686	9 609	42.5
1000	Irvine	2 836	NA	NA	2 830	4	0	1	1	11	1 258	7 476	3.7
1025	Jeffersontown	23 221	15 736	47.6	21 452	1 529	25	181	34	221	9 369	12 052	25.0
1030	Jenkins	2 751	NA	NA	2 652	85	10	4	0	6	1 182	7 193	22.1
1095	La Grange	3 853	NA	NA	3 595	235	5	8	10	26	1 522	8 649	6.7
1105	Lakeside Park	3 131	NA	NA	3 090	24	2	7	8	29	1 311	13 960	2.0
1110	Lancaster	3 421	NA	NA	3 024	388	1	7	1	7	1 546	8 261	3.7
1120	Lawrenceburg	5 911	NA	NA	5 533	341	1	11	25	43	2 459	9 698	7.9
1130	Lebanon	5 695	NA	NA	4 651	1 028	6	9	1	10	2 388	8 112	10.7
1145	Leitchfield	4 965	NA	NA	4 857	66	21	16	5	26	2 114	7 366	11.7
1160	Lexington-Fayette	225 366	204 165	10.4	190 448	30 143	351	3 713	711	2 556	97 742	11 454	736.9
1195	London	5 757	NA	NA	5 618	109	15	10	5	28	2 553	8 489	19.9
1230	Louisville	269 063	298 455	-9.8	186 208	79 783	507	1 975	590	1 756	124 018	9 129	160.9
1240	Ludlow	4 736	NA	NA	4 727	1	0	4	4	15	1 901	8 472	2.3
1247	Lyndon	8 037	NA	NA	7 463	468	7	72	27	66	4 285	10 484	8.9
1280	Madisonville	16 200	16 979	-4.6	13 997	2 104	14	74	11	96	7 146	9 764	33.3
1290	Marion	3 320	NA	NA	3 234	77	6	3	0	11	1 555	8 027	8.3

1. Codes shown are 2-digit FIPS codes for states; 4-digit census place codes for places; and 3-digit FIPS county codes followed by 3-digit census MCD codes for minor civil divisions (MCDs). MCD names are followed by county names in parentheses. 2. Hispanic persons may be of any race. 3. Dry land or land partially or temporarily covered by water.

State/Place/MCD[1] code	Place	Population: 1990	Population: Places of 10,000 or more: 1980	Population: Places of 10,000 or more: Percent change, 1980–1990	Population characteristics, 1990: Race: White	Race: Black	Race: Am. Indian, Eskimo Aleut	Race: Asian & Pacific Islander	Race: Other race	Hispanic[2]	Total housing units, 1990	Per capita income, 1985 (Dollars)	Land area,[3] 1990 (Sq. Km.)
		1	2	3	4	5	6	7	8	9	10	11	12
	KENTUCKY—Con.												
1304	Massac CDP	3 733	NA	NA	3 673	35	8	9	8	23	1 466	NA	10.0
1305	Mayfield	9 935	10 705	-7.2	8 596	1 306	8	22	3	40	4 859	9 413	16.8
1310	Maysville	7 169	NA	NA	6 127	1 012	10	13	7	18	3 355	8 964	24.9
1320	Middlesborough	11 328	12 251	-7.5	10 624	620	18	62	4	39	4 849	6 972	19.8
1323	Middletown	5 016	NA	NA	4 732	227	10	30	17	55	2 106	10 882	12.5
1360	Monticello	5 357	NA	NA	5 183	160	11	2	1	13	2 360	6 451	13.3
1370	Morehead	8 357	NA	NA	7 951	286	15	92	13	33	2 326	6 498	23.6
1375	Morganfield	3 776	NA	NA	3 162	594	7	9	4	13	1 539	9 326	5.7
1395	Mount Sterling	5 362	NA	NA	4 712	622	9	10	9	25	2 396	8 283	5.8
1400	Mount Vernon	2 654	NA	NA	2 647	1	3	2	1	16	1 146	NA	5.3
1405	Mount Washington	5 226	NA	NA	5 190	17	13	3	3	7	1 870	8 406	8.8
1420	Murray	14 439	14 248	1.3	13 421	852	13	120	33	101	5 546	8 679	19.1
1433	Newburg CDP	21 647	24 612	-12.0	10 239	11 216	26	120	46	88	8 119	6 732	14.9
1445	Newport	18 871	21 587	-12.6	18 018	717	33	62	41	90	8 059	7 305	7.1
1450	Nicholasville	13 603	10 400	30.8	12 880	653	23	31	16	54	5 220	8 855	16.0
1478	Oakbrook CDP	4 113	NA	NA	4 025	17	7	57	7	45	1 644	NA	8.8
1479	Oak Grove	2 863	NA	NA	1 923	696	36	87	121	204	1 371	NA	24.6
1485	Okolona CDP	18 902	20 039	-5.7	18 111	635	35	91	30	83	7 297	NA	17.9
1495	Owensboro	53 549	54 450	-1.7	49 802	3 445	72	172	58	211	23 074	9 233	38.8
1520	Paducah	27 256	29 315	-7.0	21 370	5 693	54	91	48	154	13 150	10 056	45.5
1525	Paintsville	4 354	NA	NA	4 308	3	10	32	1	2	2 014	10 203	11.1
1530	Paris	8 730	NA	NA	7 300	1 401	12	13	4	22	3 743	8 650	13.3
1540	Park Hills	3 321	NA	NA	3 274	23	5	16	3	15	1 529	12 107	2.0
1580	Pikeville	6 324	NA	NA	6 083	183	9	45	4	19	2 738	9 211	33.7
1595	Pleasure Ridge Park CDP	25 131	27 332	-8.1	24 586	387	36	92	30	121	9 538	NA	20.5
1605	Prestonsburg	3 558	NA	NA	3 401	120	8	26	3	21	1 516	9 280	8.2
1615	Princeton	6 940	NA	NA	6 201	707	23	7	2	18	3 168	8 911	22.5
1618	Prospect	2 788	NA	NA	2 671	49	5	58	5	27	1 089	NA	9.8
1620	Providence	4 123	NA	NA	3 385	718	7	7	6	5	1 823	7 876	15.9
1630	Radcliff	19 772	14 519	36.2	14 607	3 903	73	817	372	779	8 251	8 937	26.8
1641	Reidland CDP	4 054	NA	NA	4 013	10	1	29	1	26	1 645	NA	12.5
1650	Richmond	21 155	21 705	-2.5	18 768	2 153	43	151	40	86	7 869	6 974	22.0
1685	Russell	4 014	NA	NA	3 924	15	0	69	6	19	1 535	13 162	10.2
1695	Russellville	7 454	NA	NA	6 135	1 276	18	18	7	34	3 292	8 125	23.7
1712	St. Dennis CDP	10 326	NA	NA	7 388	2 882	14	25	17	33	4 033	NA	6.8
1715	St. Matthews	15 800	13 354	18.3	15 152	467	13	139	29	145	8 235	13 149	10.4
1760	Scottsville	4 278	NA	NA	4 128	138	4	4	4	7	1 861	7 976	14.9
1790	Shelbyville	6 238	NA	NA	4 754	1 408	6	49	21	29	2 727	8 423	11.6
1795	Shepherdsville	4 805	NA	NA	4 715	65	2	17	6	21	1 803	9 116	21.2
1805	Shively	15 535	16 725	-7.1	13 149	2 311	12	49	14	80	6 852	10 807	12.1
1840	Somerset	10 733	10 649	0.8	10 168	504	18	38	5	44	4 633	8 315	25.0
1860	Southgate	3 266	NA	NA	3 228	2	4	32	0	11	1 546	9 834	3.7
1905	Springfield	2 875	NA	NA	2 200	660	3	8	4	20	1 193	7 759	5.8
1920	Stanford	2 686	NA	NA	2 390	258	33	3	2	4	1 159	8 163	7.1
1925	Stanton	2 795	NA	NA	2 778	6	5	5	1	4	1 135	7 569	5.1
1965	Taylor Mill	5 530	NA	NA	5 485	23	2	19	1	13	2 065	10 792	16.5
1975	Tompkinsville	2 861	NA	NA	2 581	272	4	4	0	16	1 292	7 094	9.1
1995	Valley Station CDP	22 840	24 474	-6.7	22 247	431	52	63	47	143	8 168	NA	20.4
2015	Versailles	7 269	NA	NA	6 472	754	11	4	28	53	2 984	10 566	7.0
2022	Villa Hills	7 739	NA	NA	7 631	24	7	72	5	23	2 619	14 967	9.2
2025	Vine Grove	3 586	NA	NA	3 144	285	26	82	49	85	1 430	8 261	11.8
2093	Westwood CDP	5 300	NA	NA	5 262	15	4	17	2	13	2 168	NA	10.1
2140	Williamsburg	5 493	NA	NA	5 259	200	12	19	3	10	2 034	6 563	12.1
2145	Williamstown	3 023	NA	NA	3 006	2	3	11	1	8	1 296	9 871	29.0
2150	Wilmore	4 215	NA	NA	4 057	71	15	49	23	63	1 287	6 072	4.8
2155	Winchester	15 799	15 216	3.8	14 199	1 527	30	25	18	63	6 592	9 073	14.6
2195	Woodlawn-Oakdale CDP	4 954	NA	NA	4 863	77	2	6	6	28	2 096	NA	15.4
22	LOUISIANA	4 219 973	4 206 124	0.3	2 839 138	1 299 281	18 541	41 099	21 914	93 044	1 716 241	8 836	112 836.0
0005	Abbeville	11 187	12 391	-9.7	6 607	4 146	16	381	37	138	4 802	7 562	12.8
0025	Alexandria	49 188	51 565	-4.6	24 416	24 243	91	342	96	506	20 348	8 592	64.1
0040	Amite City town	4 236	NA	NA	2 234	1 990	6	4	2	98	1 524	6 146	7.7
0048	Arabi CDP	8 787	10 248	-14.3	8 610	43	28	67	39	404	3 657	NA	4.6
0050	Arcadia town	3 079	NA	NA	1 450	1 626	2	0	1	16	1 182	7 469	7.7
0064	Avondale CDP	5 813	NA	NA	4 209	782	36	723	63	347	1 849	NA	14.1
0073	Baker	13 233	12 865	2.9	9 489	3 649	30	36	29	135	4 734	9 613	17.3
0077	Ball town	3 305	NA	NA	3 261	16	12	14	2	26	1 260	9 155	20.9
0090	Bastrop	13 916	15 527	-10.4	5 892	7 974	21	21	8	65	5 402	6 215	21.5
0095	Baton Rouge	219 531	219 419	0.1	118 429	96 346	318	3 673	765	3 442	97 115	10 505	191.5
0105	Bayou Cane CDP	15 876	15 723	1.0	14 422	1 126	207	43	78	307	5 957	NA	19.8
0107	Bayou Vista CDP	4 733	NA	NA	4 424	162	100	24	23	131	1 784	NA	4.7
0109	Belle Chasse CDP	8 512	NA	NA	7 876	497	31	67	41	281	2 900	NA	64.8

1. Codes shown are 2-digit FIPS codes for states; 4-digit census place codes for places; and 3-digit FIPS county codes followed by 3-digit census MCD codes for minor civil divisions (MCDs). MCD names are followed by county names in parentheses. 2. Hispanic persons may be of any race. 3. Dry land or land partially or temporarily covered by water.

Table D. Places — **Population, Housing, Money Income, and Land Area**

State/ Place/ MCD[1] code	Place	Population: 1990	Population: Places of 10,000 or more: 1980	Population: Places of 10,000 or more: Percent change, 1980–1990	Population characteristics, 1990: Race: White	Race: Black	Race: Am. Indian, Eskimo Aleut	Race: Asian & Pacific Islander	Race: Other race	Hispanic[2]	Total housing units, 1990	Per capita income, 1985 (Dollars)	Land area,[3] 1990 (Sq. Km.)
		1	2	3	4	5	6	7	8	9	10	11	12
	LOUISIANA—Con.												
0120	Berwick town	4 375	NA	NA	3 880	403	60	25	7	78	1 730	9 344	13.1
0130	Bogalusa	14 280	16 976	-15.9	9 254	4 975	25	20	6	59	6 476	6 822	24.5
0137	Boothville-Venice CDP	2 743	NA	NA	1 810	783	80	62	8	50	974	NA	6.7
0140	Bossier City	52 721	50 861	3.7	41 817	9 521	202	794	387	1 387	21 815	9 361	98.5
0144	Boutte CDP	2 702	NA	NA	1 202	1 473	2	10	15	64	1 001	NA	13.3
0150	Breaux Bridge	6 515	NA	NA	3 542	2 955	9	2	7	65	2 588	7 391	16.7
0152	Bridge City CDP	8 327	NA	NA	4 483	3 537	65	149	93	277	3 029	NA	11.4
0153	Broadmoor CDP	3 218	NA	NA	3 154	20	3	26	15	84	1 063	NA	1.6
0155	Broussard town	3 213	NA	NA	2 332	869	4	5	3	47	1 300	8 549	7.9
0157	Brownfields CDP	5 229	NA	NA	3 860	1 338	9	19	3	29	1 921	NA	10.9
0158	Brownsville-Bawcomville CDP	7 397	NA	NA	6 506	840	34	6	11	82	2 977	NA	17.3
0175	Bunkie	5 044	NA	NA	2 816	2 172	3	0	53	103	1 945	6 375	6.9
0180	Buras-Triumph CDP	3 702	NA	NA	3 156	227	22	262	35	121	1 467	NA	13.0
0195	Carencro	5 429	NA	NA	3 471	1 940	9	0	9	54	2 145	7 412	14.3
0197	Carlyss CDP	3 305	NA	NA	3 259	20	11	8	7	40	1 255	NA	30.8
0203	Chalmette CDP	31 860	33 847	-5.9	31 143	92	98	359	168	1 572	12 380	NA	18.0
0207	Chauvin CDP	3 375	NA	NA	3 314	1	47	6	7	13	1 152	NA	12.0
0220	Church Point town	4 677	NA	NA	3 344	1 330	2	1	0	23	1 743	6 206	7.1
0223	Claiborne CDP	8 300	NA	NA	8 188	74	17	9	12	73	3 065	NA	26.0
0265	Cottonport town	2 600	NA	NA	1 277	1 317	3	1	2	25	733	NA	4.7
0280	Covington	7 691	NA	NA	5 939	1 683	25	29	15	138	3 358	10 043	17.4
0285	Crowley	13 983	16 026	-12.7	9 621	4 290	12	43	17	59	5 798	7 656	11.8
0294	Cut Off CDP	5 325	NA	NA	4 951	56	191	103	24	94	1 857	NA	33.2
0305	Delhi town	3 169	NA	NA	1 662	1 479	3	2	23	51	1 226	6 061	5.5
0315	Denham Springs	8 381	NA	NA	7 111	1 225	16	25	4	77	3 166	8 701	14.8
0320	De Quincy	3 474	NA	NA	2 779	679	9	5	2	15	1 499	7 672	7.8
0325	De Ridder	9 868	11 057	-10.8	6 173	3 522	28	100	45	193	4 139	8 311	20.2
0326	Des Allemands CDP	2 504	NA	NA	2 170	323	5	1	5	30	998	NA	17.7
0327	Destrehan CDP	8 031	NA	NA	6 999	900	14	46	72	296	2 901	NA	16.6
0340	Donaldsonville	7 949	NA	NA	3 271	4 638	4	2	34	98	2 836	6 474	6.6
0357	Dulac CDP	3 273	NA	NA	1 603	77	1 568	14	11	66	1 182	NA	58.3
0360	Eastwood CDP	2 987	NA	NA	2 756	199	8	17	7	43	1 117	NA	15.7
0361	Eden Isle CDP	3 768	NA	NA	3 651	50	12	40	15	78	2 053	NA	9.5
0362	Edgard CDP	2 753	NA	NA	202	2 549	1	0	1	4	889	NA	56.3
0372	Empire CDP	2 654	NA	NA	1 677	872	13	92	0	28	979	NA	13.8
0388	Estelle CDP	14 091	12 724	10.7	11 373	1 738	146	609	225	798	4 365	NA	13.1
0395	Eunice	11 162	12 489	-10.6	8 066	3 009	16	45	26	87	4 399	7 088	12.0
0405	Farmerville town	3 334	NA	NA	1 560	1 759	0	9	6	15	1 374	6 287	14.3
0415	Ferriday town	4 111	NA	NA	1 293	2 797	8	10	3	29	1 614	4 807	4.3
0427	Fort Polk North CDP	3 819	NA	NA	2 339	1 286	35	77	82	355	1 146	NA	10.3
0428	Fort Polk South CDP	10 911	12 498	-12.7	6 160	3 892	73	469	317	1 024	3 051	NA	16.0
0430	Franklin	9 004	NA	NA	4 996	3 919	44	23	22	87	3 365	7 508	11.4
0435	Franklinton town	4 007	NA	NA	1 965	2 033	1	8	0	11	1 512	5 726	12.4
0438	Galliano CDP	4 294	NA	NA	4 062	12	183	27	10	77	1 624	NA	21.0
0439	Gardere CDP	7 209	NA	NA	3 902	2 982	21	235	69	232	3 536	NA	8.9
0440	Garyville CDP	3 181	NA	NA	1 356	1 824	1	0	0	13	1 114	NA	48.5
0475	Gonzales	7 003	NA	NA	5 264	1 654	12	18	55	165	2 783	9 588	19.5
0490	Grambling town	5 484	NA	NA	57	5 406	5	8	8	24	1 145	5 211	12.1
0513	Gray CDP	4 260	NA	NA	2 507	1 704	33	7	9	55	1 496	NA	30.2
0525	Gretna	17 208	20 615	-16.5	10 792	5 866	69	247	234	752	7 987	8 886	9.1
0540	Hahnville CDP	2 599	NA	NA	1 344	1 234	14	1	6	40	1 016	NA	16.8
0545	Hammond	15 871	15 043	5.5	9 042	6 646	26	127	30	183	6 292	7 298	29.3
0555	Harahan	9 927	11 384	-12.8	9 814	19	30	37	27	264	4 054	12 326	5.1
0562	Harvey CDP	21 222	22 709	-6.5	12 207	7 813	112	842	248	897	9 406	NA	17.2
0570	Haynesville town	2 854	NA	NA	1 739	1 110	1	4	0	3	1 258	8 648	12.7
0595	Homer town	4 152	NA	NA	1 790	2 346	10	0	6	19	1 800	7 240	11.9
0605	Houma	30 495	32 608	-6.5	21 651	7 613	925	235	71	430	11 476	8 772	35.1
0613	Inniswold CDP	3 474	NA	NA	3 235	176	6	46	11	59	1 496	NA	5.6
0620	Iowa town	2 588	NA	NA	2 084	493	4	0	7	30	938	NA	7.2
0625	Jackson town	3 891	NA	NA	2 228	1 638	13	6	6	61	974	4 980	11.4
0630	Jeanerette	6 205	NA	NA	2 837	3 348	5	5	10	74	2 256	7 278	6.0
0634	Jefferson CDP	14 521	15 550	-6.6	11 949	2 323	33	94	122	669	7 667	NA	16.8
0640	Jena town	2 626	NA	NA	2 499	103	13	10	1	10	1 234	9 418	10.6
0645	Jennings	11 305	12 401	-8.8	8 277	2 975	14	14	25	88	4 475	7 796	26.4
0650	Jonesboro town	4 305	NA	NA	2 616	1 670	11	5	3	24	1 969	7 532	11.4
0655	Jonesville town	2 720	NA	NA	1 090	1 625	4	1	0	4	1 029	5 902	4.9
0665	Kaplan	4 535	NA	NA	3 782	714	9	19	11	40	1 956	6 690	4.5
0675	Kenner	72 033	66 382	8.5	55 765	13 021	199	1 217	1 831	7 240	27 259	10 157	39.2
0698	Lacombe CDP	6 523	NA	NA	4 611	1 820	31	12	49	142	2 637	NA	77.3
0700	Lafayette	94 440	81 961	15.2	66 867	25 679	191	1 274	429	1 614	40 379	11 876	106.0
0710	Lake Arthur town	3 194	NA	NA	2 819	365	2	6	2	3	1 344	6 945	4.8
0715	Lake Charles	70 580	75 226	-6.2	40 441	29 387	151	377	224	811	29 844	9 816	83.1
0725	Lake Providence town	5 380	NA	NA	1 127	4 208	2	19	24	54	2 050	4 625	9.3

1. Codes shown are 2-digit FIPS codes for states; 4-digit census place codes for places; and 3-digit FIPS county codes followed by 3-digit census MCD codes for minor civil divisions (MCDs). MCD names are followed by county names in parentheses. 2. Hispanic persons may be of any race. 3. Dry land or land partially or temporarily covered by water.

State/ Place/ MCD[1] code	Place	Population 1990	Places of 10,000 or more 1980	Places of 10,000 or more Percent change, 1980–1990	Race: White	Race: Black	Race: Am. Indian, Eskimo Aleut	Race: Asian & Pacific Islander	Race: Other race	Hispanic[2]	Total housing units, 1990	Per capita income, 1985 (Dollars)	Land area,[3] 1990 (Sq. Km.)
		1	2	3	4	5	6	7	8	9	10	11	12
	LOUISIANA—Con.												
0735	Laplace CDP	24 194	16 112	50.2	18 448	5 299	80	146	221	762	8 426	NA	54.8
0740	Larose CDP	5 772	NA	NA	4 753	526	268	194	31	85	2 029	NA	17.4
0750	Leesville	7 638	NA	NA	4 774	2 483	27	242	112	338	3 520	7 074	14.1
0765	Lockport town	2 503	NA	NA	2 471	13	12	2	5	40	967	NA	1.6
0790	Luling CDP	2 803	NA	NA	2 073	680	9	12	29	56	1 114	NA	9.5
0795	Lutcher town	3 907	NA	NA	1 924	1 973	2	8	0	20	1 296	7 909	8.7
0805	Mamou town	3 483	NA	NA	2 417	1 050	2	5	9	21	1 544	6 527	3.6
0810	Mandeville	7 083	NA	NA	6 486	508	15	51	23	168	3 105	12 508	11.2
0820	Mansfield	5 389	NA	NA	2 409	2 934	3	0	43	98	2 276	9 048	8.6
0830	Many town	3 112	NA	NA	1 577	1 501	26	4	4	58	1 339	7 909	6.8
0850	Marksville	5 526	NA	NA	3 521	1 957	16	20	12	263	2 058	6 654	8.0
0852	Marrero CDP	36 671	36 548	0.3	19 038	16 513	181	709	230	1 055	13 220	NA	20.9
0857	Mathews CDP	3 009	NA	NA	2 908	68	19	14	0	65	1 038	NA	13.1
0868	Meraux CDP	8 849	NA	NA	8 262	384	63	110	30	353	3 037	NA	11.8
0877	Merrydale CDP	10 395	NA	NA	2 128	8 209	4	46	8	95	3 453	NA	11.0
0882	Metairie CDP	149 428	164 160	-9.0	136 832	7 370	262	2 745	2 219	9 218	67 021	NA	60.2
0884	Mimosa Park CDP	4 516	NA	NA	4 296	155	9	33	23	147	1 591	NA	6.4
0885	Minden	13 661	15 084	-9.4	7 000	6 608	26	20	7	59	5 818	7 722	26.0
0890	Monroe	54 909	57 597	-4.7	23 783	30 504	68	465	89	425	21 610	8 020	67.8
0897	Monticello CDP	4 710	NA	NA	3 545	1 102	3	53	7	81	1 573	NA	6.2
0915	Morgan City	14 531	16 114	-9.8	10 910	3 311	173	69	68	475	5 838	10 360	15.2
0927	Moss Bluff CDP	8 039	NA	NA	7 387	579	23	19	31	89	2 832	NA	39.4
0940	Natchitoches	16 609	16 664	-0.3	8 049	8 281	45	111	123	206	6 093	7 520	26.2
0950	New Iberia	31 828	32 766	-2.9	20 441	10 605	67	628	87	725	12 426	8 652	26.3
0955	Newllano town	2 660	NA	NA	1 539	800	34	151	136	268	1 014	NA	1.8
0956	New Orleans	496 938	557 515	-10.9	173 554	307 728	759	9 678	5 219	17 238	225 573	8 975	467.9
0960	New Roads	5 303	NA	NA	2 094	3 204	2	2	1	24	1 998	7 786	11.8
0965	New Sarpy CDP	2 946	NA	NA	2 026	867	14	19	20	92	1 108	NA	4.6
0975	Norco CDP	3 385	NA	NA	2 718	630	11	17	9	41	1 371	NA	6.6
0995	Oakdale	6 832	NA	NA	4 413	2 297	22	28	72	580	2 455	5 803	11.9
1002	Oak Hills Place CDP	5 479	NA	NA	4 719	570	9	165	16	120	2 025	NA	8.0
1017	Old Jefferson CDP	4 531	NA	NA	4 250	199	9	58	15	105	1 599	NA	9.1
1025	Opelousas	18 151	18 903	-4.0	6 925	11 159	8	40	19	95	7 173	6 543	17.8
1040	Patterson	4 736	NA	NA	2 510	2 156	40	10	20	76	1 739	8 686	6.0
1048	Pierre Part CDP	3 053	NA	NA	3 043	0	5	1	4	20	1 146	NA	7.8
1055	Pineville	12 251	12 034	1.8	9 390	2 595	47	186	33	158	5 086	9 490	18.2
1075	Plaquemine	7 186	NA	NA	3 865	3 301	9	5	6	93	2 874	9 105	5.8
1100	Ponchatoula	5 425	NA	NA	3 283	2 112	23	6	1	46	2 231	6 182	9.0
1105	Port Allen	6 277	NA	NA	3 026	3 227	13	8	3	63	2 388	8 827	5.8
1115	Port Sulphur CDP	3 523	NA	NA	1 977	1 296	203	26	21	39	1 260	NA	13.9
1124	Poydras CDP	4 029	NA	NA	3 540	394	51	17	27	415	1 471	NA	10.8
1126	Prien CDP	6 448	NA	NA	6 033	338	7	48	22	99	2 362	NA	28.2
1135	Raceland CDP	5 564	NA	NA	4 362	1 161	21	3	17	61	2 077	NA	12.6
1140	Rayne	8 502	NA	NA	5 733	2 760	2	5	2	81	3 375	7 929	8.5
1145	Rayville town	4 411	NA	NA	1 514	2 893	2	0	2	22	1 631	5 069	5.6
1148	Red Chute CDP	5 431	NA	NA	5 007	354	19	34	17	93	1 965	NA	23.9
1160	Reserve CDP	8 847	NA	NA	4 691	4 076	17	12	51	173	3 325	NA	48.2
1167	River Ridge CDP	14 800	17 146	-13.7	13 104	1 551	31	48	66	440	6 194	NA	7.3
1190	Ruston	20 027	20 585	-2.7	12 793	6 789	16	323	106	263	7 669	7 826	44.8
1205	St. Martinville	7 137	NA	NA	2 874	4 228	9	10	16	84	2 633	6 780	6.2
1210	St. Rose CDP	6 259	NA	NA	3 912	2 239	19	27	62	212	2 384	NA	10.5
1227	Schriever CDP	4 958	NA	NA	3 906	970	48	28	6	56	1 813	NA	34.8
1230	Scott town	4 912	NA	NA	4 274	571	13	39	15	63	1 909	NA	16.7
1236	Shenandoah CDP	13 429	NA	NA	12 759	410	33	203	24	192	4 580	NA	16.4
1240	Shreveport	198 525	205 776	-3.5	107 838	88 860	389	1 017	421	2 156	87 473	10 240	255.4
1280	Slidell	24 124	26 718	-9.7	21 196	2 614	92	147	75	611	9 087	11 414	24.2
1291	South Vacherie CDP	3 462	NA	NA	2 358	1 101	0	2	1	19	1 139	NA	40.2
1295	Springhill	5 668	NA	NA	4 447	1 202	10	3	6	37	2 588	9 118	16.1
1310	Sulphur	20 125	19 709	2.1	19 197	777	55	41	55	230	7 812	10 041	25.2
1323	Swartz CDP	3 698	NA	NA	3 620	67	2	6	3	34	1 337	NA	14.6
1325	Tallulah	8 526	11 634	-26.7	2 249	6 243	11	7	16	59	3 241	4 500	6.2
1332	Terrytown CDP	23 787	23 548	1.0	17 913	4 699	133	705	337	1 851	9 726	NA	9.6
1335	Thibodaux	14 035	15 810	-11.2	9 461	4 442	31	81	20	165	5 454	8 110	10.0
1339	Timberlane CDP	12 614	11 579	8.9	9 773	2 092	52	538	159	778	4 499	NA	5.5
1370	Vidalia town	4 953	NA	NA	3 508	1 436	2	5	2	26	1 911	8 071	6.0
1374	Village St. George CDP	6 242	NA	NA	5 057	1 005	8	126	46	198	2 264	NA	5.7
1375	Ville Platte town	9 037	NA	NA	4 757	4 250	6	11	13	86	3 721	6 288	7.9
1380	Vinton town	3 154	NA	NA	2 505	635	2	6	6	20	1 366	8 277	11.9
1383	Violet CDP	8 574	11 678	-26.6	6 459	1 957	71	53	34	599	2 868	NA	10.5
1385	Vivian town	4 156	NA	NA	3 017	1 115	14	4	6	20	1 873	8 619	13.3
1389	Waggaman CDP	9 405	NA	NA	4 235	4 957	48	67	98	312	2 966	NA	14.4
1390	Walker town	3 727	NA	NA	3 152	567	6	2	0	30	1 391	7 484	14.9
1420	Welsh town	3 299	NA	NA	2 438	852	8	1	0	16	1 266	7 654	16.1

1. Codes shown are 2-digit FIPS codes for states; 4-digit census place codes for places; and 3-digit FIPS county codes followed by 3-digit census MCD codes for minor civil divisions (MCDs). MCD names are followed by county names in parentheses. 2. Hispanic persons may be of any race. 3. Dry land or land partially or temporarily covered by water.

State/ Place/ MCD[1] code	Place	Population			Population characteristics, 1990						Total housing units, 1990	Per capita income, 1985 (Dollars)	Land area,[3] 1990 (Sq. Km.)
			Places of 10,000 or more		Race								
		1990	1980	Percent change, 1980–1990	White	Black	Am. Indian, Eskimo Aleut	Asian & Pacific Islander	Other race	Hispanic[2]			
		1	2	3	4	5	6	7	8	9	10	11	12
	LOUISIANA—Con.												
1425	Westlake	5 007	NA	NA	4 246	735	10	4	12	53	1 904	8 894	6.0
1427	Westminster CDP	2 582	NA	NA	2 532	37	0	11	2	61	979	NA	3.0
1430	West Monroe	14 096	14 993	-6.0	11 547	2 448	40	23	38	146	6 582	10 022	18.6
1435	Westwego	11 218	12 663	-11.4	9 162	1 749	112	80	115	313	4 690	7 534	8.3
1445	Winnfield	6 138	NA	NA	3 280	2 795	20	7	36	97	2 523	5 692	8.6
1450	Winnsboro town	5 755	NA	NA	2 932	2 804	2	16	1	21	2 186	5 083	8.9
1470	Zachary	9 036	NA	NA	6 577	2 408	15	32	4	40	3 140	9 863	48.3
23	MAINE	1 227 928	1 125 043	9.1	1 208 360	5 138	5 998	6 683	1 749	6 829	587 045	9 042	79 939.2
0200	Auburn	24 309	23 128	5.1	23 934	116	51	164	44	132	10 406	9 237	154.9
0210	Augusta	21 325	21 819	-2.3	20 965	68	86	180	26	116	9 572	9 841	143.4
0270	Bangor	33 181	31 643	4.9	32 222	305	245	333	76	211	14 366	9 494	89.2
0280	Bar Harbor CDP	2 768	NA	NA	2 727	4	12	23	2	10	1 537	NA	8.2
0300	Bath	9 799	10 246	-4.4	9 472	200	25	68	34	123	4 236	9 238	23.7
0330	Belfast	6 355	NA	NA	6 312	7	22	10	4	27	2 898	7 448	88.2
0420	Biddeford	20 710	19 638	5.5	20 397	63	60	173	17	99	9 051	8 907	77.7
0560	Brewer	9 021	NA	NA	8 935	21	36	20	9	49	3 780	10 084	39.1
0680	Brunswick CDP	14 683	10 990	33.6	14 201	191	25	223	43	166	5 914	NA	32.7
0710	Bucksport CDP	2 989	NA	NA	2 954	1	10	15	9	24	1 289	NA	29.5
0770	Calais	3 963	NA	NA	3 913	5	34	7	4	17	1 773	8 412	88.2
0790	Camden CDP	4 022	NA	NA	3 993	2	15	7	5	36	2 010	NA	9.8
0840	Caribou	9 415	NA	NA	9 158	50	120	68	19	42	4 089	8 004	205.4
1250	Dexter CDP	2 650	NA	NA	2 632	2	4	10	2	18	1 238	NA	12.3
1300	Dover-Foxcroft CDP	3 077	NA	NA	3 020	3	32	20	2	16	1 288	NA	21.8
1470	Ellsworth	5 975	NA	NA	5 917	12	20	24	2	22	3 202	9 174	205.3
1530	Fairfield CDP	2 794	NA	NA	2 763	7	8	13	3	8	1 261	NA	4.8
1580	Farmington CDP	4 197	NA	NA	4 141	9	15	29	3	25	1 644	NA	10.4
1740	Gardiner	6 746	NA	NA	6 669	23	21	21	12	33	2 705	8 827	40.6
1790	Gorham CDP	3 618	NA	NA	3 575	23	6	13	1	21	1 091	NA	14.4
1920	Hallowell	2 534	NA	NA	2 506	7	7	12	2	14	1 192	10 439	15.2
1925	Hampden CDP	3 895	NA	NA	3 848	6	7	28	6	8	1 574	NA	28.7
2120	Houlton CDP	5 627	NA	NA	5 396	17	186	26	2	8	2 393	NA	19.9
2310	Kennebunk CDP	4 206	NA	NA	4 140	15	6	42	3	34	1 971	NA	17.5
2370	Kittery CDP	5 151	NA	NA	4 899	148	12	46	46	115	2 104	NA	7.3
2470	Lewiston	39 757	40 481	-1.8	39 027	267	92	274	97	284	17 118	8 796	88.3
2530	Lincoln CDP	3 399	NA	NA	3 371	2	14	12	0	3	1 454	NA	19.5
2580	Lisbon Falls CDP	4 674	NA	NA	4 574	23	23	34	20	52	1 759	NA	9.8
2645	Loring AFB CDP	7 829	NA	NA	6 802	683	49	168	127	299	1 532	NA	20.9
2740	Madawaska CDP	3 653	NA	NA	3 631	3	8	10	1	3	1 622	NA	10.8
2760	Madison CDP	2 956	NA	NA	2 940	3	8	1	4	17	1 224	NA	16.7
2980	Millinocket CDP	6 922	NA	NA	6 855	8	30	19	10	15	2 867	NA	14.1
3336	North Windham CDP	4 077	NA	NA	4 050	4	11	5	7	15	1 636	NA	18.1
3350	Norway CDP	3 023	NA	NA	3 003	2	7	9	2	6	1 373	NA	13.1
3380	Oakland CDP	3 510	NA	NA	3 485	3	6	8	8	18	1 448	NA	16.1
3400	Old Orchard Beach CDP	7 789	NA	NA	7 695	44	20	26	4	60	5 668	NA	19.3
3420	Old Town	8 317	NA	NA	7 957	37	152	159	12	56	3 547	8 697	99.2
3450	Orono CDP	9 789	NA	NA	9 447	61	75	184	22	93	2 299	NA	18.9
3680	Pittsfield CDP	3 222	NA	NA	3 198	7	2	3	12	30	1 292	NA	24.2
3750	Portland	64 358	61 572	4.5	62 161	720	262	1 071	144	513	31 293	10 386	58.6
3770	Presque Isle	10 550	11 172	-5.6	10 333	58	80	59	20	66	4 411	8 691	196.2
3890	Rockland	7 972	NA	NA	7 909	22	24	12	5	23	3 719	7 830	33.4
3950	Rumford CDP	5 419	NA	NA	5 390	5	10	8	6	33	2 623	NA	20.7
3980	Saco	15 181	12 921	17.5	15 010	44	17	95	15	83	6 826	9 774	99.7
3990	Sanford CDP	10 296	10 268	0.3	10 087	18	34	137	20	89	4 275	NA	13.2
4018	Scarborough CDP	2 586	NA	NA	2 560	4	1	19	2	6	1 169	NA	12.9
4120	Skowhegan CDP	6 990	NA	NA	6 939	3	28	16	4	15	3 124	NA	33.1
4210	South Eliot CDP	3 112	NA	NA	3 066	19	6	14	7	27	1 249	NA	18.6
4230	South Portland	23 163	22 712	2.0	22 736	68	63	266	30	165	9 713	10 311	30.8
4245	South Sanford CDP	3 929	NA	NA	3 812	10	6	98	3	34	1 635	NA	59.0
4300	Springvale CDP	3 542	NA	NA	3 414	8	16	90	14	49	1 469	NA	8.2
4560	Topsham CDP	6 147	NA	NA	5 929	73	15	99	31	98	2 285	NA	21.8
4650	Van Buren CDP	2 759	NA	NA	2 742	2	9	6	0	0	1 142	NA	9.1
4870	Waterville	17 173	17 779	-3.4	16 913	84	49	99	28	111	7 008	8 682	35.2
4960	Westbrook	16 121	14 976	7.6	15 869	99	41	92	20	78	6 617	10 219	43.7
5110	Winslow CDP	5 436	NA	NA	5 390	3	11	30	2	21	2 270	NA	15.7
5160	Winthrop CDP	2 819	NA	NA	2 784	7	12	13	3	10	1 292	NA	14.2
5250	Yarmouth CDP	3 338	NA	NA	3 314	6	3	10	5	24	1 327	NA	6.7
5290	York Harbor CDP	2 555	NA	NA	2 533	5	6	9	2	9	1 276	NA	8.3
0010	Durham town (Androscoggin)	2 842	NA	NA	2 821	10	3	7	1	9	994	NA	98.7
0010	Greene town (Androscoggin)	3 661	NA	NA	3 638	9	2	7	5	22	1 446	8 299	83.9
0010	Lisbon town (Androscoggin)	9 457	NA	NA	9 304	38	35	48	32	91	3 616	8 058	61.0
0010	Livermore Falls town (Androscoggin)	3 455	NA	NA	3 432	3	14	6	0	37	1 474	9 555	51.2

1. Codes shown are 2-digit FIPS codes for states; 4-digit census place codes for places; and 3-digit FIPS county codes followed by 3-digit census MCD codes for minor civil divisions (MCDs). MCD names are followed by county names in parentheses. 2. Hispanic persons may be of any race. 3. Dry land or land partially or temporarily covered by water.

State/ Place/ MCD[1] code	Place	Population			Population characteristics, 1990						Total housing units, 1990	Per capita income, 1985 (Dollars)	Land area,[3] 1990 (Sq. Km.)
		1990	Places of 10,000 or more		Race					Hispanic[2]			
			1980	Percent change, 1980–1990	White	Black	Am. Indian, Eskimo Aleut	Asian & Pacific Islander	Other race				
		1	2	3	4	5	6	7	8	9	10	11	12
	MAINE—Con.												
0010	Mechanic Falls town (Androscoggin)	2 919	NA	NA	2 908	0	4	2	5	11	1 118	8 077	28.8
0010	Poland town (Androscoggin)	4 342	NA	NA	4 306	13	8	14	1	10	1 895	8 669	109.6
0010	Sabattus town (Androscoggin)	3 696	NA	NA	3 682	0	5	5	4	9	1 394	7 310	66.1
0010	Turner town (Androscoggin)	4 315	NA	NA	4 176	14	8	11	106	137	1 707	8 446	154.3
0030	Fort Fairfield town (Aroostook)	3 998	NA	NA	3 945	3	45	2	3	13	1 648	7 151	198.5
0031	Fort Kent town (Aroostook)	4 268	NA	NA	4 236	8	13	10	1	10	1 634	8 182	140.3
0031	Houlton town (Aroostook)	6 613	NA	NA	6 357	19	209	26	2	8	2 774	7 884	95.2
0031	Limestone town (Aroostook)	9 922	NA	NA	8 789	734	67	191	141	320	2 434	7 169	104.7
0031	Madawaska town (Aroostook)	4 803	NA	NA	4 780	3	8	11	1	4	2 212	9 670	144.2
0033	Van Buren town (Aroostook)	3 045	NA	NA	3 022	3	9	6	5	2	1 247	6 695	87.9
0050	Bridgton town (Cumberland)	4 307	NA	NA	4 262	14	17	11	3	24	2 921	8 427	148.4
0050	Brunswick town (Cumberland)	20 906	17 366	20.4	20 088	397	50	280	91	289	8 197	10 196	121.2
0050	Cape Elizabeth town (Cumberland)	8 854	NA	NA	8 771	16	6	53	8	51	3 456	17 809	38.4
0050	Casco town (Cumberland)	3 018	NA	NA	2 998	3	8	8	1	11	1 677	NA	81.0
0050	Cumberland town (Cumberland)	5 836	NA	NA	5 788	8	11	23	6	27	2 365	15 118	67.5
0050	Falmouth town (Cumberland)	7 610	NA	NA	7 545	15	6	43	1	30	3 322	15 613	76.7
0050	Freeport town (Cumberland)	6 905	NA	NA	6 844	20	21	13	7	31	3 011	11 643	89.9
0050	Gorham town (Cumberland)	11 856	10 133	17.0	11 719	44	30	48	15	53	4 048	10 158	131.2
0050	Gray town (Cumberland)	5 904	NA	NA	5 847	19	8	26	4	27	2 836	9 285	112.0
0050	Harpswell town (Cumberland)	5 012	NA	NA	4 971	4	9	21	7	41	3 432	11 170	62.6
0050	Naples town (Cumberland)	2 860	NA	NA	2 847	4	5	2	2	12	1 946	NA	82.4
0050	New Gloucester town (Cumberland)	3 916	NA	NA	3 890	7	6	8	5	24	1 363	7 611	122.0
0050	Raymond town (Cumberland)	3 311	NA	NA	3 290	4	5	10	2	9	2 050	NA	86.1
0051	Scarborough town (Cumberland)	12 518	11 347	10.3	12 390	30	11	80	7	41	5 391	12 282	123.6
0051	Standish town (Cumberland)	7 678	NA	NA	7 629	24	6	18	1	16	3 569	9 858	156.5
0051	Windham town (Cumberland)	13 020	11 250	15.7	12 905	32	33	22	28	54	5 200	9 495	120.9
0051	Yarmouth town (Cumberland)	7 862	NA	NA	7 794	19	9	34	6	50	3 309	14 597	34.5
0070	Farmington town (Franklin)	7 436	NA	NA	7 369	9	21	34	3	32	2 877	7 821	144.4
0070	Jay town (Franklin)	5 080	NA	NA	5 045	4	10	12	9	26	2 002	9 704	125.5
0071	Wilton town (Franklin)	4 242	NA	NA	4 200	3	15	19	5	13	1 809	8 915	106.9
0090	Bar Harbor town (Hancock)	4 443	NA	NA	4 377	5	26	28	7	20	2 586	9 618	109.3
0090	Bucksport town (Hancock)	4 825	NA	NA	4 781	2	13	15	14	38	2 078	8 653	133.5
0110	China town (Kennebec)	3 713	NA	NA	3 666	1	21	21	4	16	1 703	9 083	129.1
0110	Clinton town (Kennebec)	3 332	NA	NA	3 317	4	4	5	2	14	1 226	8 457	113.7
0110	Farmingdale town (Kennebec)	2 918	NA	NA	2 876	5	20	9	8	5	1 237	10 526	29.2
0110	Litchfield town (Kennebec)	2 650	NA	NA	2 634	4	5	6	1	13	1 328	NA	97.0
0110	Monmouth town (Kennebec)	3 353	NA	NA	3 326	9	8	5	5	11	1 540	8 426	88.3
0110	Oakland town (Kennebec)	5 595	NA	NA	5 561	4	10	12	8	24	2 472	8 609	66.7
0111	Sidney town (Kennebec)	2 593	NA	NA	2 579	1	2	7	4	15	1 123	NA	109.4
0111	Vassalboro town (Kennebec)	3 679	NA	NA	3 659	1	10	7	2	18	1 602	9 081	114.7
0111	West Gardiner town (Kennebec)	2 531	NA	NA	2 517	0	3	10	1	1	1 051	NA	63.8
0111	Winslow town (Kennebec)	7 997	NA	NA	7 931	5	23	34	4	30	3 274	9 525	95.4
0111	Winthrop town (Kennebec)	5 968	NA	NA	5 909	9	15	27	8	27	2 827	10 517	80.5
0130	Camden town (Knox)	5 060	NA	NA	5 023	4	16	12	5	43	2 654	11 314	46.1
0130	Rockport town (Knox)	2 854	NA	NA	2 839	3	2	8	2	10	1 409	11 032	57.5
0130	Thomaston town (Knox)	3 306	NA	NA	3 256	14	17	16	3	14	1 212	6 929	28.3
0130	Warren town (Knox)	3 192	NA	NA	3 170	2	16	4	0	9	1 277	7 136	119.9
0150	Boothbay town (Lincoln)	2 648	NA	NA	2 634	1	6	1	6	10	1 714	NA	57.2
0150	Waldoboro town (Lincoln)	4 601	NA	NA	4 586	3	6	4	2	12	2 039	7 763	184.7
0151	Wiscasset town (Lincoln)	3 339	NA	NA	3 304	6	15	6	8	36	1 386	7 602	63.7
0170	Dixfield town (Oxford)	2 574	NA	NA	2 553	2	8	9	2	19	1 081	NA	106.7
0170	Fryeburg town (Oxford)	2 968	NA	NA	2 951	9	4	3	1	13	1 549	8 485	151.7
0170	Mexico town (Oxford)	3 344	NA	NA	3 320	1	2	21	0	6	1 459	8 752	61.0
0171	Norway town (Oxford)	4 754	NA	NA	4 725	2	8	16	3	11	2 440	8 070	116.8
0171	Oxford town (Oxford)	3 705	NA	NA	3 673	5	15	11	1	26	1 781	7 548	100.3
0171	Paris town (Oxford)	4 492	NA	NA	4 468	2	6	16	0	8	1 945	8 029	105.6
0171	Rumford town (Oxford)	7 078	NA	NA	7 035	6	11	19	7	44	3 308	9 748	178.1
0190	Dexter town (Penobscot)	4 419	NA	NA	4 397	3	7	10	2	27	2 095	8 148	91.1
0191	Glenburn town (Penobscot)	3 198	NA	NA	3 164	14	14	5	1	7	1 298	NA	70.4
0191	Hampden town (Penobscot)	5 974	NA	NA	5 911	10	10	36	7	15	2 326	10 147	98.6
0191	Hermon town (Penobscot)	3 755	NA	NA	3 721	5	15	13	1	10	1 423	8 175	93.1
0191	Holden town (Penobscot)	2 952	NA	NA	2 932	1	8	8	3	13	1 332	8 991	80.1
0191	Lincoln town (Penobscot)	5 587	NA	NA	5 550	3	21	13	0	12	2 569	7 849	175.9
0192	Milford town (Penobscot)	2 884	NA	NA	2 844	4	19	11	6	10	1 126	NA	118.1
0192	Millinocket town (Penobscot)	6 956	NA	NA	6 889	8	30	19	10	15	2 874	10 504	28.2
0192	Newport town (Penobscot)	3 036	NA	NA	3 008	5	5	13	5	10	1 496	7 155	76.4
0192	Orono town (Penobscot)	10 573	10 545	0.3	10 216	64	84	186	23	109	2 687	6 882	47.2
0192	Orrington town (Penobscot)	3 309	NA	NA	3 287	4	2	12	4	12	1 338	9 766	65.8
0210	Dover-Foxcroft town (Piscataquis)	4 657	NA	NA	4 592	3	39	21	2	22	2 128	7 291	176.8
0210	Milo town (Piscataquis)	2 600	NA	NA	2 586	3	3	7	1	5	1 235	8 091	85.0
0230	Richmond town (Sagadahoc)	3 072	NA	NA	3 025	20	9	13	5	19	1 313	7 781	78.7
0230	Topsham town (Sagadahoc)	8 746	NA	NA	8 494	80	16	125	31	110	3 243	9 445	82.9
0230	Woolwich town (Sagadahoc)	2 570	NA	NA	2 539	13	6	8	4	10	1 011	NA	90.8

1. Codes shown are 2-digit FIPS codes for states; 4-digit census place codes for places; and 3-digit FIPS county codes followed by 3-digit census MCD codes for minor civil divisions (MCDs). MCD names are followed by county names in parentheses. 2. Hispanic persons may be of any race. 3. Dry land or land partially or temporarily covered by water.

State/ Place/ MCD[1] code	Place	Population: 1990	Places of 10,000 or more: 1980	Places of 10,000 or more: Percent change, 1980–1990	Population characteristics, 1990: Race: White	Black	Am. Indian, Eskimo Aleut	Asian & Pacific Islander	Other race	Hispanic[2]	Total housing units, 1990	Per capita income, 1985 (Dollars)	Land area,[3] 1990 (Sq. Km.)
		1	2	3	4	5	6	7	8	9	10	11	12
	MAINE—Con.												
0250	Fairfield town (Somerset)	6 718	NA	NA	6 656	17	13	29	3	22	2 658	7 748	139.3
0250	Madison town (Somerset)	4 725	NA	NA	4 689	5	20	4	7	22	2 200	8 167	134.1
0251	Norridgewock town (Somerset)	3 105	NA	NA	3 084	6	11	2	2	10	1 215	7 684	129.1
0251	Pittsfield town (Somerset)	4 190	NA	NA	4 154	9	5	7	15	43	1 711	7 828	124.8
0251	Skowhegan town (Somerset)	8 725	NA	NA	8 653	5	35	28	4	15	3 895	8 430	152.8
0270	Searsport town (Waldo)	2 603	NA	NA	2 576	4	12	10	1	15	1 237	NA	74.1
0271	Winterport town (Waldo)	3 175	NA	NA	3 149	2	5	14	5	17	1 180	7 767	92.2
0291	Machias town (Washington)	2 569	NA	NA	2 541	1	9	18	0	18	1 043	NA	36.0
0310	Arundel town (York)	2 669	NA	NA	2 648	3	9	7	2	11	1 036	NA	61.9
0310	Berwick town (York)	5 995	NA	NA	5 906	6	15	65	3	23	2 222	9 179	96.1
0310	Buxton town (York)	6 494	NA	NA	6 426	20	16	31	1	25	2 362	9 244	104.9
0310	Eliot town (York)	5 329	NA	NA	5 263	25	12	21	8	52	2 038	11 485	51.1
0310	Hollis town (York)	3 573	NA	NA	3 556	2	10	3	2	22	1 254	9 014	82.9
0310	Kennebunk town (York)	8 004	NA	NA	7 907	22	14	55	6	45	3 985	12 741	90.9
0310	Kennebunkport town (York)	3 356	NA	NA	3 341	1	3	9	2	13	2 280	14 183	53.4
0310	Kittery town (York)	9 372	NA	NA	9 060	174	19	65	54	141	3 908	12 562	46.2
0310	Lebanon town (York)	4 263	NA	NA	4 242	7	1	13	0	21	1 734	7 816	141.7
0310	Limington town (York)	2 796	NA	NA	2 784	2	3	6	1	11	1 058	NA	108.7
0310	Lyman town (York)	3 390	NA	NA	3 365	5	5	11	4	15	1 473	8 728	100.9
0310	North Berwick town (York)	3 793	NA	NA	3 760	5	8	19	1	8	1 452	9 512	99.2
0311	Old Orchard Beach town (York)	7 789	NA	NA	7 695	44	20	26	4	60	5 668	9 504	19.3
0311	Sanford town (York)	20 463	18 020	13.6	19 968	37	65	356	37	180	8 326	8 310	123.8
0311	South Berwick town (York)	5 877	NA	NA	5 791	30	5	46	5	31	2 262	10 139	83.3
0311	Waterboro town (York)	4 510	NA	NA	4 486	3	10	8	3	9	2 144	8 616	143.8
0311	Wells town (York)	7 778	NA	NA	7 728	14	4	28	4	31	5 217	10 086	149.3
0311	York town (York)	9 818	NA	NA	9 742	32	14	26	4	46	6 504	12 530	142.2
24	MARYLAND	4 781 468	4 216 933	13.4	3 393 964	1 189 899	12 972	139 719	44 914	125 102	1 891 917	12 967	25 316.3
0003	Aberdeen town	13 087	11 533	13.5	9 284	3 259	51	370	123	320	5 214	10 785	13.7
0004	Aberdeen Proving Ground CDP	5 267	NA	NA	3 182	1 654	43	137	251	501	986	NA	28.2
0007	Accokeek CDP	4 477	NA	NA	3 782	531	23	121	20	84	1 585	NA	58.0
0008	Adelphi CDP	13 524	12 510	8.1	5 788	5 373	28	1 585	750	1 409	5 351	NA	7.8
0009	Andrews AFB CDP	10 228	10 064	1.6	7 091	2 516	39	385	197	548	2 341	NA	17.6
0011	Annapolis	33 187	31 740	4.6	21 552	10 964	77	445	149	483	15 252	13 874	16.4
0014	Arbutus CDP	19 750	20 163	-2.0	17 900	933	36	822	59	233	7 966	NA	16.8
0017	Arnold CDP	20 261	12 285	64.9	18 899	981	34	295	52	273	7 238	NA	28.0
0019	Ashton-Sandy Springs CDP	3 092	NA	NA	2 635	355	2	78	22	42	1 156	NA	19.6
0021	Aspen Hill CDP	45 494	47 455	-4.1	33 356	6 614	166	4 206	1 152	3 547	17 157	NA	27.1
0023	Ballenger Creek CDP	5 546	NA	NA	5 127	296	20	69	34	100	2 532	NA	14.5
0025	Baltimore	736 014	786 775	-6.5	287 753	435 768	2 555	7 942	1 996	7 602	303 706	8 647	209.3
0045	Bel Air town	8 860	NA	NA	8 409	293	13	122	23	73	3 860	13 936	6.7
0046	Bel Air North CDP	14 880	NA	NA	14 476	209	26	147	22	157	5 116	NA	42.6
0048	Bel Air South CDP	26 421	NA	NA	25 126	740	43	438	74	357	10 296	NA	41.0
0053	Beltsville CDP	14 476	12 760	13.4	10 291	2 671	32	1 228	254	629	5 503	NA	17.0
0055	Berlin town	2 616	NA	NA	1 786	804	1	20	5	12	1 101	NA	5.2
0060	Berwyn Heights town	2 952	NA	NA	2 659	88	10	161	34	102	1 030	15 585	1.7
0065	Bethesda CDP	62 936	62 736	0.3	56 226	1 889	86	4 177	558	3 729	28 253	NA	38.4
0075	Bladensburg town	8 064	NA	NA	2 182	5 412	29	160	281	436	3 574	11 118	2.6
0085	Bowie	37 589	33 695	11.6	34 341	2 144	114	854	136	828	13 066	15 473	33.3
0086	Bowleys Quarters CDP	5 595	NA	NA	5 404	148	9	29	5	18	2 435	NA	8.3
0087	Braddock Heights CDP	4 778	NA	NA	4 664	36	10	49	19	43	1 635	NA	19.7
0090	Brentwood town	3 005	NA	NA	1 454	1 243	17	127	164	415	1 081	10 436	1.0
0093	Bridgeport CDP	2 702	NA	NA	2 646	25	1	27	3	8	1 044	NA	7.2
0102	Brooklyn Park CDP	10 987	11 508	-4.5	10 644	164	64	98	17	109	4 454	NA	7.6
0110	Brunswick town	5 117	NA	NA	4 796	281	6	16	18	51	1 865	9 533	5.4
0111	Bryans Road CDP	3 809	NA	NA	2 929	782	34	55	9	54	1 351	NA	15.0
0113	Burtonsville CDP	5 853	NA	NA	4 605	582	10	608	48	204	2 159	NA	20.2
0114	Cabin John-Brookmont CDP	5 341	NA	NA	4 946	118	6	245	26	271	2 168	NA	6.8
0116	California CDP	7 626	NA	NA	6 414	961	36	170	45	167	2 907	NA	33.4
0119	Calverton CDP	12 046	NA	NA	8 521	1 812	30	1 559	124	449	4 481	NA	12.4
0120	Cambridge	11 514	11 703	-1.6	6 312	5 093	19	45	45	106	5 256	7 882	17.1
0122	Camp Springs CDP	16 392	16 118	1.7	7 398	8 306	55	530	103	316	5 676	NA	18.6
0124	Cape St. Claire CDP	7 878	NA	NA	7 596	181	21	70	10	80	2 792	NA	5.2
0125	Capitol Heights town	3 633	NA	NA	368	3 212	19	13	21	39	1 209	9 072	1.9
0128	Carmody Hills-Pepper Mill Village C..	4 815	NA	NA	131	4 638	9	19	18	43	1 478	NA	1.9
0129	Carney CDP	25 578	21 488	19.0	23 376	1 001	39	1 097	65	297	10 366	NA	18.1
0140	Catonsville CDP	35 233	33 208	6.1	31 240	3 261	73	587	72	363	14 080	NA	36.3
0167	Chesapeake Ranch Estates CDP	5 423	NA	NA	5 054	301	13	39	16	83	2 529	NA	20.5
0170	Chestertown town	4 005	NA	NA	3 138	797	10	44	16	48	1 624	10 414	6.6
0175	Cheverly town	6 023	NA	NA	3 295	2 484	8	155	81	207	2 193	16 909	3.3
0181	Chevy Chase town	2 675	NA	NA	2 606	32	2	30	5	78	1 005	NA	1.2
0182	Chevy Chase CDP	8 559	12 232	-30.0	7 897	352	11	233	66	371	3 548	NA	6.6

1. Codes shown are 2-digit FIPS codes for states; 4-digit census place codes for places; and 3-digit FIPS county codes followed by 3-digit census MCD codes for minor civil divisions (MCDs). MCD names are followed by county names in parentheses. 2. Hispanic persons may be of any race. 3. Dry land or land partially or temporarily covered by water.

State/ Place/ MCD[1] code	Place	Population: 1990	Population: Places of 10,000 or more: 1980	Population: Places of 10,000 or more: Percent change, 1980–1990	Race: White	Race: Black	Race: Am. Indian, Eskimo Aleut	Race: Asian & Pacific Islander	Race: Other race	Hispanic[2]	Total housing units, 1990	Per capita income, 1985 (Dollars)	Land area,[3] 1990 (Sq. Km.)
		1	2	3	4	5	6	7	8	9	10	11	12
	MARYLAND—Con.												
0188	Chillum CDP	31 309	32 775	-4.5	6 725	21 619	105	1 166	1 694	3 068	12 093	NA	10.6
0209	Clinton CDP	19 987	16 438	21.6	10 086	9 106	78	581	136	418	6 378	NA	27.8
0211	Clover Hill CDP	2 823	NA	NA	2 727	38	1	53	4	11	947	NA	3.5
0212	Cloverly CDP	7 904	NA	NA	5 624	1 174	7	1 010	89	240	2 493	NA	10.1
0214	Cockeysville CDP	18 668	17 013	9.7	16 630	885	37	1 063	53	282	9 346	NA	29.1
0217	Colesville CDP	18 819	14 359	31.1	12 402	3 564	27	2 634	192	611	5 995	NA	23.9
0220	College Park	21 927	23 614	-7.1	18 192	1 993	75	1 442	225	685	5 880	10 114	14.0
0227	Columbia CDP	75 883	52 518	44.5	57 507	14 020	189	3 625	542	1 935	30 651	NA	60.1
0229	Coral Hills CDP	11 032	11 602	-4.9	867	10 009	37	47	72	103	3 907	NA	3.9
0235	Cresaptown-Bel Air CDP	4 586	NA	NA	4 519	27	2	29	9	30	1 847	NA	19.3
0240	Crisfield	2 880	NA	NA	1 837	1 025	3	7	8	5	1 309	7 141	4.2
0243	Crofton CDP	12 781	12 009	6.4	11 996	561	22	173	29	208	4 718	NA	13.0
0245	Cumberland	23 706	25 928	-8.6	22 471	1 047	22	127	39	107	11 431	9 002	21.4
0247	Damascus CDP	9 817	NA	NA	9 211	378	19	161	48	209	3 315	NA	24.7
0250	Deale CDP	4 151	NA	NA	3 812	301	13	20	5	58	1 721	NA	11.2
0265	Denton town	2 977	NA	NA	2 014	934	6	12	11	31	1 217	NA	6.0
0270	District Heights	6 704	NA	NA	1 580	5 010	22	76	16	51	2 594	12 851	2.1
0271	Dodge Park CDP	4 842	NA	NA	100	4 701	12	4	25	52	1 801	NA	2.2
0275	Dundalk CDP	65 800	71 293	-7.7	61 099	4 025	246	290	140	619	26 464	NA	34.5
0290	Easton town	9 372	NA	NA	6 764	2 518	15	43	32	46	4 308	10 378	20.5
0291	East Riverdale CDP	14 187	14 117	0.5	6 543	6 129	35	680	800	1 553	5 112	NA	4.4
0294	Edgemere CDP	9 226	NA	NA	8 684	476	25	30	11	83	3 537	NA	27.9
0295	Edgewood CDP	23 903	19 455	22.9	18 924	4 044	126	446	363	687	8 408	NA	46.6
0308	Eldersburg CDP	9 720	NA	NA	9 265	309	16	123	7	82	3 288	NA	21.7
0312	Elkridge CDP	12 953	NA	NA	11 744	758	32	370	49	221	5 574	NA	20.5
0315	Elkton town	9 073	NA	NA	8 277	696	8	56	36	109	3 597	9 339	20.9
0325	Ellicott City CDP	41 396	21 784	90.0	36 517	2 151	51	2 576	101	598	15 914	NA	83.1
0335	Essex CDP	40 872	39 614	3.2	36 775	3 435	162	363	137	537	17 675	NA	24.6
0338	Fairland CDP	19 828	NA	NA	11 807	5 798	39	1 897	287	990	8 473	NA	12.9
0341	Fallston CDP	5 730	NA	NA	5 614	26	10	66	14	38	1 828	NA	22.6
0344	Ferndale CDP	16 355	14 314	14.3	14 401	1 376	60	436	82	215	6 346	NA	10.5
0346	Forest Heights town	2 859	NA	NA	791	1 942	4	99	23	81	945	13 101	1.2
0347	Forestville CDP	16 731	16 401	2.0	4 196	12 201	52	180	102	239	6 192	NA	11.7
0349	Fort Meade CDP	12 509	14 083	-11.2	8 500	3 170	64	428	347	859	3 030	NA	17.0
0353	Fort Washington CDP	24 032	NA	NA	8 629	12 539	80	2 625	159	542	7 874	NA	35.2
0355	Frederick	40 148	28 086	42.9	33 825	5 151	117	773	282	847	16 611	11 414	47.1
0358	Friendly CDP	9 028	NA	NA	2 895	5 627	47	360	99	208	2 780	NA	17.6
0365	Frostburg	8 075	NA	NA	7 660	335	8	62	10	53	3 023	7 871	7.1
0370	Fruitland	3 511	NA	NA	2 343	1 138	7	12	11	22	1 449	8 213	8.9
0385	Gaithersburg	39 542	26 424	49.6	28 531	5 094	157	4 022	1 738	3 694	16 059	14 625	23.6
0401	Garrison CDP	5 045	NA	NA	4 262	633	8	101	41	77	2 383	NA	8.1
0402	Germantown CDP	41 145	NA	NA	33 095	4 986	104	2 287	673	2 090	17 121	NA	27.8
0405	Glenarden town	5 025	NA	NA	61	4 916	8	26	14	26	1 889	10 177	2.0
0407	Glen Burnie CDP	37 305	37 263	0.1	32 185	4 212	109	650	149	503	14 664	NA	31.8
0412	Glenn Dale CDP	9 689	NA	NA	6 866	2 035	30	699	59	268	3 327	NA	21.2
0414	Goddard CDP	4 576	NA	NA	2 865	1 091	10	558	52	206	1 780	NA	6.2
0416	Golden Beach CDP	2 944	NA	NA	2 867	43	7	22	5	31	965	NA	6.7
0432	Greater Upper Marlboro CDP	11 528	NA	NA	5 180	6 073	52	157	66	193	3 614	NA	96.3
0435	Greenbelt	21 096	17 332	21.7	14 804	4 085	40	1 901	266	807	9 938	15 431	15.4
0437	Green Haven CDP	14 416	NA	NA	13 743	401	47	171	54	170	5 067	NA	8.3
0447	Green Valley CDP	9 424	NA	NA	9 176	113	14	93	28	151	2 895	NA	53.3
0450	Hagerstown	35 445	34 132	3.8	32 803	2 232	51	263	96	277	16 361	8 561	25.7
0455	Halfway CDP	8 873	NA	NA	8 609	162	18	74	10	32	3 818	NA	11.7
0460	Hampstead town	2 608	NA	NA	2 586	12	1	9	0	13	1 110	NA	5.9
0462	Hampton CDP	4 926	NA	NA	4 504	41	3	359	19	94	1 860	NA	14.8
0475	Havre de Grace	8 952	NA	NA	7 051	1 756	12	99	34	80	3 786	9 552	8.6
0493	Hillandale CDP	10 318	NA	NA	5 105	2 867	53	1 311	982	1 987	3 688	NA	5.3
0495	Hillcrest Heights CDP	17 136	17 021	0.7	1 928	15 043	24	86	55	153	7 232	NA	6.3
0502	Hillsmere Shores CDP	3 321	NA	NA	3 179	80	7	53	2	48	1 151	NA	3.5
0510	Hyattsville	13 864	12 709	9.1	8 258	4 385	54	520	647	1 187	5 773	13 329	5.5
0513	Indian Head town	3 531	NA	NA	2 554	853	48	58	18	84	1 404	NA	2.8
0517	Jessup CDP	6 537	NA	NA	2 301	4 142	39	43	12	120	393	NA	10.9
0518	Joppatowne CDP	11 084	11 348	-2.3	10 031	848	29	137	39	147	4 064	NA	17.6
0526	Kentland CDP	7 967	NA	NA	422	7 385	15	93	52	97	2 791	NA	4.3
0527	Kettering CDP	9 901	NA	NA	1 720	7 843	15	247	76	164	3 477	NA	14.1
0529	Kingsville CDP	3 550	NA	NA	3 512	2	2	31	3	23	1 281	NA	26.2
0532	Lake Shore CDP	13 269	10 181	30.3	12 943	181	42	95	8	79	4 605	NA	26.4
0534	Landover CDP	5 052	NA	NA	1 100	3 796	17	83	56	157	1 883	NA	2.1
0540	Langley Park CDP	17 474	14 038	24.5	3 699	7 594	73	1 562	4 546	6 956	5 792	NA	2.5
0542	Lanham-Seabrook CDP	16 792	15 814	6.2	9 200	6 344	60	1 048	140	488	6 001	NA	13.6
0545	Lansdowne-Baltimore Highlands CDP	15 509	16 759	-7.5	14 388	787	60	234	40	217	5 781	NA	10.6
0550	La Plata town	5 841	NA	NA	4 687	1 020	31	88	15	88	2 009	NA	12.6
0553	Largo CDP	9 475	NA	NA	1 030	8 217	33	143	52	168	3 870	NA	7.9

1. Codes shown are 2-digit FIPS codes for states; 4-digit census place codes for places; and 3-digit FIPS county codes followed by 3-digit census MCD codes for minor civil divisions (MCDs). MCD names are followed by county names in parentheses. 2. Hispanic persons may be of any race. 3. Dry land or land partially or temporarily covered by water.

State/ Place/ MCD[1] code	Place	Population: 1990	Population: Places of 10,000 or more: 1980	Population: Places of 10,000 or more: Percent change, 1980–1990	Population characteristics, 1990: Race: White	Race: Black	Race: Am. Indian, Eskimo Aleut	Race: Asian & Pacific Islander	Race: Other race	Hispanic[2]	Total housing units, 1990	Per capita income, 1985 (Dollars)	Land area,[3] 1990 (Sq. Km.)
		1	2	3	4	5	6	7	8	9	10	11	12
	MARYLAND—Con.												
0555	Laurel	19 438	12 103	60.6	15 506	2 717	42	976	197	587	9 049	13 755	8.2
0560	La Vale CDP	4 694	NA	NA	4 626	22	1	43	2	15	1 979	NA	21.0
0574	Lexington Park CDP	9 943	10 361	-4.0	7 368	2 136	55	271	113	314	3 809	NA	20.8
0575	Linganore-Bartonsville CDP	4 079	NA	NA	3 879	158	6	26	10	34	1 506	NA	40.1
0577	Linthicum CDP	7 547	NA	NA	7 284	86	9	164	4	26	2 817	NA	10.9
0579	Lochearn CDP	25 240	26 908	-6.2	7 854	17 068	48	196	74	236	9 905	NA	14.4
0592	Londontowne CDP	6 992	NA	NA	6 854	79	32	22	5	78	2 683	NA	7.8
0593	Long Meadow CDP	5 594	NA	NA	5 438	57	11	83	5	31	2 256	NA	16.4
0597	Lutherville-Timonium CDP	16 442	17 854	-7.9	15 331	228	7	850	26	254	6 596	NA	19.3
0600	Manchester town	2 810	NA	NA	2 765	17	7	20	1	3	1 039	NA	5.0
0607	Marlow Heights CDP	5 885	NA	NA	1 150	4 556	12	108	59	113	2 320	NA	5.4
0608	Marlton CDP	5 523	NA	NA	4 328	1 053	21	83	38	149	1 964	NA	15.5
0611	Maryland City CDP	6 813	NA	NA	5 489	1 039	19	181	85	226	2 620	NA	6.8
0613	Mayo CDP	2 537	NA	NA	2 442	71	12	10	2	19	1 152	NA	6.6
0614	Mays Chapel CDP	10 132	NA	NA	9 544	86	4	484	14	128	4 238	NA	9.7
0615	Middle River CDP	24 616	26 756	-8.0	22 902	1 290	102	289	33	167	9 925	NA	20.1
0627	Milford Mill CDP	22 547	20 354	10.8	8 211	13 843	61	340	92	285	9 671	NA	18.1
0631	Mitchellville CDP	12 593	NA	NA	3 428	8 515	32	538	80	233	4 422	NA	27.9
0632	Montgomery Village CDP	32 315	18 725	72.6	25 423	3 661	106	2 119	1 006	2 363	13 120	NA	16.8
0638	Mount Aetna CDP	3 608	NA	NA	3 415	146	1	38	8	49	1 641	NA	10.9
0645	Mount Airy town	3 730	NA	NA	3 581	87	13	29	20	45	1 310	NA	7.4
0650	Mount Rainier	7 954	NA	NA	2 823	4 415	22	261	433	803	3 586	10 841	1.7
0662	Naval Academy CDP	5 420	NA	NA	4 711	331	32	241	105	295	362	NA	1.4
0663	New Carrollton	12 002	12 632	-5.0	5 487	5 557	22	809	127	372	4 648	14 567	3.9
0677	North Bethesda CDP	29 656	22 714	30.6	25 316	1 151	76	2 432	681	2 262	14 026	NA	19.3
0691	North Kensington CDP	8 607	NA	NA	7 012	748	16	562	269	779	3 439	NA	4.0
0692	North Laurel CDP	15 008	NA	NA	13 210	1 130	33	558	77	332	5 842	NA	26.5
0693	North Potomac CDP	18 456	NA	NA	14 456	799	36	2 972	193	759	5 749	NA	15.6
0705	Ocean City town	5 146	NA	NA	4 956	129	23	36	2	49	25 494	14 789	11.9
0707	Ocean Pines CDP	4 251	NA	NA	4 130	79	4	32	6	34	4 184	NA	17.0
0710	Odenton CDP	12 833	13 270	-3.3	10 774	1 558	44	323	134	310	4 378	NA	34.7
0725	Olney CDP	23 019	13 026	76.7	20 120	1 493	58	1 164	184	812	7 267	NA	23.5
0735	Overlea CDP	12 137	12 965	-6.4	11 717	276	12	112	20	94	4 925	NA	8.0
0740	Owings Mills CDP	9 474	NA	NA	7 185	2 058	32	159	40	121	4 102	NA	24.9
0747	Oxon Hill-Glassmanor CDP	35 794	36 267	-1.3	6 506	27 869	120	1 011	288	674	13 698	NA	22.8
0748	Palmer Park CDP	7 019	NA	NA	142	6 801	26	28	22	31	2 224	NA	1.9
0750	Parkville CDP	31 617	35 159	-10.1	26 937	4 015	47	547	71	393	13 351	NA	11.0
0751	Parole CDP	10 054	NA	NA	9 134	752	22	133	13	109	4 534	NA	26.7
0752	Pasadena CDP	10 012	NA	NA	9 028	818	33	124	9	97	3 509	NA	19.2
0755	Perry Hall CDP	22 723	13 455	68.9	21 149	592	9	941	32	294	8 745	NA	18.1
0765	Pikesville CDP	24 815	22 555	10.0	23 647	791	19	315	43	242	11 455	NA	31.0
0772	Pleasant Hills CDP	2 591	NA	NA	2 546	28	7	10	0	12	938	NA	11.3
0775	Pocomoke City	3 922	NA	NA	2 382	1 494	24	6	16	33	1 682	8 022	5.7
0785	Poolesville town	3 796	NA	NA	3 585	122	9	47	33	130	1 172	13 429	9.0
0792	Potomac CDP	45 634	40 402	12.9	38 509	1 671	44	5 085	325	2 456	15 630	NA	82.3
0808	Pumphrey CDP	5 483	NA	NA	4 456	926	14	76	11	55	2 074	NA	6.4
0820	Randallstown CDP	26 277	25 927	1.3	16 227	9 179	61	727	83	365	9 866	NA	26.6
0823	Redland CDP	16 145	10 727	50.5	11 450	2 302	35	1 993	365	1 080	5 121	NA	17.9
0824	Reisterstown CDP	19 314	19 385	-0.4	16 048	2 560	48	545	113	406	7 801	NA	13.0
0832	Riva CDP	3 438	NA	NA	3 267	126	11	32	2	33	1 199	NA	6.5
0835	Riverdale town	5 185	NA	NA	3 200	1 645	21	193	126	304	2 190	11 811	4.1
0840	Riviera Beach CDP	11 376	NA	NA	11 078	175	18	89	16	104	4 278	NA	6.2
0850	Rockville	44 835	43 811	2.3	35 491	3 699	119	4 394	1 132	3 863	16 238	16 456	31.4
0852	Rosaryville CDP	8 976	NA	NA	6 253	2 387	44	253	39	203	3 009	NA	36.0
0853	Rosedale CDP	18 703	19 956	-6.3	16 297	2 119	35	235	17	152	7 057	NA	17.7
0856	Rossmoor CDP	6 182	NA	NA	5 667	353	2	111	49	173	4 339	NA	2.9
0857	Rossville CDP	9 492	NA	NA	7 596	1 404	36	386	70	182	4 106	NA	14.0
0858	St. Charles CDP	28 717	13 921	106.3	23 896	3 931	153	526	211	819	9 775	NA	28.4
0865	Salisbury	20 592	16 429	25.3	14 481	5 634	48	320	109	252	8 746	10 263	26.7
0870	Savage-Guilford CDP	9 669	NA	NA	7 596	1 624	26	329	94	282	3 943	NA	12.8
0875	Seat Pleasant	5 359	NA	NA	204	5 118	7	16	14	45	1 809	10 686	1.9
0882	Selby-on-the-Bay CDP	3 101	NA	NA	3 066	25	4	5	1	25	1 187	NA	8.3
0884	Severn CDP	24 499	20 134	21.7	16 562	6 545	94	1 123	175	647	8 210	NA	33.8
0885	Severna Park CDP	25 879	21 253	21.8	24 409	879	50	512	29	253	8 843	NA	33.5
0887	Shady Side CDP	4 107	NA	NA	3 464	598	20	15	10	27	1 804	NA	19.0
0900	Silver Spring CDP	76 046	72 893	4.3	49 565	17 296	221	4 202	4 762	9 905	33 494	NA	31.6
0922	South Gate CDP	27 564	24 185	14.0	23 038	3 311	82	990	143	596	11 116	NA	16.4
0924	South Kensington CDP	8 777	NA	NA	8 196	226	14	291	50	300	3 397	NA	6.3
0926	South Laurel CDP	18 591	18 034	3.1	13 004	4 290	61	966	270	714	7 861	NA	10.6
0940	Suitland-Silver Hill CDP	35 111	32 164	9.2	4 758	29 613	104	440	196	487	15 328	NA	17.2
0950	Takoma Park	16 700	16 231	2.9	9 200	6 013	61	717	709	1 619	7 133	13 905	5.2
0955	Taneytown	3 695	NA	NA	3 637	30	2	19	7	23	1 363	8 853	6.5
0958	Temple Hills CDP	6 865	NA	NA	2 568	3 978	31	200	88	194	2 972	NA	3.5

1. Codes shown are 2-digit FIPS codes for states; 4-digit census place codes for places; and 3-digit FIPS county codes followed by 3-digit census MCD codes for minor civil divisions (MCDs). MCD names are followed by county names in parentheses. 2. Hispanic persons may be of any race. 3. Dry land or land partially or temporarily covered by water.

State/ Place/ MCD[1] code	Place	Population: 1990	Population: Places of 10,000 or more: 1980	Population: Places of 10,000 or more: Percent change, 1980–1990	Population characteristics, 1990: Race: White	Race: Black	Race: Am. Indian, Eskimo Aleut	Race: Asian & Pacific Islander	Race: Other race	Hispanic[2]	Total housing units, 1990	Per capita income, 1985 (Dollars)	Land area,[3] 1990 (Sq. Km.)
		1	2	3	4	5	6	7	8	9	10	11	12
	MARYLAND—Con.												
0965	Thurmont town	3 398	NA	NA	3 374	9	1	13	1	12	1 387	10 611	6.4
0975	Towson CDP	49 445	51 083	-3.2	46 318	1 965	65	995	102	642	21 481	NA	36.4
1005	Waldorf CDP	15 058	NA	NA	12 431	2 194	89	273	71	283	5 038	NA	38.0
1007	Walker Mill CDP	10 920	10 651	2.5	755	10 045	36	40	44	98	3 744	NA	8.2
1010	Walkersville town	4 145	NA	NA	4 036	73	0	26	10	44	1 434	NA	10.4
1029	West Laurel CDP	4 151	NA	NA	3 939	102	5	94	11	70	1 368	NA	10.5
1030	Westminster	13 068	NA	NA	12 179	721	30	97	41	139	5 469	10 423	14.3
1031	Westminster South CDP	4 284	NA	NA	4 220	24	7	25	8	32	1 615	NA	10.5
1036	Wheaton-Glenmont CDP	53 720	48 598	10.5	36 013	8 686	137	5 961	2 923	6 481	19 977	NA	26.5
1037	White Marsh CDP	8 183	NA	NA	7 593	205	16	349	20	155	3 188	NA	13.7
1038	White Oak CDP	18 671	13 700	36.3	11 246	5 184	49	1 575	617	1 410	7 826	NA	12.9
1039	White Plains CDP	3 560	NA	NA	3 286	201	19	47	7	39	1 157	NA	30.3
1051	Woodlawn CDP	32 907	NA	NA	23 029	8 065	56	1 602	155	501	13 478	NA	24.9
1053	Woodlawn CDP	5 329	NA	NA	2 200	2 855	27	144	103	219	1 755	NA	3.0
1057	Woodmore CDP	2 874	NA	NA	1 670	1 065	4	113	22	75	961	NA	34.0
25	MASSACHUSETTS	6 016 425	5 737 093	4.9	5 405 374	300 130	12 241	143 392	155 288	287 549	2 472 711	12 510	20 300.3
0010	Abington CDP	13 817	13 517	2.2	13 676	48	27	37	29	94	4 955	NA	25.8
0028	Acushnet Center CDP	3 170	NA	NA	3 116	18	15	4	17	18	1 238	NA	3.8
0048	Adams CDP	6 356	NA	NA	6 318	11	4	15	8	30	3 023	NA	5.9
0080	Amesbury CDP	12 109	12 236	-1.0	11 902	88	23	66	30	82	4 865	NA	13.8
0100	Amherst CDP	17 824	17 773	0.3	15 563	786	38	1 138	299	679	3 120	NA	12.7
0119	Andover CDP	8 242	NA	NA	7 937	104	10	174	17	118	3 672	NA	9.6
0130	Arlington CDP	44 630	48 219	-7.4	42 485	598	33	1 351	163	738	19 421	NA	13.4
0190	Athol CDP	8 732	NA	NA	8 542	45	46	54	45	83	3 759	NA	21.5
0210	Attleboro	38 383	34 196	12.2	36 662	388	73	920	340	1 130	15 045	11 264	71.3
0240	Ayer CDP	2 889	NA	NA	2 511	211	15	80	72	108	1 329	NA	3.2
0265	Barnstable Village CDP	2 790	NA	NA	2 724	36	11	7	12	14	1 472	NA	17.0
0335	Bellingham CDP	4 535	NA	NA	4 408	62	18	37	10	59	1 550	NA	13.7
0350	Belmont CDP	24 720	26 100	-5.3	23 615	206	24	819	56	324	9 968	NA	12.1
0390	Beverly	38 195	37 655	1.4	37 289	328	50	388	140	439	15 652	13 907	40.0
0425	Bliss Corner CDP	4 908	NA	NA	4 799	37	4	2	66	62	2 164	NA	5.2
0440	Boston	574 283	562 994	2.0	360 875	146 945	1 884	30 388	34 191	61 955	250 863	10 774	125.4
0490	Braintree CDP	33 836	36 337	-6.9	32 964	204	32	527	109	293	12 171	NA	36.0
0510	Bridgewater CDP	7 242	NA	NA	6 944	180	15	68	35	124	2 552	NA	5.7
0540	Brockton	92 788	95 172	-2.5	74 449	12 028	269	1 589	4 453	5 860	35 376	9 944	55.6
0570	Brookline CDP	54 718	55 062	-0.6	47 839	1 696	79	4 585	519	1 596	25 353	NA	17.6
0590	Burlington CDP	23 302	23 486	-0.8	21 900	276	27	1 040	59	278	8 054	NA	30.6
0600	Buzzards Bay CDP	3 250	NA	NA	3 140	22	17	19	52	50	1 544	NA	5.1
0610	Cambridge	95 802	95 322	0.5	72 122	12 930	288	8 081	2 381	6 506	41 979	13 494	16.7
0645	Centerville CDP	9 190	NA	NA	8 977	81	25	68	39	112	5 258	NA	20.1
0690	Chelmsford CDP	32 388	31 174	3.9	31 132	156	35	988	77	320	11 817	NA	58.7
0700	Chelsea	28 710	25 431	12.9	20 005	1 492	86	1 435	5 692	9 018	11 574	8 259	5.7
0760	Chicopee	56 632	55 112	2.8	54 031	1 038	70	327	1 166	2 050	23 690	9 946	59.3
0790	Clinton CDP	7 943	12 771	-37.8	7 496	123	7	57	260	537	3 486	NA	3.7
0800	Cochituate CDP	6 046	NA	NA	5 714	78	7	224	23	81	2 249	NA	9.6
0890	Danvers CDP	24 174	24 100	0.3	23 735	124	6	241	68	259	9 119	NA	34.4
0910	Dedham CDP	23 782	25 298	-6.0	23 234	196	27	263	62	242	8 750	NA	27.1
0938	Dennis CDP	2 633	NA	NA	2 607	2	10	6	8	15	2 272	NA	12.7
0940	Dennis Port CDP	2 775	NA	NA	2 643	75	14	4	39	45	5 089	NA	7.9
1065	East Dennis CDP	2 584	NA	NA	2 526	24	6	8	20	15	1 899	NA	12.4
1080	East Falmouth CDP	5 577	NA	NA	5 142	138	54	20	223	113	4 060	NA	14.1
1105	East Harwich CDP	3 828	NA	NA	3 742	26	9	9	42	24	2 386	NA	21.4
1130	East Sandwich CDP	3 171	NA	NA	3 140	8	5	12	6	25	1 732	NA	19.2
1200	Everett	35 701	37 195	-4.0	33 381	1 131	91	641	457	1 371	15 416	10 676	8.8
1220	Fall River	92 703	92 574	0.1	90 076	952	94	1 230	351	1 577	40 375	8 050	80.3
1230	Falmouth CDP	4 047	NA	NA	3 898	46	15	22	66	63	2 972	NA	5.4
1280	Fitchburg	41 194	39 580	4.1	36 847	1 411	97	1 057	1 782	3 957	16 665	9 766	71.9
1300	Forestdale CDP	2 833	NA	NA	2 758	18	16	31	10	33	1 052	NA	9.6
1305	Fort Devens CDP	8 973	NA	NA	6 565	1 704	57	311	336	752	1 835	NA	13.4
1315	Foxborough CDP	5 706	NA	NA	5 560	34	10	80	22	54	2 570	NA	7.5
1330	Framingham CDP	64 994	65 113	-0.2	58 569	2 403	101	1 904	2 017	5 291	26 404	NA	65.1
1340	Franklin CDP	9 965	NA	NA	9 792	67	11	78	17	72	3 604	NA	10.9
1370	Gardner	20 125	17 900	12.4	19 201	403	28	182	311	558	8 654	10 314	57.5
1430	Gloucester	28 716	27 717	3.6	28 508	66	27	77	38	272	13 125	12 225	67.3
1500	Great Barrington CDP	2 810	NA	NA	2 645	126	1	17	21	72	1 373	NA	5.1
1520	Greenfield CDP	14 016	14 198	-1.3	13 678	122	33	124	59	168	6 233	NA	14.9
1710	Haverhill	51 418	46 865	9.7	48 776	1 033	96	433	1 080	2 714	21 321	11 075	86.3
1735	Hingham CDP	5 454	NA	NA	5 382	27	14	29	2	46	2 098	NA	7.7
1770	Holbrook CDP	11 041	11 140	-0.9	10 536	334	19	104	48	157	4 040	NA	19.0
1830	Holyoke	43 704	44 678	-2.2	31 938	1 571	104	356	9 735	13 573	16 917	9 611	55.1
1840	Hopedale CDP	3 961	NA	NA	3 908	14	5	31	3	18	1 492	NA	4.5

1. Codes shown are 2-digit FIPS codes for states; 4-digit census place codes for places; and 3-digit FIPS county codes followed by 3-digit census MCD codes for minor civil divisions (MCDs). MCD names are followed by county names in parentheses. 2. Hispanic persons may be of any race. 3. Dry land or land partially or temporarily covered by water.

State/ Place/ MCD[1] code	Place	Population: 1990	Population: Places of 10,000 or more: 1980	Population: Places of 10,000 or more: Percent change, 1980–1990	Population characteristics, 1990: Race: White	Race: Black	Race: Am. Indian, Eskimo Aleut	Race: Asian & Pacific Islander	Race: Other race	Hispanic[2]	Total housing units, 1990	Per capita income, 1985 (Dollars)	Land area,[3] 1990 (Sq. Km.)
		1	2	3	4	5	6	7	8	9	10	11	12
	MASSACHUSETTS—Con.												
1900	Hudson CDP	14 267	14 156	0.8	13 936	87	15	145	84	402	5 570	NA	14.8
1920	Hull CDP	10 466	NA	NA	10 267	93	22	67	17	113	5 256	NA	7.7
1950	Hyannis CDP	14 120	NA	NA	12 621	793	174	143	389	454	8 340	NA	25.4
1960	Ipswich CDP	4 132	NA	NA	4 069	26	6	18	13	33	1 883	NA	4.3
1980	Kingston CDP	4 774	NA	NA	4 694	42	5	8	25	28	2 048	NA	10.7
2030	Lawrence	70 207	63 175	11.1	45 624	4 496	367	1 358	18 362	29 237	26 915	8 624	18.0
2100	Leominster	38 145	34 508	10.5	35 506	860	71	621	1 087	3 161	15 533	11 277	74.8
2120	Lexington CDP	28 974	29 479	-1.7	26 717	313	15	1 876	53	354	10 841	NA	42.5
2150	Littleton Common CDP	2 867	NA	NA	2 824	29	2	8	4	16	1 167	NA	9.0
2170	Longmeadow CDP	15 467	16 301	-5.1	14 925	123	9	381	29	107	5 527	NA	23.4
2180	Lowell	103 439	92 418	11.9	83 859	2 474	177	11 493	5 436	10 499	40 302	10 106	35.7
2210	Lynn	81 245	78 471	3.5	67 482	6 545	227	3 003	3 988	7 432	34 670	10 607	28.0
2220	Lynnfield CDP	11 274	11 267	0.1	11 068	11	1	189	5	73	4 033	NA	26.3
2230	Malden	53 884	53 386	0.9	48 169	2 255	87	2 815	558	1 417	23 217	12 163	13.2
2260	Mansfield Center CDP	7 170	NA	NA	6 898	173	18	51	30	94	3 078	NA	7.5
2280	Marblehead CDP	19 971	20 126	-0.8	19 660	81	13	173	44	160	8 736	NA	11.7
2305	Marlborough	31 813	30 617	3.9	30 162	572	52	616	411	1 338	13 027	13 645	54.6
2310	Marshfield CDP	4 002	NA	NA	3 912	33	3	31	23	29	1 541	NA	11.2
2330	Marstons Mills CDP	8 017	NA	NA	7 715	130	50	51	71	69	3 538	NA	35.0
2350	Mattapoisett Center CDP	2 949	NA	NA	2 881	13	1	16	38	23	1 506	NA	11.5
2370	Maynard CDP	10 325	NA	NA	9 952	86	15	186	86	240	4 211	NA	13.6
2385	Medfield CDP	5 985	NA	NA	5 900	25	4	51	5	33	2 213	NA	12.8
2400	Medford	57 407	58 076	-1.2	53 622	2 336	68	1 152	229	990	22 650	12 038	21.1
2430	Melrose	28 150	30 055	-6.3	27 619	157	15	321	38	226	11 297	14 151	12.2
2490	Middleborough Center CDP	6 837	NA	NA	6 648	101	23	25	40	49	2 686	NA	10.5
2530	Milford CDP	23 339	21 730	7.4	22 401	330	36	233	339	1 004	9 168	NA	25.8
2580	Millis-Clicquot CDP	4 081	NA	NA	4 026	23	1	25	6	29	1 669	NA	6.7
2620	Milton CDP	25 725	25 860	-0.5	24 120	1 215	18	308	64	261	9 003	NA	33.8
2710	Nahant CDP	3 828	NA	NA	3 785	6	5	22	10	37	1 687	NA	3.2
2720	Nantucket CDP	3 069	NA	NA	2 911	101	3	11	43	27	3 192	NA	6.4
2750	Needham CDP	27 557	27 901	-1.2	26 724	181	15	605	32	264	10 405	NA	32.7
2770	New Bedford	99 922	98 478	1.5	87 486	4 069	404	404	7 559	6 653	41 760	8 156	52.2
2790	Newburyport	16 317	15 900	2.6	16 156	82	17	44	18	91	7 400	13 036	21.7
2830	Newton	82 585	83 622	-1.2	76 623	1 717	95	3 760	390	1 638	30 497	20 601	46.8
2850	North Adams	16 797	18 063	-7.0	16 374	219	43	91	70	199	7 230	8 839	53.0
2860	North Amherst CDP	6 239	NA	NA	4 771	247	11	937	273	453	1 871	NA	5.4
2865	Northampton	29 289	29 286	0.0	27 231	522	55	848	633	1 201	11 747	10 829	89.3
2878	North Attleborough Center CDP	16 178	NA	NA	15 833	99	11	196	39	145	6 873	NA	14.2
2889	Northborough CDP	5 761	NA	NA	5 508	51	10	171	21	67	2 121	NA	8.6
2930	North Brookfield CDP	2 635	NA	NA	2 614	6	4	8	3	14	1 088	NA	3.8
2951	North Falmouth CDP	2 625	NA	NA	2 578	16	6	16	9	18	2 139	NA	10.2
3000	North Plymouth CDP	3 450	NA	NA	3 307	84	11	37	11	52	1 544	NA	3.3
3020	North Scituate CDP	4 891	NA	NA	4 809	14	7	14	47	31	1 803	NA	10.0
3025	North Seekonk CDP	2 635	NA	NA	2 595	2	1	36	1	17	979	NA	3.4
3033	Northwest Harwich CDP	3 037	NA	NA	2 871	20	7	6	133	32	2 833	NA	20.9
3036	North Westport CDP	4 697	NA	NA	4 651	11	2	26	7	17	1 769	NA	13.4
3080	Norwood CDP	28 700	29 711	-3.4	27 716	459	37	422	66	316	11 584	NA	27.2
3125	Ocean Bluff-Brant Rock CDP	4 541	NA	NA	4 492	24	5	13	7	29	2 562	NA	5.3
3130	Ocean Grove CDP	3 169	NA	NA	3 159	2	1	2	5	7	1 294	NA	1.7
3150	Orange CDP	3 791	NA	NA	3 750	16	8	10	7	45	1 516	NA	11.2
3190	Osterville CDP	2 911	NA	NA	2 813	45	10	6	37	29	2 328	NA	14.9
3210	Oxford CDP	5 969	NA	NA	5 897	26	6	25	15	58	2 180	NA	9.1
3230	Palmer CDP	4 069	NA	NA	3 958	57	14	22	18	36	1 881	NA	10.6
3260	Peabody	47 039	45 976	2.3	45 525	570	21	509	414	1 346	18 240	12 681	42.5
3360	Pinehurst CDP	6 614	NA	NA	6 477	31	13	87	6	46	2 047	NA	8.4
3370	Pittsfield	48 622	51 974	-6.4	46 416	1 529	98	374	205	535	21 272	11 751	105.5
3400	Plymouth CDP	7 258	NA	NA	6 898	201	16	68	75	98	3 301	NA	5.9
3425	Pocasset CDP	2 756	NA	NA	2 689	35	11	8	13	25	2 143	NA	9.8
3440	Provincetown CDP	3 374	NA	NA	3 291	53	9	17	4	42	3 660	NA	4.7
3460	Quincy	84 985	84 743	0.3	77 915	928	177	5 577	388	1 197	37 732	12 840	43.5
3470	Randolph CDP	30 093	28 218	6.6	25 694	2 456	54	1 675	214	545	11 257	NA	26.1
3475	Raynham Center CDP	3 709	NA	NA	3 631	30	4	38	6	22	1 194	NA	11.0
3490	Reading CDP	22 539	22 678	-0.6	22 186	55	23	238	37	154	8 104	NA	25.7
3510	Revere	42 786	42 423	0.9	39 877	599	106	1 571	633	1 631	18 726	10 760	15.3
3578	Rockport CDP	5 448	NA	NA	5 405	14	6	19	4	30	3 193	NA	10.3
3660	Sagamore CDP	2 589	NA	NA	2 560	5	8	8	8	12	1 290	NA	8.7
3670	Salem	38 091	38 220	-0.3	35 410	1 017	106	522	1 036	2 548	17 161	11 863	21.0
3675	Salisbury CDP	3 729	NA	NA	3 706	4	9	5	5	21	2 935	NA	15.3
3700	Sandwich CDP	2 998	NA	NA	2 949	11	5	17	16	13	1 688	NA	9.4
3720	Saugus CDP	25 549	24 746	3.2	25 132	140	14	194	69	232	9 528	NA	28.5
3740	Scituate CDP	5 180	NA	NA	5 016	29	5	27	103	34	2 088	NA	10.6
3775	Sharon CDP	5 893	NA	NA	5 591	176	2	111	13	64	2 052	NA	7.7
3900	Smith Mills CDP	4 593	NA	NA	4 401	37	9	29	117	68	1 853	NA	12.3

1. Codes shown are 2-digit FIPS codes for states; 4-digit census place codes for places; and 3-digit FIPS county codes followed by 3-digit census MCD codes for minor civil divisions (MCDs). MCD names are followed by county names in parentheses. 2. Hispanic persons may be of any race. 3. Dry land or land partially or temporarily covered by water.

State/ Place/ MCD[1] code	Place	Population 1990	Places of 10,000 or more 1980	Percent change, 1980–1990	Population characteristics, 1990: Race White	Black	Am. Indian, Eskimo Aleut	Asian & Pacific Islander	Other race	Hispanic[2]	Total housing units, 1990	Per capita income, 1985 (Dollars)	Land area,[3] 1990 (Sq. Km.)
		1	2	3	4	5	6	7	8	9	10	11	12
	MASSACHUSETTS—Con.												
3910	Somerset CDP	17 655	18 813	-6.2	17 463	25	18	117	32	137	6 614	NA	21.0
3920	Somerville	76 210	77 372	-1.5	67 624	4 267	112	2 824	1 383	4 784	31 786	10 759	10.6
3932	South Amherst CDP	5 053	NA	NA	4 117	355	23	392	166	316	1 473	NA	11.0
3980	Southbridge CDP	13 631	12 882	5.8	12 026	112	22	237	1 234	2 083	5 809	NA	13.1
4003	South Dennis CDP	3 559	NA	NA	3 491	21	12	21	14	33	2 404	NA	11.5
4005	South Duxbury CDP	3 017	NA	NA	2 986	10	0	21	0	10	1 272	NA	7.7
4060	South Yarmouth CDP	10 358	NA	NA	10 136	90	14	44	74	152	7 783	NA	18.1
4070	Spencer CDP	6 306	NA	NA	6 237	16	12	12	29	72	2 671	NA	5.5
4090	Springfield	156 983	152 319	3.1	107 626	30 064	333	1 636	17 324	26 528	61 320	9 088	83.2
4130	Stoneham CDP	22 203	21 424	3.6	21 630	159	18	333	63	299	8 915	NA	15.9
4200	Swampscott CDP	13 650	13 837	-1.4	13 459	65	13	79	34	135	5 652	NA	7.9
4220	Taunton	49 832	45 001	10.7	47 484	1 000	82	227	1 039	2 362	20 281	9 742	120.7
4260	Three Rivers CDP	3 006	NA	NA	2 986	13	4	3	0	8	1 267	NA	8.3
4288	Topsfield CDP	2 711	NA	NA	2 658	16	1	31	5	17	951	NA	7.2
4330	Turners Falls CDP	4 731	NA	NA	4 627	40	17	21	26	75	2 167	NA	5.1
4410	Wakefield CDP	24 825	24 895	-0.3	24 472	109	7	204	33	189	9 520	NA	19.3
4425	Walpole CDP	5 495	NA	NA	5 415	36	2	28	14	61	2 264	NA	7.4
4440	Waltham	57 878	58 200	-0.6	52 885	1 778	74	2 055	1 086	3 239	21 723	12 897	32.9
4450	Ware CDP	6 533	NA	NA	6 397	25	27	42	42	137	2 849	NA	16.0
4468	Wareham Center CDP	2 607	NA	NA	2 473	42	5	6	81	28	1 999	NA	3.9
4530	Watertown CDP	33 284	34 384	-3.2	31 971	434	36	742	101	655	14 748	NA	10.6
4550	Webster CDP	11 849	11 175	6.0	11 401	97	55	86	210	338	5 323	NA	7.5
4570	Wellesley CDP	26 615	27 209	-2.2	25 005	416	18	1 045	131	589	8 764	NA	26.4
4610	Westborough CDP	3 917	NA	NA	3 776	42	3	39	57	78	1 749	NA	4.9
4675	West Concord CDP	5 761	NA	NA	5 037	347	16	149	212	345	1 920	NA	8.8
4690	Westfield	38 372	36 465	5.2	37 041	337	44	297	653	1 564	14 470	10 825	120.7
4775	West Springfield CDP	27 537	27 042	1.8	26 439	382	52	309	355	814	12 103	NA	43.4
4840	West Yarmouth CDP	5 409	NA	NA	5 206	105	31	22	45	86	4 939	NA	17.4
4850	Weymouth CDP	54 063	55 601	-2.8	52 777	533	73	486	194	562	21 937	NA	44.1
4870	Whitinsville CDP	5 639	NA	NA	5 574	29	7	17	12	48	2 162	NA	9.4
4883	Wilbraham CDP	3 352	NA	NA	3 261	55	1	29	6	11	1 196	NA	14.6
4920	Williamstown CDP	4 791	NA	NA	4 306	220	10	209	46	121	1 589	NA	8.9
4950	Wilmington CDP	17 654	17 471	1.0	17 371	78	17	172	16	81	5 667	NA	44.5
4960	Winchendon CDP	4 316	NA	NA	4 235	3	11	49	18	42	1 695	NA	5.9
4980	Winchester CDP	20 267	20 701	-2.1	19 484	197	16	537	33	174	7 559	NA	15.6
5000	Winthrop CDP	18 127	19 294	-6.0	17 793	129	11	127	67	240	8 113	NA	5.2
5010	Woburn	35 943	36 626	-1.9	34 717	347	57	547	275	834	14 105	12 904	32.8
5030	Worcester	169 759	161 799	4.9	147 827	7 669	540	4 770	8 953	16 258	69 336	10 454	97.3
5075	Yarmouth Port CDP	4 271	NA	NA	4 238	18	2	8	5	30	2 546	NA	15.7
0010	Barnstable town (Barnstable)	40 949	30 898	32.5	38 708	1 106	286	288	561	701	23 370	12 704	155.5
0010	Bourne town (Barnstable)	16 064	13 874	15.8	15 507	226	86	97	148	200	8 999	11 038	105.9
0010	Brewster town (Barnstable)	8 440	NA	NA	8 347	39	9	33	12	65	6 367	10 869	59.6
0010	Chatham town (Barnstable)	6 579	NA	NA	6 514	29	16	12	8	37	6 301	14 713	42.6
0010	Dennis town (Barnstable)	13 864	12 360	12.2	13 520	139	63	48	94	119	14 502	12 385	53.4
0010	Eastham town (Barnstable)	4 462	NA	NA	4 410	19	12	17	4	31	4 863	12 642	36.2
0010	Falmouth town (Barnstable)	27 960	23 640	18.3	26 438	497	176	198	651	411	18 168	12 584	114.6
0010	Harwich town (Barnstable)	10 275	NA	NA	9 888	78	23	26	260	84	8 325	11 854	54.5
0010	Mashpee town (Barnstable)	7 884	NA	NA	7 020	312	385	29	138	116	7 002	12 901	60.8
0010	Orleans town (Barnstable)	5 838	NA	NA	5 792	10	5	31	0	17	4 593	15 479	36.6
0010	Provincetown town (Barnstable)	3 561	NA	NA	3 475	56	9	17	4	46	3 802	11 320	25.0
0010	Sandwich town (Barnstable)	15 489	NA	NA	15 239	65	50	81	54	131	7 236	13 117	111.5
0010	Yarmouth town (Barnstable)	21 174	18 449	14.8	20 674	230	50	84	136	297	15 913	11 916	62.8
0030	Adams town (Berkshire)	9 445	10 381	-9.0	9 395	16	4	20	10	39	4 356	9 980	59.4
0030	Cheshire town (Berkshire)	3 479	NA	NA	3 463	4	4	7	1	26	1 358	10 695	69.8
0030	Dalton town (Berkshire)	7 155	NA	NA	7 082	32	2	33	6	40	2 733	11 960	56.5
0030	Great Barrington town (Berkshire)	7 725	NA	NA	7 402	208	8	62	45	134	3 168	10 966	117.0
0030	Lanesborough town (Berkshire)	3 032	NA	NA	2 995	14	3	16	4	25	1 292	11 218	75.2
0030	Lee town (Berkshire)	5 849	NA	NA	5 784	18	8	38	1	37	2 675	11 055	68.4
0030	Lenox town (Berkshire)	5 069	NA	NA	4 916	69	12	50	22	44	2 410	11 882	55.0
0031	Sheffield town (Berkshire)	2 910	NA	NA	2 842	53	2	12	1	13	1 460	10 253	124.7
0031	Williamstown town (Berkshire)	8 220	NA	NA	7 687	254	16	214	49	151	2 979	12 078	121.4
0050	Acushnet town (Bristol)	9 554	NA	NA	9 426	38	19	22	49	50	3 526	10 165	47.8
0050	Berkley town (Bristol)	4 237	NA	NA	4 194	11	2	7	23	36	1 411	10 476	42.8
0050	Dartmouth town (Bristol)	27 244	23 966	13.7	26 434	197	24	228	361	279	9 989	10 853	159.4
0050	Dighton town (Bristol)	5 631	NA	NA	5 578	16	12	8	17	67	1 994	10 935	58.0
0050	Easton town (Bristol)	19 807	16 623	19.2	19 192	337	21	197	60	122	6 708	13 408	73.7
0050	Fairhaven town (Bristol)	16 132	15 759	2.4	15 749	85	33	76	189	136	7 093	9 845	32.2
0050	Freetown town (Bristol)	8 522	NA	NA	8 321	46	15	33	107	65	2 906	10 373	94.8
0050	Mansfield town (Bristol)	16 568	13 453	23.2	16 052	280	28	151	57	197	6 357	12 229	53.0
0050	North Attleborough town (Bristol)	25 038	21 095	18.7	24 546	132	16	298	46	202	9 868	12 137	48.3
0050	Norton town (Bristol)	14 265	12 690	12.4	13 852	191	26	148	48	174	4 852	10 182	74.4
0050	Raynham town (Bristol)	9 867	NA	NA	9 679	83	11	76	18	86	3 515	12 167	53.1
0050	Rehoboth town (Bristol)	8 656	NA	NA	8 542	39	6	44	25	54	2 963	12 934	120.4

1. Codes shown are 2-digit FIPS codes for states; 4-digit census place codes for places; and 3-digit FIPS county codes followed by 3-digit census MCD codes for minor civil divisions (MCDs). MCD names are followed by county names in parentheses. 2. Hispanic persons may be of any race. 3. Dry land or land partially or temporarily covered by water.

State/ Place/ MCD[1] code	Place	Population			Population characteristics, 1990							Total housing units, 1990	Per capita income, 1985 (Dollars)	Land area,[3] 1990 (Sq. Km.)
		1990	Places of 10,000 or more		Race						Hispanic[2]			
			1980	Percent change, 1980–1990	White	Black	Am. Indian, Eskimo Aleut	Asian & Pacific Islander	Other race					
		1	2	3	4	5	6	7	8		9	10	11	12
	MASSACHUSETTS—Con.													
0050	Seekonk town (Bristol)	13 046	12 269	6.3	12 724	93	23	162	44		72	4 626	12 739	47.4
0050	Somerset town (Bristol)	17 655	18 813	-6.2	17 463	25	18	117	32		137	6 614	11 237	21.0
0050	Swansea town (Bristol)	15 411	15 461	-0.3	15 241	52	22	67	29		91	5 471	10 568	59.7
0051	Westport town (Bristol)	13 852	13 763	0.6	13 725	20	8	63	36		88	5 881	10 849	129.6
0070	Edgartown town (Dukes)	3 062	NA	NA	3 008	38	6	8	2		25	3 053	NA	69.9
0070	Oak Bluffs town (Dukes)	2 804	NA	NA	2 517	193	78	9	7		46	3 172	NA	19.1
0070	Tisbury town (Dukes)	3 120	NA	NA	2 931	85	71	19	14		19	2 387	12 743	17.0
0090	Amesbury town (Essex)	14 997	13 972	7.3	14 756	103	34	69	35		96	5 996	11 216	32.1
0090	Andover town (Essex)	29 151	26 370	10.5	27 706	244	36	1 097	68		433	10 892	18 373	80.3
0090	Boxford town (Essex)	6 266	NA	NA	6 140	43	6	69	8		34	2 087	19 207	62.1
0090	Danvers town (Essex)	24 174	24 100	0.3	23 735	124	6	241	68		259	9 119	13 681	34.4
0090	Essex town (Essex)	3 260	NA	NA	3 241	1	2	14	2		15	1 485	11 809	36.7
0090	Georgetown town (Essex)	6 384	NA	NA	6 344	6	9	23	2		13	2 219	13 076	33.5
0090	Groveland town (Essex)	5 214	NA	NA	5 176	8	10	16	4		27	1 813	13 291	23.2
0090	Hamilton town (Essex)	7 280	NA	NA	7 103	35	12	102	28		87	2 635	15 871	37.8
0090	Ipswich town (Essex)	11 873	11 128	6.7	11 746	44	8	51	24		77	5 162	14 067	84.5
0090	Lynnfield town (Essex)	11 274	11 267	0.1	11 068	11	1	189	5		73	4 033	20 410	26.3
0090	Manchester town (Essex)	5 286	NA	NA	5 252	2	6	23	3		19	2 315	21 330	20.3
0090	Marblehead town (Essex)	19 971	20 126	-0.8	19 660	81	13	173	44		160	8 736	19 734	11.7
0090	Merrimac town (Essex)	5 166	NA	NA	5 116	16	3	22	9		28	2 014	12 269	22.1
0090	Methuen town (Essex)	39 990	36 701	9.0	37 888	409	48	525	1 120		2 070	15 441	11 839	58.0
0091	Middleton town (Essex)	4 921	NA	NA	4 833	40	16	29	3		20	1 907	14 445	36.2
0091	Nahant town (Essex)	3 828	NA	NA	3 785	6	5	22	10		37	1 687	16 666	3.2
0091	Newbury town (Essex)	5 623	NA	NA	5 587	13	5	15	3		43	2 365	13 563	62.8
0091	North Andover town (Essex)	22 792	20 129	13.2	22 079	178	23	455	57		307	8 271	15 210	69.1
0091	Rockport town (Essex)	7 482	NA	NA	7 425	17	9	27	4		35	4 202	13 848	18.3
0091	Rowley town (Essex)	4 452	NA	NA	4 406	11	10	20	5		12	1 573	12 853	48.5
0091	Salisbury town (Essex)	6 882	NA	NA	6 831	8	20	13	10		50	4 040	9 945	40.0
0091	Saugus town (Essex)	25 549	24 746	3.2	25 132	140	14	194	69		232	9 528	12 555	28.5
0091	Swampscott town (Essex)	13 650	13 837	-1.4	13 459	65	13	79	34		135	5 652	16 618	7.9
0091	Topsfield town (Essex)	5 754	NA	NA	5 673	25	2	46	8		46	1 967	19 048	32.8
0091	Wenham town (Essex)	4 212	NA	NA	4 131	22	4	46	9		36	1 207	19 749	20.0
0091	West Newbury town (Essex)	3 421	NA	NA	3 385	20	0	15	1		17	1 147	14 423	35.0
0110	Deerfield town (Franklin)	5 018	NA	NA	4 961	13	3	34	7		38	2 083	12 975	83.6
0110	Greenfield town (Franklin)	18 666	18 436	1.2	18 208	158	48	168	84		221	8 067	10 691	56.3
0110	Montague town (Franklin)	8 316	NA	NA	8 144	47	44	43	38		111	3 727	10 493	78.8
0110	Northfield town (Franklin)	2 838	NA	NA	2 800	5	13	9	11		24	1 289	NA	89.1
0110	Orange town (Franklin)	7 312	NA	NA	7 224	34	11	29	14		88	3 106	8 560	91.6
0111	Sunderland town (Franklin)	3 399	NA	NA	3 150	79	16	91	63		168	1 504	9 755	37.3
0130	Agawam town (Hampden)	27 323	26 271	4.0	26 779	260	34	133	117		308	10 869	11 654	60.2
0130	Brimfield town (Hampden)	3 001	NA	NA	2 970	17	9	0	5		21	1 245	NA	90.0
0130	East Longmeadow town (Hampden)	13 367	12 905	3.6	13 210	74	12	56	15		61	4 796	12 693	33.6
0130	Hampden town (Hampden)	4 709	NA	NA	4 666	17	4	15	7		24	1 653	11 807	50.9
0130	Longmeadow town (Hampden)	15 467	16 301	-5.1	14 925	123	9	381	29		107	5 527	20 306	23.4
0130	Ludlow town (Hampden)	18 820	18 114	3.9	18 616	38	16	111	39		380	7 191	10 804	70.3
0130	Monson town (Hampden)	7 776	NA	NA	7 687	45	13	16	15		51	2 755	10 143	114.7
0130	Palmer town (Hampden)	12 054	11 425	5.5	11 864	90	31	43	26		72	5 061	10 599	81.7
0130	Southwick town (Hampden)	7 667	NA	NA	7 571	38	15	19	24		74	2 934	10 592	80.2
0131	West Springfield town (Hampden)	27 537	27 042	1.8	26 439	382	52	309	355		814	12 103	11 777	43.4
0131	Wilbraham town (Hampden)	12 635	12 053	4.8	12 289	155	3	166	22		101	4 631	15 473	57.6
0150	Amherst town (Hampshire)	35 228	33 229	6.0	29 930	1 626	89	2 773	810		1 669	8 816	8 371	71.7
0150	Belchertown town (Hampshire)	10 579	NA	NA	10 379	55	8	103	34		95	3 988	10 347	136.6
0150	Easthampton town (Hampshire)	15 537	15 580	-0.3	15 228	56	16	128	109		273	6 421	10 996	34.7
0150	Granby town (Hampshire)	5 565	NA	NA	5 497	15	11	30	12		67	2 004	10 833	72.2
0150	Hadley town (Hampshire)	4 231	NA	NA	4 128	16	2	75	10		24	1 715	12 591	60.4
0150	Hatfield town (Hampshire)	3 184	NA	NA	3 153	6	4	15	6		27	1 304	10 934	41.5
0150	Southampton town (Hampshire)	4 478	NA	NA	4 417	17	8	14	22		43	1 595	11 209	72.9
0150	South Hadley town (Hampshire)	16 685	16 399	1.7	16 012	177	15	400	81		210	6 233	11 574	45.9
0150	Ware town (Hampshire)	9 808	NA	NA	9 656	26	33	51	42		145	4 095	10 306	89.1
0150	Williamsburg town (Hampshire)	2 515	NA	NA	2 481	10	6	14	4		26	973	NA	66.4
0170	Acton town (Middlesex)	17 872	17 544	1.9	16 992	160	20	647	53		260	6 891	18 772	51.7
0170	Arlington town (Middlesex)	44 630	48 219	-7.4	42 485	598	33	1 351	163		738	19 421	15 541	13.4
0170	Ashby town (Middlesex)	2 717	NA	NA	2 703	6	0	8	0		27	959	NA	61.6
0170	Ashland town (Middlesex)	12 066	NA	NA	11 499	229	11	249	78		238	4 821	16 377	32.2
0170	Ayer town (Middlesex)	6 871	NA	NA	5 730	674	39	217	211		340	2 891	10 970	23.4
0170	Bedford town (Middlesex)	12 996	13 067	-0.5	12 171	351	27	401	46		190	4 602	15 984	35.6
0170	Belmont town (Middlesex)	24 720	26 100	-5.3	23 615	206	24	819	56		324	9 968	19 184	12.1
0170	Billerica town (Middlesex)	37 609	36 727	2.4	36 405	407	56	570	171		476	12 005	12 221	67.0
0170	Boxborough town (Middlesex)	3 343	NA	NA	3 212	21	3	105	2		39	1 485	19 591	26.8
0170	Burlington town (Middlesex)	23 302	23 486	-0.8	21 900	276	27	1 040	59		278	8 054	14 871	30.6
0170	Carlisle town (Middlesex)	4 333	NA	NA	4 130	9	0	186	8		36	1 495	24 213	39.8
0170	Chelmsford town (Middlesex)	32 383	31 174	3.9	31 127	156	35	988	77		320	11 815	15 399	58.7
0170	Concord town (Middlesex)	17 076	16 293	4.8	15 988	454	27	349	258		514	5 917	22 570	64.5

1. Codes shown are 2-digit FIPS codes for states; 4-digit census place codes for places; and 3-digit FIPS county codes followed by 3-digit census MCD codes for minor civil divisions (MCDs). MCD names are followed by county names in parentheses. 2. Hispanic persons may be of any race. 3. Dry land or land partially or temporarily covered by water.

State/ Place/ MCD[1] code	Place	Population 1990	Places of 10,000 or more 1980	Places of 10,000 or more Percent change, 1980–1990	Race: White	Race: Black	Race: Am. Indian, Eskimo Aleut	Race: Asian & Pacific Islander	Race: Other race	Hispanic[2]	Total housing units, 1990	Per capita income, 1985 (Dollars)	Land area,[3] 1990 (Sq. Km.)
		1	2	3	4	5	6	7	8	9	10	11	12
	MASSACHUSETTS—Con.												
0170	Dracut town (Middlesex)	25 594	21 249	20.4	25 034	140	26	314	80	241	9 279	12 253	54.1
0170	Framingham town (Middlesex)	64 989	65 113	-0.2	58 564	2 403	101	1 904	2 017	5 291	26 402	15 636	65.1
0170	Groton town (Middlesex)	7 511	NA	NA	7 378	53	15	58	7	62	2 774	14 864	84.9
0171	Holliston town (Middlesex)	12 926	12 622	2.4	12 635	132	13	123	23	152	4 413	14 277	48.5
0171	Hopkinton town (Middlesex)	9 191	NA	NA	9 022	36	8	105	20	122	3 305	15 329	68.8
0171	Hudson town (Middlesex)	17 233	16 431	4.9	16 759	148	20	213	93	465	6 685	13 117	29.8
0171	Lexington town (Middlesex)	28 974	29 479	-1.7	26 717	313	15	1 876	53	354	10 841	21 138	42.5
0171	Lincoln town (Middlesex)	7 666	NA	NA	6 935	393	8	281	49	162	2 714	24 242	37.2
0171	Littleton town (Middlesex)	7 051	NA	NA	6 917	53	7	60	14	42	2 691	15 305	43.0
0171	Maynard town (Middlesex)	10 325	NA	NA	9 952	86	15	186	86	240	4 211	13 509	13.6
0171	Natick town (Middlesex)	30 510	29 469	3.5	29 022	612	25	725	126	544	12 645	16 037	39.1
0171	North Reading town (Middlesex)	12 002	11 455	4.8	11 843	36	5	108	10	85	4 176	14 485	34.3
0171	Pepperell town (Middlesex)	10 098	NA	NA	9 924	80	10	69	15	99	3 505	12 165	58.4
0171	Reading town (Middlesex)	22 539	22 678	-0.6	22 186	55	23	238	37	154	8 104	15 253	25.7
0171	Sherborn town (Middlesex)	3 989	NA	NA	3 912	7	2	57	11	35	1 374	25 453	41.3
0171	Shirley town (Middlesex)	6 118	NA	NA	5 369	421	20	183	125	269	2 183	11 184	41.0
0172	Stoneham town (Middlesex)	22 203	21 424	3.6	21 630	159	18	333	63	299	8 915	13 869	15.9
0172	Stow town (Middlesex)	5 328	NA	NA	5 202	12	15	77	22	67	1 853	17 303	45.6
0172	Sudbury town (Middlesex)	14 358	14 027	2.4	13 714	184	16	417	27	136	4 875	21 499	63.1
0172	Tewksbury town (Middlesex)	27 266	24 635	10.7	26 580	222	42	353	69	245	8 950	12 700	53.7
0172	Townsend town (Middlesex)	8 496	NA	NA	8 388	79	4	18	7	61	2 894	11 676	85.1
0172	Tyngsborough town (Middlesex)	8 642	NA	NA	8 498	41	3	91	9	52	3 033	13 207	43.6
0172	Wakefield town (Middlesex)	24 825	24 895	-0.3	24 472	109	7	204	33	189	9 520	14 177	19.3
0172	Watertown town (Middlesex)	33 284	34 384	-3.2	31 971	434	36	742	101	655	14 748	14 304	10.6
0172	Wayland town (Middlesex)	11 874	12 162	-2.4	11 317	124	7	390	36	147	4 383	23 724	39.5
0172	Westford town (Middlesex)	16 392	13 434	22.0	16 042	37	17	270	26	162	5 530	15 635	79.3
0172	Weston town (Middlesex)	10 200	11 169	-8.7	9 625	74	0	475	26	167	3 508	35 260	44.1
0172	Wilmington town (Middlesex)	17 651	17 471	1.0	17 368	78	17	172	16	81	5 666	12 203	44.4
0172	Winchester town (Middlesex)	20 267	20 701	-2.1	19 484	197	16	537	33	174	7 559	19 738	15.6
0190	Nantucket town (Nantucket)	6 012	NA	NA	5 787	151	5	18	51	50	7 021	16 943	123.8
0210	Avon town (Norfolk)	4 558	NA	NA	4 411	102	9	26	10	36	1 666	12 065	11.3
0210	Bellingham town (Norfolk)	14 877	14 300	4.0	14 540	155	29	113	40	139	5 173	11 829	47.9
0210	Braintree town (Norfolk)	33 836	36 337	-6.9	32 964	204	32	527	109	293	12 171	13 570	36.0
0210	Brookline town (Norfolk)	54 718	55 062	-0.6	47 839	1 696	79	4 585	519	1 596	25 353	19 976	17.6
0210	Canton town (Norfolk)	18 530	18 182	1.9	17 999	237	17	224	53	150	6 789	15 066	49.0
0210	Cohasset town (Norfolk)	7 075	NA	NA	7 014	20	7	31	3	42	2 724	22 508	25.6
0210	Dedham town (Norfolk)	23 782	25 298	-6.0	23 234	196	27	263	62	242	8 750	14 769	27.1
0210	Dover town (Norfolk)	4 915	NA	NA	4 789	12	1	110	3	36	1 696	28 525	39.7
0210	Foxborough town (Norfolk)	14 637	14 148	3.5	14 366	73	18	152	28	103	5 477	13 400	52.0
0210	Franklin town (Norfolk)	22 095	18 217	21.3	21 662	149	26	222	36	143	7 692	12 383	69.3
0210	Holbrook town (Norfolk)	11 041	11 140	-0.9	10 536	334	19	104	48	157	4 040	11 334	19.0
0210	Medfield town (Norfolk)	10 531	10 220	3.0	10 354	71	5	92	9	59	3 501	17 413	37.6
0210	Medway town (Norfolk)	9 931	NA	NA	9 739	68	8	100	16	73	3 390	13 061	29.7
0210	Millis town (Norfolk)	7 613	NA	NA	7 511	34	7	51	10	60	2 832	14 151	31.5
0210	Milton town (Norfolk)	25 725	25 860	-0.5	24 120	1 215	18	308	64	261	9 003	16 534	33.8
0210	Needham town (Norfolk)	27 557	27 901	-1.2	26 724	181	15	605	32	264	10 405	20 348	32.7
0210	Norfolk town (Norfolk)	9 270	NA	NA	8 414	521	32	83	220	444	2 500	13 558	38.4
0210	Norwood town (Norfolk)	28 700	29 711	-3.4	27 716	459	37	422	66	316	11 584	13 910	27.1
0210	Plainville town (Norfolk)	6 871	NA	NA	6 766	41	1	53	10	60	2 727	12 546	28.7
0211	Randolph town (Norfolk)	30 093	28 218	6.6	25 694	2 456	54	1 675	214	545	11 257	13 149	26.1
0211	Sharon town (Norfolk)	15 517	13 601	14.1	14 650	493	6	345	23	139	5 351	17 541	60.4
0211	Stoughton town (Norfolk)	26 777	26 710	0.3	25 224	1 070	34	298	151	480	9 754	12 484	41.5
0211	Walpole town (Norfolk)	20 212	18 859	7.2	19 607	323	30	133	119	309	7 022	13 605	53.2
0211	Wellesley town (Norfolk)	26 615	27 209	-2.2	25 005	416	18	1 045	131	589	8 764	22 420	26.4
0211	Westwood town (Norfolk)	12 557	13 212	-5.0	12 314	39	2	196	6	80	4 551	19 189	28.4
0211	Weymouth town (Norfolk)	54 063	55 601	-2.8	52 777	533	73	486	194	562	21 937	12 941	44.1
0211	Wrentham town (Norfolk)	9 006	NA	NA	8 862	63	6	63	12	39	2 975	11 634	57.5
0230	Abington town (Plymouth)	13 817	13 517	2.2	13 676	48	27	37	29	94	4 955	11 532	25.8
0230	Bridgewater town (Plymouth)	21 249	17 202	23.5	19 727	1 003	62	179	278	684	6 230	10 472	71.2
0230	Carver town (Plymouth)	10 590	NA	NA	10 189	210	26	41	124	73	3 799	10 491	97.3
0230	Duxbury town (Plymouth)	13 895	11 813	17.6	13 661	126	5	72	31	94	5 141	17 654	61.5
0230	East Bridgewater town (Plymouth)	11 104	NA	NA	10 913	93	20	34	44	103	3 700	10 441	44.7
0230	Halifax town (Plymouth)	6 526	NA	NA	6 441	33	9	23	20	21	2 453	10 989	41.1
0230	Hanover town (Plymouth)	11 912	11 358	4.9	11 706	77	10	101	18	77	3 837	13 227	40.4
0230	Hanson town (Plymouth)	9 028	NA	NA	8 799	124	6	47	52	51	2 985	10 859	38.9
0230	Hingham town (Plymouth)	19 821	20 339	-2.5	19 517	91	28	160	25	165	7 161	17 840	58.2
0230	Hull town (Plymouth)	10 466	NA	NA	10 267	93	22	67	17	113	5 256	11 279	7.7
0230	Kingston town (Plymouth)	9 045	NA	NA	8 909	69	12	15	40	39	3 496	11 674	48.0
0230	Lakeville town (Plymouth)	7 785	NA	NA	7 699	25	15	32	14	51	3 138	11 205	77.4
0230	Marion town (Plymouth)	4 496	NA	NA	4 074	121	4	40	257	76	2 045	15 078	37.9
0230	Marshfield town (Plymouth)	21 531	20 910	3.0	21 163	156	28	117	67	142	8 877	13 720	73.7
0230	Mattapoisett town (Plymouth)	5 850	NA	NA	5 686	29	5	33	97	65	2 949	13 704	42.7
0230	Middleborough town (Plymouth)	17 867	16 404	8.9	17 358	274	64	66	105	170	6 395	9 694	180.2

1. Codes shown are 2-digit FIPS codes for states; 4-digit census place codes for places; and 3-digit FIPS county codes followed by 3-digit census MCD codes for minor civil divisions (MCDs). MCD names are followed by county names in parentheses. 2. Hispanic persons may be of any race. 3. Dry land or land partially or temporarily covered by water.

State/ Place/ MCD[1] code	Place	Population: 1990	Population: Places of 10,000 or more: 1980	Population: Places of 10,000 or more: Percent change, 1980–1990	Population characteristics, 1990: Race: White	Race: Black	Race: Am. Indian, Eskimo Aleut	Race: Asian & Pacific Islander	Race: Other race	Hispanic[2]	Total housing units, 1990	Per capita income, 1985 (Dollars)	Land area,[3] 1990 (Sq. Km.)
		1	2	3	4	5	6	7	8	9	10	11	12
	MASSACHUSETTS—Con.												
0230	Norwell town (Plymouth)	9 279	NA	NA	9 151	30	4	83	11	31	3 079	16 796	54.1
0230	Pembroke town (Plymouth)	14 544	13 487	7.8	14 392	73	4	59	16	65	4 881	11 422	56.6
0231	Plymouth town (Plymouth)	45 608	35 913	27.0	44 058	844	102	282	322	557	19 658	11 396	249.9
0231	Rochester town (Plymouth)	3 921	NA	NA	3 842	38	0	5	36	23	1 341	11 583	87.9
0231	Rockland town (Plymouth)	16 123	15 695	2.7	15 689	252	22	120	40	158	5 745	10 026	26.0
0231	Scituate town (Plymouth)	16 786	17 317	-3.1	16 345	65	16	76	284	126	6 983	15 717	44.5
0231	Wareham town (Plymouth)	19 232	18 457	4.2	17 329	476	99	91	1 237	580	11 383	10 315	92.7
0231	West Bridgewater town (Plymouth)	6 389	NA	NA	6 266	43	2	42	36	33	2 302	11 877	40.8
0231	Whitman town (Plymouth)	13 240	13 534	-2.2	13 058	83	26	31	42	91	4 596	10 453	18.0
0250	Winthrop town (Suffolk)	18 127	19 294	-6.0	17 793	129	11	127	67	240	8 113	13 213	5.2
0270	Ashburnham town (Worcester)	5 433	NA	NA	5 382	7	7	24	13	42	2 279	11 526	100.2
0270	Athol town (Worcester)	11 451	10 576	8.3	11 218	58	56	65	54	102	4 840	9 324	84.4
0270	Auburn town (Worcester)	15 005	14 845	1.1	14 814	49	21	102	19	85	5 892	11 890	39.8
0270	Barre town (Worcester)	4 546	NA	NA	4 485	28	1	30	2	27	1 747	10 391	114.8
0270	Blackstone town (Worcester)	8 023	NA	NA	7 898	26	11	66	22	66	2 979	9 973	28.2
0270	Bolton town (Worcester)	3 134	NA	NA	3 092	7	2	33	0	18	1 097	17 120	51.6
0270	Boylston town (Worcester)	3 517	NA	NA	3 461	20	4	26	6	16	1 362	15 352	41.5
0270	Brookfield town (Worcester)	2 968	NA	NA	2 954	9	3	2	0	10	1 240	NA	40.2
0270	Charlton town (Worcester)	9 576	NA	NA	9 527	15	7	22	5	46	3 438	9 961	110.6
0270	Clinton town (Worcester)	13 222	12 771	3.5	12 390	253	9	133	437	1 032	5 635	10 880	14.8
0270	Douglas town (Worcester)	5 438	NA	NA	5 375	9	15	22	17	59	2 191	10 052	94.2
0270	Dudley town (Worcester)	9 540	NA	NA	9 343	50	6	89	52	148	3 583	10 192	54.5
0270	Grafton town (Worcester)	13 035	11 238	16.0	12 672	178	17	151	17	174	5 035	12 759	58.9
0270	Harvard town (Worcester)	12 329	12 170	1.3	10 160	1 507	54	327	281	673	3 141	12 441	68.3
0271	Holden town (Worcester)	14 628	13 336	9.7	14 421	34	15	149	9	96	5 428	14 766	90.6
0271	Hopedale town (Worcester)	5 666	NA	NA	5 592	24	6	40	4	31	2 060	13 445	13.4
0271	Hubbardston town (Worcester)	2 797	NA	NA	2 778	8	4	4	3	27	1 025	NA	106.3
0271	Lancaster town (Worcester)	6 661	NA	NA	5 957	431	20	77	176	409	2 095	11 108	71.7
0271	Leicester town (Worcester)	10 191	NA	NA	9 972	82	16	63	58	127	3 629	10 123	60.5
0271	Lunenburg town (Worcester)	9 117	NA	NA	8 962	60	10	60	25	88	3 486	13 203	68.4
0271	Mendon town (Worcester)	4 010	NA	NA	3 955	27	6	15	7	37	1 454	13 237	46.9
0271	Milford town (Worcester)	25 355	23 414	8.3	24 382	341	36	252	344	1 022	9 819	12 046	37.8
0271	Millbury town (Worcester)	12 228	11 808	3.6	12 045	34	5	117	27	71	4 758	11 216	40.8
0271	Northborough town (Worcester)	11 929	10 568	12.9	11 319	89	20	467	34	129	4 180	16 049	48.0
0271	Northbridge town (Worcester)	13 371	12 246	9.2	13 235	57	19	38	22	108	5 013	10 417	44.5
0271	North Brookfield town (Worcester)	4 708	NA	NA	4 667	12	5	18	6	27	1 845	9 427	54.6
0271	Oxford town (Worcester)	12 588	11 673	7.8	12 369	76	18	84	41	110	4 655	10 293	69.0
0271	Paxton town (Worcester)	4 047	NA	NA	3 941	31	5	56	14	18	1 351	15 305	38.2
0272	Princeton town (Worcester)	3 189	NA	NA	3 169	4	1	15	0	24	1 103	NA	91.8
0272	Rutland town (Worcester)	4 936	NA	NA	4 852	42	5	33	4	22	1 867	10 688	91.3
0272	Shrewsbury town (Worcester)	24 146	22 674	6.5	22 885	255	13	904	89	331	10 055	14 540	53.7
0272	Southborough town (Worcester)	6 628	NA	NA	6 429	40	5	136	18	47	2 361	18 032	36.6
0272	Southbridge town (Worcester)	17 816	16 665	6.9	16 033	130	26	273	1 354	2 278	7 481	9 381	52.2
0272	Spencer town (Worcester)	11 645	10 768	8.1	11 528	28	25	28	36	100	4 770	10 432	85.1
0272	Sterling town (Worcester)	6 481	NA	NA	6 393	44	18	21	5	73	2 308	13 227	79.1
0272	Sturbridge town (Worcester)	7 775	NA	NA	7 641	37	28	51	18	59	3 180	12 903	96.9
0272	Sutton town (Worcester)	6 824	NA	NA	6 784	3	11	20	6	22	2 517	11 637	83.9
0272	Templeton town (Worcester)	6 438	NA	NA	6 391	26	3	13	5	49	2 276	9 534	83.0
0272	Upton town (Worcester)	4 677	NA	NA	4 591	31	12	34	9	33	1 895	12 876	55.7
0272	Uxbridge town (Worcester)	10 415	NA	NA	10 319	36	9	32	19	59	3 963	11 505	76.5
0272	Warren town (Worcester)	4 437	NA	NA	4 375	24	15	10	13	45	1 816	9 798	71.3
0272	Webster town (Worcester)	16 196	14 480	11.9	15 696	118	64	106	212	364	7 348	10 327	32.4
0272	Westborough town (Worcester)	14 133	13 661	3.5	13 344	240	12	420	117	279	5 767	16 342	53.2
0272	West Boylston town (Worcester)	6 611	NA	NA	6 310	88	5	45	163	185	2 276	13 568	33.4
0272	West Brookfield town (Worcester)	3 532	NA	NA	3 512	10	6	2	2	20	1 389	11 659	53.0
0272	Westminster town (Worcester)	6 191	NA	NA	6 140	12	11	19	9	37	2 405	12 236	92.0
0272	Winchendon town (Worcester)	8 805	NA	NA	8 679	22	16	64	24	86	3 349	9 269	112.1
26	MICHIGAN	9 295 297	9 262 044	0.4	7 756 086	1 291 706	55 638	104 983	86 884	201 596	3 847 926	10 902	147 135.8
0010	Adrian	22 097	21 186	4.3	19 188	723	88	172	1 926	2 958	7 842	9 426	17.9
0030	Albion	10 066	11 059	-9.0	6 673	3 096	27	74	196	473	3 656	7 371	10.9
0035	Algonac	4 551	NA	NA	4 468	6	44	13	20	44	1 771	10 427	3.6
0040	Allegan	4 547	NA	NA	4 281	186	18	22	40	85	1 853	9 361	9.5
0047	Allendale CDP	6 950	NA	NA	6 585	234	22	60	49	83	1 828	NA	59.1
0050	Allen Park	31 092	34 196	-9.1	30 465	144	66	233	184	986	12 233	13 550	18.2
0055	Alma	9 034	NA	NA	8 677	42	33	42	240	567	3 307	8 505	13.9
0065	Alpena	11 354	12 214	-7.0	11 211	27	49	61	6	53	5 002	8 423	22.0
0077	Anchorville CDP	3 202	NA	NA	3 155	5	17	7	18	48	1 446	NA	5.6
0080	Ann Arbor	109 592	107 960	1.5	89 841	9 905	386	8 424	1 036	2 827	44 010	12 911	67.1
0108	Auburn Hills	17 076	NA	NA	14 711	1 641	111	412	201	496	7 069	12 049	43.0
0125	Bad Axe	3 484	NA	NA	3 423	9	9	12	31	50	1 473	9 386	4.9
0160	Battle Creek	53 540	35 724	49.9	43 226	8 854	342	670	448	978	23 252	10 548	110.9

1. Codes shown are 2-digit FIPS codes for states; 4-digit census place codes for places; and 3-digit FIPS county codes followed by 3-digit census MCD codes for minor civil divisions (MCDs). MCD names are followed by county names in parentheses. 2. Hispanic persons may be of any race. 3. Dry land or land partially or temporarily covered by water.

State/ Place/ MCD[1] code	Place	Population 1990	Population, Places of 10,000 or more 1980	Population, Places of 10,000 or more Percent change, 1980–1990	Race: White	Race: Black	Race: Am. Indian, Eskimo Aleut	Race: Asian & Pacific Islander	Race: Other race	Hispanic[2]	Total housing units, 1990	Per capita income, 1985 (Dollars)	Land area,[3] 1990 (Sq. Km.)
		1	2	3	4	5	6	7	8	9	10	11	12
	MICHIGAN—Con.												
0165	Bay City	38 936	41 593	-6.4	36 446	953	313	174	1 050	2 189	16 372	9 539	26.9
0183	Beecher CDP	14 465	17 178	-15.8	5 559	8 390	164	19	333	638	5 192	NA	15.3
0185	Beechwood CDP	2 676	NA	NA	2 510	7	7	50	102	175	1 016	NA	4.9
0190	Belding	5 969	NA	NA	5 848	24	10	12	75	138	2 290	8 108	12.5
0200	Belleville	3 270	NA	NA	3 186	59	7	8	10	42	1 603	14 348	2.9
0215	Benton Harbor	12 818	14 707	-12.8	930	11 817	18	6	47	122	4 791	5 514	11.4
0220	Benton Heights CDP	5 465	NA	NA	2 287	3 123	34	9	12	25	2 047	NA	10.0
0230	Berkley	16 960	18 637	-9.0	16 704	27	81	120	28	187	6 729	11 994	6.8
0250	Beverly Hills village	10 610	11 675	-9.1	10 230	125	8	230	17	126	4 166	25 105	10.4
0255	Big Rapids	12 603	14 361	-12.2	11 694	634	72	119	84	197	3 548	6 534	15.4
0270	Birmingham	19 997	21 689	-7.8	19 605	87	38	254	13	155	9 764	21 460	12.4
0275	Blissfield village	3 172	NA	NA	3 061	15	13	3	80	179	1 260	9 467	5.0
0280	Bloomfield Hills	4 288	NA	NA	3 907	57	1	299	24	71	1 645	50 901	12.8
0282	Bloomfield Township CDP	42 137	42 876	-1.7	38 636	1 011	40	2 362	88	527	16 437	NA	64.6
0290	Boyne City	3 478	NA	NA	3 413	2	48	9	6	20	1 936	8 290	10.0
0310	Bridgeport CDP	8 569	NA	NA	6 596	1 433	61	25	454	793	3 233	NA	21.6
0320	Brighton	5 686	NA	NA	5 588	10	28	49	11	52	2 509	12 317	9.3
0350	Brownlee Park CDP	2 536	NA	NA	2 417	25	37	13	44	71	1 122	NA	5.1
0355	Buchanan	4 992	NA	NA	4 356	561	27	16	32	54	2 117	8 120	6.3
0363	Buena Vista CDP	8 196	NA	NA	2 477	5 040	59	13	607	875	3 203	NA	11.6
0378	Burton	27 617	29 976	-7.9	26 295	710	276	127	209	578	10 840	11 021	60.8
0385	Cadillac	10 104	10 199	-0.9	9 945	21	79	49	10	72	4 298	8 426	17.3
0402	Canton CDP	57 047	NA	NA	52 980	1 167	155	2 562	183	792	20 309	NA	93.2
0410	Carleton village	2 770	NA	NA	2 726	7	18	13	6	29	1 007	9 724	2.6
0415	Caro village	4 054	NA	NA	3 900	9	41	23	81	168	1 785	10 282	5.8
0417	Carrollton CDP	6 521	NA	NA	5 663	390	25	48	395	621	2 470	NA	8.3
0455	Cedar Springs	2 600	NA	NA	2 551	4	21	12	12	40	965	7 558	4.3
0465	Center Line	9 026	NA	NA	8 837	71	36	72	10	92	3 986	11 228	4.5
0480	Charlevoix	3 116	NA	NA	3 005	5	98	5	3	19	1 917	9 553	5.3
0485	Charlotte	8 083	NA	NA	7 903	15	44	29	92	249	3 204	9 355	14.8
0490	Cheboygan	4 999	NA	NA	4 853	3	126	14	3	22	2 215	7 146	17.2
0495	Chelsea village	3 772	NA	NA	3 716	32	13	8	3	20	1 446	11 650	6.1
0500	Chesaning village	2 567	NA	NA	2 524	0	5	2	36	77	1 046	9 668	7.8
0515	Clare	3 021	NA	NA	2 969	7	24	16	5	12	1 339	8 014	6.9
0535	Clawson	13 874	15 103	-8.1	13 660	30	37	129	18	128	5 647	12 758	5.7
0557	Clinton CDP	85 866	72 400	18.6	81 917	2 586	253	909	201	1 001	33 938	NA	73.0
0560	Clio	2 629	NA	NA	2 565	11	22	7	24	39	1 218	10 479	3.0
0565	Coldwater	9 607	NA	NA	9 392	33	56	88	38	121	3 987	9 301	17.6
0590	Comstock Northwest CDP	3 402	NA	NA	3 148	170	24	39	21	59	1 277	NA	8.2
0592	Comstock Park CDP	6 530	NA	NA	6 359	54	31	46	40	90	2 812	NA	8.2
0605	Coopersville	3 421	NA	NA	3 364	9	7	23	18	54	1 213	9 078	12.5
0620	Corunna	3 091	NA	NA	3 039	18	21	5	8	58	1 152	9 235	8.0
0638	Cutlerville CDP	11 228	NA	NA	10 835	159	80	68	86	172	4 461	NA	9.0
0650	Davison	5 693	NA	NA	5 612	8	33	15	25	85	2 612	12 030	4.6
0655	Dearborn	89 286	90 660	-1.5	87 099	494	297	837	559	2 483	36 929	13 524	63.1
0658	Dearborn Heights	60 838	67 706	-10.1	59 214	277	252	782	313	1 398	23 939	12 882	30.3
0680	Detroit	1 027 974	1 203 339	-14.6	222 316	777 916	3 655	8 461	15 626	28 473	410 027	8 852	359.3
0690	De Witt	3 964	NA	NA	3 878	25	9	13	39	112	1 347	11 403	7.4
0710	Dowagiac	6 409	NA	NA	5 186	994	141	31	57	130	2 624	7 558	10.1
0725	Dundee village	2 664	NA	NA	2 651	2	4	4	3	23	1 117	11 402	3.9
0730	Durand	4 283	NA	NA	4 209	2	20	10	42	69	1 564	9 477	4.4
0740	East Detroit	35 283	38 280	-7.8	34 819	87	132	199	46	290	13 684	11 726	13.2
0745	East Grand Rapids	10 807	10 914	-1.0	10 550	98	16	126	17	71	3 900	20 274	7.6
0765	East Lansing	50 677	51 392	-1.4	42 869	3 513	170	3 542	583	1 268	14 403	8 985	24.6
0775	East Tawas	2 887	NA	NA	2 858	3	18	6	2	9	1 580	8 144	7.5
0777	Eastwood CDP	6 340	NA	NA	5 242	947	24	48	79	168	2 748	NA	5.2
0780	Eaton Rapids	4 695	NA	NA	4 611	4	23	30	27	108	1 872	10 521	7.9
0790	Ecorse	12 180	14 447	-15.7	6 928	4 787	111	40	314	820	4 999	8 951	7.0
0793	Edgemont Park CDP	2 532	NA	NA	2 357	108	7	24	36	58	1 118	NA	2.2
0840	Escanaba	13 659	14 355	-4.8	13 280	7	317	37	18	75	6 063	8 733	30.3
0845	Essexville	4 088	NA	NA	3 985	20	25	22	36	93	1 542	10 561	3.1
0870	Fair Plain CDP	8 051	NA	NA	5 261	2 632	46	47	65	117	3 394	NA	10.9
0875	Farmington	10 132	11 022	-8.1	9 905	82	12	124	9	78	4 898	17 206	6.9
0877	Farmington Hills	74 652	58 056	28.6	70 073	1 429	129	2 870	151	887	31 171	18 260	86.2
0890	Fenton	8 444	NA	NA	8 290	35	40	38	41	98	3 395	11 749	17.0
0895	Ferndale	25 084	26 227	-4.4	24 020	348	216	358	142	426	10 207	10 649	10.0
0900	Ferrysburg	2 919	NA	NA	2 861	7	21	21	9	27	1 281	NA	7.7
0915	Flat Rock	7 290	NA	NA	7 122	52	33	42	41	139	2 829	10 585	17.4
0920	Flint	140 761	159 611	-11.8	69 788	67 485	1 045	690	1 753	4 014	58 724	10 450	87.6
0925	Flushing	8 542	NA	NA	8 424	16	19	40	43	96	3 370	13 883	11.2
0927	Forest Hills CDP	16 690	NA	NA	16 304	106	33	220	27	96	5 686	NA	127.9
0945	Fowlerville village	2 648	NA	NA	2 591	0	45	4	8	30	1 018	NA	4.4
0950	Frankenmuth	4 408	NA	NA	4 388	1	3	6	10	36	1 900	14 039	6.5

1. Codes shown are 2-digit FIPS codes for states; 4-digit census place codes for places; and 3-digit FIPS county codes followed by 3-digit census MCD codes for minor civil divisions (MCDs). MCD names are followed by county names in parentheses. 2. Hispanic persons may be of any race. 3. Dry land or land partially or temporarily covered by water.

State/ Place/ MCD[1] code	Place	Population			Population characteristics, 1990						Total housing units, 1990	Per capita income, 1985 (Dollars)	Land area,[3] 1990 (Sq. Km.)
		1990	Places of 10,000 or more		Race					Hispanic[2]			
			1980	Percent change, 1980–1990	White	Black	Am. Indian, Eskimo Aleut	Asian & Pacific Islander	Other race				
		1	2	3	4	5	6	7	8	9	10	11	12
	MICHIGAN—Con.												
0960	Franklin village	2 626	NA	NA	2 520	45	8	50	3	27	1 010	41 468	6.9
0970	Fraser	13 899	14 560	-4.5	13 665	23	68	117	26	149	5 342	11 443	10.8
0990	Fremont	3 875	NA	NA	3 825	11	7	23	9	25	1 752	10 066	7.5
1030	Garden City	31 846	35 640	-10.6	31 393	76	133	161	83	483	11 374	11 375	15.2
1035	Gaylord	3 256	NA	NA	3 214	0	19	18	5	13	1 411	7 857	6.9
1040	Gibraltar	4 297	NA	NA	4 242	7	18	18	12	41	1 662	13 562	10.0
1045	Gladstone	4 565	NA	NA	4 451	3	95	9	7	21	1 970	8 423	11.7
1050	Gladwin	2 682	NA	NA	2 645	4	10	22	1	23	1 185	NA	5.8
1070	Grand Blanc	7 760	NA	NA	7 309	219	17	183	32	90	3 299	16 635	9.5
1075	Grand Haven	11 951	11 763	1.6	11 667	59	93	87	45	145	5 218	10 659	15.0
1080	Grand Ledge	7 579	NA	NA	7 435	21	27	54	42	118	3 168	10 878	5.7
1085	Grand Rapids	189 126	181 843	4.0	144 464	35 073	1 573	2 164	5 852	9 394	73 716	9 625	114.6
1090	Grandville	15 624	12 412	25.9	15 259	112	35	160	58	215	5 871	11 555	19.5
1110	Greenville	8 101	NA	NA	7 943	14	37	42	65	197	3 389	9 529	14.3
1112	Grosse Ile CDP	9 781	NA	NA	9 374	8	35	349	15	134	3 632	NA	24.9
1115	Grosse Pointe	5 681	NA	NA	5 591	23	8	54	5	63	2 492	22 787	2.8
1120	Grosse Pointe Farms	10 092	10 551	-4.4	9 975	23	7	84	3	72	3 947	30 793	7.0
1125	Grosse Pointe Park	12 857	13 639	-5.7	12 513	112	36	176	20	185	5 009	19 631	5.6
1130	Grosse Pointe Shores village	2 955	NA	NA	2 808	11	4	124	8	42	1 094	38 202	3.0
1135	Grosse Pointe Woods	17 715	18 886	-6.2	17 422	13	9	259	12	124	6 671	21 576	8.4
1145	Hamtramck	18 372	21 300	-13.7	15 368	2 578	95	230	101	292	8 701	8 850	5.5
1150	Hancock	4 547	NA	NA	4 386	62	26	60	13	31	2 008	7 926	4.7
1170	Harper Woods	14 903	16 361	-8.9	14 584	132	27	134	26	152	6 744	12 972	6.7
1182	Harrison CDP	24 685	23 649	4.4	23 838	498	98	161	90	355	10 616	NA	36.6
1198	Haslett CDP	10 230	NA	NA	9 796	192	53	129	60	184	4 765	NA	21.6
1200	Hastings	6 549	NA	NA	6 455	8	31	31	24	83	2 618	10 142	13.6
1205	Hazel Park	20 051	20 914	-4.1	19 342	72	274	280	83	278	7 779	9 478	7.3
1225	Highland Park	20 121	27 909	-27.9	1 286	18 673	40	55	67	137	9 162	7 947	7.7
1235	Hillsdale	8 170	NA	NA	8 004	45	27	57	37	72	3 175	8 397	13.1
1240	Holland	30 745	26 281	17.0	26 971	324	103	979	2 368	4 347	11 243	10 717	36.7
1245	Holly village	5 595	NA	NA	5 439	53	35	12	56	133	2 158	10 357	7.2
1250	Holt CDP	11 744	10 097	16.3	11 361	126	48	81	128	286	4 437	NA	11.2
1270	Houghton	7 498	NA	NA	6 913	64	27	466	28	70	2 121	5 912	8.4
1271	Houghton Lake CDP	3 353	NA	NA	3 334	2	11	4	2	5	2 764	NA	15.3
1285	Howell	8 184	NA	NA	8 007	12	84	59	22	85	3 426	11 457	9.8
1300	Hudson	2 580	NA	NA	2 531	5	3	29	12	50	971	9 310	5.5
1305	Hudsonville	6 170	NA	NA	6 099	11	18	35	7	48	2 264	10 879	10.2
1310	Huntington Woods	6 419	NA	NA	6 296	30	1	75	17	59	2 411	21 307	3.8
1315	Imlay City	2 921	NA	NA	2 665	23	14	51	168	287	1 261	NA	5.8
1320	Inkster	30 772	35 190	-12.6	11 118	19 199	131	206	118	332	12 045	9 511	16.2
1325	Ionia	5 935	NA	NA	5 752	52	35	17	79	210	2 412	9 811	7.3
1330	Iron Mountain	8 525	NA	NA	8 372	13	56	61	23	66	3 789	9 205	18.7
1340	Ironwood	6 849	NA	NA	6 793	6	31	13	6	34	3 410	7 162	15.1
1345	Ishpeming	7 200	NA	NA	7 117	3	58	16	6	19	3 224	8 454	22.5
1355	Ithaca	3 009	NA	NA	2 903	1	19	7	79	122	1 198	8 227	10.0
1360	Jackson	37 446	39 739	-5.8	30 020	6 615	219	153	439	954	15 689	9 002	28.6
1363	Jenison CDP	17 882	16 330	9.5	17 625	57	19	120	61	200	5 557	NA	15.2
1370	Kalamazoo	80 277	79 722	0.7	62 039	15 053	450	1 505	1 230	2 153	31 488	10 068	63.6
1385	Keego Harbor	2 932	NA	NA	2 843	9	28	24	28	82	1 334	13 227	1.3
1392	Kentwood	37 826	30 438	24.3	34 522	2 113	159	740	292	761	16 337	11 691	54.5
1400	Kingsford	5 480	NA	NA	5 419	8	35	15	3	22	2 248	7 922	11.2
1412	K. I. Sawyer AFB CDP	6 577	NA	NA	5 828	398	46	190	115	255	1 805	NA	19.9
1433	Lake Fenton CDP	4 091	NA	NA	4 028	9	16	36	2	39	1 671	NA	14.2
1450	Lake Orion village	3 057	NA	NA	3 010	11	13	10	13	32	1 355	13 751	2.0
1475	Lambertville CDP	7 860	NA	NA	7 767	6	12	47	28	92	2 649	NA	15.7
1485	Lansing	127 321	130 414	-2.4	94 135	23 626	1 295	2 263	6 002	10 112	53 919	10 398	87.8
1490	Lapeer	7 759	NA	NA	7 240	368	62	46	43	143	3 070	9 718	14.3
1500	Lathrup Village	4 329	NA	NA	3 259	991	6	51	22	51	1 619	20 261	3.9
1535	Level Park-Oak Park CDP	3 502	NA	NA	3 286	160	11	30	15	30	1 333	NA	13.8
1550	Lincoln Park	41 832	45 105	-7.3	40 712	386	219	180	335	1 588	16 763	10 815	15.1
1565	Livonia	100 850	104 814	-3.8	98 870	265	182	1 352	181	1 355	36 641	13 934	92.5
1570	Lowell	3 983	NA	NA	3 909	10	16	18	30	56	1 510	9 320	7.3
1575	Ludington	8 507	NA	NA	8 273	41	77	30	86	176	3 955	8 695	8.7
1610	Madison Heights	32 196	35 375	-9.0	30 878	292	159	788	79	399	13 220	11 986	18.6
1625	Manistee	6 734	NA	NA	6 564	34	67	21	48	129	3 290	8 885	8.4
1630	Manistique	3 456	NA	NA	3 250	0	198	4	4	12	1 622	7 529	8.3
1660	Marine City	4 556	NA	NA	4 529	2	20	2	3	24	1 783	8 997	5.7
1675	Marquette	21 977	23 288	-5.6	20 762	621	385	162	47	129	8 216	8 081	29.5
1680	Marshall	6 891	NA	NA	6 637	96	20	30	108	229	2 894	10 127	14.6
1690	Marysville	8 515	NA	NA	8 432	4	26	37	16	74	3 518	11 943	18.0
1695	Mason	6 768	NA	NA	6 283	246	47	76	116	174	2 463	10 496	11.5
1720	Melvindale	11 216	12 322	-9.0	10 496	324	114	90	192	627	4 902	11 047	7.2
1735	Menominee	9 398	10 099	-6.9	9 290	4	70	28	6	29	4 334	9 002	13.0

1. Codes shown are 2-digit FIPS codes for states; 4-digit census place codes for places; and 3-digit FIPS county codes followed by 3-digit census MCD codes for minor civil divisions (MCDs). MCD names are followed by county names in parentheses. 2. Hispanic persons may be of any race. 3. Dry land or land partially or temporarily covered by water.

State/ Place/ MCD[1] code	Place	Population: 1990	Places of 10,000 or more: 1980	Places of 10,000 or more: Percent change, 1980–1990	Population characteristics, 1990 — Race: White	Black	Am. Indian, Eskimo Aleut	Asian & Pacific Islander	Other race	Hispanic[2]	Total housing units, 1990	Per capita income, 1985 (Dollars)	Land area,[3] 1990 (Sq. Km.)
		1	2	3	4	5	6	7	8	9	10	11	12
	MICHIGAN—Con.												
1759	Michigan Center CDP	4 863	NA	NA	4 798	7	29	13	16	47	1 976	NA	13.4
1770	Midland	38 053	37 257	2.1	36 362	654	135	728	174	638	15 447	13 621	71.5
1775	Milan	4 040	NA	NA	3 899	49	16	27	49	92	1 617	11 490	5.8
1780	Milford village	5 511	NA	NA	5 423	9	21	46	12	70	2 108	12 474	6.4
1810	Monroe	22 902	23 531	-2.7	21 359	1 057	93	193	200	415	8 840	10 491	23.3
1845	Mount Clemens	18 405	18 806	-2.1	14 774	3 274	129	80	148	334	7 727	11 008	10.9
1850	Mount Morris	3 292	NA	NA	3 131	59	45	28	29	53	1 411	10 805	3.2
1855	Mount Pleasant	23 285	23 746	-1.9	22 020	539	225	345	156	376	7 071	7 243	18.7
1870	Munising	2 783	NA	NA	2 682	2	95	4	0	4	1 268	8 722	13.9
1875	Muskegon	40 283	40 823	-1.3	28 148	10 916	390	139	690	1 416	16 019	7 827	37.2
1880	Muskegon Heights	13 176	14 611	-9.8	3 692	9 215	76	17	176	342	5 343	6 569	8.2
1890	Negaunee	4 741	NA	NA	4 678	1	48	11	3	16	2 067	8 737	35.7
1900	New Baltimore	5 798	NA	NA	5 709	27	22	30	10	48	2 459	12 014	11.9
1935	Niles	12 458	13 115	-5.0	10 685	1 542	64	51	116	285	5 473	9 247	14.5
1950	North Muskegon	3 919	NA	NA	3 853	19	14	21	12	32	1 620	14 640	4.7
1958	Northview CDP	13 712	11 662	17.6	13 252	208	19	170	63	189	5 272	NA	27.0
1960	Northville	6 226	NA	NA	6 120	9	15	72	10	48	2 583	15 605	5.2
1962	Norton Shores	21 755	22 025	-1.2	21 014	298	147	155	141	375	8 659	11 588	60.2
1965	Norway	2 910	NA	NA	2 893	1	12	2	2	3	1 311	8 332	22.8
1970	Novi	32 998	22 525	46.5	31 690	259	108	874	67	372	13 557	15 753	78.9
1985	Oak Park	30 462	31 537	-3.4	19 143	10 449	37	719	114	444	11 344	11 649	13.0
1987	Okemos CDP	20 216	NA	NA	18 244	786	76	998	112	352	7 961	NA	44.8
2035	Otsego	3 937	NA	NA	3 881	14	18	9	15	36	1 561	8 322	4.8
2055	Owosso	16 322	16 455	-0.8	15 970	23	112	82	135	392	6 716	9 703	12.6
2065	Oxford village	2 929	NA	NA	2 879	8	9	24	9	41	1 192	12 945	3.2
2100	Paw Paw village	3 169	NA	NA	3 045	66	22	15	21	63	1 390	9 728	5.0
2105	Paw Paw Lake CDP	3 782	NA	NA	3 731	8	11	7	25	50	2 150	NA	13.6
2110	Pearl Beach CDP	3 394	NA	NA	3 354	1	24	7	8	31	1 507	NA	5.5
2145	Petoskey	6 056	NA	NA	5 834	22	159	31	10	32	2 804	9 598	8.6
2175	Plainwell	4 057	NA	NA	3 999	5	26	19	8	31	1 541	9 886	5.4
2180	Pleasant Ridge	2 775	NA	NA	2 720	22	2	21	10	35	1 085	15 247	1.5
2185	Plymouth	9 560	NA	NA	9 434	29	36	43	18	105	4 528	13 468	5.8
2187	Plymouth Township CDP	23 646	NA	NA	22 860	286	58	388	54	271	9 209	NA	41.2
2200	Pontiac	71 166	76 715	-7.2	36 475	30 033	594	965	3 099	5 701	26 593	9 432	51.8
2206	Portage	41 042	38 157	7.6	38 704	1 139	147	846	206	593	16 133	12 811	83.4
2220	Port Huron	33 694	33 981	-0.8	30 342	2 296	286	198	572	1 175	14 026	9 485	20.7
2225	Portland	3 889	NA	NA	3 834	1	20	7	27	43	1 479	9 774	6.2
2282	Redford CDP	54 387	58 441	-6.9	53 342	379	199	311	156	829	20 451	NA	29.1
2305	Richmond	4 141	NA	NA	4 122	0	12	2	5	34	1 662	9 737	6.4
2310	River Rouge	11 314	12 912	-12.4	7 101	3 977	75	32	129	378	4 666	8 574	6.9
2315	Riverview	13 894	14 569	-4.6	13 353	163	34	305	39	219	5 227	12 586	11.4
2320	Rochester	7 130	NA	NA	6 883	88	15	119	25	75	3 680	15 054	10.0
2323	Rochester Hills	61 766	NA	NA	58 667	844	132	1 959	164	875	23 535	15 253	85.1
2325	Rockford	3 750	NA	NA	3 696	6	14	21	13	52	1 434	10 511	7.4
2330	Rockwood	3 141	NA	NA	3 076	2	20	33	10	41	1 135	11 011	7.0
2335	Rogers City	3 642	NA	NA	3 615	2	8	13	4	8	1 617	8 562	11.8
2340	Romeo village	3 520	NA	NA	3 256	215	13	15	21	47	1 382	13 470	5.2
2342	Romulus	22 897	24 857	-7.9	17 466	4 999	150	152	130	434	8 223	9 373	93.0
2345	Roosevelt Park	3 885	NA	NA	3 787	67	7	10	14	29	1 838	11 065	2.6
2360	Roseville	51 412	54 311	-5.3	50 007	513	234	572	86	627	20 025	10 617	25.4
2365	Royal Oak	65 410	70 893	-7.7	64 035	332	163	729	151	695	29 163	13 900	30.6
2370	Saginaw	69 512	77 508	-10.3	36 324	28 046	375	302	4 465	7 304	27 986	8 652	45.2
2371	Saginaw Township North CDP	23 018	NA	NA	21 388	763	39	496	332	733	9 486	NA	35.0
2372	Saginaw Township South CDP	13 987	NA	NA	13 197	293	43	210	244	528	6 088	NA	17.9
2380	St. Clair	5 116	NA	NA	5 059	5	11	31	10	38	2 121	13 094	7.2
2385	St. Clair Shores	68 107	76 210	-10.6	67 201	141	229	439	97	646	27 929	13 158	29.9
2390	St. Ignace	2 568	NA	NA	2 016	4	547	1	0	4	1 226	7 685	7.0
2395	St. Johns	7 284	NA	NA	7 112	9	16	47	100	221	2 870	10 306	8.1
2400	St. Joseph	9 214	NA	NA	8 743	283	20	142	26	113	4 545	13 684	8.9
2405	St. Louis	3 828	NA	NA	3 731	20	10	2	65	201	1 554	8 195	7.3
2410	Saline	6 660	NA	NA	6 481	33	25	88	33	67	2 588	12 415	10.9
2435	Sault Ste. Marie	14 689	14 448	1.7	12 439	70	2 112	41	27	81	6 013	7 885	38.4
2454	Shelby CDP	48 655	NA	NA	47 665	141	153	584	112	465	17 630	NA	90.0
2477	Shields CDP	6 634	NA	NA	6 480	36	16	29	73	170	2 372	NA	16.9
2488	Skidway Lake CDP	2 569	NA	NA	2 534	1	31	1	2	20	2 479	NA	29.4
2490	Southfield	75 728	75 568	0.2	51 409	22 053	190	1 801	275	1 300	35 054	17 068	67.9
2495	Southgate	30 771	32 058	-4.0	29 693	362	153	336	227	856	12 504	11 776	17.8
2500	South Haven	5 563	NA	NA	4 636	841	44	27	15	55	2 819	9 228	6.9
2505	South Lyon	5 857	NA	NA	5 822	3	11	16	5	31	2 485	11 749	7.0
2510	South Monroe CDP	5 266	NA	NA	5 078	80	20	52	36	87	2 087	NA	6.2
2530	Sparta village	3 968	NA	NA	3 901	2	18	16	31	68	1 585	9 977	4.9
2535	Springfield	5 582	NA	NA	5 124	329	48	41	40	95	2 409	10 196	9.8
2545	Spring Lake village	2 537	NA	NA	2 510	3	9	14	1	10	1 201	11 343	2.7

1. Codes shown are 2-digit FIPS codes for states; 4-digit census place codes for places; and 3-digit FIPS county codes followed by 3-digit census MCD codes for minor civil divisions (MCDs). MCD names are followed by county names in parentheses. 2. Hispanic persons may be of any race. 3. Dry land or land partially or temporarily covered by water.

State/ Place/ MCD[1] code	Place	Population 1990	Places of 10,000 or more 1980	Places of 10,000 or more Percent change, 1980–1990	Race White	Race Black	Race Am. Indian, Eskimo Aleut	Race Asian & Pacific Islander	Race Other race	Hispanic[2]	Total housing units, 1990	Per capita income, 1985 (Dollars)	Land area,[3] 1990 (Sq. Km.)
		1	2	3	4	5	6	7	8	9	10	11	12
	MICHIGAN—Con.												
2583	Sterling Heights	117 810	108 999	8.1	113 452	475	279	3 369	235	1 314	42 317	12 760	94.9
2600	Sturgis	10 130	NA	NA	9 919	76	29	63	43	135	4 155	9 578	13.2
2620	Swartz Creek	4 851	NA	NA	4 704	48	51	33	15	91	1 981	12 454	10.4
2633	Taylor	70 811	77 568	-8.7	66 017	2 980	407	892	515	1 991	25 727	10 117	61.2
2635	Tecumseh	7 462	NA	NA	7 231	11	32	67	121	310	2 999	11 524	12.6
2645	Temperance CDP	6 542	NA	NA	6 472	22	8	21	19	76	2 326	NA	11.9
2660	Three Rivers	7 413	NA	NA	6 529	807	21	36	20	81	3 156	8 891	10.0
2665	Traverse City	15 155	15 516	-2.3	14 865	35	139	88	28	105	6 557	9 631	21.2
2670	Trenton	20 586	22 762	-9.6	20 193	32	67	237	57	283	8 079	12 927	18.9
2675	Troy	72 884	67 102	8.6	66 701	983	115	4 943	142	927	27 197	16 945	86.9
2720	Utica	5 081	NA	NA	4 908	20	30	91	32	75	1 962	11 700	4.6
2737	Vandercook Lake CDP	4 642	NA	NA	4 544	36	26	4	32	66	1 781	NA	11.8
2740	Vassar	2 559	NA	NA	2 435	107	6	2	9	48	1 047	9 185	5.5
2773	Walker	17 279	15 088	14.5	16 806	182	76	101	114	260	7 060	10 587	65.2
2785	Walled Lake	6 278	NA	NA	6 174	7	34	60	3	25	2 884	11 801	5.9
2790	Warren	144 864	161 134	-10.1	140 995	1 047	669	1 942	211	1 583	56 189	12 546	88.8
2798	Waterford CDP	66 692	64 250	3.8	64 647	701	391	495	458	1 538	26 509	NA	81.2
2802	Waverly CDP	15 614	NA	NA	14 105	1 066	49	176	218	448	6 582	NA	14.7
2805	Wayland	2 751	NA	NA	2 712	6	24	6	3	31	1 208	NA	6.6
2810	Wayne	19 899	21 159	-6.0	17 995	1 494	146	164	100	433	7 325	10 518	15.6
2822	West Bloomfield Township CDP	54 843	41 962	30.7	50 727	1 077	66	2 842	131	668	20 494	NA	70.8
2827	Westland	84 724	84 603	0.1	80 197	2 829	467	831	400	1 594	34 514	11 669	53.0
2828	West Monroe CDP	3 919	NA	NA	3 862	9	15	8	25	69	1 524	NA	3.3
2832	Westwood CDP	8 957	NA	NA	8 250	567	11	87	42	77	4 211	NA	7.2
2840	Whitehall	3 027	NA	NA	2 934	17	31	11	34	58	1 231	9 576	7.6
2855	Whitmore Lake CDP	3 251	NA	NA	3 199	11	13	20	8	30	1 452	NA	8.1
2865	Williamston	2 922	NA	NA	2 865	12	15	6	24	69	1 268	10 843	3.8
2880	Wixom	8 550	NA	NA	8 384	27	37	76	26	103	4 475	14 250	24.3
2883	Wolf Lake CDP	4 110	NA	NA	3 970	30	61	8	41	119	1 533	NA	9.0
2895	Wolverine Lake village	4 727	NA	NA	4 693	4	10	16	4	31	1 712	15 093	3.4
2902	Woodhaven	11 631	10 902	6.7	11 169	76	45	265	76	303	4 140	11 810	16.8
2917	Wurtsmith AFB CDP	5 080	NA	NA	4 406	425	34	143	72	173	1 329	NA	18.9
2920	Wyandotte	30 938	34 006	-9.0	30 379	73	185	123	178	653	12 822	10 468	13.7
2925	Wyoming	63 891	59 616	7.2	59 752	1 736	350	955	1 098	2 234	25 056	10 327	62.9
2935	Ypsilanti	24 846	24 031	3.4	17 240	6 243	121	1 074	168	476	9 321	9 454	11.3
2940	Zeeland	5 417	NA	NA	5 178	23	8	96	112	174	2 039	10 127	7.8
0050	Allegan township (Allegan)	3 976	NA	NA	3 879	45	19	19	14	38	1 598	9 185	79.2
0050	Casco township (Allegan)	2 856	NA	NA	2 625	128	27	13	63	143	1 482	8 836	100.8
0050	Dorr township (Allegan)	5 453	NA	NA	5 360	19	43	13	18	84	1 630	8 124	93.6
0050	Fillmore township (Allegan)	2 710	NA	NA	2 626	3	5	29	47	88	933	NA	80.1
0050	Gunplain township (Allegan)	4 754	NA	NA	4 695	11	16	9	23	65	1 686	10 947	88.5
0050	Laketown township (Allegan)	4 888	NA	NA	4 500	277	18	30	63	169	1 781	13 013	56.0
0050	Lee township (Allegan)	2 672	NA	NA	2 107	437	33	8	87	174	1 417	NA	91.5
0050	Leighton township (Allegan)	3 069	NA	NA	3 034	3	18	6	8	21	1 122	9 539	90.6
0051	Otsego township (Allegan)	4 780	NA	NA	4 719	13	13	22	13	30	1 711	10 239	86.6
0051	Salem township (Allegan)	2 708	NA	NA	2 640	6	31	5	26	53	909	NA	92.6
0051	Saugatuck township (Allegan)	2 916	NA	NA	2 810	4	15	8	79	110	1 700	10 228	65.4
0051	Wayland township (Allegan)	2 569	NA	NA	2 497	4	47	3	18	46	983	NA	85.4
0070	Alpena township (Alpena)	9 602	10 152	-5.4	9 544	4	25	20	9	61	4 414	8 336	271.7
0090	Mancelona township (Antrim)	3 173	NA	NA	3 133	0	39	0	1	6	1 733	6 689	184.9
0130	Baraga township (Baraga)	2 832	NA	NA	2 328	45	447	9	3	12	1 432	6 316	481.0
0130	L'Anse township (Baraga)	3 818	NA	NA	3 360	4	450	1	3	22	1 896	7 142	644.2
0150	Barry township (Barry)	3 190	NA	NA	3 153	9	13	10	5	36	1 321	11 345	90.1
0150	Castleton township (Barry)	3 379	NA	NA	3 352	1	16	6	4	22	1 384	7 910	91.0
0150	Hastings township (Barry)	2 830	NA	NA	2 786	9	14	10	11	14	1 029	8 705	78.1
0150	Hope township (Barry)	2 993	NA	NA	2 964	3	15	8	3	13	1 541	9 494	84.4
0150	Johnstown township (Barry)	2 932	NA	NA	2 906	5	10	6	5	23	1 263	10 709	91.2
0150	Orangeville township (Barry)	2 880	NA	NA	2 793	6	10	0	71	126	1 476	8 178	87.0
0150	Prairieville township (Barry)	3 409	NA	NA	3 345	27	13	12	12	28	1 454	10 051	86.3
0150	Rutland township (Barry)	2 797	NA	NA	2 761	5	11	9	11	27	1 045	NA	91.1
0150	Thornapple township (Barry)	5 226	NA	NA	5 172	12	19	10	13	40	1 754	10 471	92.0
0150	Yankee Springs township (Barry)	2 977	NA	NA	2 969	0	4	4	0	11	1 948	NA	81.6
0170	Bangor township (Bay)	16 028	17 494	-8.4	15 693	64	72	83	116	281	6 239	10 508	36.1
0170	Beaver township (Bay)	2 810	NA	NA	2 785	0	10	2	13	47	894	8 539	91.6
0170	Fraser township (Bay)	3 680	NA	NA	3 630	4	34	1	11	55	1 362	9 337	83.7
0170	Hampton township (Bay)	9 520	10 418	-8.6	9 200	130	67	41	82	214	3 992	9 859	70.1
0170	Kawkawlin township (Bay)	4 852	NA	NA	4 765	3	44	7	33	91	1 797	9 943	84.7
0170	Monitor township (Bay)	9 512	10 143	-6.2	9 365	4	35	50	58	125	3 586	11 918	95.7
0170	Pinconning township (Bay)	2 647	NA	NA	2 575	0	37	2	33	68	1 007	9 207	94.7
0170	Portsmouth township (Bay)	3 918	NA	NA	3 837	22	13	6	40	69	1 432	10 139	51.8
0170	Williams township (Bay)	4 278	NA	NA	4 241	3	18	6	10	53	1 488	9 349	87.0
0210	Bainbridge township (Berrien)	2 865	NA	NA	2 769	25	17	7	47	96	1 311	8 345	91.1
0210	Baroda township (Berrien)	2 731	NA	NA	2 714	6	1	5	5	25	1 110	9 743	46.1

1. Codes shown are 2-digit FIPS codes for states; 4-digit census place codes for places; and 3-digit FIPS county codes followed by 3-digit census MCD codes for minor civil divisions (MCDs). MCD names are followed by county names in parentheses. 2. Hispanic persons may be of any race. 3. Dry land or land partially or temporarily covered by water.

Table D. Places — **Population, Housing, Money Income, and Land Area**

State/ Place/ MCD[1] code	Place	Population: 1990	Population: Places of 10,000 or more: 1980	Population: Places of 10,000 or more: Percent change, 1980–1990	Population characteristics, 1990: Race: White	Race: Black	Race: Am. Indian, Eskimo Aleut	Race: Asian & Pacific Islander	Race: Other race	Hispanic[2]	Total housing units, 1990	Per capita income, 1985 (Dollars)	Land area,[3] 1990 (Sq. Km.)
		1	2	3	4	5	6	7	8	9	10	11	12
	MICHIGAN—Con.												
0210	Benton Charter township (Berrien)	17 163	19 120	-10.2	9 489	7 355	97	45	177	238	7 018	7 901	84.4
0210	Berrien township (Berrien)	4 697	NA	NA	4 374	203	21	45	54	122	1 771	8 452	91.5
0210	Buchanan township (Berrien)	3 402	NA	NA	3 358	6	27	9	2	25	1 371	8 527	83.5
0210	Chikaming township (Berrien)	3 717	NA	NA	3 601	103	3	8	2	20	3 286	9 776	57.1
0210	Coloma township (Berrien)	5 123	NA	NA	5 016	25	12	10	60	122	2 338	8 987	47.2
0210	Hagar township (Berrien)	4 113	NA	NA	4 035	34	22	6	16	35	1 976	10 401	48.1
0210	Lincoln township (Berrien)	13 604	13 520	0.6	13 309	105	31	134	25	175	5 535	11 959	46.4
0210	Niles township (Berrien)	12 828	13 165	-2.6	12 269	346	106	55	52	161	4 943	9 110	97.6
0211	Oronoko township (Berrien)	9 819	10 763	-8.8	7 453	1 319	52	702	293	673	3 453	8 112	84.3
0211	Royalton township (Berrien)	3 135	NA	NA	3 027	32	3	60	13	50	1 142	11 376	46.8
0211	St. Joseph Charter township(Berrien.	9 613	NA	NA	8 780	688	33	95	17	82	3 793	12 911	17.2
0211	Three Oaks township (Berrien)	2 952	NA	NA	2 931	10	4	5	2	10	1 220	7 591	60.6
0211	Watervliet township (Berrien)	2 926	NA	NA	2 851	30	9	18	18	28	1 531	9 862	35.3
0230	Coldwater township (Branch)	4 795	NA	NA	4 101	626	25	18	25	95	1 472	9 183	73.5
0230	Quincy township (Branch)	4 003	NA	NA	3 965	3	20	13	2	27	1 836	8 424	91.4
0230	Union township (Branch)	2 976	NA	NA	2 920	0	39	17	0	29	1 179	8 642	92.4
0250	Athens township (Calhoun)	2 515	NA	NA	2 444	15	31	3	22	25	954	NA	93.6
0250	Bedford township (Calhoun)	9 810	10 157	-3.4	8 328	1 372	24	54	32	98	3 564	10 514	76.3
0250	Emmett township (Calhoun)	10 764	11 144	-3.4	10 418	129	59	82	76	148	4 296	10 660	83.5
0250	Homer township (Calhoun)	2 875	NA	NA	2 849	2	7	0	17	39	1 103	7 780	92.5
0250	Leroy township (Calhoun)	3 026	NA	NA	2 991	5	12	9	9	36	1 114	10 474	93.1
0250	Marshall township (Calhoun)	2 655	NA	NA	2 631	3	2	9	10	31	1 014	11 415	81.5
0251	Pennfield township (Calhoun)	8 386	NA	NA	8 020	250	21	65	30	118	3 550	10 843	90.1
0270	Howard township (Cass)	6 378	NA	NA	5 984	312	53	17	12	34	2 476	8 780	90.7
0270	La Grange township (Cass)	3 406	NA	NA	2 483	815	26	63	19	43	1 566	7 632	86.8
0270	Marcellus township (Cass)	2 569	NA	NA	2 527	20	10	3	9	20	1 141	NA	86.4
0270	Ontwa township (Cass)	5 592	NA	NA	5 535	24	17	9	7	42	2 404	10 852	50.6
0270	Porter township (Cass)	3 857	NA	NA	3 781	55	7	5	9	38	2 019	9 955	134.0
0270	Silver Creek township (Cass)	3 101	NA	NA	2 947	59	47	8	40	117	2 284	9 616	83.4
0270	Wayne township (Cass)	2 780	NA	NA	2 677	28	66	3	6	26	1 210	7 832	88.9
0330	Kinross township (Chippewa)	6 566	NA	NA	4 050	2 100	267	90	59	150	1 465	NA	311.0
0350	Grant township (Clare)	2 636	NA	NA	2 613	6	11	4	2	10	1 179	NA	86.2
0350	Hayes township (Clare)	3 811	NA	NA	3 768	3	24	11	5	15	3 596	6 371	81.4
0350	Surrey township (Clare)	3 221	NA	NA	3 179	9	16	7	10	31	1 771	7 775	91.4
0370	Bath township (Clinton)	6 387	NA	NA	6 193	53	44	20	77	150	2 396	10 489	93.3
0370	Bingham township (Clinton)	2 546	NA	NA	2 511	3	6	4	22	61	838	NA	85.8
0370	De Witt township (Clinton)	10 448	10 038	4.1	10 005	89	120	57	177	358	4 192	11 686	86.2
0370	Ovid township (Clinton)	3 105	NA	NA	3 048	2	3	4	48	98	1 142	9 167	92.8
0370	Victor township (Clinton)	2 784	NA	NA	2 754	6	13	5	6	37	936	NA	89.5
0370	Watertown township (Clinton)	3 731	NA	NA	3 668	15	14	17	17	44	1 286	12 855	92.5
0390	Grayling township (Crawford)	5 647	NA	NA	5 306	262	53	19	7	37	3 394	8 290	443.1
0410	Escanaba township (Delta)	3 340	NA	NA	3 266	0	63	10	1	2	1 192	7 418	155.4
0410	Wells township (Delta)	5 159	NA	NA	5 066	1	63	21	8	15	1 838	8 046	104.8
0430	Breitung township (Dickinson)	5 483	NA	NA	5 432	1	18	27	5	15	2 297	9 335	168.5
0450	Bellevue township (Eaton)	2 938	NA	NA	2 920	6	1	3	8	34	1 053	9 176	94.2
0450	Benton township (Eaton)	2 528	NA	NA	2 459	8	24	8	29	80	857	NA	88.4
0450	Delta township (Eaton)	26 129	23 822	9.7	24 170	1 316	92	241	310	648	10 757	14 321	89.4
0450	Eaton township (Eaton)	3 492	NA	NA	3 424	3	22	23	20	66	1 191	11 548	85.1
0450	Eaton Rapids township (Eaton)	3 003	NA	NA	2 917	16	8	14	48	84	1 051	10 734	88.9
0450	Oneida Charter township (Eaton)	3 228	NA	NA	3 167	14	12	13	22	48	1 109	12 447	86.8
0451	Windsor township (Eaton)	6 460	NA	NA	6 276	70	35	32	47	116	2 311	13 170	90.6
0470	Bear Creek township (Emmet)	3 469	NA	NA	3 426	4	33	6	0	13	2 101	9 010	102.6
0490	Argentine township (Genesee)	4 651	NA	NA	4 602	6	32	7	4	23	1 823	12 995	91.0
0490	Atlas township (Genesee)	5 551	NA	NA	5 480	3	27	25	16	56	1 812	12 699	91.6
0490	Clayton township (Genesee)	7 368	NA	NA	7 190	39	69	46	24	125	2 620	11 904	88.7
0490	Davison township (Genesee)	14 671	13 708	7.0	14 255	165	63	110	78	220	6 080	12 851	86.7
0490	Fenton township (Genesee)	10 055	11 744	-14.4	9 912	18	50	60	15	105	3 851	12 995	61.8
0490	Flint township (Genesee)	34 081	35 405	-3.7	30 233	2 606	324	683	235	558	14 609	13 088	61.4
0490	Flushing township (Genesee)	9 223	NA	NA	9 007	64	63	45	44	93	3 192	12 828	79.9
0490	Forest township (Genesee)	4 409	NA	NA	4 338	8	38	15	10	39	1 494	10 510	92.7
0490	Gaines township (Genesee)	5 391	NA	NA	5 306	7	48	19	11	39	1 772	10 880	91.2
0490	Genesee township (Genesee)	24 093	25 065	-3.9	21 682	1 966	223	62	160	500	9 228	10 519	76.1
0490	Grand Blanc township (Genesee)	25 392	24 413	4.0	23 447	1 241	119	452	133	420	10 017	15 408	84.6
0490	Montrose township (Genesee)	6 236	NA	NA	6 003	161	27	9	36	107	1 995	9 692	89.2
0490	Mount Morris township (Genesee)	25 198	27 928	-9.8	15 793	8 689	255	70	391	819	9 360	10 181	81.4
0491	Mundy township (Genesee)	11 511	10 786	6.7	11 184	170	55	55	47	157	4 310	13 028	92.4
0491	Richfield township (Genesee)	7 271	NA	NA	6 982	201	48	12	28	118	2 511	11 546	91.4
0491	Thetford township (Genesee)	8 333	NA	NA	7 968	243	55	24	43	129	2 909	11 058	89.8
0491	Vienna township (Genesee)	13 210	12 893	2.5	12 965	78	67	39	61	172	4 762	10 474	90.7
0550	Acme township (Grand Traverse)	3 447	NA	NA	3 386	15	14	18	14	24	1 587	10 977	65.2
0550	Blair township (Grand Traverse)	5 249	NA	NA	5 109	13	69	42	16	58	1 956	8 085	92.2
0550	East Bay township (Grand Traverse)	8 307	NA	NA	8 175	6	69	49	8	58	3 770	9 909	103.4
0550	Garfield township (Grand Traverse)	10 516	NA	NA	10 309	40	98	59	10	84	4 513	9 846	69.5

1. Codes shown are 2-digit FIPS codes for states; 4-digit census place codes for places; and 3-digit FIPS county codes followed by 3-digit census MCD codes for minor civil divisions (MCDs). MCD names are followed by county names in parentheses. 2. Hispanic persons may be of any race. 3. Dry land or land partially or temporarily covered by water.

State/ Place/ MCD[1] code	Place	Population			Population characteristics, 1990						Total housing units, 1990	Per capita income, 1985 (Dollars)	Land area,[3] 1990 (Sq. Km.)
			Places of 10,000 or more		Race								
		1990	1980	Percent change, 1980–1990	White	Black	Am. Indian, Eskimo Aleut	Asian & Pacific Islander	Other race	Hispanic[2]			
		1	2	3	4	5	6	7	8	9	10	11	12
	MICHIGAN—Con.												
0550	Green Lake township (Grand Traverse)	3 677	NA	NA	3 611	5	40	17	4	17	2 107	7 503	76.1
0550	Long Lake township (Grand Traverse)	5 977	NA	NA	5 889	1	60	23	4	33	2 621	9 102	78.0
0550	Paradise township (Grand Traverse)	2 508	NA	NA	2 480	0	18	2	8	30	912	NA	137.0
0550	Peninsula township (Grand Traverse)	4 340	NA	NA	4 300	1	11	7	21	48	2 206	13 892	72.2
0570	Wheeler township (Gratiot)	2 926	NA	NA	2 862	0	4	0	60	142	1 138	8 122	92.8
0590	Fayette township (Hillsdale)	3 190	NA	NA	3 144	24	8	3	11	29	1 303	10 200	60.2
0590	Jefferson township (Hillsdale)	3 083	NA	NA	3 073	0	6	1	3	20	1 416	6 885	92.2
0590	Somerset township (Hillsdale)	3 416	NA	NA	3 373	7	6	8	22	54	1 728	10 200	86.4
0610	Calumet township (Houghton)	7 015	NA	NA	6 960	14	30	4	7	26	3 612	6 971	86.6
0610	Portage township (Houghton)	2 941	NA	NA	2 865	5	18	51	2	8	1 500	7 911	294.5
0631	Sebewaing township (Huron)	2 937	NA	NA	2 895	0	5	3	34	60	1 317	8 870	84.4
0650	Alaiedon township (Ingham)	3 173	NA	NA	3 105	13	21	15	19	55	1 096	11 574	93.7
0650	Aurelius township (Ingham)	2 686	NA	NA	2 636	23	9	3	15	59	914	NA	94.5
0650	Delhi Charter township (Ingham)	19 190	17 144	11.9	18 577	205	75	144	189	422	7 189	11 277	74.6
0650	Lansing township (Ingham)	8 919	10 097	-11.7	8 074	513	43	105	184	440	4 355	12 687	12.8
0650	Leroy township (Ingham)	3 561	NA	NA	3 518	0	21	8	14	48	1 249	8 673	88.6
0650	Meridian township (Ingham)	35 644	28 754	24.0	32 538	1 305	169	1 373	259	736	14 811	14 544	82.4
0650	Stockbridge township (Ingham)	2 971	NA	NA	2 895	8	19	12	37	58	1 024	9 812	92.3
0650	Vevay township (Ingham)	3 668	NA	NA	3 605	10	15	2	36	74	1 256	10 822	83.7
0651	Williamstown township (Ingham)	4 285	NA	NA	4 208	26	11	20	20	52	1 509	14 860	76.4
0670	Berlin township (Ionia)	3 610	NA	NA	2 581	960	17	13	39	112	638	7 900	108.9
0670	Boston township (Ionia)	4 313	NA	NA	4 254	11	18	12	18	47	1 745	8 947	90.6
0670	Easton township (Ionia)	5 384	NA	NA	3 392	1 903	23	9	57	151	981	5 599	77.7
0670	Ionia township (Ionia)	3 153	NA	NA	3 081	7	8	11	46	86	1 186	9 886	87.8
0670	Lyons township (Ionia)	3 276	NA	NA	3 243	0	10	5	18	34	1 177	8 920	93.9
0670	Odessa township (Ionia)	3 885	NA	NA	3 755	3	12	7	108	171	1 549	9 040	92.6
0670	Orleans township (Ionia)	2 548	NA	NA	2 524	7	8	1	8	29	1 034	NA	92.0
0690	Oscoda township (Iosco)	11 958	11 376	5.1	10 995	566	103	202	92	245	5 936	6 911	315.4
0690	Plainfield township (Iosco)	3 490	NA	NA	3 451	6	27	3	3	12	3 852	7 379	268.8
0730	Chippewa township (Isabella)	4 130	NA	NA	3 627	8	449	13	33	71	1 552	7 204	93.7
0730	Coe township (Isabella)	2 967	NA	NA	2 932	3	10	14	8	31	1 154	8 605	93.8
0730	Deerfield township (Isabella)	2 598	NA	NA	2 559	4	16	11	8	19	946	NA	92.6
0730	Union township (Isabella)	5 139	NA	NA	4 939	25	94	41	40	91	1 999	8 818	75.2
0750	Blackman township (Jackson)	20 492	19 741	3.8	16 010	4 146	93	87	156	400	6 202	7 956	82.4
0750	Columbia township (Jackson)	6 308	NA	NA	6 264	2	17	21	4	41	3 181	11 773	95.1
0750	Grass Lake township (Jackson)	3 774	NA	NA	3 716	35	10	3	10	19	1 378	9 182	122.2
0750	Hanover township (Jackson)	3 710	NA	NA	3 674	7	22	2	5	27	1 375	10 140	90.6
0750	Henrietta township (Jackson)	3 858	NA	NA	3 814	8	15	2	19	42	1 489	8 858	93.9
0750	Leoni township (Jackson)	13 435	14 259	-5.8	13 189	85	57	41	63	175	5 291	9 016	127.2
0750	Napoleon township (Jackson)	6 273	NA	NA	6 172	49	21	18	13	66	2 468	9 930	76.3
0750	Norvell township (Jackson)	2 657	NA	NA	2 635	0	12	5	5	20	1 458	NA	77.7
0750	Rives township (Jackson)	4 026	NA	NA	3 988	15	8	4	11	29	1 454	9 745	93.0
0750	Sandstone township (Jackson)	3 300	NA	NA	3 267	9	11	11	2	39	1 168	9 686	94.0
0750	Spring Arbor township (Jackson)	6 939	NA	NA	6 849	25	28	22	15	60	2 504	9 456	91.7
0750	Summit township (Jackson)	21 130	22 113	-4.4	19 981	714	77	257	101	245	8 288	12 255	76.0
0751	Waterloo township (Jackson)	2 830	NA	NA	2 642	156	12	14	6	25	1 070	NA	124.1
0770	Alamo township (Kalamazoo)	3 276	NA	NA	3 205	41	8	14	8	20	1 164	10 251	94.0
0770	Brady township (Kalamazoo)	3 857	NA	NA	3 819	9	8	7	14	36	1 498	11 695	90.4
0770	Comstock township (Kalamazoo)	11 834	11 162	6.0	11 343	323	52	72	44	151	4 337	10 650	85.4
0770	Cooper township (Kalamazoo)	8 442	NA	NA	8 222	111	43	38	28	81	2 954	10 397	94.0
0770	Kalamazoo township (Kalamazoo)	20 976	20 942	0.2	18 592	1 913	88	168	215	390	9 316	11 030	30.5
0770	Oshtemo township (Kalamazoo)	13 401	10 958	22.3	12 086	949	61	235	70	181	6 525	12 303	93.2
0770	Pavilion township (Kalamazoo)	5 500	NA	NA	5 410	43	15	18	14	36	2 060	10 805	90.4
0770	Richland township (Kalamazoo)	5 099	NA	NA	5 008	46	15	20	10	42	1 944	14 025	90.1
0770	Ross township (Kalamazoo)	4 730	NA	NA	4 664	24	20	16	6	47	2 192	15 876	86.2
0770	Schoolcraft township (Kalamazoo)	6 705	NA	NA	6 595	19	27	42	22	46	2 608	11 040	89.0
0770	Texas township (Kalamazoo)	7 711	NA	NA	7 444	87	22	139	19	79	2 731	13 436	89.2
0790	Kalkaska township (Kalkaska)	4 269	NA	NA	4 202	7	43	10	7	17	1 880	8 067	182.2
0810	Ada township (Kent)	7 578	NA	NA	7 447	40	11	64	16	53	2 521	14 444	93.5
0810	Algoma township (Kent)	5 496	NA	NA	5 427	4	16	25	24	62	1 894	9 473	90.6
0810	Alpine township (Kent)	9 863	NA	NA	9 642	63	46	63	49	129	3 925	10 662	92.9
0810	Byron township (Kent)	13 235	10 104	31.0	12 987	62	56	79	51	151	4 871	10 347	94.7
0810	Caledonia township (Kent)	6 254	NA	NA	6 194	20	7	20	13	41	2 120	11 092	91.0
0810	Cannon township (Kent)	7 928	NA	NA	7 791	55	14	48	20	49	2 769	12 668	93.0
0810	Cascade township (Kent)	12 869	10 120	27.2	12 489	111	29	214	26	83	4 674	16 958	87.8
0810	Courtland township (Kent)	3 950	NA	NA	3 909	6	20	10	5	16	1 362	10 728	91.8
0810	Gaines township (Kent)	14 533	10 364	40.2	14 112	203	82	79	57	162	5 530	10 491	93.1
0810	Grand Rapids Charter township (Kent	10 760	NA	NA	10 555	56	15	102	32	91	3 764	14 501	40.9
0810	Grattan township (Kent)	2 876	NA	NA	2 840	9	9	13	5	22	1 205	10 371	90.6
0810	Lowell township (Kent)	4 774	NA	NA	4 697	17	25	27	8	48	1 543	9 322	84.5
0810	Nelson township (Kent)	3 406	NA	NA	3 371	5	19	7	4	21	1 158	8 127	93.5
0810	Oakfield township (Kent)	3 842	NA	NA	3 763	15	23	21	20	55	1 531	8 958	89.7
0811	Plainfield township (Kent)	24 946	20 608	21.1	24 325	233	48	237	103	295	9 278	11 056	91.0

1. Codes shown are 2-digit FIPS codes for states; 4-digit census place codes for places; and 3-digit FIPS county codes followed by 3-digit census MCD codes for minor civil divisions (MCDs). MCD names are followed by county names in parentheses. 2. Hispanic persons may be of any race. 3. Dry land or land partially or temporarily covered by water.

State/ Place/ MCD[1] code	Place	Population: 1990	Population: Places of 10,000 or more: 1980	Population: Places of 10,000 or more: Percent change, 1980–1990	Population characteristics, 1990: Race: White	Race: Black	Race: Am. Indian, Eskimo Aleut	Race: Asian & Pacific Islander	Race: Other race	Hispanic[2]	Total housing units, 1990	Per capita income, 1985 (Dollars)	Land area,[3] 1990 (Sq. Km.)
		1	2	3	4	5	6	7	8	9	10	11	12
	MICHIGAN—Con.												
0811	Solon township (Kent)	3 648	NA	NA	3 594	4	19	11	20	51	1 330	9 631	93.1
0811	Sparta township (Kent)	8 447	NA	NA	8 301	17	28	27	74	134	3 157	9 534	94.6
0811	Spencer township (Kent)	3 184	NA	NA	3 130	27	12	8	7	21	1 515	NA	90.9
0811	Tyrone township (Kent)	3 757	NA	NA	3 720	1	7	3	26	65	1 246	7 528	94.2
0870	Almont township (Lapeer)	4 660	NA	NA	4 598	2	16	4	40	111	1 630	10 197	95.8
0870	Attica township (Lapeer)	3 873	NA	NA	3 816	4	17	8	28	76	1 444	10 705	92.6
0870	Deerfield township (Lapeer)	4 903	NA	NA	4 826	0	24	23	30	73	1 767	9 662	92.9
0870	Dryden township (Lapeer)	3 399	NA	NA	3 381	8	7	2	1	19	1 154	11 141	92.9
0870	Elba township (Lapeer)	4 536	NA	NA	4 455	24	32	9	16	52	1 708	10 275	84.9
0870	Hadley township (Lapeer)	3 830	NA	NA	3 801	0	8	16	5	43	1 304	11 290	91.4
0870	Lapeer township (Lapeer)	4 519	NA	NA	4 452	11	9	30	17	50	1 510	12 880	82.9
0870	Marathon township (Lapeer)	4 286	NA	NA	4 229	9	19	8	21	56	1 488	9 341	86.6
0870	Mayfield township (Lapeer)	7 133	NA	NA	7 013	10	25	30	55	133	2 390	10 186	90.1
0870	Metamora township (Lapeer)	3 544	NA	NA	3 493	6	20	17	8	24	1 283	12 454	90.2
0870	North Branch township (Lapeer)	3 006	NA	NA	2 985	0	8	5	8	41	1 021	9 440	93.6
0870	Oregon township (Lapeer)	5 913	NA	NA	5 822	10	27	16	38	99	1 902	9 729	85.9
0890	Elmwood township (Leelanau)	3 427	NA	NA	3 360	7	30	16	14	45	1 515	10 667	52.2
0910	Adrian township (Lenawee)	4 336	NA	NA	4 165	14	2	33	122	262	1 505	11 186	89.9
0910	Blissfield township (Lenawee)	3 849	NA	NA	3 719	15	21	3	91	192	1 526	9 895	54.5
0910	Cambridge township (Lenawee)	4 429	NA	NA	4 366	13	21	16	13	66	2 366	9 790	82.9
0910	Clinton township (Lenawee)	3 557	NA	NA	3 533	5	7	5	7	45	1 343	11 193	46.8
0910	Madison Charter township (Lenawee)	5 351	NA	NA	4 683	332	20	18	298	582	1 681	10 449	79.6
0910	Palmyra township (Lenawee)	2 602	NA	NA	2 319	174	7	28	74	121	806	NA	95.0
0910	Raisin township (Lenawee)	5 648	NA	NA	5 490	11	19	54	74	250	1 894	9 609	93.9
0911	Rollin township (Lenawee)	3 323	NA	NA	3 291	8	3	10	11	48	2 024	11 267	87.8
0911	Woodstock township (Lenawee)	3 155	NA	NA	3 129	3	12	2	9	52	1 583	9 407	87.8
0930	Brighton township (Livingston)	14 815	11 222	32.0	14 529	71	87	111	17	128	4 874	14 368	85.8
0930	Cohoctah township (Livingston)	2 693	NA	NA	2 648	1	28	14	2	21	900	NA	98.7
0930	Deerfield township (Livingston)	3 000	NA	NA	2 978	2	11	2	7	36	1 057	10 584	94.3
0930	Genoa township (Livingston)	10 820	NA	NA	10 688	14	64	48	6	69	4 065	12 908	88.8
0930	Green Oak township (Livingston)	11 604	10 802	7.4	11 133	313	75	48	35	103	4 256	11 174	89.9
0930	Hamburg township (Livingston)	13 083	11 318	15.6	12 810	192	30	34	17	89	5 090	12 714	83.9
0930	Handy township (Livingston)	5 488	NA	NA	5 368	1	93	13	13	56	1 957	8 998	89.3
0930	Hartland township (Livingston)	6 860	NA	NA	6 795	13	17	31	4	28	2 360	12 657	94.1
0930	Howell township (Livingston)	4 298	NA	NA	4 237	7	30	15	9	37	1 360	10 124	83.0
0930	Marion township (Livingston)	4 918	NA	NA	4 884	0	13	9	12	44	1 629	9 922	92.2
0930	Oceola township (Livingston)	4 825	NA	NA	4 767	5	34	5	14	54	1 578	10 709	94.0
0930	Putnam township (Livingston)	6 183	NA	NA	6 120	4	32	18	9	44	2 264	10 546	89.0
0930	Tyrone township (Livingston)	6 854	NA	NA	6 752	16	44	16	26	51	2 352	13 155	92.3
0930	Unadilla township (Livingston)	2 949	NA	NA	2 919	9	11	0	10	32	1 096	9 849	88.1
0950	McMillan township (Luce)	2 961	NA	NA	2 763	0	197	1	0	17	1 897	7 571	1 533.3
0990	Armada township (Macomb)	4 491	NA	NA	4 442	7	12	2	28	84	1 413	10 575	94.5
0990	Bruce township (Macomb)	6 012	NA	NA	5 788	141	22	41	20	59	2 062	11 707	94.3
0990	Chesterfield township (Macomb)	25 905	18 276	41.7	25 156	384	89	216	60	297	9 594	11 370	72.3
0990	Clinton township (Macomb)	85 866	72 400	18.6	81 917	2 586	253	909	201	1 001	33 938	12 671	73.0
0990	Harrison township (Macomb)	24 685	23 649	4.4	23 838	498	98	161	90	355	10 616	13 475	36.6
0990	Lenox township (Macomb)	5 400	NA	NA	4 580	703	54	17	46	95	1 842	9 291	100.6
0990	Macomb township (Macomb)	22 714	14 230	59.6	22 322	109	58	188	37	240	7 562	12 238	94.0
0990	Ray township (Macomb)	3 230	NA	NA	3 210	1	11	4	4	27	1 076	12 149	95.4
0990	Richmond township (Macomb)	2 528	NA	NA	2 468	37	20	1	2	7	783	NA	97.0
0990	Shelby township (Macomb)	48 655	38 939	25.0	47 665	141	153	584	112	465	17 630	13 406	90.0
0991	Washington township (Macomb)	13 087	10 186	28.5	12 833	110	28	64	52	140	4 668	13 903	93.1
1010	Manistee township (Manistee)	2 952	NA	NA	2 904	3	22	9	14	54	1 343	8 344	116.2
1030	Chocolay township (Marquette)	6 025	NA	NA	5 806	45	127	43	4	47	2 340	9 844	154.5
1030	Forsyth township (Marquette)	8 775	NA	NA	8 069	328	91	203	84	206	3 904	6 962	453.9
1030	Ishpeming township (Marquette)	3 515	NA	NA	3 477	6	16	15	1	5	1 528	8 589	224.0
1030	Marquette township (Marquette)	2 757	NA	NA	2 658	2	69	21	7	17	1 131	9 087	141.8
1030	Sands township (Marquette)	2 696	NA	NA	2 502	103	42	22	27	50	717	NA	183.5
1050	Hamlin township (Mason)	2 597	NA	NA	2 574	1	4	9	9	14	1 794	10 576	71.2
1070	Big Rapids township (Mecosta)	3 100	NA	NA	2 948	87	17	30	18	40	1 194	NA	75.0
1070	Green township (Mecosta)	2 833	NA	NA	2 780	35	7	8	3	26	1 214	8 015	95.6
1090	Menominee township (Menominee)	3 956	NA	NA	3 936	0	15	5	0	6	1 657	7 996	188.7
1110	Homer township (Midland)	4 235	NA	NA	4 162	13	28	5	27	57	1 557	10 705	60.4
1110	Ingersoll township (Midland)	2 788	NA	NA	2 766	3	4	6	9	21	984	10 315	94.3
1110	Jerome township (Midland)	4 470	NA	NA	4 406	5	18	12	29	52	1 803	9 249	88.0
1110	Larkin township (Midland)	3 588	NA	NA	3 530	10	6	25	17	41	1 193	10 503	88.2
1110	Lee township (Midland)	4 017	NA	NA	3 951	7	42	1	16	36	1 395	8 509	93.2
1150	Ash township (Monroe)	7 480	NA	NA	7 373	19	41	25	22	86	2 644	10 449	89.6
1150	Bedford township (Monroe)	23 748	22 902	3.7	23 462	42	50	105	89	281	8 239	11 454	101.2
1150	Berlin township (Monroe)	6 286	NA	NA	6 210	19	25	10	22	66	2 274	10 660	83.1
1150	Dundee township (Monroe)	5 376	NA	NA	5 319	7	6	5	39	73	2 019	10 573	125.4
1150	Erie township (Monroe)	4 492	NA	NA	4 321	7	38	18	108	214	1 585	10 396	62.5
1150	Exeter township (Monroe)	3 253	NA	NA	2 942	292	7	2	10	18	1 051	10 235	94.7

1. Codes shown are 2-digit FIPS codes for states; 4-digit census place codes for places; and 3-digit FIPS county codes followed by 3-digit census MCD codes for minor civil divisions (MCDs). MCD names are followed by county names in parentheses. 2. Hispanic persons may be of any race. 3. Dry land or land partially or temporarily covered by water.

State/ Place/ MCD[1] code	Place	Population			Population characteristics, 1990						Total housing units, 1990	Per capita income, 1985 (Dollars)	Land area,[3] 1990 (Sq. Km.)
		1990	Places of 10,000 or more		Race					Hispanic[2]			
			1980	Percent change, 1980–1990	White	Black	Am. Indian, Eskimo Aleut	Asian & Pacific Islander	Other race				
		1	2	3	4	5	6	7	8	9	10	11	12
	MICHIGAN—Con.												
1150	Frenchtown township (Monroe)	18 210	18 204	0.0	17 812	175	73	68	82	271	6 881	10 152	109.1
1150	Ida township (Monroe)	4 554	NA	NA	4 506	8	24	5	11	43	1 480	10 350	95.2
1150	La Salle township (Monroe)	4 985	NA	NA	4 912	9	15	15	34	124	1 675	10 665	69.0
1150	London township (Monroe)	2 915	NA	NA	2 429	464	16	3	3	40	944	9 166	92.5
1150	Monroe township (Monroe)	11 909	11 654	2.2	11 629	98	38	69	75	215	4 585	10 332	45.1
1150	Raisinville township (Monroe)	4 634	NA	NA	4 593	13	11	12	5	34	1 492	9 453	124.8
1150	Summerfield township (Monroe)	3 076	NA	NA	3 039	8	3	11	15	26	1 019	9 902	109.4
1150	Whiteford township (Monroe)	4 433	NA	NA	4 290	92	6	10	35	89	1 577	9 823	103.2
1170	Bloomer township (Montcalm)	2 922	NA	NA	2 012	849	28	6	27	75	479	NA	91.2
1170	Cato township (Montcalm)	2 500	NA	NA	2 434	9	13	13	31	78	1 158	NA	91.4
1170	Crystal township (Montcalm)	2 541	NA	NA	2 502	0	21	4	14	35	1 467	NA	88.4
1170	Eureka township (Montcalm)	2 594	NA	NA	2 551	4	9	12	18	28	984	NA	77.0
1170	Evergreen township (Montcalm)	2 531	NA	NA	2 500	3	16	7	5	34	1 217	NA	89.8
1170	Home township (Montcalm)	2 513	NA	NA	2 440	4	19	6	44	75	1 027	7 524	93.2
1170	Montcalm township (Montcalm)	2 879	NA	NA	2 819	1	18	9	32	53	1 159	8 193	92.5
1170	Reynolds township (Montcalm)	3 028	NA	NA	2 906	23	85	7	7	39	1 234	NA	93.3
1210	Cedar Creek township (Muskegon)	2 846	NA	NA	2 769	18	31	7	21	49	1 131	NA	91.3
1210	Dalton township (Muskegon)	6 276	NA	NA	6 036	138	55	14	33	116	2 312	8 431	92.4
1210	Egelston township (Muskegon)	7 640	NA	NA	7 352	89	109	16	74	225	2 816	7 678	90.6
1210	Fruitland township (Muskegon)	4 391	NA	NA	4 283	17	64	11	16	78	1 823	9 514	94.6
1210	Fruitport township (Muskegon)	11 485	10 646	7.9	11 256	43	89	35	62	205	3 952	9 395	77.7
1210	Laketon township (Muskegon)	6 538	NA	NA	6 437	22	26	36	17	64	2 427	10 544	44.8
1210	Muskegon township (Muskegon)	15 302	14 557	5.1	14 443	515	159	46	139	363	5 742	8 204	61.7
1230	Brooks township (Newaygo)	2 728	NA	NA	2 687	2	8	7	24	53	1 671	NA	82.5
1230	Grant township (Newaygo)	2 558	NA	NA	2 371	0	2	12	173	254	960	NA	93.0
1250	Addison township (Oakland)	5 142	NA	NA	5 082	13	16	11	20	61	1 833	12 458	93.9
1250	Bloomfield township (Oakland)	42 473	42 876	-0.9	38 966	1 014	43	2 362	88	527	16 558	28 687	64.6
1250	Brandon township (Oakland)	12 051	NA	NA	11 898	10	58	52	33	128	4 172	11 758	90.8
1250	Commerce township (Oakland)	26 955	23 757	13.5	26 637	28	115	118	57	254	9 847	13 736	71.5
1250	Groveland township (Oakland)	4 705	NA	NA	4 596	43	21	17	28	99	1 576	12 409	92.2
1250	Highland township (Oakland)	17 941	16 938	5.9	17 738	46	77	43	37	166	6 271	11 133	87.3
1250	Holly township (Oakland)	8 852	NA	NA	8 509	210	40	25	68	174	3 333	11 058	90.2
1250	Independence township (Oakland)	24 722	21 537	14.8	24 305	49	97	155	116	398	8 746	14 915	92.4
1251	Lyon township (Oakland)	9 450	NA	NA	9 339	3	51	26	31	92	3 471	11 781	83.0
1251	Milford township (Oakland)	12 121	10 187	19.0	11 971	21	42	65	22	128	4 406	13 380	86.2
1251	Oakland Charter township (Oakland)	8 227	NA	NA	8 115	35	12	48	17	65	2 823	16 977	94.4
1251	Orion township (Oakland)	24 076	22 473	7.1	23 588	142	99	84	163	438	9 009	13 244	86.4
1251	Oxford township (Oakland)	11 933	10 569	12.9	11 734	37	53	72	37	160	4 376	13 453	87.8
1251	Rose township (Oakland)	4 926	NA	NA	4 770	97	21	17	21	93	1 770	13 191	90.7
1251	Royal Oak township (Oakland)	5 011	NA	NA	1 662	3 270	5	69	5	49	2 640	9 566	1.8
1251	Southfield township (Oakland)	14 255	15 078	-5.5	13 730	184	16	304	21	156	5 628	28 716	20.8
1251	Springfield township (Oakland)	9 927	NA	NA	9 704	84	53	42	44	188	3 459	11 922	92.2
1252	Waterford township (Oakland)	66 692	64 446	3.5	64 647	701	391	495	458	1 538	26 509	13 272	81.2
1252	West Bloomfield township (Oakland)	54 516	41 962	29.9	50 406	1 074	63	2 842	131	668	20 378	22 723	70.8
1252	White Lake township (Oakland)	22 608	21 890	3.3	22 162	156	132	97	61	294	8 267	12 717	87.1
1270	Grant township (Oceana)	2 578	NA	NA	2 449	3	21	9	96	124	1 016	NA	91.7
1270	Shelby township (Oceana)	3 692	NA	NA	3 363	8	26	3	292	392	1 354	7 690	93.2
1290	Mills township (Ogemaw)	3 174	NA	NA	3 134	1	35	2	2	20	3 220	5 778	89.3
1310	Ontonagon township (Ontonagon)	3 238	NA	NA	3 189	0	41	7	1	12	1 652	8 802	499.5
1350	Big Creek township (Oscoda)	2 778	NA	NA	2 751	1	20	2	4	21	2 954	NA	366.4
1370	Bagley township (Otsego)	4 929	NA	NA	4 869	8	33	15	4	24	2 595	8 384	76.4
1390	Allendale township (Ottawa)	8 022	NA	NA	7 646	235	24	67	50	84	2 154	8 060	81.1
1390	Blendon township (Ottawa)	4 740	NA	NA	4 689	7	5	12	27	49	1 425	9 001	94.6
1390	Crockery township (Ottawa)	3 599	NA	NA	3 515	33	35	3	13	39	1 310	8 192	84.7
1390	Georgetown township (Ottawa)	32 672	26 104	25.2	32 233	92	39	206	102	306	10 456	10 352	86.7
1390	Grand Haven township (Ottawa)	9 710	NA	NA	9 533	16	66	53	42	89	3 603	10 781	74.2
1390	Holland township (Ottawa)	17 523	13 722	27.7	15 981	90	58	585	809	1 623	6 416	10 331	70.6
1390	Jamestown township (Ottawa)	4 059	NA	NA	4 040	1	5	11	2	29	1 172	10 237	92.8
1390	Olive township (Ottawa)	2 866	NA	NA	2 723	72	10	11	50	124	884	NA	93.8
1390	Park township (Ottawa)	13 541	10 371	30.6	13 074	48	26	181	212	515	5 359	12 666	50.0
1390	Port Sheldon township (Ottawa)	2 929	NA	NA	2 849	6	20	43	11	73	1 295	NA	57.9
1390	Robinson township (Ottawa)	3 925	NA	NA	3 721	3	23	16	162	208	1 256	9 334	100.0
1390	Spring Lake township (Ottawa)	10 751	NA	NA	10 607	6	36	56	46	128	4 416	11 974	42.8
1390	Tallmadge township (Ottawa)	6 293	NA	NA	6 225	14	16	24	14	50	2 056	10 295	84.0
1390	Wright township (Ottawa)	3 285	NA	NA	3 199	5	8	3	70	88	959	7 896	93.7
1391	Zeeland township (Ottawa)	4 472	NA	NA	4 430	1	10	6	25	73	1 561	10 121	89.2
1430	Denton township (Roscommon)	4 290	NA	NA	4 273	0	12	2	3	18	3 998	8 058	68.3
1430	Richfield township (Roscommon)	3 413	NA	NA	3 366	3	33	4	7	25	3 448	7 113	178.5
1430	Roscommon township (Roscommon)	3 223	NA	NA	3 179	28	12	4	0	4	2 221	6 929	269.2
1450	Birch Run township (Saginaw)	5 354	NA	NA	5 299	20	19	7	9	86	1 997	10 409	92.2
1450	Bridgeport township (Saginaw)	12 747	13 978	-8.8	10 525	1 539	85	49	549	1 029	4 677	10 325	89.7
1450	Buena Vista Charter tshp (Saginaw)	10 900	12 763	-14.6	4 890	5 255	67	14	674	1 015	4 241	9 279	93.2
1450	Carrollton township (Saginaw)	6 521	NA	NA	5 663	390	25	48	395	621	2 470	10 179	8.3

1. Codes shown are 2-digit FIPS codes for states; 4-digit census place codes for places; and 3-digit FIPS county codes followed by 3-digit census MCD codes for minor civil divisions (MCDs). MCD names are followed by county names in parentheses. 2. Hispanic persons may be of any race. 3. Dry land or land partially or temporarily covered by water.

State/ Place/ MCD[1] code	Place	Population 1990	Population, Places of 10,000 or more, 1980	Population, Places of 10,000 or more, Percent change, 1980–1990	Population characteristics, 1990: Race, White	Race, Black	Race, Am. Indian, Eskimo Aleut	Race, Asian & Pacific Islander	Race, Other race	Hispanic[2]	Total housing units, 1990	Per capita income, 1985 (Dollars)	Land area,[3] 1990 (Sq. Km.)
		1	2	3	4	5	6	7	8	9	10	11	12
	MICHIGAN—Con.												
1450	Chesaning township (Saginaw)	4 904	NA	NA	4 769	6	14	10	105	178	1 835	9 370	89.8
1450	Kochville township (Saginaw)	2 740	NA	NA	2 647	48	13	14	18	59	886	9 699	48.7
1450	Maple Grove township (Saginaw)	2 830	NA	NA	2 790	17	1	1	21	31	875	9 157	92.3
1451	Richland township (Saginaw)	4 177	NA	NA	4 147	0	4	2	24	62	1 493	10 231	96.0
1451	Saginaw township (Saginaw)	37 684	38 668	-2.5	35 228	1 072	87	711	586	1 279	15 809	13 418	63.8
1451	St. Charles township (Saginaw)	3 505	NA	NA	3 438	7	24	1	35	126	1 335	8 919	95.7
1451	Spaulding township (Saginaw)	2 662	NA	NA	2 233	265	2	8	154	247	941	9 484	68.8
1451	Taymouth township (Saginaw)	4 524	NA	NA	4 405	32	42	5	40	162	1 501	8 360	92.1
1451	Thomas township (Saginaw)	10 971	11 184	-1.9	10 755	44	27	40	105	222	3 893	11 441	81.6
1451	Tittabawassee township (Saginaw)	4 627	NA	NA	4 569	12	11	9	26	91	1 712	11 599	91.1
1470	Burtchville township (St. Clair)	3 559	NA	NA	3 527	5	5	8	14	29	1 600	9 374	40.4
1470	Casco township (St. Clair)	4 552	NA	NA	4 511	2	20	7	12	47	1 502	10 250	96.5
1470	China township (St. Clair)	2 644	NA	NA	2 631	0	4	9	0	4	836	NA	89.2
1470	Clay township (St. Clair)	8 862	NA	NA	8 763	4	73	13	9	69	4 767	11 184	91.9
1470	Clyde township (St. Clair)	5 052	NA	NA	4 988	12	19	4	29	62	1 641	9 844	92.9
1470	Columbus township (St. Clair)	3 235	NA	NA	3 223	1	5	3	3	19	1 066	9 483	96.4
1470	Cottrellville township (St. Clair)	3 301	NA	NA	3 282	0	13	4	2	24	1 294	10 737	54.9
1470	East China township (St. Clair)	3 216	NA	NA	3 207	1	0	4	4	17	1 383	10 789	17.1
1470	Fort Gratiot township (St. Clair)	8 968	NA	NA	8 803	71	11	44	39	103	3 551	11 316	41.8
1470	Ira township (St. Clair)	5 587	NA	NA	5 526	8	21	10	22	58	2 396	10 765	43.9
1470	Kimball township (St. Clair)	7 247	NA	NA	7 044	114	60	7	22	93	2 538	8 050	96.5
1471	Mussey township (St. Clair)	3 113	NA	NA	2 924	6	14	5	164	195	1 107	8 657	93.2
1471	Port Huron township (St. Clair)	7 621	NA	NA	7 166	297	53	28	77	228	2 836	9 361	33.5
1471	St. Clair township (St. Clair)	4 614	NA	NA	4 579	2	6	14	13	38	1 707	12 433	100.9
1490	Burr Oak township (St. Joseph)	2 542	NA	NA	2 509	9	14	2	8	19	977	7 415	92.1
1490	Colon township (St. Joseph)	3 217	NA	NA	3 186	3	12	5	11	26	1 622	7 737	89.6
1490	Constantine township (St. Joseph)	4 152	NA	NA	4 086	20	32	7	7	47	1 603	8 162	89.5
1490	Fabius township (St. Joseph)	3 187	NA	NA	3 120	29	12	24	2	23	1 553	10 066	84.5
1490	Lockport township (St. Joseph)	3 395	NA	NA	2 933	413	13	21	15	26	1 373	9 877	77.7
1490	Mendon township (St. Joseph)	2 695	NA	NA	2 610	50	20	8	7	30	1 105	9 032	90.6
1490	Nottawa township (St. Joseph)	3 637	NA	NA	3 552	45	9	22	9	19	1 309	7 829	92.7
1490	Park township (St. Joseph)	2 769	NA	NA	2 657	92	8	4	8	30	1 030	9 442	90.9
1490	Sherman township (St. Joseph)	2 978	NA	NA	2 934	8	7	18	11	25	1 249	11 756	86.3
1490	White Pigeon township (St. Joseph)	3 654	NA	NA	3 631	6	8	7	2	28	1 747	10 015	66.1
1510	Lexington township (Sanilac)	3 028	NA	NA	2 978	0	29	5	16	78	2 004	9 090	94.1
1511	Worth township (Sanilac)	3 146	NA	NA	3 120	3	12	1	10	28	2 585	9 038	100.4
1550	Bennington township (Shiawassee)	2 726	NA	NA	2 675	4	16	13	18	45	919	10 382	94.5
1550	Burns township (Shiawassee)	3 019	NA	NA	2 980	1	24	5	9	37	1 044	10 785	91.9
1550	Caledonia township (Shiawassee)	4 514	NA	NA	4 439	3	20	28	24	52	1 644	10 367	82.0
1550	Owosso township (Shiawassee)	4 121	NA	NA	4 079	0	15	20	7	36	1 572	10 238	84.1
1550	Perry township (Shiawassee)	3 698	NA	NA	3 646	5	20	16	11	34	1 319	9 808	82.9
1550	Shiawassee township (Shiawassee)	2 731	NA	NA	2 700	0	12	5	14	31	920	9 101	95.1
1550	Venice township (Shiawassee)	2 812	NA	NA	2 778	6	18	1	9	30	1 001	10 263	97.0
1550	Vernon township (Shiawassee)	4 989	NA	NA	4 944	5	19	7	14	52	1 839	10 785	88.5
1551	Woodhull township (Shiawassee)	3 585	NA	NA	3 545	7	16	5	12	29	1 225	10 049	70.2
1570	Almer township (Tuscola)	2 628	NA	NA	2 562	5	11	13	37	52	1 019	10 174	89.7
1570	Arbela township (Tuscola)	3 182	NA	NA	3 144	13	17	7	1	24	1 071	9 551	86.6
1570	Denmark township (Tuscola)	3 369	NA	NA	3 301	1	2	39	26	72	1 292	10 433	91.3
1570	Elkland township (Tuscola)	3 430	NA	NA	3 367	5	31	20	7	38	1 402	10 545	92.2
1570	Fremont township (Tuscola)	3 153	NA	NA	3 108	1	28	10	6	37	1 106	8 544	93.1
1570	Indianfields township (Tuscola)	6 699	NA	NA	6 277	193	69	58	102	276	2 548	8 859	90.0
1570	Millington township (Tuscola)	4 199	NA	NA	4 135	11	20	15	18	46	1 516	9 880	92.6
1571	Vassar township (Tuscola)	3 866	NA	NA	3 783	7	27	3	46	84	1 339	9 245	90.4
1590	Almena township (Van Buren)	3 581	NA	NA	3 484	42	30	10	15	27	1 254	9 520	89.3
1590	Antwerp township (Van Buren)	9 293	NA	NA	8 943	114	61	30	145	297	3 280	9 268	90.4
1590	Bloomingdale township (Van Buren)	2 854	NA	NA	2 732	81	16	9	16	43	1 284	NA	88.2
1590	Columbia township (Van Buren)	2 552	NA	NA	2 332	127	24	11	58	102	1 429	NA	88.3
1590	Covert township (Van Buren)	2 855	NA	NA	1 367	1 378	25	10	75	135	1 644	6 933	90.6
1590	Decatur township (Van Buren)	3 616	NA	NA	3 306	181	56	11	62	123	1 526	7 340	91.2
1590	Geneva township (Van Buren)	3 162	NA	NA	2 620	449	28	8	57	110	1 283	7 487	91.5
1590	Hartford township (Van Buren)	3 032	NA	NA	2 800	21	55	9	147	187	1 215	7 337	88.3
1590	Lawrence township (Van Buren)	3 030	NA	NA	2 723	105	31	9	162	213	1 451	7 976	90.7
1590	Paw Paw township (Van Buren)	6 701	NA	NA	6 399	162	41	31	68	136	3 076	10 026	90.9
1590	Pine Grove township (Van Buren)	2 594	NA	NA	2 538	34	7	4	11	21	982	NA	89.2
1590	South Haven township (Van Buren)	4 185	NA	NA	3 544	561	33	20	27	83	1 867	9 400	47.4
1610	Ann Arbor township (Washtenaw)	3 793	NA	NA	3 472	127	14	167	13	51	1 712	26 362	47.7
1610	Augusta township (Washtenaw)	4 415	NA	NA	4 103	272	9	23	8	20	1 507	11 944	95.2
1610	Dexter township (Washtenaw)	4 407	NA	NA	4 333	13	27	20	14	47	1 850	12 989	79.7
1610	Lima township (Washtenaw)	2 585	NA	NA	2 553	10	8	8	6	14	977	13 178	93.9
1610	Lodi township (Washtenaw)	3 902	NA	NA	3 826	9	11	49	7	48	1 372	16 877	87.3
1610	Manchester township (Washtenaw)	3 492	NA	NA	3 453	12	12	9	6	36	1 319	12 169	98.5
1610	Northfield township (Washtenaw)	6 732	NA	NA	6 629	47	23	24	9	59	2 579	12 186	94.0
1610	Pittsfield township (Washtenaw)	17 668	12 997	35.9	13 811	2 929	62	713	153	371	7 794	14 134	72.8

1. Codes shown are 2-digit FIPS codes for states; 4-digit census place codes for places; and 3-digit FIPS county codes followed by 3-digit census MCD codes for minor civil divisions (MCDs). MCD names are followed by county names in parentheses. 2. Hispanic persons may be of any race. 3. Dry land or land partially or temporarily covered by water.

State/ Place/ MCD[1] code	Place	Population: 1990	Population: Places of 10,000 or more: 1980	Population: Places of 10,000 or more: Percent change, 1980–1990	Population characteristics, 1990: Race: White	Race: Black	Race: Am. Indian, Eskimo Aleut	Race: Asian & Pacific Islander	Race: Other race	Hispanic[2]	Total housing units, 1990	Per capita income, 1985 (Dollars)	Land area,[3] 1990 (Sq. Km.)
		1	2	3	4	5	6	7	8	9	10	11	12
	MICHIGAN—Con.												
1610	Salem township (Washtenaw)	3 734	NA	NA	3 655	53	6	16	4	31	1 258	13 305	88.8
1610	Scio township (Washtenaw)	11 077	NA	NA	10 569	262	33	186	27	111	4 266	15 851	88.5
1610	Superior township (Washtenaw)	8 720	NA	NA	6 072	2 430	41	147	30	126	3 156	12 921	91.6
1610	Sylvan township (Washtenaw)	5 827	NA	NA	5 742	45	21	15	4	46	2 189	11 149	91.1
1611	Webster township (Washtenaw)	3 235	NA	NA	3 180	17	10	27	1	36	1 173	13 348	91.3
1611	York township (Washtenaw)	6 225	NA	NA	5 196	753	64	41	171	464	1 467	10 999	91.3
1611	Ypsilanti township (Washtenaw)	45 307	44 511	1.8	35 966	8 262	167	651	261	712	18 659	11 937	78.2
1630	Brownstown township (Wayne)	18 811	18 302	2.8	17 643	502	96	469	101	490	6 751	10 984	58.2
1630	Canton township (Wayne)	57 040	48 616	17.3	52 973	1 167	155	2 562	183	792	20 307	12 608	93.2
1630	Grosse Ile township (Wayne)	9 781	NA	NA	9 374	8	35	349	15	134	3 632	18 836	24.9
1630	Grosse Pointe township (Wayne)	2 850	NA	NA	2 715	11	3	113	8	41	1 044	34 229	2.6
1631	Huron township (Wayne)	10 447	NA	NA	10 299	36	63	16	33	199	3 630	11 511	92.1
1631	Northville township (Wayne)	17 313	12 987	33.3	15 712	1 069	49	432	51	185	6 526	16 364	42.6
1631	Plymouth township (Wayne)	23 648	23 028	2.7	22 862	286	58	388	54	271	9 211	15 340	41.2
1631	Redford township (Wayne)	54 387	58 441	-6.9	53 342	379	199	311	156	829	20 451	12 099	29.1
1631	Sumpter township (Wayne)	10 891	11 112	-2.0	9 298	1 487	45	24	37	142	3 848	9 888	97.3
1631	Van Buren township (Wayne)	21 010	18 940	10.9	18 994	1 604	110	206	96	322	8 432	12 206	87.8
1650	Haring township (Wexford)	2 501	NA	NA	2 465	8	18	8	2	6	912	7 999	84.4
27	MINNESOTA	4 375 099	4 075 970	7.3	4 130 395	94 944	49 909	77 886	21 965	53 884	1 848 445	11 186	206 207.1
0020	Afton	2 645	NA	NA	2 608	6	2	19	10	20	918	16 038	65.2
0045	Albert Lea	18 310	19 200	-4.6	17 643	5	39	92	531	897	7 930	10 392	24.7
0065	Alexandria	7 838	NA	NA	7 763	3	29	33	10	40	3 741	8 739	20.9
0088	Andover	15 216	NA	NA	14 887	49	95	142	43	153	4 519	10 910	88.4
0095	Anoka	17 192	15 634	10.0	16 745	100	131	184	32	131	6 799	11 245	17.1
0102	Apple Valley	34 598	21 818	58.6	33 441	315	77	664	101	351	11 538	13 523	44.9
0110	Arden Hills	9 199	NA	NA	8 760	105	11	307	16	74	2 958	15 643	23.0
0122	Arnold CDP	2 891	NA	NA	2 831	13	32	14	1	5	1 058	NA	30.0
0150	Austin	21 907	23 006	-4.8	21 505	47	30	260	65	190	9 798	10 943	25.1
0225	Baxter	3 695	NA	NA	3 661	3	9	12	10	19	1 257	8 982	44.8
0230	Bayport	3 200	NA	NA	2 575	438	126	15	46	55	778	10 826	3.8
0270	Belle Plaine	3 149	NA	NA	3 120	1	11	15	2	9	1 146	9 497	10.5
0290	Bemidji	11 245	10 949	2.7	10 026	60	1 017	132	10	58	4 412	7 792	28.9
0300	Benson	3 235	NA	NA	3 194	0	24	14	3	17	1 484	8 640	6.5
0335	Big Lake	3 113	NA	NA	3 078	5	13	6	11	22	1 264	NA	5.5
0370	Blaine	38 975	28 558	36.5	37 866	127	306	533	143	397	13 176	11 117	87.9
0385	Bloomington	86 335	81 831	5.5	81 766	1 394	248	2 669	258	805	35 815	15 854	92.0
0390	Blue Earth	3 745	NA	NA	3 697	7	6	14	21	51	1 644	9 696	8.1
0435	Brainerd	12 353	11 489	7.5	12 081	40	151	49	32	64	5 483	8 621	17.8
0445	Breckenridge	3 708	NA	NA	3 646	2	24	17	19	35	1 619	8 609	5.9
0460	Brooklyn Center	28 887	31 230	-7.5	26 271	1 502	271	668	175	367	11 713	12 148	20.6
0465	Brooklyn Park	56 381	43 332	30.1	51 079	2 785	348	1 916	253	650	21 265	12 166	67.5
0525	Buffalo	6 856	NA	NA	6 761	7	30	44	14	37	2 608	10 410	10.3
0537	Burnsville	51 288	35 674	43.8	48 619	1 163	168	1 169	169	529	20 244	14 840	64.4
0555	Caledonia	2 846	NA	NA	2 824	0	4	18	0	1	1 189	9 955	7.4
0570	Cambridge	5 094	NA	NA	5 005	18	21	36	14	30	1 950	10 079	9.8
0585	Cannon Falls	3 232	NA	NA	3 201	0	10	19	2	13	1 282	10 808	8.8
0630	Champlin	16 849	NA	NA	16 521	65	90	133	40	132	5 532	11 560	21.2
0640	Chanhassen	11 732	NA	NA	11 448	28	39	195	22	78	4 249	15 093	53.9
0645	Chaska	11 339	NA	NA	11 125	44	25	117	28	79	4 476	12 053	35.5
0665	Chisholm	5 290	NA	NA	5 238	2	30	14	6	18	2 405	8 934	11.4
0675	Circle Pines	4 704	NA	NA	4 604	5	30	56	9	34	1 599	12 336	4.5
0750	Cloquet	10 885	11 142	-2.3	10 038	8	789	41	9	45	4 580	9 341	91.3
0790	Columbia Heights	18 910	19 978	-5.3	18 086	227	210	270	117	273	7 975	12 131	8.9
0820	Coon Rapids	52 978	35 826	47.9	51 566	255	425	575	157	496	18 098	11 614	59.1
0825	Corcoran	5 199	NA	NA	5 127	9	22	30	11	27	1 564	11 190	92.7
0837	Cottage Grove	22 935	18 994	20.7	22 144	267	68	261	195	423	7 105	11 144	88.0
0855	Crookston	8 119	NA	NA	7 849	30	101	19	120	376	3 289	9 679	12.1
0870	Crystal	23 788	25 543	-6.9	22 669	432	144	439	104	227	9 541	12 940	14.9
0930	Dayton	4 443	NA	NA	4 346	12	41	41	3	15	1 394	11 584	60.8
0935	Deephaven	3 653	NA	NA	3 591	9	3	50	0	11	1 382	26 136	6.1
0960	Delano	2 709	NA	NA	2 668	4	21	8	8	18	1 000	NA	5.0
0995	Detroit Lakes	6 635	NA	NA	6 369	11	189	32	34	75	3 375	9 920	10.5
1005	Dilworth	2 562	NA	NA	2 441	1	37	3	80	105	1 090	8 748	4.5
1040	Duluth	85 493	92 811	-7.9	81 980	747	1 837	768	161	510	36 022	10 051	175.1
1063	Eagan	47 409	20 700	129.0	44 401	1 143	157	1 492	216	595	18 450	13 424	83.5
1072	East Bethel	8 050	NA	NA	7 916	20	61	36	17	39	2 722	9 867	116.2
1075	East Grand Forks	8 658	NA	NA	8 167	38	194	35	224	613	3 500	9 515	11.5
1094	Eden Prairie	39 311	16 263	141.7	37 889	440	71	823	88	275	15 405	17 164	83.9
1105	Edina	46 070	46 073	0.0	44 774	333	65	796	102	327	20 983	24 935	40.8
1145	Elk River	11 143	NA	NA	10 989	19	53	49	33	83	3 887	10 187	110.5
1180	Ely	3 968	NA	NA	3 911	18	29	8	2	6	1 997	8 601	7.0
1220	Eveleth	4 064	NA	NA	3 971	7	65	20	1	5	1 975	9 327	16.4

1. Codes shown are 2-digit FIPS codes for states; 4-digit census place codes for places; and 3-digit FIPS county codes followed by 3-digit census MCD codes for minor civil divisions (MCDs). MCD names are followed by county names in parentheses. 2. Hispanic persons may be of any race. 3. Dry land or land partially or temporarily covered by water.

State/ Place/ MCD[1] code	Place	Population: 1990	Population: Places of 10,000 or more: 1980	Population: Places of 10,000 or more: Percent change, 1980–1990	Population characteristics, 1990: Race: White	Race: Black	Race: Am. Indian, Eskimo Aleut	Race: Asian & Pacific Islander	Race: Other race	Hispanic[2]	Total housing units, 1990	Per capita income, 1985 (Dollars)	Land area,[3] 1990 (Sq. Km.)
		1	2	3	4	5	6	7	8	9	10	11	12
	MINNESOTA—Con.												
1240	Fairmont	11 265	11 506	-2.1	11 136	5	18	53	53	93	4 989	10 594	37.3
1245	Falcon Heights	5 380	NA	NA	4 441	111	16	765	47	117	2 057	12 961	5.8
1250	Faribault	17 085	16 241	5.2	16 631	58	49	252	95	253	6 618	9 703	30.0
1255	Farmington	5 940	NA	NA	5 817	63	10	33	17	34	2 124	12 029	30.6
1275	Fergus Falls	12 362	12 519	-1.3	12 186	13	78	73	12	57	5 385	9 892	25.2
1325	Forest Lake	5 833	NA	NA	5 740	19	41	22	11	63	2 471	11 127	7.1
1385	Fridley	28 335	30 228	-6.3	27 115	277	199	636	108	295	11 418	12 850	26.2
1470	Glencoe	4 648	NA	NA	4 548	8	7	36	49	110	1 861	10 294	5.4
1480	Glenwood	2 573	NA	NA	2 567	0	3	0	3	2	1 237	9 090	8.9
1495	Golden Valley	20 971	22 775	-7.9	19 861	563	49	437	61	203	8 532	18 065	26.5
1520	Goodview	2 878	NA	NA	2 831	9	7	22	9	18	1 097	9 878	4.2
1545	Grand Rapids	7 976	NA	NA	7 801	9	137	20	9	33	3 380	9 174	15.8
1550	Granite Falls	3 083	NA	NA	3 018	1	33	7	24	28	1 401	9 376	8.9
1633	Ham Lake	8 924	NA	NA	8 801	11	44	60	8	50	2 812	10 780	89.1
1686	Hastings	15 445	12 836	20.3	15 233	48	33	99	32	76	5 547	11 106	24.2
1752	Hermantown	6 761	NA	NA	6 459	206	40	19	37	86	2 270	9 171	88.9
1765	Hibbing	18 046	21 193	-14.8	17 802	26	150	53	15	80	8 166	8 872	470.6
1835	Hopkins	16 534	15 336	7.8	15 745	254	89	373	73	191	8 572	14 377	10.6
1855	Hugo	4 417	NA	NA	4 361	5	12	35	4	15	1 440	11 220	88.0
1865	Hutchinson	11 523	NA	NA	11 359	20	19	71	54	104	4 764	11 220	14.0
1875	Independence	2 822	NA	NA	2 776	1	12	23	10	15	971	13 119	84.4
1880	International Falls	8 325	NA	NA	7 883	44	261	33	104	144	3 306	9 552	16.2
1886	Inver Grove Heights	22 477	17 147	31.1	21 830	167	116	141	223	561	8 149	12 577	74.2
1930	Jackson	3 559	NA	NA	3 390	1	6	144	18	25	1 613	9 107	9.0
1960	Jordan	2 909	NA	NA	2 874	5	11	10	9	28	1 091	10 470	5.7
1980	Kasson	3 514	NA	NA	3 473	0	5	23	13	25	1 310	9 707	3.9
2070	La Crescent	4 311	NA	NA	4 271	16	10	13	1	14	1 680	10 051	6.7
2091	Lake City	4 391	NA	NA	4 309	2	15	58	7	17	2 040	9 664	10.8
2100	Lake Elmo	5 903	NA	NA	5 804	7	8	59	25	69	2 016	13 496	61.2
2150	Lakeville	24 854	14 790	68.0	24 213	163	100	319	59	209	8 105	11 497	93.8
2200	Lauderdale	2 700	NA	NA	2 311	59	27	287	16	51	1 222	NA	1.1
2235	Le Sueur	3 714	NA	NA	3 689	2	7	13	3	15	1 519	10 824	9.4
2265	Lino Lakes	8 807	NA	NA	8 556	94	71	53	33	82	2 653	10 969	73.3
2275	Litchfield	6 041	NA	NA	5 895	9	2	36	99	162	2 519	9 641	9.3
2280	Little Canada	8 971	NA	NA	8 534	155	29	229	24	104	4 081	13 635	10.3
2285	Little Falls	7 232	NA	NA	7 128	20	45	20	19	37	3 048	8 308	12.3
2305	Long Prairie	2 786	NA	NA	2 771	0	6	4	5	15	1 259	8 689	5.7
2340	Luverne	4 382	NA	NA	4 359	4	5	6	8	18	1 994	9 436	6.2
2405	Mahtomedi	5 569	NA	NA	5 480	21	21	35	12	30	1 929	13 396	9.3
2420	Mankato	31 477	28 650	9.9	30 301	218	93	714	151	331	11 688	9 603	30.0
2430	Maple Grove	38 736	20 525	88.7	37 615	337	113	601	70	314	12 968	13 194	85.1
2455	Maplewood	30 954	26 990	14.7	29 217	781	176	628	152	479	12 120	12 363	44.9
2475	Marshall	12 023	11 161	7.7	11 743	57	41	90	92	162	4 692	9 818	19.0
2510	Medina	3 096	NA	NA	3 043	13	10	25	5	21	1 038	18 171	66.2
2520	Melrose	2 561	NA	NA	2 546	0	2	9	4	16	1 059	NA	6.9
2535	Mendota Heights	9 431	NA	NA	9 207	45	14	127	38	134	3 410	19 653	24.5
2585	Minneapolis	368 383	370 951	-0.7	288 967	47 948	12 335	15 723	3 410	7 900	172 666	12 302	142.3
2610	Minnetonka	48 370	38 683	25.0	46 950	443	85	767	125	392	20 119	18 289	70.2
2617	Minnetrista	3 439	NA	NA	3 408	5	2	22	2	15	1 272	15 773	67.6
2625	Montevideo	5 499	NA	NA	5 467	0	5	24	3	18	2 525	9 560	10.0
2635	Monticello	4 941	NA	NA	4 877	15	16	26	7	25	1 908	11 246	14.5
2645	Moorhead	32 295	29 998	7.7	30 786	152	441	355	561	890	11 511	9 487	26.1
2655	Mora	2 905	NA	NA	2 873	5	16	5	6	19	1 367	9 728	9.5
2670	Morris	5 613	NA	NA	5 391	55	28	103	36	39	2 066	8 972	10.7
2690	Mound	9 634	NA	NA	9 407	46	31	131	19	66	3 965	13 088	7.6
2695	Mounds View	12 541	12 591	-0.4	12 092	73	85	251	40	97	4 885	11 462	10.7
2700	Mountain Iron	3 362	NA	NA	3 325	1	27	8	1	2	1 422	8 579	127.8
2755	New Brighton	22 207	23 269	-4.6	21 169	169	83	717	69	181	8 811	14 055	17.2
2770	New Hope	21 853	23 087	-5.3	20 703	542	118	428	62	232	8 795	12 628	13.2
2790	Newport	3 720	NA	NA	3 544	51	37	44	44	132	1 384	10 277	9.5
2795	New Prague	3 569	NA	NA	3 551	3	2	10	3	19	1 398	10 055	6.0
2810	New Ulm	13 132	13 755	-4.5	13 028	8	9	62	25	78	5 379	9 952	22.2
2850	Northfield	14 684	12 560	16.9	14 139	106	37	314	88	201	4 288	9 289	15.9
2855	North Mankato	10 164	NA	NA	10 000	22	14	86	42	104	3 930	10 640	10.2
2860	North Oaks	3 386	NA	NA	3 205	4	9	163	5	25	1 113	28 154	18.9
2880	North St. Paul	12 376	11 921	3.8	11 950	150	67	152	57	149	4 607	11 137	7.5
2888	Oakdale	18 374	12 126	51.5	17 825	191	82	181	95	290	6 936	12 082	25.6
2890	Oak Park Heights	3 486	NA	NA	3 283	125	40	17	21	43	1 398	12 183	5.9
2925	Olivia	2 623	NA	NA	2 580	3	8	7	25	55	1 156	8 653	5.9
2940	Orono	7 285	NA	NA	7 164	28	18	55	20	58	2 787	23 627	41.8
2965	Osseo	2 704	NA	NA	2 675	7	4	9	9	21	1 034	13 804	2.0
2980	Owatonna	19 386	18 632	4.0	19 044	44	33	112	153	308	7 578	10 845	24.8
2995	Park Rapids	2 863	NA	NA	2 778	1	81	3	0	3	1 429	7 554	12.8

1. Codes shown are 2-digit FIPS codes for states; 4-digit census place codes for places; and 3-digit FIPS county codes followed by 3-digit census MCD codes for minor civil divisions (MCDs). MCD names are followed by county names in parentheses. 2. Hispanic persons may be of any race. 3. Dry land or land partially or temporarily covered by water.

State/ Place/ MCD[1] code	Place	Population: 1990	Places of 10,000 or more: 1980	Places of 10,000 or more: Percent change, 1980–1990	Population characteristics, 1990 — Race: White	Race: Black	Race: Am. Indian, Eskimo Aleut	Race: Asian & Pacific Islander	Race: Other race	Hispanic[2]	Total housing units, 1990	Per capita income, 1985 (Dollars)	Land area,[3] 1990 (Sq. Km.)
		1	2	3	4	5	6	7	8	9	10	11	12
	MINNESOTA—Con.												
3060	Pine City	2 613	NA	NA	2 592	1	13	5	2	17	1 174	NA	6.7
3080	Pipestone	4 554	NA	NA	4 344	4	134	64	8	29	2 055	9 312	11.8
3085	Plainview	2 768	NA	NA	2 744	3	9	7	5	15	1 030	NA	5.2
3105	Plymouth	50 889	31 614	61.0	48 682	821	185	1 040	161	518	19 616	16 329	85.3
3120	Princeton	3 719	NA	NA	3 690	6	20	3	0	16	1 510	8 686	9.6
3130	Prior Lake	11 482	NA	NA	11 148	47	210	65	12	85	4 177	15 418	33.9
3135	Proctor	2 974	NA	NA	2 931	8	21	9	5	20	1 245	9 641	7.8
3148	Ramsey	12 408	10 093	22.9	12 237	16	80	61	14	71	3 674	10 777	74.6
3175	Red Wing	15 134	13 720	10.3	14 768	53	215	67	31	90	6 176	10 936	90.3
3180	Redwood Falls	4 859	NA	NA	4 785	20	31	13	10	27	2 128	10 824	7.4
3210	Richfield	35 710	37 851	-5.7	33 387	932	219	1 002	170	383	16 094	13 770	17.8
3230	Robbinsdale	14 396	14 422	-0.2	13 847	249	83	172	45	131	6 155	12 980	7.2
3235	Rochester	70 745	57 890	22.2	66 650	728	214	2 926	227	822	28 961	13 380	76.3
3240	Rockford	2 665	NA	NA	2 612	12	22	10	9	17	1 016	NA	3.3
3285	Rosemount	8 622	NA	NA	8 357	55	26	155	29	85	2 866	10 774	87.3
3290	Roseville	33 485	35 820	-6.5	31 842	550	102	854	137	378	14 216	15 197	34.3
3360	St. Anthony	7 727	NA	NA	7 435	58	24	187	23	69	3 693	15 860	5.9
3370	St. Charles	2 642	NA	NA	2 494	4	9	120	15	54	1 037	NA	7.3
3380	St. Cloud	48 812	42 566	14.7	47 270	472	283	657	130	287	18 828	9 663	37.6
3382	St. Francis	2 538	NA	NA	2 476	16	33	4	9	13	800	NA	60.9
3390	St. James	4 364	NA	NA	4 078	4	9	19	254	332	1 881	8 650	5.2
3395	St. Joseph	3 294	NA	NA	3 215	32	12	29	6	38	759	5 728	2.4
3405	St. Louis Park	43 787	42 931	2.0	41 713	826	179	921	148	452	20 678	15 933	27.7
3420	St. Michael	2 506	NA	NA	2 484	0	15	7	0	13	830	NA	5.8
3425	St. Paul	272 235	270 230	0.7	223 947	20 083	3 697	19 197	5 311	11 476	117 583	11 557	136.7
3430	St. Paul Park	4 965	NA	NA	4 834	33	25	33	40	85	1 793	10 240	6.1
3435	St. Peter	9 421	NA	NA	9 212	63	37	83	26	65	2 869	8 480	13.1
3470	Sartell	5 393	NA	NA	5 339	11	15	22	6	44	1 914	10 304	7.7
3475	Sauk Centre	3 581	NA	NA	3 562	7	3	8	1	12	1 499	8 537	7.4
3480	Sauk Rapids	7 825	NA	NA	7 754	11	18	32	10	44	2 997	8 873	8.3
3485	Savage	9 906	NA	NA	9 545	74	16	246	25	89	3 395	12 831	41.2
3515	Shakopee	11 739	NA	NA	11 446	110	78	87	18	93	4 340	12 107	68.5
3535	Shoreview	24 587	17 300	42.1	23 703	183	71	559	71	228	9 280	15 511	29.0
3540	Shorewood	5 917	NA	NA	5 787	35	2	78	15	50	2 143	19 740	13.8
3565	Sleepy Eye	3 694	NA	NA	3 638	2	3	19	32	53	1 587	9 907	3.7
3595	South St. Paul	20 197	21 235	-4.9	19 725	87	101	104	180	489	8 294	11 489	14.8
3620	Spring Lake Park	6 532	NA	NA	6 249	23	38	193	29	75	2 398	11 035	5.1
3645	Staples	2 754	NA	NA	2 728	5	14	5	2	14	1 247	8 243	8.2
3670	Stewartville	4 520	NA	NA	4 482	4	16	14	4	13	1 702	9 656	4.5
3675	Stillwater	13 882	12 290	13.0	13 684	37	41	101	19	84	5 105	12 780	14.0
3760	Thief River Falls	8 010	NA	NA	7 850	9	80	31	40	92	3 630	9 550	11.6
3830	Two Harbors	3 651	NA	NA	3 633	1	12	5	0	11	1 660	9 542	8.4
3865	Vadnais Heights	11 041	NA	NA	10 637	80	33	237	54	134	4 030	11 432	18.9
3915	Virginia	9 410	11 056	-14.9	9 162	32	172	34	10	50	4 706	9 533	43.6
3930	Waconia	3 498	NA	NA	3 462	1	1	27	7	4	1 475	11 606	4.6
3935	Wadena	4 131	NA	NA	4 082	1	20	14	14	28	1 923	8 821	11.4
3945	Waite Park	5 020	NA	NA	4 912	26	26	45	11	25	2 201	9 387	5.0
4000	Waseca	8 385	NA	NA	8 277	24	22	45	17	57	3 356	10 132	8.6
4035	Wayzata	3 806	NA	NA	3 738	21	3	37	7	35	1 831	25 674	8.2
4070	West St. Paul	19 248	18 527	3.9	18 487	130	66	233	332	878	8 767	14 555	13.0
4090	White Bear Lake	24 704	22 524	9.7	24 221	87	74	253	69	272	9 465	12 889	21.2
4110	Willmar	17 531	15 895	10.3	16 836	62	122	46	465	1 205	6 985	9 914	27.6
4130	Windom	4 283	NA	NA	4 249	9	6	16	3	16	1 922	11 200	7.6
4145	Winona	25 399	25 075	1.3	24 788	167	62	314	68	218	9 682	9 252	30.7
4173	Woodbury	20 075	10 297	95.0	18 984	327	61	618	85	346	7 541	14 152	90.7
4190	Worthington	9 977	10 243	-2.6	9 347	44	62	371	153	242	4 141	9 795	18.1
0030	Columbus township (Anoka)	3 690	NA	NA	3 631	15	23	13	8	24	1 158	10 511	116.2
0030	Linwood township (Anoka)	3 588	NA	NA	3 514	10	27	33	4	36	1 315	9 666	86.4
0030	Oak Grove township (Anoka)	5 441	NA	NA	5 360	17	31	27	6	29	1 706	10 786	87.3
0070	Bemidji township (Beltrami)	2 660	NA	NA	2 471	7	171	6	5	7	966	NA	55.4
0071	Northern township (Beltrami)	3 638	NA	NA	3 448	13	150	25	2	25	1 508	9 442	72.2
0171	Thomson township (Carlton)	3 970	NA	NA	3 936	3	18	11	2	6	1 372	9 176	102.7
0250	Chisago Lake township (Chisago)	3 057	NA	NA	3 034	4	5	9	5	3	1 297	10 295	122.2
0251	Wyoming township (Chisago)	2 967	NA	NA	2 938	8	11	6	4	12	1 014	NA	77.5
0410	Alexandria township (Douglas)	4 014	NA	NA	3 982	0	17	14	1	13	1 692	10 158	64.3
0410	La Grand township (Douglas)	3 550	NA	NA	3 520	4	8	16	2	6	1 594	9 053	69.8
0590	Bradford township (Isanti)	2 637	NA	NA	2 609	10	5	9	4	13	993	NA	89.3
0611	Grand Rapids township (Itasca)	11 613	NA	NA	11 360	9	202	31	11	44	4 734	8 822	87.4
0611	Harris township (Itasca)	2 888	NA	NA	2 849	3	18	16	2	7	1 222	8 521	82.6
0671	New London township (Kandiyohi)	2 679	NA	NA	2 664	7	4	3	1	4	1 263	NA	64.8
1090	Cascade township (Olmsted)	3 128	NA	NA	2 986	15	4	117	6	22	1 092	NA	55.1
1090	Marion township (Olmsted)	5 960	NA	NA	5 884	19	21	26	10	37	2 043	10 800	89.3
1091	Rochester township (Olmsted)	3 226	NA	NA	3 171	2	2	44	7	27	1 119	15 650	62.5

1. Codes shown are 2-digit FIPS codes for states; 4-digit census place codes for places; and 3-digit FIPS county codes followed by 3-digit census MCD codes for minor civil divisions (MCDs). MCD names are followed by county names in parentheses. 2. Hispanic persons may be of any race. 3. Dry land or land partially or temporarily covered by water.

State/ Place/ MCD[1] code	Place	Population, 1990	Population, Places of 10,000 or more, 1980	Population, Places of 10,000 or more, Percent change, 1980–1990	Race, White	Race, Black	Race, Am. Indian, Eskimo Aleut	Race, Asian & Pacific Islander	Race, Other race	Hispanic[2]	Total housing units, 1990	Per capita income, 1985 (Dollars)	Land area,[3] 1990 (Sq. Km.)
		1	2	3	4	5	6	7	8	9	10	11	12
	MINNESOTA—Con.												
1230	White Bear township (Ramsey)	9 424	NA	NA	9 267	49	11	68	29	86	3 292	12 459	19.4
1373	Rice Lake township (St. Louis)	3 883	NA	NA	3 808	13	43	18	1	5	1 418	8 956	83.8
1374	White township (St. Louis)	3 668	NA	NA	3 636	0	21	7	4	6	1 665	8 671	264.2
1390	Credit River township (Scott)	2 854	NA	NA	2 831	0	1	9	13	18	882	NA	60.7
1390	Spring Lake township (Scott)	2 853	NA	NA	2 818	10	1	22	2	13	946	11 452	79.9
1410	Baldwin township (Sherburne)	2 909	NA	NA	2 893	5	5	6	0	24	1 163	NA	88.9
1410	Big Lake township (Sherburne)	4 452	NA	NA	4 414	2	18	17	1	16	1 466	10 067	114.0
1450	Avon township (Stearns)	3 385	NA	NA	3 308	30	4	34	9	21	731	NA	83.9
1452	St. Augusta township (Stearns)	2 657	NA	NA	2 648	0	3	6	0	1	796	NA	97.9
1452	St. Cloud township (Stearns)	7 549	NA	NA	7 442	24	8	64	11	23	2 344	11 335	48.7
1452	St. Joseph township (Stearns)	2 567	NA	NA	2 537	2	5	18	5	14	822	9 240	88.7
1630	Forest Lake township (Washington)	6 690	NA	NA	6 596	7	29	42	16	42	2 282	12 722	73.4
1630	Grant township (Washington)	3 778	NA	NA	3 717	12	13	26	10	23	1 195	15 046	66.8
1631	May township (Washington)	2 535	NA	NA	2 493	4	11	20	7	19	956	NA	91.4
1631	New Scandia township (Washington)	3 197	NA	NA	3 170	3	3	14	7	18	1 197	11 308	93.2
1710	Frankfort township (Wright)	2 935	NA	NA	2 901	5	7	16	6	11	888	NA	82.9
1710	Franklin township (Wright)	2 742	NA	NA	2 723	2	1	8	8	21	862	10 481	112.6
1711	Monticello township (Wright)	3 981	NA	NA	3 945	1	10	15	10	30	1 248	9 082	105.5
1711	Otsego township (Wright)	5 219	NA	NA	5 152	1	27	29	10	25	1 627	10 183	75.1
1711	Rockford township (Wright)	3 380	NA	NA	3 356	5	10	7	2	13	1 056	10 230	92.0
28	MISSISSIPPI	2 573 216	2 520 770	2.1	1 633 461	915 057	8 525	13 016	3 157	15 931	1 010 423	7 483	121 506.4
0005	Aberdeen	6 837	NA	NA	3 268	3 551	4	11	3	43	2 645	7 288	27.8
0020	Amory	7 093	NA	NA	5 225	1 838	14	4	12	32	3 019	7 957	19.6
0045	Baldwyn	3 204	NA	NA	1 881	1 316	1	6	0	2	1 280	6 648	32.0
0055	Batesville	6 403	NA	NA	3 958	2 426	3	12	4	27	2 331	7 857	30.4
0060	Bay St. Louis	8 063	NA	NA	6 522	1 451	17	48	25	186	3 561	7 962	14.8
0085	Belzoni	2 536	NA	NA	1 108	1 405	4	19	0	14	1 019	7 170	2.5
0110	Biloxi	46 319	49 311	-6.1	34 547	8 625	153	2 658	336	1 283	18 864	8 557	50.9
0130	Booneville	7 955	NA	NA	6 712	1 212	15	11	5	27	3 231	7 508	66.3
0140	Brandon	11 077	NA	NA	9 648	1 356	3	56	14	66	4 010	10 413	30.6
0150	Brookhaven	10 243	10 800	-5.2	5 607	4 599	7	29	1	20	4 196	7 819	19.0
0190	Canton	10 062	11 116	-9.5	3 264	6 753	11	31	3	16	3 592	6 158	17.7
0200	Carthage	3 819	NA	NA	2 537	1 224	53	5	0	0	1 578	7 962	24.2
0225	Clarksdale	19 717	21 111	-6.6	7 406	12 195	15	88	13	145	7 210	5 993	16.4
0235	Cleveland	15 384	14 524	5.9	8 260	7 014	5	62	43	111	5 138	7 384	18.9
0240	Clinton	21 847	14 660	49.0	17 852	3 744	19	200	32	105	7 916	11 053	61.7
0255	Collins	2 541	NA	NA	1 282	1 254	1	4	0	1	989	NA	16.9
0260	Columbia	6 815	NA	NA	4 845	1 947	6	14	3	29	2 971	8 601	15.2
0265	Columbus	23 799	27 383	-13.1	11 493	12 179	16	75	36	185	9 901	7 633	29.7
0267	Columbus AFB CDP	2 890	NA	NA	2 283	443	8	91	65	130	837	NA	18.3
0275	Corinth	11 820	13 839	-14.6	9 183	2 592	8	22	15	61	5 732	9 629	36.3
0310	Crystal Springs	5 643	NA	NA	2 690	2 934	6	10	3	29	2 075	6 251	14.0
0328	Diamondhead CDP	2 661	NA	NA	2 601	24	14	15	7	66	1 871	NA	29.4
0330	D'Iberville	6 566	13 369	-50.9	5 836	499	11	197	23	141	2 461	NA	12.3
0360	Durant	2 838	NA	NA	1 076	1 760	0	1	1	5	1 140	5 708	5.9
0385	Ellisville	3 634	NA	NA	2 667	953	1	11	2	18	1 316	5 267	14.2
0400	Escatawpa CDP	3 902	NA	NA	3 512	367	10	10	3	29	1 545	NA	16.8
0430	Flowood town	2 860	NA	NA	2 359	479	3	9	10	25	1 356	NA	42.2
0435	Forest	5 060	NA	NA	2 438	2 604	2	10	6	19	1 968	7 412	22.3
0455	Fulton	3 387	NA	NA	2 858	504	3	19	3	16	1 340	8 157	22.3
0467	Gautier	10 088	NA	NA	7 491	2 454	32	88	23	121	4 080	9 389	31.1
0495	Greenville	45 226	40 613	11.4	17 982	26 969	44	193	38	252	16 492	6 327	67.6
0505	Greenwood	18 906	20 104	-6.0	7 596	11 186	14	86	24	71	7 597	7 202	23.9
0510	Grenada	10 864	12 641	-14.1	5 462	5 350	22	21	9	34	4 382	8 187	15.2
0513	Gulf Hills CDP	5 004	NA	NA	4 329	527	8	122	18	63	1 892	NA	19.6
0515	Gulfport	40 775	39 676	2.8	28 496	11 656	114	376	133	632	18 236	9 734	58.6
0535	Hattiesburg	41 882	40 829	2.6	24 385	16 934	47	444	72	409	17 675	8 047	65.8
0540	Hazlehurst	4 221	NA	NA	1 597	2 617	0	7	0	6	1 580	7 548	11.3
0550	Hernando	3 125	NA	NA	2 252	865	2	5	1	15	1 255	8 345	8.7
0570	Hollandale	3 576	NA	NA	848	2 712	0	16	0	7	1 220	4 774	5.8
0575	Holly Springs	7 261	NA	NA	2 170	5 055	7	18	11	33	2 421	5 815	27.1
0578	Horn Lake	9 069	NA	NA	8 721	290	21	22	15	49	3 136	7 123	14.9
0585	Houston	3 903	NA	NA	2 581	1 304	6	10	2	22	1 623	8 571	18.1
0590	Indianola	11 809	NA	NA	3 959	7 794	17	24	15	65	3 883	6 847	22.3
0610	Iuka	3 122	NA	NA	2 849	266	3	3	1	9	1 461	8 130	25.0
0615	Jackson	196 637	202 893	-3.1	85 675	109 620	191	984	167	882	79 374	9 927	282.3
0630	Kosciusko	6 986	NA	NA	4 056	2 894	11	23	2	22	2 983	7 677	18.6
0653	Latimer CDP	3 222	NA	NA	3 193	16	2	8	3	21	1 123	NA	42.0
0655	Laurel	18 827	21 897	-14.0	9 719	9 055	12	31	10	75	8 381	8 786	39.9
0670	Leland	6 366	NA	NA	2 532	3 811	3	10	10	25	2 235	5 424	5.3
0690	Long Beach	15 804	NA	NA	14 504	849	36	368	47	234	6 241	9 955	26.2
0705	Louisville	7 169	NA	NA	3 578	3 574	6	11	0	37	2 829	8 107	39.1

1. Codes shown are 2-digit FIPS codes for states; 4-digit census place codes for places; and 3-digit FIPS county codes followed by 3-digit census MCD codes for minor civil divisions (MCDs). MCD names are followed by county names in parentheses. 2. Hispanic persons may be of any race. 3. Dry land or land partially or temporarily covered by water.

State/ Place/ MCD[1] code	Place	Population: 1990	Population: Places of 10,000 or more: 1980	Population: Places of 10,000 or more: Percent change, 1980–1990	Population characteristics, 1990: Race: White	Race: Black	Race: Am. Indian, Eskimo Aleut	Race: Asian & Pacific Islander	Race: Other race	Hispanic[2]	Total housing units, 1990	Per capita income, 1985 (Dollars)	Land area,[3] 1990 (Sq. Km.)
		1	2	3	4	5	6	7	8	9	10	11	12
	MISSISSIPPI—Con.												
0710	Lucedale	2 592	NA	NA	1 856	724	5	4	3	7	1 064	NA	9.8
0730	McComb	11 591	12 331	-6.0	6 197	5 355	6	19	14	53	4 969	7 990	18.9
0755	Madison	7 471	NA	NA	7 177	234	8	46	6	47	2 700	NA	28.3
0760	Magee	3 607	NA	NA	2 597	994	4	6	6	17	1 433	7 581	11.4
0805	Meridian	41 036	46 577	-11.9	22 149	18 611	55	180	41	233	17 740	8 932	92.3
0807	Meridian Station CDP	2 503	NA	NA	1 814	542	10	86	51	149	526	NA	2.7
0845	Morton	3 212	NA	NA	1 985	1 188	5	9	25	55	1 181	6 987	12.4
0850	Moss Point	17 837	18 998	-6.1	6 113	11 679	11	21	13	70	6 605	7 484	64.8
0870	Natchez	19 460	22 015	-11.6	9 596	9 796	17	44	7	97	8 660	7 880	34.2
0885	New Albany	6 775	NA	NA	4 865	1 886	3	12	9	38	2 874	8 106	25.2
0900	Newton	3 701	NA	NA	1 965	1 729	4	2	1	9	1 505	7 404	12.8
0906	North Gulfport CDP	4 966	NA	NA	154	4 800	6	4	2	6	1 862	NA	11.9
0930	Ocean Springs	14 658	14 504	1.1	13 327	907	36	353	35	217	5 971	10 251	24.2
0935	Okolona	3 267	NA	NA	1 622	1 635	3	5	2	6	1 291	6 386	16.4
0940	Olive Branch	3 567	NA	NA	2 977	560	5	8	17	18	1 392	NA	15.9
0943	Orange Grove CDP	15 676	13 476	16.3	13 006	2 303	38	281	48	243	5 778	NA	46.3
0955	Oxford	9 984	NA	NA	7 871	1 884	14	207	8	74	4 665	9 222	25.0
0975	Pascagoula	25 899	29 318	-11.7	19 998	5 557	49	239	56	252	11 053	9 565	39.3
0980	Pass Christian	5 557	NA	NA	3 532	1 712	21	285	7	59	2 823	9 995	21.8
0985	Pearl	19 588	20 778	-5.7	17 757	1 675	23	80	53	139	7 658	9 517	44.4
0995	Petal	7 883	NA	NA	7 646	202	10	14	11	28	3 180	7 611	25.0
1000	Philadelphia	6 758	NA	NA	4 158	2 439	130	24	7	44	2 875	7 869	16.2
1005	Picayune	10 633	10 361	2.6	6 706	3 878	22	23	4	74	4 322	7 114	30.6
1030	Pontotoc	4 570	NA	NA	3 774	779	8	9	0	13	1 972	9 114	24.5
1040	Poplarville	2 561	NA	NA	1 970	573	5	4	9	19	925	5 838	10.6
1075	Quitman	2 736	NA	NA	1 830	902	0	0	4	20	1 095	8 848	13.4
1093	Richland	4 014	NA	NA	3 922	61	5	21	5	9	1 620	8 910	23.8
1100	Ridgeland	11 714	NA	NA	10 191	1 412	9	79	23	110	6 141	11 291	27.9
1110	Ripley	5 371	NA	NA	4 353	1 001	4	13	0	19	2 183	6 910	29.7
1125	Rosedale	2 595	NA	NA	639	1 923	6	19	8	21	844	4 537	12.1
1135	Ruleville	3 245	NA	NA	947	2 273	0	25	0	18	1 108	5 163	6.6
1137	St. Martin CDP	6 349	NA	NA	5 689	449	18	175	18	90	2 366	NA	11.3
1180	Senatobia	4 772	NA	NA	3 336	1 421	8	5	2	26	1 637	7 625	10.2
1195	Shelby	2 806	NA	NA	355	2 431	7	4	9	26	940	5 294	7.0
1202	Shoreline Park CDP	2 775	NA	NA	2 714	23	20	8	10	72	2 142	NA	20.4
1245	Southaven	17 949	16 071	11.7	17 363	450	40	56	40	108	6 312	10 311	33.0
1250	Starkville	18 458	15 169	21.7	12 760	4 911	14	706	67	197	7 776	7 825	33.3
1345	Tupelo	30 685	23 905	28.4	23 072	7 479	20	84	30	157	12 335	10 113	132.5
1378	Vancleave CDP	3 214	NA	NA	2 854	336	17	6	1	13	1 245	NA	111.9
1385	Verona town	2 893	NA	NA	1 970	894	2	16	11	22	1 219	NA	9.3
1390	Vicksburg	20 908	25 434	-17.8	8 476	12 331	14	71	16	103	9 250	8 270	34.8
1410	Water Valley	3 610	NA	NA	2 119	1 473	8	8	2	17	1 592	6 866	18.3
1415	Waveland	5 369	NA	NA	4 675	612	10	56	16	80	2 972	8 771	17.7
1420	Waynesboro	5 143	NA	NA	2 421	2 701	3	17	1	17	2 068	6 140	17.2
1452	West Hattiesburg CDP	5 450	NA	NA	4 681	707	7	50	5	39	2 153	NA	18.3
1455	West Point	8 489	NA	NA	3 991	4 460	5	24	9	34	3 397	7 720	12.5
1460	Wiggins	3 185	NA	NA	2 215	969	1	0	0	13	1 225	6 602	11.1
1465	Winona	5 705	NA	NA	3 184	2 502	5	9	5	30	2 269	6 444	31.4
1480	Yazoo City	12 427	12 418	0.1	4 316	8 037	18	42	14	62	4 649	6 172	25.3
29	MISSOURI	5 117 073	4 916 762	4.1	4 486 228	548 208	19 835	41 277	21 525	61 702	2 199 129	10 283	178 446.0
0012	Affton CDP	21 106	23 172	-8.9	20 832	53	23	158	40	199	9 243	NA	12.8
0157	Arnold	18 828	19 141	-1.6	18 670	27	50	54	27	172	6 986	10 239	29.1
0200	Aurora	6 459	NA	NA	6 384	4	44	16	11	52	2 975	7 723	13.4
0210	Ava	2 938	NA	NA	2 907	0	18	9	4	14	1 383	7 133	7.6
0235	Ballwin	21 816	12 656	72.4	21 045	349	16	381	25	214	8 158	14 890	16.3
0252	Barnhart CDP	4 911	NA	NA	4 832	31	10	22	16	54	1 545	NA	13.3
0280	Bellefontaine Neighbors	10 922	12 082	-9.6	9 995	879	8	32	8	86	4 562	13 201	11.4
0295	Bel-Nor village	2 935	NA	NA	1 783	1 119	7	12	14	25	1 134	NA	1.7
0300	Bel-Ridge village	3 199	NA	NA	1 289	1 884	4	9	13	22	1 300	10 947	2.0
0305	Belton	18 150	12 708	42.8	17 321	425	125	139	140	426	6 854	10 416	31.4
0330	Berkeley	12 450	16 147	-22.9	4 179	8 164	21	48	38	81	4 706	9 833	12.8
0345	Bethany	3 005	NA	NA	2 980	0	13	10	2	9	1 447	9 291	11.5
0393	Black Jack	6 128	NA	NA	3 362	2 697	5	50	14	55	2 076	14 229	6.9
0425	Blue Springs	40 153	25 927	54.9	38 387	978	152	430	206	640	14 246	11 916	41.7
0445	Bolivar	6 845	NA	NA	6 695	47	49	39	15	68	2 812	7 497	11.7
0450	Bonne Terre	3 871	NA	NA	3 847	11	5	6	2	6	1 587	7 439	6.8
0455	Boonville	7 095	NA	NA	5 972	1 027	30	43	23	56	2 771	8 827	14.7
0475	Bowling Green	2 976	NA	NA	2 654	306	8	3	5	31	1 328	8 403	5.0
0495	Branson	3 706	NA	NA	3 647	2	10	25	22	50	1 915	10 817	14.8
0520	Breckenridge Hills village	5 404	NA	NA	4 300	1 001	28	45	30	68	2 243	10 197	2.2
0525	Brentwood	8 150	NA	NA	7 588	333	15	181	33	150	4 183	16 738	5.0
0530	Bridgeton	17 779	18 445	-3.6	16 830	651	32	237	29	168	7 123	14 146	37.6

1. Codes shown are 2-digit FIPS codes for states; 4-digit census place codes for places; and 3-digit FIPS county codes followed by 3-digit census MCD codes for minor civil divisions (MCDs). MCD names are followed by county names in parentheses. 2. Hispanic persons may be of any race. 3. Dry land or land partially or temporarily covered by water.

State/ Place/ MCD[1] code	Place	Population 1990	Places of 10,000 or more 1980	Places of 10,000 or more Percent change, 1980–1990	Race: White	Race: Black	Race: Am. Indian, Eskimo Aleut	Race: Asian & Pacific Islander	Race: Other race	Hispanic[2]	Total housing units, 1990	Per capita income, 1985 (Dollars)	Land area,[3] 1990 (Sq. Km.)
		1	2	3	4	5	6	7	8	9	10	11	12
	MISSOURI—Con.												
0550	Brookfield	4 888	NA	NA	4 783	88	3	4	10	36	2 469	9 501	10.8
0580	Buckner	2 873	NA	NA	2 838	5	18	5	7	26	1 069	8 898	2.8
0610	Butler	4 099	NA	NA	3 967	97	25	6	4	18	1 916	8 846	9.6
0645	California	3 465	NA	NA	3 422	22	10	10	1	4	1 562	8 211	6.5
0670	Camdenton	2 561	NA	NA	2 541	3	13	4	0	25	1 224	NA	9.0
0675	Cameron	4 831	NA	NA	4 779	32	9	7	4	20	2 142	8 663	10.5
0690	Canton	2 623	NA	NA	2 521	83	1	14	4	11	973	NA	5.0
0695	Cape Girardeau	34 438	34 361	0.2	31 065	2 771	75	445	82	192	14 627	10 130	59.6
0705	Carl Junction	4 123	NA	NA	4 035	21	54	6	7	21	1 495	8 150	11.6
0710	Carrollton	4 406	NA	NA	4 232	151	8	5	10	10	2 054	8 602	10.5
0720	Carthage	10 747	11 104	-3.2	10 216	236	102	177	16	63	4 725	9 806	16.0
0725	Caruthersville	7 389	NA	NA	5 205	2 132	9	35	8	48	2 944	6 960	12.7
0732	Castle Point CDP	4 975	NA	NA	1 298	3 626	9	30	12	27	1 602	NA	1.8
0765	Centralia	3 414	NA	NA	3 337	58	17	2	0	21	1 501	10 059	6.2
0770	Chaffee	3 059	NA	NA	3 052	2	1	4	0	2	1 363	7 874	4.6
0790	Charleston	5 085	NA	NA	3 043	2 032	2	6	2	14	1 939	6 464	9.0
0793	Chesterfield	37 991	NA	NA	35 592	902	45	1 383	69	473	14 019	NA	77.6
0805	Chillicothe	8 804	NA	NA	8 434	314	25	23	8	34	3 878	10 069	10.4
0835	Clarkson Valley	2 508	NA	NA	2 407	30	1	67	3	20	792	NA	7.0
0860	Clayton	13 874	14 219	-2.4	12 687	446	23	680	38	222	5 800	24 236	6.4
0895	Clinton	8 703	NA	NA	8 455	183	29	14	22	54	3 925	9 543	22.6
0930	Columbia	69 101	62 061	11.3	58 830	6 859	231	2 847	334	905	27 551	10 292	114.8
0942	Concord CDP	19 859	20 896	-5.0	19 633	14	18	160	34	135	7 647	NA	17.9
0977	Cottleville town	2 936	NA	NA	2 858	45	11	19	3	27	928	NA	6.2
1015	Crestwood	11 234	12 815	-12.3	11 046	62	11	93	22	102	4 591	16 333	8.3
1020	Creve Coeur	12 304	11 725	4.9	11 434	390	15	450	15	124	5 403	27 886	19.7
1045	Crystal City	4 088	NA	NA	3 718	334	7	24	5	26	1 742	10 341	6.9
1055	Cuba	2 537	NA	NA	2 529	0	4	1	3	15	1 133	NA	5.8
1105	Dellwood	5 245	NA	NA	4 730	469	12	23	11	41	2 009	12 325	2.7
1135	Desloge	4 150	NA	NA	4 131	8	5	3	3	26	1 692	8 405	5.7
1140	De Soto	5 993	NA	NA	5 865	111	6	8	3	21	2 614	8 727	8.6
1145	Des Peres	8 395	NA	NA	8 140	86	2	147	20	71	2 812	19 420	10.8
1155	Dexter	7 559	NA	NA	7 512	2	12	15	18	56	3 433	8 162	13.5
1250	East Prairie	3 416	NA	NA	3 365	35	11	4	1	7	1 420	5 880	3.4
1270	Eldon	4 419	NA	NA	4 407	0	8	4	0	19	2 119	8 221	8.1
1275	El Dorado Springs	3 830	NA	NA	3 790	0	22	10	8	25	1 890	7 358	8.1
1285	Ellisville	7 545	NA	NA	7 387	65	4	83	6	62	2 780	13 982	10.5
1355	Eureka	4 683	NA	NA	4 658	9	6	6	4	38	1 601	12 375	24.1
1370	Excelsior Springs	10 354	10 420	-0.6	9 878	314	65	44	53	92	4 229	9 512	25.1
1410	Farmington	11 598	NA	NA	10 554	908	41	62	33	89	4 128	8 580	16.5
1415	Fayette	2 888	NA	NA	2 376	492	4	11	5	17	1 140	9 152	5.8
1420	Fenton	3 346	NA	NA	3 315	3	3	22	3	29	1 143	NA	12.9
1425	Ferguson	22 286	24 740	-9.9	16 454	5 589	45	133	65	240	9 346	12 436	16.0
1435	Festus	8 105	NA	NA	7 688	346	13	28	30	60	3 292	9 573	9.2
1450	Flat River	4 823	NA	NA	4 787	10	9	11	6	13	2 086	7 434	9.2
1465	Florissant	51 206	55 372	-7.5	48 655	2 078	91	264	118	490	19 797	12 640	26.4
1497	Fort Leonard Wood CDP	15 863	21 262	-25.4	10 242	4 103	90	571	857	1 344	2 870	NA	251.7
1520	Fredericktown	3 950	NA	NA	3 905	2	15	22	6	18	1 782	6 792	8.8
1550	Frontenac	3 374	NA	NA	3 233	41	3	94	3	25	1 283	42 191	7.4
1555	Fulton	10 033	11 047	-9.2	8 808	1 121	30	56	18	49	3 750	8 670	27.5
1640	Gladstone	26 243	24 990	5.0	25 471	274	123	202	173	643	11 076	13 712	20.8
1647	Glasgow Village CDP	5 199	NA	NA	4 919	249	4	6	21	35	2 000	NA	2.4
1660	Glendale	5 945	NA	NA	5 870	36	6	20	13	50	2 326	17 993	3.3
1735	Grandview	24 967	24 502	1.9	20 193	4 232	141	234	167	381	10 315	11 641	38.2
1762	Gray Summit CDP	2 505	NA	NA	2 479	17	6	1	2	15	939	NA	20.3
1850	Hannibal	18 004	18 825	-4.4	16 686	1 142	63	80	33	87	7 896	8 594	29.3
1870	Harrisonville	7 683	NA	NA	7 557	57	25	21	23	75	3 100	10 181	17.5
1900	Hayti	3 280	NA	NA	2 129	1 137	0	14	0	9	1 415	5 666	5.6
1905	Hazelwood	15 324	12 935	18.5	13 458	1 625	24	147	70	214	6 765	14 289	12.7
1930	Hermann	2 754	NA	NA	2 734	6	6	0	8	18	1 243	9 637	5.5
1950	Higginsville	4 693	NA	NA	4 301	348	4	19	21	35	1 985	9 351	9.2
1967	High Ridge CDP	4 423	NA	NA	4 354	13	14	40	2	34	1 571	NA	9.5
2010	Hollister	2 628	NA	NA	2 607	4	10	6	1	13	1 304	NA	8.2
2122	Imperial CDP	4 156	NA	NA	4 128	0	14	11	3	26	1 564	NA	14.0
2125	Independence	112 301	111 806	0.4	108 029	1 627	684	1 097	864	2 213	48 262	11 010	202.5
2150	Jackson	9 256	NA	NA	9 110	112	10	13	11	35	3 711	9 412	21.6
2180	Jefferson City	35 481	33 618	5.5	31 523	3 580	120	164	94	275	15 437	11 516	68.9
2185	Jennings	15 905	17 026	-6.6	8 145	7 639	21	48	52	143	6 914	10 497	9.7
2205	Joplin	40 961	38 869	5.4	38 927	872	773	262	127	477	19 367	9 312	76.9
2220	Kansas City	435 146	448 154	-2.9	290 572	128 768	2 144	5 239	8 423	17 017	201 789	11 153	806.9
2235	Kennett	10 941	10 145	7.8	9 693	1 164	21	55	8	45	4 679	8 010	16.3
2270	Kinloch	2 702	NA	NA	17	2 684	1	0	0	12	990	5 822	1.9
2275	Kirksville	17 152	17 167	-0.1	16 654	208	22	208	60	156	6 927	8 078	25.4

1. Codes shown are 2-digit FIPS codes for states; 4-digit census place codes for places; and 3-digit FIPS county codes followed by 3-digit census MCD codes for minor civil divisions (MCDs). MCD names are followed by county names in parentheses. 2. Hispanic persons may be of any race. 3. Dry land or land partially or temporarily covered by water.

State/ Place/ MCD[1] code	Place	Population: 1990	Population: Places of 10,000 or more: 1980	Population: Places of 10,000 or more: Percent change, 1980–1990	Population characteristics, 1990: Race: White	Race: Black	Race: Am. Indian, Eskimo Aleut	Race: Asian & Pacific Islander	Race: Other race	Hispanic[2]	Total housing units, 1990	Per capita income, 1985 (Dollars)	Land area,[3] 1990 (Sq. Km.)
		1	2	3	4	5	6	7	8	9	10	11	12
	MISSOURI—Con.												
2280	Kirkwood	27 291	27 987	-2.5	25 415	1 619	29	201	27	188	11 699	16 426	23.4
2315	Ladue	8 847	NA	NA	8 621	63	6	156	1	72	3 384	47 790	22.3
2328	Lake St. Louis	7 400	NA	NA	7 116	175	13	74	22	118	2 910	17 260	13.2
2345	Lamar	4 168	NA	NA	4 128	4	11	17	8	23	1 887	7 946	8.8
2430	Lebanon	9 983	NA	NA	9 819	80	43	34	7	59	4 784	8 036	31.5
2435	Lee's Summit	46 418	28 742	61.5	44 997	808	141	288	184	459	18 755	12 985	153.1
2443	Lemay CDP	18 005	35 433	-49.2	17 768	110	32	48	47	223	7 774	NA	10.6
2465	Lexington	4 860	NA	NA	4 465	357	21	10	7	31	2 100	9 341	8.9
2475	Liberty	20 459	16 217	26.2	19 609	609	83	84	74	293	7 645	12 401	69.7
2545	Louisiana	3 967	NA	NA	3 652	283	12	17	3	30	1 808	9 516	6.7
2605	Macon	5 571	NA	NA	5 215	330	12	10	4	14	2 609	9 335	13.1
2620	Malden	5 123	NA	NA	3 859	1 238	15	2	9	33	2 159	6 094	15.9
2630	Manchester	6 542	NA	NA	6 103	228	5	193	13	82	2 329	15 055	5.6
2640	Maplewood	9 962	10 960	-9.1	8 232	1 425	29	240	36	127	5 432	11 086	4.0
2650	Marceline	2 645	NA	NA	2 624	9	4	1	7	28	1 262	9 106	8.4
2675	Marshall	12 711	12 781	-0.5	11 578	1 002	34	41	56	128	5 162	8 249	24.8
2680	Marshfield	4 374	NA	NA	4 326	0	32	4	12	27	1 856	7 508	11.5
2707	Maryland Heights	25 407	NA	NA	23 752	913	51	615	76	291	11 469	14 518	54.3
2715	Maryville	10 663	NA	NA	10 309	164	19	138	33	82	3 790	8 937	11.5
2745	Mehlville CDP	27 557	NA	NA	26 980	211	38	275	53	309	12 078	NA	19.1
2785	Mexico	11 290	12 276	-8.0	10 137	1 061	22	52	18	47	5 020	9 433	25.7
2850	Moberly	12 839	13 418	-4.3	11 767	930	43	69	30	111	5 834	9 565	26.1
2865	Moline Acres	2 710	NA	NA	822	1 853	4	24	7	12	1 042	11 308	1.4
2870	Monett	6 529	NA	NA	6 442	0	51	23	13	25	2 926	8 973	12.7
2875	Monroe City	2 701	NA	NA	2 433	254	5	7	2	29	1 138	9 094	8.0
2955	Mountain Grove	4 182	NA	NA	4 120	3	48	6	5	27	1 990	7 224	8.7
2975	Mount Vernon	3 726	NA	NA	3 652	14	43	11	6	46	1 617	7 975	7.4
2977	Murphy CDP	9 342	NA	NA	9 269	12	27	25	9	69	3 586	NA	10.3
3005	Neosho	9 254	NA	NA	8 821	99	190	121	23	86	4 159	8 839	34.2
3010	Nevada	8 597	NA	NA	8 433	55	52	47	10	61	3 742	8 547	15.7
3070	New Madrid	3 350	NA	NA	2 446	885	2	16	1	1	1 325	7 242	11.7
3090	Nixa	4 707	NA	NA	4 652	2	21	23	9	31	1 899	7 876	7.7
3105	Normandy	4 480	NA	NA	2 073	2 235	4	155	13	32	1 932	10 590	4.6
3110	North Kansas City	4 130	NA	NA	3 935	75	20	59	41	113	2 616	12 751	11.3
3125	Northwoods	5 106	NA	NA	555	4 538	6	3	4	22	1 830	11 423	1.8
3160	Oak Grove	4 565	NA	NA	4 495	12	17	27	14	44	1 620	8 521	9.9
3188	Oakville CDP	31 750	NA	NA	31 342	62	44	236	66	300	10 938	NA	41.6
3205	Odessa	3 695	NA	NA	3 602	67	14	5	7	23	1 556	10 661	5.8
3210	O'Fallon	18 698	NA	NA	18 297	215	68	49	69	307	6 714	10 224	41.2
3225	Olivette	7 573	NA	NA	5 850	1 505	5	196	17	57	3 187	20 233	7.2
3250	Osage Beach	2 599	NA	NA	2 560	15	11	9	4	15	2 975	NA	22.3
3275	Overland	17 987	19 543	-8.0	16 481	1 147	42	245	72	161	7 517	11 487	11.4
3285	Ozark	4 243	NA	NA	4 197	8	24	7	7	39	1 649	9 038	8.6
3290	Pacific	4 350	NA	NA	4 182	128	4	20	16	39	1 811	9 266	8.8
3295	Pagedale	3 771	NA	NA	501	3 243	9	10	8	40	1 456	8 642	3.1
3300	Palmyra	3 371	NA	NA	3 260	95	4	9	3	12	1 465	8 732	5.6
3390	Perryville	6 933	NA	NA	6 869	0	16	44	4	21	2 879	7 662	17.5
3395	Pevely	2 831	NA	NA	2 817	9	1	3	1	6	1 084	8 530	4.8
3435	Pine Lawn	5 092	NA	NA	330	4 724	6	18	14	30	1 837	7 810	1.6
3450	Platte City	2 947	NA	NA	2 841	77	8	10	11	33	1 277	NA	5.4
3470	Pleasant Hill	3 827	NA	NA	3 769	18	22	8	10	32	1 544	9 868	10.7
3480	Pleasant Valley	2 731	NA	NA	2 648	41	19	15	8	45	1 083	NA	3.5
3500	Poplar Bluff	16 996	17 139	-0.8	15 398	1 437	55	79	27	139	7 810	7 884	26.8
3510	Portageville	3 401	NA	NA	2 712	677	5	5	2	17	1 386	7 107	4.9
3515	Potosi	2 683	NA	NA	2 619	53	5	0	6	10	1 189	7 181	4.1
3610	Raymore	5 592	NA	NA	5 466	50	34	26	16	54	2 101	12 966	35.6
3615	Raytown	30 601	31 759	-3.6	29 175	994	124	157	151	441	13 216	13 164	25.7
3660	Republic	6 292	NA	NA	6 215	4	41	21	11	48	2 431	9 293	10.8
3690	Richmond	5 738	NA	NA	5 446	247	26	5	14	31	2 487	10 284	14.4
3695	Richmond Heights	10 448	11 516	-9.3	8 623	1 587	13	187	38	127	4 988	17 699	5.9
3720	Riverside	3 010	NA	NA	2 737	139	21	55	58	103	1 385	11 369	13.8
3725	Riverview village	3 242	NA	NA	2 962	264	1	6	9	18	1 502	10 336	2.1
3750	Rock Hill	5 217	NA	NA	3 447	1 698	5	54	13	62	2 126	12 311	2.8
3775	Rolla	14 090	13 303	5.9	12 984	295	46	690	75	166	5 866	9 119	20.8
3825	St. Ann	14 489	15 523	-6.7	13 304	943	45	130	67	161	6 784	11 597	8.1
3830	St. Charles	54 555	37 379	46.0	52 343	1 521	148	406	137	545	23 246	12 469	42.9
3835	St. Clair	3 917	NA	NA	3 862	30	14	4	7	22	1 604	8 364	7.2
3842	Ste. Genevieve	4 411	NA	NA	4 372	11	8	16	4	18	1 892	9 810	5.8
3855	St. James	3 256	NA	NA	3 216	11	10	12	7	14	1 415	7 132	6.7
3860	St. John	7 466	NA	NA	6 944	405	14	76	27	110	3 071	11 031	3.7
3865	St. Joseph	71 852	76 691	-6.3	68 245	2 616	236	252	503	1 586	31 276	9 382	112.3
3875	St. Louis	396 685	453 085	-12.4	202 085	188 408	950	3 733	1 509	5 124	194 919	8 799	160.4
3885	St. Peters	45 779	15 700	191.6	44 116	1 017	77	450	119	501	15 773	12 578	40.9

1. Codes shown are 2-digit FIPS codes for states; 4-digit census place codes for places; and 3-digit FIPS county codes followed by 3-digit census MCD codes for minor civil divisions (MCDs). MCD names are followed by county names in parentheses. 2. Hispanic persons may be of any race. 3. Dry land or land partially or temporarily covered by water.

State/ Place/ MCD[1] code	Place	Population: 1990	Population: Places of 10,000 or more: 1980	Population: Places of 10,000 or more: Percent change, 1980–1990	Population characteristics, 1990: Race: White	Race: Black	Race: Am. Indian, Eskimo Aleut	Race: Asian & Pacific Islander	Race: Other race	Hispanic[2]	Total housing units, 1990	Per capita income, 1985 (Dollars)	Land area,[3] 1990 (Sq. Km.)
		1	2	3	4	5	6	7	8	9	10	11	12
	MISSOURI—Con.												
3895	Salem	4 486	NA	NA	4 441	1	20	15	9	41	2 125	7 484	7.4
3906	Sappington CDP	10 917	11 388	-4.1	10 726	39	12	134	6	70	4 555	NA	13.9
3915	Savannah	4 352	NA	NA	4 314	2	18	11	7	30	1 833	9 230	7.8
3930	Scott City	4 292	NA	NA	4 280	4	5	3	0	5	1 769	8 388	10.9
3935	Sedalia	19 800	20 927	-5.4	18 524	1 078	46	87	65	181	9 314	9 678	29.1
3990	Shrewsbury	6 416	NA	NA	6 222	72	5	108	9	53	3 184	15 021	3.7
4000	Sikeston	17 641	17 421	1.3	14 577	2 936	48	40	40	95	7 329	8 194	37.5
4035	Smithville	2 525	NA	NA	2 492	11	8	14	0	12	1 016	NA	19.5
4062	Spanish Lake CDP	20 322	20 632	-1.5	16 504	3 543	46	168	61	203	8 652	NA	19.1
4075	Springfield	140 494	133 116	5.5	134 384	3 527	939	1 264	380	1 339	62 472	9 634	176.0
4160	Sugar Creek	3 982	NA	NA	3 864	11	34	26	47	111	1 748	10 398	20.8
4165	Sullivan	5 661	NA	NA	5 636	2	9	14	0	21	2 415	8 736	19.2
4190	Sunset Hills	4 915	NA	NA	4 780	55	5	66	9	36	2 033	21 178	16.0
4250	Town and Country	9 519	NA	NA	8 792	97	13	611	6	90	3 101	34 017	24.5
4260	Trenton	6 129	NA	NA	6 069	10	24	19	7	40	2 957	8 132	14.8
4275	Troy	3 811	NA	NA	3 601	160	14	11	25	58	1 630	9 849	8.2
4300	Union	5 909	NA	NA	5 794	84	13	15	3	37	2 306	9 793	10.2
4320	University City	40 087	42 738	-6.2	19 679	19 333	46	880	149	445	17 706	13 742	15.2
4345	Valley Park	4 165	NA	NA	3 955	153	16	32	9	54	1 845	8 927	6.6
4355	Vandalia	2 683	NA	NA	2 355	316	0	10	2	9	1 321	9 181	4.6
4445	Warrensburg	15 244	13 807	10.4	13 627	1 190	51	308	68	207	5 460	7 594	21.4
4450	Warrenton	3 564	NA	NA	3 481	49	7	17	10	31	1 455	9 753	13.2
4465	Washington	10 704	NA	NA	10 557	79	24	38	6	76	4 338	10 877	17.6
4485	Waynesville	3 207	NA	NA	2 699	298	28	134	48	132	1 425	10 027	12.6
4505	Webb City	7 449	NA	NA	7 275	3	131	26	14	44	3 257	8 150	17.1
4510	Webster Groves	22 987	23 097	-0.5	21 091	1 629	29	182	56	218	9 394	16 117	15.3
4520	Wellston	3 612	NA	NA	251	3 344	16	1	0	5	1 299	6 031	2.3
4535	Wentzville	5 088	NA	NA	4 300	729	14	17	28	70	1 914	9 777	25.1
4560	West Plains	8 913	NA	NA	8 779	40	49	35	10	67	4 030	7 547	21.9
4582	Whiteman AFB CDP	4 174	NA	NA	3 368	558	16	137	95	203	977	NA	13.3
4630	Windsor	3 044	NA	NA	3 004	13	14	13	0	26	1 403	8 307	6.1
4660	Woodson Terrace	4 362	NA	NA	4 184	121	15	34	8	37	1 812	12 043	2.0
30	MONTANA	799 065	786 690	1.6	741 111	2 381	47 679	4 259	3 635	12 174	361 155	8 781	376 990.9
0010	Anaconda-Deer Lodge County	10 278	12 518	-17.9	9 905	29	260	22	62	157	4 830	8 281	1 908.7
0030	Belgrade	3 411	NA	NA	3 369	3	28	5	6	57	1 290	NA	3.4
0050	Billings	81 151	66 798	21.5	76 738	439	2 569	479	926	2 481	35 964	11 002	84.4
0080	Bozeman	22 660	21 645	4.7	21 742	69	398	350	101	321	9 117	8 158	25.3
0110	Butte-Silver Bow (remainder)	33 336	37 207	-10.4	32 429	33	517	136	221	804	15 180	8 785	1 854.9
0148	Colstrip CDP	3 035	NA	NA	2 842	19	119	14	41	88	1 178	NA	14.8
0150	Columbia Falls	2 942	NA	NA	2 857	1	67	13	4	48	1 227	8 370	3.2
0160	Conrad	2 891	NA	NA	2 818	4	40	17	12	27	1 257	10 480	3.0
0170	Cut Bank	3 329	NA	NA	2 965	2	352	6	4	10	1 532	10 240	2.5
0180	Deer Lodge	3 378	NA	NA	3 283	3	55	24	13	32	1 592	9 178	3.7
0190	Dillon	3 991	NA	NA	3 871	5	77	20	18	43	1 804	7 591	4.0
0227	Evergreen CDP	4 109	NA	NA	3 965	2	111	20	11	71	1 635	NA	8.5
0280	Glasgow	3 572	NA	NA	3 341	4	198	15	14	36	1 749	9 878	3.6
0285	Glendive	4 802	NA	NA	4 725	0	49	21	7	40	2 391	9 133	8.5
0295	Great Falls	55 097	56 725	-2.9	51 301	531	2 549	458	258	926	24 157	10 381	40.0
0300	Hamilton	2 737	NA	NA	2 703	1	22	8	3	39	1 476	9 254	4.6
0305	Hardin	2 940	NA	NA	2 247	6	632	16	39	113	1 303	8 045	3.5
0320	Havre	10 201	10 891	-6.3	9 313	15	790	65	18	116	4 346	9 521	6.4
0325	Helena	24 569	23 938	2.6	23 727	55	572	145	70	326	11 053	11 019	35.0
0328	Helena Valley Southeast CDP	4 601	NA	NA	4 441	3	116	19	22	56	1 643	NA	42.1
0329	Helena Valley West Central CDP	6 327	NA	NA	6 159	3	118	35	12	52	2 281	NA	70.2
0375	Kalispell	11 917	10 648	11.9	11 586	17	220	68	26	111	5 537	10 358	11.4
0385	Laurel	5 686	NA	NA	5 595	4	50	17	20	83	2 596	8 189	4.8
0395	Lewistown	6 051	NA	NA	5 929	7	90	11	14	58	2 867	8 583	4.6
0400	Libby	2 532	NA	NA	2 474	3	41	11	3	33	1 141	8 232	2.9
0410	Livingston	6 701	NA	NA	6 546	24	60	24	47	102	3 137	9 291	6.4
0412	Lockwood CDP	3 967	NA	NA	3 734	9	148	28	48	106	1 500	NA	19.2
0416	Lolo CDP	2 746	NA	NA	2 709	4	22	5	6	31	953	NA	24.6
0418	Malmstrom AFB CDP	5 938	NA	NA	4 976	500	73	275	114	313	1 496	NA	5.1
0445	Miles City	8 461	NA	NA	8 254	7	133	19	48	124	4 006	9 846	7.9
0455	Missoula	42 918	33 387	28.5	40 983	148	1 045	622	120	551	18 488	9 532	43.1
0500	Orchard Homes CDP	10 317	10 837	-4.8	9 935	18	195	140	29	113	4 339	NA	21.0
0530	Polson	3 283	NA	NA	2 795	4	453	5	26	62	1 565	8 588	4.7
0580	Shelby	2 763	NA	NA	2 659	1	85	11	7	26	1 302	9 056	4.1
0590	Sidney	5 217	NA	NA	5 074	0	84	15	44	128	2 363	9 632	5.8
0670	Whitefish	4 368	NA	NA	4 292	3	48	14	11	62	2 259	9 846	7.8
0700	Wolf Point	2 880	NA	NA	1 924	4	923	26	3	25	1 236	8 693	2.3
31	NEBRASKA	1 578 385	1 569 825	0.5	1 480 558	57 404	12 410	12 422	15 591	36 969	660 621	10 546	199 113.2

1. Codes shown are 2-digit FIPS codes for states; 4-digit census place codes for places; and 3-digit FIPS county codes followed by 3-digit census MCD codes for minor civil divisions (MCDs). MCD names are followed by county names in parentheses. 2. Hispanic persons may be of any race. 3. Dry land or land partially or temporarily covered by water.

Table D. Places — **Population, Housing, Money Income, and Land Area**

State/ Place/ MCD[1] code	Place	Population			Population characteristics, 1990						Total housing units, 1990	Per capita income, 1985 (Dollars)	Land area,[3] 1990 (Sq. Km.)
			Places of 10,000 or more		Race								
		1990	1980	Percent change, 1980–1990	White	Black	Am. Indian, Eskimo Aleut	Asian & Pacific Islander	Other race	Hispanic[2]			
		1	2	3	4	5	6	7	8	9	10	11	12
	NEBRASKA—Con.												
0040	Alliance	9 765	NA	NA	9 184	46	295	41	199	632	4 108	11 371	12.2
0125	Auburn	3 443	NA	NA	3 420	8	7	3	5	11	1 555	11 072	3.9
0130	Aurora	3 810	NA	NA	3 775	3	3	21	8	28	1 588	9 273	4.6
0195	Beatrice	12 354	12 891	-4.2	12 178	25	66	55	30	80	5 532	11 035	17.0
0230	Bellevue	30 982	21 813	42.0	27 699	2 010	109	749	415	1 213	11 960	12 624	20.8
0285	Blair	6 860	NA	NA	6 765	47	16	16	16	37	2 717	10 458	10.5
0355	Broken Bow	3 778	NA	NA	3 714	1	55	4	4	15	1 714	8 744	4.2
0465	Central City	2 868	NA	NA	2 841	0	9	13	5	45	1 230	9 697	4.7
0475	Chadron	5 588	NA	NA	5 186	31	282	55	34	108	2 333	8 384	8.4
0478	Chalco CDP	7 337	NA	NA	7 129	59	15	91	43	147	2 399	NA	7.4
0545	Columbus	19 480	17 328	12.4	19 283	40	40	60	57	167	7 812	10 742	22.5
0590	Cozad	3 823	NA	NA	3 634	7	17	16	149	228	1 725	9 380	5.0
0620	Crete	4 841	NA	NA	4 715	12	7	90	17	40	1 865	10 988	5.4
0685	David City	2 522	NA	NA	2 507	0	7	8	0	8	1 142	8 307	3.5
0890	Fairbury	4 335	NA	NA	4 296	2	17	8	12	55	2 216	9 562	4.9
0905	Falls City	4 769	NA	NA	4 670	2	90	5	2	27	2 314	9 287	6.8
0950	Fremont	23 680	23 979	-1.2	23 362	63	92	104	59	165	9 850	10 444	17.2
0995	Gering	7 946	NA	NA	7 399	5	73	11	458	944	3 167	10 035	8.3
1030	Gothenburg	3 232	NA	NA	3 197	4	10	3	18	43	1 410	8 070	5.2
1045	Grand Island	39 386	33 180	18.7	37 830	133	127	513	783	1 887	15 855	10 453	53.2
1145	Hastings	22 837	23 045	-0.9	22 327	173	97	106	134	268	9 846	10 475	24.3
1220	Holdrege	5 671	NA	NA	5 626	3	10	13	19	60	2 526	11 486	9.0
1350	Kearney	24 396	21 158	15.3	23 736	122	67	134	337	667	9 372	9 698	22.2
1370	Kimball	2 574	NA	NA	2 547	2	7	6	12	116	1 229	9 777	4.0
1383	La Vista	9 840	NA	NA	9 327	209	46	159	99	303	3 502	9 984	4.5
1415	Lexington	6 601	NA	NA	6 452	3	28	10	108	329	2 838	9 615	7.3
1425	Lincoln	191 972	171 932	11.7	181 320	4 515	1 150	3 288	1 699	3 764	79 079	11 772	163.9
1495	McCook	8 112	NA	NA	8 007	9	17	22	57	163	3 670	11 718	13.7
1635	Minden	2 749	NA	NA	2 729	0	0	0	20	57	1 236	9 856	4.2
1695	Nebraska City	6 547	NA	NA	6 470	14	21	18	24	69	2 955	10 154	9.7
1755	Norfolk	21 476	19 449	10.4	20 863	192	168	84	169	299	8 877	10 635	23.0
1775	North Platte	22 605	24 479	-7.7	21 638	84	96	85	702	1 355	9 827	11 152	24.2
1814	Offutt AFB West CDP	10 883	NA	NA	8 616	1 484	86	423	274	632	2 835	NA	11.4
1815	Ogallala	5 095	NA	NA	4 984	6	31	13	61	194	2 276	9 556	8.5
1825	Omaha	335 795	314 267	6.9	281 603	43 989	2 274	3 412	4 517	10 288	143 612	12 886	260.7
1830	O'Neill	3 852	NA	NA	3 817	2	22	4	7	11	1 717	7 332	5.0
1915	Papillion	10 372	NA	NA	9 906	261	45	100	60	192	3 478	12 838	5.9
1980	Plattsmouth	6 412	NA	NA	6 276	24	39	30	43	97	2 495	9 346	6.9
2045	Ralston	6 236	NA	NA	6 133	30	14	33	26	107	2 437	13 324	4.2
2175	Schuyler	4 052	NA	NA	3 947	1	10	3	91	164	1 729	8 472	5.3
2185	Scottsbluff	13 711	14 156	-3.1	11 829	56	439	91	1 296	2 720	6 086	10 003	15.2
2200	Seward	5 634	NA	NA	5 582	16	9	18	9	22	2 151	10 940	4.6
2230	Sidney	5 959	NA	NA	5 762	8	42	10	137	263	2 741	11 372	15.3
2237	Skyline CDP	2 563	NA	NA	2 540	4	3	14	2	5	787	NA	8.3
2255	South Sioux City	9 677	NA	NA	8 924	63	233	126	331	545	3 816	9 350	12.1
2495	Valentine	2 826	NA	NA	2 697	1	116	12	0	7	1 332	9 660	4.6
2540	Wahoo	3 681	NA	NA	3 654	6	2	10	9	23	1 570	10 464	4.6
2590	Wayne	5 142	NA	NA	5 058	37	13	29	5	18	1 830	7 845	4.9
2620	West Point	3 250	NA	NA	3 239	1	3	4	3	6	1 388	7 797	5.2
2695	York	7 884	NA	NA	7 770	28	29	34	23	82	3 323	10 723	14.6
32	NEVADA	1 201 833	800 508	50.1	1 012 695	78 771	19 637	38 127	52 603	124 419	518 858	11 200	284 397.2
0007	Battle Mountain CDP	3 542	NA	NA	3 223	5	124	11	179	561	1 431	NA	4.7
0010	Boulder City	12 567	NA	NA	12 205	79	83	117	83	465	5 390	12 760	86.9
0025	Carson City	40 443	32 022	26.3	36 693	698	1 106	569	1 377	3 110	16 628	10 937	371.8
0032	East Las Vegas CDP	11 087	NA	NA	9 802	513	84	311	377	1 208	4 846	NA	8.1
0035	Elko	14 736	NA	NA	13 146	63	404	173	950	2 215	5 817	10 950	25.3
0040	Ely	4 756	NA	NA	4 407	12	130	27	180	506	2 098	9 567	9.1
0042	Enterprise CDP	6 412	NA	NA	6 086	91	50	84	101	389	2 506	NA	179.0
0045	Fallon	6 438	NA	NA	5 690	100	233	261	154	437	2 763	8 567	6.8
0048	Fernley CDP	5 164	NA	NA	4 898	20	86	71	89	320	2 030	NA	89.9
0053	Gardnerville Ranchos CDP	7 455	NA	NA	7 083	27	180	66	99	362	2 810	NA	38.1
0055	Hawthorne CDP	4 162	NA	NA	3 636	260	105	38	123	340	1 858	NA	3.8
0058	Henderson	64 942	24 363	166.6	59 387	1 725	635	1 316	1 879	5 280	25 400	9 572	185.3
0060	Incline Village-Crystal Bay CDP	7 119	NA	NA	6 794	23	33	83	186	480	6 255	NA	36.0
0061	Indian Hills CDP	2 544	NA	NA	2 436	3	29	28	48	168	963	NA	24.8
0063	Johnson Lane CDP	2 551	NA	NA	2 499	1	22	19	10	96	943	NA	55.3
0065	Las Vegas	258 295	164 674	56.9	202 549	29 529	2 282	9 325	14 610	32 369	109 670	10 990	215.7
0067	Laughlin CDP	4 791	NA	NA	4 546	39	48	56	102	392	2 637	NA	71.7
0076	Moapa Valley CDP	3 444	NA	NA	3 216	4	34	24	166	298	1 415	NA	22.6
0077	Nellis AFB CDP	8 377	NA	NA	6 429	1 314	67	322	245	722	2 065	NA	8.0
0078	New Washoe City CDP	2 875	NA	NA	2 776	12	44	27	16	80	1 065	NA	22.0
0080	North Las Vegas	47 707	42 739	11.6	21 578	17 827	500	1 127	6 675	10 590	15 837	7 480	157.9

1. Codes shown are 2-digit FIPS codes for states; 4-digit census place codes for places; and 3-digit FIPS county codes followed by 3-digit census MCD codes for minor civil divisions (MCDs). MCD names are followed by county names in parentheses. 2. Hispanic persons may be of any race. 3. Dry land or land partially or temporarily covered by water.

State/ Place/ MCD[1] code	Place	Population			Population characteristics, 1990						Total housing units, 1990	Per capita income, 1985 (Dollars)	Land area,[3] 1990 (Sq. Km.)
		1990	Places of 10,000 or more		Race					Hispanic[2]			
			1980	Percent change, 1980–1990	White	Black	Am. Indian, Eskimo Aleut	Asian & Pacific Islander	Other race				
		1	2	3	4	5	6	7	8	9	10	11	12
	NEVADA—Con.												
0082	Pahrump CDP	7 424	NA	NA	7 137	60	97	61	69	397	3 509	NA	717.6
0084	Paradise CDP	124 682	84 818	47.0	107 908	6 105	800	4 987	4 882	13 105	63 924	NA	123.4
0090	Reno	133 850	100 756	32.8	115 203	3 851	1 909	6 505	6 382	14 872	61 384	11 916	148.9
0100	Sparks	53 367	40 780	30.9	47 194	1 270	767	2 395	1 741	4 570	21 660	11 074	36.9
0102	Spring Creek CDP	5 866	NA	NA	5 635	12	43	34	142	302	1 914	NA	148.7
0104	Spring Valley CDP	51 726	NA	NA	46 205	1 597	245	2 631	1 048	3 564	22 236	NA	51.4
0110	Sunrise Manor CDP	95 362	44 155	116.0	77 321	9 251	939	3 987	3 864	9 394	37 264	NA	90.3
0112	Sun Valley CDP	11 391	NA	NA	10 421	139	264	165	402	1 142	4 257	NA	22.7
0114	Tonopah CDP	3 616	NA	NA	3 357	25	74	43	117	265	1 713	NA	42.0
0127	Winchester CDP	23 365	19 728	18.4	20 369	1 045	148	1 087	716	2 732	12 485	NA	11.4
0130	Winnemucca	6 134	NA	NA	5 250	15	189	35	645	1 265	2 442	9 670	19.6
33	NEW HAMPSHIRE	1 109 252	920 610	20.5	1 087 433	7 198	2 134	9 343	3 144	11 333	503 904	11 659	23 230.7
0230	Berlin	11 824	13 084	-9.6	11 712	15	21	57	19	61	5 416	9 488	159.9
0470	Claremont	13 902	14 557	-4.5	13 684	36	83	79	20	71	6 228	9 187	111.7
0520	Concord	36 006	30 400	18.4	35 350	226	101	243	86	356	15 697	11 662	166.5
0620	Derry CDP	20 446	12 248	66.9	19 893	235	49	174	95	305	8 674	NA	39.9
0650	Dover	25 042	22 387	11.9	24 390	265	53	284	50	254	11 307	10 932	69.2
0690	Durham CDP	9 236	NA	NA	8 935	59	5	224	13	79	1 569	NA	6.9
0713	East Merrimack CDP	3 656	NA	NA	3 564	57	5	27	3	43	1 696	NA	7.8
0810	Exeter CDP	9 556	NA	NA	9 406	53	10	77	10	41	4 296	NA	12.3
0830	Farmington CDP	3 567	NA	NA	3 527	6	16	9	9	24	1 443	NA	16.6
0880	Franklin	8 304	NA	NA	8 230	15	10	43	6	53	3 744	9 373	71.4
1090	Hampton CDP	7 989	NA	NA	7 911	20	8	43	7	57	3 587	NA	13.9
1130	Hanover CDP	6 538	NA	NA	5 815	245	46	413	19	148	1 490	NA	9.7
1279	Hooksett CDP	2 573	NA	NA	2 537	13	2	21	0	19	1 019	NA	12.4
1308	Hudson CDP	7 626	NA	NA	7 451	51	14	85	25	81	2 960	NA	7.9
1330	Jaffrey CDP	2 558	NA	NA	2 526	7	10	15	0	16	1 169	NA	6.5
1360	Keene	22 430	21 449	4.6	22 167	62	42	133	26	132	8 841	10 861	96.6
1390	Laconia	15 743	15 575	1.1	15 539	20	35	122	27	98	8 201	9 930	52.6
1440	Lebanon	12 183	11 134	9.4	11 884	50	32	189	28	111	5 718	11 620	104.5
1520	Littleton CDP	4 633	NA	NA	4 573	10	11	32	7	21	2 103	NA	22.3
1538	Londonderry CDP	10 114	NA	NA	9 934	42	11	98	29	125	3 472	NA	31.6
1610	Manchester	99 567	90 936	9.5	96 550	968	206	1 092	751	2 121	44 361	11 481	85.5
1710	Milford CDP	8 015	NA	NA	7 861	67	9	64	14	49	3 398	NA	14.8
1770	Nashua	79 662	67 865	17.4	75 800	1 293	177	1 536	856	2 407	33 383	13 521	80.1
1890	Newmarket CDP	4 917	NA	NA	4 645	47	12	209	4	43	2 400	NA	5.4
1910	Newport CDP	3 772	NA	NA	3 742	3	3	22	2	8	1 725	NA	26.3
2070	Peterborough CDP	2 685	NA	NA	2 622	9	2	42	10	16	1 228	NA	12.1
2093	Pinardville CDP	4 654	NA	NA	4 590	26	6	28	4	66	1 910	NA	4.1
2150	Plymouth CDP	3 967	NA	NA	3 897	19	10	39	2	18	1 066	NA	9.6
2170	Portsmouth	25 925	26 254	-1.3	24 014	1 193	71	447	200	518	11 369	10 972	40.4
2189	Raymond CDP	2 516	NA	NA	2 501	2	3	7	3	25	1 041	NA	11.9
2220	Rochester	26 630	21 560	23.5	26 291	85	54	147	53	192	11 076	9 882	117.0
2370	Somersworth	11 249	10 350	8.7	10 968	82	33	123	43	102	4 719	10 352	25.3
2385	South Hooksett CDP	3 638	NA	NA	3 577	27	2	31	1	11	1 443	NA	13.6
2480	Suncook CDP	5 214	NA	NA	5 141	25	15	25	8	29	2 246	NA	9.4
2550	Tilton-Northfield CDP	3 081	NA	NA	3 054	4	9	13	1	6	1 293	NA	7.7
2820	Wolfeboro CDP	2 783	NA	NA	2 775	2	2	4	0	19	1 758	NA	18.8
0010	Alton town (Belknap)	3 286	NA	NA	3 274	2	5	4	1	14	3 267	NA	163.5
0010	Barnstead town (Belknap)	3 100	NA	NA	3 081	9	4	6	0	17	1 861	NA	108.6
0010	Belmont town (Belknap)	5 796	NA	NA	5 738	10	29	18	1	24	2 869	10 241	79.3
0010	Gilford town (Belknap)	5 867	NA	NA	5 830	2	8	26	1	29	4 397	14 234	100.9
0010	Gilmanton town (Belknap)	2 609	NA	NA	2 597	6	2	4	0	7	1 744	NA	147.9
0010	Meredith town (Belknap)	4 837	NA	NA	4 806	9	8	11	3	26	3 720	9 788	104.1
0010	Tilton town (Belknap)	3 240	NA	NA	3 208	1	15	13	3	18	1 612	9 430	29.6
0030	Conway town (Carroll)	7 940	NA	NA	7 855	18	11	48	8	34	5 499	9 683	180.4
0030	Moultonborough town (Carroll)	2 956	NA	NA	2 935	3	6	10	2	6	3 850	NA	155.0
0030	Ossipee town (Carroll)	3 309	NA	NA	3 285	4	8	9	3	9	2 617	NA	184.3
0030	Wakefield town (Carroll)	3 057	NA	NA	3 030	11	2	10	4	9	3 158	NA	101.9
0030	Wolfeboro town (Carroll)	4 807	NA	NA	4 796	2	3	6	0	25	3 631	12 503	125.1
0050	Chesterfield town (Cheshire)	3 112	NA	NA	3 093	1	4	11	3	21	1 527	11 009	118.0
0050	Hinsdale town (Cheshire)	3 936	NA	NA	3 888	16	9	20	3	12	1 655	9 261	53.6
0050	Jaffrey town (Cheshire)	5 361	NA	NA	5 296	14	15	36	0	23	2 426	12 688	99.2
0050	Rindge town (Cheshire)	4 941	NA	NA	4 837	60	9	25	10	33	1 781	9 295	96.3
0050	Swanzey town (Cheshire)	6 236	NA	NA	6 212	8	1	13	2	16	2 582	10 006	116.5
0051	Walpole town (Cheshire)	3 210	NA	NA	3 187	3	5	9	6	10	1 465	11 770	92.1
0051	Winchester town (Cheshire)	4 038	NA	NA	3 987	13	18	20	0	16	1 673	7 602	142.3
0070	Gorham town (Coos)	3 173	NA	NA	3 153	1	2	17	0	6	1 426	9 270	82.6
0071	Lancaster town (Coos)	3 522	NA	NA	3 508	2	3	8	1	16	1 513	8 462	129.8
0090	Bristol town (Grafton)	2 537	NA	NA	2 518	5	3	8	3	8	2 250	NA	44.9
0090	Canaan town (Grafton)	3 045	NA	NA	3 034	0	3	8	0	17	1 435	NA	137.8

1. Codes shown are 2-digit FIPS codes for states; 4-digit census place codes for places; and 3-digit FIPS county codes followed by 3-digit census MCD codes for minor civil divisions (MCDs). MCD names are followed by county names in parentheses. 2. Hispanic persons may be of any race. 3. Dry land or land partially or temporarily covered by water.

State/ Place/ MCD[1] code	Place	Population: 1990	Population: Places of 10,000 or more: 1980	Population: Places of 10,000 or more: Percent change, 1980–1990	Population characteristics, 1990: Race: White	Race: Black	Race: Am. Indian, Eskimo Aleut	Race: Asian & Pacific Islander	Race: Other race	Hispanic[2]	Total housing units, 1990	Per capita income, 1985 (Dollars)	Land area,[3] 1990 (Sq. Km.)
		1	2	3	4	5	6	7	8	9	10	11	12
	NEW HAMPSHIRE—Con.												
0090	Enfield town (Grafton)	3 979	NA	NA	3 955	2	1	16	5	22	2 158	9 865	104.3
0090	Hanover town (Grafton)	9 212	NA	NA	8 435	264	47	446	20	184	2 623	12 926	127.2
0090	Haverhill town (Grafton)	4 164	NA	NA	4 145	7	6	4	2	25	2 031	9 131	132.5
0091	Littleton town (Grafton)	5 827	NA	NA	5 757	10	12	35	13	28	2 688	8 936	130.0
0091	Plymouth town (Grafton)	5 811	NA	NA	5 721	23	10	47	10	42	2 075	7 235	73.3
0110	Amherst town (Hillsborough)	9 068	NA	NA	8 947	30	5	75	11	71	3 179	18 107	88.8
0110	Bedford town (Hillsborough)	12 563	NA	NA	12 370	24	13	148	8	65	4 156	16 853	85.0
0110	Goffstown town (Hillsborough)	14 621	11 315	29.2	14 469	42	31	63	16	128	5 022	11 529	95.6
0110	Hillsborough town (Hillsborough)	4 498	NA	NA	4 456	6	9	24	3	44	2 157	10 647	113.0
0110	Hollis town (Hillsborough)	5 705	NA	NA	5 599	25	8	70	3	34	2 006	16 981	82.2
0110	Hudson town (Hillsborough)	19 530	14 022	39.3	19 136	109	28	205	52	211	6 902	13 339	73.2
0110	Litchfield town (Hillsborough)	5 516	NA	NA	5 443	35	6	30	2	48	1 845	12 322	39.1
0110	Merrimack town (Hillsborough)	22 156	15 406	43.8	21 635	220	29	230	42	216	7 915	13 595	84.5
0111	Milford town (Hillsborough)	11 795	NA	NA	11 584	101	11	75	24	73	4 793	11 587	65.3
0111	New Boston town (Hillsborough)	3 214	NA	NA	3 193	8	5	4	4	14	1 138	NA	111.0
0111	New Ipswich town (Hillsborough)	4 014	NA	NA	3 978	8	14	8	6	16	1 326	NA	84.8
0111	Pelham town (Hillsborough)	9 408	NA	NA	9 256	34	18	91	9	90	3 118	12 195	68.5
0111	Peterborough town (Hillsborough)	5 239	NA	NA	5 159	15	3	51	11	29	2 242	14 729	97.7
0111	Weare town (Hillsborough)	6 193	NA	NA	6 161	12	3	10	7	28	2 417	10 529	152.4
0111	Wilton town (Hillsborough)	3 122	NA	NA	3 074	10	10	24	4	5	1 251	11 435	66.7
0130	Allenstown town (Merrimack)	4 649	NA	NA	4 587	24	9	24	5	25	1 868	10 172	53.2
0130	Boscawen town (Merrimack)	3 586	NA	NA	3 544	16	9	16	1	20	1 221	9 539	64.0
0130	Bow town (Merrimack)	5 500	NA	NA	5 454	9	2	26	9	17	1 860	14 656	72.7
0130	Epsom town (Merrimack)	3 591	NA	NA	3 565	8	10	8	0	18	1 396	10 686	88.5
0130	Henniker town (Merrimack)	4 151	NA	NA	4 087	20	6	25	13	48	1 558	8 765	114.3
0130	Hooksett town (Merrimack)	8 767	NA	NA	8 618	48	5	89	7	42	3 484	11 407	93.8
0130	Hopkinton town (Merrimack)	4 806	NA	NA	4 782	6	1	16	1	10	1 924	15 122	112.1
0130	Loudon town (Merrimack)	4 114	NA	NA	4 095	5	8	6	0	18	1 476	NA	121.2
0130	New London town (Merrimack)	3 180	NA	NA	3 157	7	0	16	0	11	1 806	16 953	58.3
0131	Northfield town (Merrimack)	4 263	NA	NA	4 240	13	2	8	0	16	1 671	8 463	74.6
0131	Pembroke town (Merrimack)	6 561	NA	NA	6 502	22	15	12	10	39	2 536	11 461	59.1
0131	Pittsfield town (Merrimack)	3 701	NA	NA	3 682	8	5	3	3	25	1 527	9 886	61.0
0150	Atkinson town (Rockingham)	5 188	NA	NA	5 125	15	1	43	4	12	1 885	14 354	28.9
0150	Auburn town (Rockingham)	4 085	NA	NA	4 037	15	4	21	8	17	1 354	12 375	65.3
0150	Brentwood town (Rockingham)	2 590	NA	NA	2 538	19	8	11	14	18	778	NA	43.6
0150	Candia town (Rockingham)	3 557	NA	NA	3 528	12	10	5	2	17	1 192	11 950	78.6
0150	Chester town (Rockingham)	2 691	NA	NA	2 659	6	6	18	2	14	924	NA	67.1
0150	Danville town (Rockingham)	2 534	NA	NA	2 517	8	1	8	0	8	960	NA	30.3
0150	Deerfield town (Rockingham)	3 124	NA	NA	3 111	7	1	5	0	11	1 227	NA	131.9
0150	Derry town (Rockingham)	29 603	18 875	56.8	28 894	276	71	244	118	407	11 869	12 817	92.7
0150	Epping town (Rockingham)	5 162	NA	NA	5 109	12	9	17	15	44	2 059	11 706	67.4
0150	Exeter town (Rockingham)	12 481	10 989	13.6	12 297	54	13	101	16	61	5 346	12 174	50.9
0150	Fremont town (Rockingham)	2 576	NA	NA	2 550	10	3	12	1	20	920	NA	44.4
0150	Greenland town (Rockingham)	2 768	NA	NA	2 725	13	1	29	0	41	1 082	NA	27.2
0150	Hampstead town (Rockingham)	6 732	NA	NA	6 650	16	4	53	9	60	2 661	14 129	34.9
0150	Hampton town (Rockingham)	12 278	10 493	17.0	12 163	38	12	55	10	86	8 599	14 684	33.8
0150	Kingston town (Rockingham)	5 591	NA	NA	5 532	27	10	10	12	37	2 115	12 376	50.9
0150	Londonderry town (Rockingham)	19 781	13 598	45.5	19 454	79	21	188	39	185	6 739	12 948	108.3
0151	Newmarket town (Rockingham)	7 157	NA	NA	6 858	52	12	231	4	63	3 285	10 882	32.5
0151	Newton town (Rockingham)	3 473	NA	NA	3 430	16	11	3	13	36	1 251	10 728	25.7
0151	North Hampton town (Rockingham)	3 637	NA	NA	3 612	13	0	12	0	6	1 495	17 730	36.0
0151	Northwood town (Rockingham)	3 124	NA	NA	3 074	11	11	28	0	22	1 791	NA	72.5
0151	Nottingham town (Rockingham)	2 939	NA	NA	2 904	9	1	20	5	14	1 314	NA	120.4
0151	Plaistow town (Rockingham)	7 316	NA	NA	7 225	22	2	41	26	73	2 691	12 808	27.5
0151	Raymond town (Rockingham)	8 713	NA	NA	8 654	27	9	14	9	43	3 350	9 412	74.6
0151	Rye town (Rockingham)	4 612	NA	NA	4 577	10	5	19	1	8	2 443	17 512	32.7
0151	Salem town (Rockingham)	25 746	24 124	6.7	24 917	239	38	456	96	364	9 897	13 263	64.0
0151	Sandown town (Rockingham)	4 060	NA	NA	4 031	9	7	5	8	15	1 488	NA	36.0
0151	Seabrook town (Rockingham)	6 503	NA	NA	6 427	14	19	33	10	51	3 469	11 946	23.0
0151	Stratham town (Rockingham)	4 955	NA	NA	4 883	15	12	36	9	33	1 917	14 682	39.1
0151	Windham town (Rockingham)	9 000	NA	NA	8 860	43	6	80	11	54	3 327	17 756	69.4
0170	Barrington town (Strafford)	6 164	NA	NA	6 100	19	16	15	14	53	2 640	11 409	120.7
0170	Durham town (Strafford)	11 818	10 618	11.3	11 486	75	8	234	15	99	2 508	8 707	58.0
0170	Farmington town (Strafford)	5 739	NA	NA	5 681	8	19	16	15	40	2 260	8 406	96.2
0170	Lee town (Strafford)	3 729	NA	NA	3 654	17	11	46	1	23	1 393	NA	51.7
0170	Milton town (Strafford)	3 691	NA	NA	3 666	3	3	17	2	7	1 767	NA	85.8
0170	Rollinsford town (Strafford)	2 645	NA	NA	2 614	14	2	13	2	21	1 040	NA	18.9
0170	Strafford town (Strafford)	2 965	NA	NA	2 952	2	1	9	1	13	1 264	NA	127.4
0190	Charlestown town (Sullivan)	4 630	NA	NA	4 599	9	12	7	3	23	2 051	9 315	92.8
0190	Newport town (Sullivan)	6 110	NA	NA	6 066	5	10	25	4	15	2 675	9 264	112.9
0190	Sunapee town (Sullivan)	2 559	NA	NA	2 546	0	2	10	1	11	1 904	NA	54.7
34	NEW JERSEY	7 730 188	7 365 011	5.0	6 130 465	1 036 825	14 970	272 521	275 407	739 861	3 075 310	13 129	19 214.8

1. Codes shown are 2-digit FIPS codes for states; 4-digit census place codes for places; and 3-digit FIPS county codes followed by 3-digit census MCD codes for minor civil divisions (MCDs). MCD names are followed by county names in parentheses. 2. Hispanic persons may be of any race. 3. Dry land or land partially or temporarily covered by water.

State/ Place/ MCD[1] code	Place	Population 1990	Places of 10,000 or more 1980	Places of 10,000 or more Percent change, 1980–1990	Race: White	Race: Black	Race: Am. Indian, Eskimo Aleut	Race: Asian & Pacific Islander	Race: Other race	Hispanic[2]	Total housing units, 1990	Per capita income, 1985 (Dollars)	Land area,[3] 1990 (Sq. Km.)
		1	2	3	4	5	6	7	8	9	10	11	12
	NEW JERSEY—Con.												
0005	Absecon	7 298	NA	NA	6 692	313	13	239	41	154	2 771	13 811	14.8
0020	Allamuchy-Panther Valley CDP	2 764	NA	NA	2 704	17	2	29	12	68	1 355	NA	14.8
0025	Allendale borough	5 900	NA	NA	5 629	26	8	223	14	107	1 915	24 973	8.1
0050	Alpha borough	2 530	NA	NA	2 509	0	0	18	3	30	1 003	11 870	4.4
0070	Asbury Park	16 799	17 015	-1.3	5 950	9 977	49	123	700	1 533	7 692	8 338	3.7
0075	Atlantic City	37 986	40 199	-5.5	13 466	19 491	193	1 509	3 327	5 813	21 626	9 205	29.4
0085	Atlantic Highlands borough	4 629	NA	NA	4 507	76	2	26	18	84	1 932	13 493	3.2
0090	Audubon borough	9 205	NA	NA	9 094	19	13	53	26	106	3 756	11 470	3.9
0102	Avenel CDP	15 504	NA	NA	11 624	2 622	29	971	258	1 294	5 041	NA	8.9
1115	Barrington borough	6 774	NA	NA	6 541	139	12	70	12	94	2 765	11 919	4.2
1135	Bayonne	61 444	65 047	-5.5	55 571	2 895	81	1 130	1 767	5 839	26 468	11 826	14.6
1142	Beach Haven West CDP	4 237	NA	NA	4 166	7	12	42	10	57	4 514	NA	5.2
1145	Beachwood borough	9 324	NA	NA	9 144	49	6	84	41	218	3 244	9 625	7.1
1148	Beattyestown CDP	3 966	NA	NA	3 795	78	3	52	38	155	1 887	NA	7.8
1150	Beckett CDP	3 815	NA	NA	3 133	566	4	76	36	94	1 215	NA	4.6
1155	Belleville CDP	34 213	35 367	-3.3	29 447	1 254	85	2 055	1 372	3 441	14 058	NA	8.7
1160	Bellmawr borough	12 603	13 721	-8.1	12 312	117	5	115	54	201	4 789	10 191	7.9
1165	Belmar borough	5 877	NA	NA	5 486	313	4	34	40	176	3 888	12 547	2.6
1170	Belvidere town	2 669	NA	NA	2 625	12	0	25	7	35	1 084	NA	3.4
1175	Bergenfield borough	24 458	25 568	-4.3	20 526	1 026	36	2 224	646	2 253	9 035	13 713	7.5
1182	Berkeley Heights CDP	11 980	12 549	-4.5	10 995	164	2	779	40	225	3 924	NA	16.2
1190	Berlin borough	5 672	NA	NA	5 531	54	2	59	26	76	2 015	12 233	9.3
1205	Bernardsville borough	6 597	NA	NA	6 440	21	3	122	11	211	2 561	27 052	33.5
1215	Beverly	2 973	NA	NA	2 145	731	6	33	58	126	1 062	9 724	1.5
1231	Blackwood CDP	5 120	NA	NA	4 976	112	9	16	7	55	1 860	NA	3.2
1235	Bloomfield CDP	45 061	47 792	-5.7	40 130	1 937	52	2 251	691	2 311	19 293	NA	13.8
1240	Bloomingdale borough	7 530	NA	NA	7 401	30	5	65	29	234	2 916	12 329	22.8
1250	Bogota borough	7 824	NA	NA	6 972	209	30	385	228	789	2 844	13 873	2.0
1260	Boonton town	8 343	NA	NA	7 642	270	6	339	86	308	3 234	14 010	6.1
1265	Bordentown	4 341	NA	NA	3 664	616	10	24	27	84	1 897	12 752	2.4
1275	Bound Brook borough	9 487	NA	NA	8 588	217	16	231	435	1 226	3 823	13 152	4.4
1280	Bradley Beach borough	4 475	NA	NA	4 138	185	8	45	99	337	3 122	10 714	1.5
1305	Brick Township CDP	66 473	53 629	23.9	65 015	419	87	551	401	1 715	28 843	NA	68.1
1310	Bridgeton	18 942	18 795	0.8	10 365	6 996	254	153	1 174	1 829	7 142	7 883	16.1
1320	Brielle borough	4 406	NA	NA	4 121	240	10	26	9	66	1 986	18 901	4.6
1325	Brigantine	11 354	NA	NA	10 609	364	24	202	155	506	8 796	13 829	16.6
1337	Brown Mills CDP	11 429	10 568	8.1	8 034	2 284	39	704	368	885	4 007	NA	13.8
1340	Budd Lake CDP	7 272	NA	NA	6 902	155	13	152	50	252	2 694	NA	15.2
1345	Buena borough	4 441	NA	NA	3 609	205	5	30	592	905	1 761	10 192	19.7
1355	Burlington	9 835	10 246	-4.0	7 404	2 308	17	55	51	188	4 056	10 450	7.8
1365	Butler borough	7 392	NA	NA	7 274	20	4	71	23	188	2 750	13 321	5.4
1380	Caldwell CDP	7 549	NA	NA	7 166	122	6	222	33	210	3 362	NA	3.1
1390	Camden	87 492	84 910	3.0	16 620	49 362	363	1 152	19 995	27 273	30 138	5 731	22.8
1395	Cape May	4 668	NA	NA	4 172	372	19	43	62	103	4 052	10 836	6.4
1400	Cape May Court House CDP	4 426	NA	NA	3 773	547	21	75	10	35	1 859	NA	23.2
1410	Carlstadt borough	5 510	NA	NA	5 188	60	7	183	72	248	2 449	12 608	10.2
1412	Carneys Point CDP	7 686	NA	NA	6 330	1 208	18	59	71	154	3 046	NA	22.7
1415	Carteret borough	19 025	20 598	-7.6	16 040	1 108	44	766	1 067	2 760	6 811	11 757	11.3
1420	Cedar Grove CDP	12 053	12 600	-4.3	11 100	270	2	610	71	305	4 222	NA	10.7
1435	Chatham borough	8 007	NA	NA	7 805	22	1	162	17	146	3 154	21 760	6.2
1440	Cherry Hill CDP	69 319	68 785	0.8	62 236	2 243	65	4 261	514	1 380	25 773	NA	62.8
1460	Cinnaminson CDP	14 583	16 072	-9.3	13 468	772	19	260	64	204	4 877	NA	19.7
1470	Clark CDP	14 629	16 699	-12.4	14 316	15	6	240	52	428	5 638	NA	11.3
1475	Clayton borough	6 155	NA	NA	5 080	968	21	32	54	185	2 177	9 008	18.6
1477	Clearbrook Park CDP	2 853	NA	NA	2 829	12	0	11	1	20	1 864	NA	2.2
1480	Clementon borough	5 601	NA	NA	5 072	412	10	62	45	121	2 420	10 295	4.9
1485	Cliffside Park borough	20 393	21 464	-5.0	17 977	370	21	1 519	506	2 231	9 809	16 256	2.5
1487	Cliffwood Beach CDP	3 543	NA	NA	2 976	425	12	46	84	273	1 208	NA	2.5
1490	Clifton	71 742	74 388	-3.6	66 546	1 005	74	2 513	1 604	4 877	29 999	13 512	29.3
1505	Closter borough	8 094	NA	NA	6 557	92	6	1 410	29	220	2 767	17 574	8.2
1510	Collingswood borough	15 289	15 838	-3.5	14 420	465	23	246	135	393	6 734	12 085	4.7
1512	Colonia CDP	18 238	NA	NA	16 554	777	23	789	95	623	6 209	NA	10.1
1515	Concordia CDP	2 683	NA	NA	2 631	37	0	12	3	8	1 670	NA	2.8
1528	Country Lake Estates CDP	4 492	NA	NA	3 476	671	31	165	149	345	1 425	NA	2.9
1535	Cranford CDP	22 624	24 573	-7.9	21 549	689	7	331	48	541	8 405	NA	12.4
1540	Cresskill borough	7 558	NA	NA	6 459	53	0	1 026	20	238	2 600	18 745	5.5
1542	Crestwood Village CDP	8 030	NA	NA	8 004	14	1	10	1	34	6 077	NA	10.2
1544	Dayton CDP	4 321	NA	NA	3 495	308	8	475	35	175	1 562	NA	5.5
1570	Delanco CDP	3 316	NA	NA	3 267	22	2	16	9	37	1 236	NA	6.4
1585	Demarest borough	4 800	NA	NA	3 908	42	2	847	1	137	1 610	23 276	5.4
1605	Dover town	15 115	14 681	3.0	11 743	922	29	294	2 127	6 101	5 355	12 769	7.0
1620	Dumont borough	17 187	18 334	-6.3	15 679	181	18	1 174	135	931	6 328	13 811	5.1
1625	Dunellen borough	6 528	NA	NA	6 241	101	5	103	78	327	2 496	12 733	2.7

1. Codes shown are 2-digit FIPS codes for states; 4-digit census place codes for places; and 3-digit FIPS county codes followed by 3-digit census MCD codes for minor civil divisions (MCDs). MCD names are followed by county names in parentheses. 2. Hispanic persons may be of any race. 3. Dry land or land partially or temporarily covered by water.

State/ Place/ MCD[1] code	Place	Population: 1990	Population: Places of 10,000 or more: 1980	Population: Places of 10,000 or more: Percent change, 1980–1990	Population characteristics, 1990: Race: White	Population characteristics, 1990: Race: Black	Population characteristics, 1990: Race: Am. Indian, Eskimo Aleut	Population characteristics, 1990: Race: Asian & Pacific Islander	Population characteristics, 1990: Race: Other race	Population characteristics, 1990: Hispanic[2]	Total housing units, 1990	Per capita income, 1985 (Dollars)	Land area,[3] 1990 (Sq. Km.)
		1	2	3	4	5	6	7	8	9	10	11	12
	NEW JERSEY—Con.												
1642	East Brunswick CDP	43 548	37 711	15.5	38 382	969	52	3 945	200	1 246	15 395	NA	57.0
1650	East Freehold CDP	3 842	NA	NA	3 523	90	1	209	19	117	1 318	NA	7.7
1655	East Hanover CDP	9 926	NA	NA	9 112	85	3	703	23	228	3 112	NA	21.2
1665	East Orange	73 552	77 690	-5.3	5 301	66 157	311	463	1 320	2 981	28 987	8 841	10.2
1675	East Rutherford borough	7 902	NA	NA	7 209	219	12	373	89	442	3 817	12 150	9.9
1685	Eatontown borough	13 800	12 703	8.6	10 881	1 724	40	909	246	641	6 093	12 992	15.3
1690	Edgewater borough	5 001	NA	NA	4 369	154	11	371	96	534	2 827	20 001	2.2
1692	Edgewater Park CDP	8 388	NA	NA	6 746	1 449	26	112	55	218	3 224	NA	7.5
1697	Edison CDP	88 680	70 193	26.3	70 492	4 935	106	12 166	981	3 839	32 832	NA	78.2
1705	Egg Harbor City	4 583	NA	NA	3 612	509	6	33	423	959	1 750	12 172	28.8
1715	Elizabeth	110 002	106 201	3.6	72 098	21 833	297	3 002	12 772	43 050	41 315	9 572	31.9
1727	Elmwood Park borough	17 623	18 377	-4.1	16 515	146	17	601	344	1 520	6 940	12 591	6.9
1735	Emerson borough	6 930	NA	NA	6 393	71	5	431	30	207	2 257	15 695	5.8
1740	Englewood	24 850	23 701	4.8	12 217	9 808	80	1 227	1 518	3 893	9 411	17 441	12.8
1745	Englewood Cliffs borough	5 634	NA	NA	4 295	55	1	1 252	31	303	1 879	23 999	5.4
1775	Ewing CDP	34 185	34 842	-1.9	26 908	6 243	41	612	381	918	12 518	NA	39.7
1780	Fairfield CDP	7 615	NA	NA	7 345	16	7	232	15	210	2 351	NA	27.1
1785	Fair Haven borough	5 270	NA	NA	4 892	301	4	52	21	59	1 967	18 125	4.3
1790	Fair Lawn borough	30 548	32 229	-5.2	29 314	181	22	894	137	1 063	11 759	16 104	13.4
1795	Fairview borough	10 733	10 519	2.0	9 713	145	6	356	513	1 664	4 686	11 765	2.2
1796	Fairview CDP	3 853	NA	NA	3 742	20	6	65	20	98	1 318	NA	3.3
1805	Fanwood borough	7 115	NA	NA	6 413	372	2	297	31	157	2 507	16 313	3.5
1825	Flemington borough	4 047	NA	NA	3 835	93	3	102	14	70	1 854	14 694	2.8
1833	Florence-Roebling CDP	8 564	NA	NA	7 802	677	16	39	30	147	3 364	NA	5.7
1840	Florham Park borough	8 521	NA	NA	8 156	46	5	290	24	148	2 969	18 305	19.3
1846	Fords CDP	14 392	NA	NA	12 986	358	19	817	212	806	5 644	NA	6.7
1847	Forked River CDP	4 243	NA	NA	4 170	38	8	9	18	70	2 325	NA	6.7
1848	Fort Dix CDP	10 205	14 297	-28.6	5 575	3 539	77	346	668	1 347	1 273	NA	28.9
1850	Fort Lee borough	31 997	32 449	-1.4	24 704	418	18	6 505	352	1 779	16 847	22 239	6.6
1875	Franklin borough	4 977	NA	NA	4 897	26	6	23	25	141	1 970	11 084	11.6
1885	Franklin Lakes borough	9 873	NA	NA	9 204	43	16	587	23	169	3 171	30 290	24.5
1895	Freehold borough	10 742	10 020	7.2	7 892	1 962	10	293	585	1 218	4 057	11 616	5.2
1920	Garfield	26 727	26 803	-0.3	25 077	598	23	444	585	2 418	11 458	11 062	5.5
1925	Garwood borough	4 227	NA	NA	4 160	11	1	30	25	114	1 748	12 869	1.7
1935	Gibbstown CDP	3 902	NA	NA	3 854	27	5	16	0	22	1 445	NA	4.2
1940	Gilford Park CDP	8 668	NA	NA	8 499	77	14	55	23	155	4 213	NA	5.6
1950	Glassboro borough	15 614	14 574	7.1	12 291	2 893	30	234	166	452	5 440	8 737	23.9
1953	Glendora CDP	5 201	NA	NA	5 163	13	6	10	9	38	1 978	NA	2.8
1960	Glen Ridge CDP	7 076	NA	NA	6 576	226	6	231	37	166	2 470	NA	3.3
1965	Glen Rock borough	10 883	11 497	-5.3	9 979	240	2	648	14	207	3 963	19 594	7.1
1970	Gloucester City	12 649	13 098	-3.4	12 536	29	19	50	15	123	4 934	8 938	5.7
2005	Guttenberg town	8 268	NA	NA	6 549	233	27	411	1 048	3 610	4 504	18 374	0.5
2010	Hackensack	37 049	36 039	2.8	24 585	9 176	86	1 358	1 844	5 594	17 705	14 971	10.7
2015	Hackettstown town	8 120	NA	NA	7 760	119	19	181	41	258	3 202	11 487	9.6
2025	Haddonfield borough	11 628	12 336	-5.7	11 336	161	11	102	18	100	4 652	19 750	7.3
2030	Haddon Heights borough	7 860	NA	NA	7 778	35	3	36	8	57	3 154	13 274	4.0
2040	Haledon borough	6 951	NA	NA	6 411	252	12	61	215	621	2 676	11 404	3.0
2045	Hamburg borough	2 566	NA	NA	2 481	15	10	52	8	74	1 107	NA	3.0
2065	Hammonton town	12 208	12 298	-0.7	11 580	139	4	85	400	1 045	4 608	11 436	106.9
2087	Hanover Township CDP	11 538	11 846	-2.6	10 688	120	4	716	10	266	3 882	NA	27.6
2105	Harrington Park borough	4 623	NA	NA	3 965	30	0	622	6	106	1 511	19 276	4.8
2115	Harrison town	13 425	12 242	9.7	11 867	77	19	785	677	3 947	5 120	10 531	3.2
2125	Hasbrouck Heights borough	11 488	12 166	-5.6	10 866	93	6	429	94	485	4 510	15 353	3.9
2130	Haworth borough	3 384	NA	NA	2 983	56	0	327	18	93	1 142	20 401	5.1
2135	Hawthorne borough	17 084	18 200	-6.1	16 731	72	7	170	104	530	7 055	13 336	8.8
2139	Heathcote CDP	3 112	NA	NA	2 693	241	5	158	15	97	1 482	NA	6.8
2145	High Bridge borough	3 886	NA	NA	3 785	43	2	47	9	30	1 454	13 376	6.2
2147	Highland Lake CDP	4 550	NA	NA	4 512	14	4	14	6	92	2 256	NA	11.9
2150	Highland Park borough	13 279	13 396	-0.9	11 266	1 128	17	663	205	730	6 106	15 480	4.8
2155	Highlands borough	4 849	NA	NA	4 735	47	7	39	21	109	2 890	14 887	2.0
2160	Hightstown borough	5 126	NA	NA	4 281	546	17	88	194	438	2 151	14 219	3.2
2170	Hillsdale borough	9 750	10 495	-7.1	9 226	60	4	416	44	274	3 422	17 599	7.7
2175	Hillside CDP	21 044	21 440	-1.8	11 157	8 578	30	812	467	2 807	7 364	NA	7.0
2185	Hoboken	33 397	42 460	-21.3	26 374	1 843	56	1 480	3 644	10 036	17 421	9 795	3.3
2190	Ho-Ho-Kus borough	3 935	NA	NA	3 677	12	3	234	9	67	1 448	27 298	4.5
2195	Holiday City-Berkeley CDP	14 293	NA	NA	14 255	20	4	11	3	99	8 808	NA	14.9
2200	Holiday City South CDP	5 452	NA	NA	5 204	240	2	5	1	49	3 126	NA	4.8
2215	Hopatcong borough	15 586	15 531	0.4	14 964	219	14	275	114	563	6 171	12 469	28.3
2265	Irvington CDP	59 774	61 493	-2.8	13 517	41 760	142	1 313	3 042	6 315	23 792	NA	7.5
2268	Iselin CDP	16 141	NA	NA	14 116	650	17	1 243	115	521	5 994	NA	8.0
2280	Jamesburg borough	5 294	NA	NA	4 700	458	4	90	42	156	2 064	11 924	2.2
2290	Jersey City	228 537	223 532	2.2	110 263	67 864	787	25 959	23 664	55 395	90 723	8 605	38.5
2295	Keansburg borough	11 069	10 613	4.3	10 739	87	16	80	147	554	4 189	8 569	2.8

1. Codes shown are 2-digit FIPS codes for states; 4-digit census place codes for places; and 3-digit FIPS county codes followed by 3-digit census MCD codes for minor civil divisions (MCDs). MCD names are followed by county names in parentheses. 2. Hispanic persons may be of any race. 3. Dry land or land partially or temporarily covered by water.

State/ Place/ MCD[1] code	Place	Population: 1990	Population: Places of 10,000 or more: 1980	Population: Places of 10,000 or more: Percent change, 1980–1990	Population characteristics, 1990: Race: White	Race: Black	Race: Am. Indian, Eskimo Aleut	Race: Asian & Pacific Islander	Race: Other race	Hispanic[2]	Total housing units, 1990	Per capita income, 1985 (Dollars)	Land area,[3] 1990 (Sq. Km.)
		1	2	3	4	5	6	7	8	9	10	11	12
	NEW JERSEY—Con.												
2300	Kearny town	34 874	35 735	-2.4	31 556	433	59	1 638	1 188	5 950	13 435	11 333	23.7
2302	Kendall Park CDP	7 127	NA	NA	6 238	337	6	491	55	263	2 535	NA	9.6
2305	Kenilworth borough	7 574	NA	NA	7 238	188	7	90	51	394	2 844	12 270	5.5
2315	Keyport borough	7 586	NA	NA	6 708	590	25	68	195	615	3 403	10 582	3.6
2325	Kinnelon borough	8 470	NA	NA	8 219	30	9	198	14	140	2 903	21 010	47.6
2345	Lakehurst borough	3 078	NA	NA	2 607	296	13	84	78	215	1 087	8 566	2.4
2350	Lake Mohawk CDP	8 930	NA	NA	8 810	27	6	70	17	188	3 610	NA	12.8
2365	Lakewood CDP	26 095	22 863	14.1	19 117	4 937	42	293	1 706	3 481	8 544	NA	18.5
2370	Lambertville	3 927	NA	NA	3 775	116	3	19	14	78	1 818	12 743	2.9
2377	Laurence Harbor CDP	6 361	NA	NA	6 052	98	15	134	62	400	2 324	NA	7.3
2385	Lawnside borough	2 841	NA	NA	51	2 744	26	7	13	30	1 078	10 429	3.6
2390	Lawrenceville CDP	6 446	NA	NA	5 788	253	13	360	32	113	2 583	NA	12.0
2407	Leisure Knoll CDP	2 707	NA	NA	2 698	3	1	5	0	18	1 566	NA	2.3
2408	Leisuretowne CDP	2 552	NA	NA	2 536	9	3	4	0	19	1 648	NA	4.7
2410	Leisure Village CDP	4 295	NA	NA	4 126	119	3	10	37	149	3 043	NA	3.2
2412	Leisure Village West-Pine Lake Park	10 139	NA	NA	9 864	160	4	58	53	274	4 920	NA	9.9
2414	Leonardo CDP	3 788	NA	NA	3 431	296	5	24	32	147	1 007	NA	1.6
2415	Leonia borough	8 365	NA	NA	6 814	241	3	1 183	124	671	3 337	18 856	3.9
2435	Lincoln Park borough	10 978	NA	NA	10 398	104	9	399	68	381	4 020	13 436	17.4
2437	Lincroft CDP	6 193	NA	NA	5 799	70	1	318	5	124	2 088	NA	12.1
2440	Linden	36 701	37 836	-3.0	28 173	7 344	49	552	583	2 700	14 917	12 491	28.0
2445	Lindenwold borough	18 734	18 206	2.9	15 032	3 027	36	409	230	599	8 527	11 128	10.2
2450	Linwood	6 866	NA	NA	6 663	55	13	122	13	91	2 491	15 802	9.9
2462	Little Falls CDP	11 294	11 496	-1.8	10 759	194	5	217	119	411	4 460	NA	7.1
2465	Little Ferry borough	9 989	NA	NA	8 694	369	18	700	208	843	4 427	14 272	4.0
2470	Little Silver borough	5 721	NA	NA	5 629	16	1	60	15	73	2 121	19 498	7.2
2475	Livingston CDP	26 609	28 040	-5.1	23 749	288	15	2 479	78	496	8 910	NA	36.0
2485	Lodi borough	22 355	23 956	-6.7	20 032	646	21	1 084	572	2 065	9 472	12 102	5.9
2500	Long Branch	28 658	29 819	-3.9	21 064	5 589	59	421	1 525	3 888	13 632	11 360	13.5
2514	Lyndhurst CDP	18 262	20 326	-10.2	17 546	79	12	483	142	854	7 741	NA	12.0
2515	McGuire AFB CDP	7 580	NA	NA	5 190	1 855	36	254	245	520	1 829	NA	5.4
2550	Madison borough	15 850	15 357	3.2	14 562	704	12	456	116	445	5 564	19 233	10.9
2552	Madison Park CDP	7 490	NA	NA	5 491	695	10	1 107	187	788	2 968	NA	4.3
2555	Magnolia borough	4 861	NA	NA	3 896	858	14	48	45	103	1 852	10 353	2.6
2570	Manasquan borough	5 369	NA	NA	5 306	11	2	28	22	112	3 220	13 674	3.6
2605	Manville borough	10 567	11 278	-6.3	10 406	19	2	89	51	175	4 245	12 308	6.4
2612	Maple Shade CDP	19 211	20 525	-6.4	17 555	1 077	36	416	127	431	9 073	NA	10.0
2615	Maplewood CDP	21 756	22 950	-5.2	18 218	2 625	22	665	226	801	8 169	NA	10.0
2620	Margate City	8 431	NA	NA	8 285	40	9	63	34	118	6 726	19 929	3.6
2624	Marlton CDP	10 228	NA	NA	9 732	181	13	274	28	123	4 095	NA	8.4
2630	Matawan borough	9 270	NA	NA	8 304	540	17	332	77	376	3 730	14 659	5.9
2650	Maywood borough	9 473	NA	NA	8 808	161	9	397	98	561	3 778	14 194	3.3
2665	Medford Lakes borough	4 462	NA	NA	4 433	1	1	22	5	40	1 567	15 948	3.1
2670	Mendham borough	4 890	NA	NA	4 783	21	3	66	17	54	1 777	20 357	15.6
2675	Mercerville-Hamilton Square CDP	26 873	25 446	5.6	25 896	218	21	657	81	311	9 365	NA	19.9
2680	Merchantville borough	4 095	NA	NA	3 934	97	6	39	19	79	1 656	12 573	1.6
2685	Metuchen borough	12 804	13 762	-7.0	11 322	780	14	602	86	362	5 097	16 718	7.1
2700	Middlesex borough	13 055	13 480	-3.2	12 425	219	17	294	100	429	4 920	13 035	9.1
2715	Midland Park borough	7 047	NA	NA	6 845	37	12	140	13	160	2 615	14 728	4.1
2725	Millburn CDP	18 630	19 543	-4.7	17 436	224	4	921	45	312	7 108	NA	24.3
2745	Milltown borough	6 968	NA	NA	6 730	5	5	186	42	125	2 553	14 601	4.1
2750	Millville	25 992	24 815	4.7	22 522	2 195	101	155	1 019	1 974	10 150	9 952	109.7
2760	Monmouth Beach borough	3 303	NA	NA	3 259	15	1	21	7	28	1 898	24 373	2.8
2780	Montclair CDP	37 729	38 321	-1.5	24 713	11 697	93	856	370	1 249	15 069	NA	16.3
2790	Montvale borough	6 946	NA	NA	6 601	54	4	265	22	153	2 439	18 916	10.3
2800	Moonachie borough	2 817	NA	NA	2 695	23	4	68	27	152	1 117	12 286	4.5
2807	Moorestown-Lenola CDP	13 242	13 695	-3.3	12 086	886	26	215	29	134	5 248	NA	18.2
2815	Morris Plains borough	5 219	NA	NA	4 960	100	3	135	21	113	1 965	18 017	6.7
2820	Morristown town	16 189	16 614	-2.6	11 451	3 733	39	406	560	2 210	7 061	15 921	7.6
2825	Mountain Lakes borough	3 847	NA	NA	3 713	7	0	122	5	68	1 268	25 419	6.9
2830	Mountainside borough	6 657	NA	NA	6 434	45	3	164	11	126	2 454	23 500	10.4
2835	Mount Arlington borough	3 630	NA	NA	3 490	35	3	79	23	108	1 470	14 456	5.5
2840	Mount Ephraim borough	4 517	NA	NA	4 485	14	6	11	1	41	1 844	10 753	2.3
2857	Mount Holly CDP	10 639	10 818	-1.7	8 135	1 992	66	131	315	609	3 823	NA	7.5
2871	Mystic Island CDP	7 400	NA	NA	7 244	46	11	52	47	203	4 679	NA	19.9
2875	National Park borough	3 413	NA	NA	3 377	2	4	14	16	36	1 145	8 235	2.6
2885	Neptune City borough	4 997	NA	NA	4 690	157	7	77	66	139	2 298	13 545	2.3
2890	Netcong borough	3 311	NA	NA	3 196	40	2	41	32	122	1 396	12 368	2.0
2895	Newark	275 221	329 248	-16.4	78 771	160 885	649	3 281	31 635	71 761	102 473	6 494	61.7
2900	New Brunswick	41 711	41 442	0.6	23 929	12 337	130	1 651	3 664	8 063	13 556	8 701	13.5
2920	New Milford borough	15 990	16 876	-5.3	14 482	253	7	1 120	128	813	6 353	14 479	6.0
2925	New Providence borough	11 439	12 426	-7.9	10 773	62	5	560	39	309	4 325	19 515	9.5
2935	Newton town	7 521	NA	NA	7 250	160	15	54	42	189	3 115	11 439	8.0

1. Codes shown are 2-digit FIPS codes for states; 4-digit census place codes for places; and 3-digit FIPS county codes followed by 3-digit census MCD codes for minor civil divisions (MCDs). MCD names are followed by county names in parentheses. 2. Hispanic persons may be of any race. 3. Dry land or land partially or temporarily covered by water.

State/ Place/ MCD[1] code	Place	Population: 1990	Population: Places of 10,000 or more: 1980	Population: Places of 10,000 or more: Percent change, 1980–1990	Population characteristics, 1990: Race: White	Race: Black	Race: Am. Indian, Eskimo Aleut	Race: Asian & Pacific Islander	Race: Other race	Hispanic[2]	Total housing units, 1990	Per capita income, 1985 (Dollars)	Land area,[3] 1990 (Sq. Km.)
		1	2	3	4	5	6	7	8	9	10	11	12
	NEW JERSEY—Con.												
2940	North Arlington borough	13 790	16 587	-16.9	13 173	32	3	478	104	832	6 406	13 398	6.7
2952	North Bergen CDP	48 414	47 019	3.0	40 751	1 014	100	2 308	4 241	19 937	21 274	NA	13.4
2954	North Brunswick Township CDP	31 287	NA	NA	25 044	3 465	75	2 132	571	1 817	12 186	NA	31.2
2955	North Caldwell CDP	6 706	NA	NA	5 690	682	2	276	56	167	1 996	NA	7.8
2957	North Cape May CDP	3 574	NA	NA	3 464	75	13	10	12	46	2 120	NA	3.6
2960	Northfield	7 305	NA	NA	6 970	132	15	154	34	87	2 826	14 208	8.9
2965	North Haledon borough	7 987	NA	NA	7 729	97	5	45	111	337	2 574	13 575	8.9
2970	North Middletown CDP	3 160	NA	NA	3 077	10	2	38	33	140	1 146	NA	1.2
2975	North Plainfield borough	18 820	19 108	-1.5	16 200	977	15	621	1 007	2 261	7 784	14 257	7.2
2985	Northvale borough	4 563	NA	NA	4 038	20	0	475	30	248	1 556	13 702	3.4
2990	North Wildwood	5 017	NA	NA	4 930	32	22	20	13	55	7 209	10 396	4.6
2995	Norwood borough	4 858	NA	NA	4 057	55	2	725	19	135	1 608	17 682	7.1
3000	Nutley CDP	27 099	28 998	-6.5	25 130	478	11	1 275	205	887	11 001	NA	8.7
3005	Oakhurst CDP	4 130	NA	NA	4 004	12	2	105	7	73	1 411	NA	4.2
3010	Oakland borough	11 997	13 443	-10.8	11 541	130	12	278	36	326	4 019	16 053	22.3
3015	Oaklyn borough	4 430	NA	NA	4 383	23	7	13	4	47	1 887	12 161	1.6
3016	Oak Valley CDP	4 055	NA	NA	3 876	111	9	36	23	54	1 294	NA	1.8
3017	Ocean Acres CDP	5 587	NA	NA	5 512	16	2	38	19	75	2 209	NA	15.2
3020	Ocean City	15 512	13 949	11.2	14 575	764	23	77	73	203	18 880	14 455	17.9
3037	Ocean Grove CDP	4 818	NA	NA	4 548	157	6	35	72	184	3 253	NA	0.8
3040	Oceanport borough	6 146	NA	NA	5 768	249	5	88	36	114	2 149	13 610	8.3
3045	Ogdensburg borough	2 722	NA	NA	2 673	7	1	16	25	125	895	10 442	5.9
3048	Old Bridge CDP	22 151	21 815	1.5	20 518	396	18	1 028	191	845	7 145	NA	18.9
3055	Old Tappan borough	4 254	NA	NA	3 858	37	2	343	14	90	1 355	19 676	8.4
3060	Oradell borough	8 024	NA	NA	7 417	28	4	547	28	149	2 836	20 419	6.3
3065	Orange CDP	29 925	31 136	-3.9	7 169	21 045	119	385	1 207	3 237	12 318	NA	5.7
3080	Palisades Park borough	14 536	13 732	5.9	10 911	228	28	2 910	459	1 672	6 049	13 815	3.1
3085	Palmyra borough	7 056	NA	NA	6 069	887	21	38	41	130	3 035	12 369	5.1
3090	Paramus borough	25 067	26 474	-5.3	22 116	197	8	2 626	120	914	7 892	15 547	27.1
3095	Park Ridge borough	8 102	NA	NA	7 676	55	5	321	45	224	3 063	17 289	6.7
3102	Parsippany-Troy Hills Township CDP	48 478	49 868	-2.8	41 252	1 743	62	4 917	504	2 014	18 960	NA	61.9
3110	Passaic	58 041	52 463	10.6	26 304	11 955	292	4 094	15 396	29 028	19 619	8 027	8.0
3115	Paterson	140 891	137 970	2.1	57 977	50 729	436	2 024	29 725	57 711	46 138	7 216	21.9
3120	Paulsboro borough	6 577	NA	NA	4 596	1 893	31	12	45	96	2 584	9 215	5.1
3132	Pemberton Heights CDP	2 941	NA	NA	1 118	1 524	9	104	186	404	1 120	NA	2.4
3140	Pennington borough	2 537	NA	NA	2 414	61	1	56	5	29	947	NA	2.5
3145	Pennsauken CDP	34 733	33 775	2.8	27 965	5 098	128	622	920	1 693	12 713	NA	27.3
3150	Penns Grove borough	5 228	NA	NA	3 061	1 860	21	12	274	412	2 138	7 411	2.4
3155	Pennsville CDP	12 218	12 467	-2.0	12 059	22	12	97	28	92	4 826	NA	25.6
3158	Pequannock Township CDP	12 844	13 776	-6.8	12 569	34	4	209	28	261	4 385	NA	18.2
3160	Perth Amboy	41 967	38 951	7.7	25 105	4 935	173	659	11 095	23 310	15 017	9 232	12.4
3165	Phillipsburg town	15 757	16 647	-5.3	15 182	313	21	101	140	407	6 626	9 848	8.4
3180	Pine Hill borough	9 854	NA	NA	8 683	968	25	113	65	208	3 943	10 018	10.2
3195	Pitman borough	9 365	NA	NA	9 221	45	20	68	11	52	3 526	11 484	5.9
3205	Plainfield	46 567	45 555	2.2	12 338	30 573	252	493	2 911	6 996	16 063	10 835	15.6
3210	Pleasant Plains CDP	2 577	NA	NA	2 524	3	0	36	14	63	1 037	NA	3.4
3215	Pleasantville	16 027	13 435	19.3	5 825	8 826	62	293	1 021	1 690	6 759	9 063	15.0
3230	Point Pleasant borough	18 177	17 747	2.4	17 977	70	20	53	57	265	8 006	12 241	9.2
3232	Point Pleasant Beach borough	5 112	NA	NA	4 975	65	11	41	20	65	3 235	14 037	3.7
3237	Pomona CDP	2 624	NA	NA	2 366	140	2	79	37	75	918	NA	7.2
3240	Pompton Lakes borough	10 539	10 660	-1.1	10 247	57	2	161	72	314	4 056	14 438	7.7
3243	Port Monmouth CDP	3 558	NA	NA	3 486	15	0	21	36	189	1 281	NA	3.4
3248	Port Reading CDP	3 977	NA	NA	3 867	14	1	78	17	152	1 358	NA	5.8
3253	Princeton borough	12 016	12 035	-0.2	9 915	1 022	28	850	201	616	3 514	15 094	4.8
3256	Princeton North CDP	4 386	NA	NA	3 663	432	3	192	96	204	1 804	NA	4.2
3265	Prospect Park borough	5 053	NA	NA	4 467	283	7	124	172	693	1 883	10 941	1.2
3275	Rahway	25 325	26 723	-5.2	19 092	5 119	38	606	470	1 912	9 989	12 657	10.3
3277	Ramblewood CDP	6 181	NA	NA	5 872	188	2	100	19	87	2 309	NA	8.8
3280	Ramsey borough	13 228	12 899	2.6	12 447	102	21	586	72	296	4 960	17 918	14.4
3300	Raritan borough	5 798	NA	NA	5 635	11	0	116	36	191	2 371	12 152	5.3
3310	Red Bank borough	10 636	12 031	-11.6	7 325	2 809	23	189	290	623	5 112	13 710	4.6
3315	Ridgefield borough	9 996	10 294	-2.9	9 265	76	4	569	82	681	4 106	14 270	6.8
3325	Ridgefield Park village	12 454	12 738	-2.2	11 380	253	15	528	278	1 191	5 126	14 399	4.5
3335	Ridgewood village	24 152	25 208	-4.2	21 821	480	16	1 747	88	684	8 666	24 001	15.0
3340	Ringwood borough	12 623	12 625	0.0	12 043	227	123	176	54	315	4 141	13 584	64.7
3345	Rio Grande CDP	2 505	NA	NA	2 368	101	3	22	11	39	1 252	NA	6.1
3355	River Edge borough	10 603	11 111	-4.6	9 575	65	14	893	56	372	4 161	16 944	4.9
3365	Riverside CDP	7 974	NA	NA	7 702	175	6	35	56	211	3 108	NA	3.9
3375	Riverton borough	2 775	NA	NA	2 706	49	1	12	7	13	1 084	15 061	1.7
3378	River Vale CDP	9 410	NA	NA	8 752	63	5	547	43	202	3 208	NA	10.6
3380	Robertsville CDP	9 841	NA	NA	9 162	171	4	475	29	148	2 995	NA	15.4
3381	Rochelle Park CDP	5 587	NA	NA	5 266	14	9	257	41	188	2 108	NA	2.7
3390	Rockaway borough	6 243	NA	NA	5 946	72	11	155	59	291	2 355	15 487	5.4

1. Codes shown are 2-digit FIPS codes for states; 4-digit census place codes for places; and 3-digit FIPS county codes followed by 3-digit census MCD codes for minor civil divisions (MCDs). MCD names are followed by county names in parentheses. 2. Hispanic persons may be of any race. 3. Dry land or land partially or temporarily covered by water.

State/ Place/ MCD[1] code	Place	Population			Population characteristics, 1990						Total housing units, 1990	Per capita income, 1985 (Dollars)	Land area,[3] 1990 (Sq. Km.)
		1990	Places of 10,000 or more		Race					Hispanic[2]			
			1980	Percent change, 1980–1990	White	Black	Am. Indian, Eskimo Aleut	Asian & Pacific Islander	Other race				
		1	2	3	4	5	6	7	8	9	10	11	12
	NEW JERSEY—Con.												
3420	Roseland borough	4 847	NA	NA	4 634	22	0	178	13	64	1 850	20 422	9.4
3425	Roselle borough	20 314	20 641	-1.6	11 461	7 726	39	534	554	2 323	7 899	11 816	6.8
3430	Roselle Park borough	12 805	13 377	-4.3	11 797	137	6	679	186	935	5 231	13 199	3.2
3435	Rossmoor CDP	3 231	NA	NA	3 199	15	3	12	2	39	2 416	NA	2.3
3440	Rumson borough	6 701	NA	NA	6 599	23	4	70	5	71	2 621	28 517	13.5
3445	Runnemede borough	9 042	NA	NA	8 671	248	12	82	29	127	3 524	10 114	5.4
3450	Rutherford borough	17 790	19 068	-6.7	15 903	536	11	1 147	193	1 029	7 220	14 983	7.3
3455	Saddle Brook CDP	13 296	14 084	-5.6	12 715	141	17	352	71	452	5 036	NA	7.0
3460	Saddle River borough	2 950	NA	NA	2 798	13	0	137	2	56	1 072	38 040	12.9
3465	Salem	6 883	NA	NA	3 226	3 489	24	18	126	251	2 894	8 828	6.8
3475	Sayreville borough	34 986	29 969	16.7	32 576	1 130	37	1 058	185	1 404	13 347	13 414	41.8
3480	Scotch Plains CDP	21 160	20 774	1.9	17 729	2 349	37	968	77	598	7 792	NA	23.5
3500	Sea Isle City	2 692	NA	NA	2 666	7	1	13	5	18	5 991	14 035	5.7
3515	Secaucus town	14 061	13 719	2.5	12 906	336	13	691	115	1 098	6 013	15 693	15.3
3517	Sewaren CDP	2 569	NA	NA	2 422	35	1	68	43	159	946	NA	2.5
3520	Shark River Hills CDP	4 228	NA	NA	4 182	5	3	35	3	36	1 561	NA	2.2
3540	Shrewsbury borough	3 096	NA	NA	2 978	40	3	53	22	45	1 125	17 022	5.7
3544	Silverton CDP	9 175	NA	NA	8 998	36	17	95	29	229	3 942	NA	6.0
3547	Society Hill CDP	3 577	NA	NA	2 104	398	5	1 035	35	125	1 278	NA	3.6
3550	Somerdale borough	5 440	NA	NA	4 499	774	16	106	45	144	2 150	10 657	3.5
3553	Somerset CDP	22 070	21 731	1.6	12 554	7 690	37	1 276	513	1 282	8 147	NA	13.8
3555	Somers Point	11 216	10 330	8.6	10 441	457	17	215	86	313	5 449	12 337	10.4
3560	Somerville borough	11 632	11 973	-2.8	9 433	1 390	17	446	346	941	4 853	14 685	6.1
3565	South Amboy	7 863	NA	NA	7 692	24	8	91	48	246	3 057	11 349	4.0
3580	South Bound Brook borough	4 185	NA	NA	3 615	364	8	72	126	305	1 677	12 180	2.0
3600	South Orange CDP	16 390	15 864	3.3	12 560	3 064	20	560	186	536	5 488	NA	7.4
3605	South Plainfield borough	20 489	20 521	-0.2	17 995	1 297	29	822	346	905	6 823	13 104	21.6
3610	South River borough	13 692	14 361	-4.7	12 839	540	23	157	133	1 031	5 269	12 300	7.3
3615	South Toms River borough	3 869	NA	NA	2 961	725	12	45	126	262	1 133	7 813	3.0
3625	Spotswood borough	7 983	NA	NA	7 636	64	11	215	57	254	2 995	12 739	6.0
3632	Springfield CDP	13 420	13 955	-3.8	12 625	463	6	286	40	277	5 990	NA	13.3
3640	Spring Lake borough	3 499	NA	NA	3 476	3	4	10	6	32	1 890	17 691	3.4
3645	Spring Lake Heights borough	5 341	NA	NA	5 250	53	2	25	11	68	2 987	16 781	3.4
3660	Stanhope borough	3 393	NA	NA	3 281	40	8	38	26	109	1 368	14 535	4.9
3690	Stratford borough	7 614	NA	NA	7 148	321	9	99	37	125	2 881	11 100	4.1
3695	Strathmore CDP	7 060	NA	NA	6 465	196	8	346	45	231	2 388	NA	4.8
3698	Succasunna-Kenvil CDP	11 781	10 931	7.8	11 080	161	8	495	37	270	3 734	NA	17.0
3700	Summit	19 757	21 071	-6.2	17 815	1 118	16	607	201	1 044	8 003	27 444	15.7
3730	Teaneck CDP	37 825	39 007	-3.0	25 194	9 895	60	2 127	549	2 373	13 334	NA	15.7
3735	Tenafly borough	13 326	13 552	-1.7	11 281	114	2	1 855	74	467	4 898	24 368	11.9
3744	Tinton Falls borough	12 361	NA	NA	9 431	2 141	29	634	126	429	4 646	14 264	40.4
3760	Toms River CDP	7 524	NA	NA	7 120	200	24	112	68	292	3 272	NA	6.8
3765	Totowa borough	10 177	11 448	-11.1	9 854	120	8	135	60	278	3 570	12 259	10.3
3770	Trenton	88 675	92 124	-3.7	37 392	43 689	223	585	6 786	12 530	33 578	8 699	19.8
3775	Tuckerton borough	3 048	NA	NA	2 917	79	15	15	22	66	1 914	NA	9.5
3776	Turnersville CDP	3 843	NA	NA	3 581	130	4	121	7	58	1 133	NA	3.9
3777	Twin Rivers CDP	7 715	NA	NA	6 746	441	9	354	165	463	2 900	NA	3.3
3787	Union CDP	50 024	50 184	-0.3	43 277	4 694	57	1 675	321	2 239	19 334	NA	23.6
3800	Union Beach borough	6 156	NA	NA	5 972	37	10	52	85	279	2 080	9 514	4.9
3802	Union City	58 012	55 593	4.4	43 323	2 965	137	1 215	10 372	43 869	22 592	7 992	3.3
3835	Upper Saddle River borough	7 198	NA	NA	6 775	68	2	325	28	169	2 410	27 321	13.7
3845	Ventnor City	11 005	11 704	-6.0	10 468	153	21	163	200	580	7 256	14 766	5.6
3855	Verona CDP	13 597	14 166	-4.0	12 920	239	14	375	49	274	5 713	NA	7.1
3865	Villas CDP	8 136	NA	NA	8 060	21	16	27	12	63	5 549	NA	10.3
3870	Vineland	54 780	53 753	1.9	39 995	6 287	179	481	7 838	12 926	19 548	9 551	177.9
3880	Waldwick borough	9 757	10 802	-9.7	9 219	53	2	449	34	334	3 391	15 742	5.4
3890	Wallington borough	10 828	10 741	0.8	10 117	293	18	284	116	475	4 873	12 210	2.6
3900	Wanamassa CDP	4 530	NA	NA	4 371	45	3	101	10	84	1 675	NA	2.9
3905	Wanaque borough	9 711	10 025	-3.1	9 246	139	42	226	58	290	3 259	11 427	20.7
3945	Washington borough	6 474	NA	NA	6 259	127	8	34	46	160	2 787	11 569	5.1
3950	Washington Township CDP	9 245	NA	NA	8 619	78	1	526	21	274	3 190	NA	7.5
3960	Watchung borough	5 110	NA	NA	4 779	46	6	265	14	81	1 794	26 839	15.6
3970	Wayne CDP	47 025	46 474	1.2	44 675	499	33	1 469	349	1 447	16 306	NA	61.7
3975	Weehawken CDP	12 385	13 168	-5.9	10 337	557	30	334	1 127	5 132	5 583	NA	2.2
4000	West Caldwell CDP	10 422	11 407	-8.6	9 974	53	12	362	21	180	3 584	NA	13.1
4015	Westfield town	28 870	30 447	-5.2	26 408	1 323	20	1 019	100	589	10 588	21 299	17.4
4017	West Freehold CDP	11 166	NA	NA	10 297	382	7	425	55	425	4 092	NA	15.3
4020	West Long Branch borough	7 690	NA	NA	7 338	152	4	135	61	179	2 528	14 331	7.5
4025	West Milford CDP	25 430	NA	NA	24 717	262	102	231	118	542	9 411	NA	195.4
4030	West New York town	38 125	39 194	-2.7	29 249	1 524	143	743	6 466	27 930	15 794	8 804	2.6
4035	West Orange CDP	39 103	39 510	-1.0	34 269	2 240	57	2 183	354	1 728	15 256	NA	31.4
4040	West Paterson borough	10 982	11 293	-2.8	10 423	156	8	257	138	464	4 449	13 167	7.7
4045	Westville borough	4 573	NA	NA	4 457	52	5	39	20	51	1 907	10 396	2.5

1. Codes shown are 2-digit FIPS codes for states; 4-digit census place codes for places; and 3-digit FIPS county codes followed by 3-digit census MCD codes for minor civil divisions (MCDs). MCD names are followed by county names in parentheses. 2. Hispanic persons may be of any race. 3. Dry land or land partially or temporarily covered by water.

State/ Place/ MCD[1] code	Place	Population: 1990	Population: Places of 10,000 or more: 1980	Population: Places of 10,000 or more: Percent change, 1980–1990	Population characteristics, 1990: Race: White	Race: Black	Race: Am. Indian, Eskimo Aleut	Race: Asian & Pacific Islander	Race: Other race	Hispanic[2]	Total housing units, 1990	Per capita income, 1985 (Dollars)	Land area,[3] 1990 (Sq. Km.)
		1	2	3	4	5	6	7	8	9	10	11	12
	NEW JERSEY—Con.												
4060	Westwood borough	10 446	10 714	-2.5	9 333	688	15	367	43	323	4 260	15 529	6.0
4070	Wharton borough	5 405	NA	NA	4 975	141	5	171	113	636	2 122	14 194	5.7
4074	White Horse CDP	9 397	10 098	-6.9	8 872	343	3	109	70	193	3 594	NA	8.3
4077	White Meadow Lake CDP	8 002	NA	NA	7 595	91	5	286	25	241	2 769	NA	10.6
4080	Wildwood	4 484	NA	NA	3 466	854	18	17	129	318	6 269	8 013	3.4
4085	Wildwood Crest borough	3 631	NA	NA	3 579	14	1	10	27	64	4 772	11 756	3.0
4090	Williamstown CDP	10 891	NA	NA	9 386	1 285	19	77	124	268	3 938	NA	16.0
4097	Willingboro CDP	36 291	39 912	-9.1	14 401	20 350	119	696	725	1 922	11 236	NA	20.0
4105	Woodbine borough	2 678	NA	NA	1 501	804	8	18	347	441	945	5 858	20.7
4110	Woodbridge CDP	17 434	90 074	-80.6	15 086	1 029	15	985	319	1 033	7 305	NA	10.0
4115	Woodbury	10 904	10 353	5.3	8 542	2 195	21	74	72	184	4 335	11 800	5.4
4120	Woodbury Heights borough	3 392	NA	NA	3 298	59	8	26	1	19	1 130	11 618	3.2
4125	Woodcliff Lake borough	5 303	NA	NA	4 987	48	3	260	5	73	1 703	24 844	8.6
4135	Woodlynne borough	2 547	NA	NA	2 268	129	4	72	74	172	939	8 963	0.6
4140	Wood-Ridge borough	7 506	NA	NA	7 196	56	2	197	55	295	2 982	15 463	2.8
4145	Woodstown borough	3 154	NA	NA	2 747	375	3	22	7	18	1 347	12 433	4.1
4155	Wrightstown borough	3 843	NA	NA	1 976	1 452	28	146	241	435	1 339	6 008	4.5
4175	Wyckoff CDP	15 372	15 500	-0.8	14 811	79	7	451	24	249	5 248	NA	17.0
4180	Yardville-Groveville CDP	9 248	NA	NA	8 881	151	4	176	36	171	3 407	NA	8.9
4190	Yorketown CDP	6 313	NA	NA	5 928	175	1	175	34	188	1 801	NA	6.2
0010	Buena Vista township (Atlantic)	7 655	NA	NA	6 068	1 236	20	15	316	649	2 727	8 932	107.3
0010	Egg Harbor township (Atlantic)	24 544	19 381	26.6	21 324	2 292	45	604	279	747	10 018	11 699	174.3
0010	Galloway township (Atlantic)	23 330	12 100	92.8	20 665	1 717	29	624	295	861	8 869	10 969	234.1
0010	Hamilton township (Atlantic)	16 012	NA	NA	12 966	2 365	62	321	298	759	6 343	12 009	288.2
0010	Mullica township (Atlantic)	5 896	NA	NA	5 010	541	11	58	276	735	2 081	10 675	146.6
0031	Lyndhurst township (Bergen)	18 262	20 326	-10.2	17 546	79	12	483	142	854	7 741	12 793	12.0
0031	Mahwah township (Bergen)	17 905	12 127	47.6	16 227	641	240	689	108	531	7 249	19 423	67.2
0032	River Vale township (Bergen)	9 410	NA	NA	8 752	63	5	547	43	202	3 208	19 846	10.6
0032	Rochelle Park township (Bergen)	5 587	NA	NA	5 266	14	9	257	41	188	2 108	14 286	2.7
0032	Saddle Brook township (Bergen)	13 296	14 084	-5.6	12 715	141	17	352	71	452	5 036	14 149	7.1
0033	Teaneck township (Bergen)	37 825	39 007	-3.0	25 194	9 895	60	2 127	549	2 373	13 334	16 607	15.7
0033	Washington township (Bergen)	9 245	NA	NA	8 619	78	1	526	21	274	3 190	17 807	7.5
0033	Wyckoff township (Bergen)	15 372	15 500	-0.8	14 811	79	7	451	24	249	5 248	21 036	17.0
0050	Bordentown township (Burlington)	7 683	NA	NA	6 998	444	11	154	76	237	2 991	12 820	22.0
0050	Burlington township (Burlington)	12 454	11 527	8.0	9 259	2 628	38	333	196	456	4 666	11 316	34.9
0050	Chesterfield township (Burlington)	5 152	NA	NA	3 431	1 624	21	7	69	409	973	10 501	56.0
0050	Cinnaminson township (Burlington)	14 583	16 072	-9.3	13 468	772	19	260	64	204	4 877	14 631	19.7
0050	Delanco township (Burlington)	3 316	NA	NA	3 267	22	2	16	9	37	1 236	10 690	6.4
0050	Delran township (Burlington)	13 178	14 803	-11.0	11 888	915	34	296	45	157	4 656	12 365	17.2
0050	Eastampton township (Burlington)	4 962	NA	NA	4 297	440	6	173	46	195	1 988	13 579	14.8
0050	Edgewater Park township (Burlington	8 388	NA	NA	6 746	1 449	26	112	55	218	3 224	12 512	7.5
0050	Evesham township (Burlington)	35 309	21 543	63.9	33 033	1 004	33	1 122	117	476	13 268	14 218	76.5
0050	Florence township (Burlington)	10 266	NA	NA	9 414	721	17	74	40	171	3 937	11 420	25.2
0050	Hainesport township (Burlington)	3 249	NA	NA	3 166	56	4	15	8	31	1 209	10 635	16.9
0050	Lumberton township (Burlington)	6 705	NA	NA	5 876	597	9	171	52	262	2 844	12 180	33.3
0050	Mansfield township (Burlington)	3 874	NA	NA	3 794	42	3	32	3	50	1 609	13 612	56.3
0051	Maple Shade township (Burlington)	19 211	20 525	-6.4	17 555	1 077	36	416	127	431	9 073	12 134	10.0
0051	Medford township (Burlington)	20 526	17 622	16.5	20 138	87	22	235	44	200	7 116	16 038	101.8
0051	Moorestown township (Burlington)	16 116	15 604	3.3	14 735	924	28	390	39	171	6 046	19 921	38.3
0051	Mount Holly township (Burlington)	10 639	10 818	-1.7	8 135	1 992	66	131	315	609	3 823	11 245	7.5
0051	Mount Laurel township (Burlington)	30 270	17 614	71.9	27 492	1 806	42	797	133	498	12 613	15 118	56.5
0051	New Hanover township (Burlington)	9 546	14 266	-33.1	5 857	2 914	76	230	469	985	856	8 279	57.7
0051	North Hanover township (Burlington)	9 994	NA	NA	7 902	1 556	43	290	203	495	3 302	7 992	44.4
0051	Pemberton township (Burlington)	31 342	29 720	5.5	21 560	7 153	145	1 364	1 120	2 524	10 525	8 730	160.0
0051	Riverside township (Burlington)	7 974	NA	NA	7 702	175	6	35	56	211	3 108	10 276	3.9
0051	Shamong township (Burlington)	5 765	NA	NA	5 619	105	1	25	15	58	1 841	11 657	116.1
0051	Southampton township (Burlington)	10 202	NA	NA	10 028	63	16	78	17	83	4 551	12 529	114.2
0051	Springfield township (Burlington)	3 028	NA	NA	2 816	132	13	52	15	72	1 066	11 432	77.8
0051	Tabernacle township (Burlington)	7 360	NA	NA	7 172	107	4	65	12	49	2 311	11 355	128.1
0051	Westampton township (Burlington)	6 004	NA	NA	4 896	853	14	157	84	319	2 158	13 405	28.6
0051	Willingboro township (Burlington)	36 291	39 912	-9.1	14 401	20 350	119	696	725	1 922	11 236	11 520	20.0
0070	Berlin township (Camden)	5 466	NA	NA	4 617	728	4	99	18	97	1 838	9 963	8.4
0070	Cherry Hill township (Camden)	69 348	68 785	0.8	62 265	2 243	65	4 261	514	1 380	25 786	16 890	62.8
0070	Gloucester township (Camden)	53 797	45 156	19.1	49 071	3 304	86	1 094	242	790	19 893	11 402	60.2
0070	Haddon township (Camden)	14 837	15 875	-6.5	14 524	122	7	149	35	145	6 389	13 462	7.0
0071	Pennsauken township (Camden)	34 738	33 775	2.9	27 965	5 103	128	622	920	1 693	12 715	11 174	27.3
0071	Voorhees township (Camden)	24 559	12 919	90.1	20 906	1 588	21	1 919	125	474	9 905	15 897	30.0
0071	Waterford township (Camden)	10 940	NA	NA	10 279	484	14	111	52	165	3 564	9 783	93.7
0071	Winslow township (Camden)	30 087	20 034	50.2	22 431	6 905	98	341	312	924	10 493	9 869	149.4
0090	Dennis township (Cape May)	5 574	NA	NA	5 495	22	15	31	11	41	1 960	9 974	158.9
0090	Lower township (Cape May)	20 820	17 105	21.7	20 384	219	42	128	47	242	12 740	9 369	73.1
0090	Middle township (Cape May)	14 771	11 373	29.9	12 545	1 933	50	161	82	222	6 970	9 788	184.6
0090	Upper township (Cape May)	10 681	NA	NA	10 502	59	9	80	31	109	5 285	11 486	163.6

1. Codes shown are 2-digit FIPS codes for states; 4-digit census place codes for places; and 3-digit FIPS county codes followed by 3-digit census MCD codes for minor civil divisions (MCDs). MCD names are followed by county names in parentheses. 2. Hispanic persons may be of any race. 3. Dry land or land partially or temporarily covered by water.

State/ Place/ MCD[1] code	Place	Population: 1990	Population: Places of 10,000 or more: 1980	Population: Places of 10,000 or more: Percent change, 1980–1990	Population characteristics, 1990: Race: White	Race: Black	Race: Am. Indian, Eskimo Aleut	Race: Asian & Pacific Islander	Race: Other race	Hispanic[2]	Total housing units, 1990	Per capita income, 1985 (Dollars)	Land area,[3] 1990 (Sq. Km.)
		1	2	3	4	5	6	7	8	9	10	11	12
	NEW JERSEY—Con.												
0110	Commercial township (Cumberland)	5 026	NA	NA	3 962	965	23	10	66	118	2 028	7 892	84.1
0110	Deerfield township (Cumberland)	2 933	NA	NA	2 350	464	56	13	50	114	1 029	9 162	43.6
0110	Fairfield township (Cumberland)	5 699	NA	NA	2 290	2 800	392	27	190	271	1 993	7 581	109.6
0110	Hopewell township (Cumberland)	4 215	NA	NA	3 673	338	95	20	89	128	1 473	10 080	77.4
0110	Maurice River township (Cumberland)	6 648	NA	NA	4 398	1 922	50	6	272	660	1 412	7 215	241.9
0110	Upper Deerfield twnshp (Cumberland)	6 927	NA	NA	5 804	749	60	260	54	173	2 559	10 039	80.6
0130	Belleville township (Essex)	34 213	NA	NA	29 447	1 254	85	2 055	1 372	3 441	14 058	11 927	8.7
0130	Bloomfield township (Essex)	45 061	NA	NA	40 130	1 937	52	2 251	691	2 311	19 293	13 175	13.8
0130	Caldwell Borough township (Essex)	7 549	NA	NA	7 166	122	6	222	33	210	3 362	16 074	3.1
0130	Cedar Grove township (Essex)	12 053	12 600	-4.3	11 100	270	2	610	71	305	4 222	15 133	10.9
0130	City of Orange township (Essex)	29 925	NA	NA	7 169	21 045	119	385	1 207	3 237	12 318	10 499	5.7
0130	Fairfield township (Essex)	7 615	NA	NA	7 345	16	7	232	15	210	2 351	14 983	27.1
0130	Glen Ridge Borough township (Essex)	7 076	NA	NA	6 576	226	6	231	37	166	2 470	18 794	3.3
0130	Irvington township (Essex)	61 018	NA	NA	13 687	42 760	147	1 325	3 099	6 455	24 318	10 281	7.6
0130	Livingston township (Essex)	26 609	28 040	-5.1	23 749	288	15	2 479	78	496	8 910	22 118	36.0
0130	Maplewood township (Essex)	21 652	22 950	-5.7	18 177	2 578	22	655	220	780	8 132	17 014	10.0
0130	Millburn township (Essex)	18 630	19 543	-4.7	17 436	224	4	921	45	312	7 108	33 418	24.3
0130	Montclair township (Essex)	37 729	NA	NA	24 713	11 697	93	856	370	1 249	15 069	17 814	16.3
0130	North Caldwell township (Essex)	6 706	NA	NA	5 690	682	2	276	56	167	1 996	20 064	7.8
0130	Nutley township (Essex)	27 099	NA	NA	25 130	478	11	1 275	205	887	11 001	14 152	8.7
0130	South Orange Village twnshp (Essex)	16 390	15 864	3.3	12 560	3 064	20	560	186	536	5 488	22 660	7.4
0131	Verona township (Essex)	13 597	NA	NA	12 920	239	14	375	49	274	5 713	19 953	7.1
0131	West Caldwell township (Essex)	10 422	NA	NA	9 974	53	12	362	21	180	3 584	17 761	13.1
0131	West Orange township (Essex)	39 103	NA	NA	34 269	2 240	57	2 183	354	1 728	15 256	16 768	31.4
0150	Deptford township (Gloucester)	24 137	23 473	2.8	21 220	2 456	57	267	137	469	8 872	10 751	45.3
0150	East Greenwich township (Gloucester)	5 258	NA	NA	5 016	211	8	13	10	40	1 750	11 558	38.2
0150	Elk township (Gloucester)	3 806	NA	NA	3 031	726	15	3	31	75	1 380	9 631	50.8
0150	Franklin township (Gloucester)	14 482	12 396	16.8	13 138	1 090	39	59	156	400	4 878	9 465	145.1
0150	Greenwich township (Gloucester)	5 102	NA	NA	4 903	162	7	30	0	40	1 865	11 753	24.1
0150	Harrison township (Gloucester)	4 715	NA	NA	4 519	147	11	24	14	82	1 726	12 043	49.6
0150	Logan township (Gloucester)	5 147	NA	NA	4 394	627	4	78	44	130	1 725	11 828	59.0
0150	Mantua township (Gloucester)	10 074	NA	NA	9 852	131	13	57	21	111	3 619	10 972	41.2
0150	Monroe township (Gloucester)	26 703	21 639	23.4	22 874	3 325	62	256	186	556	9 622	9 876	120.6
0150	Washington township (Gloucester)	41 960	27 878	50.5	38 828	1 555	44	1 371	162	600	13 807	11 874	55.4
0151	West Deptford township (Gloucester)	19 380	18 002	7.7	18 386	748	24	178	44	248	7 638	12 471	41.2
0170	North Bergen township (Hudson)	48 414	47 019	3.0	40 751	1 014	100	2 308	4 241	19 937	21 274	11 220	13.4
0170	Weehawken township (Hudson)	12 385	13 168	-5.9	10 337	557	30	334	1 127	5 132	5 583	11 824	2.2
0190	Alexandria township (Hunterdon)	3 594	NA	NA	3 548	20	3	21	2	38	1 275	14 453	71.4
0190	Bethlehem township (Hunterdon)	3 104	NA	NA	3 073	17	1	7	6	42	1 081	13 774	54.0
0190	Clinton township (Hunterdon)	10 816	NA	NA	9 726	870	10	186	24	255	3 514	16 035	78.2
0190	Delaware township (Hunterdon)	4 512	NA	NA	4 451	26	3	30	2	52	1 636	15 374	94.6
0190	East Amwell township (Hunterdon)	4 332	NA	NA	4 247	36	9	35	5	23	1 542	14 297	74.2
0190	Franklin township (Hunterdon)	2 851	NA	NA	2 808	13	2	22	6	38	1 058	NA	59.2
0190	Holland township (Hunterdon)	4 892	NA	NA	4 856	7	3	15	11	56	1 824	13 392	61.4
0190	Kingwood township (Hunterdon)	3 325	NA	NA	3 277	22	3	15	8	49	1 227	13 710	91.7
0190	Lebanon township (Hunterdon)	5 679	NA	NA	5 598	30	6	37	8	37	2 043	14 464	82.0
0191	Raritan township (Hunterdon)	15 616	NA	NA	15 028	123	18	390	57	296	5 877	16 551	98.1
0191	Readington township (Hunterdon)	13 400	10 855	23.4	13 057	63	13	233	34	214	4 789	15 977	123.3
0191	Tewksbury township (Hunterdon)	4 803	NA	NA	4 720	33	3	45	2	56	1 752	32 651	82.0
0191	Union township (Hunterdon)	5 078	NA	NA	4 347	610	4	54	63	254	1 464	17 522	49.2
0210	East Windsor township (Mercer)	22 353	21 041	6.2	19 307	1 439	44	1 193	370	1 214	9 069	14 650	40.5
0210	Ewing township (Mercer)	34 185	34 842	-1.9	26 908	6 243	41	612	381	918	12 518	13 808	39.7
0210	Hamilton township (Mercer)	86 553	82 801	4.5	79 594	4 413	85	1 843	618	2 006	33 457	12 557	102.2
0210	Hopewell township (Mercer)	11 590	10 893	6.4	10 871	485	5	161	68	168	4 071	19 120	150.6
0210	Lawrence township (Mercer)	25 787	19 724	30.7	22 326	2 073	40	1 165	183	666	9 640	15 780	57.4
0210	Princeton township (Mercer)	13 198	13 683	-3.5	11 095	908	16	975	204	525	5 554	24 228	42.5
0210	Washington township (Mercer)	5 815	NA	NA	5 543	134	12	88	38	107	2 537	15 102	53.0
0210	West Windsor township (Mercer)	16 021	NA	NA	13 121	414	15	2 358	113	426	5 829	18 284	67.4
0230	Cranbury township (Middlesex)	2 500	NA	NA	2 296	102	3	92	7	44	922	NA	34.8
0230	East Brunswick township (Middlesex)	43 548	37 711	15.5	38 382	969	52	3 945	200	1 246	15 395	16 137	57.0
0230	Edison township (Middlesex)	88 680	70 193	26.3	70 492	4 935	106	12 166	981	3 839	32 832	15 482	78.2
0230	Monroe township (Middlesex)	22 255	15 858	40.3	21 122	700	12	384	37	411	10 303	15 998	109.4
0230	North Brunswick township (Middlesex.	31 287	22 220	40.8	25 044	3 465	75	2 132	571	1 817	12 186	15 666	31.2
0230	Old Bridge township (Middlesex)	56 475	51 515	9.6	50 511	1 894	61	3 466	543	2 829	21 116	13 583	98.5
0230	Piscataway township (Middlesex)	47 089	42 223	11.5	31 055	8 296	94	6 546	1 098	2 780	14 575	12 668	48.7
0230	Plainsboro township (Middlesex)	14 213	NA	NA	11 116	1 522	13	1 404	158	552	7 752	20 701	31.1
0231	South Brunswick township (Middlesex)	25 792	17 127	50.6	21 679	1 595	26	2 282	210	953	9 962	14 754	106.1
0231	Woodbridge township (Middlesex)	93 086	90 074	3.3	80 618	6 018	107	5 090	1 253	5 180	34 498	13 677	59.7
0250	Aberdeen township (Monmouth)	17 038	17 235	-1.1	14 244	1 943	36	580	235	850	6 170	13 756	14.4
0250	Colts Neck township (Monmouth)	8 559	NA	NA	8 008	310	10	195	36	219	2 921	21 279	81.5
0250	Freehold township (Monmouth)	24 710	19 208	28.6	22 354	1 162	17	1 047	130	856	8 673	14 722	99.8
0250	Hazlet township (Monmouth)	21 976	23 013	-4.5	20 898	188	12	750	128	822	7 298	12 416	14.6
0250	Holmdel township (Monmouth)	11 532	NA	NA	10 170	56	5	1 288	13	232	3 477	23 503	46.4

1. Codes shown are 2-digit FIPS codes for states; 4-digit census place codes for places; and 3-digit FIPS county codes followed by 3-digit census MCD codes for minor civil divisions (MCDs). MCD names are followed by county names in parentheses. 2. Hispanic persons may be of any race. 3. Dry land or land partially or temporarily covered by water.

State/ Place/ MCD[1] code	Place	Population 1990	Places of 10,000 or more 1980	Percent change, 1980–1990	Race: White	Black	Am. Indian, Eskimo Aleut	Asian & Pacific Islander	Other race	Hispanic[2]	Total housing units, 1990	Per capita income, 1985 (Dollars)	Land area,[3] 1990 (Sq. Km.)
		1	2	3	4	5	6	7	8	9	10	11	12
	NEW JERSEY—Con.												
0250	Howell township (Monmouth)	38 987	25 065	55.5	36 036	1 195	36	1 352	368	1 678	13 563	12 089	157.8
0251	Manalapan township (Monmouth)	26 716	18 914	41.2	24 802	819	14	956	125	730	9 029	14 947	79.3
0251	Marlboro township (Monmouth)	27 974	17 554	59.4	25 206	1 013	28	1 634	93	593	8 493	15 838	79.2
0251	Middletown township (Monmouth)	68 183	62 542	9.0	64 744	1 293	52	1 816	278	1 850	23 495	15 822	106.5
0251	Millstone township (Monmouth)	5 069	NA	NA	4 714	252	7	63	33	164	1 709	12 073	95.2
0251	Neptune township (Monmouth)	28 148	28 366	-0.8	17 719	9 514	88	351	476	1 173	11 786	11 458	21.2
0251	Ocean township (Monmouth)	25 058	23 570	6.3	22 641	1 314	23	933	147	667	10 011	15 572	28.6
0252	Upper Freehold township (Monmouth)	3 277	NA	NA	3 172	53	4	22	26	112	1 144	13 466	121.4
0252	Wall township (Monmouth)	20 244	18 952	6.8	19 914	116	9	172	33	212	7 896	13 970	79.3
0270	Boonton township (Morris)	3 566	NA	NA	3 420	57	1	80	8	39	1 299	20 327	22.2
0270	Chatham township (Morris)	9 361	NA	NA	8 978	42	2	318	21	179	3 729	26 463	24.2
0270	Chester township (Morris)	5 958	NA	NA	5 755	62	6	125	10	76	1 997	17 865	75.9
0270	Denville township (Morris)	13 812	14 380	-3.9	13 210	91	22	457	32	263	5 059	16 464	31.3
0270	East Hanover township (Morris)	9 926	NA	NA	9 112	85	3	703	23	228	3 112	15 049	21.2
0270	Hanover township (Morris)	11 538	11 846	-2.6	10 688	120	4	716	10	266	3 882	16 779	27.6
0270	Harding township (Morris)	3 640	NA	NA	3 583	22	2	20	13	81	1 464	46 807	52.9
0270	Jefferson township (Morris)	17 825	16 413	8.6	17 472	136	28	145	44	398	7 115	13 226	105.5
0270	Mendham township (Morris)	4 537	NA	NA	4 431	26	1	69	10	76	1 712	26 015	46.3
0271	Mine Hill township (Morris)	3 333	NA	NA	3 049	83	7	92	102	206	1 273	14 208	7.8
0271	Montville township (Morris)	15 600	14 290	9.2	14 105	172	8	1 264	51	302	5 126	18 342	48.8
0271	Morris township (Morris)	19 952	18 486	7.9	18 026	1 173	21	618	114	405	7 388	22 229	40.9
0271	Mount Olive township (Morris)	21 282	18 748	13.5	19 990	603	36	499	154	710	8 529	14 152	78.9
0271	Parsippany-Troy Hills tshp (Morris)	48 478	49 868	-2.8	41 252	1 743	62	4 917	504	2 014	18 960	15 562	61.9
0271	Passaic township (Morris)	7 826	NA	NA	7 470	43	3	292	18	204	2 804	18 626	31.3
0271	Pequannock township (Morris)	12 844	13 776	-6.8	12 569	34	4	209	28	261	4 385	15 292	18.2
0271	Randolph township (Morris)	19 974	17 828	12.0	18 152	595	12	1 064	151	651	7 240	18 142	54.3
0271	Rockaway township (Morris)	19 572	19 850	-1.4	18 387	324	28	715	118	642	7 477	15 772	109.2
0271	Roxbury township (Morris)	20 429	18 878	8.2	19 316	273	18	728	94	514	6 799	14 353	55.3
0271	Washington township (Morris)	15 592	11 402	36.7	15 062	188	13	289	40	230	5 125	15 743	116.1
0290	Barnegat township (Ocean)	12 235	NA	NA	11 854	195	13	108	65	308	4 902	9 380	87.1
0290	Berkeley township (Ocean)	37 319	23 151	61.2	36 742	388	36	88	65	561	19 873	10 507	111.1
0290	Brick township (Ocean)	66 473	53 629	23.9	65 015	419	87	551	401	1 715	28 843	11 841	68.1
0290	Dover township (Ocean)	76 371	64 455	18.5	74 154	646	101	1 138	332	1 944	35 653	11 913	106.5
0290	Jackson township (Ocean)	33 233	25 662	29.5	31 389	1 042	53	502	247	1 446	11 833	11 225	259.2
0290	Lacey township (Ocean)	22 141	14 256	55.3	21 892	68	42	93	46	358	9 513	10 780	217.6
0290	Lakewood township (Ocean)	45 048	38 464	17.1	35 937	6 356	71	641	2 043	4 650	17 888	10 716	64.3
0290	Little Egg Harbor township (Ocean)	13 333	NA	NA	13 094	91	17	69	62	303	7 194	10 491	127.2
0290	Long Beach township (Ocean)	3 407	NA	NA	3 379	3	2	9	14	41	8 836	16 219	13.8
0290	Manchester township (Ocean)	35 976	27 987	28.5	34 460	1 176	39	172	129	708	20 790	12 017	214.0
0291	Ocean township (Ocean)	5 416	NA	NA	5 362	21	9	10	14	93	2 828	11 519	53.9
0291	Plumsted township (Ocean)	6 005	NA	NA	5 739	172	19	27	48	170	2 200	9 980	103.7
0291	Stafford township (Ocean)	13 325	10 298	29.4	13 156	33	17	91	28	167	8 298	11 050	123.2
0310	Little Falls township (Passaic)	11 294	11 496	-1.8	10 759	194	5	217	119	411	4 460	14 927	7.1
0310	Wayne township (Passaic)	47 025	46 474	1.2	44 675	499	33	1 469	349	1 447	16 306	16 142	61.7
0310	West Milford township (Passaic)	25 430	22 750	11.8	24 717	262	102	231	118	542	9 411	12 719	195.4
0330	Alloway township (Salem)	2 795	NA	NA	2 541	198	21	18	17	32	1 005	9 881	85.1
0330	Carneys Point township (Salem)	8 443	NA	NA	6 984	1 280	19	82	78	182	3 328	10 902	45.3
0330	Pennsville township (Salem)	13 794	13 804	-0.1	13 564	69	15	117	29	106	5 503	11 858	59.8
0330	Pilesgrove township (Salem)	3 250	NA	NA	2 860	338	5	14	33	107	1 187	12 479	90.4
0330	Pittsgrove township (Salem)	8 121	NA	NA	7 319	640	57	58	47	140	2 788	9 456	117.7
0330	Quinton township (Salem)	2 511	NA	NA	1 981	473	12	7	38	52	997	10 001	62.6
0330	Upper Pittsgrove township (Salem)	3 140	NA	NA	2 968	111	18	16	27	45	1 129	9 560	104.0
0350	Bedminster township (Somerset)	7 086	NA	NA	6 753	119	7	185	22	149	3 757	NA	68.6
0350	Bernards township (Somerset)	17 199	12 920	33.1	16 334	295	8	525	37	331	6 658	21 136	62.1
0350	Branchburg township (Somerset)	10 888	NA	NA	10 275	147	19	434	13	171	3 944	17 376	52.5
0350	Bridgewater township (Somerset)	32 509	29 175	11.4	30 112	521	31	1 649	196	824	11 757	17 880	84.0
0350	Franklin township (Somerset)	42 780	31 296	36.7	29 885	9 135	66	3 026	668	1 913	17 080	15 114	121.2
0350	Green Brook township (Somerset)	4 460	NA	NA	4 251	41	7	139	22	120	1 458	15 177	11.9
0350	Hillsborough township (Somerset)	28 808	19 052	51.2	26 327	938	26	1 334	183	770	10 420	16 360	141.6
0350	Montgomery township (Somerset)	9 612	NA	NA	8 749	384	9	412	58	194	3 223	18 281	84.5
0351	Warren township (Somerset)	10 830	NA	NA	9 842	128	2	827	31	240	3 688	21 051	51.0
0370	Andover township (Sussex)	5 438	NA	NA	5 284	63	6	76	9	76	1 811	12 959	52.1
0370	Byram township (Sussex)	8 048	NA	NA	7 829	65	16	106	32	195	2 973	13 587	54.0
0370	Frankford township (Sussex)	5 114	NA	NA	5 067	16	6	15	10	69	2 204	12 099	88.4
0370	Fredon township (Sussex)	2 763	NA	NA	2 734	0	0	28	1	29	957	NA	45.7
0370	Green township (Sussex)	2 709	NA	NA	2 664	26	0	18	1	41	905	NA	41.8
0370	Hampton township (Sussex)	4 438	NA	NA	4 362	31	2	38	5	62	1 922	11 981	63.8
0370	Hardyston township (Sussex)	5 275	NA	NA	5 194	17	6	50	8	76	2 244	13 226	83.3
0370	Montague township (Sussex)	2 832	NA	NA	2 725	67	9	22	9	58	1 449	NA	114.0
0370	Sparta township (Sussex)	15 157	13 286	14.1	14 879	58	17	172	31	275	5 692	17 243	96.9
0371	Stillwater township (Sussex)	4 253	NA	NA	4 201	16	17	16	3	44	1 805	11 564	70.6
0371	Vernon township (Sussex)	21 211	16 302	30.1	20 932	79	27	125	48	463	8 570	12 111	177.0
0371	Wantage township (Sussex)	9 487	NA	NA	9 114	287	21	37	28	228	3 207	10 826	173.9

1. Codes shown are 2-digit FIPS codes for states; 4-digit census place codes for places; and 3-digit FIPS county codes followed by 3-digit census MCD codes for minor civil divisions (MCDs). MCD names are followed by county names in parentheses. 2. Hispanic persons may be of any race. 3. Dry land or land partially or temporarily covered by water.

State/ Place/ MCD[1] code	Place	Population			Population characteristics, 1990						Total housing units, 1990	Per capita income, 1985 (Dollars)	Land area,[3] 1990 (Sq. Km.)
			Places of 10,000 or more		Race								
		1990	1980	Percent change, 1980–1990	White	Black	Am. Indian, Eskimo Aleut	Asian & Pacific Islander	Other race	Hispanic[2]			
		1	2	3	4	5	6	7	8	9	10	11	12
	NEW JERSEY—Con.												
0390	Berkeley Heights township (Union)	11 980	12 549	-4.5	10 995	164	2	779	40	225	3 924	20 453	16.2
0390	Clark township (Union)	14 629	16 699	-12.4	14 316	15	6	240	52	428	5 638	15 540	11.3
0390	Cranford township (Union)	22 633	24 573	-7.9	21 558	689	7	331	48	543	8 407	16 254	12.5
0390	Hillside township (Union)	21 044	21 440	-1.8	11 157	8 578	30	812	467	2 807	7 364	12 025	7.0
0390	Scotch Plains township (Union)	21 160	20 774	1.9	17 729	2 349	37	968	77	598	7 792	18 823	23.5
0390	Springfield township (Union)	13 420	13 955	-3.8	12 625	463	6	286	40	277	5 990	19 387	13.3
0390	Union township (Union)	50 024	50 184	-0.3	43 277	4 694	57	1 675	321	2 239	19 334	13 838	23.6
0410	Allamuchy township (Warren)	3 484	NA	NA	3 417	19	4	30	14	75	1 623	21 090	53.2
0410	Blairstown township (Warren)	5 331	NA	NA	5 257	21	10	21	22	85	1 885	14 318	80.4
0410	Harmony township (Warren)	2 653	NA	NA	2 610	13	8	15	7	16	1 016	11 759	61.7
0410	Independence township (Warren)	3 940	NA	NA	3 833	32	5	66	4	74	1 575	12 821	51.4
0410	Knowlton township (Warren)	2 543	NA	NA	2 512	16	8	5	2	41	989	NA	64.2
0410	Lopatcong township (Warren)	5 052	NA	NA	4 943	51	1	51	6	57	2 005	12 925	18.3
0410	Mansfield township (Warren)	7 154	NA	NA	6 641	384	13	58	58	199	2 991	12 540	77.5
0411	Pohatcong township (Warren)	3 591	NA	NA	3 556	12	2	9	12	37	1 378	10 874	34.5
0411	Washington township (Warren)	5 367	NA	NA	5 245	60	3	45	14	80	1 953	13 404	45.5
0411	White township (Warren)	3 603	NA	NA	3 504	67	5	12	15	82	1 405	11 413	70.9
35	NEW MEXICO	1 515 069	1 303 303	16.2	1 146 028	30 210	134 355	14 124	190 352	579 224	632 058	8 814	314 334.1
0008	Agua Fria CDP	3 717	NA	NA	3 016	29	63	8	601	2 599	1 400	NA	6.0
0010	Alamogordo	27 596	24 024	14.9	22 834	1 668	231	520	2 343	6 899	11 974	8 923	44.3
0015	Albuquerque	384 736	331 767	16.0	301 010	11 484	11 708	6 660	53 874	132 706	166 870	11 133	342.4
0018	Anthony CDP	5 160	NA	NA	5 133	2	5	4	16	5 061	1 381	NA	2.7
0020	Artesia	10 610	10 385	2.2	8 405	155	49	24	1 977	4 128	4 510	8 559	21.3
0025	Aztec	5 479	NA	NA	4 630	11	455	16	367	1 094	2 158	7 735	10.3
0030	Bayard	2 598	NA	NA	2 244	0	15	5	334	2 234	1 028	5 737	2.2
0035	Belen	6 547	NA	NA	4 453	44	91	14	1 945	4 410	2 622	8 313	10.8
0040	Bernalillo town	5 960	NA	NA	5 116	34	124	15	671	4 447	2 179	5 976	14.3
0045	Bloomfield	5 214	NA	NA	3 828	11	696	13	666	1 414	1 846	7 442	11.6
0048	Bosque Farms village	3 791	NA	NA	3 336	18	51	17	369	966	1 384	10 895	10.1
0049	Cannon AFB CDP	3 312	NA	NA	2 663	413	35	160	41	303	759	NA	13.7
0055	Carlsbad	24 952	25 457	-2.0	20 271	643	122	163	3 753	8 331	10 575	8 606	70.6
0068	Chaparral CDP	2 962	NA	NA	2 826	46	9	13	68	1 498	1 020	NA	14.1
0069	Chimayo CDP	2 789	NA	NA	2 220	2	27	1	539	2 585	1 110	NA	17.4
0085	Clovis	30 954	31 194	-0.8	22 546	2 177	202	538	5 491	8 286	12 978	8 728	35.8
0097	Corrales village	5 453	NA	NA	5 135	20	81	37	180	1 469	2 196	11 030	27.8
0104	Deming	10 970	NA	NA	9 363	200	55	43	1 309	6 361	4 487	6 091	15.0
0111	Edgewood CDP	3 324	NA	NA	3 143	28	23	15	115	479	1 231	NA	140.5
0120	Espanola	8 389	NA	NA	7 349	51	205	15	769	7 017	3 390	7 226	19.6
0130	Eunice	2 676	NA	NA	2 584	27	23	1	41	722	1 140	9 228	7.6
0135	Farmington	33 997	31 222	8.9	26 207	277	4 696	122	2 695	5 428	13 119	9 807	60.9
0150	Gallup	19 154	18 161	5.5	9 544	223	6 363	214	2 810	6 643	6 706	7 549	28.6
0160	Grants	8 626	11 439	-24.6	7 633	125	657	56	155	4 564	3 532	6 958	35.4
0180	Hobbs	29 115	29 153	-0.1	22 916	2 168	164	138	3 729	8 771	12 327	10 198	48.9
0183	Holloman AFB CDP	5 891	NA	NA	4 334	868	49	342	298	683	1 410	NA	32.4
0211	Kirtland CDP	3 552	NA	NA	2 149	11	1 310	9	73	328	1 128	NA	15.8
0220	Las Cruces	62 126	45 060	37.9	54 791	1 211	538	690	4 896	29 124	25 676	9 290	97.1
0225	Las Vegas	14 753	14 322	3.0	9 113	104	129	91	5 316	12 096	5 716	5 687	19.2
0235	Lordsburg	2 951	NA	NA	2 614	8	12	29	288	2 084	1 204	5 714	21.6
0240	Los Alamos CDP	11 455	11 039	3.8	10 672	72	94	327	290	1 393	5 163	NA	28.1
0242	Los Chaves CDP	3 872	NA	NA	2 825	17	39	12	979	1 880	1 455	NA	30.3
0245	Los Lunas village	6 013	NA	NA	5 193	40	100	28	652	3 498	2 272	6 785	15.7
0247	Los Ranchos de Albuquerque village	3 955	NA	NA	3 346	18	43	36	512	1 351	1 581	17 524	9.5
0255	Lovington	9 322	NA	NA	6 943	258	52	17	2 052	4 160	3 700	8 294	12.5
0301	North Valley CDP	12 507	13 006	-3.8	9 063	69	232	54	3 089	6 648	4 819	NA	20.6
0304	Paradise Hills CDP	5 513	NA	NA	4 902	112	111	74	314	1 158	1 962	NA	3.8
0309	Peralta CDP	3 182	NA	NA	2 551	5	56	20	550	1 448	1 237	NA	11.8
0314	Portales	10 690	NA	NA	7 816	197	114	90	2 473	3 562	4 277	6 650	12.9
0325	Raton	7 372	NA	NA	5 978	22	37	14	1 321	3 935	3 502	8 106	18.4
0331	Rio Communities CDP	3 233	NA	NA	2 694	145	29	29	336	864	1 447	NA	15.6
0332	Rio Rancho	32 505	NA	NA	27 338	855	691	397	3 224	7 098	12 325	10 607	118.3
0334	Roswell	44 654	39 676	12.5	36 474	1 142	316	268	6 454	16 294	18 242	8 796	75.5
0340	Ruidoso village	4 600	NA	NA	4 312	14	73	13	188	777	6 677	10 804	36.7
0349	Sandia CDP	6 742	NA	NA	5 091	829	85	267	470	1 116	1 860	NA	10.8
0350	Sandia Heights CDP	3 519	NA	NA	3 420	18	28	26	27	218	1 420	NA	9.2
0359	Santa Cruz CDP	2 504	NA	NA	1 312	13	29	16	1 134	1 928	937	NA	17.5
0360	Santa Fe	55 859	48 953	14.1	45 359	332	1 249	353	8 566	26 493	24 681	11 002	94.8
0375	Santo Domingo Pueblo CDP	2 866	NA	NA	3	1	2 860	2	0	3	453	NA	5.2
0379	Shiprock CDP	7 687	NA	NA	193	17	7 439	10	28	93	2 221	NA	41.1
0380	Silver City town	10 683	NA	NA	9 936	99	80	52	516	5 667	4 255	7 316	22.8
0385	Socorro	8 159	NA	NA	6 584	79	119	200	1 177	4 282	3 502	7 346	37.3
0393	South Valley CDP	35 701	38 916	-8.3	21 928	463	596	150	12 564	25 886	12 226	NA	79.0

1. Codes shown are 2-digit FIPS codes for states; 4-digit census place codes for places; and 3-digit FIPS county codes followed by 3-digit census MCD codes for minor civil divisions (MCDs). MCD names are followed by county names in parentheses. 2. Hispanic persons may be of any race. 3. Dry land or land partially or temporarily covered by water.

State/ Place/ MCD[1] code	Place	Population			Population characteristics, 1990						Total housing units, 1990	Per capita income, 1985 (Dollars)	Land area,[3] 1990 (Sq. Km.)
		1990	Places of 10,000 or more		Race					Hispanic[2]			
			1980	Percent change, 1980–1990	White	Black	Am. Indian, Eskimo Aleut	Asian & Pacific Islander	Other race				
		1	2	3	4	5	6	7	8	9	10	11	12
	NEW MEXICO—Con.												
0400	Sunland Park	8 179	NA	NA	7 620	8	1	7	543	8 017	1 959	3 974	24.4
0405	Taos town	4 065	NA	NA	3 265	11	106	23	660	2 528	2 115	8 290	12.7
0423	Truth or Consequences	6 221	NA	NA	5 710	38	59	6	408	1 465	3 655	7 321	32.8
0425	Tucumcari	6 831	NA	NA	4 513	137	45	36	2 100	3 342	3 164	7 991	19.1
0430	Tularosa village	2 615	NA	NA	1 913	10	70	10	612	1 471	1 162	6 750	5.1
0431	University Park CDP	4 520	NA	NA	3 711	162	156	187	304	1 471	647	NA	4.1
0434	Valencia CDP	3 917	NA	NA	3 365	19	48	22	463	1 859	1 378	NA	14.3
0446	White Rock CDP	6 192	NA	NA	5 954	22	28	100	88	553	2 198	NA	18.6
0447	White Sands CDP	2 616	NA	NA	1 959	377	26	110	144	407	724	NA	6.5
0455	Zuni Pueblo CDP	5 857	NA	NA	166	10	5 669	9	3	72	1 389	NA	18.9
36	NEW YORK	17 990 455	17 558 165	2.5	13 385 255	2 859 055	62 651	693 760	989 734	2 214 026	7 226 891	11 765	122 309.7
0023	Airmont CDP	7 835	NA	NA	7 299	255	14	219	48	303	2 318	NA	12.2
0025	Akron village	2 906	NA	NA	2 866	2	33	2	3	8	1 232	9 331	5.0
0030	Albany	101 082	101 727	-0.6	76 323	20 869	277	2 326	1 287	3 183	46 199	10 675	55.4
0033	Albertson CDP	5 166	NA	NA	4 767	9	4	362	24	117	1 847	NA	1.7
0035	Albion village	5 863	NA	NA	5 165	592	36	16	54	83	2 453	10 287	7.6
0055	Alfred village	4 559	NA	NA	4 243	149	11	119	37	83	546	4 399	3.1
0090	Amityville village	9 286	NA	NA	8 330	712	22	100	122	532	3 300	14 625	5.4
0095	Amsterdam	20 714	21 872	-5.3	19 296	302	23	116	977	2 405	9 492	9 629	15.4
0140	Ardsley village	4 272	NA	NA	3 772	57	1	403	39	138	1 395	21 109	3.4
0155	Arlington CDP	11 948	11 305	5.7	10 508	907	19	411	103	349	4 501	NA	12.7
0160	Armonk CDP	2 745	NA	NA	2 614	12	0	104	15	86	957	NA	15.8
0175	Attica village	2 630	NA	NA	2 618	4	8	0	0	12	1 103	10 491	4.4
0180	Auburn	31 258	32 501	-3.8	28 738	2 129	95	162	134	673	12 682	8 763	21.7
0200	Avon village	2 995	NA	NA	2 895	49	14	25	12	34	1 166	11 530	7.8
0205	Babylon village	12 249	12 388	-1.1	11 686	354	18	127	64	480	4 536	15 664	6.2
0215	Baldwin CDP	22 719	31 630	-28.2	19 264	2 624	22	612	197	1 307	7 979	NA	7.6
0217	Baldwin Harbor CDP	7 899	NA	NA	7 552	77	5	238	27	244	2 692	NA	3.2
0220	Baldwinsville village	6 591	NA	NA	6 504	32	26	17	12	42	2 653	10 216	8.0
0225	Ballston Spa village	4 937	NA	NA	4 884	25	5	16	7	48	2 213	10 106	4.1
0232	Balmville CDP	2 963	NA	NA	2 678	155	4	63	63	165	1 154	NA	5.5
0234	Bardonia CDP	4 487	NA	NA	4 175	32	2	264	14	131	1 436	NA	6.6
0238	Barnum Island CDP	2 624	NA	NA	2 559	19	1	34	11	144	830	NA	2.4
0240	Batavia	16 310	16 703	-2.4	15 499	577	79	89	66	164	6 612	10 210	13.4
0245	Bath village	5 801	NA	NA	5 666	64	8	48	15	35	2 640	9 860	7.5
0255	Bayport CDP	7 702	NA	NA	7 453	78	3	97	71	227	2 755	NA	9.6
0260	Bay Shore CDP	21 279	10 784	97.3	17 109	2 979	47	298	846	2 696	7 938	NA	13.7
0265	Bayville village	7 193	NA	NA	7 056	15	10	86	26	281	2 703	14 600	3.6
0267	Baywood CDP	7 351	NA	NA	6 644	368	13	85	241	973	2 214	NA	5.8
0270	Beacon	13 243	12 937	2.4	10 466	1 989	12	96	680	1 870	5 039	10 063	12.3
0295	Bellmore CDP	16 438	18 106	-9.2	16 120	59	9	193	57	407	5 603	NA	6.4
0300	Bellport village	2 572	NA	NA	2 488	37	15	29	3	33	1 120	17 682	3.8
0320	Bethpage CDP	15 761	16 801	-6.2	15 326	21	8	325	81	487	5 078	NA	9.4
0321	Big Flats CDP	2 658	NA	NA	2 571	25	2	58	2	9	967	NA	10.1
0325	Binghamton	53 008	55 860	-5.1	48 733	2 594	165	1 088	428	971	24 626	10 231	26.9
0335	Blasdell village	2 900	NA	NA	2 867	5	6	6	16	69	1 222	10 977	3.0
0337	Blauvelt CDP	4 838	NA	NA	4 537	42	1	255	3	150	1 480	NA	11.8
0353	Blue Point CDP	4 230	NA	NA	4 175	19	1	14	21	100	1 548	NA	4.6
0357	Bohemia CDP	9 556	NA	NA	9 346	46	2	126	36	266	3 200	NA	22.6
0370	Brentwood CDP	45 218	44 321	2.0	33 015	6 077	171	884	5 071	15 692	12 023	NA	26.1
0372	Brewerton CDP	2 954	NA	NA	2 913	16	9	15	1	8	1 260	NA	8.2
0380	Briarcliff Manor village	7 070	NA	NA	6 528	145	2	343	52	217	2 200	25 038	15.3
0393	Brighton CDP	34 455	35 776	-3.7	31 739	1 033	47	1 466	170	564	16 068	NA	40.1
0395	Brightwaters village	3 265	NA	NA	3 196	31	2	33	3	85	1 150	19 906	2.5
0397	Brinckerhoff CDP	2 756	NA	NA	2 476	121	2	145	12	59	850	NA	2.8
0405	Brockport village	8 749	NA	NA	8 112	432	29	85	91	194	2 502	7 564	5.6
0420	Bronxville village	6 028	NA	NA	5 558	44	7	395	24	172	2 391	34 191	2.5
0425	Brookhaven CDP	3 118	NA	NA	2 933	143	13	16	13	73	1 097	NA	15.7
0430	Brookville village	3 716	NA	NA	3 046	357	6	178	129	177	622	20 865	10.4
0450	Buffalo	328 123	357 870	-8.3	212 449	100 579	2 547	3 261	9 287	16 129	151 971	8 840	105.2
0467	Calverton CDP	4 759	NA	NA	4 407	268	14	23	47	163	2 341	NA	72.5
0475	Camden village	2 552	NA	NA	2 526	7	5	9	5	10	1 025	9 988	5.9
0490	Canandaigua	10 725	10 419	2.9	10 548	100	26	37	14	84	4 717	10 816	11.9
0500	Canastota village	4 673	NA	NA	4 566	67	17	18	5	34	1 916	9 992	8.6
0515	Canton village	6 379	NA	NA	6 141	150	23	47	18	66	1 725	7 314	5.7
0523	Carle Place CDP	5 107	NA	NA	4 836	53	5	169	44	292	1 867	NA	2.4
0525	Carmel Hamlet CDP	4 800	NA	NA	4 696	44	3	35	22	115	1 728	NA	22.0
0530	Carthage village	4 344	NA	NA	4 005	184	24	83	48	100	1 751	8 168	6.5
0560	Catskill village	4 690	NA	NA	4 004	570	21	20	75	220	2 021	10 105	5.8
0575	Cayuga Heights village	3 457	NA	NA	3 068	95	4	268	22	99	1 424	20 354	4.6
0580	Cazenovia village	3 007	NA	NA	2 925	49	7	19	7	33	995	11 844	4.1
0585	Cedarhurst village	5 716	NA	NA	5 420	94	4	123	75	239	2 275	16 263	1.8

1. Codes shown are 2-digit FIPS codes for states; 4-digit census place codes for places; and 3-digit FIPS county codes followed by 3-digit census MCD codes for minor civil divisions (MCDs). MCD names are followed by county names in parentheses. 2. Hispanic persons may be of any race. 3. Dry land or land partially or temporarily covered by water.

State/ Place/ MCD[1] code	Place	Population: 1990	Places of 10,000 or more: 1980	Places of 10,000 or more: Percent change, 1980–1990	Population characteristics, 1990: Race: White	Race: Black	Race: Am. Indian, Eskimo Aleut	Race: Asian & Pacific Islander	Race: Other race	Hispanic[2]	Total housing units, 1990	Per capita income, 1985 (Dollars)	Land area,[3] 1990 (Sq. Km.)
		1	2	3	4	5	6	7	8	9	10	11	12
	NEW YORK—Con.												
0595	Centereach CDP	26 720	30 136	-11.3	25 419	518	22	554	207	1 268	7 801	NA	20.6
0600	Center Moriches CDP	5 987	NA	NA	5 401	440	17	80	49	248	2 316	NA	13.0
0604	Centerport CDP	5 333	NA	NA	5 261	16	4	49	3	72	2 042	NA	5.5
0607	Central Islip CDP	26 028	19 734	31.9	16 260	6 444	108	443	2 773	7 088	7 697	NA	15.2
0655	Cheektowaga CDP	84 387	92 145	-8.4	82 915	914	121	351	86	403	34 827	NA	65.9
0670	Chester village	3 270	NA	NA	3 012	144	27	46	41	176	1 427	NA	5.5
0672	Chestnut Ridge village	7 517	NA	NA	6 611	501	17	312	76	402	2 422	21 091	12.8
0675	Chittenango village	4 734	NA	NA	4 654	19	22	34	5	29	1 715	9 978	6.3
0725	Cobleskill village	5 268	NA	NA	5 012	136	12	51	57	135	1 665	7 060	8.1
0740	Cohoes	16 825	18 144	-7.3	16 610	107	27	45	36	109	7 639	9 780	9.7
0755	Cold Spring Harbor CDP	4 789	NA	NA	4 718	11	4	55	1	61	1 747	NA	9.6
0760	Colonie village	8 019	NA	NA	7 540	248	13	202	16	104	2 981	12 154	8.7
0765	Commack CDP	36 124	34 719	4.0	34 727	231	14	1 039	113	911	11 303	NA	31.2
0770	Congers CDP	8 003	NA	NA	7 341	100	10	465	87	373	2 635	NA	8.2
0790	Copiague CDP	20 769	20 132	3.2	18 958	971	49	220	571	2 105	7 067	NA	8.3
0793	Coram CDP	30 111	24 752	21.7	26 569	2 422	91	664	365	1 914	10 737	NA	35.7
0800	Corinth village	2 760	NA	NA	2 754	0	6	0	0	3	1 139	9 708	2.8
0805	Corning	11 938	12 953	-7.8	11 503	246	38	126	25	79	5 585	10 843	8.0
0810	Cornwall on Hudson village	3 093	NA	NA	3 045	10	8	26	4	61	1 250	13 326	5.1
0820	Cortland	19 801	20 138	-1.7	19 258	277	55	117	94	254	7 279	7 750	10.1
0830	Coxsackie village	2 789	NA	NA	2 649	111	2	13	14	72	1 245	9 470	5.6
0845	Croton-on-Hudson village	7 018	NA	NA	6 623	130	14	176	75	257	2 728	18 048	12.3
0848	Crown Heights CDP	3 200	NA	NA	2 654	369	1	144	32	136	1 041	NA	5.5
0857	Cutchogue CDP	2 627	NA	NA	2 510	91	5	20	1	70	1 586	NA	21.0
0860	Dannemora village	4 005	NA	NA	1 990	1 625	31	32	327	785	484	5 128	3.1
0865	Dansville village	5 002	NA	NA	4 927	28	5	35	7	30	2 114	10 587	6.0
0875	Deer Park CDP	28 840	30 394	-5.1	25 850	2 199	45	503	243	1 552	9 616	NA	16.1
0895	Delhi village	3 064	NA	NA	2 946	74	3	31	10	53	755	6 579	8.2
0897	Delmar CDP	8 360	NA	NA	8 193	67	7	89	4	61	3 431	NA	11.1
0900	Depew village	17 673	19 819	-10.8	17 517	78	36	33	9	75	6 892	9 934	13.1
0917	De Witt CDP	8 244	NA	NA	7 234	695	11	257	47	111	2 885	NA	8.1
0922	Dix Hills CDP	25 849	26 693	-3.2	23 812	602	28	1 336	71	744	7 698	NA	41.3
0925	Dobbs Ferry village	9 940	10 145	-2.0	8 510	593	8	691	138	482	3 781	17 732	6.3
0955	Dunkirk	13 989	15 310	-8.6	12 218	527	76	42	1 126	1 954	5 952	9 228	11.7
0965	East Aurora village	6 647	NA	NA	6 598	18	6	19	6	28	2 576	12 206	6.5
0972	Eastchester CDP	18 537	20 305	-8.7	17 099	108	3	1 281	46	459	7 884	NA	8.7
0973	East Farmingdale CDP	4 510	NA	NA	3 590	703	11	80	126	317	1 495	NA	14.0
0974	East Glenville CDP	6 518	NA	NA	6 376	42	9	81	10	53	2 189	NA	18.8
0976	East Greenbush CDP	3 784	NA	NA	3 614	82	11	73	4	51	1 450	NA	6.9
0981	East Hampton CDP	2 780	NA	NA	2 485	260	4	12	19	109	1 889	NA	14.5
0990	East Hills village	6 746	NA	NA	6 367	73	1	284	21	111	2 307	32 707	5.9
0993	East Islip CDP	14 325	13 852	3.4	13 969	49	13	199	95	469	4 670	NA	10.9
0995	East Massapequa CDP	19 550	13 987	39.8	16 760	2 129	45	374	242	1 090	6 303	NA	9.0
1000	East Meadow CDP	36 909	39 317	-6.1	33 321	1 836	26	1 302	424	1 436	11 511	NA	16.3
1005	East Middletown CDP	4 974	NA	NA	4 170	428	17	124	235	556	1 900	NA	8.6
1010	East Moriches CDP	4 021	NA	NA	3 814	85	7	85	30	156	1 542	NA	14.1
1020	East Northport CDP	20 411	20 187	1.1	19 754	153	20	356	128	598	6 970	NA	13.2
1022	East Norwich CDP	2 698	NA	NA	2 627	2	0	66	3	45	937	NA	2.7
1025	East Patchogue CDP	20 195	18 139	11.3	19 179	423	29	274	290	1 088	7 446	NA	21.5
1027	East Quogue CDP	4 372	NA	NA	4 289	45	2	22	14	69	2 985	NA	24.0
1035	East Rochester village	6 932	NA	NA	6 798	43	18	47	26	81	2 926	11 383	3.5
1040	East Rockaway village	10 152	10 917	-7.0	9 921	35	6	113	77	340	3 881	15 304	2.6
1045	East Shoreham CDP	5 461	NA	NA	5 316	41	2	86	16	140	1 671	NA	13.9
1050	East Syracuse village	3 343	NA	NA	3 275	18	27	14	9	25	1 489	10 803	4.1
1055	East Williston village	2 515	NA	NA	2 412	9	0	86	8	33	849	21 402	1.5
1060	Eden CDP	3 088	NA	NA	3 064	2	3	14	5	22	1 106	NA	13.7
1090	Ellenville village	4 243	NA	NA	3 221	530	40	55	397	1 001	1 738	10 311	23.3
1105	Elmira	33 724	35 327	-4.5	28 815	4 162	101	191	455	899	13 301	7 856	19.0
1110	Elmira Heights village	4 359	NA	NA	4 270	45	2	27	15	26	1 990	9 743	2.9
1120	Elmont CDP	28 612	27 592	3.7	21 510	4 081	79	2 108	834	3 243	9 604	NA	8.9
1125	Elmsford village	3 938	NA	NA	2 634	1 099	17	127	61	455	1 285	16 139	2.6
1128	Elwood CDP	10 916	11 847	-7.9	10 014	424	15	404	59	383	3 387	NA	12.5
1130	Endicott village	13 531	14 457	-6.4	13 068	247	21	147	48	149	6 669	11 121	8.1
1133	Endwell CDP	12 602	13 745	-8.3	12 213	138	7	214	30	106	5 373	NA	9.5
1152	Fairmount CDP	12 266	13 415	-8.6	12 049	73	50	84	10	95	4 784	NA	9.6
1155	Fairport village	5 943	NA	NA	5 829	36	10	65	3	28	2 367	12 660	4.1
1160	Fairview CDP	4 811	NA	NA	4 410	262	1	103	35	105	1 888	NA	9.0
1165	Falconer village	2 653	NA	NA	2 637	3	2	9	2	20	1 237	9 841	2.8
1170	Farmingdale village	8 022	NA	NA	7 684	62	0	169	107	601	3 314	14 282	2.9
1172	Farmingville CDP	14 842	13 398	10.8	14 406	135	12	215	74	938	4 560	NA	11.7
1185	Fayetteville village	4 248	NA	NA	4 157	15	9	59	8	28	1 840	16 990	4.4
1197	Firthcliffe CDP	4 427	NA	NA	4 300	50	3	53	21	115	1 751	NA	7.8
1205	Flanders CDP	3 231	NA	NA	2 541	616	26	28	20	99	1 459	NA	29.2

1. Codes shown are 2-digit FIPS codes for states; 4-digit census place codes for places; and 3-digit FIPS county codes followed by 3-digit census MCD codes for minor civil divisions (MCDs). MCD names are followed by county names in parentheses. 2. Hispanic persons may be of any race. 3. Dry land or land partially or temporarily covered by water.

State/ Place/ MCD[1] code	Place	Population: 1990	Population: Places of 10,000 or more: 1980	Population: Places of 10,000 or more: Percent change, 1980–1990	Population characteristics, 1990: Race: White	Race: Black	Race: Am. Indian, Eskimo Aleut	Race: Asian & Pacific Islander	Race: Other race	Hispanic[2]	Total housing units, 1990	Per capita income, 1985 (Dollars)	Land area,[3] 1990 (Sq. Km.)
		1	2	3	4	5	6	7	8	9	10	11	12
	NEW YORK—Con.												
1215	Floral Park village	15 947	16 794	-5.0	15 522	48	10	288	79	517	5 796	14 206	3.7
1225	Flower Hill village	4 490	NA	NA	4 072	39	0	355	24	154	1 506	32 184	4.2
1247	Fort Drum CDP	11 578	NA	NA	7 442	2 999	64	333	740	1 125	2 277	NA	40.7
1250	Fort Edward village	3 561	NA	NA	3 534	6	8	9	4	15	1 381	8 933	4.6
1262	Fort Salonga CDP	9 176	NA	NA	8 995	26	2	139	14	175	3 131	NA	24.0
1264	Frankfort village	2 693	NA	NA	2 689	2	0	0	2	12	1 124	8 532	2.6
1270	Franklin Square CDP	28 205	29 051	-2.9	27 463	49	14	546	133	1 004	10 111	NA	7.5
1280	Fredonia village	10 436	11 126	-6.2	10 062	166	22	114	72	203	3 548	8 298	13.4
1285	Freeport village	39 894	38 272	4.2	22 521	12 887	162	507	3 817	8 459	13 660	11 582	11.9
1310	Fulton	12 929	13 312	-2.9	12 688	72	36	81	52	181	5 536	9 971	9.7
1327	Gang Mills CDP	2 738	NA	NA	2 566	83	1	80	8	20	1 073	NA	17.1
1330	Garden City village	21 686	22 927	-5.4	20 740	263	8	624	51	528	7 716	22 832	13.8
1335	Garden City Park CDP	7 437	NA	NA	6 137	422	8	800	70	317	2 533	NA	2.5
1336	Garden City South CDP	4 073	NA	NA	3 976	6	3	67	21	141	1 437	NA	1.1
1337	Gardnertown CDP	4 209	NA	NA	3 981	133	6	36	53	243	1 565	NA	12.7
1341	Gates-North Gates CDP	14 995	15 244	-1.6	13 913	679	29	266	108	313	5 956	NA	12.1
1343	Geneseo village	7 187	NA	NA	6 885	140	22	104	36	112	1 635	7 069	6.6
1345	Geneva	14 143	15 133	-6.5	12 503	1 188	27	147	278	643	5 654	9 048	11.0
1360	Glen Cove	24 149	24 618	-1.9	20 719	1 883	32	820	695	2 774	8 798	15 178	17.2
1364	Glen Head CDP	4 488	NA	NA	4 376	13	1	64	34	150	1 651	NA	4.2
1370	Glens Falls	15 023	15 897	-5.5	14 748	175	31	42	27	158	6 569	9 573	10.0
1375	Glens Falls North CDP	7 978	NA	NA	7 851	21	8	85	13	59	3 423	NA	21.0
1377	Glenwood Landing CDP	3 407	NA	NA	3 294	4	0	85	24	84	1 273	NA	2.6
1380	Gloversville	16 656	17 836	-6.6	16 214	283	33	83	43	117	7 596	9 234	12.9
1385	Goshen village	5 255	NA	NA	4 728	381	26	49	71	205	1 877	13 394	8.3
1390	Gouverneur village	4 604	NA	NA	4 429	100	24	26	25	46	1 940	7 719	5.5
1395	Gowanda village	2 901	NA	NA	2 754	9	124	7	7	34	1 310	10 666	4.2
1405	Granville village	2 646	NA	NA	2 629	5	5	1	6	25	1 103	8 234	4.1
1410	Great Neck village	8 745	NA	NA	7 872	422	15	303	133	578	3 450	21 359	3.5
1415	Great Neck Estates village	2 790	NA	NA	2 638	57	1	87	7	129	963	34 904	2.0
1420	Great Neck Plaza village	5 897	NA	NA	5 522	119	2	129	125	481	3 612	22 226	0.8
1424	Greece CDP	15 632	16 177	-3.4	15 038	278	29	221	66	258	6 116	NA	11.3
1435	Greenlawn CDP	13 208	13 869	-4.8	10 621	2 166	22	281	118	596	4 421	NA	9.5
1443	Greenville CDP	9 528	NA	NA	7 391	192	2	1 897	46	325	3 905	NA	8.0
1450	Greenwood Lake village	3 208	NA	NA	3 168	4	4	12	20	108	1 516	14 687	5.3
1465	Halesite CDP	2 687	NA	NA	2 616	27	5	31	8	53	1 004	NA	2.2
1470	Hamburg village	10 442	10 582	-1.3	10 348	28	11	46	9	76	4 146	12 256	6.5
1480	Hamilton village	3 790	NA	NA	3 454	132	3	167	34	77	869	6 765	4.9
1500	Hampton Bays CDP	7 893	NA	NA	7 712	111	5	40	25	151	5 227	NA	29.7
1501	Hampton Manor CDP	2 600	NA	NA	2 555	27	3	10	5	14	1 038	NA	1.6
1518	Harris Hill CDP	4 577	NA	NA	4 526	10	8	29	4	26	1 702	NA	10.5
1521	Harrison village	23 308	23 046	1.1	21 684	357	17	991	259	1 145	7 984	20 182	43.6
1527	Hartsdale CDP	9 587	10 216	-6.2	7 967	695	10	767	148	498	4 226	NA	7.9
1530	Hastings-on-Hudson village	8 000	NA	NA	7 197	317	7	407	72	332	3 145	20 130	5.1
1533	Hauppauge CDP	19 750	20 960	-5.8	18 982	264	10	383	111	682	6 597	NA	28.0
1535	Haverstraw village	9 438	NA	NA	5 473	1 873	49	116	1 927	4 846	2 901	9 701	5.2
1536	Haviland CDP	3 605	NA	NA	3 456	87	4	48	10	53	1 343	NA	10.0
1538	Hawthorne CDP	4 764	NA	NA	4 555	108	4	50	47	121	1 538	NA	4.5
1545	Hempstead village	49 453	40 404	22.4	16 010	29 088	225	824	3 306	9 454	15 117	10 765	9.5
1555	Herkimer village	7 945	NA	NA	7 852	49	7	30	7	49	3 499	8 833	6.3
1563	Herricks CDP	4 097	NA	NA	3 601	13	0	472	11	126	1 419	NA	1.4
1573	Hewlett CDP	6 620	NA	NA	6 258	40	2	202	118	342	2 534	NA	2.3
1590	Hicksville CDP	40 174	43 245	-7.1	37 685	315	41	1 754	379	1 975	13 395	NA	17.6
1595	Highland CDP	4 492	NA	NA	4 294	122	5	39	32	160	1 747	NA	12.0
1600	Highland Falls village	3 937	NA	NA	3 265	532	5	67	68	233	1 708	10 847	2.9
1605	Highland Mills CDP	2 576	NA	NA	2 500	29	3	34	10	64	950	NA	4.5
1615	Hillcrest CDP	6 447	NA	NA	3 448	2 033	21	834	111	502	1 880	NA	3.3
1620	Hilton village	5 216	NA	NA	5 115	53	13	29	6	48	1 857	10 693	4.1
1631	Holbrook CDP	25 273	24 382	3.7	24 056	340	16	649	212	1 378	7 630	NA	17.7
1652	Holtsville CDP	14 972	13 515	10.8	14 546	125	17	181	103	753	4 532	NA	18.0
1655	Homer village	3 476	NA	NA	3 448	10	4	10	4	25	1 379	9 337	4.3
1665	Hoosick Falls village	3 490	NA	NA	3 449	19	5	10	7	33	1 490	9 131	4.5
1670	Hornell	9 877	10 234	-3.5	9 595	197	17	54	14	49	4 148	8 508	6.7
1675	Horseheads village	6 802	NA	NA	6 621	74	18	80	9	36	2 950	11 109	10.0
1676	Horseheads North CDP	3 003	NA	NA	2 914	42	5	33	9	17	1 078	NA	6.0
1680	Hudson	8 034	NA	NA	6 091	1 739	25	42	137	426	3 496	8 178	5.6
1685	Hudson Falls village	7 651	NA	NA	7 601	16	8	20	6	49	3 159	9 459	4.8
1695	Huntington CDP	18 243	21 752	-16.1	17 334	518	24	291	76	458	7 013	NA	19.5
1705	Huntington Station CDP	28 247	28 769	-1.8	23 091	3 596	67	527	966	3 377	9 968	NA	14.1
1706	Hurley CDP	4 644	NA	NA	4 475	36	0	118	15	42	1 733	NA	14.0
1715	Ilion village	8 888	NA	NA	8 754	41	27	26	40	88	3 586	8 637	6.4
1730	Inwood CDP	7 767	NA	NA	5 357	2 040	21	77	272	889	2 849	NA	4.3
1733	Irondequoit CDP	52 322	57 648	-9.2	50 943	703	86	329	261	752	22 151	NA	39.2

1. Codes shown are 2-digit FIPS codes for states; 4-digit census place codes for places; and 3-digit FIPS county codes followed by 3-digit census MCD codes for minor civil divisions (MCDs). MCD names are followed by county names in parentheses. 2. Hispanic persons may be of any race. 3. Dry land or land partially or temporarily covered by water.

State/ Place/ MCD[1] code	Place	Population: 1990	Population: Places of 10,000 or more: 1980	Population: Places of 10,000 or more: Percent change, 1980–1990	Population characteristics, 1990: Race: White	Race: Black	Race: Am. Indian, Eskimo Aleut	Race: Asian & Pacific Islander	Race: Other race	Hispanic[2]	Total housing units, 1990	Per capita income, 1985 (Dollars)	Land area,[3] 1990 (Sq. Km.)
		1	2	3	4	5	6	7	8	9	10	11	12
	NEW YORK—Con.												
1735	Irvington village	6 348	NA	NA	5 688	111	5	506	38	218	2 582	25 485	7.2
1737	Islandia village	2 769	NA	NA	2 425	172	5	68	99	326	930	12 549	5.8
1740	Island Park village	4 860	NA	NA	4 679	30	11	65	75	536	1 754	10 362	1.0
1742	Islip CDP	18 924	13 438	40.8	17 600	613	38	245	428	1 349	6 458	NA	14.0
1743	Islip Terrace CDP	5 530	NA	NA	5 394	23	3	46	64	236	1 667	NA	3.7
1745	Ithaca	29 541	28 732	2.8	24 166	1 916	102	2 958	399	1 068	10 075	7 675	14.1
1755	Jamestown	34 681	35 775	-3.1	32 920	900	175	157	529	1 035	15 461	8 785	22.9
1757	Jamestown West CDP	2 633	NA	NA	2 607	10	6	9	1	8	1 101	NA	6.8
1763	Jefferson Valley-Yorktown CDP	14 118	13 380	5.5	13 428	263	6	331	90	383	5 063	NA	17.9
1770	Jericho CDP	13 141	12 739	3.2	12 305	154	2	623	57	353	4 630	NA	10.3
1775	Johnson City village	16 890	17 126	-1.4	16 103	252	18	447	70	215	7 770	10 326	11.5
1780	Johnstown	9 058	NA	NA	8 863	78	17	81	19	62	3 971	9 891	12.1
1800	Kenmore village	17 180	18 474	-7.0	16 955	77	36	79	33	130	7 330	11 071	3.7
1815	Kings Park CDP	17 773	16 131	10.2	16 779	561	16	294	123	533	5 591	NA	15.5
1820	Kings Point village	4 843	NA	NA	4 561	79	4	176	23	141	1 451	41 537	8.7
1825	Kingston	23 095	24 481	-5.7	20 183	2 334	55	323	200	631	10 387	10 460	19.1
1827	Kiryas Joel village	7 437	NA	NA	7 418	2	10	6	1	124	1 332	NA	2.8
1830	Lackawanna	20 585	22 701	-9.3	18 211	1 810	31	73	460	1 048	8 986	9 328	15.9
1840	Lake Carmel CDP	8 489	NA	NA	8 315	46	21	55	52	264	3 072	NA	13.4
1845	Lake Erie Beach CDP	4 509	NA	NA	4 464	6	23	6	10	49	2 001	NA	10.0
1857	Lake Grove village	9 612	NA	NA	9 275	107	21	170	39	380	3 301	11 445	7.7
1888	Lake Ronkonkoma CDP	18 997	38 336	-50.4	18 437	152	25	289	94	724	6 265	NA	12.7
1903	Lakeview CDP	5 476	NA	NA	336	4 948	55	45	92	321	1 559	NA	2.5
1905	Lakewood village	3 564	NA	NA	3 493	14	4	50	3	19	1 629	14 059	5.1
1910	Lancaster village	11 940	13 056	-8.5	11 871	24	16	20	9	61	4 885	10 693	7.0
1913	Lansing village	3 281	NA	NA	2 613	178	11	436	43	99	1 639	15 120	12.0
1915	Larchmont village	6 181	NA	NA	5 856	85	2	185	53	295	2 336	26 984	2.8
1918	Latham CDP	10 131	11 182	-9.4	9 658	134	9	313	17	106	3 944	NA	12.4
1935	Lawrence village	6 513	NA	NA	6 229	146	12	66	60	280	2 404	27 582	9.9
1945	Le Roy village	4 974	NA	NA	4 766	161	14	24	9	36	1 991	10 651	7.0
1950	Levittown CDP	53 286	57 045	-6.6	51 883	137	31	950	285	2 184	16 988	NA	17.8
1955	Lewiston village	3 048	NA	NA	3 033	0	7	7	1	23	1 337	13 220	2.8
1960	Liberty village	4 128	NA	NA	3 399	515	8	67	139	387	1 827	9 099	6.0
1962	Lido Beach CDP	2 786	NA	NA	2 720	17	1	43	5	49	1 289	NA	4.4
1980	Lindenhurst village	26 879	26 919	-0.1	26 315	127	18	256	163	1 113	8 847	11 631	9.7
1990	Little Falls	5 829	NA	NA	5 790	5	10	22	2	30	2 709	8 501	9.8
2000	Liverpool village	2 624	NA	NA	2 570	27	8	12	7	13	1 169	12 910	2.0
2015	Lloyd Harbor village	3 343	NA	NA	3 287	14	1	35	6	56	1 106	36 141	24.2
2020	Lockport	24 426	24 844	-1.7	22 786	1 371	77	118	74	400	10 374	10 988	22.1
2027	Locust Valley CDP	3 963	NA	NA	3 588	198	1	75	101	331	1 506	NA	2.7
2035	Long Beach	33 510	34 073	-1.7	29 163	2 599	93	559	1 096	3 610	15 358	13 518	5.5
2038	Loudonville CDP	10 822	11 480	-5.7	10 264	154	7	354	43	144	3 954	NA	12.9
2040	Lowville village	3 632	NA	NA	3 530	44	5	34	19	32	1 571	11 053	5.1
2045	Lynbrook village	19 208	20 424	-6.0	18 443	104	9	408	244	941	7 406	14 370	5.2
2047	Lyncourt CDP	4 516	NA	NA	4 405	89	10	8	4	35	1 980	NA	3.0
2049	Lyndon CDP	4 593	NA	NA	4 411	50	1	115	16	43	1 811	NA	11.5
2063	Lyons village	4 280	NA	NA	3 745	462	12	15	46	105	1 752	9 314	10.5
2085	Mahopac CDP	7 755	NA	NA	7 613	34	12	58	38	223	2 972	NA	13.8
2090	Malone village	6 777	NA	NA	6 696	14	35	27	5	32	3 037	9 173	7.6
2095	Malverne village	9 054	NA	NA	8 689	118	4	212	31	345	3 178	16 202	2.7
2100	Mamaroneck village	17 325	17 616	-1.7	15 378	900	18	553	476	1 822	6 842	19 385	8.4
2110	Manhasset CDP	7 718	NA	NA	6 163	1 184	5	341	25	349	2 830	NA	6.2
2112	Manhasset Hills CDP	3 722	NA	NA	3 040	11	0	651	20	69	1 236	NA	1.5
2120	Manlius village	4 764	NA	NA	4 582	31	11	133	7	47	2 027	16 396	4.4
2130	Manorhaven village	5 672	NA	NA	4 834	48	10	469	311	931	2 325	14 659	1.2
2132	Manorville CDP	6 198	NA	NA	6 001	84	12	61	40	227	2 567	NA	66.4
2165	Massapequa CDP	22 018	24 454	-10.0	21 654	44	10	253	57	418	7 225	NA	9.4
2170	Massapequa Park village	18 044	19 779	-8.8	17 760	17	4	242	21	336	5 720	15 255	5.6
2175	Massena village	11 719	12 851	-8.8	11 419	32	204	53	11	78	5 017	10 701	11.5
2179	Mastic CDP	13 778	10 413	32.3	12 819	454	174	92	239	1 168	4 234	NA	11.5
2180	Mastic Beach CDP	10 293	NA	NA	9 920	201	21	39	112	567	4 212	NA	11.0
2195	Mattituck CDP	3 902	NA	NA	3 816	64	2	18	2	21	2 191	NA	22.4
2197	Mattydale CDP	6 418	NA	NA	6 307	59	27	20	5	64	2 693	NA	3.4
2200	Maybrook village	2 802	NA	NA	2 588	162	2	10	40	156	1 022	NA	3.4
2215	Mechanicville	5 249	NA	NA	5 228	2	6	12	1	52	2 417	11 153	2.2
2218	Medford CDP	21 274	20 418	4.2	19 693	863	49	278	391	1 746	6 458	NA	28.1
2220	Medina village	6 686	NA	NA	6 043	474	24	46	99	235	2 771	9 825	8.3
2227	Melville CDP	12 586	NA	NA	11 814	201	9	520	42	383	4 014	NA	29.3
2230	Menands village	4 333	NA	NA	3 993	246	2	70	22	78	2 283	19 695	8.3
2240	Merrick CDP	23 042	24 478	-5.9	22 431	122	7	390	92	454	7 634	NA	10.9
2254	Middle Island CDP	7 848	NA	NA	7 388	260	16	92	92	402	3 184	NA	21.4
2260	Middletown	24 160	21 454	12.6	19 853	2 684	126	342	1 155	3 217	9 475	9 874	12.8
2278	Miller Place CDP	9 315	NA	NA	9 119	59	2	95	40	242	3 039	NA	16.9

1. Codes shown are 2-digit FIPS codes for states; 4-digit census place codes for places; and 3-digit FIPS county codes followed by 3-digit census MCD codes for minor civil divisions (MCDs). MCD names are followed by county names in parentheses. 2. Hispanic persons may be of any race. 3. Dry land or land partially or temporarily covered by water.

State/ Place/ MCD[1] code	Place	Population: 1990	Population: Places of 10,000 or more: 1980	Population: Places of 10,000 or more: Percent change, 1980–1990	Population characteristics, 1990: Race: White	Race: Black	Race: Am. Indian, Eskimo Aleut	Race: Asian & Pacific Islander	Race: Other race	Hispanic[2]	Total housing units, 1990	Per capita income, 1985 (Dollars)	Land area,[3] 1990 (Sq. Km.)
		1	2	3	4	5	6	7	8	9	10	11	12
	NEW YORK—Con.												
2295	Mineola village	18 994	20 757	-8.5	18 058	190	16	476	254	1 547	7 514	14 318	4.8
2305	Minoa village	3 745	NA	NA	3 655	10	8	66	6	20	1 320	11 000	3.2
2310	Mohawk village	2 986	NA	NA	2 973	10	0	3	0	11	1 245	8 852	2.3
2320	Monroe village	6 672	NA	NA	6 415	59	4	146	48	288	2 246	12 113	8.8
2325	Monsey CDP	13 986	12 380	13.0	13 319	532	14	90	31	200	2 916	NA	6.2
2330	Montauk CDP	3 001	NA	NA	2 924	47	3	11	16	297	3 996	NA	45.2
2332	Montebello village	2 950	NA	NA	2 753	109	2	79	7	68	935	23 963	11.3
2335	Montgomery village	2 696	NA	NA	2 614	42	3	23	14	92	950	NA	3.5
2340	Monticello village	6 597	NA	NA	4 485	1 576	28	113	395	1 049	3 043	10 152	9.9
2375	Morrisville village	2 732	NA	NA	2 492	183	9	29	19	70	443	5 479	3.0
2379	Mount Ivy CDP	6 013	NA	NA	5 474	310	1	140	88	432	2 600	NA	3.8
2380	Mount Kisco village	9 108	NA	NA	7 852	749	24	276	207	1 108	3 965	15 553	8.1
2385	Mount Morris village	3 102	NA	NA	2 979	38	2	13	70	112	1 409	9 589	5.3
2388	Mount Sinai CDP	8 023	NA	NA	7 772	105	4	111	31	270	2 559	NA	15.5
2390	Mount Vernon	67 153	66 713	0.7	26 698	37 138	263	1 238	1 816	5 237	26 232	11 701	11.4
2400	Munsey Park village	2 692	NA	NA	2 568	7	0	110	7	65	837	26 138	1.3
2405	Muttontown village	3 024	NA	NA	2 688	44	0	287	5	79	951	30 905	15.8
2406	Myers Corner CDP	5 599	NA	NA	5 040	221	4	317	17	202	1 753	NA	11.0
2407	Nanuet CDP	14 065	12 578	11.8	11 405	1 591	4	898	167	759	4 948	NA	14.0
2435	Nesconset CDP	10 712	10 706	0.1	10 406	63	5	204	34	304	3 308	NA	9.9
2442	Newark village	9 849	10 017	-1.7	9 044	316	17	66	406	659	3 955	9 809	13.4
2455	Newburgh	26 454	23 438	12.9	13 557	9 208	91	136	3 462	6 143	9 995	7 642	9.9
2458	New Cassel CDP	10 257	NA	NA	2 798	6 741	43	128	547	2 066	2 642	NA	3.8
2460	New City CDP	33 673	35 859	-6.1	31 117	898	23	1 399	236	1 207	10 628	NA	40.4
2470	Newfane CDP	3 001	NA	NA	2 962	19	13	4	3	13	1 105	NA	12.1
2477	New Hempstead village	4 200	NA	NA	3 596	367	11	178	48	203	1 161	17 296	7.4
2480	New Hyde Park village	9 728	NA	NA	9 192	5	12	486	33	334	3 471	14 342	2.2
2485	New Paltz village	5 463	NA	NA	4 494	590	9	225	145	485	1 602	7 465	4.5
2495	New Rochelle	67 265	70 794	-5.0	51 141	12 166	80	1 967	1 911	7 247	26 398	17 018	26.8
2497	New Square village	2 605	NA	NA	2 573	26	0	6	0	6	445	NA	0.9
2501	New Windsor CDP	8 898	NA	NA	8 279	349	19	120	131	506	3 495	NA	9.8
2505	New York	7 322 564	7 071 639	3.5	3 827 088	2 102 512	27 531	512 719	852 714	1 783 511	2 992 169	11 188	800.2
2510	New York Mills village	3 534	NA	NA	3 507	6	5	12	4	20	1 809	11 088	2.9
2515	Niagara Falls	61 840	71 384	-13.4	50 828	9 634	1 006	163	209	739	28 635	9 333	36.4
2524	Niskayuna CDP	4 942	NA	NA	4 794	70	1	65	12	51	2 051	NA	2.6
2531	North Amityville CDP	13 849	13 140	5.4	2 403	10 797	187	128	334	1 125	4 316	NA	6.3
2532	North Babylon CDP	18 081	19 019	-4.9	17 514	170	35	265	97	745	6 123	NA	8.7
2534	North Bay Shore CDP	12 799	35 020	-63.5	8 776	1 887	30	159	1 947	4 769	3 464	NA	7.7
2535	North Bellmore CDP	19 707	20 630	-4.5	18 898	325	18	376	90	562	6 385	NA	6.8
2537	North Bellport CDP	8 182	NA	NA	4 887	2 645	102	150	398	1 370	2 231	NA	12.0
2538	North Boston CDP	2 581	NA	NA	2 569	1	5	2	4	15	953	NA	10.6
2542	Northeast Ithaca CDP	2 533	NA	NA	2 109	87	8	310	19	84	1 027	NA	3.3
2543	North Great River CDP	3 964	11 416	-65.3	3 863	17	8	37	39	215	1 125	NA	5.9
2550	North Hills village	3 453	NA	NA	3 056	28	0	362	7	72	1 572	NA	7.2
2556	North Lindenhurst CDP	10 563	11 511	-8.2	9 964	309	17	145	128	604	3 404	NA	4.9
2557	North Massapequa CDP	19 365	21 385	-9.4	19 069	33	7	203	53	454	6 114	NA	7.8
2560	North Merrick CDP	12 113	12 848	-5.7	11 664	101	4	298	46	311	3 981	NA	4.6
2565	North New Hyde Park CDP	14 359	15 114	-5.0	13 311	7	9	1 000	32	471	5 079	NA	5.1
2567	North Patchogue CDP	7 374	NA	NA	7 200	43	15	50	66	387	2 640	NA	5.5
2575	Northport village	7 572	NA	NA	7 421	47	3	91	10	153	3 010	16 779	6.0
2580	North Sea CDP	2 530	NA	NA	2 466	25	12	23	4	46	2 198	NA	23.7
2585	North Syracuse village	7 363	NA	NA	7 201	59	39	58	6	46	3 078	11 341	5.1
2590	North Tarrytown village	8 152	NA	NA	6 634	683	41	95	699	2 776	3 160	14 215	5.9
2595	North Tonawanda	34 989	35 760	-2.2	34 612	56	112	129	80	278	14 001	10 191	26.2
2600	North Valley Stream CDP	14 574	14 530	0.3	11 136	1 936	51	1 156	295	1 173	4 979	NA	4.9
2607	North Wantagh CDP	12 276	12 677	-3.2	12 013	32	8	191	32	366	4 341	NA	4.8
2610	Norwich	7 613	NA	NA	7 409	99	22	64	19	78	3 502	10 748	5.3
2630	Nyack village	6 558	NA	NA	3 934	2 456	5	103	60	299	3 026	13 171	2.0
2636	Oakdale CDP	7 875	NA	NA	7 704	71	3	79	18	173	2 772	NA	8.6
2650	Oceanside CDP	32 423	33 639	-3.6	31 560	128	40	460	235	1 251	11 152	NA	13.0
2660	Ogdensburg	13 521	12 375	9.3	11 891	1 118	100	91	321	751	4 610	8 306	13.1
2667	Old Bethpage CDP	5 610	NA	NA	5 382	69	5	141	13	77	1 862	NA	10.6
2685	Old Westbury village	3 897	NA	NA	2 842	658	8	329	60	275	1 004	36 643	22.1
2690	Olean	16 946	18 207	-6.9	16 224	456	83	103	80	144	7 351	9 013	15.4
2695	Oneida	10 850	10 810	0.4	10 614	70	91	52	23	64	4 463	9 581	57.0
2705	Oneonta	13 954	14 933	-6.6	13 400	297	20	165	72	297	4 685	7 442	11.3
2707	Orangeburg CDP	3 583	NA	NA	3 005	108	1	431	38	179	1 256	NA	8.0
2708	Orange Lake CDP	5 196	NA	NA	4 640	409	7	96	44	273	1 739	NA	13.9
2710	Orchard Park village	3 280	NA	NA	3 239	6	5	29	1	30	1 408	15 364	3.5
2725	Ossining village	22 582	20 196	11.8	15 836	5 214	57	430	1 045	3 692	8 258	14 071	8.3
2730	Oswego	19 195	19 793	-3.0	18 804	141	32	104	114	348	7 865	10 420	19.8
2750	Owego village	4 442	NA	NA	4 346	35	16	27	18	50	1 913	10 237	6.5
2758	Oyster Bay CDP	6 687	NA	NA	6 192	322	8	58	107	386	2 816	NA	3.2

1. Codes shown are 2-digit FIPS codes for states; 4-digit census place codes for places; and 3-digit FIPS county codes followed by 3-digit census MCD codes for minor civil divisions (MCDs). MCD names are followed by county names in parentheses. 2. Hispanic persons may be of any race. 3. Dry land or land partially or temporarily covered by water.

State/ Place/ MCD[1] code	Place	Population			Population characteristics, 1990						Total housing units, 1990	Per capita income, 1985 (Dollars)	Land area,[3] 1990 (Sq. Km.)
		1990	Places of 10,000 or more		Race					Hispanic[2]			
			1980	Percent change, 1980–1990	White	Black	Am. Indian, Eskimo Aleut	Asian & Pacific Islander	Other race				
		1	2	3	4	5	6	7	8	9	10	11	12
	NEW YORK—Con.												
2775	Palmyra village	3 566	NA	NA	3 502	13	10	31	10	25	1 550	11 450	3.4
2790	Patchogue village	11 060	11 291	-2.0	9 935	354	40	116	615	1 544	4 844	11 825	5.8
2798	Pearl River CDP	15 314	15 893	-3.6	14 845	61	7	357	44	403	5 503	NA	17.7
2800	Peekskill	19 536	18 236	7.1	14 295	4 143	42	437	619	1 897	8 401	11 813	11.2
2807	Pelham village	6 413	NA	NA	5 532	563	3	253	62	244	2 366	16 626	2.1
2810	Pelham Manor village	5 443	NA	NA	5 202	57	1	163	20	181	2 006	28 552	3.5
2815	Penn Yan village	5 248	NA	NA	5 150	49	8	24	17	72	2 271	9 299	5.4
2820	Perry village	4 219	NA	NA	4 171	28	1	14	5	25	1 794	8 494	5.9
2875	Plainedge CDP	8 739	NA	NA	8 528	27	3	159	22	287	2 812	NA	3.7
2880	Plainview CDP	26 207	28 037	-6.5	25 246	110	5	780	66	541	8 598	NA	14.8
2898	Plattsburgh	21 255	21 057	0.9	20 217	615	60	265	98	326	8 197	8 950	13.1
2899	Plattsburgh AFB CDP	5 483	NA	NA	4 515	662	18	182	106	291	1 333	NA	3.2
2905	Pleasantville village	6 592	NA	NA	6 201	126	2	223	40	280	2 556	18 701	4.7
2911	Pomona village	2 611	NA	NA	2 439	56	0	111	5	58	841	NA	6.3
2925	Port Chester village	24 728	23 565	4.9	19 633	2 528	24	426	2 117	7 446	9 513	11 735	6.1
2935	Port Ewen CDP	3 444	NA	NA	3 308	65	7	54	10	29	1 464	NA	5.1
2945	Port Jefferson village	7 455	NA	NA	7 066	116	6	206	61	304	2 908	15 696	7.8
2950	Port Jefferson Station CDP	7 232	17 009	-57.5	6 835	152	5	156	84	421	2 602	NA	6.8
2955	Port Jervis	9 060	NA	NA	8 674	203	33	53	97	383	3 870	8 725	6.6
2970	Port Washington CDP	15 387	14 521	6.0	13 431	449	19	1 056	432	1 523	5 712	NA	10.9
2975	Port Washington North village	2 736	NA	NA	2 531	36	3	142	24	124	1 055	19 559	1.2
2980	Potsdam village	10 251	10 635	-3.6	9 675	81	35	429	31	110	2 743	6 560	11.3
2985	Poughkeepsie	28 844	29 757	-3.1	18 859	9 078	101	439	367	1 086	13 112	11 234	13.3
3000	Pulaski village	2 525	NA	NA	2 506	1	6	10	2	8	1 147	NA	8.5
3002	Putnam Lake CDP	3 459	NA	NA	3 328	85	3	19	24	114	1 335	NA	10.0
3020	Ravena village	3 547	NA	NA	3 445	77	6	11	8	59	1 487	10 552	3.4
3033	Red Oaks Mill CDP	4 906	NA	NA	4 536	155	7	197	11	84	1 690	NA	9.1
3040	Rensselaer	8 255	NA	NA	7 789	361	27	22	56	124	3 652	9 481	7.2
3050	Rhinebeck village	2 725	NA	NA	2 619	62	0	25	19	56	1 345	14 522	4.0
3078	Ridge CDP	11 734	NA	NA	11 276	300	14	93	51	315	5 349	NA	34.2
3085	Riverhead CDP	8 814	NA	NA	6 205	2 466	46	55	42	220	3 536	NA	39.1
3100	Rochester	231 636	241 741	-4.2	141 503	73 024	1 103	4 081	11 925	20 055	101 154	9 967	92.7
3105	Rockville Centre village	24 727	25 412	-2.7	23 184	966	18	275	284	1 407	9 497	18 477	8.5
3107	Rocky Point CDP	8 596	NA	NA	8 445	35	10	73	33	309	3 870	NA	26.8
3117	Roessleville CDP	10 753	11 685	-8.0	10 287	291	18	128	29	136	4 839	NA	7.5
3120	Rome	44 350	43 826	1.2	39 657	3 526	107	565	495	1 714	16 661	8 922	194.1
3125	Ronkonkoma CDP	20 391	NA	NA	19 706	123	20	313	229	1 039	6 522	NA	21.2
3135	Roosevelt CDP	15 030	14 109	6.5	1 185	13 331	66	58	390	1 309	3 971	NA	4.6
3157	Roslyn Heights CDP	6 405	NA	NA	5 510	559	8	288	40	255	2 233	NA	3.9
3160	Rotterdam CDP	21 228	22 933	-7.4	20 918	148	24	98	40	197	8 635	NA	18.0
3180	Rye	14 936	15 083	-1.0	13 491	242	10	1 030	163	694	5 616	27 916	15.0
3182	Rye Brook village	7 765	NA	NA	7 249	117	6	297	96	387	2 835	21 774	9.0
3200	St. James CDP	12 703	12 122	4.8	12 497	54	7	120	25	269	4 428	NA	11.8
3210	Salamanca	6 566	NA	NA	6 020	20	482	23	21	36	2 834	7 596	15.5
3217	Salisbury CDP	12 226	NA	NA	11 402	52	17	656	99	590	4 101	NA	4.5
3240	Saranac Lake village	5 377	NA	NA	5 258	62	28	18	11	46	2 632	9 281	7.2
3245	Saratoga Springs	25 001	23 906	4.6	23 870	819	41	185	86	344	10 751	10 460	73.6
3250	Saugerties village	3 915	NA	NA	3 814	40	13	33	15	65	1 808	10 809	4.9
3270	Sayville CDP	16 550	12 013	37.8	16 162	94	31	233	30	372	5 560	NA	14.3
3275	Scarsdale village	16 987	17 650	-3.8	14 227	381	4	2 319	56	372	5 581	38 000	17.2
3285	Schenectady	65 566	67 972	-3.5	58 093	5 697	191	696	889	1 761	30 232	10 224	28.1
3303	Scotchtown CDP	8 765	NA	NA	7 633	636	31	227	238	801	3 056	NA	11.0
3305	Scotia village	7 359	NA	NA	7 209	60	6	71	13	84	3 176	11 117	4.4
3320	Sea Cliff village	5 054	NA	NA	4 864	92	4	54	40	199	2 066	16 577	2.8
3325	Seaford CDP	15 597	16 117	-3.2	15 299	28	8	214	48	384	5 147	NA	6.7
3327	Searingtown CDP	5 020	NA	NA	4 190	34	0	787	9	106	1 613	NA	2.4
3330	Selden CDP	20 608	17 259	19.4	19 814	307	13	306	168	1 074	6 425	NA	12.1
3335	Seneca Falls village	7 370	NA	NA	7 248	54	15	46	7	48	3 129	10 686	11.3
3338	Setauket-East Setauket CDP	13 634	10 176	34.0	12 826	193	23	533	59	316	4 595	NA	21.9
3360	Sherrill	2 864	NA	NA	2 832	3	9	13	7	10	1 126	10 726	5.1
3361	Shinnecock Hills CDP	2 847	NA	NA	2 646	153	7	25	16	105	2 261	NA	15.8
3362	Shirley CDP	22 936	18 072	26.9	21 985	413	39	224	275	1 734	7 021	NA	28.2
3380	Sidney village	4 720	NA	NA	4 603	44	16	39	18	30	2 038	9 743	6.1
3385	Silver Creek village	2 927	NA	NA	2 868	13	34	4	8	23	1 294	9 288	2.9
3400	Skaneateles village	2 724	NA	NA	2 707	6	0	10	1	12	1 223	17 539	3.5
3405	Sloan village	3 830	NA	NA	3 817	0	5	6	2	18	1 700	9 978	2.1
3410	Sloatsburg village	3 035	NA	NA	2 941	43	7	24	20	140	1 042	14 821	6.6
3415	Smithtown CDP	25 638	30 906	-17.0	25 041	100	18	406	73	621	8 360	NA	30.6
3435	Solvay village	6 717	NA	NA	6 638	15	34	15	15	125	3 115	11 485	4.3
3440	Sound Beach CDP	9 102	NA	NA	8 908	57	15	100	22	313	3 575	NA	6.9
3445	Southampton village	3 980	NA	NA	3 235	664	18	46	17	126	2 980	20 486	16.4
3465	South Farmingdale CDP	15 377	16 439	-6.5	14 945	45	8	294	85	525	4 970	NA	5.6
3475	South Glens Falls village	3 506	NA	NA	3 469	16	6	15	0	16	1 539	10 554	3.5

1. Codes shown are 2-digit FIPS codes for states; 4-digit census place codes for places; and 3-digit FIPS county codes followed by 3-digit census MCD codes for minor civil divisions (MCDs). MCD names are followed by county names in parentheses. 2. Hispanic persons may be of any race. 3. Dry land or land partially or temporarily covered by water.

State/ Place/ MCD[1] code	Place	Population: 1990	Population: Places of 10,000 or more: 1980	Population: Places of 10,000 or more: Percent change, 1980–1990	Population characteristics, 1990: Race: White	Race: Black	Race: Am. Indian, Eskimo Aleut	Race: Asian & Pacific Islander	Race: Other race	Hispanic[2]	Total housing units, 1990	Per capita income, 1985 (Dollars)	Land area,[3] 1990 (Sq. Km.)
		1	2	3	4	5	6	7	8	9	10	11	12
	NEW YORK—Con.												
3477	South Hempstead CDP	3 014	NA	NA	2 716	164	4	88	42	128	1 042	NA	1.5
3478	South Hill CDP	5 423	NA	NA	5 186	144	6	51	36	96	931	NA	15.3
3480	South Huntington CDP	9 624	14 854	-35.2	9 372	51	1	166	34	233	3 297	NA	8.7
3483	South Lockport CDP	7 112	NA	NA	6 812	199	28	44	29	82	2 842	NA	14.9
3485	South Nyack village	3 352	NA	NA	2 420	750	7	155	20	147	1 195	12 873	1.6
3490	Southold CDP	5 192	NA	NA	5 100	50	8	17	17	96	3 539	NA	27.0
3491	Southport CDP	7 753	NA	NA	7 605	111	8	15	14	25	3 233	NA	14.2
3493	South Valley Stream CDP	5 328	NA	NA	5 024	35	1	266	2	91	2 049	NA	2.2
3497	Spackenkill CDP	4 660	NA	NA	4 152	141	3	352	12	105	1 596	NA	7.5
3515	Spencerport village	3 606	NA	NA	3 571	9	6	18	2	33	1 392	13 043	3.5
3519	Springs CDP	4 355	NA	NA	4 188	59	7	55	46	201	3 459	NA	21.9
3520	Spring Valley village	21 802	20 537	6.2	10 781	9 392	78	1 134	417	1 632	8 116	13 193	5.4
3525	Springville village	4 310	NA	NA	4 268	17	9	12	4	12	1 710	9 927	9.2
3545	Stony Brook CDP	13 726	16 155	-15.0	12 922	177	18	566	43	322	4 757	NA	14.9
3550	Stony Point CDP	10 587	NA	NA	10 304	124	19	55	85	471	3 685	NA	14.2
3556	Suffern village	11 055	10 794	2.4	10 212	472	52	219	100	555	4 720	16 441	5.4
3563	Syosset CDP	18 967	NA	NA	17 337	111	5	1 468	46	395	6 342	NA	12.9
3565	Syracuse	163 860	170 105	-3.7	122 867	33 320	2 062	3 559	2 052	4 734	71 502	9 644	65.0
3573	Tappan CDP	6 867	NA	NA	5 804	143	4	856	60	357	2 225	NA	7.2
3575	Tarrytown village	10 739	10 648	0.9	9 178	769	9	444	339	1 399	4 311	17 980	7.7
3577	Terryville CDP	10 275	NA	NA	9 799	171	23	192	90	603	3 020	NA	8.3
3582	Thiells CDP	5 204	NA	NA	4 869	136	5	119	75	379	1 525	NA	4.8
3585	Thomaston village	2 612	NA	NA	2 329	50	0	189	44	240	1 043	24 388	1.1
3587	Thornwood CDP	7 025	NA	NA	6 645	138	5	174	63	175	2 203	NA	11.3
3595	Ticonderoga village	2 770	NA	NA	2 751	8	1	8	2	6	1 156	9 156	3.5
3610	Tonawanda	17 284	18 693	-7.5	17 082	28	99	60	15	118	7 062	9 922	9.8
3612	Tonawanda CDP	65 284	72 795	-10.3	63 934	475	103	669	103	490	27 259	NA	45.0
3618	Town Line CDP	2 721	NA	NA	2 707	3	3	8	0	14	893	NA	12.0
3625	Troy	54 269	56 638	-4.2	47 944	4 132	123	1 638	432	1 123	22 871	8 681	27.0
3635	Tuckahoe village	6 302	NA	NA	4 579	928	11	699	85	239	2 739	14 680	1.6
3645	Tupper Lake village	4 087	NA	NA	4 034	20	26	5	2	18	1 813	9 044	4.6
3665	Uniondale CDP	20 328	20 016	1.6	9 114	9 378	91	520	1 225	2 883	5 913	NA	6.9
3677	University Gardens CDP	4 419	NA	NA	4 008	109	0	242	60	276	1 780	NA	1.4
3690	Utica	68 637	75 632	-9.2	59 479	7 199	178	771	1 010	2 332	31 127	8 689	42.3
3693	Vails Gate CDP	3 014	NA	NA	2 652	210	4	34	114	292	1 334	NA	2.6
3698	Valley Cottage CDP	9 007	NA	NA	8 004	249	12	682	60	386	3 152	NA	11.1
3710	Valley Stream village	33 946	35 769	-5.1	32 231	149	13	1 224	329	1 514	12 165	13 861	8.9
3753	Village Green CDP	4 198	NA	NA	4 074	84	18	17	5	49	2 095	NA	3.2
3757	Viola CDP	4 504	NA	NA	4 387	70	2	33	12	67	1 370	NA	7.0
3760	Voorheesville village	3 225	NA	NA	3 171	15	8	28	3	21	1 137	13 346	8.1
3767	Wading River CDP	5 317	NA	NA	5 133	122	2	35	25	127	2 142	NA	25.4
3770	Walden village	5 836	NA	NA	5 649	65	14	49	59	238	2 264	8 954	5.1
3780	Walton village	3 326	NA	NA	3 287	13	0	23	3	14	1 496	10 043	3.9
3790	Wantagh CDP	18 567	19 817	-6.3	18 214	29	6	269	49	391	6 007	NA	9.9
3795	Wappingers Falls village	4 605	NA	NA	4 210	176	4	177	38	184	2 058	11 715	3.0
3802	Warrensburg CDP	3 204	NA	NA	3 184	5	3	12	0	16	1 381	NA	23.6
3805	Warsaw village	3 830	NA	NA	3 759	11	10	41	9	21	1 467	10 236	10.7
3810	Warwick village	5 984	NA	NA	5 620	227	49	40	48	220	2 415	11 565	5.6
3820	Washingtonville village	4 906	NA	NA	4 507	239	13	68	79	286	1 709	NA	6.7
3830	Waterloo village	5 116	NA	NA	5 042	31	3	28	12	26	1 932	9 168	5.1
3835	Watertown	29 429	27 861	5.6	27 600	1 122	150	242	315	594	12 405	9 046	22.5
3845	Watervliet	11 061	11 354	-2.6	10 772	182	25	48	34	113	5 145	10 230	3.4
3855	Waverly village	4 787	NA	NA	4 694	39	4	23	27	43	2 017	9 041	5.9
3865	Webster village	5 464	NA	NA	5 152	152	15	130	15	61	2 362	12 252	5.7
3880	Wellsville village	5 241	NA	NA	5 168	18	13	35	7	45	2 387	9 600	5.9
3881	Wesley Hills village	4 305	NA	NA	3 988	169	6	123	19	144	1 329	19 169	8.7
3885	West Babylon CDP	42 410	41 699	1.7	37 354	4 189	70	410	387	2 013	13 799	NA	20.0
3887	West Bay Shore CDP	4 907	NA	NA	4 785	15	7	73	27	182	1 788	NA	6.2
3890	Westbury village	13 060	13 871	-5.8	9 517	2 761	31	483	268	1 180	4 546	16 264	6.2
3900	West Elmira CDP	5 218	NA	NA	5 055	51	3	104	5	25	2 221	NA	7.8
3910	Westfield village	3 451	NA	NA	3 388	12	5	24	22	76	1 443	10 494	9.9
3915	West Glens Falls CDP	5 964	NA	NA	5 889	35	13	21	6	51	2 253	NA	11.9
3925	West Haverstraw village	9 183	NA	NA	7 165	1 123	27	291	577	1 697	3 281	10 099	4.0
3930	West Hempstead CDP	17 689	18 536	-4.6	16 679	348	19	509	134	707	5 992	NA	6.9
3932	West Hills CDP	5 849	NA	NA	5 627	20	2	198	2	98	1 993	NA	12.8
3935	West Islip CDP	28 419	29 533	-3.8	27 912	44	8	333	122	878	8 657	NA	16.0
3937	Westmere CDP	6 750	NA	NA	6 376	211	8	129	26	82	3 018	NA	8.2
3940	West Nyack CDP	3 437	NA	NA	3 119	85	4	189	40	152	1 118	NA	7.5
3944	West Point CDP	8 024	NA	NA	6 961	587	25	322	129	379	1 134	NA	63.0
3950	West Sayville CDP	4 680	NA	NA	4 601	25	9	31	14	94	1 884	NA	4.8
3955	West Seneca CDP	47 866	51 210	-6.5	47 314	213	89	181	69	285	17 818	NA	55.4
3957	Westvale CDP	5 952	NA	NA	5 876	10	15	44	7	45	2 209	NA	4.2
3963	Wheatley Heights CDP	5 027	NA	NA	2 830	1 855	53	176	113	436	1 449	NA	3.5

1. Codes shown are 2-digit FIPS codes for states; 4-digit census place codes for places; and 3-digit FIPS county codes followed by 3-digit census MCD codes for minor civil divisions (MCDs). MCD names are followed by county names in parentheses. 2. Hispanic persons may be of any race. 3. Dry land or land partially or temporarily covered by water.

Table D. Places — **Population, Housing, Money Income, and Land Area**

State/ Place/ MCD[1] code	Place	Population 1990	Population, Places of 10,000 or more: 1980	Population, Places of 10,000 or more: Percent change, 1980–1990	Population characteristics, 1990 — Race: White	Race: Black	Race: Am. Indian, Eskimo Aleut	Race: Asian & Pacific Islander	Race: Other race	Hispanic[2]	Total housing units, 1990	Per capita income, 1985 (Dollars)	Land area,[3] 1990 (Sq. Km.)
		1	2	3	4	5	6	7	8	9	10	11	12
	NEW YORK—Con.												
3965	Whitehall village	3 071	NA	NA	3 057	5	3	6	0	25	1 323	8 701	12.1
3970	White Plains	48 718	46 999	3.7	35 883	9 271	82	1 495	1 987	6 900	20 714	17 637	25.4
3975	Whitesboro village	4 195	NA	NA	4 125	30	4	28	8	29	1 892	9 882	2.8
3995	Williamsville village	5 583	NA	NA	5 512	28	5	36	2	15	2 613	14 090	3.2
4000	Williston Park village	7 516	NA	NA	7 211	30	7	251	17	218	2 641	14 246	1.6
4033	Woodbury CDP	8 008	NA	NA	7 555	93	4	349	7	94	2 569	NA	13.1
4040	Woodmere CDP	15 578	17 205	-9.5	14 945	178	2	367	86	330	5 308	NA	6.8
4065	Wyandanch CDP	8 950	13 215	-32.3	842	7 477	64	27	540	1 322	2 362	NA	11.5
4067	Wyantskill CDP	3 329	NA	NA	3 298	19	0	12	0	13	1 315	NA	6.3
4072	Yaphank CDP	4 637	NA	NA	4 152	427	13	24	21	195	1 506	NA	35.4
4075	Yonkers	188 082	195 351	-3.7	143 339	26 547	342	5 637	12 217	31 476	75 562	13 112	46.8
4085	Yorktown Heights CDP	7 690	NA	NA	7 125	226	3	290	46	278	2 543	NA	14.8
4090	Yorkville village	2 972	NA	NA	2 948	6	1	12	5	25	1 295	9 862	1.7
0010	Berne town (Albany)	3 053	NA	NA	3 033	13	1	6	0	11	1 372	10 547	166.0
0010	Bethlehem town (Albany)	27 552	24 296	13.4	26 576	521	28	352	75	301	10 739	15 816	126.4
0010	Coeymans town (Albany)	8 158	NA	NA	7 940	159	12	22	25	137	3 286	10 210	130.0
0010	Colonie town (Albany)	76 494	74 593	2.5	72 342	2 156	97	1 677	222	942	29 634	13 417	145.3
0010	Guilderland town (Albany)	28 764	26 515	8.5	27 629	603	28	416	88	353	12 106	13 985	150.9
0010	Knox town (Albany)	2 661	NA	NA	2 636	14	0	10	1	15	980	NA	107.5
0010	New Scotland town (Albany)	9 139	NA	NA	9 039	27	16	49	8	65	3 365	13 519	150.4
0010	Westerlo town (Albany)	3 325	NA	NA	3 305	2	6	2	10	31	1 436	9 072	149.9
0030	Alfred town (Allegany)	5 791	NA	NA	5 442	151	16	145	37	97	1 060	5 369	81.7
0030	Caneadea town (Allegany)	2 551	NA	NA	2 471	22	3	46	9	27	859	NA	92.0
0030	Cuba town (Allegany)	3 401	NA	NA	3 382	3	5	7	4	15	1 594	9 349	91.0
0031	Wellsville town (Allegany)	8 116	NA	NA	8 011	24	19	46	16	51	3 527	9 323	95.0
0070	Barker town (Broome)	2 714	NA	NA	2 669	16	20	2	7	10	963	NA	107.2
0070	Binghamton town (Broome)	5 006	NA	NA	4 853	73	5	70	5	36	1 809	12 929	66.0
0070	Chenango town (Broome)	12 310	12 233	0.6	12 168	70	10	42	20	91	4 673	11 030	88.0
0070	Colesville town (Broome)	5 590	NA	NA	5 538	18	7	25	2	32	2 068	8 602	203.4
0070	Conklin town (Broome)	6 265	NA	NA	6 160	50	9	31	15	47	2 350	9 654	63.5
0070	Dickinson town (Broome)	5 486	NA	NA	5 386	74	8	9	9	46	2 081	10 709	12.4
0070	Fenton town (Broome)	7 236	NA	NA	7 170	29	17	11	9	22	2 823	9 600	85.2
0070	Kirkwood town (Broome)	6 096	NA	NA	6 013	33	7	36	7	29	2 400	9 727	80.2
0070	Maine town (Broome)	5 576	NA	NA	5 531	18	3	23	1	21	2 073	10 555	118.4
0070	Sanford town (Broome)	2 576	NA	NA	2 566	5	3	2	0	25	1 414	8 630	233.3
0070	Triangle town (Broome)	3 006	NA	NA	2 991	1	4	10	0	5	1 139	8 850	98.7
0070	Union town (Broome)	59 786	61 179	-2.3	57 621	837	65	1 101	162	612	26 345	11 620	91.1
0070	Vestal town (Broome)	26 733	27 238	-1.9	24 860	480	16	1 203	174	479	8 976	12 279	135.1
0070	Windsor town (Broome)	6 440	NA	NA	6 392	18	6	20	4	38	2 643	8 709	237.0
0090	Allegany town (Cattaraugus)	8 327	NA	NA	8 143	52	30	95	7	57	2 591	8 272	184.4
0090	Franklinville town (Cattaraugus)	2 968	NA	NA	2 948	3	2	11	4	11	1 460	7 429	134.2
0091	Persia town (Cattaraugus)	2 530	NA	NA	2 412	8	98	6	6	27	1 077	NA	54.2
0091	Portville town (Cattaraugus)	4 397	NA	NA	4 354	26	7	2	8	27	1 662	8 742	92.3
0091	Randolph town (Cattaraugus)	2 613	NA	NA	2 579	12	11	6	5	5	1 036	8 429	93.7
0091	Yorkshire town (Cattaraugus)	3 905	NA	NA	3 859	10	9	17	10	18	1 626	7 988	95.7
0110	Aurelius town (Cayuga)	2 913	NA	NA	2 885	8	16	4	0	36	1 144	9 774	78.4
0110	Brutus town (Cayuga)	5 013	NA	NA	4 930	16	38	22	7	24	1 839	9 151	57.3
0110	Fleming town (Cayuga)	2 644	NA	NA	2 617	13	1	11	2	21	1 049	NA	56.5
0110	Moravia town (Cayuga)	3 871	NA	NA	2 961	679	4	18	209	309	1 165	8 369	75.1
0110	Owasco town (Cayuga)	3 490	NA	NA	3 466	6	1	13	4	8	1 470	11 499	54.2
0110	Sennett town (Cayuga)	2 913	NA	NA	2 839	27	5	38	4	11	953	10 626	74.6
0111	Sterling town (Cayuga)	3 285	NA	NA	3 258	11	13	0	3	7	1 761	9 352	118.2
0130	Busti town (Chautauqua)	8 050	NA	NA	7 941	28	13	62	6	40	3 552	11 823	123.7
0130	Carroll town (Chautauqua)	3 539	NA	NA	3 527	2	10	0	0	6	1 332	9 108	86.7
0130	Chautauqua town (Chautauqua)	4 554	NA	NA	4 501	21	4	16	12	40	3 820	9 397	174.1
0130	Ellery town (Chautauqua)	4 534	NA	NA	4 498	21	7	3	5	12	2 393	10 870	123.2
0130	Ellicott town (Chautauqua)	9 455	NA	NA	9 367	37	18	28	5	47	4 095	10 720	79.3
0130	Hanover town (Chautauqua)	7 380	NA	NA	7 219	41	87	13	20	50	3 417	8 644	127.7
0131	Poland town (Chautauqua)	2 604	NA	NA	2 578	4	12	7	3	14	1 032	8 626	95.0
0131	Pomfret town (Chautauqua)	14 224	14 971	-5.0	13 624	352	30	125	93	267	5 184	8 419	113.7
0131	Portland town (Chautauqua)	4 832	NA	NA	4 223	393	10	13	193	288	1 934	8 563	88.7
0131	Ripley town (Chautauqua)	2 967	NA	NA	2 951	3	6	1	6	10	1 219	7 058	126.8
0131	Sheridan town (Chautauqua)	2 582	NA	NA	2 527	15	14	21	5	24	994	10 020	96.6
0131	Stockton town (Chautauqua)	2 515	NA	NA	2 501	4	8	0	2	22	1 053	NA	122.6
0131	Westfield town (Chautauqua)	5 194	NA	NA	5 119	13	7	28	27	97	2 414	9 494	122.3
0150	Big Flats town (Chemung)	7 596	NA	NA	7 405	67	9	108	7	36	2 703	10 937	115.2
0150	Catlin town (Chemung)	2 626	NA	NA	2 588	13	5	8	12	13	985	8 102	98.5
0150	Chemung town (Chemung)	2 540	NA	NA	2 507	12	13	2	6	21	951	NA	128.0
0150	Elmira town (Chemung)	7 440	NA	NA	7 236	74	4	117	9	37	3 121	13 953	57.7
0150	Horseheads town (Chemung)	19 926	20 254	-1.6	19 422	236	30	197	41	103	8 038	10 273	92.9
0150	Southport town (Chemung)	11 571	11 586	-0.1	10 755	632	19	36	129	278	4 324	9 902	120.5
0150	Veteran town (Chemung)	3 468	NA	NA	3 417	20	3	15	13	26	1 312	9 573	99.5
0170	Afton town (Chenango)	2 972	NA	NA	2 942	3	22	3	2	20	1 256	9 044	118.9

1. Codes shown are 2-digit FIPS codes for states; 4-digit census place codes for places; and 3-digit FIPS county codes followed by 3-digit census MCD codes for minor civil divisions (MCDs). MCD names are followed by county names in parentheses. 2. Hispanic persons may be of any race. 3. Dry land or land partially or temporarily covered by water.

State/ Place/ MCD[1] code	Place	Population			Population characteristics, 1990						Total housing units, 1990	Per capita income, 1985 (Dollars)	Land area,[3] 1990 (Sq. Km.)
			Places of 10,000 or more		Race								
		1990	1980	Percent change, 1980–1990	White	Black	Am. Indian, Eskimo Aleut	Asian & Pacific Islander	Other race	Hispanic[2]			
		1	2	3	4	5	6	7	8	9	10	11	12
	NEW YORK—Con.												
0170	Bainbridge town (Chenango)	3 445	NA	NA	3 413	5	2	18	7	29	1 424	9 809	88.9
0170	Greene town (Chenango)	6 053	NA	NA	5 999	16	17	19	2	36	2 541	9 251	194.6
0170	Guilford town (Chenango)	2 875	NA	NA	2 851	13	4	5	2	21	1 293	NA	159.7
0170	New Berlin town (Chenango)	3 046	NA	NA	3 012	13	9	8	4	30	1 338	7 430	120.1
0170	Norwich town (Chenango)	4 084	NA	NA	4 044	14	12	10	4	25	1 678	9 679	108.9
0170	Oxford town (Chenango)	4 075	NA	NA	4 035	8	12	13	7	35	1 631	8 168	155.6
0171	Sherburne town (Chenango)	3 903	NA	NA	3 879	5	9	7	3	23	1 702	9 335	112.8
0190	Altona town (Clinton)	2 775	NA	NA	2 238	400	12	8	117	244	819	NA	261.7
0190	Au Sable town (Clinton)	2 870	NA	NA	2 830	17	6	10	7	29	1 203	8 524	101.3
0190	Beekmantown town (Clinton)	5 108	NA	NA	5 053	39	3	2	11	25	1 935	9 175	156.6
0190	Champlain town (Clinton)	5 796	NA	NA	5 754	11	10	12	9	37	2 543	9 871	132.6
0190	Chazy town (Clinton)	3 890	NA	NA	3 875	7	1	4	3	12	1 556	8 251	140.4
0190	Dannemora town (Clinton)	5 232	NA	NA	3 089	1 722	33	35	353	846	1 212	5 619	153.3
0190	Mooers town (Clinton)	2 995	NA	NA	2 980	3	6	5	1	20	1 170	7 740	227.1
0190	Peru town (Clinton)	6 254	NA	NA	6 131	65	16	36	6	45	2 381	9 311	205.5
0190	Plattsburgh town (Clinton)	17 231	16 394	5.1	16 016	792	32	269	122	421	5 988	8 443	119.1
0190	Saranac town (Clinton)	3 710	NA	NA	3 696	4	9	0	1	32	1 436	8 647	296.6
0190	Schuyler Falls town (Clinton)	4 787	NA	NA	4 684	60	5	32	6	43	1 706	8 474	97.0
0210	Chatham town (Columbia)	4 413	NA	NA	4 315	85	1	6	6	45	2 062	11 291	138.0
0210	Claverack town (Columbia)	6 414	NA	NA	6 284	71	8	37	14	59	2 750	9 488	123.4
0210	Copake town (Columbia)	3 118	NA	NA	3 072	18	11	4	13	35	2 089	9 013	106.1
0210	Ghent town (Columbia)	4 812	NA	NA	4 718	53	6	15	20	47	2 089	10 518	117.0
0210	Greenport town (Columbia)	4 101	NA	NA	3 936	94	11	29	31	75	1 821	11 527	48.6
0210	Kinderhook town (Columbia)	8 112	NA	NA	8 030	25	8	44	5	73	3 152	11 041	82.5
0210	Livingston town (Columbia)	3 582	NA	NA	3 506	47	3	14	12	56	1 602	8 951	99.0
0210	Stockport town (Columbia)	3 085	NA	NA	2 999	72	1	3	10	38	1 165	9 689	30.2
0230	Cortlandville town (Cortland)	8 054	NA	NA	7 933	24	17	69	11	52	3 124	10 059	129.0
0230	Homer town (Cortland)	6 508	NA	NA	6 456	16	9	22	5	39	2 465	9 295	130.5
0250	Delhi town (Delaware)	5 015	NA	NA	4 868	80	9	44	14	62	1 646	7 434	167.3
0250	Hancock town (Delaware)	3 384	NA	NA	3 301	54	14	2	13	45	2 259	8 620	412.7
0250	Middletown town (Delaware)	3 406	NA	NA	3 337	15	6	15	33	128	2 972	9 552	249.7
0250	Sidney town (Delaware)	6 667	NA	NA	6 516	64	23	43	21	42	2 995	9 289	132.6
0250	Walton town (Delaware)	5 953	NA	NA	5 889	29	2	27	6	28	2 838	9 176	251.8
0270	Amenia town (Dutchess)	5 195	NA	NA	4 876	252	8	27	32	75	1 821	8 963	112.2
0270	Beekman town (Dutchess)	10 447	NA	NA	8 888	1 350	15	148	46	883	3 176	9 071	77.7
0270	Clinton town (Dutchess)	3 760	NA	NA	3 662	52	3	31	12	74	1 544	13 200	99.6
0270	Dover town (Dutchess)	7 778	NA	NA	6 983	629	20	81	65	201	3 018	9 638	144.3
0270	East Fishkill town (Dutchess)	22 101	18 091	22.2	20 721	483	37	773	87	557	7 265	12 544	147.4
0270	Fishkill town (Dutchess)	17 655	15 506	13.9	14 543	2 470	12	404	226	1 671	5 991	13 120	71.1
0270	Hyde Park town (Dutchess)	21 230	20 737	2.4	19 823	920	17	364	106	390	7 473	12 391	95.7
0270	La Grange town (Dutchess)	13 274	12 375	7.3	12 502	286	18	405	63	286	4 553	14 570	102.8
0270	North East town (Dutchess)	2 918	NA	NA	2 838	55	5	19	1	26	1 367	10 387	112.3
0270	Pawling town (Dutchess)	5 947	NA	NA	5 806	79	9	33	20	106	2 580	13 827	114.4
0270	Pleasant Valley town (Dutchess)	8 063	NA	NA	7 813	137	9	80	24	121	3 186	13 852	85.3
0270	Poughkeepsie town (Dutchess)	40 143	39 591	1.4	36 011	2 264	36	1 595	237	982	14 329	13 271	74.5
0270	Red Hook town (Dutchess)	9 565	NA	NA	9 178	131	16	207	33	148	3 405	10 541	95.1
0270	Rhinebeck town (Dutchess)	7 558	NA	NA	7 221	224	5	67	41	154	3 047	12 470	93.9
0270	Stanford town (Dutchess)	3 495	NA	NA	3 405	61	5	7	17	45	1 564	12 067	129.5
0271	Union Vale town (Dutchess)	3 577	NA	NA	3 456	72	1	36	12	49	1 340	11 589	97.6
0271	Wappinger town (Dutchess)	26 008	26 765	-2.8	23 762	1 035	29	997	185	881	9 728	13 477	70.6
0271	Washington town (Dutchess)	4 479	NA	NA	4 285	164	6	8	16	77	2 070	15 030	153.0
0290	Alden town (Erie)	10 372	10 067	3.0	9 565	689	26	16	76	138	3 080	9 016	89.4
0290	Amherst town (Erie)	111 711	108 706	2.8	103 763	3 149	169	4 374	256	1 226	43 303	14 381	138.0
0290	Aurora town (Erie)	13 433	13 882	-3.2	13 364	25	8	28	8	62	5 128	12 413	94.3
0290	Boston town (Erie)	7 445	NA	NA	7 412	6	9	14	4	39	2 772	11 271	92.8
0290	Cheektowaga town (Erie)	99 314	109 442	-9.3	97 746	966	136	371	95	471	40 760	10 271	76.5
0290	Clarence town (Erie)	20 041	18 146	10.4	19 763	76	31	156	15	83	7 215	13 256	138.4
0290	Colden town (Erie)	2 899	NA	NA	2 889	2	2	6	0	12	1 141	10 169	92.3
0290	Collins town (Erie)	6 020	NA	NA	4 894	765	97	41	223	372	1 767	8 556	124.6
0290	Concord town (Erie)	8 387	NA	NA	8 308	28	14	21	16	30	3 274	9 546	181.6
0290	Eden town (Erie)	7 416	NA	NA	7 340	18	18	26	14	44	2 650	10 234	103.1
0290	Elma town (Erie)	10 355	10 564	-2.0	10 309	10	5	23	8	37	3 800	12 657	89.3
0290	Evans town (Erie)	17 478	17 944	-2.6	17 281	60	73	22	42	155	6 854	9 268	108.4
0290	Grand Island town (Erie)	17 561	16 770	4.7	16 946	281	43	264	27	148	6 528	12 320	74.1
0290	Hamburg town (Erie)	53 735	53 270	0.9	53 136	228	86	162	123	692	20 462	10 884	106.9
0290	Holland town (Erie)	3 572	NA	NA	3 549	3	6	14	0	14	1 343	8 873	92.4
0290	Lancaster town (Erie)	32 181	30 170	6.7	31 824	160	77	99	21	158	12 708	10 523	98.1
0291	Marilla town (Erie)	5 250	NA	NA	5 222	3	11	12	2	16	1 836	10 537	71.4
0291	Newstead town (Erie)	7 440	NA	NA	7 362	15	52	5	6	25	2 995	9 278	132.4
0291	North Collins town (Erie)	3 502	NA	NA	3 426	14	43	12	7	47	1 297	8 289	111.0
0291	Orchard Park town (Erie)	24 632	24 359	1.1	24 236	113	30	223	30	210	9 157	13 401	99.7
0291	Sardinia town (Erie)	2 667	NA	NA	2 655	0	7	5	0	8	1 001	8 996	130.3
0291	Tonawanda town (Erie)	82 464	91 269	-9.6	80 889	552	139	748	136	620	34 589	11 595	48.7

1. Codes shown are 2-digit FIPS codes for states; 4-digit census place codes for places; and 3-digit FIPS county codes followed by 3-digit census MCD codes for minor civil divisions (MCDs). MCD names are followed by county names in parentheses. 2. Hispanic persons may be of any race. 3. Dry land or land partially or temporarily covered by water.

State/ Place/ MCD[1] code	Place	Population			Population characteristics, 1990						Total housing units, 1990	Per capita income, 1985 (Dollars)	Land area,[3] 1990 (Sq. Km.)
		1990	Places of 10,000 or more		Race					Hispanic[2]			
			1980	Percent change, 1980–1990	White	Black	Am. Indian, Eskimo Aleut	Asian & Pacific Islander	Other race				
		1	2	3	4	5	6	7	8	9	10	11	12
	NEW YORK—Con.												
0291	Wales town (Erie)	2 917	NA	NA	2 898	3	8	7	1	8	1 092	10 550	92.2
0291	West Seneca town (Erie)	47 830	51 210	-6.6	47 282	213	89	177	69	285	17 807	10 463	55.4
0310	Moriah town (Essex)	4 884	NA	NA	4 705	102	21	11	45	102	2 142	7 962	172.1
0310	North Elba town (Essex)	7 870	NA	NA	6 750	875	23	101	121	552	3 733	10 042	393.4
0310	Ticonderoga town (Essex)	5 149	NA	NA	5 123	10	2	11	3	13	2 445	9 200	212.2
0330	Altamont town (Franklin)	6 199	NA	NA	6 075	77	34	10	3	38	2 991	8 830	304.7
0330	Harrietstown town (Franklin)	5 621	NA	NA	5 497	68	19	26	11	44	3 144	9 059	509.8
0330	Malone town (Franklin)	12 982	11 276	15.1	11 140	1 421	64	39	318	862	4 655	8 498	263.8
0330	Moira town (Franklin)	2 684	NA	NA	2 658	6	14	4	2	6	1 079	6 897	117.2
0350	Broadalbin town (Fulton)	4 397	NA	NA	4 365	12	3	11	6	29	2 287	9 188	82.2
0350	Johnstown town (Fulton)	6 418	NA	NA	6 341	50	6	15	6	34	2 459	8 849	182.5
0350	Mayfield town (Fulton)	5 738	NA	NA	5 706	14	6	11	1	29	2 777	9 232	151.4
0350	Northampton town (Fulton)	2 705	NA	NA	2 694	2	1	5	3	9	1 843	8 893	54.5
0350	Perth town (Fulton)	3 377	NA	NA	3 133	202	14	12	16	102	1 277	8 468	67.5
0370	Batavia town (Genesee)	6 055	NA	NA	5 926	55	16	48	10	45	2 226	9 875	125.5
0370	Bergen town (Genesee)	2 794	NA	NA	2 761	9	4	10	10	29	1 040	10 940	71.6
0370	Darien town (Genesee)	2 979	NA	NA	2 966	5	8	0	0	11	1 016	9 001	123.1
0370	Le Roy town (Genesee)	8 176	NA	NA	7 918	194	21	31	12	40	3 117	10 224	109.2
0370	Oakfield town (Genesee)	3 312	NA	NA	3 235	49	15	1	12	23	1 231	9 288	60.7
0370	Pembroke town (Genesee)	4 232	NA	NA	4 184	21	18	9	0	7	1 563	9 192	108.0
0370	Stafford town (Genesee)	2 593	NA	NA	2 549	18	18	3	5	11	1 001	10 528	80.6
0390	Athens town (Greene)	3 561	NA	NA	3 477	32	10	35	7	41	1 759	9 289	67.8
0390	Cairo town (Greene)	5 418	NA	NA	5 296	18	22	12	70	144	2 995	8 275	155.3
0390	Catskill town (Greene)	11 965	11 485	4.2	11 127	643	43	58	94	334	5 406	9 651	156.8
0390	Coxsackie town (Greene)	7 633	NA	NA	5 716	1 414	22	39	442	787	2 463	8 868	95.6
0390	Greenville town (Greene)	3 135	NA	NA	3 111	11	5	5	3	25	1 541	10 334	100.8
0390	New Baltimore town (Greene)	3 371	NA	NA	3 332	22	5	4	8	39	1 338	10 085	107.7
0430	Frankfort town (Herkimer)	7 494	NA	NA	7 463	14	4	3	10	46	2 957	9 154	96.4
0430	German Flatts town (Herkimer)	14 345	14 981	-4.2	14 187	57	27	34	40	105	5 777	8 573	87.4
0430	Herkimer town (Herkimer)	10 401	11 023	-5.6	10 293	53	7	39	9	64	4 444	8 670	81.8
0430	Manheim town (Herkimer)	3 527	NA	NA	3 507	5	1	10	4	16	1 523	7 550	75.2
0430	Schuyler town (Herkimer)	3 508	NA	NA	3 487	3	12	1	5	12	1 448	9 408	103.2
0450	Adams town (Jefferson)	4 977	NA	NA	4 937	9	16	9	6	22	1 959	8 706	109.8
0450	Alexandria town (Jefferson)	3 949	NA	NA	3 937	2	7	1	2	6	3 198	8 330	189.2
0450	Brownville town (Jefferson)	5 604	NA	NA	5 565	12	16	8	3	13	2 612	8 114	153.6
0450	Cape Vincent town (Jefferson)	2 768	NA	NA	1 823	526	6	4	409	420	2 492	NA	146.3
0450	Champion town (Jefferson)	4 574	NA	NA	4 350	143	12	28	41	98	1 837	8 416	114.8
0450	Clayton town (Jefferson)	4 629	NA	NA	4 480	92	8	10	39	83	3 014	8 362	213.9
0450	Ellisburg town (Jefferson)	3 386	NA	NA	3 367	2	9	7	1	9	1 531	7 184	220.8
0450	Hounsfield town (Jefferson)	3 089	NA	NA	3 064	7	11	7	0	2	1 607	8 926	127.6
0450	Le Ray town (Jefferson)	17 973	NA	NA	13 047	3 559	92	439	836	1 328	4 651	8 195	190.9
0450	Pamelia town (Jefferson)	2 811	NA	NA	2 707	53	14	25	12	19	988	NA	88.5
0450	Rutland town (Jefferson)	3 023	NA	NA	2 951	52	3	9	8	32	1 101	8 342	117.0
0451	Watertown town (Jefferson)	4 341	NA	NA	3 647	520	8	33	133	294	1 362	9 534	93.3
0451	Wilna town (Jefferson)	6 899	NA	NA	6 519	193	44	95	48	123	2 668	7 654	204.4
0490	Croghan town (Lewis)	3 071	NA	NA	3 058	2	0	5	6	13	1 390	7 516	464.7
0490	Denmark town (Lewis)	2 718	NA	NA	2 631	44	5	21	17	33	981	NA	131.1
0490	Lowville town (Lewis)	4 849	NA	NA	4 744	44	6	36	19	35	1 934	10 325	97.9
0490	New Bremen town (Lewis)	2 526	NA	NA	2 504	5	8	6	3	9	925	NA	143.8
0510	Avon town (Livingston)	6 283	NA	NA	6 103	104	26	34	16	57	2 425	10 782	106.6
0510	Caledonia town (Livingston)	4 441	NA	NA	4 248	152	14	16	11	16	1 656	10 823	114.3
0510	Geneseo town (Livingston)	9 178	NA	NA	8 840	164	30	108	36	114	2 548	7 850	113.9
0510	Groveland town (Livingston)	3 190	NA	NA	2 134	860	18	11	167	417	716	NA	101.4
0510	Lima town (Livingston)	4 187	NA	NA	4 115	26	6	29	11	40	1 522	9 907	82.6
0510	Livonia town (Livingston)	6 804	NA	NA	6 714	18	24	37	11	35	2 894	10 454	99.2
0510	Mount Morris town (Livingston)	4 633	NA	NA	4 487	44	8	15	79	141	1 899	9 168	131.3
0510	North Dansville town (Livingston)	5 783	NA	NA	5 705	29	7	35	7	34	2 489	10 623	25.5
0510	Nunda town (Livingston)	2 931	NA	NA	2 903	12	3	1	12	26	1 137	9 226	96.0
0510	York town (Livingston)	3 513	NA	NA	3 444	54	4	7	4	33	1 233	9 480	127.1
0530	Cazenovia town (Madison)	6 514	NA	NA	6 406	54	11	34	9	54	2 372	13 761	129.2
0530	Eaton town (Madison)	5 362	NA	NA	5 111	184	15	31	21	72	1 682	6 462	115.9
0530	Hamilton town (Madison)	6 221	NA	NA	5 842	151	5	187	36	88	1 820	7 440	107.1
0530	Lenox town (Madison)	8 621	NA	NA	8 480	78	26	25	12	55	3 635	9 490	94.3
0530	Madison town (Madison)	2 774	NA	NA	2 753	0	5	16	0	18	1 239	NA	105.9
0530	Sullivan town (Madison)	14 622	13 371	9.4	14 460	37	51	60	14	67	5 622	9 741	190.0
0550	Brighton town (Monroe)	34 455	35 776	-3.7	31 739	1 033	47	1 466	170	564	16 068	18 860	40.1
0550	Chili town (Monroe)	25 178	23 676	6.3	23 622	1 162	49	248	97	278	8 783	11 800	102.9
0550	Clarkson town (Monroe)	4 517	NA	NA	4 354	77	6	49	31	79	1 562	11 881	86.0
0550	East Rochester town (Monroe)	6 932	NA	NA	6 798	43	18	47	26	81	2 926	NA	3.5
0550	Gates town (Monroe)	28 583	29 756	-3.9	26 649	1 275	42	435	182	527	11 132	12 368	39.5
0550	Greece town (Monroe)	90 106	81 367	10.7	86 378	2 002	198	1 099	429	1 413	34 633	13 266	122.8
0550	Hamlin town (Monroe)	9 203	NA	NA	9 034	103	22	18	26	84	3 263	10 524	112.4
0550	Henrietta town (Monroe)	36 376	36 134	0.7	32 373	2 268	134	1 344	257	717	12 361	11 506	91.6

1. Codes shown are 2-digit FIPS codes for states; 4-digit census place codes for places; and 3-digit FIPS county codes followed by 3-digit census MCD codes for minor civil divisions (MCDs). MCD names are followed by county names in parentheses. 2. Hispanic persons may be of any race. 3. Dry land or land partially or temporarily covered by water.

State/ Place/ MCD[1] code	Place	Population: 1990	Population: Places of 10,000 or more: 1980	Population: Places of 10,000 or more: Percent change, 1980–1990	Population characteristics, 1990: Race: White	Race: Black	Race: Am. Indian, Eskimo Aleut	Race: Asian & Pacific Islander	Race: Other race	Hispanic[2]	Total housing units, 1990	Per capita income, 1985 (Dollars)	Land area,[3] 1990 (Sq. Km.)
		1	2	3	4	5	6	7	8	9	10	11	12
	NEW YORK—Con.												
0550	Irondequoit town (Monroe)	52 377	57 648	-9.1	50 997	704	86	329	261	752	22 177	14 168	39.5
0550	Mendon town (Monroe)	6 845	NA	NA	6 750	29	10	45	11	44	2 579	15 377	103.1
0550	Ogden town (Monroe)	16 912	14 693	15.1	16 414	263	61	123	51	211	5 982	12 751	94.8
0550	Parma town (Monroe)	13 873	12 585	10.2	13 651	117	37	55	13	94	4 907	11 906	108.6
0550	Penfield town (Monroe)	30 219	27 201	11.1	28 787	537	26	794	75	253	11 758	15 243	97.1
0550	Perinton town (Monroe)	43 015	41 802	2.9	41 222	674	53	971	95	375	16 117	15 191	88.4
0550	Pittsford town (Monroe)	24 497	26 743	-8.4	23 160	436	15	850	36	230	8 547	20 664	60.1
0550	Riga town (Monroe)	5 114	NA	NA	5 007	53	8	27	19	51	1 878	12 353	91.0
0550	Rush town (Monroe)	3 217	NA	NA	3 060	117	7	27	6	48	1 121	13 993	79.0
0550	Sweden town (Monroe)	14 181	14 859	-4.6	13 268	611	38	142	122	288	4 503	8 771	86.9
0550	Webster town (Monroe)	31 639	28 925	9.4	30 632	407	47	481	72	269	12 100	13 973	88.2
0551	Wheatland town (Monroe)	5 093	NA	NA	4 930	106	13	36	8	37	1 973	12 571	79.3
0570	Amsterdam town (Montgomery)	5 962	NA	NA	5 883	30	5	23	21	79	2 283	9 943	76.7
0570	Canajoharie town (Montgomery)	3 909	NA	NA	3 858	21	5	12	13	31	1 612	9 098	111.1
0570	Florida town (Montgomery)	2 637	NA	NA	2 610	17	1	3	6	34	1 030	9 609	130.4
0570	Minden town (Montgomery)	4 474	NA	NA	4 436	13	5	11	9	38	1 876	7 709	132.2
0570	Mohawk town (Montgomery)	3 976	NA	NA	3 883	32	17	22	22	71	1 476	8 621	89.9
0570	Palatine town (Montgomery)	2 787	NA	NA	2 767	6	2	11	1	5	1 056	8 782	106.7
0570	St. Johnsville town (Montgomery)	2 773	NA	NA	2 741	5	8	15	4	13	1 172	7 675	43.6
0590	Hempstead town (Nassau)	725 639	738 497	-1.7	605 481	87 644	1 121	17 477	13 916	48 149	246 900	14 693	311.2
0590	North Hempstead town (Nassau)	211 393	218 598	-3.3	182 710	13 922	200	11 831	2 730	12 952	77 308	21 653	138.7
0590	Oyster Bay town (Nassau)	292 657	305 796	-4.3	277 046	5 009	196	8 612	1 794	9 901	97 928	16 899	270.1
0630	Cambria town (Niagara)	4 779	NA	NA	4 740	11	17	8	3	19	1 737	10 505	103.3
0630	Hartland town (Niagara)	3 911	NA	NA	3 865	26	5	11	4	28	1 391	9 525	135.6
0630	Lewiston town (Niagara)	15 453	16 218	-4.7	15 123	127	91	94	18	145	5 383	11 965	96.4
0630	Lockport town (Niagara)	16 596	12 942	28.2	15 998	389	63	98	48	132	6 155	10 778	115.6
0630	Newfane town (Niagara)	8 996	NA	NA	8 822	89	61	17	7	42	3 547	10 822	134.3
0630	Niagara town (Niagara)	9 880	NA	NA	9 458	250	106	41	25	98	3 960	9 896	24.3
0630	Pendleton town (Niagara)	5 010	NA	NA	4 973	9	8	16	4	32	1 745	10 827	70.4
0630	Porter town (Niagara)	7 110	NA	NA	7 012	15	44	32	7	47	2 698	11 384	86.0
0630	Royalton town (Niagara)	7 453	NA	NA	7 346	53	18	27	9	28	2 743	9 978	180.9
0630	Somerset town (Niagara)	2 655	NA	NA	2 600	26	9	6	14	23	1 056	8 662	96.3
0630	Wheatfield town (Niagara)	11 125	NA	NA	11 016	34	48	21	6	44	4 237	10 343	72.3
0630	Wilson town (Niagara)	5 761	NA	NA	5 667	14	36	25	19	43	2 384	9 598	128.3
0650	Annsville town (Oneida)	2 786	NA	NA	2 708	60	7	8	3	20	993	NA	155.9
0650	Boonville town (Oneida)	4 246	NA	NA	4 227	5	5	4	5	17	1 868	8 469	186.5
0650	Camden town (Oneida)	5 134	NA	NA	5 094	17	8	10	5	31	1 957	9 313	139.9
0650	Deerfield town (Oneida)	3 942	NA	NA	3 898	20	5	18	1	11	1 352	10 124	85.3
0650	Floyd town (Oneida)	3 856	NA	NA	3 809	16	9	18	4	35	1 367	8 985	89.6
0650	Kirkland town (Oneida)	10 153	10 334	-1.8	9 907	101	6	110	29	131	3 444	11 241	87.5
0650	Lee town (Oneida)	7 115	NA	NA	6 904	110	13	61	27	55	2 545	9 869	117.0
0650	Marcy town (Oneida)	8 685	NA	NA	6 243	2 066	16	29	331	976	1 954	8 747	85.4
0650	New Hartford town (Oneida)	21 640	21 306	1.6	21 082	153	24	351	30	108	8 844	13 054	65.7
0650	Paris town (Oneida)	4 414	NA	NA	4 393	7	5	8	1	27	1 572	9 162	81.4
0651	Trenton town (Oneida)	4 682	NA	NA	4 658	13	2	7	2	17	1 842	10 181	112.2
0651	Vernon town (Oneida)	5 338	NA	NA	5 280	5	17	27	9	16	2 104	10 030	98.9
0651	Verona town (Oneida)	6 460	NA	NA	6 401	16	25	11	7	17	2 515	8 792	179.5
0651	Vienna town (Oneida)	5 564	NA	NA	5 495	17	27	17	8	32	2 690	8 064	159.2
0651	Westmoreland town (Oneida)	5 737	NA	NA	5 657	51	4	21	4	46	2 017	9 320	111.7
0651	Whitestown town (Oneida)	18 985	20 130	-5.7	18 658	189	13	90	35	133	7 649	10 701	70.4
0670	Camillus town (Onondaga)	23 625	24 376	-3.1	23 214	119	84	175	33	205	9 192	12 594	89.3
0670	Cicero town (Onondaga)	25 560	23 719	7.8	24 847	388	103	166	56	225	9 453	11 198	125.5
0670	Clay town (Onondaga)	59 749	52 792	13.2	56 795	1 691	240	871	152	592	22 187	11 850	124.3
0670	De Witt town (Onondaga)	25 148	26 868	-6.4	23 483	893	72	615	85	226	10 246	15 067	87.7
0670	Elbridge town (Onondaga)	6 192	NA	NA	6 130	6	19	20	17	50	2 322	10 160	97.3
0670	Geddes town (Onondaga)	17 677	18 485	-4.4	17 471	40	65	74	27	212	7 164	12 288	23.9
0670	LaFayette town (Onondaga)	5 105	NA	NA	4 922	47	99	30	7	29	1 825	11 107	101.7
0670	Lysander town (Onondaga)	16 346	13 897	17.6	16 073	107	58	83	25	93	6 233	11 916	160.4
0670	Manlius town (Onondaga)	30 656	28 489	7.6	29 797	183	65	579	32	214	12 136	15 406	128.5
0670	Marcellus town (Onondaga)	6 465	NA	NA	6 411	11	14	20	9	29	2 467	11 060	84.3
0670	Onondaga town (Onondaga)	18 396	17 824	3.2	17 793	269	151	154	29	96	6 800	12 584	149.5
0670	Pompey town (Onondaga)	5 317	NA	NA	5 245	16	7	48	1	14	1 936	13 208	172.0
0670	Salina town (Onondaga)	35 145	37 416	-6.1	34 179	454	127	326	59	287	14 680	11 472	35.7
0670	Skaneateles town (Onondaga)	7 526	NA	NA	7 468	17	4	34	3	40	3 179	14 333	110.5
0671	Van Buren town (Onondaga)	13 367	12 585	6.2	13 086	148	66	55	12	118	5 546	11 121	92.1
0690	Canandaigua town (Ontario)	7 160	NA	NA	7 056	48	11	35	10	67	2 743	10 497	147.3
0690	East Bloomfield town (Ontario)	3 258	NA	NA	3 208	25	13	6	6	84	1 210	10 744	86.0
0690	Farmington town (Ontario)	10 381	NA	NA	10 116	107	36	101	21	106	3 604	10 680	102.2
0690	Geneva town (Ontario)	2 967	NA	NA	2 902	51	1	13	0	16	1 360	12 494	49.5
0690	Gorham town (Ontario)	3 497	NA	NA	3 458	14	9	9	7	28	1 791	9 517	126.7
0690	Hopewell town (Ontario)	3 016	NA	NA	2 992	20	1	3	0	14	1 070	9 626	92.3
0690	Manchester town (Ontario)	9 351	NA	NA	9 254	29	37	21	10	50	3 705	9 895	97.9
0690	Naples town (Ontario)	2 559	NA	NA	2 519	12	8	15	5	27	1 095	NA	102.3

1. Codes shown are 2-digit FIPS codes for states; 4-digit census place codes for places; and 3-digit FIPS county codes followed by 3-digit census MCD codes for minor civil divisions (MCDs). MCD names are followed by county names in parentheses. 2. Hispanic persons may be of any race. 3. Dry land or land partially or temporarily covered by water.

State/ Place/ MCD[1] code	Place	Population: 1990	Population: Places of 10,000 or more: 1980	Population: Places of 10,000 or more: Percent change, 1980–1990	Population characteristics, 1990: Race: White	Race: Black	Race: Am. Indian, Eskimo Aleut	Race: Asian & Pacific Islander	Race: Other race	Hispanic[2]	Total housing units, 1990	Per capita income, 1985 (Dollars)	Land area,[3] 1990 (Sq. Km.)
		1	2	3	4	5	6	7	8	9	10	11	12
	NEW YORK—Con.												
0690	Phelps town (Ontario)	6 749	NA	NA	6 670	32	8	27	12	34	2 530	9 953	168.3
0690	Richmond town (Ontario)	3 230	NA	NA	3 210	4	5	9	2	10	1 658	10 875	109.9
0690	Seneca town (Ontario)	2 747	NA	NA	2 724	15	0	8	0	6	992	10 428	130.7
0690	Victor town (Ontario)	7 191	NA	NA	7 086	49	12	38	6	57	2 763	12 568	93.1
0690	West Bloomfield town (Ontario)	2 536	NA	NA	2 491	13	15	10	7	13	996	NA	66.1
0710	Blooming Grove town (Orange)	16 673	12 339	35.1	15 219	1 001	28	211	214	943	5 908	11 592	90.3
0710	Chester town (Orange)	9 138	NA	NA	8 650	272	32	113	71	443	3 236	12 879	65.2
0710	Cornwall town (Orange)	11 270	10 806	4.3	10 993	110	12	118	37	262	4 409	12 598	69.5
0710	Crawford town (Orange)	6 394	NA	NA	6 249	77	3	32	33	192	2 246	10 170	103.9
0710	Deerpark town (Orange)	7 832	NA	NA	7 549	169	18	35	61	273	3 114	9 238	172.0
0710	Goshen town (Orange)	11 500	10 463	9.9	10 389	825	37	129	120	516	3 702	11 960	113.9
0710	Greenville town (Orange)	3 120	NA	NA	3 011	47	7	29	26	105	1 160	NA	78.3
0710	Hamptonburgh town (Orange)	3 910	NA	NA	3 740	79	24	40	27	121	1 270	11 300	68.9
0710	Highlands town (Orange)	13 667	13 990	-2.3	11 894	1 136	36	393	208	662	3 569	9 182	80.0
0710	Minisink town (Orange)	2 981	NA	NA	2 943	19	3	11	5	81	1 023	NA	59.8
0710	Monroe town (Orange)	23 035	14 960	54.0	22 525	135	26	263	86	672	7 030	10 498	52.0
0710	Montgomery town (Orange)	18 501	16 511	12.1	17 831	361	44	109	156	656	6 803	10 009	130.6
0710	Mount Hope town (Orange)	5 971	NA	NA	4 876	949	18	54	74	780	1 633	9 169	65.3
0710	Newburgh town (Orange)	24 058	22 810	5.5	22 300	1 034	35	363	326	1 312	8 745	11 834	113.2
0710	New Windsor town (Orange)	22 937	19 502	17.6	20 950	1 231	46	341	369	1 244	8 596	10 931	90.2
0710	Tuxedo town (Orange)	3 023	NA	NA	2 961	18	0	34	10	44	1 314	19 809	123.0
0711	Wallkill town (Orange)	23 016	20 481	12.4	20 591	1 356	66	402	601	1 769	8 230	9 945	161.0
0711	Warwick town (Orange)	27 193	20 932	29.9	25 592	1 108	110	152	231	1 290	10 522	12 061	263.2
0711	Wawayanda town (Orange)	5 518	NA	NA	5 309	88	12	69	40	162	1 872	10 767	91.1
0711	Woodbury town (Orange)	8 236	NA	NA	7 944	113	17	120	42	265	3 092	12 460	93.7
0730	Albion town (Orleans)	8 178	NA	NA	6 359	1 483	62	31	243	522	2 532	9 232	65.4
0730	Carlton town (Orleans)	2 808	NA	NA	2 609	173	10	7	9	19	1 665	9 509	113.2
0730	Clarendon town (Orleans)	2 705	NA	NA	2 661	10	10	20	4	17	967	NA	91.2
0730	Gaines town (Orleans)	3 025	NA	NA	2 789	207	16	4	9	27	1 226	10 006	89.1
0730	Kendall town (Orleans)	2 769	NA	NA	2 702	28	22	10	7	17	1 058	NA	85.2
0730	Murray town (Orleans)	4 921	NA	NA	4 815	49	16	10	31	63	1 906	10 409	80.4
0730	Ridgeway town (Orleans)	7 341	NA	NA	6 878	366	29	30	38	138	2 893	9 417	129.6
0730	Shelby town (Orleans)	5 509	NA	NA	5 007	365	20	24	93	166	2 043	9 178	120.0
0750	Constantia town (Oswego)	4 868	NA	NA	4 835	5	17	5	6	24	2 083	8 904	147.3
0750	Granby town (Oswego)	7 013	NA	NA	6 931	32	20	22	8	39	2 597	9 271	116.3
0750	Hannibal town (Oswego)	4 616	NA	NA	4 570	11	15	11	9	30	1 644	8 347	116.0
0750	Hastings town (Oswego)	8 113	NA	NA	8 016	19	48	8	22	51	3 094	9 209	118.5
0750	Mexico town (Oswego)	5 050	NA	NA	5 003	13	24	7	3	18	2 105	9 748	120.0
0750	New Haven town (Oswego)	2 778	NA	NA	2 751	5	4	8	10	32	1 207	NA	80.7
0750	Oswego town (Oswego)	8 027	NA	NA	7 678	181	17	93	58	154	1 755	7 373	71.0
0750	Palermo town (Oswego)	3 582	NA	NA	3 528	11	30	10	3	22	1 182	9 119	105.2
0750	Richland town (Oswego)	5 917	NA	NA	5 869	3	18	23	4	18	2 636	9 375	148.1
0750	Sandy Creek town (Oswego)	3 454	NA	NA	3 430	3	16	4	1	14	2 465	9 413	109.5
0751	Schroeppel town (Oswego)	8 931	NA	NA	8 823	45	43	12	8	49	3 373	9 533	109.6
0751	Scriba town (Oswego)	6 472	NA	NA	6 389	17	14	34	18	57	2 602	10 826	105.1
0751	Volney town (Oswego)	5 676	NA	NA	5 620	13	12	24	7	36	2 065	9 349	125.2
0751	West Monroe town (Oswego)	4 393	NA	NA	4 343	6	39	5	0	14	1 629	8 534	87.3
0770	Milford town (Otsego)	2 845	NA	NA	2 808	8	10	10	9	54	1 400	8 520	119.4
0770	Oneonta town (Otsego)	4 963	NA	NA	4 571	327	9	23	33	100	1 981	10 890	86.9
0770	Otego town (Otsego)	3 128	NA	NA	3 082	25	3	14	4	20	1 284	9 248	116.3
0770	Otsego town (Otsego)	3 932	NA	NA	3 905	8	4	9	6	26	2 155	10 903	140.4
0771	Richfield town (Otsego)	2 711	NA	NA	2 678	7	19	7	0	7	1 355	8 067	80.1
0771	Unadilla town (Otsego)	4 343	NA	NA	4 269	38	17	16	3	27	1 849	8 967	120.2
0790	Carmel town (Putnam)	28 816	27 948	3.1	28 189	205	33	270	119	733	10 152	13 647	93.6
0790	Kent town (Putnam)	13 183	12 430	6.1	12 875	91	41	117	59	402	5 074	12 522	105.4
0790	Patterson town (Putnam)	8 679	NA	NA	8 419	163	14	49	34	213	3 172	12 405	83.6
0790	Philipstown town (Putnam)	9 242	NA	NA	8 982	113	20	90	37	218	3 805	14 650	126.5
0790	Putnam Valley town (Putnam)	9 094	NA	NA	8 844	109	8	92	41	288	3 986	14 194	107.5
0790	Southeast town (Putnam)	14 927	11 416	30.8	14 518	170	5	140	94	392	5 709	14 474	83.0
0830	Brunswick town (Rensselaer)	11 093	10 974	1.1	10 910	81	5	91	6	65	4 308	12 119	115.4
0830	East Greenbush town (Rensselaer)	14 076	12 913	9.0	13 535	264	28	221	28	160	5 556	11 953	62.3
0830	Hoosick town (Rensselaer)	6 696	NA	NA	6 624	33	7	25	7	47	2 778	8 603	163.2
0830	Nassau town (Rensselaer)	4 989	NA	NA	4 908	49	6	8	18	33	1 984	10 105	115.4
0830	North Greenbush town (Rensselaer)	10 891	10 396	4.8	10 741	84	2	57	7	49	4 090	11 478	49.1
0830	Pittstown town (Rensselaer)	5 468	NA	NA	5 416	11	19	11	11	19	1 977	9 720	159.9
0830	Poestenkill town (Rensselaer)	3 809	NA	NA	3 787	3	10	9	0	8	1 437	10 016	84.1
0830	Sand Lake town (Rensselaer)	7 642	NA	NA	7 587	10	6	38	1	53	3 120	10 472	91.2
0830	Schaghticoke town (Rensselaer)	7 574	NA	NA	7 468	60	19	24	3	39	2 660	9 740	129.3
0830	Schodack town (Rensselaer)	11 839	11 381	4.0	11 722	54	15	42	6	114	4 530	11 106	161.2
0830	Stephentown town (Rensselaer)	2 521	NA	NA	2 488	23	3	3	4	12	1 242	NA	150.2
0870	Clarkstown town (Rockland)	79 346	77 193	2.8	68 604	5 946	81	4 050	665	3 329	26 321	15 787	99.8
0870	Haverstraw town (Rockland)	32 712	31 944	2.4	25 650	3 538	83	738	2 703	7 438	10 990	11 614	58.1
0870	Orangetown town (Rockland)	46 742	48 579	-3.8	40 063	3 852	41	2 443	343	2 073	16 676	15 355	62.6

1. Codes shown are 2-digit FIPS codes for states; 4-digit census place codes for places; and 3-digit FIPS county codes followed by 3-digit census MCD codes for minor civil divisions (MCDs). MCD names are followed by county names in parentheses. 2. Hispanic persons may be of any race. 3. Dry land or land partially or temporarily covered by water.

State/ Place/ MCD[1] code	Place	Population: 1990	Population: Places of 10,000 or more: 1980	Population: Places of 10,000 or more: Percent change, 1980–1990	Population characteristics, 1990: Race: White	Race: Black	Race: Am. Indian, Eskimo Aleut	Race: Asian & Pacific Islander	Race: Other race	Hispanic[2]	Total housing units, 1990	Per capita income, 1985 (Dollars)	Land area,[3] 1990 (Sq. Km.)
		1	2	3	4	5	6	7	8	9	10	11	12
	NEW YORK—Con.												
0870	Ramapo town (Rockland)	93 861	88 976	5.5	76 067	12 986	425	3 443	940	4 336	29 794	13 425	158.6
0870	Stony Point town (Rockland)	12 814	12 838	-0.2	12 474	146	24	79	91	535	4 483	12 340	72.1
0890	Canton town (St. Lawrence)	11 120	11 532	-3.6	10 847	159	34	58	22	76	3 444	7 559	271.4
0890	Gouverneur town (St. Lawrence)	6 985	NA	NA	6 798	105	31	26	25	52	2 882	7 957	185.3
0890	Lisbon town (St. Lawrence)	3 746	NA	NA	3 724	2	13	7	0	9	1 536	7 710	280.3
0890	Louisville town (St. Lawrence)	3 040	NA	NA	2 990	4	18	27	1	8	1 297	9 981	124.7
0891	Massena town (St. Lawrence)	13 826	14 875	-7.1	13 389	33	359	34	11	81	5 884	10 314	121.6
0891	Norfolk town (St. Lawrence)	4 258	NA	NA	4 216	9	29	3	1	17	1 689	8 501	141.4
0891	Oswegatchie town (St. Lawrence)	4 036	NA	NA	3 988	11	15	20	2	16	1 740	8 778	170.5
0891	Potsdam town (St. Lawrence)	16 822	17 405	-3.3	16 146	93	59	484	40	138	5 273	7 279	262.8
0891	Stockholm town (St. Lawrence)	3 533	NA	NA	3 485	13	22	7	6	7	1 374	8 835	243.3
0910	Ballston town (Saratoga)	8 078	NA	NA	7 999	43	8	23	5	67	3 090	12 530	76.7
0910	Charlton town (Saratoga)	3 984	NA	NA	3 959	10	3	7	5	23	1 340	13 179	85.0
0910	Clifton Park town (Saratoga)	30 117	23 989	25.5	29 100	340	47	576	54	303	10 880	14 631	125.8
0910	Corinth town (Saratoga)	5 935	NA	NA	5 901	11	13	8	2	26	2 439	8 937	147.2
0910	Galway town (Saratoga)	3 266	NA	NA	3 248	6	4	7	1	16	1 699	10 178	114.0
0910	Greenfield town (Saratoga)	6 338	NA	NA	6 258	29	5	35	11	38	2 508	8 689	174.6
0910	Halfmoon town (Saratoga)	13 879	11 860	17.0	13 648	63	17	130	21	98	6 125	11 466	84.6
0910	Malta town (Saratoga)	11 709	NA	NA	11 455	131	12	89	22	152	5 053	11 481	72.6
0910	Milton town (Saratoga)	14 658	12 871	13.9	14 470	96	19	46	27	147	5 732	10 261	92.2
0910	Moreau town (Saratoga)	13 022	11 194	16.3	12 326	476	22	80	118	333	4 831	9 976	109.2
0910	Northumberland town (Saratoga)	3 645	NA	NA	3 617	16	4	7	1	20	1 240	8 471	83.8
0910	Saratoga town (Saratoga)	5 069	NA	NA	4 990	45	7	15	12	47	2 135	9 294	105.4
0910	Stillwater town (Saratoga)	7 233	NA	NA	7 162	15	18	26	12	71	2 882	9 185	107.1
0911	Waterford town (Saratoga)	8 695	NA	NA	8 577	30	9	59	20	53	3 584	11 236	17.0
0911	Wilton town (Saratoga)	10 623	NA	NA	10 400	115	9	68	31	127	3 750	9 806	92.9
0930	Duanesburg town (Schenectady)	5 474	NA	NA	5 425	24	7	17	1	19	2 059	10 637	184.5
0930	Glenville town (Schenectady)	28 771	28 519	0.9	28 299	158	22	264	28	219	11 085	12 658	129.2
0930	Niskayuna town (Schenectady)	19 048	17 471	9.0	17 999	279	10	719	41	221	7 302	17 092	36.5
0930	Rotterdam town (Schenectady)	28 395	29 451	-3.6	28 003	187	31	123	51	256	11 361	11 263	93.2
0950	Cobleskill town (Schoharie)	7 270	NA	NA	6 984	146	17	55	68	170	2 458	7 477	79.3
0950	Middleburgh town (Schoharie)	3 296	NA	NA	3 255	21	11	5	4	19	1 505	9 754	127.7
0950	Schoharie town (Schoharie)	3 369	NA	NA	3 351	10	3	2	3	21	1 344	8 286	77.2
0970	Dix town (Schuyler)	4 130	NA	NA	4 097	12	13	7	1	32	1 750	9 177	93.6
0970	Hector town (Schuyler)	4 423	NA	NA	4 388	9	7	14	5	37	2 071	8 082	265.4
0970	Montour town (Schuyler)	2 528	NA	NA	2 511	8	2	4	3	8	1 043	8 691	48.2
0990	Fayette town (Seneca)	3 636	NA	NA	3 597	15	5	12	7	16	1 609	10 169	143.0
0990	Romulus town (Seneca)	2 532	NA	NA	2 226	202	6	69	29	94	967	NA	97.9
0990	Seneca Falls town (Seneca)	9 384	NA	NA	9 236	54	24	61	9	56	4 039	10 103	62.8
0990	Waterloo town (Seneca)	7 765	NA	NA	7 613	90	8	29	25	72	3 099	9 355	56.2
1010	Addison town (Steuben)	2 645	NA	NA	2 633	4	4	2	2	22	1 119	7 745	66.4
1010	Bath town (Steuben)	12 724	12 268	3.7	12 429	166	30	68	31	69	5 059	8 694	248.7
1010	Campbell town (Steuben)	3 658	NA	NA	3 634	4	9	8	3	15	1 407	9 396	105.5
1010	Canisteo town (Steuben)	3 636	NA	NA	3 610	5	2	17	2	6	1 643	7 568	140.8
1010	Cohocton town (Steuben)	2 520	NA	NA	2 490	10	10	9	1	10	1 046	NA	145.2
1010	Corning town (Steuben)	6 367	NA	NA	6 139	162	9	54	3	28	2 520	12 140	95.6
1010	Erwin town (Steuben)	6 763	NA	NA	6 526	122	7	97	11	25	2 850	12 915	100.2
1010	Hornellsville town (Steuben)	4 149	NA	NA	4 103	9	1	32	4	22	1 735	10 011	113.0
1011	Urbana town (Steuben)	2 807	NA	NA	2 781	6	4	16	0	11	1 427	10 290	106.5
1011	Wayland town (Steuben)	4 311	NA	NA	4 228	45	15	18	5	11	1 818	8 508	101.1
1030	Babylon town (Suffolk)	202 889	203 470	-0.3	166 580	30 284	592	2 496	2 937	12 551	66 819	11 851	135.6
1030	Brookhaven town (Suffolk)	407 779	364 802	11.8	379 509	14 625	847	8 259	4 539	22 410	140 677	11 387	671.6
1030	East Hampton town (Suffolk)	16 132	14 031	15.0	15 106	703	35	136	152	812	17 068	16 152	189.8
1030	Huntington town (Suffolk)	191 474	201 512	-5.0	176 782	8 077	209	4 834	1 572	7 777	64 842	16 808	243.4
1030	Islip town (Suffolk)	299 587	298 887	0.2	261 219	20 482	572	4 761	12 553	39 135	95 314	11 521	272.5
1030	Riverhead town (Suffolk)	23 011	20 243	13.7	19 791	2 917	54	133	116	602	10 801	11 211	174.5
1030	Smithtown town (Suffolk)	113 406	116 676	-2.8	109 798	1 052	70	2 089	397	2 935	36 828	14 186	138.8
1030	Southampton town (Suffolk)	44 976	42 883	4.9	40 295	4 009	152	295	225	1 191	33 622	14 994	359.7
1030	Southold town (Suffolk)	19 836	19 172	3.5	18 964	702	29	89	52	380	12 979	13 755	139.1
1050	Bethel town (Sullivan)	3 693	NA	NA	3 457	175	12	13	36	197	3 693	8 651	221.2
1050	Callicoon town (Sullivan)	3 024	NA	NA	2 985	18	3	11	7	49	1 648	9 889	126.1
1050	Delaware town (Sullivan)	2 633	NA	NA	2 277	284	8	19	45	101	1 244	8 581	90.0
1050	Fallsburg town (Sullivan)	11 445	NA	NA	8 945	1 965	25	77	433	1 396	6 322	8 503	201.1
1050	Liberty town (Sullivan)	9 825	NA	NA	8 598	862	20	118	227	666	4 966	8 786	206.2
1050	Mamakating town (Sullivan)	9 792	NA	NA	9 435	212	21	59	65	346	5 391	9 775	249.2
1050	Neversink town (Sullivan)	2 951	NA	NA	2 922	11	2	11	5	37	1 558	9 150	214.8
1050	Rockland town (Sullivan)	4 096	NA	NA	3 959	51	9	9	68	227	2 428	8 933	244.2
1050	Thompson town (Sullivan)	13 711	13 479	1.7	10 877	2 107	31	193	503	1 563	8 331	10 120	217.8
1070	Barton town (Tioga)	8 925	NA	NA	8 786	57	25	25	32	67	3 667	8 573	153.7
1070	Candor town (Tioga)	5 310	NA	NA	5 253	37	4	13	3	46	2 041	8 568	244.9
1070	Newark Valley town (Tioga)	4 189	NA	NA	4 171	1	5	7	5	18	1 540	9 985	130.4
1070	Nichols town (Tioga)	2 525	NA	NA	2 492	9	12	9	3	16	932	8 984	87.3
1070	Owego town (Tioga)	21 279	20 471	3.9	20 808	174	34	220	43	148	8 071	11 977	269.8

1. Codes shown are 2-digit FIPS codes for states; 4-digit census place codes for places; and 3-digit FIPS county codes followed by 3-digit census MCD codes for minor civil divisions (MCDs). MCD names are followed by county names in parentheses. 2. Hispanic persons may be of any race. 3. Dry land or land partially or temporarily covered by water.

State/ Place/ MCD[1] code	Place	Population: 1990	Population: Places of 10,000 or more: 1980	Population: Places of 10,000 or more: Percent change, 1980–1990	Population characteristics, 1990: Race: White	Race: Black	Race: Am. Indian, Eskimo Aleut	Race: Asian & Pacific Islander	Race: Other race	Hispanic[2]	Total housing units, 1990	Per capita income, 1985 (Dollars)	Land area,[3] 1990 (Sq. Km.)
		1	2	3	4	5	6	7	8	9	10	11	12
	NEW YORK—Con.												
1070	Spencer town (Tioga)	2 881	NA	NA	2 827	26	5	8	15	36	1 175	8 425	128.3
1070	Tioga town (Tioga)	4 772	NA	NA	4 719	6	5	29	13	26	1 901	9 812	152.0
1090	Caroline town (Tompkins)	3 044	NA	NA	2 918	59	19	46	2	51	1 230	9 265	142.5
1090	Danby town (Tompkins)	2 858	NA	NA	2 763	57	10	20	8	14	1 087	NA	138.7
1090	Dryden town (Tompkins)	13 251	12 156	9.0	12 783	187	55	194	32	179	5 362	10 361	243.1
1090	Enfield town (Tompkins)	3 054	NA	NA	2 995	44	6	6	3	37	1 182	NA	95.5
1090	Groton town (Tompkins)	5 483	NA	NA	5 430	20	5	18	10	31	2 029	7 992	128.3
1090	Ithaca town (Tompkins)	17 797	16 022	11.1	15 803	501	26	1 336	131	515	6 193	12 203	75.4
1090	Lansing town (Tompkins)	9 296	NA	NA	8 446	265	27	506	52	142	4 135	12 142	157.3
1090	Newfield town (Tompkins)	4 867	NA	NA	4 778	42	23	11	13	35	1 988	9 612	152.5
1090	Ulysses town (Tompkins)	4 906	NA	NA	4 792	41	8	49	16	45	2 057	9 943	85.4
1110	Esopus town (Ulster)	8 860	NA	NA	8 528	183	18	100	31	116	3 443	10 508	96.5
1110	Gardiner town (Ulster)	4 278	NA	NA	4 132	91	8	36	11	119	1 910	10 868	114.8
1110	Hurley town (Ulster)	6 741	NA	NA	6 525	85	12	108	11	59	2 803	13 547	77.6
1110	Lloyd town (Ulster)	9 231	NA	NA	8 741	333	17	90	50	289	3 578	11 601	82.2
1110	Marbletown town (Ulster)	5 285	NA	NA	5 175	62	9	24	15	84	2 533	11 617	141.4
1110	Marlborough town (Ulster)	7 430	NA	NA	7 204	171	15	14	26	151	2 869	10 134	64.4
1110	New Paltz town (Ulster)	11 388	10 183	11.8	10 076	773	28	297	214	713	3 876	9 713	88.0
1110	Olive town (Ulster)	4 086	NA	NA	4 033	11	8	22	12	118	2 038	11 187	152.0
1110	Plattekill town (Ulster)	8 891	NA	NA	8 138	398	32	37	286	1 164	3 439	9 399	92.2
1110	Rochester town (Ulster)	5 679	NA	NA	5 439	138	27	31	44	182	3 227	9 236	229.0
1110	Rosendale town (Ulster)	6 220	NA	NA	6 049	103	21	27	20	128	2 645	9 958	51.6
1110	Saugerties town (Ulster)	18 467	17 975	2.7	17 967	225	50	168	57	269	7 826	10 437	167.2
1110	Shandaken town (Ulster)	3 013	NA	NA	2 952	23	12	20	6	71	2 570	9 222	310.3
1110	Shawangunk town (Ulster)	10 081	NA	NA	8 821	1 090	26	74	70	610	3 310	8 927	146.0
1110	Ulster town (Ulster)	12 329	12 297	0.3	11 689	237	22	341	40	190	5 185	11 683	69.3
1111	Wawarsing town (Ulster)	12 348	13 073	-5.5	9 888	1 683	77	136	564	1 778	5 259	8 499	338.2
1111	Woodstock town (Ulster)	6 290	NA	NA	6 025	104	26	114	21	137	3 703	14 722	174.8
1130	Chester town (Warren)	3 465	NA	NA	3 427	14	5	11	8	30	2 300	6 853	218.8
1130	Lake George town (Warren)	3 211	NA	NA	3 173	13	10	11	4	25	2 106	11 392	78.3
1130	Lake Luzerne town (Warren)	2 816	NA	NA	2 802	4	6	1	3	17	1 762	8 247	136.3
1130	Queensbury town (Warren)	22 630	19 021	19.0	22 314	80	33	174	29	173	9 632	11 536	163.2
1130	Warrensburg town (Warren)	4 174	NA	NA	4 153	5	3	13	0	20	1 977	8 118	165.0
1150	Argyle town (Washington)	3 031	NA	NA	3 019	7	2	2	1	23	1 435	8 000	146.7
1150	Fort Ann town (Washington)	6 368	NA	NA	4 137	1 884	19	11	317	979	1 667	6 505	278.9
1150	Fort Edward town (Washington)	6 330	NA	NA	6 284	9	15	16	6	53	2 361	8 215	69.6
1150	Granville town (Washington)	5 935	NA	NA	5 891	17	11	8	8	44	2 317	8 575	145.3
1150	Greenwich town (Washington)	4 557	NA	NA	4 530	6	3	14	4	28	1 861	8 511	114.0
1150	Kingsbury town (Washington)	11 851	11 602	2.1	11 775	30	13	26	7	70	4 673	8 939	103.3
1150	Salem town (Washington)	2 608	NA	NA	2 582	17	7	2	0	18	1 183	NA	135.9
1150	White Creek town (Washington)	3 196	NA	NA	3 165	10	6	13	2	18	1 335	8 489	124.0
1150	Whitehall town (Washington)	4 409	NA	NA	4 385	6	5	13	0	35	1 856	8 382	149.2
1170	Arcadia town (Wayne)	14 855	14 698	1.1	13 920	400	32	87	416	711	5 755	9 633	135.0
1170	Galen town (Wayne)	4 413	NA	NA	4 242	142	13	4	12	53	1 734	8 730	154.0
1170	Lyons town (Wayne)	6 315	NA	NA	5 681	535	19	22	58	137	2 419	9 585	96.9
1170	Macedon town (Wayne)	7 375	NA	NA	7 280	19	22	37	17	62	2 712	11 274	100.2
1170	Marion town (Wayne)	4 901	NA	NA	4 835	28	9	26	3	18	1 719	9 534	75.6
1170	Ontario town (Wayne)	8 560	NA	NA	8 369	130	30	22	9	59	3 149	11 683	83.4
1170	Palmyra town (Wayne)	7 690	NA	NA	7 602	18	21	36	13	49	3 070	10 784	86.7
1170	Sodus town (Wayne)	8 877	NA	NA	7 978	773	34	40	52	124	3 957	9 596	174.6
1170	Walworth town (Wayne)	6 945	NA	NA	6 833	64	6	24	18	56	2 314	11 741	87.6
1170	Williamson town (Wayne)	6 540	NA	NA	6 174	303	19	20	24	74	2 524	10 694	89.7
1170	Wolcott town (Wayne)	4 283	NA	NA	4 200	56	9	6	12	44	2 076	8 122	101.8
1190	Bedford town (Westchester)	16 906	15 137	11.7	14 903	1 245	39	241	478	1 223	5 987	21 986	96.5
1190	Cortlandt town (Westchester)	37 357	35 705	4.6	34 922	1 428	47	714	246	1 353	14 103	15 987	102.7
1190	Eastchester town (Westchester)	30 867	32 648	-5.5	27 236	1 080	21	2 375	155	870	13 014	21 988	12.7
1190	Greenburgh town (Westchester)	83 816	82 881	1.1	65 147	11 024	114	6 374	1 157	4 927	32 385	20 386	79.0
1190	Harrison town (Westchester)	23 308	23 046	1.1	21 684	357	17	991	259	1 145	7 984	20 182	43.6
1190	Lewisboro town (Westchester)	11 313	NA	NA	10 946	128	12	194	33	234	4 314	22 397	72.1
1190	Mamaroneck town (Westchester)	27 706	29 017	-4.5	25 295	990	28	940	453	2 005	10 833	24 678	17.1
1190	Mount Kisco town (Westchester)	9 108	NA	NA	7 852	749	24	276	207	1 108	3 965	NA	8.1
1190	Mount Pleasant town (Westchester)	40 590	39 334	3.2	35 814	2 535	115	1 079	1 047	4 137	13 198	17 195	71.7
1190	New Castle town (Westchester)	16 648	15 425	7.9	15 478	239	10	875	46	392	5 561	30 353	59.9
1190	North Castle town (Westchester)	10 061	NA	NA	9 401	236	5	362	57	378	3 522	27 265	62.4
1190	North Salem town (Westchester)	4 725	NA	NA	4 638	30	3	53	1	95	1 799	19 316	55.5
1190	Ossining town (Westchester)	34 124	30 644	11.4	26 599	5 431	64	893	1 137	4 081	12 118	16 975	30.3
1190	Pelham town (Westchester)	11 903	12 978	-8.3	10 781	620	4	416	82	425	4 386	22 478	5.6
1190	Pound Ridge town (Westchester)	4 550	NA	NA	4 399	70	9	56	16	63	1 814	29 325	59.1
1190	Rye town (Westchester)	39 524	38 896	1.6	33 267	2 857	35	1 039	2 326	8 363	15 117	15 204	18.1
1191	Scarsdale town (Westchester)	16 987	17 650	-3.8	14 227	381	4	2 319	56	372	5 581	NA	17.2
1191	Somers town (Westchester)	16 216	13 133	23.5	15 470	331	7	336	72	356	6 240	18 155	77.8
1191	Yorktown town (Westchester)	33 467	31 988	4.6	31 402	957	28	832	248	1 216	11 883	15 913	95.1
1210	Arcade town (Wyoming)	3 938	NA	NA	3 916	6	2	3	11	18	1 597	9 774	121.9

1. Codes shown are 2-digit FIPS codes for states; 4-digit census place codes for places; and 3-digit FIPS county codes followed by 3-digit census MCD codes for minor civil divisions (MCDs). MCD names are followed by county names in parentheses. 2. Hispanic persons may be of any race. 3. Dry land or land partially or temporarily covered by water.

State/ Place/ MCD[1] code	Place	Population: 1990	Population: Places of 10,000 or more: 1980	Population: Places of 10,000 or more: Percent change, 1980–1990	Population characteristics, 1990: Race: White	Race: Black	Race: Am. Indian, Eskimo Aleut	Race: Asian & Pacific Islander	Race: Other race	Hispanic[2]	Total housing units, 1990	Per capita income, 1985 (Dollars)	Land area,[3] 1990 (Sq. Km.)
		1	2	3	4	5	6	7	8	9	10	11	12
	NEW YORK—Con.												
1210	Attica town (Wyoming)	7 383	NA	NA	4 901	1 981	30	10	461	885	1 565	6 755	92.5
1210	Bennington town (Wyoming)	3 046	NA	NA	3 043	0	0	3	0	3	1 119	8 395	142.6
1210	Castile town (Wyoming)	3 042	NA	NA	3 023	6	5	7	1	9	1 700	9 186	95.9
1210	Perry town (Wyoming)	5 353	NA	NA	5 294	30	6	18	5	26	2 151	8 286	94.2
1210	Warsaw town (Wyoming)	5 342	NA	NA	5 249	13	19	52	9	29	2 048	10 205	91.8
1230	Jerusalem town (Yates)	3 784	NA	NA	3 729	25	9	12	9	36	2 358	8 203	152.5
1230	Milo town (Yates)	7 023	NA	NA	6 924	49	8	26	16	80	3 316	9 518	99.4
1230	Starkey town (Yates)	3 173	NA	NA	3 106	44	6	6	11	61	1 487	8 451	85.1
37	NORTH CAROLINA	6 628 637	5 880 416	12.7	5 008 491	1 456 323	80 155	52 166	31 502	76 726	2 818 193	9 517	126 179.9
0005	Aberdeen town	2 700	NA	NA	2 255	400	17	25	3	19	1 239	NA	8.5
0025	Ahoskie town	4 391	NA	NA	2 185	2 146	34	24	2	21	1 897	8 301	6.6
0030	Albemarle	14 939	15 110	-1.1	12 102	2 633	24	170	10	66	6 542	9 513	38.0
0040	Andrews town	2 551	NA	NA	2 451	58	23	1	18	36	1 232	NA	8.2
0055	Apex town	4 968	NA	NA	3 927	960	15	33	33	63	1 826	12 027	10.8
0065	Archdale	6 913	NA	NA	6 737	85	21	63	7	29	2 932	10 000	17.9
0075	Asheboro	16 362	15 244	7.3	13 938	2 141	47	112	124	180	7 464	10 506	30.8
0095	Asheville	61 607	53 583	15.0	48 726	12 207	165	374	135	533	29 713	10 350	90.5
0140	Ayden town	4 740	NA	NA	2 324	2 404	6	5	1	20	1 893	7 110	5.4
0215	Beaufort town	3 808	NA	NA	2 852	908	18	14	16	25	2 085	9 788	4.5
0230	Belmont	8 434	NA	NA	7 354	829	24	218	9	79	3 217	8 288	14.9
0245	Benson town	2 810	NA	NA	1 871	892	6	8	33	45	1 248	6 518	4.4
0255	Bessemer City	4 698	NA	NA	4 104	570	9	4	11	19	1 864	8 222	9.2
0262	Bethlehem CDP	3 186	NA	NA	3 163	10	4	8	1	13	1 310	NA	19.7
0285	Black Mountain town	5 418	NA	NA	4 909	440	7	56	6	28	2 519	9 580	12.5
0318	Bonnie Doone CDP	3 893	NA	NA	1 566	2 021	67	77	162	311	2 061	NA	7.9
0325	Boone town	12 915	10 191	26.7	12 169	602	24	100	20	86	4 534	6 935	14.2
0345	Brevard	5 388	NA	NA	4 552	749	10	61	16	48	2 362	8 770	8.8
0357	Brogden CDP	3 246	NA	NA	1 371	1 823	9	24	19	43	1 154	NA	5.6
0390	Burlington	39 498	37 324	5.8	30 152	8 909	78	308	51	234	17 696	10 886	52.7
0397	Butner CDP	4 679	NA	NA	2 704	1 949	8	9	9	21	1 244	NA	17.8
0408	Camp Lejeune Central CDP	36 716	30 764	19.3	24 815	9 064	267	744	1 826	3 072	4 175	NA	50.7
0415	Canton town	3 790	NA	NA	3 718	69	2	1	0	12	1 854	10 420	9.2
0430	Carolina Beach town	3 630	NA	NA	3 568	33	19	4	6	40	3 342	NA	4.4
0435	Carrboro town	11 553	NA	NA	9 066	1 930	39	427	91	199	6 108	9 934	9.1
0445	Cary town	43 858	21 708	102.0	39 374	2 417	119	1 684	264	683	18 008	15 380	80.7
0475	Chapel Hill town	38 719	32 461	19.3	31 875	4 853	123	1 684	184	607	14 850	11 954	42.8
0480	Charlotte	395 934	314 447	25.9	259 760	125 827	1 425	7 211	1 711	5 571	170 430	12 259	451.3
0490	Cherryville	4 756	NA	NA	4 311	389	9	40	7	19	2 079	10 167	9.4
0495	China Grove town	2 732	NA	NA	2 453	255	6	14	4	11	1 163	NA	3.8
0515	Clayton town	4 756	NA	NA	3 554	1 149	8	11	34	59	2 018	8 721	10.7
0518	Clemmons village	6 020	NA	NA	5 797	146	4	70	3	47	2 256	12 101	12.1
0535	Clinton	8 204	NA	NA	4 639	3 460	60	18	27	101	3 557	7 799	17.4
0565	Concord	27 347	16 942	61.4	21 495	5 623	63	150	16	150	11 616	11 190	56.5
0580	Conover	5 465	NA	NA	4 806	532	9	101	17	89	2 241	12 055	18.0
0600	Cornelius town	2 581	NA	NA	2 020	525	9	26	1	19	1 079	NA	8.6
0642	Cullowhee CDP	4 029	NA	NA	3 729	206	30	58	6	28	784	NA	8.3
0645	Dallas town	3 012	NA	NA	2 367	625	13	4	3	15	1 272	7 940	3.7
0660	Davidson town	4 046	NA	NA	3 334	639	16	50	7	48	1 332	8 646	7.7
0745	Dunn	8 336	NA	NA	4 768	3 435	61	44	28	77	3 638	8 486	13.5
0750	Durham	136 611	100 847	35.5	70 640	62 449	334	2 672	516	1 610	60 607	10 257	179.4
0763	East Flat Rock CDP	3 218	NA	NA	3 096	59	35	9	19	51	1 572	NA	8.8
0780	East Rockingham CDP	4 158	NA	NA	3 732	331	76	14	5	36	1 813	NA	8.9
0790	Eden	15 238	15 672	-2.8	12 312	2 833	26	47	20	68	6 797	8 900	30.3
0795	Edenton town	5 268	NA	NA	2 315	2 924	7	18	4	49	2 199	7 678	12.8
0805	Elizabeth City	14 292	14 004	2.1	6 722	7 448	23	69	30	100	5 800	7 507	11.7
0810	Elizabethtown town	3 704	NA	NA	1 907	1 765	12	13	7	22	1 586	6 649	9.6
0815	Elkin town	3 790	NA	NA	3 419	355	1	9	6	27	1 798	12 019	13.8
0840	Elon College town	4 394	NA	NA	3 969	388	5	24	8	20	1 113	7 387	6.5
0843	Elroy CDP	4 028	NA	NA	3 249	687	14	54	24	56	1 654	NA	17.5
0850	Enfield town	3 082	NA	NA	804	2 271	2	4	1	1	1 139	5 443	3.2
0854	Enochville CDP	2 901	NA	NA	2 870	11	4	15	1	4	1 157	NA	11.4
0856	Erwin town	4 061	NA	NA	3 543	469	21	10	18	42	1 891	9 109	8.7
0905	Farmville town	4 392	NA	NA	2 345	2 024	6	14	3	26	1 887	8 029	6.1
0910	Fayetteville	75 695	59 507	27.2	43 578	28 979	973	1 151	1 014	2 381	31 712	9 695	105.1
0927	Fletcher town	2 787	NA	NA	2 709	47	5	20	6	26	1 193	NA	12.2
0930	Forest City town	7 475	NA	NA	5 443	1 980	11	29	12	69	3 310	7 951	16.8
0931	Forest Oaks CDP	3 054	NA	NA	2 948	85	4	16	1	11	1 123	NA	13.1
0932	Fort Bragg CDP	34 744	37 834	-8.2	21 150	10 111	317	906	2 260	3 587	4 896	NA	49.2
0945	Franklin town	2 873	NA	NA	2 735	98	14	19	7	32	1 682	10 445	9.1
0965	Fuquay-Varina town	4 562	NA	NA	3 425	1 075	17	11	34	100	1 959	9 850	14.0
0966	Gamewell town	3 357	NA	NA	3 194	144	3	5	11	15	1 359	8 869	18.6
0975	Garner town	14 967	10 073	48.6	12 168	2 633	39	94	33	118	5 975	12 216	29.5

1. Codes shown are 2-digit FIPS codes for states; 4-digit census place codes for places; and 3-digit FIPS county codes followed by 3-digit census MCD codes for minor civil divisions (MCDs). MCD names are followed by county names in parentheses. 2. Hispanic persons may be of any race. 3. Dry land or land partially or temporarily covered by water.

State/ Place/ MCD[1] code	Place	Population 1990	Population – Places of 10,000 or more 1980	Population – Places of 10,000 or more Percent change, 1980–1990	Population characteristics, 1990 – Race – White	Race – Black	Race – Am. Indian, Eskimo Aleut	Race – Asian & Pacific Islander	Race – Other race	Hispanic[2]	Total housing units, 1990	Per capita income, 1985 (Dollars)	Land area,[3] 1990 (Sq. Km.)
		1	2	3	4	5	6	7	8	9	10	11	12
	NORTH CAROLINA—Con.												
0990	Gastonia	54 732	47 285	15.7	40 501	13 617	103	384	127	294	22 196	10 024	78.7
1010	Gibsonville town	3 441	NA	NA	2 795	626	10	9	1	16	1 443	8 695	5.4
1020	Glen Raven CDP	2 616	NA	NA	2 026	561	19	7	3	19	1 080	NA	11.2
1035	Goldsboro	40 709	31 895	27.6	20 490	19 314	130	539	236	599	14 345	8 040	54.5
1045	Graham	10 426	NA	NA	8 659	1 673	30	40	24	97	4 517	10 226	18.3
1055	Granite Falls town	3 253	NA	NA	3 146	88	4	3	12	17	1 366	9 140	8.5
1065	Greensboro	183 521	155 684	17.9	117 237	62 305	852	2 633	494	1 765	80 411	11 686	206.7
1070	Greenville	44 972	35 740	25.8	28 867	15 337	105	524	139	379	18 054	8 781	46.7
1088	Half Moon CDP	6 306	NA	NA	4 702	1 242	24	167	171	301	2 106	NA	16.3
1100	Hamlet	6 196	NA	NA	4 036	2 099	50	7	4	42	2 687	8 892	10.7
1130	Havelock	20 268	17 718	14.4	15 350	3 639	169	526	584	1 284	6 096	7 013	38.5
1153	Hemby Bridge CDP	2 876	NA	NA	2 727	125	11	12	1	12	956	NA	8.9
1155	Henderson	15 655	13 522	15.8	7 293	8 278	21	30	33	84	6 446	8 259	18.3
1160	Hendersonville	7 284	NA	NA	5 760	1 430	19	49	26	110	3 690	8 312	10.9
1175	Hickory	28 301	20 753	36.4	23 032	4 827	77	286	79	221	12 701	11 604	52.6
1195	High Point	69 496	63 355	9.7	47 347	20 980	375	653	141	552	29 408	10 419	111.4
1210	Hillsborough town	4 263	NA	NA	2 557	1 663	13	23	7	24	1 783	9 071	9.2
1240	Hope Mills town	8 184	NA	NA	7 282	610	140	73	79	248	3 133	9 447	11.8
1250	Hudson town	2 819	NA	NA	2 810	2	6	0	1	3	1 188	10 511	8.1
1255	Huntersville town	3 014	NA	NA	2 553	439	11	10	1	8	1 330	NA	5.0
1258	Icard CDP	2 553	NA	NA	2 548	1	2	1	1	10	1 060	NA	10.1
1280	Jacksonville	30 013	17 056	76.0	20 303	8 007	144	902	657	1 571	11 810	9 586	33.7
1285	James City CDP	4 279	NA	NA	3 459	783	8	16	13	35	1 823	NA	12.4
1290	Jamestown town	2 600	NA	NA	2 327	204	1	64	4	21	1 051	NA	5.6
1320	Kannapolis	29 696	34 564	-14.1	24 149	5 342	38	71	96	187	12 717	8 858	40.7
1340	Kernersville town	10 836	NA	NA	10 071	606	20	63	76	161	5 069	10 795	18.7
1345	Kill Devil Hills town	4 238	NA	NA	4 153	21	11	31	22	51	4 809	NA	14.2
1347	King	4 059	NA	NA	3 998	25	8	24	4	20	1 562	10 095	9.1
1350	Kings Mountain	8 763	NA	NA	6 812	1 791	17	137	6	43	3 689	9 047	15.1
1355	Kinston	25 295	25 234	0.2	10 512	14 615	34	104	30	120	10 826	8 467	34.0
1375	La Grange town	2 805	NA	NA	1 198	1 594	1	7	5	14	1 220	7 165	5.3
1420	Laurinburg	11 643	11 508	1.2	5 827	5 239	504	48	25	78	4 637	8 378	19.5
1435	Lenoir	14 192	13 748	3.2	11 864	2 240	26	40	22	76	6 338	9 437	35.2
1446	Lewisville CDP	3 206	NA	NA	3 085	96	3	20	2	21	1 337	NA	9.5
1450	Lexington	16 581	15 711	5.5	11 305	4 916	71	244	45	112	7 486	9 593	31.1
1470	Lincolnton	6 847	NA	NA	5 443	1 308	9	38	49	121	2 880	9 074	14.3
1490	Long Beach town	3 816	NA	NA	3 790	2	20	1	3	16	4 618	NA	15.9
1500	Long View town	3 229	NA	NA	2 943	228	17	31	10	16	1 474	8 790	5.7
1510	Louisburg town	3 037	NA	NA	1 920	1 097	4	15	1	21	1 064	7 122	4.9
1515	Lowell	2 704	NA	NA	2 481	207	11	0	5	6	1 124	8 592	6.8
1530	Lumberton	18 601	18 241	2.0	10 539	5 653	2 261	115	33	83	7 606	8 986	31.1
1570	Maiden town	2 574	NA	NA	2 168	375	5	2	24	83	1 023	8 706	7.3
1595	Marion	4 765	NA	NA	4 167	554	13	25	6	21	2 256	8 511	8.3
1597	Mar-Mac CDP	3 282	NA	NA	3 029	217	2	21	13	24	1 326	NA	11.5
1613	Masonboro CDP	7 010	NA	NA	6 761	194	11	37	7	56	2 687	NA	15.8
1615	Matthews town	13 651	NA	NA	13 003	467	37	132	12	121	5 330	NA	31.8
1640	Mebane	4 754	NA	NA	3 756	952	7	24	15	48	2 017	9 899	8.4
1687	Mint Hill town	11 567	NA	NA	11 212	246	46	58	5	77	4 093	13 539	46.8
1690	Mocksville town	3 399	NA	NA	2 676	701	12	9	1	10	1 514	10 673	12.9
1695	Monroe	16 127	12 639	27.6	9 397	6 483	55	95	97	215	6 347	9 420	35.9
1700	Mooresville town	9 317	NA	NA	7 088	2 139	25	44	21	45	3 808	9 273	15.3
1705	Morehead City town	6 046	NA	NA	4 877	1 066	35	52	16	56	3 206	8 265	6.8
1710	Morganton	15 085	13 763	9.6	12 520	2 319	21	208	17	58	6 558	9 931	43.3
1729	Mountain View CDP	3 697	NA	NA	3 511	146	6	33	1	11	1 311	NA	12.1
1730	Mount Airy	7 156	NA	NA	6 469	638	9	11	29	60	3 417	8 916	16.4
1740	Mount Holly	7 710	NA	NA	7 006	645	19	37	3	31	3 284	9 864	17.5
1745	Mount Olive town	4 582	NA	NA	2 156	2 405	5	10	6	18	1 853	6 507	5.9
1755	Murfreesboro town	2 580	NA	NA	1 594	914	7	59	6	14	931	7 972	4.8
1761	Myrtle Grove CDP	4 275	NA	NA	4 155	100	3	17	0	13	1 828	NA	17.8
1765	Nashville town	3 617	NA	NA	2 044	1 561	8	2	2	12	1 333	9 980	6.8
1770	New Bern	17 363	14 557	19.3	9 654	7 563	53	61	32	121	8 024	8 195	26.5
1773	New Hope CDP	5 694	NA	NA	4 837	735	10	80	32	102	2 354	NA	21.4
1774	New Hope CDP	4 491	NA	NA	3 084	1 330	11	56	10	47	1 604	NA	12.7
1785	Newport town	2 516	NA	NA	2 089	334	18	41	34	61	920	NA	5.0
1787	New River Station CDP	9 732	NA	NA	7 091	2 031	96	107	407	709	447	NA	19.8
1790	Newton	9 304	NA	NA	7 770	1 437	13	42	42	100	3 986	10 042	21.1
1811	North Hickory CDP	4 299	NA	NA	4 194	72	6	22	5	13	1 684	NA	13.5
1820	North Wilkesboro town	3 384	NA	NA	2 799	574	3	4	4	9	1 607	11 809	12.2
1847	Ogden CDP	3 228	NA	NA	3 145	56	16	7	4	23	1 319	NA	12.2
1870	Oxford	7 913	NA	NA	3 579	4 295	9	16	14	32	3 111	8 291	10.8
1897	Parkwood CDP	4 123	NA	NA	3 345	608	21	123	26	83	1 453	NA	5.3
1945	Pinehurst town	5 103	NA	NA	4 995	89	1	14	4	24	3 326	NA	28.8
1965	Pineville town	2 970	NA	NA	2 812	115	12	15	16	67	1 495	NA	7.2

1. Codes shown are 2-digit FIPS codes for states; 4-digit census place codes for places; and 3-digit FIPS county codes followed by 3-digit census MCD codes for minor civil divisions (MCDs). MCD names are followed by county names in parentheses. 2. Hispanic persons may be of any race. 3. Dry land or land partially or temporarily covered by water.

State/ Place/ MCD[1] code	Place	Population			Population characteristics, 1990						Total housing units, 1990	Per capita income, 1985 (Dollars)	Land area,[3] 1990 (Sq. Km.)
			Places of 10,000 or more		Race					Hispanic[2]			
		1990	1980	Percent change, 1980–1990	White	Black	Am. Indian, Eskimo Aleut	Asian & Pacific Islander	Other race				
		1	2	3	4	5	6	7	8	9	10	11	12
	NORTH CAROLINA—Con.												
1967	Piney Green CDP	8 999	NA	NA	6 362	2 031	57	283	266	534	3 561	NA	35.2
1980	Plymouth town	4 328	NA	NA	1 861	2 437	0	22	8	22	1 793	7 438	9.7
1992	Pope AFB CDP	2 857	NA	NA	2 044	659	18	76	60	144	472	NA	7.6
1993	Poplar Tent CDP	3 872	NA	NA	3 381	420	27	25	19	36	1 470	NA	14.2
2012	Pumpkin Center CDP	2 857	NA	NA	2 311	348	24	100	74	130	955	NA	5.6
2015	Raeford	3 469	NA	NA	1 974	1 355	109	24	7	38	1 330	8 902	7.3
2020	Raleigh	207 951	150 255	38.4	143 862	57 354	584	5 127	1 024	2 940	92 643	12 904	228.3
2030	Randleman	2 612	NA	NA	2 504	82	20	5	1	16	1 170	NA	7.1
2040	Red Springs town	3 799	NA	NA	1 553	1 965	267	13	1	14	1 549	6 653	6.2
2045	Reidsville	12 183	12 492	-2.5	7 353	4 745	15	40	30	74	5 369	9 612	20.5
2079	River Road CDP	3 892	NA	NA	2 986	898	4	3	1	13	1 799	NA	18.3
2080	Roanoke Rapids	15 722	14 702	6.9	12 849	2 719	41	100	13	78	6 738	9 014	20.1
2105	Rockingham	9 399	NA	NA	6 891	2 334	61	109	4	41	3 971	10 630	16.9
2115	Rocky Mount	48 997	41 283	18.7	24 314	24 297	122	193	71	264	20 173	10 044	64.7
2160	Roxboro	7 332	NA	NA	4 167	3 097	41	12	15	55	3 195	8 003	10.2
2167	Royal Pines CDP	4 418	NA	NA	4 311	78	3	23	3	24	1 865	NA	7.9
2180	Rutherfordton town	3 617	NA	NA	3 142	461	2	7	5	18	1 572	9 919	10.6
2187	St. Stephens CDP	8 734	10 797	-19.1	8 377	221	16	103	17	71	3 360	NA	25.7
2195	Salisbury	23 087	22 677	1.8	14 728	8 124	42	153	40	136	9 906	10 474	42.4
2210	Sanford	14 475	14 773	-2.0	9 154	5 045	85	82	109	227	6 223	9 321	36.1
2217	Sawmills town	4 088	NA	NA	4 055	1	13	9	10	17	1 598	NA	13.0
2220	Scotland Neck town	2 575	NA	NA	1 095	1 475	1	0	4	14	1 066	7 233	3.2
2229	Seagate CDP	5 444	NA	NA	5 314	79	24	18	9	37	2 259	NA	11.5
2237	Sedge Garden CDP	2 784	NA	NA	2 697	75	1	5	6	9	1 097	NA	9.4
2240	Selma town	4 600	NA	NA	2 664	1 908	7	3	18	37	1 987	7 092	8.0
2265	Shelby	14 669	15 310	-4.2	8 366	6 234	20	34	15	69	6 474	10 264	22.7
2270	Sherrills Ford CDP	3 185	NA	NA	3 056	117	6	6	0	6	2 061	NA	30.6
2275	Siler City town	4 808	NA	NA	3 393	1 293	13	8	101	184	2 027	9 803	12.0
2278	Silver Lake CDP	4 071	NA	NA	3 802	215	27	17	10	33	1 503	NA	17.0
2288	Smith Creek CDP	7 461	NA	NA	6 764	579	36	77	5	52	2 815	NA	13.8
2290	Smithfield town	7 540	NA	NA	4 730	2 654	11	50	95	153	3 278	8 820	12.2
2320	Southern Pines town	9 129	NA	NA	5 906	3 155	43	18	7	60	4 438	11 383	26.8
2329	South Gastonia CDP	5 487	NA	NA	4 981	471	13	15	7	20	2 131	NA	17.4
2370	Spencer town	3 219	NA	NA	2 467	725	13	8	6	26	1 384	9 796	5.6
2375	Spindale town	4 040	NA	NA	3 083	934	6	13	4	14	1 735	7 969	13.5
2390	Spring Lake town	7 524	NA	NA	3 044	3 787	68	324	301	567	3 090	6 123	7.8
2410	Stanley town	2 823	NA	NA	2 738	73	2	8	2	20	1 122	NA	5.1
2415	Stanleyville CDP	4 779	NA	NA	4 196	549	8	24	2	18	2 212	NA	17.5
2430	Statesville	17 567	18 607	-5.6	11 057	6 280	36	118	76	164	7 916	9 623	33.5
2470	Swannanoa CDP	3 538	NA	NA	3 386	127	12	11	2	22	1 498	NA	14.8
2495	Tarboro town	11 037	NA	NA	7 479	3 483	14	45	16	49	4 520	9 527	23.5
2510	Thomasville	15 915	14 144	12.5	11 357	4 420	72	26	40	96	6 928	8 706	26.1
2540	Trinity CDP	5 469	NA	NA	5 019	399	40	8	3	31	2 199	NA	33.5
2550	Troy town	3 404	NA	NA	2 177	1 172	43	3	9	83	1 181	8 306	6.6
2570	Valdese town	3 914	NA	NA	3 820	30	6	28	30	56	1 795	9 326	10.9
2605	Wadesboro town	3 645	NA	NA	1 926	1 698	12	8	1	10	1 552	8 392	7.7
2615	Wake Forest town	5 769	NA	NA	4 338	1 360	9	50	12	38	2 299	10 207	12.5
2625	Wallace town	2 939	NA	NA	2 134	786	10	4	5	19	1 251	9 207	5.4
2650	Warsaw town	2 859	NA	NA	1 296	1 510	14	12	27	46	1 199	7 526	6.6
2655	Washington	9 075	NA	NA	4 865	4 158	5	21	26	74	3 873	8 144	14.8
2675	Waynesville town	6 758	NA	NA	6 414	278	37	19	10	43	3 355	9 086	15.0
2687	Weddington town	3 803	NA	NA	3 651	108	14	26	4	27	1 252	NA	37.7
2688	Welcome CDP	3 377	NA	NA	3 207	146	10	9	5	8	1 357	NA	21.7
2695	Wendell town	2 822	NA	NA	2 493	315	2	9	3	10	1 141	NA	4.1
2735	Whiteville	5 078	NA	NA	3 326	1 681	41	19	11	26	2 287	8 462	9.9
2745	Wilkesboro town	2 573	NA	NA	2 251	283	0	23	16	31	1 027	NA	11.3
2750	Williamston town	5 503	NA	NA	2 668	2 820	4	9	2	15	2 327	7 344	7.6
2755	Wilmington	55 530	44 000	26.2	36 059	18 815	167	319	170	477	26 469	9 358	76.9
2760	Wilson	36 930	34 424	7.3	19 338	17 326	40	113	113	259	15 383	9 312	47.9
2768	Windemere CDP	4 604	NA	NA	4 318	244	15	24	3	39	1 807	NA	9.9
2780	Wingate town	2 821	NA	NA	2 229	551	3	22	16	23	679	7 758	3.6
2785	Winston-Salem	143 485	131 885	8.8	85 330	56 328	325	1 097	405	1 236	65 631	11 790	184.2
2790	Winterville town	2 816	NA	NA	1 622	1 175	8	10	1	11	1 104	NA	3.3
2798	Woodfin town	2 736	NA	NA	2 718	10	3	3	2	16	1 329	8 596	8.5
2813	Wrightsboro CDP	4 752	NA	NA	3 276	1 427	27	17	5	22	1 804	NA	32.0
2815	Wrightsville Beach town	2 937	NA	NA	2 921	5	2	8	1	12	2 413	17 975	3.4
2825	Yadkinville town	2 525	NA	NA	2 295	191	4	5	30	53	1 003	NA	6.7
2845	Zebulon town	3 173	NA	NA	1 847	1 307	1	0	18	27	1 233	NA	5.6
38	NORTH DAKOTA	638 800	652 717	-2.1	604 142	3 524	25 917	3 462	1 755	4 665	276 340	9 635	178 695.2
0175	Beulah	3 363	NA	NA	3 243	7	91	9	13	22	1 437	12 340	6.1
0195	Bismarck	49 256	44 485	10.7	47 615	55	1 261	219	106	325	20 038	11 836	63.0

1. Codes shown are 2-digit FIPS codes for states; 4-digit census place codes for places; and 3-digit FIPS county codes followed by 3-digit census MCD codes for minor civil divisions (MCDs). MCD names are followed by county names in parentheses. 2. Hispanic persons may be of any race. 3. Dry land or land partially or temporarily covered by water.

State/ Place/ MCD[1] code	Place	Population 1990	Population Places of 10,000 or more 1980	Population Places of 10,000 or more Percent change, 1980–1990	Population characteristics, 1990 Race White	Race Black	Race Am. Indian, Eskimo Aleut	Race Asian & Pacific Islander	Race Other race	Hispanic[2]	Total housing units, 1990	Per capita income, 1985 (Dollars)	Land area,[3] 1990 (Sq. Km.)
		1	2	3	4	5	6	7	8	9	10	11	12
	NORTH DAKOTA—Con.												
0205	Bottineau	2 598	NA	NA	2 550	5	31	11	1	6	1 164	10 705	2.7
0415	Devils Lake	7 782	NA	NA	7 200	17	532	22	11	36	3 325	9 455	13.3
0425	Dickinson	16 097	15 924	1.1	15 880	17	109	61	30	104	6 838	9 833	25.8
0545	Fargo	74 111	61 383	20.7	71 968	260	796	929	158	544	31 711	11 493	77.2
0685	Grafton	4 840	NA	NA	4 624	6	64	41	105	259	2 033	7 903	7.9
0693	Grand Forks	49 425	43 765	12.9	47 194	395	1 115	529	192	586	19 589	10 526	37.4
0694	Grand Forks AFB CDP	9 343	NA	NA	7 942	957	62	270	112	329	2 618	NA	22.0
0800	Hazen	2 818	NA	NA	2 723	4	79	11	1	8	1 118	NA	3.2
0850	Jamestown	15 571	16 280	-4.4	15 284	47	130	89	21	78	6 740	10 009	28.8
1050	Mandan	15 177	15 513	-2.2	14 778	11	338	35	15	60	5 910	9 519	25.8
1140	Minot	34 544	32 843	5.2	33 098	380	724	261	81	268	15 040	10 099	34.3
1142	Minot AFB CDP	9 095	NA	NA	7 425	986	90	289	305	522	2 575	NA	18.7
1445	Rugby	2 909	NA	NA	2 884	1	18	6	0	0	1 369	9 129	4.9
1651	Valley City	7 163	NA	NA	7 051	23	42	37	10	25	3 222	10 300	8.4
1680	Wahpeton	8 751	NA	NA	8 268	18	388	66	11	36	3 317	9 127	12.8
1715	West Fargo	12 287	10 100	21.7	12 108	12	102	26	39	88	4 574	9 559	18.3
1740	Williston	13 131	13 336	-1.5	12 539	14	517	35	26	87	6 083	11 649	18.0
39	OHIO	10 847 115	10 797 604	0.5	9 521 756	1 154 826	20 358	91 179	58 996	139 696	4 371 945	10 371	106 067.2
0010	Ada village	5 413	NA	NA	5 243	78	7	79	6	26	1 857	7 214	4.0
0035	Akron	223 019	237 177	-6.0	164 493	54 656	603	2 701	566	1 601	96 372	9 798	161.1
0055	Alliance	23 376	24 315	-3.9	20 308	2 812	56	123	77	163	9 598	8 750	21.6
0070	Amberley village	3 108	NA	NA	2 920	135	3	48	2	17	1 276	29 114	9.0
0085	Amherst	10 332	10 638	-2.9	10 164	22	16	72	58	241	3 864	11 574	18.2
0140	Archbold village	3 440	NA	NA	3 177	1	2	33	227	336	1 343	12 162	7.3
0155	Ashland	20 079	20 326	-1.2	19 507	315	30	200	27	127	8 020	9 348	24.6
0165	Ashtabula	21 633	23 449	-7.7	19 304	1 898	41	98	292	670	9 209	8 311	19.6
0180	Athens	21 265	19 743	7.7	18 910	984	28	1 241	102	252	6 098	6 647	17.6
0190	Aurora	9 192	NA	NA	9 001	110	9	66	6	48	3 478	16 280	60.3
0192	Austintown CDP	32 371	33 636	-3.8	31 239	844	57	149	82	345	13 176	NA	30.2
0193	Avon	7 337	NA	NA	7 263	26	12	27	9	71	2 425	10 342	54.1
0200	Avon Lake	15 066	13 222	13.9	14 868	32	10	139	17	134	5 588	12 710	28.8
0204	Bainbridge CDP	3 602	NA	NA	3 549	20	3	21	9	30	1 285	NA	8.7
0215	Ballville CDP	3 083	NA	NA	3 016	27	2	5	33	61	1 189	NA	7.1
0225	Baltimore village	2 971	NA	NA	2 962	4	2	3	0	20	1 180	8 840	4.4
0230	Barberton	27 623	29 751	-7.2	25 987	1 453	75	79	29	92	11 731	8 891	19.7
0235	Barnesville village	4 326	NA	NA	4 271	40	6	9	0	8	1 905	7 465	4.9
0260	Bay Village	17 000	17 846	-4.7	16 794	23	22	142	19	103	6 359	16 974	12.0
0275	Beachwood	10 677	NA	NA	9 675	847	3	147	5	62	4 732	22 984	11.9
0288	Beavercreek	33 626	31 589	6.4	32 397	309	62	786	72	342	12 148	13 417	66.7
0293	Beckett Ridge CDP	4 505	NA	NA	4 321	91	3	85	5	40	1 675	NA	12.6
0295	Bedford	14 822	15 056	-1.6	14 046	641	10	90	35	123	7 074	11 482	13.8
0300	Bedford Heights	12 131	13 214	-8.2	5 469	6 379	27	211	45	96	5 736	12 121	11.8
0305	Bellaire	6 028	NA	NA	5 663	341	4	8	12	23	2 950	7 351	4.9
0310	Bellbrook	6 511	NA	NA	6 431	20	10	40	10	44	2 254	12 299	8.1
0320	Bellefontaine	12 142	11 888	2.1	11 174	735	24	184	25	70	5 127	9 159	15.8
0330	Bellevue	8 146	NA	NA	8 077	11	3	15	40	161	3 326	9 969	9.1
0355	Belpre	6 796	NA	NA	6 565	193	10	22	6	22	3 225	9 570	6.9
0370	Berea	19 051	19 567	-2.6	17 764	1 014	36	145	92	236	7 242	11 804	14.1
0410	Bexley	13 088	13 405	-2.4	12 508	462	3	92	23	95	4 960	17 998	6.4
0412	Blacklick Estates CDP	10 080	11 232	-10.3	9 503	438	23	93	23	105	3 371	NA	6.3
0420	Blanchester village	4 206	NA	NA	4 187	5	6	7	1	19	1 598	8 426	7.6
0445	Blue Ash	11 860	NA	NA	10 969	525	12	338	16	72	4 719	14 001	19.8
0450	Bluffton village	3 367	NA	NA	3 288	32	2	36	9	30	1 225	8 721	7.7
0453	Boardman CDP	38 596	39 161	-1.4	37 864	409	21	242	60	355	16 050	NA	41.2
0454	Bolindale CDP	2 827	NA	NA	2 695	110	2	13	7	21	1 068	NA	2.5
0480	Bowling Green	28 176	25 728	9.5	26 451	742	50	600	333	625	8 964	7 599	20.5
0505	Brecksville	11 818	10 132	16.6	11 290	232	10	275	11	105	4 407	16 901	50.8
0513	Brentwood CDP	3 568	NA	NA	3 432	101	6	28	1	10	1 394	NA	10.9
0528	Bridgetown North CDP	11 748	NA	NA	11 700	14	7	23	4	35	4 607	NA	8.7
0532	Brimfield CDP	3 223	NA	NA	3 136	62	4	16	5	29	1 068	NA	10.3
0535	Broadview Heights	12 219	10 920	11.9	11 803	140	10	253	13	92	5 010	13 089	33.8
0540	Brooklyn	11 706	12 342	-5.2	11 384	107	9	122	84	229	5 239	11 680	11.1
0550	Brook Park	22 865	26 195	-12.7	22 211	319	26	181	128	365	8 036	10 260	20.2
0560	Brookville village	4 621	NA	NA	4 602	1	9	6	3	19	1 873	9 645	5.7
0570	Brunswick	28 230	28 104	0.4	27 826	124	20	217	43	227	9 444	10 668	29.8
0575	Bryan	8 348	NA	NA	8 187	7	11	32	111	270	3 556	10 664	10.3
0585	Buckeye Lake village	2 986	NA	NA	2 966	2	10	7	1	11	1 475	8 010	4.7
0595	Bucyrus	13 496	13 433	0.5	13 322	74	32	48	20	70	5 740	8 891	15.9
0620	Burlington CDP	3 003	NA	NA	2 583	412	1	3	4	15	1 195	NA	3.7
0645	Cadiz village	3 439	NA	NA	3 079	342	5	7	6	11	1 561	8 574	18.7
0670	Cambridge	11 748	13 573	-13.4	11 183	484	9	47	25	41	5 770	8 707	13.6

1. Codes shown are 2-digit FIPS codes for states; 4-digit census place codes for places; and 3-digit FIPS county codes followed by 3-digit census MCD codes for minor civil divisions (MCDs). MCD names are followed by county names in parentheses. 2. Hispanic persons may be of any race. 3. Dry land or land partially or temporarily covered by water.

State/ Place/ MCD[1] code	Place	Population 1990	Population, Places of 10,000 or more 1980	Population, Places of 10,000 or more Percent change, 1980–1990	Race: White	Race: Black	Race: Am. Indian, Eskimo Aleut	Race: Asian & Pacific Islander	Race: Other race	Hispanic[2]	Total housing units, 1990	Per capita income, 1985 (Dollars)	Land area,[3] 1990 (Sq. Km.)
		1	2	3	4	5	6	7	8	9	10	11	12
	OHIO—Con.												
0680	Campbell	10 038	11 619	-13.6	8 389	1 294	7	10	338	753	4 125	7 978	9.7
0690	Canal Fulton village	4 157	NA	NA	4 110	22	12	12	1	23	1 556	9 458	6.0
0695	Canal Winchester village	2 617	NA	NA	2 579	23	0	12	3	10	989	12 324	14.7
0700	Canfield	5 409	NA	NA	5 367	13	1	18	10	46	2 278	13 541	11.3
0705	Canton	84 161	94 730	-11.2	67 890	15 325	429	267	250	889	36 527	8 731	52.4
0715	Carey village	3 684	NA	NA	3 614	7	2	42	19	50	1 472	8 522	4.3
0720	Carlisle village	4 872	NA	NA	4 840	12	10	5	5	23	1 658	9 303	7.1
0730	Carrollton village	3 042	NA	NA	3 033	1	5	1	2	5	1 401	8 509	4.9
0760	Cedarville village	3 210	NA	NA	3 073	116	3	9	9	25	693	6 230	2.5
0765	Celina	9 650	NA	NA	9 526	6	32	38	48	134	3 951	9 516	9.4
0775	Centerville	21 082	18 886	11.6	20 303	267	17	458	37	183	8 801	15 097	23.2
0785	Chagrin Falls village	4 146	NA	NA	4 111	14	1	15	5	10	2 053	16 492	5.4
0792	Champion Heights CDP	4 665	NA	NA	4 595	45	6	13	6	32	1 774	NA	8.9
0795	Chardon village	4 446	NA	NA	4 392	12	8	33	1	32	1 817	10 103	11.9
0812	Cherry Grove CDP	4 972	NA	NA	4 838	59	4	68	3	34	1 541	NA	2.9
0840	Cheviot	9 616	NA	NA	9 457	84	7	53	15	50	4 348	10 597	3.0
0850	Chillicothe	21 923	23 420	-6.4	20 005	1 692	50	146	30	101	9 775	10 612	20.4
0863	Churchill CDP	2 691	NA	NA	2 435	215	0	24	17	43	1 098	NA	6.5
0865	Cincinnati	364 040	385 457	-5.6	220 285	138 132	660	4 030	933	2 386	169 088	10 247	200.0
0870	Circleville	11 666	11 700	-0.3	11 386	212	18	33	17	46	4 881	9 809	10.6
0900	Cleveland	505 616	573 822	-11.9	250 234	235 405	1 562	5 115	13 300	23 197	224 311	8 018	199.5
0905	Cleveland Heights	54 052	56 438	-4.2	32 534	20 054	96	1 138	230	582	21 862	13 233	21.0
0930	Clyde	5 776	NA	NA	5 629	10	11	12	114	278	2 124	9 547	8.8
0945	Coldwater village	4 335	NA	NA	4 313	0	6	4	12	24	1 547	10 694	4.2
0955	Columbiana village	4 961	NA	NA	4 949	1	3	5	3	10	2 274	9 371	9.1
0960	Columbus	632 910	564 866	12.0	471 025	142 748	1 469	14 993	2 675	6 741	278 084	9 909	494.5
0985	Conneaut	13 241	13 835	-4.3	12 993	163	23	38	24	112	5 717	8 770	68.3
1010	Cortland	5 666	NA	NA	5 571	32	7	41	15	28	2 233	11 040	9.2
1020	Coshocton	12 193	13 405	-9.0	11 899	188	18	82	6	34	5 592	10 336	19.4
1022	Covedale CDP	6 669	NA	NA	6 607	6	4	46	6	35	2 494	NA	7.1
1025	Covington village	2 603	NA	NA	2 590	1	9	0	3	18	1 032	8 902	2.6
1035	Crestline	4 934	NA	NA	4 764	130	3	24	13	22	2 153	8 699	6.0
1050	Crooksville village	2 601	NA	NA	2 597	3	0	1	0	0	1 075	7 051	3.8
1075	Cuyahoga Falls	48 950	43 890	11.5	48 017	518	65	306	44	209	21 269	11 443	66.1
1108	Day Heights CDP	2 812	NA	NA	2 774	19	9	9	1	9	942	NA	3.1
1110	Dayton	182 044	203 371	-10.5	106 258	73 595	410	1 157	624	1 356	80 370	8 621	142.5
1115	Deer Park	6 181	NA	NA	6 106	33	8	33	1	19	2 731	10 588	2.2
1125	Defiance	16 768	16 810	-0.2	14 955	390	45	78	1 300	1 998	6 475	10 842	22.5
1135	Delaware	20 030	18 780	6.7	18 847	916	35	163	69	155	7 660	9 124	27.0
1145	Delphos	7 093	NA	NA	7 066	1	5	4	17	74	2 770	8 810	5.3
1150	Delta village	2 849	NA	NA	2 759	7	6	4	73	144	1 107	9 608	5.6
1155	Dennison village	3 282	NA	NA	3 204	57	5	15	1	14	1 298	6 608	3.6
1157	Dent CDP	6 416	NA	NA	6 353	16	5	37	5	11	2 602	NA	15.4
1162	Devola CDP	2 736	NA	NA	2 685	12	1	38	0	8	1 083	NA	13.3
1169	Dillonvale CDP	4 209	NA	NA	4 152	31	10	14	2	17	1 656	NA	2.3
1180	Dover	11 329	11 782	-3.8	11 110	155	14	43	7	26	4 620	9 501	12.3
1185	Doylestown village	2 668	NA	NA	2 656	5	1	1	5	15	1 026	NA	4.1
1192	Drexel CDP	5 143	NA	NA	3 412	1 694	5	11	21	32	1 937	NA	10.6
1193	Dry Run CDP	5 389	NA	NA	5 290	14	8	74	3	46	1 701	NA	12.3
1195	Dublin	16 366	NA	NA	15 429	145	9	743	40	111	5 918	22 282	45.9
1225	East Cleveland	33 096	36 957	-10.4	1 766	31 009	37	218	66	185	15 168	8 806	8.0
1230	Eastlake	21 161	22 104	-4.3	20 866	65	33	174	23	97	7 979	9 778	16.6
1235	East Liverpool	13 654	16 687	-18.2	12 882	694	25	30	23	78	6 142	7 645	11.3
1240	East Palestine	5 168	NA	NA	5 141	6	5	3	13	36	2 097	8 601	7.2
1250	Eaton	7 396	NA	NA	7 275	66	22	22	11	30	3 083	9 762	13.3
1262	Edgewood CDP	5 189	NA	NA	5 055	68	11	35	20	60	2 212	NA	17.5
1295	Elmwood Place village	2 937	NA	NA	2 810	107	10	8	2	6	1 250	8 703	0.9
1300	Elyria	56 746	57 538	-1.4	48 219	7 763	139	303	322	855	22 544	9 744	50.3
1310	Englewood	11 432	11 329	0.9	11 132	185	12	79	24	58	4 626	11 995	13.4
1315	Enon village	2 605	NA	NA	2 548	12	1	39	5	33	1 033	13 272	3.4
1320	Euclid	54 875	59 999	-8.5	45 499	8 765	48	468	95	454	26 586	11 736	27.7
1325	Evendale village	3 175	NA	NA	2 846	154	3	164	8	26	1 026	NA	12.4
1330	Fairborn	31 300	29 702	5.4	28 913	1 290	123	814	160	418	13 288	10 517	29.0
1340	Fairfield	39 729	30 777	29.1	37 725	1 309	51	559	85	290	16 281	12 972	54.0
1343	Fairlawn	5 779	NA	NA	5 463	196	13	103	4	30	2 507	18 274	10.8
1345	Fairport Harbor village	2 978	NA	NA	2 955	13	8	0	2	11	1 337	10 017	2.7
1348	Fairview Park	18 028	19 311	-6.6	17 729	42	14	199	44	161	7 980	15 434	12.1
1380	Findlay	35 703	35 594	0.3	34 250	449	61	296	647	1 227	15 003	11 398	35.1
1381	Finneytown CDP	13 096	NA	NA	11 003	1 883	15	164	31	98	4 877	NA	10.3
1402	Forest Park	18 609	18 675	-0.4	10 114	8 134	21	256	84	170	6 902	11 571	16.4
1403	Forestville CDP	9 185	NA	NA	9 026	46	4	95	14	47	3 794	NA	9.5
1412	Fort McKinley CDP	9 740	10 161	-4.1	6 034	3 605	13	45	43	78	3 552	NA	7.4
1417	Fort Shawnee village	4 128	NA	NA	4 016	73	5	18	16	60	1 626	11 719	18.7

1. Codes shown are 2-digit FIPS codes for states; 4-digit census place codes for places; and 3-digit FIPS county codes followed by 3-digit census MCD codes for minor civil divisions (MCDs). MCD names are followed by county names in parentheses. 2. Hispanic persons may be of any race. 3. Dry land or land partially or temporarily covered by water.

State/ Place/ MCD[1] code	Place	Population: 1990	Population: Places of 10,000 or more: 1980	Population: Places of 10,000 or more: Percent change, 1980–1990	Population characteristics, 1990: Race: White	Race: Black	Race: Am. Indian, Eskimo Aleut	Race: Asian & Pacific Islander	Race: Other race	Hispanic[2]	Total housing units, 1990	Per capita income, 1985 (Dollars)	Land area,[3] 1990 (Sq. Km.)
		1	2	3	4	5	6	7	8	9	10	11	12
	OHIO—Con.												
1420	Fostoria	14 983	15 728	-4.7	13 337	977	20	60	589	1 037	6 167	9 361	18.4
1430	Franklin	11 026	10 711	2.9	10 890	87	17	28	4	15	4 208	8 591	21.1
1455	Fremont	17 648	17 834	-1.0	15 251	1 365	33	28	971	1 676	7 001	9 543	16.0
1457	Fruit Hill CDP	4 101	NA	NA	4 040	8	2	48	3	26	1 432	NA	3.2
1465	Gahanna	27 791	18 001	54.4	25 096	2 202	39	365	89	216	9 921	11 759	34.1
1475	Galion	11 859	12 391	-4.3	11 785	11	16	19	28	89	5 169	9 076	12.6
1480	Gallipolis	4 831	NA	NA	4 510	280	13	17	11	45	2 184	9 007	8.9
1495	Garfield Heights	31 739	34 938	-9.2	26 788	4 688	37	172	54	266	13 000	10 092	18.7
1505	Gates Mills village	2 508	NA	NA	2 435	5	0	52	16	29	992	NA	23.6
1510	Geneva	6 597	NA	NA	6 283	46	17	14	237	358	2 487	8 698	9.0
1525	Georgetown village	3 627	NA	NA	3 526	95	2	2	2	9	1 479	8 377	7.3
1530	Germantown	4 916	NA	NA	4 874	25	4	7	6	12	1 884	10 577	9.3
1540	Gibsonburg village	2 579	NA	NA	2 453	1	7	6	112	168	975	NA	5.6
1550	Girard	11 304	12 517	-9.7	11 000	241	19	27	17	90	4 842	9 764	12.5
1595	Golf Manor village	4 154	NA	NA	2 515	1 606	4	17	12	34	1 871	11 482	1.5
1605	Grafton village	3 344	NA	NA	2 816	487	13	6	22	55	800	NA	11.0
1620	Grandview Heights	7 010	NA	NA	6 875	43	7	49	36	87	3 013	13 278	3.4
1625	Granville village	4 353	NA	NA	4 178	115	3	50	7	35	1 127	8 944	10.6
1643	Green village	3 553	NA	NA	3 508	25	5	13	2	23	1 236	NA	7.9
1650	Greenfield	5 172	NA	NA	5 005	157	5	5	0	16	2 073	7 910	4.9
1655	Greenhills village	4 393	NA	NA	4 321	38	5	20	9	36	1 686	12 245	3.2
1657	Green Meadows CDP	2 526	NA	NA	2 474	16	2	27	7	31	941	NA	1.6
1659	Greensburg CDP	3 306	NA	NA	3 262	15	3	23	3	19	1 485	NA	23.9
1665	Greenville	12 863	12 999	-1.0	12 682	67	37	52	25	78	5 500	10 322	12.7
1673	Groesbeck CDP	6 684	NA	NA	6 453	157	4	60	10	39	2 533	NA	7.6
1675	Grove City	19 661	16 849	16.7	19 418	107	39	75	22	107	7 675	10 693	26.2
1680	Groveport village	2 948	NA	NA	2 914	12	12	6	4	14	1 137	9 447	17.8
1705	Hamilton	61 368	63 189	-2.9	56 413	4 494	93	240	128	308	25 362	9 596	51.7
1745	Harrison	7 518	NA	NA	7 472	4	7	20	15	27	2 662	9 282	9.1
1790	Heath	7 231	NA	NA	7 038	128	5	47	13	31	2 884	10 153	23.0
1810	Hicksville village	3 664	NA	NA	3 584	5	6	1	68	92	1 504	8 790	6.5
1825	Highland Heights	6 249	NA	NA	6 124	19	2	103	1	41	2 176	13 945	13.3
1830	Hilliard	11 796	NA	NA	11 579	82	19	90	26	101	4 556	9 810	22.3
1840	Hillsboro	6 235	NA	NA	5 709	454	20	43	9	23	2 721	8 922	10.4
1873	Howland Center CDP	6 732	NA	NA	6 522	107	8	91	4	56	2 372	NA	10.2
1880	Hubbard	8 248	NA	NA	8 162	51	14	14	7	58	3 376	9 567	8.0
1881	Huber Heights	38 696	35 480	9.1	35 110	2 665	96	672	153	595	14 306	10 909	53.9
1882	Huber Ridge CDP	5 255	NA	NA	5 020	155	18	33	29	75	1 800	NA	3.0
1885	Hudson village	5 159	NA	NA	5 063	16	2	75	3	42	2 294	19 067	10.5
1900	Huron	7 030	NA	NA	6 966	9	17	18	20	57	3 204	13 134	12.6
1905	Independence	6 500	NA	NA	6 427	20	2	48	3	46	2 424	13 219	24.8
1920	Ironton	12 751	14 288	-10.8	12 069	649	11	15	7	23	5 720	8 263	10.7
1932	Jackson	6 144	NA	NA	6 086	38	9	7	4	16	2 820	8 557	12.1
1955	Jefferson village	3 331	NA	NA	3 257	58	3	9	4	14	1 276	9 540	5.8
1960	Jefferson village	4 505	NA	NA	4 482	8	8	6	1	13	1 653	9 368	6.6
1995	Johnstown village	3 237	NA	NA	3 199	15	12	10	1	6	1 321	10 113	4.5
2015	Kent	28 835	26 164	10.2	25 926	2 050	49	723	87	262	9 275	8 196	22.6
2020	Kenton	8 356	NA	NA	8 204	104	18	18	12	52	3 532	8 247	7.9
2023	Kenwood CDP	7 469	NA	NA	7 037	241	6	169	16	70	3 544	NA	6.1
2025	Kettering	60 569	61 186	-1.0	59 222	437	79	746	85	477	27 096	14 751	48.3
2068	Kirtland	5 881	NA	NA	5 846	10	5	19	1	20	2 138	13 062	43.0
2088	Lake Darby CDP	2 798	NA	NA	2 723	37	1	20	17	28	821	NA	8.8
2100	Lakemore village	2 684	NA	NA	2 650	21	9	3	1	14	965	7 653	3.8
2120	Lakewood	59 718	61 963	-3.6	58 228	506	113	611	260	896	28 521	12 631	14.4
2125	Lancaster	34 507	34 953	-1.3	34 076	175	79	132	45	187	14 754	10 364	40.5
2127	Landen CDP	9 263	NA	NA	8 985	108	8	154	8	44	3 669	NA	12.5
2155	Lebanon	10 453	NA	NA	9 989	335	45	75	9	49	4 121	10 504	24.0
2195	Lexington village	4 124	NA	NA	4 072	16	2	33	1	16	1 516	10 867	7.1
2205	Lima	45 549	47 381	-3.9	33 949	10 949	102	230	319	681	18 666	8 748	32.8
2225	Lincoln Heights	4 805	NA	NA	36	4 752	5	6	6	6	1 867	6 200	1.9
2226	Lincoln Village CDP	9 958	10 548	-5.6	9 577	243	44	50	44	84	4 176	NA	4.9
2240	Lisbon village	3 037	NA	NA	2 986	29	6	14	2	6	1 261	9 159	2.9
2265	Lockland village	4 357	NA	NA	3 262	1 069	5	13	8	10	1 975	9 369	3.2
2270	Lodi village	3 042	NA	NA	3 029	1	2	7	3	9	1 271	9 374	5.6
2275	Logan	6 725	NA	NA	6 645	58	10	9	3	17	2 891	8 465	7.4
2280	London	7 807	NA	NA	7 080	660	12	35	20	49	3 202	8 807	13.0
2285	Lorain	71 245	75 416	-5.5	55 729	9 810	299	231	5 176	12 065	27 544	9 007	62.3
2287	Lordstown village	3 404	NA	NA	3 281	106	8	7	2	22	1 234	9 752	59.9
2295	Loudonville village	2 915	NA	NA	2 896	5	8	4	2	6	1 217	8 891	6.0
2300	Louisville	8 087	NA	NA	8 055	1	11	15	5	62	3 139	9 432	11.7
2305	Loveland	9 990	NA	NA	9 674	201	16	71	28	64	3 622	11 272	10.4
2350	Lyndhurst	15 982	18 092	-11.7	15 710	75	5	185	7	57	6 729	16 064	11.4
2380	McDonald village	3 526	NA	NA	3 479	30	10	4	3	20	1 225	9 743	4.3

1. Codes shown are 2-digit FIPS codes for states; 4-digit census place codes for places; and 3-digit FIPS county codes followed by 3-digit census MCD codes for minor civil divisions (MCDs). MCD names are followed by county names in parentheses. 2. Hispanic persons may be of any race. 3. Dry land or land partially or temporarily covered by water.

State/ Place/ MCD[1] code	Place	Population: 1990	Population: Places of 10,000 or more: 1980	Population: Places of 10,000 or more: Percent change, 1980–1990	Population characteristics, 1990: Race: White	Race: Black	Race: Am. Indian, Eskimo Aleut	Race: Asian & Pacific Islander	Race: Other race	Hispanic[2]	Total housing units, 1990	Per capita income, 1985 (Dollars)	Land area,[3] 1990 (Sq. Km.)
		1	2	3	4	5	6	7	8	9	10	11	12
	OHIO—Con.												
2383	Macedonia	7 509	NA	NA	7 151	266	13	71	8	24	2 497	11 841	24.8
2388	Mack North CDP	2 816	NA	NA	2 812	3	0	0	1	11	942	NA	8.0
2392	Mack South CDP	5 767	NA	NA	5 744	1	2	19	1	17	1 780	NA	9.6
2395	Madeira	9 141	NA	NA	8 913	91	1	128	8	54	3 565	16 855	8.7
2440	Mansfield	50 627	53 927	-6.1	40 870	9 153	118	310	176	475	21 909	9 814	72.3
2455	Maple Heights	27 089	29 735	-8.9	22 691	3 987	25	288	98	189	10 791	10 553	13.4
2475	Mariemont village	3 118	NA	NA	3 104	1	1	12	0	6	1 509	17 953	2.2
2480	Marietta	15 026	16 467	-8.8	14 734	193	24	62	13	72	6 481	9 341	19.9
2485	Marion	34 075	37 040	-8.0	32 277	1 438	92	154	114	289	14 243	8 502	20.8
2505	Martins Ferry	7 990	NA	NA	7 672	297	6	8	7	35	3 763	8 840	5.5
2515	Marysville	9 656	NA	NA	8 553	980	17	72	34	96	3 462	10 677	15.2
2520	Mason	11 452	NA	NA	11 295	45	18	81	13	54	4 274	12 155	31.6
2525	Massillon	31 007	30 557	1.5	27 724	3 051	74	74	84	270	12 814	9 165	34.2
2535	Maumee	15 561	15 747	-1.2	15 289	84	29	89	70	207	6 181	11 985	21.8
2545	Mayfield village	3 462	NA	NA	3 367	9	1	84	1	19	1 416	20 582	10.2
2548	Mayfield Heights	19 847	21 550	-7.9	19 000	379	8	436	24	126	10 300	13 015	10.9
2560	Medina	19 231	15 268	26.0	18 570	492	32	108	29	136	7 354	11 754	26.4
2580	Mentor	47 358	42 065	12.6	46 686	163	29	432	48	288	17 172	12 504	69.3
2595	Mentor-on-the-Lake	8 271	NA	NA	8 145	56	9	49	12	68	3 021	10 502	4.2
2610	Miamisburg	17 834	15 304	16.5	17 521	142	19	131	21	85	6 844	11 334	24.5
2615	Middleburg Heights	14 702	16 218	-9.3	14 285	108	16	273	20	108	6 312	14 134	20.9
2630	Middleport village	2 725	NA	NA	2 644	66	10	5	0	19	1 267	8 165	2.8
2635	Middletown	46 022	43 719	5.3	40 646	5 051	60	199	66	207	19 385	10 028	52.3
2665	Milford	5 660	NA	NA	5 445	175	5	22	13	44	2 779	10 472	9.4
2690	Millersburg village	3 051	NA	NA	2 987	31	7	8	18	37	1 227	8 876	4.2
2717	Mineral Ridge CDP	3 928	NA	NA	3 794	100	9	7	18	34	1 365	NA	8.5
2720	Minerva village	4 318	NA	NA	4 298	1	2	5	12	13	1 802	8 980	5.5
2730	Mingo Junction	4 297	NA	NA	4 139	121	17	10	10	41	1 878	8 462	5.7
2735	Minster village	2 650	NA	NA	2 640	0	1	7	2	6	935	10 357	4.2
2740	Mogadore village	4 008	NA	NA	3 982	4	12	6	4	14	1 509	10 841	5.4
2742	Monfort Heights East CDP	3 661	NA	NA	3 445	167	6	39	4	15	1 508	NA	4.9
2744	Monfort Heights South CDP	4 587	NA	NA	4 488	72	8	16	3	17	1 593	NA	9.0
2745	Monroe village	4 490	NA	NA	4 454	16	8	5	7	20	1 750	12 308	24.0
2760	Montgomery	9 753	10 088	-3.3	9 341	94	1	307	10	51	3 462	18 818	13.1
2765	Montpelier village	4 299	NA	NA	4 250	0	2	26	21	53	1 761	8 492	7.0
2767	Montrose-Ghent CDP	4 906	NA	NA	4 794	44	2	65	1	34	1 764	NA	25.0
2770	Moraine	5 989	NA	NA	5 704	200	15	56	14	35	2 420	9 160	17.8
2775	Moreland Hills village	3 354	NA	NA	3 211	49	1	91	2	19	1 290	23 189	18.8
2803	Mount Carmel CDP	4 462	NA	NA	4 384	46	11	14	7	34	1 677	NA	4.4
2815	Mount Gilead village	2 846	NA	NA	2 827	4	5	5	5	8	1 239	9 053	4.9
2820	Mount Healthy	7 580	NA	NA	6 372	1 137	7	38	26	46	3 497	10 603	3.7
2822	Mount Healthy Heights CDP	3 863	NA	NA	3 308	518	7	15	15	27	1 321	NA	2.0
2832	Mount Repose CDP	3 093	NA	NA	3 062	15	8	8	0	16	973	NA	3.8
2840	Mount Vernon	14 550	14 323	1.6	14 228	204	51	49	18	68	6 283	9 316	15.9
2853	Mulberry CDP	2 856	NA	NA	2 805	17	8	22	4	21	1 019	NA	3.9
2855	Munroe Falls village	5 359	NA	NA	5 242	29	1	81	6	23	1 916	12 965	7.1
2870	Napoleon	8 884	NA	NA	8 532	53	14	32	253	375	3 632	11 076	12.5
2895	Nelsonville	4 563	NA	NA	4 406	115	7	19	16	31	1 987	7 115	10.4
2925	Newark	44 389	41 200	7.7	42 605	1 424	104	172	84	295	18 967	9 919	46.7
2945	New Boston village	2 717	NA	NA	2 689	5	16	7	0	11	1 358	6 173	2.9
2950	New Bremen village	2 558	NA	NA	2 537	10	5	6	0	10	971	NA	3.1
2960	New Carlisle	6 049	NA	NA	5 977	5	19	40	8	44	2 293	9 333	4.5
2965	Newcomerstown village	4 012	NA	NA	3 859	133	10	9	1	9	1 794	7 985	6.0
2985	New Lebanon village	4 323	NA	NA	4 302	9	4	7	1	8	1 617	8 956	4.6
2990	New Lexington	5 117	NA	NA	5 102	2	9	3	1	9	2 047	7 594	4.3
2995	New London village	2 642	NA	NA	2 532	86	8	11	5	8	1 022	NA	5.3
3010	New Miami village	2 555	NA	NA	2 351	202	0	2	0	1	890	7 590	2.3
3025	New Philadelphia	15 698	16 883	-7.0	15 476	105	36	65	16	60	6 934	9 721	17.6
3050	Newton Falls	4 866	NA	NA	4 831	14	15	3	3	21	2 137	9 017	5.9
3090	Niles	21 128	23 088	-8.5	20 597	414	31	57	29	133	8 882	10 158	22.0
3095	North Baltimore village	3 139	NA	NA	3 062	1	2	20	54	96	1 238	9 106	4.4
3103	Northbrook CDP	11 471	NA	NA	10 337	994	39	71	30	98	3 987	NA	5.0
3105	North Canton	14 748	14 228	3.7	14 519	77	10	133	9	95	6 534	13 421	14.3
3110	North College Hill	11 002	11 114	-1.0	9 911	992	23	49	27	59	4 440	11 208	4.8
3120	Northfield village	3 624	NA	NA	3 497	82	5	22	18	40	1 528	10 473	2.8
3124	Northgate CDP	7 864	NA	NA	7 244	556	5	52	7	63	2 618	NA	6.5
3130	North Kingsville village	2 672	NA	NA	2 633	15	2	11	11	16	1 075	9 872	23.1
3137	North Madison CDP	8 699	NA	NA	8 657	8	11	19	4	42	3 211	NA	10.4
3145	North Olmsted	34 204	36 486	-6.3	33 223	235	39	592	115	405	13 081	12 761	29.8
3158	Northridge CDP	5 939	NA	NA	5 884	38	5	10	2	24	2 248	NA	7.9
3159	Northridge CDP	9 448	NA	NA	8 674	722	23	12	17	49	3 765	NA	5.9
3160	North Ridgeville	21 564	21 522	0.2	21 183	138	45	136	62	321	7 305	10 596	60.6
3170	North Royalton	23 197	17 671	31.3	22 656	97	17	390	37	147	9 109	12 908	55.1

1. Codes shown are 2-digit FIPS codes for states; 4-digit census place codes for places; and 3-digit FIPS county codes followed by 3-digit census MCD codes for minor civil divisions (MCDs). MCD names are followed by county names in parentheses. 2. Hispanic persons may be of any race. 3. Dry land or land partially or temporarily covered by water.

State/ Place/ MCD[1] code	Place	Population	Places of 10,000 or more		Population characteristics, 1990								
					Race								
		1990	1980	Percent change, 1980–1990	White	Black	Am. Indian, Eskimo Aleut	Asian & Pacific Islander	Other race	Hispanic[2]	Total housing units, 1990	Per capita income, 1985 (Dollars)	Land area,[3] 1990 (Sq. Km.)
		1	2	3	4	5	6	7	8	9	10	11	12
	OHIO—Con.												
3176	Northview CDP	10 337	NA	NA	9 748	410	12	162	5	64	3 798	NA	9.6
3177	Northwood	5 506	NA	NA	5 343	20	15	52	76	124	2 019	9 666	21.0
3183	Norton	11 477	12 242	-6.2	11 294	119	15	44	5	52	4 213	10 734	51.9
3185	Norwalk	14 731	14 358	2.6	14 228	344	19	48	92	269	5 954	9 734	20.6
3195	Norwood	23 674	26 342	-10.1	23 197	238	38	164	37	130	10 260	9 606	8.0
3200	Oak Harbor village	2 637	NA	NA	2 625	0	0	5	7	26	1 099	10 994	3.4
3210	Oakwood	8 957	NA	NA	8 858	31	2	55	11	56	3 822	21 238	5.7
3215	Oakwood village	3 392	NA	NA	1 712	1 650	7	12	11	23	1 354	9 214	9.0
3225	Oberlin	8 191	NA	NA	5 805	1 934	36	329	87	160	2 580	9 345	9.8
3230	Obetz village	3 167	NA	NA	3 038	105	18	2	4	29	1 180	9 223	7.1
3245	Olmsted Falls	6 741	NA	NA	6 624	31	6	45	35	97	2 514	12 832	10.7
3255	Ontario village	4 026	NA	NA	3 921	68	2	23	12	45	1 702	10 644	26.2
3260	Orange village	2 810	NA	NA	2 451	268	1	85	5	41	1 047	NA	9.4
3270	Oregon	18 334	18 649	-1.7	17 742	204	29	96	263	626	7 265	11 273	75.6
3280	Orrville	7 712	NA	NA	7 176	441	18	69	8	30	3 069	10 006	10.9
3302	Ottawa village	3 999	NA	NA	3 898	10	8	7	76	268	1 557	10 829	7.3
3305	Ottawa Hills village	4 543	NA	NA	4 360	59	4	115	5	28	1 746	27 277	4.8
3317	Overlook-Page Manor CDP	13 242	14 825	-10.7	12 747	300	24	128	43	109	5 248	NA	7.5
3325	Oxford	18 937	17 655	7.3	17 684	766	29	428	30	126	5 327	6 796	11.4
3330	Painesville	15 699	16 391	-4.2	13 387	1 997	61	64	190	389	6 404	9 635	13.4
3356	Park Layne CDP	4 795	NA	NA	4 728	21	21	22	3	36	1 618	NA	3.9
3360	Parma	87 876	92 548	-5.0	86 028	639	85	957	167	768	35 589	11 521	51.8
3365	Parma Heights	21 448	23 112	-7.2	21 083	82	23	212	48	170	9 544	12 141	10.9
3375	Pataskala village	3 046	NA	NA	3 001	22	4	4	15	24	1 233	NA	5.8
3385	Paulding village	2 605	NA	NA	2 368	107	12	0	118	246	1 105	9 782	3.3
3410	Pepper Pike	6 185	NA	NA	5 688	206	2	279	10	60	2 170	32 913	18.5
3416	Perry Heights CDP	9 055	NA	NA	8 824	171	7	39	14	68	3 459	NA	7.1
3420	Perrysburg	12 551	10 215	22.9	12 296	80	10	98	67	181	5 044	14 165	12.1
3440	Pickerington village	5 668	NA	NA	5 518	85	14	39	12	46	2 159	11 690	16.1
3455	Piqua	20 612	20 480	0.6	19 634	772	43	106	57	116	8 034	9 220	19.2
3482	Pleasant Run CDP	4 964	NA	NA	4 638	264	13	41	8	42	1 528	NA	5.4
3483	Pleasant Run Farm CDP	4 545	NA	NA	3 970	495	5	66	9	32	1 373	NA	2.9
3500	Poland village	2 992	NA	NA	2 975	4	2	9	2	8	1 144	11 635	3.2
3517	Portage Lakes CDP	13 373	11 310	18.2	13 245	43	35	46	4	37	5 865	NA	21.7
3520	Port Clinton	7 106	NA	NA	6 745	192	13	19	137	429	3 474	10 421	5.4
3530	Portsmouth	22 676	25 943	-12.6	21 308	1 172	103	76	17	93	10 758	8 838	27.9
3595	Ravenna	12 069	11 987	0.7	11 429	545	28	46	21	82	5 203	9 461	12.4
3610	Reading	12 038	12 843	-6.3	11 755	172	23	78	10	52	5 117	11 928	7.6
3635	Reynoldsburg	25 748	20 661	24.6	24 174	1 047	72	383	72	226	10 587	12 422	24.3
3638	Richfield village	3 117	NA	NA	3 084	6	11	16	0	11	1 162	12 034	20.4
3645	Richmond Heights	9 611	10 095	-4.8	8 519	743	5	336	8	64	4 503	14 223	11.3
3675	Rittman	6 147	NA	NA	6 103	3	19	10	12	41	2 329	8 947	14.5
3710	Rocky River	20 410	21 084	-3.2	20 075	39	13	263	20	155	9 691	18 683	12.3
3740	Rossford	5 861	NA	NA	5 684	88	4	51	34	84	2 442	11 711	6.7
3775	Sabina village	2 662	NA	NA	2 634	15	6	7	0	6	1 104	7 264	3.3
3780	St. Bernard	5 344	NA	NA	5 104	203	10	19	8	20	2 343	10 269	4.0
3785	St. Clairsville	5 162	NA	NA	4 953	179	6	24	0	11	2 265	11 063	5.3
3805	St. Marys	8 441	NA	NA	8 367	10	3	42	19	38	3 285	9 200	8.6
3815	Salem	12 233	12 869	-4.9	12 111	58	13	39	12	59	5 298	8 727	11.9
3830	Sandusky	29 764	31 360	-5.1	23 728	5 633	63	77	263	676	13 416	9 913	26.0
3835	Sandusky South CDP	6 336	NA	NA	5 721	542	7	43	23	44	2 147	NA	10.6
3875	Sebring	4 848	NA	NA	4 828	6	8	1	5	11	1 830	8 302	5.3
3885	Seven Hills	12 339	13 650	-9.6	12 074	14	14	224	13	56	4 584	13 415	12.9
3900	Shadyside village	3 934	NA	NA	3 928	3	1	2	0	4	1 835	9 370	2.6
3905	Shaker Heights	30 831	32 487	-5.1	20 633	9 453	61	593	91	351	13 374	22 648	16.3
3915	Sharonville	13 153	10 108	30.1	12 670	267	7	201	8	80	5 832	14 186	25.4
3943	Sheffield Lake	9 825	10 484	-6.3	9 629	78	25	42	51	241	3 542	9 848	6.5
3945	Shelby	9 564	NA	NA	9 506	12	10	24	12	39	4 012	9 668	12.2
3956	Sherwood CDP	3 709	NA	NA	3 660	17	1	26	5	31	1 222	NA	2.9
3961	Shiloh CDP	11 607	11 735	-1.1	9 781	1 651	22	120	33	133	6 226	NA	10.0
3970	Sidney	18 710	17 657	6.0	17 801	529	20	310	50	100	7 386	9 946	22.3
3975	Silver Lake village	3 052	NA	NA	3 017	2	1	31	1	15	1 274	19 942	3.7
3980	Silverton	5 859	NA	NA	2 997	2 786	3	55	18	22	2 682	10 923	2.9
4000	Solon	18 548	14 341	29.3	17 377	625	14	510	22	85	6 601	14 768	52.9
4035	South Euclid	23 866	25 713	-7.2	21 273	2 180	29	340	44	198	9 565	12 964	12.1
4040	South Lebanon village	2 696	NA	NA	2 690	0	3	3	0	4	959	7 066	2.1
4043	South Middletown CDP	3 491	NA	NA	3 470	4	7	10	0	11	1 249	NA	2.5
4050	South Point village	3 823	NA	NA	3 722	80	7	14	0	6	1 454	9 129	6.2
4055	South Russell village	3 402	NA	NA	3 377	14	1	10	0	11	1 174	24 542	10.0
4095	Springboro	6 590	NA	NA	6 499	30	14	43	4	43	2 287	12 901	17.3
4097	Springdale	10 621	10 111	5.0	8 920	1 449	7	198	47	114	4 425	12 741	12.8
4100	Springfield	70 487	72 563	-2.9	57 523	12 250	158	357	199	458	29 562	9 108	50.6
4115	Steubenville	22 125	26 400	-16.2	18 455	3 418	49	150	53	218	9 996	9 687	21.0

1. Codes shown are 2-digit FIPS codes for states; 4-digit census place codes for places; and 3-digit FIPS county codes followed by 3-digit census MCD codes for minor civil divisions (MCDs). MCD names are followed by county names in parentheses. 2. Hispanic persons may be of any race. 3. Dry land or land partially or temporarily covered by water.

State/ Place/ MCD[1] code	Place	Population: 1990	Population, places of 10,000 or more: 1980	Population, places of 10,000 or more: Percent change, 1980–1990	Population characteristics, 1990 — Race: White	Race: Black	Race: Am. Indian, Eskimo Aleut	Race: Asian & Pacific Islander	Race: Other race	Hispanic[2]	Total housing units, 1990	Per capita income, 1985 (Dollars)	Land area,[3] 1990 (Sq. Km.)
		1	2	3	4	5	6	7	8	9	10	11	12
	OHIO—Con.												
4135	Stow	27 702	25 303	9.5	26 900	298	23	449	32	142	10 462	12 260	44.4
4147	Streetsboro	9 932	NA	NA	9 781	65	17	59	10	55	3 827	9 875	62.2
4150	Strongsville	35 308	28 577	23.6	34 107	275	35	833	58	336	13 099	13 986	63.8
4155	Struthers	12 284	13 624	-9.8	11 909	279	27	11	58	194	4 948	8 169	9.7
4177	Summerside CDP	4 573	NA	NA	4 494	45	5	28	1	21	1 727	NA	5.9
4190	Swanton village	3 557	NA	NA	3 517	10	6	13	11	28	1 236	10 740	5.1
4200	Sylvania	17 301	15 527	11.4	16 782	165	21	262	71	178	6 666	15 632	15.0
4210	Tallmadge	14 870	15 269	-2.6	14 532	197	24	112	5	77	5 696	11 719	35.0
4225	The Plains CDP	2 644	NA	NA	2 600	26	6	9	3	7	1 135	NA	6.1
4227	The Village of Indian Hill	5 383	NA	NA	5 169	31	2	178	3	25	1 965	40 445	48.0
4240	Tiffin	18 604	19 549	-4.8	18 112	260	27	124	81	236	7 461	8 533	15.8
4255	Tipp City	6 027	NA	NA	5 984	0	11	29	3	27	2 642	11 126	12.8
4265	Toledo	332 943	354 635	-6.1	256 239	65 598	920	3 487	6 699	13 207	142 125	10 050	208.7
4275	Toronto	6 127	NA	NA	6 020	78	8	15	6	22	2 683	9 516	4.9
4285	Trenton	6 189	NA	NA	6 155	19	2	13	0	19	2 243	10 059	8.5
4295	Trotwood	8 816	NA	NA	4 807	3 872	27	45	65	104	3 749	10 649	15.5
4300	Troy	19 478	19 086	2.1	18 356	894	26	172	30	58	8 006	9 803	22.2
4303	Turpin Hills CDP	4 927	NA	NA	4 874	21	0	29	3	24	1 734	NA	7.7
4310	Twinsburg	9 606	NA	NA	9 069	434	10	69	24	49	3 855	11 489	31.5
4315	Uhrichsville	5 604	NA	NA	5 488	100	14	1	1	5	2 370	7 641	7.2
4320	Union	5 501	NA	NA	5 422	17	15	40	7	41	1 826	8 993	6.3
4335	Uniontown CDP	3 074	NA	NA	3 055	3	6	8	2	6	1 195	NA	6.5
4350	University Heights	14 790	15 401	-4.0	12 091	2 416	11	227	45	148	5 286	15 182	4.7
4355	Upper Arlington	34 128	35 648	-4.3	33 201	86	25	775	41	252	14 376	21 696	24.9
4360	Upper Sandusky	5 906	NA	NA	5 854	6	9	17	20	58	2 529	10 251	8.2
4365	Urbana	11 353	10 762	5.5	10 390	794	18	64	87	110	4 777	9 717	16.0
4395	Vandalia	13 882	13 161	5.5	13 693	58	22	97	12	57	5 862	12 755	28.2
4405	Van Wert	10 891	11 035	-1.3	10 510	159	20	43	159	267	4 736	10 028	13.0
4415	Vermilion	11 127	11 014	1.0	11 031	9	31	27	29	148	4 367	11 441	27.7
4445	Wadsworth	15 718	15 166	3.6	15 509	78	40	77	14	55	6 218	11 227	21.8
4460	Walbridge village	2 736	NA	NA	2 697	1	3	8	27	55	1 116	10 649	3.6
4475	Wapakoneta	9 214	NA	NA	9 116	5	19	65	9	61	3 658	9 054	11.3
4480	Warren	50 793	56 629	-10.3	39 570	10 833	92	163	135	359	21 785	10 030	41.4
4485	Warrensville Heights	15 745	16 565	-5.0	1 498	14 011	19	143	74	84	6 785	11 246	10.4
4495	Washington	12 983	12 682	2.4	12 438	431	27	74	13	35	5 394	8 010	13.5
4510	Waterville village	4 517	NA	NA	4 466	10	0	32	9	33	1 552	10 783	9.0
4515	Wauseon	6 322	NA	NA	5 876	32	20	43	351	574	2 410	9 756	11.7
4520	Waverly City	4 477	NA	NA	4 423	37	2	14	1	1	2 138	9 763	10.3
4545	Wellington village	4 140	NA	NA	4 053	61	7	9	10	30	1 609	8 940	7.3
4550	Wellston	6 049	NA	NA	6 013	16	8	8	4	27	2 505	8 351	17.9
4555	Wellsville	4 532	NA	NA	4 145	355	12	15	5	7	2 047	6 948	4.5
4570	West Carrollton City	14 403	13 148	9.5	13 902	276	23	185	17	66	6 497	12 319	16.3
4580	Westerville	30 269	23 416	29.3	29 310	525	31	351	52	216	10 521	12 442	27.3
4588	West Hill CDP	2 954	NA	NA	2 554	395	0	2	3	11	1 170	NA	4.2
4595	Westlake	27 018	19 483	38.7	26 010	162	17	780	49	255	11 014	16 871	41.2
4625	West Milton village	4 348	NA	NA	4 301	7	18	17	5	10	1 774	10 397	4.5
4645	West Portsmouth CDP	3 551	NA	NA	3 492	19	30	8	2	2	1 413	NA	12.3
4660	West Union village	3 096	NA	NA	3 071	4	12	5	4	13	1 272	7 221	5.8
4680	Wheelersburg CDP	5 113	NA	NA	5 085	8	13	6	1	5	2 074	NA	10.7
4685	Whitehall	20 572	21 299	-3.4	18 425	1 714	63	315	55	196	9 065	10 990	13.3
4690	Whitehouse village	2 528	NA	NA	2 498	3	1	8	18	25	887	NA	8.5
4691	White Oak CDP	12 430	NA	NA	12 113	161	13	132	11	50	4 846	NA	10.6
4692	White Oak East CDP	3 544	NA	NA	3 502	6	6	27	3	9	1 450	NA	2.1
4694	White Oak West CDP	2 879	NA	NA	2 839	10	5	22	3	7	1 030	NA	3.5
4695	Wickliffe	14 558	16 790	-13.3	14 047	391	9	89	22	75	5 623	10 780	12.0
4698	Wilberforce CDP	2 639	NA	NA	98	2 524	5	4	8	19	201	NA	8.0
4705	Willard	6 210	NA	NA	5 874	116	12	17	191	370	2 419	9 511	8.3
4720	Willoughby	20 510	19 329	6.1	20 126	149	28	172	35	133	8 969	12 121	26.3
4725	Willoughby Hills	8 427	NA	NA	8 070	266	4	84	3	60	4 235	15 646	27.9
4730	Willowick	15 269	17 834	-14.4	15 048	90	6	119	6	51	6 207	11 466	6.5
4740	Wilmington	11 199	10 431	7.4	10 429	645	25	84	16	39	4 635	9 500	12.9
4760	Windham village	2 943	NA	NA	2 827	98	5	12	1	12	1 328	7 175	5.5
4765	Wintersville village	4 102	NA	NA	3 792	275	13	20	2	14	1 695	9 895	6.4
4768	Withamsville CDP	2 834	NA	NA	2 813	6	3	9	3	5	1 152	NA	4.6
4774	Woodbourne-Hyde Park CDP	7 837	NA	NA	7 644	27	9	151	6	49	3 053	NA	11.9
4775	Woodlawn village	2 674	NA	NA	685	1 970	3	8	8	21	1 109	9 155	6.7
4785	Woodsfield village	2 832	NA	NA	2 815	0	14	2	1	14	1 288	9 105	5.1
4800	Wooster	22 191	19 289	15.0	21 089	775	22	260	45	140	9 015	11 112	30.6
4805	Worthington	14 869	15 016	-1.0	14 087	339	16	397	30	110	5 734	16 401	14.6
4812	Wright-Patterson AFB CDP	8 579	NA	NA	6 741	1 279	24	396	139	387	2 452	NA	30.6
4815	Wyoming	8 128	NA	NA	7 104	887	6	114	17	80	3 280	20 796	7.3
4820	Xenia	24 664	24 653	0.0	20 976	3 373	86	130	99	135	9 325	9 113	23.2
4830	Yellow Springs village	3 973	NA	NA	2 965	890	31	55	32	57	1 641	12 464	4.6

1. Codes shown are 2-digit FIPS codes for states; 4-digit census place codes for places; and 3-digit FIPS county codes followed by 3-digit census MCD codes for minor civil divisions (MCDs). MCD names are followed by county names in parentheses. 2. Hispanic persons may be of any race. 3. Dry land or land partially or temporarily covered by water.

State/ Place/ MCD[1] code	Place	Population: 1990	Population: Places of 10,000 or more: 1980	Population: Places of 10,000 or more: Percent change, 1980–1990	Population characteristics, 1990: Race: White	Race: Black	Race: Am. Indian, Eskimo Aleut	Race: Asian & Pacific Islander	Race: Other race	Hispanic[2]	Total housing units, 1990	Per capita income, 1985 (Dollars)	Land area,[3] 1990 (Sq. Km.)
		1	2	3	4	5	6	7	8	9	10	11	12
	OHIO—Con.												
4845	Youngstown	95 732	115 435	-17.1	56 777	36 487	228	289	1 951	3 820	40 802	7 968	87.5
4860	Zanesville	26 778	28 655	-6.6	23 642	2 880	141	53	62	107	11 770	8 025	27.0
40	OKLAHOMA	3 145 585	3 025 487	4.0	2 583 512	233 801	252 420	33 563	42 289	86 160	1 406 499	9 754	177 877.5
0010	Ada	15 820	15 902	-0.5	12 879	672	2 103	92	74	200	7 602	8 698	33.1
0060	Altus	21 910	23 101	-5.2	16 793	2 670	329	368	1 750	2 593	9 133	7 855	33.8
0065	Alva	5 495	NA	NA	5 316	48	81	25	25	61	2 726	10 571	6.0
0080	Anadarko	6 586	NA	NA	3 579	548	2 287	24	148	399	2 803	7 375	18.3
0085	Antlers town	2 524	NA	NA	2 123	57	338	0	6	13	1 280	6 809	5.3
0100	Ardmore	23 079	23 689	-2.6	17 861	2 711	2 101	127	279	593	10 626	10 302	126.1
0125	Atoka	3 298	NA	NA	2 512	380	399	4	3	20	1 512	7 847	14.8
0145	Bartlesville	34 256	34 568	-0.9	30 345	1 140	2 180	383	208	603	15 908	14 551	54.7
0175	Bethany	20 075	22 132	-9.3	18 508	391	643	308	225	478	8 865	11 184	13.5
0177	Bethel Acres town	2 505	NA	NA	2 353	9	132	5	6	18	948	NA	78.4
0195	Bixby	9 502	NA	NA	8 864	41	462	40	95	253	3 726	10 751	64.2
0205	Blackwell	7 538	NA	NA	6 980	6	441	25	86	182	3 636	8 541	13.0
0285	Bristow	4 062	NA	NA	3 339	360	351	2	10	28	2 009	7 281	8.1
0290	Broken Arrow	58 043	35 761	62.3	53 219	1 809	2 079	558	378	1 229	20 420	11 237	104.5
0295	Broken Bow	3 961	NA	NA	2 711	339	858	7	46	104	1 653	6 482	7.9
0435	Catoosa	2 954	NA	NA	2 568	15	357	3	11	36	1 163	NA	14.5
0455	Chandler	2 596	NA	NA	2 218	260	108	4	6	22	1 230	7 375	13.0
0465	Checotah	3 290	NA	NA	2 554	254	462	6	14	46	1 517	6 530	21.2
0485	Chickasha	14 988	15 828	-5.3	12 605	1 466	675	68	174	371	7 054	9 552	35.4
0490	Choctaw	8 545	NA	NA	7 840	120	461	55	69	243	3 080	10 477	70.3
0500	Claremore	13 280	12 085	9.9	10 608	343	2 165	84	80	220	5 590	9 217	22.6
0515	Cleveland	3 156	NA	NA	2 953	8	179	15	1	9	1 552	7 655	6.0
0520	Clinton	9 298	NA	NA	6 895	664	750	60	929	1 120	3 937	9 654	22.1
0540	Collinsville	3 612	NA	NA	3 131	5	456	12	8	35	1 542	8 803	12.9
0585	Coweta	6 159	NA	NA	5 086	248	771	16	38	73	2 406	7 660	16.2
0615	Cushing	7 218	NA	NA	6 322	292	529	23	52	114	3 754	10 261	17.7
0645	Davis	2 543	NA	NA	2 205	105	220	3	10	26	1 155	7 676	9.1
0660	Del City	23 928	28 414	-15.8	19 455	2 624	1 086	425	338	705	10 773	10 355	19.5
0680	Dewey	3 326	NA	NA	2 857	87	356	4	22	72	1 518	8 710	6.1
0720	Drumright	2 799	NA	NA	2 624	15	156	4	0	8	1 447	7 385	18.3
0725	Duncan	21 732	22 517	-3.5	19 432	925	705	118	552	748	10 401	10 424	66.8
0730	Durant	12 823	11 972	7.1	10 790	161	1 658	113	101	245	5 996	7 475	46.5
0755	Edmond	52 315	34 637	51.0	48 005	1 621	1 317	1 056	316	921	20 598	13 168	220.9
0770	Elk City	10 428	NA	NA	9 485	348	265	37	293	435	4 895	8 236	29.2
0785	El Reno	15 414	15 434	-0.1	12 444	1 387	1 217	83	283	712	6 239	8 991	206.3
0790	Enid	45 309	50 363	-10.0	41 241	1 996	1 054	570	448	961	21 680	10 852	187.0
0800	Eufaula	2 652	NA	NA	1 851	300	495	6	0	24	1 388	7 134	17.2
0820	Fairview	2 936	NA	NA	2 871	2	50	8	5	22	1 443	12 095	18.1
0865	Fort Gibson town	3 359	NA	NA	2 602	88	620	6	43	68	1 289	NA	13.7
0867	Fort Sill CDP	12 107	15 924	-24.0	6 685	4 166	145	334	777	1 212	1 372	NA	28.6
0895	Frederick	5 221	NA	NA	3 640	704	208	16	653	882	2 341	6 684	6.9
0955	Glenpool	6 688	NA	NA	5 511	161	915	68	33	110	2 437	7 708	20.4
1015	Grove	4 020	NA	NA	3 465	3	520	17	15	60	2 279	8 721	22.2
1020	Guthrie	10 518	10 312	2.0	7 939	2 019	325	54	181	303	4 502	7 741	51.5
1025	Guymon	7 803	NA	NA	7 130	14	91	16	552	977	3 495	10 228	15.5
1060	Harrah town	4 206	NA	NA	3 854	15	287	18	32	98	1 677	8 936	28.5
1090	Healdton	2 872	NA	NA	2 683	6	168	6	9	24	1 420	8 031	36.6
1095	Heavener	2 601	NA	NA	2 195	0	393	8	5	30	1 199	7 116	12.8
1110	Henryetta	5 872	NA	NA	5 148	16	655	9	44	88	2 868	7 367	14.0
1150	Hobart	4 305	NA	NA	3 468	390	207	36	204	322	2 083	7 684	5.9
1160	Holdenville	4 792	NA	NA	3 860	170	747	10	5	38	2 377	6 862	12.3
1165	Hollis	2 584	NA	NA	1 783	238	22	2	539	572	1 186	6 704	3.7
1190	Hugo	5 978	NA	NA	3 905	1 236	781	17	39	96	2 702	6 306	14.1
1205	Idabel	6 957	NA	NA	4 431	1 700	734	25	67	137	2 950	6 676	27.6
1240	Jenks	7 493	NA	NA	6 965	63	339	63	63	146	2 795	11 402	36.4
1325	Kingfisher	4 095	NA	NA	3 697	118	197	4	79	101	1 901	10 442	10.4
1405	Lawton	80 561	80 054	0.6	57 019	15 575	2 684	2 621	2 662	5 104	34 622	8 976	132.5
1435	Lindsay	2 947	NA	NA	2 772	0	157	14	4	20	1 454	8 656	6.1
1452	Lone Grove	4 114	NA	NA	3 728	100	269	5	12	32	1 608	8 491	124.6
1490	McAlester	16 370	17 255	-5.1	13 306	1 255	1 662	67	80	205	7 253	8 192	31.4
1520	Madill	3 069	NA	NA	2 534	163	279	3	90	188	1 459	9 691	6.4
1530	Mangum	3 344	NA	NA	2 870	252	49	7	166	218	1 820	7 720	4.4
1570	Marlow	4 416	NA	NA	4 120	0	261	13	22	53	2 116	6 933	9.7
1620	Miami	13 142	14 237	-7.7	10 653	179	2 198	52	60	132	6 012	8 762	24.1
1630	Midwest City	52 267	49 559	5.5	40 281	8 504	2 033	910	539	1 398	22 846	11 003	63.5
1655	Moore	40 318	35 063	15.0	36 362	719	2 136	516	585	1 353	14 824	9 758	55.7
1690	Muldrow town	2 889	NA	NA	2 264	69	546	9	1	19	1 194	6 554	8.7
1700	Muskogee	37 708	40 011	-5.8	26 025	7 108	4 145	199	231	564	17 674	8 706	89.3

1. Codes shown are 2-digit FIPS codes for states; 4-digit census place codes for places; and 3-digit FIPS county codes followed by 3-digit census MCD codes for minor civil divisions (MCDs). MCD names are followed by county names in parentheses. 2. Hispanic persons may be of any race. 3. Dry land or land partially or temporarily covered by water.

State/ Place/ MCD[1] code	Place	Population			Population characteristics, 1990						Total housing units, 1990	Per capita income, 1985 (Dollars)	Land area,[3] 1990 (Sq. Km.)
			Places of 10,000 or more		Race								
		1990	1980	Percent change, 1980–1990	White	Black	Am. Indian, Eskimo Aleut	Asian & Pacific Islander	Other race	Hispanic[2]			
		1	2	3	4	5	6	7	8	9	10	11	12
	OKLAHOMA—Con.												
1705	Mustang	10 434	NA	NA	9 821	76	394	44	99	252	3 783	10 260	31.1
1728	Newcastle	4 214	NA	NA	3 919	4	245	5	41	85	1 579	9 609	126.1
1730	New Cordell	2 903	NA	NA	2 823	3	54	5	18	49	1 487	9 772	6.7
1745	Nichols Hills	4 020	NA	NA	3 892	17	69	37	5	31	1 869	39 034	5.2
1750	Noble town	4 710	NA	NA	4 410	2	247	12	39	98	1 954	8 368	32.4
1755	Norman	80 071	67 996	17.8	70 053	2 861	3 867	2 572	718	1 904	35 650	11 236	458.5
1770	Nowata	3 896	NA	NA	2 933	255	701	0	7	34	1 894	9 812	8.1
1774	Oakhurst CDP	3 030	NA	NA	2 685	17	315	6	7	45	1 264	NA	17.4
1810	Okemah	3 085	NA	NA	2 327	59	678	11	10	32	1 528	6 583	6.7
1815	Oklahoma City	444 719	403 243	10.3	332 539	71 064	18 794	10 491	11 831	22 033	212 367	11 527	1 575.1
1820	Okmulgee	13 441	16 263	-17.4	8 487	3 217	1 634	41	62	177	6 313	7 652	33.0
1855	Owasso	11 151	NA	NA	10 246	148	664	59	34	131	4 219	10 159	15.5
1875	Pauls Valley	6 150	NA	NA	5 273	340	450	23	64	129	2 838	8 307	19.7
1880	Pawhuska	3 825	NA	NA	2 812	115	878	1	19	68	2 029	10 134	9.5
1910	Perry	4 978	NA	NA	4 549	198	176	11	44	65	2 408	9 464	15.2
1925	Piedmont	2 522	NA	NA	2 431	18	57	3	13	35	868	NA	113.3
1933	Pocola town	3 664	NA	NA	3 245	185	185	15	34	50	1 360	6 894	78.5
1935	Ponca City	26 359	26 238	0.5	23 764	773	1 455	183	184	509	12 294	11 822	45.0
1955	Poteau	7 210	NA	NA	6 473	121	590	10	16	91	3 162	8 255	73.7
1970	Pryor Creek	8 327	NA	NA	7 154	11	1 102	30	30	103	3 845	9 422	16.2
1975	Purcell	4 784	NA	NA	4 142	180	362	9	91	170	2 096	7 485	20.4
2120	Sallisaw	7 122	NA	NA	5 538	71	1 475	13	25	70	3 156	7 189	32.5
2125	Sand Springs	15 346	13 245	15.9	14 080	251	922	34	59	231	6 289	9 654	47.4
2135	Sapulpa	18 074	15 853	14.0	15 610	902	1 415	68	79	260	7 614	8 503	47.2
2150	Sayre	2 881	NA	NA	2 786	11	28	2	54	80	1 507	7 846	7.0
2165	Seminole	7 071	NA	NA	5 788	330	909	15	29	103	3 481	9 275	35.6
2195	Shawnee	26 017	26 506	-1.8	21 496	888	3 243	201	189	511	11 784	9 037	108.2
2210	Skiatook town	4 910	NA	NA	3 948	4	946	2	10	53	1 995	8 421	21.7
2260	Spencer	3 972	NA	NA	1 812	1 982	144	14	20	56	1 601	9 589	13.8
2295	Stigler	2 574	NA	NA	2 238	4	328	1	3	23	1 193	7 085	5.6
2300	Stillwater	36 676	38 268	-4.2	32 114	1 369	1 262	1 697	234	660	15 771	8 023	70.6
2305	Stilwell	2 663	NA	NA	1 444	2	1 191	4	22	49	1 103	NA	4.4
2335	Stroud	2 666	NA	NA	2 320	141	166	12	27	34	1 278	8 133	28.3
2350	Sulphur	4 824	NA	NA	4 097	60	625	8	34	71	2 199	8 045	10.9
2370	Tahlequah	10 398	NA	NA	7 101	261	2 925	40	71	184	4 579	7 201	15.3
2395	Tecumseh	5 750	NA	NA	4 929	117	684	11	9	64	2 464	7 732	39.0
2430	The Village	10 353	11 049	-6.3	8 867	1 019	281	118	68	213	4 945	13 471	6.6
2445	Tishomingo	3 116	NA	NA	2 427	186	488	5	10	52	1 363	5 952	10.5
2450	Tonkawa	3 127	NA	NA	2 880	26	192	8	21	43	1 492	8 288	5.7
2465	Tulsa	367 302	360 919	1.8	291 444	49 825	17 091	5 133	3 809	9 564	176 211	12 670	475.3
2472	Turley CDP	2 930	NA	NA	2 353	252	292	4	29	85	1 505	NA	9.6
2475	Tuttle town	2 807	NA	NA	2 604	1	190	3	9	24	1 092	8 914	41.2
2520	Vinita	5 804	NA	NA	4 410	305	1 062	14	13	55	2 617	8 327	10.9
2525	Wagoner	6 894	NA	NA	5 274	728	863	2	27	74	2 879	7 204	16.8
2540	Walters	2 519	NA	NA	2 191	3	297	1	27	64	1 230	7 489	3.8
2565	Warr Acres	9 288	NA	NA	8 421	259	329	158	121	303	4 278	12 111	7.3
2580	Watonga	3 408	NA	NA	2 604	400	317	11	76	110	1 605	8 850	5.7
2610	Weatherford	10 124	NA	NA	9 157	247	477	95	148	281	4 192	9 036	14.2
2650	Wewoka	4 050	NA	NA	2 277	998	755	14	6	17	2 010	6 757	12.5
2655	Wilburton	3 092	NA	NA	2 605	113	337	12	25	40	1 237	6 740	7.6
2685	Woodward	12 340	13 610	-9.3	11 738	25	309	60	208	407	5 616	10 098	33.8
2720	Yukon	20 935	17 112	22.3	19 634	151	636	332	182	430	7 735	11 194	66.8
41	OREGON	2 842 321	2 633 156	7.9	2 636 787	46 178	38 496	69 269	51 591	112 707	1 193 567	9 925	248 646.7
0010	Albany	29 462	26 544	11.0	28 321	100	335	378	328	887	12 322	8 828	29.7
0013	Aloha CDP	34 284	28 353	20.9	31 084	234	227	2 205	534	1 294	11 747	NA	19.2
0020	Altamont CDP	18 591	19 805	-6.1	17 477	133	619	123	239	785	7 564	NA	26.3
0040	Ashland	16 234	14 943	8.6	15 582	81	152	339	80	382	7 204	9 916	16.5
0045	Astoria	10 069	NA	NA	9 617	34	140	207	71	255	4 631	10 245	14.9
0065	Baker	9 140	NA	NA	8 945	28	77	40	50	200	4 052	8 539	17.6
0095	Beaverton	53 310	30 582	74.3	47 679	533	290	4 085	723	1 761	24 083	12 273	35.8
0100	Bend	20 469	17 263	18.6	19 959	39	174	153	144	485	9 004	9 820	34.8
0120	Brookings	4 400	NA	NA	4 229	16	84	51	20	88	2 089	9 480	7.2
0135	Burns	2 913	NA	NA	2 809	1	56	23	24	103	1 410	9 285	9.2
0145	Canby	8 983	NA	NA	8 376	6	58	145	398	755	3 245	9 474	7.6
0178	Cedar Hills CDP	9 294	NA	NA	8 504	104	55	541	90	229	4 102	NA	6.3
0179	Cedar Mill CDP	9 697	NA	NA	8 974	51	39	588	45	166	3 872	NA	10.2
0180	Central Point	7 509	NA	NA	7 289	6	63	88	63	201	2 831	8 074	6.2
0182	Chenoweth CDP	3 246	NA	NA	3 044	17	59	55	71	143	1 377	NA	15.7
0187	City of the Dalles	11 060	10 820	2.2	10 314	37	173	136	400	666	4 843	9 373	12.8
0188	Clackamas CDP	2 578	NA	NA	2 468	13	22	59	16	59	1 090	NA	5.4
0210	Coos Bay	15 076	14 424	4.5	14 285	41	372	236	142	409	6 617	8 827	27.4

1. Codes shown are 2-digit FIPS codes for states; 4-digit census place codes for places; and 3-digit FIPS county codes followed by 3-digit census MCD codes for minor civil divisions (MCDs). MCD names are followed by county names in parentheses. 2. Hispanic persons may be of any race. 3. Dry land or land partially or temporarily covered by water.

State/ Place/ MCD[1] code	Place	Population	Places of 10,000 or more		Population characteristics, 1990 — Race						Total housing units, 1990	Per capita income, 1985 (Dollars)	Land area,[3] 1990 (Sq. Km.)
		1990	1980	Percent change, 1980–1990	White	Black	Am. Indian, Eskimo Aleut	Asian & Pacific Islander	Other race	Hispanic[2]			
		1	2	3	4	5	6	7	8	9	10	11	12
	OREGON—Con.												
0215	Coquille	4 121	NA	NA	3 982	10	83	23	23	83	1 781	8 862	7.4
0220	Cornelius	6 148	NA	NA	5 354	18	70	89	617	960	2 141	8 731	4.6
0225	Corvallis	44 757	40 960	9.3	39 893	528	307	3 601	428	1 234	17 307	9 512	33.5
0230	Cottage Grove	7 402	NA	NA	7 163	16	103	78	42	162	2 925	8 630	7.0
0250	Dallas	9 422	NA	NA	9 081	17	152	63	109	230	3 672	8 037	11.1
0315	Eagle Point	3 008	NA	NA	2 884	5	57	29	33	93	1 119	7 462	4.5
0360	Eugene	112 669	105 624	6.7	105 268	1 410	1 004	3 896	1 091	3 051	47 991	10 305	98.5
0380	Florence	5 162	NA	NA	4 960	4	122	49	27	129	2 741	8 538	8.9
0385	Forest Grove	13 559	11 499	17.9	12 249	73	133	378	726	1 311	5 102	8 507	10.7
0395	Four Corners CDP	12 156	11 331	7.3	11 126	164	202	277	387	665	4 840	NA	7.8
0403	Garden Home-Whitford CDP	6 652	NA	NA	6 310	75	31	208	28	136	2 717	NA	5.5
0430	Gladstone	10 152	NA	NA	9 714	47	71	227	93	215	3 745	10 336	6.3
0455	Grants Pass	17 488	15 032	16.3	16 866	38	209	225	150	494	7 480	8 581	16.7
0462	Green CDP	5 076	NA	NA	4 923	8	81	31	33	112	1 807	NA	14.5
0465	Gresham	68 235	33 005	106.7	64 027	740	654	1 875	939	2 284	26 978	10 349	57.1
0488	Harbeck-Fruitdale CDP	3 982	NA	NA	3 883	3	44	38	14	152	1 718	NA	4.8
0500	Hayesville CDP	14 318	NA	NA	13 118	118	171	534	377	763	5 574	NA	11.5
0502	Hazelwood CDP	11 480	25 541	-55.1	10 647	123	111	553	46	323	4 568	NA	5.4
0515	Hermiston	10 040	NA	NA	8 789	88	115	195	853	1 475	4 110	8 063	14.6
0520	Hillsboro	37 520	27 664	35.6	33 235	183	209	827	3 066	4 203	13 347	9 781	49.9
0530	Hood River	4 632	NA	NA	4 193	16	56	76	291	485	2 272	9 020	5.0
0560	Independence	4 425	NA	NA	3 446	39	50	53	837	1 070	1 539	6 522	5.5
0587	Jennings Lodge CDP	6 530	NA	NA	6 189	65	49	143	84	178	2 691	NA	4.2
0605	Junction City	3 670	NA	NA	3 602	9	20	16	23	73	1 514	8 975	3.4
0615	Keizer	21 884	18 592	17.7	20 361	109	429	309	676	1 236	8 576	9 699	18.8
0620	Klamath Falls	17 737	16 661	6.5	16 180	202	699	211	445	1 054	7 832	8 276	42.5
0630	La Grande	11 766	11 354	3.6	11 218	88	134	230	96	248	4 916	8 868	10.4
0633	Lake Oswego	30 576	22 909	33.5	29 404	159	88	821	104	478	13 110	18 759	24.7
0635	Lakeview town	2 526	NA	NA	2 403	2	65	25	31	94	1 145	9 597	3.6
0640	Lebanon	10 950	10 428	5.0	10 649	18	114	86	83	231	4 554	8 003	12.5
0648	Lincoln City	5 892	NA	NA	5 699	9	76	77	31	116	4 023	8 929	13.8
0675	McMinnville	17 894	14 080	27.1	16 903	41	173	296	481	1 387	6 778	9 065	22.1
0690	Madras	3 443	NA	NA	2 794	11	163	32	443	739	1 374	NA	5.4
0720	Medford	46 951	39 603	18.6	44 501	120	565	542	1 223	2 387	19 684	10 255	47.3
0733	Metzger CDP	3 149	NA	NA	2 995	26	13	79	36	78	1 473	NA	1.9
0745	Milton-Freewater	5 533	NA	NA	4 497	3	49	13	971	1 136	2 251	7 467	4.5
0750	Milwaukie	18 692	17 931	4.2	17 851	120	121	464	136	384	8 170	11 412	12.3
0760	Molalla	3 651	NA	NA	3 447	3	38	24	139	232	1 268	7 779	4.2
0765	Monmouth	6 288	NA	NA	5 696	56	86	233	217	308	2 272	7 161	4.2
0790	Mount Angel	2 778	NA	NA	2 496	16	12	17	237	561	807	6 581	2.5
0800	Myrtle Creek	3 063	NA	NA	2 949	1	53	13	47	95	1 198	7 827	3.9
0810	Myrtle Point	2 712	NA	NA	2 589	4	91	9	19	53	1 125	8 098	4.1
0820	Newberg	13 086	10 394	25.9	12 571	31	82	167	235	803	4 673	8 427	10.9
0825	Newport	8 437	NA	NA	8 090	23	163	115	46	169	4 105	9 577	20.6
0828	North Albany CDP	4 325	NA	NA	4 212	7	29	47	30	84	1 545	NA	20.8
0830	North Bend	9 614	NA	NA	9 207	42	154	143	68	236	3 975	9 214	10.0
0842	North Springfield CDP	5 451	NA	NA	5 336	10	41	36	28	88	2 034	NA	7.2
0845	Nyssa	2 629	NA	NA	1 430	1	8	60	1 130	1 262	945	6 192	2.5
0848	Oak Grove CDP	12 576	11 640	8.0	12 050	44	71	267	144	420	5 764	NA	7.6
0849	Oak Hills CDP	6 450	NA	NA	5 767	49	18	573	43	126	2 267	NA	4.1
0855	Oakridge	3 063	NA	NA	2 942	17	46	19	39	141	1 371	8 495	3.5
0860	Oatfield CDP	15 348	NA	NA	14 836	30	78	329	75	281	5 594	NA	11.3
0865	Ontario	9 392	NA	NA	7 712	44	95	372	1 169	2 019	3 821	8 589	10.6
0870	Oregon City	14 698	14 673	0.2	14 240	49	135	177	97	317	5 675	8 973	12.2
0885	Pendleton	15 126	14 521	4.2	13 958	240	357	187	384	661	6 175	9 231	25.7
0890	Philomath	2 983	NA	NA	2 865	6	42	25	45	98	1 145	8 824	2.5
0895	Phoenix	3 239	NA	NA	3 116	8	39	28	48	136	1 425	NA	2.4
0905	Portland	437 319	366 423	19.3	370 135	33 530	5 399	23 185	5 070	13 874	198 368	10 770	322.9
0913	Powellhurst-Centennial CDP	28 756	20 132	42.8	26 860	324	288	896	388	915	11 082	NA	14.0
0930	Prineville	5 355	NA	NA	5 152	2	92	23	86	138	2 287	9 300	6.3
0942	Raleigh Hills CDP	6 066	NA	NA	5 815	20	22	162	47	99	2 712	NA	4.3
0945	Redmond	7 163	NA	NA	6 955	4	89	48	67	197	2 932	7 852	21.8
0947	Redwood CDP	3 702	NA	NA	3 621	14	36	15	16	96	1 643	NA	12.8
0950	Reedsport	4 796	NA	NA	4 600	1	93	45	57	101	2 095	8 692	5.3
0968	River Road CDP	9 443	10 370	-8.9	9 044	88	115	109	87	299	3 624	NA	6.9
0972	Rockcreek CDP	8 282	NA	NA	7 685	38	36	474	49	187	3 167	NA	5.2
0980	Roseburg	17 032	16 644	2.3	16 491	38	218	176	109	475	7 052	10 047	19.3
0982	Roseburg North CDP	6 831	NA	NA	6 649	6	90	51	35	212	2 994	NA	62.9
0995	St. Helens	7 535	NA	NA	7 303	5	106	85	36	149	3 081	8 587	9.3
1005	Salem	107 786	89 233	20.8	98 277	1 632	1 771	2 577	3 529	6 588	42 601	9 824	107.6
1015	Sandy	4 152	NA	NA	4 031	2	44	63	12	102	1 536	8 669	4.5
1017	Santa Clara CDP	12 834	14 288	-10.2	12 451	53	111	115	104	214	4 651	NA	15.1
1020	Scappoose	3 529	NA	NA	3 433	5	50	27	14	93	1 317	9 364	5.3

1. Codes shown are 2-digit FIPS codes for states; 4-digit census place codes for places; and 3-digit FIPS county codes followed by 3-digit census MCD codes for minor civil divisions (MCDs). MCD names are followed by county names in parentheses. 2. Hispanic persons may be of any race. 3. Dry land or land partially or temporarily covered by water.

State/ Place/ MCD[1] code	Place	Population: 1990	Population: Places of 10,000 or more: 1980	Population: Places of 10,000 or more: Percent change, 1980–1990	Population characteristics, 1990: Race: White	Race: Black	Race: Am. Indian, Eskimo Aleut	Race: Asian & Pacific Islander	Race: Other race	Hispanic[2]	Total housing units, 1990	Per capita income, 1985 (Dollars)	Land area,[3] 1990 (Sq. Km.)
		1	2	3	4	5	6	7	8	9	10	11	12
	OREGON—Con.												
1035	Seaside	5 359	NA	NA	5 209	17	43	53	37	102	3 608	8 387	9.5
1045	Sheridan	3 979	NA	NA	3 460	234	143	60	82	331	1 045	NA	4.5
1050	Sherwood	3 093	NA	NA	2 997	16	25	12	43	103	1 239	NA	8.3
1060	Silverton	5 635	NA	NA	5 405	7	43	18	162	357	2 225	8 220	5.0
1085	Springfield	44 683	41 621	7.4	42 607	297	681	691	407	1 299	18 121	8 206	34.8
1095	Stayton	5 011	NA	NA	4 833	4	78	34	62	156	1 915	9 075	6.6
1111	Sunnyside CDP	4 423	NA	NA	4 063	38	29	264	29	98	1 930	NA	6.6
1115	Sutherlin	5 020	NA	NA	4 856	10	73	29	52	174	2 030	7 585	13.1
1120	Sweet Home	6 850	NA	NA	6 646	11	108	50	35	136	2 834	7 678	13.8
1122	Talent	3 274	NA	NA	3 005	8	33	12	216	259	1 438	7 341	2.8
1132	Tigard	29 344	14 286	105.4	27 679	216	188	1 006	255	690	12 599	12 487	26.4
1135	Tillamook	4 001	NA	NA	3 844	4	60	43	50	108	1 733	8 462	3.9
1140	Toledo	3 174	NA	NA	3 053	1	94	12	14	61	1 246	8 842	5.0
1143	Tri-City CDP	3 585	NA	NA	3 441	1	88	39	16	70	1 333	NA	22.8
1145	Troutdale	7 852	NA	NA	7 428	144	48	169	63	251	2 509	9 948	12.9
1150	Tualatin	15 013	NA	NA	14 416	75	68	300	154	378	5 976	11 910	18.4
1160	Umatilla	3 046	NA	NA	2 546	6	49	26	419	521	1 230	7 013	7.1
1173	Veneta	2 519	NA	NA	2 402	13	75	14	15	50	932	NA	6.5
1190	Warrenton	2 681	NA	NA	2 548	3	50	63	17	42	1 131	NA	28.0
1214	West Haven-Sylvan CDP	6 009	NA	NA	5 683	51	20	225	30	85	2 745	NA	7.1
1215	West Linn	16 367	12 956	26.3	15 814	92	73	307	81	306	5 951	12 879	17.2
1222	West Slope CDP	7 959	NA	NA	7 519	74	24	297	45	134	3 675	NA	5.9
1226	White City CDP	5 891	NA	NA	5 565	29	101	40	156	321	1 664	NA	4.8
1233	Wilsonville	7 106	NA	NA	6 881	25	68	101	31	160	3 331	17 935	16.6
1235	Winston	3 773	NA	NA	3 632	9	77	31	24	102	1 459	7 667	3.3
1240	Woodburn	13 404	11 196	19.7	10 629	37	59	62	2 617	4 211	4 922	9 092	10.9
1245	Wood Village	2 814	NA	NA	2 672	25	40	30	47	107	1 122	NA	2.1
42	PENNSYLVANIA	11 881 643	11 864 720	0.1	10 520 201	1 089 795	14 733	137 438	119 476	232 262	4 938 140	10 288	116 082.8
0065	Akron borough	3 869	NA	NA	3 787	25	4	49	4	26	1 593	11 740	3.3
0095	Aldan borough	4 549	NA	NA	4 505	21	0	23	0	29	1 816	12 583	1.5
0115	Aliquippa	13 374	17 094	-21.8	9 075	4 259	9	8	23	96	6 118	9 149	10.6
0165	Allentown	105 090	103 758	1.3	90 557	5 230	186	1 414	7 703	12 274	45 636	10 575	45.9
0190	Altoona	51 881	57 078	-9.1	50 821	793	55	142	70	194	22 698	8 334	25.3
0195	Ambler borough	6 609	NA	NA	6 004	523	7	63	12	87	2 629	12 477	2.2
0205	Ambridge borough	8 133	NA	NA	7 369	674	32	27	31	125	4 078	8 731	3.8
0210	Amity Gardens CDP	2 714	NA	NA	2 592	86	3	24	9	17	968	NA	2.5
0215	Ancient Oaks CDP	2 663	NA	NA	2 589	19	6	42	7	41	857	NA	5.7
0230	Annville CDP	4 294	NA	NA	4 192	22	1	64	15	57	1 442	NA	4.0
0280	Archbald borough	6 291	NA	NA	6 271	8	6	5	1	14	2 458	8 337	43.6
0282	Ardmore CDP	12 646	NA	NA	10 816	1 639	22	152	17	162	5 567	NA	5.0
0294	Arlington Heights CDP	4 768	NA	NA	4 625	50	2	67	24	69	2 015	NA	13.7
0325	Arnold	6 113	NA	NA	5 557	523	6	17	10	24	3 022	9 140	1.9
0340	Ashland borough	3 859	NA	NA	3 850	1	2	6	0	4	1 792	8 029	4.2
0345	Ashley borough	3 291	NA	NA	3 285	3	0	3	0	10	1 433	7 916	2.4
0355	Aspinwall borough	2 880	NA	NA	2 859	4	1	12	4	24	1 532	14 356	0.9
0375	Athens borough	3 468	NA	NA	3 421	21	11	6	9	14	1 515	8 605	4.6
0402	Audubon CDP	6 328	NA	NA	5 863	281	7	151	26	94	2 459	NA	11.6
0415	Avalon borough	5 784	NA	NA	5 579	179	3	20	3	25	2 869	11 405	1.6
0430	Avoca borough	2 897	NA	NA	2 896	0	0	1	0	12	1 131	7 835	2.6
0441	Avon Heights CDP	2 714	NA	NA	2 645	24	5	13	27	93	803	NA	3.1
0455	Baden borough	5 074	NA	NA	5 031	35	2	3	3	24	2 181	9 572	5.9
0485	Baldwin borough	21 923	24 598	-10.9	21 539	251	11	91	31	106	8 917	10 798	15.0
0500	Bangor borough	5 383	NA	NA	5 338	10	6	25	4	24	2 253	9 425	3.9
0520	Barnesboro borough	2 530	NA	NA	2 526	1	0	1	2	6	1 090	8 395	4.1
0590	Beaver borough	5 028	NA	NA	4 893	113	2	9	11	39	2 365	12 033	2.4
0625	Beaver Falls	10 687	12 525	-14.7	8 767	1 820	22	30	48	87	4 667	8 241	5.5
0650	Bedford borough	3 137	NA	NA	3 096	24	0	10	7	6	1 579	10 059	2.9
0695	Bellefonte borough	6 358	NA	NA	6 310	23	2	21	2	23	2 772	9 992	4.7
0710	Bellevue borough	9 126	10 128	-9.9	8 799	259	13	34	21	41	4 779	11 234	2.6
0717	Belmont CDP	3 184	NA	NA	3 171	6	1	1	5	12	1 360	NA	4.7
0755	Bentleyville borough	2 673	NA	NA	2 618	41	6	2	6	15	1 269	8 694	9.6
0810	Berwick borough	10 976	11 850	-7.4	10 887	46	5	26	12	57	4 890	8 485	8.0
0826	Bethel Park borough	33 823	34 755	-2.7	33 172	352	17	260	22	167	12 997	13 452	30.3
0855	Bethlehem	71 428	70 419	1.4	62 540	2 080	59	1 228	5 521	9 300	28 486	10 575	49.9
0895	Birdsboro borough	4 222	NA	NA	4 185	16	3	14	4	24	1 634	11 366	3.6
0950	Blairsville borough	3 595	NA	NA	3 526	61	5	3	0	6	1 780	8 949	3.6
0955	Blakely borough	7 222	NA	NA	7 155	12	1	49	5	25	2 928	9 331	10.0
1000	Bloomsburg town	12 439	11 717	6.2	12 114	179	11	98	37	134	4 192	7 396	11.4
1012	Blue Bell CDP	6 091	NA	NA	5 648	84	0	352	7	55	2 371	NA	13.9
1052	Boothwyn CDP	5 069	NA	NA	4 891	138	1	30	9	48	2 099	NA	3.2
1065	Boyertown borough	3 759	NA	NA	3 748	3	4	4	0	7	1 713	10 908	2.1

1. Codes shown are 2-digit FIPS codes for states; 4-digit census place codes for places; and 3-digit FIPS county codes followed by 3-digit census MCD codes for minor civil divisions (MCDs). MCD names are followed by county names in parentheses. 2. Hispanic persons may be of any race. 3. Dry land or land partially or temporarily covered by water.

State/ Place/ MCD[1] code	Place	Population: 1990	Population: Places of 10,000 or more: 1980	Population: Places of 10,000 or more: Percent change, 1980–1990	Population characteristics, 1990: Race: White	Race: Black	Race: Am. Indian, Eskimo Aleut	Race: Asian & Pacific Islander	Race: Other race	Hispanic[2]	Total housing units, 1990	Per capita income, 1985 (Dollars)	Land area,[3] 1990 (Sq. Km.)
		1	2	3	4	5	6	7	8	9	10	11	12
	PENNSYLVANIA—Con.												
1070	Brackenridge borough	3 784	NA	NA	3 682	91	2	4	5	14	1 756	8 913	1.3
1075	Braddock borough	4 682	NA	NA	2 454	2 181	21	11	15	44	2 641	6 663	1.5
1095	Bradford	9 625	11 211	-14.1	9 426	68	46	56	29	77	4 477	9 072	8.9
1170	Brentwood borough	10 823	11 907	-9.1	10 756	14	13	33	7	65	4 775	11 060	3.7
1172	Bressler-Enhaut-Oberlin CDP	2 660	NA	NA	2 368	250	3	0	39	86	1 084	NA	1.5
1185	Bridgeport borough	4 292	NA	NA	4 195	58	6	30	3	50	1 895	10 380	1.7
1195	Bridgeville borough	5 445	NA	NA	5 200	227	0	16	2	15	2 617	11 624	2.8
1225	Bristol borough	10 405	10 867	-4.3	9 230	806	13	40	316	914	4 137	9 991	4.5
1230	Brittany Farms-Highlands CDP	2 747	NA	NA	2 681	29	2	34	1	18	1 146	NA	3.1
1260	Brookhaven borough	8 567	NA	NA	8 352	84	2	114	15	73	3 595	13 109	4.4
1270	Brookville borough	4 184	NA	NA	4 150	9	3	18	4	14	1 910	9 211	8.4
1275	Broomall CDP	10 930	NA	NA	10 381	85	12	443	9	108	4 280	NA	7.5
1295	Brownsville borough	3 164	NA	NA	2 792	361	1	6	4	13	1 541	7 426	2.6
1345	Bryn Mawr CDP	3 271	NA	NA	2 795	360	3	97	16	58	1 498	NA	1.6
1425	Butler	15 714	17 026	-7.7	15 352	220	36	64	42	97	7 414	9 601	7.0
1465	California borough	5 748	NA	NA	5 421	233	2	80	12	47	2 038	7 845	28.6
1510	Camp Hill borough	7 831	NA	NA	7 761	9	5	52	4	34	3 589	16 686	5.6
1530	Canonsburg borough	9 200	10 459	-12.0	8 539	621	6	18	16	42	4 086	9 155	6.0
1555	Carbondale	10 664	11 255	-5.3	10 616	10	11	21	6	55	4 489	8 487	8.4
1565	Carlisle borough	18 419	18 314	0.6	16 978	1 052	28	289	72	208	7 690	11 036	14.0
1575	Carnegie borough	9 278	10 099	-8.1	8 893	300	4	61	20	52	4 478	10 808	4.3
1580	Carnot-Moon CDP	10 187	11 102	-8.2	9 538	490	6	110	43	100	4 256	NA	12.6
1635	Castle Shannon borough	9 135	10 164	-10.1	9 049	49	7	28	2	35	4 066	11 485	4.2
1640	Catasauqua borough	6 662	NA	NA	6 529	49	5	27	52	147	2 625	10 123	3.3
1648	Cecil-Bishop CDP	2 701	NA	NA	2 675	20	0	5	1	11	974	NA	6.6
1695	Centerville borough	3 842	NA	NA	3 827	2	1	9	3	23	1 638	8 653	34.3
1740	Chalfont borough	3 069	NA	NA	3 018	25	2	23	1	35	1 144	12 459	4.3
1745	Chambersburg borough	16 647	16 174	2.9	15 084	1 196	33	143	191	302	7 618	10 018	17.8
1770	Charleroi borough	5 014	NA	NA	4 919	86	0	6	3	11	2 637	9 672	2.0
1855	Chester	41 856	45 794	-8.6	13 392	27 276	89	165	934	1 579	16 512	6 815	12.5
1860	Chesterbrook CDP	4 561	NA	NA	4 365	82	6	101	7	48	2 396	NA	4.2
1874	Chester Township CDP	5 399	NA	NA	2 429	2 892	23	28	27	92	1 879	NA	3.6
1915	Churchill borough	3 883	NA	NA	3 692	104	0	83	4	52	1 567	21 813	5.7
1920	Churchville CDP	4 255	NA	NA	4 201	13	0	38	3	34	1 180	NA	5.2
1925	Clairton	9 656	12 121	-20.3	7 054	2 557	10	10	25	57	4 676	9 154	7.2
1945	Clarion borough	6 457	NA	NA	6 207	122	7	106	15	36	1 917	6 401	3.9
1960	Clarks Summit borough	5 433	NA	NA	5 346	1	1	81	4	24	2 201	12 295	4.1
2015	Clearfield borough	6 633	NA	NA	6 538	56	7	25	7	19	3 233	9 248	4.7
2040	Clifton Heights borough	7 111	NA	NA	6 996	69	6	38	2	39	2 836	10 082	1.6
2105	Coaldale borough	2 531	NA	NA	2 518	3	1	5	4	14	1 251	7 985	5.6
2125	Coatesville	11 038	10 698	3.2	6 308	4 393	17	52	268	550	4 391	9 588	4.8
2180	Collegeville borough	4 227	NA	NA	4 097	49	2	70	9	22	1 312	10 847	4.0
2195	Collingdale borough	9 175	NA	NA	8 981	92	5	92	5	51	3 483	9 085	2.2
2198	Colonial Park CDP	13 777	NA	NA	12 694	753	12	232	86	213	6 546	NA	12.3
2205	Columbia borough	10 701	10 466	2.2	10 097	415	17	30	142	242	4 452	8 950	6.2
2220	Colwyn borough	2 613	NA	NA	2 378	201	4	18	12	11	970	9 223	0.7
2305	Connellsville	9 229	10 319	-10.6	8 776	401	9	29	14	26	4 210	7 530	5.8
2330	Conshohocken borough	8 064	NA	NA	7 453	561	13	23	14	54	3 397	10 555	2.5
2385	Coopersburg borough	2 599	NA	NA	2 545	21	6	17	10	18	958	11 279	2.4
2395	Coplay borough	3 267	NA	NA	3 202	20	9	7	29	40	1 350	11 296	1.6
2400	Coraopolis borough	6 747	NA	NA	5 860	834	9	25	19	60	3 263	10 380	3.5
2415	Cornwall borough	3 231	NA	NA	3 178	21	7	23	2	11	1 211	11 663	25.1
2417	Cornwells Heights-Eddington CDP	3 621	NA	NA	3 553	20	6	28	14	58	1 225	NA	2.6
2420	Corry	7 216	NA	NA	7 182	10	8	16	0	24	2 941	8 894	15.8
2440	Coudersport borough	2 854	NA	NA	2 832	2	7	11	2	20	1 247	7 796	14.7
2475	Crafton borough	7 188	NA	NA	7 055	86	2	39	6	40	3 384	11 107	2.9
2550	Croydon CDP	9 967	NA	NA	9 678	172	10	53	54	162	3 738	NA	6.2
2595	Curwensville borough	2 924	NA	NA	2 907	15	1	1	0	5	1 263	8 042	5.8
2615	Dallas borough	2 567	NA	NA	2 553	2	4	8	0	4	1 058	11 769	5.9
2625	Dallastown borough	3 974	NA	NA	3 943	17	3	10	1	26	1 638	10 055	1.9
2640	Danville borough	5 165	NA	NA	5 093	21	2	18	31	63	2 461	9 681	4.1
2645	Darby borough	11 140	11 513	-3.2	7 318	3 684	14	89	35	82	4 042	7 957	2.1
2650	Darby Township CDP	10 955	12 264	-10.7	6 773	4 099	24	25	34	92	3 941	NA	3.7
2775	Denver borough	2 861	NA	NA	2 832	2	0	22	5	19	1 091	NA	3.4
2795	Derry borough	2 950	NA	NA	2 939	4	5	1	1	4	1 320	8 819	2.1
2801	Devon-Berwyn CDP	5 019	NA	NA	4 694	243	0	74	8	57	1 935	NA	6.5
2810	Dickson City borough	6 276	NA	NA	6 245	8	3	16	4	43	2 795	8 746	12.2
2860	Donora borough	5 928	NA	NA	5 030	855	10	11	22	152	2 957	8 295	4.9
2865	Dormont borough	9 772	11 275	-13.3	9 592	44	3	122	11	57	4 321	10 279	1.9
2895	Downingtown borough	7 749	NA	NA	6 897	704	6	107	35	140	3 157	11 942	5.7
2900	Doylestown borough	8 575	NA	NA	8 346	90	8	107	24	103	4 100	12 906	5.6
2915	Drexel Hill CDP	29 744	NA	NA	28 957	206	20	509	52	265	12 257	NA	8.3
2945	DuBois	8 286	NA	NA	8 222	17	8	31	8	32	3 858	10 346	8.7

1. Codes shown are 2-digit FIPS codes for states; 4-digit census place codes for places; and 3-digit FIPS county codes followed by 3-digit census MCD codes for minor civil divisions (MCDs). MCD names are followed by county names in parentheses. 2. Hispanic persons may be of any race. 3. Dry land or land partially or temporarily covered by water.

State/ Place/ MCD[1] code	Place	Population: 1990	Population: Places of 10,000 or more: 1980	Population: Places of 10,000 or more: Percent change, 1980–1990	Population characteristics, 1990: Race: White	Race: Black	Race: Am. Indian, Eskimo Aleut	Race: Asian & Pacific Islander	Race: Other race	Hispanic[2]	Total housing units, 1990	Per capita income, 1985 (Dollars)	Land area,[3] 1990 (Sq. Km.)
		1	2	3	4	5	6	7	8	9	10	11	12
	PENNSYLVANIA—Con.												
3000	Dunmore borough	15 403	16 781	-8.2	15 290	53	4	47	9	81	6 307	10 002	22.6
3010	Dupont borough	2 984	NA	NA	2 980	2	1	1	0	2	1 316	8 625	3.9
3015	Duquesne	8 525	10 094	-15.5	5 813	2 624	19	19	50	62	4 106	7 899	4.7
3025	Duryea borough	4 869	NA	NA	4 861	3	1	3	1	10	2 089	8 688	14.3
3050	Eagleville CDP	3 637	NA	NA	2 907	641	5	73	11	74	1 069	NA	4.2
3200	East Greenville borough	3 117	NA	NA	3 059	22	3	16	17	42	1 135	NA	1.3
3245	East Lansdowne borough	2 691	NA	NA	2 553	20	10	105	3	30	999	9 196	0.5
3265	East McKeesport borough	2 678	NA	NA	2 621	45	6	5	1	20	1 256	9 608	1.0
3275	East Norriton CDP	13 324	12 711	4.8	12 503	557	6	243	15	85	5 201	NA	15.7
3295	Easton	26 276	26 027	1.0	22 803	2 480	44	447	502	1 159	10 309	8 490	11.0
3310	East Petersburg borough	4 197	NA	NA	4 104	32	2	41	18	32	1 601	11 471	3.3
3360	East Stroudsburg borough	8 781	NA	NA	8 317	316	14	94	40	132	2 993	8 005	7.4
3380	East Uniontown CDP	2 822	NA	NA	2 631	185	3	0	3	12	1 193	NA	5.3
3405	East York CDP	8 487	NA	NA	8 316	76	3	83	9	37	3 621	NA	7.5
3430	Ebensburg borough	3 872	NA	NA	3 809	47	3	10	3	15	1 643	10 108	4.3
3435	Economy borough	9 519	NA	NA	9 451	47	4	14	3	41	3 373	9 726	45.8
3460	Edgewood borough	3 581	NA	NA	3 428	111	2	30	10	35	1 725	13 513	1.5
3465	Edgewood CDP	2 719	NA	NA	2 713	0	1	5	0	2	1 266	NA	1.2
3475	Edinboro borough	7 736	NA	NA	7 326	270	9	120	11	33	2 030	6 319	6.0
3480	Edwardsville borough	5 399	NA	NA	5 335	38	0	20	6	30	2 553	7 923	3.1
3543	Elim CDP	3 861	NA	NA	3 828	5	2	22	4	20	1 641	NA	5.2
3560	Elizabethtown borough	9 952	NA	NA	9 742	40	17	119	34	92	3 785	10 544	6.7
3625	Ellwood City borough	8 894	NA	NA	8 792	83	4	14	1	34	3 999	8 538	6.2
3648	Emigsville CDP	2 580	NA	NA	2 496	51	1	18	14	24	1 091	NA	3.1
3655	Emmaus borough	11 157	11 001	1.4	11 031	32	1	69	24	68	4 870	12 918	7.5
3660	Emporium borough	2 513	NA	NA	2 492	7	7	2	5	1	1 220	8 076	1.9
3665	Emsworth borough	2 892	NA	NA	2 790	78	5	17	2	7	1 279	10 219	1.5
3668	Enola CDP	5 961	NA	NA	5 874	16	11	48	12	39	2 419	NA	4.8
3675	Ephrata borough	12 133	11 095	9.4	11 885	27	10	123	88	208	5 047	10 594	9.3
3685	Erie	108 718	119 123	-8.7	93 556	13 086	229	514	1 333	2 606	45 424	8 995	56.9
3700	Etna borough	4 200	NA	NA	4 156	4	1	34	5	52	1 867	8 776	1.9
3730	Exeter borough	5 691	NA	NA	5 667	13	2	7	2	24	2 255	8 334	12.1
3747	Exton CDP	2 550	NA	NA	2 438	82	3	26	1	23	1 277	NA	8.2
3795	Fairless Hills CDP	9 026	NA	NA	8 659	113	7	209	38	160	3 487	NA	5.0
3840	Fairview-Ferndale CDP	2 895	NA	NA	2 886	1	0	7	1	7	1 272	NA	2.4
3890	Farrell	6 841	NA	NA	3 951	2 865	4	9	12	33	3 030	8 116	6.0
3925	Fayetteville CDP	3 033	NA	NA	2 949	60	7	13	4	25	1 178	NA	8.4
3926	Feasterville-Trevose CDP	6 696	NA	NA	6 512	95	9	63	17	105	2 690	NA	3.4
3955	Fernway CDP	9 072	NA	NA	8 982	41	3	33	13	43	3 130	NA	13.8
3975	Fleetwood borough	3 478	NA	NA	3 443	6	0	12	17	24	1 412	11 055	2.7
3987	Flourtown CDP	4 754	NA	NA	4 625	65	1	54	9	37	1 764	NA	3.7
3990	Folcroft borough	7 506	NA	NA	7 340	97	8	53	8	48	2 623	9 815	3.5
3995	Folsom CDP	8 173	NA	NA	7 892	187	1	91	2	38	3 156	NA	3.2
4000	Ford City borough	3 413	NA	NA	3 245	153	3	2	10	18	1 701	9 083	1.7
4015	Forest Hills borough	7 335	NA	NA	7 190	101	3	37	4	25	3 159	13 412	4.0
4050	Fort Washington CDP	3 699	NA	NA	3 419	71	6	203	0	24	1 116	NA	7.1
4055	Forty Fort borough	5 049	NA	NA	5 018	9	1	14	7	23	2 126	10 404	3.5
4085	Fountain Hill borough	4 637	NA	NA	4 440	76	2	25	94	224	1 936	11 069	1.8
4105	Fox Chapel borough	5 319	NA	NA	5 072	15	7	220	5	43	1 887	42 009	20.4
4110	Frackville borough	4 700	NA	NA	4 679	1	2	16	2	27	2 049	8 117	1.5
4215	Franklin	7 329	NA	NA	7 073	207	5	22	22	34	3 430	10 037	11.8
4220	Franklin Park borough	10 109	NA	NA	9 792	96	3	209	9	55	3 420	14 298	35.1
4285	Freeland borough	3 909	NA	NA	3 881	4	4	11	9	39	1 754	8 641	1.8
4330	Fullerton CDP	13 127	NA	NA	12 437	272	6	318	94	286	6 054	NA	9.7
4365	Garden View CDP	2 687	NA	NA	2 661	6	1	19	0	5	1 159	NA	2.7
4375	Gastonville CDP	3 090	NA	NA	3 055	26	0	6	3	17	1 249	NA	7.1
4380	Geistown borough	2 749	NA	NA	2 734	5	0	9	1	8	1 133	9 536	2.8
4410	Gettysburg borough	7 025	NA	NA	6 446	381	11	68	119	232	2 812	8 664	4.2
4435	Gilbertsville CDP	3 994	NA	NA	3 960	18	0	15	1	28	1 519	NA	8.7
4450	Girard borough	2 879	NA	NA	2 847	18	3	9	2	16	1 162	9 893	6.1
4475	Glassport borough	5 582	NA	NA	5 540	23	7	7	5	41	2 508	8 803	4.4
4506	Glenolden borough	7 260	NA	NA	7 048	122	6	70	14	47	3 055	10 909	2.5
4517	Glenside CDP	8 704	NA	NA	8 295	272	8	114	15	69	3 204	NA	3.3
4565	Grantley CDP	3 069	NA	NA	2 991	37	2	26	13	33	846	NA	4.3
4610	Greencastle borough	3 600	NA	NA	3 524	59	4	10	3	22	1 614	11 490	4.1
4675	Greensburg	16 318	17 558	-7.1	15 469	655	18	105	71	134	7 552	10 283	11.0
4680	Green Tree borough	4 905	NA	NA	4 743	64	0	98	0	30	1 969	13 766	5.4
4685	Greenville borough	6 734	NA	NA	6 591	80	13	41	9	24	2 859	8 662	5.0
4745	Grove City borough	8 240	NA	NA	8 094	61	9	63	13	54	2 762	8 829	6.9
4800	Hamburg borough	3 987	NA	NA	3 973	3	2	4	5	23	1 801	10 921	4.8
4840	Hampton Township CDP	15 568	NA	NA	15 349	82	8	117	12	47	5 526	NA	41.5
4865	Hanover borough	14 399	14 890	-3.3	14 269	22	14	35	59	127	6 622	10 574	9.5
4877	Harleysville CDP	7 405	NA	NA	7 124	121	3	115	42	85	2 625	NA	10.8

1. Codes shown are 2-digit FIPS codes for states; 4-digit census place codes for places; and 3-digit FIPS county codes followed by 3-digit census MCD codes for minor civil divisions (MCDs). MCD names are followed by county names in parentheses. 2. Hispanic persons may be of any race. 3. Dry land or land partially or temporarily covered by water.

State/ Place/ MCD[1] code	Place	Population 1990	Places of 10,000 or more 1980	Places of 10,000 or more Percent change, 1980–1990	Race: White	Race: Black	Race: Am. Indian, Eskimo Aleut	Race: Asian & Pacific Islander	Race: Other race	Hispanic[2]	Total housing units, 1990	Per capita income, 1985 (Dollars)	Land area,[3] 1990 (Sq. Km.)
		1	2	3	4	5	6	7	8	9	10	11	12
	PENNSYLVANIA—Con.												
4885	Harmony Township CDP	3 694	NA	NA	3 644	42	3	4	1	24	1 534	NA	7.4
4920	Harrisburg	52 376	53 264	-1.7	22 306	26 502	147	920	2 501	4 022	24 590	9 099	21.0
4930	Harrison Township CDP	11 763	NA	NA	11 436	246	8	39	34	41	5 300	NA	18.8
4947	Harveys Lake borough	2 746	NA	NA	2 740	0	5	1	0	8	1 685	NA	13.8
4960	Hatboro borough	7 382	NA	NA	7 263	52	17	41	9	40	3 061	12 625	3.7
4965	Hatfield borough	2 650	NA	NA	2 515	44	3	66	22	50	1 172	12 018	1.6
5006	Hazleton	24 730	27 318	-9.5	24 392	51	11	166	110	249	11 343	9 198	15.5
5039	Hellertown borough	5 662	NA	NA	5 631	6	4	6	15	106	2 476	10 700	3.5
5050	Hermitage	15 300	NA	NA	14 873	325	11	76	15	55	6 359	10 554	76.9
5078	Hershey CDP	11 860	13 249	-10.5	11 349	197	11	274	29	125	5 490	NA	37.9
5108	Highspire borough	2 668	NA	NA	2 582	59	2	18	7	31	1 253	10 439	1.9
5125	Hokendauqua CDP	3 413	NA	NA	3 370	14	0	15	14	34	1 379	NA	2.9
5129	Hollidaysburg borough	5 624	NA	NA	5 557	45	11	7	4	12	2 395	10 017	6.2
5133	Homeacre-Lyndora CDP	7 511	NA	NA	7 425	44	4	34	4	26	3 283	NA	17.4
5141	Homestead borough	4 179	NA	NA	2 277	1 828	22	33	19	35	2 370	7 551	1.5
5147	Honesdale borough	4 972	NA	NA	4 938	6	8	19	1	34	2 313	10 310	10.1
5188	Horsham CDP	15 051	NA	NA	14 181	475	18	342	35	174	6 045	NA	14.2
5228	Hummelstown borough	3 981	NA	NA	3 929	8	1	41	2	22	1 838	10 364	3.3
5237	Huntingdon borough	6 843	NA	NA	6 661	134	16	26	6	37	2 715	7 930	8.9
5270	Imperial-Enlow CDP	3 449	NA	NA	3 389	44	4	11	1	26	1 491	NA	10.6
5273	Indiana borough	15 174	16 051	-5.5	14 266	538	20	282	68	134	4 803	7 442	4.6
5285	Ingram borough	3 901	NA	NA	3 792	86	2	20	1	17	1 679	10 114	1.1
5294	Irwin borough	4 604	NA	NA	4 518	67	1	13	5	22	2 289	11 099	2.3
5372	Jeannette	11 221	13 120	-14.5	10 687	485	12	11	26	26	5 159	8 867	6.2
5378	Jefferson borough	9 533	NA	NA	9 230	205	4	88	6	37	3 752	10 357	42.9
5420	Jenkintown borough	4 574	NA	NA	4 362	161	0	37	14	62	2 072	18 293	1.5
5441	Jersey Shore borough	4 353	NA	NA	4 324	15	5	8	1	6	1 816	8 281	3.2
5443	Jessup borough	4 605	NA	NA	4 577	2	5	17	4	9	1 913	8 735	17.3
5447	Jim Thorpe borough	5 048	NA	NA	5 032	8	1	7	0	20	2 098	8 052	37.5
5450	Johnsonburg borough	3 350	NA	NA	3 340	0	2	7	1	4	1 440	8 809	7.9
5453	Johnstown	28 134	35 496	-20.7	25 401	2 517	39	50	127	395	14 667	7 426	15.2
5483	Kane borough	4 590	NA	NA	4 554	6	6	9	15	24	2 018	8 790	4.0
5504	Kenhorst borough	2 918	NA	NA	2 846	24	6	37	5	20	1 286	11 447	1.5
5510	Kennedy Township CDP	7 152	NA	NA	7 088	18	1	43	2	10	2 683	NA	14.1
5516	Kennett Square borough	5 218	NA	NA	4 316	625	3	35	239	662	1 984	11 803	2.9
5530	King of Prussia CDP	18 406	NA	NA	16 876	649	44	772	65	316	8 376	NA	21.7
5537	Kingston borough	14 507	15 681	-7.5	14 307	33	8	149	10	69	6 570	11 613	5.6
5552	Kittanning borough	5 120	NA	NA	5 084	28	1	3	4	16	2 391	8 023	2.7
5579	Kulpmont borough	3 233	NA	NA	3 228	3	1	1	0	10	1 438	7 820	2.4
5580	Kulpsville CDP	5 183	NA	NA	4 819	164	1	175	24	72	2 047	NA	8.1
5582	Kutztown borough	4 704	NA	NA	4 612	37	5	41	9	31	1 805	11 047	4.1
5612	Lake City borough	2 519	NA	NA	2 505	11	1	1	1	3	921	NA	4.7
5624	Lancaster	55 551	54 725	1.5	39 368	6 802	137	1 091	8 153	11 420	22 468	8 442	19.1
5651	Lansdale borough	16 362	16 526	-1.0	15 331	336	18	600	77	324	7 009	12 252	7.9
5654	Lansdowne borough	11 712	11 891	-1.5	10 939	604	21	131	17	108	5 115	12 637	3.0
5660	Lansford borough	4 583	NA	NA	4 536	6	7	20	14	41	2 215	8 354	4.0
5675	Larksville borough	4 700	NA	NA	4 669	4	1	21	5	18	1 808	8 160	12.3
5684	Latrobe borough	9 265	10 799	-14.2	9 223	24	1	15	2	27	4 316	11 342	5.8
5687	Laureldale borough	3 726	NA	NA	3 678	21	0	9	18	36	1 643	11 375	2.1
5695	Lawnton CDP	3 221	NA	NA	2 852	293	8	59	9	44	1 373	NA	3.0
5700	Lawrence Park CDP	4 310	NA	NA	4 268	10	8	19	5	23	1 631	NA	4.8
5713	Leacock-Leola-Bareville CDP	5 685	NA	NA	5 397	23	3	223	39	108	2 142	NA	14.8
5714	Lebanon	24 800	25 711	-3.5	23 353	356	23	237	831	1 710	10 996	9 301	10.9
5723	Leechburg borough	2 504	NA	NA	2 463	32	1	3	5	6	1 243	10 216	1.2
5747	Lehighton borough	5 914	NA	NA	5 882	3	5	14	10	22	2 469	8 900	4.4
5771	Lemoyne borough	3 959	NA	NA	3 877	11	9	58	4	25	1 953	13 409	4.0
5795	Levittown CDP	55 362	NA	NA	53 929	764	72	460	137	676	18 468	NA	26.3
5801	Lewisburg borough	5 785	NA	NA	5 550	105	12	104	14	90	1 855	8 255	2.5
5807	Lewistown borough	9 341	NA	NA	9 254	53	9	23	2	15	4 476	8 328	5.2
5819	Liberty borough	2 744	NA	NA	2 698	37	0	7	2	10	1 144	9 604	3.7
5865	Lima CDP	2 670	NA	NA	2 540	100	0	25	5	14	599	NA	3.8
5893	Linglestown CDP	5 862	NA	NA	5 743	64	6	41	8	42	2 156	NA	9.7
5896	Linwood CDP	3 425	NA	NA	3 341	70	0	4	10	48	1 258	NA	1.4
5898	Lionville-Marchwood CDP	6 468	NA	NA	6 179	138	4	133	14	59	2 548	NA	6.5
5900	Lititz borough	8 280	NA	NA	8 166	38	7	57	12	55	3 217	10 931	6.0
5915	Littlestown borough	2 974	NA	NA	2 954	1	2	14	3	15	1 265	9 581	4.1
5927	Lock Haven	9 230	NA	NA	9 034	116	5	63	12	47	3 302	7 249	6.5
5974	Lorane CDP	2 580	NA	NA	2 505	42	0	27	6	19	967	NA	4.1
5985	Lower Allen CDP	6 329	NA	NA	6 119	100	3	88	19	67	2 921	NA	6.1
5990	Lower Burrell	12 251	13 200	-7.2	12 056	134	13	46	2	45	4 916	10 730	29.9
6101	Luzerne borough	3 206	NA	NA	3 197	1	3	4	1	18	1 521	8 112	1.8
6119	Lynnwood-Pricedale CDP	2 664	NA	NA	2 533	121	0	6	4	7	1 172	NA	3.3
6130	McCandless Township CDP	28 781	26 250	9.6	28 000	253	19	479	30	147	10 933	NA	42.8

1. Codes shown are 2-digit FIPS codes for states; 4-digit census place codes for places; and 3-digit FIPS county codes followed by 3-digit census MCD codes for minor civil divisions (MCDs). MCD names are followed by county names in parentheses. 2. Hispanic persons may be of any race. 3. Dry land or land partially or temporarily covered by water.

State/ Place/ MCD[1] code	Place	Population 1990	Population: Places of 10,000 or more 1980	Population: Places of 10,000 or more Percent change, 1980–1990	Population characteristics, 1990: Race: White	Black	Am. Indian, Eskimo Aleut	Asian & Pacific Islander	Other race	Hispanic[2]	Total housing units, 1990	Per capita income, 1985 (Dollars)	Land area,[3] 1990 (Sq. Km.)
		1	2	3	4	5	6	7	8	9	10	11	12
	PENNSYLVANIA—Con.												
6134	McChesneytown-Loyalhanna CDP	3 708	NA	NA	3 679	17	2	4	6	3	1 547	NA	6.0
6147	McGovern CDP	2 504	NA	NA	2 460	37	2	3	2	3	1 005	NA	4.8
6158	McKeesport	26 016	31 012	-16.1	21 310	4 482	41	48	135	315	12 535	8 628	13.0
6161	McKees Rocks borough	7 691	NA	NA	6 554	1 078	25	12	22	65	3 676	9 143	2.7
6164	McMurray CDP	4 082	NA	NA	4 009	26	4	43	0	21	1 384	NA	8.0
6167	McSherrystown borough	2 769	NA	NA	2 743	3	3	3	17	26	1 136	8 834	1.4
6169	Macungie borough	2 597	NA	NA	2 550	18	0	22	7	15	1 147	NA	2.6
6200	Mahanoy City borough	5 209	NA	NA	5 192	4	4	9	0	33	2 788	8 351	1.3
6221	Malvern borough	2 944	NA	NA	2 757	150	1	31	5	47	1 319	13 321	3.2
6233	Manheim borough	5 011	NA	NA	4 894	19	3	71	24	60	2 104	10 597	3.7
6254	Manor borough	2 627	NA	NA	2 614	3	1	5	4	7	978	NA	5.2
6260	Mansfield borough	3 538	NA	NA	3 363	130	3	33	9	34	976	6 261	4.9
6262	Maple Glen CDP	5 881	NA	NA	5 483	134	9	250	5	68	1 816	NA	8.0
6266	Marcus Hook borough	2 546	NA	NA	2 406	120	4	9	7	20	987	7 657	2.9
6272	Marietta borough	2 778	NA	NA	2 621	129	9	7	12	35	1 144	9 400	1.9
6323	Masontown borough	3 759	NA	NA	3 592	154	11	1	1	13	1 646	7 833	3.9
6348	Meadowood CDP	3 011	NA	NA	2 974	19	0	15	3	13	1 073	NA	4.0
6350	Meadville	14 318	15 544	-7.9	13 367	761	21	114	55	120	6 150	9 625	11.3
6353	Mechanicsburg borough	9 452	NA	NA	9 334	17	11	71	19	30	4 067	12 276	6.7
6360	Mechanicsville CDP	2 803	NA	NA	2 723	10	0	67	3	21	1 017	NA	5.2
6362	Media borough	5 957	NA	NA	5 035	833	10	47	32	66	3 023	13 822	1.9
6386	Meridian CDP	3 473	NA	NA	3 450	4	3	12	4	5	1 287	NA	7.3
6398	Meyersdale borough	2 518	NA	NA	2 504	2	0	11	1	7	1 058	7 903	2.2
6437	Middletown borough	9 254	10 122	-8.6	8 667	474	16	45	52	119	4 201	10 509	5.3
6438	Middletown CDP	6 866	NA	NA	6 673	81	1	46	65	216	2 444	NA	6.6
6446	Midland borough	3 321	NA	NA	2 571	699	3	12	36	122	1 688	8 486	5.3
6470	Mifflinburg borough	3 480	NA	NA	3 464	5	5	5	1	8	1 442	9 150	4.7
6518	Millersburg borough	2 729	NA	NA	2 723	3	1	2	0	10	1 294	8 603	2.0
6522	Millersville borough	8 099	NA	NA	7 593	327	9	129	41	120	2 324	7 676	5.2
6532	Millvale borough	4 341	NA	NA	4 307	11	14	9	0	29	2 078	8 206	1.7
6540	Milton borough	6 746	NA	NA	6 546	148	6	20	26	42	2 806	8 204	8.9
6544	Minersville borough	4 877	NA	NA	4 865	0	6	5	1	12	2 322	8 072	1.7
6552	Monaca borough	6 739	NA	NA	6 627	73	8	22	9	21	2 772	8 877	5.4
6556	Monessen	9 901	11 928	-17.0	8 709	1 095	6	17	74	43	4 902	9 379	7.5
6560	Monongahela	4 928	NA	NA	4 697	194	15	11	11	37	2 419	8 675	5.0
6590	Montgomeryville CDP	9 114	NA	NA	8 378	165	17	527	27	77	3 322	NA	12.4
6594	Montoursville borough	4 983	NA	NA	4 964	6	2	9	2	14	2 098	10 483	10.5
6604	Moosic borough	5 339	NA	NA	5 321	1	0	12	5	6	2 126	9 245	16.9
6622	Morrisville borough	9 765	NA	NA	8 400	1 131	5	95	134	420	4 185	11 668	4.6
6624	Morton borough	2 851	NA	NA	2 132	678	7	26	8	26	1 219	NA	0.9
6632	Mount Carmel borough	7 196	NA	NA	7 167	3	5	16	5	28	3 725	7 698	1.7
6644	Mount Joy borough	6 398	NA	NA	6 295	34	10	20	39	77	2 628	11 442	6.1
6646	Mount Lebanon CDP	33 362	34 414	-3.1	32 578	155	12	581	36	270	14 159	NA	15.7
6650	Mount Oliver borough	4 160	NA	NA	4 004	121	2	26	7	25	1 893	8 830	0.9
6652	Mount Penn borough	2 883	NA	NA	2 818	19	0	33	13	24	1 303	11 957	1.1
6662	Mount Pleasant borough	4 787	NA	NA	4 720	55	6	5	1	9	2 189	10 138	3.0
6668	Mount Union borough	2 878	NA	NA	2 538	321	3	2	14	10	1 373	7 344	2.9
6678	Muncy borough	2 702	NA	NA	2 684	1	4	8	5	11	1 150	9 957	2.2
6684	Munhall borough	13 158	14 532	-9.5	12 952	154	6	36	10	97	5 835	9 818	6.0
6685	Municipality of Monroeville borough	29 169	NA	NA	26 299	1 933	21	858	58	212	12 644	NA	51.2
6686	Municipality of Murrysville borough	17 240	16 036	7.5	16 602	84	6	534	14	85	6 217	13 459	95.5
6690	Myerstown borough	3 236	NA	NA	3 190	9	3	31	3	21	1 232	9 826	2.3
6692	Nanticoke	12 267	13 044	-6.0	12 186	20	13	34	14	79	5 635	8 123	9.1
6694	Nanty-Glo borough	3 190	NA	NA	3 189	0	0	0	1	6	1 296	7 160	4.7
6698	Narberth borough	4 278	NA	NA	4 180	24	5	58	11	57	2 044	15 357	1.3
6700	Nazareth borough	5 713	NA	NA	5 673	2	12	17	9	36	2 546	11 095	4.3
6711	Nesquehoning borough	3 364	NA	NA	3 345	1	1	13	4	11	1 527	8 443	54.8
6715	Nether Providence Township CDP	13 229	12 730	3.9	12 216	772	5	218	18	72	5 045	NA	12.2
6732	New Brighton borough	6 854	NA	NA	6 199	612	16	8	19	18	3 116	8 040	2.7
6744	New Castle	28 334	33 621	-15.7	25 937	2 268	19	63	47	141	12 463	8 351	22.1
6756	New Cumberland borough	7 665	NA	NA	7 565	19	15	51	15	52	3 410	12 946	4.3
6764	New Freedom borough	2 920	NA	NA	2 863	12	7	20	18	33	1 055	NA	5.3
6772	New Holland borough	4 484	NA	NA	4 189	37	6	155	97	199	1 885	11 267	5.4
6776	New Kensington	15 894	17 660	-10.0	14 432	1 350	13	27	72	115	7 269	10 168	10.3
6816	Newtown borough	2 565	NA	NA	2 512	24	3	24	2	21	1 104	15 547	1.4
6828	New Wilmington borough	2 706	NA	NA	2 678	10	1	14	3	5	612	6 665	2.7
6842	Norristown borough	30 749	34 684	-11.3	21 779	8 126	50	508	286	828	13 080	9 556	9.1
6850	Northampton borough	8 717	NA	NA	8 643	19	3	32	20	60	3 575	10 411	6.7
6864	North Braddock borough	7 036	NA	NA	5 401	1 609	9	3	14	53	3 347	7 824	4.0
6870	North Catasauqua borough	2 867	NA	NA	2 851	4	0	7	5	20	1 110	9 705	1.9
6882	North East borough	4 617	NA	NA	4 587	3	1	5	21	94	1 835	9 465	3.4
6922	Northumberland borough	3 860	NA	NA	3 844	5	2	7	2	22	1 718	8 986	4.1
6930	North Versailles CDP	12 302	13 294	-7.5	11 092	1 142	12	33	23	40	5 328	NA	21.0

1. Codes shown are 2-digit FIPS codes for states; 4-digit census place codes for places; and 3-digit FIPS county codes followed by 3-digit census MCD codes for minor civil divisions (MCDs). MCD names are followed by county names in parentheses. 2. Hispanic persons may be of any race. 3. Dry land or land partially or temporarily covered by water.

State/ Place/ MCD[1] code	Place	Population: 1990	Population: Places of 10,000 or more: 1980	Population: Places of 10,000 or more: Percent change, 1980–1990	Population characteristics, 1990: Race: White	Race: Black	Race: Am. Indian, Eskimo Aleut	Race: Asian & Pacific Islander	Race: Other race	Hispanic[2]	Total housing units, 1990	Per capita income, 1985 (Dollars)	Land area,[3] 1990 (Sq. Km.)
		1	2	3	4	5	6	7	8	9	10	11	12
	PENNSYLVANIA—Con.												
6932	North Wales borough	3 802	NA	NA	3 476	136	7	158	25	64	1 515	12 086	1.5
6936	Northwest Harborcreek CDP	6 662	NA	NA	6 568	69	6	13	6	21	2 283	NA	11.7
6948	Norwood borough	6 162	NA	NA	6 117	28	0	14	3	19	2 267	10 039	2.1
6970	Oakmont borough	6 961	NA	NA	6 828	72	3	50	8	19	3 177	14 184	4.2
6972	Oakwood CDP	2 541	NA	NA	2 438	95	2	3	3	3	1 026	NA	6.6
6974	O'Hara Township CDP	9 096	NA	NA	8 768	79	2	238	9	58	3 377	NA	18.2
6983	Ohioville borough	3 865	NA	NA	3 747	94	6	5	13	44	1 396	8 253	60.3
6984	Oil City	11 949	13 881	-13.9	11 831	56	14	41	7	60	5 449	9 779	11.7
6992	Old Forge borough	8 834	NA	NA	8 806	11	5	12	0	13	3 798	9 238	8.9
6995	Old Orchard CDP	2 598	NA	NA	2 535	7	3	52	1	21	935	NA	1.7
6998	Oliver CDP	3 271	NA	NA	3 086	179	1	1	4	8	1 416	NA	5.8
7006	Olyphant borough	5 222	NA	NA	5 189	11	5	15	2	25	2 229	8 999	13.9
7019	Oreland CDP	5 695	NA	NA	5 056	587	5	41	6	44	2 120	NA	3.6
7024	Orwigsburg borough	2 780	NA	NA	2 741	3	1	25	10	13	1 162	10 590	5.7
7046	Oxford borough	3 769	NA	NA	3 219	492	6	3	49	251	1 613	8 836	5.0
7056	Palmer Heights CDP	3 960	NA	NA	3 886	29	4	26	15	47	1 459	NA	3.1
7058	Palmerton borough	5 394	NA	NA	5 363	0	2	12	17	145	2 254	9 825	6.6
7060	Palmyra borough	6 910	NA	NA	6 837	24	2	42	5	40	3 120	11 621	4.8
7068	Paoli CDP	5 603	NA	NA	5 136	380	2	76	9	50	2 229	NA	5.2
7080	Parkesburg borough	2 981	NA	NA	2 725	247	5	2	2	15	1 155	9 439	3.2
7082	Park Forest Village CDP	6 703	NA	NA	6 132	172	6	356	37	83	2 656	NA	6.2
7086	Parkville CDP	6 014	NA	NA	5 952	20	10	30	2	32	2 454	NA	7.6
7093	Patterson Township CDP	3 074	NA	NA	3 050	17	2	5	0	8	1 331	NA	4.3
7102	Paxtonia CDP	4 862	NA	NA	4 614	151	9	72	16	45	2 032	NA	6.1
7104	Pen Argyl borough	3 492	NA	NA	3 450	12	1	25	4	19	1 438	10 369	3.6
7106	Penbrook borough	2 791	NA	NA	2 593	139	4	44	11	38	1 305	10 361	1.2
7136	Penndel borough	2 703	NA	NA	2 469	150	11	45	28	53	988	10 919	1.1
7138	Penn Hills CDP	51 430	57 632	-10.8	43 132	7 946	63	195	94	245	20 439	NA	49.3
7147	Penn Wynne CDP	5 807	NA	NA	5 589	99	4	110	5	38	2 289	NA	2.7
7148	Perkasie borough	7 878	NA	NA	7 794	22	9	35	18	63	3 089	12 075	6.7
7180	Philadelphia	1 585 577	1 688 210	-6.1	848 586	631 936	3 454	43 522	58 079	89 193	674 899	8 807	350.0
7186	Philipsburg borough	3 048	NA	NA	3 019	9	7	11	2	13	1 530	9 551	2.9
7188	Phoenixville borough	15 066	14 165	6.4	13 850	979	26	170	41	176	6 623	10 950	9.3
7232	Pitcairn borough	4 087	NA	NA	4 070	0	2	14	1	29	1 917	9 176	1.4
7234	Pittsburgh	369 879	423 938	-12.8	266 791	95 362	671	5 937	1 118	3 468	170 159	9 998	144.1
7238	Pittston	9 389	NA	NA	9 336	21	3	23	6	34	4 029	8 181	4.1
7245	Plains CDP	4 694	NA	NA	4 679	3	0	11	1	18	1 999	NA	3.6
7254	Pleasant Hills borough	8 884	NA	NA	8 745	64	2	71	2	44	3 515	13 210	7.1
7264	Plum borough	25 609	25 390	0.9	24 854	507	11	197	40	146	9 289	10 592	74.2
7276	Plymouth borough	7 134	NA	NA	7 095	10	8	11	10	47	3 318	7 930	2.8
7279	Plymouth Meeting CDP	6 241	NA	NA	5 818	174	10	229	10	55	2 629	NA	9.8
7300	Portage borough	3 105	NA	NA	3 097	1	0	7	0	5	1 380	8 244	1.7
7336	Port Vue borough	4 641	NA	NA	4 617	17	3	1	3	15	1 957	8 738	2.8
7340	Pottsgrove CDP	3 122	NA	NA	3 056	16	1	46	3	17	1 103	NA	7.1
7342	Pottstown borough	21 831	22 729	-4.0	19 056	2 439	35	95	206	623	9 700	9 858	12.5
7344	Pottsville	16 603	18 179	-8.7	16 190	275	23	95	20	86	7 306	8 484	10.9
7357	Progress CDP	9 654	NA	NA	8 390	1 061	11	144	48	82	4 524	NA	6.7
7362	Prospect Park borough	6 764	NA	NA	6 646	53	7	49	9	54	2 712	10 800	1.9
7370	Punxsutawney borough	6 782	NA	NA	6 751	2	10	15	4	30	3 111	8 884	8.9
7376	Quakertown borough	8 982	NA	NA	8 782	57	4	110	29	100	3 625	11 111	5.2
7385	Radnor Township CDP	28 705	27 676	3.7	26 686	906	25	1 030	58	493	10 579	NA	35.7
7402	Rankin borough	2 503	NA	NA	1 065	1 416	3	7	12	14	1 186	7 285	1.1
7418	Reading	78 380	78 686	-0.4	61 640	7 607	113	1 114	7 906	14 486	34 276	9 060	25.3
7421	Reamstown CDP	2 649	NA	NA	2 571	0	1	70	7	16	954	NA	5.9
7426	Red Lion borough	6 130	NA	NA	6 076	25	4	24	1	21	2 572	9 701	3.3
7432	Reiffton CDP	2 522	NA	NA	2 483	14	0	25	0	2	996	NA	3.6
7442	Reserve Township CDP	3 866	NA	NA	3 805	55	1	4	1	20	1 489	NA	5.2
7444	Reynoldsville borough	2 818	NA	NA	2 807	2	1	4	4	9	1 258	8 170	3.7
7457	Richboro CDP	5 332	NA	NA	5 252	2	1	70	7	30	1 548	NA	10.9
7474	Ridgway borough	4 793	NA	NA	4 759	0	1	27	6	12	2 141	9 402	6.9
7480	Ridley Park borough	7 592	NA	NA	7 488	39	4	59	2	32	3 152	13 112	2.8
7496	Roaring Spring borough	2 615	NA	NA	2 611	1	0	2	1	1	1 089	9 399	2.1
7505	Robinson Township CDP	10 830	NA	NA	10 562	136	1	102	29	49	4 498	NA	38.1
7510	Rochester borough	4 156	NA	NA	3 687	447	11	5	6	20	1 952	9 145	1.5
7524	Rockledge borough	2 679	NA	NA	2 664	3	0	10	2	9	1 119	11 626	0.9
7558	Ross Township CDP	33 482	35 102	-4.6	32 772	369	16	301	24	131	14 124	NA	37.2
7570	Royersford borough	4 458	NA	NA	4 370	52	1	31	4	30	1 942	12 348	2.0
7589	Rutherford CDP	3 481	NA	NA	3 302	149	4	17	9	67	1 404	NA	3.0
7608	St. Clair borough	3 524	NA	NA	3 517	0	2	4	1	1	1 653	7 551	3.2
7616	St. Marys borough	5 511	NA	NA	5 486	3	4	10	8	13	2 436	11 076	4.4
7649	Salunga-Landisville CDP	4 239	NA	NA	4 145	16	1	70	7	26	1 580	NA	7.9
7651	Sanatoga CDP	5 534	NA	NA	5 142	289	10	58	35	81	2 013	NA	8.8
7672	Sayre borough	5 791	NA	NA	5 698	17	14	54	8	21	2 602	8 713	5.3

1. Codes shown are 2-digit FIPS codes for states; 4-digit census place codes for places; and 3-digit FIPS county codes followed by 3-digit census MCD codes for minor civil divisions (MCDs). MCD names are followed by county names in parentheses. 2. Hispanic persons may be of any race. 3. Dry land or land partially or temporarily covered by water.

State/ Place/ MCD[1] code	Place	Population: 1990	Population: Places of 10,000 or more: 1980	Population: Places of 10,000 or more: Percent change, 1980–1990	Population characteristics, 1990: Race: White	Race: Black	Race: Am. Indian, Eskimo Aleut	Race: Asian & Pacific Islander	Race: Other race	Hispanic[2]	Total housing units, 1990	Per capita income, 1985 (Dollars)	Land area,[3] 1990 (Sq. Km.)
		1	2	3	4	5	6	7	8	9	10	11	12
	PENNSYLVANIA—Con.												
7678	Schlusser CDP	4 728	NA	NA	4 455	166	2	86	19	61	1 859	NA	6.5
7682	Schuylkill Haven borough	5 610	NA	NA	5 556	14	10	25	5	16	2 491	9 075	3.7
7696	Scottdale borough	5 184	NA	NA	5 102	69	6	0	7	16	2 289	8 605	3.0
7697	Scott Township CDP	17 118	20 413	-16.1	16 754	101	11	234	18	95	7 797	NA	10.2
7698	Scranton	81 805	88 117	-7.2	79 498	1 290	73	747	197	545	35 357	8 511	65.3
7702	Selinsgrove borough	5 384	NA	NA	5 281	29	0	32	42	80	1 839	8 872	5.0
7704	Sellersville borough	4 479	NA	NA	4 420	30	1	15	13	38	1 703	11 164	3.0
7712	Sewickley borough	4 134	NA	NA	3 589	499	2	30	14	30	2 116	13 557	2.5
7728	Shaler Township CDP	30 533	33 694	-9.4	30 212	68	10	215	28	137	11 830	NA	28.8
7730	Shamokin	9 184	10 357	-11.3	9 159	6	1	16	2	37	4 861	7 096	2.2
7737	Shanor-Northvue CDP	3 517	NA	NA	3 463	0	1	53	0	22	1 364	NA	17.4
7738	Sharon	17 493	19 057	-8.2	15 921	1 504	22	25	21	123	7 670	8 814	9.7
7742	Sharon Hill borough	5 771	NA	NA	5 279	446	11	28	7	62	2 251	10 612	2.0
7746	Sharpsburg borough	3 781	NA	NA	3 677	58	3	31	12	74	1 864	10 115	1.3
7748	Sharpsville borough	4 729	NA	NA	4 603	87	4	20	15	35	2 041	9 797	3.6
7758	Shenandoah borough	6 221	NA	NA	6 193	4	3	18	3	33	3 440	7 489	3.9
7770	Shillington borough	5 062	NA	NA	5 027	5	1	14	15	21	2 256	12 236	2.6
7771	Shiloh CDP	8 245	NA	NA	7 998	104	9	114	20	49	3 312	NA	10.9
7778	Shippensburg borough	5 331	NA	NA	5 132	108	5	73	13	30	2 366	9 946	5.2
7800	Shrewsbury borough	2 672	NA	NA	2 633	4	1	25	9	19	1 075	10 363	4.6
7816	Slatington borough	4 678	NA	NA	4 591	40	2	21	24	67	1 849	9 642	3.4
7822	Slippery Rock borough	3 008	NA	NA	2 834	65	0	103	6	18	887	7 271	4.4
7870	Somerset borough	6 454	NA	NA	6 329	48	7	47	23	48	3 100	10 523	7.1
7876	Souderton borough	5 957	NA	NA	5 724	34	6	137	56	159	2 423	11 183	2.9
7942	South Park Township CDP	14 292	NA	NA	13 773	425	4	74	16	66	5 368	NA	23.8
7972	South Williamsport borough	6 496	NA	NA	6 431	23	9	29	4	13	2 732	9 598	4.9
7998	Spring City borough	3 433	NA	NA	3 343	47	6	29	8	21	1 474	10 448	2.0
8004	Springdale borough	3 992	NA	NA	3 966	9	6	10	1	3	1 846	10 116	2.4
8010	Springetts Manor-Yorklyn CDP	3 433	NA	NA	3 044	240	8	47	94	164	1 095	NA	3.0
8015	Springfield CDP	24 160	25 326	-4.6	23 575	126	13	434	12	145	8 604	NA	16.5
8034	Spring House CDP	2 782	NA	NA	2 681	44	0	56	1	13	1 026	NA	6.7
8042	Spry CDP	4 271	NA	NA	4 193	18	1	59	0	16	1 905	NA	6.7
8050	State College borough	38 923	36 130	7.7	34 449	1 331	57	2 836	250	763	11 623	7 065	11.6
8052	Steelton borough	5 152	NA	NA	3 845	1 215	4	21	67	131	2 302	9 603	4.7
8075	Stonybrook-Wilshire CDP	4 887	NA	NA	4 741	63	8	67	8	37	1 840	NA	8.7
8080	Stowe CDP	3 598	NA	NA	3 306	250	3	28	11	36	1 406	NA	3.8
8081	Stowe Township CDP	7 681	NA	NA	7 551	99	10	10	11	39	3 674	NA	5.1
8088	Strasburg borough	2 568	NA	NA	2 538	8	1	15	6	18	1 032	NA	2.7
8098	Stroudsburg borough	5 312	NA	NA	5 005	231	5	32	39	128	2 550	10 035	4.6
8105	Sugarcreek borough	5 532	NA	NA	5 506	9	6	9	2	11	2 230	8 978	96.9
8138	Summit Hill borough	3 332	NA	NA	3 312	6	3	3	8	16	1 431	8 712	23.1
8140	Sunbury	11 591	12 292	-5.7	11 433	42	16	15	85	194	5 116	7 581	5.5
8154	Swarthmore borough	6 157	NA	NA	5 655	260	13	190	39	103	2 115	17 571	3.6
8164	Swissvale borough	10 637	11 345	-6.2	9 522	1 031	8	54	22	80	5 284	10 321	3.1
8166	Swoyersville borough	5 630	NA	NA	5 617	2	0	10	1	6	2 334	9 169	5.6
8174	Tamaqua borough	7 943	NA	NA	7 920	5	0	10	8	25	3 594	8 048	25.5
8178	Tarentum borough	5 674	NA	NA	5 550	102	10	4	8	24	2 649	8 456	3.2
8188	Taylor borough	6 941	NA	NA	6 910	2	6	16	7	8	2 828	8 132	13.5
8192	Telford borough	4 238	NA	NA	4 011	32	2	138	55	100	1 768	11 427	2.6
8213	Thompsonville CDP	3 560	NA	NA	3 512	14	0	31	3	17	1 235	NA	5.3
8216	Thorndale CDP	3 518	NA	NA	3 129	287	2	73	27	57	1 321	NA	4.5
8222	Throop borough	4 070	NA	NA	4 049	12	3	6	0	10	1 688	8 206	13.1
8231	Tinicum Township CDP	4 440	NA	NA	4 410	4	9	13	4	16	1 796	NA	14.9
8242	Titusville	6 434	NA	NA	6 367	18	12	25	12	26	2 746	8 882	7.6
8260	Towanda borough	3 242	NA	NA	3 212	4	3	14	9	26	1 464	8 835	2.9
8270	Trafford borough	3 345	NA	NA	3 318	13	3	7	4	15	1 546	11 441	3.7
8288	Trooper CDP	5 137	NA	NA	4 992	53	0	84	8	46	1 777	NA	6.1
8324	Turtle Creek borough	6 556	NA	NA	6 397	127	6	24	2	33	3 067	9 661	2.5
8335	Tyler Run-Queens Gate CDP	2 739	NA	NA	2 648	51	2	35	3	9	1 311	NA	4.0
8338	Tyrone borough	5 743	NA	NA	5 711	20	4	6	2	32	2 524	8 504	5.2
8386	Union City borough	3 537	NA	NA	3 500	8	2	24	3	12	1 477	8 004	4.9
8392	Uniontown	12 034	14 510	-17.1	10 582	1 387	16	24	25	61	5 881	9 078	5.3
8402	Upland borough	3 334	NA	NA	3 056	249	9	7	13	36	1 224	8 846	1.7
8428	Upper Providence Township CDP	9 727	NA	NA	9 268	294	6	144	15	53	3 861	NA	14.5
8430	Upper St. Clair CDP	19 692	19 023	3.5	18 935	121	21	607	8	106	6 806	NA	25.3
8488	Valley Green CDP	3 017	NA	NA	2 937	33	6	27	14	43	1 072	NA	3.6
8493	Valley View CDP	2 911	NA	NA	2 864	30	3	12	2	11	1 263	NA	2.0
8496	Vandergrift borough	5 904	NA	NA	5 725	160	4	3	12	28	2 852	8 831	3.2
8510	Verona borough	3 260	NA	NA	3 166	75	9	9	1	24	1 404	9 638	1.4
8514	Village Green-Green Ridge CDP	9 026	NA	NA	8 972	18	9	26	1	54	3 276	NA	4.7
8515	Village Shires CDP	4 364	NA	NA	4 261	18	2	77	6	23	1 770	NA	3.1
8545	Warminster Heights CDP	4 310	NA	NA	3 371	376	14	141	408	862	1 701	NA	1.6
8550	Warren	11 122	12 146	-8.4	11 040	9	29	34	10	32	5 223	9 924	7.6

1. Codes shown are 2-digit FIPS codes for states; 4-digit census place codes for places; and 3-digit FIPS county codes followed by 3-digit census MCD codes for minor civil divisions (MCDs). MCD names are followed by county names in parentheses. 2. Hispanic persons may be of any race. 3. Dry land or land partially or temporarily covered by water.

State/ Place/ MCD[1] code	Place	Population: 1990	Population: Places of 10,000 or more: 1980	Population: Places of 10,000 or more: Percent change, 1980–1990	Population characteristics, 1990: Race: White	Race: Black	Race: Am. Indian, Eskimo Aleut	Race: Asian & Pacific Islander	Race: Other race	Hispanic[2]	Total housing units, 1990	Per capita income, 1985 (Dollars)	Land area,[3] 1990 (Sq. Km.)
		1	2	3	4	5	6	7	8	9	10	11	12
	PENNSYLVANIA—Con.												
8590	Washington	15 864	18 363	-13.6	13 655	2 071	36	47	55	123	7 380	8 756	7.6
8658	Waynesboro borough	9 578	NA	NA	9 147	315	17	58	41	126	4 354	9 764	8.7
8660	Waynesburg borough	4 270	NA	NA	4 183	51	6	20	10	39	1 805	8 655	2.2
8662	Weatherly borough	2 640	NA	NA	2 618	9	0	10	3	10	994	7 918	7.8
8666	Weigelstown CDP	8 665	NA	NA	8 509	86	12	49	9	48	3 288	NA	13.2
8676	Wellsboro borough	3 430	NA	NA	3 373	24	6	26	1	5	1 516	9 727	12.7
8682	Wesleyville borough	3 655	NA	NA	3 606	28	7	3	11	31	1 538	8 843	1.4
8714	West Chester borough	18 041	17 435	3.5	13 936	3 195	34	197	679	1 366	6 457	9 579	4.8
8749	West Goshen CDP	8 948	NA	NA	8 237	461	11	191	48	171	3 431	NA	7.4
8758	West Hazleton borough	4 136	NA	NA	4 101	10	4	8	13	46	1 999	8 398	4.0
8800	West Mifflin borough	23 644	26 279	-10.0	21 793	1 761	11	52	27	85	9 948	9 822	36.7
8802	Westmont borough	5 789	NA	NA	5 735	5	1	34	14	42	2 413	16 794	6.2
8808	West Newton borough	3 152	NA	NA	3 081	64	5	2	0	9	1 453	9 485	2.9
8810	West Norriton CDP	15 209	14 034	8.4	14 297	574	2	306	30	120	6 568	NA	15.2
8828	West Pittston borough	5 590	NA	NA	5 566	7	2	13	2	6	2 411	8 893	2.1
8834	West Reading borough	4 142	NA	NA	4 016	60	9	19	38	81	1 778	9 667	1.5
8852	West View borough	7 734	NA	NA	7 673	27	2	24	8	31	3 352	10 877	2.6
8862	West Wyoming borough	3 117	NA	NA	3 105	4	2	5	1	9	1 262	8 170	9.4
8863	West Wyomissing CDP	3 097	NA	NA	3 072	16	0	7	2	20	1 331	NA	1.6
8864	West York borough	4 283	NA	NA	4 204	34	2	8	35	59	2 003	9 978	1.3
8886	Whitehall borough	14 451	15 206	-5.0	14 310	74	9	44	14	61	6 346	14 716	8.5
8896	White Oak borough	8 761	NA	NA	8 639	76	6	31	9	37	3 838	12 036	17.3
8898	Whitfield CDP	2 585	NA	NA	2 536	7	0	41	1	12	911	NA	1.7
8904	Wilkes-Barre	47 523	51 551	-7.8	45 673	1 383	43	276	148	351	20 734	8 261	17.7
8906	Wilkes-Barre Township CDP	3 572	NA	NA	3 420	45	4	95	8	25	1 685	NA	7.7
8910	Wilkinsburg borough	21 080	23 669	-10.9	9 740	11 076	55	122	87	130	11 354	10 679	6.0
8913	Wilkins Township CDP	7 487	NA	NA	7 292	120	1	49	25	30	3 325	NA	6.8
8918	Williamsport	31 933	33 401	-4.4	29 487	2 143	66	165	72	247	13 326	8 479	23.0
8922	Willow Grove CDP	16 325	NA	NA	15 576	479	9	217	44	161	6 619	NA	9.4
8924	Willow Street CDP	5 817	NA	NA	5 742	31	3	27	14	37	2 628	NA	14.1
8936	Wilson borough	7 830	NA	NA	7 504	202	5	91	28	152	3 325	10 227	3.2
8938	Windber borough	4 756	NA	NA	4 753	1	1	1	0	3	2 215	7 841	5.4
8940	Wind Gap borough	2 741	NA	NA	2 705	13	1	10	12	13	1 164	9 709	3.5
8961	Wolfdale CDP	2 906	NA	NA	2 849	46	9	1	1	10	1 164	NA	6.2
8966	Woodbourne CDP	2 953	NA	NA	2 786	65	2	87	13	44	829	NA	3.2
8977	Woodlyn CDP	10 151	NA	NA	9 434	601	12	89	15	84	4 048	NA	4.3
8979	Woodside CDP	2 947	NA	NA	2 753	43	1	148	2	30	802	NA	2.6
8992	Wormleysburg borough	2 847	NA	NA	2 751	10	6	76	4	20	1 437	16 536	2.4
9012	Wyncote CDP	2 960	NA	NA	2 849	82	2	26	1	21	1 121	NA	2.1
9013	Wyndmoor CDP	5 682	NA	NA	5 132	433	3	106	8	37	2 082	NA	4.3
9014	Wyoming borough	3 255	NA	NA	3 247	3	0	2	3	12	1 564	9 963	3.7
9016	Wyomissing borough	7 332	NA	NA	7 158	34	2	113	25	82	3 196	19 612	9.9
9028	Yeadon borough	11 980	11 727	2.2	3 820	7 915	25	147	73	107	5 019	11 514	4.2
9034	York	42 192	44 619	-5.4	30 583	8 968	98	470	2 073	3 244	18 407	8 781	13.5
9052	Youngwood borough	3 372	NA	NA	3 357	3	2	7	3	12	1 573	9 801	4.8
9056	Zelienople borough	4 158	NA	NA	4 119	21	1	10	7	22	1 838	11 119	5.5
0010	Butler township (Adams)	2 514	NA	NA	2 484	2	1	5	22	43	918	NA	62.1
0010	Conewago township (Adams)	4 532	NA	NA	4 492	0	4	12	24	43	1 657	8 852	27.1
0010	Cumberland township (Adams)	5 431	NA	NA	5 253	106	3	54	15	81	2 034	11 735	86.6
0010	Franklin township (Adams)	4 126	NA	NA	3 972	83	6	9	56	91	1 809	9 312	177.5
0011	Menallen township (Adams)	2 700	NA	NA	2 577	36	11	0	76	165	1 195	NA	110.8
0011	Mount Joy township (Adams)	2 848	NA	NA	2 777	42	2	19	8	20	1 039	9 246	67.1
0011	Mount Pleasant township (Adams)	4 076	NA	NA	4 028	12	5	22	9	23	1 463	9 094	79.2
0011	Oxford township (Adams)	3 437	NA	NA	3 403	3	0	11	20	31	1 144	NA	25.2
0011	Reading township (Adams)	3 828	NA	NA	3 805	5	2	13	3	21	1 495	9 726	68.8
0011	Straban township (Adams)	4 565	NA	NA	4 475	54	15	9	12	26	1 727	9 246	89.1
0031	Collier township (Allegheny)	4 841	NA	NA	4 680	143	2	16	0	11	1 785	9 403	36.8
0031	Elizabeth township (Allegheny)	14 712	16 255	-9.5	14 312	334	10	46	10	53	5 673	10 301	57.9
0031	Fawn township (Allegheny)	2 712	NA	NA	2 698	3	0	11	0	3	1 080	9 791	33.5
0032	Findlay township (Allegheny)	4 500	NA	NA	4 407	55	4	34	0	19	1 872	10 354	84.4
0032	Forward township (Allegheny)	3 877	NA	NA	3 827	32	5	9	4	14	1 561	9 072	49.0
0032	Hampton township (Allegheny)	15 568	14 260	9.2	15 349	82	8	117	12	47	5 526	12 875	41.5
0032	Harmar township (Allegheny)	3 144	NA	NA	3 118	5	1	18	2	4	1 530	10 982	15.5
0032	Harrison township (Allegheny)	11 763	13 252	-11.2	11 436	246	8	39	34	41	5 300	10 204	18.8
0032	Indiana township (Allegheny)	6 024	NA	NA	5 897	86	2	30	9	24	2 208	12 715	45.8
0032	Kennedy township (Allegheny)	7 265	NA	NA	7 194	19	1	46	5	10	2 726	11 346	14.1
0033	McCandless township (Allegheny)	28 781	26 250	9.6	28 000	253	19	479	30	147	10 933	15 325	42.8
0033	Marshall township (Allegheny)	4 010	NA	NA	3 963	15	0	28	4	11	1 382	13 989	40.4
0033	Moon township (Allegheny)	19 631	20 935	-6.2	18 745	630	9	198	49	175	7 857	12 631	61.4
0033	Mount Lebanon township (Allegheny)	33 362	34 414	-3.1	32 578	155	12	581	36	270	14 159	19 174	15.7
0033	North Fayette township (Allegheny)	9 537	NA	NA	9 275	200	11	49	2	50	4 037	10 662	65.0
0033	North Versailles twnshp (Allegheny)	12 302	13 294	-7.5	11 092	1 142	12	33	23	40	5 328	10 105	21.0
0034	O'Hara township (Allegheny)	9 096	NA	NA	8 768	79	2	238	9	58	3 377	17 160	18.2

1. Codes shown are 2-digit FIPS codes for states; 4-digit census place codes for places; and 3-digit FIPS county codes followed by 3-digit census MCD codes for minor civil divisions (MCDs). MCD names are followed by county names in parentheses. 2. Hispanic persons may be of any race. 3. Dry land or land partially or temporarily covered by water.

State/ Place/ MCD[1] code	Place	Population: 1990	Population: Places of 10,000 or more: 1980	Population: Places of 10,000 or more: Percent change, 1980–1990	Population characteristics, 1990: Race: White	Race: Black	Race: Am. Indian, Eskimo Aleut	Race: Asian & Pacific Islander	Race: Other race	Hispanic[2]	Total housing units, 1990	Per capita income, 1985 (Dollars)	Land area,[3] 1990 (Sq. Km.)
		1	2	3	4	5	6	7	8	9	10	11	12
	PENNSYLVANIA—Con.												
0034	Penn Hills township (Allegheny)	51 479	57 632	-10.7	43 180	7 946	63	195	95	246	20 467	10 670	49.3
0034	Pine township (Allegheny)	4 048	NA	NA	3 983	34	0	27	4	18	1 514	13 367	43.5
0034	Reserve township (Allegheny)	3 866	NA	NA	3 805	55	1	4	1	20	1 489	10 070	5.2
0034	Richland township (Allegheny)	8 600	NA	NA	8 516	40	2	37	5	49	3 201	11 498	37.7
0034	Robinson township (Allegheny)	10 830	NA	NA	10 562	136	1	102	29	49	4 498	11 455	38.1
0034	Ross township (Allegheny)	33 482	35 102	-4.6	32 772	369	16	301	24	131	14 124	13 592	37.2
0034	Scott township (Allegheny)	17 118	20 413	-16.1	16 754	101	11	234	18	95	7 797	13 119	10.2
0035	Shaler township (Allegheny)	30 533	33 694	-9.4	30 212	68	10	215	28	137	11 830	11 592	28.8
0035	South Fayette township (Allegheny)	10 329	NA	NA	9 548	671	7	93	10	31	3 775	9 728	52.7
0035	South Park township (Allegheny)	14 292	13 535	5.6	13 773	425	4	74	16	66	5 368	11 011	23.8
0035	Stowe township (Allegheny)	7 681	NA	NA	7 551	99	10	10	11	39	3 674	9 659	5.1
0035	Upper St. Clair township (Allegheny	19 692	19 023	3.5	18 935	121	21	607	8	106	6 806	21 377	25.3
0035	West Deer township (Allegheny)	11 371	10 897	4.3	11 294	31	13	27	6	33	4 304	10 032	75.1
0036	Wilkins township (Allegheny)	7 585	NA	NA	7 390	120	1	49	25	30	3 370	13 250	6.8
0050	Cowanshannock township (Armstrong)	2 813	NA	NA	2 810	3	0	0	0	10	1 145	7 296	118.1
0050	East Franklin township (Armstrong)	3 923	NA	NA	3 913	0	4	6	0	8	1 530	9 738	79.9
0050	Gilpin township (Armstrong)	2 804	NA	NA	2 758	39	2	5	0	4	1 245	8 580	42.7
0050	Kiskiminetas township (Armstrong)	5 456	NA	NA	5 417	29	2	3	5	11	2 201	8 653	105.5
0051	Manor township (Armstrong)	4 482	NA	NA	4 457	18	0	3	4	12	1 901	9 308	43.1
0051	North Buffalo township (Armstrong)	2 897	NA	NA	2 883	1	0	11	2	7	1 111	8 763	63.9
0051	Parks township (Armstrong)	2 739	NA	NA	2 609	119	1	4	6	2	1 146	8 678	36.5
0051	South Buffalo township (Armstrong)	2 687	NA	NA	2 674	6	5	2	0	10	1 009	9 803	70.1
0070	Brighton township (Beaver)	7 489	NA	NA	7 369	67	2	48	3	40	2 544	11 361	50.1
0070	Center township (Beaver)	10 742	10 733	0.1	10 454	225	5	54	4	50	3 997	9 986	39.9
0070	Chippewa township (Beaver)	6 988	NA	NA	6 899	44	3	34	8	30	2 780	10 371	42.4
0070	Daugherty township (Beaver)	3 433	NA	NA	3 383	39	2	3	6	10	1 256	9 400	25.8
0071	Franklin township (Beaver)	3 821	NA	NA	3 805	3	5	7	1	10	1 570	8 922	45.8
0071	Greene township (Beaver)	2 573	NA	NA	2 560	5	3	2	3	12	897	NA	66.9
0071	Hanover township (Beaver)	3 470	NA	NA	3 437	15	8	7	3	14	1 255	8 233	116.2
0071	Harmony township (Beaver)	3 694	NA	NA	3 644	42	3	4	1	24	1 534	10 128	7.4
0071	Hopewell township (Beaver)	13 274	14 636	-9.3	13 000	237	10	19	8	58	5 459	10 393	43.8
0071	Independence township (Beaver)	2 563	NA	NA	2 553	4	5	0	1	10	951	8 685	59.2
0072	New Sewickley township (Beaver)	6 861	NA	NA	6 834	14	5	6	2	22	2 523	8 683	84.6
0072	North Sewickley township (Beaver)	6 178	NA	NA	6 107	57	0	9	5	25	2 248	8 603	53.6
0072	Patterson township (Beaver)	3 074	NA	NA	3 050	17	2	5	0	8	1 331	11 865	4.4
0072	Raccoon township (Beaver)	3 426	NA	NA	3 419	4	3	0	0	23	1 177	9 193	48.0
0072	Rochester township (Beaver)	3 247	NA	NA	3 099	142	2	3	1	4	1 246	9 066	9.9
0072	South Beaver township (Beaver)	2 942	NA	NA	2 901	31	3	6	1	2	1 065	8 734	76.8
0090	Bedford township (Bedford)	4 945	NA	NA	4 857	57	4	23	4	24	2 292	7 848	177.7
0090	East St. Clair township (Bedford)	2 765	NA	NA	2 751	4	0	10	0	2	1 256	NA	87.7
0091	West Providence township (Bedford)	3 233	NA	NA	3 223	2	1	3	4	16	1 514	7 984	99.7
0110	Alsace township (Berks)	3 459	NA	NA	3 438	6	4	10	1	7	1 377	10 962	31.6
0110	Amity township (Berks)	6 434	NA	NA	6 267	106	12	32	17	39	2 422	11 393	47.4
0110	Bern township (Berks)	6 303	NA	NA	5 902	183	9	31	178	249	1 912	11 501	49.6
0110	Bethel township (Berks)	3 676	NA	NA	3 611	4	5	23	33	45	1 373	8 003	109.3
0110	Brecknock township (Berks)	3 770	NA	NA	3 714	23	4	26	3	43	1 332	11 532	46.2
0110	Centre township (Berks)	3 154	NA	NA	3 127	0	4	15	8	19	1 137	NA	55.5
0110	Colebrookdale township (Berks)	5 469	NA	NA	5 429	9	5	18	8	29	1 943	10 125	21.7
0110	Cumru township (Berks)	13 142	11 474	14.5	12 763	151	6	190	32	131	5 697	13 912	53.5
0110	Douglass township (Berks)	3 570	NA	NA	3 121	433	5	8	3	18	1 228	10 012	33.1
0111	Earl township (Berks)	3 016	NA	NA	3 003	4	4	2	3	13	1 108	10 154	35.9
0111	Exeter township (Berks)	17 260	14 419	19.7	16 807	247	15	148	43	139	6 780	12 163	63.1
0111	Greenwich township (Berks)	2 977	NA	NA	2 965	4	0	5	3	22	1 078	NA	81.0
0111	Hereford township (Berks)	3 026	NA	NA	2 993	4	2	15	12	27	1 106	9 430	40.0
0111	Longswamp township (Berks)	5 387	NA	NA	5 366	7	3	7	4	16	1 925	10 136	59.0
0111	Lower Alsace township (Berks)	4 627	NA	NA	4 586	17	3	12	9	46	1 984	13 347	12.2
0111	Maidencreek township (Berks)	3 397	NA	NA	3 295	13	7	31	51	127	1 259	NA	34.2
0111	Maxatawny township (Berks)	5 724	NA	NA	5 461	196	5	39	23	52	1 270	7 562	67.9
0112	Muhlenberg township (Berks)	12 636	13 031	-3.0	12 428	49	5	62	92	268	5 159	12 350	30.2
0112	Oley township (Berks)	3 362	NA	NA	3 342	10	3	7	0	11	1 281	10 871	62.7
0112	Perry township (Berks)	2 516	NA	NA	2 496	5	1	9	5	37	934	NA	47.4
0112	Richmond township (Berks)	3 439	NA	NA	3 419	4	4	5	7	20	1 343	10 726	61.2
0112	Robeson township (Berks)	5 972	NA	NA	5 913	32	6	14	7	39	2 188	10 655	93.0
0112	Rockland township (Berks)	2 675	NA	NA	2 653	2	4	9	7	12	989	NA	44.2
0112	Ruscombmanor township (Berks)	3 129	NA	NA	3 102	7	10	4	6	25	1 163	10 577	36.0
0112	South Heidelberg township (Berks)	4 382	NA	NA	4 301	54	1	13	13	55	1 475	11 574	35.7
0113	Spring township (Berks)	18 899	17 193	9.9	18 361	191	5	287	55	164	7 437	12 518	47.2
0113	Tilden township (Berks)	2 622	NA	NA	2 541	37	5	17	22	36	887	NA	49.0
0113	Tulpehocken township (Berks)	2 843	NA	NA	2 696	118	5	5	19	163	875	7 514	60.4
0113	Union township (Berks)	3 440	NA	NA	3 408	18	8	4	2	14	1 244	10 579	60.2
0113	Washington township (Berks)	2 799	NA	NA	2 766	8	7	5	13	17	969	10 593	36.3
0130	Allegheny township (Blair)	7 023	NA	NA	6 980	30	0	8	5	15	2 832	8 318	75.9
0130	Antis township (Blair)	6 176	NA	NA	6 151	11	4	9	1	15	2 440	8 847	157.4

1. Codes shown are 2-digit FIPS codes for states; 4-digit census place codes for places; and 3-digit FIPS county codes followed by 3-digit census MCD codes for minor civil divisions (MCDs). MCD names are followed by county names in parentheses. 2. Hispanic persons may be of any race. 3. Dry land or land partially or temporarily covered by water.

State/ Place/ MCD[1] code	Place	Population 1990	Population, Places of 10,000 or more 1980	Population, Places of 10,000 or more Percent change, 1980–1990	Race: White	Race: Black	Race: Am. Indian, Eskimo Aleut	Race: Asian & Pacific Islander	Race: Other race	Hispanic[2]	Total housing units, 1990	Per capita income, 1985 (Dollars)	Land area,[3] 1990 (Sq. Km.)
		1	2	3	4	5	6	7	8	9	10	11	12
	PENNSYLVANIA—Con.												
0130	Blair township (Blair)	3 994	NA	NA	3 966	4	0	21	3	4	1 577	8 541	35.2
0130	Frankstown township (Blair)	7 243	NA	NA	7 089	26	6	102	20	59	2 807	10 729	126.1
0130	Freedom township (Blair)	2 959	NA	NA	2 935	6	10	7	1	5	1 162	7 613	45.0
0130	Greenfield township (Blair)	3 802	NA	NA	3 795	1	4	2	0	5	1 604	6 532	93.0
0130	Logan township (Blair)	12 381	12 183	1.6	12 209	111	6	42	13	45	4 770	9 072	120.8
0130	Snyder township (Blair)	3 163	NA	NA	3 137	12	10	3	1	3	1 285	8 210	117.1
0150	Athens township (Bradford)	4 755	NA	NA	4 660	12	5	72	6	13	1 996	9 456	113.4
0170	Bedminster township (Bucks)	4 602	NA	NA	4 570	20	2	8	2	22	1 733	12 255	78.1
0170	Bensalem township (Bucks)	56 788	52 399	8.4	50 356	3 905	105	2 078	344	1 241	22 713	11 263	51.7
0170	Bristol township (Bucks)	57 129	58 733	-2.7	52 070	3 638	86	952	383	1 287	20 073	9 976	41.5
0170	Buckingham township (Bucks)	9 364	NA	NA	9 190	66	3	87	18	57	3 283	15 492	85.7
0170	Doylestown township (Bucks)	14 510	11 824	22.7	13 943	366	10	152	39	166	4 857	14 544	40.2
0170	East Rockhill township (Bucks)	3 753	NA	NA	3 669	48	7	22	7	16	1 359	11 183	33.5
0170	Falls township (Bucks)	34 997	36 083	-3.0	33 003	1 239	28	548	179	604	13 307	11 027	57.7
0170	Hilltown township (Bucks)	10 582	NA	NA	10 355	80	5	100	42	126	3 659	11 554	69.7
0171	Lower Makefield township (Bucks)	25 083	17 351	44.6	23 896	356	15	758	58	274	8 861	18 817	46.5
0171	Lower Southampton township (Bucks)	19 860	18 305	8.5	19 512	162	17	132	37	187	7 263	12 121	17.3
0171	Middletown township (Bucks)	43 063	34 246	25.7	41 565	675	52	653	118	531	14 942	12 265	50.2
0171	Milford township (Bucks)	7 360	NA	NA	7 279	29	3	44	5	42	2 525	10 815	72.7
0171	New Britain township (Bucks)	9 099	NA	NA	8 855	123	5	105	11	75	3 284	13 865	38.1
0171	Newtown township (Bucks)	13 685	NA	NA	13 168	221	18	261	17	181	5 329	15 383	31.0
0171	Nockamixon township (Bucks)	3 329	NA	NA	3 287	31	3	4	4	14	1 260	11 441	57.5
0171	Northampton township (Bucks)	35 406	27 392	29.3	34 656	155	16	522	57	237	11 486	13 937	66.9
0171	Plumstead township (Bucks)	6 289	NA	NA	6 214	9	9	48	9	49	2 295	11 849	70.4
0171	Richland township (Bucks)	8 560	NA	NA	8 352	64	11	105	28	97	3 344	10 793	53.1
0172	Solebury township (Bucks)	5 998	NA	NA	5 900	41	1	49	7	56	2 503	23 300	69.0
0172	Springfield township (Bucks)	5 177	NA	NA	5 116	21	1	7	32	41	1 938	13 934	79.7
0172	Tinicum township (Bucks)	4 167	NA	NA	4 104	45	3	7	8	41	1 709	13 562	78.1
0172	Upper Makefield township (Bucks)	5 949	NA	NA	5 843	29	3	67	7	48	2 024	21 560	54.2
0172	Upper Southampton township (Bucks)	16 076	15 806	1.7	15 742	123	3	172	36	116	5 918	14 084	17.1
0172	Warminster township (Bucks)	32 832	35 540	-7.6	30 989	760	45	547	491	1 166	11 207	11 415	26.4
0172	Warrington township (Bucks)	12 169	10 704	13.7	11 681	244	8	211	25	140	4 458	12 368	35.7
0172	Warwick township (Bucks)	5 915	NA	NA	5 768	30	6	102	9	70	1 981	NA	28.8
0172	West Rockhill township (Bucks)	4 518	NA	NA	4 475	20	8	13	2	37	1 684	11 094	42.2
0190	Adams township (Butler)	3 911	NA	NA	3 877	21	2	9	2	20	1 418	9 513	58.6
0190	Buffalo township (Butler)	6 317	NA	NA	6 286	15	0	15	1	19	2 321	9 246	62.6
0190	Butler township (Butler)	17 625	18 651	-5.5	17 457	72	9	64	23	60	7 051	10 888	55.9
0190	Center township (Butler)	6 239	NA	NA	6 157	10	7	62	3	26	2 436	10 196	63.1
0190	Clearfield township (Butler)	2 635	NA	NA	2 620	11	0	1	3	10	844	NA	60.5
0190	Clinton township (Butler)	2 556	NA	NA	2 551	0	2	3	0	5	962	NA	61.7
0190	Connoquenessing township (Butler)	3 093	NA	NA	3 081	5	1	2	4	5	1 247	9 111	58.2
0190	Cranberry township (Butler)	14 816	11 066	33.9	14 663	70	7	57	19	66	5 449	10 449	59.0
0191	Jackson township (Butler)	3 078	NA	NA	3 032	30	2	14	0	21	1 242	NA	54.8
0191	Jefferson township (Butler)	4 812	NA	NA	4 795	6	1	9	1	18	1 682	9 429	60.6
0191	Middlesex township (Butler)	5 578	NA	NA	5 554	12	2	7	3	34	1 990	9 880	59.5
0191	Oakland township (Butler)	2 820	NA	NA	2 815	1	2	1	1	3	973	8 471	59.4
0192	Penn township (Butler)	5 080	NA	NA	5 033	16	4	19	8	23	1 829	9 833	62.6
0192	Slippery Rock township (Butler)	4 638	NA	NA	4 482	113	6	29	8	21	1 260	6 035	66.9
0192	Summit township (Butler)	4 284	NA	NA	4 269	9	2	3	1	6	1 557	8 099	57.7
0192	Winfield township (Butler)	3 162	NA	NA	3 150	6	2	4	0	4	1 141	8 778	63.2
0210	Adams township (Cambria)	6 869	NA	NA	6 849	6	3	10	1	15	2 624	7 237	121.8
0210	Cambria township (Cambria)	6 357	NA	NA	6 223	109	6	14	5	15	2 050	6 777	127.7
0210	Cresson township (Cambria)	3 284	NA	NA	2 893	367	4	15	5	45	917	6 768	30.6
0211	East Taylor township (Cambria)	3 073	NA	NA	3 003	66	3	1	0	5	1 201	7 542	23.2
0211	Jackson township (Cambria)	5 213	NA	NA	5 203	0	2	8	0	15	1 996	7 253	125.2
0211	Lower Yoder township (Cambria)	3 342	NA	NA	3 318	14	0	9	1	38	1 544	9 180	34.5
0212	Portage township (Cambria)	4 089	NA	NA	4 080	0	0	7	2	17	1 546	7 703	63.0
0212	Richland township (Cambria)	12 777	12 940	-1.3	12 516	142	7	102	10	42	4 765	9 187	50.6
0212	Stonycreek township (Cambria)	3 562	NA	NA	3 536	15	0	6	5	9	1 587	9 173	8.8
0212	Summerhill township (Cambria)	2 798	NA	NA	2 793	0	3	0	2	4	1 064	7 185	74.5
0212	Upper Yoder township (Cambria)	5 435	NA	NA	5 395	5	2	29	4	25	2 187	10 929	30.4
0250	Franklin township (Carbon)	3 706	NA	NA	3 676	8	2	18	2	17	1 442	8 283	37.7
0250	Lower Towamensing township (Carbon)	2 948	NA	NA	2 930	0	1	0	17	52	1 123	8 297	54.6
0250	Mahoning township (Carbon)	4 198	NA	NA	4 155	6	7	30	0	17	1 617	8 920	61.1
0250	Penn Forest township (Carbon)	2 895	NA	NA	2 843	42	0	8	2	59	3 484	NA	195.7
0251	Towamensing township (Carbon)	3 111	NA	NA	3 074	4	4	19	10	35	1 272	NA	70.3
0270	Benner township (Centre)	5 085	NA	NA	4 172	853	24	12	24	104	1 289	7 320	73.9
0270	Boggs township (Centre)	2 686	NA	NA	2 679	1	4	1	1	2	998	NA	144.1
0270	College township (Centre)	6 709	NA	NA	6 492	90	8	96	23	57	2 689	11 650	47.6
0270	Ferguson township (Centre)	9 368	NA	NA	8 810	194	12	324	28	99	3 789	11 221	124.6
0270	Harris township (Centre)	4 167	NA	NA	4 094	23	4	26	20	41	1 654	13 820	82.7
0271	Patton township (Centre)	9 971	NA	NA	9 205	237	21	463	45	137	4 335	11 303	64.1
0271	Potter township (Centre)	3 020	NA	NA	3 007	1	1	10	1	10	1 331	8 445	150.5

1. Codes shown are 2-digit FIPS codes for states; 4-digit census place codes for places; and 3-digit FIPS county codes followed by 3-digit census MCD codes for minor civil divisions (MCDs). MCD names are followed by county names in parentheses. 2. Hispanic persons may be of any race. 3. Dry land or land partially or temporarily covered by water.

State/ Place/ MCD[1] code	Place	Population 1990	Places of 10,000 or more 1980	Percent change, 1980–1990	Race: White	Black	Am. Indian, Eskimo Aleut	Asian & Pacific Islander	Other race	Hispanic[2]	Total housing units, 1990	Per capita income, 1985 (Dollars)	Land area,[3] 1990 (Sq. Km.)
		1	2	3	4	5	6	7	8	9	10	11	12
	PENNSYLVANIA—Con.												
0271	Rush township (Centre)	3 411	NA	NA	3 406	1	4	0	0	4	1 578	7 706	384.3
0271	Spring township (Centre)	5 344	NA	NA	5 310	12	3	14	5	17	2 119	9 531	67.1
0271	Walker township (Centre)	2 801	NA	NA	2 795	0	3	3	0	2	1 028	8 810	105.0
0290	Birmingham township (Chester)	2 636	NA	NA	2 537	9	1	88	1	42	866	NA	16.6
0290	Caln township (Chester)	11 997	NA	NA	10 018	1 674	15	221	69	166	4 268	11 470	22.7
0290	Charlestown township (Chester)	2 754	NA	NA	2 690	37	1	25	1	31	876	15 269	32.5
0290	East Bradford township (Chester)	6 440	NA	NA	6 251	92	1	75	21	46	2 267	16 410	38.9
0290	East Brandywine township (Chester)	5 179	NA	NA	4 983	104	20	63	9	38	1 749	13 303	29.5
0290	East Caln township (Chester)	2 619	NA	NA	2 420	130	5	56	8	39	1 082	NA	9.4
0290	East Coventry township (Chester)	4 450	NA	NA	4 416	20	2	11	1	21	1 559	11 590	27.9
0290	East Fallowfield township (Chester)	4 433	NA	NA	3 998	402	5	10	18	45	1 531	10 463	40.6
0290	East Goshen township (Chester)	15 138	10 021	51.1	14 504	399	18	185	32	158	6 535	17 414	26.2
0290	East Marlborough township (Chester)	4 781	NA	NA	4 570	110	5	51	45	191	1 682	15 997	40.5
0290	East Nottingham township (Chester)	3 841	NA	NA	3 666	108	23	7	37	102	1 288	9 089	51.9
0290	East Pikeland township (Chester)	5 825	NA	NA	5 709	57	5	48	6	30	2 014	12 442	22.8
0290	Easttown township (Chester)	9 570	NA	NA	9 153	255	2	147	13	98	3 491	19 538	21.3
0290	East Vincent township (Chester)	4 161	NA	NA	3 918	194	6	21	22	27	1 550	8 550	35.1
0291	East Whiteland township (Chester)	8 398	NA	NA	7 872	307	13	175	31	139	3 001	14 002	28.5
0291	Franklin township (Chester)	2 779	NA	NA	2 712	34	0	29	4	16	942	NA	34.3
0291	Honey Brook township (Chester)	5 449	NA	NA	5 337	57	43	9	3	44	1 802	8 558	65.0
0291	Kennett township (Chester)	4 624	NA	NA	4 383	122	2	39	78	322	1 835	21 290	40.3
0291	London Britain township (Chester)	2 671	NA	NA	2 611	20	1	19	20	32	901	NA	25.6
0291	London Grove township (Chester)	3 922	NA	NA	3 667	146	1	27	81	203	1 310	11 534	44.6
0291	Lower Oxford township (Chester)	3 264	NA	NA	2 020	1 173	4	8	59	92	809	7 792	46.8
0291	New Garden township (Chester)	5 430	NA	NA	4 785	196	22	35	392	1 131	1 778	10 761	41.8
0291	New London township (Chester)	2 721	NA	NA	2 649	12	12	26	22	41	922	NA	30.7
0291	North Coventry township (Chester)	7 506	NA	NA	7 345	95	9	34	23	43	2 896	12 077	34.7
0292	Pennsbury township (Chester)	3 326	NA	NA	3 263	13	3	44	3	22	1 141	22 193	25.7
0292	Pocopson township (Chester)	3 266	NA	NA	2 930	303	4	21	8	99	830	NA	21.4
0292	Sadsbury township (Chester)	2 510	NA	NA	2 413	70	1	10	16	37	915	NA	16.2
0292	Schuylkill township (Chester)	5 538	NA	NA	5 415	61	5	54	3	51	2 115	14 685	22.2
0292	Tredyffrin township (Chester)	28 028	23 121	21.2	26 272	1 104	25	584	43	243	11 924	21 463	51.4
0292	Upper Uwchlan township (Chester)	4 396	NA	NA	4 301	45	2	45	3	43	1 390	NA	27.8
0292	Uwchlan township (Chester)	12 999	NA	NA	12 452	238	5	276	28	125	4 743	14 302	27.1
0292	Valley township (Chester)	4 007	NA	NA	2 766	1 180	3	18	40	89	1 509	9 957	15.5
0292	Wallace township (Chester)	2 541	NA	NA	2 470	50	0	18	3	25	780	NA	31.2
0292	Warwick township (Chester)	2 575	NA	NA	2 558	6	4	4	3	11	976	NA	49.7
0292	West Bradford township (Chester)	10 406	NA	NA	9 926	347	16	91	26	76	3 217	12 017	48.1
0292	West Brandywine township (Chester)	5 984	NA	NA	5 786	161	10	18	9	56	2 062	11 326	34.7
0293	West Caln township (Chester)	6 143	NA	NA	5 990	123	6	14	10	38	2 075	11 008	56.3
0293	West Goshen township (Chester)	18 082	16 164	11.9	16 885	794	13	321	69	284	6 802	13 988	30.9
0293	Westtown township (Chester)	9 937	NA	NA	9 422	327	4	168	16	84	3 279	16 569	22.7
0293	West Whiteland township (Chester)	12 403	NA	NA	11 654	521	26	159	43	164	4 900	13 977	33.6
0293	Willistown township (Chester)	9 380	NA	NA	9 117	184	1	72	6	72	3 434	19 348	47.2
0310	Clarion township (Clarion)	3 306	NA	NA	3 239	31	3	26	7	17	1 357	8 041	81.6
0330	Bradford township (Clearfield)	2 504	NA	NA	2 487	7	3	6	1	4	945	6 868	99.1
0330	Cooper township (Clearfield)	2 590	NA	NA	2 583	0	6	1	0	7	1 109	6 756	105.2
0330	Decatur township (Clearfield)	3 004	NA	NA	2 992	0	1	10	1	9	1 220	6 767	99.0
0331	Lawrence township (Clearfield)	8 000	NA	NA	7 892	65	16	24	3	12	3 204	7 918	216.4
0331	Morris township (Clearfield)	2 680	NA	NA	2 680	0	0	0	0	8	1 104	7 287	50.6
0332	Sandy township (Clearfield)	9 005	NA	NA	8 929	6	5	60	5	47	3 946	9 827	134.2
0351	Pine Creek township (Clinton)	3 188	NA	NA	3 169	5	4	10	0	1	1 251	9 254	37.3
0351	Woodward township (Clinton)	2 662	NA	NA	2 635	4	2	21	0	9	1 105	8 765	46.4
0370	Briar Creek township (Columbia)	3 010	NA	NA	2 998	6	0	5	1	16	1 182	8 007	54.6
0371	Scott township (Columbia)	4 423	NA	NA	4 359	9	4	45	6	23	1 866	10 842	18.6
0390	Hayfield township (Crawford)	2 937	NA	NA	2 918	5	1	10	3	10	1 155	8 490	100.8
0391	Sadsbury township (Crawford)	2 575	NA	NA	2 561	0	1	13	0	0	2 031	10 134	61.5
0392	Vernon township (Crawford)	5 605	NA	NA	5 496	63	7	35	4	16	2 397	9 202	76.6
0392	West Mead township (Crawford)	5 401	NA	NA	5 252	120	4	17	8	20	2 132	9 806	47.2
0410	Dickinson township (Cumberland)	3 870	NA	NA	3 826	8	1	26	9	15	1 498	9 505	118.2
0410	East Pennsboro township (Cumberland)	15 185	13 955	8.8	14 660	139	17	326	43	119	6 118	11 301	27.4
0410	Hampden township (Cumberland)	20 384	16 648	22.4	19 660	94	30	551	49	144	7 885	14 014	46.0
0410	Lower Allen township (Cumberland)	15 254	14 077	8.4	14 093	828	42	227	64	247	6 117	13 053	26.6
0410	Middlesex township (Cumberland)	5 780	NA	NA	5 674	68	4	30	4	52	2 017	10 858	67.5
0410	Monroe township (Cumberland)	5 468	NA	NA	5 407	21	8	25	7	29	2 004	12 292	67.7
0410	North Middleton twnshp (Cumberland)	9 833	NA	NA	9 350	307	8	137	31	90	3 755	10 762	60.7
0411	Shippensburg township (Cumberland)	4 606	NA	NA	4 403	137	6	47	13	42	864	5 265	6.5
0411	Silver Spring township (Cumberland)	8 369	NA	NA	8 225	14	12	118	0	19	3 254	12 078	84.2
0411	Southampton township (Cumberland)	3 552	NA	NA	3 535	5	4	6	2	4	1 253	7 466	135.9
0411	South Middleton twnshp (Cumberland)	10 340	NA	NA	10 175	68	14	67	16	62	3 939	10 535	128.2
0411	Upper Allen township (Cumberland)	13 347	10 533	26.7	13 034	88	7	196	22	65	4 539	12 515	34.3
0411	West Pennsboro township (Cumberland)	4 945	NA	NA	4 919	9	9	7	1	10	1 802	8 952	79.1
0430	Conewago township (Dauphin)	2 832	NA	NA	2 787	25	6	12	2	23	1 012	NA	43.3

1. Codes shown are 2-digit FIPS codes for states; 4-digit census place codes for places; and 3-digit FIPS county codes followed by 3-digit census MCD codes for minor civil divisions (MCDs). MCD names are followed by county names in parentheses. 2. Hispanic persons may be of any race. 3. Dry land or land partially or temporarily covered by water.

State/ Place/ MCD[1] code	Place	Population: 1990	Population: Places of 10,000 or more: 1980	Population: Places of 10,000 or more: Percent change, 1980–1990	Population characteristics, 1990: Race: White	Race: Black	Race: Am. Indian, Eskimo Aleut	Race: Asian & Pacific Islander	Race: Other race	Hispanic[2]	Total housing units, 1990	Per capita income, 1985 (Dollars)	Land area,[3] 1990 (Sq. Km.)
		1	2	3	4	5	6	7	8	9	10	11	12
	PENNSYLVANIA—Con.												
0430	Derry township (Dauphin)	18 408	18 115	1.6	17 711	251	14	376	56	185	8 164	12 676	70.5
0430	East Hanover township (Dauphin)	4 569	NA	NA	4 514	15	5	28	7	27	1 736	9 820	103.3
0430	Halifax township (Dauphin)	3 449	NA	NA	3 432	3	3	11	0	2	1 411	9 105	72.3
0430	Londonderry township (Dauphin)	4 926	NA	NA	4 877	20	6	22	1	37	2 240	10 051	59.0
0430	Lower Paxton township (Dauphin)	39 162	34 830	12.4	36 274	2 149	45	523	171	439	16 895	13 199	72.8
0430	Lower Swatara township (Dauphin)	7 072	NA	NA	6 815	158	3	78	18	77	2 683	10 533	31.4
0431	Middle Paxton township (Dauphin)	5 129	NA	NA	5 110	7	4	7	1	20	1 984	12 134	141.4
0431	South Hanover township (Dauphin)	4 626	NA	NA	4 582	19	4	17	4	19	1 630	11 745	29.5
0431	Susquehanna township (Dauphin)	18 636	18 034	3.3	15 650	2 629	24	261	72	214	8 090	13 634	34.7
0431	Swatara township (Dauphin)	19 661	18 796	4.6	17 385	1 831	25	230	190	455	7 900	11 954	34.2
0431	Upper Paxton township (Dauphin)	3 680	NA	NA	3 645	6	0	23	6	5	1 355	8 773	67.3
0431	West Hanover township (Dauphin)	6 125	NA	NA	6 028	45	6	37	9	41	2 250	10 338	60.2
0450	Aston township (Delaware)	15 080	14 530	3.8	14 950	54	12	62	2	78	5 262	11 431	14.9
0450	Bethel township (Delaware)	3 330	NA	NA	3 235	19	2	29	45	57	1 148	NA	14.7
0450	Birmingham township (Delaware)	3 118	NA	NA	3 040	15	3	59	1	22	1 288	NA	22.5
0450	Chester township (Delaware)	5 399	NA	NA	2 429	2 892	23	28	27	92	1 879	8 972	3.6
0450	Concord township (Delaware)	6 933	NA	NA	6 699	134	11	78	11	40	2 297	13 881	35.5
0450	Darby township (Delaware)	10 955	12 264	-10.7	6 773	4 099	24	25	34	92	3 941	9 641	3.7
0450	Edgmont township (Delaware)	2 735	NA	NA	2 657	14	1	58	5	28	1 265	NA	25.3
0451	Haverford township (Delaware)	49 848	52 349	-4.8	47 887	1 011	24	871	55	335	18 210	14 595	25.9
0451	Lower Chichester township (Delaware)	3 660	NA	NA	3 574	72	0	4	10	48	1 335	8 315	2.9
0451	Marple township (Delaware)	23 123	23 642	-2.2	22 098	184	25	795	21	196	8 433	14 345	26.4
0451	Middletown township (Delaware)	14 130	12 463	13.4	12 918	945	8	200	59	147	4 482	13 538	34.9
0451	Nether Providence twnshp (Delaware)	13 229	12 730	3.9	12 216	772	5	218	18	72	5 045	17 591	12.2
0451	Newtown township (Delaware)	11 366	11 775	-3.5	11 071	55	2	232	6	48	4 433	17 895	26.0
0451	Radnor township (Delaware)	28 703	27 676	3.7	26 687	906	25	1 027	58	493	10 580	19 944	35.6
0451	Ridley township (Delaware)	31 169	33 771	-7.7	29 824	1 020	16	275	34	194	12 276	11 398	13.1
0452	Springfield township (Delaware)	24 160	25 326	-4.6	23 575	126	13	434	12	145	8 604	14 389	16.5
0452	Thornbury township (Delaware)	5 056	NA	NA	2 970	1 988	20	41	37	104	1 021	10 943	23.8
0452	Tinicum township (Delaware)	4 440	NA	NA	4 410	4	9	13	4	16	1 796	10 046	14.9
0452	Upper Chichester township (Delaware)	15 004	14 377	4.4	13 672	1 193	11	106	22	160	5 749	10 951	17.4
0452	Upper Darby township (Delaware)	81 177	83 999	-3.4	75 058	2 464	89	3 405	161	822	34 115	11 831	20.4
0452	Upper Providence township (Delaware)	9 727	NA	NA	9 268	294	6	144	15	53	3 861	17 131	14.5
0470	Benzinger township (Elk)	8 509	NA	NA	8 452	5	9	40	3	11	3 085	9 045	252.9
0470	Fox township (Elk)	3 392	NA	NA	3 376	1	3	5	7	5	1 438	8 743	174.3
0470	Ridgway township (Elk)	2 617	NA	NA	2 611	3	2	1	0	2	1 127	8 611	226.1
0490	Fairview township (Erie)	7 839	NA	NA	7 738	50	0	50	1	29	2 674	14 190	72.0
0490	Girard township (Erie)	4 722	NA	NA	4 691	9	6	2	14	33	1 896	8 635	82.2
0490	Greene township (Erie)	4 959	NA	NA	4 948	2	8	1	0	6	1 676	8 589	97.1
0490	Harborcreek township (Erie)	15 108	14 644	3.2	14 772	224	18	54	40	83	5 158	9 235	88.7
0491	Lawrence Park township (Erie)	4 310	NA	NA	4 268	10	8	19	5	23	1 631	10 487	4.8
0491	McKean township (Erie)	4 503	NA	NA	4 473	9	5	12	4	9	1 578	9 079	94.8
0491	Millcreek township (Erie)	46 820	44 303	5.7	45 866	392	48	483	31	193	19 285	12 232	76.4
0491	North East township (Erie)	6 283	NA	NA	6 234	8	10	18	13	30	2 516	9 984	109.7
0491	Springfield township (Erie)	3 218	NA	NA	3 157	41	7	7	6	22	1 338	8 186	97.7
0491	Summit township (Erie)	5 284	NA	NA	5 244	24	11	4	1	7	1 977	9 462	61.8
0491	Washington township (Erie)	4 102	NA	NA	4 063	19	8	10	2	9	1 500	9 668	116.9
0491	Waterford township (Erie)	3 402	NA	NA	3 380	8	6	8	0	2	1 173	7 737	129.8
0510	Bullskin township (Fayette)	7 323	NA	NA	7 304	1	3	13	2	13	2 809	7 960	112.4
0510	Connellsville township (Fayette)	2 553	NA	NA	2 527	21	3	0	2	7	1 026	8 008	27.7
0510	Dunbar township (Fayette)	7 460	NA	NA	7 289	147	9	12	3	13	2 912	7 135	153.0
0510	Franklin township (Fayette)	2 640	NA	NA	2 608	30	0	1	1	0	1 047	7 615	76.6
0510	Georges township (Fayette)	6 525	NA	NA	6 447	64	5	9	0	3	2 522	6 786	124.2
0510	German township (Fayette)	5 596	NA	NA	5 201	383	5	3	4	33	2 211	7 142	86.3
0510	Luzerne township (Fayette)	4 904	NA	NA	4 647	246	4	2	5	15	2 027	7 392	76.6
0511	Menallen township (Fayette)	4 739	NA	NA	4 606	124	1	7	1	12	1 893	7 162	55.1
0511	North Union township (Fayette)	13 910	15 294	-9.0	13 478	397	10	14	11	50	5 761	7 581	100.2
0511	Perry township (Fayette)	2 817	NA	NA	2 713	99	1	2	2	1	1 117	7 135	51.2
0511	Redstone township (Fayette)	6 459	NA	NA	5 818	624	7	6	4	27	2 824	6 842	58.5
0511	Saltlick township (Fayette)	3 253	NA	NA	3 247	1	5	0	0	3	1 368	6 789	97.5
0511	South Union township (Fayette)	10 223	11 033	-7.3	9 890	262	3	60	8	32	4 190	9 567	43.3
0511	Springfield township (Fayette)	2 968	NA	NA	2 965	1	2	0	0	10	1 137	5 741	155.0
0511	Springhill township (Fayette)	2 800	NA	NA	2 763	20	9	0	8	23	1 112	6 465	86.7
0512	Washington township (Fayette)	4 613	NA	NA	4 534	75	0	2	2	20	1 919	8 417	24.8
0512	Wharton township (Fayette)	3 390	NA	NA	3 379	3	4	4	0	11	1 507	7 292	238.0
0550	Antrim township (Franklin)	10 107	NA	NA	9 998	50	9	19	31	49	3 652	9 436	181.5
0550	Greene township (Franklin)	11 930	11 471	4.0	11 643	185	24	54	24	115	4 897	10 110	147.0
0550	Guilford township (Franklin)	11 893	10 612	12.1	11 590	187	23	71	22	95	4 372	10 257	135.9
0550	Hamilton township (Franklin)	7 745	NA	NA	7 483	175	19	39	29	67	2 980	9 406	92.7
0550	Montgomery township (Franklin)	4 558	NA	NA	4 519	20	3	4	12	16	1 610	7 552	173.9
0550	Peters township (Franklin)	4 090	NA	NA	4 024	50	1	10	5	7	1 628	8 661	144.7
0550	Quincy township (Franklin)	5 704	NA	NA	5 609	58	2	27	8	38	1 739	7 932	115.7
0550	St. Thomas township (Franklin)	5 861	NA	NA	5 791	29	11	21	9	38	2 181	9 621	133.9

1. Codes shown are 2-digit FIPS codes for states; 4-digit census place codes for places; and 3-digit FIPS county codes followed by 3-digit census MCD codes for minor civil divisions (MCDs). MCD names are followed by county names in parentheses. 2. Hispanic persons may be of any race. 3. Dry land or land partially or temporarily covered by water.

State/ Place/ MCD[1] code	Place	Population			Population characteristics, 1990						Total housing units, 1990	Per capita income, 1985 (Dollars)	Land area,[3] 1990 (Sq. Km.)
			Places of 10,000 or more		Race								
		1990	1980	Percent change, 1980–1990	White	Black	Am. Indian, Eskimo Aleut	Asian & Pacific Islander	Other race	Hispanic[2]			
		1	2	3	4	5	6	7	8	9	10	11	12
	PENNSYLVANIA—Con.												
0550	Southampton township (Franklin)	5 484	NA	NA	5 394	61	6	15	8	32	2 107	9 063	98.4
0551	Washington township (Franklin)	11 119	NA	NA	10 780	172	18	114	35	95	4 355	10 066	100.7
0590	Cumberland township (Greene)	6 742	NA	NA	6 701	5	25	9	2	30	2 836	8 181	99.1
0590	Franklin township (Greene)	5 562	NA	NA	5 473	35	12	42	0	17	2 149	9 106	105.9
0590	Jefferson township (Greene)	2 536	NA	NA	2 446	88	0	1	1	17	1 033	8 705	56.1
0590	Morgan township (Greene)	2 887	NA	NA	2 710	149	10	8	10	26	1 037	7 744	63.6
0611	Smithfield township (Huntingdon)	4 181	NA	NA	2 719	1 439	9	2	12	59	624	NA	14.5
0630	Armstrong township (Indiana)	3 048	NA	NA	3 043	2	0	3	0	3	1 125	7 836	97.7
0630	Burrell township (Indiana)	3 669	NA	NA	3 621	34	0	12	2	11	1 501	7 934	61.4
0630	Center township (Indiana)	5 257	NA	NA	5 224	15	3	11	4	33	2 080	8 170	104.6
0630	Cherryhill township (Indiana)	2 764	NA	NA	2 751	6	3	4	0	8	978	7 682	126.4
0630	East Wheatfield township (Indiana)	2 735	NA	NA	2 734	0	1	0	0	7	1 081	6 765	69.6
0631	Green township (Indiana)	4 095	NA	NA	4 084	7	2	1	1	12	1 531	6 707	136.7
0631	Rayne township (Indiana)	3 339	NA	NA	3 326	5	1	7	0	6	1 196	8 023	122.3
0631	White township (Indiana)	13 788	13 177	4.6	13 050	470	11	220	37	79	5 777	11 140	110.3
0651	Snyder township (Jefferson)	2 535	NA	NA	2 525	0	5	3	2	6	1 041	10 521	108.2
0651	Winslow township (Jefferson)	2 526	NA	NA	2 519	0	3	4	0	7	993	7 697	117.8
0670	Fayette township (Juniata)	3 002	NA	NA	2 993	4	3	1	1	4	1 192	8 429	103.0
0690	Jefferson township (Lackawanna)	3 438	NA	NA	3 423	6	2	3	4	18	1 446	8 211	86.3
0691	Newton township (Lackawanna)	2 843	NA	NA	2 813	4	0	26	0	10	828	8 693	58.1
0691	Scott township (Lackawanna)	5 350	NA	NA	5 313	14	4	16	3	17	2 020	9 404	70.8
0691	South Abington township (Lackawanna)	6 377	NA	NA	6 201	41	13	104	18	30	2 225	11 498	23.1
0710	Bart township (Lancaster)	2 774	NA	NA	2 750	22	0	2	0	2	791	NA	41.7
0710	Brecknock township (Lancaster)	5 197	NA	NA	5 169	14	3	3	8	28	1 662	8 323	64.6
0710	Caernarvon township (Lancaster)	3 946	NA	NA	3 916	14	0	13	3	17	1 155	7 853	59.5
0710	Clay township (Lancaster)	5 050	NA	NA	4 994	5	4	33	14	36	1 669	7 330	57.6
0710	Colerain township (Lancaster)	2 867	NA	NA	2 832	18	1	12	4	14	835	NA	74.6
0710	Conestoga township (Lancaster)	3 470	NA	NA	3 448	3	2	12	5	15	1 289	10 889	37.8
0710	Conoy township (Lancaster)	2 687	NA	NA	2 671	4	9	2	1	10	953	NA	38.4
0710	Earl township (Lancaster)	5 515	NA	NA	5 444	23	1	34	13	28	1 656	7 934	56.8
0710	East Cocalico township (Lancaster)	7 809	NA	NA	7 654	11	2	125	17	64	2 824	9 396	53.4
0710	East Donegal township (Lancaster)	4 484	NA	NA	4 404	31	5	38	6	27	1 563	10 216	56.1
0710	East Drumore township (Lancaster)	3 225	NA	NA	3 202	14	5	2	2	27	968	NA	60.1
0710	East Earl township (Lancaster)	5 491	NA	NA	5 433	14	6	21	17	54	1 710	8 061	63.7
0710	East Hempfield township (Lancaster)	18 597	15 152	22.7	18 012	172	8	332	73	272	7 446	13 452	54.6
0711	East Lampeter township (Lancaster)	11 999	NA	NA	11 568	160	18	151	102	294	4 794	11 228	51.7
0711	Elizabeth township (Lancaster)	3 691	NA	NA	3 641	12	1	19	18	20	1 269	NA	45.6
0711	Ephrata township (Lancaster)	7 116	NA	NA	6 917	13	6	136	44	78	2 322	8 528	41.8
0711	Fulton township (Lancaster)	2 688	NA	NA	2 641	36	1	4	6	7	1 006	NA	67.2
0711	Lancaster township (Lancaster)	13 187	10 833	21.7	12 364	400	11	179	233	448	5 534	13 529	15.7
0711	Leacock township (Lancaster)	4 668	NA	NA	4 624	6	3	33	2	16	1 375	7 329	53.4
0711	Little Britain township (Lancaster)	2 701	NA	NA	2 670	21	4	2	4	25	855	NA	70.9
0711	Manheim township (Lancaster)	28 880	26 042	10.9	27 907	307	28	524	114	301	11 009	14 924	62.1
0711	Manor township (Lancaster)	14 130	11 474	23.1	13 782	137	11	149	51	155	5 431	11 717	99.8
0711	Martic township (Lancaster)	4 362	NA	NA	4 315	17	9	11	10	32	1 524	9 498	75.2
0712	Mount Joy township (Lancaster)	6 227	NA	NA	6 146	20	3	43	15	49	2 213	10 263	72.4
0712	Paradise township (Lancaster)	4 430	NA	NA	4 390	17	1	20	2	11	1 436	8 889	48.4
0712	Penn township (Lancaster)	6 760	NA	NA	6 675	37	8	25	15	46	2 335	11 569	76.7
0712	Pequea township (Lancaster)	4 512	NA	NA	4 461	15	1	20	15	31	1 600	11 012	35.3
0712	Providence township (Lancaster)	6 071	NA	NA	5 994	30	19	9	19	55	2 181	9 726	52.2
0712	Rapho township (Lancaster)	8 211	NA	NA	8 114	27	5	51	14	44	2 916	9 810	123.1
0712	Sadsbury township (Lancaster)	2 712	NA	NA	2 665	35	3	7	2	7	803	NA	51.2
0712	Salisbury township (Lancaster)	8 527	NA	NA	8 371	73	23	37	23	56	2 704	7 502	108.4
0712	Strasburg township (Lancaster)	3 688	NA	NA	3 680	0	0	7	1	13	1 192	9 380	51.8
0712	Upper Leacock township (Lancaster)	7 254	NA	NA	6 996	26	3	200	29	102	2 528	9 523	46.8
0712	Warwick township (Lancaster)	11 622	NA	NA	11 467	20	7	80	48	107	4 077	12 415	51.9
0712	West Cocalico township (Lancaster)	5 521	NA	NA	5 487	4	2	23	5	31	1 890	9 710	71.7
0712	West Donegal township (Lancaster)	5 605	NA	NA	5 551	12	7	29	6	34	1 631	9 907	40.8
0712	West Earl township (Lancaster)	6 434	NA	NA	6 289	11	5	103	26	61	2 033	9 523	45.7
0713	West Hempfield township (Lancaster)	12 942	NA	NA	12 451	218	6	166	101	234	4 639	10 572	48.9
0713	West Lampeter township (Lancaster)	9 865	NA	NA	9 724	56	7	39	39	80	4 109	11 699	42.6
0730	Mahoning township (Lawrence)	3 560	NA	NA	3 548	0	5	5	2	8	1 405	8 007	63.6
0730	Neshannock township (Lawrence)	8 373	NA	NA	8 244	10	8	110	1	17	3 436	13 243	44.9
0730	North Beaver township (Lawrence)	3 982	NA	NA	3 963	4	1	5	9	12	1 473	8 442	111.5
0730	Pulaski township (Lawrence)	3 469	NA	NA	3 435	20	4	10	0	19	1 261	8 073	78.9
0730	Shenango township (Lawrence)	7 187	NA	NA	7 014	144	4	5	20	40	2 667	8 503	63.1
0730	Slippery Rock township (Lawrence)	3 196	NA	NA	3 188	4	3	1	0	4	1 199	7 616	78.2
0731	Union township (Lawrence)	5 581	NA	NA	5 305	260	3	7	6	12	2 223	9 130	24.9
0731	Wayne township (Lawrence)	2 785	NA	NA	2 744	33	5	2	1	10	1 094	8 298	41.8
0750	Annville township (Lebanon)	4 294	NA	NA	4 192	22	1	64	15	57	1 442	8 654	4.0
0750	Bethel township (Lebanon)	4 343	NA	NA	4 289	15	3	14	22	42	1 575	8 228	89.9
0750	East Hanover township (Lebanon)	3 058	NA	NA	2 999	24	7	21	7	39	1 105	9 143	85.0
0750	Heidelberg township (Lebanon)	3 797	NA	NA	3 763	4	1	20	9	16	1 304	9 580	62.6

1. Codes shown are 2-digit FIPS codes for states; 4-digit census place codes for places; and 3-digit FIPS county codes followed by 3-digit census MCD codes for minor civil divisions (MCDs). MCD names are followed by county names in parentheses. 2. Hispanic persons may be of any race. 3. Dry land or land partially or temporarily covered by water.

State/ Place/ MCD[1] code	Place	Population			Population characteristics, 1990						Total housing units, 1990	Per capita income, 1985 (Dollars)	Land area,[3] 1990 (Sq. Km.)
		1990	Places of 10,000 or more		Race					Hispanic[2]			
			1980	Percent change, 1980–1990	White	Black	Am. Indian, Eskimo Aleut	Asian & Pacific Islander	Other race				
		1	2	3	4	5	6	7	8	9	10	11	12
	PENNSYLVANIA—Con.												
0750	Jackson township (Lebanon)	5 732	NA	NA	5 702	3	2	21	4	12	2 010	8 646	61.6
0750	Millcreek township (Lebanon)	2 687	NA	NA	2 675	2	4	3	3	15	968	8 373	52.7
0750	North Cornwall township (Lebanon)	4 886	NA	NA	4 676	29	4	128	49	186	2 024	12 221	24.6
0750	North Lebanon township (Lebanon)	9 741	NA	NA	9 523	47	11	83	77	173	3 695	9 371	43.8
0750	North Londonderry township (Lebanon)	5 630	NA	NA	5 575	12	1	40	2	34	2 173	10 727	27.5
0751	South Annville township (Lebanon)	3 008	NA	NA	2 977	3	0	24	4	23	1 098	10 753	50.9
0751	South Lebanon township (Lebanon)	7 491	NA	NA	7 295	76	7	57	56	149	2 465	9 996	56.4
0751	South Londonderry township (Lebanon)	4 502	NA	NA	4 467	10	5	18	2	24	1 679	10 741	62.8
0751	Swatara township (Lebanon)	3 318	NA	NA	3 287	6	1	11	13	23	1 231	8 180	54.8
0751	Union township (Lebanon)	2 755	NA	NA	2 732	9	0	11	3	21	1 106	8 550	88.9
0770	Heidelberg township (Lehigh)	3 250	NA	NA	3 204	10	7	17	12	35	1 089	9 676	63.9
0770	Lower Macungie township (Lehigh)	16 871	12 958	30.2	16 100	75	8	654	34	135	6 171	14 512	58.5
0770	Lower Milford township (Lehigh)	3 269	NA	NA	3 224	7	8	17	13	28	1 151	10 961	50.9
0770	Lynn township (Lehigh)	3 220	NA	NA	3 201	5	1	7	6	13	1 210	10 512	107.3
0770	North Whitehall township (Lehigh)	10 827	NA	NA	10 714	35	14	39	25	76	4 059	11 801	74.2
0770	Salisbury township (Lehigh)	13 401	12 259	9.3	12 922	210	6	122	141	255	5 071	13 053	28.6
0770	South Whitehall township (Lehigh)	18 261	15 919	14.7	17 757	128	9	343	24	183	6 689	14 342	44.4
0771	Upper Macungie township (Lehigh)	8 757	NA	NA	8 527	55	2	164	9	65	3 343	12 221	68.0
0771	Upper Milford township (Lehigh)	6 304	NA	NA	6 261	15	4	19	5	48	2 222	13 010	46.4
0771	Upper Saucon township (Lehigh)	9 775	NA	NA	9 675	34	4	54	8	75	3 360	12 131	63.9
0771	Washington township (Lehigh)	6 356	NA	NA	6 308	15	11	13	9	31	2 340	10 067	61.0
0771	Weisenberg township (Lehigh)	3 246	NA	NA	3 214	4	2	15	11	22	1 119	NA	69.4
0771	Whitehall township (Lehigh)	22 779	21 538	5.8	21 969	312	10	362	126	359	9 762	11 811	32.5
0790	Bear Creek township (Luzerne)	2 721	NA	NA	2 698	7	5	11	0	8	1 299	9 428	177.9
0790	Butler township (Luzerne)	6 020	NA	NA	5 487	420	10	89	14	51	2 145	7 950	86.0
0790	Dallas township (Luzerne)	7 625	NA	NA	7 518	23	2	77	5	17	2 813	10 914	48.0
0791	Fairview township (Luzerne)	3 014	NA	NA	2 952	8	2	48	4	26	1 133	12 244	25.2
0791	Foster township (Luzerne)	3 372	NA	NA	3 329	30	4	8	1	21	1 614	7 558	115.1
0791	Hanover township (Luzerne)	12 050	12 601	-4.4	11 945	72	7	19	7	53	5 106	8 365	48.7
0791	Hazle township (Luzerne)	9 323	NA	NA	9 269	13	1	21	19	39	3 836	8 495	116.3
0791	Jackson township (Luzerne)	5 336	NA	NA	3 654	1 522	18	41	101	341	907	8 306	34.6
0791	Jenkins township (Luzerne)	4 740	NA	NA	4 706	14	8	4	8	22	1 905	8 332	35.8
0791	Kingston township (Luzerne)	6 763	NA	NA	6 717	28	0	16	2	23	2 573	10 106	35.2
0792	Lehman township (Luzerne)	3 076	NA	NA	3 054	3	1	18	0	13	1 361	9 779	56.1
0792	Newport township (Luzerne)	4 593	NA	NA	4 580	3	1	4	5	22	2 082	7 638	43.1
0792	Pittston township (Luzerne)	2 725	NA	NA	2 723	1	0	1	0	3	1 022	8 409	36.9
0792	Plains township (Luzerne)	10 988	11 338	-3.1	10 936	15	1	30	6	29	4 379	8 872	33.7
0792	Ross township (Luzerne)	2 634	NA	NA	2 627	1	3	2	1	9	1 168	NA	112.0
0792	Salem township (Luzerne)	4 503	NA	NA	4 472	8	2	16	5	18	1 824	8 741	75.0
0793	Sugarloaf township (Luzerne)	3 534	NA	NA	3 498	11	1	19	5	21	1 187	10 321	57.1
0793	Wilkes-Barre township (Luzerne)	3 572	NA	NA	3 420	45	4	95	8	25	1 685	8 883	7.7
0793	Wright township (Luzerne)	4 685	NA	NA	4 610	21	9	43	2	32	1 612	9 815	34.9
0810	Clinton township (Lycoming)	3 086	NA	NA	2 659	357	22	7	41	122	872	NA	72.4
0810	Fairfield township (Lycoming)	2 580	NA	NA	2 564	1	2	11	2	11	972	NA	30.1
0810	Hepburn township (Lycoming)	2 834	NA	NA	2 819	1	4	8	2	10	1 050	9 068	43.1
0811	Loyalsock township (Lycoming)	10 644	10 763	-1.1	10 392	123	12	109	8	45	4 381	10 392	54.4
0811	Muncy Creek township (Lycoming)	3 401	NA	NA	3 387	2	2	9	1	7	1 353	8 436	52.2
0811	Old Lycoming township (Lycoming)	5 526	NA	NA	5 488	13	3	22	0	7	2 250	10 185	24.5
0812	Wolf township (Lycoming)	2 617	NA	NA	2 602	0	8	7	0	15	1 013	NA	50.6
0830	Bradford township (McKean)	5 065	NA	NA	4 968	34	15	44	4	21	1 852	9 305	143.9
0830	Foster township (McKean)	4 691	NA	NA	4 657	8	9	14	3	9	1 925	10 723	120.2
0830	Keating township (McKean)	3 070	NA	NA	3 065	1	2	0	2	7	1 277	7 303	254.2
0850	Hempfield township (Mercer)	3 826	NA	NA	3 778	10	2	36	0	0	1 503	11 534	36.6
0851	Lackawannock township (Mercer)	2 677	NA	NA	2 659	16	2	0	0	3	937	7 278	53.5
0851	Pine township (Mercer)	4 193	NA	NA	3 965	191	4	23	10	17	1 509	8 522	66.6
0851	Pymatuning township (Mercer)	3 736	NA	NA	3 680	41	0	11	4	16	1 496	7 818	42.7
0851	Shenango township (Mercer)	4 339	NA	NA	4 214	101	3	17	4	17	1 709	9 039	77.4
0851	South Pymatuning township (Mercer)	2 775	NA	NA	2 757	14	0	4	0	3	1 076	10 359	50.1
0852	West Salem township (Mercer)	3 547	NA	NA	3 535	0	6	5	1	10	1 330	8 372	95.8
0870	Armagh township (Mifflin)	3 627	NA	NA	3 618	1	1	6	1	16	1 836	7 068	240.3
0870	Brown township (Mifflin)	3 320	NA	NA	3 309	0	4	6	1	9	1 326	9 321	85.9
0870	Decatur township (Mifflin)	2 735	NA	NA	2 722	1	0	11	1	3	1 046	6 858	117.1
0870	Derry township (Mifflin)	7 650	NA	NA	7 588	21	5	32	4	26	3 055	8 738	80.6
0870	Granville township (Mifflin)	5 090	NA	NA	5 069	10	3	6	2	23	2 069	8 084	103.9
0870	Union township (Mifflin)	3 265	NA	NA	3 248	5	3	9	0	2	1 175	6 842	66.1
0870	Wayne township (Mifflin)	2 521	NA	NA	2 502	8	1	2	8	16	1 055	NA	124.0
0890	Barrett township (Monroe)	3 216	NA	NA	3 134	50	4	12	16	59	1 902	10 978	136.2
0890	Chestnuthill township (Monroe)	8 798	NA	NA	8 679	42	15	34	28	195	3 984	9 717	96.6
0890	Coolbaugh township (Monroe)	6 756	NA	NA	6 290	277	13	86	90	392	7 057	9 420	222.1
0890	Hamilton township (Monroe)	6 681	NA	NA	6 540	74	19	29	19	89	2 771	9 371	99.3
0890	Jackson township (Monroe)	3 757	NA	NA	3 688	39	6	16	8	49	1 970	NA	76.1
0890	Middle Smithfield township (Monroe)	6 382	NA	NA	6 195	103	5	48	31	161	4 526	9 866	137.6
0890	Pocono township (Monroe)	7 529	NA	NA	7 304	133	18	47	27	112	3 557	10 034	88.0

1. Codes shown are 2-digit FIPS codes for states; 4-digit census place codes for places; and 3-digit FIPS county codes followed by 3-digit census MCD codes for minor civil divisions (MCDs). MCD names are followed by county names in parentheses. 2. Hispanic persons may be of any race. 3. Dry land or land partially or temporarily covered by water.

State/ Place/ MCD[1] code	Place	Population: 1990	Population: Places of 10,000 or more: 1980	Population: Places of 10,000 or more: Percent change, 1980–1990	Population characteristics, 1990: Race: White	Race: Black	Race: Am. Indian, Eskimo Aleut	Race: Asian & Pacific Islander	Race: Other race	Hispanic[2]	Total housing units, 1990	Per capita income, 1985 (Dollars)	Land area,[3] 1990 (Sq. Km.)
		1	2	3	4	5	6	7	8	9	10	11	12
	PENNSYLVANIA—Con.												
0890	Polk township (Monroe)	4 517	NA	NA	4 479	6	7	9	16	89	2 246	8 941	77.1
0890	Ross township (Monroe)	3 696	NA	NA	3 652	16	1	19	8	48	1 416	NA	58.6
0890	Smithfield township (Monroe)	4 692	NA	NA	4 590	53	2	32	15	91	2 382	13 036	60.0
0890	Stroud township (Monroe)	10 600	NA	NA	10 261	182	4	111	42	190	4 894	11 363	80.8
0890	Tobyhanna township (Monroe)	4 318	NA	NA	4 262	35	1	16	4	73	5 671	10 029	130.8
0910	Abington township (Montgomery)	56 322	59 084	-4.7	50 374	4 605	61	1 178	104	531	22 116	15 866	40.0
0910	Cheltenham township (Montgomery)	34 923	35 509	-1.7	27 745	5 284	57	1 755	82	387	14 467	18 821	23.4
0910	Douglass township (Montgomery)	7 048	NA	NA	6 983	33	0	29	3	39	2 559	10 276	39.8
0910	East Norriton township (Montgomery)	13 324	12 711	4.8	12 503	557	6	243	15	85	5 201	13 556	15.7
0910	Franconia township (Montgomery)	7 224	NA	NA	7 096	20	2	99	7	35	2 390	12 659	35.8
0910	Hatfield township (Montgomery)	15 357	13 411	14.5	14 116	439	26	711	65	207	6 087	12 353	25.8
0910	Horsham township (Montgomery)	21 896	15 959	37.2	20 630	677	30	507	52	247	8 599	13 663	44.9
0910	Limerick township (Montgomery)	6 691	NA	NA	6 606	32	16	28	9	52	2 520	10 122	58.5
0911	Lower Frederick twnshp (Montgomery)	3 396	NA	NA	3 369	14	3	4	6	28	1 268	NA	20.7
0911	Lower Gwynedd township (Montgomery)	9 958	NA	NA	8 805	831	9	296	17	81	3 820	22 813	24.2
0911	Lower Merion township (Montgomery)	58 003	59 651	-2.8	53 988	2 603	47	1 255	110	698	23 868	26 247	61.4
0911	Lower Moreland township (Montgomery	11 768	12 511	-5.9	11 351	36	2	376	3	79	4 243	19 281	18.8
0911	Lower Pottsgrove twnshp (Montgomery	8 808	NA	NA	8 350	305	11	104	38	98	3 175	11 529	20.4
0911	Lower Providence twnshp (Montgomery	19 351	18 937	2.2	17 954	985	13	347	52	244	6 826	12 326	39.7
0911	Lower Salford township (Montgomery)	10 735	NA	NA	10 377	182	4	123	49	109	3 832	13 462	37.4
0911	Marlborough township (Montgomery)	3 116	NA	NA	3 086	15	3	10	2	18	1 140	11 308	32.5
0911	Montgomery township (Montgomery)	12 179	NA	NA	11 310	198	20	620	31	106	4 825	15 115	27.6
0911	New Hanover township (Montgomery)	5 956	NA	NA	5 891	8	4	49	4	17	2 076	11 156	56.0
0911	Perkiomen township (Montgomery)	3 200	NA	NA	3 140	27	3	20	10	21	1 240	11 281	12.6
0911	Plymouth township (Montgomery)	15 958	17 168	-7.0	14 871	535	17	520	15	121	6 392	14 104	21.8
0912	Skippack township (Montgomery)	8 790	NA	NA	5 604	2 844	53	34	255	700	1 784	9 086	35.8
0912	Springfield township (Montgomery)	19 612	20 344	-3.6	18 556	744	10	273	29	157	7 194	16 548	17.6
0912	Towamencin township (Montgomery)	14 167	11 112	27.5	13 226	351	6	550	34	136	5 389	13 502	25.1
0912	Upper Dublin township (Montgomery)	24 028	22 348	7.5	21 827	1 115	19	1 049	18	176	8 403	17 820	34.2
0912	Upper Gwynedd township (Montgomery)	12 197	NA	NA	11 117	379	5	653	43	94	4 358	14 670	21.1
0912	Upper Hanover township (Montgomery)	4 604	NA	NA	4 562	24	2	12	4	19	1 594	12 303	52.4
0912	Upper Merion township (Montgomery)	25 722	26 138	-1.6	23 678	963	62	937	82	385	11 202	16 969	43.6
0912	Upper Moreland township (Montgomery	25 313	25 874	-2.2	24 400	554	24	276	59	227	10 362	13 684	20.6
0912	Upper Pottsgrove twnshp (Montgomery	3 315	NA	NA	3 216	71	0	18	10	10	1 196	11 870	13.0
0912	Upper Providence twnshp (Montgomery	9 682	NA	NA	9 337	170	7	159	9	78	3 498	11 256	46.2
0912	Upper Salford township (Montgomery)	2 719	NA	NA	2 683	21	6	6	3	13	927	NA	23.3
0912	West Norriton township (Montgomery)	15 209	14 034	8.4	14 297	574	2	306	30	120	6 568	13 063	15.2
0912	West Pottsgrove twnshp (Montgomery)	3 829	NA	NA	3 525	257	3	28	16	43	1 500	9 050	6.1
0913	Whitemarsh township (Montgomery)	14 863	15 101	-1.6	14 278	167	16	381	21	122	5 718	18 011	37.8
0913	Whitpain township (Montgomery)	15 673	11 772	33.1	14 090	695	14	838	36	179	5 703	18 719	33.5
0913	Worcester township (Montgomery)	4 686	NA	NA	4 562	46	1	76	1	19	1 832	15 457	42.0
0930	Mahoning township (Montour)	4 134	NA	NA	4 012	42	1	74	5	31	1 299	10 269	22.3
0950	Allen township (Northampton)	2 626	NA	NA	2 612	2	0	5	7	14	943	NA	28.7
0950	Bethlehem township (Northampton)	16 425	12 094	35.8	15 879	199	5	242	100	419	5 925	11 584	37.8
0950	Bushkill township (Northampton)	5 512	NA	NA	5 475	9	1	24	3	15	1 883	10 348	65.6
0950	East Allen township (Northampton)	4 572	NA	NA	4 518	12	6	30	6	41	1 637	9 824	37.4
0950	Forks township (Northampton)	5 923	NA	NA	5 792	46	1	71	13	49	2 259	11 499	31.2
0950	Hanover township (Northampton)	7 176	NA	NA	6 924	44	3	186	19	115	2 727	15 004	17.5
0950	Lehigh township (Northampton)	9 296	NA	NA	9 233	20	6	24	13	62	3 398	9 830	76.9
0950	Lower Mount Bethel twnshp (Northamp	3 187	NA	NA	3 167	3	5	6	6	22	1 213	9 399	62.6
0950	Lower Nazareth twnshp (Northampton)	4 483	NA	NA	4 414	28	7	29	5	22	1 491	10 836	34.7
0950	Lower Saucon township (Northampton)	8 448	NA	NA	8 244	39	7	102	56	199	3 169	12 339	62.6
0951	Moore township (Northampton)	8 418	NA	NA	8 365	13	3	30	7	36	3 124	10 284	96.9
0951	Palmer township (Northampton)	14 965	13 926	7.5	14 643	127	10	146	39	135	5 647	13 637	27.8
0951	Plainfield township (Northampton)	5 444	NA	NA	5 421	6	4	9	4	23	2 051	9 160	64.1
0951	Upper Mount Bethel twnshp (Northamp	5 476	NA	NA	5 433	6	9	24	4	29	2 254	10 571	112.7
0951	Upper Nazareth twnshp (Northampton)	3 413	NA	NA	3 374	17	2	16	4	24	1 036	8 767	19.0
0951	Washington township (Northampton)	3 759	NA	NA	3 737	7	1	5	9	32	1 478	10 434	46.9
0951	Williams township (Northampton)	3 982	NA	NA	3 934	26	3	13	6	26	1 504	10 581	47.7
0970	Coal township (Northumberland)	9 922	10 984	-9.7	9 900	2	1	17	2	14	4 433	7 239	68.6
0970	Delaware township (Northumberland)	4 018	NA	NA	3 999	4	9	4	2	13	1 528	7 911	78.9
0970	Mount Carmel township (Northumberla	2 679	NA	NA	2 673	2	0	2	2	9	1 189	7 043	56.5
0970	Point township (Northumberland)	3 466	NA	NA	3 460	0	3	0	3	11	1 373	8 265	65.2
0971	Ralpho township (Northumberland)	3 625	NA	NA	3 607	1	1	16	0	17	1 448	9 532	47.8
0971	Upper Augusta township (Northumberl	2 681	NA	NA	2 601	38	2	10	30	47	1 041	9 788	52.5
0971	West Chillisquaque twnshp (Northum	3 119	NA	NA	3 082	22	2	10	3	11	1 259	7 932	33.5
0990	Carroll township (Perry)	4 597	NA	NA	4 578	5	10	4	0	33	1 660	8 903	89.1
0991	Penn township (Perry)	3 283	NA	NA	3 263	2	5	5	8	20	1 260	9 985	55.5
0991	Wheatfield township (Perry)	3 097	NA	NA	3 082	1	3	6	5	19	1 153	NA	54.2
1030	Delaware township (Pike)	3 527	NA	NA	3 446	32	3	4	42	114	2 995	NA	114.4
1030	Dingman township (Pike)	4 591	NA	NA	4 515	36	8	15	17	90	4 181	NA	150.8
1030	Lackawaxen township (Pike)	2 832	NA	NA	2 762	46	8	3	13	71	3 248	NA	203.5
1030	Lehman township (Pike)	3 055	NA	NA	2 883	97	5	49	21	171	3 975	NA	126.5

1. Codes shown are 2-digit FIPS codes for states; 4-digit census place codes for places; and 3-digit FIPS county codes followed by 3-digit census MCD codes for minor civil divisions (MCDs). MCD names are followed by county names in parentheses. 2. Hispanic persons may be of any race. 3. Dry land or land partially or temporarily covered by water.

State/ Place/ MCD[1] code	Place	Population 1990	Places of 10,000 or more: 1980	Places of 10,000 or more: Percent change, 1980–1990	Race: White	Race: Black	Race: Am. Indian, Eskimo Aleut	Race: Asian & Pacific Islander	Race: Other race	Hispanic[2]	Total housing units, 1990	Per capita income, 1985 (Dollars)	Land area,[3] 1990 (Sq. Km.)
		1	2	3	4	5	6	7	8	9	10	11	12
	PENNSYLVANIA—Con.												
1070	Butler township (Schuylkill)	4 099	NA	NA	4 090	0	0	9	0	2	1 639	8 365	69.6
1071	Hegins township (Schuylkill)	3 561	NA	NA	3 544	0	2	14	1	4	1 464	8 496	82.9
1071	North Manheim township (Schuylkill)	3 404	NA	NA	3 358	10	5	31	0	15	1 223	9 110	53.0
1072	Pine Grove township (Schuylkill)	3 699	NA	NA	3 675	0	2	21	1	12	1 473	7 681	98.9
1072	Porter township (Schuylkill)	2 560	NA	NA	2 557	0	1	1	1	4	1 086	7 737	46.4
1072	Rush township (Schuylkill)	3 472	NA	NA	3 435	8	0	22	7	28	1 460	9 516	59.0
1073	Wayne township (Schuylkill)	3 929	NA	NA	3 896	10	2	15	6	22	1 566	11 259	90.7
1073	West Brunswick township (Schuylkill	3 227	NA	NA	3 176	2	0	48	1	14	1 265	10 003	78.4
1073	West Mahanoy township (Schuylkill)	4 539	NA	NA	4 042	445	11	10	31	133	1 553	7 910	26.9
1073	West Penn township (Schuylkill)	3 693	NA	NA	3 663	7	0	14	9	29	1 493	8 690	150.7
1090	Monroe township (Snyder)	3 881	NA	NA	3 844	1	2	33	1	7	1 605	10 964	40.5
1090	Penn township (Snyder)	3 208	NA	NA	3 106	84	3	9	6	13	962	6 911	46.3
1110	Conemaugh township (Somerset)	7 737	NA	NA	7 715	3	2	12	5	29	3 070	7 877	107.0
1110	Jenner township (Somerset)	4 147	NA	NA	4 141	0	2	2	2	14	1 720	7 441	167.3
1111	Paint township (Somerset)	3 491	NA	NA	3 488	0	0	1	2	10	1 362	7 670	82.8
1111	Shade township (Somerset)	3 177	NA	NA	3 171	0	0	5	1	8	1 355	6 217	174.1
1111	Somerset township (Somerset)	8 732	NA	NA	8 659	30	3	36	4	29	3 296	7 473	165.6
1170	Charleston township (Tioga)	2 957	NA	NA	2 947	2	2	3	3	17	1 183	7 534	136.1
1170	Delmar township (Tioga)	3 048	NA	NA	3 022	7	9	10	0	8	1 329	7 702	208.3
1190	Buffalo township (Union)	2 877	NA	NA	2 856	10	4	7	0	5	1 011	7 494	79.3
1190	East Buffalo township (Union)	5 245	NA	NA	5 139	27	3	62	14	46	1 718	11 745	40.5
1190	Kelly township (Union)	4 561	NA	NA	3 638	776	35	42	70	448	1 130	6 783	44.4
1190	White Deer township (Union)	3 958	NA	NA	3 938	9	5	4	2	13	1 479	8 372	120.4
1210	Cornplanter township (Venango)	2 968	NA	NA	2 935	0	1	30	2	5	1 204	9 350	96.6
1210	Cranberry township (Venango)	7 256	NA	NA	7 224	15	8	6	3	16	2 975	8 976	182.3
1230	Conewango township (Warren)	4 475	NA	NA	4 409	31	7	24	4	12	1 713	9 616	77.6
1230	Pine Grove township (Warren)	2 756	NA	NA	2 732	2	4	18	0	4	1 101	8 919	102.8
1230	Pleasant township (Warren)	2 663	NA	NA	2 652	2	1	8	0	4	1 297	11 374	88.9
1250	Amwell township (Washington)	4 176	NA	NA	4 151	13	2	7	3	10	1 529	8 842	116.1
1250	Canton township (Washington)	9 256	10 311	-10.2	8 909	306	15	14	12	42	3 626	8 285	38.6
1250	Carroll township (Washington)	6 210	NA	NA	6 134	57	1	16	2	51	2 434	9 651	35.0
1250	Cecil township (Washington)	8 948	NA	NA	8 704	223	5	10	6	32	3 228	9 036	68.2
1250	Chartiers township (Washington)	7 603	NA	NA	7 296	282	7	8	10	5	2 964	9 989	63.5
1251	East Bethlehem township (Washington	2 799	NA	NA	2 703	90	6	0	0	3	1 271	7 573	13.2
1251	Fallowfield township (Washington)	4 972	NA	NA	4 816	141	0	11	4	17	1 927	9 420	55.1
1251	Hanover township (Washington)	2 883	NA	NA	2 855	13	3	8	4	21	1 122	9 182	123.2
1252	Mount Pleasant township (Washington	3 555	NA	NA	3 425	125	3	2	0	5	1 350	9 256	92.3
1252	North Franklin township (Washington	4 997	NA	NA	4 845	129	3	10	10	20	1 787	10 103	18.9
1252	North Strabane township (Washington	8 157	NA	NA	7 931	183	0	29	14	33	3 186	10 727	70.7
1252	Peters township (Washington)	14 467	13 104	10.4	14 279	59	4	114	11	71	5 105	15 905	50.7
1252	Smith township (Washington)	4 844	NA	NA	4 722	96	13	10	3	118	2 014	7 712	89.1
1252	Somerset township (Washington)	2 947	NA	NA	2 923	18	2	4	0	3	1 135	9 005	83.0
1252	South Franklin township (Washington	3 665	NA	NA	3 648	10	1	3	3	21	1 283	8 052	53.3
1252	South Strabane township (Washington	7 676	NA	NA	7 526	109	2	29	10	23	3 157	11 413	59.9
1252	Union township (Washington)	6 322	NA	NA	6 203	89	3	22	5	50	2 492	9 338	39.8
1270	Damascus township (Wayne)	3 081	NA	NA	3 067	4	0	8	2	22	1 956	7 581	204.6
1270	Lake township (Wayne)	3 287	NA	NA	3 254	14	3	7	9	45	3 218	NA	73.4
1271	Salem township (Wayne)	2 933	NA	NA	2 916	5	4	6	2	16	2 372	8 066	79.0
1271	Texas township (Wayne)	2 570	NA	NA	2 550	4	3	12	1	7	1 041	NA	37.5
1290	Allegheny township (Westmoreland)	7 895	NA	NA	7 803	67	5	15	5	21	2 953	9 477	79.9
1290	Derry township (Westmoreland)	15 446	16 141	-4.3	15 184	189	19	36	18	39	6 039	8 333	244.9
1290	East Huntingdon township (Westmorel	7 708	NA	NA	7 636	45	3	19	5	20	3 108	8 364	85.1
1290	Hempfield township (Westmoreland)	42 609	43 371	-1.8	41 547	747	30	247	38	158	16 100	10 437	198.4
1291	Ligonier township (Westmoreland)	6 979	NA	NA	6 952	5	2	19	1	11	3 411	12 638	237.9
1291	Mount Pleasant township (Westmoreld	11 341	11 851	-4.3	11 296	23	10	10	2	24	4 508	8 412	144.2
1291	North Huntingdon township (Westmore	28 158	31 517	-10.7	28 004	67	8	61	18	78	10 473	10 222	71.0
1292	Penn township (Westmoreland)	15 945	16 153	-1.3	15 794	73	7	63	8	59	5 640	10 234	78.6
1292	Rostraver township (Westmoreland)	11 224	11 430	-1.8	10 921	264	3	21	15	55	4 622	9 050	83.3
1292	Salem township (Westmoreland)	7 282	NA	NA	7 131	120	7	12	12	19	3 071	9 303	120.5
1292	Sewickley township (Westmoreland)	6 642	NA	NA	6 550	74	4	11	3	21	2 680	9 295	68.9
1292	South Huntingdon township (Westmore	6 352	NA	NA	6 277	60	6	9	0	28	2 557	8 463	117.2
1292	Unity township (Westmoreland)	20 109	19 964	0.7	19 935	49	8	108	9	65	7 586	10 175	173.6
1292	Washington township (Westmoreland)	7 725	NA	NA	7 641	59	7	16	2	30	2 867	10 117	82.1
1311	Tunkhannock township (Wyoming)	4 371	NA	NA	4 330	20	6	11	4	22	1 818	9 521	80.6
1330	Carroll township (York)	3 287	NA	NA	3 240	20	0	25	2	5	1 210	11 548	38.9
1330	Chanceford township (York)	5 026	NA	NA	4 983	16	7	12	8	17	1 806	9 783	125.7
1330	Codorus township (York)	3 653	NA	NA	3 636	5	0	9	3	18	1 316	10 803	86.7
1330	Conewago township (York)	4 997	NA	NA	4 896	75	5	11	10	51	1 890	9 013	63.3
1330	Dover township (York)	15 668	12 589	24.5	15 479	101	20	56	12	54	5 906	9 897	108.5
1330	East Manchester township (York)	3 714	NA	NA	3 695	4	11	2	2	17	1 449	10 314	43.1
1330	Fairview township (York)	13 258	11 941	11.0	12 831	205	19	150	53	148	5 024	11 940	92.2
1330	Franklin township (York)	3 852	NA	NA	3 828	7	6	10	1	20	1 447	10 416	49.6
1331	Heidelberg township (York)	2 622	NA	NA	2 599	10	0	12	1	8	942	NA	37.4

1. Codes shown are 2-digit FIPS codes for states; 4-digit census place codes for places; and 3-digit FIPS county codes followed by 3-digit census MCD codes for minor civil divisions (MCDs). MCD names are followed by county names in parentheses. 2. Hispanic persons may be of any race. 3. Dry land or land partially or temporarily covered by water.

State/ Place/ MCD[1] code	Place	Population: 1990	Population: Places of 10,000 or more: 1980	Population: Places of 10,000 or more: Percent change, 1980–1990	Population characteristics, 1990: Race: White	Race: Black	Race: Am. Indian, Eskimo Aleut	Race: Asian & Pacific Islander	Race: Other race	Hispanic[2]	Total housing units, 1990	Per capita income, 1985 (Dollars)	Land area,[3] 1990 (Sq. Km.)
		1	2	3	4	5	6	7	8	9	10	11	12
	PENNSYLVANIA—Con.												
1331	Hellam township (York)	5 123	NA	NA	5 064	25	7	10	17	35	2 101	11 812	71.6
1331	Hopewell township (York)	3 177	NA	NA	3 109	38	4	22	4	18	1 169	10 893	69.7
1331	Jackson township (York)	6 244	NA	NA	6 169	22	6	34	13	43	2 177	10 009	58.0
1331	Lower Windsor township (York)	7 051	NA	NA	7 008	12	8	8	15	38	2 624	8 986	65.1
1331	Manchester township (York)	7 517	NA	NA	7 342	92	6	58	19	46	2 988	11 961	41.1
1331	Manheim township (York)	2 692	NA	NA	2 671	2	11	8	0	7	897	NA	55.8
1331	Newberry township (York)	12 003	10 038	19.6	11 860	45	21	50	27	94	4 546	10 134	78.8
1332	North Codorus township (York)	7 565	NA	NA	7 518	12	3	19	13	37	2 688	10 388	83.7
1332	Paradise township (York)	3 180	NA	NA	3 153	10	1	6	10	29	1 123	10 194	52.5
1332	Peach Bottom township (York)	3 444	NA	NA	3 352	68	12	12	0	10	1 606	9 103	75.8
1332	Penn township (York)	11 658	NA	NA	11 542	21	13	65	17	74	4 540	10 207	33.0
1332	Shrewsbury township (York)	5 898	NA	NA	5 821	15	5	40	17	49	2 053	10 829	75.7
1332	Springettsbury township (York)	21 564	19 687	9.5	20 731	436	19	245	133	285	8 581	13 354	43.4
1332	Springfield township (York)	3 918	NA	NA	3 885	3	1	18	11	26	1 395	10 900	67.9
1332	Spring Garden township (York)	11 207	11 127	0.7	10 992	114	5	63	33	85	4 225	15 670	17.2
1332	Warrington township (York)	4 275	NA	NA	4 237	16	6	13	3	19	1 587	10 322	91.6
1333	West Manchester township (York)	14 369	12 728	12.9	14 015	176	16	130	32	82	6 022	11 554	52.0
1333	West Manheim township (York)	4 590	NA	NA	4 562	11	5	11	1	17	1 549	9 705	50.7
1333	Windsor township (York)	9 424	NA	NA	9 341	28	11	37	7	35	3 562	10 119	70.4
1333	York township (York)	19 231	16 893	13.8	18 864	135	9	203	20	76	8 066	13 176	66.0
44	RHODE ISLAND	1 003 464	947 154	5.9	917 375	38 861	4 071	18 325	24 832	45 752	414 572	10 892	2 706.5
0020	Barrington CDP	15 849	16 174	-2.0	15 611	52	6	152	28	125	5 822	NA	21.8
0040	Bristol CDP	21 625	20 128	7.4	21 362	99	22	100	42	410	7 959	NA	26.2
0060	Central Falls	17 637	16 995	3.8	13 656	744	47	136	3 054	5 119	7 337	7 508	3.1
0090	Cranston	76 060	71 992	5.7	72 318	1 837	139	1 348	418	1 532	30 516	11 673	74.0
0095	Cumberland Hill CDP	6 379	NA	NA	6 310	17	1	41	10	39	2 649	NA	8.4
0120	East Providence	50 380	50 980	-1.2	46 407	2 193	241	294	1 245	845	20 808	10 804	34.7
0160	Greenville CDP	8 303	NA	NA	8 196	44	5	54	4	37	3 045	NA	13.5
0250	Kingston CDP	6 504	NA	NA	6 034	149	40	245	36	141	609	NA	4.1
0277	Melville CDP	4 426	NA	NA	3 856	358	29	94	89	195	954	NA	5.7
0290	Narragansett Pier CDP	3 721	NA	NA	3 613	39	49	19	1	46	2 007	NA	9.4
0310	Newport	28 227	29 258	-3.5	25 023	2 281	210	399	314	789	13 094	11 867	20.6
0320	Newport East CDP	11 080	10 909	1.6	10 370	400	30	208	72	203	4 793	NA	14.7
0350	North Providence CDP	32 090	29 188	9.9	31 152	334	33	378	193	571	14 134	NA	14.7
0370	Pascoag CDP	5 011	NA	NA	4 985	0	9	5	12	30	1 889	NA	12.7
0380	Pawtucket	72 644	71 204	2.0	64 836	2 608	203	472	4 525	5 211	31 615	9 511	22.6
0400	Providence	160 728	156 804	2.5	112 404	23 828	1 495	9 547	13 454	24 982	66 794	9 501	47.8
0468	Tiverton CDP	7 259	NA	NA	7 204	17	13	21	4	82	2 919	NA	10.8
0475	Valley Falls CDP	11 175	10 892	2.6	11 053	21	4	32	65	275	4 293	NA	9.2
0480	Wakefield-Peacedale CDP	7 134	NA	NA	6 631	139	258	91	15	85	2 869	NA	12.6
0500	Warwick	85 427	87 123	-1.9	83 695	673	183	713	163	845	35 141	12 090	92.0
0505	Westerly CDP	16 477	14 102	16.8	16 085	118	47	205	22	159	7 019	NA	37.6
0520	West Warwick CDP	29 268	27 026	8.3	28 579	235	53	281	120	542	12 488	NA	20.5
0560	Woonsocket	43 877	45 914	-4.4	40 939	1 158	77	1 309	394	1 156	18 739	8 837	20.0
0010	Barrington town (Bristol)	15 849	16 174	-2.0	15 611	52	6	152	28	125	5 822	16 808	21.8
0010	Bristol town (Bristol)	21 625	20 128	7.4	21 362	99	22	100	42	410	7 959	9 750	26.2
0010	Warren town (Bristol)	11 385	10 640	7.0	11 277	35	11	45	17	137	4 786	10 908	15.9
0030	Coventry town (Kent)	31 083	27 065	14.8	30 771	82	32	115	83	260	11 788	10 697	154.2
0030	East Greenwich town (Kent)	11 865	10 211	16.2	11 628	49	22	159	7	77	4 663	16 155	42.7
0030	West Greenwich town (Kent)	3 492	NA	NA	3 449	11	6	21	5	13	1 370	10 195	131.1
0030	West Warwick town (Kent)	29 268	27 026	8.3	28 579	235	53	281	120	542	12 488	10 118	20.5
0050	Jamestown town (Newport)	4 999	NA	NA	4 938	32	12	10	7	45	2 517	13 259	25.1
0050	Little Compton town (Newport)	3 339	NA	NA	3 311	1	6	18	3	11	1 850	12 785	54.1
0050	Middletown town (Newport)	19 460	17 171	13.3	17 904	895	63	410	188	531	7 104	11 700	33.6
0050	Portsmouth town (Newport)	16 857	14 302	17.9	16 456	151	41	178	31	175	7 235	12 563	60.1
0050	Tiverton town (Newport)	14 312	13 526	5.8	14 206	36	20	46	4	161	5 675	10 971	76.0
0070	Burrillville town (Providence)	16 230	13 164	23.3	16 152	17	21	21	19	71	5 751	9 421	143.9
0070	Cumberland town (Providence)	29 038	27 069	7.3	28 730	71	11	116	110	440	11 217	12 198	69.4
0070	Foster town (Providence)	4 316	NA	NA	4 267	19	12	13	5	16	1 525	11 786	132.5
0070	Glocester town (Providence)	9 227	NA	NA	9 162	33	13	16	3	46	3 460	9 914	142.0
0070	Johnston town (Providence)	26 542	24 907	6.6	26 193	151	23	150	25	175	10 384	10 850	61.3
0070	Lincoln town (Providence)	18 045	16 949	6.5	17 735	41	14	189	66	183	7 281	13 082	47.2
0070	North Providence town (Providence)	32 090	29 188	9.9	31 152	334	33	378	193	571	14 134	11 799	14.7
0070	North Smithfield town (Providence)	10 497	NA	NA	10 397	17	5	69	9	56	3 835	11 728	62.3
0070	Scituate town (Providence)	9 796	NA	NA	9 719	15	2	47	13	53	3 520	11 771	126.1
0070	Smithfield town (Providence)	19 163	16 886	13.5	18 886	105	24	128	20	113	6 308	11 155	68.9
0090	Charlestown town (Washington)	6 478	NA	NA	6 284	43	103	42	6	37	4 256	10 973	95.4
0090	Exeter town (Washington)	5 461	NA	NA	5 362	41	36	17	5	30	1 919	10 526	149.5
0090	Hopkinton town (Washington)	6 873	NA	NA	6 775	19	61	17	1	45	2 662	10 024	111.3
0090	Narragansett town (Washington)	14 985	12 088	24.0	14 558	123	141	132	31	155	8 206	12 038	36.6
0090	North Kingstown town (Washington)	23 786	21 937	8.4	23 045	310	106	236	89	253	9 348	12 347	113.2
0090	Richmond town (Washington)	5 351	NA	NA	5 223	23	46	34	25	48	1 874	9 855	105.0

1. Codes shown are 2-digit FIPS codes for states; 4-digit census place codes for places; and 3-digit FIPS county codes followed by 3-digit census MCD codes for minor civil divisions (MCDs). MCD names are followed by county names in parentheses. 2. Hispanic persons may be of any race. 3. Dry land or land partially or temporarily covered by water.

State/ Place/ MCD[1] code	Place	Population: 1990	Places of 10,000 or more: 1980	Percent change, 1980–1990	Race: White	Black	Am. Indian, Eskimo Aleut	Asian & Pacific Islander	Other race	Hispanic[2]	Total housing units, 1990	Per capita income, 1985 (Dollars)	Land area,[3] 1990 (Sq. Km.)
		1	2	3	4	5	6	7	8	9	10	11	12
	RHODE ISLAND—Con.												
0090	South Kingstown town (Washington)	24 631	20 414	20.7	23 000	362	451	735	83	306	9 806	10 059	147.9
0090	Westerly town (Washington)	21 605	18 580	16.3	21 145	130	79	225	26	180	10 521	11 545	77.9
45	SOUTH CAROLINA	3 486 703	3 120 737	11.7	2 406 974	1 039 884	8 246	22 382	9 217	30 551	1 424 155	8 890	77 987.8
0005	Abbeville	5 778	NA	NA	3 142	2 624	1	10	1	15	2 471	8 164	14.9
0010	Aiken	19 872	14 978	32.7	13 519	6 132	21	128	72	170	8 543	11 471	35.2
0030	Allendale town	4 410	NA	NA	1 147	3 253	2	0	8	55	1 698	6 167	8.6
0035	Anderson	26 184	27 313	-4.1	17 043	8 971	42	80	48	139	11 503	9 561	32.1
0045	Andrews town	3 050	NA	NA	1 201	1 837	2	3	7	17	1 134	7 389	5.6
0060	Arial CDP	2 604	NA	NA	2 553	46	4	1	0	10	1 041	NA	12.9
0080	Bamberg town	3 843	NA	NA	1 823	1 991	12	11	6	12	1 443	7 027	9.1
0085	Barnwell	5 255	NA	NA	2 989	2 240	12	7	7	29	2 094	7 982	19.8
0090	Batesburg town	4 082	NA	NA	2 067	2 002	9	1	3	13	1 627	7 535	11.4
0100	Beaufort	9 576	NA	NA	6 669	2 669	42	125	71	199	4 149	10 802	22.1
0105	Belton	4 646	NA	NA	3 922	720	0	3	1	9	2 079	8 576	9.8
0106	Belvedere CDP	6 133	NA	NA	4 911	1 149	18	52	3	41	2 393	NA	10.2
0110	Bennettsville	9 345	NA	NA	3 896	5 356	63	14	16	21	3 746	7 227	13.8
0117	Berea CDP	13 535	13 164	2.8	11 827	1 533	22	52	101	371	5 629	NA	19.8
0130	Bishopville town	3 560	NA	NA	1 429	2 112	1	11	7	26	1 428	7 964	5.8
0140	Blackville town	2 688	NA	NA	724	1 962	1	0	1	6	1 016	5 832	23.7
0158	Boiling Springs CDP	3 522	NA	NA	3 318	174	3	20	7	13	1 334	NA	17.6
0176	Brookdale CDP	5 339	NA	NA	44	5 276	4	15	0	6	2 134	NA	9.8
0187	Burton CDP	6 917	NA	NA	3 955	2 743	30	97	92	214	2 702	NA	30.0
0200	Camden	6 696	NA	NA	3 792	2 889	2	7	6	23	3 041	9 330	17.2
0220	Cayce	11 163	11 701	-4.6	8 863	2 170	16	78	36	114	4 721	10 458	22.9
0222	Centerville CDP	4 866	NA	NA	4 607	226	8	12	13	29	1 833	NA	15.2
0245	Charleston	80 414	69 510	15.7	46 023	33 439	92	685	175	649	34 322	10 600	111.9
0250	Cheraw town	5 505	NA	NA	2 736	2 740	20	4	5	12	2 309	8 750	10.9
0253	Cherryvale CDP	3 061	NA	NA	1 944	1 008	9	65	35	72	1 276	NA	4.5
0260	Chester	7 158	NA	NA	2 851	4 288	5	14	0	14	2 830	7 630	8.2
0272	Clearwater CDP	4 731	NA	NA	4 183	523	14	5	6	51	1 905	NA	13.1
0275	Clemson	11 096	NA	NA	9 216	1 356	25	481	18	113	4 850	13 054	18.5
0285	Clinton	7 987	NA	NA	5 059	2 886	15	17	10	21	2 875	7 675	23.2
0295	Clover town	3 422	NA	NA	2 707	676	9	26	4	32	1 414	6 947	5.1
0305	Columbia	98 052	101 208	-3.1	52 625	42 837	341	1 399	850	1 944	36 928	8 986	303.4
0315	Conway	9 819	10 240	-4.1	5 647	4 125	6	24	17	54	3 898	8 473	14.9
0350	Darlington	7 311	NA	NA	3 304	3 971	16	14	6	31	3 040	7 998	10.6
0355	Denmark	3 762	NA	NA	622	3 139	0	0	1	7	1 535	5 799	7.9
0357	Dentsville CDP	11 839	13 579	-12.8	6 170	5 403	24	195	47	164	4 872	NA	19.1
0360	Dillon	6 829	NA	NA	4 327	2 410	48	42	2	19	2 630	7 700	11.1
0387	Dunean CDP	4 637	NA	NA	3 730	874	9	8	16	38	2 105	NA	4.3
0390	Easley	15 195	14 264	6.5	13 167	1 898	55	45	30	127	6 356	9 265	25.7
0395	East Gaffney CDP	3 278	NA	NA	2 812	449	4	10	3	17	1 333	NA	8.4
0415	Edgefield town	2 563	NA	NA	1 277	1 284	0	2	0	5	1 100	6 580	8.0
0416	Edisto CDP	2 815	NA	NA	1 085	1 720	3	7	0	10	1 105	NA	14.5
0465	Florence	29 813	30 104	-1.0	15 587	14 024	43	135	24	171	11 790	9 306	38.2
0475	Forest Acres	7 197	NA	NA	6 487	604	11	61	34	91	3 664	17 346	8.6
0478	Forestbrook CDP	2 502	NA	NA	2 261	162	10	66	3	31	1 072	NA	8.6
0490	Fort Mill town	4 930	NA	NA	4 100	804	11	7	8	37	1 989	9 601	8.1
0495	Fountain Inn town	4 388	NA	NA	2 937	1 431	1	7	12	27	1 687	8 035	12.8
0505	Gaffney	13 145	13 453	-2.3	7 854	5 135	15	127	14	40	5 450	9 159	19.1
0506	Gantt CDP	13 891	NA	NA	5 629	8 201	15	39	7	64	5 356	NA	23.1
0507	Garden City CDP	6 305	NA	NA	6 232	39	12	19	3	38	6 821	NA	13.8
0513	Georgetown	9 517	10 144	-6.2	4 307	5 155	20	24	11	45	3 866	7 902	16.9
0530	Gloverville CDP	2 753	NA	NA	2 373	359	8	4	9	24	1 190	NA	8.6
0536	Goose Creek	24 692	17 811	38.6	20 502	3 141	116	651	282	1 020	7 682	7 180	81.1
0565	Greenville	58 282	58 242	0.1	37 077	20 493	82	495	135	606	26 453	10 976	65.0
0570	Greenwood	20 807	21 613	-3.7	11 675	8 977	24	85	46	108	8 806	7 499	32.7
0575	Greer	10 322	10 525	-1.9	7 524	2 738	24	15	21	80	4 507	8 614	12.9
0580	Hampton town	2 997	NA	NA	1 910	1 081	0	5	1	11	1 255	8 869	11.4
0582	Hanahan	13 176	13 224	-0.4	11 574	1 228	50	196	128	317	5 382	12 016	24.9
0595	Hartsville	8 372	NA	NA	4 747	3 592	7	23	3	22	3 380	8 925	10.6
0619	Hilton Head Island town	23 694	11 344	108.9	21 208	2 259	34	111	82	337	21 509	19 278	108.9
0633	Homeland Park CDP	6 569	NA	NA	5 902	639	6	12	10	39	2 798	NA	12.4
0635	Honea Path town	3 841	NA	NA	3 018	810	6	5	2	20	1 701	8 746	8.6
0655	Irmo town	11 280	NA	NA	9 849	1 233	18	161	19	75	3 824	12 600	10.2
0665	Isle of Palms	3 680	NA	NA	3 669	0	1	5	5	36	3 063	14 433	11.6
0700	Johnston town	2 688	NA	NA	1 054	1 628	3	3	0	1	1 048	5 844	6.1
0707	Judson CDP	2 859	NA	NA	1 545	1 297	5	6	6	19	1 256	NA	2.1
0715	Kingstree town	3 858	NA	NA	1 582	2 264	3	7	2	14	1 578	7 394	8.1
0724	Ladson CDP	13 540	13 246	2.2	11 428	1 695	67	284	66	257	4 689	NA	22.6
0730	Lake City	7 153	NA	NA	2 378	4 756	4	15	0	26	2 720	7 006	11.4

1. Codes shown are 2-digit FIPS codes for states; 4-digit census place codes for places; and 3-digit FIPS county codes followed by 3-digit census MCD codes for minor civil divisions (MCDs). MCD names are followed by county names in parentheses. 2. Hispanic persons may be of any race. 3. Dry land or land partially or temporarily covered by water.

State/ Place/ MCD[1] code	Place	Population: 1990	Places of 10,000 or more: 1980	Places of 10,000 or more: Percent change, 1980–1990	Population characteristics, 1990: Race: White	Race: Black	Race: Am. Indian, Eskimo Aleut	Race: Asian & Pacific Islander	Race: Other race	Hispanic[2]	Total housing units, 1990	Per capita income, 1985 (Dollars)	Land area,[3] 1990 (Sq. Km.)
		1	2	3	4	5	6	7	8	9	10	11	12
	SOUTH CAROLINA—Con.												
0737	Lake Wylie CDP	2 599	NA	NA	2 562	14	5	13	5	19	1 308	NA	9.0
0745	Lancaster	8 914	NA	NA	4 660	4 218	11	15	10	28	3 703	8 851	14.0
0773	Laurel Bay CDP	4 972	NA	NA	3 329	1 314	28	155	146	298	1 564	NA	9.7
0775	Laurens	9 694	10 514	-7.8	5 607	4 064	4	14	5	29	4 017	8 200	26.5
0785	Lexington town	3 289	NA	NA	3 030	230	11	15	3	5	1 388	NA	9.6
0790	Liberty town	3 228	NA	NA	2 815	404	5	2	2	16	1 357	8 561	10.6
0802	Little River CDP	3 470	NA	NA	3 120	329	10	5	6	17	3 020	NA	20.0
0838	Lugoff CDP	3 211	NA	NA	2 656	528	17	8	2	24	1 252	NA	19.2
0870	McColl town	2 685	NA	NA	2 003	379	301	0	2	3	1 038	5 538	2.8
0890	Manning	4 428	NA	NA	1 925	2 480	3	11	9	25	1 699	8 039	6.2
0895	Marion	7 658	NA	NA	3 050	4 556	8	41	3	7	2 982	7 244	9.8
0900	Mauldin	11 587	NA	NA	9 772	1 676	18	108	13	127	4 564	11 012	17.9
0920	Moncks Corner town	5 607	NA	NA	3 793	1 772	10	9	23	42	2 170	8 881	10.8
0935	Mount Pleasant town	30 108	13 838	117.6	27 075	2 766	39	190	38	279	12 443	13 675	56.4
0940	Mullins	5 910	NA	NA	2 518	3 334	23	26	9	20	2 444	7 554	7.9
0943	Murrells Inlet CDP	3 334	NA	NA	2 904	419	4	7	0	14	1 865	NA	14.1
0945	Myrtle Beach	24 848	18 446	34.7	20 801	3 499	78	370	100	382	13 327	11 067	40.1
0955	Newberry town	10 542	NA	NA	6 068	4 373	24	59	18	73	4 243	8 554	16.1
0960	New Ellenton town	2 515	NA	NA	1 660	840	5	0	10	25	1 054	10 535	10.9
0985	North Augusta	15 351	13 593	12.9	12 763	2 393	16	152	27	103	6 810	11 593	42.4
0987	North Charleston	70 218	62 534	12.3	44 003	24 117	345	1 142	611	1 744	26 608	8 850	129.6
0990	North Hartsville CDP	2 906	NA	NA	2 290	604	6	6	0	9	1 176	NA	12.6
0991	Northlake CDP	3 162	NA	NA	2 989	151	0	21	1	8	1 406	NA	11.2
0992	North Myrtle Beach	8 636	NA	NA	8 457	132	22	22	3	57	13 336	12 290	24.2
1001	Oak Grove CDP	7 173	NA	NA	6 736	345	21	54	17	55	2 773	NA	17.5
1015	Orangeburg	13 739	14 933	-8.0	5 380	8 226	11	112	10	68	4 798	8 741	19.2
1040	Pageland town	2 666	NA	NA	1 845	808	4	7	2	5	1 060	7 608	10.6
1048	Parker CDP	11 072	NA	NA	9 955	1 052	13	8	44	138	4 673	NA	17.6
1052	Parris Island CDP	7 172	NA	NA	5 024	1 666	59	108	315	556	333	NA	31.5
1090	Pendleton town	3 314	NA	NA	2 108	1 182	10	10	4	17	1 536	7 926	9.1
1100	Pickens town	3 042	NA	NA	2 424	594	6	15	3	12	1 377	8 323	6.2
1105	Piedmont CDP	4 143	NA	NA	3 932	202	2	4	3	26	1 690	NA	23.1
1135	Port Royal town	2 985	NA	NA	1 883	1 012	12	48	30	91	1 277	8 571	7.0
1147	Red Bank CDP	5 950	NA	NA	5 411	514	13	8	4	35	2 163	NA	30.8
1148	Red Hill CDP	6 112	NA	NA	5 776	255	18	51	12	64	2 619	NA	27.7
1195	Rock Hill	41 643	35 386	17.7	25 161	15 884	186	341	71	265	15 682	8 258	60.0
1208	St. Andrews CDP	25 692	20 245	26.9	16 054	9 186	56	277	119	320	11 818	NA	20.6
1235	Saluda town	2 798	NA	NA	1 516	1 279	1	2	0	6	1 139	7 990	8.4
1242	Sans Souci CDP	7 612	NA	NA	7 060	498	20	13	21	81	3 482	NA	8.7
1250	Saxon CDP	4 002	NA	NA	2 845	1 122	7	20	8	26	1 520	NA	6.1
1270	Seneca town	7 726	NA	NA	5 167	2 509	8	18	24	68	3 367	9 419	16.4
1273	Seven Oaks CDP	15 722	16 604	-5.3	13 517	1 876	28	234	67	191	6 671	NA	21.3
1283	Shell Point CDP	2 885	NA	NA	2 512	279	3	44	47	86	1 078	NA	17.8
1290	Simpsonville town	11 708	NA	NA	10 367	1 186	24	78	53	177	4 483	9 568	14.3
1312	Socastee CDP	10 426	NA	NA	9 316	774	38	262	36	145	4 179	NA	34.7
1333	Southern Shops CDP	3 378	NA	NA	2 794	549	5	14	16	40	1 311	NA	9.2
1339	South Sumter CDP	4 371	NA	NA	444	3 917	7	1	2	5	1 467	NA	7.5
1340	Spartanburg	43 467	43 838	-0.8	23 084	19 836	46	394	107	338	17 950	9 688	46.9
1350	Springdale town	3 226	NA	NA	3 023	169	6	24	4	27	1 230	11 846	7.0
1353	Springdale CDP	2 643	NA	NA	1 967	667	5	0	4	27	1 049	NA	10.9
1390	Summerville town	22 519	NA	NA	18 153	4 018	91	167	90	332	8 834	10 410	36.1
1400	Sumter	41 943	24 896	68.5	25 087	16 042	110	487	217	661	13 650	8 621	58.9
1402	Surfside Beach town	3 845	NA	NA	3 763	33	13	23	13	42	3 128	11 555	5.0
1420	Taylors CDP	19 619	15 801	24.2	17 434	1 972	24	148	41	173	7 707	NA	28.5
1422	Tega Cay	3 016	NA	NA	2 934	43	14	24	1	29	1 168	NA	6.3
1430	Travelers Rest	3 069	NA	NA	2 688	355	3	9	14	41	1 267	10 604	9.8
1455	Union	9 836	10 512	-6.4	6 004	3 806	8	10	8	45	4 158	8 426	19.3
1462	Valencia Heights CDP	4 122	NA	NA	3 199	834	7	49	33	76	2 111	NA	2.7
1463	Valley Falls CDP	3 504	NA	NA	3 277	195	2	28	2	21	1 482	NA	13.5
1477	Wade Hampton CDP	20 014	20 180	-0.8	18 740	990	18	224	42	225	8 873	NA	22.2
1485	Walhalla town	3 755	NA	NA	3 412	280	4	17	42	165	1 726	8 385	9.6
1490	Walterboro	5 492	NA	NA	3 000	2 482	2	4	4	30	2 325	7 712	12.1
1518	Welcome CDP	6 560	NA	NA	5 850	675	6	14	15	48	2 713	NA	11.8
1520	Wellford	2 511	NA	NA	1 419	1 075	4	1	12	23	985	NA	8.6
1525	West Columbia	10 588	10 409	1.7	8 568	1 900	20	77	23	64	5 101	10 033	12.6
1535	Westminster town	3 120	NA	NA	2 687	404	1	15	13	27	1 367	7 309	9.0
1558	Wilkinson Heights CDP	3 394	NA	NA	139	3 240	11	1	3	27	1 317	NA	7.8
1565	Williamston town	3 876	NA	NA	3 109	757	0	0	10	16	1 682	8 415	8.9
1570	Williston town	3 099	NA	NA	1 702	1 384	3	5	5	11	1 267	8 808	23.0
1580	Winnsboro town	3 475	NA	NA	1 342	2 125	1	5	2	20	1 366	7 601	5.8
1589	Woodfield CDP	8 862	NA	NA	5 426	2 822	21	384	209	496	3 589	NA	7.2
1595	Woodruff town	4 365	NA	NA	3 121	1 224	9	6	5	18	1 800	8 387	9.0
1605	York	6 709	NA	NA	4 035	2 635	13	17	9	43	2 668	7 421	15.7

1. Codes shown are 2-digit FIPS codes for states; 4-digit census place codes for places; and 3-digit FIPS county codes followed by 3-digit census MCD codes for minor civil divisions (MCDs). MCD names are followed by county names in parentheses. 2. Hispanic persons may be of any race. 3. Dry land or land partially or temporarily covered by water.

State/ Place/ MCD[1] code	Place	Population 1990	Places of 10,000 or more 1980	Places of 10,000 or more Percent change, 1980–1990	Race: White	Race: Black	Race: Am. Indian, Eskimo Aleut	Race: Asian & Pacific Islander	Race: Other race	Hispanic[2]	Total housing units, 1990	Per capita income, 1985 (Dollars)	Land area,[3] 1990 (Sq. Km.)
		1	2	3	4	5	6	7	8	9	10	11	12
46	SOUTH DAKOTA	696 004	690 768	0.8	637 515	3 258	50 575	3 123	1 533	5 252	292 436	8 553	196 575.2
0005	Aberdeen	24 927	25 956	-4.0	23 925	39	812	125	26	88	10 689	9 748	21.7
0110	Belle Fourche	4 335	NA	NA	4 131	19	83	9	93	147	1 973	8 141	6.7
0147	Box Elder	2 680	NA	NA	2 263	151	141	104	21	83	1 050	6 082	8.8
0153	Brandon	3 543	NA	NA	3 520	9	6	7	1	10	1 143	9 354	7.6
0185	Brookings	16 270	14 951	8.8	15 790	73	111	284	12	53	6 012	8 263	26.9
0240	Canton	2 787	NA	NA	2 759	0	12	15	1	1	1 180	8 615	7.6
0443	Ellsworth AFB CDP	7 017	NA	NA	5 675	813	79	294	156	386	1 876	NA	4.9
0675	Hot Springs	4 325	NA	NA	3 887	20	373	26	19	77	1 872	9 292	7.4
0705	Huron	12 448	13 000	-4.2	12 170	67	134	45	32	72	5 608	10 027	15.4
0805	Lead	3 632	NA	NA	3 527	6	75	5	19	52	1 654	10 272	4.9
0870	Madison	6 257	NA	NA	6 184	11	30	21	11	20	2 613	8 384	10.0
0910	Milbank	3 879	NA	NA	3 843	2	18	11	5	8	1 711	9 457	6.3
0930	Mitchell	13 798	13 916	-0.8	13 484	22	229	49	14	36	6 064	8 345	24.3
0935	Mobridge	3 768	NA	NA	3 311	2	444	10	1	26	1 779	8 339	4.6
1085	Pierre	12 906	11 973	7.8	11 977	18	834	42	35	105	5 390	10 633	33.7
1086	Pine Ridge CDP	2 596	NA	NA	75	2	2 506	1	12	69	694	NA	5.2
1125	Rapid City	54 523	46 492	17.3	48 082	691	4 852	541	357	1 215	22 530	10 804	91.5
1126	Rapid Valley CDP	5 968	NA	NA	5 539	67	277	59	26	139	2 094	NA	27.3
1140	Redfield	2 770	NA	NA	2 757	2	9	0	2	10	1 306	9 762	4.6
1225	Sioux Falls	100 814	81 341	23.9	97 627	733	1 574	688	192	571	41 568	11 508	116.7
1240	Spearfish	6 966	NA	NA	6 724	14	176	24	28	115	2 913	8 509	9.9
1275	Sturgis	5 330	NA	NA	5 152	2	139	16	21	57	2 358	8 389	6.6
1360	Vermillion	10 034	10 136	-1.0	9 426	58	375	145	30	99	3 428	7 564	8.0
1425	Watertown	17 592	15 649	12.4	17 269	12	241	67	3	50	7 631	9 205	34.2
1500	Winner	3 354	NA	NA	3 124	0	227	1	2	9	1 540	8 004	3.7
1525	Yankton	12 703	12 011	5.8	12 312	99	255	30	7	73	5 219	9 477	19.2
47	TENNESSEE	4 877 185	4 591 036	6.2	4 048 068	778 035	10 039	31 839	9 204	32 741	2 026 067	9 290	106 758.5
0020	Alcoa	6 400	NA	NA	5 053	1 307	5	24	11	35	2 892	9 188	25.0
0050	Ashland City town	2 552	NA	NA	2 384	156	8	3	1	18	1 094	NA	9.0
0055	Athens	12 054	12 080	-0.2	10 825	1 136	18	61	14	60	5 184	8 624	31.7
0085	Bartlett town	26 989	17 170	57.2	26 022	653	23	257	34	190	8 807	12 303	37.3
0105	Belle Meade	2 839	NA	NA	2 813	14	1	10	1	5	1 149	38 365	8.1
0142	Bloomingdale CDP	10 953	12 088	-9.4	10 889	27	7	21	9	35	4 447	NA	28.7
0143	Blountville CDP	2 605	NA	NA	2 571	28	1	5	0	6	919	NA	14.8
0150	Bolivar	5 969	NA	NA	3 020	2 905	6	37	1	100	2 098	6 920	13.3
0157	Brentwood	16 392	NA	NA	15 894	260	15	213	10	82	5 514	18 286	75.2
0170	Bristol	23 421	23 986	-2.4	22 390	685	186	120	40	158	10 403	10 499	54.3
0175	Brownsville	10 019	NA	NA	4 606	5 359	12	16	26	70	3 848	7 139	18.4
0200	Camden town	3 643	NA	NA	3 438	186	2	10	7	20	1 667	9 931	12.6
0225	Centerville town	3 616	NA	NA	3 393	215	7	1	0	12	1 604	8 765	26.6
0227	Central CDP	2 635	NA	NA	2 623	1	6	1	4	6	1 130	NA	11.6
0245	Chattanooga	152 466	169 550	-10.1	99 057	51 338	329	1 478	264	974	69 601	9 340	306.7
0247	Church Hill town	4 834	NA	NA	4 722	79	6	22	5	18	2 004	9 264	16.3
0250	Clarksville	75 494	54 777	37.8	56 588	15 776	319	1 645	1 166	2 911	27 642	8 612	189.3
0255	Cleveland	30 354	26 432	14.8	27 790	2 177	81	143	163	436	13 050	10 555	51.4
0265	Clinton town	8 972	NA	NA	8 629	289	40	6	8	50	4 006	10 296	26.4
0273	Collegedale	5 048	NA	NA	4 612	171	10	121	134	246	1 641	9 127	18.7
0275	Collierville town	14 427	NA	NA	12 724	1 604	24	55	20	109	4 613	10 784	32.2
0285	Colonial Heights CDP	6 716	NA	NA	6 610	55	11	35	5	30	2 613	NA	17.2
0290	Columbia	28 583	26 372	8.4	22 451	5 888	52	109	83	212	12 142	9 579	76.2
0295	Cookeville	21 744	20 535	5.9	20 660	623	30	383	48	164	9 284	8 855	53.1
0315	Covington	7 487	NA	NA	4 307	3 145	10	19	6	25	2 920	7 675	25.1
0325	Crossville	6 930	NA	NA	6 868	2	31	19	10	25	3 054	7 415	31.6
0350	Dayton	5 671	NA	NA	5 269	350	10	23	19	23	2 306	7 678	14.2
0375	Dickson	8 791	NA	NA	7 881	829	20	37	24	63	3 818	9 130	28.6
0405	Dunlap	3 731	NA	NA	3 724	2	2	2	1	15	1 501	6 857	22.3
0420	Dyersburg	16 317	15 856	2.9	13 073	3 153	29	43	19	72	7 041	8 566	28.8
0425	Eagleton Village CDP	5 169	NA	NA	5 099	35	21	11	3	16	2 281	NA	12.0
0433	East Brainerd CDP	11 594	NA	NA	10 788	665	20	93	28	86	3 810	NA	22.5
0440	East Ridge	21 101	21 236	-0.6	20 686	112	52	240	11	96	9 631	12 208	21.6
0445	Elizabethton	11 931	12 431	-4.0	11 531	314	14	57	15	61	5 191	8 487	19.4
0480	Erwin	5 015	NA	NA	5 004	0	4	6	1	19	2 259	9 589	7.1
0490	Etowah	3 815	NA	NA	3 635	142	18	16	4	18	1 737	9 751	6.3
0495	Fairview	4 210	NA	NA	4 197	3	2	8	0	8	1 479	8 858	32.3
0499	Farragut town	12 793	NA	NA	12 242	181	18	322	30	115	4 456	14 326	41.8
0500	Fayetteville	6 921	NA	NA	5 037	1 838	7	26	13	33	3 277	8 482	17.5
0513	Forest Hills	4 231	NA	NA	4 133	38	2	57	1	33	1 597	30 723	24.0
0515	Franklin	20 098	12 407	62.0	16 289	3 615	36	103	55	185	8 748	11 071	66.1
0540	Gallatin	18 794	17 191	9.3	15 107	3 594	26	51	16	86	7 635	9 429	54.7
0555	Gatlinburg	3 417	NA	NA	3 363	2	13	38	1	25	2 923	12 363	26.0
0560	Germantown	32 893	20 459	60.8	31 299	610	63	894	27	278	11 131	19 978	39.8

1. Codes shown are 2-digit FIPS codes for states; 4-digit census place codes for places; and 3-digit FIPS county codes followed by 3-digit census MCD codes for minor civil divisions (MCDs). MCD names are followed by county names in parentheses. 2. Hispanic persons may be of any race. 3. Dry land or land partially or temporarily covered by water.

State/ Place/ MCD[1] code	Place	Population: 1990	Population: Places of 10,000 or more: 1980	Population: Places of 10,000 or more: Percent change, 1980–1990	Population characteristics, 1990: Race: White	Race: Black	Race: Am. Indian, Eskimo Aleut	Race: Asian & Pacific Islander	Race: Other race	Hispanic[2]	Total housing units, 1990	Per capita income, 1985 (Dollars)	Land area,[3] 1990 (Sq. Km.)
		1	2	3	4	5	6	7	8	9	10	11	12
	TENNESSEE—Con.												
0575	Goodlettsville	8 177	NA	NA	7 694	349	20	99	15	48	3 660	11 334	16.9
0575	Goodlettsville	3 042	NA	NA	2 983	37	0	22	0	16	1 101	NA	18.4
0600	Greenbrier town	2 873	NA	NA	2 855	6	7	1	4	19	1 111	8 445	11.5
0605	Greeneville town	13 532	14 097	-4.0	12 631	837	23	27	14	49	6 058	10 350	28.5
0611	Green Hill CDP	6 763	NA	NA	6 494	207	6	52	4	61	2 369	NA	10.0
0617	Halls CDP	6 450	10 363	-37.8	6 405	14	10	19	2	18	2 539	NA	22.6
0625	Harriman	7 119	NA	NA	6 507	574	15	13	10	27	3 234	7 164	25.4
0627	Harrison CDP	7 191	NA	NA	6 796	293	35	42	25	58	2 709	NA	19.0
0629	Harrogate-Shawanee CDP	2 657	NA	NA	2 617	11	8	18	3	18	1 035	NA	10.6
0635	Henderson	4 760	NA	NA	3 800	928	10	18	4	39	1 600	6 398	12.7
0637	Hendersonville	32 188	26 561	21.2	31 126	749	80	180	53	267	12 472	12 492	57.2
0665	Hohenwald	3 760	NA	NA	3 665	63	19	7	6	21	1 685	6 878	11.3
0672	Hopewell CDP	2 569	NA	NA	2 508	46	4	4	7	20	1 016	NA	22.4
0685	Humboldt	9 651	10 189	-5.3	5 895	3 730	10	9	7	36	4 000	7 272	19.6
0690	Huntingdon town	4 180	NA	NA	3 391	772	8	3	6	24	1 790	9 728	19.7
0705	Jackson	48 949	49 131	-0.4	28 943	19 703	39	213	51	257	20 739	9 097	104.5
0715	Jasper town	2 780	NA	NA	2 539	231	1	6	3	18	1 199	8 944	19.6
0720	Jefferson City	5 494	NA	NA	5 090	369	11	13	11	24	2 006	6 853	8.6
0730	Johnson City	49 381	39 738	24.3	45 971	2 915	98	321	76	316	21 241	10 121	79.2
0740	Jonesborough town	3 091	NA	NA	2 890	190	5	4	2	22	1 262	8 457	7.7
0750	Kingsport	36 365	32 027	13.5	34 480	1 611	41	212	21	125	16 742	11 528	83.8
0755	Kingston	4 552	NA	NA	4 316	194	5	27	10	26	2 071	10 142	9.5
0760	Knoxville	165 121	175 030	-5.7	136 604	26 053	399	1 725	340	1 099	76 453	9 438	200.1
0765	Lafayette	3 641	NA	NA	3 636	0	4	1	0	2	1 695	7 375	10.0
0770	La Follette	7 192	NA	NA	7 137	35	14	6	0	24	3 116	7 039	11.3
0784	La Vergne	7 499	NA	NA	7 071	346	30	29	23	76	2 810	9 398	42.9
0785	Lawrenceburg	10 412	10 184	2.2	9 954	394	22	38	4	42	4 711	8 794	24.5
0790	Lebanon	15 208	11 872	28.1	12 771	2 267	41	115	14	58	6 592	8 715	46.2
0795	Lenoir City	6 147	NA	NA	6 086	25	27	7	2	20	2 734	7 189	13.0
0800	Lewisburg	9 879	NA	NA	8 324	1 497	6	42	10	45	4 275	9 313	28.9
0805	Lexington	5 810	NA	NA	4 933	865	4	6	2	37	2 612	8 335	22.8
0820	Livingston town	3 809	NA	NA	3 779	26	1	1	2	7	1 679	7 418	13.2
0845	Loudon town	4 026	NA	NA	3 872	142	2	8	2	10	1 832	7 633	19.1
0850	Lynchburg, Moore County	4 721	NA	NA	4 536	174	8	2	1	20	1 912	NA	334.6
0870	McKenzie	5 168	NA	NA	4 450	702	14	0	2	19	2 158	8 888	12.2
0880	McMinnville	11 194	10 683	4.8	10 503	555	19	73	44	78	5 123	7 840	21.2
0890	Madisonville town	3 033	NA	NA	2 854	161	5	7	6	13	1 344	9 687	12.0
0895	Manchester	7 709	NA	NA	7 356	240	21	78	14	57	3 330	10 375	28.3
0900	Martin	8 600	NA	NA	6 883	1 399	18	253	47	60	3 104	6 625	18.9
0905	Maryville	19 208	17 464	10.0	18 340	603	40	204	21	102	8 280	10 666	34.9
0940	Memphis	610 337	646 356	-5.6	268 600	334 737	960	4 805	1 235	4 455	248 573	9 362	663.2
0946	Middle Valley CDP	12 255	11 420	7.3	12 002	90	15	137	11	59	4 297	NA	35.4
0947	Midway CDP	2 953	NA	NA	2 913	35	0	4	1	19	1 192	NA	18.3
0950	Milan	7 512	NA	NA	5 876	1 608	1	17	10	23	3 300	8 887	18.6
0953	Millersville	2 575	NA	NA	2 558	3	5	6	3	14	1 044	NA	19.1
0955	Millington	17 866	20 236	-11.7	14 086	2 830	139	424	387	896	4 440	7 231	27.5
0965	Monterey town	2 559	NA	NA	2 540	2	7	5	5	11	1 113	6 985	17.8
0985	Morristown	21 385	19 683	8.6	19 324	1 927	39	66	29	91	9 248	8 844	41.1
0996	Mount Carmel town	4 082	NA	NA	4 056	12	6	8	0	8	1 630	8 458	17.4
0998	Mount Juliet	5 389	NA	NA	5 199	154	12	13	11	44	1 926	11 568	30.6
1000	Mount Pleasant	4 278	NA	NA	3 141	1 118	5	12	2	13	1 879	8 297	26.3
1010	Murfreesboro	44 922	32 845	36.8	36 977	6 508	82	1 253	102	358	18 708	10 354	78.6
1016	Nashville-Davidson	488 374	455 663	7.2	360 284	118 627	1 130	6 852	1 481	4 632	219 528	11 253	1 225.9
1020	Newbern town	2 515	NA	NA	2 076	422	5	9	3	11	1 058	7 839	9.6
1030	Newport	7 123	NA	NA	6 689	395	20	14	5	40	3 171	6 919	11.2
1068	Oak Grove CDP	3 498	NA	NA	3 469	13	5	11	0	14	1 456	NA	12.4
1070	Oak Hill	4 301	NA	NA	4 198	46	3	48	6	20	1 788	22 837	20.4
1080	Oak Ridge	27 310	27 662	-1.3	24 409	2 180	97	562	62	266	12 694	13 565	221.6
1090	Oliver Springs town	3 433	NA	NA	3 295	114	14	8	2	9	1 385	8 671	11.1
1091	Oneida town	3 502	NA	NA	3 488	2	7	5	0	8	1 506	9 033	15.3
1093	Ooltewah CDP	4 903	NA	NA	4 372	473	20	30	8	44	1 847	NA	23.1
1110	Paris	9 332	10 728	-13.0	7 298	1 982	18	26	8	32	4 538	8 687	22.2
1127	Pigeon Forge	3 027	NA	NA	2 994	9	12	6	6	18	1 371	NA	15.6
1129	Pine Crest CDP	3 821	NA	NA	3 750	27	15	22	7	19	1 546	NA	7.8
1145	Portland town	5 165	NA	NA	5 058	89	8	10	0	16	2 101	9 696	17.8
1147	Powell CDP	7 534	NA	NA	7 374	100	15	31	14	27	3 023	NA	21.6
1150	Pulaski	7 895	NA	NA	5 735	2 093	16	47	4	20	3 545	8 317	10.7
1160	Red Bank	12 322	13 297	-7.3	11 464	673	18	108	59	137	6 262	11 063	16.8
1195	Ripley	6 188	NA	NA	3 382	2 777	17	9	3	47	2 490	7 243	17.7
1210	Rockwood	5 348	NA	NA	4 990	334	8	11	5	16	2 326	7 170	17.5
1215	Rogersville town	4 149	NA	NA	3 874	268	4	2	1	9	1 995	9 209	7.8
1265	Savannah	6 547	NA	NA	5 893	620	14	10	10	36	2 796	8 265	13.4
1275	Selmer town	3 838	NA	NA	3 369	443	0	26	0	14	1 780	8 445	14.0

1. Codes shown are 2-digit FIPS codes for states; 4-digit census place codes for places; and 3-digit FIPS county codes followed by 3-digit census MCD codes for minor civil divisions (MCDs). MCD names are followed by county names in parentheses. 2. Hispanic persons may be of any race. 3. Dry land or land partially or temporarily covered by water.

State/ Place/ MCD[1] code	Place	Population: 1990	Population: Places of 10,000 or more: 1980	Population: Places of 10,000 or more: Percent change, 1980–1990	Population characteristics, 1990: Race: White	Race: Black	Race: Am. Indian, Eskimo Aleut	Race: Asian & Pacific Islander	Race: Other race	Hispanic[2]	Total housing units, 1990	Per capita income, 1985 (Dollars)	Land area,[3] 1990 (Sq. Km.)
		1	2	3	4	5	6	7	8	9	10	11	12
	TENNESSEE—Con.												
1280	Sevierville town	7 178	NA	NA	7 003	89	21	61	4	42	3 321	8 890	29.9
1287	Seymour CDP	7 026	NA	NA	6 930	24	12	38	22	44	2 662	NA	32.7
1295	Shelbyville	14 049	13 530	3.8	11 475	2 390	15	120	49	92	6 163	8 528	35.7
1300	Signal Mountain town	7 034	NA	NA	6 977	17	1	34	5	36	2 718	19 327	13.1
1315	Smithville town	3 791	NA	NA	3 697	81	0	2	11	12	1 693	7 601	15.1
1320	Smyrna town	13 647	NA	NA	12 621	921	37	41	27	153	5 312	9 665	47.6
1331	Soddy-Daisy	8 240	NA	NA	8 145	64	9	17	5	24	3 356	8 998	44.9
1340	South Cleveland CDP	5 372	NA	NA	5 277	58	15	10	12	33	2 036	NA	37.0
1350	South Fulton	2 688	NA	NA	2 060	615	3	8	2	26	1 182	8 411	7.9
1360	South Pittsburg	3 295	NA	NA	2 688	599	5	2	1	9	1 444	8 197	14.8
1365	Sparta	4 681	NA	NA	4 397	264	5	11	4	17	2 034	7 995	16.2
1380	Springfield	11 227	10 814	3.8	7 800	3 392	9	18	8	55	4 530	8 220	17.8
1387	Spurgeon CDP	3 149	NA	NA	3 124	7	6	9	3	16	1 266	NA	10.3
1405	Sweetwater	5 066	NA	NA	4 621	403	7	26	9	15	2 168	8 910	17.4
1445	Trenton	4 836	NA	NA	3 273	1 539	6	16	2	15	2 150	8 446	14.1
1465	Tullahoma	16 761	15 827	5.9	15 405	1 154	27	143	32	112	7 119	9 810	57.4
1475	Union City	10 513	10 436	0.7	8 230	2 222	12	23	26	50	4 609	9 800	22.7
1488	Walnut Hill CDP	3 332	NA	NA	3 300	17	6	9	0	6	1 291	NA	15.0
1500	Waverly	3 925	NA	NA	3 446	448	7	18	6	29	1 787	8 585	21.1
1527	White House	2 987	NA	NA	2 919	55	10	2	1	14	1 122	NA	19.2
1542	Wildwood Lake CDP	2 680	NA	NA	2 655	6	8	10	1	4	1 033	NA	31.1
1545	Winchester	6 305	NA	NA	5 405	867	8	10	15	40	2 625	7 439	19.5
48	TEXAS	16 986 510	14 225 512	19.4	12 774 762	2 021 632	65 877	319 459	1 804 780	4 339 905	7 008 999	10 373	678 357.8
0010	Abernathy	2 720	NA	NA	1 834	92	17	3	774	1 210	1 034	7 360	3.1
0015	Abilene	106 654	98 312	8.5	87 888	7 474	407	1 399	9 486	16 549	44 436	9 685	267.0
0016	Abram-Perezville CDP	3 999	NA	NA	3 356	5	0	3	635	3 132	2 769	NA	17.0
0020	Addison	8 783	NA	NA	6 491	1 070	50	548	624	1 234	5 110	16 752	11.5
0035	Alamo	8 210	NA	NA	5 952	10	13	7	2 228	6 398	3 940	4 468	7.1
0040	Alamo Heights	6 502	NA	NA	6 275	11	17	24	175	651	3 381	20 380	4.8
0051	Aldine CDP	11 133	12 623	-11.8	8 571	443	48	336	1 735	2 911	4 069	NA	21.0
0055	Alice	19 788	20 961	-5.6	15 625	177	47	64	3 875	14 364	7 198	7 778	30.3
0065	Allen	18 309	NA	NA	17 061	595	111	214	328	800	6 173	12 729	49.2
0070	Alpine	5 637	NA	NA	5 378	76	10	44	129	2 562	2 436	6 950	10.4
0083	Alton	3 069	NA	NA	2 150	4	7	0	908	2 967	780	2 639	4.9
0085	Alvarado	2 918	NA	NA	2 421	335	17	2	143	326	1 163	7 834	11.3
0090	Alvin	19 220	16 514	16.4	16 311	351	91	96	2 371	4 182	7 996	10 689	47.4
0100	Amarillo	157 615	149 230	5.6	130 358	9 441	1 187	2 960	13 669	23 231	68 592	10 975	227.8
0113	Anderson Mill CDP	9 468	NA	NA	8 485	335	41	306	301	856	3 494	NA	3.9
0115	Andrews	10 678	10 996	-2.9	7 898	256	66	121	2 337	3 651	4 027	9 914	12.3
0120	Angleton	17 140	13 881	23.5	13 333	1 789	67	176	1 775	3 031	6 705	11 441	25.2
0140	Anson	2 644	NA	NA	1 874	109	4	6	651	798	1 159	7 362	5.4
0145	Anthony town	3 328	NA	NA	2 236	142	37	12	901	2 495	658	5 441	16.8
0155	Aransas Pass	7 180	NA	NA	5 903	349	31	38	859	2 541	3 155	6 957	27.0
0175	Arlington	261 721	160 113	63.5	216 284	22 009	1 323	10 271	11 834	23 312	112 767	12 796	240.9
0195	Athens	10 967	10 197	7.6	7 974	2 163	31	47	752	918	4 793	8 884	35.7
0200	Atlanta	6 118	NA	NA	4 478	1 596	8	6	30	108	2 735	8 642	29.2
0210	Austin	465 622	345 544	34.8	328 542	57 868	1 756	14 141	63 315	106 868	217 054	11 633	564.0
0230	Azle	8 868	NA	NA	8 654	43	49	26	96	249	3 476	10 206	18.5
0235	Bacliff CDP	5 549	NA	NA	5 209	26	39	90	185	464	2 508	NA	7.5
0250	Balch Springs	17 406	13 746	26.6	14 296	1 626	119	136	1 229	2 337	6 244	8 563	20.9
0255	Balcones Heights	3 022	NA	NA	2 267	203	10	15	527	1 883	1 711	12 091	1.7
0260	Ballinger	3 975	NA	NA	3 588	124	8	3	252	1 125	1 849	8 191	8.7
0285	Barrett CDP	3 052	NA	NA	87	2 954	5	0	6	24	1 077	NA	10.3
0305	Bastrop	4 044	NA	NA	2 765	850	17	16	396	621	1 826	8 926	16.1
0310	Bay City	18 170	17 837	1.9	12 045	3 182	49	259	2 635	4 809	8 189	11 382	19.0
0315	Baytown	63 850	56 923	12.2	46 590	7 672	211	479	8 898	14 784	25 020	11 333	81.1
0320	Beaumont	114 323	118 102	-3.2	62 842	47 164	243	1 905	2 169	4 919	49 021	10 139	207.3
0330	Bedford	43 762	20 821	110.2	40 625	1 156	191	1 088	702	2 023	18 848	14 992	25.9
0335	Beeville	13 547	14 574	-7.0	9 471	456	53	122	3 445	8 414	5 491	6 775	15.8
0345	Bellaire	13 842	14 950	-7.4	13 102	57	26	274	383	1 100	6 198	17 190	9.4
0355	Bellmead	8 336	NA	NA	6 586	1 064	33	19	634	1 143	3 653	7 584	16.3
0365	Bellville	3 378	NA	NA	2 751	513	11	7	96	194	1 498	12 332	6.6
0370	Belton	12 476	10 660	17.0	9 484	1 083	61	99	1 749	2 764	4 664	7 833	27.9
0380	Benbrook	19 564	13 579	44.1	17 784	765	70	656	289	780	8 377	14 647	29.4
0405	Big Lake	3 672	NA	NA	2 789	127	5	1	750	1 686	1 306	8 362	3.2
0415	Big Spring	23 093	24 804	-6.9	17 095	1 181	143	141	4 533	6 977	9 876	9 307	49.3
0430	Bishop	3 337	NA	NA	2 671	24	11	4	627	1 798	1 286	8 384	6.1
0485	Boerne	4 274	NA	NA	3 989	19	33	15	218	919	1 623	9 958	10.8
0500	Bonham	6 686	NA	NA	5 806	734	55	34	57	124	3 108	9 162	16.3
0510	Borger	15 675	15 837	-1.0	13 178	639	224	84	1 550	2 003	6 901	10 826	22.4
0520	Bowie	4 990	NA	NA	4 908	1	14	2	65	118	2 442	9 411	10.1

1. Codes shown are 2-digit FIPS codes for states; 4-digit census place codes for places; and 3-digit FIPS county codes followed by 3-digit census MCD codes for minor civil divisions (MCDs). MCD names are followed by county names in parentheses. 2. Hispanic persons may be of any race. 3. Dry land or land partially or temporarily covered by water.

Table D. Places — **Population, Housing, Money Income, and Land Area**

State/ Place/ MCD[1] code	Place	Population: 1990	Population: Places of 10,000 or more: 1980	Population: Places of 10,000 or more: Percent change, 1980–1990	Population characteristics, 1990: Race: White	Race: Black	Race: Am. Indian, Eskimo Aleut	Race: Asian & Pacific Islander	Race: Other race	Hispanic[2]	Total housing units, 1990	Per capita income, 1985 (Dollars)	Land area,[3] 1990 (Sq. Km.)
		1	2	3	4	5	6	7	8	9	10	11	12
	TEXAS—Con.												
0535	Brady	5 946	NA	NA	5 198	162	7	8	571	1 840	2 683	7 971	23.8
0545	Brazoria	2 717	NA	NA	2 244	327	25	8	113	194	1 115	10 013	4.7
0550	Breckenridge	5 665	NA	NA	4 930	228	21	24	462	667	2 834	8 144	10.7
0560	Brenham	11 952	10 966	9.0	8 629	2 802	21	152	348	536	4 794	9 028	19.1
0561	Briar CDP	3 899	NA	NA	3 810	26	8	21	34	98	1 656	NA	51.0
0565	Bridge City	8 034	NA	NA	7 883	19	22	61	49	210	3 014	9 631	15.6
0570	Bridgeport	3 581	NA	NA	3 138	24	14	0	405	673	1 390	8 847	9.0
0580	Brookshire	2 922	NA	NA	1 137	1 485	0	3	297	698	1 101	NA	9.1
0585	Brownfield	9 560	10 387	-8.0	7 076	418	29	27	2 010	3 843	3 753	8 483	13.6
0595	Brownsville	98 962	84 997	16.4	83 895	193	140	301	14 433	89 206	28 992	5 490	72.3
0605	Brownwood	18 387	19 396	-5.2	15 263	1 121	89	68	1 846	2 667	8 101	8 486	30.4
0608	Brushy Creek CDP	5 833	NA	NA	5 306	213	29	131	154	431	2 026	NA	24.1
0610	Bryan	55 002	44 337	24.1	38 437	9 452	135	851	6 127	10 892	23 007	9 395	84.6
0650	Bunker Hill Village	3 391	NA	NA	3 185	23	2	169	12	101	1 248	37 860	3.8
0655	Burkburnett	10 145	10 668	-4.9	9 605	221	104	60	155	411	4 173	9 570	24.7
0660	Burleson	16 113	11 722	37.5	15 704	26	49	99	235	544	5 855	10 161	43.5
0665	Burnet	3 423	NA	NA	2 988	99	9	13	314	511	1 670	7 391	13.5
0680	Caldwell	3 181	NA	NA	2 370	454	5	1	351	551	1 396	8 689	8.8
0695	Cameron	5 580	NA	NA	3 788	1 303	15	16	458	1 057	2 454	7 390	11.0
0696	Cameron Park CDP	3 802	NA	NA	3 115	9	7	25	646	3 651	867	NA	6.3
0702	Camp Swift CDP	2 681	NA	NA	2 115	296	37	14	219	602	821	NA	30.0
0715	Canton	2 949	NA	NA	2 839	58	17	15	20	59	1 322	10 363	9.9
0720	Canutillo CDP	4 442	NA	NA	2 529	20	9	11	1 873	3 697	1 304	NA	7.3
0725	Canyon	11 365	10 726	6.0	10 319	285	39	210	512	1 048	4 773	9 390	12.8
0727	Canyon Lake CDP	9 975	NA	NA	9 673	16	45	21	220	664	6 229	NA	374.0
0735	Carrizo Springs	5 745	NA	NA	3 597	58	13	12	2 065	4 882	1 947	5 130	8.1
0740	Carrollton	82 169	40 587	102.5	68 300	4 014	348	5 598	3 909	8 420	32 992	15 454	90.0
0745	Carthage	6 496	NA	NA	5 167	1 253	14	4	58	149	2 776	10 625	26.8
0750	Castle Hills	4 198	NA	NA	3 972	26	7	72	121	792	1 908	21 637	6.4
0765	Cedar Hill	19 976	NA	NA	16 077	2 840	73	357	629	1 612	7 040	11 901	87.1
0767	Cedar Park	5 161	NA	NA	4 825	41	22	30	243	550	1 837	10 036	19.4
0780	Center	4 950	NA	NA	3 044	1 853	2	10	41	179	2 161	7 389	16.0
0786	Central Gardens CDP	4 026	NA	NA	3 964	6	19	19	18	125	1 594	NA	6.9
0792	Channelview CDP	25 564	17 471	46.3	19 554	2 487	94	564	2 865	4 902	8 972	NA	42.4
0810	Childress	5 055	NA	NA	4 129	306	19	17	584	793	2 521	7 399	19.7
0830	Cisco	3 813	NA	NA	3 529	139	13	4	128	296	1 945	6 961	12.6
0840	Clarksville	4 311	NA	NA	2 450	1 796	10	4	51	92	1 970	6 975	7.7
0860	Cleburne	22 205	19 218	15.5	19 649	1 253	68	90	1 145	2 321	9 234	9 839	50.4
0865	Cleveland	7 124	NA	NA	4 728	2 044	20	21	311	660	2 838	7 627	11.5
0870	Clifton	3 195	NA	NA	2 921	173	1	13	87	341	1 411	8 879	4.7
0876	Cloverleaf CDP	18 230	17 317	5.3	14 507	1 566	74	249	1 834	3 723	6 913	NA	9.2
0880	Clute	8 910	NA	NA	6 259	653	42	57	1 899	3 193	3 964	8 921	12.2
0885	Clyde town	3 002	NA	NA	2 959	2	13	10	18	46	1 302	8 354	5.7
0895	Cockrell Hill	3 746	NA	NA	1 879	71	37	18	1 741	2 508	1 203	8 631	1.5
0900	Coleman	5 410	NA	NA	4 958	193	15	2	242	707	2 803	7 737	15.9
0905	College Station	52 456	37 272	40.7	43 520	3 293	108	3 428	2 107	4 679	19 845	7 558	76.3
0910	Colleyville	12 724	NA	NA	12 309	85	40	218	72	287	4 309	18 697	34.0
0920	Colorado City	4 749	NA	NA	3 727	310	6	4	702	1 637	2 166	8 221	13.7
0925	Columbus	3 367	NA	NA	2 401	688	1	8	269	373	1 627	9 308	5.9
0930	Comanche	4 087	NA	NA	3 721	12	14	2	338	875	1 885	9 367	11.4
0945	Commerce	6 825	NA	NA	5 279	1 224	23	156	143	268	3 139	7 865	16.5
0955	Conroe	27 610	18 034	53.1	20 558	3 701	72	251	3 028	4 811	11 500	10 595	54.2
0957	Converse	8 887	NA	NA	7 234	723	58	242	630	2 034	3 035	9 097	13.2
0970	Coppell	16 881	NA	NA	15 108	387	55	913	418	1 007	6 404	14 851	38.1
0975	Copperas Cove	24 079	19 469	23.7	18 084	3 969	158	901	967	2 160	9 307	8 068	24.3
0977	Corinth town	3 944	NA	NA	3 786	52	25	19	62	142	1 385	NA	20.0
0980	Corpus Christi	257 453	231 999	11.0	196 019	12 347	1 112	2 390	45 585	129 708	100 205	9 546	349.6
0990	Corsicana	22 911	21 712	5.5	15 545	5 844	69	211	1 242	2 082	9 622	9 281	53.9
0995	Cotulla	3 694	NA	NA	2 546	49	6	6	1 087	2 935	1 416	5 245	5.1
1010	Crane	3 533	NA	NA	2 367	125	7	9	1 025	1 150	1 389	8 344	2.7
1020	Crockett	7 024	NA	NA	3 724	3 107	4	24	165	322	3 142	7 522	23.0
1045	Crowley	6 974	NA	NA	6 687	23	54	28	182	404	2 430	9 759	16.4
1050	Crystal City	8 263	NA	NA	3 550	295	15	2	4 401	7 643	2 534	4 028	9.4
1055	Cuero	6 700	NA	NA	4 268	1 304	10	5	1 113	2 218	2 880	8 281	12.8
1070	Daingerfield town	2 572	NA	NA	1 870	663	6	6	27	64	1 081	7 837	5.9
1080	Dalhart	6 246	NA	NA	5 344	115	50	21	716	1 070	2 807	8 891	9.3
1085	Dallas	1 006 877	904 074	11.4	556 760	296 994	4 792	21 952	126 379	210 240	465 600	12 816	886.8
1105	Dayton	5 151	NA	NA	3 945	1 000	21	26	159	295	2 052	9 159	30.0
1110	Decatur	4 252	NA	NA	3 827	134	16	28	247	553	1 776	10 325	16.3
1115	Deer Park	27 652	22 648	22.1	25 493	299	120	325	1 415	2 987	9 127	12 721	26.8
1130	Del Rio	30 705	30 034	2.2	20 114	425	108	130	9 928	23 698	10 691	6 002	38.2
1135	Denison	21 505	23 884	-10.0	18 784	2 082	387	59	193	468	10 328	9 837	57.2
1140	Denton	66 270	48 063	37.9	54 315	6 316	299	1 860	3 480	5 937	28 791	10 854	136.3

1. Codes shown are 2-digit FIPS codes for states; 4-digit census place codes for places; and 3-digit FIPS county codes followed by 3-digit census MCD codes for minor civil divisions (MCDs). MCD names are followed by county names in parentheses. 2. Hispanic persons may be of any race. 3. Dry land or land partially or temporarily covered by water.

State/ Place/ MCD[1] code	Place	Population: 1990	Population: Places of 10,000 or more: 1980	Population: Places of 10,000 or more: Percent change, 1980–1990	Population characteristics, 1990: Race: White	Race: Black	Race: Am. Indian, Eskimo Aleut	Race: Asian & Pacific Islander	Race: Other race	Hispanic[2]	Total housing units, 1990	Per capita income, 1985 (Dollars)	Land area,[3] 1990 (Sq. Km.)
		1	2	3	4	5	6	7	8	9	10	11	12
	TEXAS—Con.												
1145	Denver City town	5 145	NA	NA	3 620	64	15	8	1 438	1 951	1 814	8 935	5.4
1155	DeSoto	30 544	15 538	96.6	23 205	6 362	100	346	531	1 520	11 650	13 928	55.9
1165	Devine	3 928	NA	NA	3 330	11	19	8	560	2 026	1 391	7 726	7.7
1168	Diboll	4 341	NA	NA	2 292	1 140	10	3	896	1 367	1 504	6 365	12.1
1180	Dickinson	9 497	NA	NA	7 655	1 269	37	64	472	1 195	3 900	12 420	16.8
1185	Dilley	2 632	NA	NA	1 652	3	4	2	971	2 109	910	4 703	4.1
1190	Dimmitt	4 408	NA	NA	2 458	193	8	14	1 735	2 170	1 642	6 498	5.0
1205	Donna	12 652	NA	NA	10 198	20	19	19	2 396	11 158	4 249	4 285	11.4
1220	Dublin	3 190	NA	NA	3 024	5	7	7	147	438	1 376	7 846	8.0
1225	Dumas	12 871	12 194	5.6	9 896	84	89	271	2 531	3 481	4 890	10 053	11.2
1230	Duncanville	35 748	27 781	28.7	29 507	4 312	125	766	1 038	2 379	13 358	14 146	29.2
1235	Eagle Lake	3 551	NA	NA	1 704	863	8	0	976	1 430	1 440	8 160	7.0
1237	Eagle Mountain CDP	5 847	NA	NA	5 089	22	23	647	66	163	2 306	NA	60.9
1240	Eagle Pass	20 651	21 407	-3.5	11 696	18	76	66	8 795	19 678	6 358	3 957	12.3
1260	Eastland	3 690	NA	NA	3 446	57	8	19	160	318	1 784	8 449	7.3
1275	Edcouch	2 878	NA	NA	2 345	0	6	2	525	2 769	827	3 610	2.0
1285	Edgecliff village	2 715	NA	NA	2 428	180	9	25	73	155	1 001	13 998	3.1
1295	Edinburg	29 885	24 075	24.1	22 191	139	55	132	7 368	25 668	9 206	6 140	36.6
1300	Edna	5 343	NA	NA	4 041	878	16	6	402	1 403	2 279	7 755	9.3
1305	El Campo	10 511	10 462	0.5	7 823	1 258	10	31	1 389	3 320	4 133	8 795	14.8
1325	Electra	3 113	NA	NA	2 846	174	32	1	60	121	1 689	8 617	6.1
1330	Elgin	4 846	NA	NA	2 584	930	18	8	1 306	1 897	1 910	7 662	7.2
1336	El Lago	3 269	NA	NA	3 174	25	1	36	33	109	1 453	16 347	1.7
1340	El Paso	515 342	425 259	21.2	396 122	17 708	2 239	5 956	93 317	355 669	168 625	7 670	635.5
1345	Elsa	5 242	NA	NA	4 072	6	0	1	1 163	5 076	1 609	3 604	3.8
1370	Ennis	13 883	12 102	14.7	9 369	2 526	28	32	1 928	2 910	5 050	9 269	43.2
1380	Euless	38 149	24 002	58.9	32 986	1 758	211	1 953	1 241	2 998	17 117	13 940	41.5
1395	Everman	5 672	NA	NA	4 256	960	16	72	368	614	2 048	10 023	4.5
1400	Fabens CDP	5 599	NA	NA	4 548	16	16	0	1 019	5 242	1 499	NA	10.2
1405	Fairfield	3 234	NA	NA	2 379	764	9	19	63	129	1 450	11 021	11.3
1415	Falfurrias	5 788	NA	NA	4 742	3	12	8	1 023	5 249	2 149	5 876	6.3
1425	Farmers Branch	24 250	24 863	-2.5	20 589	674	158	563	2 266	4 895	9 213	14 763	31.1
1430	Farmersville	2 640	NA	NA	2 111	295	2	1	231	303	1 120	NA	8.0
1453	First Colony CDP	18 327	NA	NA	14 174	875	16	2 936	326	1 192	5 976	NA	24.2
1465	Floresville	5 247	NA	NA	4 156	81	11	5	994	3 329	1 838	6 418	12.3
1467	Flower Mound town	15 527	NA	NA	14 727	321	60	156	263	658	5 366	15 837	83.0
1470	Floydada	3 896	NA	NA	2 273	238	12	7	1 366	1 682	1 641	7 005	5.2
1480	Forest Hill	11 482	11 684	-1.7	3 882	7 026	18	57	499	857	3 909	9 737	11.0
1485	Forney town	4 070	NA	NA	3 562	395	18	6	89	191	1 567	NA	19.3
1489	Fort Bliss CDP	13 915	12 687	9.7	8 448	3 976	111	439	941	2 255	2 807	NA	16.0
1493	Fort Hood CDP	35 580	31 250	13.9	19 543	12 064	282	1 260	2 431	4 405	5 618	NA	39.2
1495	Fort Stockton	8 524	NA	NA	5 296	49	30	24	3 125	5 475	3 190	7 749	11.2
1500	Fort Worth	447 619	385 166	16.2	285 549	98 532	1 914	8 910	52 714	87 345	194 429	10 515	728.0
1515	Fredericksburg	6 934	NA	NA	6 590	11	32	6	295	989	3 161	9 425	10.6
1525	Freeport	11 389	13 442	-15.3	7 086	1 739	41	32	2 491	4 395	4 835	8 787	29.7
1530	Freer	3 271	NA	NA	2 565	4	4	16	682	2 424	1 308	6 235	10.4
1531	Fresno CDP	3 182	NA	NA	1 485	581	13	7	1 096	1 510	1 069	NA	22.5
1532	Friendswood	22 814	10 719	112.8	21 404	620	68	385	337	1 386	8 048	9 379	53.7
1535	Friona	3 688	NA	NA	3 451	58	16	17	146	1 886	1 315	7 749	3.4
1540	Frisco	6 141	NA	NA	5 121	126	37	29	828	1 330	2 263	10 317	88.5
1563	Gainesville	14 256	14 081	1.2	12 424	1 005	122	105	600	920	6 421	8 876	34.9
1565	Galena Park	10 033	NA	NA	6 397	1 019	19	23	2 575	4 677	3 297	9 067	12.9
1570	Galveston	59 070	61 902	-4.6	36 315	17 161	144	1 387	4 063	12 649	30 898	10 286	119.6
1580	Garland	180 650	138 857	30.1	143 927	16 028	954	8 084	11 657	21 015	69 595	12 419	148.5
1595	Gatesville	11 492	NA	NA	7 676	2 835	76	27	878	1 368	2 909	8 733	21.3
1600	Georgetown	14 842	NA	NA	12 882	768	57	86	1 049	3 105	5 767	9 164	34.8
1605	George West	2 586	NA	NA	1 979	6	7	12	582	1 380	1 013	6 788	4.9
1610	Giddings	4 093	NA	NA	2 801	653	2	10	627	831	1 754	8 645	13.3
1620	Gilmer	4 822	NA	NA	3 725	1 016	17	4	60	126	2 140	9 551	10.2
1625	Gladewater	6 027	NA	NA	4 780	1 164	39	11	33	89	2 699	8 110	30.4
1627	Glenn Heights	4 564	NA	NA	3 766	575	33	9	181	357	1 919	NA	18.1
1655	Gonzales	6 527	NA	NA	4 414	1 035	10	11	1 057	2 651	2 619	6 804	9.0
1680	Graham	8 986	NA	NA	8 388	145	35	46	372	609	4 073	11 051	14.2
1685	Granbury	4 045	NA	NA	3 851	17	14	64	99	271	2 050	10 063	9.7
1695	Grand Prairie	99 616	71 457	39.4	75 524	9 694	774	3 002	10 622	20 467	38 721	11 072	177.4
1700	Grand Saline	2 630	NA	NA	2 510	1	8	6	105	152	1 200	8 323	5.0
1720	Grapevine	29 202	11 801	147.5	27 653	523	134	331	561	1 657	11 907	13 854	81.0
1725	Greenville	23 071	22 161	4.1	17 571	4 614	76	131	679	1 453	10 163	9 054	61.6
1745	Groesbeck	3 185	NA	NA	2 245	731	13	6	190	288	1 405	8 831	8.5
1755	Groves	16 513	17 090	-3.4	15 545	565	30	95	278	1 103	6 576	11 103	13.5
1773	Gun Barrel City town	3 526	NA	NA	3 445	39	13	17	12	56	2 130	NA	10.3
1790	Hallettsville	2 718	NA	NA	2 135	474	1	7	101	184	1 239	9 425	5.7
1800	Haltom City	32 856	29 014	13.2	29 514	419	242	1 590	1 091	2 804	14 030	10 396	32.0

1. Codes shown are 2-digit FIPS codes for states; 4-digit census place codes for places; and 3-digit FIPS county codes followed by 3-digit census MCD codes for minor civil divisions (MCDs). MCD names are followed by county names in parentheses. 2. Hispanic persons may be of any race. 3. Dry land or land partially or temporarily covered by water.

State/ Place/ MCD[1] code	Place	Population 1990	Places of 10,000 or more 1980	Percent change, 1980–1990	Race: White	Black	Am. Indian, Eskimo Aleut	Asian & Pacific Islander	Other race	Hispanic[2]	Total housing units, 1990	Per capita income, 1985 (Dollars)	Land area,[3] 1990 (Sq. Km.)
		1	2	3	4	5	6	7	8	9	10	11	12
	TEXAS—Con.												
1805	Hamilton	2 937	NA	NA	2 798	0	9	17	113	156	1 530	8 862	6.7
1810	Hamlin	2 791	NA	NA	2 144	226	9	16	396	545	1 253	8 736	13.8
1819	Harker Heights	12 841	NA	NA	10 638	1 321	77	419	386	1 179	5 182	9 900	29.6
1820	Harlingen	48 735	43 543	11.9	39 015	371	104	207	9 038	34 613	17 798	7 163	69.7
1835	Haskell	3 362	NA	NA	2 626	165	7	6	558	683	1 622	8 577	8.8
1845	Hearne	5 132	NA	NA	2 170	2 254	12	5	691	1 081	2 103	7 322	10.6
1850	Hebbronville CDP	4 465	NA	NA	3 818	2	6	3	636	4 118	1 741	NA	14.9
1860	Hedwig Village	2 616	NA	NA	2 110	45	4	176	281	552	1 033	21 058	2.2
1870	Hempstead	3 551	NA	NA	1 571	1 730	3	7	240	396	1 545	7 762	10.4
1875	Henderson	11 139	11 473	-2.9	8 049	2 703	49	16	322	588	4 856	11 765	28.3
1880	Henrietta	2 896	NA	NA	2 816	22	32	10	16	47	1 387	8 392	11.0
1885	Hereford	14 745	15 853	-7.0	10 277	296	40	37	4 095	7 625	5 404	7 843	14.5
1888	Hewitt	8 983	NA	NA	8 186	500	25	111	161	595	3 207	10 682	17.6
1895	Hidalgo	3 292	NA	NA	1 596	20	0	9	1 667	3 229	880	NA	9.0
1905	Highland Park town	8 739	NA	NA	8 558	36	12	53	80	221	3 930	35 713	5.8
1910	Highlands CDP	6 632	NA	NA	6 251	86	23	18	254	426	2 455	NA	16.0
1915	Highland Village	7 027	NA	NA	6 802	71	12	62	80	191	2 352	16 578	10.8
1925	Hillsboro	7 072	NA	NA	5 368	1 267	22	14	401	1 164	3 212	7 930	21.5
1935	Hitchcock	5 868	NA	NA	3 566	2 038	11	7	246	654	2 333	8 826	86.8
1950	Hollywood Park town	2 841	NA	NA	2 739	21	9	34	38	210	1 116	19 331	3.8
1952	Homestead Meadows CDP	4 978	NA	NA	3 791	27	16	6	1 138	3 964	1 312	NA	51.2
1955	Hondo	6 018	NA	NA	4 942	33	15	12	1 016	3 811	2 202	6 187	23.9
1970	Hooks	2 684	NA	NA	2 480	143	31	18	12	32	1 207	9 384	5.3
1975	Houston	1 630 553	1 595 167	2.2	859 069	457 990	4 126	67 113	242 255	450 483	726 435	12 115	1 398.3
1995	Humble	12 060	NA	NA	9 932	935	51	289	853	1 459	5 260	11 678	25.5
2000	Hunters Creek Village	3 954	NA	NA	3 783	11	6	116	38	135	1 460	44 908	5.0
2010	Huntsville	27 925	23 936	16.7	18 071	7 461	113	260	2 020	3 631	9 136	7 057	54.3
2015	Hurst	33 574	31 420	6.9	31 343	875	155	416	785	1 740	13 801	13 778	25.6
2020	Hutchins	2 719	NA	NA	1 329	1 062	13	32	283	463	1 128	8 237	22.0
2037	Ingleside	5 696	NA	NA	4 734	69	33	15	845	1 712	2 274	8 212	27.0
2045	Iowa Park	6 072	NA	NA	5 935	3	37	17	80	175	2 417	10 182	8.7
2060	Irving	155 037	109 943	41.0	122 068	11 653	1 006	7 146	13 164	25 238	71 059	13 175	175.1
2075	Jacinto City	9 343	NA	NA	6 377	116	47	25	2 778	4 936	3 127	9 540	4.8
2080	Jacksboro	3 350	NA	NA	3 162	50	6	8	124	158	1 659	11 301	13.5
2085	Jacksonville	12 765	12 264	4.1	8 514	3 100	40	151	960	1 409	5 045	8 494	32.7
2090	Jasper	6 959	NA	NA	3 864	2 900	13	12	170	225	2 909	7 427	19.6
2105	Jersey Village	4 826	NA	NA	4 464	57	8	242	55	201	1 543	15 882	6.5
2123	Jollyville CDP	15 206	NA	NA	13 276	715	44	619	552	1 287	6 713	NA	20.4
2135	Joshua	3 828	NA	NA	3 716	2	29	9	72	146	1 561	NA	14.8
2140	Jourdanton	3 220	NA	NA	2 763	22	22	6	407	1 555	1 172	7 645	8.5
2145	Junction	2 654	NA	NA	2 302	0	0	9	343	610	1 247	7 171	5.9
2155	Karnes City town	2 916	NA	NA	2 130	182	5	3	596	1 690	1 101	7 445	5.5
2160	Katy	8 005	NA	NA	7 090	384	26	26	479	1 063	2 954	12 083	20.8
2165	Kaufman	5 238	NA	NA	3 805	782	8	14	629	1 077	2 067	9 002	9.1
2170	Keene	3 944	NA	NA	3 290	204	21	100	329	801	1 414	8 446	6.1
2175	Keller	13 683	NA	NA	13 338	78	69	91	107	392	4 792	11 681	47.4
2195	Kenedy	3 763	NA	NA	2 571	112	25	8	1 047	2 362	1 453	7 249	8.5
2200	Kennedale	4 096	NA	NA	3 804	98	31	24	139	288	1 623	9 212	10.4
2210	Kermit	6 875	NA	NA	4 802	142	41	9	1 881	2 782	2 985	8 031	6.5
2215	Kerrville	17 384	15 276	13.8	14 883	712	51	103	1 635	3 818	8 315	10 643	40.2
2220	Kilgore	11 066	10 983	0.8	9 356	1 445	37	12	216	358	4 878	12 129	30.9
2230	Killeen	63 535	46 296	37.2	36 908	19 109	340	3 654	3 524	8 898	26 439	7 981	71.7
2233	Kingsland CDP	2 725	NA	NA	2 658	3	11	10	43	114	2 031	NA	23.4
2235	Kingsville	25 276	28 808	-12.3	16 886	951	64	395	6 980	15 765	10 100	7 619	32.9
2238	Kingwood CDP	37 397	16 267	129.9	35 609	495	79	714	500	1 650	12 810	NA	40.0
2240	Kirby	8 326	NA	NA	6 076	1 285	36	123	806	2 409	3 006	9 401	4.8
2287	Lackland AFB CDP	9 352	14 595	-35.9	7 202	1 519	53	261	317	909	894	NA	12.6
2290	Lacy-Lakeview	3 617	NA	NA	3 039	277	18	25	258	479	1 810	7 927	7.2
2300	La Feria	4 360	NA	NA	3 422	6	4	6	922	3 598	1 571	5 420	3.3
2305	La Grange	3 951	NA	NA	3 164	444	8	7	328	503	1 955	8 852	8.2
2322	La Joya	2 604	NA	NA	1 947	2	5	0	650	2 558	690	NA	5.0
2332	Lake Dallas	3 656	NA	NA	3 521	31	29	11	64	171	1 559	10 266	5.8
2340	Lake Jackson	22 776	19 102	19.2	20 376	728	71	508	1 093	2 458	8 964	14 502	35.7
2358	Lakeway	4 044	NA	NA	3 946	12	13	25	48	123	2 259	NA	9.5
2365	Lake Worth	4 591	NA	NA	4 372	15	23	42	139	306	1 778	10 796	6.5
2370	La Marque	14 120	15 361	-8.1	9 069	4 404	42	83	522	1 438	5 943	10 143	36.9
2375	Lamesa	10 809	11 790	-8.3	7 295	583	13	17	2 901	4 941	4 339	8 144	12.1
2380	Lampasas	6 382	NA	NA	5 478	138	44	43	679	1 264	2 863	8 170	14.9
2385	Lancaster	22 117	14 807	49.4	14 377	6 598	115	121	906	1 770	8 446	10 273	75.5
2390	La Porte	27 910	14 062	98.5	23 810	1 983	140	281	1 696	3 992	9 966	11 135	49.9
2400	Laredo	122 899	91 449	34.4	87 048	144	195	473	35 039	115 360	33 998	5 275	85.1
2403	Laughlin AFB CDP	2 556	NA	NA	2 064	298	16	100	78	365	659	NA	15.3
2414	League City	30 159	16 575	82.0	26 575	1 547	103	699	1 235	3 540	11 381	12 711	133.1

1. Codes shown are 2-digit FIPS codes for states; 4-digit census place codes for places; and 3-digit FIPS county codes followed by 3-digit census MCD codes for minor civil divisions (MCDs). MCD names are followed by county names in parentheses. 2. Hispanic persons may be of any race. 3. Dry land or land partially or temporarily covered by water.

State/ Place/ MCD[1] code	Place	Population 1990	Places of 10,000 or more: 1980	Places of 10,000 or more: Percent change, 1980–1990	Race: White	Race: Black	Race: Am. Indian, Eskimo Aleut	Race: Asian & Pacific Islander	Race: Other race	Hispanic[2]	Total housing units, 1990	Per capita income, 1985 (Dollars)	Land area,[3] 1990 (Sq. Km.)
		1	2	3	4	5	6	7	8	9	10	11	12
	TEXAS—Con.												
2421	Leander	3 398	NA	NA	3 101	46	13	35	203	419	1 278	NA	11.1
2440	Leon Valley	9 581	NA	NA	8 321	199	30	169	862	3 268	3 653	12 659	8.9
2445	Levelland	13 986	13 809	1.3	10 487	866	54	26	2 553	4 594	5 286	9 084	25.5
2450	Lewisville	46 521	24 273	91.7	41 226	2 159	278	892	1 966	4 026	19 724	12 349	93.3
2460	Liberty	7 733	NA	NA	6 130	1 143	9	27	424	656	3 125	10 360	92.0
2485	Littlefield	6 489	NA	NA	5 212	509	23	13	732	2 486	2 791	8 526	15.5
2487	Live Oak	10 023	NA	NA	8 539	654	48	244	538	1 941	3 671	9 560	12.1
2490	Livingston town	5 019	NA	NA	3 678	1 088	30	36	187	374	2 211	8 030	21.0
2495	Llano	2 962	NA	NA	2 873	15	8	0	66	205	1 437	8 023	8.5
2500	Lockhart	9 205	NA	NA	6 299	936	10	23	1 937	4 523	3 468	7 372	22.0
2530	Longview	70 311	62 762	12.0	53 884	13 989	308	415	1 715	2 896	30 293	10 452	135.5
2532	Lopezville CDP	2 827	NA	NA	2 222	0	4	1	600	2 763	740	NA	2.8
2546	Lost Creek CDP	4 095	NA	NA	3 863	18	12	163	39	141	1 352	NA	7.5
2565	Lubbock	186 206	173 979	7.0	144 549	15 939	570	2 617	22 531	41 916	77 852	10 067	269.7
2575	Lufkin	30 206	28 562	5.8	19 701	8 222	58	240	1 985	2 911	12 488	9 575	61.1
2580	Luling	4 661	NA	NA	3 198	549	3	2	909	1 706	2 042	6 718	7.9
2582	Lumberton	6 640	NA	NA	6 571	2	21	5	41	109	2 438	NA	23.4
2595	McAllen	84 021	66 281	26.8	59 603	288	165	576	23 389	64 672	28 597	7 941	84.0
2605	McGregor	4 683	NA	NA	3 459	729	23	4	468	856	1 876	8 004	14.0
2610	McKinney	21 283	16 256	30.9	16 152	2 742	111	111	2 167	3 598	8 539	9 506	115.0
2630	Madisonville	3 569	NA	NA	2 302	1 059	13	10	185	392	1 554	8 123	9.2
2650	Mansfield	15 607	NA	NA	14 497	420	73	62	555	1 343	5 517	11 451	100.3
2652	Manvel	3 733	NA	NA	3 498	59	17	21	138	359	1 315	11 382	74.1
2660	Marble Falls	4 007	NA	NA	3 364	117	14	11	501	725	1 840	7 129	13.9
2680	Marlin	6 386	NA	NA	3 185	2 703	7	7	484	714	3 015	7 313	11.7
2690	Marshall	23 682	24 921	-5.0	13 208	9 864	64	90	456	660	9 683	8 398	62.2
2720	Mathis	5 423	NA	NA	2 565	82	18	8	2 750	4 796	1 673	4 273	5.2
2737	Meadows	4 606	NA	NA	3 775	140	7	556	128	339	1 496	14 140	2.3
2765	Mercedes	12 694	11 851	7.1	10 208	20	11	8	2 447	11 541	4 042	4 945	19.2
2795	Mesquite	101 484	67 053	51.3	88 501	5 912	557	2 666	3 848	8 900	39 251	11 616	110.9
2800	Mexia	6 933	NA	NA	4 238	2 214	3	38	440	607	3 088	6 912	13.4
2810	Midland	89 443	70 525	26.8	71 382	8 179	332	858	8 692	19 060	38 453	14 404	170.5
2815	Midlothian	5 141	NA	NA	4 588	161	15	21	356	572	2 068	10 157	62.5
2830	Mineola	4 321	NA	NA	3 331	803	16	4	167	247	1 916	9 736	13.5
2835	Mineral Wells	14 870	14 448	2.9	12 875	765	67	151	1 012	1 830	6 256	8 297	52.7
2850	Mission	28 653	22 551	27.1	21 595	47	51	42	6 918	22 945	10 658	5 819	36.0
2852	Mission Bend CDP	24 945	NA	NA	16 896	2 777	63	3 535	1 674	3 824	8 035	NA	13.5
2855	Missouri City	36 176	24 533	47.5	21 922	10 653	102	2 261	1 238	3 346	12 346	16 123	60.1
2860	Monahans	8 101	NA	NA	6 120	385	39	20	1 537	3 060	3 305	8 695	60.5
2890	Morton	2 597	NA	NA	1 610	195	2	0	790	1 342	980	7 370	3.8
2910	Mount Pleasant	12 291	11 003	11.7	7 972	2 494	44	20	1 761	2 092	4 670	9 214	25.8
2925	Muleshoe	4 571	NA	NA	4 112	106	7	11	335	1 947	1 893	7 687	8.9
2945	Nacogdoches	30 872	27 149	13.7	22 701	6 938	64	268	901	1 562	12 253	8 457	64.6
2956	Nassau Bay	4 320	NA	NA	4 091	42	9	125	53	173	2 283	19 972	3.3
2965	Navasota	6 296	NA	NA	3 230	2 306	4	16	740	1 340	2 480	7 212	15.6
2970	Nederland	16 192	16 855	-3.9	15 719	88	47	130	208	735	6 501	11 374	12.9
2985	New Boston town	5 057	NA	NA	4 065	934	30	15	13	39	2 171	8 922	8.6
2990	New Braunfels	27 334	22 404	22.0	23 363	344	66	94	3 467	9 500	11 065	10 166	65.9
3025	Nocona	2 870	NA	NA	2 679	3	22	1	165	188	1 457	8 445	7.1
3050	North Richland Hills	45 895	30 592	50.0	42 975	832	236	754	1 098	2 681	18 121	12 939	47.2
3080	Odessa	89 699	90 027	-0.4	67 624	5 355	447	614	15 659	27 920	37 751	10 606	91.6
3115	Olney	3 519	NA	NA	3 110	97	12	2	298	400	1 793	10 032	5.3
3130	Orange	19 381	23 628	-18.0	12 563	6 450	37	195	136	457	8 532	9 201	55.5
3150	Ozona CDP	3 181	NA	NA	3 132	36	4	1	8	1 796	1 339	NA	12.1
3160	Palacios town	4 418	NA	NA	3 150	255	4	284	725	1 965	1 896	9 104	12.2
3165	Palestine	18 042	15 948	13.1	12 513	4 252	34	71	1 172	1 655	7 676	9 110	44.9
3175	Pampa	19 959	21 396	-6.7	17 634	886	182	106	1 151	1 784	9 475	10 664	22.6
3195	Paris	24 699	25 498	-3.1	18 752	5 464	240	138	105	287	11 191	8 438	70.4
3200	Pasadena	119 363	112 560	6.0	99 943	1 162	579	1 873	15 806	34 411	47 539	10 818	113.4
3215	Pearland	18 697	13 219	41.4	17 001	312	64	270	1 050	2 311	6 827	13 919	51.0
3225	Pearsall	6 924	NA	NA	4 487	166	8	19	2 244	5 529	2 281	5 563	10.9
3231	Pecan Grove CDP	9 502	NA	NA	8 717	332	23	116	314	768	3 466	NA	22.1
3235	Pecos	12 069	12 855	-6.1	11 619	336	15	31	68	8 769	4 432	7 016	18.9
3245	Perryton	7 607	NA	NA	6 602	2	95	8	900	1 382	3 301	11 040	9.2
3258	Pflugerville	4 444	NA	NA	3 854	196	23	63	308	485	1 504	NA	6.4
3260	Pharr	32 921	21 381	54.0	23 122	38	61	32	9 668	29 111	11 031	4 857	40.9
3268	Pilot Point	2 538	NA	NA	2 317	140	14	2	65	124	1 044	NA	7.6
3279	Pinehurst CDP	3 284	NA	NA	3 181	21	19	3	60	182	1 239	NA	23.4
3280	Pinehurst	2 682	NA	NA	2 470	154	1	35	22	57	1 218	9 653	4.9
3290	Piney Point Village	3 197	NA	NA	2 986	15	4	145	47	130	1 188	43 736	5.5
3295	Pittsburg	4 007	NA	NA	2 470	1 276	11	3	247	309	1 742	9 249	8.2
3305	Plainview	21 700	22 187	-2.2	13 929	1 457	96	127	6 091	9 083	8 152	8 034	33.7
3310	Plano	128 713	72 329	78.0	113 879	5 325	441	5 158	3 910	8 019	47 370	14 980	171.6

1. Codes shown are 2-digit FIPS codes for states; 4-digit census place codes for places; and 3-digit FIPS county codes followed by 3-digit census MCD codes for minor civil divisions (MCDs). MCD names are followed by county names in parentheses. 2. Hispanic persons may be of any race. 3. Dry land or land partially or temporarily covered by water.

Table D. Places — Population, Housing, Money Income, and Land Area

State/ Place/ MCD[1] code	Place	Population: 1990	Population: Places of 10,000 or more: 1980	Population: Places of 10,000 or more: Percent change, 1980–1990	Population characteristics, 1990: Race: White	Race: Black	Race: Am. Indian, Eskimo Aleut	Race: Asian & Pacific Islander	Race: Other race	Hispanic[2]	Total housing units, 1990	Per capita income, 1985 (Dollars)	Land area,[3] 1990 (Sq. Km.)
		1	2	3	4	5	6	7	8	9	10	11	12
	TEXAS—Con.												
3312	Pleasanton	7 678	NA	NA	6 238	87	29	28	1 296	3 466	2 980	7 474	16.5
3335	Port Arthur	58 724	61 251	-4.1	28 955	24 778	147	2 825	2 019	4 829	25 746	8 519	200.0
3340	Port Isabel	4 467	NA	NA	3 938	25	6	10	488	3 337	1 720	5 334	5.4
3345	Portland	12 224	12 023	1.7	11 215	100	51	60	798	2 931	4 566	11 997	15.2
3350	Port Lavaca	10 886	10 911	-0.2	7 762	509	19	330	2 266	5 076	4 319	8 836	16.6
3355	Port Neches	12 974	13 944	-7.0	12 640	39	47	129	119	421	5 246	12 246	23.6
3365	Post	3 768	NA	NA	3 289	320	8	21	130	1 170	1 547	7 462	9.7
3370	Poteet	3 206	NA	NA	2 320	3	7	0	876	2 741	1 079	5 068	4.9
3385	Prairie View	4 004	NA	NA	42	3 905	1	19	37	49	698	4 847	18.7
3390	Premont	2 914	NA	NA	2 016	8	3	13	874	2 253	1 069	7 811	4.4
3395	Presidio	3 072	NA	NA	2 384	5	7	10	666	2 916	1 049	NA	9.7
3435	Quanah	3 413	NA	NA	2 800	205	12	10	386	451	1 673	9 776	9.0
3465	Ranger	2 803	NA	NA	2 510	176	12	3	102	293	1 362	6 637	18.1
3480	Raymondville	8 880	NA	NA	6 740	54	12	10	2 064	7 790	2 838	5 238	7.0
3490	Red Oak	3 124	NA	NA	2 895	81	22	3	123	199	1 174	NA	6.9
3500	Refugio town	3 158	NA	NA	2 320	441	3	2	392	1 262	1 404	8 240	4.0
3504	Rendon CDP	7 658	NA	NA	7 195	320	11	6	126	336	2 873	NA	64.7
3520	Richardson	74 840	72 480	3.3	64 947	3 502	239	4 949	1 203	3 255	28 734	16 625	73.2
3530	Richland Hills	7 978	NA	NA	7 600	75	39	65	199	415	3 270	13 708	8.1
3540	Richmond	9 801	NA	NA	5 100	1 738	22	25	2 916	4 825	3 453	8 936	8.7
3545	Richwood	2 732	NA	NA	2 305	121	13	28	265	388	1 267	11 873	3.8
3555	Rio Grande City CDP	9 891	NA	NA	6 971	6	15	2	2 897	9 581	2 958	NA	18.6
3575	River Oaks	6 580	NA	NA	6 291	18	29	47	195	630	2 877	11 179	5.2
3595	Robinson	7 111	NA	NA	6 746	132	18	31	184	464	2 586	9 878	87.8
3600	Robstown	12 849	12 100	6.2	7 970	238	16	24	4 601	11 701	4 135	5 417	23.9
3615	Rockdale	5 235	NA	NA	4 129	815	7	5	279	887	2 358	8 866	8.1
3620	Rockport	4 753	NA	NA	3 862	92	28	265	506	1 132	2 721	9 069	15.1
3630	Rockwall	10 486	NA	NA	9 824	391	43	78	150	472	4 360	15 112	38.0
3645	Roma	8 059	NA	NA	4 533	5	10	2	3 509	7 891	2 293	2 953	6.7
3665	Rosenberg	20 183	17 995	12.2	12 869	1 584	48	76	5 606	8 920	7 420	8 226	29.2
3675	Round Rock	30 923	11 762	162.9	26 175	1 714	135	331	2 568	5 795	11 699	11 449	49.5
3685	Rowlett	23 260	NA	NA	21 058	1 252	84	325	541	1 388	8 153	12 973	48.4
3710	Rusk	4 366	NA	NA	3 248	944	24	27	123	174	1 486	7 458	17.3
3720	Sachse	5 346	NA	NA	4 983	130	38	42	153	282	1 891	NA	23.4
3725	Saginaw	8 551	NA	NA	7 948	97	54	109	343	995	3 007	9 618	19.4
3740	San Angelo	84 474	73 240	15.3	66 571	4 057	319	961	12 566	23 646	34 619	9 658	124.0
3745	San Antonio	935 933	785 809	19.1	676 082	65 884	3 303	10 703	179 961	520 282	365 414	8 499	862.6
3755	San Benito	20 125	17 988	11.9	15 256	42	29	23	4 775	17 627	6 543	5 312	23.5
3765	San Diego	4 983	NA	NA	3 734	4	7	1	1 237	4 756	1 700	5 172	4.2
3771	San Elizario CDP	4 385	NA	NA	3 528	8	31	1	817	4 260	1 069	NA	22.0
3780	Sanger	3 508	NA	NA	3 271	109	31	2	95	273	1 388	8 642	6.8
3785	San Juan	10 815	NA	NA	8 475	8	18	10	2 304	9 820	3 158	4 936	9.5
3791	San Leon CDP	3 328	NA	NA	2 927	5	16	329	51	133	1 986	NA	12.6
3795	San Marcos	28 743	23 420	22.7	22 527	1 535	66	256	4 359	10 751	10 923	6 472	45.1
3810	San Saba town	2 626	NA	NA	2 367	9	4	0	246	678	1 266	6 893	4.5
3815	Sansom Park	3 928	NA	NA	3 531	8	41	12	336	514	1 482	8 555	3.2
3822	Santa Fe	8 429	NA	NA	8 164	9	37	26	193	728	3 195	9 652	32.9
3844	Schertz	10 555	NA	NA	9 342	390	62	151	610	1 871	4 105	10 158	58.0
3854	Seabrook	6 685	NA	NA	6 157	126	34	209	159	439	3 419	13 537	14.8
3865	Seagoville	8 969	NA	NA	7 656	747	56	49	461	982	3 347	11 113	42.0
3875	Sealy	4 541	NA	NA	3 378	723	2	13	425	1 052	1 905	10 040	10.7
3880	Seguin	18 853	17 854	5.6	12 267	2 314	62	120	4 090	9 107	7 145	7 269	30.7
3884	Seminole	6 342	NA	NA	5 023	115	23	13	1 168	2 105	2 312	8 729	6.7
3885	Serenada CDP	3 242	NA	NA	3 177	11	12	13	29	91	1 092	NA	17.2
3895	Seymour	3 185	NA	NA	2 826	172	6	13	168	254	1 675	8 042	6.9
3920	Sherman	31 601	30 413	3.9	26 298	3 990	298	242	773	1 386	14 261	10 638	96.8
3935	Silsbee	6 368	NA	NA	4 368	1 951	15	12	22	128	2 659	8 388	16.7
3945	Sinton	5 549	NA	NA	3 628	210	7	16	1 688	3 760	2 031	7 332	5.7
3955	Slaton	6 078	NA	NA	4 552	591	7	4	924	2 228	2 440	7 336	14.2
3965	Smithville	3 196	NA	NA	2 326	603	2	5	260	460	1 554	7 654	6.7
3970	Snyder	12 195	12 705	-4.0	9 039	510	34	27	2 585	3 361	5 231	10 640	20.3
3971	Socorro town	22 995	NA	NA	18 071	23	68	8	4 825	21 967	5 449	NA	45.3
3990	Sonora	2 751	NA	NA	2 053	1	14	5	678	1 238	1 201	10 839	6.0
4000	South Houston	14 207	13 293	6.9	9 401	382	58	140	4 226	8 490	4 818	8 599	7.8
4005	Southlake	7 065	NA	NA	6 853	46	43	32	91	251	2 445	15 844	55.9
4025	Spearman	3 197	NA	NA	2 705	0	9	6	477	597	1 385	11 286	5.4
4035	Spring CDP	33 111	NA	NA	29 375	1 931	117	429	1 259	3 106	11 469	NA	61.8
4050	Spring Valley	3 392	NA	NA	3 266	6	2	89	29	138	1 345	22 487	3.4
4060	Stafford town	8 397	NA	NA	5 860	734	30	699	1 074	2 350	3 211	10 873	18.1
4065	Stamford	3 817	NA	NA	2 965	299	8	11	534	899	1 856	8 631	15.2
4070	Stanton	2 576	NA	NA	1 422	68	9	8	1 069	1 261	999	NA	3.7
4075	Stephenville	13 502	11 881	13.6	12 571	179	63	95	594	951	6 333	9 682	21.0
4115	Sugar Land	24 529	NA	NA	19 422	1 219	47	3 157	684	2 077	8 579	14 222	31.8

1. Codes shown are 2-digit FIPS codes for states; 4-digit census place codes for places; and 3-digit FIPS county codes followed by 3-digit census MCD codes for minor civil divisions (MCDs). MCD names are followed by county names in parentheses. 2. Hispanic persons may be of any race. 3. Dry land or land partially or temporarily covered by water.

State/ Place/ MCD[1] code	Place	Population			Population characteristics, 1990						Total housing units, 1990	Per capita income, 1985 (Dollars)	Land area,[3] 1990 (Sq. Km.)
		1990	Places of 10,000 or more		Race					Hispanic[2]			
			1980	Percent change, 1980–1990	White	Black	Am. Indian, Eskimo Aleut	Asian & Pacific Islander	Other race				
		1	2	3	4	5	6	7	8	9	10	11	12
	TEXAS—Con.												
4120	Sulphur Springs	14 062	12 804	9.8	11 793	2 004	49	45	171	478	6 375	9 679	45.2
4150	Sweeny town	3 297	NA	NA	2 594	464	6	5	228	353	1 286	11 362	4.7
4155	Sweetwater	11 967	12 242	-2.2	8 819	666	32	18	2 432	3 468	5 282	8 959	22.5
4160	Taft	3 222	NA	NA	2 336	143	8	5	730	1 978	1 210	7 726	3.9
4170	Tahoka	2 868	NA	NA	2 051	199	14	3	601	1 039	1 222	7 333	6.2
4177	Tanglewood Forest CDP	2 941	NA	NA	2 204	251	5	66	415	674	1 430	NA	4.1
4190	Taylor	11 472	10 619	8.0	7 881	1 918	19	45	1 609	3 277	4 727	8 308	27.9
4192	Taylor Lake Village	3 394	NA	NA	3 234	78	4	68	10	122	1 205	18 879	2.9
4195	Teague	3 268	NA	NA	2 502	630	5	8	123	159	1 532	8 764	9.0
4205	Temple	46 109	42 483	8.5	33 571	7 898	164	423	4 053	6 320	20 718	10 047	111.3
4215	Terrell	12 490	13 225	-5.6	7 361	4 540	31	110	448	854	4 735	7 709	45.7
4220	Terrell Hills	4 592	NA	NA	4 445	42	6	13	86	390	1 971	25 167	4.3
4225	Texarkana	31 656	31 271	1.2	19 934	11 362	115	144	101	354	14 313	8 992	54.5
4230	Texas City	40 822	41 403	-1.4	27 391	10 262	165	468	2 536	6 508	16 676	9 724	160.9
4242	The Colony	22 113	11 596	90.7	19 596	1 055	135	389	938	1 904	7 151	12 662	30.3
4243	The Woodlands CDP	29 205	NA	NA	27 531	600	61	494	519	1 743	11 389	NA	42.4
4269	Timberwood Park CDP	2 578	NA	NA	2 478	12	2	23	63	349	932	NA	51.4
4290	Tomball	6 370	NA	NA	5 629	401	19	44	277	496	2 727	10 002	25.6
4299	Town West CDP	6 166	NA	NA	4 299	364	21	880	602	1 191	1 981	NA	2.7
4320	Trinity	2 648	NA	NA	1 664	899	1	13	71	111	1 289	6 871	9.8
4323	Trophy Club town	3 922	NA	NA	3 769	66	9	52	26	107	1 583	NA	9.7
4330	Tulia	4 699	NA	NA	3 062	241	18	13	1 365	1 620	1 974	8 115	8.3
4350	Tyler	75 450	70 501	7.0	49 891	21 252	214	386	3 707	6 724	32 860	11 048	102.7
4356	Universal City	13 057	10 720	21.8	11 211	758	60	316	712	2 080	5 423	12 307	14.4
4358	University Park	22 259	22 254	0.0	21 325	245	31	493	165	567	8 983	20 146	9.6
4360	Uvalde	14 729	14 178	3.9	8 494	39	37	57	6 102	10 356	5 248	6 478	14.3
4385	Van Horn town	2 930	NA	NA	1 999	1	12	23	895	2 202	1 073	4 503	7.1
4400	Vernon	12 001	12 695	-5.5	9 195	1 277	55	79	1 395	1 847	5 379	9 212	20.9
4405	Victoria	55 076	50 695	8.6	42 362	4 373	142	227	7 972	20 847	21 802	10 179	78.0
4407	Vidor	10 935	12 043	-9.2	10 844	0	19	17	55	252	4 294	8 511	27.4
4415	Waco	103 590	101 262	2.3	70 031	23 972	291	955	8 341	16 934	45 088	8 894	196.3
4425	Wake Village	4 757	NA	NA	4 343	360	30	9	15	76	1 900	9 740	4.1
4452	Watauga	20 009	10 284	94.6	18 471	328	99	637	474	1 431	6 538	9 617	10.6
4455	Waxahachie	18 168	14 624	24.2	13 255	3 084	76	53	1 700	2 676	6 981	9 455	80.7
4460	Weatherford	14 804	12 049	22.9	13 678	404	119	94	509	951	6 577	9 466	42.2
4465	Webster	4 678	NA	NA	3 920	255	23	213	267	873	2 842	NA	13.6
4487	Wells Branch CDP	7 094	NA	NA	5 503	639	16	354	582	951	3 894	NA	5.7
4490	Weslaco	21 877	19 331	13.2	17 379	38	43	104	4 313	17 434	8 851	5 663	21.7
4500	West	2 515	NA	NA	2 321	131	1	4	58	115	1 159	NA	3.5
4510	West Columbia	4 372	NA	NA	3 257	778	18	7	312	497	1 788	9 470	6.6
4518	West Lake Hills	2 542	NA	NA	2 480	3	5	32	22	82	1 046	NA	9.6
4527	West Odessa CDP	16 568	NA	NA	13 367	105	126	28	2 942	5 331	5 978	NA	170.8
4530	West Orange	4 187	NA	NA	4 103	26	9	16	33	148	1 841	9 790	8.2
4540	West University Place	12 920	12 010	7.6	12 480	53	13	280	94	464	5 680	18 922	5.2
4550	Wharton	9 011	NA	NA	5 712	2 392	4	70	833	2 325	3 942	9 032	14.0
4575	Whitehouse	4 032	NA	NA	3 819	125	8	43	37	71	1 426	NA	7.1
4580	White Oak	5 136	NA	NA	4 988	82	34	17	15	62	1 933	10 004	23.5
4585	Whitesboro	3 209	NA	NA	3 166	3	16	7	17	41	1 465	8 752	7.1
4590	White Settlement	15 472	13 508	14.5	13 930	681	97	249	515	1 060	6 167	8 993	12.7
4605	Wichita Falls	96 259	94 201	2.2	77 415	10 788	693	1 762	5 601	9 661	40 364	10 042	140.2
4610	Willis	2 764	NA	NA	1 905	591	13	3	252	308	1 124	NA	5.3
4615	Wills Point	2 986	NA	NA	2 252	560	11	4	159	188	1 239	7 898	8.0
4630	Windcrest	5 331	NA	NA	4 855	265	13	68	130	441	2 276	21 211	4.8
4632	Windemere CDP	3 207	NA	NA	2 546	310	10	59	282	471	1 255	NA	6.6
4655	Winnsboro	2 904	NA	NA	2 701	169	5	9	20	41	1 456	8 500	8.7
4660	Winters	2 905	NA	NA	2 737	43	4	7	114	889	1 321	7 848	5.5
4690	Woodville town	2 636	NA	NA	1 850	767	7	6	6	32	1 096	8 555	8.2
4695	Woodway	8 695	NA	NA	8 443	55	20	117	60	169	3 228	13 511	17.1
4705	Wylie	8 716	NA	NA	8 268	88	62	30	268	469	3 496	11 251	42.3
4710	Yoakum	5 611	NA	NA	4 179	814	5	3	610	1 452	2 506	7 273	11.6
4720	Zapata CDP	7 119	NA	NA	5 080	0	8	8	2 023	5 789	3 151	NA	17.4
49	UTAH	1 722 850	1 461 037	17.9	1 615 845	11 576	24 283	33 371	37 775	84 597	598 388	8 535	212 815.5
0005	Alpine	3 492	NA	NA	3 455	3	11	15	8	14	792	8 240	17.9
0025	American Fork	15 696	12 564	24.9	15 334	8	66	121	167	376	4 222	6 845	15.9
0065	Blanding	3 162	NA	NA	2 134	4	971	10	43	81	907	4 940	5.0
0075	Bountiful	36 659	32 877	11.5	36 012	35	100	347	165	588	11 488	10 335	27.6
0080	Brigham City	15 644	15 596	0.3	14 822	11	261	143	407	783	5 204	9 223	32.3
0087	Canyon Rim CDP	10 527	NA	NA	10 239	30	44	143	71	202	3 932	NA	5.4
0100	Cedar City	13 443	10 972	22.5	12 824	39	458	74	48	236	4 356	7 095	29.0
0110	Centerville	11 500	NA	NA	11 321	9	30	90	50	160	3 088	9 523	15.9
0135	Clearfield	21 435	17 982	19.2	18 368	984	373	863	847	1 778	6 516	7 020	19.3

1. Codes shown are 2-digit FIPS codes for states; 4-digit census place codes for places; and 3-digit FIPS county codes followed by 3-digit census MCD codes for minor civil divisions (MCDs). MCD names are followed by county names in parentheses. 2. Hispanic persons may be of any race. 3. Dry land or land partially or temporarily covered by water.

State/ Place/ MCD[1] code	Place	Population: 1990	Population: Places of 10,000 or more: 1980	Population: Places of 10,000 or more: Percent change, 1980–1990	Population characteristics, 1990: Race: White	Race: Black	Race: Am. Indian, Eskimo Aleut	Race: Asian & Pacific Islander	Race: Other race	Hispanic[2]	Total housing units, 1990	Per capita income, 1985 (Dollars)	Land area,[3] 1990 (Sq. Km.)
		1	2	3	4	5	6	7	8	9	10	11	12
	UTAH—Con.												
0145	Clinton	7 945	NA	NA	7 503	52	20	155	215	463	2 053	7 509	14.3
0168	Cottonwood Heights CDP	28 766	22 665	26.9	28 055	65	78	394	174	648	9 101	NA	17.5
0169	Cottonwood West CDP	17 476	NA	NA	16 970	37	33	333	103	400	7 157	NA	10.0
0170	Delta	2 998	NA	NA	2 936	0	25	21	16	67	1 012	NA	7.6
0182	Draper	7 257	NA	NA	6 574	224	97	102	260	557	1 468	8 256	78.4
0196	East Millcreek CDP	21 184	24 150	-12.3	20 733	58	43	261	89	339	7 418	NA	11.5
0225	Ephraim	3 363	NA	NA	2 999	8	45	198	113	156	943	5 188	6.8
0245	Farmington	9 028	NA	NA	8 885	23	22	60	38	135	2 243	8 668	13.7
0280	Fruit Heights	3 900	NA	NA	3 846	4	9	30	11	40	1 001	9 902	5.7
0318	Granite CDP	3 300	NA	NA	3 242	12	3	33	10	39	903	NA	10.0
0320	Grantsville	4 500	NA	NA	4 330	5	59	19	87	216	1 472	8 367	44.8
0333	Harrisville	3 004	NA	NA	2 908	6	6	20	64	140	795	NA	7.2
0340	Heber	4 782	NA	NA	4 719	1	32	5	25	122	1 653	6 419	5.5
0361	Highland	5 002	NA	NA	4 956	5	8	20	13	60	1 015	NA	17.2
0371	Holladay-Cottonwood CDP	14 095	22 189	-36.5	13 822	35	20	172	46	242	4 927	NA	18.0
0377	Hooper CDP	3 468	NA	NA	3 401	1	15	18	33	57	929	NA	29.0
0395	Hurricane	3 915	NA	NA	3 839	1	30	32	13	53	1 325	NA	57.2
0405	Hyrum	4 829	NA	NA	4 654	8	62	48	57	175	1 305	6 896	9.6
0430	Kanab	3 289	NA	NA	3 227	3	34	8	17	63	1 258	NA	35.8
0445	Kaysville	13 961	NA	NA	13 695	12	46	124	84	274	3 843	8 828	24.6
0450	Kearns CDP	28 374	21 353	32.9	26 813	117	233	701	510	2 135	8 039	NA	12.6
0480	Layton	41 784	22 862	82.8	38 727	864	278	965	950	2 350	13 462	8 893	47.3
0495	Lehi	8 475	NA	NA	8 285	6	41	83	60	163	2 421	6 867	14.7
0510	Lindon	3 818	NA	NA	3 758	3	13	21	23	56	902	7 078	21.8
0512	Little Cottonwood Creek Valley CDP	5 042	NA	NA	4 957	1	8	48	28	70	1 556	NA	5.2
0520	Logan	32 762	26 844	22.0	29 933	193	412	1 673	551	1 027	11 440	7 489	36.6
0530	Maeser CDP	2 598	NA	NA	2 515	0	54	5	24	83	848	NA	16.8
0535	Magna CDP	17 829	13 138	35.7	16 795	83	144	259	548	1 488	5 534	NA	19.3
0555	Mapleton	3 572	NA	NA	3 542	0	2	6	22	69	921	7 411	23.9
0580	Midvale	11 886	10 146	17.1	10 345	46	144	460	891	1 818	4 972	8 482	8.9
0593	Millcreek CDP	32 230	NA	NA	30 052	357	333	866	622	1 797	14 530	NA	19.0
0605	Moab	3 971	NA	NA	3 767	5	148	19	32	181	1 761	8 458	7.9
0634	Mount Olympus CDP	7 413	NA	NA	7 194	6	13	178	22	91	2 550	NA	8.8
0640	Murray	31 282	25 750	21.5	29 968	205	170	463	476	1 325	12 347	10 260	24.7
0650	Nephi	3 515	NA	NA	3 445	2	43	9	16	29	1 274	7 946	9.9
0670	North Logan	3 768	NA	NA	3 691	12	16	44	5	39	985	NA	12.3
0675	North Ogden	11 668	NA	NA	11 418	23	42	113	72	212	3 238	9 063	16.0
0680	North Salt Lake	6 474	NA	NA	6 301	11	26	66	70	192	2 197	9 047	19.0
0695	Ogden	63 909	64 407	-0.8	55 885	1 741	687	1 123	4 473	7 669	27 194	9 233	67.6
0707	Oquirrh CDP	7 593	NA	NA	7 201	20	47	112	213	472	1 967	NA	6.7
0720	Orem	67 561	52 399	28.9	65 121	88	534	1 041	777	2 040	17 965	7 094	46.5
0740	Park City	4 468	NA	NA	4 378	12	23	40	15	123	5 544	16 858	21.8
0750	Payson	9 510	NA	NA	9 186	3	31	25	265	400	2 659	6 253	14.6
0765	Plain City	2 722	NA	NA	2 670	1	8	16	27	54	754	NA	8.2
0770	Pleasant Grove	13 476	10 833	24.4	13 218	11	45	60	142	330	3 549	6 976	17.8
0775	Pleasant View	3 603	NA	NA	3 538	6	17	16	26	57	1 146	10 079	17.4
0790	Price	8 712	NA	NA	8 020	33	103	75	481	899	3 410	8 673	10.7
0795	Providence	3 344	NA	NA	3 293	1	17	18	15	25	897	8 152	6.9
0800	Provo	86 835	74 108	17.2	81 683	229	929	2 374	1 620	3 623	24 578	6 347	100.0
0815	Richfield	5 593	NA	NA	5 374	1	197	3	18	76	2 067	7 729	9.0
0825	Riverdale	6 419	NA	NA	6 023	98	43	115	140	262	2 422	9 020	11.4
0835	Riverton	11 261	NA	NA	11 050	8	15	65	123	315	2 832	7 373	21.1
0840	Roosevelt	3 915	NA	NA	3 578	3	294	7	33	81	1 347	8 215	13.6
0845	Roy	24 603	19 694	24.9	23 254	237	128	425	559	1 290	7 935	9 263	17.5
0855	St. George	28 502	11 350	151.1	27 586	52	464	200	200	579	11 766	7 072	148.9
0870	Salt Lake City	159 936	163 033	-1.9	139 177	2 752	2 541	7 566	7 900	15 508	73 762	10 248	282.4
0875	Sandy	75 058	50 546	48.5	72 846	140	232	1 271	569	1 906	20 110	9 391	51.8
0905	Smithfield	5 566	NA	NA	5 426	0	12	41	87	156	1 577	7 130	10.3
0920	South Jordan	12 220	NA	NA	11 977	7	23	105	108	252	2 885	7 814	52.2
0925	South Ogden	12 105	11 346	6.7	11 528	101	45	219	212	417	4 501	10 867	8.1
0930	South Salt Lake	10 129	10 561	-4.1	8 915	134	233	349	498	981	4 984	8 513	11.6
0935	South Weber	2 863	NA	NA	2 725	17	57	33	31	88	696	NA	12.0
0940	Spanish Fork	11 272	NA	NA	11 108	1	46	28	89	247	3 363	6 978	19.7
0955	Springville	13 950	12 101	15.3	13 678	10	99	81	82	258	4 361	7 214	25.0
0975	Sunset	5 128	NA	NA	4 794	62	20	134	118	420	1 773	8 480	3.9
0980	Syracuse	4 658	NA	NA	4 510	14	17	73	44	158	1 209	7 445	15.9
0987	Taylorsville-Bennion CDP	52 351	17 448	200.0	48 980	358	327	1 513	1 173	2 918	16 509	NA	28.7
0990	Tooele	13 887	14 335	-3.1	12 981	50	154	120	582	1 564	5 190	9 807	32.2
1005	Tremonton	4 264	NA	NA	3 972	5	27	68	192	258	1 415	8 632	12.4
1022	Union CDP	13 684	NA	NA	13 170	65	44	200	205	603	5 399	NA	7.3
1024	Val Verda CDP	3 712	NA	NA	3 618	2	11	53	28	102	1 146	NA	2.0
1025	Vernal	6 644	NA	NA	6 299	6	165	44	130	264	2 845	8 447	11.8
1045	Washington	4 198	NA	NA	4 075	11	52	14	46	80	1 793	5 485	65.3

1. Codes shown are 2-digit FIPS codes for states; 4-digit census place codes for places; and 3-digit FIPS county codes followed by 3-digit census MCD codes for minor civil divisions (MCDs). MCD names are followed by county names in parentheses. 2. Hispanic persons may be of any race. 3. Dry land or land partially or temporarily covered by water.

State/ Place/ MCD[1] code	Place	Population 1990	Population: Places of 10,000 or more 1980	Population: Places of 10,000 or more Percent change, 1980–1990	Population characteristics, 1990: Race White	Race Black	Race Am. Indian, Eskimo Aleut	Race Asian & Pacific Islander	Race Other race	Hispanic[2]	Total housing units, 1990	Per capita income, 1985 (Dollars)	Land area,[3] 1990 (Sq. Km.)
		1	2	3	4	5	6	7	8	9	10	11	12
	UTAH—Con.												
1050	Washington Terrace	8 189	NA	NA	7 662	190	56	108	173	418	2 898	8 775	4.5
1070	West Bountiful	4 477	NA	NA	4 417	1	7	38	14	86	1 124	7 290	5.6
1075	West Jordan	42 892	27 192	57.7	40 324	121	272	825	1 350	2 784	11 640	7 256	69.5
1080	West Point	4 258	NA	NA	4 111	25	21	47	54	138	1 149	NA	18.6
1082	West Valley City	86 976	72 378	20.2	79 016	737	957	3 446	2 820	6 212	27 367	7 802	88.1
1083	White City CDP	6 506	NA	NA	6 284	19	16	89	98	257	1 799	NA	2.6
1095	Woods Cross	5 384	NA	NA	5 237	6	53	61	27	116	1 642	8 538	8.9
50	VERMONT	562 758	511 456	10.0	555 088	1 951	1 696	3 215	808	3 661	271 214	9 619	23 955.7
0140	Barre	9 482	NA	NA	9 405	24	20	19	14	189	4 321	9 289	10.4
0180	Bellows Falls village	3 313	NA	NA	3 285	3	8	15	2	22	1 494	8 743	3.6
0198	Bennington CDP	9 532	NA	NA	9 425	25	10	68	4	56	3 975	NA	12.6
0338	Brattleboro CDP	8 612	NA	NA	8 330	85	16	125	56	116	3 873	NA	24.7
0460	Burlington	39 127	37 712	3.8	37 876	390	123	583	155	483	15 480	9 542	27.3
0840	Essex Junction village	8 396	NA	NA	8 168	58	14	141	15	89	3 375	12 875	13.1
1528	Middlebury CDP	6 007	NA	NA	5 778	87	6	111	25	97	1 891	NA	36.0
1610	Montpelier	8 247	NA	NA	8 097	37	25	78	10	117	3 769	10 749	26.6
1730	Newport	4 434	NA	NA	4 387	13	5	15	14	28	2 128	8 300	16.2
2210	Rutland	18 230	18 436	-1.1	18 035	72	23	84	16	82	8 083	9 839	19.7
2240	St. Albans	7 339	NA	NA	7 199	16	82	27	15	40	3 241	9 068	5.2
2268	St. Johnsbury CDP	6 424	NA	NA	6 359	16	17	23	9	35	3 040	NA	33.6
2420	South Burlington	12 809	10 679	19.9	12 429	72	40	249	19	116	5 437	15 000	43.1
2440	Springfield CDP	4 207	NA	NA	4 149	1	14	40	3	22	2 000	NA	6.2
2670	Vergennes	2 578	NA	NA	2 534	9	21	13	1	13	970	NA	6.3
2875	West Brattleboro CDP	3 135	NA	NA	3 093	16	4	17	5	15	1 458	NA	25.8
3030	White River Junction CDP	2 521	NA	NA	2 467	9	14	24	7	23	1 232	NA	4.3
3160	Winooski	6 649	NA	NA	6 491	49	17	73	19	60	2 926	10 016	3.8
0010	Bristol town (Addison)	3 762	NA	NA	3 738	9	6	9	0	19	1 471	8 310	107.1
0010	Middlebury town (Addison)	8 034	NA	NA	7 798	87	6	117	26	100	2 687	8 762	101.2
0030	Bennington town (Bennington)	16 451	15 815	4.0	16 199	70	32	131	19	139	6 392	8 966	109.9
0030	Manchester town (Bennington)	3 622	NA	NA	3 590	8	3	18	3	16	2 275	12 763	109.4
0030	Pownal town (Bennington)	3 485	NA	NA	3 460	7	6	12	0	12	1 457	7 882	120.8
0030	Shaftsbury town (Bennington)	3 368	NA	NA	3 346	9	2	8	3	21	1 429	9 847	111.5
0050	Hardwick town (Caledonia)	2 964	NA	NA	2 920	0	44	0	0	15	1 275	6 038	100.0
0050	Lyndon town (Caledonia)	5 371	NA	NA	5 322	16	12	21	0	18	2 080	7 354	102.1
0050	St. Johnsbury town (Caledonia)	7 608	NA	NA	7 538	16	18	25	11	36	3 487	9 251	95.1
0070	Charlotte town (Chittenden)	3 148	NA	NA	3 120	7	2	12	7	18	1 329	14 593	107.0
0070	Colchester town (Chittenden)	14 731	12 629	16.6	14 479	81	29	126	16	136	5 922	10 803	95.7
0070	Essex town (Chittenden)	16 498	14 392	14.6	16 105	106	20	240	27	143	6 310	12 244	101.1
0070	Hinesburg town (Chittenden)	3 780	NA	NA	3 755	9	3	12	1	20	1 487	9 346	103.4
0070	Jericho town (Chittenden)	4 302	NA	NA	4 246	23	3	24	6	26	1 489	11 795	91.1
0070	Milton town (Chittenden)	8 404	NA	NA	8 343	11	23	22	5	31	3 009	9 152	134.0
0070	Richmond town (Chittenden)	3 729	NA	NA	3 696	2	12	8	11	23	1 391	11 950	82.8
0070	Shelburne town (Chittenden)	5 871	NA	NA	5 775	21	8	60	7	37	2 350	14 893	63.3
0070	Underhill town (Chittenden)	2 799	NA	NA	2 780	5	4	7	3	16	1 013	NA	132.7
0070	Williston town (Chittenden)	4 887	NA	NA	4 821	21	3	35	7	51	1 874	13 148	78.6
0110	Enosburg town (Franklin)	2 535	NA	NA	2 491	0	41	3	0	4	1 115	NA	125.8
0110	Georgia town (Franklin)	3 753	NA	NA	3 725	8	4	15	1	10	1 397	9 471	101.9
0110	Highgate town (Franklin)	3 020	NA	NA	2 911	2	93	7	7	10	1 247	NA	132.7
0110	St. Albans town (Franklin)	4 606	NA	NA	4 546	13	33	13	1	19	2 115	9 746	96.8
0110	Swanton town (Franklin)	5 636	NA	NA	5 366	6	252	10	2	14	2 423	8 744	125.4
0150	Cambridge town (Lamoille)	2 667	NA	NA	2 649	6	1	7	4	11	1 104	NA	164.7
0150	Johnson town (Lamoille)	3 156	NA	NA	3 081	5	26	22	22	34	1 097	7 338	119.8
0150	Morristown town (Lamoille)	4 733	NA	NA	4 709	7	7	10	0	14	2 080	8 055	130.2
0150	Stowe town (Lamoille)	3 433	NA	NA	3 399	4	3	24	3	13	2 830	12 309	188.3
0170	Bradford town (Orange)	2 522	NA	NA	2 504	5	7	4	2	13	1 075	NA	77.1
0170	Randolph town (Orange)	4 764	NA	NA	4 711	11	10	22	10	13	1 830	7 754	124.7
0170	Williamstown town (Orange)	2 839	NA	NA	2 833	1	1	4	0	12	1 133	NA	104.2
0190	Barton town (Orleans)	2 967	NA	NA	2 950	2	7	8	0	13	1 382	7 154	113.2
0190	Derby town (Orleans)	4 479	NA	NA	4 425	19	24	9	2	14	2 082	8 769	127.4
0210	Brandon town (Rutland)	4 223	NA	NA	4 206	3	2	10	2	9	1 654	7 780	104.0
0210	Castleton town (Rutland)	4 278	NA	NA	4 231	17	2	17	11	25	2 026	7 724	101.1
0210	Clarendon town (Rutland)	2 835	NA	NA	2 814	6	3	10	2	9	1 172	NA	81.7
0210	Fair Haven town (Rutland)	2 887	NA	NA	2 867	3	4	2	11	18	1 196	8 570	45.7
0210	Pittsford town (Rutland)	2 919	NA	NA	2 908	1	5	5	0	9	1 289	9 551	112.9
0210	Poultney town (Rutland)	3 498	NA	NA	3 470	5	4	17	2	10	1 624	8 730	113.8
0211	Rutland town (Rutland)	3 781	NA	NA	3 748	11	3	15	4	26	1 520	12 249	50.4
0230	Barre town (Washington)	7 411	NA	NA	7 372	8	8	19	4	111	2 747	10 127	79.3
0230	Berlin town (Washington)	2 561	NA	NA	2 551	0	3	7	0	31	1 022	NA	94.5
0230	Northfield town (Washington)	5 610	NA	NA	5 490	33	13	49	25	80	1 877	7 849	113.0
0230	Waterbury town (Washington)	4 589	NA	NA	4 560	8	2	15	4	20	1 956	9 066	125.1
0250	Brattleboro town (Windham)	12 241	11 835	3.4	11 913	102	20	144	62	137	5 551	10 667	82.9

1. Codes shown are 2-digit FIPS codes for states; 4-digit census place codes for places; and 3-digit FIPS county codes followed by 3-digit census MCD codes for minor civil divisions (MCDs). MCD names are followed by county names in parentheses. 2. Hispanic persons may be of any race. 3. Dry land or land partially or temporarily covered by water.

State/ Place/ MCD[1] code	Place	Population: 1990	Population: Places of 10,000 or more: 1980	Population: Places of 10,000 or more: Percent change, 1980–1990	Population characteristics, 1990: Race: White	Race: Black	Race: Am. Indian, Eskimo Aleut	Race: Asian & Pacific Islander	Race: Other race	Hispanic[2]	Total housing units, 1990	Per capita income, 1985 (Dollars)	Land area,[3] 1990 (Sq. Km.)
		1	2	3	4	5	6	7	8	9	10	11	12
	VERMONT—Con.												
0250	Rockingham town (Windham)	5 484	NA	NA	5 439	6	8	26	5	37	2 476	8 410	108.5
0250	Westminster town (Windham)	3 026	NA	NA	2 996	15	4	11	0	12	1 294	NA	119.4
0270	Chester town (Windsor)	2 832	NA	NA	2 827	2	1	1	1	10	1 527	9 031	144.8
0270	Hartford town (Windsor)	9 404	NA	NA	9 228	52	24	86	14	54	5 026	11 257	117.0
0270	Hartland town (Windsor)	2 988	NA	NA	2 961	5	4	13	5	12	1 270	NA	116.4
0270	Norwich town (Windsor)	3 093	NA	NA	3 022	20	5	38	8	17	1 382	NA	115.6
0270	Springfield town (Windsor)	9 579	10 190	-6.0	9 471	9	31	60	8	46	4 256	10 061	127.7
0271	Weathersfield town (Windsor)	2 674	NA	NA	2 664	0	5	4	1	10	1 249	8 709	113.4
0271	Windsor town (Windsor)	3 714	NA	NA	3 684	8	11	10	1	16	1 647	8 930	50.6
0271	Woodstock town (Windsor)	3 212	NA	NA	3 180	10	7	10	5	12	1 755	13 048	115.3
51	VIRGINIA	6 187 358	5 346 797	15.7	4 791 739	1 162 994	15 282	159 053	58 290	160 288	2 496 334	11 894	102 558.3
0005	Abingdon town	7 003	NA	NA	6 683	289	11	11	9	23	3 172	10 075	21.2
0025	Alexandria	111 183	103 217	7.7	76 789	24 339	333	4 632	5 090	10 778	58 252	19 783	39.6
0035	Altavista town	3 686	NA	NA	2 935	739	5	5	2	9	1 618	10 728	12.7
0042	Annandale CDP	50 975	49 524	2.9	42 154	1 946	108	5 724	1 043	3 522	20 156	NA	35.8
0052	Aquia Harbour CDP	6 308	NA	NA	5 864	291	19	107	27	131	2 021	NA	13.7
0056	Arlington CDP	170 936	152 599	12.0	130 873	17 940	537	11 560	10 026	23 089	84 847	NA	67.0
0058	Ashburn CDP	3 393	NA	NA	3 157	93	6	108	29	87	1 528	NA	17.6
0060	Ashland town	5 864	NA	NA	4 816	989	17	28	14	52	2 106	9 830	10.7
0062	Bailey's Crossroads CDP	19 507	12 564	55.3	11 562	2 177	56	2 581	3 131	5 429	8 166	NA	5.3
0064	Barracks CDP	4 710	NA	NA	3 771	440	9	440	50	89	2 228	NA	3.5
0075	Bedford	6 073	NA	NA	4 691	1 338	7	33	4	53	2 625	9 356	17.7
0081	Belle Haven CDP	6 427	NA	NA	5 695	499	11	164	58	157	3 233	NA	5.5
0085	Bellwood CDP	6 178	NA	NA	4 951	1 113	18	62	34	79	2 547	NA	15.4
0087	Bensley CDP	5 093	NA	NA	3 884	857	21	260	71	160	2 302	NA	7.5
0090	Berryville town	3 097	NA	NA	2 690	405	0	2	0	14	1 096	NA	3.4
0095	Big Stone Gap town	4 748	NA	NA	4 448	248	10	35	7	16	1 993	8 922	12.5
0100	Blacksburg town	34 590	30 638	12.9	30 243	1 477	37	2 663	170	610	11 857	8 219	48.6
0105	Blackstone town	3 497	NA	NA	1 927	1 545	1	20	4	17	1 457	7 842	5.3
0115	Bluefield town	5 363	NA	NA	5 058	231	0	73	1	16	2 346	10 686	19.8
0119	Blue Ridge CDP	2 840	NA	NA	2 760	71	3	4	2	3	1 017	NA	16.4
0122	Bon Air CDP	16 413	16 224	1.2	15 177	902	21	282	31	144	6 252	NA	22.9
0155	Bridgewater town	3 918	NA	NA	3 818	72	3	13	12	39	1 357	8 923	5.7
0160	Bristol	18 426	19 042	-3.2	17 240	1 063	13	91	19	64	8 174	9 866	30.0
0190	Buena Vista	6 406	NA	NA	6 093	282	5	21	5	12	2 494	8 361	17.7
0192	Bull Run CDP	5 525	NA	NA	4 377	764	14	228	142	239	2 878	NA	6.9
0194	Burke CDP	57 734	33 835	70.6	49 368	2 347	133	5 177	709	2 678	18 812	NA	29.7
0212	Cave Spring CDP	24 053	21 682	10.9	23 107	488	24	405	29	148	10 492	NA	30.7
0216	Centreville CDP	26 585	NA	NA	22 929	1 807	76	1 462	311	1 112	11 334	NA	25.2
0217	Chamberlayne CDP	4 577	NA	NA	2 963	1 561	6	40	7	14	1 884	NA	9.8
0218	Chantilly CDP	29 337	12 259	139.3	25 250	1 255	68	2 529	235	998	11 005	NA	30.3
0225	Charlottesville	40 341	39 916	1.1	30 684	8 561	39	935	122	476	16 785	10 733	26.6
0242	Chesapeake	151 976	114 486	32.7	107 399	41 662	444	1 899	572	1 913	55 742	10 501	882.4
0245	Chester CDP	14 986	11 728	27.8	13 288	1 395	45	220	38	183	5 839	NA	33.6
0255	Chincoteague town	3 572	NA	NA	3 515	39	9	9	0	25	3 167	NA	24.9
0260	Christiansburg town	15 004	10 345	45.0	14 149	796	2	49	8	76	6 267	9 962	35.0
0285	Clifton Forge	4 679	NA	NA	3 967	695	2	8	7	25	2 131	8 912	8.0
0315	Collinsville CDP	7 280	NA	NA	6 846	390	1	16	27	57	3 292	NA	18.9
0320	Colonial Beach town	3 132	NA	NA	2 680	402	14	28	8	19	1 924	NA	4.0
0325	Colonial Heights	16 064	16 509	-2.7	15 502	129	33	354	46	161	6 592	12 376	19.3
0332	Commonwealth CDP	5 538	NA	NA	4 454	922	3	142	17	87	2 584	NA	3.1
0334	Countryside CDP	8 349	NA	NA	7 754	322	20	214	39	234	2 942	NA	9.7
0340	Covington	6 991	NA	NA	5 953	969	6	51	12	27	3 269	9 386	11.5
0355	Culpeper town	8 581	NA	NA	6 880	1 461	46	166	28	66	3 647	10 961	17.4
0357	Dale City CDP	47 170	33 127	42.4	36 129	8 268	174	1 868	731	2 498	15 245	NA	39.3
0370	Danville	53 056	45 642	16.2	33 247	19 431	72	262	44	276	23 297	9 848	111.5
0412	Dumbarton CDP	8 526	NA	NA	6 639	1 656	43	122	66	128	4 508	NA	7.3
0414	Dumfries town	4 282	NA	NA	3 118	999	21	91	53	160	1 606	10 642	4.4
0423	Dunn Loring CDP	6 509	NA	NA	5 602	121	12	746	28	258	2 234	NA	5.3
0427	East Highland Park CDP	11 850	11 797	0.4	4 088	7 644	21	83	14	51	4 885	NA	23.2
0445	Emporia	5 306	NA	NA	2 849	2 420	11	24	2	59	2 178	8 361	17.8
0448	Ettrick CDP	5 290	NA	NA	1 371	3 857	11	30	21	47	1 599	NA	7.7
0460	Fairfax	19 622	19 390	1.2	16 830	966	43	1 409	374	1 159	7 677	16 812	16.0
0470	Falls Church	9 578	NA	NA	8 533	298	42	456	249	604	4 668	20 699	5.2
0475	Falmouth CDP	3 541	NA	NA	3 410	89	13	19	10	49	1 286	NA	8.1
0480	Farmville town	6 046	NA	NA	4 475	1 499	3	56	13	38	1 789	7 985	11.6
0491	Fishersville CDP	3 230	NA	NA	3 038	169	6	12	5	35	1 201	NA	35.5
0494	Forest CDP	5 624	NA	NA	5 332	229	9	51	3	46	2 287	NA	35.0
0496	Fort Belvoir CDP	8 590	NA	NA	5 229	2 663	55	290	353	695	2 106	NA	20.5
0497	Fort Hunt CDP	12 989	14 294	-9.1	12 220	319	19	386	45	275	4 942	NA	12.8
0498	Fort Lee CDP	6 895	NA	NA	3 266	3 036	38	214	341	581	1 495	NA	14.7
0499	Franconia CDP	19 882	NA	NA	16 328	1 749	42	1 533	230	805	8 414	NA	18.9

1. Codes shown are 2-digit FIPS codes for states; 4-digit census place codes for places; and 3-digit FIPS county codes followed by 3-digit census MCD codes for minor civil divisions (MCDs). MCD names are followed by county names in parentheses. 2. Hispanic persons may be of any race. 3. Dry land or land partially or temporarily covered by water.

State/ Place/ MCD[1] code	Place	Population 1990	Population: Places of 10,000 or more 1980	Population: Places of 10,000 or more Percent change, 1980–1990	Population characteristics, 1990: Race White	Race Black	Race Am. Indian, Eskimo Aleut	Race Asian & Pacific Islander	Race Other race	Hispanic[2]	Total housing units, 1990	Per capita income, 1985 (Dollars)	Land area,[3] 1990 (Sq. Km.)
		1	2	3	4	5	6	7	8	9	10	11	12
	VIRGINIA—Con.												
0500	Franklin	7 864	NA	NA	3 637	4 199	6	20	2	15	3 166	9 383	19.9
0505	Fredericksburg	19 027	15 322	24.2	14 468	4 115	27	205	212	463	8 063	10 506	27.2
0515	Front Royal town	11 880	11 126	6.8	10 770	1 002	18	33	57	125	4 983	9 436	24.0
0520	Galax	6 670	NA	NA	6 219	387	8	15	41	65	2 943	11 272	20.9
0538	Glen Allen CDP	9 010	NA	NA	6 124	2 754	24	81	27	53	3 514	NA	26.1
0548	Gloucester Point CDP	8 509	NA	NA	7 684	686	13	99	27	115	3 585	NA	21.7
0558	Great Falls CDP	6 945	NA	NA	6 541	37	5	349	13	170	2 308	NA	46.3
0567	Groveton CDP	19 997	18 860	6.0	14 070	3 479	56	1 428	964	1 828	7 998	NA	15.2
0590	Hampton	133 793	122 617	9.1	78 149	51 981	392	2 339	932	2 636	53 623	10 883	134.2
0600	Harrisonburg	30 707	19 671	56.1	27 968	2 018	37	469	215	481	10 900	9 158	45.5
0615	Herndon town	16 139	11 449	41.0	12 526	1 557	40	1 386	630	1 548	5 786	14 898	11.0
0620	Highland Springs CDP	13 823	12 146	13.8	8 682	4 898	66	108	69	149	5 485	NA	22.3
0637	Hollins CDP	13 305	12 287	8.3	12 712	450	16	110	17	73	5 179	NA	22.5
0638	Hollymead CDP	2 628	NA	NA	2 448	126	0	50	4	28	1 106	NA	12.6
0643	Hopewell	23 101	23 397	-1.3	16 687	5 910	64	307	133	417	9 625	9 392	26.5
0646	Huntington CDP	7 489	NA	NA	5 933	974	32	334	216	564	4 426	NA	2.0
0648	Hybla Valley CDP	15 491	15 533	-0.3	9 655	4 239	51	1 139	407	875	6 411	NA	7.9
0649	Idylwood CDP	14 710	11 982	22.8	11 165	1 197	33	1 634	681	1 791	6 423	NA	7.4
0677	Jefferson CDP	25 782	24 342	5.9	19 233	1 543	114	3 334	1 558	3 415	10 274	NA	13.2
0708	Lake Barcroft CDP	8 686	NA	NA	7 505	298	23	618	242	890	3 651	NA	6.5
0711	Lake Ridge CDP	23 862	11 072	115.5	20 773	1 995	59	737	298	936	8 488	NA	13.3
0713	Lakeside CDP	12 081	12 289	-1.7	11 226	690	19	131	15	75	5 682	NA	13.4
0714	Laurel CDP	13 011	10 569	23.1	10 636	1 955	39	342	39	146	5 771	NA	14.7
0720	Lebanon town	3 386	NA	NA	3 242	132	2	4	6	14	1 455	9 807	10.6
0725	Leesburg town	16 202	NA	NA	13 820	1 987	32	227	136	393	6 994	12 976	29.9
0730	Lexington	6 959	NA	NA	6 027	811	22	89	10	62	2 311	8 832	6.5
0732	Lincolnia CDP	13 041	10 350	26.0	9 292	1 772	48	1 414	515	1 531	5 156	NA	7.6
0739	Loch Lomond CDP	3 292	NA	NA	2 984	141	9	83	75	137	1 043	NA	1.9
0744	Lorton CDP	15 385	NA	NA	7 230	7 098	88	803	166	622	3 997	NA	32.2
0755	Luray town	4 587	NA	NA	4 276	280	6	25	0	19	2 013	9 355	12.3
0760	Lynchburg	66 049	66 743	-1.0	47 853	17 445	105	501	145	476	27 233	10 655	127.9
0772	McLean CDP	38 168	35 642	7.1	33 713	645	60	3 528	222	1 603	14 266	NA	48.0
0777	Madison Heights CDP	11 700	14 146	-17.3	9 678	1 949	38	31	4	66	4 168	NA	49.9
0780	Manassas	27 957	15 438	81.1	23 332	2 889	90	867	779	1 601	10 232	13 685	25.9
0785	Manassas Park	6 734	NA	NA	5 941	490	7	169	127	314	2 252	8 821	4.7
0787	Mantua CDP	6 804	NA	NA	5 944	193	23	599	45	201	2 645	NA	6.3
0790	Marion town	6 630	NA	NA	6 122	447	15	40	6	35	2 795	9 863	10.8
0795	Martinsville	16 162	18 149	-10.9	10 134	5 954	21	32	21	59	7 310	11 516	28.4
0798	Mechanicsville CDP	22 027	NA	NA	20 784	1 064	49	113	17	144	8 613	NA	73.6
0802	Merrifield CDP	8 399	NA	NA	6 379	496	22	1 276	226	776	3 679	NA	7.1
0818	Montclair CDP	11 399	NA	NA	10 452	572	23	273	79	313	3 616	NA	15.6
0824	Montrose CDP	6 405	NA	NA	4 089	2 210	38	49	19	47	2 760	NA	8.8
0836	Mount Vernon CDP	27 485	24 058	14.2	19 034	5 767	87	1 632	965	1 899	10 834	NA	19.7
0853	Newington CDP	17 965	NA	NA	14 611	1 601	33	1 501	219	822	6 238	NA	17.5
0860	Newport News	170 045	144 903	17.4	106 418	57 077	579	3 969	2 002	4 710	69 728	10 640	177.0
0875	Norfolk	261 229	266 979	-2.2	148 228	102 012	1 165	6 815	3 009	7 611	98 762	9 340	139.2
0883	North Springfield CDP	8 996	NA	NA	7 765	241	18	862	110	381	3 358	NA	6.3
0895	Norton	4 247	NA	NA	3 923	269	13	35	7	31	1 845	9 048	18.8
0898	Oakton CDP	24 610	19 150	28.5	21 564	1 013	63	1 507	463	1 562	9 921	NA	25.5
0920	Orange town	2 582	NA	NA	2 209	365	0	6	2	21	1 063	8 714	2.8
0960	Petersburg	38 386	41 055	-6.5	10 194	27 688	83	289	132	472	16 196	9 346	59.3
0967	Pimmit Hills CDP	6 019	NA	NA	5 222	126	29	479	163	481	2 271	NA	3.8
0980	Poquoson	11 005	NA	NA	10 728	84	24	161	8	96	3 890	12 750	40.2
0990	Portsmouth	103 907	104 577	-0.6	53 212	49 180	303	827	385	1 364	42 283	9 274	85.8
1000	Pulaski town	9 985	10 106	-1.2	9 118	828	14	21	4	45	4 376	9 036	20.3
1012	Quantico Station CDP	7 425	NA	NA	5 514	1 494	39	150	228	533	1 618	NA	18.5
1015	Radford	15 940	13 225	20.5	14 643	957	16	272	52	175	5 496	9 427	25.4
1017	Raven CDP	2 640	NA	NA	2 635	0	4	0	1	6	1 062	NA	16.7
1022	Reston CDP	48 556	36 407	33.4	39 708	5 318	88	2 560	882	2 501	19 999	NA	44.6
1030	Richlands town	4 456	NA	NA	4 442	1	5	8	0	12	1 995	6 921	6.9
1035	Richmond	203 056	219 214	-7.4	88 028	112 122	463	1 787	656	1 898	94 141	10 947	155.7
1043	Rio CDP	5 133	NA	NA	4 564	413	5	129	22	70	2 222	NA	13.6
1045	Roanoke	96 397	100 220	-3.8	71 907	23 395	165	717	213	665	44 384	10 644	111.1
1050	Rocky Mount town	4 098	NA	NA	3 191	885	0	9	13	12	1 730	9 065	11.7
1057	Rose Hill CDP	12 675	11 926	6.3	10 795	757	56	831	236	654	4 840	NA	12.0
1080	Salem	23 756	23 958	-0.8	22 473	1 065	27	165	26	111	9 609	12 214	37.7
1115	Seven Corners CDP	7 280	NA	NA	4 727	537	19	1 091	906	2 585	3 346	NA	1.8
1130	Smithfield town	4 686	NA	NA	3 056	1 603	2	19	6	30	1 859	11 551	14.3
1135	South Boston	6 997	NA	NA	4 376	2 569	11	34	7	45	2 997	9 691	14.3
1140	South Hill town	4 217	NA	NA	2 888	1 307	2	20	0	12	1 822	9 429	15.3
1145	Spotsylvania Courthouse CDP	2 694	NA	NA	2 303	329	18	20	24	48	918	NA	17.1
1150	Springfield CDP	23 706	21 435	10.6	17 273	1 564	73	4 010	786	1 772	8 790	NA	25.4
1165	Staunton	24 461	21 857	11.9	21 181	3 081	38	102	59	169	10 003	11 050	51.2

1. Codes shown are 2-digit FIPS codes for states; 4-digit census place codes for places; and 3-digit FIPS county codes followed by 3-digit census MCD codes for minor civil divisions (MCDs). MCD names are followed by county names in parentheses. 2. Hispanic persons may be of any race. 3. Dry land or land partially or temporarily covered by water.

State/ Place/ MCD[1] code	Place	Population: 1990	Population: Places of 10,000 or more: 1980	Population: Places of 10,000 or more: Percent change, 1980–1990	Population characteristics, 1990: Race: White	Race: Black	Race: Am. Indian, Eskimo Aleut	Race: Asian & Pacific Islander	Race: Other race	Hispanic[2]	Total housing units, 1990	Per capita income, 1985 (Dollars)	Land area,[3] 1990 (Sq. Km.)
		1	2	3	4	5	6	7	8	9	10	11	12
	VIRGINIA—Con.												
1172	Sterling CDP	20 512	16 080	27.6	18 118	1 154	52	963	225	717	7 344	NA	17.2
1190	Strasburg town	3 762	NA	NA	3 592	152	1	9	8	51	1 604	NA	4.9
1196	Stuarts Draft CDP	5 087	NA	NA	4 939	127	5	7	9	34	1 913	NA	25.1
1198	Sudley CDP	7 321	NA	NA	6 531	471	21	215	83	209	2 571	NA	4.0
1200	Suffolk	52 141	47 621	9.5	28 511	23 245	112	200	73	319	20 011	9 465	1 036.2
1202	Sugarland Run CDP	9 357	NA	NA	8 032	766	34	421	104	388	3 130	NA	8.4
1220	Tazewell town	4 176	NA	NA	3 773	392	4	4	3	7	1 773	9 109	10.5
1228	Timberlake CDP	10 314	NA	NA	9 868	349	6	74	17	52	4 126	NA	22.8
1240	Triangle CDP	4 740	NA	NA	3 763	807	17	103	50	178	2 195	NA	6.9
1251	Tuckahoe CDP	42 629	39 868	6.9	39 521	2 014	61	917	116	538	18 183	NA	53.3
1252	Tysons Corner CDP	13 124	10 065	30.4	11 048	522	9	1 358	187	897	7 051	NA	12.7
1254	University Heights CDP	6 900	NA	NA	5 500	796	6	562	36	100	1 019	NA	11.2
1257	Verona CDP	3 479	NA	NA	3 361	85	3	29	1	1	1 353	NA	10.2
1265	Vienna town	14 852	15 469	-4.0	12 581	610	21	1 377	263	710	5 474	18 113	11.3
1270	Vinton town	7 665	NA	NA	7 395	245	6	13	6	60	3 308	10 437	8.3
1280	Virginia Beach	393 069	262 199	49.9	316 408	54 671	1 384	17 025	3 581	12 137	147 037	12 039	643.2
1295	Warrenton town	4 830	NA	NA	3 894	882	13	20	21	61	2 105	12 245	8.9
1315	Waynesboro	18 549	15 329	21.0	16 681	1 749	34	44	41	150	7 902	10 636	36.4
1323	West Gate CDP	6 565	NA	NA	5 241	988	24	176	136	447	2 395	NA	3.0
1325	West Point town	2 938	NA	NA	2 328	559	31	17	3	23	1 184	11 618	12.2
1327	West Springfield CDP	28 126	25 012	12.5	24 045	992	87	2 639	363	1 396	10 184	NA	17.7
1340	Williamsburg	11 530	NA	NA	9 368	1 754	25	335	48	151	3 960	10 420	22.3
1345	Winchester	21 947	20 217	8.6	19 453	2 199	26	209	60	219	9 808	11 861	24.2
1355	Wise town	3 193	NA	NA	3 119	16	3	49	6	18	1 419	10 471	7.9
1357	Wolf Trap CDP	13 133	NA	NA	12 022	178	14	878	41	333	4 112	NA	24.1
1358	Woodbridge CDP	26 401	24 004	10.0	20 569	3 499	86	1 134	1 113	2 147	9 513	NA	27.1
1360	Woodstock town	3 182	NA	NA	3 062	94	3	16	7	36	1 477	9 630	8.2
1365	Wytheville town	8 038	NA	NA	7 321	663	10	39	5	35	3 528	9 924	37.0
1367	Yorkshire CDP	5 699	NA	NA	5 085	357	16	93	148	255	2 093	NA	6.1
53	WASHINGTON	4 866 692	4 132 353	17.8	4 308 937	149 801	81 483	210 958	115 513	214 570	2 032 378	10 866	172 447.2
0005	Aberdeen	16 565	18 739	-11.6	15 532	48	467	323	195	422	7 570	9 814	27.4
0017	Alderwood Manor-Bothell North CDP	22 945	16 524	38.9	21 129	228	213	1 237	138	486	8 153	NA	20.7
0030	Anacortes	11 451	NA	NA	10 945	62	192	154	98	233	4 992	11 207	28.2
0045	Arlington	4 037	NA	NA	3 920	7	41	37	32	55	1 600	8 792	14.3
0047	Artondale CDP	7 141	NA	NA	6 908	33	48	99	53	148	2 414	NA	27.4
0055	Auburn	33 102	26 417	25.3	30 571	452	689	997	393	1 010	13 977	10 771	51.0
0057	Ault Field CDP	3 795	NA	NA	2 974	401	27	211	182	295	321	NA	17.8
0059	Bangor Trident Base CDP	3 702	NA	NA	3 114	243	51	205	89	231	800	NA	7.6
0060	Battle Ground	3 758	NA	NA	3 650	10	25	32	41	109	1 376	7 606	6.6
0075	Bellevue	86 874	73 883	17.6	75 150	1 939	383	8 642	760	2 189	37 428	16 277	68.4
0080	Bellingham	52 179	45 805	13.9	48 923	411	943	1 453	449	1 256	22 114	10 037	57.0
0092	Birch Bay CDP	2 656	NA	NA	2 528	20	40	25	43	82	2 681	NA	41.4
0105	Bonney Lake	7 494	NA	NA	7 280	15	68	96	35	174	2 570	8 692	9.9
0110	Bothell	12 345	NA	NA	11 687	103	79	416	60	230	5 146	13 367	13.8
0115	Bremerton	38 142	36 209	5.3	32 011	2 719	640	2 012	760	1 848	15 693	9 778	51.5
0127	Brier	5 633	NA	NA	5 116	43	31	411	32	119	1 822	11 585	5.5
0128	Brush Prairie CDP	2 650	NA	NA	2 570	6	13	28	33	70	916	NA	20.3
0129	Bryn Mawr-Skyway CDP	12 514	11 754	6.5	8 140	2 462	123	1 596	193	402	5 245	NA	8.2
0130	Buckley	3 516	NA	NA	3 417	39	28	23	9	36	1 136	7 447	10.0
0138	Burien CDP	25 089	23 189	8.2	22 751	513	326	1 124	375	960	11 376	NA	16.6
0140	Burlington	4 349	NA	NA	3 946	18	54	47	284	527	1 816	8 980	7.8
0145	Camas	6 442	NA	NA	6 277	16	56	72	21	102	2 550	10 924	19.6
0159	Cascade-Fairwood CDP	30 107	16 939	77.7	26 159	1 043	221	2 461	223	784	11 058	NA	23.7
0160	Cascade Park East CDP	6 996	NA	NA	6 260	153	39	476	68	218	3 138	NA	4.0
0161	Cascade Park West CDP	6 656	NA	NA	6 036	143	41	370	66	195	2 741	NA	4.4
0165	Cashmere	2 544	NA	NA	2 434	0	13	11	86	135	1 057	NA	2.0
0180	Centralia	12 101	11 555	4.7	11 666	57	119	114	145	383	5 234	8 283	15.4
0185	Central Park CDP	2 669	NA	NA	2 599	0	30	31	9	23	1 072	NA	9.1
0190	Chehalis	6 527	NA	NA	6 267	54	75	70	61	190	2 694	9 333	14.5
0195	Chelan	2 969	NA	NA	2 763	3	21	36	146	178	1 664	9 135	8.1
0200	Cheney	7 723	NA	NA	6 751	129	127	592	124	240	2 733	7 361	6.7
0215	Clarkston	6 753	NA	NA	6 507	21	138	51	36	151	3 043	7 629	5.0
0217	Clarkston Heights-Vineland CDP	2 832	NA	NA	2 768	3	33	17	11	36	1 086	NA	6.9
0225	Clyde Hill town	2 972	NA	NA	2 810	8	2	152	0	22	1 081	24 815	2.7
0230	Colfax	2 713	NA	NA	2 617	1	21	65	9	25	1 241	11 504	3.8
0235	College Place	6 308	NA	NA	5 595	79	39	155	440	677	2 432	7 917	4.4
0250	Colville	4 360	NA	NA	4 156	4	121	40	39	69	1 905	8 769	5.6
0287	Country Homes CDP	5 126	NA	NA	4 918	31	45	112	20	81	1 922	NA	5.0
0292	Covington-Sawyer-Wilderness CDP	24 321	NA	NA	23 070	338	272	476	165	596	8 152	NA	52.6
0325	Des Moines	17 283	NA	NA	15 371	648	177	897	190	529	7 438	13 900	8.8
0327	Dishman CDP	9 671	10 169	-4.9	9 443	37	95	67	29	119	4 207	NA	8.8
0335	Duvall	2 770	NA	NA	2 694	7	19	16	34	72	979	NA	3.6

1. Codes shown are 2-digit FIPS codes for states; 4-digit census place codes for places; and 3-digit FIPS county codes followed by 3-digit census MCD codes for minor civil divisions (MCDs). MCD names are followed by county names in parentheses. 2. Hispanic persons may be of any race. 3. Dry land or land partially or temporarily covered by water.

State/ Place/ MCD[1] code	Place	Population: 1990	Population: Places of 10,000 or more: 1980	Population: Places of 10,000 or more: Percent change, 1980–1990	Population characteristics, 1990: Race: White	Race: Black	Race: Am. Indian, Eskimo Aleut	Race: Asian & Pacific Islander	Race: Other race	Hispanic[2]	Total housing units, 1990	Per capita income, 1985 (Dollars)	Land area,[3] 1990 (Sq. Km.)
		1	2	3	4	5	6	7	8	9	10	11	12
	WASHINGTON—Con.												
0344	Eastgate CDP	4 434	NA	NA	4 073	70	18	253	20	60	1 686	NA	3.0
0345	East Hill-Meridian CDP	42 696	NA	NA	37 970	1 081	357	2 830	458	1 222	14 777	NA	45.4
0346	East Port Orchard CDP	5 409	NA	NA	4 917	77	67	267	81	240	1 866	NA	7.3
0347	East Renton Highlands CDP	13 218	12 033	9.8	12 510	161	130	347	70	211	4 590	NA	26.6
0350	East Wenatchee	2 701	NA	NA	2 586	4	25	27	59	110	1 217	NA	2.5
0355	East Wenatchee Bench CDP	12 539	11 410	9.9	12 017	26	68	105	323	543	4 616	NA	21.1
0363	Edgewood-North Hill CDP	9 120	NA	NA	8 744	45	86	200	45	139	3 407	NA	22.5
0365	Edmonds	30 744	27 679	11.1	28 755	284	291	1 238	176	602	12 945	14 149	18.9
0378	Elk Plain CDP	12 197	NA	NA	10 933	426	173	542	123	317	4 255	NA	29.6
0380	Ellensburg	12 361	11 752	5.2	11 534	124	125	399	179	347	5 015	7 613	12.8
0382	Ellsworth North CDP	5 796	NA	NA	5 328	99	65	262	42	160	2 067	NA	3.8
0383	Ellsworth South CDP	4 423	NA	NA	4 176	30	28	154	35	103	1 825	NA	5.4
0385	Elma	3 011	NA	NA	2 863	6	39	76	27	93	1 210	8 024	3.9
0410	Enumclaw	7 227	NA	NA	7 034	16	68	66	43	114	3 031	9 986	9.8
0415	Ephrata	5 349	NA	NA	5 113	12	37	52	135	220	2 350	9 752	17.2
0417	Erlands Point-Kitsap Lake CDP	2 764	NA	NA	2 575	43	49	86	11	53	1 217	NA	5.0
0418	Esperance CDP	11 236	11 147	0.8	10 395	120	112	558	51	188	4 688	NA	5.6
0420	Everett	69 961	54 413	28.6	64 177	1 160	1 218	2 738	668	1 973	30 795	10 223	77.4
0422	Evergreen CDP	11 249	NA	NA	10 410	247	112	367	113	327	4 076	NA	11.8
0427	Fairchild AFB CDP	4 854	NA	NA	3 961	416	27	272	178	296	1 266	NA	16.8
0435	Fairview-Sumach CDP	2 749	NA	NA	1 884	63	58	17	727	856	1 087	NA	3.5
0437	Fairwood CDP	5 807	NA	NA	5 638	46	36	66	21	101	2 025	NA	9.9
0443	Federal Way CDP	67 554	NA	NA	58 537	2 709	604	4 877	827	2 210	28 087	NA	50.9
0444	Felida CDP	3 109	NA	NA	3 024	23	9	48	5	56	1 043	NA	7.2
0445	Ferndale	5 398	NA	NA	4 869	21	231	69	208	311	2 057	9 346	11.8
0450	Fife	3 864	NA	NA	3 298	166	145	160	95	273	2 152	NA	7.6
0452	Finley CDP	4 897	NA	NA	4 743	7	59	25	63	161	1 795	NA	29.7
0455	Fircrest town	5 258	NA	NA	4 934	147	20	122	35	105	2 224	14 665	2.8
0457	Five Corners CDP	6 776	NA	NA	6 456	62	58	151	49	217	2 219	NA	9.3
0465	Forks	2 862	NA	NA	2 487	64	147	50	114	197	1 042	9 082	3.9
0466	Fort Lewis CDP	22 224	23 761	-6.5	13 941	5 617	265	1 284	1 117	1 962	3 533	NA	37.1
0468	Frederickson CDP	3 502	NA	NA	3 299	51	38	83	31	93	1 213	NA	19.9
0475	Fruitvale CDP	4 125	NA	NA	3 607	37	50	38	393	487	2 024	NA	5.8
0490	Gig Harbor	3 236	NA	NA	3 147	22	8	37	22	60	1 527	NA	4.1
0500	Goldendale	3 319	NA	NA	3 071	11	106	23	108	133	1 416	8 512	5.3
0515	Grandview	7 169	NA	NA	3 875	37	29	55	3 173	3 713	2 420	7 046	12.2
0528	Green Acres CDP	4 626	NA	NA	4 492	18	66	29	21	76	1 775	NA	8.6
0531	Hadlock-Irondale CDP	2 742	NA	NA	2 622	13	68	30	9	46	1 287	NA	11.6
0538	Harbour Pointe CDP	9 107	NA	NA	8 225	95	49	671	67	253	3 069	NA	15.0
0557	Hazel Dell North CDP	6 924	15 386	-55.0	6 482	129	103	171	39	219	2 944	NA	6.9
0558	Hazel Dell South CDP	5 796	NA	NA	5 527	64	49	110	46	140	2 649	NA	5.9
0559	Highland CDP	3 656	NA	NA	3 463	26	29	34	104	156	1 163	NA	69.0
0560	Hoquiam	8 972	NA	NA	8 477	13	317	86	79	177	3 973	8 953	16.5
0582	Inglewood-Finn Hill CDP	29 132	12 467	133.7	27 205	307	188	1 236	196	564	10 361	NA	23.4
0590	Issaquah	7 786	NA	NA	7 485	30	58	188	25	163	3 348	12 219	13.2
0605	Kelso	11 820	11 129	6.2	11 175	40	250	130	225	413	4 872	8 668	20.0
0608	Kenmore CDP	8 917	NA	NA	8 175	97	54	519	72	210	3 781	NA	8.8
0610	Kennewick	42 155	34 397	22.6	37 892	476	323	837	2 627	3 684	17 209	10 523	52.1
0615	Kent	37 960	23 152	64.0	33 860	1 455	513	1 668	464	1 462	17 484	12 604	49.0
0623	Kingsgate CDP	14 259	12 652	12.7	12 599	277	103	1 109	171	409	4 852	NA	8.8
0625	Kirkland	40 052	18 779	113.3	37 154	603	240	1 741	314	947	18 061	14 781	27.7
0643	Lacey	19 279	13 940	38.3	17 131	569	206	1 166	207	668	8 081	10 037	26.2
0656	Lake Forest North CDP	8 002	NA	NA	6 979	140	77	759	47	201	2 979	NA	5.0
0657	Lake Forest Park	4 031	NA	NA	3 761	42	9	204	15	79	1 507	NA	2.8
0660	Lakeland North CDP	14 402	11 451	25.8	13 026	254	125	870	127	379	4 826	NA	17.3
0661	Lakeland South CDP	9 027	NA	NA	8 506	126	85	258	52	178	3 362	NA	15.1
0662	Lake Serene-North Lynnwood CDP	14 290	NA	NA	12 985	238	149	800	118	361	5 907	NA	15.1
0663	Lake Shore CDP	6 268	NA	NA	5 928	58	53	165	64	138	2 114	NA	4.4
0664	Lake Stevens	3 380	NA	NA	3 277	9	31	47	16	64	1 211	NA	4.3
0665	Lakewood CDP	58 412	NA	NA	43 491	7 401	794	5 577	1 149	3 220	24 230	NA	45.8
0677	Lea Hill CDP	6 876	NA	NA	6 507	68	89	158	54	143	2 334	NA	14.7
0695	Longview	31 499	31 041	1.5	29 825	170	476	672	356	644	13 441	10 638	31.1
0697	Longview Heights CDP	3 310	NA	NA	3 212	7	43	40	8	30	1 213	NA	11.0
0710	Lynden	5 709	NA	NA	5 499	4	43	78	85	154	2 167	9 139	7.1
0715	Lynnwood	28 695	22 641	26.7	25 393	563	312	2 172	255	857	11 871	10 946	18.0
0727	McChord AFB CDP	4 538	NA	NA	3 577	567	44	243	107	246	984	NA	15.0
0733	Manchester CDP	4 031	NA	NA	3 784	48	55	91	53	148	1 488	NA	7.6
0742	Marietta-Alderwood CDP	2 766	NA	NA	2 516	7	134	62	47	81	1 146	NA	15.5
0743	Martha Lake CDP	10 155	NA	NA	9 623	73	87	311	61	183	3 863	NA	12.7
0745	Marysville	10 328	NA	NA	9 810	33	247	192	46	243	4 565	9 937	12.0
0755	Medical Lake	3 664	NA	NA	3 401	128	55	63	17	157	1 055	6 219	7.8
0760	Medina	2 981	NA	NA	2 852	8	3	107	11	37	1 172	28 595	3.7
0763	Mercer Island	20 816	21 522	-3.3	18 733	300	35	1 674	74	300	8 321	21 607	16.5

1. Codes shown are 2-digit FIPS codes for states; 4-digit census place codes for places; and 3-digit FIPS county codes followed by 3-digit census MCD codes for minor civil divisions (MCDs). MCD names are followed by county names in parentheses. 2. Hispanic persons may be of any race. 3. Dry land or land partially or temporarily covered by water.

State/ Place/ MCD[1] code	Place	Population: 1990	Population: Places of 10,000 or more: 1980	Population: Places of 10,000 or more: Percent change, 1980–1990	Population characteristics, 1990: Race: White	Race: Black	Race: Am. Indian, Eskimo Aleut	Race: Asian & Pacific Islander	Race: Other race	Hispanic[2]	Total housing units, 1990	Per capita income, 1985 (Dollars)	Land area,[3] 1990 (Sq. Km.)
		1	2	3	4	5	6	7	8	9	10	11	12
	WASHINGTON—Con.												
0777	Midland CDP	5 587	NA	NA	4 858	288	112	248	81	151	2 337	NA	8.1
0778	Mill Creek	7 172	NA	NA	6 498	68	23	538	45	108	3 131	NA	7.3
0785	Milton	4 995	NA	NA	4 776	32	58	100	29	117	2 093	11 698	5.8
0786	Minnehaha CDP	9 661	NA	NA	9 153	123	97	215	73	223	3 743	NA	9.7
0790	Monroe	4 278	NA	NA	4 041	24	83	30	100	156	1 712	9 315	9.9
0795	Montesano	3 064	NA	NA	2 985	9	45	14	11	33	1 239	9 662	25.9
0805	Moses Lake	11 235	10 629	5.7	9 263	212	84	205	1 471	2 040	4 635	8 748	23.6
0807	Moses Lake North CDP	3 677	NA	NA	2 945	169	70	51	442	590	1 235	NA	15.9
0815	Mountlake Terrace	19 320	16 534	16.9	17 083	397	207	1 401	232	605	7 854	10 828	10.2
0820	Mount Vernon	17 647	13 009	35.7	15 809	78	200	245	1 315	1 921	7 167	9 760	21.8
0830	Mukilteo	7 007	NA	NA	6 695	54	51	165	42	154	2 817	NA	7.1
0845	Navy Yard City CDP	2 905	NA	NA	2 477	214	67	124	23	93	1 330	NA	2.3
0863	Newport Hills CDP	14 736	12 245	20.3	12 976	309	52	1 302	97	321	5 931	NA	15.2
0870	Normandy Park	6 709	NA	NA	6 349	53	47	230	30	96	2 628	20 002	6.2
0875	North Bend	2 578	NA	NA	2 502	18	16	21	21	55	1 097	NA	7.6
0880	North City-Ridgecrest CDP	13 832	NA	NA	11 928	325	168	1 277	134	345	5 354	NA	7.1
0881	North Creek-Canyon Park CDP	23 236	13 551	71.5	21 965	179	156	806	130	503	7 981	NA	42.8
0882	North Hill CDP	5 706	10 170	-43.9	5 325	88	51	198	44	134	2 211	NA	3.8
0883	North Marysville CDP	18 711	NA	NA	18 066	59	222	237	127	440	6 253	NA	37.7
0886	North Puyallup CDP	2 886	NA	NA	2 734	34	56	39	23	62	1 383	NA	6.9
0895	Oak Harbor	17 176	12 269	40.0	14 562	757	153	1 455	249	916	6 173	7 943	19.6
0920	Olympia	33 840	27 447	23.3	31 146	420	404	1 622	248	894	15 928	11 140	41.8
0925	Omak	4 117	NA	NA	3 411	12	585	30	79	142	1 769	9 550	4.2
0930	Opportunity CDP	22 326	21 241	5.1	21 514	163	217	304	128	366	8 917	NA	17.3
0933	Orchards North CDP	6 479	NA	NA	6 130	73	113	98	65	153	2 147	NA	9.5
0934	Orchards South CDP	12 956	NA	NA	12 126	199	151	375	105	372	4 776	NA	15.3
0945	Othello	4 638	NA	NA	2 421	15	27	66	2 109	2 188	1 637	8 902	6.0
0947	Otis Orchards-East Farms CDP	5 811	NA	NA	5 644	16	65	69	17	74	1 833	NA	18.2
0950	Pacific	4 622	NA	NA	4 251	30	71	222	48	143	1 815	NA	5.1
0953	Paine Field-Lake Stickney CDP	18 670	NA	NA	17 286	402	198	584	200	618	8 656	NA	20.0
0957	Parkland CDP	20 882	23 355	-10.6	17 972	1 069	248	1 317	276	681	7 871	NA	17.8
0958	Parkwood CDP	6 853	NA	NA	6 215	114	67	357	100	296	2 579	NA	7.1
0960	Pasco	20 337	17 944	13.3	12 179	1 147	187	502	6 322	8 300	7 698	7 695	59.1
0982	Pine Lake CDP	13 940	NA	NA	13 229	66	35	570	40	205	5 197	NA	27.5
0990	Port Angeles	17 710	17 311	2.3	16 880	70	448	249	63	288	7 833	10 041	25.3
0995	Port Angeles East CDP	2 672	NA	NA	2 610	3	38	13	8	55	1 219	NA	8.1
1000	Port Orchard	4 984	NA	NA	4 630	97	76	138	43	137	2 090	8 868	8.0
1005	Port Townsend	7 001	NA	NA	6 787	36	83	79	16	89	3 280	9 231	18.1
1010	Poulsbo	4 848	NA	NA	4 566	53	63	104	62	108	2 147	10 241	6.5
1013	Prairie Ridge CDP	8 278	NA	NA	8 019	41	98	62	58	198	2 945	NA	22.0
1020	Prosser	4 476	NA	NA	3 599	12	26	41	798	1 026	1 665	9 175	10.6
1025	Pullman	23 478	23 579	-0.4	20 654	462	138	1 994	230	536	7 546	7 874	17.3
1030	Puyallup	23 875	18 239	30.9	22 614	180	277	654	150	491	9 377	9 603	26.6
1040	Quincy	3 738	NA	NA	3 019	9	22	44	644	1 398	1 364	7 852	4.6
1055	Raymond	2 901	NA	NA	2 576	8	78	207	32	86	1 258	8 704	10.1
1065	Redmond	35 800	23 318	53.5	32 604	472	188	2 250	286	882	14 972	13 601	37.4
1070	Renton	41 688	30 612	36.2	34 790	2 731	491	3 227	449	1 234	19 243	12 279	42.1
1080	Richland	32 315	33 578	-3.8	30 053	461	220	1 071	510	983	13 872	13 878	83.0
1082	Richmond Beach-Innis Arden CDP	7 242	NA	NA	6 790	46	30	366	10	95	2 683	NA	8.0
1083	Richmond Highlands CDP	26 037	24 463	6.4	22 600	349	221	2 661	206	623	10 648	NA	13.2
1096	Riverton-Boulevard Park CDP	15 337	14 182	8.1	12 946	681	347	1 016	347	707	6 702	NA	10.9
1133	Sahalee CDP	13 951	NA	NA	13 336	117	40	386	72	268	4 593	NA	20.8
1137	Salmon Creek CDP	11 989	NA	NA	11 468	109	70	258	84	264	4 962	NA	16.3
1139	Sea-Tac CDP	22 694	NA	NA	19 629	1 029	401	1 246	389	805	10 189	NA	25.4
1140	Seattle	516 259	493 846	4.5	388 858	51 948	7 326	60 819	7 308	18 349	249 032	12 919	217.3
1150	Sedro-Woolley	6 031	NA	NA	5 677	3	87	43	221	304	2 470	7 849	8.6
1155	Selah	5 113	NA	NA	4 757	32	37	34	253	364	1 930	9 561	7.0
1160	Sequim	3 616	NA	NA	3 499	10	48	47	12	66	1 953	9 721	6.1
1165	Shelton	7 241	NA	NA	6 826	14	203	131	67	191	3 046	8 464	10.5
1167	Sheridan Beach CDP	6 518	NA	NA	5 855	102	33	485	43	115	2 691	NA	4.0
1171	Silverdale CDP	7 660	NA	NA	6 845	196	64	497	58	317	3 258	NA	13.9
1173	Silver Lake-Fircrest CDP	24 474	10 299	137.6	22 960	164	158	1 005	187	553	8 045	NA	37.2
1177	Smokey Point CDP	2 620	NA	NA	2 530	3	28	15	44	88	1 038	NA	8.7
1180	Snohomish	6 499	NA	NA	6 283	35	51	83	47	97	2 556	8 875	5.3
1200	South Broadway CDP	2 735	NA	NA	2 413	14	74	23	211	302	1 088	NA	2.6
1207	South Hill CDP	12 963	NA	NA	12 385	115	88	280	95	304	4 820	NA	18.2
1213	Spanaway CDP	15 001	NA	NA	11 944	1 158	212	1 409	278	746	5 347	NA	13.3
1220	Spokane	177 196	171 300	3.4	165 284	3 416	3 622	3 686	1 188	3 677	79 875	9 751	144.8
1245	Steilacoom town	5 728	NA	NA	4 719	530	52	324	103	260	2 371	12 516	5.4
1254	Sudden Valley CDP	2 615	NA	NA	2 522	11	23	49	10	56	1 430	NA	16.3
1268	Summit CDP	6 312	NA	NA	6 046	50	56	102	58	105	2 359	NA	12.5
1270	Sumner	6 281	NA	NA	5 978	16	105	131	51	211	2 604	9 904	9.9
1275	Sunnyside	11 238	NA	NA	5 421	33	84	73	5 627	6 423	3 576	7 091	9.3

1. Codes shown are 2-digit FIPS codes for states; 4-digit census place codes for places; and 3-digit FIPS county codes followed by 3-digit census MCD codes for minor civil divisions (MCDs). MCD names are followed by county names in parentheses. 2. Hispanic persons may be of any race. 3. Dry land or land partially or temporarily covered by water.

State/ Place/ MCD[1] code	Place	Population			Population characteristics, 1990						Total housing units, 1990	Per capita income, 1985 (Dollars)	Land area,[3] 1990 (Sq. Km.)
			Places of 10,000 or more		Race								
		1990	1980	Percent change, 1980–1990	White	Black	Am. Indian, Eskimo Aleut	Asian & Pacific Islander	Other race	Hispanic[2]			
		1	2	3	4	5	6	7	8	9	10	11	12
	WASHINGTON—Con.												
1277	Suquamish CDP	3 105	NA	NA	2 646	7	342	96	14	68	1 338	NA	17.7
1280	Tacoma	176 664	158 501	11.5	138 054	20 110	3 567	12 216	2 717	6 670	75 147	9 365	124.4
1282	Tanglewilde-Thompson Place CDP	6 061	NA	NA	4 850	373	116	597	125	357	2 193	NA	4.3
1291	Terrace Heights CDP	4 223	NA	NA	4 037	33	18	31	104	204	1 680	NA	9.6
1310	Toppenish	7 419	NA	NA	2 642	50	641	22	4 064	4 616	2 254	6 016	4.7
1311	Town and Country CDP	4 921	NA	NA	4 746	43	60	49	23	53	1 955	NA	3.7
1312	Tracyton CDP	2 621	NA	NA	2 363	69	28	142	19	76	995	NA	3.8
1315	Trentwood CDP	4 060	NA	NA	3 900	23	53	68	16	71	1 468	NA	4.6
1320	Tukwila	11 874	NA	NA	9 830	755	190	880	219	436	5 972	15 589	21.1
1325	Tumwater	9 976	NA	NA	9 487	82	111	192	104	235	4 463	10 200	25.0
1335	Union Gap	3 120	NA	NA	2 604	11	107	38	360	459	1 347	7 475	10.1
1343	University Place CDP	27 701	20 381	35.9	24 102	1 923	221	1 216	239	832	11 546	NA	20.4
1350	Vancouver	46 380	42 834	8.3	42 795	1 050	593	1 473	469	1 399	21 025	10 288	36.6
1352	Vancouver Mall CDP	6 938	NA	NA	6 456	130	74	210	68	202	2 874	NA	7.7
1354	Veradale CDP	7 836	NA	NA	7 589	36	51	131	29	111	2 724	NA	8.0
1365	Walla Walla	26 478	25 631	3.3	23 328	595	261	347	1 947	2 702	10 649	9 453	26.7
1370	Walla Walla East CDP	2 959	NA	NA	2 863	12	5	36	43	70	1 114	NA	4.9
1372	Waller CDP	6 415	NA	NA	6 095	86	90	113	31	124	2 331	NA	16.3
1373	Walnut Grove CDP	3 906	NA	NA	3 784	37	21	47	17	74	1 542	NA	8.3
1375	Wapato	3 795	NA	NA	1 193	17	309	103	2 173	2 443	1 204	6 319	2.3
1385	Washougal	4 764	NA	NA	4 629	2	59	39	35	79	2 010	9 013	6.7
1405	Wenatchee	21 756	17 257	26.1	19 932	48	240	226	1 310	1 872	9 453	9 828	15.8
1410	West Clarkston-Highland CDP	3 913	NA	NA	3 815	11	62	16	9	61	1 660	NA	5.6
1412	West Lake Sammamish CDP	6 087	NA	NA	5 608	80	24	346	29	118	2 140	NA	3.7
1413	West Lake Stevens CDP	12 453	NA	NA	11 968	71	141	197	76	265	4 412	NA	29.9
1416	West Longview CDP	3 163	NA	NA	3 042	10	52	31	28	68	1 267	NA	6.2
1418	West Pasco CDP	7 312	NA	NA	6 638	131	48	107	388	524	2 485	NA	18.0
1425	West Richland	3 962	NA	NA	3 768	38	25	80	51	120	1 564	11 963	54.4
1427	West Side Highway CDP	3 641	NA	NA	3 543	5	46	31	16	24	1 371	NA	6.5
1429	West Valley CDP	6 594	NA	NA	6 280	51	51	80	132	266	2 370	NA	8.5
1434	White Center-Shorewood CDP	20 531	19 362	6.0	15 659	791	577	3 014	490	1 056	8 218	NA	10.1
1437	White Swan CDP	2 669	NA	NA	942	8	1 535	8	176	290	765	NA	268.5
1460	Winslow	3 081	NA	NA	2 902	11	27	135	6	52	1 596	NA	4.1
1468	Woodinville CDP	23 654	NA	NA	22 611	149	126	611	157	532	7 750	NA	46.6
1470	Woodland	2 500	NA	NA	2 363	2	47	11	77	123	979	NA	4.9
1473	Woodmont Beach CDP	7 493	NA	NA	6 600	329	117	342	105	268	3 156	NA	6.1
1485	Yakima	54 827	49 826	10.0	45 258	1 315	1 108	701	6 445	8 914	22 968	9 681	38.7
54	WEST VIRGINIA	1 793 477	1 950 183	-8.0	1 725 523	56 295	2 458	7 459	1 742	8 489	781 295	8 141	62 384.2
0080	Barboursville village	2 774	NA	NA	2 751	13	2	7	1	14	1 180	9 009	7.0
0110	Beckley	18 296	20 492	-10.7	13 917	4 071	36	237	35	116	8 917	10 060	23.3
0145	Bethlehem village	2 694	NA	NA	2 630	15	1	47	1	5	1 137	10 986	9.1
0157	Blennerhassett CDP	2 924	NA	NA	2 895	13	1	14	1	5	1 064	NA	12.0
0160	Bluefield	12 756	16 060	-20.6	9 805	2 885	11	46	9	45	6 007	10 753	21.8
0195	Bridgeport	6 739	NA	NA	6 671	13	0	49	6	100	2 773	13 374	10.0
0198	Brookhaven CDP	3 836	NA	NA	3 784	25	7	16	4	24	1 589	NA	24.1
0205	Buckhannon	5 909	NA	NA	5 758	88	20	38	5	35	2 457	7 316	4.7
0280	Charleston	57 287	63 968	-10.4	48 179	8 163	108	732	105	356	28 111	12 930	76.3
0285	Charles Town	3 122	NA	NA	2 482	605	7	13	15	55	1 397	9 168	2.5
0295	Cheat Lake CDP	3 992	NA	NA	3 945	19	0	26	2	17	1 623	NA	33.2
0305	Chester	2 905	NA	NA	2 886	6	4	2	7	22	1 341	7 984	2.5
0310	Clarksburg	18 059	22 433	-19.5	17 328	636	20	54	21	252	9 241	9 526	20.3
0350	Corporation of Ranson town	2 890	NA	NA	2 470	397	3	4	16	61	1 176	NA	2.2
0365	Crab Orchard CDP	2 919	NA	NA	2 892	17	2	5	3	15	1 178	NA	6.0
0374	Cross Lanes CDP	10 878	NA	NA	10 395	301	6	149	27	65	4 465	NA	18.8
0380	Culloden CDP	2 907	NA	NA	2 883	11	3	10	0	9	1 087	NA	10.9
0425	Dunbar	8 697	NA	NA	7 970	626	7	85	9	32	4 239	11 087	7.4
0485	Elkins	7 420	NA	NA	7 257	85	19	44	15	46	3 293	7 854	7.6
0510	Fairmont	20 210	23 863	-15.3	18 717	1 343	52	73	25	127	9 958	8 613	19.5
0555	Follansbee	3 339	NA	NA	3 327	0	3	6	3	14	1 489	8 066	4.4
0640	Grafton	5 524	NA	NA	5 441	52	9	19	3	32	2 576	7 330	9.0
0735	Hinton	3 433	NA	NA	3 210	208	6	9	0	20	1 774	8 695	5.4
0749	Hooverson Heights CDP	3 056	NA	NA	3 040	4	2	9	1	11	1 143	NA	6.0
0760	Huntington	54 844	63 684	-13.9	50 739	3 700	68	255	82	295	26 674	9 577	38.6
0765	Hurricane	4 461	NA	NA	4 437	4	3	17	0	17	1 831	9 807	6.4
0805	Kenova	3 748	NA	NA	3 739	4	5	0	0	3	1 772	8 210	3.1
0815	Keyser	5 870	NA	NA	5 426	420	2	18	4	53	2 627	8 970	4.5
0845	Kingwood	3 243	NA	NA	3 206	28	1	7	1	16	1 371	9 540	6.4
0880	Lewisburg	3 598	NA	NA	3 309	271	1	14	3	18	1 757	9 733	10.4
0950	Madison	3 051	NA	NA	2 892	133	0	17	9	4	1 342	10 443	14.5
0995	Martinsburg	14 073	13 063	7.7	12 684	1 205	24	82	78	163	6 670	8 783	11.7
1095	Morgantown	25 879	27 605	-6.3	23 796	901	35	1 054	93	281	10 422	8 736	20.0

1. Codes shown are 2-digit FIPS codes for states; 4-digit census place codes for places; and 3-digit FIPS county codes followed by 3-digit census MCD codes for minor civil divisions (MCDs). MCD names are followed by county names in parentheses. 2. Hispanic persons may be of any race. 3. Dry land or land partially or temporarily covered by water.

State/ Place/ MCD[1] code	Place	Population: 1990	Population: Places of 10,000 or more: 1980	Population: Places of 10,000 or more: Percent change, 1980–1990	Population characteristics, 1990: Race: White	Race: Black	Race: Am. Indian, Eskimo Aleut	Race: Asian & Pacific Islander	Race: Other race	Hispanic[2]	Total housing units, 1990	Per capita income, 1985 (Dollars)	Land area,[3] 1990 (Sq. Km.)
		1	2	3	4	5	6	7	8	9	10	11	12
	WEST VIRGINIA—Con.												
1100	Moundsville	10 753	12 419	-13.4	10 577	138	12	21	5	121	4 618	7 845	7.4
1106	Mount Gay-Shamrock CDP	3 377	NA	NA	3 040	328	6	1	2	10	1 376	NA	28.2
1150	New Martinsville	6 705	NA	NA	6 652	8	7	34	4	13	2 776	10 141	7.2
1155	Nitro	6 851	NA	NA	6 755	74	4	15	3	21	3 065	10 068	8.9
1175	Oak Hill	6 812	NA	NA	6 467	305	13	25	2	37	3 157	9 067	10.0
1200	Paden City	2 862	NA	NA	2 857	3	2	0	0	7	1 282	9 022	2.3
1215	Parkersburg	33 862	39 967	-15.3	33 083	574	66	101	38	99	16 341	9 410	28.9
1235	Pea Ridge CDP	6 535	NA	NA	6 305	72	8	144	6	36	2 927	NA	6.3
1255	Philippi	3 132	NA	NA	3 000	73	26	20	13	41	1 342	6 903	6.7
1263	Pinch CDP	2 695	NA	NA	2 691	0	3	1	0	2	1 065	NA	9.1
1280	Point Pleasant	4 996	NA	NA	4 851	82	14	43	6	19	2 440	8 697	6.2
1300	Princeton	7 043	NA	NA	6 457	537	18	30	1	63	3 630	9 286	7.7
1335	Ravenswood	4 189	NA	NA	4 155	7	7	13	7	20	1 776	9 264	4.7
1365	Richwood	2 808	NA	NA	2 787	0	9	2	10	13	1 267	7 465	4.4
1375	Ripley	3 023	NA	NA	3 006	1	7	9	0	13	1 317	9 147	7.4
1420	St. Albans	11 194	12 402	-9.7	10 913	211	9	49	12	53	5 189	12 407	8.6
1450	Shinnston	2 543	NA	NA	2 531	7	2	3	0	42	1 162	7 779	4.1
1453	Sissonville CDP	4 290	NA	NA	4 266	10	3	4	7	23	1 650	NA	33.0
1480	South Charleston	13 645	15 968	-14.5	12 955	552	10	100	28	76	6 640	12 522	13.6
1530	Summersville town	2 906	NA	NA	2 883	1	2	18	2	17	1 295	9 856	9.1
1548	Teays Valley CDP	8 436	NA	NA	8 324	42	2	61	7	42	3 315	NA	19.3
1605	Vienna	10 862	11 618	-6.5	10 734	53	6	62	7	25	4 825	11 831	9.6
1635	Weirton	22 124	24 736	-10.6	21 064	915	21	96	28	102	9 642	10 053	46.5
1640	Welch	3 028	NA	NA	2 484	531	1	12	0	14	1 628	9 868	8.4
1645	Wellsburg	3 385	NA	NA	3 318	62	1	3	1	4	1 564	8 922	2.4
1670	Weston	4 994	NA	NA	4 915	39	16	15	9	23	2 296	7 482	4.6
1675	Westover	4 201	NA	NA	4 068	95	10	23	5	13	1 997	9 142	3.4
1690	Wheeling	34 882	43 067	-19.0	33 024	1 555	25	250	28	103	17 128	9 823	35.7
1700	White Sulphur Springs	2 779	NA	NA	2 310	455	4	7	3	28	1 394	7 777	4.4
1720	Williamson	4 154	NA	NA	3 493	609	0	41	11	14	2 011	8 623	8.4
1725	Williamstown	2 774	NA	NA	2 767	3	0	3	1	1	1 200	10 015	3.2
55	WISCONSIN	4 891 769	4 705 642	4.0	4 512 523	244 539	39 387	53 583	41 737	93 194	2 055 774	10 298	140 672.5
0025	Algoma	3 353	NA	NA	3 333	6	8	2	4	12	1 564	10 788	6.3
0027	Allouez village	14 431	14 882	-3.0	13 782	421	108	80	40	112	5 066	NA	12.0
0050	Altoona	5 889	NA	NA	5 829	7	20	20	13	37	2 397	9 901	10.6
0055	Amery	2 657	NA	NA	2 609	2	38	6	2	13	1 132	NA	7.7
0075	Antigo	8 276	NA	NA	8 157	2	83	11	23	46	3 619	8 287	14.7
0080	Appleton	65 695	59 040	11.3	63 458	163	279	1 582	213	577	25 528	11 659	44.4
0105	Ashland	8 695	NA	NA	8 124	10	510	40	11	51	3 733	7 912	34.1
0107	Ashwaubenon village	16 376	14 486	13.0	16 051	64	147	99	15	59	6 245	11 094	27.1
0150	Baraboo	9 203	NA	NA	9 076	16	69	17	25	50	3 934	10 858	12.1
0160	Barron	2 986	NA	NA	2 944	2	9	10	21	41	1 283	8 826	6.8
0180	Bayside village	4 789	NA	NA	4 587	103	4	91	4	50	1 738	28 848	6.2
0190	Beaver Dam	14 196	14 149	0.3	13 992	19	24	80	81	168	5 997	10 200	12.3
0207	Bellevue Town CDP	7 541	NA	NA	7 468	10	37	19	7	28	2 869	NA	36.9
0215	Beloit	35 573	35 207	1.0	29 104	5 575	106	412	376	691	14 033	9 539	41.9
0230	Berlin	5 371	NA	NA	5 187	1	19	90	74	112	2 245	8 738	14.8
0270	Black River Falls	3 490	NA	NA	3 331	13	135	8	3	6	1 547	9 284	7.6
0285	Bloomer	3 085	NA	NA	3 063	3	9	5	5	9	1 290	9 052	6.3
0315	Boscobel	2 706	NA	NA	2 693	1	9	1	2	8	1 141	8 693	4.7
0340	Brillion	2 840	NA	NA	2 820	0	13	3	4	13	1 069	8 892	5.9
0345	Brodhead	3 165	NA	NA	3 142	1	12	3	7	14	1 297	9 420	4.2
0355	Brookfield	35 184	34 035	3.4	34 082	136	53	859	54	260	12 254	17 135	69.5
0365	Brown Deer village	12 236	12 921	-5.3	11 159	789	21	216	51	145	5 070	14 071	11.4
0390	Burlington	8 855	NA	NA	8 690	1	12	47	105	244	3 423	10 261	9.7
0475	Cedarburg	9 895	NA	NA	9 812	13	11	37	22	89	4 036	12 734	9.2
0505	Chilton	3 240	NA	NA	3 214	0	20	5	1	13	1 287	10 526	9.3
0510	Chippewa Falls	12 727	12 263	3.8	12 603	14	53	43	14	43	5 338	9 484	25.5
0535	Clintonville	4 351	NA	NA	4 304	1	12	13	21	39	1 941	9 689	10.3
0575	Columbus	4 093	NA	NA	4 050	5	3	14	21	60	1 734	10 706	9.7
0630	Cudahy	18 659	19 547	-4.5	18 244	107	93	112	103	409	7 642	10 575	12.3
0675	De Forest village	4 882	NA	NA	4 804	16	18	14	30	48	1 757	10 154	6.2
0680	Delafield	5 347	NA	NA	5 303	5	11	19	9	39	2 172	15 359	24.1
0685	Delavan	6 073	NA	NA	5 523	64	8	50	428	661	2 427	10 167	13.1
0700	De Pere	16 569	14 892	11.3	16 324	38	152	35	20	71	5 938	11 192	21.6
0715	Dodgeville	3 882	NA	NA	3 875	3	2	0	2	8	1 573	9 890	8.6
0765	East Troy village	2 664	NA	NA	2 632	5	15	1	11	26	999	NA	6.7
0770	Eau Claire	56 856	51 516	10.4	54 042	211	332	2 150	121	343	21 880	9 162	71.7
0785	Edgerton	4 254	NA	NA	4 205	1	19	12	17	46	1 792	10 638	8.0
0810	Elkhorn	5 337	NA	NA	5 239	5	17	12	64	96	2 202	10 323	12.4
0820	Ellsworth village	2 706	NA	NA	2 674	4	12	13	3	5	1 066	NA	9.3

1. Codes shown are 2-digit FIPS codes for states; 4-digit census place codes for places; and 3-digit FIPS county codes followed by 3-digit census MCD codes for minor civil divisions (MCDs). MCD names are followed by county names in parentheses. 2. Hispanic persons may be of any race. 3. Dry land or land partially or temporarily covered by water.

State/ Place/ MCD[1] code	Place	Population 1990	Places of 10,000 or more 1980	Places of 10,000 or more Percent change, 1980–1990	Race: White	Race: Black	Race: Am. Indian, Eskimo Aleut	Race: Asian & Pacific Islander	Race: Other race	Hispanic[2]	Total housing units, 1990	Per capita income, 1985 (Dollars)	Land area,[3] 1990 (Sq. Km.)
		1	2	3	4	5	6	7	8	9	10	11	12
	WISCONSIN—Con.												
0825	Elm Grove village	6 261	NA	NA	6 122	10	7	111	11	34	2 398	28 362	8.4
0860	Evansville	3 174	NA	NA	3 152	5	5	12	0	21	1 305	11 833	4.9
0862	Evergreen CDP	3 423	NA	NA	3 391	4	9	18	1	8	1 106	NA	10.6
0903	Fitchburg	15 648	NA	NA	14 604	700	57	210	77	233	6 685	12 492	90.5
0905	Fond du Lac	37 757	35 863	5.3	36 928	112	192	292	233	575	15 176	10 200	33.1
0920	Fort Atkinson	10 227	NA	NA	10 071	13	27	67	49	125	4 074	10 305	11.2
0935	Fox Point village	7 238	NA	NA	7 091	63	3	78	3	52	2 948	29 359	7.6
0940	Franklin	21 855	16 871	29.5	20 675	818	93	179	90	357	7 753	12 622	89.7
0957	French Island CDP	4 478	NA	NA	4 420	13	14	17	14	26	1 731	NA	5.5
0990	Germantown village	13 658	10 729	27.3	13 484	58	23	67	26	77	5 100	12 038	89.1
1010	Glendale	14 088	13 882	1.5	12 961	736	15	331	45	121	5 784	15 553	15.0
1030	Grafton village	9 340	NA	NA	9 275	4	24	21	16	45	3 457	12 055	7.4
1055	Green Bay	96 466	87 899	9.7	90 888	453	2 448	2 234	443	1 063	39 726	10 662	113.5
1060	Greendale village	15 128	16 928	-10.6	14 777	22	28	263	38	178	5 745	13 797	14.5
1065	Greenfield	33 403	31 467	6.2	32 605	138	120	318	222	667	14 301	12 869	29.9
1085	Hales Corners village	7 623	NA	NA	7 502	14	19	55	33	74	3 207	14 062	8.3
1100	Hartford	8 188	NA	NA	8 085	3	16	29	55	154	3 132	10 424	12.5
1105	Hartland village	6 906	NA	NA	6 856	7	10	23	10	59	2 428	10 960	8.2
1165	Holmen village	3 220	NA	NA	3 198	1	3	16	2	12	1 160	NA	4.8
1170	Horicon	3 873	NA	NA	3 843	3	5	7	15	55	1 478	10 965	8.4
1180	Howard village	9 874	NA	NA	9 740	9	93	17	15	44	3 515	9 901	46.5
1185	Hudson	6 378	NA	NA	6 333	3	14	28	0	13	2 634	11 908	10.3
1235	Janesville	52 133	51 071	2.1	51 130	287	116	429	171	597	21 153	11 556	60.9
1240	Jefferson	6 078	NA	NA	5 924	10	27	18	99	206	2 472	9 804	10.9
1260	Kaukauna	11 982	11 312	5.9	11 634	7	101	226	14	56	4 454	9 761	12.2
1280	Kenosha	80 352	77 685	3.4	72 139	5 137	297	448	2 331	4 732	31 197	10 326	55.8
1285	Kewaskum village	2 515	NA	NA	2 489	1	5	16	4	22	944	NA	3.8
1290	Kewaunee	2 750	NA	NA	2 720	8	16	2	4	11	1 213	9 736	8.7
1295	Kiel	2 910	NA	NA	2 896	2	7	4	1	4	1 181	9 826	5.0
1300	Kimberly village	5 406	NA	NA	5 326	1	8	70	1	24	2 069	10 336	4.4
1325	La Crosse	51 003	48 347	5.5	47 830	368	229	2 474	102	447	20 897	9 701	47.5
1335	Ladysmith	3 938	NA	NA	3 779	23	30	97	9	31	1 671	8 064	9.5
1350	Lake Geneva	5 979	NA	NA	5 746	11	25	44	153	212	3 184	10 920	12.1
1355	Lake Mills	4 143	NA	NA	4 101	2	10	13	17	35	1 735	10 256	7.3
1365	Lancaster	4 192	NA	NA	4 173	3	4	12	0	4	1 766	9 914	7.0
1400	Little Chute village	9 207	NA	NA	9 161	5	26	7	8	28	3 232	10 121	9.1
1470	McFarland village	5 232	NA	NA	5 178	7	18	8	21	59	1 915	10 940	8.0
1475	Madison	191 262	170 616	12.1	173 504	8 109	752	7 471	1 426	3 877	80 047	11 824	149.6
1490	Manitowoc	32 520	32 547	-0.1	31 338	71	176	819	116	373	13 728	10 192	37.3
1505	Marinette	11 843	11 965	-1.0	11 747	5	38	27	26	49	5 268	8 716	17.2
1530	Marshfield	19 291	18 282	5.5	19 008	36	36	174	37	118	8 045	10 146	29.9
1545	Mauston	3 439	NA	NA	3 376	10	25	22	6	18	1 560	9 517	7.5
1550	Mayville	4 374	NA	NA	4 348	0	6	11	9	42	1 690	10 659	7.2
1560	Medford	4 283	NA	NA	4 255	1	8	13	6	13	1 833	10 010	8.3
1580	Menasha	14 711	14 728	-0.1	14 420	4	116	122	49	141	6 168	10 977	11.9
1585	Menomonee Falls village	26 840	27 845	-3.6	26 526	75	53	146	40	162	10 043	13 341	86.2
1590	Menomonie	13 547	12 769	6.1	12 810	163	49	474	51	111	4 539	7 557	29.2
1595	Mequon	18 885	16 189	16.7	18 172	436	18	238	21	140	6 470	19 267	119.6
1600	Merrill	9 860	NA	NA	9 777	8	29	42	4	43	4 045	8 828	17.4
1620	Middleton	13 289	11 779	12.8	12 853	170	46	169	51	124	5 895	13 480	16.7
1635	Milton	4 434	NA	NA	4 373	8	17	24	12	27	1 724	10 074	7.0
1645	Milwaukee	628 088	636 212	-1.3	398 033	191 255	5 858	11 817	21 125	39 409	254 204	9 765	248.8
1670	Monona	8 637	NA	NA	8 411	111	22	60	33	95	3 822	14 707	8.6
1675	Monroe	10 241	10 027	2.1	10 176	9	14	38	4	35	4 556	12 135	10.4
1700	Mosinee	3 820	NA	NA	3 790	3	6	2	19	32	1 478	9 258	20.0
1710	Mount Horeb village	4 182	NA	NA	4 172	2	3	4	1	22	1 638	9 535	5.8
1720	Mukwonago village	4 457	NA	NA	4 431	3	6	10	7	38	1 643	11 048	6.4
1727	Muskego	16 813	15 277	10.1	16 700	13	27	41	32	144	5 759	11 576	80.9
1745	Neenah	23 219	22 432	3.5	22 759	45	119	218	78	238	9 261	12 332	19.2
1750	Neillsville	2 680	NA	NA	2 661	3	12	4	0	10	1 199	8 278	7.0
1755	Nekoosa	2 557	NA	NA	2 463	2	12	59	21	28	1 008	10 112	8.8
1785	New Berlin	33 592	30 529	10.0	33 055	80	73	331	53	278	12 102	13 602	95.4
1795	New Holstein	3 342	NA	NA	3 323	0	13	6	0	10	1 239	9 704	5.3
1805	New London	6 658	NA	NA	6 575	7	15	23	38	96	2 694	9 134	12.7
1810	New Richmond	5 106	NA	NA	5 087	5	3	6	5	26	2 025	10 726	8.5
1825	North Fond du Lac village	4 292	NA	NA	4 248	8	18	14	4	44	1 651	9 315	4.3
1835	North Hudson village	3 101	NA	NA	3 066	4	14	14	3	10	1 122	NA	3.4
1850	Oak Creek	19 513	16 932	15.2	18 907	142	105	168	191	626	7 263	11 555	74.1
1860	Oconomowoc	10 993	NA	NA	10 938	4	7	26	18	70	4 350	11 656	15.0
1870	Oconto	4 474	NA	NA	4 407	3	33	12	19	35	1 841	8 339	17.8
1875	Oconto Falls	2 584	NA	NA	2 554	2	24	3	1	14	1 114	8 302	6.3
1887	Okauchee Lake CDP	3 819	NA	NA	3 787	11	13	6	2	21	1 607	NA	9.0
1895	Omro	2 836	NA	NA	2 785	2	21	2	26	51	1 093	7 891	5.1

1. Codes shown are 2-digit FIPS codes for states; 4-digit census place codes for places; and 3-digit FIPS county codes followed by 3-digit census MCD codes for minor civil divisions (MCDs). MCD names are followed by county names in parentheses. 2. Hispanic persons may be of any race. 3. Dry land or land partially or temporarily covered by water.

State/ Place/ MCD[1] code	Place	Population: 1990	Population: Places of 10,000 or more: 1980	Population: Places of 10,000 or more: Percent change, 1980–1990	Population characteristics, 1990: Race: White	Race: Black	Race: Am. Indian, Eskimo Aleut	Race: Asian & Pacific Islander	Race: Other race	Hispanic[2]	Total housing units, 1990	Per capita income, 1985 (Dollars)	Land area,[3] 1990 (Sq. Km.)
		1	2	3	4	5	6	7	8	9	10	11	12
	WISCONSIN—Con.												
1900	Onalaska	11 284	NA	NA	11 176	25	26	51	6	43	4 378	10 088	16.7
1915	Oregon village	4 519	NA	NA	4 482	5	5	16	11	39	1 672	10 068	6.9
1930	Oshkosh	55 006	49 620	10.9	52 945	435	273	1 201	152	456	21 827	10 058	46.5
1947	Paddock Lake village	2 662	NA	NA	2 635	0	17	3	7	61	1 074	NA	4.2
1960	Park Falls	3 104	NA	NA	3 072	3	24	5	0	19	1 308	8 756	9.2
1985	Peshtigo	3 154	NA	NA	3 141	1	10	1	1	9	1 217	9 618	7.9
1990	Pewaukee village	4 941	NA	NA	4 844	14	10	36	37	69	2 004	11 886	10.3
2020	Platteville	9 708	NA	NA	9 444	58	21	166	19	62	3 160	8 315	10.4
2021	Pleasant Prairie village	11 961	NA	NA	11 707	52	41	98	63	237	4 347	NA	83.5
2023	Plover village	8 176	NA	NA	8 067	13	19	43	34	64	2 978	9 960	20.3
2030	Plymouth	6 769	NA	NA	6 698	17	16	31	7	32	2 817	11 945	9.3
2040	Portage	8 640	NA	NA	8 302	204	45	56	33	99	3 556	9 570	21.3
2050	Port Washington	9 338	NA	NA	9 237	11	43	40	7	79	3 562	11 365	9.0
2070	Prairie du Chien	5 659	NA	NA	5 576	37	9	30	7	27	2 393	9 566	11.3
2090	Prescott	3 243	NA	NA	3 214	6	5	9	9	13	1 195	10 371	5.2
2105	Racine	84 298	85 730	-1.7	64 378	15 551	273	458	3 638	6 853	33 156	10 407	40.0
2135	Reedsburg	5 834	NA	NA	5 793	8	17	12	4	11	2 485	9 654	9.6
2155	Rhinelander	7 427	NA	NA	7 286	22	97	16	6	19	3 293	8 903	13.3
2162	Rib Mountain CDP	4 634	NA	NA	4 602	1	7	20	4	17	1 646	NA	31.5
2165	Rice Lake	7 998	NA	NA	7 901	10	33	33	21	49	3 520	9 420	16.8
2170	Richland Center	5 018	NA	NA	4 980	5	8	16	9	27	2 290	10 136	9.0
2190	Ripon	7 241	NA	NA	7 131	22	17	49	22	55	2 804	9 225	10.6
2195	River Falls	10 610	NA	NA	10 360	67	37	121	25	71	3 525	8 869	10.5
2240	Rothschild village	3 310	NA	NA	3 300	2	3	4	1	3	1 254	10 850	4.5
2255	St. Francis	9 245	10 066	-8.2	8 994	56	63	77	55	212	3 980	10 731	6.6
2265	Sauk City village	3 019	NA	NA	3 008	7	1	2	1	4	1 254	10 664	3.5
2270	Saukville village	3 695	NA	NA	3 676	1	4	12	2	18	1 273	10 334	6.2
2285	Seymour	2 782	NA	NA	2 739	0	36	6	1	7	1 059	9 501	6.5
2295	Shawano	7 598	NA	NA	7 113	19	441	14	11	56	3 249	9 301	13.5
2300	Sheboygan	49 676	48 085	3.3	46 901	104	216	1 927	528	1 252	20 588	10 585	34.3
2305	Sheboygan Falls	5 823	NA	NA	5 778	9	13	15	8	23	2 303	10 495	7.6
2325	Shorewood village	14 116	14 327	-1.5	13 585	217	24	229	61	231	6 701	16 631	4.1
2380	South Milwaukee	20 958	21 069	-0.5	20 555	68	97	114	124	393	8 428	10 643	12.4
2400	Sparta	7 788	NA	NA	7 651	77	10	32	18	83	3 266	9 635	12.7
2445	Stevens Point	23 006	22 913	0.4	22 023	118	155	643	67	196	8 627	8 864	34.6
2465	Stoughton	8 786	NA	NA	8 674	18	12	38	44	88	3 404	9 821	7.8
2480	Sturgeon Bay	9 176	NA	NA	9 037	13	81	32	13	61	4 049	9 802	24.8
2485	Sturtevant village	3 803	NA	NA	3 663	46	28	20	46	127	1 337	8 737	6.0
2495	Sun Prairie	15 333	12 931	18.6	15 049	103	52	86	43	154	5 718	10 073	18.2
2500	Superior	27 134	29 571	-8.2	26 074	144	647	229	40	141	11 684	8 935	95.7
2515	Sussex village	5 039	NA	NA	4 999	5	11	17	7	33	1 803	11 114	10.1
2535	Thiensville village	3 301	NA	NA	3 268	5	1	22	5	22	1 422	17 255	2.8
2550	Tomah	7 570	NA	NA	7 357	22	123	49	19	60	3 064	9 960	16.6
2555	Tomahawk	3 328	NA	NA	3 285	0	24	14	5	5	1 527	11 052	19.3
2575	Twin Lakes village	3 989	NA	NA	3 948	3	5	7	26	80	2 296	10 704	13.3
2580	Two Rivers	13 030	13 354	-2.4	12 718	27	75	166	44	94	5 414	9 385	14.3
2590	Union Grove village	3 669	NA	NA	3 636	5	11	1	16	90	1 321	9 912	2.8
2605	Verona	5 374	NA	NA	5 317	18	18	15	6	40	1 950	11 331	5.1
2620	Viroqua	3 922	NA	NA	3 912	1	3	6	0	9	1 870	9 721	8.0
2655	Waterloo	2 712	NA	NA	2 665	0	1	6	40	133	1 048	NA	10.1
2660	Watertown	19 142	18 113	5.7	18 902	23	64	74	79	239	7 009	9 423	25.3
2665	Waukesha	56 958	50 319	13.2	54 319	317	161	719	1 442	3 366	22 065	11 418	44.8
2670	Waunakee village	5 897	NA	NA	5 874	5	5	10	3	47	2 020	10 515	6.7
2675	Waupaca	4 957	NA	NA	4 864	1	29	10	53	91	2 190	9 203	13.5
2685	Waupun	8 207	NA	NA	7 487	608	46	19	47	160	2 828	9 352	8.0
2690	Wausau	37 060	32 426	14.3	34 485	47	261	2 216	51	242	15 318	10 732	36.5
2705	Wauwatosa	49 366	51 308	-3.8	48 042	612	89	504	119	490	20 289	15 065	34.3
2720	West Allis	63 221	63 982	-1.2	62 101	191	304	398	227	919	27 502	11 268	29.3
2730	West Bend	23 916	21 484	11.3	23 614	31	94	113	64	221	8 887	10 196	26.0
2750	West Milwaukee village	3 973	NA	NA	3 793	20	49	53	58	155	2 069	12 703	2.9
2753	Weston CDP	9 714	NA	NA	9 550	13	64	64	23	47	3 651	NA	26.5
2755	West Salem village	3 611	NA	NA	3 592	4	10	4	1	12	1 315	8 982	4.7
2775	Whitefish Bay village	14 272	14 930	-4.4	13 954	72	8	205	33	168	5 546	18 712	5.5
2795	Whitewater	12 636	11 520	9.7	11 936	304	33	231	132	295	3 831	7 329	12.5
2828	Wind Lake CDP	3 748	NA	NA	3 701	2	12	11	22	62	1 411	NA	12.2
2845	Wisconsin Rapids	18 245	17 995	1.4	17 658	18	205	305	59	133	7 833	11 103	30.3
0090	Bellevue town (Brown)	7 541	NA	NA	7 468	10	37	19	7	28	2 869	10 226	36.9
0090	Hobart town (Brown)	4 284	NA	NA	3 490	8	764	18	4	42	1 339	10 710	86.3
0091	Suamico town (Brown)	5 214	NA	NA	5 183	4	25	1	1	36	1 786	10 051	93.9
0150	Harrison town (Calumet)	3 195	NA	NA	3 182	2	6	4	1	6	1 155	11 436	92.1
0170	Eagle Point town (Chippewa)	2 542	NA	NA	2 529	0	5	7	1	6	922	8 888	160.8
0171	Hallie town (Chippewa)	4 531	NA	NA	4 489	2	16	10	14	34	1 616	8 856	56.1
0171	Lafayette town (Chippewa)	4 448	NA	NA	4 413	3	16	14	2	15	1 793	10 943	90.0

1. Codes shown are 2-digit FIPS codes for states; 4-digit census place codes for places; and 3-digit FIPS county codes followed by 3-digit census MCD codes for minor civil divisions (MCDs). MCD names are followed by county names in parentheses. 2. Hispanic persons may be of any race. 3. Dry land or land partially or temporarily covered by water.

State/ Place/ MCD[1] code	Place	Population: 1990	Population: Places of 10,000 or more: 1980	Population: Places of 10,000 or more: Percent change, 1980–1990	Population characteristics, 1990: Race: White	Population characteristics, 1990: Race: Black	Population characteristics, 1990: Race: Am. Indian, Eskimo Aleut	Population characteristics, 1990: Race: Asian & Pacific Islander	Population characteristics, 1990: Race: Other race	Population characteristics, 1990: Hispanic[2]	Total housing units, 1990	Per capita income, 1985 (Dollars)	Land area,[3] 1990 (Sq. Km.)
		1	2	3	4	5	6	7	8	9	10	11	12
	WISCONSIN—Con.												
0250	Burke town (Dane)	3 004	NA	NA	2 956	13	5	20	10	16	1 043	11 929	63.2
0250	Cottage Grove town (Dane)	3 525	NA	NA	3 495	14	7	8	1	8	1 156	10 829	89.7
0251	Dunn town (Dane)	5 274	NA	NA	5 235	3	9	23	4	21	2 122	13 018	74.3
0251	Madison town (Dane)	6 442	NA	NA	5 012	1 039	36	229	126	233	3 386	11 296	8.5
0251	Middleton town (Dane)	3 628	NA	NA	3 589	12	4	20	3	16	1 157	15 281	58.3
0252	Pleasant Springs town (Dane)	2 660	NA	NA	2 631	11	3	11	4	8	1 057	11 444	86.8
0252	Springfield town (Dane)	2 650	NA	NA	2 626	6	9	6	3	18	897	NA	93.9
0252	Westport town (Dane)	2 732	NA	NA	2 691	15	6	9	11	18	1 029	16 668	67.3
0252	Windsor town (Dane)	4 620	NA	NA	4 555	21	14	10	20	36	1 580	11 175	85.3
0270	Beaver Dam town (Dodge)	3 097	NA	NA	3 061	4	13	15	4	27	1 231	10 277	90.0
0290	Sevastopol town (Door)	2 552	NA	NA	2 539	1	6	4	2	6	1 427	10 797	134.3
0330	Menomonie town (Dunn)	2 732	NA	NA	2 649	2	2	74	5	10	972	NA	108.5
0350	Seymour town (Eau Claire)	2 757	NA	NA	2 740	0	12	2	3	10	1 025	9 648	81.2
0350	Washington town (Eau Claire)	6 226	NA	NA	6 150	8	18	46	4	14	2 193	11 653	147.5
0391	Taycheedah town (Fond du Lac)	3 383	NA	NA	3 272	91	8	7	5	24	1 180	9 820	79.9
0550	Ixonia town (Jefferson)	2 789	NA	NA	2 776	0	3	5	5	9	939	10 558	93.1
0550	Jefferson town (Jefferson)	2 673	NA	NA	2 650	4	4	8	7	15	735	7 854	113.0
0550	Koshkonong town (Jefferson)	2 984	NA	NA	2 936	14	9	14	11	18	1 269	10 839	111.5
0550	Oakland town (Jefferson)	2 526	NA	NA	2 505	0	3	6	12	25	1 207	NA	90.3
0590	Bristol town (Kenosha)	3 968	NA	NA	3 943	3	5	15	2	49	1 544	11 546	93.3
0590	Salem town (Kenosha)	7 146	NA	NA	7 076	6	24	10	30	121	3 326	10 173	77.7
0590	Somers town (Kenosha)	7 861	NA	NA	7 609	73	49	62	68	173	3 178	12 044	84.5
0590	Wheatland town (Kenosha)	3 263	NA	NA	3 224	6	12	3	18	39	1 348	8 329	61.0
0630	Campbell town (La Crosse)	4 478	NA	NA	4 420	13	14	17	14	26	1 731	10 385	10.3
0630	Onalaska town (La Crosse)	5 907	NA	NA	5 863	5	18	16	5	25	2 001	9 724	100.4
0630	Shelby town (La Crosse)	5 151	NA	NA	5 076	6	17	48	4	36	2 000	14 420	67.5
0690	Merrill town (Lincoln)	2 716	NA	NA	2 708	2	3	2	1	1	1 037	8 348	134.9
0710	Manitowoc Rapids town (Manitowoc)	2 579	NA	NA	2 550	0	4	21	4	16	798	9 337	75.5
0731	Kronenwetter town (Marathon)	4 850	NA	NA	4 811	4	10	23	2	9	1 613	10 015	135.1
0732	Rib Mountain town (Marathon)	5 605	NA	NA	5 561	2	13	24	5	19	1 945	11 223	63.7
0732	Weston town (Marathon)	11 450	11 342	1.0	11 282	13	67	65	23	50	4 236	10 004	93.0
0750	Peshtigo town (Marinette)	3 564	NA	NA	3 546	0	7	6	5	8	1 490	8 626	154.0
0780	Menominee town (Menominee)	3 890	NA	NA	416	0	3 469	0	5	55	1 742	4 857	927.2
0830	Little Suamico town (Oconto)	2 637	NA	NA	2 622	3	10	2	0	6	978	NA	96.7
0850	Minocqua town (Oneida)	3 486	NA	NA	3 454	1	22	5	4	9	3 716	10 920	390.1
0850	Pelican town (Oneida)	3 202	NA	NA	3 167	2	19	12	2	8	1 679	8 842	133.8
0870	Center town (Outagamie)	2 716	NA	NA	2 703	0	3	8	2	2	850	10 150	92.4
0870	Freedom town (Outagamie)	4 114	NA	NA	4 071	0	40	2	1	7	1 342	9 767	92.6
0870	Grand Chute town (Outagamie)	14 490	NA	NA	14 273	31	52	101	33	82	5 619	12 780	71.1
0870	Greenville town (Outagamie)	3 806	NA	NA	3 788	0	13	1	4	10	1 274	10 089	92.7
0871	Oneida town (Outagamie)	3 858	NA	NA	2 473	15	1 357	5	8	28	1 151	8 153	157.6
0890	Cedarburg town (Ozaukee)	5 334	NA	NA	5 300	10	1	22	1	17	1 654	13 926	67.2
0890	Grafton town (Ozaukee)	3 745	NA	NA	3 700	3	12	23	7	17	1 346	13 411	53.8
0970	Hull town (Portage)	5 559	NA	NA	5 494	5	28	28	4	27	1 917	10 502	76.0
1010	Burlington town (Racine)	5 833	NA	NA	5 735	3	25	28	42	83	2 528	10 131	95.1
1010	Caledonia town (Racine)	20 999	20 940	0.3	20 326	290	66	170	147	448	7 251	11 543	117.8
1010	Dover town (Racine)	3 631	NA	NA	3 507	56	19	13	36	123	1 233	7 736	91.7
1010	Mount Pleasant town (Racine)	20 084	19 324	3.9	18 639	979	25	161	280	749	8 000	12 217	92.7
1010	Norway town (Racine)	5 493	NA	NA	5 435	3	14	12	29	115	1 982	10 685	87.3
1010	Raymond town (Racine)	3 243	NA	NA	3 200	21	14	1	7	28	1 102	11 417	92.1
1010	Waterford town (Racine)	4 255	NA	NA	4 201	3	14	14	23	42	1 661	10 241	83.4
1010	Yorkville town (Racine)	2 901	NA	NA	2 871	5	10	8	7	28	998	9 991	90.5
1050	Beloit town (Rock)	6 778	NA	NA	6 148	529	21	32	48	92	2 613	10 991	68.5
1050	Fulton town (Rock)	2 867	NA	NA	2 854	3	1	3	6	27	1 240	10 695	83.0
1050	Janesville town (Rock)	3 198	NA	NA	3 026	140	12	14	6	22	965	13 381	74.9
1051	Rock town (Rock)	3 172	NA	NA	3 110	17	19	2	24	36	1 155	9 499	77.8
1090	Hudson town (St. Croix)	3 692	NA	NA	3 657	2	13	15	5	16	1 144	NA	69.2
1091	St. Joseph town (St. Croix)	2 657	NA	NA	2 618	3	4	27	5	13	974	NA	83.2
1091	Troy town (St. Croix)	2 850	NA	NA	2 827	3	10	7	3	22	1 033	NA	100.6
1130	Hayward town (Sawyer)	3 017	NA	NA	2 247	0	761	5	4	29	1 642	NA	149.5
1151	Wescott town (Shawano)	3 085	NA	NA	2 965	0	109	9	2	8	2 126	10 492	59.5
1170	Holland town (Sheboygan)	2 567	NA	NA	2 546	0	8	9	4	33	1 022	9 795	108.6
1170	Lima town (Sheboygan)	2 715	NA	NA	2 703	0	6	4	2	18	881	8 440	94.8
1170	Plymouth town (Sheboygan)	2 911	NA	NA	2 900	4	4	1	2	7	996	10 858	82.9
1171	Sheboygan town (Sheboygan)	3 866	NA	NA	3 835	1	8	17	5	22	1 419	11 684	29.4
1171	Wilson town (Sheboygan)	2 842	NA	NA	2 824	0	5	5	8	18	1 086	12 695	60.3
1250	Arbor Vitae town (Vilas)	2 531	NA	NA	2 499	1	21	10	0	2	2 041	NA	162.1
1270	Bloomfield town (Walworth)	3 723	NA	NA	3 591	108	11	3	10	47	2 074	9 178	86.6
1270	Delavan town (Walworth)	4 195	NA	NA	4 119	6	9	7	54	133	2 847	12 547	69.3
1270	East Troy town (Walworth)	3 687	NA	NA	3 587	9	18	55	18	44	1 565	10 149	81.2
1270	Geneva town (Walworth)	3 472	NA	NA	3 435	10	7	14	6	43	2 100	8 898	78.9
1270	Lyons town (Walworth)	2 579	NA	NA	2 556	2	10	1	10	27	1 061	10 408	89.9
1271	Sugar Creek town (Walworth)	2 661	NA	NA	2 605	2	5	4	45	78	1 060	9 161	87.7

1. Codes shown are 2-digit FIPS codes for states; 4-digit census place codes for places; and 3-digit FIPS county codes followed by 3-digit census MCD codes for minor civil divisions (MCDs). MCD names are followed by county names in parentheses. 2. Hispanic persons may be of any race. 3. Dry land or land partially or temporarily covered by water.

State/ Place/ MCD[1] code	Place	Population: 1990	Places of 10,000 or more: 1980	Places of 10,000 or more: Percent change, 1980–1990	Race: White	Race: Black	Race: Am. Indian, Eskimo Aleut	Race: Asian & Pacific Islander	Race: Other race	Hispanic[2]	Total housing units, 1990	Per capita income, 1985 (Dollars)	Land area,[3] 1990 (Sq. Km.)
		1	2	3	4	5	6	7	8	9	10	11	12
	WISCONSIN—Con.												
1310	Addison town (Washington)	3 051	NA	NA	3 044	0	5	1	1	6	959	9 884	93.7
1310	Barton town (Washington)	2 637	NA	NA	2 621	3	3	8	2	16	839	NA	52.0
1310	Erin town (Washington)	2 817	NA	NA	2 802	2	6	6	1	7	968	NA	92.9
1310	Farmington town (Washington)	2 523	NA	NA	2 516	1	0	4	2	10	858	NA	94.2
1310	Hartford town (Washington)	3 243	NA	NA	3 219	1	3	17	3	13	1 154	10 506	81.6
1310	Jackson town (Washington)	3 172	NA	NA	3 150	1	8	8	5	17	1 012	11 941	90.1
1310	Polk town (Washington)	3 540	NA	NA	3 524	2	4	6	4	14	1 224	10 856	86.9
1310	Richfield town (Washington)	8 993	NA	NA	8 925	16	11	32	9	26	2 980	12 159	92.9
1310	Trenton town (Washington)	4 028	NA	NA	4 005	1	9	7	6	19	1 269	10 215	88.7
1311	West Bend town (Washington)	4 607	NA	NA	4 590	0	1	14	2	11	2 006	11 430	44.4
1330	Brookfield town (Waukesha)	4 232	NA	NA	4 161	12	2	56	1	34	1 430	15 779	14.9
1330	Delafield town (Waukesha)	5 735	NA	NA	5 457	219	17	26	16	71	1 915	13 614	50.6
1330	Genesee town (Waukesha)	5 986	NA	NA	5 912	12	13	22	27	110	1 871	12 456	84.8
1330	Lisbon town (Waukesha)	8 277	NA	NA	8 198	11	33	26	9	27	2 728	12 111	82.9
1330	Merton town (Waukesha)	6 430	NA	NA	6 384	0	21	20	5	34	2 421	15 093	68.5
1331	Mukwonago town (Waukesha)	5 974	NA	NA	5 904	19	16	24	11	50	1 847	11 631	86.1
1331	Oconomowoc town (Waukesha)	7 323	NA	NA	7 264	16	20	15	8	48	2 841	12 380	77.6
1331	Ottawa town (Waukesha)	2 988	NA	NA	2 935	23	10	11	9	41	1 030	10 757	90.2
1331	Pewaukee town (Waukesha)	9 621	NA	NA	9 499	27	15	45	35	107	3 415	12 126	61.1
1331	Summit town (Waukesha)	4 003	NA	NA	3 952	23	5	16	7	31	1 596	12 718	68.0
1331	Vernon town (Waukesha)	7 549	NA	NA	7 456	27	35	20	11	76	2 267	11 153	87.7
1331	Waukesha town (Waukesha)	7 566	NA	NA	7 461	18	10	27	50	147	2 491	13 786	66.3
1350	Farmington town (Waupaca)	3 602	NA	NA	3 583	1	11	3	4	17	1 486	9 788	90.3
1390	Algoma town (Winnebago)	3 442	NA	NA	3 421	2	4	11	4	14	1 250	11 529	28.2
1390	Menasha town (Winnebago)	13 975	12 218	14.4	13 770	25	47	101	32	95	5 514	11 288	32.6
1390	Neenah town (Winnebago)	2 691	NA	NA	2 651	4	9	24	3	14	1 001	13 705	25.5
1390	Oshkosh town (Winnebago)	4 655	NA	NA	4 406	167	44	19	19	55	1 512	10 009	36.0
1410	Grand Rapids town (Wood)	7 071	NA	NA	6 993	1	17	55	5	22	2 417	11 000	58.6
1411	Saratoga town (Wood)	4 775	NA	NA	4 714	5	22	30	4	11	1 693	9 090	128.0
56	WYOMING	453 588	469 557	-3.4	427 061	3 606	9 479	2 806	10 636	25 751	203 411	9 782	251 500.8
0030	Buffalo	3 302	NA	NA	3 258	1	38	1	4	27	1 627	9 904	8.3
0045	Casper	46 742	51 016	-8.4	45 117	433	255	254	683	1 843	21 700	11 825	53.4
0050	Cheyenne	50 008	47 283	5.8	44 814	1 561	351	584	2 698	5 912	21 859	10 827	48.7
0065	Cody	7 897	NA	NA	7 776	3	56	42	20	96	3 573	10 569	23.3
0100	Douglas	5 076	NA	NA	4 870	11	44	11	140	276	2 267	9 555	13.2
0135	Evanston	10 903	NA	NA	10 575	19	89	46	174	553	4 411	9 922	24.9
0150	Fox Farm-College CDP	2 965	NA	NA	2 748	38	39	20	120	271	1 281	NA	8.7
0160	Gillette	17 635	12 134	45.3	17 165	32	209	58	171	558	7 078	12 589	33.5
0180	Green River	12 711	12 807	-0.7	11 903	40	102	58	608	1 449	4 521	10 901	29.0
0215	Jackson town	4 472	NA	NA	4 356	15	62	29	10	81	2 236	10 766	5.2
0225	Kemmerer	3 020	NA	NA	2 946	2	13	23	36	79	1 306	11 850	19.0
0245	Lander	7 023	NA	NA	6 387	8	525	30	73	181	2 890	9 628	11.0
0250	Laramie	26 687	24 410	9.3	24 857	245	201	619	765	1 778	11 076	8 495	28.8
0325	Newcastle	3 003	NA	NA	2 939	1	47	3	13	45	1 439	9 393	4.9
0355	Powell	5 292	NA	NA	5 055	7	27	27	176	390	2 175	8 151	9.2
0367	Ranchettes CDP	4 038	NA	NA	3 925	17	21	14	61	161	1 378	NA	106.7
0370	Rawlins	9 380	11 552	-18.8	8 076	90	93	57	1 064	1 911	3 948	9 595	18.5
0380	Riverton	9 202	NA	NA	8 125	27	756	60	234	598	3 870	9 352	23.6
0390	Rock Springs	19 050	19 418	-1.9	17 966	222	118	183	561	1 421	8 056	11 896	47.7
0400	Sheridan	13 900	15 087	-7.9	13 586	23	116	81	94	292	6 475	9 952	19.8
0419	South Greeley CDP	3 723	NA	NA	3 326	117	49	28	203	389	1 516	NA	5.0
0445	Thermopolis town	3 247	NA	NA	3 169	5	57	1	15	36	1 573	8 859	6.2
0450	Torrington town	5 651	NA	NA	5 290	14	26	7	314	536	2 475	8 146	5.4
0467	Warren AFB CDP	3 832	NA	NA	3 098	468	26	132	108	204	841	NA	17.0
0470	Wheatland town	3 271	NA	NA	3 232	0	8	6	25	179	1 606	9 354	10.2
0475	Worland	5 742	NA	NA	5 308	12	46	27	349	642	2 514	9 403	10.6

APPENDIX A
GEOGRAPHIC CONCEPTS AND CODES

Areas for which Data are Presented

County and City Extra presents data for States and Counties (Table A), Metropolitan Areas (Table B), Cities (Table C), and Places (Table D).

States and Counties

Data are presented for each of the 50 states and for the District of Columbia. The states are arranged alphabetically, and counties are arranged alphabetically within each state. Data are presented for 3,143 counties and county equivalents. Maps of each state, showing their counties and county equivalents, and their metropolitan areas are contained in Appendix C.

County equivalents

In Louisiana, the primary divisions of the state are known as parishes rather than counties. In Alaska, the county equivalents are the organized boroughs, together with the census areas that were developed for general statistical purposes by the State of Alaska and the U.S. Bureau of the Census. Four states—Maryland, Missouri, Nevada, and Virginia—have one or more incorporated places that are legally independent of any county and thus constitute primary divisions of their states. Similarly, the portion of Yellowstone National Park in Montana is treated as a county equivalent. Within each state, independent cities are listed alphabetically following the list of counties. A list of independent cities is given at the end of this Appendix. The District of Columbia is not divided into counties or county equivalents; data for the entire District are presented as a county equivalent.

For a number of the data series in this volume, separate data are not available for some of the smaller county equivalents. In particular, data for the smaller independent cities in Virginia often are combined with an adjacent county. Where this is known to be the case, it is indicated in the footnotes.

New counties

Two new counties have been established since 1980. In June 1981, Cibola County, New Mexico was established from part of Valencia County. In January 1983, La Paz County, Arizona was established from part of Yuma County. Data for years prior to the establishment of these two counties and some data for more recent years include these new counties in the original counties of which they were a part. Where this is known to be the case, it is indicated in the footnotes.

Alaska

Several changes in county equivalents in Alaska occurred between 1980 and 1990:

1) Aleutian Islands Census Area was replaced by Aleutians East Borough and Aleutians West Census Area.

2) Lake and Peninsula Borough was created from part of the Dillingham Census Area.

3) Northwest Arctic Borough was created from the Kobuk Census Area plus part of North Slope Borough.

Metropolitan Areas

Table B presents data for 337 metropolitan areas comprised of 249 metropolitan statistical areas (MSAs), 17 consolidated metropolitan statistical areas (CMSAs), 55 primary metropolitan statistical areas (PMSAs), and 16 New England county metropolitan areas (NECMAs). The left-hand column of each page provides an alphabetical listing of MSAs, CMSAs, and NECMAs; PMSAs are listed alphabetically under the CMSAs of which they are components.

In general, a metropolitan area is a geographic area consisting of a large population nucleus together with adjacent communities that have a high degree of economic and social integration with that nucleus. The major purpose of defining these areas is to enable all U.S. government agencies to use the same geographic definitions in tabulating and publishing data.

Metropolitan complexes with populations of one million or more may be divided into primary metropolitan statistical areas (PMSAs) with the support of local opinion. When PMSAs are defined, the larger metropolitan area of which they are components is designated a consolidated metropolitan statistical area (CMSA).

For most of the United States, metropolitan areas are defined in terms of counties because counties are the smallest geographical units for which a wide variety of statistical data can be obtained. In New England, however, the metropolitan area definitions are in terms of cities and towns because these subcounty units are of great local significance. An alternative concept for the New England states is the New England county metropolitan area (NECMA). NECMAs, rather than MSAs, CMSAs, and PMSAs, are presented for New England in this volume to enable presentation of a variety of data that are available only for counties and groups of counties.

In this publication, data for the New York-Northern New Jersey-Long Island CMSA include the Bridgeport-Stamford-Norwalk-Danbury, Connecticut NECMA. This means that all of Fairfield County, Connecticut is included; but that those parts of New Haven and Litchfield Counties that are included in Connecticut PMSAs, but not in NECMAs, are excluded from the CMSA data presented in this volume.

Cities

Table C presents data for 951 cities with 1980 populations of 25,000 or more. Corresponding data for states are also provided. The states are arranged alphabetically, and the cities are arranged alphabetically within each state.

As used in this volume, the term "city" refers to places that have been incorporated as cities, boroughs, towns, or villages under the laws of their respective states. However, towns in the New England states and New York are treated as Minor Civil Divisions (MCDs) and are not included in the cities database. Data for towns with populations of 2,500 or more in these states, as well as data for Census Designated Places (CDPs) of corresponding size, are presented in the Places database. For Hawaii, CDPs are included in the Cities table, since the U.S. Bureau of the Census does not recognize any incorporated places in Hawaii. (See the "Places" section below for discussion of MCDs and CDPs).

Places

Table D presents data for places, including Census Designated Places (CDPs), as well as incorporated places with 1990 populations of 2,500 or more. Corresponding data for states are also provided. For 12 states, Minor Civil Divisions (MCDs) are also included. Altogether, data for over 11,000 geographic areas are provided. The states are arranged alphabetically, and the places are arranged alphabetically within each state. For the 12 states for which MCD data are provided, the MCDs follow the places. The MCDs are listed alphabetically by county, with the name of the county given in parentheses following the MCD name.

Census Designated Places (CDPs)

CDPs are delineated by the U.S. Bureau of the Census, in cooperation with states and localities, as statistical counterparts of incorporated places for purposes of the decennial census. CDPs comprise densely settled concentrations of population that are identifiable by name, but are not legally incorporated places. Their boundaries, which usually coincide with visible features or the boundary of an adjacent incorporated place, have no legal status, nor do these places have officials elected to serve traditional municipal functions. CDP boundaries may change with changes in the settlement pattern; a CDP with the same name does not necessarily have the same boundaries from one census to another.

Minor Civil Divisions (MCDs)

MCDs are the primary political or administrative divisions of a county; often they are called towns or townships. In 12 states, Connecticut, Maine, Massachusetts, Michigan, Minnesota, New Hampshire, New Jersey, New York, Pennsylvania, Rhode Island, Vermont, and Wisconsin, MCDs also serve as general purpose local governments. All U.S. Bureau of the Census data products that present data for places include the MCDs in these states. Data for MCDs with populations of 2,500 or more in these 12 states are included in the Places table in this volume.

Geographic Codes

Tables A, B, C, and D provide, in one or more columns at the beginning of the table, a geographic code or codes for each area.

In Table A (States and Counties) a four-digit metropolitan area (MSA, CMSA, or NECMA) code is given in the first column for those counties that are within metropolitan areas. In the second column, a five-digit state and county code is given for each state and county. The first two digits indicate the state, the remaining three represent the county. The state code is a sequential numbering, with some gaps, of the states and the District of Columbia in alphabetical order from Alabama (01) to Wyoming (56). Within each state the counties are numbered in alphabetical order, beginning with 001, with even numbers usually omitted. Independent cities follow the counties and begin with the number 510.

These codes have been established by the U.S. government as Federal Information Processing Standards and are often referred to as "FIPS codes". They are used by U.S. government agencies and many other organizations for data presentation. They are provided in this volume for use in matching the data given here with other data sources in which counties may be identified by FIPS code. The metro area codes will also enable the user to identify the metro area of which a county is a component. Table B (Metropolitan Areas) provides the same metro area codes for each metropolitan area, and Table C (Cities) provides them for cities within metropolitan areas.

Table C (Cities) provides, in the second column, a six-digit state and place code. The first two digits identify the state and are the same as the state FIPS codes described above. The remaining four digits are place codes used by the U.S. Bureau of the Census for the 1990 Census. (In most, but not all cases, the 1990 codes are identical to the codes used for the 1980 Census and for other Bureau of the Census data products.)

Table D (Places) also provides a two-digit state code and a four-digit place code. The state code is printed only once for each state, on the data row for the state as a whole. The four digit place code, given for each place, should be used together with this state code to obtain a unique six-digit geographic identifier for each place. For MCDs, a six-digit code is given, with the first three digits identifying the county and the remaining three digits the county subdivision. Again, this six digit code should be used together with the state code to obtain a unique eight-digit geographic identifier for each MCD.

Independent Cities

Independent cities are not included in any county; data are presented separately in this volume where available.

MARYLAND:
Baltimore (Separate from Baltimore County)

MISSOURI:
St. Louis (Separate from St. Louis County)

NEVADA:
Carson City

VIRGINIA:
Alexandria
Bedford
Bristol
Buena Vista
Charlottesville
Chesapeake
Clifton Forge
Colonial Heights
Covington
Danville
Emporia
Fairfax
Falls Church
Franklin
Fredericksburg
Galax
Hampton
Harrisonburg
Hopewell
Lexington
Lynchburg
Manassas
Manassas Park
Martinsville
Newport News
Norfolk
Norton
Petersburg
Poquoson
Portsmouth
Radford
Richmond
Roanoke
Salem
South Boston
Staunton
Suffolk
Virginia Beach
Waynesboro
Williamsburg
Winchester

Appendix B
Metropolitan Statistical Areas and Components

[MSA = metropolitan statistical area; CMSA = consolidated MSA; PMSA = primary MSA; and NECMA = New England county metropolitan area. For further information, see Appendix A.]

Geographic codes: MSA/ CMSA/ PMSA/ NECMA	Geographic codes: State and County	Title and geographic components	1990 population
0040,		Abilene, TX MSA	119,655
	48 441	Taylor County	119,655
0080		Akron, OH PMSA	657,575
		(See Cleveland-Akron-Lorain CMSA)	
0120		Albany, GA MSA	112,561
	13 095	Dougherty County	96,311
	13 177	Lee County	16,250
0160		Albany-Schenectady-Troy, NY MSA	874,304
	36 001	Albany County	292,594
	36 039	Greene County	44,739
	36 057	Montgomery County	51,981
	36 083	Rensselaer County	154,429
	36 091	Saratoga County	181,276
	36 093	Schenectady County	149,285
0200		Albuquerque, NM MSA	480,577
	35 001	Bernalillo County	480,577
0220		Alexandria, LA MSA	131,556
	22 079	Rapides County	131,556
0240		Allentown-Bethlehem, PA-NJ MSA	686,688
	34 041	Warren County, NJ	91,607
	42 025	Carbon County, PA	56,846
	42 077	Lehigh County, PA	291,130
	42 095	Northampton County, PA	247,105
0280		Altoona, PA MSA	130,542
	42 013	Blair County	130,542
0320		Amarillo, TX MSA	187,547
	48 375	Potter County	97,874
	48 381	Randall County	89,673
0360		Anaheim-Santa Ana, CA PMSA	2,410,556
		(See Los Angeles-Anaheim-Riverside CMSA)	
0380		Anchorage, AK MSA	226,338
	02 020	Anchorage Borough	226,338
0400		Anderson, IN MSA	130,669
	18 095	Madison County	130,669
0405		Anderson, SC MSA	145,196
	45 007	Anderson County	145,196
0440		Ann Arbor, MI PMSA	282,937
		(See Detroit-Ann Arbor CMSA)	
0450		Anniston, AL MSA	116,034
	01 015	Calhoun County	116,034
0460		Appleton-Oshkosh-Neenah, WI MSA	315,121
	55 015	Calumet County	34,291
	55 087	Outagamie County	140,510
	55 139	Winnebago County	140,320
0480		Asheville, NC MSA	174,821
	37 021	Buncombe County	174,821
0500		Athens, GA MSA	156,267
	13 059	Clarke County	87,594
	13 157	Jackson County	30,005
	13 195	Madison County	21,050
	13 219	Oconee County	17,618
0520		Atlanta, GA MSA	2,833,511
	13 013	Barrow County	29,721
	13 035	Butts County	15,326
	13 057	Cherokee County	90,204
	13 063	Clayton County	182,052
	13 067	Cobb County	447,745
	13 077	Coweta County	53,853
	13 089	De Kalb County	545,837
	13 097	Douglas County	71,120
	13 113	Fayette County	62,415
	13 117	Forsyth County	44,083
	13 121	Fulton County	648,951
	13 135	Gwinnett County	352,910
	13 151	Henry County	58,741
	13 217	Newton County	41,808
	13 223	Paulding County	41,611
	13 247	Rockdale County	54,091
	13 255	Spalding County	54,457
	13 297	Walton County	38,586
0560		Atlantic City, NJ MSA	319,416
	34 001	Atlantic County	224,327
	34 009	Cape May County	95,089
0600		Augusta, GA-SC MSA	396,809
	13 073	Columbia County, GA	66,031
	13 189	McDuffie County, GA	20,119
	13 245	Richmond County, GA	189,719
	45 003	Aiken County, SC	120,940
0620		Aurora-Elgin, IL PMSA	356,884
		(See Chicago-Gary-Lake County CMSA)	
0640		Austin, TX MSA	781,572
	48 209	Hays County	65,614
	48 453	Travis County	576,407
	48 491	Williamson County	139,551
0680		Bakersfield, CA MSA	543,477
	06 029	Kern County	543,477
0720		Baltimore, MD MSA	2,382,172
	24 003	Anne Arundel County	427,239
	24 005	Baltimore County	692,134
	24 013	Carroll County	123,372
	24 025	Harford County	182,132
	24 027	Howard County	187,328
	24 035	Queen Anne's County	33,953
	24 510	Baltimore city	736,014
0733		Bangor, ME NECMA	146,601
	23 019	Penobscot County	146,601
0760		Baton Rouge, LA MSA	528,264
	22 005	Ascension Parish	58,214
	22 033	East Baton Rouge Parish	380,105
	22 063	Livingston Parish	70,526
	22 121	West Baton Rouge Parish	19,419
0780		Battle Creek, MI MSA	135,982

Metropolitan Statistical Areas and Components—Continued

[MSA = metropolian statistical area; CMSA = consolidated MSA; PMSA = primary MSA; and NECMA = New England county metropolitan area. For further information, see Appendix A.]

Geographic codes		Title and geographic components	1990 population
MSA/ CMSA/ PMSA/ NECMA	State and County		
	26 025	Calhoun County	135,982
0840		Beaumont-Port Arthur, TX MSA	361,226
	48 199	Hardin County	41,320
	48 245	Jefferson County	239,397
	48 361	Orange County	80,509
0845		Beaver County, PA PMSA	186,093
		(See Pittsburgh-Beaver Valley CMSA)	
0860		Bellingham, WA MSA	127,780
	53 073	Whatcom County	127,780
0870		Benton Harbor, MI MSA	161,378
	26 021	Berrien County	161,378
0875		Bergen-Passaic, NJ PMSA	1,278,440
		(See New York-Northern New Jersey-Long Island CMSA)	
0880		Billings, MT MSA	113,419
	30 111	Yellowstone County	113,419
0920		Biloxi-Gulfport, MS MSA	197,125
	28 045	Hancock County	31,760
	28 047	Harrison County	165,365
0960		Binghamton, NY MSA	264,497
	36 007	Broome County	212,160
	36 107	Tioga County	52,337
1000		Birmingham, AL MSA	907,810
	01 009	Blount County	39,248
	01 073	Jefferson County	651,525
	01 115	St. Clair County	50,009
	01 117	Shelby County	99,358
	01 127	Walker County	67,670
1010		Bismarck, ND MSA	83,831
	38 015	Burleigh County	60,131
	38 059	Morton County	23,700
1020		Bloomington, IN MSA	108,978
	18 105	Monroe County	108,978
1040		Bloomington-Normal, IL MSA	129,180
	17 113	McLean County	129,180
1080		Boise City, ID MSA	205,775
	16 001	Ada County	205,775
1123		Boston-Lawrence-Salem, MA NECMA	3,783,817
	25 009	Essex County	670,080
	25 017	Middlesex County	1,398,468
	25 021	Norfolk County	616,087
	25 023	Plymouth County	435,276
	25 025	Suffolk County	663,906
1125		Boulder-Longmont, CO PMSA	225,339
		(See Denver-Boulder CMSA)	
1140		Bradenton, FL MSA	211,707
	12 081	Manatee County	211,707
1145		Brazoria, TX PMSA	191,707
		(See Houston-Galveston-Brazoria CMSA)	
1150		Bremerton, WA MSA	189,731

Geographic codes		Title and geographic components	1990 population
MSA/ CMSA/ PMSA/ NECMA/	State and County		
	53 035	Kitsap County	189,731
1163		Bridgeport-Stamford-Norwalk-Danbury, CT PMSA	827,645
		(See New York-Northern New Jersey-Long Island CMSA)	
1240		Brownsville-Harlingen, TX MSA	260,120
	48 061	Cameron County	260,120
1260		Bryan-College Station, TX MSA	121,862
	48 041	Brazos County	121,862
1280		Buffalo, NY PMSA	968,532
		(See Buffalo-Niagara Falls CMSA)	
1282		Buffalo-Niagara Falls, NY CMSA	1,189,288
1280		Buffalo, NY PMSA	968,532
	36 029	Erie County	968,532
5700		Niagara Falls, NY PMSA	220,756
	36 063	Niagara County	220,756
1300		Burlington, NC MSA	108,213
	37 001	Alamance County	108,213
1303		Burlington, VT NECMA	137,079
	50 007	Chittenden County	131,761
	50 013	Grand Isle County	5,318
1320		Canton, OH MSA	394,106
	39 019	Carroll County	26,521
	39 151	Stark County	367,585
1350		Casper, WY MSA	61,226
	56 025	Natrona County	61,226
1360		Cedar Rapids, IA MSA	168,767
	19 113	Linn County	168,767
1400		Champaign-Urbana-Rantoul, IL MSA	173,025
	17 019	Champaign County	173,025
1440		Charleston, SC MSA	506,875
	45 015	Berkeley County	128,776
	45 019	Charleston County	295,039
	45 035	Dorchester County	83,060
1480		Charleston, WV MSA	250,454
	54 039	Kanawha County	207,619
	54 079	Putnam County	42,835
1520		Charlotte-Gastonia-Rock Hill, NC-SC MSA	1,162,093
	37 025	Cabarrus County, NC	98,935
	37 071	Gaston County, NC	175,093
	37 109	Lincoln County, NC	50,319
	37 119	Mecklenburg County, NC	511,433
	37 159	Rowan County, NC	110,605
	37 179	Union County, NC	84,211
	45 091	York County, SC	131,497
1540		Charlottesville, VA MSA	131,107
	51 003	Albemarle County	68,040
	51 065	Fluvanna County	12,429
	51 079	Greene County	10,297
	51 540	Charlottesville City	40,341
1560		Chattanooga, TN-GA MSA	433,210
	13 047	Catoosa County, GA	42,464

Metropolitan Statistical Areas and Components—Continued

[MSA = metropolian statistical area; CMSA = consolidated MSA; PMSA = primary MSA; and NECMA = New England county metropolitan area. For further information, see Appendix A.]

Geographic codes: MSA/ CMSA/ PMSA/ NECMA	Geographic codes: State and County	Title and geographic components	1990 population
	13 083	Dade County, GA	13,147
	13 295	Walker County, GA	58,340
	47 065	Hamilton County, TN	285,536
	47 115	Marion County, TN	24,860
	47 153	Sequatchie County, TN	8,863
1580		Cheyenne, WY MSA	73,142
	56 021	Laramie County	73,142
1600		Chicago, IL PMSA	6,069,974
		(See Chicago-Gary-Lake County CMSA)	
1602		Chicago-Gary-Lake County(IL), IL-IN-WI CMSA	8,065,633
0620		Aurora-Elgin, IL PMSA	356,884
	17 089	Kane County	317,471
	17 093	Kendall County	39,413
1600		Chicago, IL PMSA	6,069,974
	17 031	Cook County	5,105,067
	17 043	Du Page County	781,666
	17 111	McHenry County	183,241
2960		Gary-Hammond, IN PMSA	604,526
	18 089	Lake County	475,594
	18 127	Porter County	128,932
3690		Joliet, IL PMSA	389,650
	17 063	Grundy County	32,337
	17 197	Will County	357,313
3800		Kenosha, WI PMSA	128,181
	55 059	Kenosha County	128,181
3965		Lake County, IL PMSA	516,418
	17 097	Lake County	516,418
1620		Chico, CA MSA	182,120
	06 007	Butte County	182,120
1640		Cincinnati, OH-KY-IN PMSA	1,452,645
		(See Cincinnati-Hamilton CMSA)	
1642		Cincinnati-Hamilton, OH-KY-IN CMSA	1,744,124
1640		Cincinnati, OH-KY-IN PMSA	1,452,645
	18 029	Dearborn County, IN	38,835
	21 015	Boone County, KY	57,589
	21 037	Campbell County, KY	83,866
	21 117	Kenton County, KY	142,031
	39 025	Clermont County, OH	150,187
	39 061	Hamilton County, OH	866,228
	39 165	Warren County, OH	113,909
3200		Hamilton-Middletown, OH PMSA	291,479
	39 017	Butler County	291,479
1660		Clarksville-Hopkinsville, TN-KY MSA	169,439
	21 047	Christian County, KY	68,941
	47 125	Montgomery County, TN	100,498
1680		Cleveland, OH PMSA	1,831,122
		(See Cleveland-Akron-Lorain CMSA)	
1692		Cleveland-Akron-Lorain, OH CMSA	2,759,823
0080		Akron, OH PMSA	657,575
	39 133	Portage County	142,585
	39 153	Summit County	514,990
1680		Cleveland, OH PMSA	1,831,122
	39 035	Cuyahoga County	1,412,140
	39 055	Geauga County	81,129
	39 085	Lake County	215,499
	39 103	Medina County	122,354
4440		Lorain-Elyria, OH PMSA	271,126
	39 093	Lorain County	271,126
1720		Colorado Springs, CO MSA	397,014
	08 041	El Paso County	397,014
1740		Columbia, MO MSA	112,379
	29 019	Boone County	112,379
1760		Columbia, SC MSA	453,331
	45 063	Lexington County	167,611
	45 079	Richland County	285,720
1800		Columbus, GA-AL MSA	243,072
	01 113	Russell County, AL	46,860
	13 053	Chattahoochee County, GA	16,934
	13 215	Muscogee County, GA	179,278
1840		Columbus, OH MSA	1,377,419
	39 041	Delaware County	66,929
	39 045	Fairfield County	103,461
	39 049	Franklin County	961,437
	39 089	Licking County	128,300
	39 097	Madison County	37,068
	39 129	Pickaway County	48,255
	39 159	Union County	31,969
1880		Corpus Christi, TX MSA	349,894
	48 355	Nueces County	291,145
	48 409	San Patricio County	58,749
1900		Cumberland, MD-WV MSA	101,643
	24 001	Allegany County, MD	74,946
	54 057	Mineral County, WV	26,697
1920		Dallas, TX PMSA	2,553,362
		(See Dallas-Fort Worth CMSA)	
1922		Dallas-Fort Worth, TX CMSA	3,885,415
1920		Dallas, TX PMSA	2,553,362
	48 085	Collin County	264,036
	48 113	Dallas County	1,852,810
	48 121	Denton County	273,525
	48 139	Ellis County	85,167
	48 257	Kaufman County	52,220
	48 397	Rockwall County	25,604
2800		Fort Worth-Arlington, TX PMSA	1,332,053
	48 251	Johnson County	97,165
	48 367	Parker County	64,785
	48 439	Tarrant County	1,170,103
1950		Danville, VA MSA	108,711
	51 143	Pittsylvania County	55,655
	51 590	Danville City	53,056
1960		Davenport-Rock Island-Moline, IA-IL MSA	350,861
	17 073	Henry County, IL	51,159
	17 161	Rock Island County, IL	148,723
	19 163	Scott County, IA	150,979
2000		Dayton-Springfield, OH MSA	951,270
	39 023	Clark County	147,548
	39 057	Greene County	136,731
	39 109	Miami County	93,182
	39 113	Montgomery County	573,809
2020		Daytona Beach, FL MSA	370,712
	12 127	Volusia County	370,712
2030		Decatur, AL MSA	131,556

Metropolitan Statistical Areas and Components—Continued

[MSA = metropolian statistical area; CMSA = consolidated MSA; PMSA = primary MSA; and NECMA = New England county metropolitan area. For further information, see Appendix A.]

Geographic codes: MSA/ CMSA/ PMSA/ NECMA	Geographic codes: State and County	Title and geographic components	1990 population
	01 079	Lawrence County	31,513
	01 103	Morgan County	100,043
2040		Decatur, IL MSA	117,206
	17 115	Macon County	117,206
2080		Denver, CO PMSA	1,622,980
		(See Denver-Boulder CMSA)	
2082		Denver-Boulder, CO CMSA	1,848,319
1125		Boulder-Longmont, CO PMSA	225,339
	08 013	Boulder County	225,339
2080		Denver, CO PMSA	1,622,980
	08 001	Adams County	265,038
	08 005	Arapahoe County	391,511
	08 031	Denver County	467,610
	08 035	Douglas County	60,391
	08 059	Jefferson County	438,430
2120		Des Moines, IA MSA	392,928
	19 049	Dallas County	29,755
	19 153	Polk County	327,140
	19 181	Warren County	36,033
2160		Detroit, MI PMSA	4,382,299
		(See Detroit-Ann Arbor, MI CMSA)	
2162		Detroit-Ann Arbor, MI CMSA	4,665,236
0440		Ann Arbor, MI PMSA	282,937
	26 161	Washtenaw County	282,937
2160		Detroit, MI PMSA	4,382,299
	26 087	Lapeer County	74,768
	26 093	Livingston County	115,645
	26 099	Macomb County	717,400
	26 115	Monroe County	133,600
	26 125	Oakland County	1,083,592
	26 147	St. Clair County	145,607
	26 163	Wayne County	2,111,687
2180		Dothan, AL MSA	130,964
	01 045	Dale County	49,633
	01 069	Houston County	81,331
2200		Dubuque, IA MSA	86,403
	19 061	Dubuque County	86,403
2240		Duluth, MN-WI MSA	239,971
	27 137	St. Louis County	198,213
	55 031	Douglas County	41,758
2290		Eau Claire, WI MSA	137,543
	55 017	Chippewa County	52,360
	55 035	Eau Claire County	85,183
2320		El Paso, TX MSA	591,610
	48 141	El Paso County	591,610
2330		Elkhart-Goshen, IN MSA	156,198
	18 039	Elkhart County	156,198
2335		Elmira, NY MSA	95,195
	36 015	Chemung County	95,195
2340		Enid, OK MSA	56,735
	40 047	Garfield County	56,735
2360		Erie, PA MSA	275,572
	42 049	Erie County	275,572
2400		Eugene-Springfield, OR MSA	282,912
	41 039	Lane County	282,912
2440		Evansville, IN-KY MSA	278,990
	18 129	Posey County, IN	25,968
	18 163	Vanderburgh County, IN	165,058
	18 173	Warrick County, KY	44,920
	21 101	Henderson County, KY	43,044
2520		Fargo-Moorhead, ND-MN MSA	153,296
	27 027	Clay County, MN	50,422
	38 017	Cass County, ND	102,874
2560		Fayetteville, NC MSA	274,566
	37 051	Cumberland County	274,566
2580		Fayetteville-Springdale, AR MSA	113,409
	05 143	Washington County	113,409
2640		Flint, MI MSA	430,459
	26 049	Genesee County	430,459
2650		Florence, AL MSA	131,327
	01 033	Colbert County	51,666
	01 077	Lauderdale County	79,661
2655		Florence, SC MSA	114,344
	45 041	Florence County	114,344
2670		Fort Collins-Loveland, CO MSA	186,136
	08 069	Larimer County	186,136
2680		Ft. Lauderdale-Hollywood-Pompano Beach, FL PMSA	1,255,488
		(See Miami-Fort Lauderdale CMSA)	
2700		Fort Myers-Cape Coral, FL MSA	335,113
	12 071	Lee County	335,113
2710		Fort Pierce, FL MSA	251,071
	12 085	Martin County	100,900
	12 111	St. Lucie County	150,171
2720		Fort Smith, AR-OK MSA	175,911
	05 033	Crawford County, AR	42,493
	05 131	Sebastian County, AR	99,590
	40 135	Sequoyah County, OK	33,828
2750		Fort Walton Beach, FL MSA	143,776
	12 091	Okaloosa County	143,776
2760		Fort Wayne, IN MSA	363,811
	18 003	Allen County	300,836
	18 033	De Kalb County	35,324
	18 183	Whitley County	27,651
2800		Fort Worth-Arlington, TX PMSA	1,332,053
		(See Dallas-Fort Worth CMSA)	
2840		Fresno, CA MSA	667,490
	06 019	Fresno County	667,490
2880		Gadsden, AL MSA	99,840
	01 055	Etowah County	99,840
2900		Gainesville, FL MSA	204,111

Metropolitan Statistical Areas and Components—Continued

[MSA = metropolian statistical area; CMSA = consolidated MSA; PMSA = primary MSA; and NECMA = New England county metropolitan area. For further information, see Appendix A.]

Geographic codes: MSA/ CMSA/ PMSA/ NECMA	Geographic codes: State and County	Title and geographic components	1990 population
	12 001	Alachua County	181,596
	12 007	Bradford County	22,515
2920		Galveston-Texas City, TX PMSA (See Houston-Galveston-Brazoria CMSA)	217,399
2960		Gary-Hammond, IN PMSA (See Chicago-Gary-Lake County CMSA)	604,526
2975		Glens Falls, NY MSA	118,539
	36 113	Warren County	59,209
	36 115	Washington County	59,330
2985		Grand Forks, ND MSA	70,683
	38 035	Grand Forks County	70,683
3000		Grand Rapids, MI MSA	688,399
	26 081	Kent County	500,631
	26 139	Ottawa County	187,768
3040		Great Falls, MT MSA	77,691
	30 013	Cascade County	77,691
3060		Greeley, CO MSA	131,821
	08 123	Weld County	131,821
3080		Green Bay, WI MSA	194,594
	55 009	Brown County	194,594
3120		Greensboro-Winston Salem-High Point, NC MSA	942,091
	37 057	Davidson County	126,677
	37 059	Davie County	27,859
	37 067	Forsyth County	265,878
	37 081	Guilford County	347,420
	37 151	Randolph County	106,546
	37 169	Stokes County	37,223
	37 197	Yadkin County	30,488
3160		Greenville-Spartanburg, SC MSA	640,861
	45 045	Greenville County	320,167
	45 077	Pickens County	93,894
	45 083	Spartanburg County	226,800
3180		Hagerstown, MD MSA	121,393
	24 043	Washington County	121,393
3200		Hamilton-Middletown, OH PMSA (See Cincinnati-Hamilton CMSA)	291,479
3240		Harrisburg-Lebanon-Carlisle, PA MSA	587,986
	42 041	Cumberland County	195,257
	42 043	Dauphin County	237,813
	42 075	Lebanon County	113,744
	42 099	Perry County	41,172
3283		Hartford-New Britain-Middletown-Bristol, CT NECMA	1,123,678
	09 003	Hartford County	851,783
	09 007	Middlesex County	143,196
	09 013	Tolland County	128,699
3290		Hickory, NC MSA	221,700
	37 003	Alexander County	27,544
	37 023	Burke County	75,744
	37 035	Catawba County	118,412
3320		Honolulu, HI MSA	836,231
	15 003	Honolulu County	836,231
3350		Houma-Thibodaux, LA MSA	182,842
	22 057	Lafourche Parish	85,860
	22 109	Terrebonne Parish	96,982
3360		Houston, TX PMSA (See Houston-Galveston-Brazoria CMSA)	3,301,937
3362		Houston-Galveston-Brazoria, TX CMSA	3,711,043
1145		Brazoria, TX PMSA	191,707
	48 039	Brazoria County	191,707
2920		Galveston-Texas City, TX PMSA	217,399
	48 167	Galveston County	217,399
3360		Houston, TX PMSA	3,301,937
	48 157	Fort Bend County	225,421
	48 201	Harris County	2,818,199
	48 291	Liberty County	52,726
	48 339	Montgomery County	182,201
	48 473	Waller County	23,390
3400		Huntington-Ashland, WV-KY-OH MSA	312,529
	21 019	Boyd County, KY	51,150
	21 043	Carter County, KY	24,340
	21 089	Greenup County, KY	36,742
	39 087	Lawrence County, OH	61,834
	54 011	Cabell County, WV	96,827
	54 099	Wayne County, WV	41,636
3440		Huntsville, AL MSA	238,912
	01 089	Madison County	238,912
3480		Indianapolis, IN MSA	1,249,822
	18 011	Boone County	38,147
	18 057	Hamilton County	108,936
	18 059	Hancock County	45,527
	18 063	Hendricks County	75,717
	18 081	Johnson County	88,109
	18 097	Marion County	797,159
	18 109	Morgan County	55,920
	18 145	Shelby County	40,307
3500		Iowa CIty, IA MSA	96,119
	19 103	Johnson County	96,119
3520		Jackson, MI MSA	149,756
	26 075	Jackson County	149,756
3560		Jackson, MS MSA	395,396
	28 049	Hinds County	254,441
	28 089	Madison County	53,794
	28 121	Rankin County	87,161
3580		Jackson, TN MSA	77,982
	47 113	Madison County	77,982
3600		Jacksonville, FL MSA	906,727
	12 019	Clay County	105,986
	12 031	Duval County	672,971
	12 089	Nassau County	43,941
	12 109	St. Johns County	83,829
3605		Jacksonville, NC MSA	149,838
	37 133	Onslow County	149,838

Metropolitan Statistical Areas and Components—Continued

[MSA = metropolian statistical area; CMSA = consolidated MSA; PMSA = primary MSA; and NECMA = New England county metropolitan area. For further information, see Appendix A.]

Geographic codes: MSA/ CMSA/ PMSA/ NECMA	Geographic codes: State and County	Title and geographic components	1990 population
3610		Jamestown, NY MSA	141,895
	36 013	Chautauqua County	141,895
3620		Janesville-Beloit, WI MSA	139,510
	55 105	Rock County	139,510
3640		Jersey City, NJ PMSA	553,099
		(See New York-Northern New Jersey-Long Island CMSA)	
3660		Johnson City-Kingsport-Bristol(TN), TN-VA MSA	436,047
	47 019	Carter County, TN	51,505
	47 073	Hawkins County, TN	44,565
	47 163	Sullivan County, TN	143,596
	47 171	Unicoi County, TN	16,549
	47 179	Washington County, TN	92,315
	51 169	Scott County, VA	23,204
	51 191	Washington County, VA	45,887
	51 520	Bristol City, VA	18,426
3680		Johnstown, PA MSA	241,247
	42 021	Cambria County	163,029
	42 111	Somerset County	78,218
3690		Joliet, IL PMSA	389,650
		(See Chicago-Gary-Lake County CMSA)	
3710		Joplin, MO MSA	134,910
	29 097	Jasper County	90,465
	29 145	Newton County	44,445
3720		Kalamazoo, MI MSA	223,411
	26 077	Kalamazoo County	223,411
3740		Kankakee, IL MSA	96,255
	17 091	Kankakee County	96,255
3760		Kansas City, MO-KS MSA	1,566,280
	20 091	Johnson County, KS	355,054
	20 103	Leavenworth County, KS	64,371
	20 121	Miami County, KS	23,466
	20 209	Wyandotte County, KS	161,993
	29 037	Cass County, MO	63,808
	29 047	Clay County, MO	153,411
	29 095	Jackson County, MO	633,232
	29 107	Lafayette County, MO	31,107
	29 165	Platte County, MO	57,867
	29 177	Ray County, MO	21,971
3800		Kenosha, WI PMSA	128,181
		(See Chicago-Gary-Lake County CMSA)	
3810		Killeen-Temple, TX MSA	255,301
	48 027	Bell County	191,088
	48 099	Coryell County	64,213
3840		Knoxville, TN MSA	604,816
	47 001	Anderson County	68,250
	47 009	Blount County	85,969
	47 057	Grainger County	17,095
	47 089	Jefferson County	33,016
	47 093	Knox County	335,749
	47 155	Sevier County	51,043
	47 173	Union County	13,694
3850		Kokomo, IN MSA	96,946
	18 067	Howard County	80,827
	18 159	Tipton County	16,119
3870		La Crosse, WI MSA	97,904
	55 063	La Crosse County	97,904
3880		Lafayette, LA MSA	208,740
	22 055	Lafayette Parish	164,762
	22 099	St. Martin Parish	43,978
3920		Lafayette-West Lafayette, IN MSA	130,598
	18 157	Tippecanoe County	130,598
3960		Lake Charles, LA MSA	168,134
	22 019	Calcasieu County	168,134
3965		Lake County, IL PMSA	516,418
		(See Chicago-Gary-Lake County CMSA)	
3980		Lakeland-Winter Haven, FL MSA	405,382
	12 105	Polk County	405,382
4000		Lancaster, PA MSA	422,822
	42 071	Lancaster County	422,822
4040		Lansing-East Lansing, MI MSA	432,674
	26 037	Clinton County	57,883
	26 045	Eaton County	92,879
	26 065	Ingham County	281,912
4080		Laredo, TX MSA	133,239
	48 479	Webb County	133,239
4100		Las Cruces, NM MSA	135,510
	35 013	Dona Ana County	135,510
4120		Las Vegas, NV MSA	741,459
	32 003	Clark County	741,459
4150		Lawrence, KS MSA	81,798
	20 045	Douglas County	81,798
4200		Lawton, OK MSA	111,486
	40 031	Comanche County	111,486
4243		Lewiston-Auburn, ME NECMA	105,259
	23 001	Androscoggin County	105,259
4280		Lexington-Fayette, KY MSA	348,428
	21 017	Bourbon County	19,236
	21 049	Clark County	29,496
	21 067	Fayette County	225,366
	21 113	Jessamine County	30,508
	21 209	Scott County	23,867
	21 239	Woodford County	19,955
4320		Lima, OH MSA	154,340
	39 003	Allen County	109,755
	39 011	Auglaize County	44,585
4360		Lincoln, NE MSA	213,641
	31 109	Lancaster County	213,641
4400		Little Rock-North Little Rock, AR MS	513,117
	05 045	Faulkner County	60,006
	05 085	Lonoke County	39,268
	05 119	Pulaski County	349,660
	05 125	Saline County	64,183

Metropolitan Statistical Areas and Components—Continued

[MSA = metropolian statistical area; CMSA = consolidated MSA; PMSA = primary MSA; and NECMA = New England county metropolitan area. For further information, see Appendix A.]

Geographic codes: MSA/ CMSA/ PMSA/ NECMA	Geographic codes: State and County	Title and geographic components	1990 population
4420		Longview-Marshall, TX MSA	162,431
	48 183	Gregg County	104,948
	48 203	Harrison County	57,483
4440		Lorain-Elyria, OH PMSA	271,126
		(See Cleveland-Akron-Lorain CMSA)	
4472		Los Angeles-Anaheim-Riverside, CA CMSA	14,531,529
0360		Anaheim-Santa Ana, CA PMSA	2,410,556
	06 059	Orange County	2,410,556
4480		Los Angeles-Long Beach, CA PMSA	8,863,164
	06 037	Los Angeles County	8,863,164
6000		Oxnard-Ventura, CA PMSA	669,016
	06 111	Ventura County	669,016
6780		Riverside-San Bernardino, CA PMSA	2,588,793
	06 065	Riverside County	1,170,413
	06 071	San Bernardino County	1,418,380
4480		Los Angeles-Long Beach, CA PMSA	8,863,164
		(See Los Angeles-Anaheim-Riverside CMSA)	
4520		Louisville, KY-IN MSA	952,662
	18 019	Clark County, IN	87,777
	18 043	Floyd County, IN	64,404
	18 061	Harrison County, IN	29,890
	21 029	Bullitt County, KY	47,567
	21 111	Jefferson County, KY	664,937
	21 185	Oldham County, KY	33,263
	21 211	Shelby County, KY	24,824
4600		Lubbock, TX MSA	222,636
	48 303	Lubbock County	222,636
4640		Lynchburg, VA MSA	142,199
	51 009	Amherst County	28,578
	51 031	Campbell County	47,572
	51 680	Lynchburg City	66,049
4680		Macon-Warner Robins, GA MSA	281,103
	13 021	Bibb County	149,967
	13 153	Houston County	89,208
	13 169	Jones County	20,739
	13 225	Peach County	21,189
4720		Madison, WI MSA	367,085
	55 025	Dane County	367,085
4763		Manchester-Nashua, NH NECMA	336,073
	33 011	Hillsborough County	336,073
4800		Mansfield, OH MSA	126,137
	39 139	Richland County	126,137
4880		McAllen-Edinburg-Mission, TX MSA	383,545
	48 215	Hidalgo County	383,545
4890		Medford, OR MSA	146,389
	41 029	Jackson County	146,389
4900		Melbourne-Titusville-Palm Bay, FL MSA	398,978
	12 009	Brevard County	398,978
4920		Memphis, TN-AR-MS MSA	981,747
	05 035	Crittenden County, AR	49,939
	28 033	De Soto County, MS	67,910
	47 157	Shelby County, TN	826,330
	47 167	Tipton County, TN	37,568
4940		Merced, CA MSA	178,403
	06 047	Merced County	178,403
4992		Miami-Fort Lauderdale, FL CMSA	3,192,582
2680		Ft.Lauderdale-Hollywood-Pompano Beach, FL PMSA	1,255,488
	12 011	Broward County	1,255,488
5000		Miami-Hialeah, FL PMSA	1,937,094
	12 025	Dade County	1,937,094
5000		Miami-Hialeah, FL PMSA	1,937,094
		(See Miami-Fort Lauderdale CMSA)	
5015		Middlesex-Somerset-Hunterdon, NJ PMSA	1,019,835
		(See New York-Northern New Jersey-Long Island CMSA)	
5040		Midland, TX MSA	106,611
	48 329	Midland County	106,611
5080		Milwaukee, WI PMSA	1,432,149
		(See Milwaukee-Racine CMSA)	
5082		Milwaukee-Racine, WI CMSA	1,607,183
5080		Milwaukee, WI PMSA	1,432,149
	55 079	Milwaukee County	959,275
	55 089	Ozaukee County	72,831
	55 131	Washington County	95,328
	55 133	Waukesha County	304,715
6600		Racine, WI PMSA	175,034
	55 101	Racine County	175,034
5120		Minneaolis-St. Paul, MN-WI MSA	2,464,124
	27 003	Anoka County, MN	243,641
	27 019	Carver County, MN	47,915
	27 025	Chisago County, MN	30,521
	27 037	Dakota County, MN	275,227
	27 053	Hennepin County, MN	1,032,431
	27 059	Isanti County, MN	25,921
	27 123	Ramsey County, MN	485,765
	27 139	Scott County, MN	57,846
	27 163	Washington County, MN	145,896
	27 171	Wright County, MN	68,710
	55 109	St. Croix County, WI.	50,251
5160		Mobile, AL MSA	476,923
	01 003	Baldwin County	98,280
	01 097	Mobile County	378,643
5170		Modesto, CA MSA	370,522
	06 099	Stanislaus County	370,522
5190		Monmouth-Ocean, NJ PMSA	986,327
		(See New York-Northern New Jersey-Long Island CMSA)	
5200		Monroe, LA MSA	142,191
	22 073	Ouachita Parish	142,191
5240		Montgomery, AL MSA	292,517
	01 001	Autauga County	34,222
	01 051	Elmore County	49,210
	01 101	Montgomery County	209,085
5280		Muncie, IN MSA	119,659

Metropolitan Statistical Areas and Components—Continued

[MSA = metropolian statistical area; CMSA = consolidated MSA; PMSA = primary MSA; and NECMA = New England county metropolitan area. For further information, see Appendix A.]

Geographic codes: MSA/ CMSA/ PMSA/ NECMA	Geographic codes: State and County	Title and geographic components	1990 population
	18 035	Delaware County	119,659
5320		Muskegon, MI MSA	158,983
	26 121	Muskegon County	158,983
5345		Naples, FL MSA	152,099
	12 021	Collier County	152,099
5360		Nashville, TN MSA	985,026
	47 021	Cheatham County	27,140
	47 037	Davidson County	510,784
	47 043	Dickson County	35,061
	47 147	Robertson County	41,494
	47 149	Rutherford County	118,570
	47 165	Sumner County	103,281
	47 187	Williamson County	81,021
	47 189	Wilson County	67,675
5380		Nassau-Suffolk, NY PMSA (See New York-Northern New Jersey-Long Island CMSA)	2,609,212
5403		New Bedford-Fall River-Attleboo, MA NECMA	506,325
	25 005	Bristol County	506,325
5483		New Haven-Waterbury-Meriden, CT NECMA	804,219
	09 009	New Haven County	804,219
5523		New London-Norwich, CT NECMA	254,957
	09 011	New London County	254,957
5560		New Orleans, LA MSA	1,238,816
	22 051	Jefferson Parish	448,306
	22 071	Orleans Parish	496,938
	22 087	St. Bernard Parish	66,631
	22 089	St. Charles Parish	42,437
	22 095	St. John the Baptist Parish	39,996
	22 103	St. Tammany Parish	144,508
5600		New York, NY PMSA (See New York-Northern New Jersey-Long Island CMSA)	8,546,846
5602		New York-Northern New Jersey-Long Island, NY-NJ-CT CMSA	17,953,372
0875		Bergen-Passaic, NJ PMSA	1,278,440
	34 003	Bergen County	825,380
	34 031	Passaic County	453,060
1163		Bridgeport-Stamford-Norwalk-Danbury, CT PMSA	827,645
	09 001	Fairfield County	827,645
3640		Jersey City, NJ PMSA	553,099
	34 017	Hudson County	553,099
5015		Middlesex-Somerset-Hunterdon, NJ PMSA	1,019,835
	34 019	Hunterdon County	107,776
	34 023	Middlesex County	671,780
	34 035	Somerset County	240,279
5190		Monmouth-Ocean, NJ PMSA	986,327
	34 025	Monmouth County	553,124
	34 029	Ocean County	433,203
5380		Nassau-Suffolk, NY PMSA	2,609,212
	36 059	Nassau County	1,287,348
	36 103	Suffolk County	1,321,864
5600		New York, NY PMSA	8,546,846
	36 005	Bronx County	1,203,789
	36 047	Kings County	2,300,664
	36 061	New York County	1,487,536
	36 079	Putnam County	83,941
	36 081	Queens County	1,951,598

Geographic codes: MSA/ CMSA/ PMSA/ NECMA/	Geographic codes: State and County	Title and geographic components	1990 population
	36 085	Richmond County	378,977
	36 087	Rockland County	265,475
	36 119	Westchester County	874,866
5640		Newark, NJ PMSA	1,824,321
	34 013	Essex County	778,206
	34 027	Morris County	421,353
	34 037	Sussex County	130,943
	34 039	Union County	493,819
5950		Orange County, NY PMSA	307,647
	36 071	Orange County	307,647
5640		Newark, NJ PMSA (See New York-Northern New Jersey-Long Island CMSA)	1,824,321
5700		Niagara Falls, NY PMSA (See Buffalo-Niagara Falls CMSA)	220,756
5720		Norfolk-Virginia Beach-Newport News, VA MSA	1,396,107
	51 073	Gloucester County	30,131
	51 095	James City County	34,859
	51 199	York County	42,422
	51 550	Chesapeake City	151,976
	51 650	Hampton City	133,793
	51 700	Newport News City	170,045
	51 710	Norfolk City	261,229
	51 735	Poquoson City	11,005
	51 740	Portsmouth City	103,907
	51 800	Suffolk City	52,141
	51 810	Virginia Beach City	393,069
	51 830	Williamsburg City	11,530
5775		Oakland, CA PMSA (See San Francisco-Oakland-San Jose CMSA)	2,082,914
5790		Ocala, FL MSA	194,833
	12 083	Marion County	194,833
5800		Odessa, TX MSA	118,934
	48 135	Ector County	118,934
5880		Oklahoma City, OK MSA	958,839
	40 017	Canadian County	74,409
	40 027	Cleveland County	174,253
	40 083	Logan County	29,011
	40 087	McClain County	22,795
	40 109	Oklahoma County	599,611
	40 125	Pottawatomie County	58,760
5910		Olympia, WA MSA	161,238
	53 067	Thurston County	161,238
5920		Omaha, NE-IA MSA	618,262
	19 155	Pottawattamie County, IA	82,628
	31 055	Douglas County, NE	416,444
	31 153	Sarpy County, NE	102,583
	31 177	Washington County, NE	16,607
5950		Orange County, NY PMSA (See New York-Northern New Jersey-Long Island CMSA)	307,647
5960		Orlando, FL MSA	1,072,748
	12 095	Orange County	677,491
	12 097	Osceola County	107,728
	12 117	Seminole County	287,529
5990		Owensboro, KY MSA	87,189

Metropolitan Statistical Areas and Components—Continued

[MSA = metropolian statistical area; CMSA = consolidated MSA; PMSA = primary MSA; and NECMA = New England county metropolitan area. For further information, see Appendix A.]

Geographic codes: MSA/ CMSA/ PMSA/ NECMA	State and County	Title and geographic components	1990 population
	21 059	Daviess County	87,189
6000		Oxnard-Ventura, CA	669,016
		(See Los Angeles-Anaheim-Riverside CMSA)	
6015		Panama City, FL MSA	126,994
	12 005	Bay County	126,994
6020		Parkersburg-Marietta, WV-OH MSA	149,169
	39 167	Washington County, OH	62,254
	54 107	Wood County, WV	86,915
6025		Pascagoula, MS MSA	115,243
	28 059	Jackson County	115,243
6080		Pensacola, FL MSA	344,406
	12 033	Escambia County	262,798
	12 113	Santa Rosa County	81,608
6120		Peoria, IL MSA	339,172
	17 143	Peoria County	182,827
	17 179	Tazewell County	123,692
	17 203	Woodford County	32,653
6160		Philadelphia, PA-NJ PMSA	4,856,881
		(See Philadelphia-Wilmington-Trenton CMSA)	
6162		Philadelphia-Wilmington-Trenton, PA-NJ-DE-MD CMSA	5,899,345
6160		Philadelphia, PA-NJ PMSA	4,856,881
	34 005	Burlington County, NJ	395,066
	34 007	Camden County, NJ	502,824
	34 015	Gloucester County, NJ	230,082
	42 017	Bucks County, PA	541,174
	42 029	Chester County, PA	376,396
	42 045	Delaware County, PA	547,651
	42 091	Montgomery County, PA	678,111
	42 101	Philadelphia County, PA	1,585,577
8480		Trenton, NJ PMSA	325,824
	34 021	Mercer County	325,824
8760		Vineland-Millville-Bridgeton, NJ PMSA	138,053
	34 011	Cumberland County	138,053
9160		Wilmington, DE-NJ-MD PMSA	578,587
	10 003	New Castle County	441,946
	24 015	Cecil County	71,347
	34 033	Salem County	65,294
6200		Phoenix, AZ MSA	2,122,101
	04 013	Maricopa County	2,122,101
6240		Pine Bluff, AR MSA	85,487
	05 069	Jefferson County	85,487
6280		Pittsburgh, PA PMSA	2,056,705
		(See Pittsburg-Beaver Valley CMSA)	
6282		Pittsburgh-Beaver Valley, PA CMSA	2,242,798
0845		Beaver County, PA PMSA	186,093
	42 007	Beaver County	186,093
6280		Pittsburgh, PA PMSA	2,056,705
	42 003	Allegheny County	1,336,449
	42 051	Fayette County	145,351
	42 125	Washington County	204,584
	42 129	Westmoreland County	370,321
6323		Pittsfield, MA MSA	139,352
	25 003	Berkshire County	139,352
6403		Portland, ME MSA	243,135
	23 005	Cumberland County	243,135
6440		Portland, OR PMSA	1,239,842
		(See Portland-Vancouver CMSA)	
6442		Portland-Vancouver, OR-WA CMSA	1,477,895
6440		Portland, OR PMSA	1,239,842
	41 005	Clackamas County	278,850
	41 051	Multnomah County	583,887
	41 067	Washington County	311,554
	41 071	Yamhill County	65,551
8725		Vancouver, WA PMSA	238,053
	53 011	Clark County	238,053
6453		Portsmouth-Dover-Rochester, NH NECMA	350,078
	33 015	Rockingham County	245,845
	33 017	Strafford County	104,233
6460		Poughkeepsie, NY MSA	259,462
	36 027	Dutchess County	259,462
6483		Providence-Pawtucket-Woonsocket RI NECMA	916,270
	44 001	Bristol County	48,859
	44 003	Kent County	161,135
	44 007	Providence County	596,270
	44 009	Washington County	110,006
6520		Provo-Orem, UT MSA	263,590
	49 049	Utah County	263,590
6560		Pueblo, CO MSA	123,051
	08 101	Pueblo County	123,051
6600		Racine, WI PMSA	175,034
		(See Milwaukee-Racine CMSA)	
6640		Raleigh-Durham, NC MSA	735,480
	37 063	Durham County	181,835
	37 069	Franklin County	36,414
	37 135	Orange County	93,851
	37 183	Wake County	423,380
6660		Rapid City, SD MSA	81,343
	46 103	Pennington County	81,343
6680		Reading, PA MSA	336,523
	42 011	Berks County	336,523
6690		Redding, CA MSA	147,036
	06 089	Shasta County	147,036
6720		Reno, NV MSA	254,667
	32 031	Washoe County	254,667
6740		Richland-Kennewick-Pasco, WA MSA	150,033
	53 005	Benton County	112,560
	53 021	Franklin County	37,473
6760		Richmond-Petersburg, VA MSA	865,640
	51 036	Charles City County	6,282
	51 041	Chesterfield County	209,274
	51 053	Dinwiddie County	20,960
	51 075	Goochland County	14,163
	51 085	Hanover County	63,306
	51 087	Henrico County	217,881

Metropolitan Statistical Areas and Components—Continued

[MSA = metropolian statistical area; CMSA = consolidated MSA; PMSA = primary MSA; and NECMA = New England county metropolitan area. For further information, see Appendix A.]

Geographic codes: MSA/ CMSA/ PMSA/ NECMA	Geographic codes: State and County	Title and geographic components	1990 population
	51 127	New Kent County	10,445
	51 145	Powhatan County	15,328
	51 149	Prince George County	27,394
	51 570	Colonial Heights City	16,064
	51 670	Hopewell City	23,101
	51 730	Petersburg City	38,386
	51 760	Richmond City	203,056
6780		Riverside-San Bernardino, CA PMSA (See Los Angeles-Anaheim-Riverside CMSA)	2,588,793
6800		Roanoke, VA MSA	224,477
	51 023	Botetourt County	24,992
	51 161	Roanoke County	79,332
	51 770	Roanoke City	96,397
	51 775	Salem City	23,756
6820		Rochester, MN MSA	106,470
	27 109	Olmsted County	106,470
6840		Rochester, NY MSA	1,002,410
	36 051	Livingston County	62,372
	36 055	Monroe County	713,968
	36 069	Ontario County	95,101
	36 073	Orleans County	41,846
	36 117	Wayne County	89,123
6880		Rockford, IL MSA	283,719
	17 007	Boone County	30,806
	17 201	Winnebago County	252,913
6920		Sacramento, CA MSA	1,481,102
	06 017	El Dorado County	125,995
	06 061	Placer County	172,796
	06 067	Sacramento County	1,041,219
	06 113	Yolo County	141,092
6960		Saginaw-Bay City-Midland, MI MSA	399,320
	26 017	Bay County	111,723
	26 111	Midland County	75,651
	26 145	Saginaw County	211,946
6980		St. Cloud, MN MSA	190,921
	27 009	Benton County	30,185
	27 141	Sherburne County	41,945
	27 145	Stearns County	118,791
7000		St. Joseph, MO MSA	83,083
	29 021	Buchanan County	83,083
7040		St. Louis, MO-IL MSA	2,444,099
	17 027	Clinton County, IL	33,944
	17 083	Jersey County, IL	20,539
	17 119	Madison County, IL	249,238
	17 133	Monroe County, IL	22,422
	17 163	St. Clair County, IL	262,852
	29 071	Franklin County, MO	80,603
	29 099	Jefferson County, MO	171,380
	29 183	St. Charles County, MO	212,907
	29 189	St. Louis County, MO	993,529
	29 510	St. Louis City, MO	396,685
7080		Salem, OR MSA	278,024
	41 047	Marion County	228,483
	41 053	Polk County	49,541
7120		Salinas-Seaside-Monterey, CA MSA	355,660

Geographic codes: MSA/ CMSA/ PMSA/ NECMA/	Geographic codes: State and County	Title and geographic components	1990 population
	06 053	Monterey County	355,660
7160		Salt Lake City-Ogden, UT MSA	1,072,227
	49 011	Davis County	187,941
	49 035	Salt Lake County	725,956
	49 057	Weber County	158,330
7200		San Angelo, TX MSA	98,458
	48 451	Tom Green County	98,458
7240		San Antonio, TX MSA	1,302,099
	48 029	Bexar County	1,185,394
	48 091	Comal County	51,832
	48 187	Guadalupe County	64,873
7320		San Diego, CA MSA	2,498,016
	06 073	San Diego County	2,498,016
7360		San Francisco, CA PMSA (See San Francisco-Oakland-San Jose CMSA)	1,603,678
7362		San Francisco-Oakland-San Jose, CA CMSA	6,253,311
5775		Oakland, CA PMSA	2,082,914
	06 001	Alameda County	1,279,182
	06 013	Contra Costa County	803,732
7360		San Francisco, CA PMSA	1,603,678
	06 041	Marin County	230,096
	06 075	San Francisco County	723,959
	06 081	San Mateo County	649,623
7400		San Jose, CA PMSA	1,497,577
	06 085	Santa Clara County	1,497,577
7485		Santa Cruz, CA PMSA	229,734
	06 087	Santa Cruz County	229,734
7500		Santa Rosa-Petaluma, CA PMSA	388,222
	06 097	Sonoma County	388,222
8720		Vallejo-Fairfield-Napa, CA PMSA	451,186
	06 055	Napa County	110,765
	06 095	Solano County	340,421
7400		San Jose, CA PMSA (See San Francisco-Oakland-San Jose CMSA)	1,497,577
7480		Santa Barbara-Santa Maria-Lompoc, CA MSA	369,608
	06 083	Santa Barbara County	369,608
7485		Santa Cruz, CA PMSA (See San Francisco-Oakland-San Jose CMSA)	229,734
7490		Santa Fe, NM MSA	117,043
	35 028	Los Alamos County	18,115
	35 049	Santa Fe County	98,928
7500		Santa Rosa-Petaluma, CA PMSA (See San Francisco-Oakland-San Jose CMSA)	388,222
7510		Sarasota, FL MSA	277,776
	12 115	Sarasota County	277,776
7520		Savannah, GA MSA	242,622
	13 051	Chatham County	216,935
	13 103	Effingham County	25,687
7560		Scranton-Wilkes Barre, PA MSA	734,175
	42 037	Columbia County	63,202
	42 069	Lackawanna County	219,039

Metropolitan Statistical Areas and Components—Continued

[MSA = metropolian statistical area; CMSA = consolidated MSA; PMSA = primary MSA; and NECMA = New England county metropolitan area. For further information, see Appendix A.]

Geographic codes: MSA/ CMSA/ PMSA/ NECMA	Geographic codes: State and County	Title and geographic components	1990 population
	42 079	Luzerne County	328,149
	42 089	Monroe County	95,709
	42 131	Wyoming County	28,076
7600		Seattle, WA PMSA (See Seattle-Tacoma CMSA)	1,972,961
7602		Seattle-Tacoma, WA CMSA	2,559,164
7600		Seattle, WA PMSA	1,972,961
	53 033	King County	1,507,319
	53 061	Snohomish County	465,642
8200		Tacoma, WA PMSA	586,203
	53 053	Pierce County	586,203
7610		Sharon, PA MSA	121,003
	42 085	Mercer County	121,003
7620		Sheboygan, WI MSA	103,877
	55 117	Sheboygan County	103,877
7640		Sherman-Dension, TX MSA	95,021
	48 181	Grayson County	95,021
7680		Shreveport, LA MSA	334,341
	22 015	Bossier Parish	86,088
	22 017	Caddo Parish	248,253
7720		Sioux City, IA-NE MSA	115,018
	19 193	Woodbury County, IA	98,276
	31 043	Dakota County, NE	16,742
7760		Sioux Falls, SD MSA	123,809
	46 099	Minnehaha County	123,809
7800		South Bend-Mishawaka, IN MSA	247,052
	18 141	St. Joseph County	247,052
7840		Spokane, WA MSA	361,364
	53 063	Spokane County	361,364
7880		Springfield, IL MSA	189,550
	17 129	Menard County	11,164
	17 167	Sangamon County	178,386
7920		Springfield, MO MSA	240,593
	29 043	Christian County	32,644
	29 077	Greene County	207,949
8003		Springfield, MA MSA	602,878
	25 013	Hampden County	456,310
	25 015	Hampshire County	146,568
8050		State College, PA MSA	123,786
	42 027	Centre County	123,786
8080		Steubenville-Weirton, OH-WV MSA	142,523
	39 081	Jefferson County, OH	80,298
	54 009	Brooke County, WV	26,992
	54 029	Hancock County, WV	35,233
8120		Stockton, CA MSA	480,628
	06 077	San Joaquin County	480,628
8160		Syracuse, NY MSA	659,864
	36 053	Madison County	69,120
	36 067	Onondaga County	468,973
	36 075	Oswego County	121,771

Geographic codes: MSA/ CMSA/ PMSA/ NECMA/	Geographic codes: State and County	Title and geographic components	1990 population
8200		Tacoma, WA PMSA (See Seattle-Tacoma CMSA)	586,203
8240		Tallahassee, FL MSA	233,598
	12 039	Gadsden County	41,105
	12 073	Leon County	192,493
8280		Tampa-St. Petersburg-Clearwater, FL MSA	2,067,959
	12 053	Hernando County	101,115
	12 057	Hillsborough County	834,054
	12 101	Pasco County	281,131
	12 103	Pinellas County	851,659
8320		Terre Haute, IN MSA	130,812
	18 021	Clay County	24,705
	18 167	Vigo County	106,107
8360		Texarkana, TX-Texarkana, AR MSA	120,132
	05 091	Miller County, AR	38,467
	48 037	Bowie County, TX	81,665
8400		Toledo, OH MSA	614,128
	39 051	Fulton County	38,498
	39 095	Lucas County	462,361
	39 173	Wood County	113,269
8440		Topeka, KS MSA	160,976
	20 177	Shawnee County	160,976
8480		Trenton, NJ PMSA (See Philadelphia-Wilmington-Trenton CMSA)	325,824
8520		Tucson, AZ MSA	666,880
	04 019	Pima County	666,880
8560		Tulsa, OK MSA	708,954
	40 037	Creek County	60,915
	40 113	Osage County	41,645
	40 131	Rogers County	55,170
	40 143	Tulsa County	503,341
	40 145	Wagoner County	47,883
8600		Tuscaloosa, AL MSA	150,522
	01 125	Tuscaloosa County	150,522
8640		Tyler, TX MSA	151,309
	48 423	Smith County	151,309
8680		Utica-Rome, NY MSA	316,633
	36 043	Herkimer County	65,797
	36 065	Oneida County	250,836
8720		Vallejo-Fairfield-Napa, CA PMSA (See San Francisco-Oakland-San Jose CMSA)	451,186
8725		Vancouver, WA PMSA (See Portland-Vancouver CMSA)	238,053
8750		Victoria, TX MSA	74,361
	48 469	Victoria County	74,361
8760		Vineland-Millville-Bridgeton, NJ PMSA (See Philadelphia-Wilmington-Trenton CMSA)	138,053
8780		Visalia-Tulare-Porterville, CA MSA	311,921

Metropolitan Statistical Areas and Components—Continued

[MSA = metropolian statistical area; CMSA = consolidated MSA; PMSA = primary MSA; and NECMA = New England county metropolitan area. For further information, see Appendix A.]

Geographic codes		Title and geographic components	1990 population
MSA/ CMSA/ PMSA/ NECMA	State and County		
	06 107	Tulare County	311,921
8800		Waco, TX MSA	189,123
	48 309	McLennan County	189,123
8840		Washington, DC-MD-VA MSA	3,923,574
	11 001	District of Columbia	606,900
	24 009	Calvert County, MD	51,372
	24 017	Charles County, MD	101,154
	24 021	Frederick County, MD	150,208
	24 031	Montgomery County, MD	757,027
	24 033	Prince George's County, MD	729,268
	51 013	Arlington County, VA	170,936
	51 059	Fairfax County, VA	818,584
	51 107	Loudoun County, VA	86,129
	51 153	Prince William County, VA	215,686
	51 179	Stafford County, VA	61,236
	51 510	Alexandria City, VA	111,183
	51 600	Fairfax City, VA	19,622
	51 610	Falls Church City, VA	9,578
	51 683	Manassas City, VA	27,957
	51 685	Manassas Park City, VA	6,734
8920		Waterloo-Cedar Falls, IA MSA	146,611
	19 013	Black Hawk County	123,798
	19 017	Bremer County	22,813
8940		Wausau, WI MSA	115,400
	55 073	Marathon County	115,400
8960		West Palm Beach-Boca Raton-Del Ray, FL MSA	863,518
	12 099	Palm Beach County	863,518
9000		Wheeling, WV-OH MSA	159,301
	39 013	Belmont County, OH	71,074
	54 051	Marshall County, WV	37,356
	54 069	Ohio County, WV	50,871
9040		Wichita, KS MSA	485,270
	20 015	Butler County	50,580
	20 079	Harvey County	31,028
	20 173	Sedgwick County	403,662
9080		Wichita Falls, TX MSA	122,378
	48 485	Wichita County	122,378
9140		Williamsport, PA MSA	118,710
	42 081	Lycoming County	118,710
9160		Wilmington, DE-NJ-MD PMSA	578,587
		(See Philadelphia-Wilmington-Trenton CMSA)	
9200		Wilmington, NC MSA	120,284
	37 129	New Hanover County	120,284
9243		Worcester-Fitchburg-Leominster, MA NECMA	709,705
	25 027	Worcester County	709,705
9260		Yakima, WA MSA	188,823
	53 077	Yakima County	188,823
9280		York, PA MSA	417,848
	42 001	Adams County	78,274
	42 133	York County	339,574
9320		Youngstown-Warren, OH MSA	492,619
	39 099	Mahoning County	264,806
	39 155	Trumbull County	227,813
9340		Yuba City, CA MSA	122,643
	06 101	Sutter County	64,415
	06 115	Yuba County	58,228
9360		Yuma, AZ MSA	106,895
	04 027	Yuma County	106,895

ALABAMA - Metropolitan Statistical Areas, Counties, and Selected Places

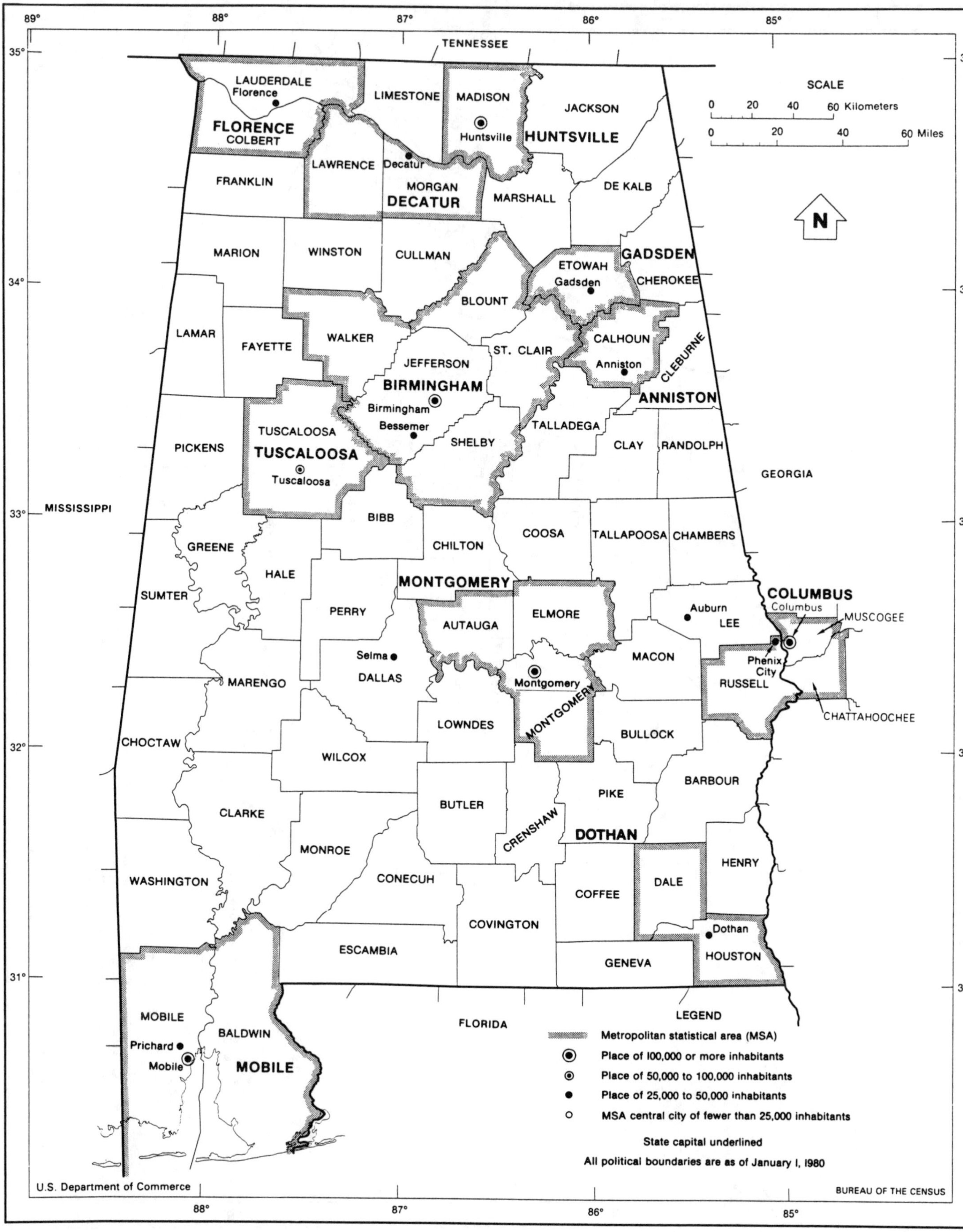

MSA boundaries are as defined on June 30, 1988

ALASKA - Metropolitan Statistical Area, Boroughs, Census Areas, and Selected Places

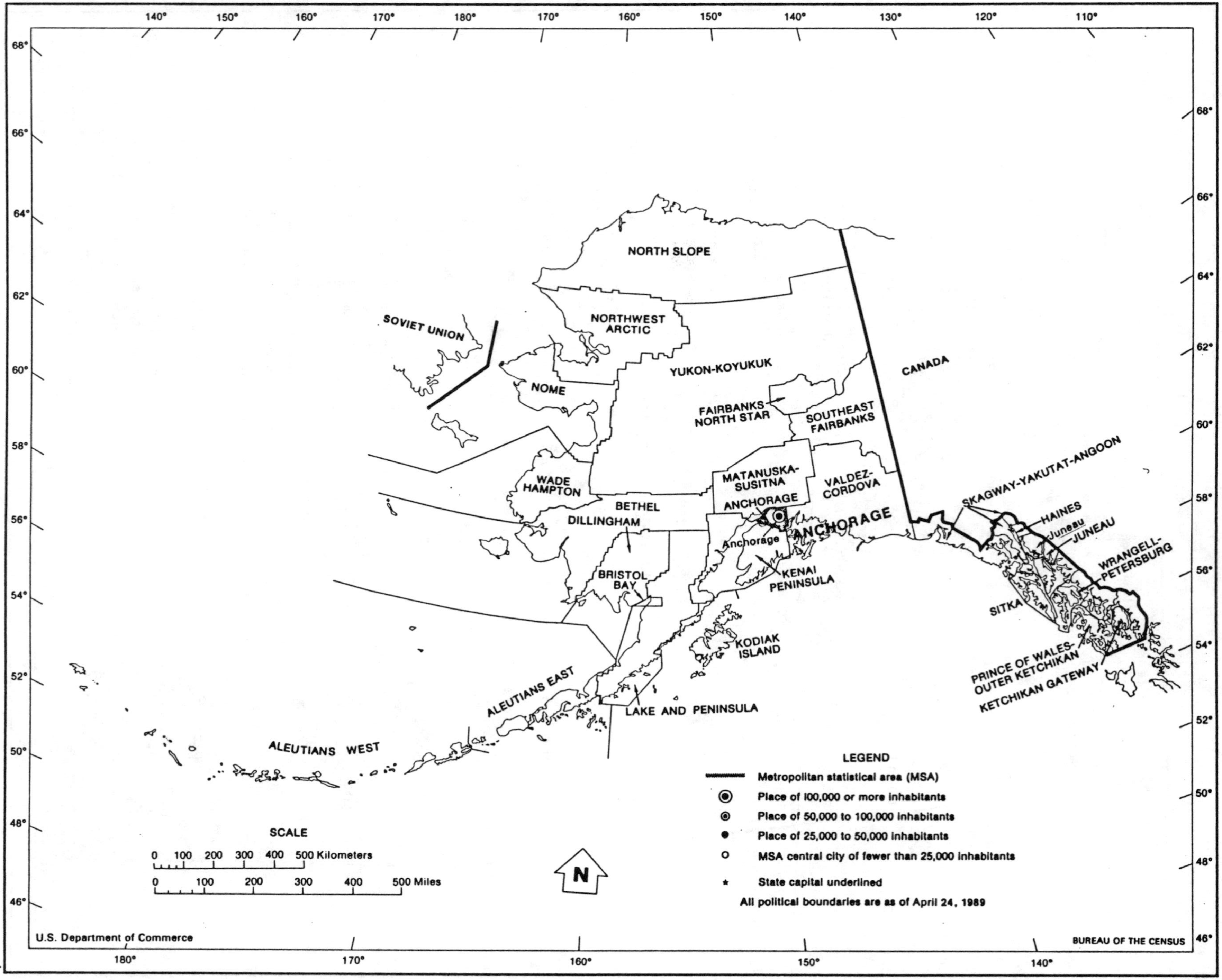

MSA boundaries are as defined on June 30, 1988

ARIZONA - Metropolitan Statistical Areas, Counties, and Selected Places

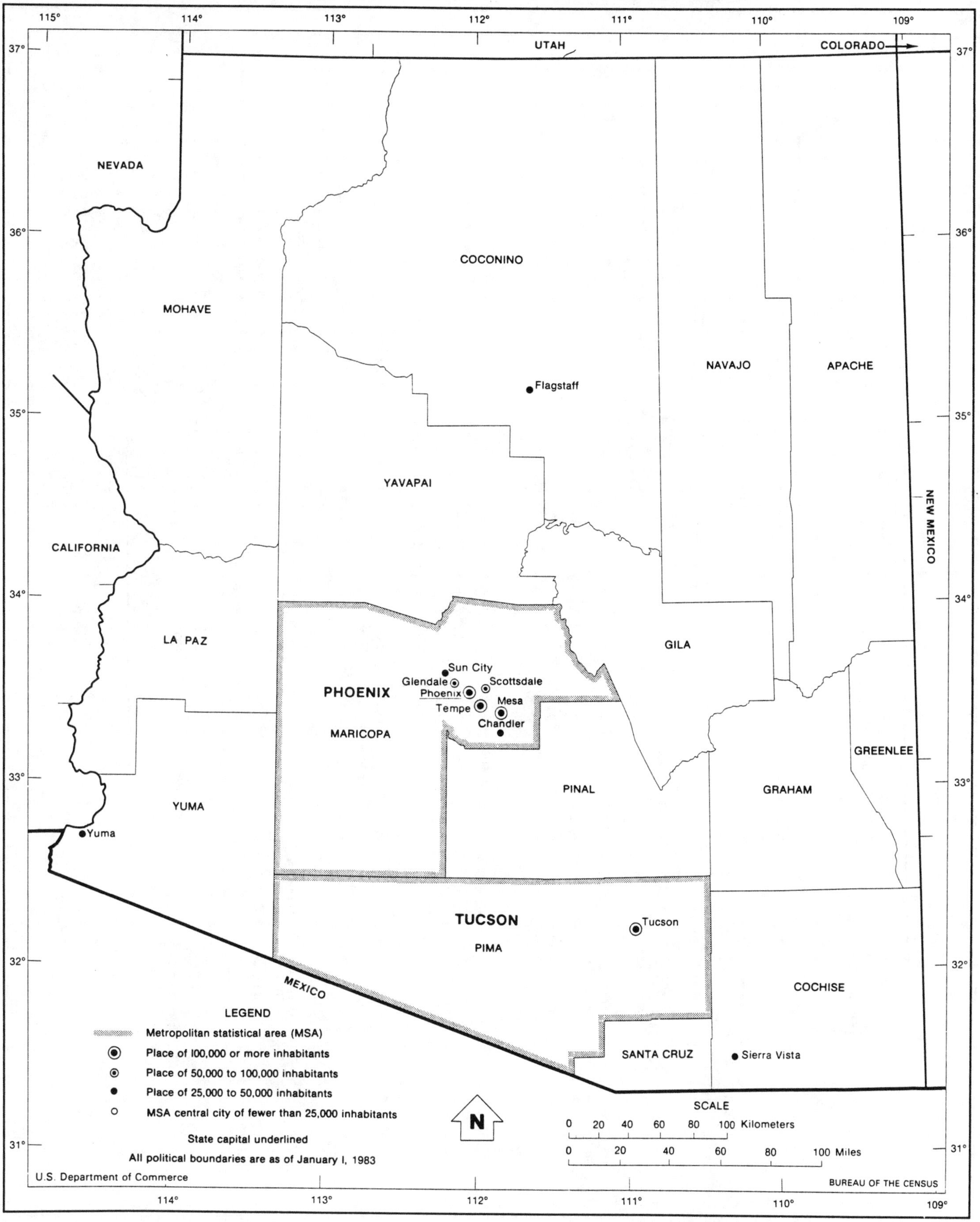

MSA boundaries are as defined on June 30, 1983

ARKANSAS - Metropolitan Statistical Areas, Counties, and Selected Places

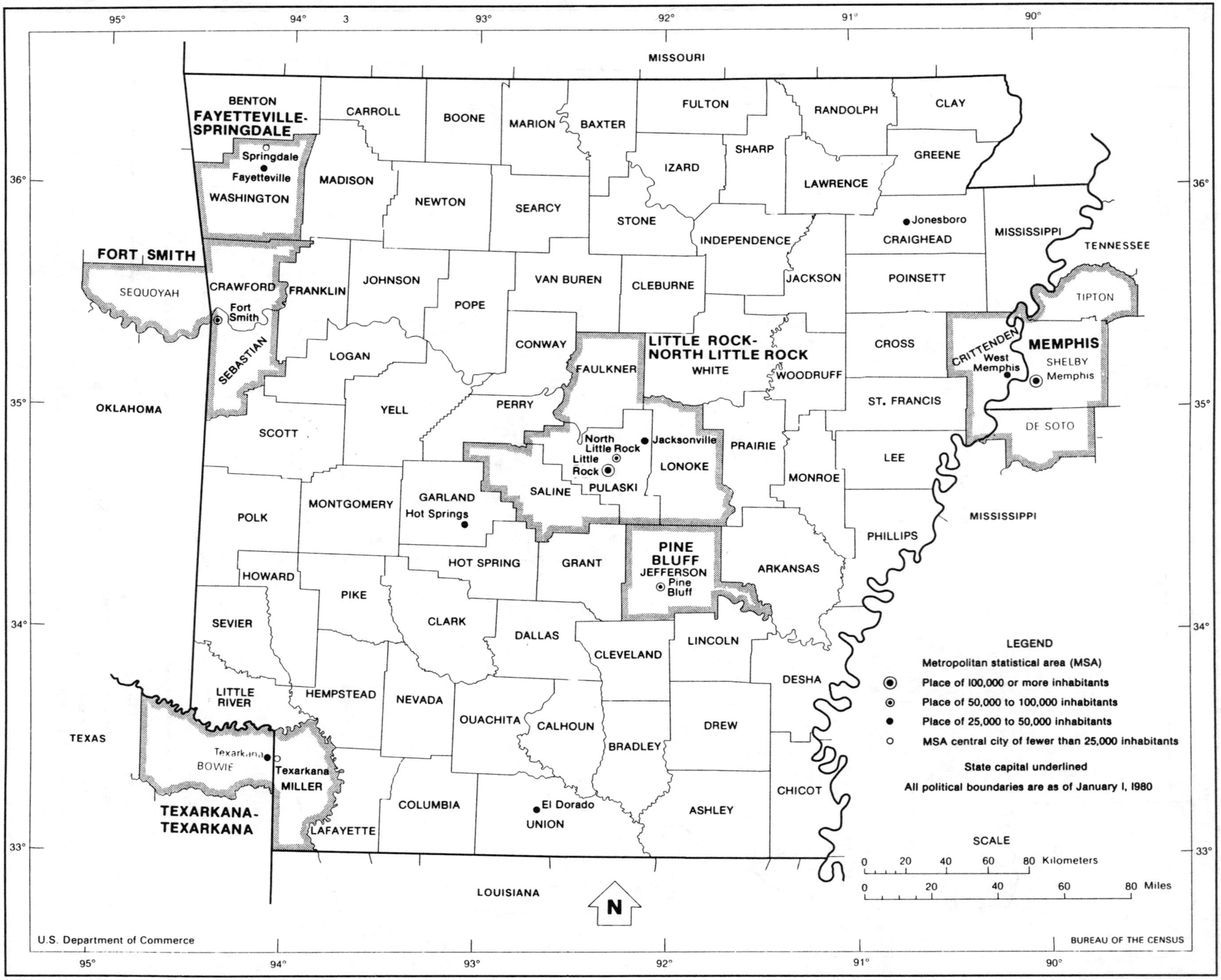

MSA boundaries are as defined on June 30, 1983

CALIFORNIA - Consolidated Metropolitan Statistical Areas, Primary Metropolitan Statistical Areas, Metropolitan Statistical Areas, Counties, and Selected Places

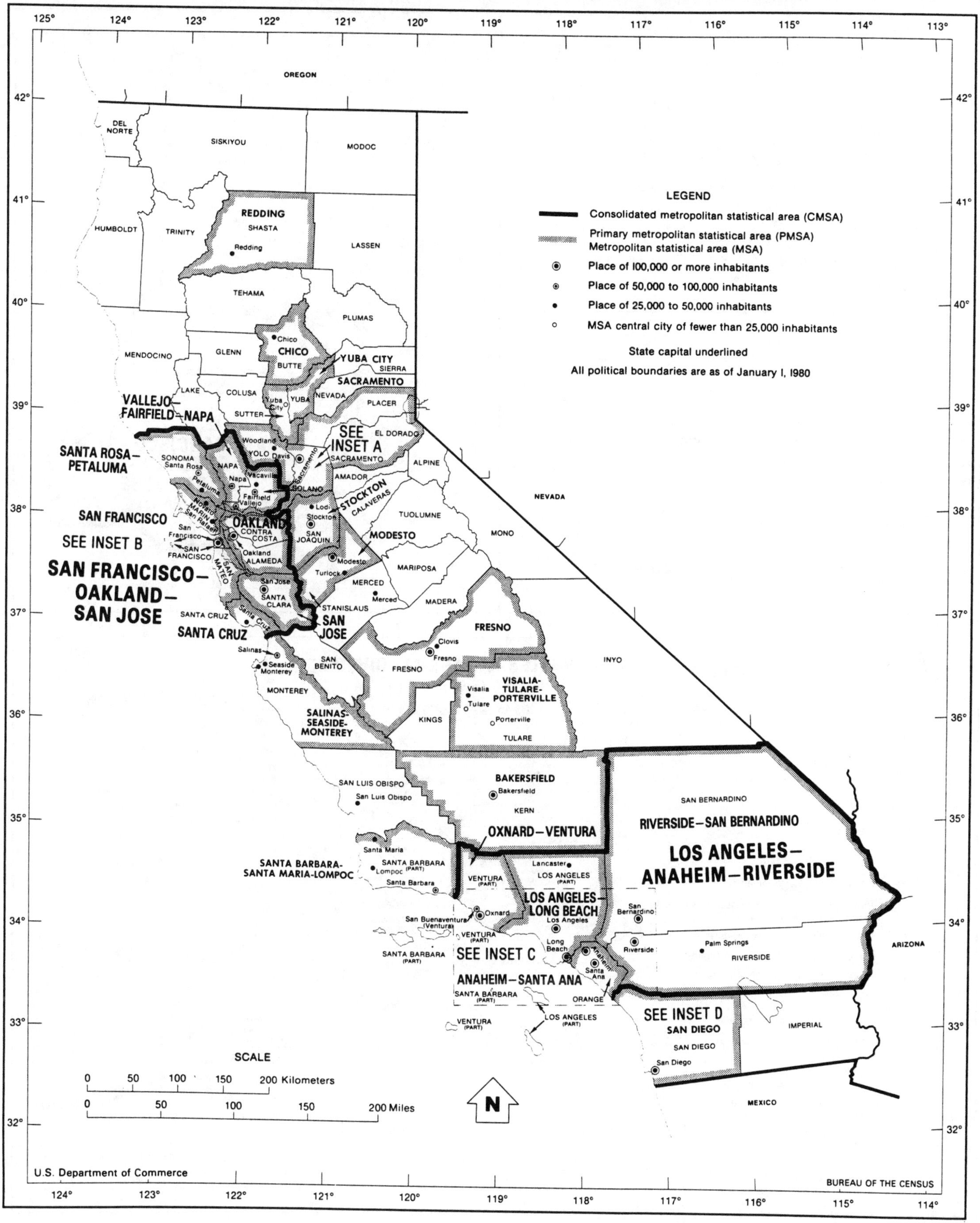

CMSA, PMSA, and MSA boundaries are as defined on June 30, 1983

CALIFORNIA - Consolidated Metropolitan Statistical Areas, Primary Metropolitan Statistical Areas, Metropolitan Statistical Areas, Counties, and Selected Places

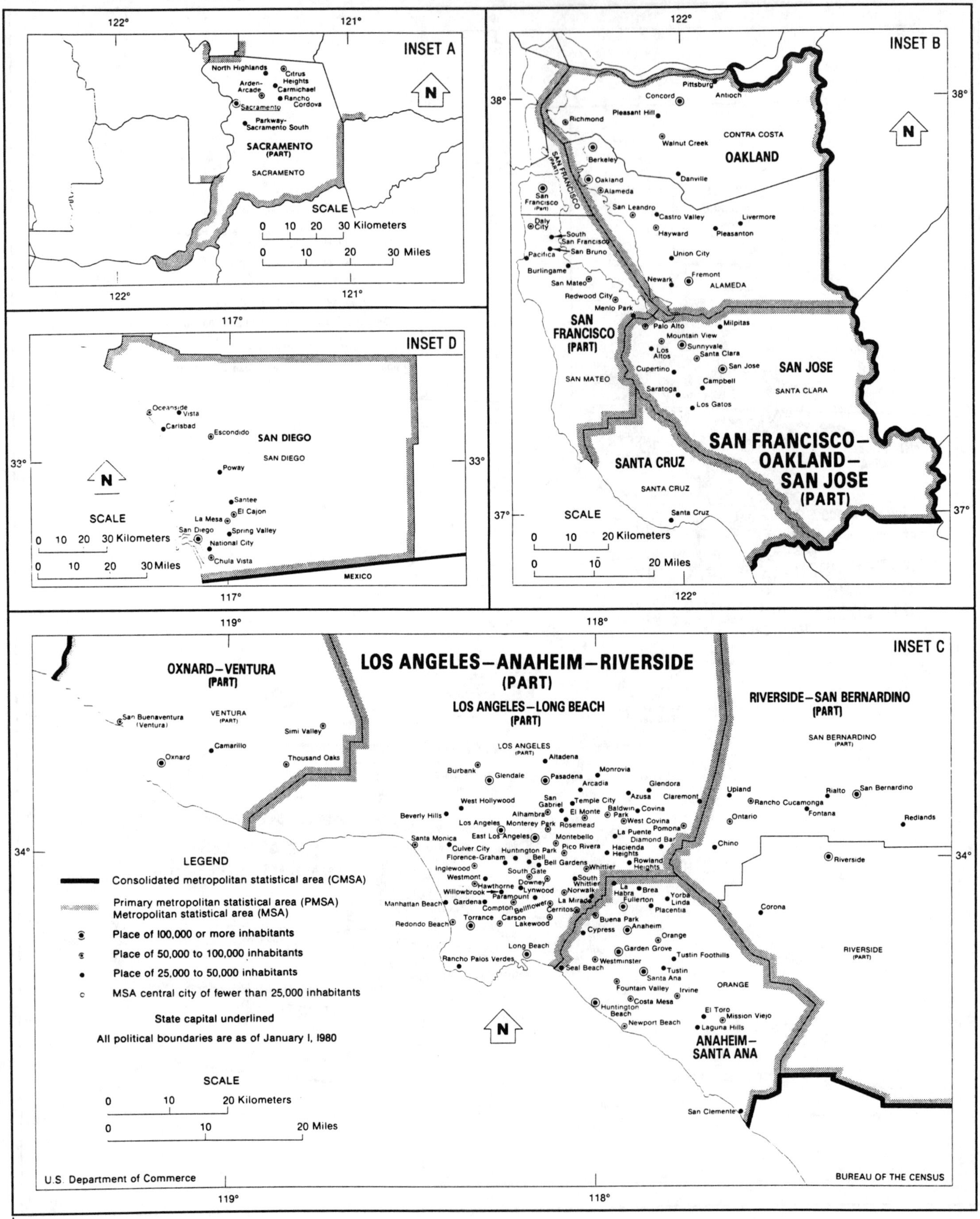

CMSA, PMSA, and MSA boundaries are as defined on June 30, 1983

COLORADO - Consolidated Metropolitan Statistical Area, Primary Metropolitan Statistical Areas, Metropolitan Statistical Areas, Counties, and Selected Places

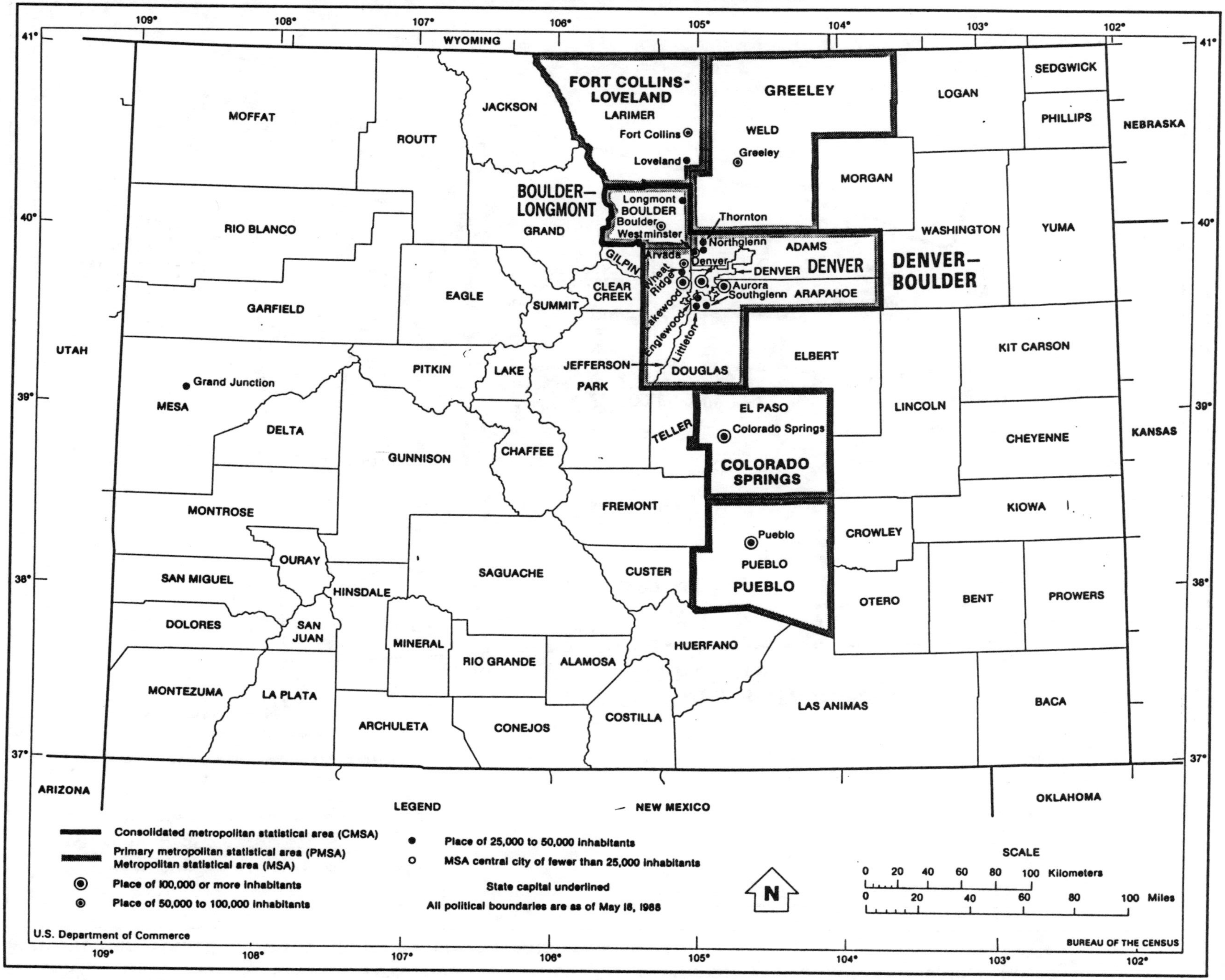

CONNECTICUT - Consolidated Metropolitan Statistical Areas, Primary Metropolitan Statistical Areas, Metropolitan Statistical Areas, Counties, and Selected Places

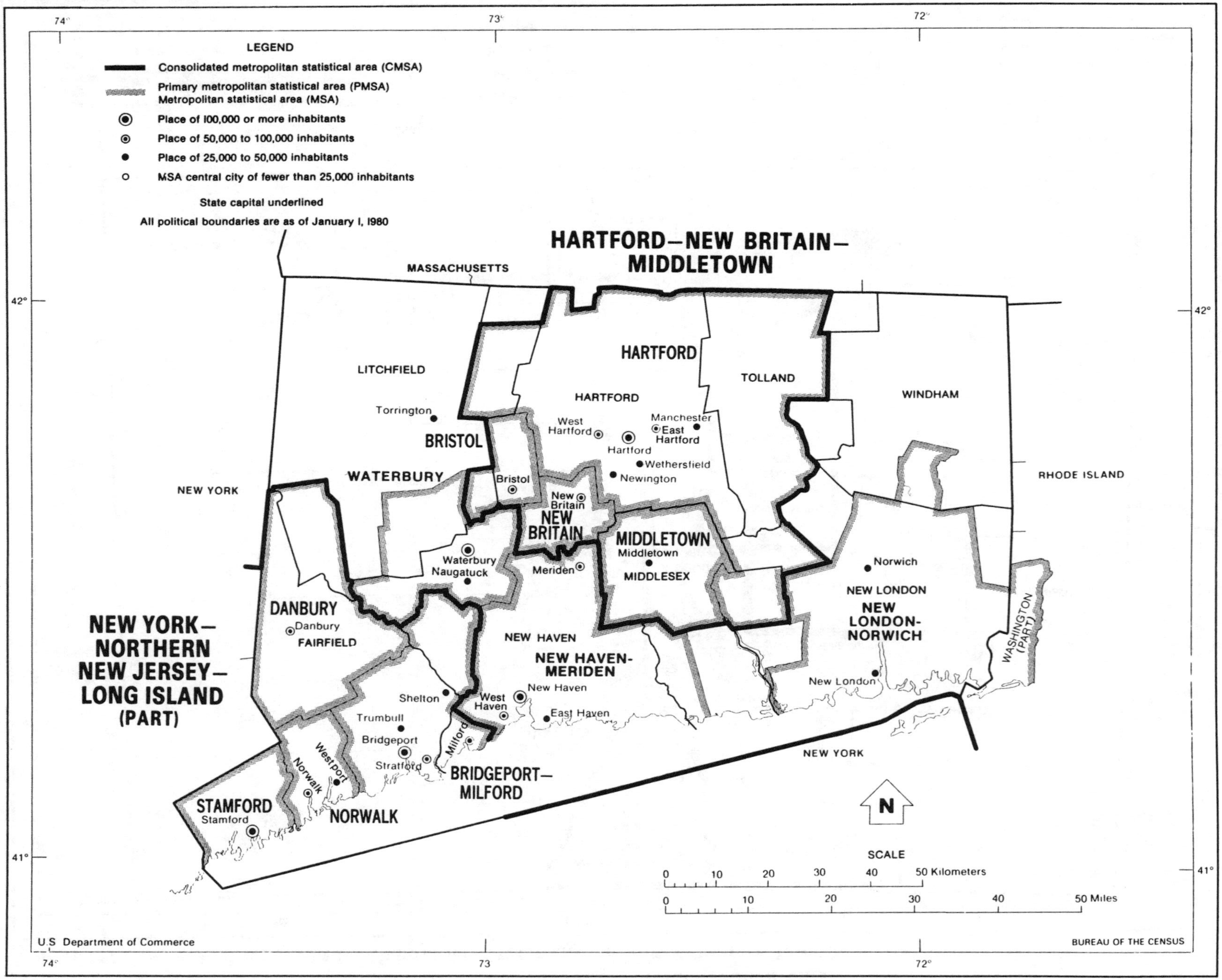

CMSA, PMSA, and MSA boundaries are as defined on June 30, 1983

DELAWARE - Consolidated Metropolitan Statistical Area, Primary Metropolitan Statistical Area, Counties, and Selected Places

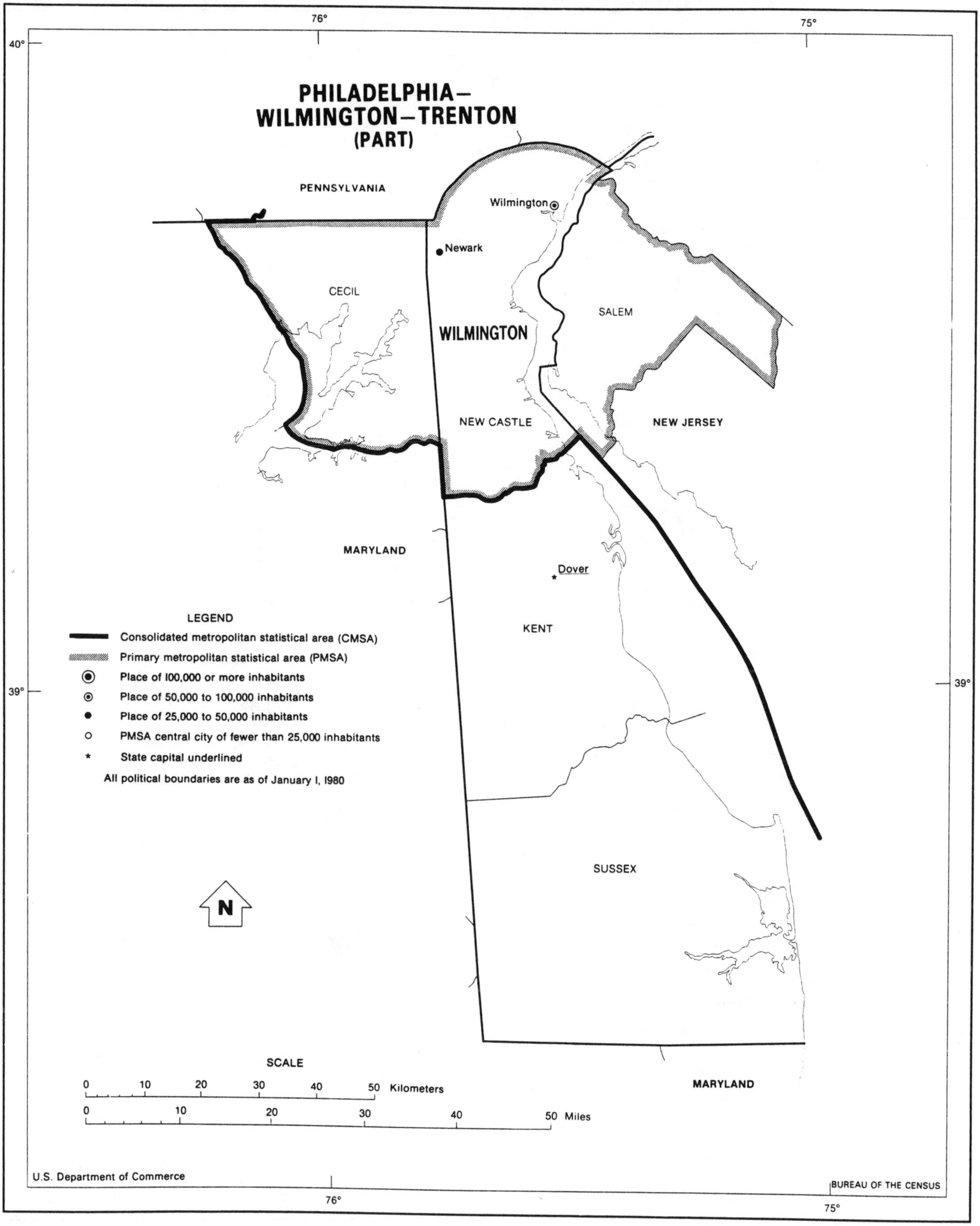

CMSA and PMSA boundaries are as defined on June 30, 1983

DISTRICT OF COLUMBIA - Metropolitan Statistical Area, Counties, Independent Cities, and Other Selected Places

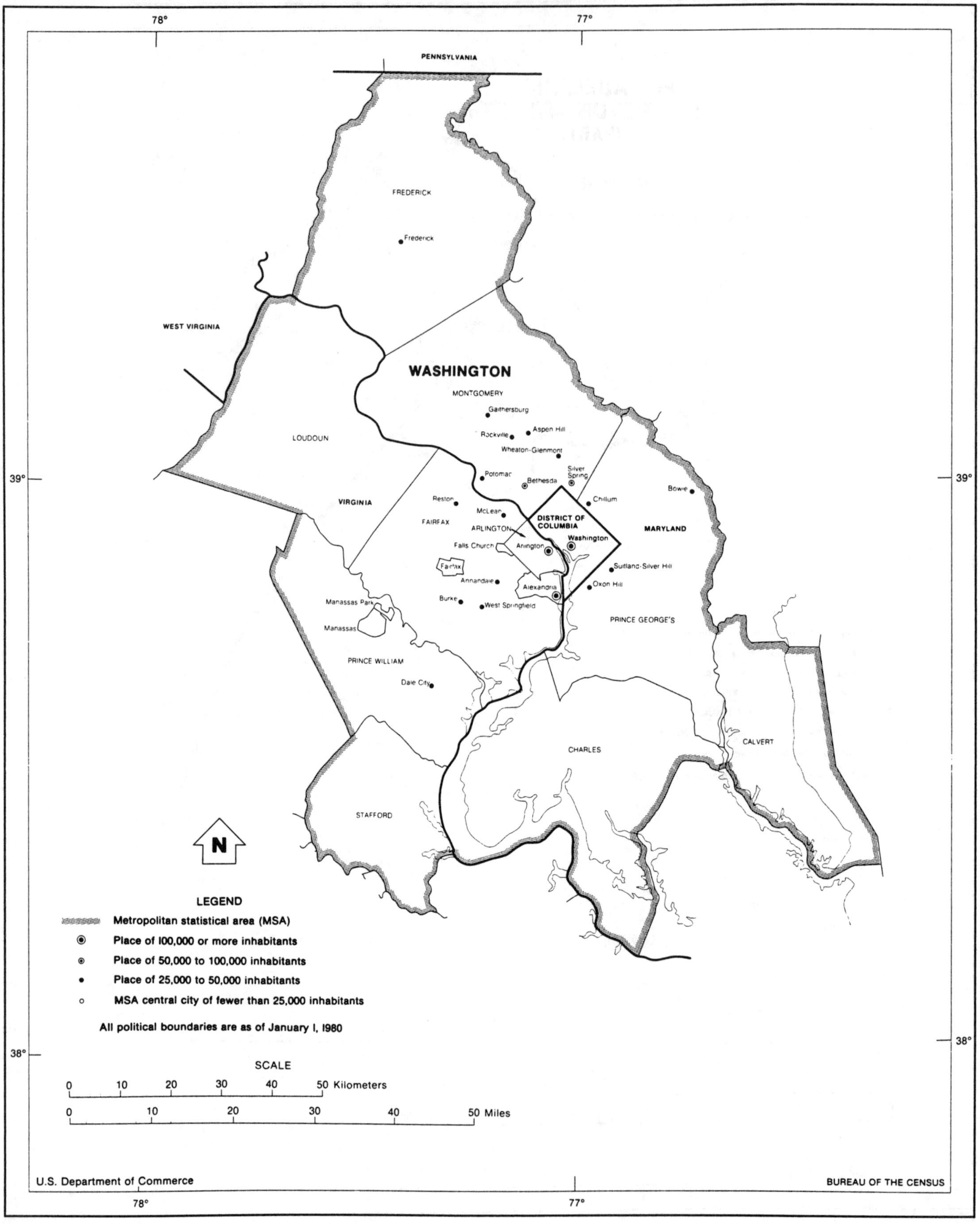

MSA boundaries are as defined on June 30, 1983

FLORIDA - Consolidated Metropolitan Statistical Area, Primary Metropolitan Statistical Areas, Metropolitan Statistical Areas, Counties, and Selected Places

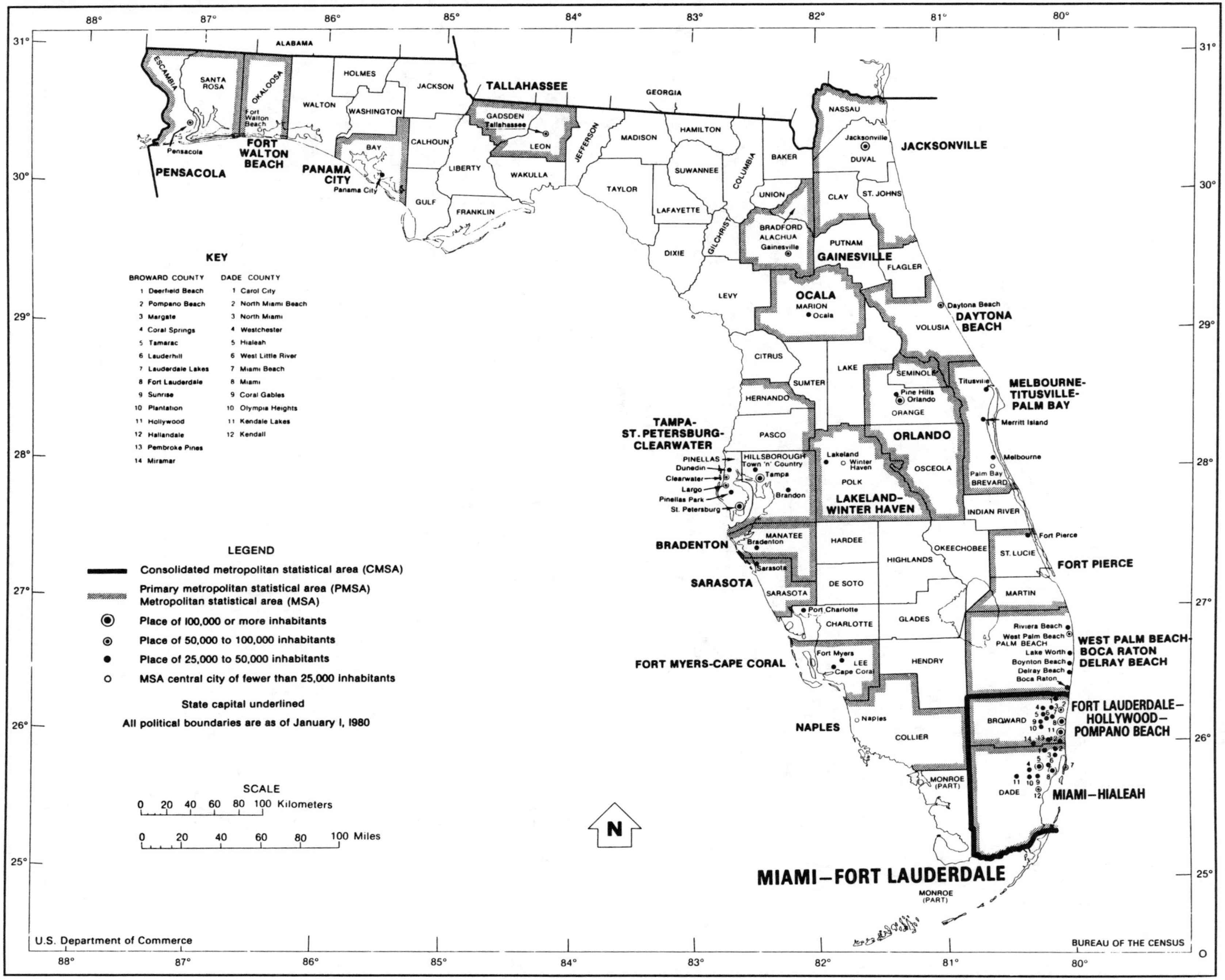

CMSA, PMSA, and MSA boundaries are as defined on June 30, 1984

GEORGIA - Metropolitan Statistical Areas, Counties, and Selected Places

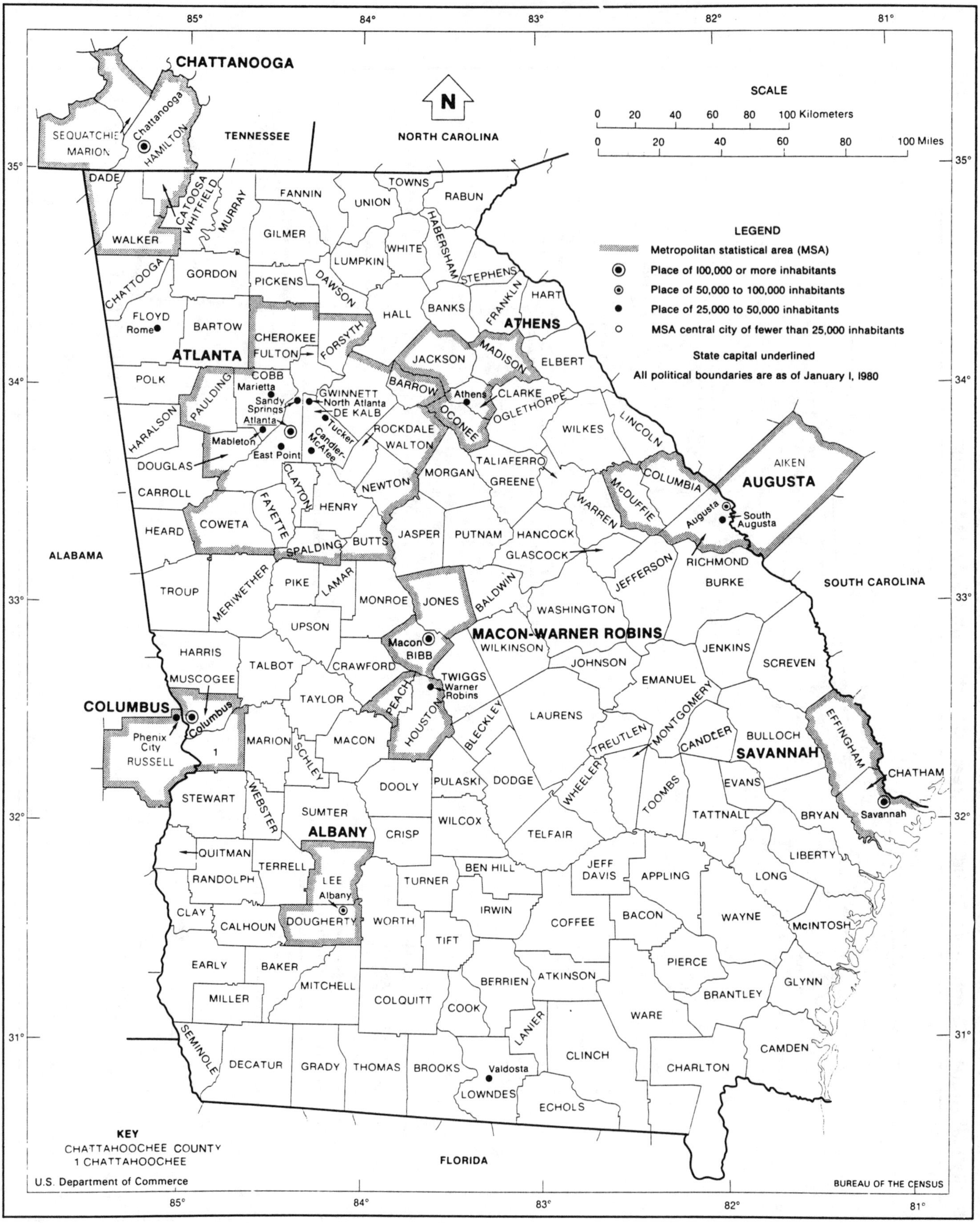

MSA boundaries are as defined on June 30, 1983

HAWAII - Metropolitan Statistical Area, Counties, and Selected Places

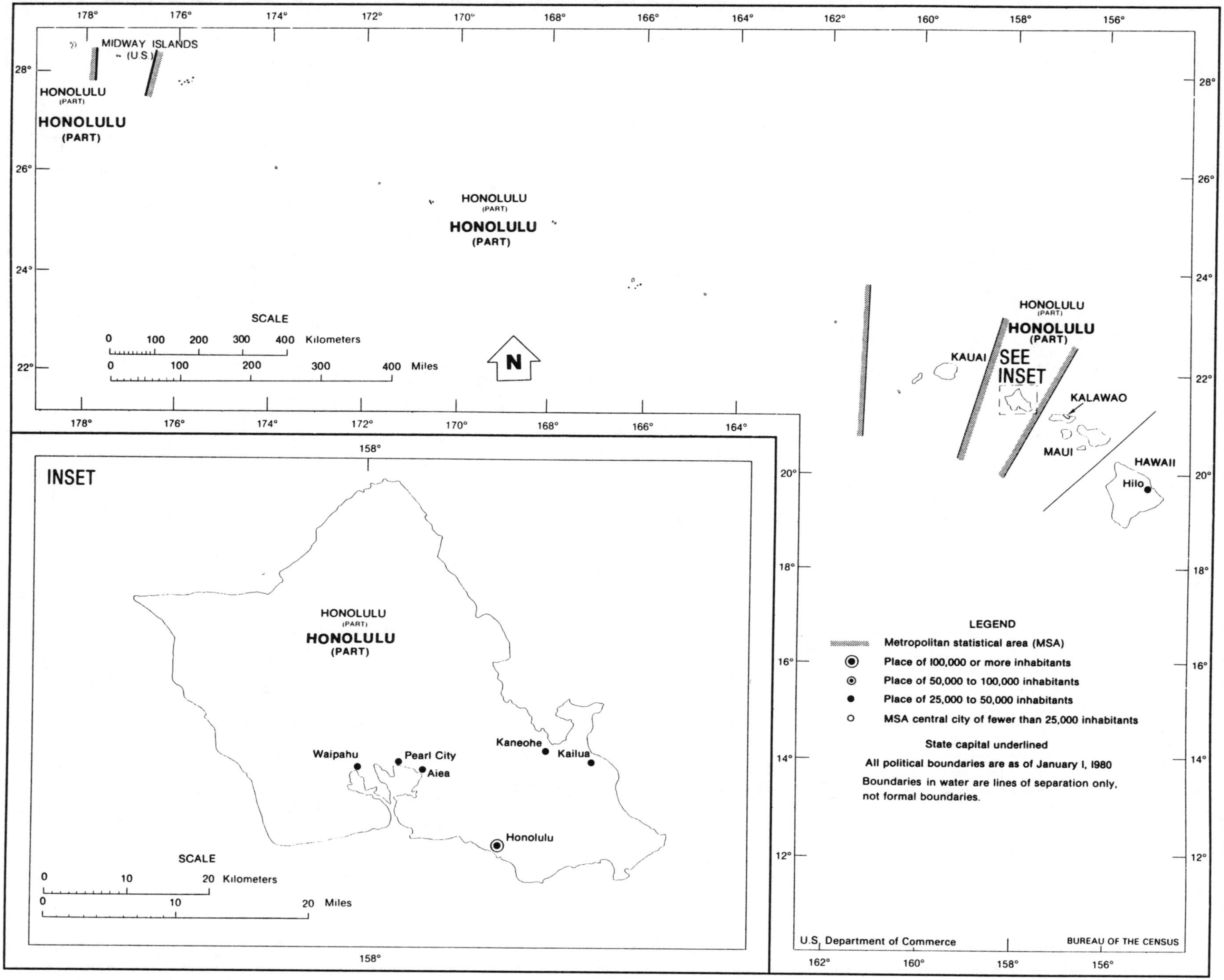

MSA boundaries are as defined on June 30, 1983

IDAHO - Metropolitan Statistical Area, Counties, and Selected Places

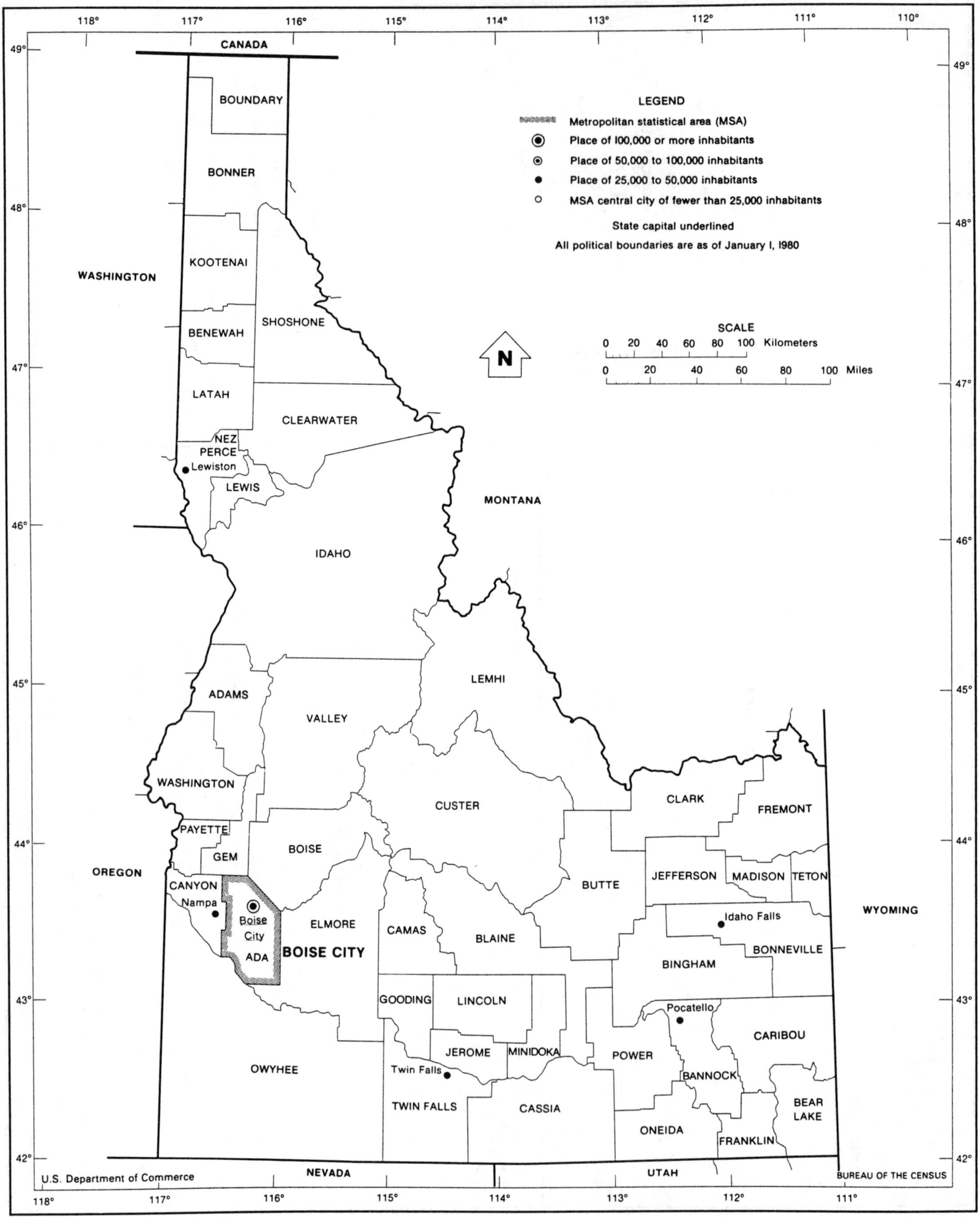

MSA boundaries are as defined on June 30, 1983

ILLINOIS - Consolidated Metropolitan Statistical Area, Primary Metropolitan Statistical Areas, Metropolitan Statistical Areas, Counties, Independent City, and Other Selected Places

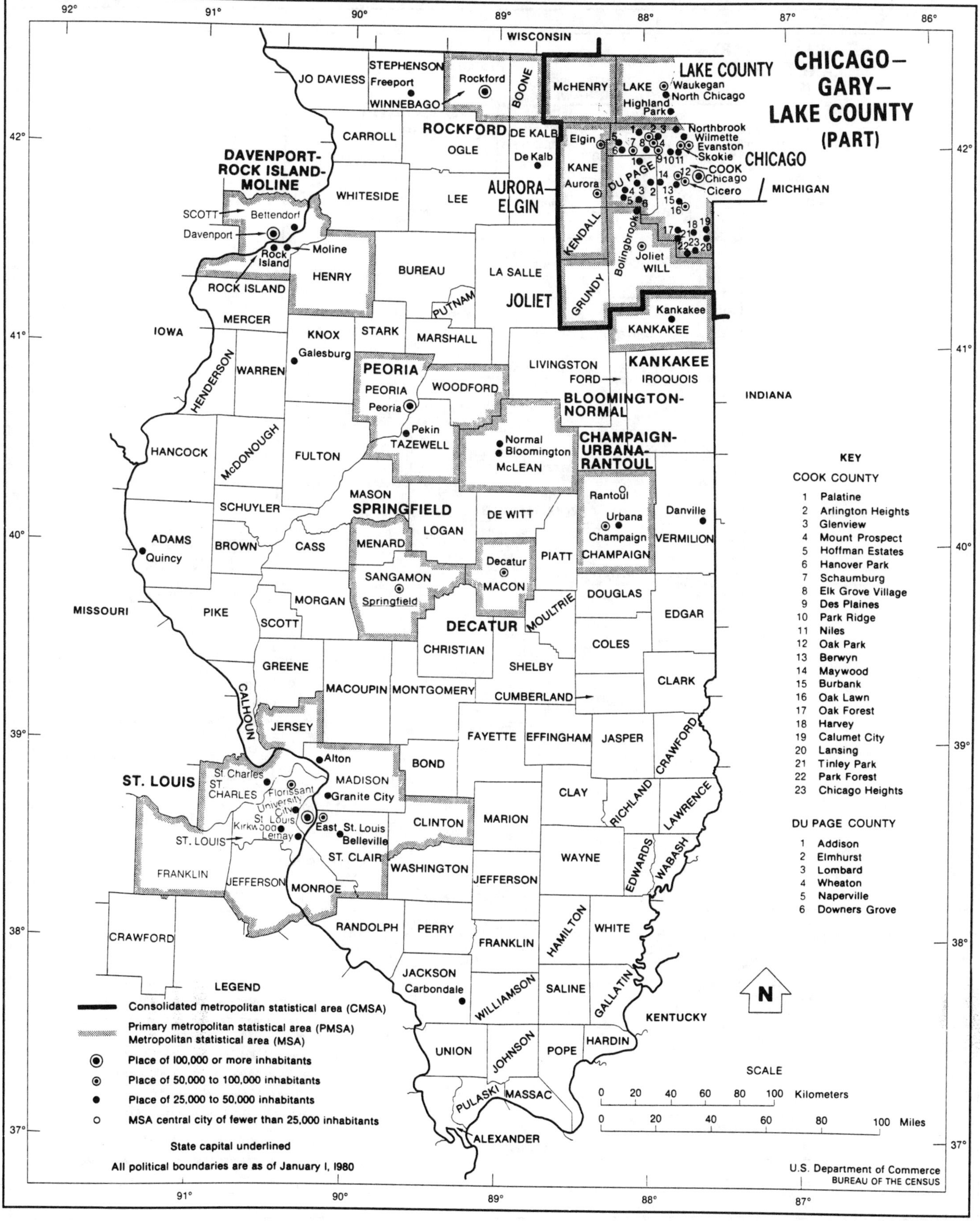

CMSA, PMSA, and MSA boundaries are as defined on June 30, 1988

INDIANA - Consolidated Metropolitan Statistical Areas, Primary Metropolitan Statistical Areas, Metropolitan Statistical Areas, Counties, and Selected Places

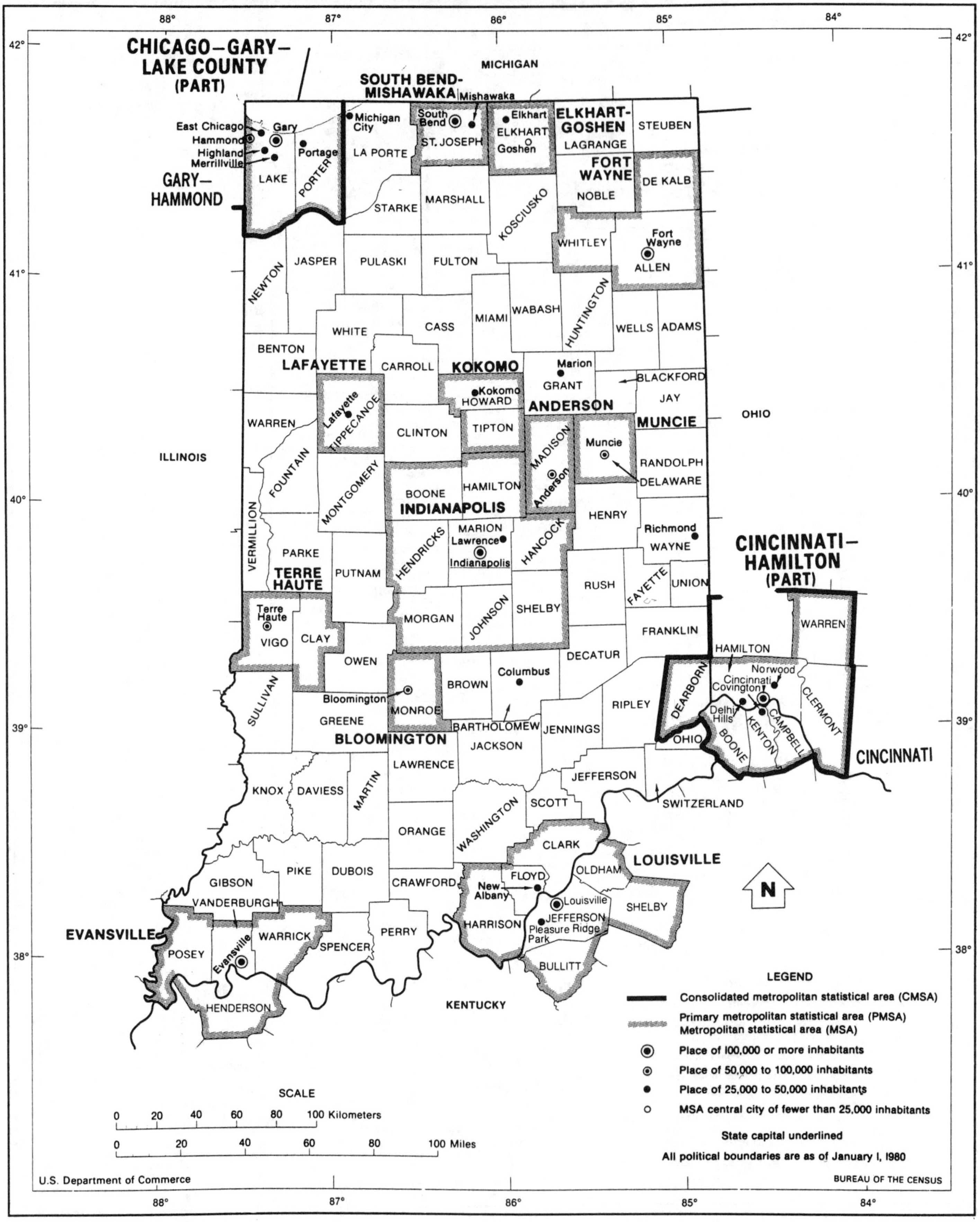

CMSA, PMSA, and MSA boundaries are as defined on June 30, 1983

IOWA - Metropolitan Statistical Areas, Counties, and Selected Places

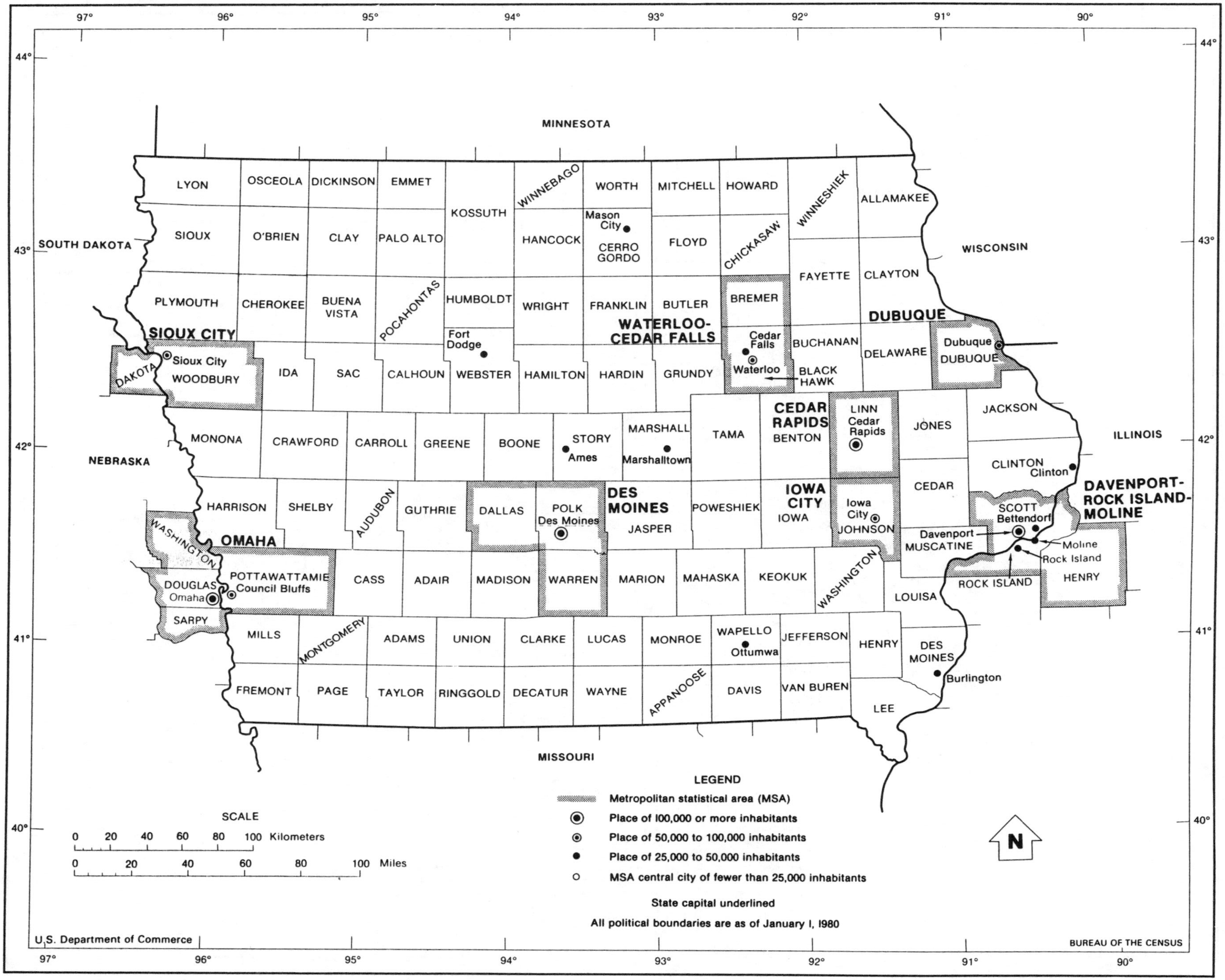

MSA boundaries are as defined on June 30, 1983

KANSAS - Metropolitan Statistical Areas, Counties, and Selected Places

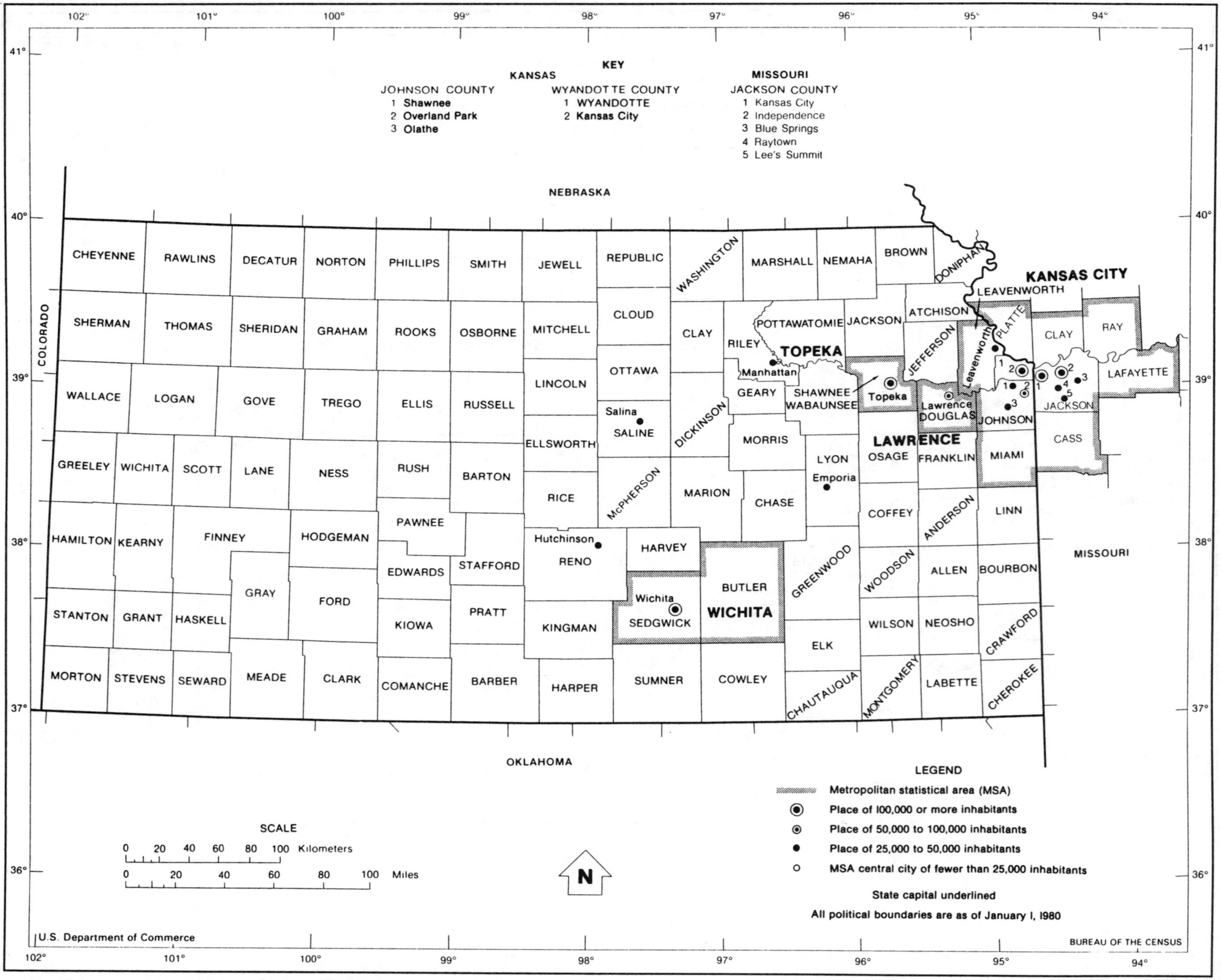

MSA boundaries are as defined on June 30, 1984

KENTUCKY - Consolidated Metropolitan Statistical Area, Primary Metropolitan Statistical Area, Metropolitan Statistical Areas, Counties, and Selected Places

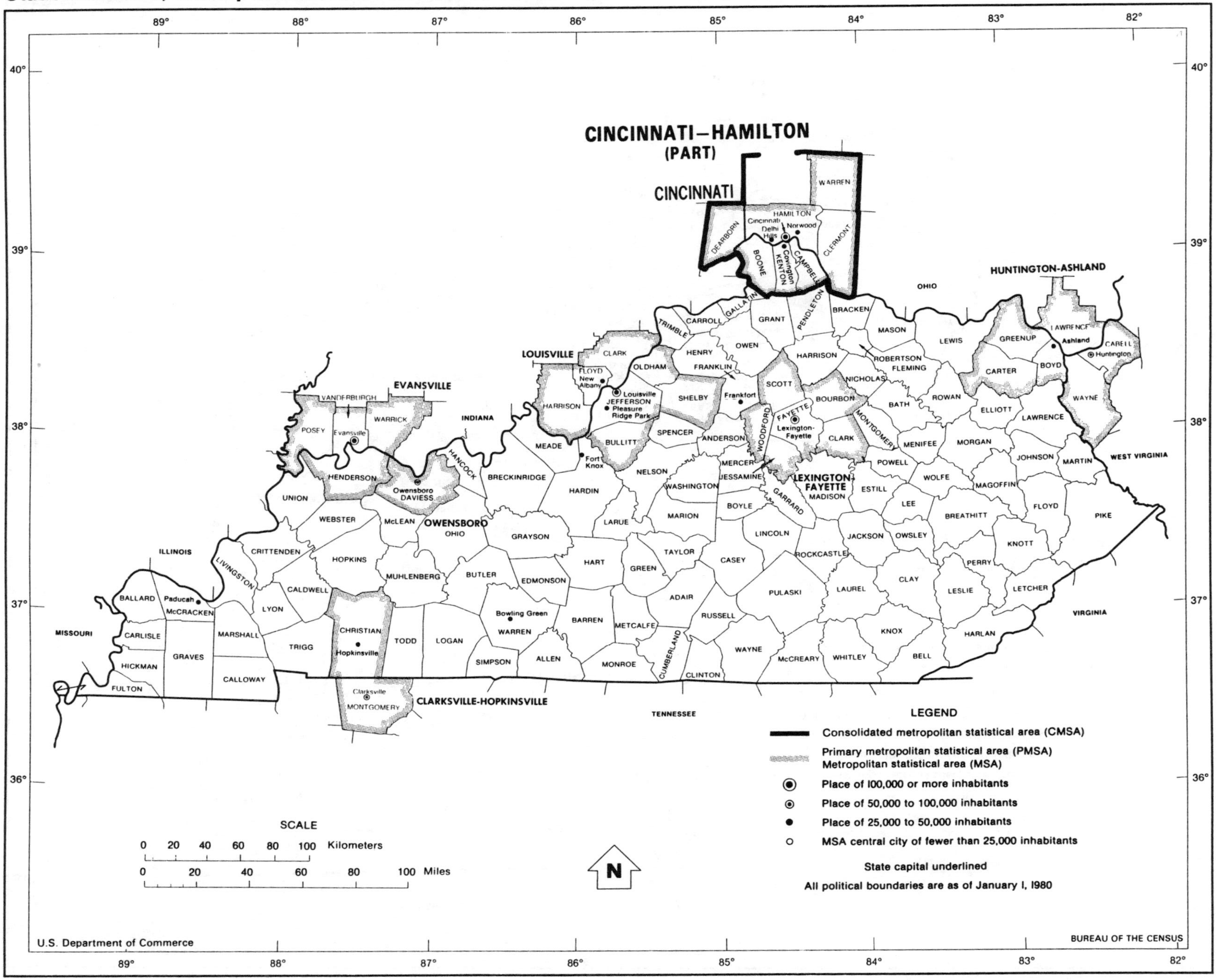

CMSA, PMSA, and MSA boundaries are as defined on June 30, 1983

LOUISIANA - Metropolitan Statistical Areas, Parishes, and Selected Places

MSA boundaries are as defined on June 30, 1983

MAINE - Metropolitan Statistical Areas, Counties, and Selected Places

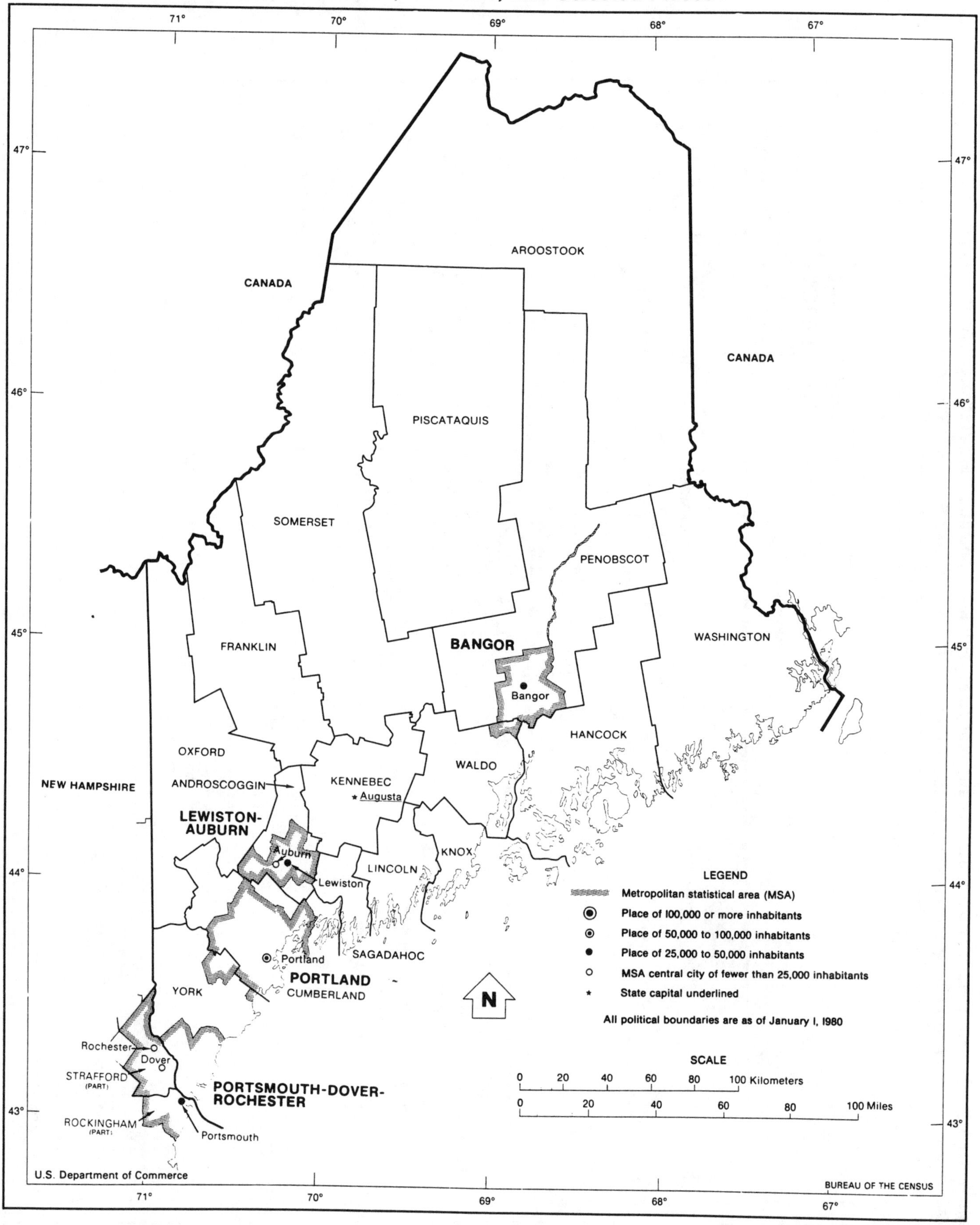

MSA boundaries are as defined on June 30, 1983

MARYLAND - Consolidated Metropolitan Statistical Area, Primary Metropolitan Statistical Area, Metropolitan Statistical Areas, Counties, Independent Cities, and Other Selected Places

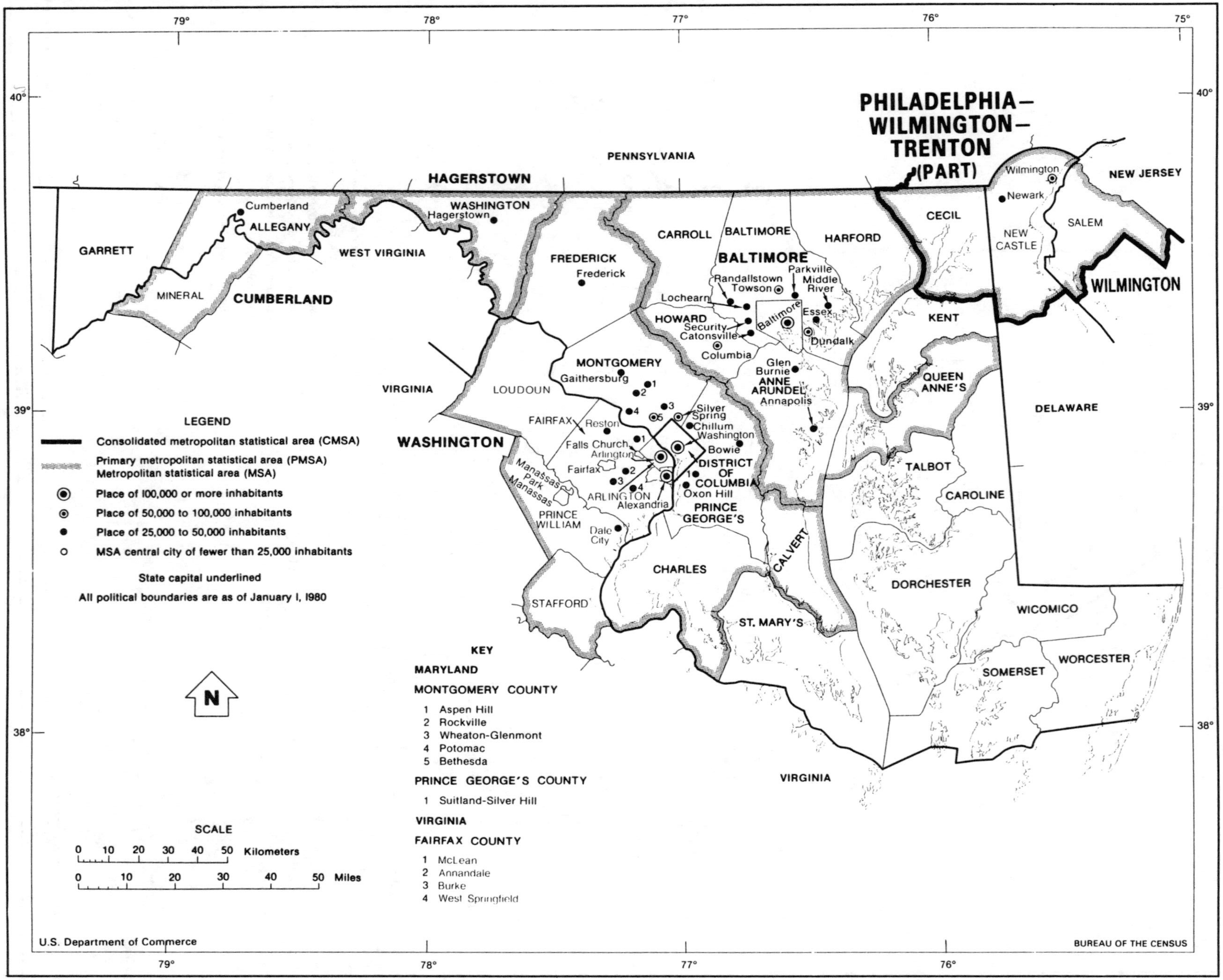

CMSA, PMSA, and MSA boundaries are as defined on June 30, 1983

MASSACHUSETTS - Consolidated Metropolitan Statistical Areas, Primary Metropolitan Statistical Areas, Metropolitan Statistical Areas, Counties, and Selected Places

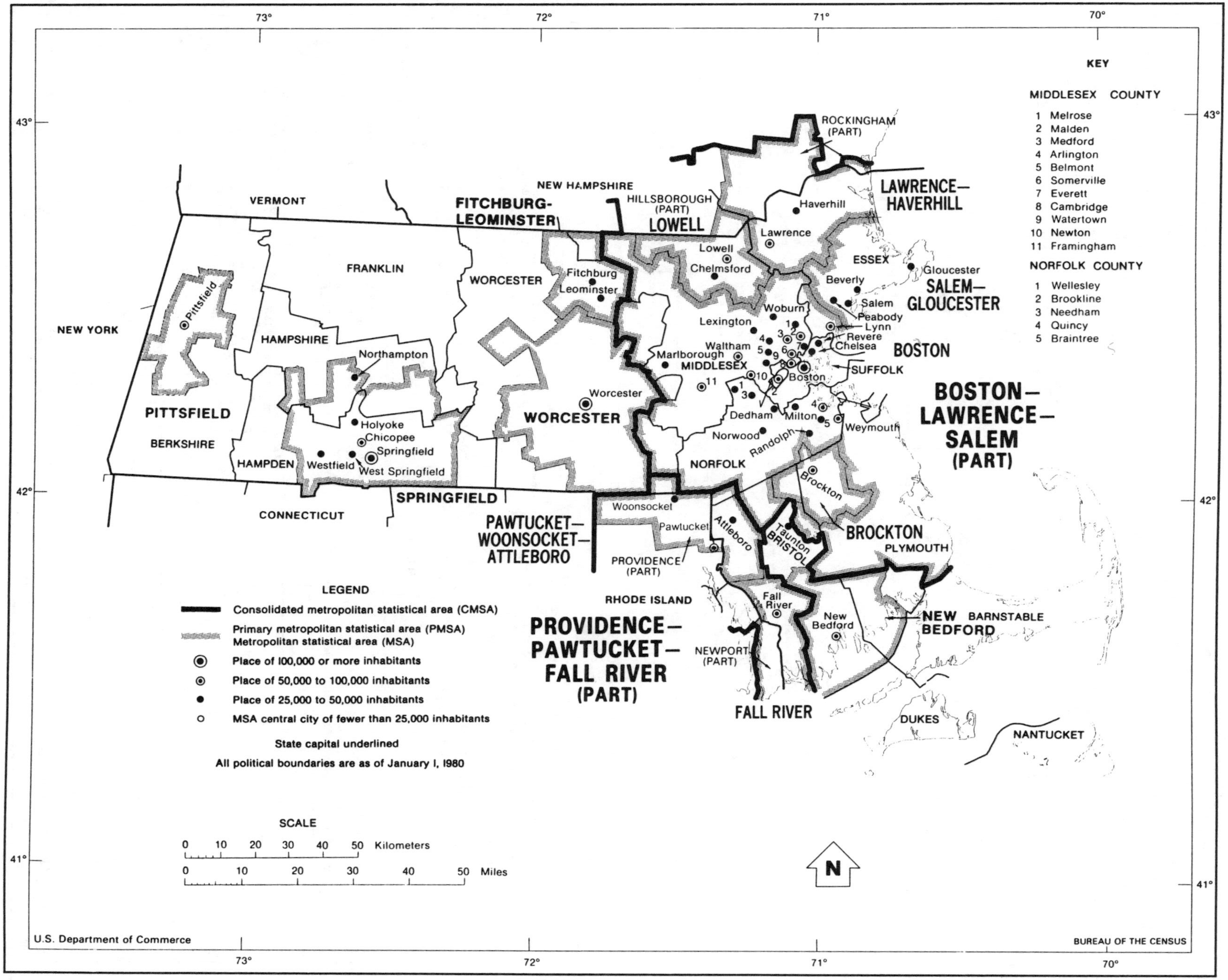

CMSA, PMSA, and MSA boundaries are as defined on June 30, 1983

MICHIGAN - Consolidated Metropolitan Statistical Area, Primary Metropolitan Statistical Areas, Metropolitan Statistical Areas, Counties, and Selected Places

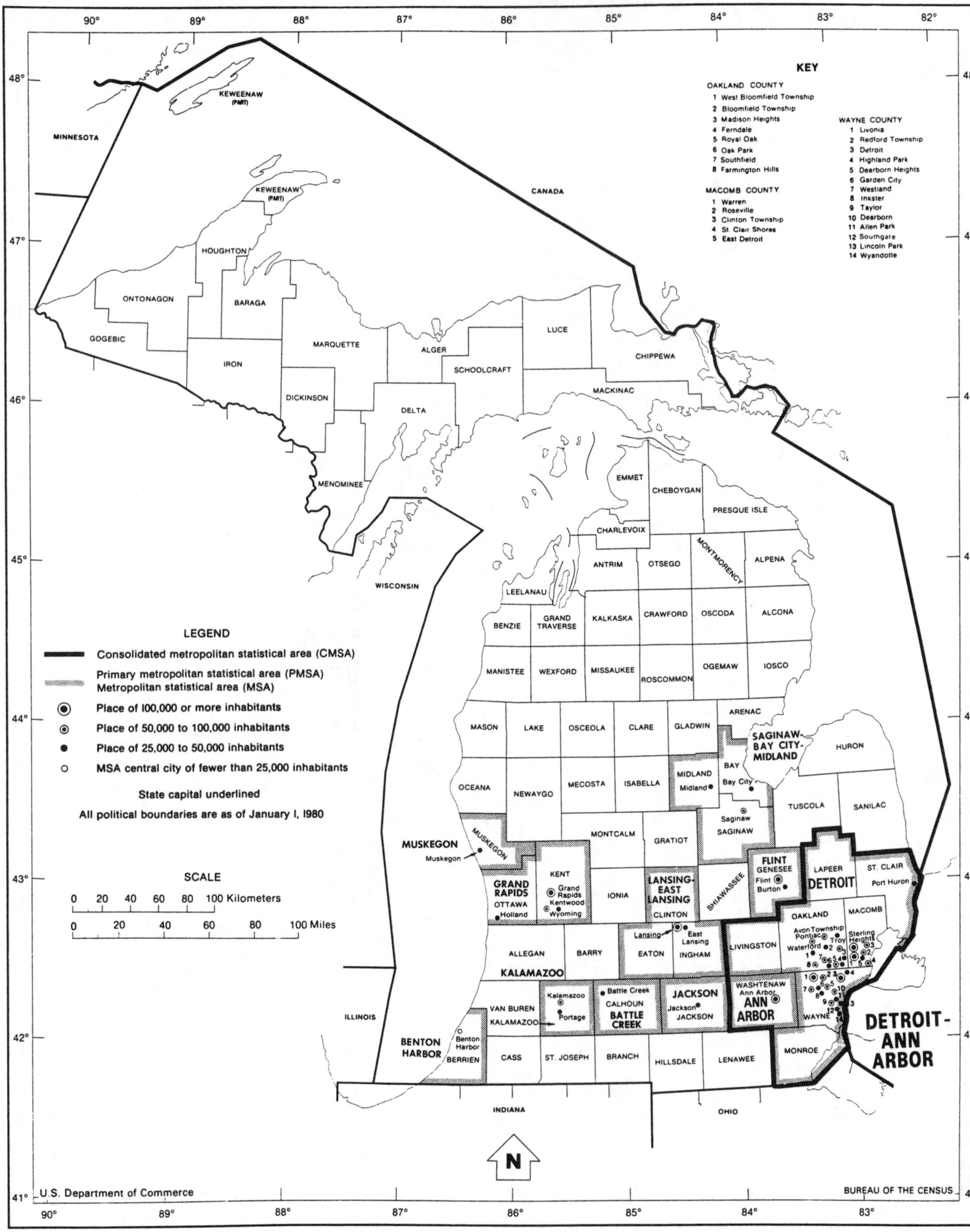

CMSA, PMSA, and MSA boundaries are as defined on June 30, 1983

MINNESOTA - Metropolitan Statistical Areas, Counties, and Selected Places

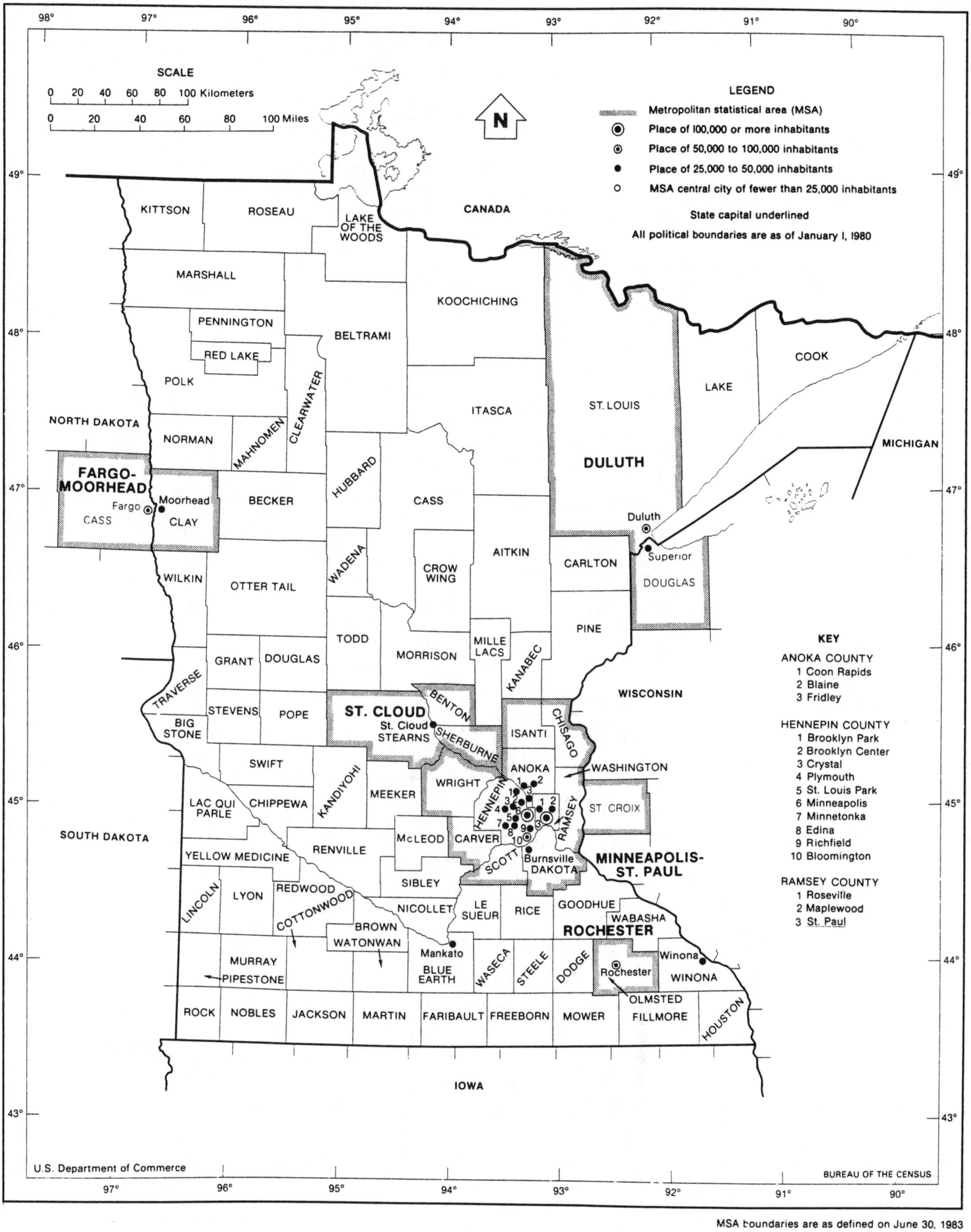

MSA boundaries are as defined on June 30, 1983

MISSISSIPPI - Metropolitan Statistical Areas, Counties, and Selected Places

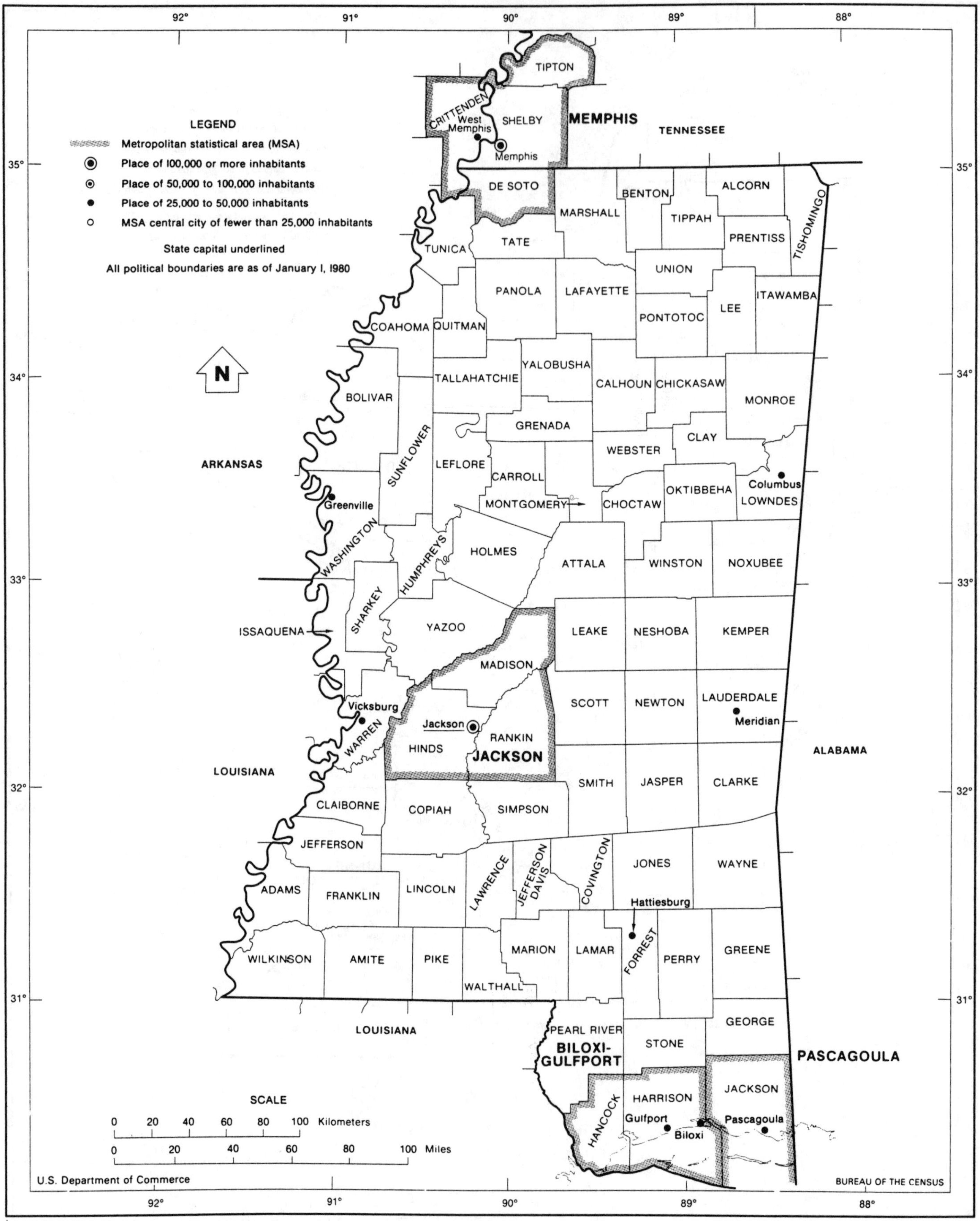

MSA boundaries are as defined on June 30, 1983

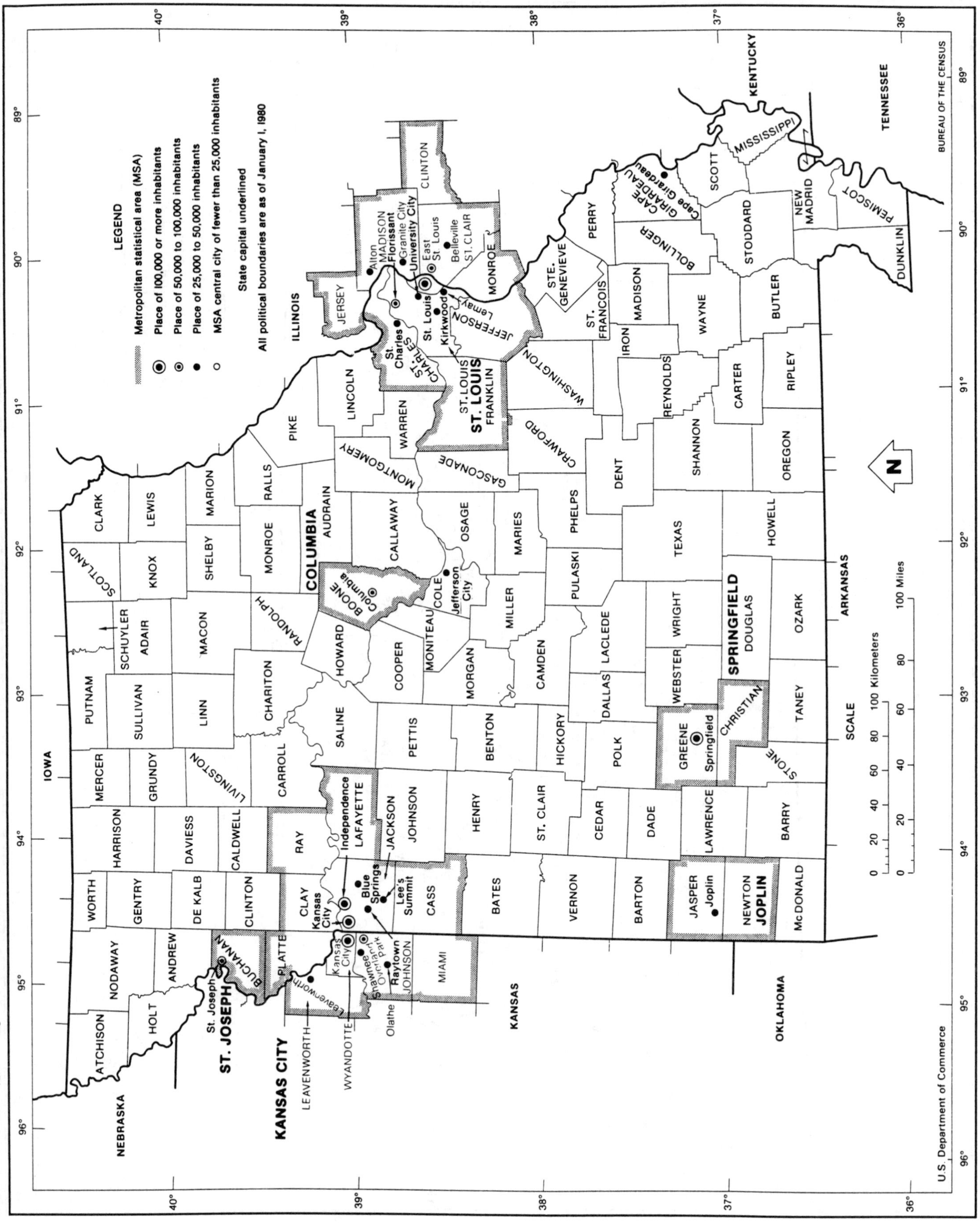
LEGEND
Metropolitan statistical area (MSA)
Place of 100,000 or more inhabitants
Place of 50,000 to 100,000 inhabitants
Place of 25,000 to 50,000 inhabitants
MSA central city of fewer than 25,000 inhabitants
State capital underlined
All political boundaries are as of January I, 1980
IOWA
ILLINOIS
KENTUCKY
TENNESSEE
ARKANSAS
OKLAHOMA
KANSAS
NEBRASKA
KANSAS CITY
ST. JOSEPH
COLUMBIA
ST. LOUIS
SPRINGFIELD
JOPLIN
SCALE
0 20 40 60 80 100 Kilometers
0 20 40 60 80 100 Miles
N
BUREAU OF THE CENSUS
U.S. Department of Commerce
MSA boundaries are as defined on June 30, 1988

MONTANA - Metropolitan Statistical Areas, Counties, and Selected Places

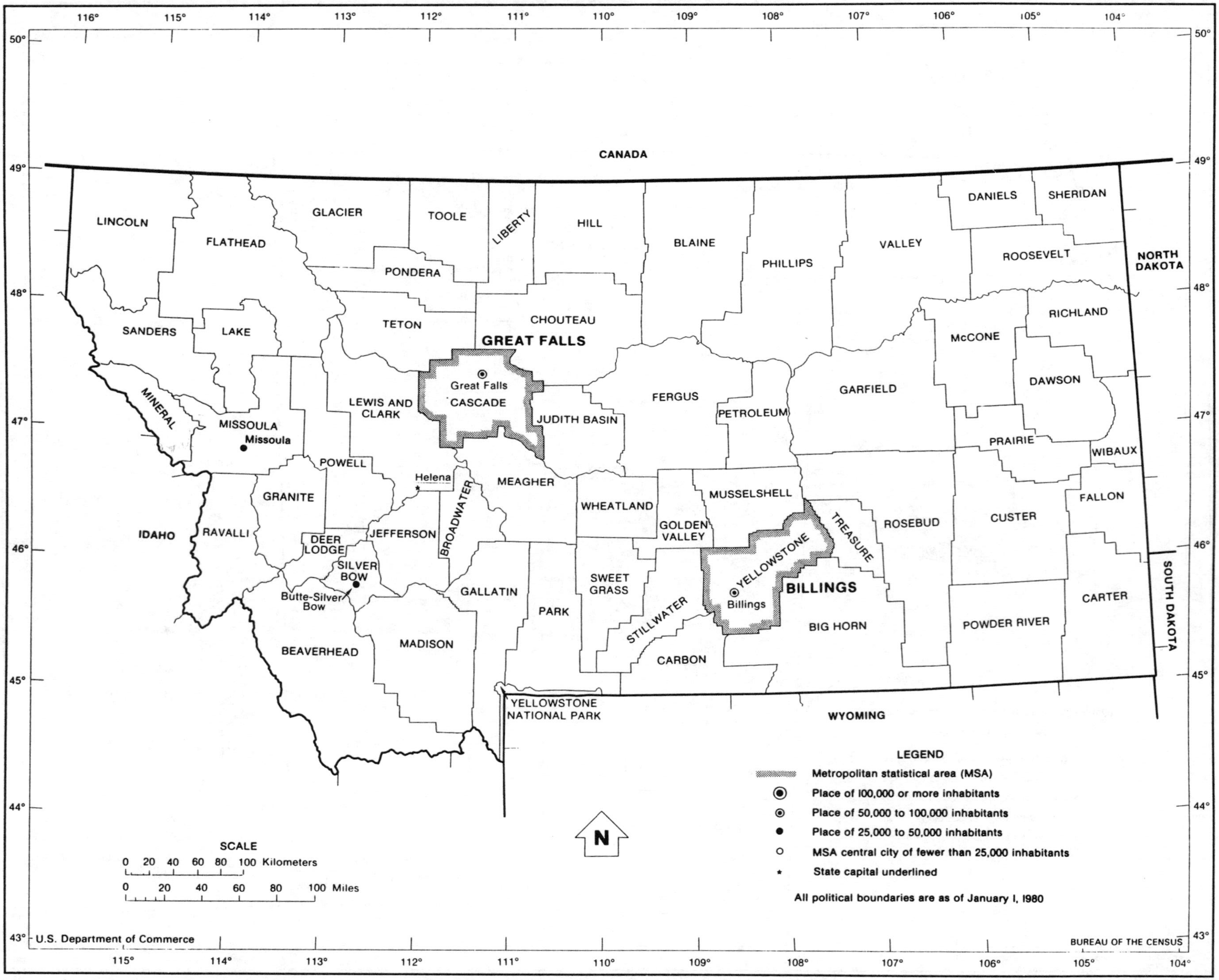
CANADA
IDAHO
NORTH DAKOTA
SOUTH DAKOTA
WYOMING
YELLOWSTONE NATIONAL PARK
LINCOLN
FLATHEAD
GLACIER
TOOLE
LIBERTY
HILL
BLAINE
PHILLIPS
VALLEY
DANIELS
SHERIDAN
ROOSEVELT
PONDERA
SANDERS
LAKE
TETON
CHOUTEAU
GREAT FALLS
Great Falls
CASCADE
MINERAL
MISSOULA
Missoula
LEWIS AND CLARK
JUDITH BASIN
FERGUS
PETROLEUM
GARFIELD
McCONE
RICHLAND
DAWSON
PRAIRIE
WIBAUX
POWELL
Helena
MEAGHER
GRANITE
RAVALLI
DEER LODGE
JEFFERSON
BROADWATER
SILVER BOW
Butte-Silver Bow
WHEATLAND
MUSSELSHELL
GOLDEN VALLEY
TREASURE
ROSEBUD
CUSTER
FALLON
YELLOWSTONE
Billings
BILLINGS
SWEET GRASS
GALLATIN
PARK
STILLWATER
CARBON
BIG HORN
POWDER RIVER
CARTER
BEAVERHEAD
MADISON
N
SCALE
0 20 40 60 80 100 Kilometers
0 20 40 60 80 100 Miles
LEGEND
Metropolitan statistical area (MSA)
Place of 100,000 or more inhabitants
Place of 50,000 to 100,000 inhabitants
Place of 25,000 to 50,000 inhabitants
MSA central city of fewer than 25,000 inhabitants
State capital underlined
All political boundaries are as of January 1, 1980
U.S. Department of Commerce
BUREAU OF THE CENSUS

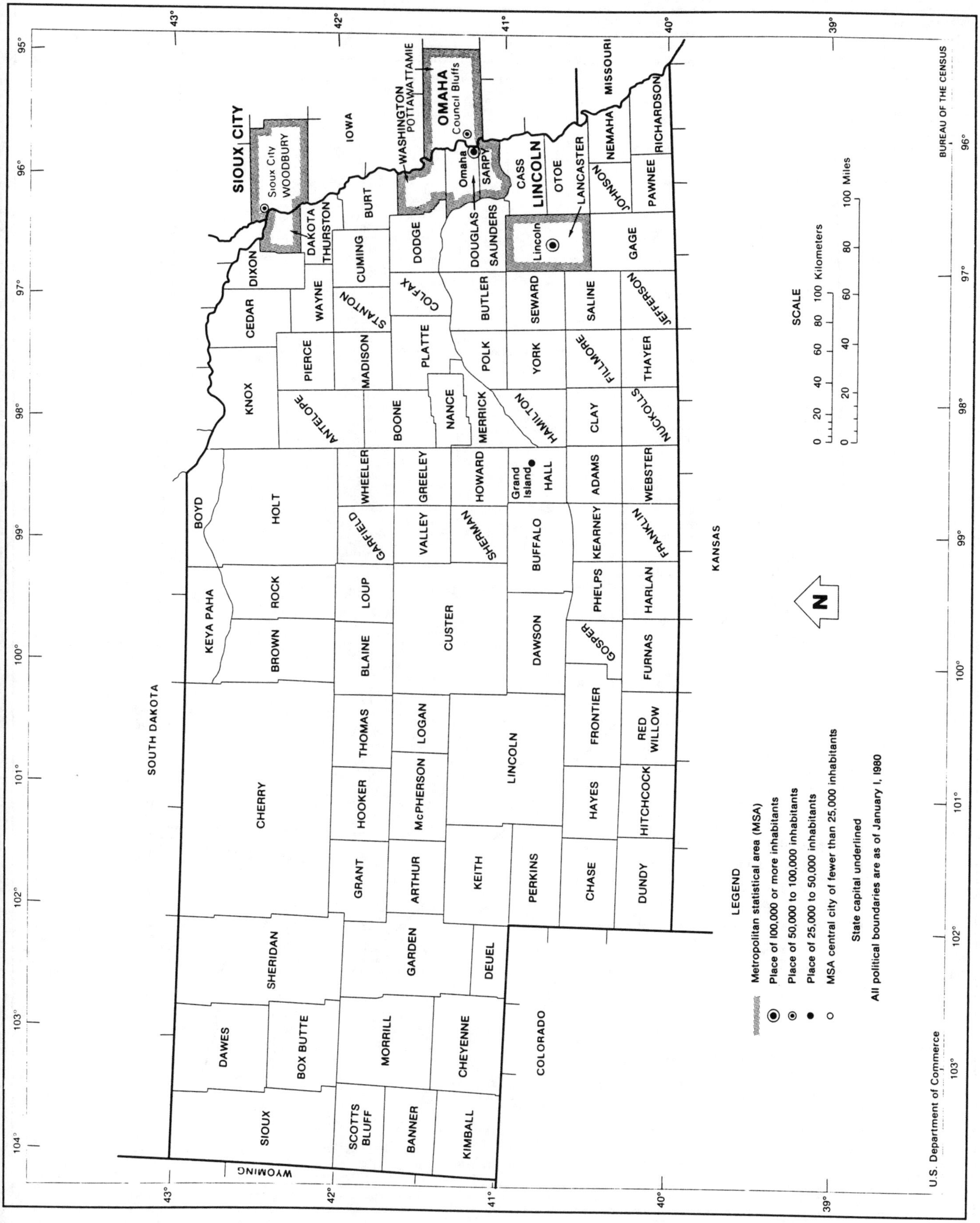
SIOUX CITY
Sioux City
WOODBURY
OMAHA
Council Bluffs
Omaha
WASHINGTON
POTTAWATTAMIE
LINCOLN
Lincoln
IOWA
MISSOURI
KANSAS
COLORADO
WYOMING
SOUTH DAKOTA
DAKOTA
THURSTON
DIXON
CEDAR
KNOX
BOYD
HOLT
KEYA PAHA
ROCK
BROWN
CHERRY
SHERIDAN
DAWES
SIOUX
BOX BUTTE
SCOTTS BLUFF
BANNER
KIMBALL
MORRILL
CHEYENNE
GARDEN
DEUEL
GRANT
ARTHUR
KEITH
PERKINS
HOOKER
McPHERSON
LINCOLN
THOMAS
LOGAN
BLAINE
LOUP
CUSTER
WHEELER
GARFIELD
GREELEY
VALLEY
HOWARD
SHERMAN
BUFFALO
DAWSON
Grand Island
HALL
ANTELOPE
BOONE
NANCE
MERRICK
PIERCE
MADISON
PLATTE
WAYNE
STANTON
CUMING
COLFAX
DODGE
BURT
DOUGLAS
SARPY
SAUNDERS
BUTLER
POLK
YORK
SEWARD
HAMILTON
CASS
OTOE
LANCASTER
SALINE
FILLMORE
CLAY
ADAMS
KEARNEY
PHELPS
GOSPER
FRONTIER
HAYES
CHASE
DUNDY
HITCHCOCK
RED WILLOW
FURNAS
HARLAN
FRANKLIN
WEBSTER
NUCKOLLS
THAYER
JEFFERSON
GAGE
JOHNSON
NEMAHA
PAWNEE
RICHARDSON
N
SCALE
0 20 40 60 80 100 Kilometers
0 20 40 60 80 100 Miles
LEGEND
Metropolitan statistical area (MSA)
Place of 100,000 or more inhabitants
Place of 50,000 to 100,000 inhabitants
Place of 25,000 to 50,000 inhabitants
MSA central city of fewer than 25,000 inhabitants
State capital underlined
All political boundaries are as of January I, 1980
U.S. Department of Commerce
BUREAU OF THE CENSUS
MSA boundaries are as defined on June 30, 1983
43° 42° 41° 40° 39°
95° 96° 97° 98° 99° 100° 101° 102° 103° 104°

NEVADA - Metropolitan Statistical Areas, Counties, Independent City, and Other Selected Places

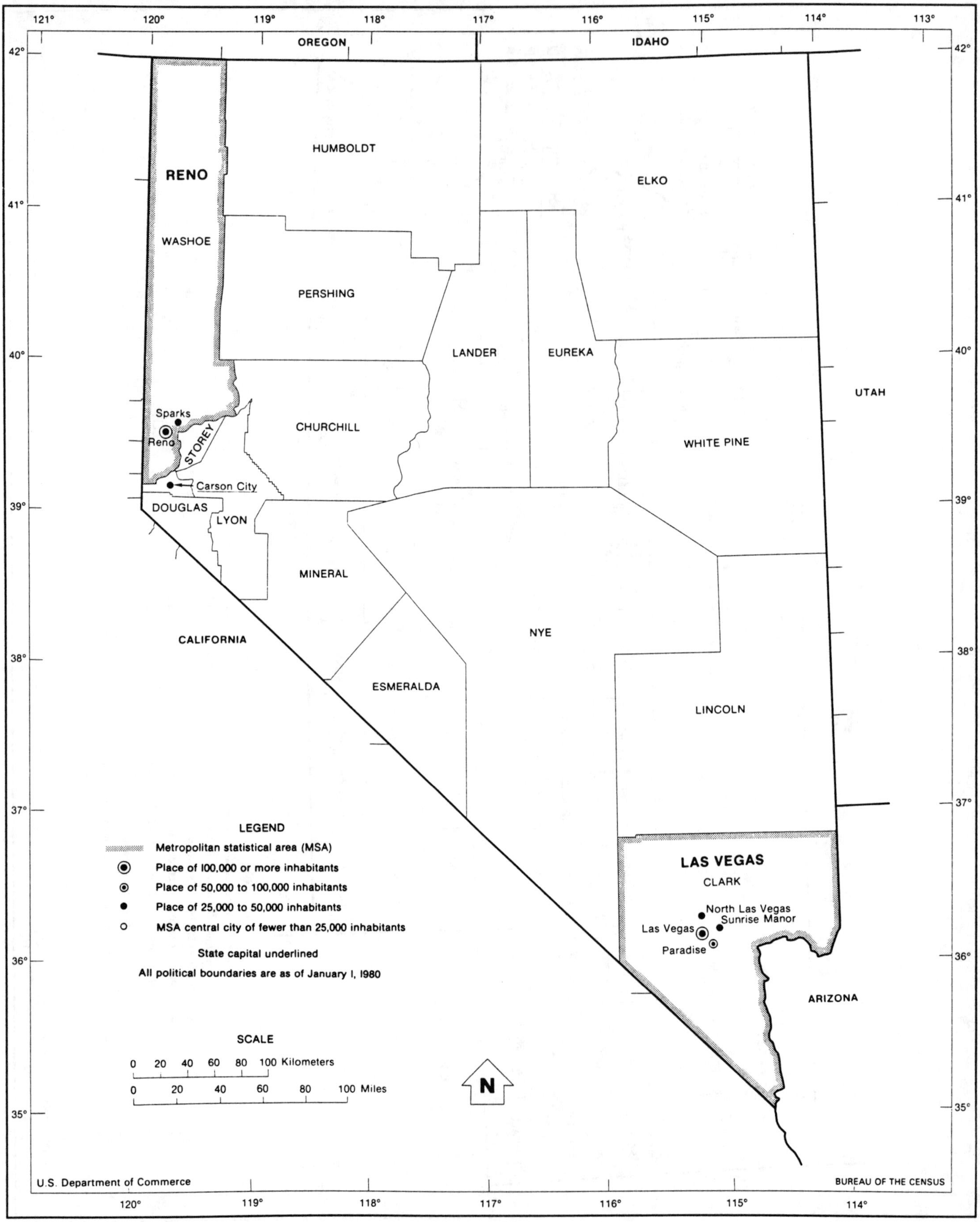

MSA boundaries are as defined on June 30, 1983

NEW HAMPSHIRE - Consolidated Metropolitan Statistical Area, Primary Metropolitan Statistical Areas, Metropolitan Statistical Areas, Counties, and Selected Places

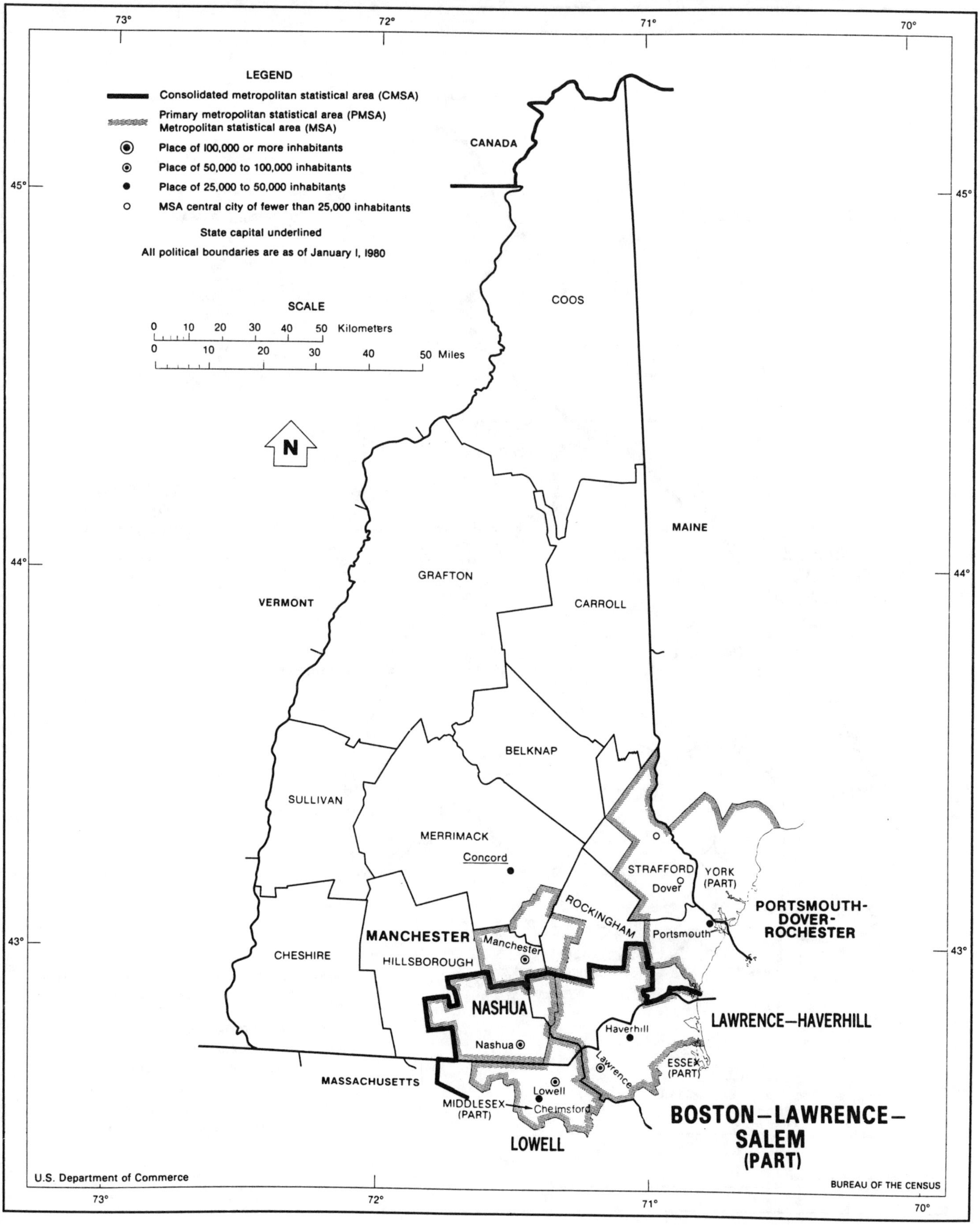

CMSA, PMSA, and MSA boundaries are as defined on June 30, 1983

NEW JERSEY-Consolidated Metropolitan Statistical Areas, Primary Metropolitan Statistical Areas, Metropolitan Statistical Areas, Counties, and Selected Places

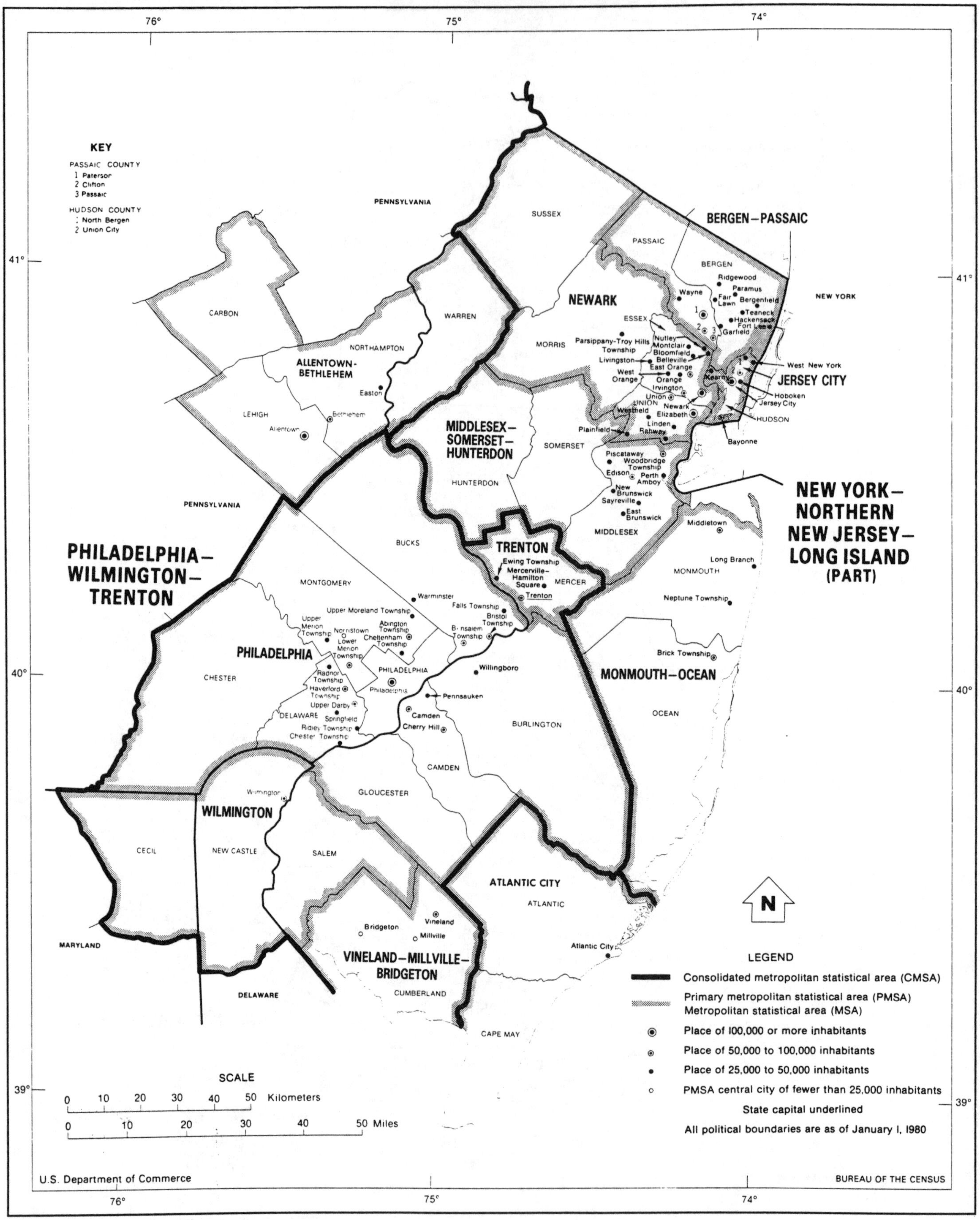

CMSA, PMSA, and MSA boundaries are as defined on June 30, 1983

NEW MEXICO - Metropolitan Statistical Areas, Counties, and Selected Places

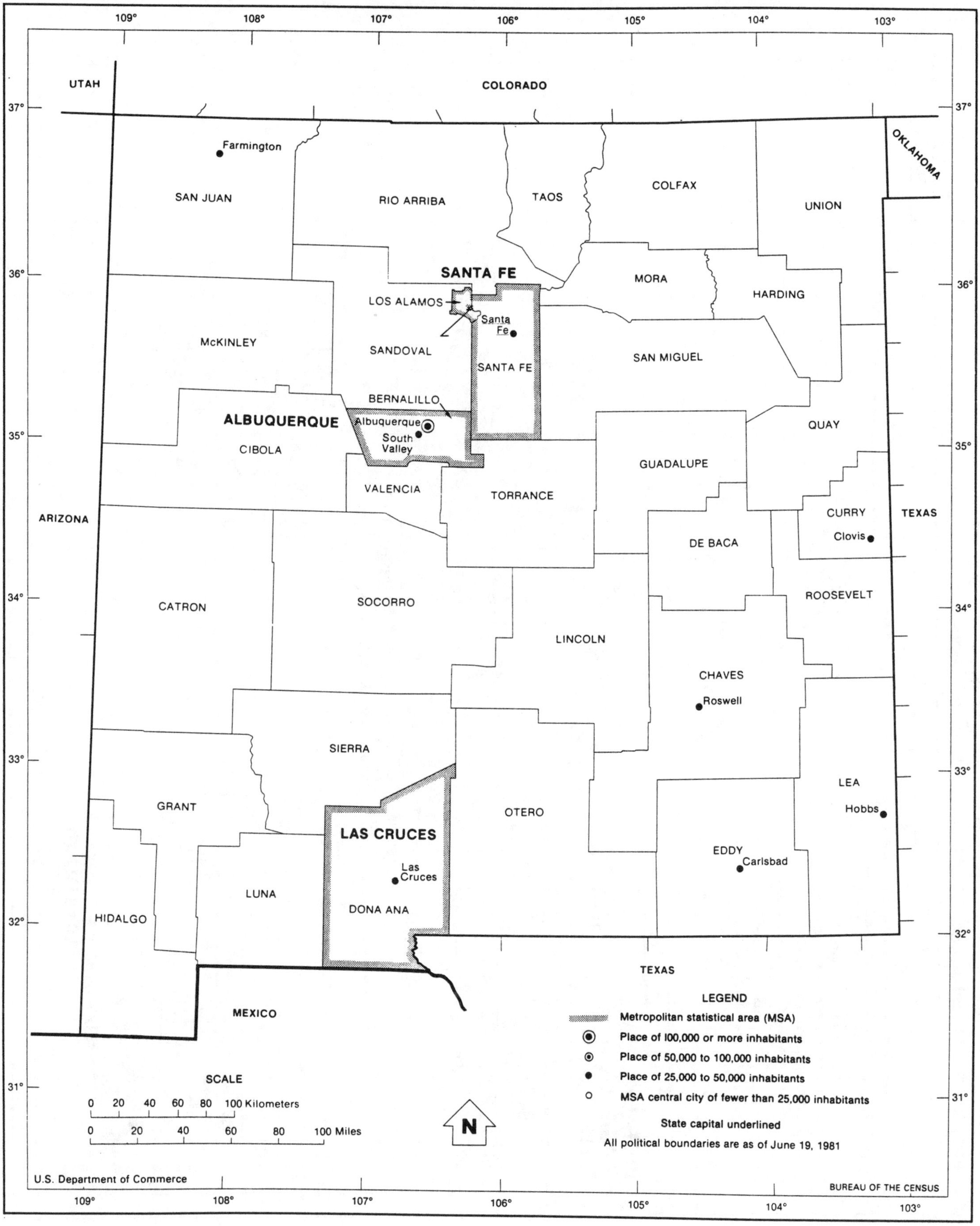

MSA boundaries are as defined on June 30, 1984

NEW YORK - Consolidated Metropolitan Statistical Areas, Primary Metropolitan Statistical Areas, Metropolitan Statistical Areas, Counties, and Selected Places

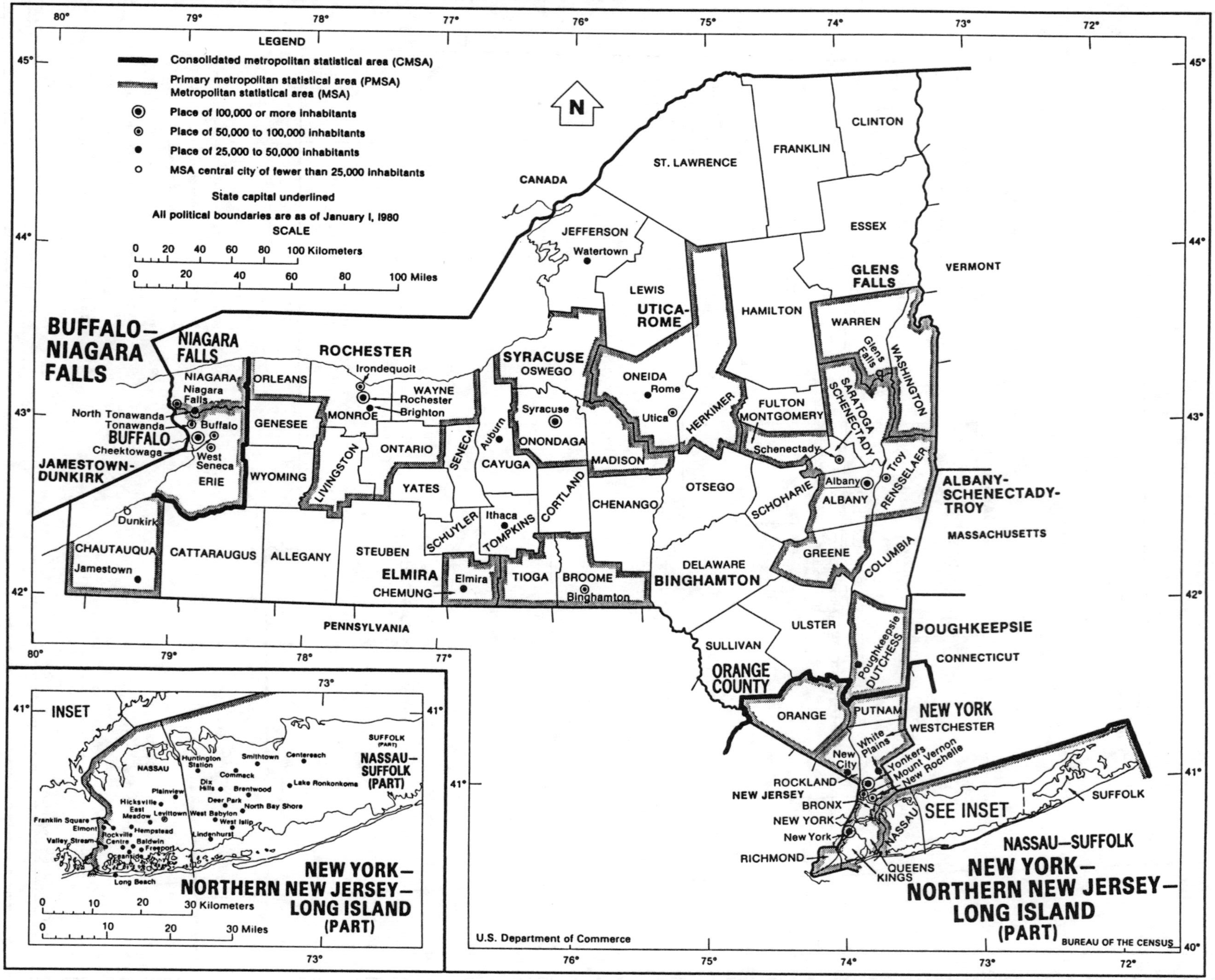

CMSA, PMSA, and MSA boundaries are as defined on June 30, 1989

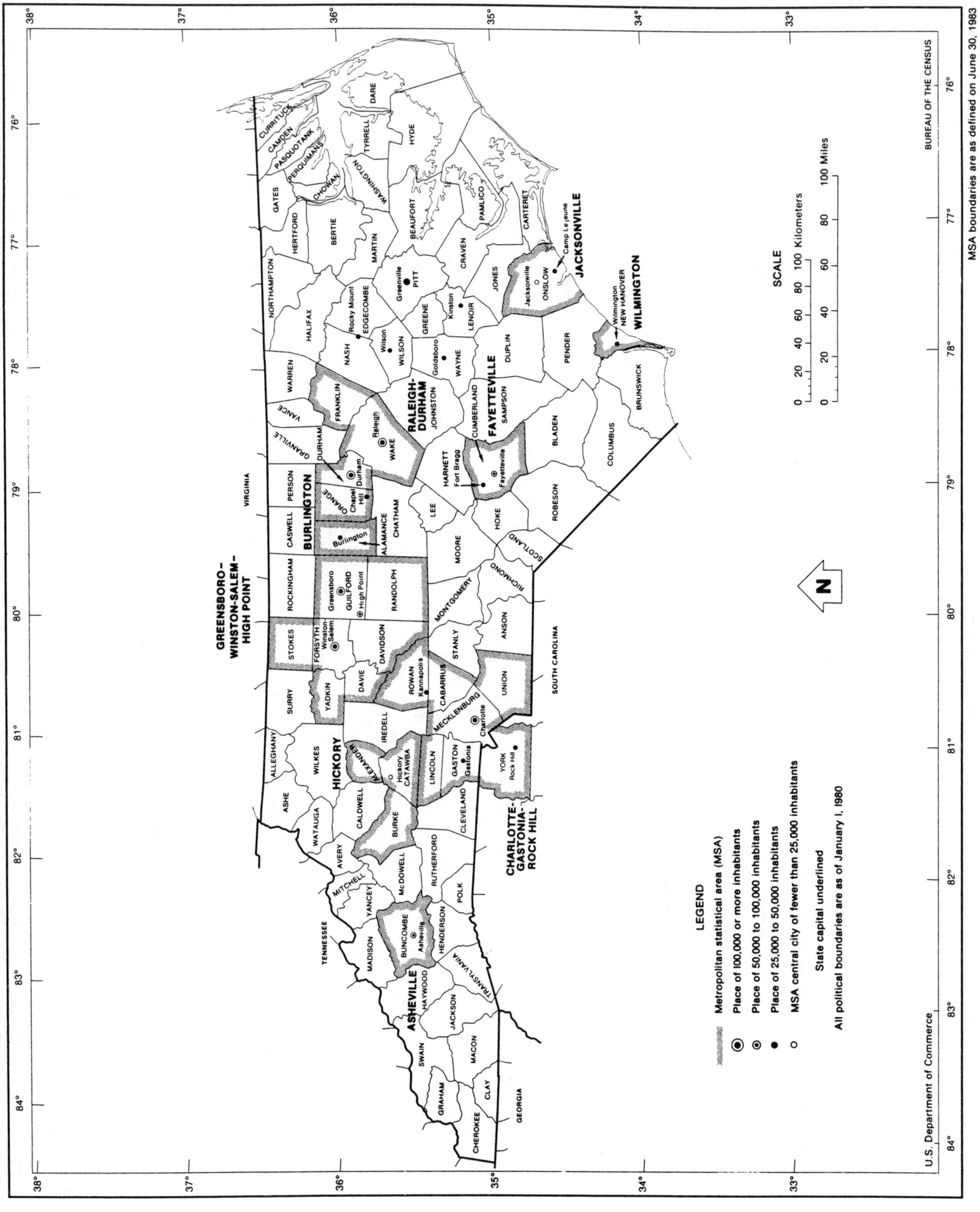
U.S. Department of Commerce
BUREAU OF THE CENSUS
MSA boundaries are as defined on June 30, 1983
LEGEND
Metropolitan statistical area (MSA)
Place of 100,000 or more inhabitants
Place of 50,000 to 100,000 inhabitants
Place of 25,000 to 50,000 inhabitants
MSA central city of fewer than 25,000 inhabitants
State capital underlined
All political boundaries are as of January I, 1980
SCALE
0 20 40 60 80 100 Miles
0 20 40 60 80 100 Kilometers
N
VIRGINIA
TENNESSEE
GEORGIA
SOUTH CAROLINA
GREENSBORO-WINSTON-SALEM-HIGH POINT
BURLINGTON
RALEIGH-DURHAM
FAYETTEVILLE
JACKSONVILLE
WILMINGTON
HICKORY
ASHEVILLE
CHARLOTTE-GASTONIA-ROCK HILL
CURRITUCK
CAMDEN
PASQUOTANK
PERQUIMANS
CHOWAN
GATES
HERTFORD
BERTIE
WASHINGTON
TYRRELL
DARE
HYDE
BEAUFORT
MARTIN
PAMLICO
CARTERET
CRAVEN
JONES
ONSLOW
NORTHAMPTON
HALIFAX
EDGECOMBE
PITT
GREENE
LENOIR
NASH
WILSON
WAYNE
DUPLIN
PENDER
NEW HANOVER
BRUNSWICK
WARREN
VANCE
FRANKLIN
GRANVILLE
DURHAM
WAKE
JOHNSTON
SAMPSON
CUMBERLAND
HARNETT
BLADEN
COLUMBUS
ROBESON
PERSON
ORANGE
CASWELL
ALAMANCE
CHATHAM
LEE
MOORE
HOKE
SCOTLAND
RICHMOND
ROCKINGHAM
GUILFORD
RANDOLPH
MONTGOMERY
ANSON
STOKES
FORSYTH
DAVIDSON
STANLY
UNION
SURRY
YADKIN
DAVIE
ROWAN
CABARRUS
MECKLENBURG
IREDELL
ALLEGHANY
WILKES
ALEXANDER
CATAWBA
LINCOLN
GASTON
YORK
ASHE
WATAUGA
CALDWELL
BURKE
CLEVELAND
AVERY
MITCHELL
YANCEY
McDOWELL
RUTHERFORD
POLK
MADISON
BUNCOMBE
HENDERSON
TRANSYLVANIA
HAYWOOD
JACKSON
SWAIN
MACON
GRAHAM
CLAY
CHEROKEE
Greenville
Rocky Mount
Wilson
Goldsboro
Kinston
Jacksonville
Camp Lejeune
Wilmington
Raleigh
Durham
Chapel Hill
Burlington
Fayetteville
Fort Bragg
Greensboro
High Point
Winston-Salem
Kannapolis
Charlotte
Gastonia
Rock Hill
Hickory
Asheville
38° 37° 36° 35° 34° 33°
76° 77° 78° 79° 80° 81° 82° 83° 84°

NORTH DAKOTA - Metropolitan Statistical Areas, Counties, and Selected Places

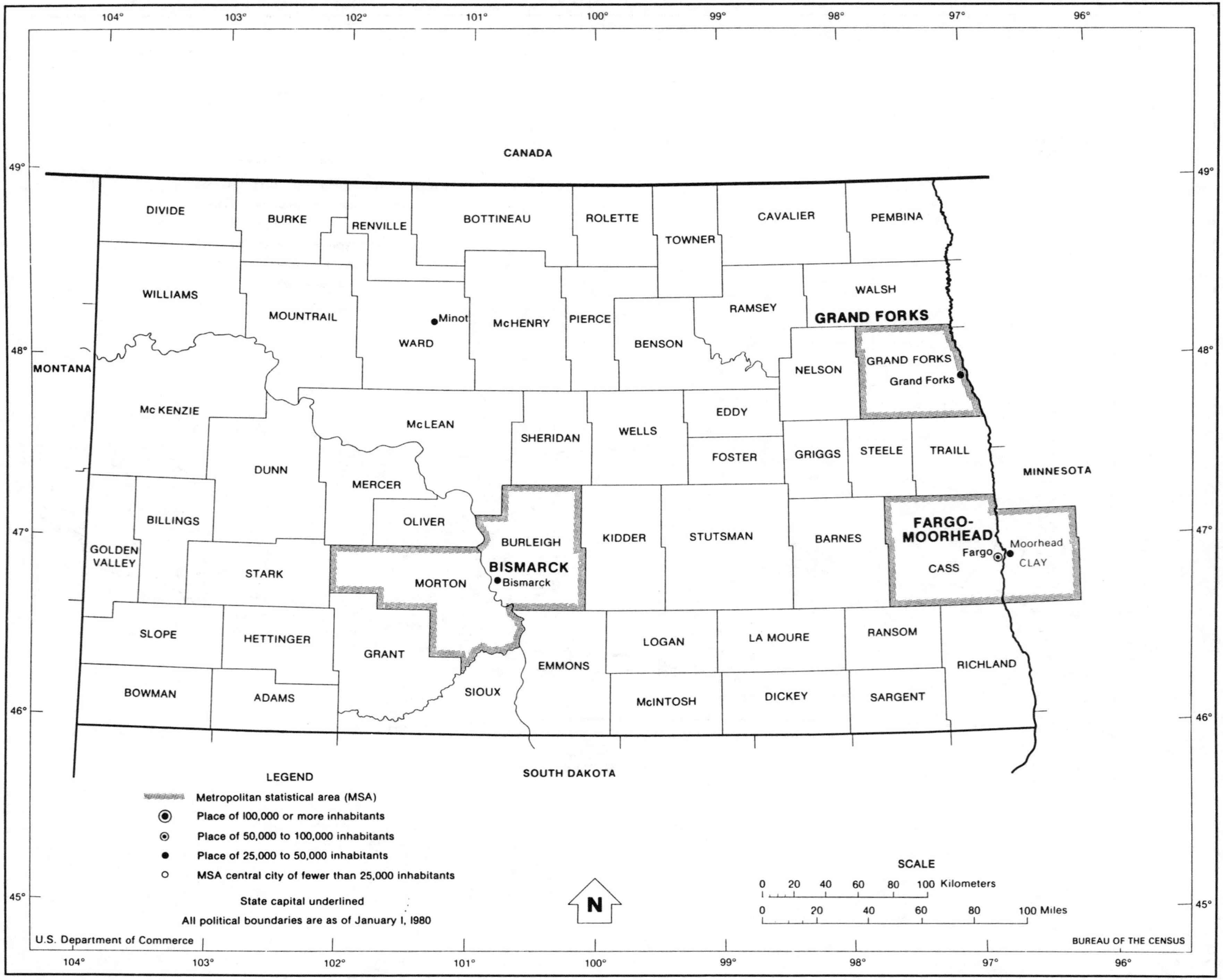

MSA boundaries are as defined on June 30, 1983

OHIO - Consolidated Metropolitan Statistical Areas, Primary Metropolitan Statistical Areas, Metropolitan Statistical Areas, Counties, and Selected Places

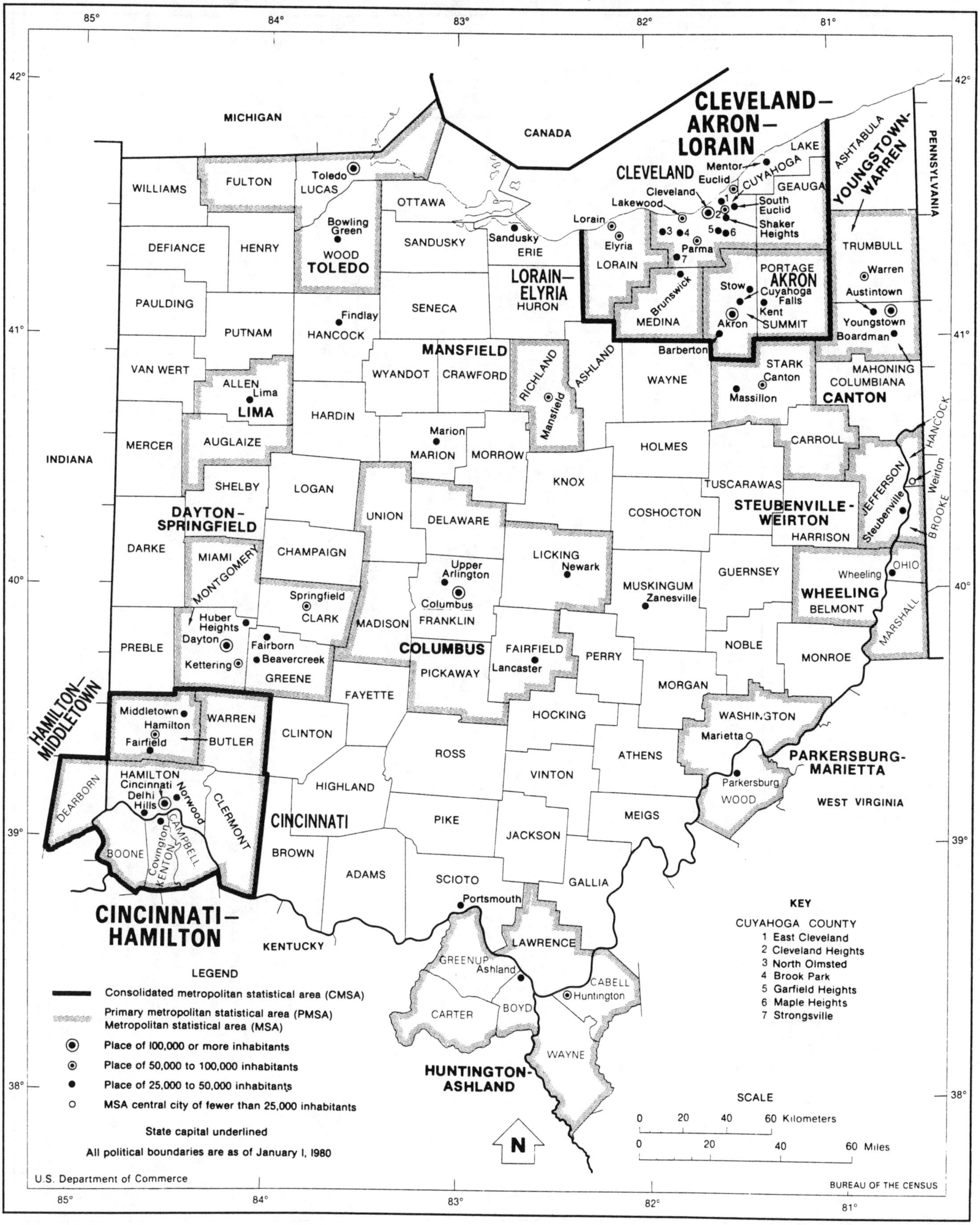

CMSA, PMSA, and MSA boundaries are as defined on June 30, 1983

OKLAHOMA - Metropolitan Statistical Areas, Counties, and Selected Places

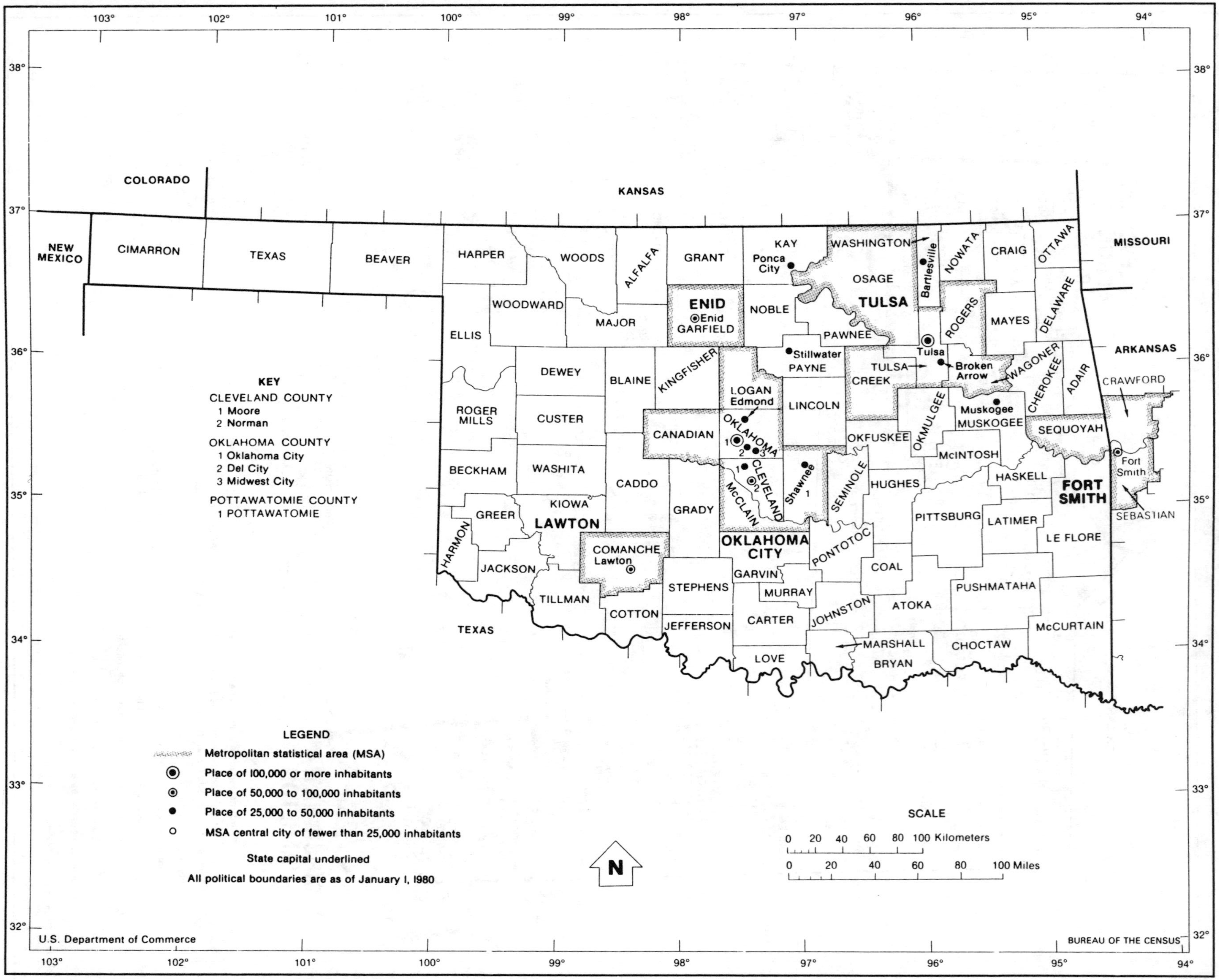

MSA boundaries are as defined on June 30, 1983

OREGON - Consolidated Metropolitan Statistical Area, Primary Metropolitan Statistical Area, Metropolitan Statistical Areas, Counties, and Selected Places

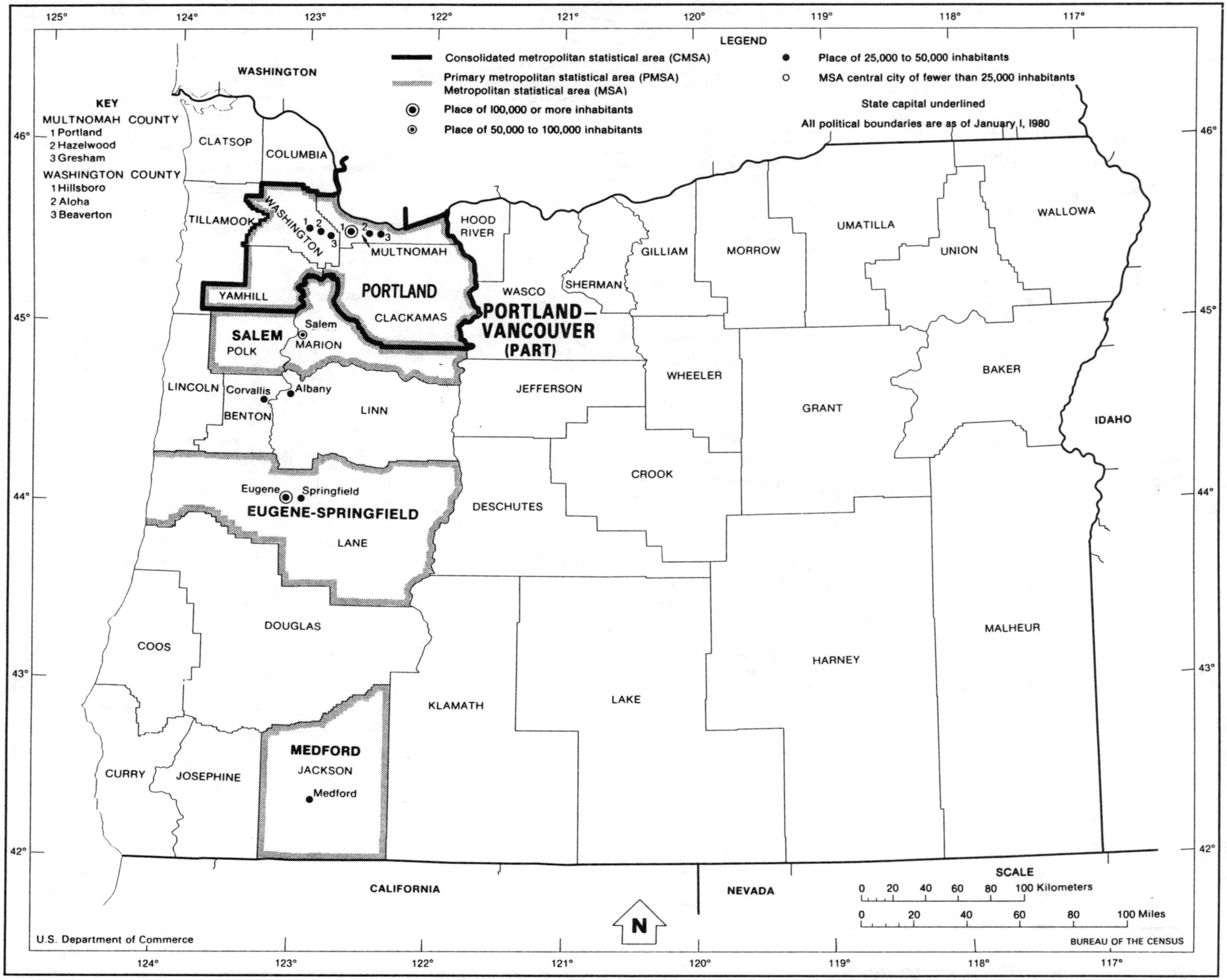

CMSA, PMSA, and MSA boundaries are as defined on June 30, 1983

PENNSYLVANIA - Consolidated Metropolitan Statistical Areas, Primary Metropolitan Statistical Areas, Metropolitan Statistical Areas, Counties, and Selected Places

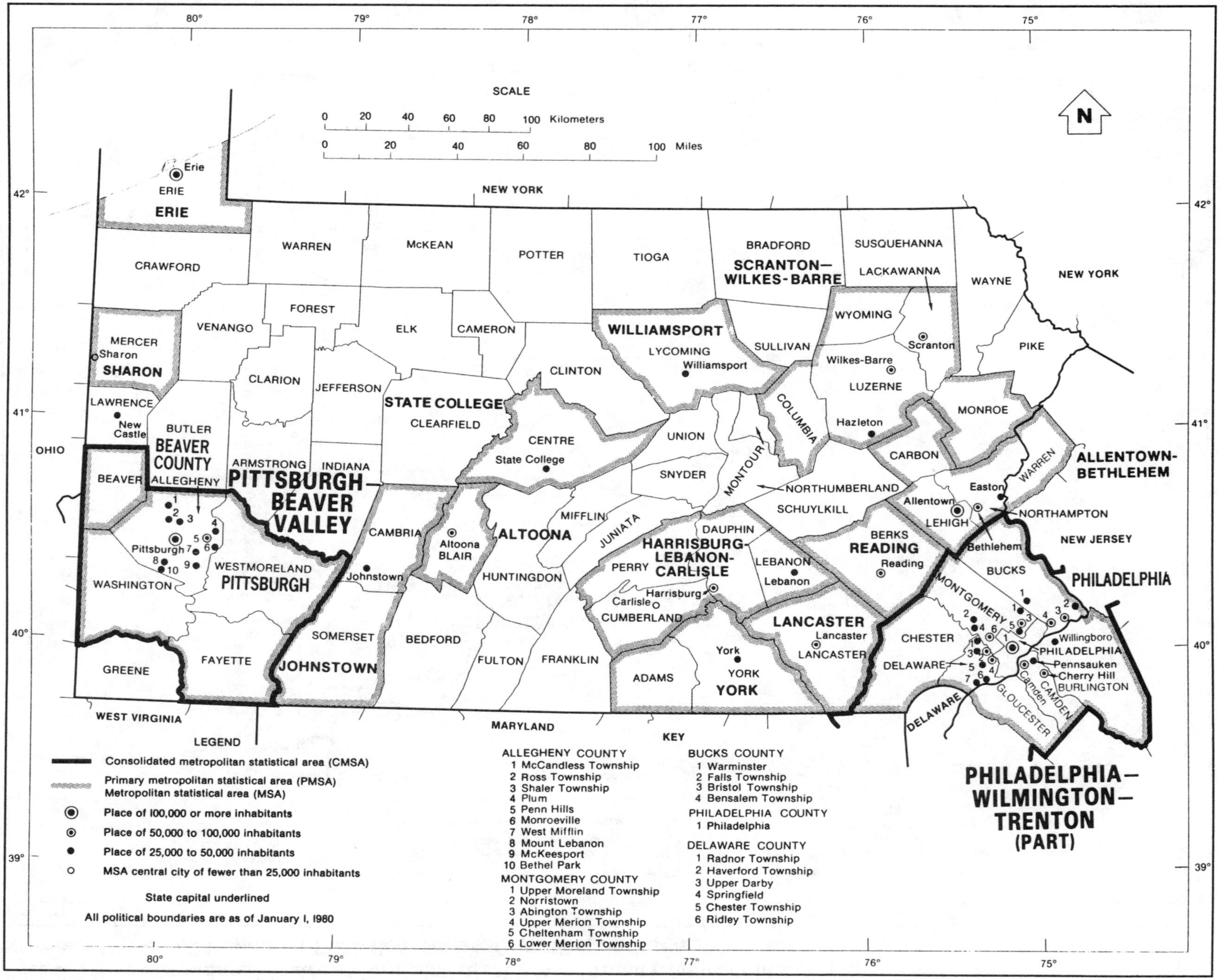

CMSA, PMSA, and MSA boundaries are as defined on June 30, 1983

RHODE ISLAND - Consolidated Metropolitan Statistical Area, Primary Metropolitan Statistical Areas, Metropolitan Statistical Area, Counties, and Selected Places

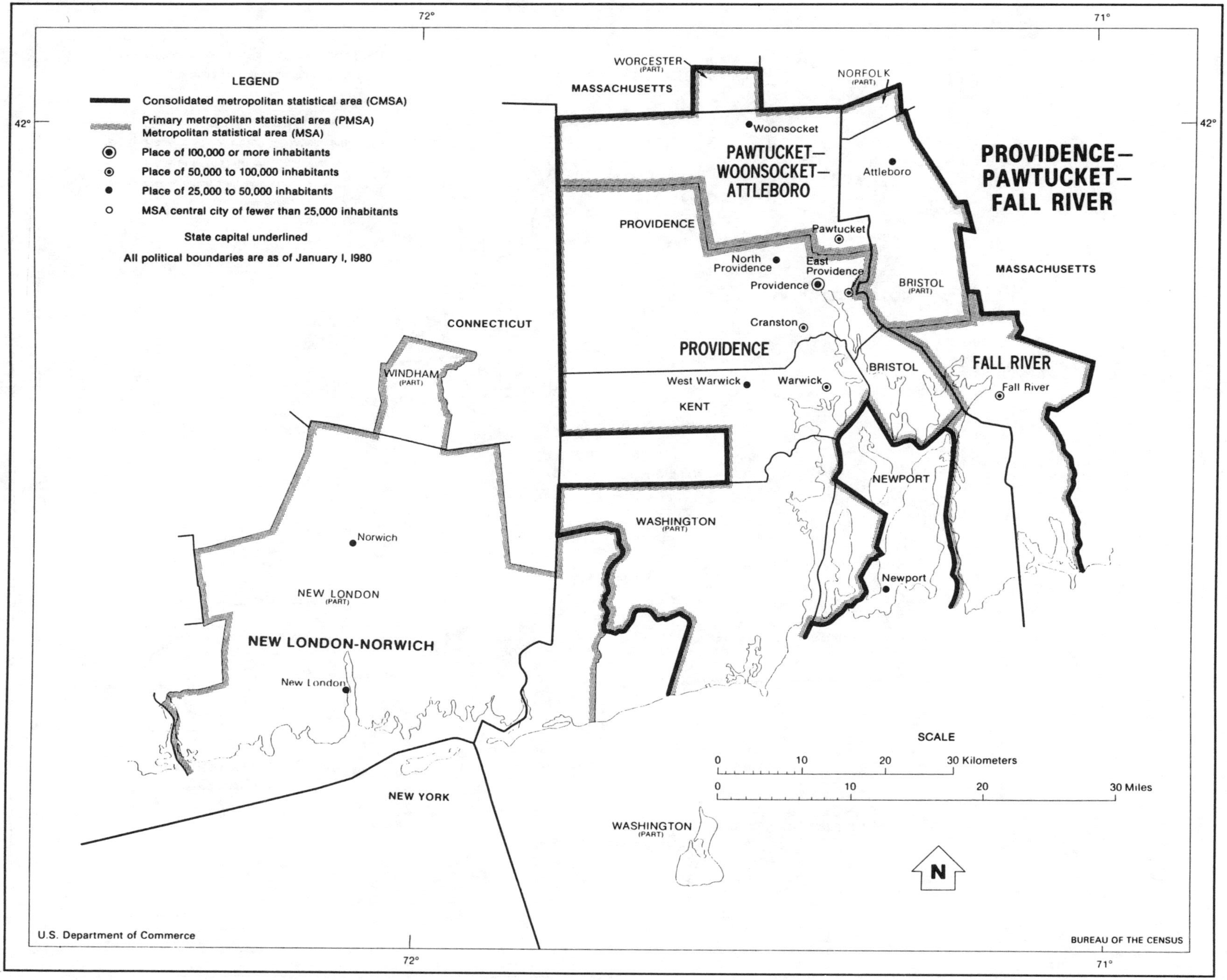

CMSA, PMSA, and MSA boundaries are as defined on June 30, 1983

SOUTH CAROLINA - Metropolitan Statistical Areas, Counties, and Selected Places

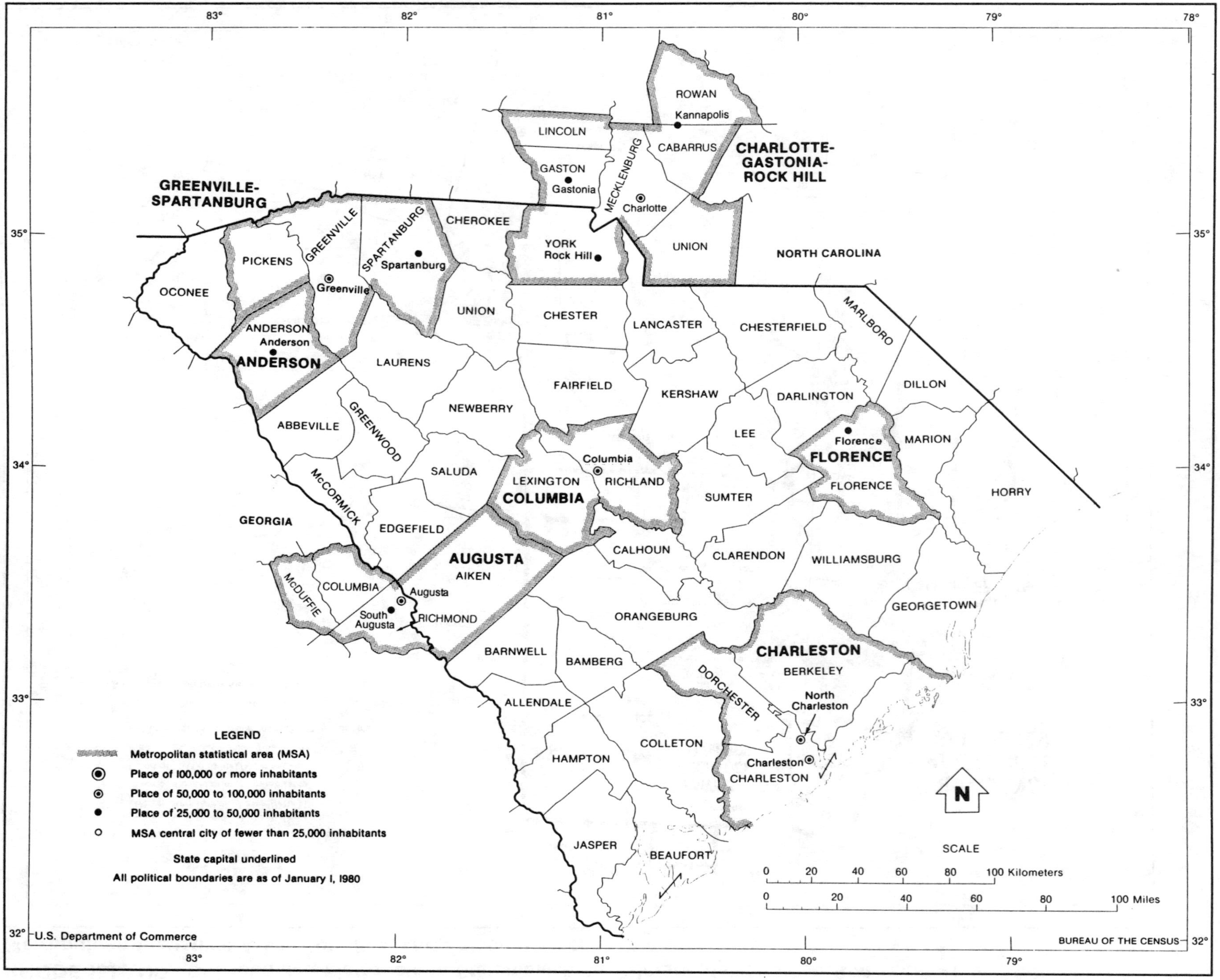

MSA boundaries are as defined on June 30, 1983

SOUTH DAKOTA - Metropolitan Statistical Area, Counties, and Selected Places

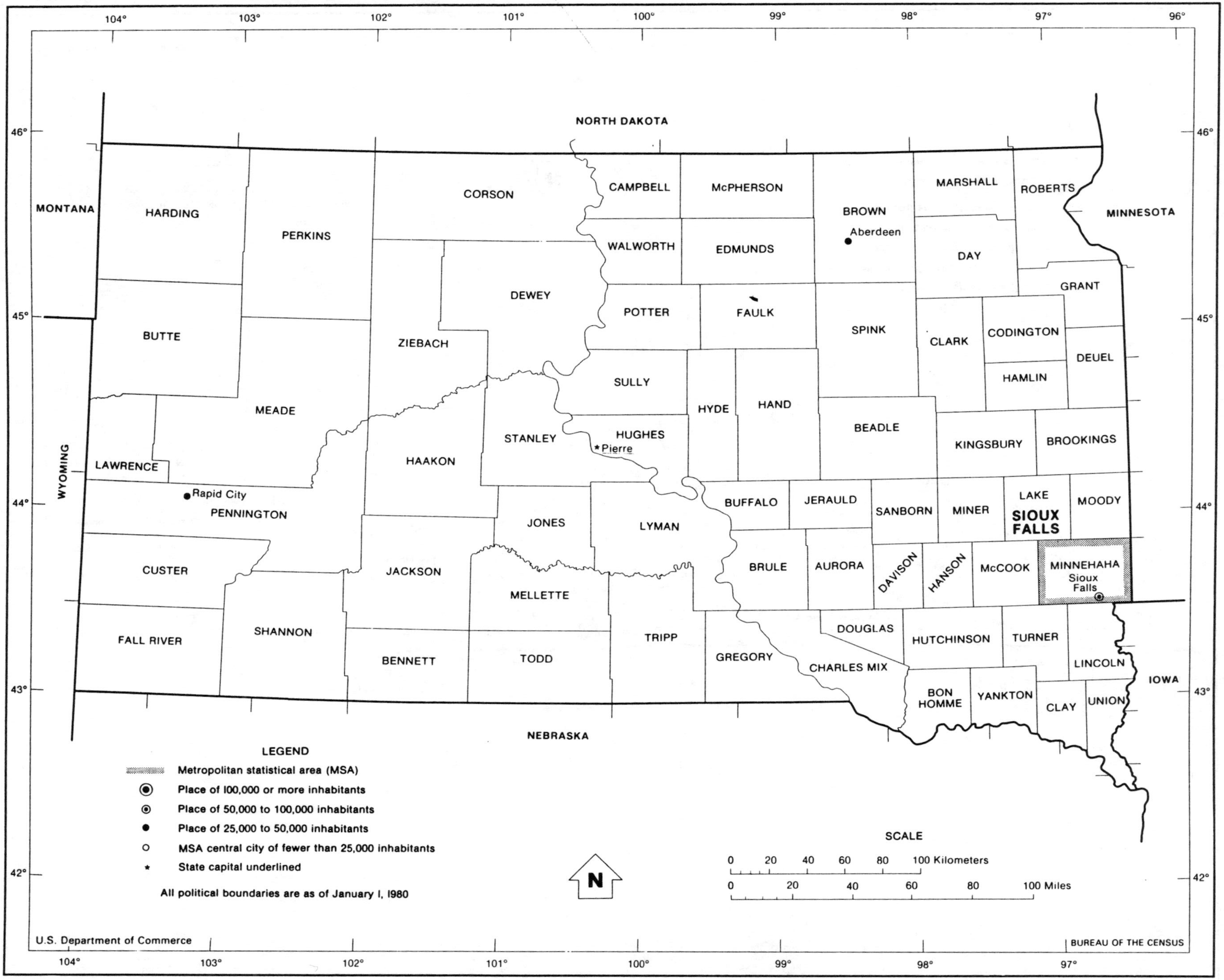

MSA boundaries are as defined on June 30, 1983

TENNESSEE - Metropolitan Statistical Areas, Counties, Independent City, and Other Selected Places

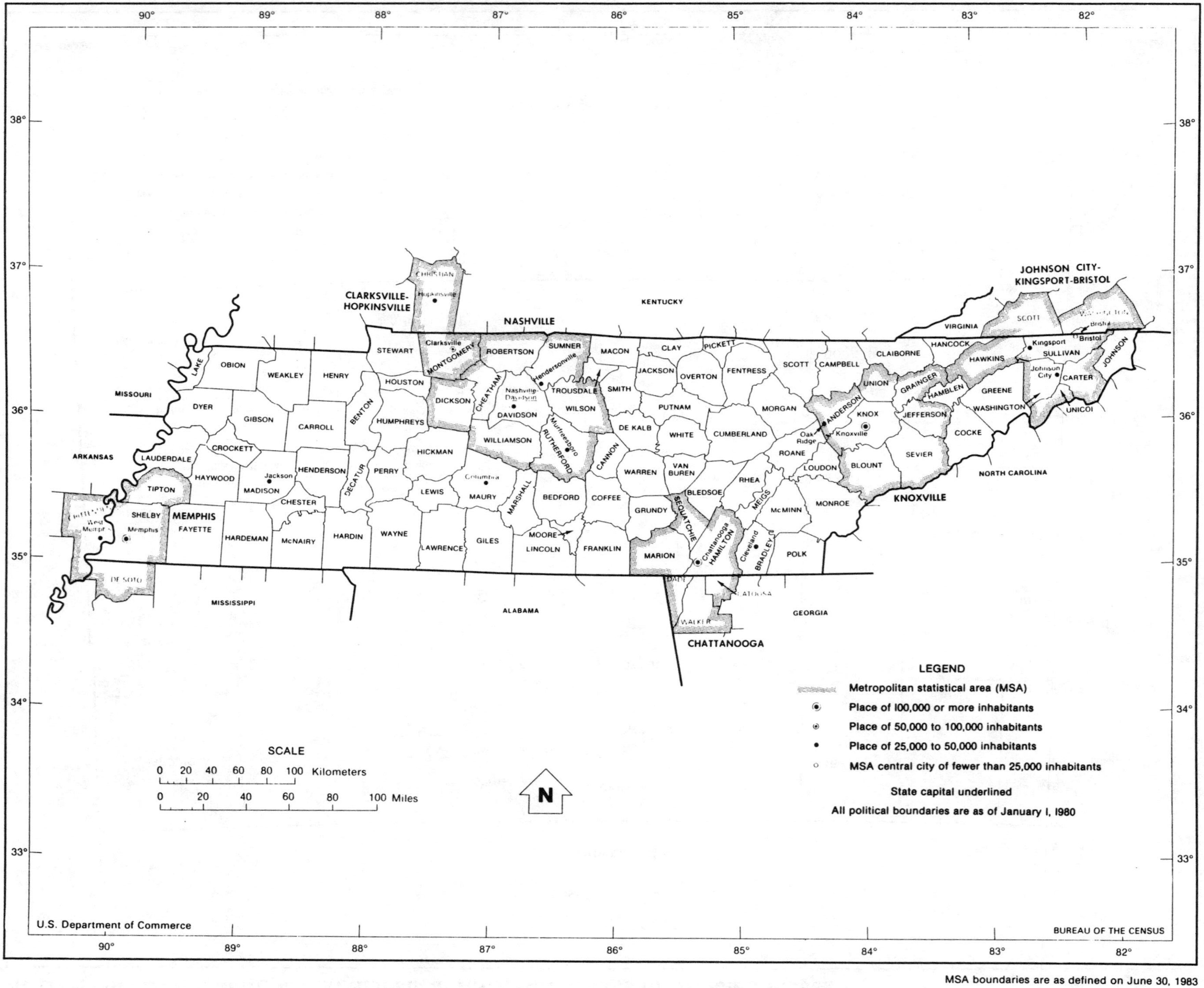

MSA boundaries are as defined on June 30, 1983

TEXAS - Consolidated Metropolitan Statistical Areas, Primary Metropolitan Statistical Areas, Metropolitan Statistical Areas, Counties, and Selected Places

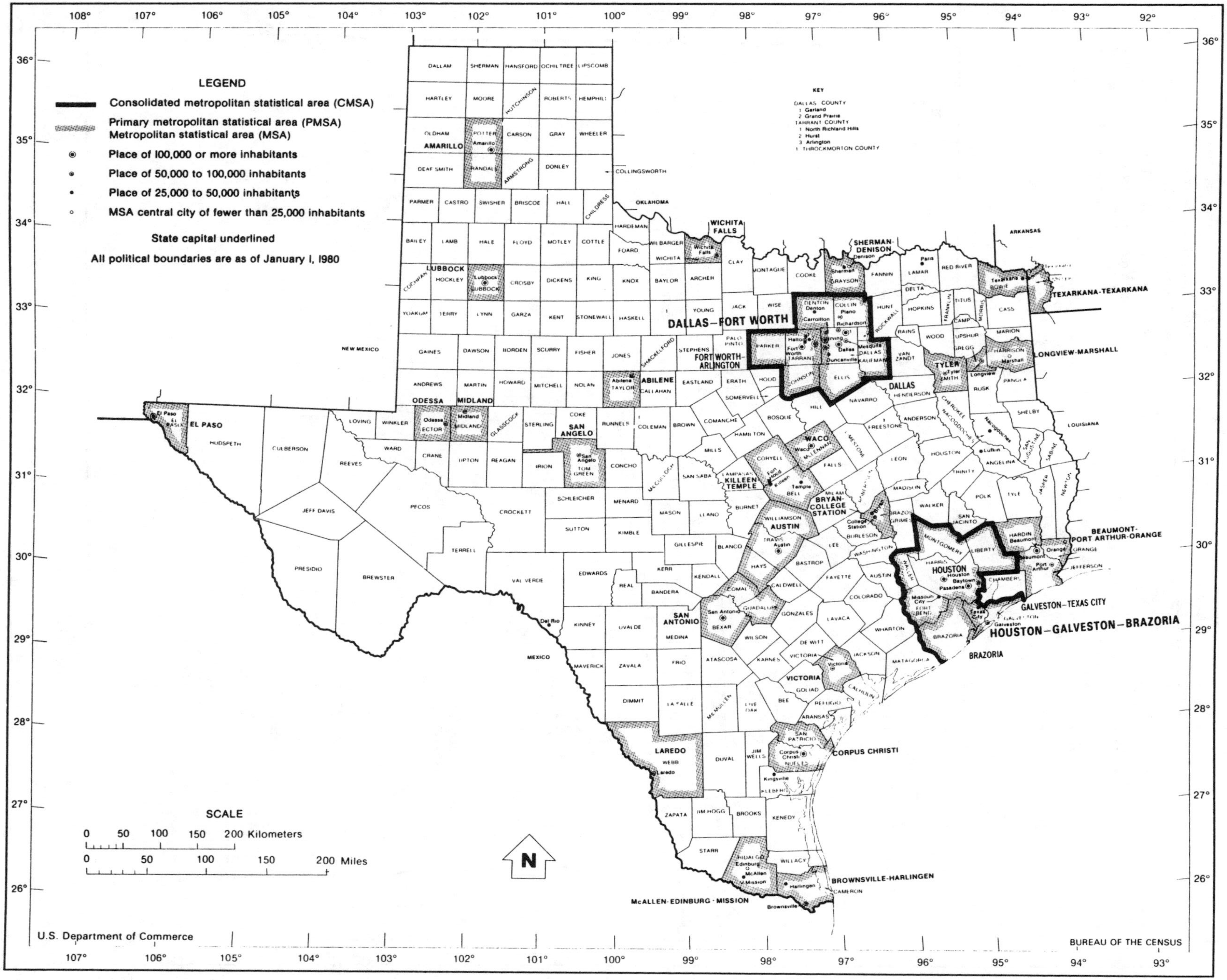

CMSA, PMSA, and MSA boundaries are as defined on June 30, 1983

UTAH - Metropolitan Statistical Areas, Counties, and Selected Places

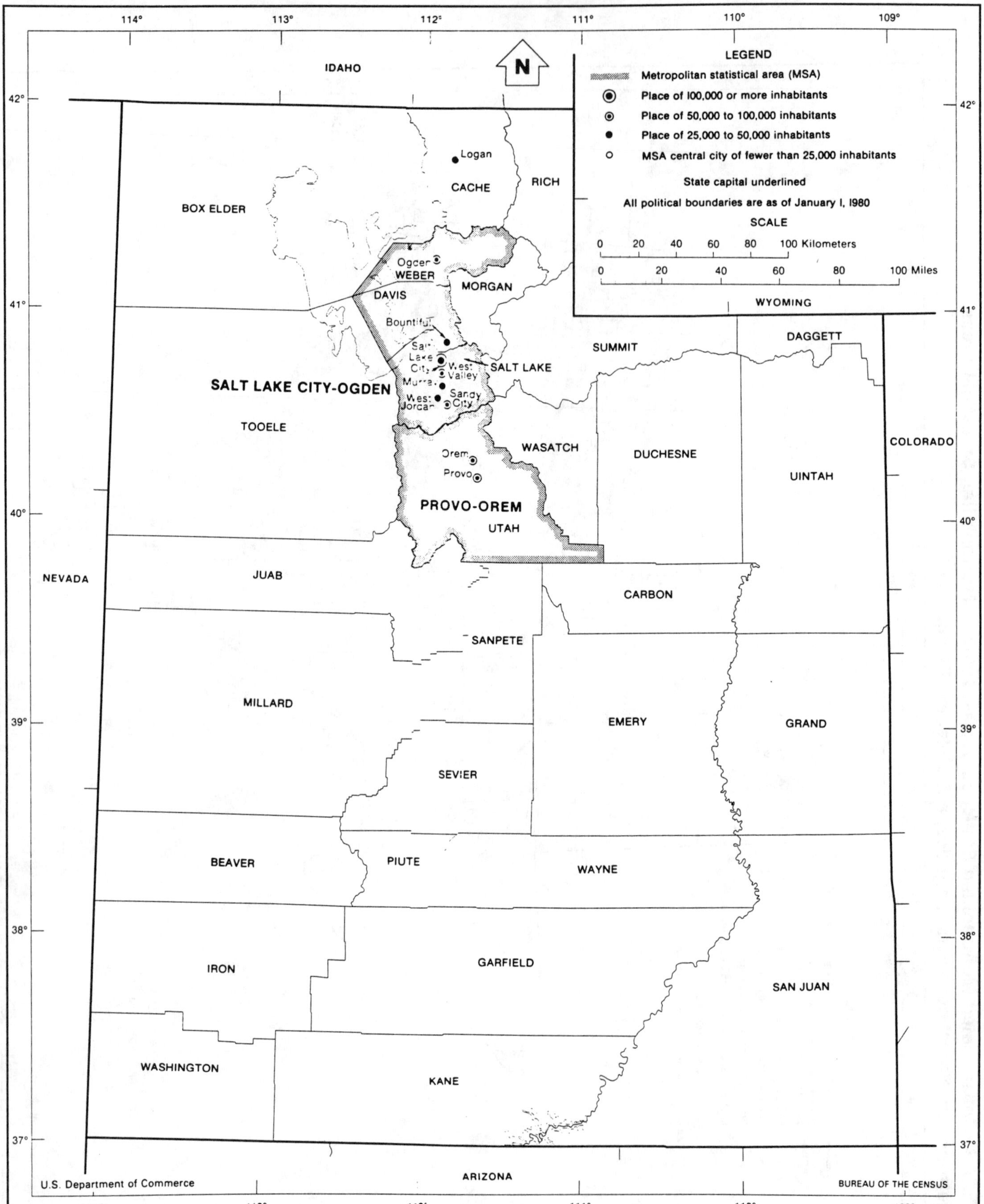

MSA boundaries are as defined on June 30, 1983

VERMONT - Metropolitan Statistical Area, Counties, and Selected Places

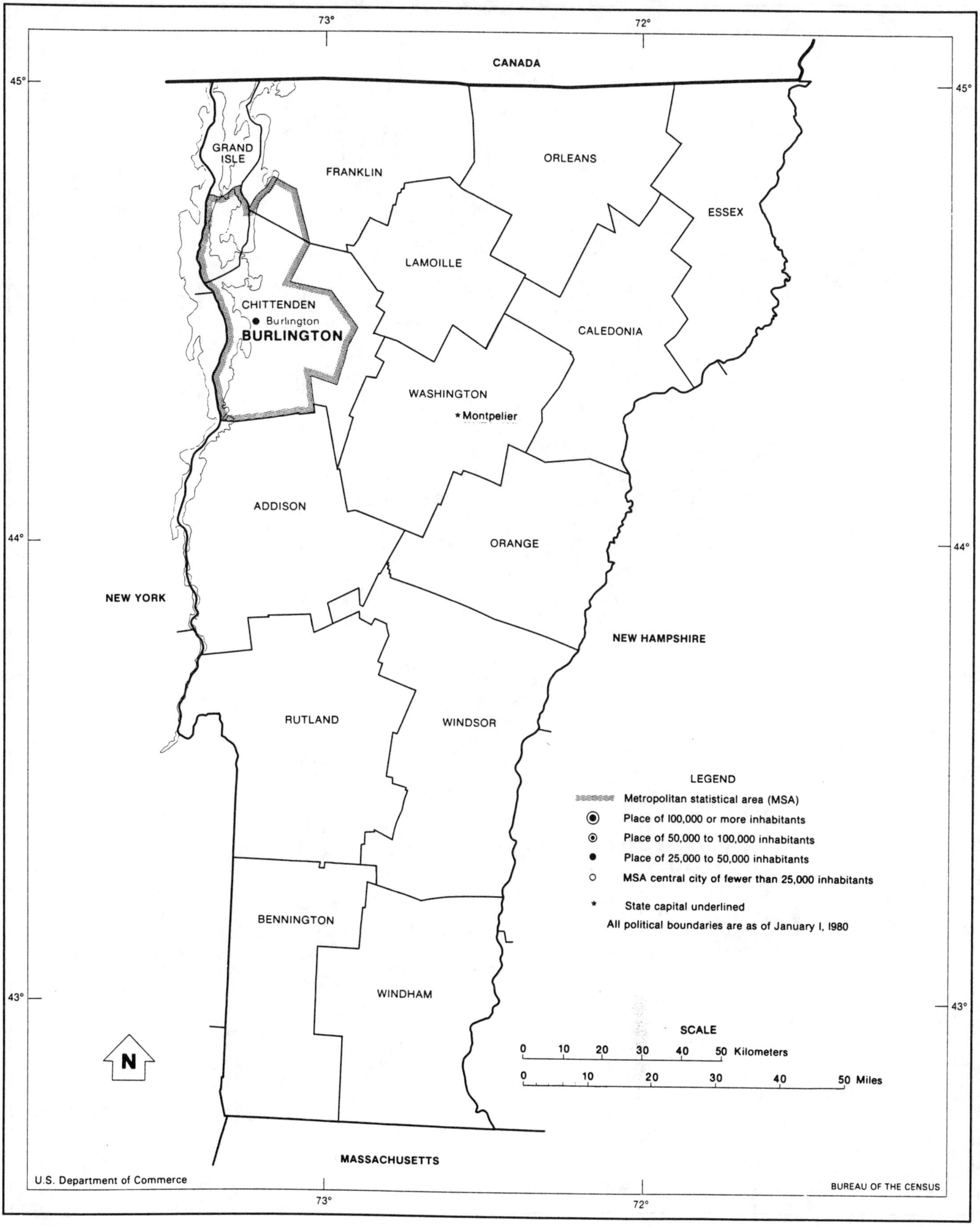

MSA boundaries are as defined on June 30, 1983

VIRGINIA - Metropolitan Statistical Areas, Counties, Independent Cities, and Other Selected Places

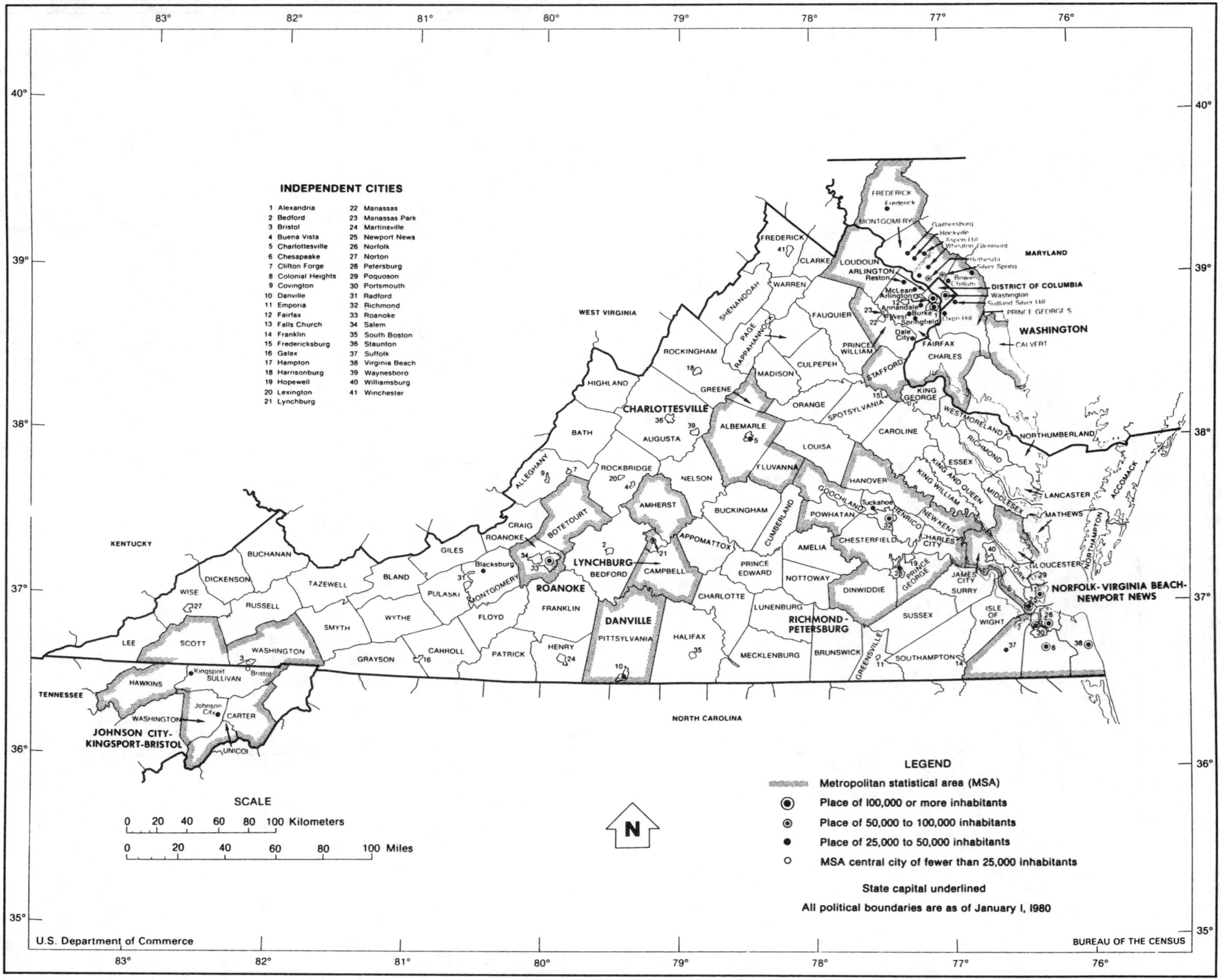

MSA boundaries are as defined on June 30, 1983

WASHINGTON - Consolidated Metropolitan Statistical Areas, Primary Metropolitan Statistical Areas, Metropolitan Statistical Areas, Counties, and Selected Places

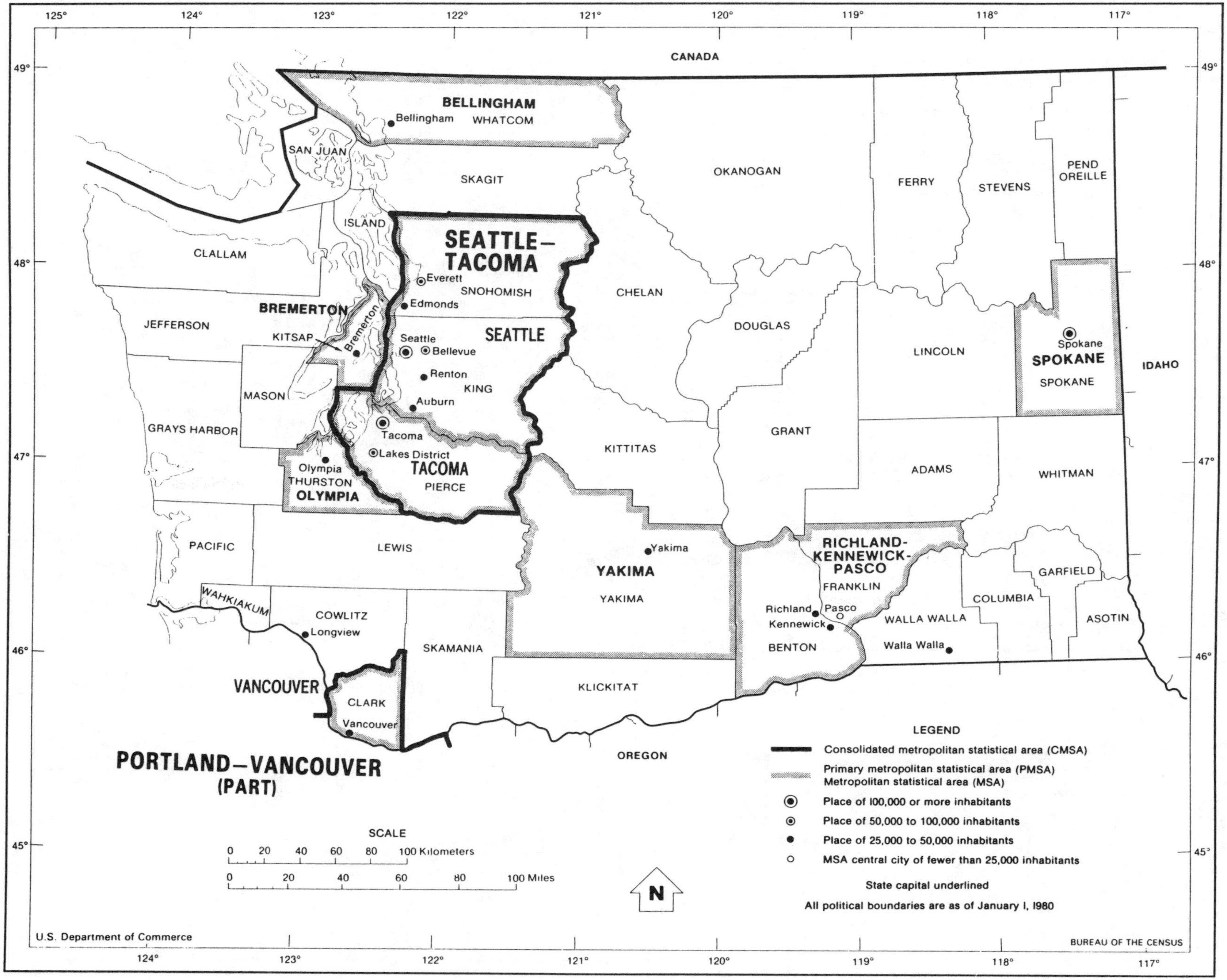

CMSA, PMSA, and MSA boundaries are as defined on June 30, 1983

WEST VIRGINIA - Metropolitan Statistical Areas, Counties, and Selected Places

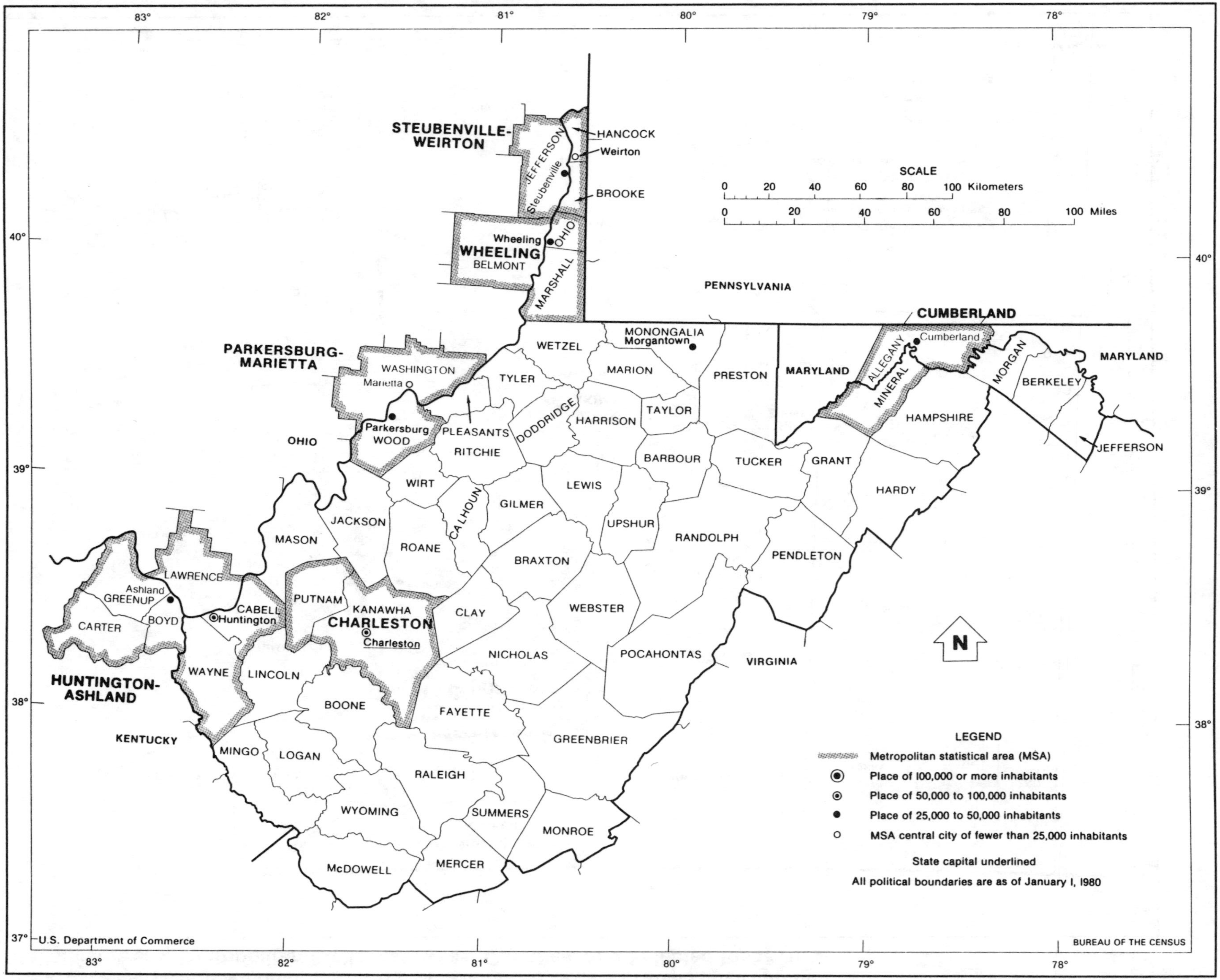

MSA boundaries are as defined on June 30, 1983

WISCONSIN - Consolidated Metropolitan Statistical Areas, Primary Metropolitan Statistical Areas, Metropolitan Statistical Areas, Counties, and Selected Places

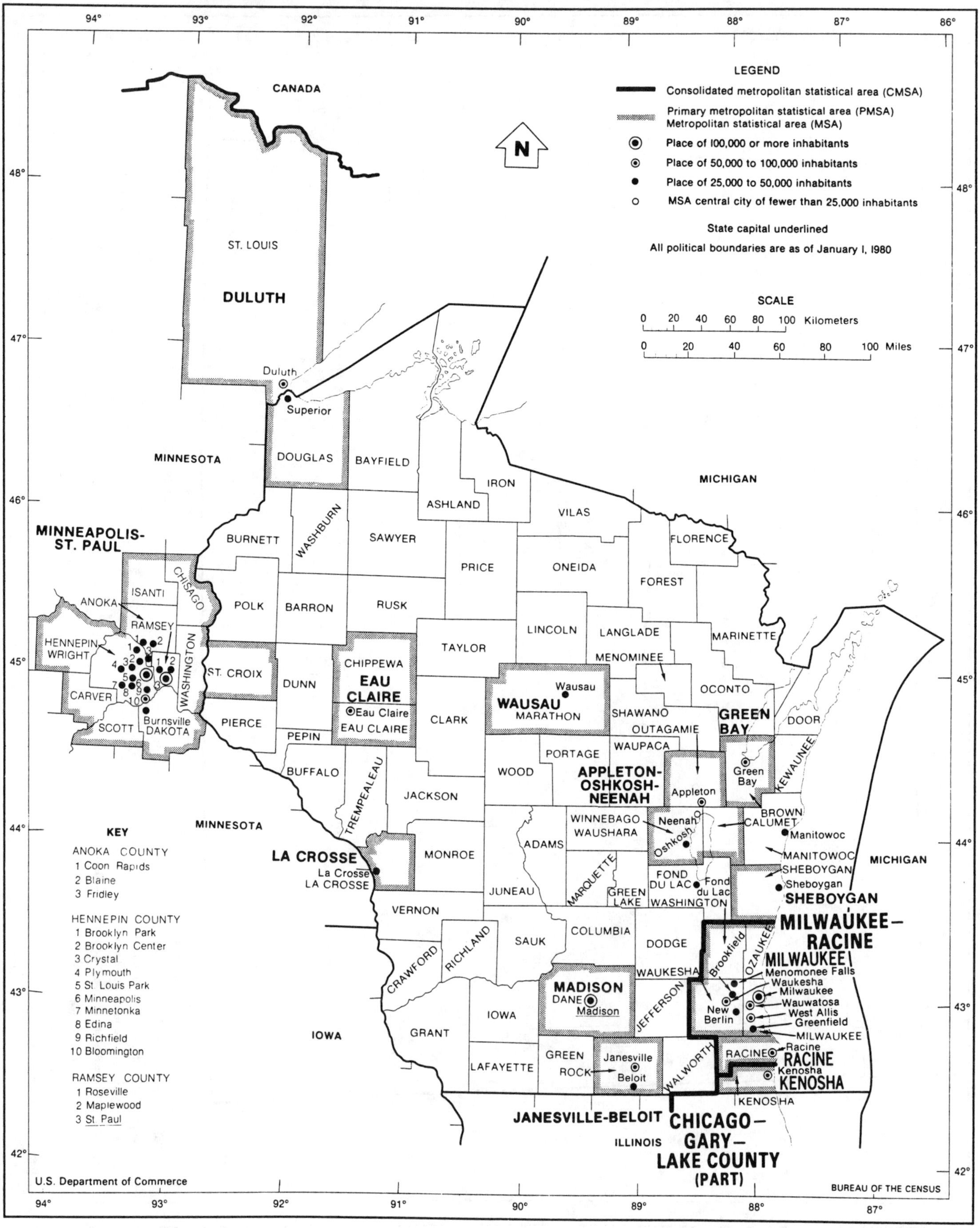

CMSA, PMSA, and MSA boundaries are as defined on June 30, 1983

WYOMING - Metropolitan Statistical Area, Counties, and Selected Places

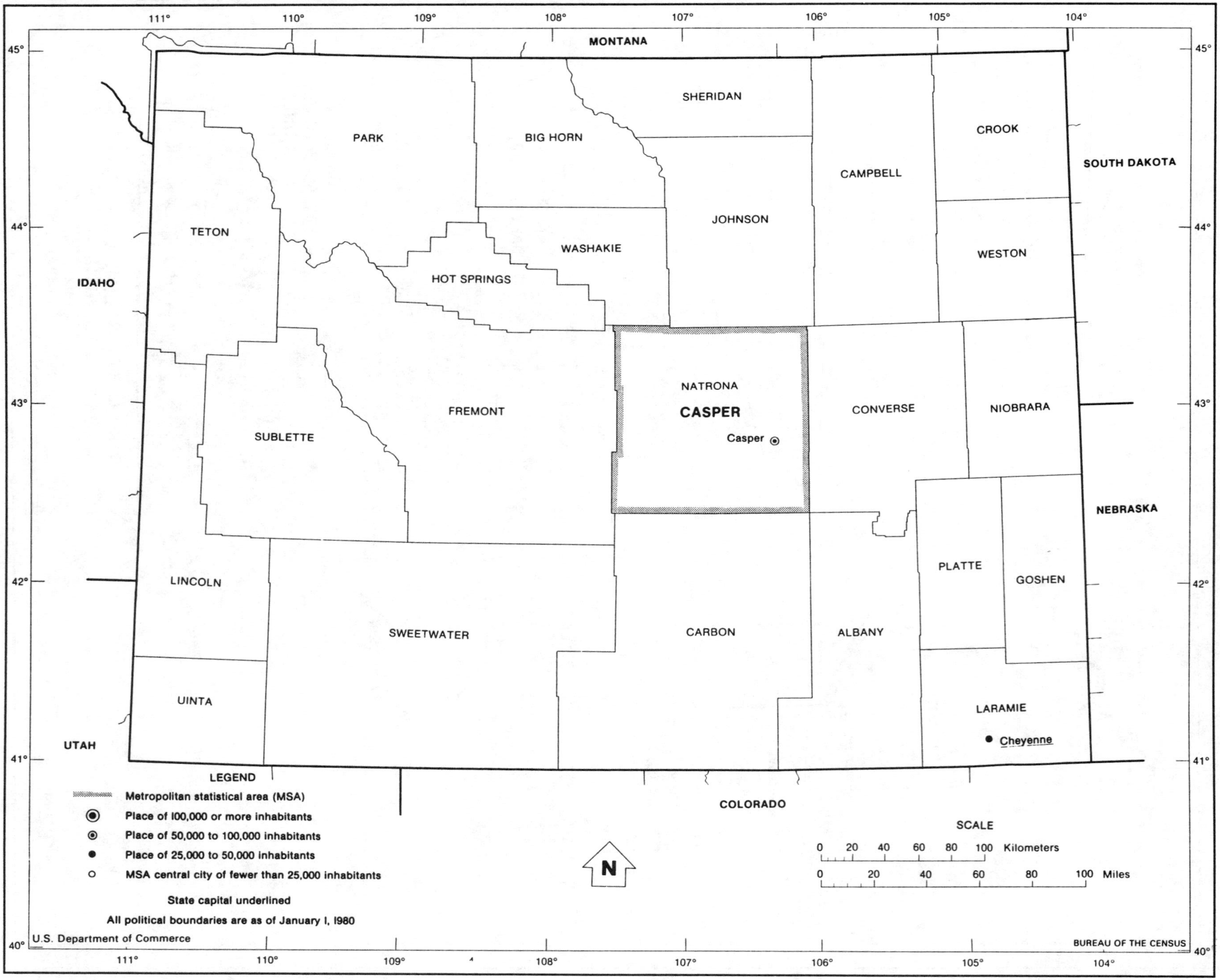

MSA boundaries are as defined on June 30, 1983

APPENDIX D
SOURCE NOTES AND EXPLANATIONS

TABLES A AND B—STATES/COUNTIES AND METRO AREAS

Table A presents 202 items for the United States as a whole, each state and the District of Columbia, and each county, county equivalent, and independent city. The counties are presented in alphabetical order within states, which are also presented alphabetically. Independent cities, which are found in Maryland, Missouri, Nevada, and Virginia are placed in alphabetical order at the end of the list of counties for those states.

Table B presents much of the same data for metropolitan areas. There are 186 items for each of the 337 metropolitan areas. In cases where particular items are not included in Table B but were included as part of the states and counties table, the corresponding item numbers have been skipped. Therefore, the item numbering for all included data remains consistent between these two tables.

LAND AREA, Items 1 & 4

Source: U.S. Bureau of the Census

Land area measurements are shown to the nearest square kilometer. Land area includes dry land and land temporarily or partially covered by water, such as marshlands, swamps, and river floodplains.

POPULATION, Items 2 & 3

Source: U.S. Bureau of the Census - 1990 Census of Population and Housing

The population data are derived from the 100 percent count from the 1990 census. The ranks are shown only for counties and independent cities.

POPULATION BY RACE, Items 5-10

Source: U.S. Bureau of the Census - 1990 Census of Population and Housing

Population by race, as defined by the Census Bureau, reflects self-identification by respondents; it does not denote any clear-cut scientific definition of biological stock. In the 1990 census, data were obtained through self-classification.

The white population is defined as persons who indicated their race as white, as well as persons who did not classify themselves in one of the specific race categories listed on the questionnaire but entered a nationality such as Canadian, German, Italian, Lebanese, or Polish.

The black population includes persons who indicated their race as black or Negro, as well as persons who did not classify themselves in one of the specific race categories but reported entries such as Black Puerto Rican, Haitian, Jamaican, Nigerian, or West Indian.

The American Indian, Eskimo, and Aleut population includes persons who indicated their race as Indian (American), Eskimo or Aleut, as well as persons who did not indicate a specific race category but reported the name of an Indian tribe.

The Asian and Pacific Islander population includes persons who indicated their race as Chinese, Filipino, Japanese, Asian Indian, Korean, Vietnamese, Hawaiian, Samoan, and Guamanian, as well as persons who provided write-in entries of such Asian and Pacific Islander groups as Cambodian, Laotian, Pakistani, and Fiji Islander. Also, persons who wrote in an entry indicating one of the specific categories were classified accordingly.

The Hispanic population is based on a complete-count question that asked respondents to identify whether they were of Spanish/Hispanic origin. Persons marking any one of the four Spanish categories (i.e., Mexican, Puerto Rican, Cuban, or other Spanish) are collectively referred to as "Hispanic." Hispanic is not a race category; Hispanic persons may be of any race.

AGE, Items 11-19

Source: U.S. Bureau of the Census - 1990 Census of Population and Housing

Age derived from the census (1990) is classified as age at last birthday (i.e., number of completed years from birth to April 1) and is based on replies to a question on month and year of birth. The percent figures are derived by dividing the sum of persons in a specified age group by the total population of a given geographic area. Data on age are based on complete counts of resident population.

POPULATION—PERCENT FEMALE, Item 20

Source: U.S. Bureau of the Census - 1990 Census of Population and Housing

The female population of a geographic area is a percent of the total population of the area.

POPULATION—COMPONENTS OF CHANGE, Items 21-29

Source: U.S. Bureau of the Census

Data on components of change cover an area's population for a specified number of years. Net migration represents the difference between the number of persons moving into a particular area and the number of persons moving away from the area. A positive figure indicates net immigration to the area; a negative figure indicates net outmigration from the area. Another measure, natural increase, is the difference between the number of births and deaths in a particular area.

HOUSEHOLDS, Items 30-34

Source: U.S. Bureau of the Census - 1990 Census of Population and Housing

A household consists of persons occupying a single housing unit. A housing unit is a house, an apartment, a group of rooms, or a single room occupied as separate living quarters. The occupants may be a single family, one person living alone, two or more families living together, or any other group of related or unrelated persons who share a housing unit. The number of households is the same as the number of year-round occupied housing units.

A family household consists of two or more persons, including the householder, who are related by birth, marriage, or adoption and who live together as one household; all such persons are considered as members of one family.

The measure of persons per household is obtained by dividing the number of persons in households by the number of households or householders. The category "Female family householder" includes only female-headed family households with no spouse present.

VITAL STATISTICS, Items 35-45

Source: U.S. National Center for Health Statistics

The registration of births, deaths, fetal deaths, and other vital events in the United States is primarily a State and local government function. The civil laws of every State provide for a continuous and permanent birth and death registration system.

Through the National Vital Statistics System, the National Center for Health Statistics (NCHS) collects and publishes data on births and deaths in the United States. The Division of Vital Statistics obtains information on births and deaths from the registration offices of all States, New York City, and the District of Columbia.

In most areas, practically all births and deaths are registered. The most recent test of the completeness of birth registration, conducted on a sample of births from 1964 to 1968, showed that 99.3 percent of all births in the United States during that period were registered. No comparable information is available for deaths, but it is generally believed that death registration in the United States is at least as complete as birth registration.

Birth and death statistics are limited to events occurring during the year. The data are by place of residence and exclude events occurring to nonresidents of the United States. Births or deaths that occur outside the United States are excluded.

Low birth weight is defined as infants weighing less than 2500 grams (5.5 pounds), at birth.

Birth and death rates represent the number of births and deaths per 1,000 resident population enumerated as of April 1 for decennial census years and estimated as of July 1 for other years.

Figures for infant deaths include deaths of children under 1 year of age; they exclude fetal deaths. The infant death rate is per 1,000 live births.

Marriage and divorce statistics are based on complete counts of events obtained from the registration offices of all States, New York City, and the District of Columbia.

State and local officials annually provide complete counts of marriages and divorces by county of occurrence and marriages by month of occurrence. From these counts, marriage and divorce totals are derived and rates computed for each Metropolitan Statistical Area (MSA) and its component counties.

Marriage and divorce statistics are limited to events occurring in the specified area during the year and include events occurring to nonresidents of the United States. Marriages or divorces that occur outside the United States are excluded. Annulments are included in the divorce statistics.

The marriage and divorce rates are based on resident population estimated as of July 1, or as of April 1 for decennial census years.

HEALTH PROFESSIONALS, Items 46 & 47

Source: American Medical Association - Data found in the U.S. Public Health Service's Area Resource File

The number of physicians represents the distribution of non-Federal physicians with known addresses who are professionally active in the United States. The source file includes information on every physician in the country. The file includes information on members and nonmembers of the AMA. It also includes graduates of foreign medical schools who are in the United States and meet U.S. education standards for primary recognition as physicians. Thus, all physicians comprising the total manpower pool are included on the file. However, the data do not include Federal physicians, non-Federal physicians who are temporarily in foreign locations, and physicians not classified by type of professional activity.

Alaska is divided into four judicial divisions; therefore, data are not available for counties in Alaska.

HOSPITALS, Items 48-50

Source: American Hospital Association - Data found in the Public Health Service's Area Resource File

Statistics for hospitals were compiled by the American Hospital Association from surveys of all hospitals in the United States and its outlying areas. They include unregistered hospitals, as well as those registered by the American Hospital Association. Hospitals were asked to report data for a full year ending September 30.

A hospital is defined as a facility with at least six beds that is licensed by the state as a hospital or that is operated as a hospital by a federal or state agency and is therefore not subject to state or local licensing laws. The data cover hospitals of all types and are fairly complete for general, tuberculosis, mental, and federal government hospitals. Institutions and services commonly referred to as convalescent and resting homes, nursing homes, infirmaries, old age homes, and sanatoriums are excluded almost entirely.

Hospital beds comprise beds, cribs, and pediatric bassinets regularly maintained (set up and staffed for use) for inpatients during the 12-month period. They exclude newborn infant bassinets. Rates are for 100,000 persons estimated as of July 1 of the year shown.

NURSING HOMES, Items 51 & 52

Source: U.S. National Center for Health Statistics

Items for nursing homes cover nursing homes as defined in the National Master Facility Inventory (NMFI), a comprehensive file of inpatient health facilities in the United States. To be included in NMFI, nursing and related care homes must have at least three inpatient beds. The minimum standards and regulations for nursing homes vary among the states so that no uniform definition is possible. Residential community care facilities in California, adult foster care homes in Michigan, adult congregate living facilities in California and Florida, and family care homes in Kentucky are not included.

CRIME, Items 53-55

Source: U.S. Federal Bureau of Investigation - Uniform Crime Reports

Through the voluntary contribution of crime statistics by law enforcement agencies across the United States, the Uniform Crime Reporting (UCR) Program provides periodic assessments of crime in the nation as measured by offenses coming to the attention of the law enforcement community. The Committee on Uniform Crime Records of the International Association of Chiefs of Police initiated this voluntary national data-collection effort in 1930. UCR Program contributors compile and submit their crime data by one of two means - either directly to the FBI or through the state UCR Programs.

Seven offenses, because of their seriousness, frequency of occurrence, and likelihood of being reported to police, were initially selected to serve as an index for evaluating fluctuations in the volume of crime. These serious crimes were murder and nonnegligent manslaughter, forcible rape, robbery, aggravated assault, burglary, larceny-theft, and motor vehicle theft. By congressional mandate, arson was added as the eighth index offense in 1979. Local totals do not include arson.

Violent offenses include four crime categories: (1) Murder and non-negligent manslaughter, as defined in the UCR Program, is the willful (non-negligent) killing of one human being by another. This offense excludes deaths caused by negligence, suicide or accident; justifiable homicides; and attempts to murder or assaults to murder. (2) Forcible rape is the carnal knowledge of a female forcibly and against her will. Assaults or attempts to commit rape by force or threat of force are also included; however, statutory rape (without force) and other sex offenses are excluded. (3) Robbery is the taking or attempting to take anything of value from the care, custody, or control of a person or persons by force or threat of force or violence and/or by putting the victim in fear. (4) Aggravated assault is an unlawful attack by one person upon another for the purpose of inflicting severe or aggravated bodily injury. This type of assault is usually accompanied by the use of a weapon or by means likely to produce death or great bodily harm. Attempts are included since an injury does not necessarily have to result when a gun, knife, or other weapon is used, which could and probably would result in a serious personal injury if the crime were successfully completed.

Rates are based on resident population enumerated as of April 1 for decennial census years and estimated as of July 1 for other years.

Data for serious crime have not been adjusted for underreporting. This may affect comparability between geographic areas or over time.

EDUCATION—PUBLIC SCHOOL ENROLLMENT, Items 56 & 57

Source: U.S. Department of Education, National Center for Education Statistics

These figures represent enrollment at all levels taught in a public school system, from prekindergarten through grade 12. However, grades 13 and 14 do appear in a few school systems containing vocational education courses, and many operating school systems offer postgraduate courses. In addition, school system enrollment figures are tabulated on the basis of the county in which the superintendent's office is located, although some parts of the system may be in other counties.

EDUCATION—ATTAINMENT, Items 58 & 59

Source: U.S. Bureau of the Census - 1980 Census of Population and Housing

Data for education in 1980 were obtained from a sample of the population as part of the 1980 Census of Population and Housing, conducted by the Bureau of the Census. Statistics for years of school completed are shown for persons 25 years old and over. The data were derived from two questions on the 1980 census questionnaire, one identifying the highest grade attended in regular school and the other asking whether the respondent finished that grade. Persons who passed a high school equivalency examination were marked "12" under the highest grade completed (if they had not completed or were not enrolled in a higher grade). Schooling received in foreign schools is reported as the equivalent grade or years in the regular American school system.

LOCAL GOVERNMENT EDUCATION EXPENDITURES, Items 60 & 61

Source: U.S. Bureau of the Census - 1982 Census of Governments

Expenditures for education represent support of schools and other educational facilities and services. Local elementary and secondary education expenditure includes all expenditure for local school systems except for interest, duplicative intergovernmental payments, and retirement benefits paid to former employees.

SOCIAL SECURITY, Items 62-64

Source: U.S. Social Security Administration

The Old-age, Survivors, and Disability Insurance Programs (OASDI) provide monthly benefits for retired and disabled workers and their dependents and to survivors of insured workers. To be eligible for benefits, a worker must have had a specified period of employment in which OASDI taxes were paid. A worker becomes eligible for full retirement benefits at age 65, although reduced benefits may be obtained up to three years earlier. Survivor benefits are payable to dependents of deceased insured workers. Disability benefits are payable to an insured worker under age 65 with a prolonged disability and to that person's dependents on the same basis as dependents of a retired worker. Also, disability benefits are payable at age 50 to the disabled widow or widower of a deceased worker who was fully insured at the time of death. A lump-sum benefit is also payable on the death of an insured worker.

Total figures represent the number of, or payments to, insured, retired, or disabled workers; the spouses, dependents, and survivors of insured persons.

SUPPLEMENTAL SECURITY INCOME, Item 65

Source: U.S. Social Security Administration

Under the direction of the Social Security Administration, the Supplemental Security Income (SSI) program provides cash payments in accordance with nationwide eligibility requirements to persons with limited income and resources who are aged, blind, or disabled. Under the SSI program, each person living in his or her own household is provided a cash payment from the federal government that is sufficient, when added to the person's countable income (the total gross money income of an individual, less certain exclusion), to bring the total monthly income up to a specified level (the federal benefit rate). If the individual or couple is living in another household, the guaranteed level is reduced by one-third.

An aged person is defined as an individual who is 65 years old or over. A blind person is anyone with vision of 20/200 or less with the use of a corrective lens in the better eye, or anyone with tunnel vision of 20 degrees or less. The disabled classification refers to any person unable to engage in any substantial gainful activity by reason of any medically determinable physical or mental impairment expected to result in death or that has lasted or can be expected to last for a continuous period of at least 12 months. For a child under 18 years, eligibility is based on disability or severity comparable with that of an adult, since the criterion of "substantial gainful activity" is inapplicable for children.

The data cover persons with federal SSI payments and/or federally administered state supplementation. States have the option to supplement the federal SSI payments for all or selected categories of recipients. The data are for persons with federal SSI payments in the following states: Alabama, Alaska, Arizona, Colorado, Connecticut, Idaho, Illinois, Indiana, Kentucky, Minnesota, Missouri, Nebraska, New Hampshire, New Mexico, North Carolina, North Dakota, Oklahoma, Oregon, South Carolina, Utah, Virginia, West Virginia (1980 only), and Wyoming; these States have State-administered supplementation. Data for Texas and West Virginia (1984 only) cover federal SSI payments only; no state supplementary payments are made.

MONEY INCOME, Items 66-71

Source: U.S. Bureau of the Census

Total money income is defined by the Bureau of the Census for statistical purposes as the sum of the following: wage or salary income; nonfarm self-employment income; net farm self-employment income; Social Security and railroad retirement income; public assistance income; and all other regularly received income such as interest, dividends, veterans' payments, pensions, unemployment compensation, and alimony. Receipts not counted as income include various "lump sum" payments such as capital gains or inheritances.

The total represents the amount of income received before deductions for personal income taxes, Social Security, bond purchases, union dues, Medicare deductions, etc.

Per capita income is based on resident population enumerated as of April 1 for decennial census years and July 1 for other years.

The constant-dollar figures are based on the annual average Consumer Price Index from the Bureau of Labor Statistics. Constant-dollar figures are estimates representing an effort to remove the effects of income changes from statistical series reported in dollar terms. However, the estimates do not reflect the price and cost-of-living differences that may exist between areas.

Families and persons were classified as below the poverty level if their total family income or unrelated individual income was less than the poverty threshold specified for the applicable family size, age of householder, and number of related children under 18 present. Poverty status is determined for all families (and by implication all family members). For persons not in families, poverty status is determined by their income in relation to the appropriate poverty threshold. Inmates of institutions, persons in military group quarters and college dormitories, and unrelated individuals under age 15 are excluded.

HOUSING, Items 72-77

Source: U.S. Bureau of the Census - 1990 Census of Population and Housing

A housing unit is a house, apartment, mobile home or trailer, group of rooms, or single room occupied or, if vacant, intended for occupancy as separate living quarters. Separate living quarters are those in which the occupants do not live and eat with any other persons in the structure and which have direct access from the outside of the building through a common hall.

The occupants of a housing unit may be a single family, one person living alone, two or more families living together, or any other group of related or unrelated persons who share living arrangements (except as described in the definition for persons "living in group quarters"). For vacant units, the criteria of separateness and direct access are applied to the intended occupants whenever possible. If that information cannot be obtained, the criteria are applied to the previous occupants. Both occupied and vacant housing units are included in the housing inventory, except recreational vehicles, tents, caves, boats, railroad cars, and the like, which are included only if they are occupied as someone's usual place of residence.

A housing unit is classified as occupied if it is the usual place of residence of the person or group of persons living in it at the time of enumeration, or if the occupants are only temporarily absent, e.g., away on vacation. A household consists of all persons who occupy a housing unit as their usual place of residence.

The percent change represents the difference in the number of total housing units in a specified area over the decade 1980-1990.

Median value is the dollar amount that divides the distribution of owner occupied housing units into two equal parts, one half of the units falling below this value and the other half exceeding it. Value is defined as the respondent's estimate of what the house would sell for if for sale. Data are presented for one-family units on less than 10 acres and with no business or medical office on the property.

Median rent is similar to median value; it represents the amount of cash rent a renter pays or the rent asked for vacant units which are being offered. Rent is to be reported only for living quarters, not for any business or other space occupied. Single family houses on lots of 10 or more acres are excluded.

CIVILIAN LABOR FORCE AND UNEMPLOYMENT, Items 78-81

Source: U.S. Bureau of Labor Statistics

Data for the civilian labor force are the product of a federal-state cooperative program in which state employment security agencies prepare labor force and unemployment estimates under concepts, definitions, and technical procedures established by the Bureau of Labor Statistics.

Unemployment data include all persons who did not work during the survey week, made specific efforts to find a job in the prior four weeks, and were available for work during the survey week (except for temporary illness). Persons waiting to be called back to a job from which they had been laid off and those waiting to report to a new job within the next 30 days are included in unemployment figures.

An explanation of the technical procedures used to develop monthly and annual local area labor force estimates appears monthly in the "Explanatory Note" for state and area unemployment data in the Bureau of Labor Statistics periodical "Employment and Earnings."

PRIVATE NONFARM ESTABLISHMENTS, Items 82-91

Source: U.S. Bureau of the Census - County Business Patterns

Data for private nonfarm employment and payroll were obtained from surveys conducted by the Bureau of the Census and Administrative records from the Internal Revenue Service (IRS). The data are reported in U.S. Bureau of the Census, "County Business Patterns."

The following types of employment are excluded from the tables: government employment, self employed persons, farm workers, and domestic service workers. Railroad employment jointly covered by social security and railroad retirement programs, employment on oceanborne vessels, and employment in foreign countries are also excluded.

Annual payroll is the combined amount of wages paid, tips reported, and other compensation, including salaries, vacation allowances, bonuses, commissions, sick leave pay, and the value of payments in-kind (such as free meals and lodging) paid to employees before deductions for Social Security, income tax, insurance, union dues, etc. All forms of compensation are included, whether or not subject to income tax or Federal Insurance Contributions Act tax, with the exception of annuities, third-party sick pay, and supplemental unemployment compensation benefits (even if income tax was withheld). For corporations, total annual payroll includes compensation paid to officers and executives; for unincorporated businesses, it does not include profit or other compensation of proprietors or partners. For single-establishment firms, annual payroll is the sum of the four quarters of total compensation. Estimating techniques based on the reporting patterns of eight quarters of administrative payroll are used to obtain payroll for those single-establishment firms' employers determined to be nonrespondents.

PERSONAL INCOME, Items 92-99

Source: U.S. Bureau of Economic Analysis

Total personal income is the current income received by residents of an area from all sources. It is measured before deductions of income and other personal taxes but after deduction of personal contributions for Social Security, government retirement, and other social insurance programs. It consists of wage and salary disbursements (covering all employee earnings, including executive salaries, bonuses, commissions, payments-in-kind, incentive payments, and tips), various types of supplementary earnings termed "other labor income", proprietors' income, rental income of persons, dividends, personal interest income, and government and business transfer payments.

Dividends are cash payments by for-profit corporations to stockholders who are U.S. residents. Interest is the monetary and imputed interest income of persons from all sources. Rent is the monetary income of persons from the rental of real property, except the income of persons primarily engaged in the real estate business, the imputed net rental income of owner-occupants of nonfarm dwellings, and the royalties received by persons.

Transfer payments are income for which services are not currently rendered. They consist of both government and business transfer payments. Government transfer payments include payments under the following programs: Federal Old-age, Survivors, Disability, and Health Insurance; unemployment insurance, railroad and government retirement; federal and state government-insured workers' compensation; veterans benefits, including veterans life insurance; food stamps; black lung; Supplemental Security Income; and Aid to Families with Dependent Children. Government payments to nonprofit institutions, other than for work under research and development contracts, are also included. The principal business transfers are corporate gifts to nonprofit institutions and consumer bad debts.

Per capita personal income is based on resident population enumerated as of April 1 for decennial census years and estimated as of July 1 for other years.

EARNINGS, Items 100-108

Source: U.S. Bureau of Economic Analysis

Earnings cover wage and salary disbursements, other labor income, and proprietors' income. Wage and salary income consists of monetary remuneration of employees, including corporate officers; commissions, tips, and bonuses; and receipts in-kind that represent income to the recipients. Retroactive wages are counted when paid rather than when earned. Other labor income includes employer contributions to private pension and welfare funds, employers' payments for privately administered workers' compensation insurance, and directors' fees. Proprietors' income is the monetary income and income in-kind of proprietorships and partnerships, including the independent professions, and of tax-exempt cooperatives.

Data for earnings obtained from the Bureau of Economic Analysis (BEA) are based on place of work. In computing personal income, BEA makes an "adjustment for residence" to earnings based on commuting patterns so that personal income is presented on a place of residence basis.

Farm earnings include the income of farm workers (wages and salaries and other labor income) and farm proprietors. Farm proprietors' income includes only the income of sole proprietorships and partnerships.

Farm earning estimates are benchmarked to data collected in the Census of Agriculture and the revised U.S. Department of Agriculture State totals of income and expense items.

Goods related industries include mining, construction, and manufacturing. Service-related and other includes private sector earnings in agricultural services, forestry and fisheries; transportation and public utilities; wholesale trade; retail trade; finance, insurance, and real estate; and services. Government earnings include all levels of government.

AGRICULTURE, Items 109-126

Source: U.S. Bureau of the Census - 1987 Census of Agriculture

The Bureau of the Census has taken a census of agriculture every ten years from 1840 to 1920 and roughly every five years from 1925 to 1987. Over time, the definition of a farm has varied. For the 1987 census, a farm is defined as any place from which $1,000 or more of agricultural products were sold or normally would have been sold during the census year.

All farms are classified by size and according to the total land area in each operation.

The term "operator" refers to a person who operates a farm, either doing the work or making day-to-day decisions about such things as planting, harvesting, feeding, marketing, etc. The operator may be the owner, a member of the owner's household, a salaried manager, a tenant, a renter, or a sharecropper. For partnerships, only one partner is counted as an operator. For census purposes, the number of operators is the same as the number of farms.

The acreage designated as "land in farms" consists primarily of agricultural land used for crops, pasture, or grazing. It also includes woodland and wasteland not actually under cultivation or used for pasture or grazing, provided it was part of the farm operator's total operation.

Land in farms is an operating-unit concept and includes land owned and operated, as well as land rented from others. Land used rent free was to be reported as land rented from others. All land in Indian reservations used for growing crops or grazing livestock was to be included as land in farms.

With few exceptions, the land in each farm was tabulated as being in the operator's principal county. The principal county was defined as the one where the largest value of agricultural products was raised or produced. It was usually the county containing all or the largest proportion of the land in the farm. For a limited number of Western States, this procedure resulted in the allocation of more land in farms to a county than the total land area of the county.

Irrigated land covers any land in farms to which water was artificially applied in the census year. Land irrigated prior to, but not in the census year is not included. Irrigation may have been used for producing a harvested crop, for pasture or grazing lands, for cultivated summer fallow, or for land planted to a crop intended for future harvest. Land flooded during high-water periods was included as irrigation only if water was diverted to agricultural lands by dams, canals, or other works.

Cropland consists of land from which crops were harvested and land that could have been used for crops without additional improvements. This includes land in nonbearing orchards and vineyards, land from which any hay was cut, land on which crops failed, idle or fallow land, and land used for grazing purposes.

Respondents were asked to report their estimate of the current market value of land and buildings owned, rented, or leased from others, and rented and leased to others. Market value refers to the respondent's estimate of what the land and buildings would sell for under current market conditions. If the value of land and buildings was not reported, it was estimated during processing by using the average value of land and buildings from similar farms in the same geographic area.

The source reports give counts of farms by value of sales of various sales-size groups. The value of farm products sold by farms represent the gross market value before taxes and production expenses of all agricultural products sold or removed from the place in 1987, regardless of who received the payment. It includes sales by the operator as well as the value of any share received by partners, landlords, contractors, and others associated with the operation. It represents the sum of all crops, including nursery products sold and livestock or poultry and their products sold. It includes income from farm-related sources such as customwork or agricultural service, income from nonfarm sources, and sales of forest products from farms and ranches. The value of agricultural products sold was collected from all operators. Where the operator failed to report a value of sales, estimates were made based on the amount of crops harvested or the number of livestock or poultry sold. Extensive estimation was required for farmers growing crops and livestock under contract.

The value of crops sold in 1987 does not necessarily represent the sales from crops harvested that year. The data include sales from crops produced in earlier years and exclude some crops produced in 1987 but held in storage and not sold in the Census year. For crops sold through a co-op that made payments in several installments, only the total value received in the Census year was to be reported. Livestock and livestock products include dairy products but exclude poultry.

MANUFACTURES, Items 127-138

Source: U.S. Bureau of the Census - 1987 Census of Manufactures

The Census of Manufactures is conducted every five years as part of the economic censuses. The census is conducted on an establishment basis. An establishment is a single physical location at which business is conducted or where services or industrial operations are performed. It is not necessarily identical with the company or enterprise, which may consist of one or more establishments. The total establishment count should be viewed as an approximation rather than a precise measurement.

The "all employees" number is the average number of production workers plus the number of other employees in mid-March. Included are all persons on paid sick leave, paid holidays, and paid vacations during the pay period. Officers of corporations are included as employees; proprietors and partners of unincorporated firms are excluded.

Payroll figures include the gross annual earnings of all employees on the payroll of operating manufacturing establishments. The definition, which is the same as the one used for calculating the Federal withholding tax, includes all forms of compensation, such as salaries, wages, commissions, dismissal pay, all bonuses, vacation and sick leave pay, and compensation-in-kind, prior to such deductions as employees' Social Security contributions, withholding taxes, group insurance, union dues, and savings bonds. The total includes salaries of officers of corporations but excludes payments to proprietors or partners of unincorporated concerns. Also excluded are payments to members of the Armed Forces and to pensioners carried on the active payroll of manufacturing establishments.

Production workers include workers (up through the line-supervisor level) engaged in fabricating, processing, assembling, inspecting, receiving, storing, handling, packing, warehousing, shipping (but not delivering), maintenance, repair, janitorial and guard services, product development, auxiliary production for plant's own use (e.g., power plant), recordkeeping, and other services closely associated with these production operations. Employees above the working supervisor level are excluded.

The number of production workers is the average for the payroll periods including the 12th of March, May, August, and November. Not included in this classification are all other employees, defined as nonproduction employees, including those engaged in factory supervision above the line-supervisor level.

Production worker hours cover hours worked or paid for at the plant, including actual overtime hours (not straight-time-equivalent hours). The data exclude hours paid for vacations, holidays, or sick leave. Production wages represent all compensation paid to production workers.

Value added by manufacture is derived by subtracting the cost of materials, supplies, containers, fuel, purchased electricity, and contract work from the value of shipments (products manufactured plus receipts for services rendered). The result of this calculation is adjusted by the addition of value added by merchandising operations (i.e., the difference between the sales value and cost of merchandise sold without further manufacture, processing or assembly) plus the net change in finished goods and work in process between the beginning- and end-of-year inventories.

Value of shipments covers the received or receivable net selling values, free on board plant (exclusive of freight charges and taxes), of all products shipped, both primary and secondary, as well as miscellaneous receipts, such as receipts for contract work performed for others, installation and repair, sales of scrap, and sales of products bought and resold without further processing. Included are all items made by or for the establishment from materials owned by it, whether sold, transferred to other plants of the same company, or shipped on consignment. The net selling value of products made in one plant on a contract basis from materials owned by another was reported by the plant providing the materials. In the case of multi-unit companies, the manufacturer was requested to report the value of products transferred to other establishments of the same company at full economic or commercial value, including not only the direct costs of production, but also a reasonable proportion of "all other costs" (including company overhead) and profit.

The aggregate of the value of shipments figure for industry groups and for all manufacturing industries includes large amounts of duplication, since the products of some industries are used as materials by others. Estimates as to the overall extent of this duplication indicate that the value of manufactured products exclusive of such duplication (the value of finished manufactures) tend to approximate two-thirds of the total value of products reported in the census of manufactures.

Data on new capital expenditures are also covered in the census. For establishments in operation and establishments under construction but not yet in operation in 1987, manufacturers were asked to report their new expenditures for (1) permanent additions and major alterations to manufacturing establishments and (2) new machinery and equipment used for replacement and additions to plant capacity if they were of the type for which depreciation accounts were ordinarily maintained. The totals for new expenditures exclude that portion of expenditures leased from nonmanufacturing concerns, new facilities owned by the federal government but operated under contract by private companies, and plant and equipment furnished to the manufacturer by communities and nonprofit organizations. Also excluded are expenditures for used plant and equipment (although reported in the census), expenditures for land, and cost of maintenance and repairs charged as current operating expenses.

BUILDING PERMITS, Items 139-146

Source: U.S. Bureau of the Census - Building Permits Survey

Figures represent private construction authorized by building permits in approximately 17,000 places in the United States. Valuation represents the cost of construction as recorded on the building permit. This figure usually excludes the cost of on-site and off-site development and improvements and the cost of heating, plumbing, electrical and elevator installations.

County, state, and U.S. totals were obtained by summing the data for permit issuing places within each jurisdiction. Thus, these totals are limited to permits issued in the 17,000 place universe covered by the Census Bureau and may not include all permits issued within the county. If a county does not contain permit-issuing places in the 17,000 place universe, an "NA" is shown. Counties with permit-issuing places that issued no permits during the period are represented by a "0".

Nonresidential construction includes amusement and recreational buildings; churches and other religious buildings; industrial buildings; office, bank and professional buildings; public works and utilities buildings; schools and other educational buildings; stores and other mercantile buildings; other nonresidential buildings, such as sheds, boathouses, barns, silos, etc.; and structures other than buildings, such as outdoor swimming pools, parking lots, patios, drive-in theatres, stadiums, grandstands, etc.

Industrial buildings include plants that produce, process, or assemble goods and materials together with any affiliated buildings such as warehouses, garages, administration buildings, etc.

Office, bank, and professional buildings include office, bank and professional buildings used primarily as offices.

Stores and other mercantile buildings include buildings used in buying, selling, distributing, or storing of merchandise and materials, or performing customer services. Any affiliated buildings are also included.

Residential building permits include buildings with any number of housing units. Hotels, apartment hotels, dormitories, fraternity houses and other nonhousekeeping residential buildings are not included in the residential detail but are included in the total (item 139).

Alterations and additions to residential buildings includes all residential housekeeping buildings and the conversion of nonresidential and nonhousekeeping buildings to residential buildings.

WHOLESALE TRADE, Items 147-150

Source: U.S. Bureau of the Census - 1987 Census of Wholesale Trade

The 1987 Census of Wholesale Trade included all establishments with one or more employees primarily engaged in selling merchandise to retailers; to industrial, commercial, institutional, farm, or professional users; or to other wholesalers; or acting as agents or brokers in buying merchandise for, or selling merchandise to, such persons or companies. The census included wholesale liquor warehouses operated by state and local governments. Excluded were warehouses and other units that serviced or were auxiliary to wholesale establishments within the same organization.

An establishment is a single physical location at which business is conducted. It is not necessarily identical with a company or enterprise, which may consist of one or more establishments. The count of establishments represents the number in business at the end of the year.

Sales figures represent sales of all establishments in business at any time during 1987. Sales include merchandise sold for cash or credit at wholesale and retail by establishments primarily engaged in wholesale trade; receipts from rental or leasing of vehicles, equipment, instruments, tools, etc.; receipts for delivery, installation, maintenance, repair, alteration, storage, and other services; and gasoline, liquor, tobacco, and other excise taxes that are paid by the manufacturer and passed on to the wholesaler. Sales figures do not include wholesale sales made by manufacturers, retailers, service establishments, or other businesses whose primary activity is other than the sales of merchandise at wholesale (e.g., service receipts, retail sales, etc.) by establishments primarily engaged in wholesale trade.

Sales are net after deductions for refunds and allowances for merchandise returned by customers. Trade-in allowances are not deducted from total sales. Total sales do not include carrying or other credit charges; sales (or other) taxes collected from customers and forwarded to taxing authorities; and nonoperating income from such sources as investments, rental or sale of real estate, etc.

Paid employees comprise all employees, including salaried officers and executives of corporations, who were on the payroll in the pay period including March 12, 1987. Included are employees on paid sick leave, paid holidays, and paid vacations. Proprietors and partners of unincorporated businesses are not included.

Annual payroll includes all forms of compensation, such as salaries, wages, commissions, bonuses, vacation allowances, sick-leave pay, and the value of payments in-kind (e.g., free meals and lodgings) paid during the year to all employees. For corporations, it includes amounts paid to officers and executives; for unincorporated businesses, it does not include profit or other compensation of proprietors or partners. Payroll is reported before deductions for Social Security, income tax, insurance, union dues, etc.

RETAIL TRADE, Items 151-162

Source: U.S. Bureau of the Census - 1987 Census of Retail Trade

The 1987 Census of Retail Trade included all establishments primarily engaged in selling merchandise for personal or household consumption and rendering services incidental to the sale of goods. The census excluded governmental organizations classified in the covered industries except for liquor stores operated by state and local governments. Data for direct sellers with no paid employees and post exchange, ship stores, and similar establishments operated on military posts by agencies of the federal government are not included. Establishments that are auxiliary (e.g., warehouses or other establishments with the primary function of providing a service) to retail establishments within the same organization are not included.

Census of retail trade figures represent a summary of reports for individual establishments rather than companies. For cases where a census report was received, separate information was obtained for each location where business was conducted. Each retail establishment was tabulated according to the physical location at which the business was conducted. When administrative records of other federal agencies were used instead of a census report, no information was available on the number of locations operated.

When two or more activities were carried on at a single location under a single ownership, all activities generally were grouped together as a single establishment. The entire establishment was classified on the basis of its major activity, and all data for it were included in that classification. However, when distinct and separate economic activities (for which different industry classification codes were appropriate) were conducted under the same ownership at a single location, and when conditions prescribed by the SIC Manual for recognizing the existence of more than one establishment were met, separate establishment reports for each of the different activities were obtained in the census.

Sales figures represent sales of all establishments in business at any time during 1987. Sales include merchandise sold for cash or credit at retail and wholesale by establishments primarily engaged in retail trade; amounts received from customers for equipment, instruments, tools, etc.; receipts for delivery, installation, maintenance, repair, alteration, storage, and other services; and gasoline, liquor, tobacco, and other excise taxes that are paid by the manufacturer or wholesaler and passed on to the retailer.

Sales are net after deduction for refunds and allowances for merchandise returned by customers. Trade-in allowances are not deducted from total sales. Total sales do not include carrying or other credit charges; sales (or other) taxes collected from customers and forwarded to taxing authorities, commissions from vending machine operators; and nonoperating income from such sources as investments, rental or sale of real estate, etc.

Sales do not include retail sales made by manufacturers, wholesalers, service establishments, or other businesses whose primary activity is other than retail trade.

Establishments with payroll are those establishments that had some paid employment during the year.

General merchandise group stores include retail stores that sell a number of lines of merchandise, such as dry goods, apparel and accessories, furniture and home furnishings, small wares, hardware, and food. The stores included in this group are known as department stores, variety stores, general merchandise stores, general stores, etc. Department stores are establishments normally employing 25 or more people, having sales of apparel and goods combined amounting to 20 percent or more of the total sales, and selling each of the following lines of merchandise: (1) furniture, home furnishings, appliances, and radio and TV sets; (2) a general line of apparel for the family; and (3) household linens and dry goods. To qualify as a department store, sales of each line must be less than 80 percent of total store sales. An establishment with total sales of $10 million or more is classified as a department store even if sales of one merchandise line exceed the maximum percent of total sales, provided that the combined sales of the other two groups are $1 million or more.

Food stores are establishments primarily engaged in selling food for home preparation and consumption. They include grocery stores; meat and fish (seafood) markets; fruit stores and vegetable markets; candy, nut, and confectionery stores; dairy products stores; retail bakeries; and establishments primarily engaged in the retail sale of specialized foods not elsewhere classified, such as eggs and poultry, health foods, spices, herbs, coffee, and tea.

Apparel and accessory stores include retail stores primarily engaged in selling clothing of all kinds and related materials for personal wear and adornment. Not included are establishments that meet the criteria for department stores or miscellaneous general merchandise stores even though most of their receipts are from the sale of apparel and apparel accessories. They consist of men's and boy's clothing and furnishing stores; women's ready-to-wear stores; women's accessory and specialty stores; children's and infant's wear stores; family clothing stores; men's, women's, children's and juvenile's, and family shoe stores; furriers and fur shops; and establishments primarily engaged in the retail sale of specialized lines of apparel and accessories not elsewhere classified, such as uniforms, bathing suits, raincoats, riding apparel, sports apparel, umbrellas, ties, and toupees. Also included are custom tailors primarily engaged in making and selling men's and women's clothing (except fur apparel) to individual order.

Eating and drinking places include retail establishments selling prepared food and drinks for consumption on the premises; they also include lunch counters and refreshment stands selling prepared foods and drinks for immediate consumption. They consist of restaurants and lunchrooms, social caterers, cafeterias, refreshment places, contract feeding, ice cream and frozen custard stands, and drinking places (alcoholic beverages).

Paid employees consist of the full-time and part-time employees, including salaried officers and executives of corporations, who were on the payroll in the pay period including March 12. Included are employees on paid sick leave, paid holidays, and paid vacations; not included are proprietors and partners of unincorporated businesses.

Payroll includes all forms of compensation such as salaries, wages, commissions, bonuses, vacation allowances, sick-leave pay, and the value of payments in kind (e.g., free meals and lodgings) paid during the year to all employees. Tips and gratuities received by employees from patrons and reported to employers are included. For corporations, it includes amounts paid to officers and executives; for unincorporated businesses, it does not include profit or other compensation of proprietors or partners. Payroll is reported before deductions for Social Security, income tax, insurance, union dues, etc.

SERVICE INDUSTRIES, Items 163-169

Source: U.S. Bureau of the Census - 1987 Census of Service Industries

The Census of Service Industries was conducted for the year 1987. Data are provided only for establishments with payroll during the year. Establishments with payroll are those that had some paid employment during the year. The data do not include establishments that are auxiliary (e.g., warehouses or other establishments with the primary function of providing a service) to service establishments within the same organization.

Total receipts include all establishments in business at any time during the year. Receipts represent the basic dollar volume measure for service establishments of firms subject to federal income tax. They include receipts from customers or clients for services rendered, from the use of facilities, and from merchandise sold during the year whether or not payment was received during the year, except for health practitioners, legal services, and architectural, engineering, and surveying services, which reported on a cash basis (payments received during the year regardless of when services were rendered). Gasoline, liquor, tobacco, and other excise taxes, which are paid by the manufacturer or wholesaler and included in the cost of goods purchased are also included.

Receipts are net after deduction for refunds and allowances for merchandise returned by customers. Receipts do not include sales, occupancy, admissions, or other taxes collected from customers and remitted directly by the firm to a local, state, or federal tax agency; nor do they include nonoperating income from such sources as interest, investments, or sale or rental of real estate.

Receipts do not include service receipts of manufacturers, wholesalers, retail establishments, or other businesses whose primary activity is other than service. They do, however, include receipts other than from services rendered (e.g., sales of merchandise to individuals or other businesses) by establishments primarily engaged in performing services and classified in the service industries.

Figures for Hotels, motels and other lodging places include hotels, rooming houses, camps, and other lodging places. This group includes establishments providing lodging, or lodging and meals. Establishments which provide accommodations for permanent residents (e.g., apartment hotels) are not included in this category.

Health services, includes establishments primarily engaged in furnishing medical, surgical, and other health services to persons. Associations or groups primarily engaged in providing medical or other health services to members are included, but those that only provide insurance covering hospitalization or medical costs are not included here.

Legal services include establishments primarily engaged in offering legal advice or legal services, the head or heads of which are members of the bar. Associations of lawyers formed solely for the sharing of expenses (including payroll) and not for the purpose of jointly practicing their profession are also included. Receipts are not applicable for these associations since their operations are funded by reimbursements from member firms and not considered operating receipts for legal services provided. Neither are such entities considered separate operating establishments; however, their payroll and employment data are included.

Paid employees consist of the full-time and part-time employees, including salaried officers and executives of corporations, who were on the payroll in the pay period including March 12. Included are employees on paid sick leave, paid holidays, and paid vacations; not included are proprietors and partners of unincorporated businesses.

Payroll includes all forms of compensation such as salaries, wages, commissions, bonuses, vacation allowances, sick-leave pay, and the value of payments in kind (e.g., free meals and lodgings) paid during the year to all employees. Tips and gratuities received by employees from patrons and reported to employers are included. For corporations, it includes amounts paid to officers and executives; for unincorporated businesses, it does not include profit or other compensation of proprietors or partners. Payroll is reported before deductions for Social Security, income tax, insurance, union dues, etc.

BANKING, Items 170 & 171

Source: U.S. Federal Deposit Insurance Corporation

Total figures for bank deposits represent deposits in all commercial and mutual savings banks in the United States. For all counties, individual banking offices -- not the combined totals of the bank -- are the source of the data. Banking office is defined to include all offices that actually hold deposits and to exclude consumer installment loan offices, computer centers, and other nondeposit installations, such as some electronic funds transfer units. It also excludes "nondeposit" trust companies.

SAVINGS CAPITAL, Items 172 & 173

Source: U.S. Federal Home Loan Bank Board

Savings capital figures for savings and loan associations, are based on the results of the survey of the dollar volume of accounts in savings and loan associations insured by the Federal Savings and Loan Insurance Corporation as of September 30. For a given county, data are presented for offices of savings and loan associations -- whether home or branch -- located in the county.

FEDERAL FUNDS AND GRANTS, Items 174-180

Source: U.S. Bureau of the Census - Consolidated Federal Funds Report

Data on Federal expenditures and obligations were obtained from a report prepared in accordance with the Consolidated Federal Funds Report (CFFR) Act of 1982 (P.L. 97-326), which specified that the following reporting systems and agencies be used as data sources: Federal Assistance Award Data System (FAADS), Federal Procurement Data System, Office of Personnel Management (OPM), and Department of Defense (DOD). In addition, several other agencies were requested to provide data, usually for selected programs. The report reflects federal government expenditures by state and territory.

Most data covering direct payments for individuals were taken from information reported to the FAADS. The two object areas of direct payments for individuals are (1) direct payments for retirement and disability benefits and (2) all other direct payments for individuals. All data represent actual expenditures during the fiscal year.

Federal funds are generally reported on the basis of obligations of government-administered funds, except deposit funds. In the federal government budget accounting system, "obligations" are funds legally set aside to be spent, but not actual expenditures. Therefore, it is possible that in some cases the dollar amounts reported for a particular program reflect obligations incurred in the current fiscal year to be spent over a period of several years.

Statistics covering procurement were provided by the United States Postal Service (USPS), for Postal Service procurement, and the Federal Procurement Data Center (FPDC), for procurement actions for all other federal agencies, including Department of Defense (DOD). Amounts provided by the USPS represent actual outlays for contractual commitments while amounts provided by the FPDC represent the value of obligations for contract actions and do not reflect actual federal government expenditures. In general, only current-year contract actions are reported for data provided by the FPDC; however, multiple-year obligations may be reported for contract actions of less than 3 years duration.

Amounts reported for salaries and wages were obtained from the Office of Personnel and Management (OPM), DOD, and USPS. The DOD provided information on military payrolls; data covering civilian employees of DOD were obtained from OPM. Amounts reported by the DOD represent estimates of fiscal year outlays by state and county. Data for Postal Service employees were provided by the USPS and were based upon place of employment (postal facility). Amounts represent actual outlays during the fiscal year, but with the national total distributed among the states and counties on an estimated basis. Data on salaries and wages for all other federal government employees (except for employees of the Central Intelligence Agency and the National Security Agency) were obtained from OPM. National totals represent actual expenditures during the fiscal year; the geographic distribution of these amounts by state and county was estimated based upon place of employment.

The principal source of grants data was the information submitted to the FAADC. The Bureau of the Census is the Executive Agent for the Office of Management and Budget and is responsible for the operation of the FAADS reporting system. The FAADS data represent the federal obligations incurred at the time the grant is awarded. The amounts reported do not represent actual expenditures since obligations in one time period may not result in outlays during the same time period. Moreover, initial amounts obligated may be adjusted at a later date, either through enhancements or obligations. The data were derived by summing the quarterly reports that covered financial assistance awarded between October 1 and September 30. All grant awards were reported by state, county, and city of the initial recipient. For many grants, this recipient is the state government even though the grant monies are subsequently distributed to county, municipal, or township governments. These "pass-through" grants generally appear in the CFFR at the state capital city (and in the associated county). No attempt is made in the CFFR to assign the dollar amounts for these pass-through programs to locations other than the state capital.

LOCAL GOVERNMENT STATISTICS, Items 181-196

Source: U.S. Bureau of the Census

Data on local governments are based on results of the 1982 Census of Governments. For each county area, the financial data comprise amounts for all local governments -- not only the county government but also any municipalities, townships, school districts, and special districts within the county. Statistics from governmental units located in two or more county areas are assigned to the county area containing the administrative office.

Revenue and expenditure items include all amounts of money received and paid out, respectively, by a government and its agencies (net of correcting transactions such as recoveries of refunds), with the exception of amounts for debt issuance and retirement and for loan and investment, agency, and private transactions.

Payments among the various funds and agencies of a particular government are excluded from revenue and expenditure items as representing internal transfers. Therefore, a government's contribution to a retirement fund that it administers is not counted as expenditure, nor is the receipt of this contribution by the retirement fund counted as revenue.

Total general revenue includes all revenue except utility, liquor stores, and insurance trust revenue. All tax revenue and intergovernmental revenue, even if designated for employee-retirement or local utility purpose, are classified as general revenue. However, to avoid duplication, revenue figures are net of reported transactions between local governments.

Intergovernmental revenue covers amounts received from the federal or state government as fiscal aid, reimbursements for performance of general government functions and specific services for the paying government, or amounts received in lieu of taxes. It excludes any amounts received from other governments for sale of property, commodities, and utility services. Figures for intergovernmental revenue from state government represent all intergovernmental revenue received from the state government, including amounts originally from the federal government but channeled through the state.

Taxes consist of compulsory contributions exacted by governments for public purposes. However, this category excludes employer and employee payments for retirement and social insurance purposes, which are classified as insurance trust revenue, and special assessments, which are classified as nontax general revenue. Property taxes are taxes conditioned on ownership of property and assessed by its value. Sales and gross receipts taxes, including "licenses" at more than normal rates, are based on volume or value of transfers of goods or services, on gross receipts, or on gross income. Related taxes are based on use, storage, production, importation, or consumption of goods. Sales and gross receipts taxes exclude dealer discounts or "commissions" allowed to merchants for collection of taxes from consumers. General sales taxes and selected taxes on sales of motor fuels, tobacco products, and other particular commodities and services are included.

Government expenditure includes all capital outlay, of which a major portion is commonly financed by borrowing, while governmental revenue does not include receipts from borrowing. Among other things, this distorts the relationship between totals of revenue and expenditure figures that are presented and renders it useless as a direct measure of the degree of budgetary "balance", as that term is generally applied.

Direct general expenditure comprises all expenditures of the local governments, excluding utility, liquor stores, and insurance trust expenditures and any intergovernmental payments.

Local government expenditures for education are mainly for provision and support of schools and other educational facilities and services, including those for educational institutions beyond the high school level operated by local governments. They cover such related services as pupil transportation; school lunch and other cafeteria operations; school health, recreation, and library services administered by local school systems; and dormitories, dining halls, and bookstores operated by public institutions of higher education.

Health and hospital expenditures include health research, clinics, nursing, immunization, and other categorical, environmental, and general health services provided by health agencies; and establishment and operation of hospital facilities, provision of hospital care, and support of other public and private hospitals.

Police protection expenditure includes police activities such as patrols, communications, custody of persons awaiting trial, and vehicular inspection.

Public welfare expenditure covers support of and assistance to needy persons contingent upon their needs. Included are cash assistance paid directly to needy persons under categorical (Old Age Assistance, Aid to Families with Dependent Children, Aid to the Blind, and Aid to the Disabled) and other welfare programs; vendor payments made directly to private purveyors for medical care, burials, and other commodities and services provided under welfare programs; welfare institutions; and any intergovernmental or other direct expenditure for welfare purposes. Pensions to former employees and other benefits not contingent on need are excluded.

Highway expenditure is for provision and maintenance of highway facilities, including toll turnpikes, bridges, tunnels, and ferries, as well as regular roads, highways, and streets. Also included are expenditures for street lighting and for snow and ice removal.

Debt outstanding includes all long-term debt obligations of the government and its agencies (exclusive of utility debt) and all interest-bearing short-term (i.e., repayable within 1 year) debt obligations remaining unpaid at the close of the fiscal year. It includes judgments, mortgages, and revenue bonds, as well as general obligation bonds, notes, and interest-bearing warrants. It includes noninterest-bearing short-term obligations, interfund obligations, amounts owed in a trust or agency capacity, advances and contingent loans from other governments, and rights of individuals to benefits from government-administered employee-retirement funds.

STATE AND LOCAL GOVERNMENT EMPLOYMENT, Items 197 & 198

Source: U.S. Bureau of Economic Analysis

Includes employment in all state and local government agencies and enterprises.

FEDERAL EMPLOYMENT, Items 199 & 200

Source: U.S. Bureau of Economic Analysis

Federal employment figures include both civilian and military, as well as persons employed in government enterprises.

ELECTION STATISTICS, Items 201 & 202

Source: Election Data Services, Washington, DC (Copyright)

The data in this report show the total vote and the percentage of the total vote won by the leading party. Sometimes the winning percentage is less than 50 percent because of votes for other parties. The data indicate the leading party by showing the letter "D" for Democrat and "R" for Republican in front of the percentage figure. In the one county where there was a tie vote the letter "T" is shown.

TABLE C—CITIES

Table C presents 134 items of data for 951 cities that had a population of 25,000 or more at the time of the 1980 census.

LAND AREA, Items 1 & 4

Source: U.S. Bureau of the Census

See the explanatory note under items 1 & 4 in the previous list of source notes for Tables A and B.

POPULATION—TOTAL PERSONS, RANK, DENSITY, CHANGE, RACE, HISPANIC ORIGIN AND AGE, Items 2 & 3, 5-14

Source: U.S Bureau of the Census - 1980 and 1990 Censuses of Population and Housing

Population change 1980-1990 (items 6-7) is calculated from 1980 and 1990 data based on city boundaries as they existed in those respective years. No attempt has been made to adjust the data to reflect boundary changes.

Also see the explanatory notes under items 2 & 3, items 5-10, items 11-19 and items 21-29 in the previous list of source notes for Tables A and B.

HOUSEHOLDS, Items 15-18

Source: U.S. Bureau of the Census - 1990 Census of Population and Housing

See the explanatory note under items 30-34 in the previous list of source notes for Tables A and B.

VITAL STATISTICS—BIRTHS AND DEATHS, Items 19-25

Source: U.S. National Center for Health Statistics

See the explanatory note under items 35-41 in the previous list of source notes for Tables A and B.

HOSPITALS—NUMBER AND NUMBER OF BEDS, Items 26-28

Source: American Hospital Association - Data found in the Public Health Service's Area Resource File

See the explanatory note under items 48-50 in the previous list of source notes for Tables A and B.

CRIME—SERIOUS CRIMES KNOWN TO THE POLICE, Items 29-31

Source: U.S. Federal Bureau of Investigation - Uniform Crime Reports

See the explanatory note under items 53-55 in the previous list of source notes for Tables A and B.

POLICE OFFICERS, Items 32 & 33

Source: Federal Bureau of Investigation

EDUCATION—ATTAINMENT, Items 34 & 35

Source: U.S. Bureau of the Census - 1980 Census of Population and Housing

See the explanatory note under items 58 & 59 in the previous list of source notes for Tables A and B.

MONEY INCOME, Items 36-41

Source: U.S. Bureau of the Census

See the explanatory note under items 66-71 in the previous list of source notes for Tables A and B.

HOUSING, Items 42-49

Source: U.S. Bureau of the Census - 1990 Census of Population and Housing

See the explanatory note under items 72-77 in the previous list of source notes for Tables A and B.

CONSTRUCTION, Items 50-53

Source: U.S. Bureau of the Census - Building Permits Survey

See the explanatory note under items 139-146 in the previous list of source notes for Tables A and B.

CIVILIAN LABOR FORCE AND UNEMPLOYMENT, Items 54-57

Source: U.S. Bureau of Labor Statistics

See the explanatory note under items 78-81 in the previous list of source notes for Tables A and B.

EMPLOYMENT, Items 58-60

Source: U.S. Bureau of the Census - 1980 Census of Population and Housing

Data on employment in 1980 are for persons 16 years old and older.

Professional, specialty and technical employees includes professional specialty occupations such as engineers, architects, and surveyors; mathematical and computer scientists; natural scientists; health diagnostic and treating occupations; teachers; as well as lawyers, judges, etc. Also included in this category are technical and related support occupations: clinical laboratory technicians, dental hygienists, health record technicians, licensed practical nurses, etc.

Precision production, craft, and operators includes occupations such as mechanics and repairers; construction trades; extractive and precision production workers, etc.; and machine operators, assemblers, and inspectors.

MANUFACTURES, Items 61-72

Source: U.S. Bureau of the Census - 1987 Census of Manufactures

See the explanatory note under items 127-138 in the previous list of source notes for Tables A and B.

WHOLESALE TRADE, Items 73-76

Source: U.S. Bureau of the Census - 1987 Census of Wholesale Trade

See the explanatory note under items 147-150 in the previous list of source notes for Tables A and B.

RETAIL TRADE, Items 77-89

Source: U.S. Bureau of the Census - 1987 Census of Retail Trade

See the explanatory note under items 151-162 in the previous list of source notes for Tables A and B.

SERVICE INDUSTRIES, Items 90-96

Source: U.S. Bureau of the Census - 1987 Census of Service Industries

See the explanatory note under items 163-169 in the previous list of source notes for Tables A and B.

FEDERAL GOVERNMENT, Items 97-99

Sources: U.S. Bureau of the Census - Consolidated Federal Funds Report and U.S. Bureau of Economic Analysis

See the explanatory notes under items 174-180, and items 199 & 200 in the previous list of source notes for Tables A and B.

CITY GOVERNMENT EMPLOYMENT, Items 100-102

Source: U.S. Bureau of the Census - *Survey of Governments, 1985: Employment Statistics*

Employment, as used in these figures, refers to all persons gainfully employed by and performing services for a city government. Employees include all persons paid for personal services performed, including persons paid from federally-funded programs, paid elected officials, persons in paid leave status, and persons paid on an annual, semiannual, quarterly, or per- meeting basis. Unpaid officials, pensioners, persons who perform work on a fee basis, and contractors and their employees are excluded from this count of employees.

FORM OF GOVERNMENT, Item 103

Source: International City Management Association, Washington, D.C., *The Municipal Yearbook, 1986* (Copyright)

Information for this item was obtained from U.S. Bureau of the Census files based on data from the International City Management Association.

CITY GOVERNMENT FINANCES, Items 104-124

Source: U.S. Bureau of the Census - Survey of Governments (1985), Finance Statistics.

Total general expenditure includes all city expenditure other than specifically enumerated kinds of expenditure classified as utility, liquor store, or employee retirement and other insurance trust expenditures.

Sewerage and sanitation includes sanitary and storm sewers, sewage disposal facilities and services, and other government activities for such purposes; sanitary engineering, smoke regulation and similar activities; and street cleaning, as well as the collection and disposal of garbage and other waste.

Parks and recreation includes cultural and scientific activities such as museums and art galleries; organized recreation, including playgrounds, playing fields, swimming pools, and bathing beaches; as well as municipal parks and special recreation facilities such as auditoriums, stadia, auto camps, recreation piers, and boat harbors.

Housing and community development includes city housing and redevelopment projects. It also includes regulation, promotion, and support of private housing and redevelopment activities. Data from Arizona, Kentucky, Michigan, New Mexico, New York, and Virginia generally include municipal housing authorities. Housing authorities for other cities are usually classified as independent governments; therefore, data for them are not included.

Also, see the explanatory notes under items 181-196 and items 197 & 198 in the previous list of source notes for Tables A and B.

CLIMATE, Items 125-131

Source: National Oceanic and Atmospheric Administration (NOAA), *Climatography of the United States*, Number 81; and *Comparative Climatic Data*, for the United States through 1981.

All climate data are average values for the 30-year period, 1951-1980.

Mean temperatures for January and July were determined by adding the average daily minimum temperatures and the average daily maximum temperatures, and dividing by two.

Temperature limits represent average daily minimum for January and average daily maximum for July.

Annual precipitation values are the average annual water equivalent of all precipitation for the 30-year period.

Heating- and cooling-degree days are used as relative measures of the energy required for the heating and cooling of buildings. One heating-degree day is accumulated for each whole degree that the mean daily temperature is below 65 degrees Fahrenheit (i.e., a mean daily temperature of 62 degrees Fahrenheit will produce 3 heating-degree days). Cooling-degree days are accumulated in similar fashion for deviations of the mean daily temperature above 65 degrees Fahrenheit.

ELECTRIC BILLS, Items 132-134

Source: U.S. Energy Information Administration, *Typical Electric Bills, 1986.*

Residential use is a classification covering electric energy supplied for residential purposes. The classification of an individual customer's account where the use is both residential and commercial is based on principal use.

Commercial refers to service to customers engaged primarily in the sales of goods and services, including institutions and government agencies.

TABLE D—PLACES

Table D presents data from the 1990 Census of Population and Housing, along with population estimates for 1986 and per capita money income estimates for 1985, for over 11,000 geographic areas with a 1980 population of 2,500 or more.

POPULATION, Items 1-3.

Source: U.S. Bureau of the Census

See explanatory notes for items 2 & 3 and items 21-29 in the list of source notes for Tables A and B.

POPULATION CHARACTERISTICS, Items 4-9

Source: U.S. Bureau of the Census - 1990 Census of Population and Housing

See explanatory note for items 5-10 in the list of source notes for Tables A and B.

TOTAL HOUSING UNITS, Item 10

Source: U.S. Bureau of the Census - 1990 Census of Population and Housing

See explanatory note for items 72-77 in the list of source notes for Tables A and B.

PER CAPITA INCOME, Item 11

Source: U.S. Bureau of the Census - Current Population Reports, Series P-26 No. 86.

Per capita income estimates are based on the population estimated as of July 1, 1986.

Also see the explanatory note for items 66-71 in the list of source notes for Tables A and B.

LAND AREA, Item 12

Source: U.S. Bureau of the Census

See explanatory note for items 1 & 4 in the list of source notes for Tables A and B.